1996
Standard Postage Stamp Catalogue

ONE HUNDRED AND FIFTY-SECOND EDITION IN SIX VOLUMES

VOLUME 5

EUROPEAN COUNTRIES and COLONIES,
INDEPENDENT NATIONS of
AFRICA, ASIA, LATIN AMERICA

R-Z

VICE PRESIDENT/PUBLISHER	Stuart J. Morrissey
EDITOR	James E. Kloetzel
ASSOCIATE EDITOR	William W. Cummings
VALUING EDITOR	Martin J. Frankevicz
NEW ISSUES EDITOR	David C. Akin
COMPUTER CONTROL COORDINATOR	Denise Oder
VALUING ANALYST	Jose R. Capote
EDITORIAL ASSISTANTS	Judith E. Bertrand, Beth Brown
CONTRIBUTING EDITOR	Joyce Nelson
ART/PRODUCTION DIRECTOR	Janine C. S. Apple
PRODUCTION COORDINATOR	Nancy S. Martin
PRODUCTION ARTIST	Meg Schultz
MARKETING/SALES DIRECTOR	William Fay
ADVERTISING	David Lodge
CIRCULATION/PRODUCT PROMOTION MANAGER	Tim Wagner

Copyright© 1995 by

Scott Publishing Co.

911 Vandemark Road, P. O. Box 828, Sidney, OH 45365-0828

A division of AMOS PRESS, INC., publishers of *Linn's Stamp News, Coin World, Cars & Parts* magazine, *Moneycard Collector* and *The Sidney Daily News.*

Table of Contents

See Volume 1A for United States and affiliated territories,
United Nations, Canada and British America.

See Volume 1B for the British Commonwealth of Nations other
than British America.

See Volumes 2, 3 and 4 for nations of Africa, Asia, Europe,
Latin America A-C, D-I and J-Q and their affiliated territories.

Copyright Notice

The contents of this book are owned exclusively by Scott Publishing Co. and all rights thereto are reserved under the Pan American and Universal Copyright Conventions.

Copyright @1995 by Scott Publishing Co., Sidney, OH. Printed in U.S.A.

COPYRIGHT NOTE

Permission is hereby given for the use of material in this book and covered by copyright if:

(a) The material is used in advertising matter, circulars or price lists for the purpose of offering stamps for sale or purchase at the prices listed therein; and

(b) Such use is incidental to the business of buying and selling stamps and is limited in scope and length, i.e., it does not cover a substantial portion of the total number of stamps issued by any country or of any special category of stamps of any country; and

(c) Such material is not used as part of any catalogue, stamp album or computerized or other system based upon the Scott catalogue numbers, or in any updated valuations of stamps not offered for sale or purchase; and

(d) Such use is not competitive with the business of the copyright owner; and

(e) Such use is for editorial purposes in publications in the form of articles or commentary, except for computer software or the serialization of books in such publications, for which separate written permission is required.

Any use of the material in this book which does not satisfy all the foregoing conditions is forbidden in any form unless permission in each instance is given in writing by the copyright owner.

Trademark Notice

The terms SCOTT, SCOTT'S, SCOTT CATALOGUE NUMBERING SYSTEM, SCOTT CATALOGUE NUMBER, SCOTT NUMBER and abbreviations thereof, are trademarks of Scott Publishing Co., used to identify its publications and its copyrighted system for identifying and classifying postage stamps for dealers and collectors. These trademarks are to be used only with the prior consent of Scott Publishing Co.

No part of this work may be reproduced in any form or by any means, electronic or mechanical, including photocopying, without permission in writing from Scott Publishing Co., P.O. Box 828, Sidney, OH 45365-0828.

ISBN 0-89487-213-3

Library of Congress Card No. 2-3301

Scott Publishing Co.

SCOTT

911 VANDEMARK ROAD, P. O. Box 828, SIDNEY, OHIO 45365-0828   513-498-0802

Dear Catalogue User:

At the beginning of each year, we get together and ask ourselves a very basic question. Why should someone buy the next edition of the Scott Catalogue? After all, in many cases a catalogue user just spent $198 for the previous edition.

What have we changed, added or improved to earn your purchase of the 1996 catalogue?

There are indeed many, many changes and improvements. So numerous I'm almost not sure where to begin. In the past I've used an imaginary snappy reporter or energetic talk show host to ask a few questions. At a recent stamp show a wag collector asked if I was going to have a man from outer space do the honors this year. Not necessary. This time I'll just ask myself the questions.

Tell us something out of the ordinary.

I'll tell you, but you won't believe it until you read it. And I dare you to read it. I'm talking about the completely revised and re-written catalogue introduction.

The new introduction is a pleasure to read and includes updated information on printing, separation and tagging.

Let's get down to the nitty-gritty. Where is the action in Volume 5?

Russia and Thailand. Russia leads the pack in Volume 5 with nearly 4,000 value changes, followed by Thailand with more than 1,700. Most of the changes in these two countries are strong increases.

In the Russia listings, there are changes starting in the mid 1930s. The Red Army set of 1938, Scott 629-635, zips to $20 mint never hinged, $9.95 unused and $5.13 used from $10 mint never hinged, $6.16 unused and $2.52 used. Scott 698-705, the 1938 Komsomol set, charges to $55 mint never hinged and $29.50 unused from $32.50 mint never hinged and $27.10 unused. The 1941 Vasili Surikov set, Scott 845-849, leaps to $40 mint never hinged, $24.25 unused and $9.75 used from $22.50 mint never hinged, $17.45 unused and $4.88 used.

Many stamps of the 1960s record sharp increases in mint never hinged condition. The 1966 World championships souvenir sheet, Scott 3232, rises to $10 from $2.50. The 1967 Flag and Arms set, Scott 3342-3357, shoots to $6.08 from $1.65. Similar strong increases are found in the issues of the 1970s and 1980s. The 1984 overprinted souvenir sheet, Scott 5171A, zips to $5 from $1.75.

Thailand again records many strong value increases, particularly in the early surcharges. Scott 6, the 1885 1 tical (in capitals) on 1 solot surcharge, moves to $450 unused and used from $300 unused and used. Scott 51, the 1898 antique lettered "1 Atts." on 12a surcharge, leaps to $325 unused and used from $65 both unused and used. The 1899 rejected design set, Scott 70-74, flies to $4,850 unused, $1,900 used from $3,250 unused and $1,240 used, and the 1932 set, Scott 225-232, hops to $147.75 unused from $83.50. The increases are also strong after the never-hinged breakpoint. The 1950 Coronation set, Scott 275-282, jumps to $88.30 from $66.25. The 1955 King Naresuan on Elephant set, Scott 304-308, leaps to $109.50 from $72.25. The 1963 Children's Day duo, Scott 412-413, doubles to $6.50 from $3.25, and the 1968 Butterfly set, Scott 509-512, shoots to $57.25 from $37.25.

What about values for countries other than Russia and Thailand?

South Viet Nam continues to post increases. The 1955 Refugees set, Scott 30-35, climbs to $89.75 mint never hinged from $79.92, and Scott 251-252, honoring the mythological founders of Viet Nam, jump to $9.55 mint never hinged from $6.

More than 1,100 changes were made in Romania. Most are found in stamps of the 1980s and the majority are sharp decreases. For example, the Flower set of 1986, Scott 3380-3385, dips to $3.85 mint never hinged from $5.38, and the 1987 Folk Costumes set, Scott 3474-3481, drops to $3.96 mint never hinged from $6.06.

Issues of the 1950s through the 1970s from St. Pierre & Miquelon increase strongly in mint never hinged condition. The 1952 Silver Fox set, Scott 343-344, rises to $5.50 from $1.80. The 1969 Buildings set, Scott 385-388, jumps to $15 from $9.90, and the 1973 Bird sextet, Scott 423-428, leaps to $15.85 from $10.08.

Many United Arab Emirates sets show increases in mint never hinged condition. The 1973 definitives, Scott 13-24, rise to $68.85 from $57.30, and the 1984 INTELSAT set, Scott 187-188, jumps to $7 from $5.25.

Are there any new listings for stamps in hinged condition?

The breakpoint for never-hinged stamps was moved in San Marino before the April 12, 1958 postage and air post stamps commemorating the Brussels World's Fair and the Milan Fair. Values for never-hinged stamps before the breakpoint have been added in San Marino and Saar. Values for hinged sets found after the breakpoint for never-hinged sets have been added for Russia's 1949 souvenir sheet marking Stalin's 70th birthday, Scott 1324, and the 1950 Moscow Skyscraper set, Scott 1518-1525.

What editorial improvements and revisions await catalogue users?

More than 2,600 stamps of North Viet Nam and the reunified Viet Nam (the Socialist Republic of Viet Nam) have been listed. The listings start with three 1951 imperforate stamps featuring Ho Chi Minh and a map of Viet Nam and continue to listings for 1994 stamps. Some sets of the 1950s are relatively expensive unused. Sets with high catalogue values include Scott 28-31, a 1956 foursome marking the return of the government to Hanoi, at $200 unused, and Scott 43-46, a set of four honoring guerrilla leader Mac Thi Buoi, at $400 unused. Scott O6-O7, two 1955 surcharges on stamps showing Ho Chi Minh, are $300 unused. Many perforated sets also exist imperforate. Values are shown for many imperforate sets, usually at a slight premium over the perforated.

In Thailand, the 1a on 3a stamp with additional large "2" surcharge which was footnoted under Scott 21 last year has become Scott 29. The stamp that was Scott 29 last year has been renumbered as Scott 30. Minor listings for se-tenant pairs of the 1963-77 semi-postals have also been added.

Illustrations have been added to aid in the identification of Thailand's Antique and Roman letter surcharges.

Issue dates have been refined in Tadjikistan and Uruguay.

Anything else?

Please be reminded that listings for Ryukyu Islands are now found in Volume 1A.

Happy Collecting!

Stuart Morrissey

Stuart Morrissey/Publisher

Acknowledgments

Our appreciation and gratitude go to the following individuals and organizations who have assisted us in preparing information included in the 1996 Scott Catalogues. Some helpers prefer anonymity. These individuals have generously shared their stamp knowledge with others through the medium of the Scott Catalogue.

Those who follow provided information that is in addition to the hundreds of dealer price lists and advertisements and scores of auction catalogues and realizations which were used in producing the Catalogue Values. It is from those noted here that we have been able to obtain information on items not normally seen in published lists and advertisements. Support from these people of course goes beyond data leading to Catalogue Values, for they also are key to editorial changes.

George F. Ackermann
A. R. Allison
B. J. Ammel
Mike Armus
Don Bakos
Alfredo V. Basurto
Jules K. Beck
Ron Bentley
Vladimir Berrio-Lemm
Kenneth R. Berry
John Birkinbine II
Rex Dean Bishop
John R. Boker, Jr.
Jeff Brasor
George W. Brett
Roger Brody
William C. Brooks VI
Randall Brooksbank
Michael Bryne
A. Bryan Camarda
Nathan Carlin
Dr. Herman J. Cestero, Jr.
E. J. Chamberlin
Richard A. Champagne
Andrew Cronin
James A. Cross
William T. Crowe
Thomas De Luca
Dan Demetriade
Brian Dias
Harry Dober
Rich Drews
Bob Dumaine
William S. Dunn
Harry A. Eisenstein
J. A. Farrington
Leon Finik
Henry Fisher
William Fletcher
Joseph E. Foley
Marvin Frey
Richard Friedberg
Huguette Gagnon
D. Scott Gallagher
Eugene A. Garrett
Peter Georgiadis
Brian M. Green
Henry Hahn
Erich E. Hamm
Dr. James B. Helme
Clifford O. Herrick
Lee H. Hill, Jr.
Dr. Eugene Holmok
Rollin C. Huggins, Jr.
W. Wilson Hulme II
Clyde Jennings
Jack Jonza
Henry Karen
Stanford M. Katz

Dr. James Kerr
Charles F. Kezbers
William Langs
Ken Lawrence
Pedro Llach
William Thomas Lockard
David MacDonnell
Robert L. Markovits
F. Brian Marshall
Clyde R. Maxwell
Timothy M. McRee
Dr. Hector Mena
Giorgio Migliavacca
Jack Molesworth
William E. Mooz
Gary M. Morris
Peter Mosiondz, Jr.
Bruce M. Moyer
Richard H. Muller
Jack Nalbandian
James Natale
Gregg Nelson
Robert Odenweller
Victor Ostolaza
Sheldon Paris
John E. Pearson
Donald J. Peterson
Vernon Pickering
Stanley M. Piller
Jon Rose
Frans H. A. Rummens
Richard H. Salz
Byron Sandfield
Jacques C. Schiff, Jr.
F. Burton Sellers
Richard Simchak
Dr. Hubert Skinner
Roger D. Skinner
Richard Stambaugh
R. J. Thoden
Scott Trepel
Ming W. Tsang
A. John Ultee
James O. Vadeboncoeur
William R. Wallace
Jerome S. Wagshal
Daniel C. Warren
Richard A. Washburn
Stephen S. Washburne
Giana Wayman
Larry S. Weiss
Nelson A. L. Weller
Hans A. Westphal
Ernest C. Wilkins
Greg Winston
Robert F. Yacano
Clarke Yarbrough
Val Zabijaka
Nathan Zankel

American Air Mail Society
Stephen Reinhard, PO Box 110,
Mineola, NY 11501

American Philatelic Society
PO Box 8000, State College, PA 16803

American Revenue Association
Bruce Miller, Suite 332,
701 South First Ave.,
Arcadia, CA 91006

American Stamp Dealers'
Association
3 School St., Glen Cove, NY 11542

American Topical Association
PO Box 630, Johnstown, PA 15907

Booklet Collectors Club
James Natale, PO Box 2461,
Cinnaminson, NJ 08077-5461

Bureau Issues Association
George V.H. Godin, PO Box 23707,
Belleville, IL 62223

Confederate Stamp Alliance
Richard L. Calhoun,
1749 W. Golf Rd., Suite 366,
Mt. Prospect, IL 60056

Errors, Freaks, and Oddities
Collectors Club
Jim McDevitt, 1903 Village Road West,
Norwood, MA 02062-2516

International Society of Worldwide
Stamp Collectors
Carol Cervenka, Route 1 Box 69A,
Caddo Mills, TX 75135

Junior Philatelists of America
Sally Horn, PO Box 850,
Boalsburg, PA 16827-0850

No-Value-Identified Collectors
Club
Albert Sauvanet, Le Clos Royal B,
Boulevard des Pas Enchantes,
44230 St. Sebastien-sur-Loire, France

Plate Number Coil Collectors Club
Joann Lenz, 37211 Alper Drive,
Sterling Heights, MI 48312-2203

Precancel Stamp Society
1750 Skippack Pk. #1603,
Center Square, PA 19422

Royal Philatelic Society
D. J. Springbett, 41 Devonshire Place,
London, U.K. W1N 1PE

Royal Philatelic Society of Canada
PO Box 929, Station Q,
Toronto ON, CANADA M4T 2P1

United Postal Stationery Society
Joann Thomas, PO Box 48,
Redlands, CA 92373

US Philatelic Classics Society
Patricia S. Walker, Briarwood,
Lisbon, MD 21765

US Possessions Philatelic Society
Charles A. Richmond, PO Box 26724,
Busch Finance Station,
Columbus, OH 43226

Society for the New Republics of
the Former USSR (Armenia, etc.)
Michael Padwee, 163 Joralemon St.,
PO Box 1520,
Brooklyn, NY 11201-1520

American Belgian Philatelic Society
Kenneth L. Costilow,
621 Virginius Dr.,
Virginia Beach, VA 23452-4417

Belize Philatelic Study Circle
Charles R. Gambill, 730 Collingswood,
Corpus Christi, TX 78412

Bermuda Collectors Society
Thomas J. McMahon, 86 Nash Road,
Purdys, NY 10578

Brazil Philatelic Association
Kurt Ottenheimer,
462 West Walnut St.,
Long Beach, NY 11561

British Caribbean Philatelic Study
Group
Gale J. Raymond, PO Box 35695,
Houston, TX 77235

British North America Philatelic
Society
Jerome C. Jarnick, 108 Duncan Drive,
Troy, MI 48098

Burma Philatelic Study Circle
A. Meech, 7208 91st Ave.,
Edmonton, AB, CANADA T6B 0R8

Canal Zone Study Group
Richard H. Salz, 60 27th Ave.,
San Francisco, CA 94121

China Stamp Society
Paul H. Gault, 140 West 18th Ave.,
Columbus, OH 43210

COPAPHIL (Colombia & Panama)
PO Box 2245, El Cajon, CA 92021

Society of Costa Rica Collectors
Dr. Hector Mena, PO Box 14831,
Baton Rouge, LA 70808

Croatian Philatelic Society (Croatia
and other Balkan areas)
Eck Spahich, 1512 Lancelot Rd.,
Borger, TX 79007

Cuban Philatelic Society of
America
PO Box 450207,
Miami, FL 33245-0207

Society for Czechoslovak Philately
Robert T. Cossaboom, PO Box 332,
Scott AFB, IL 62225

Ethiopian Philatelic Society
Huguette Gagnon, PO Box 8110-45,
Blaine, WA 98230

Falkland Islands Philatelic Study
   Group
James Driscoll, PO Box 172,
South Dennis, NJ 08245

France & Colonies Philatelic Society
Walter Parshall, 103 Spruce St.,
Bloomfield, NJ 07003

Germany Philatelic Society
PO Box 779,
Arnold, MD 21012-4779

GDR Study Group of German
   Philatelic Society
Ken Lawrence, PO Box 8040,
State College, PA 16803-8040

Great Britain Collectors Club
Frank J. Koch, PO Box 309,
Batavia, OH 45103-0309

Hellenic Philatelic Society of
   America (Greece & related areas)
Dr. Nicholas Asimakopulos,
541 Cedar Hill Ave., Wyckoff, NJ 07481

International Society of Guatemala
   Collectors
Mrs. Mae Vignola, 105 22nd Ave.,
San Francisco, CA 94116

Haiti Philatelic Society
Dwight Bishop, 16434 Shamhart Dr.,
Granada Hills, CA 91344

Hong Kong Stamp Society
Dr. An-Min Chung, 120 Deerfield Rd.,
Broomall, PA 19008

Hong Kong Collectors Club
Nikolai Lau, 6021 Yonge Street #888,
North York, ON, CANADA M2M 3W2

Hungary Philatelic Society
Thomas Phillips, PO Box 1162,
Samp Mortar Sta., Fairfield, CT 06432

India Study Circle
John Warren, PO Box 70775,
Washington, DC 20024

Society of Indochina Philatelists
Paul Blake, 1466 Hamilton Way,
San Jose, CA 95125

Iran Philatelic Study Circle
A. John Ultee, 816 Gwynne Ave.,
Waynesboro, VA 22980

Eire Philatelic Association (Ireland)
Michael J. Conway, 74 Woodside Circle,
Fairfield, CT 06430

Society of Israel Philatelists
Howard D. Chapman,
28650 Settlers Lane,
Pepper Pike, OH 44124

Italy and Colonies Study Circle
David F. Emery, PO Box 86,
Philipsburg, NJ 08865

International Society for Japanese
   Philately
Kenneth Kamholz, PO Box 1283,
Haddonfield, NJ 08033

Korea Stamp Society
William A. Matthews, PO Box 15306,
Columbus, OH 43215

Latin American Philatelic Society
Piet Steen, PO Box 6420,
Hinton, AB, CANADA T7V 1X7

Liberian Philatelic Society
William Thomas Lockard, PO Box 267,
Wellston, OH 45692

Lithuanian Philatelic Society of
   New York
Vincent M. Alones, 217 McKee St.,
Floral Park, NY 11001-1314

Plebiscite-Memel-Saar Study Group
Clay Wallace, 158 Arapaho Circle,
San Ramon, CA 94583

Mexico-Elmhurst Philatelic Society
   International
William E. Shelton, PO Box 39838,
San Antonio, TX 78218

Nepal & Tibet Philatelic Study
   Group
Roger D. Skinner,
1020 Covington Road,
Los Altos, CA 94022

American Society of Netherlands
   Philately
Jan Enthoven,
W6428 Riverview Drive,
Onalaska, WI 54650

Nicaragua Study Group
Clyde R. Maxwell, Airport Plaza,
2041 Business Center Drive,
Suite 101, Irvine, CA 92715

Society of Australasian
   Specialists/Oceania
Henry Bateman, PO Box 4862,
Monroe, LA 71211

Orange Free State Study Circle
J. R. Stroud, 28 Oxford St.,
Burnham-on-sea,
Somerset, U.K. TA8 1LQ

International Philippine Philatelic
   Society
Eugene A. Garrett, 446 Stratford Ave.,
Elmhurst, IL 60126-4123

American Society of Polar
   Philatelists (Antarctic areas)
S.H. Jacobson, PO Box 945,
Skokie, IL 60077

Pitcairn Islands Study Group
Nelson A.L. Weller,
2940 Wesleyan Lane,
Winston-Salem, NC 27106

Polonus Philatelic Society (Poland)
864 N. Ashland Ave.,
Chicago, IL 60622

International Society for
   Portuguese Philately
Michael Bryne, Adirondack Stamps,
PO Box 13100,
Mexico Beach, FL 32410

Rhodesian Study Circle
William R. Wallace, PO Box 16381,
San Francisco, CA 94116

Romanian Chapter of Croatian
   Philatelic Society
Dan Demetriade, PO Box 10182,
Detroit, MI 48210

Rossica Society of Russian Philately
Gary Combs, 8241 Chalet Ct.,
Millersville, MD 21108

Canadian Society of Russian
   Philately
Andrew Cronin,
PO Box 5722, Station A,
Toronto, ON, CANADA M5W 1P2

Ryukyu Philatelic Specialist Society
Carmine J. DiVincenzo, PO Box 381,
Clayton, CA 94517-0381

St. Helena, Ascension & Tristan
   Society
Dr. Russell V. Skavaril,
222 East Torrance Road,
Columbus, OH 43214-3834

Associated Collectors of
   El Salvador
Jeff Brasor, 7365 NW 68th Way,
Pompano Beach, FL 33067-3918

Sarawak Specialists' Society
Art Bunce, PO Box 2516,
Escondido, CA 92033

Arabian Philatelic Association
ARAMCO Box 1929,
Dhahran 31311, SAUDI ARABIA

Scandinavia Collectors Club
Robert W. Lang, PO Box 125,
Newark, DE 19715-0125

Philatelic Society for Greater
   Southern Africa
William C. Brooks VI, PO Box 2698,
San Bernardino, CA 92406-2698

Slovakia Stamp Society
Jack Benchik, PO Box 555,
Notre Dame, IN 46556

Spanish Philatelic Society
Robert H. Penn, RD #3, Box 3349-1
Bangor, PA 18013

American Helvetia Philatelic Society
   (Switzerland, Liechtenstein)
Richard T. Hall, PO Box 666,
Manhattan Beach, CA 90267-0666

Society for Thai Philately
H.R. Blakeney, PO Box 25644,
Oklahoma City, OK 73125

Tonga/Tin Can Mail Study Circle
Tom Jackson, 121 Mullinger Ct. #1A,
Schaumburg, IL 60193

Turkey and Ottoman Philatelic
   Society
Gary F. Paiste, 4249 Berritt St.,
Fairfax, VA 22030

Tuvalu & Kiribati Philatelic Society
Frank Caprio, PO Box 218071,
Nashville, TN 37221

Ukrainian Philatelic & Numismatic
   Society
Val Zabijaka, PO Box 3711,
Silver Spring, MD 20918

United Nations Philatelists
Helen Benedict,
408 S. Orange Grove Blvd.,
Pasadena, CA 91105

Vatican Philatelic Society
Louis Padavan, PO Box 127,
Remsenburg, NY 11960

Yugoslavia Study Group
Michael Lenard, 1514 North 3rd Ave.,
Wausau, WI 54401

Catalogue Information

Catalogue Value

The Scott Catalogue value is a retail value; that is, an amount you could expect to pay for a stamp in a grade of Fine to Very Fine with no faults. Any exceptions to the grade valued will be noted in the text. The value listed for any given stamp is a reference that reflects recent actual dealer selling prices for that item.

Dealer retail price lists, public auction results, published prices in advertising and individual solicitation of retail prices from dealers, collectors and specialty organizations have been used in establishing the values found in this catalogue. Scott Publishing Co. values stamps, but Scott is not a company engaged in the business of buying and selling stamps as a dealer.

Use this catalogue as a guide for buying and selling. The actual price you pay for a stamp may be higher or lower than the catalogue value because of many different factors, including the amount of personal service a dealer offers, or increased or decreased interest in the country or topic represented by a stamp or set. An item may occasionally be offered at a lower price as a "loss leader," or as part of a special sale. You also may obtain an item inexpensively at public auction because of little interest at that time or as part of a large lot.

Copies of stamps that are of a lesser grade than Fine to Very Fine, or those with condition problems, trade at lower prices than those given in this catalogue. Stamps of exceptional quality in both grade and condition often command higher prices than those listed.

Values for pre-1900 unused issues are for stamps with at least most of their original gum. Later issues are assumed to have full original gum. From breakpoints in most countries' listings, stamps are valued as never hinged, due to the wide availability of stamps in that condition. These notations are prominently placed in the listings and in the counrty information preceding the listings. Some countries also feature listings with dual values for hinged and never-hinged stamps.

Grade

A stamp's grade and condition are crucial to its value. The accompanying illustrations show examples of Fine-Very Fine stamps from different time periods, along with examples of stamps in Fine and Very Fine grades as points of reference.

FINE stamps have designs that are noticeably off center on two sides. Imperforate stamps may have small margins, and earlier issues may show the design touching one edge of the stamp. For perforated stamps, perfs may barely clear the design on one side. Used stamps may have heavier than usual cancellations.

FINE-VERY FINE stamps may be somewhat off center on one side, or slightly off center on two sides. Imperforate stamps will have two margins of at least normal size, and the design will not touch any edge. For perforated stamps, the perfs are well clear of the design, but are still noticeably off center. *However, early issues of a country may be printed in such a way that the design naturally is very close to the edges.* Used stamps will not have a cancellation that detracts from the design. This is the grade used to establish Scott Catalogue values.

VERY FINE stamps may be slightly off center on one side, but the design will be well clear of the edge. The stamp will present a nice, balanced appearance. Imperforate stamps will have three normal-sized margins. Used stamps will have light or otherwise neat cancellations.

Condition

Grade addresses only centering and (for used stamps) cancellation. *Condition* refers to factors other than grade that affect a stamp's desirability.

Factors that can increase the value of a stamp include exceptionally wide margins, particularly fresh color, the presence of selvage, and plate or die varieties. Unusual cancels on used stamps (particularly those of the 19th century) can greatly enhance their value as well.

Factors other than faults that decrease the value of a stamp include loss of original gum, regumming, a hinge remnant or foreign object adhering to the gum, natural inclusions, straight edges, and markings or notations applied by collectors or dealers.

Faults include missing pieces, tears, pin or other holes, surface scuffs, thin spots, creases, toning, short or pulled perforations, clipped perforations, oxidation or other forms of color changelings, soiling, stains, and such man-made changes as reperforations or the chemical removal or lightening of a cancellation.

Scott Publishing Co. recognizes that there is no formally enforced grading scheme for postage stamps, and that the final price you pay or obtain for a stamp will be determined by individual agreement at the time of transaction.

Fine ⟶

SCOTT CATALOGUES VALUE STAMPS IN THIS GRADE

Fine-Very Fine ⟶

Very Fine ⟶

Catalogue Listing Policy

It is the intent of Scott Publishing Co. to list all postage stamps of the world in the *Scott Standard Postage Stamp Catalogue*. The only strict criteria for listing is that stamps be decreed legal for postage by the issuing country. Whether the primary intent of issuing a given stamp or set was for sale to postal patrons or to stamp collectors is not part of our listing criteria. Scott's role is to provide basic comprehensive postage stamp information. It is up to each stamp collector to choose which items to include in a collection.

It is Scott's objective to seek reasons why a stamp should be listed, rather than why it should not. Nevertheless, there are certain types of items that will not be listed. These include the following:

1. Unissued items that are not officially distributed or released by the issuing postal authority. Even if such a stamp is "accidentally" distributed to the philatelic or even postal market, it remains unissued. If such items are officially issued at a later date by the country, they will be listed. Unissued items consist of those that have been printed and then held from sale for reasons such as change in government, errors found on stamps or something deemed objectionable about a stamp subject or design.

2. Stamps "issued" by non-existent postal entities or fantasy countries, such as Nagaland, Occusi-Ambeno, Staffa, Sedang, Torres Straits and others.

3. Semi-official or unofficial items not required for postage. Examples include items issued by private agencies for their own express services. When such items are required for delivery, or are valid as prepayment of postage, they are listed.

4. Local stamps issued for local use only. Postage stamps issued by governments specifically for "domestic" use, such as Haiti Scott 219-228, or the United States non-denominated stamps, are not considered to be locals, since they are valid for postage throughout the country of origin.

5. Items not valid for postal use. For example, a few countries have issued souvenir sheets that are not valid for postage. This area also includes a number of worldwide charity labels (some denominated) that do not pay postage.

6. Intentional varieties, such as imperforate stamps that look like their perforated counterparts and are issued in very small quantities. These are often controlled issues intended for speculation.

7. Items distributed by the issuing government only to a limited group, such as a stamp club or a single stamp dealer, and later brought to market at inflated prices. These items normally will be included in a footnote.

The fact that a stamp has been used successfully as postage, even on international mail, is not in itself sufficient proof that it was legitimately issued. Numerous examples of so-called stamps from non-existent countries are known to have been used to post letters that have successfully passed through the international mail system.

There are certain items that are subject to interpretation. When a stamp falls outside our specifications, it may be listed along with a cautionary footnote.

A number of factors are considered in our approach to analyzing how a stamp is listed. The following list of factors is presented to share with you, the catalogue user, the complexity of the listing process.

Additional printings — "Additional printings" of a previously issued stamp may range from an item that is totally different to cases where it is impossible to differentiate from the original. At least a minor number (a small-letter suffix) is assigned if there is a distinct change in stamp shade, noticeably redrawn design, or a significantly different perforation measurement. A major number (numeral or numeral and capital-letter combination) is assigned if the editors feel the "additional printing" is sufficiently different from the original that it constitutes a different issue.

Commemoratives — Where practical, commemoratives with the same theme are placed in a set. For example, the U.S. Civil War Centenniel set of 1961-65 and the Constitution Bicentennial series of 1989-90 appear as sets. Countries such as Japan and Korea issue such

material on a regular basis, with an announced, or at least predictable, number of stamps known in advance. Occasionally, however, stamp sets that were released over a period of years have been separated. Appropriately placed footnotes will guide you to each set's continuation.

Definitive sets — Blocks of numbers generally have been reserved for definitive sets, based on previous experience with any given country. If a few more stamps were issued in a set than originally expected, they often have been inserted into the original set with a capital-letter suffix, such as U.S. Scott 1059A. If it appears that many more stamps than the originally allotted block will be released before the set is completed, a new block of numbers will be reserved, with the original one being closed off. In some cases, such as the British Machin Head series or the U.S. Transportation and Great Americans series, several blocks of numbers exist. Appropriately placed footnotes will guide you to each set's continuation.

New country — Membership in the Universal Postal Union is not a consideration for listing status or order of placement within the catalogue. The index will tell you in what volume or page number the listings begin.

"No release date" items — The amount of information available for any given stamp issue varies greatly from country to country and even from time to time. Extremely comprehensive information about new stamps is available from some countries well before the stamps are released. By contrast some countries do not provide information about stamps or release dates. Most countries, however, fall between these extremes. A country may provide denominations or subjects of stamps from upcoming issues that are not issued as planned. Sometimes, philatelic agencies, those private firms hired to represent countries, add these later-issued items to sets well after the formal release date. This time period can range from weeks to years. If these items were officially released by the country, they will be added to the appropriate spot in the set. In many cases, the specific release date of a stamp or set of stamps may never be known.

Overprints — The color of an overprint is always noted if it is other than black. Where more than one color of ink has been used on overprints of a single set, the color used is noted. Early overprint and surcharge illustrations were altered to prevent their use by forgers.

Se-tenants — Connected stamps of differing features (se-tenants) will be listed in the format most commonly collected. This includes pairs, blocks or larger multiples. Se-tenant units are not always symmetrical. An example is Australia Scott 508, which is a block of seven stamps. If the stamps are primarily collected as a unit, the major number may be assigned to the multiple, with minors going to each component stamp. In cases where continuous-design or other unit se-tenants will receive significant postal use, each stamp is given a major Scott number listing. This includes issues from the United States, Canada, Germany and Great Britain, for example.

Understanding the Listings

On the following page is an enlarged "typical" listing from this catalogue. Below are detailed explanations of each of the highlighted parts of the listing.

1 **Scott number** — Scott catalogue numbers are used to identify specific items when buying, selling or trading stamps. Each listed postage stamp from every country has a unique Scott catalogue number. Therefore, Germany Scott 99, for example, can only refer to a single stamp. Although the Scott catalogue usually lists stamps in chronological order by date of issue, there are exceptions. When a country has issued a set of stamps over a period of time, those stamps within the set are kept together without regard to date of issue. This follows the normal collecting approach of keeping stamps in their natural sets.

When a country issues a set of stamps over a period of time, a group of consecutive catalogue numbers is reserved for the stamps in that set, as issued. If that group of numbers proves to be too few, capital-letter suffixes, such as "A" or "B," may be added to existing numbers to create enough catalogue numbers to cover all items in the set. A capital-letter suffix indicates a major Scott catalogue number listing. Scott uses a suffix letter only once. Therefore, a catalogue number listing with a capital-letter prefix will not also be found with the same letter (lower case) used as a minor-letter listing. If there is a Scott 16A in a set, for example, there will not also be a Scott 16a.

Suffix letters are not cumulative. A minor variety of Scott 16A would be Scott 16b, not Scott 16Ab. Any exceptions, such as Great Britain Scott 358cp, are clearly indicated.

There are times when a reserved block of Scott catalogue numbers is too large for a set, leaving some numbers unused. Such gaps in the numbering sequence also occur when the catalogue editors move an item's listing elsewhere or have removed it entirely from the catalogue. Scott does not attempt to account for every possible number, but rather attempts to assure that each stamp is assigned its own number.

Scott numbers designating regular postage normally are only numerals. Scott numbers for other types of stamps, such as air post, semi-postal, postal tax, postage due, occupation and others have a prefix consisting of one or more capital letters or a combination of numerals and capital letters.

2 **Illustration number** — Illustration or design-type numbers are used to identify each catalogue illustration. For most sets, the lowest face-value stamp is shown. It then serves as an example of the basic design approach for other stamps not illustrated. Where more than one stamp use the same illustration number, but have differences in design, the design paragraph or the description line clearly indicates the design on each stamp not illustrated. Where there are both vertical and horizontal designs in a set, a single illustration may be used, with the exceptions noted in the design paragraph or description line.

When an illustration is followed by a lower-case letter in parentheses, such as "A2(b)," the trailing letter indicates which overprint or surcharge illustration applies.

Illustrations normally are 75 percent of the original size of the stamp. An effort has been made to note all illustrations not illustrated at that percentage. Virtually all souvenir sheet illustrations are reduced even more. Overprints and surcharges are shown at 100 percent of their original size, unless otherwise noted. In some cases, the illustration will be placed above the set, between listings or omitted completely. Overprint and surcharge illustrations are not placed in this catalogue for purposes of expertizing stamps.

3 **Paper color** — The color of a stamp's paper is noted in italic type when the paper used is not white.

4 **Listing styles** — There are two principal types of catalogue listings: major and minor.

Major listings are in a larger type style than minor listings. The catalogue number is a numeral that can be found with or without a capital-letter suffix, and with or without a prefix.

Minor listings are in a smaller type style and have a small-letter suffix or (if the listing immediately follows that of the major number) may show only the letter. These listings identify a variety of the major item. Examples include perforation, color, watermark or printing method differences, multiples (some souvenir sheets, booklet panes and se-tenant combinations), and singles of multiples.

Examples of major number listings include 16, 28A, B97, C13A, 10N5, and 10N6A. Examples of minor numbers are 16a and C13b.

5 **Basic information about a stamp or set** — Introducing each stamp issue is a small section (usually a line listing) of basic information about a stamp or set. This section normally includes the date of issue, method of printing, perforation, watermark and, sometimes, some additional information of note. *Printing method, perforation and watermark apply to the following sets until a change is noted.* Stamps created by overprinting or surcharging previous issues are assumed to have the same perforation, watermark and printing method as the original. Dates of issue are as precise as Scott is able to confirm and often reflect the dates on first-day covers, rather than the actual date of release.

6 **Denomination** — This normally refers to the face value of the stamp; that is, the cost of the unused stamp at the post office at the time of issue. When a denomination is shown in parentheses, it does not appear on the stamp. This includes the non-denominated stamps of the United States, Brazil and Great Britain, for example.

7 **Color or other description** — This area provides information to solidify identification of a stamp. In many recent cases, a description of the stamp design appears in this space, rather than a listing of colors.

8 **Year of issue** — In stamp sets that have been released in a period that spans more than a year, the number shown in parentheses is the year that stamp first appeared. Stamps without a date appeared during the first year of the issue. Dates are not always given for minor varieties.

9 **Value unused and Value used** — The Scott catalogue values are based on stamps that are in a grade of Fine-Very Fine unless stated otherwise. Unused values refer to items that have not seen postal, revenue or any other duty for which they were intended. Pre-1900 unused stamps that were issued with gum must have at least most of their original gum. Later issues are assumed to have full original gum. From breakpoints specified in most countries' listings, stamps are valued as never hinged. Stamps issued without gum are noted. Modern issues with PVA or other synthetic adhesives may appear ungummed. Self-adhesive stamps are valued as appearing undisturbed on their original backing paper. For a more detailed explanation of these values, please see the "Catalogue Value," "Condition" and "Understanding Valuing Notations" elsewhere in this introduction.

In some cases, where used stamps are more valuable than unused stamps, the value is for an example with a contemporaneous cancel, rather than a modern cancel or a smudge or other unclear marking. For those stamps that were released for postal and fiscal purposes, the used value represents a postally used stamp. Stamps with revenue cancels generally sell for less.

10 **Changes in basic set information** — Bold type is used to show any changes in the basic data given for a set of stamps. This includes perforation differences from one stamp to the next or a different paper, printing method or watermark.

11 **Total value of a set** — The total value of sets of five or more stamps issued after 1900 are shown. The set line also notes the range of Scott numbers and total number of stamps included in the grouping. *Set value* is the term used to indicate the value of a stamp set when its combined total is less than the sum of the individual stamps. This happens when some of the stamps in a set have the minimum catalogue value.

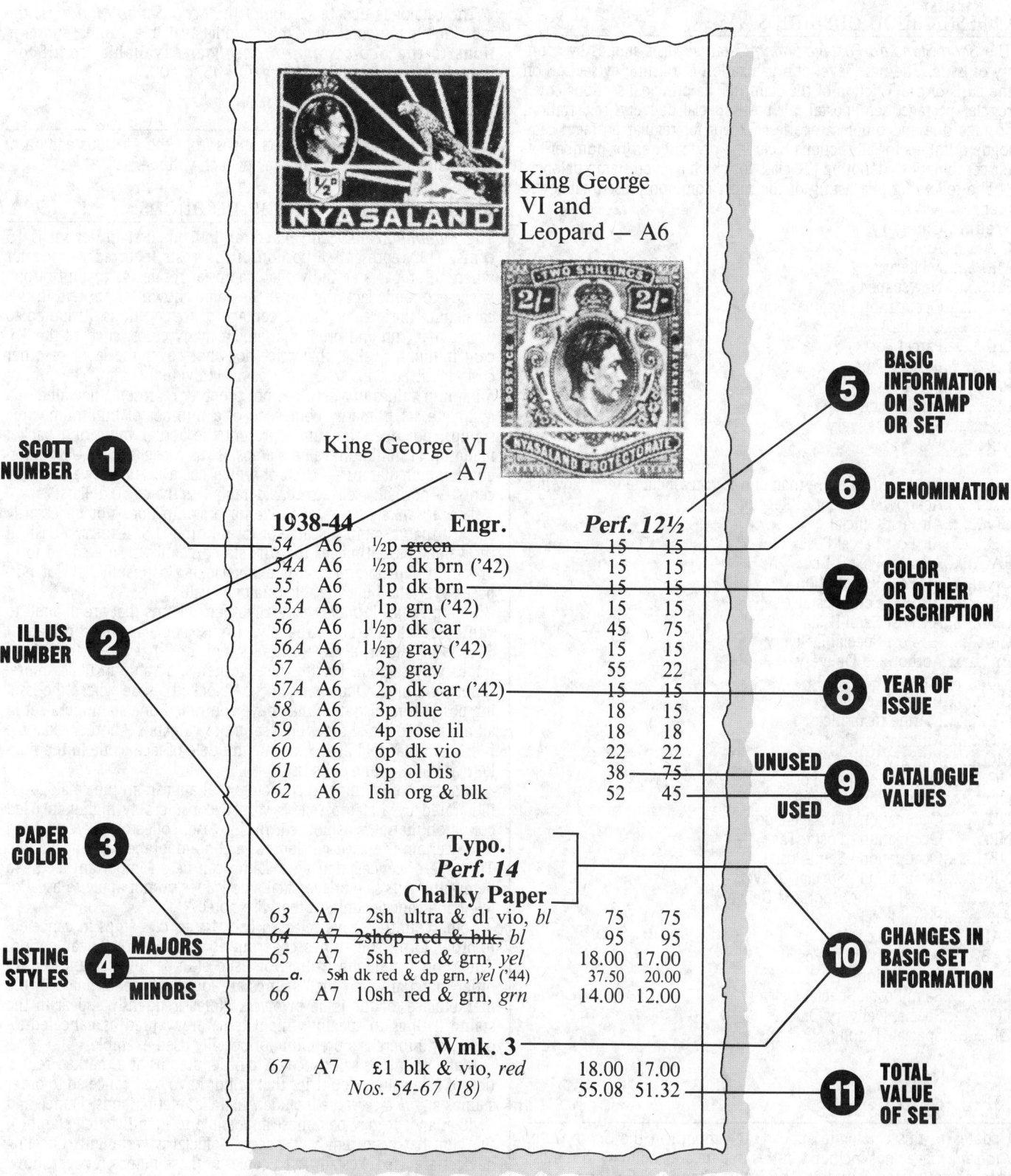

King George
VI and
Leopard — A6

King George VI
A7

5 BASIC INFORMATION ON STAMP OR SET

6 DENOMINATION

7 COLOR OR OTHER DESCRIPTION

8 YEAR OF ISSUE

9 CATALOGUE VALUES

1 SCOTT NUMBER

2 ILLUS. NUMBER

3 PAPER COLOR

4 LISTING STYLES — MAJORS / MINORS

10 CHANGES IN BASIC SET INFORMATION

11 TOTAL VALUE OF SET

1938-44　　　**Engr.**　　　**Perf. 12½**

Scott	Illus	Denom/Description	Unused	Used
54	A6	½p green	15	15
54A	A6	½p dk brn ('42)	15	15
55	A6	1p dk brn	15	15
55A	A6	1p grn ('42)	15	15
56	A6	1½p dk car	45	75
56A	A6	1½p gray ('42)	15	15
57	A6	2p gray	55	22
57A	A6	2p dk car ('42)	15	15
58	A6	3p blue	18	15
59	A6	4p rose lil	18	18
60	A6	6p dk vio	22	22
61	A6	9p ol bis	38	75
62	A6	1sh org & blk	52	45

UNUSED　　USED

Typo.
Perf. 14
Chalky Paper

Scott	Illus	Denom/Description	Unused	Used
63	A7	2sh ultra & dl vio, *bl*	75	75
64	A7	2sh6p red & blk, *bl*	95	95
65	A7	5sh red & grn, *yel*	18.00	17.00
a.		5sh dk red & dp grn, *yel* ('44)	37.50	20.00
66	A7	10sh red & grn, *grn*	14.00	12.00

Wmk. 3

Scott	Illus	Denom/Description	Unused	Used
67	A7	£1 blk & vio, *red*	18.00	17.00
		Nos. 54-67 (18)	55.08	51.32

Special Notices

Classification of stamps

The *Scott Standard Postage Stamp Catalogue* lists stamps by country of issue. The next level of organization is a listing by section on the basis of the function of the stamps. The principal sections cover regular postage, semi-postal, air post, special delivery, registration, postage due and other categories. Except for regular postage, catalogue numbers for all sections include a prefix letter (or number-letter combination) denoting the class to which a given stamp belongs.

The following is a listing of the most commonly used catalogue prefixes.

Prefix....Category
C ....Air Post
M...........Military
P............Newspaper
N ....Occupation - Regular Issues
O ....Official
Q............Parcel Post
J..............Postage Due
RA ....Postal Tax
B............Semi-Postal
E............Special Delivery
MR ....War Tax

Other prefixes used by more than one country include the following:
H ....Acknowledgment of Receipt
CO.........Air Post Official
CQ.........Air Post Parcel Post
RAC.......Air Post Postal Tax
CF..........Air Post Registration
CB ....Air Post Semi-Postal
CBO.......Air Post Semi-Postal Official
CE ....Air Post Special Delivery
EY..........Authorized Delivery
S ....Franchise
G ....Insured Letter
GY ....Marine Insurance
MC ....Military Air Post
MQ........Military Parcel Post
NC.........Occupation - Air Post
NO.........Occupation - Official
NJ..........Occupation - Postage Due
NRA.......Occupation - Postal Tax
NB ....Occupation - Semi-Postal
NE ....Occupation - Special Delivery
QY ....Parcel Post Authorized Delivery
AR ....Postal-fiscal
RAJ ....Postal Tax Due
RAB ....Postal Tax Semi-Postal
F.............Registration
EB..........Semi-Postal Special Delivery
EO ....Special Delivery Official
QE ....Special Handling

New issue listings

Updates to this catalogue appear each month in the *Scott Stamp Monthly* magazine. Included in this update are additions to the listings of countries found in the *Scott Standard Postage Stamp Catalogue* and the *Specialized Catalogue of United States Stamps*, as well as corrections and updates to current editions of this catalogue.

From time to time there will be changes in the final listings of stamps from the *Scott Stamp Monthly* to the next edition of the catalogue. This occurs as more information about certain stamps or sets becomes available.

The catalogue update section of the *Scott Stamp Monthly* is the most timely presentation of this material available. Annual subscriptions to the *Scott Stamp Monthly* are available from Scott Publishing Co., Box 828, Sidney, OH 45365-0828.

Number changes

A listing of catalogue number changes from the previous edition of the catalogue appears at the back of each volume.

Understanding valuing notations

The *minimum catalogue value* of an individual stamp or set is 15 cents. This represents a portion of the costs incurred to a dealer when he prepares an individual stamp for resale. As a point of philatelic-economic fact, the lower the value shown for an item in this catalogue, the greater the percentage of that value is attributed to dealer mark up and profit margin. In many cases, such as the 15-cent minimum value, that price does not cover the labor or other costs involved with stocking it as an individual stamp. The sum of minimum values in a set does not properly represent the value of a complete set primarily composed of a number of minimum-value stamps, nor does the sum represent the actual value of a packet made up of minimum-value stamps. Thus a packet of 1,000 different common stamps — each of which has a catalogue value of 15 cents — normally sells for considerably less than 150 dollars!

The *absence of a retail value* for a stamp does not necessarily suggest that a stamp is scarce or rare. In the U.S. listings, a dash in the value column means that the stamp is known in a stated form or variety, but information is either lacking or insufficient for purposes of establishing a usable catalogue value.

Stamp values in *italics* generally refer to items that are difficult to value accurately. For expensive items, such as those priced at $1,000 or higher, a value in italics indicates that the affected item trades very seldom. For inexpensive items, a value in italics represents a warning. One example is a "blocked" issue where the issuing postal administration may have controlled one stamp in a set in an attempt to make the whole set more valuable. Another example is an item that sold at an extreme multiple of face value in the marketplace at the time of its issue.

One type of warning to collectors that appears in the catalogue is illustrated by a stamp that is valued considerably higher in used condition than it is as unused. In this case, collectors are cautioned to be certain the used version has a contemporaneous cancellation. The type of cancellation on a stamp can be an important factor in determining its sale price. Catalogue values do not apply to fiscal or telegraph cancels, unless otherwise noted.

Some countries have released back issues of stamps in canceled-to-order form, sometimes covering at much as a 10-year period. The Scott Catalogue values for used stamps reflect canceled-to-order material when such stamps are found to predominate in the marketplace for the issue involved. Notes frequently appear in the stamp listings to specify which items are valued as canceled-to-order, or if there is a premium for postally used examples.

Many countries sell canceled-to-order stamps at a marked reduction of face value. Countries that sell or have sold canceled-to-order stamps at *full* face value include Australia, Netherlands, France and Switzerland. It may be almost impossible to identify such stamps if the gum has been removed, because official government canceling devices are used. Postally used copies of these items on cover, however, are usually worth more than the canceled-to-order stamps with original gum.

Abbreviations

Scott Publishing Co. uses a consistent set of abbreviations throughout this catalogue to conserve space, while still providing necessary information.

COLOR ABBREVIATIONS

amb .....amber	crim.....crimson	ol ....olive
anil ......aniline	cr ....cream	olvn .....olivine
ap ....apple	dk ....dark	org.......orange
aqua.....aquamarine	dl ....dull	pck ......peacock
az ....azure	dp ....deep	pnksh...pinkish
bis.......bister	db ....drab	Prus .....Prussian
bl ....blue	emer ....emerald	pur.......purple
bld ......blood	gldn .....golden	redsh ...reddish
blk ......black	grysh....grayish	res ....reseda
bril.......brilliant	grn ....green	ros ....rosine
brn.......brown	grnsh ....greenish	ryl........royal
brnsh ...brownish	hel ....heliotrope	sal........salmon
brnz....bronze	hn ....henna	saph....sapphire
brt ......bright	ind ....indigo	scar......scarlet
brnt ....burnt	int........intense	sep........sepia
car ......carmine	lav ....lavender	sien ......sienna
cer ....cerise	lem ......lemon	sil ....silver
chlky....chalky	lil ....lilac	sl ....slate
cham ...chamois	lt..........light	stl ....steel
chnt.....chestnut	mag .....magenta	turq .....turquoise
choc.....chocolate	man .....manila	ultra.....ultramarine
chr.......chrome	mar ....maroon	Ven......Venetian
cit........citron	mv ....mauve	ver ....vermilion
cl ....claret	multi ....multicolored	vio ....violet
cob ......cobalt	mlky ....milky	yel ....yellow
cop ......copper	myr......myrtle	yelsh ....yellowish

When no color is given for an overprint or surcharge, black is the color used. Abbreviations for colors used for overprints and surcharges include: "(B)" or "(Blk)," black; "(Bl)," blue; "(R)," red; and "(G)," green.

Additional abbreviations in this catalogue are shown below:

Adm. ....Administration
AFL ....American Federation of Labor
Anniv. ....Anniversary
APS ....American Philatelic Society
Assoc. ....Association
ASSR. ....Autonomous Soviet Socialist Republic
b......................Born
BEP ....Bureau of Engraving and Printing
Bicent. ....Bicentennial
Bklt.................Booklet
Brit..................British
btwn...............Between
Bur. ....Bureau
c. or ca............Circa
Cat. ....Catalogue
Cent. ....Centennial, century, centenary
CIO ....Congress of Industrial Organizations
Conf. ....Conference
Cong...............Congress
Cpl. ....Corporal
CTO ....Canceled to order
d......................Died
Dbl..................Double
EKU................Earliest known use
Engr.................Engraved
Exhib...............Exhibition
Expo................Exposition
Fed. ....Federation
GB...................Great Britain
Gen. ....General
GPO ....General post office
Horiz. ....Horizontal
Imperf.............Imperforate
Impt. ....Imprint

Intl. ....International
Invtd...............Inverted
L......................Left
Lieut., lt..........Lieutenant
Litho...............Lithographed
LL ....Lower left
LR ....Lower right
mm.................Millimeter
Ms...................Manuscript
Natl. ....National
No...................Number
NY ....New York
NYC ....New York City
Ovpt................Overprint
Ovptd. ....Overprinted
P.....................Plate number
Perf.................Perforated, perforation
Phil.................Philatelic
Photo..............Photogravure
PO ....Post office
Pr. ....Pair
P.R. ....Puerto Rico
Prec................Precancel, precanceled
Pres................President
PTT ....Post, Telephone and Telegraph
Rio..................Rio de Janeiro
Sgt...................Sergeant
Soc. ....Society
Souv. ....Souvenir
SSR.................Soviet Socialist Republic, see ASSR
St.....................Saint, street
Surch..............Surcharge
Typo................Typographed
UL ....Upper left
Unwmkd. ....Unwatermarked
UPU ....Universal Postal Union
UR ....Upper Right
US ....United States
USPOD ....United States Post Office Department
USSR ....Union of Soviet Socialist Republics
Vert. ....Vertical
VP ....Vice president
Wmk. ....Watermark
Wmkd. ....Watermarked
WWI ....World War I
WWII ....World War II

Examination

Scott Publishing Co. will not comment upon the genuineness, grade or condition of stamps, because of the time and responsibility involved. Rather, there are several expertizing groups that undertake this work for both collectors and dealers. Neither will Scott Publishing Co. appraise or identify philatelic material. The company cannot take responsibility for unsolicited stamps or covers sent by individuals.

How to order from your dealer

When ordering stamps from a dealer, it is not necessary to write the full description of a stamp as listed in this catalogue. All you need is the name of the country, the Scott catalogue number and whether the desired item is unused or used. For example, "Japan Scott 422 unused" is sufficient to identify the unused stamp of Japan listed as "422 A206 5y brown."

Basic Stamp Information

A stamp collector's knowledge of the combined elements that make a given stamp issue unique determines his or her ability to identify stamps. These elements include paper, watermark, method of separation, printing, design and gum. On the following pages each of these important areas is briefly described.

Paper

Paper is an organic material composed of a compacted weave of cellulose fibers and generally formed into sheets. Paper used to print stamps may be manufactured in sheets, or it may have been part of a large roll (called a web) before being cut to size. The fibers most often used to create paper on which stamps are printed include bark, wood, straw and certain grasses. In many cases, linen or cotton rags have been added for greater strength and durability. Grinding, bleaching, cooking and rinsing these raw fibers reduces them to a slushy pulp, referred to by paper makers as "stuff." Sizing and, sometimes, coloring matter is added to the pulp to make different types of finished paper.

After the stuff is prepared, it is poured onto sieve-like frames that allow the water to run off, while retaining the matted pulp. As fibers fall onto the screen and are held by gravity, they form a natural weave that will later hold the paper together. If the screen has metal bits that are formed into letters or images attached, it leaves slightly thinned areas on the paper. These are called watermarks.

When the stuff is almost dry, it is passed under pressure through smooth or engraved rollers - dandy rolls - or placed between cloth in a press to be flattened and dried.

Stamp paper falls broadly into two types: wove and laid. The nature of the surface of the frame onto which the pulp is first deposited causes the differences in appearance between the two. If the surface is smooth and even, the paper will be of fairly uniform texture throughout. This is known as *wove paper*. Early papermaking machines poured the pulp onto a continuously circulating web of felt, but modern machines feed the pulp onto a cloth-like screen made of closely interwoven fine wires. This paper, when held to a light, will show little dots or points very close together. The proper name for this is "wire wove," but the type is still considered wove. Any U.S. or British stamp printed after 1880 will serve as an example of wire wove paper.

Closely spaced parallel wires, with cross wires at wider intervals, make up the frames used for what is known as *laid paper*. A greater thickness of the pulp will settle between the wires. The paper, when held to a light, will show alternate light and dark lines. The spacing and the thickness of the lines may vary, but on any one sheet of paper they are all alike. See Russia Scott 31-38 for examples of laid paper.

Batonne, from the French word meaning "a staff," is a term used if the lines in the paper are spaced quite far apart, like the printed ruling on a writing tablet. Batonne paper may be either wove or laid. If laid, fine laid lines can be seen between the batons. The laid lines, which are a form of watermark, may be geometrical figures such as squares, diamonds, rectangles or wavy lines.

Quadrille is the term used when the lines in the paper form little squares. *Oblong quadrille* is the term used when rectangles, rather than squares, are formed. See Mexico-Guadalajara Scott 35-37 for examples of oblong quadrille paper.

Paper also is classified as thick or thin, hard or soft, and by color if dye is added during manufacture. Such colors may include yellowish, greenish, bluish and reddish.

Brief explanations of other types of paper used for printing stamps, as well as examples, follow.

Pelure — Pelure paper is a very thin, hard and often brittle paper that is sometimes bluish or grayish in appearance. See Serbia Scott 169-170.

Native — This is a term applied to handmade papers used to produce some of the early stamps of the Indian states. Stamps printed on native paper may be expected to display various natural inclusions that are normal and do not negatively affect value. Japanese paper, originally made of mulberry fibers and rice flour, is part of this group. See Japan Scott 1-18.

Manila — This type of paper is often used to make stamped envelopes and wrappers. It is a coarse-textured stock, usually smooth on one side and rough on the other. A variety of colors of manila paper exist, but the most common range is yellowish-brown.

Silk — Introduced by the British in 1847 as a safeguard against counterfeiting, silk paper contains bits of colored silk thread scattered throughout. The density of these fibers varies greatly and can include as few as one fiber per stamp or hundreds. U.S. revenue Scott R152 is a good example of an easy-to-identify silk paper stamp.

Silk-thread paper has uninterrupted threads of colored silk arranged so that one or more threads run through the stamp or postal stationery. See Great Britain Scott 5-6 and Switzerland Scott 14-19.

Granite — Filled with minute cloth or colored paper fibers of various colors and lengths, granite paper should not be confused with either type of silk paper. Austria Scott 172-175 and a number of Swiss stamps are examples of granite paper.

Chalky — A chalk-like substance coats the surface of chalky paper to discourage the cleaning and reuse of canceled stamps, as well as to provide a smoother, more acceptable printing surface. Because the designs of stamps printed on chalky paper are imprinted on what is often a water-soluble coating, any attempt to remove a cancellation will destroy the stamp. *Do not soak these stamps in any fluid.* To remove a stamp printed on chalky paper from an envelope, wet the paper from underneath the stamp until the gum dissolves enough to release the stamp from the paper. See St. Kitts-Nevis Scott 89-90 for examples of stamps printed on this type of chalky paper.

India — Another name for this paper, originally introduced from China about 1750, is "China Paper." It is a thin, opaque paper often used for plate and die proofs by many countries.

Double — In philately, the term double paper has two distinct meanings. The first is a two-ply paper, usually a combination of a thick and a thin sheet, joined during manufacture. This type was used experimentally as a means to discourage the reuse of stamps.

The design is printed on the thin paper. Any attempt to remove a cancellation would destroy the design. U.S. Scott 158 and other Banknote-era stamps exist on this form of double paper.

The second type of double paper occurs on a rotary press, when the end of one paper roll, or web, is affixed to the next roll to save time feeding the paper through the press. Stamp designs are printed over the joined paper and, if overlooked by inspectors, may get into post office stocks.

Goldbeater's Skin — This type of paper was used for the 1866 issue of Prussia, and was a tough, translucent paper. The design was printed in reverse on the back of the stamp, and the gum applied over the printing. It is impossible to remove stamps printed on this type of paper from the paper to which they are affixed without destroying the design.

Ribbed — Ribbed paper has an uneven, corrugated surface made by passing the paper through ridged rollers. This type exists on some copies of U.S. Scott 156-165.

Various other substances, or substrates, have been used for stamp manufacture, including wood, aluminum, copper, silver and gold foil, plastic, and silk and cotton fabrics.

Wove · Laid · Granite

Quadrille · Oblong Quadrille · Batonne

Watermarks

Watermarks are an integral part of some papers. They are formed in the process of paper manufacture. Watermarks consist of small designs, formed of wire or cut from metal and soldered to the surface of the mold or, sometimes, on the dandy roll. The designs may be in the form of crowns, stars, anchors, letters or other characters or symbols. These pieces of metal - known in the paper-making industry as "bits" - impress a design into the paper. The design sometimes may be seen by holding the stamp to the light. Some are more easily seen with a watermark detector. This important tool is a small black tray into which a stamp is placed face down and dampened with a fast-evaporating watermark detection fluid that brings up the watermark image in the form of dark lines against a lighter background. These dark lines are the thinner areas of the paper known as the watermark. Some watermarks are extremely difficult to locate, due to either a faint impression, watermark location or the color of the stamp. There also are electric watermark detectors that come with plastic filter disks of various colors. The disks neutralize the color of the stamp, permitting the watermark to be seen more easily.

Multiple watermarks of Crown Agents and Burma

Watermarks of Uruguay, Vatican City and Jamaica

WARNING: Some inks used in the photogravure process dissolve in watermark fluids (Please see the section on Soluble Printing Inks). Also, see "chalky paper."

Watermarks may be found normal, reversed, inverted, reversed and inverted, sideways or diagonal, as seen from the back of the stamp. The relationship of watermark to stamp design depends on the position of the printing plates or how paper is fed through the press. On machine-made paper, watermarks normally are read from right to left. The design is repeated closely throughout the sheet in a "multiple-watermark design." In a "sheet watermark," the design appears only once on the sheet, but extends over many stamps. Individual stamps may carry only a small fraction or none of the watermark.

"Marginal watermarks" occur in the margins of sheets or panes of stamps. They occur on the outside border of paper (ostensibly outside the area where stamps are to be printed). A large row of letters may spell the name of the country or the manufacturer of the paper. Careless press feeding may cause parts of these letters to show on stamps of the outer row of a pane.

Soluble Printing Inks

WARNING: Most stamp colors are permanent; that is, they are not seriously affected by short-term exposure to light or water. Many colors, especially of modern inks, fade from excessive exposure to light. There are stamps printed with inks that dissolve easily in water or in fluids used to detect watermarks. Use of these inks was intentional to prevent the removal of cancellations. Water affects all aniline inks, those on so-called safety paper and some photogravure printings - all such inks are known as *fugitive colors. Removal from paper of such stamps requires care and alternatives to traditional soaking.*

Separation

"Separation" is the general term used to describe methods used to separate stamps. The three standard forms currently in use are perforating, rouletting and die-cutting. These methods are done during the stamp production process, after printing. Sometimes these methods are done on-press or sometimes as a separate step. The earliest issues, such as the 1840 Penny Black of Great Britain (Scott 1), did not have any means provided for separation. It was expected the stamps would be cut apart with scissors or folded and torn. These are examples of imperforate stamps. Many stamps were first issued in imperforate formats and were later issued with perforations. Therefore, care must be observed in buying single imperforate stamps to be certain they were issued imperforate and are not perforated copies that have been altered by having the perforations trimmed away. Stamps issued imperforate usually are valued as singles. However, imperforate varieties of normally perforated stamps should be collected in pairs or larger pieces as indisputable evidence of their imperforate character.

PERFORATION

The chief style of separation of stamps, and the one that is in almost universal use today, is perforating. By this process, paper between the stamps is cut away in a line of holes, usually round, leaving little bridges of paper between the stamps to hold them together. Some types of perforation, such as hyphen-hole perfs, can be confused with roulettes, but a close visual inspection reveals that paper has been removed. The little perforation bridges, which project from the stamp when it is torn from the pane, are called the teeth of the perforation.

As the size of the perforation is sometimes the only way to differentiate between two otherwise identical stamps, it is necessary to be able to accurately measure and describe them. This is done with a perforation gauge, usually a ruler-like device that has dots or graduated lines to show how many perforations may be counted in the space of two centimeters. Two centimeters is the space universally adopted in which to measure perforations.

Perforation gauge

To measure a stamp, run it along the gauge until the dots on it fit exactly into the perforations of the stamp. If you are using a gradu-ated-line perforation gauge, simply slide the stamp along the surface until the lines on the gauge perfectly project from the center of the bridges or holes. The number to the side of the line of dots or lines that fit the stamp's perforation is the measurement. For example, an "11" means that 11 perforations fit between two centimeters. The description of the stamp therefore is "perf. 11." If the gauge of the perforations on the top and bottom of a stamp differs from that on the sides, the result is what is known as *compound perforations.* In measuring compound perforations, the gauge at top and bottom is always given first, then the sides. Thus, a stamp that measures 11 at top and bottom and 10 1/2 at the sides is "perf. 11 x 10 1/2." See U.S. Scott 632-642 for examples of compound perforations.

Stamps also are known with perforations different on three or all four sides. Descriptions of such items are clockwise, beginning with the top of the stamp.

A perforation with small holes and teeth close together is a "fine perforation." One with large holes and teeth far apart is a "coarse perforation." Holes that are jagged, rather than clean-cut, are "rough perforations." *Blind perforations* are the slight impressions left by the perforating pins if they fail to puncture the paper. Multiples of stamps showing blind perforations may command a slight premium over normally perforated stamps.

The term *syncopated perfs* describes intentional irregularities in the perforations. The earliest form was used by the Netherlands from 1925-33, where holes were omitted to create distinctive patterns. Beginning in 1992, Great Britain has used an oval perforation to help prevent counterfeiting. Several other countries have started using the oval perfs.

A new type of perforation, still primarily used for postal stationery, is known as microperfs. Microperfs are tiny perforations (in some cases hundreds of holes per two centimeters) that allows items to be intentionally separated very easily, while not accidentally breaking apart as easily as standard perforations. These are not currently measured or differentiated by size, as are standard perforations.

perce en arc · perce en lignes · perce en points · oblique roulette · perce en scie · perce serpentin

ROULETTING

In rouletting, the stamp paper is cut partly or wholly through, with no paper removed. In perforating, some paper is removed. Rouletting derives its name from the French roulette, a spur-like wheel. As the wheel is rolled over the paper, each point makes a small cut. The number of cuts made in a two-centimeter space determines the gauge of the roulette, just as the number of perforations in two centimeters determines the gauge of the perforation.

The shape and arrangement of the teeth on the wheels varies. Various roulette types generally carry French names:

Perce en lignes - rouletted in lines. The paper receives short, straight cuts in lines. This is the most common type of rouletting. See Mexico Scott 500.

Perce en points - pin-rouletted. This differs from a small perforation because no paper is removed, although round, equidistant holes are pricked through the paper. See Mexico Scott 242-256.

Perce en arc and *perce en scie* - pierced in an arc or saw-toothed designs, forming half circles or small triangles. See Hanover (German States) Scott 25-29.

Perce en serpentin - serpentine roulettes. The cuts form a serpentine or wavy line. See Brunswick (German States) Scott 13-18.

Once again, no paper is removed by these processes, leaving the stamps easily separated, but closely attached.

DIE-CUTTING

The third major form of stamp separation is die-cutting. This is a method where a die in the pattern of separation is created that later cuts the stamp paper in a stroke motion. Although some standard stamps bear die-cut perforations, this process is primarily used for self-adhesive postage stamps. Die-cutting can appear in straight lines, such as U.S. Scott 2522, shapes, such as U.S. Scott 1551, or imitating the appearance of perforations, such as New Zealand Scott 935A and 935B.

Printing Processes

ENGRAVING (Intaglio, Line-engraving, Etching)
Master die - The initial operation in the process of line engraving is making the master die. The die is a small, flat block of softened steel upon which the stamp design is recess engraved in reverse.

Master die

Photographic reduction of the original art is made to the appropriate size. It then serves as a tracing guide for the initial outline of the design. The engraver lightly traces the design on the steel with his graver, then slowly works the design until it is completed. At various points during the engraving process, the engraver hand-inks the die and makes an impression to check his progress. These are known as progressive die proofs. After completion of the engraving, the die is hardened to withstand the stress and pressures of later transfer operations.

Transfer roll

Transfer roll — Next is production of the transfer roll that, as the name implies, is the medium used to transfer the subject from the master die to the printing plate. A blank roll of soft steel, mounted on a mandrel, is placed under the bearers of the transfer press to allow it to roll freely on its axis. The hardened die is placed on the bed of the press and the face of the transfer roll is applied to the die, under pressure. The bed or the roll is then rocked back and forth under increasing pressure, until the soft steel of the roll is forced into every engraved line of the die. The resulting impression on the roll is known as a "relief" or a "relief transfer." The engraved image is now positive in appearance and stands out from the steel. After the required number of reliefs are "rocked in," the soft steel transfer roll is hardened.

Different flaws may occur during the relief process. A defective relief may occur during the rocking in process because of a minute piece of foreign material lodging on the die, or some other cause. Imperfections in the steel of the transfer roll may result in a breaking away of parts of the design. This is known as a relief break, which will show up on finished stamps as small, unprinted areas. If a damaged relief remains in use, it will transfer a repeating defect to the plate. Deliberate alterations of reliefs sometimes occur. "Altered reliefs" designate these changed conditions.

Plate — The final step in pre-printing production is the making of the printing plate. A flat piece of soft steel replaces the die on the bed of the transfer press. One of the reliefs on the transfer roll is positioned over this soft steel. Position, or layout, dots determine the correct position on the plate. The dots have been lightly marked on the plate in advance. After the correct position of the relief is

determined, the design is rocked in by following the same method used in making the transfer roll. The difference is that this time the image is being transferred from the transfer roll, rather than to it. Once the design is entered on the plate, it appears in reverse and is recessed. There are as many transfers entered on the plate as there are subjects printed on the sheet of stamps. It is during this process that double and shifted transfers occur, as well as re-entries. These are the result of improperly entered images that have not been properly burnished out prior to rocking in a new image.

Modern siderography processes, such as those used by the U.S. Bureau of Engraving and Printing, involve an automated form of rocking designs in on preformed cylindrical printing sleeves. The same process also allows for easier removal and re-entry of worn images right on the sleeve.

Transferring the design to the plate

Following the entering of the required transfers on the plate, the position dots, layout dots and lines, scratches and other markings generally are burnished out. Added at this time by the siderographer are any required *guide lines, plate numbers* or other *marginal markings.* The plate is then hand-inked and a proof impression is taken. This is known as a plate proof. If the impression is approved, the plate is machined for fitting onto the press, is hardened and sent to the plate vault ready for use.

On press, the plate is inked and the surface is automatically wiped clean, leaving ink only in the recessed lines. Paper is then forced under pressure into the engraved recessed lines, thereby receiving the ink. Thus, the ink lines on engraved stamps are slightly raised, and slight depressions (debossing) occur on the back of the stamp. Prior to the advent of modern high-speed presses and more advanced ink formulations, paper had to be dampened before receiving the ink. This sometimes led to uneven shrinkage by the time the stamps were perforated, resulting in improperly perforated stamps, or misperfs. Newer presses use drier paper, thus both *wet* and *dry printings* exist on some stamps.

Rotary Press — Until 1914, only flat plates were used to print engraved stamps. Rotary press printing was introduced in 1914, and slowly spread. Some countries still use flat-plate printing.

After approval of the plate proof, older *rotary press plates* require additional machining. They are curved to fit the press cylinder. "Gripper slots" are cut into the back of each plate to receive the "grippers," which hold the plate securely on the press. The plate is then hardened. Stamps printed from these bent rotary press plates are longer or wider than the same stamps printed from flat-plate presses. The stretching of the plate during the curving process is what causes this distortion.

Re-entry — To execute a re-entry on a flat plate, the transfer roll is re-applied to the plate, often at some time after its first use on the press. Worn-out designs can be resharpened by carefully burnishing out the original image and re-entering it from the transfer roll. If the original impression has not been sufficiently removed and the transfer roll is not precisely in line with the remaining impression, the resulting double transfer will make the re-entry obvious. If the registration is true, a re-entry may be difficult or impossible to distinguish. Sometimes a stamp printed from a successful re-entry is identified by having a much sharper and clearer impression than its neighbors. With the advent of rotary presses, post-press re-entries were not possible. After a plate was curved for the rotary press, it was impossible to make a re-entry. This is because the plate had already been bent once (with the design distorted).

However, with the introduction of the previously mentioned modern-style siderography machines, entries are made to the preformed cylindrical printing sleeve. Such sleeves are dechromed and softened. This allows individual images to be burnished out and re-entered on the curved sleeve. The sleeve is then rechromed, resulting in longer press life.

Double Transfer — This is a description of the condition of a transfer on a plate that shows evidence of a duplication of all, or a portion of the design. It usually is the result of the changing of the registration between the transfer roll and the plate during the rocking in of the original entry. Double transfers also occur when only a portion of the design has been rocked in and improper positioning is noted. If the worker elected not to burnish out the partial or completed design, a strong double transfer will occur for part or all of the design.

It sometimes is necessary to remove the original transfer from a plate and repeat the process a second time. If the finished reworked image shows traces of the original impression, attributable to incomplete burnishing, the result is a partial double transfer.

With the modern automatic machines mentioned previously, double transfers are all but impossible to create. Those partially doubled images on stamps printed from such sleeves are more than likely re-entries, rather than true double transfers.

Re-engraved — Alterations to a stamp design are sometimes necessary after some stamps have been printed. In some cases, either the original die or the actual printing plate may have its "temper" drawn (softened), and the design will be re-cut. The resulting impressions from such a re-engraved die or plate may differ slightly from the original issue, and are known as "re-engraved." If the alteration was made to the master die, all future printings will be consistently different from the original. If alterations were made to the printing plate, each altered stamp on the plate will be slightly different from each other, allowing specialists to reconstruct a complete printing plate.

Dropped Transfers — If an impression from the transfer roll has not been properly placed, a dropped transfer may occur. The final stamp image will appear obviously out of line with its neighbors.

Short Transfer — Sometimes a transfer roll is not rocked its entire length when entering a transfer onto a plate. As a result, the finished transfer on the plate fails to show the complete design, and the finished stamp will have an incomplete design printed. This is known as a "short transfer." U.S. Scott No. 8 is a good example of a short transfer.

TYPOGRAPHY (Letterpress, Surface Printing, Flexography, Dry Offset, High Etch)

Although the word "Typography" is obsolete as a term describing a printing method, it was the accepted term throughout the first century of postage stamps. Therefore, appropriate Scott listings in this catalogue refer to typographed stamps. The current term for this form of printing, however, is "letterpress."

As it relates to the production of postage stamps, letterpress printing is the reverse of engraving. Rather than having recessed areas trap the ink and deposit it on paper, only the raised areas of the design are inked. This is comparable to the type of printing seen by inking and using an ordinary rubber stamp. Letterpress includes all printing where the design is above the surface area, whether it is wood, metal or, in some instances, hardened rubber or polymer plastic.

For most letterpress-printed stamps, the engraved master is made in much the same manner as for engraved stamps. In this instance, however, an additional step is needed. The design is transferred to another surface before being transferred to the transfer roll. In this way, the transfer roll has a recessed stamp design, rather than one done in relief. This makes the printing areas on the final plate raised, or relief areas.

For less-detailed stamps of the 19th century, the area on the die not used as a printing surface was cut away, leaving the surface area raised. The original die was then reproduced by stereotyping or electrotyping. The resulting electrotypes were assembled in the required number and format of the desired sheet of stamps. The plate used in printing the stamps was an electroplate of these assembled electrotypes.

Once the final letterpress plates are created, ink is applied to the raised surface and the pressure of the press transfers the ink impression to the paper. In contrast to engraving, the fine lines of letterpress are impressed on the surface of the stamp, leaving a debossed surface. When viewed from the back (as on a typewritten page), the corresponding line work on the stamp will be raised slightly (embossed) above the surface.

PHOTOGRAVURE (Gravure, Rotogravure, Heliogravure)

In this process, the basic principles of photography are applied to a chemically sensitized metal plate, rather than photographic paper. The design is transferred photographically to the plate through a halftone, or dot-matrix screen, breaking the reproduction into tiny dots. The plate is treated chemically and the dots form depressions, called cells, of varying depths and diameters, depending on the degrees of shade in the design. Then, like engraving, ink is applied to the plate and the surface is wiped clean. This leaves ink in the tiny cells that is lifted out and deposited on the paper when it is pressed against the plate.

Gravure is most often used for multicolored stamps, generally using the three primary colors (red, yellow and blue) and black. By varying the dot matrix pattern and density of these colors, virtually any color can be reproduced. A typical full-color gravure stamp will be created from four printing cylinders (one for each color). The original multicolored image will have been photographically separated into its component colors.

For examples of the first photogravure stamps printed (1914), see Bavaria Scott 94-114.

LITHOGRAPHY (Offset Lithography, Stone Lithography, Dilitho, Planography, Collotype)

The principle that oil and water do not mix is the basis for lithography. The stamp design is drawn by hand or transferred from engraving to the surface of a lithographic stone or metal plate in a greasy (oily) substance. This oily substance holds the ink, which will later be transferred to the paper. The stone (or plate) is wet with an acid fluid, causing it to repel the printing ink in all areas not covered by the greasy substance.

Transfer paper is used to transfer the design from the original stone or plate. A series of duplicate transfers are grouped and, in turn, transferred to the final printing plate.

Photolithography — The application of photographic processes to lithography. This process allows greater flexibility of design, related to use of halftone screens combined with line work. Unlike photogravure or engraving, this process can allow large, solid areas to be printed.

Offset — A refinement of the lithographic process. A rubber-covered blanket cylinder takes the impression from the inked lithographic plate. From the "blanket" the impression is *offset* or transferred to the paper. Greater flexibility and speed are the principal reasons offset printing has largely displaced lithography. The term "lithography" covers both processes, and results are almost identical.

EMBOSSED (Relief) Printing
Embossing, not considered one of the four main printing types, is a method in which the design first is sunk into the metal of the die. Printing is done against a yielding platen, such as leather or linoleum. The platen is forced into the depression of the die, thus forming the design on the paper in relief. This process is often used for metallic inks.

Embossing may be done without color (see Sardinia Scott 4-6); with color printed around the embossed area (see Great Britain Scott 5 and most U.S. envelopes); and with color in exact registration with the embossed subject (see Canada Scott 656-657).

COMBINATION PRINTINGS
Sometimes two or even three printing methods are combined in producing stamps. In these cases, such as Austria Scott 933, the stamp's dual printing technique can be determined by studying the individual characteristics of each printing type (intaglio and offset). A few stamps, such as Singapore Scott 684-684A, combine as many as three of the four major printing types (offset, intaglio and letterpress). When this is done it often indicates the incorporation of security devices against counterfeiting.

INK COLORS
Inks or colored papers used in stamp printing often are of mineral origin, although there are numerous examples of organic-based pigments. As a general rule, organic-based pigments are far more subject to varieties and change than those of mineral-based origin.

The appearance of any given color on a stamp may be affected by many aspects, including printing variations, light, color of paper, aging and chemical alterations.

Numerous printing variations may be observed. Heavier pressure or inking will cause a more intense color, while slight interruptions in the ink feed or lighter impressions will cause a lighter appearance. Stamps printed in the same color by water-based and solvent-based inks can differ significantly in appearance. This affects several stamps in the U.S. Prominent Americans series. Hand-mixed ink formulas (primarily from the 19th century) produced under different conditions (humidity and temperature) account for notable color variations in early printings of the same stamp (see U.S. Scott 248-250, 279B, for example). Different sources of pigment can also result in significant differences in color.

Light exposure and aging are closely related in the way they affect stamp color. Both eventually break down the ink and fade colors, so that a carefully kept stamp may differ significantly in color from an identical copy that has been exposed to light. If stamps are exposed to light either intentionally or accidentally, their colors can be faded or completely changed in some cases.

Papers of different quality and consistency used for the same stamp printing may affect color appearance. Most pelure papers, for example, show a richer color when compared with wove or laid papers. See Russia Scott 181a, for an example of this effect.

The very nature of the printing processes can cause a variety of differences in shades or hues of the same stamp. Some of these shades are scarcer than others, and are of particular interest to the advanced collector.

Luminescence

All forms of tagged stamps fall under the general category of luminescence. Within this broad category is fluorescence, dealing with forms of tagging visible under longwave ultraviolet light, and phosphorescence, which deals with tagging visible only under shortwave light. Phosphorescence leaves an afterglow and fluorescence does not. These treated stamps show up in a range of different colors when exposed to UV light. The differing wavelengths of the light activates the tagging material, making it glow in various colors that usually serve different mail processing purposes.

Intentional tagging is a post-World War II phenomenon, brought about by the increased literacy rate and rapidly growing mail volume. It was one of several answers to the problem of the need for more automated mail processes. Early tagged stamps served the purpose of triggering machines to separate different types of mail. A natural outgrowth was to also use the signal to trigger machines that faced all envelopes the same way and canceled them.

Tagged stamps come many different ways and in different forms. Some tagged stamps have luminescent shapes or images imprinted on them as a form of security device. Others have blocks (United States), stripes, frames (South Africa and Canada), overall coatings (United States), bars (Great Britain and Canada) and many other types. Some types of tagging are even mixed in with the pigmented printing ink (Australia Scott 366, Netherlands Scott 478 and U.S. Scott 1359 and 2443). Each form of tagging has a different purpose, some to give different machines different types of signals, and others as adaptive forms of technological growth.

The means of applying taggant to stamps differs as much as the intended purposes for the stamps. The most common form of tagging is a coating applied to the surface of the printed stamp. Since the taggant ink is frequently invisible except under UV light, it does not interfere with the appearance of the stamp. Another common application is the use of phosphored papers. In this case the paper itself either has a coating of taggant applied before the stamp is printed or has taggant applied during the papermaking process, incorporating it into the fibers. This is currently in use in the United States. A similar form is the application of a fluorescent coating either to the finished paper or during the papermaking process. This type of tagging has been extensively used by Australia and Germany.

Many countries now use tagging in various forms to either expedite mail handling or to serve as a printing security device against counterfeiting. Following the introduction of tagged stamps for public use in 1959 by Great Britain, other countries have steadily joined the parade. Among those are Germany (1961); Canada and Denmark (1962); United States, Australia, France and Switzerland (1963); Belgium and Japan (1966); Sweden and Norway (1967); Italy (1968); and Russia (1969). Since then, many other countries have begun using forms of tagging, including Brazil, China, Czechoslovakia, Hong Kong, Guatemala, Indonesia, Israel, Lithuania, Luxembourg, Netherlands, Penrhyn Islands, Portugal, St. Vincent, Singapore, South Africa, Spain and Sweden to name a few.

In some cases, including United States, Canada, Great Britain and Switzerland, stamps were released both with and without tagging. Many of these were released during each country's experimental period. Tagged and untagged versions are listed for the aforementioned countries and are noted in some other countries' listings. For at least a few stamps, the experimentally tagged version is worth far more than its untagged counterpart, such as the 1963 experimental tagged version of France Scott 1024.

In some cases luminescent varieties of stamps were inadvertently created. Several Russian stamps, for example, sport highly fluorescent ink that was not intended as a form of tagging. Older stamps, such as early U.S. postage dues, can be positively identified by the use of UV light, since the organic ink used has become slightly fluorescent over time. Other stamps, such as Austria Scott 70a-82a (varnish bars) and Obock Scott 46-64 (printed quadrille lines), have become fluorescent over time.

Various fluorescent substances have been added to paper to make it appear brighter. These optical brightners, as they are known, greatly affect the appearance of the stamp under UV light. The brightest of these is known as Hi-Brite paper. These paper varieties are beyond the scope of the Scott Catalogue.

Shortwave UV light also is used extensively in expertizing, since each form of paper has its own fluorescent characteristics that are impossible to perfectly match. It is therefore a simple matter to detect filled thins, added perforation teeth and other alterations that involve the addition of paper. UV light also is used to examine stamps that have had cancels chemically removed and for other purposes as well.

Gum

The gum on the back of a stamp may be shiny, dull, smooth, rough, dark, white, colored or tinted. It may be obvious or virtually impossible to distinguish, as on Canada Scott 453 or Rwanda Scott 287-294. Most stamp gumming adhesives use gum arabic or dextrine as a base. Certain polymers such as polyvinyl alcohol (PVA) have been used extensively since World War II. The PVA gum used by security printers Harrison and Sons since 1968 is dull-surfaced, slightly yellowish and almost invisible.

The *Scott Standard Postage Stamp Catalogue* does not list items by types of gum. The *Scott Specialized Catalogue of United States Stamps* does differentiate among some types of gum for certain issues.

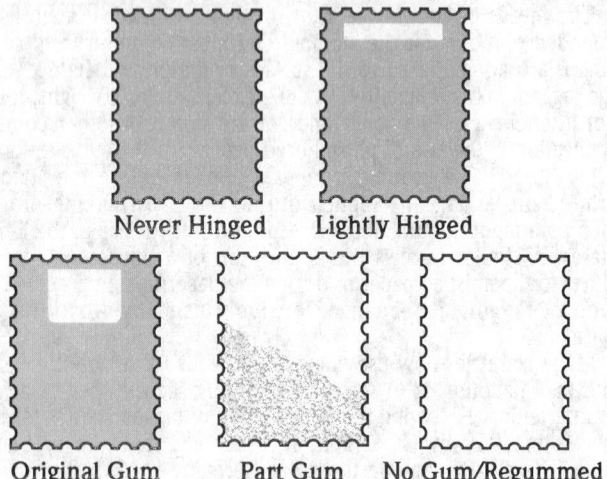

Never Hinged   Lightly Hinged

Original Gum   Part Gum   No Gum/Regummed

For purposes of determining the condition of an unused stamp, Scott Publishing Co. presents the following definitions (with accompanying illustrations): **Never Hinged (NH)** - Full original gum with no hinge mark or other blemish or disturbance. The presence of an expertizer's mark does not disqualify a stamp from this designation; **Lightly Hinged (LH)** - Full original gum with a light disturbance of the gum from the removal of a peelable hinge; **Original Gum (OG)** - Hinging and other disturbances should affect 20 percent or less of the original gum. **Part Gum (PG)** - Between 20 and 80 percent of the original gum remains. The stamp may have hinge remnants; **No Gum (NG) or Regummed (RE)** - A stamp with no gum or less than 20 percent of the original gum. A regummed stamp is considered the same as a stamp with none of its original gum for purposes of grading.

Reprints of stamps may have gum differing from the original issues. In addition, some countries have used different gum formulas for different seasons. These adhesives have different properties that may become more apparent over time.

Many stamps have been issued without gum, and the catalogue will note this fact. See United States Scott PR33-PR56. Sometimes, gum may have been removed to preserve the stamp. Germany Scott B68, for example, has a highly acidic gum that eventually destroys the stamps. This item is valued in the catalogue with gum removed.

Reprints and Reissues

These are impressions of stamps (usually obsolete) made from the original plates or stones. If they are valid for postage and reproduce obsolete issues (such as U.S.Scott 2875), the stamps are *reissues*. If they are from current issues, they are designated as *second, third,* etc., *printing*. If designated for a particular purpose, they are *special printings*.

Scott will list those reissues and reprints that are valid for postage if they differ significantly from the original printing.

When reprints are not valid for postage, but are made from original dies and plates by authorized persons, they are *official reprints*. *Private reprints* are made from original plates and dies by private hands. *Official reproductions* or imitations are made from new dies and plates by government authorization.

The U.S. government made official imitations of its first postage stamps in 1875. Produced were copies of the first two stamps (listed as Scott 3-4), reprints of the demonetized pre-1861 issues and reissues of the 1861 stamps, the 1869 stamps and the then-current 1875 denominations. An example of a private reprint is that of the New Haven, Conn., postmaster's provisional.

Most reprints differ slightly from the original stamp in some characteristic, such as gum, paper, perforation, color or watermark. Sometimes the details are followed so meticulously that only a student of that specific stamp is able to distinguish the reprint from the original.

Remainders and Canceled to Order

Some countries sell their stock of old stamps when a new issue replaces them. To avoid postal use, the *remainders* usually are canceled with a punch hole, a heavy line or bar, or a more-or-less regular-looking cancellation. The most famous merchant of remainders was Nicholas F. Seebeck. In the 1880s and 1890s, he arranged printing contracts between the Hamilton Bank Note Co., of which he was a director, and several Central and South American countries. The contracts provided that the plates and all remainders of the yearly issues became the property of Hamilton. Seebeck saw to it that ample stock remained. The "Seebecks," both remainders and reprints, were standard packet fillers for decades.

Some countries also issue stamps *canceled-to-order (CTO),* either in sheets with original gum or stuck onto pieces of paper or envelopes and canceled. Such CTO items generally are worth less than postally used stamps. In cases where the CTO material is far more prevalent in the marketplace than postally used examples, the catalogue value relates to the CTO examples, with postally used examples noted as premium items. Most CTOs can be detected by the presence of gum. However, as the CTO practice goes back at least to 1885, the gum inevitably has been soaked off some stamps so they could pass as postally used. The normally applied postmarks usually differ slightly from standard postmarks, and specialists are able to tell the difference. When applied individually to envelopes by philatelically minded persons, CTO material is known as *favor canceled* and generally sells at large discounts.

Cinderellas and Facsimiles

Cinderella is a catch-all term used by stamp collectors to describe phantoms, fantasies, bogus items, municipal issues, exhibition seals, local revenues, transportation stamps, labels, poster stamps and many other types of items. Some cinderella collectors include in their collections local postage issues, telegraph stamps, essays and proofs, forgeries and counterfeits.

A *fantasy* is an adhesive created for a nonexistent stamp-issuing authority. Fantasy items range from imaginary countries (Occusi-Ambeno, Kingdom of Sedang, Principality of Trinidad or Torres Straits), to non-existent locals (Winans City Post), or nonexistent transportation lines (McRobish & Co.'s Acapulco-San Francisco Line).

On the other hand, if the entity exists and could have issued stamps (but did not) or was known to have issued other stamps, the items are considered *bogus* stamps. These would include the Mormon postage stamps of Utah, S. Allan Taylor's Guatemala and Paraguay inventions, the propaganda issues for the South Moluccas and the adhesives of the Page & Keyes local post of Boston.

Phantoms is another term for both fantasy and bogus issues.

Facsimiles are copies or imitations made to represent original stamps, but which do not pretend to be originals. A catalogue illustration is such a facsimile. Illustrations from the Moens catalogue of the last century were occasionally colored and passed off as stamps. Since the beginning of stamp collecting, facsimiles have been made for collectors as space fillers or for reference. They often carry the word "facsimile," "falsch" (German), "sanko" or "mozo" (Japanese), or "faux" (French) overprinted on the face or stamped on the back. Unfortunately, over the years a number of these items have had fake cancels applied over the facsimile notation and have been passed off as genuine.

Forgeries and Counterfeits

Forgeries and counterfeits have been with philately virtually from the beginning of stamp production. Over time, the terminology for the two has been used interchangeably. Although both forgeries and counterfeits are reproductions of stamps, the purposes behind their creation differ considerably.

Among specialists there is an increasing movement to more specifically define such items. Although there is no universally accepted terminology, we feel the following definitions most closely mirror the items and their purposes as they are currently defined.

Forgeries (also often referred to as *Counterfeits*) are reproductions of genuine stamps that have been created to defraud collectors. Such spurious items first appeared on the market around 1860, and most old-time collections contain one or more. Many are crude and easily spotted, but some can deceive experts.

An important supplier of these early philatelic forgeries was the Hamburg printer Gebruder Spiro. Many others with reputations in this craft included S. Allan Taylor, George Hussey, James Chute, George Forune, Benjamin & Sarpy, Julius Goldner, E. Oneglia and L.H. Mercier. Among the noted 20th-century forgers were Francois Fournier, Jean Sperati and the prolific Raoul DeThuin.

Forgeries may be complete replications, or they may be genuine stamps altered to resemble a scarcer (and more valuable) type. Most forgeries, particularly those of rare stamps, are worth only a small fraction of the value of a genuine example, but a few types, created by some of the most notable forgers, such as Sperati, can be worth as much or more than the genuine. Fraudulently produced copies are known of most classic rarities and many medium-priced stamps.

In addition to rare stamps, large numbers of common 19th- and early 20th-century stamps were forged to supply stamps to the early packet trade. Many can still be easily found. Few new philatelic forgeries have appeared in recent decades. Successful imitation of well-engraved work is virtually impossible. It has proven far easier to produce a fake by altering a genuine stamp than to duplicate a stamp completely.

Counterfeit (also often referred to as *Postal Counterfeit* or *Postal Forgery*) is the term generally applied to reproductions of stamps that have been created to defraud the government of revenue. Such items usually are created at the time a stamp is current and, in some cases, are hard to detect. Because most counterfeits are seized when the perpetrator is captured, postal counterfeits, particularly used on cover, are usually worth much more than a genuine example to specialists. The first postal counterfeit was of Spain's 4-cuarto carmine of 1854 (the real one is Scott 25). Apparently, the counterfeiters were not satisfied with their first version, which is now very scarce, and they soon created an engraved counterfeit, which is common. Postal counterfeits quickly followed in Austria, Naples, Sardinia and the Roman States. They have since been created in many other countries as well, including the United States.

An infamous counterfeit to defraud the government is the 1-shilling Great Britain "Stock Exchange" forgery of 1872, used on telegraph forms at the exchange that year. The stamp escaped detection until a stamp dealer noticed it in 1898.

Fakes

Fakes are genuine stamps altered in some way to make them more desirable. One student of this part of stamp collecting has estimated that by the 1950s more than 30,000 varieties of fakes were known. That number has grown greatly since then. The widespread existence of fakes makes it important for stamp collectors to study their philatelic holdings and use relevant literature. Likewise, collectors should buy from reputable dealers who guarantee their stamps and make full and prompt refunds should a purchased item be declared faked or altered by some mutually agreed-upon authority. Because fakes always have some genuine characteristics, it is not always possible to obtain unanimous agreement among experts regarding specific items. These students may change their opinions as philatelic knowledge increases. More than 80 percent of all fakes on the philatelic market today are regummed, reperforated (or perforated for the first time), or bear forged overprints, surcharges or cancellations.

Stamps can be chemically treated to alter or eliminate colors. For example, a pale rose stamp can be re-colored to resemble a blue shade of high market value. In other cases, treated stamps can be made to resemble missing color varieties. Designs may be changed by painting, or a stroke or a dot added or bleached out to turn an ordinary variety into a seemingly scarcer stamp. Part of a stamp can be bleached and reprinted in a different version, achieving an inverted center or frame. Margins can be added or repairs done so deceptively that the stamps move from the "repaired" into the "fake" category.

Fakers have not left the backs of the stamps untouched either. They may create false watermarks, add fake grills or press out genuine grills. A thin India paper proof may be glued onto a thicker backing to create the appearance an issued stamp, or a proof printed on cardboard may be shaved down and perforated to resemble a stamp. Silk threads are impressed into paper and stamps have been split so that a rare paper variety is added to an otherwise inexpensive stamp. The most common treatment to the back of a stamp, however, is regumming.

Some in the business of faking stamps have openly advertised fool-proof application of "original gum" to stamps that lack it, although most publications now ban such ads from their pages. It is believed that very few early stamps have survived without being hinged. The large number of never-hinged examples of such earlier material offered for sale thus suggests the widespread extent of regumming activity. Regumming also may be used to hide repairs or thin spots. Dipping the stamp into watermark fluid, or examining it under longwave ultraviolet light often will reveal these flaws.

Fakers also tamper with separations. Ingenious ways to add margins are known. Perforated wide-margin stamps may be falsely represented as imperforate when trimmed. Reperforating is commonly done to create scarce coil or perforation varieties, and to eliminate the naturally occurring straight-edge stamps found in sheet margin positions of many earlier issues. Custom has made straight-edged stamps less desirable. Fakers have obliged by perforating straight-edged stamps so that many are now uncommon, if not rare.

Another fertile field for the faker is that of overprints, surcharges and cancellations. The forging of rare surcharges or overprints began in the 1880s or 1890s. These forgeries are sometimes difficult to detect, but experts have identified almost all. Occasionally, overprints or cancellations are removed to create non-overprinted stamps or seemingly unused items. This is most commonly done by removing a manuscript cancel to make a stamp resemble an unused example. "SPECIMEN" overprints may be removed by scraping and repainting to create non-overprinted varieties. Fakers use inexpensive revenues or pen-canceled stamps to generate unused stamps for further faking by adding other markings. The quartz lamp or UV lamp and a high-powered magnifying glass help to easily detect removed cancellations.

The bigger problem, however, is the addition of overprints, surcharges or cancellations - many with such precision that they are very difficult to ascertain. Plating of the stamps or the overprint can be an important method of detection.

Fake postmarks may range from many spurious fancy cancellations to a host of markings applied to transatlantic covers, to adding normally appearing postmarks to definitives of some countries with stamps that are valued far higher used than unused. With the increased popularity of cover collecting, and the widespread interest in postal history, a fertile new field for fakers has come about. Some have tried to create entire covers. Others specialize in adding stamps, tied by fake cancellations, to genuine stampless covers, or replacing less expensive or damaged stamps with more valuable ones. Detailed study of postal rates in effect at the time a cover in question was mailed, including the analysis of each handstamp used during the period, ink analysis and similar techniques, usually will unmask the fraud.

Restoration and Repairs

Scott Publishing Co. bases its catalogue values on stamps that are free of defects and otherwise meet the standards set forth earlier in this introduction. Most stamp collectors desire to have the finest copy of an item possible. Even within given grading categories there are variances. This leads to a controversial practice that is not defined in any universal manner: stamp *restoration*.

There are broad differences of opinion about what is permissible when it comes to restoration. Carefully applying a soft eraser to a stamp or cover to remove light soiling is one form of restoration, as is washing a stamp in mild soap and water to clean it. These are fairly accepted forms of restoration. More severe forms of restoration include pressing out creases or removing stains caused by tape. To what degree each of these is acceptable is dependent upon the individual situation. Further along the spectrum is the freshening of a stamp's color by removing oxide build-up or the effects of wax paper left next to stamps shipped to the tropics.

At some point in this spectrum the concept of *repair* replaces that of restoration. Repairs include filling thin spots, mending tears by reweaving or adding a missing perforation tooth. Regumming stamps may have been acceptable as a restoration or repair technique many decades ago, but today it is considered a form of fakery.

Restored stamps may or may not sell at a discount, and it is possible that the value of individual restored items may be enhanced over that of their pre-restoration state. Specific situations dictate the resultant value of such an item. Repaired stamps sell at substantial discounts from the value of sound stamps.

When the purchaser of an item has any reason to suspect that an item has been repaired, and the detection of such a repair is beyond his own ability, he should seek expert advice. There are services that specialize in giving such advice.

Terminology

Booklets — Many countries have issued stamps in small booklets for the convenience of users. This idea continues to become increasingly popular in many countries. Booklets have been issued in many sizes and forms, often with advertising on the covers, the panes of stamps or on the interleaving.

The panes used in booklets may be printed from special plates or made from regular sheets. All panes from booklets issued by the United States and many from those of other countries contain stamps that are straight edged on the sides, but perforated between. Others are distinguished by orientation of watermark or other identifying features. Any stamp-like unit in the pane, either printed or blank, that is not a postage stamp is considered to be a *label* in the catalogue listings.

Scott lists and values booklet panes only. Complete booklets are listed and valued in only a few cases, such as Grenada Scott 1055 and some forms of British prestige booklets. Individual booklet panes are listed only when they are not fashioned from existing sheet stamps and, therefore, are identifiable from their sheet stamp counterparts.

Panes usually do not have a used value assigned to them because there is little market activity for used booklet panes, even though many exist used and there is some demand for them.

Cancellations — The marks or obliterations put on stamps by postal authorities to show that they have performed service and to prevent their reuse are known as cancellations. If the marking is made with a pen, it is considered a "pen cancel." When the location of the post office appears in the marking, it is a "town cancellation." A "postmark" is technically any postal marking, but in practice the term generally is applied to a town cancellation with a date. When calling attention to a cause or celebration, the marking is known as a "slogan cancellation." Many other types and styles of cancellations exist, such as duplex, numerals, targets, fancy and others. See also "precancels," below.

Coil Stamps — These are stamps that are issued in rolls for use in dispensers, affixing and vending machines. Those coils of the United States, Canada, Sweden and some other countries are perforated horizontally or vertically only, with the outer edges imperforate. Coil stamps of some countries, such as Great Britain and Germany, are perforated on all four sides and may in some cases be distinguished from their sheet stamp counterparts by watermarks, counting numbers on the reverse or other means.

Covers — Entire envelopes, with or without adhesive postage stamps, that have passed through the mail and bear postal or other markings of philatelic interest are known as covers. Before the introduction of envelopes in about 1840, people folded letters and wrote the address on the outside. Some people covered their letters with an extra sheet of paper on the outside for the address, producing the term "cover." Used airletter sheets, stamped envelopes and other items of postal stationery also are considered covers.

Errors — Stamps that have some major, consistent unintentional deviation from the normal are considered errors. Errors include, but are not limited to, missing or wrong colors, wrong paper, wrong watermarks, inverted centers or frames on multicolor printing, inverted or missing surcharges or overprints, double impressions, missing perforations and others. Factually wrong or misspelled information, if it appears on all examples of a stamp, are not considered errors in the true sense of the word. They are errors of design. Inconsistent or randomly appearing items, such as misperfs or color shifts, are classified as freaks.

Overprints and Surcharges — Overprinting involves applying wording or design elements over an already existing stamp. Overprints can be used to alter the place of use (such as "Canal Zone" on U.S. stamps), to adapt them for a special purpose ("Porto" on Denmark's 1913-20 regular issues for use as postage due stamps, Scott J1-J7) or to commemorate a special occasion (United States Scott 647-648).

A *surcharge* is a form of overprint that changes or restates the face value of a stamp or piece of postal stationery.

Surcharges and overprints may be handstamped, typeset or, occasionally, lithographed or engraved. A few hand-written overprints and surcharges are known.

Precancels — Stamps that are canceled before they are placed in the mail are known as precancels. Precanceling usually is done to expedite the handling of large mailings and generally allow the affected mail pieces to skip certain phases of mail handling.

In the United States, precancellations generally identified the point of origin; that is, the city and state. This information appeared across the face of the stamp, usually centered between parallel lines. More recently, bureau precancels retained the parallel lines, but the city and state designations were dropped. Recent coils have a service inscription that is present on the original printing plate. These show the mail service paid for by the stamp. Since these stamps are not intended to receive further cancellations when used as intended, they are considered precancels. Such items often do not have parallel lines as part of the precancellation.

In France, the abbreviation *Affranchts* in a semicircle together with the word *Postes* is the general form of precancel in use. Belgian precancellations usually appear in a box in which the name of the city appears. Netherlands precancels have the name of the city enclosed between concentric circles, sometimes called a "lifesaver." Precancellations of other countries usually follow these patterns, but may be any arrangement of bars, boxes and city names.

Precancels are listed in the Scott catalogues only if the precancel changes the denomination (Belgium Scott 477-478); if the precanceled stamp is different from the non-precanceled version (such as untagged U.S. precancels); or if the stamp exists only precanceled (France Scott 1096-1099, U.S. Scott 2265).

Proofs and Essays — Proofs are impressions taken from an approved die, plate or stone in which the design and color are the same as the stamp issued to the public. Trial color proofs are impressions taken from approved dies, plates or stones in colors that vary from the final version. An essay is the impression of a design that differs in some way from the issued stamp. "Progressive die proofs" generally are considered to be essays.

Provisionals — These are stamps that are issued on short notice and intended for temporary use pending the arrival of regular issues. They usually are issued to meet such contingencies as changes in government or currency, shortage of necessary postage values or military occupation.

During the 1840s, postmasters in certain American cities issued stamps that were valid only at specific post offices. In 1861, postmasters of the Confederate States also issued stamps with limited validity. Both of these examples are known as "postmaster's provisionals."

Se-tenant — This term refers to an unsevered pair, strip or block of stamps that differ in design, denomination or overprint.

Unless the se-tenant item has a continuous design (see U.S. Scott 1451a, 1694a) the stamps do not have to be in the same order as shown in the catalogue (see U.S. Scott 2158a).

Specimens — The Universal Postal Union required member nations to send samples of all stamps they released into service to the International Bureau in Switzerland. Member nations of the UPU received these specimens as samples of what stamps were valid for postage. Many are overprinted, handstamped or initial-perforated "Specimen," "Canceled" or "Muestra." Some are marked with bars across the denominations (China-Taiwan), punched holes (Czechoslovakia) or back inscriptions (Mongolia).

Stamps distributed to government officials or for publicity purposes, and stamps submitted by private security printers for official approval, also may receive such defacements.

The previously described defacement markings prevent postal use, and all such items generally are known as "specimens."

Tete Beche — This term describes a pair of stamps in which one is upside down in relation to the other. Some of these are the result of intentional sheet arrangements, such as Morocco Scott B10-B11. Others occurred when one or more electrotypes accidentally were placed upside down on the plate, such as Colombia Scott 57a. Separation of the tete-beche stamps, of course, destroys the tete beche variety.

Currency Conversion

Country	Dollar	Pound	S Franc	Guilder	Yen	Lira	HK Dollar	D-Mark	Fr Franc	Cdn Dollar	Aust Dollar
Australia	1.347	2.174	1.188	0.8762	0.0161	0.0008	0.1742	0.9806	0.275	0.9936	....
Canada	1.356	2.188	1.195	0.8818	0.0162	0.0008	0.1753	0.9869	0.2768	....	1.007
France	4.899	7.903	4.318	3.186	0.058	0.0030	0.6334	3.565	....	3.613	3.636
Germany	1.374	2.217	1.211	0.894	0.016	0.0008	0.1777	....	0.2805	1.013	1.02
Hong Kong	7.734	12.476	6.817	5.029	0.0922	0.0047	....	5.628	1.578	5.703	5.739
Italy	1637.5	2641.6	1443.2	1064.8	19.53	....	211.73	1191.7	334.25	1207.5	1215.3
Japan	83.85	135.26	73.903	54.526	....	0.0512	10.844	61.02	17.116	61.8327	62.231
Netherlands	1.538	2.481	1.355	....	0.0183	0.0009	0.1988	1.119	0.3139	1.134	1.141
Switzerland	1.135	1.830	....	0.7378	0.0135	0.0007	0.1467	0.8257	0.2316	0.8367	0.8421
U.K.	0.6199	....	0.5464	0.4031	0.0074	0.0004	0.0802	0.4511	0.1265	0.4571	0.4601
U.S.	....	1.613	0.8814	0.6503	0.0119	0.0006	0.1293	0.7277	0.2041	0.7374	0.7422

Country	Currency	U.S. $ Equiv.
Romania	leu	.00052
Russia	ruble	.00019
Rwanda	franc	.0045
St. Pierre & Miquelon	French franc	.2041
St. Thomas & Prince	dobra	.00062
Salvador, El	colon	.1143
San Marino	lira	.0006
Saudi Arabia	riyal	.2666
Senegal	Community of French Africa (CFA) franc	.0020
Slovakia	koruna	.0344
Slovenia	tolar	.00895
Spain	peseta	.0082
Surinam	guilder	.0024
Sweden	krona	.1383
Switzerland	franc	.8814
Syria	piastre	.0239
Tadjikistan	ruble	.00019
Thailand	baht	.0407
Togo	CFA franc	.0020
Tunisia	dinar	1.085
Turkey	lira	.000023
Turkish Republic of Northern Cyprus	Turkish lira	.000023
Turkmenistan	ruble	.00019
Ukraine	karbovanetz	.000076
United Arab Emirates	dihram	.2724
Uruguay	nuevo peso	.1664
Uzbekistan	ruble	.00019
Vatican City	lire	.00061
Venezuela	bolivar	.0059
Wallis & Futuna	Community of French Pacific (CFP) franc	.0112
Zaire	new zaire	.00025

Colonies, Former Colonies, Offices, Territories Controlled by Parent States information can be found on page 994.

Source: *Wall Street Journal* May 8, 1995. Figures reflect values as of May 5, 1995.

Common Design Types

Pictured in this section are issues where one illustration has been used for a number of countries in the Catalogue. Not included in this section are overprinted stamps or those issues which are illustrated in each country.

EUROPA
Europa Issue, 1956

The design symbolizing the cooperation among the six countries comprising the Coal and Steel Community is illustrated in each country.

Belgium	496-497
France	805-806
Germany	748-749
Italy	715-716
Luxembourg	318-320
Netherlands	368-369

Europa Issue, 1958

"E" and Dove – CD1

European Postal Union at the service of European integration.

1958, Sept. 13

Belgium	527-528
France	889-890
Germany	790-791
Italy	750-751
Luxembourg	341-343
Netherlands	375-376
Saar	317-318

Europa Issue, 1959

6-Link Endless Chain – CD2

1959, Sept. 19

Belgium	536-537
France	929-930
Germany	805-806
Italy	791-792
Luxembourg	354-355
Netherlands	379-380

Europa Issue, 1960

19-Spoke Wheel – CD3

First anniverary of the establishment of C.E.P.T. (Conference Europeenne des Administrations des Postes et des Telecommunications.)

The spokes symbolize the 19 founding members of the Conference.

1960, Sept.

Belgium	553-554
Denmark	379
Finland	376-377

France	970-971
Germany	818-820
Great Britain	377-378
Greece	688
Iceland	327-328
Ireland	175-176
Italy	809-810
Luxembourg	374-375
Netherlands	385-386
Norway	387
Portugal	866-867
Spain	941-942
Sweden	562-563
Switzerland	400-401
Turkey	1493-1494

Europa Issue, 1961

19 Doves Flying as One – CD4

The 19 doves represent the 19 members of the Conference of European Postal and Telecommunications Administrations C.E.P.T.

1961-62

Belgium	572-573
Cyprus	201-203
France	1005-1006
Germany	844-845
Great Britain	383-384
Greece	718-719
Iceland	340-341
Italy	845-846
Luxembourg	382-383
Netherlands	387-388
Spain	1010-1011
Switzerland	410-411
Turkey	1518-1520

Europa Issue, 1962

Young Tree with 19 Leaves – CD5

The 19 leaves represent the 19 original members of C.E.P.T.

1962-63

Belgium	582-583
Cyprus	219-221
France	1045-1046
Germany	852-853
Greece	739-740
iceland	348-349
Ireland	184-185
Italy	860-861
Luxembourg	386-387
Netherlands	394-395
Norway	414-415
Switzerland	416-417
Turkey	1553-1555

Europa Issue, 1963

Stylized Links, Symbolizing Unity – CD6

1963, Sept.

Belgium	598-599
Cyprus	229-231
Finland	419
France	1074-1075
Germany	867-868
Greece	768-769
Iceland	357-358
Ireland	188-189
Italy	880-881
Luxembourg	403-404
Netherlands	416-417

Europa Issue, 1964

Symbolic Daisy – CD7

5th anniversary of the establishment of C.E.P.T. The 22 petals of the flower symbolize the 22 members of the Conference.

1964, Sept.

Austria	738
Belgium	614-615
Cyprus	244-246
France	1109-1110
Germany	897-898
Greece	801-802
Iceland	367-368
Ireland	196-197
Italy	894-895
Luxembourg	411-412
Monaco	590-591
Netherlands	428-429
Norway	458
Portugal	931-933
Spain	1262-1263
Switzerland	438-439
Turkey	1628-1629

Europa Issue, 1965

Leaves and "Fruit" – CD8

1965

Belgium	636-637
Cyprus	262-264
Finland	437
France	1131-1132
Germany	934-935
Greece	833-834
Iceland	375-376
Ireland	204-205
Italy	915-916
Luxembourg	432-433
Monaco	616-617
Netherlands	438-439
Norway	475-476
Portugal	958-960
Switzerland	469
Turkey	1665-1666

Europa Issue, 1966

Symbolic Sailboat – CD9

1966, Sept.

Andorra, French	172
Belgium	675-676
Cyprus	275-277
France	1163-1164
Germany	963-964
Greece	862-863
Iceland	384-385
Ireland	216-217
Italy	942-943
Liechtenstein	415
Luxembourg	440-441
Monaco	639-640

Norway	441-442
Switzerland	429
Turkey	1602-1603

Netherlands	441-442
Norway	496-497
Portugal	980-982
Switzerland	477-478
Turkey	1718-1719

Europa Issue, 1967

Cogwheels – CD10

1967

Andorra, French	174-175
Belgium	688-689
Cyprus	297-299
France	1178-1179
Greece	891-892
Germany	969-970
Iceland	389-390
Ireland	232-233
Italy	951-952
Liechtenstein	420
Luxembourg	449-450
Monaco	669-670
Netherlands	444-447
Norway	504-505
Portugal	994-996
Spain	1465-1466
Switzerland	482
Turkey	B120-B121

Europa Issue, 1968

Golden Key with C.E.P.T. Emblem CD11

1968

Andorra, French	182-183
Belgium	705-706
Cyprus	314-316
France	1209-1210
Germany	983-984
Greece	916-917
Iceland	395-396
Ireland	242-243
Italy	979-980
Liechtenstein	442
Luxembourg	466-467
Monaco	689-691
Netherlands	452-453
Portugal	1019-1021
San Marino	687
Spain	1526
Turkey	1775-1776

Europa Issue, 1969

"EUROPA" and "CEPT" – CD12

Tenth anniversary of C.E.P.T.

1969

Andorra, French	188-189
Austria	837
Belgium	718-719
Cyprus	326-328
Denmark	458
Finland	483
France	1245-1246
Germany	996-997
Great Britain	585
Greece	947-948
Iceland	406-407
Ireland	270-271

Italy 1000-1001
Liechtenstein 453
Luxembourg 474-475
Monaco 722-724
Netherlands 475-476
Norway 533-534
Portugal 1038-1040
San Marino 701-702
Spain 1567
Sweden 814-816
Switzerland 500-501
Turkey 1799-1800
Vatican 470-472
Yugoslavia 1003-1004

Europa Issue, 1970

Interwoven
Threads
CD13

1970
Andorra, French 196-197
Belgium 741-742
Cyprus 340-342
France 1271-1272
Germany 1018-1019
Greece 985, 987
Iceland 420-421
Ireland 279-281
Italy 1013-1014
Liechtenstein 470
Luxembourg 489-490
Monaco 768-770
Netherlands 483-484
Portugal 1060-1062
San Marino 729-730
Spain 1607
Switzerland 515-516
Turkey 1848-1849
Yugoslavia 1024-1025

Europa Issue, 1971

"Fraternity, Cooperation,
Common Effort" – CD14

1971
Andorra, French 205-206
Belgium 803-804
Cyprus 365-367
Finland 504
France 1304
Germany 1064-1065
Greece 1029-1030
Iceland 429-430
Ireland 305-306
Italy 1038-1039
Liechtenstein 485
Luxembourg 500-501
Malta 425-427
Monaco 797-799
Netherlands 488-489
Portugal 1094-1096
San Marino 749-750
Spain 1675-1676
Switzerland 531-532
Turkey 1876-1877
Yugoslavia 1052-1053

Europa Issue, 1972

EUROPA
CEPT

3F50
BELGIË·BELGIQUE

Sparkles, Symbolic of Communications
CD15

1972
Andorra, French 210-211
Andorra, Spanish 62
Belgium 825-826
Cyprus 380-382
Finland 512-513
France 1341
Germany 1089-1090
Greece 1049-1050
Iceland 439-440
Ireland 316-317
Italy 1065-1066
Liechtenstein 504
Luxembourg 512-513
Malta 450-453
Monaco 831-832
Netherlands 494-495
Portugal 1141-1143
San Marino 771-772
Spain 1718
Switzerland 544-545
Turkey 1907-1908
Yugoslavia 1100-1101

Europa Issue, 1973

Post Horn
and Arrows
CD16

1973
Andorra, French 319-320
Andorra, Spanish 76
Belgium 839-840
Cyprus 396-398
Finland 526
France 1367
Germany 1114-1115
Greece 1090-1092
Iceland 447-448
Ireland 329-330
Italy 1108-1109
Liechtenstein 528-529
Luxembourg 523-524
Malta 469-471
Monaco 866-867
Netherlands 504-505
Norway 604-605
Portugal 1170-1172
San Marino 802-803
Spain 1753
Switzerland 580-581
Turkey 1935-1936
Yugoslavia 1138-1139

PORTUGAL & COLONIES
Vasco da Gama Issue

Fleet Departing – CD20

Fleet Arriving at Calicut – CD21

Embarking at Rastello – CD22

Muse of   San Gabriel, da Gama
History – CD23   and Camoens – CD24

Archangel Gabriel,   Flagshig
the Patron Saint   San Gabriel
CD25   CD26

Vasco da
Gama
CD27

Fourth centenary of Vasco da Gama's discovery of the route to India.

1898
Azores 93-100
Macao 67-74
Madeira 37-44
Portugal 147-154
Port. Africa 1-8
Port. india 189-196
Timor 45-52

Pombal Issue
POSTAL TAX

Marquis   Planning
de   Reconstruction
Pombal   of Lisbon,1755
CD28   CD29

Pombal Monument, Lisbon – CD30

Sebastiao Jose de Carvalho e Mello,
Marquis de Pombal (1699-1782), statesman,
rebuilt Lisbon after earthquake of 1755. Tax
was for the erection of Pombal monument.
Obligatory on all mail on certain days
throughout the year.

1925
Angola RA1-RA3
Azores RA9-RA11
Cape Verde RA1-RA3
Macao RA1-RA3
Madeira RA1-RA3
Mozambique RA1-RA3
Portugal RA11-RA13
Port. Guinea RA1-RA3
Port. India RA1-RA3
St. Thomas & Prince Islands RA1-RA3
Timor RA1-RA3

Pombal Issue
POSTAL TAX DUES

CD31   CD32

CD33

1925
Angola RAJ1-RAJ3
Azores RAJ2-RAJ4
Cape Verde RAJ1-RAJ3
Macao RAJ1-RAJ3
Madeira RAJ1-RAJ3
Mozambique RAJ1-RAJ3
Portugal RAJ2-RAJ4
Port. Guinea RAJ1-RAJ3
Port. India RAJ1-RAJ3
St. Thomas & Prince Islands RAJ1-RAJ3
Timor RAJ1-RAJ3

Vasco   Mousinho de
da Gama   Albuquerque
CD34   CD35

Dam   Prince Henry the
CD36   Navigator – CD37

Affonso de   Plane over
Albuquerque   Globe
CD38   CD39

1938-39
Angola 274-291
Cape Verde 234-251
Macao 289-305
Mozambique 270-287
Port. Guinea 233-250
Port. India 439-453
St. Thomas & Prince
  Islands 302-319, 323-340
Timor 223-239

1938-39
Angola C1-C9
Cape Verde C1-C9

Macao	C7-C15
Mozambique	C1-C9
Port. Guinea	C1-C9
Port. India	C1-C8
St. Thomas & Prince Islands	C1-C18
Timor	C1-C9

Lady of Fatima Issue

Our Lady of
the Rosary,
Fatima,
Portugal
CD40

1948-49

Angola	315-318
Cape Verde	266
Macao	336
Mozambique	325-328
Port. Guinea	271
Port. India	480
St. Thomas & Prince Islands	351
Timor	254

A souvenir sheet of 9 stamps was issued in 1951 to mark the extension of the 1950 Holy Year. The sheet contains: Angola No. 316, Cape Verde No. 266, Macao No. 336, Mozambique No. 325, Portuguese Guinea No. 271, Portugese India Nos. 480, 485, St. Thomas & Prince Islands No. 351, Timor No. 254.

The sheet also contains a portrait of Pope Pius XII and is inscribed "Encerramento do Ano Santo, Fatima 1951." It was sold for 11 escudos.

Holy Year Issue

Church Bells	Angel Holding
and Dove	Candelabra
CD41	CD42

Holy Year, 1950.

1950-51

Angola	331-332
Cape Verde	268-269
Macao	339-340
Mozambique	330-331
Port. Guinea	273-274
Port. India	490-491, 496-503
St. Thomas & Prince Islands	353-354
Timor	258-259

A souvenir sheet of 8 stamps was issued in 1951 to mark the extension of the Holy Year. The sheet contains: Angola No. 331, Cape Verde No. 269, Macao No. 340, Mozambique No. 331, Portuguese Guinea No. 275, Portuguese India No. 490, St. Thomas & Prince Islands No. 354, Timor No. 258, some with colors changed. The sheet contains doves and is inscribed "Encerramento do Ano Santo, Fatima 1951." It was sold for 17 escudos.

Holy Year Conclusion Issue

Our Lady
of Fatima
CD43

Conclusion of Holy Year. Sheets contain alternate vertical rows of stamps and labels bearing quotation from Pope Pius XII, different for each colony.

1951

Angola	357
Cape Verde	270
Macao	352
Mozambique	356
Port. Guinea	275
Port. India	506
St. Thomas & Prince Islands	355
Timor	270

Medical Congress Issue

Medical
Examination
CD44

First National Congress of Tropical Medicine, Lisbon, 1952.

Each stamp has a different design.

1952

Angola	358
Cape Verde	287
Macao	364
Mozambique	359
Port. Guinea	276
Port. India	516
St. Thomas & Prince Islands	356
Timor	271

POSTAGE DUE STAMPS

CD45

1952

Angola	J37-J42
Cape Verde	J31-J36
Macao	J53-J58
Mozambique	J51-J56
Port. Guinea	J40-J45
Port. India	J47-J52
St. Thomas & Prince Islands	J52-J57
Timor	J31-J36

Sao Paulo Issue

Father Manuel de Nobrega
and View of Sao Paulo – CD46

400th anniversary of the founding of Sao Paulo, Brazil.

1954

Angola	385
Cape Verde	297
Macao	382
Mozambique	395
Port. Guinea	291
Port. India	530
St. Thomas & Prince Islands	369
Timor	279

Tropical Medicine Congress Issue

Securidaca Longipedunculata – CD47

Sixth International Congress for Tropical Medicine and Malaria, Lisbon, Sept. 1958.

Each stamp shows a different plant.

1958

Angola	409
Cape Verde	303
Macao	392
Mozambique	404
Port. Guinea	295
Port. India	569
St. Thomas & Prince Islands	371
Timor	289

Sports Issue

Flying – CD48

Each stamp shows a different sport.

1962

Angola	433-438
Cape Verde	320-325
Macao	394-399
Mozambique	424-429
Port. India	299-304
St. Thomas & Prince Islands	374-379
Timor	313-318

Anti-Malaria Issue

Anopheles Funestus and
Malaria Eradication Symbol – CD49

World Health Organization drive to eradicate malaria.

1962

Angola	439
Cape Verde	326
Macao	400
Mozambique	430
Port. India	305
St. Thomas & Prince Islands	380
Timor	319

Airline Anniversary Issue

Map of Africa, Super Constellation
and Jet Liner – CD50

Tenth anniversary of Transportes Aereos Portugueses (TAP).

1963

Angola	490
Cape Verde	327
Mozambique	434
Port. Guinea	318
St. Thomas & Prince Islands	381

National Overseas Bank Issue

Antonio Teixeira de Sousa – CD51

Centenary of the National Overseas Bank of Portugal.

1964, May 16

Angola	509
Cape Verde	328
Port. Guinea	319
St. Thomas & Prince Islands	382
Timor	320

ITU Issue

ITU Emblem and St. Gabriel CD52

Centenary of the International Communications Union.

1965, May 17

Angola	511
Cape Verde	329
Macao	402
Mozambique	464
Port. Guinea	320
St. Thomas & Prince Islands	383
Timor	321

National Revolution Issue

St. Paul's Hospital, and Commercial
and Industrial School – CD53

40th anniversary of the National Revolution.

Different buildings on each stamp.

1966, May 28

Angola	525
Cape Verde	338
Macao	403
Mozambique	465
Port. Guinea	329
St. Thomas & Prince Islands	392
Timor	322

Navy Club Issue

Mendes Barata and Cruiser
Dom Carlos I – CD54

Centenary of Portugal's Navy Club.
Each stamp has a different design.

1967, Jan. 31

Angola	527-528
Cape Verde	339-340
Macao	412-413
Mozambique	478-479
Port. Guinea	330-331
St. Thomas & Prince Islands	393-394
Timor	323-324

Admiral Coutinho Issue

Admiral Gago Coutinho and
his First Ship – CD55

Centenary of the birth of Admiral Carlos Viegas Gago Coutinho (1869-1959), explorer and aviation pioneer.

Each stamp has a different design.

1969, Feb. 17

Angola	547
Cape Verde	355
Macao	417
Mozambique	484
Port. Guinea	335
St. Thomas & Prince Islands	397
Timor	335

Administration Reform Issue

Luiz Augusto Rebello da Silva – CD56

Centenary of the administration reforms of the overseas territories.

1969, Sept. 25

Angola	549
Cape Verde	357
Macao	419
Mozambique	491
Port. Guinea	337
St. Thomas & Prince Islands	399
Timor	338

Marshal Carmona Issue

Marshal A.O. Carmona CD57

Birth centenary of Marshal Antonio Oscar Carmona de Fragoso (1869-1951), President of Portugal.

Each stamp has a different design.

1970, Nov. 15

Angola	563
Cape Verde	359
Macao	422
Mozambique	493
Port. Guinea	340
St. Thomas & Prince Islands	403
Timor	341

Olympic Games Issue

Racing Yachts and Olympic Emblem
CD59

20th Olympic Games, Munich, Aug. 26-Sept. 11.

Each stamp shows a different sport.

1972, June 20

Angola	569
Cape Verde	361
Macao	426
Mozambique	504
Port. Guinea	342
St. Thomas & Prince Islands	408
Timor	343

Lisbon-Rio de Janeiro Flight Issue

"Santa Cruz" over
Fernando de Noronha – CD60

50th anniversary of the Lisbon to Rio de Janeiro flight by Arturo de Sacadura and Coutinho, March 30-June 5, 1922.

Each stamp shows a different stage of the flight.

1972, Sept. 20

Angola	570
Cape Verde	362
Macao	427
Mozambique	505
Port. Guinea	343
St. Thomas & Prince Islands	409
Timor	344

WMO Centenary Issue

WMO Emblem – CD61

Centenary of international meterological cooperation.

1973, Dec. 15

Angola	571
Cape Verde	363
Macao	429
Mozambique	509
Port. Guinea	344
St. Thomas & Prince Islands	410
Timor	345

FRENCH COMMUNITY

Upper Volta can be found under Burkina Faso in Vol. 2

Colonial Exposition Issue

People of French Empire – CD70

Women's Heads – CD71

France Showing Way to Civilization
CD72

"Colonial Commerce" – CD73

International Colonial Exposition, Paris 1931.

1931

Cameroun	213-216
Chad	60-63
Dahomey	97-100
Fr. Guiana	152-155
Fr. Guinea	116-119
Fr. India	100-103
Fr. Polynesia	76-79
Fr. Sudan	102-105
Gabon	120-123
Guadeloupe	138-141
Indo-China	140-142
Ivory Coast	92-95
Madagascar	169-172
Martinique	129-132
Mauritania	65-68
Middle Congo	61-64
New Caledonia	176-179
Niger	73-76
Reunion	122-125
St. Pierre & Miquelon	132-135
Senegal	138-141
Somali Coast	135-138
Togo	254-257
Ubangi-Shari	82-85
Upper Volta	66-69
Wallis & Futuna Isls.	85-88

Paris International Exposition Issue
Colonial Arts Exposition Issue

"Colonial Resources"
CD74   CD77

Overseas Commerce – CD75

Exposition Building and Women – CD76

"France and the Empire" – CD78

Cultural Treasures of the Colonies
CD79

Souvenir sheets contain one imperf. stamp.

1937

Cameroun	217-222A
Dahomey	101-107
Fr. Equatorial Africa	27-32, 73
Fr. Guiana	162-168
Fr. Guinea	120-126
Fr. India	104-110
Fr. Polynesia	117-123
Fr. Sudan	106-112
Guadeloupe	148-154
Indo-China	193-199
Inini	41
Ivory Coast	152-158
Kwangchowan	132
Madagascar	191-197
Martinique	179-185
Mauritania	69-75
New Caledonia	208-214
Niger	72-83
Reunion	167-173
St. Pierre & Miquelon	165-171
Senegal	172-178
Somali Coast	139-145
Togo	258-264
Wallis & Futuna Isls.	89

Curie Issue

Pierre and Marie Curie – CD80

40th anniversary of the discovery of radium. The surtax was for the benefit of the International Union for the Control of Cancer.

1938

Cameroun	B1
Dahomey	B2
France	B76
Fr. Equatorial Africa	B1
Fr. Guiana	B3
Fr. Guinea	B2
Fr. India	B6
Fr. Polynesia	B5
Fr. Sudan	B1
Guadeloupe	B3
Indo-China	B14
Ivory Coast	B2
Madagascar	B2
Martinique	B2
Mauritania	B3
New Caledonia	B4
Niger	B1
Reunion	B4
St. Pierre & Miquelon	B3
Senegal	B3
Somali Coast	B2
Togo	B1

Caillie Issue

Rene Caille and Map of
Northwestern Africa – CD81

Death centenary of Rene Caillie (1799-1838), French explorer.

All three denominations exist with colony name omitted.

1939

Dahomey	108-110
Fr. Guinea	161-163
Fr. Sudan	113-115
Ivory Coast	160-162
Mauritania	109-111
Niger	84-86
Senegal	188-190
Togo	265-267

New York World's Fair Issue

Natives and New York Skyline – CD82

1939
Cameroun	223-224
Dahomey	111-112
Fr. Equatorial Africa	78-79
Fr. Guiana	169-170
Fr. Guinea	164-165
Fr. India	111-112
Fr. Polynesia	124-125
Fr. Sudan	116-117
Guadeloupe	155-156
Indo-China	203-204
Inini	42-43
Ivory Coast	163-164
Kwangchowan	121-122
Madagascar	209-210
Martinique	186-187
Mauritania	112-113
New Caledonia	215-216
Niger	87-88
Reunion	174-175
St. Pierre & Miquelon	205-206
Senegal	191-192
Somali Coast	179-180
Togo	268-269
Wallis & Futuna Isls.	90-91

French Revolution Issue

Storming of the Bastille – CD83

150th anniversary of the French Revolution. The surtax was for the defense of the colonies.

1939
Cameroun	B2-B6
Dahomey	B3-B7
Fr. Equatorial Africa	B4-B8, CB1
Fr. Guiana	B4-B8, CB1
Fr. Guinea	B3-B7
Fr. India	B7-B11
Fr. Polynesia	B6-B10, CB1
Fr. Sudan	B2-B6
Guadeloupe	B4-B8
Indo-China	B15-B19, CB1
Inini	B1-B5
Ivory Coast	B3-B7
Kwangchowan	B1-B5
Madagascar	B3-B7, CB1
Martinique	B3-B7
Mauritania	B4-B8
New Caledonia	B5-B9, CB1
Niger	B2-B6
Reunion	B5-B9, CB1
St. Pierre & Miquelon	B4-B8
Senegal	B4-B8, CB1
Somali Coast	B3-B7
Togo	B2-B6
Wallis & Futuna Isls.	B1-B5

Plane over Coastal Area – CD85

All five denominations exist with colony name omitted.

1940
Dahomey	C1-C5
Fr. Guinea	C1-C5
Fr. Sudan	C1-C5
Ivory Coast	C1-C5
Mauritania	C1-C5
Niger	C1-C5
Senegal	C12-C16
Togo	C1-C5

Colonial Infantryman CD86

1941
Cameroun	B13B
Dahomey	B13
Fr. Equatorial Africa	B8B
Fr. Guiana	B10
Fr. Guinea	B13
Fr. India	B13
Fr. Polynesia	B12
Fr. Sudan	B12
Guadeloupe	B10
Indo-China	B19B
Inini	B7
Ivory Coast	B13
Kwangchowan	B7
Madagascar	B9
Martinique	B9
Mauritania	B14
New Caledonia	B11
Niger	B12
Reunion	B11
St. Pierre & Miquelon	B8B
Senegal	B14
Somali Coast	B9
Togo	B10B
Wallis & Futuna Isls.	B7

Cross of Lorraine and Four-motor Plane – CD87

1941-5
Cameroun	C1-C7
Fr. Equatorial Africa	C17-C23
Fr. Guiana	C9-C10
Fr. India	C1-C6
Fr. Polynesia	C3-C9
Fr. West Africa	C1-C3
Guadeloupe	C1-C2
Madagascar	C37-C43
Martinique	C1-C2
New Caledonia	C7-C13
Reunion	C18-C24
St. Pierre & Miquelon	C1-C7
Somali Coast	C1-C7

Transport Plane CD88

Caravan and Plane CD89

1942
Dahomey	C6-C13
Fr. Guinea	C6-C13
Fr. Sudan	C6-C13
Ivory Coast	C6-C13
Mauritania	C6-C13
Niger	C6-C13
Senegal	C17-C25
Togo	C6-C13

Red Cross Issue

Marianne CD90

The surtax was for the French Red Cross and national relief.

1944
Cameroun	B28
Fr. Equatorial Africa	B38
Fr. Guiana	B12
Fr. India	B14
Fr. Polynesia	B13
Fr. West Africa	B1
Guadeloupe	B12
Madagascar	B15
Martinique	B11
New Caledonia	B13
Reunion	B15
St. Pierre & Miquelon	B13
Somali Coast	B13
Wallis & Futuna Isls.	B9

Eboue Issue

Felix Eboue – CD91

Felix Eboue, first French colonial administrator to proclaim resistance to Germany after French surrender in World War II.

1945
Cameroun	296-297
Fr. Equatorial Africa	156-157
Fr. Guiana	171-172
Fr. India	210-211
Fr. Polynesia	150-151
Fr. West Africa	15-16
Guadeloupe	187-188
Madagascar	259-260
Martinique	196-197
New Caledonia	274-275
Reunion	238-239
St. Pierre & Miquelon	322-323
Somali Coast	238-239

Victory Issue

Victory – CD92

European victory of the Allied Nations in World War II.

1946, May 8
Cameroun	C8
Fr. Equatorial Africa	C24
Fr. Guiana	C11
Fr. India	C7
Fr. Polynesia	C10
Fr. West Africa	C4
Guadeloupe	C3
Indo-China	C19
Madagascar	C44
Martinique	C3
New Caledonia	C14
Reunion	C25
St. Pierre & Miquelon	C8
Somali Coast	C8
Wallis & Futuna Isls.	C1

Chad to Rhine Issue

Leclerc's Departure from Chad – CD93

Battle at Cufra Oasis – CD94

Tanks in Action, Mareth – CD95

Normandy Invasion – CD96

Entering Paris – CD97

Liberation of Strasbourg – CD98

"Chad to the Rhine" march, 1942-44, by Gen. Jacques Leclerc's column, later French 2nd Armored Division.

1946, June 6
Cameroun	C9-C14
Fr. Equatorial Africa	C25-C30
Fr. Guiana	C12-C17
Fr. India	C8-C13
Fr. Polynesia	C11-C16
Fr. West Africa	C5-C10
Guadeloupe	C4-C9
Indo-China	C20-C25
Madagascar	C45-C50
Martinique	C4-C9
New Caledonia	C15-C20
Reunion	C26-C31
St. Pierre & Miquelon	C9-C14
Somali Coast	C9-C14
Wallis & Futuna Isls.	C2-C7

UPU Issue

French Colonials, Globe and Plane CD99

75th anniversary of the Universal Postal Union.

1949, July 4
Cameroun	C29
Fr. Equatorial Africa	C34
Fr. India	C17
Fr. Polynesia	C20
Fr. West Africa	C15
Indo-China	C26

Madagascar C55
New Caledonia C24
St. Pierre & Miquelon C18
Somali Coast C18
Togo C18
Wallis & Futuna Isls. C10

Tropical Medicine Issue

Doctor Treating Infant – CD100

The surtax was for charitable work.

1950

Cameroun B29
Fr. Equatorial Africa B39
Fr. India B15
Fr. Polynesia B14
Fr. West Africa B3
Madagascar B17
New Caledonia B14
St. Pierre & Miquelon B14
Somali Coast B14
Togo B11

Military Medal Issue

Medal, Early Marine and
Colonial Soldier – CD101

Centenary of the creation of the French Military Medal.

1952

Cameroun 332
Comoro Isls. 39
Fr. Equatorial Africa 186
Fr. India 233
Fr. Polynesia 179
Fr. West Africa 57
Madagascar 286
New Caledonia 295
St. Pierre & Miquelon 345
Somali Coast 267
Togo 327
Wallis & Futuna Isls. 149

Liberation Issue

Allied Landing, Victory Sign and
Cross of Lorraine – CD102

10th anniversary of the liberation of France.

1954, June 6

Cameroun C32
Comoro Isls. C4
Fr. Equatorial Africa C38
Fr. India C18
Fr. Polynesia C23
Fr. West Africa C17
Madagascar C57
New Caledonia C25
St. Pierre & Miquelon C19
Somali Coast C19
Togo C19
Wallis & Futuna Isls. C11

FIDES Issue

Plowmen
CD103

Efforts of FIDES, the Economic and Social Development Fund for Overseas Possessions (Fonds d' Investissement pour le Developpement Economique et Social).

Each stamp has a different design.

1956

Cameroun 326-329
Comoro Isls. 43
Fr. Polynesia 181
Madagascar 292-295
New Caledonia 303
Somali Coast 268
Togo 331

Flower Issue

Euadania
CD104

Each stamp shows a different flower.

1958-9

Cameroun 333
Comoro Isls. 45
Fr. Equatorial Africa 200-201
Fr. Polynesia 192
Fr. So. & Antarctic Terr. 11
Fr. West Africa 79-83
Madagascar 301-302
New Caledonia 304-305
St. Pierre & Miquelon 357
Somali Coast 270
Togo 348-349
Wallis & Futuna Isls. 152

Human Rights Issue

Sun, Dove and U.N. Emblem – CD105

10th anniversary of the signing of the Universal Declaration of Human Rights.

1958

Comoro Isls. 44
Fr. Equatorial Africa 202
Fr. Polynesia 191
Fr. West Africa 85
Madagascar 300
New Caledonia 306
St. Pierre & Miquelon 356
Somali Coast 274
Wallis & Futuna Isls. 153

C.C.T.A. Issue

Map of Africa & Cogwheels – CD106

10th anniversary of the Commission for Technical Cooperation in Africa south of the Sahara.

1960

Cameroun 335
Cent. African Rep. 3
Chad 66

Congo, P.R. 90
Dahomey 138
Gabon 150
Ivory Coast 180
Madagascar 317
Mali 9
Mauritania 117
Niger 104
Upper Volta 89

Air Afrique Issue, 1961

Modern and Ancient Africa,
Map and Planes – CD107

Founding of Air Afrique (African Airlines).

1961-62

Cameroun C37
Cent. African Rep. C5
Chad C7
Congo, P.R. C5
Dahomey C17
Gabon C5
Ivory Coast C18
Mauritania C17
Niger C22
Senegal C31
Upper Volta C4

Anti-Malaria Issue

Malaria Eradication Emblem – CD108

World Health Organization drive to eradicate malaria.

1962, Apr. 7

Cameroun B36
Cent. African Rep. B1
Chad B1
Comoro Isls. B1
Congo, P.R. B3
Dahomey B15
Gabon B4
Ivory Coast B15
Madagascar B19
Mali B1
Mauritania B16
Niger B14
Senegal B16
Somali Coast B15
Upper Volta B1

Abidjan Games Issue

Relay Race – CD109

Abidjan Games, Ivory Coast, Dec. 24-31, 1961.

Each stamp shows a different sport.

1962

Chad 83-84
Cent. African Rep. 19-20
Congo, P.R. 103-104
Gabon 163-164
Niger 109-111
Upper Volta 103-105

African and Malagasy Union Issue

Flag of Union – CD110

First anniversary of the Union.

1962, Sept. 8

Cameroun 373
Cent. African Rep. 21
Chad 85
Congo, P.R. 105
Dahomey 155
Gabon 165
Ivory Coast 198
Madagascar 332
Mauritania 170
Niger 112
Senegal 211
Upper Volta 106

Telstar Issue

Telstar and Globe Showing Andover
and Pleumeur-Bodou – CD111

First television connection of the United States and Europe through the Telstar satellite, July 11-12, 1962.

1962-63

Andorra, French 154
Comoro Isls. C7
Fr. Polynesia C29
Fr. So. & Antarctic Terr. C5
New Caledonia C33
Somali Coast C31
St. Pierre & Miquelon C26
Wallis & Futuna Isls. C17

Freedom From Hunger Issue

World Map and Wheat Emblem – CD112

United Nations Food and Agriculture Organization's "Freedom from Hunger" campaign.

1963, Mar. 21

Cameroun B37-B38
Cent. African Rep. B2
Chad B2
Congo, P.R. B4
Dahomey B16
Gabon B5
Ivory Coast B16
Madagascar B21
Mauritania B17
Niger B15
Senegal B17
Upper Volta B2

Red Cross Centenary Issue

Centenary Emblem – CD113

Centenary of the International Red Cross.
1963, Sept. 2
Comoro Isls. 55
Fr. Polynesia 205
New Caledonia 328
St. Pierre & Miquelon 367
Somali Coast 297
Wallis & Futuna Isls. 165

African Postal Union Issue

UAMPT Emblem, Radio Masts,
Plane and Mail – CD114

Establishment of the African and Malagasy
Posts and Telecommunications Union,
UAMPT.
1963, Sept. 8
Cameroon C47
Cent. African Rep. C10
Chad C9
Congo, P.R. C13
Dahomey C19
Gabon C13
Ivory Coast C25
Madagascar C75
Mauritania C22
Niger C27
Rwanda 36
Senegal C32
Upper Volta C9

Air Afrique Issue, 1963

Symbols of Flight – CD115

First anniversary of Air Afrique and inaugu-
ration of DC-8 service.
1963, Nov. 19
Cameroun C48
Chad C10
Congo, P.R. C14
Gabon C18
Ivory Coast C26
Mauritania C26
Niger C35
Senegal C33

Europafrica Issue

Europe and Africa Linked – CD116

Signing of an economic agreement
between the European Economic
Community and the African and Malagasy
Union, Yaoundé, Cameroun, July 20, 1963.
1963-64
Cameroun 402
Chad C11

Cent. African Rep. C12
Congo, P.R. C16
Gabon C19
Ivory Coast 217
Niger C43
Upper Volta C11

Human Rights Issue

Scales of Justice and Globe – CD117

15th anniversary of the Universal
Declaration of Human Rights.
1963, Dec. 10
Comoro Isls. 58
Fr. Polynesia 206
New Caledonia 329
St. Pierre & Miquelon 368
Somali Coast 300
Wallis & Futuna Isls. 166

PHILATEC Issue

Stamp Album, Champs Elysees Palace
and Horses of Marly – CD118

"PHILATEC," International Philatelic and
Postal Techniques Exhibition, Paris, June 5-
21, 1964.
1963-64
Comoro Isls. 60
France 1078
Fr. Polynesia 207
New Caledonia 341
St. Pierre & Miquelon 369
Somali Coast 301
Wallis & Futuna Isls. 167

Cooperation Issue

Maps of France and Africa and
Clasped Hands – CD119

Cooperation between France and the
French-speaking countries of Africa and
Madagascar.
1964
Cameroun 409-410
Cent. African Rep. 39
Chad 103
Congo, P.R. 121
Dahomey 193
France 1111
Gabon 175
Ivory Coast 221
Madagascar 360
Mauritania 181
Niger 143
Senegal 236
Togo 495

ITU Issue

Telegraph, Syncom Satellite and
ITU Emblem – CD120

Centenary of the International
Telecommunication Union.
1965, May 17
Comoro Isls. C14
Fr. Polynesia C33
Fr. So. & Antarctic Terr. C8
New Caledonia C40
New Hebrides 124-125
St. Pierre & Miquelon C29
Somali Coast C36
Wallis & Futuna Isls. C20

French Satellite A-1 Issue

Diamant Rocket and Launching
Installation – CD121

Launching of France's first satellite, Nov.
26, 1965.
1965-66
Comoro Isls. C15-C16
France 1137-1138
Fr. Polynesia C40-C41
Fr. So. & Antarctic Terr. C9-C10
New Caledonia C44-C45
St. Pierre & Miquelon C30-C31
Somali Coast C39-C40
Wallis & Futuna Isls. C22-C23

French Satellite D-1 Issue

D-1 Satellite in Orbit – CD122

Launching of the D-1 satellite at
Hammaguir, Algeria, Feb. 17, 1966.
1966
Comoro Isls. C17
France 1148
Fr. Polynesia C42
Fr. So. & Antarctic Terr. C11
New Caledonia C46
St. Pierre & Miquelon C32
Somali Coast C49
Wallis & Futuna Isls. C24

Air Afrique Issue, 1966

Planes and Air Afrique Emblem – CD123

Introduction of DC-8F planes by Air
Afrique.

1966
Cameroun C79
Cent. African Rep. C35
Chad C26
Congo, P.R. C42
Dahomey C42
Gabon C47
Ivory Coast C32
Mauritania C57
Niger C63
Senegal C47
Togo C54
Upper Volta C31

African Postal Union, 1967

Telecommunications Symbols
and Map of Africa – CD124

Fifth anniversary of the establishment of
the African and Malagasy Union of Posts and
Telecommunications, UAMPT.
1967
Cameroun C90
Cent. African Rep. C46
Chad C37
Congo, P.R. C57
Dahomey C61
Gabon C58
Ivory Coast C34
Madagascar C85
Mauritania C65
Niger C75
Rwanda C1-C3
Senegal C60
Togo C81
Upper Volta C50

Monetary Union Issue

Gold Token of the Ashantis,
17-18th Centuries – CD125

Fifth anniversary of the West African
Monetary Union.
1967, Nov. 4
Dahomey 244
Ivory Coast 259
Mauritania 238
Niger 204
Senegal 294
Togo 623
Upper Volta 181

WHO Anniversary Issue

Sun, Flowers and WHO Emblem
CD126

20th anniversary of the World Health
Organization.
1968, May 4
Afars & Issas 317
Comoro Isls. 73
Fr. Polynesia 241-242

Fr. So. & Antarctic Terr. 31
New Caledonia 367
St. Pierre & Miquelon.................................377
Wallis & Futuna Isls. 169

Human Rights Year Issue

Human Rights Flame – CD127

International Human Rights Year.
1968, Aug. 10
Afars & Issas.................................322-323
Comoro Isls. 76
Fr. Polynesia 243-244
Fr. So. & Antarctic Terr. 32
New Caledonia 369
St. Pierre & Miquelon..........................382
Wallis & Futuna Isls. 170

2nd PHILEXAFRIQUE Issue

Gabon No. 131 and Industrial Plant
CD128

Opening of PHILEXAFRIQUE, Abidjan,
Feb. 14. Each stamp shows a local scene and
stamp.
1969, Feb. 14
Cameroun...C118
Cent. African Rep.................................C65
Chad...C48
Congo, P.R..C77
Dahomey...C94
Gabon...C82
Ivory Coast...................................C38-C40
Madagascar...C92
Mali..C65
Mauritania..C80
Niger..C104
Senegal..C68
Togo...C104
Upper Volta...C62

Concorde Issue

Concorde in Flight – CD129

First flight of the prototpye Concorde
super-sonic plane at Toulouse, Mar. 1, 1969.
1969
Afars & Issas.......................................C56
Comoro Isls. C29
France..C42
Fr. Polynesia C50
Fr. So. & Antarctic Terr.........................C18
New Caledonia C63
St. Pierre & Miquelon C40
Wallis & Futuna Isls. C30

Development Bank Issue

Bank
Emblem
CD130

Fifth anniversary of the African
Development Bank.
1969
Cameroun 499
Chad..217
Congo, P.R....................................181-182
Ivory Coast...281
Mali...127-128
Mauritania...267
Niger...220
Senegal..317-318
Upper Volta..201

ILO Issue

ILO Headquarters, Geneva,
and Emblem – CD131

50th anniversary of the International Labor
Organization.
1969-70
Afars & Issas.......................................337
Comoro Isls. 83
Fr. Polynesia 251-252
Fr. So. & Antarctic Terr. 35
New Caledonia 379
St. Pierre & Miquelon...........................396
Wallis & Futuna Isls. 172

ASECNA Issue

Map of Africa, Plane and Airport – CD132

10th anniversary of the Agency for the
Security of Aerial Navigation in Africa and
Madagascar (ASECNA, Agence pour la
Securite de la Navigation Aerienne en
Afrique et a Madagascar).
1969-70
Cameroun 500
Cent. African Rep. 119
Chad..222
Congo, P.R..197
Dahomey...269
Gabon...260
Ivory Coast...287
Mali...130
Niger...221
Senegal..321
Upper Volta..204

U.P.U. Headquarters Issue

U.P.U. Headquarters and Emblem
CD133

New Universal Postal Union headquarters,
Bern, Switzerland.

1970
Afars & Issas......................................342
Algeria...443
Cameroun.....................................503-504
Cent. African Rep. 125
Chad..225
Comoro Isls. 84
Congo, P.R..216
Fr. Polyresia 261-262
Fr. So. & Antarctic Terr. 36
Gabon...258
Ivory Coast...295
Madagascar...444
Mali...134-135
Mauritania...283
New Caledonia 382
Niger..231-232
St. Pierre & Miquelon.....................397-398
Senegal..328-329
Tunisia...535
Wallis & Futuna Isls. 173

De Gaulle Issue

General de Gaulle 1940 – CD134

First anniversary of the death of Charles de
Gaulle, (1890-1970), President of France.
1971-72
Afars & Issas.................................356-357
Comoro Isls. 104-105
France..1322-1325
Fr. Polynesia 270-271
Fr. So. & Antarctic Terr. 52-53
New Caledonia 393-394
Reunion......................................377, 380
St. Pierre & Miquelon.....................417-418
Wallis & Futuna Isls. 177-178

African Postal Union Issue, 1971

Carved Stool, UAMPT Building,
Brazzaville, Congo – CD135

10th anniversary of the establishment of
the African and Malagasy Posts and
Telecommunications Union, UAMPT.
Each stamp has a different native design.
1971, Nov. 13
Cameroun C177
Cent. African Rep. C89
Chad...C94
Congo, P.R..C136
Dahomey...C146
Gabon...C120
Ivory Coast...C47
Mauritania..C113
Niger..C164
Rwanda...C8
Senegal..C105
Togo...C166
Upper Volta...C97

West African Monetary Union Issue

African Couple, City, Village and
Commemorative Coin – CD136

10th anniversary of the West African
Monetary Union.
1972, Nov. 2
Dahomey...300
Ivory Coast...331
Mauritania...299
Niger...258
Senegal..374
Togo..825
Upper Volta..280

African Postal Union Issue, 1973

Telecommunications Symbols and
Map of Africa – CD137

11th anniversary of the African and
Malagasy Posts and Telecommunications
Union (UAMPT).
1973, Sept. 12
Cameroun 574
Cent. African Rep. 194
Chad..272
Congo, P.R..289
Dahomey...311
Gabon...320
Ivory Coast...361
Madagascar...500
Mauritania...304
Niger...287
Rwanda..540
Senegal..393
Togo..849
Upper Volta..285

Philexafrique II — Essen Issue

Buffalo and Dahomey No. C33 – CD138

Wild Ducks and Baden No. 1 – CD139

Designs: Indigenous fauna, local and
German stamps.

Types CD138-CD139 printed horizontally
and vertically se-tenant in sheets of 10 (2x5).
Label between horizontal pairs alternately
commemorates Philexafrique II, Libreville,
Gabon, June 1978, and 2nd International
Stamp Fair, Essen, Germany, Nov. 1-5.
1978-1979
Benin...C285-C286
Central Africa C200-C201
Chad...C238-C239
Congo Republic C245-C246
Djibouti C121-C122
Gabon.......................................C215-C216
Ivory Coast...C64-C65
Mali C356-C357
Mauritania...............................C185-C186
Niger..C291-C292
Rwanda......................................C12-C13
Senegal.....................................C146-C147
Togo...C363-C364
Upper Volta...............................C253-C254

RAS AL KHAIMA

LOCATION — Oman Peninsula, Arabia, on Persian Gulf

GOVT. — Sheikdom under British protection

Ras al Khaima was the 7th Persian Gulf sheikdom to join the United Arab Emirates, doing so in Feb. 1972.
See United Arab Emirates.

100 Naye Paise = 1 Rupee

Catalogue values for all unused stamps in this country are for Never Hinged items.

Sheik Saqr bin Mohammed al Qasimi — A1

Seven Palm Trees — A2

Dhow — A3

Perf. 14¹/₂x14

			Unwmk.	
1964, Dec. 21		Photo.		
1	A1	5np brown & black	18	15
2	A1	15np deep blue & blk	45	22
3	A2	30np ocher & black	1.00	50
4	A2	40np blue & black	1.25	65
5	A2	75np brn red & blk	2.50	1.25
6	A3	1r lt grn & sepia	3.25	1.65
7	A3	2r brt vio & sepia	5.00	2.50
8	A3	5r blue gray & sepia	16.00	8.25
		Nos. 1-8 (8)	29.63	15.17

RIO DE ORO

LOCATION — On the northwest coast of Africa, bordering on the Atlantic Ocean

GOVT. — Spanish Colony

AREA — 71,600 sq. mi.

POP. — 24,000

CAPITAL — Villa Cisneros

Rio de Oro became part of Spanish Sahara.

100 Centimos = 1 Peseta

King Alfonso XIII A1

A2

Control Numbers on Back in Blue

1905		Unwmk.	Typo.	Perf. 14
1	A1	1c blue green	1.75	1.10
2	A1	2c claret	1.75	1.10
3	A1	3c bronze green	1.75	1.10
4	A1	4c dark brown	1.75	1.10
5	A1	5c orange red	1.75	1.10
6	A1	10c dk gray brown	1.75	1.10
7	A1	15c red brown	1.75	1.10
8	A1	25c dark blue	32.50	11.50
9	A1	50c dark green	16.00	5.25
10	A1	75c dark violet	16.00	7.50
11	A1	1p orange brown	13.00	3.25
12	A1	2p buff	35.00	17.50
13	A1	3p dull violet	27.50	7.50
14	A1	4p blue green	27.50	7.50
15	A1	5p dull blue	32.50	13.00
16	A1	10p pale red	85.00	32.50
		Nos. 1-16 (16)	297.25	113.20

For surcharges see Nos. 17, 34-36, 60-66.

No. 8 Handstamp Surcharged in Rose

a

1907

17	A1	15c on 25c dk blue	100.00	32.50

The surcharge exists inverted, double and in violet, normally positioned.

Control Numbers on Back in Blue

1907			Typo.	
18	A2	1c claret	2.00	1.40
19	A2	2c black	2.00	1.40
20	A2	3c dark brown	2.00	1.40
21	A2	4c red	2.00	1.40
22	A2	5c black brown	2.00	1.40
23	A2	10c chocolate	2.00	1.40
24	A2	15c dark blue	2.00	1.40
25	A2	25c deep green	4.75	1.40
26	A2	50c black violet	4.75	1.40
27	A2	75c orange brown	4.75	1.40
28	A2	1p orange	8.50	1.40
29	A2	2p dull violet	3.00	1.40
30	A2	3p blue green	3.00	1.40
a.		Cliché of 4p in plate of 3p	175.00	110.00
31	A2	4p dark blue	4.75	2.50
32	A2	5p red	4.75	2.50
33	A2	10p deep green	6.00	4.75
		Nos. 18-33 (16)	58.25	27.95

For surcharges see Nos. 38-43, 67-70.

**1907
10
Cens**

Nos. 9-10 Handstamp Surcharged in Red

1907

34	A1	10c on 50c dk green	45.00	10.00
a.		"10" omitted	100.00	52.50
35	A1	10c on 75c dk violet	27.50	10.00

**1908
2
Cens**

No. 12 Handstamp Surcharged in Violet

1908

36	A1	2c on 2p buff	27.50	10.50

No. 36 is found with "1908" measuring 11mm and 12mm.

Same Surcharge in Red on No. 26

38	A2	10c on 50c blk vio	20.00	4.50

A 5c on 10c (No. 23) was not officially issued.

Nos. 25, 27-28 Handstamp Surcharged Type "a" in Red, Violet or Green

1908

39	A2	15c on 25c dp grn (R)	18.00	4.00
40	A2	15c on 75c org brn (V)	25.00	5.00
a.		Green surcharge	32.50	13.00
41	A2	15c on 1p org (V)	27.50	5.00
42	A2	15c on 1p org (R)	27.50	10.00
43	A2	15c on 1p org (G)	27.50	10.00
		Nos. 39-43 (5)	125.50	34.00

As this surcharge is handstamped, it exists in several varieties: double, inverted, in pairs with one surcharge omitted, etc.

A3

1908 _Imperf._

44	A3	5c on 50c green (C)	80.00	32.50
45	A3	5c on 50c green (V)	115.00	55.00

The surcharge, which is handstamped, exists in many variations.
Nos. 44-45 are found with and without control numbers on back.

King Alfonso XIII — A4

Control Numbers on Back in Blue

1909		Typo.	Perf. 14¹/₂	
46	A4	1c red	40	32
47	A4	2c orange	40	32
48	A4	5c dark green	40	32
49	A4	10c orange red	40	32
50	A4	15c blue green	40	32
51	A4	20c dark violet	1.00	48
52	A4	25c deep blue	1.00	48
53	A4	30c claret	1.00	48
54	A4	40c chocolate	1.00	48
55	A4	50c red violet	1.40	48
56	A4	1p dark brown	2.25	1.65
57	A4	4p carmine rose	2.75	2.00
58	A4	10p claret	5.50	4.00
		Nos. 46-58 (13)	17.90	11.65

**1910
10
Céntimos**

Stamps of 1905 Handstamped in Black

1910

60	A1	10c on 5p dull bl	8.25	7.25
a.		Red surcharge	47.50	27.50
62	A1	10c on 10p pale red	8.25	6.50
a.		Violet surcharge	72.50	35.00
b.		Green surcharge	72.50	35.00
65	A1	15c on 3p dull vio	8.25	7.25
a.		Imperf.	72.50	
66	A1	15c on 4p blue grn	8.25	7.25
a.		10c on 4p bl grn	375.00	125.00

See note after No. 43.

**2
Cents**

Nos. 31 and 33 Surcharged in Red or Violet

1911-13

67	A2	2c on 4p dk blue (R)	6.50	2.50
68	A2	5c on 10p dp grn (V)	17.00	2.50

**10
Céntimos**

Nos. 29-30 Surcharged in Black

69	A2	10c on 2p dull vio	9.00	2.50
69A	A2	10c on 3p bl grn ('13)	90.00	10.50

Nos. 30, 32 Handstamped Type "a"

69B	A2	15c on 3p bl grn ('13)	72.50	6.00
70	A2	15c on 5p red	6.50	2.75
		Nos. 67-70 (6)	201.50	26.75

King Alfonso XIII
A5   A6

Control Numbers on Back in Blue

1912		Typo.	Perf. 13¹/₂	
71	A5	1c carmine rose	20	15
72	A5	2c lilac	20	15
73	A5	5c deep green	20	15
74	A5	10c red	20	15
75	A5	15c brown orange	20	15
76	A5	20c brown	20	15
77	A5	25c dull blue	20	15

78	A5	30c dark violet	20	15
79	A5	40c blue green	20	15
80	A5	50c lake	20	15
81	A5	1p red	1.50	40
82	A5	4p claret	3.25	1.65
83	A5	10p dark brown	4.50	2.00
		Nos. 71-83 (13)	11.25	5.55

For overprints see Nos. 97-109.

Control Numbers on Back in Blue

1914				Perf. 13
84	A6	1c olive black	22	15
85	A6	2c maroon	22	15
86	A6	5c deep green	22	15
87	A6	10c orange red	22	15
88	A6	15c orange red	22	15
89	A6	20c deep claret	22	15
90	A6	25c dark blue	22	15
91	A6	30c blue green	22	15
92	A6	40c brown orange	22	15
93	A6	50c dark brown	22	15
94	A6	1p dull lilac	1.65	1.25
95	A6	4p carmine rose	3.75	1.25
96	A6	10p dull violet	5.00	3.00
		Nos. 84-96 (13)	12.60	7.00

Nos. 71-83 Overprinted in 1917 Black

1917				Perf. 13¹/₂
97	A5	1c carmine rose	5.25	50
98	A5	2c lilac	5.25	50
99	A5	5c deep grn	1.00	50
100	A5	10c red	1.00	50
101	A5	15c orange brn	1.00	50
102	A5	20c brown	1.50	50
103	A5	25c dull blue	1.50	50
104	A5	30c dark violet	1.50	50
105	A5	40c blue green	1.65	50
106	A5	50c lake	1.65	50
107	A5	1p red	7.25	2.00
108	A5	4p claret	10.00	2.50
109	A5	10p dark brown	13.00	3.75
		Nos. 97-109 (13)	51.55	13.25

Nos. 97-109 exist with overprint inverted or double (value 50 percent over normal) and in dark blue (value twice normal).

King Alfonso XIII — A7

Control Numbers on Back in Blue

1919		Typo.	Perf. 13	
114	A7	1c brown	55	35
115	A7	2c claret	55	35
116	A7	5c light green	55	35
117	A7	10c carmine	55	35
118	A7	15c orange	55	35
119	A7	20c orange	55	35
120	A7	25c blue	55	35
121	A7	30c green	55	35
122	A7	40c vermilion	55	35
123	A7	50c brown	55	35
124	A7	1p lilac	3.75	2.00
125	A7	4p rose	6.00	3.50
126	A7	10p violet	7.00	5.00
		Nos. 114-126 (13)	22.25	14.00

A8

A9

Control Numbers on Back in Blue

1920				Perf. 13
127	A8	1c gray lilac	55	35
128	A8	2c rose	55	35
129	A8	5c light red	55	35
130	A8	10c lilac	55	35
131	A8	15c light brown	55	35
132	A8	20c greenish blue	55	35
133	A8	25c yellow	55	35
134	A8	30c dull blue	3.25	2.25
135	A8	40c orange	1.90	90
136	A8	50c dull rose	1.90	90
137	A8	1p gray green	1.90	90
138	A8	4p lilac rose	3.75	2.00
139	A8	10p brown	8.50	5.00
		Nos. 127-139 (13)	25.05	14.40

Control Numbers on Back in Blue

1922

140	A9	1c yellow	55	35
141	A9	2c red brown	55	35
142	A9	5c blue green	55	35
143	A9	10c pale red	55	35
144	A9	15c myrtle green	55	35
145	A9	20c turq blue	55	35
146	A9	25c deep blue	55	35
147	A9	30c deep rose	1.00	90
148	A9	40c violet	1.00	90
149	A9	50c orange	1.00	90
150	A9	1p lilac	3.25	1.40
151	A9	4p claret	5.50	3.00
152	A9	10p dark brown	8.75	5.25
		Nos. 140-152 (13)	24.35	14.80

For subsequent issues see Spanish Sahara.

RIO MUNI

LOCATION — West Africa, bordering on Cameroun and Gabon Republics
GOVT. — Province of Spain
AREA — 9,500 sq. mi.
POP. — 183,377 (1960)
CAPITAL — Bata

Rio Muni and the island of Fernando Po are the two provinces that constitute Spanish Guinea. Separate stamp issues for the two provinces were decreed in 1960.
Spanish Guinea Nos. 1-84 were used only in the territory now called Rio Muni.
Rio Muni united with Fernando Po on Oct. 12, 1968, to form the Republic of Equatorial Guinea.

100 Centimos = 1 Peseta

> Catalogue values for all unused stamps in this country are for Never Hinged items.

Boy Reading and Missionary A1

Quina Plant A2

1960 Unwmk. Photo. Perf. 13x12½

1	A1	25c dull vio bl	15	15
2	A1	50c olive brown	15	15
3	A1	75c dull grysh pur	15	15
4	A1	1p orange ver	15	15
5	A1	1.50p brt blue grn	15	15
6	A1	2p red lilac	15	15
7	A1	3p sapphire	30	15
8	A1	5p red brown	85	15
9	A1	10p lt olive grn	1.50	25
		Set value	3.10	75

1960 Perf. 13x12½

10	A2	35c shown	15	15
11	A2	80c Croton plant	15	15
		Set value	20	15

See Nos. B1-B2.

Map of Rio Muni — A3

Designs: 50c, 1p, Gen. Franco. 70c, Government Palace.

1961, Oct. 1 Perf. 12½x13

12	A3	25c gray violet	15	15
13	A3	50c olive brown	15	15
14	A3	70c brt green	15	15
15	A3	1p red orange	15	15
		Set value	32	20

25th anniversary of the nomination of Gen. Francisco Franco as Chief of State.

Rio Muni Headdress — A4

Design: 50c, Rio Muni idol.

1962, July 10 Perf. 13x12½

16	A4	25c violet	15	15
17	A4	50c green	15	15
18	A4	1p orange brown	15	15
		Set value	28	15

Issued for child welfare.

Cape Buffalo — A5

Design: 35c, Gorilla, vert.

Perf. 13x12½, 12½x13
1962, Nov. 23 Photo. Unwmk.

19	A5	15c dark olive grn	15	15
20	A5	35c magenta	15	15
21	A5	1p brown orange	20	15
		Set value	32	15

Issued for Stamp Day.

Mother and Child — A6

Father Joaquin Juanola — A7

1963, Jan. 29 Perf. 13x12½

22	A6	50c green	15	15
23	A6	1p brown orange	15	15

Issued to help the victims of the Seville flood.

1963, July 6 Perf. 13x12½

Design: 50c, Blessing hand, cross and palms.

24	A7	25c dull violet	15	15
25	A7	50c brown olive	15	15
26	A7	1p orange red	15	15
		Set value	25	15

Issued for child welfare.

Praying Child and Arms — A8

Branch of Copal Tree — A9

1963, July 12

27	A8	50c dull green	15	15
28	A8	1p redsh brown	15	15
		Set value	20	15

Issued for Barcelona flood relief.

Perf. 13x12½, 12½x13
1964, Mar. 6 Photo.

Design: 50c, Flowering quina, horiz.

29	A9	25c brt violet	15	15
30	A9	50c blue green	15	15
31	A9	1p dk carmine rose	15	15
		Set value	25	15

Issued for Stamp Day 1963.

Tree Pangolin A10

Design: 50c, Chameleon.

1964, June 1 Perf. 13x12½

32	A10	25c violet blk	15	15
33	A10	50c olive gray	15	15
34	A10	1p fawn	15	15
		Set value	26	15

Issued for child welfare.

Dwarf Crocodile A11

Designs: 15c, 70c, 3p, Dwarf crocodile. 25c, 1p, 5p, Leopard. 50c, 1.50p, 10p, Black rhinoceros.

1964, July 1

35	A11	15c lt brown	15	15
36	A11	25c violet	15	15
37	A11	50c olive	15	15
38	A11	70c green	15	15
39	A11	1p brown car	38	15
40	A11	1.50p blue green	38	15
41	A11	3p dark blue	60	15
42	A11	5p brown	1.50	60
43	A11	10p green	4.25	1.25
		Nos. 35-43 (9)	7.71	
		Set value		2.15

Greshoff's Tree Frog — A12

Stamp Day: 1p, Helmet guinea fowl, vert.

Perf. 13x12½, 12½x13
1964, Nov. 23 Photo. Unwmk.

44	A12	50c green	15	15
45	A12	1p deep claret	15	15
46	A12	1.50p blue green	15	15
		Set value	26	15

Issued for Stamp Day, 1964.

Woman's Head — A13

Woman Chemist — A14

1964 Photo. Perf. 13x12½

47	A13	50c shown	15	15
48	A14	1p shown	15	15
49	A14	1.50p Logger	15	15
		Set value	26	15

Issued to commemorate 25 years of peace.

Goliath Beetle A15

Beetle: 1p, Acridoxena hewaniana.

1965, June 1 Photo. Perf. 12½x13

50	A15	50c Prus green	15	15
51	A15	1p sepia	15	15
52	A15	1.50p black	15	15
		Set value	26	15

Issued for child welfare.

Ring-necked Pheasant — A16

Leopard and Arms of Rio Muni A17

Perf. 13x12½, 12½x13
1965, Nov. 23 Photo.

53	A16	50c grnsh gray	15	15
54	A17	1p sepia	30	15
55	A16	2.50p lilac	1.40	55
		Set value		65

Issued for Stamp Day, 1965.

Elephant and Parrot A18

Design: 1.50p, Lion and boy.

Perf. 12½x13
1966, June 1 Photo. Unwmk.

56	A18	50c olive	15	15
57	A18	1p dk purple	15	15
58	A18	1.50p brt Prus blue	15	15
		Set value	26	15

Issued for child welfare.

Water Chevrotain — A19

Designs: 40c, 4p, Tree pangolin, vert.

1966, Nov. 23 Photo. Perf. 13

59	A19	10c brown & yel brn	15	15
60	A19	40c brown & yellow	15	15
61	A19	1.50p blue & rose lilac	15	15
62	A19	4p dk bl & emerald	25	15
		Set value	40	30

Issued for Stamp Day, 1966.

A20   Potto — A21

Designs: 40c, 4p, Vine creeper.

1967, June 1   **Photo.**   *Perf. 13*
63	A20	10c green & yellow	15	15
64	A20	40c blk, rose car & grn	15	15
65	A20	1.50p blue & orange	15	15
66	A20	4p black & green	25	15
		Set value	40	30

Issued for child welfare.

1967, Nov. 23   **Photo.**   *Perf. 13*

Designs: 1p, River hog, horiz. 3.50p, African golden cat, horiz.
67	A21	1p black & red brn	15	15
68	A21	1.50p brown & grn	15	15
69	A21	3.50p org brn & grn	30	20
		Set value	42	32

Issued for Stamp Day 1967.

Zodiac Issue

Cancer — A22

Signs of the Zodiac: 1.50p, Taurus. 2.50p, Gemini.

1968, Apr. 25   **Photo.**   *Perf. 13*
70	A22	1p brt mag, *lt yel*	15	15
71	A22	1.50p brown, *pink*	15	15
72	A22	2.50p dk vio, *yel*	25	15
		Set value	36	26

Issued for child welfare.

SEMI-POSTAL STAMPS

Type of Regular Issue, 1960

Designs: 10c+5c, Croton plant. 15c+5c, Flower and leaves of croton.

1960 Unwmk. Photo.   *Perf. 13x12½*
B1	A2	10c + 5c maroon	15	15
B2	A2	15c + 5c bister brn	15	15
		Set value	15	15

The surtax was for child welfare.

Bishop Juan de Ribera — SP1

Design: 20c+5c, The clown Pablo de Valladolid by Velazquez. 30c+10c, Juan de Ribera statue.

1961   *Perf. 13x12½*
B3	SP1	10c + 5c rose brn	15	15
B4	SP1	20c + 5c dk slate grn	15	15
B5	SP1	30c + 10c olive brn	15	15
B6	SP1	50c + 20c brown	15	15
		Set value	32	24

Issued for Stamp Day, 1960.

Mandrill SP2

Design: 25c+10c, Elephant, vert.

Perf. 12½x13, 13x12½

1961, June 21   **Unwmk.**
B7	SP2	10c + 5c rose brn	15	15
B8	SP2	25c + 10c gray vio	15	15
B9	SP2	80c + 20c dk grn	15	15
		Set value	26	18

The surtax was for child welfare.

Statuette — SP3

Design: 25c+10c, 1p+10c, Male figure.

1961, Nov. 23   *Perf. 13x12½*
B10	SP3	10c + 5c rose brn	15	15
B11	SP3	25c + 10c dark pur	15	15
B12	SP3	30c + 10c olive blk	15	15
B13	SP3	1p + 10c red org	15	15
		Set value	32	24

Issued for Stamp Day 1961.

ROMANIA

Rumania, Roumania

LOCATION — Southeastern Europe, bordering on the Black Sea
GOVT. — Republic
AREA — 91,699 sq. mi.
POP. — 22,600,000 (est. 1984)
CAPITAL — Bucharest

Romania was formed in 1861 from the union of the principalities of Moldavia and Walachia in 1859. It became a kingdom in 1881. Following World War I, the original territory was considerably enlarged by the addition of Bessarabia, Bukovina, Transylvania, Crisana, Maramures and Banat. The republic was established in 1948.

40 Parale = 1 Piaster
100 Bani = 1 Leu (plural "Lei") (1868)

> Catalogue values for unused stamps in this country are for Never Hinged items, beginning with Scott 475 in the regular postage section, Scott B82 in the semi-postal section, Scott C24 in the airpost section, Scott CB1 in the airpost semipostal section, Scott J82 in the postage due section, Scott O1 in the official section, Scott RA16 in the postal tax section, and Scott RAJ1 in the postal tax postage due section.

Watermarks

Wmk. 95- Wavy   Wmk. 163- Coat of
Lines   Arms

No. 163 is not a true watermark, having been impressed after the paper was manufactured.

Wmk. 164- PR   Wmk. 165- PR
                Interlaced

Wmk. 167- Coat of Arms Covering 25
Stamps

Reduced illustration.

Wmk. 200- PR

Wmk. 225 - Crown over PTT, Multiple

Wmk. 230- Crowns and Monograms

Wmk. 276- Cross and Crown Multiple

Wmk. 289- RPR Multiple

Wmk. 358- RPR Multiple in Endless Rows

Wmk. 398- Fr Multiple

> Values of early Romanian stamps vary according to condition. Quotations for Nos. 1-14 are for fine copies. Very fine to superb specimens sell at much higher prices, and inferior or poor copies sell at reduced prices, depending on the condition of the individual specimen.

Moldavia

Coat of Arms
A1   A2

Handstamped
1858, July   **Unwmk.**   *Imperf.*
          Laid Paper
1	A1	27pa blk, *rose*	19,000	5,000.
a.		Tête bêche pair		
2	A1	54pa blue, *grn*	4,200.	2,000.
3	A1	108pa blue, *rose*	14,000.	4,500.
		Wove Paper		
4	A1	81pa blue, *bl*	21,000.	21,000.

Cut to shape or octagonally, Nos. 1-4 sell for one-fourth to one-third of these prices.

1858
      Bluish Wove Paper
5	A2	5pa black	11,500.	4,250.
a.		Tête bêche pair		
6	A2	40pa blue	125.00	85.00
a.		Tête bêche pair	650.00	1,750.
7	A2	80pa red	6,750.	300.00
a.		Tête bêche pair		

1859
      White Wove Paper
8	A2	5pa black	8,000.	4,250.
a.		Tête bêche pair		
b.		Frame broken at bottom	75.00	
c.		As "b," tête bêche pair	300.00	
9	A2	40pa blue	75.00	55.00
b.		Tête bêche pair	300.00	1,000.
10	A2	80pa red	185.00	110.00
b.		Tête bêche pair	975.00	3,000.

No. 8b has a break in the frame at bottom below "A." It was never placed in use.

Moldavia-Walachia

Coat of Arms — A3

Printed by Hand from Single Dies
1862
      White Laid Paper
11	A3	3pa orange	200.00	2,250.
a.		3pa yellow	200.00	2,250.

12	A3	6pa carmine	165.00	180.00
13	A3	6pa red	165.00	180.00
14	A3	30pa blue	45.00	60.00

White Wove Paper

15	A3	6pa org yel	30.00	90.00
a.		3pa lemon	60.00	90.00
16	A3	6pa carmine	24.00	90.00
17	A3	6pa vermilion	18.00	55.00
18	A3	30pa blue	27.50	14.00

Tête bêche pairs

11b	A3	3pa orange		
12a	A3	6pa carmine		
14a	A3	30pa blue		
15b	A3	3pa orange yellow	135.00	
16a	A3	3pa orange carmine	120.00	1,000.
17a	A3	6pa carmine	95.00	
18a	A3	6pa vermilion	72.50	
		30pa blue	105.00	

Nos. 11-18 were printed with a hand press, one at a time, from single dies. The impressions were very irregularly placed and occasionally overlapped. Sheets of 32 (4x8). The 3rd and 4th rows were printed inverted, making the second and third rows tête bêche. All values come in distinct shades, frequently even on the same sheet. The paper of this and the following issues through No. 52 often shows a bluish, grayish or yellowish tint.

1864   Typographed from Plates
White Wove Paper

19	A3	3pa yellow	22.50	1,250.
a.		Tête bêche pair	95.00	
b.		Pair, one sideways	60.00	
20	A3	6pa deep rose	2.50	
a.		Tête bêche pair	14.00	
b.		Pair, one sideways	6.75	
21	A3	30pa deep blue	3.00	21.00
a.		Tête bêche pair	15.00	
b.		Pair, one sideways	7.50	
c.		Bluish wove paper	75.00	

Stamps of 1862 issue range from very clear to blurred impressions but rarely have broken or deformed characteristics. The 1864 issue, though rarely blurred, usually have various imperfections in the letters and numbers. These include breaks, malformations, occasional dots at left of the crown or above the "R" of "PAR," a dot on the middle stroke of the "F," and many other bulges, breaks and spots of color.

The 1864 issue was printed in sheets of 40 (5x8). The first and second rows were inverted. Clichés in the third row were placed sideways, 4 with head to right and 4 with head to left, making one tête bêche pair. The fourth and fifth rows were normally placed.

No. 20 was never placed in use.

All values exist in shades, light to dark.

Counterfeit cancellations exist on #11-21.

Three stamps in this design– 2pa, 5pa, 20pa– were printed on white wove paper in 1864, but never placed in use. Value, set $5.

Romania

Prince Alexandru Ioan
Cuza — A4

TWENTY PARALES:

Type I - The central oval does not touch the inner frame. The "I" of "DECI" extends above and below the other letters.

Type II - The central oval touches the frame at the bottom. The "I" of the "DECI" is the same height as the other letters.

1865, Jan.   Unwmk.   Litho.   *Imperf.*

22	A4	2pa orange	25.00	75.00
a.		2pa yellow	21.00	90.00
b.		2pa ocher	75.00	165.00
23	A4	5pa blue	7.25	90.00
24	A4	20pa red, type I	3.00	4.75
a.		Bluish paper	120.00	
25	A4	20pa red, type II	3.00	4.75
a.		Bluish paper	120.00	

The 20pa types are found se-tenant.

White Laid Paper

26	A4	2pa orange	18.00	60.00
a.		2pa ocher	45.00	
27	A4	5pa blue	32.50	225.00

Prince
Carol — A5

Type I — A6

Type II — A7

TWENTY PARALES:

Type I - A6. The Greek border at the upper right goes from right to left.

Type II - A7. The Greek border at the upper right goes from left to right.

1866-67
Thin Wove Paper

29	A5	2pa blk, *yellow*	3.25	21.00
a.		Thick paper	27.50	165.00
30	A5	5pa blk, *dk bl*	17.00	165.00
a.		5pa black, *indigo*	60.00	300.00
b.		Thick paper	30.00	210.00
31	A6	20pa blk, *rose*, (I)	4.00	5.00
a.		Dot in Greek border, thin paper	350.00	105.00
b.		Thick paper	75.00	35.00
c.		Dot in Greek border, thick paper	100.00	60.00
32	A7	20pa blk, *rose*, (II)	5.00	5.75
a.		Thick paper	75.00	35.00

The 20pa types are found se-tenant.

Faked cancellations are known on Nos. 22-27, 29-32.

The white dot of Nos. 31a and 31c occurs in extreme upper right border.

Thick paper was used in 1866, thin in 1867.

Prince Carol
A8   A9

1868-70

33	A8	2b orange	12.00	7.00
a.		2b yellow	24.00	30.00
34	A8	3b violet ('70)	14.00	12.00
35	A8	4b dk blue	32.50	17.00
36	A8	18b scarlet	140.00	5.50
a.		18b rose	140.00	5.50

1869

37	A9	5b orange yel	35.00	13.00
a.		5b deep orange	40.00	13.00
38	A9	10b blue	17.00	7.00
a.		10b ultramarine	45.00	12.50
b.		10b indigo	50.00	17.50
40	A9	15b vermilion	40.00	10.00
41	A9	25b orange & blue	22.50	8.25
42	A9	50b blue & red	140.00	12.00
a.		50b indigo & red	185.00	12.00

No. 40 on vertically laid paper was not issued. Value $1,250.

Prince Carol
A10   A11

1871-72   *Imperf.*

43	A10	5b rose	27.50	6.50
a.		5b vermilion	30.00	7.75
44	A10	10b orange yel	40.00	12.00
a.		Vertically laid paper	275.00	250.00
45	A10	10b blue	100.00	19.00
46	A10	15b red	100.00	52.50
47	A10	25b olive brown	20.00	14.00

1872

48	A10	10b ultra	14.00	14.00
a.		Vertically laid paper	67.50	80.00
b.		10b greenish blue	95.00	20.00
49	A10	50b blue & red	30.00	150.00

No. 48 is a provisional issue printed from a new plate in which the head is placed further right. Faked cancellations are found on No. 49.

1872   *Perf. 12½*
Wove Paper

50	A10	5b rose	27.50	10.00
a.		5b vermilion	875.00	325.00
51	A10	10b blue	40.00	13.00
a.		10b ultramarine	42.50	14.00
52	A10	25b dark brown	14.00	10.00

No. 43a with faked perforation is frequently offered as No. 50a.

Paris Print, Fine Impression
1872   Typo.   *Perf. 14x13½*
Tinted Paper

53	A11	1½b brnz grn, *bluish*	2.75	28
54	A11	3b green, *bluish*	8.50	55
55	A11	5b bis, *pale buff*	5.00	42
56	A11	10b blue	5.50	42
57	A11	15b red brn, *pale buff*	55.00	2.75
58	A11	25b org, *pale buff*	60.00	3.75
59	A11	50b rose, *pale rose*	67.50	5.75

Nos. 53-59 exist imperf.

Bucharest Print, Rough Impression
Perf. 11, 11½, 13½, and Compound
1876-79

60	A11	1½b brnz grn, *bluish*	4.00	24
61	A11	5b bis, *yelsh*	12.00	30
b.		Printed on both sides		75.00
62	A11	10b bl, *yelsh* ('77)	14.00	35
a.		10b pale bl, *yelsh*	12.00	35
b.		10b dark blue, *yelsh*	17.00	48
d.		Cliché of 5b in plate of 10b ('79)		
63	A11	10b ultra, *yelsh* ('77)	20.00	48
64	A11	15b red brn, *yelsh*	40.00	60
a.		Printed on both sides		100.00
65	A11	30b org red, *yelsh* ('78)	110.00	4.75
a.		Printed on both sides		210.00

#62d has been reprinted in dark blue. The originals are in dull blue. Value of reprint, $30.

Perf. 11, 11½, 13½ and Compound
1879

66	A11	1½b blk, *yelsh*	1.75	15
b.		Imperf.		12.00
67	A11	3b ol grn, *bluish*	5.75	45
a.		Diagonal half used as a 1½b on cover		
68	A11	5b green, *bluish*	2.00	15
69	A11	10b rose, *yelsh*	6.75	15
b.		Cliché of 5b in plate of 10b	100.00	600.00
70	A11	15b rose red, *yelsh*	30.00	2.50
71	A11	25b blue, *yelsh*	24.00	2.25
72	A11	50b bister, *yelsh*	47.50	2.25

There are two varieties of the numerals on the 15b and 50b.

No. 69b has been reprinted in dark rose. Originals are in pale rose. Value of reprint, $30.

King Carol I
A12   A13

1880
White Paper

73	A12	15b brown	6.75	24
74	A12	25b blue	12.00	35

No. 74 exists imperf.

Perf. 13½, 11½ & Compound
1885-89

75	A13	1½b black	1.25	20
a.		Printed on both sides		
76	A13	3b violet	3.50	26
a.		Half used as 1½b on cover		
77	A13	5b green	35.00	2.75
78	A13	15b red brown	6.75	40
79	A13	25b blue	6.75	40

Tinted Paper

80	A13	1½b blk, *bluish*	2.50	40
81	A13	3b vio, *bluish*	3.50	55
82	A13	3b ol grn, *bluish*	3.50	26
83	A13	5b bl grn, *bluish*	3.50	40
84	A13	10b rose, *pale buff*	5.00	40
85	A13	15b red brn, *pale buff*	12.00	40
86	A13	25b bl, *pale buff*	12.00	70
87	A13	50b bis, *pale buff*	40.00	2.75

1889   Wmk. 163
Thin Pale Yellowish Paper

88	A13	1½b black	22.50	1.40
89	A13	3b violet	15.00	1.40
90	A13	5b green	15.00	1.50
91	A13	10b blue	19.00	1.40
92	A13	15b red brown	45.00	2.75
93	A13	25b dark blue	25.00	2.25

King Carol I
A14   A15

1890   *Perf. 13½, 11½ & Compound*

94	A14	1½b maroon	2.50	38
95	A14	3b violet	19.00	65
96	A14	5b emerald	5.50	55
97	A14	10b red	6.00	1.10
a.		10b rose	14.00	2.10
98	A14	15b dk brown	15.00	1.10
99	A14	25b gray blue	11.00	1.10
100	A14	50b orange	47.50	9.50

1891   Unwmk.

101	A14	1½b lilac rose	85	15
b.		Printed on both sides		65.00
102	A14	3b lilac	1.00	15
a.		3b violet	1.40	15
b.		Printed on both sides		
c.		Impressions of 5b on back	100.00	75.00
103	A14	5b emerald	1.40	18
104	A14	10b pale red	5.75	28
a.		Printed on both sides	125.00	100.00
105	A14	15b gray brown	6.50	20
106	A14	25b gray blue	4.00	20
107	A14	50b orange	45.00	1.75

Nos. 101-107 exist imperf.

1891

108	A15	1½b claret	90	40
109	A15	3b lilac	90	40
110	A15	5b emerald	2.50	1.65
111	A15	10b red	2.75	1.65
112	A15	15b gray brown	90	50

25th year of the reign of King Carol I.

1894   Wmk. 164

113	A14	3b lilac	5.00	90
114	A14	5b pale green	3.50	90
115	A14	25b gray blue	6.75	2.25
116	A14	50b orange	14.00	4.75

King Carol I
A17   A18

A19   A20

A21   A23

1893-98   Wmk. 164 & 200

117	A17	1b pale brn	50	15
118	A17	1½b black	40	15
119	A18	3b chocolate	50	15
120	A19	5b blue	60	15
a.		Cliché of the 25b in the plate of 5b	47.50	60.00
121	A19	5b yel grn ('98)	2.50	15
a.		5b emerald	3.00	15
122	A20	10b emerald	1.75	15
123	A20	10b rose ('98)	3.00	15
124	A21	15b rose	1.50	15
125	A21	15b black ('98)	3.00	18
126	A19	25b violet	1.75	15
127	A19	25b indigo ('98)	4.75	18
128	A19	40b gray grn	10.00	18
129	A19	50b orange	7.50	18
130	A23	1 l bis & rose	10.00	38
131	A23	2 l orange & brn	17.50	75
		Nos. 117-131 (15)	65.25	
		Set value		2.30

This watermark may be found in four versions (Wmks. 164, 200 and variations). The paper also varies in thickness.

A 3b orange of type A18; 10b brown, type A20; 15b rose, type A21, and 25b bright green with similar but different border, all watermarked "P R," were prepared but never issued.
Value, each $4.50.
See Nos. 132-157, 224-229. For overprints see Romanian Post Offices in the Turkish Empire Nos. 10-11.

King Carol I — A24

Perf. 11½, 13½ and Compound
1900-03 **Unwmk.**
Thin Paper, Tinted Rose on Back

132	A17	1b pale brown	50	15
133	A24	1b brown ('01)	50	15
134	A24	1b black ('03)	50	15
135	A18	3b red brown	40	15
136	A19	5b emerald	1.25	15
137	A20	10b rose	1.25	15
138	A21	15b black	85	15
139	A21	15b lil gray ('01)	1.25	15
140	A21	15b dk vio ('03)	2.50	15
141	A19	25b blue	2.50	15
142	A19	40b gray grn	6.75	15
143	A19	50b orange	6.75	15
144	A23	1 l bis & rose ('01)	15.00	15
145	A23	1 l grn & blk ('03)	12.50	35
146	A23	2 l org & brn ('01)	14.00	70
147	A23	2 l red brn & blk ('03)	14.00	70
		Nos. 132-147 (16)	80.50	
		Set value		2.50

#132 inscribed BANI; #133-134 BAN.

1900, July **Wmk. 167**

148	A17	1b pale brown	1.75	1.40
149	A18	3b red brown	1.75	1.40
150	A19	5b emerald	3.50	1.50
151	A20	10b rose	3.50	1.50
152	A21	15b black	3.50	1.50
153	A19	25b blue	8.50	2.00
154	A19	40b gray grn	14.00	2.75
155	A19	50b orange	14.00	2.75
156	A23	1 l bis & rose	17.00	3.50
157	A23	2 l orange & brn	20.00	4.00
		Nos. 148-157 (10)	87.50	22.30

Mail Coach Leaving PO — A25

1903 **Unwmk.** **Perf. 14x13½**
Thin Paper, Tinted Rose on Face

158	A25	1b gray brown	1.50	40
159	A25	3b brown violet	2.50	55
160	A25	5b pale green	5.00	95
161	A25	10b rose	4.00	95
162	A25	15b black	4.00	85
163	A25	25b blue	12.00	3.75
164	A25	40b dull green	15.00	4.50
165	A25	50b orange	25.00	6.75
		Nos. 158-165 (8)	69.00	18.70

Counterfeits are plentiful. See note after No. 172. See No. 428.

King Carol I and Façade of New Post Office — A26

1903 **Engr.** **Perf. 13½x14**
Thick Toned Paper

166	A26	15b blue	1.75	1.40
167	A26	25b blue	4.25	2.25
168	A26	40b gray grn	4.50	3.00
169	A26	50b orange	4.50	3.00
170	A26	1 l dk brown	5.25	3.00

171	A26	2 l dull red	30.00	11.50
a.		2 l orange (error)	50.00	30.00
172	A26	5 l dull violet	40.00	24.00
		Nos. 166-172 (7)	90.25	48.15

Opening of the new PO in Bucharest (Nos. 158-172).
Counterfeits exist.

Prince Carol Taking Oath of Allegiance, 1866 — A27

Prince in Royal Carriage — A28

Prince Carol at Calafat in 1877 — A29

Prince Carol Shaking Hands with His Captive, Osman Pasha — A30

Carol I as Prince in 1866 and King in 1906 — A31

Romanian Army Crossing Danube — A32

Romanian Troops Return to Bucharest in 1878 — A33

Prince Carol at Head of His Command in 1877 — A34

King Carol I at the Cathedral in 1896 — A35

King Carol I at Shrine of St. Nicholas, 1904 — A36

1906 **Engr.** **Perf. 12**

176	A27	1b bister & blk	18	15
177	A28	3b red brn & blk	22	15
178	A29	5b dp grn & blk	48	15
179	A30	10b car & blk	18	15
180	A31	15b dull vio & blk	18	15
181	A32	25b ultra & blk	1.90	60
a.		25b olive green & black	1.90	60
182	A33	40b dk brn & blk	48	30
183	A34	50b bis brn & blk	55	30
184	A35	1 l ver & blk	65	42
185	A36	2 l orange & blk	65	50
		Nos. 176-185 (10)	5.47	2.87

40 years' rule of Carol I as Prince & King.
No. 181a was never placed in use. Cancellations were by favor.

King Carol I — A37

1906

186	A37	1b bister & blk	18	15
187	A37	3b red brn & blk	55	15
188	A37	5b dp grn & blk	20	15
189	A37	10b car & blk	20	15
190	A37	15b dl vio & blk	45	15
191	A37	25b ultra & blk	5.00	1.90
192	A37	40b dk brn & blk	60	22
193	A37	50b bis brn & blk	60	22
194	A37	1 l red & blk	70	22
195	A37	2 l orange & blk	70	22
		Nos. 186-195 (10)	9.18	3.53

25th anniversary of the Kingdom.

Plowman and Angel — A38

Exposition Building — A39

Exposition Buildings
A40   A41

King Carol I — A42   Queen Elizabeth (Carmen Sylva) — A43

1906 **Typo.** **Perf. 11½, 13½**

196	A38	5b yel grn & blk	1.75	40
197	A38	10b car & blk	1.75	40
198	A39	15b vio & blk	2.50	70
199	A39	25b blue & blk	2.50	70
200	A40	30b red & blk brn	3.00	70
201	A40	40b grn & blk brn	3.00	85
202	A41	50b org & blk	3.00	1.25
203	A41	75b lt brn & dk brn	3.00	1.40
204	A42	1.50 1 red lil & blk brn	12.00	6.00
a.		Center inverted		
205	A42	2.50 1 yel & brn	12.00	6.00
a.		Center inverted		
206	A43	3 1 brn org & brn	12.00	6.00
		Nos. 196-206 (11)	56.50	24.40

General Exposition. They were sold at post offices July 29-31, 1906, and were valid only for those three days. Those sold at the exposition are overprinted "S E" in black. Remainders were sold privately, both unused and canceled to order, by the Exposition promoters.

King Carol I
A44   A45   A46

Perf. 11½, 13½ & Compound
1908-18 **Engr.**

207	A44	5b pale yel grn	1.10	15
208	A44	10b carmine	95	15
209	A45	15b purple	9.50	1.10
210	A45	25b deep blue	95	15
211	A44	40b brt green	60	15
212	A44	40b dk brn ('18)	2.75	55
213	A44	50b orange	75	15
214	A44	50b lt red ('18)	60	28
215	A44	1 l brown	95	15
216	A44	2 l red	4.25	1.10
		Nos. 207-216 (10)	22.40	3.93

Perf. 13½x14, 11½, 13½ & Compound
1909-18 **Typo.**

217	A46	1b black	15	15
218	A46	3b red brown	15	15
219	A46	5b yellow grn	15	15
220	A46	10b rose	15	15
221	A46	15b dull violet	10.50	4.75
222	A46	15b olive green	18	15
223	A46	15b red brn ('18)	48	25
		Nos. 217-223 (7)	11.76	5.75

Nos. 217-219, 222 exist imperf.
No. 219 in black is a chemical changeling.
For surcharge and overprints see Nos. 240-242, 245-247, J50-J51, RA1-RA2, RA11-RA12, Romanian Post Offices in the Turkish Empire 7-9.

Types of 1893-99
1911-19 **White Paper** **Unwmk.**

224	A17	1½b straw	70	32
225	A19	25b deep blue ('18)	35	15
226	A19	40b gray brn ('19)	70	42
227	A19	50b dull red ('19)	70	32
228	A23	1 l gray grn ('18)	1.25	25
229	A23	2 l orange ('18)	1.40	32
		Nos. 224-229 (6)	5.10	1.78

For overprints see Romanian Post Offices in the Turkish Empire Nos. 10-11.

Romania Holding Flag — A47   Romanian Crown and Old Fort on Danube — A48

Troops Crossing Danube — A49   View of Turtucaia — A50

Mircea the Great and Carol I — A51

View of Silistra — A52

Perf. 11½x13½, 13½x11½
1913, Dec. 25

230	A47	1b black	35	16
231	A48	3b ol gray & choc	80	28
232	A49	5b yel grn & blk brn	65	16
233	A50	10b org & gray	35	16
234	A51	15b bister & vio	80	28

235	A52	25b blue & choc	1.25	40
236	A49	40b bis & red vio	2.00	70
237	A48	50b yellow & bl	2.25	1.40
238	A48	1 l bl & ol bis	6.75	3.25
239	A48	2 l org red & rose	8.00	4.25
		Nos. 230-239 (10)	23.20	11.04

Romania's annexation of Silistra.

25 BANI

No. 217 Handstamped in Red

Perf. 13¹/₂x14, 11¹/₂, 13¹/₂ & Compound

1918, May 1

240	A46	25b on 1b blk	25	15

This handstamp is found inverted.

No. 219 and 220 Overprinted in Black

1918

241	A46	5b yellow green	30	18
a.		Inverted overprint	7.00	5.00
b.		Double overprint	7.00	
242	A46	10b rose	30	18
a.		Inverted overprint	7.00	5.00
b.		Double overprint	7.00	

Nos. 217, 219 and 220 Overprinted in Red or Black

1919, Nov. 8

245	A46	1b black (R)	15	15
a.		Inverted overprint	6.00	
b.		Double overprint	9.00	2.00
246	A46	5b yel grn (Bk)	15	15
a.		Inverted overprint	9.00	1.75
247	A46	10b rose (Bk)	15	15
a.		Inverted overprint	6.00	1.75
b.		Double overprint	9.00	2.00
		Set value		24

Recovery of Transylvania and the return of the King to Bucharest.

King Ferdinand
A53   A54

1920-22   Typo.

248	A53	1b black	15	15
249	A53	5b yellow grn	15	15
250	A53	10b rose	15	15
251	A53	15b red brown	45	15
252	A53	25b deep blue	95	15
253	A53	25b brown	45	15
254	A53	40b gray brown	75	15
255	A53	50b salmon	20	15
256	A53	1 l gray grn	75	15
257	A53	1 l rose	45	20
258	A53	2 l orange	75	20
259	A53	2 l dp blue	75	20
260	A53	2 l rose ('22)	1.90	1.25
		Nos. 248-260 (13)	7.85	
		Set value		2.60

Nos. 248-260 are printed on two papers: coarse, grayish paper with bits of colored fiber, and thinner white paper of better quality.

Nos. 248-251, 253 exist imperf.

TWO LEI:
Type I - The "2" is thin, with tail 2¹/₂mm wide. Top of "2" forms a hook.

Type II - The "2" is thick, with tail 3mm wide. Top of "2" forms a ball.
Type III - The "2" is similar to type II. The "E" of "LEI" is larger and about 2mm wide.

THREE LEI:
Type I - Top of "3" begins in a point. Top and middle bars of "E" of "LEI" are without serifs.
Type II - Top of "3" begins in a ball. Top and middle bars of "E" of "LEI" have serifs.

FIVE LEI:
Type I - The "5" is 2¹/₂mm wide. The end of the final stroke of the "L" of "LEI" almost touches the vertical stroke.
Type II - The "5" is 3mm wide and the lines are broader than in type I. The end of the final stroke of the "L" of "LEI" is separated from the vertical by a narrow space.

Perf. 13¹/₂x14, 11¹/₂, 13¹/₂ & Compound

1920-26

261	A54	3b black	15	15
262	A54	5b black	15	15
263	A54	10b yel grn ('25)	15	15
a.		10b olive green ('25)	35	
264	A54	25b bister brn	15	15
265	A54	25b salmon	15	15
266	A54	30b violet	20	15
267	A54	50b orange	15	15
268	A54	60b gray grn	60	30
269	A54	1 l violet	20	15
270	A54	2 l rose (I)	75	20
a.		2 l claret (I)	25.00	
271	A54	2 l lt green (II)	50	15
a.		2 l light green (I)	75	15
b.		2 l light green (III)	60	15
272	A54	3 l blue (I)	1.50	28
273	A54	3 l buff (II)	60	20
a.		3 l buff (I)	3.00	45
274	A54	3 l salmon (II)	24	15
a.		3 l salmon (I)	1.25	75
275	A54	3 l car rose (II)	45	15
276	A54	5 l emer (I)	1.25	20
277	A54	5 l lt brn (II)	45	15
a.		5 l light brown (I)	1.25	24
278	A54	6 l blue	1.75	60
279	A54	6 l carmine	2.75	95
280	A54	6 l ol grn ('26)	1.75	38
281	A54	7¹/₂ l pale bl	1.40	24
282	A54	10 l deep blue	1.40	20
		Nos. 261-282 (22)	16.69	
		Set value		4.25

#273 and 273a, also 274 and 274a, exist found se-tenant. The 50b exists in three types.
For surcharge see No. Q7.

Alba Iulia
Cathedral
A55

King
Ferdinand
A56

Coat of
Arms — A57

Queen Marie
as
Nurse — A58

Michael the Brave and
King Ferdinand
A59

King
Ferdinand
A60

Queen Marie — A61

Perf. 13¹/₂x14, 13¹/₂, 11¹/₂ & Compound

1922, Oct. 15 Photo. **Wmk. 95**

283	A55	5b black	15	15
a.		Engraver's name omitted	2.50	1.40
284	A56	25b chocolate	24	18
285	A57	50b dp green	50	24
286	A58	1 l olive grn	50	35
287	A59	2 l carmine	70	45
288	A60	3 l blue	1.40	70
289	A61	6 l violet	5.00	4.00
		Nos. 283-289 (7)	8.49	6.07

Coronation of King Ferdinand I and Queen Marie on Oct. 15, 1922, at Alba Iulia. All values exist imperforate.

King Ferdinand
A62   A63

1926, July 1 Unwmk. *Perf. 11*

291	A62	10b yellow grn	15	15
292	A62	25b orange	15	15
293	A62	50b orange brn	15	15
294	A63	1 l dk violet	15	15
295	A63	2 l dk green	15	15
296	A63	3 l brown car	15	15
297	A63	5 l black brn	15	15
298	A63	6 l dk olive	15	15
a.		6 l bright blue (error)	70.00	70.00
300	A63	9 l slate	15	15
301	A63	10 l brt blue	15	15
a.		10 l brown carmine (error)	70.00	70.00
		Nos. 291-301 (10)	1.50	1.50

60th birthday of King Ferdinand.
Exist imperf. Imperf. examples with watermark 95 are proofs.

King Carol I
and King
Ferdinand
A69

King
Ferdinand
A70

A71

1927, Aug. 1   *Perf. 13¹/₂*

308	A69	25b brown vio	20	20
309	A70	30b gray blk	20	20
310	A71	50b dk green	20	20
311	A69	1 l bluish slate	20	20
312	A70	2 l dp green	24	24
313	A70	3 l violet	32	32
314	A71	4 l dk brown	40	40
315	A71	4.50 l henna brn	1.25	1.25
316	A70	5 l red brown	40	40
317	A71	6 l carmine	85	85
318	A69	7.50 l grnsh bl	60	60
319	A69	10 l brt blue	85	85
		Nos. 308-319 (12)	5.71	5.71

50th anniversary of Romania's independence from Turkish suzerainty.
Some values exist imperf. All exist imperf. and with value numerals omitted.

King Michael
A72   A73

Perf. 13¹/₂x14 (25b, 50b); 13¹/₂

1928-29   Typo.   Unwmk.

Size: 19x25mm

320	A72	25b black	15	15
321	A72	30b fawn ('29)	20	15
322	A72	50b olive grn	15	15

Photo.

Size: 18¹/₂x24¹/₂mm

323	A73	1 l violet	20	15
324	A73	2 l dp green	24	15
325	A73	3 l brt rose	32	15
326	A73	5 l red brown	52	15
327	A73	7.50 l ultra	2.25	35
328	A73	10 l blue	1.90	18
		Nos. 320-328 (9)	5.93	
		Set value		1.10

See Nos. 343-345, 353-357. For overprints see Nos. 359-368A.

Parliament
House,
Bessarabia
A74

Designs: 1 l, 2 l, Parliament House, Bessarabia. 3 l, 5 l, 20 l, Hotin Fortress. 7.50 l, 10 l, Fortress Cetatea Alba.

1928, Apr. 29 Wmk. 95 *Perf. 13¹/₂*

329	A74	1 l deep green	50	25
330	A74	2 l deep brown	50	25
331	A74	3 l black brown	50	25
332	A74	5 l carmine lake	60	32
333	A74	7.50 l ultra	60	32
334	A74	10 l Prus blue	1.40	90
335	A74	20 l black vio	1.75	1.10
		Nos. 329-335 (7)	5.85	3.39

Reunion of Bessarabia with Romania, 10th anniv.

King Carol I
and King
Michael
A77

View of
Constanta
Harbor
A78

Trajan's
Monument
at Adam
Clisi — A79

Cernavoda
Bridge
A80

1928, Oct. 25

336	A77	1 l blue green	48	24
337	A77	2 l red brown	48	24
338	A77	3 l gray black	60	24
339	A79	5 l dull lilac	75	38
340	A79	7.50 l ultra	90	48
341	A80	10 l blue	1.25	60
342	A80	20 l carmine rose	1.90	75
		Nos. 336-342 (7)	6.36	2.83

50th anniv. of the union of Dobruja with Romania.

Michael Types of 1928-29

Perf. 13¹/₂x14

1928, Sept. 1 Typo. Wmk. 95

343	A72	25b black	35	15

Photo.

344	A73	7.50 l ultra	1.25	52
345	A73	10 l blue	2.50	35

Ferdinand I; Stephen the Great; Michael the Brave; Corvin and Constantine Brancoveanu
A81

Union with Transylvania A82

Avram Jancu A83

Prince Michael the Brave — A84

Castle Bran — A85

King Ferdinand I — A86

1929, May 10   Photo.   Wmk. 95

347	A81	1 l dark violet	1.10	60
348	A82	2 l olive green	1.10	60
349	A83	3 l violet brown	1.40	75
350	A84	4 l cerise	1.40	90
351	A85	5 l orange	1.75	90
352	A86	10 l brt blue	2.00	1.50
		Nos. 347-352 (6)	8.75	5.25

Union of Transylvania and Romania.

Michael Type of 1928

1930   Unwmk.   Perf. 14¹⁄₂x14
Size: 18x23mm

353	A73	1 l deep violet	40	15
354	A73	2 l deep green	60	15
355	A73	3 l carmine rose	1.50	15
356	A73	7.50 l ultra	2.25	35
357	A73	10 l deep blue	7.50	2.50
		Nos. 353-357 (5)	12.25	3.30

Stamps of 1928-30 **8 IUNIE 1930** Overprinted

On Nos. 320-322, 326, 328

Perf. 13¹⁄₂x14, 13¹⁄₂

1930, June 8			**Typo.**	
359	A72	25b black	18	15
360	A72	30b fawn	24	15
361	A72	50b olive green	24	15

Photo.
Size: 18¹⁄₂x24¹⁄₂mm

362	A73	5 l red brown	45	15
362A	A73	10 l brt blue	2.50	55

On Nos. 353-357
Perf. 14¹⁄₂x14
Size: 18x23mm

363	A73	1 l deep violet	24	55
364	A73	2 l deep green	24	15
365	A73	3 l carmine rose	38	15
366	A73	7.50 l ultra	1.40	35
367	A73	10 l deep blue	1.10	22

On Nos. 343-344
Perf. 13¹⁄₂x14, 13¹⁄₂
Typo.   Wmk. 95

368	A72	25b black	45	15

Photo.
Size: 18¹⁄₂x24¹⁄₂mm

368A	A73	7.50 l ultra	1.90	50
		Nos. 359-368A (12)	9.32	
		Set value		2.65

Accession to the throne by King Carol II.
This overprint exists on Nos. 323, 345.

King Carol II A87

A88

A89

Perf. 13¹⁄₂, 14, 14x13¹⁄₂
1930   Wmk. 225

369	A87	25b black	15	15
370	A87	50b chocolate	24	18
371	A87	1 l dk violet	15	15
372	A87	2 l gray green	18	15
373	A88	3 l carmine rose	35	15
374	A88	4 l orange red	35	15
375	A88	6 l carmine brn	45	15
376	A88	7.50 l ultra	50	15
377	A89	10 l deep blue	1.25	15
378	A89	16 l peacock grn	3.00	15
379	A89	20 l orange	3.50	26
		Nos. 369-379 (11)	10.12	
		Set value		95

Exist imperf. See Nos. 405-414.

A90

A91

1930, Dec. 24   Unwmk.   Perf. 13¹⁄₂

380	A90	1 l dull violet	52	15
381	A91	2 l green	52	15
382	A91	4 l vermilion	75	15
383	A91	6 l brown car	1.90	15

First census in Romania.

King Carol II — A92

King Carol I — A93

King Ferdinand — A96

King Carol II — A94

King Carol II, King Ferdinand and King Carol I — A95

1931, May 10   Photo.   Wmk. 225

384	A92	1 l gray violet	2.50	85
385	A93	2 l green	3.00	85
386	A94	6 l red brown	4.50	1.50

387	A95	10 l blue	7.50	3.00
388	A96	20 l orange	8.50	4.75
		Nos. 384-388 (5)	26.00	10.95

50th anniversary of Romanian Kingdom.

Using Bayonet — A97

Romanian Infantryman 1870 — A98

Romanian Infantry 1830 — A99

King Carol I — A100

Infantry Advance A101

King Ferdinand A102

King Carol II — A103

1931, May 10

389	A97	25b gray black	80	48
390	A98	50b dk red brn	1.25	55
391	A99	1 l gray violet	1.40	60
392	A100	2 l deep green	2.50	90
393	A101	3 l carmine rose	5.00	2.75
394	A102	7.50 l ultra	6.50	3.75
395	A103	16 l blue green	8.00	5.00
		Nos. 389-395 (7)	25.45	14.03

Centenary of the Romanian Army.

Naval Cadet Ship "Mircea" — A104

King Carol II — A108

Designs: 10 l, Ironclad. 16 l, Light cruiser. 20 l, Destroyer.

1931, May 10

396	A104	6 l red brown	3.75	1.75
397	A104	10 l blue	3.75	1.75
398	A104	16 l blue green	14.00	3.00
399	A104	20 l orange	7.50	4.00

50th anniversary of the Romanian Navy.

1931   Unwmk.   Engr.   Perf. 12

400	A108	30 l ol bis & dk bl	35	18
401	A108	50 l red & dk bl	1.25	38
402	A108	100 l dk grn & dk bl	1.50	50

Exist imperf.

Carol II, Ferdinand, Carol I — A109

1931, Nov. 1   Photo.   Wmk. 230

403	A109	16 l Prus green	6.25	25

Exists imperf.

Carol II Types of 1930-31

Perf. 13¹⁄₂, 14, 14¹⁄₂ and Compound
1932   Wmk. 230

405	A87	25b black	30	15
406	A87	50b dark brown	42	15
407	A87	1 l dark violet	75	15
408	A87	2 l gray green	75	15
409	A88	3 l carmine rose	1.25	15
410	A88	4 l orange red	2.25	15
411	A88	6 l carmine brn	4.00	15
412	A88	7.50 l ultra	6.00	38
413	A89	10 l deep blue	60.00	45
414	A89	20 l orange	60.00	5.00
		Nos. 405-414 (10)	135.72	6.88

Alexander the Good A110

King Carol II A111

1932, May   Perf. 13¹⁄₂

415	A110	6 l carmine brown	7.50	5.75

500th death anniv. of Alexander the Good, Prince of Moldavia, 1400-1432.

1932, June

416	A111	10 l brt blue	7.50	30

Exists imperf.

Cantacuzino and Gregory Ghika, Founders of Coltea and Pantelimon Hospitals A112

Session of the Congress A113

Aesculapius and Hygeia A114

1932, Sept.   Perf. 13¹⁄₂

417	A112	1 l carmine rose	4.75	3.50
418	A113	6 l deep orange	12.00	5.50
419	A114	10 l brt blue	19.00	10.00

9th Intl. History of Medicine Congress, Bucharest.

Bull's Head and Post Horn A116

Lion Rampant and Bridge A117

Dolphins
A118

Eagle and
Castles
A119

Coat of
Arms — A120

Eagle and Post
Horn — A121

Bull's Head and Post
Horn — A122

1932, Nov. 20   Typo.   Imperf.

421	A116	25b black	75	22
422	A117	1 l violet	1.10	40
423	A118	2 l green	1.40	45
424	A119	3 l car rose	1.65	60
425	A120	6 l red brown	2.25	75
426	A121	7.50 l lt blue	2.25	75
427	A122	10 l dk blue	3.00	1.10
		Nos. 421-427 (7)	12.40	4.27

75th anniv. of the first Moldavian stamps.

Mail Coach Type of 1903

1932, Nov. 20   Perf. 13½

428 A25 16 l blue green   6.75 2.50

30th anniv. of the opening of the new post office,
Bucharest, in 1903.

Arms of City of Turnu-Severin, Ruins of
Tower of Emperor Severus
A123

Inauguration
of Trajan's
Bridge
A124

Prince Carol
Landing at
Turnu-Severin
A125

Bridge over
the Danube
A126

1933, June 2   Photo.   Perf. 14½x14

429	A123	25b gray green	22	15
430	A124	50b dull blue	45	20
431	A125	1 l black brn	45	24
432	A124	2 l olive blk	1.10	35

Centenary of the incorporation in Walachia of
the old Roman City of Turnu-Severin.
Exist imperf.

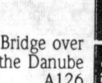

Queen
Elizabeth and
King Carol
I — A127

Profiles of
Kings Carol I,
Ferdinand
and Carol
II — A128

Castle Peles,
Sinaia
A129

1933, Aug.

433	A127	1 l dark violet	1.50	1.25
434	A128	3 l olive brown	1.50	1.25
435	A129	6 l vermilion	2.25	1.65

50th anniversary of the erection of Castle Peles,
the royal summer residence at Sinaia.
Exist imperf.

King Carol II — A130   A130   A131

King Carol II — A132

1934, Aug.   Perf. 13½

436	A130	50b brown	40	20
437	A131	2 l gray green	70	25
438	A131	4 l red	1.10	32
439	A132	6 l deep claret	3.25	20

See Nos. 446-460 for stamps inscribed "Posta."
Nos. 436, 439 exist imperf.

Child and
Grapes — A133

Woman and
Fruit — A134

1934, Sept. 14

440	A133	1 l dull green	1.40	1.10
441	A134	2 l violet brown	1.40	1.10

Natl. Fruit Week, Sept. 14-21. Exist imperf.

Crisan, Horia
and Closca
A135

1935, Feb. 28

442	A135	1 l shown	35	25
443	A135	2 l Crisan	45	38
444	A135	6 l Closca	90	50
445	A135	10 l Horia	1.75	1.00

150th anniversary of the death of three
Romanian martyrs. Exist imperf.

A139   A140

A141   A142

King Carol II — A143

Perf. 13½

		Photo.	Wmk. 230	
1935-40				
446	A139	25b black brn	15	15
447	A142	50b brown	15	15
448	A140	1 l purple	15	15
449	A141	2 l green	15	15
449A	A141	2 l dk bl grn ('40)	25	25
450	A142	3 l deep rose	15	15
450A	A142	3 l grnsh bl ('40)	30	30
451	A141	4 l vermilion	42	15
452	A140	5 l rose car ('40)	42	42
453	A143	6 l maroon	35	15
454	A140	7.50 l ultra	60	20
454A	A142	8 l magenta ('40)	60	60
455	A141	9 l brt ultra ('40)	90	90
456	A142	10 l brt blue	30	18
456A	A143	12 l sl bl ('40)	52	52
457	A139	15 l dk brn ('40)	52	52
458	A143	16 l Prus blue	60	15
459	A143	20 l orange	42	24
460	A143	24 l dk car ('40)	85	85
		Nos. 446-460 (19)	7.80	
		Set value		5.40

Exist imperf.

Nos. 454, 456
Overprinted in Red

CEHOSLOVACIA

YUGOSLAVIA

1920-1936

1936, Dec. 5

461	A140	7.50 l ultra	2.25	1.75
462	A142	10 l brt blue	2.25	1.75

16th anniversary of the Little Entente.
Overprints in silver or gold are fraudulent.

Birthplace of
Ion Creanga
A144

Ion Creanga
A145

1937, May 15

463	A144	2 l green	50	35
464	A145	3 l carmine rose	50	35
465	A144	4 l dp violet	75	50
466	A145	6 l red brown	75	65

Creanga (1837-89), writer. Exist imperf.

Cathedral at Curtea de
Arges — A146

1937, July 1

467	A146	7.50 l ultra	1.25	40
468	A146	10 l blue	2.10	35

The Little Entente (Romania, Czechoslovakia,
Yugoslavia). Exist imperf.

Souvenir Sheet

A146a

Surcharged in Black with New Values

1937, Oct. 25   Unwmk.   Perf. 13½

469	A146a	Sheet of 4	3.00	3.00
a.		2 l on 20 l orange	30	30
b.		6 l on 10 l bright blue	30	30
c.		10 l on 6 l maroon	30	30
d.		20 l on 2 l green	30	30

Promotion of the Crown Prince Michael to the
rank of Lieutenant on his 17th birthday.

Arms of Romania,
Greece, Turkey and
Yugoslavia — A147

Perf. 13x13½

1938, Feb. 10   Wmk. 230

470	A147	7.50 l ultra	75	50
471	A147	10 l blue	1.25	50

The Balkan Entente.

A148

King Carol II
A149   A150

1938, May 10   Perf. 13½

472	A148	3 l dk carmine	35	15
473	A149	6 l violet brn	35	15
474	A150	10 l blue	50	20

New Constitution of Feb. 27, 1938.

Catalogue values for unused
stamps in this section, from this
point to the end of the section, are
for Never Hinged items.

Prince Carol
at Calatorie,
1866
A151

Examining Plans
for a Monastery
A153

Prince Carol and
Carmen Sylva
(Queen Elizabeth)
A155

Sigmaringen
and Peles
Castles
A154

Prince Carol, Age
6 — A156

Equestrian
Statue — A159

Battle of Plevna
A160

On Horseback
A161

Cathedral of Curtea de
Arges — A164

King Carol I
and Queen
Elizabeth
A163

Designs: 50b, At Calafat. 4 l, In
1866. 5 l, In 1877. 12 l, in 1914.

Perf. 14, 13½

1939, Apr. 10   **Wmk. 230**

475	A151	25b olive blk	15	15
476	A151	50b violet brn	15	15
477	A153	1 l dk purple	15	15
478	A154	1.50 l green	15	15
479	A155	2 l myrtle grn	15	15
480	A156	3 l red orange	15	15
481	A156	4 l rose lake	15	15
482	A156	5 l black	15	15
483	A159	7 l olive blk	15	15
484	A160	8 l dark blue	18	15
485	A161	10 l deep mag	22	15
486	A161	12 l dull blue	30	15
487	A163	15 l ultra	38	15
488	A164	16 l Prus green	90	38
		Set value	2.80	1.30

Centenary of the birth of King Carol I.

Souvenir Sheets

1939   **Perf. 14x13½**

488A	Sheet of 3, #475-476, 478	1.50	1.50
d.	Imperf. ('40)	2.25	2.25

Perf. 14x15½

488B	Sheet of 4, #480-482, 486	1.50	1.50
e.	Imperf. ('40)	2.25	2.25
488C	Sheet of 4, #479, 483-485	1.50	1.50
f.	Imperf. ('40)	2.25	2.25

No. 488A sold for 20 l, Nos. 488B-488C for 50 l, the surtax for national defense.

Nos. 488A-488C and 488d-488f were overprinted "PRO-PATRIA 1940" to aid the armament fund. Value, set of 6, $80.

Nos. 488A-488C exist with overprint of "ROMA BERLIN 1940" and bars, but these are not recognized as having been officially issued.

Romanian
Pavilion
A165

Romanian
Pavilion
A166

1939, May 8   **Perf. 14x13½, 13½**

489	A165	6 l brown carmine	28	28
490	A166	12 l brt blue	28	28

New York World's Fair.

Mihail Eminescu
A167   A168

1939, May 22   **Perf. 13½**

491	A167	5 l olive gray	35	35
492	A168	7 l brown carmine	35	35

Mihail Eminescu, poet, 50th death anniv.

Three Types
of
Locomotives
A169

Modern Train
A170

Wood-burning
Locomotive
A171

Streamlined
Locomotive
A172

Railroad
Terminal
A173

1939, June 10   **Typo.**   **Perf. 14**

493	A169	1 l red violet	40	28
494	A170	4 l deep rose	55	28
495	A171	5 l gray lilac	60	28
496	A171	7 l claret	70	35
497	A172	12 l blue	90	90
498	A173	15 l green	2.00	1.25
		Nos. 493-498 (6)	5.15	3.34

Romanian Railways, 70th anniversary.

Arms of Romania,
Greece, Turkey and
Yugoslavia — A174

Perf. 13½

1940, May 27   **Photo.**   **Wmk. 230**

504	A174	12 l lt ultra	35	35
505	A174	16 l dull blue	35	35

The Balkan Entente.

King
Michael — A175

1940-42   **Wmk. 230**   **Perf. 14**

506	A175	25b Prus green	15	15
506A	A175	50b dk grn ('42)	15	15
507	A175	1 l purple	15	15
508	A175	2 l red orange	15	15
508A	A175	4 l slate ('42)	15	15
509	A175	5 l rose pink	15	15
509A	A175	7 l dp blue ('42)	15	15
510	A175	10 l dp magenta	24	15
511	A175	12 l dull blue	15	15
511A	A175	13 l dk vio ('42)	24	15
512	A175	16 l Prus blue	24	15
513	A175	20 l brown	1.25	15
514	A175	30 l yellow grn	15	15
515	A175	50 l olive brn	20	15
516	A175	100 l rose brown	28	15
		Set value	2.85	80

See Nos. 535A-553.

Prince Duca — A176

1941, Oct. 6   **Perf. 13½**

517	A176	6 l lt brown	15	15
518	A176	12 l dk violet	18	18
519	A176	24 l brt blue	20	20

Crossing of the Dniester River by Romanian forces invading Russia.

Nos. 517-519 each exist in an imperf., ungummed souvenir sheet of 4. These were prepared by the civil government of Trans-Dniestria to be sold for 300 lei apiece to aid the Red Cross, but were not recognized by the national government at Bucharest. The sheets reached philatelic channels in 1946.

See Nos. 554-557.

Hotin Chapel,
Bessarabia — A177   Sucevita Monastery,
Bucovina — A179

Inscribed "Basarabia" or "Bucovina" at bottom

Designs: 50b, 9.50 l, Hotin Fortress, Bessarabia. 1.50 l, Soroca Fortress, Bessarabia. 2 l, 5.50 l, Tighina Fortress, Bessarabia. 3 l, Dragomirna Monastery, Bucovina. 6.50 l, Cetatea Alba Fortress, Bessarabia. 10 l, 130 l, Putna Monastery, Bucovina. 13 l, Milisauti Monastery, Bucovina. 26 l, St. Nicholas Monastery, Suceava, Bucovina. 39 l, Rughi Monastery, Bessarabia.

1941, Dec. 1   **Perf. 13½**

520	A177	25b rose car	15	15
521	A179	50b red brn	15	15
522	A179	1 l dp vio	15	15
523	A179	1.50 l green	15	15
524	A179	2 l brn org	15	15
525	A177	3 l dk ol grn	15	15
526	A177	5 l olive blk	15	15
527	A179	5 l brown	15	15
528	A179	6.50 l magenta	28	22
529	A179	9.50 l gray blk	28	22
530	A179	10 l dk vio brn	18	15
531	A179	13 l slate blue	24	15
532	A179	17 l brn car	28	15
533	A179	26 l gray grn	35	24
534	A179	39 l bl grn	52	38
535	A179	130 l yel org	2.00	1.50
		Nos. 520-535 (16)	5.33	
		Set value		3.25

See Nos. B179-B187.

Type of 1940-42

1943-45   **Wmk. 276**   **Perf. 14**

535A	A175	25b Prus grn ('44)	15	15
536	A175	50b dk grn ('44)	15	15
537	A175	1 l dk vio ('43)	15	15
538	A175	2 l red org ('43)	15	15
539	A175	3 l red brn ('44)	15	15
540	A175	3.50 l brn ('43)	15	15
541	A175	4 l slate	15	15
542	A175	4.50 l dk brn ('43)	15	15
543	A175	5 l rose car	15	15
544	A175	6.50 l dl vio	15	15
545	A175	7 l dp bl	15	15
546	A175	10 l dp mag	15	15
547	A175	11 l brt ultra	15	15
548	A175	12 l dark blue	15	15
549	A175	15 l royal blue	15	15
550	A175	16 l dp blue	15	15
551	A175	20 l brn ('43)	15	15
551A	A175	29 l ultra ('45)	48	30
552	A175	30 l yel grn	15	15
553	A175	50 l olive blk	22	15
		Set value	1.60	1.25

Prince Duca Type of 1941

1943   **Perf. 13½**

554	A176	3 l red org	15	15
555	A176	6 l dl brn	15	15
556	A176	12 l dl vio	15	15
557	A176	24 l brt bl	22	22
		Set value	55	55

Andrei Saguna — A188

Andrei
Muresanu
A189

Transylvanians: 4.50 l, Samuel Micu. 11 l, Gheorghe Sincai. 15 l, Michael the Brave. 31 l, Gheorghe Lazar. 35 l, Avram Iancu. 41 l, Simeon Barnutiu. 55 l, Three Heroes. 61 l, Petru Maior.

1945   **Inscribed "1944"**   **Perf. 14**

558	A188	25b rose red	28	28
559	A189	50b orange	20	20
560	A189	4.50 l brown	20	20
561	A188	11 l lt ultra	20	20
562	A188	15 l Prus grn	20	20
563	A189	31 l dl vio	20	20
564	A188	35 l bl blk	20	20
565	A188	41 l olive gray	20	20
566	A189	55 l red brown	20	20
567	A189	61 l deep magenta	20	20
		Nos. 558-567,B251 (11)	2.56	2.56

Romania's liberation.

A198　　　A199

King Michael
A200　　A201

1945

			Photo.	
568	A198	50b gray blue	15	15
569	A199	1 l dl brn	15	15
570	A199	2 l violet	15	15
571	A198	2 l sepia	15	15
572	A199	4 l yel grn	15	15
573	A200	5 l dp mag	15	15
574	A198	10 l blue	15	15
575	A198	15 l magenta	15	15
576	A198	20 l dl blue	15	15
577	A200	25 l red org	15	15
578	A200	35 l brown	15	15
579	A200	40 l car rose	15	15
580	A199	50 l pale ultra	15	15
581	A199	55 l red	15	15
582	A200	75 l Prus grn	15	15
583	A201	80 l orange	15	15
584	A201	100 l dp red brn	15	15
585	A201	160 l yel grn	15	15
586	A201	200 l dk ol grn	22	15
587	A201	400 l dl vio	15	15
		Set value	1.10	1.00

Nos. 571, 573, 580, 581, 585 and 587 are printed on toned paper, Nos. 576, 577, 583, 584 and 586 on both toned and white papers, others on white paper only.

See Nos. 610-624, 651-660.

Mail Carrier
A202

Telegraph Operator
A203

Lineman
A204

Post Office, Bucharest
A205

1945, July 20　　Wmk. 276　　Perf. 13

588	A202	100 l dk brn	75	75
589	A202	100 l gray olive	75	75
590	A203	150 l brown	1.25	1.25
591	A203	150 l brt rose	1.25	1.25
592	A204	250 l lt gray ol	1.40	1.40
593	A204	250 l blue	1.40	1.40
594	A205	500 l dp mag	10.50	10.50
		Nos. 588-594 (7)	17.30	17.30

Issued in sheets of 4.

I. Ionescu, G. Titeica, A. O. Idachimescu and V. Cristescu
A207

Allegory of Learning
A208

1945, Sept. 5　　　　Perf. 13½

596	A207	2 l sepia	15	15
597	A208	80 l bl blk	15	15
		Set value	22	22

50th anniversary of "Gazeta Matematica," mathematics journal.

Cernavoda Bridge, 50th Anniv.
A209

1945, Sept. 26　　　Perf. 14

598	A209	80 l bl blk	18	15

Blacksmith and Plowman — A210

1946, Mar. 6

599	A210	80 l blue	18	15

Agrarian reform law of Mar. 23, 1945.

Atheneum, Bucharest — A211　　Numeral in Wreath — A212

Georges Enescu — A213　　Mechanic — A214

1946, Apr. 26　Photo.　Wmk. 276　Perf. 13½

600	A211	10 l dk bl	15	15
601	A212	20 l red brn	15	15
602	A212	55 l pck bl	15	15
603	A213	80 l purple	18	15
a.		Tête bêche pair	60	60
604	A212	160 l red org	15	15
		Nos. 600-604,B330-B331 (7)	2.03	
		Set value		1.65

Philharmonic Society, 25th anniv.

1946, May 1　　　　Perf. 13½x13

Labor Day: No. 606, Laborer. No. 607, Sower. No. 608, Reaper. 200 l, Students.

605	A214	10 l Prus grn	38	38
606	A214	10 l dk car rose	15	15
607	A214	20 l dl bl	38	38
608	A214	20 l dk red brn	15	15
609	A214	200 l brt red	95	95

Michael Types of 1945

1946　Wmk. 276　Photo.　Perf. 14
Toned Paper

610	A198	10 l brt red brn	15	15
611	A198	20 l vio brn	15	15
612	A201	80 l blue	15	15
613	A198	137 l yel grn	15	15
614	A201	160 l chalky bl	15	15
615	A201	200 l red org	15	15
616	A201	300 l sapphire	15	15
617	A201	360 l sepia	15	15
618	A199	400 l red org	15	15
619	A201	480 l brn red	15	15
620	A201	600 l dk ol grn	15	15
621	A201	1000 l Prus grn	15	15
622	A198	1500 l Prus grn	15	15
623	A201	2400 l magenta	15	15
624	A201	3700 l dull bl	15	15
		Set value	75	75

Demetrius Cantemir — A219　　Soccer — A222

Designs: 100 l, "Cultural Ties." 300 l, "Economic Ties."

1946, Oct. 20　　　Perf. 13½

625	A219	80 l dk brn	15	15
626	A219	100 l dp bl	15	15
627	A219	300 l bl blk	15	15
		Set value	26	26

Romania-Soviet friendship. See Nos. B338-B339.

1946, Sept. 1　　Perf. 11½, Imperf.

Designs: 20 l, Diving. 50 l, Running. 80 l, Mountain climbing.

628	A222	10 l dp blue	35	35
629	A222	20 l brt red	35	35
630	A222	50 l dp violet	35	35
631	A222	80 l chocolate	35	35
		Nos. 628-631,B340,C26,CB6 (7)	3.15	3.15

Issued in sheets of 16.

Weaving
A226　　Child Receiving Bread
A227

Transporting Relief Supplies
A228　　CGM Congress Emblem
A229

1946, Nov. 20　Photo.　Wmk. 276　Perf. 14

636	A226	80 l dk ol brn	15	15
		Set value, #636, B342-B345	50	50

Democratic Women's Org. of Romania. See No. CB7.

1947, Jan. 15　Perf. 13½x14, 14x13½

637	A227	300 l dk ol brn	15	15
638	A228	600 l magenta	15	15
		Set value		24

Social relief fund. See #B346-B348.

1947, Feb. 10　　　　Perf. 13½

639	A229	200 l blue	15	15
640	A229	300 l orange	15	15
a.		Pair, #639-640	30	30
b.		Pair, #640-641	30	30
641	A229	600 l crimson	15	15
		Set value		24

Congress of the United Labor Unions ("CGM"). Printed in sheets of 18 comprising 3 pairs of each denomination. Sheet yields 3 each of Nos. 640a and 640b.

Peace in Chariot
A230

Peace
A231　　Flags of US, Russia, GB & Romania
A232

Dove of Peace — A233

Perf. 14x13½, 13½x14
1947, Feb. 25

642	A230	300 l dl vio	15	15
643	A231	600 l dk org brn	15	15
644	A232	3000 l blue	15	15
645	A233	7200 l sage grn	15	15
		Set value	32	32

Signing of the peace treaty of Feb. 10, 1947.

King Michael — A234

1947　　　　　　Perf. 13½
Size: 25x30mm

646	A234	3000 l blue	15	15
647	A234	7200 l dl vio	15	15
648	A234	15,000 l brt bl	15	15
649	A234	21,000 l magenta	15	15
650	A234	36,000 l violet	25	15
		Nos. 646-650 (5)	85	
		Set value		48

See Nos. 661-664.

Michael Types of 1945

1947　Wmk. 276　Photo.　Perf. 14

651	A199	10 l red brn	15	15
652	A200	20 l magenta	15	15
653	A198	80 l blue	15	15
654	A199	200 l brt red	15	15
655	A198	500 l magenta	15	15
656	A199	860 l vio brn	15	15
657	A199	2500 l ultra	15	15
658	A198	5000 l sl gray	20	15
659	A198	8000 l Prus grn	35	15
660	A201	10,000 l dk brn	25	15

Type of 1947
Size: 18x21½mm

661	A234	1000 l gray bl	15	15
662	A234	5500 l yel grn	15	15
663	A234	20,000 l ol brn	15	15
664	A234	50,000 l red org	35	15
		Set value	2.00	1.00

For surcharge see No. B368.

Harvesting
Wheat
A235

Designs: 1 l, Log raft. 2 l, River steamer. 3 l,
Resita. 5 l, Cathedral of Curtea de Arges. 10 l,
View of Bucharest. 12 l, 36 l, Cernavoda Bridge.
15 l, 32 l, Port of Constantsa. 20 l, Petroleum field.

1947, Aug. 15 Perf. 14½x14
666 A235 50b red org — 15 15
667 A235 1 l red brn — 15 15
668 A235 2 l bl gray — 15 15
669 A235 3 l rose crim — 25 15
670 A235 5 l brt ultra — 30 15
671 A235 10 l brt bl — 35 15
672 A235 12 l violet — 50 15
673 A235 15 l dp ultra — 75 15
674 A235 20 l dk brn — 1.50 26
675 A235 32 l vio brn — 3.00 52
676 A235 36 l dk car rose — 3.00 26
Nos. 666-676 (11) — 10.10
Set value — 1.50

For overprints and surcharge see Nos. 684-694,
B369.

Beehive, Savings
Emblem — A236

1947, Oct. 31 Perf. 13½
677 A236 12 l dk car rose — 28 15
World Savings Day, Oct. 31, 1947.

People's Republic

Map,
Workers and
Children
A237

1948, Jan. 25 Perf. 14½x14
678 A237 12 l brt ultra — 28 15
1948 census. For surcharge see #819A.

Government
Printing Plant
and Press
A238

1948 Perf. 14½x14
670 A238 6 l magenta — 90 50
680 A238 7.50 l dk Prus grn — 50 15
b. Tête bêche pair — 1.00 90
75th anniversary of Stamp Division of Romanian
State Printing Works.
Issued: No. 680, Feb. 12; No. 679, May 20.

Romanian
and Bulgarian
Peasants
Shaking
Hands
A239

1948, Mar. 25 Wmk. 276
680A A239 32 l red brown — 35 18
Romanian-Bulgarian friendship.
For surcharge see No. 696.

Allegory of the People's
Republic — A240

1948, Apr. 8 Photo. Perf. 14x14½
681 A240 1 l car rose — 35 15
682 A240 2 l dl org — 35 18
683 A240 12 l deep blue — 50 30
New constitution.
For surcharge see No. 820.

Nos. 666 to 676
Overprinted in Black

R·P·R·

1948, Mar. Perf. 14½x14
684 A235 50b red org — 30 15
685 A235 1 l red brn — 30 15
686 A235 2 l bl gray — 55 15
687 A235 3 l rose crim — 55 15
688 A235 5 l brt ultra — 75 15
689 A235 10 l brt bl — 1.10 20
690 A235 12 l violet — 1.25 24
691 A235 15 l dp ultra — 1.25 24
692 A235 20 l dk brn — 1.50 45
693 A235 32 l vio brn — 4.25 1.50
694 A235 36 l dk car rose — 4.25 1.50
Nos. 684-694 (11) — 16.05 4.92

Romanian
Newspapers
A241

1948, Sept. 12
695 A241 10 l red brn — 28 15
Week of the Democratic Press, Sept. 12-19. See
Nos. B396-B398.

No. 680A Surcharged with New Value in
Black

1948, Aug. 17
696 A239 31 l on 32 l red brn — 55 15

Monument to
Soviet
Soldier — A242

Proclamation of
Islaz — A243

1948, Oct. 29 Photo. Perf. 14x14½
697 A242 10 l dk red — 45 30
Sheets of 50 stamps and 50 labels. See Nos.
B399-B400, CB16.

1948, June 1 Perf. 14½x14
698 A243 11 l car rose — 35 15
Nos. 698,B409-B412 (5) — 3.25 3.05
Centenary of Revolution of 1848.
For surcharge see No. 820A.

Arms of Romanian People's
Republic — A243a

1948, July 8 Wmk. 276
698A A243 50b red ("Lei 0.50") — 40 28
698B A243a 1 l red brn — 25 15
698C A243a 2 l dk grn — 25 15
698D A243a 3 l grnsh blk — 35 15
698E A243a 4 l chocolate — 35 15
698F A243a 5 l ultra — 35 15
698G A243a 10 l dp bl — 1.10 15
"Bani" instead of "Lei"
698H A243a 50b red ("Bani 0.50") — 48 15
Nos. 698A-698H (8) — 3.53
Set value — 75
See Nos. 712-717.

Nicolae
Balcescu
(1819-1852),
Writer
A244

1948, Dec. 20 Wmk. 289
699 A244 20 l scarlet — 35 15

Release from
Bondage — A245

1948, Dec. 30 Perf. 13½
700 A245 5 l brt rose — 28 15
First anniversary of the Republic.

Lenin, 25th Death
Anniv. — A246

Folk Dance — A247

1949, Jan. 21
701 A246 20 l black — 35 15
Exists imperf.

1949, Jan. 24 Perf. 13½
702 A247 10 l dp bl — 35 15
90th anniv. of the union of the Danubian
Principalities.

Ion C. Frimu
and
Revolutionary
Scene
A248

1949, Mar. 22 Perf. 14½x14
703 A248 20 l red — 35 15
Exists imperf.

Aleksander S. Pushkin,
150th Birth
Anniv. — A249

1949, May 20 Perf. 14x14½
704 A249 11 l car rose — 48 15
705 A249 30 l Prus grn — 70 28
For surcharges see Nos. 821-822.

Globe and Post
Horn — A250

Evolution of Mail Transportation — A251

Perf. 13½, 14½x14
1949, June 30 Photo. Wmk. 289
706 A250 20 l org brn — 1.50 90
707 A251 30 l brt bl — 1.10 60
UPU, 75th anniv.
For surcharges see Nos. C43-C44.

Russian
Army
Entering
Bucharest,
August, 1944
A252

1949, Aug. 23 Perf. 14½x14, Imperf.
708 A252 50 l choc, bl grn — 60 25
5th anniv. of the liberation of Romania by the
Soviet army, Aug. 1944.

"Long Live Romanian-Soviet
Amity" — A253

1949, Nov. 1 Perf. 13½x14½
709 A253 20 l dp red — 35 20
National week of Romanian-Soviet friendship celebration, Nov. 1-7, 1949. Exists imperf.

Symbols of
Transportation
A254

Joseph V. Stalin
A256

1949, Dec. 10 Perf. 13½
710 A254 11 l blue — 55 20
711 A254 20 l crimson — 55 20
Intl. Conference of Transportation Unions, Dec.
10, 1949.
Alternate vertical rows of stamps and labels in
sheet. Exist imperf.

Arms Type of 1948
1949-50 Wmk. 289 Perf. 14x13½
712 A243a 50b red ("Lei 0.50") — 35 15
713 A243a 1 l red brn — 35 15
714 A243a 2 l dk grn — 35 15
714A A243a 3 l grnsh blk — 65 15
715 A243a 5 l ultra — 50 15

716 A243a 5 l rose vio ('50)   70   15
717 A243a 10 l dp blue   90   15
       Nos. 712-717 (7)   3.80
       Set value   60

1949, Dec. 21   *Perf. 13¹/₂*
718 A256 31 l olive black   48   18

Stalin's 70th birthday. Exists imperf.

Mihail Eminescu   Poem: "Life"
    A257   A258

Designs: No. 721, "Third Letter." No. 722,
"Angel and Demon." No. 723, "Emperor and
Proletariat."

1950, Jan. 15 Photo.   Wmk. 289
719 A257 11 l blue   45   18
720 A258 11 l purple   75   22
721 A258 11 l dk grn   45   45
722 A258 11 l red brn   45   18
723 A258 11 l rose pink   45   18
       Nos. 719-723 (5)   2.55 1.21

Birth cent. of Mihail Eminescu, poet.
For surcharges see Nos. 823-827.

Fair at
Dragaica
A259

Ion Andreescu (Self-
portrait) — A260

Village
Well — A261

Perf. 14¹/₂x14, 14x14¹/₂
1950, Mar. 25
724 A259 5 l dk gray grn   45   22
725 A260 11 l ultra   75   22
726 A261 20 l brown   85   45

Birth cent. of Ion Andreescu, painter. No. 725
also exists imperf.
For surcharges see Nos. 827A-827B.

Graph and
Factories
A262

Design: 31 l, Tractor and Oil Derricks.

Inscribed: "Planul de Stat 1950."

Perf. 14¹/₂x14
1950, Apr. 23   **Wmk. 289**
727 A262 11 l red   60   18
728 A262 31 l violet   85   30

1950 plan for increased industrial production.
No. 727 exists imperf.
For surcharges see Nos. 827C-827D.

Young Man
Holding Flag
A263

Arms of
Republic
A264

1950, May 1   *Perf. 14x14¹/₂*
729 A263 31 l orange red   60   15

Labor Day, May 1. Exists imperf.
For surcharge see No. 827E.

┌─────────────────────────────────────┐
│   Canceled to Order   │
│   Canceled sets of new issues have   │
│ long been sold by the government.   │
│ Values in the second ("used") column │
│ are for these canceled-to-order   │
│ stamps. Postally used copies are   │
│ worth more.   │
└─────────────────────────────────────┘

1950   Photo.   Perf. 12¹/₂
730 A264 50b black   15   15
731 A264 1 l red   15   15
732 A264 2 l ol gray   15   15
733 A264 3 l violet   15   15
734 A264 4 l rose lilac   15   15
735 A264 5 l red brn   15   15
736 A264 6 l dp grn   15   15
737 A264 7 l vio brn   15   15
738 A264 7.50 l blue   22   15
739 A264 10 l dk brn   48   15
740 A264 11 l rose car   48   15
741 A264 15 l dp bl   28   15
742 A264 20 l Prus gray   30   15
743 A264 31 l dl grn   45   15
744 A264 36 l dk org brn   75   28
       Set value   3.65 1.00

See Nos. 947-961 which have similar design
with white denomination figures.
For overprint & surcharges see #758, 828-841.

Bugler and
Drummer
A265

Designs: 11 l, Three school children. 31 l,
Drummer, flag-bearer and bugler.

1950, May 25   *Perf. 14¹/₂x14*
745 A265 8 l blue   45   30
746 A265 11 l rose vio   75   45
747 A265 31 l org ver   1.50   90

Young Pioneers, 1st anniv.
For surcharges see Nos. 841A-841C.

Factory
Worker — A266

Aurel Vlaicu and
his First
Plane — A267

1950, July 20 Photo.   Perf. 14x14¹/₂
748 A266 11 l red brn   30   15
749 A266 11 l red   30   15
750 A266 11 l blue   30   15
751 A266 11 l blk brn   30   15

Nationalization of industry, 2nd anniv.

1950, July 22 Wmk. 289   Perf. 12¹/₂
752 A267 31 l dk grn   35   18
753 A267 61 l dk bl   40   18
754 A267 81 l ultra   40   18

Aurel Vlaicu (1882-1913), pioneer of Romanian
aviation.
For surcharges see Nos. 842-844.

Mother and   Lathe and
Child — A268   Operator — A269

1950, Sept. 9   *Perf. 13¹/₂*
755 A268 11 l rose red   30   15
756 A269 20 l dk ol brn   30   15

Congress of the Committees for the Struggle for
Peace.
For surcharge see No. 844A.

Statue of Soviet
Soldier — A270

1950, Oct. 6   *Perf. 14x14¹/₂*
757 A270 30 l red brn   48   18

Celebration of Romanian-Soviet friendship, Oct.
7-Nov. 7, 1950.

No. 741 Overprinted in   **TRĂIASCĂ**
      Carmine   **PRIETENIA**
                         ROMÂNO-
                         MAGHIĂRAI

1950, Oct. 6   *Perf. 12¹/₂*
758 A264 15 l deep blue   38   15

Romanian-Hungarian friendship.

"Agriculture," "Manufacturing" and Sports
Badge — A271

Designs: 5 l, Student workers and Sports badge.
11 l, Track team and badge. 31 l, Calisthenics and
badge.

1950, Oct. 30   *Perf. 14¹/₂x14*
759 A271 31 l rose car   60   45
760 A271 5 l red brn   45   30
761 A271 5 l brt bl   45   30
762 A271 11 l green   45   30
763 A271 31 l brn ol   1.10   75
       Nos. 750-763 (5)   3.05 2.10

For surcharge see No. 845.

ARLUS
A272

"Industry" — A273

"Agriculture"
A274 REPUBLICA POPULARA ROMANA

1950, Nov. 2   *Perf. 13¹/₂*
764 A272 11 l blue   28   15
765 A272 11 l red org   28   15

3rd Soviet-Romanian Friendship Congress.

Perf. 14x14¹/₂, 14¹/₂x14
1951, Feb. 9   Photo.   Wmk. 289
766 A273 11 l red brn   15   15
767 A274 31 l deep bl   38   16
       Set value   24

Industry and Agriculture Exposition. Exist imperf.
For surcharge see No. 846.

Ski Jump — A275   Ski
                      Descent — A276

Designs: 5 l, Skating. 20 l, Hockey. 31 l,
Bobsledding.

1951, Jan. 28   *Perf. 13¹/₂*
768 A275 4 l blk brn   30   15
769 A275 5 l vermilion   45   15
770 A276 11 l dp bl   85   22
771 A275 20 l org brn   90   48
772 A275 31 l dk gray grn   1.90   90
       Nos. 768-772 (5)   4.40 1.90

9th World University Winter Games.
For surcharges see Nos. 847-848.

Medal for
Work — A277

Orders: 4 l, Star of the Republic, Classes III, IV &
V. 11 l, Work. 35 l, Star of the Republic, Classes I
& II.

1951, May 1   *Perf. 13¹/₂*
773 A277 2 l ol gray   30   15
774 A277 4 l blue   30   15
775 A277 11 l crimson   30   15
776 A277 35 l org brn   35   19

Labor Day. Exist imperf.
For surcharges see Nos. 849-852.

Camp of
Young
Pioneers
A278

Pioneers Greeting
Stalin — A279

Admitting
New
Pioneers
A280

1951, May 8   Perf. 14x14¹/₂, 14¹/₂x14

777	A278	1 l gray grn	90	38
778	A279	1 l blue	90	15
779	A280	35 l red	75	18

Romanian Young Pioneers Organization.
For surcharge see No. 853.

Woman Orator and Flags A281

Ion Negulici A282

1951, Mar. 8   Perf. 14x14¹/₂

780	A281	1 l org brn	35	15

Woman's Day, Mar. 8. Exists imperf.

1951, June 20   Perf. 14x14¹/₂

781	A282	35 l rose red	75	45

Death cent. of Ion Negulici, painter.

Bicyclists A283

1951, July 9   Perf. 14¹/₂x14

782	A283	1 l chnt brn	1.65	50
a.		Tête bêche pair	4.00	3.25

The 1951 Bicycle Tour of Romania.

Festival Badge — A284

Boy and Girl with Flag — A285

Youths Encircling Globe — A286

1951, Aug. 1   Perf. 13¹/₂

783	A284	1 l scarlet	50	22
784	A285	5 l deep blue	50	22
785	A286	11 l deep plum	65	50

3rd World Youth Festival, Berlin.

Filimon Sarbu A287

"Romania Raising the Masses" A288

"Revolutionary Romania" — A289

1951, July 23   Perf. 14x14¹/₂

786	A287	11 l dk brn	28	15

10th death anniv. of Filimon Sarbu, patriot.

Perf. 14x14¹/₂, 14¹/₂x14
1951, July 23

787	A288	11 l yel brn	85	25
788	A288	11 l rose vio	85	25
789	A289	11 l dk grn	85	25
790	A289	11 l org red	85	25

Death cent. of C. D. Rosenthal, painter.

Scanteia Building A290

1951, Aug. 16   Perf. 14¹/₂x14

791	A290	11 l blue	35	15

20th anniv. of the newspaper Scanteia.

Miner in Dress Uniform A291

Order for National Defense A293

Design: 11 l, Miner in work clothes.

1951, Aug. 12   Perf. 14x14¹/₂

792	A291	5 l blue	24	15
793	A291	11 l plum	24	15
		Set value		20

Miner's Day. For surcharge see #854.

1951, Aug. 12   Perf. 14x14¹/₂

794	A293	10 l crimson	50	15

For surcharge see No. 855.

Choir — A294

Music Week Emblem — A295

Design: No. 796, Orchestra and dancers.

Perf. 13¹/₂
1951, Sept. 22   Photo.   Wmk. 358

795	A294	11 l blue	35	15
796	A294	11 l red brn	50	30
797	A295	11 l purple	35	15

Music Week, Sept. 22-30, 1951.

Soldier — A296

Oil Field — A297

1951, Oct. 2

798	A296	11 l blue	32	15

Army Day, Oct. 2, 1951.

1951-52

Designs: 2 l, Coal mining. 3 l, Romanian soldier. 4 l, Smelting ore. 5 l, Agricultural machinery. 6 l, Canal construction. 7 l, Agriculture. 8 l, Self-education. 11 l, Hydroelectric production. 35 l, Manufacturing.

799	A297	1 l blk brn	15	15
800	A297	2 l chocolate	15	15
801	A297	3 l scarlet	35	15
802	A297	4 l yel brn ('52)	20	15
803	A297	5 l green	35	15
804	A297	6 l brt bl ('52)	1.25	40
805	A297	7 l emerald	50	40
806	A297	8 l brn ('52)	50	40
807	A297	11 l blue	35	15
808	A297	35 l purple	1.35	80
		Nos. 799-808,C35-C36 (12)	7.30	4.70

1951-55 Five Year Plan.
2 l and 11 l exist with wmk. 289.
For surcharges see Nos. 860-869.

Arms of Soviet Union and Romania — A298

1951, Oct. 7   Wmk. 358

809	A298	4 l chnt brn, cr	35	15
810	A298	35 l org red	90	45

Month of Romanian-Soviet friendship, Oct. 7-Nov. 7.
For surcharges see Nos. 870-871.

Pavel Tcacenco A299

Railroad Conductor A300

1951, Dec. 15   Perf. 14x14¹/₂

811	A299	10 l ol brn & dk brn	35	15

Revolutionary, 26th death anniv.
For surcharge see No. 872.

1952, Mar. 24   Perf. 13¹/₂

812	A300	55b dk brn	1.50	45

Railroad Workers' Day, Feb. 16.

Ion L. Caragiale — A301

Announcing Caragiale Celebration A302

Designs: No. 814, Book and painting "1907." No. 815, Bust and wreath.

1952, Apr. 1   Perf. 13¹/₂, 14¹/₂x14
Inscribed: ". . . . I. L. Caragiale."

813	A301	55b chalky blue	85	15
814	A302	55b scarlet	85	15
815	A302	55b deep green	85	15
816	A302	1 l brown	2.50	26
		Set value		52

Birth cent. of Ion L. Caragiale, dramatist.
For surcharges see Nos. 817-819.

Types of 1952 Surcharged with New Value in Black or Carmine

1952-53

817	A302	20b on 11 l scar (As #814)	60	38
818	A302	55b on 11 l dp grn (As #815) (C)	75	50
819	A301	75b on 11 l chlky bl (C)	1.25	62

Various Issues Surcharged with New Values in Carmine or Black
On No. 678, Census
Perf. 14x13¹/₂

819A	A237	50b on 12 l ultra	6.75	3.75

On No. 683, New Constitution
Perf. 14

820	A240	50b on 12 l dp bl	2.00	1.25

On No. 698, Revolution

820A	A243	1.75 l on 11 l car rose (Bk)	25.00	12.00

On Nos. 704-705, Pushkin
1952   Wmk. 358

821	A249	10b on 11 l (Bk)	2.50	1.75
822	A249	10b on 30 l	2.50	1.75

On Nos. 719-723, Eminescu
Perf. 13¹/₂x13, 13x13¹/₂

823	A257	10b on 11 l bl	1.75	1.75
824	A258	10b on 11 l pur	1.75	1.75
825	A258	10b on 11 l dk grn	1.75	1.75
826	A258	10b on 11 l red brn (Bk)	1.75	1.75
827	A258	10b on 11 l rose pink (Bk)	1.75	1.75

On Nos. 724-725, Andreescu
Perf. 14

827A	A259	50b on 5 l dk gray grn	5.00	2.75
827B	A260	55b on 11 l ultra	5.00	2.75

On Nos. 727-728, Production Plan
Perf. 14¹/₂x14

827C	A262	20b on 11 l red (Bk)	1.75	75
827D	A262	20b on 31 l vio	1.75	75

On No. 729, Labor Day
Perf. 14

827E	A263	55b on 31 l (Bk)	2.75	2.75

On Nos. 730-739 and 741-744, National Arms
Perf. 12¹/₂

828	A264	3b on 1 l red (Bk)	70	45
829	A264	3b on 2 l ol gray (Bk)	1.10	55
830	A264	3b on 4 l rose lil (Bk)	70	30
831	A264	3b on 5 l red brn (Bk)	1.10	55
832	A264	3b on 7.50 l bl (Bk)	3.25	1.40
833	A264	3b on 10 l dk brn (Bk)	1.10	55
834	A264	55b on 50b blk brn	3.25	45
835	A264	55b on 3 l vio	3.25	45
836	A264	55b on 6 l dp grn	3.25	45
837	A264	55b on 7 l vio brn	3.25	45
838	A264	55b on 15 l dp bl	5.00	45
839	A264	55b on 20 l Prus grn	3.25	45
840	A264	55b on 31 l dl grn	3.25	45
841	A264	55b on 36 l dk org brn	5.00	45

On Nos. 745-747, Young Pioneers
Perf. 14

841A	A265	55b on 8 l	9.50	5.75
841B	A265	55b on 11 l	9.50	5.75
841C	A265	55b on 31 l (Bk)	9.50	5.75

On Nos. 752-754, Vlaicu
Perf. 12¹/₂

842	A267	10b on 3 l dk grn	1.50	75
843	A267	10b on 6 l dk bl	1.50	75
844	A267	10b on 8 l ultra	1.50	75

Original denomination canceled with an "X."

On No. 756, Peace Congress
Perf. 13¹/₂

844A	A269	20b on 20 l	2.25	1.25

On No. 759, Sports
Perf. 14¹/₂x14
845 A271 55b on 3 l (Bk)   15.00 11.50

On No. 767, Exposition
846 A274 55b on 31 l dp bl   7.50   5.75

On Nos. 771-772, Winter Games
Perf. 13¹/₂
847 A275 55b on 20 l (Bk)   20.00   8.00
848 A275 55b on 31 l   20.00   8.00

On Nos. 773-776, Labor Medals
849 A277 20b on 2 l   3.75   2.25
850 A277 20b on 4 l   3.75   2.25
851 A277 20b on 11 l   3.75   2.25
852 A277 20b on 35 l (Bk)   3.75   2.25

On Nov. 779, Young Pioneers
Perf. 14x14¹/₂
853 A280 55b on 35 l (Bk)   13.00   9.50

On No. 792, Miners' Day
854 A291 55b on 5 l bl   11.00   7.50

On No. 794, Defense Order
855 A293 55b on 10 l (Bk)   5.75   3.75

On Nos. B409-B412, 1848 Revolution
1952   **Wmk. 276**   *Perf. 13x13¹/₂*
856 SP280 1.75 l on 2 l + 2 l   9.50   3.75
857 SP281 1.75 l on 5 l + 5 l   9.50   3.75
858 SP282 1.75 l on 10 l + 10 l   9.50   3.75
859 SP280 1.75 l on 36 l + 18 l   9.50   3.75

On Nos. 799-808, 5-Year Plan
Wmk. 358   *Perf. 13¹/₂*
860 A297 35b on 1 l blk brn   1.90   65
861 A297 35b on 2 l choc   6.00   70
862 A297 35b on 3 l scar (Bk)   3.00   1.25
863 A297 35b on 4 l yel brn (Bk) 3.50   1.50
  a. Red surcharge   15.00   8.00
864 A297 35b on 5 l grn   3.00   2.00
865 A297 1 l on 6 l brt bl   4.75   3.00
866 A297 1 l on 7 l emer   3.50   1.50
867 A297 1 l on 8 l brn   3.50   2.25
868 A297 1 l on 11 l bl   4.75   1.75
869 A297 1 l on 35 l pur   4.75   1.50

Nos. 861, 868 exist with wmk. 289.

On Nos. 809-810, Romanian-Soviet Friendship
870 A298 10b on 4 l (Bk)   1.50   65
871 A298 10b on 35 l (Bk)   1.50   65

On No. 811, Tcacenco
Perf. 13¹/₂x14
872 A299 10b on 10 l   1.90   90

A302a

A303

Perf. 13¹/₂x13
1952, Apr. 14   Photo.   Wmk. 358
873 A302a 1 l Ivan P. Pavlov   1.65   50

Meeting of Romanian-Soviet doctors in Bucharest.

1952, May 1
874 A303 55b Hammer & sickle medal 75   15

Labor Day.

Medal for Motherhood
A304

Leonardo da Vinci
A305

Medals: 55b, Maternal glory. 1.75 l, Mother-Heroine.

1952, Apr. 7   Perf. 13x13¹/₂
875 A304 20b plum & sl gray   30   15
876 A304 55b henna brn   70   18
877 A304 1.75 l rose red & brn buff 1.75 40

International Women's Day.

1952, July 3
878 A305 55b purple   2.10   50

500th birth anniv. of Leonardo da Vinci.

Gogol and Scene from Taras Bulba
A306

Nikolai V. Gogol — A307

1952, Apr. 1   Perf. 13¹/₂x14, 14x13¹/₂
879 A306 55b deep blue   95   15
880 A307 1.75 l olive gray   1.40   38

Gogol, Russian writer, death cent.

Pioneers Saluting — A308

Labor Day Paraders Returning
A309

Design: 55b, Pioneers studying nature.

1952, May 21   Perf. 14
881 A308 20b brown   45   15
882 A308 55b dp grn   1.25   15
883 A309 1.75 l blue   2.10   38

Third anniversary of Romanian Pioneers.

Infantry Attack, Painting by Grigorescu — A310

Miner — A311

Design: 1.10 l, Romanian and Russian soldiers.

1952, June 7   Perf. 13x13¹/₂
884 A310 50b rose brn   45   15
885 A310 1.10 l blue   75   25
  Set value   30

Independence Proclamation of 1877, 75th anniv.

1952, Aug. 11   Wmk. 358
902 A311 20b rose red   1.25   25
903 A311 55b purple   1.25   15

Day of the Miner.

Book and Globe — A312

Students in Native Dress — A314

Chemistry Student
A313

Design: 55b, Students playing soccer.

Perf. 13¹/₂x13, 13¹/₂x14, 13x13¹/₂
1952, Sept. 5
904 A312 10b dp bl   15   15
905 A313 20b orange   70   20
906 A312 55b dp grn   2.00   25
907 A314 1.75 l rose red   3.00   50

Intl. Student Union Congr., Bucharest, Sept.

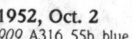
Soldier, Sailor and Aviator — A316

1952, Oct. 2   Perf. 14
909 A316 55b blue   48   18

Armed Forces Day, Oct. 2, 1952.

"Russia" Leading Peace Crusade — A317

Allegory: Romanian-Soviet Friendship — A318

1952, Oct. 7   Perf. 13¹/₂x13, 13x13¹/₂
910 A317 55b vermilion   65   18
911 A318 1.75 l blk brn   1.65   65

Month of Romanian-Soviet friendship, Oct.

Rowing on Lake Snagov — A319

Nicolae Balcescu — A320

Design: 1.75 l, Athletes marching with flags.

1952, Oct. 20
912 A319 20b dp bl   2.75   52
913 A319 1.75 l rose red   5.00   1.10

Values are for copies with poor perforations.

1952, Nov. 29
914 A320 55b gray   1.90   50
915 A320 1.75 l lemon bister 4.00   1.25

Death cent. of Nicolae Balcescu, poet.

Arms of Republic — A321

1952, Dec. 6   Wmk. 358
916 A321 55b dl grn   75   25

5th anniversary of socialist constitution.

Arms and Industrial Symbols
A322

1953, Jan. 8   Perf. 12¹/₂x13¹/₂
917 A322 55b bl, yel & red   90   35

5th anniv. of the proclamation of the People's Republic.

Matei Millo, Costache Caragiale and Aristita Romanescu
A323

1953, Feb.   Photo.   Perf. 13x13¹/₂
918 A323 55b brt ultra   1.50   35

National Theater of I. L. Caragiale, cent.

Iron Foundry Worker — A324

Worker — A325

Design: No. 921, Driving Tractor.

1953, Feb.   Perf. 13¹/₂x13, 13x13¹/₂
919 A324 55b sl grn   32   15
920 A325 55b blk brn   32   15
921 A325 55b orange   65   26
  Set value   46

3rd Congress of the Syndicate of the Romanian People's Republic.

"Strike at Grivita," Painted by G. Miclossy
A326

Arms of Romanian People's Republic
A327

1953, Feb. 16   Perf. 13x13¹/₂
922 A326 55b chestnut   1.25   15

Oil industry strike, Feb. 16, 1933, 20th anniv.

1953   Perf. 12¹/₂
923 A327 5b crimson   28   15
924 A327 55b purple   75   18
  Set value   26

Flags of
Romania and
Russia, Farm
Machinery
A328

1953, Mar. 24   *Perf. 14*
925 A328 55b dk brn, *bl*   95 24

5th anniv. of the signing of a treaty of friendship
and mutual assistance between Russia and
Romania.

Map and
Medal — A329   Rug — A330

Folk Dance
A330a

1953, Mar. 24
926 A329 55b dk gray grn   1.75 38
927 A329 55b chestnut   2.25 38

20th World Championship Table Tennis
Matches, Budapest, 1953.

1953

Designs: 10b, Ceramics. 20b, Costume of
Campulung (Muscel). 55b, Apuseni Mts. costume.

**Inscribed: "Arta Populara
Romaneasca"**

928 A330 10b dp grn   60 15
929 A330 20b red brn   1.25 15
929A A330a 35b purple   1.75 15
930 A330 55b vio bl   2.75 15
931 A330 1 l brt red vio   4.00 25
    Nos. 928-931 (5)   10.35
    Set value   60

Romanian Folk Arts.

Karl
Marx — A331   Children
Planting
Tree — A332

Physics
Class
A333

1953, May 21   *Perf. 13¹/₂x13*
932 A331 1.55 l ol brn   1.40 45

70th death anniv. of Karl Marx.

1953, May 21   *Perf. 14*

Design: 55b, Flying model planes.

933 A332 35b dp grn   1.00 15
934 A332 55b dl bl   1.40 18
935 A333 1.75 l brown   3.25 45

Women and Flags
A334   Discus Thrower
A335

Students
Offering
Teacher
Flowers
A336

1953, June 18   *Perf. 13¹/₂x13*
936 A334 55b red brn   1.00 20

3rd World Congress of Women, Copenhagen,
1953.

1953, Aug. 2 **Wmk. 358** *Perf. 14*

Designs: 55b, Students reaching toward dove.
1.75 l, Dance in local costumes.

937 A335 20b orange   52 15
938 A335 55b dp bl   90 15
939 A336 65b scarlet   1.25 38
940 A336 1.75 l red vio   3.50 50

4th World Youth Festival, Bucharest, Aug. 2-16.

Waterfall — A337   Wheat Field — A338

Design: 55b, Forester holding seedling.

1953, July 29   *Photo.*
941 A337 20b vio bl   55 15
942 A338 38b dl grn   1.40 50
943 A337 55b lt brn   1.50 22

Month of the Forest.

Vladimir V.
Mayakovsky, 60th
Birth Anniv. — A339

1953, Aug. 22
944 A339 55b brown   75 20

Miner Using
Drill
A340

1953, Sept. 19
945 A340 1.55 l slate black   1.40 40
    Miners' Day.

Arms of Republic — A342

1952-53   *Perf. 12¹/₂*
    Size: 20x24mm
947 A342 3b dp org   60 20
948 A342 5b crimson   80 15
949 A342 7b dk bl grn   80 20
950 A342 10b chocolate   1.00 15
951 A342 20b dp bl   1.25 15
952 A342 35b blk brn   2.75 15
953 A342 50b dk gray grn   3.25 15
954 A342 55b purple   7.25 15
    Size: 24x29mm
955 A342 1.10 l dk brn   6.50 28
956 A342 1.75 l violet   24.00 40
957 A342 2 l ol blk   6.50 48
958 A342 2.35 l org brn   7.75 32
959 A342 2.55 l dp org   9.75 40
960 A342 3 l dk gray grn   10.00 32
961 A342 5 l dp crim   12.00 60
    Nos. 947-961 (15)   94.20
    Set value   3.50

Stamps of similar design with value figures in
color are Nos. 730-744.

Postal
Administration
Building and
Telephone
Employees
A343

Designs: 55b, Postal Adm. Bldg. and Letter carrier. 1 l, Map and communications symbols. 1.55
l, Postal Adm. Bldg. and Telegraph employees.

1953, Oct. 20 **Wmk. 358** *Perf. 14*
964 A343 20b dk red brn   18 15
965 A343 55b ol grn   30 15
966 A343 1 l brt bl   75 15
967 A343 1.55 l rose brn   1.10 38
    Set value   70

50th anniv. of the construction of the Postal
Administration Building.

Liberation
Medal — A344   Soldier and
Flag — A345

1953, Oct. 20   *Perf. 14x13¹/₂*
968 A344 55b dk brn   70 15

9th anniv. of the liberation of Romania.

1953, Oct. 2   *Perf. 13¹/₂*
969 A345 55b olive green   70 25

Army Day, Oct. 2.

Girl with
Model Plane
A346

Civil Aviation: 20b, Parachute landing. 55b,
Glider and pilot. 1.75 l, Plane in flight.

1953, Oct. 20   *Perf. 14*
970 A346 10b org & dk gray grn   2.25 30
971 A346 20b org brn & dk ol
    grn   4.50 18
972 A346 55b dk scar & rose lil   7.25 50
973 A346 1.75 l dk rose vio & brn   9.50 75

Workers and
Flags — A347

Design: 1.55 l, Spasski Tower and lock on Volga-
Don Canal.

1953, Nov. 25   *Perf. 13x13¹/₂*
974 A347 55b brown   48 15
975 A347 1.55 l rose brown   70 25

Month of Romanian-Soviet friendship, Oct. 7-
Nov. 7.

Hemispheres and Clasped Hands — A348

Workers, Flags and
Globe — A349

1953, Nov. 25   *Perf. 14*
976 A348 55b dark olive   38 15
977 A349 1.25 l crimson   90 30

World Congress of Trade Unions.

Ciprian
Porumbescu
A350   Harvesting Machine
A351

1953, Dec. 16
978 A350 55b purple   4.00 45

Ciprian Porumbescu (1853-1883), composer.

1953, Dec. 16   *Perf. 13x13¹/₂*
    Wmk. 358

Designs: 35b, Tractor in field. 2.55 l, Cattle.

979 A351 10b sepia   28 15
980 A351 35b dk grn   38 15
981 A351 2.55 l org brn   3.50 75

Aurel
Vlaicu — A352   Lenin — A353

1953, Dec. 26   *Perf. 14*
982 A352 50b vio bl   75 18

Vlaicu, aviation pioneer, 40th death anniv.

1954, Jan. 21   *Perf. 13¹/₂*
983 A353 55b dk red brn, *buff*   75 18

30th death anniv. of Lenin.

Red Deer — A354

Designs: 55b, Children planting trees. 1.75 l, Mountain scene.

1954, Apr. 1

Yellow Surface-colored Paper

984	A354	20b dk brn	1.50	15
985	A354	55b violet	1.50	15
986	A354	1.75 l dk bl	3.25	48

Month of the Forest.

Calimanesti Rest Home — A355

Workers' Rest Homes: 1.55 l, Sinaia. 2 l, Predeal. 2.35 l, Tusnad. 2.55 l, Govora.

1954, Apr. 15   *Perf. 14*

987	A355	5b blk brn, *cream*	25	15
988	A355	1.55 l dk vio brn, *bl*	90	16
989	A355	2 l dk grn, *pink*	1.40	18
990	A355	2.35 l ol blk, *grnsh*	1.40	48
991	A355	2.55 l dk red brn, *cit*	2.00	65
	Nos. 987-991 (5)	5.95	1.62

Octav Bancila — A356

Globe, Child, Dove and Flowers — A357

1954, May 26   *Perf. 13½*

992 A356 55b red brn & dk grn   2.75 1.00

10th death anniv. of Octav Bancila, painter.

1954, June 1   *Perf. 13x13½*

993 A357 55b brown   1.25 25

Children's Day, June 1.

Girl Feeding Calf — A358

Designs: 55b, Girl holding sheaf of grain. 1.75 l, Young students.

1954, July 5   *Perf. 14*

994	A358	20b grnsh blk	25	15
995	A358	55b blue	60	18
996	A358	1.75 l car rose	1.75	32

Stephen the Great — A359

Loading Coal on Conveyor Belt — A360

1954, July 10

997 A359 55b vio brn   1.50 38

Stephen of Moldavia (1433?-1504).

1954, Aug. 8   *Perf. 13x13½*

998 A360 1.75 l black   1.50 38

Miners' Day.

Victor Babes — A361

Applicant Requesting Loan — A362

1954, Aug. 15   *Perf. 14*

999 A361 55b rose red   1.50 38

Birth cent. of Victor Babes, serologist.

1954, Aug. 20

Design: 55b, Mutual aid declaration.

1000	A362	20b dp vio	28	15
1001	A362	55b dk redsh brn	45	16
	Set value	24

5th anniv. of the Mutual Aid Organization.

Sailor and Naval Scene — A363

Monument to Soviet Soldier — A364

1954, Aug. 19   *Perf. 13x13½*

1002 A363 55b dp bl   90 25

Navy Day.

1954, Aug. 23   *Perf. 13½x13*

1003 A364 55b scar & pur   90 25

10th anniv. of Romania's liberation.

House of Culture A365

Academy of Music, Bucharest A366

Aviator A367

Designs: 55b, Scanteia building. 1.55 l, Radio station.

1954, Sept. 6   *Perf. 14, 13½x13*

1004	A365	20b vio bl	18	15
1005	A366	38b violet	40	18
1006	A365	55b vio brn	40	15
1007	A366	1.55 l red brn	75	20
	Set value	52

Publicizing Romania's cultural progress during the decade following liberation.

1954, Sept. 13   *Perf. 13½x13*
Wmk. 358

1008 A367 55b blue   90 38

Aviation Day.

Chemical Plant and Oil Derricks — A368

Dragon Pillar, Peking — A369

1954, Sept. 21   *Perf. 13x13½*

1009 A368 55b gray   1.25 25

Intl. Conference of chemical and petroleum workers, Bucharest, Sept. 1954.

1954, Oct. 7   *Perf. 14*

1010 A369 55b dk ol grn, *cr*   1.25 25

Week of Chinese Culture.

Dumitri T. Neculuta A370

ARLUS Emblem A371

1954, Oct. 17   *Perf. 13½x13*

1011 A370 55b purple   1.10 25

Neculuta, poet, 50th death anniv.

1954, Oct. 22   *Perf. 14*

Design: 65b, Romanian and Russian women embracing.

1012	A371	55b rose car	45	15
1013	A371	65b dk pur	65	18

Month of Romanian-Soviet Friendship.

Gheorghe Tattarescu A372

Barbu Iscovescu A373

1954, Oct. 24   *Perf. 13½x13*

1014 A372 55b cerise   1.40 38

Gheorghe Tattarescu (1820-1894), painter.

1954, Nov. 3   *Perf. 14*

1015 A373 1.75 l red brn   2.50 50

Death cent. of Barbu Iscovescu, painter.

Wild Boar — A374

Globe and Clasped Hands — A375

Month of the Forest: 65b, Couple planting tree. 1.20 l, Logging.

          Perf. 13½x13

1955, Mar. 15   **Wmk. 358**

1016	A374	35b brown	52	15
1017	A374	65b turq bl	90	25
1018	A374	1.20 l dk red	1.75	75

1955, Apr. 5   **Photo.**

1019 A375 25b car rose   35 15

Intl. Conference of Universal Trade Unions (Federation Syndicale Mondiale), Vienna, Apr. 1955.

Teletype — A376

Lenin — A377

1955, Dec. 20   *Perf. 13½x13*

1020 A376 50b lilac   45 18

Romanian telegraph system, cent.

1955, Apr. 22   *Perf. 13½x14*

Various Portraits of Lenin.

1021	A377	20b ol bis & brn	22	15
1022	A377	55b cop brn	40	18
1023	A377	1 l vermilion	60	22

85th anniversary of the birth of Lenin.

Chemist A378

Volleyball A379

Designs: 5b, Steelworker. 10b, Aviator. 20b, Miner. 30b, Tractor driver. 35b, Pioneer. 40b, Girl student. 55b, Mason. 1 l, Sailor. 1.55 l, Spinner. 2.35 l, Soldier. 2.55 l, Electrician.

1955-56   Wmk. 358   Perf. 14

1024	A378	3b blue	15	15
1025	A378	5b violet	15	15
1026	A378	10b chocolate	15	15
1027	A378	20b lil rose	24	15
1027A	A378	30b vio bl ('56)	40	15
1028	A378	35b grnsh bl	28	15
1028A	A378	40b slate	70	15
1029	A378	55b ol gray	40	15
1030	A378	1 l purple	75	15
1031	A378	1.55 l brn lake	1.40	15
1032	A378	2.35 l bis brn	2.10	38
1033	A378	2.55 l slate	2.25	24
	Nos. 1024-1033 (12)		8.97	
	Set value			1.15

1955, June 17

Design: 1.75 l, Woman volleyball player.

1034	A379	55b red vio, pink	1.40	50
1035	A379	1.75 l lil rose, cr	3.50	50

European Volleyball Championships, Bucharest.

Globe, Flag and Dove — A379a

Girls with Dove and Flag — A380

1955, May 7   Photo.   Perf. 13½
1035A	A379a	55b ultra	75	20

Peace Congress, Helsinki.

1955, June 1   Perf. 13½x14
1036	A380	55b dk red brn	70	20

International Children's Day, June 1.

Russian War Memorial, Berlin — A381   Theodor Aman Museum — A382

1955, May 9
1037	A381	55b dp bl	60	18

Victory over Germany, 10th anniversary.

1955, June 28   Perf. 13½, 14

Bucharest Museums: 55b, Lenin and Stalin Museum. 1.20 l, Popular Arts Museum. 1.75 l, Arts Museum. 2.55 l, Simu Museum.

1038	A382	20b rose lil	22	15
1039	A382	55b brown	28	15
1040	A382	1.20 l gray blk	45	32
1041	A382	1.75 l sl grn	80	32
1042	A382	2.55 l rose vio	1.40	38
	Nos. 1038-1042 (5)		3.15	1.32

#1038, 1040, 1042 measure 29x24½mm, #1039, 1041 32½x23mm.

Sharpshooter A383

1955, Sept. 11   Perf. 13½
1043	A383	1 l pale brn & sepia	3.25	45

European Sharpshooting Championship meeting, Bucharest, Sept. 11-18.

Fire Truck, Farm and Factory — A384

1955, Sept. 13   Wmk. 358
1044	A384	55b carmine	55	24

Firemen's Day, Sept. 13.

Bishop Dosoftei — A385   Mother and Child — A386

Romanian writers: No. 1046, Stolnicul Constantin Cantacuzino. No. 1047, Dimitrie Cantemir. No. 1048, Enachita Vacarescu. No. 1049, Anton Pann.

1955, Sept. 9   Photo.
1045	A385	55b bluish gray	55	30
1046	A385	55b dp vio	55	30
1047	A385	55b ultra	55	30
1048	A385	55b rose vio	55	30
1049	A385	55b ol gray	55	30
	Nos. 1045-1049 (5)		2.75	1.50

1955, July 7   Perf. 13½x14
1050	A386	55b ultra	60	18

World Congress of Mothers, Lausanne.

Pioneers and Train Set — A387   Rowing — A388

Designs: 20b, Pioneers studying nature. 55b, Home of the Pioneers.

1955   Perf. 12½
1051	A387	10b brt ultra	15	15
1052	A387	20b grnsh bl	45	15
1053	A387	55b dp plum	1.25	22
	Set value			35

Fifth anniversary of the Pioneer headquarters, Bucharest.

1955, Aug. 22   Perf. 13x13½
1054	A388	55b shown	3.25	48
1055	A388	1 l Sculling	6.00	70

European Women's Rowing Championship on Lake Snagov, Aug. 4-7.

Insect Pest Control A389   I. V. Michurin A390

Designs: 20b, Orchard. 55b, Vineyard. 1 l, Truck garden.

1955, Oct. 15   Perf. 14x13½
1056	A389	10b brt grn	28	15
1057	A389	20b lil rose	28	15
1058	A389	55b vio bl	70	20
1059	A389	1 l dp claret	1.25	40

Quality products of Romanian agriculture. See Nos. 1068-1071.

1955, Oct. 25   Perf. 13½x14
1060	A390	55b Prus bl	75	18

Birth cent. of I. V. Michurin, Russian agricultural scientist.

Congress Emblem — A391   Globes and Olive Branches — A392

1955, Oct. 20   Perf. 13x13½
1061	A391	20b cream & ultra	28	15

4th Soviet-Romanian Cong., Bucharest, Oct.

1955, Oct. 1   Perf. 13½x13

Design: 1 l, Three workers holding FSM banner.

1062	A392	55b dk ol grn	28	15
1063	A392	1 l ultra	45	15
	Set value			24

Intl. Trade Union Org. (Federation Syndicale Mondiale), 10th anniv.

Sugar Beets — A393   Sheep and Shepherd — A394

Designs: 20b, Cotton. 55b, Flax. 1.55l, Sun Flower.

1955, Nov. 10   Perf. 13½
1064	A393	10b plum	30	15
1065	A393	20b sl grn	42	15
1066	A393	55b brt ultra	1.25	25
1067	A393	1.55 l dk red brn	2.75	58

1955, Dec. 10   Perf. 14x13½

Stock Farming: 10b, Pigs. 35b, Cattle. 55b, Horses.

1068	A394	5b yel grn & brn	28	15
1069	A394	10b ol bis & dk vio	60	15
1070	A394	35b brick red & brn	1.25	18
1071	A394	55b dk ol bis & brn	2.50	38

Animal husbandry.

Hans Christian Andersen — A395

Portraits: 55b, Adam Mickiewicz. 1 l, Friedrich von Schiller. 1.55 l, Baron de Montesquieu. 1.75 l, Walt Whitman. 2 l, Miguel de Cervantes.

Perf. 13½x14
1955, Dec. 17   Engr.   Unwmk.
1072	A395	20b sl bl	30	15
1073	A395	55b dp ultra	50	15
1074	A395	1 l grnsh blk	65	15
1075	A395	1.55 l vio brn	1.75	38
1076	A395	1.75 l dl vio	2.00	65
1077	A395	2 l rose lake	2.00	65
	Nos. 1072-1077 (6)		7.20	2.13

Anniversaries of famous writers.

Bank Book and Savings Bank — A396

1955, Dec. 29   Photo.   Perf. 14x13½   Wmk. 358
1078	A396	55b dp vio	1.25	50
1079	A396	55b blue	60	15

Advantages of systematic saving in a bank.

Census Date — A397

Design: 1.75 l, Family group.

Inscribed: "Recensamintul Populatiei"

1956, Feb. 3   Perf. 13½
1080	A397	55b dp org	30	15
1081	A397	1.75 l emer & red brn	85	25
a.	Center inverted	200.00	200.00

National Census, Feb. 21, 1956.

Ring-necked Pheasant A398

Great Bustard — A399   Street Fighting, Paris, 1871 — A400

Animals: No. 1082, Hare. No. 1083, Bustard. 35b, Trout. 50b, Boar. No. 1087, Brown bear. 1 l, Lynx. 1.55 l, Red squirrel. 2 l, Chamois. 3.25 l, Pintail (duck). 4.25 l, Fallow deer.

1956   Wmk. 358   Perf. 14
1082	A398	20b grn & blk	1.40	32
1083	A399	20b cit & gray blk	1.40	32
1084	A399	35b brt bl & blk	1.40	32
1085	A398	50b dp ultra & brn blk	1.40	52
1086	A398	55b ol bis & ind	1.65	52
1087	A398	55b dk bl grn & dk red brn	1.65	52
1088	A398	1 l dk grn & red brn	3.00	90
1089	A399	1.55 l lt ultra & red brn	3.25	1.25
1090	A399	1.75 l sl grn & dk brn	3.75	1.75
1091	A398	2 l ultra & brn blk	14.00	6.50
1092	A398	3.25 l lt grn & blk brn	14.00	3.25
1093	A399	4.25 l brn org & dk brn	14.00	4.00
	Nos. 1082-1093 (12)		60.90	20.17

Exist imperf. in changed colors. Value, set $17.50.

1956, May 29   Perf. 13½
1094	A400	55b vermilion	70	18

85th anniversary of Commune of Paris.

Globe and Child — A400a   Oak Tree — A401

1956, June 1   Photo.   Perf. 13½x14
1095 A400a 55b dp vio   90   22

Intl. Children's Day. The sheet of 100 contains 10 labels, each with "Peace" printed on it in one of 10 languages.

1956, June 11   Litho.   Wmk. 358
Design: 55b, Logging train in timberland.
1096 A401 20b dk bl grn, *pale grn*   52   16
1097 A401 55b brn blk, *pale grn*   1.50   52

Month of the Forest.

Romanian Academy A402

1956, June 19   Photo.   Perf. 14
1098 A402 55b dk grn & dl yel   75   20

90th anniversary of Romanian Academy.

Red Cross Worker — A403   Woman Speaker and Globe — A404

1956, June 7
1099 A403 55b olive & red   1.25   38

Romanian Red Cross Congress, June 7-9.

1956, June 14
1100 A404 55b dk bl grn   70   20

Intl. Conference of Working Women, Budapest, June 14-17.

Traian Vuia and Planes — A405

1956, June 21   Perf. 13x13½
1101 A405 55b grnsh blk & brn   70   18

1st flight by Vuia, near Paris, 50th anniv.

Ion Georgescu A406

1956, June 25   Perf. 14x13½
1102 A406 55b dk red brn & dk grn   1.25   24

Ion Georgescu (1856-1898), sculptor.

White Cabbage Butterfly A407

June Bug — A408

Design: 55b, Colorado potato beetle.

Perf. 14x13½, 13½x14
1956, July 30
1103 A407 10b dp vio, pale yel & blk   2.50   28
1104 A407 55b ol blk & yel   3.75   38
1105 A408 1.75 l lt ol & dp plum   5.00   5.75
1106 A408 1.75 l gray ol & dk vio brn 5.00   70

Campaign against insect pests.

Girl Holding Sheaf of Wheat — A409   Dock Workers on Strike — A410

1956   Perf. 13½x14
1107 A409 55b "1949-1956"   1.40   25
   a.   "1951-1956" (error)   2.75   2.00

7th anniversary of collective farming.

1956, Aug. 6
1108 A410 55b dk red brn   45   15

Dock workers' strike at Galati, 50th anniv.

Title Page and Printer — A411   Maxim Gorki — A412

1956, Aug. 13   Perf. 13½
1109 A411 55b ultra   45   15

25th anniv. of the publication of "Scanteia" (The Spark).

1956, Aug. 29   Perf. 13½x14
1110 A412 55b brown   45   15

Maxim Gorki (1868-1936), Russian writer.

Theodor Aman A413   Primrose and Snowdrops A414

1956, Sept. 24   Engr.
1111 A413 55b gray blk   70   25

Aman, painter, 125th birth anniv.

1956, Sept. 26   Photo.   Perf. 14x14½
Flowers: 55b, Daffodil and violets. 1.75 l, Snapdragon and bellflowers. 3 l, Poppies and lilies of the valley.

Flowers in Natural Colors
1112 A414 5b bl, yel & red   42   16
1113 A414 55b blk, yel & red   95   26
1114 A414 1.75 l ind, pink & yel 2.75   38
1115 A414 3 l bl grn, dk bl grn & yel   3.50   55

Olympic Rings and Torch — A415   Janos Hunyadi — A416

Designs: 55b, Water polo. 1 l, Gymnastics. 1.55 l, Canoeing. 1.75 l, High jump.

1956, Oct. 25   Perf. 13½x14
1116 A415 20b vermilion   28   15
1117 A415 55b ultra   50   15
1118 A415 1 l lil rose   75   15
1119 A415 1.55 l lt bl grn   1.25   15
1120 A415 1.75 l dp pur   1.50   40
   Nos. 1116-1120 (5)   4.28   1.00

16th Olympic Games, Melbourne, 11/22-12/8.

1956, Oct.   Wmk. 358
1121 A416 55b dp vio   60   25

Janos Hunyadi (1387-1456), national hero of Hungary. No. 1121 is found se-tenant with label showing Hunyadi Castle.

Benjamin Franklin — A417   Georges Enescu as a Boy — A418

Portraits: 35b, Sesshu (Toyo Oda). 40b, G. B. Shaw. 50b, Ivan Franco. 55b, Pierre Curie. 1 l, Henrik Ibsen. 1.55 l, Fedor Dostoevski. 1.75 l, Heinrich Heine. 2.55 l, Mozart. 3.25 l, Rembrandt.

1956   Unwmk.
1122 A417 20b vio bl   18   15
1123 A417 35b rose lake   24   15
1124 A417 40b chocolate   30   15
1125 A417 50b brn blk   35   15
1126 A417 55b dk ol   35   15
1127 A417 1 l dk bl grn   70   15
1128 A417 1.55 l dp pur   95   15
1129 A417 1.75 l brt bl   1.25   22
1130 A417 2.55 l rose vio   1.75   35
1131 A417 3.25 l dk bl   1.90   90
   Nos. 1122-1131 (10)   7.97
   Set value   2.00

Great personalities of the world.

1956, Dec. 29   Engr.
Portrait: 1.75 l, Georges Enescu as an adult.
1132 A418 55b ultramarine   45   15
1133 A418 1.75 l deep claret   1.25   25

75th birth anniv. of Georges Enescu, musician and composer.

Fighting Peasants, by Octav Bancila — A419

1957, Feb. 28   Photo.   Wmk. 358
1134 A419 55b dk bl gray   75   18

50th anniversary of Peasant Uprising.

Stephen the Great — A420

1957, Apr. 24   Perf. 13½x14
1147 A420 55b brown   45   20
1148 A420 55b dk bl   70   18

Enthronement of Stephen the Great, Prince of Moldavia, 500th anniv.

Dr. George Marinescu, Marinescu Institute and Congress Emblem A421

Dr. N. Kretzulescu, Medical School, Dr. C. Davila — A422

Designs: 35b, Dr. I. Cantacuzino and Cantacuzino Hospital. 55b, Dr. V. Babes and Babes Institute.

1957, May 5   Perf. 14x13½
1149 A421 20b dp grn   22   15
1150 A421 35b dp red brn   28   15
1151 A421 55b red lil   48   22
1152 A422 1.75 l brt ultra & dk red 1.40   50

National Congress of Medical Science, Bucharest, May 5-6.
No. 1152 also for centenary of medical and pharmaceutical teaching in Bucharest. It measures 66x23mm.

Dove and Handle Bars — A423

1957, May 29   Perf. 13½x14
1153 A423 20b shown   18   15
1154 A423 55b Cyclist   48   18

10th International Bicycle Peace Race.

Woman Watching Gymnast — A424   Woman Gymnast on Bar — A425

1957, May 21   *Perf. 13½*
1155 A424 20b shown   18 15
1156 A425 35b shown   32 15
1157 A425 55b Vaulting horse   70 18
1158 A424 1.75 l Acrobat   1.75 38

European Women's Gymnastic meet, Bucharest.

Slide Rule, Caliper & Atomic Symbol — A426   Rhododendron Hirsutum — A427

Wmk. 358
1957, May 29   Photo.   *Perf. 14*
1159 A426 55b blue   60 15
1160 A426 55b brn red   1.00 22

2nd Congress of the Society of Engineers and Technicians, Bucharest, May 29-31.

1957, June 22   Litho.   Unwmk.
Carpathian Mountain Flowers: 10b, Daphne Blagayana. 20b, Lilium Bulbiferum L. 35b, Leontopodium Alpinum. 55b, Gentiana Acaulis L. 1 l, Dianthus Callizonus. 1.55 l, Primula Carpatica Griseb. 1.75 l, Anemone Montana Hoppe.

Light Gray Background
1161 A427   5b brt rose   18 15
1162 A427   10b dk grn   28 15
1163 A427   20b red org   34 15
1164 A427   35b olive   50 15
1165 A427   55b ultra   60 15
1166 A427   1 l red   95 20
1167 A427 1.55 l yellow   1.75 24
1168 A427 1.75 l dk pur   3.00 40
       Nos. 1161-1168 (8)   7.60
           Set value   1.30

Nos. 1161-1168 also come se-tenant with a decorative label.

"Oxcart" by Grigorescu A428   Nicolae Grigorescu A429

Painting: 1.75 l, Battle scene.

1957, June 29   Photo.   Wmk. 358
1169 A428 20b dk bl grn   40 15
1170 A429 55b dp brn   80 15
1171 A428 1.75 l chlky bl   2.10 60

Grigorescu, painter, 50th death anniv.

Warship — A430

1957, Aug. 3   *Perf. 13x13½*
1172 A430 1.75 l Prus bl   1.10 24
Navy Day.

Young Couple — A431

Festival Emblem A432

Folk Dance — A433

Design: 55b, Girl with flags on hoop.

Perf. 14x14½, 14x14x12½ (A432), 13½x12½ (A433)
1957, July 28
1173 A431 20b red lilac   18 15
1174 A431 55b emerald   28 15
1175 A432   1 l red orange   70 25
1176 A433 1.75 l ultra   1.25 20
           Set value   58

Moscow 1957 Youth Festival. No. 1173 measures 23x34mm, No. 1174 22x38mm.
No. 1175 was printed in sheets of 50, alternating with 40 labels inscribed "Peace and Friendship" in 20 languages.

Bugler — A434   Girl Holding Dove — A435

1957, Aug. 30   Wmk. 358   Perf. 14
1177 A434 20b brt pur   65 18
80th anniv. of the Russo-Turkish war.

1957, Sept. 3   *Perf. 13½*
1178 A435 55b Prus grn & red   65 18
Honoring the Red Cross.

Battle Scene — A436

1957, Aug. 31
1179 A436 1.75 l brown   65 24
Battle of Marasesti, 40th anniv.

Jumper and Dove — A437

Designs: 55b, Javelin thrower and bison. 1.75 l, Runner and stag.

1957, Sept. 14   Photo.   *Perf. 13½*
1180 A437 20b brt bl & blk   28 15
1181 A437 55b yel & blk   60 18
1182 A437 1.75 l brick red & blk   2.00 50

International Athletic Meet, Bucharest.

Statue of Ovid, Constanta — A438

1957, Sept. 20   Photo.   Wmk. 358
1183 A438 1.75 l vio bl   1.40 38
2000th anniv. of the birth of the Roman poet Publius Ovidius Naso.

Oil Field — A439

Design: 55b, Horse pulling drill, 1857.

1957, Oct. 5
1184 A439 20b dl red brn   20 15
1185 A439 20b indigo   20 15
1186 A439 55b vio blk   50 25
           Set value   35

Centenary of Romanian oil industry.

Congress Emblem — A440

1957, Sept. 28
1187 A440 55b ultra   42 18
4th International Trade Union Congress, Leipzig, Oct. 4-15.

Young Couple, Lenin Banner — A441   Endre Ady — A442

Designs: 35b, Lenin and Flags, horiz. 55b, Lenin statue.

1957, Nov. 6   Perf. 14x14½, 14½x14
1188 A441 10b crimson   15 15
1189 A441 35b plum   24 15
1190 A441 55b brown   35 18
           Set value   28

Russian Revolution, 40th anniversary.

1957, Dec. 5   *Perf. 14*
1191 A442 55b ol brn   55 18
Ady, Hungarian poet, 80th birth anniv.

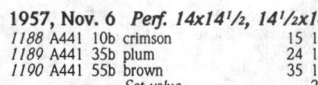

Oath of Bobilna — A443

Bobilna Monument — A444

1957, Nov. 30
1192 A443 50b deep plum   30 15
1193 A444 55b slate blue   40 15
           Set value   18

520th anniversary of the insurrection of the peasants of Bobilna in 1437.

Black-winged Stilt — A445

Animals: 10b, Great white egret. 20b, White spoonbill. 50b, Sturgeon. 55b, Ermine, horiz. 1.30 l, White pelican, horiz.

Perf. 13½x14, 14x13½
1957, Dec. 27   Photo.   Wmk. 358
1194 A445   5b red brn & gray   15 15
1195 A445   10b emer & ocher   15 15
1196 A445   20b brt red & ocher   20 15
1197 A445   50b bl grn & ocher   38 15
1198 A445   55b dp cl & gray   45 16
1199 A445 1.30 l pur & org   1.50 30
       Nos. 1194-1199,C53-C54 (8)   6.98
           Set value   1.40

Sputnik 2 and Laika A446

1957, Dec. 20   *Perf. 14x13½*
1200 A446 1.20 l bl & dk brn   1.25 38
1201 A446 1.20 l grnsh bl & choc   1.25 38

Dog Laika, "first space traveler."

Romanian Arms, Flags — A447

Designs: 55b, Arms, "Industry and Agriculture." 1.20 l, Arms, "Art, Science and Sport (soccer)."

1957, Dec. 30   *Perf. 13½*
1202 A447 25b ultra, red & ocher   18   15
1203 A447 55b dl yel   35   15
1204 A447 1.20 l crim rose   55   25
            Set value   38

Proclamation of the Peoples' Republic, 10th anniv.

Flag and
Wreath — A448

1958, Feb. 15   Unwmk.   Perf. 13½
1205 A448 1 l dk bl & red, *buff*   42   15
1206 A448 1 l brn & red, *buff*   42   15

Grivita Strike, 25th anniversary.

Television,
Radio
Antennas
A449

Design: 1.75 l, Telegraph pole and wires.

1958, Mar. 21   *Perf. 14x13½*
1207 A449 55b brt vio   30   15
1208 A449 1.75 l dp mag   80   25

Telecommunications Conference, Moscow, Dec. 3-17, 1957.

Nicolae
Balcescu — A450

Romanian Writers: 10b, Ion Creanga. 35b, Alexandru Vlahuta. 55b, Mihail Eminescu. 1.75 l, Vasile Alecsandri. 2 l, Barbu S. Delavrancea.

1958   Wmk. 358   Perf. 14x14½
1209 A450 5b bluish blk   15   15
1210 A450 10b int blk   18   15
1211 A450 35b dk bl   22   15
1212 A450 55b dk red brn   35   15
1213 A450 1.75 l blk brn   70   18
1214 A450 2 l dk sl grn   1.25 22
            Nos. 1209-1214 (6)   2.85
            Set value   70

Fencer in
Global
Mask — A451

1958, Apr. 5   *Perf. 14½x14*
1215 A451 1.75 l brt pink   1.10 25

Youth Fencing World Championships, Bucharest.

Stadium and
Health
Symbol — A452

Globe and
Dove — A453

1958, Apr. 16   *Perf. 14x14½*
1216 A452 1.20 l lt grn & red   85   18

25 years of sports medicine.

1958, May 15   Photo.
1217 A453 55b brt bl   48   15

4th Congress of the Intl. Democratic Women's Federation, June 1958.

Carl von
Linné — A454

Lepiota
Procera — A456

Portraits: 20b, Auguste Comte. 40b, William Blake. 55b, Mikhail I. Glinka. 1 l, Henry W. Longfellow. 1.75 l, Carlo Goldoni. 2 l, Jan A. Komensky.

Perf. 14x14½
1958, May 31   Unwmk.
1218 A454 10b Prus grn   15   15
1219 A454 20b brown   18   15
1220 A454 40b dp lil   28   15
1221 A454 55b dp bl   40   15
1222 A454 1 l dp mag   60   15
1223 A454 1.75 l dp vio bl   90   22
1224 A454 2 l olive   1.65 30
            Nos. 1218-1224 (7)   4.16
            Set value   90

Great personalities of the world.

1958, July   Litho.   Unwmk.
Mushrooms: 10b, Clavaria aurea. 20b, Amanita caesarea. 30b, Lactarius deliciosus. 35b, Armillaria mellea. 55b, Coprinus comatus. 1 l, Morchella conica. 1.55 l, Psalliota campestris. 1.75 l, Boletus edulis. 2 l, Cantharellus cibarius.

1225 A456 5b gray bl & brn   15   15
1226 A456 10b ol, ocher & brn   15   15
1227 A456 20b gray, red & yel   15   15
1228 A456 30b grn & dp org   18   15
1229 A456 35b lt bl & yel brn   20   15
1230 A456 55b pale grn, fawn &
             brn   35   15
1231 A456 1 l bl grn, ocher &
             brn   50   15
1232 A456 1.55 l gray, lt gray &
             pink   85   15
1233 A456 1.75 l emer, brn & buff   1.00 15
1234 A456 2 l dl bl & org yel   1.90 25
            Nos. 1225-1234 (10)   5.43
            Set value   95

Antarctic
Map and
Emil
Racovita
A457

Design: 1.20 l, Cave and Racovita.

1958, July 30   Photo.   Perf. 14½x14
1235 A457 55b indigo & lt bl   52   15
1236 A457 1.20 l ol bis & dk vio   1.00 18

90th birth anniv. of Emil Racovita, explorer and naturalist.

Armed Forces
Monument — A458

Designs: 75b, Soldier guarding industry. 1.75 l, Sailor raising flag and ship.

1958, Oct. 2   *Perf. 13½x13*
1237 A458 55b org brn   18   15
1238 A458 75b dp magenta   22   15
1239 A458 1.75 l brt blue   52   26
            Set value   40

Armed Forces Day. See No. C55.

Woman from
Oltenia — A459

Man from
Oltenia — A460

Regional Costumes: 40b, Tara Oasului. 50b, Transylvania. 55b, Muntenia. 1 l, Banat. 1.75 l, Moldavia.

1958   Unwmk.   Litho.   Perf. 13½x14
1240 A459 35b blk & red, *dl yel*   16   15
1241 A460 35b blk & red, *dl yel*   16   15
**Designs in Dark Brown and Deep
Carmine**
1242 A459 40b *pale brn*   20   15
1243 A460 40b *pale brn*   20   15
1244 A459 50b *lt lil*   24   15
1245 A460 50b *lt lil*   24   15
1246 A459 55b *gray*   38   15
1247 A460 55b *gray*   38   15
1248 A459 1 l *rose*   75   15
1249 A460 1 l *rose*   75   15
1250 A459 1.75 l *aqua*   1.00 18
1251 A460 1.75 l *aqua*   1.00 18
            Nos. 1240-1251 (12)   5.46
            Set value   1.25

Same denoms. se-tenant with label between. Exist imperf. Value, set $16.

Printer and
Hand Press
A461

Moldavia
Stamp of
1858
A462

Designs: 55b, Scissors cutting strips of 1858 stamps. 1.20 l, Postilion and mail coach. 1.30 l, Postilion blowing horn and courier on horseback. 1.75 l, 2 l, 3.30 l, Various denominations of 1858 issue.

1958, Nov. 15   Engr.   Perf. 14½x14
1252 A461 35b vio bl   22   15
1253 A461 55b dk red brn   35   15
1254 A461 1.20 l dull bl   70   15
1255 A461 1.30 l brown vio   90   16
1256 A462 1.55 l gray brn   1.00 18
1257 A462 1.75 l rose claret   1.10 25
1258 A462 2 l dull vio   1.40 48
1259 A462 3.30 l dull red brn   2.10 55
            Nos. 1252-1259 (8)   7.77
            Set value   1.80

Cent. of Romanian stamps. See No. C57. Exist imperf. Value, set $13.

Bugler
A463

Runner
A464

1958, Dec. 10   Photo.   Perf. 13½x13
1260 A463 55b crimson rose   48   18

Decade of teaching reforms.

Perf. 13½x14
1958, Dec. 9   Wmk. 358
1261 A464 1 l deep brown   90   24

Third Youth Spartacist Sports Meet.

Building and
Flag — A465

Prince Alexandru Ioan
Cuza — A466

1958, Dec. 16
1262 A465 55b dk car rose   30   15

Workers' Revolution, 40th anniversary.

Perf. 14x13½
1959, Jan. 27   Unwmk.
1263 A466 1.75 l dk blue   60   24

Centenary of the Romanian Union.

Friedrich
Handel — A467

Corn — A468

Sheep — A469

Portraits: No. 1265, Robert Burns. No. 1266, Charles Darwin. No. 1267, Alexander Popov. No. 1268, Shalom Aleichem.

1959, Apr. 25   Photo.   Perf. 13½x14
1264 A467 55b brown   32   15
1265 A467 55b indigo   32   15
1266 A467 55b slate   32   15
1267 A467 55b carmine   32   15
1268 A467 55b purple   32   15
            Nos. 1264-1268 (5)   1.60
            Set value   45

Various cultural anniversaries in 1959.

Perf. 13½x14, 14x13½
1959, June 1   Photo.   Wmk. 358

Designs: No. 1270, Sunflower and bee. No. 1271, Sugar beet and refinery. No. 1273, Cattle. No. 1274, Rooster and hens. No. 1275, Tractor and grain. No. 1276, Loaded farm wagon. No. 1277, Farm couple and "10."

1269 A468 55b brt green   25   15
1270 A468 55b red org   25   15
1271 A468 55b red lilac   25   15
1272 A469 55b olive grn   25   15
1273 A469 55b red brown   25   15
1274 A469 55b yellow brn   25   15

1275	A469	55b blue	25 15
1276	A469	55b brown	25 15

Unwmk.

1277	A469	5 l dp red lilac	2.10 65
	Nos. 1269-1277 (9)		4.10
	Set value		1.00

10th anniv. of collective farming. Sizes: #1272-1276 33x23mm; #1277 38x27mm.

Young Couple — A470

Steel Worker and Farm Woman — A471

Design: 1.60 l, Dancer in folk costume.

Perf. 13½x14

1959, July 15   Unwmk.

1278	A470	1 l brt blue	35 15
1279	A470	1.60 l car rose	70 18

7th World Youth Festival, Vienna, 7/26-8/14.

1959, Aug. 23   Litho.   Perf. 13½x14

1280	A471	55b multicolored	48 15
a.		Souvenir sheet of 1	70 26

15th anniv. of Romania's liberation from the Germans.

No. 1280a is ungummed and imperf. The blue, yellow and red vignette shows large "XV" and Romanian flag. Brown 1.20 l denomination and inscription in margin.

Prince Vlad Tepes and Document — A472

Designs: 40b, Nicolae Balcescu Street. No. 1283, Atheneum. No. 1284, Printing Combine. 1.55 l, Opera House. 1.75 l, Stadium.

1959, Sept. 20   Photo.
Centers in Gray

1281	A472	20b blue	55 15
1282	A472	40b brown	80 15
1283	A472	55b bister brn	90 22
1284	A472	55b rose lilac	1.10 22
1285	A472	1.55 l pale violet	2.50 48
1286	A472	1.75 l bluish grn	2.75 75
	Nos. 1281-1286 (6)		8.60 1.97

500th anniversary of the founding of Bucharest. See No. C71.

No. 1261 Overprinted with Shield in Silver, inscribed: "Jocurile Bucaresti Balcanice 1959"

1959, Sept. 12   Wmk. 358

1287	A464	1 l deep brown	3.25 3.25

Balkan Games.

Soccer — A473

Motorcycle Race — A474

1959   Unwmk.   Litho.   Perf. 13½

1288	A473	20b shown	18 15
1289	A474	35b shown	24 15
1290	A474	40b Ice hockey	28 15

1291	A473	55b Field ball	35 15
1292	A473	1 l Horse race	50 15
1293	A473	1.50 l Boxing	85 15
1294	A474	1.55 l Rugby	1.00 20
1295	A474	1.60 l Tennis	1.25 28
	Nos. 1288-1295,C72 (9)		6.15
	Set value		1.25

Russian Icebreaker "Lenin" A475

Perf. 14½x13½

1959, Oct. 25   Photo.

1296	A475	1.75 l blue vio	1.10 25

First atomic ice-breaker.

Stamp Album and Magnifying Glass — A476

Purple Foxglove — A477

1959, Nov. 15   Wmk. 358   Perf. 14

1297	A476	1.60 l + 40b label	1.10 38

Issued for Stamp Day.

Stamp and label were printed alternately in sheet. The 40b went to the Romanian Association of Philatelists.

1959, Dec. 15   Typo.   Unwmk.
Medicinal Flowers in Natural Colors

1298	A477	20b shown	15 15
1299	A477	40b Peppermint	22 15
1300	A477	55b Cornflower	25 15
1301	A477	55b Daisies	32 15
1302	A477	1 l Autumn crocus	42 15
1303	A477	1.20 l Monkshood	48 15
1304	A477	1.55 l Poppies	70 18
1305	A477	1.60 l Linden	80 24
1306	A477	1.75 l Dog rose	95 24
1307	A477	3.20 l Buttercup	1.75 40
	Nos. 1298-1307 (10)		6.04
	Set value		1.30

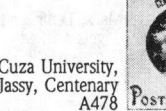

Cuza University, Jassy, Centenary A478

1960, Nov. 26   Photo.   Wmk. 358

1308	A478	55b brown	38 18

Gheorghe Cosbuc A479

Huchen (Salmon) A480

Romanian writers: 40b, Ion Luca Caragiale. 50b, Grigore Alexandrescu. 55b, Alexandru Donici. 1 l, Costache Negruzzi. 1.55 l, Dimitrie Bolintineanu.

1960, Jan. 20   Perf. 14

1309	A479	20b bluish blk	15 15
1310	A479	40b dp lilac	22 15
1311	A479	50b brown	30 15
1312	A479	55b violet brn	35 15
1313	A479	1 l violet	60 18
1314	A479	1.55 l dk blue	1.10 30
	Nos. 1309-1314 (6)		2.72
	Set value		88

1960, Feb. 1   Engr.   Unwmk.

Designs: 55b, Greek tortoise. 1.20 l, Shelduck.

1315	A480	20b blue	18 15
1316	A480	55b brown	30 15
1317	A480	1.20 l dk purple	75 15
	Nos. 1315-1317,C76-C78 (6)		4.83
	Set value		95

Woman, Dove and Globe — A481

Lenin — A482

1960, Mar. 1   Photo.   Perf. 14

1318	A481	55b violet blue	48 18

50 years of Intl. Women's Day, Mar. 8.

1960, Apr. 22   Wmk. 358   Perf. 13½

Designs: 55b, Lenin statue, Bucharest. 1.55 l, Head of Lenin.

1319	A482	40b magenta	28 15
1320	A482	55b violet blue	35 15
	Set value		20

Souvenir Sheet

1321	A482	1.55 l carmine	1.40 1.00

90th birth anniv. of Lenin.

Heroes Monument — A483

Design: 55b, Soviet war memorial.

1960, May 9   Wmk. 358   Perf. 14

1322	A483	40b vio blue	35 15
1323	A483	55b vio blue	35 25
a.		Strip of 2, #1322-1323 + label	1.65 65

15th anniversary of the liberation. Nos. 1322-1323 exist imperf., printed in deep magenta. Value, set $3.25; label strip, $4.50.

Swimming A484

Sports: 55b, Women's gymnastics. 1.20 l, High jump. 1.60 l, Boxing. 2.45 l, Canoeing.

1960, June   Unwmk.   Typo.   Perf. 14
Gray Background

1326	A484	40b blue & yel	35 25
1327	A484	55b blk, yel & emer	42 30
1328	A484	1.20 l emer & brick red	95 70
a.		Strip of 3, #1326-1328	1.75
1329	A484	1.60 l blue, yel & blk	1.75 1.25
1330	A484	2.45 l blk, emer & brick red	1.75 1.25
a.		Pair, #1329-1330 + 2 labels	3.50
	Nos. 1326-1330 (5)		5.22 3.75

17th Olympic Games, Rome, Aug. 25-Sept. 11. Nos. 1326-1330 were printed in one sheet, the top half containing No. 1328a, the bottom half No. 1330a, with gutter between. When the two strips are placed together, the Olympic rings join in a continuous design.

Exist imperf. (3.70 l replaced 2.45 l). Value, set $7.75.

Swimming — A485

Olympic Flame, Stadium — A486

Sports: 40b, Women's gymnastics. 55b, High jump. 1 l, Boxing. 1.60 l, Canoeing. 2 l, Soccer.

1960   Photo.   Wmk. 358

1331	A485	20b chalky blue	15 15
1332	A485	40b dk brn red	30 15
1333	A485	55b blue	45 15
1334	A485	1 l rose red	60 15
1335	A485	1.60 l rose lilac	75 18
1336	A485	2 l dull violet	1.40 32
	Nos. 1331-1336 (6)		3.65
	Set value		70

Souvenir Sheets
Perf. 11½

1337	A486	5 l ultra	4.50 2.25

Imperf

1338	A486	6 l dull red	7.25 3.75

17th Olympic Games.

A487

A488

Perf. 13½

1960, June 20   Unwmk.   Litho.

1339	A487	55b red org & dk car	38 18

Romanian Workers' Party, 3rd congress.

1960   Wmk. 358   Photo.   Perf. 14

Portraits: 10b, Leo Tolstoy. 20b, Mark Twain. 35b, Hokusai. 40b, Alfred de Musset. 55b, Daniel Defoe. 1 l, Janos Bolyai. 1.20 l, Anton Chekov. 1.55 l, Robert Koch. 1.75 l, Frederick Chopin.

1340	A488	10b dull pur	15 15
1341	A488	20b olive	15 15
1342	A488	35b blue	15 15
1343	A488	40b slate green	18 15
1344	A488	55b dull brn vio	42 15
1345	A488	1 l Prus blue	70 18
1346	A488	1.20 l dk car rose	90 15
1347	A488	1.55 l gray blue	1.25 15
1348	A488	1.75 l brown	1.40 25
	Nos. 1340-1348 (9)		5.30
	Set value		90

Various cultural anniversaries.

Students A489

Piano and Books A490

Designs: 5b, Diesel locomotive. 10b, Dam. 20b, Miner with drill. 30b, Ambulance and doctor. 35b, Textile worker. 50b, Nursery. 55b, Timber industry. 60b, Harvester. 75b, Feeding cattle. 1 l, Atomic reactor. 1.20 l, Oil derricks. 1.50 l, Coal mine. 1.55 l, Loading ship. 1.60 l, Athlete. 1.75 l, Bricklayer. 2 l, Steam roller. 2.40 l, Chemist. 3 l, Radio and television.

1960 **Wmk. 358 Photo.** *Perf. 14*

1349	A489	3b brt lil rose	15	15
1350	A489	5b olive bis	15	15
1351	A489	10b violet gray	15	15
1352	A489	20b blue vio	15	15
1353	A489	30b vermilion	15	15
1354	A489	35b crimson	15	15
1355	A490	40b ocher	15	15
1356	A489	50b bluish vio	16	15
1357	A489	55b blue	16	15
1358	A490	60b green	16	15
1359	A490	75b gray ol	28	15
1360	A489	1 l car rose	48	15
1361	A489	1.20 l black	38	15
1362	A489	1.50 l plum	48	15
1363	A490	1.55 l Prus grn	48	15
1364	A490	1.60 l dp blue	52	15
1365	A489	1.75 l red brown	60	15
1366	A489	2 l dk ol gray	75	15
1367	A490	2.40 l brt lilac	80	15
1368	A489	3 l grysh blue	1.00	15
		Nos. 1349-1368,C86 (21)	8.40	
		Set value		1.20

Ovid Statue at
Constanta
A491

Black Sea Resorts: 35b, Constanta harbor. 40b, Vasile Rosita beach and vase. 55b, Ionian column and Mangalia beach. 1 l, Eforie at night. 1.60 l, Eforie and sailboat.

1960, Aug. 2 **Litho.** **Unwmk.**

1369	A491	20b multicolored	15	15
1370	A491	35b multicolored	16	15
1371	A491	40b multicolored	20	15
1372	A491	55b multicolored	24	15
1373	A491	1 l multicolored	60	15
1374	A491	1.60 l multicolored	90	15
		Nos. 1369-1374,C87 (7)	3.15	
		Set value		60

Emblem — A492

Petrushka,
Russian
Puppet — A493

Designs: Various Puppets.

1960, Aug. 20 **Typo.**

1375	A492	20b multi	15	15
1376	A493	40b multi	15	15
1377	A493	55b multi	18	15
1378	A493	1 l multi	38	15
1379	A493	1.20 l multi	38	15
1380	A493	1.75 l multi	60	16
		Nos. 1375-1380 (6)	1.84	
		Set value		45

International Puppet Theater Festival.

Children on
Sled — A494

Globe and Peace
Banner — A495

Children's Sports: 35b, Boys playing ball, horiz. 55b, Ice skating, horiz. 1 l, Running. 1.75 l, Swimming, horiz.

Unwmk.

1960, Oct. 1 **Litho.** *Perf. 14*

1381	A494	20b multi	15	15
1382	A494	35b multi	15	15
1383	A494	55b multi	28	15
1384	A494	1 l multi	38	15
1385	A494	1.75 l multi	75	22
		Nos. 1381-1385 (5)	1.71	
		Set value		45

Perf. 13¹/₂x14

1960, Nov. 26 Photo. Wmk. 358

1386	A495	55b brt bl & yel	28	15

Intl. Youth Federation, 15th anniv.

Worker and
Flags
A496

Perf. 14x13

1960, Nov. 26 Litho. Unwmk.

1387	A496	55b dk car & red org	32	15

40th anniversary of the general strike.

Carp
A497

Fish: 20b, Pikeperch. 40b, Black Sea turbot. 55b, Allis shad. 1 l, Wels (catfish). 1.20 l, Sterlet. 1.60 l, Huchen (salmon).

1960, Dec. 5 **Typo.**

1388	A497	10b multi	15	15
1389	A497	20b multi	15	15
1390	A497	40b multi	24	15
1391	A497	55b multi	30	15
1392	A497	1 l multi	70	15
1393	A497	1.20 l multi	70	18
1394	A497	1.60 l multi	1.00	24
		Nos. 1388-1394 (7)	3.24	
		Set value		75

Kneeling Woman
and
Grapes — A498

Steelworker by I.
Irimescu — A499

Designs: 30b, Farmers drinking, horiz. 40b, Loading grapes into basket, horiz. 55b, Woman cutting grapes. 75b, Vintner with basket. 1 l, Woman filling basket with grapes. 1.20 l, Vintner with jug. 5 l, Antique wine jug.

1960, Dec. 20 **Litho.** *Perf. 14*

1395	A498	20b brn & gray	15	15
1396	A498	30b red org & pale grn	15	15
1397	A498	40b dp ultra & gray ol	28	15
1398	A498	55b emer & buff	38	15
1399	A498	75b dk car rose & pale grn	38	15
1400	A498	1 l Prus grn & gray ol	45	16
1401	A498	1.20 l org brn & pale bl	75	28
		Nos. 1395-1401 (7)	2.54	
		Set value		75

Souvenir Sheet

Imperf

1402	A498	5 l dk car rose & bis	3.25	1.50

Each stamp represents a different wine-growing region: Dragasani, Dealul Mare, Odobesti, Cotnari, Tirnave, Minis, Murfatlar and Pietroasa.

Perf. 13¹/₂x14, 14x13¹/₂

1961, Feb. 16 Photo. Unwmk.

Modern Sculptures: 10b, G. Doja, I. Vlad. 20b, Meeting, B. Caragea. 40b, Georges Enescu, A. Angnel. 50b, Mihail Eminescu, C. Baraschi. 55b, Peasant Revolt, 1907, M. Constantinescu, horiz.

---

1 l, "Peace," I. Jalea. 1.55 l, Building Socialism, C. Medrea. 1.75 l, Birth of an Idea, A. Szobotka.

1403	A499	5b car rose	15	15
1404	A499	10b violet	15	15
1405	A499	20b ol blk	15	15
1406	A499	40b ol bis	15	15
1407	A499	50b blk brn	18	15
1408	A499	55b org ver	18	15
1409	A499	1 l dp plum	40	15
1410	A499	1.55 l brt ultra	55	15
1411	A499	1.75 l green	85	25
		Nos. 1403-1411 (9)	2.76	
		Set value		80

Peter Poni, and
Chemical
Apparatus — A500

Romanian Scientists: 20b, A. Saligny and Danube bridge, Cernavoda. 55b, C. Budeanu and electrical formula. 1.55 l, Gh. Titeica and geometrical symbol.

1961, Apr. 11 Litho. *Perf. 13¹/₂x13*
Portraits in Brown Black

1412	A500	10b pink & vio bl	15	15
1413	A500	20b citron & mar	15	15
1414	A500	55b bl & red	22	15
1415	A500	1.55 l ocher & lil	75	16
		Set value	1.10	30

Freighter
"Galati"
A501

Ships: 40b, Passenger ship "Oltenita." 55b, Motorboat "Tomis." 1 l, Freighter "Arad." 1.55 l, Tugboat. 1.75 l, Freighter "Dobrogea."

1961, Apr. 25 **Typo.** *Perf. 14x13*

1416	A501	20b multi	18	15
1417	A501	40b multi	18	15
1418	A501	55b multi	28	15
1419	A501	1 l multi	40	15
1420	A501	1.55 l multi	55	18
1421	A501	1.75 l multi	85	25
		Nos. 1416-1421 (6)	2.44	
		Set value		70

Marx, Lenin and
Engels on Red
Flag — A502

Designs: 55b, Workers. 1 l, "Industry and Agriculture" and Workers Party Emblem.

1961, Apr. 29 **Litho.**

1422	A502	35b red, bl & ocher	16	15
1423	A502	55b mar, red & gray	24	15
		Set value		15

Souvenir Sheet

Imperf

1424	A502	1 l multi	1.25	50

40th anniv. of the Romanian Communist Party. #1424 contains one 55x33mm stamp.

Roe Deer and
Bronze Age
Hunting
Scene — A503

Lynx and Prehistoric
Hunter — A504

Designs: 35b, Boar and Roman hunter. 40b, Brown bear and Roman tombstone. 55b, Red deer, 16th cent. hunter. 75b, Red fox and feudal hunter. 1 l, Black goat and modern hunter. 1.55 l, Rabbit and hunter with dog. 1.75 l, Badger and hunter. 2 l, Roebuck and hunter.

1961, July *Perf. 13x14, 14x13*

1425	A503	10b multi	15	15
1426	A504	20b multi	18	15
1427	A504	35b multi	24	15
1428	A504	40b multi	30	15
1429	A503	55b multi	40	15
1430	A504	75b multi	60	15
1431	A503	1 l multi	75	15
1432	A503	1.55 l multi	90	15
1433	A503	1.75 l multi	1.40	25
1434	A503	2 l multi	1.65	35
		Nos. 1425-1434 (10)	6.57	
		Set value		1.20

Georges
Enescu
A505

1961, Sept. 7 **Litho.** *Perf. 14x13*

1435	A505	3 l pale vio & vio brn	1.40	25

2nd Intl. Georges Enescu Festival, Bucharest.

Peasant Playing
Panpipe — A506

Heraclitus — A507

Peasants playing musical instruments: 20b, Alpenhorn, horiz. 40b, Flute. 55b, Guitar. 60b, Bagpipe. 1 l, Zither.

Perf. 13x14, 14x13

1961 **Unwmk.** **Typo.**
Tinted Paper

1436	A506	10b multi	15	15
1437	A506	20b multi	15	15
1438	A506	40b multi	20	15
1439	A506	55b multi	38	15
1440	A506	60b multi	38	15
1441	A506	1 l multi	55	15
		Nos. 1436-1441 (6)	1.81	
		Set value		44

Perf. 13¹/₂x13

1961, Oct. 25 Photo. Wmk. 358

Portraits: 20b, Francis Bacon. 40b, Rabindranath Tagore. 55b, Domingo F. Sarmiento. 1.35 l, Heinrich von Kleist. 1.75 l, Mikhail V. Lomonosov.

1442	A507	10b maroon	15	15
1443	A507	20b brown	15	15
1444	A507	40b Prus grn	18	15
1445	A507	55b cerise	18	15
1446	A507	1.35 l brt bl	52	15
1447	A507	1.75 l purple	70	15
		Nos. 1442-1447 (6)	1.85	
		Set value		45

Swimming — A508

Gold
Medal,
Boxing
A509

Designs: No. 1449, Olympic torch. No. 1450,
Water polo, Melbourne. No. 1451, Women's high
jump, Rome.

Perf. 14x14¹⁄₂

1961, Oct. 30	Photo.		Unwmk.	
1448	A508	20b bl gray	18	15
1449	A508	20b vermilion	18	15
1450	A508	55b ultra	48	22
1451	A508	55b blue	48	22
		Set value		60

Perf. 10¹⁄₂

Size: 33x33mm

Gold Medals: 35b, Pistol shooting, Melbourne.
40b, Sharpshooting, Rome. 55b, Wrestling. 1.35 l,
Woman's high jump. 1.75 l, Three medals for
canoeing.

Medals in Ocher

1452	A509	10b Prus grn	18	15
1453	A509	35b brown	35	15
1454	A509	40b plum	38	15
1455	A509	55b org red	48	15
1456	A509	1.35 l dp ultra	80	18

Size: 46x32mm

1457	A509	1.75 l dp car rose	1.50	38
		Nos. 1452-1457 (6)	3.69	
		Set value		88

Romania's gold medals in 1956, 1960 Olympics.
#1452-1457 exist imperf. Value, set $3.75.
A souvenir sheet of one 4 l dark red & ocher was
issued. Value unused $4.25, canceled $3.25.

Congress
Emblem
A510

Primrose
A511

1961, Dec.	Litho.		Perf. 13¹⁄₂x14	
1458	A510	55b dk car rose		48 24

5th World Congress of Trade Unions, Moscow,
Dec. 4-16.

Perf. 14x13¹⁄₂, 13¹⁄₂x14

1961, Sept. 15

Designs: 20b, Sweet William. 25b, Peony. 35b,
Prickly pear. 40b, Iris. 55b, Buttercup. 1 l, Hepatica. 1.20 l, Poppy. 1.55 l, Gentian. 1.75 l, Carol
Davilla and Dimitrie Brindza. 20b, 25b, 40b, 55b,
1.20 l, 1.55 l, are vertical.

1459	A511	10b multi	15	15
1460	A511	20b multi	15	15
1461	A511	25b multi	15	15
1462	A511	35b multi	18	15
1463	A511	40b multi	22	15
1464	A511	55b multi	28	15
1465	A511	1 l multi	38	15
1466	A511	1.20 l multi	45	15
1467	A511	1.55 l multi	90	24
		Nos. 1459-1467 (9)	2.86	
		Set value		75

Souvenir Sheet

Imperf

1468	A511	1.75 l car, blk & grn	3.00 2.00

Bucharest Botanical Garden, cent.
No. 1459-1467 exist imperf. Value, set $3.

United Nations
Emblem — A512

Cock and Savings
Book — A513

Designs: 20b, Map of Balkan peninsula and
dove. 40b, Men of three races.

1961, Nov. 27			Perf. 13¹⁄₂x14	
1469	A512	20b bl, yel & pink	24	15
1470	A512	40b multi	50	15
1471	A512	55b org, lil & yel	65	18
		Set value		32

UN, 15th anniv. Nos. 1469-1470 are each
printed with alternating yellow labels.
Exist imperf. Value, set $2.75.

1962, Feb. 15	Typo.		Perf. 13¹⁄₂	

Savings Day: 55b, Honeycomb, bee and savings
book.

1472	A513	40b multi	24	15
1473	A513	55b multi	24	15
		Set value		20

Soccer Player
and Map of
Europe — A514

Wheat, Map and
Tractor — A515

1962, Apr. 20	Litho.	Perf. 13x14	
1474	A514	55b emer & red brn	48 18

European Junior Soccer Championships,
Bucharest. For surcharge see No. 1510.

1962, Apr. 27		Perf. 13¹⁄₂x14	

Designs: 55b, Medal honoring agriculture.
1.55Nl, Sheaf of wheat, hammer & sickle.

1475	A515	40b org & dk car	20	15
1476	A515	55b yel, car & brn	24	15
1477	A515	1.55 l multi	70	18
		Set value		28

Collectivization of agriculture.

Canoe Race
A516

Designs: 20b, Kayak. 40b, Eight-man shell.
55b, Two-man skiff. 1 l, Yachts. 1.20 l, Motorboats.
1.55 l, Sailboat. 3 l, Water slalom.

1962, May 15	Photo.	Perf. 14x13	
Vignette in Bright Blue			
1478	A516	10b lil rose	15	15
1479	A516	20b ol gray	15	15
1480	A516	40b red brn	15	15
1481	A516	55b ultra	22	15
1482	A516	1 l red	28	15
1483	A516	1.20 l dp plum	55	15
1484	A516	1.55 l orange	75	15
1485	A516	3 l violet	1.40	22
		Nos. 1478-1485 (8)	3.65	
		Set value		65

These stamps were also issued imperf. with color
of denomination and inscription changed. Value, set
unused $4.50, canceled $2.

Ion Luca
Caragiale — A517

Portraits: 40b, Jean Jacques Rousseau. 1.75 l,
Aleksander I. Herzen. 3.30 l, Ion Luca Caragiale
(as a young man).

1962, June 9			Perf. 13¹⁄₂x14	
1486	A517	40b dk sl grn	18	15
1487	A517	55b magenta	22	15
1488	A517	1.75 l dp bl	75	25
		Set value		38

Souvenir Sheet

Perf. 11¹⁄₂

1489	A517	3.30 l brown	3.00 1.75

Rousseau, French philosopher, 250th birth
anniv.; Caragiale, Romanian author, 50th death
anniv.; Herzen, Russian writer, 150th birth anniv.
No. 1489 contains one 2x55mm stamp.

Globes Surrounded with Flags — A518

1962, July 6	Typo.	Perf. 11	
1490	A518	55b multi	40 15

8th Youth Festival for Peace and Friendship, Helsinki, July 28-Aug. 6.

Traian
Vuia — A519

Fieldball Player
and
Globe — A520

Portraits: 20b, Al. Davila. 35b, Vasile Pirvan.
40b, Ion Negulici. 55b, Grigore Cobilcescu. 1 l,
Dr. Gheorghe Marinescu. 1.20 l, Ion Cantacuzino.
1.35 l, Victor Babes. 1.55 l, C. Levaditi.

1962, July 20	Photo.		Wmk. 358	
1491	A519	15b brown	15	15
1492	A519	20b dl red brn	15	15
1493	A519	35b brn mag	15	15
1494	A519	40b bl vio	15	15
1495	A519	55b brt bl	18	15
1496	A519	1 l dp ultra	22	15
1497	A519	1.20 l crimson	38	15
1498	A519	1.35 l Prus grn	45	15
1499	A519	1.55 l purple	90	15
		Nos. 1491-1499 (9)	2.73	
		Set value		65

Perf. 13x14

1962, May 12	Litho.	Unwmk.	
1500	A520	55b yel & vio	48 15

2nd Intl. Women's Fieldball Championships,
Bucharest.

Same Surcharged in Violet Blue:
"Campionana Mondiala 5 lei"

1962, July 31			
1501	A520	5 l on 55b yel & vio	4.25 2.10

Romanian victory in the 2nd Intl. Women's
Fieldball Championships.

Rod
Fishing — A521

Various Fishing Scenes.

1962, July 25			Perf. 14x13	
1502	A521	10b multi	15	15
1503	A521	25b multi	15	15
1504	A521	40b bl & brick red	15	15
1505	A521	55b multi	20	15
1506	A521	75b sl, gray & bl	30	15
1507	A521	1 l multi	48	15
1508	A521	1.75 l multi	75	15
1509	A521	3.25 l multi	1.40	22
		Nos. 1502-1509 (8)	3.58	
		Set value		84

No. 1474 Surcharged in Dark Blue: "1962
Campioana Europeana 2 lei"

1962, July 31			
1510	A514	2 l on 55b	1.65 1.00

Romania's victory in the European Junior Soccer
Championships, Bucharest.

Child and
Butterfly
A522

Handicraft
A523

Designs: 30b, Girl feeding bird. 40b, Boy and
model sailboat. 55b, Children writing, horiz.
1.20 l, Girl at piano, and boy playing violin. 1.55 l,
Pioneers camping, horiz.

Perf. 13x14, 14x13

1962, Aug. 25			Litho.	
1511	A522	20b lt bl, red & brn	15	15
1512	A522	30b org, bl & red brn	15	15
1513	A522	40b chalky bl, dp org & Prus bl	15	15
1514	A522	55b citron, bl & red	24	15
1515	A522	1.20 l car, brn & dk vio	38	15
1516	A522	1.55 l bis, red & vio	70	15
		Nos. 1511-1516 (6)	1.77	
		Set value		45

1962, Oct. 12		Perf. 13x14	

Designs: 10b, Food and drink. 20b, Chemical
industry. 40b, Chinaware. 55b, Leather industry.
75b, Textiles. 1.20 l, Furniture. 1.20 l, Electrical
appliances. 1.55 l, Household goods (sewing
machine and pots).

1517	A523	5b multi	15	15
1518	A523	10b multi	15	15
1519	A523	20b multi	15	15
1520	A523	40b multi	18	15
1521	A523	55b multi	18	15
1522	A523	75b multi	22	15
1523	A523	1 l multi	30	15
1524	A523	1.20 l multi	55	15
1525	A523	1.55 l multi	90	25
		Nos. 1517-1525,C126 (10)	3.68	
		Set value		95

4th Sample Fair, Bucharest.

Lenin — A524

Bull — A525

1962, Nov. 7		Perf. 10¹⁄₂	
1526	A524	55b vio bl, red & bis	35 15

Russian October Revolution, 45th anniv.

1962, Nov. 20 *Perf. 14x13, 13x14*

Designs: 20b, Sheep, horiz. 40b, Merino ram, horiz. 1 l, York pig. 1.35 l, Cow. 1.55 l, Heifer, horiz. 1.75 l, Pigs, horiz.

1527	A525	20b ultra & blk	15	15
1528	A525	40b bl, yel & sep	15	15
1529	A525	55b ocher, buff & sl grn	18	15
1530	A525	1 l gray, yel & brn	28	15
1531	A525	1.35 l dl grn, choc & blk	38	15
1532	A525	1.55 l org red, dk brn & blk	60	18
1533	A525	1.75 l dk vio bl, yel & org	75	32
		Nos. 1527-1533 (7)	2.49	
		Set value		85

Arms, Factory and Harvester A526

Perf. 14 1/2 x 13 1/2

1962, Dec. 30 Litho.

1534	A526	1.55 l multi	90	18

Romanian People's Republic, 15th anniv.

Strikers at Grivita, 1933 — A527

1963, Feb. 16 *Perf. 14x13 1/2*

1535	A527	1.75 l red, vio & yel	70	18

30th anniv. of the strike of railroad and oil industry workers at Grivita.

Tractor Driver and "FAO" Emblem A528

Tomatoes A529

Designs: 55b, Farm woman, cornfield and combine. 1.55 l, Child drinking milk and milking machine. 1.75 l, Woman with basket of grapes and vineyard.

1963, Mar. 21 Photo. *Perf. 14 1/2 x13*

1536	A528	40b vio bl	15	15
1537	A528	55b bis brn	15	15
1538	A528	1.55 l rose red	45	15
1539	A528	1.75 l green	75	25
		Set value		46

FAO "Freedom from Hunger" campaign.

Perf. 13 1/2 x14, 14x13 1/2

1963, Apr. 25 Litho. Unwmk.

Designs: 40b, Hot peppers. 55b, Radishes. 75b, Eggplant. 1.20 l, Mild peppers. 3.25 l, Cucumbers, horiz.

1540	A529	35b multi	15	15
1541	A529	40b multi	15	15
1542	A529	55b multi	16	15
1543	A529	75b multi	22	15
1544	A529	1.20 l multi	60	15
1545	A529	3.25 l multi	1.40	32
		Nos. 1540-1545 (6)	2.68	
		Set value		62

Woman Swimmer at Start — A530

Chicks — A531

Designs: 30b, Crawl, horiz. 55b, Butterfly stroke, horiz. 1 l, Backstroke, horiz. 1.35 l, Breaststroke, horiz. 1.55 l, Woman diver. 2 l, Water polo.

1963, June 15 *Perf. 13x14, 14x13*

1546	A530	25b yel brn, emer & gray	15	15
1547	A530	30b ol grn, gray & yel	15	15
1548	A530	55b bl, gray & red	18	15
1549	A530	1 l grn, gray & red	28	15
1550	A530	1.35 l ultra, car & gray	38	15
1551	A530	1.55 l pur, gray & org	70	15
1552	A530	2 l car rose, gray & org	75	35
		Nos. 1546-1552 (7)	2.59	
		Set value		75

1963, May 23 *Perf. 10 1/2*

Domestic poultry: 30b, Hen. 40b, Goose. 55b, White cock. 70b, Duck. 1 l, Hen. 1.35 l, Tom turkey. 3.20 l, Hen.

Fowl in Natural Colors; Inscription in Dark Blue

1553	A531	20b ultra	15	15
1554	A531	30b tan	15	15
1555	A531	40b org brn	15	15
1556	A531	55b brt grn	15	15
1557	A531	70b lilac	28	15
1558	A531	1 l blue	38	15
1559	A531	1.35 l ocher	55	15
1560	A531	3.20 l yel grn	1.10	38
		Nos. 1553-1560 (8)	2.91	
		Set value		75

Women and Globe — A532

1963, June 15 Photo. *Perf. 14x13*

1561	A532	55b dark blue	28	15

Intl. Women's Cong., Moscow, June 24-29.

William M. Thackeray, Writer — A533

Portraits: 50b, Eugene Delacroix, painter. 55b, Gheorghe Marinescu, physician. 1.55 l, Giuseppe Verdi, composer. 1.75 l, Stanislavski, actor and producer.

1963, July Unwmk. *Perf. 14x13*

Portrait in Black

1562	A533	40b pale vio	15	15
1563	A533	50b bis brn	18	15
1564	A533	55b olive	24	15
1565	A533	1.55 l rose brn	48	15
1566	A533	1.75 l pale vio bl	75	15
		Nos. 1562-1566 (5)	1.80	
		Set value		48

Walnuts A534

Designs: 20b, Plums. 40b, Peaches. 55b, Strawberries. 1 l, Grapes. 1.55 l, Apples. 1.60 l, Cherries. 1.75 l, Pears.

1963, Sept. 15 Litho. *Perf. 14x13 1/2*

Fruits in Natural Colors

1567	A534	10b pale yel & brn ol	15	15
1568	A534	20b pale pink & red org	15	15
1569	A534	40b lt bl & bl	15	15
1570	A534	55b dl yel & rose car	15	15
1571	A534	1 l pale vio & vio	28	15
1572	A534	1.55 l yel grn & ultra	45	15
1573	A534	1.60 l yel & bis	75	15
1574	A534	1.75 l lt bl & grn	75	15
		Nos. 1567-1574 (8)	2.83	
		Set value		58

Women Playing Volleyball and Map of Europe — A535

Designs: 40b, Three men players. 55b, Three women players. 1.75 l, Two men players. 3.20 l, Europa Cup.

1963, Oct. 22 *Perf. 13 1/2 x14*

1575	A535	5b gray & lil rose	15	15
1576	A535	40b gray & vio bl	18	15
1577	A535	55b gray & grnsh bl	30	15
1578	A535	1.75 l gray & org brn	55	15
1579	A535	3.20 l gray & vio	1.10	38
		Nos. 1575-1579 (5)	2.28	
		Set value		70

European Volleyball Championships, Oct. 22-Nov. 4.

Pine Tree, Branch and Cone — A536

Design: 1.75 l, Beech forest and branch.

1963, Dec. 5 Unwmk. *Perf. 13 1/2*

1580	A536	55b dk grn	16	15
1581	A536	1.75 l dk bl	50	15
		Set value		23

Reforestation program.

Silkworm Moth — A537

18th Century House, Ploesti — A538

Designs: 20b, Chrysalis, moth and worm. 40b, Silkworm on leaf. 55b, Bee over mountains, horiz. 60b, 1.20 l, 1.35 l, 1.60 l, Bees pollinating various flowers, horiz.

1963, Dec. 12 Litho. *Perf. 13x14*

1582	A537	10b multi	15	15
1583	A537	20b multi	15	15
1584	A537	40b multi	18	15
1585	A537	55b multi	28	15
1586	A537	60b multi	38	15
1587	A537	1.20 l multi	60	15
1588	A537	1.35 l multi	75	22
1589	A537	1.60 l multi	1.10	25
		Nos. 1582-1589 (8)	3.59	
		Set value		90

1963, Dec. 25 Engr. *Perf. 13*

Peasant Houses from Village Museum, Bucharest: 40b, Oltenia, 1875, horiz. 55b, Hunedoara, 19th Cent., horiz. 75b, Oltenia, 19th Cent. 1 l, Brasov, 1847. 1.20 l, Bacau, 19th Cent. 1.75 l, Arges, 19th Cent.

1590	A538	20b claret	15	15
1591	A538	40b blue	15	15
1592	A538	55b dl vio	18	15

1593	A538	75b green	22	15
1594	A538	1 l brn & mar	38	15
1595	A538	1.20 l gray ol	45	15
1596	A538	1.75 l dk brn & ultra	85	18
		Nos. 1590-1596 (7)	2.38	
		Set value		60

Ski Jump A539

Sports: 20b, Speed skating. 40b, Ice hockey. 55b, Women's figure skating. 60b, Slalom. 75b, Biathlon. 1 l, Bobsledding. 1.20 l, Cross-country skiing.

1963, Nov. 25 Litho. *Perf. 14*

1597	A539	10b red & dk bl	15	15
1598	A539	20b ultra & red brn	15	15
1599	A539	40b emer & red brn	20	15
1600	A539	55b vio & red brn	30	15
1601	A539	60b org & vio bl	40	15
1602	A539	75b lil rose & dk bl	50	15
1603	A539	1 l bis & vio bl	85	24
1604	A539	1.20 l grnsh bl & vio	90	35
		Nos. 1597-1604 (8)	3.45	
		Set value		1.05

9th Winter Olympic Games, Innsbruck, Jan. 29-Feb. 9, 1964.

Exist imperf. in changed colors. Value, set $5.50.

A souvenir sheet contains one imperf. 1.50 l ultramarine and red stamp showing the Olympic Ice Stadium at Innsbruck and the Winter Games emblem. Value $5.50.

Elena Teodorini as Carmen — A540

Munteanu Murgoci and Congress Emblem — A541

Designs: 10b, George Stephanescu, founder of Romanian opera. 35b, Ion Bajenaru as Petru Rares. 40b, D. Popovici as Alberich. 55b, Hariclea Darclée as Tosca. 75b, George Folescu as Boris Godunov. 1 l, Jean Athanasiu as Rigoletto. 1.35 l, Traian Grosavescu as Duke in Rigoletto. 1.55 l, N. Leonard as Hoffmann.

1964, Jan. 20 Photo. *Perf. 13*

Portrait in Dark Brown

1605	A540	10b olive	15	15
1606	A540	20b ultra	15	15
1607	A540	35b green	15	15
1608	A540	40b grnsh bl	15	15
1609	A540	55b car rose	18	15
1610	A540	75b lilac	18	15
1611	A540	1 l blue	55	15
1612	A540	1.35 l brt vio	75	15
1613	A540	1.55 l red org	85	22
		Nos. 1605-1613 (9)	3.11	
		Set value		75

1964, Feb. 5 Unwmk. *Perf. 13*

1614	A541	1.60 l brt bl, ind & bis	70	18

8th Intl. Soil Congress, Bucharest.

Asculaphid A542

Insects: 10b, Thread-waisted wasp. 35b, Wasp. 40b, Rhyparioides metelkana moth. 55b, Tussock moth. 1.20 l, Kanetisa circe butterfly. 1.55 l, Beetle. 1.75 l, Horned beetle.

1964, Feb. 20 — Litho. — Perf. 14x13
Insects in Natural Colors

1615	A542	5b pale lilac	15	15
1616	A542	10b lt bl & red	15	15
1617	A542	35b pale grn	15	15
1618	A542	40b olive green	18	15
1619	A542	55b ultra	20	15
1620	A542	1.20 l pale grn & red	40	15
1621	A542	1.55 l yel & brn	60	15
1622	A542	1.75 l orange & red	65	18
		Nos. 1615-1622 (8)	2.48	
		Set value		76

Tobacco Plant — A543

Jumping — A544

Garden flowers: 20b, Geranium. 40b, Fuchsia. 55b, Chrysanthemum. 75b, Dahlia. 1 l, Lily. 1.25 l, Day lily. 1.55 l, Marigold.

1964, Mar. 25 — Perf. 13x14

1623	A543	10b dk bl, grn & bis	15	15
1624	A543	20b gray, grn & red	15	15
1625	A543	40b pale grn, grn & red	18	15
1626	A543	55b grn, lt grn & lil	22	15
1627	A543	75b cit, red & grn	24	15
1628	A543	1 l dp cl, rose cl, grn & org	40	15
1629	A543	1.25 l sal, vio bl & grn	42	18
1630	A543	1.55 l red brn, yel & grn	55	18
		Nos. 1623-1630 (8)	2.31	
		Set value		70

Unwmk.
1964, Apr. 25 — Photo. — Perf. 13

Horse Show Events: 40b, Dressage, horiz. 1.35 l, Jumping. 1.55 l, Galloping, horiz.

1631	A544	40b lt bl, rose brn & blk	15	15
1632	A544	55b lil, red & brn	18	15
1633	A544	1.35 l brt grn, red & dk brn	55	15
1634	A544	1.55 l pale yel, bl & dp claret	80	20
		Set value		46

Hogfish A545

Mihail Eminescu A546

Fish (Constanta Aquarium): 10b, Peacock blenny. 20b, Mediterranean scad. 40b, Sturgeon. 50b, Sea horses. 55b, Yellow gurnard. 1 l, Beluga. 3.20 l, Stingray.

1964, May 10 — Litho. — Perf. 14

1635	A545	5b multi	15	15
1636	A545	10b multi	15	15
1637	A545	20b multi	15	15
1638	A545	40b multi	15	15
1639	A545	50b multi	18	15
1640	A545	55b multi	18	15
1641	A545	1 l multi	45	15
1642	A545	3.20 l multi	1.10	22
		Set value	2.20	65

1964, June 20 — Photo. — Perf. 13

Portraits: 20b, Ion Creanga. 35b, Emil Girleanu. 55b, Michelangelo. 1.20 l, Galileo Galilei. 1.75 l, William Shakespeare.

Portraits in Dark Brown

1643	A546	5b green	15	15
1644	A546	20b magenta	15	15
1645	A546	35b vermilion	25	15
1646	A546	55b bister	28	15
1647	A546	1.20 l ultra	52	16
1648	A546	1.75 l violet	90	25
		Nos. 1643-1648 (6)	2.25	
		Set value		62

50th death anniv. of Emil Girleanu, writer; the 75th death anniversaries of Ion Creanga and Mihail Eminescu, writers; and the 400th anniv. of the death of

Michelangelo and the births of Galileo and Shakespeare.

Road through Gorge — A547 High Jump — A548

Tourist Publicity: 55b, Lake Bilea and cottage. 1 l, Ski lift, Polana Brasov. 1.35 l, Ceahlaul peak and Lake Bicaz, horiz. 1.75 l, Hotel Alpin.

1964, June 29 — Engr.

1649	A547	40b rose brn	15	15
1650	A547	55b dk bl	18	15
1651	A547	1 l dl pur	30	15
1652	A547	1.35 l pale brn	45	15
1653	A547	1.75 l green	55	22
		Nos. 1649-1653 (5)	1.63	
		Set value		50

1964, July 28 — Photo.

1964 Balkan Games: 40b, Javelin throw. 55b, Running. 1 l, Discus throw. 1.20 l, Hurdling. 1.55 l, Map and flags of Balkan countries.

Size: 23x37½mm

1654	A548	30b ver, yel & yel grn	15	15
1655	A548	40b grn, yel, brn & vio	15	15
1656	A548	55b gldn brn, yel & bl grn	22	15
1657	A548	1 l brt bl, yel, brn & red	45	15
1658	A548	1.20 l pur, yel, brn & grn	55	15

Litho.
Size: 23x45mm

1659	A548	1.55 l multi	90	22
		Nos. 1654-1659 (6)	2.42	
		Set value		60

Factory — A549

Designs: 55b, Flag and Coat of Arms, vert. 75b, Combine. 1.20 l, Apartment buildings. 2 l, Flag, coat of arms, industrial and agricultural scenes. 55b, 2 l, Inscribed "A XX A aniversare a eliberarii patriei!"

1964, Aug. 23 — Photo. — Perf. 13

1660	A549	55b multi	16	15
1661	A549	60b multi	24	15
1662	A549	75b multi	24	15
1663	A549	1.20 l multi	48	15
		Set value		44

Souvenir Sheet
Imperf

1664	A549	2 l multi	1.25	55

20th anniv. of Romania's liberation. No. 1664 contains one stamp 110x70mm.

High Jump A550

Sport: 30b, Wrestling. 35b, Volleyball. 40b, Canoeing. 55b, Fencing. 1.20 l, Women's gymnastics. 1.35 l, Soccer. 1.55 l, Sharpshooting.

1964, Sept. 1 — Litho.
Olympic Rings in Blue, Yellow, Black, Green and Red

1665	A550	20b yel & blk	20	15
1666	A550	30b lilac & blk	20	15
1667	A550	35b grnsh bl & blk	20	15
1668	A550	40b pink & blk	22	15
1669	A550	55b lt yel grn & blk	32	15
1670	A550	1.20 l org & blk	65	15
1671	A550	1.35 l ocher & blk	80	22
1672	A550	1.55 l bl & blk	90	35
		Nos. 1665-1672 (8)	3.49	
		Set value		95

18th Olympic Games, Tokyo, Oct. 10-25. Nos. 1665-1669 exist imperf., in changed colors. Three other denominations exist, 1.60 l, 2 l and 2.40 l, imperf. Value, set of 8, unused $5.50, canceled $4.

An imperf. souvenir sheet contains a 3.25 l stamp showing a runner. Value unused $5.50 canceled $5.

Georges Enescu, Piano Keys and Neck of Violin — A551

Designs: 55b, Enescu at piano. 1.60 l, Enescu Festival medal. 1.75 l, Enescu bust by G. Anghel.

1964, Sept. 5 — Engr.

1673	A551	10b bl grn	15	15
1674	A551	55b vio blk	18	15
1675	A551	1.60 l dk red brn	48	20
1676	A551	1.75 l dk bl	85	22
		Set value		54

3rd Intl. Georges Enescu Festival, Bucharest, Sept., 1964.

Black Swans A552

Designs: 5b, Indian python. 35b, Ostriches. 40b, Crowned cranes. 55b, Tigers. 1 l, Lions. 1.55 l, Grevy's zebras. 2 l, Bactrian camels.

Perf. 14x13

1964, Sept. 28 — Litho. — Unwmk.

1677	A552	5b multi	15	15
1678	A552	10b multi	15	15
1679	A552	35b multi	15	15
1680	A552	40b multi	18	15
1681	A552	55b multi	22	15
1682	A552	1 l multi	38	15
1683	A552	1.55 l multi	75	16
1684	A552	2 l multi	1.00	22
		Nos. 1677-1684 (8)	2.98	
		Set value		70

Issued to publicize the Bucharest Zoo. No. 1683 inscribed "BANI."

C. Brincoveanu, Stolnicul Cantacuzino, Gheorghe Lazar and Academy A553

Designs: 40b, Alexandru Ioan Cuza, medal and University. 55b, Masks, curtain, harp, keyboard and palette, vert. 75b, Women students in laboratory and auditorium. 1 l, Savings Bank building.

Perf. 13x13½, 13½x13

1964, Oct. 14 — Photo.

1685	A553	20b multi	15	15
1686	A553	40b multi	15	15
1687	A553	55b multi	20	15
1688	A553	75b multi	24	15
1689	A553	1 l dk brn, yel & org	40	18
		Nos. 1685-1689 (5)	1.14	
		Set value		45

No. 1685 for 250th anniv. of the Royal Academy; Nos. 1686, 1688 cent. of the University of

Bucharest; No. 1687 cent. of the Academy of Art and No. 1689 cent. of the Savings Bank.

Soldier's Head and Laurel — A554

1964, Oct. 25 — Litho. — Perf. 12x12½

1690	A554	55b ultra & lt bl	28	15

Army Day.

Canadian Kayak Singles Gold Medal, Melbourne, 1956 — A555

Romanian Olympic Gold Medals: 30b, Boxing, Melbourne, 1956. 35b, Rapid Silhouette Pistol, Melbourne, 1956. 40b, Women's High Jump, Rome, 1960. 55b, Wrestling, Rome, 1960. 1.20 l, Clay Pigeon Shooting, Rome, 1960. 1.35 l, High Jump, Tokyo, 1964. 1.55 l, Javelin, Tokyo, 1964.

1964, Nov. 30 — Photo. — Perf. 13½
Medals in Gold and Brown

1691	A555	20b pink & ultra	15	15
1692	A555	30b yel grn & ultra	20	15
1693	A555	35b bluish grn & ultra	28	15
1694	A555	40b lil & ultra	40	15
1695	A555	55b org & ultra	48	15
1696	A555	1.20 l ol grn & ultra	70	18
1697	A555	1.35 l gldn brn & ultra	90	26
1698	A555	1.55 l rose lil & ultra	1.25	38
		Nos. 1691-1698 (8)	4.36	
		Set value		1.00

Romanian athletes who won gold medals in three Olympic Games. Nos. 1691-1695 exist imperf., in changed colors. Three other denominations exist, 1.60 l, 2 l and 2.40 l, imperf. Value, set of 8, unused $5.75, canceled $4.

A 10 l souvenir sheet shows the 1964 Olympic gold medal and world map. Value unused $5.50, canceled $4.

Strawberries — A556

Designs: 35b, Blackberries. 40b, Raspberries. 55b, Rose hips. 1.20 l, Blueberries. 1.35 l, Cornelian cherries. 1.55 l, Hazelnuts. 2.55 l, Cherries.

1964, Dec. 20 — Litho. — Perf. 13½x14

1703	A556	5b gray, red & grn	15	15
1704	A556	35b ocher, grn & dk vio bl	15	15
1705	A556	40b pale vio, car & grn	15	15
1706	A556	55b yel grn & red	15	15
1707	A556	1.20 l sal pink, grn, brn & ind	38	15
1708	A556	1.35 l lt bl, grn & red	42	15
1709	A556	1.55 l gldn brn, grn & ocher	75	18
1710	A556	2.55 l ultra, grn & red	1.50	25
		Nos. 1703-1710 (8)	3.65	
		Set value		75

Syncom 3 — A557

UN Headquarters,
NY — A558

Space Satellites: 40b, Syncom 3 over TV antennas. 55b, Ranger 7 reaching moon, horiz. 1 l, Ranger 7 and moon close-up, horiz. 1.20 l, Voskhod. 5 l, Konstantin Feoktistov, Vladimir M. Komarov, Boris B. Yegorov and Voskhod.

Perf. 13x14, 14x13

1965, Jan. 5   Litho.   Unwmk.
Size: 22x38mm, 38x22mm

1711	A557	30b multi	16	15
1712	A557	40b multi	35	15
1713	A557	55b multi	42	15
1714	A557	1 l multi	50	15
1715	A557	1.20 l multi, horiz.	85	15

Perf. 13½x13
Size: 52x30mm

1716	A557	5 l multi	2.00	52
		Nos. 1711-1716 (6)	4.28	
		Set value		88

For surcharge see No. 1737.

1965, Jan. 25   Perf. 12x12½
Design: 1.60 l, Arms and flag of Romania, and UN emblem.

1717	A558	55b ultra, red & gold	38	15
1718	A558	1.60 l ultra, red, gold & yel	75	16

20th anniv. of the UN and 10th anniv. of Romania's membership in the UN.

Greek Tortoise — A559

Reptiles: 10b, Bull lizard. 20b, Three-lined lizard. 40b, Sand lizard. 55b, Slow worm. 60b, Sand viper. 1 l, Desert lizard. 1.20 l, Orsini's viper. 1.35 l, Caspian whipsnake. 3.25 l, Four-lined snake.

1965, Feb. 25   Photo.   Perf. 13½

1719	A559	5b multi	15	15
1720	A559	10b multi	15	15
1721	A559	20b multi	15	15
1722	A559	40b multi	15	15
1723	A559	55b multi	18	15
1724	A559	60b multi	28	15
1725	A559	1 l multi	38	15
1726	A559	1.20 l multi	45	15
1727	A559	1.35 l multi	60	18
1728	A559	3.25 l multi	1.10	25
		Nos. 1719-1728 (10)	3.59	
		Set value		90

White Persian
Cats — A560

Designs: 1.35 l, Siamese cat. Others, Various European cats. (5b, 10b, 3.25 l, horiz.)

1965, Mar. 20   Litho.
Size: 41x29mm, 29x41mm
Cats in Natural Colors

1729	A560	5b brn org & blk	15	15
1730	A560	10b brt bl & blk	15	15
1731	A560	40b yel grn, yel & blk	15	15
1732	A560	55b rose red & blk	24	15
1733	A560	60b yel & blk	40	15
1734	A560	75b lt vio & blk	48	15
1735	A560	1.35 l red org & blk	85	15

Perf. 13x13½
Size: 62x29mm

1736	A560	3.25 l blue	1.65	35
		Nos. 1729-1736 (8)	4.07	
		Set value		88

No. 1714 Surcharged in Violet

RANGER 9
24 - 3 - 1965

5 Lei

1965, Apr. 25   Perf. 14x13

1737	A557	5 l on 1 l multi	12.50	12.50

Flight of the US rocket Ranger 9 to the moon, Mar. 24, 1965.

Dante Alighieri — A561

Portraits: 40b, Ion Bianu, philologist and historian. 55b, Anton Bacalbasa, writer. 60b, Vasile Conta, philosopher. 1 l, Jean Sibelius, Finnish composer. 1.35 l, Horace, Roman poet.

1965, May 10   Photo.   Perf. 13½
Portrait in Black

1738	A561	40b chalky blue	15	15
1739	A561	55b bister	18	15
1740	A561	60b light lilac	22	15
1741	A561	1 l dl red brn	45	15
1742	A561	1.35 l olive	60	18
1743	A561	1.75 l orange red	1.10	24
		Nos. 1738-1743 (6)	2.70	
		Set value		70

ITU Emblem, Old and New
Communication Equipment — A562

1965, May 15   Engr.

1744	A562	1.75 l ultra	90	38

ITU, centenary.

Iron
Gate,
Danube
A562a

Arms of Yugoslavia and Romania and
Djerdap Dam — A562b

Design: 55b (50d), Iron Gate hydroelectric plant and dam.

Perf. 12½x12

1965, May 20   Litho.   Unwmk.

1745	A562a	30b (25d) lt bl & grn	15	15
1746	A562a	55b (50d) lt bl & dk red	24	15
		Set value	28	15

Miniature Sheet
Perf. 13½x13

1747	A562b	Sheet of 4	2.50	2.50
a.		80b multi	22	15
b.		1.20 l multi	40	22

Issued simultaneously by Romania and Yugoslavia for the start of construction of the Iron Gate hydroelectric plant and dam. Valid for postage in both countries.
No. 1747 contains one each of Nos. 1747a, 1747b and Yugoslavia Nos. 771a and 771b. Only Nos. 1747a and 1747b were valid in Romania. Sold for 4 l. See Yugoslavia Nos. 769-771.

Small-bore Rifle
Shooting,
Kneeling — A563

Designs: 40b, Rifle shooting, prone. 55b, Rapid-fire pistol and map of Europe. 1 l, Free pistol and map of Europe. 1.60 l, Small-bore rifle, standing, and map of Europe. 2 l, 5 l, Marksmen in various shooting positions (all horizontal).

Perf. 12x12½, 12½x12

1965, May 30   Litho.   Unwmk.
Size: 23x43mm, 43x23mm

1748	A563	20b multi	15	15
1749	A563	40b dl grn, pink & blk	15	15
1750	A563	55b multi	18	15
1751	A563	1 l pale grn, blk & ocher	38	15
1752	A563	1.60 l multi	60	15

Perf. 13½
Size: 51x28mm

1753	A563	2 l multi	75	20
		Nos. 1748-1753 (6)	2.21	
		Set value		50

European Shooting Championships, Bucharest. Nos. 1749-1752 were issued imperf. in changed colors. Two other denominations exist, 3.25 l and 5 l, imperf. Value, set of 6, unused $4.25, canceled $1.75.

Fat-Frumos
and the
Giant — A564

Fairy Tales: 40b, Fat-Frumos on horseback and Ileana Cosinzeana. 55b, Harap Alb and the Bear. 1 l, "The Moralist Wolf." 1.35 l, "The Ox and the Calif." 2 l, Wolf and bear pulling sled.

1965, June 25   Photo.   Perf. 13

1756	A564	20b multi	18	15
1757	A564	40b multi	18	15
1758	A564	55b multi	22	15
1759	A564	1 l multi	40	15
1760	A564	1.35 l multi	60	15
1761	A564	2 l multi	85	22
		Nos. 1756-1761 (6)	2.43	
		Set value		52

Bee and Blossoms
A565

Space
Achievements
A566

Design: 1.60 l, Exhibition Hall, horiz.

Perf. 12x12½, 12½x12

1965, July 28   Litho.   Unwmk.

1762	A565	55b org, bl & pink	28	15
1763	A565	1.60 l multi	50	18

20th Congress of the Intl Federation of Beekeeping Assocs. (Apimondia), Bucharest, Aug. 26-31.

1965, Aug. 25   Litho.   Perf. 12x12½
Designs: 1.75 l, Col. Pavel Belyayev, Lt. Col. Alexei Leonov and Voskhod 2. 2.40 l, Early Bird over globe. 3.20 l, Lt. Col. Gordon Cooper and Lt. Com. Charles Conrad, Gemini 3 and globe.

1764	A566	1.75 l dk bl, bl & ver	80	15
1765	A566	2.40 l multi	1.10	16
1766	A566	3.20 l dk bl, lt bl & ver	2.25	15

European Quail — A567

Birds: 10b, Eurasian woodcock. 20b, Eurasian snipe. 40b, Turtle dove. 55b, Mallard. 60b, White-fronted goose. 1 l, Eurasian crane. 1.20 l, Glossy ibis. 1.35 l, Mute swan. 3.25 l, White pelican.

1965, Sept. 10   Photo.   Perf. 13½
Size: 34x34mm
Birds in Natural Colors

1767	A567	5b red brn & rose lil	15	15
1768	A567	10b red brn & yel grn	15	15
1769	A567	20b brn & bl grn	18	15
1770	A567	40b lil & org brn	22	15
1771	A567	55b brt grn & lt brn	25	15
1772	A567	60b dl org & bl	32	15
1773	A567	1 l red & lil	42	15
1774	A567	1.20 l dk brn & grn	60	15
1775	A567	1.35 l org & ultra	80	15

Size: 32x73mm

1776	A567	3.25 l ultra & sep	2.10	32
		Nos. 1767-1776 (10)	5.19	
		Set value		85

The index in each volume of the Scott Catalogue contains many listings that help identify stamps.

Marx and Lenin
A568

Vasile Alecsandri
A569

1965, Sept. 6   **Photo.**
1777 A568 55b red, blk & yel   38   18

6th Conference of Postal Ministers of Communist Countries, Peking, June 21-July 15.

1965, Oct. 9   **Unwmk.**   **Perf. 13½**
1778 A569 55b red brn, dk brn & gold   38   18

Alecsandri (1821-1890), statesman and poet.

Bird-of-Paradise
Flower — A570

Flowers from Cluj Botanical Gardens: 10b, Stanhope orchid. 20b, Paphiopedilum insigne. 30b, Zanzibar water lily, horiz. 40b, Ferocactus, horiz. 55b, Cotton blossom, horiz. 1 l, Hibiscus, horiz. 1.35 l, Gloxinia. 1.75 l, Victoria water lily, horiz. 2.30 l, Hibiscus, bird-of-paradise flower and greenhouse.

Perf. 12x12½, 12½x12
1965, Oct. 25   **Litho.**
Size: 23x43mm, 43x23mm
Flowers in Natural Colors

1779 A570	5b brown	15	15
1780 A570	10b green	15	15
1781 A570	20b dk bl	15	15
1782 A570	30b vio bl	15	15
1783 A570	40b red brn	15	15
1784 A570	55b dk red	15	15
1785 A570	1 l ol grn	30	15
1786 A570	1.35 l violet	48	15
1787 A570	1.75 l dk grn	80	15

Perf. 13½
Size: 52x30mm
1788 A570 2.30 l green   1.10   35
       Set value   3.15   85

The orchid on No. 1780 is attached to the bottom of the limb.

Running — A571

Pigeon and Post
Horn — A572

1965, Nov. 10   **Photo.**   **Perf. 13½**

1789 A571	55b shown	15	15
1790 A571	1.55 l Soccer	48	15
1791 A571	1.75 l Woman diver	55	15
1792 A571	2 l Mountaineering	60	15
1793 A571	5 l Canoeing, horiz.	1.40	30
	Nos. 1789-1793 (5)	3.18	
	Set value		68

Spartacist Games. No. 1793 commemorates the Romanian victory in the European Kayak Championships.

1965, Nov. 15   **Engr.**
Designs: 1 l, Pigeon on television antenna and post horn, horiz. 1.75 l, Flying pigeon and post horn, horiz.

1794 A572	55b + 45b label	38	15
1795 A572	1 l grn & brn	38	15
1796 A572	1.75 l ol grn & sep	85	20
	Set value		38

Issued for Stamp Day. No. 1794 is printed with alternating label showing post rider and emblem of Romanian Philatelists' Association and 45b additional charge. Stamp and label are imperf. between.

Chamois and Hunting Trophy
A573

Hunting Trophy and: 1 l, Brown bear. 1.60 l, Red deer. 1.75 l, Wild boar. 3.20 l, Antlers of red deer.

1965, Dec. 10   **Photo.**   **Perf. 13½**
Size: 37x22mm

1797 A573	55b rose lil, yel & brn	15	15
1798 A573	1 l brt grn, red & brn	28	15
1799 A573	1.60 l lt vio bl, org & brn	70	15
1800 A573	1.75 l rose, grn & blk	90	15

Size: 48x36½mm
1801 A573 3.20 l gray, gold, blk & org   1.40   30
     Nos. 1797-1801 (5)   3.43
       Set value   58

Probe III Photographing Moon — A574

Designs: 5b, Proton I space station, vert. 15b, Molniya I telecommunication satellite, vert. 3.25 l, Mariner IV and Mars picture, vert. 5 l, Gemini 5.

Perf. 12x12½, 12½x12
1965, Dec. 25   **Litho.**

1802 A574	5b multi	15	15
1803 A574	10b vio bl, red & gray	15	15
1804 A574	15b pur, gray & org	18	15
1805 A574	3.25 l vio bl, blk & red	2.25	22
1806 A574	5 l dk bl, gray & red org	3.50	45
	Nos. 1802-1806 (5)	6.23	
	Set value		80

Achievements in space research.

Cocker Spaniel — A575

Hunting Dogs: 5b, Dachshund (triangle). 40b, Retriever. 55b, Terrier. 60b, Red setter. 75b, White setter. 1.55 l, Pointers (rectangle). 3.25 l, Duck hunter with retriever (rectangle).

1965, Dec. 28   **Photo.**   **Perf. 13½**
Size: 30x42mm
1807 A575 5b multi   15   15

Size: 33½x33½mm

1808 A575	10b multi	15	15
1809 A575	40b multi	24	15
1810 A575	55b multi	35	15
1811 A575	60b multi	50	15
1812 A575	75b multi	70	15

Size: 43x28mm

1813 A575	1.55 l multi	1.40	15
1814 A575	3.25 l multi	2.75	75
	Nos. 1807-1814 (8)	6.24	
	Set value		1.20

Chessboard, Queen and Jester — A576

Chessboard and: 20b, 1.60 l, Pawn and emblem. 55b, 1 l, Rook and knight on horseback.

1966, Feb. 25   **Litho.**   **Perf. 13**

1815 A576	20b multi	15	15
1816 A576	40b multi	18	15
1817 A576	55b multi	28	15
1818 A576	1 l multi	55	15
1819 A576	1.60 l multi	1.00	15
1820 A576	3.25 l multi	2.50	65
	Nos. 1815-1820 (6)	4.66	
	Set value		1.05

Chess Olympics in Cuba.

Tractor, Grain and
Sun — A577

1966, Mar. 5
1821 A577 55b lt grn & ocher   24   15

Founding congress of the National Union of Cooperative Farms.

Gheorghe
Gheorghiu-Dej
A578

Congress
Emblem
A579

1966, Mar.   **Photo.**   **Perf. 13½**
1822 A578 55b gold & blk   30   15
   a.   5 l souvenir sheet   3.75   3.75

1st death anniv. of Pres. Gheorghe Gheorghiu-Dej (1901-65). No. 1822a contains design similar to No. 1822 with signature of Gheorghiu-Dej.

1966, Mar. 21   **Perf. 13x14½**
1823 A579 55b yel & red   30   15

1966 Congress of Communist Youth.

Folk Dancers of Moldavia — A580

Folk Dances: 40b, Oltenia. 55b, Maramaros. 1 l, Muntenia. 1.60 l, Banat. 2 l, Transylvania.

1966, Apr. 4   **Engr.**   **Perf. 13½**
Center in Black

1824 A580	30b lilac	15	15
1825 A580	40b brick red	15	15
1826 A580	55b brt bl grn	18	15
1827 A580	1 l maroon	38	15
1828 A580	1.60 l dk bl	70	15
1829 A580	2 l yel grn	1.25	30
	Nos. 1824-1829 (6)	2.81	
	Set value		55

Soccer
Game — A581

Designs: 10b, 15b, 55b, 1.75 l, Scenes of soccer play. 4 l, Jules Rimet Cup.

1966, Apr. 25   **Litho.**   **Unwmk.**

1830 A581	5b multi	15	15
1831 A581	10b multi	15	15
1832 A581	15b multi	15	15
1833 A581	55b multi	45	15
1834 A581	1.75 l multi	1.10	15
1835 A581	4 l gold & multi	2.50	60
a.	10 l souv. sheet	3.75	3.75
	Nos. 1830-1835 (6)	4.50	
	Set value		90

World Cup Soccer Championship, Wembley, England, July 11-30.
No. 1835a contains one imperf. 10 l multicolored stamp in design of 4 l, but larger (32x46mm). No gum. Issued June 20.

Symbols of
Industry — A582

Red-breasted
Flycatcher — A583

1966, May 14   **Photo.**
1836 A582 55b multi   24   15

Romanian Trade Union Congress.

1966, May 25   **Photo.**   **Perf. 13½**

Song Birds: 10b, Red crossbill. 15b, Great reed warbler. 20b, European redstart. 55b, European robin. 1.20 l, White-spotted bluethroat. 1.55 l, Yellow wagtail. 3.20 l, Common penduline tit.

1837 A583	5b gold & multi	15	15
1838 A583	10b sil & multi	15	15
1839 A583	15b gold & multi	18	15
1840 A583	20b sil & multi	18	15
1841 A583	55b sil & multi	28	15
1842 A583	1.20 l gold & multi	38	15
1843 A583	1.55 l sil & multi	1.00	30
1844 A583	3.20 l gold & multi	1.65	45
	Nos. 1837-1844 (8)	3.97	
	Set value		1.05

Venus 3
(USSR) — A584

Urechia
Nestor — A585

Designs: 20b, FR-1 (France). 1.60 l, Luna 9 (USSR). 5 l, Gemini 6 and 7 (US).

1966, June 25

1845	A584	10b dp vio, gray & red	15	15
1846	A584	20b ultra, blk & red	15	15
1847	A584	1.60 l dk bl, blk & red	55	15
1848	A584	5 l bl, blk, brn & red	1.50	48
		Set value		66

International achievements in space.

1966, June 28

Portraits: 5b, George Cosbuc. 10b, Gheorghe Sincai. 40b, Aron Pumnul. 55b, Stefan Luchian. 1 l, Sun Yat-sen. 1.35 l, Gottfried Wilhelm Leibniz. 1.60 l, Romain Rolland. 1.75 l, Ion Ghica. 3.25 l, Constantin Cantacuzino.

1849	A585	5b grn, blk & dk bl	15	15
1850	A585	10b rose car, grn & blk	15	15
1851	A585	20b grn, plum & blk	15	15
1852	A585	40b vio bl, brn & blk	15	15
1853	A585	55b brn org, bl grn & brn	20	15
1854	A585	1 l ocher, grn & blk	28	15
1855	A585	1.35 l bl & blk	35	15
1856	A585	1.60 l brt grn, dl vio & blk	55	15
1857	A585	1.75 l org, dl vio & blk	55	15
1858	A585	3.25 l bl, dk car & blk	1.00	24
		Nos. 1849-1858 (10)	3.53	
		Set value		90

Cultural anniversaries.

Country House, by Gheorghe
Petrascu — A586

Paintings: 10b, Peasant Woman, by Nicolae Grigorescu, vert. 20b, Reapers at Rest, by Camil Ressu. 55b, Man with the Blue Cap, by Van Eyck, vert. 1.55 l, Train Compartment, by Daumier. 3.25 l, Betrothal of the Virgin, by El Greco, vert.

1966, July 25   Unwmk.
Gold Frame

1859	A586	5b Prus grn & brn org	18	15
1860	A586	10b red brn & crim	18	15
1861	A586	20b brn & brt grn	18	15
1862	A586	55b vio bl & lil	26	15
1863	A586	1.55 l dk sl grn & org	1.25	38
1864	A586	3.25 l vio & ultra	2.75	1.00
		Nos. 1859-1864 (6)	4.80	1.98

See Nos. 1907-1912.

Hottonia
Palustris — A587

Marine Flora: 10b, Ceratophyllum submersum. 20b, Aldrovanda vesiculosa. 40b, Callitriche verna. 55b, Vallisneria spiralis. 1 l, Elodea Canadensis rich. 1.55 l, Hippuris vulgaris. 3.25 l, Myriophyllum spicatum.

1966, Aug. 25   Litho.   Perf. 13½
Size: 28x40mm

1865	A587	5b multi	15	15
1866	A587	10b multi	15	15
1867	A587	20b multi	15	15
1868	A587	40b multi	18	15
1869	A587	55b multi	15	15
1870	A587	1 l multi	45	15
1871	A587	1.55 l multi	70	24

Size: 28x50mm

1872	A587	3.25 l multi	1.40	38
		Nos. 1865-1872 (8)	3.33	
		Set value		90

Derivation of the
Meter — A588

Design: 1 l, Metric system symbols.

1966, Sept. 10   Photo.   Perf. 13½

1873	A588	55b salmon & ultra	24	15
1874	A588	1 l lt grn & vio	38	15
		Set value		18

Introduction of metric system in Romania, centenary.

Statue of Ovid   Line Integral
and Medical   Denoting Work
School Emblem   A590
A589

I. H. Radulescu, M. Kogalniceanu and T.
Savulescu — A591

Design: 1 l, Academy centenary medal.

1966, Sept. 30
Size: 22x27mm

1875	A589	40b lil gray, ultra, sep & gold	15	15
1876	A590	55b gray, brn, red & gold	15	15

Size: 22x34mm

1877	A589	1 l ultra, brn & gold	35	15

Size: 66x28mm

1878	A591	3 l org, dk brn & gold	95	30
		Set value		45

Centenary of the Romanian Academy.

Crawfish
A592

Molluscs and Crustaceans: 10b, Nassa reticulata, vert. 20b, Stone crab. 40b, Campylaea trizona. 55b, Helix lucorum. 1.35 l, Mytilus galloprovincialis. 1.75 l, Lymnaea stagnalis. 3.25 l, Anodonta cygnaea. (10b, 40b, 55b, 1.75 l, are snails; 1.35 l, 3.25 l, are bivalves).

1966, Oct. 15
Animals in Natural Colors

1879	A592	5b dp org	15	15
1880	A592	10b lt bl	15	15
1881	A592	20b pale lil	15	15
1882	A592	40b yel grn	15	15
1883	A592	55b car rose	20	15
1884	A592	1.35 l brt grn	45	15
1885	A592	1.75 l ultra	55	15
1886	A592	3.25 l brt org	1.40	35
		Nos. 1879-1886 (8)	3.20	
		Set value		85

Cave
Bear — A593

Prehistoric Animals: 10b, Mammoth. 15b, Bison. 55b, Cave elephant. 1.55 l, Stags. 4 l, Dinotherium.

1966, Nov. 25
Size: 36x22mm

1887	A593	5b ultra, bl grn & red brn	15	15
1888	A593	10b vio, emer & brn	15	15
1889	A593	15b ol, grn & dk brn	18	15
1890	A593	55b lil, emer & brn	30	15
1891	A593	1.55 l ultra, grn & brn	95	15

Size: 43x27mm

1892	A593	4 l rose car, grn & brn	1.50	52
		Nos. 1887-1892 (6)	3.23	
		Set value		85

Putna
Monastery,
500th
Anniv. — A594

1966   Photo.   Perf. 13½

1893	A594	2 l multi	65	15

Yuri A. Gagarin and
Vostok 1 — A595

Russian Achievements in Space: 10b, Trajectory of Sputnik 1 around globe, horiz. 25b, Valentina Tereshkova and globe with trajectory of Vostok 6. 40b, Andrian G. Nikolayev, Pavel R. Popovich and globe with trajectory of Vostok 8. 55b, Alexei Leonov walking in space.

1967, Feb. 15   Photo.   Perf. 13½

1894	A595	10b silver & multi	15	15
1895	A595	20b silver & multi	15	15
1896	A595	25b silver & multi	15	15
1897	A595	40b silver & multi	18	15
1898	A595	55b silver & multi	30	15
		Nos. 1894-1898,C163-C166 (9)	3.71	
		Set value		95

Ten years of space exploration.

Barn
Owl — A596

Birds of Prey: 20b, Eagle owl. 40b, Saker falcon. 55b, Egyptian vulture. 75b, Osprey. 1 l, Griffon vulture. 1.20 l, Lammergeier. 1.75 l, Cinereous vulture.

1967, Mar. 20   Photo.   Unwmk.
Birds in Natural Colors

1899	A596	10b vio & olive	15	15
1900	A596	20b bl & org	24	15
1901	A596	40b emer & org	18	15
1902	A596	55b yel grn & ocher	24	15
1903	A596	75b rose lil & grn	24	15
1904	A596	1 l yel org & blk	50	15
1905	A596	1.20 l claret & yel	85	15
1906	A596	1.75 l sal pink & gray	1.25	50
		Nos. 1899-1906 (8)	3.65	
		Set value		1.00

Painting Type of 1966

Paintings: 10b, Woman in Fancy Dress, by Ion Andreescu. 20b, Washwomen, by J. Al. Steriadi. 40b, Women weavers, by St. Dimitrescu, vert. 1.55 l, Venus and Amor, by Lucas Cranach, vert. 3.20 l, Hercules and the Lion of Numea, by Rubens. 5 l, Haman Asking Esther's Forgiveness, by Rembrandt, vert.

1967, Mar. 30   Perf. 13½
Gold Frame

1907	A586	10b dp bl & rose red	15	15
1908	A586	20b dp grn & bis	15	15
1909	A586	40b carmine & bl	16	15
1910	A586	1.55 l dp plum & lt ultra	52	15

1911	A586	3.20 l brown & grn	90	16
1912	A586	5 l ol grn & org	2.00	45
		Nos. 1907-1912 (6)	3.88	
		Set value		85

Mlle. Pogany,
by Brancusi
A597

Sculptures: 5b, Girl's head. 10b, The Sleeping Muse, horiz. 20b, The Infinite Column. 40b, The Kiss, horiz. 55b, Earth Wisdom (seated woman). 3.25 l, Gate of the Kiss.

1967, Apr. 27   Photo.   Perf. 13½

1913	A597	5b dl yel, blk brn & ver	15	15
1914	A597	10b bl grn, blk & lil	15	15
1915	A597	20b lt bl, blk & rose red	15	15
1916	A597	40b pink, sep & brt grn	18	15
1917	A597	55b yel grn, blk & ultra	24	15
1918	A597	1.20 l bluish lil, ol blk & org	40	18
1919	A597	3.25 l emer, blk & cer	1.10	50
		Nos. 1913-1919 (7)	2.37	
		Set value		1.00

Constantin Brancusi (1876-1957), sculptor.

Coins of
1867
A598

Design: 1.20 l, Coins of 1966.

1967, May 4

1920	A598	55b multicolored	28	15
1921	A598	1.20 l multicolored	1.10	24

Centenary of Romanian monetary system.

Infantry Soldier, by
Nicolae
Grigorescu — A599

1967, May 9

1922	A599	55b multicolored	55	18

90th anniv. of Romanian independence.

Peasants Marching, by Stefan
Luchian — A600

Painting: 40b, Fighting Peasants, by Octav Bancila, vert.

1967, May 20   Unwmk.   Perf. 13½
1923	A600	40b multicolored	28	15
1924	A600	1.55 l multicolored	1.10	70

60th anniversary of Peasant Uprising.

Centaury — A601

Carpathian Flora: 40b, Hedge mustard. 55b, Columbine. 1.20 l, Alpine violet. 1.75 l, Bell flower. 4 l, Dryas, horiz.

1967, June 10   Photo.
Flowers in Natural Colors
1925	A601	20b ocher	15	15
1926	A601	40b violet	15	15
1927	A601	55b bis & brn red	16	15
1928	A601	1.20 l yel & red brn	32	15
1929	A601	1.75 l bluish grn & car	45	15
1930	A601	4 l lt ultra	1.25	22
		Nos. 1925-1930 (6)	2.48	
		Set value		60

Fortifications, Sibiu — A602

Map of Romania and ITY Emblem — A603

Designs: 40b, Cris Castle. 55b, Wooden Church, Plopis. 1.60 l, Ruins of Nuamtulua Fortress. 1.75 l, Mogosoaia Palace. 2.25 l, Voronet Church.

1967, June 29   Photo.   Perf. 13½
Size: 33x33mm
1931	A602	20b ultra & multi	15	15
1932	A602	40b vio & multi	15	15
1933	A602	55b multi	15	15
1934	A602	1.60 l multi	38	15
1935	A602	1.75 l multi	45	15

Size: 48x36mm
1936	A602	2.25 l bl & multi	75	18
		Nos. 1931-1936 (6)	2.03	
		Set value		50

Souvenir Sheet
Imperf
1937	A603	5 l lt bl, ultra & blk	2.50	1.40

International Tourist Year.

The Attack at Marasesti, by E. Stoica A604

1967, July 24   Unwmk.   Perf. 13½
1938	A604	55b gray, Prus bl & brn	35	15

Battle of Marasesti & Oituz, 50th anniv.

Dinu Lipatti, Pianist — A605

Designs: 20b, Al. Orascu, architect. 40b, Gr. Antipa, zoologist. 55b, M. Kogalniceanu, statesman. 1.20 l, Jonathan Swift, writer. 1.75 l, Marie Curie, scientist.

1967, July 29   Photo.   Perf. 13½
1939	A605	10b ultra, blk & pur	15	15
1940	A605	20b org brn, blk & ultra	15	15
1941	A605	40b bl grn, blk & org brn	15	15
1942	A605	55b dp rose, blk & dk ol grn	20	15
1943	A605	1.20 l ol, blk & brn	35	15
1944	A605	1.75 l dl bl, blk & bl grn	70	22
		Nos. 1939-1944 (6)	1.70	
		Set value		50

Cultural anniversaries.

Wrestlers A606   Congress Emblem A607

Designs: 20b, 55b, 1.20 l, 2 l, Various fight scenes and world map (20b, 2 l horizontal); on 2 l maps are large and wrestlers small.

1967, Aug. 28
1945	A606	10b ol & multi	15	15
1946	A606	20b cit & multi	15	15
1947	A606	55b bis & multi	15	15
1948	A606	1.20 l multi	28	15
1949	A606	2 l ultra, gold & dp car	1.00	30
		Nos. 1945-1949 (5)	1.73	
		Set value		60

World Greco-Roman Wrestling Championships, Bucharest.

1967, Aug. 28
1950	A607	1.60 l lt bl, ultra & dp car	50	15

Intl. Linguists' Congress, Bucharest, Aug. 28-Sept. 2.

Ice Skating — A608

Designs: 40b, Biathlon. 55b, 5 l, Bobsledding. 1 l, Skiing. 1.55 l, Ice Hockey. 2 l, Emblem of 10th Winter Olympic Games. 2.30 l, Ski jump.

1967, Sept. 28   Photo.   Perf. 13½x13
1951	A608	20b lt bl & multi	15	15
1952	A608	40b multi	15	15
1953	A608	55b bl & multi	15	15
1954	A608	1 l lil & multi	20	15
1955	A608	1.55 l multi	30	15
1956	A608	2 l gray & multi	50	18
1957	A608	2.30 l multi	85	35
		Nos. 1951-1957 (7)	2.30	
		Set value		1.00

Souvenir Sheet
Imperf
1958	A608	5 l lt bl & multi	3.25	2.75

10th Winter Olympic Games, Grenoble, France, Feb. 6-18, 1968.
Nos. 1951-1957 issued in sheets of 10 (5x2) and 5 labels.

Curtea de Arges Monastery, 450th Anniv. — A609

1967, Nov. 1   Unwmk.   Perf. 13½
1959	A609	55b multicolored	30	15

Romanian Academy Library, Bucharest, Cent. — A610

1967, Sept. 25   Litho.
1960	A610	55b ocher, gray & dk bl	30	15

Karl Marx and Title Page — A611   Lenin — A612

1967, Nov. 4   Photo.
1961	A611	40b rose cl, blk & yel	24	15

Centenary of the publication of "Das Kapital" by Karl Marx.

1967, Nov. 3
1962	A612	1.20 l red, blk & gold	35	15

Russian October Revolution, 50th anniv.

Monorail Leaving US EXPO Pavilion A613

Designs: 1 l, EXPO emblem and atom symbol. 1.60 l, Cup, world map and EXPO emblem. 2 l, EXPO emblem.

1967, Nov. 28   Photo.
1963	A613	55b grnsh bl, vio & blk	15	15
1964	A613	1 l red, blk & gray	28	15
1965	A613	1.60 l multicolored	40	16
1966	A613	2 l multicolored	60	18
		Set value		46

EXPO '67 Intl. Exhib., Montreal, Apr. 28-Oct. 27. No. 1965 also for Romania's victory in the World Fencing Championships in Montreal.

Truck — A614   Arms of the Republic — A615

Diesel Locomotive A616   Map Showing Telephone Network A617

Designs: 10b, Communications emblem, vert. 20b, Train. 35b, Plane. 50b, Telephone, vert. 60b, Small loading truck. 1.20 l, Autobus. 1.35 l, Helicopter. 1.50 l, Trolley bus. 1.55 l, Radio station and tower. 1.75 l, Highway. 2 l, Mail truck. 2.40 l, Television tower. 3.20 l, Jet plane. 3.25 l, Steamship. 4 l, Electric train. 5 l, World map and teletype.

Photo.; Engr. (type A615)
1967-68   Perf. 13½
1967	A614	5b lt ol grn ('68)	15	15
1968	A614	10b henna brn ('68)	15	15
1969	A614	20b gray ('68)	15	15
1970	A614	35b bl blk ('68)	15	15
1971	A615	40b violet blue	15	15
1972	A614	50b orange ('68)	15	15
1973	A615	55b dull orange	15	15
1974	A614	60b orange brn ('68)	15	15

Size: 22½x28mm, 28x22½mm
1975	A616	1 l emerald ('68)	22	15
1976	A616	1.20 l red lil ('68)	28	15
1977	A617	1.35 l brt blue ('68)	30	15
1978	A616	1.50 l rose red ('68)	35	15
1979	A616	1.55 l dk brown ('68)	35	15
1980	A615	1.60 l rose red	38	15
1981	A617	1.75 l dp green ('68)	40	15
1982	A617	2 l citron ('68)	60	15
1983	A616	2.40 l dk blue ('68)	75	15
1984	A617	3 l grnsh blue	75	15
1985	A617	3.20 l ocher ('68)	1.00	15
1986	A616	3.25 l ultra ('68)	1.00	15
1987	A617	4 l lil rose ('68)	1.25	15
1988	A617	5 l violet ('68)	1.40	15
		Nos. 1967-1988 (22)	10.23	
		Set value		1.00

40th anniv. of the first automatic telephone exchange; introduction of automatic telephone service (No. 1984).
See Nos. 2078-2079, 2269-2284.

Coat of Arms, Symbols of Agriculture and Industry — A618

Designs: 55b, Coat of arms. 1.60 l, Romanian flag. 1.75 l, Coat of arms and symbols of arts and education.

1967, Dec. 26   Photo.   Perf. 13½
Size: 27x48mm
1989	A618	40b multicolored	15	15
1990	A618	55b multicolored	15	15

Size: 33½x48mm
1991	A618	1.60 l multicolored	30	18

Size: 27x48mm
1992	A618	1.75 l multicolored	50	24
		Set value		58

20th anniversary of the republic.

Souvenir Sheet

Anemones, by Stefan Luchian — A619

1968, Mar. 30   Litho.   Imperf.
1993 A619 10 l multi   4.75 4.75
   Birth centenary of Stefan Luchian, Romanian painter.

Portrait of a Lady, by Misu Popp — A620

   Paintings: 10b, The Reveille of Romania, by Gheorghe Tattarescu. 20b, Composition, by Teodorescu Sionion, horiz. 35b, The Judgment of Paris, by Hendrick van Balen, horiz. 55b, Little Girl with Red Kerchief, by Nicolae Grigorescu. 60b, The Mystical Betrothal of St. Catherine, by Lamberto Sustris, horiz. 1 l, Old Nicolas, the Zither Player, by Stefan Luchian. 1.60 l, Man with a Skull, by Dierick Bouts (?). 1.75 l, Madonna and Child with Fruit Basket, by Jan van Bylert. 2.40 l, Medor and Angelica, by Sebastiano Ricci, horiz. 3 l, Summer, by Jacob Jordaens, horiz. 3.20 l, 5 l, Ecce Homo, by Titian.

1968   Photo.   Perf. 13½
Gold Frame
Size: 28x49mm
1994 A620 10b multi   15   15
Size: 48½x36½mm, 36x48½mm
1995 A620 20b multi   15   15
1996 A620 35b multi   15   15
1997 A620 40b multi   15   15
1998 A620 55b multi   15   15
1999 A620 60b multi   18   15
2000 A620 1 l multi   28   15
2001 A620 1.60 l multi   42   15
2002 A620 1.75 l multi   42   18
2003 A620 2.40 l multi   80   30
2004 A620 3 l multi   90   50
2005 A620 3.20 l multi   1.40   70
   Nos. 1994-2005 (12)   5.15
      Set value   2.25
Miniature Sheet
Imperf
2006 A620 5 l multi   4.50 4.50
   Issue dates: 40b, 55b, 1, 1.60, 2.40, 3.20 and 5 l, Mar. 28. Others, Sept. 9.
   See Nos. 2088-2094, 2124-2130.

Human Rights Flame
A621

WHO Emblem
A622

1968, May 9   Unwmk.   Perf. 13½
2007 A621 1 l multicolored   45   15
   Intl. Human Rights Year.

1968, May 14   Photo.
2008 A622 1.60 l multi   50   15
   WHO, 20th anniversary.

"Prince Dragos Hunting Bison," by Nicolae Grigorescu — A623

1968, May 17
2009 A623 1.60 l multi   60   18
   15th Hunting Cong., Mamaia, May 23-29.

Pioneers and Liberation Monument — A624

   Pioneers: 40b, receiving scarfs. 55b, building model planes and boat. 1 l, as radio amateurs. 1.60 l, folk dancing. 2.40 l, Girl Pioneers in camp.

1968, June 9   Photo.   Perf. 13½
2010 A624 5b multi   15   15
2011 A624 40b multi   15   15
2012 A624 55b multi   16   15
2013 A624 1 l multi   30   15
2014 A624 1.60 l multi   50   15
2015 A624 2.40 l multi   70   16
   Nos. 2010-2015 (6)   1.96
      Set value   55

Ion Ionescu de la Brad — A625

   Designs: 55b, Emil Racovita. 1.60 l, Prince Mircea of Walachia.

1968
Size: 28x43mm
2016 A625 40b multicolored   20   15
2017 A625 55b green & multi   20   15
Size: 28x48mm
2018 A625 1.60 l gold & multi   45   15
      Set value   20

   Ion Ionescu de la Brad (1818-91); Emil Racovita (1868-1947), explorer and naturalist; 40b, Prince Mircea (1386-1418). Issue dates: 40b, 55b, June 24; 1.60 l, June 22.

Geranium — A626

   Designs: Various geraniums.

1968, July 20   Photo.   Perf. 13½
2019 A626 10b multicolored   15   15
2020 A626 20b multicolored   15   15
2021 A626 40b multicolored   15   15
2022 A626 55b multicolored   15   15
2023 A626 60b multicolored   15   15
2024 A626 1.20 l multicolored   26   15
2025 A626 1.35 l multicolored   35   15
2026 A626 1.60 l multicolored   75   16
      Set value   1.75 65

Avram Iancu, by B. Iscovescu and Demonstrating Students — A627

   Demonstrating Students and: 55b, Nicolae Balcescu, by Gheorghe Tattarescu. 1.60 l, Vasile Alecsandri, by N. Livaditti.

1968, July 25
2027 A627 55b gold & multi   20   15
2028 A627 1.20 l gold & multi   45   15
2029 A627 1.60 l gold & multi   70   18
      Set value   30

   120th anniversary of 1848 revolution.

Boxing — A628

Atheneum and Harp — A629

   Aztec Calendar Stone and: 10b, Javelin, Women's. 20b, Woman diver. 40b, Volleyball. 60b, Wrestling. 1.20 l, Fencing. 1.35 l, Canoeing. 1.60 l, Soccer. 5 l, Running.

1968, Aug. 28
2030 A628 10b multi   15   15
2031 A628 20b multi   15   15
2032 A628 40b multi   15   15
2033 A628 55b multi   15   15
2034 A628 60b multi   15   15
2035 A628 1.20 l multi   35   18
2036 A628 1.35 l multi   40   24
2037 A628 1.60 l multi   65   28
      Set value   1.80 1.00
Souvenir Sheet
Imperf
2038 A628 5 l multi   2.25 1.75
   19th Olympic Games, Mexico City, Oct. 12-17.

1968, Aug. 20   Litho.   Perf. 12x12½
2039 A629 55b multicolored   24   15
   Centenary of the Philharmonic Orchestra.

Globe and Emblem — A630

1968, Oct. 4   Litho.   Perf. 13½
2040 A630 1.60 l ultra & gold   50   15
   Intl. Fed. of Photograpic Art, 20th anniv.

Moldovita Monastery Church — A631

   Historic Monuments: 10b, "The Triumph of Trajan," Roman metope, vert. 55b, Cozia monastery church. 1.20 l, Court of Tirgoviste Palace. 1.55 l, Palace of Culture, Jassy. 1.75 l, Corvinus Castle, Hunedoara.

1968, Nov. 25   Engr.   Perf. 13½
2041 A631 10b dk bl, ol & brn   15   15
2042 A631 40b rose car, bl & brn   15   15
2043 A631 55b ol, brn & vio   15   15
2044 A631 1.20 l yel, mar & gray   30   15
2045 A631 1.55 l vio brn, dk bl & lt grn 50   15
2046 A631 1.75 l org, blk & ol   1.00   18
   Nos. 2041-2046 (6)   2.25
      Set value   50

Mute Swan — A632

   Protected Birds and Animals: 20b, European stilts. 40b, Sheldrakes. 55b, Egret feeding young. 60b, Golden eagle. 1.20 l, Great bustards. 1.35 l, Chamois. 1.60 l, Bison.

1968, Dec. 20   Photo.   Perf. 13½
2047 A632 10b pink & multi   15   15
2048 A632 20b multicolored   15   15
2049 A632 40b lilac & multi   15   15
2050 A632 55b olive & multi   15   15
2051 A632 60b multi   20   15
2052 A632 1.20 l multicolored   45   15
2053 A632 1.35 l blue & multi   50   15
2054 A632 1.60 l multicolored   60   16
   Nos. 2047-2054 (8)   2.35
      Set value   55

Michael the Brave's Entry into Alba Iulia, by D. Stoica — A633

   Designs: 1 l, "The Round Dance of Union," by Theodor Aman. 1.75 l, Assembly of Alba Iulia.

1968, Dec. 1   Litho.   Perf. 13½
2055 A633 55b gold & multi   20   15
2056 A633 1 l gold & multi   30   18
2057 A633 1.75 l gold & multi   40   35
   a.   Souv. sheet of 3, 2055-2057, imperf.
                                       1.50 1.50
   50th anniv. of the union of Transylvania and Romania. No. 2057a sold for 4 l.

Woman from Neamt — A634

Regional Costumes: 40b, Man from Neamt. 55b, Woman from Hunedoara. 1 l, Man from Hunedoara. 1.60 l, Woman from Brasov. 2.40 l, Man from Brasov.

1968, Dec. 28   **Perf. 12x12½**

2058	A634	5b orange & multi	15 15
2059	A634	40b blue & multi	15 15
2060	A634	55b multi	15 15
2061	A634	1 l brown & multi	26 15
2062	A634	1.60 l brown & multi	52 15
2063	A634	2.40 l multi	95 35
	Nos. 2058-2063 (6)	2.18	
	Set value		75

1969, Feb. 15

Regional Costumes: 5b, Woman from Dolj. 40b, Man from Dolj. 55b, Woman from Arges. 1 l, Man from Arges. 1.60 l, Woman from Timisoara. 2.40 l, Man from Timisoara.

2064	A634	5b multi	15 15
2065	A634	40b multi	15 15
2066	A634	55b lil & multi	15 15
2067	A634	1 l rose & multi	28 15
2068	A634	1.60 l multi	55 15
2069	A634	2.40 l brn & multi	1.00 25
	Nos. 2064-2069 (6)	2.28	
	Set value		64

Fencing A635

Sports: 20b, Women's javelin. 40b, Canoeing. 55b, Boxing. 1 l, Volleyball. 1.20 l, Swimming. 1.60 l, Wrestling. 2.40 l, Soccer.

1969, Mar. 10   **Photo.**   **Perf. 13½**
Denominations Black, Athletes in Gray

2070	A635	10b pale brown	15 15
2071	A635	20b violet	15 15
2072	A635	40b blue	15 15
2073	A635	55b red	15 15
2074	A635	1 l green	24 15
2075	A635	1.20 l brt blue	28 15
2076	A635	1.60 l cerise	48 15
2077	A635	2.40 l dp green	85 18
	Nos. 2070-2077 (8)	2.45	
	Set value		65

Type of Regular Issue

1969, Jan. 10   **Photo.**   **Perf. 13½**

2078	A614	40b Power lines	15 15
2079	A614	55b Dam	18 15
	Set value		15

Painting Type of 1968

Paintings (Nudes): 10b, Woman Carrying Jug, by Gheorghe Tattarescu. 20b, Reclining Woman, by Theodor Pallady, horiz. 35b, Seated Woman, by Nicolae Tonitza. 60b, Venus and Amor, 17th century Flemish School. 1.75 l, 5 l, Diana and Endimion, by Marco Liberi. 3 l, The Three Graces, by Alessandro Varotari.

1969, Mar. 27   **Photo.**   **Perf. 13½**
Gold Frame
Size: 37x49mm, 49x37mm

2088	A620	10b multi	15 15
2089	A620	20b multi	15 15
2090	A620	35b multi	20 15
2091	A620	60b multi	30 15
2092	A620	1.75 l multi	70 26

Size: 27½x48½mm

2093	A620	3 l multi	1.50 45
	Nos. 2088-2093 (6)	3.00	
	Set value		92

Miniature Sheet
Imperf

2094	A620	5 l multi	3.00 3.00

No. 2094 contains one stamp 36½x48½mm. with simulated perforations.
No. 2093 is incorrectly inscribed Hans von Aachen.

ILO, 50th Anniv. — A636

Symbolic Head — A637

1969, Apr. 9   **Photo.**   **Perf. 13½**

2095	A636	55b multicolored	40 15

1969, Apr. 28

2096	A637	55b ultra & multi	35 15
2097	A637	1.50 l red & multi	90 38

Romania's cultural and economic cooperation with European countries.

Communications Symbol — A638

1969, May 12   **Photo.**   **Perf. 13½**

2098	A638	55b vio bl & bluish gray	35 15

7th Session of the Conference of Postal and Telecommunications Ministers, Bucharest.

Boxers, Referee and Map of Europe A639

Map of Europe and: 40b, Two boxers. 55b, Sparring. 1.75 l, Referee declaring winner.

1969, May 24

2099	A639	35b multicolored	15 15
2100	A639	40b multicolored	15 15
2101	A639	55b multicolored	24 15
2102	A639	1.75 l blue & multi	60 18
	Set value		35

European Boxing Championships, Bucharest, May 31-June 8.

Apatura Ilia — A640

Designs: Various butterflies and moths.

1969, June 25   **Photo.**   **Perf. 13½**
Insects in Natural Colors

2103	A640	5b yellow grn	15 15
2104	A640	10b rose mag	15 15
2105	A640	20b violet	15 15
2106	A640	40b blue grn	15 15
2107	A640	55b brt blue	15 15
2108	A640	1 l blue	30 15
2109	A640	1.20 l violet bl	40 15
2110	A640	2.40 l yellow bis	80 20
	Set value	1.85	65

Communist Party Flag — A641

1969, Aug. 6   **Photo.**   **Perf. 13½**

2111	A641	55b multicolored	28 15

10th Romanian Communist Party Congress.

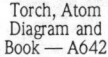

Torch, Atom Diagram and Book — A642

Broken Chain — A643

Designs: 40b, Symbols of agriculture, science and industry. 1.75 l, Pylon, smokestack and cogwheel.

1969, Aug. 10

2112	A642	35b multicolored	15 15
2113	A642	40b green & multi	15 15
2114	A642	1.75 l multicolored	50 18
	Set value		28

Exhibition showing the achievements of Romanian economy during the last 25 years.

1969, Aug. 23

Designs: 55b, Construction work. 60b, Flags.

2115	A643	10b multicolored	15 15
2116	A643	55b yellow & multi	18 15
2117	A643	60b multicolored	24 15
	Set value	46	16

25th anniversary of Romania's liberation from fascist rule.

Juggler on Unicycle — A644

Masks — A645

Circus Performers: 20b, Clown. 35b, Trapeze artists. 60b, Dressage and woman trainer. 1.75 l, Woman in high wire act. 3 l, Performing tiger and trainer.

1969, Sept. 29   **Photo.**   **Perf. 13½**

2118	A644	10b lt blue & multi	15 15
2119	A644	20b lemon & multi	15 15
2120	A644	35b lilac & multi	15 15
2121	A644	60b multicolored	16 15
2122	A644	1.75 l multicolored	55 15
2123	A644	3 l ultra & multi	90 35
	Set value	1.80	65

Painting Type of 1968

Paintings: 10b, Venetian Senator, Tintoretto School. 20b, Sofia Kretzulescu, by Gheorghe Tattarescu. 35b, Phillip IV, by Velazquez. 60b, Man Reading and Child, by Hans Memling. 1.75 l, Doamnei d'Aguesseau, by Madame Vigée-Lebrun. 3 l, Portrait of a Woman, by Rembrandt. 5 l, The Return of the Prodigal Son, by Bernardino Licinio, horiz.

1969
Gold Frame
Size: 36½x49mm

2124	A620	10b multi	15 15
2125	A620	20b multi	15 15
2126	A620	35b multi	15 15
2127	A620	60b multi	35 15
2128	A620	1.75 l multi	70 15
2129	A620	3 l multi	1.25 35
	Nos. 2124-2129 (6)	2.75	
	Set value		65

Miniature Sheet
Imperf

2130	A620	5 l gold & multi	2.00 1.50

No. 2130 contains one stamp with simulated perforations.
Issue dates: 5 l, July 31. Others, Oct. 1.

1969, Nov. 24   **Photo.**   **Perf. 13½**

2131	A645	40b Branesti	15 15
2132	A645	55b Tudora	15 15
2133	A645	1.55 l Birsesti	50 15
2134	A645	1.75 l Rudaria	60 18
	Set value		42

Armed Forces Memorial A646

1969, Oct. 25

2135	A646	55b red, blk & gold	20 15

25th anniversary of the People's Army.

Locomotives of 1869 and 1969 — A647

1969, Oct. 31

2136	A647	55b silver & multi	24 15

Bucharest-Filaret-Giurgevo railroad, cent.

A648   A649

Apollo 12 landing module.

1969, Nov. 24

2137	A648	1.50 l multi	55 50

2nd landing on the moon, Nov. 19, 1969, astronauts Captains Alan Bean, Charles Conrad, Jr. and Richard Gordon.
Printed in sheets of 4 with 4 labels (one label with names of astronauts, one with Apollo 12 emblem and 2 silver labels with picture of landing module, Intrepid).

1969, Dec. 25   **Photo.**   **Perf. 13½**

New Year: 40b, Mother Goose in Goat Disguise. 55b, Children singing and decorated tree, Sorcova. 1.50 l, Drummer and singer, Buhaiul. 2.40 l, Singer and bell ringer, Plugusorul.

2138	A649	40b bister & multi	15 15
2139	A649	55b lilac & multi	15 15
2140	A649	1.50 l blue & multi	50 15
2141	A649	2.40 l multicolored	1.00 26
	Set value		52

The Last Judgment (detail), Voronet Monastery — A650

North Moldavian Monastery Frescoes: 10b, Stephen the Great and family, Voronet. 20b, Three prophets, Sucevita. 60b, St. Nicholas (scene from his life), Sucevita, vert. 1.75 l, Siege of Constantinople, 7th century, Moldovita. 3 l, Plowman, Voronet, vert.

1969, Dec. 15

2142	A650	10b gold & multi	15	15
2143	A650	20b gold & multi	15	15
2144	A650	35b gold & multi	15	15
2145	A650	60b gold & multi	15	15
2146	A650	1.75 l gold & multi	32	15
2147	A650	3 l gold & multi	1.00	22
		Set value	1.60	55

Ice Hockey A651

Designs: 55b, Goalkeeper. 1.20 l, Two players with puck. 2.40 l, Player and goalkeeper.

1970, Jan. 20   Perf. 13½

2148	A651	20b yellow & multi	15	15
2149	A651	55b multicolored	15	15
2150	A651	1.20 l pink & multi	38	18
2151	A651	2.40 l lt blue & multi	1.00	30
		Set value		60

World Ice Hockey Championships, Bucharest and Galati, Feb. 24-Mar. 5.

Pasqueflower — A652

Flowers: 10b, Adonis vernalis. 20b, Thistle. 40b, Almond tree blossoms. 55b, Iris. 1 l, Flax. 1.20 l, Sage. 2.40 l, Peony.

1970, Feb. 25   Photo.   Perf. 13½

2152	A652	5b yellow & multi	15	15
2153	A652	10b green & multi	15	15
2154	A652	20b lt bl & multi	15	15
2155	A652	40b violet & multi	15	15
2156	A652	55b ultra & multi	15	15
2157	A652	1 l multicolored	20	15
2158	A652	1.20 l red & multi	35	15
2159	A652	2.40 l multicolored	70	20
		Set value	1.60	70

Japanese Print and EXPO '70 Emblem A653

Design: 1 l, Pagoda, EXPO '70 emblem.

1970, Mar. 23

2160	A653	20b gold & multi	15	15

Size: 29x92mm

2161	A653	1 l gold & multi	30	15
		Set value		20

EXPO '70 Intl. Exhib., Osaka, Japan, Mar. 15-Sept. 13.
A souvenir sheet exists with perforated label in pagoda design of 1 l. Issued Nov. 28, 1970. Value $1.65.

Camille, by Claude Monet (Maximum Card) — A654

1970, Apr. 19   Photo.   Perf. 13½

2162	A654	1.50 l gold & multi	45	15

Franco-Romanian Maximafil Phil. Exhib.

Cuza, by C. Popp de Szathmary A655

Lenin (1870-1924) A656

1970, Apr. 20   Perf. 13½

2163	A655	55b gold & multi	20	15

Alexandru Ioan Cuza (1820-1866), prince of Romania.

1970, Apr. 21   Photo.   Perf. 13½

2164	A656	40b dk red & multi	15	15

Map of Europe with Capital Cities A657

1970, Apr. 28

2165	A657	40b grn, brn org & blk	50	35
2166	A657	1.50 l ultra, yel brn & blk	1.00	70

Inter-European cultural and economic cooperation.

Victory Monument, Romanian and Russian Flags — A658

1970, May 9

2167	A658	55b red & multi	18	15

25th anniv. of victory over the Germans.

Greek Silver Drachm, 5th Century B.C. A659

Coins: 20b, Getic-Dacian silver didrachm, 2nd-1st centuries B.C. 35b, Emperor Trajan's copper sestertius, 106 A.D. 60b, Mircea ducat, 1400. 1.75 l, Stephen the Great's silver groschen, 1460. 3 l, Brasov klippe-taler, 1601, vert.

1970, May 15

2168	A659	10b ultra, blk & sil	15	15
2169	A659	20b hn brn, blk & sil	15	15
2170	A659	35b grn, dk brn & gold	15	15
2171	A659	60b brn, blk & sil	16	15
2172	A659	1.75 l brt bl, blk & sil	50	18
2173	A659	3 l dk car, blk & sil	1.00	26
		Nos. 2168-2173 (6)	2.11	
		Set value		65

Soccer Players and Ball — A660

Designs: Soccer ball and various scenes from soccer game.

1970, May 26   Perf. 13½

2174	A660	40b multi	15	15
2175	A660	55b multi	15	15
2176	A660	1.75 l blue & multi	45	18
2177	A660	3.30 l multi	85	30
		Set value		62

Souvenir Sheet

2178		Sheet of 4	2.00	1.50
a.		A660 1.20 l multi	28	15
b.		A660 1.50 l multi	35	18
c.		A660 1.55 l multi	38	20
d.		A660 1.75 l multi	38	20

9th World Soccer Championships for the Jules Rimet Cup, Mexico City, May 30-June 21. No. 2178 contains 4 stamps similar to Nos. 2174-2177, but with only one quarter of the soccer ball on each stamp, forming one large ball in the center of the block.

Moldovita Monastery A661

Designs: Frescoes from North Moldavian Monasteries.

1970, June 29   Perf. 13½

Size: 36½x49mm

2179	A661	10b gold & multi	15	15

Size: 27½x49mm

2180	A661	20b gold & multi	15	15

Size: 36½x49mm, 48x37mm

2181	A661	40b gold & multi	15	15
2182	A661	55b gold & multi	20	15
2183	A661	1.75 l gold & multi	38	22
2184	A661	3 l gold & multi	1.00	35
		Nos. 2179-2184 (6)	2.03	
		Set value		85

Miniature Sheet

2185	A661	5 l gold & multi	1.75	1.75

Friedrich Engels (1820-1895), German Socialist — A662

1970, July 10   Photo.   Perf. 13½

2186	A662	1.50 l multi	45	15

Aerial View of Iron Gate Power Station A663

1970, July 13

2187	A663	35b blue & multi	18	15

Hydroelectric plant at the Iron Gate of the Danube.

Cargo Ship — A664

1970, July 17

2188	A664	55b blue & multi	18	15

Romanian merchant marine, 75th anniv.

Exhibition Hall and Oil Derrick A665

1970, July 20

2189	A665	1.50 l multi	45	15

International Bucharest Fair, Oct. 13-24.

Opening of UPU Headquarters, Bern — A666

1970, Aug. 17   Photo.   Perf. 13½

2190	A666	1.50 l ultra & slate green	45	15

Education Year Emblem — A667

Iceberg Rose — A668

1970, Aug. 17

2191	A667	55b black, pur & red	18	15

International Education Year.

1970, Aug. 21

Roses: 35b, Wiener charme. 55b, Pink luster. 1 l, Piccadilly. 1.50 l, Orange Delbard. 2.40 l, Sibelius.

2192	A668	20b dk red, grn & yel	15	15
2193	A668	35b vio, yel & grn	15	15
2194	A668	55b blue, rose & grn	15	15
2195	A668	1 l grn, car rose & yel	30	15
2196	A668	1.50 l dk bl, red & grn	45	16
2197	A668	2.40 l brt bl, dp red & grn	85	22
		Nos. 2192-2197 (6)	2.05	
		Set value		65

Spaniel and Pheasant, by Jean B. Oudry A669

Paintings: 10b, The Hunt, by Domenico Brandi. 35b, The Hunt, by Jan Fyt. 60b, After the Chase, by Jacob Jordaens. 1.75 l, 5 l, Game Merchant, by Frans Snyders (horiz.). 3 l, The Hunt, by Adriaen de Gryeff. Sizes: 37x49mm (10b, 35b); 35x33mm (20b, 60b, 3 l); 49x37mm (1.75 l, 3 l).

1970, Sept. 20   Photo.   Perf. 13½

2198	A669	10b gold & multi	15	15
2199	A669	20b gold & multi	15	15
2200	A669	35b gold & multi	15	15
2201	A669	60b gold & multi	20	15
2202	A669	1.75 l gold & multi	60	30
2203	A669	3 l gold & multi	1.25	45
		Nos. 2198-2203 (6)	2.50	
		Set value		1.00

Miniature Sheet

2204	A669	5 l gold & multi	2.00	2.00

UN Emblem A670   Mother and Child A671

1970, Sept. 29

2205	A670	1.50 l lt bl, ultra & blk	45	15

25th anniversary of the United Nations.

1970, Sept. 25

Designs: 1.50 l, Red Cross relief trucks and tents. 1.75 l, Rebuilding houses.

2206	A671	55b bl gray, blk & ol	18	15
2207	A671	1.50 l, blk & car	45	15
a.		Strip of 3, #2206-2207, C179	1.40	55
2208	A671	1.75 l blue & multi	70	20
		Set value		40

Plight of the Danube flood victims.

Arabian Thoroughbred — A672

Horses: 35b, American trotter. 55b, Ghidran (Anglo-American). 1 l, Northern Moravian. 1.50 l, Trotter thoroughbred. 2.40 l, Lippizaner.

1970, Oct. 10   Photo.   Perf. 13½

2209	A672	20b blk & multi	15	15
2210	A672	35b blk & multi	15	15
2211	A672	55b blk & multi	15	15
2212	A672	1 l blk & multi	28	15

2213	A672	1.50 l blk & multi	40	15
2214	A672	2.40 l blk & multi	95	22
		Nos. 2209-2214 (6)	2.08	
		Set value		62

Ludwig van Beethoven (1770-1827), Composer — A673

1970, Nov. 2

2215	A673	55b multicolored	24	15

Abstract, by Joan Miró — A674

1970, Dec. 10   Photo.   Perf. 13½

2216	A674	3 l ultra & multi	85	70

Souvenir Sheet
Imperf

2217	A674	5 l ultra & multi	1.90	1.90

Plight of the Danube flood victims. No. 2216 issued in sheets of 5 stamps and label with signature of Miró and date of flood. No. 2217 contains one stamp with simulated perforation.

The Sense of Sight, by Gonzales Coques A675

"The Senses," paintings by Gonzales Coques (1614-1684): 20b, Hearing. 35b, Smell. 60b, Taste. 1.75 l, Touch. 3 l, Bruckenthal Museum, Sibiu. 5 l, View of Sibiu, 1808, horiz.

1970, Dec. 15   Photo.   Perf. 13½

2218	A675	10b gold & multi	15	15
2219	A675	20b gold & multi	15	15
2220	A675	35b gold & multi	15	15
2221	A675	60b gold & multi	18	15
2222	A675	1.75 l gold & multi	60	26
2223	A675	3 l gold & multi	1.00	45
		Nos. 2218-2223 (6)	2.23	
		Set value		92

Miniature Sheet
Imperf

2224	A675	5 l gold & multi	2.00	2.00

Men of Three Races A676

1971, Feb. 23   Photo.   Perf. 13½

2225	A676	1.50 l multi	45	15

Intl. year against racial discrimination.

Tudor Vladimirescu, by Theodor Aman — A677

1971, Feb. 20

2226	A677	1.50 l gold & multi	45	15

Vladimirescu, patriot, 150th death anniv.

German Shepherd A677a   lup alsacian

Dogs: 35b, Bulldog. 55b, Fox terrier. 1 l, Setter. 1.50 l, Cocker spaniel. 2.40 l, Poodle.

1971, Feb. 22

2227	A677a	20b blk & multi	15	15
2228	A677a	35b blk & multi	15	15
2229	A677a	55b blk & multi	20	15
2230	A677a	1 l blk & multi	28	15
2231	A677a	1.50 l blk & multi	40	22
2232	A677a	2.40 l blk & multi	85	42
		Nos. 2227-2232 (6)	2.03	
		Set value		95

Paris Commune A678   Congress Emblem A679

1971, Mar. 15   Photo.   Perf. 13½

2233	A678	40b multicolored	15	15

Centenary of the Paris Commune.

1971, Mar. 23

2234	A679	55b multicolored	18	15

Romanian Trade Unions Congress.

Rock Formation A680

Designs: 10b, Bicazului Gorge, vert. 55b, Winter resort. 1 l, Danube Delta view. 1.50 l, Lakeside resort. 2.40 l, Venus, Jupiter, Neptune Hotels on Black Sea.

1971, Apr. 15
Size: 23x38mm, 38x23mm

2235	A680	10b multi	15	15
2236	A680	40b multi	15	15
2237	A680	55b multi	18	15
2238	A680	1 l multi	30	15
2239	A680	1.50 l multi	50	20

Size: 76½x28mm

2240	A680	2.40 l multi	1.00	35
		Nos. 2235-2240 (6)	2.28	
		Set value		85

Tourist publicity.

Arrow Pattern A681

Design: 1.75 l, Wave pattern.

1971, Apr. 28   Photo.   Perf. 13½

2241	A681	55b multi	75	60
2242	A681	1.75 l multi	1.50	1.00

Inter-European Cultural and Economic Collaboration. Sheets of 10.

Historical Museum — A682   Demonstration, by A. Anastasiu — A684

Communist Party Emblem A683

1971, May 7   Photo.   Perf. 13½

2243	A682	55b blue & multi	15	15

For Romania's Historical Museum.

1971, May 8

Design: 35b, Reading Proclamation, by Stefan Szonyi.

2244	A684	35b multicolored	15	15
2245	A683	40b multicolored	15	15
2246	A684	55b multicolored	18	15
		Set value		15

Romanian Communist Party, 50th anniv.

Souvenir Sheets

Motra Tone, by Kole Idromeno A685

Dancing the Hora, by Theodor Aman — A686

Designs: b, Maid by V. Dimitrov-Maystora. c, Rosa Botzaris, by Joseph Stieler. d, Woman in Costume, by Katarina Ivanovic. e, Argeseanca, by Carol Popp de Szathmary. f, Woman in Modern Dress, by Calli Ibrahim.

1971, May 25   Photo.   Perf. 13½

2247	A685	Sheet of 6	3.50	3.00
a.-f.		1.20 l any single	50	38
2248	A686	5 l multicolored	2.25	2.25

Balkanphila III Stamp Exhibition, Bucharest, June 27-July 2.

No. 2247 contains 6 stamps in 3 rows and 6 labels showing exhibition emblem and "60b."

Punica Granatum L

POSTA ROMANA   b20   Pomegranate Flower — A687

Flowers: 35b, Slipperwort. 55b, Lily. 1 l, Mimulus. 1.50 l, Morning-glory. 2.40 l, Leaf cactus, horiz.

1971, June 20

2249	A687	20b ultra & multi	15	15
2250	A687	35b red & multi	15	15
2251	A687	55b ultra & multi	15	15
2252	A687	1 l car & multi	35	15
2253	A687	1.50 l car & multi	60	15
2254	A687	2.40 l ultra & multi	95	26
		Nos. 2249-2254 (6)	2.35	
		Set value		65

Nude, by Iosif Iser — A688   POSTA ROMANA   10 ฿

Paintings of Nudes: 20b, by Camil Ressu. 35b, by Nicolae Grigorescu. 60b, by Eugene Delacroix (odalisque). 1.75 l, by Auguste Renoir. 3 l, by Palma il Vecchio (Venus and Amor). 5 l, by Il Bronzino (Venus and Amor). 60b, 3 l, 5 l, horiz.

1971, July 25   Photo.   Perf. 13½
Size: 38x50mm, 49x39mm, 29x50mm (20b)

2255	A688	10b gold & multi	15	15
2256	A688	20b gold & multi	15	15
2257	A688	35b gold & multi	15	15
2258	A688	60b gold & multi	15	15
2259	A688	1.75 l gold & multi	38	18
2260	A688	3 l gold & multi	1.40	38
		Set value	2.10	75

Miniature Sheet
Imperf

2261	A688	5 l gold & multi	2.00	2.00

POSTA ROMANA   10 ฿

Ships in Storm, by B. Peters — A689

Paintings of Ships by: 20b, Ludolf Backhuysen. 35b, Andries van Eertvelt. 60b, M. W. Arnold. 1.75 l, Ivan Konstantinovich Aivazovski. 3 l, Jean Steriadi. 5 l, N. Darascu, vert.

1971, Sept. 15   Photo.   Perf. 13½

2262	A689	10b gold & multi	15	15
2263	A689	20b gold & multi	15	15
2264	A689	35b gold & multi	15	15
2265	A689	60b gold & multi	15	15
2266	A689	1.75 l gold & multi	45	20
2267	A689	3 l gold & multi	1.00	35
		Set value	1.75	75

Miniature Sheet

2268	A689	5 l gold & multi	2.00	2.00

Types of Regular Issue

Designs as Before and: 3.60 l, Mail collector. 4.80 l, Mailman. 6 l, Ministry of Posts.

1971   Photo.   Perf. 13½
Size: 16½x23mm, 23x16½mm

2269	A616	1 l emerald	22	15
2270	A617	1.20 l red lilac	28	15
2271	A617	1.35 l brt blue	30	15
2272	A616	1.50 l orange red	35	15
2273	A616	1.55 l sepia	35	15
2274	A617	1.75 l deep green	38	15
2275	A617	2 l citron	45	15
2276	A616	2.40 l dark blue	55	15
2277	A617	3 l greenish bl	70	15
2278	A617	3.20 l ocher	70	15
2279	A616	3.25 l ultra	85	15
2280	A616	3.60 l blue	1.00	15
2281	A617	4 l lilac rose	1.25	15
2282	A616	4.80 l grnsh blue	1.40	15
2283	A617	5 l violet	1.40	15
2284	A616	6 l dp magenta	1.50	15
		Nos. 2269-2284 (16)	11.68	
		Set value		80

NEAGOE BASARAB 1521-1971   60b   POSTA ROMANA

Prince Neagoe Basarab — A690

POSTA ROMANA 40 ฿

Theodor Pallady (Painter) — A691

1971, Sept. 20   Perf. 13½

2288	A690	60b gold & multi	20	15

450th anniversary of the death of Prince Neagoe Basarab of Walachia.

1971, Oct. 12   Photo.   Perf. 13½

Portraits of: 55b, Benvenuto Cellini (1500-1571), sculptor. 1.50 l, Antoine Watteau (1684-1721), painter. 2.40 l, Albrecht Dürer (1471-1528), painter.

2289	A691	40b gold & multi	15	15
2290	A691	55b gold & multi	15	15
2291	A691	1.50 l gold & multi	50	15
2292	A691	2.40 l gold & multi	1.00	26
		Set value		52

Anniversaries of famous artists.

SAPPORO'72   55 ฿   POSTA ROMANA

Proclamation of Cyrus the Great — A692

POSTA ROMANA

Figure Skating — A693

1971, Oct. 12

2293	A692	55b multicolored	18	15

2500th anniversary of the founding of the Persian empire by Cyrus the Great.

1971, Oct. 25

Designs: 20b, Ice hockey. 40b, Biathlon (skier). 55b, Bobsledding. 1.75 l, Skiing. 3 l, Sapporo '72 emblem. 5 l, Olympic flame and emblem.

2294	A693	10b lt bl, blk & red	15	15
2295	A693	20b multicolored	15	15
2296	A693	40b multicolored	15	15
2297	A693	55b lt bl, blk & red	15	15
2298	A693	1.75 l lt bl, blk & red	50	16
2299	A693	3 l lt bl, blk & red	80	28
		Set value	1.60	60

Miniature Sheet
Imperf

2300	A693	5 l multicolored	2.00	2.00

11th Winter Olympic Games, Sapporo, Japan, Feb. 3-13, 1972. Nos. 2294-2296 printed se-tenant in sheets of 15 (5x3); Nos. 2297-2298 printed se-tenant in sheets of 10 (5x2). No. 2300 contains one stamp 37x50mm.

MOLDOVITA   POSTA ROMANA ฿   10

St. George and the Dragon A694

Frescoes from North Moldavian Monasteries: 10b, 20b, 40b, Moldovita. 55b, 1.75 l, 5 l, Voronet. 3 l, Arborea, horiz.

1971, Nov. 30   Photo.   Perf. 13½

2301	A694	10b gold & multi	15	15
2302	A694	20b gold & multi	15	15
2303	A694	40b gold & multi	15	15
2304	A694	55b gold & multi	15	15
2305	A694	1.75 l gold & multi	60	18
2306	A694	3 l gold & multi	90	40
		Nos. 2301-2306 (6)	2.10	
		Set value		75

Miniature Sheet
Imperf

2307	A694	5 l gold & multi	1.90	1.50

No. 2307 contains one stamp 44x56mm.

POSTA ROMANA   40 ฿

Ferdinand Magellan A695

Designs: 55b, Johannes Kepler and observation tower. 1 l, Yuri Gagarin and rocket orbiting earth. 1.50 l, Baron Ernest R. Rutherford, atom, nucleus and chemical apparatus.

1971, Dec. 20

2308	A695	40b grn, brt rose & dk bl	15	15
2309	A695	55b lil, bl & gray grn	15	15
2310	A695	1 l violet & multi	30	15
2311	A695	1.50 l red brn, grn & bl	50	16
		Set value		38

Magellan (1480?-1521), navigator; Kepler (1571-1630), astronomer; Gagarin, 1st man in space, 10th anniv.; Ernest R. Rutherford (1871-1937), British physicist.

MATEI MILLO 54 ANI DE LA MOARTE   55 ฿   POSTA ROMANA

Matei Millo — A696

UTC   50

Young Communists Union Emblem — A697

Design: 1 l, Nicolae Iorga.

1971, Dec.

2312	A696	55b blue & multi	15	15
2313	A696	1 l purple & multi	28	15
		Set value		20

Millo (1814-1896), playwright; Iorga (1871-1940), historian and politician.

1972, Feb.

2314	A697	55b dk bl, red & gold	18	15

Young Communists Union, 50th anniv.

POSTA ROMANA   20b   LYNX LYNX

Young Animals — A698

1972, Mar. 10   Photo.   Perf. 13½

2315	A698	20b Lynx	15	15
2316	A698	35b Foxes	15	15
2317	A698	55b Roe fawns	15	15
2318	A698	1 l Wild pigs	28	15
2319	A698	1.50 l Wolves	40	20
2320	A698	2.40 l Bears	85	26
		Nos. 2315-2320 (6)	1.98	
		Set value		75

MÜNCHEN 1972   10 ฿   POSTA ROMANA

Wrestling — A699

Olympic Rings and: 20b, Canoeing. 55b, Soccer. 1.55 l, Women's high jump. 2.90 l, Boxing. 6.70 l, Field ball.

1972, Apr. 25   Photo.   Perf. 13½

2321	A699	10b yel & multi	15	15
2322	A699	20b multicolored	15	15
2323	A699	55b gray & multi	15	15
2324	A699	1.55 l grn & multi	35	18
2325	A699	2.90 l multicolored	80	24
2326	A699	6.70 l lil & multi	1.25	50
		Nos. 2321-2326 (6)	2.85	
		Set value		1.05

20th Olympic Games, Munich, Aug. 26-Sept. 10. See Nos. C186-C187.

CULTURALA · ECONOMICA · INTEREUROPEANA   POSTA ROMANA   1.75

Stylized Map of Europe and Links A700

Design: 2.90 l, Entwined arrows and links.

1972, Apr. 28

2327	A700	1.75 l dp car, gold & blk	1.10	75
2328	A700	2.90 l grn, gold & blk	1.50	1.00
a.		Pair, #2327-2328	2.60	2.00

Inter-European Cultural and Economic Collaboration.

UIC   55   POSTA ROMANA

UIC Emblem and Trains A701

1972, May 20   Photo.   Perf. 13½

2329	A701	55b dp car rose, blk & gold	18	15

50th anniv., Intl. Railroad Union (UIC).

Souvenir Sheet

"Summer," by Peter Brueghel, the
Younger — A702

1972, May 20   *Perf. 13x13½*
2330 A702 6 l gold & multi   2.00 2.00

Belgica 72, Intl. Phil. Exhib., Brussels, June 24-
July 9.

Peony — A703

Protected Flowers: 40b, Pink. 55b, Edelweiss.
60b, Nigritella rubra. 1.35 l, Narcissus. 2.90 l,
Lady's slipper.

1972, June 5   Photo.   *Perf. 13*
Flowers in Natural Colors
2331	A703	20b dk vio bl	15	15
2332	A703	40b chocolate	15	15
2333	A703	55b dp blue	15	15
2334	A703	60b dk green	18	15
2335	A703	1.35 l violet	50	18
2336	A703	2.90 l dk Prus bl	90	40
		Nos. 2331-2336 (6)	2.03	
		Set value		88

Saligny Bridge, Cernavoda — A704

Danube Bridges: 1.75 l, Giurgeni Bridge, Vadul.
2.75 l, Friendship Bridge, Giurgiu-Ruse.

1972, June 25   Photo.   *Perf. 13½*
2337	A704	1.35 l multi	35	15
2338	A704	1.75 l multi	50	15
2339	A704	2.75 l multi	85	20

North
Railroad
Station,
Bucharest,
Cent.
A705

1972, July 4
2340 A705 55b ultra & multi   24 15

Water Polo
and Olympic
Rings
A706

Olympic Rings and: 20b, Pistol shoot. 55b, Discus. 1.55 l, Gymnastics, women's. 2.75 l, Canoeing. 6.40 l, Fencing.

1972, July 5   Photo.   *Perf. 13½*
2341	A706	10b ol, gold & lil	15	15
2342	A706	20b red, gold & grn	15	15
2343	A706	55b grn, gold & brn	15	15
2344	A706	1.55 l vio, gold & ol	25	15
2345	A706	2.75 l bl, gold & gray	45	18
2346	A706	6.40 l pur, gold & gray	1.10	38
		Set value	2.00	85

20th Olympic Games, Munich, Aug. 26-Sept. 11.
See No. C187.

Stamp Printing
Press — A707

1972, July 25
2347 A707 55b multicolored   18 15

Centenary of the stamp printing office.

Stefan
Popescu, Self-
portrait
A708

1972, Aug. 10
2348	A708	55b shown	15	15
2349	A708	1.75 l Octav Bancila	28	15
2350	A708	2.90 l Gheorghe Petrascu	50	16
2351	A708	6.50 l Ion Andreescu	1.25	30
		Set value		65

Self-portraits by Romanian painters.

Runner with Torch,
Olympic
Rings — A709

City Hall
Tower,
Sibiu — A710

1972, Aug. 13
2352 A709 55b sil, bl & claret   18 15

Olympic torch relay from Olympia, Greece, to
Munich, Germany, passing through Romania.

1972   Photo.   *Perf. 13*
Designs: 1.85 l, St. Michael's Cathedral, Cluj.
2.75 l, Sphinx Rock, Mt. Bucegi, horiz. 3.35 l,
Heroes' Monument, Bucharest. 3.45 l, Sinaia Cas-
tle, horiz. 5.15 l, Hydroelectric Works, Arges, horiz.
5.60 l, Church of the Epiphany, Iasi. 6.20 l, Bran
Castle. 6.40 l, Hunedoara Castle, horiz. 6.80 l,
Polytechnic Institute, Bucharest, horiz. 7.05 l,
Black Church, Brasov. 8.45 l, Atheneum,
Bucharest. 9.05 l, Excavated Coliseum,
Sarmizegetusa, horiz. 9.10 l, Hydroelectric Station,
Iron Gate, horiz. 9.85 l, Monument, Cetatea. 11.90
l, Republic Palace, horiz. 12.75 l, Television Station.
13.30 l, Arch, Alba Iulia, horiz. 16.20 l, Clock
Tower, Sighisoara.

Size: 23x18mm, 17x24mm
2353	A710	1.85 l brt purple	35	15
2354	A710	2.75 l gray	50	15
2355	A710	3.35 l magenta	60	15
2356	A710	3.45 l green	55	15
2357	A710	5.15 l brt blue	95	15
2358	A710	5.60 l blue	1.00	15
2359	A710	6.20 l cerise	1.10	15
2360	A710	6.40 l sepia	1.25	15
2361	A710	6.80 l rose red	1.25	15
2362	A710	7.05 l black	1.40	15
2363	A710	8.45 l rose red	1.50	15
2364	A710	9.05 l dull green	1.65	15
2365	A710	9.10 l ultra	1.65	15
2366	A710	9.85 l green	1.65	15

Size: 19½x29mm, 29x21mm
2367	A710	10 l dp brown	1.90	15
2368	A710	11.90 l bluish blk	2.25	15
2369	A710	12.75 l dk violet	2.50	18
2370	A710	13.30 l dull red	2.50	20
2371	A710	16.20 l olive grn	3.00	28
		Nos. 2353-2371,C193 (20)	30.30	
		Set value		2.00

View of Satu-
Mare — A711

1972, Oct. 5
2372 A711 55b multicolored   20 15

Millennium of Satu-Mare.

Tennis
Racket
and
Davis
Cup
A712

1972, Oct. 10   *Perf. 13½*
2373 A712 2.75 l multi   75 25

Davis Cup finals between Romania and US,
Bucharest, Oct. 13-15.

Venice, by Gheorge Petrascu — A713

Paintings of Venice by: 20b, N. Darascu. 55b,
Petrascu. 1.55 l, Marius Bunescu. 2.75 l, N.
Darascu, vert. 6 l, Petrascu. 6.40 l, Marius
Bunescu.

1972, Oct. 20
2374	A713	10b gray & multi	15	15
2375	A713	20b gray & multi	15	15
2376	A713	55b gray & multi	15	15
2377	A713	1.55 l gray & multi	28	15
2378	A713	2.75 l gray & multi	55	18
2379	A713	6.40 l gray & multi	1.40	38
		Nos. 2374-2379 (6)	2.68	
		Set value		85

Souvenir Sheet
2380 A713 6 l gray & multi   2.00 2.00

Fencing, Bronze
Medal — A714

Apollo 1, 2 and
3 — A715

Designs: 20b, Team handball, bronze medal.
35b, Boxing, silver medal. 1.45 l, Hurdles,
women's, silver medal. 2.75 l, Pistol shoot, silver
medal. 6.20 l, Wrestling, gold medal.

1972, Oct. 28
2381	A714	10b red org & multi	15	15
2382	A714	20b lt grn & multi	15	15
2383	A714	35b multicolored	15	15
2384	A714	1.45 l multi	28	18
2385	A714	2.75 l ocher & multi	55	24
2386	A714	6.20 l bl & multi	1.40	48
		Nos. 2381-2386 (6)	2.68	
		Set value		1.00

Romanian medalists at 20th Olympic Games. See
No. C191. For surcharge see No. 2493.

Charity Labels
Stamp day issues frequently have an
attached, fully perforated, label with a
face value. These are Romanian Philatelic Association charity labels. They are
inscribed "AFR." The stamps are valued
with label attached. When the "label" is
part of the stamp, the stamp is listed in
the semi-postal section. See Nos. B426-
B430.

Stamp Day Semi-Postal Type of 1968
Design: Traveling Gypsies, by Emil Volkers.

1972, Nov. 15   Photo.   *Perf. 13½*
2386A SP288 1.10 l + 90b label   55 35

Stamp Day.

1972, Dec. 27   Photo.   *Perf. 13½*
2387	A715	10b shown	15	15
2388	A715	35b Grissom, Chaffee		
		and White, 1967	15	15
2389	A715	40b Apollo 4, 5, 6	15	15
2390	A715	55b Apollo 7, 8	15	15
2391	A715	1 l Apollo 9, 10	22	15
2392	A715	1.20 l Apollo 11, 12	28	15
2393	A715	1.85 l Apollo 13, 14	38	15
2394	A715	2.75 l Apollo 15, 16	60	15
2395	A715	3.60 l Apollo 17	1.10	30
		Nos. 2387-2395 (9)	3.18	
		Set value		90

Highlights of US Apollo space program.
See No. C192.

"25" and
Flags — A716

Designs: 1.20 l, "25" and national emblem.
1.75 l, "25" and factory.

1972, Dec. 25
2396	A716	55b blue & multi	18	15
2397	A716	1.20 l yel & multi	35	15
2398	A716	1.75 l ver & multi	60	18
		Set value		38

25th anniversary of the Republic.

European Bee-eater
A717

Globeflowers
A718

Nature Protection: No. 2400, Red-breasted goose. No. 2401, Penduline tit. No. 2403, Garden Turk's-cap. No. 2404, Gentian.

1973, Feb. 5   Photo.   Perf. 13
2399	A717	1.40 l gray & multi	24	15
2400	A717	1.85 l multi	35	15
2401	A717	2.75 l blue & multi	70	20
a.		Strip of 3, #2399-2401	1.40	60
2402	A718	1.40 l multi	24	15
2403	A718	1.85 l yellow & multi	35	15
2404	A718	2.75 l multi	70	20
a.		Strip of 3, #2402-2404	1.40	60

Nicolaus Copernicus — A719

1973, Feb. 19   Photo.   Perf. 13x13¹/₂
2405	A719	2.75 l multi	70	25

Nicolaus Copernicus (1473-1543), Polish astronomer. Printed with alternating label publicizing Intl. Phil. Exhib., Poznan, Aug. 19-Sept. 2.

Suceava Woman
A720

D. Paciurea (Sculptor)
A721

Regional Costumes: 40b, Suceava man. 55b, Harghita woman. 1.75 l, Harghita man. 2.75 l, Gorj woman. 6.40 l, Gorj man.

1973, Mar. 15
2406	A720	10b lt bl & multi	15	15
2407	A720	40b multicolored	15	15
2408	A720	55b bis & multi	15	15
2409	A720	1.75 l lil & multi	30	15
2410	A720	2.75 l multi	48	15
2411	A720	6.40 l multi	1.25	35
		Nos. 2406-2411 (6)	2.48	
		Set value		65

1973, Mar. 26

Portraits: 40b, I. Slavici (1848-1925), writer. 55b, G. Lazar (1779-1823), writer. 6.40 l, A. Flechtenmacher (1823-1898), composer.

2412	A721	10b multi	15	15
2413	A721	40b multi	15	15
2414	A721	55b multi	16	15
2415	A721	6.40 l multi	1.10	38
		Set value		54

Anniversaries of famous artists.

Map of Europe
A722

Design: 3.60 l, Symbol of collaboration.

1973, Apr. 28   Photo.   Perf. 13¹/₂
2416	A722	3.35 l dp bl & gold	1.10	70
2417	A722	3.60 l brt mag & gold	1.25	1.00
a.		Pair, #2416-2417	2.35	2.00

Inter-European cultural and economic cooperation. Printed in sheets of 10 with blue marginal inscription.

Souvenir Sheet

The Rape of Proserpina, by Hans von Aachen — A723

1973, May 5
2418	A723	12 l gold & multi	2.75	2.50

IBRA Munchen 1973, Intl. Stamp Exhib., Munich, May 11-20.

Prince Alexander I. Cuza — A724

Hand with Hammer and Sickle — A725

1973, May 5   Photo.   Perf. 13¹/₂
2419	A724	1.75 l multi	50	15

Alexander Ioan Cuza (1820-1873), prince of Romania, Moldavia and Walachia.

1973, May 5
2420	A725	40b gold & multi	18	15

Workers and Peasants Party, 25th anniv.

Romanian Flag, Bayonets Stabbing Swastika — A726

WMO Emblem, Weather Satellite — A727

1973, May 5
2421	A726	55b multicolored	18	15

Anti-fascist Front, 40th anniversary.

1973, June 15
2422	A727	2 l ultra & multi	50	15

Intl. meteorological cooperation, cent.

Dimitrie Ralet Holding Letter
A728

Dimitrie Cantemir
A729

Portraits with letters. 60b, Enachita Vacarescu, by A. Chladek. 1.55 l, Serdarul Dimitrie Aman, by C. Lecca.

1973, June 20
2423	A728	40b multi	15	15
2424	A728	60b multi	18	15
2425	A728	1.55 l multi	50	24
		Set value		36

"The Letter on Romanian Portraits." Socflex III Philatelic Exhibition, Bucharest, July 20-29. See Nos. B432-B433.

1973, June 25

Design: 6 l, Portrait of Cantemir in oval frame.
2426	A729	1.75 l multi	48	15

Souvenir Sheet
2427	A729	6 l multi	2.00	1.40

Dimitrie Cantemir (1673-1723), Prince of Moldavia, writer. No. 2427 contains one 38x50mm stamp.

Plate — A730

Designs: 10b, Fibulae, vert. 55b, Jug, vert. 1.55 l, Necklaces and fibula. 2.75 l, Plate, vert. 6.80 l, Octagonal bowl with animal handles. 12 l, Breastplate, vert.

1973, July 25   Photo.   Perf. 13¹/₂
2428	A730	10b vio bl & multi	15	15
2429	A730	20b green & multi	15	15
2430	A730	55b red & multi	18	15
2431	A730	1.55 l multi	35	15
2432	A730	2.75 l plum & multi	60	15
2433	A730	6.80 l multi	1.50	35
		Nos. 2428-2433 (6)	2.93	
		Set value		75

Souvenir Sheet
2434	A730	12 l multi	2.75	2.50

Roman gold treasure of Pietroasa, 4th century.

Symbolic Flower, Map of Europe
A731

Design: 5 l, Map of Europe, symbolic tree.

1973, Oct. 2   Photo.   Perf. 13¹/₂
2435	A731	2.75 l multi	1.10	70
2436	A731	5 l multi	1.75	1.00
a.		Sheet, 2 each + 2 labels	5.50	5.50

Conference for European Security and Cooperation, Helsinki, Finland, July 1973.

Jug and Cloth, Oboga — A732

Designs: 20b, Plate and Pitcher, Vama. 55b, Bowl, Marginea. 1.55 l, Pitcher and plate, Sibiu-Saschiz. 2.75 l, Bowl and jug, Pisc. 6.80 l, Figurine (fowl), Oboga.

1973, Oct. 15   Perf. 13
2437	A732	10b multi	15	15
2438	A732	20b multi	15	15
2439	A732	55b multi	18	15
2440	A732	1.55 l multi	35	15
2441	A732	2.75 l multi	60	15
2442	A732	6.80 l multi	1.50	35
		Nos. 2437-2442 (6)	2.93	
		Set value		75

Pottery and cloths from various regions of Romania.

Postilion, by A. Verona — A732a

1973, Nov. 15   Photo.   Perf. 13¹/₂
2442A	A732a	1.10 l + 90b label	38	15

Stamp Day.

Women Workers, by G. Saru
A733

Paintings of Workers: 20b, Construction Site, by M. Bunescu, horiz. 55b, Shipyard Workers, by H. Catargi, horiz. 1.55 l, Worker, by Catargi. 2.75 l, Miners, by A. Phoebus. 6.80 l, Spinner, by Nicolae Grigorescu. 12 l, Farmers at Rest, by Stefan Popescu, horiz.

1973, Nov. 26   Photo.   Perf. 13¹/₂
2443	A733	10b gold & multi	15	15
2444	A733	20b gold & multi	15	15
2445	A733	55b gold & multi	18	15
2446	A733	1.55 l gold & multi	35	15
2447	A733	2.75 l gold & multi	60	15
2448	A733	6.80 l gold & multi	1.50	35
		Nos. 2443-2448 (6)	2.93	
		Set value		75

Miniature Sheet
2449	A733	12 l gold & multi	2.50	2.25

City Hall, Craiova — A734

Tugboat under Bridge — A735

Designs: 10b, Infinite Column, by Constantin Brancusi, vert. 20b, Heroes' Mausoleum, Marasesti. 35b, Risnov Citadel. 40b, Densus Church, vert. 50b, B j Church, vert. 55b, Maldaresti Fortress. 60b, National Theater, Iasi. 1 l, Curtea-de-Arges Monastery, vert. 1.20 l, Tirgu-Mures Citadel. 1.45 l, Cargoship Dimbovita. 1.50 l, Muntenia passenger ship. 1.55 l, Three-master Mircea. 1.75 l, Motorship Transilvania. 2.20 l, Ore carrier Oltul. 3.65 l, Trawler Mures. 4.70 l, Tanker Arges.

1973-74   Photo.   Perf. 13
2450	A734	5b lake	15	15
2451	A734	10b brt blue	15	15
2452	A734	20b orange	15	15
2453	A734	35b green	15	15

2454	A734	40b dk violet	15	15
2455	A734	50b ultra	15	15
2456	A734	55b orange brn	15	15
2457	A734	60b carmine	15	15
2458	A734	1 l dp ultra	25	15
2459	A734	1.20 l olive grn	30	15
2460	A735	1.35 l gray	35	15
2461	A735	1.45 l dull blue	35	15
2462	A735	1.50 l car rose	38	15
2463	A735	1.55 l violet bl	38	15
2464	A735	1.75 l slate grn	45	15
2465	A735	2.20 l brt blue	60	15
2466	A735	3.65 l dull lilac	95	15
2467	A735	4.70 l violet brn	1.40	15
	Nos. 2450-2467 (18)		6.61	
	Set value			90

Issue dates: Nos. 2450-2459, Dec. 15, 1973. Nos. 2460-2467, Jan. 28, 1974.

POSTA ROMANA 20b
Boats at Montfleur, by Claude Monet — A736

Impressionistic paintings: 40b, Church of Moret, by Alfred Sisley, vert. 55b, Orchard in Bloom, by Camille Pissarro. 1.75 l, Portrait of Jeanne, by Pissarro, vert. 2.75 l, Landscape, by Auguste Renoir. 3.60 l, Portrait of a Girl, by Paul Cezanne, vert. 10 l, Women Taking Bath, by Renoir, vert.

1974, Mar. 15   Photo.   Perf. 13¹/₂

2468	A736	20b blue & multi	15	15
2469	A736	40b blue & multi	15	15
2470	A736	55b blue & multi	15	15
2471	A736	1.75 l blue & multi	40	15
2472	A736	2.75 l blue & multi	60	15
2473	A736	3.60 l blue & multi	80	26
	Nos. 2468-2473 (6)		2.25	
	Set value			64

Souvenir Sheet

2474	A736	10 l blue & multi	2.25	2.00

Harness Racing A737

Designs: Various horse races.

1974, Apr. 5   Photo.   Perf. 13¹/₂

2475	A737	40b ver & multi	15	15
2476	A737	55b bis & multi	15	15
2477	A737	60b multi	18	15
2478	A737	1.55 l multi	35	15
2479	A737	2.75 l multi	60	20
2480	A737	3.45 l multi	80	30
	Nos. 2475-2480 (6)		2.23	
	Set value			75

Centenary of horse racing in Romania.

Nicolae Titulescu (1883-1941) — A738

1974, Apr. 16

2481	A738	1.75 l multi	50	15

Interparliamentary Session, Bucharest, Apr. 1974. Titulescu was the first Romanian delegate to the League of Nations.

Souvenir Sheet

1850 ANI
DE LA RIDICAREA ASEZARII
NAPOCA CLVJ
LA RANG DE MVNICIPIV

Roman Memorial with First Reference to Napoca (Cluj) — A739

1974, Apr. 18   Photo.   Perf. 13

2482	A739	10 l multi	2.00	2.00

1850th anniv. of the elevation of the Roman settlement of Napoca (Cluj) to a municipality.

Stylized Map of Europe A740

Design: 3.45 l, Satellite over earth.

1974, Apr. 25   Photo.   Perf. 13¹/₂x13

2483	A740	2.20 l multi	1.25	70
2484	A740	3.45 l multi	1.50	1.00
a.	Pair, #2483-2484		2.75	2.00

Inter-European Cultural Economic Cooperation.

Young Pioneers with Banners, by Pepene Cornelia — A741

1974, Apr. 25   Photo.   Perf. 13¹/₂

2485	A741	55b multicolored	20	15

25th anniv. of the Romanian Pioneers Org.

Mail Motorboat, UPU Emblem A742

UPU Emblem and: 40b, Mail train. 55b, Mailplane and truck. 1.75 l, Mail delivery by motorcycle. 2.75 l, Mailman delivering letter to little girl. 3.60 l, Young stamp collectors. 4 l, Mail collection. 6 l, Modern post office.

1974, May 11

2486	A742	20b gray & multi	15	15
2487	A742	40b multicolored	15	15
2488	A742	55b ultra & multi	18	15
2489	A742	1.75 l multi	40	15
2490	A742	2.75 l brn & multi	60	20
2491	A742	3.60 l org & multi	85	30
	Nos. 2486-2491 (6)		2.33	
	Set value			75

Souvenir Sheet

2492		Sheet of 2	3.25	2.50
a.	A742	4 l multi		85
b.	A742	6 l multi		1.40

Centenary of Universal Postal Union.
Size of stamps of No. 2492, 28x24mm.

An imperf airmail UPU souvenir sheet of one (10 l) exists. The multicolored stamp is 49x38mm. This sheet is not known to have been sold to the public at post offices.

No. 2382 Surcharged with New Value and Overprinted: "ROMÂNIA / CAMPIOANA / MONDIALĂ / 1974"

1974, May 13

2493	A714	1.75 l on 20b multi	2.50	1.75

Romania's victory in World Handball Championship, 1974.

Soccer and Games Emblem — A743   "25" — A744

Designs: Games emblem and various scenes from soccer game.

1974, June 25   Perf. 13¹/₂

2494	A743	20b purple & multi	15	15
2495	A743	40b multi	15	15
2496	A743	55b ultra & multi	18	15
2497	A743	1.75 l brn & multi	40	15
2498	A743	2.75 l multi	60	20
2499	A743	3.60 l vio & multi	85	30
	Nos. 2494-2499 (6)		2.33	
	Set value			80

Souvenir Sheet

2500	A743	multi	2.50	2.00

World Cup Soccer Championship, Munich, June 13-July 7. No. 2500 contains one horizontal stamp 50x38mm.

An imperf. 10 l airmail souvenir sheet exists showing a globe as soccer ball and satellite. Gray blue margin showing Soccer Cup, radio tower and stadium; black control number.

1974, June 10

2501	A744	55b blue & multi	20	15

25th anniv. of the Council for Mutual Economic Assistance (COMECON).

UN Emblem and People — A745   Hand Drawing Peace Dove — A746

1974, June 25   Photo.   Perf. 13¹/₂

2502	A745	2 l multicolored	50	15

World Population Year.

1974, June 28

2503	A746	2 l ultra & multi	50	15

25 years of the National and Intl. Movement to Uphold the Cause of Peace.

Ioan, Prince of Wallachia A747   Soldier, Industry and Agriculture A748

Hunedoara Iron and Steel Works — A749

Designs: 1.10 l, Avram Iancu (1824-1872). 1.30 l, Dr. C. I. Parhon (1874-1969). 1.40 l, Bishop Dosoftei (1624-1693).

1974   Photo.   Perf. 13

2504	A747	20b blue	15	15
2505	A748	55b carmine rose	18	15
2506	A749	1 l slate green	28	15
2507	A747	1.10 l dk gray ol	28	15
2508	A747	1.30 l dp magenta	30	15
2509	A747	1.40 l dk violet	38	15
	Nos. 2504-2509 (6)		1.57	
	Set value			32

No. 2505 for Army Day, No. 2506 for 220th anniv. of Hunedoara Iron and Steel works; others for anniversaries of famous Romanians. Issue dates; 11, June 17; others June 25.

Romanians and Flags — A750

Design: 40b, Romanian and Communist flags forming "XXX," vert.

1974, Aug. 20

2510	A750	40b gold, ultra & car	15	15
2511	A750	55b yellow & multi	18	15
	Set value			15

30th anniversary of Romania's liberation from Fascist rule.

Souvenir Sheet

View, Stockholm — A751

1974, Sept. 10   Photo.   Perf. 13

2512	A751	10 l multicolored	2.00	2.00

Stockholmia 74 International Philatelic Exhibition, Stockholm, Sept. 21-29.

Thistle — A752

Nature Protection: 40b, Checkered lily. 55b, Yew. 1.75 l, Azalea. 2.75 l, Forget-me-not. 3.60 l, Pinks.

1974, Sept. 15

2513	A752	20b plum & multi	15 15
2514	A752	40b multi	15 15
2515	A752	55b multi	18 15
2516	A752	1.75 l multi	40 15
2517	A752	2.75 l brn & multi	60 20
2518	A752	3.60 l multi	85 30
		Nos. 2513-2518 (6)	2.33
		Set value	80

Isis, First Century A.D. — A753

Archaeological art works excavated in Romania: 40b, Serpent, by Glycon. 55b, Emperor Trajan, bronze bust. 1.75 l, Roman woman, statue, 3rd century. 2.75 l, Mithraic bas-relief. 3.60 l, Roman man, statue, 3rd century.

1974, Oct. 20   Photo.   *Perf. 13*

2519	A753	20b multi	15 15
2520	A753	40b ultra & multi	15 15
2521	A753	55b multi	18 15
2522	A753	1.75 l multi	40 15
2523	A753	2.75 l brn & multi	60 20
2524	A753	3.60 l multi	85 30
		Nos. 2519-2524 (6)	2.33
		Set value	80

Romanian Communist Party Emblem A754

Design: 1 l, similar to 55b.

1974, Nov. 20

2525	A754	55b blk, red & gold	18 15
2526	A754	1 l blk, red & gold	28 15
		Set value	15

9th Romanian Communist Party Congress.

Discobolus and Olympic Rings A755

1974, Nov. 11

2527	A755	2 l ultra & multi	45 15

Romanian Olympic Committee, 60th anniv.

Skylab A756

1974, Dec. 14   Photo.   *Perf. 13*

2528	A756	2.50 l multi	60 35

Skylab, manned US space laboratory. No. 2528 printed in sheets of 4 stamps and 4 labels. A 10 l imperf. souvenir sheet exists showing Skylab.

Field Ball and Games' Emblem — A757

Designs: 1.75 l, 2.20 l, Various scenes from field ball; 1.75 l, vert.

1975, Jan. 3

2529	A757	55b ultra & multi	18 15
2530	A757	1.75 l yel & multi	40 15
2531	A757	2.20 l multi	50 18
		Set value	36

World University Field Ball Championship.

Rocks and Birches, by Andreescu A758

Paintings by Ion Andreescu (1850-1882): 40b, Farm Woman with Green Kerchief. 55b, Winter in the Woods. 1.75 l, Winter in Barbizon, horiz. 2.75 l, Self-portrait. 3.60 l, Main Road, horiz.

1975, Jan. 24

2532	A758	20b multi	15 15
2533	A758	40b multi	15 15
2534	A758	55b multi	18 15
2535	A758	1.75 l multi	40 15
2536	A758	2.75 l multi	60 20
2537	A758	3.60 l multi	85 30
		Nos. 2532-2537 (6)	2.33
		Set value	80

Torch with Flame in Flag Colors and Coat of Arms — A759

1975, Feb. 1

2538	A759	40b multicolored	15 15

Romanian Socialist Republic, 10th anniv.

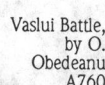

Vaslui Battle, by O. Obedeanu A760

1975, Feb. 8   Photo.   *Perf. 13½*

2539	A760	55b gold & multi	18 15

Battle at the High Bridge, Stephan the Great's victory over the Turks, 500th anniv.

Woman Spinning, by Nicolae Grigorescu A761

Michelangelo, Self-portrait A762

1975, Mar. 1

2540	A761	55b gold & multi	18 15

International Women's Year.

1975, Mar. 10

2541	A762	5 l multicolored	85 28

Michelangelo Buonarroti (1475-1564), Italian sculptor, painter and architect.
For overprint see No. 2581.

Souvenir Sheet

Escorial Palace and España 75 Emblem — A763

1975, Mar. 15   Photo.   *Perf. 13*

2542	A763	10 l multi	2.00 1.75

Espana 75 Intl. Phil. Exhib., Madrid, Apr. 4-13.

Letter with Postal Code, Pigeon A764

1975, Mar. 26   Photo.   *Perf. 13½*

2543	A764	55b blue & multi	18 15

Introduction of postal code system.

Children's Science Pavilion — A765

1975, Apr. 10   Photo.   *Perf. 13*

2544	A765	4 l multicolored	75 20

Oceanexpo 75, International Exhibition, Okinawa, July 20, 1975-Jan. 1976.

Peonies, by N. Tonitza A766

Design: 3.45 l, Chrysanthemums, by St. Luchian.

1975, Apr. 28

2545	A766	2.20 l gold & multi	85 50
2546	A766	3.45 l gold & multi	1.25 95
a.		Pair, #2545-2546	2.10 1.75

Inter-European Cultural and Economic Cooperation. Printed checkerwise in sheets of 10 (2x5).

1875 Meter Convention Emblem A767

1975, May 10   Photo.   *Perf. 13*

2547	A767	1.85 l bl, blk & gold	50 15

Cent. of Intl. Meter Convention, Paris, 1875.

Mihail Eminescu and his Home — A768

1975, June 5

2548	A768	55b multicolored	18 15

Milhail Eminescu (1850-1889), poet.

Marble Plaque and Dacian Coins 1st-2nd Centuries — A769

1975, May 26

2549	A769	55b multicolored	18 15

2000th anniv. of the founding of Alba Iulia (Apulum).

Souvenir Sheet

"On the Bank of the Seine," by Th. Pallady — A770

1975, May 26
2550 A770 10 l multicolored   2.25 1.75

ARPHILA 75, Paris, June 6-16.

Dr. Albert Schweitzer (1875-1965), Medical Missionary — A771

1974, Dec. 20   Photo.   Perf. 13½
2551 A771 40b black brown   15 15

Ana Ipatescu
A772

Policeman with Walkie-talkie
A773

1975, June 2   Photo.   Perf. 13½
2552 A772 55b lilac rose   18 15

Ana Ipatescu, fighter in 1848 revolution.

1975, Sept. 1
2553 A773 55b brt blue   20 15

Publicity for traffic rules.

Monument and Projected Reconstruction, Adam Clissi — A777

Roman Monuments: 55b, Emperor Trajan, bas-relief, vert. 1.20 l, Trajan's column, Rome, vert. 1.55 l, Governor Decibalus, bas-relief, vert. 2 l, Excavated Roman city, Turnu-Severin. 2.25 l, Trajan's Bridge, ruin and projected reconstruction. No. 2569, Roman fortifications, vert.

1975, June 26   Photo.   Perf. 13½
2563	A777	55b	red brn & blk	15	15
2564	A777	1.20 l	vio bl & blk	24	15
2565	A777	1.55 l	green & blk	24	15
2566	A777	1.75 l	dl rose & multi	35	15
2567	A777	2 l	dl yel & blk	40	15
2568	A777	2.25 l	brt bl & blk	50	18
		Nos. 2563-2568 (6)		1.88	

Set value   65

Souvenir Sheet
2569 A777 10 l multicolored   2.75 2.00

European Architectural Heritage Year.
An imperf. 10 l gold and dark brown souvenir sheet exists showing the Roman wolf suckling Romulus and Remus.
A similar souvenir sheet exists with the Roman wolf 10 l imperf. It appeared in 1978, honoring the Intl. Stamp Fair, Essen, Germany.

Michael the Brave, by Sadeler
A778

Michael the Brave Statue — A779

Designs: 1.20 l, Ottoman Messengers Offering Gifts to Michael the Brave, by Theodor Aman, horiz. 2.75 l, Michael the Brave in Battle of Calugareni, by Aman.

1975, July 7
2571	A778	55b	gold & blk	18	15
2572	A778	1.20 l	gold & multi	28	15
2573	A778	2.75 l	gold & multi	60	20
		Set value		35	

Souvenir Sheet
Imperf
2574 A779 10 l gold & multi   22.50 20.00

First political union of Romanian states under Michael the Brave, 375th anniv.
No. 2574 issued Sept. 20.

Larkspur — A780

1975, Aug. 15   Photo.   Perf. 13½
2575	A780	20b	shown	15	15
2576	A780	40b	Field poppies	15	15
2577	A780	55b	Xeranthemum annuum	18	15
2578	A780	1.75 l	Rockrose	40	15
2579	A780	2.75 l	Meadow sage	60	18
2580	A780	3.60 l	Wild chicory	85	25
		Nos. 2575-2580 (6)		2.33	
		Set value		68	

No. 2541 Overprinted in Red:

**Tîrg internaţional
de mărci poştale**

**Riccione – Italia
23–25 august 1975**

1975, Aug. 23
2581 A762 5 l multicolored   1.75 85

Intl. Phil. Exhib., Riccione, Italy, Aug. 23-25.

Map Showing Location of Craiova, 1750 — A781

Illustration reduced.

1975, Sept. 15   Photo.   Perf. 13½
2582	A781	Strip of 3		55	30
a.		20b ocher, yellow, red & black		15	15
b.		55b ocher, yellow, red & black		15	15
c.		1 l ocher, yellow, red & black		24	15

1750th anniv. of first documentation of Daco-Getian settlement of Pelendava and 500th anniversary of documentation of Craiova.
Size of Nos. 2582a, 2582c: 25x32mm; of No. 2582b: 80x32mm.

Muntenian Rug — A782

Romanian Peasant Rugs: 40b, Banat. 55b, Oltenia. 1.75 l, Moldavia. 2.75 l, Oltenia. 3.60 l, Maramures.

1975, Oct. 5   Photo.   Perf. 13½
2583	A782	20b	dk bl & multi	15	15
2584	A782	40b	black & multi	15	15
2585	A782	55b	multicolored	18	15
2586	A782	1.75 l	black & multi	40	15
2587	A782	2.75 l	multicolored	60	18
2588	A782	3.60 l	black & multi	80	22
		Nos. 2583-2588 (6)		2.28	
		Set value		65	

Minibus
A783

1975, Nov. 5   Photo.   Perf. 13½
2589	A783	20b	shown	15	15
2590	A783	40b	Gasoline truck	15	15
2591	A783	55b	Jeep	18	15
2592	A783	1.75 l	Flat-bed truck	40	15
2593	A783	2.75 l	Dacia automobile	60	18
2594	A783	3.60 l	Dump truck	85	22
		Nos. 2589-2594 (6)		2.33	
		Set value		65	

Souvenir Sheet

Winter, by Peter Brueghel, the Younger — A784

1975, Nov. 25   Photo.   Perf. 13½
2595 A784 10 l multicolored   2.50 2.00

THEMABELGA Intl. Topical Phil. Exhib., Brussels, Dec. 13-21.

Luge and Olympic Games' Emblem — A785

Innsbruck Olympic Games' Emblem and: 40b, Biathlon, vert. 55b, Woman skier. 1.75 l, Ski jump. 2.75 l, Woman figure skater. 3.60 l, Ice hockey. 10 l, Two-man bobsled.

1976, Jan. 12   Photo.   Perf. 13½
2596	A785	20b	blue & multi	15	15
2597	A785	40b	multicolored	15	15
2598	A785	55b	multicolored	18	15
2599	A785	1.75 l	ol & multi	40	15
2600	A785	2.75 l	multi	60	20
2601	A785	3.60 l	multi	80	38
		Nos. 2596-2601 (6)		2.28	
		Set value		90	

Souvenir Sheet
2602 A785 10 l multicolored   2.50 2.00

12th Winter Olympic Games, Innsbruck, Austria, Feb. 4-15. An imperf. 10 l souvenir sheet exists showing slalom; Romanian flag, Games' emblem.

Washington at Valley Forge, by W. T. Trego — A786

Paintings: 40b, Washington at Trenton, by John Trumbull, vert. 55b, Washington Crossing the Delaware, by Emanuel Leutze. 1.75 l, The Capture of the Hessians, by Trumbull. 2.75 l, Jefferson, by Thomas Sully, vert. 3.60 l, Surrender of Cornwallis at Yorktown, by Trumbull. 10 l, Signing of the Declaration of Independence, by Trumbull.

1976, Jan. 25   Photo.   Perf. 13½
2603	A786	20b	gold & multi	15	15
2604	A786	40b	gold & multi	15	15
2605	A786	55b	gold & multi	18	15
2606	A786	1.75 l	gold & multi	40	15
2607	A786	2.75 l	gold & multi	60	28
2608	A786	3.60 l	gold & multi	75	35
		Nos. 2603-2608 (6)		2.23	
		Set value		92	

Souvenir Sheet
2609 A786 10 l gold & multi   2.50 2.00

American Bicentennial. No. 2609 also for Interphil 76 Intl. Phil. Exhib., Philadelphia, Pa., May 20-June 6. Printed in horizontal rows of 4 stamps with centered label showing Bicentennial emblem.

Prayer, by
Brancusi
A787

Designs: 1.75 l, Architectural Assembly, by Brancusi. 3.60 l, Constantin Brancusi.

1976, Feb. 15   **Photo.**   *Perf. 13½*
2610	A787	55b purple & multi	18	15
2611	A787	1.75 l blue & multi	40	18
2612	A787	3.60 l multicolored	85	35

Constantin Brancusi (1876-1957), sculptor.
For surcharge see No. B440.

Anton
Davidoglu — A788

Archives
Museum — A789

Designs: 55b, Vlad Tepes. 1.20 l, Costache Negri.

1976, Feb. 25
2613	A788	40b green & multi	15	15
2614	A788	55b green & multi	18	15
2615	A788	1.20 l green & multi	28	15
2616	A789	1.75 l green & multi	40	18
		Set value	46	

Anniversaries: Anton Davidoglu (1876-1958), mathematician; Prince Vlad Tepes, commander in war against the Turks (d. 1476); Costache Negri (1812-1876), Moldavian freedom fighter; Romanian National Archives Museum, founded 1926.

Dr. Carol
Davila — A790

Vase with King
Decebalus
Portrait — A791

Designs: 1.75 l, Nurse with patient. 2.20 l, First aid.

1976, Apr. 20
2617	A790	55b multi	18	15
2618	A790	1.75 l multi	40	15
2619	A790	2.20 l yel & multi	50	15
		Set value	28	

Romanian Red Cross cent. See No. C199.

1976, May 13

Design: 3.45 l, Vase with portrait of King Michael the Bold.

2620	A791	2.20 l bl & multi	1.00	50
2621	A791	3.45 l multi	2.50	1.25

Inter-European Cultural Economic Cooperation. Nos. 2620-2621 each printed in sheets of 4 with marginal inscriptions.

Coat of Arms — A792

Spiru
Haret — A793

1976, June 12
2622	A792	1.75 l multi	40	18

1976, June 25
2628	A793	20b multicolored	15	15

Spiru Haret (1851-1912), mathematician.

Woman
Athlete — A794

Romanian Olympic Emblem and: 40b, Boxing. 55b, Team handball. 1.75 l, 2-man scull, horiz. 2.75 l, Gymnast on rings, horiz. 3.60 l, 2-man canoe, horiz. 10 l, Woman gymnast, horiz.

1976, June 25   **Photo.**   *Perf. 13½*
2629	A794	20b org & multi	15	15
2630	A794	40b multi	15	15
2631	A794	55b multi	18	15
2632	A794	1.75 l multi	40	15
2633	A794	2.75 l vio & multi	60	28
2634	A794	3.60 l bl & multi	85	46
		Nos. 2629-2634 (6)	2.33	
		Set value	1.00	

Souvenir Sheet
2635	A794	10 l rose & multi	2.50	2.00

21st Olympic Games, Montreal, Canada, July 17-Aug. 1. No. 2635 contains one stamp 49x37mm.
An imperf. airmail 10 l souvenir sheet exists showing Olympic Stadium, Montreal.

Inscribed Stone Tablets, Banat — A795

Designs: 40b, Hekate, Bacchus, bas-relief. 55b, Ceramic fragment, bowl, coins. 1.75 l, Bowl, urn and cup. 2.75 l, Sword, lance and tombstone. 3.60 l, Lances, urn. 10 l, Clay vessel and silver coins.

1976, July 25
2636	A795	20b multi	15	15
2637	A795	40b multi	15	15
2638	A795	55b org & multi	18	15
2639	A795	1.75 l multi	40	15
2640	A795	2.75 l fawn & multi	60	28
2641	A795	3.60 l multi	85	35
		Nos. 2636-2641 (6)	2.33	

		Set value	92	

Souvenir Sheet
2642	A795	10 l yel & multi	2.50	2.00

Daco-Roman archaeological treasures. No. 2642 issued Mar. 25. An imperf. 10 l souvenir sheet exists showing a silver and gold vase and silver coins.

Wolf Statue,
4th Century
Map
A796

1976, Aug. 25
2643	A796	55b multi	18	15

Founding of Buzau, 1600th anniv.

Game
A797

1976, Sept. 20
2644	A797	20b Red deer	15	15
2645	A797	40b Brown bear	15	15
2646	A797	55b Chamois	18	15
2647	A797	1.75 l Boar	40	15
2648	A797	2.75 l Red fox	60	18
2649	A797	3.60 l Lynx	85	22
		Nos. 2644-2649 (6)	2.33	
		Set value	65	

Dan
Grecu,
Bronze
Medal
A798

Nadia
Comaneci — A799

Designs: 40b, Fencing, bronze medal. 55b Gheorge Megelea (Javelin), bronze medal. 1.75 l, Handball, silver medal. 2.75 l, Boxing, 1 bronze, 2 silver medals. 3.60 l, Wrestling, silver and bronze medals. 10 l, Vasile Daba (kayak), gold and silver medals, vert.

1976, Oct. 20   **Photo.**   *Perf. 13½*
2650	A798	20b multi	15	15
2651	A798	40b car & multi	15	15
2652	A798	55b grn & multi	18	15
2653	A798	1.75 l red & multi	40	15
2654	A798	2.75 l bl & multi	60	28
2655	A798	3.60 l multi	80	40
2656	A799	5.70 l multi	1.40	48
		Nos. 2650-2656 (7)	3.68	
		Set value	1.40	

Souvenir Sheet
2657	A798	10 l multi	2.50	2.00

Romanian Olympic medalists. No. 2657 contains one 37x50mm stamp.

Milan Cathedral — A800

1976, Oct. 20   **Photo.**   *Perf. 13½*
2658	A800	4.75 l multi	1.10	38

ITALIA 76 Intl. Phil. Exhib., Milan, Oct. 14-24.

Oranges and Carnations, by
Luchian — A801

Paintings by Stefan Luchian (1868-1916): 40b, Flower arrangement. 55b, Vase with flowers. 1.75 l, Roses. 2.75 l, Cornflowers. 3.60 l, Carnations in vase.

1976, Nov. 5
2659	A801	20b multi	15	15
2660	A801	40b multi	15	15
2661	A801	55b multi	18	15
2662	A801	1.75 l multi	40	15
2663	A801	2.75 l multi	60	28
2664	A801	3.60 l multi	85	35
		Nos. 2659-2664 (6)	2.33	
		Set value	92	

Arms of Alba — A802

Designs: Arms of Romanian counties.

1976-77   **Photo.**   *Perf. 13½*
2665	A802	55b shown	25	15
2666	A802	55b Arad	25	15
2667	A802	55b Arges	25	15
2668	A802	55b Bacau	25	15
2669	A802	55b Bihor	25	15
2670	A802	55b Bistrita-Nasaud	25	15
2671	A802	55b Botosani	25	15
2672	A802	55b Brasov	25	15
2673	A802	55b Braila	25	15
2674	A802	55b Buzau	25	15
2675	A802	55b Caras-Severin	25	15
2676	A802	55b Cluj	25	15
2677	A802	55b Constanta	25	15
2678	A802	55b Covasna	25	15
2679	A802	55b Dimbovita	25	15
2680	A802	55b Dolj	25	15
2681	A802	55b Galati	25	15
2682	A802	55b Gorj	25	15
2683	A802	55b Harghita	25	15
2684	A802	55b Hunedoara	25	15
2685	A802	55b Ialomita	25	15
2686	A802	55b Iasi	25	15
2687	A802	55b Ilfov	25	15
2688	A802	55b Maramures	25	15
2689	A802	55b Mehedinti	25	15
2690	A802	55b Mures	25	15
2691	A802	55b Neamt	25	15
2692	A802	55b Olt	25	15
2693	A802	55b Prahova	25	15
2694	A802	55b Salaj	25	15
2695	A802	55b Satu-Mare	25	15
2696	A802	55b Sibiu	25	15
2697	A802	55b Suceava	25	15
2698	A802	55b Teleorman	25	15
2699	A802	55b Timis	25	15
2700	A802	55b Tulcea	25	15
2701	A802	55b Vaslui	25	15
2702	A802	55b Vilcea	25	15

2703	A802	55b Vrancea		25	15
2704	A802	55b Postal emblem		25	15
		Nos. 2665-2704 (40)		10.00	
		Set value			3.25

Sheets of 50 (10x5) contain 5 designs: Nos. 2665-2669; 2670-2674; 2675-2679; 2680-2684; 2685-2689; 2690-2694; 2695-2699; 2700-2704. Each row of 10 contains 5 pairs of each design.
Issue dates: Nos. 2665-2679, Dec. 20, 1976. Nos. 2680-2704, Sept. 5, 1977.

POSTA ROMANA   b55

Oxcart, by Grigorescu — A803

Paintings by Nicolae Grigorescu (1838-1907): 1 l, Self-portrait, vert. 1.50 l, Shepherdess. 2.15 l, Woman Spinning with Distaff. 3.40 l, Shepherd, vert. 4.80 l, Rest at Well.

1977, Jan. 20   Photo.   *Perf. 13½*

2705	A803	55b gray & multi		15	15
2706	A803	1 l gray & multi		20	15
2707	A803	1.50 l gray & multi		28	15
2708	A803	2.15 l gray & multi		38	15
2709	A803	3.40 l gray & multi		55	30
2710	A803	4.80 l gray & multi		85	38
		Nos. 2705-2710 (6)		2.41	
		Set value			1.00

Cheia Telecommunications Station — A804

1977, Feb. 1

2711	A804	55b multi	15	15

POSTA ROMANA   Red Deer A805

Protected Birds and Animals: 1 l, Mute swan. 1.50 l, Egyptian vulture. 2.15 l, Bison. 3.40 l, White-headed ruddy duck. 4.80 l, Kingfisher.

1977, Mar. 20   Photo.   *Perf. 13½*

2712	A805	55b multi		15	15
2713	A805	1 l multi		15	15
2714	A805	1.50 l multi		20	15
2715	A805	2.15 l multi		35	15
2716	A805	3.40 l multi		50	15
2717	A805	4.80 l multi		75	22
		Nos. 2712-2717 (6)		2.10	
		Set value			64

POSTA ROMANA

Calafat Artillery Unit, by Sava Hentia — A806

Paintings: 55b, Attacking Infantryman, by Oscar Obedeanu, vert. 1.50 l, Infantry Attack in Winter, by Stefan Luchian, vert. 2.15 l, Battle of Plevna (after etching). 3.40 l, Artillery, by Nicolae Ion Grigorescu. 10 l, Battle of Grivita, 1877.

1977

2718	A806	55b gold & multi		15	15
2719	A806	1 l gold & multi		15	15
2720	A806	1.50 l gold & multi		24	15
2721	A806	2.15 l gold & multi		60	15
2722	A806	3.40 l gold & multi		75	15
		Nos. 2718-2722,B442 (6)		3.14	
		Set value			70

Souvenir Sheet

2723	A806	10 l gold & multi	2.75	2.00

Centenary of Romania's independence. A 10 l imperf. souvenir sheet exists showing victorious return of army, Dobruja, 1878.
Issue dates: Nos. 2718-2722, May 9; No. 2723, Apr. 25.

Sinaia, Carpathian Mountains A807

Design: 2.40 l, Hotels, Aurora, Black Sea.

1977, May 17

2724	A807	2 l gold & multi		1.00	85
2725	A807	2.40 l gold & multi		1.40	1.25

Inter-European Cultural and Economic Cooperation. Nos. 2724-2725 printed in sheets of 4 with marginal inscriptions.

Petru Rares A808

Ion Luca Caragiale A809

1977, June 10   Photo.   *Perf. 13½*

2726	A808	40b multi	15	15

450th anniversary of the elevation of Petru Rares to Duke of Moldavia.

1977, June 10

2727	A809	55b multi	15	15

Ion Luca Caragiale (1852-1912), writer.

Red Cross Nurse, Children, Emblems A810

1977, June 10

2728	A810	1.50 l multi	35	15

23rd Intl. Red Cross Conf., Bucharest.

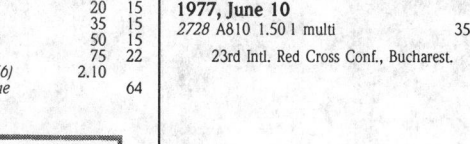

"Carpati" near Cazane, Iron Gate — A814

Designs: 1 l, "Mircesti" at Orsova. 1.50 l, "Oltenita" at Calafat. 2.15 l, Water bus at Giurgiu. 3 l, "Herculane" at Tulcea. 3.40 l, "Muntenia" in Nature preserve, Sulina. 4.80 l, Map of Danube Delta with Sulina Canal. 10 l, Danubius, god of Danube, from Trajan's Column, Rome, vert.

1977, Dec. 28

2737	A814	55b multi		15	15
2738	A814	1 l multi		15	15
2739	A814	1.50 l multi		24	15
2740	A814	2.15 l multi		40	15

Arch of Triumph, Bucharest A811

1977, June 10

2729	A811	2.15 l multi	50	15

Battles of Marasesti and Oituz, 60th anniv.

Peaks of San Marino, Exhibition Emblem — A812

1977, Aug. 28   Photo.   *Perf. 13½*

2730	A812	4 l brt bl & multi	1.00	25

Centenary of San Marino stamps, and San Marino '77 Phil. Exhib., San Marino, 8/28-9/4.

Man on Pommel Horse — A813

Gymnasts: 40b, Woman dancer. 55b, Man on parallel bars. 1 l, Woman on balance beam. 2.15 l, Man on rings. 4.80 l, Woman on double bars.

1977, Sept. 25   Photo.   *Perf. 13½*

2731	A813	20b multi		15	15
2732	A813	40b multi		15	15
2733	A813	55b multi		15	15
2734	A813	1 l multi		20	15
2735	A813	2.15 l multi		35	15
2736	A813	4.80 l multi		1.25	22
		Nos. 2731-2736 (6)		2.25	
		Set value			50

"Carpati" near Cazane, Iron Gate — A814

2741	A814	3 l multi		60	20
2742	A814	3.40 l multi		65	20
2743	A814	4.80 l multi		1.25	30
		Nos. 2737-2743 (7)		3.44	
		Set value			1.05

Souvenir Sheet

2744	A814	10 l multi	2.75	2.00

European Danube Commission.
A 10 l imperf. souvenir sheet exists showing map of Danube from Regensburg to the Black Sea.

Flag and Arms of Romania A815

Designs: 1.20 l, Computer production in Romania. 1.75 l, National Theater, Craiova.

1977, Dec. 30

2745	A815	55b multi		15	15
2746	A815	1.20 l multi		18	15
2747	A815	1.75 l multi		40	20
		Set value			32

Proclamation of Republic, 30th anniversary.

Dancers A816

Designs: Romanian male folk dancers.

1977, Nov. 28   Photo.   *Perf. 13½*

2748	A816	20b multi		15	15
2749	A816	40b multi		15	15
2750	A816	55b multi		15	15
2751	A816	1 l multi		15	15
2752	A816	2.15 l multi		38	15
2753	A816	4.80 l multi		1.25	20
		Nos. 2748-2753 (6)		2.23	
		Set value			50

Souvenir Sheet

2754	A816	10 l multi	2.00	2.00

Firiza Dam A817

Hydroelectric Stations and Dams: 40b, Negovanu. 55b, Piatra Neamt. 1 l, Izvorul Muntelui-Bicaz. 2.15 l, Vidraru. 4.80 l, Iron Gate.

1978, Mar. 10   Photo.   *Perf. 13½*

2755	A817	20b multi		15	15
2756	A817	40b multi		15	15
2757	A817	55b multi		15	15
2758	A817	1 l multi		15	15
2759	A817	2.15 l multi		35	15
2760	A817	4.80 l multi		1.00	20
		Set value			1.70	50

Soccer and Argentina '78 Emblem — A818

Designs: Various soccer scenes and Argentina '78 emblem.

1978, Apr. 15

2761	A818	55b bl & multi	15	15
2762	A818	1 l org & multi	15	15
2763	A818	1.50 l yel grn & multi	18	15
2764	A818	2.15 l ver & multi	30	15
2765	A818	3.40 l bl grn & multi	50	15
2766	A818	4.80 l lil rose & multi	1.00	22
		Nos. 2761-2766 (6)	2.28	
		Set value		56

11th World Cup Soccer Championship, Argentina '78, June 1-25. See No. C222.

King Decebalus of Dacia Statue, Deva A819

Design: 3.40 l, King Mircea the Elder of Wallachia statue, Tulcea, and ship.

1978, May 22   Photo.   Perf. 13½

2767	A819	1.30 l gold & multi	90	70
2768	A819	3.40 l gold & multi	1.65	1.25

Inter-European Cultural and Economic Cooperation. Each printed in sheet of 4.

Worker, Factory, Flag — A821   Spindle and Handle, Transilvania — A822

1978, June 11   Photo.   Perf. 13½

2770	A821	55b multi	15	15

Nationalization of industry, 30th anniv.

1978, June 20

Wood Carvings: 40b, Cheese molds, Muntenia. 55b, Spoons, Oltenia. 1 l, Barrel, Moldavia. 2.15 l, Ladle and mug, Transilvania. 4.80 l, Water bucket, Oltenia.

2771	A822	20b multi	15	15
2772	A822	40b multi	15	15
2773	A822	55b multi	15	15
2774	A822	1 l multi	15	15
2775	A822	2.15 l multi	30	15
2776	A822	4.80 l multi	1.00	22
		Set value	1.65	50

Danube Delta — A823

Tourist Publicity: 1 l, Bran Castle, vert. 1.50 l, Monastery, Suceava, Moldavia. 2.15 l, Caves, Oltenia. 3.40 l, Ski lift, Brasov. 4.80 l, Mangalia, Black Sea. 10 l, Strehaia Fortress, vert.

1978, July 20   Photo.   Perf. 13½

2777	A823	55b multi	15	15
2778	A823	1 l multi	15	15
2779	A823	1.50 l multi	20	15
2780	A823	2.15 l multi	30	15
2781	A823	3.40 l multi	50	18
2782	A823	4.80 l multi	1.00	35
		Nos. 2777-2782 (6)	2.30	
		Set value		85

Miniature Sheet

2783	A823	10 l multi	2.50	2.00

No. 2783 contains one 37x51mm stamp. Issued July 30.

Electronic Microscope A824

Designs: 40b, Hydraulic excavator. 55b, Computer center. 1.50 l, Oil derricks. 3 l, Harvester combine, horiz. 3.40 l, Petrochemical plant.

1978, Aug. 15   Photo.   Perf. 13½

2784	A824	20b multi	15	15
2785	A824	40b multi	15	15
2786	A824	55b multi	15	15
2787	A824	1.50 l multi	24	15
2788	A824	3 l multi	55	15
2789	A824	3.40 l multi	70	16
		Set value	1.70	45

Industrial development.

Polovraci Cave, Carpathians A825   "Racial Equality" A826

Caves: 1 l, Topolnita. 1.50 l, Ponoare. 2.15 l, Ratei, Mt. Bucegi. 3.40 l, Closani, Mt. Motrului. 4.80 l, Epuran. 1 l, 1.50 l, 4.80 l, Mt. Mehedinti.

1978, Aug. 25   Photo.   Perf. 13½

2790	A825	55b multi	15	15
2791	A825	1 l multi	15	15
2792	A825	1.50 l multi	20	15
2793	A825	2.15 l multi	30	15
2794	A825	3.40 l multi	50	15
2795	A825	4.80 l multi	1.00	22
		Nos. 2790-2795 (6)	2.30	
		Set value		58

1978, Sept. 28

2796	A826	3.40 l multi	50	20

Anti-Apartheid Year.

Woman Gymnast, Games' Emblem — A828

Games' Emblem and: 1 l, Running. 1.50 l, Skiing. 2.15 l, Equestrian. 3.40 l, Soccer. 4.80 l, Handball.

1978, Sept. 15

2803	A828	55b multi	15	15
2804	A828	1 l multi	15	15
2805	A828	1.50 l multi	20	15
2806	A828	2.15 l multi	30	15
2807	A828	3.40 l multi	50	15
2808	A828	4.80 l multi	1.00	26
		Nos. 2803-2808 (6)	2.30	
		Set value		72

Ptolemaic Map of Dacia A829

Designs: 55b, Meeting House of Romanian National Council, Arad. 1.75 l, Pottery vases, 8th-9th centuries, found near Arad.

1978, Oct. 21   Photo.   Perf. 13½

2809	A829	40b multi	15	15
2810	A829	55b multi	15	15
2811	A829	1.75 l multi	35	15
b.		Strip of 3, #2809-2811	50	30
		Set value	50	20

2,000th anniversary of founding of Arad.

Dacian Warrior, from Trajan's Column, Rome — A829a

1978, Nov. 5   Photo.   Perf. 13x13½

2811A	A829a	6 l + 3 l label	1.65	85

NATIONALA '78 Phil. Exhib., Bucharest. Stamp Day.

Gold Bas-relief A827

Designs: 40b, Gold armband. 55b, Gold cameo ring. 1 l, Silver bowl. 2.15 l, Eagle from Roman standard, vert. 4.80 l, Silver armband.

1978, Sept. 25

2797	A827	20b multi	15	15
2798	A827	40b multi	15	15
2799	A827	55b multi	15	15
2800	A827	1 l multi	15	15
2801	A827	2.15 l multi	30	15
2802	A827	4.80 l multi	1.00	35
		Set value	1.65	70

Daco-Roman archaeological treasures. An imperf. 10 l souvenir sheet exists showing gold helmet, vert.

Assembly at Alba Iulia, 1919 A830   Warrior, Bas-relief A831

Design: 1 l, Open book and Romanian flag.

1978, Dec. 1

2812	A830	55b gold & multi	15	15
2813	A830	1 l gold & multi	15	15
		Set value	24	15

60th anniversary of national unity.

1979   Photo.   Perf. 13½

Design: 1.50 l, Warrior on horseback, bas-relief.

2814	A831	55b multi	15	15
2815	A831	1.50 l multi	20	15
		Set value		15

2,050 years since establishment of first centralized and independent Dacian state.

"Heroes of Vaslui" — A832   Ice Hockey, Globe, Emblem — A833

Children's Drawings: 1 l, Building houses. 1.50 l, Folk music of Tica. 2.15 l, Industrial landscape, horiz. 3.40 l, winter customs, horiz. 4.80 l, Pioneer festival, horiz.

1979, Mar. 1

2816	A832	55b multi	15	15
2817	A832	1 l multi	15	15
2818	A832	1.50 l multi	20	15
2819	A832	2.15 l multi	30	15
2820	A832	3.40 l multi	50	15
2821	A832	4.80 l multi	1.00	26
		Nos. 2816-2821 (6)	2.30	
		Set value		60

International Year of the Child.

1979, Mar. 16   Photo.   Perf. 13½

Design: 3.40 l, Ice hockey players, globe and emblem.

2822	A833	1.30 l multi	28	15
2823	A833	3.40 l multi	55	20
a.		Pair, #2822-2823	85	50

European Youth Ice Hockey Championship, Miercurea-Ciuc (1.30 l) and World Ice Hockey Championship, Galati (3.40 l).

Dog's-tooth Violet — A834

Protected Flowers: 1 l, Alpine violet. 1.50 l, Linum borzaeanum. 2.15 l, Persian bindweed. 3.40 l, Primula auricula. 4.80 l, Transylvanian columbine.

1979, Apr. 25   Photo.   Perf. 13½

2824	A834	55b multi	15	15
2825	A834	1 l multi	15	15
2826	A834	1.50 l multi	20	15
2827	A834	2.15 l multi	30	15
2828	A834	3.40 l multi	50	26
2829	A834	4.80 l multi	1.00	26
		Nos. 2824-2829 (6)	2.30	
		Set value		65

Mail Coach and Post Rider, 19th Century A835

1979, May 3   Photo.   Perf. 13

2830	A835	1.30 l multi	40	24

Inter-European Cultural and Economic Cooperation. Printed in sheets of 4. See No. C231.

Oil Rig and Refinery — A836

Girl Pioneer — A837

1979, May 24   Photo.   *Perf. 13*
2832 A836 3.40 l multi   50 15

10th World Petroleum Congress, Bucharest.

1979, June 20
2833 A837 55b multi   15 15

30th anniversary of Romanian Pioneers.

Children with Flowers, IYC Emblem — A838

IYC Emblem and: 1 l, Kindergarten. 2 l, Pioneers with rabbit. 4.60 l, Drummer, trumpeters, flags.

1979, July 18   Photo.   *Perf. 13½*
2834 A838 40b multi   15 15
2835 A838 1 l multi   15 15
2836 A838 2 l multi   30 15
2837 A838 4.60 l multi   95 18
       Set value   38

International Year of the Child.

Lady in a Garden, by Tattarescu — A839

Stefan Gheorghiu — A840

Paintings by Gheorghe Tattarescu: 40b, Mountain woman. 55b, Mountain man. 1 l, Portrait of Gh. Magheru. 2.15 l, The artist's daughter. 4.80 l, Self-portrait.

1979, June 16
2838 A839 20b multi   15 15
2839 A839 40b multi   15 15
2840 A839 55b multi   15 15
2841 A839 1 l multi   15 15
2842 A839 2.15 l multi   28 15
2843 A839 4.80 l multi   90 22
       Set value   1.50 50

1979, Aug.
Designs: 55b, Gheorghe Lazar monument. 2.15 l, Lupeni monument. 4.60 l, Women in front of Memorial Arch.

2844 A840 40b multi   15 15
2845 A840 55b multi   15 15
2846 A840 2.15 l multi   30 15
2847 A840 4.60 l multi   95 18
       Set value   35

State Theater, Tirgu-Mures — A841

Modern Architecture: 40b, University, Brasov. 55b, Political Administration Buildings, Baia Mare. 1 l, Stefan Gheorghiu Academy, Bucharest. 2.15 l, Political Administration Building, Botosani. 4.80 l, House of Culture, Tirgoviste.

1979, June 25
2848 A841 20b multi   15 15
2849 A841 40b multi   15 15
2850 A841 55b multi   15 15
2851 A841 1 l multi   15 15
2852 A841 2.15 l multi   24 15
2853 A841 4.80 l multi   85 22
       Set value   1.35 50

Flags of Russia and Romania — A842

Design: 1 l, Workers' Militia, by L. Suhar, horiz.

1979, Aug. 20   Photo.   *Perf. 13½*
2854 A842 55b multi   15 15
2855 A842 1 l multi   18 15
       Set value   25 15

Liberation from Fascism, 35th anniversary.

Cargo Ship Galati — A843

Romanian Ships: 1 l, Cargo ship Bucuresti. 1.50 l, Ore carrier Resita. 2.15 l, Ore carrier Tomis. 3.40 l, Tanker Dacia. 4.80 l, Tanker Independenta.

1979, Aug. 27   Photo.   *Perf. 13½*
2856 A843 55b multi   15 15
2857 A843 1 l multi   15 15
2858 A843 1.50 l multi   18 15
2859 A843 2.15 l multi   28 15
2860 A843 3.40 l multi   45 15
2861 A843 4.80 l multi   90 25
       Nos. 2856-2861 (6)   2.11
       Set value   65

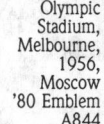

Olympic Stadium, Melbourne, 1956, Moscow '80 Emblem — A844

Moscow '80 Emblem and Olympic Stadiums: 1 l, Rome, 1960. 1.50 l, Tokyo, 1964. 2.15 l, Mexico City, 1968. 3.40 l, Munich, 1972. 4.80 l, Montreal, 1976. 10 l, Moscow, 1980.

1979, Oct. 23   Photo.   *Perf. 13½*
2862 A844 55b multi   15 15
2863 A844 1 l multi   15 15
2864 A844 1.50 l multi   20 15
2865 A844 2.15 l multi   30 15
2866 A844 3.40 l multi   50 15
2867 A844 4.80 l multi   1.00 25
       Nos. 2862-2867 (6)   2.30

Souvenir Sheet
2868 A844 10 l multi   2.50 2.00

22nd Summer Olympic Games, Moscow, July 19-Aug. 3, 1980. No. 2868 contains one 50x38mm stamp.
No. 2868 airmail.

Arms of Alba Iulia — A845

Designs: Arms of Romanian cities.

1979, Oct. 25
2869 A845 1.20 l shown   28 15
2870 A845 1.20 l Arad   28 15
2871 A845 1.20 l Bacau   28 15
2872 A845 1.20 l Baia-Mare   28 15
2873 A845 1.20 l Birlad   28 15
2874 A845 1.20 l Botosani   28 15
2875 A845 1.20 l Braila   28 15
2876 A845 1.20 l Brasov   28 15
2877 A845 1.20 l Buzau   28 15
2878 A845 1.20 l Calarasi   28 15
2879 A845 1.20 l Cluj   28 15
2880 A845 1.20 l Constanta   28 15
2881 A845 1.20 l Craiova   28 15
2882 A845 1.20 l Dej   28 15
2883 A845 1.20 l Deva   28 15
2884 A845 1.20 l Turnu-Severin   28 15
2885 A845 1.20 l Focsani   28 15
2886 A845 1.20 l Galati   28 15
2887 A845 1.20 l Gheorghe Ghe-
                 orghiu-Dej   28 15
2888 A845 1.20 l Giurgiu   28 15
2889 A845 1.20 l Hunedoara   28 15
2890 A845 1.20 l Iasi   28 15
2891 A845 1.20 l Lugoj   28 15
2892 A845 1.20 l Medias   28 15
2893 A845 1.20 l Odorheiu
                 Seguiesc   28 15

1980, Jan. 5
2894 A845 1.20 l Oradea   28 15
2895 A845 1.20 l Petrosani   28 15
2896 A845 1.20 l Piatra-Neamt   28 15
2897 A845 1.20 l Pitesti   28 15
2898 A845 1.20 l Ploiesti   28 15
2899 A845 1.20 l Resita   28 15
2900 A845 1.20 l Rimnicu-Vilcea   28 15
2901 A845 1.20 l Roman   28 15
2902 A845 1.20 l Satu-Mare   28 15
2903 A845 1.20 l Sibiu   28 15
2904 A845 1.20 l Siget-Marmatiei   28 15
2905 A845 1.20 l Sighisoara   28 15
2906 A845 1.20 l Suceava   28 15
2907 A845 1.20 l Tecuci   28 15
2908 A845 1.20 l Timisoara   28 15
2909 A845 1.20 l Tirgoviste   28 15
2910 A845 1.20 l Tirgu-Jiu   28 15
2911 A845 1.20 l Tirgu-Mures   28 15
2912 A845 1.20 l Tulcea   28 15
2913 A845 1.20 l Turda   28 15
2914 A845 1.20 l Turnu Magurele   28 15
2915 A845 1.20 l Bucharest   28 15
       Nos. 2869-2915 (47)   13.16
       Set value   3.70

A846   A847

Regional Costumes: 20b, Maramures Woman. 40b, Maramures man. 55b, Vrancea woman. 1.50 l, Vrancea man. 3 l, Padureni woman. 3.40 l, Padureni man.

1979, Oct. 27
2916 A846 20b multi   15 15
2917 A846 40b multi   15 15
2918 A846 55b multi   15 15
2919 A846 1.50 l multi   24 15
2920 A846 3 l multi   48 15
2921 A846 3.40 l multi   55 15
       Set value   1.45 45

1979, July 27
Flower Paintings by Stefan Luchian: 40b, Snapdragons. 60b, Triple chrysanthemums. 1.55 l, Potted flowers on stairs.

2922 A847 40b multi   15 15
2923 A847 60b multi   15 15
2924 A847 1.55 l multi   24 15
       Set value   42 22

Socflex, International Philatelic Exhibition, Bucharest. See Nos. B445-B446.

Souvenir Sheet

Romanian Communist Party, 12th Congress — A848

1979, Oct.
2925 A848 5 l multi   1.25 50

Figure Skating, Lake Placid '80 Emblem, Olympic Rings — A849

1979, Dec. 27   Photo.   *Perf. 13½*
2926 A849 55b shown   15 15
2927 A849 1 l Downhill skiing   15 15
2928 A849 1.50 l Biathlon   20 15
2929 A849 2.15 l Two-man bobsled-
               ding   28 15
2930 A849 3.40 l Speed skating   50 15
2931 A849 4.80 l Ice hockey   1.00 22
       Nos. 2926-2931 (6)   2.28
       Set value   60

Souvenir Sheet
2932 A849 10 l Ice hockey, diff.   2.25 1.75

13th Winter Olympic Games, Lake Placid, NY, Feb. 12-24, 1980. No. 2932 contains one 38x50mm stamp. An imperf. 10 l air post souvenir sheet exists showing four-man bobsledding.

"Calugareni", Expo Emblem — A850

1979, Dec. 29
2933 A850 55b shown   15 15
2934 A850 1 l "Orleans"   15 15
2935 A850 1.50 l #1059, type fawn   20 15
2936 A850 2.15 l #15021, type 1E   30 15
2937 A850 3.40 l "Pacific"   50 15
2938 A850 4.80 l Electric engine
               060-EA   1.00 26
       Nos. 2933-2938 (6)   2.30
       Set value   65

Souvenir Sheet
2939 A850 10 l Diesel electric   2.50 2.00

Intl. Transport Expo., Hamburg, June 8-July 1. #2939 contains one 50x40mm stamp.

Dacian Warrior,
Trajan's Column,
Rome — A851

Design: 1.50 l, Two warriors.

1980, Feb. 9　Photo.　Perf. 13¹/₂
2940	A851	55b multi	15	15
2941	A851	1.50 l multi	30	15
		Set value		16

2,050 years since establishment of first central-ized and independent Dacian state.

Kingfisher — A852

1980, Mar. 25　Photo.　Perf. 13¹/₂
2942	A852	55b shown	15	15
2943	A852	1 l Great white heron, vert.	15	15
2944	A852	1.50 l Red-breasted goose	18	15
2945	A852	2.15 l Red deer, vert.	26	15
2946	A852	3.40 l Roe deer	45	15
2947	A852	4.80 l European bison, vert.	90	26
		Nos. 2942-2947 (6)	2.09	
		Set value		65

European Nature Protection Year. A 10 l imperf. souvenir sheet exists showing bears; red control number. See No. C232.

Souvenir Sheets

George
Enescu
Playing
Violin
A853

1980, May 6
2948		Sheet of 4	1.75	1.75
a.	A853	1.30 l shown	28	16
b.	A853	1.30 l Conducting	28	16
c.	A853	1.30 l Playing piano	28	16
d.	A853	1.30 l Composing	28	16
2949		Sheet of 4	3.75	3.75
a.	A853	3.40 l Beethoven in library	80	28
b.	A853	3.40 l Portrait	80	28
c.	A853	3.40 l At piano	80	28
d.	A853	3.40 l Composing	80	28

Inter-European Cultural and Economic Cooperation.

Vallota Purpurea　　Tudor
A854　　　　　　　Vladimirescu
　　　　　　　　　　A855

1980, Apr. 10　Photo.　Perf. 13¹/₂
2050	A854	55b shown	15	15
2951	A854	1 l Eichhornia crasipes	15	15
2952	A854	1.50 l Sprekelia formosis-sima	20	15
2953	A854	2.15 l Hypericum calycinum	30	15

2954	A854	3.40 l Camellia japonica	50	15
2955	A854	4.80 l Nelumbo nucifera	1.00	25
		Nos. 2950-2955 (6)	2.30	
		Set value		65

1980, Apr. 24

Designs: 55b, Mihail Sadoveanu. 1.50 l, Battle against Hungarians. 2.15 l, Tudor Arghezi. 3 l, Horea.

2956	A855	40b multi	15	15
2957	A855	55b multi	15	15
2958	A855	1.50 l multi	20	15
2959	A855	2.15 l multi	30	15
2960	A855	3 l multi	40	18
		Set value	1.00	52

Anniversaries: 40b, Tudor Vladimirescu (1780-1821), leader of 1821 revolution; 55b, Mihail Sadoveanu (1880-1961), author; 1.50 l, Victory of Posada; 2.15 l, Tudor Arghezi (1880-1967), poet; 3 l, Horea (1730-1785), leader of 1784 uprising.

A856　　　　　　　A857

Dacian fruit bowl and cup.

1980, May 8
2961	A856	1 l multicolored	18	15

Petrodava City, 2000th anniversary.

1980, June 20　Photo.　Perf. 13¹/₂
2962	A857	55b Javelin	15	15
2963	A857	1 l Fencing	15	15
2964	A857	1.50 l Shooting	20	15
2965	A857	2.15 l Kayak	30	15
2966	A857	3.40 l Wrestling	50	15
2967	A857	4.80 l Rowing	1.00	26
		Nos. 2962-2967 (6)	2.30	
		Set value		65

Souvenir Sheet
2968	A857	10 l Handball	2.25	1.75

22nd Summer Olympic Games, Moscow, July 19-Aug. 3. No. 2968 contains one 38x50mm stamp. An imperf. 10 l air post souvenir sheet exists showing gymnast.

Congress　　　　Fireman Rescuing
Emblem — A858　　Child — A859

1980, Aug. 10　Photo.　Perf. 13¹/₂
2969	A858	55b multicolored	15	15

15th Intl. Historical Sciences Congress, Bucharest.

1980, Aug. 25
2970	A859	55b multicolored	15	15

Firemen's Day, Sept. 13.

Chinese and
Romanian Young
Pioneers at Stamp
Show — A860

1980, Sept. 18
2971	A860	1 l multicolored	20	15

Romanian-Chinese Phil. Exhib., Bucharest.

Souvenir Sheet

Parliament
Building,
Bucharest
A861

1980, Sept. 30
2972	A861	10 l multicolored	2.00	1.65

European Security Conference, Madrid. An imperf. 10 l air post souvenir sheet exists showing Plaza Mayor, Madrid.

Knights and
Chessboard
A862

1980, Oct. 1　Photo.　Perf. 13¹/₂
2973	A862	55b shown	15	15
2974	A862	1 l Rooks	15	15
2975	A862	2.15 l Man	30	15
2976	A862	4.80 l Woman	1.00	26
		Set value		45

Chess Olympiad, Valletta, Malta, Nov. 20-Dec. 8.

Dacian　　　　　Burebista
Warrior — A863　Sculpture — A864

1980, Oct. 15
2977	A863	20b shown	15	15
2978	A863	40b Moldavian soldier, 15th cent.	15	15
2979	A863	55b Walachian horseman, 17th cent.	15	15
2980	A863	1 l Flag bearer, 19th cent.	15	15
2981	A863	1.50 l Infantryman, 19th cent.	20	15
2982	A863	2.15 l Lancer, 19th cent.	30	15
2983	A863	4.80 l Mounted Elite Corps Guard, 19th cent.	1.00	35
		Set value	1.85	80

1980, Nov. 5　Photo.　Perf. 13¹/₂
2984	A864	2 l multicolored	35	15

2050 years since establishment of first central-ized and independent Dacian state.

George Oprescu　　National Dog
(1881-1969), Art　　Show — A866
Critic — A865

Famous Men: 2.15 l, Marius Bunescu (1881-1971), painter. 3.40 l, Ion Georgescu (1856-1898), sculptor.

1981, Feb. 20　Photo.　Perf. 13¹/₂
2985	A865	1.50 l multi	20	15
2986	A865	2.15 l multi	30	15
2987	A865	3.40 l multi	50	24
		Set value		48

1981, Mar. 15

Designs: Dogs. 40b, 1 l, 1.50 l, 3.40 l horiz.

2988	A866	40b Mountain sheep-dog	15	15
2989	A866	55b Saint Bernard	15	15
2990	A866	1 l Fox terrier	15	15
2991	A866	1.50 l German shepherd	20	15
2992	A866	2.15 l Boxer	30	15
2993	A866	3.40 l Dalmatian	50	16
2994	A866	4.80 l Poodle	1.00	22
		Nos. 2988-2994 (7)	2.45	
		Set value		68

River
Steamer
Stefan
cel Mare
A867

1981, Mar. 25
2995	A867	55b shown	15	15
2996	A867	1 l Vas de Supraveghere	15	15
2997	A867	1.50 l Tudor Vladimirescu	24	15
2998	A867	2.15 l Dredger Sulina	30	15
2999	A867	3.40 l Republica Populara Romana	50	24
3000	A867	4.80 l Sulina Canal	1.00	35
		Nos. 2995-3000 (6)	2.34	
		Set value		95

Souvenir Sheet
3001	A867	10 l Galati	2.50	2.00

European Danube Commission, 125th anniv. An imperf. 10 l souvenir sheet exists showing map of Danube.

Carrier
Pigeon
A868

Designs: Various carrier pigeons and doves.

1981, Apr. 15　Photo.　Perf. 13¹/₂
3002	A868	40b multi	15	15
3003	A868	55b multi	15	15
3004	A868	1 l multi	15	15
3005	A868	1.50 l multi	20	15
3006	A868	2.15 l multi	30	15
3007	A868	3.40 l multi	50	24
		Nos. 3002-3007 (6)	1.45	
		Set value		65

Romanian
Communist Party,
60th
Anniv. — A869

Singing Romania
Festival — A871

Folkdance,
Moldavia
A870

1981, Apr. 22   Photo.   Perf. 13½
3008 A869   1 l multicolored   18   15

1981, May 4   Photo.   Perf. 13½
Designs: Regional folkdances.

3009   Sheet of 4   2.50 2.50
  a. A870 2.50 l shown   45   45
  b. A870 2.50 l Transylvania   45   45
  c. A870 2.50 l Banat   45   45
  d. A870 2.50 l Muntenia   45   45
3010   Sheet of 4   2.50 2.50
  a. A870 2.50 l Maramures   45   45
  b. A870 2.50 l Dobruja   45   45
  c. A870 2.50 l Oltenia   45   45
  d. A870 2.50 l Crisana   45   45

Inter-European Cultural and Economic
Cooperation.

1981, July 15
3011 A871   55b Industry   15   15
3012 A871 1.50 l Electronics   24   15
3013 A871 2.15 l Agriculture   35   18
3014 A871 3.40 l Culture   50   30
             Set value   62

University '81
Games,
Bucharest
A872

Theodor Aman,
Artist, Birth
Sesquicentennial
A873

1981, July 17
3015 A872   1 l Book, flag   15   15
3016 A872 2.15 l Emblem   35   18
3017 A872 4.80 l Stadium, horiz.   1.00   35

1981, July 28
Aman Paintings: 40b, Self-portrait. 55b, Battle of
Giurgiu. 1 l, The Family Picnic. 1.50 l, The
Painter's Studio. 2.15 l, Woman in Interior. 3.40 l,
Aman Museum, Bucharest. 55b, 1 l, 1.50 l, 3.40 l
horiz.

3018 A873   40b multi   15   15
3019 A873   55b multi   15   15
3020 A873   1 l multi   15   15
3021 A873 1.50 l multi   28   15
3022 A873 2.15 l multi   35   18
3023 A873 3.40 l multi   60   24
        Nos. 3018-3023 (6)   1.68
             Set value   68

Thinker of Cernavoda,
3rd Cent. BC — A874

1981, July 30
3024 A874 3.40 l multi   50   24
16th Science History Congress.

Blood Donation
Campaign — A875

Romanian
Musicians — A877

Bucharest Central Military Hospital
Sesquicentennial — A876

1981, Aug. 15   Photo.   Perf. 13½
3025 A875 55b multicolored   15   15

1981, Sept. 1
3026 A876 55b multicolored   15   15

1981, Sept. 20
Designs: 40b, George Enescu (1881-1955). 55b,
Paul Constantinescu (1909-1963). 1 l, Dinu Lipatti
(1917-1950). 1.50 l, Ionel Perlea (1900-1970).
2.15 l, Ciprian Porumbescu (1853-1883). 3.40 l,
Mihail Jora (1891-1971).

3027 A877   40b multi   15   15
3028 A877   55b multi   15   15
3029 A877   1 l multi   15   15
3030 A877 1.50 l multi   28   15
3031 A877 2.15 l multi   35   18
3032 A877 3.40 l multi   50   24
        Nos. 3027-3032 (6)   1.58
             Set value   72

Stamp
Day — A879

1981, Nov. 5   Photo.   Perf. 13½
3034 A879   2 l multicolored   35   15

Children's
Games — A880

Illustrations by Eugen Palade (40b, 55b, 1 l) and
Norman Rockwell.

1981, Nov. 25
3035 A880   40b Hopscotch   15   15
3036 A880   55b Soccer   15   15
3037 A880   1 l Riding stick horse   15   15
3038 A880 1.50 l Snagging the Big
                One   24   15
3039 A880 2.15 l A Patient Friend   30   18
3040 A880   3 l Doggone It   40   20
3041 A880   4 l Puppy Love   48   35
     Nos. 3035-3041, C243 (8)   2.39
             Set value   1.25

A881   A882

1981, Dec. 28
3042 A881   55b multi   15   15
3043 A881   1 l multi   18   15
3044 A881 1.50 l multi   28   15
3045 A881 2.15 l multi   35   18
3046 A881 3.40 l multi   50   24
3047 A881 4.80 l multi   1.00   38
        Nos. 3042-3047 (6)   2.46
             Set value   1.00

Souvenir Sheet
3048 A881   10 l multi   2.00 2.00

Espana '82 World Cup Soccer.
No. 3048 contains one 38x50mm stamp. An
imperf. 10 l air post souvenir sheet exists showing
game.

1982, Jan. 30   Photo.   Perf. 13½
Designs: 1 l, Prince Alexander the Good of Mol-
davia (ruled 1400-1432). 1.50 l, Bogdan Petriceicu
Hasdeu (1838-1907), scholar. 2.15 l, Nicolae
Titulescu (1882-1941), diplomat.

3049 A882   1 l multi   20   15
3050 A882 1.50 l multi   28   15
3051 A882 2.15 l multi   38   20

Bucharest
Subway
System
A883

1982, Feb. 25
3052 A883   60b Union Square station
                entrance   15   15
3053 A883 2.40 l Heroes' Station plat-
                form   40   24
             Set value   32

60th Anniv. of
Communist Youth
Union — A884

1982
3054 A884   1 l shown   20   15
3055 A884 1.20 l Construction work-
                er   20   15
3056 A884 1.50 l Farm workers   28   15
3057 A884   2 l Research   35   18
3058 A884 2.50 l Workers   50   24
3059 A884   3 l Musicians, dancers   60   28
        Nos. 3054-3059 (6)   2.13
             Set value   94

Dog Sled
A885

1 l, 3 l, 4 l, 4.80 l, 5 l, vertical.

1982, Mar. 28   Photo.   Perf. 13½
3060 A885   55b Dog rescuing child   15   15
3061 A885   1 l Shepherd, dog   18   15
3062 A885   3 l Hunting dog   55   35
3063 A885 3.40 l shown   60   35
3064 A885   4 l Spitz, woman   70   40
3065 A885 4.80 l Guide dog, woman   80   45
3066 A885   5 l Dalmatian, girl   95   48
3067 A885   6 l Saint Bernard   1.00   40
        Nos. 3060-3067 (8)   4.93 2.73

Bran Castle,
Brasov,
1377
A886

1982, May 6
3068   Sheet of 4   2.50 2.50
  a. A886 2.50 l shown   55   55
  b. A886 2.50 l Hunedoara, Corvinilor,
                1409   55   55
  c. A886 2.50 l Sinaia, 1873   55   55
  d. A886 2.50 l Iasi, 1905   55   55
3069   Sheet of 4   2.50 2.50
  a. A886 2.50 l Neuschwanstein   55   55
  b. A886 2.50 l Stolzenfels   55   55
  c. A886 2.50 l Katz-Loreley   55   55
  d. A886 2.50 l Linderhof   55   55

Inter-European Cultural and Economic
Cooperation.

Souvenir Sheet

Constantin
Brancusi in
Paris
Studio
A887

1982, June 5
3070 A887   10 l multicolored   2.00 1.65

PHILEXFRANCE '82 Intl. Stamp Exhibition,
Paris, June 11-21.

Gloria C-16 Combine Harvester — A888

1982, June 29
3071 A888   50b shown   15   15
3072 A888   1 l Dairy farm   18   15
3073 A888 1.50 l Apple orchard   28   15
3074 A888 2.50 l Vineyard   40   20
3075 A888   3 l Irrigation   50   28
     Nos. 3071-3075, C250 (6)   2.11
             Set value   1.00

Souvenir Sheet
3076 A888   10 l Village   2.00 1.65

Agricultural modernization. No. 3076 contains
one 50x38mm stamp.

A890   A891

Resort Hotels and Beaches. 1 l, 2.50 l, 3 l, 5 l horiz.

1982, Aug. 30   Photo.   Perf. 13½

3078	A890	50b Baile Felix	15	15
3079	A890	1 l Predeal	20	15
3080	A890	1.50 l Baile Herculane	28	15
3081	A890	2.50 l Eforie Nord	40	16
3082	A890	3 l Olimp	60	20
3083	A890	5 l Neptun	95	32
		Nos. 3078-3083 (6)	2.58	
		Set value		85

1982, Sept. 6

Designs: 1 l, Legend, horiz. 1.50 l, Contrasts, horiz. 3.50 l, Relay Runner, horiz. 4 l, Genesis of Romanian People, by Sabin Balasa.

3084	A891	1 l multicolored	20	15
3085	A891	1.50 l multicolored	28	15
3086	A891	3.50 l multicolored	60	28
3087	A891	4 l multicolored	75	40
		Set value		85

Souvenir Sheet

Merry Peasant Girl, by Nicolae Grigorescu (d. 1907) A892

1982, Sept. 30   Photo.   Perf. 13½

| 3088 | A892 | 10 l multicolored | 1.75 | 1.75 |

Bucharest Intl. Fair — A893

1982, Oct. 2

| 3089 | A893 | 2 l Exhibition Hall, flag | 35 | 18 |

Savings Week, Oct. 25-31 — A894   Stamp Day — A895

1982, Oct. 25

3090	A894	1 l Girl holding bank book	18	15
3091	A894	2 l Poster	35	18
		Set value		26

1982, Nov. 10

3092	A895	1 l Woman letter carrier	18	15
3093	A895	2 l Mailman	35	18
		Set value		26

Scene from Ileana Sinziana, by Petre Ispirescu — A896

Arms, Colors, Book — A897

Fairytales: 50b, The Youngest Child and the Golden Apples, by Petre Ispirescu. 1 l, The Bear Hoaxed by the Fox, by Ion Creanga. 1.50 l, The Prince of Tear, by Mihai Eminescu. 2.50 l, The Little Bag with Two Coins Inside, by Ion Creanga. 5 l, Danila Prepeleac, by Ion Creanga.

1982, Nov. 30

3094	A896	50b multicolored	15	15
3095	A896	1 l multicolored	18	15
3096	A896	1.50 l multicolored	28	15
3097	A896	2.50 l multicolored	42	15
3098	A896	3 l multicolored	50	15
3099	A896	5 l multicolored	95	30
		Nos. 3094-3099 (6)	2.48	
		Set value		78

1982, Dec. 16

3100	A897	1 l Closed book	18	15
3101	A897	2 l Open book	35	18
		Set value		26

Natl. Communist Party Conference, Bucharest, Dec. 16-18.

A898

Designs: 50b, Wooden flask, Suceava. 1 l, Ceramic plate, Radauti. 1.50 l, Wooden scoop, Valea Mare, horiz. 2 l, Plate, jug, Vama. 3 l, Butter churn, wooden bucket, Moldavia. 3.50 l, Ceramic plates, Leheceni, horiz. 4 l, Wooden spoon, platter, Cluj. 5 l, Bowl, pitcher, Marginea. 6 l, Jug, flask, Bihor. 7 l, Spindle, shuttle, Transylvania. 7.50 l, Water buckets, Suceava. 8 l, Jug, Oboga; plate, Horezu. 10 l, Water buckets, Hunedoara, Suceava, horiz. 20 l, Wooden flask, beakers, Horezu. 30 l, Wooden spoons, Alba, horiz. 50 l, Ceramic dishes, Horezu.

1982, Dec. 22   Photo.   Perf. 13½

3102	A898	50b red orange	15	15
3103	A898	1 l dark blue	16	15
3104	A898	1.50 l orange brn	25	15
3105	A898	2 l brt blue	30	15
3106	A898	3 l olive green	45	15
3107	A898	3.50 l dk green	55	15
3108	A898	4 l lt brown	60	15
3109	A898	5 l gray blue	75	15

Size: 23x29mm, 29x23mm

3110	A898	6 l blue	90	15
3111	A898	7 l lake	1.10	15
3112	A898	7.50 l red violet	1.25	15
3113	A898	8 l brt green	1.25	15
3114	A898	10 l red	1.50	15
3115	A898	20 l purple	3.25	15
3116	A898	30 l Prus blue	4.50	38
3117	A898	50 l dark brown	8.00	65
		Nos. 3102-3117 (16)	24.96	
		Set value		2.10

35th Anniv. of Republic A899   Grigore Manolescu (1857-92), as Hamlet A900

1982, Dec. 27

3118	A899	1 l Symbols of development	18	15
3119	A899	2 l Flag	35	18
		Set value		26

1983, Feb. 28

Actors or Actresses in Famous Roles: 50b, Matei Millo (1814-1896) in The Discontented. 1 l, Mihail Pascaly (1829-1882) in Director Milo. 1.50 l, Aristizza Romanescu (1854-1918), in The Dogs. 2 l, C. I. Nottara (1859-1935) in Snowstorm. 3 l, Agatha Birsescu (1857-1939) in Medea. 4 l, Ion Brezeanu (1869-1940) in The Lost Letter. 5 l, Aristide Demetriad (1872-1930) in The Despotic Prince.

3120	A900	50b multi	15	15
3121	A900	1 l multi	18	15
3122	A900	1.50 l multi	28	15
3123	A900	2 l multi	35	15
3124	A900	2.50 l multi	42	15
3125	A900	3 l multi	50	15
3126	A900	4 l multi	70	26
3127	A900	5 l multi	85	30
		Nos. 3120-3127 (8)	3.43	
		Set value		1.15

Hugo Grotius (1583-1645), Dutch Jurist — A901

1983, Apr. 30

| 3128 | A901 | 2 l brown | 35 | 15 |

Romanian-Made Vehicles — A902

1983, May 3

3129	A902	50b ARO-10	15	15
3130	A902	1 l Dacia, 1300 station wagon	18	15
3131	A902	1.50 l ARO-242 jeep	25	15
3132	A902	2.50 l ARO-244	42	18
3133	A902	4 l Dacia 1310	70	35
3134	A902	5 l OLTCIT club passenger car	85	40
		Nos. 3129-3134 (6)	2.55	
		Set value		1.15

Johannes Kepler (1571-1630) — A903

Famous Men: No. 3135: b, Alexander von Humboldt (1769-1859), explorer. c, Goethe (1749-1832). d, Richard Wagner (1813-1883), composer. No. 3136: a, Ioan Andreescu (1850-1882), painter. b, George Constantinescu (1881-1965), engineer. c, Tudor Arghezi (1880-1967), poet. d, C.I. Parhon (1874-1969), endocrinologist.

1983, May 16

3135		Sheet of 4	2.50	2.50
a.-d.	A903	3 l multicolored	55	55
3136		Sheet of 4	2.50	2.50
a.-d.	A903	3 l multicolored	55	55

Inter-European Cultural and Economic Cooperation.

Workers' Struggle, 50th Anniv. — A904   Birds — A905

1983, July 22   Photo.   Perf. 13½

| 3137 | A904 | 2 l silver & multi | 35 | 18 |

1983, Oct. 28   Photo.   Perf. 13½

3138	A905	50b Luscinia svecica	15	15
3139	A905	1 l Sturnus roseus	16	15
3140	A905	1 l Coracias garrulus	22	15
3141	A905	2.50 l Merops apiaster	38	20
3142	A905	4 l Emberiza schoeniclus	65	35
3143	A905	5 l Lanius minor	75	42
		Nos. 3138-3143 (6)	2.31	
		Set value		1.20

Water Sports A906

1983, Sept. 16   Photo.   Perf. 13½

3144	A906	50b Kayak	15	15
3145	A906	1 l Water polo	16	15
3146	A906	1.50 l Canadian one-man canoes	22	15
3147	A906	2.50 l Diving	35	15
3148	A906	4 l Singles rowing	60	22
3149	A906	5 l Swimming	70	28
		Nos. 3144-3149 (6)	2.18	
		Set value		80

Stamp Day A907

1983, Oct. 24

| 3150 | A907 | 1 l Mailman on bicycle | 18 | 15 |
| 3151 | A907 | 3.50 l with 3 l label, flag | 1.10 | 55 |

Souvenir Sheet

| 3152 | A907 | 10 l Unloading mail plane | 1.75 | 1.75 |

#3152 is airmail, contains one 38x51mm stamp.

Geum Reptans A908

Flora (No. 3154): b, Papaver dubium. c, Carlina acaulis. d, Paeonia peregrina. e, Gentiana excisa. Fauna (No. 3155): a, Sciurus vulgaria. b, Grammia quenselii. c, Dendrocopos medius. d, Lynx. e, Tichodroma muraria.

1983, Oct. 28   Photo.   Perf. 13½

3154		Strip of 5	1.40	1.40
a.-e.	A908	1 l multicolored	24	24
3155		Strip of 5	1.40	1.40
a.-e.	A908	1 l multicolored	24	24

Issued in sheets of 15.

Lady with Feather,
by Cornelius
Baba — A909

1983, Nov. 3
3156	A909	1 l shown	18	15
3157	A909	2 l Citizens	35	15
3158	A909	3 l Farmers, horiz.	50	18
3159	A909	4 l Resting in the Field, horiz.	70	26
		Set value		64

A910   A911

1983, Nov. 30
3160	A910	1 l Banner, emblem	16	15
3161	A910	2 l Congress building, flags	30	18
		Set value		26

Pact with Romania, 65th anniv.

1983, Dec. 17

Designs: 1 l, Flags of participating countries, post office, mailman. 2 l, Congress building, woman letter carrier. 10 l, Flags, Congress building.

3162	A911	1 l multicolored	16	15
3163	A911	2 l multicolored	30	15
		Set value		20

Souvenir Sheet
| 3164 | A911 | 10 l multicolored | 1.65 | 1.65 |

BALKANFILA '83 Stamp Exhibition, Bucharest. #3164 contains one 38x50mm stamp.

Souvenir Sheet

Orient Express Centenary (Paris-Istanbul) — A912

1983, Dec. 30
| 3165 | A912 | 10 l Leaving Gara de Nord, Bucharest, 1883 | 2.50 | 2.50 |

1984 Winter
Olympics
A913

1984, Jan. 14
3166	A913	50b Cross-country skiing	15	15
3167	A913	1 l Biathlon	16	15
3168	A913	1.50 l Figure skating	22	15
3169	A913	2 l Speed skating	30	15
3170	A913	3 l Hockey	42	18
3171	A913	3.50 l Bobsledding	52	22
3172	A913	4 l Luge	60	26
3173	A913	5 l Skiing	75	32
		Nos. 3166-3173 (8)	3.12	
		Set value		1.30

A 10 l imperf souvenir sheet exists showing ski jumping.

Souvenir Sheet

Prince Alexandru Ioan Cuza,
Arms — A914

1984, Jan. 24   Photo.   Perf. 13½
| 3174 | A914 | 10 l multi | 1.75 | 1.75 |

Union of Moldavia and Walachia Provinces, 125th anniv.

Palace of Udriste
Naturel (1596-
1658), Chancery
Official — A915

Miron Costin
(1633-91),
Poet — A916

Famous Men: 1.50 l, Crisan (Marcu Giurgiu), (1733-85), peasant revolt leader. 2 l, Simion Barnutiu (1808-64), scientist. 3.50 l, Duiliu Zamfirescu (1858-1922), poet. 4 l, Nicolas Milescu (1636-1708), Court official.

1984, Feb. 8
3175	A915	50b multi	15	15
3176	A916	1 l multi	15	15
3177	A916	1.50 l multi	16	15
3178	A916	2 l multi	22	15
3179	A916	3.50 l multi	38	15
3180	A916	4 l multi	45	15
		Nos. 3175-3180 (6)	1.51	
		Set value		50

See Nos. 3210-3213.

Souvenir Sheet

15th Balkan
Chess Match,
Herculane
A917

Designs: Four successive moves culminating in checkmate.

1984, Feb. 20   Photo.   Perf. 13½
| 3181 | | Sheet of 4 | 2.25 | 2.25 |
| a.-d. | A917 | 3 l, any single | 55 | 55 |

Orsova
Bridge
A918

Bridges: No. 3182b, Arges. c, Basarabi. d, Ohaba.

No. 3183: a, Kohlbrand-Germany. b, Bosfor-Turcia. c, Europa-Austria. d, Turnului-Anglia.

1984, Apr. 24
3182		Sheet of 4	2.50	2.50
a.-d.	A918	3 l multi	55	55
3183		Sheet of 4	2.50	2.50
a.-d.	A918	3 l multi	55	55

Inter-European Cultural and Economic Cooperation.

Summer Olympics — A919

1984, May 25   Photo.   Perf. 13½
3184	A919	50b High jump	15	15
3185	A919	1 l Swimming	18	15
3186	A919	1.50 l Running	26	15
3187	A919	3 l Handball	52	30
3188	A919	4 l Rowing	70	40
3189	A919	5 l 2-man canoe	85	50
		Nos. 3184-3189 (6)	2.66	1.65

A 10 l imperf. airmail souvenir sheet exists.

Environmental Protection — A920

1984, Apr. 26   Photo.   Perf. 13½
3190	A920	1 l Sunflower	22	15
3191	A920	2 l Stag	45	15
3192	A920	3 l Fish	70	22
3193	A920	4 l Bird	90	30

Danube
Flowers — A921

45th Anniv., Youth
Anti-Fascist
Committee — A922

1984, Apr. 30   Photo.   Perf. 13½
3194	A921	50b Sagittaria sagittifolia	15	15
3195	A921	1 l Iris pseudacorus	16	15
3196	A921	1.50 l Butomus umbellatus	24	16
3197	A921	3 l Nymphaea alba, horiz.	52	25
3198	A921	4 l Nymphoides peltata, horiz.	70	32
3199	A921	5 l Nuphar luteum, horiz.	85	45
		Nos. 3194-3199 (6)	2.62	1.48

1984, Apr. 30   Photo.   Perf. 13½
| 3200 | A922 | 2 l multicolored | 40 | 16 |

25th Congress, Ear,
Nose and Throat
Medicine — A923

1984, May 30   Photo.   Perf. 13½
| 3201 | A923 | 2 l Congress seal | 40 | 16 |

Souvenir Sheets

European Soccer Cup
Championships — A923a

Soccer players and flags of: c, Romania. d, West Germany. e, Portugal. f, Spain. g, France. h, Belgium. i, Yugoslavia. j, Denmark.

1984, June 7   Photo.   Perf. 13½
3201A		Sheet of 4	2.50	2.50
c.-f.	A923a	3 l, any single	60	60
3201B		Sheet of 4	2.50	2.50
g.-i.	A923a	3 l, any single	60	60

Summer Olympics — A924

1984, July 2   Photo.   Perf. 13½
3202	A924	50b Boxing	15	15
3203	A924	1 l Rowing	16	15
3204	A924	1.50 l Team handball	25	15
3205	A924	2 l Judo	32	15
3206	A924	3 l Wrestling	50	20
3207	A924	3.50 l Fencing	65	25
3208	A924	4 l Kayak	70	28
3209	A924	5 l Swimming	85	35
		Nos. 3202-3209 (8)	3.58	
		Set value		1.40

Three imperf. 10 l souvenir sheets, one showing long jumping and two showing gymnastics exist.

Famous Romanians Type

1984, July 28   Photo.   Perf. 13½
3210	A916	1 l Micai Ciuca	18	15
3211	A916	2 l Petre Aurelian	35	15
3212	A916	3 l Alexandru Vlahuta	52	22
3213	A916	4 l Dimitrie Leonida	70	30

40th Anniv.,
Romanian
Revolution
A925

1984, Aug. 17   Photo.   Perf. 13½
| 3214 | A925 | 2 l multicolored | 35 | 15 |

Romanian Horses — A926

1984, Aug. 30   Photo.   Perf. 13½
3215	A926	50b Lippizaner	15	15
3216	A926	1 l Hutul	16	15
3217	A926	1.50 l Bucovina	24	15
3218	A926	2.50 l Nonius	40	22
3219	A926	4 l Arabian	65	32
3220	A926	5 l Romanian Mixed-breed	80	40
	Nos. 3215-3220 (6)		2.40	1.39

1784 Uprisings, 200th Anniv. — A927

1984, Nov. 1   Photo.   Perf. 13½
3221	A927	2 l Monument	30	15

Children — A928

Paintings: 50b, Portrait of Child, by T. Aman. 1 l, Shepherd, by N. Grigorescu. 2 l, Girl with Orange, by S. Luchian. 3 l, Portrait of Child, by N. Tonitza. 4 l, Portrait of Boy, by S. Popp. 5 l, Portrait of Girl, by I. Tuculescu.

1984, Nov. 10   Photo.   Perf. 13½
3222	A928	50b multicolored	15	15
3223	A928	1 l multicolored	16	15
3224	A928	2 l multicolored	35	15
3225	A928	3 l multicolored	50	22
3226	A928	4 l multicolored	70	30
3227	A928	5 l multicolored	85	38
	Nos. 3222-3227 (6)		2.71	
	Set value			1.15

Stamp Day — A929

1984, Nov. 15   Photo.   Perf. 13½
3228	A929	2 l + 1 l label	50	30

Set Values
A 15-cent minimum now applies to individual stamps and sets. Where the 15-cent minimum per stamp would increase the value of a set beyond retail, there is a "Set Value" notation giving the retail value of the set.

Souvenir Sheet

13th Party Congress A930

1984, Nov. 17   Photo.   Perf. 13½
3229	A930	10 l Party symbols	1.75	1.75

Souvenir Sheets

Romanian Medalists, 1984 Summer Olympic Games — A931

No. 3230a, Ecaterina Szabo, gymnastic floor exercise. b, 500-meter four-women kayak. c, Anisoara Stanciu, long jump. d, Greco-Roman wrestling. e, Mircea Fratica, half middleweight judo. f, Corneliu Ion, rapid fire pistol.
No. 3231a, 1000-meter two-man scull. b, Weight lifting. c, Women's relays. d, Canoeing, pair oars without coxswain. e, Fencing, team foil. f, Ecaterina Szabo, all-around gymnastics.

1984, Oct. 29   Photo.   Perf. 13½
3230		Sheet of 6	3.25	3.25
a.-f.	A931	3 l any single	52	52
3231		Sheet of 6	3.25	3.25
a.-f.	A931	3 l any single	52	52

A932   A933

Pelicans of the Danube Delta.

1984, Dec. 15
3232	A932	50b Flying	15	15
3233	A932	1 l On ground	20	15
3234	A932	1 l In water	20	15
3235	A932	2 l Nesting	40	15
	Set value			35

1984, Dec. 26
Famous Men: 50b, Dr. Petru Groza (1884-1958). 1 l, Alexandru Odobescu (1834-1895). 2 l, Dr. Carol Davila (1828-1884). 3 l, Dr. Nicolae G. Lupu (1884-1966). 4 l, Dr. Daniel Danielopolu (1884-1955). 5 l, Panait Istrati (1884-1935).

3236	A933	50b multi	15	15
3237	A933	1 l multi	16	15
3238	A933	2 l multi	35	15
3239	A933	3 l multi	50	22
3240	A933	4 l multi	70	30
3241	A933	5 l multi	85	38
	Nos. 3236-3241 (6)		2.71	
	Set value			1.15

Timisoara Power Station, Electric Street Lights, Cent. A934

1985, May 6
3255	A938	50b Nyctereutes procyonoides	15	15
3256	A938	1 l Perdix perdix	18	15
3257	A938	1.50 l Nyctea scandiaca	28	15
3258	A938	2 l Martes martes	35	15
3259	A938	3 l Meles meles	55	22
3260	A938	3.50 l Lutra lutra	70	28

1984, Dec. 29
3242	A934	1 l Generator, 1884	16	15
3243	A934	2 l Street arc lamp, Timisoara, 1884, vert.	35	16
	Set value			24

Souvenir Sheets

European Music Year A935

Composers and opera houses, No. 3244a, Moscow Theater, Tchaichovsky (1840-1893). b, Bucharest Theater, George Enescu (1881-1955). c, Dresden Opera, Wagner (1813-1883). d, Warsaw Opera, Stanislaw Moniuszko (1819-1872).
No. 3245a, Paris Opera, Gounod (1818-1893). b, Munich Opera, Strauss (1864-1949). c, Vienna Opera, Mozart (1756-1791). d, La Scala, Milan, Verdi (1813-1901).

1985, Mar. 28
3244		Sheet of 4	2.50	2.50
a.-d.	A935	3 l, any single	58	58
3245		Sheet of 4	2.50	2.50
a.-d.	A935	3 l, any single	58	58

August T. Laurian (1810-1881), Linguist and Historian — A936

Intl. Youth Year — A937

Famous men: 1 l, Grigore Alexandrescu (1810-1885), author. 1.50 l, Gheorghe Pop de Basesti (1835-1919), politician. 2 l, Mateiu Caragiale (1885-1936), author. 3 l, Gheorghe Ionescu-Sisesti (1885-1967), scientist. 4 l, Liviu Rebreanu (1885-1944), author.

1985, Mar. 29
3246	A936	50b multi	15	15
3247	A936	1 l multi	20	15
3248	A936	1.50 l multi	30	16
3249	A936	2 l multi	40	20
3250	A936	3 l multi	60	30
3251	A936	4 l multi	80	40
	Nos. 3246-3251 (6)		2.45	1.36

1985, Apr. 15
3252	A937	1 l Scientific research	16	15
3253	A937	2 l Construction	35	16

Souvenir Sheet
3254	A937	10 l Intl. solidarity	1.75	1.75

No. 3254 contains one 54x42mm stamp.

Wildlife Conservation A938

End of World War II, 40th Anniv. A939

1985, May 9
3261	A938	4 l Tetrao urogallus	75	30
3262	A938	5 l Otis tarda	90	38
	Nos. 3255-3262 (8)		3.86	1.78

1985, May 9
3263	A939	2 l War monument, natl. and party flags	35	18

Union of Communist Youth, 12th Congress — A940

1985, May 14
3264	A940	2 l Emblem	35	18

Danube-Black Sea Canal Opening, May 26, 1984 — A942

1985, June 7   Perf. 13½
3266	A942	1 l Canal, map	18	15
3267	A942	2 l Bridge over lock, Cernavoda	35	18
3268	A942	3 l Bridge over canal, Medgidea	52	26
3269	A942	4 l Agigea lock, bridge	70	35

Souvenir Sheet
3270	A942	10 l Opening ceremony, Cernavoda, Ceaucescu	1.75	1.75

No. 3270 contains one 54x42mm stamp.

Audubon Birth Bicentenary — A943

North American bird species. Nos. 3272-3275 vert.

1985, June 26
3271	A943	50b Turdus migratorius	15	15
3272	A943	1 l Pelecanus occidentalis	18	15
3273	A943	1.50 l Nyctanassa violarea	28	15
3274	A943	2 l Icterus galbula	35	18
3275	A943	3 l Podiceps grisegena	55	28
3276	A943	4 l Anas platyrhynchos	70	35
	Nos. 3271-3276 (6)		2.21	
	Set value			1.00

20th Century Paintings by Ion Tuculescu — A944

1985, July 13
3277	A944	1 l Fire, vert.	18	15
3278	A944	2 l Circuit, vert.	35	18
3279	A944	3 l Interior	55	28
3280	A944	4 l Sunset	70	35

Butterflies
A945

1985, July 15

3281	A945	50b Inachis io	15	15
3282	A945	1 l Papilio machaon	20	15
3283	A945	2 l Vanessa atalanta	40	20
3284	A945	3 l Saturnia pavonia	60	30
3285	A945	4 l Ammobiota festiva	80	40
3286	A945	5 l Smerinthus ocellatus	1.00	50
		Nos. 3281-3286 (6)	3.15	1.70

Natl. Communist Party
Achievements — A946

Natl. and party flags, and: 1 l, Transfagarasan Mountain Road. 2 l, Danube-Black Sea Canal. 3 l, Bucharest Underground Railway. 4 l, Irrigation.

1985, July 29

3287	A946	1 l multicolored	18	15
3288	A946	2 l multicolored	35	18
3289	A946	3 l multicolored	55	28
3290	A946	4 l multicolored	70	35

20th annivs.: Election of Gen.-Sec. Nicolae Ceausescu; Natl. Communist Congress.

Romanian Socialist
Constitution, 20th
Anniv. — A947

1985, Aug. 5

3291	A947	1 l Arms, wheat, dove	18	15
3292	A947	2 l Arms, eternal flame	35	18

1986 World Cup Soccer
Preliminaries — A948

Flags of participants; Great Britain, Northern Ireland, Romania, Finland, Turkey and: 50b, Sliding tackle. 1 l, Trapping the ball. 1.50 l, Heading the ball. 2 l, Dribble. 3 l, Tackle. 4 l, Scissor kick. 10 l, Dribble, diff.

1985, Oct. 15

3293	A948	50b multi	15	15
3294	A948	1 l multi	18	15
3295	A948	1.50 l multi	28	15
3296	A948	2 l multi	35	18
3297	A948	3 l multi	55	28
3298	A948	4 l multi	70	35
		Nos. 3293-3298 (6)	2.21	1.26

Souvenir Sheet

Motorcycle Centenary — A949

1985, Aug. 22 Photo. Perf. 13½

3300	A949	10 l 1885 Daimler Einspur	1.90	90

Retezat Natl. Park,
50th Anniv. — A950

1985, Aug. 29

3301	A950	50b Senecio glaberrimus	15	15
3302	A950	1 l Rupicapra rupicapra	18	15
3303	A950	2 l Centaurea retezatensis	35	18
3304	A950	3 l Viola dacica	55	28
3305	A950	4 l Marmota marmota	70	35
3306	A950	5 l Aquila chrysaetos	90	45
		Nos. 3301-3306 (6)	2.83	1.56

Souvenir Sheet

3307	A950	10 l Lynx lynx	1.90	90

No. 3307 contains one 42x54mm stamp.

Tractors Manufactured by
Universal — A951

1985, Sept. 10

3308	A951	50b 530 DTC	15	15
3309	A951	1 l 550 M HC	16	15
3310	A951	1.50 l 650 Super	24	15
3311	A951	2 l 850	32	16
3312	A951	3 l S 1801 IF	48	24
3313	A951	4 l A 3602 IF	65	32
		Nos. 3308-3313 (6)	2.00	1.17

Folk Costumes — A952

Women's and men's costumes from same region printed se-tenant, in continuous design.

1985, Sept. 28

3314	A952	50b Muscel woman	15	15
3315	A952	50b Muscel man	15	15
3316	A952	1.50 l Bistrita-Nasaud woman	28	15
3317	A952	1.50 l Bistrita-Nasaud man	28	15
3318	A952	2 l Vrancea woman	35	18
3319	A952	2 l Vrancea man	35	18
3320	A952	3 l Vilcea woman	55	25
3321	A952	3 l Vilcea man	55	25
		Nos. 3314-3321 (8)	2.66	
		Set value		1.20

Admission to UN, 30th Anniv. — A953

1985, Oct. 21

3322	A953	2 l multicolored	35	18

UN, 40th
Anniv. — A954

Mineral
Flowers — A955

1985, Oct. 21

3323	A954	2 l multicolored	35	18

1985, Oct. 28

3324	A955	50b Quartz and calcite, Herja	15	15
3325	A955	1 l Copper, Altin Tepe	20	15
3326	A955	2 l Gypsum, Cavnic	30	20
3327	A955	3 l Quartz, Ocna de Fier	60	30
3328	A955	4 l Stibium, Baiut	80	40
3329	A955	5 l Tetrahedrite, Cavnic	1.00	50
		Nos. 3324-3329 (6)	3.05	1.70

Stamp
Day — A956

1985, Oct. 29

3330	A956	2 l + 1 l label	35	18

A Connecticut Yankee in King Arthur's Court, by Mark Twain A957

The Three Brothers, by Jacob and Wilhelm Grimm — A958

Disney characters in classic fairy tales.

1985, Nov. 28

3331	A957	50b Hank Morgan awakes in Camelot	32	15
3332	A957	50b Predicts eclipse of sun	32	15
3333	A957	50b Mounting horse	32	15
3334	A957	50b Sir Sagramor	32	15
3335	A958	1 l Fencing with shadow	65	26
3336	A958	1 l Fencing, father	65	26
3337	A958	1 l Shoeing a horse	65	26
3338	A958	1 l Barber, rabbit	65	26
3339	A958	1 l Father, three sons	65	26
		Nos. 3332-3339 (8)	4.21	1.75

Souvenir Sheets

3340	A957	5 l Tournament of knights	2.75	1.40
3341	A958	5 l Cottage	2.75	1.40

Miniature Sheets

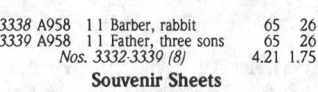

Intereuropa
1986
A959

Fauna and flora: No. 3343a, Felis silvestris. b, Mustela erminea. c, Tetrao urogallus. d, Urso arctos.

No. 3344a, Dianthus callizonus. b, Pinus cembra. c, Salix sp. d, Rose pendulina.

1986, Mar. 25 Photo. Perf. 13½

3343		Sheet of 4	2.50	2.50
a.-d.	A959	3 l, any single	60	60
3344		Sheet of 4	2.50	2.50
a.-d.	A959	3 l, any single	60	60

Inventors and Adventurers — A960

Designs: 1 l, Orville and Wilbur Wright, Wright Flyer. 1.50 l, Jacques Cousteau, research vessel Calypso. 2 l, Amelia Earhart, Lockheed Electra. 3 l, Charles Lindbergh, Spirit of St. Louis. 3.50 l, Sir Edmund Hillary (1919-), first man to reach Mt. Everest summit. 4 l, Robert Edwin Peary, Arctic explorer. 5 l, Adm. Richard Byrd, explorer. 6 l, Neil Armstrong, first man on moon.

1985, Dec. 25 Photo. Perf. 13½

3345	A960	1 l multi	30	16
3346	A960	1.50 l multi	42	20
3347	A960	2 l multi	60	30
3348	A960	3 l multi	85	42
3349	A960	3.50 l multi	1.00	50
3350	A960	4 l multi	1.10	60
3351	A960	5 l multi	1.50	70
3352	A960	6 l multi	1.65	85
		Nos. 3345-3352 (8)	7.42	3.73

Paintings by
Nicolae
Tonitza — A961

1986, Mar. 12 Photo. Perf. 13½

3353	A961	1 l Nina in Green	30	16
3354	A961	2 l Irina	60	30
3355	A961	3 l Woodman's Daughter	90	45
3356	A961	4 l Woman on the Verandah	1.25	60

Color Animated Films, 50th
Anniv. — A962

Walt Disney characters in the Band Concert, 1935.

1986, Apr. 10   Photo.   Perf. 13½
3357	A962	50b Clarabelle	25	15
3358	A962	50b Mickey Mouse	25	15
3359	A962	50b Paddy and Peter	25	15
3360	A962	50b Goofy	25	15
3361	A962	1 l Donald Duck	50	18
3362	A962	1 l Mickey Mouse, diff.	50	18
3363	A962	1 l Mickey and Donald	50	18
3364	A962	1 l Horace	50	18
3365	A962	1 l Donald and trombonist	50	18
		Nos. 3357-3365 (9)	3.50	
		Set value	1.20	

Souvenir Sheet
3366	A962	5 l Finale	2.50	85

1986 World Cup Soccer Championships, Mexico — A963

Various soccer plays and flags: 50b, Italy vs. Bulgaria. 1 l, Mexico vs. Belgium. 2 l, Canada vs. France. 3 l, Brazil vs. Spain. 4 l, Uruguay vs. Germany. 5 l, Morocco vs. Poland.

1986, May 9
3367	A963	50b multi	15	15
3368	A963	1 l multi	25	15
3369	A963	2 l multi	52	25
3370	A963	3 l multi	75	38
3371	A963	4 l multi	1.00	52
3372	A963	5 l multi	1.25	70
		Nos. 3367-3372 (6)	3.92	2.15

An imperf. 10 l airmail souvenir sheet exists picturing stadium, flags of previous winners, satellite and map.

Hotels — A964

1986, Apr. 23   Photo.   Perf. 13½
3373	A964	50b Diana, Herculane	15	15
3374	A964	1 l Termal, Felix	22	15
3375	A964	2 l Delfin, Meduza and Steaua de Mare, Eforie Nord	45	22
3376	A964	3 l Caciulata, Calimanesti Caciulata	65	32
3377	A964	4 l Palas, Slanic Moldova	90	45
3378	A964	5 l Bradet, Sovata	1.10	55
		Nos. 3373-3378 (6)	3.47	1.84

Nicolae Ceausescu, Party Flag — A965

1986, May 8   Photo.   Perf. 13½
3379	A965	2 l multicolored	60	30

Natl. Communist Party, 65th anniv.

Flowers — A966

1986, June 25   Photo.   Perf. 13½
3380	A966	50b Tulipa gesneriana	15	15
3381	A966	1 l Iris hispanica	25	15
3382	A966	2 l Rosa hybrida	50	25
3383	A966	3 l Anemone coronaria	70	35
3384	A966	4 l Freesia refracta	1.00	50
3385	A966	5 l Chrysanthemum indicum	1.25	60
		Nos. 3380-3385 (6)	3.85	2.00

Mircea the Great, Ruler of Wallachia, 1386-1418 — A967

1986, July 17   Photo.   Perf. 13½
3386	A967	2 l multicolored	60	30

Ascent to the throne, 600th anniv.

Open Air Museum of Historic Dwellings, Bucharest, 50th Anniv. — A968

1986, July 21
3387	A968	50b Alba	15	15
3388	A968	1 l Arges	22	15
3389	A968	2 l Constantia	45	22
3390	A968	3 l Timis	65	32
3391	A968	4 l Neamt	90	45
3392	A968	5 l Gorj	1.10	55
		Nos. 3387-3392 (6)	3.47	1.84

Polar Research — A969

Exploration: 50b, Julius Popper, exploration of Tierra del Fuego (1886-93). 1 l, Bazil G. Assan, exploration of Spitzbergen (1896). 2 l, Emil Racovita, Antarctic expedition (1897-99). 3 l, Constantin Dumbrava, exploration of Greenland (1927-8). 4 l, Romanians with the 17th Soviet Antarctic expedition (1971-72). 5 l, Research on krill fishing (1977-80).

1986, July 23   Photo.   Perf. 13½
3393	A969	50b multi	15	15
3394	A969	1 l multi	22	15
3395	A969	2 l multi	45	22
3396	A969	3 l multi	65	32
3397	A969	4 l multi	90	45
3398	A969	5 l multi	1.10	55
		Nos. 3393-3398 (6)	3.47	1.84

Natl. Cycling Championships A970

Various athletes.

1986, Aug. 29
3399	A970	1 l multicolored	25	15
3400	A970	2 l multicolored	50	25
3401	A970	3 l multicolored	70	35
3402	A970	4 l multicolored	1.00	50

Souvenir Sheet
3403	A970	10 l multicolored	2.50	1.25

No. 3403 contains one 42x54mm stamp.

Souvenir Sheet

Intl. Peace Year — A971

1986, July 25
3404	A971	5 l multicolored	1.25	60

Fungi — A972   A973

1986, Aug. 15
3405	A972	50b Amanita rubescens	15	15
3406	A972	1 l Boletus luridus	25	15
3407	A972	2 l Lactarius piperatus	50	25
3408	A972	3 l Lepiota clypeolaria	70	35
3409	A972	4 l Russula cyanoxantha	1.00	50
3410	A972	5 l Tremiscus helvelloides	1.25	60
		Nos. 3405-3410 (6)	3.85	2.00

1986, Nov. 10   Photo.   Perf. 13½

Famous Men: 50b, Petru Maior (c. 1761-1821), historian. 1 l, George Topirceanu (1886-1937), doctor. 2 l, Henri Coanda (1886-1972), engineer. 3 l, Constantin Budeanu (1886-1959), engineer.
3411	A973	50b dl cl, gold & dk bl		
3412	A973	1 l sl grn, gold & dk lil	15	15
3413	A973	2 l rose cl, gold & brt bl	25	15
3414	A973	3 l chlky bl, gold & choc	52	25
			70	35

UNESCO, 40th Anniv. A974

1986, Nov. 10
3415	A974	4 l multicolored	1.00	50

Stamp Day A975

1986, Nov. 15
3416	A975	2 l + 1 l label	75	35

Industry A976

1986, Nov. 28
3417	A976	50b F-300 oil rigs, vert.	15	15
3418	A976	1 l Promex excavator	22	15
3419	A976	2 l Pitesti refinery, vert.	45	22
3420	A976	3 l 110-ton dump truck	65	32
3421	A976	4 l Coral computer, vert.	90	45
3422	A976	5 l 350-megawatt turbine	1.10	55
		Nos. 3417-3422 (6)	3.47	1.84

Folk Costumes — A977

1986, Dec. 26
3423	A977	50b Capra	15	15
3424	A977	1 l Sorcova	22	15
3425	A977	2 l Plugusorul	45	22
3426	A977	3 l Buhaiul	65	32
3427	A977	4 l Caiutii	90	45
3428	A977	5 l Uratorii	1.10	55
		Nos. 3423-3428 (6)	3.47	1.84

Recycling Campaign — A978

1986, Dec. 30
3429	A978	1 l Metal	25	15
3430	A978	2 l Trees	50	25

Young Communists' League, 65th Anniv. — A979

1987, Mar. 18   Photo.   Perf. 13½
3431	A979	1 l Flags, youth	26	15
3432	A979	2 l Emblem	52	26
3433	A979	3 l Flags, youth, diff.	75	38

Miniature Sheets

Intereuropa
A980

Modern architecture: No. 3434a, Exposition Pavilion, Bucharest. b, Intercontinental Hotel, Bucharest. c, Europa Hotel, Black Sea coast. d, Polytechnic Institute, Bucharest.
No. 3435a, Administration Building, Satu Mare. b, House of Young Pioneers, Bucharest. c, Valahia Hotel, Tirgoviste. d, Caciulata Hotel, Caciulata.

1987, May 18   Photo.   Perf. 13½
3434		Sheet of 4	2.50	2.50
a.-d.	A980	3 l, any single	60	60
3435		Sheet of 4	2.50	2.50
a.-d.	A980	3 l, any single	60	60

Collective Farming, 25th Anniv. — A981

1987, Apr. 25   Photo.   Perf. 13½
3436	A981	2 l multicolored	50	25

Birch Trees by the Lakeside, by I. Andreescu — A982

Paintings in Romanian museums: 1 l, Young Peasant Girls Spinning, by N. Grigorescu. 2 l, Washerwoman, by S. Luchian. 3 l, Inside the Peasant's Cottage, by S. Dimitrescu. 4 l, Winter Landscape, by A. Ciucurencu. 5 l, Winter in Bucharest, by N. Tonitza, vert.

1987, Apr. 28
3437	A982	50b multicolored	15	15
3438	A982	1 l multicolored	18	15
3439	A982	2 l multicolored	35	18
3440	A982	3 l multicolored	55	28
3441	A982	4 l multicolored	75	38
3442	A982	5 l multicolored	1.00	52
		Nos. 3437-3442 (6)	2.98	1.66

Peasant Uprising of 1907, 80th Anniv. — A983

1987, May 30
3443	A983	2 l multicolored	50	25

Men's World Handball Championships — A984

Various plays.

1987, July 15
3444	A984	50b multi, vert.	15	15
3445	A984	1 l multi	18	15
3446	A984	2 l multi, vert.	38	18
3447	A984	3 l multi	55	28
3448	A984	4 l multi, vert.	75	38
3449	A984	5 l multi	1.00	52
		Nos. 3444-3449 (6)	3.01	1.66

A985

Natl. Currency — A986

A986 illustration reduced.

1987, July 15
3450	A985	1 l multicolored	20	15

Souvenir Sheet
3451	A986	10 l multicolored	2.00	2.00

Landscapes A987

1987, July 31   Photo.   Perf. 13½
3452	A987	50b Pelicans over the Danube Delta	15	15
3453	A987	1 l Transfagarasan Highway	18	15
3454	A987	2 l Hairpin curve, Bicazului	35	18
3455	A987	3 l Limestone peaks, Mt. Ceahlau	52	25
3456	A987	4 l Lake Capra, Mt. Fagaras	70	35
3457	A987	5 l Orchard, Borsa	90	50
		Nos. 3452-3457 (6)	2.80	1.58

A988

Scenes from Fairy Tale by Peter Ispirescu (b. 1887) — A988a

A988a illustration reduced.

1987, Sept. 25   Photo.   Perf. 13½
3458	A988	50b shown	15	15
3459	A988	1 l multi, diff.	16	15
3460	A988	2 l multi, diff.	35	16
3461	A988	3 l multi, diff.	52	25
3462	A988	4 l multi, diff.	70	35
3463	A988	5 l multi, diff.	85	40
		Nos. 3458-3463 (6)	2.73	1.46

Souvenir Sheet
3464	A988a	10 l shown	2.00	2.00

Miniature Sheets

Flora and Fauna A989

Flora: No. 3465a, Aquilegia alpina. b, Pulsatilla vernalis. c, Aster alpinus. d, Soldanella pusilla baumg. e, Lilium bulbiferum. f, Arctostaphylos uva-ursi. g, Crocus vernus. h, Crepis aurea. i, Cypripedium calceolus. j, Centaurea nervosa. k, Dryas octopetala. l, Gentiana excisa.
Fauna: No. 3466a, Martes martes. b, Felis lynx. c, Ursus maritimus. d, Lutra lutra. e, Bison bonasus. f, Branta ruficollis. g, Phoenicopterus ruber. h, Otis tarda. i, Lyrurus tetrix. j, Gypaetus barbatus. k, Vormela peregusna. l, Oxyura leucocephala.

1987, Oct. 16
Sheets of 12
3465	A989	1 l #a.-l.	3.25	1.50
3466	A989	1 l #a.-l.	3.25	1.50

Souvenir Sheet

PHILATELIA '87, Cologne — A990

1987, Oct. 19
3467		Sheet of 2 + 2 labels	3.75	3.75
a.	A990	3 l Bucharest city seal	1.90	1.90
b.	A990	3 l Cologne city arms	1.90	1.90

Locomotives A991

1987, Oct. 15
3468	A991	50b L 45 H	15	15
3469	A991	1 l LDE 125	20	15
3470	A991	2 l LDH 70	42	20
3471	A991	3 l LDE 2100	65	30
3472	A991	4 l LDE 3000	90	42
3473	A991	5 l LE 5100	1.00	50
		Nos. 3468-3473 (6)	3.32	1.72

Folk Costumes — A992

1987, Nov. 7
3474	A992	1 l Tirnave (woman)	18	15
3475	A992	1 l Tirnave (man)	18	15
3476	A992	2 l Buzau (woman)	40	18
3477	A992	2 l Buzau (man)	40	18
3478	A992	3 l Dobrogea (woman)	60	30
3479	A992	3 l Dobrogea (man)	60	30
3480	A992	4 l Ilfov (woman)	80	40
3481	A992	4 l Ilfov (man)	80	40
		Nos. 3474-3481 (8)	3.96	2.06

Stamps of same denomination se-tenant.

Postwoman Delivering Mail A993

1987, Nov. 15   Photo.   Perf. 13½
3482	A993	2 l + 1 l label	75	38

Stamp Day.

Apiculture — A994

1987, Nov. 16   Photo.   Perf. 13½
3483	A994	1 l Apis mellifica carpatica	24	15
3484	A994	2 l Bee pollinating sunflower	50	24
3485	A994	3 l Hives, Danube Delta	75	38
3486	A994	4 l Apiculture complex, Bucharest	1.00	50

1988 Winter Olympics, Calgary — A995

1987, Dec. 28   Photo.   Perf. 13½
3487	A995	50b Biathlon	15	15
3488	A995	1 l Slalom	18	15
3489	A995	1.50 l Ice hockey	30	16
3490	A995	2 l Luge	40	18
3491	A995	3 l Speed skating	60	30

3492	A995 3.50 l Women's figure skating	65 35
3493	A995 4 l Downhill skiing	80 40
3494	A995 5 l Two-man bobsled	1.00 50
	Nos. 3487-3494 (8)	4.08 2.19

An imperf. 10 l souvenir sheet picturing ski jumping also exists.

Traffic Safety
A996

Designs: 50b, Be aware of children riding bicycles in the road. 1 l, Young Pioneer girl as crossing guard. 2 l, Do not open car doors in path of moving traffic. 3 l, Be aware of pedestrian crossings. 4 l, Observe the speed limit; do not attempt curves at high speed. 5 l, Protect small children.

1987, Dec. 10   Photo.   Perf. 13¹/₂

3495	A996 50b multicolored	15 15
3496	A996 1 l multicolored	18 15
3497	A996 2 l multicolored	40 18
3498	A996 3 l multicolored	65 30
3499	A996 4 l multicolored	85 40
3500	A996 5 l multicolored	1.00 45
	Nos. 3495-3500 (6)	3.23 1.63

October Revolution, Russia, 70th
Anniv. — A997

1987, Dec. 26

3501	A997 2 l multicolored	45 22

40th Anniv. of the
Romanian
Republic — A998

1987, Dec. 30

3502	A998 2 l multicolored	45 22

70th
Birthday of
President
Nicolae
Ceausescu
A999

1988, Jan. 26

3503	A999 2 l multicolored	45 22

Pottery
A1000

1988, Feb. 26   Photo.   Perf. 13¹/₂

3504	A1000 50b Marginea	15 15
3505	A1000 1 l Oboga	18 15
3506	A1000 2 l Horezu	40 18
3507	A1000 3 l Curtea De Arges	65 30
3508	A1000 4 l Birsa	85 40
3509	A1000 5 l Vama	1.00 45
	Nos. 3504-3509 (6)	3.23 1.63

Miniature Sheets

Intereuropa
A1001

Transportation and communication: No. 3510a, Mail coach. b, ECS telecommunications satellite. c, Oltcit automobile. d, ICE high-speed electric train.
No. 3511a, Santa Maria, 15th cent. b, Cheia Ground Station satellite dish receivers. c, Bucharest subway. d, Airbus-A320.

1988, Apr. 27   Photo.   Perf. 13¹/₂

3510	Sheet of 4	2.50 2.50
a.-d.	A1001 3 l any single	60 60
3511	Sheet of 4	2.50 2.50
a.-d.	A1001 3 l any single	60 60

1988 Summer
Olympics,
Seoul — A1002

1988, Jun. 28

3512	A1002 50b Gymnastics	15 15
3513	A1002 1.50 l Boxing	30 15
3514	A1002 2 l Tennis	40 20
3515	A1002 3 l Judo	60 30
3516	A1002 4 l Running	80 40
3517	A1002 5 l Rowing	1.00 48
	Nos. 3512-3517 (6)	3.25 1.68

An imperf. 10 l souvenir sheet exists.

19th-20th Cent.
Clocks in the
Ceasului Museum,
Ploesti — A1003

1988, May 20   Photo.   Perf. 13¹/₂

3518	A1003 50b Arad Region porcelain	15 15
3519	A1003 1.50 l French bronze	32 15
3520	A1003 2 l French bronze, diff.	42 20
3521	A1003 3 l Gothic bronze	65 32
3522	A1003 4 l Saxony porcelain	85 42
3523	A1003 5 l Bohemian porcelain	1.10 52
	Nos. 3518-3523 (6)	3.49 1.76

20th Cent. timepiece (50b); others 19th cent.

Miniature Sheets

European Soccer Championships,
Germany — A1003a

Soccer players and flags of: c, Federal Republic of Germany. d, Spain. e, Italy. f, Denmark. g, England. h, Netherlands. i, Ireland. j, Soviet Union.

1988, June 9   Litho.   Perf. 13¹/₂

3523A	Sheet of 4	3.25 3.25
c.-f.	A1003a 3 l any single	80 80
3523B	Sheet of 4	3.25 3.25
g.-j.	A1003a 3 l any single	80 80

Accession of
Constanin
Brincoveanu as
Prince Regent of
Wallachia, 1688-
1714, 300th
Anniv. — A1004

1988, June 20

3524	A1004 2 l multicolored	50 25

1988 Summer Olympics, Seoul — A1005

1988, Sept. 1   Photo.   Perf. 13¹/₂

3525	A1005 50b Women's running	15 15
3526	A1005 1 l Canoeing	18 15
3527	A1005 1.50 l Women's gymnastics	28 15
3528	A1005 2 l Kayaking	40 18
3529	A1005 3 l Weight lifting	55 28
3530	A1005 3.50 l Women's swimming	60 35
3531	A1005 4 l Fencing	70 40
3532	A1005 5 l Women's rowing (double)	95 45
	Nos. 3525-3532 (8)	3.81 2.11

An imperf. 10 l souvenir sheet exists picturing women's gymnastics.

Romania-China Philatelic
Exhibition — A1006

1988, Aug. 5   Photo.   Perf. 13¹/₂

3533	A1006 2 l multicolored	50 25

Souvenir Sheet

PRAGA '88 — A1007

1988, Aug. 26

3534	A1007 5 l Carnations, by Stefan Luchian	2.00 2.00

Miniature Sheets

Orchids
A1008

No. 3535a, Oncidium lanceanum. b, Cattleya trianae. c, Sophronitis cernua. d, Bulbophyllum lobbii. e, Lycaste cruenta. f, Mormolyce ringens. g, Phragmipedium schlimii. h, Angraecum sesquipedale. i, Laelia crispa. j, Encyclia atropurpurea. k, Dendrobium nobile. l, Oncidium splendidum.
No. 3536a, Brassavola perrinii. b, Paphiopedilum maudiae. c, Sophronitis coccinea. d, Vandopsis lissochiloides. e, Phalaenopsis lueddemanniana. f, Chysis bractescens. g, Cochleanthes discolor. h, Phalaenopsis amabilis. i, Pleione pricei. j, Sobralia macrantha. k, Aspasia lunata. l, Cattleya citrina.

1988, Oct. 24

3535	Sheet of 12	3.25 3.25
a.-l.	A1008 1 l any single	24 24
3536	Sheet of 12	3.25 3.25
a.-l.	A1008 1 l any single	24 24

Miniature Sheets

Events Won by Romanian Athletes at the
1988 Seoul Olympic Games
A1009

Sporting event and medal: No. 3537a, Women's gymnastics. b, Free pistol shooting. c, Weight lifting (220 pounds). d, Featherweight boxing.
No. 3538a, Women's 1500 and 3000-meter relays. b, Women's 200 and 400-meter individual swimming medley. c, Wrestling (220 pounds). d, Rowing, coxless pairs and coxed fours.

1988, Dec. 7   Photo.   Perf. 13¹/₂

3537	Sheet of 4	3.00 3.00
a.-d.	A1009 3 l any single	75 75
3538	Sheet of 4	3.00 3.00
a.-d.	A1009 3 l any single	75 75

Stamp Day
A1010

1988, Nov. 13   Photo.   Perf. 13¹/₂

3539	A1010 2 l + 1 l label	75 38

Unitary Natl. Romanian State, 70th Anniv. A1011

1988, Dec. 29
3540	A1011	2 l multicolored	50	25

Anniversaries — A1012

Designs: 50b, Athenaeum, Bucharest. 1.50 l, Trajan's Bridge, Drobeta, on a Roman bronze sestertius used in Romania from 103 to 105 A.D. 2 l, Ruins, Suceava. 3 l, Pitesti municipal coat of arms, scroll, architecture. 4 l, Trajan's Column (detail), 113 A.D. 5 l, Gold helmet discovered in Prahova County.

1988, Dec. 30
3541	A1012	50b shown	15	15
3542	A1012	1.50 l multi	30	15
3543	A1012	2 l multi	42	20
3544	A1012	3 l multi	65	30
3545	A1012	4 l multi	85	40
3546	A1012	5 l multi	1.10	48
	Nos. 3541-3546 (6)		3.47	1.68

Athenaeum, Bucharest, cent. (50b), Suceava, the capital of Moldavia from 1401 to 1565, 600th anniv. (2 l), and Pitesti municipal charter, 600th anniv. (3 l).

Miniature Sheets

Grand Slam Tennis Championships — A1013

No. 3547: a, Men's singles, stadium in Melbourne. b, Men's singles, scoreboard. c, Mixed doubles, spectators. d, Mixed doubles, Roland Garros stadium.
No. 3548: a, Women's singles, stadium in Wimbledon. b, Women's singles, spectators. c, Men's doubles, spectators. d, Men's doubles, stadium in Flushing Meadows.

1988, Aug. 22   Photo.   Perf. 13½
3547		Sheet of 4	3.00	3.00
a.-d.	A1013	3 l any single	75	75
3548		Sheet of 4	3.00	3.00
a.-d.	A1013	3 l any single	75	75

Australian Open (Nos. 3547a-3547b), French Open (Nos. 3547c-3547d), Wimbledon (Nos. 3548a-3548b) and US Open (Nos. 3548c-3548d).

Architecture A1014

Designs: 50b, Zapodeni, Vaslui, 17th cent. 1.50 l, Berbesti, Maramures, 18th cent. 2 l, Voitinel, Suceava, 18th cent. 3 l, Chiojdu mic, Buzau, 18th cent. 4 l, Cimpanii de sus, Bihor, 19th cent. 5 l, Naruja, Vrancea, 19th cent.

1989, Feb. 8   Photo.   Perf. 13½
3549	A1014	50b multi	15	15
3550	A1014	1.50 l multi	32	18
3551	A1014	2 l multi	42	22
3552	A1014	3 l multi	65	32
3553	A1014	4 l multi	85	42
3554	A1014	5 l multi	1.10	52
	Nos. 3549-3554 (6)		3.49	1.81

Rescue and Relief Services — A1015

1989, Feb. 25
3555	A1015	50b Relief worker	15	15
3556	A1015	1 l shown	24	15
3557	A1015	1.50 l Fireman, child	38	20
3558	A1015	2 l Fireman's carry	45	24
3559	A1015	3 l Rescue team on skis	75	38
3560	A1015	3.50 l Mountain rescue	85	42
3561	A1015	4 l Water rescue	1.10	45
3562	A1015	5 l Water safety	1.25	65
	Nos. 3555-3562 (8)		5.17	2.64

Nos. 3555, 3557-3558, 3560-3561 vert.

Industries — A1016

Designs: 50b, Fasca Bicaz cement factory. 1.50 l, Bridge on the Danube near Cernavoda. 2 l, MS-2-2400/450-20 synchronous motor. 3 l, Bucharest subway. 4 l, Mangalia-Constanta ferry. 5 l, Gloria marine platform.

1989, Apr. 10   Photo.   Perf. 13½
3563	A1016	50b multi	15	15
3564	A1016	1.50 l multi	30	16
3565	A1016	2 l multi	40	20
3566	A1016	3 l multi	60	32
3567	A1016	4 l multi	80	40
3568	A1016	5 l multi	1.00	52
	Nos. 3563-3568 (6)		3.25	1.75

Anti-fascist March, 50th Anniv. A1017

1989, May 1   Photo.   Perf. 13½
3569	A1017	2 l shown	50	25

Souvenir Sheet
3570	A1017	10 l Patriots, flag	4.75	4.75

Souvenir Sheet

BULGARIA '89, Sofia, May 22-31 — A1018

Illustration reduced.

1989, May 20
3571	A1018	10 l Roses	3.00	3.00

Miniature Sheets

Intereuropa 1989 A1019

Children's activities and games: No. 3572a, Swimming. No. 3572b, Water slide. No. 3572c, Seesaw. No. 3572d, Flying kites. No. 3573a, Playing with dolls. No. 3573b, Playing ball. No. 3573c, Playing in the sand. No. 3573d, Playing with toy cars.

1989, June 15
3572		Sheet of 4	3.00	3.00
a.-d.	A1019	3 l any single	75	75
3573		Sheet of 4	3.00	3.00
a.-d.	A1019	3 l any single	75	75

Socialist Revolution in Romania, 45th Anniv. A1020

1989, Aug. 21   Photo.   Perf. 13½
3574	A1020	2 l multicolored	50	25

Cartoons — A1021

1989, Sept. 25
3575	A1021	50b Pin-pin	15	15
3576	A1021	1 l Maria	22	15
3577	A1021	1.50 l Gore and Grigore	32	16
3578	A1021	2 l Pisoiul, Balanel, Manole and Monk	42	20
3579	A1021	3 l Gruia Lui Novac	65	32
3580	A1021	3.50 l Mihaela	80	38
3581	A1021	4 l Harap alb	90	42
3582	A1021	5 l Homo sapiens	1.00	52
	Nos. 3575-3582 (8)		4.46	2.30

Romanian Writers — A1022

Portraits: 1 l, Ion Creanga (1837-1889). 2 l, Mihail Eminescu (1850-1889), poet. 3 l, Nicolae Teclu (1839-1916).

1989, Aug. 18   Photo.   Perf. 13½
3583	A1022	1 l multicolored	30	15
3584	A1022	2 l multicolored	60	28
3585	A1022	3 l multicolored	90	45

Stamp Day A1023

1989, Oct. 7
3586	A1023	2 l + 1 l label	75	38

No. 3586 has a second label picturing posthorn.

Storming of the Bastille, 1789 A1024

Emblems of PHILEXFRANCE '89 and the Revolution — A1025

Designs: 1.50 l, Gavroche. 2 l, Robespierre. 3 l, La Marseillaise, by Rouget de Lisle. 4 l, Diderot. 5 l, 1848 Uprising, Romania.

1989, Oct. 14
3587	A1024	50b shown	15	15
3588	A1024	1.50 l multicolored	30	16
3589	A1024	2 l multicolored	40	20
3590	A1024	3 l multicolored	60	30
3591	A1024	4 l multicolored	80	40
3592	A1024	5 l multicolored	1.00	50
	Nos. 3587-3592 (6)		3.25	1.71

Souvenir Sheet
3593	A1025	10 l shown	3.00	3.00

French revolution, bicent.

14th Romanian Communist Party Congress A1025a

1989, Nov. 20　　Photo.　　Perf. 13½
3593A A1025a　2 l multicolored　　50　50

Souvenir Sheet

3593B A1025a　10 l multicolored　4.75　4.75

Revolution of Dec. 22,
1989 — A1026

1990, Jan. 8　　Photo.　　Perf. 13½
3594 A1026　2 l multicolored　　40　20

World Cup Soccer Preliminaries,
Italy — A1027

Various soccer players in action.

1990, Mar. 19　　Photo.　　Perf. 13½
3595 A1027　50b multicolored　　15　15
3596 A1027　1.50 l multicolored　30　30
3597 A1027　2 l multicolored　　40　40
3598 A1027　3 l multicolored　　60　60
3599 A1027　4 l multicolored　　80　80
3600 A1027　5 l multicolored　1.00　1.00
　　Nos. 3595-3600 (6)　3.25　3.25

An imperf. 10 l airmail souvenir sheet exists.

Souvenir Sheet

First Postage Stamp, 150th
Anniv. — A1028

Illustration reduced.

1990, May 2　　Litho.　　Perf. 13½
3601 A1028　10 l multicolored　2.00　2.00

Stamp World London '90.

World Cup Soccer Championships,
Italy — A1029

Various soccer players in action.

1990, May 7　　Photo.　　Perf. 13½
3602 A1029　50b multicolored　　15　15
3603 A1029　1 l multicolored　　15　15
3604 A1029　1.50 l multicolored　15　15
3605 A1029　2 l multicolored　　18　18
3606 A1029　3 l multicolored　　28　28
3607 A1029　3.50 l multicolored　30　30

3608 A1029　4 l multicolored　　35　35
3609 A1029　5 l multicolored　　45　45
　　Set Value　1.85　1.85

An imperf. 10 l airmail souvenir sheet showing
Olympic Stadium, Rome exists.

Intl. Dog Show, Brno,
Czechoslovakia — A1030

1990, June 6
3610 A1030　50b German shepherd　15　15
3611 A1030　1 l English setter　22　22
3612 A1030　1.50 l Boxer　　32　32
3613 A1030　2 l Beagle　　45　45
3614 A1030　3 l Doberman pin-
　　　　　　　scher　　65　65
3615 A1030　3.50 l Great Dane　75　75
3616 A1030　4 l Afghan hound　90　90
3617 A1030　5 l Yorkshire terrier　1.10　1.10
　　Nos. 3610-3617 (8)　4.54　4.54

Riccione '90,
Intl.
Philatelic
Exhibition
A1031

1990, Aug. 24
3618 A1031　2 l multicolored　　50　50

See No. 3856.

Romanian-Chinese Philatelic Exhibition,
Bucharest — A1032

1990, Sept. 8　　Photo.　　Perf. 13½
3619 A1032　2 l multicolored　　18　18

Paintings
Damaged in
1989
Revolution
A1033

Designs: 50b, Old Nicolas, the Zither Player, by
Stefan Luchian. 1.50 l, Woman in Blue by Ion
Andreescu. 2 l, The Gardener by Luchian. 3 l, Vase
of Flowers by Jan Brueghel, the Elder. 4 l, Spring-
time by Peter Brueghel, the Elder, horiz. 5 l,
Madonna and Child by G. B. Paggi.

1990, Oct. 25　　Photo.　　Perf. 13½
3620 A1033　1 l multicolored　　15　15
3621 A1033　1.50 l multicolored　20　20
3622 A1033　2 l multicolored　　28　28
3623 A1033　3 l multicolored　　40　40

3624 A1033　4 l multicolored　　52　52
3625 A1033　5 l multicolored　　70　70
　　Nos. 3620-3625 (6)　2.25　2.25

Stamp
Day
A1033a

1990, Nov. 10　　Photo.　　Perf. 13½
3625A A1033a　2 l + 1 l label　25　25

Famous Romanians
A1034

Designs: 50b, Prince Constantin Cantacuzino
(1640-1716). 1.50 l, Ienachita Vacarescu (c. 1740-
1797), historian. 2 l, Titu Maiorescu (1840-1917),
writer. 3 l, Nicolae Iorga (1871-1940), historian.
4 l, Martha Bibescu (1890-1973). 5 l, Stefan
Procopiu (1890-1972), scientist.

1990, Nov. 27　　Photo.　　Perf. 13½
3626 A1034　50b sepia & dk bl　15　15
3627 A1034　1.50 l grn & brt pur　15　15
3628 A1034　2 l claret & dk bl　16　16
3629 A1034　3 l dk bl & brn　24　24
3630 A1034　4 l brn & dk bl　30　30
3631 A1034　5 l brt pur & grn　38　38
　　Nos. 3626-3631 (6)　1.38　1.38

National
Day — A1035

1990, Dec. 1　　Photo.　　Perf. 13½
3632 A1035　2 l multicolored　　25　25

No. 3594
Surcharged in
Brown

∟4
=

UN AN DE LA VICTORIA
REVOLUTIEI

1990, Dec. 22　　Photo.　　Perf. 13½
3633 A1026　4 l on 2 l　　50　50

Vincent Van Gogh, Death Cent. — A1036

Paintings: 50b, Field of Irises. 2 l, Artist's Room.
3 l, Night on the Coffee Terrace, vert. 3.50 l, Blos-
soming Fruit Trees. 5 l, Vase with Fourteen Sunflowers, vert.

1991, Mar. 29　　Photo.　　Perf. 13½
3634 A1036　50b multicolored　15　15
3635 A1036　2 l multicolored　25　25
3636 A1036　3 l multicolored　35　35
3637 A1036　3.50 l multicolored　42　42
3638 A1036　5 l multicolored　60　60
　　Nos. 3634-3638 (5)　1.77　1.77

A1037　　　　　A1038

Birds: 50b, Larus marinus. 1 l, Sterna hirundo.
1.50 l, Recurvirostra avosetta. 2 l, Stercorarius
pomarinus. 3 l, Vanellus vanellus. 3.50 l, Mergus
serrator. 4 l, Egretta garzetta. 5 l, Calidris alpina.
6 l, Limosa limosa. 7 l, Childonias hybrida.

1991, Apr. 3　　Photo.　　Perf. 13½
3639 A1037　50b ultra　　15　15
3640 A1037　1 l blue green　15　15
3641 A1037　1.50 l bister　18　18
3642 A1037　2 l dark blue　26　26
3643 A1037　3 l light green　38　38
3644 A1037　3.50 l dark green　45　45
3645 A1037　4 l purple　48　48
3646 A1037　5 l brown　65　65
3647 A1037　6 l yel brown　75　75
3648 A1037　7 l light blue　90　90
　　Nos. 3639-3648 (10)　4.35　4.35

1991, Apr. 5　　Photo.　　Perf. 13½
3649 A1038　4 l multicolored　　35　35

Easter.

Europa
A1039

1991, May 10　　Photo.　　Perf. 13½
3650 A1039　4.50 l Eutelsat I　58　58

Posthorn — A1040

1991, May 24　　Photo.　　Perf. 13½
3651 A1040　4.50 l blue　　40　40

Gymnastics — A1041

1991, June 14
3652 A1041　1 l Rings　　15　15
3653 A1041　1 l Parallel bars　15　15
3654 A1041　4.50 l Vault　50　50
3655 A1041　4.50 l Uneven parallel
　　　　　　bars　　50　50

3656 A1041	8 l	Floor exercise	90	90
3657 A1041	9 l	Balance beam	1.00	1.00
	Nos. 3652-3657 (6)		3.20	3.20

For surcharge on 5 l see No. 3735. For other surcharges see Nos. 3944, 3946.

Monasteries — A1042

1991, July 4   Photo.   Perf. 13½

3658 A1042	1 l	Curtea de Arges, vert.	15	15
3659 A1042	1 l	Putna, vert.	15	15
3660 A1042	4.50 l	Varatec, vert.	40	40
3661 A1042	4.50 l	Agapia	40	40
3662 A1042	8 l	Golia	70	70
3663 A1042	9 l	Sucevita	80	80
	Nos. 3658-3663 (6)		2.60	2.60

Hotels, Lodges, and Resorts
A1043   A1044

Designs: 1 l, Hotel Continental, Timisoara, vert. 2 l, Valea Caprei Lodge, Fagaras. 4 l, Hotel Inter-continental, Bucharest, vert. 5 l, Lebada Hotel, Crisan. 6 l, Muntele Rosu Lodge, Ciucas. 8 l, Transylvania Hotel, Cluj-Napoca. 9 l, Hotel Orizont, Predeal. 10 l, Hotel Roman, Herculane, vert. 18 l, Rarau Lodge, Rarau, vert. 20 l, Alpine Hotel, Poiana Brasov. 25 l, Constanta Casino. 30 l, Miorija Lodge, Bucegi. 45 l, Sura Dacilor Lodge, Poiana Brasov. 60 l, Valea Draganului, Tourist Complex,. 80 l, Hotel Florica, Venus Health Resort. 120 l, International Hotel, Baile Felix, vert. 160 l, Hotel Egreta, Tulcea, vert. 250 l, Motel Valea de Pesti, Valea Jiului. 400 l, Tourist Complex, Baisoara. 500 l, Hotel Bradul, Covasna. 800 l, Hotel Gorj, Tirgu Jiu.

1991   Photo.   Perf. 13½

3664 A1043	1 l	blue	15	15
3665 A1043	2 l	dark green	15	15
3666 A1043	4 l	carmine	15	15
3667 A1043	5 l	violet	15	15
3668 A1043	6 l	olive brown	15	15
3669 A1043	8 l	brown	20	20
3670 A1043	9 l	red brown	22	22
3671 A1043	10 l	olive green	25	25
3672 A1043	18 l	bright red	40	40
3673 A1043	20 l	brown org	48	48
3674 A1043	25 l	bright blue	60	60
3675 A1043	30 l	magenta	70	70
3676 A1043	45 l	dark blue	1.10	1.10
3677 A1043	60 l	brown olive	1.40	1.40
3678 A1044	80 l	purple	1.90	1.90

Size: 27x41mm, 41x27mm

3679 A1044	120 l	gray bl & dk bl vio	2.75	2.75
3680 A1044	160 l	lt ver & dk ver	3.75	3.75
3681 A1044	250 l	lt bl & dk bl	6.00	6.00
3682 A1044	400 l	tan & dk brn	10.00	10.00
3683 A1044	500 l	lt bl grn & dk bl grn	12.00	12.00
3684 A1044	800 l	pink & dk lil rose	20.00	20.00
	Nos. 3664-3684 (21)		62.50	62.50

Issue dates: 1 l, 5 l, 9 l, 10 l, Aug. 27. 2 l, 4 l, 18 l, 25 l, 30 l, Oct. 8. 6 l, 8 l, 20 l, 45 l, 60 l, 80 l, Nov. 14. 120 l, 160 l, 250 l, 400 l, 500 l, 800 l, Dec. 5.

Riccone '91, Intl. Philatelic Exhibition — A1045

1991, Aug. 27

3685 A1045	4 l multicolored		40	40

A1046   A1047

Vases: a, Decorated with birds. b, Decorated with flowers.

1991, Sept. 12

3686 A1046	5 l Pair, #a.-b.		1.00	1.00

Romanian-Chinese Philatelic Exhibition.

1991, Sept. 17

3687 A1047	1 l blue		25	25

Romanian Academy, 125th anniv.

A1048   A1049

Balkanfila '91 Philatelic Exhibition: 4 l, Flowers, by Nicu Enea. 5 l, Peasant Girl of Vlasca, by Georghe Tattarescu. 20 l, Sports Center, Bacau.

1991, Sept. 20

3688 A1048	4 l multicolored		52	52
3689 A1048	5 l multicolored		90	90

Souvenir Sheet

3690 A1048	20 l multicolored		2.00	2.00

No. 3689 printed se-tenant with 2 l Romanian Philatelic Assoc. label. No. 3690 contains one 54x42mm stamp.

Miniature Sheets

Birds: No. 3691a, Cissa erythrorhyncha. b, Malaconotus blanchoti. c, Sialia sialis. d, Sturnella neglecta. e, Harpactes fasciatus. f, Upupa epops. g, Malurus cyaneus. h, Brachypteracias squamigera. i, Leptopterus madagascariensis. j, Phoeniculus bollei. k, Melanerpes erythrocephalus. l, Pericrocotus flammeus.
No. 3692a, Melithreptus laetior. b, Rhynochetos jubatus. c, Turdus migratorius. d, Copsychus saularis. e, Monticola saxatilis. f, Xanthocephalus xanthocephalus. g, Scotopelia peli. h, Ptilogonys caudatus. i, Todus mexicanus. j, Copsychus malabaricus. k, Myzomela erythrocephala. l, Gymnostinops montezuma.

1991, Oct. 7   Sheets of 12

3691 A1049	2 l #a.-l.		3.00	3.00
3692 A1049	2 l #a.-l.		3.00	3.00

Natl. Census — A1050

1991, Oct. 15

3693 A1050	5 l multicolored		40	40

Phila Nippon '91
A1051

1991, Nov. 13   Photo.   Perf. 13½

3694 A1051	10 l	Sailing ship	1.50	1.50
3695 A1051	10 l	Bridge building	1.50	1.50

Miniature Sheets

Butterflies and Moths
A1052

Designs: No. 3696a, Ornithoptera paradisea. b, Bhutanitis lidderdalii. c, Morpho helena. d, Ornithoptera croesus. e, Phoebis avellaneda. f, Ornithoptera victoriae. g, Teinopalpus imperialis. h, Hypolimnas dexithea. i, Dabasa payeni. j, Morpho achilleana. k, Heliconius melpomene. l, Agrias claudina sardanapalus.
No. 3697a, Graellsia isabellae. b, Antocharis cardamines. c, Ammobiota festiva. d, Polygonia c-album. e, Catocala promissa. f, Rhyparia purpurata. g, Arctia villica. h, Polyommatus daphnis. i, Zerynthia polyxena. j, Daphnis nerii. k, Licaena dispar rutila. l, Pararge roxelana.

1991, Nov. 30   Photo.   Perf. 13½
Sheets of 12

3696 A1052	3 l #a.-l.		3.50	3.50
3697 A1052	3 l #a.-l.		3.50	3.50

A1053   A1054

1991, Nov. 21   Photo.   Perf. 13½

3698 A1053	1 l	Running	15	15
3699 A1053	4 l	Long jump	42	42
3700 A1053	5 l	High jump	55	55
3701 A1053	5 l	Runner in blocks	55	55
3702 A1053	9 l	Hurdles	95	95
3703 A1053	10 l	Javelin	1.10	1.10
	Nos. 3698-3703 (6)		3.72	3.72

World Track and Field Championships, Tokyo.

1991, Dec. 10   Photo.

Famous People: 1 l, Mihail Kogalniceanu (1817-1891), politician. 4 l, Nicolae Titulescu (1882-1941), politician. No. 3706, Andrei Mureseanu (1816-1863), author. No. 3707, Aron Pumnul (1818-1866), author. 9 l, George Bacovia (1881-1957), author. 10 l, Perpessicius (1891-1971), writer.

3704 A1054	1 l	multi	15	15
3705 A1054	4 l	multi	20	20
3706 A1054	5 l	multi	25	25
3707 A1054	5 l	multi	25	25
3708 A1054	9 l	multi	48	48
3709 A1054	10 l	multi	52	52
	Nos. 3704-3709 (6)		1.85	1.85

See Nos. 3759-3761, 3776-3781.

Stamp Day
A1055

1991, Dec. 20

3710 A1055	8 l multicolored		50	50

No. 3710 printed se-tenant with 2 l Romanian Philatelic Assoc. label.

Central University Library, Bucharest, Cent.
A1056

1991, Dec. 23

3711 A1056	8 l red brown		35	35

Christmas
A1057

1991, Dec. 25   Photo.   Perf. 13½

3712 A1057	8 l multicolored		50	50

See No. 3874.

1992 Winter Olympics, Albertville
A1058

1992, Feb. 1   Photo.   Perf. 13½

3713 A1058	4 l	Biathlon	15	15
3714 A1058	5 l	Alpine skiing	15	15
3715 A1058	8 l	Cross-country skiing	16	16
3716 A1058	10 l	Two-man luge	20	20
3717 A1058	20 l	Speed skating	40	40
3718 A1058	25 l	Ski jumping	52	52
3719 A1058	30 l	Ice hockey	62	62
3720 A1058	45 l	Men's figure skating	90	90
	Nos. 3713-3720 (8)		3.10	3.10

Souvenir Sheets

3721 A1058	75 l	Women's figure skating	2.50	2.50

Imperf

3722 A1058	125 l	4-Man bobsled	4.15	4.15

No. 3721 is airmail and contains one 42x54mm stamp.

Porcelain — A1059

Designs: 4 l, Sugar and cream service. 5 l, Tea service. 8 l, Goblet and pitcher, vert. 30 l, Tea service, diff. 45 l, Vase, vert.

1992, Feb. 20		Photo.	Perf. 13¹/₂	
3723	A1059	4 l multicolored	15	15
3724	A1059	5 l multicolored	15	15
3725	A1059	8 l multicolored	20	20
3726	A1059	30 l multicolored	75	75
3727	A1059	45 l multicolored	1.15	1.15
	Nos. 3723-3727 (5)		2.40	2.40

Fish
A1060

Designs: 4 l, Scomber scombrus. 5 l, Tinca tinca. 8 l, Salvelinus fontinalis. 10 l, Romanichthys valsanicola. 30 l, Chondrostoma nasus. 45 l, Mullus barbatus ponticus.

1992, Feb. 28		Photo.	Perf. 13¹/₂	
3728	A1060	4 l multicolored	16	16
3729	A1060	5 l multicolored	20	20
3730	A1060	8 l multicolored	30	30
3731	A1060	10 l multicolored	40	40
3732	A1060	30 l multicolored	1.25	1.25
3733	A1060	45 l multicolored	1.75	1.75
	Nos. 3728-3733 (6)		4.06	4.06

A1060a

1992, Mar. 11		Photo.	Perf. 13¹/₂	
3734	A1060a	90 l on 5 l multi	2.25	2.25

No. 3734 not issued without surcharge.

Olympics Type of 1991
Surcharged

90ₗ

1992, Mar. 11		Photo.	Perf. 13¹/₂	
3735	A1041	90 l on 5 l like #3657	2.25	2.25

No. 3735 not issued without surcharge.

Horses
A1061

Various stylized drawings of horses walking, running, or jumping.

1992, Mar. 17		Photo.	Perf. 13¹/₂	
3736	A1061	6 l multi, vert.	22	22
3737	A1061	7 l multi	28	28
3738	A1061	10 l multi, vert.	38	38
3739	A1061	25 l multi, vert.	95	95
3740	A1061	30 l multi	1.15	1.15
3741	A1061	50 l multi, vert.	1.90	1.90
	Nos. 3736-3741 (6)		4.88	4.88

Miniature Sheet

Discovery of America, 500th
Anniv. — A1062

Columbus and ships: a, Green background. b, Violet background. c, Blue background. d, Ship approaching island.

1992, Apr. 22		Photo.	Perf. 13¹/₂	
3742	A1062	35 l Sheet of 4, #a.-d.	6.50	6.50

Europa.

Granada '92, Philatelic
Exhibition — A1063

Designs: a, 25 l, Spain No. 1 and Romania No. 1. b, 10 l, Expo emblem. c, 30 l, Building and courtyard, Granada. (Illustration reduced).

1992, Apr. 24		Photo.	Perf. 13¹/₂	
3743	A1063	Sheet of 3, #a.-c.	1.40	1.40

Icon of Christ's
Descent into Hell,
1680 — A1064

1992, Apr. 24		Photo.	Perf. 13¹/₂	
3744	A1064	10 l multicolored	60	60

Easter.

Fire Station,
Bucharest,
Cent. — A1065

1992, May 2				
3745	A1065	10 l multicolored	60	60

Chess Olympiad, Manila — A1066

1992, June 7			Perf. 13¹/₂	
3746	A1066	10 l shown	35	35

3747	A1066	10 l Building, chess board	35	35

Souvenir Sheet

3748	A1066	75 l Shore, chess board	2.50	2.50

No. 3748 contains one 42x54mm stamp.

1992 Summer Olympics,
Barcelona — A1067

1992, July 17		Photo.	Perf. 13¹/₂	
3749	A1067	6 l Shooting, vert.	15	15
3750	A1067	7 l Weight lifting, vert.	15	15
3751	A1067	9 l Two-man canoing	15	15
3752	A1067	10 l Handball, vert.	15	15
3753	A1067	25 l Wrestling	38	38
3754	A1067	30 l Fencing	45	45
3755	A1067	50 l Running, vert.	75	75
3756	A1067	55 l Boxing	82	82
	Nos. 3749-3756 (8)		3.00	3.00

Souvenir Sheets

3757	A1067	100 l Rowing	1.50	1.50

Imperf.

3758	A1067	200 l Gymnastics	3.00	3.00

Nos. 3757-3758 are airmail. No. 3757 contains one 54x42mm stamp, No. 3758 one 40x53mm stamp.

Famous People Type of 1991

Designs: 10 l, Ion I. C. Bratianu (1864-1927), prime minister. 25 l, Ion Gh. Duca (1879-1933). 30 l, Grigore Gafencu (1892-1957), journalist and politician.

1992, July 27		Photo.	Perf. 13¹/₂	
3759	A1054	10 l green & violet	30	30
3760	A1054	25 l blue & lake	75	75
3761	A1054	30 l lake & blue	90	90

Expo
'92,
Seville
A1068

Designs: 6 l, The Thinker, Cernavoda. 7 l, Trajan's bridge, Drobeta. 10 l, Mill. 25 l, Railroad bridge, Cernavoda. 30 l, Trajan Vuia's flying machine. 55 l, Herman Oberth's rocket. 100 l, Prayer sculpture, by C. Brancusi.

1992, Sept. 1				
3762	A1068	6 l multicolored	15	15
3763	A1068	7 l multicolored	15	15
3764	A1068	10 l multicolored	18	18
3765	A1068	25 l multicolored	45	45
3766	A1068	30 l multicolored	52	52
3767	A1068	55 l multicolored	1.00	1.00
	Nos. 3762-3767 (6)		2.45	2.45

Souvenir Sheet

3768	A1068	100 l multicolored	2.00	2.00

No. 3768 contains one 42x54mm stamp.

World Post Day — A1069

1992, Oct. 9				
3769	A1069	10 l multicolored	38	38

For surcharge see No. 3945.

Discovery of America, 500th
Anniv. — A1070

Columbus and: 6 l, Santa Maria. 10 l, Nina. 25 l, Pinta. 55 l, Arrival in New World. 100 l, Sailing ship, vert.

1992, Oct. 30		Photo.	Perf. 13¹/₂	
3770	A1070	6 l multicolored	16	16
3771	A1070	10 l multicolored	28	28
3772	A1070	25 l multicolored	70	70
3773	A1070	55 l multicolored	1.50	1.50

Souvenir Sheet

3774	A1070	100 l multicolored	2.25	2.25

No. 3774 contains one 42x54mm stamp.

Romanian Postal Reorganization, 1st
Anniv. — A1071

1992, Nov. 5		Photo.	Perf. 13¹/₂	
3775	A1071	10 l multicolored	42	42

Famous People Type of 1991

Designs: 6 l, Iacob Negruzzi (1842-1932), author. 7 l, Grigore Antipa (1867-1944), naturalist. 9 l, Alexe Mateevici (1888-1917), poet. 10 l, Cezar Petrescu (1892-1961), author. 25 l, Octav Onicescu (1892-1983), mathematician. 30 l, Ecaterina Teodoroiu (1894-1917), World War I soldier.

1992, Nov. 9		Photo.	Perf. 13¹/₂	
3776	A1054	6 l green & violet	15	15
3777	A1054	7 l lilac & green	16	16
3778	A1054	9 l gray blue & purple	22	22
3779	A1054	10 l brown & blue	24	24
3780	A1054	25 l blue & brown	60	60
3781	A1054	30 l slate & blue	75	75
	Nos. 3776-3781 (6)		2.12	2.12

Wild Animals — A1072

Designs: 6 l, Haliaeetus leucocephalus, vert. 7 l, Strix occidentalis, vert. 9 l, Ursus arctos, vert. 10 l, Haematopus bachmani. 25 l, Canis lupus. 30 l, Odocoileus virginianus. 55 l, Alces alces.

1992, Nov. 16		Litho.	Perf. 13¹/₂	
3782	A1072	6 l multicolored	15	15
3783	A1072	7 l multicolored	15	15
3784	A1072	9 l multicolored	16	16
3785	A1072	10 l multicolored	18	18
3786	A1072	25 l multicolored	45	45
3787	A1072	30 l multicolored	60	60
3788	A1072	55 l multicolored	1.00	1.00
	Nos. 3782-3788 (7)		2.69	2.69

Souvenir Sheet

3789	A1072	100 l Orcinus orca	2.00	2.00

Romanian Anniversaries and Events — A1073

Designs: 7 l, Building, Galea Victoria St., 300th anniv. 9 l, Statue, School of Commerce, 600th anniv. 10 l, Curtea de Arges Monastery, 475th anniv. 25 l, School of Architecture, Bucharest, 80th anniv.

1992, Dec. 3   Photo.   Perf. 13¹/₂

3790	A1073	7 l multicolored	20	20
3791	A1073	9 l multicolored	25	25
3792	A1073	10 l multicolored	30	30
3793	A1073	25 l multicolored	75	75

Natl. Arms — A1074

1992, Dec. 7

3794	A1074	15 l multicolored	30	30

Christmas A1075

1992, Dec. 15

3795	A1075	15 l multicolored	30	30

New Telephone Numbering System — A1076

1992, Dec. 28   Photo.   Perf. 13¹/₂

3796	A1076	15 l blue, black & red	35	35

Souvenir Sheets

1992 Summer Olympics, Barcelona A1077

Designs: No. 3797a, Shooting. b, Wrestling. c, Weight lifting. d, Boxing.
No. 3798a, Women's gymnastics. b, Four-man sculls. c, Fencing. d, High jump.

1992, Dec. 30   Photo.   Perf. 13¹/₂

3797	A1077	35 l Sheet of 4, #a.-d.	3.00	3.00
3798	A1077	35 l Sheet of 4, #a.-d.	3.00	3.00

Historic Sites, Bucharest — A1078

Designs: 10 l, Mihai Voda Monastery. 15 l, Vacaresti Monastery. 25 l, Multi-purpose hall. 30 l, Mina Minovici Medical Institute.

1993, Feb. 11   Photo.   Perf. 13¹/₂

3799	A1078	10 l multicolored	18	18
3800	A1078	15 l multicolored	28	28
3801	A1078	25 l multicolored	45	45
3802	A1078	30 l multicolored	55	55

Easter — A1079

1993, Mar. 25

3803	A1079	15 l multicolored	28	28

Medicinal Plants — A1080

1993, Mar. 30

3804	A1080	10 l Crataegus monogyna	18	18
3805	A1080	15 l Gentiana phlogifolia	28	28
3806	A1080	25 l Hippophae rhamnoides	48	48
3807	A1080	30 l Vaccinium myrtillus	55	55
3808	A1080	90 l Arnica montana	95	95
3809	A1080	90 l Rosa canina	1.70	1.70
		Nos. 3804-3809 (6)	4.14	4.14

Nichita Stanescu (1933-1983), Poet — A1081

1993, Mar. 31

3810	A1081	15 l brown and blue	28	28

Souvenir Sheet

Polska '93 — A1082

1993, Apr. 28   Photo.   Perf. 13¹/₂

3811	A1082	200 l multicolored	2.25	2.25

Birds — A1083   Cats — A1084

1993, Apr. 30

3812	A1083	5 l Pica pica	15	15
3813	A1083	10 l Aquila chrysaetos	15	15
3814	A1083	15 l Pyrrhula pyrrhula	15	15
3815	A1083	20 l Upupa epops	18	18
3816	A1083	25 l Dendrocopos major	20	20
3817	A1083	50 l Oriolus oriolus	42	42
3818	A1083	65 l Loxia leucoptera	55	55
3819	A1083	90 l Hirundo rustica	80	80
3820	A1083	160 l Parus cyanus	1.40	1.40
3821	A1083	250 l Sturnus roseus	2.25	2.25
		Nos. 3812-3821 (10)	6.25	6.25

Nos. 3812-3813 are horiz.

1993, May 24   Photo.   Perf. 13¹/₂

Various cats.

3822	A1084	10 l multicolored	15	15
3823	A1084	15 l multicolored	15	15
3824	A1084	30 l multicolored	30	30
3825	A1084	90 l multicolored	95	95
3826	A1084	135 l multicolored	1.40	1.40
3827	A1084	160 l multicolored	1.65	1.65
		Nos. 3822-3827 (6)	4.60	4.60

Souvenir Sheet

Europa — A1085

Paintings and sculpture by: a, Pablo Picasso. b, Constantin Brancusi. c, Ion Irimescu. d, Alexandru Ciucurencu.

1993, May 31   Photo.   Perf. 13¹/₂

3828	A1085	280 l Sheet of 4, #a.-d.	2.75	2.75

A1086   A1087

1993, June 30   Photo.   Perf. 13¹/₂

3829	A1086	10 l Vipera berus	15	15
3830	A1086	15 l Lynx lynx	15	15
3831	A1086	25 l Tadorna tadorna	15	15
3832	A1086	75 l Hucho hucho	45	45
3833	A1086	105 l Limenitis populi	60	60
3834	A1086	280 l Rosalia alpina	1.75	1.75
		Nos. 3829-3834 (6)	3.25	3.25

Nos. 3829, 3831-3834 are horiz.

1993, June 30

3835	A1087	10 l Martes martes	15	15
3836	A1087	15 l Oryctolagus cuniculus	15	15
3837	A1087	20 l Sciurus vulgaris	15	15
3838	A1087	25 l Rupicapra rupicapra	15	15
3839	A1087	30 l Vulpes vulpes	16	16
3840	A1087	40 l Ovis ammon	22	22
3841	A1087	75 l Genetta genetta	45	45
3842	A1087	105 l Eliomys quercinus	65	65
3843	A1087	150 l Mustela ermina	85	85
3844	A1087	280 l Herpestes ichneumon	1.75	1.75
		Nos. 3835-3844 (10)	4.68	4.68

Nos. 3836, 3839, 3843-3844 are horiz.

Dinosaurs — A1088

1993, July 30   Photo.   Perf. 13¹/₂

3845	A1088	29 l Brontosaurus	16	16
3846	A1088	46 l Plesiosaurus	25	25
3847	A1088	85 l Triceratops	48	48
3848	A1088	171 l Stegosaurus	95	95
3849	A1088	216 l Tyrannosaurus	1.25	1.25
3850	A1088	319 l Archaeopteryx	2.00	2.00
		Nos. 3845-3850 (6)	5.09	5.09

Souvenir Sheet

Telafila '93, Israel-Romanian Philatelic Exhibition — A1089

Woman with Eggs, by Marcel Lancu. Illustration reduced.

1993, Aug. 21

3851	A1089	535 l multicolored	2.25	2.25

Icons — A1090

Designs: 75 l, St. Stephen. 171 l, Martyrs from Brancoveanu and Vacarescu families. 216 l, St. Anthony.

1993, Aug. 31

3852	A1090	75 l multicolored	45	45
3853	A1090	171 l multicolored	1.00	1.00
3854	A1090	216 l multicolored	1.40	1.40

Rural Mounted Police, Cent. — A1091

1993, Sept. 1

3855	A1091	29 l multicolored	22	22

Riccione '93
3–5 septembrie

No. 3618
Surcharged in
Red

1993, Sept. 3

3856	A1031	171 l on 2 l	1.10	1.10

Souvenir Sheet

Bangkok '93 — A1092

Illustration reduced.

1993, Sept. 20

3857	A1092	535 l multicolored	2.25	2.25

Famous Men — A1093

Designs: 29 l, George Baritiu (1812-93), politician. 46 l, Horia Creanga (1892-1943), architect. 85 l, Armand Calinescu (1893-1939), politician. 171 l, Dumitru Bagdasar (1893-1946), physician. 216 l, Constantin Brailoiu (1893-1958), musician. 319 l, Iuliu Maniu (1873-1953), politician.

1993, Oct. 8

3858	A1093	29 l multicolored	16	16
3859	A1093	46 l multicolored	25	25
3860	A1093	85 l multicolored	48	48
3861	A1093	171 l multicolored	95	95
3862	A1093	216 l multicolored	1.25	1.25
3863	A1093	319 l multicolored	2.00	2.00
		Nos. 3858-3863 (6)	5.09	5.09

Souvenir Sheet

Romanian Entry into Council of
Europe — A1094

1993, Nov. 26   Photo.   Perf. 13½

3864	A1094	1590 l multicolored	9.00	9.00

Expansion of
Natl. Borders,
75th Anniv.
A1095

Government leaders: 115 l, Iancu Flondor (1865-1924). 245 l, Ion I. C. Bratianu (1864-1927). 255 l, Luliu Maniu (1873-1953). 325 l, Pantelimon Halippa (1883-1979). 1060 l, King Ferdinand I (1865-1927).

1993-94

3865	A1095	115 l multicolored	50	50
3866	A1095	245 l multicolored	85	85
3867	A1095	255 l multicolored	1.00	1.00
3868	A1095	325 l multicolored	1.75	1.75

Souvenir Sheet

3869	A1095	1060 l Romania in one color	4.00	4.00
a.		Romania in four colors	10.00	10.00

No. 3869a was redrawn because of an error in the map.
Issued: No. 3869, Feb. 1994; Nos. 3865-3868, 3869a, Dec. 1, 1993.

Anniversaries and
Events — A1096

Designs: 115 l, Emblem of the Diplomatic Alliance. 245 l, Statue of Johannes Honterus, founder of first Humanitarian School. 255 l, Arms, seal of Slatina, Olt River Bridge. 325 l, Map, arms of Braila.

1993, Dec. 15

3870	A1096	115 l multicolored	50	50
3871	A1096	245 l multicolored	85	85
3872	A1096	255 l multicolored	1.00	1.00
3873	A1096	325 l multicolored	1.75	1.75

Diplomatic Alliance, 75th anniv. (#3870). Birth of Johannes Honterus, 450th anniv. (#3871). City of Slatina, 625th anniv. (#3872). County of Braila, 625th anniv. (#3873).

Christmas Type of 1991

1993, Dec. 20

3874	A1057	45 l like #3712	32	32

Insects, Wildlife from Movile
Cavern — A1097

Designs: 29 l, Clivina subterranea. 46 l, Nepa anophthalma. 85 l, Haemopis caeca. 171 l, Lascona cristiani. 216 l, Semisalsa dobrogica. 310 l, Armadilidium tabacarui. 535 l, Exploring cavern, vert.

1993, Dec. 27

3875	A1097	29 l multicolored	15	15
3876	A1097	46 l multicolored	24	24
3877	A1097	85 l multicolored	45	45
3878	A1097	171 l multicolored	85	85
3879	A1097	216 l multicolored	1.10	1.10
3880	A1097	310 l multicolored	1.50	1.50
		Nos. 3875-3880 (6)	4.29	4.29

Souvenir Sheet

3881	A1097	535 l multicolored	2.25	2.25

Alexandru Ioan
Cuza — A1098

1994, Jan. 24   Photo.   Perf. 13

3882	A1098	45 l multicolored	25	25

Historic Buildings, Bucharest — A1099

Designs: 115 l, Opera House. 245 l, Vacaresti Monastery. 255 l, Church of St. Vineri. 325 l, Dominican House, Vacaresti Monastery.

1994, Feb. 7

3883	A1099	115 l multicolored	38	18
3884	A1099	245 l multicolored	80	40
3885	A1099	255 l multicolored	85	42
3886	A1099	325 l multicolored	1.10	55
		Nos. 3883-3886 (4)	3.13	1.55

1994 Winter
Olympics,
Lillehammer
A1100

1994, Feb. 12   Perf. 13½

3887	A1100	70 l Speed skating	25	15
3888	A1100	115 l Slalom skiing	38	18
3889	A1100	125 l Bobsled	42	20
3890	A1100	245 l Biathlon	80	40
3891	A1100	255 l Ski jumping	85	42
3892	A1100	325 l Figure skating	1.10	55
		Nos. 3887-3892 (6)	3.80	1.90

Souvenir Sheet

3893	A1100	1590 l Luge	5.25	5.25

No. 3893 contains one 43x54mm stamp.

Mills — A1101

1994, Mar. 31   Perf. 13

3894	A1101	70 l Sarichioi	25	15
3895	A1101	115 l Valea Nucarilor	38	18
3896	A1101	125 l Caraorman	42	20
3897	A1101	245 l Romanii de Jos	80	40
3898	A1101	255 l Enisala, horiz.	85	42
3899	A1101	325 l Nistoresti	1.10	55
		Nos. 3894-3899 (6)	3.80	1.90

Dinosaurs — A1102

1994, Apr. 30   Photo.   Perf. 13½

3900	A1102	90 l Struthiosaurs	30	30
3901	A1102	130 l Megalosaurs	42	42
3902	A1102	150 l Parasaurolophus	48	48
3903	A1102	280 l Stenonychosaurus	90	90
3904	A1102	500 l Camarasaurus	1.60	1.60
3905	A1102	635 l Gallimimus	2.00	2.00
		Nos. 3900-3905 (6)	5.70	5.70

Romanian
Legends — A1103

Designs: 70 l, Calin the Madman. 115 l, Ileana Cosanzeana. 125 l, Ileana Cosanzeana, diff. 245 l, Ileana Cosanzeana, diff. 255 l, Agheran the Brave. 325 l, Wolf as Prince Charming, Ileana Cosanzeana.

1994, Apr. 8	**Photo.**	*Perf. 13*
3906 A1103	70 l multicolored	25 15
3907 A1103	115 l multicolored	38 18
3908 A1103	125 l multicolored	42 20
3909 A1103	245 l multicolored	80 40
3910 A1103	255 l multicolored	85 42
3911 A1103	325 l multicolored	1.10 55
Nos. 3906-3911 (6)		3.80 1.90

Easter — A1104   Trees — A1105

1994, Apr. 21
3912 A1104 60 l multicolored   25 15

Wmk. 398

1994, May 27	**Photo.**	*Perf. 13*
3913 A1105	15 l Abies alba	15 15
3914 A1105	35 l Pinus sylvestris	15 15
3915 A1105	45 l Populus alba	15 15
3916 A1105	60 l Quercus robur	15 15
3917 A1105	70 l Larix decidua	16 15
3918 A1105	125 l Fagus sylvatica	30 15
3919 A1105	350 l Acer pseudo-	
	platanus	85 42
3920 A1105	940 l Fraxinus excel-	
	sior	2.25 1.10
3921 A1105	1440 l Picea abies	3.50 1.75
3922 A1105	3095 l Tilia platyphyl-	
	los	7.50 3.75
Nos. 3913-3922 (10)		15.16 7.92

1994 World Cup
Soccer
Championships,
US — A1106

1994, June 17   **Unwmk.**
3923 A1106	90 l Group A	25 16
3924 A1106	130 l Group B	35 18
3925 A1106	150 l Group C	40 20
3926 A1106	280 l Group D	75 38
3927 A1106	500 l Group E	1.40 70
3928 A1106	635 l Group F	1.75 85
Nos. 3923-3928 (6)		4.90 2.47

Souvenir Sheet
3929 A1106 2075 l Action scene   5.25 5.25

No. 3929 is airmail and contains one 54x42mm stamp.

150 l Intl. Olympic
Committee,
Cent. — A1107

Ancient Olympians: 150 l, Torchbearer. 280 l, Discus thrower. 500 l, Wrestlers. 635 l, Arbitrator. 2075 l, Runners, emblem of Romanian Olympic Committee.

1994, June 23		
3930 A1107	150 l multicolored	40 20
3931 A1107	280 l multicolored	75 38
3932 A1107	500 l multicolored	1.40 70
3933 A1107	635 l multicolored	1.75 85
Nos. 3930-3933 (4)		4.30 2.13

Souvenir Sheet
3934 A1107 2075 l multicolored   5.25 5.25

No. 3934 contains one 54x42mm stamp. Romanian Olympic Committee, 80th anniv. (#3934).

Miniature Sheets

Mushrooms
A1108

Edible: No. 3935a, 30 l, Craterellus cornucopi-
odes. b, 60 l, Lepista nuda. c, 150 l, Boletus edulis.
d, 940 l, Lycoperdon perlatum.
Poisonous: No. 3936a, 90 l, Boletus satanas. b,
280 l, Amanita phalloides. c, 350 l, Inocybe patonil-
lardi. d, 500 l, Amanita muscaria.

1994, Aug. 8	**Photo.**	*Perf. 13½*
3935 A1108	Sheet of 4, #a.-d.	2.50 1.25
3936 A1108	Sheet of 4, #a.-d.	2.75 1.40

PHILAKOREA
'94 — A1109

1994, Aug. 16   *Perf. 13½*
3937 A1109   60 l Tuning fork   18 15

Souvenir Sheet
3938 A1109 2075 l Korean drummer   5.25 5.25

No. 3938 contains one 42x54mm stamp.

Environmental Protection in Danube River
Delta — A1110

Designs: 150 l, Huso huso. 280 l, Vipera ursini.
500 l, Haliaeetus albieilla. 635 l, Mustela lutreola.
2075 l, Periploca graeca.

1994, Aug. 31		
3939 A1110	150 l multicolored	35 18
3940 A1110	280 l multicolored	65 32
3941 A1110	500 l multicolored	1.10 55
3942 A1110	635 l multicolored	1.50 75
Nos. 3939-3942 (4)		3.60 1.80

Souvenir Sheet
3943 A1110 2075 l multicolored   4.75 4.75

No. 3943 contains one 54x42mm stamp.

150L

Nos. 3654-3655
Surcharged — a

150 LEI

1994
Posta - cea mai buna alegere
No. 3769 Surcharged — b

1994		**Perfs., Etc. as Before**	
3944 A1041(a)	150 l on 4.50 l		
	#3654	30	20
3945 A1069(b)	150 l on 10 l #3769	35	18
3946 A1041(a)	525 l on 4.50 l		
	#3655	1.10	55
Nos. 3944-3946 (3)		1.75	93

Issued: #3944, 3946 9/9/94; #3945, 10/7/94.

Circus
Animal
Acts
A1111

1994, Sept. 15	**Photo.**	*Perf. 13*
3947 A1111	90 l Elephant	22 15
3948 A1111	130 l Bear, vert.	32 16
3949 A1111	150 l Monkeys	38 20
3950 A1111	280 l Tiger	70 35
3951 A1111	500 l Lion	1.25 60
3952 A1111	635 l Horse	1.65 85
Nos. 3947-3952 (6)		4.52 2.31

20th Intl. Fair,
Bucharest — A1112

1994, Oct. 10
3953 A1112 525 l multicolored   1.25 60

**ROMANIA
&
EASTERN
EUROPE**

Albania
Bulgaria
Czechoslovakia
Hungary
Jugoslavia
Poland
Russia
& New Republics

*YEARLY UNITS.
WANTLISTS INVITED.*

Lists available at 50¢
for each country
- refundable with first order.

R.J.B. Mail Sales
P.O. Box 160
Frisco, CO 80443

Fish
A1113

World Wildlife Fund: 150 l, Acipenser ruthenus.
280 l, Acipenser guldenstaedti. 500 l, Acipenser
stellatus. 635 l, Acipenser sturio.

1994, Oct. 29	**Photo.**	*Perf. 13½*
3954 A1113	150 l multicolored	32 16
3955 A1113	280 l multicolored	60 30
3956 A1113	500 l multicolored	1.00 50
3957 A1113	635 l multicolored	1.40 70
Nos. 3954-3957 (4)		3.32 1.66

ROMANIA for beginner
and specialist!

Extensive stock of Romania includes all Scott-listed/unlisted stamps
perforated and imperforated souvenir sheets, sheetlets, mint and used.

Low price · Fast service

OLD/NEW, YEAR/THEMATIC SETS
FDC'S/CANCELS, MAXIMUM/POST CARDS.

· NEW ISSUE SERVICE ·

"I AM AT THE SOURCE"

GEORGE ARGHIR Philatelists
DETUNATA 17-27, P.O. BOX 521
RO-3400 CLUJ-NAPOCA 9, ROMANIA
TEL/FAX: +40-64-414036

Chinese-Romanian Philatelic
Exhibition — A1114

1994, Oct. 29   Photo.   Perf. 13½
3958 A1114 150 l Serpent   38   20
3959 A1114 1135 l Dragon   3.00 1.50
  a. Pair, #3958-3959 + label   3.50 3.50

Romanian
State Railway,
125th Anniv. —
A1115

1994, Oct. 31
3960 A1115 90 l multicolored   22   15

Famous
People — A1116

Designs: 30 l, Akex Drascu (1817-94). 60 l, Gh. Polizu (1819-86). 90 l, Gheorghe Tattarescu (1820-94), politician, prime minister. 150 l, Iulia Hasdeu (1869-88). 280 l, S. Mehedinti (1869-1962). 350 l, Camil Petrescu (1894-1957). 500 l, N. Paulescu (1869-1931). 940 l, L. Grigorescu (1894-1965).

1994   Photo.   Perf. 13½
3961 A1116   30 l multicolored   15   15
3962 A1116   60 l multicolored   15   15
3962a A1116 90 l multicolored   20   15
3963 A1116 150 l multicolored   32   16
3964 A1116 280 l multicolored   60   30
3965 A1116 350 l multicolored   75   38
3966 A1116 500 l multicolored   1.00   50
3967 A1116 940 l multicolored   2.00 1.00
  Nos. 3961-3967 (8)   5.17 2.79

Issued; 90 l, 12/28/94; others, 11/30/94.

Christmas — A1117

1994, Dec. 14   Perf. 13½
3968 A1117 60 l multicolored   20   15

St. Mary's Romanian Orthodox Church,
Cleveland, Ohio, 90th Anniv. — A1118

1994, Dec. 21   Photo.   Perf. 13½
3969 A1118 610 l multicolored   1.50   75

World
Tourism
Organization,
20th Anniv.
A1119

1994, Dec. 22
3970 A1119 525 l multicolored   1.25   60

Miniature Sheet

Romanian Military
Decorations — A1120

Year of medal: No. 3971a, 30 l, Distinguished Flying Cross, 1938. b, 60 l, Military Cross, 3rd class, 1916. c, 150 l, Distinguished Serivce Medal, 1st Class, 1880. d, 940 l, Order of the Romanian Star, 1877.

1994, Dec. 23
3971 A1120 Sheet of 4, #a.-d.   2.75 2.75

SEMI-POSTAL STAMPS

Queen Elizabeth   The Queen
Spinning — SP1   Weaving — SP2

Queen as War
Nurse — SP3

Perf. 11½, 11½x13½
1906, Jan. 14   Typo.   Unwmk.
B1 SP1 3b (+ 7b) brn   1.50 1.00
B2 SP1 5b (+ 10b) lt grn   1.50 1.00
B3 SP1 10b (+ 10b) rose red   5.00 2.50
B4 SP1 15b (+ 10b) vio   4.00 2.25

1906, Mar. 18
B5 SP2 3b (+ 7b) org brn   1.50 1.00
B6 SP2 5b (+ 10b) bl grn   1.50 1.00
B7 SP2 10b (+ 10b) car   5.00 2.50
B8 SP2 15b (+ 10b) red vio   4.00 2.25

Perf. 11½, 13½x11½
1906, Mar. 23
B9 SP3 3b (+ 7b) org brn   1.50 1.00
B10 SP3 5b (+ 10b) bl grn   1.50 1.00
B11 SP3 10b (+ 10b) car   5.00 2.50
B12 SP3 15b (+ 10b) red vio   4.00 2.25

Booklet panes of 4 exist of Nos. B1-B3, B5-B7, B9-B12.
Counterfeits of Nos. B1-B12 are plentiful. Copies of Nos. B1-B12 with smooth, even gum are counterfeits.

SP4

1906, Aug. 4   Perf. 12
B13 SP4 3b (+ 7b) ol brn, buff & bl   75 48
B14 SP4 5b (+ 10b) grn, rose & buff   90 48
B15 SP4 10b (+ 10b) rose red, buff & bl 1.65 1.25
B16 SP4 15b (+ 10b) vio, buff & bl   4.50 1.75

Guardian
Angel
Bringing Poor
to Crown
Princess
Marie — SP5

1907, Feb.   Engr.   Perf. 11
Center in Brown
B17 SP5 3b (+ 7b) org brn   1.50 1.25
B18 SP5 5b (+ 10b) dk grn   95   48
B19 SP5 10b (+ 10b) dk car   95   48
B20 SP5 15b (+ 10b) dl vio   75   55

Nos. B1-B20 were sold for more than face value. The surtax, shown in parenthesis, was for charitable purposes.

Map of   Stephen the
Romania — SP9   Great — SP10

Michael the Brave   Kings Carol I
SP11   and Ferdinand
                     SP12

Adam Clisi
Monument — SP13

1927, Mar. 15   Typo.   Perf. 13½
B21 SP9   1 l + 9 l lt vio   70   40
B22 SP10 2 l + 8 l Prus grn   70   40
B23 SP11 3 l + 7 l dp rose   70   40
B24 SP12 5 l + 5 l dp bl   70   40
B25 SP13 6 l + 4 l ol grn   1.90 40
  Nos. B21-B25 (5)   4.70 2.00

50th anniv. of the Royal Geographical Society. The surtax was for the benefit of that society. The stamps were valid for postage only from 3/15-4/14.

Boy Scouts in   The
Camp — SP15   Rescue — SP16

Design: 3 l+3 l, Swearing in a Tenderfoot. 4 l+4 l, Prince Nicholas Chief Scout. 6 l+6 l, King Carol II in Scout's Uniform.

1931, July 15   Photo.   Wmk. 225
B26 SP15 1 l + 1 l car rose   95   70
B27 SP16 2 l + 2 l dp grn   1.25   95
B28 SP15 3 l + 3 l ultra   1.65 1.25
B29 SP16 4 l + 4 l ol gray   1.65 1.50
B30 SP16 6 l + 6 l red brn   3.50 1.75
  Nos. B26-B30 (5)   9.00 6.15

The surtax was for the benefit of the Boy Scout organization.

Boy Scout Jamboree Issue

Scouts in Camp   Semaphore
SP20   Signaling
                   SP21

Trailing — SP22   Camp Fire — SP23

King Carol II   King Carol II
SP24   and Prince
                   Michael
                   SP25

1932, June 8   Wmk. 230
B31 SP20 25b + 25b pck grn   2.75 1.00
B32 SP21 50b + 50b brt bl   3.50 2.00
B33 SP22 1 l + 1 l ol grn   4.00 2.75
B34 SP23 2 l + 2 l org red   6.75 4.00
B35 SP24 3 l + 3 l Prus bl   12.00 8.00
B36 SP25 6 l + 6 l blk brn   14.00 10.00
  Nos. B31-B36 (6)   43.00 27.75

For overprints see Nos. B44-B49.

Tuberculosis
Sanatorium
SP26

Memorial Tablet to Postal Employees Who Died in World War I — SP27

Carmen Sylva Convalescent Home SP28

1932, Nov. 1

B37	SP26	4 l + 1 l dk grn	2.10 1.25
B38	SP27	6 l + 1 l chocolate	2.10 2.00
B39	SP28	10 l + 1 l dp bl	4.25 2.50

The surtax was given to a fund for the employees of the postal and telegraph services.

Philatelic Exhibition Issue
Souvenir Sheet

King Carol II — SP29

1932, Nov. 20 Unwmk. Imperf.

B40 SP29 6 l + 5 l dk ol grn   11.00 11.00

Intl. Phil. Exhib. at Bucharest, Nov. 20-24, 1932. Each holder of a ticket of admission to the exhibition could buy a copy of the stamp. The ticket cost 20 lei.

Roadside Shrine SP31   Woman Spinning SP33

Woman Weaving SP32

1934, Apr. 16 Wmk. 230 Perf. 13½

B41	SP31	1 l + 1 l dk brn	55 38
B42	SP32	2 l + 1 l blue	75 48
B43	SP33	3 l + 1 l slate grn	1.00 65

Weaving Exposition.

Boy Scout Mamaia Jamboree Issue

Semi-Postal Stamps o 1932 Overprinted in Black or Gold

1934, July 8

B44	SP20	25b + 25b pck grn	1.75 1.50
B45	SP21	50b + 50b brt bl (G)	2.75 1.50
B46	SP22	1 l + 1 l ol grn	3.50 2.75
B47	SP23	2 l + 2 l org red	4.00 3.50
B48	SP24	3 l + 3 l Prus bl (G)	7.75 6.75
B49	SP25	6 l + 6 l blk brn (G)	12.00 9.00
		Nos. B44-B49 (6)	31.75 25.00

Sea Scout Saluting — SP34   Scout Bugler — SP35

Sea and Land Scouts — SP36

King Carol II — SP37   Sea, Land and Girl Scouts — SP38

1935, June 8

B50	SP34	25b ol blk	90 70
B51	SP35	1 l violet	2.00 1.65
B52	SP36	2 l green	2.50 2.10
B53	SP37	6 l + 1 l red brn	3.75 2.25
B54	SP38	10 l + 2 l dk ultra	10.50 7.50
		Nos. B50-B54 (5)	19.65 14.20

Fifth anniversary of accession of King Carol II, and a national sports meeting held June 8. Surtax aided the Boy Scouts.

Nos. B50-B54 exist imperf.

King Carol II — SP39

1936, May

B55 SP39 6 l + 1 l rose car   50 35

Bucharest Exhibition and 70th anniversary of the dynasty. Exists imperf.

Girl of Oltenia — SP40   Girl of Saliste — SP42

Youth from Gorj — SP44

Designs: 1 l+1 l, Girl of Banat. 3 l+1 l, Girl of Hateg. 6 l+3 l, Girl of Neamt. 10 l+5 l, Youth and girl of Bucovina.

1936, June 8

B56	SP40	50b + 50b brown	38 25
B57	SP40	1 l + 1 l violet	38 25
B58	SP42	2 l + 1 l Prus grn	38 25
B59	SP42	3 l + 1 l car rose	38 25
B60	SP44	4 l + 2 l red org	70 52
B61	SP40	6 l + 3 l ol gray	70 60
B62	SP42	10 l + 5 l brt bl	1.40 1.10
		Nos. B56-B62 (7)	4.32 3.22

6th anniv. of accession of King Carol II. The surtax was for child welfare. Exist imperf.

Insignia of Boy Scouts SP47   SP48

Jamboree Emblem SP49   Submarine "Delfinul" SP50

1936, Aug. 20

B63	SP47	1 l + 1 l brt bl	1.90 1.50
B64	SP48	3 l + 3 l ol gray	2.75 1.90
B65	SP49	6 l + 6 l car rose	3.50 2.75

Boy Scout Jamboree at Brasov (Kronstadt).

1936, Oct.

Designs: 3 l+2 l, Training ship "Mircea." 6 l+3 l, Steamship "S.M.R."

B66	SP50	1 l + 1 l pur	1.90 1.25
B67	SP50	3 l + 1 l ultra	1.75 1.25
B68	SP50	6 l + 3 l car rose	2.50 2.50

Marine Exhibition at Bucharest. Exist imperf.

Soccer SP53

Swimming SP54

Throwing the Javelin — SP55   Skiing — SP56

King Carol II Hunting — SP57   Rowing — SP58

Horsemanship — SP59

Founding of the U.F.S.R. SP60

Start of Race — SP61   Javelin Thrower — SP62

1937, June 8 Wmk. 230 Perf. 13½

B69	SP53	25b + 25b ol blk	35 20
B70	SP54	50b + 50b brn	35 20
B71	SP55	1 l + 50b vio	35 20
B72	SP56	2 l + 4 l slate grn	35 20
B73	SP57	3 l + 1 l rose lake	45 25
B74	SP58	4 l + 1 l red org	70 28
B75	SP59	6 l + 2 l dp claret	1.00 35
B76	SP60	10 l + 4 l brt blue	1.40 1.25
		Nos. B69-B76 (8)	4.95 2.93

25th anniversary of the Federation of Romanian Sports Clubs (U.F.S.R.); 7th anniversary of the accession of King Carol II.

Exist imperf.

Designs: 4 l+1 l, Hurdling. 6 l+1 l, Finish of race. 10 l+1 l, High jump.

1937, Sept. 1 Wmk. 230 Perf. 13½

B77	SP61	1 l + 1 l purple	35 35
B78	SP62	2 l + 1 l green	45 38
B79	SP61	4 l + 1 l vermilion	55 55
B80	SP62	6 l + 1 l maroon	85 85
B81	SP61	10 l + 1 l brt bl	2.25 1.75
		Nos. B77-B81 (5)	4.45 3.88

8th Balkan Games, Bucharest. Exist imperf.

Catalogue values for unused stamps in this section, from this point to the end of the section, are for Never Hinged items.

King Carol II — SP66

1938, May 24

B82 SP66 6 l + 1 l deep magenta   42 20

Bucharest Exhibition (for local products), May 19-June 19, celebrating 20th anniversary of the union of Rumanian provinces.

Exists imperf.

Dimitrie Cantemir — SP67   Maria Doamna — SP68

Mircea the Great
SP69

Constantine
Brancoveanu
SP70

Stephen the
Great — SP71

Prince
Cuza — SP72

Michael the
Brave — SP73

Queen
Elizabeth — SP74

King Carol
II — SP75

King Ferdinand
I — SP76

King Carol I — SP77

1938, June 8   *Perf. 13½*

B83	SP67	25b + 25b ol blk	25	25
B84	SP68	50b + 50b brn	25	25
B85	SP69	1 l + 1 l blk vio	25	25
B86	SP70	2 l + 2 l yel grn	25	25
B87	SP71	3 l + 2 l dp mag	25	25
B88	SP72	4 l + 2 l scarlet	25	25
B89	SP73	6 l + 2 l vio brn	65	65
B90	SP74	7.50 l gray bl	65	65
B91	SP75	10 l brt bl	65	65
B92	SP76	16 l dk slate grn	1.10	1.10
B93	SP77	20 l vermilion	1.40	1.40
		Nos. B83-B93 (11)	5.95	5.95

8th anniv. of accession of King Carol II. Surtax was for Straja Tarii, a natl. org. for boys. Exist imperf.

"The Spring" — SP78

"Escorting
Prisoners"
SP79

"Rodica, the
Water Carrier"
SP81

Nicolae
Grigorescu
SP82

Design: 4 l+1 l, "Returning from Market."

1938, June 23   *Perf. 13½*

B94	SP78	1 l + 1 l brt bl	60	30
B95	SP79	2 l + 1 l yel grn	70	42
B96	SP79	4 l + 1 l vermilion	75	55
B97	SP81	6 l + 1 l lake	95	75
B98	SP82	10 l + 1 l brt bl	1.25	75
		Nos. B94-B98 (5)	4.25	2.77

Birth centenary of Nicolae Grigorescu, Romanian painter. Exist imperf.

St. George and the
Dragon — SP83

1939, June 8   *Photo.*

B99	SP83	25b + 25b ol gray	38	25
B100	SP83	50b + 50b brn	38	25
B101	SP83	1 l + 1 l pale vio	38	25
B102	SP83	2 l + 2 l lt grn	38	25
B103	SP83	3 l + 2 l red vio	60	25
B104	SP83	4 l + 2 l red org	80	28
B105	SP83	6 l + 2 l car rose	90	28
B106	SP83	8 l gray vio	1.00	40
B107	SP83	10 l brt bl	1.10	50
B108	SP83	12 l brt ultra	1.40	80
B109	SP83	16 l bl grn	1.65	1.00
		Nos. B99-B109 (11)	8.97	4.51

9th anniv. of accession of King Carol II. Exist imperf.

King Carol II
SP87   SP88

SP89

SP90

SP91

1940, June 8   *Perf. 13½*   *Photo.*   *Wmk. 230*

B113	SP87	1 l + 50b dl pur	25	15
B114	SP88	4 l + 1 l fawn	25	18
B115	SP89	6 l + 1 l blue	25	24
B116	SP90	8 l rose brn	38	30

B117	SP89	16 l ultra	50	38
B118	SP91	32 l dk vio brn	90	65
		Nos. B113-B118 (6)	2.53	1.90

10th anniv. of accession of King Carol II. Exist imperf.

King Carol II
SP92   SP93

1940, June 1

B119	SP92	1 l + 50b dk grn	15	15
B120	SP92	2.50 l + 50b Prus grn	18	15
B121	SP92	3 l + 1 l rose car	22	15
B122	SP92	3.50 l + 50b choc	28	18
B123	SP93	4 l + 1 l org brn	30	22
B124	SP93	6 l + 1 l sapphire	45	45
B125	SP93	9 l + 1 l brt bl	60	45
B126	SP93	14 l + 1 l dk bl grn	75	55
		Nos. B119-B126 (8)	2.93	2.00

Surtax was for Romania's air force. Exist imperf.

View of
Danube
SP94

Greco-Roman
Ruins — SP95

Designs: 3 l+1 l, Hotin Castle. 4 l+1 l, Hurez Monastery. 5 l+1 l, Church in Bucovina. 8 l+1 l, Tower. 12 l+2 l, Village church, Transylvania. 16 l+2 l, Arch in Bucharest.

1940, June 8   *Perf. 14½x14, 14x14½*
Inscribed: "Straja Tarii 8 Iunie 1940"

B127	SP94	1 l + 1 l dp vio	22	22
B128	SP95	2 l + 1 l red brn	28	28
B129	SP94	3 l + 1 l yel grn	28	28
B130	SP94	4 l + 1 l grnsh blk	35	35
B131	SP95	5 l + 1 l org ver	42	42
B132	SP95	8 l + 1 l brn car	55	55
B133	SP95	12 l + 2 l ultra	80	80
B134	SP95	16 l + 2 l dk bl gray	1.25	1.25
		Nos. B127-B134 (8)	4.15	4.15

Issued to honor Straja Tarii, a national organization for boys. Exist imperf.

King Michael
SP102

Corneliu Codreanu
SP103

1940-42   *Photo.*   *Wmk. 230*

B138	SP102	1 l + 50b yel grn	15	15
B138A	SP102	2 l + 50b yel grn	15	15
B139	SP102	2.50 l + 50b dk bl grn	15	15
B140	SP102	3 l + 1 l pur	15	15
B141	SP102	3.50 l + 50b rose pink	15	15
B141A	SP102	4 l + 50b org ver	15	15
B142	SP102	4 l + 1 l brn	15	15
B142A	SP102	5 l + 1 l dp plum	42	42
B143	SP102	6 l + 1 l lt ultra	15	15
B143A	SP102	7 l + 1 l sl grn	15	15
B143B	SP102	8 l + 1 l dp vio	15	15
B143C	SP102	12 l + 1 l brn vio	15	15

B144	SP102	14 l + 1 l brt bl	28	28
B144A	SP102	19 l + 1 l lil rose	60	60
		Set value	2.25	2.25

Issue years: #B138A, B141A, B142A, B143A, B143B, B143C, B144A, 1942; others, 1940.

1940, Nov. 8   *Unwmk.*   *Perf. 13½*
B145 SP103   7 l + 30 l dk grn   2.50   2.00

13th anniv. of the founding of the Iron Guard by Corneliu Codreanu.

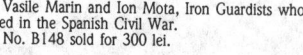

Vasile
Marin — SP104

Design: 15 l+15 l, Ion Mota.

1941, Jan. 13

B146	SP104	7 l + 7 l rose brn	48	48
B147	SP104	15 l + 15 l slate bl	1.10	1.10

Souvenir Sheet
Imperf

B148		Sheet of 2	22.50	22.50
a.		SP104 7 l + 7 l Prus green	5.75	5.75
b.		SP104 15 l + 15 l Prus green	5.75	5.75

Vasile Marin and Ion Mota, Iron Guardists who died in the Spanish Civil War.
No. B148 sold for 300 lei.

Crown, Leaves
and
Bible — SP107

Designs: 2 l+43 l, Library shelves. 7 l+38 l, Carol I Foundation, Bucharest. 10 l+35 l, King Carol I. 16 l+29 l, Kings Michael and Carol I.

Perf. 13½

1941, May 9   *Photo.*   *Wmk. 230*
Inscribed: "1891 1941"

B149	SP107	1.50 l + 43.50 l pur	30	30
B150	SP107	2 l + 43 l rose brn	30	30
B151	SP107	7 l + 38 l rose	30	30
B152	SP107	10 l + 35 l ol blk	30	30
B153	SP107	16 l + 29 l brn	30	30
		Nos. B149-B153 (5)	1.50	1.50

50th anniv. of the Carol I Foundation, established to endow research and stimulate the arts.

Same Overprinted in **CERNAUTI**
Red or Black   **5 Iulie 1941**

1941, Aug.

B154	SP107	1.50 l + 43.50 l (R)	1.40	1.40
B155	SP107	2 l + 43 l	1.40	1.40
B156	SP107	7 l + 38 l	1.40	1.40
B157	SP107	10 l + 35 l (R)	1.40	1.40
B158	SP107	16 l + 29 l	1.40	1.40

Occupation of Cernauti, Bucovina.

Same Overprinted in **CHISINAU**
Red or Black   **16 Iulie 1941**

1941, Aug.

B159	SP107	1.50 l + 43.50 l (R)	1.40	1.40
B160	SP107	2 l + 43 l	1.40	1.40
B161	SP107	7 l + 38 l	1.40	1.40
B162	SP107	10 l + 35 l (R)	1.40	1.40
B163	SP107	16 l + 29 l	1.40	1.40
		Nos. B154-B163 (10)	14.00	14.00

Occupation of Chisinau, Bessarabia.

Romanian Red Cross — SP111

1941, Aug.   **Perf. 13½**
B164	SP111	1.50 l + 38.50 l	45	45
B165	SP111	2 l + 38 l	45	45
B166	SP111	5 l + 35 l	45	45
B167	SP111	7 l + 33 l	45	45
B168	SP111	10 l + 30 l	45	45

Nos. B164-B168 (5)   2.25   2.25

Souvenir Sheet
Imperf
Without Gum
B169		Sheet of 2	6.50	6.50
a.	SP111	7 l + 33 l brown & red	1.25	1.40
b.	SP111	10 l + 30 l bright blue & red	1.25	1.40

The surtax on Nos. B164-B169 was for the Romanian Red Cross.
No. B169 sold for 200 l.

King Michael and Stephen the Great SP113

Hotin and Akkerman Castles SP114

Romanian and German Soldiers SP115

Soldiers SP116

1941, Oct. 11   **Perf. 14½x13½**
B170	SP113	10 l + 30 l ultra	50	50
B171	SP114	12 l + 28 l dl org red	50	50
B172	SP115	16 l + 24 l lt brn	50	50
B173	SP116	20 l + 20 l dk vio	50	50

For overprints see Nos. B175-B178.

Souvenir Sheet

SP118

B174	SP118	Sheet of 2	4.25	4.25
a.		16 l blue gray	38	38
b.		20 l brown carmine	38	38

Sold for 200 l. The surtax aided the Anti-Bolshevism crusade.

Nos. B170-B174 **ODESA**
Overprinted **16 Oct.1941**

1941, Oct.   **Perf. 14½x13½**
B175	SP113	10 l + 30 l ultra	60	60
B176	SP114	12 l + 28 l dl org red	60	60
B177	SP115	16 l + 24 l lt brn	60	60
B178	SP116	20 l + 20 l dk vio	60	60
a.		Sheet of 2	4.25	4.25

Occupation of Odessa, Russia.

Types of Regular Issue, 1941

Designs: 3 l+50b, Sucevita Monastery, Bucovina. 5.50 l+50b, Rughi Monastery, Soroca, Bessarabia. 5.50 l+1 l, Tighina Fortress, Bessarabia. 6.50 l+1 l, Soroca Fortress, Bessarabia. 8 l+1 l, St. Nicholas Monastery, Suceava, Bucovina. 9.50 l+1 l, Milisauti Monastery, Bucovina. 10.50 l+1 l, Putna Monastery, Bucovina. 16 l+1 l, Cetatea Alba Fortress, Bessarabia. 25 l+1 l, Hotin Fortress, Bessarabia.

1941, Dec. 1   Wmk. 230   Perf. 13½
B179	A179	3 l + 50b rose brn	18	15
B180	A179	5.50 l + 50b red org	35	18
B181	A179	5.50 l + 1 l blk	35	18
B182	A179	6.50 l + 1 l dk brn	38	35
B183	A179	8 l + 1 l lt bl	35	18
B184	A177	9.50 l + 1 l gray bl	38	28
B185	A179	10.50 l + 1 l dk bl	38	15
B186	A179	16 l + 1 l vio	50	40
B187	A179	25 l + 1 l gray blk	60	45

Nos. B179-B187 (9)   3.47   2.32

Titu Maiorescu — SP128

Statue of Miron Costin at Jassy — SP130

1942, Oct. 5
B188	SP128	9 l + 11 l dl vio	30	30
B189	SP128	20 l + 20 l yel brn	75	75
B190	SP128	20 l + 30 l blue	75	75

Souvenir Sheet
Imperf
Without Gum
B191	SP128	Sheet of 3	3.75	3.75

The surtax aided war prisoners.
No. B191 contains one each of Nos. B188-B190, imperf. Sold for 200 l.

1942, Dec.   **Perf. 13½**
B192	SP130	6 l + 44 l sepia	1.25	1.75
B193	SP130	12 l + 38 l violet	1.25	1.75
B194	SP130	24 l + 26 l blue	1.25	1.75

Anniv. of the conquest of Transdniestria, and for use only in this territory which includes Odessa and land beyond the Duiester.

Michael, Antonescu, Hitler, Mussolini and Bessarabia Map SP131

Michael, Antonescu and (inset) Stephen of Moldavia SP132

Romanian Troops Crossing Pruth River to Retake Bessarabia SP133

1942   Wmk. 230   Photo.   Perf. 13½
B195	SP131	9 l + 41 l red brn	1.25	1.75
B196	SP132	18 l + 32 l ol gray	1.25	1.75
B197	SP133	20 l + 30 l brt ultra	1.25	1.75

First anniversary of liberation of Bessarabia.

Bucovina Coats of Arms
SP134   SP135

Design: 20 l+30 l, Bucovina arms with triple-barred cross.

1942, Nov. 1
B198	SP134	9 l + 41 l brt ver	1.25	1.75
B199	SP135	18 l + 32 l blue	1.25	1.75
B200	SP135	20 l + 30 l car rose	1.25	1.75

First anniversary of liberation of Bucovina.

Andrei Muresanu — SP137

1942, Dec. 30
B201	SP137	5 l + 5 l violet	38	38

80th death anniv. of Andrei Muresanu, writer.

Avram Jancu, National Hero — SP138

1943, Feb. 15
B202	SP138	16 l + 4 l brown	50	50

Nurse Aiding Wounded Soldier SP139

1943, Mar. 1   **Perf. 14½x14**
B203	SP139	12 l + 88 l red brn & ultra	30	30
B204	SP139	16 l + 84 l brt ultra & red	30	30
B205	SP139	20 l + 80 l ol gray & red	30	30

Souvenir Sheet
Imperf
B206		Sheet of 2	1.90	1.65
a.	SP139	16 l + 84 l bright ultra & red	52	52
b.	SP139	20 l + 80 l olive gray & red	52	52

Surtax on Nos. B203-B206 aided the Romanian Red Cross.
No. B206 sold for 500 l.

Sword Hilt — SP141

Sword Severing Chain — SP142

Soldier and Family, Guardian Angel — SP143

1943, June 22   **Perf. 14x14½   Wmk. 276**
B207	SP141	36 l + 164 l brn	2.00	2.00
B208	SP142	62 l + 138 l brt bl	2.00	2.00
B209	SP143	76 l + 124 l ver	2.00	2.00

Souvenir Sheet
Imperf
B210		Sheet of 2	9.00	9.00
a.	SP143	62 l + 138 l deep blue	1.75	1.90
b.	SP143	76 l + 124 l red orange	1.75	1.90

2nd anniv. of Romania's entrance into WWII. No. B210 sold for 600 l.

Petru Maior — SP145

Horia, Closca and Crisan SP148

Designs: 32 l+118 l, Gheorghe Sincai. 36 l+114 l, Timotei Cipariu. 91 l+109 l, Gheorghe Cosbuc.

Perf. 13½; 14½x14 (No. B214)
1943, Aug. 15   Photo.   Wmk. 276
B211	SP145	16 l + 134 l red org	28	28
B212	SP145	32 l + 118 l lt bl	28	28
B213	SP145	36 l + 114 l vio	28	28
B214	SP148	62 l + 138 l car rose	28	28
B215	SP145	91 l + 109 l dk brn	28	28

Nos. B211-B215 (5)   1.40   1.40

See Nos. B219-B223.

King Michael and Ion Antonescu SP150

1943, Sept. 6
B216	SP150	16 l + 24 l blue	70	70

3rd anniv. of the government of King Michael and Marshal Ion Antonescu.

Symbols of Sports — SP151

1943, Sept. 26   **Perf. 13½**
B217	SP151	16 l + 24 l ultra	38	30
B218	SP151	16 l + 24 l red brn	38	30

The surtax was for the benefit of Romanian sports.

Portrait Type of 1943

1943, Oct. 1

Designs: 16 l+134 l, Samuel Micu. 51 l+99 l, George Lazar. 56 l+144 l, Octavian Goga. 76 l+

124 l, Simeon Barnutiu. 77 1+123 l, Andrei Saguna.

B219	SP145	16 l + 134 l red vio	24	24
B220	SP145	51 l + 99 l orange	24	24
B221	SP145	56 l + 144 l rose car	24	24
B222	SP145	76 l + 124 l slate bl	24	24
B223	SP145	77 l + 123 l brn	24	24
		Nos. B219-B223 (5)	1.20	1.20

The surtax aided refugees.

Calafat, 1877 — SP157

Designs: 2 l +2 l, World War I scene. 3.50 l+3.50 l, Stalingrad, 1943. 4 l+4 l, Tisza, 1919. 5 l+5 l, Odessa, 1941. 6.50 l+6.50 l, Caucasus, 1942. 7 l+7 l, Sevastopol, 1942. 20 l+20 l, Prince Ribescu and King Michael.

1943, Nov. 10   Photo.   Perf. 13½

B224	SP157	1 l + 1 l red brn	15	15
B225	SP157	2 l + 2 l dl vio	15	15
B226	SP157	3.50 l + 3.50 l lt ultra	15	15
B227	SP157	4 l + 4 l mag	15	15
B228	SP157	5 l + 5 l red org	25	25
B229	SP157	6.50 l + 6.50 l bl	25	25
B230	SP157	7 l + 7 l dp vio	35	35
B231	SP157	20 l + 20 l crim	45	45
		Nos. B224-B231 (8)	1.90	1.90

Centenary of Romanian Artillery.

Emblem of Romanian Engineers' Association SP165

1943, Dec. 19   Perf. 14

B232 SP165 21 l + 29 l sepia   48   40

Society of Romanian Engineers, 25th anniv.

Motorcycle, Truck and Post Horn SP166

Post Wagon SP167

Roman Post Chariot SP168

Post Rider — SP169

1944, Feb. 1   Wmk. 276   Perf. 14

B233	SP166	1 l + 49 l org red	1.10	1.10
B234	SP167	2 l + 48 l lil rose	1.10	1.10
B235	SP168	4 l + 46 l ultra	1.10	1.10
B236	SP169	10 l + 40 l dl vio	1.10	1.10

Souvenir Sheets
Perf. 14

B237		Sheet of 3	2.75	4.00
a.	SP166	1 l + 49 l orange red	70	70
b.	SP167	2 l + 48 l orange red	70	70
c.	SP168	4 l + 46 l orange red	70	70

Imperf

B238		Sheet of 3	2.75	4.00
a.	SP166	1 l + 49 l dull violet	70	70
b.	SP167	2 l + 48 l dull violet	70	70
c.	SP168	4 l + 46 l dull violet	70	70

The surtax aided communications employees. No. B238 is imperf. between the stamps. Nos. B237-B238 each sold for 200 l.

Nos. B233-B238 Overprinted

1744   1944

1944, Feb. 28

B239	SP166	1 l + 49 l org red	2.75	2.75
B240	SP167	2 l + 48 l lil rose	2.75	2.75
B241	SP168	4 l + 46 l ultra	2.75	2.75
B242	SP169	10 l + 40 l dl vio	2.75	2.75

Souvenir Sheets
Perf. 14

B243   Sheet of 3   4.75   5.25

Imperf

B244   Sheet of 3   4.75   5.25

Rugby Player SP171

Dr. N. Cretzulescu SP172

1944, Mar. 16   Perf. 15

B245 SP171 16 l + 184 l crimson   3.25   3.25

30th anniv. of the Romanian Rugby Assoc. The surtax was used to encourage the sport.

1944, Mar. 1   Photo.   Perf. 13½

B246 SP172 35 l + 65 l brt ultra   48   48

Centenary of medical teaching in Romania.

Queen Mother Helen — SP173

1945, Feb. 10

B247	SP173	4.50 l + 5.50 l multi	18	18
B248	SP173	10 l + 40 l multi	18	18
B249	SP173	15 l + 75 l multi	18	18
B250	SP173	20 l + 80 l multi	18	18

The surtax aided the Romanian Red Cross.

Kings Ferdinand and Michael and Map SP174

1945, Feb.   Perf. 14

B251 SP174 75 l + 75 l dk ol brn   48   48

Romania's liberation.

Stefan Tomsa Church, Radaseni SP175

Municipal Home SP176

Gathering Fruit — SP177

School SP178

1944   Wmk. 276   Photo.   Perf. 14

B252	SP175	5 l + 145 l brt bl	40	30
B253	SP176	12 l + 138 l car rose	40	30
B254	SP177	15 l + 135 l red org	40	30
B255	SP178	32 l + 118 l dk brn	40	30

King Michael and Carol I Foundation, Bucharest SP179

Design: 200 l, King Carol I and Foundation.

1945, Feb. 10   Perf. 13

B256	SP179	20 l + 180 l dp org	15	15
B257	SP179	25 l + 175 l slate	15	15
B258	SP179	35 l + 165 l cl brn	15	15
B259	SP179	75 l + 125 l pale vio	15	15
		Set value	32	

Souvenir Sheet
Imperf
Without Gum

B260 SP179 200 l blue   3.00   3.75

Surtax was to aid in rebuilding the Public Library, Bucharest. Nos. B256-B259 were printed in sheets of 4. No. B260 sold for 1200 l.

Ion G. Duca SP181

Designs: 16 l+184 l, Virgil Madgearu. 20 l+180 l, Nikolai Jorga. 32 l+168 l, Ilie Pintilie. 35 l+165 l, Bernath Andrei. 36 l+164 l, Filimon Sarbu.

1945, Apr. 30   Perf. 13

B261	SP181	12 l + 188 l dk bl	24	24
B262	SP181	16 l + 184 l cl brn	24	24
B263	SP181	20 l + 180 l blk brn	24	24
B264	SP181	32 l + 168 l brt red	24	24
B265	SP181	35 l + 165 l Prus bl	24	24
B266	SP181	36 l + 164 l lt vio	24	24
		Nos. B261-B266 (6)	1.44	1.44

Souvenir Sheet
Imperf

B267		Sheet of 2	10.00	11.50
a.	SP181	32 l + 168 l magenta	2.00	2.25
b.	SP181	35 l + 165 l magenta	2.00	2.25

Honoring six victims of Nazi terrorism. No. B267 sold for 1,000 l.

Books and Torch — SP188

Designs: #B269, Flags of Russia and Romania. #B270, Kremlin, Moscow. #B271, Tudor Vladimirescu and Alexander Nevsky.

1945, May 20   Perf. 14

B268	SP188	20 l + 80 l ol grn	18	18
B269	SP188	35 l + 165 l brt rose	18	18
B270	SP188	75 l + 225 l blue	18	18
B271	SP188	80 l + 420 l cl brn	18	18

Souvenir Sheet
Imperf
Without Gum

B272		Sheet of 2	5.25	6.00
a.	SP189	35 l + 165 l bright red	1.25	1.40
b.	SP190	75 l + 225 l bright red	1.25	1.40

1st Soviet-Romanian Cong., May 20, 1945. No. B272 sold for 900 l.

Karl Marx — SP193

Designs: 120 l+380 l, Friedrich Engels. 155 l+445 l, Lenin.

1945, June 30   Perf. 13½

B273	SP193	75 l + 425 l car rose	1.25	1.25
B274	SP193	120 l + 380 l bl	1.25	1.25
B275	SP193	155 l + 445 l dk vio brn	1.25	1.25

Imperf

B276	SP193	75 l + 425 l car rose	3.75	3.75
B277	SP193	120 l + 380 l dk vio brn	3.75	3.75
B278	SP193	155 l + 445 l car rose	3.75	3.75
		Nos. B273-B278 (6)	15.00	15.00

Nos. B276-B278 were printed in sheets of 4.

Woman Throwing Discus — SP196

Designs: 16 l+184 l, Diving. 20 l+180 l, Skiing. 32 l+168 l, Volleyball. 35 l+165 l, Worker athlete.

1945, Aug. 5   Wmk. 276   Photo.   Perf. 13

B279	SP196	12 l +188 l ol gray	90	90
B280	SP196	16 l +184 l lt ultra	90	90
B281	SP196	20 l +180 l dp grn	90	90
B282	SP196	32 l +168 l mag	90	90
B283	SP196	35 l +165 l brt bl	90	90

Imperf

B284	SP196	12 l +188 l org red	90	90
B285	SP196	16 l +184 l vio brn	90	90
B286	SP196	20 l +180 l dp vio	90	90
B287	SP196	32 l +168 l yel grn	90	90
B288	SP196	35 l +165 l dk ol grn	90	90
		Nos. B279-B288 (10)	9.00	9.00

Printed in sheets of 9.

Mail Plane and Bird Carrying Letter SP201

1945, Aug. 5   *Perf. 13¹/₂*
B289 SP201 200 l + 1000 l bl &
     dk bl   3.50   3.50
   a.   With label   15.00   19.00

The surtax on Nos. B279-B289 was for the Office of Popular Sports.
   Issued in sheets of 30 stamps and 10 labels, arranged 10x4 with second and fourth horizontal rows each having five alternating labels.

Agriculture and Industry United SP202

King Michael SP203

1945, Aug. 23   *Perf. 14*
B290 SP202 100 l + 400 l red   15   15
B291 SP203 200 l + 800 l blue   15   15
     Set value   20   20

The surtax was for the Farmers' Front.
For surcharges see Nos. B318-B325.

Political Amnesty SP204

Military Amnesty SP205

Agrarian Amnesty SP206

Tudor Vladimirescu SP207

Nicolae Horia SP208

Reconstruction SP209

1945, Aug.   *Perf. 13*
B292 SP204   20 l + 580 l choc   5.50   5.50
B293 SP204   20 l + 580 l mag   5.50   5.50
B294 SP205   40 l + 560 l blue   5.50   5.50
B295 SP205   40 l + 560 l sl grn   5.50   5.50
B296 SP206   55 l + 545 l red   5.50   5.50
B297 SP206   55 l + 545 l dk vio
         brn   5.50   5.50
B298 SP207   60 l + 540 l ultra   5.50   5.50
B299 SP207   60 l + 540 l choc   5.50   5.50
B300 SP208   80 l + 520 l red   5.50   5.50
B301 SP208   80 l + 520 l mag   5.50   5.50
B302 SP209 100 l + 500 l sl grn   5.50   5.50
B303 SP209 100 l + 500 l red brn   5.50   5.50
     Nos. B292-B303 (12)   66.00   66.00

1st anniv. of Romania's armistice with Russia. Issued in panes of four.
Nos. B292-B303 also exist on coarse grayish paper, ungummed (same value).

Electric Train SP210

Coats of Arms SP211

Truck on Mountain Road SP212

Oil Field — SP213

"Agriculture" SP214

1945, Oct. 1   *Perf. 14*
B304 SP210   10 l + 490 l ol grn   18   18
B305 SP211   20 l + 480 l red brn   18   18
B306 SP212   25 l + 475 l brn vio   18   18
B307 SP213   55 l + 445 l ultra   18   18
B308 SP214 100 l + 400 l brn   18   18
          Imperf
B309 SP210   10 l + 490 l blue   18   18
B310 SP211   20 l + 480 l violet   18   18
B311 SP212   25 l + 475 l bl grn   18   18
B312 SP213   55 l + 445 l gray   18   18
B313 SP214 100 l + 400 l dp mag   18   18
     Nos. B304-B313 (10)   1.80   1.80

16th Congress of the General Assoc. of Romanian Engineers.

"Brotherhood" — SP215

Designs: 160 l+1840 l, "Peace." 320 l+1680 l, Hammer crushing Nazism. 440 l+2560 l, "World Unity."

1945, Dec. 5   *Perf. 14*
B314 SP215   80 l + 920 l mag   9.25   9.25
B315 SP215 160 l + 1840 l org
         brn   9.25   9.25
B316 SP215 320 l + 1680 l vio   9.25   9.25
B317 SP215 440 l + 2560 l yel
         grn   9.25   9.25

World Trade Union Congress at Paris, Sept. 25-Oct. 10, 1945.

Nos. B290 and B291 Surcharged in Various Colors

1946, Jan. 20
B318 SP202   10 l + 90 l (Bk)   38   38
B319 SP203   10 l + 90 l (R)   38   38
B320 SP202   20 l + 80 l (G)   38   38
B321 SP203   20 l + 80 l (Bk)   38   38
B322 SP202   80 l + 120 l (Bl)   38   38
B323 SP203   80 l + 120 l (Bk)   38   38
B324 SP202 100 l + 150 l (Bk)   38   38
B325 SP203 100 l + 150 l (R)   38   38
     Nos. B318-B325 (8)   3.04   3.04

Re-distribution of Land — SP219

Sower SP220

Ox Team Drawing Hay SP221

Old and New Plowing Methods SP222

1946, Mar. 6
B326 SP219   50 l + 450 l red   15   15
B327 SP220 100 l + 900 l red vio   15   15
B328 SP221 200 l + 800 l orange   15   15
B329 SP222 400 l + 1600 l dk grn   15   15
     Set value   48   46

Agrarian reform law of Mar. 23, 1945.

Philharmonic Types of Regular Issue
     Perf. 13, 13¹/₂x13
1946, Apr. 26   **Photo.**   **Wmk. 276**
B330 A211 200 l + 800 l brt red   60   60
   a.   Sheet of 12   14.00   17.50
B331 A213 350 l + 1650 l dk bl   65   65
   a.   Sheet of 12   14.00   17.50

Issued in sheets containing 12 stamps and 4 labels, with bars of music in the margins.

Agriculture SP223

Dove SP228

Designs: 10 l+200 l, Hurdling. 80 l+200 l, Research. 80 l+300 l, Industry. 200 l+400 l, Workers and flag.

     Perf. 11¹/₂
1946, July 28   **Photo.**   **Wmk. 276**
B332 SP223   10 l + 100 l dk org
          brn & red   18   18
B333 SP223   10 l + 200 l bl & red
          brn   18   18
B334 SP223   80 l + 200 l brn vio &
          brn   18   18
B335 SP223   80 l + 300 l dk org
          brn & rose lil   18   18
B336 SP223 200 l + 400 l Prus bl &
          red   18   28
     Nos. B332-B336 (5)   90   1.00

Issued in panes of 4 stamps with marginal inscription.

1946, Oct. 20   *Perf. 13¹/₂x13, Imperf.*
B338 SP228 300 l + 1200 l scar   48   22

Souvenir Sheet
     Perf. 14x14¹/₂
B339 SP228 1000 l scarlet   1.65   2.00
Romanian-Soviet friendship. No. B339 sold for 6000 lei.

Skiing — SP230

1946, Sept. 1   *Perf. 11¹/₂, Imperf.*
B340 SP230 160 l + 1340 l dk grn   50   50
Surtax for Office of Popular Sports.

Spinning SP231

Reaping SP232

Riding — SP233

Water Carrier — SP234

1946, Nov. 20   *Perf. 14*
B342 SP231   80 l + 320 l brt red   15   15
B343 SP232 140 l + 360 l dp org   15   15
B344 SP233 300 l + 450 l brn ol   15   15
B345 SP234 600 l + 900 l ultra   15   15
     Set value   45   45

Democratic Women's Org. of Romania.

Angel with Food and Clothing SP235

Bread for Hungry Family SP236

Care for Needy SP237

1947, Jan. 15   *Perf. 13¹/₂x14*
B346 SP235 1500 l + 3500 l red org   15   15
B347 SP236 3700 l + 5300 l dp vio   15   15

     Miniature Sheet
       Imperf
     Without Gum
B348 SP237 5000 l + 5000 l ultra   1.10   1.65

Surtax helped the social relief fund.
No. B348 is miniature sheet of one.

Student
Reciting
SP238

Allegory of
Education — SP242

SP243

Designs: 300 1+300 1, Weaving class.
600 1+600 1, Young machinist. 1200 1+1200 1,
Romanian school.

Perf. 14x13¹/₂

1947, Mar. 5   Photo.   Wmk. 276

B349	SP238	200 1 + 200 1 vio bl	15	15
B350	SP238	300 1 + 300 1 red brn	15	15
B351	SP238	600 1 + 600 1 Prus grn	15	15
B352	SP238	1200 1 + 1200 1 ultra	15	15
B353	SP242	1500 1 + 1500 1 dp rose	15	15
		Set value	25	25

Souvenir Sheet
Imperf

B354	SP243	3700 1 + 3700 1 dl brn & dl bl	75	90

Romania's vocational schools, 50th anniv.

ROMANIA   Victor Babes — SP244

Designs: B356, Michael Eminescu. B357, Nicolae Grigorescu. B358, Peter Movila. B359, Aleksander S. Pushkin. B360, Mikhail V. Lomonosov.
B361, Peter I. Tchaikovsky. B362, Ilya E. Repin.

1947, Apr. 18   Perf. 14

B355	SP244	1500 1 + 1500 1 red org	15	15
B356	SP244	1500 1 + 1500 1 dk ol grn	15	15
B357	SP244	1500 1 + 1500 1 dk bl	15	15
B358	SP244	1500 1 + 1500 1 dp plum	15	15
B359	SP244	1500 1 + 1500 1 scar	15	15
B360	SP244	1500 1 + 1500 1 rose brn	15	15
B361	SP244	1500 1 + 1500 1 ultra	15	15
B362	SP244	1500 1 + 1500 1 choc	15	15
		Set value	95	95

Transportation
SP252

Labor Day: No. B364, Farmer. No. B365, Farm
woman. No. B366, Teacher and school. No. B367,
Laborer and factory.

1947, May 1

B363	SP252	1000 1 + 1000 1 dk ol brn	15	15
B364	SP252	1500 1 + 1500 1 red brn	15	15
B365	SP252	2000 1 + 2000 1 blue	15	15
B366	SP252	2500 1 + 2500 1 red vio	15	15

B367	SP252	3000 1 + 3000 1 crim rose	15	15
		Set value	50	50

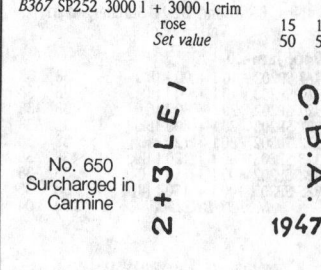

No. 650
Surcharged in
Carmine

1947, Sept. 6   Perf. 13¹/₂

B368	A234	2 1 + 3 1 on 36,000 1 vio	40	40

Balkan Games of 1947, Bucharest.

Type of 1947   **ARLUS   +5**
Surcharged in   1-7.XI.
Carmine   1947

Design: Cathedral of Curtea de Arges.

1947, Oct. 30   Imperf.

B369	A235	5 1 + 5 1 brt ultra	35	35

Soviet-Romanian Congress, Nov. 1-7.

AL XVII-LEA CONGRES   Plowing — SP257

Perf. 14x14¹/₂

1947, Oct. 5   Photo.   Wmk. 276

B370	SP257	1 1 + 1 1 shown	15	15
B371	SP257	2 1 + 2 1 Sawmill	15	15
B372	SP257	3 1 + 3 1 Refinery	15	15
B373	SP257	4 1 + 4 1 Steel mill	15	15
		Set value, #B370-B373, CB12	86	52

17th Congress of the General Assoc. of
Romanian Engineers.

Allegory of
Industry,
Science and
Agriculture
SP258

Winged Man
Holding
Hammer and
Sickle
SP259

1947, Nov. 10   Perf. 14¹/₂x14

B374	SP258	2 1 + 10 1 rose lake	15	15
B375	SP259	7 1 + 10 1 bluish blk	15	15
		Set value	24	24

2nd Trade Union Conf., Nov. 10.

SP260   SP264

Designs: 1 1+1 1, Convoy of Food for Moldavia. 2
1+2 1, "Everything for the Front-Everything for Victory." 3 1+3 1, Woman, child and hospital. 4 1+4 1,
"Help the Famine-stricken Regions." 5 1+5 ,
"Three Years of Action."

1947, Nov. 7   Perf. 14

B376	SP260	1 1 + 1 1 dk gray bl	15	15
B377	SP260	2 1 + 2 1 dk brn	15	15
B378	SP260	3 1 + 3 1 rose lake	15	15
B379	SP260	4 1 + 4 1 brt ultra	15	15
B380	SP264	5 1 + 5 1 red	15	15
		Set value	50	50

Issued in sheets of four.

Discus Thrower   Labor
SP265   SP266

Youths
Following
Filimon
Sarbu
Banner
SP269

Balkan Games of 1947: 2 1+2 1, Runner. 5 1+5 1,
Boy and girl athletes.

Perf. 13¹/₂

1948, Feb.   Wmk. 276   Photo.

B381	SP265	1 1 + 1 1 dk brn	18	18
B382	SP265	2 1 + 2 1 car lake	24	24
B383	SP265	5 1 + 5 1 blue	35	35
	Nos. B381-B383,CB13-CB14 (5)		2.67	1.84

1948, Mar. 15

Designs: 3 1+3 1, Agriculture. 5 1+5 1, Education.

B384	SP266	2 1 + 2 1 dk sl bl	25	16
B385	SP266	3 1 + 3 1 gray grn	30	15
B386	SP266	5 1 + 5 1 red brn	40	20

Imperf

B387	SP269	8 1 + 8 1 dk car rose	60	28
	Nos. B384-B387,CB15 (5)		2.40	1.29

No. B387 issued in triangular sheets of 4.

POSTA

REPUBLICA
POPULARA
ROMANA   **2+2 LEI**   Gliders — SP270

Sailboat Race
SP271   REPUBLICA POPULARA ROMANA

Designs: No. B389, Early plane. No. B390,
Plane over farm. No. B391, Transport plane.
B393, Training ship, Mircea. B394, Danube ferry.
B395, S.S. Transylvania.

1948, July 26   Perf. 14¹/₂x14¹/₂

B388	SP270	2 1 + 2 1 blue	1.25	1.25
B389	SP270	5 1 + 5 1 pur	1.25	1.25
B390	SP270	8 1 + 8 1 dk car rose	1.25	1.25
B391	SP270	10 1 + 10 1 choc	1.25	1.25
B392	SP271	2 1 + 2 1 dk grn	1.00	1.00
B393	SP271	5 1 + 5 1 slate	1.00	1.00
B394	SP271	8 1 + 8 1 brt bl	1.00	1.00
B395	SP271	10 1 + 10 1 ver	1.00	1.00
	Nos. B388-B395 (8)		9.00	9.00

Air and Sea Communications Day.

Type of Regular Issue and

SAPTAMANA PRESEI   Torch, Pen,
              Ink and Flag
              SP272

Alexandru Sahia   Romanian-Soviet
SP273   Association
              Emblem
              SP274

Perf. 14x13¹/₂, 13¹/₂x14, Imperf.

1948, Sept. 12

B396	A241	5 1 + 5 1 crimson	70	70
B397	SP272	10 1 + 10 1 violet	90	90
B398	SP273	15 1 + 15 1 blue	90	90

Week of the Democratic Press, Sept. 12-19.

1948, Oct. 29   Perf. 14

Design: 15 1+15 1, Spasski Tower, Kremlin.

B399	SP274	10 1 + 10 1 gray grn	1.25	1.25
B400	SP274	15 1 + 15 1 dp ultra	1.50	1.50

No. B399 was issued in sheets of 50 stamps and
50 labels.

Symbols of
United Labor
SP275

POSTA 10+10   Agriculture
             SP276

Industry   Automatic
SP277   Riflemen
         SP278

Soldiers Cutting
Barbed
Wire — SP279

1948, May 1   Perf. 14x13¹/₂, 13¹/₂x14

B401	SP275	8 1 + 8 1 red	2.00	2.00
B402	SP276	10 1 + 10 1 ol grn	2.00	2.00
B403	SP277	12 1 + 12 1 red brn	2.00	2.00

Labor Day, May 1. See No. CB17.

1948, May 9
Flags and Dates:
23 Aug 1944-9 Mai 1945

B404	SP278	1.50 1 + 1.50 1 shown	95	95
B405	SP279	2 1 + 2 1 shown	95	95
B406	SP279	4 1 + 4 1 Field Artillery	95	95

B407 SP279 7.50 l + 7.50 l Tank   95   95
B408 SP279   8 l + 8 l Warship   95   95
  Nos. B404-B408,CB18-CB19 (7)   9.75 9.75

Honoring the Romanian Army.

Nicolae
Balcescu
SP280

Balcescu and
Revolutionists
SP281

Balcescu,
Sandor Petöfi
and
Revolutionists
SP282

Revolution of 1848: #B412, Balcescu and
revolutionists.

1948, June 1   *Perf. 13x13¹/₂*
B409 SP280   2 l + 2 l car lake   60   60
B410 SP281   5 l + 5 l dk vio   60   60
B411 SP282 10 l + 10 l dk ol brn   60   60
B412 SP280 36 l + 18 l dp bl   1.10 1.10

For surcharges see Nos. 856-859.

Loading
Freighter
SP283

Designs: 3 l+3 l, Lineman. 11 l+11 l, Transport
plane. 15 l+15 l, Railroad train.

Wmk. 289
1948, Dec. 10   **Photo.**   *Perf. 14*
Center in Black
B413 SP283   1 l + 1 l dk grn   30   30
B414 SP283   3 l + 3 l redsh brn   38   38
B415 SP283 11 l + 11 l dp bl   1.65 1.25
B416 SP283 15 l + 15 l red   2.10 1.90
  a.   Sheet of 4   6.00 7.00

No. B416a contains four imperf. stamps similar
to Nos. B413-B416 in changed colors, center in
brown. No gum.

Runners — SP284

Parade of
Athletes
SP285

Perf. 13x13¹/₂, 13¹/₂x13
1948, Dec. 31
B421 SP284   5 l + 5 l grn   1.90 1.90
B422 SP285 10 l + 10 l brn vio   3.00 3.00
          Imperf
B423 SP284   5 l + 5 l grn   1.90 1.90
B424 SP285 10 l + 10 l red   3.00 3.00
  Nos. B421-B424,CB20-CB21 (6)   29.30 29.30

Nos. B421-B424 were issued in sheets of 4.

Souvenir Sheet

SP286

1950, Jan. 27
B425 SP286 10 l carmine   1.10 50

Philatelic exhib., Bucharest. Sold for 50 lei.

Crossing the Buzau, by Denis Auguste
Marie Raffet — SP287

1967, Nov. 15   **Engr.**   *Perf. 13¹/₂*
B426 SP287 55b + 45b ocher & indigo   40 18

Stamp Day.

Old Bucharest, 18th Century
Painting — SP288

1968, Nov. 15   **Photo.**   *Perf. 13¹/₂*
B427 SP288 55b + 45b label   40 18

Stamp Day. Label has printed perforations. See
Nos. 2386A, B428-B429.

1969, Nov. 15

Design: Courtyard, by M. Bouquet.

B428 SP288 55b + 45b label   38 15

Stamp Day. Label at right of stamp has printed
perforations.

1970, Nov. 15

Design: Mail Coach in the Winter, by Emil
Volkers.

B429 SP288 55b + 45b multi   40 15

Stamp Day.

Lady with
Letter, by Sava
Hentia — SP289

1971, Nov. 15   **Photo.**   *Perf. 13¹/₂*
B430 SP289 1.10 l + 90b multi   48 35

Stamp Day. Label portion below stamp has
printed perforations and shows Romania No. 12.

Portrait Type of Regular Issue

Designs: 4 l+2 l, Barbat at his Desk, by B.
Iscovescu. 6 l+2 l, The Poet Alecsandri with his
Family, by N. Livaditti.

1973, June 20   **Photo.**
B432 A728 4 l + 2 l multi   1.25 50
Souvenir Sheet
B433 A728 6 l + 2 l multi   1.90 1.90

No. B433 contains one 38x50mm stamp.

Map of
Europe with
Emblem
Marking
Bucharest
SP291

1974, June 25   **Photo.**   *Perf. 13¹/₂*
B435 SP291 4 l + 3 l multi   1.40 50

EUROMAX, European Exhibition of Max-
imaphily, Bucharest, Oct. 6-13.

Marketplace,
Sibiu
SP292

1974, Nov. 15   **Photo.**   *Perf. 13¹/₂*
B436 SP292 2.10 l + 1.90 l multi   90 40

Stamp Day.

No. B436 Overprinted in Red:
"EXPOZITIA FILATELICA 'NATIONALA
'74' / 15-24 noiembrie / Bucuresti"
1974, Nov. 15
B437 SP292 2.10 l + 1.90 l multi   2.50 90

NATIONALA '74 Philatelic Exhibition,
Bucharest, Nov. 15-24.

Post Office,
Bucharest
SP293

Stamp Day: 2.10 l+1.90 l, like No. B438, side
view.

1975, Nov. 15   **Photo.**   *Perf. 13¹/₂*
B438 SP293 1.50 l + 1.50 l multi   60 30
B439 SP293 2.10 l + 1.90 l multi   1.10 45

No. 2612 Surcharged and Overprinted:
"EXPOZITIA FILATELICA / BUCURESTI /
12-19.IX.1976"
1976, Sept. 12   **Photo.**   *Perf. 13¹/₂*
B440 A787 3.60 l + 1.80 l   2.10 1.25

Philatelic Exhibition, Bucharest, Sept. 12-19.

Elena Cuza, by
Theodor
Aman — SP294

Dispatch Rider
Handing Letter to
Officer — SP295

1976, Nov. 15   **Photo.**   *Perf. 13¹/₂*
B441 SP294 2.10 l + 1.90 l multi   90 45

Stamp Day.

Independence Type of 1977

Stamp Day: Battle of Rahova, after etching.

1977, May 9   **Photo.**   *Perf. 13¹/₂*
B442 A806 4.80 l + 2 l multi   1.25 35

1977, Nov.   **Photo.**   *Perf. 13¹/₂*
B443 SP295 2.10 l + 1.90 l multi   90 45

Socfilex Type of 1979

Flower Paintings by Luchian: 4 l+2 l, Field flowers. 10 l+5 l, Roses.

1979, July 27   **Photo.**   *Perf. 13¹/₂*
B445 A847 4 l + 2 l multi   1.10 38
Souvenir Sheet
B446 A847 10 l + 5 l multi   3.00 1.25

Socfilex, Oct. 26-Nov. 1, Intl. Phil. Exhib.,
Bucharest. No. B446 contains one stamp
50x38mm.

Stamp Day
SP297

1979, Dec. 12   **Photo.**   *Perf. 13¹/₂*
B447 SP297 2.10 l + 1.90 l multi   70 25

Souvenir Sheet

Stamp Day — SP298

1980, July 1   **Photo.**   *Perf. 13¹/₂*
B448 SP298 5 l + 5 l multi   2.10 2.00

December 1989 Revolution — SP299

Designs: 50b+50b, Palace on fire, Bucharest.
1 l+ 1 l, Crowd, Timisoara. 1.50 l+1 l, Soldiers &
crowd, Targu Mures. 2 l+1 l, Soldiers in Bucharest,
vert. 3 l+1 l, Funeral, Timisoara. 3.50 l+1 l, Crowd
celebrating, Brasov, vert. 4 l+1 l, Crowd with flags,
Sibiu. No. B456, Cemetery, Bucharest. No. B457,
Foreign aid.

1990, Oct. 1   **Photo.**   *Perf. 13¹/₂*
B449 SP299 50b +50b multi   15 15
B450 SP299   1 l +1 l multi   18 18
B451 SP299 1.50 l +1 l multi   22 22
B452 SP299   2 l +1 l multi   28 28
B453 SP299   3 l +1 l multi   35 35
B454 SP299 3.50 l +1 l multi   40 40
B455 SP299   4 l +1 l multi   45 45
B456 SP299   5 l +2 l multi   60 60
  Nos. B449-B456 (8)   2.63 2.63
Souvenir Sheet
B457 SP299   5 l +2 l multi   60 60

No. B457 contains one 54x42mm stamp.

Stamp Day — SP300

1992, July 15   Photo.   Perf. 13½
B458 SP300 10 l +4 l multi   38   38

For surcharge see No. B460.

Stamp
Day — SP301

1993, Apr. 26   Photo.   Perf. 13½
B459 SP301 15 l +10 l multi   15   15

No. B458 Surcharged in Red

35 ANI DE ACTIVITATE AFR-FFR
1958–1993

1993, Nov. 9   Photo.   Perf. 13½
B460 SP300 70 l + 45 l on 10 l+4 l   90   90

AIR POST STAMPS

King Carol II — AP2

1930, Oct. 4   Unwmk.
Bluish Paper
C13 AP2 1 l dk violet   70   28
C14 AP2 2 l gray green   85   28
C15 AP2 5 l red brown   1.90   55
C16 AP2 10 l brt blue   3.50   70

Junkers
Monoplane
AP3

Monoplanes
AP7

Designs: 3 l, Monoplane with biplane behind. 5
l, Biplane. 10 l, Monoplane flying leftward.

1931, Nov. 4   Wmk. 230
C17 AP3 2 l dull green   40   15
C18 AP3 3 l carmine   50   20
C19 AP3 5 l red brown   70   20
C20 AP3 10 l blue   1.65   90
C21 AP7 20 l dk violet   3.25   90
       Nos. C17-C21 (5)   6.50 1.83

Nos. C17 to C21 exist imperforate.

Souvenir Sheets

Plane
over
Resita
AP8

Plane
over
Sinaia
AP9

**   Wmk. 276**
1945, Oct. 1   Photo.   Perf. 13
Without Gum
C22 AP8 80 l slate green   5.00   5.00
Imperf
C23 AP9 80 l magenta   3.50   3.50

16th Congress of the General Assoc. of
Romanian Engineers.

Catalogue values for unused
stamps in this section, from this
point to the end of the section, are
for Never Hinged items.

Plane
AP10

Design: 500 l, Aviator and planes.

1946, Sept. 5   Perf. 13½x13
C24 AP10 200 l yel grn & bl   1.00   75
C25 AP10 500 l org red & dl bl   1.00   75

Printed in sheets of four with marginal
inscription.

Lockheed 12
Electra
AP12

CGM Congress
Emblem
AP13

1946, Oct.   Perf. 11½
C26 AP12 300 l crimson   40   40
  a.   Pair, #C26, CB6   1.25 1.25

Sheet contains 8 each of Nos. C26 and CB6,
arranged so se-tenant or normal pairs are available.

1947, Mar.   Wmk. 276   Perf. 13x14
C27 AP13 1100 l blue   28   28

Congress of the United Labor Unions ("CGM").
Printed in sheets of 15.

"May 1"
Supported by
Parachutes
AP14

Plane and
Conference
Banner
AP17

Designs: No. C29, Air Force monument. No.
C30, Plane over rural road.

1947, May 4   Perf. 11½
C28 AP14 3000 l vermilion   15   15
C29 AP14 3000 l grnsh gray   15   15
C30 AP14 3000 l blk brown   15   15

Printed in sheets of four with marginal
inscriptions.

1947, Nov. 10   Perf. 14
C31 AP17 11 l bl & dp car   25   25

2nd Trade Union Conference, Nov. 10.

Emblem of
the Republic
and Factories
AP18

Industry and
Agriculture
AP19

Transportation — AP20

**   Perf. 14x13½**
1948, Nov.22   Wmk. 289   Photo.
C32 AP18 30 l cerise   28   15
  a.   30 l carmine ('50)   38   38
C33 AP19 50 l dk slate grn   38   20
C34 AP20 100 l ultra   1.10   55

No. C32a issued May 10. For surcharges see
Nos. C37-C39.

Transportation — AP21

Design: 30 l, Agriculture.

1951-52   Wmk. 358   Perf. 13½
C35 AP21 30 l dk green ('52)   1.25 1.10
C36 AP21 50 l red brown   90   70

1951-55 Five Year Plan.
For surcharges see Nos. C40-C41.

Nos. C32-C36 Surcharged with New
Values in Blue or Carmine

1952   Wmk. 289   Perf. 14x13½
C37 AP18 3b on 30 l car (Bl)   50   25
  a.   3b on 30 l cerise (Bl)   7.25 6.50
C38 AP19 3b on 50 l dk sl grn   50   25
C39 AP20 3b on 100 l ultra   50   25

**   Perf. 13½**
**   Wmk. 358**
C40 AP21 1 l on 30 l dk grn   7.50 1.50
C41 AP21 1 l on 50 l red brn   7.50 1.50
       Nos. C37-C41 (5)   16.50 3.75

AERIANA

Nos. 706 and
707 Surcharged
in Blue or
Carmine

LEI 3

1953   Wmk. 289   Perf. 13½, 14
C43 A250 3 l on 20 l org brn   8.25 7.00
C44 A251 5 l on 30 l brt bl (C) 10.50 10.00

Plane facing right and surcharge arranged to fit
design on No. C44.

Plane over City — AP22   Sputnik 1 and
                            Earth — AP23

Designs: 55b, Plane over Mountains. 1.75 l,
over Harvest fields. 2.25 l, over Seashore.

**   Perf. 14½x14**
1956, Dec. 15   Photo.   Wmk. 358
C45 AP22 20b brt bl, org & grn   20   15
C46 AP22 55b brt bl, grn & ocher 35   15
C47 AP22 1.75 l brt bl & red org 1.25   15
C48 AP22 2.55 l brt bl & red org 1.50   38

1957, Nov. 6   Perf. 14

Design: 3.75 l, Sputniks 1 and 2 circling globe.

C49 AP23 25b brt ultra   30   15
C50 AP23 25b dk bl grn   30   15
C51 AP23 3.75 l brt ultra   1.50   38
C52 AP23 3.75 l dk bl grn   1.50   38

Nos. C49 and C51 are printed se-tenant with
gray label. Nos. C50 and C52 are printed se-tenant
with brown label. Each sheet contains 27 triptychs
with the center rows arranged tete-beche.
In 1958 Nos. C49-C52 were overprinted: 1.)
"Expozitia Universal a Bruxelles 1958" and star.
2.) Large star. 3.) Small star.

Animal Type of Regular Issue, 1957

Birds: 3.30 l, Black-headed gull, horiz. 5 l, Sea
eagle, horiz.

**   Perf. 14x13½**
1957, Dec. 27   Wmk. 358
C53 A445 3.30 l ultra & gray   1.65   28
C54 A445 5 l car & org   2.50   40

Armed Forces Type of Regular Issue

Design: Flier and planes.

Perf. 13¹/₂x13

1958, Oct. 2   Unwmk.   Photo.
C55 A458 3.30 l brt violet   90 42

Day of the Armed Forces, Oct. 2.

Earth and Sputnik 3 Orbit — AP24

1958, Sept. 20   *Perf. 14x13¹/₂*
C56 AP24 3.25 l indigo & ocher   1.75 50

Launching of Sputnik 3, May 15, 1958.

Type of Regular Issue, 1958
Souvenir Sheet

Design: Tête bêche pair of 27pa of 1858.

Perf. 11¹/₂

1958, Nov. 15   Unwmk.   Engr.
C57 A462 10 l blue   12.50 12.50

A similar sheet, printed in dull red and imperf., exists.
No. C57 was overprinted in 1959 in vermilion to commemorate the 10th anniv. of the State Philatelic Trade.
Values, $25 and $50.

Lunik I Leaving Earth AP25   Frederic Joliot-Curie AP26

1959, Feb. 4   Photo.   *Perf. 14*
C58 AP25 3.25 l vio bl, pnksh   4.50 90

Launching of the "first artificial planet of the solar system."
For surcharge see No. C70.

1959, Apr. 25   *Perf. 13¹/₂x14*
C59 AP26 3.25 l ultra   2.50 50

Frederic Joliot-Curie; 10th anniv. of the World Peace Movement.

Rock Thrush — AP27

Birds: 20b, European golden oriole. 35b, Lapwing. 40b, Barn swallow. No. C64, Goldfinch. No. C65, Great spotted woodpecker. No. C66, Great tit. 1 l, Bullfinch. 1.55 l, Long-tailed tit. 5 l, Wall creeper. Nos. C62-C67 vertical.

1959, June 25   Litho.   *Perf. 14*
Birds in Natural Colors
C60	AP27	10b gray, cr	15	15
C61	AP27	20b gray, grysh	15	15
C62	AP27	35b gray, grysh	15	15
C63	AP27	40b gray & red, pnksh	15	15
C64	AP27	55b gray, buff	22	15
C65	AP27	55b gray, grnsh	22	15
C66	AP27	55b gray & ol, grysh	22	15
C67	AP27	1 l gray and red, cr	75	15
C68	AP27	1.55 l gray & red, pnksh	90	15
C69	AP27	5 l gray, grnsh	3.75	70
		Nos. C60-C69 (10)	6.66	
		Set value		1.25

No. C58 Surcharged in Red

N.00.02.26
14-IX-1959

PRIMA RACHETA COSMICA
IN LUNA

5 LEI

1959, Sept. 14   Photo.   Unwmk.
C70 AP25 5 l on 3.25 l   4.75 1.00

1st Russian rocket to reach the moon, Sept. 14, 1959.

Miniature Sheet

Prince Vlad Tepes and Document AP28

1959, Sept. 15   Engr.   *Perf. 11¹/₂x11*
C71 AP28 20 l violet brn   45.00 45.00

500th anniv. of the founding of Bucharest.

Sport Type of Regular Issue, 1959
1959, Oct. 5   Litho.   *Perf. 13¹/₂*
C72 A474 2.80 l Boating   1.50 38

Soviet Rocket, Globe, Dog and Rabbit — AP29

Photograph of Far Side of the Moon — AP30

Design: 1.75 l, Trajectory of Lunik 3, which hit the moon.

Perf. 14, 13¹/₂ (AP30)

1959, Dec.   Photo.   Wmk. 358
C73	AP29	1.55 l dk blue	2.25	20
C74	AP30	1.60 l dk vio bl, buff	3.00	25
C75	AP29	1.75 l dk blue	3.00	25

Soviet conquest of space.

Animal Type of Regular Issue, 1960.

Designs: 1.30 l, Golden eagle. 1.75 l, Black grouse. 2 l, Lammergeier.

Unwmk.

1960, Mar. 3   Engr.   *Perf. 14*
C76	A480	1.30 l dk blue	85	22
C77	A480	1.75 l olive grn	1.25	22
C78	A480	2 l dk carmine	1.50	26

Aurel Vlaicu and Plane of 1910 AP31

Bucharest Airport and Turbo-Jet — AP32

Designs: 20b, Plane and Aurel Vlaicu. 35b, Amphibian ambulance plane. 40b, Plane spraying crops. 55b, Pilot and planes, vert. 1.75 l, Parachutes at aviation sports meet.

1960, June 15   Litho.   Unwmk.
C79	AP31	10b yellow & brn	15	15
C80	AP31	20b red org & brn	15	15

**   Photo.   Wmk. 358**
C81	AP31	35b crimson	20	15
C82	AP31	40b violet	28	15
C83	AP31	55b blue	40	15

**   Litho.   Unwmk.**
C84	AP32	1.60 l vio bl, yel & emer	95	20
C85	AP32	1.75 l bl, red, brn & pale grn	1.25	35
		Nos. C79-C85 (7)	3.38	
		Set value		80

50th anniv. of the first Romanian airplane flight by Aurel Vlaicu.
For surcharge see No. C145.

Bucharest Airport — AP33   Sputnik 4 Flying into Space — AP34

1960   Wmk. 358   Photo.   *Perf. 14*
C86 AP33 3.20 l brt ultra   1.10 15

Type of Regular Issue, 1960

Black Sea Resort: 2 l, Beach at Mamaia.

1960, Aug. 2   Litho.   Unwmk.
C87 A491 2 l grn, org & lt bl   90 18

1960, June 8   Photo.   Wmk. 358
C88 AP34 55b deep blue   1.25 24

Launching of Sputnik 4, May 15, 1960.

Saturnia Pyri — AP35   Papilio Machaon — AP36

Limenitis Populi AP37

Designs: 40b, Chrisophanus virgaureae. 1.60 l, Acherontia atropos. 1.75 l, Apatura iris, horiz.

Perf. 13, 14x12¹/₂, 14

1960, Oct. 10   Typo.   Unwmk.
C89	AP35	10b multi	15	15
C90	AP37	20b multi	15	15
C91	AP37	40b multi	15	15
C92	AP36	55b multi	28	15
C93	AP36	1.60 l multi	80	18
C94	AP36	1.75 l multi	90	18
		Nos. C89-C94 (6)	2.43	
		Set value		58

Compass Rose and Jet — AP38

Perf. 13¹/₂x14

1960, Nov. 1   Photo.   Wmk. 358
C95 AP38 55b brt bl + 45b label   48 15

Stamp Day.

Skier AP39

Slalom — AP40   Maj. Yuri A. Gagarin — AP41

Designs: 25b, Skiers going up. 40b, Bobsled. 55b, Ski jump. 1 l, Mountain climber. 1.55 l, Long-distance skier.

Perf. 14x13¹/₂, 13¹/₂x14

1961, Mar. 18   Litho.   Unwmk.
C96	AP39	10b olive & gray	15	15
C97	AP40	20b gray & dk red	15	15
C98	AP40	25b gray & bl grn	15	15
C99	AP40	40b gray & pur	15	15
C100	AP39	55b gray & ultra	20	15
C101	AP40	1 l gray & brn lake	42	15
C102	AP39	1.55 l gray & brn	75	16
		Set value	1.70	55

Exist imperf. with changed colors. Value, set $3.75.

Perf. 14x14¹/₂, 14¹/₂x14

1961, Apr. 19   Photo.   Unwmk.

Design: 3.20 l, Gagarin in space capsule and globe with orbit, horiz.

C103	AP41	1.35 l brt blue	60	15
C104	AP41	3.20 l ultra	1.25	15

No. C104 exists imperf. in dark carmine rose. Value unused $3.75, canceled $2.

Eclipse over Republic Palace Place, Bucharest AP42

Design: 1.75 l, Total Eclipse, Scinteia House and telescope.

Perf. 14x13¹/₂

1961, June 13   Wmk. 358
C106	AP42	1.60 l ultra	70	15
C107	AP42	1.75 l dk blue	70	15

Total solar eclipse of Feb. 15, 1961.

Maj. Gherman S.   Globe and
Titov — AP43   Stamps — AP44

Designs: 55b, "Peace" and Vostok 2 rocket.
1.75 l, Yuri A. Gagarin and Gherman S. Titov,
horiz.

Perf. 13¹/₂x14
1961, Sept. 11   **Unwmk.**

C108	AP43	55b dp blue	38	15
C109	AP43	1.35 l dp purple	55	15
C110	AP43	1.75 l dk carmine	90	20
		Set value	40	

Issued to honor the Russian space navigators Y.
A. Gagarin and G. S. Titov.

1961, Nov. 15   **Litho.**   **Perf. 13¹/₂x14**

C111	AP44	55b multi + 45b label	50	18

Stamp Day.

Railroad
Station,
Constanta
AP45

Buildings: 20b, Tower, RPR Palace place, vert.
55b, Congress hall, Bucharest. 75b, Mill,
Hunedoara. 1 l, Apartment houses, Bucharest. 1.20
l, Circus, Bucharest. 1.75 l, Worker's Club,
Mangalia.

Perf. 13¹/₂x14, 14x13¹/₂
1961, Nov. 20   **Typo.**

C112	AP45	20b multi	15	15
C113	AP45	40b multi	16	15
C114	AP45	55b multi	16	15
C115	AP45	75b multi	25	15
C116	AP45	1 l multi	32	15
C117	AP45	1.20 l multi	65	25
C118	AP45	1.75 l multi	95	40
		Nos. C112-C118 (7)	2.64	
		Set value	90	

Space
Exploration
Stamps and
Dove — AP46

Design: Each stamp shows a different group of
Romanian space exploration stamps.

1962, July 27   **Perf. 14x13¹/₂**

C119	AP46	35b yellow brn	15	15
C120	AP46	55b green	22	15
C121	AP46	1.35 l blue	40	16
C122	AP46	1.75 l rose red	80	28
a.		Sheet of 4	2.25	1.00
		Set value	58	

Peaceful space exploration.
No. C122a contains four imperf. stamps similar
to Nos. C119-C122 in changed colors and with one
dove covering all four stamps. Stamps are printed
together without space between.

Andrian G.
Nikolayev — AP47

Designs: 1.60 l, Globe and trajectories of Vostoks 3 and 4. 1.75 l, Pavel R. Popovich.

Perf. 13¹/₂x14
1962, Aug. 20   **Photo.**   **Unwmk.**

C123	AP47	55b purple	35	15
C124	AP47	1.60 l dark blue	1.00	22
C125	AP47	1.75 l rose claret	1.25	28

1st Russian group space flight of Vostoks 3 and 4,
Aug. 11-15, 1962.

Exhibition Hall   The Coachmen
AP48   by Szatmary
                         AP49

1962, Oct. 12   **Litho.**   **Perf. 14x13**

C126	AP48	1.60 l bl, vio bl & org	90	15

4th Sample Fair, Bucharest.

1962, Nov. 15   **Perf. 13¹/₂x14**

C127	AP49	55b + 45b label	75	24

Stamp Day. Alternating label shows No. 14 on
cover.

No. C127
Overprinted in Violet

CONFERINTA PE TARA A.F.R. BUCURESTI 30·III·1963

1963, Mar. 30

C128	AP49	55b + 45b label	1.50	1.10

Romanian Philatelists' Assoc. meeting at
Bucharest, Mar. 30. The overprint is centered on
the stamp and label, about half of it on each.

Sighisoara
Glass and
Crockery
Factory
AP50

Industrial Plants: 40b, Govora soda works. 55b,
Tirgul-Jiu wood processing factory. 1 l, Savinesti
chemical plant (synthetic fibers). 1.55 l, Hunedoara
metal factory. 1.75 l, Brazi thermal power station.

Perf. 14x13
1963, Apr. 10   **Unwmk.**   **Photo.**

C129	AP50	30b dk bl & red	15	15
C130	AP50	40b sl grn & pur	15	15
C131	AP50	55b brn red & dp bl	15	15
C132	AP50	1 l vio & brn	22	15
C133	AP50	1.55 l ver & dk bl	50	15
C134	AP50	1.75 l dk bl & mag	70	15
		Nos. C129-C134 (6)	1.87	
		Set value	50	

Industrial achievements.

Lunik 4 Approaching
Moon — AP51

1963, Apr. 29   **Perf. 13¹/₂x14**

C135	AP51	55b dk ultra & red	45	15

Imperf

C136	AP51	1.75 l vio & red	75	25

Moon flight of Lunik 4, Apr. 2, 1963.

Steam
Locomotive
AP52

Designs: 55b, Diesel locomotive. 75b, Trolley
bus. 1.35 l, Passenger ship. 1.75 l, Plane.

1963, July 10   **Litho.**   **Perf. 14¹/₂x13**

C137	AP52	40b multi	18	15
C138	AP52	55b multi	28	15
C139	AP52	75b multi	38	15
C140	AP52	1.35 l multi	70	15
C141	AP52	1.75 l multi	1.10	20
		Nos. C137-C141 (5)	2.64	
		Set value	62	

Valeri
Bykovski
AP53

Designs: 1.20 l, Bykovski, vert. 1.60 l, Tereshkova, vert. 1.75 l, Valentina Tereshkova.

1963   **Photo.**

C142	AP53	55b blue	16	15
C143	AP53	1.75 l rose red	60	18
		Set value	26	

Souvenir Sheet
Perf. 13

C144		Sheet of 2	1.95	50
a.	AP53	1.20 l ultra	50	24
b.	AP53	1.60 l ultra	50	24

Space flights of Valeri Bykovski, June 14-19, and
Valentina Tereshkova, first woman cosmonaut, June
16-19, 1963.

No. C79 Surcharged and Overprinted:
"1913-1963 50 ani de la moarte"

Unwmk.

1963, Sept. 15   **Litho.**   **Perf. 14**

C145	AP31	1.75 l on 10b	1.00	38

50th death anniv. of Aurel Vlaicu, aviation
pioneer.
Exists with "i" of "lei," missing.

Centenary Stamp
of 1958 — AP54

Stamps on Stamps: 40b, Sputnik 2 and Laika,
#1200. 55b, Yurl A. Gagarin, #C104a. 1.20 l, Niko-
layev and Popovich, #C123, C125. 1.55 l, Postal
Administration Bldg. and letter carrier, #965.

1963, Nov. 15   **Photo.**   **Perf. 14x13¹/₂**
Size: 38x26mm

C146	AP54	20b lt bl & dk brn	15	15
C147	AP54	40b brt pink & dk bl	22	15
C148	AP54	55b lt ultra & dk car rose	28	15
C149	AP54	1.20 l ocher & pur	65	15
C150	AP54	1.55 l sal pink & ol gray	65	15
		Nos. C146-C150,CB22 (6)	3.25	1.25
		Set value	88	

15th UPU Congress, Vienna.

Pavel R.
Popovich
AP55

Astronauts and flag: 5b, Yuri A. Gagarin. 10b,
Gherman S. Titov. 20b, John H. Glenn, Jr. 35b,
M. Scott Carpenter. 40b, Andrian G. Nikolayev.
60b, Walter M. Schirra. 75b, Gordon L. Cooper.
1 l, Valeri Bykovski. 1.40 l, Valentina Tereshkova.

(5b, 10b, 20b, 35b, 60b and 75b are diamond
shaped).

Perf. 13¹/₂
1964, Jan. 15   **Litho.**   **Unwmk.**
Light Blue Background

C151	AP55	5b red, yel & vio bl	15	15
C152	AP55	10b red, yel & pur	15	15
C153	AP55	20b red, ultra & ol gray	18	15
C154	AP55	35b red, ultra & sl bl	22	15
C155	AP55	40b red, yel & ultra	22	15
C156	AP55	55b red, yel & ultra	38	15
C157	AP55	60b ultra, red & sep	38	15
C158	AP55	75b red, ultra & dk bl	45	15
C159	AP55	1 l red, yel & mar	75	15
C160	AP55	1.40 l red, yel & mar	90	15
		Nos. C151-C160 (10)	3.78	
		Set value	75	

Nos. C151-C160 exist imperf. in changed colors.
Value, set $6.50
A miniature sheet contains one imperf. horizontal 2 l ultramarine and yellow stamp. Size of stamp:
59¹/₂x43mm. Value unused $7.50, canceled
$3.75

Modern and
19th Century
Post Office
Buildings
AP56

Engr. & Typo.
1964, Nov. 15   **Perf. 13¹/₂**

C161	AP56	1.60 l ultra + 40b label	75	25

Stamp Day. Stamp and label are imperf.
between.

Plane Approaching Airport and Coach
Leaving Gate — AP57

Engr. & Typo.
1966, Oct. 20   **Perf. 13¹/₂**

C162	AP57	55b + 45b label	48	15

Stamp Day.

Space Exploration Type of Regular Issue

US Achievements in Space: 1.20 l, Early Bird
satellite and globe. 1.55 l, Mariner 4 transmitting
pictures of the moon. 3.25 l, Gemini 6 & 7, rendezvous in space. 5 l, Gemini 8 meeting Agena rocket,
and globe.

1967, Feb. 15   **Photo.**   **Perf. 13¹/₂**

C163	A595	1.20 l sil & multi	25	15
C164	A595	1.55 l sil & multi	38	15
C165	A595	3.25 l sil & multi	65	15
C166	A595	5 l sil & multi	1.50	50
		Set value	70	

10 years of space exploration.

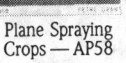

Plane Spraying
Crops — AP58

Moon, Earth
and Path of
Apollo
8 — AP59

Designs: 55b, Aerial ambulance over river,
horiz. 1 l, Red Cross and plane. 2.40 l, Biplane and
Mircea Zorileanu, aviation pioneer.

Perf. 12x12½, 12½x12

1968, Feb. 28   Litho.   Unwmk.
C167 AP58   40b bl grn, blk & yel brn   15 15
C168 AP58   55b multi   15 15
C169 AP58   1 l ultra, pale grn & red
org   28 15
C170 AP58   2.40 l brt rose lil & multi   90 30
Set value   48

1969   Photo.   Perf. 13½
Design: No. C172, Soyuz 4 and 5 over globe
with map of Russia.

C171 AP59   3.30 l multi   1.75 28
C172 AP59   3.30 l multi   1.75 28

1st manned flight around the Moon, Dec. 21-27,
1968, and the first team flights of the Russian space-
crafts Soyuz 4 and 5, Jan. 16, 1969. See note after
Hungary No. C284.
Issued in sheets of 4.
Issued: #C171, Jan. 17, #C172, Mar. 28.

Apollo 9 and
Lunar
Landing
Module over
Earth
AP60

Design: 2.40 l, Apollo 10 and lunar landing
module over moon, vert.

1969, June 15   Photo.   Perf. 13½
C173 AP60   60b multi   15 15
C174 AP60   2.40 l multi   60 25
Set value   30

US space explorations, Apollo 9 and 10.

First Man on
Moon — AP61

1969, July 24   Photo.   Perf. 13½
C175 AP61   3.30 l multi   1.10 80

Man's first landing on the moon July 20, 1969,
US astronauts Neil A. Armstrong and Col. Edwin E.
Aldrin, Jr., with Lieut. Col. Michael Collins piloting
Apollo 11. Printed in sheets of 4.

1970, June 29
Design: 1.50 l, Apollo 13 capsule splashing
down in Pacific.

C176 AP61   1.50 l multi   48 40

Flight and safe landing of Apollo 13, Apr. 11-17,
1970. Printed in sheets of 4.

BAC 1-11
Jet
AP62

Design: 2 l, Fuselage BAC 1-11 and control
tower, Bucharest airport.

1970, Apr. 6
C177 AP62   60b multi   18 15
C178 AP62   2 l multi   55 22
Set value   28

50th anniv. of Romanian civil aviation.

Flood Relief Type of Regular Issue
Design: 60b, Rescue by helicopter.

1970, Sept. 25   Photo.   Perf. 13½
C179 A671   60b bl gray, blk & ol   30 15

Issued to publicize the plight of the victims of the
Danube flood. No. C179 printed as a triptych with
Nos. 2206-2207.

Henri
Coanda's
Model Plane
AP63

1970, Dec. 1
C180 AP63   60b multicolored   25 15

Henri Coanda's first flight, 60th anniversary.

Luna 16 on
Moon
AP64

Design: No. C182, Lunokhod 1, unmanned
vehicle on moon. No. C183, US astronaut and
vehicle on moon.

1971, Mar. 5   Photo.   Perf. 13½
C181 AP64   3.30 l silver & multi   85 50
C182 AP64   3.30 l silver & multi   85 50
C183 AP64   3.30 l silver & multi   85 50

No. C181 commemorates Luna 16 Russian
unmanned, automatic moon mission, Sept. 12-24,
1970 (labels are incorrectly inscribed Oct. 12-24).
No. C182 commemorates Lunokhod 1 (Luna 17),
Nov. 10-17, 1970. Nos. C181-C182 printed in
sheets of 4 stamps, arranged checkerwise, and 4
labels. No. C183 commemorates Apollo 14 moon
landing, Jan. 31-Feb. 9. Printed in sheets of 4 with
4 labels showing portraits of US astronauts Alan B.
Shepard, Edgar D. Mitchell, Stuart A. Roosa, and
Apollo 14 emblem.

Souvenir Sheet

Cosmonauts Patsayev, Dobrovolsky and
Volkov — AP65

1971, July 26   Litho.   Perf. 13½
C184 AP65   6 l black & ultra   3.75 3.75

In memory of Russian cosmonauts Viktor I. Pat-
sayev, Georgi T. Dobrovolsky and Vladislav N.
Volkov, who died during Soyuz 11 space mission,
June 6-30, 1971.
No. C184 exists imperf. in black & blue green;
Size: 130x90mm.

Lunar Rover
on Moon
AP66

1971, Aug. 26   Photo.
C185 AP66   1.50 l blue & multi   75 60

US Apollo 15 moon mission, July 26-Aug. 7,
1971. No. C185 printed in sheets of 4 stamps and 4
labels showing astronauts David Scott, James Irwin,
Alfred Worden and Apollo 15 emblem with dates.
No. C185 exists imperf. in green & multicolored.
The sheet has a control number.

Olympic Souvenir Sheets
Designs: No. C186, Torchbearer and map of
Romania. No. C187, Soccer.

1972   Photo.   Perf. 13½
C186 A699   6 l pale grn & multi   3.75 3.75
C187 A699   6 l blue & multi   3.75 3.75

20th Olympic Games, Munich, Aug. 26-Sept. 11.
No. C186 contains one stamp 50x38mm. No.
C187 contains one stamp 48½x37mm.
Issued: No. C186, Apr. 25. No. C187, Sept. 29.
Two imperf. 6 l souvenir sheets exist, one show-
ing equestrian, the other a satellite over globe.

Lunar Rover on
Moon — AP67

1972, May 10   Photo.   Perf. 13½
C188 AP67   3 l vio bl, rose & gray grn   90 45

Apollo 16 US moon mission, Apr. 15-27, 1972.
No. C188 printed in sheets of 4 stamps and 4 gray
green and black labels showing Capt. John W.
Young, Lt. Comdr. Thomas K. Mattingly 2nd, Col.
Charles M. Duke, Jr., and Apollo 16 badge.

Aurel Vlaicu
and
Monoplane
AP68

Romanian Aviation Pioneers: 3 l, Traian Vuia and
his flying machine.

1972, Aug. 15
C189 AP68   60b multicolored   20 15
C190 AP68   3 l multicolored   85 32

**Olympic Medals Type of Regular Issue
Souvenir Sheet**
Design: Olympic silver and gold medals, horiz.

1972, Sept. 29   Litho.   Perf. 13½
C191 A714   6 l multicolored   3.00 3.00

Romanian medalists at 20th Olympic Games. An
imperf. 6 l souvenir sheet exists showing gold
medal.

**Apollo Type of Regular Issue
Souvenir Sheet**
Design: 6 l, Lunar rover, landing module, rocket
and astronauts on moon, horiz.

1972, Dec. 27   Photo.   Perf. 13½
C192 A715   6 l vio bl, bis & dl grn   3.00 3.00

No. C192 contains one stamp 48½x36mm.
An imperf. 6 l souvenir sheet exists showing
surface of moon with landing sites of last 6 Apollo
missions and landing capsule.

Type of Regular Issue, 1972
Design: Otopeni Airport, horiz.

1972, Dec. 20   Photo.   Perf. 13
Size: 29x21mm
C193 A710   14.60 l brt blue   2.75 38

Apollo and
Soyuz
Spacecraft
AP69

Design: 3.25 l, Apollo and Soyuz after link-up.

1975, July 14   Photo.   Perf. 13½
C196 AP69   1.75 l vio bl, red & ol   45 18
C197 AP69   3.25 l vio bl, red & ol   90 45

Apollo Soyuz space test project (Russo-American
cooperation), launching July 15; link-up, July 17.
Nos. C196-C197 printed in sheets of 4 stamps,
arranged checkerwise, and 4 rose lilac labels showing Apollo-Soyuz emblem.

European Security and Cooperation
Conference — AP70

1975, July 30   Photo.   Perf. 13½
C198 AP70   Sheet of 4   4.50 4.50
a.   2.75 l Map of Europe   55 55
b.   2.75 l Peace doves   55 55
c.   5 l Open book   1.00 1.00
d.   5 l Children playing   1.00 1.00

European Security and Cooperation Conference,
Helsinki, July 30-Aug. 1. No. C198b inscribed
"posta aeriana".
An imperf. 10 l souvenir sheet exists showing
Helsinki on map of Europe.

Red Cross Type of 1976
Design: Blood donors, Red Cross plane.

1976, Apr. 20   Photo.   Perf. 13½
C199 A790   3.35 l multi   70 35

De
Havilland
DH-9
AP71

Airplanes: 40b, I.C.A.R. Comercial. 60b, Douglas DC-3. 1.75 l, AN-24. 2.75 l, IL-62. 3.60 l,
Boeing 707.

1976, June 24   Photo.   Perf. 13½
C200 AP71   20b blue & multi   15 15
C201 AP71   40b blue & multi   15 15
C202 AP71   60b multi   18 15
C203 AP71   1.75 l multi   50 15
C204 AP71   2.75 l blue & multi   70 20
C205 AP71   3.60 l multi   1.00 50
Nos. C200-C205 (6)
Set value   2.68   95

Romanian Airline, 50th anniversary.

Glider I.C.A.R.-1 — AP72

Gliders: 40b, I.S.-3d. 55b, R.G.-5. 1.50 l, I.S.-11.
3 l, I.S.-29D. 3.40 l, I.S.-28B.

1977, Feb. 20   Photo.   *Perf. 13*

C206	AP72	20b multi	15	15
C207	AP72	40b multi	15	15
C208	AP72	55b multi	15	15
C209	AP72	1.50 l bl & multi	25	15
C210	AP72	3 l multi	60	15
C211	AP72	3.40 l multi	95	25
		Nos. C206-C211 (6)	2.25	
		Set value		62

Souvenir Sheet

037124

Boeing 707 over Bucharest Airport and
Pioneers — AP73

1977, June 28   Photo.   *Perf. 13½*

C212	AP73	10 l multi	2.50	2.50

European Security and Cooperation Conference,
Belgrade.
An imperf. 10 l souvenir sheet exists showing
Boeing 707, map of Europe and buildings.

Woman Letter
Carrier,
Mailbox
AP74

Design: 30 l, Plane, newspapers, letters,
packages.

1977   Photo.   *Perf. 13½*

C213	AP74	20 l multicolored	4.00	1.25
C214	AP74	30 l multicolored	5.75	2.50

Issue dates: 20 l, July 25, 30 l, Sept. 10.

LZ-1 over Friedrichshafen, 1900 — AP75

Airships: 1 l, Santos Dumont's dirigible over
Paris, 1901. 1.50 l, British R-34 over New York
and Statue of Liberty, 1919. 2.15 l, Italia over
North Pole, 1928. 3.40 l, Zeppelin LZ-127 over
Brasov, 1929. 4.80 l, Zeppelin over Sibiu, 1929.
10 l, Zeppelin over Bucharest, 1929.

1978, Mar. 20   Photo.   *Perf. 13½*

C215	AP75	60b multi	15	15
C216	AP75	1 l multi	15	15
C217	AP75	1.50 l multi	24	15
C218	AP75	2.15 l multi	32	15
C219	AP75	3.40 l multi	60	15
C220	AP75	4.80 l multi	1.25	24
		Nos. C215-C220 (6)	2.71	
		Set value		74

Souvenir Sheet

C221	AP75	10 l multi	2.75	2.75

History of airships. No. C221 contains one
stamp 50x37½mm.

Soccer Type of 1978
Souvenir Sheet

Design: 10 l, Two soccer players and Argentina
'78 emblem.

1978, Apr. 15   Photo.   *Perf. 13½*

C222	A818	10 l blue & multi	2.50	2.50

11th World Cup Soccer Championship, Argentina, June 1-25. No. C222 contains one stamp
37x50mm. A 10 l imperf. souvenir sheet exists
showing goalkeeper.

Wilbur
and
Orville
Wright,
Flyer A
AP76

Aviation History: 1 l, Louis Blériot and his plane
over English Channel, 1909. 1.50 l, Anthony Fokker and Fokker F-VII trimotor, 1926. 2.15 l, Andrei
N. Tupolev and ANT-25 monoplane, 1937. 3 l,
Otto Lilienthal and glider, 1891-96. 3.40 l, Traian
Vuia and his plane, Montesson, France, 1906.
4.80 l, Aurel Vlaicu and 1st Romanian plane, 1910.
10 l, Henri Coanda and his "jet," 1910.

1978, Dec. 18   Photo.   *Perf. 13½*

C223	AP76	55b multi	15	15
C224	AP76	1 l multi	15	15
C225	AP76	1.50 l multi	22	15
C226	AP76	2.15 l multi	35	15
C227	AP76	3 l multi	50	15
C228	AP76	3.40 l multi	60	15
C229	AP76	4.80 l multi	75	20
		Nos. C223-C229 (7)	2.72	
		Set value		65

Souvenir Sheet

C230	AP76	10 l multi	2.50	2.50

No. C230 contains one stamp 50x38mm.

Inter-Europa Type of 1979

Design: 3.40 l, Jet, mail truck and motorcycle.

1979, May 3   Photo.   *Perf. 13*

C231	A835	3.40 l multi	60	18

Animal Type of 1980
Souvenir Sheet

1980, Mar. 25   Photo.   *Perf. 13½*

C232	A852	10 l Pelicans	2.25	2.25

No. C232 contains one stamp 38x50mm.

Mercury — AP77

1981, June 30   Photo.   *Perf. 13½*

C233	AP77	55b shown	15	15
C234	AP77	1 l Venus, Earth,	15	15
		Mars		
C235	AP77	1 l Jupiter	18	15
C236	AP77	2.15 l Saturn	28	15
C237	AP77	3.40 l Uranus	45	15
C238	AP77	4.80 l Neptune, Pluto	60	30
		Nos. C233-C238 (6)	1.81	
		Set value		75

Souvenir Sheet

C239	AP77	10 l Earth	2.00	2.00

No. C239 contains one stamp 37x50mm. An
imperf. 10 l souvenir sheet exists showing planets
in orbit.

Romanian-Russian Space
Cooperation — AP78

1981   Photo.   *Perf. 13½*

C240	AP78	55b Soyuz 40	15	15
C241	AP78	3.40 l Salyut 6, Soyuz 40	40	22
		Set value		26

Souvenir Sheet

C242	AP78	10 l Cosmonauts,		
		spacecraft	2.00	2.00

No. C242 contains one stamp 50x39mm. Issue
dates: 55b, 3.40 l, May 14; 10 l, June 30.

Children's Games Type of 1981

1981, Nov. 25

C243	A880	4.80 l Flying model planes	52	30

Standard Glider — AP79

1982, June 20   Photo.   *Perf. 13½*

C244	AP79	50b shown	15	15
C245	AP79	1 l Excelsior D	15	15
C246	AP79	1.50 l Dedal I	22	15
C247	AP79	2.50 l Enthusiast	30	15
C248	AP79	4 l AK-22	50	24
C249	AP79	5 l Grifrom	70	30
		Nos. C244-C249 (6)	2.02	
		Set value		85

Agriculture Type of 1982

1982, June 29

C250	A888	4 l Helicopter spraying in-		
		secticide	60	30

Vlaicu's
Glider,
1909
AP80

Aurel Vlaicu (1882-19), Aviator: 1 l, Memorial,
Banesti-Prahova, vert. 2.50 l, Hero Aviators Memorial, by Kotzebue and Fekete, vert. 3 l, Vlaicu-1
glider, 1910.

1982, Sept. 27   Photo.   *Perf. 13½*

C251	AP80	50b multi	15	15
C252	AP80	1 l multi	15	15
C253	AP80	2.50 l multi	38	15
C254	AP80	3 l multi	45	15
		Set value		32

25th
Anniv. of
Space
Flight
AP81

Designs: 50b, H. Coanda, reaction motor, 1910.
1 l, H. Oberth, rocket, 1923. 1.50 l, Sputnik 1,
1957. 2.50 l, Vostok I, 1961. 4 l, Apollo 11, 1969.
5 l, Columbia space shuttle, 1982. 10 l, Globe.

1983, Jan. 24

C255	AP81	50b multi	15	15
C256	AP81	1 l multi	15	15
C257	AP81	1.50 l multi	20	15
C258	AP81	2.50 l multi	32	15
C259	AP81	4 l multi	50	25
C260	AP81	5 l multi	65	30
		Nos. C255-C260 (6)	1.97	
		Set value		88

Souvenir Sheet

C261	AP81	10 l multi	1.90	1.90

No. C261 contains one stamp 41x53mm.

First Romanian-
built Jet
Airliner — AP82

1983, Jan. 25   Photo.   *Perf. 13½*

C262	AP82	11 l Rombac 1-11	1.75	70

World Communications Year — AP83

1983, July 25   Photo.   *Perf. 13½*

C263	AP83	2 l Boeing 707, Postal van	45	15

40th Anniv., Intl. Civil Aviation
Organization — AP84

1984, Aug. 15   Photo.   *Perf. 13½*

C265	AP84	50b Lockheed L-14	15	15
C266	AP84	1.50 l BN-2 Islander	24	15
C267	AP84	3 l Rombac	45	24
C268	AP84	6 l Boeing 707	90	45
		Set value		85

Halley's Comet — AP85

1986, Jan. 27   Photo.   *Perf. 13½*

C269	AP85	2 l shown	30	15
C270	AP85	4 l Space probes	60	30

An imperf. 10 l air post souvenir sheet exists
showing comet and space probes, red control
number.

Souvenir Sheet

Plane of Alexandru Papana, 1936 — AP86

1986, May 15   Photo.   *Perf. 13½*

C271	AP86	10 l multi	2.75	2.75

AMERIPEX '86.

Aircraft
AP87

1987, Aug. 10

C272	AP87	50b Henri Auguste glid-		
		er, 1909	15	15
C273	AP87	1 l Sky diver, IS-28 B2		
		glider	18	15
C274	AP87	2 l IS-29 D-2 glider	35	18
C275	AP87	3 l IS-32 glider	55	28
C276	AP87	4 l IAR-35 glider	70	35
C277	AP87	5 l IS-28 M2, route	90	45
		Nos. C272-C277 (6)	2.83	1.51

1st Moon Landing, 20th Anniv. — AP88

Designs: 50b, C. Haas. 1.50 l, Konstantin Tsiolkovski (1857-1935), Soviet rocket science pioneer. 2 l, H. Oberth and equations. 3 l, Robert Goddard and diagram on blackboard. 4 l, Sergei Korolev (1906-66), Soviet aeronautical engineer. 5 l, Wernher von Braun (1912-77), lunar module.

1989, Oct. 25   **Photo.**   *Perf. 13½*
C278	AP88	50b multicolored	16	15
C279	AP88	1.50 l multicolored	45	22
C280	AP88	2 l multicolored	65	32
C281	AP88	3 l multicolored	95	45
C282	AP88	4 l multicolored	1.25	60
C283	AP88	5 l multicolored	1.50	75
	Nos. C278-C283 (6)		4.96	2.49

A 10 l souvenir sheet picturing Armstrong and *Eagle* lunar module was also issued.

Souvenir Sheet

World Stamp Expo '89, Washington, DC, Nov. 17-Dec. 3 — AP89

1989, Nov. 17   **Photo.**   *Perf. 13½*
C284	AP89	5 l Postal coach	2.00	1.00

Captured Balloons — AP90

Balloons captured by Romanian army: 30 l, German balloon, Draken, 1903. 90 l, French balloon, Caquot, 1917.

1993, Feb. 26   **Photo.**   *Perf. 13½*
C285	AP90	30 l multicolored	38	38
C286	AP90	90 l multicolored	1.10	1.10

Souvenir Sheet

European Inventions, Discoveries — AP91

Europa: a, 240 l, Hermann Oberth (1894-1989), rocket scientist. b, 2100 l, Henri Doanda (1886-1972), aeronautical engineer. Illustration reduced.

1994, May 25   **Photo.**   *Perf. 13*
C287	AP91	Sheet of 2, #a.-b. + 2 labels	7.50 7.50

ICAO, 50th Anniv. AP92

Aircraft: 110 l, Traian Vuia, 1906. 350 l, Rombac 1-11. 500 l, Boeing 737-300. 635 l, Airbus A310.

1994, Aug. 12   **Photo.**   *Perf. 13*
C288	AP92	110 l multicolored	28	15
C289	AP92	350 l multicolored	90	45
C290	AP92	500 l multicolored	1.25	60
C291	AP92	635 l multicolored	1.65	85
	Nos. C288-C291 (4)		4.08	2.05

AIR POST SEMI-POSTAL STAMPS

Catalogue values for unused stamps in this section are for Never Hinged items.

Corneliu Codreanu SPAP1

1940, Dec. 1   **Unwmk.**   **Photo.**   *Perf. 14*
CB1	SPAP1	20 l + 5 l Prus grn	1.10 1.10

Propaganda for the Rome-Berlin Axis. No. CB1 exists with overprint "1 Mai 1941 Jamboreea Nationala."

Plane over Sinaia SPAP2

Designs: 200 l+800 l, Plane over Mountains.

1945, Oct. 1   **Wmk. 276**   *Imperf.*
CB2	SPAP2	80 l + 420 l gray	70	70
CB3	SPAP2	200 l + 800 l ultra	70	70

16th Congress of the General Assoc. of Romanian Engineers.

Souvenir Sheet

Re-distribution of Land — SPAP4

1946, May 4   **Photo.**   *Perf. 14*
CB4	SPAP4	80 l blue	3.00 3.75

Agrarian reform law of Mar. 23, 1945. The sheet sold for 100 lei.

Souvenir Sheet

Plane Skywriting — SPAP5

1946, May 1   *Perf. 13*
CB5	SPAP5	200 l bl & brt red	3.75 4.50

Labor Day. The sheet sold for 10,000 lei.

Lockheed 12 Electra — SPAP6

1946, Sept. 1   *Perf. 11½*
CB6	SPAP6	300 l + 1200 l dp bl	85 85

No. CB6 exists se-tenant with No. C26. See note after No. C26. The surtax was for the Office of Popular Sports.

Miniature Sheet

Women of Wallachia, Transylvania and Moldavia — SPAP7

1946, Dec. 20   **Wmk. 276**   *Imperf.*
CB7	SPAP7	500 l + 9500 l choc & red	1.90 2.25

Democratic Women's Org. of Romania.

SPAP8

1946, Oct.   *Imperf.*
CB8	SPAP8	300 l deep plum	5.00 5.25

The surtax was for the Office of Popular Sports. Sheets of four. Stamp sold for 1300 l.

Laborer with Torch — SPAP9

1947, Mar. 1
CB9	SPAP9	3000 l + 7000 l choc	38 38

Sheets of four with marginal inscription.

Plane SPAP10   Plane above Shore Line SPAP11

1947, June 27   *Imperf.*
CB10	SPAP10	15,000 l + 15,000 l	38 38

Sheets of four with marginal inscription.

1947, May 1   *Perf. 14x13*
CB11	SPAP11	3000 l + 12,000 l bl	28 28

Planes over Mountains SPAP12   Plane over Athletic Field SPAP13

1947, Oct. 5   *Perf. 14x14½*
CB12	SPAP12	5 l + 5 l blue	52 18

17th Congress of the General Assoc. of Romanian Engineers.

Perf. 13½
1948, Feb. 20   **Photo.**   **Wmk. 276**
CB13	SPAP13	7 l + 7 l vio	80 42

Imperf
CB14	SPAP13	10 l + 10 l Prus grn	1.10 65

Balkan Games. Sheets of four with marginal inscription.

Swallow and Plane SPAP14

1948, Mar. 15   *Perf. 14x13½*
CB15	SPAP14	12 l + 12 l blue	85 50

Bucharest-Moscow Passenger Plane, Douglas DC-3 Dakota — SPAP15

1948, Oct. 29   *Perf. 14*
CB16	SPAP15	20 l + 20 l dp bl	7.25 7.25

Printed in sheets of 8 stamps and 16 small, red brown labels. Sheet yields 8 triptychs, each comprising 1 stamp flanked by label with Bucharest view and label with Moscow view.

Douglas DC-
4 — SPAP16

1948, May 1   *Perf. 13¹/₂x14*
CB17 SPAP16 20 l + 20 l blue   6.75 5.75

Issued to publicize Labor Day, May 1, 1948.

Pursuit Plane   Launching
and Victim   Model Plane
SPAP17   SPAP18

1948, May 9   *Perf. 13*
CB18 SPAP17 3 l + 3 l shown   2.25 2.25
CB19 SPAP17 5 l + 5 l Bomber   2.75 2.75

Issued to honor the Romanian army.

1948, Dec. 31   *Perf. 13x13¹/₂*
CB20 SPAP18 20 l + 20 l dp ultra   9.75 9.75

Imperf
CB21 SPAP18 20 l + 20 l Prus bl   9.75 9.75

Nos. CB20 and CB21 were issued in sheets of
four stamps, with ornamental border and "1948" in
contrasting color.

UPU Type of Air Post Issue, 1963

Design: 1.60 l+50b, Globe, map of Romania,
planes and UPU monument.

Perf. 14x13¹/₂
1963, Nov. 15   Litho.   Unwmk.
        Size: 75x27mm
CB22 AP54 1.60 l + 50b multi   1.40 50

Surtax for the Romanian Philatelic Federation.

POSTAGE DUE STAMPS

D1

Perf. 11, 11¹/₂, 13¹/₂ and Compound
1881   Typo.   Unwmk.
J1	D1	2b brown	3.25	1.00
J2	D1	5b brown	16.00	1.65
a.		Tête bêche pair	190.00	75.00
J3	D1	10b brown	21.00	1.00
J4	D1	30b brown	22.50	1.00
J5	D1	50b brown	13.00	1.00
J6	D1	60b brown	10.50	2.25

1885
J7	D1	10b pale red brown	6.00	45
J8	D1	30b pale red brown	6.00	45

1887-90
J9	D1	2b gray green	3.00	75
J10	D1	5b gray green	6.00	3.00
J11	D1	10b gray green	6.00	3.00
J12	D1	30b gray green	6.00	75

1888
J14	D1	2b green, *yellowish*	75	75
J15	D1	5b green, *yellowish*	2.25	2.25
J16	D1	10b green, *yellowish*	19.00	2.75
J17	D1	30b green, *yellowish*	11.50	1.10

1890-96   Wmk. 163
J18	D1	2b emerald	75	30
J19	D1	5b emerald	38	38
J20	D1	10b emerald	75	38
J21	D1	30b emerald	1.10	38
J22	D1	50b emerald	4.25	15
J23	D1	60b emerald	5.75	2.75

1898   Wmk. 200
J24	D1	2b blue green	30	22
J25	D1	5b blue green	60	20
J26	D1	10b blue green	75	20
J27	D1	30b blue green	75	20
J28	D1	50b blue green	3.00	60
J29	D1	60b blue green	3.75	1.40

1902-10   Unwmk.
Thin Paper, Tinted Rose on Back
J30	D1	2b green	38	15
J31	D1	5b green	20	15
J32	D1	10b green	20	15
J33	D1	30b green	35	15
J34	D1	50b green	1.75	38
J35	D1	60b green	3.75	1.90
		Nos. J30-J35 (6)	6.63	2.88

1908-11
White Paper
J36	D1	2b green	38	22
J37	D1	5b green	38	22
a.		Tête bêche pair	11.50	11.50
J38	D1	10b green	20	15
J39	D1	30b green	30	15
a.		Tête bêche pair	11.50	11.50
J40	D1	50b green	1.50	75
		Nos. J36-J40 (5)	2.76	1.49

D2

1911   Wmk. 165
J41	D2	2b dark blue, *green*	15	15
J42	D2	5b dark blue, *green*	15	15
J43	D2	10b dark blue, *green*	15	15
J44	D2	15b dark blue, *green*	15	15
J45	D2	20b dark blue, *green*	15	15
J46	D2	30b dark blue, *green*	24	15
J47	D2	50b dark blue, *green*	30	15
J48	D2	60b dark blue, *green*	38	18
J49	D2	2 l dark blue, *green*	75	42
		Nos. J41-J49 (9)	2.42	
		Set value		1.20

The letters "P.R." appear to be embossed instead
of watermarked. They are often faint or entirely
invisible.

The 20b, type D2, has two types, differing in the
width of the head of the "2." This affects Nos. J45,
J54, J58, and J63.

See Nos. J52-J77, J82, J87-J88. For overprints see
Nos. J78-J81, RAJ1-RAJ2, RAJ20-RAJ21, 3NJ1-
3NJ7.

Regular Issue of 1908   **TAXA**
Overprinted   **DE PLATA**

1918   Unwmk.
J50	A46	5b yellow green	75	25
a.		Inverted overprint	1.75	1.75
J51	A46	10b rose	75	25
a.		Inverted overprint	1.10	1.10

Postage Due Type of 1911
Wmk. 165
J52	D2	5b black, *green*	22	15
J53	D2	10b black, *green*	18	15
J54	D2	20b black, *green*	4.00	60
J55	D2	30b black, *green*	1.10	38
J55A	D2	50b black, *green*	3.00	90
		Nos. J52-J55A (5)	8.50	2.18

Perf. 11¹/₂, 13¹/₂ and Compound
1919   Unwmk.
J56	D2	5b black, *green*	15	15
J57	D2	10b black, *green*	15	15
J58	D2	20b black, *green*	55	15
J59	D2	30b black, *green*	45	15
J60	D2	50b black, *green*	1.10	38
		Nos. J56-J60 (5)	2.40	
		Set value		74

1920-26
White Paper
J61	D2	5b black	15	15
J62	D2	10b black	15	15
J63	D2	20b black	15	15
J64	D2	30b black	24	15
J65	D2	50b black	38	15
J66	D2	60b black	15	15

J67	D2	1 l black	30	15
J68	D2	2 l black	18	15
J69	D2	3 l black ('26)	18	15
J70	D2	6 l black ('26)	30	15
		Set value	1.90	50

1923-24
J74	D2	1 l black, *pale green*	24	15
J75	D2	2 l black, *pale green*	42	22
J76	D2	3 l black, *pale green* ('24)	1.10	55
J77	D2	6 l blk, *pale green* ('24)	1.40	55

Postage Due Stamps of   **8 IUNIE 1930**
1920-26 Overprinted

1930   *Perf. 13¹/₂*
J78	D2	1 l black	15	15
J79	D2	2 l black	18	15
J80	D2	3 l black	30	15
J81	D2	6 l black	45	24
		Set value	56	

Accession of King Carol II.

> Catalogue values for unused
> stamps in this section, from this
> point to the end of the section, are
> for Never Hinged items.

Type of 1911 Issue
1931   Wmk. 225
J82	D2	2 l black	70	18

D3

1932-37   Wmk. 230
J83	D3	1 l black	15	15
J84	D3	2 l black	15	15
J85	D3	3 l black ('37)	15	15
J86	D3	6 l black ('37)	15	15
		Set value	42	28

See Nos. J89-J98.

Type of 1911
1942   Typo.   *Perf. 13¹/₂*
J87	D2	50 l black	24	18
J88	D2	100 l black	38	24

Type of 1932
1946-47   Unwmk.   *Perf. 14*
J89	D3	20 l black	60	55
J90	D3	100 l black ('47)	45	24
J91	D3	200 l black	1.10	55

1946-47   Wmk. 276
J92	D3	20 l black	15	15
J93	D3	50 l black	15	15
J94	D3	80 l black	15	15
J95	D3	100 l black	18	18
J96	D3	200 l black	38	35
J97	D3	500 l black	48	48
J98	D3	5000 l black ('47)	1.25	1.25
		Nos. J92-J98 (7)	2.74	2.71

Crown and
King Michael
D3a

Perf. 14¹/₂x13¹/₂
1947   Typo.   Wmk. 276
J98A	D3a	2 l carmine	30	15
J98B	D3a	4 l gray blue	60	30
J98C	D3a	5 l black	90	45
J98D	D3a	10 l violet brown	1.50	75

Same
Overprinted

1948
J98E	D3a	2 l carmine	24	15
J98F	D3a	4 l gray blue	45	24
J98G	D3a	5 l black	60	30
J98H	D3a	10 l violet brown	1.10	52

In use, Nos. J98A-J106 and following issues were
torn apart, one half being affixed to the postage due
item and the other half being pasted into the postman's record book. Values are for unused and
canceled-to-order pairs.

Communications Badge and
Postwoman — D4

1950 Unwmk. Photo. *Perf. 14¹/₂x14*
J99	D4	2 l orange vermilion	70	70
J100	D4	4 l deep blue	70	70
J101	D4	5 l dark gray green	90	90
J102	D4	10 l orange brown	1.10	1.10

Wmk. 358
J103	D4	2 l orange vermilion	90	70
J104	D4	4 l deep blue	90	70
J105	D4	5 l dark gray green	1.25	90
J106	D4	10 l orange brown	1.65	1.25
		Nos. J99-J106 (8)	8.10	6.95

Postage Due Stamps of 1950 Surcharged
with New Values in Black or Carmine
1952   Unwmk.
J107	D4	4b on 2 l	24	24
J108	D4	10b on 4 l (C)	24	24
J109	D4	20b on 5 l (C)	45	45
J110	D4	50b on 10 l	75	75

Wmk. 358
J111	D4	4b on 2 l	22	22
J112	D4	10b on 4 l (C)	22	22
J113	D4	20b on 5 l (C)	2.50	1.25
J114	D4	50b on 10 l	3.00	1.25
		Nos. J107-J114 (8)	7.62	4.62

See note after No. J98H.

General Post Office and Post Horn — D5

1957   Wmk. 358   *Perf. 14*
J115	D5	3b brt grn	15	15
J116	D5	5b red orange	15	15
J117	D5	10b red lilac	15	15
J118	D5	20b brt red	15	15
J119	D5	40b lt bl grn	35	15
J120	D5	1 l brt ultra	1.00	16
		Set value	1.65	45

See note after No. J98H.

General Post Office and Post Horn — D6

1967, Feb. 25   Photo.   *Perf. 13*
J121	D6	3b brt grn	15	15
J122	D6	5b brt bl	15	15
J123	D6	10b lilac rose	15	15
J124	D6	20b vermilion	15	15
J125	D6	40b brown	20	15
J126	D6	1 l violet	55	15
		Set value	95	32

See note after No. J98H.

1970, Mar. 10   Unwmk.
J127	D6	3b brt grn	15	15
J128	D6	5b brt bl	15	15
J129	D6	10b lilac rose	15	15
J130	D6	20b vermilion	15	15
J131	D6	40b brown	18	15
J132	D6	1 l violet	35	15
		Set value	74	30

See note after No. J98H.

Symbols of Communications — D7

Designs: 10b, Like 5b. 20b, 40b, Pigeons, head of Mercury and post horn. 50b, 1 l, General Post Office, post horn and truck.

1974, Jan. 1		**Photo.**		**Perf. 13**
J133	D7	5b brt bl	15	15
J134	D7	10b olive	15	15
J135	D7	20b lilac rose	15	15
J136	D7	40b purple	15	15
J137	D7	50b brown	18	15
J138	D7	1 l orange	35	15
		Set value	75	35

See note after No. J98H.

1982, Dec. 23		**Photo.**		**Perf. 13½**
J139	D7	25b like #J135	15	15
J140	D7	50b like #J133	15	15
J141	D7	1 l like #J135	18	15
J142	D7	2 l like #J137	35	15
J143	D7	3 l like #J133	52	15
J144	D7	4 l like #J137	70	22
		Nos. J139-J144 (6)	2.05	
		Set value		62

See note after No. J98H.

Post Horn — D8

1992, Feb. 3		**Photo.**		**Perf. 13½**
J145	D8	4 l red	24	15
J146	D8	8 l blue	48	18

See note after No. J98H.

OFFICIAL STAMPS

Catalogue values for unused stamps in this section are for Never Hinged items.

Eagle Carrying National Emblem — O1 | Coat of Arms — O2

1929	**Photo.**	**Wmk. 95**		**Perf. 13½**
O1	O1	25b red org	25	15
O2	O1	50b dk brn	25	15
O3	O1	1 l dk vio	30	15
O4	O1	2 l ol grn	30	15
O5	O1	3 l rose car	48	15
O6	O1	4 l dk ol	48	15
O7	O1	6 l Prus bl	2.50	15
O8	O1	10 l dp bl	80	15
O9	O1	25 l car brn	1.65	1.25
O10	O1	50 l purple	4.75	3.50
		Nos. O1-O10 (10)	11.76	5.95

Type of Official Stamps of 1929 Overprinted **8 IUNIE 1930**

1930				**Unwmk.**
O11	O1	25b red org	18	15
O12	O1	50b dk brn	18	15
O13	O1	1 l dk vio	35	15
O14	O1	3 l rose car	50	15
		Set value		30

Nos. O11-O14 were not placed in use without overprint.

Same Overprint on Nos. O1-O10
Wmk. 95

O15	O1	25b red org	25	15
O16	O1	50b dk brn	25	15
O17	O1	1 l dk vio	25	15
O18	O1	2 l dp grn	25	15

O19	O1	3 l rose car	60	15
O20	O1	4 l ol blk	75	15
O21	O1	6 l Prus bl	2.00	15
O22	O1	10 l dp bl	80	15
O23	O1	25 l car brn	3.00	2.50
O24	O1	50 l purple	4.00	3.50
		Nos. O15-O24 (10)	12.15	7.20

Accession of King Carol II to the throne of Romania (Nos O11-O24).

	Perf. 13½, 13½x14½			
1931-32		**Typo.**	**Wmk. 225**	
O25	O2	25b black	22	15
O26	O2	1 l lilac	22	18
O27	O2	2 l emerald	35	35
O28	O2	3 l rose	60	60

1932		**Wmk. 230**		**Perf. 13½**
O29	O2	25b black	22	22
O30	O2	1 l violet	32	32
O31	O2	2 l emerald	48	48
O32	O2	3 l rose	60	60
O33	O2	6 l red brn	90	90
		Nos. O29-O33 (5)	2.52	2.52

PARCEL POST STAMPS

PP1

	Perf. 11½, 13½ and Compound			
1895		**Wmk. 163**		**Typo.**
Q1	PP1	25b brown red	8.75	1.50

1896				
Q2	PP1	25b vermilion	6.75	75

	Perf. 13½ and 11½x13½			
1898		**Wmk. 200**		
Q3	PP1	25b brown red	6.00	1.00
a.		Tête bêche pair		
Q4	PP1	25b vermilion	6.00	75

Thin Paper
Tinted Rose on Back

1905		**Unwmk.**		**Perf. 11½**
Q5	PP1	25b vermilion	4.50	85

1911				**White Paper**
Q6	PP1	25b pale red	4.50	85

No. 263 Surcharged in Carmine

FACTAJ
5
LEI

1928				**Perf. 13½**
Q7	A54	5 l on 10b yellow green	85	15

POSTAL TAX STAMPS

Regular Issue of 1908 Overprinted **TIMBRU DE AJUTOR**

	Perf. 11½, 13½, 11½x13½			
1915				**Unwmk.**
RA1	A46	5b green	18	15
RA2	A46	10b rose	30	15
		Set value		16

The "Timbru de Ajutor" stamps represent a tax on postal matter. The money obtained from their sale was turned into a fund for the assistance of soldiers' families.

Until 1923 the only "Timbru de Ajutor" stamps used for postal purposes were the 5b and 10b. Stamps of higher values with this inscription were used to pay the taxes on railway and theater tickets and other fiscal taxes. In 1923 the postal rate was advanced to 25b.

The Queen Weaving — PT1

1916-18				**Typo.**
RA3	PT1	5b gray blk	18	15
RA4	PT1	5b green ('18)	45	15
RA5	PT1	10b brown	30	15
RA6	PT1	10b gray blk ('18)	45	15
		Set value		45

For overprints see Nos. RA7-RA8, RAJ7-RAJ9, 3NRA1-3NRA8.

Stamps of 1916 Overprinted in Red or Black

1918				**Perf. 13½**
RA7	PT1	5b gray blk (R)	38	24
a.		Double overprint	3.00	
c.		Black overprint	4.50	
RA8	PT1	10b brn (Bk)	45	24
a.		Double overprint	4.50	
b.		Double overprint, one inverted	4.50	
c.		Inverted overprint	4.50	

Same Overprint on RA1 and RA2

1919				
RA11	A46	5b yel grn (R)	17.00	12.50
RA12	A46	10b rose (Bk)	17.00	12.50

Charity — PT3

	Perf. 13½, 11½, 13½x11½			
1921-24		**Typo.**		**Unwmk.**
RA13	PT3	10b green	15	15
RA14	PT3	25b blk ('24)	15	15
		Set value		20	15

Type of 1921-24 Issue

1928				**Wmk. 95**
RA15	PT3	25b black	75	25

Nos. RA13, RA14 and RA15 are the only stamps of type PT3 issued for postal purposes. Other denominations were used fiscally.

Catalogue values for unused stamps in this section, from this point to the end of the section, are for Never Hinged items.

Airplane PT4 | Head of Aviator PT5

1931		**Photo.**		**Unwmk.**
RA16	PT4	50b Prus bl	30	15
a.		Double impression	15.00	
RA17	PT4	1 l dk red brn	30	15
RA18	PT4	2 l ultra	60	15
		Set value		20

The use of these stamps, in addition to the regular postage, was obligatory on all postal matter for the interior of the country. The money thus obtained was to augment the National Fund for Aviation. When the stamps were not used to prepay the special tax, it was collected by means of Postal Tax Due stamps Nos. RAJ20 and RAJ21.

Nos. RA17 and RA18 were also used for other than postal tax.

1932		**Wmk. 230**		**Perf. 14 x 13½**
RA19	PT5	50b Prus bl	22	15
RA20	PT5	1 l red brn	35	15
RA21	PT5	2 l ultra	45	15
		Set value		15

The notes after No. RA18 will apply also to Nos. RA19-RA21.

After 1937 use of Nos. RA20-RA21 was limited to other than postal matter.

Nos. RA19-RA21 exist imperf.

Two stamps similar to type PT5, but inscribed "Fondul Aviatiei," were issued in 1936: 10b sepia and 20b violet.

Aviator PT6 | King Michael PT7

1937				**Perf. 13½**
RA22	PT6	50b Prus bl	15	15
RA23	PT6	1 l red brn	22	15
RA24	PT6	2 l ultra	24	15
		Set value		15

Stamps overprinted or inscribed "Fondul Aviatiei" other than Nos. RA22, RA23 or RA24 were used to pay taxes on other than postal matters.

1943	**Wmk. 276**	**Photo.**		**Perf. 14**
RA25	PT7	50b org ver	15	15
RA26	PT7	1 l lil rose	15	15
RA27	PT7	2 l brown	15	15
RA28	PT7	4 l lt ultra	15	15
RA29	PT7	5 l dull lilac	15	15
RA30	PT7	8 l yel grn	15	15
RA31	PT7	10 l blk brn	15	15
		Set value	42	42

The tax was obligatory on domestic mail.

Protection of Homeless Children — PT8

1945				
RA32	PT8	40 l Prus bl	24	18

PT9 | "Hope" — PT10

1947	**Unwmk.**	**Typo.**	**Perf. 14x14½**	
			Black Surcharge	
RA33	PT9	1 l on 2 l + 2 l pink	30	25
a.		Inverted surcharge		
RA34	PT9	5 l on 1 l + 1 l gray grn	4.50	3.75

1948				**Perf. 14**
RA35	PT10	1 l rose	1.90	15
RA36	PT10	1 l rose violet	2.10	15
		Set value		15

A 2 lei blue and 5 lei ocher in type PT10 were issued primarily for revenue purposes.

POSTAL TAX DUE STAMPS

Catalogue values for unused stamps in this section are for Never Hinged items.

Postage Due Stamps of 1911 Overprinted **TIMBRU DE AJUTOR**

Perf. 11½, 13½, 11½x13½

1915			Unwmk.	
RAJ1	D2	5b dk bl, *grn*	30	15
RAJ2	D2	10b dk bl, *grn*	30	15
a.		Wmk. 165	4.50	60
		Set value		24

PTD1   PTD2

1916		Typo.	Unwmk.	
RAJ3	PTD1	5b brn, *grn*	15	15
RAJ4	PTD1	10b red, *grn*	15	15
		Set value		24

See Nos. RAJ5-RAJ6, RAJ10-RAJ11. For overprint see No. 3NRAJ1.

1918				
RAJ5	PTD1	5b red, *grn*	18	15
a.		Wmk. 165	30	22
RAJ6	PTD1	10b brn, *grn*	18	15
a.		Wmk. 165	30	22
		Set value		20

Postal Tax Stamps of 1916, Overprinted in Red, Black or Blue   **TAXA DE PLATA**

RAJ7	PT1	5b gray blk (R)	18	15
a.		Inverted overprint		
RAJ8	PT1	10b brn (Bk)	24	15
a.		Inverted overprint		
RAJ9	PT1	10b brn (Bl)	5.00	5.00
a.		Vertical overprint	15.00	15.00

Type of 1916

1921				
RAJ10	PTD1	5b red	30	15
RAJ11	PTD1	10b brown	30	15
		Set value		24

1922-25			Typo.	
		Greenish Paper		
RAJ12	PTD2	10b brown	15	15
RAJ13	PTD2	20b brown	15	15
RAJ14	PTD2	25b brown	15	15
RAJ15	PTD2	50b brown	15	15
		Set value	36	24

1923-26				
RAJ16	PTD2	10b lt brn	15	15
RAJ17	PTD2	20b lt brn	15	15
RAJ18	PTD2	25b brown ('26)	15	15
RAJ19	PTD2	50b brown ('26)	15	15
		Set value	36	24

J82 and Type of 1911 Postage Due Stamps Overprinted in Red   **TIMBRUL AVIATIEI**

1931		Wmk. 225	Perf. 13½	
RAJ20	D2	1 l black	15	15
RAJ21	D2	2 l black	15	15
		Set value	16	15

When the Postal Tax stamps for the Aviation Fund issue (Nos. RA16 to RA18) were not used to prepay the obligatory tax on letters, etc., it was collected by affixing Nos. RAJ20 and RAJ21.

OCCUPATION STAMPS

ISSUED UNDER AUSTRIAN OCCUPATION

Emperor Karl of Austria
OS1   OS2

1917		Unwmk.	Engr.	Perf. 12½	
1N1	OS1	3b ol gray		95	60
1N2	OS1	5b ol grn		75	45
1N3	OS1	5b violet		75	45
1N4	OS1	10b org brn		15	15

1N5	OS1	12b dp bl	85	50
1N6	OS1	15b brt rose	75	45
1N7	OS1	20b red brn	15	15
1N8	OS1	25b ultra	18	20
1N9	OS1	30b slate	28	20
1N10	OS1	40b olive bis	28	20
a.		Perf. 11½	40.00	19.00
b.		Perf. 11½x12½	45.00	20.00
1N11	OS1	50b dp grn	28	20
1N12	OS1	60b rose	28	20
1N13	OS1	80b dl bl	15	15
1N14	OS1	90b dk vio	28	20
1N15	OS2	2 l rose, *straw*	40	20
1N16	OS2	3 l grn, *bl*	70	30
1N17	OS2	4 l rose, *grn*	70	30
		Nos. 1N1-1N17 (17)	7.88	4.85

Nos. 1N1-1N14 have "BANI" surcharged in red. Nos. 1N1-1N17 also exist imperforate. Value, set $20.

OS3   OS4

1918				
1N18	OS3	3b ol gray	15	15
1N19	OS3	5b ol grn	20	15
1N20	OS3	6b violet	24	24
1N21	OS3	10b org brn	26	26
1N22	OS3	12b dp bl	20	20
1N23	OS3	15b brt rose	15	15
1N24	OS3	20b red brn	15	15
1N25	OS3	25b ultra	15	15
1N26	OS3	30b slate	15	15
1N27	OS3	40b ol bis	20	20
1N28	OS3	50b dp grn	24	24
1N29	OS3	60b rose	24	24
1N30	OS3	80b dl bl	15	15
1N31	OS3	90b dk vio	20	22
1N32	OS4	2 l rose, *straw*	24	24
1N33	OS4	3 l grn, *bl*	30	30
1N34	OS4	4 l rose, *grn*	30	30
		Nos. 1N18-1N34 (17)	3.52	3.49

Exist. imperf. Value, set $17.50.

The complete series exists with "BANI" or "LEI" inverted, also with those words and the numerals of value inverted. Neither of these sets was regularly issued.

A set of 13 stamps similar to Austria Nos. M69-M81 was prepared for use in Romania in 1918, but not placed in use there. Denominations are in bani. It is reported that they were on sale after the armistice at the Vienna post office for a few days. Value $850.

ISSUED UNDER BULGARIAN OCCUPATION

Bulgarian Stamps of 1915-16 Overprinted in Red or Blue

Поща въ Ромъния
1916—1917

1916		Unwmk.	Perf. 11½, 14	
2N1	A20	1s dk blue grn (R)	15	15
2N2	A23	5s grn & vio brn (R)	1.40	38
2N3	A24	10s brn & brnsh blk (Bl)	18	15
2N4	A26	25s indigo & blk (Bl)	18	15
		Set value		62

Nos. 2N1-2N4 were used in the Dobruja district. Many varieties of overprint exist.

ISSUED UNDER GERMAN OCCUPATION

German Stamps of 1905-17 Surcharged

15 Bani
(Black)

1917		Wmk. 125	Perf. 14	
3N1	A22	15b on 15pf dk vio (R)	55	55
3N2	A16	25b on 20pf ultra (Bk)	55	55
3N3	A16	40b on 30pf org & blk, *buff* (R)	14.00	14.00

"M.V.iR." are the initials of "Militär Verwaltung in Rumänien" (Military Administration of Romania).

M.V.iR. 25 Bani

German Stamps of 1905-17 Surcharged

1917-18				
3N4	A16	10b on 10pf car	28	24
3N5	A22	15b on 15pf dk vio	2.25	2.25
3N6	A16	25b on 20pf ultra	40	40
3N7	A16	40b on 30pf org & blk, *buff*	50	50
a.		"40" omitted	50.00	67.50

Rumänien 25 Bani

German Stamps of 1905-17 Surcharged

1918				
3N8	A16	5b on 5pf grn	15	15
3N9	A16	10b on 10pf car	16	16
3N10	A22	15b on 15pf dk vio	15	15
3N11	A16	25b on 20pf bl vio	15	15
a.		25b on 20pf blue	20	20
3N12	A16	40b on 30pf org & blk, *buff*	20	20

German Stamps of 1905-17 Overprinted

Gültig 9. Armee

1918				
3N13	A16	10pf carmine	6.75	6.75
3N14	A22	15pf dk vio	10.00	10.00
3N15	A16	20pf blue	1.00	1.00
3N16	A16	30pf org & blk, *buff*	9.50	9.50

POSTAGE DUE STAMPS ISSUED UNDER GERMAN OCCUPATION

Postage Due Stamps and Type of Romania Overprinted in Red   **M.V.iR.**

Perf. 11½, 13½ and Compound

1918		Wmk. 165		
3NJ1	D2	5b dk bl, *grn*	18.00	24.00
3NJ2	D2	10b dk bl, *grn*	24.00	30.00

The 20b, 30b and 50b with this overprint are fraudulent.

		Unwmk.		
3NJ3	D2	5b dk bl, *grn*	2.25	2.25
3NJ4	D2	10b dk bl, *grn*	2.25	2.25
3NJ5	D2	20b dk bl, *grn*	2.25	2.25
3NJ6	D2	30b dk bl, *grn*	2.25	2.25
3NJ7	D2	50b dk bl, *grn*	2.25	2.25
		Nos. 3NJ1-3NJ7 (7)	53.25	65.25

POSTAL TAX STAMPS ISSUED UNDER GERMAN OCCUPATION

Romanian Postal Tax Stamps and Type of 1916

Overprinted in Red or Black

Perf. 11½, 13½ and Compound

1917			Unwmk.	
3NRA1	PT1	5b gray blk (R)	15	15
3NRA2	PT1	10b brown (Bk)	20	15

Same, Overprinted   **M.V.iR.**

1917-18				
3NRA3	PT1	5b gray blk (R)	40	15
a.		Black overprint	5.00	5.00

3NRA4	PT1	10b brown (Bk)	40	15
3NRA5	PT1	10b violet (Bk)	35	15
		Set value		28

Same, Overprinted in Red or Black

1918				
3NRA6	PT1	5b gray blk (R)	10.00	
3NRA7	PT1	10b brown (Bk)	10.00	

Same, Overprinted   **Gültig 9. Armee**

1918				
3NRA8	PT1	10b violet (Bk)	18	18

POSTAL TAX DUE STAMP ISSUED UNDER GERMAN OCCUPATION

Type of Romanian Postal Tax Due Stamp of 1916 Overprinted   **M.V.iR.**

Perf. 11½, 13½, and Compound

1918		Wmk. 165		
3NRAJ1	PTD1	10b red, *green*	2.00	2.50

ROMANIAN POST OFFICES IN THE TURKISH EMPIRE

40 Paras = 1 Piaster

King Carol I
A1   A2

Perf. 11½, 13½ and Compound

1896		Wmk. 200		
		Black Surcharge		
1	A1	10pa on 5b blue	19.00	19.00
2	A2	20pa on 10b emer	14.00	14.00
3	A1	1pia on 25b violet	14.00	14.00
		Violet Surcharge		
4	A1	10pa on 5b blue	10.00	10.00
5	A2	20pa on 10b emer	10.00	10.00
6	A1	1pia on 25b violet	10.00	10.00

Romanian Stamps of 1908-18 Overprinted in Black or Red

1919		Typo.	Unwmk.	
7	A46	5b yel grn	40	40
8	A46	10b rose	55	55
9	A46	15b red brn	55	55
10	A19	25b dp bl (R)	70	70
11	A19	40b gray brn (R)	1.40	1.40
		Nos. 7-11 (5)	3.60	3.60

All values exist with inverted overprint.

Stamps of the German Occupation of Romania can be mounted in the Scott Germany album part 2.

ROMANIAN POST OFFICES IN THE TURKISH EMPIRE POSTAL TAX STAMP

Romanian Postal Tax
Stamp of 1918
Overprinted

Perf. 11½, 11½x13½

1919		**Unwmk.**	
RA1	PT1	5b green	1.25 1.25

ROUAD, ILE
(Arwad)

LOCATION — An island in the Mediterranean, off the coast of Latakia, Syria
GOVT. — French Mandate

In 1916, while a French post office was maintained on Ile Rouad, stamps were issued by France.

25 Centimes = 1 Piaster

Stamps of French Offices in the Levant, 1902-06, Overprinted **ILE ROUAD**

Perf. 14x13½

1916, Jan. 12		**Unwmk.**	
1	A2	5c green	250.00 125.00
2	A3	10c rose red	250.00 125.00
3	A5	1pi on 25c blue	250.00 125.00

Dangerous counterfeits exist.

Stamps of French Offices in the Levant, 1902-06, **ILE ROUAD** Overprinted Horizontally

1916, Dec.			
4	A2	1c gray	45 45
5	A2	2c violet brown	45 45
6	A2	3c red orange	45 45
a.		Double overprint	40.00 40.00
7	A2	5c green	50 50
8	A3	10c rose	60 60
9	A3	15c pale red	65 65
10	A3	20c brown violet	1.00 1.00
11	A3	1pi on 25c blue	1.00 1.00
12	A3	30c violet	1.00 1.00
13	A6	40c red & pale bl	1.90 1.90
14	A6	2pi on 50c bis brn & lavender	3.00 3.00
15	A6	4pi on 1fr cl & ol grn	4.50 4.50
16	A6	20pi on 5fr dk bl & buff	14.00 14.00
		Nos. 4-16 (13)	29.50 29.50

There is a wide space between the two words of the overprint on Nos. 13 to 16 inclusive. Nos. 4, 5 and 6 are on white and coarse, grayish (G. C.) papers.
(Note on G. C. paper follows France No. 184.)

RUANDA-URUNDI
(Belgian East Africa)

LOCATION — In central Africa, bounded by Congo, Uganda and Tanganyika
GOVT. — Former United Nations trusteeship administered by Belgium
AREA — 20,540 sq. mi.
POP. — 4,700,000 (est. 1958)
CAPITAL — Usumbura

See German East Africa in Vol. 3 for stamps issued under Belgian occupation.

In 1962 the two parts of the trusteeship became independent states, the Republic of Rwanda and the Kingdom of Burundi.

100 Centimes = 1 Franc

Catalogue values for unused stamps in this country are for Never Hinged items, beginning with Scott 151 in the regular postage section, and Scott B26 in the semi-postal section.

Stamps of Belgian Congo, 1923-26, Overprinted **RUANDA URUNDI**

1924-26		**Perf. 12**	
6	A32	5c org yel	15 15
7	A32	10c green	15 15
8	A32	15c olive brn	15 15
9	A32	20c olive grn	15 15
10	A44	20c green ('26)	15 15
11	A44	25c red brown	18 15
12	A44	30c rose red	15 15
13	A32	40c olive grn ('25)	15 15
14	A32	40c violet ('25)	22 18
15	A44	50c gray blue	15 15
16	A44	50c buff ('25)	22 15
17	A44	75c red org	22 22
18	A44	75c gray blue ('25)	28 18
19	A44	1fr bister brown	30 28
20	A44	1fr dull blue ('26)	28 18
21	A44	3fr gray brown	2.25 1.50
22	A44	5fr gray	4.50 3.25
23	A44	10fr gray black	11.00 7.25
		Nos. 6-23 (18)	20.69 14.54

Belgian Congo Nos. 112-113 Overprinted **RUANDA-URUNDI** in Red or Black

1925-27		**Perf. 12½**	
24	A44	45c dk vio (R) ('27)	22 22
25	A44	60c car rose (Bk)	30 28

RUANDA

Stamps of Belgian Congo, 1923-1927, Overprinted

URUNDI

1927-29			
26	A32	10c green ('29)	15 15
27	A32	15c ol brn ('29)	60 50
28	A44	35c green	15 15
29	A44	75c salmon red	20 20
30	A44	1fr rose red	32 25
31	A32	1.25fr dull blue	45 32
32	A32	1.50fr dull blue	38 30
33	A32	1.75fr dull blue	85 55

No. 32 Surcharged **1.75**

34	A32	1.75fr on 1.50fr dl bl	38 32
		Nos. 26-34 (9)	3.48 2.74

Nos. 30 and 33 Surcharged **2**

1931			
35	A44	1.25fr on 1fr rose red	2.00 95
36	A32	2fr on 1.75fr dl bl	2.75 1.40

Porter — A1

Mountain Scene — A2

Designs: 5c, 60c, Porter. 15c, Warrior. 25c, Kraal. 40c, Cattle herders. 50c, Cape buffalo. 75c, Bahutu greeting. 1fr, Barundi women. 1.25fr, Bahutu mother. 1.50fr, 2fr, Making wooden vessel. 2.50fr, 3.25fr, Preparing hides. 4fr, Watuba potter. 5fr, Mututsi dancer. 10fr, Watusi warriors. 20fr, Urundi prince.

1931-38		**Engr.** **Perf. 11½**	
37	A1	5c dp lil rose ('38)	15 15
38	A2	10c gray	15 15
39	A2	15c pale red	15 15
40	A2	25c brn vio	15 15
41	A1	40c green	22 22
42	A2	50c gray lilac	15 15
43	A1	60c lil rose	15 15
44	A2	75c gray black	15 15
45	A2	1fr rose red	15 15
46	A1	1.25fr red brown	15 15
47	A2	1.50fr brn vio ('37)	18 15
48	A2	2fr deep blue	18 15
49	A2	2.50fr dp bl ('37)	16 16
50	A2	3.25fr brn vio	18 15
51	A2	4fr rose	24 24
52	A1	5fr gray	28 28
53	A1	10fr brn vio	50 38
54	A1	20fr brown	1.50 1.40
		Set value	4.10 3.75

For surcharges see Nos. 56-59.

King Albert Memorial Issue

King Albert — A16

1934		**Photo.**	
55	A16	1.50fr black	45 45

Stamps of 1931-38 Surcharged in Black

0F60   **0F60**

1941			
56	A1	5c on 40c green	2.25 2.25
57	A2	60c on 50c gray lil	1.50 1.50
58	A2	2.50fr on 1.50fr brn vio	1.50 1.50
59	A2	3.25fr on 2fr dp bl	6.00 6.00

Belgian Congo No. 173 Overprinted in Black **RUANDA URUNDI**

		Perf. 11	
60	A70	10c light gray	5.00 5.00

Belgian Congo Nos. 179, 181 Overprinted in Black **RUANDA URUNDI**

1941			
61	A70	1.75fr orange	3.00 3.00
62	A70	2.75fr vio bl	3.00 3.00

For surcharges see Nos. 64-65.

RUANDA URUNDI

Belgian Congo No. 168 Surcharged in Black **5 c.**

1941		**Perf. 11½**	
63	A66	5c on 1.50fr dp red brn & blk	15 15

Nos. 61-62 Surcharged with New Values and Bars in Black

1942			
64	A70	75c on 1.75fr org	1.10 1.25
65	A70	2.50fr on 2.75fr vio bl	3.00 3.00

Belgian Congo Nos. 167, 183 Surcharged in Black:

 RUANDA URUNDI

RUANDA URUNDI **2.50**

75 c. ═══

1942		**Perf. 11, 11½**	
66	A65	75c on 90c car & brn	70 65
a.		Inverted surcharge	8.00 8.00
67	A70	2.50fr on 10fr rose red	1.10 85
a.		Inverted surcharge	6.50 6.50

Oil Palms — A17

Oil Palms — A18

Watusi Chief — A19

Askari — A21

Leopard A20

Zebra — A22

Askari — A23

Design: 100fr, Watusi chief.

1942-43		**Engr.** **Perf. 12½**	
68	A17	5c red	15 15
69	A18	10c ol grn	15 15
70	A18	15c brn car	15 15
71	A18	20c dp ultra	15 15
72	A18	25c brn vio	15 15
73	A18	30c dull blue	15 15
74	A18	50c dp grn	80 15
75	A18	60c chestnut	15 15
76	A19	75c dl lil & blk	15 15
77	A19	1fr dk brn & blk	15 15

78	A19	1.25fr rose red & blk	18 15
79	A20	1.75fr dk gray brn	60 35
80	A20	2fr ocher	60 28
81	A20	2.50fr carmine	60 15
82	A21	3.50fr dk ol grn	35 20
83	A21	5fr orange	40 25
84	A21	6fr brt ultra	40 25
85	A21	7fr black	40 32
86	A21	10fr dp brn	60 35
87	A21	20fr org brn & blk	1.25 90
88	A21	50fr red & blk ('43)	1.75 1.10
89	A21	100fr grn & blk ('43)	3.50 2.75
		Nos. 68-89 (22)	12.78 8.55

Miniature sheets of Nos. 72, 76, 77 and 83 were printed in 1944 by the Belgian Government in London and given to the Belgian political review, "Message", which distributed them to its subscribers, one a month. Nos. 68-89 exist imperforate, but have no franking value. Value, set $100.
See note after Belgian Congo No. 225.
For surcharges see Nos. B17-B20.

Baluba Carving of Former King — A25

Carved Figures and Masks of Baluba Tribe: 10c, 50c, 2fr, 10fr, "Ndoha," figure of tribal king. 15c, 70c, 2.50fr, "Tshimanyi," an idol. 20c, 75c, 3.50fr, "Buangakokoma," statue of a kneeling beggar. 25c, 1fr, 5fr, "Mbuta," sacred double cup carved with two faces, Man and Woman. 40c, 1.25fr, 6fr, "Ngadimuashi," female mask. 1.50fr, 50fr, "Buadi-Muadi," mask with squared features (full face). 20fr, 100fr, "Mbowa," executioner's mask with buffalo horns.

1948-50   Unwmk.   Perf. 12x12½

90	A25	10c dp org	15 15
91	A25	15c ultra	15 15
92	A25	20c brt bl	15 15
93	A25	25c rose car	18 15
94	A25	40c violet	15 15
95	A25	50c ol brn	15 15
96	A25	70c yel grn	15 15
97	A25	75c magenta	15 15
98	A25	1fr yel org & dk vio	15 15
99	A25	1.25fr lt bl grn & mag	15 15
100	A25	1.50fr ol & mag ('50)	48 35
101	A25	2fr org & mag	15 15
102	A25	2.50fr brn red & bl grn	15 15
103	A25	3.50fr lt bl & blk	20 18
104	A25	5fr bis & mag	32 18
105	A25	6fr brn org & ind	40 15
106	A25	10fr pale vio & red brn	55 20
107	A25	20fr red org & vio brn	90 15
108	A25	50fr dp org & blk	2.50 90
109	A25	100fr crim & blk brn	4.25 2.25
		Nos. 90-109 (20)	11.43
		Set value	5.45

Nos. 102 and 105 Surcharged with New Value and Bars in Black

1949

110	A25	3fr on 2.50fr	20 15
111	A25	4fr on 6fr	15 15
112	A25	6.50fr on 6fr	25 22

St. Francis Xavier — A26   Dissotis — A27

1953   Perf. 12½x13

113	A26	1.50fr ultra & gray blk	35 35

Death of St. Francis Xavier, 400th anniv.

1953   Unwmk.   Photo.   Perf. 11½

Flowers: 15c, Protea. 20c, Vellozia. 25c, Littonia. 40c, Ipomoea. 50c, Angraecum. 60c, Euphorbia. 75c, Ochna. 1fr, Hibiscus. 1.25fr, Protea. 1.50fr, Schizoglossum. 2fr, Ansellia. 3fr, Costus. 4fr, Nymphaea. 5fr, Thunbergia. 7fr, Gerbera. 8fr, Gloriosa. 10fr, Silene. 20fr, Aristolochia.

Flowers in Natural Colors

114	A27	10c plum & ocher	15 15
115	A27	15c red & yel grn	15 15
116	A27	20c green & gray	15 15
117	A27	25c dk grn & dl org	15 15
118	A27	40c grn & sal	15 15
119	A27	50c dk car & aqua	15 15
120	A27	60c bl grn & pink	15 15
121	A27	75c dp plum & gray	15 15
122	A27	1fr car & yel	18 15
123	A27	1.25fr dk grn & bl	50 50
124	A27	1.50fr vio & ap grn	18 15
125	A27	2fr ol grn & buff	1.40 15
126	A27	3fr ol grn & pink	38 15
127	A27	4fr choc & lil	38 15
128	A27	5fr dp plum & lt bl grn	65 15
129	A27	7fr dk grn & fawn	75 28
130	A27	8fr grn & lt yel	95 32
131	A27	10fr dp plum & pale ol	1.50 15
132	A27	20fr vio bl & dl sal	2.50 42
		Nos. 114-132 (19)	10.57
		Set value	2.90

King Baudouin and Tropical Scene — A28

Designs: Various African Views.

1955   Engr. & Photo.   Portrait Photo. in Black

133	A28	1.50fr rose carmine	30 15
134	A28	3fr green	25 15
135	A28	4.50fr ultra	32 18
136	A28	6.50fr deep claret	50 25

Mountain Gorilla — A29   Cape Buffaloes — A30

Animals: 40c, 2fr, Black-and-white colobus (monkey). 50c, 6.50fr, Impalas. 3fr, 8fr, Elephants. 5fr, 10fr, Eland and Zebras. 20fr, Leopard. 50fr, Lions.

1959-61 Unwmk. Photo. Perf. 11½
Granite Paper
Size: 23x33mm, 33x23mm

137	A29	10c brn, crim, & blk brn	15 15
138	A30	20c blk, gray & ap grn	15 15
139	A29	40c mag, blk & gray grn	15 15
140	A30	50c grn, org yel & brn	15 15
141	A29	1fr brn, ultra & blk	15 15
142	A30	1.50fr blk, gray & org	16 15
143	A29	2fr grnsh bl, ind & brn	15 15
144	A30	3fr brn, dp car & blk	15 15
145	A30	5fr brn, dl yel, grn & blk	18 15
146	A30	6.50fr red, org yel & brn	28 15
147	A30	8fr bl, mag & blk	45 30
148	A30	10fr multi	45 20

Size: 45x26½mm

149	A30	20fr multi ('61)	55 45
150	A30	50fr multi ('61)	1.25 1.00
		Nos. 137-150 (14)	4.37
		Set value	2.65

For surcharge see No. 153.

Catalogue values for unused stamps in this section, from this point to the end of the section, are for Never Hinged items.

Map of Africa and Symbolic Honeycomb A31

1960   Unwmk.   Perf. 11½
Inscription in French

151	A31	3fr ultra & red	20 15

Inscription in Flemish

152	A31	3fr ultra & red	20 15

10th anniversary of the Commission for Technical Co-operation in Africa South of the Sahara (C. C. T. A.)

No. 144 Surcharged with New Value and Bars

1960

153	A30	3.50fr on 3fr	30 15

SEMI-POSTAL STAMPS

Belgian Congo Nos. B10-B11 Overprinted **RUANDA-URUNDI**

1925   Unwmk.   Perf. 12½

B1	SP1	25c + 25c car & blk	15 15
B2	SP1	25c + 25c car & blk	15 15

No. B2 inscribed "BELGISCH CONGO." Commemorative of the Colonial Campaigns in 1914-1918. Nos. B1 and B2 alternate in the sheet.

RUANDA

Belgian Congo Nos. B12-B20 Overprinted in Blue or Red

URUNDI

1930   Perf. 11½

B3	SP3	10c + 5c ver	35 35
B4	SP3	20c + 10c dk brn	70 70
B5	SP5	35c + 15c dp grn	1.40 1.40
B6	SP5	60c + 30c dl vio	1.65 1.65
B7	SP3	1fr + 50c dk car	2.50 2.50
B8	SP5	1.75fr + 75c dp bl (R)	2.75 2.75
B9	SP5	3.50fr + 1.50fr rose lake	5.75 5.75
B10	SP5	5fr + 2.50fr red brn	4.50 4.50
B11	SP5	10fr + 5fr gray blk	5.00 5.00
		Nos. B3-B11 (9)	24.60 24.60

On Nos. B3, B4 and B7 there is a space of 26mm between the two words of the overprint. The surtax was for native welfare.

Queen Astrid with Native Children — SP1

Lion of Belgium and Inscription "Belgium Shall Rise Again" — SP2

1936   Photo.

B12	SP1	1.25fr + 5c dk brn	65 55
B13	SP1	1.50fr + 10c dl rose	65 55
B14	SP1	2.50fr + 25c dk bl	75 75

Issued in memory of Queen Astrid. The surtax was for the National League for Protection of Native Children.

1942   Engr.   Perf. 12½

B15	SP2	10fr + 40fr blue	2.00 2.00
B16	SP2	10fr + 40fr dark red	2.00 2.00

Nos. 74, 78, 79 and 82 Surcharged in Red

Au profit de la Croix Rouge + 50 Fr. Ten voordeele van het Roode Kruis
a

Ten voordeele van het Roode Kruis + 100 Fr. Au profit de la Croix Rouge
b

Au profit de la Croix Rouge + 100 Fr. Ten voordeele van het Roode Kruis
c

1945   Unwmk.   Perf. 12½

B17	A18 (a)	50c + 50fr	1.10 1.40
B18	A19 (b)	1.25fr + 100fr	1.50 1.65
B19	A20 (c)	1.75fr + 100fr	1.10 1.40
B20	A21 (b)	3.50fr + 100fr	1.50 1.65

Mozart at Age 7 — SP3

Queen Elizabeth and Mozart Sonata — SP4

1956   Engr.   Perf. 11½

B21	SP3	4.50fr + 1.50fr bluish vio	90 1.00
B22	SP4	6.50fr + 2.50fr claret	2.00 2.00

200th anniv. of the birth of Wolfgang Amadeus Mozart.
Surtax for the Pro-Mozart Committee.

Nurse and Children — SP5

Designs: 4.50fr+50c, Patient receiving injection. 6.50fr+50c, Patient being bandaged.

1957   Photo.   Perf. 13x10½
Cross in Carmine

B23	SP5	3fr + 50c dk blue	55 55
B24	SP5	4.50fr + 50c dk grn	75 75
B25	SP5	6.50fr + 50c red brn	90 90

The surtax was for the Red Cross.

Catalogue values for unused stamps in this section, from this point to the end of the section, are for Never Hinged items.

Soccer — SP6

Sports: 50c+25c, High Jumper. 1.50fr+ 50c, Hurdlers. 3fr+1.25fr, Javelin thrower. 6.50fr+3.50fr, Discus thrower.

1960   **Unwmk.**   *Perf. 13½*

B26	SP6	50c + 25c int bl & maroon	15	15
B27	SP6	1.50fr + 50c dk car & blk	20	20
B28	SP6	2fr + 1fr blk & dk car	20	20
B29	SP6	3fr + 1.25fr org ver & grn	1.00	1.10
B30	SP6	6.50fr + 3.50fr ol grn & red	1.00	1.10
		Nos. B26-B30 (5)	2.55	2.75

Issued to commemorate the 17th Olympic Games, Rome, Aug. 25-Sept. 11. The surtax was for the youth of Ruanda-Urundi.

Usumbura Cathedral — SP7

Designs: 1fr+50c, 5fr+2fr, Cathedral, sideview. 1.50fr+75c, 6.50fr+3fr, Stained glass window.

1961, Dec. 18   *Perf. 11½*

B31	SP7	50c + 25c brn & buff	15	15
B32	SP7	1fr + 50c grn & pale grn	15	15
B33	SP7	1.50fr + 75c multi	15	15
B34	SP7	3.50fr + 1.50fr lt bl & brt bl	15	15
B35	SP7	5fr + 2fr car & sal	30	30
B36	SP7	6.50fr + 3fr multi	40	40
		Set value	1.05	1.05

The surtax went for the construction and completion of the Cathedral at Usumbura.

POSTAGE DUE STAMPS

RUANDA

Belgian Congo Nos. J1-J7 Overprinted   **URUNDI**

1924-27   **Unwmk.**   *Perf. 14, 14½*

J1	D1	5c blk brn	15	15
J2	D1	10c dp rose	15	15
J3	D1	15c violet	18	18
J4	D1	30c green	25	25
J5	D1	50c ultra	32	30
J6	D1	50c brt bl ('27)	32	30
J7	D1	1fr gray	38	38
		Nos. J1-J7 (7)	1.75	1.71

Belgian Congo Nos. J8- **RUANDA** J12 Overprinted in Carmine   **URUNDI**

1943   *Perf. 14x14½, 12½*

J8	D2	10c ol grn	15	15
J9	D2	20c dk ultra	15	15
J10	D2	50c green	15	15
J11	D2	1fr dk brn	18	18
J12	D2	2fr yel org	22	22
		Set value	65	65

Nos. J8-J12 values are for stamps perf. 14x14½. Those perf. 12½ sell for about three times as much.

Belgian Congo Nos. J13- **RUANDA** J19 Overprinted   **URUNDI**

1959   **Engr.**   *Perf. 11½*

J13	D3	10c ol brn	15	15
J14	D3	20c claret	15	15
J15	D3	50c green	15	15
J16	D3	1fr lt bl	15	15
J17	D3	2fr vermilion	18	18
J18	D3	4fr purple	35	35
J19	D3	6fr vio bl	45	45
		Nos. J13-J19 (7)	1.58	1.58

Both capital and lower-case U's are found in this overprint.

RUSSIA
(Union of Soviet Socialist Republics)

LOCATION — Eastern Europe and Northern Asia
GOVT. — Republic
AREA — 8,650,000 sq. mi.
POP. — 276,300,000 (est. 1985)
CAPITAL — Moscow

An empire until 1917, the government was overthrown in that year and a socialist union of republics was formed under the name of the Union of Soviet Socialist Republics. The USSR includes the following autonomous republics which have issued their own stamps: Armenia, Azerbaijan, Georgia and Ukraine.

With the breakup of the Soviet Union on Dec. 26, 1991, eleven former Soviet republics established the Commonwealth of Independent States. Stamps inscribed "Rossija" are issued by the Russian Republic.

100 Kopecks = 1 Ruble

> Catalogue values for unused stamps in this country are for Never Hinged items, beginning with Scott 1021 in the regular postage section, Scott B58 in the semi-postal section, and Scott C82 in the airpost section.

Watermarks

Wmk. 166- Colorless Numerals

Wmk. 168- Cyrillic EZGB & Wavy Lines

Initials are those of the State Printing Plant.

Wmk. 169- Lozenges

Wmk. 171- Diamonds

> Russia stamps through 1917 can be mounted in the Scott Russia album part 1.

Wmk. 170- Greek Border and Rosettes

Wmk. 226- Diamonds Enclosing Four Dots

Wmk. 293- Hammer and Sickle, Multiple

Wmk. 383- Cyrillic Letters in Shield

Empire

Coat of Arms
A1   A2   A3

Wmk. 166

1857, Dec. 10   **Typo.**   *Imperf.*

1	A1	10k brown & blue	3,500.	350.00
		Pen cancellation		175.00
		Penmark & postmark		225.00

Genuine unused copies of No. 1 are exceedingly rare. Most of those offered are used with pen cancellation removed. The unused value is for a specimen without gum. The very few known stamps with original gum sell for much more.

See Poland for similar stamp inscribed "ZALOT KOP. 10."

1858, Jan. 10   *Perf. 14½, 15*

2	A1	10k brown & blue	1,000.	100.00
3	A1	20k blue & orange	2,500.	500.00
4	A1	30k carmine & green	3,500.	1,000.

1858-64   **Unwmk.**   *Perf. 12½*
Wove Paper

5	A2	1k black & blue ('64)	32.50	16.00
a.		1k black & orange	32.50	16.00
6	A2	3k black & green ('64)	55.00	27.50
7	A2	5k black & lilac ('64)	60.00	35.00
8	A1	10k brown & blue	22.50	5.00
9	A1	20k blue & orange	125.00	22.50
a.		Half used as 10k on cover		4,000.
10	A1	30k carmine & green	100.00	50.00

1863

11	A3	5k black & blue	12.50	200.00

No. 11 was issued to pay local postage in St. Petersburg and Moscow. It is known to have been used in other cities. Copies canceled after July, 1864, are worth considerably less.

1865, June 2   *Perf. 14½, 15*

12	A2	1k black & yellow	30.00	8.00
a.		1k black & orange	30.00	8.00
13	A2	3k black & green	40.00	4.50
14	A2	5k black & lilac	50.00	5.75
15	A1	10k brown & blue	60.00	1.75
a.		Thick paper	115.00	7.50
17	A1	20k blue & orange	150.00	12.50
18	A1	30k carmine & green	175.00	22.50

1866-70   **Wmk. 168**
Horizontally Laid Paper

19	A2	1k black & yellow	2.00	22
a.		1k black & orange	2.25	50
b.		Imperf.		1,000.
c.		Vertically laid	125.00	20.00
d.		Groundwork inverted	3,000.	1,500.
e.		Thick paper	40.00	25.00
f.		As "c," imperf.	2,750.	2,250.
g.		As "b," "c" & "d"	5,000.	5,000.
20	A2	3k black & dp green	4.00	50
		3k black & yellow green	4.00	50
b.		Imperf.		1,500.
c.		Vertically laid	150.00	30.00
d.		V's in groundwork (error) ('70)	400.00	35.00
22	A2	5k black & lilac	4.75	50
a.		5k black & gray	60.00	10.00
b.		Imperf.	1,500.	750.00
c.		Vertically laid	700.00	100.00
d.		As "c," imperf.		2,750.
23	A1	10k brown & blue	12.00	85
a.		Vertically laid	65.00	8.00
b.		Center inverted		6,000.
c.		Imperf.		2,000.
24	A1	20k blue & orange	45.00	6.00
a.		Vertically laid	675.00	50.00
25	A1	30k carmine & green	55.00	17.00
a.		Vertically laid	400.00	30.00

Arms — A4

1875-79
Horizontally Laid Paper

26	A2	2k black & red	2.50	50
a.		Vertically laid	500.00	60.00
b.		Groundwork inverted		7,500.
27	A4	7k gray & rose ('79)	3.00	25
a.		Imperf.		4,250.
b.		Vertically laid	400.00	50.00
c.		Wmkd. hexagons ('79)		8,500.
d.		Center inverted		17,500.
e.		Center omitted	300.00	300.00
28	A4	8k gray & rose	3.25	75
a.		Vertically laid	450.00	60.00
b.		Imperf.		1,500.
c.		"C" instead of "B" in "Bocem"	25.00	25.00
29	A4	10k brown & rose	15.00	3.00
a.		Center inverted		8,000.
30	A4	20k blue & orange	30.00	4.25
a.		Cross-shaped "T" in bottom word	100.00	25.00
b.		Center inverted		8,000.

The hexagon watermark of No. 27c is that of revenue stamps. No. 27c exists with Perm and Riga postmarks.

Imperial Eagle and Post Horns
A5   A6

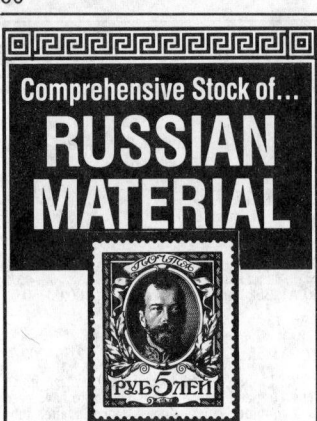

Comprehensive Stock of...

RUSSIAN MATERIAL

STAMPS, COVERS, LOCALS & ZEMSTVOS, ERRORS & VARIETIES, RARITIES

included in our...

28 PAGE FREE PRICE LIST!

•RETAIL-WHOLESALE•

LORAL

Box 740521
Rego Park, NY 11374-0521
Phone 718-699-2455
Fax 718-271-3070

RUSSIA

RARE AND CLASSIC STAMPS, POSTAL HISTORY, PROOFS. BUYING, SELLING, APPRAISALS.

For the Best Services in Classic Stamps and Postal History contact the RECOGNIZED LEADERS IN THE FIELD. Excellent stock of classic material for most countries of the World also available.

Ph. 315-422-2331, Fax 315-422-2956
10035 Carousel Center Drive
Syracuse, NY 13290-0001
Ph. 613-722-1621, Fax: 613-728-7305

THE CLASSIC COLLECTOR
LIANE & SERGIO SISMONDO
CANADIAN OFFICE: P.O. Box 6277, Station J, Ottawa, Canada K2A 1T4.

Perf. 14 to 15 and Compound
1883-88   **Wmk. 168**
Horizontally Laid Paper

31	A5	1k orange	1.00	18
a.		Imperf.	375.00	375.00
b.		Groundwork inverted	3,000.	3,000.
c.		1k yellow	1.00	25
32	A5	2k dark green	2.00	25
a.		2k yellow green ('88)	2.00	25
b.		Imperf.	375.00	350.00
c.		Wove paper	450.00	325.00
d.		Groundwork inverted		3,000.
33	A5	3k carmine	2.00	18
a.		Imperf.	400.00	400.00
b.		Groundwork inverted		3,000.
c.		Wove paper	500.00	410.00
34	A5	5k red violet	2.00	18
a.		Groundwork inverted		4,000.
35	A5	7k blue	2.00	18
a.		Imperf.	400.00	300.00
b.		Groundwork inverted	675.00	600.00
36	A6	14k blue & rose	2.50	50
a.		Imperf.	525.00	450.00
b.		Center inverted	7,000.	
c.		Diagonal half surcharge "7" in red, on cover ('84)		5,000.
37	A6	35k violet & green	15.00	2.25
38	A6	70k brown & orange	18.00	2.25

Before 1882 the 1, 2, 3 and 5 kopecks had small numerals in the background; beginning with No. 31 these denominations have a background of network, like the higher values.

No. 36c is handstamped. It is known with cancellations of Tiflis and Kutais, both in Georgia. It is believed to be of philatelic origin.

A7

1884   Perf. 13½, 13½x11½
Vertically Laid Paper

39	A7	3.50r black & gray	400.	275.
a.		Horiz. laid	6,000.	6,000.
40	A7	7r black & orange	400.	275.

Forgeries exist, especially with forged postmarks.

Imperial Eagle and Post Horns with Thunderbolts
A8   A9

With Thunderbolts Across Post Horns
Perf. 14 to 15 and Compound
1889, May 14
Horizontally Laid Paper

41	A8	4k rose	50	26
a.		Groundwork inverted		1,250.
42	A8	10k dark blue	50	18
43	A8	20k blue & carmine	2.00	30
44	A8	50k violet & green	2.25	45

Perf. 13½

45	A9	1r lt brn, brn & org	15.00	2.00
a.		Pair, imperf. between	350.00	
b.		Center omitted	250.00	250.00

See #57C, 60, 63, 66, 68, 82, 85, 87, 126, 129, 131. For surcharges see #216, 219, 223, 226.

A10   A11

A12   A13

With Thunderbolts Across Post Horns
1889-92   Perf. 14½x15
Horizontally Laid Paper

46	A10	1k orange	18	15
a.		Imperf.	250.00	250.00
47	A10	2k green	18	15
a.		Imperf.	200.00	190.00
48	A10	3k carmine	22	15
a.		Imperf.	200.00	200.00
49	A10	5k red violet	35	15
b.		Groundwork omitted	725.00	725.00
50	A10	7k dark blue	22	15
a.		Imperf.	300.00	300.00
b.		Groundwork omitted	200.00	200.00
51	A11	14k blue & rose	1.10	15
a.		Center inverted	4,000.	4,000.
52	A11	35k violet & green	3.50	60

Perf. 13½

53	A12	3.50r black & gray	18.00	4.00
54	A12	7r black & yellow	32.50	8.50
a.		Dbl. impression of black		275.00

Perf. 14 to 15 and Compound
1902-05
Vertically Laid Paper

55	A10	1k orange	15	15
a.		Imperf.	600.00	600.00
b.		Groundwork inverted	850.00	850.00
c.		Groundwork omitted	200.00	200.00
56	A10	2k yellow green	15	15
a.		2k deep green	7.50	70
b.		Groundwork inverted	600.00	300.00
c.		Groundwork inverted	850.00	850.00
d.		Groundwork double	425.00	425.00
57	A10	3k rose red	15	15
a.		Groundwork omitted	350.00	175.00
b.		Double impression	200.00	165.00
d.		Imperf.	150.00	150.00
e.		Groundwork inverted	210.00	210.00
57C	A8	4k rose red ('04)	35	15
f.		Double impression	200.00	200.00
g.		Groundwork omitted	1,500.	600.00
58	A10	5k red violet	35	15
a.		5k dull violet	4.25	2.00
b.		Groundwork inverted	750.00	750.00
c.		Imperf.	250.00	250.00
d.		Groundwork omitted	250.00	165.00
59	A10	7k dark blue	28	15
a.		Groundwork omitted	350.00	300.00
b.		Imperf.	375.00	375.00
c.		Groundwork inverted	350.00	350.00
60	A8	10k dark blue ('04)	28	15
a.		Groundwork inverted	12.50	5.00
b.		Groundwork omitted	165.00	35.00
c.		Groundwork double	165.00	35.00
61	A11	14k blue & rose	80	15
a.		Center inverted	4,750.	3,250.
b.		Center omitted	1,100.	700.00
62	A11	15k brown vio & blue ('05)	95	15
a.		Center omitted	4,000.	3,500.
b.		Center inverted		
63	A8	20k blue & car ('04)	1.00	15
64	A11	25k dull grn & lil ('05)	3.50	30
a.		Center omitted	3,250.	3,250.
b.		Center inverted	1,500.	1,500.
65	A11	35k dk vio & grn	3.50	30
a.		Center omitted		
b.		Center inverted		1,500.
66	A8	50k vio & grn ('05)	10.00	80
67	A11	70k brown & org	10.00	80

Perf. 13½

68	A9	1r lt brown, brn & orange	7.75	48
a.		Perf. 11½	350.00	50.00
b.		Perf. 13½x11½, 11½x13½	675.00	575.00
c.		Center omitted	250.00	
d.		Center omitted	250.00	250.00
e.		Center omitted	250.00	150.00
f.		Pair, imperf. btwn.	340.00	165.00
69	A12	3.50r black & gray	7.75	1.90
a.		Center omitted	5,000.	5,000.
b.		Imperf., pair	2,000.	2,000.
70	A12	7r black & yel	7.75	1.90
a.		Center inverted	4,000.	4,000.
b.		Horiz. pair, imperf. btwn.	1,600.	1,600.
c.		Imperf., pair	2,000.	2,000.

1906   Perf. 13½

71	A13	5r dk blue, grn & pale blue	22.50	3.00
a.		Perf. 11½	225.00	275.00
72	A13	10r car rose, yel & gray	50.00	5.50

The design of No. 72 differs in many details from the illustration. Nos. 71-72 were printed in sheets of 25.

See Nos. 80-81, 83-84, 86, 108-109, 125, 127-128, 130, 132-135, 137-138. For surcharges see Nos. 217-218, 220-222, 224-225, 227-229.

A14   A15

Vertical Lozenges of Varnish on Face
1909-12   **Unwmk.**   Perf. 14x14½
Wove Paper

73	A14	1k dull orange yellow	15	15
a.		1k orange yellow ('09)	20	20
c.		Double impression	85.00	85.00
74	A14	2k dull green	15	15
a.		2k green ('09)	22	22
b.		Double impression	25.00	25.00
75	A14	3k carmine	15	15
a.		3k rose red ('09)	22	22
76	A15	4k carmine	15	15
a.		4k carmine rose ('09)	22	22
77	A14	5k claret	15	15
a.		5k lilac ('12)	65	65
b.		Double impressions	22.50	22.50
78	A14	7k blue	15	15
a.		7k light blue ('09)	1.50	65
b.		Imperf.	175.00	175.00
79	A15	10k dark blue	15	15
a.		10k light blue ('09)	500.00	85.00
b.		10k pale blue	6.00	1.00
80	A11	14k dk blue & car	15	15
a.		14k blue & rose ('09)	22	22
81	A11	15k red brown & dp blue	15	15
a.		15k dull violet & blue ('09)	85	40
c.		Center omitted	115.00	85.00
d.		Center double	50.00	50.00
82	A8	20k dull bl & dk car	15	15
a.		20k blue & carmine ('10)	85	55
b.		Groundwork omitted	20.00	13.00
c.		Center double	30.00	30.00
d.		Center and value omitted	85.00	85.00
83	A11	25k dl grn & dk vio	16	16
a.		25k green & violet ('09)	32	32
b.		Center omitted	115.00	115.00
c.		Center double	25.00	25.00
84	A11	35k red brn & grn	16	16
a.		35k brown vio & yel green	52	42
b.		35k violet & green ('09)	52	42
c.		Center double	25.00	25.00
85	A8	50k red brn & grn	15	16
a.		50k violet & green ('09)	50	40
b.		Groundwork omitted	20.00	20.00
c.		Center double	32.50	32.50
d.		Center and value omitted	115.00	115.00
86	A11	70k brn & red org	15	16
a.		70k lt brown & orange ('09)	32	25
b.		Center double	40.00	40.00
c.		Center omitted	115.00	115.00

Perf. 13½

87	A9	1r pale brown, dk brn & orange	15	15
a.		1r pale brn, brn & org ('10)	25	22
b.		Perf. 12½	25	22
c.		Groundwork inverted	20.00	20.00
d.		Pair, imperf. between	22.50	22.50
e.		Center inverted	25.00	25.00
f.		Center double	16.00	16.00
		Set value	1.60	1.60

See Nos. 119-124. For surcharges see Nos. 117-118, B24-B29.

No. 87a was issued in sheets of 40 stamps, while Nos. 87 and 87b came in sheets of 50. Nos. 87g-87k are listed below No. 138a.

Nearly all values of this issue are known without the lines of varnish.

The 7k has two types:

I - The scroll bearing the top inscription ends at left with three short lines of shading beside the first letter. Four pearls extend at lower left between the leaves and denomination panel.

II - Inner lines of scroll at top left end in two curls; three pearls at lower left.

Three clichés of type II (an essay) were included by mistake in the plate used for the first printing. Value of pair, type I with type II, unused $2,500.

SURCHARGES

Russian stamps of types A6-A15 with various surcharges may be found listed under Armenia, Batum, Far Eastern Republic, Georgia, Latvia, Siberia, South Russia, Transcaucasian Federated Republics, Ukraine, Russian Offices in China, Russian Offices in the Turkish Empire and Army of the Northwest.

Peter I — A16   Alexander II — A17

Alexander III — A18   Peter I — A19

Nicholas II
A20   A21

Catherine   Nicholas I — A23
II — A22

Alexander I — A24

Alexis Mikhailovich   Paul I
A25   A26

Elizabeth   Michael
Petrovna — A27   Feodorovich — A28

The Kremlin — A29   Winter
Palace — A30

Romanov   Nicholas II — A32
Castle — A31

Without Lozenges of Varnish

				1913, Jan. 2	**Typo.**	**Perf. 13½**
88	A16	1k brown orange	25	15
89	A17	2k yellow green	25	15
90	A18	3k rose red	25	15
b.		Double impression	500.00
91	A19	4k dull red	20	15
92	A20	7k brown	20	15
b.		Double impression	350.00	350.00
93	A21	10k deep blue	40	18
94	A22	14k blue green	35	18
95	A23	15k yellow brown	70	18
96	A24	20k olive green	85	18
97	A25	25k red violet	85	32
98	A26	35k gray vio & dk grn	85	32
99	A27	50k brown & slate	1.00	42
100	A28	70k yel green & brn	2.25	1.10

Engr.

101	A29	1r deep green	8.00	4.00
102	A30	2r red brown	8.00	4.00
103	A31	3r dark violet	20.00	12.00
104	A32	5r black brown	12.00	16.00
		Nos. 88-104 (17)	56.40	39.63

Imperf., Pairs

88a	A16	1k brown orange		
90a	A18	3k rose red		
92a	A20	7k brown	850.00	

93a	A21	10k deep blue	750.00	
102a	A30	2r red brown	650.00	
103b	A31	3r dark violet	650.00	

Tercentenary of the founding of the Romanov dynasty.
See #105-107, 112-116, 139-141. For surcharges see #110-111, Russian Offices in the Turkish Empire 213-227.

Arms & 5-line Inscription on Black

				1915, Oct.	**Typo.**	**Perf. 13½**

Thin Cardboard
Without Gum

105	A21	10k blue	38	3.75
106	A23	15k brown	38	3.75
107	A24	20k olive green	38	3.75

Imperf

105a	A21	10k blue	50.00	
106a	A23	15k	32.50	40.00
107a	A24	20k	40.00	

Nos. 105-107, 112-116 and 139-141 were issued for use as paper money, but contrary to regulations were often used for postal purposes. Back inscription means: "Having circulation on par with silver subsidiary coins."

Types of 1906 Issue
Vertical Lozenges of Varnish on Face

				1915	**Perf. 13½, 13½x13**
108	A13	5r ind, grn & lt blue	20	15
a.		5r dk bl, grn & pale bl ('15)	2.50	65
b.		Perf. 12½	3.25	1.00
c.		Center double	40.00	
d.		Pair, imperf. between	200.00	
109	A13	10r car lake, yel & gray	25	20
a.		10r carmine, yel & light gray	40	25
b.		10r rose red, yel & gray ('15)	85	50
c.		10r car, yel & gray blue (error)	1,500.	
d.		Groundwork inverted	400.00	
e.		Center double	50.00	50.00

Nos. 108a and 109b were issued in sheets of 25. Nos. 108, 108b, 109 and 109a came in sheets of 50. Chemical forgeries of No. 109c exist. Genuine copies usually are centered to upper right.

Nos. 92, 94 Surcharged **10** **10**

1916

110	A20	10k on 7k brown	15	15
a.		Inverted surcharge	60.00	60.00
111	A22	20k on 14k blue green	15	15
		Set value	20	20

Types of 1913 Issue
Arms, Value & 4-line inscription on Back
Surcharged Large Numerals on Nos. 112-113

1916-17

Thin Cardboard
Without Gum

112	A16	1 on 1k brn org ('17)	28	4.50
113	A17	2 on 2k yel green ('17)	28	4.50

Without Surcharge

114	A16	1k brown orange	8.00	32.50
115	A17	2k yellow green	18.00	55.00
116	A18	3k rose red	32	4.50

See note after No. 107.

Nos. 78a, 80a Surcharged:

кoп.**10** кoп.   к.**20**к.
a   b

1917
					Perf. 14x14½
117	A14	10k on 7k lt blue	15	15
a.		Inverted surcharge	50.00	50.00
b.		Double surcharge	60.00	
118	A11	20k on 14k bl & rose	15	15
a.		Inverted surcharge	50.00	50.00
		Set value	15	15

Provisional Government
Civil War
Type of 1889-1912 Issues
Vertical Lozenges of Varnish on Face

Two types of 7r:
Type I - Single outer frame line.
Type II - Double outer frame line.

1917   Typo.   Imperf.
Wove Paper

119	A14	1k orange	15	15
120	A14	2k gray green	15	15
121	A14	3k red	15	15
122	A14	4k carmine	15	20
123	A14	5k claret	15	15
124	A15	10k dark blue	6.00	8.00

125	A11	15k red brn & dp blue	15	15
a.		Center omitted	55.00	
126	A8	20k blue & car	15	32
a.		Groundwork omitted	18.00	18.00
127	A11	25k grn & gray vio	65	1.00
128	A11	35k brown	15	32
129	A8	50k brn vio & grn	16	25
a.		Groundwork omitted	18.00	18.00
130	A11	70k brn & orange	15	40
a.		Center omitted	115.00	
131	A9	1r pale brn, brn & red org	15	15
a.		Center inverted	20.00	20.00
b.		Center omitted	20.00	20.00
c.		Center double	20.00	20.00
d.		Groundwork double	14.00	14.00
e.		Groundwork inverted	20.00	20.00
f.		Groundwork omitted	22.50	22.50
g.		Frame double	16.00	16.00
132	A13	3.50r mar & lt green	15	22
133	A13	5r dk blue, grn & pale blue	20	32
a.		5r dk bl, grn & yel (error)	1,000.	
b.		Groundwork inverted	400.00	
134	A12	7r dk green & pink (I)	65	1.00
a.		Center inverted		
135	A13	10r scarlet, yel & gray	21.00	22.50
a.		10r scarlet, green & gray (error)	1,250.	

Vertical Lozenges of Varnish on Face

				1917	**Perf. 13½, 13½x13**
137	A12	3.50r maroon & lt grn (II)	15	15
138	A12	7r dark green & pink	15	15
d.		Type I	2.00	2.00
		Set value	15	15

Perf. 12½

137a	A12	3.50r maroon & lt grn	20	15
138a	A12	7r dk grn & pink (II)	1.00	1.00

Horizontal Lozenges of Varnish on Face
Perf. 13½x13

87g	A9	1r pale brown, brn & red orange	15	15
h.		Imperf.	10.00	
i.		As "h," center omitted	22.50	
j.		As "h," center inverted	22.50	
k.		As "h," center double	22.50	
137b	A12	3.50r maroon & lt grn	20	15
d.		Imperf.	210.00	
138b	A12	7r dk grn & pink (II)	20	15
c.		Imperf.	200.00	

Nos. 87g, 137b and 138b often show the eagle with little or no embossing.

Types of 1913 Issue
Surcharge & 4-line Inscription on Back
Surcharged Large Numerals

1917

Thin Cardboard, Without Gum

139	A16	1 on 1k brown org	40	6.00
a.		Imperf.	22.50	22.50
140	A17	2 on 2k yel green	65	6.00
a.		Imperf.	22.50	22.50
b.		Surch. omitted, imperf.	45.00	45.00

Without Surcharge

141	A18	3k rose red	40	6.00
a.		Imperf.		

See note after No. 107.

Stamps overprinted with a Liberty Cap on Crossed Swords or with reduced facsimiles of pages of newspapers were a private speculation and without official sanction.

RUSSIAN TURKESTAN

25 коп.   1 рубль

Russian stamps of 1917-18 surcharged as above are frauds.

Russian Soviet Federated Socialist Republic

 ...

Severing Chain of Bondage — A33

1918   Typo.   Perf. 13½

149	A33	35k blue	15	1.25
a.		Imperf., pair	125.00	
150	A33	70k brown	15	1.25
a.		Imperf., pair	350.00	
		Set value	20	

In 1918-1922 various revenue stamps were permitted to be used for postal duty, sometimes surcharged with new values, more often not.

For surcharges see Nos. B18-B23, J1-J9 and note following No. B17.

Symbols of   Symbols of
Agriculture — A40   Industry — A41

Soviet
Symbols of
Agriculture
and Industry
A42

Science and
Arts — A43

1921   Unwmk.   Litho.   Imperf.

177	A40	1r orange	45	1.25
178	A40	2r lt brown	45	1.25
179	A41	5r dull ultra	28	32
180	A42	20r blue	1.10	3.00
a.		Pelure paper	3.25	2.75
b.		Double impression	20.00	
181	A40	100r orange	15	15
a.		Pelure paper	15	15
182	A40	200r lt brown	15	24
a.		200r olive brown	6.50	6.50
183	A43	250r dull violet	15	15
a.		Pelure paper	15	15
b.		Chalk surfaced paper	15	16
c.		Tête bêche pair	13.00	13.00
d.		Double impression	20.00	
184	A40	300r green	15	24
a.		Pelure paper	10.00	13.00
185	A41	500r blue	15	32
186	A41	1000r carmine	15	28
a.		Chalk surfaced paper	15	16
b.		Thick paper	15	16
c.		Pelure paper	15	16
		Set value	3.00	

See #203, 205. For surcharges see #191-194, 196-199, 201, 210, B40, B43-B47, J10.

New Russia
Triumphant
A44

Type I - 37½mm by 23½mm.
Type II - 38½mm by 23¼mm.

1921, Aug. 10   Wmk. 169   Engr.

187	A44	40r slate, type II	50	85
a.		Type I	75	85

For surcharges see Nos. 195, 200.

Initials Stand for
Russian Soviet
Federated Socialist
Republic — A45

1921   Litho.   Unwmk.

188	A45	100r orange	15	32
189	A45	250r violet	15	15
190	A45	1000r carmine rose	40	85

4th anniversary of Soviet Government. A 200r was not regularly issued. Value $35.

Nos. 177-179 Surcharged in Black   **5000 руб.**

1922

191 A40	5000r on 1r orange	52	60
a.	Inverted surcharge	27.50	22.50
b.	Double surcharge, red & black	27.50	22.50
c.	Pair, one without surcharge	40.00	
192 A40	5000r on 2r lt brown	90	90
a.	Inverted surcharge	20.00	15.00
b.	Double surcharge	24.00	
193 A41	5000r on 5r ultra	52	75
a.	Inverted surcharge	40.00	30.00
b.	Double surcharge	40.00	

No. 180 Surcharged

Р.С.Ф.С.Р.

5000 РУБЛЕЙ

194 A42	5000r on 20r blue	60	1.25
a.	Pelure paper	1.00	1.50
b.	Pair, one without surcharge	40.00	

Nos. 177-180, 187-187a Surcharged in Black or Red

РСФСР

10.000 р.

Wmk. Lozenges (169)

195 A44	10,000r on 40r, type I	32	45
a.	Inverted surcharge	20.00	15.00
b.	Type II	1.75	1.75
c.	"1.0000" instead of "10.000"	60.00	
d.	Double surcharge	40.00	

Red Surcharge
Unwmk.

196 A40	5000r on 1r orange	52	90
a.	Inverted surcharge	20.00	15.00
197 A40	5000r on 2r lt brown	60	1.25
a.	Inverted surcharge	40.00	30.00
198 A41	5000r on 5r ultra	60	1.25
199 A42	5000r on 20r blue	1.00	1.75
a.	Inverted surcharge	48.00	35.00

Wmk. Lozenges (169)

200 A44	10,000r on 40r, type I (R)	20	22
a.	Inverted surcharge	24.00	18.00
b.	Double surcharge	24.00	18.00
c.	With periods after Russian letters	48.00	35.00
d.	Type II	40	30
e.	As "a," type II	40.00	30.00
f.	As "c," type II	60.00	45.00

No. 183
Surcharged in
Black or Blue
Black

7500 РУБ.

1922, Mar.   Unwmk.

201 A43	7500r on 250r (Bk)	15	15
a.	Pelure paper	15	15
b.	Chalk surfaced paper	16	24
c.	Blue black surcharge	15	15
	Nos. 191-201 (11)	5.93	9.47

Nos. 201, 201a and 201b exist with surcharge inverted (value about $15 each), and double (about $25 each).

The horizontal surcharge was prepared but not issued.

Type of 1921 and

"Workers of the World Unite" A46

1922   Litho.   Wmk. 171

202 A46	5000r dark violet	35	2.00
203 A42	7500r blue	16	22
204 A46	10,000r blue	1.50	2.00

Unwmk.

205 A42	7500r blue, *buff*	16	25
a.	Double impression	17.50	
206 A46	22,500r dk violet, *buff*	24	32
	Nos. 202-206 (5)	2.41	4.79

For surcharges see Nos. B41-B42.

No. 183 Surcharged Diagonally

100,000 РУБ.

1922   Unwmk.   *Imperf.*

210 A43	100,000r on 250r	15	15
a.	Inverted surcharge	17.50	17.50
b.	Pelure paper	15	15
c.	Chalk surfaced paper	15	15
d.	As "b," inverted surcharge	17.50	20.00

Marking 5th Anniversary of October Revolution — A48

1922   A48   Typo.

211 A48	5r ocher & black	15	15
212 A48	10r brown & black	15	15
213 A48	25r violet & black	35	50
214 A48	27r rose & black	65	1.00
215 A48	45r blue & black	55	65
	Nos. 211-215 (5)	1.85	2.45

Pelure Paper

213a A48	25r violet & black	16.00
214a A48	27r rose & black	16.00
215a A48	45r blue & black	20.00

5th anniv. of the October Revolution. Sold in the currency of 1922 which was valued at 10,000 times that of the preceding years.

For surcharges see Nos. B38-B39.

Nos. 81, 82a, 85-86, 125-126, 129-130 Surcharged

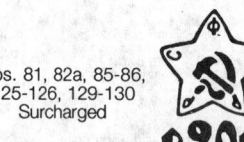

р.20р.

1922-23   Perf. 14½x15

216 A8	5r on 20k	15	40
a.	Inverted surcharge	20.00	20.00
b.	Double surcharge	30.00	30.00
217 A11	20r on 15k	25	50
a.	Inverted surcharge	32.50	32.50
218 A11	20r on 70k	15	25
a.	Inverted surcharge	10.00	12.50
b.	Double surcharge	16.00	16.00
219 A8	30r on 50k	20	40
a.	Inverted surcharge	15.00	15.00
c.	Groundwork omitted	22.50	22.50
d.	Double surcharge	13.00	13.00
220 A11	40r on 15k	15	25
a.	Inverted surcharge	15.00	15.00
b.	Double surcharge	20.00	20.00
221 A11	100r on 15k	15	25
a.	Inverted surcharge	16.00	16.00
b.	Double surcharge	20.00	20.00
222 A11	200r on 15k	15	25
a.	Inverted surcharge	15.00	15.00
b.	Double surcharge	15.00	15.00

Nos. 218-220, 222 exist in pairs, one without surcharge; Nos. 221-222 with triple surcharge; No. 221 with double surcharge, one inverted. Value, each $100.

Imperf

223 A8	5r on 20k	5.00	9.50
224 A11	20r on 15k	1,300.	
225 A11	20r on 70k	30	65
226 A8	30r on 50k brn vio & green	2.25	4.00
227 A11	40r on 15k	15	25
a.	Inverted surcharge	27.50	27.50
b.	Double surcharge	20.00	20.00
228 A11	100r on 15k	65	1.00
a.	Inverted surcharge	40.00	40.00
229 A11	200r on 15k	65	65
a.	Inverted surcharge	40.00	40.00
b.	Double surcharge	27.50	27.50
	Nos. 216-223,225-229 (13)	10.20	18.35

Counterfeits of No. 224 exist.

Worker A49   Soldier A50

1922-23   Typo.   *Imperf.*

230 A49	10r blue	15	15
231 A50	50r brown	15	15
232 A50	70r brown violet	15	15
233 A50	100r red	20	25
	Set value	50	

1923   Perf. 14x14½

234 A49	10r dp bl, perf. 13½	15	20
a.	Perf. 14	15.00	16.00
b.	Perf. 12½	1.00	85
235 A50	50r brown	15	20
a.	Perf. 12½	7.50	6.00
b.	Perf. 13½	1.50	2.00
236 A50	70r brown violet	15	20
a.	Perf. 12½	2.00	2.00
237 A50	100r red	20	30
a.	Cliché of 70r in plate of 100r	30.00	35.00
b.	Corrected cliché	75.00	100.00

No. 237b has extra broken line at right.

Soldier- Worker- Peasant
A51   A52   A53

1923   Perf. 14½x15

238 A51	3r rose	15	24
239 A52	4r brown	15	24
240 A53	5r light blue	15	24
a.	Double impression	40.00	40.00
241 A51	10r gray	15	24
a.	Double impression	16.00	
241A A51	20r brown violet	20	75
b.	Double impression	50.00	50.00
	Set value	60	

Imperf

238a A51	3r rose	10.00	20.00
239a A52	4r brown	10.00	25.00
a.	As "a," double impression	75.00	
240b A53	5r light blue	4.50	10.00
241d A51	10r gray	4.50	10.00
f.	As "d," double impression	50.00	
241c A51	20r brown violet	77.50	47.50

Stamps of 1r buff, type A52, and 2r green, type A53, perf. 12 and imperf. were prepared but not put in use. Value $1 each.

The imperfs of Nos. 238-241A were sold only by the philatelic bureau in Moscow.

Stamps of 20r, type A51, printed in gray black or dull violet are essays.

The stamps of this and the following issues were sold for the currency of 1923, one ruble of which was equal to 100 rubles of 1922 and 1,000,000 rubles of 1921.

Union of Soviet Socialist Republics

Reaping — A54   Sowing — A55

Fordson Tractor A56

Symbolical of the Exhibition — A57

1923, Aug. 19   Litho.   *Imperf.*

242 A54	1r brown & orange	80	2.00
243 A55	2r dp grn & pale grn	80	2.00
244 A56	5r dp bl & pale blue	90	2.75
245 A57	7r rose & pink	1.00	3.50

Perf. 12½, 13½

246 A54	1r brown & orange	1.75	3.50
a.	Perf. 12½	15.00	25.00

---

247 A55	2r dp grn & pale grn, perf. 12½	1.40	2.50
248 A56	5r dp bl & pale bl	1.65	4.25
a.	Perf. 13½	12.00	12.00
249 A57	7r rose & pink	2.25	5.00
a.	Perf. 12½	12.00	12.00
	Nos. 242-249 (8)	10.55	25.50

1st Agriculture and Craftsmanship Exhibition, Moscow.

Worker- Soldier- Peasant
A58   A59   A60

1923   Unwmk.   Litho.   *Imperf.*

250 A58	1k orange	55	18
251 A60	2k green	70	28
252 A59	3k red brown	70	28
253 A58	4k deep rose	70	48
254 A58	5k lilac	70	48
255 A60	6k light blue	55	22
256 A59	10k dark blue	55	22
257 A58	20k yellow green	2.25	40
258 A60	30k dark brown	3.25	1.40
259 A59	1r red & brown	4.00	1.65
	Nos. 250-259 (10)	13.95	5.59

1924   Perf. 14½x15

261 A58	4k deep rose	100.00	30.00
262 A59	10k dark blue	100.00	30.00
263 A60	30k violet	21.00	8.00
264 A59	40k slate gray	21.00	8.00

See Nos. 273-290, 304-321. For surcharges see Nos. 349-350.

Vladimir Ilyich Ulyanov (Lenin) A61   Worker A62

1924   *Imperf.*

265 A61	3k red & black	1.40	1.25
266 A61	6k red & black	1.40	1.25
267 A61	12k red & black	1.40	1.25
268 A61	20k red & black	2.75	1.40

Three printings of Nos. 265-268 differ in size of red frame.

Perf. 13½

269 A61	3k red & black	1.50	1.25
270 A61	6k red & black	1.50	1.25
271 A61	12k red & black	1.90	1.65
272 A61	20k red & black	3.00	1.90

Death of Lenin (1870-1924).
Forgeries of Nos. 265-272 exist.

Types of 1923

There are small differences between the lithographed stamps of 1923 and the typographed of 1924-25. On a few values this may be seen in the numerals.

Type A58: Lithographed. The two white lines forming the outline of the ear are continued across the cheek. Typographed. The outer lines of the ear are broken where they touch the cheek.

Type A59: Lithographed. At the top of the right shoulder a white line touches the frame at the left. Counting from the edge of the visor of the cap, lines 5, 6 and sometimes 7 touch at their upper ends. Typographed. The top line of the shoulder does not reach the frame. On the cap lines 5, 6 and 7 run together and form a white spot.

Type A60: In the angle above the first letter "C" there is a fan-shaped ornament enclosing four white dashes. On the lithographed stamps these dashes reach nearly to the point of the angle. On the typographed stamps the dashes are shorter and often only three are visible.

On unused copies of the typographed stamps the raised outlines of the designs can be seen on the backs of the stamps.

1924-25   Typo.   *Imperf.*

273 A59	3k red brown	1.40	1.00
274 A58	4k deep rose	1.40	1.00
275 A59	10k dark blue	2.25	1.00
275A A60	50k brown	350.00	25.00

Other typographed and imperf. values include: 2k green, 5k lilac, 6k light blue, 20k green and 1r red and brown. Value, unused: $150, $100, $37.50, $150, and $175.

Nos. 273-275A were regularly issued. The 7k, 8k, 9k, 30k, 40k, 2r, 3r, and 5r also exist imperf. Value, set of 8, $75.

Perf. 14½x15
Typo.

276	A58	1k orange	65.00	5.50
277	A60	2k green	65	32
278	A59	3k red brown	85	40
279	A58	4k deep rose	85	40
280	A58	5k lilac	10.00	1.40
281	A60	6k lt blue	85	40
282	A59	7k chocolate	1.00	40
283	A58	8k brown olive	1.10	70
284	A60	9k orange red	1.10	1.40
285	A59	10k dark blue	1.65	55
286	A58	14k slate blue	20.00	2.75
287	A60	15k yellow	6,000.	175.00
288	A60	20k gray green	4.00	80
288A	A60	30k violet	100.00	6.50
288B	A60	40k slate gray	100.00	6.50
289	A59	50k brown	20.00	4.00
290	A59	1r red & brown	10.00	2.00
291	A62	2r green & rose	3.25	
		Nos. 276-286,288-291 (17)	357.05	37.27

See No. 323. Forgeries of No. 287 exist.

1925
Perf. 12

276a	A58	1k orange	60	18
277a	A60	2k green	8.00	95
278a	A59	3k red brown	1.65	70
279a	A58	4k deep rose	55.00	3.25
280a	A58	5k lilac	4.00	80
282a	A59	7k chocolate	2.25	20
283a	A58	8k brown olive	80.00	7.50
284a	A60	9k orange red	13.00	5.50
285a	A59	10k dark blue	3.00	25
286a	A58	14k slate blue	2.75	40
287a	A60	15k yellow	2.75	1.00
288c	A58	20k gray green	18.00	45
288d	A60	30k violet	20.00	2.50
288e	A59	40k slate gray	15.00	2.75
289a	A59	50k brown	8.00	1.10
290a	A59	1r red & brown	275.00	150.00
		Nos. 276a-290a (16)	509.00	177.53

Soldier — A63

Worker — A64

1924-25
Perf. 13½

292	A63	3r black brn & green	11.00	4.75
a.		Perf. 10	285.00	50.00
b.		Perf. 13½x10	250.00	315.00
293	A64	5r dk bl & gray brn	32.50	9.25
a.		Perf. 10½	50.00	62.50

See Nos. 324-325.

Lenin Mausoleum, Moscow — A65

1925, Jan.   Photo.   Wmk. 170   Imperf.

294	A65	7k deep blue	2.25	2.50
295	A65	14k dark green	2.50	2.50
296	A65	20k carmine rose	2.50	2.50
297	A65	40k red brown	2.50	3.00

Perf. 13½x14

298	A65	7k deep blue	2.50	2.50
299	A65	14k dark green	2.75	2.50
300	A65	20k carmine rose	2.75	2.50
301	A65	40k red brown	2.75	3.00

First anniversary of Lenin's death.
Nos. 294-301 are found on both ordinary and thick paper. Those on thick paper sell for twice as much, except for No. 301, which is scarcer on ordinary paper.

Lenin — A66

Perf. 13½
1925, July   Engr.   Wmk. 170

302	A66	5r red brown	25.00	5.00
a.		Perf. 13½	32.50	10.00
b.		Perf. 10½ ('26)	25.00	7.00
303	A66	10r indigo	25.00	10.00
a.		Perf. 13½	150.00	82.50
b.		Perf. 10½ ('26)	20.00	10.00

Imperfs. exist. Value, set $75.
See Nos. 407-408, 621-622.

Types of 1923 Issue
1925-27   Wmk. 170   Typo.   Perf. 12

304	A58	1k orange	45	35
305	A60	2k green	45	20
306	A59	3k red brown	45	35
307	A58	4k deep rose	35	24
308	A58	5k lilac	48	24
309	A60	6k lt blue	48	24
310	A59	7k chocolate	60	16
311	A58	8k brown olive	60	16
a.		Perf. 14½x15	100.00	20.00
312	A60	9k red	90	40
313	A59	10k dark blue	90	28
a.		10k pale blue ('27)	1.65	1.00
314	A58	14k slate blue	1.10	35
315	A60	15k yellow	1.75	1.00
316	A59	18k violet	1.40	24
317	A58	20k gray green	1.65	24
318	A60	30k violet	2.00	24
319	A59	40k slate gray	2.75	35
320	A60	50k brown	4.25	35
321	A59	1r red & brown	4.25	35
a.		Perf. 14½x15	100.00	40.00
323	A62	2r green & rose red	21.00	3.75
a.		Perf. 14½x15	9.00	2.00

Perf. 13½

324	A63	3r blk brn & green	7.50	3.25
a.		Perf. 12½	30.00	10.50
325	A64	5r dark blue & gray brown	15.00	3.25
		Nos. 304-325 (21)	68.31	15.99

Nos. 304-315, 317-325 exist imperf. Value, set $75.

Mikhail V. Lomonosov and Academy of Sciences A67

1925, Sept.   Photo.   Perf. 12½, 13½

326	A67	3k orange brown	4.25	3.00
a.		Perf. 12½x12	10.50	7.50
b.		Perf. 13½x12½	42.50	27.50
c.		Perf. 13½	17.50	10.00
327	A67	15k dk olive green	4.25	3.00
a.		Perf. 13½	17.50	7.50

Russian Academy of Sciences, 200th anniv. Exist unwatermarked, on thick paper with yellow gum, perf. 13½. These are essays, later perforated and gummed.

Prof. Aleksandr S. Popov (1859-1905), Radio Pioneer — A68

1925, Oct.   Perf. 13½

328	A68	7k deep blue	2.00	1.50
329	A68	14k green	3.25	1.90

For surcharge see No. 353.

Decembrist Exiles — A69

Street Rioting in St. Petersburg — A70

Revolutionist Leaders — A71

1925, Dec. 28   Imperf.

330	A69	3k olive green	2.00	1.65
331	A70	7k brown	2.00	1.90
332	A71	14k carmine lake	3.00	2.50

Perf. 13½

333	A69	3k olive green	1.75	1.40
a.		Perf. 12½	50.00	30.00
334	A70	7k brown	1.75	1.40
335	A71	14k carmine lake	2.50	1.90
		Nos. 330-335 (6)	13.00	10.75

Centenary of Decembrist revolution.
For surcharges see Nos. 354, 357.

Revolters Parading A72

Speaker Haranguing Mob A73

Street Barricade, Moscow A74

1925, Dec. 20   Imperf.

336	A72	3k olive green	1.25	1.50
337	A73	7k brown	1.50	1.65
338	A74	14k carmine lake	2.00	2.00

Perf. 12½, 13½, 12x12½

339	A72	3k olive green	1.25	1.25
a.		Perf. 13½	4.50	4.25
340	A73	7k brown	3.25	3.00
a.		Perf. 13½	15.00	10.50
b.		Horiz. pair, imperf. btwn.	55.00	50.00
341	A74	14k carmine lake	2.00	2.00
a.		Perf. 13½	22.50	12.00
		Nos. 336-341 (6)	11.25	11.40

20th anniversary of Revolution of 1905.
For surcharges see Nos. 355, 358.

Lenin — A75

Liberty Monument, Moscow — A76

1926   Wmk. 170   Engr.   Perf. 10½

342	A75	1r dark brown	4.00	2.50
343	A75	2r black violet	6.50	4.50
a.		Perf. 12½	75.00	30.00
344	A75	3r dark green	12.00	4.50

See Nos. 406, 620.

1926, July   Litho.   Perf. 12x12½

347	A76	7k blue green & red	2.00	1.50
348	A76	14k blue green & violet	2.50	1.50

6th International Esperanto Congress at Leningrad. Exist perf. 11½.
For surcharge see No. 356.

8 КОП

Nos. 282, 282a and 310 Surcharged in Black

1927, June   Unwmk.   Perf. 14½x15

349	A59	8k on 7k chocolate	1.40	1.00
a.		Perf. 12	8.50	7.50
b.		Inverted surcharge	125.00	105.00

Perf. 12
Wmk. 170

350	A59	8k on 7k chocolate	2.00	1.10
a.		Inverted surcharge	45.00	35.00

The surcharge on Nos. 349-350 comes in two types: With space of 2mm between lines, and with space of ¾mm. The latter is much scarcer.

Same Surcharge on Stamps of 1925-26 in Black or Red
Perf. 13½, 12½, 12x12½

353	A68	8k on 7k dp bl (R)	2.25	3.50
a.		Inverted "8"	50.00	50.00
354	A70	8k on 7k brown	6.25	7.25
355	A73	8k on 7k brown	8.25	9.50
356	A76	8k on 7k blue green & red	7.00	8.50

Imperf

357	A70	8k on 7k brown	2.75	4.00
358	A73	8k on 7k brown	2.75	4.00
		Nos. 349-350,353-358 (8)	32.65	38.85

ПОЧТОВАЯ МАРКА

Postage Due Stamps of 1925 Surcharged   **КОП. 8 КОП.**

Lithographed or Typographed
1927, June   Unwmk.   Perf. 12

359	D1	8k on 1k red, typo.	1.75	1.10
a.		Litho.	100.00	100.00
360	D1	8k on 2k violet	2.50	1.75

Perf. 12, 14½x14

361	D1	8k on 3k lt blue	2.25	1.75
362	D1	8k on 7k orange	2.50	1.75
363	D1	8k on 8k green	1.75	1.10
364	D1	8k on 10k dk blue	2.25	1.65
365	D1	8k on 14k brown	1.75	1.10
		Nos. 359-365 (7)	14.75	10.10

Exist with inverted surcharge. Value each, $100.

Wmk. 170
1927, June   Typo.   Perf. 12

366	D1	8k on 1k red	1.25	1.65
367	D1	8k on 2k violet	1.25	1.65
368	D1	8k on 3k lt blue	2.00	2.00
369	D1	8k on 7k orange	2.00	2.00
370	D1	8k on 8k green	1.25	1.65
371	D1	8k on 10k dk blue	1.25	1.65
372	D1	8k on 14k brown	1.25	1.65
		Nos. 366-372 (7)	10.25	12.25

Nos. 366, 368-372 exist with inverted surcharge. Value each, $100.

Dr. L. L. Zamenhof A77

1927   Photo.   Perf. 10½

373	A77	14k yel green & brown	2.00	1.90

Unwmk.

374	A77	14k yel green & brown	2.00	1.90

40th anniversary of creation of Esperanto.
No. 374 exists perf. 10, 10x10½ and imperf. Value, imperf. pair $165.

Worker, Soldier, Peasant — A78

Worker and Sailor — A81

Lenin in Car Guarded by Soldiers A79

Smolny Institute, Leningrad A80

Map of the USSR
A82

Men of Various Soviet Republics
A83

Workers of Different Races; Kremlin in Background
A84

Typo. (3k, 8k, 18k), Engr. (7k), Litho. (14k), Photo. (5k, 28k)
Perf. 13 1/2, 12 1/2x12, 11

		1927, Oct.		**Unwmk.**
375	A78	3k bright rose	90	80
a.		Imperf., pair	215.00	
376	A79	5k deep brown	2.50	2.25
a.		Imperf.	165.00	180.00
b.		Perf. 12 1/2	20.00	27.50
c.		Perf. 12 1/2x10 1/2	22.50	16.00
377	A80	7k myrtle green	2.75	2.75
a.		Perf. 11 1/2	35.00	20.00
b.		Imperf., pair	350.00	
378	A81	8k brown & black	1.50	95
a.		Perf. 10 1/2x12 1/2	32.50	27.50
379	A82	14k dull blue & red	2.50	1.65
380	A83	18k blue	1.90	1.65
a.		Imperf.	130.00	
381	A84	28k olive brown	7.25	5.75
a.		Perf. 10	37.50	32.50
		Nos. 375-381 (7)	19.30	15.80

10th anniversary of October Revolution.
The paper of No. 375 has an overprint of pale yellow wavy lines.
No. 377b exists with watermark 170. Value, $1000.

Worker
A85

Peasant
A86

Lenin — A87

1927-28　　Typo.　　*Perf. 13 1/2*
Chalk Surfaced Paper

382	A85	1k orange	30	20
383	A86	2k apple green	30	15
385	A85	4k bright blue	30	15
386	A85	5k brown	30	15
388	A86	7k dark red ('28)	1.75	45
389	A85	8k green	90	15
391	A85	10k light brown	90	15
392	A87	14k dark green ('28)	1.25	28
393	A87	18k olive green	1.25	28
394	A87	18k dark blue ('28)	1.75	42
395	A86	20k dark gray green	1.25	28
396	A85	40k rose red	2.50	42
397	A86	50k bright blue	3.00	85
399	A85	70k gray green	3.50	85
400	A86	80k orange	4.75	1.40
		Nos. 382-400 (15)	24.00	6.18

The 1k, 2k and 10k exist imperf. Value, each $175.

Soldier and Kremlin
A88

Sailor and Flag
A89

Cavalryman
A90

Aviator
A91

1928, Feb. 6
Chalk Surfaced Paper

402	A88	8k light brown	70	28
a.		Imperf.	100.00	70.00
403	A89	14k deep blue	1.50	75
404	A90	18k carmine rose	1.65	1.40
a.		Imperf.	125.00	
405	A91	28k yellow green	2.00	1.75

10th anniversary of the Soviet Army.

Lenin Types of 1925-26
Perf. 10, 10 1/2

		1928-29　　Engr.	**Wmk. 169**	
406	A75	3r dark green ('29)	5.75	2.00
407	A66	5r red brown	6.75	2.50
408	A66	10r indigo	11.50	4.50

Bugler Sounding Assembly
A92　　　　　　A93

Perf. 12 1/2x12

		1929, Aug. 18　Photo.	**Wmk. 170**	
411	A92	10k olive brown	6.25	2.50
a.		Perf. 10 1/2	35.00	21.00
b.		Perf. 12 1/2x10 1/2x12	45.00	21.00
412	A93	14k slate	3.00	1.90
a.		Perf. 12 1/2x10 1/2x12	52.50	30.00

First All-Soviet Assembly of Pioneers.

Factory Worker — A95　　　Peasant — A96

Farm Worker — A97　　　Soldier — A98

Worker, Soldier, Peasant — A100　　　Worker — A103

Lenin — A104　　　Peasant — A107

Factory Worker — A109　　　Farm Worker — A111

Perf. 12x12 1/2

		1929-31　　Typo.	**Wmk. 170**	
413	A103	1k orange	18	15
a.		Perf. 10 1/2	20.00	13.00
b.		Perf. 14x14 1/2	50.00	35.00
414	A95	2k yellow green	18	15
415	A96	3k blue	18	15
a.		Perf. 14x14 1/2	42.50	35.00
416	A97	4k claret	30	15
417	A98	5k orange brown	30	15
a.		Imperf.	40.00	30.00
418	A100	7k scarlet	1.10	55
419	A103	10k olive green	50	15
a.		Perf. 10 1/2	27.50	22.50

Unwmk.

420	A104	14k indigo	1.10	55
a.		Perf. 10 1/2	3.00	3.25

Wmk. 170

421	A100	15k dk olive green ('30)	85	15
422	A107	20k green	85	15
a.		Perf. 10 1/2	50.00	27.50
423	A109	30k dk violet	1.40	45
424	A111	50k dp brown	1.90	1.00
425	A98	70k dk red ('30)	2.00	1.10
426	A107	80k red brown ('31)	1.90	1.10
		Nos. 413-426 (14)	12.74	5.95

Nos. 422, 423, 424 and 426 have a background of fine wavy lines in pale shades of the colors of the stamps.
See Nos. 456-466, 613A-619A. For surcharge see No. 743.

Symbolical of Industry — A112

Tractors Issuing from Assembly Line
A113

Iron Furnace (Inscription reads, "More Metal More Machines")
A114

Blast Furnace and Chart of Anticipated Iron Production — A115

		1929-30	**Perf. 12x12 1/2**	
427	A112	5k orange brown	1.25	80
428	A113	10k olive green	1.25	1.25

Perf. 12 1/2x12

429	A114	20k dull green	3.25	2.50
430	A115	28k violet black	2.00	1.40

Publicity for greater industrial production. No. 429 exists perf. 10 1/2. Value $200.

Red Cavalry in Polish Town after Battle — A116

Cavalry Charge
A117

Staff Officers of 1st Cavalry Army — A118

Plan of Action for 1st Cavalry Army — A119

		1930, Feb.	**Perf. 12x12 1/2**	
431	A116	2k yellow green	1.50	1.40
432	A117	5k light brown	1.50	1.40
433	A118	10k olive gray	3.25	2.00
434	A119	14k indigo & red	1.25	1.40

1st Red Cavalry Army, 10th anniversary.

Students Preparing a Poster Newspaper
A120

1930, Aug. 15

435	A120	10k olive green	1.25	75

Educational Exhibition, Leningrad, 7/1-8/15/30.

Telegraph Office, Moscow
A121

Lenin Hydroelectric Power Station on Volkhov River — A122

		1930　Photo.　Wmk. 169	**Perf. 10 1/2**	
436	A121	1r deep blue	4.00	3.50

Wmk. 170

437	A122	3r yel green & blk brn	4.50	2.00
		See Nos. 467, 469.		

Battleship Potemkin
A123

Inside Presnya Barricade — A124　　　Moscow Barricades in 1905 — A125

		1930　Typo.　Perf. 12x12 1/2, 12 1/2x12		
438	A123	3k red	1.40	55
439	A124	5k blue	1.40	70
440	A125	10k dk green & red	2.50	1.00

		1931	**Imperf.**	
452	A123	3k red	3.00	1.75
453	A124	5k deep blue	3.00	1.90
454	A125	10k dk green & red	4.00	2.25
		Nos. 438-454 (6)	15.30	8.15

Revolution of 1905, 25th anniversary.

Types of 1929-31 Regular Issue

		1931-32	**Imperf.**	
456	A103	1k orange	52	65
457	A95	2k yellow green	70	1.00
458	A96	3k blue	70	85
459	A97	4k claret	5.50	6.50
460	A98	5k orange brown	2.00	2.75
462	A103	10k olive green	20.00	20.00
464	A100	15k dk olive green	22.50	22.50

466	A109	30k dull violet	35.00 35.00
467	A121	1r dark blue	55.00 55.00
		Nos. 456-467 (9)	141.92 144.65

Nos. 459, 462-467 were sold only by the philatelic bureau.

Type of 1930 Issue

1931   Wmk. 170   Perf. 12x12½
469	A121	1r dark blue	1.75 75

 Maxim Gorki — A133

1932-33   Photo.
470	A133	15k dark brown	4.00 3.50
a.		Imperf.	115.00 115.00
471	A133	35k dp ultra ('33)	12.00 10.00

40th anniversary of Gorki's literary activity.

Lenin
Addressing the
People
A134

Revolution in
Petrograd
(Leningrad)
A135

Dnieper
Hydroelectric
Power
Station — A136

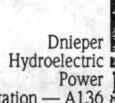

Asiatics Saluting
the Soviet
Flag — A139

Breaking Prison
Bars — A140

Designs (dated 1917 1932): 15k, Collective farm. 20k, Magnitogorsk metallurgical plant in Urals. 30k, Radio tower and heads of 4 men.

1932-33   Perf. 12½x12; 12½ (30k)
472	A134	3k dark violet	65 65
473	A135	3k dark brown	65 65
474	A136	10k ultra	1.25 1.25
475	A136	15k dark green	75 75
476	A136	20k lake ('33)	1.00 1.00
477	A136	30k dark gray ('33)	3.25 2.00
478	A139	35k gray black	65.00 52.50
		Nos. 472-478 (7)	72.55 58.80

October Revolution, 15th anniversary.

1932, Nov.   Litho.   Perf. 12½x12
479	A140	50k dark red	6.00 3.75

Intl. Revolutionaries' Aid Assoc., 10th anniv.

Trier, Birthplace of
Marx
A141

Grave,
Highgate
Cemetery,
London
A142

Design: 35k, Portrait and signature of Karl Marx (1818-1883).

Perf. 12x12½, 12½x12

1933, Mar.   Photo.
480	A141	3k dull green	3.00 1.00
481	A142	10k black brown	5.00 2.25
482	A142	35k brown violet	10.00 5.75

Fine Arts Museum, Moscow — A145

1932, Dec.   Perf. 12½
485	A145	15k black brown	15.00 13.00
486	A145	35k ultra	32.50 32.50
a.		Perf. 10½	30.00 30.00

Moscow Philatelic Exhibition, 1932.
Nos. 485 and 486 were also issued in imperf. sheets of 4 containing 2 of each value, on thick paper for presentation purposes. They were not valid for postage.

Nos. 485 and 486a Surcharged

ЛЕНИНГРАД, 1933 г.

**70
коп**

1933, Mar.   Perf. 12½
487	A145	30k on 15k black brn	26.00 20.00

Perf. 10½
488	A145	70k on 35k ultra	62.50 25.00

Leningrad Philatelic Exhibition, 1933.

Peoples of the Soviet Union

Kazaks — A146

Lezghians
A147

Tungus
A150

Crimean
Tartars — A148

Jews,
Birobidzhan
A149

Buryats — A151   Yakuts — A156

Chechens
A152

Abkhas — A153

Georgians
A154

Nientzians
A155

Great Russians — A157

Tadzhiks — A158

Transcaucasians — A159

Turkmen — A160

Ukrainians — A161

Uzbeks — A162

Byelorussians — A163

Koryaks — A164

Bashkirs
A165

Chuvashes
A166

**Perf. 12, 12x12½, 12½x12, 11x12,
12x11**

1933, Apr.   Photo.
489	A146	1k black brown	1.10 75
490	A147	2k ultra	1.10 75
491	A148	3k gray green	1.10 75
492	A149	4k gray black	1.10 75
493	A150	5k brown violet	1.10 75
494	A151	6k indigo	1.10 45
495	A152	7k black brown	1.10 45
496	A153	8k rose red	1.10 65
497	A154	9k ultra	2.00 85
498	A155	10k black brown	2.25 2.25
499	A156	14k olive green	2.00 85
500	A157	15k orange	2.25 85
501	A158	15k ultra	2.00 75
502	A159	15k dark brown	2.00 75
503	A160	15k rose red	3.00 2.00
504	A161	15k violet brown	2.25 85
505	A162	15k gray black	2.25 85
506	A163	15k dull green	2.25 85
507	A164	20k dull blue	7.00 2.00
508	A165	30k brown violet	7.00 1.65
509	A166	35k black	15.00 2.75
		Nos. 489-509 (21)	60.05 22.55

V. V. Vorovsky
A169

Designs: 3k, V. M. Volodarsky. 5k, M. S. Uritzky.

1933, Oct.   Perf. 12x12½
514	A169	1k dull green	75 55
515	A169	3k blue black	1.10 75
516	A169	5k olive brown	2.25 90

10th anniv. of the murder of Soviet Representative Vorovsky (1k). 15th anniv. of the murder of the Revolutionists Volodarsky (3k) and Uritzky (5k).
See Nos. 531-532, 580-582.

Order of the Red Banner,
15th Anniv. — A173

1933, Nov. 17   Unwmk.   Perf. 14
518	A173	20k black, red & yellow	1.50 75

No. 518, perf. 9½, is a proof.

Commissar
Schaumyan
A174

Commissar
Prokofii A.
Dzhaparidze
A175

Commissars Awaiting Execution — A176

Designs: 35k, Monument to the 26 Commissars.
40k, Worker, peasant and soldier dipping flags in
salute.

1933, Dec. 1

519	A174	4k brown	8.00	1.50
520	A175	5k dark gray	8.00	1.50
521	A176	20k purple	5.25	1.90
522	A176	35k ultra	26.00	6.25
523	A176	40k carmine	15.00	7.50
	Nos. 519-523 (5)		62.25	18.25

15th anniv. of the execution of 26 commissars at
Baku. No. 521 exists imperf.

Lenin's
Mausoleum
A179

1934, Feb. 7   Engr.   Perf. 14

524	A179	5k brown	2.25	48
a.		Imperf.	125.00	125.00
525	A179	10k slate blue	3.75	1.90
a.		Imperf.	125.00	125.00
526	A179	15k dk carmine	3.75	1.25
527	A179	20k green	3.75	1.25
528	A179	35k dark brown	6.50	2.00
	Nos. 524-528 (5)		20.00	6.88

10th anniversary of Lenin's death.

Ivan
Fedorov — A180

1934, Mar. 5

529	A180	20k carmine rose	3.50	2.50
a.		Imperf.	100.00	100.00
530	A180	40k indigo	8.50	3.50
a.		Imperf.	100.00	100.00

350th anniv. of the death of Ivan Fedorov,
founder of printing in Russia.

Portrait Type of 1933

Designs: 10k, Yakov M. Sverdlov. 15k, Victor
Pavlovich Nogin.

1934, Mar.   Photo.   Wmk. 170

531	A169	10k ultra	16.00	5.50
532	A169	15k red	19.00	9.00

Deaths of Yakov M. Sverdlov, chairman of the
All-Russian Central Executive Committee of the
Soviets, 15th anniv., Victor Pavlovich Nogin, chair-
man Russian State Textile Syndicate, 10th anniv.

Dmitri Ivanovich Mendeleev
A184   A185

1934, Sept. 15   Wmk. 170   Perf. 14

536	A184	5k emerald	4.00	1.50
537	A185	10k black brown	11.00	2.75
538	A185	15k vermilion	10.00	2.50
539	A184	20k ultra	5.75	2.50

Prof. D. I. Mendeleev (1834-1907), chemist who
discovered the Periodic Law of Classification of the
Elements.
Imperfs. exist of 5k (value $100) and 15k (value
$150).

Lenin as Child and Youth
A186   A187

Demonstration before Lenin
Mausoleum — A190

Designs: 5k, Lenin in middle age. 10k, Lenin the
orator. 30k, Lenin and Stalin.

1934, Nov. 23   Unwmk.   Perf. 14

540	A186	1k indigo & black	2.00	90
541	A187	3k indigo & black	2.00	1.10
542	A187	5k indigo & black	4.00	1.75
543	A187	10k indigo & black	3.00	1.75
544	A190	20k brn org & ultra	6.00	3.00
545	A190	30k brown org & car	18.00	7.00
	Nos. 540-545 (6)		35.00	15.50

First decade without Lenin.
See Nos. 931-935, 937.

Bombs Falling
on City
A192

"Before War and
Afterwards"
A194

Designs: 10k, Refugees from burning town. 20k,
"Plowing with the sword." 35k, "Comradeship."

1935, Jan. 1   Wmk. 170   Perf. 14

546	A192	5k violet black	5.25	3.00
547	A192	10k ultra	11.00	5.00
548	A194	15k green	13.00	5.00
549	A194	20k dark brown	11.00	5.00
550	A194	35k carmine	37.50	10.00
	Nos. 546-550 (5)		77.75	28.00

Ati-war propaganda, the designs symbolize the
horrors of modern warfare.

Subway
Tunnel — A197

Subway Station
Cross Section
A198

Subway
Station — A199

Train in Station — A200

1935, Feb. 25   Wmk. 170   Perf. 14

551	A197	5k orange	5.75	2.00
552	A198	10k dark ultra	7.25	3.50
553	A199	15k rose carmine	27.50	14.00
554	A200	20k emerald	12.00	5.50

Completion of Moscow subway.

Friedrich Engels
(1820-1895), German
Socialist and
Collaborator of
Marx — A201

1935, May   Wmk. 170   Perf. 14

555	A201	5k carmine	5.00	95
556	A201	10k dark green	2.50	1.50
557	A201	15k dark blue	5.00	1.90
558	A201	20k brown black	3.50	2.50

Running — A202

Designs: 2k, Diving. 3k, Rowing. 4k, Soccer. 5k,
Skiing. 10k, Bicycling. 15k, Tennis. 20k, Skating.
35k, Hurdling. 40k, Parade of athletes.

1935, Apr. 22   Unwmk.   Perf. 14

559	A202	1k orange & ultra	1.25	55
560	A202	2k black & ultra	1.50	55
561	A202	3k green & blk brn	3.00	1.25
562	A202	4k rose red & ultra	1.90	85
563	A202	5k pur & blk brn	1.90	85
564	A202	10k rose red & vio	7.25	2.75
565	A202	15k black & blk brn	14.00	5.75
566	A202	20k blk brn & ultra	12.00	4.00
567	A202	35k ultra & blk brn	17.50	8.25
568	A202	40k black brn & car	14.00	5.75
	Nos. 559-568 (10)		74.30	30.55

International Spartacist Games, Moscow. The
games never took place.

Silver Plate of
Sassanian
Dynasty — A212

1935, Sept. 10   Wmk. 170

569	A212	5k orange red	4.00	1.50
570	A212	10k dk yellow green	4.00	1.50
571	A212	15k dark violet	4.75	1.50
572	A212	35k black brown	7.25	2.75

3rd International Exposition of Persian Art,
Leningrad, Sept. 12-18, 1935.

Kalinin, the
Worker — A213

Mikhail
Kalinin — A216

Designs: 5k, Kalinin, the farmer. 10k, Kalinin,
the orator.

1935, Nov. 20   Unwmk.   Perf. 14

573	A213	3k rose lilac	95	52
574	A213	5k green	95	52
575	A213	10k blue slate	1.10	80
576	A216	20k brown black	2.00	1.00

60th birthday of Mikhail Kalinin, chairman of the
Central Executive Committee of the USSR.
The 20k exists imperf. Value $90.

Leo Tolstoy
A217   A218

Design: 20k, Statue of Tolstoy.

1935, Dec. 4   Perf. 14

577	A217	3k ol black & vio	90	75
578	A218	10k vio blk & blk brn	1.25	95
579	A217	20k dk grn & blk brn	3.00	2.50

Perf. 11

577a	A217	3k	2.50	60
578a	A218	10k	4.50	1.50
579a	A217	20k	7.00	1.90

25th anniv. of the death of Count Leo N. Tolstoy
(1828-1910).

Portrait Type of 1933

Designs: 2k, Mikhail V. Frunze. 4k, N. E.
Bauman. 40k, Sergei M. Kirov.

1935, Nov.   Wmk. 170   Perf. 11

580	A169	2k purple	1.40	2.75
581	A169	4k brown violet	2.25	4.50
582	A169	40k black brown	5.00	6.50

Perf. 14

580a	A169	2k	7.25	55
581a	A169	4k	10.00	55
582a	A169	40k	24.00	1.65

Death of three revolutionary heroes.
Nos. 580-582 exist imperf. but were not regularly issued. Value, set $225.

Pioneers Preventing Theft from Mailbox — A223

Designs: 3k, 5k, Pioneers preventing destruction of property. 10k, Helping recover kite. 15k, Girl Pioneer saluting.

1936, Apr.		**Unwmk.**	**Perf. 14**	
583	A223	1k yellow green	65	35
584	A223	2k copper red	2.00	35
585	A223	3k slate blue	1.00	90
586	A223	5k rose lake	85	35
587	A223	10k gray blue	2.00	1.75
588	A223	15k brown olive	10.00	6.00
		Nos. 583-588 (6)	16.50	9.70
		Perf. 11		
583a	A223	1k	1.25	35
584a	A223	2k	65	35
585a	A223	3k	3.50	45
586a	A223	5k	6.00	90
587a	A223	10k	15.00	1.10
588a	A223	15k	3.00	1.25
		Nos. 583a-588a (6)	29.40	4.40

Nikolai A. Dobrolyubov, Writer and Critic, Birth Cent. — A227

1936, Aug. 13		**Typo.**	**Perf. 11½**	
589	A227	10k rose lake	2.75	2.25
a.		Perf. 14	5.00	2.50

Aleksander Sergeyevich Pushkin A228

Statue of Pushkin, Moscow A229

Perf. 11 to 14 and Compound
1937, Feb. 1
Chalky or Ordinary Paper

590	A228	10k yellow brown	32	32
591	A228	20k Prus green	48	40
592	A228	40k rose lake	65	45
593	A229	50k blue	1.25	52
594	A229	80k carmine rose	1.90	75
595	A229	1r green	3.25	1.50
		Nos. 590-595 (6)	7.85	3.94

Souvenir Sheet
Imperf

596		Sheet of 2	4.00	17.00
a.	A228	10k brown	65	2.25
b.	A229	50k brown	65	2.25

Pushkin (1799-1837), writer and poet.

Tchaikovsky Concert Hall — A230

Designs: 5k, 15k, Telegraph Agency House. 10k, Tchaikovsky Concert Hall. 20k, 50k, Red Army Theater. 30k, Hotel Moscow. 40k, Palace of the Soviets.

1937, June		**Photo. Unwmk.**	**Perf. 12**	
597	A230	3k brown violet	65	32
598	A230	5k henna brown	65	32
599	A230	10k dark brown	1.10	32

600	A230	15k black	1.10	32
601	A230	20k olive green	65	75
602	A230	30k gray black	65	75
a.		Perf. 11	50.00	32.50
603	A230	40k violet	1.25	1.00
a.		Souv. sheet of 4, imperf.	7.50	17.00
604	A230	50k dark brown	1.25	1.00
		Nos. 597-604 (8)	7.30	4.78

First Congress of Soviet Architects. The 30k is watermarked Greek Border and Rosettes (170).
Nos. 597-601, 603-604 exist imperf. Value, each $225.

Feliks E. Dzerzhinski A235

Shota Rustaveli A236

1937, July 27		**Typo.**	**Perf. 12**	
606	A235	10k yellow brown	40	25
607	A235	20k Prus green	58	42
608	A235	40k rose lake	1.25	85
609	A235	80k carmine	1.40	1.00

Dzerzhinski, organizer of Soviet secret police, 10th death anniv. Exist imperf.

1938, Feb.		**Unwmk. Photo.**	**Perf. 12**	
610	A236	20k deep green	95	25

750th anniversary of the publication of the poem "Knight in the Tiger Skin," by Shota Rustaveli, Georgian poet.
Exists imperf. Value $135.

Statue Surmounting Pavilion A237

Soviet Pavilion at Paris Exposition A238

1938		**Typo.**		
611	A237	5k red	32	15
a.		Imperf.	50.00	
612	A238	20k rose	60	25
613	A237	50k dark blue	1.25	38

USSR participation in the 1937 International Exposition at Paris.

Types of 1929-32 and Lenin Types of 1925-26

1937-52		**Unwmk. Perf. 11½x12, 12**		
613A	A103	1k dull org ('40)	15.00	5.00
614	A95	2k yel grn ('39)	5.25	2.00
615	A97	4k claret ('40)	5.25	2.00
615A	A98	5k org brn ('46)	100.00	12.50
616	A109	10k blue ('38)	50	28
616A	A103	10k olive ('40)	90.00	12.50
616B	A109	10k black ('52)	50	35
617	A97	20k dull green	50	35
617A	A107	20k green ('39)	100.00	12.50
618	A109	30k claret ('39)	11.50	3.50
619	A104	40k indigo ('38)	2.00	90
619A	A111	50k dp brn ('40)	85	52
		Engr.		
620	A75	3r dk green ('39)	1.10	90
621	A66	5r red brn ('39)	1.75	1.25
622	A66	10r indigo ('39)	3.00	2.75

Nos. 615 to 619 exist imperforate but were not regularly issued.
No. 616B was re-issued in 1954-56 in slightly smaller format, 14½x21mm, and in gray black. See note after No. 738.

Airplane Route from Moscow to North Pole — A239

Soviet Flag and Airplanes at North Pole — A240

1938, Feb. 25		**Litho.**	**Perf. 12**	
625	A239	10k drab & black	1.40	30
626	A239	20k blue gray & blk	1.75	60
		Typo.		
627	A240	40k dull green & car	5.00	2.00
a.		Imperf.	140.00	
628	A240	80k rose car & car	1.90	1.90
a.		Imperf.	62.50	

Soviet flight to the North Pole.

Infantryman A241

Soldier A242

Stalin Reviewing Cavalry — A246

Chapayev and Boy — A247

Designs: 30k, Sailor. 40k, Aviator. 50k, Antiaircraft soldier.

1938, Mar.		**Unwmk. Photo.**	**Perf. 12**	
629	A241	10k gray blk & dk red	45	30
630	A242	20k gray blk & dk red	60	35
631	A242	30k gray blk & dk red	1.10	48
632	A242	40k gray blk & dk red	1.65	90
633	A242	50k gray blk & dk red	2.00	1.25
634	A246	80k gray blk & dk red	3.25	1.25
		Typo.		
		Perf. 12x12½		
635	A247	1r black & carmine	90	60
		Nos. 629-635 (7)	9.95	5.13
		Set, never hinged	20.00	

Workers' & Peasants' Red Army, 20th anniv.
No. 635 exists imperf. Value $125.

Aviators Chkalov, Baidukov, Beliakov and Flight Route — A248

Aviators Gromov, Danilin, Yumashev and Flight Route — A249

1938, Apr. 10			**Photo.**	
636	A248	10k black & red	75	65
637	A248	20k brown black & red	1.00	65
638	A248	40k brown & red	1.50	1.10
639	A248	50k brown vio & red	2.50	1.10
		Set, never hinged	15.00	

First Trans-Polar flight, June 18-20, 1937, from Moscow to Vancouver, Wash. Nos. 636-639 exist imperf. Value $125 each.

1938, Apr. 13				
640	A249	10k claret	1.50	60
641	A249	20k brown black	1.90	1.25
642	A249	50k dull violet	2.00	1.50
		Set, never hinged	12.00	

First Trans-Polar flight, July 12-14, 1937, from Moscow to San Jacinto, Calif. Nos. 640-642 exist imperf. Value, each $110.

Arrival of the Rescuing Ice-breakers Taimyr and Murmansk A250

Ivan Papanin and His Men Aboard Ice-breaker Yermak — A251

1938, June 21		**Typo.**	**Perf. 12, 12½**	
643	A250	10k violet brown	2.25	85
644	A250	20k dark blue	2.25	1.10
		Photo.		
645	A251	30k olive brown	5.00	1.40
646	A251	50k ultra	5.00	1.50
a.		Imperf.	135.00	
		Set, never hinged	20.00	

Rescue of Papanin's North Pole Expedition.

Arms of Uzbek — A252

Arms of USSR — A253

#650

#651

#654

#655

#656

Designs: Different arms on each stamp.

		Perf. 12, 12½		
1937-38		**Unwmk.**	**Typo.**	
647	A252	20k dp bl (Armenia)	1.00	50
648	A252	20k dull violet (Azerbaijan)	1.00	50

649	A252	20k brown orange (Byelorussia)	5.00 2.25
650	A252	20k carmine rose (Georgia)	1.10 58
651	A252	20k bl grn (Kazakh)	1.10 58
652	A252	20k emer (Kirghiz)	1.10 58
653	A252	20k yel org (Uzbek)	1.10 58
654	A252	20k blue (R.S.F.S.R.)	1.10 58
655	A252	20k claret (Tadzhik)	1.10 58
656	A252	20k car (Turkmen)	1.10 58
657	A252	20k red (Ukraine)	1.10 58

Engr.

658	A253	40k brown red	1.65 1.65
		Nos. 647-658 (12)	17.45 9.54
		Set, never hinged	30.00

Constitution of USSR. No. 649 has inscriptions in Yiddish, Polish, Byelorussian and Russian. Issue dates: 40k, 1937. Others, 1938. See Nos. 841-842.

 Nurse Weighing Child — A264

 Children at Lenin's Statue — A265

 Biology Lesson — A266

 Health Camp — A267

 Young Model Builders A268

1938, Sept. 15   Unwmk.   Perf. 12

659	A264	10k dk blue green	1.10 30
660	A265	15k dk blue green	1.10 45
661	A266	20k violet brown	1.40 45
662	A267	30k claret	1.75 80
663	A266	40k light brown	2.00 1.10
664	A268	50k deep blue	3.00 1.50
665	A268	80k light green	4.50 1.50
		Nos. 659-665 (7)	14.85 6.10
		Set, never hinged	20.00

Child welfare.

 View of Yalta A269 — Crimean Shoreline — A272

Designs: No. 667, View along Crimean shore. No. 668, Georgian military highway. No, 670, View near Yalta. No. 671, "Swallows' Nest" Castle. 20k, Dzerzhinski Rest House for workers. 30k, Sunset in Crimea. 40k, Alupka. 50k, Gursuf. 80k, Crimean Gardens. 1r, "Swallows' Nest" Castle, horiz.

Unwmk.
1938, Sept. 21   Photo.   Perf. 12

666	A269	5k brown	45 60
667	A269	5k black brown	45 60
668	A269	10k slate green	60 60
669	A272	10k brown	60 60
670	A272	15k black brown	60 60
671	A272	15k dark brown	60 60
672	A269	20k dark brown	1.00 60
673	A269	30k black brown	1.00 80
674	A269	40k brown	1.50 80
675	A272	50k dp slate green	1.50 1.65
676	A269	80k brown	2.25 1.65
677	A272	1r slate green	5.00 2.75
		Nos. 666-677 (12)	15.55 11.85
		Set, never hinged	25.00

 Children Flying Model Plane — A281

 Glider — A282

 Captive Balloon — A283

 Dirigible over Kremlin — A284

 Parachute Jumpers — A285

 Hydroplane A286

 Balloon in Flight — A287

 Balloon Ascent — A288

 Four-motor Plane — A289

Unwmk.
1938, Oct. 7   Typo.   Perf. 12

678	A281	5k violet brown	70 55
679	A282	10k olive gray	70 55
680	A283	15k pink	1.25 55
681	A284	20k deep blue	1.25 55
682	A285	30k claret	1.90 95
683	A286	40k deep blue	2.25 95
684	A287	50k blue green	4.50 1.40
685	A288	80k brown	4.00 2.50
686	A289	1r blue green	5.25 2.00
		Nos. 678-686 (9)	21.80 10.00
		Set, never hinged	40.00

For overprints see Nos. C76-C76D.

 Sokol Terminal A291

 Kiev Station A292

Mayakovsky Station, Moscow Subway — A290

 Dynamo Station — A293

 Train in Tunnel — A294

 Revolution Square Station — A295

Unwmk.
1938, Nov. 7   Photo.   Perf. 12

687	A290	10k deep red violet	1.50 80
688	A291	15k dark brown	1.40 80
689	A292	20k black brown	1.90 80
690	A293	30k dark red violet	1.90 80
691	A294	40k black brown	1.90 1.25
692	A295	80k dark brown	1.90 1.65
		Nos. 687-692 (6)	10.50 6.10
		Set, never hinged	15.00

Second line of the Moscow subway opening.

 Girl with Parachute A296

 Young Miner A297

 Harvesting A298

Designs: 50k, Students returning from school. 80k, Aviator and sailor.

1938, Dec. 7   Typo.   Perf. 12

693	A296	20k deep blue	75 35
694	A297	30k deep claret	75 35
695	A298	40k violet brown	95 35
696	A296	50k deep rose	1.25 70
697	A298	80k brown	3.75 1.00
		Nos. 693-697 (5)	7.45 2.75
		Set, never hinged	12.50

20th anniv. of the Young Communist League (Komsomol).

 Diving A301

 Discus Thrower A302

Designs: 15k, Tennis. 20k, Acrobatic motorcyclists. 30k, Skier. 40k, Runners. 50k, Soccer. 80k, Physical culture.

Unwmk.
1938, Dec. 28   Photo.   Perf. 12

698	A301	5k scarlet	1.75 55
699	A302	10k black	1.75 55
700	A302	15k brown	2.00 55
701	A302	20k green	2.00 90
702	A302	30k dull violet	5.25 1.00
703	A302	40k deep green	6.25 1.40
704	A302	50k blue	5.25 1.00
705	A302	80k deep blue	5.25 1.75
		Nos. 698-705 (8)	29.50 7.70
		Set, never hinged	55.00

 Gorki Street, Moscow — A309

 Dynamo Subway Station A315

 Foundryman A316

Moscow scenes: 20k, Council House & Hotel Moscow. 30k, Lenin Library. 40k, Crimea Bridge. 50k, Bridge over Moscow River. 80k, Khimki Station.

Paper with network as in parenthesis

1939, Mar.   Typo.   Perf. 12

706	A309	10k brn (red brown)	70 35
707	A309	20k dk sl grn (lt blue)	85 35
708	A309	30k brn vio (red brn)	85 80
709	A309	40k blue (lt blue)	1.50 80
710	A309	50k rose lake (red brn)	2.50 1.00
711	A309	80k gray ol (lt blue)	2.75 1.00
712	A315	1r dk blue (lt blue)	4.50 1.65
		Nos. 706-712 (7)	13.65 5.95

"New Moscow." On 30k, denomination is at upper right.

1939, Mar.

713	A316	15k dark blue	55 30
		Never hinged	1.00
a.		Imperf.	20.00
		Never hinged	50.00

 Statue on USSR Pavilion — A317

USSR
Pavilion — A318

1939, May Photo.
714 A317 30k indigo & red 28 15
a. Imperf. ('40) 55 35
715 A318 50k blue & bister brn 32 24
a. Imperf. ('40) 60 45
Set, never hinged 75

Russia's participation in the NY World's Fair.

Paulina Osipenko A318a   Marina Raskova A318b

Design: 60k, Valentina Grizodubova.

1939, Mar.
718 A318a 15k green 1.25 60
719 A318b 30k brown violet 1.25 60
720 A318b 60k red 2.75 1.10
Set, never hinged 7.50

Non-stop record flight from Moscow to the Far East.
Exist imperf. Value, each $250.

Shevchenko, Early Portrait A319   Monument at Kharkov A321

Design: 30k, Shevchenko portrait in later years.

1939, Mar. 9
721 A319 15k black brn & blk 1.00 42
722 A319 30k dark red & blk 1.00 42
723 A321 60k green & dk brn 2.75 1.75
Set, never hinged 8.00

Taras G. Shevchenko (1814-1861), Ukrainian poet and painter.

Milkmaid with Prize Cow — A322

Tractor-plow at Work on Abundant Harvest — A323

Designs: 20k, Shepherd tending sheep. No. 727, Fair pavilion. No. 728, Fair emblem. 45k, Turkmen picking cotton. 50k, Drove of horses. 60k, Symbolizing agricultural wealth. 80k, Kolkhoz girl with sugar beets. 1r, Hunter with Polar foxes.

1939, Aug.
724 A322 10k rose pink 42 15
725 A323 15k red brown 42 15
726 A323 20k slate black 42 15
727 A322 30k purple 42 15

728 A322 30k red orange 42 15
729 A322 45k dark green 55 55
730 A322 50k copper red 55 55
731 A322 60k bright purple 1.00 75
732 A322 80k dark violet 1.00 75
733 A322 1r dark blue 2.00 90
Nos. 724-733 (10) 7.20 4.25
Set, never hinged 12.50

Soviet Agricultural Fair.

Worker-Soldier-Aviator
A331   A332   A333

Arms of USSR
A334   A335

1939-43 Unwmk. Typo. Perf. 12
734 A331 5k red 15 15
735 A332 15k dark green 22 24
736 A333 30k deep blue 22 24
737 A334 60k fawn ('43) 60 24

Photo.
738 A335 60k rose carmine 48 35
Nos. 734-738 (5) 1.67 1.22
Set, never hinged 2.00

No. 734 was re-issued in 1954-56 in slightly smaller format: 14x21½mm, instead of 14¾x22¼mm. Other values reissued in smaller format: 10k, 15k, 20k, 25k, 30k, 40k and 1r. (See notes following Nos. 622, 1260, 1347 and 1689.)

No. 416 Surcharged with New Value in Black

1939 Wmk. 170
743 A97 30k on 4k claret 7.50 7.50
Never hinged 12.50
a. Unwmkd. 35.00 25.00

M.E. Saltykov (N. Shchedrin)
A336   A337

1939, Sept. Typo. Unwmk.
745 A336 15k claret 30 15
746 A337 30k dark green 45 20
747 A336 45k olive gray 75 22
748 A337 60k dark blue 95 32
Set, never hinged 3.00

Mikhail E. Saltykov (1826-89), writer & satirist who used pen name of N. Shchedrin.

Sanatorium of the State Bank — A338

Designs: 10k, 15k, Soviet Army sanatorium. 20k, Rest home, New Afyon. 30k, Clinical Institute. 50k, 80k, Sanatorium for workers in heavy industry. 60k, Rest home, Sukhumi.

1939, Nov. Photo. Perf. 12
749 A338 5k dull brown 40 20
750 A338 10k carmine 40 20
751 A338 15k yellow green 40 20
752 A338 20k dk slate green 40 20
753 A338 30k bluish black 40 20
754 A338 50k gray black 85 30
755 A338 60k brown violet 1.00 45
756 A338 80k orange red 1.25 60
Nos. 749-756 (8) 5.10 2.35
Set, never hinged 12.00

Mikhail Y. Lermontov (1814-1841), Poet and Novelist, in 1837 — A346

Portrait in 1838 — A347   Portrait in 1841 — A348

1939, Dec.
757 A346 15k indigo & sepia 80 45
758 A347 30k dk grn & dull blk 2.00 65
759 A348 45k brick red & indigo 1.65 95
Set, never hinged 6.00

Nikolai Chernyshevski A349   Anton Chekhov A350

1939, Dec. Photo.
760 A349 15k dark green 35 22
761 A349 30k dull violet 35 45
762 A349 60k Prus green 75 45
Set, never hinged 3.00

50th anniversary of the death of Nikolai Chernyshevski, scientist and critic.

1940, Feb. Unwmk. Perf. 12
Design: 20k, 30k, Portrait with hat.
763 A350 10k dark yellow green 25 22
764 A350 15k ultra 25 22
765 A350 20k violet 50 42
766 A350 30k copper brown 1.00 55
Set, never hinged 3.00

Chekhov (1860-1904), playwright.

Welcome to Red Army by Western Ukraine and Western Byelorussia A352

Designs: 30k, Villagers welcoming tank crew. 50k, 60k, Soldier giving newspapers to crowd. 1r, Crowd waving to tank column.

1940, Apr.
767 A352 10k deep rose 35 20
768 A352 30k myrtle green 35 20
769 A352 50k gray black 65 45
770 A352 60k indigo 65 45
771 A352 1r red 1.00 90
Nos. 767-771 (5) 3.00 2.20
Set, never hinged 6.00

Liberation of the people of Western Ukraine and Western Byelorussia.

Ice-breaker "Josef Stalin," Captain Beloussov and Chief Ivan Papanin A356

Vadygin and Papanin A358

Map of the Drift of the Sedov and Crew Members — A359

Design: 30k, Icebreaker Georgi Sedov, Captain Vadygin and First Mate Trofimov.

1940, Apr.
772 A356 15k dull yel green 1.40 55
773 A356 30k dull purple 2.75 55
774 A358 50k copper brown 2.25 55
775 A359 1r dark ultra 4.50 1.65
Set, never hinged 15.00

Heroism of the Sedov crew which drifted in the Polar Basin for 812 days.

Vladimir V. Mayakovsky
A360   A361

1940, June
776 A360 15k deep red 30 15
777 A360 30k copper brown 52 22
778 A361 60k dark gray blue 60 32
779 A361 80k bright ultra 52 32
Set, never hinged 3.00

Mayakovsky, poet (1893-1930).

K.A. Timiryazev and Academy of Agricultural Sciences A362

In the Laboratory of Moscow University A363

Last Portrait — A364

Monument in Moscow — A365

1940, June
780 A362 10k indigo 35 22
781 A363 15k purple 35 30
782 A364 30k dk violet brown 35 30
783 A365 60k dark green 1.40 55
Set, never hinged 3.00

20th anniversary of the death of K. A. Timiryasev, scientist and professor of agricultural and biological sciences.

Relay Race — A366

Sportswomen Marching A367

Children's Sport Badge — A368

Skier — A369

Throwing the Grenade A370

1940, July 21

784	A366	15k carmine rose	70	24
785	A367	30k sepia	1.50	24
786	A368	50k dk violet blue	1.65	60
787	A369	60k dk violet blue	2.25	60
788	A370	1r grayish green	3.75	1.25
		Nos. 784-788 (5)	9.85	2.93
		Set, never hinged	13.00	

2nd All-Union Physical Culture Day.

Tchaikovsky Museum at Klin — A371

Tchaikovsky & Passage from his Fourth Symphony — A372

Peter Ilich Tchaikovsky and Excerpt from Eugene Onegin — A373

1940, Aug. Unwmk. Typo. Perf. 12

789	A371	15k Prus green	95	35
790	A372	20k brown	95	35
791	A372	30k dark blue	95	35
792	A371	50k rose lake	95	50
793	A373	60k red	1.10	75
		Nos. 789-793 (5)	4.90	2.30
		Set, never hinged	8.50	

Tchaikovsky (1840-1893), composer.

Volga Provinces Pavilion A374

Northeast Provinces Pavilion — A376

ПАВИЛЬОН МОСКОВСКОЙ, РЯЗАНСКОЙ И ТУЛЬСКОЙ ОБЛ.
#797

ПАВИЛЬОН УКРАИНСКОЙ ССР
#798

ПАВИЛЬОН БЕЛОРУССКОЙ ССР
#799

ПАВИЛЬОН АЗЕРБАЙДЖАНСКОЙ ССР
#800

ПАВИЛЬОН ГРУЗИНСКОЙ ССР
#801

ПАВИЛЬОН АРМЯНСКОЙ ССР
#802

У ВХОДА В ПАВИЛЬОН УЗБЕКСКОЙ ССР
#803

ПАВИЛЬОН ТУРКМЕНСКОЙ ССР
#804

ПАВИЛЬОН ТАДЖИКСКОЙ ССР
#805

ПАВИЛЬОН КИРГИЗСКОЙ ССР
#806

ПАВИЛЬОН КАЗАХСКОЙ ССР
#807

ПАВИЛЬОН КАРЕЛО-ФИНСКОЙ ССР
#808

1940, Oct. Photo.

794	A374	10k shown	1.00	45
795	A374	15k Far East Provinces	1.00	45
796	A376	30k shown	1.00	60
797	A376	30k Central Regions	1.00	60
798	A376	30k Ukrainian	1.00	60
799	A376	30k Byelorussian	1.00	60
800	A376	30k Azerbaijan	1.00	60
801	A374	30k Georgian	1.00	60
802	A376	30k Armenian	1.00	60
803	A376	30k Uzbek	1.00	60
804	A374	30k Turkmen	1.00	60
805	A376	30k Tadzhik	1.00	60
806	A376	30k Kirghiz	1.50	1.25
807	A376	30k Kazakh	1.50	1.25
808	A376	30k Karelian Finnish	1.50	1.25
809	A376	50k Main building	95	60
810	A376	60k Mechanizaton Pavilion, Stalin statue	2.25	1.25
		Nos. 794-810 (17)	20.75	13.15
		Set, never hinged	35.00	

All-Union Agricultural Fair.
Nos. 796-808 printed in three sheet formats with various vertical and horizontal se-tenant combinations.

Monument to Red Army Heroes — A391

Map of War Operations and M. V. Frunze — A393

Heroic Crossing of the Sivash A394

Designs: 15k, Grenade thrower. 60k, Frunze's headquarters, Stroganovka. 1r, Victorious soldier.

1940 Imperf.

811	A391	10k dark green	50	30
812	A391	15k orange ver	50	30
813	A393	30k dull brown & car	50	30
814	A394	50k violet brn	50	38
815	A394	60k indigo	50	60
816	A391	1r gray black	1.25	60
		Nos. 811-816 (6)	3.75	2.48
		Set, never hinged	5.00	

20th anniversary of battle of Perekop.
Nos. 811-816 were also issued perf. 12. Set price about 25% more.

Coal Miners — A397

Blast Furnace — A398

Bridge over Moscow-Volga Canal — A399

Three New Type Locomotives A400

Workers on a Collective Farm — A401

Automobiles and Planes — A402

Oil Derricks — A403

1941, Jan. Perf. 12

817	A397	10k deep blue	25	16
818	A398	15k dark violet	25	16
819	A399	20k deep blue	25	16
820	A400	30k dark brown	32	20
821	A401	50k olive brown	32	40
822	A402	60k olive brown	52	52
823	A403	1r dark blue green	1.00	80
		Nos. 817-823 (7)	2.91	2.40
		Set, never hinged	6.00	

Soviet industries.

Troops on Skis — A404

Sailor — A405

Soldiers with Cannon A406

Designs: 20k, Cavalry. 30k, Machine gunners. 45k, Army horsemen. 50k, Aviator. 1r, 3r, Marshal's Star.

1941-43

824	A404	5k dark violet	48	15
825	A405	10k deep blue	48	15
826	A406	15k brt yellow green	18	15
827	A404	20k vermilion	18	15
828	A404	30k dull brown	18	15
829	A406	45k gray green	60	30
830	A404	50k dull blue	35	40
831	A404	1r dull blue green	48	55
831A	A404	3r myrtle grn ('43)	1.90	1.10
		Nos. 824-831A (9)	4.83	3.10
		Set, never hinged	6.00	

Army & Navy of the USSR, 23rd anniv.

Battle of Ismail A412

Field Marshal Aleksandr Suvorov A413

1941 Unwmk. Perf. 12

832	A412	10k dark green	40	30
833	A412	15k carmine rose	55	45
834	A413	30k blue black	80	65
835	A413	1r olive brown	1.65	90
		Set, never hinged	5.00	

150th anniversary of the capture of the Turkish fortress, Ismail.

Kirghiz Horse Breeder A414

Kirghiz Miner — A415

1941, Mar.

836	A414	15k dull brown	90	45
837	A415	30k dull purple	1.25	60
		Set, never hinged	3.50	

15th anniversary of the Kirghizian Soviet Socialist Republic.

Prof. N. E.
Zhukovski
A416

Zhukovski
Lecturing
A418

Military Air
Academy
A417

1941, Mar.
838	A416	15k deep blue	45	22
839	A417	30k carmine rose	45	35
840	A418	50k brown violet	75	42
		Set, never hinged	2.50	

Prof. Zhukovski, scientist (1847-1921).

Arms Type of 1938

Design: Arms of Karelian-Finnish Soviet Socialist Republic.

1941, Mar.
841	A252	30k rose	60	35
842	A252	45k dark blue green	90	60
		Set, never hinged	2.00	

1st anniversary of the Karelian-Finnish Soviet Socialist Republic.

Spasski Tower,
Kremlin
A420

Kremlin and Moscow
River
A421

1941, May   Typo.   Unwmk.
843	A420	1r dull red	45	35
844	A421	2r brown orange	1.10	70
		Set, never hinged	2.00	

"Suvorov's
March through
the Alps, 1799"
A422

Vasili Ivanovich
Surikov, Self-
portrait
A424

"Stepan Rasin on
the Volga" — A423

1941, June   Photo.   Perf. 12
845	A422	20k black	1.25	75
846	A423	30k scarlet	2.00	1.25
847	A422	50k dk violet brown	4.00	2.25
848	A423	1r gray green	6.00	2.50
849	A424	2r brown	11.00	3.00
		Nos. 845-849 (5)	24.25	9.75
		Set, never hinged	40.00	

Surikov (1848-1916), painter.

Mikhail Y. Lermontov.
Poet, Death
Centenary — A425

1941, July
850	A425	15k Prus green	4.25	1.65
851	A425	30k dark violet	5.75	2.25
		Set, never hinged	15.00	

Visitors in Lenin
Museum
A426

Lenin Museum
A427

1941-42
852	A426	15k rose red	1.25	2.00
853	A427	30k dark violet ('42)	5.00	4.00
854	A426	45k Prus green	2.25	2.25
855	A427	1r orange brn ('42)	6.50	4.00
		Set, never hinged	25.00	

Fifth anniversary of Lenin Museum.

Mother's Farewell to a
Soldier Son ("Be a
Hero!") — A428

1941, Aug.
856	A428	30k carmine	10.00	10.00
		Never hinged	15.00	

Alisher
Navoi — A429

People's
Militia — A430

1942, Jan.
857	A429	30k brown	5.75	4.50
858	A429	1r dark violet	9.00	7.50
		Set, never hinged	20.00	

500th anniversary of the birth of Alisher Navoi, Uzbekian poet.

1941, Dec.   Typo.
859	A430	30k dull blue	30.00	30.00
		Never hinged	50.00	

Junior Lieutenant
Talalikhin
Ramming
German Plane in
Midair — A431

Captain Gastello
and Burning Plane
Diving into
Enemy Gasoline
Tanks — A432

Major General
Dovator and
Cossack Cavalry
in
Action — A433

Shura Chekalin
Fighting Nazi
Soldiers — A434

Nazi Soldiers Leading Zoya
Kosmodemjanskaja to her Death — A435

1942-44   Unwmk.   Photo.   Perf. 12
860	A431	20k bluish black	80	20
860A	A431	30k Prus grn ('44)	80	20
861	A432	30k bluish black	80	20
861A	A432	30k dp ultra ('44)	80	20
862	A433	30k black	80	20
863	A434	30k black	80	20
863A	A434	30k brt yel green ('44)	80	20
864	A435	30k black	80	20
864A	A435	30k rose vio ('44)	80	20
865	A434	1r slate green	3.75	1.75
866	A435	2r slate green	6.00	2.50
		Nos. 860-866 (11)	16.95	6.05
		Set, never hinged	10.00	

Issued to honor Soviet heroes.
For surcharges see Nos. C80-C81.

Anti-tank
Artillery
A436

Signal Corps in
Action
A437

Defense of
Leningrad
A440

Guerrilla
Fighters — A438

War
Worker — A439

Red Army
Scouts — A441

1942-43
867	A436	20k black	40	40
868	A437	30k sappire	70	48
869	A438	30k Prus green ('43)	70	48
870	A439	30k dull red brn ('43)	70	48
871	A440	60k blue black	1.75	1.60
872	A441	1r black brown	3.00	2.40
		Nos. 867-872 (6)	7.25	5.84
		Set, never hinged	10.00	

Women
Workers and
Soldiers
A442

Flaming Tank
A443

Women
Preparing Food
Shipments
A444

Sewing
Equipment for
Red
Army — A445

Anti-Aircraft
Battery in
Action — A446

1942-43   Typo.   Unwmk.
873	A442	20k dark blue	40	40
874	A443	20k dull rose violet	40	40
875	A444	30k brown violet ('43)	40	40
876	A445	45k dull rose red	85	85
877	A446	45k deep dull blue ('43)	85	85
		Nos. 873-877 (5)	2.90	2.90
		Set, never hinged	30.00	

Manufacturing
Explosives
A447

Designs: 10k, Agriculture. 15k, Group of Fighters. 20k, Storming the Palace. 30k, Lenin and Stalin. 60k, Tanks. 1r, Lenin. 2r, Revolution scene.

Inscribed: "1917 XXV 1942"

1943, Jan.   Photo.   Perf. 12
878	A447	5k black brown	18	15
879	A447	10k black brown	18	15
880	A447	15k blue black	18	15
881	A447	20k blue black	30	15
882	A447	30k black brown	30	15
883	A447	60k black brown	60	25
884	A447	1r dull red brown	95	50
885	A447	2r black	2.25	90
		Nos. 878-885 (8)	4.94	2.40
		Set, never hinged	10.00	

25th anniversary of October Revolution.

Mount St. Elias,
Alaska — A455

Bering Sea and
Bering's
Ship — A456

1943, Apr.
886	A455	30k chalky blue	40	15
887	A456	60k Prus green	65	15
888	A455	1r yellow green	1.40	38
889	A456	2r bister brown	2.75	65
		Set, never hinged	10.00	

200th anniv. of the death of Vitus Bering, explorer (1681-1741).

Medical
Corpsmen and
Wounded
Soldier — A457

Trench
Mortar — A458

Army
Scouts — A459

Repulsing Enemy
Tanks — A460

Snipers — A461

1943

890	A457	30k myrtle green	25	22
891	A458	30k brown bister	25	22
892	A459	30k myrtle green	25	22
893	A460	60k myrtle green	75	75
894	A461	60k chalky blue	75	75
	Nos. 890-894 (5)		2.25	2.16
	Set, never hinged		5.00	

Maxim Gorki
(1868-1936),
Writer — A462

1943, June

895	A462	30k green	35	15
896	A462	60k slate black	45	22
	Set, never hinged		1.00	

Patriotic War
Medal
A463

Order of Field
Marshal Suvorov
A464

1943, July   Engr.

897	A463	1r black	1.00	1.00
898	A464	10r dk olive green	4.00	4.00
	Set, never hinged		6.00	

Sailors — A465

Designs: 30k, Navy gunner and warship. 60k,
Soldiers and tank.

1943, Oct.   Photo.

899	A465	20k golden brown	15	15
900	A465	30k dark myrtle green	15	15
901	A465	60k brt yellow green	30	18
902	A465	3r chalky blue	85	40
	Set, never hinged		2.50	

25th anniv. of the Red Army and Navy.

Karl Marx   Vladimir V.
A468   Mayakovsky
                       A469

1943, Sept.

903	A468	30k blue black	40	25
904	A468	60k dk slate green	60	25
	Set, never hinged		1.50	

125th anniv. of the birth of Karl Marx.

1943, Oct.

905	A469	30k red orange	30	25
906	A469	60k deep blue	40	25
	Set, never hinged		1.00	

Mayakovsky, poet, 50th birth anniv.

Flags of US,
Britain, and
USSR — A470

1943, Nov.

907	A470	30k black, dp red & dk blue	60	32
908	A470	3r sl blue, red & lt blue	2.50	85
	Set, never hinged		3.50	

The Tehran conference.

Ivan Turgenev (1818-
83), Poet — A471

1943, Oct.

909	A471	30k myrtle green	3.25	3.25
910	A471	60k dull purple	4.25	4.25
	Set, never hinged		12.50	

Map of
Stalingrad
A472

Harbor of
Sevastopol and
Statue of
Lenin — A473

Leningrad
A474

Odessa — A475

1944, Mar.   Perf. 12

911	A472	30k dull brown & car	25	15
912	A473	30k dark blue	25	15
913	A474	30k dk slate green	25	15
914	A475	30k yel green	25	15
	Set, never hinged		1.50	

Honoring the defenders of Stalingrad, Leningrad,
Sevastopol and Odessa.
See No. 959.
No. 911 measures 33x22mm and also exists in
smaller size: 32x21½mm.

USSR War
Heroes — A476

1944, Apr.

915	A476	30k deep ultra	35	25
	Never hinged		50	

Sailor Loading   Tanks — A478
Gun — A477

Soldier
Bayoneting a
Nazi
A479

Infantryman
A480

Soldier Throwing Hand
Grenade — A481

1943-44   Photo.

916	A477	15k deep ultra	15	15
917	A478	20k red orange ('44)	15	15
918	A479	30k dull brn & dk red ('44)	20	15
919	A480	1r brt yel green	55	35
920	A481	2r Prus green ('44)	85	70
	Nos. 916-920 (5)		1.90	1.50
	Set, never hinged		3.00	

25th anniversary of the Young Communist
League (Komsomol).

Flags of US, USSR, Great
Britain — A482

1944, May 30   Unwmk.   Perf. 12

921	A482	60k black, red & blue	60	30
922	A482	3r dk bl, red & lt bl	3.25	1.10
	Set, never hinged		4.75	

Day of the Nations United Against Germany,
June 14, 1944.

Patriotic War   Order of Prince
Order — A483   Alexander
                         Nevsky — A484

Order of Field   Order of Field
Marshal Suvorov   Marshal Kutuzov
A485   A486

Paper with network as in parenthesis

1944   Typo.   Perf. 12, Imperf.

923	A483	15k dull red *(rose)*	15	15
924	A484	20k blue *(lt blue)*	18	15
925	A485	30k green *(green)*	20	16
926	A486	60k dull red *(rose)*	45	35
	Set, never hinged		1.75	

Order of   Order of Prince,
Patriotic   Alexander
War — A487   Nevski — A488

Order of Field   Order of Field
Marshal Kutuzov   Marshal
A489   Suvorov
                          A490

1944, June   Unwmk.   Engr.   Perf. 12

927	A487	1r black	22	18
928	A488	3r blue black	55	42
929	A489	5r dark olive green	95	60
930	A490	10r dark red	1.65	70
	Set, never hinged		4.00	

Types of 1934, Inscribed 1924-1944 and

Lenin's Mausoleum — A491

Designs: 30k (No. 931), 3r, Lenin and Stalin.
50k, Lenin in middle age. 60k, Lenin, the orator.

1944, June — Photo.

931	A190	30k orange & car	15	18
932	A186	30k slate & black	15	18
933	A187	45k slate & black	22	28
934	A187	50k slate & black	25	28
935	A187	60k slate & black	28	28
936	A491	1r indigo & brown black	65	40
937	A190	3r bl blk & dull org	1.75	85
	Nos. 931-937 (7)		3.45	
	Set value			1.00
	Set, never hinged		5.00	

20 years without Lenin.

Nikolai Rimski-Korsakov
A492   A493

1944, June — Perf. 12, Imperf.

938	A492	30k gray black	18	15
939	A493	60k slate green	30	15
940	A492	1r brt blue green	38	15
941	A493	3r purple	65	20
	Set value			55
	Set, never hinged		2.50	

Rimski-Korsakov (1844-1909), composer.

N.A. Schors
A494

Sergei A.
Chaplygin
A497

Heroes of the 1918 Civil War: No. 943, V.I. Chapayev. No. 944, S.G. Lazho.

1944, Sept. — Perf. 12

942	A494	30k gray black	25	15
943	A494	30k dark slate green	25	15
944	A494	30k brt yellow green	25	15
	Set value			36
	Set, never hinged		1.00	

See Nos. 1209-1211, 1403.

1944, Sept.

945	A497	30k gray	22	15
946	A497	1r lt brown	85	18
	Set value			26
	Set, never hinged		1.50	

75th anniversary of the birth of Sergei A. Chaplygin, scientist and mathematician.

Khanpasha
Nuradilov
A498

A. Matrosov
A499

F.
Louzan — A500

M. S. Polivanova
and N. V.
Kovshova
A501

Pilot B. Safonov — A502

1944, July

947	A498	30k slate green	15	15
948	A499	60k dull purple	30	24
949	A500	60k dull blue	30	24
950	A501	60k bright green	30	24
951	A502	60k slate black	45	24
	Nos. 947-951 (5)		1.50	1.11
	Set, never hinged		3.00	

Soviet war heroes.

Ilya E.
Repin — A503

Ivan A.
Krylov — A505

"Cossacks' Reply
to Sultan
Mohammed
IV" — A504

1944, Nov. — Perf. 12½, Imperf.

952	A503	30k slate green	30	18
953	A504	50k dk blue green	42	18
954	A504	60k chalky blue	42	18
955	A503	1r dk orange brown	60	20
956	A504	2r dark purple	1.25	30
	Nos. 952-956 (5)		2.99	1.04
	Set, never hinged		4.00	

I. E. Repin (1844-1930), painter.

1944, Nov. — Perf. 12

957	A505	30k yellow brown	15	15
958	A505	1r dk violet blue	24	15
	Set value			25
	Set, never hinged		55	

Krylov, fable writer, death centenary.

Leningrad Type
Souvenir Sheet

1944, Dec. 6 — Imperf.

959		Sheet of 4	4.00	3.75
	Never hinged		6.00	
a.	A474 30k dark slate green		40	40

Liberation of Leningrad, Jan. 27, 1944.

Partisan
Medal — A507

Order for
Bravery — A508

Order of Bogdan
Chmielnicki
A509

Order of Victory
A510

Order of
Ushakov
A511

Order of
Nakhimov
A512

Paper with network as in parenthesis
Perf. 12½, Imperf.

1945, Jan. — Typo.   Unwmk.

960	A507	15k black (green)	16	15
961	A508	30k dp blue (lt blue)	16	15
962	A509	45k dk blue	20	15
963	A510	60k dl rose (pale rose)	28	15
964	A511	1r dull blue (green)	40	18
965	A512	1r yel green (blue)	40	18
	Nos. 960-965 (6)		1.60	96
	Set, never hinged		3.00	

Aleksandr S.
Griboedov
A513

Red Army
Soldier
A514

1945, Jan. — Photo.   Perf. 12½

966	A513	30k dk slate green	28	18
967	A513	60k gray brown	55	28
	Set, never hinged		1.25	

Griboedov (1795-1829), poet & statesman.

1945, Mar.

968	A514	60k gray blk & henna	48	55
969	A514	3r gray blk & henna	1.50	1.10
	Set, never hinged		3.00	

Souvenir Sheet
Imperf

970		Sheet of 4	25.00	25.00
	Never hinged		30.00	
a.	A514 3r gray brown & henna		7.50	7.50

Second anniv. of victory at Stalingrad.

Order for
Bravery
A516

Order of Bogdan
Chmielnicki
A517

Order of Victory — A518

1945 — Engr.   Perf. 12

971	A516	1r indigo	35	15
972	A517	2r black	75	25
973	A518	3r henna	1.25	40
	Set, never hinged		3.25	

See Nos. 1341-1342. For overprints see Nos. 992, 1709.

A519

A520

A521

A522

A523

Battle
Scenes — A524

1945, Apr. — Photo.   Perf. 12½

974	A519	20k sl grn, org red & black	18	18
975	A520	30k blue blk & dull orange	20	20
976	A521	30k blue black	20	20
977	A522	60k orange red	35	35
978	A523	1r slate green & org red	52	52
979	A524	1r slate green	52	52
	Nos. 974-979 (6)		1.97	1.97
	Set, never hinged		3.50	

Red Army successes against Germany.

Parade in Red
Square, Nov. 7,
1941 — A525

Designs: 60k, Soldiers and Moscow barricade, Dec. 1941. 1r, Air battle, 1941.

1945, June

980	A525	30k dk blue violet	25	25
981	A525	60k olive black	42	42
982	A525	1r black brown	1.40	1.40
	Set, never hinged			

3rd anniversary of the victory over the Germans before Moscow.

Elite Guard
Badge and
Cannons
A528

Motherhood
Medal
A529

Stamps of Russia can be mounted in the annual Scott Russia and Commonwealth of Independent States supplement.

Motherhood Glory Order — A530

Mother-Heroine Order — A531

1945, Apr. **Typo.**
983 A528 60k red   40 25
    Never hinged   80

1945 **Perf. 12½, Imperf.**
Paper with network as in parenthesis
Size: 22x33¼mm
984 A529 20k brown (lt blue)   15 15
985 A530 30k yel brown (green)   22 15
986 A531 60k dull rose (pale rose)   40 15

Perf. 12½
Engr.
Size: 20x38mm
986A A529 1r blk brn (green)   40 15
986B A530 2r dp bl (lt blue)   89 32
986C A531 3r brn red (lt blue)   1.00 60
    Nos. 984-986C (6)   3.06 1.52
    Set, never hinged   4.00

Academy Building, Moscow A532

Academy at Leningrad and M. V. Lomonosov A533

1945, June **Photo.** **Perf. 12½**
987 A532 30k blue violet   35 15
    a. Horiz. pair, imperf. between 3.25
988 A533 2r grnsh black   1.25 55
    Set, never hinged   2.00

Academy of Sciences, 220th anniv.

Popov and his Invention A534

Aleksandr S. Popov A535

1945, July **Unwmk.**
989 A534 30k dp blue violet   42 16
990 A534 60k dark red   85 24
991 A535 1r yellow brown   1.50 35
    Set, never hinged   3.50

50th anniversary of the "invention of radio" by A. S. Popov.

ПРАЗДНИК ПОБЕДЫ

No. 973 Overprinted in Blue

9 мая 1945 года

1945, Aug. **Perf. 12**
992 A518 3r henna   1.00 50
    Never hinged   1.50

Victory of the Allied Nations in Europe.

Iakovlev Fighter — A536

Petliakov-2 Dive Bombers A537

Ilyushin-2 Bombers A538

Designs: Nos. 992A, 995, Iakovlev Fighter. Nos. 992B, 1000, Petliakov-2 dive bombers. Nos. 992C, 996, Ilyushin-2 bombers. Nos. 992D, 993, Petliakov-8 heavy bomber. Nos. 992E, 1001, Tupolev-2 bombers. Nos. 992F, 997, Ilyushin-4 bombers. Nos. 992G, 999, Polikarpov-2 biplane. Nos. 992H, 998, Lavochkin-7 fighters. Nos. 992I, 994, Iakovlev fighter in action.

1945-46 **Unwmk.** **Photo.** **Perf. 12**
992A A536 5k dk violet ('46)   30 18
992B A537 10k hn brn ('46)   30 18
992C A538 15k hn brn ('46)   40 18
992D A536 15k Prus brn ('46)   40 18
992E A538 20k gray brn ('46)   45 24
992F A538 30k violet ('46)   45 24
992G A538 30k brown ('46)   45 24
992H A538 50k blue vio ('46)   95 58
992I A536 60k dl bl vio ('46)   95 58
993 A536 1r gray black   2.00 1.25
994 A536 1r henna brown   2.00 1.25
995 A536 1r brown   2.00 1.25
996 A538 1r deep brown   2.00 1.25
997 A538 1r int black   2.00 1.25
998 A538 1r orange ver   2.00 1.25
999 A538 1r bright green   2.00 1.25
1000 A538 1r deep brown   2.00 1.25
1001 A538 1r violet blue   2.00 1.25
    Nos. 992A-1001 (18)   22.65 13.85
    Set, never hinged   30.00

Issue dates: Nos. 992A-992I, Mar. 26. Nos. 993-1001, Aug. 19.

Lenin
A545   A546

Various Lenin Portraits
Dated "1870-1945"

1945, Sept. **Perf. 12½**
1002 A545 30k bluish black   25 15
1003 A546 50k gray brown   30 15
1004 A546 60k orange brown   40 18
1005 A546 1r greenish black   65 22
1006 A546 3r sepia   2.00 60
    Nos. 1002-1006 (5)   3.60 1.30
    Set, never hinged   5.00

75th anniversary of the birth of Lenin.

Prince M. I. Kutuzov A550

Aleksandr Ivanovich Herzen A551

1945, Sept. 16
1007 A550 30k blue violet   35 20
1008 A550 60k brown   65 30
    Set, never hinged   1.50

Field Marshal Prince Mikhail Illarionovich Kutuzov (1745-1813).

1945, Oct. 26
1009 A551 30k dark brown   35 20
1010 A551 2r greenish black   1.10 40
    Set, never hinged   2.00

75th anniversary of the death of A. I. Herzen, author and revolutionist.

Ilya Mechnikov A552

Friedrich Engels A553

1945, Nov. 27
1011 A552 30k brown   35 20
1012 A552 1r greenish black   70 40
    Set, never hinged   2.00

Ilya I. Mechnikov, zoologist and bacteriologist (1845-1916).

1945, Nov. **Unwmk.** **Perf. 12½**
1013 A553 30k dark brown   45 20
1014 A553 60k Prussian green   60 30
    Set, never hinged   1.25

125th anniversary of the birth of Friedrich Engels, collaborator of Karl Marx.

Tank Leaving Assembly Line — A554

Designs: 30k, Harvesting wheat. 60k, Airplane designing. 1r, Moscow fireworks.

1945, Dec. 25 **Photo.**
1015 A554 20k indigo & brown   42 22
1016 A554 30k black & orange brn 42 22
1017 A554 60k brown & green   75 24
1018 A554 1r dk blue & orange   1.40 35
    Set, never hinged   6.00

Artillery Observer and Guns — A558

Heavy Field Pieces — A559

1945, Dec.
1019 A558 30k brown   45 35
1020 A559 60k sepia   1.00 65
    Set, never hinged   2.50

Artillery Day, Nov. 19, 1945.

> Catalogue values for unused stamps in this section, from this point to the end of the section, are for Never Hinged items.

Victory Medal — A560

Soldier with Victory Flag — A561

1946, Jan. 23
1021 A560 30k dk violet   30 20
1022 A560 30k brown   30 20
1023 A560 30k greenish black   65 20
1024 A560 60k henna   65 20
1025 A561 60k black & dull red   65 20
    Nos. 1021-1025 (5)   2.55 1.00

Arms of USSR — A562

Red Square — A563

1946, Feb. 10
1026 A562 30k henna   25 25
1027 A563 45k violet   35 25
1028 A562 60k greenish black   70 30

Elections to the Supreme Soviet of the USSR, Feb. 10, 1946.

Artillery in Victory Parade — A564

Victory Parade — A565

1946, Feb. 23
1029 A564 60k dark brown   50 20
1030 A564 2r dull violet   1.00 25
1031 A565 3r black & red   1.40 40

Issued to publicize the Victory Parade held in Moscow, June 24, 1945.

Order of Lenin — A566

Order of Red Star — A567

Medal of Hammer and Sickle A568

Order of Token of Veneration A569

Gold Star
Medal — A570

Order of Red
Banner — A571

Order of the Red
Workers'
Banner — A572

Paper with network as in parenthesis
1946 Unwmk. Typo. Perf. 12½x12

1032	A566	60k myrtle grn (green)	1.00 50
1033	A567	60k dk vio brn (brown)	1.00 50
1034	A568	60k plum (pink)	1.00 50
1035	A569	60k dp blue (green)	1.00 50
1036	A570	60k dk car (salmon)	1.00 50
1037	A571	60k red (salmon)	1.00 50
1038	A572	60k dk brn vio (buff)	1.00 50
		Nos. 1032-1038 (7)	7.00 3.50

See Nos. 1650-1654.

Workers'
Achievement of
Distinction
A573

Workers'
Gallantry
A574

Marshal's
Star — A575

Defense of
Soviet Trans-
Arctic
Regions — A576

Meritorious
Service in Battle
A577

Defense of
Caucasus
A578

Defense of
Moscow
A579

Bravery
A580

Paper with network as in parenthesis
1946

1039	A573	60k choc (salmon)	1.10 75
1040	A574	60k brown (salmon)	1.10 75
1041	A575	60k blue (pale blue)	1.10 75
1042	A576	60k dk green (green)	1.10 75
1043	A577	60k dk blue (green)	1.10 75
1044	A578	60k dk yel grn (grn)	1.10 75
1045	A579	60k car (pink)	1.10 75
1046	A580	60k dk violet (blue)	1.10 75
		Nos. 1039-1046 (8)	8.80 6.00

A581

Maxim
Gorki — A582

1946, June 18   Photo.

1047	A581	30k brown	15 15
1048	A582	60k dark green	55 15

10th anniversary of the death of Maxim Gorki
(Alexei M. Peshkov).

Kalinin
A583

Chebyshev
A584

1946, June

1049 A583 20k sepia   50 25

Mikhail Ivanovich Kalinin (1875-1946).

1946, May 25

1050	A584	30k brown	50 15
1051	A584	60k gray brown	65 15

Pafnuti Lvovich Chebyshev (1821-94),
mathematician.

View of
Sukhumi — A585

Sanatorium at
Sochi — A587

Designs: 30k, Promenade at Gagri. 45k, New
Afyon Sanatorium.

1946, June 18

1052	A585	15k dark brown	25 15
1053	A585	30k dk slate green	30 15
1054	A587	30k dark green	30 15
1055	A585	45k chestnut brown	50 16
		Set value	52

All-Union Parade of Physical
Culturists — A589

1946, July 21

1056 A589 30k dark green   4.00 2.25

Tank
Divisions in
Red Square
A590

1946, Sept. 8

1057	A590	30k dark green	60 32
1058	A590	60k brown	95 48

Honoring Soviet tankmen.

Belfry of Ivan
the Great,
Kremlin
A591

Bolshoi Theater,
Moscow
A592

Hotel
Moscow — A593

Red
Square
A597

Spasski Tower and
Statues of Minin and
Pozharski — A598

Designs (Moscow scenes): 20k, Bolshoi Theater,
Sverdlov Square. 45k, View of Kremlin. 50k, Lenin
Museum.

1946, Sept. 5

1059	A591	5k brown	28 15
1060	A592	10k sepia	48 15
1061	A593	15k chestnut	48 15
1062	A593	20k light brown	48 15
1063	A593	45k dark green	85 18
1064	A593	50k brown	85 25
1065	A597	60k blue violet	1.25 25
1066	A598	1r chestnut brown	1.75 25
		Nos. 1059-1066 (8)	6.42 1.53

Workers'
Achievement of
Distinction — A599

Workers'
Gallantry — A600

Partisan of the
Patriotic
War — A601

Defense of Soviet
Trans-Arctic
Regions — A602

Meritorious Service
in Battle — A603

Defense of
Caucasus — A604

Defense of
Moscow — A605

Bravery — A606

1946, Sept. 5   Engr.

1067	A599	1r dark violet brown	65 45
1068	A600	1r dark carmine	65 45
1069	A601	1r carmine	65 45
1070	A602	1r blue black	65 45
1071	A603	1r black	65 45
1072	A604	1r black brown	65 45
1073	A605	1r olive black	65 45
1074	A606	1r deep claret	65 45
		Nos. 1067-1074 (8)	5.20 3.60

See Nos. 1650-1654.

Give the
Country Each
Year: 127
Million Tons
of Grain — A607

60 Million Tons
of Oil — A608

60 Million Tons
of Steel — A610

500 Million
Tons of
Coal — A609

50 Million Tons
of Cast
Iron — A611

Perf. 12¹/₂x12

1946, Oct. 6	Photo.	Unwmk.		
1075	A607	5k olive brown	15	15
1076	A608	10k dk slate green	15	15
1077	A609	15k brown	15	15
1078	A610	20k dk blue violet	15	15
1079	A611	30k brown	32	16
		Set value	72	58

Symbols of Transportation, Map and
Stamps — A612

Early Soviet
Stamp — A613

Stamps of Soviet Russia — A614

1946, Nov. 6			**Perf. 12¹/₂**	
1080	A612	15k black & dk red	90	55
a.		Sheet of 4, imperf.	50.00	50.00
1081	A613	30k dk green & brn	1.40	60
a.		Sheet of 4, imperf.	50.00	50.00
1082	A614	60k dk green & blk	1.90	80
a.		Sheet of 4, imperf.	50.00	50.00

1st Soviet postage stamp, 25th anniv.

Lenin and
Stalin — A615

1946	Photo.	**Perf. 12¹/₂, Imperf.**		
1083	A615	30k dp brown org	1.25	1.25
a.		Sheet of 4, imperf.	25.00	17.50
1084	A615	30k dk green	1.25	1.25

29th anniversary of October Revolution.
Issue dates: Nos. 1083-1084 imperf., Nov. 6;
perf., Dec. 18. No. 1083a, June, 1947.

Dnieprostroy Dam and Power
Station — A616

1946, Dec. 23			**Perf. 12¹/₂**	
1085	A616	30k sepia	65	42
1086	A616	60k chalky blue	1.00	60

Aleksandr P. Karpinsky
A617

Nikolai A.
Nekrasov
A618

1947, Jan. 17			Unwmk.	
1087	A617	30k dark green	65	30
1088	A617	50k sepia	1.00	45

Karpinsky (1847-1936), geologist.

Canceled to Order
Canceled sets of new issues have
long been sold by the government. Values in the second ("used") column are
for these canceled-to-order stamps.
Postally used copies are worth more.

1946, Dec. 4				
1089	A618	30k sepia	40	20
1090	A618	60k brown	60	30

Nikolai A. Nekrasov (1821-1878), poet.

Lenin's
Mausoleum — A619

Lenin — A620

1947, Jan. 21				
1091	A619	30k slate blue	60	25
1092	A619	30k dark green	60	25
1093	A620	50k dark brown	85	25

23rd anniversary of the death of Lenin.
See Nos. 1197-1199.

F. P. Litke and
Sailing
Vessel — A621

N. M.
Przewalski, Mare
and
Foal — A622

1947, Jan. 27				
1094	A621	20k blue violet	38	16
1095	A621	20k sepia	38	16
1096	A622	60k olive brown	80	32
1097	A622	60k sepia	80	32

Soviet Union Geographical Society, cent.

Nikolai E.
Zhukovski
(1847-1921),
Scientist
A623

1947, Jan. 17				
1098	A623	30k sepia	42	20
1099	A623	60k blue violet	55	30

Stalin Prize
Medal — A624

1946, Dec. 21		Photo.		
1100	A624	30k black brown	1.50	60

Russian Soldier
A625

Military
Instruction
A626

Aviator, Sailor
and
Soldier — A627

Perf. 12x12¹/₂, 12¹/₂x12, Imperf.

1947, Feb. 23			Unwmk.	
1101	A625	20k sepia	32	20
1102	A626	30k slate blue	32	20
1103	A627	30k brown	32	20

29th anniversary of the Soviet Army.

Reprints
From here through 1953 many sets
exist in two distinct printings from different plates.

Arms of:

Russian Socialist
Federated Soviet
Republic — A628

Armenian
SSR — A629

Azerbaijan
SSR — A630

Byelorussian
SSR — A631

Estonian
SSR — A632

Georgian
SSR — A633

Karelo Finnish
SSR — A634

Kazakh
SSR — A635

Kirghiz
SSR — A636

Latvian
SSR — A637

Lithuanian
SSR — A638

Moldavian
SSR — A639

Tadzhkistan
SSR — A640

Turkmen
SSR — A641

Ukrainian
SSR — A642

Uzbek
SSR — A643

Soviet Union — A644

1947	Unwmk.	Photo.	**Perf. 12¹/₂**	
1104	A628	30k henna brown	40	25
1105	A629	30k chestnut	40	25
1106	A630	30k olive brown	40	25
1107	A631	30k olive green	40	25
1108	A632	30k violet black	40	25
1109	A633	30k dark vio brown	40	25
1110	A634	30k dark violet	40	25
1111	A635	30k deep orange	40	25
1112	A636	30k dark violet	40	25
1113	A637	30k yellow brown	40	25
1114	A638	30k dark olive green	40	25
1115	A639	30k dark vio brown	40	25
1116	A640	30k dark green	40	25
1117	A641	30k gray black	40	25
1118	A642	30k blue violet	42	25
1119	A643	30k brown	35	25

Litho.

1120	A644	1r dk brn, bl, gold & red	1.25	85
		Nos. 1104-1120 (17)	7.62	4.85

Aleksander S. Pushkin (1799-1837), Poet — A645

1947, Feb. **Photo.** *Perf. 12*
1121 A645 30k sepia 55 24
1122 A645 50k dk yellow green 75 26

Classroom A646

Parade of Women — A647

1947, Mar. 11
1123 A646 15k bright blue 1.00 60
1124 A647 30k red 1.25 90

Intl. Day of Women, Mar. 8, 1947.

Moscow Council Building A648

1947 *Perf. 12 1/2*
1125 A648 30k sep, gray blue & brick red 1.00 38

30th anniversary of the Moscow Soviet. Exists imperf. The imperf. exists also with gray blue omitted.
Both perf. and imperf. stamps exist in two sizes: 40x27mm and 41x27mm.

May Day Parade in Red Square A649

1947, June 10 *Perf. 12 1/2*
1126 A649 30k scarlet 42 35
1127 A649 1r dk olive green 1.10 55

Labor Day, May 1, 1947.

Nos. 1062 and 1064 to 1066 Overprinted in Red
800 лет Москвы 1147-1947 гг.

1947, Sept. *Perf. 12 1/2x12*
1128 A593 20k lt brown 75 15
1129 A593 50k brown 95 50
1130 A597 60k blue violet 1.25 60
1131 A598 1r chestnut brown 2.00 70

Overprint arranged in 4 lines on No. 1131.

Crimea Bridge, Moscow — A650

Gorki Street, Moscow A651

View of Kremlin, Moscow — A652

Designs: No. 1134, Central Telegraph Building. No. 1135, Kiev Railroad Station. No. 1136, Kazan Railroad Station. No. 1137, Kaluga St. No. 1138, Pushkin Square. 50k, View of Kremlin. No. 1141, Grand Kremlin Palace. No. 1142, "Old Moscow," by Vasnetsov. No. 1143, St. Basil Cathedral. 2r, View of Kremlin. 3r, View of Kremlin. 5r, Hotel Moscow and government building.

1947 **Photo.** *Perf. 12 1/2*
Various Frames, Dated 1147-1947
1132 A650 5k dk bl & dk brn 32 24
1133 A651 10k red brown & brn black 32 24
1134 A650 30k brown 45 24
1135 A650 30k dk Prus blue 45 24
1136 A650 30k ultra 45 24
1137 A650 30k dp yel green 45 24
1138 A651 30k yel green 45 24
1139 A650 50k dp yel green 60 35
1140 A652 60k red brown & brn blk 70 35
1141 A651 60k gray blue 70 35
1142 A651 1r dark violet 1.50 85
Typo.
Colors: Blue, Yellow and Red
1143 A651 1r multicolored 1.50 85
1144 A651 2r multicolored 2.75 1.75
1145 A650 3r multicolored 5.25 1.75
  a. Souv. sheet of 4, imperf. 25.00 20.00
1146 A650 5r multicolored 8.75 3.00
  Nos. 1132-1146 (15) 24.64 10.93

Nos. 1128-1146 for founding of Moscow, 800th anniv.
Nos. 1143-1146 were printed in a single sheet containing a row of each denomination plus a row of labels.

Karamyshevsky Dam — A653

Map Showing Moscow-Volga Canal — A654

Designs: No. 1148, Direction towers, Yakromsky Lock. 45k, Yakromsky Pumping Station. 50k, Khimki Station. 1r, Lock #8.

1947, Sept. 7 **Photo.**
1147 A653 30k sepia 65 15
1148 A653 30k red brown 65 15
1149 A653 45k henna brown 65 15
1150 A653 50k bright ultra 65 15
1151 A654 60k bright rose 65 15
1152 A653 1r violet 90 35
  Nos. 1147-1152 (6) 4.15 1.10

Moscow-Volga Canal, 10th anniversary.

Elektrozavodskaya Station — A655

Mayakovsky Station — A656

Planes and Flag — A657

Designs (Moscow Subway scenes): No. 1154, Ismailovsky Station. No. 1155, Sokol Station. No. 1156, Stalinsky Station. No. 1158, Kiev Station.

1947, Sept.
1153 A655 30k sepia 65 24
1154 A655 30k blue black 65 24
1155 A655 45k yellow brown 90 24
1156 A655 45k deep violet 90 24
1157 A656 60k henna brown 1.50 28
1158 A656 60k deep yellow green 1.50 28
  Nos. 1153-1158 (6) 6.10 1.52

1947, Sept. 1
1159 A657 30k deep violet 35 15
1160 A657 1r bright ultra 85 18

Day of the Air Fleet. For overprints see Nos. 1246-1247.

Spasski Tower, Kremlin — A658

Perf. 12 1/2
1947, Nov. **Unwmk.** **Typo.**
1161 A658 60k dark red 5.00 2.50

See No. 1260.

Agave Plant at Sukhumi A659

Gullripsh Sanatorium, Sukhumi A660

Peasants', Livadia — A661

New Riviera — A662

1947, Nov. **Photo.**
Russian sanatoria: No. 1166, Abkhasia, New Afyon. No. 1167, Kemeri, near Riga. No. 1168, Kirov Memorial, Kislovodsk. No. 1169, Voroshilov Memorial, Sochi. No. 1170, Riza, Gagri. No. 1171, Zapadugol, Sochi.

1162 A659 30k dark green 30 15
1163 A660 30k violet 30 15
1164 A661 30k olive 30 15
1165 A662 30k brown 30 15
1166 A660 30k red brown 30 15
1167 A660 30k black violet 30 15
1168 A660 30k bright ultra 30 15
1169 A660 30k dk brown violet 30 15
1170 A659 30k dk yel green 30 15
1171 A660 30k sepia 30 15
  Nos. 1162-1171 (10) 3.00
  Set value 1.25

Blast Furnaces, Constantine A663

Tractor Plant, Kharkov — A664

Tractor Plant, Stalingrad A665

Maxim Gorki Theater, Stalingrad A666

Designs: 20k, No. 1180, Kirov foundry, Makeevka. Nos. 1175, 1179, Agricultural machine plant, Rostov.

1947, Nov. *Perf. 12 1/2, Imperf.*
1172 A663 15k yellow brown 15 15
1173 A663 20k sepia 15 15
1174 A663 30k violet brown 30 18
1175 A663 30k dark green 30 18
1176 A664 30k brown 30 18
1177 A665 30k black brown 30 18
1178 A666 60k violet brown 65 32
1179 A665 60k violet brown 65 32
1180 A663 1r orange red 1.00 45
1181 A664 1r red 1.00 45
1182 A665 1r violet 1.00 45
  Nos. 1172-1182 (11) 5.80 3.01

Reconstruction of war-damaged cities and factories, and as Five-Year-Plan publicity.

Revolutionists — A667

Designs: 30k, No. 1185, Revolutionists. 50k, 1r, Industry. No. 1186, 2r, Agriculture.

1947, Nov. *Perf. 12 1/2, Imperf.*
Frame in Dark Red
1183 A667 30k greenish black 28 15
1184 A667 50k blue black 42 25
1185 A667 60k brown black 55 35
1186 A667 60k brown 55 52

1187	A667	1r black	90	65
1188	A667	2r greenish black	1.75	90
		Nos. 1183-1188 (6)	4.45	2.82

30th anniversary of October Revolution.

Palace of the Arts
(Winter Palace)
A668

Peter I
Monument
A669

Designs (Leningrad in 1947): 60k, Sts. Peter and Paul Fortress. 1r, Smolny Institute.

1948, Jan. 10   *Perf. 12¹/₂*

1189	A668	30k violet	80	40
1190	A669	50k dk slate green	1.50	45
1191	A668	60k sepia	1.50	75
1192	A669	1r dk brown violet	2.50	1.10

5th anniversary of the liberation of Leningrad from the German blockade.

Government
Building,
Kiev — A670

Designs: 50k, Dnieprostroy Dam. 60k, Wheat field and granary. 1r, Steel mill and coal mine.

1948, Jan. 25   *Perf. 12¹/₂*

1193	A670	30k indigo	1.00	25
1194	A670	50k violet	1.50	28
1195	A670	60k golden brown	2.00	32
1196	A670	1r sepia	3.25	65

30th anniversary of the Ukrainian Soviet Socialist Republic.

Lenin Types of 1947
Inscribed "1924-1948"

1948, Jan. 21   **Unwmk.**

1197	A619	30k brown violet	95	55
1198	A619	60k dark gray blue	2.00	70
1199	A620	60k deep yellow green	2.00	70

24th anniversary of the death of Lenin.

Vasili I.
Surikov — A672

Soviet Soldier
and
Artillery — A675

Fliers and
Planes — A676

1948, Feb. 15   **Photo.**   *Perf. 12*

| 1201 | A672 | 30k red brown | 1.25 | 75 |
| 1202 | A672 | 60k dark green | 2.50 | 1.25 |

Vasili Ivanovich Surikov, artist, birth cent.

1948, Feb. 23

Designs: No. 1206, Soviet sailor. 60k, Military class.

1205	A675	30k brown	1.10	50
1206	A675	30k gray	1.10	50
1207	A676	30k violet blue	1.10	50
1208	A676	60k red brown	1.75	75

Hero Types of 1944

Designs: No. 1209, N.A. Schors. No. 1210, V.I. Chapayev. No. 1211, S.G. Lazho.

1948, Feb. 23

1209	A494	60k deep green	1.00	65
1210	A494	60k yellow brown	1.00	65
1211	A494	60k violet blue	1.00	65

Nos. 1205-1211 for 30th anniv. of the Soviet army.

Karl Marx, Friedrich
Engels and
Communist
Manifesto — A677

1948, Apr.

| 1212 | A677 | 30k black | 30 | 15 |
| 1213 | A677 | 50k henna brown | 50 | 18 |

Centenary of the Communist Manifesto.

Miner — A678

Marine — A679

Aviator — A680

Woman
Farmer — A681

Arms of USSR
A682

Scientist
A683

Spasski Tower,
Kremlin — A684

Soldier — A685

1948   **Photo.**

1214	A678	5k sepia	1.25	75
1215	A679	10k violet	1.25	75
1216	A680	15k bright blue	1.65	1.10
1217	A681	20k brown	1.75	1.25
1218	A682	30k henna brown	1.90	1.25
1219	A683	45k brown violet	2.75	1.90
1220	A684	50k bright blue	4.25	3.25
1221	A685	60k bright green	6.25	4.75
		Nos. 1214-1221 (8)	21.05	15.00

See Nos. 1306, 1343-1347, 1689.

May
Day
Parade
in Red
Square
A686

1948, June 5   *Perf. 12*

| 1222 | A686 | 30k deep carmine rose | 1.00 | 80 |
| 1223 | A686 | 60k bright blue | 2.00 | 1.25 |

Labor Day, May 1, 1948.

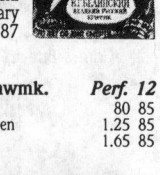

Vissarion G. Belinski
(1811-48), Literary
Critic — A687

1948, June 7   Unwmk.   *Perf. 12*

1224	A687	30k brown	80	85
1225	A687	50k dark green	1.25	85
1226	A687	60k purple	1.65	85

Aleksandr N. Ostrovski
A690   A691

1948, June 10   Photo.   *Perf. 12*

1227	A690	30k bright green	1.90	65
1228	A691	60k brown	2.25	1.10
1229	A691	1r brown violet	3.75	1.90

Ostrovski (1823-1886), playwright.
Exist imperf. Value, set $75.

Ivan I. Shishkin
(1832-1898),
Painter — A692

"Field of
Rye," by
Shishkin
A693

Design: 60k, "Bears in a Forest," by Shishkin.

Photo. (30k, 1r), Typo. (50k, 60k)
1948, June 12

1230	A692	30k dk grn & vio brn	1.75	60
1231	A693	50k multicolored	2.25	60
1232	A693	60k multicolored	4.00	75
1233	A692	1r brown & blue blk	6.00	1.10

Industrial
Expansion
A694

Public
Gathering at
Leningrad
A695

Photo., Frames Litho. in Carmine
1948, June 25

1234	A694	15k red brown	1.65	85
1235	A695	30k slate	2.25	1.25
1236	A694	60k brown black	3.50	1.90

Industrial five-year plan.

Planting
Crops — A696

Designs: No. 1238, 1r, Gathering vegetables. 45k, No. 1241, Baling cotton. No. 1242, Harvesting grain.

1948, July 12   **Photo.**

1237	A696	30k carmine rose	22	22
1238	A696	30k blue green	22	22
1239	A696	45k red brown	40	30
1240	A696	50k brown black	50	30
1241	A696	60k dark green	50	30
1242	A696	60k dk blue green	50	30
1243	A696	1r purple	85	50
		Nos. 1237-1243 (7)	3.19	2.14

Agricultural five-year plan.

Arms and
Citizens of
USSR — A697

Soviet
Miners — A698

Photo., Frames Litho. in Carmine
1948, July 25

| 1244 | A697 | 30k slate | 1.40 | 65 |
| 1245 | A697 | 60k greenish black | 1.65 | 85 |

25th anniv. of the USSR.

Nos. 1159 and 1160 Overprinted
in Red

ИЮЛЬ
1948
года

1948, Aug. 24   *Perf. 12¹/₂*

| 1246 | A657 | 30k deep violet | 1.75 | 1.25 |
| 1247 | A657 | 1r bright ultra | 1.75 | 1.25 |

Air Fleet Day, 1948. On sale one day.

1948, Aug.   Photo.   *Perf. 12¹/₂x12*

Miner's Day, Aug. 29: 60k, Scene in mine. 1r, Miner's badge.

1248	A698	30k blue	25	15
1249	A698	60k purple	50	20
1250	A698	1r green	80	25

A. A. Zhdanov
A699

Soviet Sailor
A700

1948, Sept. 3

| 1251 | A699 | 40k slate | 75 | 35 |

Andrei A. Zhdanov, statesman, 1896-1948.

1948, Sept. 12   *Perf. 12*

| 1252 | A700 | 30k blue green | 1.00 | 1.25 |
| 1253 | A700 | 60k bright blue | 3.00 | 2.00 |

Navy Day, Sept. 12.

Slalom
A701

Motorcyclist
A702

Designs: No. 1254, Foot race. 30k, Soccer game. 45k, Motorboat race. 50k, Diving.

1948, Sept. 15   Perf. 12½x12

1253A	A701	15k dark blue	95	24
1254	A702	15k violet	95	24
1254A	A702	20k dk slate blue	1.10	24
1255	A701	30k brown	1.25	24
1256	A701	45k sepia	1.40	24
1257	A702	50k blue	2.25	32
		Nos. 1253A-1257 (6)	7.90	1.52

Tankmen
Group — A703

Design: 1r, Tank parade.

1948, Sept. 25

1258	A703	30k sepia	2.00	1.25
1259	A703	1r rose	5.25	1.65

Day of the Tankmen, Sept. 25.

Spasski Tower Type of 1947

1948   Litho.   Perf. 12x12½

1260	A658	1r brown red	1.10	30

No. 1260 was re-issued in 1954-56 in slightly smaller format: 14½x21½mm, instead of 14¾x22mm and in a paler shade. See note after No. 738.

Train — A704

Transportation 5-year plan: 60k, Auto and bus at intersection. 1r, Steamships at anchor.

1948, Sept. 30 Photo.   Perf. 12½x12

1261	A704	30k brown	3.25	1.40
1262	A704	50k dark green	4.50	1.65
1263	A704	60k blue	7.50	1.65
1264	A704	1r blue violet	9.50	2.75

Horses — A705

Livestock 5-year plan: 60k, Dairy farm.

1948, Sept. 30   Perf. 12

1265	A705	30k slate gray	1.50	1.10
1266	A705	60k bright green	2.50	1.75
1267	A705	1r brown	3.50	2.25

Pouring Molten
Metal — A706

Heavy
Machinery
Plant — A707

Designs: 60k, 1r, Iron pipe manufacture.

1948, Oct. 14   Perf. 12½

1268	A706	30k purple	1.25	60
1269	A706	30k brown	1.50	80
1270	A706	60k carmine	1.75	1.25
1271	A706	1r dull blue	3.50	2.00

1948, Oct. 14

Design: 60k, Pump station interior.

1272	A707	30k purple	90	45
1273	A707	50k sepia	1.75	1.10
1274	A707	60k brown	2.25	1.25

Nos. 1268-1274 publicize the 5-year plan for steel, iron and machinery industries.

Khachatur Abovian
(1809-1848), Armenian
Writer and Poet — A708

1948, Oct. 16   Perf. 12x12½

1275	A708	40k purple	2.75	2.50
1276	A708	50k deep green	3.25	2.50

Farkhatz
Hydroelectric
Station — A709

Design: 60k, Zouiev Hydroelectric Station.

1948, Oct. 24   Perf. 12½

1277	A709	30k green	95	85
1278	A709	60k red	2.25	1.50
1279	A709	1r carmine rose	4.00	2.50

Electrification five-year plan.

Coal
Mine — A710

Designs: #1282, 1r, Oil field and tank cars.

1948, Oct. 24

1280	A710	30k sepia	1.90	60
1281	A710	60k brown	2.00	90
1282	A710	60k red brown	2.00	90
1283	A710	1r blue green	4.00	2.00

Coal mining and oil production 5-year plan.

Flying Model
Planes — A712

Pioneers
Saluting — A714

Marching
Pioneers
A713

Designs: 60k, Pioneer bugler. 1r, Pioneers at campfire.

1948, Oct. 26   Perf. 12½

1284	A712	30k dark blue green	3.25	2.00
1285	A713	45k dark violet	4.25	2.25
1286	A714	45k deep carmine	4.25	2.25

1287	A714	60k deep ultra	5.25	3.25
1288	A713	1r deep blue	13.00	5.50
		Nos. 1284-1288 (5)	30.00	15.25

Young Pioneers, a Soviet youth organization, and governmental supervision of children's summer vacations.

Marching
Youths
A715

Farm
Girl — A716

League Members
and Flag — A717

Designs: 50k, Communist students. 1r, Flag and badges. 2r, Young worker.

1948, Oct. 29   Perf. 12½
Inscribed: "1918 1948 XXX"

1289	A715	20k violet brown	80	80
1290	A716	25k rose red	1.25	1.00
1291	A716	40k brown & red	1.90	1.25
1292	A715	50k blue green	3.25	1.65
1293	A717	1r multicolored	6.00	3.50
1294	A716	2r purple	12.00	7.00
		Nos. 1289-1294 (6)	25.20	15.20

30th anniversary of the Young Communist League (Komsomol).

Stage of
Moscow Art
Theater — A719

K. S. Stanislavski,
V. I. Nemirovich
Danchenko — A720

1948, Nov. 1   Perf. 12½

1295	A719	40k gray blue	2.25	1.50
1296	A720	1r violet brown	3.00	2.50

Moscow Art Theater, 50th anniv.

Flag and Moscow
Buildings — A721

1948, Nov. 7   Perf. 12½

1297	A721	40k red	1.50	1.25
1298	A721	1r green	2.25	1.75

31st anniversary of October Revolution.

House of Unions,
Moscow
A722

Player's Badge
(Rook and
Chessboard)
A723

1948, Nov. 20   Perf. 12½

1299	A722	30k greenish blue	65	35
1300	A723	40k violet	1.50	45
1301	A722	50k orange brown	2.00	60

16th Chess Championship.

Artillery
Salute — A724

1948, Nov. 19   Perf. 12½

1302	A724	30k blue	1.25	1.00
1303	A724	1r rose carmine	1.75	1.65

Artillery Day, Nov. 19, 1948.

Vasili Petrovich
Stasov — A725

Stasov and Barracks of
Paul's Regiment,
Petrograd — A726

1948, Nov. 27   Unwmk.

1304	A725	40k brown	1.00	50
1305	A726	1r sepia	2.00	75

Stasov (1769-1848), architect.

Arms Type of 1948

1948   Litho.   Perf. 12x12½

1306	A682	40k brown red	3.50	20

Y. M. Sverdlov
Monument
A727

Design: 40k, Lenin Street, Sverdlovsk.

1948   Photo.   Perf. 12½

1307	A727	30k blue	18	15
1308	A727	40k purple	30	15
1309	A727	1r bright green	65	15
		Set value		35

225th anniv. of the city of Sverdlovsk (before 1924, Ekaterinburg). Exist imperf.

"Swallow's
Nest," Crimea
A729

Hot Spring,
Piatigorsk
A730

Shoreline, Sukhumi — A731   Tree-lined Walk, Sochi — A732

Formal Gardens, Sochi — A733

Stalin Highway, Sochi — A734

Colonnade, Kislovodsk — A735

Seascape, Gagri — A736

1948, Dec. 30   *Perf. 12 1/2*
1310	A729	40k brown	65	15
1311	A730	40k bright red violet	65	15
1312	A731	40k dark green	65	15
1313	A732	40k violet	65	15
1314	A733	40k dark purple	65	15
1315	A734	40k dark blue green	65	15
1316	A735	40k bright blue	65	15
1317	A736	40k dark blue green	65	15
		Nos. 1310-1317 (8)	5.20	1.20

Byelorussian S.S.R. Arms — A737

1949, Jan. 4
1318	A737	40k henna brown	1.50	90
1319	A737	1r blue green	3.50	1.75

Byelorussian SSR, 30th anniv.

Mikhail V. Lomonosov — A738   Lomonosov Museum, Leningrad — A739

1949, Jan. 10
1320	A738	40k red brown	1.10	90
1321	A738	50k green	1.50	90
1322	A739	1r deep blue	3.00	2.25

Cape Dezhnev (East Cape) — A740

Design: 1r, Map and Dezhnev's ship.

1949, Jan. 30
1323	A740	40k olive green	5.50	3.25
1324	A740	1r gray	9.50	6.50

300th anniv. of the discovery of the strait between Asia and America by S. I. Dezhnev.

Souvenir Sheet

A741

1949, Dec.   *Imperf.*
1325	A741	Sheet of 4	125.00	125.00
a.		40k Stalin's birthplace, Gorki	12.00	18.00
b.		40k Lenin & Stalin, Leningrad, 1917	12.00	18.00
c.		40k Lenin & Stalin, Gorki	12.00	18.00
d.		40k Marshal Stalin	12.00	18.00
		Hinged	85.00	

70th birthday of Joseph V. Stalin.

Lenin Mausoleum — A742

1949, Jan. 21   *Perf. 12 1/2*
1326	A742	40k ol green & org brown	2.25	1.50
1327	A742	1r gray black & org brown	5.00	2.75
a.		Sheet of 4	150.00	150.00

25th anniversary of the death of Lenin. No. 1327a exists imperf. Value $425.

Admiral S. O. Makarov — A743   Kirov Military Medical Academy — A744

Professors Botkin, Pirogov and Sechenov — A745

1949, Mar. 15
1328	A743	40k blue	1.65	90
1329	A743	1r red brown	2.25	1.40

Centenary of the birth of Admiral Stepan Osipovich Makarov, shipbuilder.

1949, Mar. 24
1330	A744	40k red brown	1.40	1.00
1331	A745	50k blue	2.00	1.50
1332	A744	1r blue green	3.00	2.25

150th anniversary of the foundation of Kirov Military Medical Academy, Leningrad.

Soviet Soldier — A746

1949, Mar. 16   Photo.
1333	A746	40k rose red	5.00	4.50

31st anniversary of the Soviet army.

Textile Weaving — A747   Political Leadership — A748

Designs: 25k, Preschool teaching, No. 1337, School teaching, No. 1338, Farm women. 1r, Women athletes.

1949, Mar. 8   *Perf. 12 1/2*
Inscribed: "8 МАРТА 1949г"
1334	A747	20k dark violet	15	15
1335	A747	25k blue	28	15
1336	A747	40k henna brown	42	15
1337	A747	50k slate gray	70	28
1338	A747	50k brown	70	28
1339	A747	1r green	1.65	45
1340	A748	2r copper red	2.50	1.40
		Nos. 1334-1340 (7)	6.40	2.86

International Women's Day, Mar. 8.

Medal Types of 1945

1948-49   Engr.
1341	A517	2r green ('49)	1.75	85
1341A	A517	2r violet brown	6.75	6.00
1342	A518	3r brown car ('49)	2.25	85

For overprint see No. 1709.

Types of 1948

1949   Litho.   *Perf. 12x12 1/2*
1343	A678	15k black	32	15
1344	A681	20k green	32	15
1345	A680	25k dark blue	50	15
1346	A683	30k brown	60	20
1347	A684	50k deep blue	1.50	55
		Nos. 1343-1347 (5)	3.24	1.20

The 20k, 25k and 30k were re-issued in 1954-56 in slightly smaller format. The 20k measures 14x21mm, instead of 15x22mm; 25k, 14 1/2x21mm, instead of 14 1/2x21 3/4mm, and 30k, 14 1/2x21mm, instead of 15x22mm.

The smaller-format 20k is olive green, the 25k, slate blue. The 15k was reissued in 1959 (?) in smaller format: 14x21mm, instead of 14 1/2x22mm. See note after No. 738.

See No. 1709.

Vasili R. Williams (1863-1939), Agricultural Scientist — A749

1949, Apr. 18   Photo.   *Perf. 12 1/2*
1348	A749	25k blue green	1.50	1.25
1349	A749	50k brown	2.50	1.90

Russian Citizens and Flag — A750   A. S. Popov and Radio — A751

Popov Demonstrating Radio to Admiral Makarov — A752

1949, Apr. 30   *Perf. 12 1/2*
1350	A750	40k scarlet	1.00	65
1351	A750	1r blue green	2.00	1.25

Labor Day, May 1, 1949.

1949, May   Unwmk.
1352	A751	40k purple	1.25	48
1353	A752	50k brown	2.00	65
1354	A751	1r blue green	4.00	1.25

54th anniversary of Popov's discovery of the principles of radio.

Soviet Publications — A753

Reading Pravda — A754

1949, May 4
1355	A753	40k crimson	1.75	1.25
1356	A754	1r dark violet	2.75	1.50

Soviet Press Day.

Ivan V. Michurin — A755   A. S. Pushkin, 1822 — A756

Pushkin Reading Poem — A757

1949, July 28
1357	A755	40k blue gray	1.75	50
1358	A755	1r bright green	3.50	1.10

Michurin (1855-1925), agricultural scientist.

1949, June   Unwmk.

Designs: No. 1360, Pushkin portrait by Kiprensky, 1827. 1r, Pushkin Museum, Boldino.
1359	A756	25k indigo & sepia	60	55
1360	A756	40k org brn & sepia	1.50	1.25
a.		Souv. sheet of 4, 2 each #1361, 1363, imperf.	30.00	16.00
1361	A757	40k brn red & dk violet	1.50	1.40
1362	A757	1r choc & slate	3.25	3.00
1363	A757	2r brown & vio bl	5.50	5.00
		Nos. 1359-1363 (5)	12.35	11.20

150th anniversary of the birth of Aleksander S. Pushkin.

Horizontal rows of Nos. 1361 and 1363 contain alternate stamps and labels.

No. 1360a issued July 20.

River Tugboat — A758

Design: 1r, Freighter, motorship "Bolshaya Volga."

1949, July, 13

1364	A758	40k slate blue	3.00 2.75
1365	A758	1r red brown	4.50 4.00

Centenary of the establishment of the Sormovo Machine and Boat Works.

VCSPS No. 3, Kislovodsk A759

State Sanatoria for Workers: No. 1367, Communications, Khosta. No. 1368, Sanatorium No. 3, Khosta. No. 1369, Electric power, Khosta. No. 1370, Sanatorium No. 1, Kislovodsk. No. 1371, State Theater, Sochi. No. 1372, Frunze Sanatorium, Sochi. No. 1373, Sanatorium at Machindzhaury. No. 1374, Clinical, Chaltubo. No. 1375, Sanatorium No. 41, Zheleznovodsk.

1949, Sept. 10   Photo.   Perf. 12½

1366	A759	40k violet	25 15
1367	A759	40k black	25 15
1368	A759	40k carmine	25 15
1369	A759	40k blue	25 15
1370	A759	40k violet brown	25 15
1371	A759	40k red orange	25 15
1372	A759	40k dark brown	25 15
1373	A759	40k green	25 15
1374	A759	40k red brown	25 15
1375	A759	40k blue green	25 15
	Nos. 1366-1375 (10)		2.50
	Set value		1.00

Regatta — A760

Designs (Sports, "1949"): 25k, Kayak race. 30k, Swimming. 40k, Bicycling. No. 1380, Soccer. 50k, Mountain climbing. 1r, Parachuting. 2r, High jump.

1949, Aug. 7

1376	A760	20k bright blue	38 30
1377	A760	25k blue green	50 15
1378	A760	30k violet	70 15
1379	A760	40k red brown	95 15
1380	A760	40k green	95 15
1381	A760	50k dk blue gray	1.00 15
1382	A760	1r carmine rose	1.65 60
1383	A760	2r gray black	3.75 80
	Nos. 1376-1383 (8)		9.88
	Set value		1.70

V. V. Dokuchayev and Fields — A761

1949, Aug. 8

1384	A761	40k brown	40 30
1385	A761	1r green	85 50

Vasili V. Dokuchayev (1846-1903), pioneer soil scientist.

Vasili Bazhenov and Lenin Library, Moscow A762

1949, Aug. 14   Photo.   Perf. 12½

1386	A762	40k violet	90 28
1387	A762	1r red brown	1.65 40

Bazhenov, architect, 150th death anniv.

A. N. Radishchev A763   Ivan P. Pavlov A764

1949, Aug. 31

1388	A763	40k blue green	1.10 75
1389	A763	1r gray	2.50 1.65

200th anniversary of the birth of Aleksandr N. Radishchev, writer.

1949, Sept. 30   Unwmk.

1390	A764	40k deep brown	50 25
1391	A764	1r gray black	1.25 35

Pavlov (1849-1936), Russian physiologist.

Globe Encircled by Letters A765

1949, Oct.   Perf. 12½

1392	A765	40k org brn & indigo	50 15
a.		Imperf.	3.00 2.25
1393	A765	50k indigo & gray vio	50 15
a.		Imperf.	3.00 2.25

75th anniv. of the UPU.

Cultivators A766

Map of European Russia — A767

Designs: No. 1395, Peasants in grain field. 50k, Rural scene. 2r, Old man and children.

1949, Oct. 18   Perf. 12½

1394	A766	25k green	60 42
1395	A766	40k violet	1.25 85
1396	A767	40k gray grn & blk	1.25 85
1397	A766	50k deep blue	1.75 1.10
1398	A766	1r gray black	3.00 1.90
1399	A766	2r dark brown	7.00 4.50
	Nos. 1394-1399 (6)		14.85 9.62

Encouraging agricultural development. Nos. 1394, 1398, 1399 measure 33x19mm. Nos. 1395, 1397 measure 33x22mm.

Maly (Little) Theater, Moscow A768

M. N. Ermolova, I. S. Mochalov, A. N. Ostrovski, M. S. Shchepkin and P. M. Sadovsky A769

1949, Oct. 27

1400	A768	40k green	80 25
1401	A768	50k red orange	1.00 25
1402	A769	1r deep brown	1.90 45

125th anniversary of the Maly Theater (State Academic Little Theater).

Chapayev Type of 1944

1949, Oct. 22   Photo.

1403	A494	40k brown orange	4.50 2.75

30th anniversary of the death of V. I. Chapayev, a hero of the 1918 civil war.

Portrait and outer frame same as type A494. Dates "1919 1949" are in upper corners. Other details differ.

125th Anniv. of the Birth of Ivan Savvich Nikitin, Russian Poet (1824-1861) — A770

1949, Oct. 24   Unwmk.

1404	A770	40k brown	80 18
1405	A770	1r slate blue	1.25 30

Spasski Tower and Russian Citizens A771

1949, Oct. 29   Perf. 12½

1406	A771	40k brown orange	2.75 1.50
1407	A771	1r deep green	4.75 2.50

October Revolution, 32nd anniversary.

Sheep, Cattle and Farm Woman A772

1949, Nov. 2

1408	A772	40k chocolate	50 15
1409	A772	1r violet	1.00 28

Encouraging better cattle breeding in Russia.

Arms and Flag of USSR — A773

1949, Nov. 30   Engr.   Perf. 12

1410	A773	40k carmine	7.00 3.25

Constitution Day.

Electric Trolley Car — A774   Ski Jump — A775

Designs: 40k, 1r, Diesel train. 50k, Steam train.

1949, Nov. 19   Photo.   Perf. 12½

1411	A774	25k red	90 15
1412	A774	40k violet	1.10 15
1413	A774	50k brown	1.75 15
1414	A774	1r Prus green	4.00 32

1949, Nov. 12   Unwmk.

Designs: 40k, Girl on rings. 50k, Ice hockey. 1r, Weight lifter. 2r, Wolf hunt.

1415	A775	20k dark green	70 15
1416	A775	40k orange red	1.25 15
1417	A775	50k deep blue	2.00 15
1418	A775	1r red	2.50 25
1419	A775	2r violet	5.50 80
	Nos. 1415-1419 (5)		11.95 1.50

Textile Mills — A776

Designs: 25k, Irrigation system. 40k, 1r, Government buildings, Stalinabad. 50k, University of Medicine.

1949, Dec. 7   Photo.   Perf. 12

1420	A776	20k blue	38 15
1421	A776	25k green	42 15
1422	A776	40k red orange	50 20
1423	A776	50k violet	75 24
1424	A776	1r gray black	1.40 48
	Nos. 1420-1424 (5)		3.45 1.22

Tadzhik Republic, 20th anniv.

"Russia" versus "War" — A777   Byelorussians and Flag — A778

1949, Dec. 25

1425	A777	40k rose carmine	40 15
1426	A777	50k blue	55 22

Issued to portray Russia as the defender of world peace.

1949, Dec. 23   Unwmk.

Design: No. 1428, Ukrainians and flag.

Inscribed: "1939 1949"

1427	A778	40k orange red	3.00 2.25
1428	A778	40k deep orange	3.00 2.25

Return of western territories to the Byelorussian and Ukrainian Republics, 10th anniv.

Teachers College A779

Designs: 25k, State Theater. No. 1431, Government House. No. 1432, Navol Street, Tashkent. 1r, Fergana Canal. 2r, Kuigonyarsk Dam.

1950, Jan. 3

1429	A779	20k blue	35 15
1430	A779	25k gray black	35 15
1431	A779	40k red orange	75 22
1432	A779	40k violet	75 22
1433	A779	1r green	1.75 40
1434	A779	2r brown	3.50 50
	Nos. 1429-1434 (6)		7.45 1.64

Uzbek Republic, 25th anniversary.

Lenin at Razliv — A780

Lenin's Office, Kremlin A781

Design: 1r, Lenin Museum.

1950, Jan. Unwmk. Litho. Perf. 12
1435 A780 40k dk green & dk brn   55   15
1436 A781 50k dk brn, red brn & green 90   20
1437 A781 1r dk brn, dk grn & cream   1.65 30

26th anniversary of the death of Lenin.

Textile Factory, Ashkhabad A782

Designs: 40k, 1r, Power dam and Turkmenian arms. 50k, Rug making.

1950, Jan. 7   Photo.
1438 A782 25k gray black   75   55
1439 A782 40k brown   1.10   85
1440 A782 50k green   1.65 1.25
1441 A782 1r purple   3.50 2.50

Turkmen Republic, 25th anniversary.

Motion Picture Projection A783

1950, Feb.
1442 A783 25k brown   10.00 4.00

Soviet motion picture industry, 30th anniv.

Voter A784

Kremlin A785

1950, Mar. 8
1443 A784 40k green, yellow   2.00 1.50
1444 A785 1r rose carmine   3.00 2.50

Supreme Soviet elections, Mar. 12, 1950.

Market value for a particular scarce stamp may remain relatively low if few collectors want it.

Morozov Monument, Moscow A786

Globes and Communication Symbols A787

1950, Mar. 16   Perf. 12½
1445 A786 40k black brn & red   2.50 1.75
1446 A786 1r dk green & red   5.00 3.00

Unveiling of a monument to Pavlik Morozov, Pioneer.

1950, Apr. 1
1447 A787 40k deep green   2.25 2.00
1448 A787 50k deep blue   2.75 2.00

Meeting of the Post, Telegraph, Telephone and Radio Trade Unions.

State Polytechnic Museum A788

State Museum of Oriental Cultures A789

State University Museum — A790

Pushkin Museum A791

Museums: No. 1451, Tretiakov Gallery. No. 1452, Timiryazev Biology Museum. No. 1453, Lenin Museum. No. 1454, Museum of the Revolution. No. 1456, State History Museum.

Inscribed: "МОСКВА 1949" in Top Frame
1950, Mar. 28   Litho.   Perf. 12½
Multicolored Centers
1449 A788 40k dark blue   1.10   25
1450 A789 40k dark blue   1.10   25
1451 A789 40k green   1.10   25
1452 A789 40k dark brown   1.10   25
1453 A789 40k olive brown   1.10   25
1454 A789 40k claret   1.10   25
1455 A790 40k red   1.10   25
1456 A790 40k chocolate   1.10   25
1457 A791 40k brown violet   1.10   25
   Nos. 1449-1457 (9)   9.90 2.25

Soviets of Three Races A792

A. S. Shcherbakov A793

Design: 1r, Four Russians and communist banner, horiz.

1950, May 1   Photo.   Perf. 12½
1458 A792 40k org red & gray   2.50 1.65
1459 A792 1r red & gray black   5.00 3.25

Labor Day, May 1, 1950.

1950, May   Unwmk.
1460 A793 40k black, pale blue   90   70
1461 A793 1r dk green, buff   1.90 1.75

Shcherbakov, political leader (1901-1945).

Monument A794

Victory Medal A795

**   Perf. 12x12½**
1950   Photo.   Wmk. 293
1462 A794 40k dk brown & red   3.50 2.25
**   Unwmk.**
1463 A795 1r carmine rose   4.00 2.75

5th Intl. Victory Day, May 9, 1950.

A. V. Suvorov A796

Farmers Studying Agronomic Techniques A797

Designs: 50k, Suvorov crossing Alps, 32½x47mm. 60k, Badge, flag and marchers, 24x39½mm. 2r, Suvorov facing left, 19x33½mm.

**Various Designs and Sizes
Dated "1800 1950"**
1950   Perf. 12, 12½x12
1464 A796 40k blue, pink   1.40   75
1465 A796 50k brown, pink   1.75   90
1466 A796 60k gray black, pale gray   2.00 2.00
1467 A796 1r dk brn, lemon   3.50 2.00
1468 A796 2r greenish blue   6.25 5.00
   Nos. 1464-1468 (5)   14.90 10.65

Field Marshal Count Aleksandr V. Suvorov (1730-1800), 150th death anniv.

1950, June   Perf. 12½

Designs: No. 1470, 1r, Sowing on collective farm.

1469 A797 40k dk grn, pale grn 1.25   65
1470 A797 40k gray black, buff 1.25   65
1471 A797 1r blue, lemon   3.50 1.65

George M. Dimitrov A798

Opera and Ballet Theater, Baku A799

1950, July 2
1472 A798 40k gray black, citron 1.00   70
1473 A798 1r gray blk, salmon   2.50 1.40

Dimitrov (1882-1949), Bulgarian-born revolutionary leader and Comintern official.

1950, July   Photo.   Perf. 12½
Designs: 40k, Azerbaijan Academy of Science. 1r, Stalin Avenue, Baku.

1474 A799 25k dp green, citron   65   52
1475 A799 40k brown, pink   1.65   95
1476 A799 1r gray black, buff   4.75 3.50

Azerbaijan SSR, 30th anniversary.

Victory Theater A800

Lenin Street A801

Designs: 50k, Gorky Theater. 1r, Monument marking Stalingrad defense line.

1950, June
1477 A800 20k dark blue   60   40
1478 A801 40k green   1.10   80
1479 A801 50k red orange   1.50 1.25
1480 A801 1r gray   3.25 2.50

Restoration of Stalingrad.

Moscow Subway Stations: "Park of Culture" A802

Designs: No. 1482, Kaluzskaya station. No. 1483, Taganskaya. No. 1484, Kurskaya. No. 1485, Paveletskaya. No. 1486, Park of Culture. No. 1487, Taganskaya.

1950, July 30
**   Size: 33½x23mm**
1481 A802 40k deep carmine   90   15
1482 A802 40k dark green, buff 90   15
1483 A802 40k deep blue   90   15
1484 A802 1r dark brn, citron 1.90   52
1485 A802 1r purple   1.90   52
1486 A802 1r dark green, citron 1.90 52
**   Size: 33x18½mm**
1487 A802 1r black, pink   1.75   38
   Nos. 1481-1487 (7)   10.15 2.39

Socialist Peoples and Flags A803

1950, Aug. 4   Unwmk.   Perf. 12½
1488 A803 40k multicolored   90   15
1489 A803 50k deep blue, buff 1.90   20
1490 A803 1r multicolored   2.00   30

Trade Union Building, Riga — A804

Opera and Ballet Theater, Riga — A805

Designs: 40k, Latvian Cabinet building. 50k, Monument to Jan Rainis. 1r, Riga State Univ. 2r, Latvian Academy of Sciences.

1950   Photo.   Perf. 12½
1491 A804 25k dark brown   65   20
1492 A804 40k scarlet   90   48
1493 A804 50k dark green   2.00   48
1494 A805 60k deep blue   2.25   48

1495 A805	1r lilac	3.50 1.00
1496 A804	2r sepia	6.00 1.25
Nos. 1491-1496 (6)		15.30 3.89

Latvian SSR, 10th anniv.

Lithuanian Academy of Sciences — A806   Marite Melnik — A807

Design: 1r, Cabinet building.

1950
1497 A806	25k deep blue, *bluish*	1.40 48
1498 A807	40k brown	2.75 1.00
1499 A806	1r scarlet	6.00 2.50

Lithuanian SSR, 10th anniv.

Stalingrad Square, Tallinn A808   Victor Kingisepp A809

Designs: 40k, Government building, Tallinn. 50k, Estonia Theater, Tallinn.

1950
1500 A808	25k dark green	1.25 80
1501 A808	40k scarlet	1.50 95
1502 A808	50k blue, *yellow*	2.50 1.40
1503 A809	1r brown, *blue*	4.50 3.00

Estonian SSR, 10th anniv.

Citizens Signing Appeal for Peace A810   Children and Governess A811

Design: 50k, Peace Demonstration.

1950, Oct. 16   **Photo.**
1504 A810	40k red, *salmon*	75 70
1505 A811	40k black	75 70
1506 A811	50k dark red	1.40 1.00
1507 A810	1r brown, *salmon*	2.25 2.00

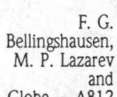

F. G. Bellingshausen, M. P. Lazarev and Globe — A812

Route of Antarctic Expedition — A813

1950, Oct. 25   **Unwmk.**   **Perf. 12½**
Blue Paper
1508 A812	40k dark carmine	14.00 7.50
1509 A813	1r purple	26.00 7.50

130th anniversary of the Bellingshausen-Lazarev expedition to the Antarctic.

M. V. Frunze — A814   M. I. Kalinin — A815

1950, Oct. 31
1510 A814	40k blue, *buff*	2.50 1.75
1511 A814	1r brown, *blue*	6.00 4.00

Frunze, military strategist, 25th death anniv.

1950, Nov. 20   **Engr.**
1512 A815	40k deep green	90 65
1513 A815	1r reddish brown	2.00 1.10
1514 A815	5r violet	4.50 2.00

75th anniversary of the birth of M. I. Kalinin, Soviet Russia's first president.

Gathering Grapes — A816

Armenian Government Building A817   G. M. Sundukian A818

1950, Nov. 29   **Photo.**   **Perf. 12½**
1515 A816	20k dp blue, *buff*	1.50 65
1516 A817	40k red org, *blue*	2.50 1.25
1517 A818	1r ol gray, *yellow*	6.00 3.00

Armenian Republic, 30th anniv. 1r also for birth of Sundukian, playwright.

Apartment Building, Koteljnicheskaya Quay — A819   Hotel, Kalanchevkaya Square — A820

Various Buildings
Inscribed: "Mockba, 1950"

1950, Dec. 2   **Unwmk.**
1518 A819	1r red brown, *buff*	19.00 15.00
1519 A819	1r gray black	19.00 15.00
1520 A819	1r brown, *blue*	19.00 15.00
1521 A819	1r dk green, *blue*	19.00 15.00
1522 A820	1r dp blue, *buff*	19.00 15.00
1523 A820	1r black, *buff*	19.00 15.00
1524 A820	1r red orange	19.00 15.00
1525 A819	1r dk grn, *yellow*	19.00 15.00
Nos. 1518-1525 (8)		152.00 120.00
Set, hinged		125.00

Skyscrapers planned for Moscow.

Spasski Tower, Kremlin — A821

1950, Dec. 4
1526 A821	1r dk grn, red brn & yel brown	10.00 3.00

October Revolution, 33rd anniversary.

Golden Autumn by Levitan — A822

I. I. Levitan (1861-90), Painter — A823

1950, Dec. 6   **Litho.**   **Perf. 12½**
1527 A822	40k multicolored	4.25 55

Perf. 12
Photo.
1528 A823	50k red brown	5.75 55

Black Sea by Aivazovsky — A824

Ivan K. Aivazovsky (1817-1900) Painter — A825

Design: 50k, "Ninth Surge."

1950, Dec. 6   **Litho.**
Multicolored Centers
1529 A824	40k chocolate	1.10 15
1530 A824	50k chocolate	1.10 40
1531 A825	1r indigo	1.50 90

Flags and Newspapers Iskra and Pravda — A826   Presidium of Supreme Soviet, Alma-Ata — A827

Design: 1r, Flag and profiles of Lenin and Stalin.

1950, Dec. 23   **Photo.**
1532 A826	40k gray blk & red	13.00 7.00
1533 A826	1r dk brn & red	17.00 11.00

1st issue of the newspaper Iskra, 50th anniv.

1950, Dec. 27

Design: 1r, Opera and Ballet Theater.

Inscribed: "ALMA-ATA" in Cyrillic
1534 A827	40k gray black, *blue*	7.25 50
1535 A827	1r red brn, *yellow*	7.50 2.50

Kazakh Republic, 30th anniversary. Cyrillic charcters for "ALMA-ATA" are above building in vignette on 40k, immediately below building on right on 1r.

Decembrists and Senatskaya Square, Leningrad A828

1950, Dec. 30   **Unwmk.**
1536 A828	1r black brn, *yellow*	7.00 4.00

Decembrist revolution of 1825.

Lenin at Razliv A829

Design: 1r, Lenin and young communists.

1951, Jan. 21   **Litho.**   **Perf. 12½**
Multicolored Centers
1537 A829	40k olive green	2.25 30
1538 A829	1r indigo	3.75 70

27th anniversary of the death of Lenin.

Mountain Pasture — A830

Government Building, Frunze — A831

1951, Feb. 2   **Photo.**   **Perf. 12½**
1539 A830	25k dk brown, *blue*	2.25 1.10
1540 A831	40k dp green, *blue*	2.75 1.65

Kirghiz Republic, 25th anniv.

Government Building, Tirana — A832

1951, Jan. 6   **Unwmk.**   **Perf. 12**
1541 A832	40k green, *bluish*	10.00 7.00

Honoring the Albanian People's Republic.

Bulgarians Greeting Russian Troops — A833

Lenin Square, Sofia — A834

Design: 60k, Monument to Soviet soldiers.

1951, Jan. 13
1542 A833 25k gray black, *bluish* 1.75 75
1543 A834 40k org red, *salmon* 3.25 1.50
1544 A834 60k blk brn, *salmon* 5.00 2.25

Honoring the Bulgarian People's Republic.

Choibalsan State University — A835

State Theater, Ulan Bator A836

Mongolian Republic Emblem and Flag — A837

1951, Mar. 12
1545 A835 25k purple, *salmon* 55 45
1546 A836 40k dp orange, *yellow* 1.10 45
1547 A837 1r multicolored 2.75 1.50

Honoring the Mongolian People's Republic.

D. A. Furmanov (1891-1926) Writer — A838

Furmanov at Work — A839

1951, Mar. 17   Perf. 12½
1548 A838 40k brown 2.00 65
1549 A839 1r gray black, *buff* 3.00 1.00

Russian War Memorial, Berlin — A840

1951, Mar. 21   Perf. 12
1550 A840 40k dk gray grn & dk red 4.00 1.00
1551 A840 1r brown blk & red 8.00 2.00

Stockholm Peace Conference.

Kirov Machine Works A841

1951, May 19   Photo.   Perf. 12½
1552 A841 40k brown, *cream* 3.00 2.00

Kirov Machine Works, 150th anniv.

Bolshoi Theater, Moscow — A842

Russian Composers A843

1951, May   Unwmk.
1553 A842 40k multicolored 3.50 42
1554 A843 1r multicolored 7.00 85

Bolshoi Theater, Moscow, 175th anniv.

Liberty Bridge, Budapest A844

Monument to Liberators A845

Budapest Buildings: 40k, Parliament. 60k, National Museum.

1951, June 9   Perf. 12
1555 A844 25k emerald 55 22
1556 A844 40k bright blue 90 40
1557 A844 60k sepia 1.25 1.00
1558 A845 1r sepia, *salmon* 2.25 1.65

Honoring the Hungarian People's Republic.

Harvesting Wheat — A846

Designs: 40k, Apiary. 1r, Gathering citrus fruits. 2r, Cotton picking.

1951, June 25
1559 A846 25k dark green 45 28
1560 A846 40k green, *bluish* 60 28
1561 A846 1r brown, *yellow* 1.65 75
1562 A846 2r dk green, *salmon* 3.25 1.25

Kalinin Museum, Moscow A847

Mikhail I. Kalinin A848

F. E. Dzerzhinski A849

Design: 1r, Kalinin statue.

1951, Aug. 4   Perf. 12x12½, 12½x12
1563 A847 20k orange brn & black 38 25
1564 A848 40k dp green & choc 75 38
1565 A848 1r vio blue & gray 1.50 75

5th anniv. of the death of Kalinin.

1951, Aug. 4   Engr.   Perf. 12x12½
Design: 1r, Profile of Dzerzhinski.
1566 A849 40k brown red 1.75 80
1567 A849 1r gray black 2.75 1.25

25th death anniv. of F. E. Dzerzhinski.

Aleksandr M. Butlerov — A850

A. Kovalevski — A850a

P. K. Kozlov — A850b

N. S. Kurnakov — A850c

P. N. Lebedev A850d

N. I. Lobachevski A850e

A. N. Lodygin — A850f

A. N. Svertzov — A850g

K. E. Tsiolkovsky A850h

A. A. Aliabiev A851

Russian Scientists: No. 1570 Sonya Kovalevskaya. No. 1572, S. P. Krasheninnikov. No. 1577, D. I. Mendeleev. No. 1578, N. N. Miklukho-Maklai. No. 1580, A. G. Stoletov. No. 1581, K. A. Timiryasev. No. 1583, P. N. Yablochkov.

1951, Aug. 15   Photo.   Perf. 12½
1568 A850 40k org red, *bluish* 1.40 25
1569 A850a 40k dk blue, *salmon* 90 15
1570 A850 40k purple, *salmon* 90 15
1571 A850b 40k orange red 90 15
1572 A850 40k purple 90 15
1573 A850c 40k brown, *salmon* 90 15
1574 A850d 40k blue 90 15
1575 A850e 40k brown 90 15
1576 A850f 40k green 90 15
1577 A850 40k deep blue 90 15
1578 A850 40k org red, *salmon* 90 15
1579 A850g 40k sepia, *salmon* 90 15
1580 A850 40k green, *salmon* 90 15
1581 A850 40k brown, *salmon* 90 15
1582 A850h 40k gray black, *blue* 1.40 25
1583 A850 40k sepia 90 15
Nos. 1568-1583 (16) 15.40 2.60

Two printings exist in differing stamp sizes of most of this issue.

1951, Aug. 28
Design: No. 1585, V. S. Kalinnikov.
1584 A851 40k brown, *salmon* 6.00 4.00
1585 A851 40k gray, *salmon* 10.00 6.00

Russian composers.

Opera and Ballet Theater, Tbilisi — A852

Gathering Citrus Fruit — A853

Designs: 40k, Principal street, Tbilisi. 1r, Picking tea.

1951   Unwmk.   Perf. 12½
1586 A852 20k dp green, *yellow* 60 35
1587 A853 25k pur, org & brn 80 35
1588 A853 40k dk brn, *blue* 1.75 75
1589 A853 1r red brn & dk grn 4.00 1.75

Georgian Republic, 30th anniversary.

Emblem of Aviation Society — A854

Planes and Emblem A855

Designs: 60k, Flying model planes. 1r, Parachutists.

1951, Sept. 19   Litho.   Perf. 12½
Dated: "1951"

1590 A854 40k multicolored   75   15
1591 A854 60k emer, lt bl & brn   1.40   28
1592 A854 1r blue, sal & lilac   2.00   45
1593 A855 2r multicolored   4.50   80

Promoting interest in aviation.

Victor M. Vasnetsov
(1848-1926),
Painter — A856

Three Heroes, by Vasnetsov — A857

1951, Oct. 15
1594 A856 40k dk bl, brn & buff   1.25   25
1595 A857 1r multicolored   1.90   1.00

Hydroelectric Station,
Lenin and
Stalin — A858

Design: 1r, Spasski Tower, Kremlin.

1951, Nov. 6   Photo.   Perf. 12½
Dated: "1917-1951"

1596 A858 40k blue vio & red   4.75   1.50
1597 A858 1r dk brown & red   7.25   2.50

34th anniversary of October Revolution.

Map, Dredge and
Khakhovsky
Hydroelectric
Station — A859

Map,
Volga
Dam and
Tugboat
A860

Designs (each showing map): 40k, Stalingrad Dam. 60k, Excavating Turkmenian canal. 1r, Kuibyshev dam.

1951, Nov. 28   Perf. 12½
1598 A859 20k multicolored   3.25   1.65
1599 A860 30k multicolored   4.50   2.25
1600 A860 40k multicolored   7.00   3.75
1601 A860 60k multicolored   8.00   4.25
1602 A860 1r multicolored   17.00   8.50
    Nos. 1598-1602 (5)   39.75   20.40

Flag and Citizens
Signing Peace Appeal
A861

M. V.
Ostrogradski
A862

1951, Nov. 30   Perf. 12½
1603 A861 40k gray & red   10.00   7.00

Third All-Union Peace Conference.

1951, Dec. 10   Unwmk.
1604 A862 40k black brn, pink   7.50   3.50

150th anniversary of the birth of Mikhail V. Ostrogradski, mathematician.

Monument to
Jan Zizka,
Prague — A863

Monument to Soviet
Liberators — A864

Designs: 25k, Monument to Soviet Soldiers, Ostrava. 40k, Julius Fucik. 60k, Smetana Museum, Prague.

1951, Dec. 10   Perf. 12½
1605 A863 20k vio blue, sal   3.00   1.25
1606 A863 25k copper red, yel   3.25   1.50
1607 A863 40k red orange, sal   4.50   1.75
1608 A863 60k brnsh gray, buff   6.00   2.50
1609 A864 1r brnsh gray, buff   13.00   5.25
    Nos. 1605-1609 (5)   29.75   12.25

Soviet-Czechoslovakian friendship.

Volkhovski
Hydroelectric
Station and
Lenin Statue
A865

1951, Dec. 19
1610 A865 40k dk bl, gray & yel   90   20
1611 A865 1r pur, gray & yel   2.00   55

25th anniv. of the opening of the Lenin Volkhovski hydroelectric station.

Lenin as a
Schoolboy — A866

Horizontal Designs: 60k, Lenin among children. 1r, Lenin and peasants.

1952, Jan. 24   Photo.   Perf. 12½
Multicolored Centers

1612 A866 40k dk blue green   1.75   25
1613 A866 60k violet blue   2.25   38
1614 A866 1r orange brown   3.25   45

28th anniversary of the death of Lenin.

Semenov
A867

Kovalevski
A868

1952, Feb. 1
1615 A867 1r sepia, blue   4.00   3.50

Petr Petrovich Semenov-Tianshanski (1827-1914), traveler and geographer who explored the Tian Shan mountains.

1952, Mar. 3   Unwmk.
1616 A868 40k sepia, yellow   10.00   8.00

V. O. Kovalevski (1843-1883), biologist and palaeontologist.

Skaters
A869

1952, Mar. 3
1617 A869 40k shown   1.25   22
1618 A869 60k Skiers   2.25   32

N. V. Gogol and Characters from "Taras Bulba" — A870

Designs: 60k, Gogol and V. G. Belinski. 1r, Gogol and Ukrainian peasants.

1952, Mar. 4
Dated: "1852-1952"

1619 A870 40k sepia, blue   75   15
1620 A870 60k blk, dk brown & brown org   1.25   15
1621 A870 1r multicolored   1.50   24
    Set value   38

Death centenary of N. V. Gogol, writer.

G. K.
Ordzhonikidze
A871

Workers and
Soviet Flag
A872

Workers' Rest
Home
A873

1952, Apr. 23   Photo.   Perf. 12½
1622 A871 40k dp green, pink   1.50   1.25
1623 A871 1r sepia, blue   2.25   1.50

15th anniv. of the death of Grigori K. Ordzhonikidze, Georgian party worker.

1952, May 15   Unwmk.

Designs: No. 1626, Aged citizens. No. 1627, Schoolgirl.

1624 A872 40k red & blk, cream   4.50   3.25
1625 A873 40k red & dk grn, pale gray   4.50   3.25
1626 A873 40k red & brown, pale gray   4.50   3.25
1627 A872 40k red & black, pale gray   4.50   3.25

Adoption of Stalin constitution., 15th anniv

A. S. Novikov-Priboy and Ship — A874

1952, June 5
1628 A874 40k blk, pale cit & bl grn   50   15

Novikov-Priboy, writer, 75th birthanniv.

150th anniv. of Birth
of Victor Hugo (1802-
1855), French
Writer — A875

1952, June 5   Unwmk.   Perf. 12½
1629 A875 40k brn org, gray & black   50   15

Julaev — A876

Sedov — A877

1952, June 28
1630 A876 40k rose red, pink   50   15

200th anniversary of the birth of Salavat Julaev, Bashkir hero who took part in the insurrection of 1773-1775.

1952, July 4
1631 A877 40k dk bl, dk brn & blue green   7.50   3.00

Georgi J. Sedov, Arctic explorer (1877-1914).

Arms and Flag
of Romania
A878

University Square,
Bucharest
A879

Design: 60k, Monument to Soviet soldiers.

1952, July 26
1632 A878 40k multicolored   80   28
1633 A878 60k dk green, pink   1.25   60
1634 A879 1r bright ultra   1.65   1.25

Zhukovski
A880

Ogarev
A881

Design: No. 1636, K. P. Bryullov.

1952, July 26   **Pale Blue Paper**
1635 A880 40k gray black   75 28
1636 A880 40k brt blue green   75 28
    V. A. Zhukovski, poet, and Bryullov, painter (1799-1852).

1952, Aug. 29
1637 A881 40k deep green   50 25
    75th anniversary of the death of N. P. Ogarev, poet and revolutionary.

Uspenski — A882   Nakhimov — A883

1952, Sept. 4
1638 A882 40k indigo & dk brown   50 25
    Gleb Ivanovich Uspenski (1843-1902), writer.

1952, Sept. 9
1639 A883 40k multicolored   80 60
    Adm. Paul S. Nakhimov (1802-1855).

University
Building,
Tartu — A884

1952, Oct. 2
1640 A884 40k black brn, *salmon* 2.50 1.00
    150th anniversary of the enlargement of the University of Tartu, Estonia.

Kajum Nasyri
A885

A. N.
Radishchev
A886

1952, Nov. 5
1641 A885 40k brown, *yellow*   2.50 1.25
    Nasyri (1825-1902), Tartar educator.

1952, Oct. 23
1642 A886 40k black, brn & dk red   90 85
    Radishchev, writer, 150th death anniv.

M.S. Joseph Stalin
at Entrance to
Volga-Don
Canal — A887

Design: 1r, Lenin, Stalin and red banners.

1952, Nov. 6   **Perf. 12½**
1643 A887 40k multicolored   1.90 1.25
1644 A887 1r brown, red & yel   3.50 2.75
    35th anniversary of October Revolution.

Pavel
Fedotov — A888

V. D.
Polenov — A889

"Moscow Courtyard" — A890

1953, Nov. 26
1645 A888 40k red brn & black   50 25
    Centenary of the death of Pavel Andreievitch Fedotov (1815-1852), artist.

1952, Dec. 6
1646 A889 40k red brown & buff   75 30
1647 A890 1r multicolored   1.75 55
    Polenov, artist, 25th death anniv.

A. I. Odoyevski (1802-
39) Poet — A891

1952, Dec. 8
1648 A891 40k gray blk & red orange 75 25

D. N. Mamin-
Sibiryak
A892

1952, Dec. 15
1649 A892 40k dp green, *cream*   75 25
    Centenary of the birth of Dimitrii N. Mamin-Sibiryak (1852-1912), writer.

Composite Medal Types of 1946
Frames as A599-A606
Centers as Indicated

Medals: 1r, Token of Veneration. 2r, Red Star. 3r, Red Workers' Banner. 5r, Red Banner. 10r, Lenin.

1952-59		**Engr.**	**Perf. 12½**	
1650	A569	1r dark brown	7.00	7.00
1651	A567	2r red brown	1.00	55
1652	A572	3r dp blue violet	1.50	95
1653	A571	5r dk carmine ('53)	1.90	95
1654	A566	10r bright rose	3.50	1.90
a.		10r dull red ('59)	3.00	1.50
		Nos. 1650-1654 (5)	14.90	11.35

Vladimir M. Bekhterev
(1857-1927),
Neuropathologist
A893

1952, Dec. 24   **Photo.**
1655 A893 40k vio bl, slate & blk 60 28

Byelorusskaya Station — A894

Designs (Moscow Subway stations): 40k, Botanical Garden Station. 40k, Novoslobodskaya Station. 40k, Komsomolskaya Station.

1952, Dec. 30
          Multicolored Centers
1656 A894 40k dull violet   60 15
1657 A894 40k light ultra   60 15
1658 A894 40k blue gray   60 15
1659 A894 40k dull green   60 15
    a. Horiz. strip of 4, #1656-1659 2.50 2.00

USSR
Emblem
and Flags of
16 Union
Republics
A895

1952, Dec. 30
1660 A895 1r grn, dk red & brn   2.25 1.50
    30th anniversary of the USSR.

Lenin — A896

1953, Jan. 26
1661 A896 40k multicolored   3.50 2.75
    29 years without Lenin.

Stalin Peace
Medal — A897

Valerian V.
Kuibyshev — A898

1953, Apr. 30   **Perf. 12½**
1662 A897 40k red brn, bl & dull
          yel   10.00 6.00

1953, June 6
1663 A898 40k red brn & black   95 55
    Kuibyshev (1888-1935), Bolshevik leader.

A899

A900

1953, July 21
1664 A899 40k buff & dk brown   95 75
    Nikolai G. Chernyshevski (1828-1889), writer and radical leader; exiled to Siberia for 24 years.

1953, July 19
1665 A900 40k ver & gray brown   2.50 1.00
    60th anniv. of the birth of Vladimir V. Mayakovsky, poet.

Tsymijanskaja Dam — A901

Volga-Don Canal: No. 1666, Lock No. 9, Volga-Don Canal. No. 1667, Lock 13. No. 1668, Lock 15. No. 1669, Volga River lighthouse. No. 1671, M. S. "Joseph Stalin" in canal.

1953, Aug. 29   **Litho.**
1666 A901 40k multicolored   1.00 15
1667 A901 40k multicolored   1.00 15
1668 A901 40k multicolored   1.00 15
1669 A901 40k multicolored   1.00 15
1670 A901 40k multicolored   1.00 15
1671 A901 1r multicolored   2.25 50
    Nos. 1666-1671 (6)   7.25
    Set value   1.00

V. G.
Korolenko — A902

Leo N.
Tolstoy — A903

1953, Aug. 29 Photo. Perf. 12x12½
1672 A902 40k brown   75 25
    V. G. Korolenko (1853-1921), writer.

1953, Sept.   **Perf. 12**
1673 A903 1r dark brown   4.00 3.50
    125th anniversary of the birth of Count Leo N. Tolstoy, writer.

Moscow University and Two Youths — A904

Nationalities of the Soviet Union — A905

Design: 1r, Komsomol badge and four orders.

1953, Oct. 29   Perf. 12¹/₂x12
1674 A904 40k multicolored   2.50 1.40
1675 A904 1r multicolored   4.50 1.90

35th anniversary of the Young Communist League (Komsomol).

1953, Nov. 6

Design: 60k, Lenin and Stalin at Smolny monastery.

1676 A905 40k multicolored   4.50 2.75
1677 A905 60k multicolored   10.00 5.50

36th anniversary of October Revolution. No. 1676 measures 25¹/₂x38mm; No. 1677, 25¹/₂x42mm.

Lenin and His Writings — A906

Design: 1r, Lenin facing left and pages of "What to Do."

1953
1678 A906 40k multicolored   3.50 2.50
1679 A906 1r dk brn, org brn & red   7.50 3.50

The 40k was issued on Nov. 12 for 50th anniv. of the formation of the Communist Party. The 1r Dec. 14 for 50th anniv. of the 2nd congress of the Russian Socialist Party.

Lenin Statue — A907

Peter I Statue, Decembrists' Square — A908

Leningrad Views: Nos. 1681 & 1683, Admiralty building. Nos. 1685 & 1687, Smolny monastery.

1953, Nov. 23
1680 A907 40k brn blk, *yellow*   1.75 1.10
1681 A907 40k vio brn, *yellow*   1.75 1.10
1682 A907 40k dk brn, *pink*   1.75 1.10
1683 A907 40k brn blk, *cream*   1.75 1.10
1684 A908 1r dk brn, *blue*   4.00 2.75
1685 A908 1r dk green, *pink*   4.00 2.75
1686 A908 1r violet, *yellow*   4.00 2.75
1687 A908 1r blk brn, *blue*   4.00 2.75
Nos. 1680-1687 (8)   23.00 15.40

See Nos. 1944-1945, 1943a.

"Pioneers", and Model of Lomonosov Moscow University A909

Aleksandr S. Griboedov, Writer (1795-1829) A910

1953, Dec. 22   Litho.   Perf. 12
1688 A909 40k dk sl grn, dk brn & red   2.50 1.00

Arms Type of 1948

1954-57
1689 A682 40k scarlet   1.00 50
   a.   8 ribbon turns on wreath at left ('54)   4.25 1.65

No. 1689 was re-issued in 1954-56 typographed in slightly smaller format: 14¹/₂x21³/₄mm, instead of 14³/₄x21³/₄mm, and in a lighter shade. See note after No. 738.
No. 1689 has 7 ribbon turns on left side of wreath.

1954, Mar. 4   Photo.
1690 A910 40k dp claret, *cream*   70 20
1691 A910 1r black, *green*   1.40 32

Kremlin View — A911

V. P. Chkalov — A912

1954, Mar. 7   Litho.   Perf. 12¹/₂x12
1692 A911 40k red & gray   4.00 2.50

1954 elections to the Supreme Soviet.

1954, Mar. 16   Perf. 12
1693 A912 1r gray, vio bl & dk brown   3.50 60

50th anniversary of the birth of Valeri P. Chkalov (1904-1938), airplane pilot.

Lenin — A913

Lenin at Smolny A914

Designs: No. 1696, Lenin's home (later museum), Ulyanovsk. No. 1697, Lenin addressing workers. No. 1698, Lenin among students, University of Kazan.

1954, Apr. 16   Photo.
1694 A913 40k multicolored   3.00 45
   Size: 38x27¹/₂mm
1695 A914 40k multicolored   3.00 45
1696 A914 40k multicolored   3.00 45

   Size: 48x35mm
1697 A914 40k multicolored   3.00 45
1698 A914 40k multicolored   3.00 45
Nos. 1694-1698 (5)   15.00 2.25

30th anniversary of the death of Lenin. For overprint see No. 2060.

Joseph V. Stalin — A915

1954, Apr. 30   Unwmk.   Perf. 12
1699 A915 40k dark brown   5.00 1.50

First anniversary of the death of Stalin.

Supreme Soviet Buildings in Kiev and Moscow A916

T. G. Shevchenko Statue, Kharkov — A917

Designs: No. 1701, University building, Kiev. No. 1702, Opera, Kiev. No. 1703, Ukranian Academy of Science. No. 1705, Bogdan Chmielnicki statue, Kiev. No. 1706 Flags of Soviet Russia and Ukraine. No. 1707, T. G. Shevchenko statue, Kanev. No. 1708, Chmielnicki proclaming reunion of Ukraine and Russia, 1654.

1954, May 10   Litho.
   Size: 37¹/₂x26mm, 26x37¹/₂mm
1700 A916 40k red brn, sal, cream & black   95 15
1701 A916 40k ultra, vio bl & brn   95 15
1702 A916 40k red brn, buff, blue brown   95 15
1703 A916 40k org brn, cream & grn   95 18
1704 A917 40k rose red, blk, yel & brown   1.25 18
1705 A917 60k multicolored   1.25 30
1706 A917 1r multicolored   2.75 48
   Size: 42x28mm
1707 A916 1r multicolored   1.90 48
   Size: 45x29¹/₂mm
1708 A916 1r multicolored, *pink*   2.75 48

300-ЛЕТИЕ

No. 1341 Overprinted in Carmine

ВОССОЕДИНЕННЯ УКРАИНЫ С РОССИЕЙ

1709 A517 2r green   6.25 1.65
Nos. 1700-1709 (10)   19.95 4.20

300th anniversary of the union between the Ukraine and Russia.

Sailboat Race — A918

Basketball — A919

Sports: No. 1711, Hurdle race. No. 1712, Swimmers. No. 1713, Cyclists. No. 1714, Track. No. 1715, Skier. No. 1716, Mountain climbing.

1954, May 29
   Frames in Orange Brown
1710 A918 40k blue & black   1.10 15
1711 A918 40k vio gray & blk   1.10 15
1712 A918 40k dk blue & black   1.10 15
1713 A918 40k dk brn & buff   1.10 15
1714 A918 40k black brn & buff   1.10 15
1715 A918 1r blue & black   2.25 25
1716 A918 1r blue & black   2.25 25
1717 A919 1r dk brn & brn   2.25 25
Nos. 1710-1717 (8)   12.25 1.50

For overprint see No. 2170.

Cattle A920

Designs: No. 1719, Potato planting and cultivation. No. 1720, Kolkhoz hydroelectric station.

1954, June 8
1718 A920 40k brn, cream, ind & blue gray   1.65 85
1719 A920 40k gray grn, buff & brown   1.65 85
1720 A920 40k blk, bl grn & vio bl   1.65 85

Anton P. Chekhov, Writer, 50th Death Anniv. — A921

1954, July 15
1721 A921 40k green & black brn   55 50

F. A. Bredichin, V. J. Struve, A. A. Belopolski and Observatory A922

1954, July 26
1722 A922 40k vio bl, blk & blue   5.00 1.00

Restoration of Pulkov Observatory.

Mikhail I. Glinka, Composer, 150th Birth Anniv. — A923

Pushkin and
Zhukovsky
Visiting
Glinka
A924

1954, July 26
1723 A923 40k dp cl, pink & blk
                      brown   4.50   35
1724 A924 60k multicolored   5.50   60

Nikolai A.
Ostrovsky
A925

Monument to
Sunken Ships
A926

Defenders of
Sevastopol
A927

1954, Sept. 29   Photo.   Perf. 12¹/₂x12
1725 A925 40k brn, dark red & yel   65   20

Ostrovsky (1904-1936), blind writer.

1954, Oct. 17   Perf. 12¹/₂
Design: 1r, Admiral P. S. Nakhimov.
1726 A926 40k blue grn, blk & ol
                      brown   48   15
1727 A927 60k org brn, blk & brn   65   20
1728 A926 1r brn, blk & ol green 1.25 35

Centenary of the defense of Sevastopol during
the Crimean War.

Sculpture at
Exhibition
Entrance — A928

Agriculture
Pavilion
A929

Cattle
Pavilion
A929a

Designs: No. 1732, Machinery pavilion. No.
1733, Main entrance. No. 1734, Main pavilion.

Perf. 12¹/₂, 12¹/₂x12, 12x12¹/₂
1954, Nov. 5   Litho.
Size: 26x37mm
1729 A928 40k multicolored   42   15

Size: 40x29mm
1730 A929 40k multicolored   42   15
1731 A929a 40k multicolored   42   15
1732 A929 40k multicolored   42   15
Size: 40¹/₂x33mm
1733 A929 1r multicolored   85   32
Size: 28¹/₂x40¹/₂mm
1734 A928 1r multicolored   85   32
Nos. 1729-1734 (6)   3.38 1.24

1954 Agricultural Exhibition.

Marx, Engels, Lenin
and Stalin — A930

1954, Nov. 6   Photo.   Perf. 12¹/₂x12
1735 A930 1r dk brn, pale org & red 3.50 2.75

37th anniversary of October Revolution.

Kazan University
Building — A931

1954, Nov. 11   Perf. 12x12¹/₂
1736 A931 40k deep blue   50   25
1737 A931 60k claret   70   42

Founding of Kazan University, 150th anniv.

Salome
Neris
A932

1954, Nov. 17   Perf. 12¹/₂x12
1738 A932 40k red org & ol gray 2.00 40

50th anniversary of the birth of Salome Neris
(1904-1945), Lithuanian poet.

Vegetables and
Garden
A933

Cultivating Flax — A934

Designs: No. 1741, Tractor plowing field. No.
1742, Loading ensilage.

1954, Dec. 12   Litho.   Perf. 12x12¹/₂
1739 A933 40k multicolored   90   15
1740 A934 40k multicolored   90   15
1741 A933 40k multicolored   90   15
1742 A934 60k multicolored   1.25 24

Joseph
Stalin — A935

Anton G.
Rubinstein — A936

1954, Dec. 21   Engr.   Perf. 12¹/₂x12
1743 A935 40k rose brown   60   48
1744 A935 1r dark blue   1.25 60

Birth of Joseph V. Stalin, 75th anniv.

1954, Dec. 30   Photo.
1745 A936 40k claret, gray & blk 4.00 35

Rubinstein, composer, 125th birth anniv.

Vsevolod M. Garshin
(1855-1888),
Writer — A937

Lithographed and Photogravure
1955, Mar. 2   Unwmk.   Perf. 12
1746 A937 40k buff, blk brn & green 75 25

K. A.
Savitsky and
Painting
A938

1955, Mar. 21   Photo.
1747 A938 40k multicolored   1.00   28
   a.   Sheet of 4, black inscription 30.00 25.00
   b.   As "a," red brn inscription   30.00 25.00

K. A. Savitsky (1844-1905), painter.
Size: Nos. 1747a, 1747b, 152x108mm.

Globe and Clasped
Hands — A939

1955, Apr. 9   Litho.
1748 A939 40k multicolored   35   25

International Conference of Public Service
Unions, Vienna, April 1955.

Poets Pushkin
and
Mickiewicz
A940

Brothers in Arms
Monument,
Warsaw — A941

Palace of
Culture and
Science,
Warsaw
A942

Copernicus,
Painting by
Jan Matejko
(in
Medallion)
A943

Unwmk.
1955, Apr. 22   Photo.   Perf. 12
1749 A940 40k chalky blue, vio &
                      black   1.25   25
1750 A941 40k violet black   1.25   25
1751 A942 1r brt red & gray black 2.50 65
1752 A943 1r multicolored   2.50   65

Polish-USSR treaty of friendship, 10th anniv.

Lenin at Shushinskoe — A944

Lenin at Secret
Printing House
A945

Friedrich von
Schiller
A946

Design: 1r, Lenin and Krupskaya with peasants at
Gorki, 1921.

1955, Apr. 22
Frame and Inscription in Dark Red
1753 A944 60k multicolored   1.00   40
1754 A944 1r multicolored   2.00   45
1755 A945 1r multicolored   2.00   45

85th anniversary of the birth of Lenin.

1955, May 10
1756 A946 40k chocolate   50   25

150th anniversary of the death of Friedrich von
Schiller, German poet.

A. G. Venezianov and "Spring on the
Land" — A947

1955, June 21   **Photo.**
1757 A947 1r multicolored   1.75   60
   a.   Souvenir sheet of 4   20.00   12.50

Venezianov, painter, 175th birth anniv.

Anatoli K. Liadov (1855-1914), Composer A948

1955, July 5   **Litho.**
1758 A948 40k red brn, blk & lt brn   2.00   25

Aleksandr Popov — A949

Lenin — A950

Storming the Winter Palace A951

1955, Nov. 5

Portraits Multicolored
1759 A949 40k light ultra   75   20
1760 A949 1r gray brown   1.50   35

60th anniv. of the construction of a coherer for detecting Hertzian electromagnetic waves by A. S. Popov, radio pioneer.

1955, Nov. 6

Design: 1r, Lenin addressing the people.
1761 A950 40k multicolored   1.10   30
1762 A951 40k multicolored   1.10   30
1763 A951 1r multicolored   2.75   65

38th anniversary of October Revolution.

Apartment Houses, Magnitogorsk A952

1955, Nov. 29
1764 A952 40k multicolored   3.00   25

25th anniversary of the founding of the industrial center, Magnitogorsk.

Arctic Observation Post — A953

Design: 1r, Scientist at observation post.

1955, Nov. 29   **Perf. 12½x12**
1765 A953 40k multicolored   1.25   20
1766 A953 60k multicolored   3.50   30
1767 A953 1r multicolored   5.25   45
   a.   Souvenir sheet of 4 ('58)   30.00   25.00

Publicizing the Soviet scientific drifting stations at the North Pole.
In 1962, No. 1767a was overprinted in red "1962" on each stamp and, in the lower sheet margin, a three-line Russian inscription meaning "25 years from the beginning of the work of "NP-1" station."

Sheet value, $35 unused, $27.50 canceled.

Fedor Ivanovich Shubin (1740-1805), Sculptor — A954

1955, Dec. 22   **Perf. 12**
1768 A954 40k green & multi   30   15
1769 A954 1r brown & multi   60   20

Federal Socialist Republic Pavilion (R.S.F.S.R.) A955

ПАВИЛЬОН ТАДЖИКСКОЙ ССР
#1771

ПАВИЛЬОН БЕЛОРУССКОЙ ССР
#1772

ПАВИЛЬОН АЗЕРБАЙДЖАНСКОЙ ССР
#1773

ПАВИЛЬОН ГРУЗИНСКОЙ ССР
#1774

ПАВИЛЬОН АРМЯНСКОЙ ССР
#1775

ПАВИЛЬОН ТУРКМЕНСКОЙ ССР
#1776

ПАВИЛЬОН УЗБЕКСКОЙ ССР
#1777

ПАВИЛЬОН УКРАИНСКОЙ ССР
#1778

ПАВИЛЬОН КАЗАХСКОЙ ССР
#1779

ПАВИЛЬОН КИРГИЗСКОЙ ССР
#1780

ПАВИЛЬОН КАРЕЛО ФИНСКОЙ ССР
#1781

ПАВИЛЬОН МОЛДАВСКОЙ ССР
#1782

ПАВИЛЬОН ЭСТОНСКОЙ ССР
#1783

ПАВИЛЬОН ЛАТВИЙСКОЙ ССР
#1784

ПАВИЛЬОН ЛИТОВСКОЙ ССР
#1785

Designs: Pavilions.

1955   **Litho.**   **Unwmk.**
Centers in Natural Colors; Frames in Blue Green and Olive
1770 A955 40k shown   45   15
   a.   Sheet of 4   15.00   9.50
1771 A955 40k Tadzhik   45   15
1772 A955 40k Byelorussian   45   15
   a.   Sheet of 4   15.00   9.50
1773 A955 40k Azerbaijan   45   15
1774 A955 40k Georgian   45   15

1775 A955 40k Armenian   45   15
1776 A955 40k Turkmen   45   15
1777 A955 40k Uzbek   45   15
1778 A955 40k Ukrainian   45   15
   a.   Sheet of 4   15.00   9.50
1779 A955 40k Kazakh   45   15
1780 A955 40k Kirghiz   45   15
1781 A955 40k Karelo-Finnish   45   15
1782 A955 40k Moldavian   45   15
1783 A955 40k Estonian   45   15
1784 A955 40k Latvian   45   15
1785 A955 40k Lithuanian   45   15
   Nos. 1770-1785 (16)   7.20
     Set value   1.60

All-Union Agricultural Fair.
Nos. 1773-1785 were printed in sheets containing various stamps, providing a variety of horizontal se-tenant pairs and strips.

Lomonosov Moscow State University, 200th Anniv. A956

Design: 1r, New University buildings.

1955, June 9   **Perf. 12**
1786 A956 40k multicolored   65   15
   a.   Sheet of 4 ('56)   4.50   11.50
1787 A956 1r multicolored   1.40   25
   a.   Sheet of 4 ('56)   9.00   19.00

Vladimir V. Mayakovsky A957

1955, May 31
1788 A957 40k multicolored   1.00   25

Mayakovsky, poet, 25th death anniv.

Race Horse — A958

Trotter — A959

1956, Jan. 9
1789 A958 40k dark brown   50   15
1790 A958 60k Prus grn & blue green   90   18
1791 A959 1r dull pur & blue vio   1.65   30

International Horse Races, Moscow, Aug. 14-Sept. 4, 1955.

Alexei N. Krylov (1863-1945), Mathematician, Naval Architect — A960

Symbol of Spartacist Games, Stadium and Factories — A961

1956, Jan. 9
1792 A960 40k gray, brown & black   38   15

1956, Jan. 18
1793 A961 1r red vio & lt grn   55   25

5th All-Union Spartacist Games of Soviet Trade Union sport clubs, Moscow, Aug. 12-18, 1955.

Atomic Power Station A962

Design: 60k, Atomic Reactor.

1956, Jan. 31
1794 A962 25k multicolored   40   16
1795 A962 60k multicolored   1.25   25
1796 A962 1r multicolored   2.25   38

Establishment of the first Atomic Power Station of the USSR Academy of Science. Inscribed in Russian: "Atomic Energy in the service of the people."

Statue of Lenin, Kremlin and Flags — A963

Khachatur Abovian — A964

1956, Feb.
1797 A963 40k multicolored   50   15
1798 A963 1r ol, buff & red org   70   18
     Set value   26

20th Congress of the Communist Party of the Soviet Union.

1956, Feb. 25   **Unwmk.**   **Perf. 12**
1799 A964 40k black brn, *bluish*   1.25   25

Abovian, Armenian writer, 150th birth anniv.

Buying Sets
It is often less expensive to purchase complete sets than individual stamps that make up the set. Set values are provided for many such sets.

Workers with   Nikolai A.
Red   Kasatkin — A966
Flag — A965

1956, Mar. 14
1800 A965 40k multicolored   1.50 25
    Revolution of 1905, 50th anniversary.

1956, Apr. 30
1801 A966 40k carmine lake   50 25
    Kasatkin (1859-1930), painter.

"On the Oka
River"
A967

1956, Apr. 30
       Center Multicolored
1802 A967 40k bister & black   1.10 15
1803 A967 1r ultra & black   2.00 28
    A. E. Arkhipov, painter.

I. P.   V. G.
Kulibin — A968   Perov — A969

"Birdcatchers" — A970

1956, May 12
1804 A968 40k multicolored   75 25
    Kulibin, inventor, 220th birth anniv.

1956, May 12
    Painting: No. 1807, "Hunters at Rest."
       Multicolored Centers
1805 A969 40k green   1.00 15
1806 A970 1r brown   2.00 30
1807 A970 1r orange brown   2.00 30
    Vassili Grigorievitch Perov (1833-82), painter.

Ural
Pavilion
A971

#1809

#1810

#1811

#1812

#1813

#1814

#1815

#1816

#1817

#1818

#1819

#1820

Pavilions: No. 1809, Tatar Republic. No. 1810,
Volga District. No. 1811, Central Black Earth Area.
No. 1812, Northeastern District. No. 1813, North-
ern Caucasus. No. 1814, Bashkir Republic. No.
1815, Far East. No. 1816, Central Asia. No. 1817,
Young Naturalists. No. 1818, Siberia. No. 1819,
Leningrad and Northwestern District. No. 1820,
Moscow, Tula, Kaluga, Ryazan and Bryansk
Districts.

1956, Apr. 25
       Multicolored Centers
1808 A971 1r yel green & pale yel   95 15
1809 A971 1r blue grn & pale yel   95 15
1810 A971 1r dk blue grn & pale
        yel   95 15
1811 A971 1r dk bl grn & yel grn   95 15
1812 A971 1r dk blue grn & buff   95 15
1813 A971 1r ol gray & pale yel   95 15
1814 A971 1r olive & yellow   95 15
1815 A971 1r olive grn & lemon   95 15
1816 A971 1r olive brn & lemon   95 15
1817 A971 1r olive brn & lemon   95 15
1818 A971 1r brown & yellow   95 15
1819 A971 1r redsh brown & yel   95 15
1820 A971 1r dk red brn & yel   95 15
    Nos. 1808-1820 (13)   12.35
    Set value   1.55

    All-Union Agricultural Fair, Moscow.
    Six of the Pavilion set were printed se-tenant in
one sheet of 30 (6x5), the strip containing Nos.
1809, 1816, 1817, 1813, 1818 and 1810 in that
order. Two others, Nos. 1819-1820, were printed
se-tenant in one sheet of 35.

Lenin   Lobachevski
A972   A973

1956, May 25
1821 A972 40k lilac & multi   3.00 2.00
    86th anniversary of the birth of Lenin.

1956, June 4
1822 A973 40k black brown   35 15
    Nikolai Ivanovich Lobachevski (1793-1856),
mathematician.

Nurse and
Textile
Factory
A974

    Design: 40k, First Aid instruction.

1956, June 4   **Unwmk.**
1823 A974 40k lt ol grn, grnsh bl & red   40 15
1824 A974 40k red brn, lt bl & red   40 15
    Red Cross and Red Crescent. No. 1823 measures
37x25mm; No. 1824, 40x28mm.

V. K.   I. M.
Arseniev — A975   Sechenov — A976

1956, June 15   Litho.   Perf. 12
1825 A975 40k violet, black & rose   40 15
    Arseniev (1872-1930), explorer and writer.

1956, June 15
1826 A976 40k multicolored   40 15
    I. M. Sechenov (1829-1905), physiologist.

A. K. Savrasov,
Painter — A977

1956, June 22
1827 A977 1r dull yel & brown   1.00 20

I. V.
Michurin,
Scientist,
Birth
Centenary
A978

    Design: 60k, I. V. Michurin with Pioneers.

1956, June 22
       Center Multicolored
1828 A978 25k dark brown   60 15
1829 A978 60k green & lt blue   90 20
1830 A978 1r light blue   2.00 50
    Nos. 1828 and 1830 measure 32x25mm. No.
1829 measures 47x26mm.

Nadezhda K.
Krupskaya
A979

1956, June 28
1831 A979 40k brn, lt blue & pale
        brown   2.00 75
    Krupskaya (1869-1939), teacher and wife of
Lenin.
    See Nos. 1862, 1886, 1983, 2028.

S. M.   N. S.
Kirov — A980   Leskov — A981

1956, June 28
1832 A980 40k red, buff & brown   38 15
    Kirov, revolutionary (1886-1934).

1956, July 10
1833 A981 40k olive bister & brn   15 15
1834 A981 1r green & dk brown   60 40
    Nikolai S. Leskov (1831-1895), novelist.

Aleksandr A. Blok
(1880-1921),
Poet — A982

1956, July 10
1835 A982 40k olive & brn, *cream*   35 15

Farm
Machinery
Factory
A983

1956, July 23   Perf. 12½x12
1836 A983 40k multicolored   25 15
    Rostov Farm Machinery Works, 25th anniv.

A984

1956, July 23   **Unwmk.**
1837 A984 40k brown & rose violet   60 15
    G. N. Fedotova (1846-1925), actress. See No.
2026.

P. M.
Tretiakov and
Art Gallery
A985

"The Rooks Have
Arrived" by A. K.
Savrasov — A986

1956, July 31   *Perf. 12*
1838 A985 40k multicolored   3.00 25
1839 A986 40k multicolored   3.00 25

Tretiakov Art Gallery, Moscow, cent.

Relay
Race — A987

Volleyball — A988

Designs: No. 1842, Rowing. No. 1843, Swimming. No. 1844, Medal with heads of man and woman. No. 1845, Tennis. No. 1846, Soccer. No. 1847, Fencing. No. 1848, Bicycle race. No. 1849, Stadium and flag. No. 1850, Diving. No. 1851, Boxing. No. 1852, Gymnast. 1r, Basketball.

1956, Aug. 5
1840 A987 10k carmine rose   18 15
1841 A988 25k dk orange brn   32 15
1842 A988 25k grn, blue & lt brn   32 15
1843 A988 25k brt grnsh blue   32 15
1844 A988 40k org, pink, bis & yellow   48 15
1845 A988 40k orange brown   48 15
1846 A987 40k brt yel grn & dk brown   48 15
1847 A987 40k grn, brt grn & dk brn, *grnsh*   48 15
1848 A987 40k blue green   48 15
1849 A987 40k brt yel grn & red   48 15
1850 A988 40k greenish blue   48 15
1851 A988 60k violet   80 15
1852 A988 60k brt violet   80 15
1853 A987 1r red brown   1.25 32
   Nos. 1840-1853 (14)   7.35
   Set value   1.25

All-Union Spartacist Games, Moscow, Aug. 5-16.

Parachute Landing
A989

Building under
Construction
A990

1956, Aug. 5   *Perf. 12x12¹/₂*
1854 A989 40k multicolored   40 15

Third World Parachute Championships, Moscow, July 1956.

1956   Photo.   *Perf. 12*

Builders' Day: 60k, Building a factory. 1r, Building a dam.

1855 A990 40k deep orange   32 15
1856 A990 60k brown carmine   65 15
1857 A990 1r intense blue   95 15
   Set value   28

Ivan
Franko — A991

Makhmud
Aivazov — A992

1956, Aug. 27
1858 A991 40k deep claret   40 15
1859 A991 1r bright blue   80 18

Franko, writer (1856-1916).

1956, Aug. 27

Two types:
I - Three lines in panel with "148."
II - Two lines in panel with "148."

1860 A992 40k emerald (II)   5.00 3.00
   a.   Type I   20.00 17.50

148th birthday of Russia's oldest man, an Azerbaijan collective farmer.

Robert Burns, Scottish
Poet, 160th Death
Anniv. — A993

1956-57   Photo.
1861 A993 40k yellow brown   4.00 1.25
   Engr.
1861A A993 40k lt ultra & brn ('57)   1.90 85

For overprint see No. 2174.

Portrait Type of 1956

Portrait: Lesya Ukrainka (1871-1913), Ukrainian writer.

1956, Aug. 27   Litho.
1862 A979 40k olive, blk & brown   1.00 25

Statue of
Nestor — A995

A. A.
Ivanov — A996

1956, Sept. 22   *Perf. 12x12¹/₂*
1863 A995 40k multicolored   1.25 15
1864 A995 1r multicolored   1.25 15

900th anniversary of the birth of Nestor, first Russian historian.

1956, Sept. 22   Unwmk.
1865 A996 40k gray & brown   35 15

Aleksandr Andreevich Ivanov (1806-58), painter.

I. E. Repin and "Volga River
Boatmen" — A997

"Cossacks Writing a Letter to the Turkish
Sultan" — A998

1956, Aug. 21
   Multicolored Centers
1866 A997 40k org brn & black   3.25 45
1867 A998 1r chalky blue & blk   6.50 55

Ilya E. Repin (1844-1930), painter.

Chicken Farm
A999

Designs: No. 1869, Harvest. 25k, Harvesting corn. No. 1871, Women in corn field. No. 1872, Farm buildings. No. 1873, Cattle. No. 1874, Farm workers, inscriptions and silos.

1956, Oct. 7
1868 A999 10k multicolored   15 15
1869 A999 10k multicolored   15 15
1870 A999 25k multicolored   28 15
1871 A999 40k multicolored   58 15
1872 A999 40k multicolored   58 15
1873 A999 40k multicolored   58 15
1874 A999 40k multicolored   58 15
   Nos. 1868-1874 (7)   2.90 1.05

Nos. 1868, 1872 and 1873 measure 37x25¹/₂mm. Nos. 1869-1871 measure 37x27¹/₂mm. No. 1874 measures 37x21mm.

Benjamin
Franklin — A1000

G. B
Shaw — A1000a

Dostoevski — A1000b

Portraits: No. 1876 Sesshu (Toyo Oda). No. 1877, Rembrandt. No. 1879, Mozart. No. 1880, Heinrich Heine. No. 1882, Ibsen. No. 1883, Pierre Curie.

1956, Oct. 17   Photo.
   Size: 25x37mm
1875 A1000 40k copper brown   1.25 42
1876 A1000 40k brt orange   1.00 22
1877 A1000 40k black   1.25 22
1878 A1000a 40k black   1.00 22
   Size: 21x32mm
1879 A1000 40k grnsh blue   1.00 22
1880 A1000 40k violet   1.00 22
1881 A1000b 40k green   1.00 22
1882 A1000 40k brown   1.00 22
1883 A1000 40k brt green   1.25 42
   Nos. 1875-1883 (9)   9.75 2.38

Great personalities of the world.

Demand, as well as supply, determine a stamp's market value.

Antarctic Bases
A1001

G. I. Kotovsky
A1002

1956, Oct. 22   Litho.   *Perf. 12x12¹/₂*
1884 A1001 40k slate, grnsh bl & red   85 32

Soviet Scientific Antarctic Expedition.

1956, Oct. 30
1885 A1002 40k magenta   85 15

75th anniv. of the birth of G. I. Kotovsky (1881-1925), military commander.

Portrait Type of 1956

Portrait: Julia A. Zemaite (1845-1921), Lithaunian novelist.

1956, Oct. 30   *Perf. 12*
1886 A979 40k lt ol green & brn   45 25

Fedor A.
Bredichin
(1831-1904),
Astronomer
A1004

1956, Oct. 30
1887 A1004 40k sepia & ultra   2.50 75

Field Marshal Count
Aleksandr V. Suvorov
(1730-1800) — A1005

1956, Nov. 17   Engr.
1888 A1005 40k orange & maroon   30 15
1889 A1005 1r ol & dk red brn   60 15
1890 A1005 3r lt red brn & black   1.65 65

Shatura
Power Station
A1006

1956   Litho.   *Perf. 12¹/₂x12*
1891 A1006 40k multicolored   60 20

30th anniv. of the Shatura power station.

Kryakutni's
Balloon,
1731
A1007

1956, Nov. 17
1892 A1007 40k lt brn, sep & yel   90 20

225th anniv. of the 1st balloon ascension of the Russian inventor, Kryakutni.

A1008

1956, Dec. 3   Unwmk.   Perf. 12
1893 A1008 40k ultra & brown   35   20

Yuli M. Shokalski (1856-1940), oceanographer and geodesist.

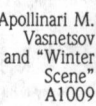

Apollinari M. Vasnetsov and "Winter Scene" A1009

1956, Dec. 30
1894 A1009 40k multicolored   75   25

Vasnetsov (1856-1933), painter.

Indian Building and Books — A1010

Ivan Franko — A1011

1956, Dec. 26
1895 A1010 40k deep carmine   35   20

Kalidasa, 5th century Indian poet.

1956, Dec. 26   Engr.
1896 A1011 40k dk slate green   35   20

Ivan Franko, Ukrainian writer.
See Nos. 1858-1859.

Leo N. Tolstoy A1012

Portraits of Writers: No. 1898, Mikhail V. Lomonosov. No. 1899, Aleksander S. Pushkin. No. 1900, Maxim Gorki. No. 1901, Shota Rustaveli. No. 1902, Vissarion G. Belinski. No. 1903, Mikhail Y. Lermontov, poet, and Darjal Ravine in Caucasus.

1956-57   Litho.   Perf. 12¹/₂x12
Size: 37¹/₂x27¹/₂mm
1897 A1012 40k brt grnsh blue & brown   35   15
1898 A1012 40k dk red, ol & brn olive   35   15
Size: 35¹/₂x25¹/₂mm
1899 A1012 40k dk gray blue & brown   35   15
1900 A1012 40k black & brn car   35   15
1901 A1012 40k ol, brn & ol gray   35   15
1902 A1012 40k bis, dl vio & brn ('57)   35   15
1903 A1012 40k indigo & ol ('57)   35   15
       Nos. 1897-1903 (7)   2.45
            Set value   75

Famous Russian writers.
See Nos. 1960-1962, 2031, 2112.

Fedor G. Volkov and Theater A1013

1956, Dec. 31   Unwmk.
1904 A1013 40k magenta, gray & yel   35   20

200th anniversary of the founding of the St. Petersburg State Theater.

Vitus Bering and Map of Bering Strait A1016

1957, Feb. 6
1905 A1016 40k brown & blue   75   20

275th anniversary of the birth of Vitus Bering, Danish navigator and explorer.

Dmitri I. Mendeleev A1017

Mikhail I. Glinka A1018

1957, Feb. 6   Perf. 12x12¹/₂
1906 A1017 40k gray & gray brn   1.00   25

D. I. Mendeleev (1834-1907), chemist.

1957, Feb. 23   Perf. 12

Design: 1r, Scene from opera Ivan Susanin.

1907 A1018 40k dk red, buff & sep   40   15
1908 A1018 1r multicolored   65   20

Mikhail I. Glinka (1804-1857), composer.

Emblem — A1019

Emblem — A1020

1957, Feb. 23
1909 A1019 40k dk blue, red & ocher   35   16

All-Union festival of Soviet Youth, Moscow.

1957, Feb. 24   Photo.

Designs: 40k, Player. 60k, Goalkeeper.

1910 A1020 25k deep violet   48   15
1911 A1020 40k bright blue   48   15
1912 A1020 60k emerald   48   15

23rd Ice Hockey World Championship Games in Moscow.

Dove and Festival Emblem — A1021

Assembly Line — A1022

1957   Litho.   Perf. 12
1913 A1021 40k multicolored   25   15
1914 A1021 60k multicolored   35   15

6th World Youth Festival, Moscow. Exist imperf. Value, each $30.

1957, Mar. 15
1915 A1022 40k Prus green & dp org   30   15

Moscow Machine Works centenary.

Black Grouse A1023

Axis Deer — A1024

Animals: 10k, Gray partridge. No. 1918, Polar bear. No. 1920, Bison. No. 1921, Mallard. No. 1922, European elk. No. 1923, Sable.

1957, Mar. 28
Center in Natural Colors
1916 A1024 10k yel brown   65   15
1917 A1023 15k brown   65   15
1918 A1024 15k slate blue   70   15
1919 A1024 20k red orange   70   15
1920 A1023 30k ultra   70   15
1921 A1023 30k dk olive grn   70   15
1922 A1023 40k dk olive grn   1.75   30
1923 A1024 40k violet blue   1.75   30
       Nos. 1916-1923 (8)   7.60   1.50

See Nos. 2213-2219, 2429-2431.

Wooden Products, Hohloma A1025

National Handicrafts: No. 1925, Lace maker, Vologda. No. 1926, Bone carver, North Russia. No. 1927, Woodcarver, Moscow area. No. 1928, Rug weaver, Turkmenistan. No. 1929, Painting.

1957-58   Unwmk.
1924 A1025 40k red org, yel & black   1.50   24
1925 A1025 40k brt car, yel & brown   1.50   24
1926 A1025 40k ultra, buff & gray   1.50   24
1927 A1025 40k brn, pale yel & hn brown   1.50   24
1928 A1025 40k buff, brn, bl & org ('58)   1.90   40
1929 A1025 40k multicolored ('58)   1.90   40
       Nos. 1924-1929 (6)   9.80   1.76

Aleksei N. Bach A1026

G. V. Plekhanov A1027

1957, Apr. 6   Litho.   Perf. 12
1930 A1026 40k ultra, brn & buff   50   15

Aleksei Nikolaievtch Bach, biochemist (1857-1946).

1957, Apr. 6   Engr.
1931 A1027 40k dull purple   35   15

Georgi Valentinovich Plekhanov (1856-1918), political philosopher.

Leonhard Euler A1028

1957, Apr. 17   Litho.
1932 A1028 40k lilac & gray   55   20

Leonhard Euler (1707-1783), Swiss mathematician and physicist.

Lenin — A1029

Youths of All Races Carrying Festival Banner — A1030

Designs: No. 1934, Lenin talking to soldier and sailor. No. 1935, Lenin building barricades.

1957, Apr. 22
Multicolored Centers
1933 A1029 40k magenta & bister   40   15
1934 A1029 40k magenta & bister   40   15
1935 A1029 40k magenta & bister   40   15

87th anniversary of the birth of Lenin.

1957, May 27   Perf. 12x12¹/₂

Design: 20k, Sculptor with motherhood statue. 40k, Young couples dancing. 1r, Festival banner and fireworks over Moscow University.

1936 A1030 10k emerald, pur & yel   15   15
1937 A1030 20k multicolored   15   15
1938 A1030 25k emerald, pur & yel   20   15
1939 A1030 40k rose, bl grn & bis brn   30   15
1940 A1030 1r multicolored   30   15
       Nos. 1936-1940 (5)   1.30
            Set value   40

6th World Youth Festival in Moscow. The 10k, 20k, and 1r exist imperf. Value each about $15.

Marine Museum
Place and
Neva — A1031

Henry
Fielding — A1032

Designs: No. 1942, Lenin monument. No. 1943, Nevski Prospect and Admiralty.

1957, May 27   Photo.   Perf. 12
1941 A1031 40k blue green   25 15
1942 A1031 40k reddish brown   25 15
1943 A1031 40k bluish violet   25 15
  a.   Souv. sheet of 3, red border   7.50 4.00
         Set value   35

250th anniversary of Leningrad.
No. 1943a contains imperf. stamps similar to #1941, 1680 (in reddish brown), 1943, and is for 40th anniv. of the October Revolution. Issued Nov. 7, 1957. A similar sheet is listed as No. 2002a.

Type of 1953 Overprinted   250 лет
in Red   Ленинграда

Designs: No. 1944, Peter I Statue, Decembrists' Square. No. 1945, Smolny Institute.

1957, May 27   Perf. 12¹/₂x12
1944 A908 1r black brn, *greenish*   45 15
1945 A908 1r green, *pink*   45 15

250th anniversary of Leningrad.
The overprint is in one line on No. 1945.

1957, June 20   Litho.
1946 A1032 40k multicolored   35 15

Fielding (1707-54), English playwright, novelist.

William
Harvey — A1033

M. A.
Balakirev — A1034

1957, May 20   Photo.
1947 A1033 40k brown   35 15

300th anniversary of the death of the English physician William Harvey, discoverer of blood circulation.

1957, May 20   Engr.
1948 A1034 40k bluish black   35 15

Balakirev, composer (1836-1910).

A. I. Herzen
and N. P.
Ogarev
A1035

1957, May 20   Litho.
1949 A1035 40k blk vio & dk ol gray   35 15

Centenary of newspaper Kolokol (Bell).

Kazakhstan Workers'
Medal — A1036

1957, May 20
1950 A1036 40k lt blue, blk & yel   35 15

A1037   A1037a   A1037b

Portraits: No. 1951, A. M. Liapunov. No. 1952, V. Mickevicius Kapsukas, writer. No. 1953, G. Bashindchagian, Armenian painter. No. 1954, Yakub Kolas, Byelorussian poet. No. 1955, Carl von Linné, Swedish botanist.

1957   Various Frames   Photo.
1951 A1037   40k dull red brown   2.00 1.25
1952 A1037a 40k sepia   2.00 1.25
1953 A1037   40k sepia   2.00 1.25
1954 A1037b 40k gray   2.00 1.25
1955 A1037   40k brown black   2.00 1.25
    Nos. 1951-1955 (5)   10.00 6.25

See Nos. 2036-2038, 2059.

Bicyclist
A1038

1957, June 20   Litho.
1956 A1038 40k claret & vio blue   50 15

10th Peace Bicycle Race.

Telescope — A1039

Designs: No. 1958, Comet and observatory. No. 1959, Rocket leaving earth.

1957, July 4
    Size: 25¹/₂x37mm
1957 A1039 40k brn, ocher & blue   1.00 25
1958 A1039 40k indigo, lt bl & yel 1.00 25

    Size: 14¹/₂x21mm
1959 A1039 40k blue violet   1.00 25

International Geophysical Year, 1957-58. See Nos. 2089-2091.

Folksinger
A1040

1957, May 20
1960 A1040 40k multicolored   35 15

"The Song of Igor's Army," Russia's oldest literary work.

Taras G.
Shevchenko,
Ukrainian
Poet — A1041

Design: #1962, Nikolai G. Chernyshevski, writer and politician.

1957, July 20
1961 A1041 40k green & dk red brn   25 15
1962 A1041 40k orange brn & green   25 15
    Set value   24

Woman Gymnast — A1043

Designs: 25k, Wresting. No. 1965, Stadium. No. 1966, Youths of three races. 60k, Javelin thrower.

1957, July 15   Litho.   Perf. 12
1963 A1043 20k bluish vio & org brn 20 15
1964 A1043 25k brt grn & claret   20 15
1965 A1043 40k Prus bl, ol & red   32 15
1966 A1043 40k crimson & violet   32 15
1967 A1043 60k ultra & brown   42 15
    Nos. 1963-1967 (5)   1.46
    Set value   55

Third International Youth Games, Moscow.

Javelin
Thrower — A1044

Designs: No. 1969, Sprinter. 25k, Somersault. No. 1971, Boxers. No. 1972, Soccer players, horiz. 60k, Weight lifter.

1957, July 20   Unwmk.
1968 A1044 20k lt ultra & ol blk   18 15
1969 A1044 20k brt grn, red vio &
              black   18 15
1970 A1044 25k orange, ultra & blk   18 15
1971 A1044 40k rose vio & blk   45 15
1972 A1044 40k dp pink, bl, buff &
              black   45 15
1973 A1044 60k lt violet & brn   95 15
    Nos. 1968-1973 (6)   2.39
    Set value   65

Success of Soviet athletes at the 16th Olympic Games, Melbourne.

Kupala
A1045

Kremlin
A1046

1957, July 27   Photo.
1974 A1045 40k dark gray   1.00 60

Yanka Kupala (1882-1942), poet.

1957, July 27   Litho.
Moscow Views: No. 1976, Stadium. No. 1977, University. No. 1978, Bolshoi Theater.

Center in Black
1975 A1046 40k dull red brown   22 15
1976 A1046 40k brown violet   22 15
1977 A1046 1r red   52 20
1978 A1046 1r brt violet blue   52 20

Sixth World Youth Festival, Moscow.

Lenin
Library — A1047

1957, July 27   Photo.
1979 A1047 40k brt grnsh blue   20 15
  a.   Souvenir sheet of 2, light blue,
         imperf.   12.00 12.00

Intl. Phil. Exhib., Moscow, July 29-Aug. 11. No. 1979 exists imperf. Value $10.

Pierre Jean de
Beranger — A1048

Globe, Dove and
Olive
Branch — A1049

1957, Aug. 9
1980 A1048 40k brt blue green   20 15

Beranger (1780-1857), French song writer.

1957, Aug. 8   Litho.
1981 A1049 40k bl, grn & bis brn   1.40 30
1982 A1049 1r violet, grn & brn   3.50 55

Publicity for world peace.

Portrait Type of 1956

Portrait: 40k, Clara Zetkin (1857-1933), German communist.

1957, Aug. 9
1983 A979 40k gray blue, brn & blk 1.00 20

Krenholm
Factory,
Narva — A1050

1957, Sept. 8   Photo.
1984 A1050 40k black brown   1.00 15

Centenary of Krenholm textile factory, Narva, Estonia.

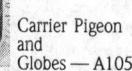
Carrier Pigeon
and
Globes — A1051

1957, Sept. 26   Unwmk.   Perf. 12
1985 A1051 40k blue   15 15
1986 A1051 60k lilac   25 15
    Set value   22

Intl. Letter Writing Week, Oct. 6-12.

Wyborshez
Factory, Lenin
Statue — A1052

1957, Sept. 23   **Litho.**
1987 A1052 40k dark blue   50 15

Krasny Wyborshez factory, Leningrad, cent.

Vladimir Vasilievich
Stasov (1824-1906),
Art and Music
Critic — A1053

1957, Sept. 23   **Engr.**
1988 A1053 40k brown   30 15
1989 A1053 1r bluish black   60 15

Congress Emblem
A1054

1957, Oct. 7   Litho.   Perf. 12
1990 A1054 40k gray blue & blk, *bluish* 25 15

4th International Trade Union Congress, Leipzig,
Oct. 4-15.

Konstantin E.
Tsiolkovsky and
Rockets — A1055

1957, Oct. 7
1991 A1055 40k dk blue & pale brown 1.40 60

Tsiolkovsky (1857-1935), rocket and astronautics
pioneer.
For overprint see No. 2021.

Sputnik 1
Circling
Globe — A1056

Turbine Wheel,
Kuibyshev
Hydroelectric
Station — A1057

1957   **Photo.**
1992 A1056 40k indigo, *bluish*   55 30
1993 A1056 40k bright blue   55 30

Launching of first artificial earth satellite, Oct. 4.
Issue dates: No. 1992, Nov. 5; No. 1993, Dec. 28.

1957, Nov. 20   **Litho.**
1994 A1057 40k red brown   18 15

All-Union Industrial Exhib. See #2030.

Meteor
A1058

Lenin
A1059

1957, Nov. 20
1995 A1058 40k multicolored   50 15

Falling of Sihote Alinj meteor, 10th anniv.

1957, Oct. 30   **Engr.**

Design: 60k, Lenin reading Pravda, horiz.

1996 A1059 40k blue   38 15
1997 A1059 60k rose red   42 15
         Set value   25

40th anniversary of October Revolution.

Students and
Moscow
University
A1060

Worker and Railroad
A1061

Designs: No. 1999, Red flag and Lenin. No.
2000, Lenin addressing workers and peasants. 60k,
Harvester.

Perf. 12¹/₂x12, 12x12¹/₂, 12¹/₂
1957, Oct. 15   **Litho.**
1998 A1060 10k buff, sepia & red   15 15
1999 A1060 40k buff, red, sep & yel 24 15
2000 A1060 40k red, black & yellow   24 15
2001 A1061 40k red, yellow & green   24 15
2002 A1061 60k red, ocher & vio brn 32 15
  a. Souvenir sheet of 3, #2000-2002,
         imperf.   7.50 5.00
      Nos. 1998-2002 (5)   1.19
         Set value   35

40th anniv. of the October Revolution. A similar
sheet is listed as No. 1943a.
Nos. 1998-2002 exist imperf.

Federal Socialist
Republic
A1062

Uzbek Republic
A1063

Designs (Republic): No. 2005, Tadzhik (building
and peasant girl). No. 2006, Byelorussia (truck).
No. 2007, Azerbaijan (buildings). No. 2008, Georgia (valley, palm and couple). No. 2009, Armenia,
(fruit, power line and mountains). No. 2010, Turkmen (couple and lambs). No. 2011, Ukraine (farmers). No. 2012, Kazakh (harvester and combine).
No. 2013, Kirghiz (horseback rider and building).
No. 2014, Moldavia (automatic sorting machine).
No. 2015, Estonia (girl in national costume). No.
2016, Latvia (couple, sea and field). No. 2017, Lithuania (farm and farmer couple).

1957, Oct. 25
2003 A1062 40k multicolored   65 32
2004 A1063 40k multicolored   65 32
2005 A1062 40k multicolored   65 32
2006 A1062 40k multicolored   65 32
2007 A1062 40k multicolored   65 32
2008 A1062 40k multicolored   65 32
2009 A1062 40k multicolored   65 32
2010 A1062 40k multicolored   65 32
2011 A1063 40k multicolored   65 32
2012 A1062 40k multicolored   65 32
2013 A1062 40k multicolored   65 32
2014 A1062 40k multicolored   65 32

2015 A1063 40k multicolored   65 32
2016 A1062 40k multicolored   65 32
2017 A1062 40k multicolored   65 32
     Nos. 2003-2017 (15)   9.75 4.80

40th anniversary of the October Revolution.

Artists and
Academy of
Art — A1064

Red Army
Monument,
Berlin — A1065

Monument: 1r, Worker and Peasant monument,
Moscow.

1957, Dec. 16
2018 A1064 40k black, *pale salmon* 16 15
2019 A1065 60k black   20 15
2020 A1065 1r black, *pink*   32 15
         Set value   32

200th anniversary of the Academy of Arts, Leningrad. Artists on 40k are K. P. Bryulov, Ilya Repin
and V. I. Surikov.

No. 1991
Overprinted in
Black

4/X-57 г. Первый в мире
искусств. спутник Земли

1957, Nov. 28
2021 A1055 40k   10.00 5.00

Launching of Sputnik 1.

Ukrainian Arms,
Symbolic Figures
A1066

1957, Dec. 24
2022 A1066 40k yellow, red & blue   30 15

Ukrainian Soviet Republic, 40th anniv.

Edvard Grieg
A1067

Giuseppe
Garibaldi
A1068

1957, Dec. 24   **Photo.**
2023 A1067 40k black, *buff*   1.00 20

Grieg, Norwegian composer, 50th death anniv.

1957, Dec. 24   **Litho.**
2024 A1068 40k plum, lt grn & blk   35 15

Garibaldi, (1807-1882) Italian patriot.

V. L.
Borovikovsky
A1069

Kuibyshev
Hydroelectric Station
and Dam
A1070

1957, Dec. 24   **Photo.**
2025 A1069 40k brown   35 15

Vladimir Lukich Borovikovsky (1757-1825),
painter.

Portrait Type of 1956

Portrait: 40k, Mariya Nikolayevna Ermolova
(1853-1928), actress.

1957, Dec. 28   **Litho.**
2026 A984 40k red brn & brt violet   50 15

1957, Dec. 28
2027 A1070 40k dark blue, *buff*   35 15

Type of 1956

Portrait: 40k, Rosa Luxemburg (1870-1919),
German socialist.

1958, Jan. 8
2028 A979 40k blue & brown   75 60

Chi Pai-shih
A1070a

Flag and Symbols
of Industry
A1070b

1958, Jan. 8   **Photo.**
2029 A1070a 40k deep violet   50 25

Chi Pai-shih (1860-1957), Chinese painter.

1958, Jan. 8   **Litho.**
2030 A1070b 60k gray vio, red & black 50 15

All-Union Industrial Exhib. Exists imperf.

Aleksei N.
Tolstoi, Novelist
& Dramatist
(1883-1945)
A1071

1958, Jan. 28   Photo.   Perf. 12
2031 A1071 40k brown olive   35 20

See Nos. 2112, 2175-2178C.

Symbolic Figure Greeting
Sputnik 2 — A1072

1957-58   Litho.
Figure in Buff

2032	A1072	20k black & rose	25 15
2033	A1072	40k black & grn ('58)	35 15
2034	A1072	60k black & lt brn ('58)	55 18
2035	A1072	1r black & blue	70 24
		Set value	60

Launching of Sputnik 2, Nov. 3, 1957.

Small Portrait Type of 1957

Portraits: No. 2036, Henry W. Longfellow, American poet. No. 2037, William Blake, English artist, poet, mystic. No. 2038, E. Sharents, Armenian poet.

1958, Mar.   Unwmk.   *Perf. 12*
Various Frames

2036	A1037	40k gray black	1.65 50
2037	A1037	40k gray black	1.65 50
2038	A1037	40k sepia	1.65 50

Victory at Pskov — A1073   Soldier and Civilian A1074

Designs: No. 2040, Airman, sailor and soldier. No. 2042, Sailor and soldier. 60k, Storming of Berlin Reichstag building.

1958, Feb. 21

2039	A1073	25k multicolored	22 15
2040	A1073	40k multicolored	40 15
2041	A1074	40k multicolored	40 15
2042	A1074	40k multicolored	40 15
2043	A1073	60k multicolored	75 15
		Nos. 2039-2043 (5)	2.17
		Set value	35

40th anniversary of Red Armed Forces.

Peter Ilich Tchaikovsky — A1075

Swan Lake Ballet A1076

Design: 1r, Tchaikovsky, pianist and violinist.

1958, Mar. 18

2044	A1075	40k grn, bl, brn & red	45 15
2045	A1076	40k grn, ultra, red & yel	45 15
2046	A1075	1r lake & emerald	1.25 25
		Set value	45

Honoring Tchaikovsky and for the Tchaikovsky competitions for pianists and violinists. Exist imperf. Value, set $10.

Nos. 2044-2045 were printed in sheets of 30, including 15 stamps of each value and 5 se-tenant pairs.

V. F. Rudnev — A1077   Maxim Gorki — A1078

1958, Mar. 25   Unwmk.

2047	A1077	40k green, blk & ocher	38 15

Rudnev, naval commander.

1958, Apr. 3   Litho.   *Perf. 12*

2048	A1078	40k multicolored	18 15

Gorki, writer, 90th birth anniv.

Spasski Tower A1079   Russian Pavilion, Brussels A1080

1958, Apr. 9

2049	A1079	40k dp violet, *pinkish*	22 15
2050	A1079	60k rose red	32 15

13th Congress of the Young Communist League (Komsomol).

1958, Apr.

2051	A1080	10k multicolored	15 15
2052	A1080	40k multicolored	30 15
		Set value	15

Universal and International Exhibition at Brussels. Exist imperf. Value $2.

Lenin — A1081   Jan A. Komensky (Comenius) — A1082

1958, Apr. 22   Engr.

2053	A1081	40k dk blue gray	22 15
2054	A1081	60k rose brown	30 15
2055	A1081	1r brown	52 15
		Set value	30

88th anniversary of the birth of Lenin.

1958, May 5

Portrait: Nos. 2056-2058, Karl Marx.

2056	A1081	40k brown	15 15
2057	A1081	60k dark blue	30 15
2058	A1081	1r dark red	60 15
		Set value	32

140th anniversary of the birth of Marx.

1958, Apr. 17   Photo.

2059	A1082	40k green	30 32

No. 1695 Overprinted in Blue   200 лет Академии художеств СССР. 1957

1958, Apr. 22

2060	A914	40k multicolored	2.50 1.00

Academy of Arts, Moscow, 200th anniv.

Lenin Order A1083   Carlo Goldoni A1084

1958, Apr. 30   Litho.

2061	A1083	40k brown, yellow & red	35 20

1958, Apr. 28   Photo.

2062	A1084	40k blue & dk gray	35 20

Carlo Goldoni, Italian dramatist.

Radio Tower, Ship and Planes — A1085

1958, May 7

2063	A1085	40k blue green & red	1.50 35

Issued for Radio Day, May 7.

Globe and Dove A1086   Ilya Chavchavadze A1087

1958, May 6   Litho.

2064	A1086	40k blue & black	16 15
2065	A1086	60k ultra & black	25 15
		Set value	20

4th Congress of the Intl. Democratic Women's Federation, June, 1958, at Vienna.

1958, May 12   Photo.

2066	A1087	40k black & blue	25 15

50th anniversary of the death of Ilya Chavchavadze, Georgian writer.

Flags and Communication Symbols A1088

1958-59   Litho.

2067	A1088	40k blue, red, yel & blk	2.50 2.00
a.		Red half of Czech flag at bottom	2.50 2.00

Communist ministers' meeting on social problems in Moscow, Dec. 1957.

On No. 2067, the Czech flag (center flag in vertical row of five) is incorrectly pictured with red stripe on top. This error is corrected on No. 2067a.

Bugler — A1089   Children of Three Races — A1090

Pioneers: 25k, Boy with model plane.

1958, May 29   Unwmk.   *Perf. 12*

2068	A1089	10k ultra, red & red brn	15 15
2069	A1089	25k ultra, yel & red brn	15 15
		Set value	22 15

1958, May 29

Design: No. 2071, Child and bomb.

2070	A1090	40k car, ultra & brn	15 15
2071	A1090	40k carmine & brown	15 15
		Set value	20

Intl. Day for the Protection of Children.

Soccer Players and Globe A1091   Rimski-Korsakov A1092

1958, June 5

2072	A1091	40k blue, red & buff	16 15
2073	A1091	60k blue, red & buff	35 15
		Set value	22

6th World Soccer Championships, Stockholm, June 8-29. Exist imperf. Value $4.

1958, June 5   Photo.

2074	A1092	40k blue & brown	50 15

Nikolai Andreevich Rimski-Korsakov (1844-1908), composer.

Girl Gymnast — A1093

Design: No. 2076, Gymnast on rings and view.

1958, June 24   Litho.

2075	A1093	40k ultra, red & buff	30 15
2076	A1093	40k blue, red buff & grn	30 15
		Set value	20

14th World Gymnastic Championships, Moscow, July 6-10.

Bomb, Globe, Atom, Sputniks, Ship A1094

1958, July 1

2077	A1094	60k dk blue, blk & org	38 15

Conference for peaceful uses of atomic energy, held at Stockholm.

Street Fighters — A1095   Congress Emblem — A1097

Moscow State University A1096

1958, July 5
2078 A1095 40k red & violet blk   18   15

Communist Party in the Ukraine, 40th anniv.

1958, July 8   *Perf. 12*
2079 A1096 40k red & blue   22   15
2080 A1097 60k lt grn, blue & red   35   15
   a.   Souvenir sheet of 2   7.00   5.50

5th Congress of the International Architects' Organization, Moscow.
No. 2080a contains Nos. 2079-2080, imperf., with background design in yellow, brown, blue and red. Issued Sept. 8, 1958.

Young Couple A1098

1958, June 25
2081 A1098 40k blue & ocher   15   15
2082 A1098 60k yel green & ocher   28   15
     Set value   18

Day of Soviet Youth.

Sputnik 3 Leaving Earth A1099   Sadriddin Aini A1100

1958, June 16
2083 A1099 40k vio blue, grn & rose   60   20

Launching of Sputnik 3, May 15. Printed in sheets with alternating labels, giving details of launching.

1958, July 15
2084 A1100 40k rose, black & buff   30   15

80th birthday of Aini, Tadzhik writer.

Emblem A1101

1958, July 21   **Typo.**   *Perf. 12*
2085 A1101 40k lilac & blue   25   15

1st World Trade Union Conference of Working Youths, Prague, July 14-20.

Type of 1958-59 and

TU-104 and Globe — A1102

Design: 1r, Turbo-propeller liner AN-10.

1958, Aug.   **Litho.**
2086 A1102 60k blue, red & bis   22   15
2087 A1123 1r yel, red & black   38   15
     Set value   24

Soviet civil aviation. Exist imperf. Value, set $5.50. See Nos. 2147-2151.

L. A. Kulik — A1103

1958, Aug. 12
2088 A1103 40k sep, bl, yel & claret   60   15

50th anniv. of the falling of the Tungus meteor and the 75th anniv. of the birth of L. A. Kulik, meteorist.

IGY Type of 1957

Designs: No. 2089, Aurora borealis and camera. No. 2090, Schooner "Zarja" exploring earth magnetism. No. 2091, Weather balloon and radar.

1958, July 29
     Size: 25 1/2x37mm
2089 A1039 40k blue & brt yel   38   15
2090 A1039 40k blue green   38   15
2091 A1039 40k bright ultra   38   15
     Set value   30

International Geophysical Year, 1957-58.

Crimea Observatory A1104   Moscow University A1105

Design: 1r, Telescope.

1958, Aug.   **Photo.**
2092 A1104 40k brn & brt grnsh bl   35   15
2093 A1105 60k lt blue, vio & yel   50   15
2094 A1104 1r dp blue & org brn   60   18

10th Congress of the International Astronomical Union, Moscow.

Postilion, 16th Century A1106

Designs: #2095, 15th cent. letter writer. #2097, A. L. Ordyn-Natshokin and sleigh mail coach, 17th cent. No. 2098, Mail coach and post office, 18th cent. #2099, Troika, 19th cent. #2100, Lenin stamp, ship and Moscow University. #2101, Jet plane and postilion. #2102, Leningrad Communications Museum, vert. #2103, V. N. Podbielski and letter carriers. #2104, Mail train. #2105, Loading mail on plane. #2106, Ship, plane, train and globe.

1958, Aug. Unwmk. Litho.   *Perf. 12*
2095 A1106 10k red, blk, yel & lilac   15   15
2096 A1106 10k multicolored   15   15
2097 A1106 25k ultra & slate   22   15
2098 A1106 25k black & ultra   22   15
2099 A1106 40k car lake & brn black   28   15
2100 A1106 40k black, mag & brn   28   15
2101 A1106 40k red, org & gray   28   15
2102 A1106 40k salmon & brown   28   15
2103 A1106 60k grnsh blue & red lil   42   16
2104 A1106 60k grnsh bl & lilac   42   16
2105 A1106 1r multicolored   65   25
2106 A1106 1r multicolored   65   25
     Nos. 2095-2106 (12)   4.00
     Set value   1.65

Centenary of Russian postage stamps.
Two imperf. souvenir sheets exist, measuring 155x106mm. One contains one each of Nos. 2095-2099, with background design in red, ultramarine, yellow and brown. The other contains one each of Nos. 2100, 2103-2106, with background design in

---

blue, gray, ocher, pink and brown. Value for both, $10 unused, $6.50 canceled.
Nos. 2096, 2100-2101 exist imperf. Value each $3.25.

M. I. Chigorin A1107   Golden Gate, Vladimir A1108

1958, Aug. 30   **Photo.**
2107 A1107 40k black & emerald   35   20

50th anniversary of the death of M. I. Chigorin, chess player.

1958, Aug. 23   **Litho.**

Design: 60k, Gorki Street with trolley bus and truck.

2108 A1108 40k multicolored   15   15
2109 A1108 60k lt violet, yel & blk   25   15
     Set value   16

850th anniv. of the city of Vladimir.

Nurse Bandaging Man's Leg — A1109

Design: No. 2111, Hospital and people of various races.

1958, Sept. 15
2110 A1109 40k multicolored   20   15
2111 A1109 40k olive, lemon & red   20   15
     Set value   20

40 years of Red Cross-Red Crescent work.

Portrait Type of 1958

Portrait: Mikhail E. Saltykov (Shchedrin), writer.

1958, Sept. 15
2112 A1071 40k brn black & mar   32   15

Rudagi A1110   V. V. Kapnist A1111

1958, Oct. 10   **Litho.**   *Perf. 12*
2113 A1110 40k multicolored   20   15

1100th anniversary of the birth of Rudagi, Persian poet.

1958, Sept. 30
2114 A1111 40k blue & gray   20   15

200th anniversary of the birth of V. V. Kapnist, poet and dramatist.

Book, Torch, Lyre, Flower — A1112

1958, Oct. 4
2115 A1112 40k red org, ol & blk   20   15

Conf. of Asian & African Writers, Tashkent.

Chelyabinsk Tractor Factory — A1113

Designs: No. 2117, Zaporozstal foundry. No. 2118, Ural machine building plant.

1958, Oct. 20   **Photo.**
2116 A1113 40k green & yellow   16   15
2117 A1113 40k brown red & yel   16   15
2118 A1113 40k blue   16   15
     Set value   20

Pioneers of Russian Industry.

Ancient Georgian on Horseback A1114

1958, Oct. 18   **Litho.**
2119 A1114 40k ocher, ultra & red   75   15

1500th anniv. of Tbilisi, capital of Georgia.

Red Square, Moscow — A1115

#2121

#2124

#2127

#2128

#2131

Capitals of Soviet Republics: #2121, Lenin Square, Alma Ata. #2122, Lenin statue, Ashkhabad. #2123, Lenin statue, Tashkent. #2124, Lenin Square, Stalinabad. #2125, Rustaveli Ave., Tbilisi. #2126, View from Dvina River, Riga. #2127, University Square, Frunze. #2128, View, Yerevan. #2129, Communist Street, Baku. #2130, Lenin Prospect, Kishinev. #2131, Round Square, Minsk. #2132, Viru Gate, Tallinn. #2133, Main Street, Kiev. #2134, View, Vilnius.

1958   **Engr.**
2120 A1115 40k violet   50   15
2121 A1115 40k brt blue green   50   15
2122 A1115 40k greenish gray   50   15
2123 A1115 40k dark gray   50   15
2124 A1115 40k blue   50   15
2125 A1115 40k violet blue   50   15
2126 A1115 40k brown red   50   15
2127 A1115 40k dk blue gray   50   15
2128 A1115 40k brown   50   15
2129 A1115 40k purple   50   15
2130 A1115 40k olive   50   15
2131 A1115 40k gray brown   50   15
2132 A1115 40k emerald   50   15
2133 A1115 40k lilac rose   50   15
2134 A1115 40k orange ver   50   15
     Nos. 2120-2134 (15)   7.50   2.25

See No. 2836.

Young Civil War
Soldier,
1919 — A1116

Designs: 20k, Industrial brigade. 25k, Youth in World War II. 40k, Girl farm worker. 60k, Youth building new towns. 1r, Students, fighters for culture.

1958, Oct. 25   **Litho.**

2135	A1116	10k multicolored	18	15
2136	A1116	20k multicolored	20	15
2137	A1116	25k multicolored	30	15
2138	A1116	40k multicolored	32	15
2139	A1116	60k multicolored	52	15
2140	A1116	1r multicolored	1.25	25
		Nos. 2135-2140 (6)	2.77	
		Set value	58	

40th anniversary of the Young Communist League (Komsomol).

Marx and
Lenin — A1117

Lenin, Intellectual,
Peasant and
Miner — A1118

1958, Oct. 31

2141	A1117	40k multicolored	20	15
2142	A1118	1r multicolored	40	15
		Set value	22	

41st anniversary of Russian Revolution.

Torch, Wreath and
Family
A1119

Sergei Esenin
A1120

1958, Nov. 5

2143	A1119	60k blk, beige & dull bl	35	15

10th anniversary of the Universal Declaration of Human Rights.

1958, Nov. 29

2144	A1120	40k multicolored	35	15

Sergei Esenin (1895-1925), poet.

G. K.
Ordzhonikidze
A1121

Kuan Han-ching
A1122

1958, Dec. 12   *Perf. 12*

2145	A1121	40k multicolored	22	15

G. K. Ordzhonikidze (1886-1937), Georgian party worker.

1958, Dec. 5

2146	A1122	40k dk blue & gray	22	15

700th anniversary of the theater of Kuan Han-ching, Chinese dramatist.

Airliner IL-14 and
Globe — A1123

Soviet civil aviation: No. 2148, Jet liner TU-104. No. 2149, Turbo-propeller liner TU-114. 60k, Jet liner TU-110. 2r, Turbo-propeller liner IL-18.

1958-59

2147	A1123	20k ultra, black & red	15	15
2148	A1123	40k bl grn, blk & red	24	15
2149	A1123	40k brt bl, blk & red	24	15
2150	A1123	60k rose car & black	25	15
2151	A1123	2r plum, red & black ('59)	65	20
		Nos. 2147-2151 (5)	1.53	
		Set value	48	

Exist imperf.; value $10.
See Nos. 2086-2087.

Eleonora
Duse — A1124

John
Milton — A1125

1958, Dec. 26

2152	A1124	40k blue green & gray	20	15

Duse, Italian actress, bith cent.

1958, Dec. 17

2153	A1125	40k brown	20	15

John Milton (1608-1674), English poet.

K. F. Rulye
A1126

Fuzuli
A1127

1958, Dec. 26

2154	A1126	40k ultra & black	20	15

Rulye, educator, death cent.

1958, Dec. 23   **Photo.**

2155	A1127	40k grnsh blue & brown	20	15

400th anniv. of the death of Fuzuli (Mehmet Suleiman Oglou), Turkish poet.

Census Emblem
and
Family — A1128

Lunik and
Sputniks over
Kremlin — A1129

Design: No. 2157, Census emblem.

1958, Dec.   **Litho.**

2156	A1128	40k multicolored	20	15
2157	A1128	40k yel, gray, bl & red	20	15
		Set value	20	

1959 Soviet census.

1959, Jan.   **Unwmk.**   *Perf. 12*

Designs: 40k, Lenin and view of Kremlin. 60k, Workers and Lenin power plant on Volga.

2158	A1129	40k multicolored	30	15
2159	A1129	60k multicolored	45	20
2160	A1129	1r red, yel & vio bl	1.25	35

21st Cong. of the Communist Party and "the conquest of the cosmos by the Soviet people."

Lenin Statue, Minsk
Buildings — A1130

Atomic
Icebreaker
"Lenin"
A1131

1958, Dec. 20

2161	A1130	40k red, buff & brown	22	15

Byelorussian Republic, 40th anniv.

1958, Dec. 31

Design: 60k, Diesel Locomotive "TE-3."

2162	A1131	40k multicolored	48	18
2163	A1131	60k multicolored	70	25

Shalom
Aleichem
A1132

Evangelista
Torricelli
A1133

1959, Feb. 10

2164	A1132	40k chocolate	35	15

Aleichem, Yiddish writer, birth cent.

1959, Feb.

Scientists: #2166, Charles Darwin, English biologist. #2167, N. F. Gamaleya, microbiologist.

Various Frames

2165	A1133	40k blue green & blk	25	15
2166	A1133	40k chalky blue & brn	25	15
2167	A1133	40k dk red & black	25	15
		Set value	30	

Woman Skater
A1134

Frederic Joliot-
Curie
A1135

1959, Feb. 5

2168	A1134	25k ultra, black & ver	20	15
2169	A1134	40k ultra & black	35	15
		Set value	20	

Women's International Ice Skating Championships, Sverdlovsk.

No. 1717 Overprinted
in Orange Brown

Победа
баскетбольной
команды СССР.
Чили 1959 г.

1959, Feb. 12

2170	A919	1r	5.00	4.00

"Victory of the USSR Basketball Team - Chile 1959." However, the 3rd World Basketball Championship honors went to Brazil when the Soviet team was disqualified for refusing to play Nationalist China.

1959, Mar. 3   **Litho.**   *Perf. 12*

2171	A1135	40k turq bl & gray brn, beige	30	18

Joliot-Curie (1900-58), French scientist.

Selma Lagerlöf
A1136

Peter Zwirka
A1137

1959, Feb. 26

2172	A1136	40k red brown & black	25	15

Lagerlöf (1858-1940), Swedish writer.

1959, Mar. 3

2173	A1137	40k hn brn & blk, yel	25	15

Zwirka (1909-1947), Lithuanian writer.

No. 1861A Overprinted in Red: "1759
1959"

1959, Feb. 26   **Engr.**

2174	A993	40k lt ultra & brown	10.00	7.50

200th anniversary of the birth of Robert Burns, Scottish poet.

Type of 1958

Russian Writers: No. 2175, A. S. Griboedov. No. 2176, A. N. Ostrovski. No. 2177, Anton Chekhov. No. 2178, I. A. Krylov. No. 2178A, Nikolai V. Gogol. No. 2178B, S. T. Aksakov. No. 2178C, A. V. Koltzov. poet, and reaper.

1959   **Litho.**

2175	A1071	40k buff, cl, blk & violet	28	20
2176	A1071	40k vio & brown	28	20
2177	A1071	40k slate & hn brn	28	20
2178	A1071	40k ol bister & brn	28	20
2178A	A1071	40k ol, gray & bis	28	20
2178B	A1071	40k brn, vio & bis	28	20
2178C	A1071	40k violet & black	28	20
		Nos. 2175-2178C (7)	1.96	1.40

No. 2178A for the 150th birth anniv. of Nikolai V. Gogol, writer, No. 2178B the centenary of the death of S. T. Aksakov, writer.

A. S. Popov and Rescue from Ice Float — A1138

Design: 60k, Radio broadcasting "Peace" in five languages.

1959, Mar. 13
2179 A1138 40k brn, blk & dk blue   35 15
2180 A1138 60k multicolored   55 20

Centenary of the birth of A. S. Popov, pioneer in radio research.

M.S. Rossija at Odessa — A1139

Ships: 10k, Steamer, Vladivostok-Petropavlovsk-Kamchatka line. 20k, M.S. Feliks Dzerzhinski, Odessa-Latakia line. No. 2184, Ship, Murmansk-Tyksi line. 60k, M.S. Mikhail Kalinin at Leningrad. 1r, M.S. Baltika, Leningrad-London line.

1959   Litho.   Unwmk.
2181 A1139 10k multicolored   15 15
2182 A1139 20k red, lt grn & dk bl   16 15
2183 A1139 40k multicolored   20 15
2184 A1139 40k blue, buff & red   20 15
2185 A1139 60k bl grn, red & buff   32 15
2186 A1139 1r ultra, red & yel   48 15
    Nos. 2181-2186 (6)   1.51
    Set value   48

Honoring the Russian fleet.

Globe and Luna 1 — A1140

Luna 1, launched Jan. 2, 1959: No. 2188, Globe and route of Luna 1.

1959, Apr. 13
2187 A1140 40k red brown & rose   40 15
2188 A1140 40k ultra & blue   40 15
    Set value   24

Saadi and "Gulistan" A1141

1959, Mar. 20   Photo.
2189 A1141 40k dk blue & black   25 22

Persian poet Saadi (Muslih-ud-Din) and 700th anniv. of his book, "Gulistan" (1258).

Suahan S. Orbeliani   Drawing by
A1142   Korin
                           A1143

1959, Apr. 2
2190 A1142 40k dull rose & black   20 18

Orbeliani (1658-1725), Georgian writer.

1959, Apr. 10   Litho.
2191 A1143 40k multicolored   18 18

Ogata Korin (1653?-1716), Japanese artist.

Lenin   Cachin
A1144   A1146

1959, Apr. 17   Engr.
2192 A1144 40k sepia   18 18

89th anniversary of the birth of Lenin.

1959, Apr. 27   Photo.
2194 A1146 60k dark brown   18 18

Marcel Cachin (1869-1958), French Communist Party leader.

Joseph Haydn   Alexander von
A1147   Humboldt
                           A1148

1959, May 8
2195 A1147 40k dk bl, gray & brn black 50 15

Sesquicentennial of the death of Joseph Haydn, Austrian composer.

1959, May 6
2196 A1148 40k violet & brown   22 15

Alexander von Humboldt, German naturalist and geographer, death centenary.

Three Races   Mountain
Carrying Flag of   Climber
Peace   A1150
A1149

1959, Apr. 30   Litho.
2199 A1149 40k multicolored   60 15

10th anniv. of World Peace Movement.

1959, May 15

Sports and Travel: No. 2201, Tourists reading map. No. 2202, Canoeing, horiz. No. 2203, Skiers.

2200 A1150 40k multicolored   20 15
2201 A1150 40k multicolored   20 15
2202 A1150 40k multicolored   20 15
2203 A1150 40k multicolored   20 15
    Set value   28

I. E. Repin   N. Y. Coliseum
Statue, Moscow   and Spasski Tower
A1151   A1152

Statues: No. 2205, Lenin, Ulyanovsk. 20k, V. V. Mayakovsky, Moscow. 25k, Alexander Pushkin, Leningrad. 60k, Maxim Gorki, Moscow. 1r, Tchaikovsky, Moscow.

1959   Photo.   Unwmk.
2204 A1151 10k ocher & sepia   15 15
2205 A1151 10k red & black   15 15
2206 A1151 20k violet & sepia   15 15
2207 A1151 25k grnsh blue & blk   15 15
2208 A1151 60k lt green & slate   22 15
2209 A1151 1r lt ultra & gray   35 15
    Set value   1.00 50

1959, June 25   Litho.   Perf. 12
2210 A1152 20k multicolored   22 15
2211 A1152 40k multicolored   30 15
  a. Souv. sheet of 1, imperf.   2.50 1.00
    Set value   20

Soviet Exhibition of Science, Technology and Culture, New York, June 20-Aug. 10. No. 2211a issued July 20.

Animal Types of 1957

Animals: 20k, Hare. No. 2214, Siberian horse. No. 2215, Tiger. No. 2216, Red squirrel. No. 2217, Pine marten. No. 2218, Hazel hen. No. 2219, Mute swan.

1959-60   Litho.   Perf. 12
Center in Natural Colors
2213 A1023 20k vio blue ('60)   22 15
2214 A1023 25k blue black   22 15
2215 A1023 25k brown   22 15
2216 A1023 40k deep green   28 15
2217 A1023 40k dark green   28 15
2218 A1024 60k dark green   32 15
2219 A1023 1r bright blue   40 30
    Nos. 2213-2219 (7)   1.94
    Set value   1.00

Louis Braille   Musa Djalil
A1153   A1154

1959, July 16
2220 A1153 60k blue grn, bis & brn   30 15

150th anniversary of the birth of Louis Braille, French educator of the blind.

1959, July 16   Photo.
2221 A1154 40k violet & black   22 15

Musa Djalil, Tatar poet.

Sturgeon — A1155

1959, July 16
2222 A1155 40k shown   22 15
2223 A1155 60k Chum salmon   30 15
    Set value   20

See Nos. 2375-2377.

Gymnast
A1156

Statues: No. 2205, Lenin, Ulyanovsk. 20k, V. V.

Athletes Holding   Globe and
Trophy   Hands
A1157   A1158

Designs: 25k, Runner. 60k, Water polo.

1959, Aug. 7
2224 A1156 15k lilac rose & gray   15 15
2225 A1156 25k yel green & red brn   15 15
2226 A1157 30k brt red & gray   16 15
2227 A1156 60k blue & org yel   28 15
    Set value   32

2nd National Spartacist Games.

1959, Aug. 12   Litho.
2228 A1158 40k yel, blue & red   20 15

2nd Intl. Conf. of Public Employees Unions.

Cathedral and Modern   Schoolboys in
Building   Workshop
A1159   A1160

1959, Aug. 21   Unwmk.   Perf. 12
2229 A1159 40k blue, ol, yel & red   20 15

1100th anniv. of the city of Novgorod.

1959, Aug. 27   Photo.

Design: 1r, Workers in night school.

2230 A1160 40k dark purple   16 15
2231 A1160 1r dark blue   52 15
    Set value   18

Strengthening the connection between school and life.

Glacier Survey   Rocket and
A1161   Observatory
                           A1162

Designs: 25k, Oceanographic ship "Vityaz" and map. 40k, Plane over Antarctica, camp and emperor penguin.

1959
2232 A1161 10k blue green   15 15
2233 A1161 25k brt blue & red   28 15
2234 A1161 40k ultra & red   50 15
2235 A1162 1r ultra & buff   1.40 30
    Set value   48

Intl. Geophysical Year. 1st Russian rocket to reach the moon, Sept. 14, 1959 (#2235).

Workers and
Farmers
Holding
Atom
Symbol
A1163

1959, Sept. 23   Litho.
2236 A1163 40k red org & bister   25   15

All-Union Economic Exhibition, Moscow.

Russian and
Chinese
Students
A1164

Design: 40k, Russian miner and Chinese steel
worker.

1959, Sept. 25   Litho.   Perf. 12
2237 A1164 20k multicolored   25   15
2238 A1164 40k multicolored   35   15
     Set value   20

People's Republic of China, 10th anniv.

Letter Carrier   Makhtumkuli
A1165   A1166

1959, Sept.
2239 A1165 40k dk car rose & black   15   15
2240 A1165 60k blue & black   30   15
     Set value   15

Intl. Letter Writing Week, Oct. 4-10.

1959, Sept. 30   Photo.
2241 A1166 40k brown   25   15

225th anniversary of the birth of Makhtumkuli,
Turkmen writer.

East German Emblem   City Hall, East
and Workers — A1167   Berlin — A1168

1959, Oct. 6   Litho.
2242 A1167 40k multicolored   22   15
              Photo.
2243 A1168 60k dp claret & buff   35   15
     Set value   15

German Democratic Republic, 10th anniv.

Steel
Production — A1169

7-Year Production Plan (Industries): #2244,
Chemicals. #2245, Spasski Tower, hammer and
sickle. #2246, Home building. #2247, Meat production, woman with farm animals. #2248,
Machinery. #2249, Grain production, woman tractor driver. #2250, Oil. #2251, Textiles. #2252,
Steel. #2253, Coal. #2254, Iron. #2255, Electric
power.

1959-60   Litho.
2244 A1169 10k vio, grnsh blue &
           maroon   15   15
2245 A1169 10k orange & dk car   15   15
2246 A1169 15k brn, yel & red   15   15
2247 A1169 15k brn, grn & mar   15   15
2248 A1169 20k bl grn, yel & red   15   15
2249 A1169 20k green, yel & red   15   15
2250 A1169 30k lilac, sal & red   15   15
2251 A1169 30k gldn brn, lil, red &
           green ('60)   20   15
2252 A1169 40k vio bl, yel & org   20   15
2253 A1169 40k dk blue, pink & dp
           rose   20   15
2254 A1169 60k org red, yel, bl &
           maroon   28   15
2255 A1169 60k ultra, buff & red   28   15
     Set value   1.90   85

Arms of   Path of Luna 3
Tadzhikistan   and Electronics
A1170   Laboratory
                 A1171

1959, Oct. 13
2258 A1170 40k red, emer, ocher &
           black   35   15

Tadzhikistan statehood, 30th anniversary.

1959, Oct. 12
2259 A1171 40k violet   48   22

Flight of Luna 3 around the moon, Oct. 4, 1959.

Red Square,
Moscow
A1172

1959, Oct. 26   Engr.
2260 A1172 40k dark red   20   15

42nd anniversary of October Revolution.

US
Capitol,
Globe
and
Kremlin
A1173

1959, Oct. 27   Photo.
2261 A1173 60k blue & yellow   28   15

Visit of Premier Nikita Khrushchev to the US,
Sept., 1959.

Helicopter
A1174

Designs: 25k, Diver. 40k, Motorcyclist. 60k,
Parachutist.

1959, Oct. 28
2262 A1174 10k vio blue & maroon   15   15
2263 A1174 25k blue & brown   16   15
2264 A1174 40k red brn & indigo   20   15
2265 A1174 60k blue & ol bister   28   15
     Set value   32

Honoring voluntary aides of the army.

Moon, Earth
and Path of
Rocket
A1175

Design: No. 2267, Kremlin and diagram showing
rocket and positions of moon and earth.

1959, Nov. 1   Litho.
2266 A1175 40k bl, dk bl, red & bis   40   15
2267 A1175 40k gray, pink & red   40   15
     Set value   24

Landing of the Soviet rocket on the moon, Sept.
14, 1959.

Sandor Petőfi   Victory Statue
A1176   and View of
               Budapest
               A1177

1959, Nov. 9   Perf. 12x12¹/₂, 12¹/₂x12
2268 A1176 20k gray & ol bister   15   15
2269 A1177 40k multicolored   18   15
     Set value   20

Soviet-Hungarian friendship.
For overprint see No. 2308.

Manolis Glezos and   A. A.
Acropolis   Voskresensky
A1178   A1179

1959, Nov. 12   Photo.   Perf. 12x12¹/₂
2270 A1178 40k ultra & brown   6.00   4.75

Manolis Glezos, Greek communist.

1959, Dec. 7   Perf. 12¹/₂x12
2271 A1179 40k ultra & brown   25   15

Voskresensky, chemist, 150th birth anniv.

Chusovaya River,
Ural — A1180

Designs: No. 2273, Lake Ritza, Caucasus. No.
2274, Lena River, Siberia. No. 2275, Seashore, Far
East. No. 2276, Lake Iskander, Central Asia. No.
2277, Lake Baikal, Siberia. No. 2278, Belukha
Mountain, Altai range. No. 2279, Gursuf region,
Crimea. No. 2280, Crimea.

1959, Dec.   Engr.   Perf. 12¹/₂
2272 A1180 10k purple   15   15
2273 A1180 10k rose carmine   15   15
2274 A1180 25k dark blue   15   15
2275 A1180 25k olive   15   15
2276 A1180 25k dark red   15   15
2277 A1180 40k claret   25   15

2278 A1180 60k Prus blue   30   15
2279 A1180 1r olive green   40   15
2280 A1180 1r deep orange   40   15
    Nos. 2272-2280 (9)   2.10   80
     Set value   80

"Trumpeters of 1st   Farm
Cavalry" by M. Grekov   Woman
A1181   A1182

1959, Dec. 30   Litho.   Perf. 12¹/₂x12
2283 A1181 40k multicolored   30   22

40th anniversary of the 1st Cavalry.

1958-60   Engr.   Perf. 12¹/₂

Designs: 25k, Architect. 60k, Steel worker.

2286 A1182 20k slate grn ('59)   1.65   52
2287 A1182 25k sepia ('59)   1.65   85
2288 A1182 60k carmine   15.00   4.25

         Perf. 12x12¹/₂   Litho.
2290 A1182 20k green ('60)   15   15
2291 A1182 25k sepia ('60)   18   15
2292 A1182 60k vermilion ('59)   45   15
2293 A1182 60k blue ('60)   25   15
    Nos. 2286-2293 (7)   19.33   6.22

M. V. Frunze   Gabrichevsky
A1183   A1184

1960, Jan. 25   Photo.   Perf. 12¹/₂
2295 A1183 40k dark red brown   24   15

75th anniv. of the birth of Mikhail V. Frunze
(1885-1925), revolutionary leader.

         Perf. 12¹/₂x12
1960, Jan. 30   Unwmk.
2296 A1184 40k brt violet & brown   24   15

Centenary of the birth of G. N. Gabrichevski,
microbiologist.

Anton Chekhov
and Moscow
Home — A1185

Design: 40k, Chekhov in later years, and Yalta
home.

1960, Jan. 20   Litho.   Perf. 12x12¹/₂
2297 A1185 20k red, gray & vio blue   15   15
2298 A1185 40k dk blue, buff & brn   20   15
     Set value   15

Anton P. Chekhov (1860-1904), playwright.

Komissar-
zhevskaya
A1186

Ice Hockey
A1187

1960, Feb. 5   Photo.   *Perf. 12¹/₂x12*
2299 A1186 40k chocolate   20 15
Vera Komissarzhevskaya (1864-1910), actress.

1960, Feb. 18   Litho.   *Perf. 11¹/₂*
Sports: 25k, Speed skating. 40k, Skier. 60k, Woman figure skater. 1r, Ski jumper.
2300 A1187 10k ocher & vio blue   15 15
2301 A1187 25k multicolored   16 15
2302 A1187 40k org, rose lil & vio blue   24 15
2303 A1187 60k vio, green & buff   32 15
2304 A1187 1r blue, green & brn   48 20
Nos. 2300-2304 (5)   1.35
Set value   56
8th Olympic Winter Games, Squaw Valley, Calif., Feb. 18-29.

Sword- into-
Plowshare Statue, UN,
NY — A1188

1960   *Perf. 12x12¹/₂*
2305 A1188 40k grnsh bl, yel & brown   32 15
    a.   Souvenir sheet   1.00 45
No. 2305a for Premier Nikita Khrushchev's visit to the 15th General Assembly of the UN in NYC.

Women of Various
Races — A1189

1960, Mar. 8
2306 A1189 40k multicolored   20 15
50 years of Intl. Woman's Day, Mar. 8.

Planes in
Combat and
Timur Frunze
A1190

1960, Feb. 23   *Perf. 12¹/₂x12*
2307 A1190 40k multicolored   20 15
Lieut. Timur Frunze, World War II hero.

No. 2269 Overprinted in   15 лет
Red   освобождения
                             Венгрии

1960, Apr. 4
2308 A1177 40k multicolored   1.40 1.00
15th anniversary of Hungary's liberation from the Nazis.

Lunik 3 Photographing
Far Side of
Moon — A1191

Design: 60k, Far side of the moon.

1960   Photo.   *Perf. 12x12¹/₂*
2309 A1191 40k pale bl, dk bl & yel   50 15

Litho.
2310 A1191 60k lt bl, dk bl & citron   50 15
Photographing of the far side of the moon, Oct. 7, 1959.

Lenin as
Child
A1192

Various Lenin Portraits and: 20k, Lenin with children and Christmas tree. 30k, Flag, workers and ship. 40k, Kremlin, banners and marchers. 60k, Map of Russia, buildings and ship. 1r, Peace proclamation and globe.

1960, Apr. 10   Litho.   *Perf. 12¹/₂x12*
2311 A1192 10k multicolored   15 15
2312 A1192 20k red, green & blk   15 15
2313 A1192 30k multicolored   15 15
2314 A1192 40k multicolored   15 15
2315 A1192 60k multicolored   30 15
2316 A1192 1r red, vio bl & brn   45 15
Nos. 2311-2316 (6)   1.35
Set value   50
90th anniversary of the birth of Lenin.

Steelworker
A1193

Government House,
Baku
A1194

1960, Apr. 30   Photo.
2317 A1193 40k brown & red   15 15
Industrial overproduction by 50,000,000r during the 1st year of the 7-year plan.

1960, Apr.   Litho.   *Perf. 12x12¹/₂*
2318 A1194 40k bister & brown   32 22
Azerbaijan, 40th anniv.
For surcharge see #2898.

Brotherhood Monument,
Prague — A1195

Design: 60k, Charles Bridge, Prague.

1960, Apr. 29   Photo.   *Perf. 12¹/₂x12*
2319 A1195 40k brt blue & black   15 15
2320 A1195 60k black brn & yellow   35 15
Set value   16
Czechoslovak Republic, 15th anniv.

Radio Tower and Popov Central Museum
of Communications, Leningrad — A1196

1960, May 6   Litho.
2321 A1196 40k blue, ocher & brn   25 15
Radio Day.

Gen. I. D. Tcherniakovski and
Soldiers — A1197

1960, May 4
2322 A1197 1r multicolored   60 15
Gen. I. D. Tcherniakovski, World War II hero and his military school.

Robert Schumann
A1198

Yakov M.
Sverdlov
A1199

1960, May 20   Photo.   *Perf. 12x12¹/₂*
2323 A1198 40k ultra & black   15 15
150th anniversary of the birth of Robert Schumann, German composer.

1960, May 24   *Perf. 12¹/₂x12*
2324 A1199 40k dk brown & org brn   15 15
Sverdlov (1885-1919), 1st USSR Pres.

Stamp of 1957
Under
Magnifying
Glass — A1200

1960, May 28   Litho.   *Perf. 11¹/₂*
2325 A1200 60k multicolored   28 15
Stamp Day.

Karl Marx Avenue, Petrozavodsk, Karelian
Autonomous Republic — A1201

#2327

#2329

#2330

#2332

#2333

#2339

#2341

#2342

Capitals, Soviet Autonomous Republics: No. 2327, Lenin street, Batum, Adzhar. No. 2328, Cultural Palace, Izhevsk, Udmurt. No. 2329, August street, Grozny, Chechen-Ingush. No. 2330, Soviet House, Cheboksary, Chuvash. No. 2331, Buinak Street, Makhachkala, Dagestan. No. 2332, Soviet street, Ioshkar Ola, Mari. No. 2333, Chkalov street, Dzaudzhikau, North Ossetia. No. 2334, October street, Yakutsk, Yakut. No. 2335, House of Ministers, Nukus, Kara-Kalpak.

1960   Engr.   *Perf. 12¹/₂*
2326 A1201 40k Prus green   30 15
2327 A1201 40k violet blue   30 15
2328 A1201 40k green   30 15
2329 A1201 40k maroon   30 15
2330 A1201 40k dull red   30 15
2331 A1201 40k carmine   30 15
2332 A1201 40k dark brown   30 15
2333 A1201 40k orange brown   30 15
2334 A1201 40k dark blue   30 15
2335 A1201 40k brown   30 15
Nos. 2326-2335 (10)   3.00
Set value   1.20
See Nos. 2338-2344C. For overprints see Nos. 2336-2337.

No. 2326 Overprinted in   40 лет
Red   КАССР
                          8.VI.1960

1960, June 4
2336 A1201 40k Prus green   1.75 1.25
Karelian Autonomous Rep., 40th anniv.

No. 2328
Overprinted in   40 лет Удмуртской АССР
Red   4/XI 1960.

1960, Nov. 4
2337 A1201 40k green   2.25 1.25
Udmurt Autonomous Rep., 40th anniv.

1961-62   Perf. 12¹/₂, 12¹/₂x12

Capitals, Soviet Autonomous Republics: No. 2338, Rustaveli Street, Sukhumi, Abkhazia. No. 2339, House of Soviets, Nalchik, Kabardino-Balkar. No. 2340, Lenin Street, Ulan-Ude, Buriat. No. 2341, Soviet Street, Syktyvkar, Komi. No. 2342, Lenin Street, Nakhichevan, Nakhichevan. No. 2343, Elista, Kalmyk. No. 2344, Ufa, Bashkir. No. 2344A, Lobachevsky Square, Kazan, Tartar. No. 2344B, Kizil, Tuvinia. No. 2344C, Saransk, Mordovia.

2338	A1201	4k orange ver	25	15
2339	A1201	4k dark violet	25	15
2340	A1201	4k dark blue	25	15
2341	A1201	4k gray	25	15
2342	A1201	4k dk car rose	25	15
2343	A1201	4k olive green	25	15
2344	A1201	4k dull purple	25	15
2344A	A1201	4k grnsh blk ('62)	25	15
2344B	A1201	4k claret ('62)	25	15
2344C	A1201	4k deep green ('62)	25	15
		Nos. 2338-2344C (10)	2.50	
		Set value		1.00

Denominations of Nos. 2338-2344C are in the revalued currency.

Children's Friendship A1202

Drawings by Children: 20k, Collective farm, vert. 25k, Winter joys. 40k, "In the Zoo."

Perf. 12x12¹/₂, 12¹/₂x12

1960, June 1   Litho.

2345	A1202	10k multicolored	15	15
2346	A1202	20k multicolored	15	15
2347	A1202	25k multicolored	15	15
2348	A1202	40k multicolored	16	15
		Set value	50	30

Lomonosov University and Congress Emblem A1203

1960, June 17   Photo.   Perf. 12¹/₂x12

2349	A1203	60k yellow & dk brown	28	15

1st congress of the International Federation for Automation Control, Moscow.

Sputnik 4 and Globe — A1204

1960, June 17   Perf. 12x12¹/₂

2350	A1204	40k vio blue & dp org	75	35

Launching on May 15, 1960, of Sputnik 4, which orbited the earth with a dummy cosmonaut.

Kosta Hetagurov (1859-1906), Ossetian Poet — A1205

1960, June 20   Litho.   Perf. 12¹/₂

2351	A1205	40k gray blue & brown	25	15

Flag and Tallinn, Estonia — A1206

Soviet Republics, 20th Annivs.: No. 2353, Flag and Riga, Latvia. No. 2354, Flag and Vilnius, Lithuania.

Perf. 12x12¹/₂, 12¹/₂ (#2353)

1960   Photo.

2352	A1206	40k red & ultra	15	15

Typo.

2353	A1206	40k blue, gray & red	15	15

Litho.

2354	A1206	40k blue, red & green	15	15
		Set value		20

Cement Factory, Belgorod A1207

Design: 40k, Factory, Novy Krivoi.

1960, June 28   Perf. 12¹/₂x12

2355	A1207	25k ultra & black	15	15
2356	A1207	40k rose brown & black	15	15
		Set value	22	15

"New buildings of the first year of the seven-year plan."

Automatic Production Line and Roller Bearing A1208

Design: No. 2358, Automatic production line and gear.

1960, June 13   Perf. 11¹/₂

2357	A1208	40k rose violet	15	15
2358	A1208	40k Prus green	15	15
		Set value	24	15

Publicizing mechanization and automation of factories.

Running A1209

Sports: 10k, Wrestling. 15k, Basketball. 20k, Weight lifting. 25k, Boxing. No. 2364, Fencing. No. 2365, Diving. No. 2366, Women's gymnastics. 60k, Canoeing. 1r, Steeplechase.

1960, Aug. 1   Litho.   Perf. 11¹/₂

2359	A1209	5k multicolored	18	15
2360	A1209	10k brn, blue & yel	18	15
2361	A1209	15k multicolored	18	15
2362	A1209	20k blk, crim & sal	18	15
2363	A1209	25k lake, sl & rose	18	15
2364	A1209	40k vio bl, bl & bis	18	15
2365	A1209	40k vio, gray & pink	18	15
2366	A1209	40k multicolored	18	15
2367	A1209	40k multicolored	28	15
2368	A1209	1r brown, lilac & pale green	60	25
		Nos. 2359-2368 (10)	2.32	
		Set value		1.00

17th Olympic Games, Rome, Aug. 25-Sept. 11.

No. 2365 Overprinted in Red   Международная ярмарка в Риччоне

1960, Aug. 23

2369	A1209	40k	3.00	3.00

12th San Marino-Riccione Stamp Fair.

Kishinev, Moldavian Republic A1210

1960, Aug. 2   Perf. 12x12¹/₂

2370	A1210	40k multicolored	25	15

20th anniversary of Moldavian Republic.

Tractor and Factory — A1211   Book Museum, Hanoi — A1212

Perf. 12x12¹/₂, 12¹/₂x12

1960, Aug. 25

2371	A1211	40k green, ocher & blk	15	15
2372	A1212	60k blue, lilac & brn	22	15
		Set value		16

15th anniversary of North Viet Nam.

Gregory N. Minkh, Microbiologist, 125th Birth Anniv. — A1213

1960, Aug. 25   Photo.   Perf. 12¹/₂x12

2373	A1213	60k bister brn & dk brn	32	15

"March," by I. I. Levitan A1214

1960, Aug. 29

2374	A1214	40k ol bister & black	40	15

I. I. Levitan, painter, birth cent.

Fish Type of 1959

Designs: 20k, Pikeperch. 25k, Fur seals. 40k, Ludogan whitefish.

1960, Sept. 3   Perf. 12¹/₂

2375	A1155	20k blue & black	15	15
2376	A1155	25k vio gray & red brn	15	15
2377	A1155	40k rose lilac & purple	15	15
		Set value	36	24

Forest by I. I. Shishkin — A1215

1960, Aug. 29   Engr.

2378	A1215	1r red brown	80	15

5th World Forestry Congress, Seattle, Wash., Aug. 29-Sept. 10.

Globe with USSR and Letter — A1216

1960, Sept. 10   Litho.   Perf. 12x12¹/₂

2379	A1216	40k multicolored	15	15
2380	A1216	60k multicolored	22	15
		Set value		16

Intl. Letter Writing Week, Oct. 3-9.

Farmer, Worker, Scientist A1217

1960, Oct. 4   Typo.   Perf. 12¹/₂

2381	A1217	40k multicolored	15	15

Kazakh SSR, 40th anniv.

Globes and Olive Branch — A1218

1960, Sept. 29   Litho.   Perf. 12¹/₂x12

2382	A1218	60k pale vio, bl & gray	28	15

World Federation of Trade Unions, 15th anniv.

Kremlin, Sputnik 5 and Dogs Belka and Strelka A1219

1960, Sept. 29   Photo.

2383	A1219	40k brt pur & yellow	55	15
2384	A1219	1r blue & salmon	85	22

Flight of Sputnik 5, Aug. 19-20, 1960.

Passenger Ship "Karl Marx" — A1220

Ships: 40k, Turbo-electric ship "Lenin." 60k, Speedboat "Raketa" (Rocket).

1960, Oct. 24   Litho.   Perf. 12x12¹/₂

2385	A1220	25k blue, blk, red & yel	15	15
2386	A1220	40k blue, black & red	30	15
2387	A1220	60k blue, black & rose	35	15
		Set value		28

A. N. Voronikhin
and Kasansky
Cathedral,
Leningrad
A1221

1960, Oct. 24   Photo.
2388 A1221 40k gray & brn black   15 15
Voronikhin, architect, 200th birth anniv.

J. S.
Gogebashvili
A1222

1960, Oct. 29
2389 A1222 40k dk gray & magenta   30 15
120th anniversary of the birth of J. S.
Gogebashvili, Georgian teacher and publicist.

Red Flag, Electric
Power Station and
Factory — A1223

1960, Oct. 29   Litho.
2390 A1223 40k red, yel & brown   22 15
43rd anniversary of October Revolution.

Leo
Tolstoy — A1224

Designs: 40k, Tolstoy in Yasnaya Polyana. 60k,
Portrait, vert.

Perf. 12x12½, 12½x12
1960, Nov. 14
2391 A1224 20k violet & brown   15 15
2392 A1224 40k blue & lt brown   15 15
2393 A1224 60k dp claret & sepia   25 15
         Set value   44 24
50th anniversary of the death of Count Leo Tolstoy, writer.

Yerevan,
Armenian
Republic
A1225

1960, Nov. 14   Perf. 12x12½
2394 A1225 40k bl, red, buff & brn 15 15
Armenian Soviet Rep., 40th anniv.

The Scott International album provides spaces for an extensive representative collection of the world's
postage stamps.

Friedrich Engels
A1226

Badge of Youth
Federation
A1227

1960, Nov. 25   Engr.   Perf. 12½
2395 A1226 60k slate   38 25
Friedrich Engels, 140th birth anniv.

1960, Nov. 2   Litho.
2396 A1227 60k brt pink, blk & yel 38 15
Intl. Youth Federation, 15th anniv.

40-ton Truck
MAL-530
A1228

Automotive Industry: 40k, "Volga" car. 60k,
"Moskvitch 407" car. 1r, "Tourist LAS-697" Bus.

1960, Oct. 29 Photo. Perf. 12x12½
2397 A1228 25k ultra & gray   15 15
2398 A1228 40k ol bister & ultra   15 15
2399 A1228 60k Prus green & dp car 30 15
Litho.
2400 A1228 1r multicolored   52 15
         Set value   38

N. I. Pirogov
A1229

Friendship
University and
Students
A1230

1960, Dec. 13 Photo. Perf. 12½x12
2401 A1229 40k green & brn black   25 15
Pirogov, surgeon, 125th birth anniv.

1960, Nov.   Perf. 12½x12½
2402 A1230 40k brown carmine   25 15
Completion of Friendship of Nations University
in Moscow.
For surcharge see No. 2462.

Mark Twain
A1231

1960, Nov. 30   Perf. 12½x12
2403 A1231 40k dp orange & brown   50 40
Mark Twain, 125th birth anniv.

Dove and Globe
A1232

Akaki Zeretely
A1233

1960, Oct. 29   Photo.
2404 A1232 60k maroon & gray   25 15
Intl. Democratic Women's Fed, 15th anniv.

1960, Dec. 27
2405 A1233 40k violet & black brn 32 15
Zeretely, Georgian poet, 120th birth anniv.

Frederic Chopin,
after Delacroix
A1234

1960, Dec. 24   Perf. 12x11½
2406 A1234 40k bister & brown   32 15
Chopin, Polish composer, 150th birth anniv.

North Korean Flag
and Flying
Horse — A1235

Crocus — A1236

1960, Dec. 24 Litho.   Perf. 12½x12
2407 A1235 40k multicolored   25 15
15th anniversary of "the liberation of the Korean
people by the Soviet army."

1960   Perf. 12x12½
Asiatic Flowers: No. 2409, Tulip. No. 2410, Trol-
lius. No. 2411, Tulip. No. 2412, Ginseng. No.
2413, Iris. No. 2414, Hypericum. 1r, Dog rose.

Flowers in Natural Colors
2408 A1236 20k green & violet   22 15
2409 A1236 20k vio blue & black   22 15
2410 A1236 25k gray   28 15
2411 A1236 40k ol bister & black   32 15
2412 A1236 40k green & blk, wmkd. 32 15
2413 A1236 60k yel, green & red   70 15
2414 A1236 60k bluish grn & blk   70 15
2415 A1236 1r slate green & blk   1.10 15
      Nos. 2408-2415 (8)   3.86
         Set value   60
The watermark on No. 2412 consists of vertical
rows of chevrons.

Lithuanian
Costumes
A1237

Regional Costumes: 60k, Uzbek.

Perf. 12½ (10k), 11½ (60k)
1960, Dec. 24   Typo.   Unwmk.
2416 A1237 10k multicolored   25 15
2417 A1237 60k multicolored   1.00 15
         Set value   16

Currency Revalued
1961-62   Litho.   Perf. 11½
Regional Costumes: No. 2418, Moldavia. No.
2419, Georgia. No. 2420, Ukrainia. No. 2421,
White Russia. No. 2422, Kazakhstan. No. 2422A,
Latvia. 4k, Koryak. 6k, Russia. 10k, Armenia. 12k,
Estonia.

2418 A1237 2k buff, brn & ver   15 15
2419 A1237 2k red, brn, ocher &
                  black   15 15
2420 A1237 3k ultra, buff, red &
                  brown   22 15
2421 A1237 3k red org, ocher &
                  black   22 15
2422 A1237 3k buff, brn, grn &
                  red   22 15
2422A A1237 3k org red, gray ol &
                  blk ('62)   22 15
2423 A1237 4k multicolored   45 15
2424 A1237 6k multicolored   55 25
2425 A1237 10k brn, ol bis & ver-
                  milion   80 30
2426 A1237 12k red, ultra & black 1.10 40
      Nos. 2418-2426 (10)   4.08
         Set value   1.70
See Nos. 2723-2726.

Lenin and
Map Showing
Electrification
A1238

1961   Perf. 12½x12
2427 A1238 4k blue, buff & brown   15 15
2428 A1238 10k red org & blue blk 38 25
State Electrification Plan, 40th anniv. (in 1960).

Animal Types of 1957
1961, Jan. 7   Perf. 12½
2429 A1024 1k Brown bear   15 15
2430 A1023 6k Beaver   70 35
2431 A1023 10k Roe deer   90 55

Georgian Flag
and Views
A1239

1961, Feb. 15   Perf. 12½x12
2432 A1239 4k multicolored   30 15
40th anniv. of Georgian SSR.

Nikolai D. Zelinski
A1240

N. A.
Dobrolyubov
A1241

1961, Feb. 6 Photo. Perf. 12x12½
2433 A1240 4k rose violet   30 15
Zelinski, chemist, birth cent.

1961, Feb. 5   Perf. 11½x12
2434 A1241 4k brt blue & brown   40 15
Nikolai A. Dobrolyubov, journalist and critic
(1836-1861).

A1242

A1243

Designs: 3k, Cattle. 4k, Tractor in cornfield. 6k, Mechanization of Grain Harvest. 10k, Women picking apples.

1961		Perf. 12x12¹/₂, 12x11¹/₂		
2435	A1242	3k blue & magenta	25	15
2436	A1242	4k green & dk gray	25	15
2437	A1242	6k vio blue & brn	60	15
2438	A1242	10k maroon & ol grn	80	15
		Set value		32

Agricultural development.

Perf. 12x12¹/₂; 12x11¹/₂ (Nos. 2439A, 2442 & 12k)

1961-65   **Unwmk.**

Designs: 1k, "Labor" Holding Peace Flag. 2k, Harvester and silo. 3k, Space rockets. 4k, Arms and flag of USSR. 6k, Spasski tower. 10k, Workers' monument. 12k, Minin and Pozharsky Monument and Spasski tower. 16k, Plane over power station and dam.

Engr.

2439	A1243	1k olive bister	1.90	15

Litho.

2439A	A1243	1k olive bister	75	15
2440	A1243	2k green	18	15
2441	A1243	3k dk violet	2.50	15

Engr.

2442	A1243	3k dk violet	4.25	95

Litho.

2443	A1243	4k red	75	15
2443A	A1243	4k org brn ('65)	95	35
2444	A1243	5k vermilion	6.75	65
2445	A1243	6k dk car rose	1.90	15
2446	A1243	10k orange	3.50	15

Photo.

2447	A1243	12k brt magenta	3.50	30

Litho.

2448	A1243	16k ultra	5.25	1.10
	Nos. 2439-2448 (12)		32.18	4.40

V. P. Miroshnitchenko — A1244

1961, Feb. 23   **Photo.**   **Perf. 12¹/₂x12**

2449	A1244	4k violet brn & slate	25	15

Soldier hero of World War II.
See Nos. 2570-2571.

Taras G. Shevchenko and Birthplace A1245

Shevchenko Statue, Kharkov A1246

Andrei Rubljov A1247

Design: 6k, Book, torch and Shevchenko with beard.

Perf. 12¹/₂, 11¹/₂x12

1961, Mar.   **Litho.; Photo. (4k)**

2450	A1245	3k brown & violet	30	15
2451	A1246	4k red orange & gray	60	20
2452	A1246	6k black, grn & red brn	85	22

Shevchenko, Ukrainian poet, death cent. No. 2452 was printed with alternating green and black label, containing a quotation. See No. 2852.

1961, Mar. 13   **Litho.**   **Perf. 12¹/₂x12**

2453	A1247	4k ultra, bister & brn	15	15

Rubljov, painter, 600th birth anniv.

N. V. Sklifosovsky A1248

Robert Koch A1249

1961, Mar. 26   **Photo.**   **Perf. 11¹/₂x12**

2454	A1248	4k ultra & black	15	15

Sklifosovsky, surgeon, 125th birth anniv.

1961, Mar. 26

2455	A1249	6k dark brown	15	15

Koch, German microbiologist, 59th death anniv.

Globe and Sputnik 8 — A1250

Design: 10k, Space probe and its path to Venus.

1961, Apr.   **Litho.**   **Perf. 11¹/₂**

2456	A1250	6k dk & lt blue & org	55	20

Photo.

2457	A1250	10k vio blue & yel	75	30

Launching of the Venus space probe, Feb. 12, 1961.

Open Book and Globe A1251

1961, Apr. 7   **Litho.**   **Perf. 12¹/₂x12**

2458	A1251	6k ultra & sepia	70	15

Centenary of the children's magazine "Around the World."

Musician, Dancers and Singers A1252

1961, Apr. 7   **Unwmk.**

2459	A1252	4k yel, red & black	40	15

Russian National Choir, 50th anniv.

African Breaking Chains and Map A1253

Design: 6k, Globe, torch and black and white handshake.

1961, Apr. 15   **Perf. 12¹/₂**

2460	A1253	4k multicolored	30	15
2461	A1253	6k blue, purple & org	30	15
		Set value		25

Africa Day and 3rd Conference of Independent African States, Cairo, Mar. 25-31.

No. 2402 Surcharged in Red

'4 коп.

имени Патриса Лумумбы 1961 г.

1961, Apr. 15   **Photo.**   **Perf. 12x12¹/₂**

2462	A1230	4k on 40k brown car	70	15

Naming of Friendship University, Moscow, in memory of Patrice Lumumba, Premier of Congo.

Maj. Yuri A. Gagarin A1254

Designs: 6k, Kremlin, rockets and radar equipment. 10k, Rocket, Gagarin with helmet and Kremlin.

1961, Apr.   **Perf. 11¹/₂ (3k), 12¹/₂x12**

2463	A1254	3k Prus blue	24	15

Litho.

2464	A1254	6k blue, violet & red	58	15
2465	A1254	10k red, blue grn & brn	1.10	35

1st man in space, Yuri A. Gagarin, Apr. 12, 1961. No. 2464 printed with alternating light blue and red label. Nos. 2463-2465 exist imperf. Value $1.75.

Lenin — A1255

Rabindranath Tagore — A1256

1961, Apr. 22   **Litho.**   **Perf. 12x12¹/₂**

2466	A1255	4k dp car, salmon & blk	15	15

91st anniversary of Lenin's birth.

1961, May 8   **Engr.**   **Perf. 11¹/₂x12**

2467	A1256	6k bis, maroon & blk	15	15

Tagore, Indian poet, birth cent.

The Hunchbacked Horse — A1257

Fairy Tales: 1k, The Geese and the Swans. 3k, Fox, Hare and Cock. 6k, The Peasant and the Bear. 10k, Ruslan and Ludmilla.

1961   **Litho.**   **Perf. 12¹/₂**

2468	A1257	1k multicolored	15	15
2469	A1257	3k multicolored	50	30
2470	A1257	4k multicolored	15	15
2471	A1257	6k multicolored	52	35
2472	A1257	10k multicolored	65	38
	Nos. 2468-2472 (5)		1.97	1.33

"Man Conquering Space" — A1258

Design: 6k, Giuseppe Garibaldi.

1961, May 24   **Photo.**

2481	A1258	4k orange brown	22	15
2482	A1258	6k lilac & salmon	45	15
		Set value		18

International Labor Exposition, Turin.

Lenin A1259

Patrice Lumumba A1260

Various portraits of Lenin.

1961   **Photo.**   **Perf. 12¹/₂x12**
Olive Bister Frame

2483	A1259	20k dark green	85	85
2484	A1259	30k dark blue	1.90	1.90
2485	A1259	50k rose red	2.75	2.75

1961, May 29   **Litho.**

2486	A1260	2k yellow & brown	15	15

Lumumba (1925-61), premier of Congo.

Kindergarten A1261

Children's Day: 3k, Young Pioneers in camp. 4k, Young Pioneers, vert.

Perf. 12¹/₂x12, 12x12¹/₂

1961, May 31   **Photo.**

2487	A1261	2k orange & ultra	15	15
2488	A1261	3k ol bister & purple	15	15
2489	A1261	4k red & gray	15	15
		Set value		28	26

Dog Zvezdochka and Sputnik 10 — A1263

Sputniks 9 and 10: 4k, Dog Chernushka and Sputnik 9, vert.

1961, June 8   **Litho.**   **Perf. 12¹/₂, 11¹/₂**

2491	A1263	2k vio, Prus blue & blk	35	15

Photo.

2492	A1263	4k Prus blue & brt grn	35	15

124 RUSSIA

A1265

A1266

Engraved and Photogravure

1961, June 13   *Perf. 11¹/₂x12*
2493 A1265 4k carmine & black   30 15

150th anniversary of the birth of Vissarion G. Belinski, author and critic.

1961, June 22   Litho.   *Perf. 12¹/₂*
2494 A1266 4k black, red & yel   30 15

Lt. Gen. D. M. Karbishev, who was tortured to death in the Nazi prison camp at Mauthausen, Austria.

Hydro-meteorological Map and Instruments — A1267

1961, June 21   *Perf. 12x12¹/₂*
2495 A1267 6k ultra & green   50 15

40th anniversary of hydro-meteorological service in Russia.

Gliders — A1268

Designs: 6k, Motorboat race. 10k, Motorcycle race.

1961, July 5   Photo.   *Perf. 12¹/₂*
2497 A1268   4k dk slate grn & crim   30 15
       Litho.
2498 A1268 6k slate & vermilion   38 15
2499 A1268 10k slate & vermilion   1.25 15
       Set value   28

USSR Technical Sports Spartakiad.

 (see below)

Javelin Thrower A1269

1961, Aug. 8   Photo.   *Perf. 12¹/₂x12*
2500 A1269 6k dp carmine & pink   15 15

7th Trade Union Spartacist Games.

S. I. Vavilov A1270

Vazha Pshavela A1271

1961, July 25
2501 A1270 4k lt green & sepia   15 15

Vavilov, president of Academy of Science.

1961   Photo.   *Perf. 11¹/₂x12*
2502 A1271 4k dk brown & cream   35 15

Pshavela, Georgian poet, birth cent.

Scientists at Control Panel for Rocket — A1272

Globe and Youth Activities A1273

Design: 2k, Men pushing tank into river.

1961   Unwmk.   *Perf. 11¹/₂*
2503 A1273 2k orange & sepia   15 15
2504 A1272 4k lilac & dk green   35 15
2505 A1273 6k ultra & citron   45 15
       Set value   22

International Youth Forum, Moscow.

Arms of Mongolian Republic and Sukhe Bator Statue A1274

1961, July 25   Litho.   *Perf. 12¹/₂x12*
2506 A1274 4k multicolored   40 15

Mongol national revolution, 40th anniv.

Knight Kalevipoeg A1275

Symbols of Biochemistry A1276

1961, July 31
2507 A1275 4k black, blue & yel   15 15

1st publication of "Kalevipoeg," Estonian national saga, recorded by R. K. Kreutzwald, Estonian writer, cent.

1961, July 31
2508 A1276 6k multicolored   35 15

5th Intl. Biochemistry Congress, Moscow.

Major Titov and Vostok 2 — A1277

Design: 4k, Globe with orbit and cosmonaut.

1961, Aug.   Photo.   *Perf. 11¹/₂*
2509 A1277 4k vio blue & dp plum   25 15
2510 A1277 6k brown, grn & org   35 15

1st manned space flight around the world, Maj. Gherman S. Titov, Aug. 6-7, 1961. Nos. 2509-2510 exist imperf. Value, set $2.50.

A. D. Zacharov and Admiralty Building, Leningrad A1278

1961, Aug. 8   *Perf. 12x11¹/₂*
2511 A1278 4k blue, dk brn & buff   15 15

Zacharov (1761-1811), architect.

Defense of Brest, 1941 A1279

Designs: No. 2512, Defense of Moscow. No. 2514, Defense of Odessa. No. 2514A, Defense of Sevastopol. No. 2514B, Defense of Leningrad. No. 2514C, Defense of Kiev. No. 2514D, Battle of the Volga (Stalingrad).

1961-63   Photo.   *Perf. 12¹/₂x12*
2512   A1279 4k blk & red brn
           (Moscow)   35   15
           Litho.
2513   A1279 4k (Brest)   35   15
2514   A1279 4k (Odessa)   35   15
2514A A1279 4k (Sevastopol;'62)   35   15
2514B A1279 4k brn, dl bl & bis (Le-
           ningrad;'63)   35   15
2514C A1279 4k blk & multi
           (Kiev;'63)   35   15
2514D A1279 4k dl org & multi (Vol-
           ga;'63)   35   15
      Nos. 2512-2514D (7)   2.45
       Set value   84

"War of Liberation," 1941-1945.
See Nos. 2757-2758.

Students' Union Emblem — A1280

1961, Aug. 8   Litho.   *Perf. 12¹/₂*
2515 A1280 6k ultra & red   35 15

15th anniversary of the founding of the International Students' Union.

Soviet Stamps A1281

Stamps and background different on each denomination.

1961, Aug.   *Perf. 12¹/₂x12*
2516 A1281 2k multicolored   20 15
2517 A1281 4k multicolored   38 24
2518 A1281 6k multicolored   50 30
2519 A1281 10k multicolored   75 38

40 years of Soviet postage stamps.

Nikolai A. Schors Statue, Kiev — A1282

Statue: 4k, Gregori I. Kotovski, Kishinev.

1961   Photo.   *Perf. 11¹/₂x12*
2520 A1282 2k lt ultra & sepia   30 15
2521 A1282 4k rose vio & sepia   30 15
       Set value   15

Letters and Means of Transportation A1283

1961, Sept. 15   *Perf. 11¹/₂*
2522 A1283 4k dk car & black   30 15

International Letter Writing Week.

Angara River Bridge, Irkutsk A1284

1961, Sept. 15   Litho.   *Perf. 12¹/₂x12*
2523 A1284 4k ol bis, lilac & black   15 15

300th anniversary of Irkutsk.

Lenin, Marx, Engels and Marchers — A1285

Designs: 3k, Obelisk commemorating conquest of space and Moscow University. No. 2526, Harvester combine. No. 2527, Industrial control center. No. 2528, Worker pointing to globe.

1961   **Litho.**
2524 A1285 2k ver, yel & brown   38   24
2525 A1285 3k org & deep blue   65   24
2526 A1285 4k mar, bis & red
           brown   38   24
2527 A1285 4k car rose, brn, org &
           blue   38   24
2528 A1285 4k red & dk brown   38   24
      Nos. 2524-2528 (5)   2.17 1.20

22nd Congress of the Communist Party of the USSR, Oct. 17-31.

Soviet Soldier
Monument,
Berlin — A1286

1961, Sept. 28 Photo.   Perf. 12x12½
2529 A1286 4k red & gray violet   40 15

10th anniversary of the International Federation
of Resistance, FIR.

Workers
Studying
Mathematics
A1287

Designs: 2k, Communist labor team. 4k, Workers around piano.

1961, Sept. 28 Litho.   Perf. 12½x12
2530 A1287 2k plum & red, cream   15 15
2531 A1287 3k brn & red, yellow   15 15
2532 A1287 4k vio blue & red, cr   20 15
           Set value   24

Publicizing Communist labor teams in their
efforts for labor, education and relaxation.

Rocket and Stars — A1288

**Engraved on Aluminum Foil
1961, Oct. 17   Perf. 12½**
2533 A1288 1r black & red   9.00 4.25

Soviet scientific and technical achievements in
exploring outer space.

Overprinted in Red   XXII съезд
                       КПСС

1961, Oct. 23
2534 A1288 1r black & red   10.00 4.50

Communist Party of the USSR, 22nd cong.

Amangaldi   Franz Liszt
Imanov   A1290
A1289

1961, Oct. 25 Photo.   Perf. 11½x12
2535 A1289 4k green, buff & brn   15 15

Amangaldi Imanov (1873-1919), champion of
Soviet power in Kazakhstan.

1961, Oct. 31   Perf. 12x11½
2536 A1290 4k mar, dk brn & ocher   50 15

Liszt, composer, 150th birth anniv.

Flags and
Slogans
A1291

1961, Nov. 4   Perf. 11½
2537 A1291 4k red, yel & dark red   50 15

44th anniversary of October Revolution.

Hand Holding   Congress Emblem
Hammer   A1293
A1292

Designs: Nos. 2538, 2542, Congress emblem.
Nos. 2539, 2543, African breaking chains. No.
2541, Three hands holding globe.

1961, Nov.   Perf. 12, 12½, 11½
2538 A1293 2k scarlet & bister   16 15
2539 A1293 2k dk purple & gray   16 15
2540 A1292 4k plum, org & blue   32 15
2541 A1292 4k blk, lt blue & pink   38 15
2542 A1293 6k grn, bister & red   70 15
2543 A1293 6k ind, dull yel & red   48 15
     Nos. 2538-2543 (6)   2.20
           Set value   60

Fifth World Congress of Trade Unions, Moscow,
Dec. 4-16.

Lomonosov   Hands Holding
Statue   Hammer and
A1294   Sickle
                 A1295

Designs: 6k, Lomonosov at desk. 10k,
Lomonosov, his birthplace and Leningrad Academy
of Science, horiz.

Perf. 11½x12, 12x11½
1961, Nov. 19   Photo. & Engr.
2544 A1294 4k Prus blue, yel grn &
                  brown   25 15
2545 A1294 6k green, yel & black   40 15
2546 A1294 10k mar, slate & brn   95 22
           Set value   38

250th anniversary of the birth of M. V.
Lomonosov, scientist and poet.

1961, Nov. 27 Litho.   Perf. 12x12½
2547 A1295 4k red & yellow   30 15

USSR constitution, 25th anniv.

Romeo and Juliet   Linemen — A1297
Ballet — A1296

Ballets: 2k, Red Flower. 3k, Paris Flame. 10k,
Swan Lake.

1961-62   Perf. 12x12½
2548 A1296 2k brn, car & lt green
                  ('62)   15 15
2549 A1296 3k multicolored ('62)   16 15
2550 A1296 6k dk brn, bis & vio   40 15
2551 A1296 10k blue, pink & dk brn   60 15
           Set value   30

Honoring the Russian Ballet.

1961   Perf. 12½
2552 A1297 3k shown   18 15
2553 A1297 4k Welders   26 15
2554 A1297 6k Surveyor   32 15
           Set value   20

Honoring self-sacrificing work of youth in the 7-
year plan.

Andrejs Pumpurs
(1841-1902),
Latvian Poet and
Satirist — A1298

1961, Dec. 20   Perf. 12x11½
2555 A1298 4k gray & claret   30 15

Bulgarian
Couple,
Flag,
Emblem and
Building
A1299

1961, Dec. 28   Perf. 12½x12
2556 A1299 4k multicolored   30 15

Bulgarian People's Republic, 15th anniv.

Fridtjof
Nansen
A1300

1961, Dec. 30 Photo.   Perf. 11½
2557 A1300 6k dk blue & brown   1.50 52

Centenary of the birth of Fridtjof Nansen, Norwegian Polar explorer.

Mihael Ocipovich Dolivo-
Dobrovolsky — A1301

1962, Jan. 25   Perf. 12x11½
2558 A1301 4k bister & dk blue   15 15

Dolivo-Dobrovolsky, scientist and electrical engineer, birth cent.

Woman and
Various
Activities
A1302

1962, Jan. 26   Perf. 11½
2559 A1302 4k bister, blk & dp org   15 15

Honoring Soviet Women.

Aleksander S. Pushkin,
125th Death
Anniv. — A1303

1962, Jan. 26 Litho.   Perf. 12½x12
2560 A1303 4k buff, dk brown & ver   15 15

Dancers
A1304

1962, Feb. 6   Perf. 12x12½
2561 A1304 4k bister & ver   15 15

State ensemble of folk dancers, 25th anniv.

Speed Skating,
Luzhniki
Stadium
A1305

Perf. 11½
1962, Feb. 17 Unwmk.   Photo.
2562 A1305 4k orange & ultra   32 15

International Winter Sports Championships,
Moscow, 1962.

No. 2562   СОВЕТСКИЕ КОНЬКОБЕЖЦЫ—
Overprinted   НЕМПИОНЫ
               МИРА

1962, Mar. 3
2563 A1305 4k orange & ultra   1.50 35

Victories of I. Voronina and V. Kosichkin, world
speed skating champions, 1962.

Ski Jump
A1305a

Design: 10k, Woman long distance skier, vert.

1962, May 31   Perf. 11½
2564 A1305a 2k ultra, brown & red   15 15
2565 A1305a 10k org, ultra & black   25 15
            Set value   32 16

International Winter Sports Championships,
Zakopane, 1962.

Hero Type of 1961

Designs: 4k, V. S. Shalandin. 6k, Magomet
Gadgiev.

1962, Feb. 22   Perf. 12½x12
2570 A1244 4k dk blue & brown   1.50 75
2571 A1244 6k brn & slate grn   1.50 75

Soldier heroes of World War II.

Skier
A1306

1962, Mar. 3   *Perf. 11¹/₂*
2572 A1306 4k shown   28   15
2573 A1306 6k Ice hockey   35   15
2574 A1306 10k Ice skating   80   16

First People's Winter Games, Sverdlovsk.
For overprints see Nos. 2717, 3612.

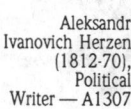

Aleksandr
Ivanovich Herzen
(1812-70),
Political
Writer — A1307

1962, Mar. 28 Litho. *Perf. 12x12¹/₂*
2575 A1307 4k ultra, black & buff   20   15

Lenin
A1308

Vostok 1
A1309

Design: 6k, Lenin, horiz.

Perf. 12x12¹/₂, 12¹/₂x12
1962, Mar. 28
2576 A1308 4k brown, red & yel   30   15
2577 A1308 6k blue, org & brn   30   15
              Set value   20

14th congress of the Young Communist League
(Komsomol).

1962, Apr. Unwmk. *Perf. 11x11¹/₂*
2578 A1309 10k multicolored   1.00   50

1st anniv. of Yuri A. Gagarin's flight into space.
No. 2578 was printed in sheets of 20 stamps
alternating with 20 labels.
No. 2578 was also issued imperf. Value $1.50.

Bust of
Tchaikovsky — A1310

1962, Apr. 19 Photo. *Perf. 11¹/₂x12*
2579 A1310 4k blue, black & bis   15   15

Second International Tchaikovsky Competition in
Moscow.

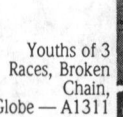

Youths of 3
Races, Broken
Chain,
Globe — A1311

1962, Apr. 19   *Perf. 11¹/₂*
2580 A1311 6k black, brn & yel   15   15

International Day of Solidarity of Youth against
Colonialism.

15-Cent Minimum Value
*The minimum value for a single
stamp is 15 cents. This value
reflects the costs of handling
inexpensive stamps.*

Ulyanov (Lenin)
Family Portrait
A1312

Lenin — A1313

1962, Apr. 21   *Perf. 12x11¹/₂*
2581 A1312 4k gray, red & dk brn   20   15
Typographed and Emboss
Perf. 12¹/₂
2582 A1313 10k dk red, gray & blk   40   15
  a.   Souv. sheet of 2, perf. 12 ('64) 2.50 60
              Set value   17

92nd anniversary of the birth of Lenin.
No. 2582a for 94th anniv. of the birth of Lenin.
Issued Nov. 6, 1964.

Cosmos 3 Satellite — A1314

1962, Apr. 26 Litho. *Perf. 12¹/₂x12*
2586 A1314 6k blk, lt blue & vio   50   15

Cosmos 3 earth satellite launching, Apr. 24.

Charles Dickens
A1315

Karl Marx
Monument,
Moscow
A1316

Portrait: No. 2589, Jean Jacques Rousseau.

1962, Apr. 29
2588 A1315 6k blue, brn & pur   35   15
Perf. 11¹/₂x12
Photo.
2589 A1315 6k gray, lilac & brn   35   15
              Set value   20

Charles Dickens, English writer, 150th birth
anniv. and Jean Jacques Rousseau, French writer,
250th birth anniv.

1962, Apr. 29   *Perf. 12x12¹/₂*
2590 A1316 4k deep ultra & gray   30   15

Pravda, Lenin,
Revolutionists
A1317

Lenin Reading
Pravda
A1318

Designs: No. 2592, Pravda, Lenin and rocket.

1962, May 4   Litho.
2591 A1317 4k black, bister & red   30   15
2592 A1317 4k red, black & ocher   30   15
Perf. 11¹/₂
Photo.
2593 A1318 4k ocher, dp cl & red   30   15

50th anniversary of Pravda, Russian newspaper
founded by Lenin.

Malaria
Eradication
Emblem and
Mosquito
A1319

1962
2594 A1319 4k Prus blue, red & blk   45   15
2595 A1319 6k ol green, red & blk   45   15
              Set value   15

WHO drive to eradicate malaria. Issue dates: 4k,
May 6; 6k, June 23.
No. 2595 exists imperf. Value $1.

Pioneers
Taking
Oath
before
Lenin and
Emblem
A1320

Designs (Emblem and): 3k, Lenja Golikov and
Valja Kotik. No. 2598, Pioneers building rocket
model. No. 2599, Red Cross, Red Crescent and
nurse giving health instruction. 6k, Pioneers of
many races and globe.

1962, May 19 Litho. *Perf. 12¹/₂x12*
2596 A1320 2k green, red & brn   15   15
2597 A1320 3k multicolored   20   15
2598 A1320 4k multicolored   25   15
2599 A1320 4k multicolored   25   15
2600 A1320 6k multicolored   45   15
  Nos. 2596-2600 (5)   1.30
              Set value   46

All-Union Lenin Pioneers, 40th anniv.

Mesrob
A1321

Ivan A.
Goncharov
A1322

1962, May 27 Photo. *Perf. 12¹/₂x12*
2601 A1321 4k yellow & dk brown   75   15

"1600th" anniversary of the birth of Bishop Mesrob (350?-439), credited as author of the Armenian
and Georgian alphabets.

1962, June 18
2602 A1322 4k gray & brown   30   15

Ivan Aleksandrovich Goncharov (1812-91), novelist, 150th birth anniv.

Volleyball
A1323

Louis Pasteur
A1324

Designs: 2k, Bicyclists, horiz. 10k, Eight-man
shell. 12k, Goalkeeper, soccer, horiz. 16k,
Steeplechase.

1962, June 27   *Perf. 11¹/₂*
2603 A1323 2k lt brn, blk & ver   20   15
2604 A1323 4k brn org, black & buff   28   15
2605 A1323 10k ultra, black & yel   70   15
2606 A1323 12k lt blue, brn & yel   90   15
2607 A1323 16k lt green, blk & red   1.10   15
  Nos. 2603-2607 (5)   3.18
              Set value   50

Intl. Summer Sports Championships, 1962.

1962, June 30   *Perf. 12¹/₂x12*
2608 A1324 6k black & brown org   15   15

Invention of the sterilization process by Louis
Pasteur, French chemist, cent.

Library, 1862
A1325

Design: No. 2610, New Lenin Library.

1962, June 30   Photo.
2609 A1325 4k slate & black   15   15
2610 A1325 4k slate & black   15   15
  a.   Pair, #2609-2610   30   15
              Set value   15

Centenary of the Lenin Library, Moscow.

Auction Building and Ermine — A1326

1962, June 30   Litho.
2611 A1326 6k multicolored   40   15

International Fur Auction, Leningrad.

Young Couple,
Lenin,
Kremlin — A1327

Workers of Three
Races and
Dove — A1328

1962, June 30   *Perf. 12x12¹/₂*
2612 A1327 2k multicolored   30   15
2613 A1328 4k multicolored   30   15
              Set value   17   15

Program of the Communist Party of the Soviet
Union for Peace and Friendship among all people.

Hands
Breaking Bomb
A1329

1962, July 7   **Perf. 11½**
2614 A1329 6k blue, blk & olive   30 15

World Congress for Peace and Disarmament, Moscow, July 9-14.

Yakub Kolas
and Yanka
Kupala
A1330

1962, July 7   **Photo.**   **Perf. 12½x12**
2615 A1330 4k henna brn & buff   30 15

Byelorussian poets. Kolas (1882-1956), and Kupala (1882-1942).

Alepker
Sabir — A1331

Cancer Congress
Emblem — A1332

1962, July 16   **Perf. 11½**
2616 A1331 4k buff, dk brn & blue   30 15

Sabir, Azerbaijan poet & satirist, (1862-1911).

1962, July 16   **Litho.**   **Perf. 12½**
2617 A1332 6k grnsh blue, blk & red   35 15

8th Anti-Cancer Cong., Moscow, July 1962.

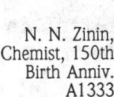

N. N. Zinin,
Chemist, 150th
Birth Anniv.
A1333

1962, July 16   **Photo.**   **Perf. 12x11½**
2618 A1333 4k violet & dk brown   35 15

I. M. Kramskoy,
Painter
A1334

I. D. Shadr, Sculptor
A1335

M. V. Nesterov,
Painter — A1336

Perf. 11½x12, 12x12½
1962, July 28
2619 A1334 4k gray, mar & dk brn   35 15
2620 A1335 4k black & red brown   35 15
2621 A1336 4k multicolored   35 15
     Set value   20

Vostok 2 Going into
Space — A1337

Perf. 11½
1962, Aug. 7   **Unwmk.**   **Photo.**
2622 A1337 10k blk, lilac & blue   60 15
2623 A1337 10k blk, orange & blue   60 15

1st anniv. of Gherman Titov's space flight. Issued imperf. on Aug. 6. Value, set $4.50.

Friendship
House,
Moscow
A1338

1962, Aug. 15   **Perf. 12x12½**
2624 A1338 6k ultra & gray   15 15

Kremlin and Atom Symbol — A1339

Design: 6k, Map of Russia, atom symbol and "Peace" in 10 languages.

1962, Aug. 15   **Litho.**   **Perf. 12½x12**
2625 A1339 4k multicolored   35 15
2626 A1339 6k multicolored   35 15

Use of atomic energy for peace.

Andrian G.
Nikolayev
A1340

Cosmonauts in Space Helments — A1341

"To Space" Monument
by G.
Postnikov — A1342

Design: No. 2628, Pavel R. Popovich, with inscription at left and dated "12-15-VIII, 1962."

1962   **Photo.**   **Perf. 11½**
2627 A1340 4k blue, brn & red   32 15
2628 A1340 4k blue, brn & red   32 15

Perf. 12½x12
Litho.
1962   A1341 6k dk bl, lt bl, org & yellow   95 15
2629 A1341 6k dk bl, lt bl, org & yellow   95 15

Perf. 11½
Photo.
2630 A1342 6k brt blue & multi   90 15
2631 A1342 10k violet & multi   95 15
    Nos. 2627-2631 (5)   3.44
     Set value   54

Souvenir Sheet

Design: 1r, Monument and portraits of Gagarin, Titov, Nikolayev and Popovich.

1962, Nov. 27   **Litho.**   **Perf. 12½**
2631A A1342 1r brt bl, blk & sil   5.00 3.50

Nos. 2627-2631A honor the four Russian "conquerors of space," with Nos. 2627-2629 for the 1st group space flight, by Vostoks 3 and 4, Aug. 11-15, 1962. Also issued imperf.
For overprint see No. 2662.

Carp and
Bream — A1343

Design: 6k, Freshwater salmon.

1962, Aug. 28   **Photo.**   **Perf. 11½x12**
2632 A1343 4k blue & orange   20 15
2633 A1343 6k blue & orange   42 15
     Set value   15

Fish preservation in USSR.

Feliks E.
Dzerzhinski
A1344

1962, Sept. 6   **Litho.**   **Perf. 12½x12**
2634 A1344 4k ol green & dk blue   15 15

Dzerzhinski (1877-1926), organizer of Soviet secret police, 85th birth anniv.

O. Henry and
New York
Skyline
A1345

1962, Sept. 10   **Photo.**   **Perf. 12x11½**
2635 A1345 6k yel, red brn & black   15 15

O. Henry (William Sidney Porter, 1862-1910), American writer.

Barclay de
Tolly,
Mikhail I.
Kutuzov,
Petr I.
Bagration
A1346

Designs: 4k, Denis Davidov leading partisans. 6k, Battle of Borodino. 10k, Wasilisa Kozhina and partisans.

1962, Sept. 25   **Perf. 12½x12**
2636 A1346 3k orange brown   25 15
2637 A1346 4k ultra   25 15
2638 A1346 6k blue gray   60 15
2639 A1346 10k violet   70 15
     Set value   35

War of 1812 against the French, 150th anniv.

Street in
Vinnitsa
A1347

1962, Sept. 25   **Photo.**
2640 A1347 4k yel bister & black   15 15

Town of Vinnitsa, Ukraine, 600th anniv.

"Mail and
Transportation"
A1348

1962, Sept. 25   **Perf. 11½**
2641 A1348 4k blue grn, blk & lilac   15 15

Intl. Letter Writing Week, Oct. 7-13.

Cedar — A1349

Construction
Worker — A1350

Plants: 4k, Canna. 6k, Arbutus. 10k, Chrysanthemum.

1962, Sept. 27   **Engr. & Photo.**
2642 A1349 3k ver, black & green   24 15
2643 A1349 4k multicolored   24 15
2644 A1349 6k multicolored   24 15
2645 A1349 10k multicolored   65 15
     Set value   30

Nikitsky Botanical Gardens, 150th anniv.

1962, Sept. 29   **Litho.**   **Perf. 12x12½**

Designs: No. 2647, Hiker. No. 2648, Surgeon. No. 2649, Worker and lathe. No. 2650, Farmer's wife. No. 2651, Textile worker. No. 2652, Teacher.

2646 A1350 4k org, gray & vio blue   15 15
2647 A1350 4k yel, gray, grn & blue   15 15
2648 A1350 4k grn, gray & lilac rose   15 15
2649 A1350 4k ver, gray & lilac   15 15
2650 A1350 4k blue, gray & emer   15 15
2651 A1350 4k brt pink, gray & vio   15 15
2652 A1350 4k yel, gray, dp vio, red & brown   15 15
     Set value   70 35

Sputnik and
Stars
A1351

1962, Oct. 4   **Perf. 12½x12**
2653 A1351 10k multicolored   90 25

5th anniversary, launching of Sputnik 1.

M. F. Ahundov,
Azerbaijan Poet and
Philosopher, 150th
Birth Anniv. — A1352

1962, Oct. 2   **Photo.**
2654 A1352 4k lt green & dk brown   30 15

Farm and Young Couple with Banner A1353

Designs: No. 2656, Tractors, map and surveyor. No. 2657, Farmer, harvester and map.

1962, Oct. 18   Litho.   Perf. 12¹/₂x12
2655 A1353 4k multicolored   70 40
2656 A1353 4k multicolored   70 40
2657 A1353 4k brown, yel & red   70 40

Honoring pioneer developers of virgin soil.

N. N. Burdenko A1354

V. P. Filatov A1355

1962, Oct. 20   Perf. 12¹/₂x12
2658 A1354 4k red brn, lt blue & blk   30 15
2659 A1355 4k multicolored   30 15
        Set value   15

Scientists and academicians.

Lenin Mausoleum, Red Square — A1356

1962, Oct. 26   Litho.
2660 A1356 4k multicolored   35 15

92nd anniversary of Lenin's birth.

Worker, Flag and Factories — A1357

1962, Oct. 29   Perf. 12x12¹/₂
2661 A1357 4k multicolored   15 15

45th anniv. of the October Revolution.

No. 2631 Overprinted in Dark Violet

1962, Nov. 3   Photo.   Perf. 11¹/₂
2662 A1342 10k violet & multi   2.50 90

Launching of a rocket to Mars.

Togolok Moldo (1860-1942), Kirghiz Poet — A1358

Sajat Nova (1712-1795), Armenian Poet — A1359

1962, Nov. 17   Perf. 12x12¹/₂
2663 A1358 4k brn red & black   15 15
2664 A1359 4k ultra & black   15 15
        Set value   24 15

Arms, Hammer & Sickle and Map of USSR A1360

1962, Nov. 17   Perf. 11¹/₂
2665 A1360 4k red, orange & dk red   15 15

USSR founding, 40th anniv.

Space Rocket, Earth and Mars — A1361

1962, Nov. 17   Perf. 12¹/₂x12
        Size: 73x27mm
2666 A1361 10k purple & org red   80 25

Launching of a space rocket to Mars, Nov. 1, 1962.

Electric Power Industry — A1362

Designs: No. 2668, Machines. No. 2669, Chemicals and oil. No. 2670, Factory construction. No. 2671, Transportation. No. 2672, Telecommunications and space. No. 2673, Metals. No. 2674, Grain farming. No. 2675, Dairy, poultry and meat.

1962   Litho.   Perf. 12¹/₂x12
2667 A1362 4k ultra, red, blk & gray   35 15
2668 A1362 4k ultra, gray, yel & cl   35 15
2669 A1362 4k yel, pink, blk, gray & brown   35 15
2670 A1362 4k yel, blue, red brn & gray   35 15
2671 A1362 4k mar, yel, red & blue   35 15
2672 A1362 4k brt yel, blue & brn   35 15
2673 A1362 4k lil, org, yel & dk brn   15
2674 A1362 4k vio, bis, org red & dk brown   35 15
2675 A1362 4k emer, dk brn, brn & gray   35 15
        Nos. 2667-2675 (8)   2.80
        Set value   45

"Great decisions of the 22nd Communist Party Congress" and Russian people at work.
Issue dates: Nos. 2667-2669, Nov. 19. Others, Dec. 28.

Queen, Rook and Knight — A1363

Perf. 12¹/₂
1962, Nov. 24   Unwmk.   Photo.
2676 A1363 4k orange yel & black   50 25

30th Russian Chess Championships.

Gen. Vasili Blucher A1364

1962, Nov. 27   Perf. 11¹/₂
2677 A1364 4k multicolored   15 15

General Vasili Konstantinovich Blucher (1889-1938).

V. N. Podbelski (1887-1920), Minister of Posts A1365

1962, Nov. 27   Perf. 12¹/₂x12
2678 A1365 4k red brn, gray & black   15 15

Makharenko A1366

Gaidar A1367

1962, Nov. 30   Perf. 11¹/₂x12
2679 A1366 4k multicolored   15 15
2680 A1367 4k multicolored   15 15
        Set value   20 15

A. S. Makharenko (1888-1939) and Arkadi Gaidar (1904-1941), writers.

Dove and Globe A1368

1962, Dec. 22   Litho.   Perf. 12¹/₂x12
2681 A1368 4k multicolored   30 15

New Year 1963. Has alternating label inscribed "Happy New Year!" Issued imperf. on Dec. 20. Value 75 cents.

D. N. Prjanishnikov A1369

Rose-colored Starlings A1370

1962, Dec. 22   Perf. 12x12¹/₂
2682 A1369 4k multicolored   30 15

Prjanishnikov, founder of Russian agricultural chemistry.

1962, Dec. 26   Photo.   Perf. 11¹/₂

Birds: 4k, Red-breasted geese. 6k, Snow geese. 10k, White storks. 16k, Greater flamingos.

2683 A1370 3k green, blk & pink   15 15
2684 A1370 4k brn, blk & dp org   20 15
2685 A1370 6k gray, black & red   25 15
2686 A1370 10k blue, black & red   65 15
2687 A1370 16k lt blue, rose & blk 1.10 24
        Nos. 2684-2687 (4)   2.20
        Set value   55

FIR Emblem — A1371

1962, Dec. 26   Perf. 12x12¹/₂
2688 A1371 4k violet & red   30 15
2689 A1371 6k grnsh blue & red   30 15
        Set value   15

4th Cong. of the Intl. Federation of Resistance.

Map of Russia, Bank Book and Number of Savings Banks A1372

Design: 6k, as 4k, but with depositors.

1962, Dec. 30   Litho.   Perf. 12¹/₂x12
2690 A1372 4k multicolored   30 15
2691 A1372 6k multicolored   30 15
        Set value   15

40th anniv. of Russian savings banks.

Rustavsky Fertilizer Plant — A1373

Hydroelectric Power Stations: No. 2693, Bratskaya. No. 2964, Volzhskaya.

1962, Dec. 30   Photo.   Perf. 12¹/₂
2692 A1373 4k ultra, lt blue & black   25 15
2693 A1373 4k yel grn, bl grn & blk   25 15
2694 A1373 4k gray bl, brt bl & blk   25 15
        Set value   15

Stanislavski A1374

Serafimovich A1375

Perf. 12¹/₂
1963, Jan. 15   Unwmk.   Engr.
2695 A1374 4k slate green   30 15

Stanislavski (professional name of Konstantin Sergeevich Alekseev, 1863-1938), actor, producer and founder of the Moscow Art Theater.

1963, Jan. 19   Photo.   Perf. 11¹/₂
2696 A1375 4k mag, dk brn & gray   30 15

A. S. Serafimovich (1863-1949), writer.

Children in Nursery A1376

Designs: No. 2698, Kindergarten. No. 2699, Pioneers marching and camping. No. 2700, Young people studying and working.

1963, Jan. 31
2697 A1376 4k brn org, org red & black   32 15
2698 A1376 4k blue, mag & orange   32 15
2699 A1376 4k brt green, red & brn   32 15
2700 A1376 4k multicolored   32 15
        Set value   28

Wooden Dolls and Toys, Russia — A1377

National Handicrafts: 6k, Pottery, Ukraine. 10k, Bookbinding, Estonia. 12k, Metalware, Dagestan.

1963, Jan. 31   Litho.   Perf. 12x12½
2701	A1377	4k multicolored	15 15
2702	A1377	6k multicolored	20 15
2703	A1377	10k multicolored	42 15
2704	A1377	12k ultra, org & black	58 15
		Set value	28

Gen. Mikhail N. Tukhachevski A1378

Designs: No. 2706, U. M. Avetisian. No. 2707, A. M. Matrosov. No. 2708, J. V. Panfilov. No. 2709, Y. F. Fabriscius.

Perf. 12½x12
1963, Feb.   Photo.   Unwmk.
2705	A1378	4k blue grn & slate grn	30 15
2706	A1378	4k org brown & black	30 15
2707	A1378	4k ultra & dk brown	30 15
2708	A1378	4k dp rose & black	30 15
2709	A1378	4k rose lilac & vio blue	30 15
	Nos. 2705-2709 (5)		1.50
		Set value	35

45th anniv. of the Soviet Army and honoring its heroes. No. 2705 for Gen. Mikhail Nikolaevich Tukhachevski (1893-1937).

M. A. Pavlov A1379

E. O. Paton and Dnieper Bridge, Kiev A1379a

Portraits: #2711, I. V. Kurchatov. #2712, V. I. Vernadski. #2713, Aleksei N. Krylov. #2714, V. A. Obrutchev, geologist.

1963   Perf. 11½x12
Size: 21x32mm
2710	A1379	4k gray, buff & dk bl	15 15
2711	A1379	4k slate & brown	15 15

Perf. 12
2712	A1379	4k lilac gray & lt brn	15 15

Perf. 11½
Size: 23x34½mm
2713	A1379	4k dk blue, sep & red	15 15
2714	A1379	4k brn ol, gray & red	15 15
2715	A1379a	4k grnsh bl, blk & red	15 15
		Set value	60 30

Members of the Russian Academy of Science. No. 2715 for Eugene Oskarovich Paton (1870-1953), bridge building engineer.

Winter Sports A1380

1963, Feb. 28   Perf. 11½
2716	A1380	4k brt blue, org & blk	15 15

5th Trade Union Spartacist Games. Printed in sheets of 50 (5x10) with every other row inverted.

No. 2573 Overprinted

Советские
хоккеисты-
чемпионы
мира
и Европы.
Стокгольм
1963 г.

1963, Mar. 20
2717	A1306	6k Prus blue & plum	1.00 40

Victory of the Soviet ice hockey team in the World Championships, Stockholm. For overprint see No. 3612.

Victor Kingisepp A1381

Blaumanis A1382

1963, Mar. 24   Perf. 12x12½
2718	A1381	4k blue gray & choc	15 15

75th anniversary of the birth of Victor Kingisepp, communist party leader.

1963, Mar. 24   Perf. 12½x12
2719	A1382	4k ultra & dk red brn	15 15

Centenary of the birth of Rudolfs Blaumanis (1863-1908), Latvian writer.

Flower and Globe — A1383

Designs: 6k, Atom diagram and power line. 10k, Rocket in space.

1963, Mar. 26   Perf. 11½
2720	A1383	4k red, ultra & green	22 15
2721	A1383	6k red, green & lilac	32 15
2722	A1383	10k red, vio & lt blue	80 15
		Set value	24

"World without Arms and Wars." The 10k exists imperf. Value $1.50. For overprint see No. 2754.

Costume Type of 1960-62

Regional Costumes: 3k, Tadzhik. No. 2724, Kirghiz. No. 2725, Azerbaijan. No. 2726, Turkmen.

1963, Mar. 31   Litho.   Perf. 11½
2723	A1237	3k blk, red, ocher & org	40 15
2724	A1237	4k brown, ver, ocher & ultra	50 15
2725	A1237	4k blk, ocher, red & grn	50 15
2726	A1237	4k red, lil, ocher & blk	50 15
		Set value	20

Lenin — A1384

1963, Mar. 30   Engr.   Perf. 12
2727	A1384	4k red & brown	1.25 60

93rd anniversary of the birth of Lenin.

Luna 4 Approaching Moon — A1385

1963, Apr. 2   Photo.
2728	A1385	6k black, lt blue & red	50 15

Soviet rocket to the moon, Apr. 2, 1963. Exists imperforate. Value, $1.25.
For overprint see No. 3160.

Woman and Beach Scene A1386

Designs: 4k, Young man's head and factory. 10k, Child's head and kindergarden.

1963, Apr. 7   Litho.   Perf. 12½x12
2729	A1386	2k multicolored	30 25
2730	A1386	4k multicolored	30 25
2731	A1386	10k multicolored	42 25

15th anniversary of World Health Day.

Sputnik and Earth — A1387

Designs: No. 2733, Vostok 1, earth and moon. No. 2734, Rocket and Sun.

1963, Apr. 12
2732	A1387	10k blk, blue & lil rose	1.25 35
	a.	"10k" blue	1.25 35
	b.	Pair, #2732-2732a	2.50 75
2733	A1387	10k lil rose, blue & blk	1.25 35
	a.	"10k" lilac rose	1.25 35
	b.	Pair, #2733-2733a	2.50 75
2734	A1387	10k black, red & yellow	1.25 35
	a.	"10k" yellow	1.25 35
	b.	Pair, #2734-2734a	2.50 75

Cosmonauts' Day.

Demian Bednii (1883-1945), Poet — A1388

Soldiers on Horseback and Cuban Flag — A1389

1963, Apr. 13   Photo.
2735	A1388	4k brown & black	30 15

1963, Apr. 25   Perf. 11½

Soviet-Cuban friendship: 6k, Cuban flag, hands with gun and book. 10k, Cuban and USSR flags and crane lifting tractor.
2736	A1389	4k black, red & ultra	25 15
2737	A1389	6k black, red & ultra	25 15
2738	A1389	10k red, ultra & black	50 15
		Set value	22

Karl Marx A1390

Hasek A1391

1963, May 9   Perf. 12x12½
2739	A1390	4k dk red brn & black	15 15

145th anniversary of the birth of Marx.

1963, Apr. 29   Perf. 11½x12
2740	A1391	4k black	15 15

Jaroslav Hasek (1883-1923), Czech writer.

Moscow P.O. for Foreign Mail — A1392

1963, May 9   Perf. 11½
2741	A1392	6k brt violet & red brn	15 15

5th Conference of Communications Ministers of Socialist countries, Budapest.

King and Pawn A1393

Designs: 6k, Queen and bishop. 16k, Rook and knight.

1963, May 22   Photo.
2742	A1393	4k multicolored	22 15
2743	A1393	6k ultra, brt pink & grnsh blue	35 15
2744	A1393	16k brt plum, brt pink & black	90 15
		Set value	24

25th Championship Chess Match, Moscow. Exists imperf., issued May 18. Value $2.

Richard Wagner — A1394

Boxers — A1395

Design: No. 2745A, Giuseppe Verdi.

1963   Unwmk.   Perf. 11¹/₂x12
2745 A1394 4k black & red   50 25
2745A A1394 4k red & violet brn   50 25

150th annivs. of the births of Wagner and Verdi, German and Italian composers.

1963, May 29   Litho.   Perf. 12¹/₂

Design: 6k, Referee proclaiming victor.

2746 A1395 4k multicolored   15 15
2747 A1395 6k multicolored   15 15
       Set value   15

15th European Boxing Championships, Moscow.

Valeri Bykovski — A1396

Valentina Tereshkova — A1397

Designs: No. 2749, Tereshkova. No. 2751, Bykovski. No. 2752, Symbolic man and woman fliers. No. 2753, Tereshkova, vert.

Litho. (A1396); Photo. (A1397)
1963   Perf. 12¹/₂x12, 12x12¹/₂
2748 A1396 4k multicolored   25 15
2749 A1396 4k multicolored   25 15
  a.   Pair #2748-2749   50 15
2750 A1397 6k grn & dk car rose   25 15
2751 A1397 6k purple & brown   20 15
2752 A1397 10k blue & red   85 15
2753 A1396 10k multicolored   1.50 35
       Nos. 2748-2753 (6)   3.30
       Set value   95

Space flights of Valeri Bykovski, June 14-19, and Valentina Tereshkova, 1st woman cosmonaut, June 16-19, 1963, in Vostoks 5 and 6.
No. 2749a has continuous design. Nos. 2750-2753 exist imperf. Value $3.

No. 2720 Overprinted in Red

Всемирный конгресс женщин.

1963, June 24   Photo.   Perf. 11¹/₂
2754 A1383 4k red, ultra & green   50 25

Intl. Women's Cong., Moscow, June 24-29.

Globe, Camera and Film — A1398

1963, July 7   Photo.   Perf. 11¹/₂
2755 A1398 4k gray & ultra   40 30

3rd International Film Festival, Moscow.

Vladimir V. Mayakovsky, Poet, 70th Birth Anniv. — A1399

1963, July 19   Engr.   Perf. 12¹/₂
2756 A1399 4k red brown   15 15

Tanks and Map A1400

Design: 6k, Soldier, tanks and flag.

1963, July   Litho.   Perf. 12¹/₂x12
2757 A1400 4k sepia & orange   30 25
2758 A1400 6k org, slate green & blk 30 25

20th anniversary of the Battle of Kursk in the "War of Liberation," 1941-1945.

Bicyclist — A1401

Sports: 4k, Long jump. 6k, Women divers, horiz. 12k, Basketball. 16k, Soccer.

Perf. 12¹/₂x12, 12x12¹/₂
1963, July 27
2759 A1401 3k multicolored   15 15
2760 A1401 4k multicolored   15 15
2761 A1401 6k multicolored   25 15
2762 A1401 12k multicolored   45 15
2763 A1401 16k multicolored   60 15
  a.   Souvenir sheet of 4, imperf. 2.00 75
       Nos. 2759-2763 (5)   1.60
       Set value   45

3rd Spartacist Games.
Exist imperf. Value $2.
No. 2763a contains stamps similar to the 3k, 4k, 12k and 16k, with colors changed. Issued Dec. 22.

Ice Hockey — A1402

Lenin — A1403

1963, July 27   Photo.
2764 A1402 6k red & gray blue   50 25

World Ice Hockey Championship, Stockholm.
For overprint see No. 3012.

1963, July 29
2765 A1403 4k red & black   15 15

60th anniversary of the 2nd Congress of the Social Democratic Labor Party.

Freighter and Relief Shipment A1404

Design: 12k, Centenary emblem.

1963, Aug. 8   Perf. 12¹/₂
2766 A1404 6k Prus green & red   35 15
2767 A1404 12k dark blue & red   80 15
       Set value   18

Centenary of International Red Cross.

Lapp Reindeer Race A1405

Designs: 4k, Pamir polo, vert. 6k, Burjat archery. 10k, Armenian wrestling, vert.

1963, Aug. 8   Perf. 11¹/₂
2768 A1405 3k lt vio bl, brn & red 25 15
2769 A1405 4k bis brn, red & blk   30 15
2770 A1405 6k yel, black & red   30 15
2771 A1405 10k sepia, blk & dk red 45 15
       Set value   35

A. F. Mozhaisky (1825-1890), Pioneer Airplane Builder A1406

Aviation Pioneers: 10k, P. N. Nesterov (1887-1914), pioneer stunt flyer. 16k, N. E. Zhukovski (1847-1921), aerodynamics pioneer, and pressurized air tunnel.

1963, Aug. 18   Engr. & Photo.
2772 A1406 6k black & brt blue   22 15
2773 A1406 10k black & brt blue   55 25
2774 A1406 16k black & brt blue   90 25

Alexander S. Dargomyzhski and Scene from "Rusalka" A1408

S. S. Gulak-Artemovsky and Scene from "Cossacks on the Danube" A1409

Design: No. 2777, Georgi O. Eristavi and theater.

Perf. 11¹/₂x12, 12x12¹/₂
1963, Sept. 10   Photo.
2776 A1408 4k violet & black   28 15
2777 A1408 4k gray violet & brn   28 15
2778 A1409 4k red & black   28 15
       Set value   15

Dargomyzhski, Ukrainian composer; Eristavi, Georgian writer, and Gulak-Artemovsky, Ukrainian composer, 150th birth annivs.

Map of Antarctica, Penguins, Research Ship and Southern Lights A1410

Designs: 4k, Map, southern lights and snocats (trucks). 6k, Globe, camp and various planes. 12k, Whaler and whales.

1963, Sept. 16   Litho.   Perf. 12¹/₂x12
2779 A1410 3k multicolored   18 15
2780 A1410 4k multicolored   30 15
2781 A1410 6k violet, blue & red   45 15
2782 A1410 12k multicolored   1.50 25
       Set value   28

"The Antarctic - Continent of Peace."

Letters, Globe, Plane, Train and Ship — A1411

1963, Sept. 20   Photo.   Perf. 11¹/₂
2783 A1411 4k violet, black & org 15 15

International Letter Writing Week.

Denis Diderot — A1412

Gleb Uspenski — A1414

1963, Oct. 10   Unwmk.   Perf. 11¹/₂
2784 A1412 4k dk blue, brn & yel bister 15 15

Denis Diderot (1713-84), French philosopher and encyclopedist.

1963, Oct. 10

Portraits: No. 2787, N. P. Ogarev. No. 2788, V. Brusov. No. 2789, F. Gladkov.

2786 A1414 4k buff, red brn & dk brown 40 15
2787 A1414 4k black & pale green   40 15
2788 A1414 4k car, brown & gray   40 15
2789 A1414 4k car, ol brown & gray 40 15
       Set value   20

Gleb Ivanovich Uspenski (1843-1902), historian and writer; Ogarev, politician, 150th birth anniv.; Brusov, poet, 90th birth anniv., Fyodor Gladkov (1883-1958), writer.

"Peace" Worker, Student, Astronaut and Lenin — A1415

Kirghiz Academy and Spasski Tower — A1416

Designs: No. 2794, "Labor," automatic controls. No. 2795, "Liberty," painter, lecturer, newspaper man. No. 2796, "Equality," elections, regional costumes. No. 2797, "Brotherhood," Recognition of achievement. No. 2798, "Happiness," Family.

1963, Oct. 15   Litho.   Perf. 12¹/₂x12
2793 A1415 4k dk red, red & blk   45 35
2794 A1415 4k red, dk red & blk   45 35
2795 A1415 4k dk red, red & blk   45 35
2796 A1415 4k red, dk red & blk   45 35
2797 A1415 4k dk red, red & blk   45 35

2798 A1415 4k dk red, red & blk   45   35
   a. Strip of 6, #2793-2798   2.75 2.25
   Nos. 2793-2798 (6)   2.70 2.10

Proclaiming Peace, Labor, Liberty, Equality, Brotherhood and Happiness.

1963, Oct. 22   *Perf. 12x12¹/₂*
2799 A1416 4k red, yel & vio blue   15   15

Russia's annexation of Kirghizia, cent.

Lenin and Young Workers
A1417

Design: No. 2801, Lenin and Palace of Congresses, the Kremlin.

1963, Oct. 24   Photo.   *Perf. 11¹/₂*
2800 A1417 4k crimson & black   15   15
2801 A1417 4k carmine & black   15   15
   Set value   20   15

13th Congr. of Soviet Trade Unions, Moscow.

Olga Kobylyanskaya, Ukrainian Novelist, Birth Cent. — A1418

1963, Oct. 24   *Perf. 11¹/₂x12*
2802 A1418 4k tan & dk car rose   50   25

Ilya Mechnikov
A1419

Cruiser Aurora and Rockets
A1420

Designs: 6k, Louis Pasteur. 12k, Albert Calmette.

1963, Oct. 28   *Perf. 12*
2803 A1419 4k green & bister   20   25
2804 A1419 6k purple & bister   30   25
2805 A1419 12k blue & bister   1.00 25

Pasteur Institute, Paris, 75th anniv; 12k for Albert Calmette (1863-1933), bacteriologist.

1963, Nov. 1
2806 A1420 4k mar, blk, gray & red orange   38   15
2807 A1420 4k mar, blk, gray & brt rose red   38   15
   Set value   20

Development of the Armed Forces, and 46th anniv. of the October Revolution. The bright rose red ink of No. 2807 is fluorescent.

Mausoleum Gur Emi, Samarkand — A1421

Designs (Architecture in Samarkand, Uzbekistan): No. 2809, Shahi-Zind Mosque. 6k, Registan Square.

1963, Nov. 14   Litho.   *Perf. 12*
   Size: 27¹/₂x27¹/₂mm
2808 A1421 4k blue, yel & red brn   28   15

2809 A1421 4k blue, yel & red brn   28   15
   Size: 55x27¹/₂mm
2810 A1421 6k blue, yel & red brn   70   15
   Set value   24

Proclamation, Spasski Tower and Globe — A1422

1963, Nov. 15 Photo.   *Perf. 12x11¹/₂*
2811 A1422 6k purple & lt blue   50   15

Signing of the Nuclear Test Ban Treaty between the US and the USSR.

Pushkin Monument, Kiev
A1423

M. S. Shchepkin
A1424

Portrait: No. 2814, V. L. Durov (1863-1934), circus clown.

1963   Engr.   *Perf. 12x12¹/₂*
2812 A1423 4k dark brown   15   15
2813 A1424 4k brown   15   15
2814 A1424 4k brown black   15   15
   Set value   30   15

No. 2813 for M. S. Shchepkin, actor, 75th birth anniv.

Yuri M. Steklov, 1st Editor of Izvestia, 90th Birth Anniv. — A1425

1963, Nov. 17   Photo.   *Perf. 11¹/₂*
2815 A1425 4k black & lilac rose   15   15

Vladimir G. Shuhov and Moscow Radio Tower — A1426

1963, Nov. 17   *Perf. 12¹/₂x12*
2816 A1426 4k green & black   15   15

Shuhov, scientist, 110th birth anniv.

USSR and Czech Flags, Kremlin and Hradcany
A1427

1963, Nov. 25   *Perf. 11¹/₂*
2817 A1427 6k red, ultra & brown   40   25

Russo-Czechoslovakian Treaty, 20th anniv.

Fyodor A. Poletaev — A1428

1963, Nov. 25 Litho.   *Perf. 12¹/₂x12*
2818 A1428 4k multicolored   40   30

F. A. Poletaev, Hero of the Soviet Union, National Hero of Italy, and holder of the Order of Garibaldi.

Julian Grimau and Worker Holding Flag — A1429

1963, Nov. 29   Photo.   *Perf. 11¹/₂*
   Flag and Name Panel Embossed
2819 A1429 6k vio black, red & buff   15   15

Spanish anti-fascist fighter Julian Grimau.

Rockets, Sky and Tree — A1430

"Happy New Year!" — A1431

1963, Dec. 12 Litho.   *Perf. 12x12¹/₂*
2820 A1430 6k multicolored   15   15

   Photogravure and Embossed
1963, Dec. 20   *Perf. 11¹/₂*
2821 A1431 4k grn, dk blue & red   15   15
2822 A1431 6k dk bl & fluor. rose red 15   15
   Set value   15

Nos. 2820-2822 issued for New Year 1964.

Mikas J. Petrauskas, Lithuanian Composer, 90th Birth Anniv. — A1432

1963, Dec. 20   Photo.   *Perf. 11¹/₂x12*
2823 A1432 4k brt green & brown   75   35

Topaz — A1433

Precious stones of the Urals: 4k, Jasper. 6k, Amethyst. 10k, Emerald. 12k, Rhodonite. 16k, Malachite.

1963, Dec. 26   Litho.   *Perf. 12*
2824 A1433 2k brn, yel & blue   25   15
2825 A1433 4k multicolored   70   15
2826 A1433 6k red & purple   60   15
2827 A1433 10k multicolored   1.00 15
2828 A1433 12k multicolored   1.25 15
2829 A1433 16k multicolored   1.40 15
   Nos. 2824-2829 (6)   5.20
   Set value   58

Coat of Arms and Sputnik — A1434

Rockets: No. 2831, Luna I. No. 2832, Rocket around the moon. No. 2833, Vostok I, first man in space. No. 2834, Vostok III & IV. No. 2835, Vostok VI, first woman astronaut.

1963, Dec. 27   Litho. & Embossed
2830 A1434 10k red, gold & gray   50   20
2831 A1434 10k red, gold & gray   50   20
2832 A1434 10k red, gold & gray   50   20
2833 A1434 10k red, gold & gray   50   20
2834 A1434 10k red, gold & gray   50   20
2835 A1434 10k red, gold & gray   50   20
   a. Vert. strip of 6, #2830-2835   3.00 1.25
   Nos. 2830-2835 (6)   3.00 1.20

Soviet achievements in space.

Dyushambe, Tadzhikistan — A1435

1963, Dec. 30   Engr.
2836 A1435 4k dull blue   50   30

No. 2836 was issued after Stalinabad was renamed Dyushambe.
For overprint see No. 2943.

Flame, Broken Chain and Rainbow — A1436

1963, Dec. 30   Litho.
2837 A1436 6k multicolored   50   25

15th anniversary of the Universal Declaration of Human Rights.

F. A. Sergeev — A1437

1963, Dec. 30 Photo.   *Perf. 12x12¹/₂*
2838 A1437 4k gray & red   35   25

80th anniversary of the birth of the revolutionist Artjem (F. A. Sergeev).

Sun and Radar — A1438

Designs: 6k, Sun and Earth, vert. 10k, Earth and Sun.

1964, Jan. 1   Photo.   *Perf. 11¹/₂*
2839 A1438 4k brt mag, org & black   25   25
2840 A1438 6k org yel, red & blue   40   25
2841 A1438 10k blue, vio & orange   45   25

International Quiet Sun Year, 1964-65.

Christian
Donalitius
A1439

1964, Jan. 1   Unwmk.   Perf. 12
2842 A1439 4k green & black   15 15

Lithuanian poet Christian Donalitius (Donelaitis),
250th birth anniv.

Women's
Speed Skating
A1440

Designs: 4k, Women's cross country skiing. 6k,
1964 Olympic emblem and torch. 10k, Biathlon.
12k, Figure skating pair.

1964, Feb. 4   Perf. 11½, Imperf.
2843 A1440 2k ultra, blk & lilac rose   22 15
2844 A1440 4k lilac rose, blk & ultra   25 15
2845 A1440 6k dk blue, red & blk   30 18
2846 A1440 10k green, lilac & blk   52 22
2847 A1440 12k lilac, black & grn   75 25
     Nos. 2843-2847 (5)   2.04 95

9th Winter Olympic Games, Innsbruck Jan. 29-
Feb. 9, 1964. See Nos. 2865, 2867-2870.

Anna S.
Golubkina
(1864-1927),
Sculptor
A1441

1964, Feb. 4   Photo.
2848 A1441 4k gray, brown & buff   15 15

150 років з дня
народження.
1964 р.

Ovpt. on
#2450 in Red

Taras G.
Shevchenko — A1443

Designs: 4k, Shevchenko statue, Kiev. 10k,
Shevchenko by Ilya Repin. (Portrait on 6k by I.
Kremsko.)

1964   Litho.   Perf. 12
2852 A1245 3k brown & violet   22 15
Engr.
2853 A1443 4k magenta   22 15
2854 A1443 4k deep green   35 15
2855 A1443 6k red brown   35 15
2856 A1443 6k indigo   35 15
Photo.
2857 A1443 10k bister & brown   85 15
2858 A1443 10k buff & dull violet   85 15
     Nos. 2852-2858 (7)   3.19
     Set value   52

Shevchenko, Ukrainian poet, 150th birth anniv.
Issue dates: Nos. 2852, 2857-2858, Feb. 22.
Others, Mar. 1.

K. S. Zaslonov
К.С.ЗАСЛОНОВ A1444

Soviet Heroes: No. 2860, N. A. Vilkov. No.
2861, J. V. Smirnov. No. 2862, V. S. Khorujaia

(heroine). No. 2862A, I. M. Sivko. No. 2862B, I. S.
Polbin.

1964-65   Photo.
2859 A1444 4k hn brn & brn blk   15 15
2860 A1444 4k Prus bl & vio blk   15 15
2861 A1444 4k brn red & indigo   15 15
2862 A1444 4k bluish gray & dk
                brown   15 15
2862A A1444 4k lilac & black ('65)   15 15
2862B A1444 4k blue & dk brn ('65)   15 15
     Set value   60 42

Printer Inking
Form, 16th
Century
A1445

Design: 6k, Statue of Ivan Fedorov, first Russian
printer.

1964, Mar. 1   Litho.   Unwmk.
2863 A1445 4k multicolored   15 15
2864 A1445 6k multicolored   15 15
     Set value   22 15

400th anniv. of book printing in Russia.

Nos. 2843-2847 Overprinted

Советские
женщины-
конькобежцы—
сильнейшие
в мире

and

Ice Hockey
A1446

Olympic Gold
Medal, "11
Gold, 8 Silver,
6 Bronze"
A1447

Design: 3k, Ice hockey.

1964, Mar. 9   Photo.   Perf. 11½
2865 A1440 2k ultra, blk & lilac rose   20 15
2866 A1440 3k blk, bl grn & red   24 15
2867 A1440 4k lil rose, blk & ultra   30 15
2868 A1440 6k dk bl, red & blk   70 15
2869 A1440 10k grn, lil & blk   80 15
2870 A1440 12k lilac, black & grn   90 15
Perf. 12
2871 A1447 16k org red & gldn brown   1.25 25
     Nos. 2865-2871 (7)   4.39
     Set value   88

Soviet victories at the 9th Winter Olympic
Games.
On Nos. 2865, 2867-2870 the black overprints
commemorate victories in various events and are
variously arranged in 3 to 6 lines, with "Innsbruck"
in Russian added below "1964" on 2k, 4k, 10k and
12k.

Rubber
Industry — A1448

Regular and
Volunteer
Militiamen — A1449

Designs: No. 2873, Textile industry. No. 2874,
Cotton, wheat, corn and helicopter spraying land.

1964   Litho.   Perf. 12x12½
2872 A1448 4k org, lilac, ultra & blk   15 15
2873 A1448 4k org, blk, grn & ultra   15 15
2874 A1448 4k dull yel, ol, red & bl   15 15
     Set value   30 15

Importance of the chemical industry to the Soviet
economy.
Issue dates: No. 2872, Feb. 10. Nos. 2873-2874,
Mar. 27.

1964, Mar. 27   Photo.   Perf. 12
2875 A1449 4k red & deep ultra   30 30

Day of the Militia.

Sailor and
Odessa
Lighthouse
A1450

Liberation Monument,
Minsk — A1451

Design: No. 2877, Lenin statue and Leningrad.

1964   Litho.   Perf. 12½x12
2876 A1450 4k red, lt grn, ultra & black 15 15
2877 A1450 4k red, yel, grn, brn & black 15 15
2878 A1451 4k bl, gray, red & emer   15 15
     Set value   30 15

Liberation of Odessa (#2876), Leningrad
(#2877), Byelorussia (#2878), 20th anniv.
Issue dates: #2876, Apr. 10. #2877, May 9.
#2878, June 30.

First Soviet
Sputniks
A1452

F. A. Tsander
A1453

Lenin
A1454

Designs: 6k, Mars 1 spacecraft. No. 2886, Konstantin E. Tsiolkovsky. No. 2887, N. I. Kibaltchitch.
No. 2888, Statue honoring 3 balloonists killed in
1934 accident. 12k, Gagarin and Kosmos 3.

Perf. 11½, Imperf.
1964, Apr.   Photo.
2883 A1452 4k red org, blk & blue
                green   25 15
2884 A1452 6k dk blue & org red   50 15
2885 A1453 10k grn, blk & fluor.
                pink   60 15
2886 A1453 10k dk bl grn, blk &
                fluor. pink   60 15
2887 A1453 10k lilac, blk & lt grn   60 15
2888 A1453 10k blue & black   60 15
2889 A1452 12k blue grn, org brn &
                black   60 25
     Nos. 2883-2889 (7)   3.75
     Set value   1.00

Leaders in rocket theory and technique.

Engraved and Photogravure
1964-65   Perf. 12x11½
2890 A1454 4k blk, buff & lilac rose   4.50 2.00
    a. Re-engraved ('65)   3.50 2.00

94th anniversary of the birth of Lenin.
On No. 2890a, the portrait shading is much
heavier. Lines on collar are straight and unbroken,
rather than dotted.
For souvenir sheet see No. 2582a.

William
Shakespeare,
400th Birth
Anniv.
A1455

1964, Apr. 23   Perf. 11½
2891 A1455 10k gray & red brown   60 25

See Nos. 2985-2986.

"Irrigation" — A1456

1964, May 12   Litho.   Perf. 12x12½
2892 A1456 4k multicolored   15 15

Я.Б. ГАМАРНИК A1457

Perf. 12½x11½
1964, May 12   Photo.
2893 A1457 4k blue & gray brown   15 15

Y. B. Gamarnik, army commander, 70th birth
anniv..

D. I.
Gulia — A1458

Portraits: No. 2895, Hamza Hakim-Zade Nijazi.
No. 2896, Saken Seifullin. No. 2896A, M. M. Kotsyubinsky. No. 2896B, Stepanos Nazaryan. No.
2896C, Toktogil Satyiganov.

Engraved and Photogravure
1964   Unwmk.   Perf. 12x11½
2894 A1458 4k green, buff & blk   15 15
2895 A1458 4k red, buff & black   15 15
2896 A1458 4k brn, ocher, buff &
                black   15 15
2896A A1458 4k brn lake, blk & buff   15 15
2896B A1458 4k blue, pale bl, blk & buff 15 15
2896C A1458 4k red brown & black   15 15
     Set value   60 30

Abkhazian poet Gulia, 90th birth anniv.;
Uzbekian poet and composer Nijazi, 75th birth
anniv.; Kazakian poet Seifullin, 70th birth anniv.;
Ukrainian writer Kotsyubinsky (1864-1913); Arme-
nian writer Nazaryan (1814-1879); Kirghiz poet
Satylganov (1864-1933).

Arkadi Gaidar
(1904-41)
A1459

Writers: No. 2897A, Nikolai Ostrovsky (1904-36) and battle scene (portrait at left).

1964		Photo.	Perf. 12	
2897	A1459	4k red orange & gray	15	15
		Engr.		
2897A	A1459	4k brown lake & black	15	15
		Set value	20	15

No. 2318 Surcharged:

150 лет вхождения
в состав России
1964

4
коп.

1964, May 27		Litho.	Perf. 12	
2898	A1194	4k on 40k bister & brn	3.00	15

Azerbaijan's joining Russia, 150th anniv.

"Romania"
A1460

Elephant
A1461

Designs: No. 2900, "Poland," (map, Polish eagle, industrial and agricultural symbols). No. 2901, "Bulgaria" (flag, rose, industrial and agricultural symbols). No. 2902, Soviet and Yugoslav soldiers and embattled Belgrade. No. 2903, "Czechoslovakia" (view of Prague, arms, Russian soldier and woman). No. 2903A, Map and flag of Hungary, Liberty statue. No. 2903B, Statue of Russian Soldier and Belvedere Palace, Vienna. No. 2904, Buildings under construction, Warsaw; Polish flag and medal.

1964-65		Litho.	Perf. 12	
2899	A1460	6k gray & multi	15	15
2900	A1460	6k ocher, red & brn	15	15
2901	A1460	6k tan, grn & red	15	15
2902	A1460	6k gray, blk, dl bl, ol & red	15	15
2903	A1460	6k ultra, black & red ('65)	15	15
2903A	A1460	6k brn, red & green ('65)	15	15
2903B	A1460	6k dp org, gray bl & black ('65)	15	15
2904	A1460	6k blue, red, yel & bister ('65)	15	15
		Nos. 2899-2904 (8)	1.20	
		Set value		55

20th anniversaries of liberation from German occupation of Romania, Poland, Bulgaria, Belgrade, Czechoslovakia, Hungary, Vienna and Warsaw.

Perf. 12x12½, 12½x12, Imperf.

1964			Photo.	

Designs: 2k, Giant panda, horiz. 4k, Polar bear. 6k, European elk. 10k, Pelican. 12k, Tiger. 16k, Lammergeier.

Size: 25x36mm, 36x25mm

2905	A1461	1k red & black	15	15
2906	A1461	2k tan & black	15	15
		Perf. 12		
		Size: 26x28mm		
2907	A1461	4k grnsh gray, black & tan	15	15
		Perf. 12x12½		
		Size: 25x36mm		
2908	A1461	6k ol, dk brn & tan	22	15
		Perf. 12		
		Size: 26x28mm		
2909	A1461	10k ver, gray & black	38	15
		Perf. 12½x12, 12x12½		
		Size: 36x25mm, 25x36mm		
2910	A1461	12k brn, ocher & blk	70	15
2911	A1461	16k ultra, blk, bis & yellow	65	15
		Nos. 2905-2911 (7)	2.40	
		Set value		60

100th anniv. of the Moscow zoo.
Issue dates: Perf., June 18. Imperf., May.

Leningrad Post Office
A1462

1964, June 30		Litho.	Perf. 12	
2912	A1462	4k citron, black & red	15	15

Leningrad postal service, 250th anniv.

Corn
A1463

Thorez
A1464

1964		Photo.	Perf. 11½, Imperf.	
2913	A1463	2k shown	15	15
2914	A1463	3k Wheat	15	15
2915	A1463	4k Potatoes	20	15
2916	A1463	6k Beans	25	15
2917	A1463	10k Beets	30	15
2918	A1463	12k Cotton	60	15
2919	A1463	16k Flax	90	15
		Nos. 2913-2919 (7)	2.55	
		Set value		55

Issue dates: Perf., July 10. Imperf., June 25.

1964, July 31				
2920	A1464	4k black & red	75	25

Maurice Thorez, chairman of the French Communist party.

Equestrian and Russian Olympic Emblem
A1465

Designs: 4k, Weight lifter. 6k, High jump. 10k, Canoeing. 12k, Girl gymnast. 16k, Fencing.

1964, July			Perf. 11½, Imperf.	
2921	A1465	3k lt yel grn, red, brn & black	15	15
2922	A1465	4k yel, black & red	20	15
2923	A1465	6k lt blue, blk & red	25	15
2924	A1465	10k bl grn, red & blk	50	15
2925	A1465	12k gray, black & red	60	15
2926	A1465	16k lt ultra, blk & red	75	15
		Nos. 2921-2926 (6)	2.45	
		Set value		55

18th Olympic Games, Tokyo, Oct. 10-25, 1964.
Two 1r imperf. souvenir sheets exist, showing emblem, woman gymnast and stadium. Size: 91x71mm.
Value, red sheet, $4.75 unused, $1.75 canceled; green sheet, $165 unused, $225 canceled.

Three Races — A1466

Jawaharlal Nehru — A1467

1964, Aug. 8		Photo.	Perf. 12	
2929	A1466	6k orange & black	40	35

International Congress of Anthropologists and Ethnographers, Moscow.

1964, Aug. 20			Perf. 11½	
2930	A1467	4k brown & black	40	15

Prime Minister Nehru of India (1889-1964).

Conquest of Space

A souvenir sheet, issued Aug. 20, 1964, celebrates the Conquest of Space. It carries six perforated, multicolored 10k stamps with different, interlocking designs picturing Soviet rockets and spacecraft. Size of sheet, 141x110mm. Value, $3.75 unused, $1.50 canceled. Sheet also exists on glossy paper. Value, $10 unused, $6 canceled.

Marx and Engels
A1468

A. V. Vishnevsky
A1469

Designs: No. 2932 Lenin and title page of "CPSS Program." No. 2933, Worker breaking chains around the globe. No. 2934, Title pages of "Communist Manifesto" in German and Russian. No. 2935, Globe and banner inscribed "Workers of the World Unite."

1964, Aug. 27		Photo.	Perf. 11½x12	
2931	A1468	4k red, dk red & brown	15	15
2932	A1468	4k red, brn & slate	15	15
2933	A1468	4k blue, fluor. brt rose & black	15	15
		Perf. 12½x12		
		Litho.		
2934	A1468	4k ol black, blk & red	15	15
2935	A1468	4k blue, red & ol bister	15	15
		Set value	50	35

Centenary of First Socialist International.

1964		Photo.	Perf. 11½	

Portraits: No. 2937, N. A. Semashko. No. 2938, D. Ivanovsky.

Size: 23½x35mm

2936	A1469	4k gray & brown	15	15
2937	A1469	4k buff, sepia & red	15	15
		Litho.		
		Size: 22x32½mm		
2938	A1469	4k tan, gray & brown	15	15
		Set value	30	15

90th birth annivs. Vishnevsky, surgeon, and Semashko, founder of the Russian Public Health Service; Ivanovsky (1864-1920), physician.

Palmiro Togliatti (1893-1964), General Secretary of the Italian Communist Party — A1470

1964, Sept. 15			Perf. 12½x12	
2939	A1470	4k black & red	15	15

Letter, Aerogram and Globe
A1471

1964, Sept. 20			Litho.	
2940	A1471	4k tan, lilac rose & ultra	15	15

Intl. Letter Writing Week, Oct. 5-11.

Arms of German Democratic Republic, Factories, Ship and Train — A1472

1964, Oct. 7			Perf. 12	
2942	A1472	6k blk, yel, red & bister	15	15

German Democratic Republic, 15th anniv.

No. 2836 Overprinted in Red

40 лет Советскому Таджикистану
1964 год

1964, Oct. 7			Engr.	
2943	A1435	4k dull blue	1.75	1.00

40th anniversary of Tadzhik Republic.

Woman Holding Bowl of Grain and Fruit
A1473

Uzbek Farm Couple and Arms — A1474

Turkmen Woman Holding Arms — A1475

1964, Oct.			Litho.	
2944	A1473	4k red, green & brn	40	15
2945	A1474	4k red yel & claret	40	15
2946	A1475	4k red, black & red brn	30	20

40th anniv. of the Moldavian, Uzbek and Turkmen Socialist Republics.
Issue dates: #2944, Oct. 7. Others, Oct. 26.

Soldier and Flags
A1476

1964, Oct. 14				
2947	A1476	4k red, bis, dk brn & bl	15	15

Liberation of the Ukraine, 20th anniv.

Mikhail Y. Lermontov (1814-41), Poet — A1477

Designs: 4k, Birthplace of Tarchany. 10k, Lermontov and Vissarion G. Belinski.

1964, Oct. 14		Engr.; Litho. (10k)		
2948	A1477	4k violet black	15	15
2949	A1477	6k black	24	15
2950	A1477	10k dk red brn & buff	70	15
		Set value		18

Hammer and
Sickle
A1478

1964, Oct. 14   **Litho.**
2951 A1478 4k dk blue, red, ocher &
                    yellow   15 15

47th anniversary of October Revolution.

Col. Vladimir M.
Komarov
A1479

Komarov, Feoktistov and
Yegorov — A1480

Designs: No. 2953, Boris B. Yegorov, M.D. No.
2954, Konstantin Feoktistov, scientist. 10k, Spacecraft Voskhod I and cosmonauts. 50k, Red flag with
portraits of Komarov, Feoktistov and Yegorov, and
trajectory around earth.

Perf. 11½ (A1479), 12½x12
1964   **Photo.**
2952 A1479 4k bl grn, blk & org   20 15
2953 A1479 4k bl grn, blk & org   20 15
2954 A1479 4k bl grn, blk & org   20 15
                    Size: 73x23mm
2955 A1480 6k vio & dk brn   24 15
2956 A1480 10k dp ultra & pur   85 15
                    Imperf
                    Litho.
                    Size: 90x45½mm
2957 A1480 50k vio, red & gray   5.00 1.40
            Nos. 2952-2957 (6)   6.69
                    Set value   1.75

3-men space flight of Komarov, Yegorov and
Feoktistov, Oct. 12-13. Dates of issue: #2952-2954,
Oct. 19; #2955, Oct. 17; #2956, Oct. 13; #2957,
Nov. 20.

A. I. Yelizarova-
Ulyanova
A1482

Portrait: #2961, Nadezhda K. Krupskaya.

1964, Nov. 6   Photo.   Perf. 11½
2960 A1482 4k brn, org & indigo   15 15
2961 A1482 4k indigo, red & brn   15 15
                    Set value   20 15

Yelizarova-Ulyanova, Lenin's sister, birth cent. &
Krupskaya, Lenin's wife, 95th birth anniv.

Farm Woman,   Mushrooms
Sheep, Flag of   A1484
Mongolia
A1483

1964, Nov. 20   Litho.   Perf. 12
2962 A1483 6k multicolored   15 15

Mongolian People's Republic, 40th anniv.

1964, Nov. 25   Litho.   Perf. 12
Designs: Various mushrooms.
2963 A1484 2k ol grn, red brn & yel-
                    low
2964 A1484 4k green & yellow   15 15
2965 A1484 6k bluish grn, brn & yel-
                    low   50 15
2966 A1484 10k grn, org red & brn   65 15
2967 A1484 12k ultra, yel & green   1.25 15
            Nos. 2963-2967 (5)   2.70
                    Set value   56

Nos. 2963-2967 exist varnished, printed in
sheets of 25 with 10 labels in outside vertical rows.
Issued Nov. 30. Value, set $5.

A. P.
Dovzhenko
A1485

Design: 6k, Scene from "Tchapaev" (man and
boy with guns).

1964, Nov. 30   Photo.   Perf. 12
2968 A1485 4k gray & dp ultra   40 25
2968A A1485 6k pale olive & blk   40 25

Dovzhenko (1894-1956), film producer, and
30th anniv. of the production of the film
"Tchapaev."

"Happy New   V. J. Struve
Year"   A1487
A1486

Photogravure and Engraved
1964, Nov. 30   Perf. 11½
2969 A1486 4k multicolored   50 30

New Year 1965. The bright rose ink is
fluorescent.

1964-65   Photo.   Perf. 12½x11½
Portraits: No. 2971, N. P. Kravkov. No. 2971A,
P. K. Sternberg. No. 2971B, Ch. Valikhanov. No.
2971C, V. A. Kistjakovski.

2970 A1487 4k slate bl & dk brn   65 15
                    Litho.
2971 A1487 4k brn, red & black   32 15
                    Photo.
                    Perf. 11½
2971A A1487 4k dk blue & dk brn   32 15
                    Perf. 12
2971B A1487 4k rose vio & black   32 15
                    Litho.
2971C A1487 4k brn vio, blk & cit   32 15
            Nos. 2970-2971C (5)   1.93
                    Set value   35

Astronomer Struve (1793-1864), founder of
Pulkov Observatory; Kravkov (1865-1924), phar-
macologist; Sternberg (1865-1920), astronomer;
Valikhanov (1835-1865), Kazakh scientist;
Kistjakovski (1865-1952), chemist.

Issue dates: #2970, Nov. 30. #2971, Jan. 31,
1965. #2971A-2971B, Sept. 21, 1965. #2971C,
Dec. 24.

S. V. Ivanov
and Skiers
A1488

1964, Dec. 22   Engr.   Perf. 12½
2972 A1488 4k black & brown   50 30

S. V. Ivanov (1864-1910), painter.

Chemical Industry: Fertilizers and Pest
Control — A1489

Importance of the chemical industry for the
national economy: 6k, Synthetics factory.

1964, Dec. 25   Photo.   Perf. 12
2973 A1489 4k olive & lilac rose   15 15
2974 A1489 6k dp ultra & black   15 15
                    Set value   15

European
Cranberries — A1490

Wild Berries: 3k, Huckleberries. 4k, Mountain
ash. 10k, Blackberries. 16k, Cranberries.

1964, Dec. 25   Perf. 11½x12
2975 A1490 1k pale green & car   15 15
2976 A1490 3k gray, vio bl & grn   20 15
2977 A1490 4k gray, org red &
                    brown   24 15
2978 A1490 10k lt grn, dk vio blue &
                    claret   40 15
2979 A1490 16k gray, brt green & car
                    rose   50 15
            Nos. 2975-2979 (5)   1.49
                    Set value   38

Academy of
Science Library
A1491

1964, Dec. 25   Typo.   Perf. 12x12½
2980 A1491 4k black, pale grn & red   15 15

250th anniv. of the founding of the Academy of
Science Library, Leningrad.

Congress Palace,   Khan
Kremlin — A1492   Tengri — A1493

1964, Dec. 25
2981 A1492 1r dark blue   4.50 1.00

1964, Dec. 29   Photo.   Perf. 11½
Mountains: 6k, Kazbek, horiz. 12k, Twin peaks
of Ushba.

2982 A1493 4k grnsh bl, vio bl & buff   15 15
2983 A1493 6k yel, dk brn & ol   15 15
2984 A1493 12k lt yel, grn & pur   40 15
                    Set value   24

Development of mountaineering in Russia.

Portrait Type of 1964

Design: 6k, Michelangelo. 12k, Galileo.

Engraved and Photogravure
1964, Dec. 30   Perf. 11½
2985 A1455 6k sep, red brn & org   15 25
2986 A1455 12k dk brown & green   1.25 25

Michelangelo Buonarotti, artist, 400th death
anniv. and Galileo Galilei, astronomer and physicist, 400th birth anniv.

Helmet
A1494

Treasures from Kremlin Treasury: 6k, Saddle.
10k, Jeweled fur crown. 12k, Gold ladle. 16k,
Bowl.

1964, Dec. 30   Litho.
2987 A1494 4k multicolored   20 15
2988 A1494 6k multicolored   30 15
2989 A1494 10k multicolored   45 15
2990 A1494 12k multicolored   1.10 15
2991 A1494 16k multicolored   1.25 15
            Nos. 2987-2991 (5)   3.30
                    Set value   44

Dante — A1495   Blood
                          Donor — A1496

1965, Jan. 29   Photo.   Perf. 11½
2995 A1495 4k dk red brn & ol bis   35 25

Dante Alighieri (1265-1321), Italian poet.

1965, Jan. 31   Litho.   Perf. 12
Honoring blood donors: No. 2997, Hand holding
carnation, and donors' emblem.

2996 A1496 4k dk car, red, vio bl & bl   15 15
2997 A1496 4k brt grn, red & dk grn   15 15
                    Set value   20 15

Bandy — A1497   Police
                          Dog — A1498

Design: 6k, Figure skaters and Moscow Sports
Palace.

1965, Feb.   Photo.   Perf. 11½x12
2998 A1497 4k blue, red & yellow   15 15
2999 A1497 6k green, blk & red   15 15
                    Set value   15

4k issued Feb. 21, for the victory of the Soviet
team in the World Bandy Championship, Moscow,
Feb. 21-27; 6k issued Feb. 12, for the European
Figure Skating Championship. For overprint see No.
3017.

**Perf. 12x11½, 11½x12 (Photo.
stamps); 12x12½, 12½x12 (Litho.)**
Photo., Litho. (1k, 10k, 12k, 16k)
1965, Feb. 26

Dogs: 1k, Russian hound. 2k, Irish setter. No.
3003, Pointer. No. 3004, Fox terrier. No. 3005,
Sheepdog. No. 3006, Borzoi. 10k, Collie. 12k,
Husky. 16k, Caucasian sheepdog. (1k, 2k, 4k, 12k
and No. 3006 horiz.)

3000 A1498 1k black, yel & mar   18 15
3001 A1498 2k ultra, blk & red
                    brown   22 15
3002 A1498 3k blk, ocher & org
                    red   24 15
3003 A1498 4k org, yel grn & blk   35 15
3004 A1498 4k brn, blk & lt grn   35 15
3005 A1498 6k chalky blue, sep &
                    red   45 15
3006 A1498 6k chalky bl, org brn &
                    black   45 15
3007 A1498 10k yel green, ocher &
                    red   85 16

3008	A1498	12k gray, blk & ocher	95 20
3009	A1498	16k multicolored	1.10 24
		Nos. 3000-3009 (10)	5.14
		Set value	1.25

Richard Sorge (1895-1944), Soviet spy and Hero of the Soviet Union — A1499

1965, Mar. 6   Photo.   Perf. 12x12½

3010 A1499 4k henna brn & black   50 30

Communications Symbols — A1500

1965, Mar. 6   Perf. 12½x12

3011 A1500 6k grnsh blue, vio & brt purple   50 30

Intl. Telecommunication Union, cent.

No. 2764 Overprinted   ТАМПЕРЕ 1965 г.

1965, Mar. 20   Photo.   Perf. 12

3012 A1402 6k red & gray blue   1.00 30

Soviet victory in the European and World Ice Hockey Championships.

Lt. Col. Alexei Leonov Taking Movies in Space — A1501

Design: 1r, Leonov walking in space and Voskhod 2.

1965, Mar. 23   Photo.   Perf. 12
Size: 73x23mm

3015 A1501 10k brt ultra, org & gray   80 35

First man walking in space, Lt. Col. Alexei Leonov, Mar. 17, 1965 ("18 March" on stamp). Exists imperf. Value $1.

Souvenir Sheet

1965, Apr. 12   Litho.

3016 A1501 1r multicolored   5.50 1.75

Space flight of Voskhod 2. No. 3016 contains one 81x27mm stamp.

No. 2999 Overprinted   Советские фигуристы—чемпионы мира в парном катании

1965, Mar. 26   Perf. 11½x12

3017 A1497 6k green, black & red   80 25

Soviet victory in the World Figure Skating Championships.

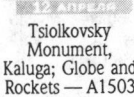

Flags of USSR and Poland — A1502

1965, Apr. 12   Photo.   Perf. 12

3018 A1502 6k bister & red   50 15

20th anniversary of the signing of the Polish-Soviet treaty of friendship, mutual assistance and postwar cooperation.

Tsiolkovsky Monument, Kaluga; Globe and Rockets — A1503

Rockets, Radio Telescope, TV Antenna — A1504

Designs: 12k, Space monument, Moscow. 16k, Cosmonauts' monument, Moscow. No. 3023, Globe with trajectories, satellite and astronauts.

1965, Apr. 12   Perf. 11½

3019	A1503	4k pale grn, black & brt rose	20 15
3020	A1503	12k vio, pur & brt rose	50 15
3021	A1503	16k multicolored	80 15

Lithographed on Aluminum Foil
Perf. 12½x12

3022	A1504	20k black & red	4.00 2.50
3023	A1504	20k blk, blue & red	4.00 2.50
		Nos. 3019-3023 (5)	9.50 5.45

National Cosmonauts' Day. On Nos. 3019-3021 the bright rose is fluorescent.

Lenin A1505

1965, Apr. 16   Engr.   Perf. 12

3024 A1505 10k tan & indigo   50 25

95th anniversary of the birth of Lenin.

Poppies A1506

Soviet Flag, Broken Swastikas, Fighting in Berlin A1507

Flowers: 3k, Daisies. 4k, Peony. 6k, Carnation. 10k, Tulips.

1965, Apr. 23   Photo.   Perf. 11

3025	A1506	1k maroon, red & grn	15 15
3026	A1506	3k dk brn, yel & grn	15 15
3027	A1506	4k blk, grn & lilac	20 15

3028	A1506	6k dk sl grn, grn & red	28 15
3029	A1506	10k dk plum, yel & grn	45 16
		Nos. 3025-3029 (5)	1.23
		Set value	50

1965   Perf. 11½

Designs: 2k, "Fatherland Calling!" (woman with proclamation) by I. Toidze. 3k, "Attack on Moscow" by V. Bogatkin. No. 3033, "Rest after the Battle" by Y. Neprintsev. No. 3034, "Mother of Partisan" by S. Gerasimov. 6k, "Our Flag - Symbol of Victory" (soldiers with banner) by V. Ivanov. 10k, "Tribute to the Hero" (mourners at bier) by F. Bogorodsky. 12k, "Invincible Nation and Army" (worker and soldier holding shell) by V. Koretsky. 16k, "Victory celebration on Red Square" by K. Yuan. 20k, Soldier and symbols of war.

3030	A1507	1k red, black & gold	25 15
3031	A1507	2k crim, blk & gold	25 15
3032	A1507	3k ultra & gold	30 15
3033	A1507	4k green & gold	45 15
3034	A1507	4k violet & gold	45 15
3035	A1507	6k dp claret & gold	60 15
3036	A1507	10k plum & gold	1.25 15
3037	A1507	12k black, red & gold	1.40 15
3038	A1507	16k lilac rose & gold	1.50 15
3039	A1507	20k red, black & gold	2.50 30
		Nos. 3030-3039 (10)	8.95
		Set value	95

20th anniv. of the end of World War II. Issued Apr. 25-May 1.

Souvenir Sheet

From Popov's Radio to Space Telecommunications — A1508

1965, May 7   Litho.   Perf. 11½

3040 A1508 1r blue & multi   5.50 2.50

70th anniv. of Aleksandr S. Popov's radio pioneer work. No. 3040 contains 6 labels without denominations or country name.

Marx, Lenin and Crowd with Flags — A1509

1965, May 9   Photo.   Perf. 12x12½

3041 A1509 6k red & black   15 15

6th conference of Postal Ministers of Communist Countries, Peking, June 21-July 15.

Bolshoi Theater, Moscow — A1510

1965, May 20   Perf. 11x11½

3042 A1510 6k grnsh blue, bis & blk   15 15

International Theater Day.

Col. Pavel Belyayev A1511

Design: No. 3044, Lt. Col. Alexei Leonov.

1965, May 23   Perf. 12x11½

3043 A1511 6k magenta & silver   15 15
3044 A1511 6k purple & silver   15 15

Space flight of Voshkod 2, Mar. 18-19, 1965, and the 1st man walking in space, Lt. Col. Alexei Leonov.

Sverdlov A1512

Grothewohl A1513

Portrait: No. 3046, Juldash Akhunbabaev.

Photogravure and Engraved
1965, May 30   Perf. 11½x12

3045 A1512 4k orange brn & blk   60 30
3046 A1512 4k lt violet & blk   60 30

Yakov M. Sverdlov, 1885-1919, 1st pres. of USSR, and J. Akhunbabaev, 1885-1943, pres. of Uzbek Republic.

1965, June 12   Photo.   Perf. 12

3051 A1513 4k black & magenta   15 15

Otto Grotewohl, prime minister of the German Democratic Republic (1894-1964).

Maurice Thorez A1514

Communication by Satellite A1515

1965, June 12

3052 A1514 6k brown & red   15 15

Maurice Thorez (1900-1964), chairman of the French Communist party.

1965, June 15   Litho.

Designs: No. 3054, Pouring ladle, steel mill and map of India. No. 3055, Stars, satellites and names of international organizations.

3053	A1515	3k olive, blk & gold	25 15
3054	A1515	6k emer, dk grn & gold	25 15
3055	A1515	6k vio blue, gold & blk	25 15
		Set value	18

Emphasizing international cooperation through communication, economic cooperation and international organizations.

Symbols of Chemistry A1516

1965, June 15   Photo.   Perf. 11½

3056 A1516 4k blk, brt rose & brt bl   30 15

20th Cong. of the Intl. Union of Pure and Applied Chemistry (IUPAC), Moscow. The bright rose ink is fluorescent.

V. A.
Serov — A1517

Design: 6k, Full-length portrait of Feodor Chalia-pin, the singer, by Serov.

1965, June 25   Typo.   Perf. 12½
3057 A1517 4k red brn, buff & black   30 25
3058 A1517 6k olive bister & black   30 25

Serov (1865-1911), historical painter.

Abay
Kunanbaev,
Kazakh Poet
A1518

Designs (writers and poets): No. 3060, Vsevolod Ivanov (1895-1963). No. 3060A, Eduard Vilde, Estonian writer. No. 3061, Mark Kropivnitsky, Ukrainian playwright. No. 3062, Manuk Apeghyan, Armenian writer and critic. No. 3063, Musa Djalil, Tartar poet. No. 3064, Hagop Hagopian, Armenian poet. No. 3064A, Djalil Mamedkulizade, Azerbaijan writer.

1965-66   Photo.   Perf. 12½x12
3059 A1518 4k lt violet & blk   40 28
3060 A1518 4k rose lilac & blk   40 28
3060A A1518 4k gray & black   40 28
3061 A1518 4k black & org brn   40 28
          Perf. 12½
          Typo.
3062 A1518 4k crim, blue grn &
              blk   40 28
          Perf. 11½
      Photogravure and Engraved
3063 A1518 4k black & org brn
              ('66)   40 28
3064 A1518 4k green & blk ('66)   40 28
          Photo.
3064A A1518 4k Prus green & blk
              ('66)   40 28
      Nos. 3059-3064A (8)   3.20 2.24

Sizes: Nos. 3059-3062, 38x25mm. Nos. 3063-3064A, 35x23mm.

Jan Rainis
A1518a

1965, Sept. 8   Photo.   Perf. 12½x12
3064B A1518a 4k dull blue & black   35 25

Rainis (1865-1929), Latvian playwright. "Rainis" was pseudonym of Jan Plieksans.

Film, Screen,
Globe and
Star
A1519

1965, July 5   Litho.   Perf. 12
3065 A1519 6k brt blue, gold & blk   35 15

4th Intl. Film Festival, Moscow: "For Humanism in Cinema Art, for Peace and Friendship among Nations."

Concert Bowl,
Tallinn
A1520

"Lithuania" — A1521

"Latvia"
A1522

1965, July   Perf. 12x11½, 11½x12
3066 A1520 4k ultra, blk, red & ocher   15 15
3067 A1521 4k red & brown   15 15
3068 A1522 4k yel, red & blue   15 15
          Set value   30 15

25th anniversaries of Estonia, Lithuania and Latvia as Soviet Republics. Issue dates: No. 3066, July 7; No. 3067, July 14; No. 3068, July 16.

"Keep
Peace" — A1523

Protesting Women and
Czarist Eagle — A1524

1965, July 10   Photo.   Perf. 11x11½
3069 A1523 6k yellow, black & blue   40 15

1965, July 20   Litho.   Perf. 11½
Designs: No. 3071, Soldier attacking distributor of handbills. No. 3072, Fighters on barricades with red flag. No. 3073, Monument for sailors of Battleship "Potemkin," Odessa.

3070 A1524 4k black, red & ol grn   25 15
3071 A1524 4k red, ol green & blk   25 15
3072 A1524 4k red, black & brn   25 15
3073 A1524 4k red & violet blue   25 15
          Set value   20

60th anniversary of the 1905 revolution.

Values quoted in this catalogue are for stamps graded Fine-Very Fine and with no faults. An illustrated guide to grade is provided in the "Catalogue Information" section of the Introduction.

Gheorghe Gheorghiu-Dej
(1901-1965), President
of Romanian State
Council (1961-
1965) — A1525

1965, July 26   Photo.   Perf. 12
3074 A1525 4k black & red   30 15

Relay Race
A1526

Sport: No. 3076, Bicycle race. No. 3077, Gymnast on vaulting horse.

1965, Aug. 5   Litho.   Perf. 12½x12
3075 A1526 4k vio blue, bis brn & red
              brown   30 15
3076 A1526 4k buff, red brn, gray & ma-
              roon   30 15
3077 A1526 4k bl, mar, buff & lt brn   35 15
          Set value   15

8th Trade Union Spartacist Games.

Electric
Power — A1527

Designs: 2k, Metals in modern industry. 3k, Modern chemistry serving the people. 4k, Mechanization, automation and electronics. 6k, New materials for building industry. 10k, Mechanization and electrification of agriculture. 12k, Technological progress in transportation. 16k, Application of scientific discoveries to industry.

1965, Aug. 5   Photo.   Perf. 12x11½
3078 A1527 1k olive, bl & blk   16 15
3079 A1527 2k org, blk & yel   16 15
3080 A1527 3k yel, vio & bister   16 15
3081 A1527 4k ultra, ind & red   22 15
3082 A1527 6k ultra & bister   32 15
3083 A1527 10k yel, orange & red
              brown   70 15
3084 A1527 12k Prus blue & red   80 15
3085 A1527 16k rose lilac, blk & vio-
              let blue   1.25 30
      Nos. 3078-3085 (8)   3.77
          Set value   84

Creation of the material and technical basis of communism.

Gymnast
A1528

Javelin and
Running
A1529

Design: 6k, Bicycling.

1965, Aug. 12   Perf. 11½
3086 A1528 4k multi & red   25 15
3087 A1528 6k gmsh bl, red & brn   25 15
          Set value   15

9th Spartacist Games for school children.

1965, Aug. 27
Designs: 6k, High jump and shot put. 10k, Hammer throwing and hurdling.

3088 A1529 4k brn, lilac & red   25 15
3089 A1529 6k brn, yel green & red   25 15
3090 A1529 10k brn, chlky bl & red   60 15
          Set value   22

US-Russian Track and Field Meet, Kiev.

Worker and
Globe — A1530

Flag of North Viet
Nam, Factory and
Palm — A1531

Designs: No 3092, Heads of three races and torch. No. 3093, Woman with dove.

1965, Sept. 1
3091 A1530 6k dk purple & tan   30 15
3092 A1530 6k brt bl, brn & red org   30 15
3093 A1530 6k Prus green & tan   30 15
          Set value   20

Intl. Fed. of Trade Unions (#3091), Fed. of Democratic Youth (#3092), Democratic Women's Fed. (#3093), 20th annivs.

1965, Sept. 1   Litho.   Perf. 12
3094 A1531 6k red, yel, brn & gray   50 30

Republic of North Viet Nam, 20th anniv.

Scene from
Film
"Potemkin"
A1532

Film Scenes: 6k, "Young Guard." 12k, "Ballad of a Soldier."

1965, Sept. 29   Litho.   Perf. 12½x12
3095 A1532 4k blue, blk & red   32 25
3096 A1532 6k multicolored   32 25
3097 A1532 12k multicolored   55 25

Post Rider, 16th Century — A1533

History of the Post: No. 3099, Mail coach, 17th-18th centuries. 2k, Train, 19th century. 4k, Mail truck, 1920. 6k, Train, ship and plane. 12k, New Moscow post office, helicopter, automatic sorting and cancelling machines. 16k, Lenin, airport and map of USSR.

1965   Photo.   Unwmk.   Perf. 11½x12
3098 A1533 1k org brn, dk gray & dk
              green   15 15
3099 A1533 1k gray, ocher & dk
              brown   15 15
3100 A1533 2k dl lil, brt bl & brn   20 15
3101 A1533 4k bis, rose lake & blk   28 15
3102 A1533 6k pale brn, Prus grn &
              black   40 15
3103 A1533 12k lt ultra, lt brn & blk   60 15
3104 A1533 16k gray, rose red & vio
              black   70 15
      Nos. 3098-3104 (7)   2.48
          Set value   50

For overprint see No. 3175.

Atomic
Icebreaker
"Lenin"
A1534

Designs: No. 3106, Icebreakers "Taimir" and
"Vaigitch." 6k, Dickson Settlement. 10k, Sailing
ships "Vostok" and "Mirni," Bellinghausen-Lazarew
expedition, and icebergs. 16k, Vostok South Pole
station.

1965, Oct. 23   Litho.   Perf. 12
Size: 37x25mm
3106 A1534 4k blue, black & org   25   25
3107 A1534 4k blue, black & org   25   25
  a.   Pair #3106-3107   60   50
3108 A1534 6k sepia & dk violet   65   25
Size: 33x33mm
3109 A1534 10k red, black & buff   80   25
Size: 37x25mm
3110 A1534 16k vio blk & red brn   1.00   25
  Nos. 3106-3110 (5)   2.95 1.25

Scientific conquests of the Arctic and Antarctic.
No. 3107a has continuous design.

Souvenir Sheet

Basketball,
Map of
Europe and
Flags
A1535

1965, Oct. 29   Litho.   Imperf.
3111 A1535 1r multicolored   4.00 1.00

14th European Basketball Championship,
Moscow.

Timiryazev Agriculture Academy,
Moscow — A1536

1965, Oct. 30   Photo.   Perf. 11
3112 A1536 4k brt car, gray & vio bl   30 15

Agriculture Academy, Moscow, cent.

Souvenir Sheet

Lenin
A1537

Lithographed and Engraved
1965, Oct. 30   Imperf.
3113 A1537 10k sil, blk & dp org   2.00 60

48th anniv. of the October Revolution.

Nicolas Poussin (1594-
1665), French
Painter — A1538

1965, Nov. 16   Photo.   Perf. 11½
3114 A1538 4k gray blue, dk bl & dk
            brown   30 15

Kremlin
A1539

1965, Nov. 16   Perf. 12x11½
3115 A1539 4k black, ver & silver   30 15

New Year 1966.

Mikhail
Ivanovich Kalinin
(1875-1946),
USSR President
(1923-1946)
A1540

1965, Nov. 19   Perf. 12½
3116 A1540 4k dp claret & red   30 15

Klyuchevskaya Sopka — A1541

Kamchatka Volcanoes: 12k, Karumski erupting,
vert. 16k, Koryakski snowcovered.

1965, Nov. 30   Litho.   Perf. 12
3117 A1541 4k multicolored   18 15
3118 A1541 12k multicolored   45 15
3119 A1541 16k multicolored   75 15
  Set value   30

October Subway Station,
Moscow — A1542

Subway Stations: No. 3121, Lenin Avenue, Moscow. No. 3122, Moscow Gate, Leningrad. No.
3123, Bolshevik Factory, Kiev.

1965, Nov. 30   Engr.
3120 A1542 6k indigo   30 25
3121 A1542 6k brown   30 25
3122 A1542 6k gray brown   30 25
3123 A1542 6k slate green   30 25

Buzzard — A1543

Birds: 2k, Kestrel. 3k, Tawny eagle. 4k, Red kite.
10k, Peregrine falcon. 12k, Golden eagle, horiz.
14k, Lammergeier, horiz. 16k, Gyrfalcon.

1965   Photo.   Perf. 11½x12
3124 A1543 1k gray grn & black   15 15
3125 A1543 2k pale brn & blk   15 15
3126 A1543 3k lt ol grn & black   15 15
3127 A1543 4k lt gray brn & blk   30 15
3128 A1543 10k lt vio brn & blk   55 10
3129 A1543 12k blue & black   75 20
3130 A1543 14k bluish gray & blk   80 25
3131 A1543 16k dl red brn & blk   85 15
  Nos. 3124-3131 (8)   3.70
  Set value   1.25

Issue dates: 4k, 10k, Nov. 1k 2k, 12k, 14k, Dec.
24. 3k, 16k, Dec. 29.

Red Star
Medal, War
Scene and
View of
Kiev — A1544

Red Star Medal, War Scene and view of: No.
3133, Leningrad. No. 3134, Odessa. No. 3135,
Moscow. No. 3136, Brest Litovsk. No. 3137,
Volgograd (Stalingrad). No. 3138, Sevastopol.

1965, Dec.   Perf. 11½
Red, Gold and:
3132 A1544 10k brown   42 15
3133 A1544 10k dark blue   42 15
3134 A1544 10k Prussian blue   42 15
3135 A1544 10k dark violet   42 15
3136 A1544 10k dark brown   42 15
3137 A1544 10k black   42 15
3138 A1544 10k gray   42 15
  Nos. 3132-3138 (7)   2.94
  Set value   48

Honoring the heroism of various cities during
World War II. Nos. 3136-3138 issued Dec. 30,
others, Dec. 20.

Map and Flag of
Yugoslavia, and
National Assembly
Building — A1545

1965, Dec. 30   Litho.   Perf. 12
3139 A1545 6k vio blue, red & bis   40 15

Republic of Yugoslavia, 20th anniv.

Collective Farm
Watchman by
S.V. Gerasimov
A1547

Painting: 16k, "Major's Courtship" by Pavel
Andreievitch Fedotov, horiz.

1965, Dec. 31   Engr.
3145 A1547 12k red & sepia   1.10 25
3146 A1547 16k red & dark blue   1.40 50

Painters: Gerasimov, 80th birth anniv; Pavel A.
Fedotov (1815-52).

Microscope and
Moscow
University
A1548

Congress Emblems: No. 3148, Turkeys, geese,
chicken and globe. No. 3149, Crystals. No. 3150,
Oceanographic instruments and ship. No. 3151,
Mathematical symbols.

1966   Photo.   Perf. 11½
3147 A1548 6k dull blue, blk & red   25 15
3148 A1548 6k gray, pur & black   25 15
3149 A1548 6k ol bister, blk & blue   25 15
3150 A1548 6k grnsh blue & blk   25 15
3151 A1548 6k dull yel, red brn & blk 25 15
  Nos. 3147-3151 (5)   1.25
  Set value   35

Intl. congresses to be held in Moscow: 9th Cong.
of Microbiology (#3147); 13th Cong. on Poultry
Raising (#3148); 7th Cong. on Crystallography
(#3149); 2nd Intl. Cong. of Oceanography (#3150);
Intl. Cong. of Mathematicians (#3151).
See Nos. 3309-3310.

Mailman and Milkmaid, 19th Century
Figurines — A1549

1966, Jan. 28   Litho.
3152 A1549 6k shown   25 25
3153 A1549 10k Tea set   35 25

Bicentenary of Dimitrov Porcelain Works.

Romain
Rolland (1866-
1944), French
Writer
A1550

Portrait: No. 3155, Eugène Pottier (1816-1887),
French poet and author of the "International."

1966   Photo. & Engr.   Perf. 11½
3154 A1550 4k dk blue & brn org   15 15
3155 A1550 4k sl, red & dk red brn   15 15
  Set value   20 15

Horseback Rider,
and Flags of
Mongolia and
USSR — A1551

1966, Jan. 31   Litho.   Perf. 12½x12
3159 A1551 4k red, ultra & vio brn   35 25

20th anniversary of the signing of the Mongolian-
Soviet treaty of friendship and mutual assistance.

No. 2728
Overprinted in
Silver

„ЛУНА-9" — НА ЛУНЕ!
3.2. 1966

1966, Feb. 5   Photo.   Perf. 12
3160 A1385 6k blk, lt blue & red   2.50 1.10

1st soft landing on the moon by Luna 9, Feb. 3,
1966.

Map of Antarctica With Soviet
Stations — A1552

Diesel Ship "Ob" and Emperor
Penguins — A1553

Design: No. 3164, Snocat tractors and aurora
australis.

1966, Feb. 14   Photo.   Perf. 11
3162 A1552 10k sky bl, sil & dk car   65 25
3163 A1553 10k silver & dk car   65 25
3164 A1553 10k dk car, sil & sky bl   65 25
　　a.　　Strip of 3, #3162-31264   2.00 75

10 years of Soviet explorations in Antarctica. No.
3162 has horizontal rows of perforation extending
from either mid-side up to the map.

Lenin
A1554

1966, Feb. 22   Photo.   Perf. 12x11½
3165 A1554 10k grnsh black & gold   65 25
3166 A1554 10k dk red & silver   65 25

96th anniversary of the birth of Lenin.

N.Y. Iljin,   Kremlin Congress
Guardsman   Hall
A1555   A1556

Soviet Heroes: #3168, Lt. Gen. G. P.
Kravchenko. #3169, Pvt. Anatoli Uglovsky.

1966   Perf. 11½x12
3167 A1555 4k dp org & vio black   30 25
3168 A1555 4k grnsh blue & dk pur   30 25
3169 A1555 4k green & brown   30 25

1966, Feb. 28   Typo.   Perf. 12
3172 A1556 4k gold, red & lt ultra   30 15

23rd Communist Party Congress.

Hamlet and
Queen from
Film "Hamlet"
A1557

Film Scene: 4k, Two soldiers from "The Quick
and the Dead."

1966, Feb. 28   Litho.
3173 A1557 4k red, black & olive   35 15
3174 A1557 10k ultra & black   35 15

No. 3104   Учредительная конференция
Overprinted   Всесоюзного общества
                  филателистов. 1966

1966, Mar. 10   Photo.   Perf. 11½x12
3175 A1533 16k multicolored   1.50 1.00

Constituent assembly of the All-Union Society of
Philatelists, 1966.

Emblem and Skater — A1558

Designs: 6k, Emblem and ice hockey. 10k,
Emblem and slalom skier.

1966, Mar. 11   Perf. 11
3176 A1558 4k ol, brt ultra & red   32 15
3177 A1558 6k bluish lilac, red & dk
               brown   50 15
3178 A1558 10k lt bl, red & dk brn   65 15
　　　　　　Set value   24

Second Winter Spartacist Games, Sverdlovsk.
The label-like upper halves of Nos. 3176-3178 are
separated from the lower halves by a row of
perforations.

Electric
Locomotive
A1559

Designs: 6k, Map of the Lenin Volga-Baltic
Waterway, Admiralty, Leningrad, and Kremlin.
10k, Ship passing through lock in waterway, vert.
12k, M.S. Aleksander Pushkin. 16k, Passenger liner
and globe.

1966   Litho.   Perf. 12½x12, 12x12½
3179 A1559 4k multicolored   15 15
3180 A1559 6k gray, ultra, red &
               black   15 15
3181 A1559 10k Prus bl, gray brn &
               black   42 15
3182 A1559 12k blue, ver & black   40 15
3183 A1559 16k blue & multi   55 20
　　　　Nos. 3179-3183 (5)   1.67
　　　　　　Set value   58

Modern transportation. Dates of issue: #3179-
3181, Aug. 6; #3182-3183, Mar. 25.

Supreme Soviet   Sergei M.
Building, Frunze   Kirov
A1560   A1561

1966, Mar. 25   Photo.   Perf. 12
3184 A1560 4k deep red   35 25

40th anniv. of the Kirghiz Republic.

1966   Engr.   Perf. 12
Portraits: No. 3186, Grigori Ordzhonikidze. No.
3187, Ion Yakir.

3185 A1561 4k dk red brown   50 25
3186 A1561 4k slate green   50 25
3187 A1561 4k dark gray violet   50 25

Kirov (1886-1934), revolutionist and Secretary of
the Communist Party Central Committee; Ordzhonikidze (1886-1937), a political leader of the Red
Army and government official; Yakir, military leader
in October Revolution, 70th birth anniv.
Issue dates: No. 3185, Mar. 27. No. 3186, June
22. No. 3187, July 30.

Souvenir Sheet

Lenin — A1563

Embossed and Typographed
1966, Mar. 29   Imperf.
3188 A1563 50k red & silver   3.00 90

23rd Communist Party Congress.

Aleksandr E. Fersman
(1883-1945),
Mineralogist — A1564

Soviet Scientists: #3190, D. K. Zabolotny (1866-
1929), microbiologist. #3191, M. A. Shatelen
(1866-1957), physicist. #3191A, Otto Yulievich
Schmidt (1891-1956), scientist and arctic explorer.

1966, Mar. 30   Litho.   Perf. 12½x12
3189 A1564 4k vio blue & multi   50 25
3190 A1564 4k red brown & multi   50 25
3191 A1564 4k lilac & multi   50 25
3191A A1564 4k Prus blue & brown   50 25

Luna 10 Automatic Moon
Station — A1565

Overprinted in Red:
„Луна-10"—XXIII съезду КПСС

1966, Apr. 8   Typo.   Imperf.
3192 A1565 10k gold, blk, brt bl & brt
               rose   1.50 60

Launching of the 1st artificial moon satellite,
Luna 10. The bright rose ink is fluorescent on Nos.
3192-3194.

Type A1565 Without Overprint

Design: 12k, Station on moon.

1966, Apr. 12   Perf. 12
3193 A1565 10k multicolored   40 30
3194 A1565 12k multicolored   60 30

Day of Space Research, Apr. 12, 1966.

Molniya 1 and   Ernst Thälmann
Television Screens   A1567
A1566

1966, Apr. 12   Litho.   Perf. 12½
3195 A1566 10k gold, blk, brt bl & red   50 25

Launching of the communications satellite
"Lightning I," Apr. 23, 1965.

1966-67   Engr.   Perf. 12½x12
Portraits: No. 3197, Wilhelm Pieck. No. 3198,
Sun Yat-sen. No. 3199, Sen Katayama.

3196 A1567 6k rose claret   50 25
3197 A1567 6k blue violet   50 25
3198 A1567 6k reddish brown   50 25

Photo.
3199 A1567 6k gray green ('67)   50 25

Thälmann (1886-1944), German Communist
leader; Pieck (1876-1960), German Dem. Rep.
Pres.; Sun Yat-sen (1866-1925), leader of the Chinese revolution; Katayama (1859-1933), founder of
Social Democratic Party in Japan in 1901.
Issue dates: #3196, Apr. 16. #3197-3198, June
22. #3199, Nov. 2, 1967.

Soldier, 1917,
and Astronaut
A1568

1966, Apr. 30   Litho.   Perf. 11½
3200 A1568 4k brt rose & black   30 15

15th Congress of the Young Communist League
(Komsomol).

---

*The first value column gives the cat-
alogue value of an unused stamp,
the second that of a used stamp.*

Ice Hockey Player A1569

1966, Apr. 30
3201 A1569 10k red, ultra, gold & black 40 25

Soviet victory in the World Ice Hockey Championships. For souvenir sheet see No. 3232. For overprint see No. 3315.

Nicolai Kuznetsov — A1570

Heroes of Guerrilla Warfare during WWII (Gold Star of Hero of the Soviet Union and): No. 3203, Imant Sudmalis. No. 3204, Anya Morozova. No. 3205, Filipp Strelets. No. 3206, Tikhon Rumazhkov.

1966, May 9 Photo. Perf. 12x12¹/₂
3202 A1570 4k green & black 15 15
3203 A1570 4k ocher & black 15 15
3204 A1570 4k blue & black 15 15
3205 A1570 4k brt rose & black 15 15
3206 A1570 4k violet & black 15 15
　　　　　　Set value 50 25

Peter I. Tchaikovsky A1571

Designs: 4k, Moscow State Conservatory and Tchaikovsky monument. 16k, Tchaikovsky House, Klin.

1966, May 26 Typo. Perf. 12¹/₂
3207 A1571 4k red, yel & black 25 25
3208 A1571 6k yel, red & black 38 30
3209 A1571 16k red, bluish gray & black 85 35

Third International Tchaikovsky Contest, Moscow, May 30-June 29.

Runners — A1572

Designs: 6k, Weight lifters. 12k, Wrestlers.

1966, May 26 Photo. Perf. 11x11¹/₂
3210 A1572 4k emer, olive & brn 20 15
3211 A1572 6k org, black & lt brn 28 15
3212 A1572 12k grnsh bl, brn ol & black 45 15
　　　　　　Set value 22

No. 3210, Znamensky Brothers Intl. Track Competitions; No. 3211, Intl. Weightlifting Competitions; No. 3212, Intl. Wrestling Competitions for Ivan Poddubny Prize.

Jules Rimet World Soccer Cup, Ball and Laurel A1573

Chessboard, Gold Medal, Pawn and King — A1574

Designs: No. 3214, Soccer. 12k, Fencers. 16k, Fencer, mask, foil and laurel branch.

1966, May 31 Litho. Perf. 11¹/₂
3213 A1573 4k rose red, gold & black 20 15
3214 A1573 6k emer, tan, blk & red 30 15
3215 A1574 6k brn, gold, blk & white 30 15
3216 A1573 12k brt blue, ol & blk 70 15
3217 A1573 16k multicolored 75 16
　　　　Nos. 3213-3217 (5) 2.25
　　　　　　Set value 48

Nos. 3213-3214 for World Cup Soccer Championship, Wembley, England, July 11-30; No. 3215 the World Chess Title Match between Tigran Petrosian and Boris Spassky; Nos. 3216-3217 the World Fencing Championships. For souvenir sheet see No. 3232.

Sable and Lake Baikal, Map of Barguzin Game Reserve — A1575

Design: 6k, Map of Lake Baikal region and Game Reserve, brown bear on lake shore.

1966, June 25 Photo. Perf. 12
3218 A1575 4k steel blue & black 35 25
3219 A1575 6k rose lake & black 35 25

Barguzin Game Reserve, 50th anniv.

Pink Lotus — A1576

Designs: 6k, Palms and cypresses. 12k, Victoria cruziana.

1966, June 30 Perf. 11¹/₂
3220 A1576 3k green, pink & yel 16 15
3221 A1576 6k grnsh bl, ol brn & dk brn 28 15
3222 A1576 12k multicolored 50 15
　　　　　　Set value 24

Sukhum Botanical Garden, 125th anniv.

Dogs Ugolek and Veterok after Space Flight — A1577

Designs: No. 3224, Diagram of Solar System, globe and medal of Venus 3 flight. No. 3225, Luna 10, earth and moon.

1966, July 15 Perf. 12x11¹/₂
3223 A1577 6k ocher, ind & org brn 30 15
3224 A1577 6k crim, blk & silver 30 15
　　　　　Perf. 12x12¹/₂
3225 A1577 6k dk blue & bister brn 30 15
　　　　　　Set value 20

Soviet achievements in space.

Itkol Hotel, Mount Cheget and Map of Russia A1578

Arch of General Headquarters, Winter Palace and Alexander Column — A1579

Resort Areas: 4k, Ship on Volga River and Zhigul Mountain. 10k, Castle, Kislovodsk. 12k, Ismail Samani Mausoleum, Bukhara, Uzbek. 16k, Hotel Caucasus, Sochi.

Perf. 12¹/₂x12, 12¹/₂ (6k)
1966　　　　　　　　　**Litho.**
3226 A1578 1k multicolored 15 15
3227 A1578 4k multicolored 15 15
3228 A1579 6k multicolored 15 15
3229 A1578 10k multicolored 24 15
3230 A1578 12k multicolored 38 15
3231 A1578 16k multicolored 52 15
　　　　Nos. 3226-3231 (6) 1.59
　　　　　　Set value 48

Issue dates: 10k, Sept. 14. Others, July 20.

Souvenir Sheet

A1580

1966, July 26 Litho. Perf. 11¹/₂
3232 A1580 Sheet of 4 10.00 1.75
　a. 10k Fencers 2.00 42
　b. 10k Chess 2.00 42
　c. 10k Soccer cup 2.00 42
　d. 10k Ice hockey 2.00 42

World fencing, chess, soccer and ice hockey championships.
See Nos. 3201, 3213-3217.

Congress Emblem, Congress Palace and Kremlin Tower — A1581

1966, Aug. 6 Photo. Perf. 11¹/₂x12
3233 A1581 4k brown & yellow 30 15

Consumers' Cooperative Societies, 7th Cong.

Dove, Crane, Russian and Japanese Flags A1582

1966, Aug. 9 Perf. 12¹/₂x11¹/₂
3234 A1582 6k gray & red 40 25

Soviet-Japanese friendship, and 2nd meeting of Russian and Japanese delegates at Khabarovsk.

"Knight Fighting with Tiger" by Rustaveli — A1583

Designs: 4k, Shota Rustaveli, bas-relief. 6k, "Avtandil at a Mountain Spring." 50k, Shota Rustaveli Monument and design of 3k stamp.

Perf. 11¹/₂x12¹/₂
1966, Aug. 31　　　　　　　**Engr.**
3235 A1583 3k black, *olive green* 25 15
3236 A1583 4k brown, *yellow* 25 15
3237 A1583 6k bluish black, *lt ultra* 35 15
　　　　　　Set value 16

Souvenir Sheet
Imperf
Engraved and Photogravure
3238 A1583 50k slate green & bis 3.00 1.25

800th anniv. of the birth of Shota Rustaveli, Georgian poet, author of "The Knight in the Tiger's Skin." No. 3238 contains one 32x49mm stamp; dark green margin with design of 6k stamp.

Coat of Arms and Fireworks over Moscow A1584

Lithographed (Lacquered)
1966, Sept. 14　　　　　**Perf. 11¹/₂**
3239 A1584 4k multicolored 30 15

49th anniversary of October Revolution.

Grayling A1585

Designs (Fish and part of design of 6k stamp): 4k, Sturgeon. 6k, Trawler, net and map of Lake Baikal, vert. 10k, Two Baikal cisco. 12k, Two Baikal whitefish.

1966, Sept. 25   Photo. & Engr.

3240 A1585	2k multicolored	15	15
3241 A1585	4k multicolored	16	15
3242 A1585	6k multicolored	24	15
3243 A1585	10k multicolored	50	15
3244 A1585	12k gray, dk grn & red brown	55	15
	Nos. 3240-3244 (5)	1.60	
	Set value		45

Fish resources of Lake Baikal.

Map of Russia and Symbols of
Transportation and
Communication — A1586

Designs (map of Russia and): No. 3246, Technological education. No. 3247, Agriculture and mining. No. 3248, Increased productivity through five-year plan. No. 3249, Technology and inventions.

1966, Sept. 29   Photo.   Perf. 11½x12

3245 A1586	4k ultra & silver	30	15
3246 A1586	4k car & silver	30	15
3247 A1586	4k red brown & silver	30	15
3248 A1586	4k red & silver	30	15
3249 A1586	4k dp green & silver	30	15
	Nos. 3245-3249 (5)	1.50	
	Set value		25

23rd Communist Party Congress decisions.

Government
House,
Kishinev,
and
Moldavian
Flag
A1587

1966, Oct. 8   Litho.   Perf. 12½x12

3250 A1587 4k multicolored   50 30

500th anniversary of Kishinev.

Symbolic Water
Cycle — A1588

1966, Oct. 12   Perf. 11½

3251 A1588 6k multicolored   35 15

Hydrological Decade (UNESCO), 1965-1974.

Nikitin Monument in
Kalinin, Ship's Prow and
Map — A1589

1966, Oct. 12   Photo.

3252 A1589 4k multicolored   40 25

Afanasii Nikitin's trip to India, 500th anniv.

Scene from
Opera "Nargiz"
by M.
Magomayev
A1590

Design: No. 3254, Scene from opera "Kerogli" by Y. Gadjubekov (knight on horseback and armed men).

1966, Oct. 12

3253 A1590	4k black & ocher	30	15
3254 A1590	4k blk & blue green	30	15
a.	Pair, #3253-3254	60	15
	Set value		15

Azerbaijan opera. Printed in checkerboard arrangement.

Fighters
A1591

1966, Oct. 26

3255 A1591 6k red, blk & ol bister   40 15

30th anniversary of Spanish Civil War.

National Militia
A1592

Protest Rally
A1592a

1966, Oct. 26   Litho.   Perf. 12x12½

3256 A1592 4k red & dark brown   35 15

25th anniv. of the National Militia.

1966, Oct. 26   Perf. 12

3256A A1592a 6k yel, black & red   40 25

"Hands off Viet Nam!"

Soft Landing on
Moon, Luna 9
A1593

Symbols of Agriculture
and Chemistry
A1594

Designs: 1k, Congress Palace, Moscow, and map of Russia. 3k, Boy, girl and Lenin banner. 4k, Flag. 6k, Plane and Ostankino Television Tower. 10k, Soldier and Soviet star. 12k, Steel worker. 16k, "Peace," woman with dove. 20k, Demonstrators in Red Square, flags, carnation and globe. 50k, Newspaper, plane, train and Communications Ministry. 1r, Lenin and industrial symbols.

1966   Litho.   Perf. 12
Inscribed "1966"

3257 A1593	1k dk red brown	15	15
3258 A1593	2k violet	15	15
3259 A1593	3k red lilac	15	15
3260 A1593	4k bright red	15	15
3261 A1593	6k ultra	20	15
3262 A1593	10k olive	40	15
3263 A1593	12k red brown	80	15
3264 A1593	16k violet blue	85	15

Perf. 11½
Photo.

3265 A1594	20k bis, red & dk bl	1.25	15
3266 A1594	30k dp grn & green	1.65	28
3267 A1594	50k blue & violet bl	3.50	35
3268 A1594	1r black & red	5.50	55
	Nos. 3257-3268 (12)	14.75	
	Set value		1.75

No. 3260 was issued on fluorescent paper in 1969.
See Nos. 3470-3481.

Ostankino Television
Tower, Molniya 1
Satellite and
Kremlin — A1595

1966, Nov. 19   Litho.   Perf. 12

3273 A1595 4k multicolored   35 15

New Year, 1967, the 50th anniversary of the October Revolution.

Diagram of Luna 9 Flight — A1596

Arms of Russia and
Pennant Sent to
Moon — A1597

Design: No. 3276, Luna 9 and photograph of moonscape.

1966, Nov. 25   Typo.   Perf. 12

3274 A1596	10k black & silver	50	25
3275 A1597	10k red & silver	50	25
3276 A1596	10k black & silver	50	25
a.	Strip of 3, #3274-3276	1.50	75

Soft landing on the moon by Luna 9, Jan. 31, 1966, and the television program of moon pictures on Feb. 2.

Battle of Moscow, 1941 — A1598

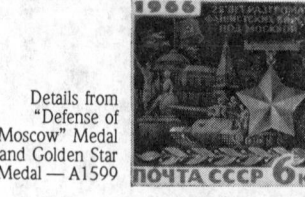

Details from
"Defense of
Moscow" Medal
and Golden Star
Medal — A1599

25th anniv. of Battle of Moscow: 10k, Sun rising over Kremlin. Ostankino Tower, chemical plant and rockets.

Perf. 12, 11½ (A1599)
1966, Dec. 1

			Photo.
3277 A1598	4k red brown	20	15
3278 A1599	6k bister & brown	45	15
3279 A1598	10k dp bister & yellow	60	15
	Set value		26

Cervantes and
Don Quixote
A1600

1966, Dec. 15   Photo.   Perf. 11½

3280 A1600 6k gray & brown   30 15

Miguel Cervantes Saavedra (1547-1616), Spanish writer.

Bering's Ship and Map of Voyage to
Commander Islands — A1601

Far Eastern Territories: 2k, Medny Island and map. 4k, Petropavlosk-Kamchatski Harbor. 6k, Geyser, Kamchatka, vert. 10k, Avachinskaya Bay, Kamchatka. 12k, Fur seals, Bering Island. 16k, Guillemots in bird sanctuary, Kuril Islands.

1966, Dec. 25   Perf. 12

3281 A1601	1k bister & multi	15	15
3282 A1601	2k bister & multi	15	15
3283 A1601	4k dp blue & multi	22	15
3284 A1601	6k multicolored	32	15
3285 A1601	10k dp blue & multi	45	15
3286 A1601	12k olive & multi	80	15
3287 A1601	16k lt blue & multi	90	15
	Nos. 3281-3287 (7)	2.99	
	Set value		55

Communications
Satellite,
Molniya 1
A1602

Design: No. 3289, Luna 11 moon probe, moon, earth and Soviet emblem.

1966, Dec. 29   Photo.   Perf. 12x11½

3288 A1602	6k blk, vio bl & brt rose	40	15
3289 A1602	6k black & brt rose	40	15
	Set value		15

Issued to publicize space explorations. The bright rose is fluorescent.

Golden Stag, Scythia, 6th Century
B.C. — A1603

Treasures from the Hermitage, Leningrad: 6k, Silver jug, Persia, 5th Century A.D. 10k, Statue of Voltaire by Jean Antoine Houdon. 12k, Malachite vase, Ural, 1840. 16k, "The Lute Player," by Michelangelo de Caravaggio. (6k, 10k, 12k are vertical).

1966, Dec. 29   Engr.   Perf. 12

3200 A1603	4k yellow & black	20	15
3291 A1603	6k gray & black	30	15
3292 A1603	10k dull vio & black	50	20
3293 A1603	12k emer & black	75	28
3294 A1603	16k ocher & black	85	32
	Nos. 3290-3294 (5)	2.60	1.10

Sea Water
Converter and
Pavilion at
EXPO
'67 — A1604

Designs (Pavilion and): 6k, Splitting atom, vert.
10k, "Proton" space station. 30k, Soviet pavilion.

1967, Jan. 25   Litho.   Perf. 12
3295 A1604 4k multicolored   25   15
3296 A1604 6k multicolored   25   15
3297 A1604 10k multicolored   30   15
    Set value   22

Souvenir Sheet
3298 A1604 30k multicolored   2.50 1.25

EXPO '67, Intl. Exhib., Montreal, 4/28-10/27.

1st Lieut. B.
I. Sizov
A1605

Design: No. 3300, Sailor V. V. Khodyrev.

1967, Feb. 16   Photo.   Perf. 12x11½
3299 A1605 4k dull yel & ocher   25   25
3300 A1605 4k gray & dk gray   25   25

Heroes of World War II.

Woman's Head and Pavlov
Shawl — A1606

1967, Feb. 16   Perf. 11
3301 A1606 4k violet, red & green 30   15

International Woman's Day, Mar. 8.

Movie Camera and
Film — A1607

1967, Feb. 16   Photo.   Perf. 11½
3302 A1607 6k multicolored   40   25

5th Intl. Film Festival, Moscow, July 5-20.

Trawler Fish Factory and Fish — A1608

Designs: No. 3304, Refrigerationship. No. 3305,
Crab canning ship. No. 3306, Fishing trawler. No.
3307, Black Sea seiner.

1967, Feb. 28   Litho.   Perf. 12x11½
Ships in Black and Red
3303 A1608 6k blue & gray   40   25
3304 A1608 6k blue & gray   40   25
3305 A1608 6k blue & gray   40   25
3306 A1608 6k blue & gray   40   25
3307 A1608 6k blue & gray   40   25
  a. Vert. strip of 5, #3303-3307   2.00 1.25
    Nos. 3303-3307 (5)   2.00 1.25

Soviet fishing industry.

Newspaper Forming
Hammer and Sickle,
Red Flag — A1609

1967, Mar. 13   Litho.   Perf. 12x12½
3308 A1609 4k cl brn, red, yel & brn 30 15

50th anniversary of newspaper Izvestia.

Congress Type of 1966

Congress Emblems and: No. 3309, Moscow
State University, construction site and star. No.
3310, Pile driver, mining excavator, crossed ham-
mers, globe and "V."

1967, Mar. 10   Photo.   Perf. 11½
3309 A1548 6k ultra, brt blue & blk   30 15
3310 A1548 6k blk, org red & blue   30 15
    Set value   15

Intl. congresses to be held in Moscow: 7th General Assembly Session of the Intl. Standards Association (#3309); 5th Intl. Mining Cong. (#3310).

International Tourist Year Emblem and
Travel Symbols — A1610

1967, Mar. 10   Perf. 11
3314 A1610 4k black, sky bl & silver 30 15

International Tourist Year, 1967.

No. 3201 Overprinted   **Вена - 1967**

1967, Mar. 29   Litho.   Perf. 11½
3315 A1569 10k multicolored   1.50 75

Victory of the Soviet team in the Ice Hockey
Championships, Vienna, Mar. 18-29. Overprint
reads: "Vienna-1967."

Space Walk — A1611

Designs: 10k, Rocket launching from satellite.
16k, Spaceship over moon, and earth.

1967, Mar. 30   Litho.   Perf. 12
3316 A1611 4k bister & multi   25   15
3317 A1611 10k black & multi   70   15
3318 A1611 16k lilac & multi   1.00 30
    Set value   50

National Cosmonauts' Day.

Lenin as
Student, by V.
Tsigal
A1612

Sculptures of Lenin: 3k, Monument at Ulyanovsk
by M. Manizer. 4k, Lenin in Razliv, by V. Pinchuk,
horiz. 6k, Head, by G. Neroda. 10k, Lenin as
Leader, statue, by N. Andreyev.

1967   Photo.   Perf. 12x11½, 11½x12
3319 A1612 2k ol grn, sepia & buff   15 15
3320 A1612 3k maroon & brown   18 15
3321 A1612 4k ol black & gold   28 15
3322 A1612 6k dk bl, silver & blk   40 15
3323 A1612 10k sil, gray bl & blk   75 15
3323A A1612 10k gold, gray & black   75 15
    Nos. 3319-3323A (6)   2.51
    Set value   40

97th anniversary of the birth of Lenin.
Issued: No. 3323A, Oct. 25. Others, Apr. 22.

Lt. M. S.
Kharchenko
and Battle
Scenes
A1613

Designs: No. 3325, Maj. Gen. S. V. Rudnev. No.
3326, M. Shmyrev.

1967, Apr. 24   Perf. 12x11½
3324 A1613 4k brt purple & ol bis   25 15
3325 A1613 4k ultra & ol bister   25 15
3326 A1613 4k org brn & ol bister   25 15
    Set value   15

Partisan heroes of WWII.

Marshal S. S. Biryuzov,
Hero of the Soviet
Union — A1614

1967, May 9   Photo.   Perf. 12
3327 A1614 4k ocher & slate green   40 40

Driver
Crossing Lake
Ladoga
A1615

1967, May 9   Perf. 11½
3328 A1615 4k plum & blue gray   30 15

25th anniversary of siege of Leningrad.

Views of Old
and New Minsk
A1616

1967, May 9
3329 A1616 4k slate green & black   35 15

900th anniversary of Minsk.

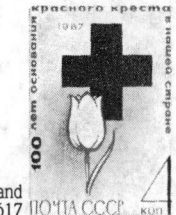

Red Cross and
Tulip — A1617

1967, May 15   Perf. 12
3330 A1617 4k yel brown & red   30 15

Centenary of the Russian Red Cross.

Stamps of
1918 and
1967
A1618

1967   Photo.   Perf. 11½
3331 A1618 20k blue & black   90 30
  a. Souv. sheet of 2, imperf.   4.00 1.25

All-Union Philatelic Exhibition "50 Years of the
Great October," Moscow, Oct. 1-10. Se-tenant with
label showing exhibition emblem.
Issue dates: 20k, May 25. Sheet, Oct. 1.
No. 3331 was re-issued Oct. 3 with "Oct. 1-10"
printed in blue on the label. Value $1.

Komsomolsk-on-Amur and Map of Amur
River — A1619

1967, June 12   Perf. 12x12½
3332 A1619 4k red & brown   40 15

35th anniv. of the Soviet youth town, Komsomolsk-on-Amur. Printed with label showing boy
and girl of Young Communist League and tents.

Souvenir Sheet

Sputnik Orbiting Earth — A1620

1967, June 24   Litho.   Perf. 13x12
3333 A1620 30k black & multi   2.50 1.10

10th anniv. of the launching of Sputnik 1, the 1st
artificial satellite, Oct. 4, 1957.

Motorcyclist
A1621

Photogravure and Engraved
1967, June 24   Perf. 12x11½
3334 A1621 10k multicolored   40 15

Intl. Motor Rally, Moscow, July 19.

G. D. Gai (1887-1937), Corps Commander of the First Cavalry, 1920 — A1622

1967, June 30   Photo.   Perf. 12
3335 A1622 4k red & black   30   15

Children's Games Emblem and Trophy A1623

1967, July 8   Perf. 11½
3336 A1623 4k silver, red & black   30   15

10th National Athletic Games of School Children, Leningrad, July, 1967.

Games Emblem and Trophy A1624

Designs: No. 3338, Cup and dancer. No. 3339, Cup and bicyclists. No. 3340, Cup and diver.

1967, July 20
3337 A1624 4k silver, red & black   15   15
3338 A1624 4k silver, red & black   15   15
  a.   Pair, #3337-3338   20   15
3339 A1624 4k silver, red & black   15   15
3340 A1624 4k silver, red & black   15   15
  a.   Pair, #3339-3340   20   15
        Set value   40   20

4th Natl. Spartacist Games, & USSR 50th anniv. Se-tenant in checkerboard arrangement.

V. G. Klochkov (1911-41), Hero of the Soviet Union A1625

1967, July 20   Perf. 12½x12
3341 A1625 4k red & black   40   25

Alternating label shows citation.

Soviet Flag, Arms and Moscow Views A1626

Arms of USSR and Laurel — A1627

АРМЯНСКАЯ ССР
ՀԱՅԿԱԿԱՆ ՍՍՀ

#3343

АЗЕРБАЙДЖАНСКАЯ ССР
АЗӘРБАЈҸАН ССР

#3344

БЕЛОРУССКАЯ ССР
БЕЛАРУСКАЯ ССР

#3345

ГРУЗИНСКАЯ ССР
საქართველოს სსრ

#3347

КИРГИЗСКАЯ ССР
КЫРГЫЗ ССР

#3349

МОЛДАВСКАЯ ССР
РСС МОЛДОВЕНЯСКЭ

#3352

ТАДЖИКСКАЯ ССР
РСС ТОҶИКИСТОН

#3353

ТУРКМЕНСКАЯ ССР
ТҮРКМЕНИСТАН ССР

#3354

УКРАИНСКАЯ ССР
УКРАЇНСЬКА РСР

#3355

УЗБЕКСКАЯ ССР
ЎЗБЕКИСТОН ССР

#3356

Flag, Crest and Capital of Republic.

1967, Aug. 4   Litho.   Perf. 12½x12
3342 A1626 4k shown   38   15
3343 A1626 4k Armenia   38   15
3344 A1626 4k Azerbaijan   38   15
3345 A1626 4k Byelorussia   38   15
3346 A1626 4k Estonia   38   15
3347 A1626 4k Georgia   38   15
3348 A1626 4k Kazakhstan   38   15
3349 A1626 4k Kirghizia   38   15
3350 A1626 4k Latvia   38   15
3351 A1626 4k Lithuania   38   15
3352 A1626 4k Moldavia   38   15
3353 A1626 4k Tadzhikistan   38   15
3354 A1626 4k Turkmenistan   38   15
3355 A1626 4k Ukraine   38   15
3356 A1626 4k Uzbekistan   38   15
3357 A1627 4k red, gold & black   38   15
     Nos. 3342-3357 (16)   6.08
           Set value   75

50th anniversary of October Revolution.

Communication Symbols A1628

1967, Aug. 16   Photo.   Perf. 12
3358 A1628 4k crimson & silver   1.50   15

Development of communications in USSR.

Flying Crane, Dove and Anniversary Emblem A1629

1967, Aug. 20   Perf. 12½x12
3359 A1629 16k silver, red & blk   50   30

Russo-Japanese Friendship Meeting, held at Khabarovsk. Emblem is for 50th anniv. of October Revolution.

Karl Marx and Title Page of "Das Kapital" — A1630

1967, Aug. 22   Engr.   Perf. 12½x12
3360 A1630 4k sepia & dk red   40   30

Centenary of the publication of "Das Kapital" by Karl Marx.

Russian Checkers Players — A1631

Design: 6k, Woman gymnast.

Photogravure and Engraved
1967, Sept. 9   Perf. 12x11½
3361 A1631 1k lt brn, dp brn & sl   30   15
3362 A1631 6k ol bister & maroon   30   15
           Set value   15

World Championship of Russian Checkers (Shashki) at Moscow, and World Championship of Rhythmic Gymnastics.

Javelin — A1632

1967, Sept. 9   Engr.   Perf. 12x12½
3363 A1632 2k shown   25   15
3364 A1632 3k Running   25   15
3365 A1632 4k Jumping   25   15
           Set value   15

Europa Cup Championships, Kiev, Sept. 15-17.

Ice Skating and Olympic Emblem A1633

Designs: 3k, Ski jump. 4k, Emblem of Winter Olympics, vert. 10k, Ice hockey. 12k, Long-distance skiing.

Photogravure and Engraved
1967, Sept. 20   Perf. 11½
3366 A1633 2k gray, black & blue   16   15
3367 A1633 3k bis, ocher, blk &
               green   16   15
3368 A1633 4k gray, bl, red & blk   20   15
3369 A1633 10k bis, brn, bl & blk   50   15
3370 A1633 12k gray, blk, lilac &
               green   65   15
     Nos. 3366-3370 (5)   1.67
           Set value   32

10th Winter Olympic Games, Grenoble, France, Feb. 6-18, 1968.

Silver Fox A1634   Young Guards Memorial A1635

Fur-bearing Animals: 2k, Arctic blue fox, horiz. 6k, Red fox, horiz. 10k, Muskrat, horiz. 12k, Ermine. 16k, Sable. 20k, Mink, horiz.

1967, Sept. 20   Photo.
3371 A1634 2k brn, blk & gray blue   18   15
3372 A1634 4k tan, dk brn & gray
               blue   28   15
3373 A1634 6k gray grn, ocher &
               black   45   15
3374 A1634 10k yel grn, dk brn &
               ocher   75   15
3375 A1634 12k lilac, blk & bis   80   15
3376 A1634 16k org, brn & black   90   15
3377 A1634 20k gray blue, blk & dk
               brown   1.10   30
     Nos. 3371-3377 (7)   4.46
           Set value   85

International Fur Auctions in Leningrad.

1967, Sept. 23
3378 A1635 4k magenta, org & blk   30   15

25th anniv. of the fight of the Young Guards at Krasnodon against the Germans.

Map of Cedar Valley Reservation and Snow Leopard — A1636

1967, Oct. 14   Perf. 12
3379 A1636 10k ol bister & black   40   15

Far Eastern Cedar Valley Reservation.

Planes and Emblem A1637

1967, Oct. 14   Perf. 11½
3380 A1637 6k dp blue, red & gold   30   15

French Normandy-Neman aviators, who fought on the Russian Front, 25th anniv.

Militiaman and Soviet Emblem A1638

1967, Oct. 14   Perf. 12½x12
3381 A1638 4k ver & ultra   30   15

50th anniversary of the Soviet Militia.

Space Station Orbiting Moon — A1639

Science Fiction: 6k, Explorers on the moon, horiz. 10k, Rocket flying to the stars. 12k, Landscape on Red Planet, horiz. 16k, Satellites from outer space.

1967 Litho. Perf. 12x12¹⁄₂, 12¹⁄₂x12

3382	A1639	4k multicolored	16	15
3383	A1639	6k multicolored	32	15
3384	A1639	10k multicolored	50	15
3385	A1639	12k multicolored	65	15
3386	A1639	16k multicolored	85	20
	Nos. 3382-3386 (5)		2.48	
	Set value			60

Emblem of USSR and Red Star — A1640

Lenin Addressing 2nd Congress of Soviets, by V. A. Serov — A1641

Builders of Communism, by L. M. Merpert and Y. N. Skripkov — A1641a

Paintings: #3389, Lenin pointing to Map, by L. A. Schmatjko, 1957. #3390, The First Cavalry Army, by M. B. Grekov, 1924. #3391, Working Students on the March, by B. V. Yoganson, 1928. #3392, Russian Friendship for the World, by S. M. Karpov, 1924. #3393, Five-Year Plan Morning, by Y. D. Romas, 1934. #3394, Farmers' Holiday, by S. V. Gerasimov, 1937. #3395, Victory in the Great Patriotic War, by Y. K. Korolev, 1965.

Lithographed and Embossed
1967, Oct. 25 Perf. 11¹⁄₂

3387	A1640	4k gold, yel, red & dk brown	15	15
3388	A1641	4k gold & multi	15	15
3389	A1641	4k gold & multi	15	15
3390	A1641	4k gold & multi	15	15
3391	A1641	4k gold & multi	15	15
3392	A1641	4k gold & multi	15	15
3393	A1641	4k gold & multi	15	15
3394	A1641	4k gold & multi	15	15
3395	A1641	4k gold & multi	15	15
3396	A1641a	4k gold & multi	15	15
a.	Souvenir sheet of 2		3.00	1.00
	Set value		1.00	50

50th anniversary of October Revolution. No. 3396a contains two 40k imperf. stamps similar to Nos. 3388 and 3396. Issued Nov. 5.

Souvenir Sheet

Hammer, Sickle and Sputnik — A1642

1967, Nov. 5 Engr. Perf. 12¹⁄₂x12
3397 A1642 1r lak   5.00 2.00

50th anniv. of the October Revolution. Margin contains "50" as a watermark.

Ostankino Television Tower — A1643

1967, Nov. 5 Litho. Perf. 11¹⁄₂
3398 A1643 16k gray, org & black   60 25

Jurmala Resort and Hepatica A1644

Health Resorts of the Baltic Region: 6k, Narva-Joesuu and Labrador tea. 10k, Druskininkai and cranberry blossoms. 12k, Zelenogradsk and Scotch heather, vert. 16k, Svetlogorsk and club moss, vert.

Perf. 12¹⁄₂x12, 12x12¹⁄₂
1967, Nov. 30 Litho.
Flowers in Natural Colors

3399	A1644	4k blue & black	16	15
3400	A1644	6k ocher & black	38	15
3401	A1644	10k green & black	42	15
3402	A1644	12k gray olive & blk	45	15
3403	A1644	16k brown & black	65	15
	Nos. 3399-3403 (5)		2.06	
	Set value			52

Emergency Commission Emblem — A1645

1967, Dec. 11 Photo. Perf. 11¹⁄₂
3404 A1645 4k ultra & red   30 15

50th anniversary of the All-Russia Emergency Commission (later the State Security Commission).

Hotel Russia and Kremlin A1646

1967, Dec. 14
3405 A1646 4k silver, dk brn & brt pink 30 15

New Year 1968. The pink is fluorescent.

1967, Dec. 14

Soldiers, Sailors, Congress Building, Kharkov, and Monument to the Men of Arsenal — A1647

Designs: 6k, Hammer and sickle and scenes from industry and agriculture. 10k, Ukrainians offering bread and salt, Monument of the Unknown Soldier, Kiev, and Lenin monument in Zaporozhye.

1967, Dec. 20 Litho. Perf. 12¹⁄₂

3406	A1647	4k multicolored	30	15
3407	A1647	6k multicolored	30	15
3408	A1647	10k multicolored	35	15
	Set value			17

50th anniv. of the Ukrainian SSR.

Three Kremlin Towers A1648

Kremlin: 6k, Cathedral of the Annunciation, horiz. 10k, Konstantin and Elena, Nabatnaya and Spasski towers. 12k, Ivan the Great bell tower. 16k, Kutafya and Troitskaya towers.

Engraved and Photogravure
Perf. 12x11¹⁄₂, 11¹⁄₂x12
1967, Dec. 25

3409	A1648	4k dk brn & claret	15	15
3410	A1648	6k dk brn, yel & grn	18	15
3411	A1648	10k maroon & slate	52	15
3412	A1648	12k sl green, yel & vio	60	15
3413	A1648	16k brn, pink & red	80	15
	Nos. 3409-3413 (5)		2.25	
	Set value			34

Coat of Arms, Lenin's Tomb and Rockets A1649

Designs: No. 3415, Agricultural Progress: Wheat, reapers and silo. No. 3416, Industrial Progress: Computer tape, atom symbol, cogwheel and factories. No. 3417, Scientific Progress: Radar, microscope, university buildings. No. 3418, Communications progress: Ostankino TV tower, railroad bridge, steamer and Aeroflot emblem, vert.

1967, Dec. 25 Engr. Perf. 12¹⁄₂

3414	A1649	4k maroon	15	15
3415	A1649	4k green	15	15
3416	A1649	4k red brown	15	15
3417	A1649	4k violet blue	15	15
3418	A1649	4k dark blue	15	15
	Set value		50	25

Material and technical basis of Russian Communism.

Monument to the Unknown Soldier, Moscow — A1650

1967, Dec. 25
3419 A1650 4k carmine   35 25

Dedication of the Monument of the Unknown Soldier of WWII in the Kremlin Wall.

Seascape by Ivan Aivazovsky — A1651

Paintings: 3k, Interrogation of Communists by B. V. Yoganson, 1933. #3422, The Lacemaker, by V. A. Tropinin, 1823, vert. #3423, Bread-makers, by T. M. Yablonskaya, 1949. #3424, Alexander Nevsky, by P. D. Korin, 1942-43, vert. #3425, The Boyar Morozov Going into Exile by V. I. Surikov, 1887. #3426, The Swan Maiden, by M. A. Vrubel, 1900, vert. #3427, The Arrest of a Propagandist by Ilya E. Repin, 1878. 16k, Moscow Suburb in February by G. G. Nissky, 1957.

Perf. 12¹⁄₂x12, 12x12¹⁄₂, 12, 11¹⁄₂
1967, Dec. 29 Litho.
Size: 47x33mm, 33x47mm

3420	A1651	3k multicolored	15	15
3421	A1651	4k multicolored	15	15
3422	A1651	4k multicolored	15	15

Size: 60x35mm, 35x60mm

3423	A1651	6k multicolored	16	15
3424	A1651	6k multicolored	16	15
3425	A1651	6k multicolored	16	15

Size: 47x33mm, 33x47mm

3426	A1651	10k multicolored	35	15
3427	A1651	10k multicolored	35	15
3428	A1651	16k multicolored	45	18
	Nos. 3420-3428 (9)		2.08	
	Set value			80

Tretiakov Art Gallery, Moscow.

Globe, Wheel and Workers of the World — A1652

1968, Jan. 18 Photo. Perf. 12
3429 A1652 6k ver & green   35 15

14th Trade Union Congress.

Lt. S. Baikov and Velikaya River Bridge A1653

Heroes of WWII (War Memorial and): #3431. Lt. A. Pokalchuk. #3432, P. Gutchenko.

1968, Jan. 20 Perf. 12¹⁄₂x12

3430	A1653	4k blue gray & black	30	15
3431	A1653	4k rose & black	30	15
3432	A1653	4k gray green & black	30	15
	Set value			15

Thoroughbred and Horse Race — A1654

Horses: 6k, Arab mare and dressage, vert. 10k, Orlovski trotters. 12k, Altekin horse performing, vert. 16k, Donskay race horse.

1968, Jan. 23 Perf. 11¹⁄₂

3433	A1654	4k ultra, blk & red lil	16	15
3434	A1654	6k crim, blk & ultra	25	15
3435	A1654	10k grnsh blue, blk & orange	38	15
3436	A1654	12k org brn, black & apple green	52	15
3437	A1654	16k ol grn, blk & red	70	15
	Nos. 3433-3437 (5)		2.01	
	Set value			45

Horse breeding.

Maria I. Ulyanova (1878-1937), Lenin's Sister — A1655

1968, Jan. 30   *Perf. 12x12¹/₂*
3438 A1655 4k indigo & pale green   30 15

Soviet Star and Flags of Army, Air Force and Navy — A1656

Lenin Addressing Troops in 1919 — A1657

Designs: No. 3441, Dneprostroi Dam and sculpture "On Guard." No. 3442, 1918 poster and marching volunteers. No. 3443, Red Army entering Vladivostok, 1922, and soldiers' monument in Primorie. No. 3444, Poster "Red Army as Liberator," Western Ukraine. No. 3445, Poster "Westward," defeat of German army. No. 3446, "Battle of Stalingrad" monument and German prisoners of war. No. 3447, Victory parade on Red Square, May 24, 1945, and Russian War Memorial, Berlin. Nos. 3448-3449, Modern weapons and Russian flag.

1968, Feb. 20 Typo.   *Perf. 12x12¹/₂*
3439 A1656 4k gold & multi   15 15
              Photo.
              Perf. 11¹/₂x12
3440 A1657 4k blk, red, pink & silver 15 15
3441 A1657 4k gold, black & red   15 15
              Litho.
              Perf. 12¹/₂x12
3442 A1657 4k yel grn, blk, red & buff 15 15
3443 A1657 4k grn, dk brn, red & bis   15 15
3444 A1657 4k green & multi   15 15
3445 A1657 4k yel green & multi   15 15
       Perf. 11¹/₂x12, 12x11¹/₂
              Photo.
3446 A1657 4k blk, silver & red   15 15
3447 A1657 4k gold, blk, pink & red   15 15
3448 A1656 4k black, red & silver   15 15
              Set value   1.00 50

              Souvenir Sheet
1968, Feb. 23   Litho.   Imperf.
3449 A1656 1r blk, silver & red   3.50 1.50

50th anniv. of the Armed Forces of the USSR. No. 3449 contains one 25x37¹/₂mm stamp with simulated perforations.

New issue listings, plus the most interesting read in the hobby, characterize the "Scott Stamp Monthly". For more information, please call 1-800-488-5351.

Maxim Gorki (1868-1936), Writer — A1658

1968, Feb. 29 Photo.   Perf. 12
3450 A1658 4k gray ol & dk brown   30 15

Fireman, Fire Truck and Boat — A1659

Link-up of Cosmos 186 and 188 Satellites — A1660

1968, Mar. 30 Photo. Perf. 12x12¹/₂
3451 A1659 4k red & black   30 15

50th anniversary of Soviet Fire Guards.

1968, Mar. 30   Perf. 11¹/₂
3452 A1660 6k blk, dp lilac rose & gold 30 15

First link-up in space of two satellites, Cosmos 186 and Cosmos 188, Oct. 30, 1967.

N. N. Popudrenko A1661

Design: No. 3453, P. P. Vershigora.

1968, Mar. 30   Perf. 12¹/₂x12
3453 A1661 4k gray green & black   30 15
3454 A1661 4k lt purple & black   30 15
              Set value   15

Partisan heroes of World War II.

Globe and Hand Shielding from War — A1662

1968, Apr. 11   Perf. 11¹/₂
3455 A1662 6k sil, mar, ver & black   50 35

Emergency session of the World Federation of Trade Unions and expressing solidarity with the people of Vietnam.

Space Walk — A1663

Designs: 6k, Docking operation of Kosmos 186 and Kosmos 188. 10k, Exploration of Venus.

1968, Apr. 12   Litho.
3456 A1663 4k multicolored   15 15
3457 A1663 6k multicolored   16 15
3458 A1663 10k multicolored   32 15
  a. Block of 3, #3456-3458 + 3 labels 75 50
              Set value   22

National Astronauts' Day.

Lenin, 1919 — A1664

Lenin Portraits: No. 3460, Addressing crowd on Red Square, Nov. 7, 1918. No. 3461, Full-face portrait, taken in Petrograd, Jan. 1918.

Engraved and Photogravure
1968, Apr. 16   Perf. 12x11¹/₂
3459 A1664 4k gold, brown & red   30 15
3460 A1664 4k gold, red & black   30 15
3461 A1664 4k gold, brn, buff & red   30 15
              Set value   15

98th anniversary of the birth of Lenin.

Alisher Navoi, Uzbek Poet, 525th Birth Anniv. — A1665

1968, Apr. 29 Photo. Perf. 12x12¹/₂
3462 A1665 4k deep brown   30 15

Karl Marx (1818-83) A1666

1968, May 5   Engr.   Perf. 11¹/₂x12
3463 A1666 4k black & red   30 15

Frontier Guard — A1667   Jubilee Badge — A1668

1968, May 22 Photo.   Perf. 11¹/₂
3464 A1667 4k sl green, ocher & red   25 15
3465 A1668 6k sl grn, blk & red brn   25 15
              Set value   25

Russian Frontier Guards, 50th anniv.

Crystal and Congress Emblem A1669

Congress Emblems and: No. 3467, Power lines and factories. No. 3468, Ground beetle. No. 3469, Roses and carbon rings.

1968, May 30
3466 A1669 6k blue, dk blue & grn   25 15
3467 A1669 6k orange, gold & dk brn   25 15
3468 A1669 6k red brn, gold & blk   25 15
3469 A1669 6k lilac rose, org & blk   25 15
              Set value   50

Intl. congresses, Leningrad: 8th Cong. for Mineral Research; 7th World Power Conf.; 13th Entomological Cong.; 4th Cong. for the Study of Volatile Oils.

              Types of 1966
Designs as before.

1968, June 20   Engr.   Perf. 12
3470 A1593 1k dk red brown   15 15
3471 A1593 2k deep violet   15 15
3472 A1593 3k plum   20 15
3473 A1593 4k bright red   20 15
3474 A1593 6k blue   40 15
3475 A1593 10k olive   60 15
3476 A1593 12k red brown   75 15
3477 A1593 16k violet blue   90 15
              Perf. 12¹/₂
3478 A1594 20k red   1.00 15
3479 A1594 30k bright green   1.65 16
3480 A1594 50k violet blue   2.75 32
              Perf. 12x12¹/₂
3481 A1594 1r gray, red brn &
              black   6.00 50
  Nos. 3470-3481 (12)   14.75
              Set value   1.50

Sadriddin Aini A1670

1968, June 30 Photo. Perf. 12¹/₂x12
3482 A1670 4k olive bister & maroon   30 15

Aini (1878-1954), Tadzhik poet.

Post Rider and C.C.E.P. Emblem A1671

Design: No. 3484, Modern means of communications (train, ship, planes and C.C.E.P. emblem).

1968, June 30
3483 A1671 6k gray & red brown   30 15
3484 A1671 6k orange brn & bister   30 15

Annual session of the Council of the Consultative Commission on Postal Investigation of the UPU (C.C.E.P.), Moscow, Sept. 20-Oct. 5.

Bolshevik Uprising, Kiev — A1672

1968, July 5   Perf. 11¹/₂
3485 A1672 4k gold, red & plum   30 15

Ukrainian Communist Party, 50th anniv.

Athletes
A1673

1968, July 9
3486 A1673 4k yel, dp car & bister 30 15

1st Youth Summer Sports Games for 50th anniv. of the Leninist Young Communists League.

Field Ball — A1674

Table Tennis
A1675

Designs: 6k, 20th Baltic Regatta. 10k, Soccer player and cup. 12k, Scuba divers.

Perf. 12x12¹/₂, 12¹/₂x12
1968, July 18 Litho.
3487 A1674 2k red & multi 15 15
3488 A1675 4k purple & multi 15 15
3489 A1674 6k blue & multi 24 15
3490 A1674 10k multicolored 32 15
3491 A1675 12k green & multi 45 15
  Nos. 3487-3491 (5) 1.31
    Set value 35

European youth sports competitions.

Rhythmic
Gymnast
A1676

Olympic Sports: 6k, Weight lifting. 10k, Rowing. 12k, Women's hurdling. 16k, Fencing. 40k, Running.

1968, July 31 Photo. *Perf. 11¹/₂*
Gold Background
3492 A1676 4k blue & green 18 15
3493 A1676 6k dp rose & purple 30 15
3494 A1676 10k yel green & green 52 15
3495 A1676 12k orange & red brn 60 15
3496 A1676 16k ultra & pink 70 15
  Nos. 3492-3496 (5) 2.30
    Set value 40

Souvenir Sheet
Perf. 12¹/₂x12
Lithographed and Photogravure
3497 A1676 40k gold, grn, org & gray 1.75 1.00

19th Olympic Games, Mexico City, Oct. 12-27.

Gediminas Tower,
Vilnius — A1677

1968, Aug. 14 Photo. *Perf. 11¹/₂*
3498 A1677 4k magenta, tan & red 30 15

Soviet power in Lithuania, 50th anniv.

Tbilisi State
University
A1678

1968, Aug. 14 *Perf. 12*
3499 A1678 4k slate grn & lt brn 30 15

Tbilisi State University, Georgia, 50th anniv.

Laocoon — A1679

1968, Aug. 16 *Perf. 11¹/₂*
3500 A1679 6k sepia, blk & mar 3.00 2.00

"Promote solidarity with Greek democrats."

Red Army Man, Cavalry Charge and Order
of the Red Banner of Battle — A1680

Designs: 3k, Young man and woman, Dnepro-stroi Dam and Order of the Red Banner of Labor. 4k, Soldier, storming of the Reichstag, Berlin, and Order of Lenin. 6k, "Restoration of National Economy" (workers), and Order of Lenin. 10k, Young man and woman cultivating virgin land and Order of Lenin. 50k, like A1680.

1968, Aug. 25 Litho. *Perf. 12¹/₂x12*
3501 A1680 2k gray, red & ocher 15 15
3502 A1680 3k multicolored 15 15
3503 A1680 4k org, ocher & rose car 15 15
3504 A1680 6k multicolored 15 15
3505 A1680 10k olive & multi 16 15
    Set value 54 25

Souvenir Sheet
Imperf
3506 A1680 50k ultra, red & bister 2.50 1.00

50th anniv. of the Lenin Young Communist League, Komsomol.

Chemistry
Institute and
Dimeric
Molecule
A1681

1968, Sept. 3 Photo. *Perf. 11¹/₂*
3507 A1681 4k vio bl, dp lil rose & black 30 15

50th anniversary of Kurnakov Institute for General and Inorganic Chemistry.

Letter,
Compass Rose,
Ship and Plane
A1682

Compass Rose
and Stamps of
1921 and 1965
A1683

1968, Sept. 16 Photo. *Perf. 11¹/₂*
3508 A1682 4k dk car rose, brn & brt red 30 15
3509 A1683 4k dk blue, blk & bister 30 15
    Set value 15

No. 3508 for Letter Writing Week, Oct. 7-13, and No. 3509 for Stamp Day and the Day of the Collector.

The 26 Baku
Commissars,
Sculpture by
Merkurov
A1684

1968, Sept. 20
3510 A1684 4k multicolored 40 15

50th anniversary of the shooting of the 26 Commissars, Baku, Sept. 20, 1918.

Toyvo Antikaynen (1898-1941), Finnish Workers' Organizer — A1685

1968, Sept. 30 *Perf. 12*
3511 A1685 6k gray & sepia 60 15

Russian Merchant
Marine Emblem
A1686

1968, Sept. 30 *Perf. 12x11¹/₂*
3512 A1686 6k blue, red & indigo 40 15

Russian Merchant Marine.

Order of the October
Revolution
A1687

Pavel P.
Postyshev
A1688

Typographed and Embossed
1968, Sept. 30 *Perf. 12x12¹/₂*
3513 A1687 4k gold & multi 35 25

51st anniv. of the October Revolution. Printed with alternating label.

1968-70 Engr. *Perf. 12¹/₂x12*
Designs: No. 3515, Stepan G. Shaumyan (1878-1918). No. 3516, Amkal Ikramov. (1898-1938). No. 3516A, N. G. Markin (1893-1918). No. 3516B, P. E. Dybenko (1889-1938). No. 3516C, S. V. Kosior (1889-1939). No. 3516D, Vasili Kikvidze (1895-1919).

Size: 21¹/₂x32¹/₂mm
3514 A1688 4k bluish black 42 15
3515 A1688 4k bluish black 42 15
3516 A1688 4k gray black 42 15
3516A A1688 4k black 42 15
3516B A1688 4k dark car ('69) 42 15
3516C A1688 4k indigo ('69) 42 15
3516D A1688 4k dk brown ('70) 42 15
  Nos. 3514-3516D (7) 2.94
    Set value 35

Honoring outstanding workers for the Communist Party and the Soviet State.

Issue dates: #3514-3516, Sept. 30, 1968. #3516A, Dec. 31, 1968. #3516D, Sept. 24, 1970. Others, May 15, 1969. See #3782.

American
Bison and
Zebra
A1689

Designs: No. 3518, Purple gallinule and lotus. No. 3519, Great white egrets, vert. No. 3520, Ostrich and golden pheasant, vert. No. 3521, Eland and guanaco. No. 3522, European spoonbill and glossy ibis.

Perf. 12¹/₂x12, 12x12¹/₂
1968, Oct. 16 Litho.
3517 A1689 4k ocher, brn & blk 20 15
3518 A1689 4k ocher & multi 20 15
3519 A1689 6k olive & black 30 15
3520 A1689 6k gray & multi 30 15
3521 A1689 10k dp green & multi 45 15
3522 A1689 10k emerald & multi 45 15
  Nos. 3517-3522 (6) 1.90
    Set value 42

Askania Nova and Astrakhan state reservations.

Ivan S. Turgenev
(1818-83),
Writer — A1690

Warrior, 1880 B.C.
and Mt.
Ararat — A1691

1968, Oct. 10 Engr. *Perf. 12x12¹/₂*
3523 A1690 4k green 4.50 35

Engraved and Photogravure
1968, Oct. 18 *Perf. 11¹/₂*
Design: 12k, David Sasountsi monument, Yerevan, and Mt. Ararat.
3524 A1691 4k blk & dk blue, *gray* 25 15
3525 A1691 12k dk brn & choc, *bis* 35 15
    Set value 15

Yerevan, capital of Armenia, 2,750th anniv.

First Radio
Tube
Generator and
Laboratory
A1692

1968, Oct. 26 Photo. *Perf. 11¹/₂*
3526 A1692 4k dk blue, dp bis & blk 30 15

50th anniversary of Russia's first radio laboratory at Gorki (Nizhni Novgorod).

Prospecting
Geologist and
Crystals
A1693

Designs: 6k, Prospecting for metals: seismographic test apparatus with shock wave diagram, plane and truck. 10k, Oil derrick in the desert.

1968, Oct. 31   Litho.   Perf. 11½
3527 A1693 4k blue & multi   38 15
3528 A1693 6k multicolored   20 15
3529 A1693 10k multicolored   52 16
            Set value   30

Geology Day. Printed with alternating label.

Borovoe,
Kazakhstan
A1694

Landscapes: #3531, Djety-Oguz, Kirghizia, vert.
#3532, Issyk-kul Lake, Kirghizia. #3533, Borovoe,
Kazakhstan, vert.

Perf. 12½x12, 12x12½
1968, Nov. 20   Typo.
3530 A1694 4k dk red brn & multi   15 15
3531 A1694 4k gray & multi   15 15
3532 A1694 6k dk red brn & multi   15 15
3533 A1694 6k black & multi   15 15
            Set value   48 20

Recreational areas in the Kazakh and Kirghiz
Republics.

Medals and Cup, Riccione, 1952, 1961
and 1965 — A1695

Designs: 4k, Medals, Eiffel Tower and Arc de
Triomphe, Paris, 1964. 6k, Porcelain plaque, gold
medal and Brandenburg Gate, Debria, Berlin, 1950,
1959. 12k, Medal and prize-winning stamp #2888,
Buenos Aires. 16k, Cups and medals, Rome, 1952,
1954. 20k, Medals, awards and views, Vienna,
1961, 1965. 30k, Trophies, Prague, 1950, 1955,
1962.

1968, Nov. 27 Photo. Perf. 11½x12
3534 A1695 4k dp cl, sil & blk   15 15
3535 A1695 6k dl bl, gold & blk   24 15
3536 A1695 10k light ultra, gold &
                 black   40 15
3537 A1695 12k blue, silver & blk   48 15
3538 A1695 16k red, gold & black   55 15
3539 A1695 20k bright blue, gold &
                 black   70 15
3540 A1695 30k orange brown, gold &
                 black   1.00 30
        Nos. 3534-3540 (7)   3.52
            Set value   75

Awards to Soviet post office at foreign stamp
exhibitions.

Worker with   V. K. Lebedinsky
Banner — A1696   and Radio
                         Tower — A1697

1968, Nov. 29   Perf. 12x12½
3541 A1696 4k red & black   50 35

Estonian Workers' Commune, 50th anniv.

1968, Nov. 29   Perf. 11½x12
3542 A1697 4k gray grn, blk & gray   50 25

V. K. Lebedinsky (1868-1937), scientist.

Souvenir Sheet

Communication via Satellite — A1698

1968, Nov. 29   Litho.   Perf. 12
3543 A1698 Sheet of 3   3.00 70
    a.   16k Molniya I   70 15
    b.   16k Map of Russia   70 15
    c.   16k Ground Station "Orbite"   70 15

Television transmission throughout USSR with
the aid of the earth satellite Molniya I.

Sprig, Spasski
Tower, Lenin
Univ. and
Library — A1699

1968, Dec. 1   Perf. 11½
3544 A1699 4k ultra, sil, grn & red   60 30

New Year 1969.

Maj. Gen. Georgy
Beregovoi — A1700

1968, Dec. 14   Photo.   Perf. 11½
3545 A1700 10k Prus blue, blk & red   40 25

Flight of Soyuz 3, Oct. 26-30.

Rail-laying
and Casting
Machines
A1701

Soviet railroad transportation: 4k, Railroad map
of the Soviet Union and Train.

1968, Dec. 14   Perf. 12½x12
3546 A1701 4k rose mag & orange   15 15
3547 A1701 10k brown & emerald   16 15
            Set value   22 15

Newspaper Banner and
Monument — A1702

1968, Dec. 23   Perf. 11½
3548 A1702 4k tan, red & dk brn   35 25

Byelorussian communist party, 50th anniv.

The Reapers, by
A. Venetzianov
A1703

Knight at the Crossroads, by Viktor M.
Vasnetsov — A1704

Paintings: 2k, The Last Day of Pompeii, by Karl
P. Bryullov. 4k, Capture of a Town in Winter, by
Vasili I. Surikov. 6k, On the Lake, by I.I. Levitan.
10k, Alarm, 1919 (family), by K. Petrov-Vodkin.
16k, Defense of Sevastopol, 1942, by A. Deineka.
20k, Sculptor with a Bust of Homer, by G. Korzhev.
30k, Celebration on Uristsky Square, 1920, by G.
Koustodiev. 50k, Duel between Peresvet and
Chelubey, by Avilov.

Perf. 12x12½, 12½
1968, Dec. 25   Litho.
3549 A1703 1k multicolored   15 15
3550 A1704 2k multicolored   15 15
3551 A1704 3k multicolored   17 15
3552 A1704 4k multicolored   22 15
3553 A1704 6k multicolored   35 15
3554 A1703 10k multicolored   55 15
3555 A1704 16k multicolored   60 15
3556 A1703 20k multicolored   65 15
3557 A1704 30k multicolored   85 28
3558 A1704 50k multicolored   1.65 40
        Nos. 3549-3558 (10)   5.34
            Set value   1.20

Russian State Museum, Leningrad.

House, Zaoneje,
1876 — A1705

Russian Architecture: 4k, Carved doors, Gorki
Oblast, 1848. 6k, Castle, Kizhi, 1714. 10k, Fortress
wall, Rostov-Yaroslav, 16th-17th centuries. 12k,
Gate, Tsaritsino, 1785. 16k, Architect Rossi Street,
Leningrad.

1968, Dec. 27 Engr. Perf. 12x12½
3559 A1705 3k dp brown, ocher   22 15
3560 A1705 4k green, yellow   22 15
3561 A1705 6k violet, gray violet   35 15
3562 A1705 10k dl bl, grnsh gray   45 15
3563 A1705 12k car, gray   55 15
3564 A1705 16k black, yellow   70 15
        Nos. 3559-3564 (6)   2.49
            Set value   40

Banners of Young Communist League,
October Revolution Medal — A1707

1968, Dec. 31   Litho.   Perf. 12
3566 A1707 12k red, yel & black   40 30

Award of Order of October Revolution to the
Young Communist League on its 50th anniversary.

Soldiers on
Guard — A1708

1969, Jan. 1   Perf. 12x12½
3567 A1708 4k orange & claret   30 15

Latvian Soviet Republic, 50th anniv.

Revolutionaries and Monument — A1709

Designs: 4k, Partisans and sword. 6k, Workers
and Lenin Medals.

1969, Jan.   Photo.   Perf. 11½
3568 A1709 2k ocher & rose claret   25 15
3569 A1709 4k ocher & red   25 15
3570 A1709 6k dk olive, mag & red   25 15
            Set value   15

Byelorussian Soviet Republic, 50th anniv.

Souvenir Sheet

Vladimir Shatalov, Boris Volynov, Alexei S.
Elisseyev, Evgeny Khrunov — A1710

1969, Jan. 22   Imperf.
3571 A1710 50k dp bis & dk brn   4.00 1.25

1st team flights of Soyuz 4 and 5, Jan. 16, 1969.

Leningrad
University
A1711

1969, Jan. 23 Photo. Perf. 12½x12
3572 A1711 10k black & maroon   40 15

University of Leningrad, 150th anniv.

Ivan A. Krylov   Nikolai Filchenkov
A1712   A1713

1969, Feb. 13   Litho.   Perf. 12x12½
3573 A1712 4k black & multi   50 30

Krylov (1769?-1844), fable writer.

1969   Photo.

Designs: No. 3575, Alexander Kosmodemian-sky. No. 3575A, Otakar Yarosh, member of Czechoslovak Svoboda Battalion.

3574	A1713	4k dull rose & black	15	15
3575	A1713	4k emerald & dk brn	15	15
3575A	A1713	4k blue & black	15	15
		Set value	25	15

Heroes of World War II. Issue dates: #3575A, May 9. Others, Feb. 23.

"Shoulder to the Wheel," Parliament, Budapest A1714

Design: "Shoulder to the Wheel" is a sculpture by Zigmond Kisfaludi-Strobl.

1969, Mar. 21   Typo.   Perf. 11½

3576 A1714 6k black, ver & lt grn   30   15

Hungarian Soviet Republic, 50th anniv.

Oil Refinery and Salavat Tualeyev Monument — A1715

1969, Mar. 22   Litho.   Perf. 12

3577 A1715 4k multicolored   20   15

50th anniv. of the Bashkir Autonomous Socialist Republic.

Sergei P. Korolev, Sputnik 1, Space Monument, Moscow — A1716

Vostok on Launching Pad — A1717

Natl. Cosmonauts' Day: No. 3579, Zond 2 orbiting moon, and photograph of earth made by Zond 5. 80k, Spaceship Soyuz 3.

Perf. 12½x12, 12x12½

1969, Apr. 12   Litho.

3578	A1716	10k black, vio & grn	25	15
3579	A1716	10k dk brn, yel & brn red	25	15
3580	A1717	10k multicolored	25	15
		Set value		20

Souvenir Sheet
Perf. 12

3581 A1716 80k vio, green & red   3.00 1.25

No. 3581 contains one 37x24mm stamp.

Lenin University, Kazan, and Kremlin A1718

Lenin House, Kuibyshev A1718a

Lenin House, Pskov A1718b

Lenin House, Shushensko A1718c

Smolny Institute, Leningrad A1718d

Designs (Places Connected with Lenin): No. 3586, Straw Hut, Razliv. No. 3587, Lenin Museum, Gorki. No. 3589, Lenin's room, Kremlin. No. 3590, Lenin Museum, Ulyanovsk. No. 3591, Lenin House, Ulyanovsk.

1969   Photo.   Perf. 11½

3582	A1718	4k pale rose & multi	15	15
3583	A1718a	4k beige & multi	15	15
3584	A1718b	4k bister brn & multi	15	15
3585	A1718c	4k gray vio & multi	15	15
3586	A1718	4k violet & multi	15	15
3587	A1718	4k blue & multi	15	15
3588	A1718d	4k brick red & multi	15	15
3589	A1718	4k rose red & multi	15	15
3590	A1718	4k lt red brn & multi	15	15
3591	A1718	4k dull green & multi	15	15
		Set value	85	50

99th anniv. of the birth of Lenin.

Telephone, Transistor Radio and Trademark A1719

1969, Apr. 25   Perf. 12½x12

3592 A1719 10k sepia & dp org   40   15

50th anniversary of VEF Electrical Co.

ILO Emblem and Globe — A1720

1969, May 9   Perf. 11

3593 A1720 6k car rose & gold   35   15

50th anniversary of the ILO.

Suleiman Stalsky A1721

1969, May 15   Photo.   Perf. 12½x12

3595 A1721 4k tan & ol green   40   25

Stalsky (1869-1937), Dagestan poet.

Yasnaya Polyana Rose — A1722

Flowers: 4k, "Stroynaya" lily. 10k, Cattleya orchid. 12k, "Listopad" dahlia. 14k, "Ural Girl" gladioli.

1969, May 15   Litho.   Perf. 11½

3596	A1722	2k gray & multi	15	15
3597	A1722	4k gold & multi	15	15
3598	A1722	10k gold & multi	24	15
3599	A1722	12k gold & multi	38	15
3600	A1722	14k gold & multi	38	15
		Nos. 3596-3600 (5)	1.30	
		Set value		35

Work of the Botanical Gardens of the Academy of Sciences.

Ukrainian Academy of Sciences A1723

1969, May 22   Photo.   Perf. 12½x12

3601 A1723 4k brown & yellow   50   25

Ukrainian Academy of Sciences, 50th anniv.

Film, Camera and Medal — A1724

Ballet Dancers A1725

1969, June 3   Litho.   Perf. 12x12½

3602	A1724	6k rose car, blk & gold	20	15
3603	A1725	6k dk brown & multi	20	15
		Set value		15

Intl. Film Festival in Moscow, and 1st Intl. Young Ballet Artists' Competitions.

Congress Emblem and Cell Division A1726

Estonian Singer and Festival Emblem A1727

1969, June 10   Photo.   Perf. 11½

3605 A1726 6k dp claret, lt bl & yel   50   30

Protozoologists, 3rd Intl. Cong., Leningrad.

1969, June 14   Perf. 12x12½

3606 A1727 4k ver & bister   50   25

Centenary of the Estonian Song Festival.

Mendeleev and Formula with Author's Corrections — A1728

Design: 30k, Dmitri Ivanovich Mendeleev, vert.

Engraved and Lithographed
1969, June 20   Perf. 12

3607 A1728 6k brown & rose   50   30

Souvenir Sheet

3608 A1728 30k carmine rose   3.00 1.25

Cent. of the Periodic Law (classification of elements), formulated by Dimitri I. Mendeleev (1834-1907). No. 3608 contains one engraved 29x37mm stamp.

Hand Holding Peace Banner and World Landmarks A1729

1969, June 20   Photo.   Perf. 11½

3609 A1729 10k blue, dk brn & gold   40   25

20th anniversary of the Peace Movement.

Laser Beam Guiding Moon Rocket — A1730

1969, June 20

3610 A1730 4k silver, black & red   50   25

Soviet scientific inventions, 50th anniv.

Ivan Kotlyarevski (1769-1838), Ukrainian Writer A1731

Typographed and Photogravure

1969, June 25   *Perf. 12½x12*
3611 A1731 4k blk, olive & lt brn   50 25

No. 2717 Overprinted in Стокгольм. 1969
Vermilion

1969, June 25   Photo.   Perf. 11½
3612 A1306 6k Prus blue & plum   2.50 1.50

Soviet victory in the Ice Hockey World Championships, Stockholm, 1969.

"Hill of Glory" Monument and Minsk Battle Map — A1732

1969, July 3   Litho.   Perf. 12x12½
3613 A1732 4k red & olive   15 15

25th anniv. of the liberation of Byelorussia from the Germans.

Eagle, Flag and Map of Poland — A1733

Design: No. 3615, Hands holding torch, flags of Bulgaria and USSR, and Bulgarian coat of arms.

1969, July 10   Photo.   Perf. 12
3614 A1733 6k red & bister   60 15
Litho.
3615 A1733 6k bis, red, green & blk 60 15
          Set value   15

25th anniv. of the Polish Republic; liberation of Bulgaria from the Germans.

Monument to 68 Heroes A1734

1969, July 15   Photo.   Perf. 12
3616 A1734 4k red & maroon   50 30

25th anniversary of the liberation of Nikolayev from the Germans.

Old Samarkand A1735

Design: 6k, Intourist Hotel, Samarkand.

1969, July 15   Typo.
3617 A1735 4k multicolored   30 15
3618 A1735 6k multicolored   30 15
          Set value   15

2500th anniversary of Samarkand.

Volleyball A1736

Munkascy & "Woman Churning Butter" A1737

Design: 6k, Kayak race.

Photogravure and Engraved

1969, July 20   Perf. 11½
3619 A1736 4k dp org & red brn   35 15
3620 A1736 6k multicolored   35 15
          Set value   15

Championships: European Junior Volleyball; European Rowing.

1969, July 20   Photo.
3621 A1737 6k dk brn, blk & org 40 25

Mihaly von Munkascy (1844-1900), Hungarian painter.

Miners' Monument — A1738

1969, July 30
3622 A1738 4k silver & magenta   35 20

Centenary of the founding of the city of Donetsk, in the Donets coal basin.

Machine Gun Cart, by Mitrofan Grekov — A1739

1969, July 30   Engr.   Perf. 12½x12
3623 A1739 4k red brown & brn red 40 25

First Mounted Army, 50th anniv.

Barge Pullers Along the Volga, by Repin — A1740

Ilya E. Repin (1844-1930), Self-portrait A1741

Repin Paintings: 6k, "Not Expected." 12k, Confession. 16k, Dnieper Cossacks.

Perf. 12½x12, 12x12½
1969, Aug. 5   Litho.
3624 A1740 4k multicolored   22 15
3625 A1740 6k multicolored   30 15
3626 A1741 10k bis, red brn & blk 30 15
3627 A1740 12k multicolored   42 15
3628 A1740 16k multicolored   52 15
      Nos. 3624-3628 (5)   1.68
          Set value   34

Runner A1742

Komarov A1743

Design: 10k, Athlete on rings.

1969, Aug. 9   Perf. 12x12½
3629 A1742 4k red, green & blk   25 25
3630 A1742 10k green, lt blue & blk 25 25

Souvenir Sheet
Imperf
3631 A1742 20k red, bister & blk 1.75 60

9th Trade Union Spartakiad, Moscow.

1969, Aug. 22   Photo.   Perf. 12x11½
3632 A1743 4k olive & brown   30 15

V. L. Komarov (1869-1945), botanist.

Hovannes Tumanian, Armenian Landscape A1744

1969, Sept. 1   Typo.   Perf. 12½x12
3633 A1744 10k blk & peacock blue 40 25

Tumanian (1869-1923), Armenian poet.

Turkmenian Wine Horn, 2nd Century — A1745

Mahatma Gandhi — A1746

Designs: 6k, Persian Simurg vessel (giant anthropomorphic bird), 13th century. 12k, Head of goddess Kannon, Korea, 8th century. 16k, Bodhisattva, Tibet, 7th century. 20k, Statue of Ebisu and fish (tai), Japan, 17th century.

1969, Sept. 3   Litho.   Perf. 12x12½
3634 A1745 4k blue & multi   22 15
3635 A1745 6k lilac & multi   32 15
3636 A1745 12k red & multi   55 15
3637 A1745 16k blue vio & multi   65 16
3638 A1745 20k pale grn & multi   85 24
      Nos. 3634-3638 (5)   2.59 85

Treasures from the State Museum of Oriental Art.

1969, Sept. 10   Engr.
3639 A1746 6k deep brown   40 35

Centenary of the birth of Mohandas K. Gandhi (1869-1948), leader in India's fight for independence.

Black Stork Feeding Young A1747

Belovezhskaya Forest reservation: 6k, Doe and fawn (red deer). 10k, Fighting bison. 12k, Lynx and cubs. 16k, Wild pig and piglets.

1969, Sept. 10   Photo.   Perf. 12
Size: 75x23mm, 10k; 35x23mm, others
3640 A1747 4k blk, yel grn & red 15 15
3641 A1747 6k blue grn, dk brn & ocher 20 15
3642 A1747 10k dk brn, dull org & dp org 50 15
3643 A1747 12k dk & yel green, brn & gray 50 15
3644 A1747 16k gray, yel grn & dk brown 60 15
      Nos. 3640-3644 (5)   1.95
          Set value   38

Komitas A1748

1969, Sept. 18   Typo.   Perf. 12½x12
3645 A1748 6k blk, gray & salmon 50 30

Komitas (S. N. Sogomonian, 1869-1935), Armenian composer.

Lisa Chaikina A1749

A. Cheponis, J. Aleksonis and G. Borisa A1750

Design: No. 3647, Major S. I. Gritsevets and fighter planes.

1969, Sept. 20   Photo.   Perf. 12½x12
3646 A1749 4k olive & brt green   30 15
3647 A1749 4k gray & black   30 15
Perf. 11½
3648 A1750 4k hn brn, brn & buff   30 18
          Set value   40

Heroes of the Soviet Union.

Ivan Petrovich Pavlov — A1751

East German Arms, TV Tower and Brandenburg Gate — A1752

1969, Sept. 26
3649 A1751 4k multicolored   40 25

Pavlov (1849-1936), physiologist.

1969, Oct. 7   Litho.
3650 A1752 6k red, black & yel   35 25

German Democratic Republic, 20th anniv.

Aleksei V. Koltsov — A1753

National Emblem — A1754

1969, Oct. 14   Photo.   Perf. 12x12½
3652 A1753 4k lt blue & brown   40 25

Aleksei Vasilievich Koltsov (1809-42), poet.

1969, Oct. 14   Perf. 12x11½
3653 A1754 4k gold & red   50 30

25th anniversary of the liberation of the Ukraine from the Nazis.

Stars, Hammer and Sickle — A1755

1969, Oct. 21   Typo.   Perf. 11½
3654 A1755 4k vio blue, gold, yel & red 40 25

52nd anniversary of October Revolution.

Georgy Shonin and Valery Kubasov — A1756

Designs: No. 3656, Anatoly Filipchenko, Vladislav Volkov and Viktor Gorbatko. No. 3657, Vladimir Shatalov and Alexey Elisyev.

1969, Oct. 22   Photo.   Perf. 12½x12
3655 A1756 10k black & gold   30 15
3656 A1756 10k black & gold   30 15
3657 A1756 10k black & gold   30 15
  a. Strip of 3, #3655-3657   1.25 25
     Set value   20

Group flight of the space ships Soyuz 6, Soyuz 7 and Soyuz 8, Oct. 11-13.

Lenin as a Youth A1757

1969, Oct. 25   Engr.   Perf. 11½
3658 A1757 4k dark red, pink   40 25

1st Soviet Youth Philatelic Exhibition, Kiev, dedicated to Lenin's 100th birthday.

Emblem of Communications Unit of Army — A1758

1969, Oct. 30   Photo.
3659 A1758 4k dk red, red & bister   40 25

50th anniversary of the Communications Troops of Soviet Army.

Souvenir Sheet

Lenin and Quotation — A1759

Lithographed and Embossed
1969, Nov. 6   Imperf.
3660 A1759 50k red, gold & pink   2.25 90

52nd anniv. of the October Revolution.

Cover of "Rules of the Kolkhoz" and Farm Woman's Monument A1760

1969, Nov. 18   Photo.   Perf. 12½x12
3661 A1760 4k brown & gold   40 25

3rd All Union Collective Farmers' Congress, Moscow, Nov.-Dec.

Vasilissa, the Beauty, by Ivan Y. Bilibin — A1761

Designs (Book Illustrations by Ivan Y. Bilibin): 10k, Marya Morevna. 16k, Finist, the Fine Fellow, horiz. 20k, The Golden Cock. 50k, The Sultan and the Czar. The inscriptions on the 16k and 20k are transposed. 4k, 10k, 16k are fairy tales; 20k and 50k are tales by Pushkin.

1969, Nov. 20   Litho.   Perf. 12
3662 A1761 4k gray & multi   22 20
3663 A1761 10k gray & multi   60 50
3664 A1761 16k gray & multi   75 75
3665 A1761 20k gray & multi   85 85
3666 A1761 50k gray & multi   3.00 1.40
  a. Strip of 5, #3662-3666   5.50 4.50
     Nos. 3662-3666 (5)   5.42 3.70

Illustrator and artist Ivan Y. Bilibin.

USSR Emblems Dropped on Venus, Radar Installation and Orbits — A1762

Design: 6k, Interplanetary station, space capsule and orbits.

1969, Nov. 25   Photo.   Perf. 12x11½
3667 A1762 4k bister, black & red   25 15
3668 A1762 6k gray, lilac rose & blk 25 15
     Set value   15

Completion of the fights of the space stations Venera 5 and Venera 6.

Flags of USSR and Afghanistan A1763

Russian State Emblem and Star A1764

1969, Nov. 30   Photo.   Perf. 11½
3669 A1763 6k red, black & green   35 25

50th anniversary of diplomatic relations between Russia and Afghanistan.

Coil Stamp
1969, Nov. 13   Perf. 11x11½
3670 A1764 4k red   60 30

MiG Jet and First MiG Fighter Plane — A1765

1969, Dec. 12   Perf. 11½x12
3671 A1765 6k red, black & gray   40 25

Soviet aircraft builders.

Lenin and Flag — A1766

Typographed and Lithographed
1969, Dec. 25   Perf. 11½
3672 A1766 4k gold, blue, red & blk 40 25

Happy New Year 1970, birth cent. of Lenin.

Antonov 2 — A1767

Aircraft: 3k, PO-2. 4k, ANT-9. 6k, TsAGI 1-EA. 10k, ANT-20 "Maxim Gorki." 12k, Tupolev-104. 16k, MiG-10 helicopter. 20k, Ilyushin-62. 50k, Tupolev-144.

Photogravure and Engraved
1969   Perf. 11½x12
3673 A1767 2k bister & multi   15 15
3674 A1767 3k multicolored   15 15
3675 A1767 4k multicolored   15 15
3676 A1767 6k multicolored   24 15
3677 A1767 10k lt vio & multi   40 15
3678 A1767 12k multicolored   55 15
3679 A1767 16k multicolored   65 15
3680 A1767 20k multicolored   70 15
     Nos. 3673-3680 (8)   2.99
     Set value   60

Souvenir Sheet
Imperf
3681 A1767 50k blue & multi   2.50 1.00

History of national aeronautics and aviation. No. 3681 margin contains signs of the zodiac, partly overlapping the stamp.
Issue dates: Nos. 3679 and 3681, Dec. 31; others Dec. 25.

Photograph of Earth by Zond 7 — A1768

Designs: No. 3683a, same as 10k. No. 3683b, Photograph of moon.

1969, Dec. 26   Photo.   Perf. 12x11½
3682 A1768 10k black & multi   40 30
Souvenir Sheet
Imperf
Litho.
3683   Sheet of 2   4.00 2.00
  a. A1768 50k indigo & multi   1.65 90
  b. A1768 50k dark brown & multi   1.65 90

Space explorations of the automatic stations Zond 6, Nov. 10-17, 1968, and Zond 7, Aug. 8-14, 1969. No. 3683 contains 27x40mm stamps with simulated perforations.

Model Aircraft — A1769

Technical Sports: 4k, Motorboats. 6k, Parachute jumping.

1969, Dec. 26   Engr.   Perf. 12½x12
3684 A1769 3k bright magenta   25 15
3685 A1769 4k dull blue green   25 15
3686 A1769 6k red orange   25 15
     Set value   35

Romanian Arms and Soviet War Memorial, Bucharest — A1770

1969, Dec. 31   Photo.   Perf. 11½
3687 A1770 6k rose red & brown   60   35

25th anniversary of Romania's liberation from fascist rule.

Ostankino Television Tower, Moscow — A1771

1969, Dec. 31   Typo.   Perf. 12
3688 A1771 10k multicolored   60   35

Lenin, by N. Andreyev — A1772

Paintings: No. 3690, Lenin at Marxist Meeting, St. Petersburg, by A. Moravov (behind table). No. 3691, Lenin at Second Party Day, by Y. Vinogradov (next to table). No. 3692, First Day of Soviet Power, by F. Modorov (leading crowd). No. 3693, Conversation with Lenin, by A. Shirokov (in front of red table). No. 3694, Farmers' Delegation Meeting Lenin, by Modorov (seated at desk). No. 3695, With Lenin, by V. A. Serov (with cap, in background). No. 3696, Lenin on May 1, 1920, by I. Brodsky (with cap, in foreground). No. 3697, Builder of Communism, by a group of painters (in red). No. 3698, Mastery of Space, by A. Deyneka (rockets).

1970, Jan. 1   Litho.   Perf. 12
3689 A1772 4k multicolored   15   15
3690 A1772 4k multicolored   15   15
3691 A1772 4k multicolored   15   15
3692 A1772 4k multicolored   15   15
3693 A1772 4k multicolored   15   15
3694 A1772 4k multicolored   15   15
3695 A1772 4k multicolored   15   15
3696 A1772 4k multicolored   15   15
3697 A1772 4k multicolored   15   15
3698 A1772 4k multicolored   15   15
          Set value   1.00   50

Centenary of birth of Lenin (1870-1924).

Map of Antarctic, "Mirny" and "Vostok" A1773

Design: 16k, Camp and map of the Antarctic with Soviet Antarctic bases.

1970, Jan. 27   Photo.   Perf. 11½
3699 A1773 4k multicolored   25   25
3700 A1773 16k multicolored   70   25

150th anniversary of the Bellingshausen-Lazarev Antarctic expedition.

F. W. Sychkov and "Tobogganing" — A1774

1970, Jan. 27   Perf. 12½x12
3701 A1774 4k sepia & vio blue   40   25

F. W. Sychkov (1870-1958), painter.

Col. V. B. Borsoyev — A1775

Design: No. 3703, Sgt. V. Peshekhonov.

1970, Feb. 10   Perf. 12x12½
3702 A1775 4k brown olive & brn   30   15
3703 A1775 4k dark gray & plum   30   15
          Set value   15

Heroes of the Soviet Union.

Geographical Society Emblem and Globes A1776

Torch of Peace A1777

1970, Feb. 26   Photo.   Perf. 11½
3704 A1776 6k bis, Prus bl & dk brn   40   30

Russian Geographical Society, 125th anniv.

1970, Mar. 3   Litho.   Perf. 12
3705 A1777 6k blue green & tan   30   15

Intl. Women's Solidarity Day, Mar. 8.

Symbols of Russian Arts and Crafts — A1778

Lenin — A1780

Lenin — A1779

Designs: 6k, Russian EXPO '70 pavilion. 10k, Boy holding model ship.

1970, Mar. 10   Photo.   Perf. 11½
3706 A1778 4k dk blue grn, red & black   25   15
3707 A1778 6k blk, silver & red   25   15
3708 A1778 10k vio blue, sil & red   25   15
          Set value   16

Souvenir Sheet
Engr. & Litho.
Perf. 12x12½
3709 A1779 50k dark red   2.00   1.00

EXPO '70 International Exhibition, Osaka, Japan, Mar. 15-Apr. 13.

1970, Mar. 14   Photo.   Perf. 11½
3710 A1780 4k red, black & gold   40   30

Souvenir Sheet
Photogravure and Embossed
Imperf
3711 A1780 20k red, black & gold   2.00   1.00

USSR Philatelic Exhibition dedicated to the centenary of the birth of Lenin.

Friendship Tree, Sochi — A1781

1970, Mar. 18   Litho.   Perf. 11½
3712 A1781 10k multicolored   50   30

Friendship among people. Printed with alternating label.

National Emblem, Hammer and Sickle, Oil Derricks A1782

1970, Mar. 18   Photo.   Perf. 11½
3713 A1782 4k dk car rose & gold   35   25

Azerbaijan Republic, 50th anniversary.

Ice Hockey Players A1783

1970, Mar. 18
3714 A1783 6k blue & slate green   35   15

World Ice Hockey Championships, Sweden.

Overprinted in Upper Right Corner with Orange Cyrillic Inscription in 5 Vertical Lines

1970, Apr. 1   Photo.   Perf. 11½
3715 A1783 6k blue & slate green   40   25

Soviet hockey players as the tenfold world champions.

D. N. Medvedev A1784

Hungarian Arms, Budapest Landmarks A1786

Worker, Books, Globes and UNESCO Symbol A1785

Portrait: No. 3717, K. P. Orlovsky.

1970, Mar. 26   Engr.   Perf. 12x12½
3716 A1784 4k chocolate   25   15
3717 A1784 4k dk redsh brown   25   15
          Set value   15

Heroes of the Soviet Union.

1970, Mar. 26   Photo.   Perf. 12½x12
3718 A1785 6k car lake & ocher   30   15

UNESCO-sponsored Lenin Symposium, Tampere, Finland, Apr. 6-10.

1970, Apr. 4   Typo.   Perf. 11½
3719 A1786 6k multicolored   30   15

Liberation of Hungary, 25th anniv. See No. 3738.

Cosmonauts' Emblem A1787

1970, Apr. 12   Litho.   Perf. 11½
3720 A1787 6k buff & multi   30   15

Cosmonauts' Day.

The only revenue stamps listed in this catalogue are those also authorized for prepayment of postage.

Lenin, 1891 — A1788

Order of Victory — A1789

Designs: Various portraits of Lenin.

Lithographed and Typographed
1970, Apr. 15   **Perf. 12x12½**

3721 A1788	2k green & gold	15	15
3722 A1788	2k ol gray & gold	15	15
3723 A1788	4k vio blue & gold	15	15
3724 A1788	4k lake & gold	15	15
3725 A1788	6k red brn & gold	15	15
3726 A1788	6k lake & gold	15	15
3727 A1788	10k dk brn & gold	18	15
3728 A1788	10k dark rose brown & gold	22	15
3729 A1788	12k blk, sil & gold	28	15

Photo.
3730 A1788	12k red & gold	28	15
	Set value	1.50	1.00

Souvenir Sheet
1970, Apr. 22   **Litho.**   **Typo.**

3731 A1788 20k blk, silver & gold   1.50 70

Cent. of the birth of Lenin. Issued in sheets of 8 stamps surrounded by 16 labels showing Lenin-connected buildings, books, coats of arms and medals. No. 3731 contains one stamp in same design as No. 3729.

1970, May 8   **Photo.**   **Perf. 11½**

Designs: 2k, Monument to the Unknown Soldier, Moscow. 3k, Victory Monument, Berlin-Treptow. 4k, Order of the Great Patriotic War. 10k, Gold Star of the Order of Hero of the Soviet Union and Medal of Socialist Labor. 30k, Like 1k.

3732 A1789	1k red lilac, gold & gray	15	15
3733 A1789	2k dark brown, gold & red	15	15
3734 A1789	3k dark brown, gold & red	15	15
3735 A1789	4k dark brown, gold & red	15	15
3736 A1789	10k red lil, gold & red	32	15
	Set value	75	26

Souvenir Sheet
Imperf.

3737 A1789 30k dark red, gold & gray 2.00 60

25th anniv. of victory in WWII. No. 3737 has simulated perforations.

Arms-Landmark Type of 1970
Design: Czechoslovakia arms and view of Prague.

1970, May 8   **Typo.**   **Perf. 12½**

3738 A1786 6k dk brown & multi   35 15

25th anniversary of the liberation of Czechoslovakia from the Germans.

Young Fighters, and Youth Federation Emblem A1791

1970, May 20   **Litho.**   **Perf. 12**

3739 A1791 6k blue & black   30 15

25th anniversary of the World Federation of Democratic Youth.

Lenin A1792

1970, May 20   **Photo.**   **Perf. 11½**

3740 A1792 6k red   30 15

Intl. Youth Meeting dedicated to the cent. of the birth of Lenin, UN, NY, June 1970.

Komsomol Emblem with Lenin A1793

1970, May 20   **Litho.**   **Perf. 12**

3741 A1793 4k red, yel & purple   30 15

16th Congress of the Young Communist League, May 26-30.

Hammer and Sickle Emblem and Building of Supreme Soviet in Kazan — A1794

#3744

#3744B

#3744C

Designs (Hammer-Sickle Emblem and Supreme Soviet Building in): No. 3743, Petrozavodsk. No. 3744, Cheboksary. No. 3744A, Elista. No. 3744B, Izhevsk. No. 3744C, Yoshkar-Ola.

1970   **Engr.**   **Perf. 12x12½**

3742	A1794	4k violet blue	50 15
3743	A1794	4k green	50 15
3744	A1794	4k dark carmine	50 15
3744A	A1794	4k red	50 15
3744B	A1794	4k dark green	50 15
3744C	A1794	4k dark carmine	50 15
	Nos. 3742-3744C (6)		3.00
	Set value		30

50th annivs. of the Tatar (#3742), Karelian (#3743), Chuvash (#3744), Kalmyk (#3744A), Udmurt (#3744B) and Mari (#3744C) autonomous SSRs.

Issue dates: No. 3742, May 27; No. 3743, June 5; No. 3744, June 24; Nos. 3744A-3744B, Oct. 22; No. 3744C, Nov. 4.

See Nos. 3814-3823, 4286, 4806.

Soccer — A1795

Sword into Plowshare Statue, UN, NY — A1796

Design: 10k, Woman athlete on balancing bar.

1970, May 31   **Photo.**   **Perf. 11½**

3745 A1795	10k lt gray & brt rose	40	15
3746 A1795	16k dk grn & org brn	65	15
	Set value		17

17th World Gymnastics Championships, Ljubljana, Oct. 22-27; 9th World Soccer Championships for the Jules Rimet Cup, Mexico City, May 29-June 21.

1970, June 1   **Litho.**   **Perf. 12x12½**

3747 A1796 12k gray & lake   50 25

25th anniversary of the United Nations.

Soyuz 9, Andrian Nikolayev, Vitaly Sevastyanov A1797

1970, June 7   **Photo.**   **Perf. 12x11½**

3748 A1797 10k multicolored   40 15

424 hour space flight of Soyuz 9, June 1-19.

Friedrich Engels A1798

1970, June 16   **Engr.**   **Perf. 12x12½**

3749 A1798 4k chocolate & ver   35 15

Friedrich Engels (1820-1895), German socialist, collaborator with Karl Marx.

Armenian Woman and Symbols of Agriculture and Industry A1799

Design: No. 3751, Kazakh woman and symbols of agriculture and industry.

1970, June 16   **Photo.**   **Perf. 11½**

3750 A1799	4k red brn & silver	30	30
3751 A1799	4k brt rose lilac & gold	30	30

50th anniversaries of the Armenian (No. 3750) and the Kazakh (No. 3751) Soviet Socialist Republics.

Missile Cruiser "Grozny" — A1800

Soviet Warships: 3k, Cruiser "Aurora." 10k, Cruiser "October Revolution." 12k, Missile cruiser "Varyag." 20k, Atomic submarine "Leninsky Komsomol."

1970, July 26   **Photo.**   **Perf. 11½x12**

3752 A1800	3k lilac, pink & blk	16	15
3753 A1800	4k yellow & black	24	15
3754 A1800	10k rose & black	45	15
3755 A1800	12k buff & dk brown	45	15
3756 A1800	20k blue grn, dk brn & vio blue	90	15
	Nos. 3752-3756 (5)		2.20
	Set value		36

Navy Day.

Soviet and Polish Workers and Flags A1801

"History," Petroglyphs, Sputnik and Emblem A1802

1970, July 26   **Perf. 12**

3757 A1801 6k red & slate   30 15

25th anniversary of the Treaty of Friendship, Collaboration and Mutual Assistance between USSR and Poland.

1970, Aug. 16   **Perf. 11½**

3758 A1802 4k red brn, buff & blue   40 25

13th International Congress of Historical Sciences in Moscow.

Mandarin Ducks A1803

Animals from the Sikhote-Alin Reserve: 6k, Pine marten. 10k, Asiatic black bear, vert. 16k, Red deer. 20k, Ussurian tiger.

Perf. 12½x12, 12x12½
1970, Aug. 19   **Litho.**

3759 A1803	4k multicolored	17	15
3760 A1803	6k multicolored	25	15
3761 A1803	10k multicolored	28	15
3762 A1803	16k ultra & multi	42	15
3763 A1803	20k gray & multi	60	16
	Nos. 3759-3763 (5)		1.72
	Set value		48

Keep up to date with all new stamp issues by subscribing to the "Scott Stamp Monthly". Please call 1-800-488-5351 for more information.

Magnifying Glass over
Stamp, and
Covers — A1804

Pioneers'
Badge — A1805

1970, Aug. 31   Photo.   Perf. 12x12½
3764 A1804 4k red & silver   50 25

2nd All-Union Philatelists' Cong., Moscow.

1970, Sept. 24   Photo.   Perf. 11½

Soviet general education: 2k, Lenin and Children, monument. 4k, Star and scenes from play
"Zarnitsa."

3765 A1805	1k gray, red & gold	25	15
3766 A1805	2k brn red & slate grn	25	15
3767 A1805	4k lt ol, car & gold	25	15
	Set value		15

Yerevan
University
A1806

1970, Sept. 24   Photo.   Perf. 12½x12
3768 A1806 4k ultra & salmon pink   30 15

Yerevan State University, 50th anniv.

Library Bookplate,
Vilnius
University — A1807

Woman Holding
Flowers — A1808

1970, Oct.   Typo.   Perf. 12x12½
3772 A1807 4k silver, gray & blk   50 25

Vilnius University Library, 400th anniv.

1970, Oct. 30   Photo.
3773 A1808 6k blue & lt brown   30 15

25th anniversary of the International Democratic
Federation of Women.

Farm Woman, Cattle Farm — A1809

Designs: No. 3775, Farmer and mechanical farm
equipment. No. 3776, Farmer, fertilization equipment and plane.

1970, Oct. 30   Perf. 11½x12
3774 A1809	4k olive, yellow & red	15	15
3775 A1809	4k ocher, yellow & red	15	15
3776 A1809	4k lt vio, yellow & red	15	15
	Set value	25	15

Aims of the new agricultural 5-year plan.

Lenin — A1810

Lithographed and Embossed
1970, Nov. 3   Perf. 12½x12
3777 A1810 4k red & gold   30 15

Souvenir Sheet
3778 A1810 30k red & gold   1.75 75

53rd anniv. of the October Revolution.

**50 лет
ленинскому плану
ГОЭЛРО ● 1970**

No. 3389
Overprinted in Gold

1970, Nov. 3   Perf. 11½
3779 A1641 4k gold & multi   75 75

50th anniversary of the GOELRO Plan for the
electrification of Russia.

Spasski Tower and Fir
Branch
A1811

A. A. Baykov
A1812

1970, Nov. 23   Litho.   Perf. 12x12½
3780 A1811 6k multicolored   30 15

New Year, 1971.

1970, Nov. 25   Photo.   Perf. 12½x12
3781 A1812 4k sepia & golden brn   30 15

Baykov (1870-1946), metallurgist and
academician.

Portrait Type of 1968

Portrait: No. 3782, A. D. Tsyurupa.

1970, Nov. 25   Photo.   Perf. 12x12½
3782 A1688 4k brown & salmon   35 25

Tsyurupa (1870-1928), First Vice Chairman of
the Soviet of People's Commissars.

Vasily Blazhenny
Church, Red
Square — A1813

Tourist publicity: 6k, Performance of Swan Lake.
10k, Two deer. 12k, Folk art. 14k, Sword into
Plowshare statue, by E. Vouchetich, and museums.
16k, Automobiles and woman photographer.

Photogravure and Engraved
1970, Nov. 29   Perf. 12x11½
Frame in Brown Orange
3783 A1813	4k multicolored	15	15
3784 A1813	6k multicolored	16	15
3785 A1813	10k brn org & sl green	35	15
3786 A1813	12k multicolored	45	15

3787 A1813	14k multicolored	50	18
3788 A1813	16k multicolored	65	18
	Nos. 3783-3788 (6)	2.26	
	Set value		75

Daisy
A1814

1970, Nov. 29   Litho.   Perf. 11½
3789 A1814	4k shown	15	15
3790 A1814	6k Dahlia	15	15
3791 A1814	10k Phlox	35	15
3792 A1814	12k Aster	45	15
3793 A1814	16k Clementis	75	15
	Nos. 3789-3793 (5)	1.85	
	Set value		44

UN Emblem, African
Mother and Child,
Broken
Chain — A1815

1970, Dec. 10   Photo.   Perf. 12x12½
3794 A1815 10k blue & dk brown   50 15

United Nations Declaration on Colonial Independence, 10th anniversary.

Ludwig van
Beethoven
(1770-1827),
Composer
A1816

1970, Dec. 16   Engr.   Perf. 12½x12
3795 A1816 10k deep claret, pink   50 30

Skating — A1817

Luna
16 — A1818

Design: 10k, Skiing.

1970, Dec. 18   Photo.   Perf. 11½
3796 A1817	4k light gray, ultra & dark red	20	15
3797 A1817	10k light gray, brt green & brown	30	15
	Set value		15

1971 Trade Union Winter Games.

1970, Dec.   Photo.   Perf. 11½

Designs: No. 3799, 3801b, Luna 16 leaving
moon. No. 3800, 3801c, Capsule landing on earth.
No. 3801a, like No. 3798.

3798 A1818	10k gray blue	35	15
3799 A1818	10k dk purple	35	15
3800 A1818	10k gray blue	35	15
	Set value		20

Souvenir Sheet
3801	Sheet of 3	4.00	1.00
a.	A1818 20k blue	70	25
b.	A1818 20k dark purple	70	25
c.	A1818 20k blue	70	25

Luna 16 unmanned, automatic moon mission,
Sept. 12-24, 1970.
Nos. 3801a-3801c have attached labels (no perf.
between vignette and label). Issue dates: No. 3801,
Dec. 18; Nos. 3798-3800, Dec. 28.

The Conestabile
Madonna, by
Raphael
A1819

Paintings: 4k, Apostles Peter and Paul, by El
Greco. 10k, Perseus and Andromeda, by Rubens,
horiz. 12k, The Prodigal Son, by Rembrandt. 16k,
Family Portrait, by van Dyck. 20k, The Actress
Jeanne Samary, by Renoir. 30k, Woman with Fruit,
by Gauguin. 50k, The Litte Madonna, by da Vinci.
All paintings from the Hermitage in Leningrad,
except 20k from Pushkin Museum, Moscow.

Perf. 12x12½, 12½x12
1970, Dec. 23   Litho.
3802 A1819	3k gray & multi	15	15
3803 A1819	4k gray & multi	18	15
3804 A1819	10k gray & multi	45	15
3805 A1819	12k gray & multi	45	15
3806 A1819	16k gray & multi	55	15
3807 A1819	20k gray & multi	75	15
3808 A1819	30k gray & multi	1.65	25
	Nos. 3802-3808 (7)	4.18	
	Set value		80

Souvenir Sheet
Imperf
3809 A1819 50k gold & multi   3.00 90

Harry Pollyt
and Shipyard
A1820

1970, Dec. 31   Photo.   Perf. 12
3810 A1820 10k maroon & brown   40 30

Pollyt (1890-1960), British labor leader.

International
Cooperative
Alliance — A1821

1970, Dec. 31   Perf. 11½x12
3811 A1821 12k yel green & red   40 30

Intl. Cooperative Alliance, 75th anniv.

Lenin
A1822

1971, Jan. 1   Perf. 12
3812 A1822 4k red & gold   15 15

Year of the 24th Congress of the Communist
Party of the Soviet Union.

Georgian Republic Flag — A1823

1971, Jan. 12   Litho.   Perf. 11½
3813 A1823 4k ol bister & multi   15 15

Georgian SSR, 50th anniversary.

Republic Anniversaries Type of 1970

No. 3816

No. 3818

Designs (Hammer-Sickle Emblem and): No. 3814, Supreme Soviet Building, Makhachkala. No. 3815, Fruit, ship, mountain, conveyor. No. 3816, Grapes, refinery, ship. No. 3817, Supreme Soviet Building, Nalchik. No. 3818, Supreme Soviet Building, Syktyvkar, and lumber industry. No. 3819, Natural resources, dam, mining. No. 3820, Industrial installations and natural products. No. 3821, Ship, "industry." No. 3822, Grapes, pylons and mountains. No. 3823, Kazbek Mountain, industrial installations, produce.

1971-74   Engr.   Perf. 12x12½
3814 A1794 4k dk blue green   15 15
3815 A1794 4k rose red   15 15
3816 A1794 4k red   15 15
3817 A1794 4k blue   15 15
3818 A1794 4k green   15 15
3819 A1794 4k brt bl ('72)   15 15
3820 A1794 4k car rose ('72)   15 15
3821 A1794 4k brt ultra ('73)   15 15
3822 A1794 4k golden brn ('74)   15 15
Litho.
3823 A1794 4k dark red ('74)   15 15
Set value   80 50

50th annivers. of Dagestan (#3814), Abkazian (#3815), Adzhar (#3816), Kabardino-Balkarian (#3817), Komi (#3818), Yakut (#3819), Checheno-Ingush (#3820), Buryat (#3821), Nakhichevan (#3822), and North Ossetian (#3823) autonomous SSRs.
No. 3823 also for bicentenary of Ossetia's union with Russia.
Issue dates: #3814, Jan. 20. #3815, Mar. 3. #3816, June 16. #3817-3818, Aug. 17. #3819, Apr. 20. #3820, Nov. 22. #3821, May 24. #3822, Feb. 6. #3823, July 7.

Tower of Genoa, Cranes, Hammer and Sickle — A1824

Palace of Culture, Kiev — A1825

1971, Jan. 28   Typo.   Perf. 12
3824 A1824 10k dk red, gray & yel   30 15

Founding of Feodosiya, Crimea, 2500th anniv.

1971, Feb. 16   Photo.   Perf. 11½
3825 A1825 4k red, bister & blue   15 15

Ukrainian Communist Party, 24th cong.

N. Gubin, I. Chernykh, S. Kosinov A1826

1971, Feb. 16   Perf. 12½x12
3826 A1826 4k slate grn & vio brn   15 15

Heroes of the Soviet Union.

"Industry and Agriculture" A1827

Lesya Ukrayinka A1828

1971, Feb. 16   Perf. 12x12½
3827 A1827 6k olive bister & red   15 15

State Planning Organization, 50th anniv.

1971, Feb. 25
3828 A1828 4k orange red & bister   15 15

Ukrayinka (1871-1913), Ukrainian poet.

"Summer" Dance — A1829

Dancers of Russian Folk Dance Ensemble: No. 3830, "On the Skating Rink." No. 3831, Ukrainian dance "Hopak." No. 3832, Adzharian dance. No. 3833, Gypsy dance.

1971, Feb. 25   Litho.   Perf. 12½x12
3829 A1829 10k bister & multi   40 15
3830 A1829 10k olive & multi   40 15
3831 A1829 10k olive bis & multi   40 15
3832 A1829 10k gray & multi   40 15
3833 A1829 10k grnsh gray & multi   40 15
Nos. 3829-3833 (5)   2.00
Set value   35

Luna 17 on Moon A1830

Designs: No. 3835, Ground control. No. 3836, Separation of Lunokhod 1 and carrier. No. 3835, Lunokhod 1 in operation.

1971, Mar. 16   Photo.   Perf. 11½
3834 A1830 10k dp violet & sepia   32 15
3835 A1830 12k dk blue & sepia   50 15
3836 A1830 12k dk blue & sepia   50 15
3837 A1830 16k dp violet & sepia   60 15
a.   Souv. sheet of 4, #3834-3837   2.50 1.00
Set value   50

Luna 17 unmanned, automated moon mission, Nov. 10-17, 1970.

Paris Commune A1831

Industry, Science, Culture A1832

1971, Mar. 18   Litho.   Perf. 12
3838 A1831 6k red & black   30 15

Centenary of the Paris Commune.

1971, Mar. 29   Perf. 11½
3839 A1832 6k bister, brn & red   15 15

24th Communist Party Cong., Mar. 30-Apr. 3.

Yuri Gagarin Medal A1833

1971, Mar. 30   Photo.   Perf. 11½
3840 A1833 10k brown & lemon   40 15

10th anniv. of man's first flight into space.

Space Research A1834

1971, Mar. 30
3841 A1834 12k slate blue & vio brn   40 15

Cosmonauts' Day, Apr. 12.

E. Birznieks-Upitis A1835

Bee and Blossom A1836

1971, Apr. 1   Perf. 12x12½
3842 A1835 4k red brown & gray   15 15

Birznieks-Upitis (1871-1960), Latvian writer.

1971, Apr. 1   Perf. 11½
3843 A1836 6k olive & multi   15 15

23rd International Beekeeping Congress, Moscow, Aug. 22-Sept. 2.

Souvenir Sheet

Cosmonauts and Spacecraft — A1837

Designs: 10k, Vostok. No. 3844b, Yuri Gagarin. No. 3844c, First man walking in space. 16k, First orbital station.

1971, Apr. 12   Litho.   Perf. 12
3844 A1837 Sheet of 4   3.00 1.00
a.   10k violet brown   42 18
b.-c.   12k Prussian green   45 18
d.   16k violet brown   50 18

10th anniv. of man's 1st flight into space. Size of stamps: 26x19mm.

Lenin Memorial, Ulyanovsk — A1838

1971, Apr. 16   Photo.   Perf. 12
3845 A1838 4k cop red & ol bister   15 15

Lenin's birthday. Memorial was built for centenary celebration of his birth.

Lt. Col. Nikolai I. Vlasov — A1839

Khafiz Shirazi — A1840

1971, May 9   Photo.   Perf. 12x12½
3846 A1839 4k gray olive & brn   30 15

Hero of the Soviet Union.

1971, May 9   Litho.
3847 A1840 4k olive, brn & black   15 15

650th anniversary of the birth of Khafiz Shirazi, Tadzhik-Persian poet.

GAZ-66 — A1841

Soviet Cars: 3k, BelAZ-540 truck. No. 3850, Moskvich-412. No. 3851, ZAZ-968. 10k, Volga.

1971, May 12   Photo.   Perf. 11x11½
3848 A1841 2k yellow & multi   15 15
3849 A1841 3k lt blue & multi   15 15
3850 A1841 4k lt lilac & multi   15 15
3851 A1841 4k lt gray & multi   16 15
3852 A1841 10k lt lilac & multi   16 15
Set value   48 26

15-Cent Minimum Value
The minimum catalogue value is 15 cents. Separating se-tenant pieces into individual stamps does not increase the value of the stamps since demand for the separated stamps may be small.

Bogomolets
A1842

Satellite
A1843

1971, May 24   **Photo.**   *Perf. 12*
3853 A1842 4k orange & black   15 15
A. A. Bogomolets, physician, 90th birth anniv.

1971, June 9   *Perf. 11½*
3854 A1843 6k blue & multi   15 15
15th General Assembly of the International Union of Geodesics and Geophysics.

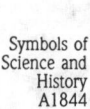

Symbols of
Science and
History
A1844

1971, June 9   *Perf. 12*
3855 A1844 6k green & gray   15 15
13th Congress of Science History.

Oil Derrick &
Symbols
A1845

1971, June 9   *Perf. 11½*
3856 A1845 6k multicolored   20 15
8th World Oil Congress.

Sukhe Bator Monument — A1846

1971, June 16   **Typo.**   *Perf. 12*
3857 A1846 6k red, gold & black   15 15
50th anniversary of Mongolian revolution.

Monument of
Defenders of
Liepaja
A1847

1971, June 21   **Photo.**
3858 A1847 4k gray, black & brn   30 25
30th anniversary of the defense of Liepaja (Libau) against invading Germans.

Map of
Antarctica and
Station
A1848

Weather Map,
Plane, Ship and
Satellite
A1849

Engraved and Photogravure
1971, June 21   *Perf. 11½*
3859 A1848 6k black, grn & ultra   50 30
Antarctic Treaty pledging peaceful uses of & scientific co-operation in Antarctica, 10th anniv.

1971, June 21
3860 A1849 10k black, red & ultra   50 30
50th anniversary of Soviet Hydrometeorological service.

FIR Emblem,
"Homeland" by E.
Vouchetich
A1850

1971, June 21 Photo.   *Perf. 12x12½*
3861 A1850 6k dk red & slate   15 15
International Federation of Resistance Fighters (FIR), 20th anniversary.

Discus and
Running
A1851

Designs: 4k, Archery (women). 6k, Dressage. 10k, Basketball. 12k, Wrestling.

Lithographed and Engraved
1971, June 24   *Perf. 11½*
3862 A1851 3k violet blue, *rose*   15 15
3863 A1851 4k slate grn, *pale pink*   20 15
3864 A1851 6k red brn, *apple grn*   28 15
3865 A1851 10k dk pur, *gray blue*   40 15
3866 A1851 12k red brn, *yellow*   50 15
Nos. 3862-3866 (5)   1.53
Set value   28
5th Summer Spartakiad.

Benois
Madonna, by
da Vinci
A1852

Paintings: 4k, Mary Magdalene, by Titian. 10k, The Washerwoman, by Jean Simeon Chardin, horiz. 12k, Portrait of a Young Man, by Frans Hals. 14k, Tancred and Arminia, by Nicolas Poussin, horiz. 16k, Girl with Fruit, by Murillo. 20k, Girl with Ball, by Picasso.

Perf. 12x12½, 12½x12
1971, July 7   Litho.
3867 A1852 2k bister & multi   15 15
3868 A1852 4k bister & multi   16 15
3869 A1852 10k bister & multi   40 15
3870 A1852 12k bister & multi   45 15
3871 A1852 14k bister & multi   52 15
3872 A1852 16k bister & multi   65 15
3873 A1852 20k bister & multi   75 20
Nos. 3867-3873 (7)   3.08
Set value   72
Foreign master works in Russian museums.

Kazakhstan
Flag, Lenin
Badge
A1853

1971, July 7   **Photo.**   *Perf. 11½*
3874 A1853 4k blue, red & brown   15 15
50th anniversary of the Kazakh Communist Youth League.

Star Emblem
and Letters
A1854

1971, July 14
3875 A1854 4k oliver, blue & black   15 15
International Letter Writing Week.

Nikolai A.
Nekrasov, by
Ivan N.
Kramskoi
A1855

Portraits: No. 3877, Aleksandr Spendiarov, by M. S. Saryan. 10k, Fedor M. Dostoevski, by Vassili G. Perov.

1971, July 14   Litho.   *Perf. 12x12½*
3876 A1855 4k citron & multi   25 15
3877 A1855 4k gray blue & multi   25 15
3878 A1855 10k multicolored   30 15
Set value   16
Nikolai Alekseevitch Nekrasov (1821-1877), poet, Fedor Mikhailovich Dostoevski (1821-1881), novelist, Spendiarov (1871-1928), Armenian composer.
See Nos. 4056-4057.

Zachary Paliashvili
(1871-1933), Georgian
Composer and
Score — A1856

1971, Aug. 3   **Photo.**   *Perf. 12x12½*
3879 A1856 4k brown   15 15

Gorki Kremlin,
Stag and
Hydrofoil
A1857

1971, Aug. 3   Litho.   *Perf. 12*
3880 A1857 16k multicolored   60 25
Gorki (formerly Nizhni Novgorod), 750th anniv. See Nos. 3889, 3910-3914.

Federation
Emblem and
Students
A1858

1971, Aug. 3   **Photo.**   *Perf. 11½*
3881 A1858 6k ultra & multi   15 15
Intl. Students Federation, 25th anniv.

Common
Dolphins
A1859

Sea Mammals: 6k, Sea otter. 10k, Narwhals. 12k, Walrus. 14k, Ribbon seals.

Photogravure and Engraved
1971, Aug. 12   *Perf. 11½*
3882 A1859 4k silver & multi   15 15
3883 A1859 6k silver & multi   15 15
3884 A1859 10k silver & multi   20 15
3885 A1859 12k silver & multi   24 15
3886 A1859 14k silver & multi   28 15
Nos. 3882-3886 (5)   1.02
Set value   36

Miner's Star of
Valor — A1860

1971, Aug. 17   **Photo.**   *Perf. 11½*
3887 A1860 4k bister, black & red   15 15
250th anniversary of the discovery of coal in the Donets Basin.

Ernest
Rutherford and
Diagram of
Movement of
Atomic
Particles
A1861

1971, Aug. 24   **Photo.**   *Perf. 12*
3888 A1861 6k magenta & dk ol   15 15
Rutherford (1871-1937), British physicist.

Gorki and Gorki Statue — A1862

1971, Sept. 14   *Perf. 11¹/₂*
3889 A1862 4k steel blue & multi   15 15

Gorki (see #3880).

Troika and Spasski Tower A1863

1971, Sept. 14
3890 A1863 10k black, red & gold   30 15

New Year 1972.

Automatic Production Center — A1864

Designs: No. 3892, Agricultural development. No. 3893, Family in shopping center. No. 3894, Hydro-generators, thermoelectric station. No. 3895, Marchers, flags, books inscribed Marx and Lenin.

1971, Sept. 29 Photo. *Perf. 12x11¹/₂*
3891 A1864 4k purple, red & blk   15 15
3892 A1864 4k ocher, red & brn   15 15
3893 A1864 4k yel, olive & red   15 15
3894 A1864 4k bister, red & brn   15 15
3895 A1864 4k ultra, red & slate   15 15
          Set value   50 25

Resolutions of 24th Soviet Union Communist Party Congress.

The Meeting, by Vladimir Y. Makovsky A1865

Ivan N. Kramskoi, Self-portrait — A1866

Paintings: 4k, Woman Student, by Nikolai A. Yaroshenko. 6k, Woman Miner, by Nikolai A. Kasatkin. 10k, Harvest, by G. G. Myasoyedov, horiz. 16k, Country Road, by A. K. Savrasov. 20k, Pine Forest, by I. I. Shishkin, horiz.

Perf. 12x12¹/₂, 12¹/₂x12
1971, Oct. 14   **Litho.**
Frame in Light Gray
3896 A1865 2k multicolored   15 15
3897 A1865 4k multicolored   20 15
3898 A1865 6k multicolored   30 15
3899 A1865 10k multicolored   60 15

3900 A1865 16k multicolored   65 15
3901 A1865 20k multicolored   1.25 16
          Nos. 3896-3901 (6)   3.15
          Set value   52

Souvenir Sheet
Lithographed and Gold Embossed
3902 A1866 50k dk green & multi   2.00 60

History of Russian painting.

V. V. Vorovsky, Bolshevik Party Leader and Diplomat, Birth Cent. — A1867

1971, Oct. 14   Engr.   *Perf. 12*
3903 A1867 4k red brown   15 15

Cosmonauts Dobrovolsky, Volkov and Patsayev — A1868

1971, Oct. 20 Photo. *Perf. 11¹/₂x12*
3904 A1868 4k black, lilac & org   15 15

In memory of cosmonauts Lt. Col. Georgi T. Dobrovolsky, Vladislav N. Volkov and Viktor I. Patsayev, who died during the Soyuz 11 space mission, June 6-30, 1971.

Order of October Revolution A1869

1971, Oct. 20   Litho.   *Perf. 12*
3905 A1869 4k red, yel & black   15 15

54th anniversary of October Revolution.

E. Vakhtangov and "Princess Turandot" A1870 — Dzhambul Dzhabayev A1871

Designs: No. 3907, Boris Shchukin and scene from "Man with Rifle (Lenin)," horiz. No. 3908, Ruben Simonov and scene from "Cyrano de Bergerac," horiz.

Perf. 12x12¹/₂, 12¹/₂x12
1971, Oct. 26   **Photo.**
3906 A1870 10k maroon & red brn   35 15
3907 A1870 10k brown & dull yel   35 15
3908 A1870 10k red brown & ocher   35 15
          Set value   20

Vakhtangov Theater, Moscow, 50th anniv.

1971, Nov. 16   *Perf. 12x12¹/₂*
3909 A1871 4k orange & brown   30 25

Dzhabayev (1846-1945), Kazakh poet.

Gorki Kremlin Type, 1971

Designs: 3k, Pskov Kremlin and Velikaya River. 4k, Novgorod Kremlin and eternal flame memorial. 6k, Smolensk Fortress and liberation monument. 10k, Kolomna Kremlin and buses. 50k, Moscow Kremlin.

1971, Nov. 16   Litho.   *Perf. 12*
3910 A1857 3k multicolored   15 15
3911 A1857 4k multicolored   15 15
3912 A1857 6k gray & multi   15 15
3913 A1857 10k olive & multi   16 15
          Set value   40 22

Souvenir Sheet
Engraved and Lithographed
Perf. 11¹/₂
3914 A1857 50k yellow & multi   1.75 1.00

Historic buildings. No. 3914 contains one 21¹/₂x32mm stamp.

William Foster, View of New York — A1872

1971   Litho.   *Perf. 12*
3915 A1872 10k brown & black ("- 1961")   50 25
     a.   "-1964"   10.00 7.25

William Foster (1881-1961), chairman of Communist Party of US.
No. 3915a was issued Nov. 16 with incorrect death date (1964). No. 3915, with corrected date (1961), was issued Dec. 8.

Aleksandr Fadeyev and Cavalrymen A1873

1971, Nov. 25 Photo. *Perf. 12¹/₂x12*
3916 A1873 4k slate & orange   30 25

Aleksandr Fadeyev (1901-1956), writer.

Amethyst and Diamond Brooch — A1874

Precious Jewels: No. 3918, Engraved Shakh diamond, India, 16th century. No. 3919, Diamond daffodils, 18th century. No. 3920, Amethyst and diamond pendant. No. 3921, Diamond rose made for centenary of Lenin's birth. 30k, Diamond and pearl pendant.

1971, Dec. 8   Litho.   *Perf. 11¹/₂*
3917 A1874 10k brt blue & multi   32 15
3918 A1874 10k dk red & multi   32 15
3919 A1874 10k grnsh black & multi   32 15
3920 A1874 20k grnsh black & multi   70 22
3921 A1874 20k rose red & multi   70 22
3922 A1874 30k black & multi   1.10 38
          Nos. 3917-3922 (6)   3.46
          Set value   1.00

Souvenir Sheet

Workers with Banners, Congress Hall and Spasski Tower — A1875

1971, Dec. 15 Photo. *Perf. 11x11¹/₂*
3923 A1875 20k red, pale green & brown   2.00 1.00

See note after No. 3895. No. 3923 contains one partially perforated stamp.

Vanda Orchid — A1876

Flowers: 1k, #3929b, shown. 2k, Anthurium. 4k, #3929c, Flowering crab cactus. 12k, #3929a, Amaryllis. 14k, #3929d, Medinilla magnifica.

1971, Dec. 15 Litho. *Perf. 12x12¹/₂*
3924 A1876 1k olive & multi   15 15
3925 A1876 2k green & multi   15 15
3926 A1876 4k blue & multi   15 15
3927 A1876 12k multicolored   48 15
3928 A1876 14k multicolored   55 15
          Nos. 3924-3928 (5)   1.48
          Set value   40

Miniature Sheet
Perf. 12
3929   Sheet of 4   2.00 90
a.-d.   A1876 10k any single   40 25

Nos. 3929a-3929d have white background, black frame line and inscription. Size of stamps 19x57mm.
Issue dates: Nos. 3924-3928, Dec. 15; No. 3929, Dec. 30.

Peter I Reviewing Fleet, 1723 — A1877

History of Russian Fleet: 4k, Oriol, first ship built in Eddinovo, 1668, vert. 10k, Battleship Poltava, 1712, vert. 12k, Armed ship Ingermanland, 1715, vert. 16k, Frigate Vladimir, 1848.

Perf. 11¹/₂x12, 12x11¹/₂
1971, Dec. 15   **Engr. & Photo.**
3930 A1877 1k multicolored   30 25
3931 A1877 4k brown & multi   35 25
3932 A1877 10k multicolored   75 35
3933 A1877 12k multicolored   75 35
3934 A1877 16k lt green & multi   1.50 40
          Nos. 3930-3934 (5)   3.65 1.60

Ice Hockey A1878

1971, Dec. 15   Litho.   *Perf. 12¹/₂*
3935 A1878 6k multicolored   30 25

25th anniversary of Soviet ice hockey.

Oil Rigs and Causeway in Caspian Sea — A1879

1971, Dec. 30   *Perf. 11¹/₂*
3936 A1879 4k dp blue, org & blk   15 15

Baku oil industry.

G. M. Krzhizhanovsky (1872-1959), Scientist and Co-worker with Lenin — A1880

1972, Jan. 5   Engr.   Perf. 12
3937 A1880 4k yellow brown   15 15

Alexander Scriabin
A1881

Bering's Cormorant
A1882

1972, Jan. 6   Photo.   Perf. 12x12½
3938 A1881 4k indigo & olive   30 25

Scriabin (1872-1915), composer.

1972, Jan. 12   Perf. 11½
Birds: 6k, Ross' gull, horiz. 10k, Barnacle geese. 12k, Spectacled eiders, horiz. 16k, Mediterranean gull.

3939 A1882   4k dk grn, blk & yel   16 15
3940 A1882   6k indigo, pink & blk   24 15
3941 A1882 10k grnsh blue, blk & brown   50 15
3942 A1882 12k multicolored   55 15
3943 A1882 16k ultra, gray & red   30 20
         Nos. 3939-3943 (5)   1.75
         Set value   52

Waterfowl of the USSR.

Speed Skating — A1883

Heart, Globe and Exercising Family — A1884

Designs (Olympic Rings and): 6k, Women's figure skating. 10k, Ice hockey. 12k, Ski jump. 16k, Long-distance skiing. 50k, Sapporo '72 emblem.

1972, Jan. 20   Litho.   Perf. 12x12½
3944 A1883   4k bl grn, red & brn   15 15
3945 A1883   6k yel grn, blue & dp orange   15 15
3946 A1883 10k vio, bl & dp org   25 15
3947 A1883 12k light blue, blue & brick red   30 15
3948 A1883 16k gray, bl & brt rose   50 20
         Nos. 3944-3948 (5)   1.35
         Set value   50

Souvenir Sheet
3949 A1883 50k multicolored   1.50 75

11th Winter Olympic Games, Sapporo, Japan, Feb. 3-13.
For overprint see No. 3961.

1972, Feb. 9   Photo.
3950 A1884 4k brt green & rose red   15 15

Heart Week sponsored by the WHO.

Leipzig Fair Emblem and Soviet Pavilion
A1885

Hammer, Sickle and Cogwheel Emblem
A1886

1972, Feb. 22   Perf. 11½
3951 A1885 16k red & gold   60 25

50th anniversary of the participation of the USSR in the Leipzig Trade Fair.

1972, Feb. 29   Perf. 12x12½
3952 A1886 4k rose red & lt brown   15 15

15th USSR Trade Union Congress, Moscow, March 1972.

Aloe
A1887

Aleksandra Kollontai
A1888

Medicinal Plants: 2k, Horn poppy. 4k, Groundsel. 6k, Orthosiphon stamineus. 10k, Nightshade.

1972, Mar. 14 Litho. Perf. 12x12½
Flowers in Natural Colors
3953 A1887   1k olive bister   15 15
3954 A1887   2k slate green   15 15
3955 A1887   4k brt purple   15 15
3956 A1887   6k violet blue   20 16
3957 A1887 10k dk brown   40 22
         Nos. 3953-3957 (5)   1.05
         Set value   70

1972, Mar. 20 Engr. Perf. 12½x12
Portraits: No. 3959, Georgy Chicherin. No. 3960, Kamo (pseudonym of S.A. Ter-Petrosyan).

3958 A1888 4k red brown   15 15
3959 A1888 4k claret   15 15
3960 A1888 4k olive bister   15 15
         Set value   20 15

Outstanding workers of the Communist Party of the Soviet Union and for the State.

No. 3949 Overprinted in Margin
Souvenir Sheet

СОВЕТСКИЕ СПОРТСМЕНЫ
ЗАВОЕВАЛИ
8 ЗОЛОТЫХ
МЕДАЛЕЙ,
5 СЕРЕБРЯНЫХ,
3 БРОНЗОВЫХ.

1972, Mar. 20 Litho. Perf. 12x12½
3961 A1883 50k multicolored   4.00 2.00

Victories of Soviet athletes in the 11th Winter Olympic Games (8 gold, 5 silver, 3 bronze medals). For similar overprints see Nos. 4028, 4416.

Orbital Station Salyut and Spaceship Soyuz Docking Above Earth — A1889

Designs: No. 3963, Mars 2 approaching Mars, and emblem dropped on Mars. 16k, Mars 3, which landed on Mars, Dec. 2, 1971.

1971, Apr. 5   Photo.   Perf. 11½x12
3962 A1889   6k vio, blue & silver   20 15
3963 A1889   6k purple, ocher & sil   20 15
3964 A1889 16k pur, blue & silver   1.00 15
         Set value   24

Cosmonauts' Day.

Shield and Products of Izhory Factory
A1890

1972, Apr. 20   Perf. 12½x12
3965 A1890 4k purple & silver   15 15

250th anniversary of Izhory Factory, founded by Peter the Great.

Leonid Sobinov in "Eugene Onegin," by Tchaikovsky
A1891

1972, Apr. 20
3966 A1891 10k dp brown & buff   30 15

Sobinov (1872-1934), opera singer.

Book, Torch, Children and Globe
A1892

1972, May 5   Perf. 11½
3967 A1892 6k brn, grnsh bl & buff   15 15

International Book Year 1972.

Girl in Laboratory and Pioneers
A1893

Designs: 1k, Pavlik Morosov (Pioneer hero). Pioneers saluting and banner. 3k, Pioneers with wheelbarrow, Chukchi boy, and Chukotka Pioneer House. 4k, Pioneer Honor Guard and Parade. 30k, Pioneer Honor Guard, vert.

1972, May 10
3968 A1893   1k red & multi   15 15
3969 A1893   2k multicolored   15 15
3970 A1893   3k multicolored   15 15
3971 A1893   4k gray & multi   15 15
         Set value   26 20

Souvenir Sheet
Perf. 12x12½
3972 A1893 30k multicolored   2.00 75

50th anniversary of the Lenin Pioneer Organization of the USSR.

Pioneer Bugler
A1894

1972, May 27   Photo.   Perf. 11½
3973 A1894 4k red, ocher & plum   15 15

2nd Youth Philatelic Exhibition, Minsk, and 50th anniv. of Lenin Pioneer Org.

M. S. Ordubady (1872-1950), Azerbaijan Writer and Social Worker — A1895

1972, May 25   Perf. 12x12½
3974 A1895 4k orange & rose brn   30 15

Globe
A1896

1972, May 25   Perf. 11½
3975 A1896 6k multicolored   60 30

European Safety and Cooperation Conference, Brussels.

Cossack Leader, by Ivan Nikitin — A1897

Paintings: 4k, Fedor G. Volkov (actor), by Anton Losenko. 6k, V. Majkov (poet), by Fedor Rokotov. 10k, Nikolai I. Novikov (writer), by Dimitri Levitsky. 12k, Gavriil R. Derzhavin (poet, civil servant), by Vladimir Borovikovsky. 16k, Peasants' Supper, by Mikhail Shibanov, horiz. 20k, View of Moscow, by Fedor Alexeyev, horiz.

Perf. 12x12½, 12½x12
1972, June 7   Litho.
3976 A1897   2k gray & multi   15 15
3977 A1897   4k gray & multi   15 15
3978 A1897   6k gray & multi   24 15
3979 A1897 10k gray & multi   40 15
3980 A1897 12k gray & multi   45 15
3981 A1897 16k gray & multi   70 18
3982 A1897 20k gray & multi   95 26
         Nos. 3976-3982 (7)   3.04
         Set value   78

History of Russian painting. See Nos. 4036-4042, 4074-4080, 4103-4109.

George Dimitrov
A1898

Fencing, Olympic Rings
A1899

1972, June 15 Photo. Perf. 12½x12
3983 A1898 6k brown & ol bister   30 15

Dimitrov (1882-1949), Bulgarian Communist Party leader and Premier.

1972, July 1   Perf. 12x11½

Designs (Olympic Rings and): 6k, Women's gymnastics. 10k, Canoeing. 14k, Boxing. 16k, Running. 50k, Weight lifting.

3984 A1899	4k brt mag & gold	15	15
3985 A1899	6k dp green & gold	18	15
3986 A1899	10k brt blue & gold	55	15
3987 A1899	14k Prus blue & gold	60	15
3988 A1899	16k red & gold	85	15
Nos. 3984-3988 (5)		2.33	
Set value			40

Souvenir Sheet
Perf. 11½

3989 A1899	50k gold & multi	2.00	80

20th Olympic Games, Munich, Aug. 26-Sept. 11. #3989 contains one 25x35mm stamp.
For overprint see No. 4028.

Congress Palace, Kiev — A1900

1972, July 1   Photo. & Engr.
3990 A1900	6k Prus blue & bister	15	15

9th World Gerontology Congress, Kiev, July 2-7.

Roald Amundsen, "Norway," Northern Lights A1901

1972, July 13   Photo.   Perf. 11½
3991 A1901	6k vio blue & dp bister	30	25

Roald Amundsen (1872-1928), Norwegian polar explorer.

17th Century House, Chernigov A1902

Designs: 4k, Market Square, Lvov, vert. 10k, Kovnirov Building, Kiev. 16k, Fortress, Kamenets-Podolski, vert.

Perf. 12x12½, 12½x12
1972, July 18   Litho.
3992 A1902	4k citron & multi	15	15
3993 A1902	6k gray & multi	15	15
3994 A1902	10k ocher & multi	40	15
3995 A1902	16k salmon & multi	60	15
Set value			26

Historic and architectural treasures of the Ukraine.

Asoka Pillar, Indian Flag, Red Fort, New Delhi A1903

1972, July 27   Photo.   Perf. 11½
3996 A1903	6k dk blue, emer & red	15	15

25th anniversary of India's independence.

Miners' Emblem A1904

1972, Aug. 10
3997 A1904	4k violet gray & red	15	15

25th Miners' Day.

Far East Fighters' Monument — A1905

Designs: 4k, Monument for Far East Civil War heroes, industrial view. 6k, Vladivostok rostral column, Pacific fleet ships.

1972, Aug. 10
3998 A1905	3k red org, car & black	15	15
3999 A1905	4k yel, sepia & blk	15	15
4000 A1905	6k pink, dk car & black	15	15
Set value		30	16

50th anniversary of the liberation of the Far Eastern provinces.

Boy with Dog, by Murillo A1906

Paintings from the Hermitage, Leningrad: 4k, Breakfast, Velazquez. 6k, Milkmaid's Family, Louis Le Nain. 16k, Sad Woman, Watteau. 20k, Moroccan Saddling Steed, Delacroix. 50k, Self-portrait, Van Dyck. 4k, 6k horiz.

Perf. 12½x12, 12x12½
1972, Aug. 15   Litho.
4001 A1906	4k multicolored	15	15
4002 A1906	6k multicolored	22	15
4003 A1906	10k multicolored	35	15
4004 A1906	16k multicolored	50	15
4005 A1906	20k multicolored	75	18
Nos. 4001-4005 (5)		1.97	
Set value			48

Souvenir Sheet
Perf. 12
4006 A1906	50k multicolored	2.50	1.00

Sputnik 1 — A1907

1972, Sept. 14   Litho.   Perf. 12x11½
4007 A1907	6k shown	15	15
4008 A1907	6k Launching of Vostok 2	15	15
4009 A1907	6k Lenov floating in space	15	15
4010 A1907	6k Lunokhod on moon	15	15
4011 A1907	6k Venera 7 descending to Venus	15	15
4012 A1907	6k Mars & descending to Mars	15	15
Nos. 4007-4012 (6)		90	
Set value			50

15 years of space era. Sheets of 6.

Konstantin Aleksandrovich Mardzhanishvili (1872-1933), Theatrical Producer — A1908

1972, Sept. 20   Engr.   Perf. 12x12½
4013 A1908	4k slate green	30	25

Museum Emblem, Communications Symbols — A1909

1972, Sept. 20   Photo.   Perf. 11½
4014 A1909	4k slate green & multi	15	15

Centenary of the A. S. Popov Central Museum of Communications.

"Stamp" and Topical Collecting Symbols A1910

Engraved and Lithographed
1972, Oct. 4   Perf. 12
4015 A1910	4k yel, black & red	15	15

Philatelic Exhibition in honor of 50th anniversary of the USSR.

Lenin A1911

1972, Oct. 12   Photo.   Perf. 11½
4016 A1911	4k gold & red	15	15

55th anniversary of October Revolution.

Militia Badge — A1912   Arms of USSR — A1913

1972, Oct. 12
4017 A1912	4k gold, red & dk brn	15	15

55th anniv. of the Militia of the USSR.

1972, Oct. 28   Perf. 12x11½

USSR, 50th anniv.: #4019, Arms and industrial scene. #4020, Arms, Supreme Soviet, Kremlin. #4021, Lenin. #4022, Arms, worker, book (Constitution). 30k, Coat of arms and Spasski Tower, horiz.

4018 A1913	4k multicolored	15	15
4019 A1913	4k multicolored	15	15
4020 A1913	4k multicolored	15	15
4021 A1913	4k multicolored	15	15
4022 A1913	4k multicolored	15	15

Set value		40	25

Souvenir Sheet
Lithographed; Embossed
Perf. 12
4023 A1913	30k red & gold	1.50	40

Kremlin and Snowflake A1914   Savings Bank Book A1915

Engraved and Photogravure
1972, Nov. 15   Perf. 11½
4024 A1914	6k multicolored	15	15

New Year 1973.

1972, Nov. 15   Photo.   Perf. 12x12½
4025 A1915	4k lilac & slate	15	15

50th anniv. of savings banks in the USSR.

Soviet Olympic Emblem and Laurel — A1916

Design: 30k, Soviet Olympic emblem and obverse of gold, silver and bronze medals.

1972, Nov. 15   Perf. 11½
4026 A1916	20k brn ol, red & gold	50	40
4027 A1916	30k dp car, gold & brn	1.00	60

No. 3989 Overprinted in Red

СЛАВА
СОВЕТСНИМ ОЛИМПИЙЦАМ,
ЗАВОЕВАВШИМ
50 ЗОЛОТЫХ, 27 СЕРЕБРЯНЫХ
И 22 БРОНЗОВЫЕ НАГРАДЫ!

Souvenir Sheet
4028 A1899	50k gold & multi	3.00	1.25

Soviet medalists at 20th Olympic Games.

Battleship Peter the Great, 1872 — A1917

History of Russian Fleet: 3k, Cruiser Varyag, 1899. 4k, Battleship Potemkin, 1900. 6k, Cruiser Ochakov, 1902. 10k, Mine layer Amur, 1907.

Engraved and Photogravure
1972, Nov. 22   Perf. 11½x12
4029 A1917	2k multicolored	32	15
4030 A1917	3k multicolored	32	15
4031 A1917	4k multicolored	45	15
4032 A1917	6k multicolored	70	15
4033 A1917	10k multicolored	1.10	15
Nos. 4029-4033 (5)		2.89	
Set value			35

Grigory S. Skovoroda
A1918

Child Reading Traffic Rules
A1919

1972, Dec. 7 Engr. Perf. 12
4034 A1918 4k dk violet blue 30 15

Grigory S. Skovoroda (1722-1794), Ukrainian philosopher and humanist.

1972, Dec. 7 Photo. Perf. 11½
4035 A1919 4k Prus blue, blk & red 15 15

Traffic safety campaign.

Russian Painting Type of 1972

Paintings: 2k, Meeting of Village Party Members, by E. M. Cheptsov, horiz. 4k, Pioneer Girl, by Nicolai A. Kasatkin. 6k, Woman Delegate, by G. G. Ryazhsky. 10k, Winter's End, by K. F. Yuon, horiz. 16k, The Partisan A. G. Lunev, by N. I. Strunnikov. 20k, Igor E. Grabar, self-portrait. 50k, Blue Space (seascape with flying geese), by Arcadia A. Rylov, horiz.

Perf. 12x12½, 12½x12
1972, Dec. 7 Litho.
4036 A1897 2k olive & multi 15 15
4037 A1897 4k olive & multi 15 15
4038 A1897 6k olive & multi 15 15
4039 A1897 10k olive & multi 38 15
4040 A1897 16k olive & multi 55 15
4041 A1897 20k olive & multi 80 22
 Nos. 4036-4041 (6) 2.18
  Set value 64

Souvenir Sheet
Perf. 12
4042 A1897 50k multicolored 2.00 1.25

History of Russian painting.

Symbolic of Theory and Practice — A1920

Engraved and Photogravure
1972, Dec. 7 Perf. 11½
4043 A1920 4k sl grn, yel & red brn 30 15

Centenary of Polytechnic Museum, Moscow.

Venus 8 and Parachute
A1921

1972, Dec. 28 Photo. Perf. 11½
4044 A1921 6k dl cl, bl & blk 30 15
Souvenir Sheet
Imperf
4045 Sheet of 2 9.00 3.00
 a. A1921 50k Venus 8 2.50 90
 b. A1921 50k Mars 3 2.50 90

Soviet space research. No. 4045 contains 2 40x20mm stamps with simulated perforations.

Globe, Torch and Palm — A1922

1973, Jan. 5 Perf. 11x11½
4046 A1922 10k tan, vio blue & red 35 30

15th anniversary of Afro-Asian Peoples' Solidarity Organization (AAPSO).

I. V. Babushkin
A1923

"30," Map and Admiralty Tower, Leningrad
A1924

1973, Jan. 10 Engr. Perf. 12
4047 A1923 4k greenish black 15 15

Babushkin (1873-1906), revolutionary.

1973, Jan. 10 Photo. Perf. 11½
4048 A1924 4k pale brown, ocher & black 15 15

30th anniversary of the breaking of the Nazi blockade of Leningrad.

TU-154 Turbojet Passenger Plane — A1925

1973, Jan. 10 Litho. Perf. 12
4049 A1925 6k multicolored 15 15

50th anniversary of Soviet Civil Aviation.

Gediminas Tower, Flag, Modern Vilnius
A1926

1973, Jan. 10 Photo. Perf. 11½
4050 A1926 10k gray, red & green 40 30

650th anniversary of Vilnius.

Heroes' Memorial, Stalingrad — A1927

Designs (Details from Monument): 3k, Man with rifle and "Mother Russia," vert. 10k, Mourning mother and child. 12k, Arm with torch, vert. No. 4055a, Red star, hammer and sickle emblem and statuary like 3k. No. 4055b, "Mother Russia," vert.

1973, Feb. 1 Litho. Perf. 11½
4051 A1927 3k dp orange & black 25 15
4052 A1927 4k dp yellow & black 25 15
4053 A1927 10k olive & multi 25 15
4054 A1927 12k dp car & black 25 15
  Set value 50

Souvenir Sheet
Perf. 12x12½, 12½x12
4055 Sheet of 2 1.50 75
 a.-b. A1927 20k any single 45 20

30th anniversary of the victory over the Germans at Stalingrad. No. 4055 contains 2 40x18mm stamps.

Large Portrait Type of 1971

Designs: 4k, Mikhail Prishvin (1873-1954), author. 10k, Fedor Chaliapin (1873-1938), opera singer, by K. Korovin.

1973 Litho. Perf. 11½x12
4056 A1855 4k pink & multi 15 15
4057 A1855 10k lt blue & multi 16 15
  Set value 22 15

Issue dates: 4k, Feb. 1; 10k, Feb. 8.

"Mayakovsky Theater"
A1928

"Mossovet Theater"
A1929

1973, Feb. 1 Photo. Perf. 11½
4058 A1928 10k red, gray & indigo 30 15
4059 A1929 10k red, mag & gray 30 15
  Set value

50th anniversary of the Mayakovsky and Mossovet Theaters in Moscow.

Copernicus and Solar System
A1930

1973, Feb. 8 Engr. & Photo.
4060 A1930 10k ultra & sepia 40 25

500th anniversary of the birth of Nicolaus Copernicus (1473-1543), Polish astronomer.

Ice Hockey
A1931

Design: 50k, Two players, vert.

1973, Mar. 14 Photo. Perf. 11½
4061 A1931 10k gold, blue & sepia 40 25
Souvenir Sheet
4062 A1931 50k bl grn, gold & sep 2.00 1.00

European and World Ice Hockey Championships, Moscow.
See No. 4082.

Athletes and Banners of Air, Land and Naval Forces — A1932

Tank, Red Star and Map of Battle of Kursk — A1933

1973, Mar. 14
4063 A1932 4k bright blue & multi 30 15

Sports Society of Soviet Army, 50th anniv.

1973, Mar. 14
4064 A1933 4k gray, black & red 30 15

30th anniversary of Soviet victory in the Battle of Kursk during World War II.

Nikolai E. Bauman (1873-1905), Bolshevist Revolutionary — A1934

1973, Mar. 20 Engr. Perf. 12½x12
4065 A1934 4k brown 30 15

Red Cross and Red Crescent — A1935

Designs: 6k, Theater curtain and mask. 16k, Youth Festival emblem and young people.

1973, Mar. 20 Photo. Perf. 11
4066 A1935 4k gray green & red 15 15
4067 A1935 6k violet blue & red 20 15
4068 A1935 16k multicolored 70 15
  Set value 22

Union of Red Cross and Red Crescent Societies of the USSR, 50th anniv.; 15th Cong. of the Intl. Theater Institute; 10th World Festival of Youth and Students, Berlin.

Aleksandr N. Ostrovsky, by V. Perov
A1936

1973, Apr. 5 Litho. Perf. 12x12½
4069 A1936 4k tan & multi 30 15

Ostrovsky (1823-1886), dramatist.

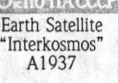

Earth Satellite "Interkosmos" A1937

Lunokhod 2 on Moon and Lenin Moon Plaque A1938

1973, Apr. 12   Photo.   Perf. 11½
4070	A1937	6k brn ol & dull claret	15	15
4071	A1938	6k vio blue & multi	15	15
		Set value		15

Souvenir Sheets
Perf. 12x11½
4072		Sheet of 3, purple & multi	2.50	1.00
a.	A1938	20k Lenin plaque	52	30
b.	A1938	20k Lunokhod 2	52	30
c.	A1938	20k Telecommunications	52	35
4073		Sheet of 3, slate grn & multi	2.50	1.00
a.	A1938	20k Lenin plaque	52	30
b.	A1938	20k Lunokhod 2	52	30
c.	A1938	20k Telecommunications	52	30

Cosmonauts' Day. No. 4070 for cooperation in space research by European communist countries. Souvenir sheets contain 3 50x21mm stamps.

Russian Painting Type of 1972

Paintings: 2k, Guitarist, V. A. Tropinin. 4k, Young Widow, by P. A. Fedotov. 6k, Self-portrait, by O. A. Kiprensky. 10k, Woman with Grapes ("An Afternoon in Italy") by K. P. Bryullov. 12k, Boy with Dog ("That was my Father's Dinner"), by A. Venetsianov. 16k, "Lower Gallery of Albano," by A. A. Ivanov. 20k, Soldiers ("Conquest of Siberia"), by V. I. Surikov, horiz.

Perf. 12x12½, 12½x12
1973, Apr. 18   Litho.
4074	A1897	2k gray & multi	15	15
4075	A1897	4k gray & multi	15	15
4076	A1897	6k gray & multi	22	15
4077	A1897	10k gray & multi	42	22
4078	A1897	12k gray & multi	60	22
4079	A1897	16k gray & multi	65	26
4080	A1897	20k gray & multi	80	32
		Nos. 4074-4080 (7)	2.99	1.47

Athlete, Ribbon of Lenin Order — A1939

1973, Apr. 18   Photo.   Perf. 11½
4081	A1939	4k blue, red & ocher	15	15

50th anniversary of Dynamo Sports Society.

No. 4062 with Blue Green Inscription and Ornaments Added in Margin
Souvenir Sheet
1973, Apr. 26   Photo.   Perf. 11½
4082	A1931	50k bl grn, gold & sep	5.00	2.00

Soviet victory in European and World Ice Hockey Championships, Moscow.

"Mikhail Lermontov," Route Leningrad to New York — A1940

1973, May 20   Photo.   Perf. 11½
4083	A1940	16k multicolored	60	25

Inauguration of transatlantic service Leningrad to New York.

Ernest E. T. Krenkel, Polar Stations and Ship Chelyuskin A1941

1973, May 20   Litho. & Engr.
4084	A1941	4k dull blue & olive	40	30

Krenkel (1903-1971), polar explorer.

Emblem and Sports — A1942

Singers — A1943

1973, May 20   Litho.   Perf. 12x12½
4085	A1942	4k multicolored	15	15

Sports Association for Labor and Defense.

1973, May 24
4086	A1943	10k multicolored	35	25

Centenary of Latvian Song Festival.

Throwing the Hammer — A1944

Designs: 3k, Athlete on rings. 4k, Woman diver. 16k, Fencing. 50k, Javelin.

1973, June 14   Litho.   Perf. 11½
4087	A1944	2k lemon & multi	15	15
4088	A1944	3k blue & multi	15	15
4089	A1944	4k citron & multi	15	15
4090	A1944	16k lilac & multi	35	15
		Set value	54	25

Souvenir Sheet
4091	A1944	50k gold & multi	1.75	1.25

Universiad, Moscow, 1973.

Souvenir Sheet

Valentina Nikolayeva-Tereshkova — A1945

1973, June 14   Photo.   Perf. 12x11½
4092	A1945	Sheet of 3 + label	3.00	1.25
a.		20k as cosmonaut	55	25
b.		20k with Indian and African women	55	25
c.		20k with daughter	55	25

Flight of the 1st woman cosmonaut, 10th anniv.

European Bison — A1946

1973, July 26   Photo.   Perf. 11x11½
4093	A1946	1k shown	15	15
4094	A1946	3k Ibex	15	15
4095	A1946	4k Caucasian snowcock	20	15
4096	A1946	6k Beaver	35	15
4097	A1946	10k Deer and fawns	50	15
		Nos. 4093-4097 (5)	1.35	
		Set value		34

Caucasus and Voronezh wildlife reserves.

Party Membership Card with Lenin Portrait — A1947

1973, July 26   Litho.   Perf. 11½
4098	A1947	4k multicolored	15	15

70th anniversary of 2nd Congress of the Russian Social Democratic Workers' Party.

Abu-al-Rayhan al-Biruni (973-1048), Arabian (Persian) Scholar and Writer — A1948

1973, Aug. 9   Engr.   Perf. 12x12½
4099	A1948	6k red brown	15	15

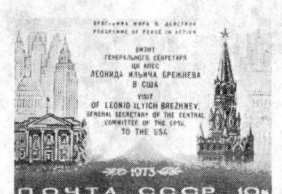

White House, Spasski Tower, Hemispheres — A1949

Designs: No. 4101, Eiffel Tower, Spasski Tower, globe. No. 4102, Schaumburg Palace, Bonn, Spasski Tower, globe. Stamps show representative buildings of Moscow, Washington, New York, Paris and Bonn.

1973, Aug. 10   Photo.   Perf. 11½x12
4100	A1949	10k magenta & multi	50	50
4101	A1949	10k brown & multi	50	50
4102	A1949	10k dp car & multi	50	50
a.		Souv. sheet of 3 + 3 labels	2.50	2.50

Visit of General Secretary Leonid I. Brezhnev to Washington, Paris and Bonn. Nos. 4100-4102 each printed with se-tenant label with different statements by Brezhnev in Russian and English, French and German, respectively.

No. 4102a contains 4k stamps similar to Nos. 4100-4102 in changed colors. Issued Nov. 26. See Nos. 4161-4162.

Russian Painting Type of 1972

Paintings: 2k, S. T. Konenkov, sculptor, by P. D. Korin. 4k, Tractor Operators at Supper, by A. A. Plastov. 6k, Letter from the Front, by A. I. Laktionov. 10k, Mountains, by M. S. Saryan. 16k, Wedding on a Future Street, by Y. I. Pimenov. 20k, Ice Hockey, mosaic by A. A. Deineka. 50k, Lenin at 3rd Congress of Young Communist League, by B. V. Yoganson.

1973, Aug. 22   Litho.   Perf. 12x12½
Frame in Light Gray
4103	A1897	2k multicolored	15	15
4104	A1897	4k multicolored	16	15
4105	A1897	6k multicolored	18	15
4106	A1897	10k multicolored	35	15
4107	A1897	16k multicolored	60	15
4108	A1897	20k multicolored	70	15
		Nos. 4103-4108 (6)	2.14	
		Set value		50

Souvenir Sheet
Perf. 12
4109	A1897	50k multicolored	2.00	1.25

History of Russian Painting.

Museum, Tashkent A1950

Y. M. Steklov A1951

1973, Aug. 23   Photo.   Perf. 12x12½
4110	A1950	4k multicolored	15	15

Lenin Central Museum, Tashkent branch.

1973, Aug. 27   Photo.   Perf. 11½x12
4111	A1951	4k multicolored	15	15

Steklov (1873-1941), party worker, historian, writer.

Book, Pen and Torch — A1952

Echinopanax Elatum — A1953

1973, Aug. 31   Perf. 11½
4112	A1952	6k multicolored	15	15

Conf. of Writers of Asia & Africa, Alma-Ata.

1973, Sept. 5   Litho.   Perf. 12x12½

Medicinal Plants: 2k, Ginseng. 4k, Orchis maculatus. 10k, Arnica montana. 12k, Lily of the valley.
4113	A1953	1k yellow & multi	15	15
4114	A1953	2k lt blue & multi	15	15
4115	A1953	4k gray & multi	15	15
4116	A1953	10k sepia & multi	30	15
4117	A1953	12k green & multi	55	15
		Nos. 4113-4117 (5)	1.30	
		Set value		28

Imadeddin Nasimi, Azerbaijani Poet, 600th Birth Anniv. — A1954

1973, Sept. 5   Engr.
4118	A1954	4k sepia	30	15

Cruiser Kirov — A1955

Soviet Warships: 4k, Battleship October Revolution. 6k, Submarine Krasnogvardeyets. 10k, Torpedo boat Soobrazitelny. 16k, Cruiser Red Caucasus.

Engraved and Photogravure
1973, Sept. 12   **Perf. 11½x12**
4119	A1955	3k violet & multi	15	15
4120	A1955	4k green & multi	15	15
4121	A1955	6k multicolored	20	15
4122	A1955	10k blue grn & multi	30	15
4123	A1955	16k multicolored	50	20
		Nos. 4119-4123 (5)	1.30	
		Set value		48

Globe and Red Flag Emblem — A1956

1973, Sept. 25   **Photo.**   **Perf. 11½**
4124	A1956	6k gold, buff & red	15	15

15th anniversary of the international communist review "Problems of Peace and Socialism," published in Prague.

Emelyan I. Pugachev and Peasant Army — A1957

Engraved and Photogravure
1973, Sept. 25   **Perf. 11½x12**
4125	A1957	4k brn, bister & red	15	15

Bicentenary of peasant revolt of 1773-75 led by Emelyn Ivanovich Pugachev.

Crystal, Institute Emblem and Building A1958

1973, Oct. 5   **Perf. 11½**
4126	A1958	4k black & multi	15	15

Leningrad Mining Institute, 150th anniv.

15-Cent Minimum Value
The minimum catalogue value is 15 cents. Separating se-tenant pieces into individual stamps does not increase the value of the stamps since demand for the separated stamps may be small.

Palm, Globe, Flower A1959

Elena Stasova A1960

1973, Oct. 5   **Photo.**
4127	A1959	6k red, gray & dk blue	15	15

World Cong. of Peace-loving Forces, Moscow.

1973, Oct. 5   **Perf. 11½x12**
4128	A1960	4k deep claret	15	15

Elena Dmitriyevna Stasova (1873-1966), communist party worker.
See Nos. 4228-4229.

Order of Friendship A1961

1973, Oct. 5   **Litho.**   **Perf. 12**
4129	A1961	4k red & multi	15	15

56th anniv. of the October Revolution. Printed se-tenant with coupon showing Arms of USSR and proclamation establishing Order of Friendship of People, in 1972, on the 50th anniv. of the USSR.

Marshal Malinovsky A1962

Ural Man, Red Guard, Worker A1963

1973, Oct. 5   **Engr.**
4130	A1962	4k slate	15	15

Rodion Y. Malinovsky (1898-1967).
See Nos. 4203-4205.

1973, Oct. 17   **Photo.**   **Perf. 11½**
4131	A1963	4k red, gold & black	15	15

250th anniversary of the city of Sverdlovsk.

Dimitri Cantemir (1673-1723), Prince of Moldavia, Writer — A1964

1973, Oct. 17   **Engr.**   **Perf. 12x12½**
4132	A1964	4k rose claret	15	15

Salvador Allende (1908-73), Pres. of Chile A1965

1973, Nov. 26   **Photo.**   **Perf. 11½**
4133	A1965	6k rose brn & black	15	15

Spasski Tower, Kremlin A1966

Nariman Narimanov A1967

1973, Nov. 30   **Litho.**   **Perf. 12x12½**
4134	A1966	6k brt blue & multi	15	15

New Year 1974.

1973, Nov. 30   **Engr.**   **Perf. 12**
4135	A1967	4k slate green	15	15

Nariman Narimanov (1870-1925), Chairman of Executive Committee of USSR.

Russo-Balt, 1909 — A1968

Designs: 3k, AMO-F15 truck, 1924. 4k, Spartak, NAMI-I car, 1927. 12k, Ya-6 autobus, 1929. 16k, GAZ-A car, 1932.

1973, Nov. 30   **Photo.**   **Perf. 12x11½**
4136	A1968	2k purple & multi	15	15
4137	A1968	3k olive & multi	15	15
4138	A1968	4k ocher & multi	15	15
4139	A1968	12k vio blue & multi	42	15
4140	A1968	16k red & multi	75	15
		Nos. 4136-4140 (5)	1.62	
		Set value		34

Development of Russian automotive industry.
See Nos. 4216-4220, 4325-4329, 4440-4444.

Still Life, by Frans Snyders — A1969

Paintings: 6k, Woman Trying on Earrings, by Rembrandt, vert. 10k, Sick Woman and Physician, by Jan Steen, vert. 12k, Still Life with Sculpture, by Jean-Baptiste Chardin, vert. 14k, Lady in Garden, by Claude Monet. 16k, Young Love, by Jules Bastien-Lepage, vert. 20k Girl with Fan, by Auguste Renoir, vert. 50k, Flora, by Rembrandt, vert.

Perf. 12x11½, 11½x12
1973, Dec. 12   **Litho.**
4141	A1969	4k bister & multi	15	15
4142	A1969	6k bister & multi	22	15
4143	A1969	10k bister & multi	40	15
4144	A1969	12k bister & multi	42	15
4145	A1969	14k bister & multi	50	15
4146	A1969	16k bister & multi	55	15
4147	A1969	20k bister & multi	80	15
		Nos. 4141-4147 (7)	2.94	
		Set value		80

Souvenir Sheet
Perf. 12
4148	A1969	50k multicolored	2.00	1.00

Foreign paintings in Russian museums.

Pablo Picasso (1881-1973), Painter — A1970

1973, Dec. 20   **Photo.**   **Perf. 12x11½**
4149	A1970	6k gold, slate grn & red	15	15

Organ Pipes and Dome, Riga — A1971

Designs: No. 4151, Small Trakai Castle, Lithuania. No. 4152, Great Sea Gate, Tallinn, Estonia. 10k, Town Hall and "Old Thomas" weather vane, Tallinn.

1973, Dec. 20   **Engr.**   **Perf. 12x12½**
4150	A1971	4k blk, red & slate grn	15	15
4151	A1971	4k gray, red & buff	15	15
4152	A1971	4k black, red & grn	15	15
4153	A1971	10k sep, grn, red & blk	24	15
		Set value	45	22

Architecture of the Baltic area.

I. G. Petrovsky A1972

L. A. Artsimovich A1973

Portraits: No. 4154, I. G. Petrovsky (1901-1973), mathematician, rector of Moscow State University. No. 4155, L. A. Artsimovich (1909-1973), physician, academician. No. 4156, K. D. Ushinsky (1824-1874), teacher. No. 4157, M. D. Millionschikov (1913-1973), vice president of Academy of Sciences.

1973-74   **Photo.**   **Perf. 11½**
4154	A1972	4k orange & multi	15	15
4155	A1973	4k blk brn & olive	15	15

Engr.
Perf. 12½x12
4156	A1973	4k multicolored	15	15

Litho.
Perf. 12
4157	A1973	4k multicolored	15	15
		Set value	28	20

Issue dates: No. 4154, Dec. 28, 1973. Others, Feb. 6, 1974.

Flags of India and USSR, Red Fort, Taj Mahal and Kremlin — A1974

Design: No. 4162, Flags of Cuba and USSR, José Marti Monument, Moncada Barracks and Kremlin.

1973-74   **Litho.**   *Perf. 12*
4161	A1974	4k lt ultra & multi	15	15
4162	A1974	4k lt green & multi ('74)	15	15
		Set value	15	15

Visit of General Secretary Leonid I. Brezhnev to India and Cuba. Nos. 4161-4162 each printed with se-tenant label with different statements by Brezhnev in Russian and Hindi, and Russian and Spanish respectively.

Red Star, Soldier, Newspaper — A1975

1974, Jan. 1   **Photo.**   *Perf. 11x11½*
4166	A1975	4k gold, red & black	15	15

50th anniversary of the Red Star newspaper.

Victory Monument, Peter-Paul Fortress, Statue of Peter I — A1976

1974, Jan. 16   **Litho.**   *Perf. 11½*
4167	A1976	4k multicolored	15	15

30th anniversary of the victory over the Germans near Leningrad.

Oil Workers, Refinery A1977

Comecon Building A1978

1974, Jan. 16   **Photo.**   *Perf. 11½*
4168	A1977	4k dull blue, red & blk	15	15

10th anniversary of the Tyumen oilfields.

1974, Jan. 16   **Photo.**   *Perf. 11½*
4169	A1977	16k red brn, olive & red	35	25

25th anniversary of the Council for Mutual Economic Assistance.

Skaters and Rink, Medeo A1979

1974, Jan. 28
4170	A1979	6k slate, brn red & blue	15	15

European Women's Skating Championships, Medeo, Alma-Ata.

Art Palace, Leningrad, Academy, Moscow A1980

1974, Jan. 30   **Photo. & Engr.**
4171	A1980	10k multicolored	35	25

25th anniversary of the Academy of Sciences of the USSR.

3rd Winter Spartiakad Emblem A1981

Young People and Emblem A1982

1974, Mar. 20   **Photo.**   *Perf. 11½*
4172	A1981	10k gold & multi	35	25

Third Winter Spartiakad.

1974, Mar. 20   **Photo. & Engr.**
4173	A1982	4k multicolored	15	15

Youth scientific-technical work.

Azerbaijan Theater — A1983

1974, Mar. 20   **Photo.**   *Perf. 11½*
4174	A1983	6k org, red brn & brn	30	25

Centenary of Azerbaijan Theater.

Meteorological Satellite "Meteor" A1984

Cosmonauts V. G. Lazarev and O. G. Makarov and Soyuz 12 — A1985

Design: No. 4177, Cosmonauts P. I. Klimuk and V. V. Lebedev, and Soyuz 13.

1974, Mar. 27   *Perf. 11½*
4175	A1984	6k violet & multi	15	15

Perf. 12x11½
4176	A1985	10k grnsh blue & multi	35	15
4177	A1985	10k dull yel & multi	35	15
		Set value		18

Cosmonauts' Day.

Odessa by Moonlight, by Aivazovski — A1986

Seascapes by Aivazovski: 4k, Battle of Chesma, 1848, vert. 6k, St. George's Monastery. 10k, Stormy Sea. 12k, Rainbow (shipwreck). 16k, Shipwreck. 50k, Portrait of Aivazovski, by Kramskoy, vert.

Perf. 12x11½, 11½x12
1974, Mar. 30   **Litho.**
4178	A1986	2k gray & multi	15	15
4179	A1986	4k gray & multi	16	15
4180	A1986	6k gray & multi	35	15
4181	A1986	10k gray & multi	50	15
4182	A1986	12k gray & multi	55	15
4183	A1986	16k gray & multi	85	24
		Nos. 4178-4183 (6)	2.56	
		Set value		60

Souvenir Sheet
4184	A1986	50k multi	1.75	90

Ivan Konstantinovich Aivazovski (1817-1900), marine painter. Sheets of Nos. 4178-4183 each contain 2 labels with commemorative inscriptions. See Nos. 4230-4234.

Young Man and Woman, Banner A1987

1974, Mar. 30   **Litho.**   *Perf. 12½x12*
4185	A1987	4k red, yel & brown	15	15

17th Cong. of the Young Communist League.

Lenin, by V. E. Tsigal A1988

1974, Mar. 30
4186	A1988	4k yel, red & brown	15	15

50th anniversary of naming the Komsomol (Young Communist League) after Lenin.

Souvenir Sheet

Lenin at the Telegraph, by Igor E. Grabar — A1989

1974, Apr. 16   **Litho.**   *Perf. 12*
4187	A1989	50k multicolored	1.50	90

104th anniv. of the birth of Lenin.

Rainbow, Swallow over Clouds — A1990

Congress Emblem and Clover — A1991

Designs (EXPO '74 Emblem and): 6k, Fish in water. 10k, Crystal. 16k, Rose. 20k, Fawn. 50k, Infant.

1974, Apr. 24   **Photo.**   *Perf. 11½*
4188	A1990	4k lilac & multi	15	15
4189	A1990	6k multicolored	20	15
4190	A1990	10k multicolored	32	15
4191	A1990	16k blue & multi	48	15
4192	A1990	20k citron & multi	55	16
		Nos. 4188-4192 (5)	1.70	
		Set value		52

Souvenir Sheet
Litho.
Perf. 12x12½
4193	A1990	50k blue & multi	1.50	80

EXPO '74 World's Fair, theme "Preserve the Environment," Spokane, WA, May 4-Nov. 4.

1974, May 7   **Photo.**   *Perf. 11½*
4194	A1991	4k green & multi	15	15

12th International Congress on Meadow Cultivation, Moscow, 1974.

"Cobblestones, Weapons of the Proletariat," by I. D. Shadra A1992

1974, May 7
4195	A1992	4k gold, red & olive	15	15

50th anniversary of the Lenin Central Revolutionary Museum of the USSR.

Saiga — A1993

Fauna of USSR: 3k, Koulan (wild ass). 4k, Desman. 6k, Sea lion. 10k, Greenland whale.

1974, May 22   **Litho.**   *Perf. 11½*
4196	A1993	1k olive & multi	15	15
4197	A1993	3k green & multi	15	15
4198	A1993	4k multicolored	20	15
4199	A1993	6k multicolored	32	15
4200	A1993	10k muiticolored	50	15
		Nos. 4196-4200 (5)	1.32	
		Set value		30

Peter Ilich Tchaikovsky A1994

1974, May 22   **Photo.**   *Perf. 11½*
4201	A1994	6k multicolored	25	20

5th International Tchaikovsky Competition, Moscow.

Souvenir Sheet

Aleksander S. Pushkin, by O. A.
Kiprensky — A1995

1974, June 4   Litho.   Imperf.
4202 A1995 50k multicolored   1.75 80

Aleksander S. Pushkin (1799-1837).

Marshal Type of 1973

Designs: #4203, Marshal F. I. Tolbukhin (1894-1949); #4204, Admiral I. S. Isakov (1894-1967); #4205, Marshal S. M. Budenny (1883-1973).

1974   Engr.   Perf. 12
4203 A1962 4k olive green   15 15
4204 A1962 4k indigo   15 15
4205 A1962 4k slate green   15 15
    Set value   20 15

Issue dates: No. 4203, June 5; No. 4204, July 18; No. 4205, Aug. 20.

Stanislavski and Nemirovich-
Danchenko — A1996

1974, June 12   Litho.   Perf. 12
4211 A1996 10k yel, black & dk red   35 15

75th anniv. of the Moscow Arts Theater.

Runner, Track,
Open Book
A1997

1974, June 12   Photo.   Perf. 11½
4212 A1997 4k multicolored   15 15

13th Natl. School Spartakiad, Alma-Ata.

Railroad
Car — A1998

1974, June 12
4213 A1998 4k multicolored   30 25

Egorov Railroad Car Factory, cent.

Victory   Liberation
Monument,   Monument,
Minsk — A1999   Poltava — A2000

Design: No. 4215, Monument and Government House, Kiev.

1974, June 20
4214 A1999 4k violet, black & yel   15 15
4215 A1999 4k blue, black & yel   15 15
    Set value   15 15

30th anniversary of liberation of Byelorussia (No. 4214), and of Ukraine (No. 4215).
    Issue dates: #4214, June 20; #4215, July 18.

Automotive Type of 1973

Designs: 2k, GAZ AA truck, 1932. 3k, GAZ 03-30 bus, 1933. 4k, Zis 5 truck, 1933. 14k, Zis 8 bus, 1934. 16k, Zis 101 car, 1936.

1974, June 20   Perf. 12x11½
4216 A1968 2k brown & multi   15 15
4217 A1968 3k multicolored   15 15
4218 A1968 4k orange & multi   15 15
4219 A1968 14k multicolored   50 15
4220 A1968 16k multicolored   60 15
    Nos. 4216-4220 (5)   1.55
    Set value   40

Soviet automotive industry.

1974, July 7   Perf. 11½
4221 A2000 4k dull red & sepia   15 15

800th anniversary of city of Poltava.

Nike
Monument,
Warsaw and
Polish Flag
A2001

1974, July 7   Litho.   Perf. 12½x12
4222 A2001 6k olive & red   15 15

Polish People's Republic, 30th anniversary.

Mine Layer — A2002

Soviet Warships: 4k, Landing craft. 6k, Anti-submarine destroyer and helicopter. 16k, Anti-submarine cruiser.

Engraved and Photogravure
1974, July 25   Perf. 11½x12
4223 A2002 3k multicolored   15 15
4224 A2002 4k multicolored   16 15
4225 A2002 6k multicolored   40 15
4226 A2002 16k multicolored   75 15
    Set value   32

Pentathlon
A2003

1974, Aug. 7   Photo.   Perf. 11½
4227 A2003 16k gold, blue & brown   50 25

World Pentathlon Championships, Moscow.

Portrait Type of 1973

Portraits: No. 4228, Dimitri Ulyanov (1874-1943). Soviet official and Lenin's brother. No. 4229, V. Menzhinsky (1874-1934), Soviet official.

1974, Aug. 7   Engr.   Perf. 12½x12
4228 A1960 4k slate green   25 20
Litho.
Perf. 12x11½
4229 A1960 4k rose lake   25 20

Painting Type of 1974

Russian paintings: 4k, Lilac, by W. Kontchalovski. 6k, "Towards the Wind" (sailboats), by E.

Kalnins. 10k, "Spring" (girl and landscape), by O. Zardarjan. 16k, Northern Harbor, G. Nissky. 20k, Kirghiz Girl, by S. Tchnikov, vert.

Perf. 12x11½, 11½x12
1974, Aug. 20   Litho.
4230 A1986 4k gray & multi   15 15
4231 A1986 6k gray & multi   18 15
4232 A1986 10k gray & multi   35 15
4233 A1986 16k gray & multi   52 15
4234 A1986 20k gray & multi   75 16
    Nos. 4230-4234 (5)   1.95
    Set value   50

Printed in sheets of 18 stamps and 2 labels.

Page of First   Monument,
Russian   Russian and
Primer — A2004   Romanian
                       Flags — A2005

1974, Aug. 20   Photo.   Perf. 11½
4235 A2004 4k black, red & gold   15 15

1st printed Russian primer, 400th anniv.

1974, Aug. 23
4236 A2005 6k dk blue, red & yel   15 15

Romania's liberation from Fascist rule, 30th anniversary.

Vitebsk
A2006

1974, Sept. 4   Litho.   Perf. 12
4237 A2006 4k dk car & olive   15 15

Millennium of city of Vitebsk.

Kirghiz Republic
A2007

50th Anniv. of Founding of Republics (Flags, industrial and agricultural themes): No. 4239, Moldavia. No. 4240, Turkmen. No. 4241, Uzbek. No. 4242, Tadzhik.

1974, Sept. 4   Perf. 11½x11
4238 A2007 4k vio blue & multi   15 15
4239 A2007 4k maroon & multi   15 15
4240 A2007 4k yellow & multi   15 15
4241 A2007 4k green & multi   15 15
4242 A2007 4k lt blue & multi   15 15
    Set value   50 25

Arms and Flag of
Bulgaria — A2008

Photogravure and Engraved
1974, Sept. 4   Perf. 11½
4243 A2008 6k gold & multi   15 15

30th anniv. of the Bulgarian revolution.

Arms of DDR
and Soviet
War Memorial,
Treptow
A2009

1974, Sept. 4   Photo.
4244 A2009 6k multicolored   15 15

German Democratic Republic, 25th anniv.

Souvenir Sheet

Soviet Stamps and Exhibition
Poster — A2010

1974, Sept. 4   Litho.   Perf. 12x12½
4245 A2010 50k multicolored   7.50 3.00

3rd Cong. of the Phil. Soc. of the USSR.

Maly State
Theater — A2011

1974, Oct. 3   Photo.   Perf. 11x11½
4246 A2011 4k red, black & gold   15 15

150th anniversary of the Lenin Academic Maly State Theater, Moscow.

"Guests from Overseas," by N. K.
Roerich — A2012

1974, Oct. 3   Litho.   Perf. 12
4247 A2012 6k multicolored   15 15

Nicholas Konstantin Roerich (1874-1947), painter and sponsor of Roerich Pact and Banner of Peace.

UPU Monument,
Bern, and Arms
of
USSR — A2013

Development of Postal Service — A2014

UPU Cent: No. 4248, Ukrainian coat of arms, letters, UPU emblem and headquarters, Bern. No. 4249, Arms of Byelorussia, UPU emblem, letters, stagecoach and rocket.

Photogravure and Engraved

1974, Oct. 9			**Perf. 12x11½**	
4248	A2013	10k red & multi	35	15
4249	A2013	10k red & multi	35	15
4250	A2013	10k red & multi	35	15
		Set value		30

Souvenir Sheet
Typo.
Perf. 11½x12

4251	A2014	Sheet of 3	7.50	3.00
a.		30k Jet and UPU emblem	2.00	80
b.		30k Mail coach and UPU emblem	2.00	80
c.		40k UPU emblem	2.00	80

Order of Labor, 1st, 2nd and 3rd Grade A2015

KAMAZ Truck Leaving Kama Plant — A2016

Design: #4254, Nurek Hydroelectric Plant.

1974, Oct. 16		**Litho.**	**Perf. 12½x12**	
4252	A2015	4k multicolored	15	15
4253	A2016	4k multicolored	15	15
4254	A2016	4k multicolored	15	15
		Set value	20	15

Space Stations Mars 4-7 over Mars — A2017

P. R. Popovitch, Y. P. Artyukhin and Soyuz 14 — A2018

Design: No. 4257, Cosmonauts G. V. Sarafanov and L. S. Demin, Soyuz 15, horiz.

Perf. 12x11½, 11½

1974, Oct. 28			**Photo.**	
4255	A2017	6k multicolored	25	15
4256	A2018	10k multicolored	38	15
4257	A2018	10k multicolored	38	15
		Set value		25

Russian explorations of Mars (6k); flight of Soyuz 14 (No. 4256) and of Soyuz 15, Aug. 26-28 (No. 4257).

Mongolian Flag and Arms A2019

1974, Nov. 14		**Photo.**	**Perf. 11½**	
4258	A2019	6k gold & multi	15	15

Mongolian People's Republic, 50th anniv.

Guards' Ribbon, Estonian Government Building, Tower — A2020

1974, Nov. 14				
4259	A2020	4k multicolored	15	15

Liberation of Estonia, 30th anniversary.

Tanker, Passenger and Cargo Ships A2021

1974, Nov. 14		**Typo.**	**Perf. 12½x12**	
4260	A2021	4k multicolored	15	15

USSR Merchant Marine, 50th anniversary.

Spasski Tower Clock A2022

1974, Nov. 14		**Litho.**	**Perf. 12**	
4261	A2022	4k multicolored	30	15

New Year 1975.

The Fishmonger, by Pieters A2023

Paintings: 4k, The Marketplace, by Beukelaer, 1564, horiz. 10k, A Drink of Lemonade, by Gerard Terborch. 14k, Girl at Work, by Gabriel Metsu. 16k, Saying Grace, by Jean Chardin. 20k, The Spoiled Child, by Jean Greuze. 50k, Self-portrait, by Jacques Louis David.

Perf. 12x12½, 12½x12

1974, Nov. 20			**Litho.**	
4262	A2023	4k bister & multi	15	15
4263	A2023	6k bister & multi	25	15
4264	A2023	10k bister & multi	35	15
4265	A2023	14k bister & multi	50	15
4266	A2023	16k bister & multi	55	20
4267	A2023	20k bister & multi	75	30
		Nos. 4262-4267 (6)	2.55	
		Set value		88

Souvenir Sheet
Perf. 12

4268	A2023	50k multicolored	1.50	75

Foreign paintings in Russian museums. Printed in sheets of 16 stamps and 4 labels.

Morning Glory — A2024

Ivan Nikitin — A2025

Designs: Flora of the USSR.

1974, Nov. 20			**Perf. 12x12½**	
4269	A2024	1k red brn & multi	15	15
4270	A2024	2k green & multi	15	15
4271	A2024	4k multicolored	16	15
4272	A2024	10k brown & multi	50	15
4273	A2024	12k dk blue & multi	55	15
		Nos. 4269-4273 (5)	1.51	
		Set value		40

1974, Dec. 11		**Photo.**	**Perf. 11½**	
4274	A2025	4k gray green, grn & blk	30	25

Ivan S. Nikitin (1824-1861), poet.

Leningrad Mint — A2026

Photogravure and Engraved

1974, Dec. 11			**Perf. 11**	
4275	A2026	6k silver & multi	15	15

250th anniversary of the Leningrad Mint.

Mozhajsky Plane, 1882 — A2027

Early Russian Aircraft: No. 4277, Grizidubov-N biplane, 1910. No. 4278, Russia-A, 1910. No. 4279, Russian Vityaz (Sikorsky), 1913. No. 4280, Grigorovich flying boat, 1914.

1974, Dec. 25		**Photo.**	**Perf. 11½x12**	
4276	A2027	6k olive & multi	16	15
4277	A2027	6k ultra & multi	16	15
4278	A2027	6k magenta & multi	16	15
4279	A2027	6k red & multi	16	15
4280	A2027	6k brown & multi	16	15
		Nos. 4276-4280 (5)	80	
		Set value		35

Russian aircraft history, 1882-1914.

Sports and Sport Buildings, Moscow — A2028

1974, Dec. 25			**Perf. 11½**	
4281	A2028	Sheet of 4	2.50	50
a.		10k Woman gymnast	42	15
b.		10k Running	42	15
c.		10k Soccer	42	15
d.		10k Canoeing	42	15

Moscow preparing for Summer Olympic Games, 1980.

Rotary Press, Masthead A2029

1975, Jan. 20				
4282	A2029	4k multicolored	15	15

Komsomolskaya Pravda newspaper, 50th anniv.

Masthead and Pioneer Emblems A2030

Spartakiad Emblem and Skiers A2031

1975, Jan. 20				
4283	A2030	4k red, blk & silver	15	15

50th anniversary of the newspaper Pioneers' Pravda.

1975, Jan. 20				
4284	A2031	4k blue & multi	15	15

8th Winter Spartakiad of USSR Trade Unions.

Games' Emblem, Hockey Player and Skier A2032

1975, Jan. 20				
4285	A2032	16k multicolored	50	25

5th Winter Spartakiad of Friendly Armies, Feb. 23-Mar. 1.

Republic Anniversaries Type of 1970

Design (Hammer-Sickle Emblem and): No. 4286, Landscape and produce.

1975, Jan. 24		**Engr.**	**Perf. 12x12½**	
4286	A1794	4k green	30	15

50th anniversary of Karakalpak Autonomous Soviet Socialist Republic.

David, by Michelangelo — A2033

Michelangelo,
Self-portrait
A2034

Designs (Works by Michelangelo): 6k, Squatting
Boy. 10k, Rebellious Slave. 14k, The Creation of
Adam. 20k, Staircase, Laurentian Library, Florence.
30k, The Last Judgment.

Lithographed and Engraved
1975, Feb. 27   Perf. 12½x12

4296	A2033	4k slate grn & grn	15 15
4297	A2033	6k red brn & bister	22 15
4298	A2033	10k slate grn & grn	42 20
a.		Min. sheet, 2 each #4296-4298	1.50 65
4299	A2033	14k red brn & bister	65 20
4300	A2033	20k slate grn & grn	90 40
4301	A2033	30k red brn & bister	1.10 60
a.		Min. sheet, 2 each #4299-4301	5.00 2.00
		Nos. 4296-4301 (6)	3.44 1.70

Souvenir Sheet
Perf. 12x11½

4302 A2034 50k gold & multi   3.00 80

Michelangelo Buonarroti (1475-1564), Italian
sculptor, painter and architect. Issued only in the
min. sheets of 6.

Mozhajski, Early Plane and Supersonic Jet
TU-144 — A2035

1975, Feb. 27   Photo.   Perf. 12x11½
4303 A2035 6k violet blue & ocher   15 15

A. F. Mozhajski (1825-1890), pioneer aircraft
designer, birth sesquicentennial.

"Metric
System"
A2036

1975, Mar. 14   Perf. 11½
4304 A2036 6k blk, vio blue & org   15 15

Intl. Meter Convention, Paris, 1875, cent.

Spartakiad
Emblem and
Sports
A2037

1975, Mar. 14
4305 A2037 6k red, silver & black   15 15

6th Summer Spartakiad.

Liberation
Monument,
Parliament,
Arms — A2038

Charles Bridge
Towers, Arms
and
Flags — A2039

1975, Mar. 14
4306	A2038	6k gold & multi	15 15
4307	A2039	6k gold & multi	15 15
		Set value	15

30th anniv. of liberation from fascism, Hungary
(#4306) & Czechoslovakia (#4307).

Flags of France and
USSR
A2040

Yuri A. Gagarin,
by L. Kerbel
A2041

A. V. Filipchenko, N.N. Rukavishnikov,
Russo-American Space Emblem, Soyuz
16 — A2042

1975, Mar. 25   Litho.   Perf. 12
4308 A2040 6k lilac & multi   15 15

50th anniv. of the establishment of diplomatic
relations between France and USSR, 1st foreign recognition of Soviet State.

Perf. 11½x12, 12x11½
1975, Mar. 28   Photo.
Cosmonauts' Day: 10k, A. A. Gubarev, G. M.
Grechko aboard Soyuz 17 & orbital station Salyut 4.

4309	A2041	6k blue, silver & red	20 15
4310	A2042	10k black, blue & red	40 15
4311	A2042	16k multicolored	50 15
		Set value	22

Warsaw Treaty
Members'
Flags — A2043

1975, Apr. 16   Litho.   Perf. 12
4312 A2043 6k multicolored   30 15

Signing of the Warsaw Treaty (Bulgaria, Czechoslovakia, German Democratic Rep., Hungary,
Poland, Romania, USSR), 20th anniv.

Lenin on Steps
of Winter
Palace, by V. G.
Zyplakow
A2044

1975, Apr. 22   Perf. 12x12½
4313 A2044 4k multicolored   30 15

105th anniversary of the birth of Lenin.

Communications Emblem and Exhibition
Pavilion — A2045

1975, Apr. 22   Perf. 11½
4314 A2045 6k ultra, red & silver   15 15

International Communications Exhibition,
Sokolniki Park, Moscow, May 1975.

Lenin and Red Flag
A2046

War Memorial,
Berlin-Treptow
A2048

Order of Victory — A2047

1975, Apr. 22   Typo.   Perf. 12
4315	A2046	4k shown	15 15
4316	A2046	4k Eternal Flame and guard	15 15
4317	A2046	4k Woman munitions worker	15 15
4318	A2046	4k Partisans	15 15
4319	A2046	4k Soldier destroying swastika	15 15
4320	A2046	4k Soldier with gun and banner	15 15
		Set value	60 30

Souvenir Sheet
Litho., Typo. & Photo.
Imperf
4321 A2047 50k multicolored   5.00 3.00

World War II victory, 30th anniversary.

1975, Apr. 25   Litho.   Perf. 12x12½
4322 A2048 6k buff & multi   15 15

Souvenir Sheet
4323 A2048 50k dull blue & multi   3.00 60

Socfilex 75 Intl. Phil. Exhib. honoring 30th
anniv. of WWII victory, Moscow, May 8-18.

Soyuz-Apollo Docking Emblem and
Painting by Cosmonaut A. A.
Leonov — A2049

1975, May 8   Photo.   Perf. 12x11½
4324 A2049 20k multicolored   75 35

Russo-American space cooperation.

Automobile Type of 1973
Designs: 2k, GAZ-M-I car, 1936. 3k, 5-ton
truck, YAG-6, 1936. 4k, ZIZ-16, autobus, 1938.
12k, KIM-10 car, 1940. 16k, GAZ-67B jeep, 1943.

1975, May 23   Photo.   Perf. 12x11½
4325	A1968	2k dp org & multi	15 15
4326	A1968	3k green & multi	15 15
4327	A1968	4k dk green & multi	15 15
4328	A1968	12k maroon & multi	30 15
4329	A1968	16k olive & multi	45 15
		Set value	1.00 36

Canal, Emblem,
Produce — A2050

1975, May 23   Perf. 11½
4330 A2050 6k multicolored   15 15

9th Intl. Congress on Irrigation and Drainage,
Moscow, and International Commission on Irrigation and Drainage, 25th anniv..

Flags and
Arms of
Poland and
USSR,
Factories
A2051

1975, May 23
4331 A2051 6k multicolored   15 15

Treaty of Friendship, Cooperation and Mutual
Assistance between Poland & USSR, 30th anniv.

Man in Space
and
Earth — A2052

1975, May 23
4332 A2052 6k multicolored   15 15

First man walking in space, Lt. Col. Alexei Leonov, 10th anniversary.

Yakov M. Sverdlov
(1885-1919), Organizer
and Early Member of
Communist
Party — A2053

1975, June 4
4333 A2053 4k multicolored   30 15

Congress, Emblem, Forest and — A2054

1975, June 4
4334 A2054 6k multicolored   15 15

8th International Congress for Conservation of Plants, Moscow.

Symbolic Flower with Plants and Emblem A2055

1975, June 20   Litho.   Perf. 11½
4335 A2055 6k multicolored   15 15

12th International Botanical Congress.

Souvenir Sheet

UN Emblem A2056

1975, June 20   Photo.   Perf. 11½x12
4336 A2056 50k gold & blue   2.50 1.00

30th anniversary of United Nations.

Globe and Film — A2057

1975, June 20   Photo.   Perf. 11½
4337 A2057 6k multicolored   15 15

9th Intl. Film Festival, Moscow, 1975.

Soviet and American Astronauts and Flags — A2058

Apollo and Soyuz After Link-up and Earth — A2059

Soyuz Launch — A2060

Designs: No. 4340, Spacecraft before link-up, earth and project emblem. 50k, Soviet Mission Control Center.

1975, July 15   Litho.   Perf. 11½
4338 A2058 10k multicolored   45 15
4339 A2059 12k multicolored   65 18
4340 A2059 12k multicolored   65 18
a.   Vert. pair, #4339-4340   1.40 38
4341 A2060 16k multicolored   75 38

Souvenir Sheet
Photo.
Perf. 12x11½
4342 A2058 50k multicolored   2.75 1.25

Apollo-Soyuz space test project (Russo-American space cooperation), launching, July 15; link-up July 17.

No. 4342 contains one 50x21mm stamp.
See US Nos. 1569-1570.

Sturgeon, Caspian Sea, Oceanexpo 75 Emblem — A2061

Designs (Oceanexpo 75 Emblem and): 4k, Saltwater shell, Black Sea. 6k, Eel, Baltic Sea. 10k, Sea duck, Arctic Sea. 16k, Crab, Far Eastern waters. 20k, Chrisipther (fish), Pacific Ocean.

1975, July 22   Photo.   Perf. 11
4343 A2061 3k multicolored   15 15
4344 A2061 4k multicolored   15 15
4345 A2061 6k green & multi   32 20
4346 A2061 10k dk blue & multi   45 28
4347 A2061 16k purple & multi   65 30
4348 A2061 20k multicolored   80 65
Nos. 4343-4348 (6)   2.52 1.73
Souvenir Sheet
Perf. 12x11½
4349   Sheet of 2   2.50 90
a.   A2061 30k Dolphin rising   1.00 30
b.   A2061 30k Dolphin diving   1.00 30

Oceanexpo 75, 1st Intl. Oceanographic Exhib., Okinawa, July 20, 1975-Jan. 1976. No. 4349 contains 55x25mm stamps.

Parade, Red Square, 1941, by K. F. Yuon — A2062

Paintings: 2k, Morning of Industrial Moscow, by Yuon. 6k, Soldiers Inspecting Captured Artillery, by Lansere. 10k, Excavating Metro Tunnel, by Lansere. 16k, Pushkin and His Wife at Court Ball, by Ulyanov, vert. 20k, De Lauriston at Kutuzov's Headquarters, by Ulyanov.

1975, July 22   Perf. 12½x11½
                                    Litho.
4350 A2062 1k gray & multi   15 15
4351 A2062 2k gray & multi   15 15
4352 A2062 6k gray & multi   18 15
4353 A2062 10k gray & multi   35 15
4354 A2062 16k gray & multi   65 22
4355 A2062 20k gray & multi   75 30
Nos. 4350-4355 (6)   2.23
Set value   75

Konstantin F. Yuon (1875-1958), Yevgeni Y. Lansere (1875-1946), Nikolai P. Ulyanov (1875-1949).

Finlandia Hall, Map of Europe, Laurel A2063

Chuyrlenis, Waves and Lighthouse A2064

1975, Aug. 18   Photo.   Perf. 11½
4356 A2063 6k brt blue, gold & blk   15 15

European Security and Cooperation Conference, Helsinki, July 30-Aug. 1. Printed se-tenant with label with quotation by Leonid I. Brezhnev, first secretary of Communist party.

1975, Aug. 20   Photo. & Engr.
4357 A2064 4k grn, indigo & gold   50 15

M. K. Chuyrlenis, Lithuanian composer, birth centenary.

Avetik Isaakyan, by Martiros Sar'yan A2065

1975, Aug. 20   Litho.   Perf. 12x12½
4358 A2065 4k multicolored   15 15

Isaakyan (1875-1957), Armenian poet.

Jacques Duclos A2066

al-Farabi A2067

1975, Aug. 20   Photo.   Perf. 11½x12
4359 A2066 6k maroon & silver   15 15

Duclos (1896-1975), French labor leader.

1975, Aug. 20   Perf. 11½
4360 A2067 6k grnsh blue, brn & bis   15 15

Nasr al-Farabi (870?-950), Arab philosopher.

Male Ruffs A2068

1975, Aug. 25   Litho.   Perf. 12½x12
4361 A2068 1k shown   15 15
4362 A2068 4k Altai roebuck   15 15
4363 A2068 6k Siberian marten   18 15
4364 A2068 10k Old squaw (duck)   38 15
4365 A2068 16k Badger   55 15
Nos. 4361-4365 (5)   1.41
Set value   42

Berezina River and Stolby wildlife reservations, 50th anniversary.

A2069

A2070

Designs: #4366, Flags of USSR, North Korea, arms of N. K., Liberation monument, Pyongyang. #4367, Flags of USSR, North Viet Nam, arms of N.V., industrial development.

1975, Aug. 28   Perf. 12
4366 A2069 6k multicolored   30 15
4367 A2070 6k multicolored   30 15
Set value   15

Liberation of North Korea from Japanese occupation (#4366); and establishment of Democratic Republic of Viet Nam (#4367), 30th anniys.

P. Klimuk and V. Sevastyanov, Soyuz 18 and Salyut 4 Docking — A2071

1975, Sept. 12   Photo.   Perf. 12x11½
4368 A2071 10k ultra, blk & dp org   30 15

Docking of space ship Soyuz 18 and space station Salyut 4.

S. A. Esenin and Birches A2072

Photogravure and Engraved
1975, Sept. 12   Perf. 11½
4369 A2072 6k brown & ocher   15 15

Sergei A. Esenin (1895-1925), poet.

Standardization Symbols A2073

1975, Sept. 12   Photo.   Perf. 11½
4370 A2073 4k red & multi   15 15

USSR Committee for Standardization of Communications Ministry, 50th anniversary.

Karakul Lamb
A2074

1975, Sept. 22   Photo.   Perf. 11½
4371 A2074 6k black, yel & grn   15 15

3rd International Symposium on astrakhan production, Samarkand, Sept. 22-27.

Dr. M. P.   Exhibition Emblem
Konchalovsky   A2076
A2075

1975, Sept. 30   Perf. 11½x12
4372 A2075 4k brown & red   15 15

Konchalovsky (1875-1942), physician.

1975, Sept. 30   Perf. 11½
4373 A2076 4k deep blue & red   15 15

3rd All-Union Youth Phil. Exhib., Erevan.

IWY Emblem and   Yugoslavian Flag
Rose   and Parliament
A2077   A2078

1975, Sept. 30   Litho.   Perf. 12x11½
4374 A2077 6k multicolored   15 15

International Women's Year 1975.

1975, Sept. 30   Photo.   Perf. 11½
4375 A2078 6k gold, red & blue   15 15

Republic of Yugoslavia, 30th anniv.

Illustration from   Mikhail
1938 Edition, by   Ivanovich
V. A. Favorsky   Kalinin
A2079   A2080

1975, Oct. 20   Typo.   Perf. 12
4376 A2079 4k buff, red & black   30 15

175th anniversary of the 1st edition of the old Russian saga "Slovo o polku Igoreve."

1975, Oct. 20   Engr.   Perf. 12

Portrait: No. 4378, Anatoli Vasilievich Lunacharski.

4377 A2080 4k sepia   15 15
4378 A2080 4k sepia   15 15
      Set value   20 15

Kalinin (1875-1946), chairman of Central Executive Committee and Presidium of Supreme Soviet;

Lunacharski (1875-1933), writer, commissar for education.

Hand Holding Torch and Lenin
Quotation — A2081

1975, Oct. 20   Engr.
4379 A2081 4k red & olive   15 15

First Russian Revolution (1905), 70th anniv.

Building Baikal-
Amur Railroad
A2082

Novolipetsk   Nevynomyssk
Metallurgical   Chemical Plant,
Plant   Fertilizer Formula
A2083   A2084

1975, Oct. 30   Photo.   Perf. 11½
4380 A2082 4k gold & multi   15 15
4381 A2083 4k red, gray & sl green   15 15
4382 A2084 4k red, blue & silver   15 15
      Set value   30 15

58th anniversary of October Revolution.

Bas-relief of Decembrists and "Decembrists
at the Senate Square," by D. N.
Kardovsky — A2085

1975, Nov. 12   Litho. & Engr.
4383 A2085 4k gray & multi   15 15

Sesquicentennial of Decembrist rising.

Star and
"1976" — A2086

1975, Nov. 12   Litho.   Perf. 12x12½
4384 A2086 4k green & multi   35 15

New Year 1976.

Village Street, by
F. A. Vasilev
A2087

Paintings by Vasilev: 4k, Road in Birch Forest. 6k, After the Thunderstorm. 10k, Swamp, horiz. 12k, In the Crimean Mountains. 16k, Meadow, horiz. 50k, Self-portrait.

Perf. 12x12½, 12½x12
1975, Nov. 25
4385 A2087 2k gray & multi   15 15
4386 A2087 4k gray & multi   15 15
4387 A2087 6k gray & multi   30 15
4388 A2087 10k gray & multi   45 15
4389 A2087 12k gray & multi   55 15
4390 A2087 16k gray & multi   70 22
      Nos. 4385-4390 (6)   2.30
      Set value   60

Souvenir Sheet
Perf. 12
4391 A2087 50k gray & multi   2.25 90

Fedor Aleksandrovich Vasilev (1850-1873), landscape painter. Nos. 4385-4390 printed in sheets of 7 stamps and one label.

Landing
Capsule, Venus
Surface, Lenin
Banner
A2088

1975, Dec. 8   Photo.   Perf. 11½
4392 A2088 10k multicolored   35 25

Flights of Soviet interplanetary stations Venera 9 and Venera 10.

Gabriel
Sundoukian
A2089

1975, Dec. 8   Litho.   Perf. 12
4393 A2089 4k multicolored   50 30

Sundoukian (1825-1912), Armenian playright.

Polar Poppies,
Taiga — A2090

Regional Flowers: 6k, Globeflowers, tundra. 10k, Buttercups, oak forest. 12k, Wood anemones, steppe. 16k, Eminium Lehmannii, desert.

Photogravure and Engraved
1975, Dec. 25   Perf. 12x11½
4394 A2090 4k black & multi   15 15
4395 A2090 6k black & multi   22 15
4396 A2090 10k black & multi   32 15
4397 A2090 12k black & multi   40 15
4398 A2090 16k black & multi   50 22
      Nos. 4394-4398 (5)   1.59
      Set value   60

A. L. Mints (1895-1974),
Academician — A2091

1975, Dec. 31   Photo.   Perf. 11½x12
4399 A2091 4k dp brown & gold   15 15

Demon, by A.
Kochupalov
A2092

Paintings: 6k, Vasilisa the Beautiful, by I. Vakurov. 10k, Snow Maiden, by T. Zubkova. 16k, Summer, by K. Kukulieva. 20k, The Fisherman and the Goldfish, by I. Vakurov, horiz.

1975, Dec. 31   Litho.   Perf. 12
4400 A2092 4k bister & multi   15 15
4401 A2092 6k bister & multi   22 15
4402 A2092 10k bister & multi   35 15
4403 A2092 16k bister & multi   45 15
4404 A2092 20k bister & multi   55 25
   a.   Strip of 5, #4400-4404   1.75 60
         Nos. 4400-4404 (5)   1.72
         Set value   56

Palekh Art State Museum, Ivanov Region.

Wilhelm Pieck (1876-
1960), Pres. of German
Democratic
Republic — A2093

1976, Jan. 3   Engr.   Perf. 12½x12
4405 A2093 6k bluish black   20 15

M. E. Saltykov-Shchedrin, by I.N.
Kramskoi — A2094

1976, Jan. 14   Litho.   Perf. 12x12½
4406 A2094 4k multicolored   15 15

Mikhail Evgrafovich Saltykov-Shchedrin (1826-1889), writer and revolutionist.

Congress Emblem A2095

Lenin Statue, Kiev A2096

1976, Feb. 2   Photo.   Perf. 11½
4407 A2095 4k red, gold & mar   15 15

Souvenir Sheet
Perf. 11½x12
4408 A2095 50k red, gold & mar   2.00 65

25th Congress of the Communist Party of the Soviet Union.

1976, Feb. 2   Perf. 11½
4409 A2096 4k red, black & blue   15 15

Ukrainian Communist Party, 25th Congress.

Ice Hockey, Games' Emblem A2097

Designs (Winter Olympic Games' Emblem and): 4k, Cross-country skiing. 6k, Figure skating, pairs. 10k, Speed skating. 20k, Luge. 50k, Winter Olympic Games' emblem, vert.

1976, Feb. 4   Litho.   Perf. 12½x12
4410 A2097 2k multicolored   15 15
4411 A2097 4k multicolored   15 15
4412 A2097 6k multicolored   32 15
4413 A2097 10k multicolored   45 15
4414 A2097 20k multicolored   95 30
   Nos. 4410-4414 (5)   2.02
     Set value   58

Souvenir Sheet
Perf. 12x12½
4415 A2097 50k vio bl, org & red   2.00 1.00

12th Winter Olympic Games, Innsbruck, Austria, Feb. 4-15. No. 4415 contains one stamp; silver and violet blue margin showing designs of Nos. 4410-4414. Size: 90x80mm.

No. 4415 Overprinted in Red
Souvenir Sheet

СЛАВА
СОВЕТСКОМУ
СПОРТУ!

СПОРТСМЕНЫ СССР
ЗАВОЕВАЛИ
13 ЗОЛОТЫХ,
6 СЕРЕБРЯНЫХ,
8 БРОНЗОВЫХ
МЕДАЛЕЙ!

1976, Mar. 24
4416 A2097 50k multicolored   6.00 4.00

Success of Soviet athletes in 12th Winter Olympic Games. Translation of overprint: "Glory to Soviet Sport! The athletes of the USSR have won 13 gold, 6 silver and 8 bronze medals."

K.E. Voroshilov — A2098

1976, Feb. 4   Engr.   Perf. 12
4417 A2098 4k slate green   40 15

Kliment Efremovich Voroshilov (1881-1969), pres. of revolutionary military council, commander of Leningrad front, USSR pres. 1953-60. See Nos. 4487-4488.

Flag over Kremlin Palace of Congresses, Troitskaya Tower — A2099

Photogravure on Gold Foil
1976, Feb. 24   Perf. 12x11½
4418 A2099 20k gold, green & red   4.00 2.00

25th Congress of the Communist Party of the Soviet Union (CPSU).

Lenin on Red Square, by P. Vasiliev — A2100

1976, Mar. 10   Litho.   Perf. 12½x12
4419 A2100 4k yellow & multi   15 15

106th anniversary of the birth of Lenin.

Atom Symbol and Dubna Institute — A2101

1976, Mar. 10   Photo.   Perf. 11½
4420 A2101 6k vio bl, red & silver   16 15

Joint Institute of Nuclear Research, Dubna, 20th anniversary.

Bolshoi Theater — A2102

1976, Mar. 24   Litho.   Perf. 11x11½
4421 A2102 10k yel, blue & dk brn   30 15

Bicentenary of Bolshoi Theater.

Back from the Fair, by Konchalovsky — A2103

Paintings by P. P. Konchalovsky: 2k, The Green Glass. 6k, Peaches. 10k, Meat, Game and Vegetables. 20k, Self-portrait, 1943, vert.

1976, Apr. 6   Perf. 12½x12, 12x12½
4422 A2103 1k yellow & multi   15 15
4423 A2103 2k yellow & multi   15 15
4424 A2103 6k yellow & multi   28 15
4425 A2103 16k yellow & multi   70 16
4426 A2103 20k yellow & multi   85 30
   Nos. 4422-4426 (5)   2.13
     Set value   62

Birth centenary of P. P. Konchalovsky.

Vostok, Salyut-Soyuz Link-up — A2104

Yuri A. Gagarin A2105

Designs: 6k, Meteor and Molniya Satellites, Orbita Ground Communications Center. 10k, Cosmonauts on board Salyut space station and Mars planetary station. 12k, Interkosmos station and Apollo-Soyuz linking.

Lithographed and Engraved
1976, Apr. 12   Perf. 11½
4427 A2104 4k multicolored   16 15
4428 A2104 6k multicolored   22 15
4429 A2104 10k multicolored   35 15
4430 A2104 12k multicolored   55 20
     Set value   48

Souvenir Sheet
Engr.   Perf. 12
4431 A2105 50k black   10.00 2.00

1st manned flight in space, 15th anniv.

I. A. Dzhavakhishvili A2106

Samed Vurgun and Derrick A2107

1976, Apr. 20   Photo.   Perf. 11½x12
4432 A2106 4k multicolored   15 15

Dzhavakhishvili (1876-1940), scientist.

1976, Apr. 20   Perf. 11½
4433 A2107 4k multicolored   15 15

Vurgun (1906-56), natl. poet of Azerbaijan.

USSR Flag, Worker and Farmer Monument — A2108

1976, May 12   Litho.   Perf. 11½x12
4434 A2108 4k multicolored   15 15

1st All-Union Festival of Amateur Artists.

FIP Emblem — A2109

1976, May 12   Photo.   Perf. 11½
4435 A2109 6k ultra & carmine   15 15

Intl. Federation of Philately, 50th anniv.

Souvenir Sheet

V. A. Tropinin, Self-portrait — A2110

1976, May 12   Litho.   Perf. 12
4436 A2110 50k multicolored   2.00 1.00

Vasily Andreevich Tropinin (1776-1857), painter.

Emblem, Dnieper Bridge A2111

Dr. N. N. Burdenko A2112

1976, May 20   Photo.   Perf. 11½
4437 A2111 4k Prus blue, gold & blk   15 15

Bicentenary of Dnepropetrovsk.

1976, May 20   Perf. 11½x12
4438 A2112 4k deep brown & red   15 15

Burdenko (1876-1946), neurosurgeon.

K. A. Trenev (1876-1945), Playwright — A2113

1976, May 20   Perf. 11½
4439 A2113 4k black & multi   15 15

Automobile Type of 1973

Designs: 2k, ZIS-110 passenger car. 3k, GAZ-51 Gorky truck. 4k, GAZ-M-20 Pobeda passenger car. 12k, ZIS-150 Moscow Motor Works truck. 16k, ZIS-154 Moscow Motor Works bus.

1976, June 15   Photo.   Perf. 12x11½
4440 A1968 2k grnsh bl & multi   18 15
4441 A1968 3k bister & multi   20 15
4442 A1968 4k dk blue & multi   20 15

4443	A1968	12k brown & multi	60	15
4444	A1968	16k deep car & multi	80	16
	Nos. 4440-4444 (5)		1.98	
	Set value			42

Canoeing
A2114

Designs (USSR National Olympic Committee Emblem and): 6k, Basketball, vert. 10k, Greco-Roman wrestling. 14k, Women's discus, vert. 16k, Target shooting. 50k, Olympic medal, obverse and reverse.

Perf. 12¹/₂x12, 12x12¹/₂
1976, June 23   **Litho.**

4445	A2114	4k red & multi	15	15
4446	A2114	6k red & multi	18	15
4447	A2114	10k red & multi	45	15
4448	A2114	14k red & multi	60	15
4449	A2114	16k red & multi	65	22
	Nos. 4445-4449 (5)		2.03	
	Set value			60

Souvenir Sheet

| 4450 | A2114 | 50k red & multi | 3.00 | 75 |

21st Olympic Games, Montreal, Canada, July 17-Aug. 1.
For overprint see No. 4472.

Electric Trains, Overpass
A2115

1976, June 23   Photo.   Perf. 11¹/₂

| 4451 | A2115 | 4k multicolored | 15 | 15 |

Electrification of USSR railroads, 50th anniversary.

L. Emilio
Rekabarren
A2116

1976, July 6

| 4452 | A2116 | 6k gold, red & blk | 15 | 15 |

Luis Emilio Rekabarren (1876-1924), founder of Chilean Communist Party.

L. M.
Pavlichenko — A2117

1976, July 6

| 4453 | A2117 | 4k dp brn, silver & yel | 15 | 15 |

Ljudmilla Mikhajlovna Pavlichenko (1916-1974), WWII heroine, Komsomol, War Veterans and Women's Committee member.

New Partner, by
P. A. Fedotov
A2118

Paintings: 4k, The Fastidious Fiancée, horiz. 6k, Aristocrat's Breakfast. 10k, Gamblers, horiz. 16k, The Outing. 50k, Self-portrait.

Perf. 12x12¹/₂, 12¹/₂x12
1976, July 15   **Litho.**

4454	A2118	2k black & multi	15	15
4455	A2118	4k black & multi	15	15
4456	A2118	6k black & multi	20	15
4457	A2118	10k black & multi	45	15
4458	A2118	16k black & multi	65	22
	Nos. 4454-4458 (5)		1.60	
	Set value			50

Souvenir Sheet
Perf. 12

| 4459 | A2118 | 50k multicolored | 4.00 | 75 |

Pavel Andreevich Fedotov (1815-1852), painter. Nos. 4454-4458 each printed in sheets of 20 stamps and center label with black commemorative inscription.

S. S. Nametkin   Squacco Heron
A2119   A2120

1976, July 20   Photo.   Perf. 11¹/₂x12

| 4460 | A2119 | 4k blue, black & buff | 15 | 15 |

Sergei Semenovich Nametkin (1876-1950), organic chemist.

1976, Aug. 18   Litho.   Perf. 12x12¹/₂

Waterfowl: 3k, Arctic loon. 4k, European coot. 6k, Atlantic puffin. 10k, Slender-billed gull.

4465	A2120	1k dk green & multi	15	15
4466	A2120	3k ol green & multi	15	15
4467	A2120	4k orange & multi	15	15
4468	A2120	6k purple & multi	15	15
4469	A2120	10k brt blue & multi	20	15
	Set value		54	35

Nature protection.

Peace
Dove — A2121

1976, Aug. 25   Photo.   Perf. 11¹/₂

| 4470 | A2121 | 4k salmon, gold & blue | 15 | 15 |

2nd Stockholm appeal and movement to stop arms race.

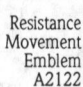

Resistance
Movement
Emblem
A2122

1976, Aug. 25

| 4471 | A2122 | 6k dk blue, black & gold | 15 | 15 |

Intl. Resistance Movement Fed., 25th anniv.

"Industry" — A2126

No. 4450 Overprinted in Gold in Margin
Souvenir Sheet

СПОРТСМЕНЫ
СССР
ЗАВОЕВАЛИ
47 ЗОЛОТЫХ,
43 СЕРЕБРЯНЫХ
И **35** БРОНЗОВЫХ
МЕДАЛЕЙ!

СОВЕТСКОМУ
СПОРТУ
СЛАВА!

The two parts of the overprint have been moved closer together to fit the column.

1976, Aug. 25   Litho.   Perf. 12¹/₂x12

| 4472 | A2114 | 50k red & multi | 4.50 | 75 |

Victories of Soviet athletes in 21st Olympic Games (47 gold, 43 silver and 35 bronze medals).

Flags of India and   UN, UNESCO
USSR — A2123   Emblems, Open
                          Book — A2124

1976, Sept. 8   **Perf. 12**

| 4473 | A2123 | 4k multicolored | 15 | 15 |

Friendship and cooperation between USSR and India.

1976, Sept. 8   Engr.   Perf. 12x12¹/₂

| 4474 | A2124 | 16k multicolored | 40 | 30 |

UNESCO, 30th anniv.

B. V. Volynov, V. M. Zholobov, Star
Circling Globe — A2125

1976, Sept. 8   Photo.   Perf. 12x11¹/₂

| 4475 | A2125 | 10k brn, blue & black | 50 | 35 |

Exploits of Soyuz 21 and Salyut space station.

1976, Sept. 17

4476	A2126	4k shown	15	15
4477	A2126	4k Farm industry	15	15
4478	A2126	4k Science	15	15
4479	A2126	4k Transport & communications	15	15
4480	A2126	4k Intl. cooperation	15	15
	Set value		45	40

25th Congress of the Communist Party of the Soviet Union.

Au (woman), by
I. V. Markichev
A2127

Paintings: 2k, Plower, by I. I. Golikov, horiz. 12k, Firebird, by A. V. Kotuhin, horiz. 14k, Festival, by A. I. Vatagin. 20k, Victory, by I. I. Vakurov.

Perf. 12¹/₂x12, 12x12¹/₂
1976, Sept. 22   **Litho.**

4481	A2127	2k black & multi	20	15
4482	A2127	4k black & multi	25	15
4483	A2127	12k black & multi	1.10	15
4484	A2127	14k black & multi	1.25	15
4485	A2127	20k black & multi	1.65	33
	Nos. 4481-4485 (5)		4.45	
	Set value			70

Palekh Art State Museum, Ivanov Region.

Shostakovich,
Score from
7th
Symphony,
Leningrad
A2128

1976, Sept. 25   Engr.   Perf. 12¹/₂x12

| 4486 | A2128 | 6k dk vio blue | 15 | 15 |

Dimitri Dimitrievich Shostakovich (1906-1975), composer.

Voroshilov Type of 1976

Portraits: #4487, Zhukov. #4488, Rokossovsky.

1976, Oct. 7   Engr.   Perf. 12

4487	A2098	4k slate green	15	15
4488	A2098	4k brown	15	15
	Set value		16	15

Marshal Georgi Konstantinovich Zhukov (1896-1974), commander at Stalingrad and Leningrad and Deputy of Supreme Soviet; Marshal Konstantin K. Rokossovsky (1896-1968), commander at Stalingrad.

Intercosmos-14
A2129

Designs: 10k, India's satellite Arryabata. 12k, Soyuz-19 and Apollo before docking. 16k, French satellite Aureole and Northern Lights. 20k, Docking of Soyuz-Apollo, Intercosmos-14 and Aureole.

1976, Oct. 15   Photo.   Perf. 11¹/₂

4489	A2129	6k black & multi	15	15
4490	A2129	10k black & multi	28	15
4491	A2129	12k black & multi	42	15
4492	A2129	16k black & multi	50	15
4493	A2129	20k black & multi	65	20
	Nos. 4489-4493 (5)		2.00	
	Set value			60

Interkosmos Program for Scientific and Experimental Research.

Vladimir I.
Dahl — A2130

Photogravure and Engraved
1976, Oct. 15   *Perf. 11½*
4494 A2130 4k green & dk grn   15 15

Vladimir I. Dahl (1801-1872), physician, writer, compiled Russian Dictionary.

Electric Power
Industry
A2131

Designs: No. 4496, Balashovo textile mill. No. 4497, Laying of drainage pipes and grain elevator.

1976, Oct. 20   Photo.   *Perf. 11½*
4495 A2131 4k dk blue & multi   15 15
4496 A2131 4k rose brn & multi   15 15
4497 A2131 4k slate grn & multi   15 15
          Set value   24 24

59th anniversary of the October Revolution.

Petrov Tumor Research   M. A. Novinski
Institute   A2133
A2132

1976, Oct. 28
4498 A2132 4k vio blue & gold   50 15
          Perf. 11½x12
4499 A2133 4k dk brn, buff & blue   40 15
          Set value   15

Petrov Tumor Research Institute, 50th anniversary, and 135th birth anniversary of M. A. Novinski, cancer research pioneer.

Aviation
Emblem, Gakkel
VII,
1911 — A2134

Russian Aircraft (Russian Aviation Emblem and): 6k, Gakkel IX, 1912. 12k, I. Steglau No. 2, 1912. 14k, Dybovski's Dolphin, 1913. 16k, Iliya Muromets, 1914.

Lithographed and Engraved
1976, Nov. 4   *Perf. 12x12½*
4500 A2134 3k multicolored   15 15
4501 A2134 6k multicolored   20 15
4502 A2134 12k multicolored   65 32
4503 A2134 14k multicolored   75 35
4504 A2134 16k multicolored   80 50
          Nos. 4500-4504 (5)   2.55 1.47

See Nos. C109-C120.

Saffron — A2135

Flowers of the Caucasus: 2k, Pasqueflowers. 3k, Gentian. 4k, Columbine. 6k, Checkered lily.

1976, Nov. 17   *Perf. 12x11½*
4505 A2135 1k multicolored   15 15
4506 A2135 2k multicolored   15 15
4507 A2135 3k multicolored   15 15
4508 A2135 4k multicolored   15 15
4509 A2135 6k multicolored   15 15
          Set value   38 28

Spasski Tower
Clock,
Greeting Card
A2136

1976, Nov. 25   Litho.   *Perf. 12½x12*
4510 A2136 4k multicolored   15 15

New Year 1977.

Parable of the Workers in the Vineyard, by
Rembrandt — A2137

Rembrandt Paintings in Hermitage: 6k, birth anniversary. 10k, 14k, Holy Family, vert. 20k, Rembrandt's brother Adrian, 1654, vert. 50k, Artaxerxes, Esther and Haman.

Perf. 12½x12, 12x12½
1976, Nov. 25   **Photo.**
4511 A2137   4k multicolored   15   15
4512 A2137   6k multicolored   20   15
4513 A2137 10k multicolored   50   15
4514 A2137 14k multicolored   65   15
4515 A2137 20k multicolored   90   30
          Nos. 4511-4515 (5)   2.40
          Set value   65

Souvenir Sheet
4516 A2137 50k multicolored   4.00 1.25

Rembrandt van Rijn (1606-69). Nos. 4511 and 4515 printed in sheets of 7 stamps and decorative label.

Armed Forces   Worker and Farmer,
Order — A2138   by V. I.
                       Muhina — A2139

Marx and Lenin, by   Council for Mutual
Fridman and   Economic Aid
Belostotsky   Building
A2140   A2141

Lenin, 1920   Globe and Sputnik
Photograph   Orbits
A2142   A2143

Designs: 2k, Golden Star and Hammer and Sickle medals. 4k, Coat of arms and "CCCP." 6k, TU-154 plane, globe and airmail envelope. 10k, Order of Labor. 12k, Space exploration medal with Gagarin portrait. 16k, Lenin Prize medal.

1976   Engr.   *Perf. 12x12½*
4517 A2138 1k greenish black   15 15
4518 A2138 2k brt magenta   15 15
4519 A2139 3k red   15 15
4520 A2138 4k brick red   15 15
4521 A2139 6k Prus blue   22 15
4522 A2138 10k olive green   42 15
4523 A2139 12k violet blue   50 15
4524 A2139 16k deep green   60 15
          Perf. 12½x12
4525 A2140 20k brown red   80 15
4526 A2141 30k brick red   1.10 15
4527 A2142 50k brown   1.90 15
4528 A2143 1r dark blue   4.00 15
          Nos. 4517-4528 (12) 10.14
          Set value   70

Issue dates: #4517-4524, Dec. 17. #4525-4528, Aug. 10.
See #4596-4607. For overprint see #5720.

Luna 24
Emblem and
Moon Landing
A2144

1976, Dec. 17   Photo.   *Perf. 11½*
4531 A2144 10k multicolored   30 15

Moon exploration of automatic station Luna 24.

Icebreaker "Pilot" — A2145

Icebreakers: 6k, Ermak, vert. 10k, Fedor Litke. 16k, Vladimir Ilich, vert. 20k, Krassin.

Perf. 12x11½, 11½x12
1976, Dec. 22   **Litho. & Engr.**
4532 A2145 4k multicolored   15 15
4533 A2145 6k multicolored   18 15
4534 A2145 10k multicolored   42 15
4535 A2145 16k multicolored   55 22
4536 A2145 20k multicolored   70 28
          Nos. 4532-4536 (5)   2.00
          Set value   75

See Nos. 4579-4585.

Soyuz 22 Emblem, Cosmonauts V. F.
Bykofsky and V. V. Aksenov — A2146

1976, Dec. 28   Photo.   *Perf. 12x11½*
4537 A2146 10k multicolored   30 25

Soyuz 22 space flight, Sept. 15-23.

Society
Emblem — A2147

1977, Jan. 1   *Perf. 11½*
4538 A2147 4k multicolored   15 15

Red Banner Voluntary Soc., supporting Red Army, Navy & Air Force, 50th anniv.

S. P. Korolev,
Vostok Rocket
and Satellite
A2148

1977, Jan. 12
4539 A2148 4k multicolored   15 15

Sergei Pavlovich Korolev (1907-1966), creator of first Soviet rocket space system.

Globe and
Palm
A2149

1977, Jan. 12
4540 A2149 4k multicolored   15 15

World Congress of Peace Loving Forces, Moscow, Jan. 1977.

Sedov and "St.
Foka"
A2150

1977, Jan. 25   Photo.   *Perf. 11½*
4541 A2150 4k multicolored   15 15

G.Y. Sedov (1877-1914), polar explorer and hydrographer.

Worker and   Ship Sailing Across
Farmer   the
Monument and   Oceans — A2152
Izvestia Front
Page — A2151

1977, Jan. 25
4542 A2151 4k silver, black & red   15 15

60th anniversary of newspaper Izvestia.

1977, Jan. 25
4543 A2152 6k deep blue & gold   30 15

24th Intl. Navigation Cong., Leningrad.

Congress Hall and Troitskaya Tower, Kremlin
A2153

Marshal Leonid A. Govorov (1897-1955)
A2154

1977, Feb. 9   Photo.   Perf. 11½
4544 A2153 4k red, gold & black   15 15

16th Congress of USSR Trade Unions.

1977   Engr.   Perf. 12

Marshals of the Soviet Union: No. 4546, Ivan S. Koniev. No. 4547, K. A. Merezhkov. No. 4548, W. D. Sokolovsky.

4545 A2154 4k brown   15 15
4546 A2154 4k slate green   15 15
4547 A2154 4k brown   15 15
4548 A2154 4k black   15 15
      Set value   38 24

Issue dates: #4545, Feb. 9. Others, June 7.

Academy, Crest, Anchor and Ribbons
A2155

Photogravure and Engraved
1977, Feb. 9   Perf. 11½
4549 A2155 6k multicolored   15 15

A. A. Grechko Naval Academy, Leningrad, sesquicentennial.

Jeanne Labourbe
A2156

Queen and Knights
A2157

1977, Feb. 25   Photo.   Perf. 11½
4550 A2156 4k multicolored   15 15

Jeanne Labourbe (1877-1919), leader of French communists in Moscow.

1977, Feb. 25
4551 A2157 6k multicolored   30 15

4th European Chess Championships.

Cosmonauts V. D. Zudov and V. I. Rozhdestvensky — A2158

1977, Feb. 25   Perf. 12x11½
4552 A2158 10k multicolored   15 15

Soyuz 23 space flight, Oct. 14-16, 1976.

A. S. Novikov-Priboy (1877-1944), Writer — A2159

1977, Mar. 16   Photo.   Perf. 11½
4553 A2159 4k multicolored   15 15

Welcome, by M. N. Soloninkin
A2160

Folk Tale Paintings from Fedoskino Artists' Colony: 6k, Along the Street, by V. D. Antonov, horiz. 10k, Northern Song, by J. V. Karapaev. 12k, Tale of Czar Saltan, by A. I. Kozlov. 14k, Summer Troika, by V. A. Nalimov, horiz. 16k, Red Flower, by V. D. Lipitsky.

Perf. 12x12½, 12½x12
1977, Mar. 16   Litho.
4554 A2160 4k black & multi   15 15
4555 A2160 6k black & multi   35 15
4556 A2160 10k black & multi   65 15
4557 A2160 12k black & multi   80 15
4558 A2160 14k black & multi   90 15
4559 A2160 16k black & multi   1.00 15
      Nos. 4554-4559 (6)   3.85
      Set value   60

Lenin on Red Square, by K.V. Filatov — A2161

1977, Apr. 12   Perf. 12½x11½
4560 A2161 4k multicolored   15 15

107th anniversary of the birth of Lenin.

Electricity Congress Emblem
A2162

1977, Apr. 12   Photo.   Perf. 11½
4561 A2162 6k blue, red & gray   15 15

World Electricity Congress, Moscow 1977.

Yuri Gagarin, Sputnik, Soyuz and Salyut — A2163

1977, Apr. 12   Perf. 12x11½
4562 A2163 6k multicolored   15 15

Cosmonauts' Day.

N. I. Vavilov
A2164

Feliks E. Dzerzhinski
A2165

1977, Apr. 26   Photo.   Perf. 11½
4563 A2164 4k multicolored   15 15

Vavilov (1887-1943), agricultural geneticist.

1977, May 12   Engr.   Perf. 12½x12
4564 A2165 4k black   30 15

Feliks E. Dzerzhinski (1877-1926), organizer and head of secret police (OGPU).

Saxifraga Sibirica — A2166

Siberian Flowers: 3k, Dianthus repena. 4k, Novosieversia glactalis. 6k, Cerasticum maxinicem. 16k, Golden rhododendron.

1977, May 12   Litho.   Perf. 12x12½
4565 A2166 2k multicolored   15 15
4566 A2166 3k multicolored   18 15
4567 A2166 4k multicolored   20 15
4568 A2166 6k multicolored   30 15
4569 A2166 16k multicolored   80 16
      Nos. 4565-4569 (5)   1.63
      Set value   38

V. V. Gorbatko, Y. N. Glazkov, Soyuz 24 Rocket
A2167

1977, May 16   Photo.   Perf. 12x11½
4570 A2167 10k multicolored   40 25

Space explorations of cosmonauts on Salyut 5 orbital station, launched with Soyuz 24 rocket.

Film and Globe — A2168

1977, June 21   Photo.   Perf. 11½
4571 A2168 6k multicolored   15 15

10th Intl. Film Festival, Moscow 1977.

Lion Hunt, by Rubens — A2169

Rubens Paintings, Hermitage, Leningrad: 4k, Lady in Waiting, vert. 10k, Workers in Quarry. 12k, Alliance of Water and Earth, vert. 20k, Landscape with Rainbow. 50k, Self-portrait.

Perf. 12x12½, 12½x12
1977, June 24   Litho.
4572 A2169 4k yellow & multi   15 15
4573 A2169 6k yellow & multi   18 15
4574 A2169 10k yellow & multi   38 15
4575 A2169 12k yellow & multi   50 15
4576 A2169 20k yellow & multi   75 30
      Nos. 4572-4576 (5)   1.96
      Set value   55

Souvenir Sheet
4577 A2169 50k yellow & multi   2.50 80

Peter Paul Rubens (1577-1640), painter. Sheets of No. 4575 contain 2 labels with commemorative inscriptions and Atlas statue from Hermitage entrance.

Souvenir Sheet

Judith, by Giorgione
A2170

1977, July 15   Litho.   Perf. 12x12½
4578 A2170 50k multicolored   2.00 1.00

Il Giorgione (1478-1511), Venetian painter.

Icebreaker Type of 1976

Icebreakers: 4k, Aleksandr Sibiryakov. 6k, Georgi Sedov. 10k, Sadko. 12k, Dezhnev. 14k, Siberia. 16k, Lena. 20k, Amguyema.

Lithographed and Engraved
1977, July 27   Perf. 12x11½
4579 A2145 4k multicolored   15 15
4580 A2145 6k multicolored   15 15
4581 A2145 10k multicolored   32 15
4582 A2145 12k multicolored   38 18
4583 A2145 14k multicolored   45 22
4584 A2145 16k multicolored   50 32
4585 A2145 20k multicolored   65 45
      Nos. 4579-4585 (7)   2.60 1.62

Souvenir Sheet

Icebreaker Arctica — A2171

Lithographed and Engraved
1977, Sept. 15   Perf. 12½x12
4586 A2171 50k multicolored   9.00 5.00

Arctica, first ship to travel from Murmansk to North Pole, Aug. 9-17.

View and Arms
of Stavropol
A2172

Stamps and
Exhibition
Emblem
A2173

1977, Aug. 16   Photo.   *Perf. 11½*
4587 A2172 6k multicolored   15 15
    200th anniversary of Stavropol.

1977, Aug. 16
4588 A2173 4k multicolored   15 15

October Revolution Anniversary Philatelic Exhibition, Moscow.

Yuri A. Gagarin and
Spacecraft — A2174

Designs: No. 4590, Alexei Leonov floating in space. No. 4591, Orbiting space station, cosmonauts at control panel. Nos. 4592-4594, Various spacecraft: No. 4592, International cooperation for space research; No. 4593, Interplanetary flights; No. 4594, Exploring earth's atmosphere.   50k, "XX," laurel, symbolic Sputnik with Red Star.

1977, Oct. 4   Photo.   *Perf. 11½x12*
4589 A2174 10k sepia & multi   25 15
4590 A2174 10k gray & multi   25 15
4591 A2174 10k gray green & multi   25 15
4592 A2174 20k green & multi   60 35
4593 A2174 20k violet blue & multi   60 35
4594 A2174 20k bister & multi   60 35
    Nos. 4589-4594 (6)   2.55 1.50
Souvenir Sheet
4595 A2174 50k claret & gold   7.50 7.50

20th anniv. of space research. No. 4595 contains one stamp, size: 22x32mm.

Types of 1976

Designs: 15k, Communications emblem and globes; others as before.

1977-78   Litho.   *Perf. 12x12½*
4596 A2138 1k olive green   15 15
4597 A2138 2k lilac rose   15 15
4598 A2139 3k brick red   15 15
4599 A2138 4k vermilion   15 15
4600 A2139 6k Prus blue   18 15
4601 A2138 10k gray green   40 15
4602 A2139 12k vio blue   42 15
4602A A2139 15k blue ('78)   55 15
4603 A2139 16k slate green   60 15
    Perf. 12½x12
4604 A2140 20k brown red   75 15
4605 A2141 30k dull brick red   1.00 15
4606 A2142 50k brown   2.00 15
4607 A2143 1r dark blue   3.75 15
    Nos. 4596-4607 (13)   10.25
    Set value   75

Nos. 4596-4602A, 4604-4607 were printed on dull and shiny paper.
For overprint see No. 5720.

Souvenir Sheet

Bas-relief, 12th Century, Cathedral of St.
Dimitri, Vladimir — A2175

Designs: 6k, Necklace, Ryazan excavations, 12th century. 10k, Mask, Cathedral of the Nativity, Suzdal, 13th century. 12k, Archangel Michael, 15th century icon. 16k, Chalice by Ivan Fomin, 1449. 20k, St. Basil's Cathedral, Moscow, 16th century.

1977, Oct. 12   Litho.   *Perf. 12*
4608   Sheet of 6   2.50 1.25
  a. A2175 4k gold & black   15
  b. A2175 6k gold & multi   18
  c. A2175 10k gold & multi   35
  d. A2175 12k gold & multi   42
  e. A2175 16k gold & multi   45
  f. A2175 20k gold & multi   60

Masterpieces of old Russian culture.

Fir, Snowflake,
Molniya
Satellite — A2176

1977, Oct. 12   *Perf. 12x12½*
4609 A2176 4k multicolored   30 15

New Year 1978.

Cruiser Aurora
and
Torch — A2177

60th Anniversary of
Revolution
Medal — A2178

60th Anniv. of October Revolution: #4611, Lenin speaking at Finland Station (monument), 1917. #4612, 1917 Peace Decree, Brezhnev's book about Lenin. #4613, Kremlin tower with star and fireworks.

1977, Oct. 26   Photo.   *Perf. 12x11½*
4610 A2177 4k gold, red & black   15 15
4611 A2177 4k gold, red & black   15 15
4612 A2177 4k gold, red & black   15 15
4613 A2177 4k gold, red & black   15 15
    Set value   32 24
Souvenir Sheet
    Perf. 11½
4614 A2178 30k gold, red & black   1.50 70

Flag of USSR, Constitution (Book) with
Coat of Arms — A2179

Designs: No. 4616, Red banner, people and cover of constitution. 50k, Constitution, Kremlin and olive branch.

1977, Oct. 31   Litho.   *Perf. 12½x12*
4615 A2179 4k red, black & yel   15 15
4616 A2179 4k red, black & yel   15 15
    Set value   16 15
Souvenir Sheet
    Perf. 11½x12½
Lithographed and Embossed
4617 A2179 50k red, gold & yel   1.75 1.00

Adoption of new constitution. No. 4617 contains one 70x50mm stamp.

Souvenir Sheet

Leonid Brezhnev
A2180

Lithographed and Embossed
1977, Nov. 2   *Perf. 11½x12*
4618 A2180 50k gold & multi   1.75 1.00

Adoption of new constitution, General Secretary Brezhnev, chairman of Constitution Commission.

Postal Official and Postal Code — A2181

Mail Processing (Woman Postal Official and): No. 4620, Mail collection and Moskvich 430 car. No. 4621, Automatic letter sorting machine. No. 4622, Mail transport by truck, train, ship and planes. No. 4623, Mail delivery in city and country.

Lithographed and Engraved
1977, Nov. 16   *Perf. 12½x12*
4619 A2181 4k multicolored   15 15
4620 A2181 4k multicolored   15 15
4621 A2181 4k multicolored   15 15
4622 A2181 4k multicolored   15 15
4623 A2181 4k multicolored   15 15
    Set value   40 30

Capital, Asoka
Pillar, Red
Fort — A2182

Proclamation
Monument,
Charkov — A2183

1977, Dec. 14   Photo.   *Perf. 11½*
4624 A2182 6k maroon, gold & red   15 15
    30th anniversary of India's independence.

1977, Dec. 14   Litho.   *Perf. 12x12½*
4625 A2183 6k multicolored   15 15

60th anniv. of Soviet power in the Ukraine.

Lebetina Viper — A2184

Protected Fauna: 1k to 12k, Venomous snakes, useful for medicinal purposes. 16k, Polar bear and cub. 20k, Walrus and calf. 30k, Tiger and cub.

Photogravure and Engraved
1977, Dec. 16   *Perf. 11½x12*
4626 A2184 1k black & multi   15 15
4627 A2184 4k black & multi   15 15
4628 A2184 6k black & multi   18 15
4629 A2184 10k black & multi   35 15
4630 A2184 12k black & multi   42 15
4631 A2184 16k black & multi   55 18
4632 A2184 20k black & multi   75 25
4633 A2184 30k black & multi   1.00 35
    Nos. 4626-4633 (8)   3.55
    Set value   1.15

Wheat, Combine,
Silos — A2185

Congress Palace,
Spasski
Tower — A2186

1978, Jan. 27   Photo.   *Perf. 11½*
4634 A2185 4k multicolored   15 15

Gigant collective grain farm, Rostov Region, 50th anniversary.

1978, Jan. 27   Litho.   *Perf. 12x12½*
4635 A2186 4k multicolored   15 15

Young Communist League, Lenin's Komsomol, 60th anniv. and its 25th Cong.

The Scott Catalogue value is a retail value; that is, what you could expect to pay for the stamp in a grade of Fine-Very Fine. The value listed reflects recent actual dealer selling prices.

Liberation Obelisk, Emblem, Dove — A2187

1978, Jan. 27   Photo.   Perf. 11½
4636 A2187 6k multicolored   15 15

8th Congress of International Federation of Resistance Fighters, Minsk, Belorussia.

Soldiers Leaving for the Front — A2188

Designs: No. 4638, Defenders of Moscow Monument, Lenin banner. No. 4639, Soldier as defender of the people.

1978, Feb. 21   Litho.   Perf. 12½x12
4637 A2188 4k red & multi   15 15
4638 A2188 4k red & multi   15 15
4639 A2188 4k red & multi   15 15
             Set value   24 18

60th anniversary of USSR Military forces.

Morning, by Kustodiev — A2189

Kustodiev Paintings: 4k, Celebration in Village. 6k, Shrovetide (winter landscape). 12k, Merchant's Wife Drinking Tea. 20k, Bolshevik. 50k, Self-portrait, vert.

1978, Mar. 3   Perf. 11½
             Size: 70x33mm
4640 A2189 4k lilac & multi   15 15
4641 A2189 6k lilac & multi   18 15
             Size: 47x32mm
             Perf. 12½x12
4642 A2189 10k lilac & multi   40 15
4643 A2189 12k lilac & multi   50 15
4644 A2189 20k lilac & multi   70 25
             Nos. 4640-4644 (5)   1.93
             Set value   60

             Souvenir Sheet
             Perf. 11½x12½
4644A A2189 50k lilac & multi   1.75 75

Boris Mikhailovich Kustodiev (1878-1927), painter. Nos. 4640-4643 have se-tenant label showing museum where painting is kept. No. 4644A has label giving short biography.

Docking in Space, Intercosmos Emblem A2190

Designs: 6k, Rocket, Soviet Cosmonaut Aleksei Gubarev and Czechoslovak Capt. Vladimir Remek on launching pad. 32k, Weather balloon, helicopter, Intercosmos emblem, USSR and Czechoslovakian flags.

1978, Mar. 10   Litho.   Perf. 12x12½
4645 A2190 6k multicolored   15 15
4646 A2190 15k multicolored   45 15
4647 A2190 32k multicolored   1.00 38
             Set value   58

Intercosmos, Soviet-Czechoslovak cooperative space program.

Festival Emblem — A2191

1978, Mar. 17   Litho.   Perf. 12x12½
4648 A2191 4k blue & multi   15 15

11th Youth & Students' Cong., Havana.

Tulip, Bolshoi Theater A2192

Moscow Flowers: 2k, Rose "Moscow morning" and Lomonosov University. 4k, Dahlia "Red Star" and Spasski Tower. 10k, Gladiolus "Moscovite" and VDNH Building. 12k, Ilich anniversary iris and Lenin Central Museum.

1978, Mar. 17   Perf. 12½x12
4649 A2192 1k multicolored   15 15
4650 A2192 2k multicolored   15 15
4651 A2192 4k multicolored   15 15
4652 A2192 10k multicolored   20 15
4653 A2192 12k multicolored   25 15
             Set value   64 38

IMCO Emblem and Waves — A2193

1978, Mar. 17   Litho.   Perf. 12x12½
4654 A2193 6k multicolored   15 15

Intergovernmental Maritime Consultative Org., 20th anniv., and World Maritime Day.

Spaceship, Orbits of Salyut 5, Soyuz 26 and 27 A2194

World Federation of Trade Unions Emblem A2195

1978, Apr. 12   Photo.   Perf. 12
4655 A2194 6k blue, dk blue & gold   15 15

Cosmonauts' Day, Apr. 12.

1978, Apr. 16   Perf. 12
4656 A2195 6k multicolored   15 15

9th World Trade Union Congress, Prague.

2-2-0 Locomotive, 1845, Petersburg and Moscow Stations — A2196

Locomotives: 1k, 1st Russian model by E. A. and M. W. Cherepanov, vert. 2k, 1-3-0 freight, 1845. 16k, Aleksandrov 0-3-0, 1863. 20k, 2-2-0 passenger and Sergievsk Pustyn platform, 1863.

1978, Apr. 20   Litho.   Perf. 11½
4657 A2196 1k orange & multi   15 15
4658 A2196 2k ultra & multi   15 15
4659 A2196 3k yellow & multi   15 15
4660 A2196 16k green & multi   58 20
4661 A2196 20k rose & multi   70 25
             Nos. 4657-4661 (5)   1.73
             Set value   60

             Souvenir Sheet

Lenin, by V. A. Serov A2197

1978, Apr. 22   Perf. 12x12½
4662 A2197 50k multicolored   1.50 75

108th anniversary of the birth of Lenin.

Soyuz and Salyut 6 Docking in Space — A2198

Y. V. Romanenko and G. M. Grechko — A2199

1978, June 15   Perf. 12
4663 A2198 15k multicolored   50 20
4664 A2199 15k multicolored   50 20

Photographic survey and telescopic observations of stars by crews of Soyuz 26, Soyuz 27 and Soyuz 28, Dec. 10, 1977-Mar. 16, 1978. Nos. 4663-4664

printed se-tenant with label showing schematic pictures of various experiments.

Space Meteorology, Rockets, Spaceship, Earth — A2200

Designs (Intercosmos Emblem and): No. 4666, Natural resources of earth and Soyuz. No. 4667, Space communications, "Orbita" Station and Molnyia satellite. No. 4668, Man, earth and Vostok. 50k, Study of magnetosphere, Prognoz over earth.

1978, June 23   Perf. 12x12½
4665 A2200 10k green & multi   25 15
4666 A2200 10k blue & multi   25 15
4667 A2200 10k violet & multi   25 15
4668 A2200 10k rose lilac & multi   25 15
             Set value   40

             Souvenir Sheet
             Perf. 11½x12½
4669 A2200 50k multicolored   1.50 75

Space explorations of the Intercosmos program. #4669 contains one 36x51mm stamp.

Soyuz Rocket on Carrier — A2201

Designs (Flags of USSR and Poland, Intercosmos Emblem): 15k, Crystal, spaceship (Sirena, experimental crystallogenesis in space). 32k, Research ship "Cosmonaut Vladimir Komarov", spaceship, world map and paths of Salyut 6, Soyuz 29-30.

1978,   Litho.   Perf. 12½x12
4670 A2201 6k multicolored   15 15
4671 A2201 15k multicolored   40 15
4672 A2201 32k multicolored   80 40

Intercosmos, Soviet-Polish cooperative space program. Issue dates: 6k, June 28. 15k, June 30. 32k, July 5.

Lenin, Awards Received by Komsomol A2202

Kamaz Car, Train, Bridge, Hammer and Sickle A2203

1978, July 5   Perf. 12x12½
4673 A2202 4k multicolored   15 15
4674 A2203 4k multicolored   15 15
             Set value   20 15

Leninist Young Communist League (Komsomol), 60th anniv. (#4673); Komsomol's participation in 5-year plan (#4674).
    For overprint see No. 4703.

M. V. Zaharov
A2204

Torch, Flags of
Participants
A2205

1978, July 5   Engr.   Perf. 12
4675 A2204 4k sepia   15 15

M. V. Zaharov (1898-1972), Marshal of the
Soviet Union.

1978, July 25   Litho.   Perf. 12x12¹/₂
4676 A2205 4k multicolored   15 15

Construction of Soyuz gas-pipeline (Friendship
Line), Orenburg. Flags of participating countries
shown: Bulgaria, Hungary, German Democratic
Republic, Poland, Romania, USSR, Czechoslovakia.

Harvey
A2206

N. G. Chernyshevsky
A2207

1978, July 25   Perf. 12
4677 A2206 6k blue, black & dp grn   15 15

Dr. William Harvey (1578-1657), discoverer of
blood circulation.

1978, July 30   Engr.   Perf. 12x12¹/₂
4678 A2207 4k brown, yellow   15 15

Nikolai Gavilovich Chernyshevsky (1828-1889),
revolutionary.

Whitewinged
Petrel
A2208

Antarctic Fauna: 1k, Crested penguin, horiz. 4k,
Emperor penguin and chick. 6k, White-blooded
pikes. 10k, Sea elephant, horiz.

Perf. 12x11¹/₂, 11¹/₂x12
1978, July 30   Litho.
4679 A2208 1k multicolored   18 15
4680 A2208 3k multicolored   32 15
4681 A2208 4k multicolored   32 15
4682 A2208 6k multicolored   45 15
4683 A2208 10k multicolored   75 15
     Nos. 4679-4683 (5)   2.02
          Set value   32

The Red Horse, by Petrov-Votkin — A2209

Paintings by Petrov-Votkin: 6k, Mother and
Child, Petrograd, 1918. 10k, Death of the Commissar. 12k, Still-life with Fruit. 16k, Still-life with Tea-
pot and Flowers. 50k, Self-portrait, 1918, vert.

1978, Aug. 16   Litho.   Perf. 12¹/₂x12
4684 A2209 4k silver & multi   15 15
4685 A2209 6k silver & multi   22 15
4686 A2209 10k silver & multi   52 15
4687 A2209 12k silver & multi   70 15
4688 A2209 16k silver & multi   80 20
     Nos. 4684-4688 (5)   2.39
          Set value   55

Souvenir Sheet
Perf. 11¹/₂x12
4689 A2209 50k silver & multi   1.75 1.00

Kozma Sergeevich Petrov-Votkin (1878-1939),
painter. Nos. 4684-4688 have se-tenant labels. No.
4689 has label the size of stamp.

Soyuz 31 in
Shop,
Intercosmos
Emblem, USSR
and DDR
Flags — A2210

Designs (Intercosmos Emblem, USSR and Ger-
man Democratic Republic Flags and): 15k, Pamir
Mountains photographed from space; Salyut 6,
Soyuz 29 and 31 complex and spectrum. 32k,
Soyuz 31 docking, photographed from Salyut 6.

1978   Litho.   Perf. 12x12¹/₂
4690 A2210 6k multicolored   15 15
4691 A2210 15k multicolored   85 15
4692 A2210 32k multicolored   1.65 45
          Set value   65

Intercosmos, Soviet-East German cooperative
space program.
Issue dates: 6k, Aug. 27. 15k, Aug. 31. 32k,
Sept. 3.

PRAGA '78
Emblem,
Plane, Radar,
Spaceship
A2211

Photogravure and Engraved
1978, Aug. 29   Perf. 11¹/₂
4693 A2211 6k multicolored   15 15

PRAGA '78 International Philatelic Exhibition,
Prague, Sept. 8-17.

Leo Tolstoi
(1828-1910),
Novelist and
Philosopher
A2212

1978, Sept. 7   Engr.   Perf. 12x12¹/₂
4694 A2212 4k slate green   1.25 90

Stag, Conference
Emblem — A2213

1978   Photo.   Perf. 11¹/₂
4695 A2213 4k multicolored   15 15

14th General Assembly of the Society for Wildlife
Preservation, Ashkhabad.

Bronze Figure,
Erebuni, 8th
Century
A2214

Armenian Architecture: 6k, Etchmiadzin Cathedral, 4th century. 10k, Stone crosses, Dzaghkatzor,
13th century. 12k, Library, Erevan, horiz. 16k,
Lenin statue, Lenin Square, Erevan, horiz.

1978   Litho.   Perf. 12x12¹/₂, 12¹/₂x12
4696 A2214 4k multicolored   15 15
4697 A2214 6k multicolored   18 15
4698 A2214 10k multicolored   30 15
4699 A2214 12k multicolored   38 15
4700 A2214 16k multicolored   48 16
     Nos. 4696-4700 (5)   1.49
          Set value   50

Issued: 4k, 10k, 16k, Sept. 12; others, Oct. 14.

Memorial,
Messina,
Russian
Warships
A2215

1978, Sept. 12   Photo.   Perf. 11¹/₂
4701 A2215 6k multicolored   15 15

70th anniversary of aid given by Russian sailors
during Messina earthquake.

Communications
Emblem, Ostankino
TV Tower — A2216

1978, Sept. 20   Photo.   Perf. 11¹/₂
4702 A2216 4k multicolored   15 15

Organization for Communication Cooperation of
Socialist Countries, 20th anniv.

No. 4673
Overprinted

ФИЛЬВЫСТАВКА .60 лет ВЛКСМ"

МОСКВА. 1978

1978, Sept. 20   Litho.   Perf. 12x12¹/₂
4703 A2202 4k multicolored   1.25 70

Philatelic Exhibition for the Leninist Young Communist League.

Souvenir Sheet

Diana, by Paolo Veronese — A2217

1978, Sept. 28   Litho.   Perf. 12x11¹/₂
4704 A2217 50k multicolored   1.50 1.00

Veronese (1528-88), Italian painter.

Kremlin, Moscow
A2218

S. G. Shauyan
A2219

Souvenir Sheet
Lithographed and Embossed
1978, Oct. 7   Perf. 11¹/₂x12
4705 A2218 30k gold & multi   1.00 65

Russian Constitution, 1st anniversary.

1978, Oct. 11   Engr.   Perf. 12¹/₂x12
4706 A2219 4k slate green   15 15

Stepan Georgevich Shauyan (1878-1918), Communist Party functionary.

Ferry, Russian and Bulgarian Colors — A2220

Hammer and Sickle, Flags — A2221

1978, Oct. 14   Photo.   *Perf. 11¹/₂*
4707 A2220 6k multicolored   15 15
Opening of Ilychovsk-Varna Ferry.

1978, Oct. 26   Photo.   *Perf. 11¹/₂*
4708 A2221 4k gold & multi   15 15
61st anniversary of October Revolution.

Silver Gilt Cup, Novgorod, 12th Century — A2222

Old Russian Art: 10k, Pokrowna Nerli Church, 12th century, vert. 12k, St. George Slaying the Dragon, icon, Novgorod, 15th century, vert. 16k, The Czar, cannon, 1586.

Perf. 12¹/₂x12, 12x12¹/₂
1978, Nov. 28   Litho.
4709 A2222 6k multicolored   15 15
4710 A2222 10k multicolored   40 15
4711 A2222 12k multicolored   50 15
4712 A2222 16k multicolored   60 20
              Set value   48

Oncology Institute, Emblem — A2223

Savior Tower, Kremlin — A2224

1978, Dec. 1   Photo.   *Perf. 11¹/₂*
4713 A2223 4k multicolored   15 15
P.A. Herzen Tumor Institute, 75th anniv.

1978, Dec. 20 Litho. *Perf. 12x12¹/₂*
4714 A2224 4k silver, blue & red   15 15
New Year 1979.

Nestor Pechersky, Chronicler, c. 885 — A2225

History of Postal Service: 6k, Birch bark letter and stylus. 10k, Messenger with trumpet and staff, from 14th century Psalm book. 12k, Winter traffic, from 16th century book by Sigizmund Gerberstein. 16k, Prikaz post office, from 17th century icon.

Lithographed and Engraved
1978, Dec. 20   *Perf. 12¹/₂x12*
4715 A2225 4k multicolored   15 15
4716 A2225 6k multicolored   18 15
4717 A2225 10k multicolored   48 15
4718 A2225 12k multicolored   52 15
4719 A2225 16k multicolored   65 20
        Nos. 4715-4719 (5)   1.98
              Set value   55

Kovalenok and Ivanchenkov, Salyut 6-Soyuz — A2226

1978, Dec. 20 Photo. *Perf. 11¹/₂x12*
4720 A2226 10k multicolored   30 15
Cosmonauts V. V. Kovalenok and A. S. Ivanchenkov spent 140 days in space, June 15-Nov. 2, 1978.

Vasilii Pronchishchev — A2227

Icebreakers: 6k, Captain Belousov, 1954, vert. 10k, Moscow. 12k, Admiral Makarov, 1974. 16k, Lenin, 1959, vert. 20k, Nuclear-powered Arctica.

Perf. 11¹/₂x12, 12x11¹/₂
1978, Dec. 20   Photo. & Engr.
4721 A2227 4k multicolored   15 15
4722 A2227 6k multicolored   15 15
4723 A2227 10k multicolored   32 15
4724 A2227 12k multicolored   40 15
4725 A2227 16k multicolored   50 20
4726 A2227 20k multicolored   60 22
        Nos. 4721-4726 (6)   2.12
              Set value   76

Souvenir Sheet

Mastheads and Globe with Russia — A2228

1978, Dec. 28   Litho.   *Perf. 12*
4727 A2228 30k multicolored   1.00 35
Distribution of periodicals through the Post and Telegraph Department, 60th anniversary.

Cuban Flags Forming Star — A2229

1979, Jan. 1   Photo.   *Perf. 11¹/₂*
4728 A2229 6k multicolored   15 15
Cuban Revolution, 20th anniversary.

Russian and Byelorussian Flags, Government Building, Minsk A2230

1979, Jan. 1
4729 A2230 4k multicolored   15 15
Byelorussian SSR and Byelorussian Community Party, 60th anniv.

Ukrainian and Russian Flags, Reunion Monument — A2231

1979, Jan. 16
4730 A2231 4k multicolored   30 15
Reunion of Ukraine & Russia, 325th anniv.

Old and New Vilnius University Buildings A2232

1979, Jan. 16   Photo. & Engr.
4731 A2232 4k black & salmon   15 15
400th anniversary of University of Vilnius.

Bulgaria No. 1 and Exhibition Hall A2233

1979, Jan. 25 Litho. *Perf. 12¹/₂x12*
4732 A2233 15k multicolored   35 15
Filaserdica '79 Philatelic Exhibition, Sofia, for centenary of Bulgarian postal service.

Sputniks, Soviet Radio Hams Emblem — A2234

1979, Feb. 23   Photo.   *Perf. 11¹/₂*
4733 A2234 4k multicolored   15 15
Sputnik satellites Radio 1 and Radio 2, launched, Oct. 1978.

1-3-0 Locomotive, 1878 — A2235

Locomotives: 3k, 1-4-0, 1912. 4k, 2-3-1, 1915. 6k, 1-3-1, 1925. 15k, 1-5-0, 1947.

1979, Feb. 23   Litho.   *Perf. 11¹/₂*
4734 A2235 2k multicolored   15 15
4735 A2235 3k multicolored   15 15
4736 A2235 4k multicolored   16 15
4737 A2235 6k multicolored   24 15
4738 A2235 15k multicolored   65 18
        Nos. 4734-4738 (5)   1.35
              Set value   50

Souvenir Sheet

Medal for Land Development A2236

1979, Mar. 14   *Perf. 11¹/₂x12¹/₂*
4739 A2236 50k multicolored   1.50 75
25th anniv. of drive to develop virgin lands.

Venera 11 and 12 over Venus — A2237

1979, Mar. 16   Photo.   *Perf. 11¹/₂*
4740 A2237 10k multicolored   30 15
Interplanetary flights of Venera 11 and Venera 12, December 1978.

Albert Einstein, Equation and Signature A2238

1979, Mar. 16
4741 A2238 6k multicolored   30 15
Einstein (1879-1955), theoretical physicist.

Congress Emblem A2239

1979, Mar. 16
4742 A2239 6k multicolored   15 15
21st World Veterinary Congress, Moscow.

"To Arms," by R. Berens A2240

1979, Mar. 21
4743 A2240 4k multicolored   15 15
Soviet Republic of Hungary, 60th anniv.

RUSSIA   175

Salyut 6, Soyuz, Research Ship,
Letters — A2241

1979, Apr. 12   Litho.   *Perf. 11¹/₂x12*
4744 A2241 15k multicolored   50 15
Cosmonauts' Day.

Souvenir Sheet

Ice Hockey — A2242

1979, Apr. 14   Photo.   *Perf. 12x11¹/₂*
4745 A2242 50k multicolored   1.50 75
World and European Ice Hockey Championships,
Moscow, Apr. 14-27.
For overprint see No. 4751.

Souvenir Sheet

Lenin
A2243

1979, Apr. 18
4746 A2243 50k red, gold & brown   1.50 75
109th anniversary of the birth of Lenin.

Astronauts' Training   Exhibition
Center — A2244   Emblem — A2245

Design: 32k, Astronauts, landing capsule, radar,
helicopter and emblem.

1979, Apr. 12   Litho.   *Perf. 11¹/₂*
4747 A2244 6k multicolored   15 15
4748 A2244 32k multicolored   1.10 40
            Set value   45
Joint Soviet-Bulgarian space flight.

1979, Apr. 18   Photo.   *Perf. 11¹/₂*
4749 A2245 15k sil, red & vio blue   60 15
National USSR Exhibition in the United Kingdom. Se-tenant label with commemorative
inscription.

Blast Furance, Pushkin
Theater, "Tent"
Sculpture — A2246

1979, May 24   Photo.   *Perf. 11¹/₂*
4750 A2246 4k multicolored   15 15
50th anniversary of Magnitogorsk City.

Souvenir Sheet

No. 4745   СОВЕТСКИЕ ХОККЕИСТЫ—
Overprinted in ЧЕМПИОНЫ МИРА
Margin in Red   И ЕВРОПЫ

1979, May 24   *Perf. 12x11¹/₂*
4751 A2242 50k multicolored   3.00 80
Victory of Soviet team in World and European Ice
Hockey Championships.

Infant, Flowers, IYC
Emblem — A2247

1979, June   Litho.   *Perf. 12x12¹/₂*
4752 A2247 4k multicolored   15 15
International Year of the Child.

Horn Player and Bears Playing Balalaika,
Bogorodsk Wood Carvings — A2248

Folk Art: 3k, Decorated wooden bowls, Khokh-
loma. 4k, Tray decorated with flowers, Zhestovo.
6k, Carved bone boxes, Kholmogory. 15k, Lace,
Vologda.

1979, June 14   Litho.   *Perf. 12¹/₂x12*
4753 A2248 2k multicolored   15 15
4754 A2248 3k multicolored   15 15
4755 A2248 4k multicolored   15 15
4756 A2248 6k multicolored   20 15
4757 A2248 15k multicolored   48 24
       Nos. 4753-4757 (5)   1.13
            Set value   60

V. A. Djanibekov,
O. G. Makarov,
Spacecraft
A2249

1979, June   *Perf. 12x11¹/₂*
4758 A2249 4k multicolored   35 15
Flights of Soyuz 26-27 and work on board of
orbital complex Salyut 26-27.

COMECON   Scene from
Building,   "Potemkin" and
Members'   Festival
Flags — A2250   Emblem — A2251

1979, June 26   *Perf. 12*
4759 A2250 16k multicolored   50 20
Council for Mutual Economic Aid of Socialist
Countries, 30th anniversary.

Photogravure and Engraved
1979, July   *Perf. 11¹/₂*
4760 A2251 15k multicolored   50 15
11th International Film Festival, Moscow, and
60th anniversary of Soviet film industry.

Lenin Square
Station,
Tashkent
A2252

1979, July   Litho.   *Perf. 12*
4761 A2252 4k multicolored   15 15
Tashkent subway.

Souvenir Sheets

Atom Symbol,   USSR Philatelic
Factories,   Society
Dam — A2253   Emblem — A2254

1979, July 23   Photo.   *Perf. 11¹/₂x12*
4762 A2253 30k multicolored   1.00 45
50th anniversary of 1st Five-Year Plan.

1979, July 25   Litho.   *Perf. 12x12¹/₂*
4763 A2254 50k gray grn & red   1.50 70
4th Cong. of USSR Phil. Soc., Moscow.

Exhibition
Hall, Scene
from
"Chapayev"
A2255

1979, Aug. 8   Photo.   *Perf. 11¹/₂*
4764 A2255 4k multicolored   15 15
60th anniversary of Soviet Film and Exhibition of
History of Soviet Film.

Roses, by P. P. Konchalovsky,
1955 — A2256

Russian Flower Paintings: 1k, Flowers and Fruit,
by I. F. Khrutsky, 1830. 2k, Phlox, by I. N. Kramskoi, 1884. 3k, Lilac, by K. A. Korovin, 1915. 15k,
Bluebells, by S. V. Gerasimov, 1944. 2k, 3k, 15k,
vert.

Perf. 12¹/₂x12, 12x12¹/₂
1979, Aug. 16   Litho.
4765 A2256 1k multicolored   15 15
4766 A2256 2k multicolored   15 15
4767 A2256 3k multicolored   15 15
4768 A2256 15k multicolored   40 30
4769 A2256 32k multicolored   75 55
            Set value   1.35 1.00

John   Soviet Circus
McClean — A2257   Emblem — A2258

1979, Aug. 29   Litho.   *Perf. 11¹/₂*
4770 A2257 4k red & black   15 15
John McClean (1879-1923), British Communist
labor leader.

1979, Sept.
4771 A2258 4k multicolored   15 15
Soviet Circus, 60th anniversary.

Friendship — A2259

Children's Drawings: 3k, Children and Horses.
4k, Dances. 15k, The Excursion.

1979, Sept. 10   *Perf. 12¹/₂x12*
4772 A2259 2k multicolored   15 15
4773 A2259 3k multicolored   15 15
4774 A2259 4k multicolored   15 15
4775 A2259 15k multicolored   30 20
            Set value   52 38
International Year of the Child.

Oriolus oriolus — A2260

Birds: 3k, Dendrocopus minor. 4k, Parus cristatus. 10k, Tyto alba. 15k, Caprimulgus europaeus.

1979, Sept. 18
4776	A2260	2k multicolored	15	15
4777	A2260	3k multicolored	15	15
4778	A2260	4k multicolored	15	15
4779	A2260	10k multicolored	32	15
4780	A2260	15k multicolored	50	20
	Nos. 4776-4780 (5)		1.27	
	Set value			52

German Arms, Marx, Engels, Lenin, Berlin A2261

1979, Oct. 7   Photo.   Perf. 11½
4781	A2261	6k multicolored	15	15

German Democratic Republic, 30th anniv.

Valery Ryumin, Vladimir Lyakhov, Salyut 6 — A2262

Design: No. 4783, Spacecraft.

1979, Oct. 10   Perf. 12x11½
4782	A2262	15k multicolored	35	25
4783	A2262	15k multicolored	35	25
a.		Pair, #4782-4783	70	50

175 days in space, Feb. 25-Aug. 19. No. 4783a has continuous design.

Star — A2264   Hammer and Sickle — A2265

1979, Oct. 18   Perf. 11½
4784	A2264	4k multicolored	15	15

USSR Armed Forces, 60th anniversary.

1979, Oct. 18
4785	A2265	4k multicolored	15	15

October Revolution, 62nd anniversary.

Katherina, by T. G. Shevchenko A2266

Ukrainian Paintings: 3k, Working Girl, by K.K. Kostandi. 4k, Lenin's Return to Petrograd, by A.M. Lopuhov. 10k, Soldier's Return, by N.V. Kostesky. 15k, Going to Work, by M.G. Belsky.

1979, Nov. 18   Litho.   Perf. 12x12½
4786	A2266	2k multicolored	15	15
4787	A2266	3k multicolored	15	15
4788	A2266	4k multicolored	15	15
4789	A2266	10k multicolored	20	15
4790	A2266	15k multicolored	30	20
	Set value		72	52

Shabolovka Radio Tower, Moscow — A2267   Mischa Holding Stamp — A2268

1979, Nov. 28   Photo.   Perf. 12
4791	A2267	32k multicolored	1.00	50

Radio Moscow, 50th anniversary.

1979, Nov. 28   Perf. 12x12½
4792	A2268	4k multicolored	50	15

New Year 1980.

Hand Holding Peace Message — A2269   Policeman, Patrol Car, Helicopter — A2270

Peace Program in Action: No. 4794, Hands holding cultural symbols. No. 4795, Hammer and sickle, flag.

1979, Dec. 5   Litho.   Perf. 12
4793	A2269	4k multicolored	15	15
4794	A2269	4k multicolored	15	15
4795	A2269	4k multicolored	15	15
	Set value		26	24

1979, Dec. 20   Perf. 12x12½
Traffic Safety: 4k, Car, girl and ball. 6k, Speeding cars.
4796	A2270	3k multicolored	15	15
4797	A2270	4k multicolored	15	15
4798	A2270	6k multicolored	15	15
	Set value		28	22

Vulkanolog — A2271

Research Ships and Portraits: 2k, Professor Bogorov. 4k, Ernst Krenkel. 6k, Vladislav Volkov. 10k, Cosmonaut Yuri Gagarin. 15k, Academician E.B. Kurchatov.

Lithographed and Engraved
1979, Dec. 25   Perf. 12x11½
4799	A2271	1k multicolored	15	15
4800	A2271	2k multicolored	15	15
4801	A2271	4k multicolored	15	15
4802	A2271	6k multicolored	18	15
4803	A2271	10k multicolored	32	15
4804	A2271	48k multicolored	48	20
	Nos. 4799-4804 (6)		1.43	
	Set value			60

See Nos. 4881-4886.

Souvenir Sheet

Explorers Raising Red Flag at North Pole — A2272

1979, Dec. 25   Photo.   Perf. 11½x12
4805	A2272	50k multicolored	2.00	75

Komsomolskaya Pravda North Pole expedition.

Type of 1970
Design: 4k, Coat of arms, power line, factories.

1980, Jan. 10   Litho.   Perf. 12x12½
4806	A1794	4k carmine	15	15

Mordovian Autonomous SSR, 50th anniv.

Freestyle Skating A2273

Perf. 12x12½, 12½x12
1980, Jan. 22
4807	A2273	4k Speed skating	15	15
4808	A2273	6k shown	15	15
4809	A2273	10k Ice hockey	25	15
4810	A2273	15k Downhill skiing	35	25
4811	A2273	20k Luge, vert.	50	35
	Nos. 4807-4811 (5)		1.40	
	Set value			90

Souvenir Sheet
4812	A2273	50k Cross-country skiing, vert.	1.75	1.00

13th Winter Olympic Games, Lake Placid, NY, Feb. 12-24.

Nikolai Ilyitch Podvoiski (1880-1948), Revolutionary — A2274

1980, Feb. 16   Engr.   Perf. 12½x12
4813	A2274	4k claret brown	15	15

Rainbow, by A.K. Savrasov — A2275

Paintings: No. 4815, Summer Harvest, by A.G. Venetsianov, vert. No. 4816, Old Erevan, by M.S. Saryan.

1980, Mar. 4   Litho.   Perf. 11½
4814	A2275	6k multicolored	25	15
4815	A2275	6k multicolored	25	15
4816	A2275	6k multicolored	25	15
	Set value			24

Souvenir Sheet

Cosmonaut Alexei Leonov — A2276

1980, Mar. 18   Litho.   Perf. 12½x12
4817	A2276	50k multicolored	1.75	75

Man's first walk in space (Voshkod 2, Mar. 18-19, 1965).

Georg Ots, Estonian Artist A2277   Lenin Order, 50th Anniversary A2278

1980, Mar. 21   Engr.
4818	A2277	4k slate blue	15	15

1980, Apr. 6   Photo.   Perf. 11½
4819	A2278	4k multicolored	15	15

Souvenir Sheet

Cosmonauts, Salyut 6 and Soyuz — A2279

1980, Apr. 12   Litho.   Perf. 12
4820	A2279	50k multicolored	1.50	1.00

Intercosmos cooperative space program.

Flags and Arms of Azerbaijan, Government House — A2280

"Mother Russia," Fireworks over Moscow — A2282

Lenin, 110th Birth Anniversary — A2281

1980, Apr. 22   Photo.
4821 A2280 4k multicolored   15   15

Azerbaijan Soviet Socialist Republic, Communist Party of Azerbaijan, 60th anniv.

Souvenir Sheet
1980, Apr. 22   Perf. 12x11½
4822 A2281 30k multicolored   1.25   75

1980, Apr. 25   Litho.

Designs: No. 4824, Soviet War Memorial, Berlin, raising of Red flag. No. 4825, Parade, Red Square, Moscow.

4823 A2282 4k multicolored   15   15
4824 A2282 4k multicolored   15   15
4825 A2282 4k multicolored   15   15
     Set value   24   24

35th anniv. of victory in World War II.

Workers' Monument A2283

"XXV" A2284

1980, May 12   Litho.   Perf. 12
4826 A2283 4k multicolored   15   15

Workers' Delegates in Ivanovo-Voznesensk, 75th anniversary.

1980, May 14   Photo.   Perf. 11½
4827 A2284 32k multicolored   1.25   75

Signing of Warsaw Pact (Bulgaria, Czechoslovakia, German Democratic Rep., Hungary, Poland, Romania, USSR), 25th anniv.

YaK-24 Helicopter, 1953 — A2285

1980, May 15   Litho.   Perf. 12½x12
4828 A2285 1k shown   15   15
4829 A2285 2k MI-8, 1962   15   15
4830 A2285 3k KA-26, 1965   15   15
4831 A2285 6k MI-6, 1957   15   15
4832 A2285 15k MI-10   40   25
4833 A2285 32k V-12   80   55
     Set value   1.50   1.05

David Anacht, Illuminated Manuscript A2286

Emblem, Training Lab A2287

1980, May 16   Perf. 12
4834 A2286 4k multicolored   15   15

David Anacht, Armenian philosopher, 1500th birth anniversary.

1980, June 4
4835 A2287 6k shown   15   15
4836 A2287 15k Cosmonauts meeting   40   25
4837 A2287 32k Press conference   80   55

Intercosmos cooperative space program (USSR-Hungary).

Polar Fox A2288

1980, June 25   Litho.   Perf. 12x12½
4838 A2288 2k Dark silver fox,vert.   15   15
4839 A2288 4k shown   15   15
4840 A2288 6k Mink   15   15
4841 A2288 10k Azerbaijan nutria, vert.   20   15
4842 A2288 15k Black sable   30   20
     Set value   78   55

Factory, Buildings, Arms of Tatar A.S.S.R. A2289

1980, June 25   Perf. 12
4843 A2289 4k multicolored   15   15

Tatar Autonomous SSR, 60th anniv.

College — A2290

Ho Chi Minh — A2291

1980, July 1   Photo.   Perf. 11½
4844 A2290 4k multicolored   15   15

Bauman Technological College, Moscow, 150th anniversary.

1980, July 7
4845 A2291 6k multicolored   15   15

Red Flag, Lithuanian Arms, Flag, Red Guards Monument A2292

1980, July 12   Litho.   Perf. 12
4846 A2292 4k multicolored   15   15

Lithuanian SSR, 40th anniv.

Russian Flag and Arms, Latvian Flag, Monument, Buildings A2293

Design: No. 4848, Russian flag and arms, Estonian flag, monument, buildings.

1980, July 21   Litho.   Perf. 12
4847 A2293 4k multicolored   15   15
4848 A2293 4k multicolored   15   15
     Set value   20   16

Restoration of Soviet power.

Cosmonauts Boarding Soyuz — A2294

1980, July 24   Perf. 12x12½
4849 A2294 6k shown   15   15
4850 A2294 15k Working aboard spacecraft   45   25
4851 A2294 32k Return flight   80   55

Center for Cosmonaut Training, 20th anniv.

Avicenna (980-1037), Philosopher and Physician — A2295

Photogravure and Engraved
1980, Aug. 16   Perf. 11½
4852 A2295 4k multicolored   15   15

Soviet Racing Car KHADI-7 — A2296

1980, Aug. 25   Litho.   Perf. 12
4853 A2296 2k shown   15   15
4854 A2296 6k KHADI-10   15   15
4855 A2296 15k KHADI-113   50   30
4856 A2296 30k KHADI-133   90   65
     Set value   1.05

Kazakhstan Republic, 60th Anniversary A2297

1980, Aug. 26
4857 A2297 4k multicolored   50   15

Ingres, Self-portrait, and Nymph — A2298

1980, Aug. 29   Perf. 12x12½
4858 A2298 32k multicolored   1.00   50

Jean Auguste Dominique Ingres (1780-1867), French painter.

Morning on the Field of Kulikovo, by A. Bubnov — A2299

1980, Sept. 6   Litho.   Perf. 12
4859 A2299 4k multicolored   15   15

Battle of Kulikovo, 600th anniversary.

Town Hall, Tartu — A2300

1980, Sept. 15   Photo.   Perf. 11½
4860 A2300 4k multicolored   15   15

Tartu, 950th anniversary.

Y.V. Malyshev,
V.V. Aksenov
A2301

1980, Sept. 15   Litho.   Perf. 12x12¹/₂
4861 A2301 10k multicolored   30 25
Soyuz T-2 space flight.

Flight Training, Yuri
Gagarin — A2302

1980, Sept. 15   Photo.   Perf. 11¹/₂x12
4862 A2302   6k shown   15 15
4863 A2302 15k Space walk   40 25
4864 A2302 32K Endurance test   80 45

Gagarin Cosmonaut Training Center, 20th
anniversary.

Cosmonauts
Training
A2303

Designs (Intercosmos Emblem, Flags of USSR and
Cuba and): 15k, Inside weightless cabin. 32k,
Landing.

1980, Sept. 15   Litho.   Perf. 12x12¹/₂
4865 A2303   6k multicolored   15 15
4866 A2303 15k multicolored   40 25
4867 A2303 32k multicolored   80 45

Intercosmos cooperative space program (USSR-
Cuba).

October
Revolution,
63rd
Anniversary
A2304

1980, Sept. 20   Photo.   Perf. 11¹/₂
4868 A2304 6k multicolored   15 15

David Gurumishvily
(1705-1792),
Poet — A2305

1980, Sept. 20
4869 A2305 6k multicolored   15 15

Family with Serfs, by N.V. Nevrev (1830-
1904) — A2305a

Design: No. 4869B, Countess Tarakanova, by
K.D. Flavitsky (1830-1866), vert.

1980, Sept. 25   Litho.   Perf. 11¹/₂
4869A A2305a 6k multicolored   15 15
4869B A2305a 6k multicolored   15 15
            Set value   24 16

A.F. Joffe (1880-1960),
Physicist — A2306

1980, Sept. 29
4870 A2306 4k multicolored   15 15

Siberian Pine
A2307

1980, Sept. 29   Litho.   Perf. 12¹/₂x12
4871 A2307   2k shown   15 15
4872 A2307   4k Oak   15 15
4873 A2307   6k Lime tree, vert.   15 15
4874 A2307 10k Sea bucthorn   20 15
4875 A2307 15k European ash   30 20
            Set value   75 55

A.M. Vasilevsky (1895-
1977), Soviet
Marshal — A2308

1980, Sept. 30   Engr.   Perf. 12
4876 A2308 4k dark green   15 15

Souvenir Sheet

Mischa Holding
Olympic
Torch — A2309

1980, Nov. 24   Perf. 12x12¹/₂
4877 A2309 1r multicolored   7.50 1.75

Completion of 22nd Summer Olympic Games,
Moscow, July 19-Aug. 3.

A.V. Suvorov
(1730-1800),
General and
Military Theorist
A2310

1980, Nov. 24   Engr.
4878 A2310 4k slate   15 15

A2311

1980, Nov. 24   Litho.   Perf. 12
4879 A2311 4k multicolored   50 15

Armenian SSR & Armenian Communist Party,
60th annivs.

Aleksandr Blok (1880-
1921), Poet — A2312

1980, Nov. 24
4880 A2312 4k multicolored   15 15

Research Ship Type of 1979
Lithographed and Engraved
1980, Nov. 24   Perf. 12x11¹/₂
4881 A2271   2k Aju Dag, Fleet arms   15 15
4882 A2271   3k Valerian Urywaev   15 15
4883 A2271   4k Mikhail Somov   15 15
4884 A2271   6k Sergei Korolev   15 15
4885 A2271 10k Otto Schmidt   20 15
4886 A2271 15k Ustislav Kelgysh   30 20
            Set value   82 60

For overprint see No. 5499.

Russian   Soviet Medical College,
Flag   50th Anniversary
A2313   A2314

1980, Dec. 1   Engr.   Perf. 12x12¹/₂
4887 A2313 3k orange red   15 15

1980, Dec. 1   Photo.   Perf. 11¹/₂
4888 A2314 4k multicolored   15 15

New Year
1981
A2315

1980, Dec. 1   Litho.   Perf. 12
4889 A2315 4k multicolored   15 15

Lenin,
Electrical Plant
A2316

1980, Dec. 18
4890 A2316 4k multicolored   15 15

60th anniversary of GOELRO (Lenin's electro-
economic plan).

A.N. Nesmeyanov (1899-
1980),
Chemist — A2317

1980, Dec. 19   Perf. 12¹/₂x12
4891 A2317 4k multicolored   15 15

Nagatinski Bridge, Moscow — A2318

Photogravure and Engraved
1980, Dec. 23   Perf. 11¹/₂x12
4892 A2318   4k shown   15 15
4893 A2318   6k Luzhniki Bridge   15 15
4894 A2318 15k Kalininski Bridge   30 20
            Set value   50 35

S.K. Timoshenko
A2319

Flags of India and
USSR, Government
House, New Delhi
A2320

1980, Dec. 25   Engr.   Perf. 12
4895 A2319 4k rose lake   15 15

Timoshenko (1895-1970), Soviet marshal.

1980, Dec. 30   Litho.   Perf. 12x12½
4896 A2320 4k multicolored   50 35

Visit of Pres. Brezhnev to India. Printed se-tenant with inscribed label.

Mirny Base — A2321

1981, Jan. 5   Perf. 12
4897 A2321 4k shown   15 15
4808 A2321 6k Earth station, rocket 15 15
4899 A2321 15k Map, supply ship 30 20
　　　　Set value   50 35

Soviet Antarctic research, 25th anniv.

Dagestan Soviet Socialist Republic, 60th Anniversary A2322

1981, Jan. 20
4900 A2322 4k multicolored   15 15

Bandy World Championship, Cheborovsk A2323

1981, Jan. 20
4901 A2323 6k multicolored   15 15

26th Congress of Ukrainian Communist Party. A2324

1981, Jan. 23   Photo.   Perf. 11½
4902 A2324 4k multicolored   15 15

Lenin, "XXVI" A2325

Lenin and Congress Building — A2326

Banner and Kremlin — A2327

1981   Photo.   Perf. 11½
4903 A2325 4k multicolored   15 15

Photogravure and Embossed
1982   Perf. 11½x12
4904 A2326 20k multicolored   1.50 75

Souvenir Sheet
Litho.
Perf. 12x12½
4905 A2327 50k multicolored   1.50 75

26th Communist Party Congress. Issue dates: 4k, 20k, Jan. 22; 50k, Feb. 16.

Mstislav V. Keldysh A2328

Freighter, Flags of USSR and India A2329

Perf. 11½x12
1981, Feb. 10   Photo.   Engr.
4906 A2328 4k multicolored   15 15

Mstislav Vsevolodovich Keldysh (1911-1978), mathematician.

1981, Feb. 10   Litho.   Perf. 12
4907 A2329 15k multicolored   50 30

Soviet-Indian Shipping Line, 25th anniv.

Baikal-Amur Railroad and Map A2330

10th Five-Year Plan Projects (1976-1980): No. 4909, Gas plant, Urengoi (spherical tanks). No. 4910, Enisei River power station (dam). No. 4911, Atomic power plant. No. 4912, Paper mill. No. 4913, Coal mining, Ekibstyi.

1981, Feb. 18   Perf. 12½x12
4908 A2330 4k multicolored   15 15
4909 A2330 4k multicolored   15 15
4910 A2330 4k multicolored   15 15
4911 A2330 4k multicolored   15 15
4912 A2330 4k multicolored   15 15
4913 A2330 4k multicolored   15 15
　　　　Set value   50 48

Georgian Soviet Socialist Republic, 60th Anniv. A2331

1981, Feb. 25   Perf. 12
4914 A2331 4k multicolored   15 15

Abkhazian Autonomous Soviet Socialist Republic, 60th Anniv. A2332

1981, Mar. 4
4915 A2332 4k multicolored   15 15

Communica-tions Institute A2333

Satellite, Radio Operator A2334

1981, Mar. 12   Photo.   Perf. 11½
4916 A2333 4k multicolored   15 15

Moscow Electrotechnical Institute of Communications, 60th anniv.

1981, Mar. 12
4917 A2334 4k multicolored   35 25

30th All-Union Amateur Radio Designers Exhibition.

Cosmonauts L.I. Popov and V.V. Rumin A2335

1981, Mar. 20   Litho.   Perf. 12
4918 A2335 15k shown   40 25
4919 A2335 15k Spacecraft complex 60 25
　a.　Pair, #4918-4919 + label   1.00 50

185-day flight of Cosmos 35-Salyut 6-Cosmos 37 complex, Apr. 9-Oct. 11, 1980. No. 4919a has a continuous design.

Cosmonauts O. Makarov, L. Kizim and G. Strekalov — A2336

1981, Mar. 20   Perf. 12½x12
4920 A2336 10k multicolored   24 15

Soyuz T-3 flight, Nov. 27-Dec. 10, 1980.

Lift-Off, Baikonur Base — A2337

1981, Mar. 23
4921 A2337 6k shown   15 15
4922 A2337 15k Mongolians watching flight on TV 40 25
4923 A2337 32k Re-entry   80 48

Intercosmos cooperative space program (USSR-Mongolia).

Vitus Bering — A2338

Yuri Gagarin and Earth — A2339

Yuri Gagarin — A2340

1981, Mar. 25   Engr.   Perf. 12x12½
4924 A2338 4k dark blue   15 15

Bering (1680-1741), Danish navigator.

1981, Apr. 12   Photo.   Perf. 11½x12
4925 A2339 6k shown   15 15
4926 A2339 15k S.P. Korolev (craft designer) 40 25
4927 A2339 32k Monument   80 48

Souvenir Sheet
4928 A2340 50k shown   5.00 1.00

Soviet space flights, 20th anniv. Nos. 4925-4927 each se-tenant with label.

Salyut Orbital Station, 10th Anniv. of Flight — A2341

1981, Apr. 19   Litho.   Perf. 12x12½
4929 A2341 32k multicolored   1.00 50

Souvenir Sheet

111th Birth
Anniv. of
Lenin — A2342

1981, Apr. 22   Perf. 11¹/₂x12¹/₂
4930 A2342 50k multicolored   1.50   60

Sergei Prokofiev
(1891-1953),
Composer
A2343

New Hofburg
Palace, Vienna
A2344

1981, Apr. 23   Engr.   Perf. 12
4931 A2343 4k dark purple   40   25

1981, May 5   Litho.
4932 A2344 15k multicolored   50   22

WIPA 1981 Phil. Exhib., Vienna, May 22-31.

Adzhar
Autonomous
Soviet Socialist
Republic, 60th
Anniv.
A2345

1981, May 7
4933 A2345 4k multicolored   15   15

Centenary of
Welding
(Invented by
N.N.
Benardos)
A2346

Lithographed and Engraved
1981, May 12   Perf. 11¹/₂
4934 A2346 6k multicolored   15   15

Intl. Architects Union,
14th Congress,
Warsaw — A2347

1981, May 12   Photo.
4935 A2347 15k multicolored   50   25

Albanian Girl,
by A.A. Ivanov
A2348

Paintings: No. 4937, Horseman, by F.A.
Roubeau. No. 4938, The Demon, by M.A. Wrubel,
horiz. No. 4939, Sunset over the Sea, by N.N. Ge,
horiz.

1981, May 15   Litho.   Perf. 12x12¹/₂
4936 A2348 10k multicolored   25   15
4937 A2348 10k multicolored   25   15
4938 A2348 10k multicolored   25   15
4939 A2348 10k multicolored   25   15

Cosmonauts in
Training
A2349

1981, May 15
4940 A2349   6k shown   15   15
4941 A2349 15k In space   40   25
4942 A2349 32k Return   80   48

Intercosmos cooperative space program (USSR-Romania).

Dwarf
Primrose
A2350

Flowers of the Carpathian Mountains: 6k, Great
carline thistle. 10k, Mountain parageum. 15k,
Alpine bluebell. 32k, Rhododendron kotschyi.

1981, May 20   Perf. 12
4943 A2350   4k multicolored   15   15
4944 A2350   6k multicolored   15   15
4945 A2350 10k multicolored   25   15
4946 A2350 15k multicolored   40   25
4947 A2350 32k multicolored   80   48
          Nos. 4943-4947 (5)   1.75 1.18

Luigi Longo, Italian
Labor Leader, 1st Death
Anniv. — A2351

1981, May 24   Photo.   Perf. 11¹/₂
4948 A2351 6k multicolored   15   15

Nizami
Gianshevi
(1141-1209),
Azerbaijan
Poet
A2352

1981, May 25   Photo. & Engr.
4949 A2352 4k multicolored   15   15

A2353   A2354

1981, June 18   Litho.   Perf. 12
4950 A2353   4k Running   15   15
4951 A2353   6k Soccer   15   15
4952 A2353 10k Discus throwing   30   15
4953 A2353 15k Boxing   45   30
4954 A2353 32k Diving   85   50
          Nos. 4950-4954 (5)   1.90 1.25

1981, July 6
4955 A2354 6k multicolored   15   15

Mongolian Revolution, 60th anniv.

12th Intl. Film Festival,
Moscow — A2355

1981, July 6   Photo.   Perf. 11¹/₂
4956 A2355 15k multicolored   50   25

River Tour
Boat Lenin
A2356

1981, July 9   Litho.   Perf. 12¹/₂
4957 A2356   4k shown   15   15
4958 A2356   6k Cosmonaut Gagarin   15   15
4959 A2356 15k Valerian Kuibyshev   40   25
4960 A2356 32k Freighter Baltijski   90   48
          Set value   88

Icebreaker Maligin — A2357

Photogravure and Engraved
1981, July 9   Perf. 11¹/₂x12
4961 A2357 15k multicolored   50   25

26th Party Congress Resolutions (Intl.
Cooperation) — A2358

1981, July 15   Photo.   Perf. 12x11¹/₂
4962 A2358 4k shown   15   15
4963 A2358 4k Industry   15   15
4964 A2358 4k Energy   15   15
4965 A2358 4k Agriculture   15   15
4966 A2358 4k Communications   15   15
4967 A2358 4k Arts   15   15
          Nos. 4962-4967 (6)   90
          Set value   48

I.N. Ulyanov (Lenin's
Father), 150th Anniv.
of Birth — A2359

1981, July 25   Engr.   Perf. 11¹/₂
4968 A2359 4k multicolored   15   15

Leningrad Theater,
Sesquicentennial — A2360

1981, Aug. 12   Photo.   Perf. 11¹/₂
4969 A2360 6k multicolored   15   15

A.M.
Gerasimov,
Artist, Birth
Centenary
A2361

1981, Aug. 12   Litho.   Perf. 12
4970 A2361 4k multicolored   15   15

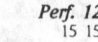

Physical Chemistry Institute, Moscow
Academy of Science, 50th Anniv.
A2362

1981, Aug. 12   Photo.   Perf. 11¹/₂
4971 A2362 4k multicolored   15   15

Siberian
Tit — A2363

Designs: Song birds.

Perf. 12¹/₂x12, 12x12¹/₂
1981, Aug. 20   Litho.
4972 A2363   6k shown   15   15
4973 A2363 10k Tersiphone paradisi,
               vert.   32   15
4974 A2363 15k Emberiza jankovski   42   25
4975 A2363 20k Sutora webbiana,
               vert.   55   30
4976 A2363 32k Saxicola torquata,
               vert.   90   45
          Nos. 4972-4976 (5)   2.34 1.30

60th Anniv. of Komi Autonomous Soviet Socialist Republic A2364

1981, Aug. 22   *Perf. 12*
4977 A2364 4k multicolored   35 15

Svyaz-'81 Intl. Communications Exhibition — A2365

Photogravure and Engraved
1981, Aug. 22   *Perf. 11½*
4978 A2365 4k multicolored   15 15

60th Anniv. of Kabardino-Balkar Autonomous Soviet Socialist Republic — A2366

1981, Sept. 1   Litho.   *Perf. 12*
4979 A2366 4k multicolored   15 15

War Veterans' Committee, 25th Anniv. — A2367

Schooner Kodor — A2368

1981, Sept. 1   Photo.   *Perf. 11½*
4980 A2367 4k multicolored   15 15

Perf. 12½x12, 12x12½
1981, Sept. 18   **Litho.**
Designs: Training ships. 4k, 6k, 15k, 20k, horiz.

4981 A2368	4k 4-masted bark Tovarich I	15	15
4982 A2368	6k Barkentine Vega I	15	15
4983 A2368	10k shown	30	15
4984 A2368	15k 3-masted bark Tovarich	40	30
4985 A2368	20k 4-masted bark Kruzenstern	50	35
4986 A2368	32k 4-masted bark Sedov	75	50
Nos. 4981-4986 (6)		2.25	1.60

A2369   A2370

1981, Oct. 10   *Perf. 12*
4987 A2369 4k multicolored   15 15
Kazakhstan's Union with Russia, 250th Anniv.

1981, Oct. 10   Photo.   *Perf. 11½*
4988 A2370 4k multicolored   75 50
Mikhail Alekseevich Lavrentiev (1900-80), mathematician.

64th Anniv. of October Revolution — A2371

1981, Oct. 15   **Litho.**
4989 A2371 4k multicolored   15 15

Ekran Satellite TV Broadcasting System A2372

1981, Oct. 15   *Perf. 12*
4990 A2372 4k multicolored   15 15

A2373

A2374

1981, Oct. 15
4991 A2373 10k multicolored   30 15
4992 A2374 10k multicolored   30 15
Salyut 6-Soyuz flight of V.V. Kovalionok and V.P. Savinykh.

Пабло Пикассо 1881-1973
1981 ПОЧТА СССР к50
A2375

ПОЧТА СССР-1981
4
С.Д.МЕРКУРОВ
A2376

Souvenir Sheet
1981, Oct. 25   *Perf. 12x12½*
4993 A2375 50k multicolored   2.75 90
Birth centenary of Pablo Picasso.

Photogravure and Engraved
1981, Nov. 5   *Perf. 11½*
4994 A2376 15k multicolored   15 15
Sergei Dmitrievich Merkurov (1881-1952), artist.

Autumn, by Nino Pirosmanas, 1913 — A2377

Paintings: 6k, Guriyka, by M.G. Kokodze, 1921. 10k, Fellow Travelers, by U.M. Dzhaparidze, 1936, horiz. 15k, Shota Rustaveli, by S.S. Kobuladze, 1938. 32k, Collecting Tea, by V.D. Gudiashvili, 1964, horiz.

Perf. 12x12½, 12½x12
1981, Nov. 5   **Litho.**
4995 A2377 4k multicolored   15 15
4996 A2377 6k multicolored   20 15
4997 A2377 10k multicolored   48 15
4998 A2377 15k multicolored   65 25
4999 A2377 32k multicolored   1.40 48
Nos. 4995-4999 (5)   2.88 1.18

New Year 1982 — A2378

1981, Dec. 2   Litho.   *Perf. 12*
5000 A2378 4k multicolored   15 15

Public Transportation 19th-20th Cent. — A2379

Photogravure and Engraved
1981, Dec. 10   *Perf. 11½x12*
5001 A2379 4k Sled   15 15
5002 A2379 6k Horse-drawn trolley 15 15
5003 A2379 10k Coach   28 15
5004 A2379 15k Taxi, 1926   40 25
5005 A2379 20k Bus, 1926   50 30
5006 A2379 32k Trolley, 1912   80 50
Nos. 5001-5006 (6)   2.28 1.50

Souvenir Sheet

Kremlin and New Delhi Parliament — A2380

1981, Dec. 17   **Photo.**
5007 A2380 50k multicolored   50 75
1st direct telephone link with India. Labels show Brezhnev and Mrs. Gandhi talking on telephone.

A2381

A2382

1982, Jan. 11   Litho.   *Perf. 12*
5008 A2381 4k multicolored   15 15
5009 A2382 4k multicolored   15 15
      Set value   16 16
60th anniv. of Checheno-Ingush Autonomous SSR and of Yakutsk Autonomous SSR.

1500th Anniv. of Kiev — A2383

1982, Jan. 12   Photo.   *Perf. 11½x12*
5010 A2383 10k multicolored   30 25

A2384   A2385

1982, Jan. 12   *Perf. 11½*
5011 A2384 4k multicolored   15 15
S.P. Korolev (1907-66), rocket designer.

1982, Jan. 20   Litho.   *Perf. 12*
5012 A2385 6k multicolored   15 15
Nazym Khikmet (1902-1963), Turkish poet.

10th World Trade Union Congress, Havana — A2386

1982, Feb. 1   Photo.   *Perf. 11½*
5013 A2386 15k multicolored   50 25

Find what you're looking for in the "Scott Stamp Monthly". New issue and topical listings, as well as fascinating features, are found in each issue. Please call 1-800-488-5351 for more information.

17th Soviet Trade
Union
Congress — A2387

1982, Feb. 10   **Litho.**
5014 A2387 4k multicolored   15 15

Edouard
Manet (1832-
1883)
A2388

1982, Feb. 10   **Perf. 12x12½**
5015 A2388 32k multicolored   1.00 45

Equestrian
Sports
A2389

1982, Feb. 16   Photo.   Perf. 11½
5016 A2389 4k Hurdles   15 15
5017 A2389 6k Riding   15 15
5018 A2389 15k Racing   30 20
              Set value   50 35

2nd Death Anniv. of
Marshal Tito of
Yugoslavia — A2390

1982, Feb. 25   Litho.   Perf. 12
5019 A2390 6k olive black   15 15

350th Anniv.
of State
University of
Tartu
A2392

1982, Mar. 4   Photo.   Perf. 11½
5020 A2392 4k multicolored   15 15

9th Intl.
Cardiologists
Congress,
Moscow
A2393

1982, Mar. 4
5021 A2393 15k multicolored   50 22

Souvenir Sheet

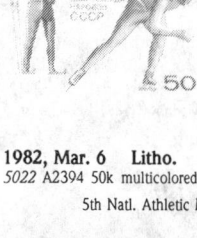

Biathlon,
Speed
Skating
A2394

1982, Mar. 6   Litho.   Perf. 12½x12
5022 A2394 50k multicolored   1.50 70
          5th Natl. Athletic Meet.

Blueberry   Venera 13 and
Bush — A2395   Venera 14
                     Flights — A2396

1982, Mar. 10   Litho.   Perf. 12x12½
5023 A2395 4k Blackberries   15 15
5024 A2395 6k shown   15 15
5025 A2395 10k Cranberries   32 15
5026 A2395 15k Cherries   45 25
5027 A2395 32k Strawberries   1.00 45
          Nos. 5023-5027 (5)   2.07 1.15

1982, Mar. 10   Photo.   Perf. 11½
5028 A2396 10k multicolored   30 25

Marriage
Ceremony, by
W.W. Pukirev
(1832-1890)
A2397

Paintings: No. 5030, M.I. Lopuchino, by Vladimir Borowikowsky (1757-1825). No. 5031, E.W.
Davidov, by O.A. Kiprensky (1782-1836). No.
5032, Landscape.

1982, Mar. 18   **Perf. 12**
5029 A2397 6k multicolored   15 15
5030 A2397 6k multicolored   15 15
5031 A2397 6k multicolored   15 15
5032 A2397 6k multicolored   15 15
              Set value   48 32

K.I. Tchukovsky (1882-
1969), Writer — A2398

1982, Mar. 31   **Engr.**
5033 A2398 4k black   15 15

Cosmonauts' Day — A2399

1982, Apr. 12   Photo.   Perf. 12x11½
5034 A2399 6k multicolored   15 15

Souvenir Sheet

112th Birth Anniv. of
Lenin — A2400

1982, Apr. 22   Photo.   Perf. 11½x12
5035 A2400 50k multicolored   1.50 70

A2401   A2402

1982, Apr. 25   Engr.   Perf. 12
5036 A2401 4k brown   15 15
   V.P. Soloviev-Sedoi (1907-79), composer.

1982, Apr. 25
5037 A2402 6k green   15 15
   G. Dimitrov (1882-1949), 1st Bulgarian Prime
Minister.

Kremlin Tower,   70th Anniv. of Pravda
Moscow   Newspaper
A2403   A2404

1982   Litho.   Perf. 12½x12
5038 A2403 45k brown   1.10 70
   a.   Engraved   1.10 70
   Issue dates: #5038, Apr. 25. #5038a, Oct. 12.

1982, May 5   Photo.   Perf. 12x11½
5039 A2404 4k multicolored   15 15

A2405   A2406

1982, May 10   **Perf. 11½**
5040 A2405 6k multicolored   15 15
   UN Conf. on Human Environment, 10th anniv.

1982, May 19
5041 A2406 4k multicolored   15 15
          Pioneers' Org., 60th anniv.

A2407   A2408

1982, May 19
5042 A2407 4k multicolored   15 15
          Communist Youth Org., 19th Cong.

1982, May 19
5043 A2408 15k multicolored   50 25
          ITU Delegates Conf., Nairobi.

TUL-80 Electric Locomotive — A2409

1982, May 20   **Perf. 12x11½**
5044 A2409 4k shown   15 15
5045 A2409 6k TEP-75 diesel   18 15
5046 A2409 10k TEP-7 diesel   38 15
5047 A2409 15k WL-82m electric   58 25
5048 A2409 32k EP-200 electric   1.25 48
          Nos. 5044-5048 (5)   2.54 1.18

1982 World Cup — A2410

1982, June 4   **Perf. 11½x12**
5049 A2410 20k olive & purple   60 28

Grus
Monacha — A2411

18th Ornithological Congress, Moscow: Rare birds.

1982, June 10 Litho. Perf. 12x12½
5050	A2411	2k shown	15	15
5051	A2411	4k Haliaeetus pelagicus	15	15
5052	A2411	6k Eurynorhynchus	15	15
5053	A2411	10k Eulabeia indica	30	15
5054	A2411	15k Chettusia gregaria	40	30
5055	A2411	32k Ciconia boyciana	80	50
		Nos. 5050-5055 (6)	1.95	
		Set value		1.15

Komomolsk-on-Amur City, 50th Anniv. — A2412

Photogravure and Engraved
1982, June 10 Perf. 11½
5056	A2412	4k multicolored	15	15

Tatchanka, by M.B. Grekov (1882-1934) — A2413

1982, June 15 Litho. Perf. 12½x12
5057	A2413	6k multicolored	15	15

2nd UN Conference on Peaceful Uses of Outer Space, Vienna, Aug. 9-21 — A2414

1982, June 15 Photo. Perf. 11½
5058	A2414	15k multicolored	50	22

Intercosmos Cooperative Space Program (USSR-France) — A2415

1982 Litho. Perf. 12½x12
5059	A2415	6k Cosmonauts	15	15
5060	A2415	20k Rocket, globe	65	30
5061	A2415	45k Satellites	1.40	70

Souvenir Sheet
5062	A2415	50k Emblem, satellite	1.50	75

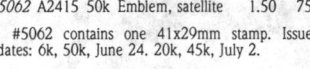

#5062 contains one 41x29mm stamp. Issue dates: 6k, 50k, June 24. 20k, 45k, July 2.

The Legend of the Goldfish, by P. Sosin, 1968 — A2416

Lacquerware Paintings, Ustera: 10k, Minin's Appeal to Count Posharski, by J. Phomitchev, 1953. 15k, Two Peasants, by A. Kotjagin, 1933. 20k, The Fisherman, by N. Klykov, 1933, 32k, The Arrest of the Propagandists, by N. Shishakov, 1968.

1982, July 6 Litho. Perf. 12½x12
5063	A2416	6k multicolored	15	15
5064	A2416	10k multicolored	32	15
5065	A2416	15k multicolored	42	15
5066	A2416	20k multicolored	65	30
5067	A2416	32k multicolored	95	45
		Nos. 5063-5067 (5)	2.49	1.30

Telephone Centenary — A2417

1982, July 13 Perf. 12
5068	A2417	4k Phone, 1882	15	15

P. Schilling's Electro-magnetic Telegraph Sesquicentennial — A2418

Photogravure and Engraved
1982, July 16 Perf. 11½
5069	A2418	6k Voltaic cells	15	15

Intervision Gymnastics Contest A2419

1982, Aug. 10 Photo.
5070	A2419	15k multicolored	50	30

Mastjahart Glider, 1923 A2420

Gliders.

1982, Aug. 20 Litho. Perf. 12½x12
5071	A2420	4k shown	15	15
5072	A2420	6k Red Star, 1930	15	15
5073	A2420	10k ZAGI-1, 1934	30	15

Size: 60x28mm
Perf. 11½x12
5074	A2420	20k Stakhanovets, 1939	50	15
5075	A2420	32k Troop carrier GR-29, 1941	80	50
		Nos. 5071-5075 (5)	1.90	
		Set value		92

See Nos. 5118-5122.

 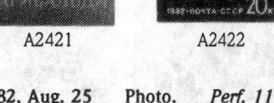

A2421 A2422

1982, Aug. 25 Photo. Perf. 11½
5076	A2421	6k multicolored	15	15

Garibaldi (1807-1882).

1982, Aug. 30
5077	A2422	20k multicolored	75	30

Intl. Atomic Energy Authority, 25th Anniv.

A2423 A2424

1982, Sept. 10 Engr. Perf. 12
5078	A2423	4k red brown	15	15

Marshal B.M. Shaposhnikov (1882-1945).

1982, Sept. 10 Photo. Perf. 11½
5079	A2424	6k King	25	15
5080	A2424	6k Queen	25	15
		Set value		16

World Chess Championship. See #5084.

A2425 A2426

1982, Sept. 10
5081	A2425	6k multicolored	15	15

African Natl. Congress, 70th Anniv.

1982, Sept. 17 Engr. Perf. 12½x12
5082	A2426	4k green	15	15

S.P. Botkin (1832-89), physician.

Souvenir Sheet

25th Anniv. of Sputnik — A2427

1982, Sept. 17 Litho. Perf. 12x12½
5083	A2427	50k multicolored	5.00	85

No. 5079 Overprinted in Gold for Karpov's Victory

1982, Sept. 22 Photo. Perf. 11½
5084	A2424	6k multicolored	60	30

World War II Warships — A2428

Photogravure and Engraved
1982, Sept. 22 Perf. 11½x12
5085	A2428	4k Submarine S-56	15	15
5086	A2428	6k Minelayer Gremjashtsky	15	15
5087	A2428	15k Mine sweeper T-205	50	30
5088	A2428	20k Cruiser Red Crimea	60	35
5089	A2428	45k Sebastopol	1.40	70
		Nos. 5085-5089 (5)	2.80	1.65

65th Anniv. of October Revolution — A2429

1982, Oct. 12 Litho. Perf. 12
5090	A2429	4k multicolored	15	15

House of the Soviets, Moscow — A2430

60th Anniv. of USSR: No. 5092, Dnieper Dam, Komosomol Monument, Statue of worker. No. 5093, Soviet War Memorial, resistance poster. No. 5094, Worker at podium, decree text. No. 5095, Workers' Monument, Moscow, Rocket, jet. No. 5096, Arms, Kremlin.

1982, Oct. 25 Photo. Perf. 11½x12
5091	A2430	10k multicolored	25	15
5092	A2430	10k multicolored	25	15
5093	A2430	10k multicolored	25	15
5094	A2430	10k multicolored	25	15
5095	A2430	10k multicolored	25	15
5096	A2430	10k multicolored	65	15
		Nos. 5091-5096 (6)	1.90	90

No. 5095 Overprinted in Red for All-Union Philatelic Exhibition, 1984

Всесоюзная
филателистическая
выставка

1982, Nov. 10
5097	A2430	10k multicolored	75	15

Portrait of an Actor, by Domenico Fetti — A2431

Paintings from the Hermitage: 10k, St. Sebastian, by Perugino. 20k, The Danae, by Titian, horiz. 45k,

Portrait of a Woman, by Correggio. No. 5102, Portrait of a Young Man, by Capriola. No. 5103a, Portrait of a Young Woman, by Melzi.

1982, Nov. 25   Litho.   Perf. 12x12½
5098 A2431 4k multicolored   15   15
5099 A2431 10k multicolored   40   15
5100 A2431 20k multicolored   65   35
5101 A2431 45k multicolored   1.25   70
5102 A2431 50k multicolored   1.25   75
    Nos. 5098-5102 (5)   3.70 2.10

Souvenir Sheet
5103   Sheet of 2   4.50 1.65
   a.   A2431 50k multicolored   1.00   65

See Nos. 5129-5134, 5199-5204, 5233-5238, 5310-5315, 5335-5340.

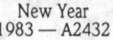

New Year
1983 — A2432

60th Anniv. of
USSR — A2433

1982, Dec. 1
5104 A2432 4k multicolored   15   15

Souvenir Sheet
1982, Dec. 3   Perf. 12½x12
5105 A2433 50k multicolored   1.50   90

Souvenir Sheet

Mountain Climbers Scaling Mt.
Everest — A2434

1982, Dec. 20   Photo.   Perf. 11½x12
5106 A2434 50k multicolored   2.50 1.10

Lighthouses
A2435

Mail Transport
A2436

1982, Dec. 29   Litho.   Perf. 12
5107 A2435 6k green & multi   15   15
5108 A2435 6k lilac & multi   15   15
5109 A2435 6k salmon & multi   15   15

5110 A2435 6k lt gldn brn & multi   15   15
5111 A2435 6k lt brown & multi   15   15
    Set value   60   40

See Nos. 5179-5183, 5265-5269.

1982, Dec. 22   Perf. 12
5112 A2436 5k greenish blue   50   15

1983, May 20   Litho.   Perf. 12
5113 A2436 5k blue   1.00   15

Iskra Newspaper
Masthead
A2438

Fedor P. Tolstoi
A2439

1983, Jan. 5   Litho.   Perf. 12x12½
5114 A2438 4k multicolored   15   15

80th anniv. of 2nd Social-Democratic Workers' Party.

1983, Jan. 5   Photo.   Perf. 11½
5115 A2439 4k multicolored   15   15

Tolstoi (1783-1873), painter.

65th Anniv. of
Armed
Forces — A2440

60th Anniv. of
Aeroflot
Airlines — A2441

1983, Jan. 25   Litho.   Perf. 12
5116 A2440 4k multicolored   15   15

Souvenir Sheet
1983, Feb. 9   Perf. 12x12½
5117 A2441 50k multicolored   1.50 1.00

Glider Type of 1982
1983, Feb. 10   Perf. 12½x12
5118 A2420 2k A-9, 1948   15   15
5119 A2420 4k KAJ-12, 1957   15   15
5120 A2420 6k A-15, 1960   15   15
5121 A2420 20k SA-7, 1970   50   35
5122 A2420 45k LAJ-12, 1979   1.10   70
    Nos. 5118-5122 (5)   2.05
    Set value   1.25

Tashkent Bimillenium — A2442

1983, Feb. 17   Perf. 12½x12
5123 A2442 4k View   15   15

B.N. Petrov
(1913-1980),
Scientist
A2443

Holy Family, by
Raphael
A2444

1983, Feb. 17
5124 A2443 4k multicolored   15   15

1983, Feb. 17   Perf. 12x12½
5125 A2444 50k multicolored   1.50 1.00

Soyuz T-7-
Salyut 7-Soyuz
T-5 Flight
A2445

1983, Mar. 10   Perf. 12x12½
5126 A2445 10k L. Popov, A. Serebrav,
           S. Savitskaya   30   15

Souvenir Sheet

World Communications Year — A2446

1983, Mar. 10   Photo.   Perf. 11½
5127 A2446 50k multicolored   1.50 1.25

A.W. Aleksandrov, Natl. Anthem
Composer — A2447

1983, Mar. 22   Litho.   Perf. 12
5128 A2447 4k multicolored   15   15

Hermitage Type of 1982

Rembrandt Paintings, Hermitage, Leningrad: 4k, Portrait of an Old Woman. 10k, Portrait of a Learned Man. 20k, Old Warrior. 45k, Portrait of Mrs. B. Martens Doomer. No. 5133, Sacrifice of Abraham. No. 5134a, Portrait of an Old Man in a Red Garment.

**   Perf. 12x12½**
1983, Mar. 25   Wmk. 383
5129 A2431 4k multicolored   15   15
5130 A2431 10k multicolored   30   15
5131 A2431 20k multicolored   60   35
5132 A2431 45k multicolored   1.40   90
5133 A2431 50k multicolored   1.50   95
    Nos. 5129-5133 (5)   3.95 2.50

Souvenir Sheet
Lithographed and Embossed
5134   Sheet of 2 + label   4.00 3.00
   a.   A2431 50k multicolored   1.65   70

Souvenir Sheet

Cosmonauts' Day — A2449

**   Perf. 12½x12**
1983, Apr. 12   Litho.   Unwmk.
5135 A2449 50k Soyuz T   7.50 2.00

Souvenir Sheet

113th Birth Anniv. of
Lenin — A2450

Photogravure and Engraved
1983, Apr. 22   Perf. 11½x12
5136 A2450 50k multicolored   1.50   70

A2451

Salyut 7-Soyuz 7 211-Day Flight — A2452

1983, Apr. 25   Litho.   Perf. 12½x12
5137 A2451 10k A. Berezovoy, V.
            Lebedev   30   25
5138 A2452 10k Spacecraft   30   25
   a.   Pair, #5137-5138   60   50

Exists se-tenant with label.

Karl Marx
(1818-1883)
A2453

1983, May 5   Perf. 12x12½
5139 A2453 4k multicolored   15   15

View of Rostov-on-Don — A2454

1983, May 5   Photo.   *Perf. 11¹/₂*
5140 A2454 4k multicolored   15 15

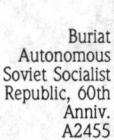
Buriat Autonomous Soviet Socialist Republic, 60th Anniv. A2455

1983, May 12   Litho.   *Perf. 12*
5141 A2455 4k multicolored   15 15

Kirov Opera and Ballet Theater, Leningrad, 200th Anniv. — A2456

Photogravure and Engraved
1983, May 12   *Perf. 11¹/₂x12*
5142 A2456 4k multicolored   20 20

Emblem of Motorcycling, Auto Racing, Shooting, Motorboating, Parachuting Organization — A2457

1983, May 20   Litho.   *Perf. 11¹/₂*
5143 A2457 6k multicolored   25 20

A.I. Khachaturian (1903-1978), Composer A2458

1983, May 25   Engr.   *Perf. 12¹/₂x12*
5144 A2458 4k violet brown   35 25

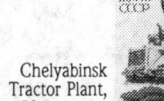
Chelyabinsk Tractor Plant, 50th Anniv. A2459

1983, June 1   Photo.   *Perf. 11¹/₂*
5145 A2459 4k multicolored   15 15

Simon Bolivar Bicentenary A2460

Photogravure and Engraved
1983, June 10   *Perf. 12*
5146 A2460 6k brown & dk brown   15 15

City of Sevastopol, 200th Anniv. — A2461

1983, June 14   Photo.   *Perf. 11¹/₂x12*
5147 A2461 5k multicolored   25 15

Spring Flowers — A2462

1983, June 14   Litho.   *Perf. 12x12¹/₂*
5148 A2462 4k multicolored   15 15
5149 A2462 6k multicolored   15 15
5150 A2462 10k multicolored   30 15
5151 A2462 15k multicolored   40 30
5152 A2462 20k multicolored   50 35
        Nos. 5148-5152 (5)   1.50
        Set value   95

Valentina Tereshkova's Spaceflight, 20th Anniv. — A2463

1983, June 16   Litho.   *Perf. 12*
5153 A2463 10k multicolored   35 15
  a.   Miniature sheet of 8

A2464   A2465

Photogravure and Engraved
1983, June 20   *Perf. 11¹/₂*
5154 A2464 4k multicolored   15 15
P.N. Pospelov (1898-1979), academician.

1983, June 21   Photo.   *Perf. 11¹/₂*
5155 A2465 4k multicolored   20 20

10th European Cong. of Rheumatologists.

13th International Film Festival, Moscow A2466

1983, July 7   Litho.   *Perf. 12*
5156 A2466 20k multicolored   60 25

Ships of the Soviet Fishing Fleet — A2467

Photogravure and Engraved
1983, July 20   *Perf. 12x11¹/₂*
5157 A2467 4k Two trawlers   15 15
5158 A2467 6k Refrigerated trawler   18 15
5159 A2467 10k Large trawler   55 15
5160 A2467 15k Large refrigerated
                     ship   58 25
5161 A2467 20k Base ship   75 32
        Nos. 5157-5161 (5)   2.21
        Set value   85

E.B. Vakhtangov (1883-1922), Actor and Producer A2468

1983, July 20   Photo.   *Perf. 11¹/₂*
5162 A2468 5k multicolored   15 15

"USSR-1" Stratospheric Flight, 50th Anniv. — A2469

1983, July 25   Photo.   *Perf. 12*
5163 A2469 20k multicolored   60 40
  a.   Miniature sheet of 8

Food Fish A2470

Designs 4k, Oncorhynchus nerka. 6k, Perciformes. 15k, Anarhichas minor. 20k, Neogobius fluviatilis, 45k, Platichthys stellatus.

1983, Aug. 5   Litho.   *Perf. 12¹/₂x12*
5164 A2470 4k multicolored   15 15
5165 A2470 6k multicolored   15 15
5166 A2470 15k multicolored   52 38
5167 A2470 20k multicolored   65 42
5168 A2470 45k multicolored   1.40 90
        Nos. 5164-5168 (5)   2.87 2.00

A2471

Moscow Skyline — A2472

1983, Aug. 18   Photo.   *Perf. 11¹/₂*
5169 A2471 6k multicolored   15 15
Souvenir Sheet
5170 A2472 50k cobalt blue   1.50 80
SOZPHILEX '83 Philatelic Exhibition.

Miniature Sheet

First Russian Postage Stamp, 125th Anniv. A2473

Photogravure and Engraved
1983, Aug. 25   *Perf. 11¹/₂x12*
5171 A2473 50k pale yel & black   1.50 70

No. 5171 Ovptd. on Margin in Red for the 5th Philatelic Society Congress

V СЪЕЗД ВОФ. МОСКВА. ОКТЯБРЬ 1984 г.

1984, Oct. 1
5171A A2473 50k pale yel & black   5.00 4.50

Namibia Day A2474

Palestinian Solidarity A2475

1983, Aug. 26   Photo.   *Perf. 11¹/₂*
5172 A2474 5k multicolored   15 15

1983, Aug. 29   Photo.   *Perf. 11¹/₂*
5173 A2475 5k multicolored   15 15

1st European Championship of Radio-Telegraphy, Moscow — A2476

1983, Sept. 1   Photo.   *Perf. 11¹/₂*
5174 A2476 6k multicolored   15 15

A2477

1983, Sept. 2   Photo.   Perf. 12x11¹/₂
5175 A2477 10k multicolored   30   15

4th UNESCO Council on Communications Development.

Muhammad Al-Khorezmi, Uzbek Mathematician, 1200th Birth Anniv. — A2478

Photogravure and Engraved
1983, Sept. 6   Perf. 11¹/₂
5176 A2478 4k multicolored   15   15

Marshal A.I. Egorov (1883-1939) A2479

Union of Georgia and Russia, 200th Anniv. A2480

1983, Sept. 8   Engr.   Perf. 12
5177 A2479 4k brown violet   15   15

1983, Sept. 8   Photo.   Perf. 11¹/₂
5178 A2480 6k multicolored   15   15

Lighthouse Type of 1982

Baltic Sea lighthouses.

1983, Sept. 19   Litho.   Perf. 12
5179 A2435 1k Kipu   15   15
5180 A2435 5k Keri   15   15
5181 A2435 10k Stirsudden   25   15
5182 A2435 12k Tahkun   30   16
5183 A2435 20k Tallinn   50   25
    Nos. 5179-5183 (5)   1.35
    Set value   66

Early Spring, by V.K. Bjalynitzky-Birulja, 1912 — A2481

Paintings by White Russians: 4k, Portrait of the Artist's Wife with Fruit and Flowers, by J.F. Krutzky, 1838. 15k, Young Partisan, by E.A. Zaitsev, 1943. 20k, Partisan Madonna, by M.A. Savitsky, 1967. 45k, Harvest, by V.K. Tsvirko, 1972. 15k, 20k, vert.

Perf. 12¹/₂x12, 12¹/₂x12¹/₂
1983, Sept. 28
5184 A2481 4k multicolored   15   15
5185 A2481 6k multicolored   15   15
5186 A2481 15k multicolored   40   30

5187 A2481 20k multicolored   50   35
5188 A2481 45k multicolored   1.10   70
    Nos. 5184-5188 (5)   2.30 1.65

Hammer and Sickle Steel Mill, Moscow, Centenary A2482

1983, Oct. 1   Photo.   Perf. 11¹/₂
5189 A2482 4k multicolored   15   15

Natl. Food Program A2483

1983, Oct. 10
5190 A2483 5k Wheat production   15   15
5191 A2483 5k Cattle, dairy products 15 15
5192 A2483 5k Produce   15   15
    Set value   30   20

A2484   A2485

1983, Oct. 12   Litho.   Perf. 12
5193 A2484 4k multicolored   15   15

October Revolution, 66th anniv.

1983, Oct. 12   Engr.   Perf. 12x12¹/₂
5194 A2485 4k dark brown   15   15

Ivan Fedorov, first Russian printer (Book of the Apostles), 400th death anniv.

Urengoy-Uzgorod Transcontinental Gas Pipeline Completion — A2486

1983, Oct. 12   Photo.   Perf. 12x11¹/₂
5195 A2486 5k multicolored   15   15

A2487   A2488

1983, Oct. 19   Litho.   Perf. 12
5196 A2487 4k multicolored   15   15

A.W. Sidorenko (1917-82), geologist.

1983, Oct. 19   Photo.   Perf. 11¹/₂
5197 A2488 5k Demonstration   15   15

Campaign Against Nuclear Weapons.

Machtumkuli, Turkmenistan Poet, 250th Birth Anniv. — A2489

1983, Oct. 27   Photo.
5198 A2489 5k multicolored   15   15

Hermitage Painting Type of 1982

Paintings by Germans: 4k, Madonna and Child with Apple Tree, by Lucas Cranach the Elder. 10k, Self-portrait, by Anton R. Mengs. 20k, Self-portrait, by Jurgen Owen. 45k, Sailboat, by Caspar David Friedrich. No. 5203, Rape of the Sabines, by Johann Schoenfeld, horiz. No. 5204a, Portrait of a Young Man, by Hans Holbein.

Perf. 12x12¹/₂, 12¹/₂x12
1983, Nov. 10   Litho.
5199 A2431 4k multicolored   15   15
5200 A2431 10k multicolored   40   15
5201 A2431 20k multicolored   60   35
5202 A2431 45k multicolored   1.25   70
5203 A2431 50k multicolored   1.50   75
    Nos. 5199-5203 (5)   3.90 2.10
          Souvenir Sheet
5204   Sheet of 2   4.00 2.50
  a.   A2431 50k multicolored   1.65   65

Physicians Against Nuclear War Movement A2490

1983, Nov. 17   Photo.   Perf. 11¹/₂
5205 A2490 5k Baby, dove, sun   15   15

Sukhe Bator (1893-1923), Mongolian People's Rep. Founder — A2491

1983, Nov. 17
5206 A2491 5k Portrait   15   15

New Year 1984 A2492

1983, Dec. 1
5207 A2492 5k Star, snowflakes   15   15

Newly Completed Buildings, Moscow — A2493

Perf. 12¹/₂x12, 12¹/₂x12¹/₂
1983, Dec. 15   Engr.
5208 A2493 3k Children's Musical
            Theater   15   15
5209 A2493 4k Tourist Hotel, vert. 15   15
5210 A2493 6k Council of Minis-
            ters   16   15

5211 A2493 20k Ismaelovo Hotel   70   32
5212 A2493 45k Novosti Press Agen-
            cy   1.50   70
    Nos. 5208-5212 (5)   2.66
    Set value   1.25

A2494   A2495

Souvenir Sheet
1983, Dec. 20   Photo.   Perf. 11¹/₂
5213 A2494 50k multicolored   5.00 5.00

Environmental Protection Campaign.

1984, Jan. 1
5214 A2495 4k multicolored   15   15

Moscow Local Broadcasting Network, 50th anniv.

European Women's Skating Championships A2496

1984, Jan. 1   Perf. 12x11¹/₂
5215 A2496 5k multicolored   15   15

Cuban Revolution, 25th Anniv. A2497

1984, Jan. 1   Perf. 11¹/₂
5216 A2497 5k Flag, "25"   15   15

World War II Tanks — A2498

1984, Jan. 25   Litho.   Perf. 12¹/₂x12
5217 A2498 10k KW   30   15
5218 A2498 10k IS-2   30   15
5219 A2498 10k T-34   30   15
5220 A2498 10k ISU-152   30   15
5221 A2498 10k SU-100   30   15
    Nos. 5217-5221 (5)   1.50   75

1984 Winter Olympics — A2499

1984, Feb. 8   Photo.   Perf. 11¹/₂x12
5222 A2499 5k Biathlon   15   15
  a.   Miniature sheet of 8

5223	A2499	10k Speed skating	38 15
a.		Miniature sheet of 8	
5224	A2499	20k Hockey	75 32
a.		Miniature sheet of 8	
5225	A2499	45k Figure skating	1.40 70
a.		Miniature sheet of 8	

Moscow Zoo, 120th
Anniv. — A2500

1984, Feb. 16   Litho.   Perf. 12½x12

5226	A2500	2k Mandrill	15 15
5227	A2500	3k Gazelle	15 15
5228	A2500	4k Snow leopard	15 15
5229	A2500	5k Crowned crane	15 15
5230	A2500	20k Macaw	40 25
		Set value	70 50

Yuri Gagarin (1934-68) — A2501

1984, Mar. 9   Engr.   Perf. 12½x12

5231	A2501	15k Portrait, Vostok	50 35
a.		Miniature sheet of 8	

Souvenir Sheet

Mass Development of
Virgin and Unused
Land, 30th
Anniv. — A2502

1984, Mar. 14   Photo.   Perf. 11½x12

5232	A2502	50k multicolored	1.50 75

Hermitage Painting Type of 1982

Paintings by English Artists: 4k, E.K. Vorontsova, by George Hayter. 10k, Portrait of Mrs. Greer, by George Romney. 20k, Approaching Storm, by George Morland, horiz. 45k, Portrait of an Unknown Man, by Marcus Gheeraerts Jr. No. 5237, Cupid and Venus, by Joshua Reynolds. No. 5238a, Portrait of a Lady in Blue, by Thomas Gainsborough.

Perf. 12x12½, 12½x12

1984, Mar. 20   Litho.   Wmk. 383

5233	A2431	4k multicolored	15 15
5234	A2431	10k multicolored	38 15
5235	A2431	20k multicolored	60 35
5236	A2431	45k multicolored	1.40 70
5237	A2431	1.65k multicolored	1.65 75
		Nos. 5233-5237 (5)	4.18 2.10

Souvenir Sheet

5238		Sheet of 2	5.00 1.70
a.	A2431	50k multicolored	2.00 65

Nos. 5233-5237 each se-tenant with label showing text and embossed emblem.

S.V.
Ilyushin — A2503

Andrei S.
Bubnov — A2504

Perf. 11½

1984, Mar. 23   Photo.   Unwmk.

5239	A2503	5k Aircraft designer, (1894-1977)	30 15

1984, Apr. 3   Perf. 11½x12

5240	A2504	5k Statesman, (1884-1940)	15 15

Intercosmos
Cooperative
Space Program
(USSR-India)
A2505

Designs: 5k, Weather Station M-100 launch. 20k, Geodesy (satellites, observatory). 45k, Rocket, satellites, dish antenna. 50k, Flags, cosmonauts.

1984   Perf. 12x11½

5241	A2505	5k multicolored	15 15
5242	A2505	20k multicolored	75 32
5243	A2505	45k multicolored	1.65 70

Souvenir Sheet

5244	A2505	50k multicolored	1.50 75

No. 5244 contains one 25x36mm stamp. Issue dates: 50k, Apr. 5; others, Apr. 3.

Cosmonauts' Day — A2506

1984, Apr. 12   Perf. 11½x12

5245	A2506	10k Futuristic spaceman	50 30

Tchelyuskin Arctic Expedition, 50th
Anniv. — A2507

Photogravure and Engraved

1984, Apr. 13   Perf. 11½x12

5246	A2507	6k Ship	15 15
a.		Miniature sheet of 8	
5247	A2507	15k Shipwreck	52 25
a.		Miniature sheet of 8	
5248	A2507	45k Rescue	1.50 70
a.		Miniature sheet of 8	

Souvenir Sheet
Photo.

5249	A2507	50k Hero of Soviet Union medal	1.50 70

First HSU medal awarded to rescue crew. No. 5249 contains one 27x39mm stamp.

Souvenir Sheet

114th Birth
Anniv. of Lenin
A2508

Perf. 11½x12½

1984, Apr. 22   Litho.

5250	A2508	50k Portrait	1.50 70

Aquatic
Plants — A2509

Soviet Peace
Policy — A2510

1984, May 5   Perf. 12x12½, 12½x12

5251	A2509	1k Lotus	15 15
5252	A2509	2k Euriola	15 15
5253	A2509	3k Water lilies, horiz.	15 15
5254	A2509	10k White nymphaea	20 15
a.		Miniature sheet of 8	
5255	A2509	20k Marshflowers, horiz.	40 25
		Set value	78 55

1984, May 8   Photo.   Perf. 11½

5256	A2510	5k Marchers, banners (at left)	15 15
5257	A2510	5k Text	15 15
5258	A2510	5k Marchers, banners (at right)	15 15
		Set value	30 20

Nos. 5256-5258 se-tenant.

A2511   A2512

1984, May 15   Photo.   Perf. 11½

5259	A2511	10k multicolored	30 25

E.O. Paton Institute of Electric Welding, 50th anniv.

1984, May 21

5260	A2512	10k multicolored	30 30

25th Conf. for Electric and Postal Communications Cooperation.

A2513   A2514

1984, May 29

5261	A2513	5k violet brown	15 15

Maurice Bishop, Grenada Prime Minister (1944-83).

1984, May 31

5262	A2514	5k multicolored	15 15

V.I. Lenin Central Museum, 60th anniv.

City of Archangelsk,
400th Anniv. — A2515

1984, June 1   Photo. & Engr.

5263	A2515	5k multicolored	15 15

European Youth
Soccer
Championship
A2516

1984, June 1   Photo.   Perf. 12x11½

5264	A2516	15k multicolored	50 30

Lighthouse Type of 1982

Far Eastern seas lighthouses.

1984, June 14   Litho.   Perf. 12

5265	A2435	1k Petropavlovsk	15 15
5266	A2435	2k Tokarev	15 15
5267	A2435	4k Basargin	15 15
5268	A2435	5k Kronitsky	15 15
5269	A2435	10k Marekan	20 15
		Set value	48 38

Salyut 7-Soyuz T-9 150-Day
Flight — A2517

1984, June 27   Litho.   Perf. 12

5270	A2517	15k multicolored	50 30

A2518

Photogravure and Engraved

1984, July 1   Perf. 11½

5271	A2518	10k multicolored	30 25

Morflot, Merchant & Transport Fleet, 60th anniv.

60th Anniv. of Awarding V.I. Lenin Name
to Youth Communist League — A2519

1984, July 1   Photo.   Perf. 11½x12
5272 A2519 5k multicolored   15 15

Liberation of
Byelorussia, 40th
Anniv. — A2520

1984, July 3   Photo.   Perf. 12x11½
5273 A2520 5k multicolored   15 15

CMEA Conference,
Moscow — A2521

1984, June 12   Photo.   Perf. 11½
5274 A2521 5k CMEA Building & Kremlin   15 15

A2522   A2523

1984, July 20   Photo.   Perf. 11½
5275 A2522 5k Convention seal   15 15

27th Intl. Geological Cong., Moscow.

1984, July 22   Photo.   Perf. 11½
5276 A2523 5k Arms, draped flag   15 15

People's Republic of Poland, 40th anniv.

B. V. Asafiev
(1884-1949),
Composer
A2524

1984, July 25   Engr.   Perf. 12½x12
5277 A2524 5k greenish black   15 15

Relations
with Mexico,
60th Anniv.
A2525

1984, Aug. 4   Litho.   Perf. 12
5278 A2525 5k USSR, Mexican flags   15 15

Miniature Sheet

Russian Folk
Tales — A2526

Designs: a, 3 archers. b. Prince and frog. c, Old
man and prince. d, Crowd and swans. e, Wolf and
men. f, Bird and youth. g, Youth on white horse. h,
Couple with Tsar. i, Village scene. j, Man on black
horse. k, Old man. l, Young woman.

1984, Aug. 10   Litho.   Perf. 12x12½
5279   Sheet of 12   5.00 2.50
a.-l. A2526 5k, any single   30   15

Friendship
'84 Games
A2527

1984, Aug. 15   Photo.   Perf. 11½
5280 A2527 1k Basketball   15   15
5281 A2527 5k Gymnastics, vert.   15   15
5282 A2527 10k Weightlifting   25   15
5283 A2527 15k Wrestling   38   20
5284 A2527 20k High jump   50   25
      Nos. 5280-5284 (5)   1.43
           Set value   70

A2528   A2529

1984, Aug. 23   Litho.   Perf. 12
5285 A2528 5k Flag, monument   15   15

Liberation of Romania, 40th anniv.

1984, Sept. 5   Litho.   Perf. 12½x12
Subjects: 35k, 3r, Environmental protection. 2r,
Arctic development. 5r, World peace.
5286 A2529 35k Sable   65   48
5287 A2529 2r Ship, arctic map   3.50 2.50
           Engr.
5288 A2529 3r Child and globe   5.75 3.25
5289 A2529 5r Palm frond and
               globe   9.00 5.75

See Nos. 6016B-6017A.

A2530   A2531

1984, Sept. 7   Photo.   Perf. 11½
5290 A2530 15k Motherland statue,
                Volgograd   50 30
5291 A2530 15k Spasski Tower, Moscow 50 30

World Chess Championships.

1984, Sept. 9   Photo.   Perf. 11½
5292 A2531 5k Bulgarian arms   15   15

Bulgarian Revolution, 40th anniv.

Ethiopian
Revolution,
10th Anniv.
A2532

1984, Sept. 12   Litho.   Perf. 12
5293 A2532 5k Ethiopian flag, seal 15   15

Novokramatorsk Machinery Plant, 50th
Anniv. — A2533

Photogravure and Engraved
1984, Sept. 20   Perf. 11½
5294 A2533 5k Excavator   15   15

Nakhichevan
ASSR, 60th
Anniv.
A2534

1984, Sept. 20   Litho.   Perf. 12
5295 A2534 5k Arms   15   15

Television
from Space,
25th Anniv.
A2535

1984, Oct. 4   Photo.   Perf. 11½
5296 A2535 5k Luna 3   15   15
5297 A2535 20k Venera 9   55   30
5298 A2535 45k Meteor satellite   1.25 60
           Souvenir Sheet
           Perf. 11½x12
5299 A2535 50k Camera, space
                walker, vert.   1.50 75

No. 5299 contains one 26x37mm stamp.

German
Democratic
Republic, 35th
Anniv.
A2536

1984, Oct. 7   Photo.   Perf. 11½
5300 A2536 5k Flag, arms   15   15

Ukrainian
Liberation, 40th
Anniv.
A2537

1984, Oct. 8   Photo.   Perf. 12x11½
5301 A2537 5k Motherland statue, Kiev 15 15

Soviet
Republics and
Parties, 60th
Anniv.
A2538

Flags and Arms: No. 5302, Moldavian SSR. No.
5303, Kirgiz SSR. No. 5304, Tadzhik SSR. No.
5305, Uzbek SSR. No. 5306, Turkmen SSR.

1984   Litho.   Perf. 12
5302 A2538 5k multicolored   15   15
5303 A2538 5k multicolored   15   15
5304 A2538 5k multicolored   15   15
5305 A2538 5k multicolored   15   15
5306 A2538 5k multicolored   15   15
           Set value   50   35

Issue dates: No. 5302, Oct. 12; Nos. 5303-
5304, Oct. 14, Nos. 5305-5306, Oct. 27.

A2539   A2540

1984, Oct. 23   Photo.   Perf. 11½
5307 A2539 5k Kremlin, 1917 flag   15   15

October Revolution, 67th anniv.

1984, Nov. 6   Photo.   Perf. 11½
5308 A2540 5k Aircraft, spacecraft 15 15

M. Frunze Institute of Aviation and
Cosmonautics.

Baikal - Amur
Railway
Completion
A2541

1984, Nov. 7   Photo.   Perf. 11½
5309 A2541 5k Workers, map, engine 30   15

Hermitage Type of 1982

Paintings by French Artists: 4k, Girl in a Hat, by
Jean Louis Voille. 10k, A Stolen Kiss, by Jean-
Honore Fragonard. 20k, Woman Combing her Hair,
by Edgar Degas. 45k, Pigmalion and Galatea, by

Francois Boucher. 50k, Landscape with Polyphenus, by Nicholas Poussin. No. 5315a, Child with a Whip, by Pierre-Auguste Renoir.

Perf. 12x12½, 12½x12
1984, Nov. 20 Litho.
5310	A2431	4k multicolored	15 15
5311	A2431	10k multi, horiz.	32 15
5312	A2431	20k multicolored	55 42
5313	A2431	45k multi, horiz.	1.25 75
5314	A2431	50k multi, horiz.	1.40 90
	Nos. 5310-5314 (5)		3.67 2.37

Souvenir Sheet
5315		Sheet of 2	3.50 2.00
a.	A2431	50k multicolored	1.00 60

Mongolian Peoples' Republic, 60th Anniv. — A2542

1984, Nov. 26 Photo. **Perf. 11½**
5316 A2542 5k Mongolian flag, arms 30 15

New Year 1985 — A2543

1984, Dec. 4 Litho. **Perf. 11½**
5317 A2543 5k Kremlin, snowflakes 15 15
a. Miniature sheet of 8

Souvenir Sheet

Environmental Protection — A2544

1984, Dec. 4 Litho. **Perf. 12½x12**
5318 A2544 50k Leaf, pollution sources 1.50 75

Russian Fire Vehicles — A2545

Photogravure and Engraved
1984, Dec. 12 **Perf. 12x11½**
5319	A2545	3k Crew wagon, 19th cent.	15 15
5320	A2545	5k Pumper, 19th cent.	16 15
5321	A2545	10k Ladder truck, 1904	35 15
5322	A2545	15k Pumper, 1904	52 22
5323	A2545	20k Ladder truck, 1913	65 28
	Nos. 5319-5323 (5)		1.83
	Set value		75

See Nos. 5410-5414.

Intl. Venus-Halley's Comet Project — A2546

1984, Dec. 15 Photo. **Perf. 12x11½**
5324 A2546 15k Satellite, flight path 60 35
a. Miniature sheet of 8

Indira Gandhi (1917-1984), Indian Prime Minister — A2547

1984, Dec. 28 Litho. **Perf. 12**
5325 A2547 5k Portrait 1.00 75

1905 Revolution A2548

1985, Jan. 22 Photo. **Perf. 11½**
5326 A2548 5k Flag, Moscow memorial 15 15

A2549   A2550

1985, Jan. 24
5327 A2549 5k multicolored 15 15

Patrice Lumumba Peoples' Friendship University, 25th Anniv.

1985, Feb. 2
5328 A2550 5k bluish, blk & ocher 15 15

Mikhail Vasilievich Frunze (1885-1925), party leader.

Karakalpak ASSR, 60th Anniv. A2551

1985, Feb. 16 **Perf. 12**
5329 A2551 5k Republic arms 15 15

10th Winter Spartakiad of Friendly Armies — A2552

1985, Feb. 23 **Perf. 11½**
5330 A2552 5k Hockey player, emblem 15 15

Kalevala, 150th Anniv. A2553

1985, Feb. 25 Litho. **Perf. 12**
5331 A2553 5k Rune singer, frontispiece 15 15

Finnish Kalevala, collection of Karelian epic poetry compiled by Elias Lonrot.

A2554   A2555

1985, Mar. 3 Engr. **Perf. 12½x12**
5332 A2554 5k rose lake 15 15

Yakov M. Sverdlov (1885-1919), party leader.

1985, Mar. 6 Photo. **Perf. 11½**
5333 A2555 5k Pioneer badge, awards 15 15

Pionerskaya Pravda, All-Union children's newspaper, 60th Anniv.

Maria Alexandrovna Ulyanova (1835-1916), Lenin's Mother — A2556

1985, Mar. 6 Engr. **Perf. 12½x12**
5334 A2556 5k black 30 15

Hermitage Type of 1982

Paintings by Spanish artists: 4k, The Young Virgin Praying, vert., by Francisco de Zurbaran (1598-1664). 10k, Still-life, by Antonio Pereda (c. 1608-1678). 20k, The Immaculate Conception, vert., by Murillo (1617-1682). 45k, The Grinder, by Antonio Puga. No. 5339, Count Olivares, vert., by Diego Velazques (1599-1660). No. 5340a, Portrait of the actress Antonia Zarate, vert., by Goya (1746-1828).

Perf. 12x12½, 12½x12
1985, Mar. 14 Litho. **Wmk. 383**
5335	A2431	4k multicolored	15 15
5336	A2431	10k multicolored	30 15
5337	A2431	20k multicolored	50 40
5338	A2431	45k multicolored	1.25 90
5339	A2431	50k multicolored	1.40 95
	Nos. 5335-5339 (5)		3.60 2.55

Souvenir Sheet
Lithographed and Embossed
5340		Sheet of 2 + label	3.00 2.00
a.	A2431	50k multicolored	1.10 75

EXPO '85, Tsukuba, Japan — A2557

Soviet exhibition, Expo '85 emblems and: 5k, Cosmonauts in space. 10k, Communications satellite. 20k, Alternative energy sources development. 45k, Future housing systems.

Perf. 12x11½
1985, Mar. 17 Photo. Unwmk.
5341	A2557	5k multicolored	16 15
5342	A2557	10k multicolored	30 18
5343	A2557	20k multicolored	55 45
5344	A2557	45k multicolored	1.25 90

Souvenir Sheet
5345 A2557 50k Soviet exhibition emblem, globe 1.50 90

Souvenir Sheet

Johann Sebastian Bach (1685-1750), Composer A2558

Photogravure and Engraved
1985, Mar. 21 **Perf. 12x11½**
5346 A2558 50k black 1.50 1.00

A2559   A2560

1985, Apr. 4 Litho. **Perf. 12**
5347 A2559 5k Natl. crest, Budapest memorial 15 15

Hungary liberated from German occupation, 40th Anniv.

1985, Apr. 5 Photo. **Perf. 11½**
5348 A2560 15k Emblem 40 34

Society for Cultural Relations with Foreign Countries, 60th anniv.

Victory over Fascism, 40th Anniv. A2561

Designs: No. 5349, Battle of Moscow, soldier, Kremlin, portrait of Lenin. No. 5350, Soldier, armed forces. No. 5351, Armaments production, worker. No. 5352, Partisan movement, cavalry. No. 5353, Berlin-Treptow war memorial, German Democratic Republic. No. 5354, Order of the Patriotic War, second class.

1985, Apr. 20 **Perf. 12x11½**
5349	A2561	5k multicolored	30 15
5350	A2561	5k multicolored	30 15
5351	A2561	5k multicolored	30 15
5352	A2561	5k multicolored	30 15
5353	A2561	5k multicolored	30 15
	Nos. 5349-5353 (5)		1.50
	Set value		35

Souvenir Sheet
Perf. 11½
5354 A2561 50k multicolored 1.50 52

No. 5354 contains one 28x40mm stamp.

No. 5353 Ovptd. in Red for 40th Year Since World War II Victory All-Union Philatelic Exhibition

„40 лет Великой Победы"

1985, Apr. 29   Photo.   Perf. 12x11½
5354A A2561 5k brn lake, gold & vermilion   50 50

Yuri Gagarin Center for Training Cosmonauts, 25th Anniv. — A2562

Cosmonauts day: Portrait, cosmonauts, Soyuz-T spaceship.

1985, Apr. 12   Photo.   Perf. 11½x12
5355 A2562 15k multicolored   50 25
a.   Miniature sheet of 8

12th World Youth Festival, Moscow A2563

1985, Apr. 15   Litho.   Perf. 12x12½
5356 A2563 1k Three youths   15 15
5357 A2563 3k African girl   16 15
5358 A2563 5k Girl, rainbow   20 15
5359 A2563 20k Asian youth, camera   95 35
5360 A2563 45k Emblem   2.25 75
Nos. 5356-5360 (5)   3.71
Set value   1.30

Souvenir Sheet

1985, July 4
5361 A2563 30k Emblem   2.00 1.00

115th Birth Anniv. of Lenin — A2564

Portrait and: No. 5362, Lenin Museum, Tam-pere, Finland. No. 5363, Memorial apartment, Paris, France.

1985, Apr. 22   Photo.   Perf. 11½x12
5362 A2564 5k multicolored   15 15
5363 A2564 5k multicolored   15 15
Set value   20 15

Souvenir Sheet
Litho.
Perf. 12x12½
5364 A2564 30k Portrait   1.50 1.00

No. 5364 contains one 30x42mm stamp.

Order of Victory — A2565

Photogravure and Engraved
1985, May 9   Perf. 11½
5365 A2565 20k sil, royal bl, dk red &
gold   60 35

Allied World War II victory over Germany and Japan, 40th anniv.

A2566   A2567

1985, May 9   Litho.   Perf. 12½x12
5366 A2566 5k Arms   15 15

Liberation of Czechoslovakia from German occu-pation, 40th Anniv.

1985, May 14   Photo.   Perf. 11½
5367 A2567 5k Flags of member nations 15 15

Warsaw Treaty Org., 30th anniv.

Mikhail Alexandrovich Sholokhov (1905-1984), Novelist & Nobel Laureate — A2568

Portraits and book covers: No. 5368, Tales from the Don, Quiet Flows the Don, A Human Tragedy. No. 5369, The Quiet Don, Virgin Lands Under the Plow, Thus They Have Fought for Their Homeland. No. 5370, Portrait.

1985, May 24   Litho.   Perf. 12½x12
5368 A2568 5k reddish brn, cream &
gold   15 15
5369 A2568 5k chest, yel brn & gold 15 15

Photo.
Perf. 12x11½
Size: 37x52mm
5370 A2568 5k brn, gold & black 15 15
Set value   30 24

INTERCOSMOS Project Halley-Venus — A2570

1985, June 11   Litho.   Perf. 12
5372 A2570 15k Spacecraft, satellites,
Venus   50 25
a.   Miniature sheet of 8

Artek Pioneer Camp, 60th Anniv. A2571

1985, June 14   Photo.   Perf. 11½
5373 A2571 4k Camp, badges, Lenin Pioneers emblem   50 15

Mutiny on the Battleship Potemkin, 80th Anniv. — A2572

Photogravure and Engraved
1985, June 16   Perf. 11½x12
5374 A2572 5k dk red, gold & black 30 15

Miniature Sheet

Soviet Railways Rolling Stock — A2573

Designs: a, Electric locomotive WL 80-R (grn). b, Tanker car (bl). c, Refrigerator car (bl). d, Sleeper car (brn). e, Tipper car (brn). f, Box car (brn). g, Shunting diesel locomotive (bl). h, Mail car (grn).

1985, June 15   Engr.   Perf. 12½x12
5375   Sheet of 8   2.50 1.65
a.-h. A2573 10k any single   25 15

Cosmonauts L. Kizim, V. Soloviov, O. Atkov and Salyut-7 Spacecraft — A2574

1985, June 25   Litho.
5376 A2574 15k multicolored   50 25
a.   Miniature sheet of 8

Soyuz T-10, Salyut-7 and Soyuz T-11 flights, Feb. 8-Oct. 2, 1984.

Beating Sword into Plowshares, Sculpture Donated to UN Hdqtrs. by USSR — A2575

Photogravure and Engraved
1985, June 26   Perf. 11½
5377 A2575 45k multicolored   1.50 75

UN 40th anniv.

Intl. Youth Year — A2576

1985, June 26   Photo.   Perf. 12
5378 A2576 10k multicolored   30 25

Medicinal Plants from Siberia — A2577

1985, July 10   Litho.   Perf. 12½x12
5379 A2577 2k O. dictiocarpum   15 15
5380 A2577 3k Thermopsis lanceo-
lata   15 15
5381 A2577 5k Rosa acicularis lindi 15 15
5382 A2577 20k Rhaponticum
carthamoides   80 40
5383 A2577 45k Bergenia crassifolia
fritsch   1.65 75
Nos. 5379-5383 (5)   2.90
Set value   1.30

Cosmonauts V. A. Dzhanibekov, S. E. Savistskaya, and I. P. Volk, Soyuz T-12 Mission, July 17-29, 1984 — A2578

1985, July 17
5384 A2578 10k multicolored   40 15
a.   Miniature sheet of 8

1st woman's free flight in space.

Caecilienhof Palace, Potsdam, Flags of UK, USSR, & US — A2579

Finlandia Hall, Helsinki — A2580

1985, July 17
5385 A2579 15k multicolored   50 24

Potsdam Conference, 40th anniv.

1985, July 25   Photo.   Perf. 11½
5386 A2580 20k multicolored   50 30

Helsinki Conference on European security and cooperation, 10th anniv.

Flags of USSR, North Korea, Liberation Monument in Pyongyang — A2581

1985, Aug. 1
5387 A2581 5k multicolored   15 15
Socialist Rep. of North Korea, 40th anniv.

Endangered Wildlife A2582

Designs: 2k, Sorex bucharensis, vert. 3k, Cardiocranius paradoxus. 5k, Selevinia betpakdalensis, vert. 20k, Felis caracal. 45k, Gazella subgutturosa. 50k, Panthera pardus.

Perf. 12x12¹/₂, 12¹/₂x12
1985, Aug. 15   **Litho.**
5388 A2582 2k multicolored   15 15
5389 A2582 3k multicolored   15 15
5390 A2582 5k multicolored   15 15
        Size: 47x32mm
5391 A2582 20k multicolored   75 35
  a.   Miniature sheet of 8
5392 A2582 45k multicolored   1.65 75
      Nos. 5388-5392 (5)   2.85
              Set value   1.25
        Souvenir Sheet
5393 A2582 50k multicolored   2.50 75

Youth World Soccer Cup Championships, Moscow — A2583

1985, Aug. 24   **Perf. 12**
5394 A2583 5k multicolored   30 25

Alexander G. Stakhanov, Coal Miner & Labor Leader A2584

1985, Aug. 30   Photo.   Perf. 11¹/₂
5395 A2584 5k multicolored   15 15
Stakhanovite Movement for high labor productivity, 50th anniv.

Bryansk Victory Memorial, Buildings, Arms A2585

1985, Sept. 1
5396 A2585 5k multicolored   30 25
Millennium of Bryansk.

Socialist Republic of Vietnam, 40th Anniv. — A2586

1985, Sept. 2   Litho.   Perf. 12¹/₂x12
5397 A2586 5k Arms   15 15

A2587

1985, Sept. 2   Photo.   Perf. 11¹/₂
5398 A2587 10k multicolored   50 15
1985 World Chess Championship match, A. Karpov Vs. G. Kasparov, Moscow.

Lutsk City, Ukrainian SSR, 900th Anniv. — A2588

1985, Sept. 14
5399 A2588 5k Lutsk Castle   15 15

Open Book, the Weeping Jaroslavna and Prince Igor's Army — A2589

Photogravure and Engraved
1985, Sept. 14   Perf. 11¹/₂x12
5400 A2589 10k multicolored   35 15
The Song of Igor's Campaign, epic poem, 800th anniv.

Sergei Vasilievich Gerasimov (1885-1964), Painter — A2590

1985, Sept. 26   Perf. 12x11¹/₂
5401 A2590 5k Portrait   15 15

October Revolution, 68th Anniv. — A2591

UN 40th Anniv. — A2592

1985, Oct. 10   Photo.   Perf. 11¹/₂
5402 A2591 5k multicolored   15 15

1985, Oct. 24
5403 A2592 15k multicolored   50 25

Krushjanis Baron (1835-1923), Latvian Folklorist — A2593

Lithographed and Engraved
1985, Oct. 31
5404 A2593 5k beige & black   30 15

Lenin, Laborer Breaking Chains A2594

1985, Nov. 20   Photo.
5405 A2594 5k multicolored   15 15
Petersburg Union struggle for liberation of the working classes, founded by Lenin, 90th anniv.

Largest Soviet Telescope, 10th Anniv. — A2595

1985, Nov. 20   Engr.   Perf. 12¹/₂x12
5406 A2595 10k dark blue   50 25
Soviet Observatory inauguration.

A2596   A2597

1985, Nov. 25   Photo.
5407 A2596 5k multicolored   15 15
Angolan Independence, 10th anniv.

1985, Nov. 29   Perf. 11¹/₂
5408 A2597 5k multicolored   15 15
Socialist Federal Republic of Yugoslavia, 40th anniv.

New Year — A2598   Samantha Smith — A2599

1985, Dec. 3   Litho.   Perf. 12
5409 A2598 5k multicolored   15 15
  a.   Miniature sheet of 8

        Vehicle Type of 1984
1985, Dec. 18   Photo.   Perf. 12x11¹/₂
5410 A2545 3k AMO-F15, 1926   15 15
5411 A2545 5k PMZ-1, 1933   15 15
5412 A2545 10k AC-40, 1977   42 15
5413 A2545 20k AL-30, 1970   70 35
5414 A2545 45k AA-60, 1978   1.40 70
      Nos. 5410-5414 (5)   2.82
              Set value   1.30

1985, Dec. 25   Perf. 12
5415 A2599 5k vio blue, choc & ver   50 15
American student invited to meet with Soviet leaders in 1984.

A2600   A2601

1985, Dec. 30   Litho.
5416 A2600 5k multicolored   15 15
N.M. Emanuel (1915-1984), chemist.

1985, Dec. 30
5417 A2601 5k Sightseeing   20 15
5418 A2601 5k Sports   20 15
              Set value   20
Family leisure activities.

Intl. Peace Year — A2602

1986, Jan. 2   Photo.   Perf. 11¹/₂
5419 A2602 20k brt blue, bluish grn & silver   60 30

Flags, Congress Palace, Carnation A2603

Lenin, Troitskaya Tower, Congress Palace A2604

Lenin — A2605

1986, Jan. 3
5420 A2603 5k multicolored   15   15
Photogravure and Engraved
Perf. 12x11½
5421 A2604 20k multicolored   70   28
                    Set value   35
Souvenir Sheet
Photo.
Perf. 11½
5422 A2605 50k multicolored   1.75 70
27th Communist Party Congress.

A2606   A2607

1986, Jan. 10   **Perf. 11½x12**
5423 A2606 15k multicolored   50   25
Modern Olympic Games, 90th anniv.

Perf. 12½x12, 12x12½
1986, Jan. 15   **Litho.**
Flora of Russian Steppes, different.
5424 A2607 4k multicolored   15   15
5425 A2607 5k multi, horiz.   15   15
5426 A2607 10k multicolored   30   15
5427 A2607 15k multicolored   40   30
5428 A2607 20k multicolored   50   35
  a.   Miniature sheet of 8   1.50
       Nos. 5424-5428 (5)
       Set value   92

Vodovzvodnaya Tower,
Grand Kremlin
Palace — A2608

1986, Jan. 20   **Perf. 12½x12**
5429 A2608 50k grayish green   1.50 70

Voronezh City, 400th
Anniv. — A2609

1986, Feb. 20   **Perf. 11½**
5430 A2609 5k multicolored   30   15

A2610   A2611

1986, Feb. 20   Engr.   Perf. 12
5431 A2610 10k bluish black   35   15
Bela Kun (1886-1939), Hungarian party leader.

1986, Feb. 28   Perf. 12½x12
5432 A2611 5k grayish black   15   15
Karolis Pozhela (1896-1926), Lithuanian party
founder.

Intercosmos Project Halley, Final
Stage — A2612

1986, Mar. 6   Litho.   Perf. 12
5433 A2612 15k Vega probe, comet   50   25
  a.   Miniature sheet of 8
Souvenir Sheet
Perf. 12½x12
5434 A2612 50k Vega I, comet   1.75 75
No. 5434 contains one 42x30mm stamp.

Butterflies
A2613

1986, Mar. 18   Perf. 12x12½
5435 A2613 4k Utetheisa pulchella 15   15
5436 A2613 5k Allancastria caucasi-
           ca   15   15
5437 A2613 10k Zegris eupheme   38   16
5438 A2613 15k Catocala sponsa   50   50
5439 A2613 20k Satyrus bischoffi   65   55
  a.   Miniature sheet of 8
       Nos. 5435-5439 (5)   1.83 1.51

EXPO '86,   A2615
Vancouver — A2614

1986, Mar. 25   Photo.   Perf. 12x11½
5440 A2614 20k Globe, space station 75 30

1986, Mar. 27   Engr.   Perf. 12½x12
5441 A2615 5k black   30   15
S.M. Kirov (1886-1934), party leader.

Cosmonauts' Day — A2616

Designs: 5k, Konstantin E. Tsiolkovsky (1857-
1935), aerodynamics innovator, and futuristic space
station. 10k, Sergei P. Korolev (1906-1966), rocket
scientist, and Vostok spaceship, vert. 15k, Yuri
Gagarin, 1st cosmonaut, Sputnik I and Vega probe.

Perf. 12½x12, 12x12½
1986, Apr. 12   **Litho.**
5442 A2616 5k multicolored   15   15
  a.   Miniature sheet of 8
5443 A2616 10k multicolored   25   15
  a.   Miniature sheet of 8
5444 A2616 15k multicolored   35   25
  a.   Miniature sheet of 7 + label
       Set value   45
No. 5444 printed se-tenant with label picturing
Vostok and inscribed for the 25th anniv. of first
space flight.

1986 World Ice Hockey Championships,
Moscow — A2617

1986, Apr. 12   Photo.   Perf. 11½
5445 A2617 15k multicolored   50   25

Ernst Thalmann
(1886-1944), German
Communist
Leader — A2618

1986, Apr. 16   Engr.   Perf. 12½x12
5446 A2618 10k dark red brown   30   15
5447 A2618 10k reddish brown   30   15

Lenin, 116th Birth Anniv. — A2619

Portraits and architecture: No. 5448, Socialist-
Democratic People's House, Prague. No. 5449,
Lenin Museum, Leipzig. No. 5450, Lenin Museum,
Poronino, Poland.

1986, Apr. 22   Photo.   Perf. 11½x12
5448 A2619 5k multicolored   15   15
5449 A2619 5k multicolored   15   15
5450 A2619 5k multicolored   15   15
       Set value   30   20

Tambov City,
350th Anniv.
A2620

1986, Apr. 27   **Perf. 11½**
5451 A2620 5k Buildings, city arms 15 15

Soviet Peace
Fund, 25th
Anniv.
A2621

1986, Apr. 27
5452 A2621 10k lt chalky bl, gold & brt
           ultra   40   15

29th World Cycle   Toadstools
Race, May 6-22   A2623
A2622

1986, May 6
5453 A2622 10k multicolored   40   15

1986, May 15   Litho.   Perf. 12
5454 A2623 4k Amanita phalloides   15   15
5455 A2623 5k Amanita muscaria   15   15
5456 A2623 10k Amanita pantherina 42   15
5457 A2623 15k Tylopilus felleus   55   30
5458 A2623 20k Hypholoma fascicu-
           lare   70   35
       Nos. 5454-5458 (5)   1.97
       Set value   95

A2624   A2625

1986, May 19   Photo.   Perf. 11½
5459 A2624 10k multicolored   35   15
UNESCO Campaign, Man and Biosphere,

1986, May 20
5460 A2625 10k multicolored   35   15
9th Soviet Spartakiad.

A2626   A2627

Design: Lenin's House, Eternal Glory and V. I.
Chapaiev monuments, Gorky State Academic
Drama Theater.

1986, May 24
5461 A2626 5k multicolored   15   15
City of Kuibyshev, 400th anniv.

1986, May 25
5462 A2627 5k multicolored   15   15
"COMMUNICATION '86, Moscow."

1986 World Cup Soccer Championships, Mexico — A2628

Designs: 5k, 10k, Various soccer plays. 15k, World Cup on FIFA commemorative gold medal.

1986, May 31
5463	A2628	5k multicolored	15	15
a.		Miniature sheet of 8		
5464	A2628	10k multicolored	25	15
a.		Miniature sheet of 8		
5465	A2628	15k multicolored	40	25
a.		Miniature sheet of 8		
		Set value		45

Paintings in the Tretyakov Gallery, Moscow — A2629

Designs: 4k, Lane in Albano. 1837, by M.I. Lebedev, vert. 5k, View of the Kremlin in Foul Weather, 1851, by A.K. Savrasov. 10k, Sunlit Pine Trees, 1896, by I.I. Shishkin, vert. 15k, Return, 1896, by A.E. Arkhipov, vert. 45k, Wedding Procession in Moscow, the 17th Century, 1901, by A.P. Ryabushkin.

Perf. 12x12¹/₂, 12¹/₂x12
1986, June 11   **Litho.**
5466	A2629	4k multicolored	15	15
5467	A2629	5k multicolored	15	15
5468	A2629	10k multicolored	32	15

Size: 74x37mm
Perf. 11¹/₂
5469	A2629	5k multicolored	42	30
5470	A2629	45k multicolored	1.25	75
		Nos. 5466-5470 (5)	2.29	1.50

Irkutsk City, 300th Anniv. — A2630   UNESCO Projects in Russia — A2632

Goodwill Games, Moscow, July 5-20 A2631

1986, June 28   **Photo.**   *Perf. 11¹/₂*
5471	A2630	5k multicolored	15	15

1986, July 4   **Photo.**   *Perf. 11¹/₂*
5472	A2631	10k Prus bl, gold & blk	35	15
5473	A2631	10k brt blue, gold & blk	35	15

1986, July 15
Designs: 5k, Information sciences. 10k, Geological correlation. 15k, Inter-governmental oceanographic commission. 35k, Intl. hydrologic program.
5474	A2632	5k multicolored	15	15
5475	A2632	10k multicolored	38	15
5476	A2632	15k multicolored	50	30
5477	A2632	35k multicolored	95	55

Tyumen, 400th Anniv. A2633

1986, July 27
5478	A2633	5k multicolored	15	15

A2634   A2635

1986, Aug. 1   **Photo.**   *Perf. 11¹/₂*
5479	A2634	10k multicolored	35	15

Olof Palme (1927-86), Prime Minister of Sweden.

1986, Aug. 8
5480	A2635	15k multicolored	50	25

10th World Women's Basketball Championships, Moscow, Aug. 15-17.

Natl. Sports Committee Intl. Alpinist Camps — A2636

1986, Sept. 5   **Litho.**   *Perf. 12*
5481	A2636	4k Mt. Lenin	15	15
5482	A2636	5k Mt. E. Korzhenev-skaya	15	15
a.		Miniature sheet of 8		
5483	A2636	10k Mt. Belukha	42	15
5484	A2636	15k Mt. Communism	55	30
5485	A2636	30k Mt. Elbrus	1.00	50
		Nos. 5481-5485 (5)	2.27	1.25

See Nos. 5532-5535.

Souvenir Sheet

Red Book, Rainbow, Earth A2637

1986, Sept. 10   *Perf. 11¹/₂*
5486	A2637	50k multicolored	1.75	75

Nature preservation.

A2638   A2640

A2639

1986, Sept. 13   **Photo.**
5487	A2638	5k multicolored	15	15

Chelyabinsk, 250th anniv.

1986, Sept. 23
5488	A2639	15k multicolored	38	25

Mukran, DDR to Klaipeda, Lithuania, Train Ferry, inauguration.

1986, Sept. 26
5489	A2640	5k multicolored	15	15

Siauliai, Lithuanian SSR, 750th anniv.

Trucks — A2641

1986, Oct. 15   *Perf. 11¹/₂x12*
5490	A2641	4k Ural-375D, 1964	15	15
5491	A2641	5k GAZ-53A, 1965	15	15
5492	A2641	10k KrAZ-256B, 1966	30	15
a.		Miniature sheet of 8		
5493	A2641	15k MAZ-515B, 1974	40	30
5494	A2641	20k ZIL-133GY, 1979	50	35
		Nos. 5490-5494 (5)	1.50	
		Set value		95

A2642   A2643

Design: Lenin Monument in October Square, Kremlin, Moscow.

1986, Oct. 1   **Litho.**   *Perf. 12*
5495	A2642	5k multicolored	15	15

October Revolution, 69th anniv.

1986, Oct. 10   **Photo.**   *Perf. 11¹/₂*
5496	A2643	5k Icebreaker, helicopters	15	15
5497	A2643	10k Mikhail Somov port side	20	15
a.		Pair, #5496-5497	30	20
b.		Miniature sheet of 8, 4 each		
		Set value		20

Souvenir Sheet
Perf. 12¹/₂x11¹/₂
5498	A2643	50k Trapped in ice	2.25	65

Mikhail Somov trapped in the Antarctic No. 5497a has a continuous design. No. 5498 contains one 51¹/₂x36¹/₂mm stamp.

No. 4883 Ovptd. in Black for Rescue of the Mikhail Somov

15.III—26.VII.1985
Дрейф во льдах Антарктики

Lithographed & Engraved
1986, Oct. 10   *Perf. 12x11¹/₂*
5499	A2271	4k multicolored	75	15

Locomotives — A2644

1986, Oct. 15   **Litho.**   *Perf. 12*
5500	A2644	4k EU 684-37, 1929	15	15
5501	A2644	5k FD 21-3000, 1941	15	15
5502	A2644	10k OV-5109, 1907	55	15
a.		Miniature sheet of 8		
5503	A2644	20k C017-1613, 1944	95	40
5504	A2644	30k FDP 20-578, 1941	1.25	65
		Nos. 5500-5504 (5)	3.05	1.50

Grigori Konstantinovich Ordzhonikidze (1886-1937), Communist Party Leader — A2645

1986, Oct. 18   **Engr.**   *Perf. 12¹/₂x12*
5505	A2645	5k dark blue green	15	15

A.G. Novikov (1896-1984), Composer A2646

1986, Oct. 30
5506	A2646	5k brown black	15	15

A2647   A2648

1986, Nov. 4   **Photo.**   *Perf. 11¹/₂*
5507	A2647	10k blue & silver	35	15

UNESCO, 40th anniv.

1986, Nov. 12
5508	A2648	5k lt grnsh gray & black	15	15

Sun Yat-sen (1866-1925), Chinese statesman.

Mikhail Vasilyevich Lomonosov, Scientist A2649

1986, Nov. 19   **Engr.**   *Perf. 12x12¹/₂*
5509	A2649	5k dk violet brown	15	15

Aircraft by A.S. Yakovlev — A2650

1986, Nov. 25　Photo.　Perf. 11½x12
5510	A2650	4k 1927		15	15
5511	A2650	5k 1935		15	15
a.		Miniature sheet of 8			
5512	A2650	10k 1946		40	15
5513	A2650	20k 1972		65	35
5514	A2650	30k 1981		95	50
		Nos. 5510-5514 (5)		2.30	1.30

New Year
1987 — A2651　　　　　A2652

1986, Dec. 4　Litho.　Perf. 11½
5515	A2651	5k Kremlin towers		15	15
a.		Miniature sheet of 8			

1986, Dec. 12　Photo.　Perf. 11½x12

Red banner and: No. 5516, Computers. No. 5517, Engineer, computer, dish receivers. No. 5518, Aerial view of city. No. 5519, Council for Mutual Economic Assistance building, workers. No. 5520, Spasski Tower, Kremlin Palace.

5516	A2652	5k multicolored		15	15
5517	A2652	5k multicolored		15	15
5518	A2652	5k multicolored		15	15
5519	A2652	5k multicolored		15	15
5520	A2652	5k multicolored		15	15
		Set value		50	35

27th Communist Party Cong., Feb. 25-Mar. 6.

A2653　　　　　A2654

1986, Dec. 24　Engr.　Perf. 12½x12
5521	A2653	5k black		15	15

Alexander Yakovlevich Parkhomenko (1886-1921), revolution hero.

1986, Dec. 25　Photo.　Perf. 11½
5522	A2654	5k brown & buff		15	15

Samora Moises Machel (1933-1986) Pres. of Mozambique.

Miniature Sheet

Palace Museums in Leningrad — A2655

1986, Dec. 25　Engr.　Perf. 12
5523		Sheet of 5 + label		3.00	1.40
a.	A2655	5k State Museum, 1898		15	15
b.	A2655	10k The Hermitage, 1764		32	15

c.	A2655	15k Petrodvorets, 1728	45	30
d.	A2655	20k Yekaterininsky, 1757	55	35
e.	A2655	50k Pavlovsk, restored c. 1945	1.25	75

18th Soviet Trade
Unions Congress,
Feb. 24-28 — A2656

1987, Jan. 7　Photo.　Perf. 11½
5524	A2656	5k multicolored		15	15

Butterflies
A2657

1987, Jan. 15　Litho.　Perf. 12x12½
5525	A2657	4k Atrophaneura alcinous		15	15
5526	A2657	5k Papilio machaon		15	15
5527	A2657	10k Papilio alexanor		30	15
5528	A2657	20k Papilio maackii		40	30
5529	A2657	30k Iphiclides podalirius		75	50
		Nos. 5525-5529 (5)		1.75	1.25

A2658　　　　　A2659

1987, Jan. 31　　　Perf. 12½x12
5530	A2658	5k multicolored		15	15

Karlis Miyesniyek (1887-1977), Artist.

1987, Feb. 4　　　Perf. 12
5531	A2659	5k buff & lake		15	15

Stasis Shimkus (1887-1943), composer.

Alpinist Camps Type of 1986
1987, Feb. 4
5532	A2636	4k Chimbulak Gorge		15	15
5533	A2636	10k Shavla Gorge		30	15
5534	A2636	20k Mts. Donguz-orun, Nakra-tau		50	35
5535	A2636	35k Mt. Kazbek		75	55

Vasily Ivanovich
Chapayev (1887-
1919), Revolution
Hero — A2660

1987, Feb. 9　　　Engr.
5536	A2660	5k dark red brown		15	15

Heino Eller
(1887-1970),
Estonian
Composer
A2661

1987, Mar. 7　Litho.　Perf. 12
5537	A2661	5k buff & brown		15	15

A2662　　　　　A2663

1987, Mar. 8　Photo.　Perf. 11½
5538	A2662	5k multicolored		15	15

Souvenir Sheet
Perf. 11½x12
5539	A2662	50k "XX," and colored bands		1.75	75

All-Union Leninist Young Communist League 20th Congress, Moscow. No. 5539 contains one 26x37mm stamp.

Photogravure and Engraved
1987, Mar. 20　　　Perf. 11½
5540	A2663	5k buff & sepia		15	15

Iosif Abgarovich rbeli (1887-1961), first president of the Armenian Academy of Sciences.

World Wildlife Fund — A2664

Polar bears.

1987, Mar. 25　Photo.　Perf. 11½x12
5541	A2664	5k multicolored		15	15
a.		Miniature sheet of 8			
5542	A2664	10k multicolored		30	15
a.		Miniature sheet of 8			
5543	A2664	20k multicolored		70	40
a.		Miniature sheet of 8			
5544	A2664	35k multicolored		1.00	75
a.		Miniature sheet of 8			

Cosmonauts'
Day — A2665　　　　UN Emblem,
　　　　　　　　　　ESCAP
　　　　　　　　　Headquarters,
　　　　　　　　　Bangkok — A2666

1987, Apr. 12　　　Perf. 11½
5545	A2665	10k Sputnik, 1957		35	15
5546	A2665	10k Vostok 3 and 4, 1962		35	15
5547	A2665	10k Mars 1, 1962		35	15
a.		Miniature sheet of 8			

1987, Apr. 21
5548	A2666	10k multicolored		30	15

UN Economic and Social Commission for Asia and the Pacific, 40th anniv.

Lenin, 117th Birth Anniv. — A2667

Paintings: No. 5549, Lenin's Birthday, by N.A. Sysoyev. No. 5550, Lenin with Delegates at the 3rd Congress of the Soviet Young Communist League, by P.O. Belousov. No. 5551a, Lenin's Underground Activity (Lenin, lamp), by D.A. Nalbandyan. No. 5551b, Before the Assault (Lenin standing at table), by S.P. Viktorov. No. 5551c, We'll Show the Earth the New Way (Lenin, soldiers, flags), by A.G. Lysenko. No. 5551d, Lenin in Smolny, October 1917 (Lenin seated), by M.G. Sokolov. No. 5551e, Lenin, by N.A. Andreyev.

1987, Apr. 22　Litho.　Perf. 12½x12
5549	A2667	5k multicolored		15	15
5550	A2667	5k multicolored		15	15
		Set value		20	15

Souvenir Sheet
Perf. 12
5551		Sheet of 5		1.75	75
a.-e.	A2667	10k any single		30	15

Sizes: Nos. 5551a-5551d, 40x28mm; No. 5551e, 40x56mm.

A2668

1987, May 5　Photo.　Perf. 11½
5552	A2668	10k multicolored		30	15

European Gymnastics Championships, Moscow, May 18-26.

Bicycle
Race — A2669　　　　Fauna — A2670

1987, May 6
5553	A2669	10k multicolored		30	15

40th Peace Bicycle Race, Poland-Czecholsovakia-German Democratic Republic, May.

Perf. 12½x12 (#5554), 12x12½
1987, May 15　　　Litho.
5554	A2670	5k Menzbira marmot		15	15
a.		Miniature sheet of 8			
5555	A2670	10k Bald badger, horiz.		30	15
		Size: 32x47mm			
5556	A2670	15k Snow leopard		40	25
		Set value			45

Passenger Ships — A2671

1987, May 20　Photo.　Perf. 12x11½
5557	A2671	5k Maxim Gorki		15	15
5558	A2671	10k Alexander Pushkin		35	15
a.		Miniature sheet of 8			
5559	A2671	30k The Soviet Union		1.10	45

Paintings by
Foreign Artists in
the Hermitage
Museum
A2672

Designs: 4k, Portrait of a Woman, by Lucas Cranach Sr. (1472-1553). 5k, St. Sebastian, by Titian. 10k, Justice, by Durer. 30k, Adoration of the Magi, by Pieter Brueghel the Younger (c. 1564-1638). 50k, Ceres, by Rubens.

Perf. 12x12¹/₂, 12¹/₂x12

1987, June 5   **Litho.**

5560	A2762	4k multicolored	15	15
5561	A2762	5k multicolored	15	15
5562	A2762	10k multicolored	38	15
5563	A2762	30k multicolored	90	50
5564	A2762	50k multicolored	1.65	75
		Nos. 5560-5564 (5)	3.23	1.70

Tolyatti City, 250th Anniv. — A2673

Design: Zhiguli car, Volga Motors factory, Lenin Hydroelectric plant.

1987, June 6   **Photo.**   *Perf. 11¹/₂*

5565	A2673	5k multicolored	15	15

Aleksander Pushkin (1799-1837), Poet — A2674

1987, June 6   **Litho.**

5566	A2674	5k buff, yel brn & deep brown	15	15

Printed se-tenant with label.

A2675   A2676

1987, June 7   **Engr.**   *Perf. 12¹/₂x12*

5567	A2675	5k black	15	15

Maj.-Gen. Sidor A. Kovpak (1887-1967), Vice-Chairman of the Ukranian SSR.

1987, June 23   **Photo.**   *Perf. 11¹/₂*

5568	A2676	10k multicolored	30	15

Women's World Congress on Nuclear Disarmament, Moscow, June 23-27.

Tobolsk City, 400th Anniv. — A2677

Frelimo, 25th Anniv. — A2678

Design: Tobolsk kremlin, port, theater and Ermak Monument.

1987, June 25

5569	A2677	5k multicolored	15	15

1987, June 25

5570	A2678	5k Flag of Congo, man	15	15
5571	A2678	5k Flags of Frelimo, USSR	15	15
a.		Pair, #5570-5571	20	15
		Set value	20	15

Mozambique-USSR Peace Treaty, 10th anniv. No. 5571a has continuous design.

Ferns — A2679   A2680

1987, July 2   **Litho.**   *Perf. 12*

5572	A2679	4k Scolopendrium vulgare	15	15
5573	A2679	5k Ceterach officinarum	15	15
5574	A2679	10k Salvinia natans, horiz.	38	15
5575	A2679	15k Matteuccia struthiopteris	50	30
5576	A2679	50k Adiantum pedatum	1.40	75
		Nos. 5572-5576 (5)	2.58	1.50

1987, July 3

Designs: #5577, Kremlin and 2000 Year-old Coin of India. #5578, Red Fort, Delhi, Soviet hammer & sickle.

5577	A2680	5k shown	15	15
5578	A2680	5k muticolored	15	15
a.		Pair, #5577-5578	20	15
		Set value	20	15

Festivals 1987-88: India in the USSR (No. 5577) and the USSR in India (No. 5578).

15th Intl. Film Festival, July 16-17, Moscow — A2681

1987, July 6   **Photo.**   *Perf. 11¹/₂*

5579	2681	10k multicolored	35	15

Joint Soviet-Syrian Space Flight — A2682

Mir Space Station — A2683

Flags, Intercosmos emblem and: 5k, Cosmonaut training and launch. 10k, Mir space station, Syrian parliament and cosmonauts. 15k, Gagarin Memorial, satellite dishes and cosmonauts wearing space suits.

1987   **Litho.**   *Perf. 12x12¹/₂*

5580	A2682	5k multicolored	15	15
5581	A2682	10k multicolored	25	15
5582	A2682	15k multicolored	40	25
		Set value		45

Souvenir Sheet

5583	A2683	50k multicolored	1.75	75

Issue dates: 5k, July 22; 10k, July 24; 15k, 50k July 30.

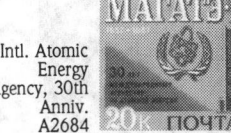

Intl. Atomic Energy Agency, 30th Anniv. A2684

1987, July 29   **Photo.**   *Perf. 11¹/₂*

5584	A2684	20k multicolored	60	30

14th-16th Century Postrider — A2685

Designs: 5k, 17th cent. postman and 17th cent. kibitka (sled). 10k, 16th-17th cent. ship and 18th cent. packet. 30k, Railway station and 19th cent. mailcars. 35k, AMO-F-15 bus and car, 1905. 50k, Postal headquarters, Moscow, and modern postal delivery trucks.

Photo. & Engr.

1987, Aug. 25   *Perf. 11¹/₂x12*

5585	A2685	4k buff & black	15	15
5586	A2685	5k buff & black	15	15
5587	A2685	10k buff & black	32	15
5588	A2685	30k buff & black	1.00	50
5589	A2685	35k buff & black	1.10	55
		Nos. 5585-5589 (5)	2.72	1.50

Souvenir Sheet

5590	A2685	50k pale yel, dull gray grn & blk	1.75	90

A2686

October Revolution, 70th Anniv. — A2687

Paintings by Russian artists: No. 5591, Long Live the Socialist Revolution! by V.V. Kuznetsov. No. 5592, V.I. Lenin Proclaims the Soviet Power (Lenin pointing), by V.A. Serov. No. 5593, V.I. Lenin (with pencil), by P.V. Vasiliev. No. 5594, On the Eve of the Storm (Lenin, Trotsky, Dzerzhinski), by V.V. Pimenov. No. 5585, Taking the Winter Palace by Storm, by V.A. Serov.

1987, Aug. 25   **Litho.**   *Perf. 12¹/₂x12*

5591	A2686	5k shown	15	15
5592	A2686	5k multicolored	15	15
5593	A2686	5k multicolored	15	15

Size: 70x33mm
Perf. 11¹/₂

5594	A2686	5k multicolored	15	15
5595	A2686	5k multicolored	15	15
		Set value	50	35

Souvenir Sheet
Photo. & Engr.
Perf. 12x11¹/₂

5596	A2687	30k gold & black	1.50	45

For overprint see No. 5604.

Souvenir Sheet

Battle of Borodino, 175th Anniv. — A2688

1987, Sept. 7   **Litho.**   *Perf. 12¹/₂x12*

5597	A2688	1r black, yel brn & blue gray	3.00	1.50

A2689   A2690

1987, Sept. 18   **Engr.**

5598	A2689	5k intense blue	15	15

Pavel Petrovich Postyshev (1887-1939), party leader.

1987, Sept. 19   **Photo.**   *Perf. 11¹/₂*

Design: 5k, Monument to founder Yuri Dolgoruki, by sculptor S. Orlov, A. Antropov, N. Stamm and architect V. Andreyev, in Sovetskaya Square, and buildings in Moscow.

5599	A2690	5k dark red brn, cream & dark orange	15	15

Moscow, 840th anniv.

Scientists — A2691

Designs: No. 5600, Muhammed Taragai Ulugh Begh (1394-1449), Uzbek astronomer and mathematician. No. 5601, Sir Isaac Newton (1642-1727), English physicist and mathematician. No. 5602, Marie Curie (1867-1934), physicist, chemist, Nobel laureate.

1987, Oct. 3   **Photo. & Engr.**

5600	A2691	5k dark blue, org brn & black	15	15
5601	A2691	5k dull grn, blk & dark ultra	15	15
5602	A2691	5k brown & deep blue	15	15
		Set value	30	20

Nos. 5600-5602 each printed se-tenant with inscribed label.

Souvenir Sheet

COSPAS-SARSAT Intl. Satellite System for Tracking Disabled Planes and Ships — A2692

1987, Oct. 15   Photo.
5603 A2692 50k multicolored   2.25 75

No. 5595 Overprinted in Gold

**Всесоюзная
филателистическая выставка
„70 лет Великого Октября"**

1987, Oct. 17   Litho.
5604 A2686 5k multicolored   1.00 15

All-Union Philatelic Exhibition and the 70th Anniv. of the October Revolution.

My Quiet Homeland, by V.M. Sidorov — A2693

The Sun Above Red Square, by P.P. Ossovsky — A2694

Paintings by Soviet artists exhibited at the 7th Republican Art Exhibition, Moscow, 1985: 4k, There Will be Cities in the Taiga, by A.A. Yakovlev. 5k, Mother, by V.V. Shcherbakov. 30k, On Jakutian Soil, by A.N. Osipov. 35k, Ivan's Return, by V.I. Yerofeyev.

Perf. 12x12½, 12½x12
1987, Oct. 20
5605 A2693 4k multi, vert.   15   15
5606 A2693 5k multi, vert.   15   15
5607 A2693 10k shown   40   15
5608 A2693 30k multicolored   90   50
5609 A2693 35k multicolored   1.00   55
    Nos. 5605-5609 (5)   2.60 1.50

Souvenir Sheet
Perf. 11½x12½
5610 A2694 50k multicolored   2.50 1.00

John Reed (1887-1920), American Journalist — A2695

1987, Oct. 22   Perf. 11½
5611 A2695 10k buff & dark brown   40   15

Samuil Yakovlevich Marshak (1887-1964), Author — A2696

1987, Nov. 3   Engr.   Perf. 12½x12
5612 A2696 5k deep claret   15   15

A2697

1987, Nov. 8
5613 A2697 5k slate blue   50   15

Ilja Grigorjevich Chavchavadze (1837-1907), Georgian author.

A2698   A2699

1987, Nov. 19   Photo.   Perf. 11½
5614 A2698 5k black & brown   15   15

Indira Gandhi (1917-1984).

1987, Nov. 25   Perf. 12½x12
5615 A2699 5k black   15   15

Vadim Nikolaevich Podbelsky (1887-1920), revolution leader.

A2700   A2701

1987, Nov. 25
5616 A2700 5k dark blue gray   15   15

Nikolai Ivanovich Vavilov (1887-1943), botanist.

Photo. & Engr.
1987, Nov. 25   Perf. 11½

Modern Science: 5k, TOKAMAK, a controlled thermonuclear reactor. 10k, Kola Project (Earth strata study). 20k, RATAN-600 radiotelescope.

5617 A2701 5k grnsh gray & brown   15   15
5618 A2701 10k dull grn, lt blue gray & dark blue   35   15
5619 A2701 20k gray olive, blk & buff 70   15
         Set value   50

US and Soviet Flags, Spasski Tower and US Capitol — A2702

1987, Dec. 17   Photo.
5620 A2702 10k multicolored   50   15

INF Treaty (eliminating intermediate-range nuclear missiles) signed by Gen.-Sec. Gorbachev and Pres. Reagan, Dec. 8.

New Year 1988
A2703

1987, Dec. 2   Litho.   Perf. 12x12½
5621 A2703 5k Kremlin   15   15
  a.   Miniature sheet of 8

Marshal Ivan Khristoforovich Bagramyan (1897-1982) — A2704

1987, Dec. 2   Engr.   Perf. 12½x12
5622 A2704 5k black   15   15

Miniature Sheet

18th-19th Cent. Naval Commanders and War Ships — A2705

Designs: 4k, Adm. Grigori Andreyevich Spiridov (1713-1790), Battle of Chesmen. 5k, Fedor Fedorovich Ushakov (1745-1817), Storming of Corfu. 10k, Adm. Dimitiri Nikolayevich Senyavin (1763-1831) and flagship at the Battle of Afon off Mt. Athos. 25k, Mikhail Petrovich Lazarev (1788-1851), Battle of Navarin. 30k, Adm. Pavel Stepanovich Nakhimov (1802-1855), Battle of Sinop.

1987, Dec. 22
5623   Sheet of 5 + label   2.50 1.25
  a. A2705 4k dark blue & indigo   15   15
  b. A2705 5k maroon & indigo   15   15
  c. A2705 10k maroon & indigo   35   15
  d. A2705 25k dark blue & indigo   80   38
  e. A2705 30k dark blue & indigo   1.00   50

No. 5623 contains corner label (LR) picturing ensign of period Russian Navy vessels and anchor. See No. 5850.

A2706   A2707

1987, Dec. 26   Photo.   Perf. 11½
5624 A2706 10k multicolored   35   15

Asia-Africa Peoples Solidarity Organization, 30th anniv.

1988, Jan. 4   Photo.   Perf. 11½
5625 A2707 10k #149, #150 UR   50   15
5626 A2707 10k #150, #149 UR   50   15
  a.   Pair, #5625-5626   1.00   30

1st Soviet Postage Stamp, 70th anniv. Lettering in brown on No. 5625, in blue on No. 5626.

A2708   A2709

1988, Jan. 4
5627 A2708 5k Biathlon   15   15
         Miniature sheet of 8
5628 A2708 10k Cross-country skiing 30   15
         Miniature sheet of 8
5629 A2708 15k Slalom   40   30
         Miniature sheet of 8
5630 A2708 20k Pairs figure skating 50   35
         Miniature sheet of 8
5631 A2708 30k Ski jumping   70   48
  a.   Miniature sheet of 8
       Nos. 5627-5631 (5)   2.05 1.43
Souvenir Sheet
5632 A2708 50k Ice hockey, horiz.   1.50 1.00

1988 Winter Olympics, Calgary. For overprint see No. 5665.

1988, Jan. 7
5633 A2709 35k blue & gold   1.00 65

World Health Org., 40th anniv.

Lord Byron (1788-1824), English Poet — A2710

Photo. & Engr.
1988, Jan. 22   Perf. 12x11½
5634 A2710 15k Prus blue, blk & grn black   50   30

A2711   A2712

1988, Jan. 27   Photo.   Perf. 11½
5635 A2711 20k multicolored   60 40

Cultural, Technical and Educational Agreement with the US, 30th anniv.

1988, Feb. 5
5636 A2712 5k black & tan   15 15

G.I. Lomov-Oppokov (1888-1938), party leader. See Nos. 5649, 5660, 5666, 5673, 5700, 5704, 5721, 5812.

Animated Soviet Cartoons — A2713

1988, Feb. 18   Litho.   Perf. 12½x12
5637 A2713 1k Little Humpback
          Horse, 1947   15 15
5638 A2713 3k Winnie-the-Pooh,
          1969   15 15
5639 A2713 4k Gena, the Crocodile,
          1969   15 15
5640 A2713 5k Just you Wait! 1969   15 15
5641 A2713 10k Hedgehog in the
          Mist, 1975   30 20
          Set value   70 48
Souvenir Sheet
5642 A2713 30k Post, 1929   1.00 60

A2714   A2715

1988, Feb. 21   Photo.   Perf. 11½
5643 A2714 10k buff & black   30 20

Mikhail Alexandrovich Bonch-Bruevich (1888-1940), broadcast engineer.

1988, Feb. 25
5644 A2715 15k blk, brt blue & dark red 50 30
a.   Miniature sheet of 8

Intl. Red Cross and Red Crescent Organizations, 125th annivs.

World Speed Skating Championships, Mar. 5-6, Alma-Ata — A2716

1988, Mar. 13   Photo.   Perf. 11½
5645 A2716 15k blk, vio & brt blue   45 30

No. 5645 printed se-tenant with label picturing Alma-Ata skating rink, Medeo.

A2717

1988, Mar. 13   Litho.   Perf. 12½x12
5646 A2717 10k dark olive green   30 20

Anton Semenovich Makarenko (1888-1939), teacher, youth development expert.

A2718   A2719

1988, Mar. 17   Engr.   Perf. 12x12½
5647 A2718 5k gray black   15 15

Franzisk Skorina (b. 1488), 1st printer in Byelorussia.

1988, Mar. 22   Photo.   Perf. 11½
5648 A2719 5k multicolored   15 15

Labor Day.

Party Leader Type of 1988
1988, Mar. 24   Engr.   Perf. 12
5649 A2712 5k dark green   15 15

Victor Eduardovich Kingisepp (1888-1922).

Organized Track and Field Events in Russia, Cent. A2721

1988, Mar. 24   Photo.   Perf. 11½
5650 A2721 15k multicolored   50 30

Marietta Sergeyevna Shaginyan (1888-1982), Author A2722

1988, Apr. 2   Litho.   Perf. 12½x12
5651 A2722 10k brown   30 20

Soviet-Finnish Peace Treaty, 40th Anniv. A2723

1988, Apr. 6   Photo.   Perf. 11½
5652 A2723 15k multicolored   50 30

Cosmonaut's Day — A2724

Victory, 1948, Painted by P.A. Krivonogov — A2725

Design: MIR space station, Soyuz TM transport ship, automated cargo ship Progress and Quant module.

1988, Apr. 12   Perf. 11½x12
5653 A2724 15k multicolored   50 30
a.   Miniature sheet of 8

1988, Apr. 20   Litho.   Perf. 12x12½
5654 A2725 5k multicolored   15 15

Victory Day (May 9).

Sochi City, 150th Anniv. A2726

1988, Apr. 20   Photo.   Perf. 11½
5655 A2726 5k multicolored   15 15

Branches of the Lenin Museum — A2727

Portrait of Lenin and: No. 5656, Central museum, Moscow, opened May 15, 1926. No. 5657, Branch, Leningrad, opened in 1937. No. 5658, Branch, Kiev, opened in 1938. No. 5659, Branch, Krasnoyarsk, opened in 1987.

1988, Apr. 22   Litho.   Perf. 12
5656 A2727 5k vio brown & gold   15 15
5657 A2727 5k brn vio, vio brown &
          gold   15 15
5658 A2727 5k deep brown olive & gold 15 15
5659 A2727 5k dark green & gold   15 15
a.   Block of 4, Nos. 5656-5659   60 40
          Set value   40

See Nos. 5765-5767, 5885-5887.

Party Leader Type of 1988
1988, Apr. 24   Photo.   Perf. 11½
5660 A2712 5k blue black   15 15

Ivan Alexeyevich Akulov (1888-1939).

A2729   Karl Marx — A2730

1988, Apr. 30
5661 A2729 20k multicolored   65 42

EXPO '88, Brisbane, Australia.

1988, May 5   Engr.   Perf. 12
5662 A2730 5k chocolate   15 15

Social and Economic Reforms — A2731

Designs: No. 5663, Cruiser Aurora, revolutionary soldiers, workers and slogans Speeding Up, Democratization, and Glasnost against Kremlin Palace. No. 5664, Worker, agriculture and industries.

1988, May 5   Photo.   Perf. 12x11½
5663 A2731 5k multicolored   15 15
5664 A2731 5k multicolored   15 15
          Set value   20

No. 5632 Ovptd. in Dark Red

Спортсмены СССР завоевали 11 золотых, 9 серебряных и 9 бронзовых медалей!

Souvenir Sheet
1988, May 12   Photo.   Perf. 11½
5665 A2708 50k multicolored   2.00 1.25

Victory of Soviet athletes at the 1988 Winter Olympics, Calgary. No. 5665 overprinted below stamp on souvenir sheet margin. Soviet sportsmen won 11 gold, 9 silver and 9 bronze medals.

Party Leader Type of 1988
1988, May 19   Engr.   Perf. 12
5666 A2712 5k black   15 15

Nikolai Mikhailovich Shvernik (1888-1970).

Hunting Dogs — A2733

Designs: 5k, Russian borzoi, fox hunt. 10k, Kirghiz greyhound, falconry. 15k, Russian retrievers. 20k, Russian spaniel, duck hunt. 35k, East Siberian husky, bear hunt.

1988, May 20   Litho.
5667 A2733 5k multicolored   16 15
5668 A2733 10k multicolored   35 22
5669 A2733 15k multicolored   55 32
5670 A2733 20k multicolored   80 50
5671 A2733 35k multicolored   1.25 80
          Nos. 5667-5671 (5)   3.11 1.99

A2734   A2736

1988, May 29   Photo.   Perf. 11½
5672 A2734 5k multicolored   30 15

Soviet-US Summit Conf., May 29-June 2, Moscow.

Party Leader Type of 1988
1988, June 6   Engr.   Perf. 12
5673 A2712 5k brown black   15 15

Valerian Vladimirovich Kuibyshev (1888-1935).

1988, June 7   Photo.   Perf. 11½
Design: Flags, Mir space station and Soyuz TM spacecraft.
5674 A2736 15k multicolored   50 32

Shipka '88, USSR-Bulgarian joint space flight, June 7.

A2737

A2738

Design: Natl. & Canadian flags, skis & obe.

1988, June 16
5675 A2737 35k multicolored   1.25   80

Soviet-Canada transarctic ski expedition, May-Aug.

1988, June 16
5676 A2738 5k multicolored   15   15

For a world without nuclear weapons.

ПОЧТА СССР·1988   A2739

A2740 5к

19th All-union Communist Party Conference, Moscow — A2741

1988, June 16   **Perf. 12**
5677 A2739 5k multicolored   15   15
    Photo.
    Perf. 11½
5678 A2740 5k multicolored   15   15
    Set value   20
    Souvenir Sheet
    Perf. 11½x12
5679 A2741 50k multicolored   1.75 1.00

1988 Summer Olympics, Seoul A2742

1988, June 29   **Litho.**   **Perf. 12**
5680 A2742 5k Hurdling   15   15
    a.   Miniature sheet of 8
5681 A2742 10k Long jump   35   25
    a.   Miniature sheet of 8
5682 A2742 15k Basketball   55   40
    a.   Miniature sheet of 8
5683 A2742 20k Rhythmic gymnastics   70   50
    a.   Miniature sheet of 8
5684 A2742 30k Swimming   1.00   70
    a.   Miniature sheet of 8
    Nos. 5680-5684 (5)   2.75 2.00
    Souvenir Sheet
5685 A2742 50k Soccer   1.75 1.10

For overprint see No. 5722.

Phobos Intl. Space Project — A2743

Flowers Populating Deciduous Forests — A2744

1988, July 7   **Photo.**   **Perf. 11½x12**
5686 A2743 10k Satellite, space probe   30   20

For the study of Phobos, a satellite of Mars.

1988, July 7   **Litho.**   **Perf. 12**
5687 A2744 5k Campanula latifolia   15   15
5688 A2744 10k Orobus vernus, horiz.   35   25
5689 A2744 15k Pulmonaria obscura   50   35
5690 A2744 20k Lilium martagon   65   45
5691 A2744 35k Ficaria verna   1.10   75
    Nos. 5687-5691 (5)   2.75 1.95

A2745

НЕЛЬСОН МАНДЕЛА
A2746

1988, July 14   **Photo.**   **Perf. 11½**
5692 A2745 5k multicolored   15   15

Leninist Young Communist League (Komsomol), 70th anniv. For overprint see No. 5699.

1988, July 18
5693 A2746 10k multicolored   30   20

Nelson Mandela (b. 1918), South African anti-apartheid leader

Paintings in the Timiriazev Equestrian Museum of the Moscow Agricultural Academy — A2747

Paintings: 5k, *Light Gray Arabian Stallion*, by N.E. Sverchkov, 1860. 10k, *Konvoets*, a Kabardian, by M.A. Vrubel, 1882, vert. 15k, *Horsewoman Riding an Orlov-Rastopchinsky*, by N.E. Sverchkov. 20k, *Letuchka*, a Gray Orlov Trotter, by V.A. Serov, 1886, vert. 30k, *Sardar*, an Akhaltekinsky Stallion, by A.B. Villevalde, 1882.

1988, July 20   **Litho.**   **Perf. 12½x12**
5694 A2747 5k multicolored   15   15
5695 A2747 10k multicolored   30   20
5696 A2747 15k multicolored   45   30
5697 A2747 20k multicolored   60   40
5698 A2747 30k multicolored   1.00   70
    Nos. 5694-5698 (5)   2.50 1.75

No. 5692 Ovptd. for the All-Union Philatelic Exhibition, Moscow, Aug. 10-17   **Филвыставка. Москва**

1988, Aug. 10   **Photo.**   **Perf. 11½**
5699 A2745 5k multicolored   40   28

Party Leader Type of 1988

1988, Aug. 13   **Engr.**   **Perf. 12½x12**
5700 A2712 5k black   15   15

Petr Lazarevich Voykov (1888-1927), economic and trade union plenipotentiary.

Intl. Letter-Writing Week
A2749

1988, Aug. 25   **Photo.**   **Perf. 11½**
5701 A2749 5k blue grn & dark blue green   15   15

A2750

A2751

1988, Aug. 29
5702 A2750 15k Earth, Mir space station and Soyuz-TM   50   30

Soviet-Afghan joint space flight.

1988, Sept. 1   **Photo.**   **Perf. 11½**
5703 A2751 10k multicolored   30   20

Problems of Peace and Socialism magazine, 30th anniv.

Party Leader Type of 1988

1988, Sept. 13   **Engr.**   **Perf. 12**
5704 A2712 5k black   15   15

Emmanuil Ionovich Kviring (1888-1937).

A2753

A2753a

A2753c

A2753b

A2753d

Designs: No. 5705, *Ilya Muromets*, Russian lore. No. 5706, *Ballad of the Cossack Golota*, Ukrainian lore. No. 5707, *Musician-Magician*, a Byelorussian fairy tale. No. 5708, *Koblandy-batyr*, a poem from Kazakh. No. 5709, *Alpamysh*, a fairy tale from Uzbek.

    Perf. 12x12½, 12½x12
1988, Sept. 22   **Litho.**
5705 A2753 10k multicolored   30   20
5706 A2753a 10k multicolored   30   20
5707 A2753b 10k multicolored   30   20
5708 A2753c 10k multicolored   30   20
5709 A2753d 10k multicolored   30   20
    Nos. 5705-5709 (5)   1.50 1.00

Nos. 5705-5709 each printed se-tenant with inscribed labels. See note A2795.

Appeal of the Leader, 1947, by I.M. Toidze
A2754

1988, Oct. 5   **Perf. 12x12½**
5710 A2754 5k multicolored   15   15

October Revolution, 71st anniv.

А.Т. БОЛОТОВ
A2755

А.Н. ТУПОЛЕВ
A2756

1988, Oct. 18   **Engr.**   **Perf. 12**
5711 A2755 10k black   30   20

Andrei Timofeyevich Bolotov (1738-1833), agricultural scientist, publisher.

1988, Oct. 18
5712 A2756 10k steel blue   30   20

Andrei Nikolayevich Tupolev (1888-1972), aeronautical engineer.

A2757   A2758

Design: 20k, Map of expedition route, atomic icebreaker *Sibirj* and expedition members.

1988, Oct. 25   **Litho.**
5713 A2757 20k multicolored   60   40

North Pole expedition (in 1987).

1988, Oct. 30   **Engr.**
5714 A2758 5k brown black   16   15

Dmitry F. Ustinov (1908-84), minister of defense.

Soviet-Vietnamese Treaty, 10th Anniv. — A2759

1988, Nov. 3   Photo.   Perf. 11½
5715 A2759 10k multicolored   30   20

State Broadcasting and Sound Recording Institute, 50th Anniv. A2760

1988, Nov. 3
5716 A2760 10k multicolored   30   20

UN Declaration of Human Rights, 40th Anniv. A2761

1988, Nov. 21
5717 A2761 10k multicolored   30   20

New Year 1989 — A2762

Design: Preobrazhensky Regiment bodyguard riding to announce Peter the Great's decree to celebrate new year's eve as of January 1, 1700.

1988, Nov. 24   Litho.   Perf. 12x11½
5718 A2762 5k multicolored   16   15

Soviet-French Joint Space Flight A2763

1988, Nov. 26   Photo.   Perf. 11½
5719 A2763 15k Space walkers   45   30

No. 4607 Overprinted in Red

★
КОСМИЧЕСКАЯ
ПОЧТА

1988, Dec. 16   Litho.   Perf. 12½x12
5720 A2143 1r dark blue   3.50 2.25

Space mail.

Party Leader Type of 1988

1988, Dec. 16   Engr.
5721 A2712 5k slate green   15   15

Martyn Ivanovich Latsis (1888-1938).

Souvenir Sheet

СПОРТСМЕНЫ СССР ЗАВОЕВАЛИ 55 ЗОЛОТЫХ, 31 СЕРЕБРЯНУЮ И 46 БРОНЗОВЫХ МЕДАЛЕЙ СЕУЛ • 1988

No. 5685 Overprinted in Bright Blue

1988, Dec. 20   Litho.   Perf. 12
5722 A2742 50k multicolored   1.50 1.00

Victory of Soviet athletes at the 1988 Summer Olympics, Seoul. Overprint on margin of No. 5722 specifies that Soviet athletes won 55 gold, 31 silver and 46 bronze medals.

Post Rider A2765

Fountains of Petrodvorets A2766

Designs: 3k, Cruiser *Aurora*. 4k, Spasski Tower, Lenin Mausoleum. 5k, Natl. flag, crest. 10k, *The Worker and the Collective Farmer*, 1935, sculpture by V.I. Mukhina. 15k, Satellite dish. 20k, Lyre, art tools, quill pen, parchment (arts and literature). 25k, *Discobolus*, 5th cent. sculpture by Myron (c. 480-440 B.C.). 30k, Map of the Antarctic, penguins. 35k, *Mercury*, sculpture by Giambologna (1529-1608). 50k, White cranes (nature conservation). 1r, UPU emblem.

1988, Dec. 22   Engr.   Perf. 12x11½
5723 A2765 1k dark brown   15   15
5724 A2765 3k dark blue green   15   15
5725 A2765 4k indigo   15   15
5726 A2765 5k red   15   15
5727 A2765 10k claret   30   20
5728 A2765 15k deep blue   45   30
5729 A2765 20k olive gray   60   40
5730 A2765 25k dark green   75   50
5731 A2765 30k dark blue   90   60
5732 A2765 35k dark red brown   1.05   70
5733 A2765 50k sapphire   1.50 1.00

Perf. 12x12½
5734 A2765 1r blue gray   3.00 2.00
    Nos. 5723-5734 (12)   9.15 6.30

See Nos. 5838-5849, 5981-5987.

1988, Dec. 25   Engr.   Perf. 11½x12
Designs: 5k, Samson Fountain, 1723, and Great Cascade. 10k, Adam Fountain, 1722, and sculptures, 1718, by D. Bonazza. 15k, Golden Mountain Cascade, by N. Miketti (1721-1723) and M.G. Zemtsov. 30k, Roman Fountains, 1763. 50k, Oak Tree Fountain, 1735.

5735 A2766 5k myrtle green   15   15
5736 A2766 10k myrtle green   30   20
5737 A2766 15k myrtle green   45   30
5738 A2766 30k myrtle green   90   60
5739 A2766 50k myrtle green   1.50 1.00
  a.   Pane of 5, #5735-5739   3.30 2.20
    Nos. 5735-5739 (5)   3.30 2.25

Panes have photogravure margin. Panes are printed bilaterally and separated in the center by perforations so that stamps in the 2nd pane are arranged in reverse order from the 1st pane.

19th Communist Party Congress — A2767

1988, Dec. 30   Photo.   Perf. 12x11½
Multicolored and:
5740 A2767 5k deep car (power)   15   15
5741 A2767 5k deep blue vio (industry)   15   15
5742 A2767 5k green (land)   15   15
    Set value   30

Souvenir Sheet

Inaugural Flight of the *Buran* Space Shuttle, Nov. 15 — A2768

1988, Dec. 30   Perf. 11½x12
5743 A2768 50k multicolored   1.50 1.00

Luna 1, 30th Anniv. — A2769

1989, Jan. 2   Photo.   Perf. 11½
5744 A2769 15k multicolored   50   30

Jalmari Virtanen (1889-1939), Karelian Poet — A2770

1989, Jan. 8
5745 A2770 5k olive brown   15   15

Council for Mutual Economic Assistance, 40th Anniv. A2771

1989, Jan. 8
5746 A2771 10k multicolored   30   20

Environmental Protection — A2772

1989, Jan. 18   Litho.   Perf. 12½x12
5747 A2772 5k Forest   15   15
5748 A2772 10k Arctic deer   30   20
5749 A2772 15k Stop desert encroachment   45   30

Nos. 5747-5749 printed se-tenant with inscribed labels picturing maps.

Samovars — A2773

Samovars in the State Museum, Leningrad: 5k, Pear-shaped urn, late 18th cent. 10k, Barrel-shaped urn by Ivan Listisin, early 19th cent. 20k, "Kabachok" urn by the Sokolov Bros., Tula, c. 1830. 30k, Vase-shaped urn by the Nikolari Malikov Studio, Tula, c. 1840.

1989, Feb. 8   Photo.   Perf. 11½
5750 A2773 5k multicolored   15   15
5751 A2773 10k multicolored   30   20
5752 A2773 20k multicolored   60   40
5753 A2773 30k multicolored   90   60

Modest Petrovich Mussorgsky (1839-1881), Composer — A2774

1989, Feb. 15   Litho.   Perf. 12½x12
5754 A2774 10k dull vio & vio brn   30   20

P.E. Dybenko (1889-1938), Military Commander — A2775

1989, Feb. 28   Engr.   Perf. 12
5755 A2775 5k black   15   15

T.G. Shevchenko (1814-1861), Poet A2776

1989, Mar. 6   Litho.   Perf. 11½
5756 A2776 5k pale grn, blk & brn   15   15

Cultivated Lilies — A2777

1989, Mar. 15   Perf. 12½x12
5757 A2777 5k Lilium speciosum   15   15
5758 A2777 10k African queen   30   20
5759 A2777 15k Eclat du soir   45   30
5760 A2777 30k White tiger   90   60

Souvenir Sheet

Labor Day, Cent. — A2778

1989, Mar. 25   *Perf. 11¹⁄₂x12*
5761 A2778 30k multicolored   1.00 60

*Victory
Banner*, by P.
Loginov and
V. Pamfilov
A2779

1989, Apr. 5 Litho. *Perf. 12x12¹⁄₂*
5762 A2779 5k multicolored   15 15

World War II Victory Day.

Cosmonauts' Day — A2780

Illustration reduced.

1989, Apr. 12 Photo. *Perf. 11x11¹⁄₂*
5763 A2780 15k Mir space station   45 30

A2781

1989, Apr. 14   *Perf. 11¹⁄₂*
5764 A2781 10k multicolored   30 20

Bering Bridge Soviet-American Expedition, Anadyr and Kotzebue.

Type of 1988

Portraits and branches of the Lenin Central Museum: No. 5765, Kazan. No. 5766, Kuibyshev. No. 5767, Frunze.

1989, Apr. 14 Litho. *Perf. 12*
5765 A2727 5k rose brown & multi   15 15
5766 A2727 5k olive gray & multi   15 15
5767 A2727 5k deep brown & multi   15 15
                Set value   30

Lenin's 119th Birth Anniv.

Souvenir Sheet

Launch of Interplanetary Probe
Phobos — A2783

1989, Apr. 24   *Perf. 11¹⁄₂x12*
5768 A2783 50k multicolored   1.50 1.00

A2784   A2785

1989, May 5 Photo. *Perf. 11¹⁄₂*
5769 A2784 5k multicolored   15 15

Hungarian Soviet Republic, 70th anniv.

1989, May 5 Photo. & Engr.
5770 A2785 5k multicolored   15 15

Volgograd, 400th anniv.

Honeybees — A2786

1989, May 18 Litho. *Perf. 12*
5771 A2786 5k Drone   16 15
5772 A2786 10k Workers, flowers,
              man-made hive   32 20
5773 A2786 20k Worker collecting
              pollen   65 40
5774 A2786 35k Queen, drones,
              honeycomb   1.15 78

Photography,
150th Anniv.
A2787

1989, May 24 Photo. *Perf. 11¹⁄₂*
5775 A2787 5k multicolored   15 15

I.A. Kuratov (1839-1875),
Author — A2788

1989, June 26 Litho. *Perf. 12¹⁄₂x12*
5776 A2788 5k dark golden brown   18 15

Jean Racine
(1639-1699),
French
Dramatist
A2789

Photo. & Engr.
1989, June 16   *Perf. 12x11¹⁄₂*
5777 A2789 15k multicolored   50 32

Europe, Our   Mukhina, by
Common   Nesterov — A2791
Home — A2790

Designs: 5k, Map of Europe, stylized bird. 10k, Crane, two men completing a bridge, globe. 15k, Stork's nest, globe.

1989, June 20 Photo. *Perf. 11¹⁄₂*
5778 A2790 5k multicolored   16 15
5779 A2790 10k multicolored   32 20
5780 A2790 15k multicolored   48 32

1989, June 25 Litho. *Perf. 12x12¹⁄₂*
5781 A2791 5k chalky blue   18 15

Vera I. Mukhina (1889-1953), sculptor.

13th World Youth and
Student Festival,
Pyongyang — A2792

1989, July 1 Litho. *Perf. 12*
5782 A2792 10k multicolored   32 20

Ducks
A2793

1989, July 1
5783 A2793 5k *Tadorna tadorna*   16 15
5784 A2793 15k *Anas crecca*   32 20
5785 A2793 20k *Tadorna ferruginea*   65 50
  a.   Min. sheet, 2 5k, 4 15k, 3 20k   4.25 3.00

French
Revolution,
Bicent.
A2794

Designs: 5k, PHILEXFRANCE '89 emblem and Storming of the Bastille. 15k, Marat, Danton, Robespierre. 20k, "La Marseillaise," from the Arc de Triomphe carved by Francois Rude (1784-1855).

Photo. & Engr., Photo. (15k)
1989, July 7   *Perf. 11¹⁄₂*
5786 A2794 5k multicolored   16 15
5787 A2794 15k multicolored   48 32
5788 A2794 20k multicolored   65 42
  a.   Miniature sheet of 8

A2795   A2795a

A2795b   A2795c

Folklore and
Legends — A2795d

Designs: No. 5789, *Amiraniani*, Georgian lore. No. 5790, *Koroglu*, Azerbaijan lore. No. 5791, *Fir, Queen of the Grass-snakes*, Lithuanian lore. No. 5792, *Mioritsa*, Moldavian lore. No. 5793, *Lach-plesis*, Latvian lore.

1989, July 12 Litho. *Perf. 12x12¹⁄₂*
5789 A2795 10k multicolored   32 20
5790 A2795a 10k multicolored   32 20
5791 A2795b 10k multicolored   32 20
5792 A2795c 10k multicolored   32 20
5793 A2795d 10k multicolored   32 20
  Nos. 5789-5793 (5)   1.60 1.00

Each printed with a se-tenant label. See types A2753-A2753d & #5890-5894.

Tallinn Zoo, 50th   Intl. Letter
Anniv. — A2796   Writing
              Week — A2797

1989, July 20 Photo. *Perf. 11¹⁄₂*
5794 A2796 10k Lynx   32 20

1989, July 20 Litho. *Perf. 12*
5705 A2797 5k multicolored   16 15

Pulkovskaya Observatory, 150th
Anniv. — A2798

Photo. & Engr.
1989, July 20   Perf. 11½
5796 A2798 10k multicolored   32 20

Souvenir Sheet

ПОЧТА СССР 1989 50к

Peter the Great and Battle Scene — A2799

1989, July 27   Photo.   Perf. 11½x12
5797 A2799 50k dk blue & dk brn   1.75 1.15

Battle of Hango, 275th anniv.

City of Nikolaev, Bicent. A2800

ПОЧТА СССР 5

1989, Aug. 3   Photo.   Perf. 11½
5798 A2800 5k multicolored   18 15

80th Birth Anniv. of Kwame Nkrumah, 1st Pres. of Ghana — A2801

КВАМЕ НКРУМА

1989, Aug. 9
5799 A2801 10k multicolored   32 20

6th Congress of the All-Union Philatelic Soc., Moscow A2802

1989, Aug. 9   Perf. 12
5800 A2802 10k blue, blac & pink   32 20

Printed se-tenant with label picturing simulated stamps and congress emblem.

James Fenimore Cooper (1789-1851), American Novelist A2803

Photo. & Engr.
1989, Aug. 19   Perf. 12x11½
5801 A2803 15k multicolored   48 32

А2804

Soviet Circus Performers — A2805

Performers and scenes from their acts: 1k, V.L. Durov, clown and trainer. 3k, M.N. Rumyantsev, clown. 4k, V.I. Filatov, bear trainer. 5k, E.T. Kio, magician. 10k, V.E. Lazarenko, acrobat and clown. 30k, Moscow Circus, Tsvetnoi Boulevard.

1989, Aug. 22   Litho.   Perf. 12
5802 A2804 1k multicolored   15 15
5803 A2804 3k multicolored   15 15
5804 A2804 4k multicolored   15 15
5805 A2804 5k multicolored   16 15
5806 A2804 10k multicolored   32 20
           Set value   75 50

Souvenir Sheet
Perf. 12x12½
5807 A2805 30k multicolored   1.05 70

А2806   А2807

1989, Aug. 25   Photo.   Perf. 11½
5808 A2806 15k multicolored   48 32

5th World Boxing Championships, Moscow.

1989, Oct. 5   Litho.   Perf. 12x12½

Design: Demonstration of the First Radio Receiver, 1895, by N. Sysoev.

5809 A2807 10k multicolored   32 20

Aleksandr Popov (1859-1905), inventor of radio in Russia.

А2808   А2811

Polish People's Republic, 45th Anniv. A2809

1989, Oct. 7   Photo.   Perf. 11½
5810 A2808 5k multicolored   16 15

German Democratic Republic, 40th anniv.

1989, Oct. 7
5811 A2809 5k multicolored   16 15

Party Leader Type of 1988

1989, Oct. 10   Engr.   Perf. 12
5812 A2712 5k black   16 15

S.V. Kosior (1889-1939).

1989, Oct. 10
5813 A2811 15k dark red brown   48 32

Jawaharlal Nehru, 1st prime minister of independent India.

Guardsmen of October, by M.M. Chepik A2812

1989, Oct. 14   Litho.   Perf. 12½x12
5814 A2812 5k multicolored   16 15

October Revolution, 72nd anniv.

Kosta Khetagurov (1859-1906), Ossetic Poet A2813

1989, Oct. 14
5815 A2813 5k dark red brown   16 15

А2814   А2815

1989, Oct. 14   Photo.   Perf. 11½
5816 A2814 5k buff, sepia & black   16 15

Li Dazhao (1889-1927), communist party leader of China.

1989, Oct. 20   Engr.   Perf. 12
5817 A2815 5k black   16 15

Jan Karlovich Berzin (1889-1938), army intelligence leader.

Russian — A2816

Musical Instruments: No. 5819, Byelorussian. No. 5820, Ukrainian. No. 5821, Uzbek.

Photo. & Engr.
1989, Oct. 20   Perf. 12x11½
Denomination Color
5818 A2816 10k blue   32 20
5819 A2816 10k brown   32 20
5820 A2816 10k lemon   32 20
5821 A2816 10k blue green   32 20

See Nos. 5929-5932, 6047-6049.

Scenes from Novels by James Fenimore Cooper A2817

Designs: No. 5822, The Hunter, (settlers, canoe). No. 5823, Last of the Mohicans (Indians, settlers). No. 5824, The Pathfinder, (couple near cliff). No. 5825, The Pioneers (women, wild animals). No. 5826, The Prairie (injured Indians, horse).

1989, Nov. 17   Litho.   Perf. 12x12½
5822 A2817 20k multicolored   65 42
5823 A2817 20k multicolored   65 42
5824 A2817 20k multicolored   65 42
5825 A2817 20k multicolored   65 42
5826 A2817 20k multicolored   65 42
  a.   Strip of 5, #5822-5826   3.25 2.10

Printed se-tenant in a continuous design.

Monuments — A2818

Designs: No. 5827, Pokrovsky Cathedral, St. Basil's, statue of K. Minin and D. Pozharsky, Moscow. No. 5828, Petropavlovsky Cathedral, statue of Peter the Great, Leningrad. No. 5829, Sofiisky Cathedral, Bogdan Chmielnicki monument, Kiev. No. 5830, Khodzha Akhmed Yasavi Mausoleum, Turkestan. No. 5831, Khazret-Khyzr Mosque, Samarkand.

1989, Nov. 20   Perf. 11½
Color of "Sky"
5827 A2818 15k tan   48 32
5828 A2818 15k gray green   48 32
5829 A2818 15k blue green   48 32
5830 A2818 15k violet blue   48 32
5831 A2818 15k bright blue   48 32
  Nos. 5827-5831 (5)   2.40 1.60

New Year 1990 A2819

1989, Nov. 22   Perf. 12
5832 A2819 5k multicolored   16 15

Space Achievements
A2820

Designs: Nos. 5833, 5837a, Unmanned Soviet probe on the Moon. Nos. 5834, 5837b, American astronaut on Moon, 1969. Nos. 5835, 5837c, Soviet cosmonaut and American astronaut on Mars. Nos. 5836, 5837d, Mars, planetary body, diff.

1989, Nov. 24

5833	A2820	25k multicolored	80	55
5834	A2820	25k multicolored	80	55
5835	A2820	25k multicolored	80	55
5836	A2820	25k multicolored	80	55
a.		Block of 4, #5833-5836	3.25	2.20

Souvenir Sheet
Imperf

5837		Sheet of 4	3.25	2.20
a.-d.		A2820 25k any single	80	50

World Stamp Expo '89, Washington DC, Nov. 17-Dec. 3; 20th UPU Cong. See US No. C126.

Type of 1988
Dated 1988

1989, Dec. 25   Litho.   Perf. 12x12½

5838	A2765	1k dark brown	15	15
5839	A2765	3k dark blue green	15	15
5840	A2765	4k indigo	15	15
5841	A2765	5k red	15	15
5842	A2765	10k claret	30	20
5843	A2765	15k deep blue	45	30
5844	A2765	20k olive gray	60	40
5845	A2765	25k dark green	75	50
5846	A2765	30k dark blue	90	60
5847	A2765	35k dark red brown	1.05	70
5848	A2765	50k sapphire	1.50	1.00
5849	A2765	1r blue gray	3.00	2.00
		Nos. 5838-5849 (12)	9.15	6.30

Admirals Type of 1987
Miniature Sheet

Admirals and battle scenes: 5k, V.A. Kornilov (1806-1854). 10k, V.I. Istomin (1809-1855). 15k, G.I. Nevelskoi (1813-1876). 20k, G.I. Butakov (1820-1882). 30k, A.A. Popov (1821-1898). 35k, Stepan O. Makarov (1849-1904).

1989, Dec. 28   Engr.   Perf. 12½x12

5850		Sheet of 6	3.75	2.45
a.	A2705	5k brown & Prus blue	16	15
b.	A2705	10k brown & Prus blue	32	20
c.	A2705	15k dark blue & Prus blue	48	32
d.	A2705	20k dark blue & Prus blue	65	42
e.	A2705	30k brown & Prus blue	95	65
f.	A2705	35k brown & Prus blue	1.10	75

Global
Ecology — A2821

Designs: 10k, Flower dying, industrial waste entering the environment. 15k, Bird caught in industrial waste, Earth. 20k, Sea of chopped trees.

1990, Jan. 5   Photo.   Perf. 11½

5851	A2821	10k multicolored	32	20
5852	A2821	15k multicolored	50	32
5853	A2821	20k multicolored	65	42

Capitals of the Republics

A2822   A2822a   A2822b

A2822c   A2822d   A2822e

A2822f   A2822g   A2822h

A2822i   A2822j   A2822k

A2822l   A2822m   A2822n

1990, Jan. 18   Litho.   Perf. 12x12½

5854	A2822	5k Moscow	16	15
5855	A2822a	5k Tallinn	16	15
5856	A2822b	5k Riga	16	15
5857	A2822c	5k Vilnius	16	15
5858	A2822d	5k Minsk	16	15
5859	A2822e	5k Kiev	16	15
5860	A2822f	5k Kishinev	16	15
5861	A2822g	5k Tbilisi	16	15
5862	A2822h	5k Yerevan	16	15
5863	A2822i	5k Baku	16	15
5864	A2822j	5k Alma-Ata	16	15
5865	A2822k	5k Tashkent	16	15
5866	A2822l	5k Frunze	16	15
5867	A2822m	5k Ashkhabad	16	15
5868	A2822n	5k Dushanbe	16	15
		Nos. 5854-5868 (15)	2.40	
		Set value		1.50

ХО ШИ МИН

A2823   A2824

1990, Feb. 3   Perf. 11½

5869	A2823	10k black & brown	35	24

Ho Chi Minh (1890-1969).

1990, Feb. 3   Photo.

5870	A2824	5k multicolored	18	15

Vietnamese Communist Party, 60th anniv.

Owls — A2825

Perf. 12x12½, 12½x12
1990, Feb. 8   Litho.

5871	A2825	10k Nyctea scandiaca	32	20
5872	A2825	20k Bubo bubo, vert.	65	42
5873	A2825	55k Asio otus	1.75	1.15

Penny Black, 150th Anniv. A2826

Emblems and various Penny Blacks: No. 5875, Position TP. No. 5876, Position TF. No. 5877, Position AH. No. 5878, Position VK. No. 5879, Position AE.

1990, Feb. 15   Photo.   Perf. 11½

5874	A2826	10k shown	32	20
5875	A2826	20k gold & black	65	42
5876	A2826	20k gold & black	65	42
5877	A2826	35k multicolored	1.10	75
5878	A2826	35k multicolored	1.10	75
		Nos. 5874-5878 (5)	3.82	2.54

Souvenir Sheet
Perf. 12x11½

5879	A2826	1r dk green & blk	3.25	2.20

Stamp World London '90 (35k).
No. 5879 contains one 37x26mm stamp.

ITU, 125th
Anniv.
A2827

1990, Feb. 20   Photo.   Perf. 11½

5880	A2827	20k multicolored	68	45

Labor
Day — A2828

1990, Mar. 28   Photo.   Perf. 11½

5881	A2828	5k multicolored	18	15

Victory, 1945,
by A. Lysenko
A2829

1990, Mar. 28   Litho.   Perf. 12x12½

5882	A2829	5k multicolored	18	15

End of World War II, 45th anniv.

Mir Space
Station,
Cosmonaut
A2830

1990, Apr. 12

5883	A2830	20k multicolored	65	46

Cosmonauts' Day.

Lenin, 120th Birth
Anniv. — A2831

1990, Apr. 14   Engr.   Perf. 11½

5884	A2831	5k red brown	18	15

LENINIANA '90 all-union philatelic exhibition.

Lenin Birthday Type of 1988

Portrait of Lenin and: No. 5885, Lenin Memorial (birthplace), Ulyanovsk. No. 5886, Branch of the Central Lenin Museum, Baku. No. 5887, Branch of the Central Lenin Museum, Tashkent.

1990, Apr. 14   Litho.   Perf. 12

5885	A2727	5k dark car & multi	18	15
5886	A2727	5k rose vio & multi	18	15
5887	A2727	5k dark grn & multi	18	15
		Set value		36

Lenin, 120th Birth Anniv.

Tchaikovsky,
Scene from
Iolanta
A2832

1990, Apr. 25   Engr.   Perf. 12½x12

5888	A2832	15k black	45	30

Tchaikovsky (1840-1893), composer.

Kalmyk Legend
Dzhangar, 550th
Anniv. — A2833

1990, May 22   Litho.   Perf. 12x12½

5889	A2833	10k black & black brown	32	22

Folklore Type of 1989

Designs: No. 5890, *Manas*, Kirghiz legend (Warrior with saber leading battle). No. 5891, *Guraguli*, Tadzhik legend (Armored warriors and elephant). No. 5892, *David Sasunsky*, Armenian legend (Men, arches, vert.). No. 5893, *Cerogly*, Turkmen legend (Sleeping woman, man with lute, vert.). No. 5894, *Kalevipoeg*, Estonian legend (Man with boards, vert.). Nos. 5890-5894 printed se-tenant with descriptive label.

Perf. 12½x12, 12x12½
1990, May 22

5890	A2795	10k multicolored	32	22
5891	A2795	10k multicolored	32	22
5892	A2795	10k multicolored	32	22
5893	A2795	10k multicolored	32	22
5894	A2795	10k multicolored	32	22
		Nos. 5890-5894 (5)	1.60	1.10

World Cup Soccer Championships, Italy
1990 — A2834

Various soccer players.

1990, May 25   Perf. 12x12½

5895	A2834	5k multicolored	18	15
5896	A2834	10k multicolored	32	22
5897	A2834	15k multicolored	45	30

5898	A2834	25k multicolored	80	52
5899	A2834	35k multicolored	1.10	72
a.		Strip of 5, #5895-5899	2.85	2.00

A2835

1990, June 5   Litho.   Perf. 11¹/₂

5900	A2835	15k multicolored	45	30

Final agreement, European Conference on Security and Cooperation, 15th anniv.

45th World Shooting Championships, Moscow — A2836

1990, June 5   Photo.

5901	A2836	15k multicolored	45	30

Cooperation in Antarctic Research A2837

1990, June 13   Litho.   Perf. 12x12¹/₂

5902	A2837	5k Scientists on ice	18	15
5903	A2837	50k Krill	1.80	1.20
a.		Souv. sheet of 2, #5902-5903	2.00	

See Australia Nos. 1182-1183.

Goodwill Games A2838

1990, June 14   Litho.   Perf. 11¹/₂

5904	A2838	10k multicolored	36	24

Souvenir Sheet

Battle of the Neva River, 750th Anniv. — A2839

1990, June 20   Litho.   Perf. 12¹/₂x12

5905	A2839	50k multicolored	1.80	1.20

Duck Conservation A2840

1990, July 1   Litho.   Perf. 12

5006	A2840	5k Anas platyrhychos	18	15
5007	A2840	15k Bucephala clangula	55	36
5008	A2840	20k Netta rufina	72	48

Poultry A2841

1990, July 1   Perf. 12x12¹/₂

5009	A2841	5k Obroshinsky geese	18	15
5010	A2841	10k Adler rooster & hen	36	24
5011	A2841	15k North Caucasian turkeys	55	36

Spaso-Efrosinievsky Monastery, Polotsk — A2842

Statue of Nicholas Baratashvili and Pantheon, Mtasminda A2843

Palace of Shirvanshahs, Baku A2844

Statue of Stefan III the Great, Kishinev A2845

St. Nshan's Church, Akhpat A2846

Historic Architecture: No. 5915, Cathedral, Vilnius. No. 5917, St. Peter's Church, Riga. No. 5919, Niguliste Church, Tallinn.

1990, Aug. 1   Litho.   Perf. 11¹/₂

5912	A2842	15k multicolored	55	36
5913	A2843	15k multicolored	55	36
5914	A2844	15k multicolored	55	36
5915	A2842	15k multicolored	55	36
5916	A2845	15k multicolored	55	36
5917	A2842	15k multicolored	55	36
5918	A2846	15k multicolored	55	36
5919	A2842	15k multicolored	55	36
		Nos. 5912-5919 (8)	4.40	2.88

See Nos. 5968-5970.

Prehistoric Animals — A2847

1990, Aug. 15

5920	A2847	1k Sordes	15	15
5921	A2847	3k Chalicotherium	15	15
5922	A2847	5k Indricotherium	18	15
5923	A2847	10k Saurolophus	36	24
5924	A2847	20k Thyestes	72	48
		Nos. 5920-5924 (5)	1.56	
		Set value		95

Nos. 5921-5923 vert.

Indian Child's Drawing of the Kremlin A2848

Designs: No. 5926, Russian child's drawing of India.

1990, Aug. 15   Perf. 12

5925	A2848	10k multicolored	36	24
5926	A2848	10k multicolored	36	24
a.		Pair, #5925-5926	72	48

See India Nos. 1318-1319.

A2849   A2850

1990, Sept. 12   Engr.   Perf. 12x11¹/₂

5927	A2849	5k blue	18	15

Letter Writing Week.

1990, Sept. 12   Perf. 11¹/₂

5928	A2850	5k multicolored	18	15

Traffic safety.

Musical Instruments Type of 1989

Musical Instruments: No. 5929, Kazakh. No. 5930, Georgian. No. 5931, Azerbaijanian. No. 5932, Lithuanian.

Photo. & Engr.

1990, Sept. 20   Perf. 12x11¹/₂

Denomination Color

5929	A2816	10k brown	36	24
5930	A2816	10k green	36	24
5931	A2816	10k orange	36	24
5932	A2816	10k blue	36	24

Killer Whales A2855

Northern Sea Lions A2856

Sea Otter A2857

Common Dolphin A2858

1990, Oct. 3   Litho.   Perf. 12x11¹/₂

5933	A2855	25k multicolored	82	54
5934	A2856	25k multicolored	82	54
5935	A2857	25k multicolored	82	54
5936	A2858	25k multicolored	82	54

See US Nos. 2508-2511.

A2859   A2860

Design: Lenin Among the Delegates to the 2nd Congress of Soviets, by S.V. Gerasimov.

1990, Oct. 10   Litho.   Perf. 12x12¹/₂

5937	A2859	5k multicolored	18	15

October Revolution, 73rd Anniv.

1990, Oct. 22   Perf. 12

Nobel Laureates in Literature: #5938, Ivan A. Bunin (1870-1953). #5939, Boris Pasternak (1890-1960). #5940, Mikhail A. Sholokov (1905-1984).

5938	A2860	15k brown olive	55	36
5939	A2860	15k bluish black	55	36
5940	A2860	15k black	55	36

Submarines — A2861

1990, Nov. 14   Litho.   Perf. 12

5941	A2861	5k Sever-2	18	15
5942	A2861	10k Tinro-2	36	24
5943	A2861	15k Argus	55	36
5944	A2861	25k Paisis	90	60
5945	A2861	35k Mir	1.25	84
		Nos. 5941-5945 (5)	3.24	2.19

A2862   A2863

Armenia-Mother Monument by E. Kochar.

1990, Nov. 27   Litho.   Perf. 11¹/₂

5946	A2862	10k multicolored	36	24

Armenia '90 Philatelic Exhibition.

1990, Nov. 29   Photo.   Perf. 11¹/₂

Soviet Agents: #5947, Rudolf I. Abel (1903-71). #5948, Kim Philby (1912-88). #5949, Konon T. Molody (1922-70). #5950, S.A. Vaupshasov (1899-1976). #5951, I.D. Kudrya (1912-42).

5947	A2863	5k black & brown	18	15
5948	A2863	5k black & bluish blk	18	15
5949	A2863	5k black & yel brown	18	15
5950	A2863	5k black & yel green	18	15
5951	A2863	5k black & brown	18	15
		Nos. 5947-5951 (5)	90	
		Set value		60

Joint Soviet-Japanese Space
Flight — A2864

1990, Dec. 2   Litho.   Perf. 12
5952 A2864 20k multicolored   72   48

Happy New Year — A2865

Illustration reduced.

1990, Dec. 3   Perf. 11½
5953 A2865 5k multicolored   18   15
  b.   Miniature sheet of 8

Charter for a New
Europe — A2865a

1990, Dec. 31   Litho.   Perf. 11½
5953A A2865a 30k Globe, Eiffel
                Tower   1.10   80

Marine
Life
A2866

1991, Jan. 4   Litho.   Perf. 12
5954 A2866 4k Rhizostoma pulmo   15   15
5955 A2866 5k Anemonia sulcata   18   15
5956 A2866 10k Squalus acanthias   36   24
5957 A2866 15k Engraulis encrasico-
                lus   55   40
5958 A2866 20k Tursiops truncatus   72   48
       Nos. 5954-5958 (5)   1.96 1.42

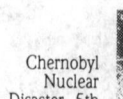

Chernobyl
Nuclear
Disaster, 5th
Anniv.
A2867

1991, Jan. 22   Perf. 11½
5959 A2867 15k multicolored   55   40

Sorrento
Coast with
View of
Capri, 1826,
by S.F.
Shchedrin
(1791-1830)
A2868

Evening in
the Ukraine,
1878, by
A.I.
Kuindzhi
(1841-1910)
A2869

Paintings: No. 5961, New Rome, St. Angel's Castle, 1823, by Shchedrin. No. 5963, Birch Grove, 1879, by Kuindzhi.

1991, Jan. 25   Perf. 12½x12
5960 A2868 10k multicolored   36   24
5961 A2868 10k multicolored   36   24
  a.   Pair, #5960-5961+label   72   48
5962 A2869 10k multicolored   36   24
5963 A2869 10k multicolored   36   24
  a.   Pair, #5962-5963+label   72   48

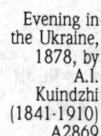

Paul Keres
(1916-1975),
Chess
Grandmaster
A2870

1991, Jan. 7   Litho.   Perf. 11½
5964 A2870 15k dark brown   54   40

Environmental
Protection
A2871

Designs: 10k, Bell tower near Kaliazin, Volga River region. 15k, Lake Baikal. 20k, Desert zone of former Aral Sea.

1991, Feb. 5   Litho.   Perf. 11½
5965 A2871 10k multicolored   36   24
5966 A2871 15k multicolored   54   40
5967 A2871 20k multicolored   72   48

Moslem Tower,   Mukhammed
Uzgen, Kirghizia   Bashar
A2872   Mausoleum,
                       Tadzhikstan
                       A2873

Talkhatan-baba Mosque,
Turkmenistan
A2874

1991, Mar. 5
5968 A2872 15k multicolored   18   15
5969 A2873 15k multicolored   18   15
5970 A2874 15k multicolored   18   15

       See Nos. 5912-5919.

Russian Settlements in America — A2875

Designs: 20k, G. I. Shelekhov (1747-1795), Alaska colonizer. 30k, A. A. Baranov, (1746-1819), first governor of Russian America. 50k, I. A. Kuskov, founder of Ross, California.

1991, Mar. 14   Perf. 12x11½
5971 A2875 20k brt blue & black   72   48
5972 A2875 30k olive brn & blk   1.10   80
5973 A2875 50k red brn & black   1.80 1.20

Yuri A.   No. 5977c
Gagarin — A2876   Inscription

1991, Apr. 6   Perf. 11½x12
5974 A2876 25k Pilot   90   70
5975 A2876 25k Cosmonaut   90   70
5976 A2876 25k Pilot, wearing hat   90   70
5977 A2876 25k As civilian   90   70
  a.   Block of 4, #5974-5977   3.60   2.80
  b.   Sheet of 4, #5974-5977, imperf.   3.60   2.80
  c.   As "b," inscribed   3.60   2.80
  d.   Sheet, 2 each, #5974-5977, Perf.
        12x11½   7.20   5.50

#5977b-5977c have simulated perforations.

May 1945 by
A. and S.
Tkachev
A2877

1991, Apr. 10   Perf. 12
5978 A2877 5k multicolored   18   15

       World War II Victory Day.

Asia and Pacific
Transport Network,
10th Anniv. — A2878

1991, Apr. 15   Perf. 11½
5979 A2878 10k multicolored   15   15

Type of 1988
Dated 1991

Designs: 2k, Early ship, train, and carriage. 7k, Airplane, helicopter, ocean liner, cable car, van. 12k, Space shuttle. 13k, Space station.

1991, Apr. 15   Litho.   Perf. 12x12½
5984 A2765 2k orange brown   15   15
5985 A2765 7k bright blue   25   20
  a.   Perf. 12x11½, photo.   25   20
5986 A2765 12k dk lilac rose   45   30
5987 A2765 13k deep violet   50   35

For surcharges see Tadjikistan Nos. 10-11.

Lenin, 121st
Birth Anniv.
A2879

Painting: Lenin working on "Materialism and Empirical Criticism" by P.P. Belousov.

1991, Apr. 22   Litho.   Perf. 12
5992 A2879 5k multicolored   18   15

Sergei
Prokofiev
(1891-1953),
Composer
A2880

1991, Apr. 23   Perf. 12½x12
5993 A2880 15k brown   54   40

Orchids — A2881   A2882

1991, May 7   Perf. 12
5994 A2881 3k Cypripedium calce-
                olus   15   15
5995 A2881 5k Orchis purpurea   18   15
5996 A2881 10k Ophrys apifera   36   24
5997 A2881 25k Calypso bulbosa   72   48
5998 A2881 25k Epipactis palustris   90   60
       Nos. 5994-5998 (5)   2.31 1.62

1991, May 14

Nobel Prize Winners: #5999, Ivan P. Pavlov (1849-1936), 1904, Physiology. #6000, Elie Metchnikoff (1845-1916), 1908, Physiology. #6001, Andrei D. Sakharov, (1921-89), 1975, Peace.

5999 A2882 15k black   54   40
6000 A2882 15k black   54   40
6001 A2882 15k blue black   54   40

William
Saroyan
(1908-1981),
American
Writer
A2883

1991, May 22   Perf. 11½
6002 A2883 1r multicolored   3.60 2.75

       See US No. 2538.

Russia-Great
Britain Joint
Space Mission
A2884

1991, May 18   Litho.   Perf. 12
6003 A2884 20k multicolored   72   48

Cultural
Heritage
A2885

Designs: 10k, Miniature from "Ostomirov Gospel," by Sts. Cyril & Methodius, 1056-1057. 15k, "Russian Truth," manuscript, 11th-13th century by Jaroslav Mudrin. 20k, Sergei Radonezhski by Troitse Sergeiev Lavra, 1424. 25k, Trinity, icon by Andrei Rublev, c. 1411. 30k, Illustration from "Book of the Apostles," by Ivan Feodorov and Petr Mstislavetz, 1564.

1991, June 20   Litho.   Perf. 12x12½

6004	A2885	10k multicolored	36	24
6005	A2885	15k multicolored	55	40
6006	A2885	20k multicolored	72	48
6007	A2885	25k multicolored	90	60
6008	A2885	30k multicolored	1.10	80
a.		Strip of #6004-6008	3.63	2.52
		Nos. 6004-6008 (5)	3.63	2.52

Ducks
A2886

Designs: 5k, Anas acuta. 15k, Aythya marila. 20k, Oxyura leucocephala.

1991, July 1   Perf. 12

6009	A2886	5k multicolored	18	15
6010	A2886	15k multicolored	54	40
6011	A2886	20k multicolored	72	48
a.		Min. sheet of 9, 2 #6009, 4 #6010, 3 #6011	4.75	3.30

Airships
A2887

Designs: 1k, Albatross, 1910, vert. 3k, GA-42, 1987, vert. 4k, Norge, 1923. 5k, Victory, 1944. 20k, Graf Zeppelin, 1928.

1991, July 18

6012	A2887	1k multicolored	15	15
6013	A2887	3k multicolored	15	15
6014	A2887	4k multicolored	15	15
6015	A2887	5k multicolored	18	15
6016	A2887	20k multicolored	72	48
a.		Miniature sheet of 8		
		Nos. 6012-6016 (5)	1.35	
		Set value		68

Types of 1984

1991-92   Litho.   Imperf.

6016B	A2529	2r Ship, Arctic map	40	20

Perf. 12½x12

6017	A2529	3r Child & globe	1.25	82
6017A	A2529	5r Palm frond and globe	5.80	3.90

Issued: 3r, June 25; 5r, Nov. 10. 2r, Apr. 20, 1992.

Conf. on Security and Cooperation in Europe — A2088

1991, July 1   Photo.   Perf. 11½

6018	A2888	10k multicolored	15	15

Bering & Chirikov's Voyage to Alaska, 250th Anniv. — A2889

Design: No. 6020, Sailing ship, map.

1991, July 27   Perf. 12x11½

6019	A2889	30k multicolored	36	24
6020	A2889	30k multicolored	36	24

A2890

A2891

1991, Aug. 1   Perf. 12

6021	A2890	30k multicolored	36	24

Ukrainian declaration of sovereignty.

1991, Aug. 1   Perf. 12x11½

6022	A2891	7k brown	15	15

Letter Writing Week.

1992 Summer Olympic Games, Barcelona
A2892

1991, Sept. 4   Litho.   Perf. 12x12½

6023	A2892	10k Canoeing	15	15
a.		Miniature sheet of 8		
6024	A2892	20k Running	22	15
a.		Miniature sheet of 8		
6025	A2892	30k Soccer	36	22
a.		Miniature sheet of 8		
		Set value		32

Victims of Aug. 1991 Failed Coup — A2893

Citizens Protecting Russian "White House" — A2893a

1991, Oct. 11   Litho.   Perf. 11½

6026	A2893	7k Vladimir Usov, b. 1954	15	15
6027	A2893	7k Illya Krichevsky, b. 1963	15	15
6028	A2893	7k Dmitry Komar, b. 1968	15	15
		Set value	24	15

Souvenir Sheet

6029	A2893a	50k multicolored	60	36

USSR-Austria Joint Space Mission
A2894

1991, Oct. 2   Litho.   Perf. 11½

6030	A2894	20k multicolored	24	15

Folk Holidays

Ascension, Armenia
A2895

New Year, Azerbaijan
A2895a

Ivan Kupala Day, Byelorussia
A2895b

Berikaoba, Georgia
A2895d

New Year, Estonia
A2895c

Kazakhstan — A2895e

Kys Kumai, Kirgizia
A2895f

Ivan Kupala Day, Latvia
A2895g

Palm Sunday, Lithuania
A2895h

Plugushorul, Moldavia
A2895i

Shrovetide, Russia
A2895j

New Year, Tadzhikistan
A2895k

Spring Tulips, Uzbekistan
A2895n

Harvest, Turkmenistan — A2895l

Christmas, Ukraine — A2895m

Perf. 12x12½, 12½x12

1991, Oct. 4   Litho.

6031	A2895	15k multicolored	18	15
6032	A2895a	15k multicolored	18	15
6033	A2895b	15k multicolored	18	15
6034	A2895c	15k multicolored	18	15
6035	A2895d	15k multicolored	18	15
6036	A2895e	15k multicolored	18	15
6037	A2895f	15k multicolored	18	15
6038	A2895g	15k multicolored	18	15
6039	A2895h	15k multicolored	18	15
6040	A2895i	15k multicolored	18	15
6041	A2895j	15k multicolored	18	15
6042	A2895k	15k multicolored	18	15
6043	A2895l	15k multicolored	18	15
6044	A2895m	15k multicolored	18	15
6045	A2895n	15k multicolored	18	15
a.		Min. sheet, 2 each #6031-6045	11.25	
		Nos. 6031-6045 (15)	2.70	
		Set value		1.35

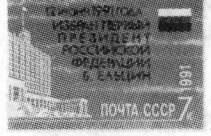

A2896

1991, Oct. 29   Litho.   Perf. 11½

6046	A2896	7k multicolored	15	15

Election of Boris Yeltsin, 1st president of Russian Republic, June 12, 1991.

Musical Instruments Type of 1989

Musical Instruments: No. 6048, Moldavia. No. 6049, Latvia. No. 6050, Kirgiz.

Photo. & Engr.

1991, Nov. 19   Perf. 12x11½

Denomination Color

6047	A2816	10k red	15	15
6048	A2816	10k brt greenish blue	15	15
6049	A2816	10k red lilac	15	15
		Set value	36	36

New Year 1992 — A2897

1991, Dec. 8   Litho.   Perf. 12x12½

6050	A2897	7k multicolored	15	15

A2899

A2900

Russian Historians: #6052, V. N. Tatischev (1686-1750). #6053, N. M. Karamzin (1766-1826). #6054, S. M. Soloviev (1820-79). #6055, V. O. Kluchevski (1844-1911).

1991, Dec. 12   **Photo. & Engr.**
6052	A2899	10k multicolored	15	15
6053	A2899	10k multicolored	15	15
6054	A2899	10k multicolored	15	15
6055	A2899	10k multicolored	15	15
		Set value	48	48

With the breakup of the Soviet Union on Dec. 26, 1991, eleven former Soviet republics established the Commonwealth of Independent States. Stamps inscribed "Rossija" are issued by the Russian Republic.

1992, Jan. 10   **Litho.**   *Perf. 11¹/₂x12*
6056	A2900	14k Cross-country skiing, ski jumping	15	15
a.		Miniature sheet of 8		
6057	A2900	1r Freestyle skiing	20	15
a.		Miniature sheet of 8		
6058	A2900	2r Bobsleds	40	24
a.		Miniature sheet of 8		
		Set value	64	38

1992 Winter Olympics, Albertville.

Souvenir Sheet

Battle on the Ice, 750th Anniv. — A2901

1992, Feb. 20   **Litho.**   *Perf. 12¹/₂x12*
6059	A2901	50k multicolored	15	15

A2902

Designs: 10k, Golden Portal, Vladimir. 15k, Kremlin, Pskov. 20k, Georgy the Victor. 25k, 55k, Triumph Gate, Moscow. 30k, "Millennium of Russia," by M.O. Mikeshin, Novgorod. 50k, St. George Slaying the Dragon. 60k, Minin-Posharsky Monument, Moscow. 80k, "Millenium of Russia," by M.O. Mikeshin, Novgorod. 1r, Church, Kizki. 1.50r, Monument to Peter the Great, St. Petersburg. 2r, St. Basil's Cathedral, Moscow. 3r, Tretyakov Gallery, Moscow. 5r, Morosov House, Moscow. 10r, St. Isaac's Cathedral, St. Petersburg. 25r, Monument to Yuri Dolgoruky, Moscow. 100r, Kremlin, Moscow.

Perf. 12¹/₂x12, 11¹/₂x12 (15k, 25k, 3r)
1992   **Litho.**
6060	A2902	10k salmon	15	15
6060A	A2902	15k dark brown	15	15
6061	A2902	20k red	15	15
6062	A2902	25k red brown	15	15
6063	A2902	30k black	15	15
6064	A2902	50k dark blue	15	15
6065	A2902	55k dark blue green	15	15
6066	A2902	60k blue green	15	15
6066A	A2902	80k lake	15	15
6067	A2902	1r yel brown	15	15
6067A	A2902	1.50r olive	22	15
6068	A2902	2r lilac	45	35
6068A	A2902	3r red	30	22
6069	A2902	5r dark brown	75	55
6070	A2902	10r bright blue	1.50	1.00

6071	A2902	25r dark red	3.75	2.75
6071A	A2902	100r bright olive	15.00	10.00
	Nos. 6060-6071A (17)		23.47	16.52

Issue date: 20k, 30k, Feb. 26. 10k, 60k, 2r, Apr. 20. 25r, May 25. 10r, 100r, May. 1r, 1.50r, 5r, June 25. 55k, Aug. 11. 50k, 80k, Aug. 18. 15k, 25k, 3r, Sept. 10.
See Nos. 6111-6121.

Victory by N. N. Baskakov — A2903

1992, Mar. 5   *Perf. 12x12¹/₂*
6072	A2903	5k multicolored	15	15

End of World War II, 47th anniv.

Prioksko-Terrasny Nature Reserve — A2904

1992, Mar. 12   *Perf. 12*
6073	A2904	50k multicolored	15	15

Russia-Germany Joint Space Mission — A2905

1992, Mar. 17
6074	A2905	5r multicolored	1.00	60

Souvenir Sheet

Discovery of America, 500th Anniv. — A2906

1992, Mar. 18   *Perf. 12x11¹/₂*
6075	A2906	3r Ship, Columbus	60	38

Characters from Children's Books — A2907

1992, Apr. 22   **Litho.**   *Perf. 12*
6076	A2907	25k Pinocchio	15	15
6077	A2907	30k Cipollino	15	15
6078	A2907	35k Dunno	15	15
6079	A2907	50k Karlson	15	15
		Set value	30	22

Space Accomplishments A2908

Designs: No. 6081, Astronaut, Russian space station and space shuttle. No. 6082, Sputnik, Vostok, Apollo Command and Lunar modules. No. 6083, Soyuz, Mercury and Gemini spacecraft.

1992, May 29   **Litho.**   *Perf. 11¹/₂x12*
6080	A2908	25r multicolored	1.00	75
6081	A2908	25r multicolored	1.00	75
6082	A2908	25r multicolored	1.00	75
6083	A2908	25r multicolored	1.00	75
a.		Block of 4, #6080-6083	4.00	3.00

See US Nos. 2631-2634.

1992 Summer Olympics, Barcelona A2909

Perf. 11¹/₂x12, 12x11¹/₂
1992, June 5   **Photo.**
6084	A2909	1r Team handball, vert.	15	15
a.		Miniature sheet of 8	85	65
6085	A2909	2r Fencing	20	15
a.		Miniature sheet of 8	1.70	1.30
6086	A2909	3r Judo	30	22
a.		Miniature sheet of 8	2.50	1.90

Explorers — A2910

Designs: 55r, L. A. Zagoskin, Alaska-Yukon. 70r, N. N. Miklucho-Maklai, New Guinea. 1r, G. I. Langsdorf, Brazil.

1992, June 23   **Litho.**   *Perf. 12x11¹/₂*
6087	A2910	55k multicolored	15	15
6088	A2910	70k multicolored	15	15
6089	A2910	1r multicolored	15	15
		Set value	38	28

Ducks A2911

1992, July 1   *Perf. 12*
6090	A2911	1r Anas querquedula	15	15
6091	A2911	2r Aythya ferina	20	15
6092	A2911	3r Anas falcata	30	22
a.		Min. sheet of 9, 3 #6090, 4 #6091, 2 #6092	3.40	

The Saviour, by Andrei Rublev A2912

1992, July 3   *Perf. 12x12¹/₂*
6093	A2912	1r multicolored	15	15
a.		Miniature sheet of 8	2.00	

The Taj Mahal Mausoleum in Agra, by Vasili Vereshchagin (1842-1904) — A2913

Design: No. 6095, Let Me Approach (detail), by Vereshchagin.

1992, July 3   *Perf. 12¹/₂x12*
6094	A2913	1.50r multicolored	15	15
6095	A2913	1.50r multicolored	15	15
a.		Pair, #6094-6095 + label	30	22

Cathedral of the Assumption, Moscow — A2914   Cathedral of the Annunciation, Moscow — A2915

Design: No. 6098, Archangel Cathedral, Moscow.

1992, Sept. 3   **Litho.**   *Perf. 11¹/₂*
6096	A2914	1r multicolored	15	15
a.		Miniature sheet of 9	55	
6097	A2915	1r multicolored	15	15
a.		Miniature sheet of 9	55	
6098	A2915	1r multicolored	15	15
a.		Miniature sheet of 9	55	
		Set value	18	15

The Nutcracker, by Tchaikovsky, Cent. A2916

Designs: No. 6099, Nutcrackers, one holding rifle. No. 6100, Nutcrackers, diff. No. 6101, Pas de deux before Christmas tree. No. 6102, Ballet scene.

1992, Nov. 4   **Litho.**   *Perf. 12¹/₂x12*
6099	A2916	10r multicolored	38	28
6100	A2916	10r multicolored	38	28
6101	A2916	25r multicolored	1.00	75
6102	A2916	25r multicolored	1.00	75
a.		Block of 4, #6099-6102	2.75	2.10

A2917   A2918

A2919   A2920

Christmas

Icons: No. 6103, Joachim and Anna, 16th cent. No. 6104, Madonna and Child, 14th cent. No. 6105, Archangel Gabriel, 14th cent. No. 6106, St. Nicholas, 16th cent.

1992, Nov. 27 *Perf. 11½*

6103	A2917	10r multicolored	45	32
6104	A2918	10r multicolored	45	32
6105	A2919	10r multicolored	45	32
6106	A2920	10r multicolored	45	32
a.		Block of 4, #6103-6106	1.80	1.30

See Sweden Nos. 1979-1982.

New Year
1993 — A2921

1992, Dec. 2 Litho. *Perf. 12x12½*

6107	A2921	50k multicolored	18	15
a.		Miniature sheet of 9	1.65	

Discovery of America,
500th Anniv. — A2922

1992, Dec. 29 *Perf. 11½x12*

6108	A2922	15r Flags, sculpture	38	28

Monuments Type of 1992

Designs: 4r, Church, Kizki. 6r, Monument to Peter the Great, St. Petersburg. 15r, 45r, The Horsebreaker, St. Petersburg. 50r, Kremlin, Rostov. 75r, Monument to Yuri Dolgoruky, Moscow. 150r, Golden Gate of Vladimir. 250r, Church, Bogolubova. 300r, Monument of Minin and Pozharsky. 500r, Lomonosov University, Moscow. 1000r, Fortress of St. Peter and St. Paul, St. Petersburg.

Litho., Photo. (50r, 250r, 500r)
1992-95 *Perf. 12½x12*

6109	A2902	4r red brown	15	15
6110	A2902	6r gray blue	15	15
6111	A2902	15r brown	38	28
a.		Photo.	38	28
6113	A2902	45r slate	1.15	82
6114	A2902	50r purple	1.30	95
6115	A2902	75r red brown	1.95	1.40
6118	A2902	150r blue	38	22
6119	A2902	250r green	6.50	4.75
6120	A2902	300r red brown	77	45
6121	A2902	500r violet	13.00	9.50

Perf. 12x11½

6123	A2902	1000r slate	65	48

Values are as of date issued. Denominations still available may be sold at much lower prices.
Issued: #6111a, 6114, 6119, 6121, 12/25/92; #6109-6110, 6/4/93; No. 6113, 6115, 1/25/93; 150r, 300r, 12/30/93; 1000r, 1/27/95.
This is an expanding set. Numbers may change.

Marius Petipa (1818-1910),
Choreographer — A2923

Ballets: No. 6126, Paquita (1847). No. 6127, Sleeping Beauty (1890). No. 6128, Swan Lake (1895). No. 6129, Raymonda (1898).

1993, Jan. 14 Litho. *Perf. 12½x12*

6126	A2923	25r multicolored	42	28
6127	A2923	25r multicolored	42	28
6128	A2923	25r multicolored	42	28
6129	A2923	25r multicolored	42	28
a.		Block of 4, #6126-6129	1.75	1.15

A2924

Characters from Children's Books: a, 2r, Scrub and Rub. b, 3r, Big Cockroach. c, 10r, The Buzzer Fly. d, 15r, Doctor Doolittle. e, 25r, Barmalei.

1993, Feb. 25 Litho. *Perf. 12½x12*

6130	A2924	Strip of 5, #a.-e.	85	65

No. 6130 printed in continuous design.

City of Vyborg, 700th
Anniv. — A2925

1993, Mar. 18 Photo. *Perf. 11½x12*

6131	A2925	10r Vyborg Castle	40	28

Battle of Kursk,
50th Anniv.
A2926

1993, Mar. 25 *Perf. 12x12½*

6132	A2926	10r multicolored	20	15

Victory Day.

Flowers — A2927

1993, Mar. 25 *Perf. 12½x12*

6133	A2927	10r Saintpaulia ionantha	15	15
6134	A2927	15r Hibiscus rosa-sinensis	15	15
6135	A2927	25r Cyclamen persicum	22	15
6136	A2927	50r Fuchsia hybrida	45	30
6137	A2927	100r Begonia semperflorens	90	60
		Nos. 6133-6137 (5)	1.87	1.35

See Nos. 6196-6200.

Communications
Satellites — A2928

1993, Apr. 12 Photo. *Perf. 11½*

6138	A2928	25r Molniya-3	20	15
6139	A2928	45r Ekran-M	35	25
6140	A2928	50r Gorizont	40	28
6141	A2928	75r Luch	60	40
6142	A2928	100r Express	80	52
		Nos. 6138-6142 (5)	2.35	1.60

Souvenir Sheet
Perf. 12x11½

6143	A2928	250r Ground station, horiz.	2.10	1.40

No. 6143 contains one 37x26mm stamp.

Antique
Silver — A2929

Designs: 15r, Snuff box, 1820, mug, 1849. 25r, Tea pot, 1896-1908. 45r, Vase, 1896-1908. 75r, Tray, candlestick holder, 1896-1908. 100r, Coffee pot, cream and sugar set, 1852. 250r, Sweet dish, 1896-1908, biscuit dish, 1844.

1993, May 5 Litho. *Perf. 11½*

6144	A2929	15r multicolored	15	15
6145	A2929	25r multicolored	25	15
6146	A2929	45r multicolored	45	30
6147	A2929	75r multicolored	75	50
6148	A2929	100r multicolored	1.00	65
		Nos. 6144-6148 (5)	2.60	1.75

Souvenir Sheet
Perf. 12½x12

6149	A2929	250r multicolored	2.50	1.65

No. 6149 contains one 52x37mm stamp.

Novgorod Kremlin
A2930   A2931

Designs: No. 6150, Kremlin towers, 14th-17th cent. No. 6151, St. Sofia's Temple, 11th cent. No. 6152, Belfry of St. Sophia's, 15th-18th cent. 250r, Icon, "Sign of the Virgin," 12th cent.

1993, June 4 Litho. *Perf. 12*

6150	A2930	25r multicolored	25	16
6151	A2931	25r multicolored	25	16
6152	A2931	25r multicolored	25	16

Souvenir Sheet
Perf. 12½x12

6153	A2930	250r multicolored	2.50	1.65

No. 6153 contains one 42x30mm stamp.

Russian-Danish
Relations, 500th
Anniv. — A2932

1993, June 17 *Perf. 11½*

6154	A2932	90r green & light green	52	35

See Denmark No. 985.

Ducks
A2933

Designs: 90r, Somateria stelleri. 100r, Somateria mollissima. 250r, Somateria spectabilis.

1993, July 1 Litho. *Perf. 12*

6155	A2933	90r multicolored	16	15
6156	A2933	100r multicolored	18	15
6157	A2933	250r multicolored	45	30
a.		Min. sheet, 4 each #6155-6156, 1 #6157	5.00	
		Set value		52

Sea Life
A2934

1993, July 6

6158	A2934	50r Pusa hispida	25	16
6159	A2934	60r Paralithodes brevipes	32	22
6160	A2934	90r Todarodes pacificus	48	35
6161	A2934	100r Oncorhynchus masu	52	38
6162	A2934	250r Fulmarus glacialis	1.25	90
		Nos. 6158-6162 (5)	2.82	2.01

Natl. Museum of
Applied Arts and Folk
Crafts,
Moscow — A2935

Designs: No. 6163, Skopino earthenware candlestick. No. 6164, Painted tray, horiz. No. 6165, Painted box, distaff. No. 6166, Enamel icon of St. Dmitry of Solun. 250r, Fedoskino lacquer miniature Easter egg depicting the Resurrection.

Perf. 12x12½, 12½x12

1993, Aug. 11 Litho.

6163	A2935	50r multicolored	25	15
6164	A2935	50r multicolored	25	15
6165	A2935	100r multicolored	52	35
6166	A2935	100r multicolored	52	35
6167	A2935	250r multicolored	1.25	80
		Nos. 6163-6167 (5)	2.79	1.80

Goznak (Bank
Note Printer and
Mint), 175th
Anniv. — A2936

1993, Sept. 2 Litho. *Perf. 12*

6168	A2936	100r multicolored	48	36

Shipbuilders — A2937

Designs: No. 6169, Peter the Great (1672-1725), Goto Predestinatsia. No. 6170, K.A. Shilder (1786-1854), first all-metal submarine. No. 6171, I.A. Amosov (1800-1878), screw steamship Archimedes. No. 6172, I.G. Bubnov (1872-1919), submarine Bars. No. 6173, B.M. Malinin (1889-1949), submarine Dekabrist. No. 6174, A.I. Maslov (1894-1968), cruiser Kirov.

1993, Sept. 7

6169	A2937	100r multicolored	52	35
6170	A2937	100r multicolored	52	35
6171	A2937	100r multicolored	52	35
6172	A2937	100r multicolored	52	35
6173	A2937	100r multicolored	52	35
6174	A2937	100r multicolored	52	35
a.		Block of 6, #6169-6174	3.25	2.25

RUSSIA is our specialty!

If you collect Russia, Russia Area or Zemstvos you need our BIG 20-Page Russia Update. It offers a tremendous selection of singles, sets and year units – mint and cancelled. Your Satisfaction Guaranteed!

Your copy of the Update is $2.00 (Refundable) by mail. Free by telephone! 1-800-747-7763.

The Stamp Professor

**Dr. Frederic G. Bean
1500C E. 79th Street
Bloomington, MN 55425**

ASDA APS   VISA
ROSSICA   MasterCard

Selling? We buy Russia Area stamps and Postal History. Ship, write or call 1-800-747-7763. Prompt, fair offers.

RUSSIA!

**Extensive Stock of
RUSSIA AND
RELATED AREAS**
Mint and Used
Low Prices! Fast Service!

**SEND FOR A
FREE 50-PAGE
PRICE LIST OF
RUSSIA AND
WORLDWIDE!**

ALMAZ CO., Dept. VR
P.O. Box 100-812,
Vanderveer Station
Brooklyn, NY 11210
Tel./FAX (718) 241-6360

Moscow Kremlin
A2938   A2939

Designs: No. 6175, Granovitaya Chamber (1487-91). No. 6176, Church of Rizpolozheniye (1484-88). No. 6177, Teremnoi Palace (1635-36).

1993, Oct. 28   Litho.   Perf. 12
6175 A2938 100r multicolored   40   25
6176 A2939 100r multicolored   40   25
6177 A2939 100r multicolored   40   25

Panthera Tigris
A2940

Designs: 100r, Adult in woods. 250r, Two cubs. 500r, Adult in snow.

1993, Nov. 25   Litho.   Perf. 12¹/₂x12
6178 A2940 50r multicolored   15   15
6179 A2940 100r multicolored   25   16
6180 A2940 250r multicolored   60   40
6181 A2940 500r multicolored 1.25   85
  a.   Block of 4, #6178-6181   2.25 1.50
  b.   Miniature sheet, 2 #6181a   4.50

World Wildlife Fund.

New Year 1994 — A2941

1993, Dec. 2   Photo.   Perf. 11¹/₂
6182 A2941 25r multicolored   22   15
  a.   Sheet of 8   1.75

A2942   Wildlife — A2943

1993, Nov. 25   Photo.   Perf. 11¹/₂x12
6183 A2942 90r gray, black & red   35   20

Prevention of AIDS.

1993, Dec. 30   Litho.   Perf. 12¹/₂x12
6184 A2943 250r Phascolarctos
                 cinereus   45   28
6185 A2943 250r Monachus schauin-
                 slandi   45   28
6186 A2943 250r Haliaeetus
                 leucocephalus   45   28
6187 A2943 250r Elephas maximus   45   28
6188 A2943 250r Grus vipio   45   28
6189 A2943 250r Ailuropoda mela-
                 noleuca   45   28
6190 A2943 250r Phocoenoides dalli   45   28
6191 A2943 250r Eschrichtius robus-
                 tus   45   28
  a.   Miniature sheet of 8, #6184-6191   6.00
       Nos. 6184-6191 (8)   3.60 2.24

Nikolai Rimsky-Korsakov (1844-1908),
Scene from "Sadko" — A2944

Scenes from operas: No. 6193, "Golden Cockerel," 1907. No. 6194, "The Czar's Bride," 1898. No. 6195, "The Snow Maiden," 1881.

1994, Jan. 20   Litho.   Perf. 12¹/₂x12
6192 A2944 250r multicolored   45   28
6193 A2944 250r multicolored   45   28
6194 A2944 250r multicolored   45   28
6195 A2944 250r multicolored   45   28
  a.   Block of 4, #6192-6195   1.80 1.15

Flower Type of 1993

Designs: 50r, Epiphyllum peacockii. No. 6197, Mammillaria swinglei. No. 6198, Lophophora williamsii. No. 6199, Opuntia basilaris. No. 6200, Selenicereus grandiflorus.

1994, Feb. 25   Litho.   Perf. 12¹/₂x12
6196 A2927 50r multicolored   15   15
6197 A2927 100r multicolored   18   15
6198 A2927 100r multicolored   18   15
6199 A2927 250r multicolored   48   28
6200 A2927 250r multicolored   48   28
       Nos. 6196-6200 (5)   1.47 1.01

York Cathedral,   Metropolis Church,
Great   Athens — A2946
Britain — A2945

Gothic Church,   Notre Dame
Roskilde,   Cathedral,
Denmark — A2947   Paris — A2948

St. Peter's Basilica,   Cologne Cathedral,
Vatican   Germany — A2950
City — A2949

St. Basil's   Seville Cathedral,
Cathedral,   Spain — A2952
Moscow — A2951

Design: No. 6207, St. Patrick's Cathedral, New York, US.

1994, Mar. 24   Litho.   Perf. 12x12¹/₂
6201 A2945 150r multicolored   22   15
6202 A2946 150r multicolored   22   15
6203 A2947 150r multicolored   22   15
6204 A2948 150r multicolored   22   15
6205 A2949 150r multicolored   22   15
6206 A2950 150r multicolored   22   15
6207 A2951 150r multicolored   22   15
6208 A2951 150r multicolored   22   15
6209 A2952 150r multicolored   22   15
  a.   Miniature sheet of 9, #6201-6209   2.00
       Nos. 6201-6209 (9)   1.98 1.35

Space Research
A2953

Designs: 100r, TS-18 Centrifuge, Soyuz landing module during re-entry. 250r, Soyuz spacecraft docked at Mir space station. 500r, Training in hydrolaboratory, cosmonaut during space walk.

1994, Apr. 12   Litho.   Perf. 12x11¹/₂
6210 A2953 100r multicolored   16   15
6211 A2953 250r multicolored   42   30
6212 A2953 500r multicolored   85   60

Liberation of
Russian
Areas, 50th
Anniv.
A2954

Battle maps and: a, Katyusha rockets, liberation of Russia. b, Russian fighter planes, liberation of Ukraine. c, Combined offensive, liberation of Belarus.

1994, Apr. 26   Perf. 12
6213 A2954 100r Block of 3 + label   48   32

See Belarus No. 78, Ukraine No. 195.

Russian Architecture
A2955

Structure, architect: 50r, Krasniye Vorota, Moscow, Prince D.V. Ukhtomsky (1719-74). 100r, Academy of Science, St. Petersburg, Giacomo Quarenghi (1744-1817). 150r, Trinity Cathedral, St. Petersburg, V.P. Stasov (1769-1848). 300r, Church of Christ the Saviour, Moscow, K.A. Ton (1794-1881).

1994, May 25   Litho.   Perf. 12¹/₂x12
6214 A2955 50r lt brown & blk   15   15
6215 A2955 100r red brown & blk   15   15
6216 A2955 150r olive green & blk   22   15
6217 A2955 300r gray violet & blk   48   32

Painting Type of 1992

Paintings by V. D. Polenov (1844-1927): No. 6218, Christ and the Adultress, 1886-87. No. 6219, Golden Autumn, 1893.

1994, June 1   Litho.   Perf. 12¹/₂x12
6218 A2913 150r multicolored   25   16
6219 A2913 150r multicolored   25   16
  a.   Pair, #6218-6219 + label   50   32

Ducks
A2956

1994, July 1   *Perf. 12*
6220	A2956	150r Anas penelope	22	15
6221	A2956	250r Aythya fuligula	38	25
6222	A2956	300r Anas formosa	48	32
a.		Min. sheet, 3 #6220, 4 #6221, 2 #6222	3.00	2.00
b.		As "a," overprinted	3.00	2.00

No. 6222b is overprinted in sheet margin: "World Philatelic Exhibition Moscow-97" in Cyrillic and Latin with four exhibition emblems.

A2957   A2958

1994, July 5   **Photo.**   *Perf. 11½x12*
6223	A2957	100r multicolored	18	15

1994 Goodwill Games, St. Petersburg.

1994, July 5   **Litho.**   *Perf. 12*

Nobel Prize Winners in Physics: No. 6224, P.L. Kapitsa (1894-1984). No. 6225, P.A. Cherenkov (1904-90).
6224	A2958	150r sepia	24	15
6225	A2958	150r sepia	24	15

Intl. Olympic Committee, Cent. A2959

1994, July 5
6226	A2959	250r multicolored	32	16

Russian Postal Day — A2960

1994, July 8   *Perf. 11½x12*
6227	A2960	125r multicolored	20	15

Porcelain A2961

Designs: 50r, Snuff box, 1752. 100r, Candlestick, 1750-1760. 150r, Statue of watercarrier, 1818. 250r, Vase, 19th cent. 300r, Statue of lady with mask, 1910. 500r, Monogramed dinner service, 1848.

1994, Aug. 10   **Litho.**   *Perf. 11½*
6228	A2961	50r multicolored	15	15
a.		Min. sheet of 9	70	65
b.		As "a," overprinted	70	65
6229	A2961	100r multicolored	15	15
6230	A2961	150r multicolored	22	15
6231	A2961	250r multicolored	38	25
6232	A2961	300r multicolored	45	30
		Nos. 6228-6232 (5)	1.35	1.00

Souvenir Sheet
6233	A2961	500r multicolored	75	75

No. 6228b is overprinted in sheet margin: "World Philatelic Exhibition Moscow 97" in Cyrillic and Latin with four exhibition logos.

Integration of Tuva into Russia, 50th Anniv. — A2962

1994, Oct. 13   **Photo.**   *Perf. 11½12*
6234	A2962	125r multicolored	16	15

Russian Voyages of Exploration — A2963

Sailing ships and: No. 6235, V.M. Golovnin, Kurile Islands expedition, 1811. No. 6236, I.F. Kruzenstern, trans-global expedition, 1803-06. No. 6237, F.P. Wrangel, North American expedition, 1829-35. No. 6238, F.P. Litke, Novaya Zemlya expedition, 1821-24.

Photo. & Engr.

1994, Nov. 22   *Perf. 12x11½*
6235	A2963	250r multicolored	20	15
6236	A2963	250r multicolored	20	15
a.		Miniature sheet of 8	1.60	1.10
6237	A2963	250r multicolored	20	15
6238	A2963	250r multicolored	20	15
		Nos. 6235-6238 (4)	80	60

Russian Fleet, 300th anniv. (#6236a).

New Year 1995 — A2964

1994, Dec. 6   **Photo.**   *Perf. 12x11½*
6239	A2964	125r multicolored	16	15
a.		Min. sheet of 8	1.25	80

Alexander Griboedov (1795-1829), Poet, Diplomat A2965

1995, Jan. 5   **Litho.**   *Perf. 11½*
6240	A2965	250r sepia & black	22	15

No. 6240 printed se-tenant with label.

A2966

Mikhail Fokine (1880-1942), Choreographer — A2967

Scenes from ballets: No. 6241, Scheherazade. No. 6242, The Fire Bird. No. 6243, Petrouchka.

1995, Jan. 18   **Litho.**   *Perf. 12½x12*
6241	A2966	500r multicolored	35	25
6242	A2967	500r multicolored	35	25
6243	A2967	500r multicolored	35	25
a.		Block of 3 + label	1.05	75

Mikhail Kutuzov (1745-1813), Field Marshal — A2968

1995, Jan. 20
6244	A2968	300r multicolored	22	15
a.		Miniature sheet of 8	1.75	1.25

16th-17th Cent. Architecture, Moscow A2969

Designs: 125r, English Yard, Varvarka St. 250r, Averki Kirillov's house, Bersenevskaya Embankment. 300r, Volkov's house, Kharitonievsky Lane.

1995, Feb. 15   **Litho.**   *Perf. 12½12*
6245	A2969	125r multicolored	15	15
6246	A2969	250r multicolored	25	15
6247	A2969	300r multicolored	30	15
		Nos. 6245-6247 (3)	70	45

UN Fight Against Drug Abuse — A2970

1995, Mar. 1   *Perf. 12½x12*
6248	A2970	150r multicolored	16	15

Endangered Species A2971

Designs: a, Lake. b, Pusa hispida. c, Lynx. d, River, trees.

1995, Mar. 1   *Perf. 12x12½*
6249	A2971	250r Block of 4, #a.-d.	75	50

Nos. 6249a-6249b, 6249c-6249d are continuous designs. See Finland No. 960.

End of World War II, 50th Anniv. A2972

Designs: No. 6250, Churchill, Roosevelt, Stalin at Yalta. No. 6251, Ruins of Reichstag, Berlin. No. 6252, Monument to concentration camp victims. No. 6253, Tomb of the Unknown Soldier, Moscow, vert. No. 6254, Potsdam Conference, map of divided Germany, vert. No. 6255, Russian planes over Manchuria. No. 6256, Victory parade, Moscow, vert.

1995, Apr. 7   *Perf. 12x12½, 12½x12*
6250	A2972	250r multicolored	25	15
6251	A2972	250r multicolored	25	15
6252	A2972	250r multicolored	25	15
6253	A2972	250r multicolored	25	15

1967-1994 RUSSIAN YEAR SETS
(ALL ★★ MNH)

YEAR	PRICE	YEAR	PRICE	YEAR	PRICE	YEAR	PRICE
1967	$25.75	1974	$28.50	1981	$32.75	1988	$36.50
1968	32.00	1975	35.00	1982	29.25	1989	28.00
1969	26.50	1976	38.50	1983	32.75	1990	30.75
1970	25.00	1977	46.00	1984	32.75	1991	34.50
1971	25.00	1978	41.75	1985	25.00	1992	26.50
1972	25.75	1979	44.50	1986	25.00	1993	42.50
1973	25.50	1980	41.75	1987	27.00	1994	47.50

PRICES AVAILABLE ★★ 1960-1966 YEAR SETS - ASK!

COMPLETE ★★ 1961-1992 (32 years of Soviet Stamps)

SPECIAL! ONLY $1250. WHILE THEY LAST!
Includes all Scott-listed stamps, MNH, F-VF with many extras either unlisted or footnoted, e.g., 1962 red ovpt Arctic Souvenir Sheet, 1964 Tokyo Olympic green (Scott Cat. $175.00) Souvenir Sheet. Also some imperfs and paper varieties. A great opportunity to get a great collection.

SEND TO:

Rossica

M & W BROOKS

P.O. Box 630218 / Kappock St. / Spuyten Duyvil Sta.
Riverdale, New York 10463   **Phone or Fax: 718-548-4297**

TERMS: 1) Payment with order / U.S. check or money order only. 2) N.Y.S. residents add 8¼% sales tax. 3) Orders under $50 add $3.00 for postage and insurance. We guarantee service. Best stamp quality, knowledge, reliability and satisfaction.

NEW REPUBLICS, UKRAINE & LOCAL POSTS 1991-1994

NOW AVAILABLE: #1-Russian Republics, Crimea & Local Posts, over 150 page pricelist catalogue, ONLY $19.50. #2 - Ukraine & Local Posts, over 150 page catalogue also $19.50. SPECIAL-BOTH CATALOGUES for $39.50.
All cat. prices include postage. (Cost of catalogue(s) refundable upon a minimum $200 purchase in one order.) NOTE: some issues and Republics have questionable status. We try to list everything as we receive it and let time be the judge.

6254	A2972	250r multicolored	25	15
6255	A2972	250r multicolored	25	15
	Nos. 6250-6255 (6)		1.50	
	Set value			75

Souvenir Sheet
Perf. 11½x12

6256	A2972	500r multicolored	50	50

No. 6256 contains one 37x52mm stamp.

Year Sets

Year set values are determined from price lists offering complete sets for each year. Not all dealers offer these sets. Values may be lower or higher than the total value of the individual stamps. Contents of the sets being offered may differ. First number is typical number of stamps in set, second number is number of souvenir sheets. Miniature sheets of 8 are not included.

1975	107 + 7	45.00
1976	121 + 10	65.00
1977	116 + 8	70.00
1978	127 + 9	65.00
1979	92 + 8	55.00
1980	108 + 6	60.00
1981	106 + 5	40.00
1982	99 + 7	42.50
1983	92 + 9	45.00
1984	116 + 9	60.00
1985	85 + 8	37.50
1986	105 + 4	32.50
1987	97 + 8	37.50
1988	126 + 8	55.00
1989	114 + 6	32.50
1990	113 + 5	40.00
1991	104 + 4	30.00
1992	77 + 3	32.50

SEMI-POSTAL STAMPS

Empire

Admiral Kornilov Monument, Sevastopol — SP1

Pozharski and Minin Monument, Moscow — SP2

Statue of Peter the Great, Leningrad — SP3

Alexander II Memorial and Kremlin, Moscow — SP4

Perf. 11½ to 13½ and Compound

1905		Typo.	Unwmk.	
B1	SP1	3k red, brn & grn	2.75	2.25
a.		Perf. 13½x11½	175.00	145.00
b.		Perf. 13½	27.50	27.50
c.		Perf. 11½x13½	200.00	165.00
B2	SP2	5k lilac, vio & straw	2.00	1.75
B3	SP3	7k lt bl, dk bl & pink	2.75	2.25
a.		Perf. 13½	42.50	42.50
B4	SP4	10k lt blue, dk bl & yel	4.00	3.25

These stamps were sold for 3 kopecks over face value. The surtax was donated to a fund for the orphans of soldiers killed in the Russo-Japanese war.

Ilya Murometz Legendary Russian Hero — SP5

Designs: 3k, Don Cossack Bidding Farewell to His Sweetheart. 7k, Symbolical of Charity. 10k, St. George Slaying the Dragon.

1914			Perf. 11½, 12½	
B5	SP5	1k red brn & dk grn, straw	40	45
B6	SP5	3k mar & gray grn, pink	40	45
B7	SP5	7k dk brn & dk grn, buff	40	45
B8	SP5	10k dk blue & brn, blue	1.90	2.25

Perf. 13½

B5a	SP5	1k	30	45
B6a	SP5	3k	27.50	32.50
B7a	SP5	7k	24	45
B8a	SP5	10k	5.75	7.25

1915			White Paper	
B9	SP5	1k orange brn & gray		24 35
B10	SP5	3k car & gray black		30 45
B12	SP5	7k dk brown & dk green		4.25
B13	SP5	10k dk blue & brown		18 35

These stamps were sold for 1 kopeck over face value. The surtax was donated to charities connected with the war of 1914-17.

No. B12 not regularly issued.

Nos. B5-B13 exist imperf. Value each, $150 unused, $250 canceled.

Russian Soviet Federated Socialist Republic
Volga Famine Relief Issue

Relief Work on Volga River — SP9

Administering Aid to Famine Victim — SP10

1921		Litho.	Imperf.	
B14	SP9	2250r green	3.00	6.50
a.		Pelure paper	60.00	55.00
B15	SP9	2250r deep red	2.50	4.50
a.		Pelure paper	7.50	12.50
B16	SP9	2250r brown	2.50	11.00
B17	SP10	2250r dark blue	6.00	14.00

Forged cancels and counterfeits of Nos. B14-B17 are plentiful.

Stamps of type A33 with this overprint were not charity stamps nor did they pay postage in any form.

They represent taxes paid on stamps exported from or imported into Russia. In 1925 the semi-postal stamps of 1914-15 were surcharged for the same purpose. Stamps of the regular issues 1918 and 1921 have also been surcharged with inscriptions and new values, to pay the importation and exportation taxes.

Nos. 149-150 Surcharged in Black, Red, Blue or Orange

Р. С. Ф. С. Р.
ГОЛОДАЮЩИМ
250 р.+250 р

1922, Feb.			Perf. 13½	
B18	A33	100r + 100r on 70k	60	1.65
a.		"100 p. + p. 100"	55.00	65.00
B19	A33	100r + 100r on 70k (R)	60	1.65
B20	A33	100r + 100r on 70k (Bl)	30	85
B21	A33	250r + 250r on 35k	30	85
B22	A33	250r + 250r on 35k (R)	60	1.65
B23	A33	250r + 250r on 35k (O)	1.10	3.25
	Nos. B18-B23 (6)		3.50	9.90

Issued to raise funds for Volga famine relief. Nos. B18-B22 exist with surcharge inverted. Values $20 to $40.

Regular Issues of 1909-18 Overprinted

РСФСР
Филателия
—Детям—
19-8-22

1922, Aug. 19			Perf. 14	
B24	A14	1k orange	175.00	175.00
B25	A14	2k green	15.00	25.00
B26	A14	3k red	12.00	25.00
B27	A14	5k claret	15.00	25.00
B28	A15	10k dark blue	15.00	25.00

Imperf

B29	A14	1k orange	175.00	200.00
	Nos. B24-B29 (6)		407.00	475.00

The overprint means "Philately for the Children." The stamps were sold at five million times their face values and 80% of the amount was devoted to child welfare. The stamps were sold only at Moscow and for one day.

Exist with overprint reading up. Counterfeits exist including those with overprint reading up. Reprints exist.

Worker and Peasant (Industry and Agriculture) — SP11

Allegory: Agriculture Will Help End Distress SP12

Star of Hope, Wheat and Worker-Peasant Handclasp — SP13

Sower — SP14

1922		Litho.	Imperf.	
		Without Gum		
B30	SP11	2t (2000r) green	8.50	20.00
B31	SP12	2t (2000r) rose	14.00	32.50
B32	SP13	4t (4000r) rose	14.00	32.50
B33	SP14	6t (6000r) green	14.00	32.50

Nos. B30-B33 exist with double impression. Value, each $100.

Counterfeits of Nos. B30-B33 exist.

Miniature copies of Nos. B30-B33 exist, taken from the 1933 Soviet catalogue.

Automobile SP15

Steamship SP16

Railroad Train SP17

Airplane SP18

1922			Imperf.	
B34	SP15	light violet	15	15
B35	SP16	violet	15	15
B36	SP17	gray blue	15	15
B37	SP18	blue gray	1.25	3.00

Inscribed "For the Hungry." Each stamp was sold for 200,000r postage and 50,000r charity. Counterfeits of Nos. B34-B37 exist.

1 мая 1923 г.

Nos. 212, 183, 202 Surcharged in Bronze, Gold or Silver

Филателия—трудящимся.

2 р.+2 р.

1923			Imperf.	
B38	A48	1r +1r on 10r	125.00	125.00
a.		Inverted surcharge	250.00	250.00
B39	A48	1r +1r on 10r (G)	20.00	30.00
a.		Inverted surcharge	250.00	250.00
B40	A43	2r +2r on 250r	16.00	25.00
a.		Pelure paper	20.00	22.50
b.		Inverted surcharge	200.00	200.00
c.		Double surcharge		
		Wmk. 171		
B41	A46	4r +4r on 5000r	14.00	22.50
a.		Date spaced "1 923"	165.00	165.00
b.		Inverted surcharge	265.00	265.00
B42	A46	4r +4r on 5000r (S)	400.00	350.00
a.		Inverted surcharge	850.00	850.00
b.		Date spaced "1 923"	850.00	850.00
c.		As "b," inverted surch.	3,200.	
	Nos. B38-B42 (5)		575.00	552.50

The inscriptions mean "Philately's Contribution to Labor." The stamps were on sale only at Moscow and for one day. The surtax was for charitable purposes.

Counterfeits of No. B42 exist.

Leningrad Flood Issue

C.C.C.P.
пострадавшему
от наводнения
Ленинграду.
Nos. 181-182,
184-186
Surcharged

7 к. + 20 к.

1924	Unwmk.		Imperf.
B43 A40	3k + 10k on 100r	80	1.25
a.	Pelure paper	3.00	4.00
b.	Inverted surcharge	85.00	85.00
B44 A40	7k + 20k on 200r	80	1.25
a.	Inverted surcharge	105.00	105.00
B45 A40	14k + 30k on 300r	90	2.50
a.	Pelure paper	215.00	215.00

Similar Surcharge in Red or Black

B46 A41	12k + 40k on 500r (R)	1.65	2.50
a.	Double surcharge	115.00	115.00
b.	Inverted surcharge	115.00	115.00
B47 A41	20k + 50k on 1000r	1.10	2.50
a.	Thick paper	11.50	18.00
b.	Pelure paper	20.00	25.00
c.	Chalk surface paper	10.00	12.50
	Nos. B43-B47 (5)	5.25	10.00

The surcharge on Nos. B43 to B45 reads: "S.S.S.R. For the sufferers by the inundation at Leningrad." That on Nos. B46 and B47 reads: "S.S.S.R. For the Leningrad Proletariat, 23, IX, 1924."

No. B46 is surcharged vertically, reading down, with the value as the top line.

Orphans
SP19

Lenin as a Child
SP20

1926	Typo.		Perf. 13½
B48 SP19	10k brown	3.25	3.00
B49 SP20	20k deep blue	4.00	4.25
	Wmk. 170		
B50 SP19	10k brown	1.00	90
B51 SP20	20k deep blue	1.50	1.65

Two kopecks of the price of each of these stamps was donated to organizations for the care of indigent children.

Types of 1926 Issue

1927			
B52 SP19	8k + 2k yel green	70	35
B53 SP20	18k + 2k deep rose	1.75	1.00

Surtax was for child welfare.

Industrial Training
SP21

Agricultural Training
SP22

		Perf. 10, 10½, 12½	
1929-30	Photo.		Unwmk.
B54 SP21	10k +2k ol brn & org brn	2.50	2.50
a.	Perf. 10½	52.50	52.50
B55 SP21	10k +2k ol grn ('30)	1.50	1.25
B56 SP22	20k +2k blk brn & bl, perf. 10½	2.00	3.50
a.	Perf. 12½	35.00	35.00
b.	Perf. 10	10.00	10.00
B57 SP22	20k +2k bl grn ('30)	2.00	3.50

Surtax was for child welfare.

> Catalogue values for unused stamps in this section, from this point to the end of the section, are for Never Hinged items.

"Montreal Passing Torch to Moscow" — SP23

Moscow '80 Olympic Games Emblem — SP24

22nd Olympic Games, Moscow, 1980: 16k+6k, like 10k+5k. 60k+30k, Aerial view of Kremlin and Moscow '80 emblem.

1976, Dec. 28	Litho.		Perf. 12x12½
B58 SP23	4k + 2k multi	22	16
B59 SP24	10k + 5k multi	42	32
B60 SP24	16k + 6k multi	85	40

Souvenir Sheet
Photo.
Perf. 11½

B61 SP23	60k + 30k multi	2.25	1.65

Greco-Roman Wrestling — SP25

Moscow '80 Emblem and: 6k+3k, Free-style wrestling. 10k+5k, Judo. 16k+6k, Boxing. 20k+10k, Weight lifting.

1977, June 21	Litho.		Perf. 12½x12
B62 SP25	4k + 2k multi	18	15
B63 SP25	6k + 3k multi	28	18
B64 SP25	10k + 5k multi	40	28
B65 SP25	16k + 6k multi	60	35
B66 SP25	20k + 10k multi	80	45
	Nos. B62-B66 (5)	2.26	1.41

Perf. 12½x12, 12x12½
1977, Sept. 22

Designs: 4k+2k, Bicyclist. 6k+3k, Woman archer, vert. 10k+5k, Sharpshooting. 16k+6k, Equestrian. 20k+10k, Fencer. 50k+25k, Equestrian and fencer.

B67 SP25	4k + 2k multi	18	15
B68 SP25	6k + 3k multi	25	20
B69 SP25	10k + 5k multi	38	28
B70 SP25	16k + 6k multi	55	35
B71 SP25	20k + 10k multi	70	45
	Nos. B67-B71 (5)	2.06	1.43

Souvenir Sheet
Perf. 12½x12

B72 SP25	50k + 25k multi	3.00	1.65

1978, Mar. 24   Perf. 12½x12

Designs: 4k+2k, Swimmer at start. 6k+3k, Woman diver, vert. 10k+5k, Water polo. 16k+6k, Canoeing. 20k+10k, Canadian single. 50k+25k, Start of double scull race.

B73 SP25	4k + 2k multi	15	15
B74 SP25	6k + 3k multi	25	15
B75 SP25	10k + 5k multi	40	22
B76 SP25	16k + 6k multi	55	28
B77 SP25	20k + 10k multi	70	45
	Nos. B73-B77 (5)	2.05	1.25

Souvenir Sheet

B78 SP25	50k + 25k grn & blk	2.50	2.50

Star-class Yacht SP26

Women's Gymnastics SP27

Keel Yachts and Moscow '80 Emblem: 6k+3k, Soling class. 10k+5k, Centerboarder 470. 16k+6k, Finn class. 20k+10k, Flying Dutchman class. 50k+25k, Catamaran Tornado, horiz.

1978, Oct. 26	Litho.		Perf. 12x12½
B79 SP26	4k + 2k multi	15	15
B80 SP26	6k + 3k multi	25	15
B81 SP26	10k + 5k multi	40	18
B82 SP26	16k + 6k multi	55	28
B83 SP26	20k + 10k multi	70	38
	Nos. B79-B83 (5)	2.05	1.14

Souvenir Sheet
Perf. 12½x12

B84 SP26	50k + 25k multi	2.50	1.40

1979, Mar. 21   Litho.   Perf. 12x12½

Designs: 6k+3k, Man on parallel bars. 10k+5k, Man on horizontal bar. 16k+6k, Woman on balance beam. 20k+10k, Woman on uneven bars. 50k+25k, Man on rings.

B85 SP27	4k + 2k multi	15	15
B86 SP27	6k + 3k multi	25	15
B87 SP27	10k + 5k multi	40	18
B88 SP27	16k + 6k multi	55	28
B89 SP27	20k + 10k multi	70	38
	Nos. B85-B89 (5)	2.05	1.14

Souvenir Sheet
Perf. 12½x12

B90 SP25	50k + 25k multi	2.00	1.40

1979, June   Perf. 12½x12, 12x12½

Designs: 4k+2k, Soccer. 6k+3k, Basketball. 10k+5k, Women's volleyball. 16k+6k, Handball. 20k+10k, Field hockey.

B91 SP25	4k + 2k multi	15	15
B92 SP27	6k + 3k multi	22	15
B93 SP27	10k + 5k multi	40	18
B94 SP27	16k + 6k multi	55	28
B95 SP25	20k + 10k multi	70	38
	Nos. B91-B95 (5)	2.02	1.14

22nd Olympic Games, Moscow, July 19-Aug. 3, 1980.

Running, Moscow '80 Emblem SP27a

1980	Litho.		Perf. 12½x12, 12x12½
B96 SP27a	4k + 2k shown	15	15
B97 SP27a	4k + 2k Pole vault	15	15
B98 SP27a	6k + 3k Discus	25	15
B99 SP27a	6k + 3k Hurdles	25	15
B100 SP27a	10k + 5k Javelin	42	18
B101 SP27a	10k + 5k Walking, vert.	42	18
B102 SP27a	16k + 6k Hammer throw	70	28
B103 SP27a	16k + 6k High jump	70	28
B104 SP27a	20k + 10k Shot put	90	38
B105 SP27a	20k + 10k Long jump	90	38
	Nos. B96-B105 (10)	4.84	2.28

Souvenir Sheet

B106 SP27a	50k + 25k Relay race	2.00	1.00

22nd Olympic Games, Moscow, July 19-Aug. 3. Issued: Nos. B96, B99, B101, B103, B105, Feb. 6; others, Mar. 12.

Moscow '80 Emblem, Relief from St. Dimitri's Cathedral, Arms of Vladimir — SP28

Moscow '80 Emblem and: No. B108, Bridge over Klyazma River and Vladimir Hotel. No. B109, Relief from Nativity Cathedral and coat of arms (falcon), Suzdal. No. B110, Tourist complex and Pozharski Monument, Suzdal. No. B111, Frunze Monument, Ivanovo, torch and spindle. No. B112, Museum of First Soviets, Fighters of the Revolution Monument, Ivanovo.

Photogravure and Engraved

1977, Dec. 30		Perf. 11½x12
B107 SP28	1r + 50k multi	2.00	90
B108 SP28	1r + 50k multi	2.00	90
B109 SP28	1r + 50k multi	2.00	90
B110 SP28	1r + 50k multi	2.00	90
B111 SP28	1r + 50k multi	2.00	90
B112 SP28	1r + 50k multi	2.00	90
	Nos. B107-B112 (6)	12.00	5.40

"Tourism around the Golden Ring."

Fortifications and Arms of Zagorsk — SP29

Moscow '80 Emblem and (Coat of Arms design): No. B114, Gagarin Palace of Culture and new arms of Zagorsk (building & horse). No. B115, Rostov Kremlin with St. John the Divine Church and No. B116, View of Rostov from Nero Lake (deer). No. B117, Alexander Nevski and WWII soldiers' monuments, Pereyaslav and No. B118, Peter the Great monument, Pereyaslav (lion & fish). No. B119, Tower and wall of Monastery of the Transfiguration, Jaroslaw and No. B120, Dock and monument for Soviet heroes, Jaroslaw (bear).

1978		Perf. 12x11½
	Multicolored and:	
B113 SP29	1r + 50k gold	2.00	80
B114 SP29	1r + 50k silver	2.00	80
B115 SP29	1r + 50k silver	2.00	80
B116 SP29	1r + 50k silver	2.00	80
B117 SP29	1r + 50k gold	2.00	80
B118 SP29	1r + 50k gold	2.00	80
B119 SP29	1r + 50k gold	2.00	80
B120 SP29	1r + 50k silver	2.00	80
	Nos. B113-B120 (8)	16.00	6.40

Issue dates: Nos. B113-B116, Oct. 16; Nos. B117-B120, Dec. 25.

1979		Perf. 12x11½

Moscow '80 Emblem and: No. B121, Narikaly Fortress, Tbilisi, 4th century. No. B122, Georgia Philharmonic Concert Hall, "Muse" sculpture, Tbilisi. No. B123, Chir-Dor Mosque, 17th century, Samarkand. No. B124, Peoples Friendship Museum, "Courage" monument, Tashkent. No. B125, Landscape, Erevan. B126, Armenian State Opera and Ballet Theater, Erevan.

	Multicolored and:		
B121 SP29	1r+50k sil, bl circle	2.25	1.40
B122 SP29	1r+50k gold, yel circle	2.25	1.40
B123 SP29	1r+50k sil, bl 8-point star	2.25	1.40
B124 SP29	1r+50k gold, red 8-point star	2.25	1.40
B125 SP29	1r+50k sil, bl diamond	2.25	1.40
B126 SP29	1r+50k gold, red diamond	2.25	1.40
	Nos. B121-B126 (6)	13.50	8.40

Issue dates: Nos. B121-B124, Sept. 5; Nos. B125-B126, Oct.

Kremlin SP29a

Kalinin Prospect,
Moscow
SP29b

Admiralteistvo,
St. Isaak
Cathedral,
Leningrad
SP29c

World War II
Defense
Monument,
Leningrad
SP29d

Bogdan
Khmelnitisky
Monument, St.
Sophia's
Monastery
Kiev — SP29e

Metro Bridge,
Dnieper River,
Kiev — SP29f

Palace of Sports,
Obelisk,
Minsk — SP29g

Republican House
of
Cinematography,
Minsk — SP29h

Vyshgorodsky
Castle, Town
Hall,
Tallinn — SP29i

Viru Hotel,
Tallinn — SP29j

1980   **Perf. 12x11¹/₂**

Moscow '80 Emblem, Coat of Arms,

B127	SP29a	1r + 50k multi	1.90	75
B128	SP29b	1r + 50k multi	1.90	75
B129	SP29c	1r + 50k multi	2.25	90
B130	SP29d	1r + 50k multi	2.25	90
B131	SP29e	1r + 50k multi	2.25	90
B132	SP29f	1r + 50k multi	2.25	90
B133	SP29g	1r + 50k multi	2.25	90
B134	SP29h	1r + 50k multi	2.25	90
B135	SP29i	1r + 50k multi	2.25	90
B136	SP29j	1r + 50k multi	2.25	90
		Nos. B127-B136 (10)	21.80	8.70

Tourism. Issue dates: #B127-B128, Feb. 29.
#B129-B130, Mar. 25; #B131-B136, Apr. 30.

Soviet Culture Fund — SP30

Art treasures: No. B137, *Z.E. Serebriakova*,
1910, by O.K. Lansere, vert. No. B138, *Boyar's
Wife Examining an Embroidery Design*, 1905, by
K.V. Lebedev. No. B139, *Talent*, 1910, by N.P.
Bogdanov-Belsky, vert. No. B140, *Trinity*, 15th-
16th cent., Novgorod School, vert.

Perf. 12x12¹/₂, 12¹/₂x12
1988, Aug. 22   **Litho.**

B137	SP30	10k +5k multi	48	32
B138	SP30	15k +7k multi	70	45
B139	SP30	30k +15k multi	1.40	95
	Souvenir Sheet			
B140	SP30	1r +50k multi	4.50	3.00

SP31   SP33

Lenin
Children's
Fund
SP32

1988, Oct. 20   **Litho.**   **Perf. 12**

B141	SP31	10k +5k Bear	45	30
B142	SP31	10k +5k Wolf	45	30
B143	SP31	20k +10k Fox	90	60
B144	SP31	20k +10k Boar	90	60
B145	SP31	20k +10k Lynx	90	60
a.		Block of 5+label, #B141-B145	3.75	2.50
		Nos. B141-B145 (5)	3.60	2.40

Zoo Relief Fund. See Nos. B152-B156, B166-
B168.

1988, Dec. 12   **Litho.**   **Perf. 12**

Children's drawings and fund emblem: No.
B146, Skating Rink. No. B147, Rooster. No. B148,
May (girl and flowers).

B146	SP32	5k +2k multi	22	15
B147	SP32	5k +2k multi	22	15
B148	SP32	5k +2k multi	22	15
a.		Block of 3+label, #B146-B148	68	45

See Nos. B169-B171.

1988, Dec. 27   **Perf. 12¹/₂x12**

Designs: No. B149, Tigranes I (c. 140-55 B.C.),
king of Armenia, gold coin. No. B150, St. Ripsime
Temple, c. 618. No. B151, *Virgin and Child*, fresco
(detail) by Ovnat Ovnatanyan, 18th cent., Echmia-
dzin Cathedral.

B149	SP33	20k +10k multi	90	60
B150	SP33	30k +15k multi	1.35	90
B151	SP33	50k +25k multi	2.25	1.50
a.		Block of 3+label, #B149-B151	4.50	3.00

Armenian earthquake relief. For surcharges see
Nos. B173-B175.

Zoo Relief Type of 1988
1989, Mar. 20   **Litho.**   **Perf. 12**

B152	SP31	10k+5k Marten	45	30
B153	SP31	10k+5k Squirrel	45	30
B154	SP31	20k+10k Hare	90	60
B155	SP31	20k+10k Hedgehog	90	60
B156	SP31	20k+10k Badger	90	60
a.		Block of 5+label, #B152-B156	3.60	2.50
		Nos. B152-B156 (5)	3.60	2.40

Lenin Children's Fund Type of 1988

Fund emblem and children's drawings: No.
B157, Rabbit. No. B158, Cat. No. B159, Doctor.
Nos. B157-B159 vert.

1989, June 14   **Litho.**   **Perf. 12**

B157	SP32	5k +2k multi	24	16
B158	SP32	5k +2k multi	24	16
B159	SP32	5k +2k multi	24	16
a.		Block of 3+label, #B157-B159	72	48

Surtax for the fund.

Soviet Culture
Fund — SP34

Paintings and porcelain: No. B160, *Village Market*, by A. Makovsky. No. B161, *Lady Wearing a*

Hat, by E. Zelenin. No. B162, *Portrait of the
Actress Bazhenova*, by A. Sofronova. No. B163,
Two Women, by H. Shaiber. No. B164, Popov por-
celain coffee pot and plates, 19th cent.

1989   **Litho.**   **Perf. 12x12¹/₂**

B160	SP34	4k +2k multi	20	15
B161	SP34	5k +2k multi	25	15
B162	SP34	10k +5k multi	60	32
B163	SP34	20k +10k multi	1.10	65
B164	SP34	30k +15k multi	1.75	95
		Nos. B160-B164 (5)	3.90	2.22

Souvenir Sheet

Nature Conservation — SP35

1989, Dec. 14   **Photo.**   **Perf. 11¹/₂**
B165 SP35 20k + 10k Swallow   1.25   1.25

Surtax for the Soviet Union of Philatelists.

Zoo Relief Type of 1988
1990, May 4   **Litho.**   **Perf. 12**

B166	SP31	10k +5k *Aquila chrysaetos*	45	30
B167	SP31	20k +10k *Falco cherrug*	98	65
B168	SP31	20k +10k *Corvus corax*	98	65
a.		Block of 3 + label, #B166-B168	2.50	1.65

Nos. B166-B168 horiz.

Lenin's Children Fund Type of 1988

Designs: No. B169, Clown. No. B170, Group of
women. No. B171, Group of children. Nos. B169-
B171, vert.

1990, July 3   **Litho.**   **Perf. 12**

B169	SP32	5k +2k multi	22	15
B170	SP32	5k +2k multi	22	15
B171	SP32	5k +2k multi	22	15
a.		Block of 3, #B169-B171 + label	66	42

Nature Conservation — SP36

1990, Sept. 12   **Litho.**   **Perf. 12**
B172 SP36 20k +10k multi   1.10   1.10

Surtax for Soviet Union of Philatelists.

Nos. B149-B151 Overprinted

Филателистическая   Восстановление,
    выставка   милосердие,
„Армения-90"   помощь
    #B173   #B174-B175

1990, Nov. 24   Litho.   Perf. 12x12½

B173	SP33	20k +10k multi	1.10 75
B174	SP33	30k +15k multi	1.65 1.10
B175	SP33	50k +25k multi	2.75 1.80
a.		Block of 3+label, #B173-B175	5.50 3.75

Armenia '90 Philatelic Exhibition.

Soviet Culture Fund — SP37

Paintings by N. K. Roerich: 10k+5k, Unkrada, 1909. 20k+10k, Pskovo-Pechorsky Monastery, 1907.

1990, Dec. 20   Litho.   Perf. 12½x12

B176	SP37	10k +5k multi	55 35
B177	SP37	20k +10k multi	1.10 75

Souvenir Sheet

Joys of All Those Grieving, 18th Cent. — SP38

1990, Dec. 23   Perf. 12½x12

B178	SP38	50k +25k multi	2.75 2.75

Surtax for Charity and Health Fund.

Ciconia Ciconia SP39

1991, Feb. 4   Litho.   Perf. 12

B179	SP39	10k +5k multi	55 36

Surtax for the Zoo Relief Fund.

Souvenir Sheet

USSR Philatelic Society, 25th Anniv. — SP40

1991, Feb. 15   Perf. 12½x12½

B180	SP40	20k +10k multi	1.10 1.10

The Universe by V. Lukianets SP41

Painting by V. Lukianets: No. B182, Another Planet.

1991, June 1   Litho.   Perf. 12½x12

B181	SP41	10k +5k multi	18 15
B182	SP41	10k +5k multi	18 15
		Set value	18

SP42   SP43

1991, July 10   Perf. 12x12½

B183	SP42	20k +10k multi	36 24

Surtax for Soviet Culture Fund.

1991, July 10   Perf. 12

B184	SP43	20k +10k multi	36 24

Surtax for Soviet Charity & Health Fund

Souvenir Sheet

SP44

1992, Jan. 22   Litho.   Perf. 12½x12

B185	SP44	3r +50k multi	70 70

Surtax for Nature Preservation.

AIR POST STAMPS

AP1   Fokker F-111 — AP2

Plane Overprint in Red

1922   Unwmk.   Imperf.

C1	AP1	45r green & black	7.50 10.00

5th anniversary of October Revolution.
No. C1 was on sale only at the Moscow General Post Office. Counterfeits exist.

1923   Photo.

C2	AP2	1r red brown	2.75
C3	AP2	3r deep blue	3.25
C4	AP2	5r green	3.25
a.		Wide "5"	500.00
C5	AP2	10r carmine	2.25

Nos. C2-C5 were not placed in use.

Nos. C2-C5 Surcharged **10 коп. зол.**

1924

C6	AP2	5k on 3r dp blue	1.00 1.00
C7	AP2	10k on 5r green	1.00 1.00
a.		Wide "5"	250.00 250.00
b.		Inverted surcharge	450.00 450.00
C8	AP2	15k on 1r red brown	1.00 1.00
a.		Inverted surcharge	500.00 500.00
C9	AP2	20k on 10r car	1.00 1.00
a.		Inverted surcharge	500.00 500.00

Airplane over Map of World — AP3

1927, Septz. 1   Litho.   Perf. 13x12

C10	AP3	10k dk bl & yel brn	5.50 3.75
C11	AP3	15k dp red & ol grn	6.75 6.75

1st Intl. Air Post Cong. at The Hague, initiated by the USSR.

Graf Zeppelin and "Call to Complete 5-Year Plan in 4 Years" — AP4

1930   Photo.   Wmk. 226   Perf. 12½

C12	AP4	40k dk & dl blue	16.00 10.00
a.		Perf. 10½	22.50 19.00
b.		Imperf.	700.00 700.00
C13	AP4	80k dk car & rose	18.00 15.00
a.		Perf. 10½	20.00 10.00
b.		Imperf.	700.00 700.00

Flight of the Graf Zeppelin from Friedrichshafen to Moscow and return.

Symbolical of Airship Communication from the Tundra to the Steppes — AP5

Airship over Dneprostroi Dam — AP6

Airship over Lenin Mausoleum — AP7

Airship Exploring Arctic Regions — AP8

Constructing an Airship — AP9

1931-32   Wmk. 170   Photo.   Imperf.

C15	AP5	10k dark violet	15.00 16.00

Litho.

C16	AP6	15k gray blue	15.00 22.50

Typo.

C17	AP7	20k dk carmine	15.00 22.50

Photo.

C18	AP8	50k black brown	15.00 22.50
C19	AP9	1r dark green	15.00 22.50
		Nos. C15-C19 (5)	75.00 106.00

Perf. 10½, 12, 12½ and Compound

Litho.

C20	AP5	10k dark violet	4.75 2.50

Litho.

C21	AP6	15k gray blue	9.00 3.75

Typo.

C22	AP7	20k dk carmine	6.50 2.00
a.		20k light red	7.50 3.00

Photo.

C23	AP8	50k black brown	4.75 2.00
a.		50k gray blue (error)	200.00 200.00
C24	AP9	1r dark green	5.50 2.00

Perf. 12½
Unwmk.
Engr.

C25	AP6	15k gray blk ('32)	1.00 50
a.		Perf. 10½	400.00 110.00
b.		Perf. 14	57.50 37.50
c.		Imperf.	325.00
		Nos. C20-C25 (6)	31.50 12.75

The 11½ perforation on Nos. C20-C25 is of private origin.

North Pole Issue

Graf Zeppelin and Icebreaker "Malygin" Transferring Mail — AP10

1931   Wmk. 170   Imperf.

C26	AP10	30k dark violet	12.00 9.25
C27	AP10	35k dark green	12.00 9.25
C28	AP10	1r gray black	12.00 9.25
C29	AP10	2r deep ultra	15.00 12.00

Perf. 12x12½

C30	AP10	30k dark violet	20.00 20.00
C31	AP10	35k dark green	20.00 20.00
C32	AP10	1r gray black	20.00 20.00
C33	AP10	2r deep ultra	20.00 20.00

Map of Polar Region, Airplane and Icebreaker "Sibiryakov" — AP11

1932   Wmk. 170   Perf. 12, 10½

C34	AP11	50k carmine rose	24.00 15.00
a.		Perf. 10½	775.00 775.00
b.		Perf. 10½x12	1,200.
C35	AP11	1r green	24.00 15.00
a.		Perf. 12	125.00 40.00

2nd International Polar Year in connection with flight to Franz-Josef Land.

Stratostat "U.S.S.R." AP12   Furnaces of Kuznetsk AP13

1933   Photo.   Perf. 14

C37	AP12	5k ultra	40.00 8.50
a.		Vert. pair, imperf. btwn.	500.00
C38	AP12	10k carmine	40.00 8.50
a.		Horiz. pair, imperf. btwn.	500.00
C39	AP12	20k violet	22.50 8.50

Ascent into the stratosphere by Soviet aeronauts, Sept. 30th, 1933.

1933   Wmk. 170   Perf. 14

Designs: 10k, Oil wells. 20k, Collective farm. 50k, Map of Moscow-Volga Canal project. 80k, Arctic cargo ship.

C40	AP13	5k ultra	10.00 4.75
C41	AP13	10k green	10.00 4.75
C42	AP13	20k carmine	20.00 9.00
C43	AP13	50k dull blue	26.00 9.00
C44	AP13	80k purple	20.00 9.00
		Nos. C40-C44 (5)	86.00 36.50

Unwmk.

C45	AP13	5k ultra	10.50	3.00
C46	AP13	10k green	10.50	3.00
a.		Horiz. pair, imperf. btwn.	375.00	150.00
C47	AP13	20k carmine	15.00	5.00
C48	AP13	50k dull blue	27.50	10.50
C49	AP13	80k purple	20.00	5.00
		Nos. C45-C49 (5)	83.50	26.50

10th anniversary of Soviet civil aviation and air-mail service. Counterfeits exist.

I. D. Usyskin — AP18

Designs: 10k, A. B. Vasenko. 20k, P. F. Fedoseinko.

1934		**Wmk. 170**	**Perf. 11**	
C50	AP18	5k vio brown	11.50	3.25
C51	AP18	10k brown	32.50	3.25
C52	AP18	20k ultra	32.50	3.25

			Perf. 14	
C50a	AP18	5k	110.00	95.00
C51a	AP18	10k	185.00	185.00
C52a	AP18	20k	225.00	225.00

Honoring victims of the stratosphere disaster. See Nos. C77-C79.

Airship "Pravda" — AP19

Airship Landing — AP20

Airship "Voroshilov" — AP21

Sideview of Airship — AP22

Airship "Lenin" — AP23

1934			**Perf. 14**	
C53	AP19	5k red orange	12.50	2.25
C54	AP20	10k claret	12.50	3.50
C55	AP21	15k brown	12.50	4.50
C56	AP22	20k black	27.50	7.00
C57	AP23	30k ultra	50.00	7.00
		Nos. C53-C57 (5)	115.00	24.25

Capt. V. Voronin and "Chelyuskin" — AP24

Prof. Otto Y. Schmidt AP25

A. V. Lapidevsky AP26

S. A. Levanevsky AP27

"Schmidt Camp" — AP28

Designs: 15k, M. G. Slepnev. 20k, I. V. Doronin. 25k, M. V. Vodopianov. 30k, V. S. Molokov. 40k, N. P. Kamanin.

1935			**Perf. 14**	
C58	AP24	1k red orange	5.00	2.50
C59	AP25	3k rose carmine	6.00	2.50
C60	AP26	5k emerald	5.00	2.50
C61	AP27	10k dark brown	6.00	2.50
C62	AP27	15k black	7.25	2.50
C63	AP27	20k deep claret	10.00	4.75
C64	AP27	25k indigo	25.00	9.25
C65	AP27	30k dull green	35.00	11.00
C66	AP27	40k purple	25.00	7.00
C67	AP28	50k dark ultra	25.00	9.25
		Nos. C58-C67 (10)	149.25	53.75

Aerial rescue of ice-breaker Chelyuskin crew and scientific expedition.

No. C61 Surcharged in Red

Перелет Москва— Сан-Франциско через Сев. полюс 1935

1р.

1935, Aug.				
C68	AP27	1r on 10k dk brn	150.00	175.00
a.		Inverted surcharge	3,200.	3,200.
b.		Small Cyrillic "f"	275.00	300.00

Issued in commemoration of the Moscow-San Francisco flight. Counterfeits exist.

Single-Engined Monoplane — AP34

Five-Engined Transport — AP35

Designs: 20k, Twin-engined cabin plane. 30k, Four-motored transport. 40k, Single-engined amphibian. 50k, Twin-motored transport. 80k, Eight-motored transport.

1937		**Unwmk.**	**Perf. 12**	
C69	AP34	20k yel brn & blk	1.00	75
a.		Imperf.		175.00
C70	AP34	20k gray grn & blk	1.00	75
C71	AP34	30k red brn & blk	1.25	75
C72	AP34	40k vio brn & blk	1.75	95
C73	AP34	50k dk vio & blk	3.00	1.50
C74	AP35	80k bl vio & brn	2.75	1.50
C75	AP35	1r black, brown & buff	7.50	3.00
a.		Sheet of 4, imperf.	50.00	85.00
		Nos. C69-C75 (7)	18.25	9.20
		Set, never hinged	35.00	

Jubilee Aviation Exhib., Moscow, Nov. 15-20. Vertical pairs, imperf. between, exist for No. C71, value $100; No. C73, value $90.

Types of 1938 Regular Issue Overprinted in Various Colors

18 АВГУСТА ДЕНЬ АВИАЦИИ СССР

1939			**Typo.**	
C76	A282	10k red (C)	1.40	42
C76A	A285	30k blue (R)	1.40	42
C76B	A286	40k dull green (Br)	1.40	42
C76C	A287	50k dull violet (R)	2.25	55
C76D	A289	1r brown (Bl)	3.00	1.75
		Nos. C76-C76D (5)	9.45	3.56
		Set, never hinged	15.00	

Soviet Aviation Day, Aug. 18, 1939.

Types of 1934 with "30.1.1944" Added at Lower Left

Designs: No. C77, P. F. Fedoseinko. No. C78, I. D. Usyskin. No. C79, A. B. Vasenko.

1944		**Photo.**	**Perf. 12**	
C77	AP18	1r deep blue	1.50	60
C78	AP18	1r slate green	1.50	60
C79	AP18	1r brt yellow green	1.50	75
		Set, never hinged	5.50	

1934 stratosphere disaster, 10th anniv.

Nos. 860A and 861A Surcharged in Red

АВИАПОЧТА 1944 г. 1 РУБЛЬ

1944, May 25				
C80	A431	1r on 30k Prus green	50	15
C81	A432	1r on 30k deep ultra	50	15
		Set, never hinged	1.25	

Catalogue values for unused stamps in this section, from this point to the end of the section, are for Never Hinged items.

Planes and Soviet Air Force Flag — AP42

1948, Dec. 10		**Litho.**	**Perf. 12½**	
C82	AP42	1r dark blue	2.50	1.00

Air Force Day.

Plane over Zages, Caucasus AP43

Plane over Farm Scene AP44

Map of Russian Air Routes and Transport Planes — AP45

Designs: No. C85, Sochi, Crimea. No. C86, Far East. No. C87, Leningrad. 2r, Moscow. 3r, Arctic.

		Perf. 12x12½		
1949, Nov. 9		**Photo.**	**Unwmk.**	
C83	AP43	50k red brn, lemon	1.10	65
C84	AP44	60k sepia, pale buff	2.25	1.25
C85	AP44	1r org brn, yelsh	2.25	1.25
C86	AP43	1r blue, bluish	2.25	1.25
C87	AP43	1r red brn, pale fawn	2.25	1.25
C88	AP45	1r blk, ultra & red, gray	4.75	2.25
C89	AP43	2r org brn, bluish	7.00	3.25
C90	AP43	3r dk green, bluish	11.50	5.50
		Nos. C83-C90 (8)	33.35	16.65

Plane and Mountain Stream AP46

Globe and Plane AP47

Design: 1r, Plane over river.

1955		**Litho.**	**Perf. 12½x12**	
C91	AP46	1r multicolored	1.75	55
C92	AP47	2r black & yel grn	2.50	75

For overprints see Nos. C95-C96.

1955, May 31			**Photo.**	
C93	AP47	2r chocolate	1.75	55
C94	AP47	2r deep blue	1.75	55

Nos. C91 and C92 Overprinted in Red

„Сев. полюс" — Москва 1955 г.

		Perf. 12x12½		
1955, Nov. 22		**Litho.**	**Unwmk.**	
C95	AP46	1r multicolored	2.75	2.00
C96	AP46	2r black & yel grn	4.75	3.00

Issued for use at the scientific drifting stations North Pole-4 and North Pole-5. The inscription reads "North Pole-Moscow, 1955." Counterfeits exist.

Arctic Camp AP48

1956, June 8			**Perf. 12½x12**	
C97	AP48	1r blue, grn, brn, yel & red	1.50	65

Opening of scientific drifting station North Pole-6.

Helicopter over
Kremlin
AP49

Air Force
Emblem and
Arms of
Normandy
AP50

1960, Mar. 5   **Photo.**   *Perf. 12*
C98 AP49 60k ultra   1.00   28

Surcharged with New Value, Bars and
"1961"

1961, Dec. 20
C99 AP49 6k on 60k ultra   80   28

1962, Dec. 30   **Unwmk.**   *Perf. 11½*
C100 AP50 6k blue grn, ocher & carmine 60 15

French Normandy-Neman Escadrille, which
fought on the Russian front, 20th anniv.

Jet over Map
Showing
Airlines in
USSR — AP51

Designs: 12k, Aeroflot emblem and globe. 16k,
Jet over map showing Russian international airlines.

1963, Feb.
C101 AP51 10k red, blk & tan   60   18
C102 AP51 12k blue, red, tan & blk   85   22
C103 AP51 16k blue, blk & red   1.00   35

Aeroflot, the civil air fleet, 40th anniv.

Tupolev 134 at Sheremetyevo Airport,
Moscow — AP52

Civil Aviation: 10k, An-24 (Antonov) and
Vnukovo Airport, Moscow. 12k, Mi-10 (Mil helicopter) and Central Airport, Moscow. 16k, Be-10
(Beriev) and Chinki Riverport, Moscow. 20k, Antei
airliner and Domodedovo Airport, Moscow.

1965, Dec. 31
C104 AP52 6k org, red & vio   28   15
C105 AP52 10k lt green, org red &
     gray   45   15
C106 AP52 12k lilac, dk sep & lt grn   45   15
C107 AP52 16k lilac, lt brn, red & grn   70   15
C108 AP52 20k org red, pur & gray   85   22
    Nos. C104-C108 (5)   2.73
       Set value   70

Aviation Type of 1976

Aviation 1917-1930 (Aviation Emblem and): 4k,
P-4 BIS biplane, 1917. 6k, AK-1 monoplane, 1924.
10k, R-3 (ANT-3) biplane, 1925. 12k, TB-1 (ANT-4)
monoplane, 1925. 16k, R-5 biplane, 1929. 20k,
Shcha-2 amphibian, 1930.

Lithographed and Engraved
1977, Aug. 16   *Perf. 12x11½*
C109 A2134 4k multicolored   15   15
C110 A2134 6k multicolored   15   15
C111 A2134 10k multicolored   28   15
C112 A2134 12k multicolored   30   15
C113 A2134 16k multicolored   .45   30
C114 A2134 20k multicolored   65   15
    Nos. C109-C114 (6)   1.98 1.25

1978, Aug. 10

Designs: 4k, PO-2 biplane, 1928. 6k, K-5 passenger plane, 1929. 10k, TB-3, cantilever monoplane,
1930. 12k, Stal-2, 1931. 16k, MBR-2 hydroplane,
1932. 20k, I-16 fighter plane, 1934.

C115 A2134 4k multicolored   15   15
C116 A2134 6k multicolored   15   15
C117 A2134 10k multicolored   32   15

C118 A2134 12k multicolored   35   15
C119 A2134 16k multicolored   45   15
C120 A2134 20k multicolored   60   25
    Nos. C115-C120 (6)   2.02
       Set value   75

Aviation 1928-1934.

Jet and Compass
Rose — AP53

1978, Aug. 4   **Litho.**   *Perf. 12*
C121 AP53 32k dark blue   80   28

Aeroflot Plane AH-28 — AP54

Designs: Various Aeroflot planes.

Photogravure and Engraved
1979   *Perf. 11½x12*
C122 AP54 2k shown   15   15
C123 AP54 3k YAK-42   15   15
C124 AP54 10k T4-154   30   15
C125 AP54 15k IL76 transport   45   15
C126 AP54 32k IL86 jet liner   85   45
    Nos. C122-C126 (5)   1.90
       Set value   82

AIR POST OFFICIAL STAMPS

Used on mail from Russian embassy in
Berlin to Moscow. Surcharged on Consular
Fee stamps. Currency: the German mark.

OA1

Surcharge in Carmine

1922, July   **Litho.**   *Perf. 13½*
Bicolored Burelage
CO1 OA1 12m on 2.25r   67.50
CO2 OA1 24m on 3r   67.50
CO3 OA1 120m on 2.25r   77.50
CO4 OA1 600m on 3r   97.50
CO5 OA1 1200m on 10k   135.00
CO6 OA1 1200m on 50k   6,500.
CO7 OA1 1200m on 2.25r   375.00
CO8 OA1 1200m on 3r   650.00

Three types of each denomination, distinguished
by shape of "C" in surcharge and length of second
line of surcharge. Used copies have pen or crayon
cancel. Forgeries exist.

SPECIAL DELIVERY STAMPS

Motorcycle
Courier — SD1

Express Truck — SD2

Design: 80k, Locomotive.

     Perf. 12½x12, 12x12½
1932   **Photo.**   **Wmk. 170**
E1 SD1 5k dull brown   7.50   6.25
E2 SD2 10k violet brown   9.75   6.25
E3 SD2 80k dull green   24.00 12.50

Used values are for c-t-o.

POSTAGE DUE STAMPS

Доплата
3 коп.
золотом

Regular Issue of 1918
Surcharged in Red or
Carmine

1924-25   **Unwmk.**   *Perf. 13½*
J1 A33 1k on 35k blue   15   90
J2 A33 3k on 35k blue   15   90
J3 A33 5k on 35k blue   15   90
  a.   Imperf.   60.00
J4 A33 8k on 35k blue ('25)   24   90
  a.   Imperf.   40.00
J5 A33 10k on 35k blue   15   1.10
  a.   Pair, one without surcharge   25.00
J6 A33 12k on 70k brown   15   90
J7 A33 14k on 35k blue ('25)   15   90
  a.   Imperf.   65.00
J8 A33 32k on 35k blue   15   1.10
J9 A33 40k on 35k blue   15   1.10
  a.   Imperf.   60.00
       Set value   1.15

Surcharge is found inverted on Nos. J1-J2, J4, J6-
J9; value $25-$50. Double on Nos. J2, J4-J6; value,
$40-$50.

ДОПЛАТА

Regular Issue of
1921 Surcharged in
Violet

1 коп.

1924   **Imperf.**
J10 A40 1k on 100r orange   3.50   6.00
  a.   1k on 100r yellow   4.00 12.50
  b.   Pelure paper   4.00 12.50
  c.   Inverted surcharge   67.50

D1

Lithographed or Typographed
1925   *Perf. 12*
J11 D1 1k red   2.00   1.50
J12 D1 2k violet   1.00   2.25
J13 D1 3k light blue   1.00   2.25
J14 D1 7k orange   1.00   2.25
J15 D1 8k green   1.00   3.00
J16 D1 10k dark blue   1.65   4.50
J17 D1 14k brown   2.00   4.50
    Nos. J11-J17 (7)   9.65 20.25

       Perf. 14½x14
J13a D1 3k   4.00   6.00
J14a D1 7k   8.25 12.50
J16a D1 10k   32.50 40.00
J17a D1 14k   2.25   3.50

1925   **Wmk. 170**   **Typo.**   *Perf. 12*
J18 D1 1k red   45   85
J19 D1 2k violet   45   85
J20 D1 3k light blue   60   1.10
J21 D1 7k orange   60   1.10
J22 D1 8k green   60   1.10

J23 D1 10k dark blue   75   1.65
J24 D1 14k brown   1.10   2.25
    Nos. J18-J24 (7)   4.55   8.90

For surcharges see Nos. 359-372.

WENDEN (LIVONIA)

A former district of Livonia, a province of
the Russian Empire, which became part of
Latvia, under the name of Vidzeme.

Used values for Nos. L2-L12 are for
pen-canceled copies. Postmarked
specimens sell for considerably more.

A1

1862   **Unwmk.**   **Imperf.**
L1 A1 (2k) blue   3.50
  a.   Tête bêche pair   17.50

No. L1 may have been used for a short period of
time but withdrawn because of small size.

A2   A3

1863
L2 A2 (2k) rose & black   150.00 150.00
  a.   Background inverted   275.00 275.00
L3 A3 (4k) blue grn & blk   70.00 70.00
  a.   (4k) yellow green & black   150.00 150.00
  b.   Half used as 2k on cover   1,800.
  c.   Background inverted   150.00 150.00
  d.   As "a," background inverted   210.00 210.00

The official imitations of Nos. L2 and L3 have a
single instead of a double hyphen after
"WENDEN."

Coat of Arms
A4   A5   A6

1863-71
L4 A4 (2k) rose & green   27.50 14.00
  a.   Yellowish paper
  b.   Green frame around central oval   37.50 21.00
  c.   Tête bêche pair   1,800.
L5 A5 (2k) rose & grn ('64)   70.00 57.50
L6 A6 (2k) rose & green   21.00 21.00

Official imitations of Nos. L4b and L5 have a
rose instead of a green line around the central
oval. The first official imitation of No. L6 has the
central oval 5½mm instead of 6¼mm wide; the
second imitation is less clearly printed than the
original and the top of the "f" of "Briefmarke" is
too much hooked.

Coat of Arms
A7   A8

1872-75   *Perf. 12½*
L7 A7 (2k) red & green   25.00 21.00
L8 A8 2k yel grn & red ('75)   7.00   8.00
  a.   Numeral in upper right corner re-
     sembles an inverted "3"   27.50 27.50

Reprints of No. L8 have no horizontal lines in
the background. Those of No. L8a have the
impression blurred and only traces of the horizontal lines.

A9

Wenden
Castle — A10

1878-80

L9	A9	2k green & red	7.00 8.00
a.		Imperf.	
L10	A9	2k blk, grn & red ('80)	7.00 8.00
a.		Imperf., pair	27.50

No. L9 has been reprinted in blue green and yellow green with perforation 11½ and in gray green with perforation 12½ or imperforate.

1884			*Perf. 11½*
L11	A9	2k black, green & red	2.50 2.50
a.		Green omitted	21.00
b.		Arm inverted	21.00
c.		Arm double	27.50
d.		Imperf., pair	21.00

1901			*Engr.*
L12	A10	2k dk green & brown	3.50 3.50
a.		Tête bêche pair	
b.		Imperf., pair	20.00

OCCUPATION STAMPS

Issued under Finnish Occupation

Finnish Stamps of 1917-18 Overprinted **Aunus**

1919		**Unwmk.**	*Perf. 14*
N1	A19	5p green	12.50 12.50
N2	A19	10p rose	12.50 12.50
N3	A19	20p buff	12.50 12.50
N4	A19	40p red violet	12.50 12.50
N5	A19	50p orange brn	100.00 100.00
N6	A19	1m dl rose & blk	105.00 105.00
N7	A19	5m violet & blk	325.00 325.00
N8	A19	10m brown & blk	575.00 575.00
		Nos. N1-N8 (8)	1,155. 1,155.

"Aunus" is the Finnish name for Olonets, a town of Russia.

Counterfeits overprints exist.

Issued under German Occupation

Germany Nos. 506 to 523 Overprinted in Black **OSTLAND**

1941-43		**Unwmk. Typo.**	*Perf. 14*
N9	A115	1pf gray black	15 15
N10	A115	3pf light brown	15 15
N11	A115	4pf slate	15 15
N12	A115	5pf dp yellow green	15 15
N13	A115	6pf purple	15 15
N14	A115	8pf red	15 15
N15	A115	10pf dk brown ('43)	15 1.00
N16	A115	12pf carmine ('43)	15 1.00

		Engr.	
N17	A115	10pf dark brown	20 25
N18	A115	12pf brt carmine	20 25
N19	A115	15pf brown lake	15 15
N20	A115	16pf peacock grn	15 15
N21	A115	20pf blue	15 15
N22	A115	24pf orange brown	15 15
N23	A115	25pf brt ultra	15 15
N24	A115	30pf olive green	15 15
N25	A115	40pf brt red violet	15 15
N26	A115	50pf myrtle green	15 15
N27	A115	60pf dk red brown	15 15
N28	A115	80pf indigo	15 15
		Set value	1.50 3.40

Issued for use in Estonia, Latvia and Lithuania.

Same Overprinted in Black **UKRAINE**

		Typo.	
N29	A115	1pf gray black	15 15
N30	A115	3pf lt brown	15 15
N31	A115	4pf slate	15 15
N32	A115	5pf dp yel green	15 15
N33	A115	6pf purple	15 15
N34	A115	8pf red	15 15
N35	A115	10pf dk brown ('43)	15 1.00
N36	A115	12pf carmine ('43)	15 1.00

		Engr.	
N37	A115	10pf dk brown	25 35
N38	A115	12pf brt carmine	25 35
N39	A115	15pf brown lake	15 15
N40	A115	16pf peacock green	15 15
N41	A115	20pf blue	15 15
N42	A115	24pf orange brown	15 15

N43	A115	25pf bright ultra	15 15
N44	A115	30pf olive green	15 15
N45	A115	40pf brt red violet	15 15
N46	A115	50pf myrtle green	15 15
N47	A115	60pf dk red brown	15 15
N48	A115	80pf indigo	15 15
		Set value	1.50 3.60

ARMY OF THE NORTHWEST

(Gen. Nicolai N. Yudenich)

Russian Stamps of 1909-18 Overprinted in Black or Red **СѢВ.Зап. армія**

On Stamps of 1909-12
Perf. 14 to 15 and Compound

1919, Aug. 1

1	A14	2k green	2.50 4.25
2	A14	5k claret	2.50 4.25
3	A15	10k dk blue (R)	2.75 5.00
4	A11	15k red brn & bl	2.75 5.00
5	A8	20k blue & car	5.00 7.50
6	A11	25k grn & gray violet	8.50 12.00
7	A8	50k brn vio & grn	5.00 6.25

Perf. 13½

8	A9	1r pale brn, dk brn & org	10.50 14.00
9	A13	10r scar, yel & gray	30.00 52.50

On Stamps of 1917
Imperf

10	A14	3k red	1.40 3.50
11	A12	3.50r mar & lt grn	17.50 27.50
12	A13	5r dk blue, grn & pale bl	14.00 25.00
13	A12	7r dk green & pink	77.50 125.00

No. 2 Surcharged
Perf. 14, 14½x15

14	A14	10k on 5k claret	1.75 3.75
		Nos. 1-14 (14)	181.65 295.50

Nos. 1-14 exist with inverted overprint or surcharge. The 1, 3½, 5, 7 and 10 rubles with red overprint are trial printings (value $40 each). The 20k on 14k, perforated, and the 1, 2, 5, 15, 70k and 1r imperforate were overprinted but never placed in use. Value: $80, $30, $40, $40, $40 and $60.

These stamps were in use from Aug. 1 to Oct. 15, 1919.

Counterfeits of Nos. 1-14 abound.

ARMY OF THE NORTH

A1

A2

A3

A4

A5

1919, Sept. Typo. Imperf.

1	A1	5k brown violet	15 70
2	A2	10k blue	15 70
3	A3	15k yellow	15 70
4	A4	20k rose	15 70
5	A5	50k green	15 70
		Nos. 1-5 (5)	75 3.50

The letters OKCA are the initials of Russian words meaning "Special Corps, Army of the North". The stamps were in use from about the end of September to the end of December, 1919.

(General Miller)

A set of seven stamps of this design was prepared in 1919, but not issued.

RUSSIAN OFFICES ABROAD

For various reasons the Russian Empire maintained Post Offices to handle its correspondence in several foreign countries. These were similar to the Post Offices in foreign countries maintained by other world powers.

OFFICES IN CHINA

100 Kopecks = 1 Ruble
100 Cents = 1 Dollar (1917)

Russian Stamps Overprinted in Blue or Red

КИТАЙ

On Issues of 1889-92
Horizontally Laid Paper

1899-1904 Wmk. 168 Perf. 14½x15

1	A10	1k orange (Bl)	50 65
2	A10	2k yel green (R)	50 65
3	A10	3k carmine (Bl)	50 65
4	A10	5k red violet (Bl)	50 65
5	A10	7k dk blue (R)	1.25 2.00
6	A8	10k dk blue (Bl)	1.25 2.00
7	A8	50k vio & grn (Bl) ('04)	4.00 4.50

Perf. 13½

8	A9	1r lt brn, brn & org (Bl) ('04)	21.00 22.50
		Nos. 1-8 (8)	29.50 33.60

On Issues of 1902-05
Vertically Laid Paper
Perf. 14½ to 15 and Compound

1904-08

Overprinted in Black, Red or Blue

9	A8	4k rose red (Bl)	2.00 2.50
10	A10	7k dk blue (R)	10.00 12.50
11	A8	10k dk blue (R)	775.00 850.00
a.		Groundwork inverted	3,250.
12	A11	14k bl & rose (R)	5.00 3.50
13	A11	15k brn vio & blue (Bl) ('08)	5.00 4.50
14	A8	20k blue & car (Bl)	1.50 2.50
15	A11	25k dull grn & lil (R) ('08)	10.00 6.50
16	A11	35k dk vio & grn (R)	2.50 3.25
17	A8	50k vio & grn (Bl)	42.50 55.00
18	A11	70k brn & org (Bl)	10.00 12.50

Perf. 13½

19	A9	1r lt brn, brn & org (Bl)	15.00 11.50
20	A12	3.50r blk & gray (R)	9.50 10.00
21	A13	5r dk bl, grn & pale bl (R) ('07)	7.50 10.00
22	A12	7r blk & yel (Bl)	12.50 10.00
23	A13	10r scar, yel & gray (Bl) ('07)	40.00 50.00
		Nos. 9-10,12-23 (14)	173.00 194.25

On Issues of 1909-12
Wove Paper
Lozenges of Varnish on Face

1910-16 Unwmk. Perf. 14x14½

24	A14	1k orange yel (Bl)	25 32
25	A14	1k org yel (Bl Bk)	3.50 5.00
26	A14	2k green (Bk)	25 32
27	A14	2k green (Bl)	4.00 6.25
a.		Double ovpt. (Bk and Bl)	
28	A14	3k rose red (Bl)	25 32
29	A14	3k rose red (Bk)	7.25 10.00
30	A15	4k carmine (Bl)	25 32
31	A15	4k carmine (Bk)	5.00 7.25
32	A14	7k lt blue (Bk)	25 32
33	A15	10k blue (Bk)	25 32
34	A11	14k blue & rose (Bk)	55 65
35	A11	14k blue & rose (Bl)	3.25 4.50
36	A11	15k dl vio & bl (Bk)	32 65
37	A8	20k blue & car (Bk)	32 65
38	A11	25k green & vio (Bl)	2.25 3.25
39	A11	25k grn & vio (Bk)	55 1.65
40	A11	35k vio & grn (Bk)	25 32
41	A11	35k vio & grn (Bl)	25 32
42	A8	50k vio & grn (Bk)	25 32
43	A8	50k brn vio & grn (Bk)	11.50 16.00
44	A11	70k lt brn & org (Bl)	25 32

Perf. 13½

45	A9	1r brn, brn & org (Bl)	1.00 1.10
47	A13	5r dk bl, grn & pale bl (R)	7.25 8.25
		Nos. 24-47 (22)	48.99 68.08

Russian Stamps of 1902-12 Surcharged:

1 CENT — a
10 CENTS — b
1 DOLLAR — c

On Stamps of 1909-12

1917 Perf. 11½, 13½, 14, 14½x15

50	A14(a)	1c on 1k dl org yel	50 4.00
51	A14(a)	2c on 2k dull grn	50 4.00
52	A14(a)	3c on 3k car	50 4.00
a.		Inverted surcharge	65.00
b.		Double surcharge	150.00
53	A15(a)	4c on 4k car	1.00 3.25
54	A14(a)	5c on 5k claret	1.00 11.50
55	A15(b)	10c on 10k dk blue	1.00 11.50
a.		Inverted surcharge	85.00 85.00
b.		Double surcharge	115.00
56	A11(b)	14c on 14k dk blue & carmine	1.00 8.50
a.		Imperf.	6.00
b.		Inverted surcharge	100.00
57	A11(a)	15c on 15k brn lilac & dp blue	1.00 11.50
58	A8(b)	20c on 20k bl & car	1.00 11.50
59	A11(a)	25c on 25k grn & violet	1.00 11.50
60	A11(a)	35c on 35k brn vio & green	1.25 11.50
a.		Inverted surcharge	27.50
61	A8(a)	50c on 50k brn vio & green	1.10 11.50
62	A11(a)	70c on 70k brn & red orange	1.10 11.50
63	A9(c)	$1 on 1r pale brn, brn & org	1.10 11.50
		Nos. 50-63 (14)	13.05

On Stamps of 1902-05
Vertically Laid Paper
Perf. 11½, 13, 13½, 13½x11½
Wmk. Wavy Lines (168)

64	A12	$3.50 on 3.50r blk & gray	7.00 32.50
65	A13	$5 on 5r dk bl, grn & pale blue	7.00 32.50
66	A12	$7 on 7r blk & yel	6.75 32.50

On Stamps of 1915
Unwmk. Perf. 13½
Wove Paper

68	A13	$5 on 5r ind, grn & lt blue	13.00 42.50
a.		Inverted surcharge	125.00
70	A13	$10 on 10r car lake, yel & gray	12.50 100.00
		Nos. 64-70 (5)	44.75

The surcharge on Nos. 64-70 is in larger type than on the $1.

Russian Stamps of 1909-18 Surcharged in Black or Red **2 Cent.**

On Stamps of 1909-12

1920 Perf. 14, 14½x15

72	A14	1c on 1k dull org yellow	32.50 37.50
73	A14	2c on 2k dull grn (R)	16.00 15.00
74	A14	3c on 3k car	16.00 15.00
75	A14	4c on 4k car	16.00 15.00
a.		Inverted surcharge	130.00
76	A14	5c on 5k claret	16.00 15.00
77	A15	10c on 10k dk bl (R)	100.00 57.50
78	A14	10c on 10k on 7k blue	95.00 57.50

On Stamps of 1917-18
Imperf

79	A14	1c on 1k orange	22.50 15.00
a.		Inverted surcharge	45.00 75.00
80	A14	5c on 5k claret	30.00 30.00
a.		Inverted surcharge	140.00
b.		Double surcharge	200.00
c.		Surcharged "Cent" only	95.00
		Nos. 72-80 (9)	344.00

OFFICES IN THE TURKISH EMPIRE

Various powers maintained post offices in the Turkish Empire before World War I by authority of treaties which ended with the

signing of the Treaty of Lausanne in 1923. The foreign post offices were closed Oct. 27, 1923.

100 Kopecks = 1 Ruble
40 Paras = 1 Piaster (1900)

Coat of Arms
A1

1863 Unwmk. Typo. Imperf.
1 A1 6k blue 275.00 1,000.
a. 6k light blue, thin paper 350.00 1,350.
b. 6k dark blue, chalky paper 90.00

A2   A3

1865 Litho.
2 A2 (2k) brown & blue 700.00 625.00
3 A3 (20k) blue & red 900.00 850.00

Twenty-eight varieties of each.

A4   A5   A6

1866 Horizontal Network
4 A4 (2k) rose & pale bl 35.00 52.50
5 A5 (20k) dp blue & rose 55.00 57.50

1867 Vertical Network
6 A4 (2k) rose & pale bl 70.00 87.50
7 A5 (20k) dp blue & rose 100.00 150.00

The initials inscribed on Nos. 2 to 7 are those of the Russian Company of Navigation and Trade. Stamps of Russian Offices in the Turkish Empire overprinted with these initials were used in the Ukraine and are listed under that country.
The official imitations of Nos. 2 to 7 are on yellowish white paper. The colors are usually paler than those of the originals and there are minor differences in the designs.

Horizontally Laid Paper
1868 Typo. Wmk. 168 Perf. 11½
8 A6 1k brown 35.00 19.00
9 A6 3k green 35.00 19.00
10 A6 5k blue 35.00 19.00
11 A6 10k car & green 35.00 19.00

Colors of Nos. 8-11 dissolve in water.

1872-90 Perf. 14½x15
12 A6 1k brown 6.25 3.00
13 A6 3k green 20.00 2.00
14 A6 5k blue 3.75 1.00
15 A6 10k pale red & grn ('90) 1.00 50
b. 10k carmine & green 11.00 3.75

Vertically Laid Paper
12a A6 1k 37.50 12.50
13a A6 3k 37.50 12.50
14a A6 5k 37.50 12.50
15a A6 10k 87.50 30.00

Nos. 12-15 exist imperf.

No. 15 Surcharged in Black or Blue:

a   b   c

1876
16 A6(a) 8k on 10k (Bk) 60.00 45.00
a. Vertically laid
b. Inverted surcharge 375.00
17 A6(a) 8k on 10k (Bl) 85.00 65.00
a. Vertically laid
b. Inverted surcharge

1879
18 A6(b) 7k on 10k (Bk) 85.00 65.00
a. Vertically laid
b. Inverted surcharge
19 A6(b) 7k on 10k (Bl) 100.00 85.00
a. Vertically laid
b. Inverted surcharge
19C A6(c) 7k on 10k (Bl) 700.00 550.00
19D A6(c) 7k on 10k (Bk) 550.00 500.00

Nos. 16-19D have been extensively counterfeited.

1879 Perf. 14½x15
20 A6 1k black & yellow 3.00 1.50
a. Vertically laid 9.00 7.50
21 A6 2k black & rose 4.50 4.25
a. Vertically laid 10.00 6.00
22 A6 7k carmine & gray 6.50 1.75
a. Vertically laid 27.50 12.50

1884
23 A6 1k orange 45 28
24 A6 2k green 70 40
25 A6 5k pale red violet 2.75 95
26 A6 7k blue 1.40 40

Nos. 23-26 imperforate are believed to be proofs. No. 23 surcharged "40 PARAS" is bogus, though some copies were postally used.

Russian Company of Navigation and Trade

Р.О.П.и.Т.

This overprint, in two sizes, was privately applied in various colors to Russian Offices in the Turkish Empire stamps of 1900-1910.
See Ukraine.

A7   A8   A9

A10   A11

Surcharged in Blue, Black or Red
1900
Horizontally Laid Paper
27 A7 4pa on 1k orange (Bl) 15 15
a. Inverted surcharge 30.00 30.00
28 A7 4pa on 1k orange (Bk) 15 15
a. Inverted surcharge 30.00 30.00
29 A7 10pa on 2k green 22 22
a. Inverted surcharge
30 A8 1pi on 10k dk blue 50 60
a. Inverted surcharge

1903-05
Vertically Laid Paper
31 A7 10pa on 2k yel green 30 50
a. Inverted surcharge 70.00
32 A8 20pa on 4k rose red (Bl) 30 50
a. Inverted surcharge 25.00
33 A8 1pi on 10k dk blue 30 50
a. Groundwork inverted +55.00 17.50
34 A8 2pi on 20k blue & car (Bk) 70 1.00
35 A8 5pi on 50k brn vio & grn 1.75 2.00
36 A9 7pi on 70k brn & org (Bl) 2.00 3.00

Perf. 13½
37 A10 10pi on 1r lt brn, brn & org (Bl) 3.25 4.75
38 A10 35pi on 3.50r blk & gray 9.75 13.00
39 A11 70pi on 7r blk & yel 11.20 15.00
Nos. 31-39 (9) 29.55 40.25

A12

A13   A14

Wove Paper
Lozenges of Varnish on Face
1909 Unwmk. Perf. 14½x15
40 A12 5pa on 1k orange 24 35
41 A12 10pa on 2k green 30 52
a. Inverted surcharge 7.25 8.50
42 A12 20pa on 4k carmine 60 90
43 A12 1pi on 10k blue 65 1.00
44 A12 5pi on 50k vio & grn 1.40 1.75
45 A12 7pi on 70k brn & org 2.00 2.75

Perf. 13½
46 A13 10pi on 1r brn & org 3.00 5.00
47 A14 35pi on 3.50r mar & lt grn 10.50 14.00
48 A14 70pi on 7r dk grn & pink 18.00 25.00
Nos. 40-48 (9) 36.69 51.27

50th anniv. of the establishing of the Russian Post Offices in the Levant.

Nos. 40-48 Overprinted with Names of Various Cities
Overprinted "Constantinople"
Black Overprint
1909-10 Perf. 14½x15
61 A12 5pa on 1k 15 28
62 A12 10pa on 2k 15 28
63 A12 20pa on 4k 28 45
64 A12 1pi on 10k 30 52
65 A12 5pi on 50k 60 90
66 A12 7pi on 70k 1.40 2.00

"Consnantinople"
61a A12 5pa on 1k 1.65
62a A12 10pa on 2k 1.25
63a A12 20pa on 4k 2.00
64a A12 1pi on 10k 2.75
65a A12 5pi on 50k 2.75
66a A12 7pi on 70k 5.00

"Constantinopie"
61b A12 5pa on 1k 1.65
62b A12 10pa on 2k 2.00
63b A12 20pa on 4k 2.00
64b A12 1pi on 10k 2.75
65b A12 5pi on 50k 2.75
66b A12 7pi on 70k 5.00

Perf. 13½
67 A13 10pi on 1r 5.50 8.75
a. "Constanttnople" 14.00
68 A14 35pi on 3.50r 16.00 27.50
69 A14 70pi on 7r 30.00 42.50

Overprinted "Constautinople"
68a A14 35pi on 3.50r 32.50
69a A14 70pi on 7r 60.00

Overprinted "Constantjnople"
68b A14 35pi on 3.50r 32.50
69b A14 70pi on 7r 60.00

Blue Overprint
Perf. 14½x15
70 A12 5pa on 1k 2.50 3.50
a. "Constanninople" 8.00
Nos. 61-70 (26) 273.43 86.68

Overprinted "Jaffa"
Black Overprint
71 A12 5pa on 1k 1.40 2.50
a. Inverted overprint 11.50
72 A12 10pa on 2k 1.75 2.75
a. Inverted overprint 11.50
73 A12 20pa on 4k 2.00 3.50
a. Inverted overprint 27.50
74 A12 1pi on 10k 2.50 3.50
a. Double overprint 32.50
75 A12 5pi on 50k 6.00 7.00
76 A12 7pi on 70k 7.25 9.75

Perf. 13½
77 A13 10pi on 1r 24.00 37.50
78 A14 35pi on 3.50r 60.00 87.50
79 A14 70pi on 7r 80.00 125.00

Blue Overprint
Perf. 14½x15
80 A12 5pa on 1k 4.00 6.25
Nos. 71-80 (10) 188.90 285.25

Overprinted "Ierusalem"
Black Overprint
81 A12 5pa on 1k 1.50 2.00
a. Inverted overprint 13.00
b. "erusalem" 8.25
82 A12 10pa on 2k 2.00 3.00
a. Inverted overprint 13.00
b. "erusalem" 8.25
83 A12 20pa on 4k 3.00 4.00
a. Inverted overprint 13.00
b. "erusalem" 8.25
84 A12 1pi on 10k 3.00 4.00
a. Inverted overprint 11.50
85 A12 5pi on 50k 5.00 8.00
a. "erusalem" 22.50
86 A12 7pi on 70k 10.00 13.00
a. "erusalem" 22.50

Perf. 13½
87 A13 10pi on 1r 32.50 42.50
88 A14 35pi on 3.50r 75.00 90.00
89 A14 70pi on 7r 90.00 125.00

Blue Overprint
Perf. 14½x15
90 A12 5pa on 1k 4.50 6.50
Nos. 81-90 (10) 226.50 298.00

Overprinted "Kerassunde"
Black Overprint
91 A12 5pa on 1k 28 42
a. Inverted overprint 8.75
92 A12 10pa on 2k 28 45
a. Inverted overprint 8.75
93 A12 20pa on 4k 42 60
a. Inverted overprint 10.50
94 A12 1pi on 10k 52 70
95 A12 5pi on 50k 1.00 1.25
96 A12 7pi on 70k 1.40 2.00

Perf. 13½
97 A13 10pi on 1r 5.50 7.75
98 A14 35pi on 3.50r 17.50 21.00
99 A14 70pi on 7r 25.00 30.00

Blue Overprint
Perf. 14½x15
100 A12 5pa on 1k 3.75 5.50
Nos. 91-100 (10) 55.65 69.67

Overprinted "Mont Athos"
Black Overprint
101 A12 5pa on 1k 30 60
b. Inverted overprint 14.00
102 A12 10pa on 2k 30 60
b. Inverted overprint 14.00
103 A12 20pa on 4k 35 65
b. Inverted overprint 15.00
104 A12 1pi on 10k 60 85
b. Double overprint 22.50
105 A12 5pi on 50k 2.00 2.50
106 A12 7pi on 70k 3.00 4.25
b. Pair, one without "Mont Athos" 16.00

Perf. 13½
107 A13 10pi on 1r 10.00 12.50
108 A14 35pi on 3.50r 22.50 27.50
109 A14 70pi on 7r 40.00 55.00

Blue Overprint
Perf. 14½x15
110 A12 5pa on 1k 3.50 6.25
Nos. 101-110 (10) 82.55 110.70

"Mont Atho"
101a A12 5pa on 1k 13.00
102a A12 10pa on 2k 13.00
103a A12 20pa on 4k 13.00
104a A12 1pi on 10k 20.00
c. As "a," double overprint 85.00
105a A12 5pi on 50k 27.50
106a A12 7pi on 70k 40.00
110a A12 5pa on 1k 11.50

Overprinted   G. Ллонz

111 A12 5pa on 1k 35 55
112 A12 10pa on 2k 35 55
113 A12 20pa on 4k 45 90
114 A12 1pi on 10k 90 1.75
115 A12 5pi on 50k 1.75 2.75
116 A12 7pi on 70k 3.00 5.00

Perf. 13½
117 A13 10pi on 1r 18.00 25.00
Nos. 111-117 (7) 24.80 36.50

The overprint is larger on No. 117.

Overprinted "Salonique"
Black Overprint
Perf. 14½x15
131 A12 5pa on 1k 30 60
a.   6.50
b. Pair, one without overprint
132 A12 10pa on 2k 45 90
a. Inverted overprint 10.00
133 A12 20pa on 4k 60 90
a. Inverted overprint 13.00
134 A12 1pi on 10k 60
135 A12 5pi on 50k 1.25 1.75
136 A12 7pi on 70k 2.50 3.00

Perf. 13½
137 A13 10pi on 1r 12.00 15.00
138 A14 35pi on 3.50r 27.50 32.50
139 A14 70pi on 7r 40.00 50.00

Blue Overprint
Perf. 14½x15
140 A12 5pa on 1k — 6.00 7.25
Nos. 131-140 (10) — 91.20 112.80

Overprinted "Smyrne"
Black Overprint
141 A12 5pa on 1k — 24 45
  a. Double overprint — 5.00
  b. Inverted overprint
142 A12 10pa on 2k — 24 45
  a. Inverted overprint — 8.25
143 A12 20pa on 4k — 45 60
  a. Inverted overprint — 10.00
144 A12 1pi on 10k — 45 75
145 A12 5pi on 50k — 90 1.50
146 A12 7pi on 70k — 1.75 3.00

Perf. 13½
147 A13 10pi on 1r — 9.00 10.50
148 A14 35pi on 3.50r — 18.00 21.00
149 A14 70pi on 7r — 27.00 32.50

Blue Overprint
Perf. 14½x15
150 A12 5pa on 1k — 3.25 4.75
Nos. 141-150 (10) — 61.28 75.50

"Smyrn"
141c A12 5pa on 1k — 3.50 4.00
142b A12 10pa on 2k — 3.25 4.00
143b A12 20pa on 4k — 3.25 4.00
144a A12 1pi on 10k — 4.50 5.75
145a A12 5pi on 50k — 4.50 5.25
146a A12 7pi on 70k — 6.50 6.50

Overprinted "Trebizonde"
Black Overprint
151 A12 5pa on 1k — 24 45
  a. Inverted overprint — 4.50
152 A12 10pa on 2k — 24 45
  a. Inverted overprint — 6.50
  b. Pair, one without "Trebizonde"
153 A12 20pa on 4k — 45 40
  a. Inverted overprint — 10.00
154 A12 1pi on 10k — 45 75
  a. Pair, one without "Trebizonde" — 27.50
155 A12 5pi on 50k — 1.00 1.50
156 A12 7pi on 70k — 1.75 3.00

Perf. 13½
157 A13 10pi on 1r — 9.00 10.50
158 A14 35pi on 3.50r — 18.00 21.00
159 A14 70pi on 7r — 27.50 32.50

Blue Overprint
Perf. 14½x15
160 A12 5pa on 1k — 3.25 4.75
Nos. 151-160 (10) — 61.88 75.30

On Nos. 158 and 159 the overprint is spelled "Trebisonde".

Overprinted "Beyrouth"
Black Overprint
1910
161 A12 5pa on 1k — 22 45
162 A12 10pa on 2k — 22 45
  a. Inverted overprint — 20.00
163 A12 20pa on 4k — 40 60
164 A12 1pi on 10k — 40 75
165 A12 5pi on 50k — 80 1.50
166 A12 7pi on 70k — 1.65 3.00

Perf. 13½
167 A13 10pi on 1r — 8.25 10.50
168 A14 35pi on 3.50r — 18.00 21.00
169 A14 70pi on 7r — 25.00 32.50
Nos. 161-169 (9) — 52.94 70.75

Overprinted "Dardanelles"
Perf. 14½x15
171 A12 5pa on 1k — 22 45
172 A12 10pa on 2k — 22 45
  a. Pair, one without overprint
173 A12 20pa on 4k — 40 60
  a. Inverted overprint — 10.00
174 A12 1pi on 10k — 40 75
175 A12 5pi on 50k — 80 1.50
176 A12 7pi on 70k — 1.65 3.00

Perf. 13½
177 A13 10pi on 1r — 8.25 10.25
178 A14 35pi on 3.50r — 16.00 21.00
179 A14 70pi on 7r — 25.00 32.50
  a. Center and ovpt. inverted
Nos. 171-179 (9) — 52.94 70.50

Overprinted "Metelin"
Perf. 14½x15
181 A12 5pa on 1k — 28 60
  a. Inverted overprint — 10.00
182 A12 10pa on 2k — 28 60
  a. Inverted overprint — 13.00
183 A12 20pa on 4k — 55 90
  a. Inverted overprint — 13.00
184 A12 1pi on 10k — 55 90
185 A12 5pi on 50k — 1.10 1.75
186 A12 7pi on 70k — 2.25 3.50

Perf. 13½
187 A13 10pi on 1r — 11.00 15.00
188 A14 35pi on 3.50r — 25.00 32.50
189 A14 70pi on 7r — 35.00 45.00
Nos. 181-189 (9) — 76.01 100.75

Overprinted "Rizeh"
Perf. 14½x15
191 A12 5pa on 1k — 22 45
  a. Inverted overprint — 6.50
192 A12 10pa on 2k — 22 45
  a. Inverted overprint — 10.00
193 A12 20pa on 4k — 40 60
  a. Inverted overprint — 10.00
194 A12 1pi on 10k — 40 60
195 A12 5pi on 50k — 80 1.50
196 A12 7pi on 70k — 1.65 3.00

Perf. 13½
197 A13 10pi on 1r — 8.25 10.50
198 A14 35pi on 3.50r — 16.00 21.00
199 A14 70pi on 7r — 25.00 32.50
Nos. 191-199 (9) — 52.94 70.60

Nos. 61-199 for the establishing of Russian Post Offices in the Levant, 50th anniv.

A15   A16   A17

Vertically Laid Paper
1910 Wmk. 168 Perf. 14½x15
200 A15 20pa on 5k red violet (Bl) — 38 50

Wove Paper
Vertical Lozenges of Varnish on Face
1910 Unwmk. Perf. 14x14½
201 A16 5pa on 1k org yel (Bl) — 15 22
202 A16 10pa on 2k green (R) — 15 22
203 A17 20pa on 4k car rose (Bl) — 15 22
204 A17 1pi on 10k blue (R) — 15 22
205 A8 5pi on 50k vio & grn (Bl) — 38 60
206 A9 7pi on 70k lt brn & org (Bl) — 42 65

Perf. 13½
207 A10 10pi on 1r pale brn, brn & org (Bl) — 50 75
Nos. 201-207 (7) — 1.90 2.88

Russian Stamps of 1909-12 Surcharged in Black:

20 PARA — No. 208
1½ PIASTRE — Nos. 209-212

1912 Perf. 14x14½
208 A14 20pa on 5k claret — 15 20
209 A11 1½pi on 15k dl vio & blue — 18 24
210 A8 2pi on 20k bl & car — 18 30
211 A11 2½pi on 25k grn & vio — 25 42
  a. Double surcharge — 50.00 50.00
212 A11 3½pi on 35k vio & grn — 38 55
Nos. 208-212 (5) — 1.14 1.71

Russia Nos. 88-91, 93, 95-104 Surcharged:

PARA 5 (c) **PARA 10** (d)
1 PIASTRE (e) **1 PIAS 1½ TRE** (f)
(g) **30 PIASTRES**

1913 Perf. 13½
213 A16(c) 5pa on 1k — 15 15
214 A17(d) 10pa on 2k — 15 15
215 A18(c) 15pa on 3k — 15 15
216 A19(c) 20pa on 4k — 15 16
217 A21(e) 1pi on 10k — 18 20
218 A23(f) 1½pi on 15k — 40 52
219 A24(f) 2pi on 20k — 40 52
220 A25(f) 2½pi on 25k — 55 70
221 A26(f) 3½pi on 35k — 1.40 1.40
222 A27(e) 5pi on 50k — 1.65 1.75
223 A28(f) 7pi on 70k — 6.50 7.00
224 A29(g) 10pi on 1r — 6.50 7.00
225 A30(e) 20pi on 2r — 1.40 1.40
226 A31(g) 30pi on 3r — 2.00 2.00
227 A32(e) 50pi on 5r — 57.50 62.50
Nos. 213-227 (15) — 79.08 85.60

Romanov dynasty tercentenary.
Forgeries exist of overprint on No. 227.

Russia Nos. 75, 71, 72 Surcharged:

15 PARA (h) **PIAS 50 TRES** (i)

Perf. 14x14½
Wove Paper
228 A14(h) 15pa on 3k — 15 15

Perf. 13, 13½
230 A13(i) 50pi on 5r — 4.50 10.00

Vertically Laid Paper
Wmk. Wavy Lines (168)
231 A13(i) 100pi on 10r — 9.00 20.00
  a. Double surcharge — 24.00 40.00

No. 228 has lozenges of varnish on face but No. 230 has not.

Wrangel Issues

For the Posts of Gen. Peter Wrangel's army and civilian refugees from South Russia, interned in Turkey, Serbia, etc.

Very few of the Wrangel overprints were actually sold to the public, and many of the covers were made up later with the original cancels. Reprints abound. Values probably are based on sales of reprints in most cases.

ПОЧТА
РУССКОИ
АРМІИ
1.000
РУБЛЕЙ

Russian Stamps of 1902-18 Surcharged in Blue, Red or Black

On Russia Nos. 69-70
Vertically Laid Paper
1921 Wmk. 168 Perf. 13½
232 A12 10,000r on 3.50r — 8.25 8.25
233 A12 10,000r on 7r — 6.50 6.50
234 A12 20,000r on 3.50r — 13.00 13.00
235 A12 20,000r on 7r — 6.50 6.50

On Russia Nos. 71-86, 87a, 117-118, 137-138
Wove Paper
Perf. 14x14½, 13½
Unwmk.
236 A14 1000r on 1k — 32 32
237 A14 1000r on 2k (R) — 32 32
237A A14 1000r on 2k (Bk) — 4.50 4.50
238 A14 1000r on 3k — 15 15
  a. Inverted surcharge — 65 65
239 A15 1000r on 4k — 15 15
  a. Inverted surcharge — 65 65
240 A14 1000r on 5k — 15 15
  a. Inverted surcharge — 65 65
241 A14 1000r on 7k — 15 15
  a. Inverted surcharge — 65 65
242 A15 1000r on 10k — 15 15
  a. Inverted surcharge — 65 65
243 A14 1000r on 10k on 7k — 15 15
244 A14 5000r on 3k — 15 15
245 A11 5000r on 14k — 1.00 1.00
246 A11 5000r on 15k — 15 15
  a. "PYCCKIN" — 2.00 2.00
247 A8 5000r on 20k — 35 35
  a. "PYCCKIN" — 2.00 2.00
248 A11 5000r on 20k on 14k — 35 35
249 A11 5000r on 25k — 15 15
250 A11 5000r on 35k — 15 15
  a. Inverted surcharge — 65 65
  b. New value omitted
251 A8 5000r on 50k — 15 15
  a. Inverted surcharge
252 A11 5000r on 70k — 15 15
  a. Inverted surcharge — 1.00 1.00
253 A9 10,000r on 1r (Bl) — 15 15
254 A9 10,000r on 1r (Bk) — 80 80
255 A13 10,000r on 3.50r — 32 32
256 A13 10,000r on 5r — 4.75 4.75
257 A13 10,000r on 10r — 40 40
258 A9 20,000r on 1r — 25 25
259 A12 20,000r on 3.50r — 25 25
  a. Inverted surcharge — 3.25 3.25
  b. New value omitted — 27.50 27.50
260 A12 20,000r on 7r — 9.50 9.50
261 A13 20,000r on 10r — 20 20
Nos. 236-261 (27) — 25.26 25.31

On Russia No. 104
261A A32 20,000r on 5r

On Russia Nos. 119-123, 125-135
Imperf
262 A14 1000r on 1k — 22 25
263 A14 1000r on 2k (R) — 22 25
263A A14 1000r on 2k (Bk) — 25 32
264 A14 1000r on 3k — 22 25
265 A15 1000r on 4k — 6.50 6.50
266 A14 1000r on 5k — 22 25
267 A14 5000r on 3k — 22 25
268 A14 5000r on 15k — 22 30
268A A8 5000r on 20k — 10.00
268B A11 5000r on 25k — 10.00
269 A11 5000r on 35k — 50 52
270 A8 5000r on 50k — 50 52
271 A11 5000r on 70k — 20 22
272 A9 10,000r on 1r (Bl) — 15 15
  a. Inverted surcharge — 1.00 65

273 A9 10,000r on 1r (Bk) — 22 25
274 A12 10,000r on 3.50r — 22 25
275 A13 10,000r on 5r — 85 1.00
276 A13 10,000r on 7r — 5.25 5.25
276A A13 10,000r on 10r — 32.50
277 A9 20,000r on 1r (Bl) — 15 15
  a. Inverted surcharge — 1.00 1.00
278 A9 20,000r on 1r (Bk) — 22 25
279 A12 20,000r on 3.50r — 85 1.00
280 A12 20,000r on 5r — 16 20
281 A12 20,000r on 7r — 4.00 4.00
281A A13 20,000r on 10r — 32.50
Nos. 262-268,269-276,277-281 (21) — 21.40 22.18

A18   A19

On Postal Savings Stamps
Perf. 14½x15
Wmk. 171
282 A18 10,000r on 1k red, buff — 16 20
283 A19 10,000r on 5k grn, buff — 15 15
  a. Inverted surcharge — 2.75
284 A19 10,000r on 10k brn, buff — 15 15
  a. Inverted surcharge — 2.75
Set value — 26 30

On Stamps of Russian Offices in Turkey
On No. 38-39
Vertically Laid Paper
Wmk. Wavy Lines (168)
284B A11 20,000r on 35pi on 3.50r
284C A11 20,000r on 70pi on 7r

On Nos. 200-207
Vertically Laid Paper
284D A15 1000r on 20pa on 5k — 1.10 1.10

Wove Paper
Unwmk.
285 A16 1000r on 5pa on 1k — 35 35
286 A16 1000r on 10pa on 2k — 35 35
287 A17 1000r on 20pa on 4k — 28 28
288 A17 1000r on 1pi on 10k — 35 35
289 A8 5000r on 5pi on 50k — 38 38
290 A9 5000r on 7pi on 70k — 38 38
291 A10 10,000r on 10pi on 1r — 1.50 1.50
  a. Inverted surcharge — 4.75 4.75
  b. Pair, one without surcharge — 4.75 4.75
292 A10 20,000r on 10pi on 1r — 28 28
  a. Inverted surcharge — 4.75 4.75
  b. Pair, one without surcharge — 4.75 4.75
Nos. 284D-292 (9) — 4.97 4.97

On Nos. 208-212
293 A14 1000r on 20pa on 5k — 38 38
294 A11 5000r on 1½pi on 15k — 38 38
295 A8 5000r on 2pi on 20k — 38 38
296 A11 5000r on 2½pi on 25k — 38 38
297 A11 5000r on 3½pi on 35k — 48 48
Nos. 293-297 (5) — 2.00 2.00

On Nos. 228, 230-231
298 A14 1000r on 15pa on 3k — 28 28
299 A13 10,000r on 50pi on 5r — 8.50 8.50
300 A13 10,000r on 100pi on 10r — 10.50 10.50
301 A13 20,000r on 50pi on 5r — 28 28
302 A13 20,000r on 100pi on 10r — 10.50 10.50
Nos. 298-302 (5) — 30.06 30.06

On Stamps of South Russia
Denikin Issue
Imperf
303 A5 5000r on 5k org — 15 15
  a. Inverted surcharge
304 A5 5000r on 10k green — 15 15
305 A5 5000r on 15k red — 15 15
306 A5 5000r on 35k lt bl — 15 15
307 A5 5000r on 70k dk blue — 15 15
307A A5 10,000r on 70k dk blue — 5.25 5.25
308 A6 10,000r on 1r brn & red — 16 20
309 A6 10,000r on 2r gray vio & yel — 25 28
  a. Inverted surcharge — 1.25 1.25
310 A6 10,000r on 3r dull rose & grn — 45 50
311 A6 10,000r on 5r slate & vio — 50 50
312 A6 10,000r on 7r gray grn & rose — 10.00 10.00
313 A6 10,000r on 10r red & gray — 45 50
314 A6 20,000r on 1r brn & red — 15 15
315 A6 20,000r on 2r gray vio & yel — 3.25 3.25
  a. Inverted surcharge — 5.00 5.00
315B A6 20,000r on 2r gray vio & yel (Bk) — 20 22
316 A6 20,000r on 3r dull rose & grn (Bl) — 5.25 5.25
316A A6 20,000r on 3r dull rose & grn (Bk) — 2.75 2.75
317 A6 20,000r on 5r slate & vio — 20 22

318	A6	20,000r on 7r gray grn & rose	6.50 6.50
319	A6	20,000r on 10r red & gray	20 22
		Nos. 303-319 (20)	36.31 36.59

Trident Stamps of Ukraine Surcharged in Blue, Red, Black or Brown

1921 *Perf. 14, 14½x15*

320	A14	10,000r on 1k org	15 15
321	A14	10,000r on 2k grn	65 85
322	A14	10,000r on 3k red	15 15
a.		Inverted surcharge	1.25 1.25
323	A15	10,000r on 4k car	15 15
324	A14	10,000r on 5k cl	20 22
325	A14	10,000r on 7k lt bl	15 15
a.		Inverted surcharge	1.25 1.25
326	A15	10,000r on 10k dk bl	15 15
a.		Inverted surcharge	1.25 1.25
327	A14	10,000r on 10k on 7k lt bl	15 15
a.		Inverted surcharge	1.25 1.25
328	A8	20,000r on 20k bl & car (Br)	15 15
a.		Inverted surcharge	1.25 1.25
329	A8	20,000r on 20k bl & car (Bk)	15 16
a.		Inverted surcharge	1.25 1.25
330	A11	20,000r on 20k on 14k bl & rose	15 20
331	A11	20,000r on 35k red brn & grn	10.00 10.00
332	A8	20,000r on 50k brn vio & grn	15 15
a.		Inverted surcharge	1.25 1.25
		Nos. 320-332 (13)	12.35 12.63

Imperf

333	A14	10,000r on 1k org	15 15
a.		Inverted surcharge	1.65
334	A14	10,000r on 2k grn	32 32
335	A14	10,000r on 3k red	15 15
336	A8	20,000r on 20k bl & car	18 18
337	A11	20,000r on 35k red brn & grn	4.00 4.00
338	A8	20,000r on 50k brn vio & grn	32 32
		Nos. 333-338 (6)	5.12 5.12

There are several varieties of the trident surcharge on Nos. 320 to 338.

Same Surcharge on Russian Stamps On Stamps of 1909-18
Perf. 14x14½

338A	A14	10,000r on 1k dl org yel	45 25
339	A14	10,000r on 2k dl grn	45 25
340	A14	10,000r on 3k car	15 15
341	A15	10,000r on 4k car	15 15
342	A14	10,000r on 5k dk cl	15 15
343	A14	10,000r on 7k blue	18 15
344	A15	10,000r on 10k dk bl	45 30
344A	A14	10,000r on 10k on 7k bl	90 55
344B	A11	20,000r on 14k dk bl & car	5.00 2.75
345	A11	20,000r on 15k red brn & dp bl	18 15
346	A8	20,000r on 20k dl bl & dk car	15 15
347	A11	20,000r on 20k on 14k dk bl & car	90 55
348	A11	20,000r on 35k red brn & grn	35 22
349	A8	20,000r on 50k brn vio & grn	35 22
349A	A11	20,000r on 70k brn & red org	45 32
		Nos. 338A-349A (15)	10.09 6.24

On Stamps of 1917-18
Imperf

350	A14	10,000r on 1k org	24 20
351	A14	10,000r on 2k gray grn	24 20
352	A14	10,000r on 3k red	24 20
353	A15	10,000r on 4k car	7.75 5.25
354	A14	10,000r on 5k claret	24 20
355	A11	20,000r on 15k red brn & dp bl	24 20
356	A8	20,000r on 50k brn vio & grn	70 55
357	A11	20,000r on 70k brn & org	35 32
		Nos. 350-357 (8)	10.00 7.12

Same Surcharge on Stamps of Russian Offices in Turkey
On Nos. 40-45
Perf. 14½x15

358	A12	10,000r on 5pa on 1k	2.50 1.65
359	A12	10,000r on 10pa on 2k	2.50 1.65
360	A12	10,000r on 20pa on 4k	2.50 1.65
361	A12	10,000r on 1pi on 10k	2.50 1.65
362	A12	20,000r on 5pi on 50k	2.50 1.65
363	A12	20,000r on 7pi on 70k	2.50 1.65
		Nos. 358-363 (6)	15.00 9.90

On Nos. 201-206

364	A16	10,000r on 5pa on 1k	32 32
365	A16	10,000r on 10pa on 2k	32 32
366	A17	10,000r on 20pa on 4k	32 32
367	A17	10,000r on 1pi on 10k	32 32
368	A8	20,000r on 5pi on 50k	32 32
369	A9	20,000r on 7pi on 70k	32 32
		Nos. 364-369 (6)	1.92 1.92

On Nos. 228, 208-212, Stamps of 1912-13

370	A14	10,000r on 15pa on 3k	20 20
371	A14	10,000r on 20pa on 5k	32 32
372	A11	20,000r on 1½pi on 15k	32 32
373	A8	20,000r on 2pi on 20k	40
374	A11	20,000r on 2½pi on 25k	40
375	A11	20,000r on 3½pi on 35k	40

Same Surcharge on Stamp of South Russia, Crimea Issue

376	A8	20,000r on 5r on 20k bl & car	16.00
		Nos. 370-376 (7)	18.04

RWANDA
(Rwandaise Republic)

LOCATION — Central Africa, adjoining the ex-Belgian Congo, Tanganyika, Uganda and Burundi
GOVT. — Republic
AREA — 10,169 sq. mi.
POP. — 5,650,000 (est. 1984)
CAPITAL — Kigali

Rwanda was established as an independent republic on July 1, 1962. With Burundi, it had been a UN trusteeship territory administered by Belgium.
See Ruanda-Urundi.

100 Centimes = 1 Franc

Catalogue values for all unused stamps in this country are for Never Hinged items.

Watermark

Wmk. 368- JEZ Multiple

Gregoire Kayibanda and Map of Africa — A1

Design: 40c, 1.50fr, 6.50fr, 20fr, Rwanda map spotlighted, "R" omitted.

Perf. 11½
1962, July 1 Unwmk. Photo.

1	A1	10c brown & gray grn	15 15
2	A1	40c brown & rose lil	15 15
3	A1	1fr brown & blue	60 30
4	A1	1.50fr brown & lt brn	15 15
5	A1	3.50fr brown & dp org	15 15
6	A1	6.50fr brown & lt vio bl	18 15
7	A1	10fr brown & citron	20 15
8	A1	20fr brown & rose	42 16
		Set value	1.65 80

Map of Africa and Symbolic Honeycomb A2

Ruanda-Urundi Nos. 151-152 Overprinted with Metallic Frame Obliterating Previous Inscription and Denomination. Black Commemorative Inscription and "REPUBLIQUE RWANDAISE." Surcharged with New Value.

1963, Jan. 28 Unwmk. Perf. 11½

9	A2	3.50fr sil, blk, ultra & red	15 15
10	A2	6.50fr brnz, blk, ultra & red	70 70
11	A2	10fr stl bl, blk, ultra & red	20 20
12	A2	20fr sil, blk, ultra & red	38 38

Rwanda's admission to UN, Sept. 18, 1962.

Stamps of Ruanda-Urundi, 1953, Overprinted

Littonia — A3

Designs as before.

1963, Mar. 21 Unwmk. Perf. 11½
Flowers in Natural Colors; Metallic and Black Overprint

13	A3	25c dk grn & dl org	15 15
14	A3	40c green & salmon	15 15
15	A3	60c bl grn & pink	15 15
16	A3	1.25fr dk green & blue	70 70
17	A3	1.50fr violet & apple grn	55 55
18	A3	2fr on 1.50fr vio & ap grn	80 80
19	A3	4fr on 1.50fr vio & ap grn	80 80
20	A3	5fr dp plum & lt bl grn	80 80
21	A3	7fr dk green & fawn	80 80
22	A3	10fr dp plum & pale ol	80 80
		Nos. 13-22 (10)	5.70 5.70

The overprint consists of silver panels with black lettering. The panels on No. 19 are bluish gray.

Imperforates exist of practically every issue, starting with Nos. 23-26, except Nos. 36, 55-69, 164-169.

Wheat Emblem, Bow, Arrow, Hoe and Billhook A4

1963, July 1 Photo. Perf. 13½

23	A4	2fr brown & green	15 15
24	A4	4fr magenta & ultra	15 15
25	A4	7fr red & gray	15 15
26	A4	10fr olive grn & yel	55 38
		Set value	85 55

FAO "Freedom from Hunger" campaign.
The 20fr leopard and 50fr lion stamps of Ruanda-Urundi, Nos. 149-150, overprinted "Republique Rwandaise" at top and "Contre la Faim" at bottom, were intended to be issued Mar. 21, 1963, but were not placed in use.

Coffee — A5

Designs: 10c, 40c, 4fr, Coffee. 20c, 1fr, 7fr, Bananas. 30c, 2fr, 10fr, Tea.

1963, July 1 Perf. 11½

27	A5	10c violet bl & brn	15 15
28	A5	20c slate & yellow	15 15
29	A5	30c vermilion & grn	15 15
30	A5	40c dp green & brown	15 15
31	A5	1fr maroon & yellow	15 15
32	A5	2fr dk blue & green	65 52
33	A5	4fr red & brown	15 15
34	A5	7fr yellow grn & yellow	16 15
35	A5	10fr violet & green	25 15
		Set value	1.35 1.00

First anniversary of independence.

African Postal Union Issue
Common Design Type
1963, Sept. 8 Unwmk. Perf. 12½

36	CD114	14fr black, ocher & red	55 50

Post Horn and Pigeon — A6

1963, Oct. 25 Photo. Perf. 11½

37	A6	50c ultra & rose	15 15
38	A6	1.50fr brown & blue	50 40
39	A6	3fr dp plum & gray	15 15
40	A6	20fr green & yellow	35 18
		Set value	95 65

Rwanda's admission to the UPU, Apr. 6.

Scales, UN Emblem and Flame — A7

1963, Dec. 10 Unwmk. Perf. 11½

41	A7	5fr crimson	15 15
42	A7	6fr brt purple	42 30
43	A7	10fr brt blue	22 15
		Set value	50

15th anniversary of the Universal Declaration of Human Rights.

Children's Clinic — A8

Designs: 20c, 7fr, Laboratory examination, horiz. 30c, 10fr, Physician examining infant. 40c, 20fr, Litter bearers, horiz.

1963, Dec. Photo.

44	A8	10c yel org, red & brn blk	15 15
45	A8	20c grn, red & brn blk	15 15
46	A8	30c bl, red & brn blk	15 15
47	A8	40c red lil, red & brn	15 15
48	A8	2fr bl grn, red brn & blk	50 42
49	A8	7fr ultra, red & blk	15 15
50	A8	10fr red brn, red & brn blk	20 15
51	A8	20fr dp org, red & brn	40 15
		Set value	1.40 95

Centenary of the International Red Cross.

Map of Rwanda and Woman at Water Pump — A9

1964, May 4 Unwmk. Perf. 11½

52	A9	3fr lt grn, dk brn & ultra	15 15
53	A9	7fr pink, dk brn & ultra	30 18
54	A9	10fr yel, dk brn & ultra	42 30
		Set value	75 52

Souvenir Sheet
Imperf

54A	A9	25fr lilac, bl, brn & blk	2.50 2.50

UN 4th World Meteorological Day, Mar. 23.

Ruanda-Urundi Nos. 138-150, 153
Overprinted "REPUBLIQUE RWANDAISE",
Some Surcharged, in Silver and Black

Buffaloes — A10

Designs: 10c, 20c, 30c, Buffaloes. 40c, 2fr,
Black-and-white colobus (monkey). 50c, 7.50fr,
Impalas. 1fr, Mountain gorilla. 3fr, 4fr, 8fr, African
elephants. 5fr, 10fr, Eland and zebras. 20fr, Leopard. 50fr, Lions. 40c, 1fr and 2fr are vertical.

1964, June 29   Photo.   Perf. 11½
Size: 33x23mm, 23x33mm

55	A10	10c on 20c gray, ap grn & blk	15	15
56	A10	20c blk, gray & ap grn	15	15
57	A10	30c on 1.50fr blk, gray & org	15	15
58	A10	40c mag, blk & gray grn	15	15
59	A10	50c grn, org yel & brn	15	15
60	A10	1fr ultra, blk & brn	15	15
61	A10	2fr grnsh bl, ind & brn	15	15
62	A10	3fr brn, dp car & blk	15	15
63	A10	4fr on 3.50fr on 3fr brn, dp car & blk	24	15
64	A10	5fr brn, dl yel, grn & blk	22	15
65	A10	7.50fr on 6.50fr red, org yel & brn	45	15
66	A10	8fr blue, mag & blk	3.00	2.50
67	A10	10fr brn, dl yel, brt pink & blk	60	15

Size: 45x26½mm

68	A10	20fr hn brn, ocher & blk	1.00	52
69	A10	50fr dp blue & brown	1.65	1.25
		Nos. 55-69 (15)	8.36	
		Set value		5.00

Boy with Crutch
and Gatagara
Home — A11

Basketball — A12

Designs: 40c, 8fr, Girls with sewing machines,
horiz. 4fr, 10fr, Girl on crutches, map of Rwanda
and Gatagara Home.

1964, Nov. 10   Photo.   Perf. 11½

70	A11	10c lilac blk brn	15	15
71	A11	40c blue & blk brn	15	15
72	A11	4fr org red & blk brn	15	15
73	A11	7.50fr yel grn & blk brn	22	18
74	A11	8fr bister & blk brn	1.10	75
75	A11	10fr magenta & blk brn	32	20
		Nos. 70-75 (6)	2.09	
		Set value		1.30

Gatagara Home for handicapped children.

1964, Dec. 8   Litho.   Perf. 13½

Sport: 10c, 4fr, Runner, horiz. 30c, 20fr, High
jump, horiz. 40c, 50fr, Soccer.

Size: 26x38mm

76	A12	10c gray, sl & dk grn	15	15
77	A12	20c pink, sl & rose red	15	15
78	A12	30c lt grn, sl & grn	15	15
79	A12	40c buff, sl & brn	15	15
80	A12	4fr vio gray, sl & vio	15	15
81	A12	5fr pale grn, sl & yel grn	1.50	1.50
82	A12	20fr pale lil, sl & red lil	38	32
83	A12	50fr gray, sl & dk gray	90	75
a.		Souvenir sheet of 4	5.00	5.00
		Set value	3.00	2.80

18th Olympic Games, Tokyo, Oct. 10-25. No.
83a contains 4 stamps (10fr, soccer; 20fr, basketball; 30fr, high jump; 40fr, runner). Size of stamps:
28x38mm.

Quill, Books, Radical
and Retort — A13

Medical
School and
Student with
Microscope
A14

Designs: 30c, 10fr, Scales, hand, staff of Mercury
and globe. 40c, 12fr, View of University.

1965, Feb. 22   Engr.   Perf. 11½

84	A13	10c multicolored	15	15
85	A14	20c multicolored	15	15
86	A13	30c multicolored	15	15
87	A14	40c multicolored	15	15
88	A13	5fr multicolored	15	15
89	A14	7fr multicolored	15	15
90	A13	10fr multicolored	80	70
91	A14	12fr multicolored	22	15
		Set value	1.40	1.15

National University of Rwanda at Butare.

Abraham
Lincoln, Death
Cent. — A15

1965, Apr. 15   Photo.   Perf. 13½

92	A15	10c emerald & dk red	15	15
93	A15	20c red brn & dk bl	15	15
94	A15	30c brt violet & red	15	15
95	A15	40c brt grnsh bl & red	15	15
96	A15	7fr orange brn & pur	16	15
97	A15	40fr black & brt grn	1.65	60
		Set value	2.00	90

Souvenir Sheet

98	A15	50fr red lilac & red	1.90	1.90

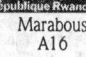

Marabous
A16

Zebras
A17

Designs: 30c, Impalas. 40c, Crowned cranes,
hippopotami and cattle egrets. 1fr, Cape buffalos.
3fr, Cape hunting dogs. 5fr, Yellow baboons. 10fr,
Elephant and map of Rwanda with location of park.
40fr, Anhinga, great anad reed cormorants. 100fr,
Lions.

1965, Apr. 28   Photo.   Perf. 11½
Size: 32x23mm

99	A16	10c multicolored	15	15
100	A17	20c multicolored	15	15
101	A16	30c multicolored	15	15
102	A17	40c multicolored	15	15
103	A16	1fr multicolored	15	15
104	A17	3fr multicolored	15	15
105	A16	5fr multicolored	2.50	90
106	A17	10fr multicolored	16	15

Size: 45x26mm

107	A17	40fr multicolored	65	25
108	A17	100fr multicolored	1.60	20
		Nos. 99-108 (10)	5.81	
		Set value		1.70

Kagera National Park publicity.

Telstar and
ITU Emblem
A18

Design: 40c, 50fr, Syncom satellite. 60fr, old
and new communications equipment.

1965   Unwmk.   Perf. 13½

109	A18	10c red brn, ultra & car	15	15
110	A18	40c violet, emer & yel	15	15
111	A18	4.50fr blk, car & dk bl	1.00	42
112	A18	50fr dk brn, yel grn & brt grn	75	18
		Set value		70

Souvenir Sheet

113	A18	60fr blk brn, org brn & bl	1.90	1.90

ITU, centenary. Issue dates: No. 113, July 19.
Others, May 17.

Papilio Bromius
Chrapkowskii
Suffert — A19

Cattle, ICY
Emblem and Map
of Africa — A20

Various butterflies and moths in natural colors.

1965-66   Photo.   Perf. 12½

114	A19	10c black & yellow	15	15
115	A19	15c black & dp org ('66)	15	15
116	A19	20c black & lilac	15	15
117	A19	30c black & red lil	15	15
118	A19	35c dk brn & dk bl ('66)	15	15
119	A19	40c black & Prus bl	15	15
120	A19	1.50fr black & grn ('66)	15	15
121	A19	3fr dk brn & ol grn ('66)	1.40	55
122	A19	4fr black & red brn	80	40
123	A19	10fr black & pur ('66)	20	15
124	A19	50fr black & brown	60	22
125	A19	100fr dk brn & bl ('66)	1.60	55
		Set value	4.90	2.10

The 15c, 20c, 40c, 1.50fr, 10fr and 50fr are
horizontal.

1965, Oct. 25   Unwmk.   Perf. 12

ICY Emblem, Map of Africa and: 40c, Tree and
lake. 4.50fr, Gazelle under tree. 45fr, Mount
Ruwenzori.

126	A20	10c olive bis & bl grn	15	15
127	A20	40c lt ultra, red brn & grn	15	15
128	A20	4.50fr brt grn, red & brn	80	40
129	A20	45fr rose claret	70	25
		Set value		75

John F.
Kennedy
(1917-1963)
A21

1965, Nov. 22   Photo.   Perf. 11½

130	A21	10c brt grn & dk brn	15	15
131	A21	40c brt pink & dk brn	15	15
132	A21	50c dk blue & dk brn	15	15
133	A21	1fr gray ol & dk brn	15	15
134	A21	8fr violet & dk brn	1.40	1.00
135	A21	50fr gray & dk brn	1.00	80
		Set value	2.50	2.00

Souvenir Sheet

136		Sheet of 2	6.75	6.75
a.	A21	40fr orange & dark brown	3.00	3.00
b.	A21	60fr ultra & dark brown	3.00	3.00

Madonna — A22

1965, Dec. 20

137	A22	10c gold & dk green	15	15
138	A22	40c gold & dk brn red	15	15
139	A22	50c gold & dk blue	15	15
140	A22	4fr gold & slate	50	45
141	A22	6fr gold & violet	15	15
142	A22	30fr gold & dk brown	42	40
		Set value	1.10	1.00

Christmas.

Father Joseph Damien and Lepers — A23

Designs: 40c, 45fr, Dr. Albert Schweitzer and
Hospital, Lambarene.

1966, Jan. 31   Perf. 11½

143	A23	10c ultra & red brn	15	15
144	A23	40c dk red & vio bl	15	15
145	A23	4.50fr slate & brt grn	22	15
146	A23	45fr dk & hn brn	1.50	80
		Set value		95

Issued for World Leprosy Day.

Pope Paul VI, St. Peter's, UN Headquarters
and Statue of Liberty — A24

Design: 40c, 50fr, Pope Paul VI, Papal arms and
UN emblem.

1966, Feb. 28   Photo.   Perf. 12

147	A24	10c henna brn & slate	15	15
148	A24	40c brt blue & slate	15	15
149	A24	4.50fr lilac & slate	1.10	1.10
150	A24	50fr brt green & slate	90	35

Visit of Pope Paul VI to the UN, New York City,
Oct. 4, 1965.

Globe Thistle — A25

Flowers: 20c, Blood lily. 30c, Everlasting. 40c,
Natal plum. 1fr, Tulip tree. 3fr, Rendle orchid. 5fr,
Aloe. 10fr, Ammocharis tinneana. 40fr, Coral tree.
100fr, Caper. (20c, 40c, 1fr, 3fr, 5fr, 10fr are
vertical).

1966, Mar. 14   Perf. 11½
Granite Paper

151	A25	10c lt blue & multi	15	15
152	A25	20c orange & multi	15	15
153	A25	30c car rose & multi	15	15
154	A25	40c green & multi	15	15
155	A25	1fr multicolored	15	15
156	A25	3fr indigo & multi	15	15
157	A25	5fr multicolored	3.00	1.90
158	A25	10fr blue grn & multi	22	15

159	A25	40fr brown & multi	75 38
160	A25	100fr dk bl grn & multi	1.90 1.10
a.		Miniature sheet	4.00 3.00
		Nos. 151-160 (10)	6.77
		Set value	3.75

No. 160a contains one 100fr stamp in changed color, bright blue and multicolored.

Opening of WHO Headquarters, Geneva — A26

1966, May 1   Litho.   Perf. 12½x12

161	A26	2fr lt olive green	15 15
162	A26	3fr vermilion	16 16
163	A26	5fr violet blue	15 15
		Set value	28 28

Soccer — A27

Mother and Child, Planes Dropping Bombs — A28

Designs: 20c, 9fr, Basketball. 30c, 50fr, Volleyball.

1966, May 30   Photo.   Perf. 15x14

164	A27	10c dl grn, ultra & blk	15 15
165	A27	20c crimson, grn & blk	15 15
166	A27	30c bl, brt rose lil & blk	15 15
167	A27	40c yel bis, grn & blk	15 15
168	A27	9fr gray, red lil & blk	16 15
169	A27	50fr rose lil, Prus bl & blk	90 80
		Set value	1.25 1.10

National Youth Sports Program.

1966, June 29   Perf. 13½
Design and Inscription Black and Red

170	A28	20c rose lilac	15 15
171	A28	30c yellow green	15 15
172	A28	50c lt ultra	15 15
173	A28	6fr yellow	15 15
174	A28	15fr blue green	55 20
175	A28	18fr lilac	50 35
		Set value	1.25 75

Campaign against nuclear weapons.

A29   A30

Global soccer ball.

1966, July   Perf. 11½

176	A29	20c org & indigo	15 15
177	A29	30c lilac & indigo	15 15
178	A29	50c brt grn & indigo	15 15
179	A29	6fr brt rose & indigo	22 15
180	A29	12fr lt vio brn & ind	65 25
181	A29	25fr ultra & indigo	80 50
		Set value	1.80 95

World Soccer Cup Championship, Wembley, England, July 11-30.

1966, Oct. 24   Engr.   Perf. 14

Designs: 10c, Mikeno Volcano and crested shrike, horiz. 40c, Nyamilanga Falls. 4.50fr, Gahinga and Muhabura volcanoes and lobelias, horiz. 55fr, Rusumu Falls.

182	A30	10c green	15 15
183	A30	40c brown carmine	15 15
184	A30	4.50fr violet blue	45 35
185	A30	55fr red lilac	50 35
		Set value	1.00 75

UNESCO Emblem, African Artifacts and Musical Clef — A31

UNESCO 20th Anniv.: 30c, 10fr, Hands holding primer showing giraffe and zebra. 50c, 15fr, Atom symbol and power drill. 1fr, 50fr, Submerged sphinxes and sailboat.

1966, Nov. 4   Photo.   Perf. 12

186	A31	20c brt rose & dk bl	15 15
187	A31	30c grnsh blue & blk	15 15
188	A31	50c ocher & blk	15 15
189	A31	1fr violet & blk	15 15
190	A31	5fr yellow grn & blk	15 15
191	A31	10fr brown & blk	16 16
192	A31	15fr red lilac & dk bl	50 30
193	A31	50fr dull bl & blk	55 45
		Set value	1.45 1.15

Rock Python — A32

Snakes: 20c, 20fr, Jameson's mamba. 30c, 3fr, Rock python. 50c, Gabon viper. 1fr, Black-lipped spitting cobra. 5fr, African sand snake. 70fr, Egg-eating snake. (20c, 50c, 3fr and 20fr are horizontal.)

1967, Jan. 30   Photo.   Perf. 11½

194	A32	20c red & black	15 15
195	A32	30c bl, dk brn & yel	15 15
196	A32	50c yel grn & multi	15 15
197	A32	1fr lt lil, blk & bis	15 15
198	A32	3fr lt vio, dk brn & yel	15 15
199	A32	5fr yellow & multi	16 15
200	A32	20fr pale pink & multi	80 60
201	A32	70fr pale vio, brn & blk	1.20 65
		Set value	2.40 1.60

Ntaruka Hydroelectric Station and Tea Flowers — A33

Designs: 30c, 25fr, Transformer and chrysanthemums (pyrethrum). 50c, 50fr, Sluice and coffee.

1967, Mar. 6   Photo.   Perf. 13½

202	A33	20c maroon & dp bl	15 15
203	A33	30c black & red brn	15 15
204	A33	50c brown & violet	15 15
205	A33	4fr dk grn & dp plum	15 15
206	A33	25fr violet & sl grn	30 30
207	A33	50fr dk blue & brn	90 90
		Set value	1.35 1.35

Ntaruka Hydroelectric Station.

Souvenir Sheets

Cogwheels — A34

1967, Apr. 15   Engr.   Perf. 11½

208	A34	100fr dk red brown	2.00 2.00
209	A34	100fr brt rose lilac	2.00 2.00

7th "Europa" Phil. Exhib. and the Philatelic Salon of African States, Naples, Apr. 8-16.

Souvenir Sheet

African Dancers and EXPO '67 Emblem — A35

1967, Apr. 28   Perf. 11½

210	A35	180fr dark purple	3.00 3.00

EXPO '67, Intl. Exhib., Montreal, Apr. 28-Oct. 27.
A similar imperf. sheet has the stamp in violet brown.

St. Martin, by Van Dyck and Caritas Emblem — A36

Paintings: 40c, 15fr, Rebecca at the Well, by Murillo, horiz. 60c, 18fr, St. Christopher, by Dierick Bouts. 80c, 26fr, Job and his Friends, by Il Calabrese (Mattia Preti), horiz.

Perf. 13x11, 11x13
1967, May 8   Photo.
Black Inscription on Gold Panel

211	A36	20c dark purple	15 15
212	A36	40c blue green	15 15
213	A36	60c rose carmine	15 15
214	A36	80c deep blue	15 15
215	A36	9fr redsh brown	75 42
216	A36	15fr orange ver	26 15
217	A36	18fr dk olive grn	32 15
218	A36	26fr dk carmine rose	42 30
		Set value	1.90 1.15

Issued to publicize the work of Caritas-Rwanda, Catholic welfare organization.

Round Table Emblem and Zebra — A37

Round Table Emblem and: 40c, Elephant. 60c, Cape buffalo. 80c, Antelope. 18fr, Wheat. 100fr, Palm tree.

1967, July 31   Photo.   Perf. 14

219	A37	20c gold & multi	15 15
220	A37	40c gold & multi	15 15
221	A37	60c gold & multi	15 15
222	A37	80c gold & multi	15 15
223	A37	18fr gold & multi	28 16
224	A37	100fr gold & multi	1.60 65
		Set value	2.00 1.00

Rwanda Table No. 9 of Kigali, a member of the Intl. Round Tables Assoc.

EXPO '67 Emblem, Africa Place and Dancers and Drummers — A38

EXPO '67 Emblem, Africa Place and: 30c, 3fr, Drum and vessels. 50c, 40fr, Two dancers. 1fr, 34fr, Spears, shields and bow.

1967, Aug. 10   Perf. 12

225	A38	20c brt blue & sepia	15 15
226	A38	30c brt rose lil & sepia	15 15
227	A38	50c orange & sepia	15 15
228	A38	1fr green & sepia	15 15
229	A38	3fr violet & sepia	15 15
230	A38	15fr emerald & sepia	16 15
231	A38	34fr rose red & sepia	50 35
232	A38	40fr grnsh bl & sepia	65 38
		Set value	1.50 1.00

Lions Emblem, Globe and Zebra — A39

1967, Oct. 16   Photo.   Perf. 13½

233	A39	20c lilac, bl & blk	15 15
234	A39	80c lt grn, bl & blk	15 15
235	A39	1fr rose car, bl & blk	15 15
236	A39	8fr bister, bl & blk	15 15
237	A39	10fr ultra, bl & blk	15 15
238	A39	50fr yel grn, bl & blk	90 65
		Set value	1.30 1.00

50th anniversary of Lions International.

Woodland Kingfisher — A40

Birds: 20c, Red bishop, vert. 60c, Red-billed quelea, vert. 80c, Double-toothed barbet. 2fr, Pin-tailed whydah, vert. 3fr, Solitary cuckoo. 18fr, Green wood hoopoe, vert. 25fr, Blue-collared bee-eater. 80fr, Regal sunbird, vert. 100fr, Red-shouldered widowbird.

1967, Dec. 18   *Perf. 11½*
239 A40 20c multicolored   15 15
240 A40 40c multicolored   15 15
241 A40 60c multicolored   15 15
242 A40 80c multicolored   15 15
243 A40 2fr multicolored   15 15
244 A40 3fr multicolored   15 15
245 A40 18fr multicolored   40 15
246 A40 25fr multicolored   45 16
247 A40 80fr multicolored   1.20 60
248 A40 100fr multicolored   1.75 70
         Set value   4.10 1.80

Souvenir Sheet

X° JEUX OLYMPIQUES D'HIVER

GRENOBLE 1968

Ski Jump, Speed Skating — A41

1968, Feb. 12 Photo.   Perf. 11½
249   Sheet of 2   2.00 2.00
 a.   A41 50fr bl, blk & grn (skier)   75 75
 b.   A41 50fr grn, blk & bl (skater) 75 75
 c.   Souv. sheet of 2, #249a at right 2.00 2.00

10th Winter Olympic Games, Grenoble, France, Feb. 6-18.

Runner, Mexican Sculpture and Architecture — A42

Sport and Mexican Art: 40c, Hammer throw, pyramid and animal head. 60c, Hurdler and sculptures. 80c, Javelin and sculptures.

1968, May 27   Photo.   Perf. 11½
250 A42 20c ultra & multi   15 15
251 A42 40c multicolored   15 15
252 A42 60c lilac & multi   15 15
253 A42 80c orange & multi   20 20
         Set value   50 50

19th Olympic Games, Mexico City, Oct. 12-27.

Souvenir Sheet

XIX JEUX OLYMPIQUES

REPUBLIQUE RWANDAISE

19th Olympic Games, Mexico City — A43

Designs: a, 8fr, Soccer. b, 10fr, Mexican horseman and cactus. c, 12fr, Field hockey. d, 18fr, Cathedral, Mexico City. e, 20fr, Boxing. f, 30fr, Modern buildings, musical instruments and vase.

1967, May 27   Photo.   Perf. 11½
         Granite Paper
254 A43   Sheet of 6, #a.-f.   2.75 2.75

Three sets of circular gold "medal" overprints with black inscriptions were applied to the six stamps of No. 254 to honor 18 Olympic winners. Issued Dec. 12, 1968. Value $10.

Souvenir Sheet

Martin Luther King, Jr. — A44

1968, July 29   Engr.   Perf. 13½
255 A44 100fr sepia   2.25 1.75

Rev. Dr. Martin Luther King, Jr. (1929-1968), American civil rights leader. See No. 406.

Diaphant Orchid — A45

Flowers: 40c, Pharaoh's scepter. 60c, Flower of traveler's-tree. 80c, Costus afer. 2fr, Banana tree flower. 3fr, Flower and fruit of papaw tree. 18fr, Clerodendron. 25fr, Sweet potato flowers. 80fr, Baobab tree flower. 100fr, Passion flower.

1968, Sept. 9   Litho.   Perf. 13
256 A45 20c lilac & multi   15 15
257 A45 40c multicolored   15 15
258 A45 60c bl grn & multi   15 15
259 A45 80c multicolored   15 15
260 A45 2fr brt yellow & multi   15 15
261 A45 3fr multicolored   15 15
262 A45 18fr multicolored   25 15
263 A45 25fr gray & multi   35 16
264 A45 80fr multicolored   1.40 55
265 A45 100fr multicolored   1.60 70
         Set value   3.90 1.80

Equestrian and "Mexico 1968" — A46

Designs: 40c, Judo and "Tokyo 1964." 60c, Fencing and "Rome 1960." 80c, High jump and "Berlin 1936." 38fr, Women's diving and "London 1908 and 1948." 60fr, Weight lifting and "Paris 1900 and 1924."

1968, Oct. 24   Litho.   Perf. 14x13
266 A46 20c orange & sepia   15 15
267 A46 40c grnsh bl & sepia   15 15
268 A46 60c car rose & sepia   15 15
269 A46 80c ultra & sepia   15 15
270 A46 38fr red & sepia   55 25
271 A46 60fr emerald & sepia   1.00 50
         Set value   1.70 90

19th Olympic Games, Mexico City, Oct. 12-27.

Tuareg, Algeria — A47

African National Costumes: 40c, Musicians, Upper Volta. 60c, Senegalese women. 70c, Girls of Rwanda going to market. 8fr, Young married couple from Morocco. 20fr, Nigerian officials in state dress.

40fr, Man and women from Zambia. 50fr, Man and woman from Kenya.

1968, Nov. 4   Litho.   Perf. 13
272 A47 30c multicolored   15 15
273 A47 40c multicolored   15 15
274 A47 60c multicolored   15 15
275 A47 70c multicolored   15 15
276 A47 8fr multicolored   15 15
277 A47 20fr multicolored   30 16
278 A47 40fr multicolored   60 35
279 A47 50fr multicolored   70 50
         Set value   1.85 1.25

Souvenir Sheet

Nativity, by Giorgione — A48

1968, Dec. 16   Engr.   Perf. 11½
280 A48 100fr green   2.50 2.50

Christmas.
See Nos. 309, 389, 422, 494, 564, 611, 713, 787, 848, 894.

Singing Boy, by Frans Hals — A49

Paintings and Music: 20c, Angels' Concert, by van Eyck. 40c, Angels' Concert, by Matthias Grunewald. 60c, No. 283a, Singing Boy, by Frans Hals. 80c, Lute Player, by Gerard Terborch. 2fr, The Fifer, by Manet. 6fr, No. 286a, Young Girls at the Piano, by Renoir.

1969, Mar. 31   Photo.   Perf. 13
281 A49 20c gold & multi   15 15
282 A49 40c gold & multi   15 15
283 A49 60c gold & multi   15 15
 a.   Souvenir sheet, 75fr   1.40 1.40
284 A49 80c gold & multi   15 15
285 A49 2fr gold & multi   15 15
286 A49 6fr gold & multi   15 15
 a.   Souvenir sheet, 75fr   1.40 1.40
         Set value, #281-286,
         C6-C7   3.00 2.25

Tuareg Men — A50

African Headdresses: 40c, Ovambo woman, South West Africa. 60c, Guinean man and Congolese woman. 80c, Dagger dancer, Guinean forest area. 8fr, Mohammedan Nigerians. 20fr, Luba dancer, Kabondo, Congo. 40fr, Senegalese and Gambian women. 80fr, Rwanda dancer.

1969, May 29   Litho.   Perf. 13
287 A50 20c multicolored   15 15
288 A50 40c multicolored   15 15
289 A50 60c multicolored   15 15
290 A50 80c multicolored   15 15
291 A50 8fr multicolored   15 15

292 A50 20fr multicolored   30 16
293 A50 40fr multicolored   65 35
294 A50 80fr multicolored   1.40 60
         Set value   2.65 1.35

See #398-405. For overprints see #550-557.

The Moneylender and his Wife, by Quentin Massys — A51

Design: 70fr, The Moneylender and his Wife, by Marinus van Reymerswaele.

1969, Sept. 10 Photo.   Perf. 13
295 A51 30fr silver & multi   60 42
296 A51 70fr gold & multi   1.40 1.00

5th anniv. of the African Development Bank. Printed in sheets of 20 stamps and 20 labels with commemorative inscription.
For overprints see Nos. 612-613.

Souvenir Sheet

First Man on the Moon — A52

1969, Oct. 9   Engr.   Perf. 11½
297 A52 100fr blue gray   1.60 1.60

See note after Mali No. C80. See No. 407.

Camomile and   Worker with
Health   Pickaxe and
Emblem — A53   Flag — A54

Medicinal Plants and Health Emblem: 40c, Aloe. 60c, Cola. 80c, Coca. 3fr, Hagenia abissinica. 75fr, Cassia. 80fr, Cinchona. 100fr, Tephrosia.

1969, Nov. 24   Photo.   Perf. 13
         Flowers in Natural Colors
298 A53 20c gold, blue & blk   15 15
299 A53 40c gold, yel grn & blk   15 15
300 A53 60c gold, pink & blk   15 15
301 A53 80c gold, green & blk   15 15
302 A53 3fr gold, orange & blk   15 15
303 A53 75fr gold, yel & blk   1.40 55

304	A53	80fr gold, lilac & blk		1.50	65
305	A53	100fr gold, dl yel & blk		1.75	80
		Nos. 298-305 (8)		5.40	
		Set value			2.20

For overprints & surcharge see #534-539, B1.

1969, Nov.   **Photo.**   *Perf. 11½*

306	A54	6fr brt pink & multi		15	15
307	A54	18fr ultra & multi		38	20
308	A54	40fr brown & multi		70	42

10th anniversary of independence.
For overprints see Nos. 608-610.

Christmas Type of 1968
Souvenir Sheet

Design: "Holy Night" (detail), by Correggio.

1969, Dec. 15   **Engr.**   *Perf. 11½*

309	A48	100fr ultra		2.75	2.75

The Cook, by
Pierre
Aertsen — A55

Paintings: 20c, Quarry Worker, by Oscar Bonnevalle, horiz. 40c, The Plower, by Peter Brueghel, horiz 60c, Fisherman, by Constantin Meunier. 80c, Slipway, Ostende, by Jean van Noten, horiz. 10fr, The Forge of Vulcan, by Velasquez, horiz. 50fr, "Hiercheuse" (woman shoveling coal), by Meunier. 70fr, Miner, by Pierre Paulus.

1969, Dec. 22   **Photo.**   *Perf. 13½*

310	A55	20c gold & multi		15	15
311	A55	40c gold & multi		15	15
312	A55	60c gold & multi		15	15
313	A55	80c gold & multi		15	15
314	A55	8fr gold & multi		20	15
315	A55	10fr gold & multi		22	15
316	A55	50fr gold & multi		1.00	55
317	A55	70fr gold & multi		1.40	70
		Set value		3.00	1.60

ILO, 50th anniversary.

Napoleon Crossing
St. Bernard, by
Jacques L.
David — A56

Paintings of Napoleon Bonaparte (1769-1821): 40c, Decorating Soldier before Tilsit, by Jean Baptiste Debret. 60c, Addressing Troops at Augsburg, by Claude Gautherot. 80c, First Consul, by Jean Auguste Ingres. 8fr, Battle of Marengo, by Jacques Auguste Pajou. 20fr, Napoleon Meeting Emperor Francis II, by Antoine Jean Gros. 40fr, Gen. Bonaparte at Arcole, by Gros. 80fr Coronation, by David.

1969, Dec. 29

318	A56	20c gold & multi		15	15
319	A56	40c gold & multi		15	15
320	A56	60c gold & multi		15	15
321	A56	80c gold & multi		15	15
322	A56	8fr gold & multi		24	15
323	A56	20fr gold & multi		50	28
324	A56	40fr gold & multi		1.00	55
325	A56	80fr gold & multi		2.00	1.10
		Nos. 318-325 (8)		4.34	
		Set value			2.20

Epsom Derby, by Gericault — A57

Paintings of Horses: 40c, Horses Emerging from the Sea, by Delacroix. 60c, Charles V at Muhlberg, by Titian, vert. 80c, Amateur Jockeys, by Edgar Degas, 8fr, Horsemen at Rest, by Philips Wouwerman. 20fr, Imperial Guards Officer, by Géricault, vert. 40fr, Friends of the Desert, by Oscar Bonnevalle. 80fr, Two Horses (detail from the Prodigal Son), by Rubens.

1970, Mar. 31   **Photo.**   *Perf. 13½*

326	A57	20c gold & multi		15	15
327	A57	40c gold & multi		15	15
328	A57	60c gold & multi		15	15
329	A57	80c gold & multi		15	15
330	A57	8fr gold & multi		15	15
331	A57	20fr gold & multi		40	16
332	A57	40fr gold & multi		70	35
333	A57	80fr gold & multi		1.40	65
		Set value		2.80	1.40

Souvenir Sheet

Fleet in Bay of Naples, by Peter Brueghel,
the Elder — A58

1970, May 2   **Engr.**   *Perf. 11½*

334	A58	100fr brt rose lilac		2.00	2.00

10th Europa Phil. Exhib., Naples, Italy, May 2-10. Copies of No. 334 were trimmed to 68x58mm and overprinted in silver or gold "NAPLES 1973" on the stamp, and "Salon Philatelique des Etats Africains / Exposition du Timbre-Poste Europa" in October, 1973.

Soccer and
Mexican
Decorations — A59

Tharaka Meru
Woman, East
Africa — A60

Designs: Various scenes from soccer game and pre-Columbian decorations.

1970, June 15   **Photo.**   *Perf. 13*

335	A59	20c gold & multi		15	15
336	A59	30c gold & multi		15	15
337	A59	50c gold & multi		15	15
338	A59	1fr gold & multi		15	15
339	A59	6fr gold & multi		15	15
340	A59	18fr gold & multi		40	16
341	A59	30fr gold & multi		60	40
342	A59	90fr gold & multi		1.75	70
		Set value			

9th World Soccer Championships for the Jules Rimet Cup, Mexico City, May 30-June 21.

1970, June 1   **Litho.**

African National Costumes: 30c, Musician with wooden flute, Niger. 50c, Woman water carrier, Tunisia. 1fr, Ceremonial costumes, North Nigeria.

3fr, Strolling troubadour "Griot," Mali. 5fr, Quipongos women, Angola. 50fr, Man at prayer, Mauritania. 90fr, Sinehatiali dance costumes, Ivory Coast.

343	A60	20c multi		15	15
344	A60	30c multi		15	15
345	A60	50c multi		15	15
346	A60	1fr multi		15	15
347	A60	3fr multi		15	15
348	A60	5fr multi		15	15
349	A60	50fr multi		90	42
350	A60	90fr multi		1.60	70
		Set value		2.75	1.40

For overprints and surcharges see Nos. 693-698, B2-B3.

Flower Arrangement, Peacock, EXPO '70
Emblem — A61

EXPO Emblem and: 30c, Torii and Camellias, by Yukihiko Yasuda. 50c, Kabuki character and Woman Playing Samisen, by Nampu Katayama. 1fr, Tower of the Sun, and Warrior Riding into Water. 3fr, Pavilion and Buddhist deity. 5fr, Pagoda and modern painting by Shuho Yamakawa. 20fr, Japanese inscription "Omatsuri" and Osaka Castle. 70fr, EXPO '70 emblem and Warrior on Horseback.

1970, Aug. 24   **Photo.**   *Perf. 13*

351	A61	20c gold & multi		15	15
352	A61	30c gold & multi		15	15
353	A61	50c gold & multi		15	15
354	A61	1fr gold & multi		15	15
355	A61	3fr gold & multi		15	15
356	A61	5fr gold & multi		15	15
357	A61	20fr gold & multi		32	25
358	A61	70fr gold & multi		1.00	50
		Set value		1.60	1.00

EXPO '70 International Exhibition, Osaka, Japan, Mar. 15-Sept. 13.

Young Mountain Gorillas — A62

Designs: Various Gorillas. 40c, 80c, 2fr, 100fr are vertical.

1970, Sept. 7

359	A62	20c olive & blk		15	15
360	A62	40c brt rose lil & blk		15	15
361	A62	60c blue, brn & blk		15	15
362	A62	80c org brn & blk		15	15
363	A62	1fr dp car & blk		15	15
364	A62	2fr black & multi		15	15
365	A62	15fr sepia & blk		40	20
366	A62	100fr brt bl & blk		2.50	1.50
		Set value		3.10	1.50

Pierre J. Pelletier
and Joseph B.
Caventou — A63

Designs: 20c, Cinchona flower and bark. 80c, Quinine powder and pharmacological vessels. 1fr, Anopheles mosquito. 3fr, Malaria patient and nurse. 25fr, "Malaria" (mosquito).

1970, Oct. 27   **Photo.**   *Perf. 13*

367	A63	20c silver & multi		15	15
368	A63	80c silver & multi		15	15
369	A63	1fr silver & multi		15	15
370	A63	3fr silver & multi		15	15
371	A63	25fr silver & multi		50	25
372	A63	70fr silver & multi		1.40	60
		Set value		2.10	1.00

150th anniv. of the discovery of quinine by Pierre Joseph Pelletier (1788-1842) and Joseph Bienaimé Caventou (1795-1877), French pharmacologists.

Apollo
Spaceship — A64

Apollo Spaceship: 30c, Second stage separation. 50c, Spaceship over moon surface. 1fr, Landing module and astronauts on moon. 3fr, Take-off from moon. 5fr, Return to earth. 10fr, Final separation of nose cone. 80fr, Splashdown.

1970, Nov. 23   **Photo.**   *Perf. 13*

373	A64	20c silver & multi		15	15
374	A64	30c silver & multi		15	15
375	A64	50c silver & multi		15	15
376	A64	1fr silver & multi		15	15
377	A64	3fr silver & multi		15	15
378	A64	5fr silver & multi		15	15
379	A64	10fr silver & multi		16	15
380	A64	80fr silver & multi		1.20	90
		Set value		1.70	1.25

Conquest of space.

Franklin D. Roosevelt and Brassocattleya
Olympia Alba — A65

Designs: Various portraits of Franklin D. Roosevelt and various orchids.

1970, Dec. 21   **Photo.**   *Perf. 13*

381	A65	20c blue, blk & brn		15	15
382	A65	30c car rose, blk & brn		15	15
383	A65	50c dp org, blk & brn		15	15
384	A65	1fr green, blk & brn		15	15
385	A65	2fr maroon, blk & grn		15	15
386	A65	6fr lilac & multi		15	15
387	A65	30fr bl, blk & sl grn		60	30
388	A65	60fr lil rose, blk & sl grn		1.25	50
		Set value		2.10	1.00

Pres. Franklin D. Roosevelt, 25th death anniv.

Christmas Type of 1968
Souvenir Sheet

Design: 100fr, Adoration of the Shepherds, by José de Ribera, vert.

1970, Dec. 24   **Engr.**   *Perf. 11½*

389	A48	100fr Prus blue		2.00	2.00

Pope Paul VI — A66

Portraits of Popes: 20c, John XXIII, 1958-1963. 30c, Pius XII, 1939-1958. 40c, Pius XI, 1922-39. 1fr, Benedict XV, 1914-22. 18fr, St. Pius X, 1903-14. 20fr, Leo XIII, 1878-1903. 60fr, Pius IX, 1846-78.

1970, Dec. 31   **Photo.**   *Perf. 13*

390	A66	10c gold & dk brn		15	15
391	A66	20c gold & dk grn		15	15
392	A66	30c gold & dp claret		15	15
393	A66	40c gold & indigo		15	15

394	A66	1fr gold & dk pur	15	15
395	A66	18fr gold & purple	35	16
396	A66	20fr gold & org brn	42	25
397	A66	60fr gold & blk brn	1.10	60
		Set value	2.00	1.20

Centenary of Vatican I, Ecumenical Council of the Roman Catholic Church, 1869-70.

Headdress Type of 1969

African Headdresses: 20c, Rendille woman. 30c, Young Toubou woman, Chad. 50c, Peul man, Niger. 1fr, Young Masai man, Kenya. 5fr, Young Peul girl, Niger. 18fr, Rwanda woman. 25fr, Man, Mauritania. 50fr, Rwanda women with pearl necklaces.

1971, Feb. 15   Litho.   Perf. 13

398	A50	20c multi	15	15
399	A50	30c multi	15	15
400	A50	50c multi	15	15
401	A50	1fr multi	15	15
402	A50	5fr multi	15	15
403	A50	18fr multi	30	20
404	A50	25fr multi	45	25
405	A50	50fr multi	1.00	50
		Set value	2.00	1.15

M. L. King Type of 1968
Souvenir Sheet

Design: 100fr, Charles de Gaulle (1890-1970), President of France.

1971, Mar. 15   Engr.   Perf. 13½

406	A44	100fr ultra	2.00	1.50

Astronaut Type of 1969 Inscribed in Dark Violet with Emblem and: "APOLLO / 14 / SHEPARD / ROOSA / MITCHELL"

1971, Apr. 15   Engr.   Perf. 11½
Souvenir Sheet

407	A52	100fr brown orange	4.00	3.50

Apollo 14 US moon landing, Jan. 31-Feb. 9.

Beethoven, by Christian Horneman — A67

Beethoven Portraits: 30c, Joseph Stieler. 50c, by Ferdinand Schimon. 3fr, by H. Best. 6fr, by W. Fassbender. 90fr, Beethoven's Funeral Procession, by Leopold Stöber.

1971, July 5   Photo.   Perf. 13

408	A67	20c gold & multi	15	15
409	A67	30c gold & multi	15	15
410	A67	50c gold & multi	15	15
411	A67	3fr gold & multi	15	15
412	A67	6fr gold & multi	15	15
413	A67	90fr gold & multi	1.90	1.00
		Set value	2.25	1.20

Ludwig van Beethoven (1770-1827), composer.

Equestrian A68

Olympic Sports: 30c, Runner at start. 50c, Basketball. 1fr, High jump. 8fr, Boxing. 10fr, Pole vault. 20fr, Wrestling. 60fr, Gymnastics (rings).

1971, Oct. 25   Photo.   Perf. 13

414	A68	20c gold & black	15	15
415	A68	30c gold & dp rose lil	15	15
416	A68	50c gold & vio bl	15	15
417	A68	1fr gold & dp grn	15	15
418	A68	8fr gold & henna brn	16	15
419	A68	10fr gold & purple	22	15
420	A68	20fr gold & dp brn	40	22
421	A68	60fr gold & Prus bl	1.20	50
		Set value	2.15	1.10

20th Summer Olympic Games, Munich, Aug. 26-Sept. 10, 1972.

Christmas Type of 1968
Souvenir Sheet

Design: 100fr, Nativity, by Anthony van Dyck, vert.

1971, Dec. 20   Engr.   Perf. 11½

422	A48	100fr indigo	2.00	2.00

Adam by Dürer — A69

Paintings by Albrecht Dürer (1471-1528), German painter and engraver: 30c, Eve. 50c, Hieronymus Holzschuher, Portrait. 1fr, Lamentation of Christ. 3fr, Madonna with the Pear. 5fr, St. Eustace. 20fr, Sts. Paul and Mark. 70fr, Self-portrait, 1500.

1971, Dec. 31   Photo.   Perf. 13

423	A69	20c gold & multi	15	15
424	A69	30c gold & multi	15	15
425	A69	50c gold & multi	15	15
426	A69	1fr gold & multi	15	15
427	A69	3fr gold & multi	15	15
428	A69	5fr gold & multi	15	15
429	A69	20fr gold & multi	42	22
430	A69	70fr gold & multi	1.40	90
		Set value	2.10	1.35

A 600fr on gold foil honoring Apollo 15 was issued Jan. 15, 1972.

Guardsmen Exercising A70

National Guard Emblem and: 6fr, Loading supplies. 15fr, Helicopter ambulance. 25fr, Health Service for civilians. 50fr, Guardsman and map of Rwanda, vert.

1972, Feb. 7   Perf. 13½x14, 14x13½

431	A70	4fr dp org & multi	15	15
432	A70	6fr yellow & multi	15	15
433	A70	15fr lt blue & multi	22	15
434	A70	25fr red & multi	45	25
435	A70	50fr multicolored	90	60
		Nos. 431-435 (5)	1.87	1.30

"The National Guard serving the nation." For overprints see Nos. 559-563.

Ice Hockey, Sapporo Olympics Emblem A71

1972, Feb. 12   Perf. 13x13½

436	A71	20c shown	15	15
437	A71	30c Speed skating	15	15
438	A71	50c Ski jump	15	15
439	A71	1fr Men's figure skating	15	15
440	A71	6fr Cross-country skiing	15	15
441	A71	12fr Slalom	25	16
442	A71	20fr Bobsledding	45	26
443	A71	60fr Downhill skiing	1.40	90
		Set value	2.35	1.55

11th Winter Olympic Games, Sapporo, Japan, Feb. 3-13.

 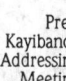

Antelopes and Cercopithecus — A72

1972, Mar. 20   Photo.   Perf. 13

444	A72	20c shown	15	15
445	A72	30c Buffaloes	15	15
446	A72	50c Zebras	15	15
447	A72	1fr Rhinoceroses	15	15
448	A72	2fr Wart hogs	15	15
449	A72	6fr Hippopotami	15	15
450	A72	18fr Hyenas	35	20
451	A72	32fr Guinea fowl	60	38
452	A72	60fr Antelopes	1.20	70
453	A72	80fr Lions	1.60	1.00
		Set value	4.00	2.50

Akagera National Park.

A73   A74

Family raising flag of Rwanda.

1972, Apr. 4   Perf. 13x12½

454	A73	6fr dk red & multi	15	15
455	A73	18fr green & multi	35	20
456	A73	60fr brown & multi	1.10	70

10th anniversary of the Referendum establishing Republic of Rwanda.

1972, May 17   Photo.   Perf. 13

Birds: 20c, Common Waxbills and Hibiscus. 30c, Collared sunbird. 50c, Variable sunbird. 1fr, Greater double-collared sunbird. 4fr, Ruwenzori puff-back flycatcher. 6fr, Red-billed fire finch. 10fr, Scarlet-chested sunbird. 18fr, Red-headed quelea. 60fr, Black-headed gonolek. 100fr, African golden oriole.

457	A74	20c dl grn & multi	15	15
458	A74	30c buff & multi	15	15
459	A74	50c yellow & multi	15	15
460	A74	1fr lt blue & multi	15	15
461	A74	4fr dl rose & multi	15	15
462	A74	6fr lilac rose & multi	15	15
463	A74	10fr pink & multi	16	15
464	A74	18fr gray & multi	35	20
465	A74	60fr multicolored	1.20	70
466	A74	100fr violet & multi	1.75	1.20
		Set value	3.75	2.40

Belgica '72 Emblem, King Baudouin, Queen Fabiola, Pres. and Mrs. Kayibanda — A75

1972, June 24   Photo.   Perf. 13
Size: 37x34mm

467	A75	18fr Rwanda landscape	38	20
468	A75	22fr Old houses, Bruges	45	22

Size: 50x34mm

469	A75	40fr shown	80	40
a.		Strip of 3, #467-469	1.65	1.00

Belgica '72 Intl. Phil. Exhib., Brussels, June 24-July 9.

Pres. Kayibanda Addressing Meeting A76

Pres. Grégoire Kayibanda: 30c, promoting officers of National Guard. 50c, with wife and children. 6fr, casting vote. 10fr, with wife and dignitaries at Feast of Justice. 15fr, with Cabinet and members of Assembly. 18fr, taking oath of office. 50fr, Portrait, vert.

1972, July 4

470	A76	20c gold & slate grn	15	15
471	A76	30c gold & dk pur	15	15
472	A76	50c gold & choc	15	15
473	A76	6fr gold & Prus bl	15	15
474	A76	10fr gold & dk pur	20	15
475	A76	15fr gold & dk bl	30	15
476	A76	18fr gold & brn	42	20
477	A76	50fr gold & Prus bl	1.00	60
		Set value	2.10	1.25

10th anniversary of independence.

Equestrian, Olympic Emblems A77

Olympic Emblems, Stadium, TV Tower and: 30c, Hockey. 50c, Soccer. 1fr, Broad jump. 6fr, Bicycling. 18fr, Yachting. 30fr, Hurdles. 44fr, Gymnastics, women's.

1972, Aug. 16   Photo.   Perf. 14

478	A77	20c dk brn & gold	15	15
479	A77	30c vio bl & gold	15	15
480	A77	50c dk green & gold	15	15
481	A77	1fr dp claret & gold	15	15
482	A77	6fr black & gold	15	15
483	A77	18fr brown & gold	30	20
484	A77	30fr dk vio & gold	60	30
485	A77	44fr Prus bl & gold	80	40
		Set value	2.00	1.25

20th Olympic Games, Munich, Aug. 26-Sept. 11.

Relay (Sport) and UN Emblem — A78

1972, Oct. 23   Photo.   Perf. 13

486	A78	20c shown	15	15
487	A78	30c Musicians	15	15
488	A78	50c Dancers	15	15
489	A78	1fr Operating room	15	15
490	A78	6fr Weaver & painter	15	15
491	A78	18fr Classroom	16	20
492	A78	24fr Laboratory	55	25
493	A78	50fr Hands of 4 races reaching for equality	1.00	60
		Nos. 486-493 (8)	2.46	1.80

Fight against racism.

Christmas Type of 1968
Souvenir Sheet

Design: 100fr, Adoration of the Shepherds, by Jacob Jordaens, vert.

1972, Dec. 11   Perf. 11½

494	A48	100fr red brown	2.00	2.00

Phymateus Brunneri — A79

Designs: Various insects. 30c, 1fr, 6fr, 22fr, 100fr, vertical.

1973, Jan. 31   **Photo.**   **Perf. 13**

495	A79	20c multi	15	15
496	A79	30c multi	15	15
497	A79	50c multi	15	15
498	A79	1fr multi	15	15
499	A79	2fr multi	15	15
500	A79	6fr multi	15	15
501	A79	18fr multi	35	20
502	A79	22fr multi	42	20
503	A79	70fr multi	1.40	80
504	A79	100fr multi	2.00	1.20
	Nos. 495-504 (10)		5.07	
	Set value			2.60

Souvenir Sheet
Perf. 14

505	A79	80fr like 20c	1.75	1.75

No. 505 contains one stamp 43½x33½mm.

Emile Zola, by Edouard Manet — A80

Paintings Connected with Reading, and Book Year Emblem: 30c, Rembrandt's Mother. 50c, St. Jerome Removing Thorn from Lion's Paw, by Colantonio. 1fr, Apostles Peter and Paul, by El Greco. 2fr, Virgin and Child with Book, by Roger van der Weyden. 6fr, St. Jerome in his Cell, by Antonella de Messina. 40fr, St. Barbara, by Master of Flemalle. No. 513, Don Quixote, by Otto Bonevalle. No. 514, Pres. Kayibanda reading book.

1973, Mar. 12   **Photo.**   **Perf. 13**

506	A80	20c gold & multi	15	15
507	A80	30c gold & multi	15	15
508	A80	50c gold & multi	15	15
509	A80	1fr gold & multi	15	15
510	A80	2fr gold & multi	15	15
511	A80	6fr gold & multi	15	15
512	A80	40fr gold & multi	65	32
513	A80	100fr gold & multi	1.65	75
	Set value		2.60	1.30

Souvenir Sheet
Perf. 14

514	A80	100fr gold, bl & ind	1.65	1.25

International Book Year.

Longombe — A81   Rubens and Isabella Brandt, by Rubens — A82

Designs: Musical instruments of Central and West Africa.

1973, Apr. 9   **Photo.**   **Perf. 13½**

515	A81	20c shown	15	15
516	A81	30c Horn	15	15
517	A81	50c Xylophone	15	15
518	A81	1fr Harp	15	15

519	A81	4fr Alur horns	15	15
520	A81	6fr Drum, bells and horn	15	15
521	A81	18fr Large drums (Ngoma)	30	16
522	A81	90fr Toba	1.60	80
	Set value		2.20	1.25

1973, May 11

Paintings from Old Pinakothek, Munich (IBRA Emblem and): 30c, Young Man, by Cranach. 50c, Woman Peeling Turnips, by Chardin. 1fr, The Abduction of Leucippa's Daughters, by Rubens. 2fr, Virgin and Child, by Filippo Lippi. 6fr, Boys Eating Fruit, by Murillo. 40fr, The Lovesick Woman, by Jan Steen. No. 530, Jesus Stripped of His Garments, by El Greco. No. 531, Oswalt Krehl, by Dürer.

523	A82	20c gold & multi	15	15
524	A82	30c gold & multi	15	15
525	A82	50c gold & multi	15	15
526	A82	1fr gold & multi	15	15
527	A82	2fr gold & multi	15	15
528	A82	6fr gold & multi	15	15
529	A82	40fr gold & multi	70	35
530	A82	100fr gold & multi	1.90	80
	Set value		2.90	1.40

Souvenir Sheet

531	A82	100fr gold & multi	2.00	1.60

IBRA München 1973 Intl. Phil. Exhib., Munich, May 11-20. No. 531 contains one stamp 40x56mm.

Map of Africa and Peace Doves — A83

Design: 94fr, Map of Africa and hands.

1973, July 23   **Photo.**   **Perf. 13½**

532	A83	6fr gold & multi	16	15
533	A83	94fr gold & multi	1.90	1.50

Org. for African Unity, 10th anniv.
For overprints see Nos. 895-896.

Nos. 298-303 Overprinted in Blue, Black, Green or Brown: "SECHERESSE / SOLIDARITE AFRICAINE"

1973, Aug. 23   **Photo.**   **Perf. 13**

534	A53	20c multi (Bl)	15	15
535	A53	40c multi (Bk)	15	15
536	A53	60c multi (Bl)	15	15
537	A53	80c multi (G)	15	15
538	A53	3fr multi (G)	15	15
539	A53	75fr multi (Br)	1.50	90
	Nos. 534-539,B1 (7)		4.75	
	Set value			3.35

African solidarity in drought emergency.

African Postal Union Issue
Common Design Type

1973, Sept. 12   **Engr.**   **Perf. 13**

540	CD137	100fr dp brn, bl & brn	2.00	1.60

Six-lined Distichodus — A84

African Fish: 30c, Little triggerfish. 50c, Spotted upside-down catfish. 1fr, Nile mouthbreeder. 2fr, African lungfish. 6fr, Pareutropius mandevillei. 40fr, Congo characin. 100fr, Like 20c. 150fr, Julidochromis ornatus.

1973, Sept. 3   **Photo.**   **Perf. 13**

541	A84	20c gold & multi	15	15
542	A84	30c gold & multi	15	15
543	A84	50c gold & multi	15	15
544	A84	1fr gold & multi	15	15
545	A84	2fr gold & multi	15	15
546	A84	6fr gold & multi	15	15
547	A84	40fr gold & multi	70	40
548	A84	150fr gold & multi	3.00	1.50
	Set value		4.00	2.15

Souvenir Sheet

549	A84	100fr gold & multi	2.00	2.00

No. 549 contains one stamp 48x29mm.

QUINZAINE AFRICAINE BRUXELLES 15/30 SEPT. 1973

Nos. 398-405 Overprinted in Black, Silver, Green or Blue

1973, Sept. 15   **Litho.**

550	A50	20c multi (Bk)	15	15
551	A50	30c multi (S)	15	15
552	A50	50c multi (Bk)	15	15
553	A50	1fr multi (G)	15	15
554	A50	5fr multi (S)	15	15
555	A50	18fr multi (Bk)	35	20
556	A50	25fr multi (Bk)	50	25
557	A50	50fr multi (Bl)	1.20	55
	Set value		2.35	1.20

Africa Weeks, Brussels, Sept. 15-30, 1973. On the 30c, 1fr and 25fr the text of the overprint is horizontal.

Nos. 431-435 Overprinted in Gold

Perf. 13½x14, 14x13½

1973, Oct. 31   **Photo.**

559	A70	4fr dp org & multi	15	15
560	A70	6fr yellow & multi	15	15
561	A70	15fr lt blue & multi	42	27
562	A70	25fr red & multi	70	40
563	A70	50fr multicolored	1.50	80
	Nos. 559-563 (5)		2.92	1.77

25th anniv. of the Universal Declaration of Human Rights.

Christmas Type of 1968
Souvenir Sheet

Design: 100fr, Adoration of the Shepherds, by Guido Reni.

1973, Dec. 15   **Engr.**   **Perf. 11½**

564	A48	100fr brt violet	2.00	2.00

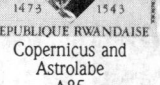

Copernicus and Astrolabe A85   Pres. Juvénal Habyarimana A86

Designs: 30c, 18fr, 100fr, Portrait. 50c, 80fr, Copernicus and heliocentric system. 1fr, like 20c.

1973, Dec. 26   **Photo.**   **Perf. 13**

565	A85	20c silver & multi	15	15
566	A85	30c silver & multi	15	15
567	A85	50c silver & multi	15	15
568	A85	1fr gold & multi	15	15
569	A85	18fr gold & multi	22	20
570	A85	80fr gold & multi	1.20	80
	Set value		1.60	1.10

Souvenir Sheet

571	A85	100fr gold & multi	2.00	2.00

Nicolaus Copernicus (1473-1543), Polish astronomer.

1974, Apr. 8   **Photo.**   **Perf. 11½**
Black Inscriptions

572	A86	1fr bister & sepia	15	15
573	A86	2fr ultra & sepia	15	15
574	A86	5fr rose red & sep	15	15
575	A86	6fr grnsh bl & sep	15	15
576	A86	26fr lilac & sepia	45	30
577	A86	60fr ol grn & sepia	1.20	65
	Set value		1.90	1.10

Souvenir Sheet

Christ Between the Thieves (Detail), by Rubens — A87

1974, Apr. 12   **Engr.**   **Perf. 11½**

578	A87	100fr sepia	4.00	4.00

Easter.

Yugoslavia-Zaire Soccer Game — A88

Designs: Games' emblem and soccer games.

1974, July 6   **Photo.**   **Perf. 13½**

579	A88	20c shown	15	15
580	A88	40c Netherlands-Sweden	15	15
581	A88	60c Germany (Fed.)-Australia	15	15
582	A88	80c Haiti-Argentina	15	15
583	A88	2fr Brazil-Scotland	15	15
584	A88	6fr Bulgaria-Uruguay	15	15
585	A88	40fr Italy-Poland	70	40
586	A88	50fr Chile-Germany (DDR)	1.00	65
	Set value		2.00	1.30

World Cup Soccer Championship, Munich, June 13-July 7.

Marconi's Laboratory Yacht "Elletra" — A89

Designs: 30c, Marconi and steamer "Carlo Alberto." 50c, Marconi's wireless apparatus and telecommunications satellites. 4fr, Marconi and globes connected by communications waves. 35fr, Marconi's radio, and radar. 60fr, Marconi and transmitter at Poldhu, Cornwall. 50fr, like 20c.

1974, Aug. 19   **Photo.**   **Perf. 13½**

587	A89	20c violet, blk & grn	15	15
588	A89	30c green, blk & vio	15	15
589	A89	50c yellow, blk & lil	15	15
590	A89	4fr salmon, blk & bl	15	15
591	A89	35fr lilac, blk & yel	60	40
592	A89	60fr blue, blk & brnz	1.20	70
	Set value		2.00	1.25

Souvenir Sheet

593	A89	50fr gold, blk & lt bl	1.20	1.20

Guglielmo Marconi (1874-1937), Italian electrical engineer and inventor.

The Flute Player,
by J.
Leyster — A90

Messenger
Monk — A91

Paintings: 20c, Diane de Poitiers, Fontainebleau
School. 50c, Virgin and Child, by David. 1fr, Triumph of Venus, by Boucher. 10fr, Seated Harlequin, by Picasso. 18fr, Virgin and Child, 15th century. 20fr, Beheading of St. John, by Hans Fries.
50fr, Daughter of Andersdotter, by J. F. Höckert.

1974, Sept. 23   Photo.   Perf. 14x13
594 A90 20c gold & multi   15   15
595 A90 30c gold & multi   15   15
596 A90 50c gold & multi   15   15
597 A90 1fr gold & multi   15   15
598 A90 10fr gold & multi   16   15
599 A90 18fr gold & multi   30   16
600 A90 20fr gold & multi   35   22
601 A90 50fr gold & multi   1.00   60
         Set value   2.00 1.25

INTERNABA 74 Intl. Phil. Exhib., Basel, June 7-
10, and Stockholmia 74, Intl. Phil. Exhib., Stockholm, Sept. 21-29.
Six multicolored souvenir sheets exist containing
two 15fr stamps each in various combinations of
designs of Nos. 594-601. One souvenir sheet of
four 25fr stamps exists with designs of Nos. 595,
597, 599 and 601.

1974, Oct. 9   Perf. 14
UPU Emblem and Messengers: 30c, Inca. 50c,
Morocco. 1fr, India. 18fr, Polynesia. 80fr, Rwanda.

602 A91 20c gold & multi   15   15
603 A91 30c gold & multi   15   15
604 A91 50c gold & multi   15   15
605 A91 1fr gold & multi   15   15
606 A91 18fr gold & multi   42   38
607 A91 80fr gold & multi   1.65 1.60
         Set value   2.25 2.10

Centenary of Universal Postal Union.

Nos. 306-308
Overprinted

1974, Dec. 16   Photo.   Perf. 11½
608 A54 6fr brt pink & multi   3.50 3.50
609 A54 18fr ultra & multi   3.50 3.50
610 A54 40fr brn & multi   3.75 3.75

15th anniversary of independence.

Christmas Type of 1968
Souvenir Sheet

Design: 100fr, Adoration of the Kings, by Joos
van Cleve.

1974, Dec. 23   Engr.   Perf. 11½
611 A48 100fr slate green   4.00 4.00

Nos. 295-296 Overprinted: "1974 / 10e
Anniversaire"

1974, Dec. 30   Photo.   Perf. 13
612 A51 30fr sil & multi   55   55
613 A51 70fr gold & multi   1.10 1.10

African Development Bank, 10th anniversary.

Uganda Kob — A92

Antelopes: 30c, Bongos, horiz. 50c, Rwanda
antelopes. 1fr, Young sitatungas, horiz. 4fr, Greater
kudus. 10fr, Impalas, horiz. 34fr, Waterbuck. 40fr,
Impalas. 60fr, Greater kudu. 100fr, Derby's elands,
horiz.

1975, Mar. 17   Photo.   Perf. 13
614 A92 20c multi   15   15
615 A92 30c multi   15   15
616 A92 50c multi   15   15
617 A92 1fr multi   15   15
618 A92 4fr multi   15   15
619 A92 10fr multi   15   15
620 A92 34fr multi   50   25
621 A92 100fr multi   1.65   75
         Set value   2.50 1.30

Miniature Sheets
622 A92 40fr multi   2.75 2.75
623 A92 60fr multi   2.75 2.75

Miniature Sheets

The Burial of Jesus, by Raphael — A93

1975, Apr. 1   Photo.   Perf. 13x14
624 A93 20fr shown   1.00 1.00
625 A93 30fr Pietá, by Cranach the
         Elder   1.20 1.20
626 A93 50fr by van der Weyden   1.20 1.20
627 A93 100fr by Bellini   1.20 1.20

Easter. Size of stamps: 40x52mm.
See Nos. 681-684.

Souvenir Sheets

Prince
Balthazar
Charles, by
Velazquez
A94

Paintings: 30fr, Infanta Margaret of Austria, by
Velazquez. 50fr, The Divine Shepherd, by Murillo.
100fr, Francisco Goya, by V. Lopez y Portana.

1975, Apr. 4   Photo.   Perf. 13
628 A94 20fr multi   1.00 1.00
629 A94 30fr multi   1.20 1.20
630 A94 50fr multi   1.20 1.20
631 A94 100fr multi   1.20 1.20

Espana 75 Intl. Phil. Exhib., Madrid, Apr. 4-13.
Size of stamps: 38x48mm. See Nos. 642-643. For
overprints see Nos. 844-847.

Pyrethrum (Insect
Powder) — A95

1975, Apr. 14   Perf. 13
632 A95 20c shown   15   15
633 A95 30c Tea   15   15
634 A95 50c Coffee (beans and pan)   15   15
635 A95 4fr Bananas   15   15
636 A95 10fr Corn   16   15
637 A95 12fr Sorghum   20   15
638 A95 26fr Rice   45   25
639 A95 47fr Coffee (workers and
         beans)   1.10   45
         Set value   2.10 1.05

**Souvenir Sheets
Perf. 13½**
640 A95 25fr like 50c   65   65
641 A95 75fr like 47fr   1.60 1.60

Year of Agriculture and 10th anniversary of
Office for Industrialized Cultivation.

Souvenir Sheets
Painting Type of 1975

Paintings: 75fr, Louis XIV, by Hyacinthe Rigaud.
125fr, Cavalry Officer, by Jean Gericault.

1975, June 6   Photo.   Perf. 13
642 A94 75fr multi   1.60 1.60
643 A94 125fr multi   3.00 3.00

ARPHILA 75, Intl. Philatelic Exhibition, Paris,
June 6-16. Size of stamps: 38x48mm.

Nos. 390-397 Overprinted: "1975 /
ANNEE / SAINTE"

1975, June 23   Photo.   Perf. 13
644 A66 10c gold & dk brn   15   15
645 A66 20c gold & dk grn   15   15
646 A66 30c gold & dp claret   15   15
647 A66 40c gold & indigo   15   15
648 A66 1fr gold & dk pur   15   15
649 A66 18fr gold & purple   30   15
650 A66 20fr gold & org brn   40   20
651 A66 60fr gold & blk brn   1.50   80
         Set value   2.40 1.30

Holy Year 1975.

White Pelicans — A96

Designs: African birds.

1975, June 20
652 A96 20c shown   15   15
653 A96 30c Malachite kingfisher   15   15
654 A96 50c Goliath herons   15   15
655 A96 1fr Saddle-billed storks   15   15
656 A96 4fr African jacana   15   15
657 A96 10fr African anhingas   20   15
658 A96 34fr Sacred ibis   60   15
659 A96 80fr Hartlaub ducks   1.60   80
         Set value   2.60 1.40

Miniature Sheets
660 A96 40fr Flamingoes   1.20 1.20
661 A96 60fr Crowned cranes   1.60 1.60

Globe Representing
Races and WPY
Emblem — A97

The Bath, by Mary
Cassatt and IWY
Emblem — A98

World Population Year: 26fr, Population graph
and emblem. 34fr, Globe with open door and
emblem.

1975, Sept. 1   Photo.   Perf. 13½x13
662 A97 20fr dp bl & multi   38   20
663 A97 26fr dl red brn & multi   50   25
664 A97 34fr yel & multi   70   35

1975, Sept. 15   Perf. 13
IWY Emblem and: 30c, Mother and Infant Son,
by Julius Gari Melchers. 50c, Woman with Milk
Jug, by Jan Vermeer. 1fr, Water Carrier, by Goya.
8fr, Rwanda woman cotton picker. 12fr, Scientist
with microscope. 18fr, Mother and child. 25fr,
Empress Josephine, by Pierre-Paul Prud'hon. 40fr,
Madame Vigee-Lebrun and Daughter, self-portrait.
60fr, Woman carrying child on back and water jug
on head.

665 A98 20c gold & multi   15   15
666 A98 30c gold & multi   15   15
667 A98 50c gold & multi   15   15
668 A98 1fr gold & multi   15   15
669 A98 8fr gold & multi   15   15
670 A98 12fr gold & multi   20   15
671 A98 18fr gold & multi   30   15
672 A98 60fr gold & multi   1.20   60
         Set value   2.00 1.15

**Souvenir Sheets
Perf. 13½**
673 A98 25fr multi   6.50 6.50
674 A98 40fr multi   6.50 6.50

International Women's Year. Nos. 673-674 each
contain one stamp 37x49mm.

Owl, Quill and
Book — A99

Designs: 30c, Hygiene emblem. 1.50fr, Kneeling woman holding scales of Justice. 18fr, Chemist
in laboratory. 26fr, Symbol of commerce and chart.
34fr, University Building.

1975, Sept. 29   Perf. 13
675 A99 20c pur & multi   15   15
676 A99 30c ultra & multi   15   15
677 A99 1.50fr lilac & multi   15   15
678 A99 18fr blue & multi   30   15
679 A99 26fr olive & multi   45   25
680 A99 34fr blue & multi   70   35
         Set value   1.55   65

National Univ. of Rwanda, 10th anniv.

Souvenir Sheets
Painting Type of 1975

Paintings by Jan Vermeer (1632-1675): 20fr,
Man and Woman Drinking Wine. 30fr, Young
Woman Reading Letter. 50fr, Painter in his Studio.
100fr, Young Woman Playing Virginal.

1975, Oct. 13   Photo.   Perf. 13x14
681 A93 20fr multi   40   40
682 A93 30fr multi   60   60
683 A93 50fr multi   1.00 1.00
684 A93 100fr multi   2.00 2.00

Size of stamps: 40x52mm.

Waterhole and Impatiens
Stuhlmannii — A100

Designs: 30c, Antelopes, zebras, candelabra cactus. 50c, Brush fire, and tapinanthus prunifolius. 5fr, Bulera Lake and Egyptian white lotus. 8fr, Erosion prevention and protea madiensis. 10fr, Marsh and melanthera brownei. 26fr, Landscape, lobelias and senecons. 100fr, Sabyinyo Volcano and polystachya kermesina.

1975, Oct. 25   *Perf. 13*
685	A100	20c blk & multi	15	15
686	A100	30c blk & multi	15	15
687	A100	50c blk & multi	15	15
688	A100	5fr blk & multi	15	15
689	A100	8fr blk & multi	15	15
690	A100	10fr blk & multi	16	15
691	A100	26fr blk & multi	50	25
692	A100	100fr blk & multi	1.90	1.00
		Set value	2.90	1.60

Nature protection.
For overprints see Nos. 801-808.

Nos. 343-348
Overprinted

**SECHERESSE
SOLIDARITE
1975**

1975, Nov. 10   Litho.   *Perf. 13*
693	A60	20c multi	15	15
694	A60	30c multi	15	15
695	A60	50c multi	15	15
696	A60	1fr multi	15	15
697	A60	3fr multi	15	15
698	A60	5fr multi	15	15
		Set value, #693-698,		
		B2-B3	3.80	2.75

African solidarity in drought emergency.

Fork-lift
Truck on
Airfield
A101

Designs: 30c, Coffee packing plant. 50c, Engineering plant. 10fr, Farmer with hoe, vert. 35fr, Coffee pickers, vert. 54fr, Mechanized harvester.

Wmk. JEZ Multiple (368)
1975, Dec. 1   Photo.   *Perf. 14x13½*
699	A101	20c gold & multi	15	15
700	A101	30c gold & multi	15	15
701	A101	50c gold & multi	15	15
702	A101	10fr gold & multi	16	15
703	A101	35fr gold & multi	60	35
704	A101	54fr gold & multi	1.00	55
		Set value	1.90	1.10

Basket Carrier and
Themabelga
Emblem — A102

Themabelga Emblem and: 30c, Warrior with shield and spear. 50c, Woman with beads. 1fr, Indian woman. 5fr, Male dancer with painted body. 7fr, Woman carrying child on back. 35fr, Male dancer with spear. 51fr, Female dancers.

1975, Dec. 8   Unwmk.   *Perf. 13½*
705	A102	20c blk & multi	15	15
706	A102	30c blk & multi	15	15
707	A102	50c blk & multi	15	15

708	A102	1fr blk & multi	15	15
709	A102	5fr blk & multi	15	15
710	A102	7fr blk & multi	15	15
711	A102	35fr blk & multi	60	35
712	A102	51fr blk & multi	90	50
		Set value	1.90	1.10

THEMABELGA Intl. Topical Philatelic Exhibition, Brussels, Dec. 13-21.

Christmas Type of 1968

Design: 100fr, Adoration of the Kings, by Peter Paul Rubens.

1975, Dec. 22   Engr.   *Perf. 11½*
713	A48	100fr brt rose lil	3.50	3.50

Dr.
Schweitzer,
Keyboard,
Score
A103

Albert Schweitzer and: 30c, 5fr, Lambaréné Hospital. 50c, 10fr, Organ pipes from Strassbourg organ, and score. 1fr, 80fr, Dr. Schweitzer's house, Lambaréné. 3fr, like 20c.

1976, Jan. 30   Photo.   *Perf. 13½*
714	A103	20c maroon & pur	15	15
715	A103	30c grn & pur	15	15
716	A103	50c brn org & pur	15	15
717	A103	1fr red lil & pur	15	15
718	A103	3fr vio bl & pur	15	15
719	A103	5fr brn & pur	15	15
720	A103	10fr bl & pur	20	15
721	A103	80fr ver & pur	1.40	80
		Set value	1.95	1.10

World Leprosy Day.
For overprints see Nos. 788-795.

Surrender at
Yorktown
A104

American Bicentennial (Paintings): 30c, Instruction at Valley Forge. 50c, Presentation of Captured Colors at Yorktown. 1fr, Washington at Fort Lee. 18fr, Washington Boarding British Warship. 26fr, Washington Studying Battle Plans at Night. 34fr, Washington Firing Cannon. 40fr, Washington Crossing the Delaware. 100fr, Sailing Ship "Bonhomme Richard," vert.

1976, Mar. 22   Photo.   *Perf. 13x13½*
722	A104	20c gold & multi	15	15
723	A104	30c gold & multi	15	15
724	A104	50c gold & multi	15	15
725	A104	1fr gold & multi	15	15
726	A104	18fr gold & multi	35	16
727	A104	26fr gold & multi	42	22
728	A104	34fr gold & multi	60	35
729	A104	40fr gold & multi	65	40
		Set value	2.20	1.30

Souvenir Sheet
Perf. 13½
730	A104	100fr gold & multi	2.50	2.50

Sister Yohana, First   Yachting — A106
Nun — A105

Designs: 30c, Abdon Sabakati, one of first converts. 50c, Father Alphonse Brard, first Superior of Save Mission. 4fr, Abbot Balthazar Gafuku, one of first priests. 10fr, Msgr. Bigirumwami, first bishop. 25fr, Save Church, horiz. 60fr, Kabgayi Cathedral, horiz.

Perf. 13x13½, 13½x13
1976, Apr. 26   Photo.
731	A105	20c multi	15	15
732	A105	30c multi	15	15
733	A105	50c multi	15	15
734	A105	4fr multi	15	15
735	A105	10fr multi	20	15
736	A105	25fr multi	45	25
737	A105	60fr multi	1.00	60
		Set value	1.90	1.10

50th anniv. of the Roman Catholic Church of Rwanda.

Montreal Games Emblem and: 30c, Steeplechase. 50c, Long jump. 1fr, Hockey. 10fr, Swimming. 18fr, Soccer. 29fr, Boxing. 51fr, Vaulting.

738	A106	20c gray & dk car	15	15
739	A106	30c gray & Prus bl	15	15
740	A106	50c gray & blk	15	15
741	A106	1fr gray & pur	15	15
742	A106	10fr gray & ultra	25	15
743	A106	18fr gray & dk brn	35	16
744	A106	29fr gray & blk	60	25
745	A106	51fr gray & slate grn	90	50
		Set value	2.25	1.15

21st Olympic Games, Montreal, Canada, July 17-Aug. 1.

First
Message,
Manual
Switchboard
A107

Designs: 30c, Telephone, 1876 and interested crowd. 50c, Telephone c. 1900, and woman making a call. 1fr, Business telephone exchange, c. 1905. 4fr, "Candlestick" phone, globe and A. G. Bell. 8fr, Dial phone and Rwandan man making call. 26fr, Telephone, 1976, satellite and radar. 60fr, Push-button telephone, Rwandan international switchboard operator.

1976, June 21   Photo.   *Perf. 14*
746	A107	20c dl red & indigo	15	15
747	A107	30c grnsh bl & indigo	15	15
748	A107	50c brn & indigo	15	15
749	A107	1fr org & indigo	15	15
750	A107	4fr lilac & indigo	15	15
751	A107	8fr grn & indigo	20	15
752	A107	26fr dl red & indigo	50	25
753	A107	60fr vio & indigo	1.10	60
		Set value	2.00	1.10

Centenary of first telephone call by Alexander Graham Bell, Mar. 10, 1876.

Type of 1976 Overprinted in Silver with Bicentennial Emblem and "Independence Day"

Designs as before.

1976, July 4   *Perf. 13x13½*
754	A104	20c silver & multi	15	15
755	A104	30c silver & multi	15	15
756	A104	50c silver & multi	15	15
757	A104	1fr silver & multi	15	15
758	A104	18fr silver & multi	35	25
759	A104	26fr silver & multi	50	25
760	A104	34fr silver & multi	60	35
761	A104	40fr silver & multi	65	40
		Set value	2.25	1.40

Independence Day.

Soccer, Montreal
Olympic
Emblem — A108

Montreal Olympic Games Emblem and: 30c, Shooting. 50c, Woman canoeing. 1fr, Gymnast. 10fr, Weight lifting. 12fr, Diving. 26fr, Equestrian. 50fr, Shot put.

1976, Aug. 1   Photo.   *Perf. 13½x13*
762	A108	20c multi	15	15
763	A108	30c multi	15	15
764	A108	50c multi	15	15
765	A108	1fr multi	15	15

766	A108	10fr multi	16	15
767	A108	12fr multi	20	15
768	A108	26fr multi	42	15
769	A108	50fr multi	1.00	50
		Set value	1.95	1.10

Souvenir Sheet

Designs: Various phases of hurdles race, horiz.

770		Sheet of 4	3.00	3.00
a.	A108	20fr Start	35	35
b.	A108	30fr Sprint	55	55
c.	A108	40fr Hurdle	70	70
d.	A108	60fr Finish	1.00	1.00

21st Olympic Games, Montreal, Canada, July 17-Aug. 1.

Apollo and
Soyuz Take-
offs, Project
Emblem
A109

Designs: 30c, Soyuz in space. 50c, Apollo in space. 1fr, Apollo. 2fr, Spacecraft before docking. 12fr, Spacecraft after docking. 30fr, Astronauts visiting in docked spacecraft. 54fr, Apollo splashdown.

1976, Oct. 29   Photo.   *Perf. 13½x14*
771	A109	20c multi	15	15
772	A109	30c multi	15	15
773	A109	50c multi	15	15
774	A109	1fr multi	15	15
775	A109	2fr multi	15	15
776	A109	12fr multi	25	15
777	A109	30fr multi	60	30
778	A109	54fr multi	90	55
		Set value	2.00	1.15

Apollo Soyuz space test program (Russo-American cooperation), July 1975.
For overprints see Nos. 836-843.

Eulophia   Hands and Symbols
Cucullata — A110   of Learning — A111

Orchids: 30c, Eulophia streptopetala. 50c, Disa Stairsii. 1fr, Aerangis kotschyana. 10fr, Eulophia abyssinica. 12fr, Bonatea steudneri. 26fr, Ansellia gigantea. 50fr, Eulophia angolensis.

1976, Nov. 22   Photo.   *Perf. 14x13½*
779	A110	20c multi	15	15
780	A110	30c multi	15	15
781	A110	50c multi	15	15
782	A110	1fr multi	15	15
783	A110	10fr multi	16	15
784	A110	12fr multi	25	15
785	A110	26fr multi	50	25
786	A110	50fr multi	1.00	50
		Set value	2.05	1.10

Christmas Type of 1968
Souvenir Sheet

Design: Nativity, by Francois Boucher.

1976, Dec. 20   Engr.   *Perf. 11½*
787	A48	100fr brt ultra	3.00	3.00

Nos. 714-721 Overprinted: "JOURNEE / MONDIALE / 1977"

1977, Jan. 29   Photo.   *Perf. 13½*
788	A103	20c mar & pur	15	15
789	A103	30c grn & pur	15	15
790	A103	50c brn org & pur	15	15
791	A103	1fr red lil & pur	15	15
792	A103	3fr vio bl & pur	15	15
793	A103	5fr brn & pur	16	15
794	A103	10fr bl & pur	25	15
795	A103	80fr ver & pur	1.40	80
		Set value	2.00	1.15

World Leprosy Day.

1977, Feb. 7   Litho.   Perf. 12½

Designs: 26fr, Hands and symbols of science. 64fr, Hands and symbols of industry.

796 A111	10fr multi	20	15
797 A111	26fr multi	52	38
798 A111	64fr multi	90	75

10th Summit Conference of the African and Malagasy Union, Kigali, 1976.

Souvenir Sheets

Descent from the Cross, by Rubens A112

Easter: 25fr, Crucifixion, by Rubens.

1977, Apr. 27   Photo.   Perf. 13

| 799 A112 | 25fr multi | 60 | 60 |
| 800 A112 | 75fr multi | 1.50 | 1.50 |

Size of stamp: 40x40mm.

Nos. 685-692 Overprinted

CONFERENCE MONDIALE DE L'EAU

1977, May 2

801 A100	20c blk & multi	15	15
802 A100	30c blk & multi	15	15
803 A100	50c blk & multi	15	15
804 A100	5fr blk & multi	20	15
805 A100	8fr blk & multi	30	15
806 A100	10fr blk & multi	30	15
807 A100	26fr blk & multi	90	45
808 A100	100fr blk & multi	3.00	1.90
Nos. 801-808 (8)		5.15	3.25

World Water Conference.

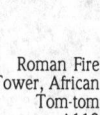

Roman Fire Tower, African Tom-tom A113

ITU Emblem and: 30c, Chappe's optical telegraph and postillion. 50c, Morse telegraph and code. 1fr, Tug Goliath laying cable in English Channel. 4fr, Telephone, radio, television. 18fr, Kingsport (US space exploration ship) and Marots communications satellite. 26fr, Satellite tracking station and O.T.S. satellite. 50fr, Mariner II, Venus probe.

1977, May 23   Litho.   Perf. 12½

809 A113	20c multi	15	15
810 A113	30c multi	15	15
811 A113	50c multi	15	15
812 A113	1fr multi	15	15
813 A113	4fr multi	15	15
814 A113	18fr multi	45	22
815 A113	26fr multi	62	32
816 A113	50fr multi	1.25	62
Set value		2.60	1.35

World Telecommunications Day.

Souvenir Sheets

Amsterdam Harbor, by Willem van de Velde, the Younger A114

Design: 40fr, The Night Watch, by Rembrandt.

1977, May 26   Photo.   Perf. 13½

| 817 A114 | 40fr multi | 80 | 80 |
| 818 A114 | 60fr multi | 1.20 | 1.20 |

AMPHILEX '277 Intl. Philatelic Exhibition, Amsterdam, May 27-June 5. Size of stamp: 38x49mm.

Road to Calvary, by Rubens — A115

Paintings by Peter Paul Rubens (1577-1640): 30c, Judgment of Paris, horiz. 50c, Marie de Medicis. 1fr, Heads of Black Men, horiz. 4fr, 26fr, Details from St. Ildefonso triptych. 8fr, Helene Fourment and her Children, horiz. 60fr, Helene Fourment.

1977, June 13   Perf. 14

819 A115	20c gold & multi	15	15
820 A115	30c gold & multi	15	15
821 A115	50c gold & multi	15	15
822 A115	1fr gold & multi	15	15
823 A115	4fr gold & multi	15	15
824 A115	8fr gold & multi	20	15
825 A115	26fr gold & multi	50	25
826 A115	60fr gold & multi	1.20	60
Set value		2.15	1.10

Souvenir Sheet

Viking on Mars A116

1977, June 27   Photo.   Perf. 13

| 827 A116 | 100fr multi | 5.00 | 5.00 |

US Viking landing on Mars, first anniv.

RWANDA

Crested Eagle — A117

Birds of Prey: 30c, Snake eagle. 50c, Fish eagle. 1fr, Monk vulture. 3fr, Red-tailed buzzard. 5fr, Yellow-beaked kite. 20fr, Swallow-tailed kite. 100fr, Bateleur.

1977, Sept. 12   Litho.   Perf. 14

828 A117	20c multi	15	15
829 A117	30c multi	15	15
830 A117	50c multi	15	15
831 A117	1fr multi	15	15
832 A117	3fr multi	15	15

833 A117	5fr multi	15	15
834 A117	20fr multi	42	22
835 A117	100fr multi	2.00	1.00
Set value		2.75	1.45

Nos. 771-778 Overprinted: "in memoriam / WERNHER VON BRAUN / 1912-1977"

1977, Sept. 19   Photo.   Perf. 13½x14

836 A109	20c multi	15	15
837 A109	30c multi	15	15
838 A109	50c multi	15	15
839 A109	1fr multi	15	15
840 A109	2fr multi	15	15
841 A109	12fr multi	22	15
842 A109	30fr multi	60	30
843 A109	54fr multi	1.20	60
Set value		2.25	1.20

Wernher von Braun (1912-1977), space and rocket expert.

Nos. 628-631 Gold Embossed "ESPAMER '77" and ESPAMER Emblem
Souvenir Sheets

1977, Oct. 3   Photo.   Perf. 13

844 A94	20fr multi	50	50
845 A94	30fr multi	75	75
846 A94	60fr multi	1.25	1.25
847 A94	100fr multi	2.50	2.50

ESPAMER '77, International Philatelic Exhibition, Barcelona, Oct. 7-13.

Christmas Type of 1968
Souvenir Sheet

Design: 100fr, Nativity, by Peter Paul Rubens.

1977, Dec. 12   Engr.   Perf. 13½

| 848 A48 | 100fr violet blue | 3.00 | 3.00 |

Marginal inscription typographed in red.

Boy Scout Playing Flute A118   Chimpanzees A119

Designs: 30c, Campfire. 50c, Bridge building. 1fr, Scouts with unit flag. 10fr, Map reading. 18fr, Boating. 26fr, Cooking. 44fr, Lord Baden-Powell.

1978, Feb. 20   Litho.   Perf. 12½

849 A118	20c yel grn & multi	15	15
850 A118	30c blue & multi	15	15
851 A118	50c lilac & multi	15	15
852 A118	1fr blue & multi	15	15
853 A118	10fr pink & multi	20	15
854 A118	18fr lt grn & multi	38	18
855 A118	26fr orange & multi	55	25
856 A118	44fr salmon & multi	90	45
Set value		2.20	1.15

10th anniversary of Rwanda Boy Scouts.

1978, Mar. 20   Photo.   Perf. 13½x13

Designs: 30c, Gorilla. 50c, Colobus monkey. 3fr, Galago. 10fr, Cercopithecus monkey (mone). 26fr, Potto. 60fr, Cercopithecus monkey (griuet). 150fr, Baboon.

857 A119	20c multi	15	15
858 A119	30c multi	15	15
859 A119	50c multi	15	15
860 A119	3fr multi	15	15
861 A119	10fr multi	20	15
862 A119	26fr multi	55	25
863 A119	60fr multi	1.20	55
864 A119	150fr multi	3.00	1.50
Nos. 857-864 (8)		5.55	
Set value			2.50

Euporus Strangulatus — A120

Coleoptera: 30c, Rhina afzelii, vert. 50c, Pentalobus palini. 3fr, Corynodes dejeani, vert. 10fr, Mecynorhina torquata. 15fr, Mecocerus rhombeus, vert. 20fr, Macrotoma serripes. 25fr, Neptunides stanleyi, vert. 26fr, Petrognatha gigas. 100fr, Eudicella gralli, vert.

1978, May 22   Litho.   Perf. 14

865 A120	20c multi	15	15
866 A120	30c multi	15	15
867 A120	50c multi	15	15
868 A120	3fr multi	15	15
869 A120	10fr multi	20	15
870 A120	15fr multi	30	20
871 A120	20fr multi	40	25
872 A120	25fr multi	50	28
873 A120	26fr multi	52	30
874 A120	100fr multi	2.00	1.40
Nos. 865-874 (10)		4.52	
Set value			2.75

Crossing "River of Poverty" A121

Emblem and: 10fr, 60fr, Men poling boat, facing right. 26fr, like 4fr.

1978, May 29   Perf. 12½

875 A121	4fr multi	15	15
876 A121	10fr multi	20	15
877 A121	26fr multi	52	30
878 A121	60fr multi	1.20	80

Natl. Revolutionary Development Movement (M.R.N.D.).

Soccer, Rimet Cup, Flags of Netherlands and Peru — A122

11th World cup, Argentina, June 1-25, (Various Soccer Scenes and Flags of): 30c, Sweden & Spain. 50c, Scotland & Iran. 2fr, Germany & Tunisia. 3fr, Italy & Hungary. 10fr, Brazil and Austria. 34fr, Poland & Mexico. 100fr, Argentina & France.

1978, June 19   Perf. 13

879 A122	20c multi	15	15
879A A122	30c multi	15	15
879B A122	50c multi	15	15
880 A122	2fr multi	15	15
881 A122	3fr multi	15	15
882 A122	10fr multi	15	15
883 A122	34fr multi	50	32
884 A122	100fr multi	1.50	1.00
Set value		2.35	1.60

Wright Brothers, Flyer I — A123

History of Aviation: 30c, Santos Dumont and Canard 14, 1906. 50c, Henry Farman and Voisin No. 1, 1908. 1fr, Jan Olieslaegers and Bleriot, 1910. 3fr, Marshal Balbo and Savoia S-17, 1919. 10fr, Charles Lindbergh and Spirit of St. Louis, 1927. 55fr, Hugo Junkers and Junkers JU52/3, 1932. 60fr, Igor Sikorsky and Sikorsky VS 300, 1939. 130fr, Concorde over New York.

1978, Oct. 30   Litho.   Perf. 13½x14

885 A123	20c multi	15	15
886 A123	30c multi	15	15
887 A123	50c multi	15	15
888 A123	1fr multi	15	15
889 A123	3fr multi	15	15
890 A123	10fr multi	20	15
891 A123	55fr multi	1.10	70
892 A123	60fr multi	1.20	80
Set value		2.70	1.80

Souvenir Sheet
Perf. 13x13½
893 A123 130fr multi   2.25 2.25

No. 893 contains one stamp 47x35mm.

Christmas Type of 1968
Souvenir Sheet

Design: 200fr, Adoration of the Kings, by Albrecht Dürer, vert.

1978, Dec. 11   Engr.   *Perf. 11½*
894 A48 200fr brown   4.00 4.00

Nos. 532-533, Overprinted "1963 1978" in Black or Blue

1978, Dec. 18   Photo.   *Perf. 13½*
895 A83 6fr multi (Bk)   16 15
896 A83 94fr multi (Bl)   1.90 1.25

Org. for African Unity, 15th anniv.

Goats
A124

Designs: 20c, Ducks, vert. 50c, Cock and chickens, vert. 4fr, Rabbits. 5fr, Pigs, vert. 15fr, Turkey. 50fr, Sheep and cattle, vert. Bull.

1978, Dec. 28   Litho.   *Perf. 14*
897 A124 20c multi   15 15
898 A124 30c multi   15 15
899 A124 50c multi   15 15
900 A124 4fr multi   15 15
901 A124 5fr multi   15 15
902 A124 15fr multi   30 20
903 A124 50fr multi   1.00 65
904 A124 75fr multi   1.50 1.00
    Set value   3.10 2.05

Husbandry Year.

Papilio
Demodocus
A125

Butterflies: 30c, Precis octavia. 50c, Charaxes smaragdalis. 4fr, Charaxes guderiana. 15fr, Colotis evippe. 30fr, Danaus limniace. 50fr, Byblia acheloia. 150fr, Utetheisa pulchella.

1979, Feb. 19   Photo.   *Perf. 14½*
905 A125 20c multi   15 15
906 A125 30c multi   15 15
907 A125 50c multi   15 15
908 A125 4fr multi   15 15
909 A125 15fr multi   30 20
910 A125 30fr multi   60 40
911 A125 50fr multi   1.00 65
912 A125 150fr multi   3.00 2.00
    Nos. 905-912 (8)   5.50 3.85

Euphorbia
Grantii,
Weavers
A126

Design: 60fr, Drummers and Intelsat IV-A.

1979, June 8   Photo.   *Perf. 13*
913 A126 40fr multi   80 55
914 A126 60fr multi   1.20 80

Philexafrique II, Libreville, Gabon, June 8-17.

Entandrophragma Excelsum — A127

Trees and Shrubs: 20c, Polyscias fulva. 50c, Ilex mitis. 4fr, Kigelia Africana. 15fr, Ficus thonningi. 20fr, Acacia Senegal. 50fr, Symphonia globulifera. 110fr, Acacia sieberana. 20c, 50c, 15fr, 50fr, vertical.

1979, Aug. 27   *Perf. 14*
915 A127 20c multi   15 15
916 A127 30c multi   15 15
917 A127 50c multi   15 15
918 A127 4 fr multi   15 15
919 A127 15fr multi   22 15
920 A127 20fr multi   30 20
921 A127 50fr multi   75 50
922 A127 110fr multi   1.65 1.10
    Nos. 915-922 (8)   3.52
    Set value   2.10

Black and
White Boys,
IYC Emblem
A128

Designs: 26fr, 100fr, Children of various races, diff., vert.

1979, Nov. 19   Photo.
923 A128   Block of 8   4.50 3.00
   a.   26fr, any single   55 38
924 A128 42fr multi   80 55

Souvenir Sheet
925 A128 100fr multi   2.00 1.50

Intl. Year of the Child. No. 923 printed in sheets of 16 (4x4).

Basket
Weaving
A129

Perf. 12½x13, 13x12½
1979, Dec. 3   Litho.
926 A129 50c shown   15 15
927 A129 1.50fr Wood carving, vert.   15 15
928 A129 2fr Metal working   15 15
929 A129 10fr Jewelry, vert.   20 15
930 A129 20fr Straw plaiting   40 20
931 A129 26fr Wall painting, vert.   55 25
932 A129 40fr Pottery   80 40
933 A129 100fr Smelting, vert.   2.00 1.00
    Nos. 926-933 (8)   4.40
    Set value   2.00

Souvenir Sheet

Children of Different Races, Christmas Tree — A130

1979, Dec. 24   Engr.   *Perf. 12*
934 A130 200fr ultra & dp mag   6.00 3.00

Christmas; Intl. Year of the Child.

German East
Africa #N5,
Hill — A131   RWANDA   20c

Sir Rowland Hill (1795-1879), originator of penny postage, and Stamps of Ruanda-Urundi or: 30c, German East Africa #N23. 50c, German East Africa #NB9. 3fr, #25. 10fr, #42. 26fr, #123. 100fr, #B28.

1979, Dec. 31   Litho.   *Perf. 14*
935 A131 20c multi   15 15
936 A131 30c multi   15 15
937 A131 50c multi   15 15
938 A131 3fr multi   15 15
939 A131 10fr multi   22 15
940 A131 26fr multi   65 25
941 A131 50fr multi   1.50 60
942 A131 100fr multi   2.50 1.00
    Nos. 935-942 (8)   5.47
    Set value   2.10

Sarothrura
Pulchra
A132

Birds of the Nyungwe Forest: 20c Ploceus alienus, vert. 30c, Regal sunbird, vert. 3fr, Tockus alboterminatus. 10fr, Pygmy owl, vert. 26fr, Emerald cuckoo. 60fr, Finch, vert. 100fr, Stepanoaetus coronatus, vert.

Perf. 13½x13, 13x13½
1980, Jan. 7   Photo.
943 A132 20c multi   15 15
944 A132 30c multi   15 15
945 A132 50c multi   15 15
946 A132 3fr multi   15 15
947 A132 10fr multi   22 15
948 A132 26fr multi   65 25
949 A132 60fr multi   1.50 60
950 A132 100fr multi   2.50 1.00
    Nos. 943-950 (8)   5.47
    Set value   2.10

First Footstep
on Moon,
Spacecraft
A133

Spacecraft and Moon Exploration: 1.50fr, Descent onto lunar surface. 8fr, American flag. 30fr, Solar panels. 50fr, Gathering soil samples. 60fr, Adjusting sun screen. 200fr, Landing craft.

1980, Jan. 31   Photo.   *Perf. 13x13½*
951 A133 50c multi   15 15
952 A133 1.50fr multi   15 15
953 A133 8fr multi   20 15
954 A133 30fr multi   70 30
955 A133 50fr multi   1.40 50
956 A133 60fr multi   1.50 60
    Nos. 951-956 (6)   4.10
    Set value   1.55

Souvenir Sheet
957 A133 200fr multi   5.00 2.00

Apollo 11 moon landing, 10th anniv. (1979).

Globe, Butare and
1905 Chicago Club
Emblems — A134

Rotary International, 75th Anniversary (Globe, Emblems of Butare or Kigali Clubs and): 30c, San

Francisco, 1908. 50c, Chicago, 1910. 4fr, Buffalo, 1911. 15fr, London, 1911. 20fr, Glasgow, 1912. 50fr, Bristol, 1917. 60fr, Rotary International, 1980.

1980, Feb. 23   Litho.   *Perf. 13*
958 A134 20c multi   15 15
959 A134 30c multi   15 15
960 A134 50c multi   15 15
961 A134 4fr multi   15 15
962 A134 15fr multi   30 15
963 A134 20fr multi   40 20
964 A134 50fr multi   1.00 50
965 A134 60fr multi   1.20 60
    Nos. 958-965 (8)   3.50
    Set value   1.60

Gymnast,
Moscow '80
Emblem
A135

1980, Mar. 10   *Perf. 12½*
966 A135 20c shown   15 15
967 A135 30c Basketball   15 15
968 A135 50c Bicycling   15 15
969 A135 3fr Boxing   15 15
970 A135 20fr Archery   50 20
971 A135 26fr Weight lifting   65 25
972 A135 50fr Javelin   1.25 50
973 A135 60fr Fencing   2.50 1.00
    Nos. 966-973 (8)   5.50
    Set value   2.10

22nd Summer Olympic Games, Moscow, July 19-Aug. 3.

Souvenir Sheet

Amalfi Coast, by Giacinto Gigante — A136

1980, Apr. 28   Photo.   *Perf. 13½*
974 A136 200fr multi   5.75 2.50

20th Intl. Philatelic Exhibition, Europa '80, Naples, Apr. 26-May 4.

Geaster
Mushroom
A137

1980, July 21   Photo.   *Perf. 13½*
975 A137 20c shown   15 15
976 A137 30c Lentinus atrobrunneus   15 15
977 A137 50c Gomphus stereoides   15 15
978 A137 4fr Cantharellus cibarius   15 15
979 A137 10fr Stilbothamnium dybowskii   22 15
980 A137 15fr Xeromphalina tenuipes   38 15
981 A137 70fr Podoscypha elegans   1.60 70
982 A137 100fr Mycena   2.25 1.00
    Nos. 975-982 (8)   5.05
    Set value   2.10

Still
Life,
by
Renoir
A138

Impressionist Painters: 30c, 26fr, At the Theater, by Toulouse-Lautrec, vert. 50c, 10fr, Seaside Garden, by Monet. 4fr, Mother and Child, by Mary

Cassatt, vert. 5fr, Starry Night, by Van Gogh. 10fr, Dancers at their Toilet, by Degas, vert. 50fr, The Card Players, by Cezanne. 70fr, Tahitian Women, by Gauguin, vert. 75fr, like 20c. 100fr, In the Park, by Seurat.

1980, Aug. 4   Litho.   Perf. 14

983	A138	20c multi	15	15
984	A138	30c multi	15	15
985	A138	50c multi	15	15
986	A138	4fr multi	15	15
a.		Sheet of 2, 4fr, 20fr	70	70
987	A138	5fr multi	15	15
a.		Sheet of 2, 5fr, 75fr	2.00	2.00
988	A138	10fr multi	22	15
a.		Sheet of 2, 10fr, 70fr	2.00	2.00
989	A138	50fr multi	1.40	50
a.		Sheet of 2, 50fr, 10fr	1.50	1.50
990	A138	70fr multi	1.60	70
991	A138	100fr multi	2.25	1.00
		Nos. 983-991 (9)	6.22	
		Set value		2.50

Souvenir Sheet

Virgin of the Harpies, by Andrea Del Sarto — A139

Photogravure and Engraved
1980, Dec. 22   Perf. 11½

992	A139	200fr multi	5.00	3.00

Christmas.

Belgian War of Independence, Engraving — A140

Belgian Independence Sesquicentennial: Engravings of War of Independence.

1980, Dec. 29   Litho.   Perf. 12½

993	A140	20c pale grn & brn	15	15
994	A140	30c brn org & brn	15	15
995	A140	50c lt bl & brn	15	15
996	A140	0fr yel & brn	18	15
997	A140	10fr brt lil & brn	20	15
998	A140	20fr ap grn & brn	40	20
999	A140	70fr pink & brn	1.40	70
1000	A140	90fr lem & brn	1.75	90
		Nos. 993-1000 (8)	4.38	
		Set value		2.10

Swamp Drainage A141

1980, Dec. 31   Photo.   Perf. 13½

1001	A141	20c shown	15	15
1002	A141	30c Fertilizer shed	15	15
1003	A141	1.50fr Rice fields	15	15
1004	A141	8fr Tree planting	20	15
1005	A141	10fr Terrace planting	28	15
1006	A141	40fr Farm buildings	1.10	55
1007	A141	90fr Bean cultivation	2.50	1.25
1008	A141	100fr Tea cultivation	2.75	1.40
		Nos. 1001-1008 (8)	7.28	3.95

Soil Conservation Year.

Pavetta Rwandensis A142

1981, Apr. 6   Photo.   Perf. 13x13½

1009	A142	20c shown	15	15
1010	A142	30c Cyrtorchis praetermissa	15	15
1011	A142	50c Pavonia urens	15	15
1012	A142	4fr Cynorkis kassnerana	15	15
1013	A142	5fr Gardenia ternifolia	15	15
1014	A142	10fr Leptactina platyphylla	25	15
1015	A142	20fr Lobelia petiolata	50	25
1016	A142	40fr Tapinanthus brunneus	1.00	50
1017	A142	70fr Impatiens niamniamensis	1.75	90
1018	A142	150fr Dissotis rwandensis	3.75	1.90
		Nos. 1009-1018 (10)	8.00	
		Set value		3.80

Girl Knitting — A143

SOS Children's Village: Various children.

1981, Apr. 27   Perf. 13

1019	A143	20c multi	15	15
1020	A143	30c multi	15	15
1021	A143	50c multi	15	15
1022	A143	1fr multi	15	15
1023	A143	8fr multi	18	15
1024	A143	10fr multi	22	15
1025	A143	70fr multi	1.50	70
1026	A143	150fr multi	3.25	1.50
		Nos. 1019-1026 (8)	5.75	
		Set value		2.50

Carolers, by Norman Rockwell A144

Designs: Saturday Evening Post covers by Norman Rockwell.

1981, May 11   Litho.   Perf. 13½x14

1027	A144	20c multi	15	15
1028	A144	30c multi	15	15
1029	A144	50c multi	15	15
1030	A144	1fr multi	15	15
1031	A144	8fr multi	16	15
1032	A144	20fr multi	40	20
1033	A144	50fr multi	1.00	50
1034	A144	70fr multi	1.40	70
		Set value	3.10	1.60

Cerval A145

Designs: Meat-eating animals.

1981, June 29   Photo.   Perf. 13½x14

1035	A145	20c shown	15	15
1036	A145	30c Jackals	15	15
1037	A145	2fr Genet	15	15
1038	A145	2.50fr Banded mongoose	15	15
1039	A145	10fr Zorille	20	15
1040	A145	15fr White-cheeked otter	30	15
1041	A145	70fr Golden wild cat	1.40	70
1042	A145	200fr Hunting dog, vert.	4.00	2.00
		Nos. 1035-1042 (8)	6.50	
		Set value		3.10

RWANDA
Drummer Sending Message — A146

1981, Sept. 1   Litho.   Perf. 13

1043	A146	20c shown	15	15
1044	A146	30c Map, communication waves	15	15
1045	A146	2fr Jet, radar screen	15	15
1046	A146	2.50fr Satellite, teletape	15	15
1047	A146	10fr Dish antenna	25	15
1048	A146	15fr Ship, navigation devices	38	18
1049	A146	70fr Helicopter	1.75	90
1050	A146	200fr Satellite with solar panels	5.00	2.50
		Nos. 1043-1050 (8)	7.98	
		Set value		2.80

1500th Birth Anniv. of St. Benedict A147

Paintings and Frescoes of St. Benedict: 20c, Leaving his Parents, Mt. Oliveto Monastery, Maggiore. 30c, Oldest portrait, 10th cent., St. Chrisogone Church, Rome, vert. 50c, Portrait, Virgin of the Misericord polyptich, Borgo San Sepolcro. 4fr, Giving the Rules of the order to his Monks, Mt. Oliveto Monastery. 5fr, Monks at their Meal, Mt. Oliveto Monastery. 20fr, Portrait, 13th cent., Lower Chruch of the Holy Spirit, Subiaco, vert. 70fr, Our Lady in Glory with Sts. Gregory and Benedict, San Gimigniao, vert. 100fr, Priest Carrying Easter Meal to St. Benedict, by Jan van Coninxloo, 16th cent.

Perf. 13½x13, 13x13½
1981, Nov. 30   Photo.

1051	A147	20c multi	15	15
1052	A147	30c multi	15	15
1053	A147	50c multi	15	15
1054	A147	4fr multi	15	15
1055	A147	5fr multi	15	15
1056	A147	20fr multi	40	20
1057	A147	70fr multi	1.40	65
1058	A147	100fr multi	2.00	2.00
		Nos. 1051-1058 (8)	4.55	
		Set value		3.00

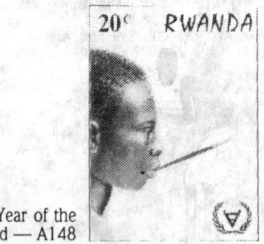

Intl. Year of the Disabled — A148

1981, Dec. 7   Litho.   Perf. 13

1059	A148	20c Painting	15	15
1060	A148	30c Soccer	15	15
1061	A148	4.50fr Crocheting	15	15
1062	A148	5fr Painting vase	15	15
1063	A148	10fr Sawing	20	15
1064	A148	60fr Sign language	1.20	65
1065	A148	70fr Doing puzzle	1.40	80
1066	A148	100fr Juggling	2.00	1.10
		Nos. 1059-1066 (8)	5.40	
		Set value		2.80

Souvenir Sheet

Christmas A149

Photo. & Engr.
1981, Dec. 21   Perf. 13½

1067	A149	200fr Adoration of the Kings, by van der Goes	4.00	2.00

Natl. Rural Water Supply Year — A150

1981, Dec. 28   Litho.   Perf. 12½

1068	A150	20c Deer drinking	15	15
1069	A150	30c Women carrying water, vert.	15	15
1070	A150	50c Pipeline	15	15
1071	A150	10fr Filing pan, vert.	20	15
1072	A150	19fr Drinking	40	22
1073	A150	70fr Mother, child, vert.	1.40	65
1074	A150	100fr Lake pumping station, vert.	2.00	1.00
		Nos. 1068-1074 (7)	4.45	
		Set value		2.10

World Food Day, Oct. 16, 1981 A151

1982, Jan. 25   Litho.   Perf. 13

1075	A151	20c Cattle	15	15
1076	A151	30c Bee	15	15
1077	A151	50c Fish	15	15
1078	A151	1fr Avocados	15	15
1079	A151	8fr Boy eating banana	16	15
1080	A151	50fr Sorghum	40	20
1081	A151	70fr Vegetables	1.40	65
1082	A151	100fr Balanced diet	2.00	1.00
		Nos. 1075-1082 (8)	4.56	
		Set value		2.10

Hibiscus Berberidifolius A152

1982, June 14   Litho.   Perf. 13

1083	A152	20c shown	15	15
1084	A152	30c Hypericum lanceolatum, vert.	15	15
1085	A152	50c Canarina eminii	15	15
1086	A152	4fr Polygala ruwenxoriensis	15	15
1087	A152	10fr Kniphofia grantii, vert.	20	15
1088	A152	35fr Euphorbia candelabrum, vert.	70	35
1089	A152	70fr Disa erubescens, vert.	1.40	65
1090	A152	80fr Gloriosa simplex	1.60	1.00
		Nos. 1083-1090 (8)	4.50	
		Set value		2.20

20th Anniv. of Independence — A153

1982, June 28
1091	A153	10fr	Flags	20	15
1092	A153	20fr	Hands releasing doves	40	20
1093	A153	30fr	Flag, handshake	60	30
1094	A153	50fr	Govt. buildings	1.00	50

1982 World Cup — A154

Designs: Various soccer players.

1982, July 6   *Perf. 14x14½*
1095	A154	20c	multi	15	15
1096	A154	30c	multi	15	15
1097	A154	1.50fr	multi	15	15
1098	A154	8fr	multi	16	15
1099	A154	10fr	multi	20	15
1100	A154	20fr	multi	40	20
1101	A154	70fr	multi	1.40	65
1102	A154	90fr	multi	1.90	90
		Nos. 1095-1102 (8)		4.51	
		Set value			2.00

TB Bacillus Centenary — A155

1982, Nov. 22   Litho.   *Perf. 14½*
1103	A155	10fr	Microscope, slide	20	15
1104	A155	20fr	Serum, slide	40	20
1105	A155	70fr	Lungs, slide	1.40	65
1106	A155	100fr	Koch	2.00	1.00

Souvenir Sheets

Madam Recamier, by David — A156

PHILEXFRANCE '82 Intl. Stamp Exhibition, Paris, June 11-21: No. 1108, St. Anne and Virgin and Child with Franciscan Monk, by H. van der Goes. No. 1109, Liberty Guiding the People, by Delacroix. No. 1110, Pygmalion, by P. Delvaux.

1982, Dec. 11   *Perf. 13½*
1107	A156	40fr	multi	80	42
1108	A156	40fr	multi	80	42
1109	A156	60fr	multi	1.20	55
1110	A156	60fr	multi	1.20	55

Souvenir Sheet

Rest During the Flight to Egypt, by Murillo A157

1982, Dec. 20   Photo. & Engr.
1111	A157	200fr	carmine rose	4.00	2.00

Christmas.

10th Anniv. of UN Conference on Human Environment — A158

1982, Dec. 27   Litho.   *Perf. 14*
1112	A158	20c	Elephants	15	15
1113	A158	30c	Lion	15	15
1114	A158	50c	Flower	15	15
1115	A158	4fr	Bull	15	15
1116	A158	5fr	Deer	15	15
1117	A158	10fr	Flower, diff.	20	15
1118	A158	20fr	Zebras	40	20
1119	A158	40fr	Crowned cranes	80	40
1120	A158	50fr	Bird	1.00	50
1121	A158	70fr	Woman pouring coffee beans	1.40	65
		Nos. 1112-1121 (10)		4.55	
		Set value			2.00

Scouting Year A159

Perf. 13½x14½

1983, Jan. 17   Photo.
1122	A159	20c	Animal first aid	15	15
1123	A159	30c	Camp	15	15
1124	A159	1.50fr	Campfire	15	15
1125	A159	8fr	Scout giving sign	16	15
1126	A159	10fr	Knot	20	15
1127	A159	20fr	Camp, diff.	40	20
1128	A159	70fr	Chopping wood	1.40	65
1129	A159	90fr	Sign, map	1.75	90
		Nos. 1122-1129 (8)		4.36	
		Set value			2.00

For overprints see Nos. 1234-1241.

Nectar-sucking Birds — A160

Perf. 14x14½, 14½x14

1983, Jan. 31   Litho.
1130	A160	20c	Angola nectar bird	15	15
1131	A160	30c	Royal nectar birds	15	15
1132	A160	50c	Johnston's nectar bird	15	15
1133	A160	4fr	Bronze nectar birds	15	15
1134	A160	5fr	Collared souimangas	15	15
1135	A160	10fr	Blue-headed nectar bird	30	15
1136	A160	20fr	Purple-bellied nectar bird	40	20
1137	A160	40fr	Copper nectar birds	80	40
1138	A160	50fr	Olive-bellied nectar birds	1.00	50
1139	A160	70fr	Red-breasted nectar bird	1.40	65
		Nos. 1130-1139 (10)		4.65	
		Set value			2.00

30c, 4fr, 10fr, 40fr, 70fr horiz. Inscribed 1982.

Soil Erosion Prevention A161

1983, Feb. 14   *Perf. 14½*
1140	A161	20c	Driving cattle	15	15
1141	A161	30c	Pineapple field	15	15
1142	A161	50c	Interrupted ditching	15	15
1143	A161	9fr	Hedges, ditches	18	15
1144	A161	10fr	Reafforestation	20	15
1145	A161	20fr	Anti-erosion barriers	40	20
1146	A161	30fr	Contour planting	60	30
1147	A161	50fr	Terracing	1.00	50
1148	A161	60fr	Protection of river banks	1.20	60
1149	A161	70fr	Fallow, planted strips	1.40	65
		Nos. 1140-1149 (10)		5.43	
		Set value			2.50

For overprints & surcharges see #1247-1255.

Cardinal Cardijn (1882-1967) A162   Gorilla A163

Young Catholic Workers Movement Activities. Inscribed 1982.

1983, Feb. 22   *Perf. 12½x13*
1150	A162	20c	Feeding ducks	15	15
1151	A162	30c	Harvesting bananas	15	15
1152	A162	50c	Carrying melons	15	15
1153	A162	10fr	Teacher	25	15
1154	A162	19fr	Shoemakers	50	22
1155	A162	20fr	Growing millet	50	25
1156	A162	70fr	Embroidering	1.75	80
1157	A162	80fr	shown	2.00	1.00
		Nos. 1150-1157 (8)		5.45	2.87

1983, Mar. 14   *Perf. 14*

Various gorillas. Nos. 1158-1163 horiz.
1158	A163	20c	multi	15	15
1159	A163	30c	multi	15	15
1160	A163	9.50fr	multi	18	15
1161	A163	10fr	multi	20	15
1162	A163	20fr	multi	40	20
1163	A163	30fr	multi	60	30
1164	A163	60fr	multi	1.20	60
1165	A163	70fr	multi	1.40	65
		Nos. 1158-1165 (8)		4.28	2.35

Souvenir Sheet

The Granduca Madonna, by Raphael A164

Typo. & Engr.   *Perf. 11½*
1166	A164	200fr	multi	2.50	1.40

Christmas.

Local Trees — A165

1984, Jan. 15   Litho.   *Perf. 13½x13*
1167	A165	20c	Hagenia abyssinica	15	15
1168	A165	30c	Dracaena steudneri	15	15
1169	A165	50c	Phoenix reclinata	15	15
1170	A165	10fr	Podocarpus milanjianus	15	15
1171	A165	19fr	Entada abyssinica	25	15
1172	A165	70fr	Parinari excelsa	90	45
1173	A165	100fr	Newtonia buchananii	1.40	65
1174	A165	200fr	Acacia gerrardi, vert.	2.50	1.40
		Nos. 1167-1174 (8)		5.65	
		Set value			2.80

World Communications Year — A166

1984, May 21   Litho.   *Perf. 12½*
1175	A166	20c	Train	15	15
1176	A166	30c	Ship	15	15
1177	A166	4.50fr	Radio	15	15
1178	A166	10fr	Telephone	15	15
1179	A166	15fr	Mail	20	15
1180	A166	50fr	Jet	65	35
1181	A166	70fr	Satellite, TV screen	90	45
1182	A166	100fr	Satellite	1.40	65
		Nos. 1175-1182 (8)		3.75	
		Set value			1.75

1st Manned Flight Bicent. — A167

Historic flights: 20c, Le Martial, Sept. 19, 1783. 30c, La Montgolfiere, Nov. 21, 1783. 50c, Charles and Robert, Dec. 1, 1783, and Blanchard, Mar. 2, 1784. 9fr, Jean-Pierre Blanchard and wife in balloon. 10fr, Blanchard and Jeffries, 1785. 50fr, E. Demuyter, 1937. 80fr, Propane gas balloons. 200fr, Abruzzo, Anderson and Newman, 1978.

1984, June 4   Litho.   *Perf. 13*
1183	A167	20c	multi	15	15
1184	A167	30c	multi	15	15
1185	A167	50c	multi	15	15
1186	A167	9fr	multi	15	15
1187	A167	10fr	multi	15	15
1188	A167	50fr	multi	65	35
1189	A167	80fr	multi	1.00	50
1190	A167	200fr	multi	2.50	1.40
		Nos. 1183-1190 (8)		4.90	
		Set value			2.50

1984 Summer Olympics A168

1984, July 16   *Perf. 14*
1191 A168 20c Equestrian   15   15
1192 A168 30c Wind surfing   15   15
1193 A168 50c Soccer   15   15
1194 A168 9fr Swimming   15   15
1195 A168 10fr Field hockey   15   15
1196 A168 40fr Fencing   55   25
1197 A168 80fr Running   1.10   55
1198 A168 200fr Boxing   2.50 1.40
        Nos. 1191-1198 (8)   4.90
            Set value   2.45

Zebras and
Buffaloes
A169

1984, Nov. 26   Litho.   *Perf. 13*
1199 A169 20c Zebra with colt   15   15
1200 A169 30c Buffalo with calf,
                  vert.   15   15
1201 A169 50c Two zebras, vert.   15   15
1202 A169 9fr Zebras fighting   15   15
1203 A169 10fr Buffalo, vert.   15   15
1204 A169 80fr Zebra herd   1.00   55
1205 A169 100fr Zebra, vert.   1.25   60
1206 A169 200fr Buffalo   2.50 1.25
        Nos. 1199-1206 (8)   5.50
            Set value   2.65

Souvenir Sheet

Christmas
1984 — A170

1984, Dec. 24   Typo. & Engr.
1207 A170 200fr Virgin and Child,
                   by Correggio   3.50 2.25

Gorilla Gorilla Beringei — A171

1985, Mar. 25   Litho.   *Perf. 13*
1208 A171 10fr Adults and young   15   15
1209 A171 15fr Adults   20   15
1210 A171 25fr Female holding
                  young   35   16
1211 A171 30fr Three adults   40   20
            Set value   52

Souvenir Sheet
Perf. 11½x12
1212 A171 200fr Baby climbing
                   branch, vert.   2.50 1.40

No. 1212 contains one 37x52mm stamp.

Self-Sufficiency in Food
Production — A172

Designs: 20c, Raising chickens and turkeys.
30c, Pineapple harvest. 50c, Animal husbandry.
9fr, Grain products. 10fr, Education. 50fr, Sowing
grain. 80fr, Food reserves. 100fr, Banana harvest.

1985, Mar. 30
1213 A172 20c multi   15   15
1214 A172 30c multi   15   15
1215 A172 50c multi   15   15
1216 A172 9fr multi   15   15
1217 A172 10fr multi   15   15
1218 A172 50fr multi   65   35
1219 A172 80fr multi   1.00   50
1220 A172 100fr multi   1.40   65
        Nos. 1213-1220 (8)   3.80
            Set value   1.75

Natl.
Redevelopment
Movement, 10th
Anniv. — A173

1985, July 5
1221 A173 10fr multi   15   15
1222 A173 30fr multi   40   20
1223 A173 70fr multi   90   45

UN, 40th
Anniv.
A174

1985, July 25
1224 A174 50fr multi   65   35
1225 A174 100fr multi   1.40   65

Audubon Birth Bicent. — A175

Illustrations of North American bird species by
John J. Audubon.

1985, Sept. 18
1226 A175 10fr Barn owl   15   15
1227 A175 20fr White-faced owl   25   15
1228 A175 40fr Red-breasted hum-
                  mingbird   55   25
1229 A175 80fr Warbler   1.00   50

Intl.
Youth
Year
A176

1985, Oct. 14
1230 A176 7fr Education and agricul-
                  ture   15   15
1231 A176 9fr Bicycling   15   15
1232 A176 44fr Construction   55   28
1233 A176 80fr Schoolroom   1.00   50
            Set value   90

Nos. 1122-1129 Ovptd. in Green or Rose
Violet with the Girl Scout Trefoil and
"1910/1985"

1985, Nov. 25   *Perf. 13½x14½*
1234 A159 20c multi   15   15
1235 A159 30c multi (RV)   15   15
1236 A159 1.50fr multi   15   15
1237 A159 8fr multi (RV)   15   15
1238 A159 10fr multi   15   15
1239 A159 20fr multi   25   15

1240 A159 70fr multi (RV)   90   45
1241 A159 90fr multi   1.10   60
            Set value   2.60 1.40

Natl. Girl Scout Movement, 75th anniv.

Souvenir Sheet

Adoration of the Magi, by Titian — A177

Photo. & Engr.
1985, Dec. 24   *Perf. 11½*
1242 A177 200fr violet   3.00 2.00

Christmas.

Transportation and
Communication — A178

1986, Jan. 27   Litho.   *Perf. 13*
1243 A178 10fr Articulated truck   15   15
1244 A178 30fr Hand-canceling letters   40   20
1245 A178 40fr Kigali Satellite Station   55   25
            Size: 52x34mm
1246 A178 80fr Kayibanda Airport,
                  Kigali   1.00   50

Nos. 1141-1149 Surcharged or Ovptd.
with Silver Bar and "ANNEE 1986 /
INTENSIFICATION AGRICOLE"

1986, May 5   Litho.   *Perf. 14½*
1247 A161 9fr #1143   18   15
1248 A161 10fr on 30c #1141   20   15
1249 A161 10fr on 50c #1142   20   15
1250 A161 10fr #1144   20   15
1251 A161 20fr #1145   40   20
1252 A161 30fr #1146   60   30
1253 A161 50fr #1147   1.00   50
1254 A161 60fr #1148   1.20   60
1255 A161 70fr #1149   1.40   70
        Nos. 1247-1255 (9)   5.38 2.90

1986 World Cup
Soccer
Championships,
Mexico — A179

Various soccer plays, natl. flags.

1986, June 16   *Perf. 13*
1256 A179 2fr Morocco, England   15   15
1257 A179 4fr Paraguay, Iraq   15   15
1258 A179 5fr Brazil, Spain   15   15
1259 A179 10fr Italy, Argentina   20   15
1260 A179 40fr Mexico, Belgium   80   40
1261 A179 45fr France, USSR   90   45
        Nos. 1256-1261 (6)   2.35
            Set value   1.05

For overprints see Nos. 1360-1365.

Akagera Natl. Park — A180

1986, Dec. 15   Litho.   *Perf. 13*
1262 A180 4fr Antelopes   15   15
1263 A180 7fr Shoebills   15   15
1264 A180 9fr Cape elands   18   15
1265 A180 10fr Giraffe   20   15
1266 A180 80fr Elephants   1.60   80
1267 A180 90fr Crocodiles   1.80   90
            Size: 48x34mm
1268 A180 100fr Weaver birds   2.00 1.00
1269 A180 100fr Pelican, zebras   2.00 1.00
        Nos. 1262-1269 (8)   8.08 4.30

Nos. 1268-1269 printed se-tenant in a continuous design with label picturing map on right.

Christmas,
Intl. Peace
Year
A181

1986, Dec. 24   Litho.   *Perf. 13*
1270 A181 10fr shown   20   15
1271 A181 15fr Dove, Earth   30   15
1272 A181 30fr like 10fr   60   30
1273 A181 70fr like 15fr   1.40   70

UN Child Survival
Campaign — A182

1987, Feb. 13
1274 A182 4fr Breast feeding   15   15
1275 A182 6fr Rehydration therapy   15   15
1276 A182 10fr Immunization   20   15
1277 A182 70fr Growth monitoring   1.40   70
            Set value   90

Year of Natl. Self-sufficiency in Food
Production — A183

1987, June 15   Litho.   *Perf. 13*
1278 A183 5fr Farm   15   15
1279 A183 7fr Storing produce   15   15
1280 A183 40fr Boy carrying basket
                  of fish, produce   80   40
1281 A183 60fr Tropical fruit   1.20   60

Nos. 1279-1281 vert.

Natl. Independence, 25th Anniv. — A184

Designs: 10fr, Pres. Habyarimana, soldiers, farmers. 40fr, Pres. officiating government session. 70fr, Pres., Pope John Paul II. 100fr, Pres., vert.

1987, July 1
1283	A184	10fr multi	20	15
1284	A184	40fr multi	80	40
1285	A184	70fr multi	1.40	70
1286	A184	100fr multi	2.00	1.00

Fruit
A185

1987, Sept. 28
1287	A185	10fr Bananas, vert.	20	15
1288	A185	40fr Pineapples	80	40
1289	A185	80fr Papayas	1.60	80
1290	A185	90fr Avocados	1.80	90
1291	A185	100fr Strawberries, vert.	2.00	1.00
		Nos. 1287-1291 (5)	6.40	3.25

Leopards — A186

1987, Nov. 18   Litho.   Perf. 13
1292	A186	50fr Female, cub	1.00	50
1293	A186	50fr Three cubs playing	1.00	50
1294	A186	50fr Adult attaching gazelle	1.00	50
1295	A186	50fr In tree	1.00	50
1296	A186	50fr Leaping from tree	1.00	50
a.		Strip of 5, Nos. 1292-1296	5.00	2.50
		Nos. 1292-1296 (5)	5.00	2.50

Intl. Year of the Volunteer — A187

1987, Dec. 12
1297	A187	5fr Constructing village water system	15	15
1298	A187	12fr Education, vert.	24	15
1299	A187	20fr Modern housing, vert.	40	20
1300	A187	60fr Animal husbandry, vert.	1.20	60
		Set value		96

Souvenir Sheet

Virgin and Child, by Fra Angelico (c. 1387-1455) A188

1987, Dec. 24   Engr.   Perf. 11½
1301	A188	200fr deep mag & dull blue	4.00	2.00

Christmas.

Maintenance of the Rural Economy Year — A189

1988, June 13   Litho.   Perf. 13
1302	A189	10fr Furniture store	26	15
1303	A189	40fr Dairy farm	1.05	52
1304	A189	60fr Produce market	1.60	80
1305	A189	80fr Fruit market	2.10	1.05

Primates, Nyungwe Forest A190

1988, Sept. 15   Litho.   Perf. 13
1306	A190	2fr Chimpanzee	15	15
1307	A190	3fr Black and white colobus	15	15
1308	A190	10fr Pygmy galago	25	15
1309	A190	90fr Cercopithecidae ascagne	2.35	1.20
		Set value		1.40

1988 Summer Olympics, Seoul A191

1988, Sept. 19
1310	A191	5fr Boxing	15	15
1311	A191	7fr Relay	18	15
1312	A191	8fr Table tennis	22	15
1313	A191	10fr Women's running	28	15
1314	A191	90fr Hurdles	2.35	1.20
		Nos. 1310-1314 (5)	3.18	1.80

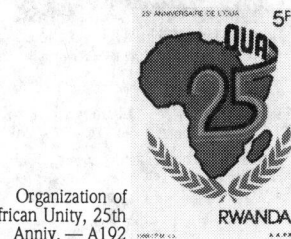

Organization of African Unity, 25th Anniv. — A192

1988, Nov. 30   Litho.   Perf. 13
1315	A192	5fr shown	15	15
1316	A192	7fr Handskake, map	18	15
1317	A192	8fr "OAU" in brick, map	20	15
1318	A192	90fr Slogan	2.35	1.20

Souvenir Sheet

NOËL 1988

Detail of The Virgin and the Soup, by Paolo Veronese — A193

1988, Dec. 23   Engr.   Perf. 13½
1319	A193	200fr lt vio, grnsh bl & lake	5.25	5.25

Christmas. Margin is typographed.

Intl. Red Cross and Red Crescent Organizations, 125th Annivs. — A194

1988, Dec. 30   Litho.   Perf. 13
1320	A194	10fr Refugees	25	15
1321	A194	30fr First aid	78	40
1322	A194	40fr Elderly	1.05	52
1323	A194	100fr Travelling doctor	2.60	1.30
		Nos. 1322-1323 vert.		

Medicinal Plants — A195

1989, Feb. 15   Litho.   Perf. 13
1324	A195	5fr Plectranthus barbatus	15	15
1325	A195	10fr Tetradenia riparia	28	15
1326	A195	20fr Hygrophila auriculata	55	28
1327	A195	40fr Datura stramonium	1.10	55
1328	A195	50fr Pavetta ternifolia	1.40	70
		Nos. 1324-1328 (5)	3.48	1.83

Interparliamentary Union, Cent. — A196

1989, Oct. 20   Litho.   Perf. 13
1329	A196	10fr shown	30	16
1330	A196	30fr Hills, lake	90	50
1331	A196	70fr Hills, stream	2.10	1.15
1332	A196	90fr Sun rays, hills	2.75	1.50

Souvenir Sheet

NOËL 1989

L'Adoration des Mages
P.P. RUBENS
(1577-1640)
Musées Royaux des Beaux-Arts Bruxelles

Christmas — A197

Adoration of the Magi by Rubens.

1989, Dec. 29   Engr.   Perf. 11½
1333	A197	100fr blk, red & grn	3.40	3.40

Rural Organization Year — A198

Designs: 10fr, Making pottery. 70fr, Carrying produce to market. 90fr, Firing clay pots. 100fr, Clearing land.

CAMPO RODAN
RUE DU LOMBARD 9
1000 BRUSSELS, BELGIUM
PHONE: 011-32-2-514-5292
FAX: 011-32-2-514-5415

Specialists in...
BELGIUM
and former territories:
RWANDA
CONGA - ZAIRE
KATANGA
SOUTH KASAI
RUANDA
URUNDI
BURUNDI
LUXEMBOURG
EUROPE

Charge it! We accept:

1989, Dec. 29   Litho.   _Perf. 13¹/₂x13_

1334	A198	10fr multi	35	18
1335	A198	70fr multi, vert.	2.35	1.30
1336	A198	90fr multi	3.00	1.65
1337	A198	200fr multi	6.75	3.75

Revolution, 30th Anniv. (in 1989) — A199

Designs: 10fr, Improved living conditions. 60fr, Couple, farm tools. 70fr, Modernization. 100fr, Flag, map, native.

1990, Jan. 22   _Perf. 13_

1338	A199	10fr multi	35	18
1339	A199	60fr multi, vert.	2.05	1.10
1340	A199	70fr multi	2.35	1.30
1341	A199	100fr multi	3.35	1.85

Inscribed 1989.

French Revolution, Bicent. (in 1989) — A200

Paintings of the Revolution: 10fr, Triumph of Marat by Boilly. 60fr, Rouget de Lisle singing La Marseillaise by Pils. 70fr, Oath of the Tennis Court by David. 100fr, Trial of Louis XVI by Court.

1990, Jan. 22

1342	A200	10fr multicolored	35	18
1343	A200	60fr multicolored	2.05	1.10
1344	A200	70fr multicolored	2.35	1.30
1345	A200	100fr multicolored	3.35	1.85

Inscribed 1989.

African Development Bank, 25th Anniv. (in 1989) — A201

1990, Feb. 22   _Perf. 13¹/₂x13_

1346	A201	10fr Building construction	35	18
1347	A201	20fr Harvesting	70	40
1348	A201	40fr Cultivation	1.35	75
1349	A201	90fr Building, truck, harvesters	3.00	1.65

Belgica '90, Intl. Philatelic Exhibition — A202

Illustration reduced.

1990, May 21   Litho.   _Imperf._

1350	A202	100fr Great Britain #1	3.50	1.75
1351	A202	100fr Belgium #B1011	3.50	1.75
1352	A202	100fr Rwanda #516	3.50	1.75

Visit of Pope John Paul II A203

1990, Aug. 27   Litho.   _Perf. 13¹/₂x13_

1353	A203	10fr shown	35	18
1354	A203	70fr Holding crucifix	2.30	1.25

Souvenir Sheet
Perf. 11¹/₂

1355	A203	100fr Hands together	3.25	1.75

No. 1355 contains one 36x51mm stamp.

Intl. Literacy Year A204

Designs: 10fr, Teacher at blackboard. 20fr, Teacher seated at desk. 50fr, Small outdoor class. 90fr, Large outdoor class.

1991, Jan. 25   Litho.   _Perf. 13¹/₂x13_

1356	A204	10fr multicolored	20	15
1357	A204	20fr multicolored	40	25
1358	A204	50fr multicolored	95	55
1359	A204	90fr multicolored	1.75	95

I T A L I A 90

Nos. 1256-1261 Ovptd. in Black on Silver

1990, May 25   Litho.   _Perf. 13_

1360	A179	2fr on No. 1256	15	15
1361	A179	4fr on No. 1257	15	15
1362	A179	5fr on No. 1258	15	15
1363	A179	10fr on No. 1259	28	15
1364	A179	40fr on No. 1260	1.15	58
1365	A179	45fr on No. 1261	1.30	65
		Nos. 1360-1365 (6)	3.18	
		Set value		1.60

Self-help Organizations — A205

1991, Jan. 25   Litho.   _Perf. 13¹/₂x13_

1366	A205	10fr Tool making	28	15
1367	A205	20fr Animal husbandry	58	30
1368	A205	50fr Textile manufacturing	1.40	70
1369	A205	90fr Road construction	2.50	1.35

Dated 1990.

SEMI-POSTAL STAMPS

No. 305 Surcharged in Black and Overprinted in Brown: "SECHERESSE/SOLIDARITE AFRICAINE"

1973, Aug. 23   Photo.   _Perf. 13_

B1	A53	100fr + 50fr multi	2.50	2.25

African solidarity in drought emergency.

Nos. 349-350 Surcharged and Overprinted Like Nos. 693-698

1975, Nov. 10   Litho.   _Perf. 13_

B2	A60	50fr + 25fr multi	1.50	1.00
B3	A60	90fr + 25fr multi	2.00	1.50

African solidarity in drought emergency.

AIR POST STAMPS

African Postal Union Issue, 1967
Common Design Type

1967, Sept. 18   Engr.   _Perf. 13_

C1	CD124	6fr brown, rose cl & gray	15	15
C2	CD124	18fr brt lil, ol brn & plum	40	30
C3	CD124	30fr green, dp bl & red	65	55

PHILEXAFRIQUE Issue

Alexandre Lenoir, by Jacques L. David — AP1

1968, Dec. 30   Photo.   _Perf. 12¹/₂_

C4	AP1	100fr emerald & multi	1.90	80

Issued to publicize PHILEXAFRIQUE, Philatelic exhibition in Abidjan, Feb. 14-23, 1969. Printed with alternating emerald label.

2nd PHILEXAFRIQUE Issue

Ruanda-Urundi No. 123, Cowherd and Lake Victoria — AP2

1969, Feb. 14   Litho.   _Perf. 14_

C5	AP2	50fr multicolored	90	80

Issued to commemorate the opening of PHILEX-AFRIQUE, Abidjan, Feb. 14.

Painting Type of Regular Issue

Paintings and Music: 50fr, The Music Lesson, by Fragonard. 100fr, Angels' Concert, by Memling, horiz.

1969, Mar. 31   Photo.   _Perf. 13_

C6	A49	50fr gold & multi	80	38
C7	A49	100fr gold & multi	1.90	1.60

African Postal Union Issue, 1971
Common Design Type

Design: Woman and child of Rwanda and UAMPT Building, Brazzaville, Congo.

1971, Nov. 13   _Perf. 13x13¹/₂_

C8	CD135	100fr blue & multi	1.75	1.75

No. C8 Overprinted in Red

a

LIÈGE ACCUEILLE LES PAYS DE LANGUE FRANCAISE
1973
b

1973, Sept. 17   Photo.   _Perf. 13x13¹/₂_

C9	CD135(a)	100fr multi	2.00	2.00
C10	CD135(b)	100fr multi	2.00	2.00
a.		Pair, #C9-C10	4.00	4.00

3rd Conference of French-speaking countries, Liège, Sept. 15-Oct. 14. Overprints alternate checkerwise in same sheet.

Sassenage Castle, Grenoble — AP3

1977, June 20   Litho.   _Perf. 12¹/₂_

C11	AP3	50fr multi	1.25	1.00

10th anniversary of International French Language Council.

Philexafrique II-Essen Issue
Common Design Types

Designs: No. C12, Okapi, Rwanda #239. No. C13, Woodpecker, Oldenburg #4.

1978, Nov. 1   Litho.   _Perf. 12¹/₂_

C12	CD138	30fr multi	60	50
C13	CD139	30fr multi	60	50
a.		Pair, #C12-C13	1.25	1.00

SAAR

LOCATION — On the Franco-German border southeast of Luxembourg
GOVT. — A German state
POP. — 1,400,000 (1959)
AREA — 991 sq. mi.
CAPITAL — Saarbrücken

A former German territory, the Saar was administered by the League of Nations 1920-35. After a January 12, 1935, plebiscite, it returned to Germany, and the use of German stamps was resumed. After World War II, France occupied the Saar and later established a protectorate. The provisional semi-independent State of Saar was established Jan. 1, 1951. France returned the Saar to the German Federal Republic Jan. 1, 1957.

Saar stamps were discontinued in 1959 and replaced by stamps of the German Federal Republic.

100 Pfennig = 1 Mark
100 Centimes = 1 Franc (1921)

Watermark

Wmk. 285- Marbleized Pattern

Sarre

German Stamps of
1906-19 Overprinted

Perf. 14, 14½

			Wmk. 125	
1920, Jan. 30				
1	A22	2pf gray	75	1.90
b.		Double overprint	725.00	1,200.
2	A22	2½pf gray	1.00	3.00
3	A16	3pf brown	40	1.25
4	A16	5pf green	15	22
b.		Double overprint	240.00	400.00
5	A22	7½pf orange	22	35
6	A16	10pf carmine	15	22
b.		Double overprint	240.00	400.00
7	A22	15pf dk violet	15	20
a.		Double overprint	225.00	360.00
8	A16	20pf blue violet	15	30
a.		Double overprint	180.00	300.00
9	A16	25pf org & blk, yel	9.00	10.00
10	A16	30pf org & blk, buff	15.00	17.50
11	A22	35pf red brown	15	25
12	A16	40pf lake & blk	24	35
13	A16	50pf pur & blk, buff	16	30
14	A16	60pf red violet	22	35
15	A16	75pf green & blk	25	28
16	A16	80pf lake & blk, rose	150.00	150.00

Three types of overprint exist on Nos. 1-5, 12, 13; two types on Nos. 6-11, 14-16.

Inverted Overprint

1a	A22	2pf gray	75.00	125.00
2a	A22	2½pf gray	110.00	180.00
3a	A16	3pf brown	100.00	160.00
4a	A16	5pf green	200.00	325.00
5a	A22	7½pf orange	150.00	240.00
6a	A16	10pf carmine	150.00	240.00
9a	A16	25pf org & blk, yel	275.00	400.00
11a	A22	35pf red brown	135.00	225.00
12a	A16	40pf lake & blk	130.00	200.00
13a	A16	50pf pur & blk, buff	150.00	240.00
15a	A16	75pf green & blk	72.50	125.00

Sarre

Overprinted

17	A17	1m carmine rose	16.00	22.50
a.		Inverted overprint	325.00	525.00
b.		Double overprint	450.00	725.00
		Nos. 1-17 (28)	1,741.	2,743.

The 3m type A19 exists with this overprint but was not issued.
Overprint forgeries exist.

Sarre

Bavarian Stamps of
1914-16 Overprinted

Perf. 14x14½

			Wmk. 95	
1920, Mar. 1				
19	A10	2pf gray	1,000.	4,000.
20	A10	3pf brown	100.00	525.00
21	A10	5pf yellow grn	40	85
a.		Double overprint	400.00	900.00
22	A10	7½pf green	40.00	150.00
23	A10	10pf carmine rose	40	85
a.		Double overprint	150.00	265.00
24	A10	15pf vermilion	6.00	20.00
a.		Double overprint	175.00	315.00
25	A10	15pf carmine	35	90
26	A10	20pf blue	35	90
a.		Double overprint	150.00	265.00
27	A10	25pf gray	3.75	8.50
28	A10	30pf orange	4.00	7.50
30	A10	40pf olive green	4.50	7.50
31	A10	50pf red brown	60	90
a.		Double overprint	100.00	150.00
32	A10	60pf dark green	2.00	5.00

Sarre

Overprinted

Perf. 11½

35	A11	1m brown	10.00	18.00
a.		1m dark brown	11.50	19.00
36	A11	2m violet	45.00	70.00
37	A11	3m scarlet	75.00	110.00

SARRE

Overprinted

38	A12	5m deep blue	625.00	900.00
39	A12	10m yellow green	110.00	150.00
a.		Double overprint	9,000.	15,000.

Nos. 19, 20 and 22 were not officially issued, but were available for postage. Examples are known legitimately used on cover. The 20m type A12 was also overprinted in small quantity.
Overprint forgeries exist.

German Stamps of
1906-20 Overprinted **SAARGEBIET**

Perf. 14, 14½

			Wmk. 125	
1920, Mar. 26				
41	A16	5pf green	15	20
42	A16	5pf red brown	28	26
43	A16	10pf carmine	15	20
44	A16	10pf orange	20	16
45	A22	15pf dk violet	15	20
46	A16	20pf blue violet	15	20
47	A16	20pf green	30	26
a.		Double overprint		
48	A16	30pf org & blk, buff	18	20
a.		Double overprint	55.00	
49	A16	30pf dull blue	40	40
50	A16	40pf lake & blk	18	20
51	A16	40pf carmine rose	60	40
52	A16	50pf pur & blk, buff	20	20
a.		Double overprint	55.00	
53	A16	60pf red violet	32	25
54	A16	75pf green & blk	32	25
a.		Double overprint	90.00	
55	A17	1.25m green	90	70
56	A17	1.50m yellow brn	90	70
57	A21	2.50m lilac rose	2.75	7.00
58	A16	4m black & rose	5.00	14.00
a.		Double overprint	20.00	
		Nos. 41-58 (18)	13.13	25.78

On No. 57 the overprint is placed vertically at each side of the stamp.
Counterfeit overprints exist.

Inverted Overprint

41a	A16	5pf green	12.50	125.00
43a	A16	10pf carmine	13.00	
44a	A16	10pf orange	8.50	
45a	A22	15pf dark violet	13.00	175.00
46a	A16	20pf blue violet	12.50	
48b	A16	30pf org & blk, buff		
50a	A16	40pf lake & blk		
52b	A16	50pf pur & blk, buff		
53a	A16	60pf red violet	35.00	150.00
54b	A16	75pf green & black	90.00	
55a	A17	1.25m green	70.00	
56a	A17	1.50m yellow brown	60.00	

SARRE ❀ ❀

20

SAARGEBIET

Germany No. 90
Surcharged in Black

1921, Feb.

65	A16	20pf 75pf grn & blk	30	75
a.		Inverted surcharge	16.00	25.00
b.		Double surcharge	42.50	70.00

Mark 5 Mark

Germany No. 120
Surcharged

SAARGEBIET

66	A22	5m on 15pf vio brn	3.75	10.00
67	A22	10m on 15pf vio brn	5.00	11.00

Forgeries exist of Nos. 66-67.

Saar stamps can be mounted in the Scott Germany album part 2.

Old Mill near Mettlach — A3

Miner at Work — A4

Entrance to Reden Mine — A5

Saar River Traffic — A6

Saar River near Mettlach — A7

Slag Pile at Völklingen — A8

Signal Bridge, Saarbrücken — A9

Church at Mettlach — A10

"Old Bridge," Saarbrücken — A11

Cable Railway at Ferne — A12

Colliery Shafthead — A13

Saarbrücken City Hall — A14

Pottery at Mettlach — A15

St. Ludwig's Cathedral — A16

Presidential Residence, Saarbrücken — A17

Burbach Steelworks, Dillingen A18

1921	**Unwmk.**	**Typo.**	**Perf. 12½**	
68	A3	5pf ol grn & vio	16	18
a.		Tête bêche pair	3.50	8.75
c.		Center inverted	50.00	
69	A4	10pf orange & ultra	16	20
70	A5	20pf green & slate	25	40
a.		Tête bêche pair	5.50	15.00
c.		Perf. 10½	13.00	55.00
d.		As "c," tête bêche pair	60.00	190.00
71	A6	25pf brn & dk bl	25	50
a.		Tête bêche pair	6.50	17.50

72	A7	30pf gray grn & brn	22	25
a.		Tête bêche pair	5.50	15.00
c.		30pf ol grn & blk	1.65	10.00
d.		As "c," tête bêche pair	10.50	27.50
e.		As "c," imperf., pair	175.00	350.00
73	A8	40pf vermilion	22	20
a.		Tête bêche pair	13.00	37.50
74	A9	50pf gray & blk	50	1.10
75	A10	60pf red & dk brn	1.10	1.25
76	A11	80pf deep blue	45	50
a.		Tête bêche pair	18.00	50.00
77	A12	1m lt red & blk	45	50
a.		1m grn & blk	675.00	
78	A13	1.25m lt brn & dk grn	70	75
79	A14	2m red & black	2.00	1.90
80	A15	3m brown & dk ol	2.50	5.00
a.		Center inverted	85.00	
81	A16	5m yellow & vio	6.25	9.00
82	A17	10m grn & red brn	8.25	11.00
83	A18	25m ultra, red & blk	26.00	40.00
		Nos. 68-83 (16)	49.46	72.73

Values for tête bêche are for vertical pair. Horizontal pairs sell for about twice as much.
The ultramarine ink on No. 69 appears to be brown where it overlays the orange.
Exist imperf. but were not regularly issued.

Nos. 70-83 Surcharged in Red, Blue or Black

5 cent.   **1 Fr.**
a   b

5 FRANKEN
c

1921, May 1				
85	A5(a)	3c on 20pf (R)	18	22
a.		Tête bêche pair	3.50	10.00
d.		Perf. 10½	3.25	16.00
e.		As "d," tête bêche pair	15.00	37.50
86	A6(a)	5c on 25pf (R)	15	35
a.		Tête bêche pair	60.00	190.00
87	A7(a)	10c on 30pf (Bl)	20	22
a.		Tête bêche pair	3.50	10.00
b.		Inverted surcharge	80.00	225.00
88	A8(a)	15c on 40pf (Bk)	30	22
a.		Tête bêche pair	55.00	190.00
b.		Inverted surcharge	80.00	225.00
89	A9(a)	20c on 50pf (R)	20	15
90	A10(a)	25c on 60pf (Bl)	35	15
91	A11(a)	30c on 80pf (Bk)	95	42
a.		Tête bêche pair	9.00	25.00
c.		Inverted surcharge	80.00	225.00
d.		Double surcharge	80.00	225.00
92	A12(a)	40c on 1m (Bl)	1.40	32
a.		Inverted surcharge	80.00	225.00
93	A13(a)	50c on 1.25m (Bk)	2.00	55
b.		Perf. 10½	45.00	75.00
94	A14(a)	75c on 2m (Bl)	2.00	75
95	A15(b)	1fr on 3m (Bl)	2.50	1.40
96	A16(b)	2fr on 5m (Bl)	7.25	3.50
97	A17(b)	3fr on 10m (Bk)	8.00	11.00
b.		Double surcharge	165.00	375.00
98	A18(c)	5fr on 25m (Bl)	12.00	17.50
		Nos. 85-98 (14)	37.48	36.75

In these surcharges the period is occasionally missing and there are various wrong font and defective letters.
Values for tête bêche are for vertical pairs. Horizontal pairs sell for about twice as much.
Nos. 85-89, 91, 93, 97-98 exist imperf. but were not regularly issued.

Cable Railway, Ferne — A19

Miner at Work — A20

"Old Bridge," Saarbrücken A21

Saarbrücken City Hall — A22

Slag Pile at
Völklingen — A23

Pottery at
Mettlach — A24

Saar River
Traffic — A25

St. Ludwig's
Cathedral — A26

Colliery
Shafthead — A27

Mettlach
Church — A28

Burbach
Steelworks,
Dillingen
A29

Perf. 12¹/₂x13¹/₂, 13¹/₂x12¹/₂

1922-23 Typo.

99	A19	3c ol grn & straw	30	26
100	A20	5c orange & blk	24	15
101	A21	10c blue green	24	15
102	A19	15c deep brown	40	15
103	A19	15c orange ('23)	2.75	22
104	A22	20c dk bl & lem	2.25	15
105	A22	20c brt bl & straw ('23)	3.00	22
106	A22	25c red & yellow	2.75	1.00
107	A22	25c mag & straw ('23)	2.25	15
108	A23	30c carmine & yel	40	30
109	A24	40c brown & yel	65	15
110	A25	50c dk bl & straw	65	15
111	A24	75c dp grn & straw	7.00	10.00
112	A24	75c blk & straw ('23)	19.00	1.50
113	A26	1fr brown red	2.25	15
114	A27	2fr deep violet	3.50	1.25
115	A28	3fr org & dk grn	3.50	1.25
116	A29	5fr brn & red brn	14.00	24.00
		Nos. 99-116 (18)	65.13	41.35

Nos. 99 to 116 exist imperforate but were not
regularly issued in that condition.
For overprints see Nos. O1-O15.

Madonna of
Blieskastel — A30

Perf. 13¹/₂x12¹/₂

1925, Apr. 9 Photo.
Size: 23x27mm

118	A30	45c lake brown	2.50	2.50

Size: 31¹/₂x36mm
Perf. 12

119	A30	10fr black brown	8.50	21.00

Nos. 118-119 exist imperf. but were not regularly issued.
For overprint see No. 154.

Market
Fountain, St.
Johann — A31

View of Saar
Valley — A32

Colliery
Shafthead
A35

Burbach
Steelworks
A36

Designs: 15c, 75c, View of Saar Valley. 20c,
40c, 90c, Scene from Saarlouis fortifications. 25c,
50c, Tholey Abbey.

1927-32 Perf. 13¹/₂

120	A31	10c deep brown	48	15
121	A32	15c olive black	32	42
122	A32	20c brown orange	30	15
123	A32	25c bluish slate	38	18
124	A31	30c olive green	48	15
125	A32	40c olive brown	38	15
126	A32	50c magenta	48	15
127	A35	60c red org ('30)	95	15
128	A32	75c brown violet	45	15
129	A35	80c red orange	2.00	4.50
130	A32	90c deep red ('32)	5.00	10.50
131	A35	1fr violet	1.65	18
132	A36	1.50fr sapphire	2.75	18
133	A36	2fr brown red	2.75	18
134	A36	3fr dk olive grn	6.00	40
135	A36	5fr deep brown	7.75	3.50
		Nos. 120-135 (16)	32.12	21.09

For surcharges and overprints see Nos. 136-153,
O16-O26.

60 cent.

Nos. 126 and 129
Surcharged

════

1930-34

136	A32	40c on 50c mag ('34)	75	70
137	A35	60c on 80c red orange	75	1.25

Plebiscite Issue
Stamps of 1925-32 Overprinted in Various
Colors

VOLKSABSTIMMUNG
1935

Perf. 13¹/₂, 13¹/₂x13, 13x13¹/₂
1934, Nov. 1

139	A31	10c brown (Br)	40	32
140	A32	15c black grn (G)	40	32
141	A32	20c brown org (O)	32	40
142	A32	25c bluish sl (Bl)	55	70
143	A31	30c olive grn (G)	30	30
144	A32	40c olive brn (Br)	32	40
145	A32	50c magenta (R)	70	70
146	A35	60c red orange (V)	32	30
147	A32	75c brown violet (V)	70	30
148	A32	90c deep red (R)	70	80
149	A35	1fr violet (V)	85	80
150	A36	1.50fr sapphire (Bl)	1.25	1.75
151	A36	2fr brown red (R)	1.75	2.25
152	A36	3fr dk ol grn (G)	3.00	5.00
153	A36	5fr dp brown (Br)	14.00	16.00

Size: 31¹/₂x36mm
Perf. 12

154	A30	10fr black brn (Br)	18.00	30.00
		Nos. 139-154 (16)	43.56	60.84

French Administration

Miner — A37

Steel
Workers — A38

Harvesting Sugar
Beets — A39

Mettlach
Abbey — A40

Marshal Ney — A41

Saar River
near
Mettlach
A42

1947 Unwmk. Photo. Perf. 14

155	A37	2pf gray	15	15
156	A37	3pf orange	15	30
157	A37	6pf dk Prus grn	15	15
158	A37	8pf scarlet	15	15
159	A37	10pf rose violet	15	15
160	A38	15pf brown	15	30
161	A38	16pf ultra	15	15
162	A38	20pf brown rose	15	15
163	A38	24pf dp brown org	15	15
164	A39	25pf cerise	30	10.00
165	A39	30pf lt olive grn	15	30
166	A39	40pf orange brn	15	15
167	A39	50pf blue violet	30	10.00
168	A40	60pf violet	30	10.00
169	A40	80pf dp orange	15	22
170	A41	84pf brown	15	22
171	A42	1m gray green	15	30
		Set value	1.70	
		Set, never hinged	2.00	

Nos. 155-162, 164-171 exist imperf.

Types of 1947

1947 Wmk. 285

172	A37	12pf olive green	15	15
173	A39	45pf crimson	20	7.50
174	A40	75pf brt blue	15	20
		Set value	30	
		Set, never hinged	50	

Nos. 172-174 exist imperf.

Types of 1947 Surcharged with New
Value, Bars and Ornament in Black or Red

1947, Nov. 27 Unwmk.
Printing II

175	A37	10c on 2pf gray	15	25
176	A37	60c on 3pf orange	15	25
177	A37	1fr on 10pf rose vio	15	25
178	A37	2fr on 12pf ol grn	15	75
179	A38	3fr on 15pf brown	15	25
180	A38	4fr on 16pf ultra	15	2.00
181	A38	5fr on 20pf brn rose	15	50
182	A38	6fr on 24pf dp brn org	15	25
183	A39	9fr on 30pf lt ol grn	22	3.00
184	A39	10fr on 50pf bl vio (R)	28	5.00
185	A40	14fr on 60pf violet	35	2.50
186	A41	20fr on 84pf brown	25	3.75
187	A42	50fr on 1m gray grn	95	6.25
		Set value	2.55	
		Set, never hinged	3.50	

Printing I

175a	A37	10c on 2pf gray	75.00	200.00
176a	A37	60c on 3pf orange	60.00	525.00
177a	A37	1fr on 10pf rose vio	5.00	8.75
178a	A37	2fr on 12pf ol grn, wmk. 285	25	50
179a	A38	3fr on 15pf brown	400.00	1,200.
180a	A38	4fr on 16pf ultra	9.00	65.00
181a	A38	5fr on 20pf brn rose	35.00	2,000.
182a	A38	6fr on 24pf dp brn org	25	1.00
183a	A39	9fr on 30pf lt ol grn	37.50	475.00
184a	A39	10fr on 50pf bl vio (R)	380.00	4,000.
185a	A40	14fr on 60pf violet	90.00	575.00
186a	A41	20fr on 84pf brown	2.00	3.75
187a	A42	50fr on 1m gray grn	35.00	275.00
		Nos. 175a-187a (13)	1,129.	

Printing I was surcharged on Nos. 155-171. The
crossbar of the A's in SAAR is high on the 10c, 60c,
1fr, 2fr, 9fr and 10fr; numeral "1" has no base serif
on the 3fr and 4fr; wide space between vignette
and SAAR panel; 1m inscribed "1M."
Printing II was surcharged on a special printing of
the basic stamps, with details of design that differ
on each denomination. The "A" crossbar is low on
10c, 60c, 1fr, 2fr, 9fr, 10fr; numeral "1" has base
serif on 3fr and 4fr; narrow space between vignette
and SAAR panel; 1m inscribed "1SM."
Inverted surcharges exist on Nos. 175-187 and
175a-187a.

French Protectorate

Clasped
Hands
A43

Colliery
Shafthead
A44

Designs: 2fr, 3fr, Worker. 4fr, 5fr, Girl gathering
wheat. 6fr, 9fr, Miner. 14fr, Smelting. 20fr, Reconstruction. 50fr, Mettlach Abbey portal.

Perf. 14x13, 13
1948, Apr. 1 Engr. Unwmk.

188	A43	10c henna brn	22	85
189	A43	60c dk Prus grn	22	85
190	A43	1fr brown blk	15	15
191	A43	2fr rose car	15	15
192	A43	3fr black brn	15	15
193	A43	4fr red	15	15
194	A43	5fr red violet	15	15
195	A43	6fr henna brown	20	15
196	A43	9fr dk Prus grn	1.65	15
197	A44	10fr dark blue	90	18
198	A44	14fr dk vio brn	1.25	45
199	A44	20fr henna brn	2.25	45
200	A44	50fr blue blk	5.00	1.40
		Nos. 188-200 (13)	12.44	5.23
		Set, never hinged	32.50	

Map of the
Saar — A45

1948, Dec. 15 Photo. Perf. 13¹/₂x13

201	A45	10fr dark red	85	1.10
202	A45	25fr deep blue	1.25	2.50
		Set, never hinged	4.00	

French Protectorate establishment, 1st anniv.

Caduceus, Microscope,
Bunsen Burner and
Book — A46

1949, Apr. 2 Perf. 13x13¹/₂

203	A46	15fr carmine	1.75	18
		Never hinged	4.00	

Issued to honor Saar University.

Ludwig van
Beethoven — A47

Laborer Using
Spade — A51

Saarbrücken
A52

Designs: 10c, Building trades. 1fr, 3fr, Gears, factories. 5fr, Dumping mine waste. 6fr, 15fr, Coal mine interior. 8fr, Communications symbols. 10fr, Emblem of printing. 12fr, 18fr, Pottery. 25fr, Blast furnace worker. 45fr, Rock formation "Great Boot." 60fr, Reden Colliery, Landsweiler. 100fr, View of Weibelskirchen.

1949-51   Unwmk.   Perf. 13x13¹/₂

204	A47	10c violet brn	15	85
205	A47	60c gray ('51)	15	85
206	A47	1fr carmine lake	60	15
207	A47	3fr brown ('51)	2.75	22
208	A47	5fr dp violet ('51)	80	15
209	A47	6fr Prus grn ('51)	4.25	20
210	A47	8fr olive grn ('51)	28	20
211	A47	10fr orange ('50)	1.50	15
212	A47	12fr dk green	5.25	15
213	A47	15fr red ('50)	2.75	15
214	A47	18fr brn car ('51)	1.00	2.50

Perf. 13¹/₂

215	A51	20fr gray ('50)	65	15
216	A51	25fr violet blue	6.50	15
217	A52	30fr red brown ('51)	5.50	30
218	A52	45fr rose lake ('51)	1.90	32
219	A51	60fr deep green ('51)	1.90	75
220	A51	100fr brown	2.75	1.00
		Nos. 204-220 (17)	38.68	8.24
		Set, never hinged	95.00	

Peter
Wust — A54

St. Peter — A55

1950, Apr. 3
221 A54 15fr carmine rose   1.75 *4.00*
  Never hinged   5.50

Peter Wust (1884-1940), Catholic philosopher.

1950, June 29   Engr.   Perf. 13
222 A55 12fr deep green   1.75 *4.50*
223 A55 15fr red brown   2.00 *4.50*
224 A55 25fr blue   3.75 *7.50*
  Set, never hinged   16.00

Holy Year, 1950.

Street in
Ottweiler
A56

Symbols of the Council of
Europe
A57

1950, July 10   Photo.   Perf. 13x13¹/₂
225 A56 10fr orange brown   1.50 *4.50*
  Never hinged   3.25

400th anniversary of the founding of Ottweiler.

1950, Aug. 8   Perf. 13¹/₂
226 A57 25fr deep blue   18.00 8.00
  Never hinged   42.50

Issued to commemorate the Saar's admission to the Council of Europe. See No. C12.

Post Rider and Guard — A62

1951, Apr. 29   Engr.   Perf. 13
227 A62 15fr dk violet brn   3.00 *10.00*
  Never hinged   5.50

Issued to publicize Stamp Day, 1951.

"Agriculture and
Industry" and Fair
Emblem — A63

Tower of
Mittelbexbach
and
Flowers — A67

1951, May 12   Photo.   Perf. 13x13¹/₂
228 A63 15fr dk gray grn   85 *3.00*
  Never hinged   2.25

1951 Fair at Saarbrücken.

1951, June 9   Engr.   Perf. 13
229 A67 15fr dark green   85 60
  Never hinged   2.25

Issued to publicize the Exhibition of Gardens and Flowers, Bexbach, 1951.

Refugees
A68

Globe & Stylized Fair
Building
A69

1952, May 2   Unwmk.   Perf. 13
230 A68 15fr bright red   1.00 75
  Never hinged   1.75

Issued to honor the Red Cross.

1952, Apr. 26
231 A69 15fr red brown   1.00 75
  Never hinged   1.75

1952 Fair at Saarbrücken.

Mine
Shafts — A70

Ludwig's
Gymnasium
A71

General Post
Office — A72

Reconstruction of St.
Ludwig's Cathedral
A73

"SM"
Monogram
A74

Designs: 3fr, 18fr, Bridge building. 6fr, Transporter bridge, Mettlach. 30fr, Saar University Library.

1952-55   Engr.

232	A70	1fr dk bl grn ('53)	15	15
233	A71	2fr purple ('53)	15	15
234	A72	3fr dk car rose ('53)	15	15
235	A72	5fr dk grn (no inscription)	1.90	15
236	A72	5fr dk grn ("Hauptpostamt Saarbrücken") ('54)	15	15
237	A72	6fr vio brn ('53)	15	15
238	A71	10fr brn ol ('53)	20	15
239	A72	12fr green ('53)	20	15
240	A70	15fr blk brn (no inscription)	2.75	15
241	A70	15fr blk brn ("Industrie-Landschaft") ('53)	1.25	15
242	A70	15fr dp car ('55)	15	15
243	A72	18fr dk rose brn ('55)	90	3.00
244	A72	30fr ultra ('53)	28	40
245	A73	500fr brn car ('53)	4.75	30.00
		Nos. 232-245 (14)	13.13	35.05
		Set, never hinged	32.50	

For overprints see Nos. 257-259.

1953, Mar. 23
246 A74 15fr dark ultra   1.00 75
  Never hinged   1.75

1953 Fair at Saarbrücken.

Bavarian and
Prussian
Postilions
A75

1953, May 3
247 A75 15fr deep blue   1.75 *5.00*
  Never hinged   2.75

Stamp Day.

Fountain and Fair
Buildings — A76

1954, Apr. 10
248 A76 15fr deep green   85 50
  Never hinged   1.75

1954 International Fair at Saarbrücken.

Post Coach and Post Bus of 1920 — A77

1954, May 9   Engr.
249 A77 15fr red   1.65 *5.50*
  Never hinged   2.75

Stamp Day, May 9, 1954.

Madonna and
Child, Holbein
A78

Designs: 10fr, Sistine Madonna, Raphael. 15fr, Madonna and Child with pear, Durer.

1954, Aug. 14
250 A78 5fr deep carmine   32 *1.25*
251 A78 10fr dark green   45 *1.65*
252 A78 15fr dp violet bl   70 *2.25*
  Set, never hinged   2.75

Centenary of the promulgation of the Dogma of the Immaculate Conception.

Cyclist and
Flag — A79

Symbols of Industry and
Rotary Emblem — A80

1955, Feb. 28   Photo.   Perf. 13x13¹/₂
253 A79 15fr multicolored   15 35

World championship cross country bicycle race.

1955, Feb. 28
254 A80 15fr orange brown   15 35
  Never hinged   25

Rotary International, 50th anniversary.

Flags of Participating
Nations — A81

1955, Apr. 18   Photo.   Perf. 13x13¹/₂
255 A81 15fr multicolored   15 35
  Never hinged   25

1955 International Fair at Saarbrücken.

Postman at
Illingen
A82

Unwmk.

1955, May 8   Engr.   Perf. 13
256 A82 15fr deep claret   30 1.10
    Never hinged   60

Issued to publicize Stamp Day, 1955.

Nos. 242-244 Overprinted
"VOLKSBEFRAGUNG 1955"

1955, Oct. 22
257 A70 15fr deep carmine   15 24
258 A72 18fr dk rose brn   15 26
259 A72 30fr ultra   15 50
    Set value   22
    Set, never hinged   50

Plebiscite, Oct. 23, 1955.

Symbols of Industry   Radio Tower,
and the Fair   Saarbrücken
A83   A84

1956, Apr. 14   Photo.   Perf. 11½
260 A83 15fr dk brn red & yel grn 15 25
    Never hinged   20

Intl. Fair at Saarbrücken, Apr. 14-29, 1956.

1956, May 6
Granite Paper
261 A84 15fr grn & grnsh bl   15 25
    Never hinged   20

Stamp Day.

German Administration

Arms of   Pres. Theodor
Saar — A85   Heuss — A86

Perf. 13x13½
1957, Jan. 1   Litho.   Wmk. 304
262 A85 15fr brick red & blue   15 20
    Never hinged   15

Return of the Saar to Germany.

1957   Typo.   Perf. 14
Size: 18x22mm
263 A86 1(fr) brt green   15 15
264 A86 2(fr) brt violet   15 15
265 A86 3(fr) bister brown   15 15
266 A86 4(fr) red violet   15 48
267 A86 5(fr) lt olive green   15 15
268 A86 6(fr) vermilion   15 15
269 A86 10(fr) gray   15 22
270 A86 12(fr) deep orange   15 15
271 A86 15(fr) lt blue green   15 15
272 A86 18(fr) carmine rose   28 05
273 A86 25(fr) brt lilac   15 38

Engr.
274 A86 30(fr) pale purple   15 48
275 A86 45(fr) gray olive   48 1.50
276 A86 50(fr) violet brn   48 70
277 A86 60(fr) dull rose   65 1.75
278 A86 70(fr) red orange   1.25 2.75
279 A86 80(fr) olive green   48 1.75
280 A86 90(fr) dark gray   1.10 2.75

Size: 24x29mm
281 A86 100(fr) dk carmine   90 4.75
282 A86 200(fr) violet   2.75 13.00
    Nos. 263-282 (20)   10.02 32.74
    Set, never hinged   18.00

See Nos. 289-308.

Steel   Merzig Arms and St.
Industry — A87   Peter's
                   Church — A88

Perf. 13x13½
1957, Apr. 20   Litho.   Wmk. 304
284 A87 15fr gray & magenta   15 20
    Never hinged   15

The 1957 Fair at Saarbrücken.

1957, May 25   Perf. 14
285 A88 15fr blue   15 20
    Never hinged   15

Centenary of the town of Merzig.

"United
Europe" — A89

Lithographed; Tree Embossed
Perf. 14x13½
1957, Sept. 16   Unwmk.
286 A89 20fr orange & yel   15 55
287 A89 35fr violet & pink   25 65
    Set, never hinged   50

Europa, publicizing a united Europe for peace
and prosperity.

Carrier
Pigeons — A90

Wmk. 304
1957, Oct. 5   Litho.   Perf. 14
288 A90 15fr dp carmine & blk   15 15
    Never hinged   15

Issued for International Letter Writing Week,
Oct. 6-12.

Redrawn Type of 1957; "F" added after
denomination

1957   Wmk. 304   Litho.   Perf. 14
Size: 18x22mm
289 A86 1fr gray green   15 15
290 A86 3fr blue   15 15
291 A86 5fr olive   15 15
292 A86 6fr lt brown   15 30
293 A86 10fr violet   15 18
294 A86 12fr brown org   15 18
295 A86 15fr dull green   18 18
296 A86 18fr gray   75 2.25
297 A86 20fr lt olive grn   42 1.25
298 A86 25fr orange brn   28 30
299 A86 30fr rose lilac   35 30
300 A86 35fr brown   85 1.25
301 A86 45fr lt blue grn   60 1.75
302 A86 50fr dk red brown   35 85
303 A86 70fr brt green   1.65 2.25
304 A86 80fr chalky blue   1.10 2.25
305 A86 90fr rose carmine   1.90 3.75

Engr.
Size: 24x29mm
306 A86 100fr orange   1.65 3.25
307 A86 200fr brt green   3.25 10.00
308 A86 300fr brt green   3.75 12.50
    Nos. 289-308 (20)   17.98 43.24
    Set, never hinged   37.50

"Max and
Moritz" — A91

Design: 15fr, Wilhelm Busch.

Perf. 13½x13
1958, Jan. 9   Litho.   Wmk. 304
309 A91 12fr lt ol grn & blk   15 15
310 A91 15fr red & black   15 22
    Set value   18
    Set, never hinged   22

50th anniversary of the death of Wilhelm Busch,
humorist.

"Prevent Forest
Fires" — A92

1958, Mar. 5   Perf. 14
311 A92 15fr brt red & blk   15 20
    Never hinged   15

Issued to aid in the prevention of forest fires.

Rudolf
Diesel
A93

1958, Mar. 18   Engr.
312 A93 12fr dk blue grn   15 20
    Never hinged   15

Centenary of the birth of Rudolf Diesel, inventor.

Fair Emblem and   View of Homburg
City Hall,   A95
Saarbrücken
A94

1958, Apr. 10   Litho.   Perf. 14
313 A94 15fr dull rose   15 20
    Never hinged   15

1958 Fair at Saarbrücken.

1958, June 14   Engr.   Wmk. 304
314 A95 15fr gray green   15 20
    Never hinged   15

400th anniversary of Homburg.

Turner Emblem   Herman Schulze-
A96   Delitzsch
                   A97

1958, July 21   Litho.   Perf. 13½x14
315 A96 12fr gray, blk & dl grn   15 20
    Never hinged   15

150 years of German Turners and the 1958 Turner Festival.

1958, Aug. 29   Engr.   Wmk. 304
316 A97 12fr yellow green   15 20
    Never hinged   15

150th anniv. of the birth of Schultze-Delitzsch,
founder of German trade organizations.

Europa Issue, 1958
Common Design Type
1958, Sept. 13   Litho.
Size: 24½x30mm
317 CD1 12fr yellow grn & bl   25 50
318 CD1 30fr lt blue & red   32 65
    Set, never hinged   95

Issued to show the European Postal Union at the
service of European integration.

Jakob   Old and New City
Fugger — A98   Hall and Burbach
                   Mill — A99

Perf. 13x13½
1959, Mar. 6   Wmk. 304
319 A98 15fr dk red & blk   15 15
    Never hinged   15

500th anniv. of the birth of Jakob Fugger the
Rich, businessman and banker.

1959, Apr. 1   Engr.   Perf. 14x13½
320 A99 15fr light blue   15 20
    Never hinged   15

Greater Saarbrucken, 50th anniversary.

Hands Holding   Alexander von
Merchandise   Humboldt
A100   A101

1959, Apr. 1   Litho.
321 A100 15fr deep rose   15 15
    Never hinged   15

1959 Fair at Saarbrucken.

1959, May 6   Engr.   Perf. 13½x14
322 A101 15fr blue   15 20
    Never hinged   15

Cent. of the death of Alexander von Humboldt,
naturalist and geographer.

SEMI-POSTAL STAMPS

Red Cross Dog   Maternity Nurse
Leading Blind   with Child — SP4
Man — SP1

SAAR

239

Designs: #B2, Nurse and invalid. #B3, Children
getting drink at spring.

1926, Oct. 25   *Perf. 13½*   Photo.
    Unwmk.

B1	SP1	20c + 20c dk ol grn	6.00	12.00
B2	SP1	40c + 40c dk brn	6.75	13.00
B3	SP1	50c + 50c red org	6.75	13.00
B4	SP4	1.50fr + 1.50fr brt bl	13.00	30.00

Nos. B1-B4 Overprinted   1927-28

1927, Oct. 1

B5	SP1	20c + 20c dk ol grn	10.00	14.00
B6	SP1	40c + 40c dk brn	9.25	19.00
B7	SP1	50c + 50c red org	8.00	13.00
B8	SP4	1.50fr + 1.50fr brt bl	12.00	37.50

"The Blind Beggar"
by
Dyckmans — SP5

"Almsgiving" by
Schiestl — SP6

"Charity" by
Raphael — SP7

1928, Dec. 23   Photo.

B9	SP5	40c (+40c) blk brn	11.00	19.00
B10	SP5	50c (+50c) brn rose	11.00	19.00
B11	SP5	1fr (+1fr) dl vio	11.00	19.00
B12	SP6	1.50fr (+1.50fr) cob bl	11.00	19.00
B13	SP6	2fr (+2fr) red brn	12.50	20.00
B14	SP6	3fr (+3fr) dk ol grn	12.50	20.00
B15	SP7	10fr (+10fr) dk brn	350.00	2,750.
		Nos. B9-B15 (7)	419.00	

"Orphaned" by
Kaulbach — SP8

"St. Ottilia" by
Feuerstein — SP9

"Madonna" by
Ferruzzio — SP10

1929, Dec. 22

B16	SP8	40c (+15c) ol grn	1.75	3.25
B17	SP8	50c (+20c) cop red	3.50	5.00
B18	SP8	1fr (+50c) vio brn	3.50	6.50
B19	SP9	1.50fr (+75c) Prus bl	3.50	6.50
B20	SP9	2fr (+1fr) brn car	3.50	6.75
B21	SP9	3fr (+2fr) sl grn	6.00	14.00
B22	SP10	10fr (+8fr) blk brn	40.00	80.00
		Nos. B16-B22 (7)	61.75	

"The Safety-Man"
SP11

"The Good
Samaritan"
SP12

"In the
Window" — SP13

1931, Jan. 20

B23	SP11	40c (+15c)	7.25	17.50
B24	SP11	60c (+20c)	7.25	17.50
B25	SP12	1fr (+50c)	7.25	27.50
B26	SP11	1.50fr (+75c)	10.00	27.50
B27	SP12	2fr (+1fr)	10.00	27.50
B28	SP12	3fr (+2fr)	14.00	27.50
B29	SP13	10fr (+10fr)	67.50	175.00
		Nos. B23-B29 (7)	123.25	

St. Martin of
Tours — SP14

Designs: #B33-B35, "Charity." #B36, "The
Widow's Mite."

1931, Dec. 23

B30	SP14	40c (+15c)	12.00	25.00
B31	SP14	60c (+20c)	12.00	25.00
B32	SP14	1fr (+50c)	14.00	37.50
B33	SP14	1.50fr (+75c)	17.00	37.50
B34	SP14	2fr (+1fr)	18.00	37.50
B35	SP14	3fr (+3fr)	26.00	75.00
B36	SP14	5fr (+5fr)	75.00	225.00
		Nos. B30-B36 (7)	174.00	

Ruins at
Kirkel — SP17

Illingen Castle,
Kerpen — SP23

Designs: 60c, Church at Blie. 1fr, Castle
Ottweiler. 1.50fr, Church of St. Michael, Saar-
brucken. 2fr, Statue of St. Wendel. 3fr, Church of
St. John, Saarbrucken.

1932, Dec. 20

B37	SP17	40c (+15c)	8.50	16.00
B38	SP17	60c (+20c)	8.50	16.00
B39	SP17	1fr (+50c)	13.00	30.00
B40	SP17	1.50fr (+75c)	20.00	37.50
B41	SP17	2fr (+1fr)	20.00	37.50
B42	SP17	3fr (+2fr)	47.50	125.00
B43	SP23	5fr (+5fr)	82.50	200.00
		Nos. B37-B43 (7)	200.00	

Scene of
Neunkirchen
Disaster
SP24

1933, June 1

B44	SP24	60c (+ 60c) org red	12.50	16.00
B45	SP24	3fr (+ 3fr) ol grn	30.00	42.50
B46	SP24	5fr (+ 5fr) org brn	32.50	60.00

The surtax was for the aid of victims of the
explosion at Neunkirchen, Feb. 10.

"Love" — SP25

Designs: 60c, "Anxiety." 1fr, "Peace." 1.50fr,
"Solace." 2fr, "Welfare." 3fr, "Truth." 5fr, Figure
on Tomb of Duchess Elizabeth of Lorraine

1934, Mar. 15   Photo.

B47	SP25	40c (+15c) blk brn	5.00	10.00
B48	SP25	60c (+20c) red org	5.00	10.00
B49	SP25	1fr (+50c) dl vio	6.75	12.50
B50	SP25	1.50fr (+75c) blue	12.50	22.50
B51	SP25	2fr (+1fr) car rose	11.50	22.50
B52	SP25	3fr (+2fr) ol grn	12.50	22.50
B53	SP25	5fr (+5fr) red brn	27.50	50.00
		Nos. B47-B53 (7)	80.75	

Nos. B47-B53 Overprinted like Nos. 139-
154 in Various Colors Reading up

1934, Dec. 1   *Perf. 13x13½*

B54	SP25	40c (+15c) (Br)	3.75	9.00
B55	SP25	60c (+20c) (R)	3.75	9.00
B56	SP25	1fr (+50c) (V)	7.25	17.50
B57	SP25	1.50fr (+75c) (Bl)	7.25	17.50
B58	SP25	2fr (+1fr) (R)	9.25	24.00
B59	SP25	3fr (+2fr) (G)	8.50	22.50
B60	SP25	5fr (+5fr) (Br)	14.00	30.00
		Nos. B54-B60 (7)	53.75	

French Protectorate

Various Flood Scenes
SP32   SP33

Perf. 13½x13, 13x13½
1948, Oct. 12   Photo.
Inscribed "Hochwasser-Hilfe 1947-48"

B61	SP32	5fr + 5fr dl grn	1.65	18.00
B62	SP33	6fr + 4fr dk vio	1.65	18.00
B63	SP32	12fr + 8fr red	2.00	26.00
B64	SP33	18fr + 12fr bl	3.00	30.00
a.		Souv. sheet of 4, #B61-B64, imperf.	265.00	2,000.
		Never hinged	550.00	
		Nos. B61-B64,CB1 (5)	23.30	187.00
		Set, never hinged	44.50	

The surtax was for flood relief.

Hikers and
Ludweiler
Hostel — SP34

Designs: No. B66, Hikers approaching Weiss-
kirchen Hostel.

1949, Jan. 11   *Perf. 13½x13*

B65	SP34	8fr + 5fr dk grn	1.25	3.50
B66	SP34	10fr + 7fr dk grn	1.25	2.75
		Set, never hinged	4.50	

The surtax aided youth hostels.

Mare and
Foal — SP35

Design: No. B68, Jumpers.

1949, Sept. 25   *Perf. 13½*

B67	SP35	15fr + 5fr brn red	5.75	20.00
B68	SP35	25fr + 15fr blue	7.25	21.00
		Set, never hinged	26.00	

Day of the Horse, Sept. 25, 1949.

Detail from "Moses
Striking the
Rock" — SP36

Designs: No. B70, "Christ at the Pool of
Bethesda." No. B71, "The Sick Child." No. B72,
"St. Thomas of Villeneuve." No. B73, Madonna of
Blieskastel.

1949, Dec. 20   Engr.   *Perf. 13*

B69	SP36	8fr + 2fr indigo	4.25	27.50
B70	SP36	15fr + 3fr dk grn	5.00	30.00
B71	SP36	15fr + 5fr brn lake	7.25	52.50
B72	SP36	25fr + 10fr dp ultra	10.50	80.00
B73	SP36	50fr + 20fr choc	19.00	110.00
		Nos. B69-B73 (5)	46.00	
		Set, never hinged	92.50	

Adolph
Kolping
SP37

Relief for the
Hungry
SP38

1950, Apr. 3   Photo.   *Perf. 13x13½*

B74	SP37	15fr + 5fr car rose	13.00	50.00
		Never hinged	24.00	

Engraved and Typographed
1950, Apr. 28   *Perf. 13*

B75	SP38	25fr + 10fr dk brn car & red	13.00	42.50
		Never hinged	24.00	

Stagecoach — SP39

1950, Apr. 22   Engr.

B76	SP39	15fr + 15fr brn red & dk brn	25.00	85.00
		Never hinged	52.50	

Stamp Day, Apr. 27, 1950. Sold at the exhibition and to advance subscribers.

Lutwinus
Seeking
Admission to
Abbey
SP40

Designs: 12fr+3fr, Lutwinus Building Mettlach
Abbey. 15fr+5fr, Lutwinus as Abbot. 25fr+10fr,
Bishop Lutwinus at Rheims. 50fr+20fr, Aid to the
poor and sick.

1950, Nov. 10   Unwmk.   *Perf. 13*

B77	SP40	8fr + 2fr dk brn	3.25	17.00
B78	SP40	12fr + 3fr dk grn	3.25	17.00
B79	SP40	15fr + 5fr red brn	4.00	24.00

B80 SP40 25fr + 10fr blue   6.00   *40.00*
B81 SP40 50fr + 20fr brn car   8.25   *60.00*
    Nos. B77-B81 (5)   24.75
    Set, never hinged   40.00

The surtax was for public assistance.

Mother and Child — SP41

John Calvin and Martin Luther — SP42

1951, Apr. 28

B82 SP41 10fr + 10fr dk grn & car 12.00 *35.00*
    Never hinged   21.00

The surtax was for the Red Cross.

1951, Apr. 28

B83 SP42 15fr + 5fr blk brn   90   *3.50*
    Never hinged   1.40

375th anniversary of the Reformation in Saar.

"Mother" SP43

Runner with Torch SP44

Paintings: 15fr+5fr, "Before the Theater." 18fr+7fr, "Sisters of Charity." 30fr+10fr, "The Good Samaritan." 50fr+20fr, "St. Martin and Beggar."

1951, Nov. 3

B84 SP43 12fr + 3fr dk grn   2.75 *10.00*
B85 SP43 15fr + 5fr pur   2.75 *10.00*
B86 SP43 18fr + 7fr dk red   3.25 *13.00*
B87 SP43 30fr + 10fr dp bl   5.25 *20.00*
B88 SP43 50fr + 20fr blk brn   12.50 *42.50*
    Nos. B84-B88 (5)   26.50
    Set, never hinged   42.50

1952, Mar. 29   Unwmk.   *Perf. 13*

Design: 30fr+5fr, Hand with olive branch, and globe.

B89 SP44 15fr + 5fr dp grn   1.40   *6.25*
B90 SP44 30fr + 5fr dp bl   1.65   *8.75*
    Set, never hinged   5.50

XV Olympic Games, Helsinki, 1952.

Postrider Delivering Mail — SP45

1952, Mar. 30

B91 SP45 30fr + 10fr dark blue   4.75 *17.50*
    Never hinged   7.50

Stamp Day, Mar. 29, 1952.

Count Stroganoff as a Boy — SP46

Henri Dunant — SP47

Portraits: 18fr+7fr, The Holy Shepherd by Murillo. 30fr+10fr, Portrait of a Boy by Georg Melchior Kraus.

1952, Nov. 3

B92 SP46 15fr + 5fr dk brn   1.90   *6.75*
B93 SP46 18fr + 7fr brn lake   2.50   *9.25*
B94 SP46 30fr + 10fr dp bl   2.75 *10.50*
    Set, never hinged   14.00

The surtax was for child welfare.

1953, May 3   Cross in Red

B95 SP47 15fr + 5fr blk brn   1.00   *4.00*
    Never hinged   1.75

Clarice Strozzi by Titian — SP48

Children of Rubens SP49

Portrait: 30fr+10fr, Rubens' son.

1953, Nov. 16

B96 SP48 15fr + 5fr purple   90   *3.00*
B97 SP49 18fr + 7fr dp claret   90   *3.50*
B98 SP48 30fr + 10fr dp ol grn   1.75   *5.50*
    Set, never hinged   7.00

The surtax was for child welfare.

St. Benedict Blessing St. Maurus — SP50

Child and Cross — SP51

1953, Dec. 18   Litho.

B99 SP50 30fr + 10fr black   1.00   *4.50*
    Never hinged   1.90

The surtax was for the abbey at Tholey.

1954, May 10   Engr.

B100 SP51 15fr + 5fr chocolate   1.25   *4.25*
    Never hinged   2.00

The surtax was for the Red Cross.

Street Urchin with Melon, Murillo — SP52

Nurse Holding Baby — SP53

Paintings: 10fr+5fr, Maria de Medici, Bronzino. 15fr+7fr, Baron Emil von Maucler, Dietrich.

1954, Nov. 15

B101 SP52 5fr + 3fr red   18   *50*
B102 SP52 10fr + 5fr dk grn   22   *60*
B103 SP52 15fr + 7fr purple   28   *75*
    Set, never hinged   1.10

The surtax was for child welfare.

Perf. 13x13½

1955, May 5   Photo.   Unwmk.

B104 SP53 15fr + 5fr blk & red   15   *45*
    Never hinged   25

The surtax was for the Red Cross.

Dürer's Mother, Age 63 — SP54

Etchings by Dürer: 10fr+5fr, Praying hands. 15fr+7fr, Old man of Antwerp.

1955, Dec. 10   Engr.   *Perf. 13*

B105 SP54 5fr + 3fr dk grn   20   *45*
B106 SP54 10fr + 5fr ol grn   40   *90*
B107 SP54 15fr + 7fr ol bis   50 *1.10*
    Set, never hinged   1.75

The surtax was for public assistance.

First Aid Station, Saarbrücken, 1870 — SP55

1956, May 7

B108 SP55 15fr + 5fr dk brn   15   *30*
    Never hinged   20

The surtax was for the Red Cross.

"Victor of Benevent" SP56

Winterberg Monument SP57

1956, July 25   Unwmk.   *Perf. 13*

B109 SP56 12fr + 3fr dk yel grn & bl grn 15 *28*
B110 SP56 15fr + 5fr brn vio & brn   15   *28*
    Set value   24
    Set, never hinged   50

Issued to publicize the forthcoming 16th Olympic Games at Melbourne, Nov. 22-Dec. 8, 1956.

1956, Oct. 29

B111 SP57 5fr + 2fr green   15   *15*
B112 SP57 10fr + 3fr red lilac   15   *28*
B113 SP57 15fr + 5fr brown   15   *28*
    Set value   22
    Set, never hinged   48

The surtax was for the rebuilding of monuments.

"La Belle Ferronnière" by da Vinci — SP58

Designs: 10fr + 5fr, "Saskia" by Rembrandt. 15fr+7fr, "Family van Berchem," by Frans Floris. (Detail: Woman playing Spinet.)

1956, Dec. 10

B114 SP58 5fr + 3fr deep blue   15   *15*
B115 SP58 10fr + 5fr deep claret   15   *24*
B116 SP58 15fr + 7fr dark green   15   *40*
    Set value   34
    Set, never hinged   52

The surtax was for charitable works.

German Administration

Miner with Drill — SP59

"The Fox who Stole the Goose" — SP60

Designs: 6fr+4fr, Miner. 15fr+7fr, Miner and conveyor. 30fr+10fr, Miner and coal elevator.

Wmk. 304

1957, Oct. 1   Litho.   *Perf. 14*

B117 SP59 6fr + 4fr bis brn & blk   15   *15*
B118 SP59 12fr + 6fr blk & yel grn   15   *16*
B119 SP59 15fr + 7fr blk & red   15   *38*
B120 SP59 30fr + 10fr blk & bl   18   *45*
    Set value   46
    Set, never hinged   70

The surtax was for independent welfare organizations.

1958, Apr. 1   Wmk. 304   *Perf. 14*

Design: 15fr+7fr, "A Hunter from the Palatinate."

B121 SP60 12fr + 6fr brn red, grn & blk 15 *18*
B122 SP60 15fr + 7fr grn, red, blk & gray 15 *24*
    Set value   16
    Set, never hinged   28

The surtax was to finance young peoples' study trip to Berlin.

Friedrich Wilhelm Raiffeisen SP61

Dairy Maid SP62

Designs: 15fr+7fr, Girl picking grapes. 30fr+10fr, Farmer with pitchfork.

1958, Oct. 1   Wmk. 304   *Perf. 14*

B123 SP61 6fr + 4fr gldn brn & dk brn 15 *15*
B124 SP62 12fr + 6fr grn, red & yel   15   *15*
B125 SP62 15fr + 7fr red, yel & bl   18   *30*

B126 SP62 30fr + 10fr bl & ocher   22   40
    Set value   56
    Set, never hinged   95

The surtax was for independent welfare organizations.

AIR POST STAMPS

Airplane over Saarbrücken AP1

Perf. 13½
1928, Sept. 19   Unwmk.   Photo.
C1 AP1 50c brown red   2.50   1.75
C2 AP1 1fr dark violet   3.00   2.25

For overprints see Nos. C5, C7.

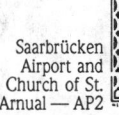

Saarbrücken Airport and Church of St. Arnual — AP2

1932, Apr. 30
C3 AP2 60c orange red   4.00   2.50
C4 AP2 5fr dark brown   35.00   60.00

For overprints see Nos. C6, C8.

Nos. C1-C4 Overprinted like Nos. 139-154 in Various Colors

1934, Nov. 1   Perf. 13½, 13½x13
C5 AP1 50c brn red (R)   4.00   5.25
C6 AP2 60c org red (O)   2.75   2.50
C7 AP1 1fr dk vio (V)   6.00   7.25
C8 AP2 5fr dk brn (Br)   8.50   9.50

French Protectorate

Shadow of Plane over Saar River — AP3

      Unwmk.
1948, Apr. 1   Engr.   Perf. 13
C9 AP3 25fr red   2.50   1.90
C10 AP3 50fr dk Prus grn   1.40   95
C11 AP3 200fr rose car   13.00   16.00
    Set, never hinged   27.50

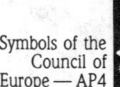

Symbols of the Council of Europe — AP4

1950, Aug. 8   Photo.   Perf. 13½
C12 AP4 200fr red brown   85.00   140.00
    Never hinged   150.00

Saar's admission to the Council of Europe.

AIR POST SEMI-POSTAL STAMP

French Protectorate

Flood Scene SPAP1

Perf. 13½x13
1948, Oct. 12   Photo.   Unwmk.
CB1 SPAP1 25fr + 25fr sep   15.00   95.00
    Never hinged   27.50
a.   Souvenir sheet of 1   200.00   1,500.
    Never hinged   450.00

The surtax was for flood relief.

OFFICIAL STAMPS

Regular Issue of 1922-1923 Overprinted Diagonally in Red or Blue

DIENSTMARKE

Perf. 12½x13½, 13½x12½
1922-23   Unwmk.
O1 A19 3c ol grn & straw (R)   52   19.00
O2 A20 5c org & blk (R)   25   18
O3 A21 10c bl grn (R)   25   15
O4 A19 15c dp brn (Bl)   25   15
O5 A19 15c org (Bl) ('23)   1.65   25
O6 A22 20c dk bl & lem (Bl)   25   15
O7 A22 20c brt bl & straw (R)   1.65   25
     ('23)
O8 A22 25c red & yel (Bl)   2.50   65
O9 A22 25c mag & straw (Bl)   1.65   22
     ('23)
O10 A23 30c car & yel (Bl)   25   15
O11 A24 40c brn & yel (Bl)   42   15
O12 A25 50c dk bl & straw (R)   42   15
O13 A24 75c dp grn & straw (R)   10.50   12.50
O14 A24 75c blk & straw (R) ('23)   3.00   1.25
O15 A26 1fr brn red (Bl)   4.50   1.40
    Nos. O1-O15 (15)   28.06   36.60

Inverted overprints exist on 10c, 20c, 30c, 50c and 1fr. Double overprints exist on Nos. O4, O6 and 1fr.

Regular Issue of 1927-30 Overprinted in Various Colors

DIENSTMARKE

1927-34   Perf. 13½
O16 A31 10c dp brn (Bl) ('34)   1.00   1.25
O17 A32 15c ol blk (Bl) ('34)   1.50   4.25
O18 A32 20c brn org (Bk) ('31)   1.00   80
O19 A32 25c bluish sl (Bl)   1.50   2.75
O20 A31 30c ol grn (C)   1.10   15
O21 A32 40c ol brn (C)   85   15
O22 A32 50c mag (Bl)   85   15
O23 A35 60c red org (Bk) ('30)   60   18
O24 A32 75c brn vio (C)   70   35
O25 A35 1fr vio (RO)   1.50   15
O26 A36 2fr brn red (Bl)   1.50   22
    Nos. O16-O26 (11)   12.10   12.65

The overprint listed is at a 23 to 25-degree angle. Also at 32-degree angle on Nos. O20-O22, O24-O26.
The overprint on Nos. O16 and O20 is known only inverted. Nos. O21-O26 exist with double overprint.

French Protectorate

Arms — O1

1949, Oct. 1   Engr.   Perf. 14x13
O27 O1 10c deep carmine   20   11.00
O28 O1 30c blue black   15   12.00
O29 O1 1fr Prus green   15   15
O30 O1 2fr orange red   85   55
O31 O1 5fr blue   25   22
O32 O1 10fr black   40   50
O33 O1 12fr red violet   3.25   3.75
O34 O1 15fr indigo   40   20
O35 O1 20fr green   90   55
O36 O1 30fr violet rose   1.10   2.00
O37 O1 50fr purple   1.10   1.90
O38 O1 100fr red brown   40.00   100.00
    Nos. O27-O38 (12)   48.75
    Set, never hinged   100.00

STE.-MARIE DE MADAGASCAR

LOCATION — An island off the east coast of Madagascar
GOVT. — French Possession
AREA — 64 sq. mi.
POP. — 8,000 (approx.)

In 1896 Ste.-Marie de Madagascar was attached to the colony of Madagascar for administrative purposes.

100 Centimes = 1 Franc

Navigation and Commerce — A1

1894 Unwmk. Typo. Perf. 14x13½
Name of Colony in Blue or Carmine
1 A1 1c black, *lil bl*   55   55
2 A1 2c brown, *buff*   60   60
3 A1 4c claret, *lavender*   2.40   2.00
4 A1 5c green, *grnsh*   5.50   4.00
5 A1 10c black, *lavender*   5.50   4.25
6 A1 15c blue   11.00   11.00
7 A1 20c red, *green*   10.00   7.00
8 A1 25c black, *rose*   8.00   6.00
9 A1 30c brown, *bister*   5.50   4.50
10 A1 40c red, *straw*   5.75   4.50
11 A1 50c carmine, *rose*   22.50   18.00
12 A1 75c violet, *org*   40.00   20.00
13 A1 1fr brnz grn, *straw*   20.00   14.00
    Nos. 1-13 (13)   137.30   96.40

Perf. 13½x14 stamps are counterfeits.

These stamps were replaced by those of Madagascar.

ST. PIERRE & MIQUELON

LOCATION — Two small groups of islands off the southern coast of Newfoundland
GOVT. — Formerly a French colony, now a Department of France
AREA — 93 sq. mi.
POP. — 6,051 (est. 1984)
CAPITAL — St. Pierre

The territory of St. Pierre and Miquelon became a Department of France in July 1976.

100 Centimes = 1 Franc

> Catalogue values for unused stamps in this country are for Never Hinged items, beginning with Scott 300 in the regular postage section, Scott B13 in the semi-postal section, Scott C1 in the airpost section, and Scott J68 in the postage due section.

Stamps of French Colonies Handstamp Surcharged in Black

1885   Unwmk.   Imperf.
1 A8 05c on 40c ver, *straw*   45.00   22.50
2 A8 10c on 40c ver, *straw*   12.00   9.00
a.   "M" inverted   110.00   75.00
3 A8 15c on 40c ver, *straw*   12.00   9.00

Nos. 2 and 3 exist with "SPM" 17mm wide instead of 15½mm.
Nos. 1-3 exist with surcharge inverted and with it doubled.

Handstamp Surcharged in Black

05
S P M
b

25
S P M
c

25
d

S P M

1885
4 A8 (b) 05c on 35c blk, *yel*   55.00   40.00
5 A8 (b) 05c on 75c car, *rose*   150.00   90.00
6 A8 (b) 05c on 1fr brnz grn, *straw*   12.00   11.00
7 A8 (c) 25c on 1fr brnz grn, *straw*   5,750.   1,600.
8 A8 (d) 25c on 1fr brnz grn, *straw*   2,100.   1,100.

Nos. 7 and 8 exist with surcharge inverted, and with it vertical. No. 7 exists with "S P M" above "25" (the handstamping was done in two steps).

1885   Perf. 14x13½
9 A9 (c) 5c on 2c brn, *buff*   4,250.   1,750.
10 A9 (d) 5c on 4c cl, *lav*   225.00   150.00
11 A9 (b) 05c on 20c red, *grn*   12.00   11.00

No. 9 surcharge is always inverted. No. 10 exists with surcharge inverted.

P D
5
A15

1886, Feb.   Typo.   Imperf.
      Without Gum
12 A15 5c black   650.00
13 A15 10c black   800.00
14 A15 15c black   500.00

"P D" are the initials for "Payé a destination." Excellent forgeries exist.

Stamps of French Colonies Surcharged in Black

15 c.   **15 c.**
S P M   **S P M**
e   f

1891   Perf. 14x13½
15 A9 (e) 15c on 30c brn, *bis*   17.50   15.00
a.   Inverted surcharge   120.00   90.00
16 A9 (e) 15c on 35c blk, *org*   375.00   250.00
a.   Inverted surcharge   400.00   325.00
17 A9 (f) 15c on 35c blk, *org*   800.00   500.00
a.   Inverted surcharge   1,400.   800.00
18 A9 (e) 15c on 40c red, *straw*   40.00   32.50
a.   Inverted surcharge   100.00   90.00

Stamps of French Colonies Overprinted in Black or Red

1891, Oct. 15
19 A9 1c blk, *lil bl*   4.50   4.00
a.   Inverted overprint   12.50   12.50
20 A9 1c blk, *lil bl* (R)   4.25   4.25
a.   Inverted overprint   9.00   9.00
21 A9 2c brn, *buff*   4.50   4.00
a.   Inverted overprint   12.50   12.50
22 A9 2c brn, *buff* (R)   10.00   10.00
a.   Inverted overprint   27.50   27.50
23 A9 4c cl, *lav*   4.50   4.00
a.   Inverted overprint   14.00   14.00
24 A9 4c cl, *lav* (R)   8.00   8.00
a.   Inverted overprint   22.50   22.50
25 A9 5c grn, *grnsh*   4.50   4.00
a.   Double surcharge   40.00

26	A9	10c blk, *lav*	14.00	11.00
a.		Inverted overprint	32.50	32.50
27	A9	10c blk, *lav* (R)	7.00	7.00
a.		Inverted overprint	22.50	22.50
28	A9	15c blk, *blue*	9.00	6.25
29	A9	20c red, *grn*	27.50	25.00
30	A9	25c blk, *rose*	11.00	9.00
31	A9	30c brn, *bis*	45.00	37.50
32	A9	35c vio, *org*	275.00	165.00
a.		Double surcharge	82.50	
33	A9	40c red, *straw*	35.00	25.00
34	A9	75c car, *rose*	45.00	40.00
a.		Inverted overprint	100.00	100.00
35	A9	1fr brnz grn, *straw*	27.50	25.00
a.		Inverted overprint	82.50	82.50

Numerous varieties of mislettering occur in the preceding overprint: "S," "ST," "P," "M," "ON," or "." missing; "-" instead of "ON"; "=" instead of "-." These varieties command values double or triple those of normal stamps.

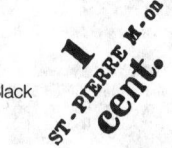

Surcharged in Black

1891-92

36	A9	1c on 5c grn, *grnsh*	4.25	4.00
37	A9	1c on 10c blk, *lav*	5.25	4.25
38	A9	1c on 25c blk, *rose* ('92)	4.00	3.25
39	A9	2c on 10c blk, *lav*	4.00	3.25
a.		Double surcharge	42.50	
40	A9	2c on 15c bl	3.00	3.00
41	A9	2c on 25c blk, *rose* ('92)	3.00	3.00
42	A9	4c on 20c red, *grn*	3.00	3.00
43	A9	4c on 25c blk, *rose* ('92)	3.00	3.00
44	A9	4c on 30c brn, *bis*	9.00	8.00
45	A9	4c on 40c red, *straw*	12.00	7.00
		Nos. 36-45 (10)	50.50	41.75

See note after No. 35.

Surcharged

j   k

1892, Nov. 4

46	A9 (j)	1c on 5c grn, *grnsh*	5.00	4.25
47	A9 (j)	2c on 5c grn, *grnsh*	5.00	4.25
48	A9 (j)	4c on 5c grn, *grnsh*	5.00	4.25
49	A9 (k)	1c on 25c blk, *rose*	2.50	2.50
50	A9 (k)	2c on 25c blk, *rose*	2.50	2.50
51	A9 (k)	4c on 25c blk, *rose*	2.50	2.50
		Nos. 46-51 (6)	22.50	20.25

See note after No. 35.

Postage Due Stamps of French Colonies Overprinted in Red

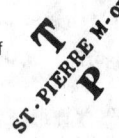

1892, Dec. 1   *Imperf.*

52	D1	10c black	15.00	15.00
53	D1	20c black	9.00	9.00
54	D1	30c black	10.00	10.00
55	D1	40c black	10.00	10.00
56	D1	60c black	45.00	45.00

Black Overprint

57	D1	1fr brown	65.00	65.00
58	D1	2fr brown	120.00	120.00
59	D1	5fr brown	225.00	225.00
		Nos. 52-59 (8)	499.00	499.00

See note after No. 35. "T P" stands for "Timbre Poste."

Navigation and Commerce — A16

1892-1908   Typo.   *Perf. 14x13½*

60	A16	1c blk, *lil bl*	40	40
61	A16	2c brown, *buff*	40	40
62	A16	4c claret, *lav*	80	70
63	A16	5c green, *grnsh*	1.00	1.00
64	A16	5c yel grn ('08)	1.65	1.40
65	A16	10c black, *lav*	2.50	2.25
66	A16	10c red ('00)	2.25	80
67	A16	15c bl, quadrille paper	25.00	3.40
68	A16	15c gray, *lt gray* ('00)	42.50	25.00
69	A16	20c red, *grn*	11.00	8.25
70	A16	25c black, *rose*	4.00	1.20
71	A16	25c blue ('00)	7.00	5.00
72	A16	30c brown, *bis*	4.00	2.00
73	A16	35c blk, *yel* ('06)	3.75	3.00
74	A16	40c red, *straw*	3.50	2.00
75	A16	50c car, *rose*	21.00	16.00
76	A16	50c brown, *az* ('00)	16.00	14.00
77	A16	75c violet, *org*	14.00	11.00
78	A16	1fr brnz grn, *straw*	11.00	6.00
		Nos. 60-78 (19)	150.00	101.80

Perf. 13½x14 stamps are counterfeits.
For surcharges and overprints see Nos. 110-120, Q1-Q2.

Fisherman A17

Fulmar Petrel — A18

Fishing Schooner A19

1909-30

79	A17	1c orange red & ol	15	15
80	A17	2c olive & dp bl	15	15
81	A17	4c violet & ol	15	15
82	A17	5c bl grn & ol grn	20	20
83	A17	5c blue & blk ('22)	15	15
84	A17	10c car rose & red	20	20
85	A17	10c bl grn & ol grn ('22)	15	15
86	A17	10c bister & mag ('25)	20	20
86A	A17	15c dl vio & rose ('17)	20	15
87	A17	20c bis brn & vio brn	45	45
88	A18	25c dp blue & blue	80	60
89	A18	25c ol brn & bl grn ('22)	22	22
90	A18	30c orange & vio brn	45	45
91	A18	30c rose & dull red ('22)	15	15
92	A18	30c red brn & bl ('25)	15	15
93	A18	30c gray grn & bl grn ('26)	28	28
94	A18	35c ol grn & vio brn	20	20
95	A18	40c vio brn & ol grn	1.25	80
96	A18	45c violet & ol grn	28	28
97	A18	50c olive & ol grn	55	55
98	A18	50c bl & pale bl ('22)	45	45
99	A18	50c yel brn & mag ('25)	25	25
100	A18	60c bl & ver ('25)	28	28
101	A18	65c vio & org brn ('28)	50	50
102	A18	75c brown & olive	55	55
103	A18	90c brn red & org red ('30)	10.00	10.00
104	A19	1fr vio brn & dp bl	1.40	1.20
105	A19	1.10fr bl grn & org red ('28)	1.50	1.50
106	A19	1.50fr bl & dp bl ('30)	4.00	4.00
107	A19	2fr violet & brn	1.40	1.25
108	A19	3fr red violet ('30)	4.00	4.00
109	A19	5fr vio brn & ol grn	4.50	3.00
		Nos. 79-109 (32)	35.16	32.56

For overprints and surcharges see Nos. 121-131, 206C-206D, B1-B2, Q3-Q5.

Stamps of 1892-1906 Surcharged in Carmine or Black

05   10

1912

110	A16	5c on 2c brn, *buff*	80	80
111	A16	5c on 4c cl, *lav* (C)	15	15
112	A16	5c on 15c bl (C)	15	15
113	A16	5c on 20c red, *grn*	15	15
114	A16	5c on 25c blk, *rose* (C)	15	15
115	A16	5c on 30c brn, *bis* (C)	25	25
116	A16	5c on 35c blk, *yel* (C)	40	40
117	A16	10c on 40c red, *straw*	15	15
118	A16	10c on 50c car, *rose*	28	28
119	A16	10c on 75c dp vio, *org*	65	65
120	A16	10c on 1fr brnz grn, *straw*	80	80
		Nos. 110-120 (11)	3.93	3.93

Two spacings between the surcharged numerals are found on Nos. 110 to 120.

Stamps and Types of 1909-17 Surcharged with New Value and Bars in Black, Blue (Bl) or Red

1924-27

121	A17	25c on 15c dl vio & rose ('25)	20	20
a.		Double surcharge	70.00	
b.		Triple surcharge	70.00	
122	A19	25c on 2fr vio & lt brn (Bl)	20	20
123	A19	25c on 5fr brn & ol grn (Bl)	20	20
a.		Triple surcharge	65.00	
124	A18	65c on 45c vio & ol grn ('25)	45	45
125	A18	85c on 75c brn & ol ('25)	45	45
126	A18	90c on 75c brn red & dp org ('27)	80	80
127	A19	1.25fr on 1fr dk bl & ultra (R) ('26)	70	70
128	A19	1.50fr on 1fr ultra & dk bl ('27)	1.40	1.40
129	A19	3fr on 5fr ol brn & red vio ('27)	80	80
130	A19	10fr on 5fr ver & ol grn ('27)	6.50	6.50
131	A19	20fr on 5fr vio & ver ('27)	9.00	9.00
		Nos. 121-131 (11)	20.70	20.70

Colonial Exposition Issue
Common Design Types

1931, Apr. 13   Engr.   *Perf. 12½*
Name of Country in Black

132	CD70	40c deep green	90	90
133	CD71	50c violet	90	90
134	CD72	90c red orange	90	90
135	CD73	1.50fr dull blue	90	90

Map and Fishermen — A20

Lighthouse and Fish — A21

Fishing Steamer and Sea Gulls — A22

Perf. 13½x14, 14x13½

1932-33   Typo.

136	A20	1c red brn & ultra	15	15
137	A21	2c black & dk grn	15	15
138	A22	4c magenta & ol brn	15	15
139	A22	5c violet & dk brn	15	15
140	A21	10c red brn & blk	15	15
141	A21	15c dk blue & vio	40	40
142	A20	20c black & red org	40	40
143	A21	25c lt vio & lt grn	40	40
144	A22	30c dk grn & bl grn	40	40
145	A22	40c dp bl & dk brn	55	55
146	A21	45c ver & dp grn	55	55
147	A22	50c dk brn & dk grn	55	55
148	A22	65c ol brn & org	65	65
149	A20	75c grn & red org	65	65
150	A20	90c dull red & red	70	70
151	A21	1fr org brn & org red	55	55
152	A20	1.25fr dp bl & lake ('33)	70	70
153	A20	1.50fr dp blue & blue	70	70
154	A21	1.75fr blk & dk brn ('33)	90	90
155	A22	2fr bl blk & Prus bl	3.75	3.75
156	A21	3fr dp grn & dk brn	4.50	4.50
157	A21	5fr brn red & dk brn	9.00	9.00
158	A22	10fr dk grn & grn	27.50	27.50
159	A20	20fr ver & dp grn	27.50	27.50
		Nos. 136-159 (24)	81.10	81.10

For overprints and surcharges see Nos. 160-164, 207-221.

Nos. 147, 149, 153-154, 157 Overprinted in Black, Red or Blue

JACQUES CARTIER

1534 - 1934		1534-1934
p		q

1934, Oct. 18

160	A21(p)	50c (Bk)	80	80
161	A20(q)	75c (Bk)	1.20	1.20
162	A20(p)	1.50fr (Bk)	1.20	1.20
163	A22(p)	1.75fr (R)	1.50	1.50
164	A21(p)	5fr (Bl)	12.00	12.00
		Nos. 160-164 (5)	16.70	16.70

400th anniv. of the landing of Jacques Cartier.

Paris International Exposition Issue
Common Design Types

1937   *Perf. 13*

165	CD74	20c deep violet	65	65
166	CD75	30c dark green	65	65
167	CD76	40c carmine rose	65	65
168	CD77	50c dk brown & blue	65	65
169	CD78	90c red	65	65
170	CD79	1.50fr ultra	65	65
		Nos. 165-170 (6)	3.90	3.90

Colonial Arts Exhibition Issue
Souvenir Sheet
Common Design Type

1937   *Imperf.*

171	CD78	3fr dark ultra	2.25	2.25

Dog Team — A23

Port St. Pierre — A24

Tortue Lighthouse A25

Soldiers' Bay at Langlade A26

1938-40   Photo.   *Perf. 13½x13*

172	A23	2c dk blue green	15	15
173	A23	3c brown violet	15	15
174	A23	4c dk red violet	15	15
175	A23	5c carmine lake	15	15
176	A23	10c bister brown	15	15
177	A23	15c red violet	15	15
178	A23	20c blue violet	15	15
179	A23	25c Prus blue	80	80
180	A24	30c dk red violet	15	15
181	A24	35c deep green	20	20
182	A24	40c slate blue ('40)	15	15
183	A24	45c deep green ('40)	20	20
a.		Value omitted	35.00	
184	A24	50c carmine rose	15	15
185	A24	55c Prus blue	1.00	1.00
186	A24	60c violet ('39)	20	20
187	A24	65c brown	1.65	1.65
188	A24	70c orange yel ('39)	20	20
189	A25	80c violet	35	35
190	A25	90c ultra ('39)	20	20
191	A25	1fr brt pink	4.00	4.00
192	A25	1fr pale ol grn ('40)	20	20
193	A25	1.25fr rose violet ('39)	60	60
194	A25	1.40fr dk brown ('40)	15	15
195	A25	1.50fr blue green	20	20
196	A25	1.60fr rose violet ('40)	25	25
197	A25	1.75fr deep blue	55	55
198	A26	2fr rose violet	15	15
199	A26	2.25fr brt blue ('39)	28	28
200	A26	2.50fr orange yel ('40)	45	45
201	A26	3fr gray brown	15	15
202	A26	5fr henna brown	40	40

203	A26	10fr dk bl, *bluish*	55	55
204	A26	20fr slate green	65	65
		Nos. 172-204 (33)	14.88	14.88

For overprints and surcharges see Nos. 222-255, 260-299, B9-B10.

New York World's Fair Issue
Common Design Type

1939, May 10   Engr.   Perf. 12½x12

205	CD82	1.25fr carmine lake	40	40
206	CD82	2.25fr ultra	40	40

For overprints and surcharges see Nos. 256-259.

Lighthouse
on
Cliff — A27

1941   Engr.   Perf. 12½x12

206A	A27	1fr dull lilac	25
206B	A27	2.50fr blue	25

Nos. 206A-206B were issued by the Vichy government and were not placed on sale in the colony. Stamps of types A23 and A26 without "RF" monogram were issued in 1941-1944 by the Vichy government, but were not sold in the colony.

Free French Administration
The circumstances surrounding the overprinting and distribution of these stamps were most unusual. Practically all of the stamps issued in small quantities, with the exception of Nos. 260 to 299, were obtained by speculators within a few days after issue. At a later date, the remainders were taken over by the Free French Agency in Ottawa, Canada, by whom they were sold at a premium for the benefit of the Syndicat des Oeuvres Sociales. Large quantities appeared on the market in 1991, including many "errors."
Excellent counterfeits of these surcharges and overprints are known.

Nos. 86 and 92 Overprinted in Black

FRANCE LIBRE

a

F. N. F. L.

1942   Unwmk.   Perf. 14x13½

206C	A17	10c	625.00	625.00
206D	A18	30c	650.00	650.00

The letters "F. N. F. L." are the initials of "Forces Navales Francaises Libres" or "Free French Naval Forces."

Same Overprint in Black on Nos. 137-139, 145-148, 151, 154-155, 157

207	A21	2c	125.00	125.00
208	A22	4c	22.50	22.50
208A	A22	5c	475.00	475.00
209	A22	40c	7.00	7.00
210	A21	45c	90.00	90.00
211	A21	50c	3.50	3.50
212	A22	65c	16.00	16.00
213	A21	1fr	165.00	165.00
214	A22	1.75fr	3.50	3.50
215	A22	2fr	3.50	3.50
216	A22	5fr	150.00	150.00

**FRANCE
LIBRE**

Nos. 142, 149, 152-153
Overprinted in Black

F N F L

Perf. 13½x14

216A	A20	20c	190.00	190.00
217	A20	75c	9.00	9.00
218	A20	1.25fr	9.00	9.00
218A	A20	1.50fr	225.00	225.00

On Nos. 152, 149 Surcharged with New Value and Bars

219	A20	10fr on 1.25fr	18.00	18.00
220	A20	20fr on 75c	25.00	25.00

No. 154 Surcharged in Red

**5 fr
FRANCE LIBRE
F. N. F. L.**

Perf. 14x13½

221	A22	5fr on 1.75fr	5.00	5.00

Stamps of 1938-40 Overprinted type "a" in Black

Perf. 13½x13

222	A23	2c dk blue grn	225.00	225.00
223	A23	3c brown violet	70.00	70.00
224	A23	4c dk red violet	57.50	57.50
225	A23	5c carmine lake	450.00	450.00
226	A23	10c bister brown	4.50	4.50
227	A23	15c red violet	950.00	950.00
228	A23	20c blue violet	95.00	95.00
229	A23	25c Prus blue	4.50	4.50
230	A24	35c deep green	450.00	450.00
231	A24	40c slate blue	4.50	4.50
232	A24	45c deep green	4.50	4.50
233	A24	55c Prus blue	6,000.	6,000.
234	A24	60c violet	375.00	375.00
235	A24	65c brown	8.50	8.50
236	A24	70c orange yellow	17.50	17.50
237	A24	80c violet	225.00	225.00
238	A25	90c ultra	6.75	6.75
239	A25	1fr pale ol grn	5.00	5.00
240	A25	1.25fr brt rose	5.00	5.00
241	A25	1.40fr dark brown	5.00	5.00
242	A25	1.50fr blue green	425.00	425.00
243	A25	1.60fr rose violet	4.50	4.50
244	A26	2fr rose violet	30.00	30.00
245	A26	2.25fr brt blue	4.50	4.50
246	A26	2.50fr orange yel	5.00	5.00
247	A26	3fr gray brown	7,000.	7,000.
248	A26	5fr henna brown	1,300.	1,300.
248A	A26	20fr slate grn	600.00	600.00

Nos. 176, 190 Surcharged in Black

FRANCE LIBRE

F. N. F. L.

20 c

249	A23	20c on 10c	3.50	3.50
250	A23	30c on 10c	3.50	3.50
251	A25	60c on 90c	4.25	4.25
252	A23	1.50fr on 10c	7.00	7.00
253	A23	2.50fr on 10c	7.00	7.00
254	A23	10fr on 10c	30.00	30.00
255	A25	20fr on 90c	32.50	32.50

**New York World's Fair Issue
Overprinted type "a" in Black**

Perf. 12½x12

256	CD82	1.25fr carmine lake	4.75	4.75
257	CD82	2.25fr ultra	4.75	4.75

2 fr 50

Nos. 205-206 Surcharged

**FRANCE LIBRE
F. N. F. L.**

258	CD82	2.50fr on 1.25fr	6.25	6.25
259	CD82	3fr on 2.25fr	6.25	6.25

Noël 1941

Stamps of 1938-40 Overprinted in Carmine

**FRANCE LIBRE
F. N. F. L.**

1941   Perf. 13½x13

260	A23	10c bister brn	20.00	20.00
261	A23	20c blue violet	20.00	20.00
262	A23	25c Prus blue	20.00	20.00
263	A24	40c slate blue	20.00	20.00
264	A24	45c deep green	20.00	20.00
265	A24	65c brown	20.00	20.00
266	A24	70c orange yel	20.00	20.00
267	A25	80c violet	20.00	20.00
268	A25	90c ultra	20.00	20.00
269	A25	1fr pale ol grn	20.00	20.00
270	A25	1.25fr brt rose	20.00	20.00
271	A25	1.40fr dk brown	20.00	20.00
272	A25	1.60fr rose violet	22.50	22.50
273	A25	1.75fr brt blue	22.50	22.50
274	A26	2fr rose violet	22.50	22.50
275	A26	2.25fr brt blue	22.50	22.50
276	A26	2.50fr orange yel	22.50	22.50
277	A26	3fr gray brown	22.50	22.50

Same Surcharged in Carmine with New Values

278	A23	10fr on 10c bister brn	37.50	37.50
279	A25	20fr on 90c ultra	37.50	37.50
		Nos. 260-279 (20)	450.00	450.00

Stamps of 1938-40 Overprinted in Black

280	A23	10c bister brn	26.00	26.00
281	A23	20c blue violet	26.00	26.00
282	A23	25c Prus blue	26.00	26.00
283	A24	40c slate blue	26.00	26.00
284	A24	45c deep green	26.00	26.00
285	A24	65c brown	26.00	26.00
286	A24	70c orange yel	26.00	26.00
287	A25	80c violet	26.00	26.00
288	A25	90c ultra	26.00	26.00
289	A25	1fr pale ol grn	26.00	26.00
290	A25	1.25fr brt rose	26.00	26.00
291	A25	1.40fr dk brown	26.00	26.00
292	A25	1.60fr rose violet	26.00	26.00
293	A25	1.75fr brt blue	475.00	475.00
294	A26	2fr rose vio	26.00	26.00
295	A26	2.25fr brt blue	26.00	26.00
296	A26	2.50fr orange yel	26.00	26.00
297	A26	3fr gray brown	26.00	26.00

Same Surcharged in Black with New Values

298	A23	10fr on 10c bister brn	75.00	75.00
299	A25	20fr on 90c ultra	75.00	75.00
		Nos. 280-299 (20)	1,067.	1,067.

Christmas Day plebiscite ordered by Vice Admiral Emile Henri Muselier, commander of the Free French naval forces (Nos. 260-299).

> **Catalogue values for unused stamps in this section, from this point to the end of the section, are for Never Hinged items.**

St. Malo
Fishing
Schooner
A28

1942   Photo.   Perf. 14x14½

300	A28	5c dark blue	15	15
301	A28	10c dull pink	15	15
302	A28	25c brt green	15	15
303	A28	30c slate black	15	15
304	A28	40c brt grnsh blue	15	15
305	A28	60c brown red	15	15
306	A28	1fr dark violet	20	20
307	A28	1.50fr brt red	40	40
308	A28	2fr brown	20	20
309	A28	2.25fr brt ultra	40	40
310	A28	4fr dk orange	20	20
311	A28	5fr dp plum	20	20
312	A28	10fr lt ultra	45	45
313	A28	20fr dark green	65	65
		Set value	3.00	3.00

50c

Nos. 300, 302, 309 Surcharged in Carmine or Black

1945

314	A28	50c on 5c (C)	15	15
315	A28	70c on 5c (C)	15	15
316	A28	80c on 5c (C)	15	15
317	A28	1.20fr on 5c (C)	15	15
318	A28	2.40fr on 25c	15	15
319	A28	3fr on 25c	15	15
320	A28	4.50fr on 25c	35	15
321	A28	15fr on 2.50fr (C)	60	60
		Set value	1.50	1.30

Eboue Issue
Common Design Type

1945   Engr.   Perf. 13

322	CD91	2fr black	28	28
323	CD91	25fr Prussian green	45	45

Nos. 322 and 323 exist imperforate.

Soldiers' Bay — A29

Fishing
Industry
Symbols
A30

Fishermen
A31

Weighing the
Catch — A32

Fishing Boat
and Dinghy
A33

Storm-swept
Coast — A34

1947, Oct. 6   Engr.   Perf. 12½

324	A29	10c chocolate	15	15
325	A29	30c violet	15	15
326	A29	40c rose lilac	15	15
327	A29	50c intense blue	15	15
328	A30	60c carmine	15	15
329	A30	80c brt ultra	15	15
330	A30	1fr dk green	15	15
331	A31	1.20fr blue grn	22	22
332	A31	1.50fr black	22	22
333	A31	2fr red brown	22	22
334	A32	3fr rose violet	70	70
335	A32	3.60fr dp brown org	45	45
336	A32	4fr sepia	45	45
337	A33	5fr orange	40	40
338	A33	6fr blue	55	55
339	A33	10fr Prus green	70	70
340	A34	15fr dk slate grn	90	90
341	A34	20fr vermilion	80	80
342	A34	25fr dark green	90	90
		Nos. 324-342 (19)	7.56	7.56

Imperforates
Most stamps of St. Pierre and Miquelon from 1947 onward exist imperforate in issued and trial colors, and also in small presentation sheets in issued colors.

Silver
Fox — A35

1952, Sept. 10   Unwmk.   Perf. 13

343	A35	8fr dk brown	2.50	65
344	A35	17fr blue	3.00	80

Military Medal Issue
Common Design Type

1952, Dec. 1   Engr. & Typo.

345	CD101	8fr multicolored	6.00	2.25

Fish Freezing Plant — A36

1955-56   **Engr.**
346 A36 30c ultra & dk blue   22   15
347 A36 50c gray, blk & sepia   22   15
348 A36 3fr purple   40   22
349 A36 40fr Prussian blue   2.00 1.20

Issued: 40fr, July 4; others, Oct. 22, 1956.

FIDES Issue

Fish Freezer "Le Galantry" A37

Perf. 13x12½
1956, Feb. 20   Unwmk.
350 A37 15fr blk brn & chestnut   1.75 60

See note in Common Design section after CD103.

Codfish A38

Design: 4fr, 10fr, Lighthouse and fishing fleet.

1957, Nov. 4   Perf. 13
351 A38 40c dk brn & grnsh bl   18   15
352 A38 1fr brown & green   22   15
353 A38 2fr indigo & dull blue   42   15
354 A38 4fr maroon, car & pur   48   20
355 A38 10fr grnsh bl, dk bl & brn 1.00   40
      Nos. 351-355 (5)   2.30 1.05

Human Rights Issue
Common Design Type
1958, Dec. 10   Engr.   Perf. 13
356 CD105 20fr red brn & dk blue   2.00 70

Flower Issue
Common Design Type
1959   Photo.   Perf. 12½x12
357 CD104 5fr Spruce   1.65 45

Ice Hockey A39

Mink — A40

1959, Sept. 14   Engr.   Perf. 13
358 A39 20fr multicolored   1.75 50
359 A40 25fr indigo, yel grn & brn 3.00 70

Cypripedium Acaule — A41

Eider Ducks — A42

Flower: 50fr, Calopogon pulchellus.

1962, Apr. 24   Unwmk.   Perf. 13
360 A41 25fr grn, org & car rose   2.75 50
361 A41 50fr green & car lake   5.25 90

See No. C24.

1963, Mar. 4   Perf. 13

Birds: 1fr, Rock ptarmigan. 2fr, Ringed plovers. 6fr, Blue-winged teal.

362 A42 50c blk, ultra & ocher   42   15
363 A42 1fr red brn, ultra & rose   75   15
364 A42 2fr blk, dk bl & bis   1.25 25
365 A42 6fr multicolored   3.00 60

Albert Calmette A43

1963, Aug. 5   Engr.
366 A43 30fr dk brn & dk blue   6.00 90

Albert Calmette, bacteriologist, birth cent.

Red Cross Centenary Issue
Common Design Type
1963, Sept. 2   Unwmk.   Perf. 13
367 CD113 25fr ultra, gray & car   5.00 65

Human Rights Issue
Common Design Type
1963, Dec. 10   Unwmk.   Perf. 13
368 CD117 20fr org, bl & dk brn   2.25 65

Philatec Issue
Common Design Type
1964, Apr. 4   Engr.
369 CD118 60fr choc, grn & dk bl   5.00 2.25

Rabbits — A44

1964, Sept. 28   Perf. 13
370 A44 3fr shown   1.10   20
371 A44 4fr Fox   1.10   20
372 A44 5fr Roe deer   2.25   40
373 A44 34fr Charolais bull   6.25 1.20

Airport and Map of St. Pierre and Miquelon A45

Designs: 40fr, Television tube and tower, and map. 48fr, Map of new harbor of St. Pierre.

1967   Engr.   Perf. 13
374 A45 30fr ind, bl & dk red   3.75   55
375 A45 40fr sl grn, ol & dk red 4.75   60
376 A45 48fr dk red, brn & sl bl 5.50   80

Issue dates: 30fr, Oct. 23; 40fr, Nov. 20; 48fr, Sept. 25.

WHO Anniversary Issue
Common Design Type
1968, May 4   Engr.   Perf. 13
377 CD126 10fr multicolored   4.75   55

René de Chateaubriand and Map of Islands — A46

Designs: 4fr, J. D. Cassini and map. 15fr, Prince de Joinville, François F. d'Orleans (1818-1900), ships and map. 25fr, Admiral Gauchet, World War I warship and map.

1968, May 20   Photo.   Perf. 12½x13
378 A46 4fr multicolored   2.25   55
379 A46 6fr multicolored   3.50   60
380 A46 15fr multicolored   4.50   80
381 A46 25fr multicolored   4.75 1.20

Human Rights Year Issue
Common Design Type
1968, Aug. 10   Engr.   Perf. 13
382 CD127 20fr bl, ver & org yel 5.25   45

Belle Rivière, Langlade A47

Design: 15fr, Debon Brook, Langlade.

1969, Apr. 30   Engr.   Perf. 13
Size: 36x22mm
383 A47 5fr bl, sl grn & brn   3.00   30
384 A47 15fr brn, bl & dl grn   3.75   45

See Nos. C41-C42.

Treasury A48

Designs: 25fr, Scientific and Technical Institute of Maritime Fishing. 30fr, Monument to seamen lost at sea. 60fr, St. Christopher College.

1969, May 30   Engr.   Perf. 13
385 A48 10fr brt bl, cl & blk   1.50   22
386 A48 25fr dk bl, brt bl & brn red 3.00 45
387 A48 30fr blue, grn & gray   4.50   60
388 A48 60fr brt bl, brn red & blk 6.00 1.00

Ringed Seals — A49

Designs: 3fr, Sperm whales. 4fr, Pilot whales. 6fr, Common dolphins.

1969, Oct. 6   Engr.   Perf. 13
389 A49 1fr lil, vio brn & red brn 3.00 40
390 A49 3fr bl grn, ind & red   3.00   40
391 A49 4fr ol, gray grn & mar 3.50   55
392 A49 6fr brt grn, pur & red 5.25   60

L'Estoile and Granville, France — A50

Designs: 40fr, "La Jolie" and St. Jean de Luz, France, 1750. 48fr, "Le Juste" and La Rochelle, France, 1860.

1969, Oct. 13   Engr.   Perf. 13
393 A50 34fr grn, mar & sl grn 5.25   80
394 A50 40fr brn red, lem & sl grn 7.25 1.20
395 A50 48fr multicolored   11.00 1.60

Historic ships connecting St. Pierre and Miquelon with France.

ILO Issue
Common Design Type
1969, Nov. 24
396 CD131 20fr org, gray & ocher 4.50 55

UPU Headquarters Issue
Common Design Type
1970, May 20   Engr.   Perf. 13
397 CD133 25fr dk car, brt bl & brn 4.25 55
398 CD133 34fr maroon, brn & gray 6.75 70

Rowers and Globe — A51

1970, Oct. 13   Photo.   Perf. 12½x12
399 A51 20fr lt grnsh bl & brn   4.00   45

World Rowing Championships, St. Catherine.

Blackberries — A52

1970, Oct. 20   Engr.   Perf. 13
400 A52 3fr shown   1.10   16
401 A52 4fr Strawberries   1.25   22
402 A52 5fr Raspberries   1.65   30
403 A52 6fr Blueberries   2.00   40

Ewe and Lamb — A53

Designs: 30fr, Animal quarantine station. 34fr, Charolais bull. 48fr, Refrigeration ship and slaughterhouse.

1970   Engr.   Perf. 13
404 A53 15fr plum, grn & olive 3.75   45
405 A53 30fr sl, bis brn & ap grn 4.25   45
406 A53 34fr red lil, org brn & emer 6.75 1.20
407 A53 48fr multicolored   5.00   80

Issue dates: 48fr, Nov. 10; others, Dec. 8.

Saint François d'Assise 1900 — A54

Ships: 35fr, Sainte Jehanne, 1920. 40fr, L'Aventure, 1950. 80fr, Commandant Bourdais, 1970.

1971, Aug. 25
408 A54 30fr Prus bl & hn brn   4.75   60
409 A54 35fr Prus bl, lt grn & ol brn 6.25 70
410 A54 40fr sl grn, bl & dk brn 8.50 1.00
411 A54 80fr dp grn, bl & blk   9.50 1.40

Deep-sea fishing fleet.

"Aconit" and Map of Islands — A55

1971, Sept. 27   Engr.   Perf. 13
412 A55 22fr shown   7.25   80
413 A55 25fr Alysse   10.00 1.40
414 A55 50fr Mimosa   15.00 1.60

Rallying of the Free French forces, 30th anniv.

Ship's Bell — A56

St. Pierre Museum: 45fr, Old chart and sextants, horiz.

1971, Oct. 25 Photo. *Perf. 12½x13*
415 A56 20fr gray & multi   2.75   55
416 A56 45fr red brn & multi   4.50   70

De Gaulle Issue
Common Design Type

Designs: 35fr, Gen. de Gaulle, 1940. Pres. de Gaulle, 1970.

1971, Nov. 9 Engr. *Perf. 13*
417 CD134 35fr vermilion & blk   6.75 1.50
418 CD134 45fr vermilion & blk   10.00 2.00

Haddock A57

Fish: 3fr, Hippoglossoides platessoides. 5fr, Sebastes mentella. 10fr, Codfish.

1972, Mar. 7
419 A57   2fr vio bl, ind & pink   2.75   20
420 A57   3fr grn & gray olive   3.25   25
421 A57   5fr Prus bl & brick red   3.50   30
422 A57 10fr grn & slate grn   5.00   42

Oldsquaws — A58

Birds: 10c, 70c, Puffins. 20c, 90c, Snow owl. 40c, like 6c. Identification of birds on oldsquaw and puffin stamps transposed.

1973, Jan. 1 Engr. *Perf. 13*
423 A58   6c Prus bl, pur & brn   60   15
424 A58 10c Prus bl, blk & org   1.00   20
425 A58 20c ultra, bis & dk vio   1.00   20
426 A58 40c pur, sl grn & brn   2.50   32
427 A58 70c brt grn, blk & org   3.25   55
428 A58 90c Prus bl, bis & pur   7.50   90
      Nos. 423-428 (6)   15.85 2.32

Indoor Swimming Pool — A59

Design: 1fr, Cultural Center of St. Pierre.

1973, Sept. 25 Engr. *Perf. 13*
429 A59 60c brn, brt bl & dk car   3.00   35
430 A59   1fr bl grn, ocher & choc 4.50   60

Opening of Cultural Center of St. Pierre.

Map of Islands, Weather Balloon and Ship, WMO Emblem — A60

1974, Mar. 23 Engr. *Perf. 13*
431 A60 1.60fr multicolored   6.00 1.20

World Meteorological Day.

Gannet Holding Letter — A61

1974, Oct. 9 Engr. *Perf. 13*
432 A61 70c blue & multi   2.75   42
433 A61 90c red & multi   3.00   50

Centenary of Universal Postal Union.

Clasped Hands over Red Cross — A62

Hands Putting Money into Fish-shaped Bank — A63

1974, Oct. 15 Photo. *Perf. 12½x13*
434 A62 1.50fr multicolored   5.00   70

Honoring blood donors.

1974, Nov. 15 Engr. *Perf. 13*
435 A63 50c ocher & vio bl   2.50   35

St. Pierre Savings Bank centenary.

Church of St. Pierre and Seagulls — A64

Designs: 10c, Church of Miquelon and fish. 20c, Church of Our Lady of the Sailors, and fishermen.

1974, Dec. 9 Engr. *Perf. 13*
436 A64   6c multicolored   1.50   16
437 A64 10c multicolored   1.50   16
438 A64 20c multicolored   3.00   35

Danaus Plexippus A65

Design: 1fr, Vanessa atalanta, vert.

1975, July 17 Litho. *Perf. 12½*
439 A65   1fr blue & multi   5.00   60
440 A65 1.20fr green & multi   6.00   70

Pottery — A66

Mother and Child, Wood Carving — A67

1975, Oct. 20 Engr. *Perf. 13*
441 A66 50c ol, brn & choc   2.50   45
442 A67 60c blue & dull yel   2.50   45

Local handicrafts.

Pointe Plate Lighthouse and Murres — A68

Designs: 10c, Galantry lighthouse and Atlantic puffins. 20c, Cap Blanc lighthouse, whale and squid.

1975, Oct. 21
443 A68   6c vio bl, blk & lt grn   *1.40* 15
444 A68 10c lil rose, blk & dk ol *1.90* 16
445 A68 20c blue, indigo & brn   *3.00* 28

Georges Pompidou (1911-74), Pres. of France — A68a

1976, Feb. 17 Engr. *Perf. 13*
446 A68a 1.10fr brown & slate   4.00   60

Georges Pompidou (1911-1974), President of France.

Washington and Lafayette, American Flag — A69

1976, July 12 Photo. *Perf. 13*
447 A69   1fr multicolored   2.50   60

American Bicentennial.

Woman Swimmer and Maple Leaf — A70

Design: 70c, Basketball and maple leaf, vert.

1976, Aug. 10 Engr. *Perf. 13*
448 A70 70c multicolored   2.00   40
449 A70 2.50fr multicolored   6.50 1.20

21st Olympic Games, Montreal, Canada, July 17-Aug. 1.

Vigie Dam A71

1976, Sept. 7 Engr. *Perf. 13*
450 A71 2.20fr multicolored   4.00 1.25

Croix de Lorraine — A72

Fishing Vessels: 1.40fr, Goelette.

1976, Oct. 5 Photo. *Perf. 13*
451 A72 1.20fr multicolored   2.50   70
452 A72 1.40fr multicolored   3.00 1.00

France Nos. 1783-1784, 1786-1789, 1794, 1882, 1799, 1885, 1802, 1889, 1803-1804 and 1891 Ovptd. "SAINT PIERRE / ET / MIQUELON"

1986, Feb. 4 Engr. *Perf. 13*
453 A915   5c dark green   15   15
454 A915 10c dull red   15   15
455 A915 20c brt green   15   15
456 A915 30c orange   15   15
457 A915 40c brown   15   15
458 A915 50c lilac   15   15
459 A915   1fr olive green   26   26
460 A915 1.80fr emerald   48   48
461 A915   2fr brt yellow grn   52   52
462 A915 2.20fr red   55   55
463 A915   3fr chocolate brn   80   80
464 A915 3.20fr sapphire   85   85
465 A915   4fr brt carmine   1.00 1.00
466 A915   5fr gray blue   1.40 1.40
467 A915 10fr purple   2.75 2.75
      Nos. 453-467 (15)   9.51 9.51

Discovery of St. Pierre & Miquelon by Jacques Cartier, 450th Anniv. — A73

1986, June 11 Engr. *Perf. 13*
476 A73 2.20fr sep, sage grn & redsh brn 65 65

Statue of Liberty, Cent. — A74

1986, July 4
477 A74 2.50fr Statue, St. Pierre Harbor 70 70

Values quoted in this catalogue are for stamps graded Fine-Very Fine and with no faults. An illustrated guide to grade is provided in the "Catalogue Information" section of the Introduction.

Fishery Resources — A75

Holy Family, Stained Glass by J. Balmet — A76

1986-89   Engr.   Perf. 13
478	A75	1fr bright red	28 28
479	A75	1.10fr brt orange	35 35
480	A75	1.30fr dark red	40 40
481	A75	1.40fr violet	42 42
482	A75	1.40fr dark red	45 45
483	A75	1.50fr brt ultra	50 50
484	A75	1.60fr emerald grn	48 48
485	A75	1.70fr green	55 55

Nos. 478-485 (8)   3.43 3.43

Issue dates: 1fr, No. 481, Oct. 22; 1.10fr, 1.50fr, Oct. 17, 1987; 1.30fr, 1.60fr, Aug. 7, 1988; No. 482, 1.70fr, July 14, 1989.

1986, Dec. 10   Litho.   Perf. 13
486 A76 2.20fr multicolored   70 70

Christmas.

Hygrophorus Pratensis A77

1987-90   Engr.   Perf. 12½
487 A77 2.50fr shown   75 75
488 A77 2.50fr Russula paludosa britz   85 85
489 A77 2.50fr Tricholoma virgatum   80 80
490 A77 2.50fr Hydnum repandum   82 82

Issue dates: No. 487, Feb. 14; No. 488, Jan. 29, 1988; No. 489, Jan. 28, 1989; No. 490, Jan. 17, 1990.

Dr. François Dunan (1884-1961), Clinic — A78

1987, May 5   Engr.   Perf. 13
491 A78 2.20fr brt bl, blk & dk red brn   70 70

Transat Yacht Race, Lorient to St. Pierre to Lorient A79

1987, May 18
492 A79 5fr dp ultra, dk rose brn & brt bl   2.00 2.00

Visit of Pres. Mitterand A80

1987, May 29   Litho.   Perf. 12½x13
493 A80 2.20fr dull ultra, gold & scar   70 70

Marine Slip, Cent. — A81

1987, June 20   Litho.   Perf. 13
494 A81 2.50fr pale sal & dk red brn   65 65

Stern Trawler La Normande — A82

1987-91   Photo.
495 A82 3fr shown   1.25 1.25
496 A82 3fr Le Marmouset   95 95
497 A82 3fr Le Malabar   95 95
498 A82 3fr St. Denis, St. Pierre   1.20 1.20
499 A82 3fr Cryos   1.10 1.10

Nos. 495-499 (5)   5.45 5.45

Issue dates: No. 495, Oct. 14; No. 496, Sept. 28, 1988. No. 497, Nov. 2, 1989. No. 498, Oct. 29, 1990; No. 499, Nov. 12, 1991.
This is an expanding set. Numbers will change when complete.

St. Christopher and the Christ Child, Stained Glass Window and Scout Emblem — A83

1987, Dec. 9   Litho.   Perf. 13
503 A83 2.20fr multicolored   80 80

Christmas, Scout movement in St. Pierre & Miquelon, 50th anniv.

The Great Barachoise Nature Reserve — A84

1987, Dec. 16   Engr.   Perf. 13x12½
504 A84 3fr Horses, waterfowl   1.50 1.50
505 A84 3fr Waterfowl, seals   1.50 1.50
a. Pair, #504-505 + label   3.25 3.25

No. 505a is in continuous design.

1988, Nov. 2
506 A84 2.20fr Ross Cove   75 75
507 A84 13.70fr Caope Perce   4.75 4.75
a. Pair, #506-507 + label   5.75 5.75

No. 507a is in continuous design.

1988 Winter Olympics, Calgary A86

1988, Mar. 5   Engr.   Perf. 13
508 A86 5fr brt ultra & dark red   1.90 1.90

Louis Thomas (1887-1976), Photographer A87

1988, May 4   Engr.   Perf. 13
509 A87 2.20fr blk, dk ol bis & Prus bl   70 70

France No. 2105 Overprinted "ST-PIERRE ET MIQUELON"

1988, July 25   Engr.   Perf. 13
510 A1107 2.20fr ver, blk & violet blue   70 70

Seizure of Schooner Nellie J. Banks, 50th Anniv. A88

1988, Aug. 7
511 A88 2.50fr brn, vio blue & brt blue   75 75

The Nellie J. Banks was seized by Canada for carrying prohibited alcohol in 1938.

Christmas — A89

1988, Dec. 17   Litho.   Perf. 13
512 A89 2.20fr multicolored   70 70

Judo Competitions in St. Pierre & Miquelon, 25th Anniv. A90

1989, Mar. 4   Engr.   Perf. 13
513 A90 5fr brn org, blk & yel grn   1.65 1.65

French Revolution Bicent.; 40th Anniv. of the UN Declaration of Human Rights (in 1988) — A91

1989   Engr.   Perf. 12½x13
514 A91 2.20fr Liberty   72 72
515 A91 2.20fr Equality   72 72
516 A91 2.20fr Fraternity   72 72

Issue dates: No. 514, Mar. 28; No. 515, May 9; No. 516, June 19.

Souvenir Sheet

French Revolution, Bicent. — A92

Designs: a, Bastille, liberty tree. b, Bastille, ship. c, Building, revolutionaries raising flag and liberty tree. d, Revolutionaries, building with open doors.

1989, July 14   Engr.   Perf. 13
517 A92 Sheet of 4 + 2 labels   6.40 6.40
a.-d. 5fr any single   1.60 1.60

Heritage of Ile aux Marins — A93

Designs: 2.20fr, Coastline, ships in harbor, girl in boat, fish. 13.70fr, Coastline, ships in harbor, boy flying kite from boat, map of Ile aux Marins.

1989, Sept. 9   Engr.   Perf. 13x12½
518 A93 2.20fr multi   70 70
519 A93 13.70fr multi   4.25 4.25
a. Pair, #518-519 + label   5.00

Nos. 519a is in continuous design.

George Landry and Bank Emblem
A95

1989, Nov. 8   Engr.   Perf. 13
520 A95 2.20fr bl & golden brn   72 72

Bank of the Islands, cent.

Christmas — A96

1989, Dec. 2   Litho.   Perf. 13
521 A96 2.20fr multicolored   72 72

France Nos. 2179-2182, 2182A-2186, 2188-2189, 2191-2194, 2204B, 2331, 2333, 2336, 2338, 2342 Ovptd. "ST-PIERRE / ET / MIQUELON"

1990-94   Engr.   Perf. 13
522	A1161	10c brown black	15	15
523	A1161	20c light green	15	15
524	A1161	50c bright violet	18	18
527	A1161	1fr orange	36	36
528	A1161	2fr apple grn	72	72
528A	A1161	2fr blue	75	75
529	A1161	2.10fr green	75	75
530	A1161	2.20fr green	80	80
531	A1161	2.30fr red	82	82
531A	A1161	2.40fr emerald	85	85
532	A1161	2.50fr red	1.00	1.00
533	A1161	3.20fr bright blue	1.10	1.10
534	A1161	3.40fr blue	1.25	1.25
534A	A1161	3.50fr apple green	1.25	1.25
535	A1161	3.80fr bright pink	1.35	1.35
536	A1161	4fr brt lil rose	1.50	1.50
536A	A1161	4.20fr rose lilac	1.60	1.60
536B	A1161	4.40fr blue	1.50	1.50
537	A1161	5fr dull blue	1.80	1.80
538	A1161	10fr violet	3.60	3.60
539	A1161	(2.50fr) red	90	90

Booklet Stamps
Self-Adhesive
Die Cut
542	A1161	2.50fr red	95	95
a.		Booklet pane of 10	9.50	
		Nos. 522-542 (22)	23.33	23.33

Issued: 2.30fr, 1/2/90; 2.10fr, 2/5/90; 10c, 20c, 50c, 3.20fr, 3.80fr, 3/26/90; 1fr, 5fr, #528, 7/16/90; #532, 2.20fr, 12/2/91; 3.40fr, 4fr, 1/13/92, #542, 1992; 4.20fr, 1/13/93; #539, 6/6/93; 2.40fr, 3.50fr, 4.40fr, 10/6/93; #528A, 8/22/94.
This is an expanding set. Numbers will change again if necessary.

A97   A98

1990, June 18   Perf. 13
546 A97 2.30fr Charles de Gaulle   82 82

De Gaulle's call for French Resistance, 50th anniv.

1990, Nov. 22
547 A98 1.70fr red, claret & blue   68 68
548 A98 2.30fr red, claret & blue   95 95
a.   Pair, #547-548 + label   1.65 1.65

25 Kilometer Race of Miquelon
A99

1990, June 25
549 A99 5fr Runner, map   1.80 1.80

Micmac Canoe, 1875 — A100

1990, July 31   Engr.   Perf. 13x13½
550 A100 2.50fr multicolored   95 95

Views of St. Pierre — A101

Harbor scene.

1990, Oct. 24   Engr.   Perf. 13x12½
551 A101 2.30fr bl, grn & brn   90 90
552 A101 14.50fr bl, grn & brn   5.75 5.75
a.   Pair, #551-552 + label   6.75 6.75

No. 552a is in continous design.

Christmas — A103

1990, Dec. 15   Litho.
553 A103 2.30fr multicolored   95 95

Papilio Brevicaudata — A104

1991-92   Litho.   Perf. 13
554 A104 2.50fr multicolored   95 95
    Perf. 12
555 A104 3.60fr Aeshna Eremita, Nuphar Variegatum   1.40 1.40

Issued: 2.50fr, Jan. 16; 3.60fr, Mar. 9, 1992.
This is an expanding set. Numbers will change again if necessary.

Marine Tools, Sailing Ship
A105

1991, Mar. 6   Litho. & Engr.   Perf. 13
559 A105 1.40fr yellow & green   55 55
560 A105 1.70fr yellow & red   65 65

Scenic Views
A106

Designs: Nos. 548, 552, Saint Pierre. Nos. 549, 553, Ile aux Marins. Nos. 550, 554, Langlade. Nos. 551, 555, Miquelon.

1991, Apr. 17   Engr.   Perf. 13
561	A106	1.70fr blue	65	65
562	A106	1.70fr blue	65	65
563	A106	1.70fr blue	65	65
564	A106	1.70fr blue	65	65
a.		Strip of 4, #561-564	2.60	2.60
565	A106	2.50fr red	95	95
566	A106	2.50fr red	95	95
567	A106	2.50fr red	95	95
568	A106	2.50fr red	95	95
a.		Strip of 4, #565-568	3.80	3.80
		Nos. 561-568 (8)	6.40	6.40

Lyre Music Society, Cent. — A107

1991, June 21   Engr.   Perf. 13
569 A107 2.50fr multicolored   85 85

Newfoundland Crossing by Rowboat "Los Gringos" — A108

1991, Aug. 3   Engr.   Perf. 13x12½
570 A108 2.50fr multicolored   85 85

Basque Sports
A109

1991, Aug. 24   Perf. 13
571 A109 5fr red & green   1.70 1.70

Natural Heritage — A110

Designs: 2.50fr, Fishermen. 14.50fr, Shoreline, birds.

1991, Oct. 21   Engr.   Perf. 13x12½
572 A110 2.50fr multicolored   90 90
573 A110 14.50fr multicolored   5.10 5.10
a.   Pair, #572-573 + label   6.00 6.00

No. 573a is in continuous design.

Central Economic Cooperation Bank, 50th Anniv. — A111

1991, Dec. 2   Engr.   Perf. 13x12½
574 A111 2.50fr 1941 100fr note   1.00 1.00

Christmas — A112

1991, Dec. 23   Litho.   Perf. 13
575 A112 2.50fr multicolored   1.00 1.00

Christmas Day Plebescite, 50th anniv.

Vice Admiral Emile Henri Muselier (1882-1965), Commander of Free French Naval Forces
A113

1992, Jan. 13   Litho.   Perf. 13
576 A113 2.50fr multicolored   1.00 1.00

1992 Winter Olympics, Albertville
A114

1992, Feb. 10   Engr.   Perf. 13
577 A114 5fr vio bl, blue & mag   1.95 1.95

Caulking Tools, Bow of Ship
A115

Perf. 13x12½
1992, Apr. 6   Litho. & Engr.
578 A115 1.50fr pale bl gray & brown   55 55
579 A115 1.80fr pale bl gray & blue   65 65

Lighthouses A116

Designs: a, Galantry. b, Feu Rouge. c, Pointe-Plate. d, Ile Aux Marins.

1992, July 8 **Litho.** ***Perf. 13***
580 A116 2.50fr Strip of 4, #a.-d. 4.00 4.00

Natural Heritage — A117

1992, Aug. 17 **Engr.** ***Perf. 13x12½***
581 A117 2.50fr Langlade 1.25 1.25
582 A117 15.10fr Doulisie Valley 7.50 7.50
a. Pair, #581-582 + label 8.75 8.75

No. 582a is in continuous design.
See Nos. 593-594, 605-606.

Discovery of America, 500th Anniv. — A118

Photo. & Engr.
1992, Oct. 12 ***Perf. 13x12½***
583 A118 5.10fr multicolored 2.00 2.00

Le Baron de L'Esperance A119

1992, Nov. 23 **Engr.** ***Perf. 13***
584 A119 2.50fr claret, brown & blue 95 95

Christmas — A120

1992, Dec. 9 **Litho.** ***Perf. 13***
585 A120 2.50fr multicolored 90 90

Commander R. Birot (1906-1942) A121

1993, Jan. 13
586 A121 2.50fr multicolored 90 90

Deep Sea Diving A122

1993, Feb. 10 **Engr.** ***Perf. 12***
587 A122 5fr multicolored 1.75 1.75

A123

A124

Monochamus Scutellatus, Cichorium Intybus.

1993, Mar. 10 **Litho.** ***Perf. 13½x13***
588 A123 3.60fr multicolored 1.25 1.25

See No. 599.

1993, Apr. 7 **Litho.** ***Perf. 13½x13***
Slicing cod.

589 A124 1.50fr green & multi 55 55
590 A124 1.80fr red & multi 68 68

Move to the Magdalen Islands, Quebec, by Miquelon Residents, Bicent. — A125

1993, June 6 **Engr.** ***Perf. 13***
591 A125 5.10fr brown, blue & green 2.00 2.00

Fish — A126

Designs: a, Capelin. b, Ray. c, Halibut (fletan). d, Toad fish (crapaud).

1993, July 28 **Photo.** ***Perf. 13***
592 A126 2.80fr Strip of 4, #a.-d. 3.75 3.75

Natl. Heritage Type of 1992

1993, Aug. 23 **Engr.** ***Perf. 13x12½***
593 A117 2.80fr Miquelon 1.00 1.00
594 A117 16fr Otter pool 5.75 5.75
a. Pair, #593-594 + label 6.75 6.75

No. 594a is a continuous design.

Commissioner's Residence — A127

1993, Oct. 7 **Engr.** ***Perf. 13***
595 A127 3.70fr multicolored 1.25 1.25

Christmas — A128

1993, Dec. 13 **Litho.** ***Perf. 13***
596 A128 2.80fr multicolored 95 95

Commander Louis Blaison (1906-1942), Submarine Surcouf A129

1994, Jan. 17 **Litho.** ***Perf. 13***
597 A129 2.80fr multicolored 95 95

Petanque World Championships — A130

1994, Feb. 14 **Engr.** ***Perf. 12½x12***
598 A130 5.10fr multicolored 1.75 1.75

Insect and Flower Type of 1993

Design: 3.70fr, Cristalis tenax, taraxacum officinale, horiz.

1994, Mar. 14 **Litho.** ***Perf. 13x13½***
599 A123 3.70fr multicolored 1.25 1.25

Drying Codfish, 1905 — A131

1994, Apr. 11 **Litho.** ***Perf. 13***
600 A131 1.50fr black & blue green 55 55
601 A131 1.80fr multicolored 65 65

Women's Right to Vote, 50th Anniv. A132

1994, Apr. 25
602 A132 2.80fr multicolored 1.00 1.00

Hospital Ship St. Pierre, Cent. — A133

1994, July 4
603 A133 2.80fr multicolored 1.00 1.00

Souvenir Sheet

Ships A134

Designs: a, Miquelon. b, Isle of St. Pierre. c, St. George XII. d, St. Eugene IV.

1994, July 11 ***Perf. 12***
604 Sheet of 4 5.00 5.00
a.-b. A134 2.80fr any single 1.00 1.00
c.-d. A134 3.70fr any single 1.50 1.50

Natural Heritage Type of 1992

1994, Aug. 22 **Engr.** ***Perf. 13***
605 A117 2.80fr Woods 1.10 1.10
606 A117 16fr "The Hat" 6.50 6.50
a. Pair, #605-606 + label 7.60 7.60

SCOTT
Catalogue Tabs
Scott Catalogue Tabs make referencing listings quick and easy. The peel-and-stick tabs feature country names and specialty areas for each volume of the catalogue. Tabs are sold separately for each volume of the catalogue. Each tab set is priced at *$2.95*. Scott Catalogue Tabs are available from your favorite stamp dealer or direct from:
Scott Publishing Co.
Box 828 Sidney OH 45365-0828
1-800-572-6885

Parochial School
A135

1994, Oct. 10   Engr.   Perf. 13
607 A135 3.70fr multicolored   1.40 1.40

Stamp Show
A136

1994, Oct. 17
608 A136 3.70fr green, yellow & blue   1.40 1.40

Chirstmas — A137   NOËL 1994 2,80

1994, Nov. 28   Litho.   Perf. 13
609 A137 2.80fr multicolored   1.10 1.10

Louis Pasteur (1822-95)
A138

1995, Jan. 16   Litho.   Perf. 13
610 A138 2.80fr multicolored   1.10 1.10

Triathlon
A139
Le Triathlon

1995, Feb. 13   Engr.   Perf. 12
611 A139 5.10fr multicolored   2.00 2.00

Dicranum Scoparium & Cladonia Cristatella — A140

1995   Litho.   Perf. 13
612 A140 3.70fr multicolored   1.50 1.50

SEMI-POSTAL STAMPS

Regular Issue of 1909-17
Surcharged in Red   +5c

1915-17   Unwmk.   Perf. 14x13½
B1 A17 10c + 5c car rose & red   35 35
B2 A17 15c + 5c dl vio & rose ('17)   45 45

Curie Issue
Common Design Type
1938, Oct. 24   Engr.   Perf. 13
B3 CD80 1.75fr + 50c brt ultra   5.25 5.25

French Revolution Issue
Common Design Type
1939, July 5   Photo.
Name and Value Typo. in Black
B4 CD83 45c + 25c green   3.00 3.00
B5 CD83 70c + 30c brown   3.00 3.00
B6 CD83 90c + 35c red org   3.00 3.00
B7 CD83 1.25fr + 1fr rose pink   3.00 3.00
B8 CD83 2.25fr + 2fr blue   3.00 3.00
    Nos. B4-B8 (5)   15.00 15.00

Common Design Type and

Sailor of Landing Force — SP1   Dispatch Boat "Ville d'Ys" — SP2

1941   Photo.   Perf. 13½
B8A SP1 1fr + 1fr red   60
B8B CD86 1.50fr + 3fr maroon   60
B8C SP2 2.50fr + 1fr blue   60

Nos. B8A-B8C were issued by the Vichy government, and were not placed on sale in the colony. Nos. 206A-206B were surcharged "OEUVRES COLONIALES" and surtax (including change of denomination of the 2.50fr to 50c). These were issued in 1944 by the Vichy government and not placed on sale in the colony.

Nos. 239, 246 With Additional Surcharge in Carmine

+ 50c

ŒUVRES SOCIALES

+

1942   Unwmk.   Perf. 13½x13
B9 A25 1fr + 50c   18.00 18.00
B10 A26 2.50fr + 1fr   18.00 18.00

Catalogue values for unused stamps in this section, from this point to the end of the section, are for Never Hinged items.

Red Cross Issue
Common Design Type
1944   Perf. 14½x14
B13 CD90 5fr + 20fr dp ultra   40 40

Surtax for the French Red Cross and national relief.

Tropical Medicine Issue
Common Design Type
1950, May 15   Engr.   Perf. 13
B14 CD100 10fr + 2fr red brn & red   3.00 3.00

The surtax was for charitable work.

AIR POST STAMPS

Catalogue values for unused stamps in this section are for Never Hinged items.

Common Design Type
Perf. 14½x14
1942, Aug. 17   Photo.   Unwmk.
C1 CD87 1fr dark orange   15 15
C2 CD87 1.50fr bright red   15 15
C3 CD87 5fr brown red   16 16
C4 CD87 10fr black   25 25
C5 CD87 25fr ultra   30 30
C6 CD87 50fr dark green   45 45
C7 CD87 100fr plum   70 70
    Nos. C1-C7 (7)   2.16 2.16

Victory Issue
Common Design Type
1946, May 8   Engr.   Perf. 12½
C8 CD92 8fr deep claret   42 42

Chad to Rhine Issue
Common Design Types
1946, June 6
C9 CD93 5fr brown red   70 50
C10 CD94 10fr lilac rose   70 50
C11 CD95 15fr gray blk   90 65
C12 CD96 20fr violet   90 65
C13 CD97 25fr chocolate   1.40 1.00
C14 CD98 50fr grnsh blk   1.40 1.00
    Nos. C9-C14 (6)   6.00 4.30

Plane, Sailing Vessel and Coast — AP2

AP3

AP4

1947, Oct. 6
C15 AP2 50fr yel grn & rose   4.25 1.50
C16 AP3 100fr dk blue grn   6.75 2.25
C17 AP4 200fr bluish blk & brt rose   14.00 3.25

UPU Issue
Common Design Type
1949, July 4   Engr.   Perf. 13
C18 CD99 25fr multicolored   7.50 4.50

Liberation Issue
Common Design Type
1954, June 6
C19 CD102 15fr sepia & red   4.00 4.00

10th anniversary of the liberation of France.

Plane over St. Pierre Harbor — AP6

1956, Oct. 22
C20 AP6 500fr ultra & indigo   32.50 12.50

Dog and Village — AP7

Design: 100fr, Caravelle over archipelago.

1957, Nov. 4   Unwmk.   Perf. 13
C21 AP7 50fr gray, brn blk & bl   24.00 9.00
C22 AP7 100fr black & gray   11.00 4.50

Anchors and Torches — AP8

1959, Sept. 14   Engr.   Perf. 13
C23 AP8 200fr dk pur, grn & claret   8.00 3.00

Approval of the constitution and the vote which confirmed the attachment of the islands to France.

Pitcher Plant — AP9

1962, Apr. 24   Unwmk.   Perf. 13
C24 AP9 100fr green, org & car   7.00 1.50

Gulf of St. Lawrence and Submarine "Surcouf" — AP10

Perf. 13½x12½
1962, July 24   Photo.
C25 AP10 500fr dk red & blue   90.00 60.00

20th anniv. of St. Pierre & Miquelon's joining the Free French.

Telstar Issue
Common Design Type
1962, Nov. 22   Engr.   Perf. 13
C26 CD111 50fr Prus grn & bister   4.00 2.25

Arrival of Governor Dangeac, 1763 — AP11

1963, Aug. 5   Unwmk.   Perf. 13
C27 AP11 200fr dk bl, sl grn & brn   12.00 3.50

Bicentenary of the arrival of the first French governor.

Jet Plane and Map of Maritime Provinces and New England — AP12

1964, Sept. 28   Engr.   Perf. 13
C28 AP12 100fr choc & Prus bl   7.50 3.00

Inauguration of direct airmail service between St. Pierre and New York City.

ITU Issue
Common Design Type

1965, May 17
C29 CD120 40fr org brn, dk bl & lil rose   12.00 3.50

French Satellite A-1 Issue
Common Design Type

Designs: 25fr, Diamant rocket and launching installations. 30fr, A-1 satellite.

1966, Jan. 24   Engr.   Perf. 13
C30 CD121 25fr dk brn, dk bl & rose cl   4.25 2.00
C31 CD121 30fr dk bl, rose cl & dk brn   4.25 2.00
    a.   Strip of 2, #C30-C31 + label   9.00 4.50

French Satellite D-1 Issue
Common Design Type

1966, May 23   Engr.   Perf. 13
C32 CD122 48fr brt grn, ultra & rose claret   5.00 2.25

Arrival of Settlers — AP13

1966, June 22   Photo.   Perf. 13
C33 AP13 100fr multicolored   8.00 2.25

150th anniv. of the return of the islands of St. Pierre and Miquelon to France.

Front Page of Official Journal and Printing Presses — AP14

1966, Oct. 20   Engr.   Perf. 13
C34 AP14 60fr dk bl, lake & dk pur   5.00 1.25

Centenary of the Government Printers and the Official Journal.

Map of Islands, Old and New Fishing Vessels — AP15

Design: 100fr, Cruiser Colbert, maps of Brest, St. Pierre and Miquelon.

1967, July 20   Engr.   Perf. 13
C35 AP15 25fr dk bl, gray & crim   16.00 7.00
C36 AP15 100fr multicolored   30.00 15.00

Visit of President Charles de Gaulle.

Speed Skater and Olympic Emblem — AP16

Design: 60fr, Ice hockey goalkeeper and Olympic emblem.

1968, Apr. 22   Photo.   Perf. 13
C37 AP16 50fr ultra & multi   5.00 1.20
C38 AP16 60fr green & multi   7.00 1.50

10th Winter Olympic Games, Grenoble, France, Feb. 6-18.

War Memorial, St. Pierre — AP17

1968, Nov. 11   Photo.   Perf. 12½
C39 AP17 500fr multicolored   17.00 10.00

World War I armistice, 50th anniv.

Concorde Issue
Common Design Type

1969, Apr. 17   Engr.   Perf. 13
C40 CD129 34fr dk brown & olive   19.00 5.00

Scenic Type of Regular Issue, 1969.

Designs: 50fr, Grazing horses, Miquelon. 100fr, Gathering driftwood on Mirande Beach, Miquelon.

1969, Apr. 30   Engr.   Perf. 13
Size: 47½x27mm
C41 A47 50fr ultra, brn & olive   9.00 2.00
C42 A47 100fr dk brn, bl & slate   16.00 4.50

L'Esperance Leaving Saint-Malo, 1600 — AP18

1969, June 16   Engr.   Perf. 13
C43 AP18 200fr blk, grn & dk red   25.00 3.00

Pierre Loti and Sailboats — AP19

1969, June 23
C44 AP19 300fr lemon, choc & Prus bl   24.00 6.00

Loti (1850-1923), French novelist and naval officer.

EXPO Emblem and "Mountains" by Yokoyama Taikan — AP20

Design: 34fr, Geisha, rocket and EXPO emblem, vert.

1970, Sept. 8   Engr.   Perf. 13
C45 AP20 34fr dp claret, ol & ind   6.00 1.00
C46 AP20 85fr orange, ind & car   13.00 2.00

EXPO '70 Intl. Exposition, Osaka, Japan, Mar. 15-Sept. 13.

Etienne François Duke of Choiseul and his Ships — AP21

Designs: 50fr, Jacques Cartier, ship and landing party. 60fr, Sebastien Le Gonrad de Sourdeval, ships and map of islands.

1970, Nov. 25
Portrait in Lake
C47 AP21 25fr lilac & Prus bl   5.50 60
C48 AP21 50fr sl grn & red lil   5.50 1.50
C49 AP21 60fr red lil & sl grn   12.50 1.50

De Gaulle, Cross of Lorraine, Sailor, Soldier, Coast Guard — AP22

1972, June 18   Engr.   Perf. 13
C50 AP22 100fr lilac, brn & grn   16.00 3.00

Charles de Gaulle (1890-1970), French pres.

Louis Joseph de Montcalm — AP23

Designs: 2fr, Louis de Buade Frontenac, vert. 4fr, Robert de La Salle.

1973, Jan. 1
C51 AP23 1.60fr multicolored   3.00 60
C52 AP23 2fr multicolored   4.00 80
C53 AP23 4fr multicolored   9.50 1.60

Transall C 160 over St. Pierre — AP24

1973, Oct. 16   Engr.   Perf. 13
C54 AP24 10fr multicolored   27.50 7.00

Arms and Map of Islands, Fish and Bird — AP25

1974, Nov. 5   Photo.   Perf. 13
C55 AP25 2fr gold & multi   8.00 1.00

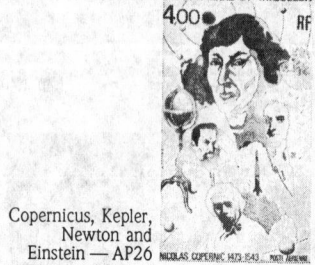

Copernicus, Kepler, Newton and Einstein — AP26

1974, Nov. 26   Engr.
C56 AP26 4fr multicolored   10.00 2.00

Nicolaus Copernicus (1473-1543), Polish astronomer.

Type of 1909, Cod and ARPHILA Emblem — AP27

1975, Aug. 5   Engr.   Perf. 13
C57 AP27 4fr ultra, red & indigo   13.00 2.50

ARPHILA 75, International Philatelic Exhibition, Paris, June 6-16.

Judo, Maple Leaf, Olympic Rings — AP28

1975, Nov. 18   Engr.   Perf. 13
C58 AP28 1.90fr red, blue & vio   7.00 1.20

Pre-Olympic Year.

Concorde — AP29

1976, Jan. 21   Engr.   Perf. 13
C59 AP29 10fr red, blk & slate   20.00 6.00

1st commercial flight of supersonic jet Concorde from Paris to Rio, Jan. 21.

A. G. Bell, Telephone and Satellite AP30

1976, June 22   Litho.   Perf. 12½
C60 AP30 5fr vio bl, org & red   7.00 2.75

Centenary of first telephone call by Alexander Graham Bell, Mar. 10, 1876.

Aircraft — AP31

1987, June 30   Engr.   Perf. 13
C61 AP31 5fr Hawker-Siddeley H. S. 748, 1987   1.75 1.75
C62 AP31 10fr Latecoere 522, 1939   3.35 3.35

Hindenburg — AP32

Designs: 10fr, Douglas DC3, 1948-1988. 20fr, Piper Aztec.

1988-89   Engr.   Perf. 13
C63 AP32 5fr multicolored   1.40 1.40
C64 AP32 10fr multicolored   3.00 3.00
C65 AP32 20fr multicolored   6.50 6.50

Issued: 20fr, May 31, 1989; others, June 22.

Flying Flea, Bird — AP33

1990, May 21   Engr.
C66 AP33 5fr multicolored   1.75 1.75

Piper Tomahawk — AP34

1991, May 29   Engr.   Perf. 13
C67 AP34 10fr multicolored   3.85 3.85

Radio-controlled Model Airplanes — AP35

1992, May 11   Engr.   Perf. 13
C68 AP35 20fr brown, red & org   7.75 7.75

Migratory Birds — AP36

Photo. & Engr.
1993, May 17   Perf. 13x12½
C69 AP36 5fr Puffin   1.85 1.85
C70 AP36 10fr Golden plover   3.70 3.70

AIR POST SEMI-POSTAL STAMPS

V4

Stamps of the design shown above and stamp of Cameroun type V10 inscribed "St. Pierre-et-Miquelon" were issued in 1942 by the Vichy Government, but were not placed on sale in the Colony.

POSTAGE DUE STAMPS

Postage Due Stamps of French Colonies Overprinted in Red

1892   Unwmk.   Imperf.
J1 D1 5c black   25.00 25.00
J2 D1 10c black   6.25 6.25
J3 D1 15c black   6.25 6.25
J4 D1 20c black   6.25 6.25
J5 D1 30c black   6.25 6.25
J6 D1 40c black   6.25 6.25
J7 D1 60c black   27.50 27.50

Black Overprint
J8 D1 1fr brown   55.00 55.00
J9 D1 2fr brown   55.00 55.00
    Nos. J1-J9 (9)   193.75 193.75

These stamps exist with and without hyphen. See note after No. 59.

SAINT-PIERRE -ET- MIQUELON

Postage Due Stamps of France, 1893-1924, Overprinted

1925-27   Perf. 14x13½
J10 D2 5c blue   20 20
J11 D2 10c dark brown   20 20
J12 D2 20c olive green   28 28
J13 D2 25c rose   28 28
J14 D2 30c red   40 40
J15 D2 45c blue green   40 40
J16 D2 50c brown vio   80 80
J17 D2 1fr red brn, straw   1.00 1.00
J18 D2 3fr magenta ('27)   3.50 3.50

SAINT-PIERRE -ET-MIQUELON
Surcharged
2 francs à percevoir

J19 D2 60c on 50c buff   80 80
J20 D2 2fr on 1fr red   1.25 1.25
    Nos. J10-J20 (11)   9.11 9.11

Newfoundland Dog — D3

1932, Dec. 5   Typo.
J21 D3 5c dk blue & blk   60 60
J22 D3 10c green & blk   60 60
J23 D3 20c red & blk   80 80
J24 D3 25c red vio & blk   80 80
J25 D3 30c orange & blk   1.50 1.50
J26 D3 45c lt blue & blk   1.50 1.50
J27 D3 50c blue grn & blk   3.00 3.00
J28 D3 60c brt rose & blk   4.00 4.00
J29 D3 1fr yellow brn & blk   9.00 9.00
J30 D3 2fr dp violet & blk   15.00 15.00
J31 D3 3fr dk brown & blk   15.00 15.00
    Nos. J21-J31 (11)   51.80 51.80

For overprints and surcharge see Nos. J42-J46.

Codfish — D4

1938, Nov. 17   Photo.   Perf. 13
J32 D4 5c gray black   15 15
J33 D4 10c dk red violet   15 15
J34 D4 15c slate green   15 15
J35 D4 20c deep blue   15 15
J36 D4 30c rose carmine   15 15
J37 D4 50c dk blue green   15 15
J38 D4 60c dk blue   20 20
J39 D4 1fr henna brown   25 25
J40 D4 2fr gray brown   1.10 1.10
J41 D4 3fr dull violet   1.50 1.50
    Set value   3.40 3.40

For overprints see Nos. J48-J67.

Type of Postage Due Stamps of 1932 Overprinted in Black   **FRANCE LIBRE F. N. F. L.**

1942   Unwmk.   Perf. 14x13½
J42 D3 25c red vio & blk   140.00 140.00
J43 D3 30c orange & blk   140.00 140.00
J44 D3 50c blue grn & blk   550.00 550.00
J45 D3 2fr dp vio & bl blk   18.00 18.00

Same Surcharged in Black

3 fr FRANCE LIBRE F. N. F. L.

J46 D3 3fr on 2fr dp vio & blk   9.00 9.00
a.   "F.N.F.L." omitted   4.00 4.00
    Nos. J42-J46 (5)   857.00 857.00

Postage Due Stamps of 1938 Overprinted in Black   **NOËL 1941 F N F L**

1942   Perf. 13
J48 D4 5c gray black   10.00 10.00
J49 D4 10c dk red violet   10.00 10.00
J50 D4 15c slate green   10.00 10.00
J51 D4 20c deep blue   10.00 10.00
J52 D4 30c rose carmine   10.00 10.00
J53 D4 50c dk blue green   17.50 17.50
J54 D4 60c dark blue   45.00 45.00
J55 D4 1fr henna brown   55.00 55.00

J56 D4 2fr gray brown   55.00 55.00
J57 D4 3fr dull violet   62.50 62.50
    Nos. J48-J57 (10)   285.00 285.00

Christmas Day plebiscite ordered by Vice Admiral Emile Henri Muselier, commander of the Free French naval forces.

Postage Due Stamps of 1938 Overprinted in Black   **FRANCE LIBRE F N F L**

1942
J58 D4 5c gray black   19.00 19.00
J59 D4 10c dk red violet   2.50 2.50
J60 D4 15c slate green   2.50 2.50
J61 D4 20c deep blue   2.50 2.50
J62 D4 30c rose carmine   2.50 2.50
J63 D4 50c dk blue green   2.50 2.50
J64 D4 60c dark blue   2.50 2.50
J65 D4 1fr henna brown   7.75 7.75
J66 D4 2fr gray brown   7.75 7.75
J67 D4 3fr dull violet   275.00 275.00
    Nos. J58-J67 (10)   324.50 324.50

> Catalogue values for unused stamps in this section, from this point to the end of the section, are for Never Hinged items.

Arms and Fishing Schooner — D5

1947, Oct. 6   Engr.   Perf. 13
J68 D5 10c deep orange   15 15
J69 D5 30c deep ultra   15 15
J70 D5 50c dk blue green   15 15
J71 D5 1fr deep carmine   15 15
J72 D5 2fr dk green   15 15
J73 D5 3fr violet   35 35
J74 D5 4fr chocolate   40 40
J75 D5 5fr yellow green   40 40
J76 D5 10fr black brown   45 45
J77 D5 20fr orange red   55 55
    Nos. J68-J77 (10)   2.90 2.90

Newfoundland Dog — D6

1973, Jan. 1   Engr.   Perf. 13
J78 D6 2c brown & blk   25 25
J79 D6 10c purple & blk   38 38
J80 D6 20c grnsh bl & blk   90 90
J81 D6 30c dk car & blk   2.00 2.00
J82 D6 1fr blue & blk   5.00 5.00
    Nos. J78-J82 (5)   8.53 8.53

France Nos. J106-J115 Overprinted "ST-PIERRE ET MIQUELON" Reading Up in Red

1986, Sept. 15   Engr.   Perf. 13
J83 D8 10c multicolored   15 15
J84 D8 20c multicolored   15 15
J85 D8 30c multicolored   15 15
J86 D8 40c multicolored   15 15
J87 D8 50c multicolored   15 15
J88 D8 1fr multicolored   30 30
J89 D8 2fr multicolored   60 60
J90 D8 3fr multicolored   90 90
J91 D8 4fr multicolored   1.20 1.20
J92 D8 5fr multicolored   1.50 1.50
    Nos. J83-J92 (10)   5.25 5.25

PARCEL POST STAMPS

COLIS POSTAUX

No. 65 Overprinted

1901   Unwmk.   Perf. 14x13½
Q1 A16 10c black, lavender   40.00 40.00
a.   Inverted overprint

No. 66 Overprinted Colis Postaux

Q2	A16	10c red	7.00 7.00

Nos. 84 and 87 Overprinted

Colis Postaux

1917-25

Q3	A17	10c	80 80
a.		Double overprint	22.50
Q4	A17	20c ('25)	65 65
a.		Double overprint	40.00 40.00

No. Q4 with FRANCE LIBRE Additional Overprint in Black F. N. F. L.

1942

Q5	A17	20c	425.00 250.00

ST. THOMAS AND PRINCE ISLANDS

Democratic Republic of Sao Tome and Principe

LOCATION — Two islands in the Gulf of Guinea, 125 miles off the west coast of Africa
GOVT. — Republic
AREA — 372 sq. mi.
POP. — 102,000 (est. 1984)
CAPITAL — Sao Tome

This colony of Portugal became a province, later an overseas territory, and achieved independence on July 12, 1975.

1000 Reis = 1 Milreis
100 Centavos = 1 Escudo (1913)
100 Cents = 1 Dobra (1977)

Catalogue values for unused stamps in this country are for Never Hinged items, beginning with Scott 353 in the regular postage section, Scott J52 in the postage due section, and Scott RA4 in the postal tax section.

Portuguese Crown — A1   King Luiz — A2

5, 25, 50 REIS:
Type I - "5" is upright.
Type II - "5" is slanting.

10 REIS:
Type I - "1" has short serif at top.
Type II - "1" has long serif at top.

40 REIS:
Type I - "4" is broad.
Type II - "4" is narrow.

Perf. 12½, 13½

1869-75 Unwmk. Typo.

1	A1	5r black, I	2.00 1.90
a.		Type II	
2	A1	10r yellow, I	14.00 8.50
a.		Type II	17.50 10.50
3	A1	20r bister	3.50 2.75
4	A1	25r rose, I	1.25 1.10
		25r red	4.50 1.50
5	A1	40r blue ('75), I	4.75 3.50
a.		Type II	5.50 4.50
6	A1	50r gray grn, II	8.00 6.00
a.		Type I	15.00 14.00
7	A1	100r gray lilac	6.00 5.50
8	A1	200r red orange ('75)	8.25 6.25
9	A1	300r chocolate ('75)	8.25 7.00

1881-85

10	A1	10r gray grn, I	8.00 6.75
a.		Type II	9.50 6.00
b.		Perf. 13½, I	11.00 8.00
11	A1	20r car rose ('85)	3.50 3.00
12	A1	25r vio ('85), II	2.25 1.75
13	A1	40r yel buff, II	5.00 4.00
a.		Perf. 13½	6.00 4.50
14	A1	50r dk blue, I	2.50 2.25
a.		Type II	2.50 2.25

For surcharges and overprints see Nos. 63-64, 129-129B, 154.
Nos. 1 to 14 inclusive have been reprinted on stout white paper, ungummed, with rough perforation 13½, also on ordinary paper with shiny white gum and clean-cut perforation 13½ with large holes.

Typo., Head Embossed

1887 Perf. 12½, 13½

15	A2	5r black	3.00 2.50
16	A2	10r green	4.25 2.50
17	A2	20r brt rose	4.25 3.00
a.		Perf. 12½	55.00 55.00
18	A2	25r violet	4.25 1.65
19	A2	40r brown	4.25 2.25
20	A2	50r blue	4.25 2.50
21	A2	100r yellow brn	4.25 2.00
22	A2	200r gray lilac	15.00 10.50
23	A2	300r orange	15.00 10.50

For surcharges and overprints see Nos. 24-26, 62, 65-72, 130-131, 155-158, 234-237.
Nos. 15, 16, 19, 21, 22, and 23 have been reprinted in paler colors than the originals, with white gum and cleancut perforation 13½. Value $1.50 each.

Nos. 16-17, 19 Surcharged:

5 réis (a)   cinco réis (b)   Rs.50 (c)

1889-91 Without Gum

24	A2(a)	5r on 10r	35.00 20.00
25	A2(b)	5r on 20r	25.00 20.00
26	A2(c)	50r on 40r ('91)	225.00 70.00

Varieties of Nos. 24-26, including inverted and double surcharges, "5" inverted, "Cinoc" and "Cinco," were deliberately made and unofficially issued.

King Carlos
A6   A7

1895 Typo. Perf. 11½, 12½

27	A6	5r yellow	60 45
28	A6	10r red lilac	95 75
29	A6	15r red brown	1.40 1.10
30	A6	20r lavender	1.50 1.10
31	A6	25r green	1.50 75
32	A6	50r light blue	1.65 70
a.		Perf. 13½	2.00 1.50
33	A6	75r rose	3.75 3.25
34	A6	80r yellow grn	7.25 6.25
35	A6	100r brn, yel	3.50 3.00
36	A6	150r car, rose	6.00 5.00
37	A6	200r dk bl, bl	7.75 6.50
38	A6	300r dk bl, sal	8.50 7.75

For surcharges and overprints see Nos. 73-84, 132-137, 159-165, 238-243, 262-264, 268-274.

1898-1903 Perf. 11½
Name and Value in Black except 500r

39	A7	2½r gray	25 25
40	A7	5r orange	25 20
41	A7	10r lt green	25 20
42	A7	15r brown	2.00 1.75
43	A7	15r gray grn ('03)	1.10 1.10
44	A7	20r gray violet	90 50
45	A7	25r sea green	70 25
46	A7	25r carmine ('03)	1.10 50
47	A7	50r blue	65 30
48	A7	50r brown ('03)	4.50 4.50
49	A7	65r dull blue ('03)	10.00 9.00
50	A7	75r rose	10.00 6.50
51	A7	75r red lilac ('03)	1.75 1.40
52	A7	80r brt violet	5.00 5.00
53	A7	100r dk blue, bl	2.50 2.00
54	A7	115r org brn, pink ('03)	7.00 8.00
55	A7	130r brn, straw ('03)	7.00 6.00
56	A7	150r brn, buff	2.75 2.25
57	A7	200r red lil, pnksh	4.75 2.75
58	A7	300r dk blue, rose	5.50 5.00
59	A7	400r dull bl, straw ('03)	10.00 8.50
60	A7	500r blk & red, bl ('01)	7.25 5.00
61	A7	700r vio, yelsh ('01)	16.00 12.00
		Nos. 39-61 (23)	101.20 82.75

For overprints and surcharges see Nos. 86-105, 116-128, 138-153, 167-169, 244-249, 255-261, 265-267.

Stamps of 1869-95 Surcharged in Red or Black

1902

On Stamp of 1887

62	A2	130r on 5r blk (R)	6.00 5.00
a.		Perf. 13½	32.50 32.50

On Stamps of 1869

63	A1	115r on 50r grn	10.00 7.50
64	A1	400r on 10r yel	25.00 12.00
a.		Double surcharge	

On Stamps of 1887

65	A2	65r on 20r rose	6.25 4.50
a.		Perf. 13½	8.50 7.00
66	A2	65r on 25r violet	4.50 4.00
a.		Inverted surcharge	
67	A2	65r on 100r yel brn	4.50 4.75
68	A2	115r on 10r blue grn	4.50 4.00
69	A2	115r on 300r orange	4.50 4.00
70	A2	130r on 200r gray lil	6.00 5.00
71	A2	400r on 40r brown	8.00 7.00
72	A2	400r on 50r blue	14.00 12.00
a.		Perf. 13½	110.00 90.00

On Stamps of 1895

73	A6	65r on 5r yellow	4.00 3.00
74	A6	65r on 10r red vio	4.00 3.00
75	A6	65r on 15r choc	4.00 3.00
76	A6	65r on 20r lav	4.00 3.00
77	A6	115r on 25r grn	4.00 3.00
78	A6	115r on 150r car, rose	4.00 3.00
79	A6	115r on 200r bl, bl	4.00 4.00
80	A6	130r on 75r rose	4.00 4.00
81	A6	130r on 100r brn, yel	4.00 3.50
a.		Double surcharge	
82	A6	130r on 300r bl, sal	4.00 3.00
83	A6	400r on 50r lt blue	1.10 95
a.		Perf. 13½	2.00 1.65
84	A6	400r on 80r yel grn	2.00 1.50

On Newspaper Stamp No. P12

85	N3	400r on 2½r brown	1.10 95
a.		Double surcharge	
		Nos. 62-85 (24)	137.45 103.65

Reprints of Nos. 63, 64, 67, 71, and 72 have shiny white gum and clean-cut perf. 13½.

Stamps of 1898 Overprinted PROVISORIO

1902

86	A7	15r brown	2.00 1.50
87	A7	25r sea green	2.00 1.25
88	A7	50r blue	2.25 1.50
89	A7	75r rose	5.00 3.50

No. 49 Surcharged in Black 50 RÉIS

1905

90	A7	50r on 65r dull blue	3.25 2.75

Stamps of 1898-1903 Overprinted in Carmine or Green REPUBLICA

1911

91	A7	2½r gray	25 20
a.		Inverted overprint	15.00 11.00
92	A7	5r orange	25 20
93	A7	10r lt green	25 20
a.		Inverted overprint	15.00 12.00
94	A7	15r gray green	25 20
95	A7	20r gray violet	25 20
96	A7	25r carmine (G)	60 20
97	A7	50r brown	25 20
a.		Inverted overprint	15.00 12.00
98	A7	75r red lilac	38 20
99	A7	100r dk bl, bl	60 50
a.		Inverted overprint	17.50 14.00
100	A7	115r org brn, pink	1.10 95
101	A7	130r brown, straw	1.10 95
102	A7	200r red lil, pnksh	6.00 4.25
103	A7	400r dull blue, straw	1.40 1.00
104	A7	500r blk & red, bl	1.40 1.00
105	A7	700r violet, yelsh	1.40 1.00
		Nos. 91-105 (15)	15.48 11.25

King Manuel II — A8

Overprinted in Carmine or Green

1912 Perf. 11½, 12

106	A8	2½r violet	15 15
a.		Double overprint	16.00 16.00
b.		Double overprint, one inverted	
107	A8	5r black	15 15
108	A8	10r gray green	15 15
a.		Double overprint	14.00 14.00
109	A8	20r carmine (G)	1.00 75
110	A8	25r violet brn	60 45
111	A8	50r dk blue	60 55
112	A8	75r bister brn	90 55
113	A8	100r brn, lt grn	1.10 50
114	A8	200r dk grn, sal	2.00 1.40
115	A8	300r black, azure	2.00 2.00
		Nos. 106-115 (10)	8.65 6.65

Stamps of 1898-1905 Overprinted in Black REPUBLICA

1913

On Stamps of 1898-1903

116	A7	2½r gray	1.00 1.00
a.		Double overprint	15.00 15.00
b.		Inverted overprint	12.00 12.00
117	A7	5r orange	1.25 1.00
118	A7	15r gray green	22.50 17.50
a.		Inverted overprint	
119	A7	20r gray violet	1.50 1.50
a.		Inverted overprint	
120	A7	25r carmine	5.75 4.50
a.		Inverted overprint	
b.		Double overprint	
121	A7	75r red lilac	5.00 5.00
122	A7	100r bl, bluish	6.50 7.50
123	A7	115r org brn, pink	37.50 35.00
a.		Double overprint	75.00 60.00
124	A7	130r brn, straw	13.00 13.00
125	A7	200r red lil, pnksh	14.00 13.00
126	A7	400r dl bl, straw	14.00 12.50
127	A7	500r blk & red, gray	35.00 42.50
128	A7	700r vio, yelsh	47.50 40.00

On Provisional Issue of 1902

129	A1	115r on 50r green	110.00 85.00
a.		Inverted overprint	
129B	A1	400r on 10r yellow	375.00 375.00
130	A2	115r on 10r blue grn	2.75 2.50
a.		Inverted overprint	
131	A2	400r on 50r blue	75.00 75.00
132	A6	115r on 25r green	2.00 1.75
a.		Inverted overprint	
133	A6	115r on 150r car, rose	42.50 40.00
a.		Inverted overprint	
134	A6	115r on 200r bl, bl	2.50 2.00
135	A6	130r on 75r rose	2.25 2.00
136	A6	400r on 50r lt bl	4.00 4.00
a.		Perf. 13½	7.50 7.50
137	A6	400r on 80r yel grn	5.00 4.25

Same Overprint on Nos. 86, 88, 90

138	A7	15r brown	2.00 1.75
139	A7	50r blue	2.25 2.00
140	A7	50r on 65r dull bl	16.00 12.00

No. 123-125, 130-131 and 137 were issued without gum.

Stamps of 1898-1905 Overprinted in Black REPUBLICA

On Stamps of 1898-1903

141	A7	2½r gray	60 50
a.		Inverted overprint	
b.		Double overprint	11.00 11.00
c.		Double overprint inverted	
142	A7	5r orange	27.50 22.50
143	A7	15r gray green	1.75 1.50
a.		Inverted overprint	
144	A7	20r gray violet	140.00 75.00
a.		Inverted overprint	

145	A7	25r carmine	37.50	27.50
a.		Inverted overprint		
146	A7	75r red lilac	2.75	2.25
147	A7	100r blue, *bl*	2.25	1.75
148	A7	115r org brn, *pink*	10.00	8.00
a.		Inverted overprint		
149	A7	130r brown, *straw*	8.00	7.00
a.		Inverted overprint		
150	A7	200r red lil, *pnksh*	2.50	1.75
a.		Inverted overprint		
151	A7	400r dull bl, *straw*	10.00	8.00
152	A7	500r blk & red, *gray*	9.00	8.50
153	A7	700r violet, *yelsh*	9.00	8.50

On Provisional Issue of 1902

154	A1	115r on 50r green	150.00	110.00
155	A2	115r on 10r bl grn	2.50	2.25
156	A2	115r on 300r orange	175.00	125.00
157	A2	130r on 5r black	175.00	125.00
158	A2	400r on 50r blue	125.00	90.00
159	A6	115r on 25r green	2.00	1.75
160	A6	115r on 150r car, *rose*	2.50	2.25
a.		"REPUBLICA" inverted		
161	A6	115r on 200r bl, *bl*	2.50	2.25
162	A6	130r on 75r rose	2.25	2.00
a.		Inverted surcharge		
163	A6	130r on 100r brn, *yel*	400.00	450.00
164	A6	400r on 50r lt bl	3.50	3.00
a.		Perf. 13½	17.50	6.00
165	A6	400r on 80r yel grn	2.50	2.25
166	N3	400r on 2½r brn	2.00	1.75

Same Overprint on Nos. 86, 88, 90

167	A7	15r brown	1.50	1.25
a.		Inverted overprint		
168	A7	50r blue	1.50	1.25
a.		Inverted overprint		
169	A7	50r on 65r dull bl	2.25	1.50

Most of Nos. 141-169 were issued without gum.

Vasco da Gama Issue of Various Portuguese Colonies Surcharged as

REPUBLICA S.TOMÉ E PRINCIPE ¼ C.

On Stamps of Macao

170	CD20	¼c on ½a bl grn	2.00	2.00
171	CD21	½c on 1a red	2.00	2.00
172	CD22	1c on 2a red vio	2.00	2.00
173	CD23	2½c on 4a yel grn	2.00	2.00
174	CD24	5c on 8a dk bl	2.00	2.00
175	CD25	7½c on 12a vio brn	2.75	2.75
176	CD26	10c on 16a bis brn	2.00	2.00
177	CD27	15c on 24a bister	2.00	2.00
		Nos. 170-177 (8)	16.75	16.75

On Stamps of Portuguese Africa

178	CD20	¼c on 2½r bl grn	1.40	1.40
179	CD21	½c on 5r red	1.40	1.40
180	CD22	1c on 10r red vio	1.40	1.40
181	CD23	2½c on 25r yel grn	1.40	1.40
182	CD24	5c on 50r dk bl	1.40	1.40
183	CD25	7½c on 75r vio brn	1.75	1.75
184	CD26	10c on 100r bis brn	1.40	1.40
185	CD27	15c on 150r bister	1.40	1.40
		Nos. 178-185 (8)	11.55	11.55

On Stamps of Timor

186	CD20	¼c on ½a bl grn	1.75	1.50
187	CD21	½c on 1a red	1.75	1.50
188	CD22	1c on 2a red vio	1.75	1.50
a.		Double surcharge		
189	CD23	2½c on 4a yel grn	1.75	1.50
190	CD24	5c on 8a dk bl	1.75	2.00
191	CD25	7½c on 12a vio brn	2.25	2.00
192	CD26	10c on 16a bis brn	1.75	1.50
193	CD27	15c on 24a bister	1.75	1.50
		Nos. 186-193 (8)	14.50	13.00
		Nos. 170-193 (24)	42.80	41.30

Ceres — A9

1914-26 Typo. Perf. 12x11½, 15x14
Name and Value in Black

194	A9	¼c olive brown	15	15
195	A9	½c black	15	15
196	A9	1c blue green	65	65
197	A9	1c yellow grn ('22)	15	15
198	A9	1½c lilac brn	15	15
199	A9	2c carmine	15	15
200	A9	2c gray ('26)	20	20
201	A9	2½c lt violet	15	15
202	A9	3c orange ('22)	20	20
203	A9	4c rose ('22)	20	20
204	A9	4½c gray ('22)	20	20
205	A9	5c deep blue	45	35
206	A9	5c brt blue ('22)	20	20
207	A9	6c lilac ('22)	20	20
208	A9	7c ultra ('22)	20	20
209	A9	7½c yellow brn	20	20
210	A9	8c slate	20	20
211	A9	10c orange brn	25	25
212	A9	12c blue green ('22)	50	45
213	A9	15c plum	2.00	1.65

214	A9	15c brown rose ('22)	25	25
215	A9	20c yellow green	1.75	1.10
216	A9	24c ultra ('26)	3.50	3.00
217	A9	25c choc ('26)	3.50	3.00
218	A9	30c brown, *grn*	2.25	1.75
219	A9	30c gray grn ('22)	50	40
220	A9	40c brown, *pink*	2.00	1.75
221	A9	40c turq bl ('22)	55	50
222	A9	50c orange, *sal*	4.50	3.50
223	A9	50c lt violet ('26)	75	60
224	A9	60c dk blue ('22)	1.25	90
225	A9	60c rose ('26)	2.00	2.00
226	A9	80c brt rose ('22)	1.65	50
227	A9	1e green, *blue*	4.00	3.50
228	A9	1e pale rose ('22)	2.25	1.40
229	A9	1e blue ('26)	2.25	1.90
230	A9	2e dk violet ('22)	2.75	1.65
231	A9	5e buff ('26)	20.00	12.50
232	A9	10e pink ('26)	30.00	20.00
233	A9	20e pale turq ('26)	55.00	50.00
		Nos. 194-233 (40)	147.25	116.25

Perforation and paper variations command a premium for some of Nos. 194-233.
For surcharges see Nos. 250-253, 281-282.

Preceding Issues Overprinted in Carmine

REPUBLICA

1915
On Provisional Issue of 1902

234	A2	115r on 10r green	2.25	2.00
235	A2	115r on 300r org	2.25	1.75
236	A2	130r on 5r black	4.00	3.00
237	A2	130r on 200r gray lil	1.50	1.25
238	A6	115r on 25r green	60	45
239	A6	115r on 150r car, *rose*	60	45
240	A6	115r on 200r bl, *bl*	60	45
241	A6	130r on 75r rose	60	45
242	A6	130r on 100r brn, *yel*	1.40	1.40
243	A6	130r on 300r bl, *sal*	1.10	90

Same Overprint on Nos. 88 and 90

244	A7	50r blue	90	60
245	A7	50r on 65r dull bl	90	60
		Nos. 234-245 (12)	16.70	13.30

2½ C.

REPUBLICA

No. 86 Overprinted in Blue and Surcharged in Black

1919

246	A7	2½c on 15r brown	60	55

No. 91 Surcharged in ½ C. Black

247	A7	½c on 2½r gray	3.00	2.75
248	A7	1c on 2½r gray	2.25	2.00
249	A7	2½c on 2½r gray	1.10	65

No. 194 Surcharged in Blue ½

250	A9	½c on ¼c ol brn	2.00	1.75
251	A9	2c on ¼c ol brn	2.25	1.90
252	A9	2½c on ¼c ol brn	6.00	5.00

No. 201 Surcharged in Black $04 Centavos

253	A9	4c on 2½c lt vio	90	75
		Nos. 246-253 (8)	18.10	15.35

Nos. 246-253 were issued without gum.

Stamps of 1898-1905 Overprinted in Green or Red

REPUBLICA

1920
On Stamps of 1898-1903

255	A7	75r red lilac (G)	55	50
256	A7	100r blue, *blue* (R)	80	75
257	A7	115r org brn, *pink* (G)	1.65	1.40
258	A7	130r brn, *straw* (G)	65.00	50.00
259	A7	200r red lil, *pnksh* (G)	1.65	1.00
260	A7	500r blk, & red, *gray* (G)	1.10	1.00
261	A7	700r vio, *yelsh* (G)	1.65	1.25

On Stamps of 1902

262	A6	115r on 25r grn (R)	90	60
263	A6	115r on 200r bl, *bl* (R)	1.10	1.00
264	A6	130r on 75r rose (G)	1.65	1.50

On Nos. 88-89

265	A7	50r blue (R)	1.25	1.10
266	A7	75r rose (R)	7.50	7.00

On No. 90

267	A7	50r on 65r dl bl (R)	8.00	7.00
		Nos. 255-257,259-267 (12)	27.80	24.10

Nos. 238-243 Surcharged in Blue or Red

DEZ CENTAVOS

1923

			Without Gum	
268	A6	10c on 115r on 25r (Bl)	50	40
269	A6	10c on 115r on 150r (Bl)	50	40
270	A6	10c on 115r on 200r (R)	50	40
271	A6	10c on 130r on 75r (Bl)	50	40
272	A6	10c on 130r on 100r (Bl)	50	40
273	A6	10c on 130r on 300r (R)	50	40
		Nos. 268-273 (6)	3.00	2.40

Nos. 268-273 are usually stained and discolored.

República

Nos. 84-85 Surcharged

40 C.

1925

274	A6	40c on 400r on 80r yel grn	90	45
275	N3	40c on 400r on 2½r brn	90	45

Nos. 228 and 230 Surcharged

70 C.

1931

281	A9	70c on 1e pale rose	2.00	1.25
282	A9	1.40e on 2e dk vio	2.75	2.50

Ceres — A11

1934 Typo. Perf. 12x11½ Wmk. 232

283	A11	1c bister	20	20
284	A11	5c olive brown	20	20
285	A11	10c violet	20	20
286	A11	15c black	25	25
287	A11	20c gray	25	25
288	A11	30c dk green	35	30
289	A11	40c red orange	35	30
290	A11	45c brt blue	55	40
291	A11	50c brown	55	30
292	A11	60c olive grn	40	30
293	A11	70c brown org	70	45
294	A11	80c emerald	40	30
295	A11	85c deep rose	2.75	2.00
296	A11	1e maroon	75	60
297	A11	1.40e dk green	2.25	1.65

298	A11	2e dk violet	3.25	1.50
299	A11	5e apple green	7.50	4.25
300	A11	10e olive bister	17.50	10.00
301	A11	20e orange	60.00	30.00
		Nos. 283-301 (19)	98.40	53.35

Common Design Types Inscribed "S. Tomé"

1938 Unwmk. Perf. 13½x13
Name and Value in Black

302	CD34	1c gray green	15	15
303	CD34	5c orange brown	20	20
304	CD34	10c dk carmine	30	30
305	CD34	15c dk violet brn	30	30
306	CD34	20c slate	30	30
307	CD35	30c rose violet	30	30
308	CD35	35c brt green	55	45
309	CD35	40c brown	55	45
310	CD35	50c brt red vio	55	45
311	CD36	60c gray black	90	70
312	CD36	70c brown violet	90	70
313	CD36	80c orange	90	70
314	CD36	1e red	2.25	1.10
315	CD37	1.75e blue	1.75	1.00
316	CD37	2e brown car	11.00	6.50
317	CD37	5e olive green	11.00	6.50
318	CD38	10e blue violet	14.00	7.75
319	CD38	20e red brown	22.50	8.00
		Nos. 302-319 (18)	68.40	35.85

Marble Column and Portuguese Arms with Cross — A12

1938 Perf. 12½

320	A12	80c blue green	1.40	1.10
321	A12	1.75e deep blue	6.50	3.25
322	A12	20e brown	25.00	12.00

Visit of the President of Portugal in 1938.

Common Design Types Inscribed "S. Tomé e Principe"

1939 Perf. 13½x13
Name and Value in Black

323	CD34	1c gray grn	18	15
324	CD34	5c orange brn	18	15
325	CD34	10c dk carmine	18	15
326	CD34	15c dk vio brn	18	15
327	CD34	20c slate	18	15
328	CD35	30c rose violet	22	15
329	CD35	35c brt green	22	15
330	CD35	40c brown	22	15
331	CD35	50c brt red vio	22	18
332	CD36	60c gray black	70	60
333	CD36	70c brown violet	80	70
334	CD36	80c orange	80	70
335	CD36	1e red	70	40
336	CD37	1.75e blue	95	50
337	CD37	2e brown car	1.90	1.40
338	CD37	5e olive green	3.75	2.75
339	CD38	10e blue violet	8.50	3.50
340	CD38	20e red brown	11.00	5.75
		Nos. 323-340 (18)	30.88	17.68

Cola Nuts — A13

UPU Symbols — A14

Designs: 10c, Breadfruit. 30c, Annona. 50c, Cacao pods. 1e, Coffee. 1.75e, Dendem. 2e, Avocado. 5e, Pineapple. 10e, Mango. 20e, Coconuts.

1948 Litho. Perf. 14½

341	A13	5c black & yellow	30	30
342	A13	10c black & buff	40	30
343	A13	30c indigo & gray	1.50	1.25
344	A13	50c brown & yellow	1.50	1.25
345	A13	1e red & rose	3.00	1.75
346	A13	1.75e gray & blue	4.00	3.25
347	A13	2e black & grn	3.00	1.50
348	A13	5e brown & lil rose	7.00	4.00
349	A13	10e black & pink	10.00	7.50
350	A13	20e black & gray	35.00	20.00
a.		Sheet of 10, #341-350	90.00	90.00
		Nos. 341-350 (10)	65.70	41.10

No. 350a sold for 42.50 escudos.

Lady of Fatima Issue
Common Design Type

1948, Dec. — Unwmk.
351 CD40 50c purple — 5.25 4.50

> Catalogue values for unused stamps in this section, from this point to the end of the section, are for Never Hinged items.

1949 — Unwmk. — *Perf. 14*
352 A14 3.50e black & gray — 4.00 3.00

UPU, 75th anniv.

Holy Year Issue
Common Design Types

1950 — *Perf. 13x13½*
353 CD41 2.50e blue — 2.75 1.50
354 CD42 4e orange — 4.50 3.50

Holy Year Extension Issue
Common Design Type

1951 — *Perf. 14*
355 CD43 4e ind & bl gray — 2.75 2.00

Medical Congress Issue
Common Design Type

1952 — *Perf. 13½*
356 CD44 10c Clinic — 30 30

Joao de
Santarem
A15

Jeronymos Convent
A16

Portraits: 30c, Pero Escobar. 50c, Fernao de Po 1e, Alvaro Esteves. 2e, Lopo Goncalves. 3.50e, Martim Fernandes.

1952 — Unwmk. — Litho. — *Perf. 14*
Centers Multicolored
357 A15 10c cream & choc — 15 15
358 A15 30c pale grn & dk grn — 15 15
359 A15 50c gray & dk gray — 15 15
360 A15 1e gray bl & dk bl — 60 15
361 A15 2e lil gray & vio brn — 45 15
362 A15 3.50e buff & choc — 60 25
Nos. 357-362 (6) — 2.10
Set value — 65

For overprints and surcharges see Nos. 423, 425, 428-429, 432, 450-457, 474-481.

1953 — *Perf. 13x13½*
363 A16 10c dk brown & gray — 15 15
364 A16 50c brn org & org — 50 40
365 A16 3e blue blk & gray blk — 2.00 80

Exhib. of Sacred Missionary Art, Lisbon, 1951.

Stamp Centenary Issue

Stamp of Portugal and Arms of Colonies — A17

1953 — Photo. — *Perf. 13*
366 A17 50c multicolored — 75 60

Centenary of Portugal's first postage stamps.

Presidential Visit Issue

Map and
Plane — A18

1954 — Typo. & Litho. — *Perf. 13½*
367 A18 15c blk, bl, red & grn — 20 15
368 A18 5e brown, green & red — 1.10 80

Visit of Pres. Francisco H. C. Lopes.

Sao Paulo Issue
Common Design Type

1954 — Litho.
369 CD46 2.50e bl, gray bl & blk — 55 35

Fair Emblem, Globe and Arms — A19

1958 — Unwmk. — *Perf. 12x11½*
370 A19 2.50e multicolored — 60 50

World's Fair at Brussels.

Tropical Medicine Congress Issue
Common Design Type

Design: Cassia occidentalis.

1958 — *Perf. 13½*
371 CD47 5e pale grn, brn, yel, grn & red — 2.00 1.75

Compass Rose — A20

Going to Church — A21

1960 — Litho. — *Perf. 13½*
372 A20 10e gray & multi — 1.00 40

500th death anniv. of Prince Henry the Navigator.

1960 — *Perf. 14½*
373 A21 1.50e multicolored — 40 30

10th anniv. of the Commission for Technical Cooperation in Africa South of the Sahara (C.C.T.A.).

Sports Issue
Common Design Type

Sports: 50c, Angling. 1e, Gymnast on rings. 1.50e, Handball. 2e, Sailing. 2.50e, Sprinting. 20e, Skin diving.

1962, Jan. 18 — Litho. — *Perf. 13½*
Multicolored Design
374 CD48 50c gray green — 15 15
a. "$50 CORREIOS" omitted
375 CD48 1e lt lilac — 60 22
376 CD48 1.50e salmon — 60 22
377 CD48 2e blue — 75 35
378 CD48 2.50e gray green — 95 50
379 CD48 20e dark blue — 2.25 1.65
Nos. 374-379 (6) — 5.30 3.09

On No. 374a, the blue impression, including imprint, is missing.
For overprint see No. 449.

Anti-Malaria Issue
Common Design Type

Design: Anopheles gambiae.

1962 — Unwmk. — *Perf. 13½*
380 CD49 2.50e multicolored — 1.15 80

Airline Anniversary Issue
Common Design Type

1963 — Unwmk. — *Perf. 14½*
381 CD50 1.50e pale blue & multi — 60 50

National Overseas Bank Issue
Common Design Type

Design: Francisco de Oliveira Chamico.

1964, May 16 — *Perf. 13½*
382 CD51 2.50e multicolored — 70 50

ITU Issue
Common Design Type

1965, May 17 — Litho. — *Perf. 14½*
383 CD52 2.50e tan & multi — 1.50 1.00

Infantry Officer, 1788 — A22

Designs: 35c, Sergeant with lance, 1788. 40c, Corporal with pike, 1788. 1e, Private with musket, 1788. 2.50e, Artillery officer, 1806. 5e, Private, 1811. 7.50e, Private, 1833. 10e, Lancer officer, 1834.

1965, Aug. 24 — Litho. — *Perf. 13½*
384 A22 20c multicolored — 16 15
385 A22 35c multicolored — 16 15
386 A22 40c multicolored — 22 16
387 A22 1e multicolored — 1.10 50
388 A22 2.50e multicolored — 1.10 50
389 A22 5e multicolored — 1.65 1.25
390 A22 7.50e multicolored — 2.00 1.90
391 A22 10e multicolored — 2.50 2.00
Nos. 384-391 (8) — 8.89 6.61

On No. 374a, the blue impression, including imprint, is missing. For overprints and surcharges see Nos. 424, 426-427, 435, 458-463, 482-485, 489-490.

National Revolution Issue
Common Design Type

Design: 4e, Arts and Crafts School and Anti-Tuberculosis Dispensary.

1966, May 28 — Litho. — *Perf. 11½*
392 CD53 4e multicolored — 75 50

Navy Club Issue
Common Design Type

Designs: 1.50e, Capt. Campos Rodrigues and ironclad corvette Vasco da Gama. 2.50e, Dr. Aires Kopke, microscope and tsetse fly.

1967, Jan. 31 — Litho. — *Perf. 13*
393 CD54 1.50e multicolored — 90 50
394 CD54 2.50e multicolored — 1.40 75

Valinhos Shrine, Children and Apparition
A23

Cabral Medal, from St. Jerome's Convent
A24

1967, May 13 — Litho. — *Perf. 12½x13*
395 A23 2.50e multicolored — 30 25

50th anniv. of the apparition of the Virgin Mary to 3 shepherd children, Lucia dos Santos, Francisco and Jacinta Marto, at Fatima.

1968, Apr. 22 — Litho. — *Perf. 14*
396 A24 1.50e blue & multi — 45 30

500th birth anniv. of Pedro Alvares Cabral, navigator who took possession of Brazil for Portugal.

Admiral Coutinho Issue
Common Design Type

Design: 2e, Adm. Coutinho, Cago Coutinho Island and monument, vert.

1969, Feb. 17 — Litho. — *Perf. 14*
397 CD55 2e multicolored — 50 35

Vasco da Gama's Fleet — A25

Manuel Portal of Guarda Episcopal See — A26

1969, Aug. 29 — Litho. — *Perf. 14*
398 A25 2.50e multicolored — 75 50

Vasco da Gama (1469-1524), navigator.

Administration Reform Issue
Common Design Type

1969, Sept. 25 — Litho. — *Perf. 14*
399 CD56 2.50e multicolored — 50 35

For overprint see No. 430.

1969, Dec. 1 — Litho. — *Perf. 14*
400 A26 4e multicolored — 50 35

500th birth anniv. of King Manuel I.

Pero Escobar, Joao de Santarem and Map of Islands — A27

Pres. Américo Rodrigues Thomaz — A28

1970, Jan. 25 — Litho. — *Perf. 14*
401 A27 2.50e lt blue & multi — 35 30

500th anniv. of the discovery of St. Thomas and Prince Islands.

1970 — Litho. — *Perf. 12½*
402 A28 2.50e multicolored — 35 30

Visit of Pres. Américo Rodrigues Thomaz of Portugal.

Marshal Carmona Issue
Common Design Type

Design: 5e, Antonio Oscar Carmona in dress uniform.

1970, Nov. 15 — Litho. — *Perf. 14*
403 CD57 5e multicolored — 75 55

Coffee Plant and Stamps — A29

Descent from the Cross — A30

Designs: 1.50e, Postal Administration Building and stamp No. 1, horiz. 2.50e, Cathedral of St. Thomas and stamp No. 2.

1970, Dec.   *Perf. 13¹/₂*
404 A29   1e multicolored   25   15
405 A29   1.50e multicolored   35   15
406 A29   2.50e multicolored   60   20

Centenary of St. Thomas and Prince Islands postage stamps.

1972, May 25   **Litho.**   *Perf. 13*
407 A30   20e lilac & multi   2.50   1.90

4th centenary of publication of The Lusiads by Luiz Camoens.

Olympic Games Issue
Common Design Type

Design: 1.50e, Track and javelin, Olympic emblem.

1972, June 20   *Perf. 14x13¹/₂*
408 CD59   1.50e multicolored   35   25

Lisbon-Rio de Janeiro Flight Issue
Common Design Type

Design: 2.50e, "Lusitania" flying over warship at St. Peter Rocks.

1972, Sept. 20   **Litho.**   *Perf. 13¹/₂*
409 CD60   2.50e multicolored   35   25

WMO Centenary Issue
Common Design Type

1973, Dec. 15   **Litho.**   *Perf. 13*
410 CD61   5e dull grn & multi   60   50

For overprint see No. 434.

Republic

Flags of Portugal and St. Thomas & Prince — A31

1975, July 12   **Litho.**   *Perf. 13¹/₂*
411 A31   3e gray & multi   40   40
412 A31   10e yellow & multi   1.00   30
413 A31   20e lt blue & multi   2.00   50
414 A31   50e salmon & multi   3.50   2.25

Argel Agreement, granting independence, Argel, Sept. 26, 1974.
For overprints see Nos. 675-678.

Man and Woman with St. Thomas & Prince Flag — A32

1975, Dec. 21
415 A32   1.50e pink & multi   15   15
416 A32   4e multicolored   40   20
417 A32   7.50e org & multi   75   40
418 A32   20e blue & multi   1.75   1.00
419 A32   50e ocher & multi   4.00   2.00
    Nos. 415-419 (5)   7.05   3.75

Proclamation of Independence, Dec. 7, 1975.

Chart and Hand — A33

1975, Dec. 21   **Litho.**   *Perf. 13¹/₂*
420 A33   1e ocher & multi   15   15
421 A33   1.50e multicolored   20   15
422 A33   2.50e orange & multi   30   15
     Set value   36

National Reconstruction Fund.

****

Stamps of 1952-1973 Overprinted

Rep. Democr.

12-7-75

1977   **Litho.**   *Perf. 13¹/₂, 14, 13*
423 A15   10c multi (#357)
424 A22   20c multi (#384)
425 A15   30c multi (#358)
426 A22   35c multi (#385)
427 A22   40c multi (#386)
428 A15   50c multi (#359)
429 A15   1e multi (#360)
430 CD56   2.50e multi (#399)
431 A27   2.50e multi (#401)
432 A15   3.50e multi (#362)
433 A26   4e multi (#400)
434 CD61   5e multi (#410)
435 A22   5.50e multi (#390)
436 A20   10e multi (#372)
     (14)   15.00
     Nos. 423-436

The 10c, 30c, 50c, 1e, 3.50e, 10e issued with glassine interleaving stuck to back.

Pres. Manuel Pinto da Costa and Flag — A34

Designs: 3.50e, 4.50e, Portuguese Governor handing over power. 12.50e, like 2e.

1977, Jan.   *Perf. 13¹/₂*
437 A34   2e yellow & multi   20   15
438 A34   3.50e blue & multi   25   15
439 A34   4.50e red & multi   35   15
440 A34   12.50e multicolored   90   35

1st anniversary of independence.

Some of the unvalued sets that follow may not have been issued by the government.

Peter Paul Rubens (1577-1640), Painter — A35

Details from or entire paintings: 1e (60x44mm), Diana and Calixto, horiz. 5e (60x36mm), The Judgement of Paris, horiz. 10e (60x28mm), Diana and her Nymphs Surprised by Fauns, horiz. 15e (40x64mm), Andromeda and Perseus. 20e (40x64mm), The Banquet of Tereo. 50e (32x64mm) Fortuna.
No. 447a, 20e, (30x40mm) like #445. No. 447b, 75e, (40x30mm) The Banquet of Tereo, diff.

1977, June 28   **Litho.**   *Perf. 13¹/₂*
441 A35   1e multicolored
442 A35   5e multicolored
443 A35   10e multicolored
444 A35   15e multicolored
445 A35   20e multicolored
446 A35   50e multicolored

Souvenir Sheet
Perf. 14
447 A35   Sheet of 2, #a.-b.

See type A40 for Rubens stamps without "$" in denomination.

Ludwig van Beethoven — A36

Designs: a, 20e, Miniature, 1802, by C. Hornemann. b, 30e, Life mask, 1812, by F. Klein. c, 50e, Portrait, 1818, by Ferdinand Schimon.

1977, June 28   *Perf. 13¹/₂*
448 A36   Strip of 3, #a.-c.

For overprint see No. 617.

No. 379 Ovptd. "Rep. Democr. / 12-7-77"

1977, July 12
449 CD48   20e multicolored

Pairs of Nos. 358-359, 357, 362, 384-386 Overprinted Alternately in Black

     a   b

1977, Oct. 19   **Litho.**   *Perf. 14, 13¹/₂*
450 A15(a)   3e on 30c multi
451 A15(b)   3e on 30c multi
452 A15(a)   5e on 50c multi
453 A15(b)   5e on 50c multi
454 A15(a)   10e on 10c multi
455 A15(b)   10e on 10c multi
456 A15(a)   15e on 3.50e multi
457 A15(b)   15e on 3.50e multi
458 A22(a)   20e on 20c multi
459 A22(b)   20c on 20c multi
460 A22(a)   35e on 35c multi
461 A22(b)   35e on 35c multi
462 A22(a)   40e on 40c multi
463 A22(b)   40e on 40c multi

Centenary of membership in UPU. Overprints "a" and "b" alternate in sheets. Nos. 450-457 issued with glassine interleaving stuck to back.
These overprints exist in red on Nos. 452-453, 458-463 and on 1e on 10c, 3.50e and 30e on 30c.

Mao Tse-tung (1893-1976), Chairman, People's Republic of China — A37

1977, Dec.   **Litho.**   *Perf. 13¹/₂x14*
464 A37   50d multicolored   5.50
   a.   Souvenir sheet   7.50

For overprint see No. 597.

Lenin — A38

Russian Supersonic Plane — A39

Designs: 40d, Rowing crew. 50d, Cosmonaut Yuri A. Gagarin.

1977, Dec.   *Perf. 13¹/₂x14, 14x13¹/₂*
465 A38   15d multicolored   75
466 A39   30d multicolored   1.50
467 A39   40d multicolored   2.00
468 A38   50d red & black   2.50
   a.   Sheet of 4, #465-468

60th anniv. of Russian October Revolution.
For overprints see Nos. 592-595.

Paintings by Rubens — A40

Designs: 5d, 70d, Madonna and Standing Child. 10d, Holy Family. 25d, Holy Family, diff. 50d, Madonna and Child.

Perf. 13¹/₂, 13¹/₂x14 (50d)
1977, Dec.
Size: 31x47mm (50d)
469 A40   5d multicolored
470 A40   10d multicolored
471 A40   25d multicolored
472 A40   50d multicolored
473 A40   70d multicolored
   a.   Sheet of 4, #469-471, #473

Pairs of Nos. 357-359, 362, 384-385 Surcharged

3
PRÉMIO NOBEL DE PAZ 1954
a

3
UNHCR
#475

5
UNICEF
#477

10
OIT
#479

15
AMNESTY INTER- NATIONAL
#481

20
COMITE INTERNAC. DA CRUZ VERMELHA
#483, 485

1978, May 25   *Perf. 14½, 13½*
474 A15 (a)   3d on 30c #358
475 A15   3d on 30c #358
476 A15 (a)   5d on 50c #359
477 A15   5d on 50c #359
478 A15 (a) 10d on 10c #357
479 A15   10d on 10c #357
480 A15 (a) 15d on 3.50e #362
481 A15   15d on 3.50e #362
482 A22 (a) 20d on 20c #384
483 A22   20d on 20c #384
484 A22 (a) 35d on 35c #385
485 A22   35d on 35c #385

Overprints for each denomination alternate on sheet. Nos. 474-481 issued with glassine interleaving stuck to back.

Flag of St. Thomas and Prince Islands — A41

Designs: Nos. 487, 487a, Map of Islands, vert. No. 488, Coat of arms, vert.

Perf. 14x13½, 13½x14
1978, July 12
486 A41 5d multi   40
487 A41 5d multi   40
   a.   Souvenir sheet, 50d   4.25
488 A41 5d multi   40
   a.   Strip of 3, #486-488   1.25

Third anniversary of independence. Printed in sheets of 9. No. 487a contains one imperf. stamp.

No. 386 Surcharged

3º ANIV. DA ENTRADA NA ONU 1975/1978
#489

1975 1978
#490

1978, Sept. 3   Litho.   *Perf. 13½*
489 A22 40d on 40e #386
490 A22 40d on 40e #386

Membership in United Nations, 3rd anniv.

Miniature Sheets

Tahitian Women with Fan, by Paul Gauguin — A42

Paintings: No. 491b, Still Life, by Matisse. c, Barbaric Tales, by Gauguin. d, Portrait of Armand Roulin, by Van Gogh. e, Abstract, by Georges Braque.

No. 492a, 20d, like #491c. b, 30d, Horsemen on the Beach, by Gauguin.

1978, Nov. 1   *Perf. 14*
491 A42 10d Sheet of 9, #e., 2 each #a.-d.
Imperf
492 A42   Sheet of 3, #491a, 492a-492b
No. 492 has simulated perfs and exists with green margin and without simulated perfs and stamps in different order.

Miniature Sheet

UPU, Centennial — A43

Designs: Nos. 493a, Emblem, yellow & black. b, Emblem, green & black. c, Emblem, blue & black. d, Emblem, red & black. e, Concorde, balloon. f, Sailing ship, satellite. g, Monorail, stagecoach. h, Dirigible, steam locomotive. 50d, like #487g.

1978, Nov. 1   *Perf. 14*
493 A43   Sheet of 12, #a.-d., 2 each, #e.-h.
a.-d.   5d any single
e.-h.   15d any single
Souvenir Sheet
494 A43 50d multicolored

For overprint see No. 706.

Miniature Sheets

New Currency, 1st Anniv. A44

Obverse and reverse of bank notes: #a, 1000d. b, 50d. c, 500d. d, 100d. e, Obverse of 50c, 1d, 2d, 5d, 10d, 20d coins.

1978, Dec. 15   *Perf. 13½*
Sheet of 9
495 A44 5d #e., 2 each #a.-d.
496 A44 8d #e., 2 each #a.-d.

World Cup Soccer Championships, Argentina — A45

Various soccer plays: No. 497a, Two players in yellow shirts, one in blue. b, Two players in blue shirts, one in white. c, Six players, referee. d, Two players. No. 498a, Seven players. b, Two players at goal. c, Six players.

1978, Dec. 15   *Perf. 14*
497 A45   3d Block of 4, #a.-d.
498 A45 25d Strip of 3, #a.-c.

Souvenir sheets of one exist.

Overprinted with Names of Winning Countries

Campeão Mundial URUGUAY 1930/50

No. 499b, ITALIA, 1934/38. c, BRASIL, 1958/62/70. d, ALEMANIA 1954/74. No. 500a, INGLATERRA, 1966. b, Vencedores 1978 / 1o ARGENTINA / 2o HOLANDA / 3o BRASIL. c, ARGENTINA 1978.

1979, June 1   Litho.   *Perf. 14*
499 A45   3d Block of 4, #a.-d.
500 A45 25d Strip of 3, #a.-c.

Souvenir sheets of one exist.

Butterflies A46

Flowers — A47

Designs: 50c, Charaxes odysseus. 1d, Crinum giganteum. No. 503a, Quisqualis indica. b, Tecoma stans. c, Nerium oleander. d, Pyrostegia venusta. 10d, Hypolimnas salmacis thomensis. No. 505a, Charaxes monteiri, male. b, Charaxes monteiri, female. c, Papilio leonidas thomasius. d, Crenis boisduvali insularis. 25d, Asystasia gangetica. No. 507, Charaxes varanes defulvata. Nos. 508, Hibiscus mutabilis.

Perf. 15, 15x14½ (#503), 14½x15 (#505)
1979, June 8
501 A46 50c multicolored
502 A47   1d multicolored
503 A47   8d Block of 4, #a.-d.
504 A46 10d multicolored
505 A46 11d Block of 4, #a.-d.
506 A47 25d multicolored
Souvenir Sheets
Perf. 15
507 A46 50d multicolored
Imperf
508 A47 50d multicolored

No. 508 contains one 30x46mm stamp with simulated perforations.

Intl. Communications Day — A48

1979, July 6   *Perf. 13*
509 A48   1d shown
510 A48 11d CCIR emblem
   a.   Pair, #509-510 + label
511 A48 14d Syncom, 1963
512 A48 17d Symphony, 1975
   a.   Pair, #511-512 + label

Intl. Advisory Council on Radio Commmunications (CCIR), 50th anniv. (#510).

Intl. Year of the Child A49

Designs: 1d, Child's painting of bird. 7d, Young Pioneers. 14d, Children coloring on paper. 17d, Children eating fruit. 50d, Children from different countries joining hands.

1979, July 6
513 A49   1d multicolored
514 A49   7d multicolored
515 A49 14d multicolored
516 A49 17d multicolored
Size: 100x100mm
Imperf
517 A49 50d multicolored

Souvenir Sheets

Sir Rowland Hill, 1795-1879 — A50

1979, Sept. 15   *Perf. 15*
518 A50 25d DC-3 Dakota
Perf. 14
519 A50 25d Graf Zeppelin, vert.

First Air Mail Flight, Lisbon to St. Thomas & Prince, 30th anniv. (#518), Brasiliana '79 Intl. Philatelic Exhibition and 18th UPU Congress (#519). See Nos. 528-533 for other stamps inscribed "Historia da Aviancao." For overprint see No. 700.

Albrecht Durer, 450th Death Anniv. — A51

Portraits: No. 520, Willibald Pirckheimer. No. 521, Portrait of a Negro. 1d, Portrait of a Young Man, facing right. 7d, Adolescent boy. 8d, The Negress Catherine. No. 525, Girl with Braided Hair. No. 526, Self-portrait as a Boy. No. 527, Feast of the Holy Family.

1979   *Perf. 14*
Background Color
520 A51 50c blue green
521 A51 50c orange
522 A51   1d blue
523 A51   7d brown
524 A51   8d red
525 A51 25d lilac
Souvenir Sheets
Perf. 13½
526 A51 25d lil, buff & blk
Perf. 13½x14
527 A51 25d blk, lil & buff

Issue dates: Nos. 520-526, Nov. 29. No. 527, Dec. 25. No. 527 contains one 35x50mm stamp. Christmas, Intl. Year of the Child (#527). For overprint see No. 591.

History of
Aviation
A52

1979, Dec. 21   *Perf. 15*
528 A52   50c Wright Flyer i
529 A52   1d Sikorsky VS 300
530 A52   5d Spirit of St. Louis
531 A52   7d Dornier DO X
532 A52   8d Santa Cruz Fairey III D
533 A52   17d Space Shuttle

See No. 518 for souvenier sheet inscribed "Historia da Aviancao."

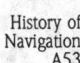

History of
Navigation
A53

1979, Dec. 21
534 A53   50c Caravel, 1460
535 A53   1d Portuguese galleon, 1560
536 A53   3d Sao Gabriel, 1497
537 A53   5d Caravelao Navio Dos
538 A53   8d Caravel Redonda, 1512
539 A53   25d Galley Fusta, 1540

Size: 129x98mm
Imperf
540 A53   25d Map of St. Thomas & Prince, 1602

Birds — A54

1979, Dec. 21   *Perf. 14*
541 A54   50c Serinus rufobrunneus
542 A54   50c Euplectes aureus
543 A54   1d Alcedo leucogaster nais
544 A54   7d Dreptes thomensis
545 A54   8d Textor grandis
546 A54   100d Speirops lugubris

Souvenir Sheet
Perf. 14½
547 A54   25d Treron S. thomae

No. 546 is airmail.

Fish
A55

1979, Dec. 28   *Perf. 14*
548 A55   50c Cypselurus lineatus
549 A55   1d Canthidermis maculatus
550 A55   5d Diodon hystrix
551 A55   7d Ostracion tricornis
552 A55   8d Rhinecanthus aculeatus
553 A55   50d Chaetodon striatus

Souvenir Sheet
Perf. 14½
554 A55   25d Holocentrus axensionis

No. 553 is airmail.

Balloons — A56

Designs: 50c, Blanchard, 1784. 1d, Lunardi II, 1785. 3d, Von Lutgendorf, 1786. 7d, John Wise "Atlantic," 1859. 8d, Salomon Anree "The Eagle," 1896. No. 560, Stratospheric balloon of Prof. Piccard, 1931. No. 561, Indoor demonstration of hot air balloon, 1709, horiz.

1979, Dec. 28   *Perf. 15*
555 A56   50c multicolored
556 A56   1d multicolored
557 A56   3d multicolored
558 A56   7d multicolored
559 A56   8d multicolored
560 A56   25d multicolored

Souvenir Sheet
Perf. 14
560A A56   25d multicolored

No. 560A contains one 50x38mm stamp.

Dirigibles
A57

Designs: 50c, Dupuy de Lome, 1872. 1d, Paul Hanlein, 1872. 3d, Gaston brothers, 1882. 7d, Willows II, 1909. 8d, Ville de Lucerne, 1910. 17d, Mayfly, 1910.

1979, Dec. 28   *Perf. 15*
561 A57   50c multicolored
562 A57   1d multicolored
563 A57   3d multicolored
564 A57   7d multicolored
565 A57   8d multicolored
566 A57   17d multicolored

1980
Olympics,
Lake Placid &
Moscow
A58

Olympic Venues: 50c, Lake Placid, 1980. Nos. 568, 572a, Mexico City, 1968. Nos. 569, 572b, Munich, 1972. Nos. 570, 572c, Montreal, 1976. Nos. 571, 572d, Moscow, 1980.

1980, June 13   Litho.   *Perf. 15*
567 A58   50c multicolored
568 A58   11d multicolored
569 A58   11d multicolored
570 A58   11d multicolored
571 A58   11d multicolored

Souvenir Sheet
572 A58   7d Sheet of 4, #a.-d.

Proclamation Type of 1975 and

Sir Rowland
Hill (1795-
1879)
A59

Sir Rowland Hill and: 50c, #1. 1d, #415. 8d, #411. No. 571, #449. No. 572, #418.

1980, June 1   *Perf. 15*
573 A59   50c multicolored
574 A59   1d multicolored
575 A59   8d multicolored
576 A59   20d multicolored

Souvenir Sheet
Imperf
577 A32   20d multicolored

No. 577 contains one 38x32mm stamp with simulated perforations.

Moon
Landing,
10th Anniv.
(in 1979)
A60

Designs: 50c, Launch of Apollo 11, vert. 1d, Astronaut on lunar module ladder, vert. 14d, Setting up research experiments. 17d, Astronauts, experiment. 25d, Command module during reentry.

1980, June 13   *Perf. 15*
578 A60   50c multicolored
579 A60   1d multicolored
580 A60   14d multicolored
581 A60   17d multicolored

Souvenir Sheet
582 A60   25d multicolored

Miniature Sheet

Independence, 5th
Anniv. — A61

Designs: No. 583a, US #1283B. b, Venezuela #C942. c, Russia #3710. d, India #676. e, T. E. Lawrence (1888-1935). f, Ghana #106. g, Russia #2486. h, Algeria #624. i, Cuba #1318. j, Cape Verde #366. k, Mozambique #617. l, Angola #601. 25d, King Amador.

1980, July 12   *Perf. 13*
583 A61   5d Sheet of 12, #a.-l. + 13 labels

Souvenir Sheet
Perf. 14
584 A61   25d multicolored

No. 584 contains one 35x50mm stamp. For overprint see No. 596.

No. 527 Ovptd. "1980" on Stamp and Intl. Year of the Child emblem in Sheet Margin

1980, Dec. 25   *Perf. 14*
591 A51   25d on No. 527

Christmas.

Nos. 465-468a
Overprinted in Black or
Silver

1981, Feb. 2   *Perf. 13½x14, 14x13½*
592 A38   15d on #465 (S)
593 A39   30d on #466 (S)
594 A39   40d on #467
595 A38   50d on #468
    a.   on No. 468a

No. 584 Ovptd. with UN and Intl. Year of the Child emblems and Three Inscriptions

1981, Feb. 2   *Perf. 14*
596 A61   25d on No. 584

Nos. 464-464a Ovptd. in Silver and Black "UNIAO / SOVIETICA / VENCEDORA / 1980" with Olympic emblem and "JOGOS OLIMPICOS DE MOSCOVO 1980"

1981, May 15   *Perf. 13½x14*
597 A37   50d on #464
    a.   on #464a

Mammals — A65

1981, May 22   *Perf. 14*
598 A65   50c Crocidura thomensis
599 A65   50c Mustela nivalis
600 A65   1d Viverra civetta
601 A65   7d Hipposioleros fuliginosus
602 A65   8d Rattus norvegicus
603 A65   14d Eidolon helvum

Souvenir Sheet
Perf. 14½
604 A65   25d Cercopithecus mona

Shells
A66

Designs: No. 611a, 10d, Bolinus cornutus, diff. b, 15d, Conus genuanus.

1981, May 22   *Perf. 14*
605 A66   50c Haxaplex hoplites
606 A66   50c Bolinus cornutus
607 A66   1d Cassis tessellata
608 A66   1.50d Harpa doris
609 A66   11d Strombus latus
610 A66   17d Cymbium glans

Souvenir Sheet
Perf. 14½
611 A66   Sheet of 2, #a.-b.

Johann Wolfgang
von Goethe
(1749-1832),
Poet — A67

Design: 75d, Goethe in the Roman Campagna, by Johann Heinrich W. Tischbein.

1981, Nov. 14   *Perf. 14*
612 A67   25d multicolored

Souvenir Sheet
613 A67   75d multicolored

PHILATELIA '81, Frankfurt/Main, Germany.

Tito — A68

1981, Nov. 14   *Perf. 12¹/₂x13*
614 A68 17d Wearing glasses
615 A68 17d shown
  a.   Sheet of 2, #614-615

Souvenir Sheet
Perf. 14x13¹/₂
616 A68 75d In uniform

Nos. 614-615 issued in sheets of 4 each plus label. For overprints see Nos. 644-646.

No. 448 Ovptd. in White

*Casamento do Príncipe
Carlos e Lady Diana*

1981, Nov. 28   *Perf. 13¹/₂*
617 A36   Strip of 3, #a.-c.

Wedding of Prince Charles and Lady Diana. On No. 617 the white overprint was applied by a thermographic process producing a shiny, raised effect.

Overprint exists in gold.

World Chess
Championships
A69

Chess pieces: No. 618, Egyptian. No. 619, Two Chinese, green. No. 620, Two Chinese, red. No. 621, English. No. 622, Indian. No. 623, Scandinavian. 75d, Khmer.
No. 624a, Anatoly Karpov. b, Victor Korchnoi.

1981, Nov. 28   Litho.   Perf. 14
618 A69 1.50d multicolored
619 A69 1.50d multicolored
620 A69 1.50d multicolored
621 A69 1.50d multicolored
622 A69 30d multicolored
623 A69 30d multicolored
624 A69 30d Pair, #a.-b.

Souvenir Sheet
625 A69 75d multicolored

Nos. 618-623 exist in souvenir sheets of one. No. 624 exists in souvenir sheet with simulated perfs. Nos. 618-625 exist imperf.

No. 624 Ovptd. in red "ANATOLIJ KARPOV / Campeao Mundial / de Xadrez 1981"

1981, Dec. 10   *Perf. 14*
627 A69 30d Pair, #a.-b.

Exists in souvenir sheet with simulated perfs or imperf.

S. TOMÉ E PRÍNCIPE

Pablo
Picasso — A70

Paintings: 14d, The Old and the New Year. No. 629a, Young Woman. b, Child with Dove. c, Paul de Pierrot with Flowers. d, Francoise, Claude, and Paloma.
No. 630a, Girl. b, Girl with Doll. 75d, Father, Mother and Child.

1981, Dec. 10   *Perf. 14x13¹/₂*
628 A70 14d multicolored
629 A70 17d Strip of 4, #a.-d.
630 A70 20d Pair, #a.-b.

Souvenir Sheet
Perf. 13¹/₂
631 A70 75d multicolored

Intl. Year of the Child. Christmas (#628, 631). No. 630 is airmail.
Nos. 628, 629a-629d, 630a-630b exist in souvenir sheets of one. No. 631 contains one 50x60mm stamp.
See Nos. 683-685.

Intl. Year of the
Child — A71

Paintings: No. 632a, Girl with Dog, by Thomas Gainsborough. b, Miss Bowles, by Sir Joshua Reynolds. c, Sympathy, by Riviere. d, Master Simpson, by Devis. e. Two Boys with Dogs, by Gainsborough.
No. 633a, Girl feeding cat. b, Girl wearing cat mask. c, White cat. d, Cat wearing red bonnet. e, Girl teaching cat to read.
No. 634a, Boy and Dog, by Picasso. b, Clipper, by Picasso.
No. 635a, Two white cats. b, Himalayan cat.

1981, Dec. 30   *Perf. 14*
632 A71 1.50d Strip of 5, #a.-e.
633 A71 1.50d Strip of 5, #a.-e.
634 A71 50d Pair, #a.-b.
635 A71 50d Pair, #a.-b. + label

Souvenir Sheets
Perf. 13¹/₂
636 A71 75d Girl with dog
637 A71 75d Girl with cat

Nos. 636-637 contain one 30x40mm stamp.

2nd Central Africa
Games, Luanda,
Angola — A73

Designs: No. 638a, Shot put. b, Discus. c, High jump. d, Javelin.
50d, Team handball. 75d, Runner.

1981, Dec. 30   *Perf. 13¹/₂x14*
638 A73 17d Strip of 4, a.-d.

---

639 A73 50d multicolored

Souvenir Sheet
640 A73 75d multicolored

World Food
Day — A74

Designs: No. 641a, Ananas sativus. b, Colocasia esculenta. c, Artocarbus altilis.
No. 642a, Mangifera indica. b, Theobroma cacao. c, Coffea arabica. 75d, Musa sapientum.

1981, Dec. 30
641 A74 11d Strip of 3, #a.-c.
642 A74 30d Strip of 3, #a.-c.

Souvenir Sheet
643 A74 75d multicolored

Nos. 614-616 Ovptd. in
Black

1982, May 25   *Perf. 12¹/₂x13*
644 A68 17d on #614
645 A68 17d on #615
  a.   On #615a

Souvenir Sheet
Perf. 14
646 A68 75d on #616

World Cup Soccer
Championships,
Spain — A75

Emblem and: No. 647a, Goalie in blue shirt jumping to catch ball. b, Two players, yellow, red shirts. c, Two players, black shirts. d, Goalie in green shirtcatching ball.
No. 648a, Player dribbling. b, Goalie facing opponent.
No. 649, Goalie catching ball from emblem in front of goal. No. 650, Like #649 with continuous design.

1982, June 21   *Perf. 13¹/₂x14*
647 A75 15d Strip of 4, #a.-d.
648 A75 25d Pair, #a.-b.

Souvenir Sheets
649 A75 75d multicolored
650 A75 75d multicolored

Nos. 648a-648b are airmail. Nos. 647a-647d, 648a-648b exist in souvenir sheets of one.

S. TOMÉ E PRÍNCIPE
A76

SÃO TOMÉ E PRÍNCIPE
A77

Transportation: No. 651, Steam locomotive, TGV train. No. 652, Propeller plane and Concorde.

1982, June 21   *Perf. 12¹/₂x13*
651 A76 15d multicolored
652 A76 15d multicolored
  a.   Souv. sheet of 2, #651-652

PHILEXFRANCE '82.

1982, July 31
653 A77 25d multicolored

Robert Koch, discovery of tuberculosis bacillus, cent.

Goethe,
150th
Anniv. of
Death
A78

1982, July 31   *Perf. 13x12¹/₂*
654 A78 50d multicolored

Souvenir Sheet
655 A78 10d like #654

A79

A80

1982, July 31   *Perf. 12¹/₂x13*
656 A79 75d multicolored

Souvenir Sheet
657 A79 10d Sheet of 1
657A A79 10d Sheet of 2, purple &
                  multi

Princess Diana, 21st birthday. No. 657A exists with red violet inscriptions and different central flower.

1982, July 31

Boy Scouts, 75th Anniv.: 15d, Cape of Good Hope #178-179. 30d, Lord Baden-Powell, founder of Boy Scouts.

658 A80 15d multicolored
659 A80 30d multicolored
  a.   Souv. sheet of 2, #658-659 + label

Nos. 658-659 exits in sheets of 4 each plus label.

A81

A82

Caricatures by Picasso: No. 660a, Musicians. b, Stravinsky.

1982, July 31
660 A81 30d Pair, #a.-b.

Souvenir Sheet
661 A81 5d like #660b

Igor Stravinsky (1882-1971), composer.

1982, July 31

George Washington, 250th Anniv. of Birth: Nos. 662, 663b, Washington, by Gilbert Stuart. Nos. 663, 663c, Washington, by Roy Lichtenstein.

662 A82 30d multicolored
663 A82 30d blk & pink

Souvenir Sheet
663A A82 5d Sheet of 2, #b.-c.

Dinosaurs — A83

Designs: No. 670a, 25d, Pteranodon. b, 50d, Stenopterygius.

1982, Nov. 30   *Perf. 14x13½*
664 A83   6d Parasaurolophus
665 A83   16d Stegosaurus
666 A83   16d Triceratops
667 A83   16d Brontosaurus
668 A83   16d Tyrannosaurus rex
669 A83   50d Dimetrodon
      Souvenir Sheet
670 A83   Sheet of 2, #a.-b.

Charles Darwin, cent. of death (#670).

Explorers — A84

Explorers and their ships. 50c, Thor Heyerdahl, Kon-tiki. No. 672a, Magellan, Carrack. b, Drake, Golden Hind. c, Columbus, Santa Maria. d, Leif Eriksson, Viking longship. 50d, Capt. Cook, Endeavour.

1982, Dec. 21   *Litho.*
671 A84   50c multicolored
672 A84   18d Strip of 4, #a.-d.
673 A84   50d multicolored
      Souvenir Sheet
674 A85   75d multicolored

Departure of Marco Polo from Venice — A85

Nos. 411-414 Ovptd. with Assembly Emblem and "2o ANIVERSARIO DA 1a ASSEMBLEIA DA J.M.L.S.T.P." in Silver

1982, Dec. 24   *Perf. 13½x14*
675 A31   3d on #411
676 A31   10d on #412
677 A31   20d on #413
678 A31   50d on #414

MLSTP 3rd Assembly — A86

1982, Dec. 24   *Perf. 13½x14*
679 A86   8d bl & multi
680 A86   12d grn & multi
681 A86   16d brn org & multi
682 A86   30d red lilac & multi

    Picasso Painting Type of 1981

Designs: No. 683a, Lola. b, Aunt Pepa. c, Mother. d, Lola with Mantilla.
No. 684a, Corina Romeu. b, The Aperitif. 75d, Holy Family in Egypt, horiz.

1982, Dec. 24
683 A70   18d Strip of 4, #a.-d.
684 A70   25d Pair, #a.-b.
      Souvenir Sheet
      Perf. 14x13½
685 A70   75d multicolored

Intl. Women's Year (#683-684), Christmas (#685).

Locomotives — A87

Designs: 9d, Class 231K, France, 1941. No. 687a, First steam locomotive, Great Britain, 1825. b, Class 59, Africa, 1947. c, William Mason, US, 1850. d, Mallard, Great Britain, 1938. 50d, Henschel, Portugal, 1929. 75d, Locomotive barn, Swindon, Great Britain.

1982, Dec. 31   *Perf. 14x13½*
686 A87   9d multicolored
687 A87   16d Strip of 4, #a.-d.
688 A87   50d multicolored
      Souvenir Sheet
689 A87   75d multicolored

Easter — A88

Paintings: No. 690a, St. Catherine, by Raphael. b, St. Margaret, by Raphael.
No. 691a, Young Man with a Pointed Beard, by Rembrandt. b, Portrait of a Young Woman, by Rembrandt.
No. 692a, Rondo (Dance of the Italian Peasants), by Rubens, horiz. b, The Garden of Love, by Rubens, horiz.
No. 693, Samson and Delilah, by Rubens. No. 694, Descent from the Cross, by Rubens.
No. 695a, Elevation of the Cross, by Rembrandt. b, Descent from the Cross, by Rembrandt.
Nos. 696a, 697, The Crucifixion, by Raphael. Nos. 696b, 698, The Transfiguration, by Raphael.

1983, May 9   *Perf. 13½x14, 14x13½*
690 A88   16d Pair, #a.-b.
691 A88   16d Pair, #a.-b.
692 A88   16d Pair, #a.-b.
693 A88   18d multicolored
694 A88   18d multicolored
695 A88   18d Pair, #a.-b.
696 A88   18d multicolored
      Souvenir Sheets
697 A88   18d vio & multi
698 A88   18d multicolored

Souvenir sheets containing Nos. 690a-690b, 691a-691b, 692a-692b, 693, 694, 695a-695b exist.

BRASILIANA '83, Rio de Janeiro — A89

Santos-Dumont dirigibles: No. 699a, #5. b, #14 with airplane.

1983, July 29   *Litho.*   *Perf. 13½*
699 A89   25d Pair, #a.-b.

First manned flight, bicent.

No. 519 Overprinted with Various Designs

1983, July 29   *Litho.*   *Perf. 14*
      Souvenir Sheet
700 A50   25d multicolored

BRASILIANA '83.

First Manned Flight, Bicent. — A90

Designs: No. 701a, Wright Flyer No. 1, 1903. b, Alcock & Brown Vickers Vimy, 1919.
No. 702a, Bleriot monoplane, 1909. b, Boeing 747, 1983.
No. 703a, Graf Zeppelin, 1929. b, Montgolfiere brother's balloon, 1783. No. 704, Pierre Testu-Brissy. 60d, Flight of Vincent Lunardi's second balloon, vert.

1983, Sept. 16   *Perf. 14x13½*
701 A90   18d Pair, #a.-b.
702 A90   18d Pair, #a.-b.
703 A90   20d Pair, #a.-b.
704 A90   20d multicolored
      Souvenir Sheet
      Perf. 13½x14
705 A90   60d multicolored

Individual stamps from Nos. 701-704 exist in souvenir sheets of 1.

Nos. 493e, 493a, 493e (#706a) and 493g, 493c, 493g (#706b) Ovptd. in Gold with UPU and Philatelic Salon Emblems and:
"SALON DER PHILATELIE ZUM / XIX WELTPOSTKONGRESS / HAMBURG 1984" Across Strips of Three Stamps
Nos. 493f, 493b, 493f (#706c) 493h, 493d, 493h (#706d) Ovptd. in Gold with UPU and Philatelic Salon Emblems and:
"19TH CONGRESSO DA / UNIAO POSTAL UNIVERSAL / HAMBURGO 1984" Across Strips of Three Stamps

1983, Dec. 24   *Perf. 14*
706 A43   Sheet of 12, #a.-d.

Overprint is 91x30mm. Exists imperf with silver overprint.

Christmas — A91

Paintings: No. 707, Madonna of the Promenade, 1518, by Raphael. No. 708, Virgin of Guadalupe, 1959, by Salavador Dali.

1983, Dec. 24   *Perf. 12½x13*
707 A91   30d multicolored
708 A91   30d multicolored

Nos. 707-708 exist in souvenir sheets of 1.

Automobiles — A92

Designs: No. 709a, Renault, 1912. b, Rover Phaeton, 1907.
No. 710a, Morris, 1913. b, Delage, 1910.
No. 711a, Mercedes Benz, 1927. b, Mercedes Coupe, 1936.
No. 712a, Mercedes Cabriolet, 1924. b, Mercedes Simplex, 1902.
75d, Peugeot Daimler, 1894.

1983, Dec. 28   *Perf. 14x13½*
709 A92   12d Pair, #a.-b.
710 A92   12d Pair, #a.-b.
711 A92   20d Pair, #a.-b.
712 A92   20d Pair, #a.-b.
      Souvenir Sheet
713 A92   75d multicolored

Nos. 709-712 exist as souvenir sheets. No. 713 contains one 50x41mm stamp.

Medicinal Plants — A93

1983, Dec. 28   *Perf. 13½*
714 A93   50c Cymbopogon citratus
715 A93   1d Adenoplus breviflorus
716 A93   5.50d Bryophillum pinatum
717 A93   15.50d Buchholzia coriacea
718 A93   16d Hiliotropium indicum
719 A93   20d Mimosa pigra
720 A93   46d Piperonia pallucila
721 A93   50d Achyranthes aspera

1984 Olympics, Sarajevo and Los Angeles — A94

Designs: No. 722, Pairs' figure skating.

No. 723a, Downhill skiing. b, Speed skating. c, Ski jumping.
No. 724, Equestrian.
No. 725a, Cycling. b, Rowing. c, Hurdling.
No. 726a, Bobsled. b, Women's archery.

1983, Dec. 29   *Perf. 13¹/₂x14*
722 A94 16d multicolored
723 A94 16d Strip of 3, #a.-c.
724 A94 18d multicolored
725 A94 18d Strip of 3, #a.-c.
       Souvenir Sheet
726 A94 30d Sheet of 2, #a.-b.

Souvenir sheets of 2 exist containing Nos. 722 and 723b, 723a and 723c, 724 and 725b, 725a and 725c.

Birds — A95

1983, Dec. 30   *Perf. 13¹/₂*
727 A95 50c Spermestes cucullatus
728 A95 1d Xanthophilus princeps
729 A95 1.50d Thomasophantes sanctithomae
730 A95 2d Quelea erythrops
731 A95 3d Textor velatus peixotoi
732 A95 4d Anabathmis hartlaubii
733 A95 5.50d Serinus mozambicus santhome
734 A95 7d Estrilda astrild angolensis
735 A95 10d Horizorhinus dohrni
       Size: 30x43mm
736 A95 11d Zosterops ficedulinus
737 A95 12d Prinia molleri
738 A95 14d Chrysococcyx cupreus insularum
739 A95 15.50d Halcyon malimhicus dryas
740 A95 16d Turdus olivaceofuscus
741 A95 17d Oriolus crassirostris
742 A95 18.50d Dicrurus modestus
743 A95 20d Columba thomensis
744 A95 25d Stigmatopelia senegalensis thome
       Size: 31x47mm
       Perf. 13¹/₂x14
745 A95 30d Chaetura thomensis
746 A95 42d Onychognatus fulgidus
747 A95 46d Lamprotornis ornatus
748 A95 100d Tyto alba thomensis
       Souvenir Sheet

ESPANA '84, Madrid — A96

Paintings: a, 15.50d, Paulo Riding Donkey, by Picasso. b, 16d, Abstract, by Miro. c, 18.50d, My Wife in the Nude, by Dali.

1984, Apr. 27   *Perf. 13¹/₂x14*
749 A96 Sheet of 3, #a.-c.

LUBRAPEX '84, Lisbon — A97

Children's drawings: 16d, Children watching play. 30d, Adults.

1984, May 9   *Perf. 13¹/₂*
750 A97 16d multicolored
751 A97 30d multicolored

Intl. Maritime Organization, 25th Anniv. — A98

Ships: Nos. 752a, 753a, Phoenix, 1869. 752b, 753b, Hamburg, 1893. 752c, 753c, Prince Heinrich, 1900.
No. 754a, Leopold, 1840. b, Stadt Schaffhausen, 1851. c, Crown Prince, 1890. d, St. Gallen, 1905.
No. 755a, Elise, 1816. b, De Zeeuw, 1824. c, Friedrich Wilhelm, 1827. d, Packet Hansa.
No. 756a, Savannah, 1818. b, Chaperone, 1884. c, Alida, 1847. d, City of Worcester, 1881.
No. 757, Ferry, Lombard Bridge, Hamburg, c. 1900. No. 758, Train, coaches on bridge, c. 1880, vert. No. 759, Windmill, bridge, vert. No. 760, Queen of the West. No. 761, Bremen. No. 762, Union.

1984, June 19 Litho. *Perf. 14x13¹/₂*
752 A98 50c Strip of 3, #a.-c.
753 A98 50c Strip of 3, #a.-c.
754 A98 7d Piece of 4, #a.-d.
    e. Souv. sheet of 2, #754a-754b
    f. Souv. sheet of 2, #754c-754d
755 A98 8d Piece of 4, #a.-d.
    e. Souv. sheet of 2, #755a-755b
    f. Souv. sheet of 2, #755c-755d
756 A98 15.50d Piece of 4, #a.-d.
    e. Souv. sheet of 2, #756a, 756d
    f. Souv. sheet of 2, #756b-756c
       Souvenir Sheets
       Perf. 14x13¹/₂, 13¹/₂x14
757 A98 10d multicolored
758 A98 10d multicolored
759 A98 10d multicolored
       Perf. 13¹/₂
760 A98 15d multicolored
761 A98 15d multicolored
762 A98 15d multicolored

Nos. 757-759 exist imperf in different colors. Nos. 760-762 contain one 60x33mm stamp each. Nos. 753a-753c have UPU and Hamburg Philatelic Salon emblems and are additionally inscribed "PARTICIPACAO DE S. TOME E PRINCIPE / NO CONGRESSO DA U.P.U. EM HAMBURGO."
Sheets containing Nos. 754-756 contain one lable.

Natl. Campaign Against Malaria A99

1984, Sept. 30   *Perf. 13¹/₂*
764 A99 8d Malaria victim
765 A99 16d Mosquito, DDT, vert.
766 A99 30d Exterminator, vert.

A100   A101

World Food Day: 8d, Emblem, animals, produce. 16d, Silhouette, animals. 46d, Plowed field, produce. 30d, Tractor, field, produce, horiz.

1984, Oct. 16
767 A100 8d multicolored
768 A100 16d multicolored
769 A100 46d multicolored
       Souvenir Sheet
770 A100 30d multicolored

1984, Nov. 5

Mushrooms: 10d, Coprinus micaceus. 20d, Amanita rubescens. 30d, Armillariella mellea. 50d, Hygrophorus chrysodon, horiz.

771 A101 10d multicolored
772 A101 20d multicolored
773 A101 30d multicolored
       Souvenir Sheet
774 A101 50d multicolored

Christmas — A102

Designs: 30d, Candles, offering, stable. 50d, Stable, Holy Family, Kings.

1984, Dec. 25
775 A102 30d multicolored
       Souvenir Sheet
776 A102 50d multicolored

No. 776 contains one 60x40mm stamp.

Conference of Portuguese Territories in Africa — A103

1985, Feb. 14
777 A103 25d multicolored

Reinstatement of Flights from Lisbon to St. Thomas, 1st Anniv. — A104

Designs: 25d, Douglas DC-3, map of northwest Africa. 30d, Air Portugal Douglas DC-8. 50d, Fokker Friendship.

1985, Dec. 6 Litho. *Perf. 13¹/₂*
778 A104 25d multicolored
779 A104 30d multicolored
       Souvenir Sheet
779A A104 50d multicolored

Flowers   Mushrooms
A105   A106

1985, Dec. 30   *Perf. 11¹/₂x12*
780 A105 16d Flowering cactus
781 A105 20d Sunflower
782 A105 30d Porcelain rose

1986, Sept. 18   *Perf. 13¹/₂*
783 A106 6d Fistulina hepatica
784 A106 25d Collybia butyracea
785 A106 30d Entoloma clypeatum
       Souvenir Sheet
786 A106 75d Cogumelos II

No. 786 exists with margins trimmed on four sides removing the control number.

Miniature Sheet

World Cup Soccer, Mexico A107

Designs: No. 787a, Top of trophy. b, Bottom of trophy. c, Interior of stadium. d, Exterior of stadium.

1986, Oct. 1
787 A107 25d Sheet of 4, #a.-d.

For overprints see Nos. 818-818A.

Miniature Sheet

1988 Summer Olympics, Seoul A108

Seoul Olympic Games emblem, and: No. 788a, Map of North Korea. b, Torch. c, Olympic flag, map of South Korea. d, Text.

1986, Oct. 2
788 A108 25d Sheet of 4, #a.-d.

Halley's Comet — A109

Designs: No. 789a, 5d, Challenger space shuttle, 1st launch. b, 6d, Vega probe. c, 10d, Giotto probe. d, 16d, Comet over Nuremberg, A.D. 684. 90d, Comet, Giotto probe, horiz.

1986, Oct. 27
789 A109 Sheet of 4, #a.-d.+5 labels
       Souvenir Sheet
790 A109 90d multicolored

Automobiles
A110

Designs: No. 791a, 50c, Columbus Monument, Barcelona. b, 6d, Fire engine ladder truck, c. 1900. c, 16d, Fire engine, c. 1900. d, 30d, Fiat 18 BL Red Cross ambulance, c. 1916.

1986, Nov. 1
791 A110   Sheet of 4, #a.-d.+5 labels

Railway
Stations and
Signals
A111

Designs: 50c, London Bridge Station, 1900. 6d, 100-300 meter warning signs. 20d, Signal lamp. 50d, St. Thomas & Prince Station.

1986, Nov. 2   *Perf. 13½*
792 A111   50c multicolored
793 A111   6d multicolored
794 A111   20d multicolored
Souvenir Sheet
795 A111   50d multicolored

LUBRAPEX '86,
Brazil — A112

Exhibition emblem and: No. 796a, 1d, Line fisherman on shore. b, 1d, Line fisherman in boat. c, 2d, Net fisherman. d, 46d, Couple trap fishing, lobster.

1987, Jan. 15
796 A112   Sheet of 4, #a.-d.+2 labels

Intl. Peace
Year — A113

Designs: 8d, Mahatma Gandhi. 10d, Martin Luther King, Jr. 16d, Red Cross, Intl. Peace Year, UN, UNESCO, Olympic emblems and Nobel Peace Prize medal. 20d, Albert Luthuli. 75d, Peace Dove, by Picasso.

1987, Jan. 15
797 A113   8d bl, blk & pur
798 A113   10d bl, blk & grn
799 A113   16d multicolored
800 A113   20d multicolored
Souvenir Sheet
801 A113   75d multicolored

Christmas
1986 — A114

Paintings by Albrecht Durer: No. 802a, 50c, Virgin and Child. b, 1d, Madonna of the Carnation. c, 16d, Virgin and Child, diff. d, 20d, The Nativity. 75d, Madonna of the Goldfinch.

1987, Jan. 15
802 A114   Strip of 4, #a.-d.
Souvenir Sheet
803 A114   75d multicolored

Fauna
and
Flora
A115

Birds: a, 1d, Agapornis fischeri. b, 2d, Psittacula krameri. c, 10d, Psittacus erithacus. d, 20d, Agapornis personata psittacidae.
Flowers: e, 1d, Passiflora caerulea. f, 2d, Oncidium nubigenum. g, 10d, Helicontia wagneriana. h, 20d, Guzmania liguiata.
Butterflies: i, 1d, Aglais urticae. j, 2d, Pieris brassicae. k, 10d, Fabriciana niobe. l, 20d, Zerynthia polyxena.
Dogs: m, 1d, Sanshu. n, 2d, Hamiltonstovare. o, 10d, Gran spitz. p, 20d, Chow-chow.

1987, Oct. 15   *Perf. 14x13½*
804 A115   Sheet of 16, #a.-p.

Sports Institute,
10th
Anniv. — A116

Designs: No. 805a, 50c, Three athletes. b, 20d, Map of St. Thomas and Prince, torchbearers. c, 30d, Volleyball, soccer, team handball and basketball players.
50d, Bjorn Borg.

1987, Oct. 30
805 A116   Strip of 3, #a.-c.
Souvenir Sheet
Perf. 13½x14
806 A116   50d Sheet of 1 + label

Miniature Sheet

Discovery of
America, 500th
Anniv. (in
1992) — A117

Emblem and: No. 807a, 15d, Columbus with globe, map and arms. b, 20d, Battle between Spanish galleon and pirate ship. c, 20d, Columbus landing in New World. 100d, Model ship, horiz.

1987, Nov. 3   *Perf. 13½x14*
807 A117   Sheet of 3, #a.-c. + 3 labels
Souvenir Sheet
Perf. 14x13½
808 A117   100d multicolored

Mushrooms — A118

Designs: No. 809a, 6d, Calocybe ionides. b, 25d, Hygrophorus coccineus. c, 30d, Boletus versipellis. 35d, Morchella vulgaris, vert.

1987, Nov. 10   *Perf. 14x13½*
809 A118   Strip of 3, #a.-c.
Souvenir Sheet
Perf. 13½x14
810 A118   35d multicolored

Locomotives — A119

Designs: No. 811a, 5d, Jung, Germany. b, 10d, Mikado 2413. c, 20d, Baldwin, 1920. 50d, Pamplona Railroad Station, 1900.

1987, Dec. 1   Litho.   *Perf. 14x13½*
811 A119   Strip of 3, #a.-c.
Souvenir Sheet
812 A119   50d multicolored

Miniature Sheet

Christmas
A120

Paintings of Virgin and Child by: No. 813a, 1d, Botticelli. b, 5d, Murillo. c, 15d, Raphael. d, 20d, Memling.
50d, Unkmown artist, horiz.

1987, Dec. 20   *Perf. 13½x14*
813 A120   Sheet of 4, #a.-d.
Souvenir Sheet
Perf. 14x13½
814 A120   50d multicolored

World Boy Scout Jamboree, Australia,
1987-88 — A121

1987, Dec. 30   *Perf. 14x13½*
815 A121   50c multicolored

Russian
October
Revolution,
70th Anniv.
A122

1988   **Litho.**   *Perf. 12*
816 A122   25d Lenin addressing revolutionaries   1.20

Souvenir Sheet

Lubrapex '88 — A123

1988, May   *Perf. 14x13½*
817 A123   80d Trolley

Nos. 787a-787d Ovptd.
"CAMPEONATO MUNDIAL / DE FUTEBOL MEXICO '86 / ALEMANHA / SUBCAMPIAO" in Silver (#818) or Same with "ARGENTINA / CAMPIAO" Instead in Gold (#818A) Across Four Stamps

1988, Aug. 15   *Perf. 13½*
818   A107   25d Block of 4 (S)
818A A107   25d Block of 4 (G)

Medicinal
Plants — A108

Mushrooms
A109

Medicinal plants: No. 819a, 5d, Datura metel. b, 5d, Salaconta. c, 5d, Cassia occidentalis. d, 10d, Solanum ovigerum. e, 20d, Leonotis nepetifolia.
Mushrooms: No. 820a, 10d, Rhodopaxillus nudus. b, 10d, Volvaria volvacea. c, 10d, Psalliota bispora. d, 10d, Pleurotus ostreatus. e, 20d, Clitocybe geotropa.

1988, Oct. 26   *Perf. 13½x14*
819 A108   Strip of 5, #a.-e.
820 A109   Strip of 5, #a.-e.
Souvenir Sheets
821 A108   35d Hiersas durero
822 A109   35d Mushroom on wood

Miniature Sheets

Passenger Trains — A110

Designs: No. 823a, Swiss Federal Class RE 6/6, left. b, Class RE 6/6, right.
No. 824a, Japan Natl. Class EF 81, left. b, Class EF 81, right.
No. 825a, German Electric E 18, 1930, left. b, E 18, 1930, right.
60d, Japan Natl. Class 381 Electric.

1988, Nov. 4   *Perf. 14x13¹/₂*
823 A110 10d Sheet of 4, 2 each
     #a.-b + 2 labels
824 A110 10d Sheet of 4, 2 each
     #a.-b + 2 labels
825 A110 10d Sheet of 4, 2 each
     #a.-b + 2 labels

Souvenir Sheet

826 A110 60d multicolored

Butterflies
A111

Various flowers and: No. 827a, White and brown spotted butterfly. b, Dark brown and white butterfly, flower stigma pointing down. c, Brown and white butterfly, flower stigma pointing down.
50d, Brown, white and orange butterly.

1988, Nov. 25   *Perf. 13¹/₂x14*
827 A111 10d Strip of 3, #a.-c.

Souvenir Sheet

828 A111 50d multicolored

Ferdinand von Zeppelin (1838-1917) — A112

Berlin, 750th Anniv. — A113

Designs: No. 829a, Sailing ship, dirigible L23. b, Dirigibles flying over British merchant ships. c, Rendezvous of zeppelin with Russian ice breaker Malygin.
No. 830a, Airship Le Jeune at mooring pad, Paris, 1903, vert. b, von Zeppelin, vert.

     Perf. 14x13¹/₂, 13¹/₂x14
1988, Nov. 25
829 A112 10d Strip of 3, #a.-c.
830 A112 10d Pair, #a.-b.

Souvenir Sheet

831 A113 50d multicolored

Natl.
Arms — A114

Automatic Telephone Exchange Linking the Islands, 1st Anniv. — A115

1988, Dec. 15   *Perf. 13¹/₂*
832 A114 10d multicolored
833 A115 25d multicolored

Olympics Games, Seoul, Barcelona and Albertville — A116

World Cup Soccer Championships, Italy, 1990 — A117

Designs: No. 834, View of Barcelona, Cobi. No. 835, Barcelona Games emblem, vert. No. 836, Gold medal from 1988 Seoul games, vert. No. 837, Emblems of 1988 and 1992 games. No. 838, Bear on skis, Albertville, 1992. No. 839, Soccer ball. No. 840, Italy '90 Championships emblem, vert. No. 841, World Cup Trophy, vert. No. 842, Transfer of Olympic flag during Seoul closing ceremony. No. 843, Olympic pins. No. 844, like #838. No. 845, Soccer balls as hemispheres of globe.

     Perf. 14x13¹/₂, 13¹/₂x14
1988, Dec. 15
834 A116 5d multicolored
835 A116 5d multicolored
836 A116 5d multicolored
837 A116 5d multicolored
838 A116 5d grn & multi
839 A117 5d multicolored
840 A117 5d multicolored
841 A117 5d multicolored

Souvenir Sheets
     Perf. 14x13¹/₂

842 A116 50d multicolored
843 A116 50d multicolored
844 A116 50d blue & multi
845 A117 50d multicolored

No. 842 exists with Olympic emblems in gold or silver. No. 845 exists with marginal inscriptions in gold or silver. See Nos. 876-877 for souvenir sheets similar in design to No. 840.

Intl. Boy Scout Jamboree, Australia, 1987-88 — A118

Designs: No. 846a, Campfire. b, Scout emblem, pitched tents, flag. c, Scout emblem, tent flaps, flag, axe.
110d, Trefoil center point, horiz.

1988, Dec. 15   *Perf. 13¹/₂x14*
846 A118 10d Strip of 3, #a.-c.

Souvenir Sheet
     Perf. 14x13¹/₂

847 A118 110d multicolored

Intl. Red Cross, 125th Anniv. — A119

Designs: No. 848a, 50c, Patient in hospital. b, 5d, Transporting victims. c, 20d, instructing workers. 50d, Early mail train, horiz.

1988, Dec. 15   *Perf. 13¹/₂x14*
848 A119   Strip of 3, #a.-c.

Souvenir Sheet
     Perf. 14x13¹/₂

849 A119 50d multicolored

No. 848c is airmail.

Miniature Sheet

Christmas — A120

Paintings: No. 850a, 10d, Madonna and Child with St. Anthony Abbot and the Infant Baptism, by Titian. b, 10d, Madonna and Child with St. Catherine and a Rabbit, by Titian. c, 10d, Nativity Scene, by Rubens. d, 30d, Adoration of the Magi, by Rubens. 50d, The Annunciation (detail), by Titian, vert.

1988, Dec. 23   *Perf. 14x13¹/₂*
850 A120   Sheet of 4, #a.-d.

Souvenir Sheet
     Perf. 13¹/₂x14

851 A120 50d multicolored

Titian, 500th anniv. of birth. Country name does not appear on No. 850d.

French Revolution, Bicent. — A121

Designs: No. 852, Eiffel Tower, Concorde, stylized doves, flag. No. 853 Eiffel Tower, flag, stylized doves. No. 854, Eiffel Tower, flag, stylized doves, TGV train, vert. 50d, TGV train.

     Perf. 14x13¹/₂, 13¹/₂x14
1989, July 14   *Litho.*
852 A121 10d multicolored
853 A121 10d multicolored
854 A121 10d multicolored

Souvenir Sheet

855 A121 50d multicolored

Keep up to date with all new stamp issues by subscribing to the "Scott Stamp Monthly". Please call 1-800-488-5351 for more information.

Fruit — A122

1989, Sept. 15   *Perf. 13¹/₂x14*
856 A122 50c Chapu-chapu
857 A122 1d Guava
858 A122 5d Mango
859 A122 10d Carambola
860 A122 25d Nona
861 A122 50d Avacado
862 A122 50d Cajamanga

     Perf. 14x13¹/₂
863 A122 60d Jackfruit
864 A122 100d Cacao
865 A122 250d Bananas
866 A122 500d Papaya

Souvenir Sheet
     Perf. 13¹/₂x14

867 A122 1000d Pomegranate

Nos. 863-866 are horiz.

Orchids — A123

Designs: No. 868, Dendrobium phalaenopsis. No. 869, Catteleya granulosa. 50d, Diothonea imbricata and maxillaria eburnea.

1989, Oct. 15   *Perf. 13¹/₂x14*
868 A123 20d multicolored
869 A123 20d multicolored

Souvenir Sheet

870 A123 50d multicolored

Hummingbirds — A124

Designs: No. 871, Topaza bella, sappho sparganura, vert. No. 872, Petasophores anais. No. 873, Lophornis adorabilis, chalcostigma herrani, vert. 50d, Oreotrochilus chimborazo.

     Perf. 13¹/₂x14, 14x13¹/₂
1989, Oct. 15
871 A124 20d multicolored
872 A124 20d multicolored
873 A124 20d multicolored

Souvenir Sheet
     Perf. 14x13¹/₂

874 A124 50d multicolored

Miniature Sheet

1990 World Cup
Soccer
Championships,
Italy — A125

Program covers: No. 875a, 10d, Globe and soccer ball, 1962. b, 10d, Foot kicking ball, 1950. c, 10d, Abstract design, 1982. d, 20d, Player kicking ball, 1934.
No. 876a, Character emblem, horiz. b, USA 94, horiz. 50d, like #876a, horiz.

1989, Oct. 24   *Perf. 13¹/₂x14*
875 A125   Block of 4, #a.-d.
Souvenir Sheets
Perf. 14x13¹/₂
876 A125 25d Sheet of 2, #a.-b.
877 A125 50d blue & multi

1992 Summer Olympics,
Barcelona — A126

Perf. 13¹/₂x14, 14x13¹/₂
1989, Oct. 24
878 A126 5d Tennis, vert.
879 A126 5d Basketball, vert.
880 A126 5d Running
881 A126 35d Baseball, vert.
Souvenir Sheet
Perf. 14x13¹/₂
882 A126 50d Sailing

Nos. 878-881 exist in souvenir sheets of one. No country name of souvenir sheet of one of No. 878.

Locomotives — A127

Perf. 14x13¹/₂, 13¹/₂x14
1989, Oct. 27
884 A127 20d Japan
885 A127 20d Philippines
886 A127 20d Spain, vert.
887 A127 20d India
888 A127 20d Asia
Souvenir Sheets
889 A127 50d Garratt, Africa
890 A127 50d Trans-Gabon, vert.

Nos. 884-888 exist in souvenir sheets of one.

Ships
A128

Designs: No. 891, Merchant ships at sea, 16th cent. No. 892, Caravels, merchant ships in harbor, 16th cent. No. 893, Three merchant ships at sea, 18th cent. No. 894, War ships, 18th cent. No. 895, Four merchant ships, 18th cent. No. 896, Passenger liner, Port of Hamburg. No. 897, German sailing ship, 17th cent., vert.

1989, Oct. 27   *Perf. 14x13¹/₂*
891 A128 20d multicolored
892 A128 20d multicolored
893 A128 20d multicolored
894 A128 20d multicolored
895 A128 20d multicolored
Souvenir Sheets
896 A128 50d multicolored
Perf. 13¹/₂x14
897 A128 50d multicolored

Discovery of America, 500th anniv., in 1992 (#891-895) and Hamburg, 800th anniv. (#891-897).
Nos. 891-895 exist in souvenir sheets of one.

Butterflies
A129

1989, Dec. 20   *Perf. 13¹/₂x14*
898 A129 20d Tree bark
899 A129 20d Leaves
900 A129 20d Flowers
901 A129 20d Bird
902 A129 20d Blades of grass
Souvenir Sheet
903 A129 100d yel, brn & multi

Nos. 898-902 exist in souvenir sheets of one.

African
Development
Bank, 25th
Anniv. — A130

1989, Dec. 20   *Perf. 13¹/₂x14*
904 A130 25d blk, lt bl & grn

World Telecommunications Day — A131

1989, Dec. 20   *Perf. 14x13¹/₂*
905 A131 60d multicolored
Souvenir Sheet
Perf. 13¹/₂x14
906 A131 100d Early Bird satellite, vert.

Christmas
A132

Paintings: No. 907, Adoration of the Magi (detail), by Durer. No. 908, Young Virgin Mary, by Titian. No. 909, Adoration of the King, by Rubens. No. 910, Sistine Madonna, by Raphael. 100d, Madonna and Child Surrounded by Garland and Boy Angels, by Rubens.

1989, Dec. 23   *Perf. 13¹/₂x14*
907 A132 25d multicolored
908 A132 25d multicolored
909 A132 25d multicolored
910 A132 25d multicolored
Souvenir Sheet
911 A132 100d multicolored

Nos. 907-910 exist in souvenir sheets of one.

Expedition of
Sir Arthur
Eddington to
St. Thomas
and Prince,
70th Anniv.
A133

Designs: No. 912, Albert Einstein with Eddington. No. 913, Locomotive on Prince Island. No. 914, Roca Sundy railway station.

1990   **Litho.**   *Perf. 13¹/₂*
912 A133 60d multicolored
913 A133 60d multicolored
914 A133 60d multicoloed
  a.   Souvenir sheet of 3, #912-914

A134   Orchids — A135

Independence, 15th Anniv.: a, Map, arms. b, Map, birds carrying envelope. c, Flag.

1990, July 12   *Perf. 13¹/₂*
Souvenir Sheet
916 A134 50d Sheet of 3, #a.-c.

1990, Sept. 15 Litho. *Perf. 13¹/₂*
917 A135 20d Eulophia guineensis
918 A135 20d Ancistrochilus
919 A135 20d Oeceoclades maculata
920 A135 20d Vanilla imperialis
921 A135 20d Ansellia africana
Souvenir Sheets
Perf. 14x13¹/₂
922 A135 50d Angraecum distichum, horiz.
923 A135 50d Polystachya affinis, horiz.

Expo '90, Intl. Garden and Greenery Exposition, Osaka.

Locomotives — A136

1990, Sept. 28   *Perf. 14x13¹/₂*
924 A136 5d Bohemia, 1923-41
925 A136 20d W. Germany, 1951-56
926 A136 25d Mallet, 1896-1903
927 A136 25d Russia, 1927-30
928 A136 25d England, 1927-30
Souvenir Sheets
929 A136 50d Camden-Amboy, 1834-38
930 A136 50d Stockton-Darlington, 1825

Souvenir Sheet

Iberoamericana '90 Philatelic
Exposition — A137

1990, Oct. 7
931 A137 300d Armas Castle

1990 World Cup
Soccer
Championships,
Italy — A138

Designs: No. 932, German team with World Cup Trophy. No. 933, Two players with ball. No. 934, Three players with ball. No. 935, Italian player. No. 936, US Soccer Federation emblem and team members, horiz. No. 937, World Cup Trophy, horiz.

1990, Oct. 15   *Perf. 13¹/₂*
932 A138 25d multicolored
933 A138 25d multicolored
934 A138 25d multicolored
935 A138 25d multicolored
Souvenir Sheets
Perf. 14x13¹/₂
936 A138 50d multicolored
937 A138 50d multicolored

Mushrooms
A139

1990, Nov. 2   *Perf. 13¹/₂x14*
938 A139 20d Boletus aereus
939 A139 20d Coprinus micaceus
940 A139 20d Pholiota spectabilis
941 A139 20d Krombholzia aurantiaca
942 A139 20d Stropharia aeruginosa
Souvenir Sheets
Perf. 14x13¹/₂
943 A139 50d Hypholoma capnoides
944 A139 50d Pleurotus ostreatus

Nos. 943-944 horiz. See Nos. 1014-1020.

Butterflies — A140

1990, Nov. 2　*Perf. 14x13¹/₂, 13¹/₂x14*
945 A140 15d Megistanis baeotus
946 A140 15d Ascia vamillae
947 A140 15d Danaus chrysippus
948 A140 15d Morpho menelaus
949 A140 15d Papilio rutulus, vert.
950 A140 25d Papilio paradiesa

Souvenir Sheets
951 A140 50d Parnassius clodius, vert.
952 A140 50d Papilio macmaon, vert.

Presenting Gifts to the Newborn King — A141

Christmas: No. 954, Nativity scene. No. 955, Adoration of the Magi. No. 956, Flight into Egypt. No. 957, Adoration of the Magi, diff. No. 958, Portrait of Artist's Daughter Clara (detail), by Rubens, horiz.

1990, Nov. 30　*Perf. 13¹/₂x14*
953 A141 25d multicolored
954 A141 25d multicolored
955 A141 25d multicolored
956 A141 25d multicolored

Souvenir Sheets
957 A141 50d multicolored

Perf. 14x13¹/₂
958 A141 50d multicolored

Death of Rubens, 350th anniv. (#958).

Anniversaries and Events — A142

1990, Dec. 15　*Perf. 13¹/₂x14*
959 A142 20d shown

Souvenir Sheets
Perf. 14x13¹/₂, 13¹/₂x14 (#962, 964)
960 A142 50d Oath of Confederation
961 A142 50d Pointed roof
962 A142 50d William Tell statue, vert.
963 A142 50d Brandenburg Gate
964 A142 50d Penny Black, vert.
965 A142 100d bank note

Swiss Confederation, 700th anniv. (#959-962). Brandenburg Gate, 200th anniv. (#963). First postage stamp, 150th anniv. (#964). Independence of St. Thomas and Prince, 15th anniv. (#965).

Paintings — A143

Designs: No. 966, The Bathers, by Renoir. No. 967, Girl Holding Mirror for Nude, by Picasso, vert. No. 968, Nude, by Rubens, vert. No. 969, Descent from the Cross (detail), by Rubens, vert. No. 970, Nude, by Titian, vert. No. 971, Landscape, by Durer. No. 972, Rowboats, by Van Gogh. No. 973, Nymphs, by Titian. No. 974, Bather, by Titian, vert. No. 975, Postman Joseph Roulin (detail), by Van Gogh, vert. No. 976, The Abduction of the Daughters of Leucippus, by Rubens, vert. No. 977, Nude, by Titian, vert., diff.

Perf. 14x13¹/₂, 13¹/₂x14
1990, Dec. 15
966 A143 10d multicolored
967 A143 10d multicolored
968 A143 10d multicolored
969 A143 10d multicolored
970 A143 10d multicolored
971 A143 20d multicolored
972 A143 20d multicolored
973 A143 25d multicolored
974 A143 25d multicolored

Souvenir Sheets
Perf. 13¹/₂x14
975 A143 50d multicolored
976 A143 50d multicolored
977 A143 50d multicolored

Rubens, 350th anniv. of death (#968-969, 976). Titian, 500th anniv. of death (#970, 973-974, 977). Van Gogh, centennial of death (#972, 975).
See No. 958 for other souvenir sheet for Rubens death anniv.

S. TOMÉ E PRÍNCIPE

Flora and Fauna — A144

Designs: 1d, Gecko. 5d, Cobra. 10d, No. 980, Sea turtle. No. 981, Fresh water turtle. No. 982, Civet. 70d, Civet in tree. No. 984, Civet with young. No. 985, Civet in den.
Psittacus erithacus: 80d, In tree, vert. 100d, On branch with wings spread, vert. 250d, Feeding young, vert. No. 989, Three in flight, vert.

1991, Feb. 2　*Perf. 14x13¹/₂*
978 A144 1d multicolored
979 A144 5d multicolored
980 A144 10d multicolored
981 A144 50d multicolored
982 A144 50d multicolored
983 A144 70d multicolored
984 A144 75d multicolored
985 A144 75d multicolored

Perf. 13¹/₂x14
986 A144 80d multicolored
987 A144 100d multicolored
988 A144 250d multicolored
989 A144 500d multicolored

Souvenir Sheets
990 A144 500d Orchid, vert.
991 A144 500d Rose, vert.

See Nos. 1054I-1054L.

Locomotives — A145

1991, May 7　*Perf. 14x13¹/₂, 13¹/₂x14*
992 A145 75d shown
993 A145 75d North America, vert.
994 A145 75d Germany, vert.

995 A145 75d New Delhi, vert.
996 A145 75d Brazil, vert.
997 A145 200d Two leaving terminal

Souvenir Sheets
998 A145 500d Engine 120, vert.
999 A145 500d Engine 151-001

Birds — A146

1991, July 8　*Perf. 13¹/₂x14*
1000 A146 75d Psittacula kuhlii
1001 A146 75d Plydolophus rosaceus
1002 A146 75d Falco tinnunculus
1003 A146 75d Platycercus palliceps
1004 A146 200d Marcrocercus aracanga

Souvenir Sheets
1005 A146 500d Ramphastos culmenatus
1006 A146 500d Strix nyctea

Paintings — A147

Designs: 50d, Venus and Cupid, by Titian. No. 1008, Horse's Head (detail), by Rubens. No. 1009, Child's face (detail), by Rubens. 100d, Spanish Woman, by Picasso. 200d, Man with Christian Flag, by Titian. No. 1012, Study of a Negro, by Rubens. No. 1013, Madonna and Child, by Raphael.

1991, July 31
1007 A147 50d multicolored
1008 A147 75d multicolored
1009 A147 75d multicolored
1010 A147 100d multicolored
1011 A147 200d multicolored

Souvenir Sheets
1012 A147 500d multicolored
1013 A147 500d multicolored

Mushroom Type of 1990
1991, Aug. 30
1014 A139 50d Clitocybe geotropa
1015 A139 50d Lepiota procera
1016 A139 75d Boletus granulatus
1017 A139 125d Coprinus comatus
1018 A139 200d Amanita rubescens

Souvenir Sheets
1019 A139 500d Armillariella mellea

Perf. 14x13¹/₂
1020 A139 500d Nictalis parasitica, horiz.

Flowers — A148

Designs: No. 1022, Zan tedeschia elliotiana. No. 1023, Cyrtanthes pohliana. No. 1024, Phalaenopsis lueddemanniana. No. 1025, Haemanthus katharinae. 500d, Arundina graminifolia.

1991, Sept. 9　*Perf. 13¹/₂x14*
1021 A148 50d shown
1022 A148 50d multicolored
1023 A148 100d multicolored
1024 A148 100d multicolored
1025 A148 200d multicolored

Souvenir Sheet
1026 A148 500d multicolored

Souvenir Sheet

Iberoamericano '92 Intl. Philatelic Exhibition — A149

1991, Oct. 11　Litho.　*Perf. 14x13¹/₂*
1027 A149 800d multicolored

Discovery of America, 500th Anniv. (in 1992) — A150

1991, Oct. 12　*Perf. 13¹/₂x14*
1028 A150 50d Columbus
1029 A150 50d Sailing ship
1030 A150 75d Sailing ship, diff.
1031 A150 125d Landing in New World
1032 A150 200d Pointing the way

Souvenir Sheet
Perf. 14x13¹/₂
1033 A150 500d Columbus' fleet, horiz.

Butterflies — A151

1991, Oct. 16　*Perf. 14x13¹/₂*
1034 A151 125d Limentis popul
1035 A151 125d Pavon inachis io

Souvenir Sheet
Perf. 13¹/₂x14
1036 A151 500d Zerynthia polyxena

Phila Nippon '91.

1991, Nov. 15　*Perf. 14x13¹/₂*
1037 A151 125d Macaon papilio machaon
1038 A151 125d Gran pavon
1039 A151 125d Pavon inachis io, diff.
1040 A151 125d Artia caja

Souvenir Sheet
Perf. 13¹/₂x14
1041 A151 500d Unnamed butterfly, vert.

Christmas.

Landmarks — A152

Fauna — A153

Landmarks of France: No. 1042, Ile de France, vert. No. 1043, Chenonceau Castle. No. 1044, Azay-le-Rideau Castle. No. 1045, Chambord Castle. No. 1046, Chaumont Castle. No. 1047, Fountainebleau Palace.
Animals and birds: No. 1048a, Weasel, monkey. b, Civet, rats. c, Goat, cow. d, Rabbits, wildcat. e, Parrot, black bird. f, White bird, multicolored bird.

Perf. 13¹/₂x14, 14x13¹/₂
1991, Nov. 15
1042-1048 A152   25d Set of 7
Souvenir Sheet
1049   A152 500d Paris map, 1615

Express Mail Service from St. Thomas and Prince — A154

1991   Litho.   Perf. 14
1050 A154 3000d multicolored

Souvenir Sheets

1991 Intl. Olympic Committee Session, Birmingham A154a

Designs: No. 1050A, IOC emblem, Birmingham Session. No. 1050B, 1998 Winter Olympics emblem, Nagano. No. 1050C, 1998 Winter Olympics mascot.

1992   Litho.   Perf. 14
1050A A154a 800d multicolored
1050B A154a 800d multicolored
1050C A154a 800d multicolored

Souvenir Sheet

IBEREX '91 — A154b

1992
1050D A154b 800d multicolored

Souvenir Sheet

1992 Winter Olympics, Albertville — A154c

1992
1050E A154c 50d Olympic medals

No. 1050E exists with pictures of different medalists in sheet margin: Blanca Fernandez, Spain; Alberto Tomba, Italy; Mark Kirchner, Germany; Torgny Mogren, Norway.

1992 Summer Olympics, Barcelona A154d

View of earth from space with: No. 1050F, High jumper. No. 1050G, Roller hockey player. No. 1050H, Equestrian. No. 1050I, Kayaker. No. 1050J, Weight lifter. No. 1050K, Archer. No. 1050L, Michael Jordan, horiz.

1992
1050F-1050K A154d 50d Set of 6
Souvenir Sheet
1050L A154d 50d multicolored

Whales — A155

Designs: No. 1051, Orcinus orca. No. 1052, Orcinus orca, two under water. No. 1053, Pseudoraca crassidens. No. 1054, Pseudoraca crassidens, three under water.

1992   Litho.   Perf. 14
1051-1054 A155 450d Set of 4

World Wildlife Fund.

Visit of Pope John Paul II A155a

Designs: No. 1054c, Flags, Pope. No. 1054d, Church with two steeples. No. 1054e, Church, diff. No. 1054f, Pope, vert. No. 1054g, Church, blue sky, vert. No. 1054h, Church, closer view, vert.

1992, Apr. 19   Litho.   Perf. 14
Sheets of 4
1054A A155a 200d 2 #1054c, 1 each #d.-e.
1054B A155a 200d 2 #1054f, 1 each #g.-h.

Flora and Fauna Type of 1991

Designs: No. 1054I, 1000d, Brown & white bird, vert. No. 1054J, 1500d, Yellow flower, vert. No. 1054K, 2000d, Red flower, vert. No. 1054L, 2500d, Black bird, vert.

1992, Apr. 19
1054I-1054L A144 Set of 4

Souvenir Sheet

Olymphilex '92 — A156

Olympic athletes: a, Women's running. b, Women's gymnastics. c, Earvin "Magic" Johnson.

1992, July 29
1055 A156 300d Sheet of 3, #a.-c.

Mushrooms A157

Designs: 75d, Leccinum ocabrum. 100d, Amanita spissa, horiz. 125d, Strugilomyces floccopus. 200d, Suillus luteus. 500d, Agaricus siluaticus. No. 1061, Amanita pantherma, horiz. No. 1062, Agaricus campestre.

1992, Sept. 5   Perf. 14
1056 A157   75d multicolored
1057 A157 100d multicolored
1058 A157 125d multicolored
1059 A157 200d multicolored
1060 A157 500d multicolored
Souvenir Sheets
Perf. 14x13¹/₂, 13¹/₂x14
1061 A157 1000d multicolored
1062 A157 1000d multicolored

Birds — A158

Designs: 75d, Paradisea regie, pipra rupicole. 100d, Trogon pavonis. 125d, Paradisea apoda. 200d, Pavocriotctus. 500d, Ramphatos maximus. No. 1068, Woodpecker. No. 1069, Picus major.

1992, Sept. 15   Perf. 14
1063 A158   75d multicolored
1064 A158 100d multicolored
1065 A158 125d multicolored
1066 A158 200d multicolored
1067 A158 500d multicolored
Souvenir Sheets
Perf. 13¹/₂x14
1068 A158 1000d multicolored
1069 A158 1000d multicolored

Marcelo da Veiga (1892-1976), Writer A159

Designs: a, 10d. b, 40d. c, 50d. d, 100d.

1992, Oct. 3   Perf. 13¹/₂
1070 A159 Sheet of 4, #a.-d.

Locomotives — A160

Designs: 75d, 100d, 125d, 200d, 500d, Various locomotives. No. 1076, Steam train arriving at station. No. 1077, Engineer, stoker in locomotive cab.

1992, Oct. 3   Perf. 14x13¹/₂
1071 A160   75d black
1072 A160 100d black
1073 A160 125d black
1074 A160 200d black
1075 A160 500d black
Souvenir Sheets
1076 A160 1000d black
1077 A160 1000d black

Butterflies and Moths — A161

Designs: 75d, Chelonia purpurea. 100d, Hoetera philocteles. 125d, Attacus pavonia major. 200d, Ornithoptera urvilliana. 500d, Acherontia atropos. No. 1083, Peridromia amphinome, vert. No. 1084, Uramia riphacus, vert.

1992, Oct. 18   Perf. 14x13¹/₂
1078 A161   75d multicolored
1079 A161 100d multicolored
1080 A161 125d multicolored
1081 A161 200d multicolored
1082 A161 500d multicolored

Souvenir Sheets
Perf. 13¹/₂x14

1083 A161 1000d multicolored
1084 A161 1000d multicolored

1992, 1996 Summer Olympics, Barcelona
and Atlanta — A162

Designs: 50d, Wind surfing. No. 1086, Wrestling. No. 1087, Women's 4x100 meters relay. No. 1088, Swimming. No. 1089, Equestrian, vert. No. 1090, Field hockey. No. 1091, Men's 4x100 meters relay, vert. No. 1092, Mascots for Barcelona and Atlanta. No. 1093, Opening ceremony, Barcelona.
No. 1094, Atlanta '96 Emblem, vert. No. 1095, Archer lighting Olympic Flame with flaming arrow, vert. No. 1096, Transfer of Olympic Flag, closing ceremony, vert. No. 1097, Gymnastics.

1992, Oct. 1   Litho.   Perf. 14
1085 A162   50d multicolored
1086 A162 300d multicolored
1087 A162 300d multicolored
1088 A162 300d multicolored
1089 A162 300d multicolored
1090 A162 300d multicolored
1091 A162 300d multicolored
1092 A162 300d multicolored
1093 A162 300d multicolored

Souvenir Sheets
1094 A162 800d multicolored
1095 A162 1000d multicolored
1096 A162 1000d multicolored

Perf. 13¹/₂
1097 A162 1000d multicolored

A number has been reserved for an additional souvenir sheet with this set.

Butterflies — A163   Flowers — A164

Designs: No. 1099, White butterfly. No. 1100, Black and orange butterfly. No. 1101, Pink flower, black, white, red and blue butterfly. No. 1102, Black and white butterfly on right side of flower stem. No. 1103, Yellow and black butterfly. 2000d, Iris flower, black butterfly wing, horiz.

1993, May 26   Litho.   Perf. 14
1099-1103 A163 500d Set of 5

Souvenir Sheet
1104   A163 2000d multicolored

1993, June 18
1105 A164 500d Fucinho de porco
1106 A164 500d Heliconia
1107 A164 500d Gravo nacional
1108 A164 500d Tremessura
1109 A164 500d Anturius

Souvenir Sheet
1110 A164 2000d Girassol

Miniature Sheet

Union of Portuguese Speaking Capitals — A165

Designs: a, 100d, Emblem. b, 150d, Grotto. c, 200d, Statue of Christ the Redeemer, Rio de Janeiro. d, 250d, Skyscraper. e, 250d, Monument. f, 300d, Building with pointed domed roof. g, 350d, Municipal building. h, 400d, Square tower. i, 500d, Residence, flag, truck.

1993, July 30
1111 A165   Sheet of 9, #a.-i.

Brasiliana '93.

Birds — A166

Designs: No. 1112, Cecia. No. 1113, Sui-sui. No. 1114, Falcon. No. 1115, Parrot. No. 1116, Heron.

1993, June 15   Litho.   Perf. 14
1112-1116 A166 500d Set of 5

Souvenir Sheet
1117   A166 1000d Macaw, toucan, horiz.

Dinosaurs — A167

Designs: No. 1118, Lystrosaurus. No. 1119, Patagosaurus. No. 1120, Shonisaurus ictiosaurios, vert. No. 1121, Dilophosaurus, vert. No. 1122, Dicraeosaurus, vert. No. 1123, Tyrannosaurus rex, vert.

1993, July 21
1118-1123 A167 500d Set of 6

Souvenir Sheets
1124 A167 1000d Protoavis
1125 A167 1000d Brachiosaurus

Mushrooms A168

Designs: No. 1126, Agrocybe aegerita. No. 1127, Psalliota arvensis. No. 1128, Coprinus comatus.

No. 1129, Hygrophorus psittacinus. No. 1130, Amanita caesarea.
No. 1131, Ramaria aurea. No. 1132, Pluteus murinus, horiz.

1993, May 25   Litho.   Perf. 14
1126-1130 A168 800d Set of 5

Souvenir Sheets
1131-1132 A168 2000d Set of 2

Locomotives — A169

Nos. 1133-1137, Various views of small diesel locomotive.
Nos. 1138-1139, Various steam locomotives, vert.

1993, June 16
1133-1137 A169 800d Set of 5

Souvenir Sheets
1138-1139 A169 2000d Set of 2

1994 World Cup Soccer Championships,
US — A170

Designs: No. 1140, Team photo. Nos. 1141-1147, Players in action.
No. 1148, Fans, faces painted as flags. No. 1149, Stylized player.

1994, July 6
1140-1147 A170 800d Set of 8

Souvenir Sheets
1148-1149 A170 2000d Set of 2

UPU Congress — A171

1994, Aug. 16
1150 A171 1000d shown

Souvenir Sheet
1151 A171 2000d Ship

AIR POST STAMPS

Common Design Type
Inscribed "S. Tomé"
1938   Perf. 13¹/₂x13
Name and Value in Black

C1 CD39 10c scarlet   30.00 22.50
C2 CD39 20c purple   15.00 11.00
C3 CD39 50c orange   1.50 1.25
C4 CD39 1e ultra   2.50 2.00
C5 CD39 2e lilac brown   3.75 3.00
C6 CD39 3e dark green   5.75 4.00
C7 CD39 5e red brown   7.50 6.50
C8 CD39 9e rose carmine   8.50 6.50
C9 CD39 10e magenta   9.50 6.50
    Nos. C1-C9 (9)   84.00 63.25

Common Design Type
Inscribed "S. Tomé e Principe"
1939   Engr.   Unwmk.
Name and Value Typo. in Black

C10 CD39 10c scarlet   38   25
C11 CD39 20c purple   38   25
C12 CD39 50c orange   38   25
C13 CD39 1e deep ultra   38   25
C14 CD39 2e lilac brown 1.40 1.10
C15 CD39 3e dark green   2.00 1.25
C16 CD39 5e red brown   2.75 1.75
C17 CD39 9e rose carmine 4.75 2.50
C18 CD39 10e magenta   5.50 2.50
    Nos. C10-C18 (9)   17.92 10.10

No. C16 exists with overprint "Exposicao International de Nova York, 1939-1940" and Trylon and Perisphere.

POSTAGE DUE STAMPS

"S. Thomé" — D1

1904   Unwmk.   Typo.   Perf. 12
J1 D1   5r yellow green   55   55
J2 D1 10r slate   65   65
J3 D1 20r yellow brown   65   65
J4 D1 30r orange   80   65
J5 D1 50r gray brown   1.40 1.40
J6 D1 60r red brown   1.75 1.65
J7 D1 100r red lilac   2.75 1.75
J8 D1 130r dull blue   4.00 3.25
J9 D1 200r carmine   4.00 3.50
J10 D1 500r gray violet   6.50 5.00
    Nos. J1-J10 (10)   23.05 19.05

Overprinted in
Carmine or Green

REPUBLICA

1911
J11 D1   5r yellow green   25   25
J12 D1 10r slate   25   25
J13 D1 20r yellow brown   25   25
J14 D1 30r orange   25   25
J15 D1 50r gray brown   25   25
J16 D1 60r red brown   60   60
J17 D1 100r red lilac   70   70
J18 D1 130r dull blue   70   70
J19 D1 200r carmine (G)   70   70
J20 D1 500r gray violet   1.10 1.10
    Nos. J11-J20 (10)   5.05 5.05

Nos. J1-J10 Overprinted
in Black

REPUBLICA

1913   Without Gum
J21 D1   5r yellow green   3.75 3.75
J22 D1 10r slate   5.00 4.50
J23 D1 20r yellow brown   2.50 2.50
J24 D1 30r orange   2.50 2.50
J25 D1 50r gray brown   2.50 2.50
J26 D1 60r red brown   3.00 3.00
J27 D1 100r red lilac   5.00 4.00
J28 D1 130r dull blue   21.00 21.00
 a. Inverted overprint   40.00 40.00
J29 D1 200r carmine   27.50 22.50
J30 D1 500r gray violet   30.00 27.50
    Nos. J21-J30 (10)   102.75 93.75

Nos. J1-J10
Overprinted in Black

REPUBLICA

1913   Without Gum
J31 D1   5r yellow green   1.75 1.75
 a. Inverted overprint
J32 D1 10r slate   2.25 2.25
J33 D1 20r yellow brown   1.75 1.75

J34	D1	30r orange	1.75	1.75
a.		Inverted overprint		
J35	D1	50r gray brown	1.75	1.75
J36	D1	60r red brown	2.75	2.25
J37	D1	100r red lilac	2.75	2.25
J38	D1	130r dull blue	2.75	2.75
J39	D1	200r carmine	4.50	3.50
J40	D1	500r gray violet	13.00	13.00
		Nos. J31-J40 (10)	35.00	33.00

No. J5 Overprinted "Republica" in Italic Capitals like Regular Issue in Green

1920			**Without Gum**	
J41	D1	50r gray brn	40.00	35.00

"S. Tomé" — D2

1921		**Typo.**	**Perf. 11½**	
J42	D2	½c yellow green	20	15
J43	D2	1c slate	20	15
J44	D2	2c orange brown	20	15
J45	D2	3c orange	20	15
J46	D2	5c gray brown	20	15
J47	D2	6c lt brown	20	15
J48	D2	10c red violet	20	15
J49	D2	13c dull blue	25	20
J50	D2	20c carmine	25	20
J51	D2	50c gray	35	40
		Nos. J42-J51 (10)	2.25	1.85

In each sheet one stamp is inscribed "S. Thomé" instead of "S. Tomé." Value, set of 10, $60.

> Catalogue values for unused stamps in this section, from this point to the end of the section, are for Never Hinged items.

Common Design Type
Photo. & Typo.

1952		**Unwmk.**	**Perf. 14**	
		Numeral in Red, Frame Multicolored		
J52	CD45	10c chocolate	15	15
J53	CD45	30c red brown	15	15
J54	CD45	50c dark blue	15	15
J55	CD45	1e dark blue	25	25
J56	CD45	2e olive green	60	60
J57	CD45	5e black brown	1.25	1.25
		Nos. J52-J57 (6)	2.55	2.55

NEWSPAPER STAMPS

N1   N2

		Perf. 11½, 12½ and 13½		
1892		**Without Gum**	**Unwmk.**	
		Black Surcharge		
P1	N1	2½r on 10r green	95.00	55.00
P2	N1	2½r on 20r rose	125.00	57.50
P3	N2	2½r on 10r green	125.00	57.50
P4	N2	2½r on 20r rose	125.00	57.50
		Green Surcharge		
P5	N1	2½r on 5r black	67.50	30.00
P6	N1	2½r on 20r rose	125.00	57.50
P8	N2	2½r on 5r black	125.00	60.00
P9	N2	2½r on 10r green	125.00	62.50
P10	N2	2½r on 20r rose	125.00	77.50

Both surcharges exist on No. 18 in green.

N3   d

1893		**Typo.**	**Perf. 11½, 13½**	
P12	N3	2½r brown		45 40

For surcharges and overprints see Nos. 85, 166, 275, P13.

No. P12 Overprinted Type "d" in Blue

1899				
		Without Gum		
P13	N3	2½r brown	25.00	16.00

POSTAL TAX STAMPS

Pombal Issue
Common Design Types

1925		**Unwmk.**	**Perf. 12½**	
RA1	CD28	15c orange & black	45	45
RA2	CD29	15c orange & black	45	45
RA3	CD30	15c orange & black	45	45

Certain revenue stamps (5e, 6e, 7e, 8e and other denominations) were surcharged in 1946 "Assistencia", 2 bars and new values (1e and 1.50e) and used as postal tax stamps.

> Catalogue values for unused stamps in this section, from this point to the end of the section, are for Never Hinged items.

PT1   0$50

1948-58		**Typo.**	**Perf. 12x11½**	
		Denomination in Black		
RA4	PT1	50c yellow grn	4.00	1.10
RA5	PT1	1e carmine rose	4.25	1.50
RA6	PT1	1e emerald ('58)	1.75	75
RA7	PT1	1.50e bister brown	2.50	1.90

Denominations of 2e and up were used only for revenue purposes. No. RA6 lacks "Colonia de" below coat of arms.

Type of 1958 Surcharged

um escudo   Um escudo

1$00   1$00

m   n

1964-65		**Typo.**	**Perf. 12x11½**	
RA8	PT1(m)	1e on 5e org yel	12.00	12.00
RA9	PT1(n)	1e on 5e org yel ('65)	4.50	4.50

The basic 5e orange yellow does not carry the words "Colonia de."

No. RA6 Surcharged: "Um escudo"

1965				
RA10	PT1	1e emerald	2.00	2.00

1$00

Type of 1948 Surcharged

UM
ESCUDO

1965		**Typo.**	**Perf. 12x11½**	
RA11	PT1	1e emerald		40 40

POSTAL TAX DUE STAMPS

Pombal Issue
Common Design Types

1925		**Unwmk.**	**Perf. 12½**	
RAJ1	CD31	30c orange & black	75	75
RAJ2	CD32	30c orange & black	75	75
RAJ3	CD33	30c orange & black	75	75

SALVADOR, EL

LOCATION — On the Pacific coast of Central America, between Guatemala, Honduras and the Gulf of Fonseca
GOVT. — Republic
AREA — 8,236 sq. mi.
POP. — 5,300,000 (est. 1984)
CAPITAL — San Salvador

8 Reales = 100 Centavos = 1 Peso
100 Centavos = 1 Colón

> Catalogue values for unused stamps in this country are for Never Hinged items, beginning with Scott 589 in the regular postage section, Scott C85 in the airpost section, and Scott O362 in the official section.

Watermarks

Wmk. 117- Liberty Cap   Position of wmk. on reprints

Wmk. 172- Honeycomb

Wmk. 173- S

Wmk. 240- REPUBLICA DE EL SALVADOR in Sheet

Wmk. 269- REPUBLICA DE EL SALVADOR

Volcano San Miguel — A1

1867		**Unwmk.**	**Engr.**	**Perf. 12**	
1	A1	½r blue		65	75
2	A1	1r red		65	65
3	A1	2r green		1.50	2.00
4	A1	4r bister		3.50	3.00

Nos. 1-4 when overprinted "Contra Sello" and shield with 14 stars, are telegraph stamps. For similar overprint see Nos. 5-12.

Nos. 1-4 Handstamped

1874					
5	A1	½r blue		6.50	3.50
6	A1	1r red		6.50	3.50
7	A1	2r green		6.50	3.50
8	A1	4r bister		19.00	17.50

Nos. 1-4 Handstamped

9	A1	½r blue		3.75	2.00
10	A1	1r red		3.75	2.00
11	A1	2r green		3.75	2.00
12	A1	4r bister		7.50	5.00

The overprints on Nos. 5-12 exist double. Counterfeits are plentiful.

Coat of Arms
A2   A3

A4   A5

A6

1879		**Litho.**	**Perf. 12½**	
13	A2	1c green	2.00	90
a.		Invtd. "V" for 2nd "A" in "SALVADOR"	4.00	2.00
b.		Invtd. "V" for "A" in "REPUBLICA"	4.00	2.00
c.		Invtd. "V" for "A" in "UNIVERSAL"	4.00	2.00
14	A3	2c rose	2.75	1.50
a.		Invtd. scroll in upper left corner	8.00	5.00

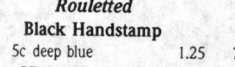

15	A4	5c blue	5.00 1.25
a.		5c ultra	8.00 4.00
16	A5	10c black	10.00 3.50
17	A6	20c violet	16.00 10.00
		Nos. 13-17 (5)	35.75 17.15

There are fifteen varieties of the 1c and 2c, twenty-five of the 5c and five each of the 10 and 20c.

In 1881 the 1c, 2c and 5c were redrawn, the 1c in fifteen varieties and the 2c and 5c in five varieties each.

No. 15 comes in a number of shades from light to dark blue.

These stamps, when overprinted "Contra sello" and arms, are telegraph stamps.
For overprints see Nos. 25D-25E, 28A-28C.

Allegorical Figure of El Salvador — A7   Volcano — A8

1887   Engr.   Perf. 12
18	A7	3c brown	38 18
a.		Imperf., pair	2.50 2.50
19	A8	10c orange	3.00 90

For surcharges and overprints see Nos. 25, 26C-28, 30-32.

A9   A10

1888   Rouletted
20	A9	5c deep blue	30 25

For overprints see Nos. 35-36.

1889   Perf. 12
21	A10	1c green	15
22	A10	2c scarlet	15

Same Overprinted with Heavy Bar Obliterating "UNION POSTAL DEL"
23	A10	1c green	30 25
24	A10	2c scarlet	30

Nos. 21, 22 and 24 were never placed in use.
For overprints see Nos. 26, 29.

No. 18 Surcharged   **1 centavo**

Type I - thick numerals, heavy serifs.
Type II - thin numerals, straight serifs.
25	A7	1c on 3c brn, type II	65 50
a.		Double surcharge	1.50
b.		Triple surcharge	3.50
c.		Type I	65

The 1c on 2c scarlet is bogus.

Handstamped   **1889.**

1889
Violet Handstamp
25D	A2	1c green	12.50 12.50
25E	A6	20c violet	30.00 30.00
26	A10	1c green, #23	1.00 90
26C	A7	1c on 3c, #27	20.00 20.00
27	A7	3c brown	1.00 90
28	A8	10c orange	5.00 4.00

Black Handstamp
28A	A2	1c green	15.00 14.00
28B	A3	2c rose	17.50 17.50
28C	A6	20c violet	30.00 30.00
29	A10	1c green, #23	1.25 1.00
30	A7	3c brown	1.25 1.00
31	A7	1c on 3c, #27	17.50 17.50
32	A8	10c orange	4.50 3.50

Rouletted
Black Handstamp
35	A9	5c deep blue	1.25 75

Violet Handstamp
36	A9	5c deep blue	1.25 75

The 1889 handstamps as usual, are found double, inverted, etc. Counterfeits are plentiful.

A13   A14

1890   Engr.   *Perf. 12*
38	A13	1c green	15 15
39	A13	2c bis brn	15 15
40	A13	3c yellow	15 15
41	A13	5c blue	15 15
42	A13	10c violet	15 15
43	A13	20c orange	15 20
44	A13	25c red	50 1.00
45	A13	50c claret	15 65
46	A13	1p carmine	15 1.50
		Set value	1.08

The issues of 1890 to 1898 inclusive were printed by the Hamilton Bank Note Co., New York, to the order of N. F. Seebeck, who held a contract for stamps with the government of El Salvador. This contract gave the right to make reprints of the stamps and such were subsequently made in some instances, as will be found noted in italic type.

Used values of 1890-1898 issues are for stamps with genuine cancellations applied while the stamps were valid. Various counterfeit cancellations exist.

1891
47	A14	1c vermilion	15 15
48	A14	2c yellow green	15 15
49	A14	3c violet	15 15
50	A14	5c carmine lake	15 15
51	A14	10c blue	15 15
52	A14	11c violet	15 15
53	A14	20c green	15 32
54	A14	25c yellow brown	15 38
55	A14	50c dark blue	15 90
56	A14	1p dark brown	15 1.50
		Set value	1.20

For surcharges see Nos. 57-59.
Nos. 47 and 56 have been reprinted in thick toned paper with dark gum.

A15

Nos. 48, 49 Surcharged in Black or Violet:

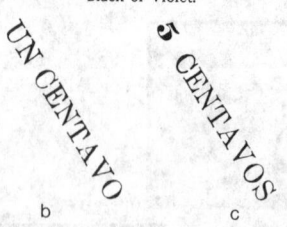

b   c

1891
57	A15	1c on 2c yellow grn	2.25 2.00
a.		Inverted surcharge	4.00
58	A14 (b)	1c on 2c yellow grn	1.65 1.40
59	A14 (c)	5c on 3c violet	4.00 3.25

Landing of Columbus — A18

1892   Engr.
60	A18	1c blue green	15 15
61	A18	2c orange brown	15 15
62	A18	3c ultra	15 15
63	A18	5c gray	15 15
64	A18	10c vermilion	15 15
65	A18	11c brown	15 38
66	A18	20c orange	15 38
67	A18	25c maroon	15 45
68	A18	50c yellow	15 90
69	A18	1p carmine lake	15 1.25
		Set value	1.20

400th anniversary of the discovery of America by Columbus.

Nos. 63, 66-67 Surcharged

UN CENTAVO   Nos. 70, 72
UN CENTAVO   Nos. 73-75

Surcharged in Black, Red or Yellow

1892
70	A18	1c on 5c gray (Bk) (down)	1.00 65
a.		Surcharge reading up	1.75 1.10
72	A18	1c on 5c gray (R) (up)	1.00 80
a.		Surcharge reading down	
73	A18	1c on 20c org (Bk)	1.25 75
a.		Inverted surcharge	3.50 2.50
b.		"V" of "CENTAVO" inverted	3.50 2.50

Similar Surcharge in Yellow or Blue, "centavo" in lower case letters
74	A18	1c on 25c mar (Y)	1.50 1.25
a.		Inverted surcharge	2.50 2.50
75	A18	1c on 25c mar (Bl)	200.00 200.00
a.		Double surcharge (Bl + Bk)	225.00 225.00

Counterfeits exist of Nos. 75 and 75a. Nos. 75, 75a have been questioned.

Gen. Carlos Ezeta — A21

1893   Engr.
76	A21	1c blue	15 15
77	A21	2c brown red	15 15
78	A21	3c purple	15 15
79	A21	5c deep brown	15 15
80	A21	10c orange brown	15 15
81	A21	11c vermilion	15 22
82	A21	20c green	15 28
83	A21	25c dk olive gray	15 38
84	A21	50c red orange	15 50
85	A21	1p black	15 75
		Set value	1.20

For surcharge see No. 89.

Founding City of Isabela — A22   Columbus Statue, Genoa — A23

Departure from Palos — A24

1893
86	A22	2p green	75
87	A23	5p violet	75
88	A24	10p orange	75

Nos. 86 to 88 commemorate the discoveries by Columbus. No. 86 is known on cover, but experts

---

are not positive that Nos. 87 and 88 were postally used.

No. 77 Surcharged "UN CENTAVO"

1893
89	A21	1c on 2c brown red	50 42
a.		"CENTNVO"	3.00 3.00

Liberty A26   Columbus before Council of Salamanca A27

Columbus Protecting Indian Hostages — A28

Columbus Received by Ferdinand and Isabella — A29

1894, Jan.
91	A26	1c brown	15 15
92	A26	2c blue	15 15
93	A26	3c maroon	15 15
94	A26	5c orange brn	15 15
95	A26	10c violet	15 15
96	A26	11c vermilion	15 25
97	A26	20c dark blue	15 32
98	A26	25c orange	15 38
99	A26	50c black	15 65
100	A26	1p slate blue	15 90
101	A27	2p deep blue	75
102	A28	5p carmine lake	75
103	A29	10p deep brown	75
		Nos. 91-103 (13)	3.75

Nos. 101-103 for the discoveries by Columbus. Experts are not positive that these were postally used.

No. 96 Surcharged   **1 Centavo**

1894, Dec.
104	A26	1c on 11c vermilion	1.50 65
a.		"Ccntavo"	20.00 20.00
b.		Double surcharge	

Coat of Arms
A31   A32

Arms Overprint in Second Color Various Frames

1895, Jan. 1
105	A31	1c olive & green	20 20
106	A31	2c dk green & bl	20 20
a.		2c dark green & green	1.00 85
107	A31	3c brown & brown	20 20
108	A31	5c blue & brown	20 20
109	A31	10c orange & brn	20 25
110	A31	12c magenta & brn	20 30
111	A31	15c ver & ver	20 35
112	A31	20c yellow & brn	20 42
a.		Inverted overprint	2.00
113	A31	24c violet & brn	20 45
114	A31	30c dp blue & blue	20 50
115	A31	50c carmine & brn	20 65
116	A31	1p black & brn	20 90
		Nos. 105-116 (12)	2.40 4.62

As printed, Nos. 105-116 portrayed Pres. Antonio Ezeta, brother of Gen. Carlos Ezeta. Before issuance, Ezeta's overthrow caused the government to obliterate his features with the national arms overprint. The 3c, 10c, 30c exist without overprint. Value $1 each.

Reprints of 2c are in dark yellow green on thick paper. Value 15 cents.

1895   Engr.   Perf. 12

117	A32	1c olive	60	50
118	A32	2c dk blue grn	15	15
119	A32	3c brown	15	15
120	A32	5c blue	15	15
121	A32	10c orange	65	30
122	A32	12c claret	65	30
123	A32	15c vermilion	15	30
124	A32	20c deep green	18	50
125	A32	24c violet	18	50
126	A32	30c deep blue	15	45
127	A32	50c carmine lake	1.00	1.25
128	A32	1p gray black	1.25	1.75
		Nos. 117-128 (12)	5.26	6.30

The reprints are on thicker paper than the originals, and many of the shades differ. Value 15c each.

Nos. 122, 124-126 Surcharged in Black or Red:

UN centavo

1895

129	A32	1c on 12c claret (Bk)	1.00	90
130	A32	1c on 24c violet	1.00	90
131	A32	1c on 30c dp blue	1.00	90
132	A32	2c on 20c dp green	1.00	90
133	A32	3c on 30c dp blue	1.25	1.10
a.		Double surcharge	4.50	
		Nos. 129-133 (5)	5.25	4.70

"Peace" — A45

1896, Jan. 1   Engr.   Unwmk.

134	A45	1c blue	15	15
135	A45	2c dark brown	15	15
136	A45	3c blue green	15	15
137	A45	5c brown olive	15	15
138	A45	10c yellow	15	20
139	A45	12c dark blue	75	90
140	A45	15c brt ultra	15	20
a.		15c light violet	1.00	2.00
141	A45	20c magenta	65	50
142	A45	24c vermilion	15	25
143	A45	30c orange	15	42
144	A45	50c black brn	15	50
145	A45	1p rose lake	15	90
		Nos. 134-145 (12)	2.90	4.47

The frames of Nos. 134-145 differ slightly on each denomination.
For overprints see Nos. O1-O12, O37-O48.

Wmk. 117

| 145B | A45 | 2c dark brown | 20 | 20 |

The 1c, 2c, 12c, 20c, 30c, 50c and 1p on unwatermarked paper and the 2c on watermarked have been reprinted. The paper is thicker than that of the originals and the shades are different. The watermark is always upright on original stamps of Salvador, sideways on the reprints. Value 15c each.

Coat of Arms — A46   "White House" — A47

Locomotive — A48   Mt. San Miguel — A49

Ocean Steamship
A50   A51

Post Office — A52   Lake Ilopango — A53

Atehausillas Waterfall — A54   Coat of Arms — A55

Coat of Arms — A56   Columbus — A57

1896

146	A46	1c emerald	18	18
147	A47	2c lake	18	18
148	A48	3c yellow brn	18	18
149	A49	5c deep blue	18	18
150	A50	10c brown	18	18
151	A51	12c slate	18	18
152	A52	15c blue green	18	25
153	A53	20c carmine rose	18	30
154	A54	24c violet	18	38
155	A55	30c deep green	18	38
156	A56	50c orange	18	38
157	A57	100c dark blue	18	90
		Nos. 146-157 (12)	2.16	3.67

Nos. 146-157 exist imperf.

Unwmk.

157B	A46	1c emerald	15	15
157C	A47	2c lake	15	15
157D	A48	3c yellow brn	15	15
157E	A49	5c deep blue	15	15
157F	A50	10c brown	18	18
157G	A51	12c slate	15	18
157I	A52	15c blue green	22	25
157J	A53	20c carmine rose	15	38
157K	A54	24c violet	50	90
157M	A55	30c deep green	15	65
157N	A56	50c orange	15	65
157O	A57	100c dark blue	15	1.10
		Nos. 157B-157O (12)	2.25	4.89

See Nos. 159-170L. For surcharges and overprints see Nos. 158, 158D, 171-174C, O13-O36, O49-O72, O79-O126.

The 15c, 30c, 50c and 100c have been reprinted on watermarked and the 1c, 2c, 3c, 5c, 12c, 20c, 24c and 100c on unwatermarked paper. The papers of the reprints are thicker than those of the originals and the shades are different. Value, set of 12, $1.20.

Black Surcharge on Nos. 154, 157K

Quince centavos

1896   Wmk. 117

158	A54	15c on 24c violet	4.00	4.00
a.		Double surcharge		
b.		Inverted surcharge	8.50	

Unwmk.

| 158D | A54 | 15c on 24c violet | 4.00 | 3.00 |

Exist spelled "Qnince."

Types of 1896

1897   Engr.   Wmk. 117

159	A46	1c scarlet	15	15
160	A47	2c yellow grn	15	15
161	A48	3c bister brn	15	15
162	A49	5c orange	15	15
163	A50	10c blue grn	15	15
164	A51	12c blue	42	30
165	A52	15c black	2.50	2.00
166	A53	20c slate	15	15

167	A54	24c yellow	15	25
168	A55	30c rose	15	20
169	A56	50c violet	18	50
170	A57	100c brown lake	2.50	2.00
		Nos. 159-170 (12)	6.80	6.15

Unwmk.

170A	A46	1c scarlet	15	15
170B	A47	2c yellow grn	15	15
170C	A48	3c bister brn	15	15
170D	A49	5c orange	15	15
170E	A50	10c blue grn	75	50
170F	A51	12c blue	75	75
170G	A52	15c black	2.00	2.00
170H	A53	20c slate	15	25
170I	A54	24c yellow	15	50
170J	A55	30c rose	1.90	1.25
170K	A56	50c violet	90	90
170L	A57	100c brown lake	6.25	6.25
		Nos. 170A-170L (12)	13.45	13.00

The 1c, 2c, 3c, 5c, 12c, 15c, 50c and 100c have been reprinted on watermarked and the entire issue on unwatermarked paper. The papers of the reprints are thicker than those of the originals. Value, set of 20, $2.

Surcharged in Red or Black

TRECE centavos

1897   Wmk. 117

171	A54	13c on 24c yel (R)	2.50	2.50
172	A55	13c on 30c rose (Bk)	2.50	2.50
173	A56	13c on 50c vio (Bk)	2.50	2.50
174	A57	13c on 100c brn lake (Bk)	2.50	2.50

Unwmk.

174A	A54	13c on 24c yel (R)	2.50	2.50
174B	A55	13c on 30c rose (Bk)	2.50	2.50
174C	A56	13c on 50c vio (Bk)	2.50	2.50

Coat of Arms of "Republic of Central America" — A59

ONE CENTAVO:
Originals: The mountains are outlined in red and blue. The sea is represented by short red and dark blue lines on a light blue background.
Reprints: The mountains are outlined in red only. The sea is printed in green and dark blue, much blurred.

FIVE CENTAVOS:
Originals: The sea is represented by horizontal and diagonal lines of dark blue on a light blue background.
Reprints: The sea is printed in green and dark blue, much blurred. The inscription in gold is in thicker letters.

1897   Litho.

| 175 | A59 | 1c bl, gold, rose & grn | 50 | 1.00 |
| 176 | A59 | 5c rose, gold, bl & grn | 50 | 1.50 |

Forming of the "Republic of Central America." For overprints see Nos. O73-O76.
Stamps of type A59 formerly listed as "Type II" are now known to be reprints.

Allegory of Central American Union — A60

1898   Engr.   Wmk. 117

177	A60	1c orange ver	18	15
178	A60	2c rose	18	18
179	A60	3c pale yel grn	18	18
180	A60	5c blue green	18	15
181	A60	10c gray blue	18	18
182	A60	12c violet	18	25
183	A60	13c brown lake	18	18
184	A60	20c deep blue	18	30
185	A60	24c deep ultra	18	35
186	A60	26c bister brn	18	40
187	A60	50c orange	18	75
188	A60	1p yellow	18	1.00
		Nos. 177-188 (12)	2.16	4.07

For overprints and surcharges see Nos. 189-198A, 224-241, 269A-269B, O129-O142.
The entire set has been reprinted on unwatermarked paper and all but the 12c and 20c on watermarked paper. The shades of the reprints are not the same as those of the originals, and the paper is thicker. Value, set of 22, $2.25.

No. 180 Overprinted Vertically, up or down in Black, Violet, Red, Magenta and Yellow

Transito Territorial

1899

189	A60	5c blue grn (Bk)	7.50	6.25
a.		Italic 3rd "r" in "Territorial"	12.50	12.50
b.		Double ovpt. (Bk + Y)	37.50	37.50
190	A60	5c blue grn (V)	82.50	82.50
191	A60	5c blue grn (R)	70.00	70.00
191A	A60	5c blue grn (M)	70.00	70.00
191B	A60	5c blue grn (Y)	75.00	75.00

Counterfeits exist.

Nos. 177-184 Overprinted in Black

1899

192	A60	1c orange ver	1.00	50
193	A60	2c rose	1.25	1.00
194	A60	3c pale yel grn	1.25	50
195	A60	5c blue green	1.25	50
196	A60	10c gray blue	2.00	1.25
197	A60	12c violet	3.25	2.50
198	A60	13c brown lake	3.25	2.00
198A	A60	20c deep blue	100.00	100.00
		Nos. 192-198A (8)	113.25	108.25

Counterfeits exist of the "wheel" overprint used in 1899-1900.

Ceres ("Estado") — A61

Inscribed: "Estado de El Salvador"

1899   Unwmk.   Litho.   Perf. 12

199	A61	1c brown	15	
200	A61	2c gray green	15	
201	A61	3c blue	15	
202	A61	5c brown org	15	
203	A61	10c chocolate	15	
204	A61	12c dark green	15	
205	A61	13c deep rose	15	
206	A61	24c light blue	15	
207	A61	26c carmine rose	15	
208	A61	50c orange red	15	
209	A61	100c violet	15	
		Set value		1.10

#208-209 were probably not placed in use.
For overprints and surcharges see Nos. 210-223, 242-252D, O143-O185.

Same, Overprinted

Red Overprint

| 210 | A61 | 1c brown | 50.00 | 32.50 |

Blue Overprint

211	A61	1c brown	50	15
212	A61	5c brown org	50	20
212A	A61	10c chocolate	5.00	3.50

Black Overprint

213	A61	1c brown	50	15
214	A61	2c gray grn	75	15
215	A61	3c blue	75	25
216	A61	5c brown org	35	15
217	A61	10c chocolate	50	15
218	A61	12c dark green	1.25	50
219	A61	13c deep rose	1.10	65
220	A61	24c light blue	12.50	10.00
221	A61	26c car rose	3.25	2.00
222	A61	50c orange red	3.25	2.75
223	A61	100c violet	3.25	3.25
		Nos. 213-223 (11)	27.45	20.00

"Wheel" overprint exists double and triple.

No. 177 Handstamped **1900**

1900   Wmk. 117

| 224 | A60 | 1c orange ver | 1.00 | 1.00 |

No. 177 Overprinted **1900**

| 225 | A60 | 1c orange ver | 12.50 | 12.50 |

1900

Stamps of 1898
Surcharged in Black

1 centavo

1900

226	A60	1c on 10c gray blue	5.00	4.25
a.		Inverted surcharge	7.50	6.50
227	A60	1c on 13c brn lake	275.00	
228	A60	2c on 12c vio	17.50	12.50
a.		"eentavo"		
b.		Inverted surcharge		
c.		"centavos"	30.00	
d.		As "c," double surcharge		
e.		Vertical surcharge		
229	A60	2c on 13c brn lake	2.00	1.75
a.		"eentavo"	3.25	2.75
b.		Inverted surcharge	5.00	4.00
c.		"1900" omitted		
230	A60	2c on 20c dp blue	2.00	2.00
a.		Inverted surcharge	3.25	3.25
230B	A60	2c on 26c bis brn	175.00	175.00
231	A60	3c on 12c vio	37.50	37.50
a.		"eentavo"		
b.		Inverted surcharge	35.00	35.00
c.		Double surcharge		
232	A60	3c on 50c org	10.00	10.00
a.		Inverted surcharge	10.00	10.00
233	A60	5c on 12c vio		
234	A60	5c on 24c ultra	11.00	11.00
a.		"eentavo"		
b.		"centavos"	11.00	
235	A60	5c on 26c bis brn	37.50	37.50
a.		Inverted surcharge	35.00	35.00
236	A60	5c on 1p yel	15.00	15.00
a.		Inverted surcharge	15.00	15.00

With Additional Overprint in Black

237	A60	2c on 12c vio	2.50	2.50
a.		Inverted surcharge	2.50	2.50
b.		"eentavo"	8.00	
c.		"centavos" (plural)	75.00	
d.		"1900" omitted		
237H	A60	3c on 13c brn lake		
238	A60	3c on 12c vio	42.50	42.50
a.		"eentavo"	35.00	35.00
239	A60	5c on 26c bis brn	67.50	67.50
a.		Inverted surcharge		

Vertical Surcharge
"Centavos" in the Plural

240	A60	2c on 12c vio	95.00	95.00
b.		Without wheel		
240A	A60	5c on 24c dp ultra	95.00	95.00

With Additional Overprint in Black

241	A60	5c on 12c vio	17.50	17.50
a.		Surcharge reading downward		

Counterfeits exist of the surcharges on Nos. 226-241 and the "wheel" overprint on Nos. 237-239, 241.

Same Surcharge on Stamps of 1898
Without Wheel

1900   **Unwmk.**

242	A61	1c on 13c dp rose	40	40
a.		Inverted surcharge	75	75
b.		"eentavo"	75	75
c.		"ecntavo"	1.25	75
d.		"1 centavo 1"	4.00	3.00
e.		Double surcharge		
243	A61	2c on 12c dk grn	1.75	1.25
a.		Inverted surcharge	2.50	2.50
b.		"eentavo"		
244	A61	2c on 13c dp rose	1.00	75
a.		"eentavo"	1.25	1.25
b.		Inverted surcharge	1.40	1.40
c.		Inverted surcharge		
245	A61	3c on 12c dk grn	1.00	85
a.		Inverted surcharge	2.00	1.50
b.		"eentavo"	4.00	4.00
c.		Double surcharge	2.00	

With Additional Overprint in Black

246	A61	1c on 2c gray grn	25	15
a.		"eentavo"	90	65
b.		Inverted surcharge	4.00	3.00
247	A61	1c on 13c dp rose	1.00	85
a.		"eentavo"	4.00	
b.		"1 centavo 1"		
248	A61	2c on 12c dk grn	1.40	1.00
a.		"eentavo"	4.00	
b.		Inverted surcharge	1.25	1.25
c.		Double surcharge	2.00	
249	A61	2c on 13c dp rose	42.50	
a.		"eentavo"		
b.		Double surcharge	75.00	75.00
250	A61	3c on 12c dk grn	1.40	90
a.		Inverted surcharge	1.50	1.25
b.		"eentavo"	2.50	2.25
c.		Date double	4.00	
251	A61	5c on 24c lt bl	2.50	1.25
a.		"eentavo"	4.00	4.00
252	A61	5c on 26c car rose	1.10	1.00
a.		Inverted surcharge	4.00	2.50
b.		"eentavo"	1.75	1.50

252D	A61	5c on 1c on 26c car rose		
		Nos. 246-248,250-252 (6)	7.65	5.15

Counterfeits exist of the surcharges on Nos. 242-252D and the "wheel" overprint on Nos. 246-252D.

Ceres
("Republica") — A63

There are two varieties of the 1c, type A63, one with the word "centavo" in the middle of the label (#253, 263, 270, 299, 305, 326), the other with "centavo" nearer the left end than the right (#270, 299, 305, 326).

The stamps of type A63 are found in a great variety of shades. Stamps of type A63 without handstamp were not regularly issued.

Handstamped in Violet or
Black

Inscribed: "Republica de El Salvador"

1900

253	A63	1c blue green	20	20
a.		1c yellow green	20	20
254	A63	2c rose	30	20
255	A63	3c gray black	20	20
256	A63	5c pale blue	50	35
a.		5c deep blue	50	35
257	A63	10c deep blue	60	45
258	A63	12c yel green	60	45
259	A63	13c yel brown	50	45
260	A63	24c gray	4.00	4.00
261	A63	26c yel brown	1.75	1.75
262	A63	50c rose red	1.75	1.50
		Nos. 253-262 (10)	10.40	9.55

For overprints and surcharges see Nos. 263-269, 270-282, 293A-311B, 317, 326-335, O223-O242, O258-O262, O305-O312.

Handstamped in Violet
or Black

263	A63	1c lt green	1.75	1.75
264	A63	2c pale rose	1.75	1.75
265	A63	3c gray black	1.75	75
266	A63	5c slate blue	1.75	50
267	A63	10c deep blue	50.00	42.50
268	A63	13c yellow brn	12.50	8.75
269	A63	50c dull rose	1.75	1.75
		Nos. 263-269 (7)	71.25	57.75

Handstamped on 1898 Stamps
Wmk. 117

269A	A60	2c rose	30.00	30.00
269B	A60	10c gray blue	30.00	30.00

The overprints on Nos. 253 to 269B are handstamped and, as usual with that style of overprint, are to be found double, inverted, omitted, etc.

Stamps of Type A63
Overprinted in Black

1900   **Unwmk.**

270	A63	1c light green	20	15
271	A63	2c rose	20	15
272	A63	3c gray black	20	15
273	A63	5c pale blue	20	15
a.		5c dark blue	20	15
274	A63	10c deep blue	40	15
a.		10c pale blue	30	15
275	A63	12c light green	40	30
276	A63	13c yellow brown	20	15
277	A63	24c gray	40	40
278	A63	26c yellow brown	50	50
		Nos. 270-278 (9)	2.70	2.10

This overprint is known double, inverted, etc.

Nos. 271-273 Surcharged in Black

1902

280	A63	1c on 2c rose	2.75	2.25
281	A63	1c on 3c black	2.00	1.40
282	A63	1c on 5c blue	1.25	1.00

Morazán
Monument — A64

Perf. 14, 14½

1903   **Engr.**   **Wmk. 173**

283	A64	1c green	35	15
284	A64	2c carmine	35	15
285	A64	3c orange	80	50
286	A64	5c dark blue	35	15
287	A64	10c dull violet	35	15
288	A64	12c slate	40	15
289	A64	13c red brown	40	18
290	A64	24c scarlet	2.50	15
291	A64	26c yellow brn	2.50	1.25
292	A64	50c bister	1.25	75
293	A64	100c grnsh blue	3.75	2.50
		Nos. 283-293 (11)	13.00	7.18

For surcharges and overprint see Nos. 312-316, 318-325, O253.

Stamps of 1900 with Shield in Black
Overprinted:

1905   1905
(5¾x13½mm)   (5x14¾mm)
a   b

1905   1905
(4½x16mm)   (4½x13½mm)
c   d

(5x14½mm) — e   **1905**

1905-06   **Unwmk.**   **Perf. 12**
Blue Overprint

293A	A63 (a)	2c rose		
294	A63 (a)	3c gray blk	4.00	3.00
a.		Without shield		
295	A63 (a)	5c blue	4.50	3.00

Purple Overprint

296	A63 (b)	3c gray blk (Shield in purple)	4.50	4.00
296A	A63 (b)	5c bl (Shield in purple)	3.25	3.00
297	A63 (b)	3c gray blk	6.00	4.50
298	A63 (b)	5c blue	4.00	3.00

Black Overprint

298A	A63 (b)	5c blue		

Blue Overprint

299	A63 (c)	1c green	4.50	3.00
299B	A63 (c)	2c rose	40	35
a.		"1905" vert.	80	
300	A63 (c)	5c blue	1.25	60
301	A63 (c)	10c deep blue	75	60

Black Overprint

302	A63 (c)	2c rose	3.00	1.50
303	A63 (c)	5c blue	12.50	12.50
304	A63 (c)	10c deep blue	4.00	3.50

Blue Overprint

305	A63 (d)	1c green	5.00	3.50
306	A63 (d)	2c rose (ovpt. vert.)	3.00	1.50
a.		Overprint horiz.		
306B	A63 (d)	3c gray black	5.00	1.75
307	A63 (d)	5c blue	2.50	1.00

Blue Overprint

311	A63 (e)	2c rose	2.50	2.00
a.		Without shield	4.00	3.00

Black Overprint

311B	A63 (e)	5c blue	20.00	19.00

These overprints are found double, inverted, omitted, etc. Counterfeits exist.

Regular Issue of 1903 Surcharged with
New Values:

UN CENTAVO   5 CENTAVOS
f   g

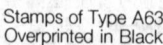

1 CENTAVO 1
h

1905-06   Wmk. 173   Perf. 14, 14½
Black Surcharge

312	A64 (f)	1c on 2c car	40	25
a.		Double surcharge	3.00	

Red Surcharge

312B	A64 (g)	5c on 12c slate	75	50
c.		Double surcharge		
d.		Black surcharge	3.50	3.50
e.		As "d," double surcharge		

Blue Handstamped Surcharge

313	A64 (h)	1c on 2c car	25	15
314	A64 (h)	1c on 10c vio	20	15
315	A64 (h)	1c on 12c sl ('06)	1.00	50
316	A64 (h)	1c on 13c red brn	4.00	3.25

No. 271 with Handstamped Surcharge
in Blue
Unwmk.

317	A63 (h)	1c on 2c rose	42.50	37.50

The "h" is handstamped in strips of four stamps each differing from the others in the size of the upper figures of value and in the letters of the word "CENTAVO", particularly in the size of the "N" and the "O" of that word. The surcharge is known inverted, double, etc.

Regular Issue of 1903 with Handstamped
Surcharge:

5
i

j   k

Wmk. 173
Red Handstamped Surcharge

318	A64 (i)	5c on 12c slate	2.25	1.50
319	A64 (j)	5c on 12c slate	2.25	1.75
a.		Blue surcharge		

Blue Handstamped Surcharge

320	A64 (k)	5c on 12c slate	2.00	1.75

One or more of the numerals in the handstamped surcharges on Nos. 318, 319 and 320 are frequently omitted, inverted, etc.

Surcharged:

6 6   1 1

6 CENTAVOS 6
l   m

Blue Handstamped Surcharge

321	A64 (l)	6c on 12c slate	50	30
322	A64 (l)	6c on 13c red brn	1.00	42

Red Handstamped Surcharge

323	A64 (l)	6c on 12c slate	17.50	12.00

Type "l" is handstamped in strips of four varieties, differing in the size of the numerals and letters. The surcharge is known double and inverted.

Black Surcharge

324	A64 (m)	1c on 13c red brn	1.50	1.00
b.		Double surcharge	4.00	3.00
c.		Right "1" & dot omitted		
		Both numerals omitted		
325	A64 (m)	3c on 13c red brn	50	38

Stamps of 1900, with
Shield in Black,
Overprinted — n   **01905**

1905 — **Unwmk.** — **Perf. 12**
Blue Overprint

326	A63 (n)	1c green	4.50	3.25
a.	Inverted overprint			
327	A63 (n)	2c rose	3.25	3.25
a.	Vertical overprint		6.00	5.00
327B	A63 (n)	3c black	30.00	27.50
327C	A63 (n)	5c blue	12.50	10.00
328	A63 (n)	10c deep blue	6.00	4.50

Black Overprint

328A	A63 (n)	10c deep blue	7.50	4.50

Counterfeits of Nos. 326-335 abound.

Stamps of 1900, with Shield in Black
Surcharged or Overprinted:

1906

1906 — **Blue and Black Surcharge**

329	A63 (o)	2c on 26c brn org	50	40
a.	"2" & dot double		7.50	7.50
330	A63 (o)	3c on 26c brn org	4.00	3.25
a.	"3" & dot double			

Black Surcharge or Overprint

331	A63 (o)	3c on 26c brn org	3.00	2.50
a.	Disks & numerals omitted			
b.	"3" and disks double			
c.	"1906" omitted			
333	A63 (p)	10c deep blue	1.75	1.40
334	A63 (p)	10c deep blue	1.25	1.25
334A	A63 (q)	26c brown org	22.50	20.00
a.	"1906" in blue			

No. 257 Overprinted in Black

335	A63 (q)	10c dp bl (Shield in violet)	17.50	15.00
a.	Overprint type "p"			

There are numerous varieties of these surcharges and overprints.

Pres. Pedro José
Escalón — A65

1906 — **Engr.** — **Perf. 11½**
Glazed Paper

336	A65	1c green & blk	15	15
a.	Thin paper		75	75
337	A65	2c red & blk	15	15
338	A65	3c yellow & blk	15	15
339	A65	5c ultra & blk	15	15
a.	5c dark blue & black		15	15
340	A65	6c carmine & blk	15	15
341	A65	10c violet & blk	15	15
342	A65	12c violet & blk	15	15
343	A65	13c dk brn & blk	15	15
345	A65	24c carmine & blk	35	35
346	A65	26c choc & blk	35	35
347	A65	50c yellow & blk	35	45
348	A65	100c blue & blk	3.00	3.00
	Nos. 336-348 (12)		5.25	5.35

All values of this set are known imperforate but are not believed to have been issued in this condition.

See Nos. O263-O272. For overprints and surcharges see Nos. 349-354.

The entire set has been reprinted. The shades of the reprints differ from those of the originals, the paper is thicker and the perforation 12. Value, set of 12, $1.20.

Nos. 336-338 Overprinted
in Black

1907

349	A65	1c green & blk	25	25
a.	Shield in red		3.50	

350	A65	2c red & blk	25	25
a.	Shield in red		3.50	
351	A65	3c yellow & blk	25	25

Reprints of Nos. 349 to 351 have the same characteristics as the reprints of the preceding issue. Value, set of 3, 15c.

Stamps of 1906
Surcharged with
Shield and

 1

352	A65	1c on 5c ultra & blk	15	15
a.	1c on 5c dark blue & black		15	15
b.	Inverted surcharge			
c.	Double surcharge			
352D	A65	1c on 6c rose & blk	20	20
d.	Double surcharge		1.25	1.25
353	A65	2c on 6c rose & blk	2.00	1.00
354	A65	10c on 6c rose & blk	50	35

The above surcharges are frequently found with the shield double, inverted, or otherwise misplaced.

National Palace — A66

Overprinted with Shield in Black

1907 — **Engr.** — **Unwmk.**
Paper with or without colored dots

355	A66	1c green & blk	15	15
356	A66	2c red & blk	15	15
357	A66	3c yellow & blk	15	15
358	A66	5c blue & blk	15	15
a.	5c ultramarine & black		15	15
359	A66	6c ver & blk	15	15
a.	Shield in red		3.75	
360	A66	10c violet & blk	15	15
361	A66	12c violet & blk	15	15
362	A66	13c sepia & blk	15	15
363	A66	24c rose & blk	15	15
364	A66	26c yel brn & blk	30	20
365	A66	50c orange & blk	50	35
a.	50c yellow & black		3.50	
366	A66	100c turq bl & blk	1.00	50
	Nos. 355-366 (12)		3.15	
	Set value			1.70

Most values exist without shield, also with shield inverted, double, and otherwise misprinted. Many of these were never sold to the public.

See 2nd footnote following No. 421.
See Nos. 369-373, 397-401. For surcharges and overprints see Nos. 367-368A, 374-77, 414-421, 443-444, J71-J74, J76-J80, O329-O331.

UN CENTAVO

No. 356 With Additional
Surcharge in Black

1908

367	A66	1c on 2c red & blk	25	25
a.	Double surcharge		1.00	1.00
b.	Inverted surcharge		50	50
c.	Double surcharge, one inverted		50	50
d.	Red surcharge			

UN CENTAVO

Same Surcharged in
Black or Red

368	A66	1c on 2c	19.00	17.50
368A	A66	1c on 2c (R)	27.50	25.00

Counterfeits exist of the surcharges on Nos. 368-368A.

Type of 1907

1909 — **Engr.** — **Wmk. 172**

369	A66	1c green & blk	15	15
370	A66	2c rose & blk	15	15
371	A66	3c yellow & blk	25	15
372	A66	5c blue & blk	25	15
373	A66	10c violet & blk	30	20
	Nos. 369-373 (5)		1.10	
	Set value			70

The note after No. 366 will apply here also.

1821

Nos. 355, 369 — **15 septiembre**
Overprinted in Red

1909

1909, Sept. — **Unwmk.**

374	A66	1c green & blk	2.25	1.10
a.	Inverted overprint		10.00	

Wmk. 172

375	A66	1c green & blk	1.75	1.40
a.	Inverted overprint			

88th anniv. of El Salvador's independence.

2 CENTAVOS

Nos. 362, 364
Surcharged

1909

1909 — **Unwmk.**

376	A66	2c on 13c sep & blk	1.50	1.25
a.	Inverted surcharge			
377	A66	3c on 26c yel brn & blk	1.75	1.40
a.	Inverted surcharge			

A67   A68

Design: Pres. Fernando Figueroa.

1910 — **Engr.** — **Wmk. 172**

378	A67	1c sepia & blk	15	15
379	A67	2c dk grn & blk	15	15
380	A67	3c orange & blk	15	15
381	A67	4c carmine & blk	15	15
a.	4c scarlet & black		15	15
382	A67	5c purple & blk	15	15
383	A67	6c scarlet & blk	15	15
384	A67	10c purple & blk	15	15
385	A67	12c dp bl & blk	15	15
386	A67	17c ol grn & blk	15	15
387	A67	19c brn red & blk	15	15
388	A67	26c choc & blk	15	15
389	A67	50c yellow & blk	15	15
390	A67	100c turq bl & blk	15	15
	Set value		1.60	1.45

1911 — **Unwmk.**

Designs: 5c, José Matías Delgado. 6c, Manuel José Arce. 12c, Centenary Monument.

Paper with colored dots

391	A68	5c dp blue & brn	15	15
392	A68	6c orange & brn	15	15
393	A68	12c violet & brn	15	15

Wmk. 172

394	A68	5c dp blue & brn	15	15
395	A68	6c orange & brn	15	15
396	A68	12c violet & brn	15	15
	Set value		54	60

Centenary of the insurrection of 1811.

Palace Type of 1907 without Shield

1911

Paper without colored dots

397	A66	1c scarlet	15	15
398	A66	2c chocolate	25	25
a.	Paper with brown dots			
399	A66	13c deep green	15	15
400	A66	24c yellow	15	15
401	A66	50c dark brown	15	15
	Set value		70	70

José Matías   Manuel José
Delgado   Arce
A71   A72

Francisco   Rafael Campo
Morazán   A74
A73

Trinidad   Monument of
Cabañas   Gerardo Barrios
A75   A76

Centenary   National Palace
Monument   A78
A77

Rosales   Coat of
Hospital — A79   Arms — A80

1912 — **Unwmk.** — **Perf. 12**

402	A71	1c dp bl & blk	20	15
403	A72	2c bis brn & blk	25	15
404	A73	5c scarlet & blk	25	15
405	A74	6c dk grn & blk	20	15
406	A75	12c ol grn & blk	1.00	18
407	A76	17c violet & slate	60	15
408	A77	19c scar & slate	1.25	20
409	A78	29c org & slate	1.50	20
410	A79	50c blue & slate	1.75	38
411	A80	1col black & slate	2.50	75
	Nos. 402-411 (10)		9.50	2.46

Juan Manuel   Pres. Manuel E.
Rodríguez   Araujo
A81   A82

1914 — **Perf. 11½**

412	A81	10c orange & brn	2.50	75
413	A82	25c purple & brn	2.50	75

Type of 1907 without Shield **1915**
Overprinted in Black

1915

Paper overlaid with colored dots

414	A66	1c gray green	15	15
415	A66	2c red	15	15
416	A66	5c ultra	15	15
417	A66	6c pale blue	15	15
418	A66	10c yellow	60	30
419	A66	12c brown	50	15
420	A66	50c violet	15	15
421	A66	100c black brn	1.40	1.40
	Nos. 414-421 (8)		3.25	
	Set value			2.25

Varieties such as center omitted, center double, center inverted, imperforate exist with or without date, date inverted, date double, etc., but are believed to be entirely unofficial.

Preceding the stamps with the "1915" overprint a quantity of stamps of this type was overprinted with the letter "S." Evidence is lacking that they were ever placed in use. The issue was demonetized in 1916.

National Theater — A83

Various frames.

1916		Engr.	Perf. 12	
431	A83	1c deep green	15	15
432	A83	2c vermilion	15	15
433	A83	5c deep blue	15	15
434	A83	6c gray violet	25	15
435	A83	10c black brn	25	15
436	A83	12c violet	2.50	50
437	A83	17c orange	35	15
438	A83	25c dk brown	80	20
439	A83	29c black	5.00	75
440	A83	50c slate	2.50	1.50
		Nos. 431-440 (10)	12.10	
		Set value		3.40

Watermarked letters which occasionally appear are from the papermaker's name.

For surcharges and overprints see Nos. 450-455, 457-466, O332-O341.

Nos. O324-O325 with "OFICIAL" Barred out in Black

1917				
441	O3	2c red	45	45
a.		Double bar		
442	O3	5c ultramarine	50	35
a.		Double bar		

Regular Issue of 1915 Overprinted "OFICIAL" and Re-overprinted in Red

CORRIENTE

443	A66	6c pale blue	65	50
a.		Double bar		
444	A66	12c brown	85	65
a.		Double bar		
b.		"CORRIENTE" inverted		

Same Overprint in Red On Nos. O323-O327

445	O3	1c gray green	1.75	1.25
a.		"CORRIENTE" inverted		
b.		Double bar		
c.		"CORRIENTE" omitted		
446	O3	2c red	1.75	1.25
a.		Double bar		
447	O3	5c ultra	9.00	6.00
a.		Double bar, both in black		
448	O3	10c yellow	1.00	50
a.		Double bar		
b.		"OFICIAL" and bar omitted		
449	O3	50c violet	50	50
a.		Double bar		
		Nos. 443-449 (7)	15.50	10.65

Nos. O334-O335 Overprinted or Surcharged in Red:

Corriente	Un Centavo
a	b

450	A83	(a) 5c deep blue	1.50	1.00
a.		"CORRIENTE" double		
451	A83	(b) 1c on 6c gray vio	1.00	75
a.		"CORRIERTE"		
b.		"CORRIENRE"	5.00	
c.		"CORRIENTE" double		

No. 434 Surcharged in Black

1

452	A83	1c on 6c gray vio	1.75	1.00
1918				
a.		Double surcharge		
b.		Inverted surcharge		

No. 434 Surcharged in Black

1 Centavo 1

1918				
453	A83	1c on 6c gray vio	1.50	75
a.		"Centado"	2.25	1.50
b.		Double surcharge	2.50	1.75
c.		Inverted surcharge		

No. 434 Surcharged in Black or Red

CENTAVO

454	A83	1c on 6c gray vio	4.00	3.25
a.		Double surcharge		
b.		Inverted surcharge	5.00	5.00
455	A83	1c on 6c gray vio (R)	4.00	3.25
a.		Double surcharge		
b.		Inverted surcharge	5.00	5.00

Counterfeits exist of Nos. 454-455.

Pres. Carlos
Meléndez — A85

1919			Engr.	
456	A85	1col dk blue & blk	50	50

For surcharge see No. 467.

No. 437 Surcharged in Black

1

1 Centavo 1

1919				
457	A83	1c on 17c orange	20	15
a.		Inverted surcharge	75	75
b.		Double surcharge	75	75

Nos. 435-436, 438, 440 Surcharged in Black or Blue

1

1 Centavo 1

2

2 centavos 2

VALE
5 Centavos

6

SEIS

1920-21				
458	A83	1c on 12c violet	20	15
a.		Double surcharge	1.00	1.00
459	A83	2c on 10c dk brn	25	15
460	A83	5c on 50c slate ('21)	40	15
461	A83	6c on 25c dk brn (Bl) ('21)	40	20

Same Surch. in Black on No. O337

462	A83	1c on 12c violet	1.00	1.00
a.		Double surcharge		

No. 460 surcharged in yellow and 461 surcharged in red are essays.

No. 462 is due to some sheets of Official Stamps being mixed with the ordinary 12c stamps at the time of surcharging. The error stamps were sold to the public and used for ordinary postage.

Surcharged in Red:

15

Types:

15 **15** **15** **15**
I   II   III   IV

463	A83	15c on 29c blk (III) ('21)	1.00	38
a.		Double surcharge	2.00	
b.		Type I	1.50	1.00
c.		Type II	1.00	75
d.		Type IV	2.50	

35
Treinta y cinco

Surcharged in Blue or Black

464	A83	26c on 29c blk (Bl)	1.00	60
466	A83	35c on 50c slate (Bk)	1.00	60

One stamp in each row of ten of No. 464 has the "t" of "cts" inverted and one stamp in each row of No. 466 has the letters "c" in "cinco" larger than the normal.

No. 464 surcharged in green or yellow and the 35c on 29c black are essays.

60

No. 456
Surcharged in Red

CENTAVOS

467	A85	60c on 1col dk bl & blk	30	25

Setting includes three types of numerals and "CENTAVOS" measuring from 16mm to 20mm wide.

Un centavo
1919

A93

1921				
468	A93	1c on 1c ol grn	15	15
a.		Double surcharge	75	
469	A93	1c on 5c yellow	15	15
a.		Inverted surcharge		
b.		Double surcharge		

470	A93	1c on 10c blue	15	15
a.		Double surcharge	50	
471	A93	1c on 25c green	15	15
a.		Double surcharge		
472	A93	1c on 50c olive	15	15
a.		Double surcharge		
473	A93	1c on 1p gray blk	18	18
a.		Double surcharge		
		Set value	50	50

The frame of No. 473 differs slightly from the illustration.

Setting includes many wrong font letters and numerals.

Francisco Menéndez A94	Manuel José Arce A95

Confederation Coin — A96	Delgado Addressing Crowd — A97

Coat of Arms of Confederation A98	Francisco Morazán A99

Independence Monument A100	Columbus A101

1921			Engr.	Perf. 12
474	A94	1c green	25	15
475	A95	2c black	25	15
476	A96	5c orange	1.00	15
477	A97	6c carmine rose	50	15
478	A98	10c deep blue	50	15
479	A99	25c olive grn	2.50	15
480	A100	60c violet	6.00	50
481	A101	1col black brn	10.00	75
		Nos. 474-481 (8)	21.00	
		Set value		1.70

For overprints and surcharges see Nos. 481A-485, 487-494, 506, O342-O349.

Nos. 474-477 Overprinted in Red, Black or Blue

CENTENARIO   **CENTENARIO**
a   b

1921				
481A	A94	(a) 1c green (R)	5.00	4.00
481B	A95	(a) 2c black (R)	5.00	4.00
481C	A96	(b) 5c orange (Bk)	5.00	4.00
481D	A97	(b) 6c car rose (Bl)	5.00	4.00

Centenary of independence.

No. 477 Surcharged:

5

a **5**   **5**

5

b

1923
482	A97 (a)	5c on 6c	35	15
483	A97 (b)	5c on 6c	30	15
484	A97 (b)	20c on 6c	35	25

Nos. 482-484 exist with double surcharge.

10

No. 475 Surcharged in Red

1923
485	A95	10c on 2c black	50	15

José Simeón Cañas y Villacorta — A102

1923   Engr.   Perf. 11½
486	A102	5c blue	50	25

Centenary of abolition of slavery.
For surcharge see No. 571.

6   6

Nos. 479, 481
Surcharged in Red or Black

Seis centavos

1924   Perf. 12
487	A99	1c on 25c ol grn (R)	15	15
a.		Numeral at right inverted		
b.		Double surcharge		
488	A99	6c on 25c ol grn (R)	20	15
489	A99	20c on 25c ol grn (R)	50	25
490	A101	20c on 1col blk brn (Bk)	65	38

Nos. 476, 478 Surcharged:

1

6   6

centavo

Centavos

1924
491	A96	1c on 5c orange (Bk)	35	20
492	A98	6c on 10c dp bl (R)	35	20

Nos. 491-492 exist with double surcharge.
A stamp similar to No. 492 but with surcharge "6 centavos 6" is an essay.

2

No. 476 Surcharged

Dos centavos

1924
493	A96	2c on 5c orange	35	25
a.		Top ornament omitted	2.00	2.00

---

15 Sept.
1874 — 1924
No. 480 Surcharged:

5   5

U. P. U.
CINCO CENTAVOS

1924
Red Surcharge
494	A100	5c on 60c violet	4.25	3.25
a.		"1781" for "1874"	10.00	8.75
b.		"1934" for "1924"	10.00	8.75

Universal Postal Union, 50th anniversary.
This stamp with black surcharge is an essay.
Copies have been passed through the post.

Daniel Hernández Monument A106

National Gymnasium A107

Atlacatl — A108

Conspiracy of 1811 — A109

Bridge over Lempa River — A110

Map of Central America — A111

Balsam Tree — A112

Tulla Serra — A114

Columbus at La Rábida — A115

Coat of Arms — A116

Photogravure; Engraved (35c, 1col)
1924-25   Perf. 12½; 14 (35c, 1col)
495	A106	1c red violet	15	15
496	A107	2c dark red	25	15
497	A108	3c chocolate	15	15
498	A109	5c olive blk	15	15
499	A110	6c grnsh blue	25	15
500	A111	10c orange	60	15
a.		"ATLANT CO"	5.25	5.25
501	A112	20c deep green	1.00	25
502	A114	35c scar & grn	2.50	38
503	A115	50c orange brown	2.00	30
504	A116	1col grn & vio ('25)	3.00	30
		Nos. 495-504 (10)	10.05	
		Set value		1.70

For overprints and surcharges see Nos. 510-511, 520-534, 585, C1-C10, C19, O350-O361, RA1-RA4.

No. 480 Surcharged in Red

Dos centavos

1925, Aug.   Perf. 12
506	A100	2c on 60c violet	1.25	1.25

City of San Salvador, 400th anniv.
The variety with dates in black is an essay.

View of San Salvador — A118

1925   Photo.   Perf. 12½
507	A118	1c blue	65	65
508	A118	2c deep green	65	65
509	A118	3c Mahogany red	65	65

No. 506 and Nos. 507 to 509 were issued to commemorate the fourth centenary of the founding of the City of San Salvador.

Black Surcharge
Exposición Santaneca
Julio de 1928

3   ,,,,   3

1928, July 17
510	A111	3c on 10c orange	65	50
a.		"ATLANT CO"	12.50	12.50

Industrial Exhibition, Santa Ana, July 1928.

Red Surcharge

1928
511	A109	1c on 5c olive black	25	20
a.		Bar instead of top left "1"	38	25

Pres. Pío Romero Bosque, Salvador, and Pres. Lázaro Chacón, Guatemala A121

1929   Litho.   Perf. 11½
Portraits in Dark Brown
512	A121	1c dull violet	25	25
a.		Center inverted	12.50	12.50
513	A121	3c bister brn	25	25
a.		Center inverted	37.50	37.50
514	A121	5c gray grn	25	25
515	A121	10c orange	25	25

Issued to celebrate the opening of the international railroad connecting El Salvador and Guatemala.
Nos. 512-515 exist imperforate. No. 512 in the colors of No. 515.

Tomb of Menéndez A122

1930, Dec. 3
516	A122	1c violet	2.50	2.25
517	A122	3c brown	2.50	2.25
518	A122	5c dark green	2.50	2.25
519	A122	10c yellow brn	2.50	2.25

Centenary of the birth of General Francisco Menéndez.

Stamps of 1924-25 Issue Overprinted **1932**

1932   Perf. 12½, 14
520	A106	1c deep violet	15	15
521	A107	2c dark red	20	15
522	A108	3c chocolate	30	15
523	A109	5c olive blk	30	15
524	A110	6c deep blue	35	15
525	A111	10c orange	1.00	15
a.		"ATLANT CO"	7.50	6.25
526	A112	20c deep green	1.50	45
527	A114	35c scar & grn	2.25	75
528	A115	50c orange brown	3.00	1.00
529	A116	1col green & vio	5.00	2.25
		Nos. 520-529 (10)	14.05	5.35

Values are for the overprint measuring 7½x3mm. It is found in two other sizes: 7½x3¼mm and 8x3mm.

Types of 1924-25
Surcharged with New Values in Red or Black

1934   Perf. 12½
530	A109	2(c) on 5c grnsh blk	15	15
a.		Double surcharge		
531	A111	3(c) on 10c org (Bk)	15	15
a.		"ATLANT CO"	4.00	4.00

Nos. 503, 504, 502 Surcharged with New Values in Black
Perf. 12½, 14½
532	A115	2(c) on 50c	30	15
a.		Double surcharge	3.00	
533	A116	8(c) on 1col	15	15
534	A114	15(c) on 35c	30	18
		Nos. 530-534 (5)	1.05	
		Set value		55

Police Barracks — A123

Two types of the 2c:
Type I - The clouds have heavy lines of shading.
Type II - The lines of shading have been removed from the clouds.

Perf. 12½
1934-35   Wmk. 240   Litho.
535	A123	2c gray brn, type I	20	15
a.		2c brown, type II	20	15
536	A123	5c car, type II	20	15
537	A123	8c lt ultra, type II	20	15
		Nos. 535-537,C33-C35 (6)	3.10	
		Set value		1.35

Discus Thrower A124

1935, Mar. 16   Engr.   Unwmk.
538	A124	5c carmine	2.00	1.65
539	A124	8c blue	2.25	1.90
540	A124	10c orange yel	2.75	2.00
541	A124	15c bister	3.25	2.25
542	A124	37c green	4.00	3.25
		Nos. 538-542 (5)	14.25	11.05

Issued to commemorate the 3rd Central American Games. See Nos. C36-C40.

Same Overprinted **HABILITADO** in Black

1935, June 27

543	A124	5c carmine	2.75	2.00
544	A124	8c blue	4.00	2.00
545	A124	10c orange yel	4.00	2.00
546	A124	15c bister	4.00	2.50
547	A124	37c green	6.50	4.00
		Nos. 543-547 (5)	21.25	13.00

See Nos. C41-C45.

Flag of El	Tree of San
Salvador	Vicente
A125	A126

1935, Oct. 26   Litho.   Wmk. 240

548	A125	1c gray blue	15	15
549	A125	2c black brn	15	15
550	A125	3c plum	16	15
551	A125	5c rose carmine	25	15
552	A125	8c ultra	30	15
553	A125	15c fawn	40	25
		Nos. 548-553,C46 (7)	1.91	
		Set value		75

1935, Dec. 26

Numerals in Black, Tree in Yellow Green

554	A126	2c black brn	50	25
555	A126	3c dk blue grn	50	30
556	A126	5c rose red	50	35
557	A126	8c dark blue	50	40
558	A126	15c brown	50	50
		Nos. 554-558 (5)	2.50	1.80

Tercentenary of San Vicente. See Nos. C47-C51.

Volcano of	Wharf at
Izalco — A127	Cutuco — A128

Doroteo	Parade Ground
Vasconcelos	A130
A129	

Dr. Tomás G.	Sugar
Palomo — A131	Mill — A132

Coffee at	Gathering
Pier — A133	Balsam — A134

Pres. Manuel E.
Araujo — A135

1935, Dec.   Engr.   Unwmk.

559	A127	1c deep violet	15	15
560	A128	2c chestnut	15	15
561	A129	3c green	15	15
562	A130	5c carmine	40	15
563	A131	8c dull blue	15	15
564	A132	10c orange	25	15
565	A133	15c dk olive bis	40	15
566	A134	50c indigo	2.00	1.25
567	A135	1col black	5.00	3.00
		Nos. 559-567 (9)	8.65	
		Set value		4.70

Paper has faint imprint "El Salvador" on face.
For surcharges and overprint see Nos. 568-570, 573, 583-584, C52.

Stamps of 1935 Surcharged with New Value in Black

1938   Perf. 12½

568	A130	1c on 5c carmine	15	15
569	A132	3c on 10c orange	15	15
570	A133	8c on 15c dk ol bis	18	15
		Set value		26

No. 486 Surcharged with New Value in Red

1938   Perf. 11½

571	A102	3c on 5c blue	18	18

Centenary of the death of José Simeón Cañas, liberator of slaves in Latin America.

Map of Flags of US and El
Salvador — A136

Engraved and Lithographed

1938, Apr. 21   Perf. 12

572	A136	8c multicolored	38	30

150th anniv. of US Constitution. See No. C61.

No. 560 Surcharged with New Value in Black

1938   Perf. 12½

573	A128	1c on 2c chestnut	15	15

Indian Sugar
Mill — A137

Designs: 2c, Indian women washing. 3c, Indian girl at spring. 5c, Indian plowing. 8c, Izote flower. 10c, Champion cow. 20c, Extracting balsam. 50c, Maquilishuat in bloom. 1col, Post Office, San Salvador.

1938-39   Engr.   Perf. 12

574	A137	1c dark violet	15	15
575	A137	2c dark green	15	15
576	A137	3c dark brown	25	15
577	A137	5c scarlet	25	15
578	A137	8c dark blue	1.25	15
579	A137	10c yel org ('39)	2.00	15
580	A137	20c bis brn ('39)	1.75	20
581	A137	50c dull blk ('39)	2.25	45
582	A137	1col black ('39)	2.00	75
		Nos. 574-582 (9)	10.05	
		Set value		1.85

For surcharges & overprints see #591-592, C96.

25 Sept.
1939   1939

Nos. 566-567, 504
Surcharged in Red

BATALLA
SAN PEDRO PERULAPAN
₡ 0.50

1939, Sept. 25   Perf. 12½, 14

583	A134	8c on 50c indigo	25	15
584	A135	10c on 1col blk	38	15
585	A116	50c on 1col grn & vio	2.50	2.50

100th anniversary of the battle of San Pedro Perulapán.

Sir Rowland
Hill — A146

1940, Mar. 1   Perf. 12½

586	A146	8c dk bl, lt bl & blk	2.50	50

Centenary of the postage stamp. See Nos. C69-C70.

Statue of
Christ and
San
Salvador
Cathedral
A147

A148

Wmk. 269

1942, Nov. 23   Engr.   Perf. 14

587	A147	8c deep blue	50	20

Souvenir Sheet
Imperf
Without Gum
Lilac Tinted Paper

588	A148	Sheet of 4	12.00	12.00
a.		8c deep blue	3.50	3.50
b.		30c red orange	3.50	3.50

Nos. 587-588 were issued to commemorate the first Eucharistic Congress of Salvador. See No. C85. No. 588 contains two No. 587 and two No. C85, imperf.

> Catalogue values for unused stamps in this section, from this point to the end of the section, are for Never Hinged items.

Cuscatlán Bridge, Pan-American
Highway — A149

Arms Overprint at Right in Carmine
Perf. 12½

1944, Nov. 24   Unwmk.   Engr.

589	A149	8c dk bl & blk	16	15

See No. C92.

Gen. Juan José
Canas — A150

1945, June 9

590	A150	8c blue	15	15

No. 575 Surcharged in Black

1 1
a   *b*

1944-46

591	A137(a)	1(c) on 2c dk grn	15	15
592	A137(b)	1(c) on 2c dk grn ('46)	15	15
		Set value	24	15

Lake of	Ceiba Tree
Ilopango	A152
A151	

Water Carriers — A153

1946-47   Litho.   Wmk. 240

593	A151	1c bl ('47)	15	15
594	A152	2c lt bl grn ('47)	20	15
595	A153	5c carmine	15	15
		Set value	40	18

Isidro
Menéndez — A154

Designs: 2c, Cristano Salazar. 3c, Juan Bertis. 5c, Francisco Duenas, 8c, Ramon Belloso. 10c, Jose Presentacion Trigueros. 20c, Salvador Rodriguez Gonzalez. 50c, Francisco Castaneda. 1col, David Castro.

1947   Unwmk.   Engr.   Perf. 12

596	A154	1c car rose	15	15
597	A154	2c dp org	15	15
598	A154	3c violet	15	15
599	A154	5c slate gray	15	15
600	A154	8c dp bl	15	15
601	A154	10c bis brn	16	15
602	A154	20c green	28	15
603	A154	50c black	65	30
604	A154	1col scarlet	1.40	40
		Set value	2.80	1.10

For surcharges and overprints see Nos. 621-626, 634, C118-C120, O362-O368.

Manuel José
Arce — A163

1948, Feb. 25   Perf. 12½

605	A163	8c deep blue	28	15

See Nos. C108-C110.

President Roosevelt Presenting Awards for Distinguished Service — A164

President Franklin D. Roosevelt — A165

A166

Designs: 8c, Pres. and Mrs. Roosevelt. 15c, Mackenzie King, Roosevelt and Winston Churchill. 20c, Roosevelt and Cordell Hull. 50c, Funeral of Pres. Roosevelt.

1948, Apr. 12
Various Frames; Center in Black

606	A164	5c dk bl	15	15
607	A164	8c green	15	15
608	A165	12c violet	20	15
609	A164	15c vermilion	24	18
610	A164	20c car lake	28	20
611	A164	50c gray	70	45
		Nos. 606-611 (6)	1.72	1.28

Souvenir Sheet
Perf. 13½

612	A166	1col ol grn & brn	1.90	1.40

3rd anniv. of the death of F. D. Roosevelt. See Nos. C111-C117.

Torch and Winged Letter — A167

Perf. 12½
1949, Oct. 9   Unwmk.   Engr.

613	A167	8c blue	42	15

75th anniv. of the UPU. See #C122-C124.

Workman and Soldier Holding Torch — A168

Wreath and Open Book — A169

1949, Dec. 15   Litho.   Perf. 10½

614	A168	8c blue	30	15

1st anniversary of the Revolution of Dec. 14, 1948. See Nos. C125-C129.

Perf. 11½
1952, Feb. 14   Photo.   Unwmk.
Wreath in Dark Green

615	A169	1c yel grn	15	15
616	A169	2c magenta	15	15
617	A169	5c brn red	15	15
618	A169	10c yellow	15	15
619	A169	20c gray grn	20	15
620	A169	1col dp car	1.00	75
		Set value	1.45	1.10

Constitution of 1950. See Nos. C134-C141.

Nos. 598, 600 and 603 Surcharged with New Values in Various Colors

1952-53   Perf. 12½

621	A154	2c on 3c vio (C)	15	15
622	A154	2c on 8c dp bl (C)	15	15
623	A154	3c on 8c dp bl (G)	15	15
624	A154	5c on 8c dp bl (O)	15	15
625	A154	7c on 8c dp bl (Bk)	15	15
626	A154	10c on 50c blk (O) ('53)	20	15
		Set value	78	50

Nos. C106 and C107 Surcharged and "AEREO" Obliterated in Various Colors

1952-53   Wmk. 240

627	AP31	2c on 12c choc (Bl)	15	15
628	AP32	2c on 14c dk bl (R) ('53)	15	15
629	AP31	5c on 12c choc (Bl)	15	15
630	AP32	10c on 14c dk bl (C)	15	15
		Set value	48	40

José Marti — A170

Perf. 10½
1953, Feb. 27   Litho.   Unwmk.

631	A170	1c rose red	15	15
632	A170	2c bl grn	15	15
633	A170	10c dk vio	16	15
		Nos. 631-633,C142-C144 (6)	1.43	
		Set value		75

Issued to commemorate the centenary of the birth of José Marti, Cuban patriot.

No. 598 Overprinted in Carmine

"IV Congreso Médico Social Panamericano 15 / 19 Abril, 1953"

1953, June 19   Perf. 12½

634	A154	3c violet	20	15

Issued to commemorate the 4th Pan-American Congress of Social Medicine, San Salvador, April 16-19, 1953. See No. C146.

Signing of Act of Independence A171

Capt. Gen. Gerardo Barrios A172

1953, Sept. 15   Litho.   Perf. 11½

635	A171	1c rose pink	15	15
636	A171	2c dp bl grn	15	15
637	A171	3c purple	15	15
638	A171	5c dp bl	15	15
639	A171	7c lt brn	15	15
640	A171	10c ocher	20	15
641	A171	20c dp org	28	15
642	A171	50c green	60	30
643	A171	1col gray	1.25	90
		Set value, #635-643, C147-C150	3.60	2.45

132nd anniversary of the Act of Independence, Sept. 15, 1821.

1953, Dec. 1   Perf. 11½

Portrait: 3c, 7c, 10c, 22c, Francisco Morazan, (facing left).

Black Overprint ("C de C")

644	A172	1c green	15	15
645	A172	2c blue	15	15
646	A172	3c green	15	15
647	A172	5c carmine	15	15
648	A172	7c blue	15	15
649	A172	10c carmine	16	15
650	A172	20c violet	20	15
651	A172	22c violet	28	20
		Set value	1.00	65

The overprint "C de C" is a control indicating "Tribunal of Accounts." A double entry of this overprint occurs twice in each sheet of each denomination.
For overprint see No. 729.

Coastal Bridge — A173

Motherland and Liberty A174

Census Allegory A175

Balboa Park A176

Designs: Nos. 654, 655, National Palace. Nos. 659, 665, Izalco Volcano. Nos. 660, 661, Guayabo dam. No. 666, Lake Ilopango. No. 669, Housing development. Nos. 670, 673, Coast guard boat. No. 671, Modern highway.

Perf. 11½
1954, June 1   Unwmk.   Photo.

652	A173	1c car rose & brn	15	15
653	AP43	1c ol & bl gray	15	15
654	A173	1c pur & pale lil	15	15
655	A173	2c yel grn & lt gray	15	15
656	A174	2c car lake	15	15
657	A175	2c org red	15	15
658	AP44	3c maroon	15	15
659	A173	3c bl grn & bl	16	15
660	A174	3c dk gray & vio	15	15
661	A174	5c red vio & vio	15	15
662	AP44	5c emerald	15	15
663	A176	7c magenta & buff	16	15
664	AP43	7c bl grn & gray bl	16	15
665	A173	7c pur & brn & org	16	15
666	A173	10c car lake	16	15
667	AP46	10c red, dk brn & bl	16	15
668	A174	10c dk bl grn	16	15
669	A174	20c org & cr	32	15
670	A173	22c gray vio	32	25
671	A176	50c dk gray & brn	65	28
672	AP46	1col brn org, dk brn & bl	1.25	75
673	A173	1col brt bl	1.25	50
		Nos. 652-673 (22)	6.41	
		Set value		3.00

See Nos. C151-C165. For surcharges and overprints see Nos. 692-693, 736, C193.

Capt. Gen. Gerardo Barrios — A177

Coffee Picker — A178

Perf. 12½
1955, Dec. 20   Wmk. 269   Engr.

674	A177	1c red	15	15
675	A177	2c yel grn	15	15
676	A177	3c vio bl	16	15
677	A177	20c violet	20	15
		Nos. 674-677,C166-C167 (6)	1.06	
		Set value		60

Perf. 13½
1956, June 20   Litho.   Unwmk.

678	A178	3c bis brn	15	15
679	A178	5c red org	15	15
680	A178	10c dk bl	16	15
681	A178	2col dk red	1.65	1.00
		Nos. 678-681,C168-C172 (9)	6.50	
		Set value		3.50

Centenary of Santa Ana Department. For overprint see No. C187.

Map of Chalatenango — A179

1956, Sept. 14

682	A179	2c blue	15	15
683	A179	7c rose red	28	25
684	A179	50c yel brn	48	30
		Nos. 682-684,C173-C178 (9)	3.07	
		Set value		2.00

Centenary of Chalatenango Department (in 1955). For surcharge see No. 694.

Coat of Arms of Nueva San Salvador — A180

Perf. 12½
1957, Jan. 3   Wmk. 269   Engr.

685	A180	1c rose red	15	15
686	A180	2c green	15	15
687	A180	3c violet	15	15
688	A180	7c red org	32	25
689	A180	10c ultra	15	15
690	A180	50c pale brn	40	30
691	A180	1col dl red	85	65
		Nos. 685-691,C179-C183 (12)	5.69	
		Set value		3.40

Centenary of the founding of the city of Nueva San Salvador (Santa Tecla).
For surcharges and overprints see Nos. 695-696, 706, 713, C194-C195, C197-C199.

Nos. 664-665, 683 and 688 Surcharged with New Value in Black

1957   Unwmk.   Photo.   Perf. 11½

692	A173	6c on 7c bl grn & gray bl	30	30
693	A173	6c on 7c org brn & org	30	30

1957   Litho.   Perf. 13½

694	A179	6c on 7c rose red	20	15

Perf. 12½
1957-58   Wmk. 269   Engr.

695	A180	5c on 7c red org ('58)	25	15
696	A180	6c on 7c red org	30	16
		Nos. 692-696 (5)	1.35	1.06

El Salvador Intercontinental Hotel — A181

Perf. 11½
1958, June 28   Unwmk.   Photo.
Granite Paper
Vignette in Green, Dark Blue & Red

697	A181	3c brown	15	15
698	A181	6c crim rose	15	15
699	A181	10c brt bl	15	15
700	A181	15c brt grn	18	15
701	A181	20c lilac	30	16
702	A181	30c brt yel grn	42	22
		Set value	1.18	68

Presidents Eisenhower and Lemus and Flags A182

1959, Dec. 14   Granite Paper
Design in Ultramarine, Dark Brown,
Light Brown and Red

703	A182	3c pink	18	15
704	A182	6c green	18	15
705	A182	10c crimson	28	15
	Nos. 703-705,C184-C186 (6)		1.38	
		Set value		60

Visit of Pres. José M. Lemus of El Salvador to the US, Mar. 9-21.

No. 686 Overprinted: "5 Enero 1960 XX Aniversario Fundacion Sociedad Filatelica de El Salvador"

1960   Wmk. 269   Engr.   Perf. 12½

706	A180	2c green	15	15

Philatelic Association of El Salvador, 20th anniv.

Apartment Houses A183

1960   Unwmk.   Photo.   Perf. 11½
Multicolored Centers; Granite Paper

707	A183	10c scarlet	15	15
708	A183	15c brt pur	15	15
709	A183	25c brt yel grn	24	15
710	A183	30c Prus bl	26	16
711	A183	40c olive	42	25
712	A183	80c dk bl	75	75
	Nos. 707-712 (6)		1.97	1.61

Issued to publicize the erection of multifamily housing projects in 1958.
For surcharges see Nos. 730, 733.

No. 686 Surcharged with New Value

1960   Wmk. 269   Engr.   Perf. 12½

713	A180	1c on 2c grn	15	15

Poinsettia — A184

Perf. 11½
1960, Dec.   Unwmk.   Photo.
Granite Paper
Design in Slate Green, Red
and Yellow

714	A184	3c yellow	15	15
715	A184	6c salmon	20	15
716	A184	10c grnsh bl	28	15
717	A184	15c pale vio bl	32	15
	Nos. 714-717,C188-C191 (8)		2.42	1.50

Miniature Sheet

718	A184	40c silver	65	50

Nos. 718 and C192 exist with overprints for: 1- 1st Central American Philatelic Cong., July, 1961. 2- Death of General Barrios, 96th anniv. 3- Cent. of city of Ahuachapan. 4- Football (soccer) games. 5- 4th Latin American Cong. of Pathological Anatomy and 10th Central American Medical Cong., Dec., 1963. 6- Alliance for Progress, 2nd anniv.
For surcharge see No. C196.

Fathers Nicolas, Vicente and Manuel Aguilar A185

Parish Church, San Salvador, 1808 A186

Designs: 5c, 6c, Manuel José Arce, José Matias Delgado and Juan Manuel Rodriguez. 10c, 20c, Pedro Pablo Castillo, Domingo Antonio de Lara and Santiago José Celis. 50c, 80c, Monument to the Fathers, Plaza Libertad.

Perf. 11½
1961, Nov. 5   Unwmk.   Photo.

719	A185	1c gray & dk brn	15	15
720	A185	2c rose & dk brn	15	15
721	A185	5c pale brn & dk ol grn	18	15
722	A185	6c brt pink & dk brn	20	15
723	A185	10c bl & dk brn	20	15
724	A185	20c vio & dk brn	28	15
725	A186	30c brt bl & vio	40	16
726	A186	40c brn org & sep	55	20
727	A186	50c bl grn & sep	75	40
728	A186	80c gray & ultra	1.25	75
	Nos. 719-728 (10)		4.11	
		Set value		1.95

Sesquicentennial of the first cry for Independence in Central America.
For surcharges and overprints see Nos. 731-732, 734-735, 737, 760, 769, 776.

No. 651 Overprinted: "III Exposición Industrial Centroamericana Diciembre de 1962"

1962, Dec. 21   Litho.   Perf. 11½

729	A172	22c violet	28	20

Issued to publicize the 3rd Central American Industrial Exposition. See Nos. C193-C195.

Nos. 708, 726-728 and 673 Surcharged

1962-63   Photo.

730	A183	6c on 15c ('63)	28	15
731	A186	6c on 40c ('63)	28	15
732	A186	6c on 50c ('63)	28	15
733	A183	10c on 15c	28	15
734	A186	10c on 50c ('63)	28	15
735	A186	10c on 80c ('63)	28	15
736	A173	10c on 1col ('63)	28	15
	Nos. 730-736 (7)		1.96	
		Set value		88

Surcharge includes bars on Nos. 731-734, 736; dot on Nos. 730, 735.

No. 726 Overprinted in Arc: "CAMPAÑA MUNDIAL CONTRA EL HAMBRE"

1963, Mar. 21

737	A186	40c brn org & sepia	70	40

FAO "Freedom from Hunger" campaign.

Coyote — A187

Christ on Globe — A188

Designs: 2c, Spider monkey, vert. 3c, Raccoon. 5c, King vulture, vert. 6c, Brown coati. 10c, Kinkajou.

1963   Photo.   Perf. 11½

738	A187	1c lil, blk, ocher & brn	15	15
739	A187	2c lt grn & blk	15	15
740	A187	3c fawn, dk brn & buff	15	15
741	A187	5c gray grn, ind, red & buff	15	15
742	A187	6c rose lil, blk, brn & buff	15	15
743	A187	10c lt bl, brn & buff	15	15
		Set value	45	30

See Nos. C200-C207.

1964-65   Perf. 12x11½

744	A188	6c bl & brn	15	15
745	A188	10c bl & bis	15	15

		Set value	18	15

Miniature Sheets
Imperf

746	A188	60c bl & brt pur	60	60
a.		Marginal ovpt. La Union	1.25	1.25
b.		Marginal ovpt. Usulutan	1.25	1.25
c.		Marginal ovpt. La Libertad	1.25	1.25

2nd Natl. Eucharistic Cong., San Salvador, Apr. 16-19.
Nos. 746a, 746b and 746c commemorate the centenaries of the Departments of La Union, Usulután and La Libertad.
Issue dates: Nos. 744-746, Apr. 16, 1964. Nos. 746a-746b, June 22, 1965, No. 746c, Jan. 28, 1965.
See Nos. C208-C210. For overprints see Nos. C232, C238.

Pres. John F. Kennedy A189

Perf. 11½x12
1964, Nov. 22   Unwmk.

747	A189	6c buff & blk	15	15
748	A189	10c tan & blk	16	15
749	A189	50c pink & blk	50	22
	Nos. 747-749,C211-C213 (6)		1.61	
		Set value		80

Miniature Sheet
Imperf

750	A189	70c dp grn & blk	65	50

President John F. Kennedy (1917-1963).
For overprints & surcharge see #798, 843, C259.

Water Lily — A190

1965, Jan. 6   Photo.   Perf. 12x11½

751	A190	3c shown	15	15
752	A190	5c Maquilishuat	15	15
753	A190	6c Cinco negritos	15	15
754	A190	30c Hortensia	20	15
755	A190	40c Maguey	60	18
756	A190	60c Geranium	65	20
		Set value	1.60	60

See Nos. C215-C220. For overprints and surcharges see Nos. 779, C243, C348-C349.

ICY Emblem — A191

1965, Apr. 27   Photo.   Perf. 11½x12
Design in Brown and Gold

757	A191	5c dp yel	15	15
758	A191	6c dp rose	15	15
759	A191	10c gray	15	15
	Set value, #757-759,			
	C221-C223		80	50

International Cooperation Year.
For overprints see Nos. 764, 780, C227, C244, C312.

No. 728 Overprinted in Red: "1er. Centenario Muerte / Cap. Gral. Gerardo Barrios / 1865 1965 / 29 de Agosto"

1965   Unwmk.   Perf. 11½

760	A186	80c gray & ultra	65	50
a.		"Garl." instead of "Gral."	1.00	1.00

Cent. of the death of Capt. Gen. Gerardo Barrios.

Francisco Antonio Gavidia A192

Fair Emblem A193

Perf. 11½x12
1965, Sept. 24   Photo.   Unwmk.
Portrait in Natural Colors

761	A192	2c blk & rose vio	15	15
762	A192	3c blk & org	16	15
763	A192	6c blk & lt ultra	16	15
	Nos. 761-763,C224-C226 (6)		2.16	
		Set value		1.00

Issued to honor Francisco Antonio Gavidia, philosopher.
For surcharges see Nos. 852-853.

No. 759 Overprinted in Carmine: "1865 / 12 de Octubre / 1965 / Dr. Manuel Enrique Araujo"

1965, Oct. 12

764	A191	10c brn, gray & gold	15	15

Centenary of the birth of Manuel Enrique Araujo, president of Salvador, 1911-1913. See No. C227.

1965, Nov. 5   Photo.   Perf. 12x11½

765	A193	6c yel & multi	15	15
766	A193	10c multi	15	15
767	A193	20c pink & multi	20	15
	Nos. 765-767,C228-C230 (6)		4.56	3.27

Issued to publicize the International Fair of El Salvador, Nov. 5-Dec. 4, 1965.
For overprints and surcharge see Nos. 784, C246, C311, C323.

WHO Headquarters, Geneva A194

1966, May 20   Photo.   Unwmk.

768	A194	15c beige & multi	16	15

Inauguration of WHO Headquarters, Geneva. See No. C231. For overprints and surcharges see Nos. 778, 783, 864, C242, C245, C322.

No. 728 Overprinted in Red: "Mes de Conmemoracion / Civica de la Independencia / Centroamericana / 19 Sept. / 1821 1966"

1966, Sept. 19   Photo.   Perf. 11½

769	A186	80c gray & ultra	52	50

Issued to publicize the month of civic commemoration of Central American independence.

UNESCO Emblem A195

1966, Nov. 4   Unwmk.   Perf. 12

770	A195	20c gray, blk & vio bl	16	15
771	A195	1col emer, blk & vio bl	85	40

20th anniv. of UNESCO.
See Nos. C233-C234. For surcharges see Nos. 853A, C352.

Map of Central America, Flags and Cogwheels A196

1966, Nov. 27   **Litho.**   *Perf. 12*
772 A196   6c multi   15   15
773 A196   10c multi   15   15
    Nos. 772-773,C235-C237 (5)   1.16
    Set value   82

Issued to commemorate the 2nd International Fair of El Salvador, Nov. 5-27.

José Simeon Cañas Pleading for Indian Slaves — A197

1967, Feb. 18   **Litho.**   *Perf. 11½*
774 A197   6c yel & multi   15 15
775 A197   10c lil rose & multi   15 15
    Set value   22 15

Father José Simeon Cañas y Villacorta, D.D. (1767-1838), emancipator of the Central American slaves.
See Nos. C239-C240. For surcharges see Nos. 841A-842, 891, C403-C405.

No. 726 Overprinted in Red: "XV Convención de Clubes / de Leones, Región de / El Salvador-11 y 12 / de Marzo de 1967"

1967   **Photo.**
776 A186   40c brn org & sep   48 25

Issued to publicize the 15th Convention of Lions Clubs of El Salvador, March 11-12.

Volcano San Miguel A198

1967, Apr. 14   **Photo.**   *Perf. 13*
777 A198   70c lt rose lil & brn   1.00 60

Centenary of stamps of El Salvador.
See No. C241. For surcharges see Nos. 841, C320, C350.

No. 768 Overprinted in Red: "VIII CONGRESO / CENTROAMERICANO DE / FARMACIA Y BIOQUIMICA / 5 di 11 Noviembre de 1967"

1967, Oct. 26   **Photo.**   *Perf. 12x11½*
778 A194   15c multi   16 15

Issued to publicize the 8th Central American Congress for Pharmacy and Biochemistry. See No. C242.

No. 751 Overprinted in Red: "I Juegos / Centroamericanos y del / Caribe de Basquetbol / 25 Nov. al 3 Dic. 1967"

1967, Nov. 15
779 A190   3c dl grn, brn, yel & org   15 15

Issued to publicize the First Central American and Caribbean Basketball Games, Nov. 25-Dec. 3. See No. C243.

No. 757 Overprinted in Carmine: "1968 / AÑO INTERNACIONAL DE / LOS DERECHOS HUMANOS"

1968, Jan. 2   **Photo.**   *Perf. 11½x12*
780 A191   5c dp yel, brn & gold   15 15

Issued for International Human Rights Year 1968. See No. C244.

Weather Map, Satellite and WMO Emblem — A199

1968, Mar. 25   **Photo.**   *Perf. 11½x12*
781 A199   1c multi   15 15
782 A199   30c multi   30 15
    Set value   16

World Meteorological Day, Mar. 25.

No. 768 Overprinted in Red: "1968 / XX ANIVERSARIO DE LA / ORGANIZACION MUNDIAL / DE LA SALUD"

1968, Apr. 7   *Perf. 12x11½*
783 A194   15c multi   20 20

20th anniv. of WHO. See No. C245.

No. 765 Overprinted in Red: "1968 / Año / del Sistema / del Crédito / Rural"

1968, May 6   **Photo.**   *Perf. 12x11½*
784 A193   6c yel & multi   15 15

Rural credit system. See No. C246.

Alberto Masferrer — A200   Scouts Helping to Build — A201

1968, June 22   **Litho.**   *Perf. 12x11½*
785 A200   2c multi   15   15
786 A200   6c multi   15   15
787 A200   25c vio & multi   32   15
    Set value, #785-787,   68   38
    C247-C248

Issued to commemorate the centenary of the birth of Alberto Masferrer, philosopher and scholar. For surcharges and overprints see Nos. 819, 843A, 890, C297.

1968, July 26   **Litho.**   *Perf. 12*
788 A201   25c multi   24 15

Issued to publicize the 7th Inter-American Boy Scout Conference, July-Aug., 1968. See No. C249.

Map of Central America, Flags and Presidents of US, Costa Rica, Salvador, Guatemala, Honduras and Nicaragua — A202

1968, Dec. 5   **Litho.**   *Perf. 14½*
789 A202   10c tan & multi   15 15
790 A202   15c multi   16 15
    Set value   20

Meeting of Pres. Lyndon B. Johnson with the presidents of the Central American republics (J. J. Trejos, Costa Rica; Fidel Sanchez Hernandez, Salvador; J. C. Mendez Montenegro, Guatemala; Osvaldo López Arellano, Honduras; Anastasio Somoza Debayle, Nicaragua), San Salvador, July 5-8, 1968. See Nos. C250-C251.

Heliconius Charithonius A203

Various Butterflies.

1969   **Litho.**   *Perf. 12*
791 A203   5c bluish lil, blk & yel   15   15
792 A203   10c beige & multi   15   15
793 A203   30c lt grn & multi   24   15
794 A203   50c tan & multi   40   18
    Nos. 791-794,C252-C255 (8)   11.40 7.13

For surcharge see No. C353.

Red Cross Activities A204

1969   **Litho.**   *Perf. 12*
795 A204   10c lt bl & multi   15   15
796 A204   20c pink & multi   15   15
797 A204   40c lil & multi   28   15
    Nos. 795-797,C256-C258 (6)   4.92 3.60

Issued to commemorate the 50th anniversary of the League of Red Cross Societies.

No. 749 Overprinted in Green: "Alunizaje / Apolo-11 / 21 Julio / 1969"

1969, Sept.   **Photo.**   *Perf. 11½x12*
798 A189   50c pink & blk   40 30

Man's first landing on the moon, July 20, 1969. See note after US No. C76.
The same overprint in red brown and pictures of the landing module and the astronauts on the moon were applied to the margin of No. 750.
See No. C259.

Social Security Hospital A205

1969, Oct. 24   **Litho.**   *Perf. 11½*
799 A205   6c multi   15   15
800 A205   10c multi, diff.   15   15
801 A205   30c multi, diff.   28   15
    Nos. 799-801,C260-C262 (6)   7.33 4.45

For surcharges see Nos. 857, C355.

ILO Emblem — A206

1969   **Litho.**   *Perf. 13*
802 A206   10c yel & multi   15 15

50th anniv. of the ILO. See No. C263.

Chorros Spa A207

Views: 40c, Jaltepeque Bay. 80c, Fountains, Amapulapa Spa.

1969, Dec. 19   **Photo.**   *Perf. 12x11½*
803 A207   10c blk & multi   15   15
804 A207   40c blk & multi   32   25
805 A207   80c blk & multi   65   50
    Nos. 803-805,C264-C266 (6)   2.06 1.65

Tourism.

Euchroma Gigantea — A208

Insects: 25c, Grasshopper. 30c, Digger wasp.

1970, Feb. 24   **Litho.**   *Perf. 11½x11*
806 A208   5c lt bl & multi   15   15
807 A208   25c dl yel & multi   20   15
808 A208   30c dl rose & multi   28   15
    Nos. 806-808,C267-C269 (6)   8.03 4.95

For surcharges see Nos. C371-C373.

Map and Arms of Salvador, National Unity Emblem A209

1970, Apr. 14   **Litho.**   *Perf. 14*
809 A209   10c yel & multi   15   15
810 A209   40c pink & multi   48   15
    Set value   20

Salvador's support of universal human rights. See Nos. C270-C271. For overprints and surcharge see Nos. 823, C301, C402.

Soldiers with Flag — A210

Design: 30c, Anti-aircraft gun.

1970, May 7   *Perf. 12*
811 A210   10c green & multi   15   15
812 A210   30c lemon & multi   30   15
    Nos. 811-812,C272-C274 (5)   1.38
    Set value   58

Issued for Army Day, May 7. For overprints see Nos. 836, C310.

National Lottery Headquarters — A211

1970, July 15   **Litho.**   *Perf. 12*
813 A211   20c lt vio & multi   16 15

National Lottery centenary. See No. C291.

UN and Education Year Emblems A212

1970, Sept. 11   **Litho.**   *Perf. 12*
814 A212   50c multi   40 15
815 A212   1col multi   85 45

Issued for International Education Year. See Nos. C292-293.

Map of Salvador, Globe and Cogwheels A213

1970, Oct. 28   Litho.   Perf. 12
816 A213 5c pink & multi   15 15
817 A213 10c buff & multi   15 15
           Set value   16 15

4th International Fair, San Salvador. See Nos. C294-C295.

Beethoven — A214

1971, Feb. 22   Litho.   Perf. 13½
818 A214 50c ol, brn & yel   50 20

Second International Music Festival. See No. C296. For overprint see No. 833.

No. 787 Overprinted: "Año / del Centenario de la / Biblioteca Nacional / 1970"
1970, Nov. 25   Perf. 12x11½
819 A200 25c vio & multi   20 18

Cent. of the National Library. See No. C297.

Maria Elena   Pietà, by
Sol — A215   Michelangelo — A216

1971, Apr. 1   Litho.   Perf. 14
820 A215 10c lt grn & multi   15 15
821 A215 30c multi   20 15
           Set value   28 25

Maria Elena Sol, Miss World Tourism, 1970-71. See Nos. C298-C299. For overprint see No. 832.

1971, May 10
822 A216 10c sal & vio brn   15 15

Mother's Day, 1971. See No. C300.

1867
CIV Aniversario*
No. 810 Overprinted **Fundación de la**
in Red   **Policía Nacional**
                     6-Julio
                     1971

1971, July 6   Litho.   Perf. 14
823 A209 40c pink & multi   35 18

104th anniversary of National Police. See No. C301.

Tiger Sharks A217

1971, July 28
824 A217 10c shown   15 15
825 A217 40c Swordfish   20 20
           Set value   26 28

See Nos. C302-C303.

Declaration of Independence — A218

Designs: Various sections of Declaration of Independence of Central America.

1971   Perf. 13½x13
826 A218 5c yel grn & blk   15 15
827 A218 10c brt rose & blk   15 15
828 A218 15c dp org & blk   15 15
829 A218 20c dp red lil & blk   15 15
           Set value, #826-829,
           C304-C307   1.70 1.30

Sesquicentennial of independence of Central America.
For overprints see Nos. C321, C347.

Izalco Church A219

Design: 30c, Sonsonate Church.

1971, Aug. 21   Litho.   Perf. 13x13½
830 A219 20c blk & multi   20 15
831 A219 30c pur & multi   30 15

See Nos. C308-C309.

No. 821 Overprinted in Carmine: "1972 Año de Turismo / de las Américas"
1972, Nov. 15   Litho.   Perf. 14
832 A215 30c multi   20 15

Tourist Year of the Americas, 1972.

No. 818 Overprinted **III Festival Internacional de Música 9 - 25 - Febrero - 1973.**
in Red

1973, Feb. 5   Litho.   Perf. 13½
833 A214 50c ol, brn & yel   25 20

3rd International Music Festival, Feb. 9-25. See No. C313.

Lions International Emblem — A220

1973, Feb. 20   Litho.   Perf. 13
834 A220 10c pink & multi   15 15
835 A220 25c lt bl & multi   15 15
           Set value   15 15

31st Lions International District "D" Convention, San Salvador, May 1972. See Nos. C314-C315.

No. 812 Overprinted: "1923 1973 / 50 AÑOS FUNDACION / FUERZA AEREA"
1973, Mar. 20   Litho.   Perf. 12
836 A210 30c lem & multi   18 18

50th anniversary of Salvadorian Air Force.

Hurdling A221

Designs (Olympic Emblem and): 10c, High jump. 25c, Running. 60c, Pole vault.

1973, May 21   Litho.   Perf. 13
837 A221 5c lil & multi   15 15
838 A221 10c dl org & multi   15 15
839 A221 25c bl & multi   15 15
840 A221 60c ultra & multi   28 25
           Nos. 837-840,C316-C319 (8)   3.48
           Set value   2.25

20th Olympic Games, Munich, Aug. 26-Sept. 11, 1972.

No. 777 Surcharged:

10 CTS.

1973, Dec.   Photo.   Perf. 13
841 A198 10c on 70c multi   15 15

See No. C320.

Nos. 774, C240 Surcharged with New Value and Overprinted "1823-1973 / 150 Aniversario Liberación / Esclavos en Centroamérica"
1973-74   Litho.   Perf. 11½
841A A197 5c on 6c multi ('74)   15 15
842 A197 10c on 45c multi   15 15

Sesquicentennial of the liberation of the slaves in Central America. On No. 841A two bars cover old denomination. On No. 842 "Aereo" is obliterated with a bar and old denomination with two bars.

Nos. 747 and 786 Surcharged:

5 CTS.

1974   Photo.   Perf. 11½x12
843 A189 5c on 6c buff & blk   15 15

Litho.   Perf. 12x11½
843A A200 5c on 6c multi   15 15
           Set value   16 15

No. 843A has one obliterating rectangle and sans-serif "5."
Issued: No. 843, Apr. 22. No. 843A, June 21.

Rehabilitation Institute Emblem — A222

1974, Apr. 30   Litho.   Perf. 13
844 A222 10c multi   15 15

10th anniversary of the Salvador Rehabilitation Institute. See No. C324.

INTERPOL Headquarters, Saint-Cloud, France — A223

1974, Sept. 2   Litho.   Perf. 12½
845 A223 10c multi   15 15

50th anniv. of Intl. Criminal Police Organization (INTERPOL). See No. C341.

UN and FAO Emblems — A224

1974, Sept. 2   Litho.   Perf. 12½
846 A224 10c bl, dk bl & gold   15 15

World Food Program, 10th anniversary. See No. C342.

25c Silver Coin, 1914 — A225

1974, Nov. 19   Litho.   Perf. 12½x13
848 A225 10c shown   15 15
849 A225 15c 50c silver, 1953   15 15
850 A225 25c 25c silver, 1943   15 15
851 A225 30c 1c copper, 1892   15 15
           Set value, #848-851,
           C343-C346   1.80 1.25

No. 763 Surcharged

XII Serie Ajedrez de Centro America y del Caribe Oct. 1974
5 cts.

1974, Oct. 14   Photo.   Perf. 11½x12
852 A192 5c on 6c multi   15 15

12th Central American and Caribbean Chess Tournament, Oct. 1974.

¢ 0.10

No. 762 and 771 Surcharged

Footnotes near stamp listings often refer to other stamps of the same design.

1974-75   *Perf. 11¹/₂x12, 12*
853 A192 10c on 3c multi   15 15
853A A195 25c on 1col multi ('75)   15 15
       Set value   16 15

Bar and surcharge on one line on No. 853A.
Issued: #853, Dec. 19; #853A, Jan. 13.

UPU
Emblem — A226

1975, Jan. 22   **Litho.**   *Perf. 13*
854 A226 10c bl & multi   15 15
855 A226 60c bl & multi   24 30
       Set value   28 35

Cent. of UPU. See Nos. C356-C357.

Acajutla
Harbor — A227

1975, Feb. 17
856 A227 10c blue & multi   15 15

See No. C358.

¢ 0.05

No. 799
Surcharged

1975   **Litho.**   *Perf. 11¹/₂*
857 A205 5c on 6c multi   15 15

Central Post
Office, San
Salvador
A228

1975, Apr. 25   **Litho.**   *Perf. 13*
858 A228 10c bl & multi   15 15

See No. C359.

Map of
Americas
and El
Salvador,
Trophy
A229

1975, June 25   **Litho.**   *Perf. 12¹/₂*
859 A229 10c red org & multi   15 15
860 A229 40c yel & multi   25 25
       Set value   32

El Salvador, site of 1975 Miss Universe Contest.
See Nos. C360-C361.

Claudia Lars, Poet,
and IWY
Emblem — A230

1975, Sept. 4   **Litho.**   *Perf. 12¹/₂*
861 A230 10c yel & bl blk   15 15

International Women's Year 1975. See Nos.
C362-C363.

Nurses Attending
Patient — A231

1975, Oct. 24   **Litho.**   *Perf. 12¹/₂*
862 A231 10c lt grn & multi   15 15

Nurses' Day. See No. C364. For overprint see
No. 868.

Congress
Emblem — A232

1975, Nov. 19   **Litho.**   *Perf. 12¹/₂*
863 A232 10c yel & multi   15 15

15th Conference of Inter-American Federation of
Securities Enterprises, San Salvador, Nov. 16-20.
See No. C365.

No. 768 Overprinted in Red: "XVI /
CONGRESO MEDICO /
CENTROAMERICANO / SAN SALVADOR,
/ EL SALVADOR, / DIC. 10-13, 1975"

1975, Nov. 26 Photo.   *Perf. 12x11¹/₂*
864 A194 15c beige & multi   15 15

16th Central American Medical Congress, San
Salvador, Dec. 10-13.

Flags of Participants,
Arms of
Salvador — A233

1975, Nov. 28   **Litho.**   *Perf. 12¹/₂*
865 A233 15c blk & multi   15 15
866 A233 50c brn & multi   20 20
       Set value   26 24

8th Ibero-Latin-American Dermatological Congress, San Salvador, Nov. 28-Dec. 3. See Nos.
C366-C367.

Jesus and Caritas
Emblem — A234

1975, Dec. 18   **Litho.**   *Perf. 13¹/₂*
867 A234 10c dl red & mar   15 15

7th Latin American Charity Congress, San Salvador, Nov. 1971. See No. C368.

No. 862 Overprinted: "III CONGRESO /
ENFERMERIA / CENCAMEX 76"

1976, May 10   **Litho.**   *Perf. 12¹/₂*
868 A231 10c lt grn & multi   15 15

CENCAMEX 76, 3rd Nurses' Congress.

Map of El
Salvador — A235

1976, May 18
869 A235 10c vio bl & multi   15 15

10th Congress of Revenue Collectors (Centro
Interamericano de Administradores Tributarios,
CIAT), San Salvador, May 16-22. See No. C382.

Flags of
Salvador
and US,
Torch,
Map of
Americas
A236

The Spirit of '76,
by Archibald M.
Willard — A237

1976, June 30   **Litho.**   *Perf. 12¹/₂*
870 A236 10c yel & multi   15 15
871 A237 40c multi   16 15
       Set value   20 18

American Bicentennial. See #C383-C384.

American Crocodile — A238

1976, Sept. 23   **Litho.**   *Perf. 12¹/₂*
872 A238 10c shown   18 15
873 A238 20c Green iguana   15 15
874 A238 30c Iguana   25 25
       Nos. 872-874,C385-C387 (6)   1.41 1.38

Post-classical Vase,
San
Salvador — A239

Pre-Columbian Art: 15c, Brazier with classical
head, Tazumal. 40c, Vase with classical head,
Tazumal.

1976, Oct. 11   **Litho.**   *Perf. 12¹/₂*
875 A239 10c multi   15 15
876 A239 15c multi   15 15
877 A239 40c multi   32 32
       Nos. 875-877,C388-C390 (6)   1.77 1.42

For overprint see No. C429.

Fair
Emblem — A240

1976, Oct. 25   **Litho.**   *Perf. 12¹/₂*
878 A240 10c multi   15 15
879 A240 30c gray & multi   24 24
       Set value   32 32

7th International Fair, Nov. 5-22. See Nos.
C391-C392.

Child under
Christmas
Tree — A241

1976, Dec. 16   **Litho.**   *Perf. 11*
880 A241 10c yel & multi   15 15
881 A241 15c buff & multi   15 15
882 A241 30c vio & multi   24 24
883 A241 40c pink & multi   32 32
       Nos. 880-883,C393-C396 (8)   2.56 1.96

Christmas 1976.

Rotary Emblem,
Map of
Salvador — A242

1977, June 20   **Litho.**   *Perf. 11*
884 A242 10c multi   15 15
885 A242 15c multi   15 15
       Set value   20 20

San Salvador Rotary Club, 50th anniversary. See
Nos. C397-C398.

Cerron
Grande
Hydroelectric
Station
A243

Designs: No. 887, 15c, Central sugar refinery,
Jiboa. 30c, Radar station, Izalco, vert.

1977, June 29   *Perf. 12¹/₂*
886 A243 10c multi   15 15
887 A243 10c multi   15 15
888 A243 15c multi   15 15
889 A243 30c multi   24 15
       Nos. 886-889,C399-C401 (7)   1.89
                                                   1.00

Industrial development. Nos. 886-889 have colorless overprint in multiple rows: GOBIERNO DEL
SALVADOR.

Nos. 785 and 774 Surcharged with New
Value and Bar

1977, June 30   *Perf. 12x11¹/₂, 11¹/₂*
890 A200 15c on 2c multi   15 15
891 A197 25c on 6c multi   20 15
       Set value   15

Microphone, ASDER Emblem A244

1977, Sept. 14   Litho.   Perf. 14
892 A244 10c multi   15 15
893 A244 15c multi   15 15
    Set value   20 20
Broadcasting in El Salvador, 50th anniversary (Asociacion Salvadoreño de Empresa Radio). See Nos. C406-C407.

Wooden Drum A245

Design: 10c, Flute and recorder.

1978, Aug. 29   Litho.   Perf. 12½
894 A245 5c multi   15 15
895 A245 10c multi   15 15
    Nos. 894-895,C433-C435 (5)   1.50
    Set value   80

For surcharge see No. C492.

"Man and Engineering" A246

1978, Sept. 12   Litho.   Perf. 13½
896 A246 10c multi   15 15
4th National Engineers' Congress, San Salvador, Sept. 18-23. See No. C436.

Izalco Station — A247

1978, Sept. 14   Perf. 12½
897 A247 10c multi   15 15
Inauguration of Izalco satellite earth station, Sept. 15, 1978. See No. C437.

Fair Emblem — A248

1978, Oct. 30   Litho.   Perf. 12½
898 A248 10c multi   15 15
899 A248 20c multi   16 16
    Set value   24 24
8th International Fair, Nov. 3-20. See Nos. C440-C441.

Henri Dunant, Red Cross Emblem A249

1978, Oct. 30   Perf. 11
900 A249 10c multi   15 15
Henri Dunant (1828-1910), founder of the Red Cross. See No. C442.

World Map and Cotton Boll — A250

1978, Nov. 22   Perf. 12½
901 A250 15c multi   15 15
International Cotton Consulting Committee, 37th Meeting, San Salvador, Nov. 27-Dec. 2. See No. C443.

Nativity, Stained-glass Window A251

1978, Dec. 5   Litho.   Perf. 12½
902 A251 10c multi   15 15
903 A251 15c multi   15 15
    Set value   20 20
Christmas 1978. See Nos. C444-C445.

Athenaeum Coat of Arms — A252

1978, Dec. 20   Litho.   Perf. 14
904 A252 5c multi   15 15
Millennium of Castilian language. See No. C446.

Postal Service and UPU Emblems A253

1979, Apr. 2   Litho.   Perf. 14
905 A253 10c multi   15 15
Centenary of Salvador's membership in Universal Postal Union. See No. C447.

"75," Health Organization and WHO Emblems A254

1979, Apr. 7   Perf. 14x14½
906 A254 10c multi   15 15
Pan-American Health Organization, 75th anniversary. See No. C448.

Flame and Pillars — A255

1979, May 25   Litho.   Perf. 12½
907 A255 10c multi   15 15
908 A255 15c multi   15 15
    Set value   20 20
Social Security 5-year plan, 1978-1982. See Nos. C449-C450.

Pope John Paul II, Map of Americas — A256

1979, July 12   Litho.   Perf. 14½x14
909 A256 10c multi   15 15
910 A256 20c multi   16 15
    Set value   24 15
See Nos. C454-C455.

Mastodon A257

1979, Sept. 7   Litho.   Perf. 14
911 A257 10c shown   15 15
912 A257 20c Saber-toothed tiger   16 16
913 A257 30c Toxodon   24 24
    Nos. 911-913,C458-C460 (6)   2.55 1.85

Salvador Flag, José Aberiz and Proclamation — A258

1979, Sept. 14   Perf. 14½x14
914 A258 10c multi   15 15
National anthem centenary. See No. C461.

Cogwheel around Map of Americas — A259

1979, Oct. 19   Litho.   Perf. 14½x14
915 A259 10c multi   15 15
8th COPIMERA Congress (Mechanical, Electrical and Allied Trade Engineers), San Salvador, Oct. 22-27. See No. C462.

Children of Various Races, IYC Emblem A260

Children and Nurses, IYC Emblem — A261

Perf. 14x14½, 14½x14
1979, Oct. 29
916 A260 10c multi   15 15
917 A261 15c multi   15 15
    Set value   20 20
International Year of the Child.

Map of Central and South America, Congress Emblem — A262

1979, Nov. 1   Litho.   Perf. 14½x14
918 A262 10c multi   15 15
5th Latin American Clinical Biochemistry Congress, San Salvador, Nov. 5-10. See No. C465.

Coffee Bushes in Bloom, Coffee Association Emblem A263

Salvador Coffee Association, 50th Anniversary: 30c, Planting coffee bushes, vert. 40c, Coffee berries.

Perf. 14x14½, 14½x14
1979, Dec. 18
919 A263 10c multi   15 15
920 A263 30c multi   24 24
921 A263 40c multi   32 32
    Nos. 919-921,C466-C468 (6)   2.51 1.91

10c Children, Dove and Star — A264

1979, Dec. 18   Perf. 14¹/₂x14
922 A264 10c multi   15 15
Christmas 1979.

Hoof and Mouth
Disease
Prevention
A265

1980, June 3   Litho.   Perf. 14¹/₂x14
923 A265 10c multi   15 15
See No. C469.

Anadara
Grandis
A266

1980, Aug. 12   Perf. 14x14¹/₂
924 A266 10c shown   15 15
925 A266 30c Ostrea iridescens   24 24
926 A266 40c Turitello leucostoma   32 32
Nos. 924-926,C470-C473 (7)   2.36 1.96

Quetzal (Pharomachrus mocino) — A267

1980, Sept. 10   Litho.   Perf. 14x14¹/₂
927 A267 10c shown   15 15
928 A267 20c Penelopina nigra   16 16
Nos. 927-928,C474-C476 (5)   1.51 1.11

Local Snakes
A268

1980, Nov. 12   Litho.   Perf. 14x14¹/₂
929 A268 10c Tree snake   15 15
930 A268 20c Water snake   16 16
Set value   24 24
See Nos. C477-C478.

A269   A270

1980, Nov. 26   Litho.   Perf. 14
931 A269 15c multi   15 15
932 A269 20c multi   16 16
Corporation of Auditors, 50th anniv. See Nos.
C479-C480.

1980, Dec. 5   Litho.   Perf. 14
933 A270 5c multi   15 15
934 A270 10c multi   15 15
Set value   15 15
Christmas. See Nos. C481-C482.

A271   A272

Dental association emblems.

1981, June 18   Litho.   Perf. 14
935 A271 15c lt yel grn & blk   15 15
Dental Society of Salvador, 50th anniv.; Odonto-
logical Federation of Central America and Panama,
25th anniv. See No. C494.

1981, Aug. 14   Litho.   Perf. 14x14¹/₂
Design: Hands reading braille book.
936 A272 10c multi   15 15
Nos. 936,C495-C498 (5)   2.15 1.50
Intl. Year of the Disabled.

A273   A274

1981, Aug. 28   Litho.   Perf. 14x14¹/₂
937 A273 10c multi   15 15
Roberto Quinonez Natl. Agriculture College,
25th anniv. See No. C499.

1981, Sept. 16   Litho.   Perf. 14x14¹/₂
938 A274 10c multi   15 15
World Food Day. See No. C500.

1981 World
Cup
Preliminaries
A275

1981, Nov. 27   Litho.   Perf. 14x14¹/₂
939 A275 10c shown   15 15
940 A275 40c Cup soccer ball, flags   32 25
Set value   40 32
See Nos. C505-C506.

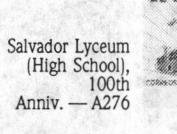

Salvador Lyceum
(High School),
100th
Anniv. — A276

1981, Dec. 17   Litho.   Perf. 14
941 A276 10c multi   15 15
See No. C507.

Pre-Columbian
Stone
Sculptures — A277

1982, Jan. 22   Litho.   Perf. 14
942 A277 10c Axe with bird's head   15 15
943 A277 20c Sun disc   16 16
944 A277 40c Stele Carving with ef-
             figy   32 32
Nos. 942-944,C508-C510 (6)   1.73 1.43

Scouting
Year — A278

1982, Mar. 17 Litho. Perf. 14¹/₂x14
945 A278 10c shown   15 15
946 A278 30c Girl Scout helping woman 24 24
See Nos. C511-C512.

Armed
Forces
A279

1982, May 7   Litho.   Perf. 14x13¹/₂
947 A279 10c multi   15 15
See No. C514.

1982 World
Cup
A280

1982, July 14   Perf. 14x14¹/₂
948 A280 10c Team, emblem   15 15
See Nos. C518-C520.

10th International
Fair — A281

1982, Oct. 14   Litho.   Perf. 14
949 A281 10c multi   15 15
See No. C524.

Christmas
1982 — A282

1982, Dec. 14   Litho.   Perf. 14
950 A282 5c multi   15 15
See No. C528.

Dancers, Pre-Colombian Ceramic
Design — A283

1983, Feb. 18   Litho.   Perf. 14
951 A283 10c shown   15 15
952 A283 20c Sower   16 16
953 A283 25c Flying Man   20 20
954 A283 60c Hunters   50 50
955 A283 60c Hunters, diff.   50 50
956 A283 1col Procession   80 80
957 A283 1col Procession, diff.   80 80
Nos. 951-957 (7)   3.11 3.11
Nos. 953-957 airmail. Stamps of same denomination se-tenant.

Visit of Pope
John Paul
II — A284

1983, Mar. 4   Litho.   Perf. 14
958 A284 25c shown   20 20
959 A284 60c Monument to the Divine
             Savior, Pope   50 40

Salvadoran Air
Force, 50th
Anniv.
A285

1983, Mar. 24   Litho.   Perf. 14
960 A285 10c Ricardo Aberle   15 15
961 A285 10c Air Force Emblem   15 15
962 A285 10c Enrico Massi   15 15
a.   Strip of 3, #960-962   24 24
963 A285 10c Juan Ramon Munes   15 15
964 A285 10c American Air Force Coop-
             eration Emblem   15 15

965 A285 10c Belisario Salazar   15   15
  a.   Strip of 3, #963-965   24   24
         Set value   48   48

Arranged se-tenant horizontally with two Nos.
960 or 963 at left and two Nos. 962 or 965 at
right.

A286   A287

Local butterflies.

1983, May 31   Litho.   Perf. 14
966   Pair   15   15
  a.   A286 5c Papilio torquatus   15   15
  b.   A286 5c Metamorpha steneles   15   15
967   Pair   16   16
  a.   A286 10c Papilio torquatus, diff. 15   15
  b.   A286 10c Anaea marthesia   15   15
968   Pair   24   24
  a.   A286 15c Prepona brooksiana   15   15
  b.   A286 15c Caligo atreus   15   15
969   Pair   40   40
  a.   A286 25c Morpho peleides   20   20
  b.   A286 25c Dismorphia praxinoe   20   20
970   Pair   80   80
  a.   A286 50c Morpho polyphemus   40   40
  b.   A286 50c Metamorphia epaphus   40   40
         Nos. 966-970 (5)   1.75 1.75

1983, June 23   Litho.   Perf. 14
971 A287 75c multi   60   50

Simon Bolivar, 200th birth anniv.

A288   A289

1983, July 21   Litho.   Perf. 14
972 A288 10c Dr. Jose Mendoza, col-
         lege emblem   15   15

Salvador Medical College, 40th anniv.

Perf. 13¹/₂x14, 14x13¹/₂
1983, Oct. 30   Litho.
973 A289 10c multi   15   15
974 A289 50c multi, horiz.   40   40

Centenary of David J. Guzman national museum.
50c airmail.

World Communications Year — A290

Designs: 10c, Gen. Juan Jose Canas, Francisco
Duenas (organizers of First natl. telegraph service),
Morse key, 1870. 25c, Mailman delivering letters,
vert. 50c, Post Office sorting center, San Salvador.
25c, 50c airmail.

Perf. 14x13¹/₂, 13¹/₂x14
1983, Nov. 23   Litho.
975 A290 10c multi   15   15
976 A290 25c multi   20   20
977 A290 50c multi   40   30

A291   A292

Perf. 13¹/₂x14, 14x13¹/₂
1983, Nov. 30
978 A291 10c Dove over globe   15   15
979 A291 25c Creche figures, horiz.   20   20
         Set value   28   28

Christmas. 25c is airmail.

1983, Dec. 13
980 A292 10c Vehicle exhaust   15   15
981 A292 15c Fig tree   15   15
982 A292 25c Rodent   20   20
         Set value   40   40

Environmental protection. 15c, 25c airmail.

Philatelists' Day — A293   Corn — A294

1984, Jan. 5   Perf. 14x13¹/₂
983 A293 10c No. 1   15   15

1984, Feb. 21 Litho.   Perf. 14¹/₂x14
984 A294 10c shown   15   15
985 A294 15c Cotton   15   15
986 A294 25c Coffee beans   15   15
987 A294 50c Sugar cane   20   15
988 A294 75c Beans   30   22
989 A294 1col Agave   40   30
990 A294 5col Balsam   2.00 1.50
         Nos. 984-990 (7)   3.35 2.62

See Nos. 1047-1051.

Caluco
Church,
Sonsonate
A295

1984, Mar. 30   Perf. 14x13¹/₂
991 A295 5c shown   15   15
992 A295 10c Salcoatitan, Sonsonate   15   15
993 A295 15c Huizucar, La Libertad   15   15
994 A295 25c Santo Domingo, Son-
         sonate   15   15
995 A295 50c Pilar, Sonsonate   20   15
996 A295 75c Nahuizalco, Sonsonate   30   22
         Set value   75   60

Nos. 993-996 airmail.

Central
Reserve Bank
of Salvador,
50th Anniv.
A296

1984, July 17 Litho.   Perf. 14x14¹/₂
997 A296 10c First reserve note   15   15
998 A296 25c Bank, 1959   15   15
         Set value   15   15

25c airmail.

1984 Summer
Olympics
A297

Perf. 14x13¹/₂, 13¹/₂x14
1984, July 20
999 A297 10c Boxing   15   15
1000 A297 25c Running, vert.   15   15
1001 A297 40c Bicycling   16   15
1002 A297 50c Swimming   20   15
1003 A297 75c Judo, vert.   30   22
1004 A297 1col Pierre de Coubertin   40   30
         Set value   1.20 90

Nos. 1000-1004 airmail.
For surcharge see No. C536A.

Govt. Printing
Office
Building
Opening
A298

1984, July 27   Perf. 14x13¹/₂
1005 A298 10c multi   15   15

5th of
November
Hydroelectric
Plant — A299

Designs: 55c, Cerron Grande Plant. 70c,
Ahuachapan Geothermal Plant. 90c, Mural. 2col,
15th of September Plant. 7c, 90c, 2 col airmail.

1984, Sept. 13 Litho.   Perf. 14x14¹/₂
1006 A299 20c multi   15   15
1007 A299 55c multi   22   18
1008 A299 70c multi   28   22
1009 A299 90c multi   36   28
1010 A299 2col multi   80   60
         Nos. 1006-1010 (5)   1.81 1.43

Boys Playing
Marbles — A300

1984, Oct. 16   Perf. 14¹/₂x14
1011 A300 55c shown   22   18
1012 A300 70c Spinning top   28   22
1013 A300 90c Flying kite   36   28
1014 A300 2col Top, diff.   80   60

11th
International
Fair — A301

1984, Oct. 31 Litho.   Perf. 14x14¹/₂
1015 A301 25c shown   15   15
1016 A301 70c Fairgrounds   28   22
         Set value   30

70c airmail.

Los Chorros
Tourist Center
A302

1984, Nov. 23 Litho.   Perf. 14x14¹/₂
1017 A302 15c shown   15   15
1018 A302 25c Plaza las Americas   15   15
1019 A302 70c El Salvador Interna-
         tional Airport   28   22
1020 A302 90c El Tunco Beach   36   28
1021 A302 2col Sihuatehuacan Tour-
         ist Center   80   60
         Nos. 1017-1021 (5)   1.74
         Set value   1.20

The Paper of
Papers, 1979,
by Roberto A.
Galicia (b.
1945)
A302a

Paintings by natl. artists: 20c, The White Nun,
1939, by Salvador Salazar Arrue (b. 1899), vert.
70c, Supreme Elegy to Masferrer, 1968, by Antonio
G. Ponce (b. 1938), vert. 90c, Transmutation,
1979, by Armando Solis (b. 1940). 2 col, Figures at
Theater, 1959, by Carlos Canas (b. 1924), vert.

1984, Dec. 10   Perf. 14
1021A A302a 20c multi   15   15
1021B A302a 55c multi   22   16
1021C A302a 70c multi   28   22
1021D A302a 90c multi   35   26
1021E A302a 2col multi   75   60
         Nos. 1021A-1021E (5)   1.75 1.39

Nos. 1021B-1021E are airmail. 70c and 2col
issued with overprinted silver bar and corrected
inscription in black; copies exist without overprint.

Christmas
1984 — A303

1984, Dec. 19   Litho.
1022 A303 25c Glass ornament   15   15
1023 A303 70c Ornaments, dove   28   22
         Set value   30

No. 1023 airmail.

Birds — A304

1984, Dec. 21 Litho.   Perf. 14¹/₂x14
1024 A304 15c Lepidocolaptes affinis   15   15
1025 A304 25c Spodiornis rusticus
         barriliensis   15   15
1026 A304 55c Claravis mondetoura   22   18
1027 A304 70c Hylomanes momotu-
         la   28   22
1028 A304 90c Xenotriccus cal-
         izonus   36   28
1029 A304 1col Cardellina rubrifrons   45   35
         Nos. 1024-1029 (6)   1.61
         Set value   1.15

Nos. 1026-1029 airmail.

Salvador
Bank
Centenary
A305

1985, Feb. 6   Litho.   Perf. 14
1030 A305 25c Stock certificate   15 15

Mortgage Bank,
50th
Anniv. — A306

1985, Feb. 20   Litho.   Perf. 14
1031 A306 25c Mortgage   15 15

Intl. Youth
Year — A307

1985, Feb. 28   Litho.   Perf. 14
1032 A307 25c IYY emblem   15 15
1033 A307 55c Woodcrafting   22 18
1034 A307 70c Professions symbol-
             ized   28 22
1035 A307 1.50col Youths marching   60 45

Nos. 1033-1035 airmail.

Archaeology
A308

1985, Mar. 6   Litho.   Perf. 14¹/₂x14
1036 A308 15c Pre-classical figure   15 15
1037 A308 20c Engraved vase   15 15
1038 A308 25c Post-classical ceramic   15 15
1039 A308 55c Post-classical figure   22 18
1040 A308 70c Late post-classical
             deity   28 22
1041 A308 1col Late post-classical
             figure   40 30
          Set value   1.12 88

Souvenir Sheet
Rouletted 13¹/₂
1042 A308 2col Tazumal ruins,
             horiz.   80 60

Nos. 1039-1041 airmail. No. 1042 has enlarge-
ment of stamp design in margin.

Natl. Red
Cross,
Cent. — A309

1985, Mar. 13   Litho.   Perf. 14
1043 A309 25c Anniv. emblem vert.   15 15
1044 A309 55c Sea rescue   20 15
1045 A309 70c Blood donation service   25 20
1046 A309 90c First aid, ambulance,
             vert.   35 26

Nos. 1044-1046 are airmail.

Agriculture Type of 1984
1985   Perf. 14¹/₂x14
1047 A294 55c Cotton   20 15
1048 A294 70c Corn   25 20
1049 A294 90c Sugar cane   35 26
1050 A294 2col Beans   75 60
1051 A294 10col Agave   4.00 3.00
          Nos. 1047-1051 (5)   5.55 4.21

Issue dates: 55c, 70c, 90c, Apr. 4. 2col, 10col,
Sept. 4.

Child
Survival
A310

Children's drawings.

1985, May 3   Litho.   Perf. 14x14¹/₂
1052 A310 25c Hand, houses   15 15
1053 A310 55c House, children   20 15
1054 A310 70c Boy, girl holding hands   25 20
1055 A310 90c Oral vaccination   35 28

Nos. 1053-1055 are airmail.

Salvador
Army
A311

1985, May 17   Perf. 14
1056 A311 25c Map   15 15
1057 A311 70c Recruit, natl. flag   25 20
          Set value   26

No. 1057 is airmail.

Inauguration of
Pres. Duarte, 1st
Anniv. — A312

1985, June 28   Perf. 14¹/₂x14
1058 A312 25c Flag, laurel, book   15 15
1059 A312 70c Article I, Constitution   25 20

Inter-American Development Bank, 25th
Anniv. — A313

Bank emblem and: 25c, Central Hydro-electric
Dam, power station. 70c, Map of Salvador. 1col,
Natl. arms.

1985, July 5   Perf. 14x13¹/₂
1060 A313 25c multi   15 15
1061 A313 70c multi   25 20
1062 A313 1col multi   38 30

Nos. 1061-1062 are airmail.

Fish — A314

1985, Sept. 30   Perf. 14x14¹/₂
1064 A314 25c Cichlasoma
             trimaculatum   15 15
1065 A314 55c Rhamdia
             guatemalensis   20 15
1066 A314 70c Poecilia sphenops   25 20
1067 A314 90c Cichlasoma
             nigrofasciatum   35 28
1068 A314 1col Astyanax fas-
             ciatus   38 30
1069 A314 1.50col Dormitator la-
             tifrons   60 42
          Nos. 1064-1069 (6)   1.93 1.50

Nos. 1065-1069 are airmail.

UNFAO, 40th
Anniv. — A315

1985, Oct. 16   Perf. 14¹/₂x14
1070 A315 20c Cornucopia   15 15
1071 A315 40c Centeotl, Nahuat god of
             corn   15 15
          Set value   22 18

Dragonflies
A316

Designs: 25c, Cordulegaster godmani mclachlan.
55c, Libellula herculea karsch. 70c, Cora marina
selys. 90c, Aeshna cornigera braver. 1col, Mecisto-
gaster ornata rambur. 1.50col, Hetaerina
smaragdalis de marmels.

1985, Dec. 9   Perf. 14x14¹/₂
1072 A316   25c multi   15 15
1073 A316   55c multi   20 15
1074 A316   70c multi   25 20
1075 A316   90c multi   35 28
1076 A316   1col multi   38 30
1077 A316   1.50col multi   60 42
          Nos. 1072-1077 (6)   1.93 1.50

Nos. 1073-1077 are airmail.
For surcharge see No. C544.

Summer, 1984,
by Roberto
Huezo (b.1947)
A317

Paintings by natl. artists: 25c, Profiles, 1978, by
Rosa Mena Valenzuela (b. 1924), vert. 70c, The
Deliverance, 1984, by Fernando Llort (b. 1949).
90c, Making Tamale, 1975, by Pedro A. Garcia (b.
1930). 1col, Warm Presence, 1984, by Miguel A.
Orellana (b. 1929), vert. Nos. 1079-1082 are
airmail.

1985, Dec. 18   Perf. 14
1078 A317 25c multi   15 15
1079 A317 55c multi   20 15
1080 A317 70c multi   25 20
1081 A317 90c multi   35 26
1082 A317 1col multi   38 30
          Nos. 1078-1082 (5)   1.33 1.06

San Vincente
de Austria y
Lorenzana
City, 350th
Anniv.
A318

1985, Dec. 20
1083 A318 15c Tower, vert.   15 15
1084 A318 20c Cathedral   15 15
          Set value   15 15

Intl. Peace Year
1986 — A319

1986, Feb. 21   Litho.   Perf. 14
1085 A319 15c multi   15 15
1086 A319 70c multi   50 38

Postal Code
Inauguration
A320

1986, Mar. 14   Litho.   Perf. 14x14¹/₂
1087 A320 20c Domestic mail   16 15
1088 A320 25c Intl. mail   18 15

Radio El
Salvador, 60th
Anniv.
A321

1986, Mar. 21
1089 A321 25c Microphone   18 15
1090 A321 70c Map   50 38

No. 1090 is airmail.

Mammals
A322

1986, May 30   Litho.   Perf. 14x14¹/₂
1091 A322 15c Felis wiedii   15 15
1092 A322 20c Tamandua te-
             tradactyla   16 15
1093 A322 1col Dasypus novemcinc-
             tus   80 60
1094 A322 2col Pecarii tajacu   1.60 1.20

Nos. 1093-1094 are airmail.

1986 World Cup Soccer Championships, Mexico — A323

Designs: 70c, Flags, mascot. 1col, Players, Soccer Cup, vert. 2col, Natl. flag, player dribbling, vert. 5col, Goal, emblem.

1986, June 6   Perf. 14x14¹/₂, 14¹/₂x14

1095	A323	70c multi	55	42
1096	A323	1col multi	80	60
1097	A323	2col multi	1.60	1.20
1098	A323	5col multi	4.00	3.00

Teachers — A324

1986, June 30   Litho.   Perf. 14¹/₂x14

1099	A324	20c Dario Gonzalez	15	15
1100	A324	20c Valero Lecha	15	15
1101	A324	40c Marcelino G. Flamenco	20	15
1102	A324	40c Camilo Campos	20	15
1103	A324	70c Saul Flores	32	24
1104	A324	70c Jorge Larde	32	24
1105	A324	1col Francisco Moran	48	35
1106	A324	1col Mercedes M. De Luarca	48	35
		Nos. 1099-1106 (8)	2.30	1.78

Stamps of the same denomination printed setenant. Nos. 1103-1106 are airmail.

Pre-Hispanic Ceramic Seal, Cara Sucia, Ahuachapan, Tlaloc Culture (300 B.C.-A.D. 1200) — A325

1986, July 23   Litho.   Perf. 13¹/₂

1107	A325	25c org & brn	15	15
1108	A325	55c grn, org & brn	25	18
1109	A325	70c pale gray, org & brn	32	24
1110	A325	90c pale yel, org & brn	45	32
1111	A325	1col pale grn, org & brn	48	35
1112	A325	1.50col pale pink, org & brn	70	52
		Nos. 1107-1112 (6)	2.35	1.76

Nos. 1108-1112 are airmail.

World Food Day — A326

1986, Oct. 30   Litho.   Perf. 14x14¹/₂

1113	A326	20c multi	16	15

Flowers A327

1986, Sept. 30   Perf. 14

1114	A327	20c Spathiphyllum phrynifolium, vert.		
1115	A327	25c Asclepias curassavica	15	15
1116	A327	70c Tagetes tenuifolia	32	24
1117	A327	1col Ipomoea tiliacea, vert.	48	35
		Set value		76

Nos. 1116-1117 are airmail.

Christmas A328

Perf. 14x14¹/₂, 14¹/₂x14

1986, Dec. 10   Litho.

1118	A328	25c Candles, vert.	15	15
1119	A328	70c Doves	32	24

No. 1119 is airmail.

Crafts — A329

1986, Dec. 18

1120	A329	25c Basket-making	15	15
1121	A329	55c Ceramicware	25	18
1122	A329	70c Guitars, vert.	32	24
1123	A329	1col Baskets, diff.	48	35

Christmas A330

Paintings: 25c, Church, by Mario Araujo Rajo, vert. 70c, Landscape, by Francisco Reyes.

1986, Dec. 22

1124	A330	25c multi	15	15
1125	A330	70c multi	32	24

No. 1125 is airmail.

Promotion of Philately A331

1987, Mar. 10   Litho.   Perf. 14¹/₂x14

1126	A331	25c multi	15	15

Intl. Aid Following Earthquake, Oct. 10, 1986 — A332

1987, Mar. 25

1127	A332	15c multi	15	15
1128	A332	70c multi	32	24
1129	A332	1.50col multi	70	52
1130	A332	5col multi	2.40	1.80

Orchids — A333

1987, June 8   Litho.   Perf. 14¹/₂x14

1131	A333	20c Maxillaria tenuifolia	15	15
1132	A333	20c Ponthieva maculata	15	15
1133	A333	25c Meiracyllium trinasutum	15	15
1134	A333	25c Encyclia vagans	15	15
1135	A333	70c Encyclia cochleata	32	24
1136	A333	70c Maxillaria atrata	32	24
1137	A333	1.50col Sobrialia xantholeuca	70	52
1138	A333	1.50col Encyclia microcharis	70	52
		Nos. 1131-1138 (8)	2.64	
		Set value		1.85

Nos. 1133-1138 horiz. Stamps of the same denomination printed se-tenant. Nos. 1135-1138 are airmail.

Teachers — A334

Designs: No. 1139, C. de Jesus Alas, music. No. 1140, Luis Edmundo Vasquez, medicine. No. 1141, David Rosales, law. No. 1142, Guillermo Trigueros, medicine. No. 1143, Manuel Farfan Castro, history. No. 1144, Iri Sol, voice. No. 1145, Carlos Arturo Imendia, primary education. No. 1146, Benjamin Orozco, chemistry.

1987, June 30   Litho.   Perf. 14¹/₂x14

1139	A334	15c greenish blue & blk	15	15
1140	A334	15c greenish blue & blk	15	15
1141	A334	20c beige & blk	15	15
1142	A334	20c beige & blk	15	15
1143	A334	70c yel org & blk	32	24
1144	A334	70c yel org & blk	32	24
1145	A334	1.50col lt blue grn & blk	70	52
1146	A334	1.50col lt blue grn & blk	70	52
		Nos. 1139-1146 (8)	2.64	
		Set value		1.80

Stamps of the same denomination printed se-tenant. Nos. 1143-1146 are airmail.

10th Pan American Games, Indianapolis A335

Perf. 14¹/₂x14, 14x14¹/₂

1987, July 31

1147	A335	20c Emblem, vert.	15	15
1148	A335	20c Table tennis, vert.	15	15
1149	A335	25c Wrestling	15	15
1150	A335	25c Fencing	15	15
1151	A335	70c Softball	32	24
1152	A335	70c Equestrian	32	24
1153	A335	5col Weight lifting, vert.	2.35	1.75
1154	A335	5col Hurdling, vert.	2.35	1.75
		Nos. 1147-1154 (8)	5.94	4.58

Stamps of the same denomination are printed se-tenant. Nos. 1151-1154 are airmail.

Prior Nicolas Aguilar (1742-1818) A336

Famous men: 20c, Domingo Antonio de Lara (1783-1814), aviation pioneer. 70c, Juan Manuel Rodrigues (1771-1837), president who abolished slavery. 1.50col, Pedro Pablo Castillo (1780-1814), patriot.

1987, Sept. 11   Litho.   Perf. 14¹/₂x14

1155	A336	15c multi	15	15
1156	A336	20c multi	15	15
1157	A336	70c multi	32	24
1158	A336	1.50col multi	70	52
		Set value		90

Nos. 1157-1158 are airmail.

World Food Day A337

1987, Oct. 16   Perf. 14x14¹/₂

1159	A337	50c multi	24	18

Paintings by Salarrue — A338

Perf. 14¹/₂x14, 14x14¹/₂

1987, Nov. 30

1160	A338	25c Self-portrait	15	15
1161	A338	70c Lake	32	24

No. 1161 is airmail.
See Nos. 1186-1189.

Christmas 1987 — A339

Designs: 25c, Virgin of Perpetual Sorrow, stained-glass window. 70c, The Three Magi, figurines.

1987, Nov. 18   Perf. 14x14¹/₂

1162	A339	25c multi	15	15
1163	A339	70c multi	32	24

No. 1163 is airmail.

Pre-Columbian
Musical
Instruments
20c. A340

Designs: 20c, Pottery drum worn around neck. No. 1165, Frieze picturing pre-Columbian musicians, from a Salua culture ceramic vase, c. 700-800 A.D. (left side), vert. No. 1166, Frieze (right side), vert. 1.50col, Conch shell trumpet.

Perf. 14x14½, 14½x14

1987, Dec. 14			Litho.	
1164	A340	20c multi	15	15
1165	A340	70c multi	32	24
1166	A340	70c multi	32	24
1167	A340	1.50col multi	70	52

Nos. 1165-1167 are airmail. Nos. 1165-1166 are printed se-tenant in a continuous design.

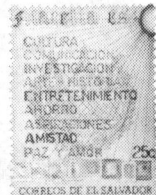

Promotion of
Philately — A341

1988, Jan. 20		Litho.	Perf. 14	
1168	A341	25c multi	15	15

Young
Entrepreneurs
of El Salvador
A342

1988			Perf. 14x14½	
1169	A342	25c multi	15	15

St. John Bosco
(1815-88)
A343

1988, Mar. 15		Litho.	Perf. 14x14½	
1170	A343	20c multi	15	15

Environmental
Protection
A344

1988, June 3		Litho.	Perf. 14x14½	
1171	A344	20c Forests	15	15
1172	A344	70c Forests and rivers	35	28
		Set value		35

No. 1172 is airmail.

1988-1992
Summer
Olympics,
Seoul and
Barcelona
A345

1988, Aug. 31		Litho.	Perf. 13½	
1173	A345	1col High jump		
1174	A345	1col Javelin		
1175	A345	1col Shooting		
1176	A345	1col Wrestling		
1177	A345	1col Basketball		
a.		Strip of 5, Nos. 1173-1177		
b.		Min. sheets of 5 + 5 labels		

1178 A345 2col Torch

Souvenir Sheets

Printed in sheets of 10 containing 2 each Nos. 1173-1177.
No. 1177b exists in 2 forms: 1st contains labels picturing 1988 Summer Games emblem or character trademark; 2nd contains labels picturing the 1992 Summer Games emblem or character trademark.
No. 1178 exists in 2 forms: 1st contains 1988 Games emblem; 2nd contains 1992 Games emblem.
Some, or all, of this issue seem not to have been available to the public.

World Food
Day — A346

1988, Oct. 11		Litho.	Perf. 14x14½	
1179	A346	20c multi	15	15

13th Intl. Fair,
Nov. 23-Dec.
11 — A347

1988, Oct. 25			Perf. 14½x14	
1180	A347	70c multi	35	28

Child Protection
A348

1988, Nov. 10				
1181	A348	15c Flying kite	15	15
1182	A348	20c Child hugging adult's leg	15	15
		Set value	18	15

Christmas
A349

Paintings by Titian: 25c, Virgin and Child with the Young St. John and St. Anthony. 70c, Virgin

and Child in Glory with St. Francis and St. Alvise, vert.

Perf. 14x14½, 14½x14

1988, Nov. 15				
1183	A349	25c multi	15	15
1184	A349	70c multi	35	28
		Set value		36

70c is airmail.

Return to Moral
Values — A350

1988, Nov. 22			Perf. 14½x14	
1185	A350	25c multi	15	15

Art Type of 1987

Paintings by Salvadoran artists: 40c, Esperanza de los Soles, by Victor Rodriguez Preza. 1col, Shepherd's Song, by Luis Angel Salinas, horiz. 2col, Children, by Julio Hernandez Aleman, horiz. 5col, El Nino de Las Alcancias, by Camilo Minero. Nos. 1187-1189 are airmail.

Perf. 14½x14, 14x14½

1988, Nov. 30				
1186	A338	40c multi	20	15
1187	A338	1col multi	50	38
1188	A338	2col multi	1.00	75
1189	A338	5col multi	2.50	1.90

A351

Discovery of America, 500th Anniv. (in 1992) — A352

Ruins and artifacts: a, El Tazumul. b, Multicolored footed bowl. c, San Andres. d, Two-color censer. e, Sihuatan. f, Carved head of the God of Lluvia. g, Cara Sucia. h, Man-shaped vase. i, San Lorenzo. j, Multicolored pear-shaped vase. 2col, Christopher Columbus.

1988, Dec. 21			Perf. 14x14½	
1190		Sheet of 10	5.00	3.80
a.-j.		A351 1col any single	50	38

Souvenir Sheet
Roulette 13½

| 1191 | A352 | 2col vermilion | 1.00 | 75 |

UN
Declaration of
Human Rights,
40th Anniv.
A353

1988, Dec. 9			Perf. 14½x14, 14x14½	
1192	A353	25c Family, map, emblem, vert.	15	15
1193	A353	70c shown	35	28
		Set value		36

70c is airmail.

World Wildlife
Fund — A354

Felines: a, Felis wiedii laying on tree branch. b, Felis wiedii sitting on branch. c, Felis pardalis laying in brush. d, Felis pardalis standing on tree branch.

1988			Perf. 14½x14	
1194		Strip of 4	82	60
a.-b.	A354	25c any single	15	15
c.-d.	A354	55c any single	28	21

World
Meteorological
Organization,
40th
Anniv. — A355

1989, Feb. 3		Litho.	Perf. 14½x14	
1195	A355	15c shown	15	15
1196	A355	20c Wind gauge	15	15
		Set value	18	15

Meteorology in El Salvador, cent.

Promotion of
Philately
A356

1989, Mar. 15		Litho.	Perf. 14½x14	
1197	A356	25c Philatelic Soc. emblem	15	15

See No. 1230.

Natl. Fire
Brigade, 106th
Anniv.
A357

1989, June 19		Litho.	Perf. 14x14½	
1198	A357	25c Fire truck	15	15
1199	A357	70c Firemen	35	28
		Set value		36

French
Revolution,
Bicent.
A358

1989, July 12

1200	A358	90c Anniv. emblem	45	35
1201	A358	1col Storming of the Bastille	48	38

Souvenir Sheets

Stamps on Stamps
A359

Statues of Queen Isabella and Christopher Columbus
A360

Designs: a, #88. b, #101. c, #86. d, #102. e, #87. f, #103.

1989, May 31   Litho.   Perf. 14x14½
Miniature Sheet

1202	Sheet of 6	1.20	90
a.-f.	A359 50c any single	20	15

Souvenir Sheet
Rouletted 13½

1203	A360 2col shown	78	58

Discovery of America, 500th anniv. (in 1992). No. 1203 exists in two forms: margin pictures Natl. Palace with either 500th anniv. emblem or anniv. emblem and "92" at lower right.

Signing Act of Independence
A361

1989, Sept. 1   Perf. 14x14½

1204	A361	25c shown	15	15
1205	A361	70c Flag, natl. seal, heroes	28	20
		Set value		28

Natl. independence, 168th anniv. No. 1205 is airmail.

Demographic Assoc., 27th Anniv.
A362

1989, July 26

1206	A362 25c multi		15	15

1990 World Cup Soccer Championships, Italy — A363

Soccer ball, flags of Salvador and: No. 1207, US No. 1208, Guatemala. No. 1209, Costa Rica. No. 1210, Trinidad & Tobago. 55c, Trinidad & Tobago, Guatemala, US, Costa Rica. 1col, Soccer ball, Cuscatlan Stadium.

1989, Sept. 1   Litho.   Perf. 14x14½

1207	A363	20c shown	15	15
1208	A363	20c multicolored	15	15
a.		Pair, #1207-1208	20	20
1209	A363	25c multicolored	15	15
1210	A363	25c multicolored	15	15
a.		Pair, #1209-1210	25	25
1211	A363	55c multicolored	25	18
1212	A363	1col multicolored	48	36
		Set value	1.15	86

Beatification of Marcellin Champagnat, Founder of the Marist Brothers Order
A364

1989, Sept. 28

1213	A364	20c multicolored	16	15

America Issue — A365

UPAE emblem and pre-Columbian artifacts: 25c, *The Cultivator*, rock painting. 70c, Ceramic urn.

1989, Oct. 12

1214	A365	25c multicolored	15	15
1215	A365	70c multicolored	35	28

World Food Day — A366

Perf. 14x14½, 14½x14
1989, Oct. 16   Litho.

1216	A366	15c shown	15	15
1217	A366	55c Aspects of agriculture, vert.	28	20
		Set value	36	26

Children's Rights — A367

1989, Oct. 26   Litho.   Perf. 14½x14

1218	A367	25c multicolored	18	15

Creche Figures — A368

1989, Dec. 1

1219	A368	25c shown	15	15
1220	A368	70c Holy Family, diff.	35	28

Christmas.

Birds of Prey — A369

Perf. 14½x14, 14x14½
1989, Dec. 20

1221	A369	70c *Sarcoramphus papa*	35	28
1222	A369	1col *Polyborus plancus*	50	38
1223	A369	2col *Accipiter striatus*	1.00	75
1224	A369	10col *Glaucidium brasilianum*	5.00	3.75

Nos. 1221 and 1223 vert.

Tax Court, 50th Aniv.
A370

1990, Jan. 12   Litho.   Perf. 14x14½

1225	A370	50c multicolored	20	16

Lord Baden-Powell, 133rd Birth Anniv. — A371

1990, Feb. 23   Perf. 14½x14

1226	A371	25c multicolored	18	15

Intl. Women's Day — A372

1990, Mar. 8   Litho.   Perf. 14½x14

1227	A372	25c multicolored	15	15

Type of 1989 and

Hour Glass — A373

1990   Perf. 14½x14

1228	A373	25c multicolored	15	15
1229	A373	55c multicolored	22	16
		Set value		24

Souvenir Sheet
Rouletted 13½ with Simulated Perfs.

1230	A356 2col blk & pale blue	78	58

Philatelic Soc., 50th anniv. Nos. 1229-1230 are airmail.

Fight Against Addictions
A375

1990, Apr. 26   Litho.   Perf. 14x14½

1231	A375	20c Alcohol	15	15
1232	A375	25c Smoking	15	15
1233	A375	1.50col Drugs	55	42
		Set value	68	52

No. 1233 is airmail.

La Prensa, 75th Anniv. — A376

1990, May 14   Litho.   Perf. 14½x14

1234	A376	15c multicolored	15	15
1235	A376	25c "75", newspaper	15	15
		Set value		20

55c. A377

World Cup Soccer Championships, Italy — A378

Soccer player and flags of: No. 1236, Argentina, USSR, Cameroun, Romania. No. 1237, Italy, US, Austria, Czechoslovakia. No. 1238, Brazil, Costa Rica, Sweden, Scotland. No. 1239, Germany, United Arab Emirates, Yugoslavia, Colombia. No. 1240, Belgium, Spain, Korea, Uruguay. No. 1241, England, Netherlands, Ireland, Egypt.

1990, June 15   Perf. 14x14½

1236	A377	55c multicolored	25	18
1237	A377	55c multicolored	25	18
1238	A377	70c multicolored	35	25
1239	A377	70c multicolored	35	25
1240	A377	1col multicolored	50	38
1241	A377	1col multicolored	50	38
1242	A378	1.50col multicolored	75	58
	Nos. 1236-1242 (7)		2.95	2.20

For surcharge see No. 1245.

Christopher Columbus
A379

Columbus, Map — A380

Stained glass window: b, Queen Isabella. c, Columbus' Arms. d, Discovery of America 500th anniv. emblem. e, One boat of Columbus' fleet. f, Two boats.

1990, July 30   Litho.   Perf. 14
Miniature Sheet
1243   Sheet of 6   3.00 2.30
a.-f. A379 1col any single   50   38
Souvenir Sheet
Rouletted 13 1/2
1244 A380 2col multicolored   1.10   82
See Nos. 1283-1284.

No. 1239 Surcharged in Black

90c.   ▬

1991, Feb.   Litho.   Perf. 14x14 1/2
1245 A377 90c on 70c multi   45   25

World Summit for
Children — A381

1990, Sept. 25   Perf. 14 1/2x14
1246 A381 5col blk, gold & dk bl   2.75 2.00

First Postage
Stamps, 150th
Anniv.
A382

Designs: a, Sir Rowland Hill. b, Penny Black. c, No. 21. d, Central Post Office. e, No. C124.

1990, Oct. 5   Litho.   Perf. 14
1247   Sheet of 5 + label   4.65 3.50
a.-e. A382 2col any single   95   70

World Food
Day — A383

1990, Oct. 16   Litho.   Perf. 14
1248 A383 5col multicolored   2.35 1.75

San Salvador
Electric Light
Co.,
Cent. — A384

1990, Oct. 30
1249 A384 20c shown   15   15
1250 A384 90c Lineman, power lines 45   35

America
Issue
A385

1990, Oct. 11   Litho.   Perf. 14x14 1/2
1251 A385 25c Chichontepec Volcano 15   15
1252 A385 70c Lake Coatepeque   35   25

Chamber of
Commerce,
75th Anniv.
A386

1990, Nov. 22
1253 A386 1 col blk, gold & bl   48   35

Traffic
Safety — A387

Design: 40c, Intersection, horiz.

Perf. 14 1/2x14, 14x14 1/2
1990, Nov. 13
1254 A387 25c multicolored   15   15
1255 A387 40c multicolored   20   15

Butterflies
A388

Perf. 14x14 1/2, 14 1/2x14
1990, Nov. 28
1256 A388 15c Eurytides calliste   15   15
1257 A388 20c Papilio garamas
               amerias   15   15
1258 A388 25c Papilio garamas   15   15
1259 A388 55c Hypanartia godmani   28   20
1260 A388 70c Anaea excellens   35   30
1261 A388 1col Papilio pilumnus   50   38
       Nos. 1256-1261 (6)   1.58
       Set value   1.10
Souvenir Sheet
Roulette 13 1/2
1262 A388 2col Anaea proserpina   1.00   78
Nos. 1259-1261 are vert.

University of El
Salvador, 150th
Anniv. — A389

1991, Feb. 27   Litho.   Perf. 14 1/2x14
1263 A389 25c shown   15   15
1264 A389 70c Sun, footprints,
               hand   35   30
1265 A389 1.50col Dove, globe   75   65

Christmas
A390

Perf. 14x14 1/2, 14 1/2x14
1990, Dec. 7   Litho.
1266 A390 25c shown   15   15
1267 A390 70c Nativity, vert.   35   30

Month of the
Elderly — A391

1991, Jan. 31   Perf. 14 1/2x14
1268 A391 15c purple & blk   15   15

Restoration of
Santa Ana
Theater
A392

1991, Apr. 12   Perf. 14
1269 A392 20c Interior   15   15
1270 A392 70c Exterior   35   30
       Set value   35

Amphibians
A393

Designs: 25c, Smilisca baudinii. 70c, Eleutherodactylus rugulosus. 1col, Plectrohyla guatemalensis. 1.50col, Agalychnis moreletii.

1991, May 29   Litho.   Perf. 14x14 1/2
1271 A393 25c multicolored   15   15
1272 A393 70c multicolored   35   30
1273 A393 1col multicolored   50   38
1274 A393 1.50col multicolored   75   65

Aid for
Children's
Village
A394

Designs: 90c, Children playing outdoors.

1991, June 21   Litho.   Perf. 14x14 1/2
1275 A394 20c multicolored   15   15
1276 A394 90c multicolored   42   35

United
Family — A395

1991, June 28   Litho.   Perf. 14 1/2x14
1277 A395 50c multicolored   25   15

Birds — A396

1991, Aug. 30
1278 A396 20c Melanotis hy-
                poleucus   15   15
1279 A396 25c Agelaius phoeniceus 15   15
1280 A396 70c Campylorhynchus
                rufinucha   35   30
1281 A396 1col Cissilopha melano-
                cyanea   50   38
1282 A396 5col Chiroxiphia linearis 2.35 1.75
       Nos. 1278-1282 (5)   3.50 2.73

Discovery of America, 500th Anniv. Type of 1990

Designs: No. 1283a, Hourglass, chart. b, Chart, ship's sails. c, Sailing ship near Florida. d, Corner of chart, ships. e, Compass rose, Cuba, Yucatan Peninsula. f, South America, "500" emblem. No. 1284, Sail, landfall.

1991, Sept. 16   Litho.   Perf. 14
Miniature Sheet
1283 A379 1col Sheet of 6, #a.-f. 3.00 1.50
Souvenir Sheet
Rouletted 6 1/2
1284 A380 2col multicolored   1.00   50

America
Issue — A397

Designs: 25c, Battle of Acaxual. 70c, First missionaries in Cuzcatlan.

1991, Oct. 11   Litho.   Perf. 14x14 1/2
1285 A397 25c multicolored   15   15
1286 A397 70c multicolored   35   30

World Food
Day — A398

1991, Oct. 16   **Perf. 14¹/₂x14**
1287 A398 50c multicolored   25   15

Wolfgang
Amadeus
Mozart, Death
Bicent.
A399

1991, Oct. 23   **Perf. 14x14¹/₂**
1288 A399 1col multicolored   50   38

Christmas
A400

Perf. 14¹/₂x14, 14x14¹/₂
1991, Nov. 13   **Litho.**
1289 A400 25c Nativity scene, vert.   15   15
1290 A400 70c Children singing   38   30

Total Solar
Eclipse, July
11 — A401

1991, Dec. 17   **Perf. 14x14¹/₂**
1291 A401 70c shown   38   30
1292 A401 70c Eastern El Salvador   38   30
   a.   Pair, #1291-1292   76   60

No. 1292a has continous design.

Red Cross Life
Guards
A402

1992, Feb. 28 **Litho.** **Perf. 14x14¹/₂**
1293 A402 3col Rescue   1.50 1.15
1294 A402 4.50col Swimming com-
              petition   2.25 1.70

Lions Clubs in El
Salvador, 50th
Anniv. — A403

1992, Mar. 13   **Perf. 14¹/₂x14**
1295 A403 90c multicolored   45   35

Protect the
Environment — A404

Designs: 60c, Man riding bicycle. 80c, Children
walking outdoors. 1.60col, Sower in field. 3col,
Clean water. 2.20col, Natural foods. 5col,
Recycling center. 10col, Conservation of trees and
nature. 25col, Wildlife protection.

1992, Apr. 6 **Litho.** **Perf. 14x14¹/₂**
1298 A404   60c   multi   30   22
1299 A404   80c   multi   40   30
1300 A404   1.60col multi   80   60
1302 A404   2.20col multi   1.10   85
1303 A404   3col   multi   1.50 1.15
1304 A404   5col   multi   2.50 1.90
1305 A404   10col   multi   5.00 3.75
1307 A404   25col   multi   12.50 9.40
       Nos. 1298-1307 (8)   24.10 18.17

This is an expanding set. Numbers may change.

Physicians
A405

Designs: 80c, Dr. Roberto Orellana Valdes. 1col,
Dr. Carlos Gonzalez Bonilla. 1.60col, Dr. Andres
Gonzalo Funes. 2.20col, Dr. Joaquin Coto.

1992, Apr. 30
1308 A405   80c   multicolored   40   30
1309 A405   1col multicolored   50   38
1310 A405   1.60col multicolored   80   60
1311 A405   2.20col multicolored   1.10   85

Women's Auxiliary
of St. Vincent of
Paul Society,
Cent. — A406

1992, Mar. 10 **Litho.** **Perf. 14¹/₂x14**
1312 A406 80c multicolored   45   38

Population and
Housing
Census — A407

Design: 80c, Globe showing location of El
Salvador.

1992, June 29 **Litho.** **Perf. 14¹/₂x14**
1313 A407 60c multicolored   35   30
1314 A407 80c multicolored   45   38

1992 Summer
Olympics,
Barcelona — A408

1992, July 17 **Litho.** **Perf. 14¹/₂x14**
1315 A408   60c Hammer throw   35   30
1316 A408   80c Volleyball   45   38
1317 A408   90c Shot put   75   58
1318 A408 2.20col Long jump   1.30   65
1319 A408   3col Vault   1.75   85
1320 A408   5col Balance beam   3.00 1.50
       Nos. 1315-1320 (6)   7.60 4.26

Simon
Bolivar — A409

1992, July 24
1321 A409 2.20col multicolored   1.30 65

A410

Discovery of America, 500th
Anniv. — A411

Designs: No. 1322, European and Amerindian
faces. No. 1323, Ship in person's eye. No. 1324,
Ship at sea. No. 1325, Ship, satellite over Earth.
3col, Cross, Indian pyramid.

1992, Aug. 28 **Litho.** **Perf. 14x14¹/₂**
1322 A410 1col multicolored   58   30
1323 A410 1col multicolored   58   30
        Perf. 14¹/₂x14¹/₂
1324 A410 1col multicolored   58   30
1325 A410 1col multicolored   58   30
   a.   Min. sheet of 8, 2 each #1322-
          1325   4.65 2.40
        Souvenir Sheet
        Rouletted 13¹/₂
1326 A411 3col multicolored   1.75 85

Immigrants to
El Salvador
A412

Designs: No. 1327, Feet walking over map. No.
1328, Footprints leading to map.

1992, Sept. 16 **Litho.** **Perf. 14x14¹/₂**
1327 A412 2.20col multicolored   1.15 58
1328 A412 2.20col multicolored   1.15 58
   a.   Pair, #1327-1328   2.30 1.15

General Francisco
Morazan (1792-
1842)
A413

1992, Sept. 28   **Perf. 14¹/₂x14**
1329 A413 1col multicolored   58   30

Association of
Salvadoran
Broadcasters
A414

1992, Oct. 3
1330 A414 2.20col multicolored   1.15 58

Salvadoran Radio Day, Intl. Radio Day.

Discovery of
America, 500th
Anniv.
A415

ScottMounts
more mount for the money

- Identical in appearance with more expensive mounts.
- Center-split across the back for easy insertion of stamps,
  ScottMounts prevent chemical deterioration and eliminate tears.
- Made of 100% inert polystrol foil, ScottMounts are available in
  your choice of clear or black backs.
- Why pay more? Why settle for less? Discover the quality and value
  ScottMounts have to offer.

Available from your local dealer or direct from:
Scott Publishing Co., P.O. Box 828,
Sidney, OH 45365-0828

1992, Oct. 13   Litho.   *Perf. 14x14¹/₂*
1331 A415   80c Indian artifacts   45   22
1332 A415   2.20col Map, ship   1.25   62

Exfilna
'92 — A416

1992, Oct. 22   *Perf. 14x14¹/₂*
1333 A416   5col multicolored   2.75   1.38

Discovery of America, 500th Anniv.

Peace in El Salvador A417

1992, Oct. 30
1334 A417   50c black, blue & yellow   28   15

Christmas A418

Perf. 14x14¹/₂, 14¹/₂x14
1992, Nov. 23   Litho.
1335 A418   80c shown   45   22
1336 A418   2.20col Nativity, vert.   1.25   62

Wildlife A419

Designs: 50c, Tapirus bairdii. 70c, Chironectes minimus. 1col, Eira barbara. 3col, Felis yagouaroundi. 4.50col, Odocoileus virginianus.

1993, Jan. 15   Litho.   *Perf. 14x14¹/₂*
1337 A419   50c multicolored   28   15
1338 A419   70c multicolored   40   20
1339 A419   1col multicolored   58   30
1340 A419   3col multicolored   1.70   85
1341 A419   4.50col multicolored   2.50   1.25
   Nos. 1337-1341 (5)   5.46   2.75

Month of the Elderly A420

Design: 2.20col, Boy, old man holding tree.

1993, Jan. 27
1342 A420   80c black   45   22
1343 A420   2.20col multicolored   1.25   62

Agape Social Welfare Organization A421

Designs: a, Divine Providence Church. b, People, symbols of love and peace.

1993, Mar. 4   Litho.   *Perf. 14x14¹/₂*
1344 A421   1col Pair, #a.-b.   45   22

Secretary's Day — A422

1993, Apr. 26   Litho.   *Perf. 14x14¹/₂*
1345 A422   1col multicolored   45   22

Benjamin Bloom Children's Hospital A423

1993, June 18   Litho.   *Perf. 14x14¹/₂*
1346 A423   5col multicolored   2.25   1.15

Visit by Mexican President Carlos Salinas de Gortari A424

1993, July 14
1347 A424   2.20col multicolored   1.00   50

Aquatic Birds — A425

1993, Sept. 28   Litho.   *Perf. 14x14¹/₂*
1348 A425   80c Casmerodius al-
      bus   18   15
1349 A425   1col Mycteria america-
      na   22   15
1350 A425   2.20col Ardea herodias   50   25
1351 A425   5col Ajaja ajaja   1.10   58

Pharmacy Review Commission, Cent. — A426

1993, Oct. 6
1352 A426   80c multicolored   18   15

America Issue — A427

Endangered species: 80c, Dasyprocta punctata. 2.20col, Procyon lotor.

1993, Oct. 11   Litho.   *Perf. 14x14¹/₂*
1353 A427   80c multicolored   18   15
1354 A427   2.20col multicolored   50   25

Fifth Central America Games — A428

Designs: 50c, Mascot, torch. 1.60col, Emblem. 2.20col, Mascot, map of Central America, horiz. 4.50col, Map of El Salvador, mascot, horiz.

Perf. 14¹/₂x14, 14x14¹/₂
1993, Oct. 29   Litho.
1355 A428   50c multicolored   15   15
1356 A428   1.60col multicolored   38   18
1357 A428   2.20col multicolored   50   25
1358 A428   4.50col multicolored   1.00   50

Miniature Sheet

Medicinal Plants — A429

Designs: a, Solanum mammosum. b, Hamelia patens. c, Tridex procumbens. d, Calea urticifolia. e, Ageratum conyzoides. f, Pluchea odorata.

1993, Dec. 10   Litho.   *Perf. 14¹/₂x14*
1359 A429   1col Sheet of 6, #a.-f.   1.25   65

Christmas A430

1993, Nov. 23   *Perf. 14x14¹/₂*
1360 A430   80c Holy Family   30   15
1361 A430   2.20col Nativity Scene   85   42

Alberto Masferrer (1868-1932), Writer — A431

1993, Nov. 30
1362 A431   2.20col multicolored   85   42

Intl. Year of the Family — A432

1994, Feb. 28   Litho.   *Perf. 14¹/₂x14*
1363 A432   2.20col multicolored   85   42

Military Hospital, Cent. — A433

1994, Apr. 27   Litho.   *Perf. 14*
1364 A433   1col shown   22   15
1365 A433   1col Hospital building   22   15

City of Santa Ana, Cent. — A434

Designs: 60c, Arms of Department of Santa Ana. 80c, Inscription honoring heroic deeds of 44 patriots.

1994, Apr. 29   Litho.   *Perf. 14*
1366 A434   60c multicolored   15   15
1367 A434   80c multicolored   18   15

1994 World Cup Soccer Championships, US — A435

Soccer plays, flags from: 60c, Romania, Colombia, Switzerland, US. 80c, Sweden, Cameroun, Russia, Brazil. 1col, South Korea, Spain, Bolivia, Germany. 2.20col, Bulgaria, Nigeria, Greece, Argentina. 4.50col, Mexico, Norway, Ireland, Italy. 5col, Saudi Arabia, Netherlands, Morocco, Belgium.

1994, June 6   Litho.   *Perf. 14*
1368 A435   60c multicolored   15   15
1369 A435   80c multicolored   18   15
1370 A435   1col multicolored   22   15
1371 A435   2.20col multicolored   48   24
1372 A435   4.50col multicolored   1.00   50
1373 A435   5col multicolored   1.10   55
   Nos. 1368-1373 (6)   3.13   1.74

Plaza of Sovereign Military Order of Malta A436

1994, June 24   Litho.   *Perf. 14*
1374 A436   2.20col multicolored   48   24

Traditions
A437

Designs: 1col, Tiger and deer dance. 2.20col, Spotted bull dance.

1994, June 30

1375	A437	1col multicolored	22	15
1376	A437	2.20col multicolored	48	24

Nutritional
Plants — A438

1994, Aug. 29   Litho.   Perf. 14

1377	A438	70c Capsicum annuum	15	15
1378	A438	80c Theobroma cacao	18	15
1379	A438	1col Ipomoea batatas	22	15
1380	A438	5col Chamaedorea tepejilote	1.10	55

Postal
Transport
Vehicles
A439

1994, Oct. 11   Litho.   Perf. 14

1381	A439	80c Jeep	40	20
1382	A439	2.20col Train	1.10	55

America issue.

22nd Bicycle Race
of El Salvador
A440

1994, Oct. 26

1383	A440	80c multicolored	40	20

16th Intl. Fair of
El Salvador
A441

1994, Oct. 31

1384	A441	5col multicolored	2.50	1.25

Christmas
A442

1994, Nov. 16

1385	A442	80c shown	40	20
1386	A442	2.20col Magi, Christ child	1.10	55

Beetles — A443

1994, Dec. 16   Litho.   Perf. 14

1387	A443	80c Cotinis mutabilis	18	15
1388	A443	1col Phyllophaga	22	15
1389	A443	2.20col Galofa	50	25
1390	A443	5col Callipogon barbatus	1.10	55
		Nos. 1387-1390 (4)	2.00	1.10

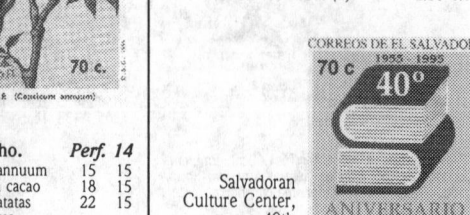

Salvadoran
Culture Center,
40th
Anniv. — A444

1995, Mar. 24   Litho.   Perf. 14½x14

1391	A444	70c shown	16	15
1392	A444	1col "40" emblem	22	15

AIR POST STAMPS

Regular Issue of
1924-25   **Servicio Aéreo**
Overprinted in Black
or Red

First Printing.

15c on 10c: "15 QUINCE 15" measures 22½mm.

20c: Shows on the back of the stamp an albino impression of the 50c surcharge.

25c on 35c: Original value canceled by a long and short bar.

40c on 50c: Only one printing.

50c on 1col: Surcharge in dull orange red.

Perf. 12½, 14

1929, Dec. 28   Unwmk.

C1	A112	20c dp green (Bk)	3.25	3.25
a.		Red overprint	425.00	425.00

Counterfeits exist of No. C1a.

With Additional Surcharge of New Values and Bars in Black or Red

C3	A111	15c on 10c orange	50	50
a.		"ALTANT CO"	14.00	14.00
C4	A114	25c on 35c scar & grn	1.25	1.25
a.		Bars inverted	7.50	7.50
C5	A115	40c on 50c org brn	50	35
C6	A116	50c on 1col grn & vio (R)	8.00	6.50

Second Printing.

15c on 10d: "15 QUINCE 15" measures 20½mm.

20c: Has not the albino impression on the back of the stamp.

25c on 35c: Original value cancelled by two bars of equal length.

50c on 1col: Surcharge in carmine rose.

1930, Jan. 10

C7	A112	20c deep green	45	45
C8	A111	15c on 10c org	45	45
a.		"ATLANT CO"	17.50	
b.		Double surcharge	10.00	
c.		As "a" double surcharge	75.00	
d.		Pair, one without surcharge	175.00	
C9	A114	25c on 35c scar & grn	38	38
C10	A116	50c on 1col grn & vio (C)	90	90
a.		Without bars over "UN COLON"	2.50	
b.		As "a," without block over "1"	2.50	

Numerous wrong font and defective letters exist in both printings of the surcharges.

No. C10 with black surcharge is bogus.

Mail Plane over
San
Salvador — AP1

1930, Sept. 15   Engr.   Perf. 12½

C11	AP1	15c deep red	15	15
C12	AP1	20c emerald	18	15
C13	AP1	25c brown violet	18	15
C14	AP1	40c ultra	32	15
		Set value		32

Simón
Bolivar — AP2

1930, Dec. 17   Litho.   Perf. 11½

C15	AP2	15c deep red	3.75	2.75
a.		"15" double	82.50	
C16	AP2	20c emerald	3.75	2.75
C17	AP2	25c brown violet	3.75	2.75
a.		Vert. pair, imperf. btwn.	110.00	
b.		Imperf., pair		
C18	AP2	40c dp ultra	3.75	2.75

Centenary of death of Simón Bolivar. Counterfeits of Nos. C15-C18 exist.

No. 504 Overprinted in
Red

1931, June 29   Engr.   Perf. 14

C19	A116	1col green & vio	2.50	2.00

Tower of La Merced
Church — AP3

1931, Nov. 5   Litho.   Perf. 11½

C20	AP3	15c dark red	2.50	2.00
a.		Imperf., pair	50.00	
C21	AP3	20c blue green	2.50	2.00
C22	AP3	25c dull violet	2.50	2.00
a.		Vert. pair, imperf. btwn.	110.00	
C23	AP3	40c ultra	2.50	2.00
a.		Imperf., pair	60.00	

120th anniv. of the 1st movement toward the political independence of El Salvador. In the tower of La Merced Church (AP3) hangs the bell which José Matias Delgado-called the Father of his Country-rang to initiate the movement for liberty.

José Matías
Delgado
AP4

Airplane and
Caravels of
Columbus
AP5

1932, Nov. 12   Wmk. 271   Perf. 12½

C24	AP4	15c dull red & vio	75	75
C25	AP4	20c blue grn & bl	1.00	1.00
C26	AP4	25c dull vio & brn	1.00	1.00
C27	AP4	40c ultra & grn	1.25	1.25

1st centenary of the death of Father José Matías Delgado, who is known as the Father of El Salvadoran Political Emancipation.

Nos. C24-C27 show cheek without shading in the 72nd stamp of each sheet.

1933, Oct. 12   Wmk. 240   Perf. 13

C28	AP5	15c red orange	2.00	1.40
C29	AP5	20c blue green	2.00	1.40
C30	AP5	25c lilac	2.00	1.40
C31	AP5	40c ultra	2.00	1.40
C32	AP5	1col black	2.00	1.40
		Nos. C28-C32 (5)	10.00	7.00

441st anniversary of the sailing of Chistopher Columbus from Palos, Spain, for the New World.

Police Barracks Type

1934, Dec. 16   Perf. 12½

C33	A123	25c lilac	40	15
C34	A123	30c brown	60	30
a.		Imperf., pair	42.50	
C35	A123	1col black	1.50	65

Runner
AP7

1935, Mar. 16   Engr.   Unwmk.

C36	AP7	15c carmine	2.75	2.75
C37	AP7	25c violet	2.75	2.75
C38	AP7	30c brown	2.50	2.00
C39	AP7	55c blue	12.00	10.00
C40	AP7	1col black	9.00	8.00
		Nos. C36-C40 (5)	29.00	25.50

Issued in commemoration of the Third Central American Games.

For overprints and surcharge see Nos. C41-C45, C53.

Same Overprinted HABILITADO
in Black

1935, June 27

C41	AP7	15c carmine	2.75	1.25
C42	AP7	25c violet	2.75	1.25
C43	AP7	30c brown	2.75	1.25
C44	AP7	55c blue	18.00	15.00
C45	AP7	1col black	9.00	8.00
		Nos. C41-C45 (5)	35.25	26.75

Flag of El Salvador Type

1935, Oct. 26   Litho.   Wmk. 240

C46	A125	30c black brown	50	15

Tree of San Vicente Type

1935, Dec. 26   Perf. 12½

**Numerals in Black,
Tree in Yellow Green**

C47	A126	10c orange	80	70
C48	A126	15c brown	80	70
C49	A126	20c dk blue grn	80	70
C50	A126	25c dark purple	80	70
C51	A126	30c black brown	80	70
		Nos. C47-C51 (5)	4.00	3.50

Tercentenary of San Vicente.

No. 565 Overprinted in AEREO
Red

1937   Engr.   Unwmk.

C52	A133	15c dk olive bis	20	15
a.		Double overprint	25.00	

No. C44 Surcharged in Red 30

C53	AP7	30c on 55c blue	1.75	75

Panchimalco
Church
AP10

1937, Dec. 3   Engr.   Perf. 12

C54	AP10	15c orange yel	20	15
C55	AP10	20c green	20	15
C56	AP10	25c violet	20	15
C57	AP10	30c brown	20	15
C58	AP10	.40c blue	20	15

C59 AP10 1col black	90	25
C60 AP10 5col rose carmine	3.00	2.00
Nos. C54-C60 (7)	4.90	3.05

US Constitution Type of Regular Issue

1938, Apr. 22   Engr. & Litho.
C61 A136 30c multicolored   60   50

José Simeón Cañas Villacorta — AP12

1938, Aug. 18   Engr.
C62 AP12 15c orange	75	75
C63 AP12 20c brt green	90	75
C64 AP12 30c redsh brown	90	75
C65 AP12 1col black	3.00	2.50

José Simeón Cañas y Villacorta (1767-1838), liberator of slaves in Central America.

Golden Gate Bridge, San Francisco Bay AP13

1939, Apr. 14   Perf. 12½
C66 AP13 15c dull yel & blk	20	15
C67 AP13 30c dk brown & blk	25	15
C68 AP13 40c dk blue & blk	38	20
Set value		40

Golden Gate International Exposition, San Francisco.
For surcharges see Nos. C86-C91.

Sir Rowland Hill Type

1940, Mar. 1   Engr.
C69 A146 30c dk brn, buff & blk	3.25	1.25
C70 A146 80c org red & blk	8.00	6.00

Centenary of the postage stamp. Covers postmarked Feb. 29 were predated. Actual first day was Mar. 1.

Map of the Americas, Figure of Peace, Plane — AP15

1940, May 22   Perf. 12
C71 AP15 30c brown & blue	25	20
C72 AP15 80c dk rose & blk	50	42

Pan American Union, 50th anniversary.

Coffee Tree in Bloom — AP16   Coffee Tree with Ripe Berries — AP17

1940, Nov. 27
C73 AP16 15c yellow orange	1.00	18
C74 AP16 20c deep green	1.25	15
C75 AP16 25c dark violet	1.50	38

C76 AP17 30c copper brown	1.75	18
C77 AP17 1col black	5.25	45
Nos. C73-C77 (5)	10.75	1.34

Juan Lindo, Gen. Francisco Mallespin and New National University of El Salvador — AP18

Designs (portraits changed): 40c, 80c, Narciso Monterey and Antonio José Canas. 60c, 1col, Isidro Menéndez and Chrisanto Salazar.

1941, Feb. 16   Perf. 12½
C78 AP18 20c dk grn & rose lake	80	52
C79 AP18 40c ind & brn org	80	52
C80 AP18 60c dl pur & brn	80	52
C81 AP18 80c hn brn & dk bl grn	2.00	1.40
C82 AP18 1col blk & org	2.00	1.40
C83 AP18 2col yel org & rose vio	2.00	1.40
a. Min. sheet of 6, #C78-C83, perf. 11½	9.25	9.25
Nos. C78-C83 (6)	8.40	5.76

Centenary of University of El Salvador. Stamps from No. C83a, perf. 11½, sell for about the same values as the perf. 12½ stamps.

Catalogue values for unused stamps in this section, from this point to the end of the section, are for Never Hinged items.

Map of El Salvador AP20

Wmk. 269
1942, Nov. 25   Engr.   Perf. 14
C85 AP20 30c red org	50	30
a. Horiz. pair, imperf. between	100.00	

First Eucharistic Cong. of El Salvador. See No. 588.

Nos. C66 to C68 Surcharged with New Values in Dark Carmine **15**

1943   Unwmk.   Perf. 12½
C86 AP13 15c on 15c dl yel & blk	28	20
C87 AP13 20c on 30c dk brn & blk	40	30
C88 AP13 25c on 40c dk bl & blk	65	50

Nos. C66 to C68 Surcharged with New Values in Dark Carmine **15**

1944
C89 AP13 15c on 15c dl yel & blk	32	22
C90 AP13 20c on 30c dk brn & blk	52	30
C91 AP13 25c on 40c dk bl & blk	65	30

Bridge Type of Regular Issue Arms Overprint at Right in Blue Violet
1944, Nov. 24   Engr.
C92 A149 30c crim rose & blk   32   15

No. C92 exists without overprint, but was not issued in that form.

Presidential Palace AP22

National Theater AP23

National Palace AP24

1944, Dec. 22   Perf. 12½
C93 AP22 15c red vio	15	15
C94 AP23 20c dk bl grn	16	15
C95 AP24 25c dl vio	20	15
Set value		24

For surcharge and overprint see Nos. C145-C146.

No. 582 Overprinted in Red **Aéreo**

1945, Aug. 23   Perf. 12
C96 A137 1col black   60   22

Juan Ramon Uriarte — AP25

Perf. 12½
1946, Jan. 1   Wmk. 240   Typo.
C97 AP25 12c dk bl	16	15
C98 AP25 14c dp vio	16	15
Set value		15

Mayan Pyramid, St. Andrés Plantation AP26

Municipal Children's Garden, San Salvador AP27

Civil Aeronautics School, Ilopango Airport AP28

1946, May 1   Unwmk.
C99 AP26 30c rose car	16	15
C100 AP27 40c dp ultra	16	15
C101 AP28 1col black	85	30
Set value		45

For surcharge see No. C121.

Alberto Masferrer — AP29

1946, July 19   Litho.   Wmk. 240
C102 AP29 12c carmine	20	15
C103 AP29 14c dl grn	20	15
a. Imperf., pair	10.00	
Set value		18

Souvenir Sheets

AP30

Designs: 40c, Charles I of Spain. 60c, Juan Manuel Rodriguez. 1col, Arms of San Salvador. 2col, Flag of El Salvador.

Perf. 12, Imperf.
1946, Nov. 8   Engr.   Unwmk.
C104 AP30 Sheet of 4	2.50	2.50
a. 40c brown	42	42
b. 60c carmine	42	42
c. 1col green	42	42
d. 2col ultramarine	42	42

4th cent. of San Salvador's city charter. The imperf. sheets are without gum.

Felipe Soto — AP31   Alfredo Espino — AP32

Perf. 12½
1947, Sept. 11   Wmk. 240   Litho.
C106 AP31 12c chocolate	20	15
C107 AP32 14c dark blue	16	15
Set value		18

For surcharges see Nos. 627-630.

Arce Type of Regular Issue
1948, Feb. 26   Engr.   Unwmk.
C108 A163 12c green	16	15
C109 A163 14c rose car	24	15
C110 A163 1col violet	2.25	1.40

Cent. of the death of Manuel José Arce (1783-1847). "Father of Independence" and 1st pres. of the Federation of Central America.

Roosevelt Types of Regular Issue
Designs: 12c, Pres. Franklin D. Roosevelt. 14c, Pres. Roosevelt presenting awards for distinguished service. 20c, Roosevelt and Cordell Hull. 25c, Pres. and Mrs. Roosevelt. 1col, Mackenzie King, Roosevelt and Winston Churchill. 2col, Funeral of Pres. Roosevelt. 4col, Pres. and Mrs. Roosevelt.

1948, Apr. 12   Engr.   Perf. 12½
Various Frames, Center in Black
C111 A165 12c green	32	25
C112 A164 14c olive	32	25
C113 A164 20c chocolate	32	25
C114 A164 25c carmine	32	25
C115 A164 1col vio brn	1.35	75
C116 A164 2col bl vio	2.25	1.40
Nos. C111-C116 (6)	4.88	3.00

Souvenir Sheet
Perf. 13½
C117 A166 4col gray & brn   4.00   3.00

Nos. 599, 601 and 604 Overprinted in Carmine or Black **Aéreo**

1948, Sept. 7   Perf. 12½
C118 A154 5c slate gray	15	15
C119 A154 10c bis brn	15	15
C120 A154 1col scar (Bk)	1.20	50
Set value		60

No. C99 Surcharged in Black
1949, July 23
C121 AP26 10(c) on 30c rose car   16   15

UPU Type of Regular Issue
1949, Oct. 9   Engr.   Perf. 12½
C122 A167 5c brown	15	15
C123 A167 10c black	16	15
C124 A167 1col purple	5.25	5.25

Flag and Arms of El
Salvador — AP38

1949, Dec. 15   *Perf. 10½*
**Flag and Arms in Blue,
Yellow and Green**

C125 AP38	5c ocher	15	15
C126 AP38	10c dk grn	20	15
a.	Yellow omitted	20.00	
C127 AP38	15c violet	28	15
C128 AP38	1col rose	60	40
C129 AP38	5col red vio	5.00	3.75
	Nos. C125-C129 (5)	6.23	4.60

Issued to commemorate the 1st anniversary of
the Revolution of Dec. 14, 1948.

Isabella I of   Flag, Torch and
Spain — AP39   Scroll — AP40

1951, Apr. 28   Litho.   Unwmk.
**Background in Ultramarine,
Red and Yellow**

C130 AP39	10c green	32	15
C131 AP39	20c purple	32	15
a.	Horiz. pair, imperf. between	25.00	
C132 AP39	40c rose car	32	15
C133 AP39	1col blk brn	1.25	50

Issued to commemorate the 500th anniversary of
the birth of Queen Isabella I of Spain. Nos. C130-
C133 exist imperforate.

1952, Feb. 14   Photo.   *Perf. 11½*
Flag in Blue

C134 AP40	10c brt bl	15	15
C135 AP40	15c chocolate	16	15
C136 AP40	20c dp bl	16	15
C137 AP40	25c gray	16	15
C138 AP40	40c purple	32	20
C139 AP40	1col red org	65	38
C140 AP40	2col org brn	2.25	1.75
C141 AP40	5col vio bl	2.25	90
	Nos. C134-C141 (8)	6.10	3.83

Constitution of 1950.

Marti Type of Regular Issue Inscribed
"Aereo"

1953, Feb. 27   Litho.   *Perf. 10½*

C142 AP170	10c dk pur	16	15
C143 AP170	20c dl brn	16	15
C144 AP170	1col dl org	65	38
	Set value		58

No. C95 Surcharged "C 0.20" and
Obliterations in Red

1953, Mar. 20   *Perf. 12½*

C145 AP24	20c on 25c dl vio	28	15

No. C95	"IV Congreso Medico
Overprinted in	Social Panamericano
Carmine	16 / 19 Abril, 1953"

1953, June 19

C146 AP24	25c dl vio	40	18

See note after No. 634.

Bell Tower, La
Merced
Church — AP42

1953, Sept. 15   *Perf. 11½*

C147 AP42	5c rose pink	15	15
C148 AP42	10c dp bl grn	15	15
C149 AP42	20c blue	20	15
C150 AP42	1col purple	65	50
	Set value	1.00	74

132nd anniv. of the Act of Independence, Sept.
15, 1821.

Postage Types and

Fishing
Boats — AP43

Gen. Manuel José
Arce — AP44

ODECA
Officials and
Flag — AP46

Designs: No. C155, National Palace. No. C157,
Coast guard boat. No. C158, Lake Ilopango. No.
C160, Guayabo dam. No. C161, Housing develop-
ment. No. C162, Modern highway. No. C164,
Izalco volcano.

Perf. 11½
1954, June 1   Unwmk.   Photo.

C151 AP43	5c org brn & cr	20	15
C152 AP175	5c brt car	20	15
C153 AP44	10c gray bl	24	15
C154 AP178	10c pur & lt brn	24	15
C155 AP43	10c ol & bl gray	24	15
C156 AP46	10c bl grn, dk grn & bl	24	15
C157 AP43	10c rose car	30	15
C158 AP43	15c dk gray	35	15
C159 AP173	20c pur & gray	42	15
C160 AP46	25c bl grn & bl	42	15
C161 AP46	30c mag & sal	48	15
C162 AP176	40c brt org & brn	65	25
C163 AP174	80c red brn	1.40	90
C164 AP43	1col magenta & sal	1.65	90
C165 AP174	2col orange	3.00	90
	Nos. C151-C165 (15)	10.03	
	Set value		3.75

Barrios Type of Regular Issue, 1955

1955, Dec. 20   Wmk. 269   Engr.

C166 AP177	20c brown	16	15
C167 AP177	30c dp red lil	24	15

Santa Ana Type of Regular Issue, 1956

Perf. 13½

1956, June 20   Unwmk.   Litho.

C168 AP178	5c org brn	15	15
C169 AP178	10c green	15	15
C170 AP178	40c red lil	24	15
C171 AP178	80c emerald	60	38
C172 AP178	5col gray bl	3.25	1.75
	Nos. C168-C172 (5)	4.39	2.58

For overprint see No. C187.

Chalatenango Type of Regular Issue, 1956

1956, Sept. 14

C173 AP179	10c brt rose	15	15
C174 AP179	15c orange	16	15
C175 AP179	20c lt ol grn	16	15
C176 AP179	25c dl pur	32	18
C177 AP179	50c org brn	52	40
C178 AP179	1col brt vio bl	85	65
	Nos. C173-C178 (6)	2.16	
	Set value		1.45

Nueva San Salvador Type of Regular Issue,
1957

Perf. 12½

1957, Jan. 3   Wmk. 269   Engr.

C179 A180	10c pink	15	15
C180 A180	20c dl red	20	15
C181 A180	50c pale org red	32	22

C182 A180	1col lt grn	85	45
C183 A180	2col org red	2.00	1.25
	Nos. C179-C183 (5)	3.52	2.22

For overprints see Nos. C195, C198.

Lemus' Visit Type of Regular Issue, 1959
Perf. 11½

1959, Dec. 14   Unwmk.   Photo.
Granite Paper

**Design in Ultramarine, Dark Brown
Light Brown and Red**

C184 A182	15c red	20	15
C185 A182	20c green	24	15
C186 A182	30c carmine	30	18
	Set value		38

No. C169 Overprinted in Red: "ANO
MUNDIAL DE LOS REFUGIADOS 1959-
1960"

1960, Apr. 7   Litho.   *Perf. 13½*

C187 A178	10c green	24	15

World Refugee Year, 7/1/59-6/30/60.

Type of Regular Issue, 1960
Poinsettia
Perf. 11½

1960, Dec. 17   Unwmk.   Photo.
Granite Paper

**Design in Slate Green,
Red and Yellow**

C188 A184	20c rose lil	28	15
C189 A184	30c gray	32	20
C190 A184	40c lt gray	32	20
C191 A184	50c sal pink	55	35

Miniature Sheet
Imperf

C192 A184	60c gold	65	35

See note after No. 718.
For surcharge see No. C196.

Nos. 672, 691 and C183 Overprinted: "III
Exposición Industrial Centroamericana
Diciembre de 1962" with "AEREO" Added
on Nos. 672, 691

1962, Dec. 21   *Perf. 11½, 12½*

C193 A174	1col brn org, dk brn & bl	1.00	75
C194 A180	1col dl red	50	32
C195 A180	2col org red	1.00	65

Issued to publicize the 3rd Central American
Industrial Exposition.

For surcharges see Nos. C197, C199.

Nos. C189, C194, C182 and C195
Surcharged

1963

C196 A184	10c on 30c multi	16	15
C197 A180	10c on 1col dl red	16	15
C198 A180	10c on 1col lt grn	1.10	25
C199 A180	10c on 2col org red	1.10	25
	Set value		70

Surcharges include: "X" on No. C196; two dots
and bar at bottom on No. C197. Heavy bar at
bottom on No. C198. On No. C199, the four-line
"Exposition" overprint is lower than on No. C195.

Turquoise-browed Motmot — AP49

Birds: 5c, King vulture (vert., like No. 741). 6c,
Yellow-headed parrot, vert. 10c, Spotted-breasted
oriole. 30c, Greattailed grackle. 40c, Great curassow, vert. 50c, Magpie-jay. 80c, Golden-fronted
woodpecker, vert.

1963   Unwmk.   Photo.   *Perf. 11½*
Birds in Natural Colors

C200 AP49	5c gray grn & blk	15	15
C201 AP49	6c tan & bl	15	15
C202 AP49	10c lt bl & blk	15	15
C203 AP49	20c gray & brn	24	15
C204 AP49	30c ol bis & blk	38	15
C205 AP49	40c pale & dk vio	50	20
C206 AP49	50c lt grn & blk	55	25
C207 AP49	80c vio bl & blk	1.00	60
	Nos. C200-C207 (8)	3.12	
	Set value		1.45

Eucharistic Congress Type of Regular Issue,
1964

1964-65   *Perf. 12x11½*

C208 A188	10c slate grn & bl	15	15
C209 A188	25c red & blue	20	15
	Set value		16

Miniature Sheets
Imperf

C210 A188	80c bl & grn	65	65
a.	Marginal ovpt. La Union	85	85
b.	Marginal ovpt. Usulutan	85	85
c.	Marginal ovpt. La Libertad	85	85

See note after No. 746.
Issue dates: Nos. C208-C210, Apr. 16, 1964.
Nos. C210a-C210b, June 22, 1965, 210c, Jan. 28,
1965.
For overprints see Nos. C232, C238.

Kennedy Type of Regular Issue

1964, Nov. 22   *Perf. 11½x12*

C211 A189	15c gray & blk	16	15
C212 A189	20c sage grn & blk	24	15
C213 A189	40c yel & blk	40	22
	Set value		44

Miniature Sheet
Imperf

C214 A189	80c grnsh bl & blk	1.00	75

For overprint see No. C259.

Flower Type of Regular Issue

1965, Jan. 6   Photo.   *Perf. 12x11½*

C215 A190	10c Rose	15	15
C216 A190	15c Platanillo	15	15
C217 A190	25c San Jose	20	15
C218 A190	40c Hibiscus	28	18
C219 A190	45c Veranera	40	20
C220 A190	70c Fire flower	55	32
	Nos. C215-C220 (6)	1.73	
	Set value		95

For overprint and surcharges see Nos. C243,
C348-C349.

ICY Type of Regular Issue
Perf. 11½x12

1965, Apr. 27   Photo.   Unwmk.
Design in Brown and Gold

C221 A191	15c light blue	15	15
C222 A191	30c dull lilac	20	15
C223 A191	50c ocher	32	22
	Set value		38

For overprints see Nos. C227, C244, C312.

Gavidia Type of Regular Issue

1965, Sept. 24   Photo.   Unwmk.
Portraits in Natural Colors

C224 A192	10c blk & green	16	15
C225 A192	20c blk & bister	28	15
C226 A192	1col blk & rose	1.25	50
	Set value		70

No. C223 Overprinted in Green: "1865 /
12 de Octubre / 1965 / Dr. Manuel
Enrique Araujo"

1965, Oct. 12   *Perf. 11½x12*

C227 A191	50c brn, ocher & gold	42	40

See note after No. 764.

Fair Type of Regular Issue, 1965

1965, Nov. 5   *Perf. 12x11½*

C228 A193	20c bl & multi	16	15
C229 A193	80c multi	65	42
C230 A193	5col multi	3.25	2.25

For overprint see No. C311.

WHO Type of Regular Issue

1966, May 20   Photo.   Unwmk.

C231 A194	50c multi	42	22

For overprints see Nos. C242, C245.

No. C209 Overprinted in Dark Green:
"1816 1966 / 150 años / Nacimiento /
San Juan Bosco"

1966, Sept. 3   Photo.   *Perf. 12x11½*

C232 A188	25c red & blue	32	25

150th anniv. of the birth of St. John Bosco
(1815-88), Italian priest, founder of the Salesian
Fathers and Daughters of Mary.

UNESCO Type of Regular Issue

1966, Nov. 4   Photo.   *Perf. 12*

C233 A195	30c tan, blk & vio bl	32	15
C234 A195	2col emer, blk & vio bl	1.65	1.00

For surcharge see No. C352.

Fair Type of Regular Issue, 1966

1966, Nov. 27   Litho.   *Perf. 12*
C235 A196 15c multi   16 15
C236 A196 20c multi   20 15
C237 A196 60c multi   50 38

No. C209 Overprinted: "IX-Congreso / Interamericano / de Educacion / Católica / 4 Enero 1967"

1967, Jan. 4   Photo.   *Perf. 12x11¹/₂*
C238 A188 25c red & bl   32 25

Issued to publicize the 9th Inter-American Congress for Catholic Education.

Cañas Type of Regular Issue

1967, Feb. 18   Litho.   *Perf. 11¹/₂*
C239 A197 5c multi   15 15
C240 A197 45c lt bl & multi   55 35
    Set value   40

For surcharges see Nos. C403-C405.

Volcano Type of Regular Issue

1967, Apr. 14   Photo.   *Perf. 13*
C241 A198 50c ol gray & brn   50 22

For surcharges see Nos. C320, C350.

No. C231 Overprinted in Red: "VIII CONGRESO / CENTROAMERICANO DE / FARMACIA & B10QUIMICA / 5 di 11 Noviembre de 1967"

1967, Oct. 26   Photo.   *Perf. 12x11¹/₂*
C242 A194 50c multi   42 40

Issued to publicize the 8th Central American Congress for Pharmacy and Biochemistry.

No. C217 Overprinted in Red: "I Juegos / Centroamericanos y del / Caribe de Basquetbol / 25 Nov. al 3 Dic. 1967"

1967, Nov. 15
C243 A190 25c bl, yel & grn   25 25

First Central American and Caribbean Basketball Games, Nov. 25-Dec. 3.

No. C222 Overprinted in Carmine: "1968 / AÑO INTERNACIONAL DE / LOS DERECHOS HUMANOS"

1968, Jan. 2   Photo.   *Perf. 11¹/₂x12*
C244 A191 30c dl lil, brn & gold   40 30

International Human Rights Year 1968.

No. C231 Overprinted in Red: "1968 / XX ANIVERSARIO DE LA / ORGANIZACION MUNDIAL / DE LA SALUD"

1968, Apr. 7   *Perf. 12x11¹/₂*
C245 A194 50c multi   50 50

20th anniv. of WHO.

No. C229 Overprinted in Red: "1968 / Año / del Sistema / del Crédito / Rural"

1968, May 6   Photo.   *Perf. 12x11¹/₂*
C246 A193 80c multi   65 50

Rural credit system.

Masferrer Type of Regular Issue

1968, June 22   Litho.   *Perf. 12x11¹/₂*
C247 A200 5c brn & multi   15 15
C248 A200 15c grn & multi   15 15
    Set value   22 15

For overprint see No. C297.

Scouts Hiking AP50

1968, July 26   Litho.   *Perf. 12*
C249 AP50 10c multi   15 15

Issued to publicize the 7th Inter-American Boy Scout Conference, July-Aug., 1968.

Presidents' Meeting Type of Regular Issue

1968, Dec. 5   Litho.   *Perf. 14¹/₂*
C250 A202 20c salmon & multi   15 15
C251 A202 1col lt bl & multi   75 50
    Set value   56

Butterfly Type of Regular Issue

Designs: Various butterflies.

1969   Litho.   *Perf. 12*
C252 A203 20c multi   16 15
C253 A203 1col multi   65 35
C254 A203 2col multi   1.65 1.00
C255 A203 10col gray & multi   8.00 5.00

For surcharge see No. C353.

Red Cross, Crescent and Lion and Sun Emblems — AP51

1969   Litho.   *Perf. 11*
C256 AP51 30c yel & multi   24 15
C257 AP51 1col multi   85 50
C258 AP51 4col multi   3.25 2.50

Issued to commemorate the 50th anniversary of the League of Red Cross Societies.
For surcharges see Nos. C351, C354.

No. C213 Overprinted in Green: "Alunizaje / Apolo-11 / 21 Julio / 1969"

1969, Sept.   Photo.   *Perf. 11¹/₂x12*
C259 A189 40c yel & blk   30 30

Man's 1st landing on the moon, July 20, 1969. See note after US No. C76.
The same overprint in red brown and pictures of the landing module and the astronauts on the moon were applied to the margin of No. C214.

Hospital Type of Regular Issue

Design: Benjamin Bloom Children's Hospital.

1969, Oct. 24   Litho.   *Perf. 11¹/₂*
C260 A205 1col multi   85 50
C261 A205 2col multi   1.65 1.00
C262 A205 5col multi   4.25 2.50

For surcharge see No. C355.

ILO Type of Regular Issue

1969   Litho.   *Perf. 13*
C263 A206 50c lt bl & multi   40 18

Tourist Type of Regular Issue

Views: 20c, Devil's Gate. 35c, Ichanmichen Spa. 60c, Aerial view of Acajutla Harbor.

1969, Dec. 19   Photo.   *Perf. 12x11¹/₂*
C264 A207 20c blk & multi   16 15
C265 A207 35c blk & multi   28 20
C266 A207 60c blk & multi   50 40

Insect Type of Regular Issue, 1970

1970, Feb. 24   Litho.   *Perf. 11¹/₂x11*
C267 A208 2col Bee   1.65 1.00
C268 A208 3col Elaterida   2.50 1.50
C269 A208 4col Praying mantis   3.25 2.00

For surcharges see Nos. C371-C373.

Human Rights Type of Regular Issue

Design: 20c, 80c, Map and arms of Salvador and National Unity emblem similar to A209, but vertical.

1970, Apr. 14   Litho.   *Perf. 14*
C270 A209 20c bl & multi   16 15
C271 A209 80c bl & multi   80 40
    Set value   45

For overprint & surcharge see #C301, C402.

Army Type of Regular Issue

Designs: 20c, Fighter plane. 40c, Gun and crew. 50c, Patrol boat.

1970, May 7   *Perf. 12*
C272 A210 20c gray & multi   16 15
C273 A210 40c grn & multi   35 15
C274 A210 50c bl & multi   42 15
    Set value   32

For overprint see No. C310.

Brazilian Team, Jules Rimet Cup — AP52

Designs: Soccer teams and Jules Rimet Cup.

1970, May 25   Litho.   *Perf. 12*
C275 AP52 1col Belgium   1.00 65
C276 AP52 1col Brazil   1.00 65
C277 AP52 1col Bulgaria   2.00 1.00
C278 AP52 1col Czechoslovakia   1.00 65
C279 AP52 1col Germany (Fed. Rep.) 1.00 65
C280 AP52 1col Britain   1.00 65
C281 AP52 1col Israel   1.00 65
C282 AP52 1col Italy   1.00 65
C283 AP52 1col Mexico   1.00 65
C284 AP52 1col Morocco   1.00 65
C285 AP52 1col Peru   1.00 65
C286 AP52 1col Romania   1.00 65
C287 AP52 1col Russia   1.00 65
C288 AP52 1col Salvador   1.00 65
C289 AP52 1col Sweden   1.00 65
C290 AP52 1col Uruguay   1.00 65
    Nos. C275-C290 (16)   17.00 10.75

Issued to publicize the 9th World Soccer Championships for the Jules Rimet Cup, Mexico City, May 30-June 21, 1970.
For overprints see Nos. C325-C340.

Lottery Type of Regular Issue

1970, July 15   Litho.   *Perf. 12*
C291 A211 80c multi   65 25

Education Year Type of Regular Issue

1970, Sept. 11   Litho.   *Perf. 12*
C292 A212 20c pink & multi   16 15
C293 A212 2col buff & multi   1.65 1.00

Fair Type of Regular Issue

1970, Oct. 28   Litho.   *Perf. 12*
C294 A213 20c multi   24 15
C295 A213 30c yel & multi   32 15
    Set value   15

Music Type of Regular Issue

Design: 40c, Johann Sebastian Bach, harp, horn and music.

1971, Feb. 22   Litho.   *Perf. 13¹/₂*
C296 A214 40c gray & multi   38 18

For overprint see No. C313.

No. C247 Overprinted: "Año / del Centenario de la / Biblioteca Nacional / 1970"

1970, Nov. 25   *Perf. 12x11¹/₂*
C297 A200 5c brn & multi   15 15

Miss Tourism Type of Regular Issue

1971, Apr. 1   Litho.   *Perf. 14*
C298 A215 20c lil & multi   15 15
C299 A215 60c gray & multi   45 30
    Set value   38

Pietà Type of Regular Issue

1971, May 10
C300 A216 40c lt yel grn & vio brn 32 20

No. C270 Overprinted in Red Like No. 823

1971, July 6   Litho.   *Perf. 14*
C301 A209 20c bl & multi   18 25

Fish Type of Regular Issue

Designs: 30c, Smalltooth sawfish. 1col, Atlantic sailfish.

1971, July 28
C302 A217 30c lilac & multi   18 25
C303 A217 1col multi   65 50

Independence Type of Regular Issue

Designs: Various sections of Declaration of Independence of Central America.

1971   Litho.   *Perf. 13¹/₂x13*
C304 A218 30c bl & blk   20 15
C305 A218 40c brn & blk   30 20
C306 A218 50c yel & blk   38 25
C307 A218 60c gray & blk   50 35
  a. Souvenir sheet of 8   1.75 1.65

No. C307a contains 8 stamps with simulated perforations similar to Nos. 826-829, C304-C307.
For overprints see Nos. C311, C347.

Church Type of Regular Issue

Designs: 15c, Metapan Church. 70c, Panchimalco Church.

1971, Aug. 21   Litho.   *Perf. 13x13¹/₂*
C308 A219 15c ol & multi   15 15
C309 A219 70c multi   55 35

No. C274   1951-12 Octubre-1971
Overprinted in   XX Aniversario
Red   MARINA NACIONAL

1971, Oct. 12   Litho.   *Perf. 12*
C310 A210 50c bl & multi   38 30

National Navy, 20th anniversary.

No. C229 Overprinted: "V Feria / Internacional / 3-20 Noviembre / de 1972"

1972, Nov. 3   Photo.   *Perf. 12x11¹/₂*
C311 A193 80c multi   90 50

5th Intl. Fair, El Salvador, Nov. 3-20.

No. C223 Overprinted in Red

1972 - XXX Aniversario
Creacion Instituto
Interamericano de
Ciencias Agricolas

1972, Nov. 30   Photo.   *Perf. 11¹/₂x12*
C312 A191 50c ocher, brn & gold   42 30

30th anniversary of the Inter-American Institute for Agricultural Sciences.

No. C296 Overprinted   III Festival Internacional de Música 9 - 25 - Febrero - 1973.

1973, Feb. 5   Litho.   *Perf. 13¹/₂*
C313 A214 40c gray & multi   30 25

3rd International Music Festival, Feb. 9-29.

Lions Type of Regular Issue

Designs: 20c, 40c, Map of El Salvador and Lions International Emblem.

1973, Feb. 20   Litho.   *Perf. 13*
C314 A220 20c gray & multi   15 15
C315 A220 40c multi   30 20

Olympic Type of Regular Issue

Designs: 20c, Javelin, women's. 80c, Discus, women's. 1col, Hammer throw. 2col, Shot put.

1973, May 21   Litho.   *Perf. 13*
C316 A221 20c lt grn & multi   15 15
C317 A221 80c sal & multi   55 35
C318 A221 1col ultra & multi   65 50
C319 A221 2col multi   1.40 90

No. C241 Surcharged Like No. 841

1973, Dec.   Photo.   *Perf. 13*
C320 A198 25c on 50c multi   15 15

No. C307a Overprinted: "Centenario / Cuidad / Santiago de Maria / 1874 1974"
Souvenir Sheet

1974, Mar. 7   Litho.   *Imperf.*
C321 A218 Sheet of 8   1.00 1.00

Centenary of the City Santiago de Maria. The overprint is so arranged that each line appears on a different pair of stamps.

No. C231 Surcharged in Red

25 cts.

1974, Apr. 22   Photo.   Perf. 12x11½
C322 A194 25c on 50c multi   15 15

10 CTS.

No. C229
Surcharged

1974, Apr. 24
C323 A193 10c on 80c multi   15 15

Rehabilitation Type of 1974

1974, Apr. 30   Litho.   Perf. 13
C324 A222 25c multi   20 15

Nos. C275-C290 Overprinted

ALEMANIA 1974

1974, June 4   Litho.   Perf. 12
C325 AP52 1col Belgium   65   50
C326 AP52 1col Brazil   65   50
C327 AP52 1col Bulgaria   65   50
C328 AP52 1col Czech.   65   50
C329 AP52 1col Germany   65   50
C330 AP52 1col Britain   65   50
C331 AP52 1col Israel   65   50
C332 AP52 1col Italy   65   50
C333 AP52 1col Mexico   65   50
C334 AP52 1col Morocco   65   50
C335 AP52 1col Peru   65   50
C336 AP52 1col Romania   65   50
C337 AP52 1col Russia   65   50
C338 AP52 1col Salvador   65   50
C339 AP52 1col Sweden   65   50
C340 AP52 1col Uruguay   65   50
  Nos. C325-C340 (16)   10.40 8.00

World Cup Soccer Championship, Munich, June 13-July 7.

INTERPOL Type of 1974

1974, Sept. 2   Litho.   Perf. 12½
C341 A223 25c multi   20 20

FAO Type of 1974

1974, Sept. 2   Litho.   Perf. 12½
C342 A224 25c bl, dk bl & gold   20 15

Coin Type of 1974

1974, Nov. 19   Litho.   Perf. 12½x13
C343 A225 20c 1p silver, 1892   16 15
C344 A225 40c 20c silver, 1828   32 20
C345 A225 50c 20p gold, 1892   50 25
C346 A225 60c 20col gold, 1925   50 30

No. C307a Overprinted: "X ASAMBLEA
GENERAL DE LA CONFERENCIA /
INTERAMERICANA DE SEGURIDAD
SOCIAL Y XX / REUNION DEL COMITE
PERMANENTE INTERAMERICANO / DE
SEGURIDAD SOCIAL, 24 -- 30
NOVIEMBRE 1974"

1974, Nov. 18   Litho.   Imperf.
Souvenir Sheet
C347 A218   Sheet of 8   1.75 1.75

Social Security Conference, El Salvador, Nov. 24-30. The overprint is so arranged that each line appears on a different pair of stamps.

Issues of 1965-69 Surcharged

₡ 0.10

₡ 0.10

a   b

c   ₡ 0.25

₡ 0.25

d

1974-75
C348 A190(a) 10c on 45c #C219   15 15
C349 A190(a) 10c on 70c #C220   15 15
C350 A198(b) 10c on 50c #C241   15 15
C351 AP51(d) 25c on 1col #C257   20 20
C352 A195(c) 25c on 2col #C234
                            ('75) 32 18
C353 A203(d) 25c on 2col #C254
                            ('75) 20 20
C354 AP51(d) 25c on 4col #C258   20 20
C355 A205(d) 25c on 5col #C262   20 20
             Set value   1.35 1.20

No. C353 has new value at left and 6 vertical bars. No. C355 has 7 vertical bars.

UPU Type of 1975

1975, Jan. 22   Litho.   Perf. 13
C356 A226 25c bl & multi   20 15
C357 A226 30c bl & multi   24 20

Acajutla Harbor Type of 1975

1975, Feb. 17
C358 A227 15c bl & multi   15 15

Post Office Type of 1975

1975, Apr. 25   Litho.   Perf. 13
C359 A228 25c bl & multi   20 15

Miss Universe Type of 1975

1975, June 25   Perf. 12½
C360 A229 25c multi   20 15
C361 A229 60c lil & multi   50 40

Women's Year Type and

IWY
Emblem — AP53

1975, Sept. 4   Litho.   Perf. 12½
C362 A230 15c bl & bl blk   15 15
C363 AP53 25c yel grn & blk   20 15
            Set value   20

International Women's Year 1975.

Nurse Type of 1975

1975, Oct. 24   Litho.   Perf. 12½
C364 A231 25c lt blue & multi   20 15

Printers' Congress Type of 1975

1975, Nov. 19   Litho.   Perf. 12½
C365 A232 30c green & multi   24 24

Dermatologists' Congress Type, 1975

1975, Nov. 28
C366 A233 20c blue & multi   16 15
C367 A233 30c red & multi   24 15

Caritas Type of 1975

1975, Dec. 18   Litho.   Perf. 13½
C368 A234 20c bl & vio bl   16 15

UNICEF
Emblem — AP54

1975, Dec. 18
C369 AP54 15c lt grn & sil   15 15
C370 AP54 20c dl rose & sil   16 15

UNICEF, 25th anniv. (in 1971).

Nos. C267-C269 Surcharged

25c.

1976, Jan. 14   Perf. 11½x11
C371 A208 25c on 2col multi   20 15
C372 A208 25c on 3col multi   20 15
C373 A208 25c on 4col multi   20 15

Caularthron
Bilamellatum
AP55

Designs: Orchids.

1976, Feb. 19   Litho.   Perf. 12½
C374 AP55 25c shown   20 20
C375 AP55 25c Oncidium oli-
               ganthum   20 20
C376 AP55 25c Epidendrum radi-
               cans   20 20
C377 AP55 25c Epidendrum vitel-
               linum   20 20
C378 AP55 25c Cyrtopodium
               punctatum   20 20
C379 AP55 25c Pleurothallis schiedei 20 20
C380 AP55 25c Lycaste cruenta   20 20
C381 AP55 25c Spiranthes speciosa 20 20
       Nos. C374-C381 (8)   1.60 1.60

CIAT Type of 1976

1976, May 18   Litho.   Perf. 12½
C382 A235 50c org & multi   40 15

Bicentennial Types of 1976

1976, June 30   Litho.   Perf. 12½
C383 A236 25c multi   20 15
C384 A237 5col multi   3.75 2.50

Reptile Type of 1976

Reptiles: 15c, Green fence lizard. 25c, Basilisk. 60c, Star lizard.

1976, Sept. 23   Litho.   Perf. 12½
C385 A238 15c multi   15 15
C386 A238 25c multi   20 20
C387 A238 60c multi   48 48

Archaeology Type of 1976

Pre-Columbian Art: 25c, Brazier with pre-classical head, El Trapiche. 50c, Kettle with pre-classical head, Atiquizaya. 70c, Classical whistling vase, Tazumal.

1976, Oct. 11   Litho.   Perf. 12½
C388 A239 25c multi   20 15
C389 A239 50c multi   40 25
C390 A239 70c multi   55 40

For overprint see No. C429.

Fair Type of 1976

1976, Oct. 25   Litho.   Perf. 12½
C391 A240 25c multi   20 15
C392 A240 70c yel & multi   55 40

Christmas Type of 1976

1976, Dec. 16   Litho.   Perf. 11
C393 A241 25c bl & multi   20 15
C394 A241 50c multi   40 25
C395 A241 60c multi   50 30
C396 A241 75c red & multi   60 40

Rotary Type of 1977

1977, June 20   Litho.   Perf. 11
C397 A242 25c multi   20 15
C398 A242 1col multi   80 50

Industrial Type of 1977

Designs: 25c, Radar station, Izalco (vert.). 50c, Central sugar refinery, Jiboa. 75c, Cerron Grande hydroelectric station.

1977, June 29   Perf. 12½
C399 A243 25c multi   20 15
C400 A243 50c multi   40 15
C401 A243 75c multi   60 40

Nos. C399-C401 have colorless overprint in multiple rows: GOBIERNO DEL SALVADOR.

Nos. C271 and C239 Surcharged with
New Value and Bar

1977   Perf. 14, 11½
C402 A209 25c on 80c multi   22 15
C403 A197 30c on 5c multi   25 15
C404 A197 40c on 5c multi   30 20
C405 A197 50c on 5c multi   40 25

Broadcasting Type of 1977

1977, Sept. 14   Litho.   Perf. 14
C406 A244 20c multi   15 15
C407 A244 25c multi   20 15

Symbolic
Chessboard and
Emblem — AP56

1977, Oct. 20   Litho.   Perf. 11
C408 AP56 25c multi   20 15
C409 AP56 50c multi   40 25

El Salvador's victory in International Chess Olympiad, Tripoli, Libya, Oct. 24-Nov. 15, 1976.

Soccer — AP57

Boxing
AP58

1977, Nov. 16   Litho.   Perf. 16
C410 AP57 10c shown   15   15
C411 AP57 10c Basketball   15   15
C412 AP57 15c Javelin   15   15
C413 AP57 15c Weight lifting 15   15
C414 AP57 20c Volleyball   16   15
C415 AP58 20c shown   16   15
C416 AP57 25c Baseball   20   15
C417 AP58 25c Softball   20   15
C418 AP57 30c Swimming   24   20
C419 AP58 30c Fencing   24   20
C420 AP58 40c Bicycling   32   25
C421 AP58 50c Rifle shooting 40   30
C422 AP58 50c Women's tennis 40   30
C423 AP57 60c Judo   48   35
C424 AP58 75c Wrestling   60   40
C425 AP58 1col Equestrian hurdles 80 50
C426 AP58 1col Woman gymnast 80   50
C427 AP58 2col Table tennis 1.65 1.00
    Nos. C410-C427 (18)   7.25 5.20

Size: 100x119mm
C428 AP57 5col Games' poster 4.00 4.00

2nd Central American Olympic Games, San Salvador, Nov. 25-Dec. 4.

No. C390 Overprinted in Red:
"CENTENARIO / CIUDAD DE /
CHALCHUAPA / 1878-1978"

1978, Feb. 13   Litho.   Perf. 12½
C429 A239 70c multi   55 55

Centenary of Chalchuapa.

Map of South
America,
Argentina '78
Emblem — AP59

1978, Aug. 15   Litho.   Perf. 11
C430 AP59 25c multi   20 15
C431 AP59 60c multi   50 40
C432 AP59 5col multi   4.00 3.00

11th World Cup Soccer Championship, Argentina, June 1-25.

Musical Instrument Type of 1978

Designs: 25c, Drum, vert. 50c, Hollow rattles. 80c, Xylophone.

1978, Aug. 29   *Perf. 12¹/₂*
C433 A245 25c multi   20 15
C434 A245 50c multi   40 15
C435 A245 80c multi   60 40

For surcharge see No. C492.

Engineering Type of 1978
1978, Sept. 12   Litho.   *Perf. 13¹/₂*
C436 A246 25c multi   15 15

Izalco Station Type of 1978
1978, Sept. 14   *Perf. 12¹/₂*
C437 A247 75c multi   60 40

Softball, Bat and Globes AP60

Fair Type, 1978
1978, Oct. 17   Litho.   *Perf. 12¹/₂*
C438 AP60 25c pink & multi   20 15
C439 AP60 1col yel & multi   80 50

4th World Softball Championship for Women, San Salvador, Oct. 13-22.

Fair Type, 1978
1978, Oct. 30   Litho.   *Perf. 12¹/₂*
C440 A248 15c multi   15 15
C441 A248 25c multi   20 15

Red Cross Type, 1978
1978, Oct. 30   *Perf. 11*
C442 A249 25c multi   20 15

Cotton Conference Type, 1978
1978, Nov. 22   *Perf. 12¹/₂*
C443 A250 40c multi   32 20

Christmas Type, 1978
1978, Dec. 5   Litho.   *Perf. 12¹/₂*
C444 A251 25c multi   20 15
C445 A251 1col multi   80 50

Athenaeum Type 1978
1978, Dec. 20   Litho.   *Perf. 14*
C446 A252 25c multi   20 15

UPU Type of 1979
1979, Apr. 2   Litho.   *Perf. 14*
C447 A253 75c multi   60 40

Health Organization Type of 1979
1979, Apr. 7   *Perf. 14x14¹/₂*
C448 A254 25c multi   20 15

Social Security Type of 1979
1979, May 25   Litho.   *Perf. 12¹/₂*
C449 A255 25c multi   20 15
C450 A255 1col multi   80 50

Games Emblem — AP61

1979, July 12   Litho.   *Perf. 14¹/₂x14*
C451 AP61 25c multi   20 15
C452 AP61 40c multi   30 20
C453 AP61 70c multi   55 40

8th Pan American Games, Puerto Rico, July 1-15. For surcharge see No. C493.

Pope John Paul II Type of 1979
Design: 60c, 5col, Pope John Paul II and pyramid, horiz.

1979, July 12
C454 A256 60c multi   50 30
C455 A256 5col multi   4.00 2.50

"25," Family and Map of Salvador — AP62

1979, May 14   Litho.   *Perf. 14x14¹/₂*
C456 AP62 25c blk & bl   20 15
C457 AP62 60c blk & lil rose   50 35

Social Security, 25th anniversary.

Pre-Historic Animal Type, 1979
1979, Sept. 7   Litho.   *Perf. 14*
C458 A257 15c Mammoth   15 15
C459 A257 25c Giant anteater, vert.   20 15
C460 A257 2 col Hyenas   1.65 1.00

National Anthem Type, 1979
1979, Sept. 14   *Perf. 14¹/₂x14*
C461 A258 40c Jose Aberiz, score   30 20

COPIMERA Type, 1979
1979, Oct. 19   Litho.   *Perf. 14¹/₂x14*
C462 A259 50c multi   40 25

Circle Dance, IYC Emblem — AP63

Children's Village and IYC Emblems AP64

1979, Oct. 29
C463 AP63 25c multi   20 15
C464 AP64 30c vio & blk   24 20

International Year of the Child.

Biochemistry Type of 1979
1979, Nov. 1   Litho.   *Perf. 14¹/₂x14*
C465 A262 25c multi   20 15

Coffee Type of 1979
Designs: 50c, Picking coffee. 75, Drying coffee beans. 1col, Coffee export.

     Perf. 14x14¹/₂, 14¹/₂x14
1979, Dec. 18
C466 A263 50c multi   40 25
C467 A263 75c multi   60 40
C468 A263 1 col multi   80 55

Hoof and Mouth Disease Type of 1980
1980, June 3   Litho.   *Perf. 14¹/₂x14*
C469 A265 50c multi   50 30

Shell Type of 1980
1980, Aug. 12   *Perf. 14x14¹/₂*
C470 A266 15c Hexaplex regius   15 15
C471 A266 25c Polinices helicoides   20 15
C472 A266 75c Jenneria pustulata   50 40
C473 A266 1 col Pitar lupanaria   80 55

Birds Type
1980, Sept. 10   Litho.   *Perf. 14x14¹/₂*
C474 A267 25c Aulacorhynchus prasinus   20 15
C475 A267 50c Strix varia fulvescens   40 25
C476 A267 75c Myadestes unicolor   60 40

Snake Type of 1980
1980, Nov. 12   Litho.   *Perf. 14x14¹/₂*
C477 A268 25c Rattlesnake   20 15
C478 A268 50c Coral snake   40 25

Auditors Type
1980, Nov. 26   Litho.   *Perf. 14*
C479 A269 50c multi   40 25
C480 A269 75c multi   60 40

Christmas Type
1980, Dec. 5   Litho.   *Perf. 14*
C481 A270 25c multi   20 15
C482 A270 60c multi   50 30

Intl. Women's Decade, 1976-85 — AP65

1981, Jan. 30   *Perf. 14¹/₂x14*
C483 AP65 25c olive green & blk   20 15
C484 AP65 1 col orange & black   80 50

Protected Animals AP66

1981, Mar. 20   Litho.   *Perf. 14x14¹/₂*
C485 AP66 25c Ateles geoffroyi   20 15
C486 AP66 40c Lepisosteus tropicus   30 22
C487 AP66 50c Iguana iguana   40 25
C488 AP66 60c Eretmochelys imbricata   50 35
C489 AP66 75c Spizaetus ornatus   60 40
Nos. C485-C489 (5)   2.00 1.37

Heinrich von Stephan, 150th Birth Anniv. — AP67

1981, May 18   Litho.   *Perf. 14¹/₂x14*
C490 AP67 15c multi   15 15
C491 AP67 2 col multi   1.65 1.00

Nos. C435, C453 Surcharged
     Perf. 12¹/₂, 14¹/₂x14
1981, May 18   Litho.
C492 A245 50c on 80c, #C435   40 25
C493 AP61 1 col on 70c, #C453   80 55

Dental Associations Type
1981, June 18   Litho.   *Perf. 14*
C494 A271 5 col bl & blk   4.00 3.00

IYD Type of 1981
1981, Aug. 14   Litho.   *Perf. 14x14¹/₂*
C495 A272 25c like #936   20 15
C496 A272 50c Emblem   40 25
C497 A272 75c like #936   60 40
C498 A272 1 col like # C496   80 55

Quinonez Type
1981, Aug. 28   Litho.   *Perf. 14x14¹/₂*
C499 A273 50c multi   40 25

World Food Day Type
1981, Sept. 16   Litho.   *Perf. 14x14¹/₂*
C500 A274 25c multi   20 15

Land Registry Office, 100th Anniv. — AP68

1981, Oct. 30   Litho.   *Perf. 14x14¹/₂*
C501 AP68 1 col multi   80 55

TACA Airlines, 50th Anniv. AP69

1981, Nov. 10   Litho.   *Perf. 14*
C502 AP69 15c multi   15 15
C503 AP69 25c multi   20 15
C504 AP69 75c multi   60 40

World Cup Preliminaries Type
1981, Nov. 27   Litho.   *Perf. 14x14¹/₂*
C505 A275 25c Like No. 939   20 15
C506 A275 75c Like No. 940   60 40

Lyceum Type
1981, Dec. 17   Litho.   *Perf. 14*
C507 A276 25c multi   20 15

Sculptures Type
1982, Jan. 22   Litho.   *Perf. 14*
C508 A277 25c Palm leaf with effigy   20 15
C509 A277 30c Jaguar mask   25 20
C510 A277 80c Mayan flint carving   65 45

Scouting Year Type of 1982
1982, Mar. 17   Litho.   *Perf. 14¹/₂x14*
C511 A278 25c Baden-Powell   20 15
C512 A278 50c Girl Scout, emblem   40 25

TB Bacillus Cent. — AP70   Symbolic Design — AP71

1982, Mar. 24   *Perf. 14*
C513 AP70 50c multi   40 25

Armed Forces Type of 1982
1982, May 7   Litho.   *Perf. 14x14¹/₂*
C514 A279 25c multi   20 15

1982, May 14   *Perf. 14*
C515 AP71 75c multi   60 40

25th anniv. of Latin-American Tourist Org. Confederation (COTAL).

14th World Telecommunications Day — AP72

1982, May 17   *Perf. 14x14¹/₂*
C516 AP72 15c multi   15 15
C517 AP72 2col multi   1.65 1.00

World Cup Type of 1982
1982, July 14
C518 A280 25c Team, emblem   20 15
C519 A280 60c Map, cup   50 35
Size: 67x47mm
     Perf. 11¹/₂
C520 A280 2col Team, emblem, diff. 1.65 1.00

1982 World
Cup — AP73

Flags or Arms of Participating Countries;
#C521a, C522a, Italy. #C521b, C522c, Germany.
#C521c, C522e, Argentina. #C521d, C522m,
England. #C521e, C522o, Spain. #C521f, C522q,
Brazil. #C521g, C522b, Poland. #C521h, C522d,
Algeria. #C521i, C522f, Belgium. #C521j, C522n,
France. #C521k, C522p, Honduras. #C521l,
C522r, Russia. #C521m, C522g, Peru. #C521n,
C522i, Chile. #C521o, C522k, Hungary. #C521p,
C522s, Czechoslovakia. #C521q, C522u, Yugosla-
via. #C521r, C522w, Scotland. #C521s, C522h,
Cameroun. #C521t, C522j, Austria. #C521u,
C522l, Salvador. #C521v, C522t, Kuwait.
#C521w, C522v, Ireland. #C521x, C522x, New
Zealand.

1982, Aug. 26
C521		Sheet of 24	3.00	
a.-x.	AP73	15c Flags	15	15
C522		Sheet of 24	5.00	
a.-x.	AP73	25c Arms	20	15

Salvador Team, Cup, Flags — AP74

1982, Aug. 26   Litho.   Perf. 11½
C523	AP74	5col multi	4.00 2.50

International Fair Type
1982, Oct. 14   Litho.   Perf. 14
C524	A281	15c multi	15 15

World Food
Day — AP75

1982, Oct. 21   Litho.   Perf. 14
C525	AP75	25c multi	20 15

St. Francis of Assisi,   Natl. Labor
800th Birth Anniv.   Campaign
AP76   AP77

1982, Nov. 10   Litho.   Perf. 14
C526	AP76	1col multi	80 60

1982, Nov. 30   Litho.   Perf. 14x14½
C527	AP77	50c multi	40 25

Christmas Type
1982, Dec. 14   Litho.   Perf. 14
C528	A282	25c multi, horiz.	20 15

Salvadoran
Paintings
AP78

Designs: No. C529, The Pottery of Paleca, by
Miguel Ortiz Villacorta. No. C530, The Rural
School, by Luis Caceres Madrid. No. C531, To the
Wash, by Julia Diaz. No. C532, "La Pancha" by
Jose Mejia Vides. No. C533, Boats Near The
Beach, by Raul Elas Reyes. No. C534, The Mule-
teers, by Canjura.

Perf. 14x13½, 13½x14
1983, Oct. 18   Litho.
C529	AP78	25c multi	20	15
C530	AP78	25c multi	20	15
C531	AP78	75c multi, vert.	60	40
C532	AP78	75c multi, vert.	60	40
C533	AP78	1col multi, vert.	80	55
C534	AP78	1col multi, vert.	80	55
		Nos. C529-C534 (6)	3.20	2.20

Stamps of the same denomination are se-tenant.

Fishing
Industry — AP79

1983, Dec. 20   Litho.   Perf. 14½x14
C535	AP79	25c Fisherman	20 15
C536	AP79	75c Feeding fish	60 40

No. 999 Surcharged

₡1.00
AÉREO

1985, Apr. 10   Litho.   Perf. 14
C536A	A297	1col on 10c multi	80 50

Natl. Constitution,
Cent. — AP80

1986, Aug. 29   Litho.   Perf. 14
C537	AP80	1col multi	48 35

Hugo Lindo
(1917-1985),
Writer — AP81

1986, Nov. 10   Litho.   Perf. 14½x14
C538	AP81	1col multi	48 35

Central American
Economic
Integration Bank,
25th
Anniv. — AP82

1986, Nov. 20
C539	AP82	1.50col multi	70 52

12th Intl. Fair,
Feb. 14-Mar. 1
AP83

1987, Jan. 20   Litho.   Perf. 14½x14
C540	AP83	70c multi	32 24

Intl. Year of
Shelter for the
Homeless
AP84

Perf. 14x14½, 14½x14
1987, July 15   Litho.
C541	AP84	70c shown	32 24
C542	AP84	1col Emblem, vert.	45 35

Miniature Sheet

Discovery of
America,
500th Anniv.
(in 1992)
AP85

15th cent. map of the Americas (details) and: a,
Ferdinand. b, Isabella. c, Caribbean. d, Ships, coat
of arms. e, Base of flagstaff. f, Ships. g, Pre-Columbian statue. h, Compass. i, Anniv. emblem. j,
Columbus rose.

1987, Dec. 21   Litho.   Perf. 14
C543		Sheet of 10	4.50 3.50
a.-j.	AP85	1col any single	45 35

No. 1075 Surcharged

₡5.⁰⁰

1988, Oct. 28   Litho.   Perf. 14x14½
C544	A316	5col on 90c multi	2.35 1.75

PRENFIL '88, Nov. 25-Dec. 2, Buenos Aire.

Organization of
American
States 18th
General
Assembly, Nov.
14-19 — AP86

1988, Nov. 19
C545	AP86	70c multi	38 28

Handicapped
Soccer
Championships
AP87

1990, May 2   Litho.   Perf. 14½x14
C546	AP87	70c multicolored	34 25

REGISTRATION STAMPS

Gen. Rafael Antonio
Gutiérrez — R1

1897   Engr.   Wmk. 117   Perf. 12
F1	R1	10c dark blue	125.00	
F2	R1	10c brown lake	15	
		Unwmk.		
F3	R1	10c dark blue	20	
F4	R1	10c brown lake	15	

Nos. F1 and F3 were probably not placed in use
without the overprint "FRANQUEO OFICIAL"
(Nos. O127-O128).
*The reprints are on thick unwatermarked paper.
Value, set of 2, 16c.*

ACKNOWLEDGMENT OF RECEIPT STAMPS

AR1

1897   Engr.   Wmk. 117   Perf. 12
H1	AR1	5c dark green	15
		Unwmk.	
H2	AR1	5c dark green	15
		Set value	18

*No. H2 has been reprinted on thick paper. Value
15c.*

POSTAGE DUE STAMPS

D1

1895   Unwmk.   Engr.   Perf. 12
J1	D1	1c olive green	15	15
J2	D1	2c olive green	15	15
J3	D1	3c olive green	15	15

J4	D1	5c olive green	15	15
J5	D1	10c olive green	15	15
J6	D1	15c olive green	15	15
J7	D1	25c olive green	15	18
J8	D1	50c olive green	15	25
		Set value	85	1.05

See Nos. J9-J56. For overprints see Nos. J57-J64, O186-O214.

1896   **Wmk. 117**

J9	D1	1c red	20	20
J10	D1	2c red	20	20
J11	D1	3c red	20	25
J12	D1	5c red	20	25
J13	D1	10c red	20	25
J14	D1	15c red	20	30
J15	D1	25c red	20	30
J16	D1	50c red	20	35
		Nos. J9-J16 (8)	1.60	2.10

Unwmk.

J17	D1	1c red	15	15
J18	D1	2c red	15	15
J19	D1	3c red	15	15
J20	D1	5c red	15	15
J21	D1	10c red	15	15
J22	D1	15c red	15	15
J23	D1	25c red	15	15
J24	D1	50c red	15	18
		Set value	80	1.00

Nos. J17 to J24 exist imperforate.

1897

J25	D1	1c deep blue	15	15
J26	D1	2c deep blue	15	15
J27	D1	3c deep blue	15	15
J28	D1	5c deep blue	15	15
J29	D1	10c deep blue	15	15
J30	D1	15c deep blue	15	15
J31	D1	25c deep blue	15	15
J32	D1	50c deep blue	15	20
		Set value	80	1.00

1898

J33	D1	1c violet	20	
J34	D1	2c violet	20	
J35	D1	3c violet	20	
J36	D1	2c violet	20	
J37	D1	10c violet	20	
J38	D1	15c violet	20	
J39	D1	25c violet	20	
J40	D1	50c violet	20	
		Nos. J33-J40 (8)	1.60	

Reprints of Nos. J1 to J40 are on thick paper, often in the wrong shades and usually with the impression somewhat blurred. Value, set of 40, $2, watermarked or unwatermarked.

1899   **Wmk. 117 Sideways**

J41	D1	1c orange	15	
J42	D1	2c orange	15	
J43	D1	3c orange	15	
J44	D1	5c orange	15	
J45	D1	10c orange	15	
J46	D1	15c orange	15	
J47	D1	25c orange	15	
J48	D1	50c orange	15	
		Set value	80	

Unwmk.
Thick Porous Paper

J49	D1	1c orange	15	
J50	D1	2c orange	15	
J51	D1	3c orange	15	
J52	D1	5c orange	15	
J53	D1	10c orange	15	
J54	D1	15c orange	15	
J55	D1	25c orange	15	
J56	D1	50c orange	15	
		Set value	80	

Nos. J41-J56 were probably not put in use without the wheel overprint.

Nos. J49-J56 Overprinted in Black

1900

J57	D1	1c orange	50	
J58	D1	2c orange	50	
J59	D1	3c orange	50	
J60	D1	5c orange	75	
J61	D1	10c orange	1.00	
J62	D1	15c orange	1.00	
J63	D1	25c orange	1.25	
J64	D1	50c orange	1.50	
		Nos. J57-J64 (8)	7.00	

See note after No. 198A.

Morazán
Monument — D2

Perf. 14, 14½

1903   **Engr.**   **Wmk. 173**

J65	D2	1c yellow green	1.25	1.00
J66	D2	2c carmine	2.00	1.50
J67	D2	3c orange	2.00	1.50
J68	D2	5c dark blue	2.00	1.50
J69	D2	10c dull violet	2.00	1.50
J70	D2	25c blue green	2.00	1.50
		Nos. J65-J70 (6)	11.25	8.50

Nos. 355, 356, 358 **DEFICIENCIA**
and 360 Overprinted **DE FRANQUEO**

1908   **Unwmk.**   **Perf. 11½**

J71	A66	1c green & blk	38	35
J72	A66	2c red & blk	30	25
J73	A66	5c blue & blk	75	50
J74	A66	10c violet & blk	1.10	1.00

Same Overprint on No. O275

J75	O3	3c yellow & blk	75	65
		Nos. J71-J75 (5)	3.28	2.75

Deficiencia de franqueo

Nos. 355-358, 360
Overprinted

J76	A66	1c green & blk	25	25
J77	A66	2c red & blk	30	30
J78	A66	3c yellow & blk	35	35
J79	A66	5c blue & blk	50	50
J80	A66	10c violet & blk	1.00	1.00
		Nos. J76-J80 (5)	2.40	2.40

It is now believed that stamps of type A66, on paper with Honeycomb watermark, do not exist with genuine overprints of the types used for Nos. J71-J80.

Pres. Fernando
Figueroa — D3

1910   **Engr.**   **Wmk. 172**

J81	D3	1c sepia & blk	15	15
J82	D3	2c dk grn & blk	15	15
J83	D3	3c orange & blk	15	15
J84	D3	4c scarlet & blk	15	15
J85	D3	5c purple & blk	15	15
J86	D3	12c deep blue & blk	15	15
J87	D3	24c brown red & blk	15	15
		Set value	62	62

OFFICIAL STAMPS

Overprint Types

a   b

c   d   e

---

f   g

Punch with 12 small holes

Type "c" is called the "wheel" overprint.

Nos. 134-157O Overprinted Type a

1896   **Unwmk.**   **Perf. 12**

O1	A45	1c blue	15	
O2	A45	2c dk brown	15	
a.		Double overprint		
O3	A45	3c blue grn	30	
O4	A45	5c brown ol	15	
O5	A45	10c yellow	15	
O6	A45	12c dk blue	15	
O7	A45	15c blue vio	15	
O8	A45	20c magenta	30	
O9	A45	24c vermilion	15	
O10	A45	30c orange	30	
O11	A45	50c black brn	15	
O12	A45	1p rose lake	15	
		Nos. O1-O12 (12)	2.25	

The 1c has been reprinted on thick unwatermarked paper. Value 15c.

Wmk. 117

O13	A46	1c emerald	15	
O14	A47	2c lake	15	
O15	A48	3c yellow brn	15	
a.		Inverted overprint	1.00	
O16	A49	5c dp blue	15	
O17	A50	10c brown	15	
a.		Inverted overprint	1.25	
O18	A51	12c slate	15	
O19	A52	15c blue grn	15	
O20	A53	20c car rose	15	
a.		Inverted overprint		
O21	A54	24c violet	15	
O22	A55	30c dp green	15	
O23	A56	50c orange	15	
O24	A57	100c dk blue	20	
		Nos. O13-O24 (12)	1.85	

Unwmk.

O25	A46	1c emerald	15	
a.		Double overprint		
O26	A47	2c lake	15	
O27	A48	3c yellow brn	15	
O28	A49	5c dp blue	85	
O29	A50	10c brown	15	
a.		Inverted overprint		
O30	A51	12c slate	15	
O31	A52	15c blue grn	22	
O32	A53	20c car rose	15	
a.		Inverted overprint		
O33	A54	24c violet	42	
O34	A55	30c dp green	15	
O35	A56	50c orange	85	
O36	A57	100c dk blue	1.10	
		Nos. O25-O36 (12)	4.49	

The 3, 5, 10, 12, 15, 20, 24, 30 and 100c have been reprinted on thick unwatermarked paper and the 15c, 50c and 100c on thick watermarked paper. Value, set of 12, $1.20.

Nos. 134-145 Handstamped Type b in
Black or Violet

1896

O37	A45	1c blue	7.50	
O38	A45	2c dk brown	7.50	
O39	A45	3c blue green	7.50	
O40	A45	5c brown olive	7.50	
O41	A45	10c yellow	8.75	
O42	A45	12c dk blue	11.50	
O43	A45	15c blue violet	11.50	
O44	A45	20c magenta	11.50	
O45	A45	24c vermilion	11.50	
O46	A45	30c orange	11.50	
O47	A45	50c black brown	15.00	
O48	A45	1p rose lake	15.00	
		Nos. O37-O48 (12)	126.25	

Reprints of the 1c and 2c on thick paper exist with this handstamp. Value, set of 2, 20c.

Forged overprints exist of Nos. O37-O78, O103-O126 and of the higher valued stamps of O141-O214.

Nos. 146-157F, 157I-157O, 158D
Handstamped Type b in Black or Violet

1896   **Wmk. 117**

O49	A46	1c emerald	6.25	
O50	A47	2c lake	6.25	
O51	A48	3c yellow brn	6.25	
O52	A49	5c deep blue	6.25	
O53	A50	10c brown	6.25	
O54	A51	12c slate	10.00	

O55	A52	15c blue green	11.50	
O56	A53	20c carmine rose	11.50	
O57	A54	24c violet	11.50	
O58	A55	30c deep green	11.50	
O59	A56	50c orange	11.50	
O60	A57	100c dark blue	11.50	
		Nos. O49-O60 (12)	110.25	

Unwmk.

O61	A46	1c emerald	6.25	
O62	A47	2c lake	6.25	
O63	A48	3c yellow brn	6.25	
O64	A49	5c deep blue	6.25	
O65	A50	10c brown	8.75	
O66	A52	15c blue green	11.50	
O67	A58	15c on 24c vio	11.50	
O68	A53	20c carmine rose	11.50	
O69	A54	24c violet	11.50	
O70	A55	30c deep green	11.50	
O71	A56	50c orange	12.50	
O72	A57	100c dark blue	12.50	
		Nos. O61-O72 (12)	116.25	

Nos. 175-176 Overprinted Type a in Black

1897

O73	A59	1c bl, gold, rose & grn	25	
O74	A59	5c rose, gold, bl & grn	25	

These stamps were probably not officially issued.

Nos. 175-176 Handstamped Type b in
Black or Violet

1900

O75	A59	1c bl, gold, rose & grn	17.50	
O76	A59	5c rose, gold, bl & grn	17.50	

Nos. 159-170L Overprinted Type a in
Black

1897   **Wmk. 117**

O79	A46	1c scarlet	15	
O80	A47	2c yellow green	1.25	
O81	A48	3c bister brown	50	
O82	A49	5c orange	15	15
O83	A50	10c blue green	15	
O84	A51	12c blue	25	
O85	A52	15c black	25	50
O86	A53	20c slate	15	
O87	A54	24c yellow	18	
a.		Inverted overprint		
O88	A55	30c rose	50	
O89	A56	50c violet	1.25	1.00
O90	A57	100c brown lake	1.75	
		Nos. O79-O90 (12)	6.53	

Unwmk.

O91	A46	1c scarlet	15	
O92	A47	2c yellow green	30	
O93	A48	3c bister brown	20	
O94	A49	5c orange	15	18
O95	A50	10c blue green	65	
O96	A51	12c blue	65	
O97	A52	15c black	75	
O98	A53	20c slate	15	38
O99	A54	24c yellow	15	38
O100	A55	30c rose	15	38
O101	A56	50c violet	65	
O102	A57	100c brown lake	38	1.00
		Nos. O91-O102 (12)	4.33	

All values have been reprinted on thick paper without watermark and the 1c, 12c, 15c and 100c on thick paper with watermark. Value, set of 16, $1.60.

Nos. 159-170L Handstamped Type b in
Violet or Black

1897   **Wmk. 117**

O103	A46	1c scarlet	7.50	
O104	A47	2c yellow green	7.50	
O105	A48	3c bister brown	7.50	
O106	A49	5c orange	7.50	
O107	A50	10c blue green	8.75	
O108	A51	12c blue		
O109	A52	15c black		
O110	A53	20c slate	15.00	
O111	A54	24c yellow	17.50	
O112	A55	30c rose		
O113	A56	50c violet		
O114	A57	100c brown lake		

Unwmk.

O115	A46	1c scarlet	7.50	
O116	A47	2c yellow grn	7.50	
O117	A48	3c bister brn	7.50	
O118	A49	5c orange	7.50	
O119	A50	10c blue green	7.50	
O120	A51	12c blue		
O121	A52	15c black		
O122	A53	20c slate		
O123	A54	24c yellow		
O124	A55	30c rose	15.00	
O125	A56	50c violet		
O126	A57	100c brown lake	17.50	

Reprints of the 1 and 15c on thick watermarked paper and the 12, 30, 50 and 100c on thick unwatermarked paper are known with this overprint. Value, set of 6, 60c.

Nos. F1, F3 Overprinted Type a in Red
Wmk. 117
O127 R1 10c dark blue   15
Unwmk.
O128 R1 10c dark blue   20

The reprints are on thick paper. Value 15c. Originals of the 10c brown lake Registration Stamp and the 5c Acknowledgment of Receipt stamp are believed not to have been issued with the "FRANQUEO OFICIAL" overprint. They are believed to exist only as reprints.

Nos. 177-188 Overprinted Type a

1898			Wmk. 117
O129	A60	1c orange ver	15
O130	A60	2c rose	15
O131	A60	3c pale yel grn	1.40
O132	A60	5c blue green	15
O133	A60	10c gray blue	15
O134	A60	12c violet	1.40
O135	A60	13c brown lake	20
O136	A60	20c deep blue	15
O137	A60	24c ultra	15
O138	A60	26c bister brn	20
O139	A60	50c orange	15
O140	A60	1p yellow	20
		Nos. O129-O140 (12)	4.45

Reprints of the above set are on thick paper. Value, set of 12, $1.20, with or without watermark.

No. 177 Handstamped Type b in Violet
O141 A60 1c orange ver   30.00

No. O141 with Additional Overprint Type c in Black
O142 A60 1c orange ver

Counterfeits exist of the "wheel" overprint.

Nos. 204-205, 207 and 209 Overprinted Type a

1899			Unwmk.
O143	A61	12c dark green	
O144	A61	13c deep rose	
O145	A61	26c carmine rose	
O146	A61	100c violet	

Nos. O143-O144 Punched With Twelve Small Holes
O147 A61 12c dark green
O148 A61 13c deep rose

Official stamps punched with twelve small holes were issued and used for ordinary postage.

Nos. 199-209 Overprinted Type d

1899
Blue Overprint

O149	A61	1c brown	15
O150	A61	2c gray green	15
O151	A61	3c blue	15
O152	A61	5c brown orange	15
O153	A61	10c chocolate	15
O154	A61	13c deep rose	15
O155	A61	26c carmine rose	15
O156	A61	50c orange red	15
O157	A61	100c violet	15

Black Overprint

O158	A61	3c blue	15
O159	A61	12c dark green	15
O160	A61	24c lt blue	15
		Set value	1.20

Nos. O149 to O160 were probably not placed in use.

With Additional Overprint Type c in Black

O161	A61	1c brown	40	35
O162	A61	2c gray green	60	50
O163	A61	3c blue	40	35
O164	A61	5c brown org	40	35
O165	A61	10c chocolate	50	40
O166	A61	12c dark green		
O167	A61	13c deep rose	1.00	85
O168	A61	24c lt blue	15.00	15.00
O169	A61	26c carmine rose	1.00	60
O170	A61	50c orange red	1.00	85
O171	A61	100c violet	1.25	85
		Nos. O161-O165,O167-O171 (10)	21.55	20.10

Nos. O149-O155, O159-O160 Punched With Twelve Small Holes
Blue Overprint

O172	A61	1c brown	90	30
O173	A61	2c gray green	1.10	30
O174	A61	3c blue	1.50	1.25
O175	A61	5c brown org	2.00	1.00
O176	A61	10c chocolate	2.50	1.75
O177	A61	13c deep rose	2.50	1.25
O177A	A61	24c lt blue		
O178	A61	26c carmine rose	25.00	12.00

Black Overprint

O179	A61	12c dark green	2.00	1.50
		Nos. O172-O177,O178-O179 (8)	37.50	19.35

It is stated that Nos. O172-O214 inclusive were issued for ordinary postage and not for use as official stamps.

Nos. O161-O167, O169 Overprinted Type c in Black

O180	A61	1c brown	1.25	1.10
O180A	A61	2c gray green		
O181	A61	3c blue		
O182	A61	5c brown orange	1.25	
O182A	A61	10c chocolate		
O182B	A61	12c dark green		
O183	A61	13c deep rose	4.00	2.00
O184	A61	26c carmine rose		

Overprinted Types a and e in Black
O185 A61 100c violet

Nos. J49-J56 Overprinted Type a in Black

1900			
O186	D1	1c orange	22.50
O187	D1	2c orange	22.50
O188	D1	3c orange	22.50
O189	D1	5c orange	22.50
O190	D1	10c orange	22.50
O191	D1	15c orange	50.00
O192	D1	25c orange	50.00
O193	D1	50c orange	50.00
		Nos. O186-O193 (8)	262.50

Nos. O194-O189, O191-O193 Overprinted Type c in Black

O194	D1	1c orange	
O195	D1	2c orange	12.50
O196	D1	3c orange	
O197	D1	5c orange	
O198	D1	15c orange	12.50
O199	D1	25c orange	15.00
O200	D1	50c orange	135.00

Nos. O186-O189 Punched With Twelve Small Holes

O201	D1	1c orange	25.00
O202	D1	2c orange	25.00
O203	D1	3c orange	25.00
O204	D1	5c orange	25.00

Nos. O201-O204 Overprinted Type c in Black

O205	D1	1c orange	9.00	6.50
O206	D1	2c orange		6.50
O207	D1	3c orange		6.50
O208	D1	5c orange	9.00	6.50

Overprinted Type a in Violet and Type c in Black

O209	D1	2c orange	12.50
a.	Inverted overprint		
O210	D1	3c orange	
O211	D1	10c orange	3.00

Nos. O186-O188 Handstamped Type e in Violet

O212	D1	1c orange	9.00	7.50
O213	D1	2c orange	9.00	7.50
O214	D1	3c orange	9.00	9.00

See note after No. O48.

Type of Regular Issue of 1900 Overprinted Type a in Black

O223	A63	1c lt green	35	35
a.	Inverted overprint			
O224	A63	2c rose	40	35
a.	Inverted overprint			1.75
O225	A63	3c gray black	25	25
a.	Overprint vertical			
O226	A63	5c blue	25	25
O227	A63	10c blue	70	70
a.	Inverted overprint			
O228	A63	12c yellow grn	70	70
O229	A63	13c yellow brn	70	70
O230	A63	24c gray black	50	70
O231	A63	26c yellow brn	25.00	20.00
a.	Inverted overprint			
O232	A63	50c dull rose		
a.	Inverted overprint			
		Nos. O223-O231 (9)	28.85	24.00

Nos. O223-O224, O231-O232 Overprinted Type f in Violet

O233	A63	1c lt green	4.75	4.00
O234	A63	2c rose	25.00	
a.	"FRANQUEO OFICIAL" inverted			
O235	A63	26c yellow brown	50	50
O236	A63	50c dull rose	75	55

Nos. O223, O225-O228, O232 Overprinted Type g in Black

O237	A63	1c lt green	5.00	5.00
O238	A63	3c gray black		
O239	A63	5c blue		
O240	A63	10c blue		

O241	A63	12c yellow green	

Violet Overprint
O242 A63 50c dull rose   10.00

The shield overprinted on No. O242 is of the type on No. O212.

O1

1903		Wmk. 173	Perf. 14, 14½	
O243	O1	1c yellow green	35	25
O244	O1	2c carmine	35	20
O245	O1	3c orange	1.00	85
O246	O1	5c dark blue	35	20
O247	O1	10c dull violet	50	35
O248	O1	13c red brown	50	35
O249	O1	15c yellow brown	3.25	1.75
O250	O1	24c scarlet	35	35
O251	O1	50c bister	50	35
O252	O1	100c grnsh blue	50	75
		Nos. O243-O252 (10)	7.65	5.40

For surcharges see Nos. O254-O257.

No. 285 Handstamped Type b in Black
1904
O253 A64 3c orange   35.00

2   2

Nos. O246-O248 Surcharged in Black

1905				
O254	O1	2c on 5c dk bl	3.25	2.75
O255	O1	3c on 5c dk bl		
a.	Double surcharge			
O256	O1	3c on 10c dl vio	9.00	6.00
O257	O1	3c on 13c red brn	85	70

A 2c surcharge of this type exists on No. O247.

No. O225 Overprinted in Blue

1905   **1905**
a   b

1905			Unwmk.	
O258	A63(a)	3c gray black	2.00	1.75
O259	A63(b)	3c gray black	1.75	1.50

Nos. O224-O225 Overprinted in Blue

1906   **1906**
c   d

1906				
O260	A63(c)	2c rose	11.25	10.00
O261	A63(c)	3c gray black	1.25	1.00
a.	Overprint "1906" in blk			
O262	A63(d)	3c gray black	1.40	1.25

Escalón — O2   National Palace — O3

1906		Engr.	Perf. 11½	
O263	O2	1c green & blk	15	15
O264	O2	2c carmine & blk	15	15
O265	O2	3c yellow & blk	15	15
O266	O2	5c blue & blk	15	32
O267	O2	10c violet & blk	15	15
O268	O2	13c dk brown & blk	15	15
O269	O2	15c red org & blk	20	15
O270	O2	24c carmine & blk	25	20

O271	O2	50c orange & blk	25	65
O272	O2	100c dk blue & blk	25	2.00
		Nos. O263-O272 (10)	1.85	4.07

The centers of these stamps are also found in blue black.

Nos. O263 to O272 have been reprinted. The shades differ, the paper is thicker and the perforation 12. Value, set of 10, 50c.

1908				
O273	O3	1c green & blk	15	15
O274	O3	2c red & blk	15	15
O275	O3	3c yellow & blk	15	15
O276	O3	5c blue & blk	15	15
O277	O3	10c violet & blk	15	15
O278	O3	13c violet & blk	20	15
O279	O3	15c pale brn & blk	15	15
O280	O3	24c rose & blk	15	15
O281	O3	50c yellow & blk	15	15
O282	O3	100c turq blue & blk	20	15
		Set value	1.10	90

For overprints see Nos. 441-442, 445-449, J75, O283-O292, O323-O328.

Nos. O273-O282 Overprinted Type g in Black

O283	O3	1c green & blk	85
O284	O3	2c red & blk	1.00
O285	O3	3c yellow & blk	1.00
O286	O3	5c blue & blk	1.25
O287	O3	10c violet & blk	1.25
O288	O3	13c violet & blk	1.50
O289	O3	15c pale brn & blk	1.50
O290	O3	24c rose & blk	2.00
O291	O3	50c yellow & blk	2.50
O292	O3	100c turq & blk	3.00
		Nos. O283-O292 (10)	15.85

Pres. Figueroa — O4

1910		Engr.	Wmk. 172	
O293	O4	2c dk green & blk	15	15
O294	O4	3c orange & blk	15	15
O295	O4	4c scarlet & blk	15	15
a.	4c carmine & black			
O296	O4	5c purple & blk	15	15
O297	O4	6c scarlet & blk	15	15
O298	O4	10c purple & blk	15	15
O299	O4	12c dp blue & blk	15	15
O300	O4	17c olive grn & blk	15	15
O301	O4	19c brn red & blk	15	15
O302	O4	29c choc & blk	15	15
O303	O4	50c yellow & blk	15	15
O304	O4	100c turq & blk	15	15
		Set value	1.00	1.00

Regular Issue, Type A63, Overprinted or Surcharged:

OFICIAL
a

3
b

OFICIAL
c

UN COLON

1911			Unwmk.	
O305	A63(a)	1c lt green	15	15
O306	A63(b)	3c on 13c yel brn	15	15
O307	A63(b)	5c on 10c dp bl	15	15
O308	A63(a)	10c deep blue	15	15
O309	A63(a)	12c lt green	15	15
O310	A63(a)	13c yellow brn	15	15
O311	A63(b)	50c on 10c dp bl	15	15
O312	A63(c)	1col on 13c yel brn	15	15
		Set value	68	68

O5   O6

1914   Typo.   Perf. 12
**Background in Green, Shield and
"Provisional" in Black**

O313	O5	2c yellow brn	15	15
O314	O5	3c yellow	15	15
O315	O5	5c dark blue	15	15
O316	O5	10c red	15	15
O317	O5	12c green	15	15
O318	O5	17c violet	15	15
O319	O5	50c brown	15	15
O320	O5	100c dull rose	15	15
		Set value	64	64

Stamps of this issue are known imperforate or
with parts of the design omitted or misplaced.
These varieties were not regularly issued.

1914   Typo.

O321	O6	2c blue green	15	15
O322	O6	3c orange	15	15
		Set value	16	16

Type of Official Stamps of 1908 With Two
Overprints

1915

1915

O323	O3	1c gray green	30	25
a.		"1915" double		
b.		"OFICIAL" inverted		
O324	O3	2c red	30	25
O325	O3	5c ultra	30	25
O326	O3	10c yellow	30	25
a.		Date omitted		
O327	O3	50c violet	60	50
O328	O3	100c black brown	1.25	1.00
		Nos. O323-O328 (6)	3.05	2.50

Same Overprint on #414, 417, 429

O329	A66	1c gray green	1.65	1.65
O330	A66	6c pale blue	50	40
a.		6c ultramarine		
O331	A66	12c brown	60	60

Nos. O323-O327, O329-O331 exist imperforate.
Nos. O329-O331 exist with "OFICIAL" inverted
and double. See note after No. 421.

Nos. 431-440 Overprinted
in Blue or Red

1916

O332	A83	1c deep green	15	15
O333	A83	2c vermilion	35	15
O334	A83	5c dp blue (R)	25	15
O335	A83	6c gray vio (R)	15	15
O336	A83	10c black brown	15	15
O337	A83	12c violet	40	25
O338	A83	17c orange	15	15
O339	A83	25c dark brown	15	15
O340	A83	29c black (R)	15	15
O341	A83	50c slate (R)	15	15
		Set value	1.60	1.00

Nos. 474-481 Overprinted

OFICIAL   **OFICIAL**

a   b

1921

O342	A94(a)	1c green	15	15
O343	A95(a)	2c black	15	15
a.		Inverted overprint		
O344	A96(b)	5c orange	20	15
O345	A97(a)	6c carmine rose	15	15
O346	A98(a)	10c deep blue	20	15
O347	A99(a)	25c olive green	50	25
O348	A100(a)	60c violet	62	50
O349	A101(a)	1col black brown	65	65
		Nos. O342-O349 (8)	2.62	
		Set value		1.90

Nos. 498 and 500
Overprinted in Black or **OFICIAL**
Red

1925

O350	A109	5c olive black	35	15
O351	A111	10c orange (R)	50	15
a.		"ATLANT CO"	7.50	6.25
		Set value		22

Inverted overprints exist.

Regular Issue of 1924-25   **OFICIAL**
Overprinted in Black or
Red

1927

O352	A106	1c red violet	20	15
O353	A107	2c dark red	40	25
O354	A109	5c olive blk (R)	40	25
O355	A110	6c dp blue (R)	3.00	2.50
O356	A111	10c orange	50	30
a.		"ATLANT CO"	12.50	11.50
O357	A116	1col grn & vio (R)	1.50	1.00
		Nos. O352-O357 (6)	6.00	4.45

Inverted overprints exist on 1c, 2c, 5c, 10c.

Regular Issue of 1924-25   **OFICIAL**
Overprinted in Black

1932   Perf. 12½

O358	A106	1c deep violet	20	15
O359	A107	2c dark red	40	25
O360	A109	5c olive black	20	15
O361	A111	10c orange	70	30
a.		"ATLANT CO"	14.00	12.50

> Catalogue values for unused
> stamps in this section, from this
> point to the end of the section, are
> for Never Hinged items.

Regular Issue of
1947 Overprinted in   **OFICIAL**
Black or Red

1948   Unwmk.   Engr.   Perf. 12

O362	A154	1c carmine rose	42.50	19.00
O363	A154	2c deep orange	42.50	19.00
O364	A154	5c slate gray (R)	42.50	19.00
O365	A154	10c bister brn (R)	42.50	19.00
O366	A154	20c green (R)	42.50	19.00
O367	A154	50c black (R)	42.50	19.00
		Nos. O362-O367 (6)	255.00	114.00

No. 602 Surcharged in Carmine and Black

1 CTS

OFICIAL

1964(?)

O368	A154	1c on 20c green	

The X's are black, the rest carmine.

PARCEL POST STAMPS

Mercury — PP1

1895   Unwmk.   Engr.   Perf. 12

Q1	PP1	5c brown orange	25
Q2	PP1	10c dark blue	25
Q3	PP1	15c red	25
Q4	PP1	20c orange	25
Q5	PP1	50c blue green	25
		Nos. Q1-Q5 (5)	1.25

POSTAL TAX STAMPS

Nos. 503, 501
Surcharged

**EDIFICIOS
POSTALES
1**

1931   Unwmk.   Perf. 12½

RA1	A115	1c on 50c org brn	20	15
		Double surcharge	2.00	2.00
RA2	A112	2c on 20c dp grn	20	15
		Set value		20

Nos. 501, 503
Surcharged

**EDIFICIOS
POSTALES
₡ 0.01**

RA3	A112	1c on 20c dp grn	20	15
RA4	A115	2c on 20c org brn	20	15
a.		Without period in "0.02"	1.25	
		Set value		20

The use of these stamps was obligatory, in addition to the regular postage, on letters and other
postal matter. The money obtained from their sale
was to be used to erect a new post office in San
Salvador.

SAMOA

LOCATION — An archipelago in the South
Pacific Ocean, east of Fiji
GOVT. — Former monarchy and (partially)
former German possession
AREA — 1,130 sq. mi.
POP. — 39,000 (est. 1910)
CAPITAL — Apia

In 1861-99, Samoa was an independent
kingdom under the influence of the US, to
which the harbor of Pago Pago had been
ceded, and that of Great Britain and Germany. In 1898 a disturbance arose, resulting
in the withdrawal of Great Britain, and the
partitioning of the islands between Germany
and the US.   Early in World War I the
islands under German domination were
occupied by New Zealand troops and in
1920 the League of Nations declared them a
mandate to New Zealand.   See Vol. 1B for
British issues.

12 Pence = 1 Shilling
20 Shillings = 1 Pound
100 Pfennig = 1 Mark (1900)

Watermark

Wmk. 62- NZ and
Star Wide Apart

Issues of the Kingdom

A1

Type I - Line above "X" is usually unbroken. Dots
over "SAMOA" are uniform and evenly spaced.
Upper right serif of "M" is horizontal.
Type II - Line above "X" is usually broken. Small
dot near upper right serif of "M."
Type III - Line above "X" roughly retouched.
Upper right serif of "M" bends down.
Type IV - Speck of color on curved line below
center of "M."

Perf. 12, 12½
1877-82   Litho.   Unwmk.

1	A1	1p blue (III) ('79)	17.50	22.50
a.		1p ultra (III) ('79)	19.00	27.50
b.		1p ultra (III) ('78)	67.50	65.00
c.		1p ultra (III) ('77)	200.00	82.50
2	A1	2p lilac rose (IV) ('82)	17.50	
3	A1	3p ver (III) ('79)	20.00	22.50
a.		3p brt scarlet (III) ('79)	20.00	22.50
b.		3p scarlet (II)	210.00	72.50
c.		3p deep scarlet (I) ('77)	90.00	72.50
4	A1	6p violet (III) ('79)	20.00	22.50
a.		6p violet (I) ('78)	150.00	85.00
b.		6p violet (I) ('77)	210.00	90.00
5	A1	9p yel brn (IV) ('80)	32.50	82.50
a.		9p orange brown (IV) ('80)	32.50	82.50
6	A1	1sh org yel (II) ('78)	60.00	60.00
a.		1sh dull yellow (II) ('77)	35.00	32.50
7	A1	2sh dp brown (III) ('79)	77.50	82.50
a.		2sh red brown (II) ('78)	200.00	175.00
b.		2sh brown (II) ('78)	200.00	175.00
8	A1	5sh yel grn (III) ('79)	425.00	500.00
a.		5sh deep green (II) ('78)	425.00	500.00
b.		5sh gray green (II) ('78)	1,000.	1,250.

The 1p often has a period after "PENNY." The
2p was never placed in use.
Imperforates of this issue are proofs.
Sheets of the first issue were not perforated
around the outer sides. All values except the 2p
were printed in sheets of 10 (2x5). The 1p, 3p and
6p type I and the 1p type III were also printed in
sheets of 20 (4x5), and six stamps on each of these
sheets were perforated all around. The 2p was
printed in sheets of 21 (3x7) and five stamps in the
second row were perforated all around. These are
the only varieties of the original stamps which have
not one or two imperforate edges.
Reprints are of type IV and nearly always perforated on all sides. They have a spot of color at the
edge of the panel below the "M." This spot is not
on any originals except the 2p, which may be
distinguished by its color, and the 9p which may
be distinguished by having a rough blind perf. 12.

Palms — A2   King Malietoa
Laupepa — A3

1895-99   Typo.   Wmk. 62   Perf. 11

9	A2	½p brown vio ('95)	60	1.25
10	A2	½p green ('99)	42	55
11	A2	1p green ('95)	90	1.25
12	A2	1p red brown ('99)	40	50
13	A2	2p brt yellow ('95)	90	90
14	A3	2½p rose ('92)	75	75
15	A3	2½p blk, perf. 10x11 ('96)	1.10	1.10
a.		Perf. 11 ('95)	75.00	65.00
16	A2	4p blue ('95)	1.00	1.25
17	A2	6p maroon ('95)	1.10	3.00
18	A2	1sh rose ('95)	1.40	4.50
19	A2	2sh6p red violet ('95)	4.50	9.00
c.		Vert. pair, imperf. btwn.	400.00	
		Nos. 9-19 (11)	13.07	24.05

1886-92   Perf. 12½

9a	A2	½p brown violet	10.00	15.00
11a	A2	1p green	5.50	11.00
13a	A2	2p orange	5.50	5.50
14a	A3	2½p rose ('92)	95	1.90
16a	A2	4p blue	5.00	5.50
17a	A2	6p maroon		650.00
18a	A2	1sh rose	20.00	7.75
c.		Diagonal half used as 6p on cover		350.00
19a	A2	2sh6p purple	30.00	22.50
		Nos. 9a-16a,18a-19a (7)	76.95	68.65

1887-92   Perf. 12x11½

9b	A2	½p brown violet	18	18
11b	A2	1p green	4.50	1.10
13b	A2	2p brown orange	5.50	1.65
14b	A3	2½p rose ('92)	165.00	2.75
16b	A2	4p blue	82.50	3.25
17b	A2	6p maroon	11.00	5.50
18b	A2	1sh rose	8.25	2.75
19b	A2	2sh6p red violet	8.75	1.40
		Nos. 9b-19b (8)	285.68	18.58

Three forms of watermark 62 are found on
stamps of type A2: 1. Wide "N Z" and wide star,
6mm apart (used 1886-87). 2. Wide "N Z" and
narrow star, 4mm apart (1890). 3. Narrow "NZ"
and narrow star, 7mm apart (1890-1900). The
2½p has only the last form.
For surcharges and overprints see Nos. 20-22,
24-38.

No. 14a Handstamp Surcharged in Black
or Red

**FIVE
PENCE**   **FIVE
PENCE**

a   b

Column 1 — SAMOA

c **5d**

1893   **Perf. 12x11½**
20	A2(a)	5p on 4p blue (bar 16mm)	37.50 37.50
21	A2(b)	5p on 4p blue	45.00 50.00
22	A2(c)	5p on 4p blue (R)	10.00 10.00

As the surcharges on Nos. 20-21 were hand-stamped in two steps and on No. 22 in three steps, various varieties exist.

Flag Design — A7

1894-95   **Typo.**   **Perf. 11½x12**
23	A7	5p vermilion	5.00 2.50
a.		Perf. 11 ('95)	1.50 7.00

Types of 1887-1895 Surcharged in Blue, Black, Red or Green:

Surcharged
1½d. d   **R 3d.** e

1895   **Perf. 11**
24	A2(d)	1½p on 2p orange (Bl)	1.50 1.50
a.		1½p on 2p brn org, perf. 12x11½ (Bl)	2.00 2.00
b.		1½p on 2p yel, "2" ends with vertical stroke	1.00 1.00
25	A2(e)	3p on 2p orange (Bk)	2.00 2.00
a.		3p on 2p brn org, perf. 12x11½ (Bk)	3.00 3.00
b.		3p on 2p yel, perf. 11 (Bk)	30.00 30.00
c.		Vert. pair, imperf. btwn.	425.00

1898-1900   **Perf. 11**
26	A2(d)	2½p on 1sh rose (Bk)	95 95
a.		Double surcharge	425.00
27	A2(d)	2½p on 2shóp vio (Bk)	3.75 5.50
28	A2(d)	2½p on 1p bl grn (R)	40 80
a.		Inverted surcharge	425.00
29	A2(d)	2½p on 1sh rose (R)	5.50 6.00
30	A2(e)	3p on 2p org (G)	60

No. 30 was a re-issue, available for postage.

Stamps of 1886-99 Overprinted in Red or Blue

PROVISIONAL GOVT.

1899
31	A2	½p green (R)	20 22
32	A2	1p red brown (Bl)	20 22
33	A2	2p orange (R)	32 40
a.		2p yellow	40 50
34	A2	4p blue (R)	32 40
35	A7	5p scarlet (Bl)	38 38
36	A2	6p maroon (Bl)	52 70
37	A2	1sh rose (Bl)	1.25 1.40
38	A2	2shóp violet (R)	2.25 2.50
		Nos. 31-38 (8)	5.44 6.22

In 1900 the Samoan islands were partitioned between the US and Germany. The American part has since used US stamps.

Issued under German Dominion

A10   A11

Stamps of Germany Overprinted
1900   **Unwmk.**   **Perf. 13½x14½**
51	A10	3pf dark brown	9.25 8.50
52	A10	5pf green	13.00 10.50
53	A11	10pf carmine	9.25 10.50
54	A11	20pf ultra	18.00 18.00
55	A11	25pf orange	45.00 47.50
56	A11	50pf red brown	45.00 40.00
		Nos. 51-56 (6)	139.50 135.00

Kaiser's Yacht "Hohenzollern"
A12   A13

1900   **Typo.**   **Perf. 14**
57	A12	3pf brown	1.00 65
58	A12	5pf green	1.25 65
59	A12	10pf carmine	1.25 65
60	A12	20pf ultra	80 1.25
61	A12	25pf org & blk, yel	1.40 10.00
62	A12	30pf org & blk, sal	1.25 10.00
63	A12	40pf lake & blk	1.25 10.00
64	A12	50pf org & blk, sal	1.50 10.00
65	A12	80pf lake & blk, rose	3.25 22.50

Perf. 14½x14   **Engr.**
66	A13	1m carmine	3.50 45.00
67	A13	2m blue	4.75 70.00
68	A13	3m black vio	7.25 100.00
69	A13	5m slate & car	150.00 415.00
		Nos. 57-69 (13)	178.45

1915   **Wmk. 125**   **Typo.**   **Perf. 14**
70	A12	3pf brown	1.25
71	A12	5pf green	1.75
72	A12	10pf carmine	1.75

Perf. 14½x14   **Engr.**
73	A13	5m slate & car	22.50

Nos. 70-73 were never put in use.

SAN MARINO

LOCATION — Eastern Italy, about 20 miles inland from the Adriatic Sea
GOVT. — Republic
AREA — 24.1 sq. mi.
POP. — 21,622 (1981)
CAPITAL — San Marino

100 Centesimi = 1 Lira

Catalogue values for unused stamps in this country are for Never Hinged items, beginning with Scott 412 in the regular postage section, Scott B39 in the semi-postal section, Scott C97 in the airpost section, Scott E26 in the special delivery section, and Scott Q40 in the parcel post section.

Watermarks

Wmk. 140- Crown

Wmk. 174- Coat of Arms   Wmk. 217- Three Plumes

Wmk. 277- Winged Wheel   Wmk. 303- Multiple Stars

Wmk. 339- Triskelion

Values of San Marino Nos. 1-28, 72 are for specimens in fine condition with original gum. Very fine to superb stamps sell at higher prices. Copies without gum or with perforations cutting into the design sell at lower prices, depending on the condition of the individual specimen.

Coat of Arms
A1   A2

1877-99   **Typo.**   **Wmk. 140**   **Perf. 14**
1	A1	2c green	3.50 1.00
2	A1	2c blue ('94)	3.00 1.75
3	A1	2c claret ('95)	2.50 1.75
4	A2	5c orange ('90)	27.50 3.75
5	A2	5c olive grn ('92)	1.75 85
6	A2	5c green ('99)	1.50 65
7	A2	10c ultra	27.50 3.75
a.		10c blue ('90)	110.00 16.00
8	A2	10c dk green ('92)	1.90 1.00
9	A2	10c claret ('99)	1.50 90
10	A2	15c claret ('94)	45.00 11.00
11	A2	20c vermilion	4.50 1.50
12	A2	20c lilac ('95)	1.90 1.50
13	A2	25c maroon ('90)	27.50 5.00
14	A2	25c blue ('99)	1.65 1.10
15	A2	30c brown	165.00 16.00
16	A2	30c org red ('92)	2.50 1.75
17	A2	40c violet	165.00 16.00
18	A2	40c dk brown ('92)	1.75 1.75
19	A2	45c gray grn ('92)	1.90 1.75
20	A2	65c red brown ('92)	2.25 1.75
21	A2	1 l car & yel ('92)	900.00 225.00
22	A2	1 l lt blue ('95)	800.00 200.00
23	A2	2 l brn & yel ('94)	24.00 20.00
24	A2	5 l vio & gar ('94)	55.00 55.00

See Nos. 911-915.

Nos. 7a, 15, 11 Surcharged in Black   **C mi. 5**

1892
25	A2	5c on 10c blue	21.00 5.00
a.		Inverted surcharge	21.00 5.00
b.		5c on 10c ultramarine	6,750. 1,250.
c.		As "b," inverted surch.	6,750. 1,250.
26	A2	5c on 30c brown	175.00 22.50
a.		Inverted surcharge	175.00 22.50
b.		Double surch., one inverted	175.00 50.00
c.		Double invtd. surcharge	175.00 35.00
27	A2	10c on 20c ver	13.00 1.00
a.		Inverted surcharge	16.00 1.90
b.		Double surch., one inverted	15.00 7.00
c.		Double surcharge	15.00 7.00

Ten to twelve varieties of each surcharge.

No. 11 Surcharged **10**   10

1892
28	A2	10c on 20c ver	75.00 1.75

Government Palace and Portraits of Regents, Tonnini and Marcucci
A6   A7

Portraits of Regents and View of Interior of Palace — A8

Perf. 15½
1894, Sept. 30   **Litho.**   **Wmk. 174**
29	A6	25c blue & dk brn	1.50 38
30	A7	50c dull red & dk brn	4.50 1.00
31	A8	1 l green & dk brown	4.50 1.00

Opening of the new Government Palace and the installation of the new Regents.

Statue of Liberty — A9

Wmk. 140
1899-1922   **Typo.**   **Perf. 14**
32	A9	2c brown	55 45
33	A9	2c claret ('22)	15 15
34	A9	5c brown org	1.00 90
35	A9	5c olive grn ('22)	15 15
36	A9	10c brown org ('22)	15 15
37	A9	20c dp brown ('22)	15 15
38	A9	25c ultra ('22)	18 18
39	A9	45c red brown ('22)	45 45
		Nos. 32-39 (8)	2.78 2.58

Numeral of Value — A10   Mt. Titano — A11

1903-25   **Perf. 14, 14½x14**
40	A10	2c violet	4.50 60
41	A10	2c orange brn ('21)	15 15
42	A11	5c blue grn	1.50 30
43	A11	5c olive grn ('21)	15 15
44	A11	5c red brn ('25)	15 15
45	A11	10c claret	1.50 30
46	A11	10c brown org ('21)	15 15
47	A11	10c olive grn ('25)	15 15
48	A11	15c blue grn ('22)	15 15
49	A11	15c brown vio ('25)	15 15
50	A11	20c brown orange	25.00 7.25
51	A11	20c brown org ('21)	15 15
52	A11	20c blue grn ('25)	15 15
53	A11	25c blue	5.50 1.25
54	A11	25c gray ('21)	15 15
55	A11	25c violet ('25)	15 15
56	A11	30c brown red	2.25 2.50
57	A11	30c claret ('21)	16 16
58	A11	30c orange ('25)	3.75 45
59	A11	40c orange red	3.50 3.00
60	A11	40c dp rose ('21)	18 18
61	A11	40c brown ('25)	16 16
62	A11	45c yellow	3.50 3.00
63	A11	50c brown vio ('23)	28 28
64	A11	50c gray blk ('25)	16 16
65	A11	60c brown red ('25)	18 18
66	A11	65c chocolate	3.50 3.00
67	A11	80c blue ('21)	32 32
68	A11	90c brown ('23)	32 32
69	A11	1 l olive green	7.75 4.00
70	A11	1 l ultra ('21)	32 32
71	A11	1 l lt blue ('25)	22 22
72	A11	2 l violet	300.00 90.00
73	A11	2 l orange ('21)	7.00 7.25
74	A11	2 l lt green ('25)	1.00 1.00

75	A11	5 l slate	50.00	40.00
76	A11	5 l ultra ('25)	5.00	5.00
		Nos. 40-76 (37)	429.20	172.85

For overprints and surcharges see Nos. 77, 93-96, 107, 188-189, B1-B2, E2, E4.

1905

No. 50 Surcharged

15

1905, Sept. 1
77	A11	15c on 20c brown org	2.75	1.50
a.		Large "5" in "1905"	13.00	7.75

Coat of Arms
A12   A13

Two types:
I - Width 18½mm.
II - Width 19mm.

1907-10   Unwmk.   Engr.   Perf. 12
78	A12	1c brown, II ('10)	75	55
a.		Type I	1.50	75
79	A13	15c gray, I	6.00	1.10
a.		Type II ('10)	65.00	5.00

Cent. 20

No. 79a Surcharged in Brown

1918

1918, Mar. 15
80	A13	20c on 15c gray	1.25	1.25

St. Marinus — A14

Perf. 14½x14, 14x14½
1923, Aug. 11   Typo.   Wmk. 140
81	A14	30c dark brown	20	28

San Marino Intl. Exhib. of 1923. Proceeds from the sale of this stamp went to a mutual aid society.

Italian Flag and Views of Arbe and Mt. Titano A15

1923, Aug. 6
82	A15	50c olive green	20	28

Presentation to San Marino of the Italian flag which had flown over the island of Arbe, the birthplace of the founder of San Marino. Inscribed on back: "V. Moraldi dis. Blasi inc. Petiti impr.-Roma."

Mt. Titano and Sword — A16

1923, Sept. 29   Perf. 14x14½
83	A16	1 l dark brown	3.00	3.00

In honor of the San Marino Volunteers who were killed or wounded in WWI.

Giuseppe Garibaldi A17

Allegory-San Marino Sheltering Garibaldi A18

1924, Sept. 25   Perf. 14
84	A17	30c dark violet	32	32
85	A17	50c olive brown	32	32
86	A17	60c dull red	90	90
87	A18	1 l deep blue	1.50	1.50
88	A18	2 l gray green	1.75	1.75
		Nos. 84-88 (5)	4.79	4.79

75th anniv. of Garibaldi's taking refuge in San Marino.

Semi-Postal Stamps of 1918 Surcharged with New Values and Bars

Cmi 30

1924, Oct. 9
89	SP1	30c on 45c yel brn & blk	22	22

Surcharged

LIRE   UNA

••••••••••••••••••••••••••

90	SP2	60c on 1 l bl grn & blk	2.25	2.25
91	SP2	1 l on 2 l vio & blk	5.25	5.25
92	SP2	2 l on 3 l red brn & blk	4.50	4.50

Lire 1,20

Nos. 67 and 68 Surcharged in Black or Red

1926, July 1
93	A11	75c on 80c blue	30	30
94	A11	1.20 l on 90c brown	30	30
95	A11	1.25 l on 90c brn (R)	1.00	1.00
96	A11	2.50 l on 80c blue (R)	1.40	1.40

Antonio Onofri — A19

A20

Unwmk.
1926, July 29   Engr.   Perf. 11
97	A19	10c dk blue & blk	15	15
98	A19	20c olive grn & blk	45	40
99	A19	45c dk vio & blk	22	22
100	A19	65c green & blk	22	22
101	A19	1 l orange & blk	1.40	1.40
102	A19	2 l red vio & blk	1.40	1.40
		Nos. 97-102 (6)	3.84	3.79

For surcharges see Nos. 104-106, 181-182.

Perf. 14½x14
1926, Nov. 25   Wmk. 140
103	A20	1.85 l on 60c violet	30	30

Nos. 101 and 102 Surcharged **1,25**

1927, Mar. 10   Unwmk.   Perf. 11
104	A19	1.25 l on 1 l	1.10	1.10
105	A19	2.50 l on 2 l	3.00	3.00
106	A19	5 l on 2 l	17.00	17.00

Type of Special Delivery Stamp of 1923 Surcharged

L. 1,75

1927, Sept. 15   Wmk. 140   Perf. 14
107	A11	1.75 l on 50c on 25c vio	45	45

The 50c on 25c violet was not issued without 1.75-lire surcharge.

War Memorial A21

Unwmk.
1927, Sept. 28   Engr.   Perf. 12
108	A21	50c brown violet	60	60
109	A21	1.25 l blue	1.10	1.10
110	A21	10 l gray	8.25	8.25

Erection of a cenotaph in memory of the San Marino volunteers in WWI.

Capuchin Church and Convent A22

Design: 2.50 l, 5 l, Death of St. Francis.

1928, Jan. 2
111	A22	50c red	6.75	1.40
112	A22	1.25 l dp blue	1.10	1.10
113	A22	2.50 l dk brown	1.10	1.10
114	A22	5 l dull violet	9.25	9.25

7th centenary of the death of St. Francis of Assisi. For surcharges see Nos. 183-184.

The Rocca (State Prison) — A24

Government Palace — A25

Statue of Liberty — A26

1929-35   Wmk. 217
115	A24	5c vio brn & ultra	15	15
116	A24	10c bl gray & red vio	30	15
117	A24	15c dp org & emer	15	15
118	A24	20c dk bl & org red	15	15
119	A24	25c grn & gray blk	15	15
120	A24	30c gray brn & red	15	15
121	A24	50c red vio & ol gray	15	15
122	A24	75c dp red & gray blk	15	15
123	A25	1 l dk brn & emer	15	15
124	A25	1.25 l dk blue & blk	15	15
125	A25	1.75 l green & org	15	15
126	A25	2 l bl gray & red	15	15
127	A25	2.50 l car rose & ultra	15	15
128	A25	3 l dp org & bl	15	15
129	A25	3.70 l ol blk & red brn ('35)	18	18
130	A26	5 l dk vio & dk grn	20	20
131	A26	10 l bis brn & dk bl	95	95
132	A26	15 l green & red vio	7.25	7.25
133	A26	20 l dk blue & red	125.00	125.00
		Nos. 115-133 (19)	135.83	135.68

General Post Office — A27

San Marino-Rimini Electric Railway — A28

1932, Feb. 4
134	A27	20c blue green	2.00	85
135	A27	50c dark red	3.25	1.75
136	A27	1.25 l dark blue	100.00	45.00
137	A27	1.75 l dark brown	32.50	24.00
138	A27	2.75 l dark violet	10.50	9.00
		Nos. 134-138 (5)	148.25	80.60

Opening of new General Post Office. For surcharges see Nos. 151-160.

1932, June 11
139	A28	20c deep green	55	55
140	A28	50c dark red	80	80
141	A28	1.25 l dark blue	1.40	1.40
142	A28	5 l deep brown	18.00	16.00

Opening of the new electric railway between San Marino and Rimini.

Giuseppe Garibaldi A29

Garibaldi's Arrival at San Marino A30

1932, July 30
143	A29	10c violet brown	60	60
144	A29	20c violet	28	28
145	A29	25c green	52	52
146	A29	50c yellow brn	1.25	1.25
147	A30	75c dark red	1.25	1.25
148	A30	1.25 l dark blue	1.90	1.90
149	A30	2.75 l brown orange	9.00	9.00
150	A30	5 l olive green	110.00	110.00
		Nos. 143-150 (8)	124.80	124.80

Garibaldi (1807-1882), Italian patriot.

Nos. 138 and 137 Surcharged

50 CENT
28 MAGGIO 1933   CONVEGNO FILATELICO

1933, May 27
151	A27	25c on 2.75 l	45	45
152	A27	50c on 1.75 l	1.75	1.75
153	A27	75c on 2.75 l	7.00	7.00
154	A27	1.25 l on 1.75 l	125.00	125.00

Convention of philatelists, San Marino, May 28.

MOSTRA FILATELICA 12-27 APRILE 1934

Nos. 134-137
Surcharged in Black

1934, Apr. 12

155	A27	25c on 1.25 l	48	48
156	A27	50c on 1.75 l	70	70
157	A27	75c on 50c	2.00	2.00
158	A27	1.25 l on 20c	13.00	13.00

San Marino's participation (with a philatelic pavilion) in the 15th annual Trade Fair at Milan, Apr. 12-27.

Nos. 136 and 138 Surcharged Wheel and New Value

1934, Apr. 12

159	A27	3.70 l on 1.25 l	40.00	40.00
160	A27	3.70 l on 2.75 l	40.00	40.00

Ascent to Mt. Titano A31

Unwmk.

1935, Feb. 7　　Engr.　　Perf. 14

161	A31	5c choc & blk	15	15
162	A31	10c dk vio & blk	15	15
163	A31	20c orange & blk	15	15
164	A31	25c green & blk	15	15
165	A31	50c olive bis & blk	20	20
166	A31	75c brown red & blk	1.25	1.25
167	A31	1.25 l blue & blk	2.50	2.50
		Nos. 161-167 (7)	4.55	4.55

12th anniv. of the founding of the Fascist Movement.

Melchiorre Delfico — A32　　Statue of Delfico — A33

1935, Apr. 15　　Wmk. 217　　Perf. 12
Center in Black

169	A32	5c brown lake	15	15
170	A32	7½c lt brown	15	15
171	A32	10c dk blue grn	15	15
172	A32	15c rose carmine	4.00	80
173	A32	20c orange	15	15
174	A32	25c green	15	15
175	A32	30c dull violet	15	15
176	A33	50c olive green	65	52
177	A33	75c red	3.50	3.50
178	A33	1.25 l dark blue	80	80
179	A33	1.50 l dk brown	9.50	9.50
180	A33	1.75 l brown org	15.00	15.00
		Nos. 169-180 (12)	34.35	31.02

Melchiorre Delfico (1744-1835), historian.
For surcharges see Nos. 202, 277.

Nos. 99-100 Surcharged in Black 80

1936, Apr. 14　　Unwmk.　　Perf. 11

181	A19	80c on 45c dk vio & blk	1.10	1.10
182	A19	80c on 65c grn & blk	1.10	1.10

Nos. 112-113 Surcharged in Black

 L. 2,05

1936, Aug. 23　　　　Perf. 12

183	A22	2.05 l on 1.25 l	3.25	3.25
184	A22	2.75 l on 2.50 l	14.00	14.00

Souvenir Sheet

Design from Base of Roman Column A34

1937, Aug. 23　　Engr.　　Wmk. 217

185	A34	5 l steel blue	8.50	8.50

Unveiling of the Roman Column at San Marino. The date "1636 d. F. R." means the 1,636th year since the founding of the republic.
No. 185 was privately surcharged "+ 10 L 1941."

Souvenir Sheets

Abraham Lincoln — A35

1938, Apr. 7　　Wmk. 217　　Perf. 13

186	A35	3 l dark blue	85	85
187	A35	5 l rose red	9.50	9.50

Dedication of a Lincoln bust, Sept. 3, 1937.

No. 49 and Type of 1925 Surcharged with New Value in Black

1941　　Wmk. 140　　Perf. 14

188	A11	10c on 15c brown vio	15	15
189	A11	10c on 30c brown org	55	40

Flags of Italy and San Marino — A36

Harbor of Arbe — A37

1942　　　　Photo.

190	A36	10c yel brn & brn org	15	15
191	A36	15c brn & red brn	15	15
192	A36	20c gray grn & gray blk	15	15
193	A36	25c green & blue	15	15
194	A36	50c brn red & brn	15	15
195	A36	75c red & gray blk	15	15
196	A37	1.25 l bl & gray bl	15	15
197	A37	1.75 l brn & grnsh blk	22	22
198	A37	2.75 l bis brn & gray bl	38	38
199	A37	5 l green & brown	2.25	2.25
		Set value	3.35	3.45

Return of the Italian flag to Arbe.

San Marino stamps can be mounted in the annual Scott San Marino supplement.

GIORNATA FILATELICA RIMINI · SAN MARINO

No. 190 Surcharged in Black

3 AGOSTO 1942 (1641 d. F. R.)

C.——30

1942, July 30

200	A36	30c on 10c	28	28

Rimini-San Marino Stamp Day, Aug. 3.

No. 192 Surcharged with New Value and Bars in Black

1942, Sept. 14

201	A36	30c on 20c	20	20

No. 177 Surcharged with New Value in Black

1942, Sept. 28　　Wmk. 217　　Perf. 12

202	A33	20 l on 75c red & blk	6.75	6.75

Printing Press and Newspaper A38

Newspapers — A39

1943, Apr. 12　　Wmk. 140　　Photo.　　Perf. 14

203	A38	10c deep green	15	15
204	A38	15c bister	15	15
205	A38	20c dk orange brn	15	15
206	A38	30c dk rose vio	15	15
207	A38	50c blue black	15	15
208	A38	75c red orange	15	15
209	A39	1.25 l blue	15	15
210	A39	1.75 l deep violet	15	15
211	A39	5 l slate	18	18
212	A39	10 l dark brown	1.75	1.75
		Set value	2.45	2.60

Nos. 206 and 207 Overprinted in Red

GIORNATA FILATELICA RIMINI - SAN MARINO 5 LUGLIO 1943 (1642 d. F. R.)

1943, July 1

213	A38	30c dk rose vio	15	15
214	A38	50c blue black	15	15
		Set value	20	20

Rimini-San Marino Stamp Day, July 5.

A40　　　　A41

Overprinted in Black: "28 LVGLIO 1943 1642 F. R."

1943, Aug. 27

215	A40	5c brown	15	15
216	A40	10c orange red	15	15
217	A40	20c ultra	15	15
218	A40	25c deep green	15	15
219	A40	30c brown carmine	15	15
220	A40	50c deep violet	15	15
221	A40	75c car rose	15	15

222	A41	1.25 l sapphire	15	15
223	A41	1.75 l red org	15	15
224	A41	2.75 l dk red brn	18	18
225	A41	5 l green	45	45
226	A41	10 l violet	75	75
227	A41	20 l slate blue	1.90	1.90
		Set value	3.90	4.00

This series was prepared to commemorate the 20th anniversary of fascism, but as Mussolini was overthrown July 25, 1943, it was converted by overprinting to commemorate the downfall of fascism.
Overprint on Nos. 222-227 adds "d." before "F.R."
Nos. 215-227 exist without overprint (not regularly issued). Value of set $45.
See Nos. C26-C33.

A42　　　　A43

Overprinted "Governo Provvisorio" in Black

1943, Aug. 27

228	A42	5c brown	15	15
229	A42	10c orange red	15	15
230	A42	20c ultra	15	15
231	A42	25c deep green	15	15
232	A42	30c brown carmine	15	15
233	A42	50c deep violet	15	15
234	A42	75c carmine rose	15	15
235	A43	1.25 l sapphire	15	15
236	A43	1.75 l red orange	30	30
237	A43	5 l green	55	55
238	A43	20 l slate blue	1.90	1.90
		Set value	3.20	3.35

See Nos. C34-C39.

Souvenir Sheets

A44

Perf. 14, Imperf.

1945, Mar. 15　　Photo.　　Unwmk.

239	A44	Sheet of 3	27.50	27.50
a.		10 l dull blue	6.00	6.00
b.		15 l dull green	6.00	6.00
c.		25 l dull red brown	6.00	6.00

Sheets contain a papermaker's watermark, "Hammermill Bond, Made in U.S.A."
Nos. 239, 241 and C40 were issued to commemorate the 50th anniv. of the reconstruction of the Government Palace.

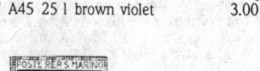

Government Palace — A45

1945, Mar. 15　　Wmk. 140　　Perf. 14

241	A45	25 l brown violet	3.00	3.00

Coat of Arms of Faetano — A46

Coats of Arms: 20c, 60c, 25 l, Montegiardino. 40c, 5 l, 50 l, San Marino. 80c, 2 l-4 l, Fiorentino. 10 l, Borgomaggiore. 20 l, Serravalle.

1945-46   Wmk. 277

242	A46	10c dark blue	15	15
243	A46	20c vermilion	15	15
244	A46	40c deep orange	15	15
245	A46	60c slate black	15	15
246	A46	80c dark green	15	15
247	A46	1 l dk car rose	15	15
248	A46	1.20 l deep violet	15	15
249	A46	2 l chestnut	15	15
250	A46	3 l dp blue ('46)	15	15
250A	A46	4 l red org ('46)	15	15
251	A46	5 l dark brown	15	15
251A	A46	15 l dp blue ('46)	65	1.10

Lithographed and Engraved

252	A46	10 l brt red & brown	1.50	1.10
253	A46	20 l brt red & ultra	2.75	1.65
254	A46	20 l org brn & ultra ('46)	2.75	1.65
a.		Vert. pair, imperf. btwn.	175.00	
255	A46	25 l hn brn & ultra ('46)	2.75	1.90

Size: 22x27mm

256	A46	50 l ol brn & ultra ('46)	3.00	5.75
		Nos. 242-256 (17)	15.05	14.80

Nos. 252-256 are in sheets of 10 (2x5). Values: Nos. 252, 254-255, $60 each. No. 253, $90, No. 256, $200.

For surcharges see Nos. 258-259, B26.

UNUS IN UNIVERSO ANIMUS

POSTE REPUBLICA DI S. MARINO

"Dawn of New Hope" — A52

Engr. & Litho.
1946   Unwmk.   Perf. 14

257	A52	100 l dull yel & brn vio	3.25	3.25
i.		Vert. pair, imperf. btwn.	175.00	

UN Relief and Rehabilitation Administration. Sheets of 10 with blue coat of arms in top margin.

Franklin D. Roosevelt and Flags of San Marino and US — A52a

Designs: 1 l, 50 l, Quotation on Liberty, from Franklin D. Roosevelt. 2 l, 100 l, Roosevelt portrait, vert. 5 l, 15 l, Roosevelt and flags (as shown).

Wmk. 277
1947, May 3   Photo.   Perf. 14

257A	A52a	1 l bister & brn	15	15
257B	A52a	2 l blue & sepia	15	15
257C	A52a	5 l violet & multi	15	15
257D	A52a	15 l green & multi	15	15
257E	A52a	50 l vermilion & brn	45	45
257F	A52a	100 l violet & sepia	65	65
		Set value	1.35	1.35

Franklin D. Roosevelt (1882-1945), 32nd president of the US. See Nos. C51A-C51H. For surcharges see Nos. 257G-257I, C51I-C51K.

Nos. 257A-257C Surcharged with New Value

1947, June 16

257G	A52a	3 l on 1 l	25	25
257H	A52a	4 l on 2 l	25	25
257I	A52a	6 l on 5 l	25	25
		Nos. 257G-257I,C51I-C51K (6)	1.59	1.59

No. 250A Surcharged with New Value in Black

1947, June 16   Wmk. 277

258	A46	6(l) on 4 l red org	15 15

No. 250A Surcharged in Black

259	A46	21 l on 4 l red org	50	60

REP. DI SAN MARINO

LIRE 1 POSTE

"St. Marinus Raising the Republic" by Girolamo Batoni — A53

Wmk. 217
1947, July 18   Engr.   Perf. 12

260	A53	1 l brt grn & vio	15	15
261	A53	2 l purple & olive	15	15
262	A53	4 l vio brn & dk bl grn	15	15
263	A53	10 l org & bl blk	15	15
264	A53	25 l carmine & purple	40	55
265	A53	50 l dk bl grn & brn	9.00	8.25
		Nos. 260-265,C52-C53 (8)	13.00	12.40

For overprints and surcharges see Nos. 294-295, B27-B38, C56.

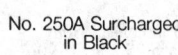

CENTENARIO DEL FRANCOBOLLO 1847-1947 U.S.A.

United States 1847 Stamp — A54

United States Stamps of 1847 and 1869 — A55

CENTENARIO DEL FRANCOBOLLO 1847-1947 U.S.A.

REPUBBLICA DI S. MARINO

A56

Wmk. 277
1947, Dec. 24   Photo.   Perf. 14

266	A54	2 l red vio & dk brn	15	15
267	A55	3 l sl gray, dp ultra & car	15	15
268	A54	6 l dp bl & dk gray grn	15	15
269	A56	15 l vio, dp ultra & car	18	22
270	A55	35 l dk brn, dp ultra & car	60	60
271	A56	50 l sl grn, dp ultra & car	85	90
		Nos. 266-271,C55 (7)	6.08	6.17

1st United States postage stamps, cent.

POST RESPUBLICA S.

REPUBBLICA DI SAN MARINO

Laborer and San Marino Flag — A57

1948, June 3

272	A57	5 l brown	15	15
273	A57	8 l green	15	18
274	A57	30 l crimson	20	24
275	A57	50 l red brn & rose lil	1.40	1.40

Engr.

276	A57	100 l dk bl & dp vio	19.00	19.00
		Nos. 272-276 (5)	20.90	20.97

See Nos. 373-374.

No. 172 Surcharged with New Value and Ornaments in Black

1948   Wmk. 217   Perf. 12

277	A32	100 l on 15c	21.00 21.00

REPUBBLICA DI S. MARINO   LIRE 1

Government Palace — A58

REPUBBLICA DI S. MARINO   LIRE 8

Mt. Titano, Distant View — A59

Various Views of San Marino.

1949-50   Wmk. 277   Photo.   Perf. 14

278	A58	1 l black & blue	15	15
279	A58	2 l violet & car	15	15
280	A58	3 l violet & ultra	15	15
281	A58	4 l black & vio	15	15
282	A58	5 l violet & brn	15	15
283	A58	6 l dp blue & sep	15	18
284	A59	8 l blk brn & yel brn	15	24
285	A59	10 l brn blk & bl	15	15
286	A58	12 l brt rose & vio	35	52
287	A58	15 l vio & brt rose	52	75
288	A58	20 l dp bl & brn ('50)	3.25	1.00
289	A58	35 l green & violet	1.90	1.90
290	A58	50 l brt rose & yel brn	75	1.00
291	A58	55 l dp bl & dl grn ('50)	10.50	11.00

Perf. 14x13½
Engr.

292	A59	100 l blk brn & dk grn	42.50	22.50
293	A59	200 l dp blue & brn	47.50	32.50
		Nos. 278-293 (16)	108.47	72.49

Nos. 260 and 261 Overprinted in Black

Giornata Filatelica San Marino-Riccione 28-6-1949

1949, June 28   Wmk. 217

294	A53	1 l brt green & vio	15	15
295	A53	2 l purple & olive	15	15
		Set value	20	18

San Marino-Riccione Stamp Day, June 28.

1849   1949   L. 1   R.S.M.

Francesco Nullo — A60

Designs: 1 l, 20 l, Francesco Nullo. 2 l, 5 l, Anita Garibaldi. 3 l, 50 l, Giuseppe Garibaldi. 4 l, 15 l, Ugo Bassi.

Wmk. 277
1949, July 31   Photo.   Perf. 14
Size: 22x28mm

296	A60	1 l blk & car lake	15	15
297	A60	2 l red brn & blue	15	15
298	A60	3 l car lake & dk grn	15	15
299	A60	4 l violet & dk brn	15	15

Size: 26½x36½mm

300	A60	5 l purple & dk brn	15	15
301	A60	15 l car lake & gray bl	70	70
302	A60	20 l violet & car lake	1.10	1.10
303	A60	50 l red brn & violet	12.00	12.00
		Nos. 296-303 (8)	14.55	14.55

Centenary of Garibaldi's escape to San Marino. See Nos. C57-C61, 404-410.

RSM 75° ANNIVERSARIO UNIONE POSTALE UNIVERSALE 100

Stagecoach on Road from San Marino A61

1949, Dec. 29   Engr.

304	A61	100 l blue & gray vio	5.00	5.00
		Sheet of 6	100.00	100.00

UPU, 75th anniversary.

R.S.M. CROCE ROSSA SAMMARINESE   L.25

A62

R.S.M. CROCE ROSSA SAMMARINESE   L.100

A63a

R.S.M. CROCE ROSSA SAMMARINESE   L.75

A63

Perf. 13½x14, 14x13½
1951, Mar. 15   Engr.   Wmk. 277
Sky and Cross in Carmine

305	A62	25 l dk brn & red vio	3.00	3.00
306	A63	75 l org brn & dk brn	3.75	3.75
307	A63a	100 l dk brn & gray blk	5.50	5.50

Issued to honor the San Marino Red Cross.

REP DI SAN MARINO   L 1

Christopher Columbus A64

Designs: 2 l, 25 l, Columbus on his ship. 3 l, 10 l, 20 l, Landing of Columbus. 4 l, 15 l, 80 l, Pioneers trading with Indians. 5 l, 200 l, Columbus and map of Americas.

1952, Jan. 28   Photo.   Perf. 14

308	A64	1 l brn org & dk grn	15	15
309	A64	2 l dk brown & vio	15	15
310	A64	3 l violet & dk brn	15	15
311	A64	4 l blue & org brn	15	15
312	A64	5 l grn & dk bl grn	15	15
313	A64	10 l dk brown & blk	15	20
314	A64	15 l carmine & blk	18	18

Engr.

315	A64	20 l dp bl & dk bl grn	30	35
316	A64	25 l vio brn & blk brn	1.25	1.00
317	A64	60 l choc & vio bl	3.00	3.00
318	A64	80 l gray & blk	6.00	6.00
319	A64	200 l Prus brn & dp ultra	14.00	14.00
		Nos. 308-319,C80 (13)	39.63	39.48

Issued to honor Christopher Columbus.

Type of 1952 in New Colors Overprinted in Black or Red

FIERA DI TRIESTE 1952

1952, June 29   Photo.

320	A64	1 l vio & dk brn	15	15
321	A64	2 l carmine & blk	15	15
322	A64	3 l grn & dk bl grn (R)	15	15
323	A64	4 l dk brn & blk	15	15
324	A64	5 l purple & vio	15	20
325	A64	10 l bl & org brn (R)	1.00	1.00
326	A64	15 l org brn & blue	2.75	2.75
		Nos. 320-326,C81 (8)	16.50	16.55

4th Intl. Sample Fair of Trieste.

REPUBLICA DI SAN MARINO   LIRE 1

Discobolus — A65

REP DI S. MARINO   LIRE 2

Tennis A66

Model
Airplane — A67

Designs: 3 l, Runner. 4 l, Cyclist. 5 l, Soccer.
25 l, Shooting. 100 l, Roller skating.

1953, Apr. 20   Wmk. 277   Perf. 14

327	A65	1 l dk brn & blk	15	15
328	A66	2 l black & brown	15	15
329	A65	3 l blk & grnsh bl	15	15
330	A66	4 l blk & brt bl	15	15
331	A66	5 l dk brn & sl grn	15	15
332	A67	10 l dp blue & crim	15	28
333	A67	25 l blk & dk brn	1.10	1.10
334	A66	100 l dk brn & slate	2.75	2.75
		Nos. 327-334,C90 (9)	44.75	44.88

See No. 438.

Type of 1953
Overprinted in
Black

GIORNATA FILATELICA
S. MARINO · RICCIONE
24 AGOSTO 1953

1953, Aug. 24

335	A66	100 l grn & dk bl grn	12.00	12.00

San Marino-Riccione Stamp Day, Aug. 24.

Narcissus
A68

Flowers: 2 l, Tulips. 3 l, Oleanders. 4 l, Cornflowers. 5 l, Carnations. 10 l, Irises. 25 l, Cyclamen.
80 l, Geraniums. 100 l, Roses.

1953, Dec. 28   Photo.

336	A68	1 l multicolored	15	15
337	A68	2 l multicolored	15	15
338	A68	3 l multicolored	15	15
339	A68	4 l multicolored	15	15
340	A68	5 l multicolored	15	15
341	A68	10 l multicolored	15	24
342	A68	25 l multicolored	1.75	1.75
343	A68	80 l multicolored	8.75	8.75
344	A68	100 l multicolored	11.00	11.00
		Nos. 336-344 (9)	22.40	22.49

Walking Racer — A69

Fencing
A70

Sports: 3 l, Boxing. 4 l, 200 l, 250 l, Gymnastics.
5 l, Motorcycling. 8 l, Javelin-throwing. 12 l, Auto-
mobiling. 25 l, Wrestling. 80 l, Walk racer.

1954-55   Photo.   Wmk. 277

345	A69	1 l violet & cer	15	15
346	A70	2 l dk green & vio	15	15
347	A70	3 l brn & brn org	15	15
348	A69	4 l dk bl & brt bl	15	15
349	A70	5 l dk grn & dk brn	15	15
350	A70	8 l lilac rose & pur	15	20
351	A69	12 l black & crim	15	15
352	A69	25 l bl & dk bl grn	20	20
353	A69	80 l dk bl & bl grn	38	38
354	A69	200 l violet & brn	2.25	2.25

Perf. 12½x13
Engr.

355	A69	250 l multi ('55)	27.50	27.50
		Sheet of 4 (#355)	180.00	180.00
		Nos. 345-355 (11)	31.38	31.48

A71

A72

Liberty statue and Government palace.

1954, Dec. 16   Perf. 13x13½

356	A71	20 l choc & blue	20	22
357	A71	60 l car & dk grn	75	75

See No. C92.

1955, Aug. 27   Wmk. 303   Perf. 14

358	A72	100 l gray blk & bl	2.50	2.50
		Never hinged	3.75	

7th San Marino-Riccione Stamp Fair. See No.
385.

Murata Nuova
Bridge — A73

View of La
Rocca — A74

Design: 15 l, Government Palace.

1955, Nov. 15   Perf. 14
Size: 22x27½mm; 27½x22mm

359	A73	5 l blue & brown	15	15
360	A74	10 l org & bl car	15	15
361	A74	15 l Prus grn & car	15	15
362	A73	25 l dk brn & vio	15	15
363	A74	35 l vio & red car	15	15
		Set value	46	46
		Set, never hinged	1.00	

See Nos. 386-388, 636-638.

Ice Skater — A75

Skier — A76

Designs: 3 l, 50 l, Tobogganing. 4 l, Skier going
downhill. 5 l, 100 l, Ice Hockey player. 10 l, Girl
ice skater.

1955, Dec. 15   Wmk. 303   Perf. 14

364	A75	1 l brown & yellow	15	15
365	A76	2 l brt blue & red	15	15
366	A76	3 l blk brn & lt brn	15	15
367	A76	4 l brown & green	15	15
368	A76	5 l ultra & sal pink	15	15
369	A76	10 l ultra & pink	15	15
370	A76	25 l gray blk & red	60	60
371	A76	50 l brown & indigo	1.40	1.40
372	A76	100 l blk & Prus grn	3.25	3.25
		Nos. 364-372,C95 (10)	15.65	15.65
		Set, never hinged	35.00	

7th Winter Olympic Games at Cortina
d'Ampezzo, Jan. 26-Feb. 5, 1956.

For surcharge see No. C96.

Type of 1948 Inscribed: "50th
Anniversario Arengo 25 Marzo 1906"

1956, Mar. 24   Wmk. 303   Perf. 14

373	A57	50 l sapphire	4.00	5.00
		Never hinged	5.00	

50th anniv. of the meeting of the heads of families (Arengo), the beginning of the democratic era in
San Marino.

Type of 1948 inscribed: "Assistenza
Invernale"

1956, Mar. 24   Photo.

374	A57	50 l dark green	4.00	5.00
		Never hinged	5.00	

Issued to publicize the Winterhelp charity.

Pointer and
Arms — A77

Dogs: 2 l, Russian greyhound. 3 l, Sheep dog. 4 l,
English greyhound. 5 l, Boxer. 10 l, Great Dane.
25 l, Irish setter. 60 l, German shepherd. 80 l,
Scotch collie. 100 l, Hunting hound.

1956, June 8   Wmk. 303   Perf. 14

375	A77	1 l ultra & brown	15	15
376	A77	2 l car lake & bl gray	15	15
377	A77	3 l ultra & brown	15	15
378	A77	4 l grnsh bl & gray vio	15	15
379	A77	5 l car lake & dk brn	15	15
380	A77	10 l ultra & brown	15	15
381	A77	25 l dk blue & multi	18	18
382	A77	60 l car lake & multi	1.40	1.40
383	A77	80 l dk blue & multi	1.75	1.75
384	A77	100 l car lake & multi	2.75	2.75
		Nos. 375-384 (10)	6.98	6.98
		Set, never hinged	17.50	

Sailboat Type of 1955

1956   Wmk. 303   Perf. 14

385	A72	100 l brown & bl grn	1.50	1.75
		Never hinged	2.00	

8th San Marino-Riccione Stamp Fair.

Types of 1955 with added inscription:
"Congresso Internaz. Periti Filatelici San
Marino-Salsomaggiore 6-8 Ottobre 1956."

Designs: 20 l, La Rocca. 80 l, Murata Nuova
Bridge. 100 l, Government palace.

1956, Oct. 6   Perf. 14
Size: 26x36mm; 36x26mm

386	A74	20 l blue & brown	38	28
387	A73	80 l vio & red car	1.50	1.40
388	A74	100 l org & bl grn	1.65	1.65
		Set, never hinged	4.25	

Intl. Philatelic Congress, San Marino, Oct. 6-8.

Street and Borgo
Maggiore
Church — A78

Hospital
Street — A79

Views: 3 l, Gate tower. 20 l, Covered Market of
Borgo Maggiore. 125 l, View from South Bastion.

1957, May 9   Photo.   Wmk. 303

389	A78	2 l dk grn & rose red	15	15
390	A78	3 l blue & brown	15	15
391	A78	20 l dk blue green	18	15
392	A79	60 l brn & blue vio	75	65

Engr.

393	A78	125 l dk blue & blk	32	28
		Nos. 389-393 (5)	1.55	1.38
		Set, never hinged	2.00	

See Nos. 473-476, 633-635.

Daisies and View of San
Marino — A80

Flowers: 2 l, Primrose. 3 l, Lily. 4 l Orchid. 5 l,
Lily of the Valley. 10 l, Poppy. 25 l, Pansy. 60 l,
Gladiolus. 80 l, Wild Rose. 100 l, Anemone.

Wmk. 303
1957, Aug. 31   Photo.   Perf. 14
Flowers in Natural Colors

394	A80	1 l dk vio blue	15	15
395	A80	2 l dk vio blue	15	15
396	A80	3 l dk vio blue	15	15
397	A80	4 l dk vio blue	15	15
398	A80	5 l dk vio blue	15	15
399	A80	10 l blue, buff & lilac	15	15
400	A80	25 l blue, yel & lilac	15	15
401	A80	60 l blue, yel & dl red brn	28	24
402	A80	80 l blue & dl red brn	40	35
403	A80	100 l bl, yel & dl red brn	90	90
		Set value	2.15	2.05
		Set, never hinged	3.25	

Type of 1949 Inscribed:
"Commemorazione 150 Nascita G.
Garibaldi."

Portraits: 2 l, 50 l, Anita Garibaldi. 3 l, 25 l,
Francesco Nullo. 4 l, 100 l, Giuseppe Garibaldi.
15 l, Ugo Bassi.

1957, Dec. 12   Wmk. 303   Perf. 14
Size: 22x28mm

404	A60	2 l vio & dull bl	15	15
405	A60	3 l lake & dk grn	15	15
406	A60	5 l brn & ol gray	15	15

Size: 26½x37mm

407	A60	15 l blue & vio	15	15
408	A60	25 l green & dk gray	15	30
409	A60	50 l violet & brn	85	1.50
410	A60	100 l brown & vio	85	1.50
		Set value	2.00	
		Set, never hinged	3.50	

Nos. 409-410 are printed se-tenant.
Birth of Giuseppe Garibaldi, 150th anniv.

Panoramic
View — A81

1958, Feb. 27   Engr.   Perf. 14

411	A81	500 l green & blk	37.50	37.50
		Never hinged	85.00	
		Sheet of 6	300.00	275.00

Catalogue values for unused
stamps in this section, from this
point to the end of the section, are
for Never Hinged items.

Fair Emblem and San
Marino Peaks — A82

1958, Apr. 12   Photo.   Perf. 14

412	A82	40 l yel green & brn	22	15
413	A82	60 l brt blue & mar	30	28

World's Fair, Brussels, Apr. 17-Oct. 19.

Madonna and Fair Entrance A83

Design: 60 l, View of Fair Grounds.

1958, Apr. 12
414	A83	15 l yellow, grn & bl	20	15
415	A83	60 l green & rose red	70	60

San Marino's 10th participation in the Milan Fair. See No. C97.

Wheat — A84

Designs: 2 l, 125 l, Corn. 3 l, 80 l, Grapes. 4 l, 25 l, Peaches. 5 l, 40 l, Plums.

1958, Aug. 30   Wmk. 303   Perf. 14
416	A84	1 l dk blue & yel org	15	15
417	A84	2 l dk green & red org	15	15
418	A84	3 l blue & ocher	15	15
419	A84	4 l green & rose car	15	15
420	A84	5 l blue, yel & grn	15	15
421	A84	15 l ultra & brn org	15	15
422	A84	25 l multicolored	15	15
423	A84	40 l multicolored	32	22
424	A84	80 l multicolored	65	45
425	A84	125 l bl, grn & org ver	2.75	1.75
		Set value	4.20	2.90

Bay and Stamp of Naples A85

1958, Oct. 8   Photo.
426	A85	25 l lilac & red brn	32	30

Centenary of the stamps of Naples. See No. C100.

Pierre de Coubertin — A86

Portraits: 3 l, Count Alberto Bonacossa. 5 l, Avery Brundage. 30 l, Gen. Carlo Montu. 60 l, J. Sigfrid Edstrom. 80 l, Henri de Baillet Latour.

1959, May 19   Wmk. 303   Perf. 14
427	A86	2 l brn org & blk	15	15
428	A86	3 l lilac & gray brn	15	15
429	A86	5 l blue & dk grn	15	15
430	A86	30 l violet & blk	15	15
431	A86	60 l dk grn & gray brn	22	18
432	A86	80 l car rose & dp grn	22	18
		Set value, #427-432, C106	1.65	1.45

Leaders of the Olympic movement; 1960 Olympic Games, Rome. See Nos. 1060-1062.

Lincoln and his Praise of San Marino, May 7, 1861 — A87

Lincoln Portraits and: 10 l, Map of San Marino. 15 l, Government palace. 70 l, San Marino peaks, vert.

1959, July 1   Perf. 14
433	A87	5 l brown & blk	15	15
434	A87	10 l blue grn & ultra	15	15
435	A87	15 l gray & green	15	15
		Perf. 13x13½		
		Engr.		
436	A87	70 l violet	95	75
		Set value	1.20	1.00

Birth sesquicentennial of Abraham Lincoln. See No. C108.

Arch of Augustus, Rimini, and Romagna ½b Stamp A88

1959, Aug. 29   Photo.   Perf. 14
437	A88	30 l black & brown	22	16

Centenary of the first stamps of Romagna. See No. C109.

Type of 1953 Inscribed: "Universiade Torino"

1959, Aug. 29   Wmk. 303   Perf. 14
438	A65	30 l red orange	60	40

Turin University Sports Meet, Aug. 27-Sept. 6.

Messina Cathedral Portal and Stamp of Sicily 1859 — A89

Stamp of Sicily and: 2 l, Greek temple, Selinus. 3 l, Erice Church. 4 l, Temple of Concordia, Agrigento. 5 l, Ruins of Castor and Pollux Temple, Agrigento. 25 l, San Giovanni degli Eremiti Church. 60 l, Greek theater, Taormina, horiz.

1959, Oct. 16
439	A89	1 l ocher & dk brn	15	15
440	A89	2 l olive & dk red	15	15
441	A89	3 l blue & slate	15	15
442	A89	4 l red & brown	15	15
443	A89	5 l dull bl & rose lil	15	15
444	A89	25 l multicolored	22	18
445	A89	60 l multicolored	25	22
		Set value, #439-445, C110	1.95	1.45

Centenary of stamps of Sicily.

Golden Oriole — A90

Nightingale — A91   Shot Put — A92

Birds: 3 l, Woodcock. 4 l, Hoopoe. 5 l, Red-legged partridge. 10 l, Goldfinch. 25 l, European Kingfisher. 60 l, Ringnecked pheasant. 80 l, Green woodpecker. 110 l, Red-breasted flycatcher.

1960, Jan. 28   Photo.   Perf. 14
Centers in Natural Colors
446	A90	1 l blue	15	15
447	A91	2 l green & red	15	15
448	A90	3 l green & red	15	15
449	A91	4 l dk green & red	15	15
450	A90	5 l dark green	15	15
451	A91	10 l blue & red	15	15
452	A91	25 l grnsh blue	26	20
453	A90	60 l blue & red	1.40	1.00
454	A91	80 l Prus blue & red	2.25	1.90
455	A91	110 l blue & red	2.75	2.25
		Nos. 446-455 (10)	7.56	6.25

1960, May 23   Wmk. 303   Perf. 14

Sports: 2 l, Gymnastics. 3 l, Walking. 4 l, Boxing. 5 l, Fencing, horiz. 10 l, Bicycling. 15 l, Hockey, horiz. 25 l, Rowing, horiz. 60 l, Soccer. 110 l, Equestrian, horiz.

456	A92	1 l car rose & vio	15	15
457	A92	2 l gray & org	15	15
458	A92	3 l brn ol & pur	15	15
459	A92	4 l rose red & brn	15	15
460	A92	5 l brown & blue	15	15
461	A92	10 l red brn & bl	15	15
462	A92	15 l emer & lilac	15	15
463	A92	25 l bl grn & org	15	15
464	A92	60 l dp grn & org	15	15
465	A92	110 l emer, red & blk	15	15
		Set of 3 souvenir sheets	7.00	7.00
		Set value, #456-465, C111-C114	1.65	1.45

17th Olympic Games, Rome, Aug. 25-Sept. 11. Souvenir sheets are: (1.) Sheet of 4, one each of 1 l, 2 l, 3 l and 60 l, all printed in deep green and brown. (2.) Sheet of 4, one each of 4 l and 10 l plus a 20 l and 40 l in designs of Nos. C111-C112 but without "Posta Aerea" inscribed-all 4 printed in rose red and brown. (3.) Sheet of 6, one each of 5 l, 15 l, 25 l and 110 l plus an 80 l and 125 l in designs of Nos. C113-C114 but without "Posta Aerea"- all 6 printed in emerald and brown.

Mt. Titano — A93

Founder Melvin Jones and Lions Headquarters A94

Designs (Lions Emblem and): 60 l, Government Palace and statue of Liberty. 115 l, Clarence L. Sturm, president. 150 l, Finis E. Davis, vice president.

1960, July 1   Photo.   Wmk. 303
466	A93	30 l red brn & dk bl	15	15
467	A94	45 l bl vio & bis brn	50	50
468	A93	60 l dull rose & bl	15	15
469	A94	115 l green & blk	50	50
470	A94	150 l brn & dk bl	3.50	2.75
		Nos. 466-470,C115 (6)	9.80	8.05

Lions Intl.; founding of the Lions Club of San Marino.

Beach of Riccione and San Marino Peaks — A95

1960, Aug. 27   Perf. 14
471	A95	30 l multicolored	45	32

12th San Marino-Riccione Stamp Day, Aug. 27. See No. C116.

Boy with Basket of Fruit, by Caravaggio — A96

1960, Dec. 29   Wmk. 303   Perf. 14
472	A96	200 l multicolored	6.50	4.75

350th anniversary of the death of Michelangelo da Caravaggio (Merisi), painter.

Types of 1957

Views: 1 l, Hospital street. 4 l, Government building. 80 l, Gate tower. 115 l, Covered market of Borgo Maggiore.

1961, Feb. 16   Perf. 14
473	A79	1 l dk blue grn	15	15
474	A78	4 l dk blue & blk	15	15
475	A78	30 l brt vio & brn	70	28
476	A78	115 l brown & blue	42	35
		Set value	1.25	75

Hunting Roebuck A97

Hunting Scenes (16th-18th century): 2 l, Falconer, vert. 3 l, Wild boar hunt. 4 l, Duck shooting with crossbow. 5 l, Stag hunt. 10 l, Mounted falconer, vert. 30 l, Hunter with horn and dogs. 60 l, Hunter with rifle and dog, vert. 70 l, Hunter and beater. 115 l, Duck hunt.

Wmk. 303
1961, May 4   Photo.   Perf. 14
477	A97	1 l lil rose & vio bl	15	15
478	A97	2 l gray, dk red & blk	15	15
479	A97	3 l red org, brn & blk	15	15
480	A97	4 l lt bl, red & blk	15	15
481	A97	5 l yellow grn & brn	15	15
482	A97	10 l org, blk, brn & vio	15	15
483	A97	30 l yel, bl & dk grn	15	15
484	A97	60 l ocher, brn, blk & red	16	16
485	A97	70 l green, blk & car	24	24
486	A97	115 l brt pink, blk & dk bl	42	42
		Set value	1.25	1.25

Mt. Titano and Cancelled Stamp of Sardinia, 1862 A98

Photogravure and Embossed
1961, Sept. 5   Wmk. 303   Perf. 13
487	A98	30 l multicolored	60	60
488	A98	70 l multicolored	1.25	1.25
489	A98	200 l multicolored	65	65

Cent. of Independence Phil. Exhib., Turin, 1961.

Europa Issue, 1961

View of San Marino — A99

Wmk. 339
1961, Oct. 20   Photo.   Perf. 13
490	A99	500 l brn & blue grn	9.75	9.75
		Sheet of 6	55.00	55.00

King Enzo's Palace
and Neptune
Fountain,
Bologna — A100

Views of Bologna: 70 l, Loggia dei Mercanti.
100 l, Two Towers.

1961, Nov. 25   Wmk. 339   Perf. 14

491	A100	30 l grnsh bl & blk	15	15
492	A100	70 l dk ol grn & blk	15	15
493	A100	100 l red brown & blk	18	18
		Set value	40	40

Bophilex, philatelic exhibition, Bologna.

Duryea,
1892 — A101

Automobiles (pre-1910): 2 l, Panhard-Levassor.
3 l, Peugeot. 4 l, Daimler. 5 l, Fiat, vert. 10 l,
Decauville. 15 l, Wolseley. 20 l, Benz. 25 l, Napier.
30 l, White, vert. 50 l, Oldsmobile. 70 l, Renault,
vert. 100 l, Isotta Fraschini. 115 l, Bianchi. 150 l,
Alfa.

1962, Jan. 23   Wmk. 303   Perf. 14

494	A101	1 l red brn & bl	15	15
495	A101	2 l ultra & org brn	15	15
496	A101	3 l black, brn & org	15	15
497	A101	4 l gray & dk red	15	15
498	A101	5 l violet & org	15	15
499	A101	10 l black & org	15	15
500	A101	15 l black & ver	15	15
501	A101	20 l black & ultra	15	15
502	A101	25 l gray & org	15	15
503	A101	30 l black & ocher	15	15
504	A101	50 l black & brt pink	18	18
505	A101	70 l black, gray & grn	18	18
506	A101	100 l black, yel & car	18	18
507	A101	115 l blk, org & bl grn	18	18
508	A101	150 l multicolored	45	45
		Set value	2.00	2.00

Wright Plane,
1904 — A102

Historic Planes (1907-1910): 2 l, Ernest Archdea-
con. 3 l, Albert and Emile Bonnet-Labranche. 4 l,
Glenn Curtiss. 5 l, Farman. 10 l, Louis Bleriot. 30 l,
Hubert Latham. 60 l, Alberto Santos Dumont. 70 l,
Alliott Verdon Roe. 115 l, Faccioli.

Wmk. 339
1962, Apr. 4   Photo.   Perf. 14

509	A102	1 l blk & dull yel	15	15
510	A102	2 l red brn & grn	15	15
511	A102	3 l red brn & gray grn	15	15
512	A102	4 l brown & blk	15	15
513	A102	5 l magenta & blue	15	15
514	A102	10 l ocher & bl grn	15	15
515	A102	30 l ocher & ultra	15	15
516	A102	60 l black & ocher	22	22
517	A102	70 l dp orange & blk	30	30
518	A102	115 l blk, grn & ocher	75	75
		Set value	1.75	1.75

Mountaineer
Descending — A103

Designs: 2 l, View of Sassolungo. 3 l, Mt. Titano.
4 l, Three Peaks of Javaredo. 5 l, Matterhorn. 15 l,

Skier on downhill run. 30 l, Climbing an overhang.
40 l, Cutting steps in ice. 85 l, Giant's Tooth. 115 l,
Mt. Titano.

1962, June 14   Wmk. 339   Perf. 14

519	A103	1 l bis brn & blk	15	15
520	A103	2 l Prus grn & blk	15	15
521	A103	3 l lilac & blk	15	15
522	A103	4 l brt bl & blk	15	15
523	A103	5 l dp org & blk	15	15
524	A103	15 l org yel & blk	15	15
525	A103	30 l carmine & blk	15	15
526	A103	40 l grnsh bl & blk	15	15
527	A103	85 l lt green & blk	18	18
528	A103	115 l vio bl & blk	28	28
		Set value	1.00	1.00

Hunter with
Dog — A104

Modern Hunting Scenes: 2 l, Hound master on
horseback, vert. 3 l, Duck hunt. 4 l, Stag hunt. 5 l,
Partridge hunt. 15 l, Lapwing (hunt). 50 l, Wild
duck hunt. 70 l, Duck hunt from boat. 100 l, Boar
hunt. 150 l, Pheasant hunt, vert.

1962, Aug. 25   Photo.   Perf. 14

529	A104	1 l brown & yel grn	15	15
530	A104	2 l dk bl & org	15	15
531	A104	3 l blk & Prus bl	15	15
532	A104	4 l black & brown	15	15
533	A104	5 l brn & yel grn	15	15
534	A104	15 l blk & org brn	15	15
535	A104	50 l brn, dp grn & blk	15	15
536	A104	70 l grn, sal pink & blk	15	15
537	A104	100 l blk, brick red & sep	18	18
538	A104	150 l grn, lil & blk	22	22
		Set value	1.00	1.00

Europa Issue, 1962

Mt. Titano and
"Europa"
A105

1962, Oct. 25   Wmk. 339

539	A105	200 l gray & car	1.75	1.75
		Sheet of 6	12.50	12.50

Egyptian
Cargo
Ship — A106

Ancient Ships: 2 l, Greece, 2nd Cent. B.C. 3 l,
Roman galley. 4 l, Vikings, 10th Cent. 5 l, "Santa
Maria," 1492. 10 l, Cypriote galleon, vert. 30 l,
Galley, 1600. 60 l, "Sovereign of the Seas," 1637,
vert. 70 l, Danish ship, 1750, vert. 115 l, Frigate,
1850.

1963, Jan. 10

540	A106	1 l blue & org yel	15	15
541	A106	2 l mag, tan & brn	15	15
542	A106	3 l brown & lil rose	15	15
543	A106	4 l vio brn & gray	15	15
544	A106	5 l brown & yellow	15	15
545	A106	10 l brn & brt yel grn	15	15
546	A106	30 l blk, bl & sep	60	45
547	A106	60 l lt vio bl & yel grn	45	45
548	A106	70 l blk, gray & dl red	45	45
549	A106	115 l blk, brn & gray bl	1.25	1.40
		Set value	3.20	3.20

Lady with Veil, by
Raphael — A107

Jousting with
"Saracen,"
Arezzo — A108

Paintings by Raphael: 70 l, Self-portrait. 100 l,
St. Barbara from Sistine Madonna. 200 l, Portrait of
a Young Woman (Maddalena Strozzi).

Wmk. 339
1963, Mar. 28   Photo.   Perf. 14
Size: 26¹/₂x37mm

550	A107	30 l multicolored	32	32
551	A107	70 l multicolored	15	15
552	A107	100 l multicolored	20	20

Size: 26¹/₂x44mm

553	A107	200 l multicolored	38	38

1963, June 22   Wmk. 339   Perf. 14

Medieval "Knightly Games": 2 l, French knights,
horiz. 3 l, Crossbow contest. 4 l, English knight
receiving lance, horiz. 5 l, Tournament, Florence.
10 l, Jousting with "Quintana," Ascoli Piceno. 30 l,
"Quintana," Foligno, horiz. 60 l, Race through
Siena. 70 l, Tournament, Malpaga, horiz. 115 l,
Knights challenging.

554	A108	1 l lilac rose	15	15
555	A108	2 l slate	15	15
556	A108	3 l black	15	15
557	A108	4 l violet	15	15
558	A108	5 l rose violet	15	15
559	A108	10 l dull green	15	15
560	A108	30 l red brown	15	15
561	A108	60 l Prus green	15	15
562	A108	70 l brown	15	15
563	A108	115 l black	15	15
		Set value	75	75

Butterfly — A109

St. Marinus Statue,
Government
Palace — A110

Designs: Various butterflies. 70 l, 115 l, horiz.

Wmk. 339
1963, Aug. 31   Photo.   Perf. 14

564	A109	25 l multicolored	16	16
565	A109	30 l multicolored	16	16
566	A109	60 l multicolored	18	18
567	A109	70 l multicolored	20	20
568	A109	115 l multicolored	32	32
		Nos. 564-568 (5)	1.02	1.02

1963, Aug. 31

569	A110	100 l shown	25	25
570	A110	100 l Modern fountain	25	25

San Marino-Riccione Stamp Fair.

Europa Issue, 1963

Flag and
"E" — A111

1963, Sept. 21   Wmk. 339   Perf. 14

571	A111	200 l blue & brn org	40	40

Women's
Hurdles
A112

Sports: 2 l, Pole vaulting, vert. 3 l, Women's
relay race. 4 l, Men's high jump. 5 l, Soccer. 10 l,
Women's high jump. 30 l, Women's discus throw,
vert. 60 l, Women's javelin throw. 70 l, Water polo.
115 l, Hammer throw.

1963, Sept. 21

572	A112	1 l org & red brn	15	15
573	A112	2 l lt grn & dk brn	15	15
574	A112	3 l bl & dk brn	15	15
575	A112	4 l dp bl & dk brn	15	15
576	A112	5 l red & dk brn	15	15
577	A112	10 l lil rose & cl	15	15
578	A112	30 l gray & red brn	15	15
579	A112	60 l brt yel & dk brn	15	15
580	A112	70 l brt bl & dk brn	15	15
581	A112	115 l grn & dk brn	15	15
		Set value	55	55

Publicity for 1964 Olympic Games.

Modern
Pentathlon
A113

Designs: 1 l, Runner, vert. 2 l, Woman gymnast,
vert. 3 l, Basketball, vert. 5 l, Dual rowing. 15 l,
Broad jumper. 30 l, Swimmer in racing dive. 70 l,
Woman sprinter. 120 l, Bicycle racers, vert. 150 l,
Fencers, vert.

Inscribed "Tokio, 1964"

1964, June 25   Wmk. 339   Perf. 14

582	A113	1 l brn & yel grn	15	15
583	A113	2 l blk & red brn	15	15
584	A113	3 l blk & brown	15	15
585	A113	4 l blk & org red	15	15
586	A113	5 l blk & brt bl	15	15
587	A113	15 l dk brn & org	15	15
588	A113	30 l dk vio & bl	15	15
589	A113	70 l red brn & grn	15	15
590	A113	120 l brn & brt bl	15	15
591	A113	150 l blk & crimson	15	15
		Set value	85	85

18th Olympic Games, Tokyo, Oct. 10-25.

Same Inscribed "Verso Tokio"

1964, June 25   Photo.

592	A113	30 l indigo & lilac	15	15
593	A113	70 l brn & Prus grn	16	16
		Set value	25	25

"Verso Tokyo" Stamp Exhibition at Rimini, Italy,
June 25-July 6.

Murray-Blenkinsop Locomotive,
1812 — A114

History of Locomotive: 2 l, Puffing Billy, 1813.
3 l, Locomotion I, 1825. 4 l, Rocket, 1829. 5 l,
Lion, 1838. 15 l, Bayard, 1839. 70 l, Crampton,
1849. 50 l, Little England, 1851. 90 l, Spitfire, c.
1860. 110 l, Rogers, c. 1865.

1964, Aug. 29   Wmk. 339   Perf. 14

594	A114	1 l blk & buff	15	15
595	A114	2 l blk & green	15	15
596	A114	3 l blk & rose lilac	15	15
597	A114	4 l blk & yellow	15	15
598	A114	5 l blk & salmon	15	15
599	A114	15 l blk & yel grn	15	15
600	A114	20 l blk & dp pink	15	15
601	A114	50 l blk & pale bl	15	15
602	A114	90 l blk & yel org	35	35
603	A114	110 l blk & brt bl	60	60
		Set value	1.50	1.50

Baseball Players A115

1964, Aug. 29   **Photo.**
604 A115 30 l shown   16 16
605 A115 70 l Pitcher   16 16

8th European Baseball Championship, Milan.

Europa Issue, 1964

"E" and Globe A116

1964, Oct. 15   **Wmk. 339**   **Perf. 14**
606 A116 200 l dk blue & red   55 55

President John F. Kennedy (1917-1963) A117

Design: 130 l, John F. Kennedy and American flag, vert.

1964, Nov. 22   **Photo.**   **Perf. 14**
607 A117 70 l multicolored   16 16
608 A117 130 l multicolored   24 24

Start of Bicycle Race from Government Palace — A118

Rooks on Chessboard — A120

Brontosaurus A119

Designs: 70 l, Cyclists (going right) and view of San Marino. 200 l, Cyclists (going left) and view of San Marino.

1965, May 15   **Photo.**   **Wmk. 339**
609 A118 30 l sepia   15 15
610 A118 70 l deep claret   15 15
611 A118 200 l rose red   22 22
     Set value   40 40

48th Bicycle Tour of Italy.

1965, June 30   **Wmk. 339**   **Perf. 14**

Dinosaurs: 2 l, Brachiosaurus, vert. 3 l, Pteranodon. 4 l, Elasmosaurus. 5 l, Tyrannosaurus. 10 l, Stegosaurus. 75 l, Thaumatosaurus victor. 100 l, Iguanodon. 200 l, Triceratops.

612 A119 1 l dk brn & emer   15 15
613 A119 2 l blk & sl bl   15 15
614 A119 3 l sl grn, ol grn & yel   15 15
615 A119 4 l brn & slate bl   15 15
616 A119 5 l claret & grn   15 15
617 A119 10 l claret & grn   15 15
618 A119 75 l dk bl & bl grn   30 30
619 A119 100 l green & claret   30 30
620 A119 200 l brown & grn   45 45
     Set value   1.50 1.50

Europa Issue, 1965
1965, Aug. 28   **Photo.**   **Perf. 14**
621 A120 200 l brown & multi   28 28

Dante by Gustave Doré A121

Doré's Illustrations for Divina Commedia: 90 l, Charon ferrying boat across Acheron. 130 l, Eagle carrying Dante from Purgatory to Paradise. 140 l, Dante with Beatrice examined by Sts. Peter, James and John on faith.

     Perf. 14x14½
1965, Nov. 20   **Engr.**   **Wmk. 339**
     Center in Brown Black

622 A121 40 l indigo   15 15
623 A121 90 l car rose   15 15
624 A121 130 l red brown   15 15
625 A121 140 l ultra   18 18
     Set value   55 55

Dante Alighieri (1265-1321), poet.

Stylized Peaks, Flags of Italy and San Marino A122

1965, Nov. 25   **Photo.**   **Perf. 14**
626 A122 115 l grn, red, ocher & bl   18 18

Visit of Giuseppe Saragat, president of Italy.

Trotter A123

Horses: 20 l, Cross Country, vert. 40 l, Hurdling. 70 l, Gallop. 90 l, Steeplechase. 170 l, Polo, vert.

     Perf. 14x13, 13x14
1966, Feb. 28   **Photo.**   **Wmk. 339**
627 A123 10 l multicolored   15 15
628 A123 20 l multicolored   15 15
629 A123 40 l multicolored   15 15
630 A123 70 l multicolored   15 15
631 A123 90 l multicolored   15 15
632 A123 170 l multicolored   18 18
     Set value   64 64

Scenic Types of 1955-57

Designs: 5 l, Hospital Street. 10 l, Gate tower. 15 l, View from South Bastion. 40 l, Murata Nuova Bridge. 90 l, View of La Rocca. 140 l, Government Palace.

1966, Mar. 29   **Wmk. 339**   **Perf. 14**
633 A79 5 l blue & brn   15 15
634 A78 10 l dk sl grn & bl grn   15 15
635 A78 15 l dk brn & vio   15 15
636 A77 40 l dk pur & brick red   15 15
637 A74 90 l blk & dull bl   15 15
638 A74 140 l violet & org   15 15
     Set value   45 45

"Bella" by Titian A124

Titian Paintings: 90 l, 100 l, Details from "The Education of Love." 170 l, Detail from "Sacred and Profane Love."

1966, June 16   **Wmk. 339**   **Perf. 14**
639 A124 40 l multicolored   15 15
640 A124 90 l multicolored   15 15
641 A124 100 l multicolored   15 15
642 A124 170 l multicolored   22 22
     Set value   54 54

Stone Bass — A125

Fish: 2 l, Cuckoo wrasse. 3 l, Dolphin. 4 l, John Dory. 5 l, Octopus, vert. 10 l, Orange scorpionfish. 40 l, Electric ray, vert. 90 l, Jellyfish, vert. 115 l, Sea Horse, vert. 130 l, Dentex.

     Perf. 14x13½, 13½x14
1966, Aug. 27   **Photo.**   **Wmk. 339**
643 A125 1 l multicolored   15 15
644 A125 2 l multicolored   15 15
645 A125 3 l multicolored   15 15
646 A125 4 l multicolored   15 15
647 A125 5 l multicolored   15 15
648 A125 10 l multicolored   15 15
649 A125 40 l multicolored   15 15
650 A125 90 l multicolored   15 15
651 A125 115 l multicolored   15 15
652 A125 130 l multicolored   15 15
     Set value   85 85

Europa Issue, 1966

Our Lady of Europe A126

1966, Sept. 24   **Wmk. 339**   **Perf. 14**
653 A126 200 l multicolored   25 25

Peony and Mt. Titano — A127

Flowers and Various Views of Mt. Titano: 10 l, Bell flowers. 15 l, Pyrenean poppy. 20 l, Purple nettle. 40 l, Day lily. 140 l, Gentian. 170 l, Thistle.

     Wmk. 339
1967, Jan. 12   **Photo.**   **Perf. 14**
654 A127 5 l multicolored   15 15
655 A127 10 l multicolored   15 15
656 A127 15 l multicolored   15 15
657 A127 20 l multicolored   15 15
658 A127 40 l multicolored   15 15

659 A127 140 l multicolored   15 15
660 A127 170 l multicolored   15 15
     Set value   70 70

St. Marinus — A128

The Return of the Prodigal Son — A129

Design: 170 l, St. Francis. The paintings are by Giovanni Francesco Barbieri (1591-1666).

     Wmk. 339
1967, Mar. 16   **Photo.**   **Perf. 14**
661 A128 40 l multicolored   15 15
662 A128 170 l multicolored   20 20
663 A129 190 l multicolored   22 22
   a.   Strip of 3, #661-663   55 55

Map Showing Members of CEPT — A130

Amanita Caesarea — A131

Europa Issue, 1967
1967, May 5   **Wmk. 339**   **Perf. 14**
664 A130 200 l sl grn & brn org   25 20

1967, June 15   **Photo.**   **Perf. 14**

Various Mushrooms.

665 A131 5 l multicolored   15 15
666 A131 15 l multicolored   15 15
667 A131 20 l multicolored   15 15
668 A131 40 l multicolored   15 15
669 A131 50 l multicolored   15 15
670 A131 170 l multicolored   15 15
     Set value   55 55

Amiens Cathedral A132

Designs: 40 l, Siena Cathedral. 80 l, Toledo Cathedral. 90 l, Salisbury Cathedral. 170 l, Cologne Cathedral.

     Wmk. 339
1967, Sept. 21   **Engr.**   **Perf. 14**
671 A132 20 l dk vio, bister   15 15
672 A132 40 l slate grn, bis   15 15
673 A132 80 l slate bl, bis   15 15
674 A132 90 l sepia, bis   15 15
675 A132 170 l deep plum, bis   16 16
     Set value   55 55

Crucifix of Santa Croce, by Cimabue — A133

1967, Dec. 5   Wmk. 339   Perf. 15
676 A133 300 l brn & vio blue   40   40

The Crucifix of Santa Croce, by Giovanni Cimabue (1240-1302), was severely damaged in the Florentine flood of Nov. 1966.

Coat of Arms — A134

Coats of Arms: 3 l, Penna Rossa. 5 l, Fiorentino. 10 l, Montecerreto. 25 l, Serravalle. 35 l, Montegiardino. 50 l, Faetano. 90 l, Borgo Maggiore. 180 l, Montelupo. 500 l, State arms of San Marino.

Perf. 13x13½
1968, Mar. 14   Litho.   Wmk. 339
677 A134   2 l multi   15   15
678 A134   3 l multi   15   15
679 A134   5 l multi   15   15
680 A134   10 l multi   15   15
681 A134   25 l multi   15   15
682 A134   35 l multi   15   15
683 A134   50 l multi   15   15
684 A134   90 l multi   15   15
685 A134 180 l multi   15   15
686 A134 500 l multi   48   48
          Set value   1.15 1.15

Europa Issue, 1968
Common Design Type
1968, Apr. 29   Engr.   Perf. 14x13½
Size: 37x27½mm
687 CD11 250 l cl brn   38   38

"Battle of San Romano" (Detail), by Paolo Uccello — A135

Designs: Details from "The Battle of San Romano," by Paolo Uccello (1397-1475).

Photogravure and Engraved
1968, June 14   Wmk. 339   Perf. 14
688 A135   50 l pale lil & blk   15   15
689 A135   90 l pale lil & blk, vert. 15 15
690 A135 130 l pale lil & blk   15   15
691 A135 230 l pale pink & blk   30   30
          Set value   60   60

The Mystic Nativity, by Botticelli, Detail A136

Wmk. 339
1968, Dec. 5   Engr.   Perf. 14
602 A136   50 l dark blue   15   15
603 A136   90 l deep claret   15   15
604 A136 180 l sepia   25   25
          Set value   45   45

Christmas.

"Peace" by Lorenzetti A137

Designs: 80 l, "Justice." 90 l, "Moderation." 180 l, View of Siena, 14th century, horiz. All designs are from the "Good Government" frescoes by Ambrogio Lorenzetti in the Town Hall of Siena.

Wmk. 339
1969, Feb. 13   Engr.   Perf. 14
695 A137   50 l dark blue   15   15
696 A137   80 l brown   15   15
697 A137   90 l dk blue vio   15   15
698 A137 180 l magenta   22   22
          Set value   48   48

Young Soldier, by Bramante — A138

Designs: 90 l, Old Soldier, by Bramante. Designs are from murals in the Pinakotheke of Brear, Milan.

1969, Apr. 28   Photo.   Perf. 14
699 A138   50 l multicolored   15   15
700 A138   90 l multicolored   15   15
          Set value   22   22

Bramante (1444-1514), Italian architect and painter.

Europa Issue, 1969
Common Design Type
1969, Apr. 28   Engr.   Perf. 14x13
Size: 37x27mm
701 CD12   50 l dull green   15   15
702 CD12 180 l rose claret   15   18

Charabanc A139

Coaches, 19th Century: 10 l, Barouche. 25 l, Private drag. 40 l, Hansom cab. 50 l, Curricle. 90 l, Wagonette. 180 l, Spider phaeton.

Perf. 14½x14
1969, June 25   Photo.   Unwmk.
703 A139   5 l blk, ocher & dk bl 15   15
704 A139   10 l blk, grn & pur   15   15
705 A139   25 l dk grn, pink & brn 15   15
706 A139   40 l ind, lil & lt brn   15   15
707 A139   50 l blk, dl yel & dk bl 15   15
708 A139   90 l blk, yel grn & brn 15   15
709 A139 180 l multi   15   15
          Set value   60   60

Pier at Rimini A140

Paintings by R. Viola: 20 l, Mt. Titano. 200 l, Pier at Riccione, horiz.

1969, Sept. 17   Unwmk.   Perf. 14
710 A140   20 l multicolored   15   15
711 A140 180 l multicolored   20   20
712 A140 200 l multicolored   24   24

"Faith" by Raphael — A141

Designs: 180 l, "Hope" by Raphael. 200 l, "Charity" by Raphael.

Perf. 13½x14
1969, Dec. 10   Engr.   Wmk. 339
713 A141   20 l dl pur & sal   15   15
714 A141 180 l dl pur & lt grn   20   20
715 A141 200 l dp pur & bis   24   24

Signs of the Zodiac A142

Perf. 14x13½
1970, Feb. 18   Photo.   Unwmk.
716 A142   1 l Aries   15   15
717 A142   2 l Taurus   15   15
718 A142   3 l Gemini   15   15
719 A142   4 l Cancer   15   15
720 A142   5 l Leo   15   15
721 A142   10 l Virgo   15   15
722 A142   15 l Libra   15   15
723 A142   20 l Scorpio   15   15
724 A142   70 l Sagittarius   15   15
725 A142   90 l Capricorn   15   15
726 A142 100 l Aquraius   15   15
727 A142 180 l Pisces   24   24
          Set value   1.10 1.10

Fleet in Bay of Naples, by Peter Brueghel, the Elder — A143

Unwmk.
1970, Apr. 30   Photo.   Perf. 14
728 A143 230 l multi   40   40

10th Europa Phil. Exhib., Naples, May 2-10.

Europa Issue, 1970
Common Design Type
1970, Apr. 30   Perf. 14x13½
Size: 36x27mm
729 CD13   90 l brt yel grn & red   15   15
730 CD13 180 l ocher & red   20   20

St. Francis' Gate and Rotary Emblem — A144   Woman with Mandolin, by Tiepolo — A145

Design: 220 l, Rocca (State Prison) and Rotary emblem.

1970, June 25   Photo.   Perf. 13½x14
731 A144 180 l multi   25   25
732 A144 220 l multi   30   30

65th anniv. of Rotary Intl.; 10th anniv. of the San Marino Rotary Club.

1970, Sept. 10   Unwmk.   Perf. 14
Paintings by Tiepolo: 180 l, Woman with Parrot. 220 l, Rinaldo and Armida Surprised, horiz.

Size: 26½x37½mm
733 A145   50 l multi   15   15
734 A145 180 l multi   22   22

Size: 56x37½mm
735 A145 220 l multi   30   30
a.   Strip of 3, #733-735   70   70

Giambattista Tiepolo (1696-1770), Venetian painter.

Black Pete — A146

Walt Disney and Jungle Book Scene A147

Disney Characters: 2 l, Gyro Gearloose. 3 l, Pluto. 4 l, Minnie Mouse. 5 l, Donald Duck. 10 l, Goofy. 15 l, Scrooge McDuck. 50 l, Huey, Louey and Dewey. 90 l, Mickey Mouse.

Perf. 13x14, 14x13
1970, Dec. 22   Photo.
736 A146   1 l multi   15   15
737 A146   2 l multi   15   15
738 A146   3 l multi   15   15
739 A146   4 l multi   15   15
740 A146   5 l multi   15   15
741 A146   10 l multi   15   15
742 A146   15 l multi   15   15
743 A146   50 l multi   20   20
744 A146   90 l multi   38   38
745 A147 220 l multi   4.50 4.50
       Nos. 736-745 (10)   6.13 6.13

Honoring Walt Disney (1901-1966), cartoonist and film maker.

Customhouse Dock, by Canaletto — A148

Paintings by Canaletto: 180 l, Grand Canal between Balbi Palace and Rialto Bridge. 200 l, St. Mark's and Doges' Palace.

1971, Mar. 23   Unwmk.   Perf. 14

746	A148	20 l multi	15	15
747	A148	180 l multi	30	30
748	A148	200 l multi	32	32

Save Venice campaign.

Europa Issue, 1971
Common Design Type

1971, May 29   Perf. 13¹/₂x14
Size: 27¹/₂x23mm

749	CD14	50 l org & blue	15	15
750	CD14	90 l blue & org	18	18

Congress Emblem and Hall, San Marino
Flag — A149

Design: 90 l, Detail from Government Palace door, Congress and San Marino emblems, vert.

1971, May 29   Photo.   Perf. 12

751	A149	20 l vio & multi	15	15
752	A149	90 l ol & multi	15	15
753	A149	180 l multi	22	22
		Set value	42	42

Italian Philatelic Press Union Congress, San Marino, May 29-30.

Duck-shaped Jug with Flying Lasa — A150

Etruscan Art, 6th-3rd Centuries B.C.: 80 l, Head of Mercury, vert. 90 l, Sarcophagus of a married couple, vert. 180 l, Chimera.

Photo. & Engr.
1971, Sept. 16   Perf. 14

754	A150	50 l blk & org	15	15
755	A150	80 l blk & lt grn	15	15
756	A150	90 l blk & lt bl	15	15
757	A150	180 l blk & org	22	22
		Set value	58	58

Tiger Lily
A151

Venus, by
Botticelli
A152

1971, Dec. 2   Photo.   Perf. 11¹/₂

758	A151	1 l shown	15	15
759	A151	2 l Phlox	15	15
760	A151	3 l Carnations	15	15
761	A151	4 l Globe flowers	15	15
762	A151	5 l Thistles	15	15
763	A151	10 l Peonies	15	15
764	A151	15 l Hellebore	15	15
765	A151	50 l Anemones	15	15
766	A151	90 l Gaillardia	15	15
767	A151	220 l Asters	20	20
		Set value	70	70

1972, Feb. 23   Perf. 14, 13x14 (180 l)

Details from La Primavera, by Sandro Botticelli: 180 l, Three Graces. 220 l, Spring.

Sizes: 50 l, 220 l, 21x37mm;
180 l, 27x37mm

768	A152	50 l gold & multi	15	15
769	A152	180 l gold & multi	22	22
770	A152	220 l gold & multi	30	30

Europa Issue 1972
Common Design Type

1972, Apr. 27   Perf. 11¹/₂
Granite Paper
Size: 22¹/₂x33mm

771	CD15	50 l org & multi	15	15
772	CD15	90 l bl & multi	15	15
		Set value	25	25

St. Marinus
Taming
Bear — A153

Designs: 55 l, Donna Felicissima asking St. Marinus for mercy for her sons. 100 l, St. Marinus turning archers to stone. 130 l, Felicissima giving mountains to St. Marinus to establish Republic.

Photo. & Engr.
1972, Apr. 27   Perf. 14

773	A153	25 l dl yel & blk	15	15
774	A153	55 l sal pink & blk	15	15
775	A153	100 l dl bl & blk	15	15
776	A153	130 l citron & blk	15	15
		Set value	38	38

Allegories of San Marino after 16th century paintings.

Italian House
Sparrow — A154

1972, June 30   Photo.   Perf. 11¹/₂
Granite Paper

777	A154	1 l shown	15	15
778	A154	2 l Firecrest	15	15
779	A154	3 l Blue tit	15	15
780	A154	4 l Ortolan bunting	15	15
781	A154	5 l White-spotted bluethroat	15	15
782	A154	10 l Bullfinch	15	15
783	A154	25 l Linnet	15	15
784	A154	50 l Black-eared wheater	15	15
785	A154	90 l Sardinian warbler	15	15
786	A154	220 l Greenfinch	24	24
		Set value	80	80

Young Man, Heart,
Emblem — A155

Italian Philatelic
Federation
Emblem — A156

Design: 90 l, Heart disease victim, horiz.

Perf. 13¹/₂x14, 14x13¹/₂
1972, Aug. 26

787	A155	50 l lt bl & multi	15	15
788	A155	90 l ocher & multi	16	16

World Heart Month.

1972, Aug. 26   Perf. 13¹/₂x14

789	A156	25 l gold & ultra	15	15

Honoring veterans of Philately.

5c Coin,
1864
A157

Coins: 10 l, 10c coin, 1935. 15 l, 1 lira, 1906. 20 l, 5 lire, 1898. 25 l, 5 lire, 1937. 50 l, 10 lire, 1932. 55 l, 20 lire, 1938. 220 l, 20 lire, 1925.

1972, Dec. 15   Litho.   Perf. 12¹/₂x13

790	A157	5 l gray, blk & brn	15	15
791	A157	10 l org, blk & sil	15	15
792	A157	15 l brt rose, blk & sil	15	15
793	A157	20 l lil, blk & sil	15	15
794	A157	25 l vio, blk & sil	15	15
795	A157	50 l brt bl, blk & sil	15	15
796	A157	55 l ocher, blk & sil	15	15
797	A157	220 l emer, blk & gold	22	22
		Set value	74	74

New
York,
1673
A158

Design: 300 l, View of New York from East River, 1973.

1973, Mar. 9   Photo.   Perf. 11¹/₂
Granite Paper

798	A158	200 l bis, ocher & ol grn	32	32
799	A158	300 l bl, lil & blk	40	40
a.		Pair, #798-799	80	80

New York, 300th anniv. Printed checkerwise.

Rotary Press, San
Marino
Towers — A159

Gymnasts and
Olympic
Rings — A160

1973, May 10   Photo.   Perf. 13x14

800	A159	50 l multi	15	15

Tourist Press Congress, San Marino.

1973, May 10   Unwmk.

801	A160	100 l grn & multi	18	18

5th Youth Games.

Europa Issue 1973
Common Design Type

1973, May 10   Perf. 11¹/₂
Size: 32¹/₂x23mm

802	CD16	20 l sal & multi	16	16
803	CD16	180 l lt bl & multi	85	85

Grapes — A161

1973, July 11   Photo.   Perf. 11¹/₂

804	A161	1 l shown	15	15
805	A161	2 l Tangerines	15	15
806	A161	3 l Apples	15	15
807	A161	4 l Plums	15	15
808	A161	5 l Strawberries	15	15
809	A161	10 l Pears	15	15
810	A161	25 l Cherries	15	15
811	A161	50 l Pomegranate	15	15
812	A161	90 l Apricots	15	15
813	A161	220 l Peaches	15	15
		Set value	70	70

Arc-en-Ciel,
France
A162

Famous Aircraft: 55 l, Macchi Castoldi, Italy. 60 l, Antonov, USSR. 90 l, Spirit of St. Louis, US. 220 l, Handley Page, Great Britain.

1973, Aug. 31   Photo.   Perf. 14x13¹/₂

814	A162	25 l ocher, vio bl & gold	15	15
815	A162	55 l gray, vio bl & gold	15	15
816	A162	60 l rose, vio bl & gold	15	15
817	A162	90 l lem, vio bl & gold	15	15
818	A162	220 l org, vio bl & gold	22	22
		Set value	55	55

Crossbowman,
Serravalle
Castle — A163

Designs: 10 l, Crossbowman, Pennarossa Castle. 15 l, Drummer, Montegiardino Castle. 20 l, Trumpeter, Fiorentino Castle. 30 l, Crossbowman, Borga Maggiore Castle. 50 l, Trumpeter, Guaita Castle. 80 l, Crossbowman, Faetano Castle. 200 l, Crossbowman, Montelupo Castle.

1973, Nov. 7   Photo.   Perf. 13¹/₂

819	A163	5 l blk & multi	15	15
820	A163	10 l blk & multi	15	15
821	A163	15 l blk & multi	15	15
822	A163	20 l blk & multi	15	15
823	A163	30 l blk & multi	15	15
824	A163	40 l blk & multi	15	15
825	A163	50 l blk & multi	15	15
826	A163	80 l blk & multi	15	15
827	A163	200 l blk & multi	20	20
		Set value	88	88

San Marino victories in the Crossbow Tournament, Massa Marittima, July 15, 1973.

Attendants, by Gentile
Fabriano — A164

Christmas: Details from Adoration of the Kings, by Gentile Fabriano (1370-1427).

1973, Dec. 19   Photo.   Perf. 11¹/₂

828	A164	5 l shown	15	15
829	A164	30 l King	15	15
830	A164	115 l King	15	15
831	A164	250 l Horses	22	22
		Set value	52	52

Shield, 16th
Century — A165

16th Century Armor: 5 l, Round shield. 10 l, German full armor. 15 l, Helmet with intricate etching. 20 l, Horse's head armor "Massimiliano." 30 l, Decorated helmet with Sphinx statuette on top. 50 l, Pommeled sword and gauntlets. 80 l, Sparrow-beaked helmet. 250 l, Sforza round shield.

Engr. & Litho.

1974, Mar. 12   *Perf. 13*

832	A165	5 l	blk, lt grn & buff	15 15
833	A165	10 l	blk, buff & bl	15 15
834	A165	15 l	blk, bl & ultra	15 15
835	A165	20 l	blk, tan & ultra	15 15
836	A165	30 l	blk & lt bl	15 15
837	A165	50 l	blk, rose & ultra	15 15
838	A165	80 l	blk, gray & grn	15 15
839	A165	250 l	blk & yel	22 22
			Set value	78 78

Head of Woman, by
Emilio Greco — A166

Europa: 200 l, Nude, by Emilio Greco (head shown on 100 l).

Engr. & Litho.

1974, May 9   *Perf. 13x14*

840	A166	100 l	buff & blk	16 16
841	A166	200 l	pale grn & blk	32 32

Yachts at
Riccione and
San Marino
Peaks — A167

1974, July 18   **Photo.**   *Perf. 11½*
Granite Paper

842	A167	50 l	ultra & multi	18 18

26th San Marino-Riccione Stamp Day.

Arms of San
Sepolcro — A168

Designs: Coats of arms of participating cities.

1974, July 18   *Perf. 12*

843	A168	15 l	shown	60 60
844	A168	20 l	Massa Marittima	60 60
845	A168	50 l	San Marino	60 60
846	A168	115 l	Gubbio	60 60
847	A168	300 l	Lucca	60 60
a.		Strip of 5, #843-847		3.00 3.00
		Nos. 843-847 (5)		3.00 3.00

9th Crossbow Tournament, San Marino.

UPU
Emblem
A169

1974, Oct. 9   **Photo.**   *Perf. 11½*
Granite Paper

848	A169	50 l	multi	15 15
849	A169	90 l	grn & multi	15 15
			Set value	22 22

Centenary of Universal Postal Union.

Mt. Titano and
Hymn by
Tommaseo — A170

Niccolo
Tommaseo — A171

1974, Dec. 12   **Photo.**   *Perf. 13½x14*

850	A170	50 l	lt grn, blk & red	15 15
851	A171	150 l	yel, grn & blk	18 18
			Set value	24 24

Tommaseo (1802-1874), Italian writer.

Virgin and Child,
14th Century
Wood
Panel — A172

1974, Dec. 12   *Perf. 11½*

852	A172	250 l	gold & multi	35 35

Christmas.

"Refuge in San
Marino" — A173

1975, Feb. 20   **Photo.**   *Perf. 13½x14*

853	A173	50 l	multi	15 15

Flight of 100,000 refugees from Romagna to San Marino, 30th anniversary.

Musicians, from Leopard Tomb,
Tarquinia — A174

Etruscan Art: 30 l, Chariot race, from Tomb on the Hill, Chiusi. 180 l, Achilles and Troilus, from Bulls' Tomb, Tarquinia. 220 l, Dancers, from Triclinium Tomb, Tarquinia.

Litho. & Engr.

1975, Feb. 20   *Perf. 14*

854	A174	20 l	multi	15 15
855	A174	30 l	multi	15 15
856	A174	180 l	multi	15 15
857	A174	220 l	multi	28 28
			Set value	60 60

Europa Issue 1975

St. Marinus, by Guercino (Francesco
Barbieri)

A175   A176

1975, May 14   **Photo.**   *Perf. 11½*
Granite Paper

858	A175	100 l	multi	15 15
859	A176	200 l	multi	25 25

The Lamentation, by
Giotto — A177

Frescoes by Giotto (details): 40 l, Mary and Jesus (Flight into Egypt). 50 l, Heads of four angels (Flight into Egypt). 100 l, Mary Magdalene (Noli Me Tangere), horiz. 500 l, Angel and the elect (Last Judgment), horiz.

1975, July 10   **Photo.**   *Perf. 11½*
Granite Paper

860	A177	10 l	gold & multi	15 15
861	A177	40 l	gold & multi	15 15
862	A177	50 l	gold & multi	15 15
863	A177	100 l	gold & multi	15 15
864	A177	500 l	gold & multi	52 52
			Set value	95 95

Holy Year.

Tokyo, 1835, Woodcut by
Hiroshige — A178

Design: 300 l, Tokyo, Business District, 1975.

1975, Sept. 5   **Photo.**   *Perf. 11½*
Granite Paper

865	A178	200 l	multi	28 28
866	A178	300 l	multi	42 42

Nos. 865-866 printed se-tenant checkerwise in sheets of 50.

Aphrodite
A179

1975, Sept. 19   **Photo.**   *Perf. 11½*

867	A179	50 l	vio, blk & gray	20 20

Europa '75 Philatelic Exhibition, Naples.

Multiple
Crosses — A180

1975, Sept. 19

868	A180	100 l	blk, dp org & vio	15 15

EUROCOPHAR Intl. Pharmaceutical Cong.

Angel — A181   Doni
Madonna — A182

Christmas: 100 l, Head of Virgin, from Doni Madonna by Michelangelo.

1975, Dec. 3   **Photo.**   *Perf. 11½*
Granite Paper

869	A181	50 l	multi	15 15
870	A181	100 l	multi	15 15
871	A182	250 l	multi	60 60
a.		Strip of 3, #869-871		80 80

Woman on Balcony,
by Gentilini — A183

Two Women,
by Gentilini
A184

Design: 230 l, Woman (same as right head on 150 l) and IWY emblem, by Franco Gentilini.

1975, Dec. 3
Granite Paper

872	A183	70 l	bl & multi	15 15
873	A184	150 l	multi	15 15
874	A183	230 l	multi	25 25

International Women's Year.

Modesty, by
Emilio
Greco — A185

Capitol,
Washington,
D.C. — A186

"Civic Virtues": 20 l, Temperance. 50 l, Fortitude. 100 l, Altruism. 150 l, Hope. 220 l, Prudence. 250 l, Justice. 300 l, Faith. 500 l, Honesty. 1000 l, Industry. Designs show drawings of women's heads by Emilio Greco.

1976, Mar. 4   Photo.   Perf. 11½
Granite Paper

875	A185	10 l buff & blk	15	15
876	A185	20 l pink & blk	15	15
877	A185	50 l grnsh & blk	15	15
878	A185	100 l salmon & blk	15	15
879	A185	150 l lilac & blk	16	16
880	A185	220 l gray & blk	25	25
881	A185	250 l yel & multi	35	35
882	A185	300 l gray & blk	38	38
883	A185	500 l yel & blk	60	60
884	A185	1000 l gray & blk	1.25	1.25
		Nos. 875-884 (10)	3.59	3.59

See Nos. 900-905, 931-933.

1976, May 29   Photo.   Perf. 11½

Arms of San Marino and: 150 l, Statue of Liberty. 180 l, Independence Hall, Philadelphia.

885	A186	70 l multi	15	15
886	A186	150 l multi	16	16
887	A186	180 l multi	22	22

American Bicentennial.

Montreal Olympic Games Emblem A187

1976, May 29

888	A187	150 l crim & blk	20	20

21st Olympic Games, Montreal, Canada, 7/17-8/1.

Decorated Plate — A188

Europa: 180 l, Seal of San Marino.

1976, July 8   Photo.   Perf. 11½
Granite Paper

889	A188	150 l multi	22	22
890	A188	180 l bl, sil & blk	22	22

"Unity" — A189   "Peaks of San Marino" — A190

1976, July 8   Perf. 13½x14

891	A189	150 l vio blk, yel & red	22	22

United Mutual Aid Society, centenary.

1976, Oct. 14   Photo.   Perf. 13x14

892	A190	150 l blk & multi	22	22

ITALIA 76 Intl. Phil. Exhib., Milan, Oct. 14-24.

Children and UNESCO Emblem A191

1976, Oct. 14   Perf. 11½
Granite Paper

893	A191	180 l multi	22	22
894	A191	220 l multi	25	25

UNESCO, 30th anniv.

Annunciation (detail), by Titian — A192

Design: 300 l, Virgin and Child, by Titian.

Litho. & Engr.
1976, Dec. 15   Perf. 13x14

895	A192	150 l multi	15	15
896	A192	300 l multi	42	42
a.		Pair, #895-896	65	65

Christmas.

Exhibition Emblem A193

1977, Jan. 28   Photo.   Perf. 11½
Granite Paper

897	A193	80 l multi	15	15
898	A193	170 l multi	15	15
899	A193	200 l multi	24	24

San Marino 77 Phil. Exhib. See No. C133.

Civic Virtues Type of 1976

Designs: 70 l, Fortitude. 90 l, Prudence. 120 l, Altruism. 160 l, Temperance. 170 l, Hope. 320 l, Faith.

1977, Apr. 14   Photo.   Perf. 11½
Granite Paper

900	A185	70 l pink & blk	15	15
901	A185	90 l buff & blk	15	15
902	A185	120 l lt bl & blk	15	15
903	A185	160 l lt grn & blk	22	22
904	A185	170 l cream & blk	22	22
905	A185	320 l lil & blk	40	40
		Set value	1.12	1.12

San Marino, after Ghirlandaio A194

Europa: 200 l, San Marino, detail from painting by Guercino.

1977, Apr. 14
Granite Paper

906	A194	170 l multi	24	24
907	A194	200 l multi	28	28

Vertical Flying Machine, by da Vinci — A195

Litho. & Engr.
1977, June 6   Perf. 13x14

908	A195	120 l multi	18	18

Centenary of Enrico Forlanini's experiments with vertical flight.

University Square, Bucharest, 1877 — A196

Design: 400 l, National Theater and Intercontinental Hotel, 1977.

1977, June 6   Photo.   Perf. 11½
Granite Paper

909	A196	200 l bis & multi	28	28
910	A196	400 l lt bl & multi	40	40
a.		Pair, #909-910	68	58

Centenary of Romanian independence. Printed checkerwise.

Type A2 of 1877 — A197

1977, June 15   Engr.   Perf. 15x14½

911	A197	40 l slate grn	15	15
912	A197	70 l deep blue	15	15
913	A197	170 l red	30	30
914	A197	500 l brown	52	52
915	A197	1000 l purple	1.00	1.00
		Nos. 911-915 (5)	2.12	2.12

Centenary of San Marino stamps.

St. Marinus, by Retrosi — A198   Medicinal Plants — A199

Souvenir Sheet
1977, Aug. 28   Photo.   Perf. 11½
Granite Paper

916	A198	Sheet of 5	8.50	8.50
a.		1000 l single stamp	1.65	1.65

Centenary of San Marino stamps; San Marino '77 Phil. Exhib., Aug. 28-Sept. 4.

1977, Oct. 19   Photo.   Perf. 11½

917	A199	170 l multi	22	22

Congress of Italian Pharmacists' Union. Design shows high mallow, tilia, camomile, borage, centaury and juniper.

Woman Attacked by Octopus, Emblem A200

1977, Oct. 19

918	A200	200 l multi	25	25

World Rheumatism Year.

Virgin Mary — A201   San Francisco Gate — A202

Christmas: 230 l, Palm, olive and star. 300 l, Angel.

1977, Dec. 5   Photo.   Perf. 11½

919	A201	170 l sil, gray & blk	20	20
920	A201	230 l sil, gray & blk	25	25
921	A201	300 l sil, gray & blk	30	30
a.		Strip of 3, #919-921	75	75

1978, May 30   Photo.   Perf. 11½

Europa: 200 l, Ripa Gate.

922	A202	170 l lt bl & dk bl	20	20
923	A202	200 l buff & brn	28	28

Baseball Player and Diamond — A203   Feather, WHO Emblem — A204

1978, May 30

924	A203	90 l multi	15	15
925	A203	120 l multi	18	18

World Baseball Championships.

1978, May 30

926	A204	320 l multi	38	38

Fight against hypertension.

ITU Emblem, Waves Coming from 3 Peaks — A205

1978, July 26   Photo.   Perf. 11½

927	A205	10 l car & yel	15	15
928	A205	200 l vio bl & lt bl	30	30
		Set value	35	35

Membership in ITU.

Seagull and Falcon, 3 Peaks A206

1978, July 26
929 A206　120 l multi　　　　15　15
930 A206　170 l multi　　　　22　22

30th San Marino-Riccione Stamp Day.

Civic Virtues Type of 1976

Drawings by Emilio Greco: 5 l, Wisdom. 35 l, Love. 2000 l, Faithfulness.

1978, Sept. 28　Photo.　Perf. 11½
Granite Paper
931 A185　5 l lt vio & blk　　15　15
932 A185　35 l gray & blk　　15　15
933 A185　2000 l yel & blk　2.25　2.25

Christmas A207

1978, Dec. 6　Photo.　Perf. 14x13½
941 A207　10 l Holly leaves　15　15
942 A207　120 l Stars　　　　15　15
943 A207　170 l Snowflakes　24　24
　　　　Set value　　　　　　40　40

Globe and Woman Holding Torch — A208

1978, Dec. 6　　　　Perf. 11½x12
944 A208　200 l multi　　　　22　22

Universal Declaration of Human Rights, 30th anniversary.

First San Marino Autobus, 1915 — A209

Europa: 220 l, Maii coach, 1895.

1979, Mar. 29　Photo.　Perf. 11½x12
945 A209　170 l multi　　　　28　28
946 A209　220 l multi　　　　35　35

Albert Einstein (1879-1955), Theoretical Physicist A210

1979, Mar. 29　　　　Perf. 11½
947 A210　120 l gray, lt & dk brn　20　20

San Marino Crossbow Federation Emblem — A211

Maigret — A212

1979, July 12　Litho.　Perf. 14x13
948 A211　120 l multi　　　　20　20

14th Crossbow Tournament.

Litho. & Engr.
1979, July 12　　　　Perf. 13x14

Fictional Detectives: 80 l, Perry Mason. 150 l, Nero Wolfe. 170 l, Ellery Queen. 220 l, Sherlock Holmes.

949 A212　10 l multi　　　　15　15
950 A212　80 l multi　　　　15　15
951 A212　150 l multi　　　20　20
952 A212　170 l multi　　　20　20
953 A212　220 l multi　　　32　32
　　Nos. 949-953 (5)　　　1.02　1.02

Girl Holding Bird — A213

IYC Emblem, Paintings by Marina Busignani: 120 l, 170 l, 220 l, Children and birds, diff. 350 l, Mother nursing child.

1979, Sept. 6　Litho.　Perf. 11½
954 A213　20 l multi　　　　15　15
955 A213　120 l multi　　　15　15
956 A213　170 l multi　　　20　20
957 A213　220 l multi　　　24　24
958 A213　350 l multi　　　35　35
　　　　Set value　　　　　95　95

St. Apollonia, 15th Century Woodcut — A214

Chestnut Tree, Deer — A216

Waterskier A215

1979, Sept. 6　　　　Photo.
959 A214　170 l multi　　　　20　20

13th Biennial Intl. Congress of Stomatology.

1979, Sept. 6
960 A215　150 l multi　　　　20　20

European Waterskiing Championship.

1979, Oct. 25　Photo.　Perf. 11½

Protected Trees and Animals or Birds: 10 l, Cedar of Lebanon, falcon. 35 l, Dogwood, racoon. 50 l, Banyan, tiger. 70 l, Umbrella pine, hoopoe. 90 l, Siberian spruce, marten. 100 l, Eucalyptus, koala bear. 120 l, Date palm, camel. 150 l, Sugar maple, beaver. 170 l, Adansonia, elephant.

961 A216　5 l multi　　　　15　15
962 A216　10 l multi　　　15　15
963 A216　35 l multi　　　15　15
964 A216　50 l multi　　　15　15
965 A216　70 l multi　　　15　15
966 A216　90 l multi　　　15　15
967 A216　100 l multi　　15　15
968 A216　120 l multi　　15　15
969 A216　150 l multi　　18　18
970 A216　170 l multi　　22　22
　　　　Set value　　　1.05　1.05

Holy Family, by Antonio Alberto de Ferrara, 15th Century Fresco — A217

Christmas (de Ferrara Fresco): 80 l, St. Joseph. 170 l, Infant Jesus. 220 l, One of the Three Kings.

1979, Dec. 6　Photo.　Perf. 12
971 A217　80 l multi　　　15　15
972 A217　170 l multi　　24　24
973 A217　220 l multi　　28　28
974 A217　320 l multi　　32　32

Disturbing Muses, by Giorgio de Chirico — A218

1979, Dec.
975 A218　40 l shown　　　　15　15
976 A218　150 l Ancient horses　18　18
977 A218　170 l Self-portrait　22　22

Giorgio de Chirico, Italian surrealist painter.

St. Benedict, 15th Century Fresco — A219

Fight Against Cigarette Smoking — A220

1980, Mar. 27　Photo.　Perf. 12x11½
Granite Paper
978 A219　170 l multi　　　　22　22

St. Benedict of Nursia, 1500th birth anniversary.

1980, Mar. 27

Designs: Sketches of smokers and cigarettes by Giuliana Consilivio.

979 A220　120 l multi　　　15　15
980 A220　220 l multi　　　40　40
981 A220　520 l multi　　　65　65

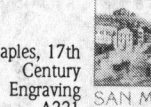

Naples, 17th Century Engraving A221

1980, Mar. 27　　　　Perf. 14x13½
982 A221　170 l multi　　　　25　25

20th Intl. Phil. Exhib., Europa '80, Naples, Apr. 26-May 4.

View of London, 1850 — A222

1980, May 8　　　　Perf. 11½x12
983 A222　200 l shown　　　24　24
984 A222　400 l London, 1980　55　55
a.　Pair, #983-984　　　80　80

London 1980 Intl. Stamp Exhib., May 6-14. Printed checkerwise.
See Nos. 1001-1002, 1032-1033, 1054-1055, 1069-1070, 1098-1099, 1110-1111, 1141-1142.

Giovanbattista Belluzzi (1506-1554), Military Architect A223

Europa: 220 l, Antonio Orafo (1460-1552), goldsmith and jeweler.

1980, May 8　　　　Perf. 11½
985 A223　170 l multi　　　　22　22
986 A223　220 l multi　　　　30　30

Bicycling — A224

1980, July 7　Photo.　Perf. 11½
Granite Paper
987 A224　70 l shown　　　　15　15
988 A224　90 l Basketball　　15　15
989 A224　170 l Running　　28　28
990 A224　350 l Gymnast　　42　42
991 A224　450 l High jump　55　55
　　Nos. 987-991 (5)　　1.55　1.55

22nd Summer Olympic Games, Moscow, July 19-Aug. 3.

Ancient Fortifications A225

Weight Lifting A226

Photogravure and Engraved
1980, Sept. 18   *Perf. 13¹/₂x14*
992 A225 220 l multi   32 32

World Tourism Conf., Manila, Sept. 27.

1980, Sept. 18 Photo.   *Perf. 14x13¹/₂*
993 A226 170 l multi   22 22

European Junior Weight Lifting Championship, Sept.

Robert Stolz, "Philatelic Waltz" Score A227

Photo. & Engr.
1980, Sept. 18   *Perf. 14*
994 A227 120 l lt bl & blk   22 22

Robert Stolz (1880-1975) composer.

Madonna of the Harpies, by Andrea Del Sarto — A228

Annunciation by Del Sarto (Details): 250 l, Virgin Mary. 500 l, Angel.

1980, Dec. 11   *Perf. 13¹/₂*
995 A228 180 l multi   25 25
996 A228 250 l multi   38 38
997 A228 500 l multi   75 75

Christmas; 450th death anniv. of Del Sarto.

St. Joseph's Eve Bonfire — A229   Intl. Year of the Disabled — A230

Europa Issue 1981
1981, Mar. 24 Photo.   *Perf. 12*
Granite Paper
998 A229 200 l shown   24 24
999 A229 300 l San Marino Day fireworks   40 40

1981, May 15 Photo.   *Perf. 11¹/₂*
Granite Paper
1000 A230 300 l multi   38 38

Exhibition Type of 1980
Design: St. Charles' Square, Vienna, by Jakob Alt, 1817.

1981, May 15
Granite Paper
1001 A222 200 l shown   28 28
1002 A222 300 l Vienna, 1981   38 38
  a. Pair, #1001-1002   70 70

WIPA '81 Intl. Phil. Exhib., Vienna, May 22-31.

Woman Playing Flute — A232   Grand Prix Motorcycle Race — A233

Designs: Drawings based on Roman sculptures.

1981, July 10 Photo.   *Perf. 11¹/₂*
Granite Paper
1003 A232 300 l shown   48 48
1004 A232 550 l Soldier   80 80
1005 A232 1500 l Shepherd   1.40 1.40
  a. Souv. sheet of 3, #1003-1005   3.00 3.00

Virgil's birth bimillennium. No. 1005a has continuous design.

1981, July 10 Litho.   *Perf. 14x15*
1006 A233 200 l multi   22 22

Natl. Urban Development Plan (Housing) — A234

1981, Sept. 22   **Photo.**
Granite Paper
1007 A234 20 l shown   15 15
1008 A234 80 l Parks   15 15
1009 A234 400 l Energy plants   45 45
  Set value   60 60

European Junior Judo Championship, Oct. 30-Nov. 1 — A235

1981, Sept. 22 Photo.   *Perf. 11¹/₂*
Granite Paper
1010 A235 300 l multi   42 42

World Food Day — A236

1981, Oct. 23
Granite Paper
1011 A236 300 l multi   42 42

A237   A238

Designs: 150 l, Child Holding a Dove, by Pablo Picasso (1881-1973). 200 l, Homage to Picasso, by Renato Guttuso.

1981, Oct. 23
Granite Paper
1012 A237 150 l multi   20 20
1013 A237 200 l multi   28 24

Photo. & Engr.
1981, Dec. 15   *Perf. 13¹/₂*
Christmas; 500th Birth Anniv. of Benvenuto Tisi da Garafalo Adoration of the Kings and St. Bartholomew): 200 l, One of the Three Kings with Goblet, by Garafalo. 300 l, King with a Jar. 600 l, Virgin and Child.
1014 A238 200 l multi   24 24
1015 A238 300 l multi   35 35
1016 A238 600 l multi   75 75

Postal Stationery Centenary A239

1982, Feb. 19 Photo.   *Perf. 12*
1017 A239 200 l multi   22 22

Savings Bank Centenary A240

1982, Feb. 19
1018 A240 300 l multi   38 38

Europa 1982 — A241

Designs: 300 l, Convocation of the Assembly of Heads of Families, 1906. 450 l, Napoleons's Treaty of Friendship offer, 1797.

1982, Apr. 21 Photo.   *Perf. 11¹/₂*
Granite Paper
1019 A241 300 l multi   48 48
1020 A241 450 l multi   75 75

Archimedes A242   800th Birth Anniv. of St. Francis of Assisi A243

1982, Apr. 21 Photo.   *Perf. 14x13¹/₂*
1021 A242 20 l shown   15 15
1022 A242 30 l Copernicus   15 15
1023 A242 40 l Newton   15 15
1024 A242 50 l Lavoisier   15 15
1025 A242 60 l Marie Curie   15 15
1026 A242 100 l Robert Koch   15 15
Litho. & Engr.
1027 A242 200 l Thomas Edison   16 16
1028 A242 300 l Guglielmo Marconi   38 38
1029 A242 450 l Hippocrates   75 75
Engr.
1030 A242 5000 l Galileo   6.00 6.00
  Nos. 1021-1030 (10)   8.19 8.19

See Nos. 1041-1046.

1982, June 10   **Photo.**
1031 A243 200 l multi   25 25

Exhibition Type of 1980
1982, June 10
1032 A222 300 l Notre Dame, 1806   35 35
1033 A222 450 l 1982   55 55
  a. Pair, #1032-1033   90 90

PHILEXFRANCE '82 Stamp Exhibition, Paris, June 11-21.

Visit of Pope John Paul II — A245   Natl. Flags of ASCAT Members — A246

1982, Aug. 29 Litho.   *Perf. 13¹/₂x14*
1034 A245 900 l multi   1.00 1.00

1982, Sept. 1 Photo.   *Perf. 11¹/₂*
Granite Paper
1035 A246 300 l multi   40 40

Inaugural Meeting of ASCAT (Assoc. of Editors of Philatelic Catalogues), 1977.

15th Amnesty Intl. Congress, Rimini, Italy, Sept. 9-15 — A247   Christmas — A248

1982, Sept. 1   **Unwmk.**
1036 A247 700 l blk & red   80 80

Photo. & Engr.
1982, Dec. 15 *Perf. 13¹/₂*

Paintings by Gregorio Sciltian (b. 1900).

1037	A248	200 l Angel	25	25
1038	A248	300 l Virgin and Child	38	38
1039	A248	450 l Angel, diff.	55	55

Secondary School Centenary — A249

Auguste Piccard — A251

3rd Formula One Grand Prix — A250

1983, Feb. 24 Photo. *Perf. 13¹/₂x14*

1040	A249	300 l Begni Building	35	35

Scientist Type of 1982
1983, Apr. 21 *Perf. 14x13¹/₂*

1041	A242	150 l Alexander Fleming	15	15
1042	A242	250 l Alessandro Volta	35	35
1043	A242	350 l Evangelista Torricelli	52	52
1044	A242	400 l Carolus Linnaeus	55	55
1045	A242	1000 l Pythagoras	1.00	1.00
1046	A242	1400 l Leonardo da Vinci	1.50	1.50
		Nos. 1041-1046 (6)	4.07	4.07

1983, Apr. 20 Photo. *Perf. 14x13¹/₂*

1047	A250	50 l multi	15	15
1048	A250	350 l multi	40	40

Perf. 12x11¹/₂

1983, Apr. 20 **Granite Paper**

1049	A251	400 l Aerostat	90	90
1050	A251	500 l Bathyscaph	1.10	1.10

Europa. Piccard (1884-1962), Swiss scientist.

World Communications Year — A252

1983, Apr. 28 Engr. *Perf. 14x13*

1051	A252	400 l Ham radio operator	50	50
1052	A252	500 l Mailman	60	60

Manned Flight Bicentenary — A253

Lithographed and Engraved
1983, May 22 *Perf. 13¹/₂x14*

1053	A253	500 l Montgolfiere, 1783	60	60

Exhibition Type of 1980
Designs: Botafogo Bay and Monte Corcovado, Rio de Janeiro.

1983, July 29 Photo. *Perf. 11¹/₂x12*
Granite Paper

1054	A222	400 l 1845	50	50
1055	A222	1400 l 1983	1.65	1.65

Se-tenant. BRASILIANA '83 Intl. Stamp Show, Rio de Janeiro, July 29-Aug. 7.

20th Anniv. of World Food Program A255

1983, Sept. 29 Photo. *Perf. 14x13¹/₂*

1056	A255	500 l multi	60	60

Christmas — A256

Flag-wavers Group, 2nd Anniv. — A257

Paintings, Raphael (1483-1520): 300 l, Our Lady of the Grand Duke. 400 l, Our Lady of the Goldfinch. 500 l, Our Lady of the Chair.

Photo. & Engr.
1983, Dec. 1 *Perf. 13¹/₂*

1057	A256	300 l multi	38	38
1058	A256	400 l multi	45	45
1059	A256	500 l multi	55	55
a.		Strip of 3, #1057-1059	1.40	1.40

Olympic Type of 1959
IOC Presidents: 300 l, Demetrius Vikelas, 1894-96. 400 l, Lord Killanin. 550 l, Antonio Samaranch, 1984.

1984, Feb. 8 Photo. *Perf. 14x13¹/₂*

1060	A86	300 l multi	35	35
1061	A86	400 l multi	48	48
1062	A86	550 l multi	65	65

Litho. & Engr.
1984, Apr. 27 *Perf. 13x14*

1063	A257	300 l Flag	35	35
1064	A257	400 l Flags	48	48

Europa (1959-1984) A258

1984, Apr. 27 Photo. *Perf. 11¹/₂*
Granite Paper

1065	A258	400 l multi	80	80
1066	A258	550 l multi	95	95

A259

A260

1984, June 14 Photo. *Perf. 13¹/₂x14*

1067	A259	450 l multi	55	55

Motorcross Grand Prix, Baldasserona.

Souvenir Sheet
1984, June 14 Litho. *Perf. 13x14*

1068		Sheet of 2	2.00	2.00
a.	A260	550 l Man	70	70
b.	A260	1000 l Woman	1.25	1.25

1984 Summer Olympics.

Exhibition Type of 1980
Ausipex '84: Views of Melbourne. Se-tenant.

1984, Sept. 21 Photo. *Perf. 11¹/₂*
Granite Paper

1069	A222	1500 l 1839	2.00	2.00
1070	A222	2000 l 1984	2.75	2.75

Visit of Italian Pres. Pertini A262

1984, Oct. 20 Photo. *Perf. 14x13¹/₂*

1071	A262	1950 l multi	3.00	2.75

School and Philately — A263

Christmas — A264

Sketches by Jacovitti.

1984, Oct. 30 *Perf. 13¹/₂x14*

1072	A263	50 l Universe	15	15
1073	A263	100 l Evolution	15	15
1074	A263	150 l Environment	24	24
1075	A263	200 l Mankind	25	25
1076	A263	450 l Science	60	60
1077	A263	550 l Philosophy	70	70
		Nos. 1072-1077 (6)	2.09	2.09

1984, Dec. 5 Litho. *Perf. 13¹/₂x14*

Details of Madonna of San Girolamo by Correggio, 1527.

1078	A264	400 l multi	55	55
1079	A264	450 l multi	60	60
1080	A264	550 l multi	80	80
a.		Strip of 3, #1078-1080	2.00	2.00

Composers and Music — A265

Olympiad of the Small States, May 23-26 — A266

Europa: 450 l, Johann Sebastian Bach (1685-1750), Toccata and Fugue. 600 l, Vincenzo Bellini (1801-1835), Norma.

1985, Mar. 18 Photo. *Perf. 12*

1081	A265	450 l ocher & gray blk	1.00	1.00
1082	A265	600 l yel grn & gray blk	1.25	1.25

1985, May 16 Litho. *Perf. 13¹/₂x14*

Sportphilex '85: Natl. Olympic Committee and Sportphilex '85 emblems, flags of Andorra, Cyprus, Iceland, Liechtenstein, Luxembourg, Malta, Monaco, San Marino.

1083	A266	50 l Diving	15	15
1084	A266	350 l Running	45	45
1085	A266	400 l Rifle shooting	52	52
1086	A266	450 l Cycling	60	60
1087	A266	600 l Handball	80	80
		Nos. 1083-1087 (5)	2.52	2.52

Emigration — A267

Intl. Youth Year — A268

1985, May 16

1088	A267	600 l Birds migrating	80	80

1985, June 24 Photo. *Perf. 12*
Granite Paper

1089	A268	400 l Boy, dove	55	55
1090	A268	600 l Girl, dove, horse	85	85

Helsinki Conference, 10th Anniv. — A269

City Hall, by Renzo Bonelli, Camera Lens. — A270

1985, June 24 *Perf. 13¹/₂x14*

1091	A269	600 l Sapling, sunburst, clouds	80	80

1985, June 24 *Perf. 13¹/₂x14¹/₂*

1092	A270	450 l multi	60	60

Intl. Fed. of Photographic Art, 18th Congress.

World Angling Championships, Arno River, Florence, Sept. 14-15 — A271

1985, Sept. 11 Photo. *Perf. 14¹/₂x15*

1093	A271	600 l Hooked fish	80	80

Alessandro Manzoni (1785-1873), Novelist & Poet — A272

19th century engravings from Manzoni's I Promessi Sposi (1825-27): 400 l, Don Abbondio encounters Don Rodrigo's henchmen. 450 l, The attempt to force the curate to perform a dubious marriage ceremony. 600 l, The Plague at Milan.

1985, Sept. 11 Engr. *Perf. 14x13¹/₂*

1094	A272	400 l multi	55	55
1095	A272	450 l multi	60	60
1096	A272	600 l multi	85	85

Intl. Feline
Fed. Congress
A273

Mosaic detail: Cat, Natl. Museum, Naples.

1985, Oct. 25   Photo.   *Perf. 12*
Granite Paper
1097 A273 600 l multi   85 85

Exhibition Type of 1980

ITALIA '85: Views of the Colosseum, Rome.

1985, Oct. 25   *Perf. 11¹/₂x12*
Granite Paper
1098 A222 1000 l multi   1.25 1.25
1099 A222 1500 l multi   1.90 1.90
   a.   Pair, #1098-1099   3.25 3.25

Christmas
A275

Photo. & Engr.
1985, Dec. 3   *Perf. 14*
1100 A275 400 l Angel   60 60
1101 A275 450 l Mother and Child   70 70
1102 A275 600 l Angel, diff.   90 90
   a.   Strip of 3, #1100-1102   2.25 2.25

Hospital,
Cailungo
A276

1986, Mar. 6   Photo.   *Perf. 12x11¹/₂*
1103 A276 400 l multi   60 60
1104 A276 650 l multi   85 85

Natl. social security org., ISS, 30th anniv., and
World Health Day.

Halley's
Comet — A277

Designs: 550 l, Giotto space probe. 1000 l, Adoration of the Magi, by Giotto (1276-1337).

1986, Mar. 6   *Perf. 11¹/₂x12*
1105 A277 550 l multi   75 75
1106 A277 1000 l multi   1.35 1.35

Deer
A278

3rd Veterans World
Table Tennis
Championships
A279

Europa Issue 1986
1986, May 22   Photo.   *Perf. 13¹/₂x14*
1107 A278 550 l shown   3.25 3.25
1108 A278 650 l Falcon   3.75 3.75

1986, May 22   Engr.
1109 A279 450 l dp mag, dk chlky bl &
                  ultra   62 62

AMERIPEX '86, Chicago, May 22-June
1 — A280

Views of Old Water Tower, Chicago: 2000 l,
Lithograph, 1870, by Charles Shober. 3000 l, Photograph, 1986.

**   *Perf. 11¹/₂x12***
1986, May 22   Photo.   Unwmk.
1110 A280 2000 l multi   2.75 2.75
1111 A280 3000 l multi   4.25 4.25
   a.   Pair, #1110-1111   7.00 7.00

Intl. Peace
Year — A281

1986, July 10   Photo.   *Perf. 11¹/₂x12*
1112 A281 550 l multi   75 75

Souvenir Sheet

Terra Cotta Statuary,
Tomb of Emperor
Qin Shi Huang Di
(259-210
B.C.) — A282

Litho. & Engr.
1986, July 10   *Perf. 13¹/₂*
1113   Sheet of 3   4.50 4.50
   a. A282 550 l Bearded man   75 75
   b. A282 650 l Horse, horiz.   88 88
   c. A282 2000 l Bearded man, diff. 2.75 2.75

Normalization of diplomatic relations with the
People's Republic of China, 15th anniv.

UNICEF, 40th
Anniv.
A283

European Boccie
Championships
A284

1986, Sept 16   Photo.   *Perf. 12*
1114 A283 650 l multi   95 95

1986, Sept. 16   *Perf. 14x15*
1115 A284 550 l multi   80 80

Choral Society,
25th
Anniv. — A285

Christmas — A286

Painting (detail): Apollo Dancing with the Muses,
by Giulio Romano (1492-1546).

1986, Sept. 16
1116 A285 450 l multi   75 75

Photo. & Engr.
1986, Nov. 26   *Perf. 14*
Design: Oil on wood triptych, 15th cent., by
Hans Memling (1435-1494), Kunsthistorisches
Museum, Vienna.

1117 A286 450 l St. John the Baptist 75 75
1118 A286 550 l Virgin and Child   90 90
1119 A286 650 l St. John the Evan-
                  gelist   1.10 1.10
   a.   Strip of 3, #1117-1119   2.75 2.75

Europa Issue 1987

Our Lady of
Consolation Church,
Borgomaggiore
A287

Church designed by Giovanni Michelucci, architect: 600 l, Architect's sketch of interior. 700 l,
Actual interior.

1987, Mar. 12   Photo.   *Perf. 12*
1120 A287 600 l multi   3.25 3.25
1121 A287 700 l multi   3.75 3.75

Motoring
Events
A288

Designs: 500 l, 80th anniv., Peking-Paris Race.
600 l, 15th San Marino Rally. 700 l, Mille Miglia
Race, 60th anniv.

1987, Mar. 12   *Perf. 11¹/₂*
1122 A288 500 l multi   80 80
1123 A288 600 l multi   95 95
1124 A288 700 l multi   1.10 1.10

Sculptures, Open-
air Museum
A289

Seventh Natl. Art
Biennale
A290

**   *Perf. 14¹/₂x13¹/₂***
1987, June 13   Photo.
1125 A289   50 l Reffi Busignani   15 15
1126 A289 100 l Bini   16 16
1127 A289 200 l Guguianu   32 32
1128 A289 300 l Berti   48 48
1129 A289 400 l Crocetti   62 62

1130 A289   500 l Berti, diff.   78 78
1131 A289   600 l Messina   90 90
1132 A289 1000 l Minguzzi   1.50 1.50
1133 A289 2200 l Greco   3.50 3.50
1134 A289 10000 l Sassu   15.50 15.50
   Nos. 1125-1134 (10)   23.91 23.91

1987, June 13   *Perf. 11¹/₂*
Abstract works: 500 l, Dal Diario del Brasile-
foresta Vergine, by Emilio Vedova. 600 l, Inven-
zione Cromatica con Brio, by Corrado Cagli.

Granite Paper
1135 A290 500 l multi   78 78
1136 A290 600 l multi   90 90

Air Club of San
Marino Ultra-
lightweight
Aircraft — A291

1987, June 13
Granite Paper
1137 A291 600 l multi   90 90

Mahatma
Gandhi
A292

1987, Aug. 2 Photo. *Perf. 14x13¹/₂*
1138 A292 500 l Gandhi Square, bust 78 78

A293   A294

1987, Aug. 29   *Perf. 12*
Granite Paper
1139 A293 600 l Olympic emblem, ath-
                  lete   90 90

OLYMPHILEX '87, Rome.

1987, Aug. 29   Granite Paper
1140 A294 700 l ultra, blk & red   1.00 1.00

First Representation of San Marino at the Mediterranean Games, Syria, Sept. 11-15.

Exhibition Type of 1980

HAFNIA '87: Views of Copenhagen (1836-
1986), as seen from the Round Tower.

1987, Oct. 16 Photo. *Perf. 11¹/₂x12*
Granite Paper
1141 A222 1200 l multi   1.90 1.90
1142 A222 2200 l multi, diff.   3.50 3.50
   a.   Pair, #1141-1142   5.50 5.50

Christmas — A296

High Speed
Train — A297

Details from Triptych of Cortona and The Annunciation, by Fra Angelico (c. 1400-1455), Diocesan
Museum of Cortona: No. 1143, Angel. No. 1144,

316

SAN MARINO

Madonna and child. No. 1145, Saint. Printed setenant.

Photo. & Engr.
1987, Nov. 12   *Perf. 13½*
1143 A296 600 l multi   98   98
1144 A296 600 l multi   98   98
1145 A296 600 l multi   98   98
  a. Strip of 3, #1143-1145   3.00 3.00

Europa Issue 1988
1988, Mar. 17 Photo. *Perf. 12*
Granite Paper
1146 A297 600 l shown   2.25 2.25
1147 A297 700 l Fiber optics   2.75 2.75

Promote Stamp
Collecting
A298

Stamps, cancellations, covers: 50 l, Nos. 81, B25 and 859. 150 l, No. C11. 300 l, Nos. 349 and 1006. 350 l, Nos. 944 and 1031. 1000 l, Nos. 303, 1081 and 308.

1988, Mar. 17   *Perf. 11½*
Granite Paper
1148 A298 50 l multi   15   15
1149 A298 150 l multi   24   24
1150 A298 300 l multi   50   50
1151 A298 350 l multi   58   58
1152 A298 1000 l multi   1.60 1.60
  Nos. 1148-1152 (5)   3.07 3.07

See Nos. 1179-1183, 1225-1229.

A299   A300

Historic sites and distinguished professors: 550 l, Carlo Malagola. 650 l, Pietro Ellero. 1300 l, Giosue Carducci (1835-1907), professor of literary history, 1861-1904, and Nobel Prize winner for literature, 1906. 1700 l, Giovanni Pascoli (1855-1912), lyric poet, Pascoli's successor as professor at Bologna.

1988, May 7 Photo. *Perf. 13½x14*
1153 A299 550 l multi   85   85
1154 A299 650 l multi   1.00 1.00
1155 A299 1300 l multi   1.90 1.90
1156 A299 1700 l multi   2.50 2.50

Bologna University, 900th anniv.

1988, July 8 Photo. *Perf. 13½x14*
Posters from Fellini Films: 300 l, La Strada. 900 l, La Dolce Vita. 1200 l, Amarcord.
1157 A300 300 l multi   45   45
1158 A300 900 l multi   1.35 1.35
1159 A300 1200 l multi   1.80 1.80

Federico Fellini, Italian film director and winner of the 1988 San Marino Prize.
See Nos. 1187-1190, 1202-1204.

Mt. Titano
and Sand
Dunes of the
Adriatic Coast
A301

1988, July 8   *Perf. 14x13½*
1160 A301 750 l multi   1.10 1.10

40th Stamp Fair, Riccione.

Souvenir Sheet

1988 Summer Olympics, Seoul — A302

1988, Sept. 19 Photo. *Perf. 13½x14*
1161 A302 Sheet of 3   4.00 4.00
  a. 650 l Running   95   95
  b. 750 l Hurdles   1.10 1.10
  c. 1300 l Gymnastics   1.90 1.90

Intl. AIDS
Congress,
San Marino,
Oct. 10-14
A303

1988, Sept. 19   *Perf. 14x13½*
1162 A303 250 l shown   38   38
1163 A303 350 l "AIDS"   52   52
1164 A303 650 l Virus, knot   95   95
1165 A303 1000 l Newspaper   1.50 1.50

Kurhaus Scheveningen, The
Hague — A304

Perf. 11½x12
1988, Oct. 18 Photo. Granite Paper
1166 A304 1600 l Lithograph, c.
    1885   2.35 2.35
1167 A304 3000 l 1988   4.40 4.40
  a. Pair, #1166-1167   6.75 6.75

FILACEPT '88, Holland.
See Nos. 1190-1191.

Christmas
A305

Paintings by Melozzo da Forli (1438-1494): No. 1168, Angel with Violin, Vatican Art Gallery. No. 1169, Angel of the Annunciation, Uffizi Gallery, Florence. No. 1170, Angel with Mandolin, Vatican Art Gallery.

1988, Dec. 9 Photo. *Perf. 13½*
Size of No. 1169: 21x40mm
1168 A305 650 l multi   1.05 1.05
1169 A305 650 l multi   1.05 1.05
1170 A305 650 l multi   1.05 1.05
  a. Strip of 3, #1168-1168 3.25 3.25

Europa Issue 1989
Souvenir Sheet

Children's Games — A306

1989, Mar. 31 Photo. *Perf. 13½x14*
1171   Sheet of 2   7.00 7.00
  a. A306 650 l Sledding   3.25 3.25
  b. A306 750 l Hopscotch 3.75 3.75

Nature
Conservation
A307

Illustrations by contest-winning youth: 200 l, Federica Sparagna. 500 l, Giovanni Monteduro. 650 l, Rosa Mannarino.

1989, Mar. 31   *Perf. 14x13½*
1172 A307 200 l multi   30   30
1173 A307 500 l multi   75   75
1174 A307 650 l multi   95   95

Sporting Anniversaries and Events — A308

1989, May 13 Photo. *Perf. 12*
Granite Paper
1175 A308 650 l Olympics   98   98
1176 A308 750 l Soccer   1.15 1.15
1177 A308 850 l Tennis   1.25 1.25
1178 A308 1300 l Car racing   1.95 1.95

Natl. Olympic Committee, 30th anniv. (650 l); admission of San Marino Soccer Federation to the UEFA and FIFA (750 l); San Marino '89, the tennis grand prix (850 l); Grand Prix of San Marino, Imola (1300 l).

Stamp Collecting Type of 1988
Covers and canceled stamps (postal history): 100 l, No. 916a with Iserravalle cancel, Sept. 1, 1977. 200 l, No. 1151 with Montegiardino cancel, May 3, 1986. 400 l, Italy No. 47 canceled on San Marino parcel card #422, 1895. 500 l, Type SP3 essay proposed by Martin Riester di Parigi, March 1865. 1000 l, Stampless cover, 1862.

1989, May 13 Granite Paper *Perf. 12*
1179 A298 100 l multi   15   15
1180 A298 200 l multi   30   30
1181 A298 400 l multi   60   60
1182 A298 500 l multi   75   75
1183 A298 1000 l multi   1.50 1.50
  Nos. 1179-1183 (5)   3.30 3.30

French Revolution,
Bicent. — A309

1989, July 7 Litho. *Perf. 12½x13*
1184 A309 700 l The Tennis Court
    Oath   1.00 1.00
1185 A309 1000 l Arrest of Louis
    XVI   1.50 1.50
1186 A309 1800 l Napoleon   2.75 2.75

Show Business Type of 1988
Scenes from: 1200 l, Marguerite et Armand. 1500 l, Apollon Musagete. 1700 l, Valentino.

1989, Sept. 18 Photo. *Perf. 13½x14*
1187 A300 1200 l multi   1.80 1.80
1188 A300 1500 l multi   2.25 2.25
1189 A300 1700 l multi   2.55 2.55

Rudolf Nureyev, Russian ballet dancer and winner of the 1989 San Marino Prize.
See Nos. 1187-1189, 1202-1204.

Exhibition Type of 1988
Views of The Capitol, Washington, DC.: 2000 l, In 1850. 2500 l, In 1989.

1989, Nov. 17 Photo. *Perf. 11½*
Granite Paper
1190 A304 2000 l multi   3.00 3.00
1191 A304 2500 l multi   3.75 3.75
  a. Pair, #1190-1191   6.75 6.75

World Stamp Expo '89.

A310   A311

Christmas: Panels from a Polyptych, c. 1540, by Coda Studio of Rimini, in the Church of the Servants of Mary, Valdragone.

1989, Nov. 17
Size of No. 1193: 50x40mm
Granite Paper
1192 A310 650 l Angel   95   95
1193 A310 650 l Holy family   95   95
1194 A310 650 l Praying Madonna 95   95
  a. Strip of 3, #1192-1194 3.00 3.00

1990, Feb. 22 Photo. *Perf. 13½x14*
Europa: Post offices.
1195 A311 700 l Palazzetto delle
    Poste, 1842   1.10 1.10
1196 A311 800 l Dogana   1.30 1.30

A312   A313

Design: The Martyrdom of Saint Agatha, by Giambattista Tiepolo, and occupation force departing by the Porta del Loco.

1990, Feb. 22 Granite Paper *Perf. 12*
1197 A312 3500 l multicolored 5.50 5.50

Liberation from Cardinal Alberoni's occupation force, 250th anniv.

Perf. 11½x12
1990, Mar. 23   Photo.
Granite Paper
European Tourism Year: No. 1198, The republic pinpointed on a map of Italy. No. 1199, San Marino atop Mt. Titano in proximity to other cities in the region. No. 1200, Rocca Guaita, San Marino.
1198 A313 600 l shown   95   95
1199 A313 600 l multicolored   95   95
1200 A313 600 l multicolored   95   95

See Nos. 1209a, 1260-1262.

Souvenir Sheet

1990 World Cup Soccer Championships, Italy — A314

Various athletes: a, Germany. b, Italy. c, Great Britain. d, Uruguay. e, Brazil. f, Argentina.

1990, Mar. 23		Perf. 13¹/₂x14	
1201	Sheet of 6	6.25	6.25
a.-f.	A314 700 l any single	1.00	1.00

Show Business Type of 1988

Scenes from: 600 l, *Hamlet.* 700 l, *Richard III* 1500 l, *Marathon Man.*

1990, May 3	Photo.	Perf. 13¹/₂x14	
1202	A300 600 l multi	98	98
1203	A300 700 l multi	1.15	1.15
1204	A300 1500 l multi	2.45	2.45

Sir Laurence Olivier (1907-1989), British actor, winner of the 1990 San Marino Prize. Name misspelled "Lawrence" on the stamps.

President of Italy, State Visit — A315

1990, June 11	Litho.	Perf. 13x12¹/₂	
1205	A315 600 l multicolored	98	98

Statue of Saint Marinus — A316

Designs: No. 1207, Liberty statue. No. 1208, Government Palace. No. 1209, Flag of San Marino.

1990, June 11	Photo.	Perf. 11¹/₂	
Granite Paper			
Booklet Stamps			
1206	A316 50 l multicolored	15	15
1207	A316 50 l multicolored	15	15
1208	A316 50 l multicolored	15	15
1209	A316 50 l multicolored	15	15
a.	Bklt. pane of 7, #1198-1200, perf. 11¹/₂ vert., #1206-1209	3.20	
	Set value	32	32

See Nos. 1256-1259.

Discovery of America, 500th Anniv. (in 1992) A317

1990, Sept. 6	Litho.	Perf. 13x12¹/₂	
1210	A317 1500 l Artifacts, map	1.90	1.90
1211	A317 2000 l Native plants, map	2.50	2.50

See Nos. 1230-1231.

Pinocchio, by Carlo Collodi (1826-1890) — A318

Cartoon style drawings from Pinocchio.

1990, Sept. 6	Photo.	Perf. 11¹/₂x12	
Granite Paper			
1212	A318 250 l shown	40	40
1213	A318 400 l Geppetto	65	65
1214	A318 450 l Blue fairy	75	75
1215	A318 600 l Cat & wolf	95	95

Flora and Fauna — A319

Designs: 200 l, Papilio machaon, Ephedra major. 300 l, Apoderus coryli, Corylus avellana. 500 l, Eliomys quercinus, Quercus ilex. 1000 l, Lacerta viridis, Ophrys bertolonii. 2000 l, Regulus ignicapillus, Pinus nigra.

1990, Oct. 31	Photo.	Perf. 14x13¹/₂	
1216	A319 200 l multicolored	30	30
1217	A319 300 l multicolored	45	45
1218	A319 500 l multicolored	75	75
1219	A319 1000 l multicolored	1.50	1.50
1220	A319 2000 l multicolored	3.00	3.00
	Nos. 1216-1220 (5)	6.00	6.00

A320   A321

Christmas: Cuciniello Crib, San Martino Museum of Naples.

1990, Oct. 31		Perf. 11¹/₂	
Granite Paper			
1221	A320 750 l shown	1.25	1.25
1222	A320 750 l Nativity, diff.	1.25	1.25
a.	Pair, #1221-1222	2.50	2.50

1991, Feb. 12	Photo.	Perf. 13¹/₂x14	
1223	A321 750 l Ariane 4 rocket	3.50	3.50
1224	A321 800 l ERS-1 satellite	3.75	3.75

Europa.

Stamp Collecting Type of 1988

Areas of philately: 100 l, Stamp store. 150 l, Clubs. 200 l, Exhibitions. 450 l, Albums, catalogues. 1500 l, Magazines, books.

1991, Feb. 12		Perf. 12	
Granite Paper			
1225	A298 100 l multicolored	16	16
1226	A298 150 l multicolored	24	24
1227	A298 200 l multicolored	32	32
1228	A298 450 l multicolored	75	75
1229	A298 1500 l multicolored	2.25	2.25
	Nos. 1225-1229 (5)	3.72	3.72

Italian Philatelic Press Union, 25th anniv. (No. 1229).

Discovery of America Type

1991, Mar. 22	Litho.	Perf. 13¹/₂x12	
1230	A317 750 l Map, instruments	1.10	1.10
1231	A317 3000 l Columbus' fleet	4.50	4.50

1992 Summer Olympics, Barcelona A323

Olympic torch relay.

1991, Mar. 22		Perf. 15x14	
1232	A323 400 l Athens	60	60
1233	A323 600 l San Marino	90	90
1234	A323 2000 l Barcelona	3.00	3.00

Basketball, Cent. — A324   Fauna — A325

Designs: 750 l, James Naismith (1861-1939), creator of basketball, players.

1991, June 4	Photo.	Perf. 13¹/₂x14	
1235	A324 650 l multicolored	1.05	1.05
1236	A324 750 l multicolored	1.20	1.20

1991, June 4		Perf. 14x13¹/₂	
1237	A325 500 l House cat	75	75
1238	A325 550 l Hamster on wheel	85	85
1239	A325 700 l Great Dane, poodle	1.10	1.10
1240	A325 1000 l Tropical fish	1.50	1.50
1241	A325 1200 l Birds in cage	1.75	1.75
	Nos. 1237-1241 (5)	5.95	5.95

Children's Day.
See Nos. 1251-1255.

James Clerk Maxwell (1831-1879), Physicist A326

1991, Sept. 24	Photo.	Perf. 14x13¹/₂	
1242	A326 750 l multicolored	1.20	1.20

Radio, cent. (in 1995).
See Nos. 1263, 1279, 1300.

Souvenir Sheet

Birth of New Europe — A327

Designs: No. 1243a, Dove, broken chains, Brandenburg Gate. b, Pres. Gorbachev, rainbow, Pres. Bush. c, Flower, broken barbed wire, map.

1991, Sept. 24		Litho.	
1243	A327 1500 l Sheet of 3, #a.-c.	7.20	7.20

Christmas — A328

Different winter views of 10th century La Rocca fortress.

1991, Nov. 13	Litho.	Perf. 14¹/₂	
1244	A328 600 l multicolored	95	95
1245	A328 750 l multicolored	1.10	1.10
1246	A328 1200 l multicolored	1.90	1.90

No. 1246 is airmail.

Gioachino Rossini (1792-1868), Composer — A329

Designs: 750 l, Bianca e Falliero, Rossini opera festival 1989. 1200 l, The Barber of Seville, La Scala 1982-83.

1992, Feb. 3	Photo.	Perf. 14x13¹/₂	
1247	A329 750 l multicolored	1.20	1.20
1248	A329 1200 l multicolored	2.00	2.00

Discovery of America, 500th Anniv. A330

Designs: 1500 l, Columbus, ships at anchor, natives. 2000 l, Map of voyages.

1992, Feb. 3	Litho.	Perf. 12	
1249	A330 1500 l multicolored	2.50	2.50
1250	A330 2000 l multicolored	3.35	3.35

Fauna Type of 1991

Flora.

1992, Mar. 26	Litho.	Perf. 13¹/₂	
1251	A325 50 l Roses	15	15
1252	A325 200 l House plant	32	32
1253	A325 300 l Orchids	50	50
1254	A325 450 l Cacti	75	75
1255	A325 5000 l Geraniums	8.25	8.25
	Nos. 1251-1255 (5)	9.97	9.97

Tourism Types of 1990

Designs: No. 1256, Crossbowman. No. 1257, Tennis player. No. 1258, Motorcyclist. No. 1259, Race car. No. 1260, Couple in moonlight. No. 1261, Man in restaurant. No. 1262, Woman reading beneath umbrella.

1992, Mar. 26		Perf. 14¹/₂x13¹/₂	
Booklet Stamps			
1256	A316 50 l multicolored	15	15
1257	A316 50 l multicolored	15	15
1258	A316 50 l multicolored	15	15
1259	A316 50 l multicolored	15	15

		Perf. 13¹/₂ Vert.	
1260	A313 600 l multicolored	95	95
1261	A313 600 l multicolored	95	95
1262	A313 600 l multicolored	95	95
a.	Bklt. pane, 1 each #1256-1262+label	3.35	
	Set value	3.35	3.35

Physicist Type of 1991

Design: Heinrich Rudolf Hertz (1857-94).

1992, Mar. 26	Photo.	Perf. 14x13¹/₂	
1263	A326 750 l multicolored	1.20	1.20

Radio, cent. (in 1995).

Discovery of America, 500th Anniv. — A331

1992, May 22   Photo.   Perf. 12x11½
Granite Paper

1264	A331	750 l Globe, ship at sea	1.20 1.20
1265	A331	850 l Ship in egg	1.40 1.40

Europa.

Souvenir Sheet

1992 Summer Olympics, Barcelona — A332

Designs: a, Soccer. b, Shooting. c, Swimming. d, Running.

1992, May 22   Litho.   Perf. 14

1266	A332	1250 l Sheet of 4, #a.-d.	8.00 8.00

Mushrooms — A333

Designs: Nos. 1267, Poisonous mushrooms. No. 1268a, Edible mushrooms in bowl. No. 1268b, Edible mushrooms on table.

SAN MARINO

BUYING AND SELLING,
QUALITY STAMPS OF
SAN MARINO MINT
NEVER HINGED OR LH.
THE ITALIAN AREA
INCLUDING
VATICAN CITY,
TRIESTE A & B -
Whether buying or selling,
my prices are very reasonable.

EUROPE

From Andorre to Turkey,
including
The English Area,
Mint Never Hinged Sets.

My buy-sell price list contains well
over 12,000 sets, all kinds of topicals, where you will find my selling prices, and the price I pay for
each set that I need.

**SEND A #10 55¢ SASE
TODAY FOR YOUR FREE
COPY OF OUR PRICE LIST!
You will be glad you did.**

F. COPPOLA

P.O. Box 181022
Utica, MI 48318-1022

1992, Sept. 18   Photo.   Perf. 11½x12
Granite Paper

1267	A333	Pair	80 80
a.-b.		250 l any single	40 40
1268	A333	Pair	1.15 1.15
a.-b.		350 l any single	56 56

Admission to the UN — A334

Designs: a, Arms of San Marino, buildings. b, UN emblem, buildings.

1992, Sept. 18   Litho.   Perf. 12x12½

1269	A334	Pair	3.20 3.20
a.-b.		1000 l any single	1.60 1.60

The Sacred
Conversation, by
Piero della
Francesca (1420-
1492)
A335

Christmas: a, Entire painting. b, Detail of faces. c, Detail of dome.

1992, Nov. 16   Litho.   Perf. 14½

1270		Triptych	3.60 3.60
a.-c.	A335	750 l any single	1.20 1.20

Contemporary
Art — A336

Paintings: 750 l, Stars, by Nicola de Maria. 850 l, Abstract face, by Mimmo Paladino.

1993, Jan. 29   Litho.   Perf. 11½

1271	A336	750 l multicolored	1.20 1.20
1272	A336	850 l multicolored	1.40 1.40

Europa.

1993 Sporting
Events — A337

1993, Jan. 29   Perf. 13½x14

1273	A337	300 l Tennis	48 48
1274	A337	400 l Cross-country skiing	65 65
1275	A337	550 l Women running	90 90
1276	A337	600 l Fisherman	1.00 1.00
1277	A337	700 l Men running	1.15 1.15
1278	A337	1300 l Sailboat, runners	2.10 2.10
		Nos. 1273-1278 (6)	6.28 6.28

No. 1273, Youth Games. No. 1274-1275, European Youth Olympic Days. No. 1276, World Championships for Freshwater Angling Clubs, Ostellato, Italy. No. 1277, Games of Small European Countries, Malta. No. 1278, Mediterranean Games, Roussillon, France.

Physicists Type of 1991

Design: 750 l, Edouard Branly (1844-1940).

1993, Mar. 26   Photo.   Perf. 14x13½

1279	A326	750 l multicolored	95 95

Radio, cent. (in 1995).

Souvenir Sheet

Inauguration of State Television — A338

Designs: a, 100-meter finals, World Track Championships, Tokyo, 1991. b, San Marino. c, Neil Armstrong on moon, 1969.

1993, Mar. 26   Litho.   Perf. 13½

1280		Sheet of 3	7.50 7.50
a.-c.	A338	2000 l any single	2.50 2.50

Soaking may affect the hologram on #1280b.

Butterflies — A339

1993, May 26   Litho.   Perf. 14x15

1281	A339	250 l Iphiclides podalirius	38 38
1282	A339	250 l Colias crocea	38 38
1283	A339	250 l Nymphalis antiopa	38 38
1284	A339	250 l Melitaea cinxia	38 38
a.		Block or strip of 4, #1281-1284	1.55 1.55

World Wildlife Fund.

Miniature Sheet

United
Europe — A340

Village of Europe: No. 1285a, Denmark. b, England. c, Ireland. d, Luxembourg. e, Germany. f, Netherlands. g, Belgium. h, Portugal. i, Italy. j, Spain. k, France. l, Greece.

1993, May 26   Perf. 13½x14

1285	A340	750 l Sheet of 12	13.00 13.00
a.		Any single, #a.-l.	1.00 1.00

Famous
Men — A341

Designs: 550 l, Carlo Goldoni (1707-93), playwright, vert. 650 l, Horace (65-8BC), poet and satirist, vert. 850 l, Claudio Monteverdi (1567-1643), composer. 1850 l, Guy de Maupassant (1850-93), writer.

1993, Sept. 17   Litho.   Perf. 13½x14

1286	A341	550 l multicolored	85 85
1287	A341	650 l multicolored	1.00 1.00
1288	A341	850 l multicolored	1.25 1.25
1289	A341	1850 l multicolored	2.75 2.75

Christmas
A342

Designs: 600 l, San Marino in winter, vert.
Paintings by Gerard van Honthorst: 750 l, Adoration of the Child. 850 l, Adoration of the Shepherds, vert.

1993, Nov. 12   Litho.   Perf. 14½

1290	A342	600 l multicolored	70 70
1291	A342	750 l multicolored	90 90
1292	A342	850 l multicolored	1.00 1.00

10th Intl.
Dog Show
A343

Designs: 350 l, Dachshund. 400 l, Afghan hound. 450 l, Belgian tervueren shepherd dog. 500 l, Boston terrier. 550 l, Mastiff. 600 l, Alaskan malamute.

1994, Jan. 31   Litho.   Perf. 15x14

1293	A343	350 l multicolored	42 42
1294	A343	400 l multicolored	48 48
1295	A343	450 l multicolored	55 55
1296	A343	500 l multicolored	60 60
1297	A343	550 l multicolored	65 65
1298	A343	600 l multicolored	70 70
		Nos. 1293-1298 (6)	3.40 3.40

Souvenir Sheet

1994 Winter
Olympics,
Lillehammer
A344

Designs: a, 90-meter ski jump. b, Downhill skiing. c, Giant slalom skiing. d, Pairs figure skating.

1994, Jan. 31   Perf. 13½

1299	A344	750 l 2 each #a.-d.	7.25 7.25

Physicists Type of 1991

Design: 750 l, Aleksandr Stepanovich Popov (1859-1905).

1994, Mar. 11   Photo.   Perf. 14x13½

1300	A326	750 l multicolored	90 90

Radio Cent. (in 1995).

Gardens — A345

1994, Mar. 11   Litho.   Perf. 13

1301	A345	100 l Gate	15 15
1302	A345	200 l Grape arbor	25 25
1303	A345	300 l Well	35 35
1304	A345	450 l Gazebo	55 55
1305	A345	1850 l Pond	2.25 2.25
		Nos. 1301-1305 (5)	3.55 3.55

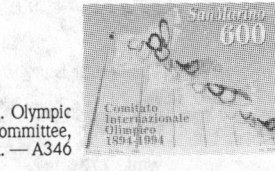

Intl. Olympic
Committee,
Cent. — A346

1994, Mar. 11   Photo.   Perf. 14x13½
1306 A346 600 l multicolored   70   70

1994 World Cup
Soccer
Championships,
US — A347

Various soccer plays: a, Two players, one with #8
on shirt. b, Player in blue shirt kicking ball upward.
c, Player heading ball. d, Players, one with #6 on
shirt. e, Goal keeper.

1994, May 23   Litho.   Perf. 14
1307 A347 600 l Strip of 5, #a.-e.   3.50 3.50

No. 1307 has a continuous design.

Europa — A348

Ulysses spacecraft and: 750 l, Flight path around
Sun and Jupiter. 850 l, Sun.

1994, May 23
1308 A348 750 l multicolored   1.00 1.00
1309 A348 850 l multicolored   1.25 1.25

Inauguration
of
Government
Building,
Cent.
A349

Designs: 150 l, Exterior in shade, vert. 600 l,
Exterior in sunshine, vert. 650 l, Clock tower.
1000 l, Interior.

Perf. 13½x13, 13x13½
1994, Sept. 30   Litho.
1310 A349 150 l multicolored   20   20
1311 A349 600 l multicolored   75   75
1312 A349 650 l multicolored   85   85
1313 A349 1000 l multicolored   1.25 1.25
        Nos. 1310-1313 (4)   3.05 3.05

Dedication
of St.
Mark's
Basilica,
900th
Anniv.
A350

1994, Oct. 8   Photo.   Perf. 13½x13
1314 A350 750 l multicolored   1.10 1.10
  a.   Souvenir sheet of 2, tete beche 2.25 2.25

No. 1314 printed with se-tenant label. No.
1314a contains No. 1314 and Italy No. 2003. Only
No. 1314 was valid for postage in San Marino.

Touring Club of
Italy, Cent. — A351

Vehicles traveling on road in middle of flower
field: a, Traffic cop, bus. b, Tandem tanker truck. c,
Sailboat, volcano. d, Truck loaded with animals,
camper, fish in lake.

1994, Nov. 18   Litho.   Perf. 14x13½
1315   Block of 4   5.00 5.00
  a.-d. A351 1000 l any single   1.25 1.25

No. 1315 is a continuous design.

A352   A353

The Enthroned Madonna and Child with Saints,
by Giovanni Santi (1440-1494) (Christmas): 600 l,
Drummer, piper. 750 l, Madonna and Child. 850 l,
Piper, harpist.

1994, Nov. 18   Perf. 14x15
1316 A352 600 l multicolored   75   75
1317 A352 750 l multicolored   90   90
1318 A352 850 l multicolored   1.00 1.00
        Nos. 1316-1318 (3)   2.65 2.65

1995, Feb. 10   Photo.   Perf. 13x14
1319 A353 100 l Cycling   15   15
1320 A353 500 l Volleyball   65   65
1321 A353 650 l Speed skater   80   80
1322 A353 850 l Runner   1.10 1.10
        Nos. 1319-1322 (4)   2.70 2.70

Sporting Events of 1995: Junior World Cycling
Championships, Forli, San Marino (#1319). Volley-
ball, cent. (#1320). Men's Speed Skating World
Championships, Baselga di Pine, Italy (#1321).
World Track & Field Championships, Goteborg,
Sweden (#1322).

European Nature
Conservation
Year — A354

Nature scenes with flowers, water: a, Snails,
dragonfly, fish. b, Frog, snake. c, Ladybugs, butterfly. d, Ducklings, frog. e, Ducks, snail.

1995, Feb. 10
1323 A354 600 l Strip of 5, #a.-e. 3.75 3.75

No. 1323 is a continuous design.

UN, 50th
Anniv. — A355

Designs: 550 l, UN emblem surrounded by people. 600 l, Emblem in center of rose. 650 l, Hourglass shaped from halves of globe. 1200 l, "50,"
Emblem, rainbow.

1995, Mar. 24   Litho.   Perf. 14x15
1324 A355 550 l multicolored   65   65
1325 A355 600 l multicolored   70   70
1326 A355 650 l multicolored   75   75
1327 A355 1200 l multicolored   1.40 1.40
        Nos. 1324-1327 (4)   3.50 3.50

Peace &
Freedom
A356

1995, Mar. 24   Perf. 15x14
1328 A356 750 l shown   90   90
1329 A356 850 l Sheep, meadow   1.00 1.00

Europa.

SEMI-POSTAL STAMPS

Regular Issue of 1903 Surcharged:
1917   1917

Pro combattenti   Pro combattenti

= 25   Cent.   50
    a   b

1917, Dec. 15   Wmk. 140   Perf. 14
B1 A10(a) 25c on 2c vio   90   90
B2 A11(b) 50c on 2 l vio   13.00 13.00

Statue of Liberty — SP1

View of San
Marino
SP2

1918, June 1   Typo.
B3 SP1 2c dl vio & blk   15   15
B4 SP1 5c bl grn & blk   15   15
B5 SP1 10c lake & blk   15   15
B6 SP1 20c brn org & blk   15   15
B7 SP1 25c ultra & blk   25   25

B8 SP1 45c yel brn & blk   25   25
B9 SP2 1 l bl grn & blk   5.75 5.75
B10 SP2 2 l vio & blk   4.25 4.25
B11 SP2 3 l claret & blk   4.25 4.25
        Nos. B3-B11 (9)   15.35 15.35

These stamps were sold at an advance of 5c each
over face value, the receipts from that source being
devoted to the support of a hospital for Italian
soldiers.

For surcharges see Nos. 89-92.

**3
Novembre
1918**

Nos. B6-B8
Overprinted

1918, Dec. 12
B12 SP1 20c brn org & blk   75   75
B13 SP1 25c ultra & blk   75   75
B14 SP1 45c yel brn & blk   75   75

Overprinted **3 Novembre 1918**

B15 SP2 1 l blue grn & blk   75   75
B16 SP2 2 l violet & blk   5.00 5.00
B17 SP2 3 l claret & blk   5.00 5.00
        Nos. B12-B17 (6)   13.00 13.00

Celebration of Italian Victory over Austria.
Inverted overprints were privately produced.

Coat of   Liberty
Arms   SP4
SP3

1923, Sept. 20   Engr.
B18 SP3 5c + 5c olive grn   15   15
B19 SP3 10c + 5c orange   15   15
B20 SP3 15c + 5c dk green   15   15
B21 SP3 25c + 5c brn lake   40   40
B22 SP3 45c + 5c vio brn   70   70
B23 SP3 50c + 5c gray   50   50
B24 SP4 1 l + 5c blk & bl   1.25 1.25
        Nos. B18-B24 (7)   3.30 3.05

New issue listings, plus
the most interesting read in
the hobby, characterize the
"Scott Stamp Monthly".
For more information,
please call 1-800-488-5351.

**FILATELIA RIVA RENO
PAYING TOP PRICES • SERIOUS BUYER...
TRIESTE ZONE A – ZONE B
SAN MARINO, VATICAN and ITALY**
**Collections, Lots, Accumulations,
Postal History & Covers**
- A.M.G. - Italian Social Republic - Italian Offices Abroad
BEFORE SELLING, ASK US!
Don't hesitate! Call or fax for our...top buying prices
and quick payment in US funds!
NEW ISSUE SERVICE!
• Special Conditions for Dealers •
Filatelia Riva Reno di Luciano Morselli
Via Galliera, 23 - 40121 Bologna - Italy
FAX +39-51-232180 • TEL +39-51-237480

american philatelic society
borsa filatelica nazionale milano
feder. nazion. comm. filatelici italiani-roma
philatelic traders' society
verband des deutschen briefm. handels
american stamp dealers association

St. Marinus — SP5

Wmk. 140

1944, Apr. 25   Photo.   Perf. 14

B25	SP5	20 l + 10 l gldn brn	90	50
		Sheet of 8	27.50	27.50

The surtax was used for workers' houses. See No. CB1.

No. 256 Surcharged in Red "L. 10"

1946, Aug. 24   Unwmk.

B26	A46	50 l + 10 l	5.00	5.00
		Sheet of 10	575.00	575.00

Third Philatelic Day, Rimini. The surtax was for the exhibition.

Air Post Types of 1946 Surcharged "CONVEGNO FILATELICO / 30 NOVEMBRE 1946 / + LIRE 25" (or "LIRE 50") in Red or Violet

1946, Nov. 30   Wmk. 277

B26A	AP7	3 l + 25 l dk brn (R)	25	18
B26B	AP8	5 l + 25 l red org (V)	25	18
B26C	AP6	10 l + 50 l ultra (R)	2.75	2.50

Inscription "Posta Aerea" does not appear on these stamps.

No. 260 Surcharged in + Black

1947, Nov. 13   Wmk. 217   Perf. 12

B27	A53	1 l + 1 l brt grn & vio	15	15
B28	A53	1 l + 2 l brt grn & vio	15	15
B29	A53	1 l + 3 l brt grn & vio	15	15
B30	A53	1 l + 4 l brt grn & vio	15	15
B31	A53	1 l + 5 l brt grn & vio	15	15
a.		Strip of 5, #B27-B31	1.00	1.00

Surcharged on No. 261

B32	A53	2 l + 1 l pur & olive	15	15
B33	A53	2 l + 2 l pur & olive	15	15
B34	A53	2 l + 3 l pur & olive	15	15
B35	A53	2 l + 4 l pur & olive	15	15
B36	A53	2 l + 5 l pur & olive	15	15
a.		Strip of 5, #B32-B36	1.00	1.00

Surcharged on No. 262

B37	A53	4 l + 1 l	3.00	3.25
B38	A53	4 l + 2 l	3.00	3.25
a.		Pair, #B37-B38	12.00	12.00
		Set value	6.60	7.25

Surcharges on Nos. B27-B38 are arranged consecutively, changing from ascending to descending order of denomination on alternate rows in the sheet.

Catalogue values for unused stamps in this section, from this point to the end of the section, are for Never Hinged items.

Refugee Boy — SP6

1982, Dec. 15   Photo.   Perf. 11½

B39	SP6	300 l + 100 l multi	48	48

Surcharge was for refugee support.

AIR POST STAMPS

View of San Marino AP1

Wmk. 217

1931, June 11   Engr.   Perf. 12

C1	AP1	50c blue grn	45	45
C2	AP1	80c red	65	65
C3	AP1	1 l bister brn	65	65
C4	AP1	2 l brt violet	90	90
C5	AP1	2.60 l Prus bl	7.00	7.00
C6	AP1	3 l dk gray	7.00	7.00
C7	AP1	5 l olive grn	1.75	1.75
C8	AP1	7.70 l dk brown	2.25	2.25
C9	AP1	9 l dp orange	2.75	2.75
C10	AP1	10 l dk blue	135.00	135.00
		Nos. C1-C10 (10)	158.40	158.40

Exist imperf.

Graf Zeppelin Issue

Stamps of Type AP1 Surcharged in Blue or Black

1933, Apr. 28

C11	AP1	3 l on 50c org	65	45.00
C12	AP1	5 l on 80c ol grn	27.50	45.00
C13	AP1	10 l on 1 l dk bl (Bk)	27.50	57.50
C14	AP1	12 l on 2 l yel brn	27.50	70.00
C15	AP1	15 l on 2.60 l dl red (Bk)	27.50	80.00
C16	AP1	20 l on 3 l bl grn (Bk)	27.50	90.00
		Nos. C11-C16 (6)	138.15	387.50

Exist imperf.

Nos. C1 and C2 Surcharged

1936, Apr. 14

C17	AP1	75c on 50c blue grn	2.75	2.75
C18	AP1	75c on 80c red	7.75	7.75

Nos. C5 and C6 Surcharged with New Value and Bars

1941, Jan. 12

C19	AP1	10 l on 2.60 l	100.00	100.00
C20	AP1	10 l on 3 l	24.00	24.00

View of Arbe — AP2

Wmk. 140

1942, Mar. 16   Photo.   Perf. 14

C21	AP2	25c brn & gray blk	15	15
C22	AP2	50c grn & brn	15	15
C23	AP2	75c gray bl & red brn	16	16
C24	AP2	1 l ocher & brn	28	28
C25	AP2	5 l bis brn & bl	3.50	3.50
		Nos. C21-C25 (5)	4.24	4.24

Return of the Italian flag to Arbe.

San Marino Map, Fasces and Wing AP3

San Marino Map, Fasces and Wing AP4

Overprinted "28 LVGLIO 1943 1642 d. F. R." in Black

1943, Aug. 27

C26	AP3	25c yellow org	15	15
C27	AP3	50c car rose	15	15
C28	AP3	75c dark brown	15	15
C29	AP3	1 l dk rose vio	15	15
C30	AP3	2 l sapphire	15	92
C31	AP3	5 l orange red	28	28
C32	AP3	10 l deep green	75	75
C33	AP3	20 l black	2.25	2.75
		Nos. C26-C33 (8)	4.03	5.30

See footnote after No. 227. Nos. C26-C33 exist without overprint (not regularly issued). Value $2,250.

Overprinted "GOVERNO PROVVISORIO"

1943, Aug. 27

C34	AP4	25c yellow org	15	15
C35	AP4	50c car rose	15	15
C36	AP4	75c dark brown	15	15
C37	AP4	1 l dk rose vio	15	15
C38	AP4	5 l orange red	38	38
C39	AP4	20 l black	1.90	1.90
		Nos. C34-C39 (6)	2.88	2.88

Government Palace — AP5

Planes over Mt. Titano — AP8

Gulls and San Marino Skyline AP6

Plane and View of San Marino AP7

Plane over Globe — AP9

1945, Mar. 15   Photo.

C40	AP5	25 l bister brn	2.50	2.50

See note after No. 239.

Photo., Engr. (20 l, 50 l)

1946-47   Unwmk.   Perf. 14

C41	AP6	25c blue blk	15	15
C42	AP7	75c red org	15	15
C43	AP6	1 l brown	15	15
C44	AP7	2 l dull green	15	15
C45	AP7	3 l violet	15	15
C46	AP8	5 l violet blue	15	15
C47	AP6	10 l crimson	15	16
C48	AP8	20 l brown lake	1.50	1.75
C49	AP8	35 l orange red	3.50	3.25
C50	AP8	50 l dk yellow grn	3.50	3.25
C51	AP9	100 l sepia ('47)	1.25	1.25
		Nos. C41-C51 (11)	10.80	10.56

Some values exist imperforate.
Issue dates: 35 l, Nov. 3, 1946; 100 l, Mar. 27, 1947; others, Aug. 8, 1946.

For surcharges and overprint see Nos. B26A-B26C, C54.

Roosevelt Type of Regular Issue, 1947

F. D. Roosevelt and: 1 l, 31 l, 50 l, Eagle. 2 l, 20 l, 100 l, San Marino arms. 5 l, 200 l, Flags of San Marino and US, vert.

Wmk. 277

1947, May 3   Photo.   Perf. 14

C51A	A52a	1 l dp ultra & sep	15	15
C51B	A52a	2 l org red & sep	15	15
C51C	A52a	5 l multicolored	15	15
C51D	A52a	20 l choc & sepia	15	15
C51E	A52a	31 l orange & sepia	28	28
C51F	A52a	50 l dk car & sepia	35	40
C51G	A52a	100 l blue & sepia	60	85
C51H	A52a	200 l multicolored	9.50	6.50
		Nos. C51A-C51H (8)	11.33	8.63

Nos. C51A-C51E, C51H exist imperf. Value, set $105.

Nos. C51A-C51C Surcharged

1947, June 16

C51I	A52a	3 l on 1 l dp ultra & sep	28	28
C51J	A52a	4 l on 2 l org red & sep	28	28
C51K	A52a	6 l on 5 l multicolored	28	28

St. Marinus Type of Regular Issue, 1947

Wmk. 217

1947, July 18   Engr.   Perf. 12

Center in Bright Blue

C52	A53	25 l deep orange	1.00	1.00
C53	A53	50 l red brown	2.00	2.00

No. C51 Overprinted in Red

Giornata Filatelica
Rimini - San Marino
18 Luglio 1947

1947, July 18   Unwmk.   Perf. 14

C54	AP9	100 l sepia	70	70
a.		Double overprint	22.50	
b.		Inverted overprint	65.00	

Rimini Phil. Exhib., July 18-20.

US No. 1 and Mt. Titano AP11

Wmk. 277

1947, Dec. 24   Engr.   Perf. 14

C55	AP11	100 l dk pur & dk brn	4.00	4.00
a.		Imperf.	47.50	
		Sheet of 10	1,250.	

1st US postage stamps, cent.

No. 264 Surcharged "POSTA AEREA" and New Value in Black

1948, Oct. 9   Wmk. 217   Perf. 12

C56	A53	200 l on 25 l	12.00	12.00

Giuseppe and Anita Garibaldi Entering San Marino — AP12

Wmk. 277

1949, June 28   Photo.   Perf. 14

Size: 27½x22mm

C57	AP12	2 l brn red & ultra	15	15
C58	AP12	3 l dk green & sepia	15	15
C59	AP12	5 l dk bl grn & ultra	15	20

Size: 37x22mm

C60	AP12	25 l dk green & vio	1.00	1.00
C61	AP12	65 l grnsh blk & gray blk	5.00	5.00
		Nos. C57-C61 (5)	6.45	6.50

Garibaldi's escape to San Marino, cent.

Stagecoach on Road from San Marino AP13

1950, Feb. 9   Engr.   Perf. 14
C62 AP13 200 l deep blue   1.40   1.40
  a. Perf. 13½x14 ('51)   2.75   2.75
     As "a," sheet of 6   22.50 22.50
  b. Imperf ('51)   11.50 11.50
     As "b," sheet of 6   90.00 90.00

UPU, 75th anniv. No. C62 was issued in sheets of 25; Nos. C62a and C62b in sheets of 6. See No. C75.

AP14

AP15

AP16

Various Views of San Marino.

1950, Apr. 12   Photo.   Perf. 14
Size: 27½x21½mm, 21½x27½mm
C63 AP14   2 l vio & dp grn   15   15
C64 AP14   3 l blue & brown   15   15
C65 AP15   5 l brn blk & rose
             red   15   15
C66 AP14 10 l grnsh blk & bl   20   24
C67 AP14 15 l grnsh blk & vio   22   30
Size: 36x26½mm, 26½x36mm
C68 AP15 55 l dp bl & dp grn   8.75 7.25
C69 AP14 100 l car & gray   2.25 2.25
C70 AP15 250 l violet & brn   8.75 7.25
Engr.
C71 AP16 500 l bl, dk grn & vio
             brn   55.00 55.00
     Nos. C63-C71 (9)   75.62 72.74

See No. C78. For overprints and surcharges see Nos. C72-C74, C76, C79.

Types of 1950 Overprinted in Black, Blue or Brown

XXVIII FIERA INTERNAZIO-NALE DI MILANO APRILE 1950

1950, Apr. 12   Photo.
New Colors; Sizes as Before
C72 AP15   5 l dp bl & dp grn   15   15
C73 AP14 15 l car & gray (Bl)   60   55
C74 AP15 55 l vio & brn (Br)   2.50 2.50

The overprint is arranged differently on each denomination.
San Marino's participation in the 28th Intl. Fair of Milan, Apr., 1950.

Stagecoach Type of 1950

1951, Jan. 31   Engr.   Perf. 13½x14
C75 AP13 300 l multi   11.00 11.00
     Sheet of 6   100.00 100.00
  a. Imperf.   100.00 100.00

No. C71 Surcharged in Black "Giornata Filatelica San Marino-Riccione 20-8-1951," New Value and Bars

1951, Aug. 20   Perf. 14
C76 AP16 300 l on 500 l   22.50 22.50

Flag and Plane — AP17

1951, Nov. 22   Engr.   Wmk. 277
C77 AP17 1000 l multi   200.00 200.00
     Sheet of 6   5,250. 4,250.

Type of 1950

1951, Apr. 28   Photo.   Perf. 14
Size: 36x26½mm
C78 AP16 500 l dk grn & brn   75.00 75.00
     Sheet of 6   1,000. 1,000.

Pro-alluvionati itai i 1951

No. C70 Surcharged in Black

100
≡

1951, Dec. 6
C79 AP15 100 l on 250 l   3.75 3.75

Issued to raise funds for flood victims in northern Italy.

Columbus, Globe, Statue of Liberty and Buildings AP18

1952, Jan. 28   Engr.
C80 AP18 200 l dk bl & blk   14.00 14.00

Issued to honor Christopher Columbus.

Type of 1952
Overprinted in Red   FIERA DI TRIESTE 1952

1952, June 29
C81 AP18 200 l blk brn & choc   12.00 12.00

4th Intl. Sample Fair of Trieste.

Cyclamen — AP19

Flowers and Seacoast — AP20

Designs: 2 l, As Nos. C85 to C87 with flowers omitted. 3 l, Rose.

1952, Aug. 25   Photo.   Perf. 10x14
C82 AP19 1 l pur & lil rose   15   15
C83 AP19 2 l blue & bl grn   15   15
C84 AP19 3 l dk brn & red   15   15
Perf. 14
C85 AP20 5 l rose lil & brn   15   15
C86 AP20 25 l vio & bl grn   22   30

Perf. 13
Engr.
C87 AP20 200 l multicolored   22.50 22.50
     Sheet of 6, #C87   300.00 300.00
     Nos. C82-C87 (6)   23.32 23.40

Riccione Phil. Exhib., Aug. 25, 1952.

Plane Making Photographic Survey AP21

Design: 75 l, Aerial survey, seen through window.

1952, Nov. 17   Photo.   Perf. 14
C88 AP21 25 l olive green   90   90
C89 AP21 75 l red brn & pur   3.50 3.50

Aerial photographic survey of San Marino, 1952.

Skier AP22

1953, Apr. 20   Engr.
C90 AP22 200 l bl grn & dk grn   40.00 40.00
     Sheet of 6   600.00 600.00

Plane and Arms of San Marino AP23

1954, Apr. 5
C91 AP23 1000 l dk blue & brn   65.00 65.00
     Sheet of 6   575.00 575.00

Type of Regular Issue, 1954

1954, Dec. 16   Photo.   Perf. 13
C92 A71 120 l dp bl & red brn   1.10 1.10

Hurdler AP25

1955, June 26   Wmk. 303   Perf. 14
C93 AP25 80 l shown   85   65
C94 AP25 120 l Relay   85   90
     Set, never hinged   2.75

San Marino's first Intl. Exhib. of Olympic Stamps, June.

Ski Jumper AP26

1955, Dec. 15
C95 AP26 200 l blk & red org   9.50 9.50

7th Winter Olympic Games at Cortina d'Ampezzo, Jan. 26-Feb. 5, 1956.

No. 372 Overprinted in Upper Right Corner with Plane and "Posta Aerea"

1956, Dec. 10
C96 A76 100 l blk & Prus grn   95 1.25
     Never hinged   1.25

Catalogue values for unused stamps in this section, from this point to the end of the section, are for Never Hinged items.

Helicopter, Plane and Modernistic Building — AP27

Wmk. 303
1958, Apr. 12   Photo.   Perf. 14
C97 AP27 125 l lt blue & brn   2.00 2.00

10th participation in Milan Fair.
See Nos. 414-415.

View of San Marino AP28

Design: 300 l, Road from Mt. Titano.

Wmk. 303
1958, June 23   Engr.   Perf. 13
C98 AP28 200 l brn & dk blue   2.00 2.00
C99 AP28 300 l magenta & vio   2.00 2.00
  a. Strip, Nos. C98, C99 + label 4.50 4.50

Printed in sheets containing 20 each of Nos. C98 and C99 flanking a center label with San Marino coat of arms. Nos. C98 and C99 also come se-tenant in sheet.

Naples Stamps Type of Regular Issue

Design: Bay of Naples and 50g stamp of Naples.

1958, Oct. 8   Photo.   Perf. 14
C100 A85 125 l brn & red brn   1.65 1.65

Sea Gull — AP29

Birds: 10 l, Falcon. 15 l, Mallard. 120 l, Stock dove. 250 l, Barn swallow.

1959, Feb. 12   Perf. 14
C101 AP29   5 l green & gray   15   15
C102 AP29 10 l blue & org brn   15   15
C103 AP29 15 l red & multi   15   15
C104 AP29 120 l rose red, yel & gray
             blk   45   35
C105 AP29 250 l dp grn, yel & blk 1.25 1.10
     Set value   1.90 1.70

Pierre de Coubertin AP30

Wmk. 303
1959, May 19   Engr.   Perf. 13
C106 AP30 120 l sepia   1.00   85

Pierre de Coubertin; 1960 Olympic Games in Rome.

Alitalia
Viscount Over
San Marino
AP31

1959, June 3   Photo.   Perf. 14
C107 AP31 120 l bright violet   1.75 1.10
First flight San Marino-Rimini-London.

Lincoln Type of Regular Issue, 1959
Design: Abraham Lincoln and San Marino peaks.

1959, July 1   Engr.   Perf. 14x13
C108 A87 200 l dark blue   3.50 2.50

Romagna Stamps Type
Design: Bologna view, 3b Romagna stamp.

Wmk. 303
1959, Aug. 29   Photo.   Perf. 14
C109 A88 120 l blk & blue grn   2.25 1.65

Sicily Stamps Type
Design: Fishing boats, Monte Pellegrino and 50g
stamp of Sicily, horiz.

1959, Oct. 16
C110 A89 200 l multicolored   1.25 75

Olympic Games Type
Sports: 20 l, Basketball. 40 l, Sprint race. 80 l,
Swimming, horiz. 125 l, Target shooting, horiz.

1960, May 23   Wmk. 303   Perf. 14
C111 A92 20 l lilac   15 15
C112 A92 40 l bis brn & dk red   22 22
C113 A92 80 l ultra & buff   32 30
C114 A92 125 l ver & dk brn   40 22
Souvenir sheets are valued and described below
No. 465.

Lions Intl. Type
Design: 200 l, Globe and Lions emblem.

1960, July 1   Photo.
C115 A94 200 l ol grn, brn & ultra   5.00 4.00

12th Stamp Fair Type
1960, Aug. 27   Wmk. 303   Perf. 14
C116 A95 125 l multicolored   1.40 1.25

Helicopter
and Mt.
Titano
AP32

1961, July 6   Engr.   Perf. 14
C117 AP32 1000 l rose carmine   37.50 27.50
     Sheet of 6   240.00 175.00

Tupolev TU-
104A
AP33

Planes: 10 l, Boeing 707, vert. 15 l, Douglas DC-
8. 25 l, Boeing 707. 50 l, Vickers Viscount 837.
75 l, Caravelle, vert. 120 l, Vickers VC10. 200 l, D.
H. Comet 4C. 300 l, Boeing 727. 500 l, Rolls Royce
Dart turbo-prop. 1000 l, Boeing 707.

1963-65   Wmk. 339   Photo.   Perf. 14
C118 AP33   5 l blue & vio brn   15 15
C119 AP33 10 l org & dk bl   15 15
C120 AP33 15 l violet & buff   15 15
C121 AP33 25 l violet & car   15 15
C122 AP33 50 l grnsh bl & red   15 15
C123 AP33 75 l emer & dp org   15 15
C124 AP33 120 l vio bl & red   28 28
C125 AP33 200 l brt yel & blk   22 22
C126 AP33 300 l orange & blk   25 25
              Perf. 13
C127 AP33 500 l multicolored   3.50 3.50
     Sheet of 4   14.00 14.00

C128 AP33 1000 l lil rose, ultra &
                  yel   2.50 2.50
     Sheet of 4   21.00 21.00
Nos. C118-C128 (11)   7.65 7.65
Issued: Nos. C118-C126, Dec. 5, 1963. No.
C127, Mar. 4, 1965. No. C128, Mar. 12, 1964.

Mt. Titano and
Flight
Symbolized
AP34

1972, Oct. 25   Unwmk.   Perf. 11½
Granite Paper
C129 AP34 1000 l multi   1.00 90

Glider
AP35

Designs: Each stamp shows a different type of air
current in background.

1974, Oct. 9   Photo.   Perf. 11½
Granite Paper
C130 AP35 40 l multicolored   15 15
C131 AP35 120 l multicolored   15 15
C132 AP35 500 l multicolored   50 50
50th anniversary of gliding in Italy.

San Marino 77 Type of 1977
1977, Jan. 28   Photo.   Perf. 11½
C133 A193 200 l multicolored   22 22

Wright Brothers' Flyer
A — AP36

1978, Sept. 28   Photo.   Perf. 11½
C134 AP36 10 l multicolored   15 15
C135 AP36 50 l multicolored   15 15
C136 AP36 200 l multicolored   22 22
              Set value   35 35
75th anniversary of first powered flight.

AIR POST SEMI-POSTAL STAMP

View of San
Marino
APSP1

Wmk. 140
1944, Apr. 25   Photo.   Perf. 14
CB1 APSP1 20 l + 10 l ol grn   90 90
     Sheet of 8   22.50 22.50
The surtax was used for workers' houses.

SPECIAL DELIVERY STAMPS

SD1

Unwmk.
1907, Apr. 25   Engr.   Perf. 12
E1 SD1 25c carmine   5.25 2.50
For surcharges see Nos. E3, E5.

Type of Regular Issue **ESPRESSO**
of 1903 Overprinted

Perf. 14½x14
1923, May 30   Wmk. 140
E2 A11 60c violet   30 30

Type of 1907 Issue Surcharged

Cent. 60

1923, July 26   Perf. 14
E3 SD1 60c on 25c carmine   30 30
  a. Vert. pair, imperf. between   20.00

No. E2 Surcharged **Lire 1,25**

1926, Nov. 25   Perf. 14½x14
E4 A11 1.25 l on 60c violet   45 45

No. E3 Surcharged

L 1,25

▌▌▌▌▌▌▌▌▌▌▌▌▌▌▌▌▌▌▌▌▌▌▌▌▌

1927, Sept. 15
E5 SD1 1.25 l on 60c on 25c   35 35
  a. Inverted surcharge   8.50
  b. Vert. pair, imperf. between   42.50
  c. Double surcharge   65.00

Statue of Liberty and View of San Marino
SD2

Wmk. 217
1929, Aug. 29   Engr.   Perf. 12
E6 SD2 1.25 l green   16 16

Overprinted in Red **UNION
                      POSTALE UNIVERSELLE**

E7 SD2 2.50 l deep blue   55 55

Arms of San
Marino
SD3

Wmk. 140
1943, Sept.   Photo.   Perf. 14
E8 SD3 1.25 l green   15 15
E9 SD3 2.50 l reddish orange   15 15
              Set value   22 22

View of San
Marino
SD4

Pegasus
SD5

1945-46   Photo.   Wmk. 140
E12 SD4 2.50 l deep green   15 15
E13 SD4   5 l deep orange   15 15
              Unwmk.
E14 SD4   5 l carmine rose   70 50
              Wmk. 277
E15 SD4 10 l sapphire ('46)   1.75 1.25
              Engr.
              Unwmk.
E16 SD5 30 l deep ultra ('46)   4.00 4.00
      Nos. E12-E16 (5)   6.75 6.05
See Nos. E22-E23. For surcharges see Nos. E17-
E21, E24-E25.

Nos. E14 and E15 Surcharged in Black

▨▨

L. 15

1947   Unwmk.   Perf. 14
E17 SD4 15 l on 5 l car rose   25 20
              Wmk. 277
E18 SD4 15 l on 10 l saph   25 20

No. E16 Surcharged with New Value and
Bars in Carmine
1947-48   Unwmk.
E19 SD5 35 l on 30 l ('48)   18.00 18.00
E20 SD5 60 l on 30 l   3.00 3.00
E21 SD5 80 l on 30 l ('48)   8.50 10.00

Types of 1945-46
1950, Dec. 11   Photo.   Wmk. 277
E22 SD4 60 l rose brown   3.50 3.50
E23 SD5 80 l deep blue   3.50 3.50
      Set, never hinged   17.00

Nos. E22-E23 Surcharged with New Value
and Three Bars
1957, Dec. 12   Perf. 14
E24 SD4 75 l on 60 l rose brn   1.50 1.50
E25 SD5 100 l on 80 l dp blue   1.50 1.50
      Set, never hinged   5.00

| Catalogue values for unused |
| stamps in this section, from this |
| point to the end of the section, are |
| for Never Hinged items. |

Crossbow
SD6

Design: No. E27, "Espresso" at left; crossbow
casts two shadows.

1965, Aug. 28   Photo.   Wmk. 339
E26 SD6 120 l on 75 l blk, gray & yel 15 15
E27 SD6 135 l on 100 l blk & org   18 18

Without Surcharge
Design: 80 l, 100 l, "Espresso" at left; crossbow
casts two shadows.

1966, Mar. 29
E28 SD6 75 l blk, gray & yel   15 15
E29 SD6 80 l blk & lilac   15 15
E30 SD6 100 l blk & orange   18 18

SEMI-POSTAL SPECIAL DELIVERY STAMP

SPSD1

Wmk. 140

1923, Sept. 20   Engr.   *Perf. 14*

EB1	SPSD1	60c + 5c brown red	75	75

POSTAGE DUE STAMPS

D1

Wmk. 140

1897-1920   Typo.   *Perf. 14*

J1	D1	5c bl grn & dk brn	15	15
J2	D1	10c bl grn & dk brn	15	15
a.		Numerals inverted	12.00	12.00
J3	D1	30c bl grn & dk brn	15	15
J4	D1	50c bl grn & dk brn	50	50
a.		Numerals inverted	12.00	12.00
J5	D1	60c bl grn & dk brn	1.50	2.00
J6	D1	1 l cl & dk brn	1.00	1.00
J7	D1	3 l cl & dk brn ('20)	3.00	3.75
J8	D1	5 l cl & dk brn	14.00	12.50
J9	D1	10 l cl & dk brn	5.00	6.25
		Nos. J1-J9 (9)	25.45	26.45

See Nos. J10-J36. For surcharges see Nos. J37-J60, J64.

1924

J10	D1	5c rose & brown	15	15
J11	D1	10c rose & brown	15	15
J12	D1	30c rose & brown	15	15
J13	D1	50c rose & brown	15	15
J14	D1	60c rose & brown	1.25	1.25
J15	D1	1 l green & brown	1.50	1.50
J16	D1	3 l green & brown	6.25	6.25
J17	D1	5 l green & brown	7.25	7.25
J18	D1	10 l green & brown	60.00	60.00
		Nos. J10-J18 (9)	76.85	76.85

1925-39   *Perf. 14*

J19	D1	5c blue & brn	15	15
a.		Numerals inverted	14.00	14.00
J20	D1	10c blue & brn	15	15
a.		Numerals inverted	14.00	14.00
J21	D1	15c blue & brn ('39)	15	15
J22	D1	20c blue & brn ('39)	15	15
J23	D1	25c blue & brn ('39)	15	15
J24	D1	30c blue & brn	15	15
J25	D1	40c blue & brn ('39)	1.00	1.00
J26	D1	50c blue & brn	15	15
a.		Numerals inverted	14.00	14.00
J27	D1	60c blue & brn	52	52
J28	D1	1 l buff & brn	1.25	52
J29	D1	2 l buff & brn ('39)	52	52
J30	D1	3 l buff & brn	17.50	13.00
J31	D1	5 l buff & brn	5.25	2.50
J32	D1	10 l buff & brn	8.75	4.00
J33	D1	15 l buff & brn ('28)	52	52
J34	D1	25 l buff & brn ('28)	14.00	10.50
J35	D1	30 l buff & brn ('28)	2.50	4.50
J36	D1	50 l buff & brn ('28)	4.00	5.25
		Nos. J19-J36 (18)	56.86	44.11

Postage Due Stamps of 1925 Surcharged in Black and Silver

1931, May 18

J37	D1	15c on 5c bl & brn	15	15
J38	D1	15c on 10c bl & brn	15	15
J39	D1	15c on 30c bl & brn	15	15
J40	D1	20c on 5c bl & brn	15	15
J41	D1	20c on 10c bl & brn	15	15
J42	D1	20c on 30c bl & brn	15	15
J43	D1	25c on 5c bl & brn	48	26
J44	D1	25c on 10c bl & brn	48	26
J45	D1	25c on 30c bl & brn	5.50	3.25
J46	D1	40c on 5c bl & brn	32	15
J47	D1	40c on 10c bl & brn	38	15
J48	D1	40c on 30c bl & brn	38	15
J49	D1	2 l on 5c bl & brn	14.00	14.00
J50	D1	2 l on 10c bl & brn	30.00	19.00
J51	D1	2 l on 30c bl & brn	25.00	16.00
		Nos. J37-J51 (15)	77.44	54.12

Nos. J19, J24-J25, J30, J34, J33, J22 Surcharged in Black   **Lire 1**

Perf. 14, 14½x14

1936-40   Wmk. 140

J52	D1	10c on 5c ('38)	55	55
J53	D1	25c on 30c ('38)	4.25	4.25
J54	D1	50c on 5c ('37)	4.25	4.00
J55	D1	1 l on 30c	13.00	3.25
J56	D1	1 l on 40c ('40)	4.25	3.00
J57	D1	1 l on 3 l ('37)	11.00	1.10
J58	D1	1 l on 25 l ('39)	27.50	6.75
J59	D1	2 l on 15 l ('38)	13.00	8.00
J60	D1	3 l on 20c ('40)	15.00	13.00
		Nos. J52-J60 (9)	92.80	43.90

D6   Coat of Arms — D7

1939   Typo.   *Perf. 14*

J61	D6	5c blue & brown	15	15

Nos. J61 and J36 Surcharged with New Values and Bars

1940-43

J62	D6	10c on 5c	38	38
J63	D6	50c on 5c	1.50	75
J64	D1	25 l on 50 l ('43)	1.75	1.75

Unwmk.

1945, June 7   Photo.   *Perf. 14*

J65	D7	5c dk green	15	15
J66	D7	10c orange brn	15	15
J67	D7	15c rose red	15	15
J68	D7	20c dp ultra	15	15
J69	D7	25c dk purple	15	15
J70	D7	30c rose lake	15	15
J71	D7	40c bister	15	15
J72	D7	50c slate blk	15	15
J73	D7	60c chestnut	15	15
J74	D7	1 l dp orange	15	15
J75	D7	2 l carmine	15	15
J76	D7	5 l dull violet	15	15
J77	D7	10 l dark blue	15	22
J78	D7	20 l dark green	4.50	4.00
J79	D7	25 l red orange	4.50	4.00
J80	D7	50 l dark brown	4.50	4.00
		Nos. J65-J80 (16)	15.45	14.02

PARCEL POST STAMPS

These stamps were used by affixing them to the way bill so that one half remained on it following the parcel, the other half staying on the receipt given the sender. Most used halves are right halves. Complete stamps were and are obtainable canceled, probably to order. Both unused and used values are for complete stamps.

PP1

Engraved, Typographed

1928, Nov. 22   Unwmk.   *Perf. 12*

Pairs are imperforate between

Q1	PP1	5c blk brn & bl	15	15
a.		Imperf.	12.00	
Q2	PP1	10c dk bl & bl	15	15
Q3	PP1	20c gray blk & bl	15	15
a.		Imperf.	12.00	
Q4	PP1	25c car & blue	15	15
Q5	PP1	30c ultra & blue	15	15
Q6	PP1	50c orange & bl	15	15
Q7	PP1	60c rose & blue	15	15
Q8	PP1	1 l violet & brn	15	15
a.		Imperf.	12.00	
Q9	PP1	2 l green & brn	24	24
Q10	PP1	3 l bister & brn	32	32
Q11	PP1	4 l gray & brn	42	42
Q12	PP1	10 l rose lilac & brn	85	85
Q13	PP1	12 l red brn & brn	3.25	3.25
Q14	PP1	15 l olive grn & brn	6.75	6.75
a.		Imperf.	12.00	
Q15	PP1	20 l brn vio & brn	7.25	7.25
		Nos. Q1-Q15 (15)	20.28	20.28

Halves Used

Q1-Q8		15
Q9-Q10		15
Q11		19
Q12		35

Q13		65
Q14		2.75
Q15		3.00

1945-46   Wmk. 140   *Perf. 14*

Pairs are perforated between

Q16	PP1	5c rose vio & red org	15	15
Q17	PP1	10c red org & blk	15	15
Q18	PP1	20c dark red & grn	15	15
Q19	PP1	25c yel & blk	15	15
Q20	PP1	30c red vio & org red	15	15
Q21	PP1	50c dull pur & blk	15	15
Q22	PP1	60c rose lake & blk	15	15
Q23	PP1	1 l brown & dp bl	15	15
Q24	PP1	2 l dk brn & dk bl	15	15
Q25	PP1	3 l olive brn & brn	15	15
Q26	PP1	4 l blue grn & brn	15	15
Q27	PP1	10 l bl blk & brt pur	15	15
Q28	PP1	12 l myr grn & dl bl	1.90	1.25
Q29	PP1	15 l green & purple	1.75	1.10
Q30	PP1	20 l rose lil & brn	1.25	85
Q31	PP1	25 l dp car & ultra ('46)	24.00	22.50
Q32	PP1	50 l yel & dp org ('46)	27.50	27.50
		Nos. Q16-Q32 (17)	58.20	55.00

Halves Used

Q16-Q27		15
Q28		15
Q29		15
Q30		15
Q31		25
Q32		50

Nos. Q32 and Q31 Surcharged with New Value and Wavy Lines in Black

1948-50

Q33	PP1	100 l on 50 l	35.00	37.50
		Half, used		1.00
Q34	PP1	200 l on 25 l ('50)	72.50	77.50
		Half, used		1.00

1953, Mar. 5   Wmk. 277   *Perf. 13½*

Pairs Perforated Between

Q35	PP1	10 l dk grn & rose lil	17.00	6.25
		Half, used		1.00
Q36	PP1	300 l purple & lake	110.00	110.00
		Half, used		1.00

1956   Wmk. 303   *Perf. 13½*

Q37	PP1	10 l gray & brt pur	35	30
		Half, used		15
Q38	PP1	50 l yel & dp org	1.10	1.00
		Half, used		15

No. Q38 Surcharged with New Value and Wavy Lines In Black

Q39	PP1	100 l on 50 l	1.25	1.10
		Half, used		25

> Catalogue values for unused stamps in this section, from this point to the end of the section, are for Never Hinged items.

1960-61

Q40	PP1	300 l violet & brn	55.00	55.00
		Half, used		50
Q41	PP1	500 l dk brn & car ('61)	3.25	3.00
		Half, used		15

1965-72   Wmk. 339   *Perf. 13½*

Pairs Perforated Between

Q42	PP1	10 l gray & brt pur	15	15
Q43	PP1	50 l yellow & red org	15	15
Q44	PP1	100 l on 50 l yel & red org	1.40	1.40
Q45	PP1	300 l violet & brown	45	45
Q46	PP1	500 l brn & red ('72)	8.25	8.25
Q47	PP1	1000 l bl grn & lt red brn ('67)	90	90
		Nos. Q42-Q47 (6)	11.30	11.30

Halves Used

Q42-Q43		15
Q44-Q45		15
Q46		20
Q47		45

SASENO

LOCATION — An island in the Adriatic Sea, lying at the entrance of Valona Bay, Albania

GOVT. — Former Italian possession

AREA — 2 sq. mi.

Italy occupied this Albanian islet in 1914, and returned it to Albania in 1947.

100 Centesimi = 1 Lira

> Used values in italics are for postally used stamps. CTO's or stamps with fake cancels sell for about the same as unused, hinged stamps.

Italian Stamps of 1901-22 Overprinted   **SASENO**

1923   Wmk. 140   *Perf. 14*

1	A48	10c claret	2.50	*8.25*
2	A48	15c slate	2.50	*8.25*
3	A50	20c brown orange	2.50	*8.25*
4	A49	25c blue	2.50	*8.25*
5	A49	30c yellow brown	2.50	*8.25*
6	A49	50c violet	2.50	*8.25*
7	A49	60c carmine	2.50	*8.25*
8	A46	1 l brown & green	2.50	*8.25*
a.		Double overprint	70.00	
		Nos. 1-8 (8)	20.00	

Superseded by postage stamps of Italy.

1996 Vol. 5 Number Changes

324 SAUDI ARABIA

SAUDI ARABIA

LOCATION — Southwestern Asia, on the Arabian Peninsula between the Red Sea and the Persian Gulf
GOVT. — Kingdom
AREA — 927,000 sq. mi.
POP. — 8,400,000 (est. 1984)
CAPITAL — Riyadh

In 1916 the Grand Sherif of Mecca declared the Sanjak of Hejaz independent of Turkish rule. In 1925, Ibn Saud, then Sultan of the Nejd, captured the Hejaz after a prolonged siege of Jedda, the last Hejaz stronghold.

The resulting Kingdom of the Hejaz and Nejd was renamed Saudi Arabia in 1932.

40 Paras = 1 Piaster = 1 Guerche (Garch, Qirsh)
11 Guerche = 1 Riyal (1928)
110 Guerche = 1 Sovereign (1931)
440 Guerche = 1 Sovereign (1952)
20 Piasters (Guerche) = 1 Riyal (1960)
100 Halalas = 1 Riyal (1976)

Catalogue values for unused stamps in this country are for Never Hinged items, beginning with Scott 178 in the regular postage section, Scott C1 in the airpost section, Scott J28 in the postage due section, Scott O7 in official section, and Scott RA6 in the postal tax section.

Watermarks

Wmk. 337- Crossed Swords and Palm Tree

Wmk. 361- Crossed Swords, Palm Tree and Arabic Inscription

HEJAZ

Sherifate of Mecca

Adapted from Carved Door Panels of Mosque El Salih Talay, Cairo — A1

Taken from Page of Koran in Mosque of El Sultan Barquq, Cairo — A2

Taken from Details of an Ancient Prayer Niche in the Mosque of El Amri at Qus in Upper Egypt — A3

		Perf. 10, 12		
1916, Oct.			**Unwmk.**	**Typo.**
L1	A1	¼pi green	45.00	35.00
L2	A2	½pi red	45.00	32.50
a.		Perf. 10	120.00	100.00
L3	A3	1pi blue	12.00	12.00
a.		Perf. 12	150.00	150.00
b.		Perf. 10x12		850.00

Exist imperf. Forged perf. exist.
See Nos. L5-L7, L10-L12. For overprints see Nos. L16-L18, L26-L28, L52-L54, L57-L59, L61-L66, L67, L70-L72, L77-L81, 37.

Central Design Adapted from a Koran Design for a Tomb. Background is from Stone Carving on Entrance Arch to the Ministry of Wakfs — A4

				Roulette 20
1916-17				
L4	A4	⅛pi orange ('17)	4.00	1.50
L5	A1	¼pi green	5.00	1.50
L6	A2	½pi red	6.00	1.50
L7	A3	1pi blue	6.00	1.50

See No. L9. For overprints and surcharge see Nos. L15a, L16c, L17b, L18d, L25, L51, L56, L69, 33.

Adapted from Stucco Work above Entrance to Cairo R. R. Station — A5

Adapted from First Page of the Koran of Sultan Farag — A6

				Serrate Roulette 13
1917				
L8	A5	1pa lilac brown	3.00	1.50
L9	A4	⅛pi orange	3.00	1.50
L10	A1	¼pi green	3.00	1.50
L11	A2	½pi red	3.00	1.50
L12	A3	1pi blue	3.00	1.50
L13	A6	2pi magenta	20.00	10.00
		Nos. L8-L13 (6)	35.00	17.50

Designs A1-A6 are inscribed "Hejaz Postage."
For overprints and surcharge see Nos. L14-L24, L29-L31, L55, L60, L66B, L73-L75, 32, 38.

Kingdom of the Hejaz
Stamps of 1917-18 Overprinted in Black, Red or Brown:

				Serrate Roulette 13
1921, Dec. 21				
L14	A5	1pa lilac brown	30.00	15.00
L15	A4	⅛pi orange	60.00	17.50
a.		Inverted overprint	100.00	
b.		Double overprint	200.00	
c.		Roulette 20	600.00	
d.		As "c," invtd. overprint		1,500.
L16	A1	¼pi green	12.00	6.00
a.		Inverted overprint	100.00	
b.		Double overprint	200.00	
c.		Roulette 20	600.00	
d.		As "c," invtd. overprint		
L17	A2	½pi red	15.00	7.50
a.		Inverted overprint	150.00	85.00
b.		Roulette 20	600.00	
L18	A3	1pi blue (R)	12.00	7.00
a.		Brown overprint	27.50	20.00
b.		Black overprint	35.00	30.00

c.		As "b." invtd. overprint	400.00	
d.		Roulette 20	700.00	
L19	A6	2pi magenta	17.50	10.00
		Nos. L14-L19 (6)	146.50	63.00

Nos. L15-L17, L18b and L19 exist with date (1340) omitted at left or right side.
Some values exist with gold overprint.
Forgeries of Nos. L14-L23 abound.

No. L14 With Additional Surcharge:

a   b

L22	A5(a)	½pi on 1pa	300.00	140.00
L23	A5(b)	1pi on 1pa	300.00	140.00

Stamps of 1917-18 Overprinted in Black

1922, Jan. 7				
L24	A5	1pa lilac brown	3.25	3.00
a.		Inverted overprint	150.00	
b.		Double overprint	100.00	
c.		Double ovpt., one inverted	200.00	
L25	A4	⅛pi orange	10.00	7.00
a.		Inverted overprint	100.00	
b.		Double ovpt., one inverted	200.00	
L26	A1	¼pi green	3.25	3.00
a.		Inverted overprint	100.00	
b.		Double ovpt., one inverted	200.00	
L27	A2	½pi red	2.50	2.00
a.		Inverted overprint	100.00	
b.		Double ovpt., one inverted	200.00	
L28	A3	1pi blue	2.50	90
a.		Double overprint	90.00	
b.		Inverted overprint	150.00	
L29	A6	2pi magenta	7.25	6.00
a.		Double overprint	150.00	

With Additional Surcharge of New Value

L30	A5(a)	½pi on 1pa lilac brn	22.50	15.00
L31	A5(b)	1pi on 1pa lilac brn	2.50	1.00
a.		Inverted surcharge	100.00	
b.		Double surcharge	90.00	
c.		Dbl. surch., one invtd., ovpt. invtd.		
		Nos. L24-L31 (8)	53.75	37.90

The 1921 and 1922 overprints read: "The Government of Hashemite Arabia, 1340."
The overprint on No. L28 in red is bogus.
Forgeries abound.

Types A7 and A8 are valued in fine condition.

Arms of Sherif of Mecca — A7

1922, Feb.			**Typo.**	**Perf. 11½**
L32	A7	⅛pi red brown	2.00	50
L34	A7	½pi red	2.00	50
L35	A7	1pi dark blue	2.00	50
L36	A7	1½pi violet	2.00	50
L37	A7	2pi orange	2.00	50
L38	A7	3pi olive brown	2.00	50
L39	A7	5pi olive green	2.00	60
		Nos. L32-L39 (7)	14.00	3.60

Values are for copies with perfs touching the design.
Numerous shades exist. Exist imperf.
Forgeries exist, usually perf. 11.
Reprints of Nos. L32, L35 exist; paper and shades differ.
See Nos. L48A-L49. For surcharges and overprints see Nos. L40-L48, L76, L82-L159, 7-20, 38A-48, 55A-58A, LJ11-LJ16, LJ26-LJ39, J1-J8, J10-J11, P1-P3, Jordan 64-72, 91, 103-120, J1-J17, O1.

Stamps of 1922 Surcharged with New Values in Arabic:

c   d

1923
L40	A7(c)	¼pi on ⅛pi org brn	35.00	5.00
a.		Double surcharge		
b.		Double inverted surcharge		
c.		Double surch., one invtd.		
L41	A7(d)	10pi on 5pi ol grn	30.00	10.00
a.		Double surch., one invtd.		
b.		Inverted surcharge		

Forgeries exist.

Caliphate Issue

Stamps of 1922 Overprinted in Gold

1924
L42	A7	⅛pi orange brown	3.50	
L43	A7	½pi red	3.50	
L44	A7	1pi dark blue	3.50	
L45	A7	1½pi violet	3.50	
L46	A7	2pi orange	3.50	
L47	A7	3pi olive brown	4.00	
L48	A7	5pi olive green	4.00	
		Nos. L42-L48 (7)	25.50	

Assumption of the Caliphate by King Hussein in Mar., 1924. The overprint reads "In commemoration of the Caliphate, Shaaban, 1342."
The overprint was typographed in black and dusted with "gold" powder while wet. It exists inverted on the 1pi, 2pi and 5pi. Inverted overprints on other values are forgeries.
The overprint is 18-20mm wide. The 1st setting of the ½p is 16mm.
Forgeries exist.
Nos. L43-L44, L46 exist with postage due overprint as on Nos. LJ11-LJ13.

Type of 1922 and

Arms of Sherif of Mecca — A8

1924				**Perf. 11½**
L48A	A7	¼pi yellow green	5.50	90
b.		Tête bêche pair	30.00	
L49	A7	3pi brown red	10.00	4.00
a.		3pi dull red	5.00	5.00
L50	A8	10pi vio & dk brn	5.00	4.00
a.		Center inverted	00.00	15.00
b.		Center omitted	75.00	
c.		10pi purple & sepia	5.00	4.00

Nos. L48A, L50, L50a exist imperf.
Reprints, official and unofficial, of Nos. L48A-L50 exist; paper and shades differ.
Forgeries exist, usually perf. 11.
For overprint see Nos. L76A, Jordan 121.

Jedda Issues
Stamps of 1916-17 Overprinted

The control overprints on Nos. L51-L159 read: "Hukumat al Hejaziyeh, 5 Rabi al'awwal 1343" (The Hejaz Government, October 4, 1924). This is the date of the accession of King Ali.
Counterfeits exist of all Jedda overprints.

Jedda issues were also used in Medina and Yambo. Used values for #L51-L186 and LJ17-LJ39 are for genuine cancels. Privately applied cancels read "Mekke" (bilingual or all Arabic), often with wrong dates as early as 1916. These are worth half the used values.

Red Overprint

1925, Jan.				**Roulette 20**
L51	A4	⅛pi orange	15.00	15.00
a.		Inverted overprint	100.00	
b.		Ovptd. on face and back	200.00	
L52	A1	¼pi green	15.00	15.00
a.		Inverted overprint	65.00	
b.		Double overprint	60.00	
c.		Double overprint, one invtd.	150.00	
L53	A2	½pi red	75.00	75.00
a.		Inverted overprint	165.00	
L54	A3	1pi blue	35.00	35.00
a.		Inverted overprint	150.00	

b. Double ovpt., one invtd. 140.00

Serrate Roulette 13

L55	A5	1pa lilac brown	14.00	14.00
a.		Inverted overprint	75.00	
b.		Double overprint	65.00	
c.		Ovptd. on face and back	200.00	
L56	A4	1/8pi orange	37.50	37.50
a.		Inverted overprint	90.00	
L57	A1	1/4pi green	22.50	22.50
a.		Pair, one without overprint	1,750.	
b.		Inverted overprint	50.00	
c.		Double ovpt., one inverted	300.00	
L58	A2	1/2pi red	30.00	30.00
a.		Inverted overprint	150.00	
L59	A3	1pi blue	35.00	35.00
a.		Inverted overprint	110.00	
L60	A6	2pi magenta	40.00	40.00
a.		Inverted overprint	150.00	

Gold Overprint
Roulette 20

L61	A1	1/4pi green	2,500.	2,500.

Serrate Roulette 13

L62	A1	1/4pi green	25.00	25.00
a.		Inverted overprint	110.00	

The overprint on No. L61 was typographed in red or blue (No. L62 only in red) and dusted with "gold" powder while wet.

Blue Overprint
Roulette 20

L63	A1	1/4pi green	25.00	25.00
a.		Inverted overprint	90.00	
b.		Ovptd. on face and back	90.00	
L64	A2	1/2pi red, invtd. ovpt.	90.00	90.00
a.		Upright overprint	150.00	

Serrate Roulette 13

L65	A1	1/4pi green	18.00	18.00
a.		Inverted overprint	75.00	
b.		Vertical overprint	1,000.	
L66	A2	1/2pi red	30.00	30.00
a.		Inverted overprint	100.00	
L66B	A6	2pi mag., invtd. ovpt.	1,500.	

Blue overprint on Nos. L4, L8, L9 are bogus.

Same Overprint in Blue on Provisional Stamps of 1922
Overprinted on No. L17

L67	A2	1/2pi red	2,750.

Overprinted on Nos. L24-L29

L68	A5	1pa lilac brn	175.00	175.00
L69	A4	1/8pi orange	2,000.	2,000.
a.		Inverted overprint		
L70	A1	1/4pi green	72.50	72.50
a.		Inverted overprint	800.00	
L71	A2	1/2pi red	95.00	95.00
a.		Inverted overprint	900.00	
L72	A3	1pi blue	125.00	125.00
L73	A6	2pi magenta	175.00	175.00
a.		Inverted overprint	1,500.	

Same Overprint on Nos. L30 and L31

L74	A5(a)	1/2pi on 1pa	100.00	100.00
L75	A5(b)	1/2pi on 1pa	85.00	85.00
a.		Inverted overprint	650.00	

Same Overprint in Blue Vertically, Reading Up or Down, on Stamps of 1922-24
Perf. 11 1/2

L76	A7	1/2pi red	1,000.	1,000.
L76A	A8	10pi vio & dk brn	2,000.	2,000.

Nos. L5, L10 Overprinted in Blue or Red

Roulette 20

L77	A1	1/4pi green (Bl)	200.00	200.00
L78	A1	1/4pi green (R)	275.00	275.00

Serrate Roulette 13

L79	A1	1/4pi green (Bl)	100.00	100.00
L80	A1	1/4pi green (R)	65.00	65.00

Nos. L77-L80 exist with overprint reading up or down. It reads up in illustration.

Nos. L10, L32-L39, L48A, L49a, L50 Overprinted

Serrate Roulette 13
Red Overprint (vertical)

L81	A1	1/4pi green	1,000.

Overprint on No. L81 also exists horizontal and inverted.

Perf. 11 1/2
Blue Overprint

L82	A7	1/8pi red brown	6.00	6.00
a.		Inverted overprint	50.00	
L83	A7	1/2pi red	8.00	8.00
a.		Double overprint	75.00	
b.		Inverted overprint	50.00	50.00
c.		Double ovpt., one invtd.	75.00	
d.		Overprint reading up		
L84	A7	1pi dark blue		
a.		Inverted overprint	50.00	
L85	A7	1 1/2pi violet	12.00	12.00
a.		Inverted overprint	50.00	
L86	A7	2pi orange	12.00	12.00
a.		Double ovpt., one invtd.	75.00	
b.		Inverted overprint	50.00	
c.		Double overprint	75.00	
L87	A7	3pi olive brown	10.00	10.00
a.		Inverted overprint	50.00	
b.		Double ovpt., one invtd.	75.00	
c.		Overprint reading up	175.00	
d.		Dbl. ovpt., both invtd.	100.00	
L88	A7	3pi dull red	12.00	12.00
a.		Inverted overprint	50.00	
b.		Double ovpt., one invtd.	75.00	
L89	A7	5pi olive green	12.00	12.00
a.		Inverted overprint	50.00	

Several values exist in pairs, one without overprint.

Black Overprint

L90	A7	1/8pi red brown		
L91	A7	1/2pi red	5.00	5.00
a.		Inverted overprint	65.00	
L92	A7	1pi dark blue		
L93	A7	1 1/2pi violet	13.00	13.00
a.		Inverted overprint	75.00	
L94	A7	2pi orange	8.00	8.00
a.		Inverted overprint	50.00	
L95	A7	3pi olive brown	6.00	6.00
a.		Inverted overprint	75.00	75.00
L96	A7	3pi dull red	8.00	8.00
a.		Inverted overprint	50.00	
L97	A7	5pi olive green	10.00	10.00
a.		Inverted overprint	50.00	

Red Overprint

L98	A7	1/8pi red brn, invtd.		
L99	A7	1/4pi yellow grn	17.50	17.50
a.		Tête bêche pair	30.00	
b.		Inverted overprint	50.00	
L100	A7	1/2pi red		
a.		Inverted overprint		
L101	A7	1pi dark blue	9.00	9.00
a.		Inverted overprint	50.00	
b.		Double ovpt., one invtd.	35.00	
L102	A7	1 1/2pi violet	5.00	5.00
a.		Inverted overprint	50.00	
L103	A7	2pi orange	13.00	13.00
a.		Inverted overprint	50.00	
b.		Overprint reading up	175.00	
L104	A7	3pi olive brown	13.00	13.00
a.		Inverted overprint	50.00	
L105	A7	3pi dull red, invtd.		
L106	A7	5pi olive green	8.00	8.00
a.		Inverted overprint	50.00	
b.		Overprint reading up	100.00	
c.		Center inverted	100.00	
L107	A8	10pi vio & dk brn	17.50	17.50
a.		Inverted overprint	50.00	
b.		Center inverted	100.00	
c.		As "b," invtd. ovpt.	150.00	

Gold Overprint

L108	A7	1/8pi red brown	30.00	30.00
L109	A7	1/2pi red	30.00	30.00
L110	A7	1pi dark blue	30.00	30.00
L111	A7	1 1/2pi violet	125.00	125.00
L112	A7	2pi orange	100.00	100.00
L113	A7	3pi olive brown	37.50	37.50
L114	A7	3pi dull red	110.00	110.00
L115	A7	5pi olive green	95.00	95.00

Inverted overprints are forgeries.

Same Overprint on Nos. L42-L48
Blue Overprint

L116	A7	1/8pi red brown	47.50	47.50
a.		Double ovpt., one invtd.	300.00	
L117	A7	1/2pi red	90.00	90.00
L118	A7	1pi dark blue	60.00	60.00
L119	A7	1 1/2pi violet	72.50	72.50
a.		Overprint reading up		
L120	A7	2pi orange	300.00	300.00
a.		Inverted overprint	475.00	
L121	A7	3pi olive brown	125.00	125.00
a.		Inverted overprint	200.00	
L122	A7	5pi olive green	42.50	42.50
a.		Inverted overprint	225.00	

Black Overprint

L123	A7	1/8pi red brown	47.50	47.50
L125	A7	1 1/2pi violet	150.00	150.00
a.		Inverted overprint	250.00	
L127	A7	3pi olive brown	125.00	125.00
a.		Inverted overprint	250.00	
L128	A7	5pi olive green	150.00	150.00
a.		Inverted overprint	250.00	

Red Overprint

L129	A7	1pi dark blue	100.00	100.00
L130	A7	1 1/2pi violet	125.00	125.00
L131	A7	2pi orange	100.00	100.00

Overprints on stamps or in colors other than those listed are forgeries.

Stamps of 1922-24 Surcharged

a

and Handstamped

b

1pi   10pi

1925		**Litho.**	**Perf. 11 1/2**	
L135	A7	1/4pi on 1/4pi on 1/8pi red brn	52.50	52.50
b.		1pi on 1/4pi on 1/8pi red brown		
L136	A7	1/4pi on 1/4pi on 1/2pi red	32.50	32.50
c.		1pi on 1/4pi on 1/2pi	60.00	60.00
L138	A7	1pi on 1pi on 2pi orange	32.50	32.50
a.		1/4pi on 1/4pi on 2pi org	100.00	
b.		10pi on 1pi on 2pi org	50.00	
c.		1pi on 1pi on 2pi org	100.00	
L139	A7	1pi on 1pi on 3pi ol brn	24.00	24.00
L140	A7	1pi on 1pi on 3pi dl red	37.50	37.50
b.		1/4pi on 1pi on 3pi dl red		
L141	A7	10pi on 10pi on 5pi ol grn	18.00	18.00
b.		10pi on 10 pi on 5 pi		
		Nos. L135-L141 (6)	197.00	197.00

The printed surcharge (a) reads "The Hejaz Government. October 4, 1924," with new denomination in third line. This surcharge alone was used for the first issue (Nos. L135a-L141a). The new denomination was so small and indistinct that its equivalent in larger characters was soon added by handstamp (b) at bottom of each stamp for the second issue (Nos. L135-L141).

The handstamped surcharge (b) is found double, inverted, etc. It is also known in dark violet.

Without Handstamp "b"

L135a	A7	1/4pi on 1/4pi on 1/8pi red brn	100.00
L136b	A7	1/4pi on 1/4pi on 1/2pi red	100.00
L138e	A7	1pi on 1pi on 2pi orange	100.00
L139a	A7	1pi on 1pi on 3pi olive brn	100.00
L140a	A7	1pi on 1pi on 3pi dull red	100.00
L141a	A7	10pi on 10pi on 5pi olive grn	100.00
		Nos. L135a-L141a (6)	600.00

Stamps of 1922-24 Surcharged

Black Surcharge

L142	A7	1/4pi on 1/2pi red	8.00	8.00
a.		Inverted surcharge	40.00	
L143	A7	1/4pi on 1/2pi red	8.00	8.00
a.		Inverted surcharge	40.00	
L144	A7	1pi on 1/2pi red	8.00	8.00
a.		Inverted surcharge	25.00	
L145	A7	1pi on 1 1/2pi violet	8.00	8.00
a.		Inverted surcharge	35.00	
L146	A7	1pi on 2pi orange	8.00	8.00
a.		"10pi"	85.00	
b.		Inverted surcharge	40.00	
L147	A7	1pi on 3pi olive brn	8.00	8.00
a.		"10pi"	75.00	
b.		Inverted surcharge		
L148	A7	10pi on 5pi olive grn	15.00	15.00
a.		Inverted surcharge	65.00	

Blue Surcharge

L149	A7	1/8pi on 1/2pi red	12.00	12.00
a.		Inverted surcharge	65.00	
L150	A7	1/4pi on 1/2pi red	12.00	12.00
a.		Inverted surcharge	50.00	
L151	A7	1pi on 1/2pi red	12.00	12.00
a.		Inverted surcharge	50.00	
b.		Double surcharge		
L152	A7	1pi on 1 1/2pi violet	12.00	12.00
a.		Inverted surcharge	65.00	
b.		Double surcharge		
L153	A7	1pi on 2pi orange	12.00	12.00
a.		"10pi"	70.00	
b.		Inverted surcharge	65.00	
L154	A7	1pi on 3pi olive brn	25.00	25.00
a.		"10pi"	85.00	
b.		Inverted surcharge	70.00	

L155	A7	10pi on 5pi olive grn	27.50	27.50
a.		Inverted surcharge	60.00	

Red Surcharge

L156	A7	10pi on 1 1/2pi violet	25.00	25.00
a.		Inverted surcharge	80.00	
L157	A7	10pi on 2pi orange	25.00	25.00
a.		"10pi"	80.00	
b.		Inverted surcharge	80.00	
L158	A7	10pi on 3pi olive brn	25.00	25.00
a.		"10pi"	100.00	
b.		Inverted surcharge	80.00	
L159	A7	10pi on 5pi olive grn	25.00	25.00
a.		Inverted surcharge	80.00	

The "10pi" surcharge is found inverted on Nos. L146a, L147a. The existence of genuine inverted "10pi" surcharges on Nos. L153a, L154a, L157a and L158a is in doubt.

King Ali Issue

A9

A10

A11

A12

1925, May-June			**Perf. 11 1/2**	
		Black Overprint		
L160	A9	1/8pi chocolate	1.65	1.65
L161	A9	1/4pi ultra	1.65	1.65
L162	A9	1/2pi car rose	1.65	1.65
L163	A10	1pi yellow green	2.00	2.00
L164	A10	1 1/2pi orange	2.00	2.00
L165	A10	2pi blue	2.50	2.50
L166	A11	3pi dark green	2.50	2.50
L167	A11	5pi orange brn	2.50	2.50
L168	A12	10pi red & green	5.00	5.00
a.		Center inverted	75.00	

Red Overprint

L169	A9	1/8pi chocolate	3.00	3.00
L170	A9	1/4pi ultra	1.75	1.75
L171	A10	1pi yellow green	2.25	2.25
L172	A10	1 1/2pi orange	2.25	2.25
L173	A10	2pi deep blue	2.75	2.75
L174	A11	3pi dark green	3.00	3.00
a.		Horiz. pair, imperf. vert.		
L175	A11	5pi orange brown	3.00	3.00
L176	A12	10pi red & green	6.00	6.00

Blue Overprint

L177	A9	1/8pi chocolate	2.00	2.00
L179	A9	1/2pi car rose	2.00	2.00
L180	A10	1pi yellow green	2.00	2.00
L181	A10	1 1/2pi orange	2.00	2.00
L182	A11	3pi dark green	2.00	2.00
L183	A11	5pi orange brn	6.00	6.00
L184	A12	10pi red & green	8.00	8.00
L185	A12	10pi red & org	275.00	275.00

Without Overprint

L186	A12	10pi red & green	7.50	7.50
a.		Dbl. impression of center	100.00	

The overprint in the tablets on Nos. L160-L185 reads: "5 Rabi al'awwal, 1343" (Oct. 5, 1924), the date of the accession of King Ali.

The tablet overprints vary slightly in size. Each is found reading upward or downward and at either side of the stamp. These control overprints were first applied in Jedda by the government press. They were later made from new plates by the stamp printer in Cairo. In the Jedda overprint, the bar over the "0" figure extends to the left. Some values exist with 13m or 15mm instead of 18mm between tablets. They sell for more. The lines of the Cairo overprinting are generally wider, but more lightly printed, usually appearing slightly grayish and the bar is at center right. The Cairo overprints are believed not to have been placed in use.

Imperforates exist.

Nos. L160-L168 are known with the overprints spaced as on type D3 and aligned horizontally.

Copies of these stamps (perforated or imperforate) without the overprint, except No. L186 were not regularly issued and not available for postage.

No. L185 without overprint is a proof. Two sheets were overprinted by error and were put on sale with the ordinary stamps.

The ¼pi with blue overprint is bogus.

No. L186 in other colors are color trials.

For overprints see #58B-58C, Jordan 122-129.

NEJDI ADMINISTRATION OF HEJAZ

Handstamped in Blue, Red, Black or Violet

The overprint reads: "1343. Barid al Sultanat at Nejdia" (1925. Post of the Sultanate of Nejd).

The overprints on this and succeeding issues are handstamped and, as usual, are found double, inverted, etc. These variations are scarce.

1925, Mar.-Apr.   Unwmk.   Perf. 12

On Stamp of Turkey, 1915, With Crescent and Star in Red

1	A22	5pa ocher (Bl)	37.50	30.00
2	A22	5pa ocher (R)	25.00	22.50
3	A22	5pa ocher (Bk)	30.00	25.00
4	A22	5pa ocher (V)	25.00	20.00

On Stamp of Turkey, 1913

5	A28	10pa green (Bl)	22.50	18.00
6	A28	10pa green (R)	17.50	14.00

On Stamps of Hejaz, 1922-24
Perf. 11½

7	A7	⅛pi red brn (R)	25.00	25.00
8	A7	⅛pi red brn (Bk)	35.00	35.00
9	A7	⅛pi red brn (V)	25.00	25.00
10	A7	⅛pi car (R)	30.00	30.00
11	A7	⅛pi car (Bk)	35.00	35.00
12	A7	⅛pi car (V)	27.50	27.50
13	A7	½pi red (Bl)	22.50	22.50
14	A7	½pi red (V)	17.50	17.50
15	A7	1½pi vio (R)	25.00	25.00
16	A7	2pi yel buff (R)	60.00	60.00
a.		2pi orange (R)	40.00	
17	A7	2pi yel buff (V)	60.00	60.00
a.		2pi orange (V)	35.00	35.00
18	A7	3pi brn red (Bl)	30.00	30.00
19	A7	3pi brn red (R)	22.50	22.50
20	A7	3pi brn red (V)	25.00	25.00

Many Hejaz stamps of the 1922 type were especially printed for this and following issues. The reimpressions are usually more clearly printed, in lighter shades than the 1922 stamps, and some are in new colors.

Counterfeits exist.

Arabic Inscriptions
R1   R2

On Hejaz Bill Stamp

22	R1	1pi violet (R)	15.00	15.00

On Hejaz Notarial Stamps

23	R2	1pi violet (R)	20.00	20.00
24	R2	2pi blue (R)	30.00	30.00
25	R2	2pi blue (V)	27.50	27.50

For overprint see No. 49.

Locomotive — R3

On Hejaz Railway Tax Stamps

26	R3	1pi blue (R)	37.50	10.00
27	R3	2pi ocher (R)	47.50	15.00
28	R3	2pi ocher (V)	37.50	10.00
29	R3	3pi lilac (R)	37.50	22.50
		Nos. 1-20,22-29 (28)	850.00	724.50

There are two types of basic stamps.
For overprints and surcharges see Nos. 34, 50-54, 55, 59-68, J12-J15.

Pilgrimage Issue

Various Stamps Handstamp Surcharged in Blue and Red in Types "a" and "b" and with Tablets with New Values

a   b

Surcharge "a" reads: "Tezkar al Hajj al Awwal Fi 'ahd al Sultanat al Nejdia, 1343" (Commemorating the first pilgrimage under the Nejdi Sultanate, 1925).

"b" reads: "Al Arba" (Wednesday.)

1925, July 1   Perf. 12
On Stamps of Turkey, 1913

30	A28	1pi on 10pa grn (Bl & R)	75.00	60.00
31	A30	5pi on 1pi bl (Bl & R)	75.00	60.00

On Stamps of Hejaz, 1917-18
Serrate Roulette 13

32	A5	2pi on 1pa lil brn (R & Bl)	95.00	75.00
33	A4	4pi on ¼pi org (R & Bl)	350.00	350.00

On Hejaz Railway Tax Stamp
Perf. 11½

34	R3	3pi lilac (Bl & R)	75.00	40.00
		Nos. 30-34 (5)	670.00	585.00

No. 30 with handstamp "a" in black was a favor item.

Handstamped in Blue, Red, Black or Violet

This overprint has practically the same meaning as that described over No. 1. The Mohammedan year (1343) is omitted.

This handstamp is said to be in private hands at this time. Extreme caution is advised before buying rare items.

1925, July-Aug.   Perf. 12
On Stamp of Turkey, 1915, with Crescent and Star in Red

35	A22	5pa ocher (Bl)	25.00	25.00

On Stamps of Turkey, 1913

36	A28	10pa green (R)	20.00	20.00
a.		Black overprint	80.00	

On Stamps of Hejaz, 1922 (Nos. L28-L29)
Serrate Roulette 13

37	A3	1pi blue (R)	60.00	75.00
38	A6	2pi magenta (Bl)	60.00	75.00

On Stamps of Hejaz, 1922-24
Perf. 11½

38A	A7	⅛pi red brn (Bk)	4,750.	
38B	A7	⅛pi red brn (Bl)	4,000.	
39	A7	½pi red (Bl)	10.00	10.00
a.		Imperf., pair	25.00	25.00
39B	A7	½pi red (Bk)	20.00	20.00
c.		Imperf., pair	40.00	40.00
40	A7	1pi gray vio (R)	30.00	30.00
a.		1pi black violet (R)	45.00	
41	A7	1½pi dk red (R)	30.00	30.00
a.		1½pi brick red (Bk)	50.00	
42	A7	2pi yel buff (Bl)	50.00	50.00
a.		2pi orange (Bl)	60.00	60.00
43	A7	3pi deep vio (Bl)	55.00	55.00
44	A7	3pi brown red (Bl)	30.00	30.00
45	A7	5pi scarlet (Bl)	37.50	37.50
		Nos. 35-38,39-45 (12)	427.50	457.50

Overprint on Nos. 38A, 39B, 39C is blue-black.
See note above No. 35.

With Additional Surcharge of New Value Typo. in Black:

c   d

e

Color in parenthesis is that of overprint on basic stamp.

46	A7(c)	1pi on ½pi (Bl)	10.00	2.00
a.		Imperf., pair	30.00	
b.		Ovpt. & surch. inverted		
47	A7(d)	1½pi on ½pi (Bl)	15.00	8.00
a.		Imperf., pair	30.00	
b.		Black overprint	20.00	
48	A7(e)	2pi on 3pi (Bl)	15.00	15.00

Several variations in type settings of "c," "d" and "e" exist, including inverted letters and values.

On Hejaz Notarial Stamp

49	R2	2pi blue (Bk)	20.00	20.00

On Hejaz Railway Tax Stamps

50	R3	1pi blue (R)	25.00	25.00
51	R3	1pi blue (Bk)	30.00	10.00
52	R3	2pi ocher (Bl)	27.50	10.00
53	R3	3pi lilac (Bl)	22.50	22.50
54	R3	5pi green (Bl)	20.00	20.00

Hejaz Railway Tax Stamp Handstamped in Black

This overprint reads: "Al Saudia. - Al Sultanat al Nejdia." (The Saudi Sultanate of Nejd.)

1925-26

55	R3	1pi blue	250.00	

On Nos. L34, L36-L37, L41

55A	A7	½ pi red	375.00	
56	A7	1½pi violet	375.00	
a.		Violet overprint	375.00	
57	A7	2pi orange	375.00	
57A	A7	10pi on 5pi ol grn	375.00	

On Nos. L95 and L97

Color in parentheses is that of rectangular overprint on basic stamp

58	A7	3pi olive brn (Bk)	375.00	
58A	A7	5pi olive grn (Bk)	375.00	

On Nos. L162-L163, L173
Perf. 11½

58B	A9	½pi car rose (Bk)	375.00	
58C	A10	1pi yellow grn (Bk)	210.00	
58D	A10	2pi blue (Bk)	375.00	

Nos. 55-58D were provisionally issued at Medina after its capitulation.

Specialists question the status of unused examples of Nos. 55-58D.

This overprint exists on Nos. L160-L161, L164-L172, L174-L175, L180-L183. These 17 are known as bogus items, but may exist genuine.

No. L161 (¼pi) is known with a similar but larger overprint. It is a forgery.

Lithographed overprints are forgeries.

The illustrated overprint is not genuine.

Medina Issue

Hejaz Railway Tax Stamps Handstamped

and Handstamp Surcharged in Various Colors

The large overprint reads: "The Nejdi Posts - 1344 - Commemorating Medina, the Illustrious". The tablet shows the new value.

1925

59	R3	1pi on 10pi vio (Bk & V)	50.00	60.00
60	R3	2pi on 50pi lt bl (R & Bl)	50.00	60.00
61	R3	3pi on 100pi red brn (Bl & Bk)	50.00	60.00
62	R3	4pi on 500pi dull red (Bl & Bk)	50.00	60.00
63	R3	5pi on 1000pi dp red (Bl & Bk)	50.00	60.00
		Nos. 59-63 (5)	250.00	300.00

Jedda Issue

Hejaz Railway Tax Stamps Handstamped and Tablet with New Value in Various Colors

This handstamp reads: "Commemorating Jedda - 1344 - The Nejdi Posts."

1925

64	R3	1pi on 10pi vio (Bk & Bl)	60.00	60.00
65	R3	2pi on 50pi lt bl (R & Bk)	60.00	60.00
66	R3	3pi on 100pi red brn (R & Bl)	60.00	60.00
67	R3	4pi on 500pi dl red (Bk & Bl)	60.00	60.00
68	R3	5pi on 1000pi dp red (Bk & Bl)	60.00	60.00
		Nos. 64-68 (5)	300.00	300.00

Nos. 59-63 and 64-68 were prepared in anticipation of the surrender of Medina and Jedda.

Kingdom of Hejaz-Nejd

Arabic Inscriptions and Value — A1

A2

Inscriptions in upper tablets: "Barid al Hejaz wa Nejd" (Posts of the Hejaz and Nejd)

1926, Feb.   Typo.   Unwmk.   Perf. 11

69	A1	¼pi violet	12.50	9.25
70	A1	½pi gray	12.50	9.25
71	A1	1pi deep blue	16.00	11.00
72	A2	2pi blue green	13.00	9.25
73	A2	3pi carmine	16.00	10.00
74	A2	5pi maroon	8.25	6.25
		Nos. 69-74 (6)	78.25	54.75

Nos. 69-71, 74 exist imperf. Value, each $32.50.
Used values are for favor cancels.

1926, Mar.   Perf. 11

75	A1	¼pi orange	6.25	3.50
76	A1	½pi blue green	2.50	1.50
77	A1	1pi carmine	1.90	1.50
78	A2	2pi violet	2.50	1.50
79	A2	3pi dark blue	2.50	1.50
80	A2	5pi lt brown	6.25	3.50
a.		5pi olive brown		
		Nos. 75-80 (6)	21.90	12.75

Nos. 75-80 also exist with perf. 14, 14x11, 11x14 and imperf. All of these sell for 10 times the values quoted.

Counterfeits of types A1 and A2 are perf. 11½. They exist with and without overprints.

Types A1 and A2 in colors other than listed are proofs.

Pan-Islamic Congress Issue
Stamps of 1926 Handstamped

1926   Perf. 11

92	A1	¼pi orange	5.25	3.00
93	A1	½pi blue green	5.25	3.00
94	A1	1pi carmine	5.25	3.00
95	A2	2pi violet	5.25	3.00
96	A2	3pi dark blue	5.25	3.00
97	A2	5pi light brown	5.25	3.00
		Nos. 92-97 (6)	31.50	18.00

The overprint reads: "al Mootamar al Islami 20 Zilkada, Sanat 1344". (The Islamic Congress, June 1, 1926.)

See counterfeit note after No. 80.

Tughra of King Abdul
Aziz — A3

1926-27   Typo.   Perf. 11½
98 A3	⅛pi ocher	3.50	50
99 A3	¼pi gray green	4.00	1.25
100 A3	½pi dull red	4.00	1.25
101 A3	1pi deep violet	4.00	1.25
102 A3	1½pi gray blue	12.00	2.00
103 A3	3pi olive green	10.00	4.00
104 A3	5pi brown orange	20.00	5.00
105 A3	10pi dark brown	60.00	6.00
	Nos. 98-105 (8)	117.50	21.25

Inscription at top reads: "Al Hukumat al Arabia" (The Arabian Government). Inscription below tughra reads: "Barid al Hejaz wa Nejd" (Post of the Hejaz and Nejd).

Stamps of 1926-27
Handstamped in Black
or Red

1927
107 A3	⅛pi ocher	12.00	5.00
108 A3	¼pi gray grn	12.00	5.00
109 A3	½pi dull red	12.00	5.00
110 A3	1pi deep violet	12.00	5.00
111 A3	1½pi gray bl (R)	12.00	5.00
112 A3	3pi olive green	12.00	5.00
113 A3	5pi brown orange	12.00	5.00
114 A3	10pi dark brown	12.00	5.00
	Nos. 107-114 (8)	96.00	40.00

The overprint reads: "In commemoration of the Kingdom of Nejd and Dependencies, 25th Rajab 1345."

Turkey No. 258
Surcharged in Violet

1927 (?)   Perf. 12
115 A28 1g on 10pa green

The authenticity of this stamp has been questioned. Similar surcharges of 6g and 20g were made in red, but were not known to have been issued.

A4   A5

1929-30   Typo.   Perf. 11½
117 A4	1¾g gray blue	20.00	2.50
119 A4	20g violet	25.00	4.50
120 A4	30g green	40.00	12.50

1930   Perf. 11, 11½
125 A5	½g rose	15.00	3.00
126 A5	1½g violet	15.00	2.00
127 A5	1¾g ultra	15.00	2.50
128 A5	3½g emerald	15.00	4.00

Perf. 11
129 A5	5g black brown	25.00	6.00
	Nos. 125-129 (5)	85.00	17.50

Anniversary of King Ibn Saud's accession to the throne of the Hejaz, January 8, 1926.

A6   A7

1931-32   Perf. 11½
130 A6	⅛g ocher ('32)	14.00	2.50
131 A6	¼g blue green	14.00	2.00
133 A6	1¾g ultra	18.00	2.50

1932   Perf. 11½
135 A7	¼g blue green	6.00	2.00
a.	Perf 11		
136 A7	½g scarlet	17.50	3.00
a.	Perf 11		
137 A7	2¼g ultra	42.50	5.00
a.	Perf 11		

Kingdom of Saudi Arabia

A8

1934, Jan.   Perf. 11½, Imperf.
138 A8	¼g yellow green	8.00	8.00
139 A8	½g red	8.00	8.00
140 A8	1½g light blue	15.00	15.00
141 A8	3g blue green	15.00	15.00
142 A8	3½g ultra	27.50	6.00
143 A8	5g yellow	35.00	30.00
144 A8	10g red orange	67.50	
145 A8	20g bright violet	85.00	
146 A8	¼s claret	165.00	
147 A8	30g dull violet	100.00	
148 A8	½s chocolate	375.00	
149 A8	1s violet brown	750.00	
	Nos. 138-149 (12)	1,651.	

Proclamation of Emir Saud as Heir Apparent of Arabia. Perf. and imperf. stamps were issued in equal quantities.

Tughra of King
Abdul Aziz — A9

1934-57   Perf. 11, 11½
159 A9	⅛g yellow	3.50	40
160 A9	¼g yellow grn	3.50	40
161 A9	½g rose red ('43)	2.75	15
a.	½g dark carmine	13.00	1.50
162 A9	⅞g lt blue ('56)	4.50	50
163 A9	1g blue green	3.50	40
164 A9	2g olive grn ('57)	7.25	2.00
a.	2g olive bister ('57)	27.50	8.00
165 A9	2⅞g violet ('57)	4.50	50
166 A9	3g ultra ('38)	4.50	20
a.	3g light blue	22.50	2.00
167 A9	3½g lt ultra	18.00	2.00
168 A9	5g orange	4.50	50
169 A9	10g violet	15.00	1.50
170 A9	20g purple brn	22.50	1.00
a.	20g purple black	22.50	2.50
171 A9	100g red vio ('42)	72.50	4.50
172 A9	200g vio brn ('42)	90.00	6.00
	Nos. 159-172 (14)	256.50	20.05

The ½g has two types differing in position of the tughra.
No. 162 measures 31x22mm. No. 164 30½x21½mm. No. 165, 30½x22mm. No. 166 30x21mm. No. 171, 31x22mm. No. 172, 30½x21½mm. Rest of set, 29x20½mm. Grayish paper was used in 1946-49 printings.
No. 168 exists with pin-perf 6.
For overprint see No. J24.

Yanbu Harbor near
Radwa — A10

1945   Typo.   Perf. 11½
173 A10	½g brt carmine	6.50	25
174 A10	3g lt ultra	8.25	1.00
175 A10	5g purple	25.00	1.25
176 A10	10g dk brown vio	55.00	3.00

Meeting of King Abdul Aziz and King Farouk of Egypt at Jebal Radwa, Saudi Arabia, Jan. 24, 1945.

Map of Saudi Arabia   Type II (Flag
Type I (Flag   inscriptions
inscriptions   scratched out)
intact) — A11

1946   Unwmk.   Perf. 11½
177 A11	½g magenta (II)	17.50	1.00
a.	Type I	60.00	1.00
b.	Type I, perf. 11	50.00	10.00
c.	Type II, perf. 11	75.00	

Return of King Ibn Saud from Egypt.
This stamp was required on all mail during Jan.-July. It may be a postal tax stamp.

> Catalogue values for unused stamps in this section, from this point to the end of the section, are for Never Hinged items.

Arms of Saudi
Arabia and
Afghanistan
A12

1950, Mar.   Perf. 11
178 A12	½g carmine	7.50	1.00
179 A12	3g violet blue	12.50	1.00

Visit of Zahir Shah of Afghanistan, March 1950. One 3g in each sheet inscribed POSTFS, value $50.

Old City Walls,
Riyadh — A13

1950
Center in Red Brown
180 A13	½g magenta	4.00	15
181 A13	1g lt blue	7.50	15
182 A13	3g violet	11.00	50
183 A13	5g vermilion	24.00	1.00
184 A13	10g green	45.00	2.50
a.	Singular "guerche" in Arabic	325.00	40.00
	Nos. 180-184 (5)	91.50	4.30

50th lunar anniversary of King Ibn Saud's capture of Riyadh, Jan. 16, 1902.
No. 184a: On the 3g, 5g and 10g the currency is expressed in the plural in both French (grouche) and Arabic. One stamp in each sheet of 20 (4x5), position 11, of the 10g shows the Arabic characters in the singular form of "guerche," as on the ½g and 1g.

Arms of Saudi
Arabia and
Jordan — A14

1951, Nov.   Perf. 11
185 A14	½g carmine	5.25	1.00
a.	"BOYAUME"	225.00	
186 A14	3g violet blue	16.00	1.50
a.	"BOYAUME"	225.00	

Visit of King Tallal of Jordan, Nov. 1951.

Bedouins and
Train — A15

SAUDI ARABIA
RARE AND CLASSIC STAMPS, POSTAL HISTORY, PROOFS. BUYING, SELLING, APPRAISALS.
For the Best Services in Classic Stamps and Postal History contact the RECOGNIZED LEADERS IN THE FIELD. Excellent stock of classic material for most countries of the World also available.
THE CLASSIC COLLECTOR
LIANE & SERGIO SISMONDO
Ph. 315-422-2331, Fax 315-422-2956
10035 Carousel Center Drive
Syracuse, NY 13290-0001
CANADIAN OFFICE: P.O. Box 6277, Station J, Ottawa, Canada K2A 1T4. Ph. 613-722-1621, Fax: 613-728-7305

Saudi Arabia & Middle East
Hundreds of specialized, rare and unusual lots
Varieties, Errors, Proofs, Essays & Covers
in our Mail Sale Catalogs
Serious Collectors, whether Buying or Selling, must see this *extensively illustrated* catalog.
Write, call or fax for a **Free Sample**
Filatco
The Middle East Specialists
P.O. Box 1461, Dept. K, Appleton, WI 54913 U.S.A.
Tel: 414-735-0701   Fax: 414-735-9453

1952, June   Engr.   Perf. 12

187	A15	½q redsh brown	4.75	75
188	A15	1q deep green	4.75	75
189	A15	3q violet	9.50	50
190	A15	10q rose pink	19.00	3.50
191	A15	20q blue	40.00	7.50
		Nos. 187-191 (5)	78.00	13.00

Inaugural trip over the Saudi Government Railroad between Riyadh and Dammam.

Saudi Arabia Arms and Lebanon Emblem — A16

1953, Feb.   Typo.   Perf. 11

192	A16	½g carmine	5.25	1.00
193	A16	3g violet blue	10.50	1.50

Visit of President Camille Chamoun of Lebanon.

Arms of Saudi Arabia and Emblem of Pakistan — A17

1953, Mar.

194	A17	½g dark carmine	6.75	1.00
195	A17	3g violet blue	14.00	1.50

Visit of Gov.-Gen. Ghulam Mohammed of Pakistan.

Saudi Arabia

Free Price List

Classic to Modern Sets & Singles

We Buy!

Saudi Arabia and all Worldwide • Better Stamps • Collections • Rarities • Covers

For buying or selling Saudi Arabia and all other U.S. & Worldwide call

1-800-9-4-STAMP

(1-800-947-8267)

VISA MasterCard DISCOVER AMERICAN EXPRESS

Henry Gitner Philatelists, Inc.

P.O. Box 3077-S
Middletown, NY 10940
Tel: 914-343-5151
Fax: 914-343-0068

Philately – The Quiet Excitement!

Arms of Saudi Arabia and Jordan — A18

Globe — A18a

1953, July   Unwmk.

196	A18	½g carmine	5.00	1.00
a.		"GOERCHE"	125.00	
197	A18	3g violet blue	15.00	1.50

Visit of King Hussein of Jordan, July, 1953.

1955, July   Litho.

198	A18a	½g emerald	2.75	50
199	A18a	3g violet	7.50	1.00
200	A18a	4g orange	11.00	2.50

Issued to commemorate the founding of the Arab Postal Union, July 1, 1954.

Ministry of Communications Building, Riyadh — A19

1960, Apr. 12   Photo.   Perf. 13

201	A19	2p bright blue	75	15
202	A19	5p deep claret	1.50	20
203	A19	10p dark green	3.75	50

Arab Postal Union Conference, at Riyadh, Apr. 11. Imperfs. exist.

Arab League Center, Cairo A20

1960, Mar. 22   Perf. 13x13½

204	A20	2p dull grn & blk	2.00	20

Opening of the Arab League Center and the Arab Postal Museum in Cairo. Exists imperf.

Radio Tower and Waves A21

1960, June 4

205	A21	2p red & black	2.00	25
206	A21	5p brown blk & mar	3.00	30
207	A21	10p bluish blk & ultra	5.00	70

1st international radio station in Saudi Arabia. Imperfs. exist.

Map of Palestine, Refugee Camp and WRY Emblem — A22

1960, Oct. 30   Litho.   Perf. 13

208	A22	2p dark blue	40	15
209	A22	8p lilac	40	15
210	A22	10p green	1.25	20
		Set value		40

World Refugee Year, July 1, 1959-June 30, 1960. Imperfs. exist.

Wadi Hanifa Dam, near Riyadh — A23   Gas-Oil Separating Plant, Buqqa — A24

Type I (Saud Cartouche) (Illustrated over No. 286)

1960-62   Unwmk.   Photo.   Perf. 14
Size: 27½x22mm

211	A23	½p bis brn & org	1.40	15
212	A23	1p ol bis & pur	1.40	15
213	A23	2p blue & sepia	1.40	15
214	A23	3p sepia & blue	1.40	15
215	A23	4p sepia & ocher	1.40	15
216	A23	5p blk & dk violet	1.40	15
217	A23	6p brn blk & car rose	1.40	20
a.		6p black & carmine rose	1.65	35
		('62)		
218	A23	7p red & gray ol	1.40	15
219	A23	8p dk bl & brn blk	1.40	30
220	A23	9p org brn & scar	1.40	30
c.		9p yel brn & metallic red	1.65	50
221	A23	10p emer grn & mar	1.40	20
		('62)		
222	A23	10p blue green & maroon	1.65	35
223	A23	20p brown & green	2.00	75
224	A23	50p black & brown	4.00	25
225	A23	75p brown & gray	22.50	2.00
226	A23	100p dk bl & grn bl	60.00	2.25
		200p lilac & green	55.00	2.50
			85.00	6.50
		Nos. 211-226 (16)	242.15	15.80

1960-61

227	A24	½p maroon & org	1.25	15
228	A24	1p blue & red org	1.25	15
229	A24	2p vermilion & blue	1.25	15
230	A24	3p lilac & brt grn	1.25	15
231	A24	4p yel grn & lilac	1.25	15
232	A24	5p dk gray & brn red	1.25	15
233	A24	6p brn org & dk vio	1.25	15
234	A24	7p vio & dull grn	1.25	15
235	A24	8p blue grn & gray	1.25	20
236	A24	9p ultra & sepia	3.50	20
237	A24	10p dk blue & rose	1.90	35
238	A24	20p org brn & blk	7.00	50
239	A24	50p red & brn grn	20.00	1.50
240	A24	75p red & blk brn	30.00	3.00
241	A24	100p dk bl & red brn	47.50	2.75
242	A24	200p dk gray & ol grn	80.00	6.50
		Nos. 227-242 (16)	201.15	16.20

Nearly all of Nos. 211-242 exist imperf; probably not regularly issued.
See Nos. 258-273, 286-341, 393-450, 461-483.

Dammam Port — A25

Wmk. 337
1961, Aug. 16   Litho.   Perf. 13

243	A25	3p lilac	1.75	20
244	A25	6p light blue	2.50	30
245	A25	8p dark green	4.25	40

Expansion of the port of Dammam. Imperf min. sheets of 4 were for presentation purposes and have wmk. sideways.

Globe, Radio and Telegraph A26

Arab League Building, Cairo — A27

Malaria Eradication Emblem — A28

Perf. 13x13½
1961, Aug. 7   Photo.   Unwmk.

246	A26	3p dull purple	1.50	15
247	A26	6p gray black	2.50	30
248	A26	8p brown	4.00	50

Arab Union of Telecommunications. Imperfs. exist.

1962, Apr. 22   Wmk. 337   Perf. 13

249	A27	3p olive green	1.25	20
250	A27	6p carmine rose	2.50	30
251	A27	8p slate blue	3.75	40

Arab League Week, Mar. 22-28.

Imperforate or missing-color varieties of Nos. 249-285 and 344-353 were not regularly issued, except No. 255a.

1962, May 7   Litho.   Wmk. 337

252	A28	3p red org & blue	85	15
253	A28	6p emerald & Prus bl	1.25	25
254	A28	8p black & lil rose	1.90	40
a.		Souv. sheet of 3, #252-254, imperf.	15.00	15.00

WHO drive to eradicate malaria.
Nos. 252-254 are known unofficially overprinted with new dates only or with "AIR MAIL" and two plane silhouettes.
A 4p exists as an essay.

Koran — A29

1963, Mar. 12   Wmk. 337   Perf. 11

255	A29	2½p lilac rose & pink	1.00	15
256	A29	7½p blue & pale grn	2.00	35
257	A29	9½p green & gray	3.00	40

First anniversary of the Islamic Institute, Medina. A 3p exists as an essay. Copies of the 2½p exist with virtually all the pink background omitted. No copies are known with the pink completely omitted.

Dam Type of 1960 Redrawn
Type I (Saud Cartouche)

Perf. 13½x13
1963-65   Wmk. 337   Litho.
Size: 28½x23mm

258	A23	½p bis brn & org	10.00	75

Nos. 258, 264-265 are widely spaced in the sheet, producing large margins.

Perf. 14
Photo.
Size: 27½x22mm

259	A23	½p bis brn & org ('65)	15.00	1.50
260	A23	3p sepia & blue	6.00	60
261	A23	4p sepia & ocher ('64)	8.00	80
262	A23	5p black & dk vio	8.00	80
263	A23	20p dk carmine & grn	15.00	1.50
		Nos. 258-263 (6)	62.00	5.95

A 1p was prepared but not issued. It is known only imperf.

Gas-Oil Plant Type of 1960 Redrawn
Type I (Saud Cartouche)

Perf. 13½x13
1963-65   Wmk. 337   Litho.
Size: 28½x23mm

264	A24	½p maroon & orange	9.25	1.00
265	A24	1p blue & red org ('64)	4.25	30

Photo.
Perf. 14
Size: 27¹/₂x22mm

266	A24	¹/₂p mar & org ('64)	7.00	50
267	A24	1p blue & red org	5.75	30
268	A24	3p lilac & brt grn	14.00	1.00
269	A24	4p yel grn & lilac	8.25	50
270	A24	5p dk gray & brn red	8.25	50
271	A24	6p brn org & dk vio ('65)	12.00	70
272	A24	8p dull grn & blk	20.00	1.25
273	A24	9p blue & sepia	20.00	1.50
		Nos. 264-273 (10)	108.75	7.55

The 3p, 4p and 6p exist imperf.

Hands Holding Wheat Emblem A30

1963, Mar. 21   **Litho.**   *Perf. 11*

274	A30	2¹/₂p lilac rose & rose	1.25	15
275	A30	7¹/₂p brt lilac & pink	1.25	30
276	A30	9p red brn & lt blue	2.50	35

FAO "Freedom from Hunger" campaign. The 3p imperf in various colors are essays.

Jet over Dhahran Airport — A31   Flame — A32

1963, July 27   **Litho.**   *Perf. 13*

277	A31	1p blue gray & ocher	1.25	15
278	A31	3¹/₂p ultra & emer	2.50	20
279	A31	6p emerald & rose	4.25	15
a.		"Thahran" for "Dharan" in Arabic	6.00	
280	A31	7¹/₂p lilac rose & lt bl	4.25	30
281	A31	9¹/₂p ver & dull vio	6.00	40
		Nos. 277-281 (5)	18.25	1.30

Opening of the US-financed terminal of the Dhahran Airport and inauguration of international jet service.

On No. 279a the misspelling consists of an omitted dot over character near top left in one horiz. row of five.

1964, Apr.   **Wmk. 337**   *Perf. 13x13¹/₂*

282	A32	3p lil, pink & Prus bl	3.25	15
283	A32	6p yel grn, lt bl & Prus bl	4.25	25
284	A32	9p brn, buff & Prus bl	8.50	40

15th anniv. of the signing of the Universal Declaration of Human Rights.

The 3p in other colors is an essay.

King Faisal and Arms of Saudi Arabia A33

1964, Nov.   **Litho.**   *Perf. 13*

285	A33	4p dk blue & emerald	4.50	15

Issued to commemorate the installation of Prince Faisal ibn Abdul Aziz as King, Nov. 2, 1964.

King Saud's Cartouche — Type I   King Faisal's Cartouche — Type II

Redrawn Dam Type of 1960
Type I (Saud Cartouche)

1965-70   **Litho.**   **Unwmk.**   *Perf. 14*
Size: 27x22mm

286	A23	1p olive bis & pur	20.00	1.00
287	A23	2p dk blue & sep	4.00	25
288	A23	3p sepia & blue	4.00	30
289	A23	4p sepia & ocher	7.00	30
290	A23	5p black & dk vio	5.00	30
291	A23	6p black & car rose	12.00	60
292	A23	7p brown & gray	12.00	30
293	A23	8p blue & gray	65.00	5.00
294	A23	9p org brn & scar	60.00	5.00
295	A23	10p blue grn & mar	65.00	3.00
296	A23	11p red & yel grn	5.25	2.00
297	A23	12p orange & dk bl	5.25	30
298	A23	13p dk olive & rose	5.25	40
299	A23	14p org brn & yel grn	5.25	40
300	A23	15p sepia & gray grn	5.25	2.00
301	A23	16p dk red & dl vio	6.75	45
302	A23	17p rose lil & dk bl	6.75	2.25
303	A23	18p green & brt bl	6.75	45
304	A23	19p black & bister	9.00	50
305	A23	20p brown & green	11.00	1.00
306	A23	23p mar & lilac	9.00	2.00
307	A23	24p ver & blue	9.00	60
308	A23	26p olive & yel	11.00	75
309	A23	27p ultra & red brn	11.00	75
310	A23	31p gray & dull bl	11.00	80
311	A23	33p ol grn & lilac	11.00	80
312	A23	100p dk bl & grnsh bl	325.00	50.00
313	A23	200p dull lilac & grn	325.00	50.00
		Nos. 286-313 (28)	1,032.	131.50

A 50p exists but was never placed in use.

Issue years: 1966, 2p, 4p, 10p-20p, 1968, 6p-9p. 1970, 100p-200p.

Redrawn Gas-Oil Plant Type of 1960
Type I (Saud Cartouche)

1964-70   **Litho.**   **Unwmk.**
Size: 27x22mm

314	A24	1p blue & red org	8.00	20
315	A24	2p vermilion & bl	12.00	20
316	A24	3p lilac & brt grn	5.00	15
317	A24	4p yel grn & lilac	7.25	20
318	A24	5p dl gray vio & dk red brn	26.00	2.00
319	A24	6p brn org & dk vio	55.00	5.00
320	A24	7p vio & dull grn	30.00	2.00
321	A24	8p blue grn & gray	6.75	30
322	A24	9p ultra & sepia	14.00	30
323	A24	10p dk blue & rose	375.00	35.00
324	A24	11p olive & orange	4.50	30
325	A24	12p bister & green	4.50	30
326	A24	13p rose red & dk bl	4.50	40
327	A24	14p vio & lt brown	6.00	40
328	A24	15p rose red & sep	6.75	50
329	A24	16p green & rose red	9.00	50
330	A24	17p car rose & red brn	14.00	1.50
331	A24	18p gray & ultra	9.00	60
332	A24	19p brown & yellow	9.00	60
333	A24	20p dull org & dk gray	30.00	2.00
334	A24	23p orange & car	8.00	70
335	A24	24p emer & org yel	9.00	80
336	A24	26p lilac & red brn	12.00	80
337	A24	27p ver & dk gray	12.00	80
338	A24	31p dull grn & car	21.00	1.50
339	A24	33p red brn & gray	19.00	1.50
340	A24	50p red brn & dull grn	350.00	50.00
341	A24	200p dk gray & ol gray	350.00	50.00
		Nos. 314-341 (28)	1,417.	159.05

A 100p exists but was never placed in use.

Issue years: 1965, 4p, 8p, 9p, 23p-33p. 1966, 1p, 2p, 5p, 11p-14p, 16p-20p. 1967, 15p. 1968, 6p, 7p. 1969, 50p. 1970, 200p. Others, 1964.

Holy Ka'aba, Mecca — A34

1965, Apr. 17   **Wmk. 337**   *Perf. 13*

344	A34	4p salmon & blk	3.50	20
345	A34	6p brt pink & blk	5.50	25
346	A34	10p yel grn & blk	7.75	40

Mecca Conf. of the Moslem World League.

Arms of Saudi Arabia and Tunisia A35

1965, Apr.   **Litho.**

347	A35	4p car rose & sil	3.00	20
348	A35	8p red lilac & sil	3.75	35
349	A35	10p ultra & sil	5.50	40

Issued to commemorate the visit of Pres. Habib Bourguiba of Tunisia, Feb. 22-26.

Highway, Hejaz Mountains — A36

1965, June 2   **Wmk. 337**   *Perf. 13*

350	A36	2p red & blk	1.75	30
351	A36	4p blue & blk	2.75	40
352	A36	6p lilac & blk	3.75	50
353	A36	8p brt green & blk	5.50	60

Opening of highway from Mecca to Tayif.

ICY Emblem A37

1965, Nov. 13   **Unwmk.**   *Perf. 13*

354	A37	1p yellow & dk brn	1.50	15
355	A37	2p orange & ol grn	1.50	15
356	A37	3p lt blue & gray	1.50	15
357	A37	4p orange & dk sl grn	1.50	20
358	A37	10p orange & magenta	4.00	50
		Nos. 354-358 (5)	10.00	
		Set value		95

International Cooperation Year, 1965.

ITU Emblem, Old and New Communication Equipment — A38

1965, Dec. 22   **Litho.**   *Perf. 13*

359	A38	3p blue & blk	2.25	15
360	A38	4p lilac & dk grn	2.25	15
361	A38	8p emerald & dk brn	2.25	35
362	A38	10p dull org & dk grn	2.25	40

Centenary of the ITU.

Library Aflame and Lamp A39

1966, Jan.   **Litho.**   *Perf. 12x12¹/₂*

363	A39	1p orange	1.50	15
364	A39	2p dark red	1.50	15
365	A39	3p red violet	2.25	15
366	A39	4p violet	3.00	20
367	A39	5p lilac rose	5.25	35
368	A39	6p vermilion	8.75	50
		Nos. 363-368 (6)	22.25	1.50

Burning of the Library of Algiers, June 2, 1962. Nos. 363-368 were withdrawn from sale Jan. 26, 1966, due to incorrect Arabic inscriptions. Later some values were inadvertently again placed in use.

Arab Postal Union Emblem — A40   Dagger in Map of Palestine — A41

1966, Mar. 15   **Litho.**   *Perf. 14*

369	A40	3p dull pur & ol	1.10	15
370	A40	4p dp blue & ol	1.10	15
371	A40	6p maroon & ol	4.50	25
372	A40	7p dp green & ol	4.50	35

10th anniversary (in 1964) of the Arab Postal Union. Printed in sheets of two panes, so horizontal gutter pairs exist.

1966, Mar. 19   **Litho.**   *Perf. 13*

373	A41	2p yel grn & blk	1.50	15
374	A41	4p lt brown & blk	3.00	15
375	A41	6p dull blue & blk	4.75	25
376	A41	8p ocher & blk	6.50	35

Deir Yassin massacre, Apr. 9, 1948.

Emblems of World Boy Scout Conference and Saudi Arabian Scout Association A42

1966, Mar. 23   **Unwmk.**

377	A42	4p yel, blk, grn & gray	5.00	50
378	A42	8p yel, blk, org & lt bl	5.00	50
379	A42	10p yel, blk, sal & bl	10.00	75

Arab League Rover Moot (Boy Scout Jamboree).

WHO Headquarters, Geneva, and Flag — A43

1966, May   **Litho.**   *Perf. 13*

380	A43	4p aqua & multi	1.25	15
381	A43	6p yel brn & multi	2.50	25
382	A43	10p pink & multi	5.00	40

Opening of the WHO Headquarters, Geneva.

UNESCO Emblem — A44

1966, Sept.   **Unwmk.**   *Perf. 12*

383	A44	1p apple grn & multi	1.40	15
384	A44	2p dull org & multi	1.40	15
385	A44	3p lilac rose & multi	1.90	15
386	A44	4p pale green & multi	1.90	15
387	A44	10p gray & multi	2.75	40
		Nos. 383-387 (5)	9.35	
		Set value		80

20th anniv. of UNESCO.

Radio Tower, Telephone and Map of Arab Countries — A45

1966, Nov. 7   Litho.   Perf. 12½
Design in Black, Carmine & Yellow

388 A45	1p vio blue	1.75	15
389 A45	2p bluish lilac	1.75	15
390 A45	4p rose lilac	3.50	15
391 A45	6p lt olive grn	3.50	30
392 A45	7p gray green	4.50	40
	Nos. 388-392 (5)	15.00	1.15

Issued to publicize the 8th Congress of the Arab Telecommunications Union, Riyadh.

Redrawn Dam Type of 1960
Type II (Faisal Cartouche)
(Illustrated over No. 286)

1966-76   Litho. Unwmk.   Perf. 14
Size: 27x22mm

393 A23	1p ol bis & pur	175.00	25.00
394 A23	2p dk blue & sep	21.00	1.65
395 A23	3p blk & dk bl	12.00	90
396 A23	4p sepia & ocher	17.00	45
397 A23	5p blk & dk vio	45.00	8.25
398 A23	6p blk & car rose	35.00	7.50
399 A23	7p sepia & gray	20.00	90
400 A23	8p dk blue & gray	12.00	50
401 A23	9p org brn & scar	8.25	90
402 A23	10p blue grn & mar	17.00	1.50
403 A23	11p red & yel grn	12.00	1.50
404 A23	12p orange & dk bl	7.25	1.50
405 A23	13p blk & rose	24.00	1.50
406 A23	14p org brn & yel grn	21.00	1.50
407 A23	15p sep & gray grn	21.00	2.00
408 A23	16p dk red & dl vio	30.00	3.50
409 A23	17p rose lil & dk bl	35.00	2.00
410 A23	18p green & brt bl	25.00	2.75
411 A23	19p black & bister	8.00	90
412 A23	20p brown & grn	80.00	2.50
413 A23	23p maroon & lil	300.00	5.00
414 A23	24p ver & blue	57.50	6.00
415 A23	26p olive & yel	9.25	80
416 A23	27p ultra & red brn	8.50	80
417 A23	33p ol grn & lilac	47.50	2.50
419 A23	50p black & brown	190.00	40.00
420 A23	100p dk bl & grnsh bl	300.00	50.00
421 A23	200p dull lilac & grn	300.00	80.00
	Nos. 393-421 (28)	1,838.	253.40

A 31p has been reported.

Issue years: 1966, 1p. 1967, 2p, 10p. 1968, 3p, 4p, 6p, 7p, 20p. 1969, 5p, 8p. 1970, 9p, 23p. 1972, 12p, 15p, 16p. 1973, 11p. 1974, 17p, 50p-200p. 1975, 13p, 14p, 19p, 24p-33p. 1976, 18p.

Redrawn Gas-Oil Plant Type of 1960
Type II (Faisal Cartouche)

1966-78   Unwmk.
Size: 27x22mm

422 A24	1p bl & red org	40.00	3.00
423 A24	2p ver & dull bl	7.75	30
424 A24	3p lilac & brt grn	15.00	60
425 A24	4p grn & dull lil	9.00	30
426 A24	5p dl gray vio & dk red brn	42.50	2.00
427 A24	6p brn org & dull pur	26.00	4.00
428 A24	7p vio & dull grn	35.00	30
429 A24	8p bl grn & grnsh gray	6.00	30
430 A24	9p ultra & sep	5.00	30
431 A24	10p dk blue & rose	5.00	60
432 A24	11p olive & orange	80.00	8.00
433 A24	12p bister & grn	5.00	80
434 A24	13p rose red & dk bl	47.50	30
435 A24	14p vio & lt brn	45.00	2.50
436 A24	15p car & sepia	15.00	70
437 A24	16p grn & rose red	15.00	80
438 A24	17p car rose & red brn	11.00	60
439 A24	18p gray & ultra	15.00	1.65
440 A24	19p brown & yellow	18.00	1.65
441 A24	20p brn org & gray	13.00	1.65
442 A24	23p orange & car	30.00	2.00
443 A24	24p emer & org yel	10.00	80
444 A24	26p lilac & red brn	200.00	
445 A24	27p ver & dk gray	12.00	4.00
446 A24	31p green & rose car	12.00	80
447 A24	33p brown & gray	22.50	1.25
448 A24	50p red brn & dl grn	375.00	150.00
449 A24	100p dk bl & red brn	325.00	45.00
450 A24	200p dk gray & ol gray	400.00	62.50
	Nos. 422-450 (29)	1,870.	

Issue years: 1967, 20p. 1968, 3p, 5p-9p, 15p, 16p. 1969, 100p. 1970, 11p, 14p, 200p. 1973,

13p, 18p, 24p. 1974, 19p, 50p. 1975, 12p, 17p, 27p-33p. 1978, 26p. Others, 1966.

Emblem of Saudi Arabian Scout Association — A46

Meteorological Instruments and WMO Emblem — A47

1967, Mar. 28   Litho.   Perf. 13½
Emblem in Green, Red, Yellow & Black

451 A46	1p dk blue & blk	2.25	15
452 A46	2p blue grn & blk	2.25	15
453 A46	3p lt blue & blk	3.25	15
454 A46	4p rose brn & blk	4.25	15
455 A46	6p brown & blk	9.50	50
	Nos. 451-455 (5)	21.50	1.10

2nd Arabic League Rover Moot, Mecca, March 13-28.

1967, July   Unwmk.   Perf. 13

456 A47	1p brt magenta	1.40	15
457 A47	2p violet	2.50	15
458 A47	3p olive	2.50	15
459 A47	4p blue green	8.00	15
460 A47	10p brown	11.00	35
	Nos. 456-460 (5)	25.40	
	Set value		70

Issued for World Meteorological Day.

Redrawn Dam Type of 1960
Type II (Faisal Cartouche)

1968-76   Wmk. 361   Litho.   Perf. 14

461 A23	1p ol bis & pur ('71)	1,250.	300.00
462 A23	2p dk blue & sep	32.50	2.00
463 A23	3p blk & dk bl	22.50	1.00
464 A23	4p sepia & ocher	200.00	32.50
465 A23	5p blk & dk vio	27.50	2.00
466 A23	6p blk & car rose	26.00	1.50
467 A23	7p sepia & gray	40.00	3.00
468 A23	8p dk bl & gray	20.00	1.00
469 A23	9p org brn & ver	72.50	7.00
470 A23	10p bl grn & mar	50.00	4.00
471 A23	11p red & yel grn	60.00	6.00
472 A23	12p org & sl bl	55.00	5.00
473 A23	13p black & rose	75.00	7.50

Issue years: 1968, 2p, 10p. 1969, 3p. 1970, 8p. 1971, 1p, 5p. 1972, 6p, 7p, 11p, 12p. 1973, 4p. 1974, 13p. 1976, 9p.

Redrawn Gas-Oil Plant Type of 1960
Type II (Faisal Cartouche)

1968-76   Perf. 14

474 A24	1p bl & red org	10.50	1.00
475 A24	2p ver & dl bl	6.25	50
476 A24	4p grn & dl lil	80.00	8.00
477 A24	5p dk brn & red brn ('73)	22.50	1.50
478 A24	6p brn org & dk vio ('73)	27.50	2.00
479 A24	9p dk bl & sep ('76)	45.00	4.00
480 A24	10p dk bl & rose	9.50	70
481 A24	11p ol & org ('72)	32.50	2.00
482 A24	12p bis & grn ('72)	35.00	3.00
483 A24	23p org & car ('74)	60.00	3.00
	Nos. 474-483 (10)	328.75	25.70

Map Showing Dammam to Jedda Road, and Dates — A48

Wmk. 361
1968, Aug.   Litho.   Perf. 14

484 A48	1p yellow & multi	1.50	15
485 A48	2p orange & multi	1.50	15
486 A48	3p multicolored	3.00	15

487 A48	4p multicolored	3.00	15
488 A48	10p multicolored	9.00	40
	Nos. 484-488 (5)	18.00	
	Set value		75

Issued to commemorate the completion of the trans-Saudi Arabia highway in 1967.

Several positions in the sheet have the dots representing Dammam and Riyadh omitted. Most had the dots added by pen before issuance.

Prophet's Mosque, Medina — A49

New Arcade, Mecca Mosque — A50

Perf. 13½x14
1968-76   Litho.   Wmk. 361

489 A49	1p org & grn, wmk. 337 ('70)	3.00	30
490 A49	2p red brn & grn ('72)	4.75	40
a.	Wmk. 337 ('71)	7.00	30
b.	As "a," redrawn	200.00	
491 A49	3p vio & grn ('72)	4.25	40
a.	Wmk. 337 ('70)	3.00	30
492 A49	4p ocher & green	4.75	40
a.	Redrawn, wmk. 361 ('72)	6.00	50
b.	Redrawn, wmk. 337		
493 A49	5p dp lil rose & grn, wmk. 337 ('71)	10.00	1.00
494 A49	6p blk & grn ('73)	12.00	1.00
a.	6p gray & green ('76)	20.00	1.00
495 A49	10p brown & green	15.00	1.00
a.	Redrawn		
496 A49	20p dk brn & grn ('70)	20.00	2.00
a.	Redrawn		
497 A49	50p sepia & grn ('75)	20.00	6.50
498 A49	100p dk bl & grn ('75)	25.00	5.00
499 A49	200p red & grn ('75)	25.00	7.00
	Nos. 489-499 (11)	143.75	25.00

See redrawn note following No. 526. No. 494 exists imperf.

1968-69

500 A50	3p dp org & gray ('69)	400.00	100.00
501 A50	4p green & gray	5.75	50
502 A50	10p magenta & gray	9.25	1.00

Expansion of Prophet's Mosque — A51

Madayin Saleh — A52

1968-76

503 A51	1p org & grn ('72)	5.00	25
504 A51	2p brn & grn ('72)	8.00	25
505 A51	3p blk & grn ('69)	7.00	40
b.	3p gray & green ('76)	20.00	2.00
c.	As No. 505, redrawn		
506 A51	4p org & grn ('70)	7.00	50
507 A51	5p red & grn ('76)	7.50	75
508 A51	6p Prus bl & grn ('72)	10.00	1.00
509 A51	8p rose red & grn ('76)	25.00	2.00
510 A51	10p brn red & grn ('76)	9.25	60
b.	10p orange & green ('76)	20.00	1.00
511 A51	20p vio & grn ('74)	20.00	2.50
	Nos. 503-511 (9)	98.75	8.25

Wmk. 337

503a A51	1p	5.50	40
504a A51	2p ('70)	7.50	35
b.	As "a," redrawn	40.00	
505a A51	3p ('71)	8.00	80
d.	As "a," redrawn		
506a A51	4p ('72)	5.00	50
		10.00	
507a A51	5p ('72)	5.00	50
508a A51	6p ('72)	7.00	60
510a A51	10p ('72)	12.00	70
c.	As "a," redrawn		
511a A51	20p ('72)	9.25	80

See redrawn note following No. 526.

1968-75

512 A52	2p ultra & bis brn ('70)	22.50	4.00
513 A52	4p dk & lt brown	5.50	80
514 A52	7p org & lt brn ('75)	55.00	10.00
515 A52	10p sl grn & lt brn	14.00	2.00
516 A52	20p lil rose & brn ('71)	15.00	1.50

Arabian Stallion — A53

Camels and Oil Derrick — A54

517 A53	4p mag & org brn	5.50	80
518 A53	10p blk & org brn	16.00	3.00
519 A53	14p bl & ocher ('71)	25.00	6.00
520 A53	20p ol grn & ocher ('71)	10.50	2.00

1969-71

521 A54	4p dk pur & redsh brn ('71)	20.00	4.00
522 A54	10p ultra & hn brn	14.00	3.00

Holy Ka'aba, Mecca — A55

Numeral & "Postage" on Gray Background, 8p on White

1969-75

523 A55	4p dp grn & blk ('70)	8.50	80
a.	Redrawn, value corner white ('74)	17.50	3.00
524 A55	6p dp lil rose & blk ('71)	5.00	40
a.	Value corner white ('74)	25.00	3.00
525 A55	8p red & blk ('75)	30.00	3.00
526 A55	10p org & blk ('69)	17.50	1.50
a.	Redrawn, value corner white ('74)	15.00	2.00
b.	Redrawn ('75)		

On the original stamps the knob-shaped Arabic letter, located under the two square dots in the middle of the top panel, has a small central dot. The dot often is missing.

On the redrawn stamps the dot has been enlarged into a conspicuous irregular oval. The 3p also has a period added after the value and the 4p has the "4" under the "T" instead of the "S." There are other small differences.

Rover Moot Badge — A56

Perf. 13½x14
1969, Feb. 19   Litho.   Wmk. 337

607 A56	1p orange & multi	1.65	15
608 A56	4p dull purple & multi	5.00	20
609 A56	10p orange brn & multi	14.00	60

3rd Arab League Rover Moot, Mecca, Feb. 19-Mar. 3.

Traffic Light and Intersection — A57

1969, Feb.   Wmk. 361   Perf. 13½

610 A57	3p dl bl, red & brt bl grn	2.25	15
a.	3p dull blue, red & gray green	6.75	1.00
611 A57	4p org brn, red & gray grn	2.25	15
612 A57	10p dl pur, red & gray grn	4.50	50

Issued for Traffic Day.

WHO Emblem — A58

1969, Oct. 20   Wmk. 337   Perf. 14
613 A58 4p lt bl, vio bl & yel   7.50 15

20th anniv. (in 1968) of WHO.

Islamic Conference Emblem A59

1970, Mar. 23   Litho.   Wmk. 361
614 A59 4p blue & black   3.00 15
615 A59 10p yellow bis & blk   4.75 45

Islamic Conference of Foreign Ministers, Jedda, March 1970.

Open Book and Satellite Earth Receiving Station — A60

Perf. 14x13½
1970, Aug. 1   Litho.   Wmk. 337
616 A60 4p violet bl & multi   4.75 15
617 A60 10p green & multi   9.50 50

World Telecommunications Day.

Steel Rolling Mill, Jedda — A61

1970, Oct. 26   Wmk. 337   Perf. 13½
618 A61 3p yellow org & multi   2.75 15
619 A61 4p violet & multi   4.25 15
620 A61 10p brt green & multi   7.25 50

Inauguration of 1st steel mill in Saudi Arabia.

Rover Moot Emblem — A62

1971, Feb.   Litho.   Perf. 14
621 A62 10p brt blue & multi   8.75 75

4th Arab League Rover Moot, 1971.

Telecommunications Symbol — A63

1971, May 17   Wmk. 337   Perf. 14
622 A63 4p blue & blk   1.90 15
623 A63 10p lilac & blk   4.00 40

World Telecommunications Day.

University Minaret — A64

Arab League Emblem — A65

Wmk. 337; Wmk. 361 (4p)
1971, Aug.   Litho.   Perf. 14
624 A64 3p brt green & black   1.40 15
625 A64 4p brown & black   2.75 15
626 A64 10p blue & black   5.75 50

King Abdul Aziz National University.

1971, Nov.   Wmk. 337   Perf. 13½
627 A65 10p multicolored   5.25 40

Arab League Week.

Education Year Emblem — A66

OPEC Emblem — A67

1971, Nov.   Litho.
628 A66 4p apple grn & brn red   5.25 15

International Education Year 1970.

1971, Dec.   Perf. 14
629 A67 4p light blue   6.50 15

10th anniversary of OPEC (Organization of Petroleum Exporting Countries).

Globe — A68

1972, Aug.   Wmk. 361   Perf. 14
630 A68 4p multicolored   6.00 15

4th World Telecommunications Day.

Telephone — A69

1972, Oct.   Wmk. 337, 361 (5p)
631 A69 1p red, blk & grn   1.90 15
632 A69 4p dk grn, blk & grn   1.90 15
633 A69 5p lil, blk & grn   3.75 20
634 A69 10p tan, blk & grn   7.50 50

Inauguration of automatic telephone system (1969).

Writing Hand — A70

1972, Sept. 8   Litho.   Wmk. 361
635 A70 10p multicolored   8.75 35

World Literacy Day, Sept. 8.

Holy Ka'aba and Grand Mosque, Mecca — A71

Designs (Rover Moot Emblem and): 4p, Prophet's Mosque, Medina. 10p, Plains of Arafat.

1973
636 A71 4p lt blue & multi   3.25 20
637 A71 6p lilac & multi   6.50 30
638 A71 10p salmon & multi   10.00 60

5th Arab League Rover Moot.

Globe and Map of Palestine A71a

1973   Litho.   Wmk. 361   Perf. 14
639 A71a 4p black, yel & red   3.25 15
640 A71a 10p blue, yel & red   6.75 40

Palestine Week.

Leaf and Emblem — A72

1973
641 A72 4p yellow & multi   7.00 25

International Hydrological Decade 1965-74.

Arab Postal Union Emblem — A73

1973, Dec.   Litho.   Perf. 14
642 A73 4p sepia & multi   4.75 25
643 A73 10p purple & multi   10.00 50

25th anniversary (in 1971) of the Conference of Sofar, Lebanon, establishing the Arab Postal Union.

Balloons and Pacifier — A74

1973, Dec.
644 A74 4p lt blue & multi   7.50 15

Universal Children's Day (stamp dated 1971).

Arab Postal and UPU Emblems A75

1974, July 7   Wmk. 361   Perf. 14
645 A75 3p yellow & multi   50.00 2.50
646 A75 4p rose & multi   50.00 5.00
647 A75 10p lt green & multi 50.00 7.50

Centenary of the Universal Postal Union.

Handshake and UNESCO Emblem — A76

1974, May 21   *Perf. 13½*
648 A76 4p orange & multi   2.50 25
649 A76 10p green & multi   10.50 75

International Book Year, 1972.

Desalination
Plant — A77

1974, Sept. 3   Wmk. 361   Perf. 14
650 A77 4p dp orange & bl   2.25 15
651 A77 6p emerald & vio   4.75 25
652 A77 10p rose red & blk   7.25 50

Opening (in 1971) of sea water desalination plant, Jedda.

A78   A79

Design: INTERPOL emblem.

1974, Nov. 1
653 A78 4p ocher & ultra   7.75 20
654 A78 10p emerald & ultra   16.00 50

50th anniversary (in 1973) of International Criminal Police Organization.

1974, Oct. 26   Litho.   Wmk. 361

APU emblem, tower and letter.

655 A79 4p multicolored   10.00 15

Arab Consultative Council for Postal Studies, 3rd session.

UPU
Headquarters,
Bern — A80

1974, Nov. 15   *Perf. 13½*
656 A80 3p orange & multi   3.00 25
657 A80 4p lilac & multi   6.25 50
658 A80 10p blue & multi   8.75 1.25

Opening of new Universal Postal Union Headquarters, Bern, May 1970.

Tank, Planes,
Rockets and
Flame — A81

1974, Dec. 15   *Perf. 14*
659 A81 3p slate & multi   2.00 15
660 A81 4p brown & multi   4.25 25
661 A81 10p lilac & multi   12.50 75

King Faisal Military Cantonment, 1971.

A82   A84

A83

Red Crescent flower.

1974, Dec. 17   Perf. 14x14½
662 A82 4p gray & multi   2.00 25
663 A82 4p lt green & multi   5.00 50
664 A82 10p lt blue & multi   10.00 1.00

Saudi Arabian Red Crescent Society, 10th anniversary (in 1973).

1974, Dec. 23   Wmk. 361   Perf. 14

Saudi Arabian scout emblem and minarets.

665 A83 4p brown & multi   4.75 20
666 A83 6p blue blk & multi   9.25 30
667 A83 10p purple & multi   14.00 60

6th Arab League Rover Moot, Mecca.

1975, Mar. 31   Perf. 14x13½

Design: Reading braille.

668 A84 4p multicolored   4.00 25
669 A84 10p multicolored   9.50 50

Day of the Blind.

Anemometer and Weather Balloon with
UN Emblem — A85

Perf. 13½x14
1975, May 8   Litho.   Wmk. 361
670 A85 4p multicolored   8.75 25

Centenary (in 1973) of International Meteorological Cooperation.

King Faisal — A86   Conference
                          Emblem — A87

1975, July 6   Unwmk.   Perf. 14
671 A86 4p green & rose brn   3.00 25
672 A86 10p violet & green   4.00 75
673 A86 23p dk green & vio   8.00 1.25

Miniature Sheet
Imperf
674 A86 40p Prus bl & ocher   400.00

King Faisal ibn Abdul-Aziz Al Saud (1906-1975).
Size of No. 674: 71x80mm.

1975, July 11   Perf. 14
675 A87 10p rose brn & blk   6.00 50

6th Islamic Conference of Foreign Ministers, Jedda, July 12.

Wheat and
Sun — A88

1975, Sept. 17   Litho.   Wmk. 361
676 A88 4p lilac & multi   2.50 20
677 A88 10p blue & multi   7.50 40

Charity Society, 20th anniversary.

Holy Ka'aba, Globe, Clasped Hands — A89

1975, Sept. 17   Perf. 14
678 A89 4p olive bis & multi   7.00 15
679 A89 10p orange & multi   14.00 35

Conference of Moslem Organizations, Mecca, Apr. 6-10, 1974.

Saudia Tri-Star and DC-3 — A90

1975, Sept.   Litho.   Unwmk.
680 A90 4p buff & multi   7.00 20
681 A90 10p lt blue & multi   14.00 50

Saudia, Saudi Arabian Airline, 30th anniversary.

Conference
Centers in
Mecca and
Riyadh — A91

1975, Sept.   Perf. 14
682 A91 10p multicolored   10.00 50

Friday Mosque, Medina, and Juwatha
Mosque, al-Hasa — A92

1975, Oct. 26   Litho.   Unwmk.
683 A92 4p green & multi   6.75 25
684 A92 10p vermilion & multi   9.50 50

Ancient Islamic holy places.

FAO Emblem — A93

1975, Oct. 26
685 A93 4p gray & multi   3.75 20
686 A93 10p buff & multi   11.00 50

World Food Program, 10th anniversary (in 1973). Stamps are dated 1973.

Conference Emblem — A94

1976, Mar. 20   Unwmk.   Perf. 14
687 A94 4p multicolored   14.00 25

Islamic Solidarity Conference of Science and Technology.

Saudi Arabia Map, Transmission Tower, TV
Screen — A95

1976, May 26   Litho.   Perf. 14
688 A95 4p multicolored   14.00 25

Saudi Arabian television, 10th anniversary.

Grain, Atom
Symbol,
Graph — A96

1976, June 28   Litho.   Perf. 14
689 A96 20h yellow & multi   3.75 25
690 A96 50h yellow & multi   6.25 50

Second Five-year Plan.

Holy
Ka'aba — A97

Two types:
I - "White" minarets. Gray vignette.
II - Black minarets and vignette. Design redrawn, strengthened, darkened, clarified.

1976-79   Litho.   Wmk. 361   *Perf. 14*
Type II

691	A97	5h lilac & blk	16	15
692	A97	10h lt violet & blk	25	15
693	A97	15h salmon & blk	35	15
694	A97	20h lt bl & blk, II	4.75	20
a.		Type I	4.25	20
695	A97	25h yellow & blk	5.50	20
696	A97	30h gray grn & blk	1.10	15
697	A97	35h bister & blk	1.50	15
698	A97	40h lt green & blk	90	15
a.		Type I ('77)	3.50	20
b.		Imperf., pair, II	6.75	30
			125.00	
699	A97	45h dull rose & blk	1.00	15
700	A97	50h pink & blk	1.10	15
703	A97	65h gray blue & blk	1.40	15
710	A97	1r lt yel grn & blk	2.00	20
711	A97	2r green & black	7.25	35
		Nos. 691-711 (13)	24.76	
		Set value		2.00

Imperfs of Nos. 691-711 other than No. 698b were not regularly issued.
Issue years: 20h, 1977; 5h-15h, 25h-50h, 1r, 1978; 65h, 2r, 1979.
See Nos. 872-882, 961-968.

Quba Mosque, Medina, built 622 — A98

1976-77
719	A98	20h orange & blk	2.25	15
720	A98	50h emer & lilac ('77)	4.25	20
a.		Imperf., pair		

Reissued in 1978 in different shades.

Globe, Telephones 1876 and 1976 A100

1976, July 17   Unwmk.   *Perf. 13½*
721 A100 50h multicolored   7.00 30

Centenary of first telephone call by Alexander Graham Bell, Mar. 10, 1876.

Arab Leaders A101

1976, Oct. 30   Litho.   *Perf. 14*
722 A101 20h ultra & emerald   5.75 25

Arab Summit Conference, Riyadh, October. Leaders pictured: Pres. Elias Sarkis, Lebanon; Pres. Anwar Sadat, Egypt; Pres. Hafez al Assad, Syria; King Khalid, Saudi Arabia; Amir Sabah, Kuwait; Yasir Arafat, Palestine Liberation Organization chairman.

WHO Emblem and Eye — A102

1976, Nov. 28   Litho.   *Perf. 14*
723 A102 20h multicolored   12.00 15
World Health Day; Prevention of Blindness.

Holy Ka'aba — A103

1976, Nov. 28   Unwmk.
724 A103 20h multicolored   7.50 20
50th anniversary of installation of new covering of Holy Ka'aba, Mecca.

Conference Emblem A104

Unwmk.
1977, Feb. 18   Litho.   *Perf. 14*
725 A104 20h multicolored   7.75 15
Islamic Jurisprudence Conference, Riyadh, Oct. 24-Nov. 2, 1976.

A105   A106

Design: Sharia College emblem.

1977, Feb. 25   *Perf. 14*
726 A105 4p multicolored   7.00 15
25th anniversary (in 1974) of the founding of Sharia (Islamic Law) College, Mecca.

1977
727	A106	20h dk brn & brt grn	2.00	15
a.		Incorrect date	25.00	
728	A106	80h bl blk & brt grn	4.00	50
a.		Incorrect date	25.00	

2nd anniversary of installation of King Khalid ibn Abdul-Aziz. Nos. 727a-728a (illustrated), issued Mar. 3, have incorrect Arabic date in bottom panel, last characters of 2nd and 3rd rows identical "ir." Stamps withdrawn after a few days and replaced Aug. 14 with corrected date, last characters in 3rd row changed to "ro."

Diesel Train and Map of Route — A107

1977, May 23   Litho.   *Perf. 14*
729 A107 20h multicolored   20.00 15
Dammam-Riyadh railroad, 25th anniversary.

Arabic Ornament and Names — A108

Designs (Names from Left to Right): UL, Malik Ben Anas (715-795). UR, Mohammad Ben Idris Al-Shafi'i (767-820). LL, Abu Hanifa an-Nu'man (699-767). LR, Ahmed Ben Hanbal (780-855).

1977, Aug. 15   Litho.   *Perf. 14*
730	A108	Block of 4	32.50	2.25
a.-d.		20h, single stamp	3.00	25

Famous Imams (7th-9th centuries), founders of traditional schools of Islamic jurisprudence. Sheets of 60.

Al Khafji Oil Rig — A109

1976-80   Wmk. 361
731	A109	5h vio blue & org	15	15
732	A109	10h yellow grn & org	15	15
733	A109	15h brown & orange	15	15
734	A109	20h green & orange	18	15
735	A109	25h dk purple & org	22	15
736	A109	30h blue & orange	25	15
737	A109	35h sepia & orange	30	15
a.		Imperf., pair	300.00	
738	A109	40h magenta & orange	30	15
a.		40h dull purple & org	200.00	
739	A109	45h violet & orange	40	20
740	A109	50h rose & orange	45	20
a.		50h dull org & org (error)	75.00	7.50
741	A109	55h grnsh bl & org	22.50	4.00
743	A109	65h sepia & orange	1.25	35
750	A109	1r gray & orange	1.50	60
751	A109	2r dk vio & org ('80)	3.25	1.00
		Nos. 731-751 (14)	31.05	7.55

All values exist with extra dot in Arabic "Al Khafji." The 20, 25, 50, 65h and 1r were retouched to remove the dot.
Color of flame varies from light orange to vermilion. See Nos. 885-892.
Imperfs of other values are believed not to have been regularly issued.

Mohenjo-Daro Ruins — A110

1977, Oct. 23   Litho.   Unwmk.
761 A110 50h multicolored   7.75 30
UNESCO campaign to save Mohenjo-Daro excavations in Pakistan.

Idrisi's World Map, 1154 — A111

1977, Nov. 1   Litho.   *Perf. 14*
762 A111 20h multicolored   2.00 15
763 A111 50h multicolored   4.00 35
First International Symposium on Studies in the History of Arabia at the University of Riyadh, Apr. 23-26, 1977.

King Faisal Specialist Hospital, Riyadh — A112

1977, Nov. 13   Litho.   Unwmk.
764 A112 20h multicolored   3.25 20
765 A112 50h multicolored   5.25 35

Conference Emblem — A113

1978, Jan. 24   Litho.   *Perf. 14*
766 A113 20h vio blue & yel   4.50 15
1st World Conf. on Moslem Education.

APU Emblem, Members' Flags — A114

1978, Jan. 21
767 A114 20h multicolored   1.75 15
768 A114 80h multicolored   4.00 50
25th anniversary of Arab Postal Union.

Taif-Abha-Gizan Highway — A115

1978, Oct. 15   Litho.   Perf. 14
769 A115 20h multicolored   2.00 15
770 A115 80h multicolored   4.00 40

Inauguration of Taif-Abha-Gizan highway.

Pilgrims, Mt. Arafat and Holy Ka'aba — A116

Unwmk.
1978, Nov. 6   Litho.   Perf. 14
771 A116 20h multicolored   1.90 15
772 A116 80h multicolored   3.75 40

Pilgrimage to Mecca.

Gulf Postal Organization Emblem — A117

1979, Feb. 6   Litho.   Perf. 14
773 A117 20h multicolored   1.65 15
774 A117 50h multicolored   3.25 25

First Conference of Gulf Postal Organization, Baghdad.

Saudi Arabia No. 129, King Abdul Aziz ibn Saud A118

Unwmk.
1979, June 4   Litho.   Perf. 14
775 A118 20h multicolored   1.50 15
776 A118 50h multicolored   3.25 25
777 A118 115h multicolored   5.25 58

Souvenir Sheet
Imperf
778 A118 100h multicolored   100.00

1st commemorative stamp, 50th anniv. No. 778 contains one stamp with simulated perforations. Size: 101x76mm.

Crown Prince Fahd — A119

1979, June 25   Perf. 14
779 A119 20h multicolored   2.00 15
780 A119 50h multicolored   4.00 25

Crown Prince Fahd ibn Abdul Aziz.

Dome of the Rock, Jerusalem A120

1979, July 2   Wmk. 361
781 A120 20h multi (shades)   1.75 25

Imperfs. exist. See No. 866.

Gold Door, Holy Ka'aba — A121

1979, Oct. 13   Litho.   Perf. 14
782 A121 20h multicolored   1.75 15
783 A121 80h multicolored   4.00 40

Installation of new gold doors. Imperfs. exist.

Pilgrims at Holy Ka'aba, Mecca Mosque — A122

1979, Oct. 27
784 A122 20h multicolored   1.25 15
785 A122 50h multicolored   3.00 25

Pilgrimage to Mecca. Imperfs. exist.

Birds in Trees, IYC Emblem — A123

IYC Emblem and: 50h, Child's drawing.

1980, Feb. 17   Litho.   Perf. 14
786 A123 20h multicolored   11.00 15
787 A123 50h multicolored   18.00 25

International Year of the Child (1979). Imperfs. exist.

King Abdul Aziz ibn Saud on Horseback, Saudi Flag — A124

1980, Apr. 5   Litho.   Perf. 14
788 A124 20h multicolored   1.50 15
789 A124 80h multicolored   3.50 40

Saudi Arabian Army, 80th anniv. (1979). Imperfs. exist.

Arab League, 35th Anniversary A125

Smoke Entering Lungs, WHO Emblem A127

International Bureau of Education, 50th Anniversary A126

1980, Apr. 27   Litho.   Perf. 14
790 A125 20h multicolored   2.00 15

Imperfs. exist.

1980, May 4
791 A126 50h multicolored   2.50 25

Imperfs. exist.

1980, May 20
792 A127 20h shown   1.50 15
793 A127 50h Cigarette, horiz.   3.50 25

Anti-smoking campaign. Imperfs. exist.

20th Anniversary of OPEC — A128

Design: 50h, Workers holding OPEC emblem (Organization of Petroleum Exporting Countries).

1980, Sept. 1   Litho.   Perf. 14
794 A128 20h multicolored   1.50 15
795 A128 50h multi, vert.   3.00 25

Pilgrims Arriving at Jedda Airport A129

1980, Oct. 18
796 A129 20h multicolored   1.00 15
797 A129 50h multicolored   2.00 25

Pilgrimage to Mecca.

Conference Emblem A130

Holy Ka'aba, Mecca Mosque — A131

Hegira, 1500th Anniv. A132

1981, Jan. 25   Litho.   Perf. 14
798 A130 20h shown   1.10 15
799 A131 20h shown   1.10 15
800 A131 20h Prophet's Mosque, Medina   1.10 15
801 A131 20h Dome of the Rock, Jerusalem   1.10 15
    Set value   40

Third Islamic Summit Conference, Mecca.

1981, Jan. 26
802 A132 20h multicolored   85 15
803 A132 50h multicolored   1.65 25
804 A132 80h multicolored   3.25 40

Souvenir Sheet
805 A132 300h multicolored

Industry Week — A133

1981, Feb. 21
806 A133 20h multicolored   80 15
807 A133 80h multicolored   2.50 40

Line Graph and Telephone A134

Map of Saudi Arabia, Microwave Tower A135

1981, Feb. 28
808 A134 20h shown   30 15
809 A135 80h shown   2.50 40
810 A134 115h Earth satellite station   2.75 55

Souvenir Sheets
811 A134 100h like #808
812 A134 100h like #809
813 A134 100h like #810

Ministry of Posts and Telecommunications achievements.

Arab City Day — A135a

1981, Apr. 2   Litho.   Perf. 14
814 A135a 20h multicolored   40 15
815 A135a 65h multicolored   1.25 32
816 A135a 80h multicolored   1.65 40
817 A135a 115d multicolored   2.25 60

Jedda Airport
Opening
A136

1981, Apr. 12
818 A136 20h shown   70   15
819 A136 80h Plane over airport, diff.   2.75 40

1982 World Cup   Intl. Year of the
Soccer Preliminary   Disabled — A138
Games — A137

1981, July 26   Litho.   Perf. 14
820 A137 20h multicolored   1.90 15
821 A137 80h multicolored   3.50 40

1981, Aug. 5
822 A138 20h Reading braille   1.75 15
823 A138 50h Man weaving rug   2.75 25

3rd Five-year
Plan (1981-
1985)
A139

1981, Sept. 5
824 A139 20h multicolored   1.50 15

King Abdul
Aziz, Map of
Saudi Arabia
A140

1981, Sept. 23   Litho.   Perf. 14
825 A140   5h multicolored   15   15
826 A140 10h multicolored   15   15
827 A140 15h multicolored   16   15
828 A140 20h multicolored   30   15
829 A140 50h multicolored   75   25
830 A140 65h multicolored   1.10   32
831 A140 80h multicolored   2.75   40
832 A140 115h multicolored   3.25   58
       Nos. 825-832 (8)   8.61
         Set value   1.80
Souvenir Sheet
Imperf
833 A140 10r multicolored   80.00

50th anniv. of kingdom. No. 833 shows king,
map, document. Size: 100x75mm.

Pilgrimage to
Mecca
A141

1981, Oct. 7
834 A141 20h multicolored   1.75 15
835 A141 65h multicolored   3.50 32

World Food
Day — A142

1981, Oct. 16
836 A142 20h multicolored   1.40 15

2nd Session of the
Gulf Cooperative
Council Summit
Conference, Riyadh,
Nov. 10 — A143

1981, Nov. 10   Litho.   Perf. 14
837 A143 20h multicolored   80   15
838 A143 80h multicolored   2.50   40

King Saud
University,
25th Anniv.
A144

1982, Mar. 10   Litho.   Perf. 14
839 A144 20h multicolored   80   15
840 A144 50h multicolored   1.65   25

New
Regional
Postal
Centers
A145

1982, July 14   Litho.   Perf. 14
841 A145 20h Riyadh P.O.   38   15
842 A145 65h Jedda   1.25   32
843 A145 80h Dammam   1.65   40
844 A145 115h Automated sorting   2.00   58

Four 300h souvenir sheets exist in same designs
as Nos. 841-844 respectively.

Riyadh Television
Center — A146

1982, Sept. 4
845 A146 20h multicolored   1.40 15

25th Anniv. of
King's Soccer
Cup — A147

1982, Sept. 8
846 A147 20h multicolored   95   15
847 A147 65h multicolored   1.90   32

30th Anniv. of
Arab Postal
Union — A148

1982, Sept. 8
848 A148 20h Emblem   80   15
849 A148 65h Map, vert.   2.00   32

Pilgrimage to
Mecca
A149

1982, Sept. 26
850 A149 20h multicolored   90   15
851 A149 50h multicolored   1.90   25

World
Standards
Day — A150

1982, Oct. 14
852 A150 20h multicolored   1.40 15

World Food
Day — A151

1982, Oct. 16
853 A151 20h multicolored   1.40 15

Coronation
of King
Fahd, June
14, 1982
A152

Installation
of Crown
Prince
Abdullah,
June 14,
1982
A153

1983, Feb. 12   Litho.   Perf. 14
854 A152 20h multicolored   30   15
855 A153 20h multicolored   30   15
856 A152 50h multicolored   70   25
857 A153 50h multicolored   70   25
858 A152 65h multicolored   1.00   32
859 A153 65h multicolored   1.00   32
860 A152 80h multicolored   1.25   40
861 A153 80h multicolored   1.25   40
862 A152 115h multicolored   1.75   60
863 A153 115h multicolored   1.75   60
       Nos. 854-863 (10)   10.00 3.44

Two one-stamp souvenir sheets contain Nos.
862-863, perf. 12½.

6th Anniv. of United Arab Shipping
Co. — A154

Various freighters.

1983, Aug. 9   Litho.   Perf. 14
864 A154 20h multicolored   15   15
865 A154 65h multicolored   40   20
         Set value   26

Dome of the
Rock,
Jerusalem
A155

1983, Sept.   Wmk. 361   Perf. 12
866 A155 20h multicolored   15   15
         See No. 781.

Pilgrimage to
Mecca
A156

1983, Sept. 16   Litho.   Perf. 14
867 A156 20h brt blue & multi   25   15
868 A156 65h dk black & multi   85   20
         Set value   26

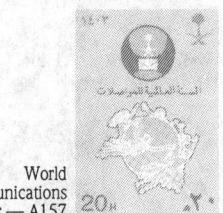

World
Communications
Year — A157

1983, Oct. 8   Litho.   Perf. 14
869 A157 20h Post and UPU emblems   15   15
870 A157 80h Telephone and ITU em-
             blems   48   24
         Set value   30

Holy Ka'ba Type of 1976
Type II
Perf. 14x13½
1982-86   Litho.   Wmk. 361
Size: 26x21mm

872 A97 10h lt vio & blk ('83)   15   15
   a.   Perf. 12, unwmkd. ('87)   15   15
873 A97 15h sal & blk, perf. 12 ('85) 15   15
874 A97 20h lt blue & blk   20   15
   a.   Perf. 12 ('84)   20   15
   b.   Perf. 12, unwmkd.   15   15
   c.   Perf. 13½   25   15
880 A97 50h pink & blk ('83)   50   15
   a.   Perf. 13½   50   15
   b.   Perf. 12 ('86)   30   15
881 A97 65h gray bl & blk   65   15
   a.   Perf. 13½   65   15
   b.   Perf. 12 ('84)   65   15
   c.   Perf. 12, unwmkd. ('84)   65   15
882 A97 1r lt yel grn & blk   1.00   20
   a.   Perf. 13½   1.00   20
   b.   Perf. 12 ('83)   1.00   20
   c.   Perf. 12, unwmkd. ('85)   1.00   20
       Nos. 872-882 (6)   2.65
         Set value   60

Counterfeits of the 1r are perf. 11.

Al Khafji Oil Rig Type of 1976
Perf. 14x13½

1982-84   Litho.   Wmk. 361
Size: 26x21mm

885	A109	5h vio bl & org	15	15
886	A109	10h yel grn & org	15	15
887	A109	15h bis brn & org	15	15
888	A109	20h green & org	15	15
890	A109	50h rose & org	30	15
891a	A109	65h sepia & orange	3.00	1.50
892	A109	1r gray & org	60	30

Perf. 13½

885a	A109	5h	15	15
886a	A109	10h	15	15
887a	A109	15h	15	15
888a	A109	20h	15	15
890a	A109	50h	15	15
891	A109	65h sepia & org ('84)	40	20
892a	A109	1r	60	30

1983   Perf. 12

886b	A109	10h	15	15
887b	A109	15h	15	15
888b	A109	20h	15	15
889	A109	25h dk pur & org	15	15
890b	A109	50h	30	15
891b	A109	65h	40	20
892b	A109	1r	60	30
		Set value	1.50	75

Opening of King Khalid International Airport — A158

1983, Nov. 16   Litho.   Perf. 13½x14

893	A158	20h shown	15	15
894	A158	65h blue & multi	40	20
		Set value		26

World Food Day — A159

1983, Nov. 29   Litho.   Perf. 14

895	A159	20h Wheat, Irrigation, Silos	15	15

Aqsa Mosque, Jerusalem A160

1983, Dec. 13   Litho.   Perf. 14

896	A160	20h multicolored	15	15

Old and Modern Riyadh — A161

Shobra Palace, Taif — A162

Old and New Jedda (Waterfront) — A163

1984-92   Litho.   Wmk. 361   Perf. 12

900	A161	20h lilac rose & multi	15	15
901	A162	20h Prus grn & multi	15	15
907	A161	50h black & multi	30	15
908	A162	50h brown & multi	75	38

Unwmk.

908A	A161	50h multicolored	52	26
908B	A162	50h multicolored	75	38
909	A163	50h multicolored	1.00	50
909A	A162	75h multicolored	75	38
909B	A163	75h pink & multi	1.00	50
909C	A161	75h green & multi	75	38
910	A162	150h green & multi	1.65	82
911	A161	150h pink & multi	1.65	82
911A	A163	150h green & multi	1.70	85
		Nos. 900-911A (13)	11.12	5.72

Issued: #900, 6/27/84; #901, 10/13/84; #907, 8/29/84; #908, 3/10/87; #910, 9/3/87; #908B, 11/3/87; #911, 5/4/88; #909, 911A, 1/31/89; #909A, 1990; #908A, 909B, 1991; #909C, 1992. This is an expanding set. Numbers will change if necessary.

Estate Development Fund, 10th Anniv. A165

1984, July 28   Unwmk.

912	A165	20h multicolored	35	15

Opening of Solar Village, near Al-Eyenah A166

1984, Aug. 14   Litho.   Perf. 12

913	A166	20h multicolored	15	15
914	A166	80h Stylized sun, solar panels	60	24
		Set value		30

Imperf
Size: 81x81mm

915	A166	100h like 20h		12.50
916	A166	100h like 80h		12.50

Pilgrimage to Mecca — A167

1984, Sept. 4   Litho.   Perf. 14

917	A167	20h brown & multi	25	15

Perf. 12

918	A167	65h olive gray & multi	80	20
		Set value		26

Participation of Saudi Arabian Soccer Team in 1984 Olympics — A168

1984, Sept. 25   Litho.   Perf. 12

919	A168	20h blue & multi	25	15
920	A168	115h green & multi	1.00	35
		Set value		40

"Games" and "Olympiad" are misspelled on both stamps.

World Food Day — A169

1984, Oct. 16   Litho.   Perf. 12

921	A169	20h multicolored	35	15

Beginning with Nos. 922-923 some issues are printed in sheets that have labels inscribed in Arabic. Generally there are from 2 to 6 labels per sheet. Stamps with label attached command a premium.

90th Anniv. International Olympic Committee A170

1984, Dec. 23   Litho.   Perf. 12

922	A170	20h multicolored	15	15
923	A170	50h multicolored	60	15
		Set value		15

Launch of ARABSAT — A171

1985, Feb. 9   Litho.   Perf. 12

924	A171	20h ARABSAT, view of Earth	90	15

7th Holy Koran Competition A172

1985, Feb. 10   Litho.   Perf. 12

925	A172	20h multicolored	25	15
926	A172	65h multicolored	75	20
		Set value		26

4th Five-Year Development Plan, 1985-1990 A173

Portrait of King Fahd, industry emblems and: 20h, Dhahran Harbor, Jubail. 50h, Television tower, earth receiver, microwave tower. 65h, Agriculture. 80h, Harbor, Yanbu.

1985, Mar. 23   Litho.   Perf. 13x12

927	A173	20h multicolored	48	15
928	A173	50h multicolored	1.25	15
929	A173	65h multicolored	1.40	20
930	A173	80h multicolored	1.90	22
a.		Block of 4, #927-930	5.00	75
		Set value		62

Intl. Youth Year — A174

1985, May 4   Perf. 12

931	A174	20h multicolored	18	15
932	A174	80h multicolored	70	22
		Set value		28

Self-sufficiency in Wheat Production — A175

1985, May 4

933	A175	20h multicolored	48	15

East-West Pipeline — A176

1985, June 9

934	A176	20h Tanker loading berth, Yanbu	25	15
935	A176	65h Pipeline, map	75	20
		Set value		26

Shuttle Launch — A177

Shuttle, Missions Emblem — A178

1985, July 7
936 A177 20h multicolored 25 15
937 A178 115h multicolored 1.25 32
Set value 38

Prince Sultan Ibn Salman Al-Saud, 1st Arab-Moslem astronaut, on Discovery 51-G.

UN, 40th Anniv. A179

1985, July 15
938 A179 20h multicolored 60 15

Highway, Map, Holy Ka'aba in Mecca to Prophet's Mosque in Medina — A180

1985, July 22
939 A180 20h multicolored 25 15
940 A180 65h multicolored 75 20
Set value 26

Mecca-Medina Highway opening, Oct. 11, 1984.

Post Code Inauguration — A181

1985, July 24
941 A181 20h Covers 25 15

1984 Asian Soccer Cup Victory A182

1985, July 30
942 A182 20h multicolored 18 15
943 A182 65h multicolored 48 20
944 A182 115h multicolored 1.00 32
Set value 58

Pilgrimage to Mecca — A183

1985, Aug. 25 Litho. Perf. 12
945 A183 10h multicolored 15 15
946 A183 15h multicolored 20 15
947 A183 20h multicolored 25 15
948 A183 65h multicolored 75 20
Set value 35

1st Gulf Olympics Day, Riyadh, May 2 A184

1985, Sept. 8
949 A184 20h multicolored 25 15
950 A184 115h multicolored 1.25 32
Set value 38

World Food Day — A185

1985, Oct. 16
951 A185 20h multicolored 20 15
952 A185 65h multicolored 65 20
Set value 26

King Abdul Aziz, Masmak Fort and Horsemen — A186

1985, Dec. 1
953 A186 15h multicolored 15 15
954 A186 20h multicolored 15 15
955 A186 65h multicolored 38 20
956 A186 80h multicolored 45 22
Set value 52

Intl. Conference on the History of King Abdul Aziz Al-Sa'ud, Riyadh. An imperf. souvenir sheet showing smaller versions of Nos. 953-956 and the conference emblem exists. Sold for 10r.

King Fahd Koran Publishing Center, Medina — A187

1985, Dec. 18
957 A187 20h multicolored 15 15
958 A187 65h multicolored 52 20
Set value 26

OPEC, 25th Anniv. A188

1985, Dec. 24
959 A188 20h multicolored 15 15
960 A188 65h multicolored 52 20
Set value 26

Holy Ka'aba Type of 1976
Type II
Booklet Stamps

1986, Feb. 17 Litho. Perf. 12
Size: 29x19mm
961 A97 10h lt vio & blk
a. Booklet pane of 4 24.00
965 A97 20h bluish grn & blk
968 A97 50h pink & black
a. Bklt. pane of 4, #961, 2 #965, #968 37.50

Due to vending machine breakdowns, distribution of this set has been very limited. The government does have stocks of these stamps but they are not currently being sold.
This is an expanding set. Numbers will change if necessary.

A189 A191

A190

1986, Jan. 8 Litho. Perf. 12
971 A189 20h multicolored 15 15
Intl. Peace Year.

1986, Mar. 24 Perf. 14, 12 (65h)
972 A190 20h multicolored 18 15
a. Perf. 12 18 15
973 A190 65h multicolored 55 20
Set value 26

Riyadh Municipality, 50th aAnniv.

1986, Apr. 21 Perf. 12
974 A191 20h multicolored 15 15
975 A191 50h multicolored 28 15
20

UN child survival campaign.

General Establishment for Electric Power, 10th Anniv. A192

1986, Apr. 26
976 A192 20h multicolored 15 15
977 A192 65h multicolored 38 20
Set value 26

Continental Maritime Cable Inauguration — A193

1986, June 1 Litho. Perf. 12
978 A193 20h multicolored 30 15
979 A193 50h multicolored 75 15
Set value 20

Natl. Guard Housing Project, Riyadh, Inauguration A194

1986, July 19
980 A194 20h multicolored 32 15
981 A194 65h multicolored 1.10 20
Set value 26

Islamic Arch, Holy Ka'aba — A195

1986-92 Litho. Perf. 12
984 A195 30h black & bluish grn 18 15
985 A195 40h black & lilac rose 22 15
986 A195 50h black & brt green 75 38
987 A195 75h black & Prus bl 90 45
a. Perf. 13½x14 75 38
989 A195 150h black & rose lilac 1.80 90
a. Perf. 13½x14 1.50 75
Nos. 984-989 (5) 3.85 2.03

Issue dates: 30h, 40h, Aug. 5. 75h, 150h, July 30, 1990. 50h, Oct. 9, 1990. #987a, June 13, 1992. #989a, June 6, 1992.
This is an expanding set. Numbers will change if necessary.

Pilgrimage to Mecca — A196

Designs of: a, A116. b, A129. c, A156. d, A149. e, A141. f, A122. g, A183. h, A167.

1986, Aug. 13 Litho. Perf. 12
1002 Block of 8 12.00 12.00
a.-h. A196 20h, any single

Discovery of Oil, 50th Anniv. — A197 World Food Day — A198

1986, Sept. 16
1003 A197 20h Well, refinery 30 15
1004 A197 65h Well, map 85 18
Set value 24

Because of difficulty in separation most copies have damaged perfs.

1986, Oct. 18
1005 A198 20h shown 15 15
1006 A198 115h Stylized plant 85 32
Set value 38

Massacre of Palestinian Refugees, Sept. 17, 1982 — A199

1986, Nov. 1 Litho. Perf. 12
1007 A199 80h multicolored 65 32
1008 A199 115h multicolored 95 48

Definitive stamps generally do not have an official date of issue. Any dates shown probably reflect sales at the Riyadh or Dammam post offices only.

Saudi Universities

Imam Mohammed ibn Saud — A200

Umm al-Qura — A201

King Saud — A202

King Fahd Petroleum and Minerals — A203

King Faisal — A204

King Abdul Aziz — A205

Medina Islamic — A206

1986-91

1009	A200	15h sage grn & blk	15	15
1010	A200	20h ultra & black	16	15
1010A	A200	50h ultra & black	45	22
1011	A200	65h brt blue & blk	52	25
1011A	A200	75h brt blue & blk	75	38
1012	A200	100h rose & black	80	40
1013	A200	150h rose claret & blk	1.40	70
1014	A201	50h ultra & black	55	28
1015	A201	65h brt blue & blk	75	25
1016	A201	75h brt blue & blk	75	38
1017	A201	100h dull rose & blk	1.10	55
1018	A201	150h rose claret & blk	1.65	82
1020	A202	50h ultra & black	60	30
1021	A202	75h brt blue & blk	75	38
1022	A202	100h dull rose & blk	1.10	55
1023	A202	150h rose claret & blk	1.50	75
1025	A203	50h ultra & black	45	22
1026	A203	75h brt blue & blk	75	38
1027	A203	150h rose claret & blk	1.40	70
1029	A204	50h ultra & black	45	22
1029A	A204	75h brt blue & blk	75	38
1030	A204	150h rose claret & blk	1.50	50
1033	A205	50h ultra & black	45	22
1033A	A205	75h brt blue & blk	75	38
1034	A205	150h rose claret & blk	1.50	75
1036	A206	50h ultra & black	50	17
1036A	A206	75h brt blue & blk	75	38
1037	A206	150h rose claret & blk	1.40	22
		Nos. 1009-1037 (28)	23.63	11.03

Issue dates: Nos. 1009-1012, Nov. 26. No. 1017, Mar. 29. No. 1022, July 22. Nos. 1014, 1018, Aug. 8. Nos. 1013, 1027, 1037, Jan. 31, 1989. Nos. 1025, 1029, 1033, Feb. 25, 1989. No. 1015, Mar. 1989. No. 1030, Apr. 29, 1989. No. 1036, July 4, 1989. Nos. 1023, 1034, Apr. 29, 1989. No. 1010A, Feb. 25, 1989. No. 1020, 1989. Nos. 1011A, 1016, 1026, 1990. Nos. 1021, 1029A, 1033A, 1036A, 1991.

This is an expanding set. Numbers will change if necessary.

Saudi-Bahrain Highway Inauguration — A207

1986, Nov. 26   Perf. 14
1039	Strip of 2	32	16
a.-b.	A207 20h any single	16	15

Printed se-tenant in a continuous design.

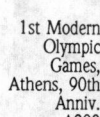

1st Modern Olympic Games, Athens, 90th Anniv. A208

1986, Dec. 27
1040	A208 20h multicolored	16	15
1041	A208 100h multicolored	80	40

General Petroleum and Minerals Organization (Petromin), 25th Anniv. A209

Unwmk.
1987, Feb. 23   Litho.   Perf. 12
1042	A209 50h multicolored	55	28
1043	A209 100h multicolored	1.10	55

Restoration and Expansion of Quba Mosque, Medina — A210

Design: View of mosque and model of expanded mosque.

1987, Mar. 21
1044	A210 50h multicolored	75	28
1045	A210 75h multicolored	1.10	40

Vocational Training A211

Designs: a, Welding. b, Drill press operation. c, Lathe operation. d, Electrician.

Unwmk.
1987, Apr. 8   Litho.   Perf. 12
1046	Block of 4	5.60	2.80
a.-d.	A211 50h any single	1.40	70

Cairo Exhibition — A212

Design: Desert fortifications in silhouette, Riyadh television tower, King Khalid Intl. Airport hangars and pyramid of Giza.

Unwmk.
1987, June 17   Litho.   Perf. 12
1047	A212 50h multicolored	58	30
1048	A212 75h multicolored	88	45

A213

Inauguration of King Fahd Telecommunications Center, Jedda — A214

1987, July 21
1049	A213 50h multicolored	58	30
1050	A214 75h multicolored	88	45

Afghan Resistance Movement — A215

1987, July 25
1051	A215 50h multicolored	55	28
1052	A215 100h multicolored	1.10	55

Pilgrimage to Mecca — A216

Design: View of Ihram and Meqat Wadi Muhrim Mosque from Wadi Muhrim Meqat.

1987, Aug. 3
1053	A216 50h multicolored	58	30
1054	A216 75h multicolored	88	45
1055	A216 100h multicolored	1.15	58

Home for Disabled Children, 1st Anniv. — A217

1987, Oct. 3
1056	A217 50h multicolored	52	25
1057	A217 75h multicolored	78	40

World Post Day — A218

1987, Oct. 10
1058	A218 50h multicolored	55	28
1059	A218 150h multicolored	1.60	80

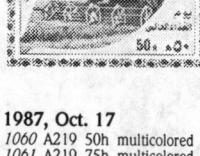

World Food Day — A219

1987, Oct. 17
1060	A219 50h multicolored	52	25
1061	A219 75h multicolored	78	40

Social Welfare Society, 25th Anniv. — A220

Dome of the Rock — A221

1987, Oct. 26
1062	A220 50h multicolored	60	30
1063	A220 75h multicolored	1.20	60

1987, Dec. 5
1064	A221 75h multicolored	85	42
1065	A221 150h multicolored	1.70	85

Restoration and Expansion of the Prophet's Mosque, Medina — A222

1987, Dec. 15   Perf. 14
1066	A222 50h multicolored	52	25
1067	A222 75h multicolored	78	40
1068	A222 150h multicolored	1.55	78

An imperf. 300h souvenir sheet exists.

Battle of Hattin, 800th Anniv. A223

Design: Warriors in silhouette and Dome of the Rock.

1987, Dec. 21   Perf. 12
1069	A223 75h multicolored	82	40
1070	A223 150h multicolored	1.65	82

Saladin's conquest of Jerusalem.

A224

A225

1987, Dec. 26
1071	A224 50h multicolored	60	30
1072	A224 75h multicolored	88	45

8th session of the Supreme Council of the Gulf Cooperation Council.

1988, Feb. 13 Litho. *Perf. 12*
1073 A225 50h multicolored 1.00 50
1074 A225 75h multicolored 1.50 75

3rd Regional Highways Conf. of the Middle East.

A226

Inauguration of King Fahd Intl.
Stadium — A227

1988, Mar. 2
1075 A226 50h multicolored 62 30
1076 A227 150h multicolored 1.85 95

Blood
Donation — A228

1988, Apr. 13 Litho. *Perf. 12*
1077 A228 50h multicolored 62 30
1078 A228 75h multicolored 92 45

WHO, 40th Anniv. — A229

1988, Apr. 7
1079 A229 50h multicolored 62 30
1080 A229 75h multicolored 92 45

King Fahd, Custodian of the Holy
Mosques — A230

Design: King Fahd and mosques at Medina and
Mecca.

1988, Apr. 23 Litho. *Perf. 12*
1081 A230 50h multicolored 50 25
1082 A230 75h multicolored 75 38
1083 A230 150h multicolored 1.50 75

A 75h souvenir sheet exists containing an
enlarged version of No. 1082. Sold for 3r.

Environmental
Protection — A231

1988, June 5
1084 A231 50h multicolored 52 25
1085 A231 75h multicolored 78 40

Palestinian
Uprising,
Gaza and the
West Bank
A232

1988, July 10
1086 A232 75h multicolored 75 38
1087 A232 150h multicolored 1.50 75

Pilgrimage to Mecca — A233

1988, July 23 Litho. *Perf. 12*
1088 A233 50h multicolored 62 30
1089 A233 75h multicolored 92 45

World Food
Day — A234

1988, Oct. 16 Litho. *Perf. 12*
1090 A234 50h multicolored 52 25
1091 A234 75h multicolored 78 40

Qiblatain Mosque Expansion — A235

1988, Nov. 9
1092 A235 50h multicolored 52 25
1093 A235 75h multicolored 80 40

5th World Youth Soccer Championships,
Riyadh, Dammam, Jedda and Taif — A250

1989, Feb. 16 Litho. *Perf. 12*
1094 A250 75h multicolored 75 25
1095 A250 150h multicolored 1.50 50

World Health
Day — A251

1989, Apr. 8 Litho. *Perf. 12*
1096 A251 50h multicolored 52 25
1097 A251 75h multicolored 80 40

Sea Water Desalination Plant — A252

1989, May 30 Litho. *Perf. 12*
1098 A252 50h multicolored 55 28
1099 A252 75h multicolored 85 44

Proclamation
of the State of
Palestine,
Nov. 15,
1988
A253

1989, June 6 Litho. *Perf. 12*
1100 A253 50h multicolored 50 17
1101 A253 75h multicolored 75 25

Pilgrimage to Mecca — A254

Design: Al-Tan'eem Mosque, Mecca.

1989, July 12 Litho. *Perf. 12*
1102 A254 50h multicolored 50 17
1103 A254 75h multicolored 75 25

World Food
Day — A255

1989, Oct. 16 Litho. *Perf. 12*
1104 A255 75h multicolored 70 35
1105 A255 150h multicolored 1.40 70

Holy Mosque Expansion — A256

1989, Dec. 30 Litho. *Perf. 12*
1106 A256 50h multicolored 52 25
1107 A256 75h multicolored 78 40
1108 A256 150h multicolored 1.55 78

Youth Soccer Cup   UNESCO World
Championships   Literacy Year
A257   A258

1989, Dec. 20
1109 A257 75h multicolored 72 35
1110 A257 150h multicolored 1.45 72

1990, Jan. 9
1111 A258 50h multicolored 55 28
1112 A258 75h multicolored 82 40

World Health Day — A259

Unwmk.
1990, Apr. 7 Litho. *Perf. 12*
1113 A259 75h multicolored 70 35
1114 A259 150h multicolored 1.40 70

Flowers — A262

1990
1115 Block of 21 8.40
a.-u. A262 50h any single 40 20
1116 Block of 21 12.25
a.-u. A262 75h any single 58 30
1117 Block of 21 24.25
a.-u. A262 150h any single 1.15 58

21 Different species pictured on the sheets.
Issue dates: 50h, 75h, Feb. 6; 150h, Jan. 17.

Islamic
Conference,
20th Anniv.
A263

1990, Feb. 7 Litho. *Perf. 12*
1118 A263 75h bl & multi 50 25
1119 A263 150h gray & multi 1.00 50

Islamic
Heritage
A264

Designs: b, Arabic script in rectangle. c, Circular
design. d, Mosque and minaret.

1990, July 29
1120 Block of 4 3.60 1.80
a.-d. A264 75h any single 90 45

Horses
A265

1990, Apr. 14

Color of Horse

1121	Block of 4	2.40	1.20
a.	A265 50h white, red tassels on bridle	60	30
b.	A265 50h black	60	30
c.	A265 50h white, brown bridle	60	30
d.	A265 50h chestnut	60	30
1122	A265 50h like #1121d	60	30
1123	A265 75h like #1121b	90	45
1124	A265 100h like #1121a	1.20	60
1125	A265 150h like #1121c	1.80	90

No. 1121 has white border on two sides. Nos. 1122-1125 have white border on four sides.

Pilgrimage to Mecca — A266

1990, June 28

1126	A266	75h multicolored	80	40
1127	A266	150h multicolored	1.60	80

Television
Tower — A267

1990, July 21

1128	A267	75h multicolored	80	40
1129	A267	150h multicolored	1.60	80

Saudi Arabian
Airlines
Route
Map — A268

1990, Sept. 3

1130	A268	75h Global routes	75	36
1131	A268	75h Domestic routes	75	36
a.		Pair, #1130-1131	1.50	75
1132	A268	150h like #1130	1.50	75
1133	A268	150h like #1131	1.50	75
a.		Pair, #1132-1133	3.00	1.50

World Food
Day — A269

1990, Oct. 16   Litho.   *Perf. 12*

1134	A269	75h multicolored	75	36
1135	A269	150h multicolored	1.50	75

Organization
of Petroleum
Exporting
Countries
(OPEC), 30th
Anniv.
A270

1990, Sept. 26

1136	A270	75h multicolored	75	36
1137	A270	150h multicolored	1.50	75

Fifth Five Year
Development
Plan — A271

Designs: a, Oil refinery, irrigation, and oil storage tanks. b, Radio tower, highway, and mine. c, Monument, sports stadium, and vocational training. d, Television tower, environmental protection, and modern architecture.

1990, Oct. 30

1138	A271	75h Block of 4, #a.-d.	3.00	1.50

Battle of
Badr,
624 — A272

1991, Apr. 3   Litho.   *Perf. 12*

1139	A272	75h org, dk grn & grn	70	35
1140	A272	150h lt bl, dk bl & grn	1.40	70

A273   A274

1991, Apr. 9

1141	A273	75h multicolored	70	35
1142	A273	150h multicolored	1.40	70

World Health Day.

1991   Litho.   *Perf. 12*

Animals: a, k, Impala. b, l, Ibex. c, m, Oryx. d, n, Fox. e, o, Bat. f, p, Hyena. g, q, Cat. h, r, Dugong. i, s, Leopard.

Blocks of 9

1143	A274	25h Block, #a.-i.	2.40	1.20
1144	A274	50h Block, #a.-i.	4.80	2.40
1145	A274	75h Block, #a.-i.	7.25	3.65
1146	A274	100h Block, #a.-i.	9.50	4.75
1146J	A274	150h Block, #k.-s.	14.50	11.00
t.		Perf 14x13½	14.50	11.00

Issued: #1143-1146, May 1; #1146J, Dec. 1. No. 1146J exists imperf.

Pilgrimage to Mecca — A275

1991, June 20   Litho.   *Perf. 14*

1147	A275	75h blue & multi	70	35
1148	A275	150h green & multi	1.40	70

World Telecommunications Day — A276

1991, June 3   *Perf. 12*

1149	A276	75h multicolored	70	35
1150	A276	150h multicolored	1.40	70

A277   A278

1991, May 11

1151	A277	75h multicolored	1.00	50
1152	A277	150h multicolored	2.00	1.00

Liberation of Kuwait.

1991, Sept. 8   Litho.   *Perf. 12*

1153	A278	75h blue & multi	1.00	50
1154	A278	150h buff & multi	2.00	1.00

Literacy Day.

A279   A281

A280

1991, Oct. 16   Litho.   *Perf. 12*

1155	A279	75h green & multi	80	40
1156	A279	150h orange & multi	1.60	80

World Food Day.

1991, Dec. 7

1157	A280	75h green & multi	80	40
1158	A280	150h dk blue & multi	1.60	80

Childrens' Day.

1992, Apr. 8   Litho.   *Perf. 12*

1159	A281	75h lt blue & multi	75	38
1160	A281	150h lt orange & multi	1.50	75

World Health Day.

War Between
the Arabs of
Medina and
Mecca, 624-
630
A282

1992, Apr. 18

1161	A282	75h lt orange & green	75	38
1162	A282	150h lt bl, dk bl & grn	1.50	75

Pilgrimage to
Mecca
A283

Unwmk.

1992, June 9   Litho.   *Perf. 12*

1163	A283	75h lt blue & multi	75	38
1164	A283	150h lt orange & multi	1.50	75

Population and Housing Census — A284

1992, Sept. 26   Litho.   *Perf. 14*

1165	A284	75h blue & multi	68	35
1166	A284	150h org yellow & multi	1.35	70

World Food
Day — A285

1992, Oct. 17   *Perf. 12*

1167	A285	75h Vegetables	68	35
1168	A285	150h Fruits	1.35	70

Consultative
Council — A286

Document: a, 12 lines. b, 13 lines. c, 11 lines. 5r, Scrolls of 12, 11, & 13 lines.

1992, Dec. 12   Litho.   *Perf. 12*

1169	A286	75h Strip of 3, #a.-c.	2.10	1.05
1170	A286	150h Strip of 3, #a.-c.	4.00	2.00

Imperf

Size: 120x79mm

1170A	A286	5r multicolored	17.00	8.50

Birds — A287

Designs (75h/150h, 100h, 25h): a, k, c, Woodpecker. b, l, d, Arabian bustard. c, m, e, Lark. d, n, f, Turtle dove. e, o, g, Heron. f, p, h, Partridge. g, q, i, Hoopoe. h, r, j, Falcon. i, s, k, Houbara bustard. Illustration reduced.

1992-94   *Perf. 14x13½*
Blocks of 9

1170B	A287	25h #c.-k.	2.25	2.25
1171	A287	75h #a.-i.	6.65	3.30
1171J	A287	100h #k.-s.	8.00	4.00
t.		Perf. 12	8.00	4.00
1172	A287	150h #a.-i.	13.00	6.50
j.		Perf. 12	13.00	6.50

Issued: 150h, 3/18/92; 75h, 7/14/92; 100h, 3/1/93; 25h, 1994; #1171t, 1172j, 8/94.

World Health Day — A288

1993, Apr. 7   Litho.   *Perf. 12*

1173	A288	75h red & multi	70	35
1174	A288	150h blue & multi	1.40	70

King Fahd Championship Soccer Cup — A289

1993, Mar. 15

1175	A289	75h green & multi	70	35
1176	A289	150h rose red & multi	1.40	70

Pilgrimage to Mecca — A290

1993, May 30   Litho.   *Perf. 12*

1177	A290	75h green & multi	68	35
1178	A290	150h blue & multi	1.35	68

Intl. Telecommunications Day — A291

1993, May 17
Inscription Color

1179	A291	75h dark blue	68	35
1180	A291	150h red lilac	1.35	68

Battle of Alkandk A292

1993, May 15

1181	A292	75h light orange & grn	68	35
1182	A292	150h lt bl, dk bl & grn	1.35	68

World Food Day — A293

1993, Dec. 14   Litho.   *Perf. 12*

1183	A293	75h black & multi	70	35
1184	A293	150h red & multi	1.40	70

World Dental Health Day — A294

1994, Apr. 9   Litho.   *Perf. 12*

1185	A294	75h multicolored	70	35
1186	A294	150h multicolored	1.40	70

Intl. Olympic Committee, Cent. — A295

1994, Apr. 23   Litho.   *Perf. 12*

1187	A295	75h blue & multi	70	35
1188	A295	150h red & multi	1.40	70

Battle of Kaben A296

1994, June 14   Litho.   *Perf. 12*

1189	A296	75h bister & green	70	35
1190	A296	150h silver, blue & green	1.40	70

Pilgrimage to Mecca — A297

1994, May 14

1191	A297	75h green & multi	70	35
1192	A297	150h red & multi	1.40	70

Consultative Council — A298

Design: 150h, Different view of building, inscription tablet at right.

1994, July 12   Litho.   *Perf. 12*

1193	A298	75h multicolored	70	35
1194	A298	150h multicolored	1.40	70
a.		Souv. sheet of 2, #1193-1194, imperf.		

No. 1194a sold for 5r.

A299

1994 World Soccer Cup Championships, US — A300

1994, June 18

1195	A299	75h multicolored	70	35
1196	A300	150h multicolored	1.40	70

King Aziz Port — A301

1994   Litho.   *Perf. 12*

1197	A301	75h multicolored	70	35

A302

World Food Day — A303

1994   Litho.   *Perf. 12*

1198	A302	75h Green house	70	35
1199	A303	150h Foods	1.40	70

AIR POST STAMPS

Catalogue values for unused stamps in this section are for Never Hinged items.

Airspeed Ambassador Airliner — AP1

1949-58   Unwmk.   Typo.   *Perf. 11*

C1	AP1	1g blue green	2.25	15
C2	AP1	3g ultra	2.75	15
a.		3g blue ('58)	11.50	1.00
C3	AP1	4g orange	2.75	15
C4	AP1	10g purple	7.75	15
C5	AP1	20g brn vio ('58+)	7.00	20
a.		20g chocolate ('49)	14.00	50
C6	AP1	100g violet rose	70.00	7.00
		Nos. C1-C6 (6)	92.50	7.80

Imperfs. exist, not regularly issued.
The 1st printings are on grayish paper and sell for more.
No. C3 exists with pin-perf 6.
+ The date for No. C5 is not definite.

Saudi Airlines Convair 440 — AP2

Type I (Saud Cartouche)
(Illustrated over No. 286)

1960-61   Photo.   *Perf. 14*

C7	AP2	1p dull pur & grn	60	15
C8	AP2	2p grn & dull pur	60	15
C9	AP2	3p brn red & bl	60	15
C10	AP2	4p bl & dull pur	60	15
C11	AP2	5p grn & rose red	60	15
C12	AP2	6p ocher & slate	1.00	20
C13	AP2	8p rose & gray ol	1.25	20
C14	AP2	9p purple & red brn	1.75	20
C15	AP2	10p blk & dl red brn	5.00	45
C16	AP2	15p bl & bis brn	5.00	20
C17	AP2	20p bis brn & emer	5.00	40
C18	AP2	30p sep & Prus grn	12.50	1.00
C19	AP2	50p green & indigo	25.00	75
C20	AP2	100p gray & dk brn	50.00	2.00
C21	AP2	200p dk vio & black	75.00	3.00
		Nos. C7-C21 (15)	184.50	9.15

Nos. C7-C18 exist imperf., probably not regularly issued.

1963-64   Photo.   Wmk. 337
Size: 27½x22mm

C24	AP2	1p lilac & green	2.50	15
C25	AP2	2p green & dull pur	9.50	20
C26	AP2	4p blue & dull pur	3.50	15
C27	AP2	6p ocher & slate	9.50	80
C28	AP2	8p rose & gray olive	18.00	1.50
C29	AP2	9p pur & red brn ('64)	12.00	1.00
		Nos. C24-C29 (6)	55.00	3.80

Redrawn
Perf. 13½x13

1964   Wmk. 337   Litho.
Size: 28½x23mm

C30	AP2	3p brn red & dull bl	5.25	50
C31	AP2	10p blk & dk red brn	8.25	80
C32	AP2	20p bis brn & emer	17.50	1.75

Nos. C30-C32 are widely spaced in the sheet, producing large margins.

Saudi Airline Boeing 720-B Jet — AP3

Type I (Saud Cartouche)
(Illustrated over No. 286)

1965-70   Unwmk.   Litho.   *Perf. 14*

C33	AP3	1p lilac & green	70.00	3.00
C34	AP3	2p grn & dull pur	2,500.	100.00
C35	AP3	3p rose lil & dull bl	10.50	15
C36	AP3	4p blue & dull pur	6.00	15
C37	AP3	5p ol & rose red	2,000.	450.00

C38	AP3	6p ocher & slate	110.00	2.00
C39	AP3	7p rose & ol gray	7.00	40
C40	AP3	8p rose & gray ol	90.00	2.00
C41	AP3	9p purple & red brn	7.50	30
C42	AP3	10p blk & dk red brn	100.00	6.00
C43	AP3	11p green & bister	90.00	20.00
C44	AP3	12p orange & gray	7.00	30
C45	AP3	13p dk green & yel grn	7.00	30
C46	AP3	14p dk blue & org	7.00	40
C47	AP3	15p blue & bis brn	82.50	6.00
C48	AP3	16p black & ultra	10.00	50
C49	AP3	17p bister & sepia	7.50	40
C50	AP3	18p dk bl & yel grn	7.50	40
C51	AP3	19p car & dp org	8.75	50
C52	AP3	20p bis brn & emer	150.00	7.00
C53	AP3	23p olive & bister	165.00	12.00
C54	AP3	24p dk blue & sep	7.50	50
C55	AP3	26p ver & blue grn	7.50	50
C56	AP3	27p ol brn & ap grn	7.75	50
C57	AP3	31p car rose & rose red	8.00	60
C58	AP3	33p red & dull pur	13.00	60

The 50p, 100p and 200p exist but were not placed in use.
Issue years: 1966, 1p, 3p, 7p, 10p, 12p-14p, 16p-19p. 1969, 5p, 11p. 1970, 2p, 6p, 8p, 15p, 20p. Others, 1965.

Type II (Faisal Cartouche)

1966-78   Unwmk.   Litho.   Perf. 14

C59	AP3	1p dull pur & grn	21.00	1.00
C60	AP3	2p green & dull pur	22.50	1.50
C61	AP3	3p brn red & dull bl	22.50	50
C62	AP3	4p blue & dull pur	10.00	25
C63	AP3	5p ol & rose red	2,000.	500.00
C64	AP3	6p ocher & slate	140.00	10.00
C65	AP3	7p rose & ol gray	62.50	7.00
C66	AP3	8p rose & gray ol	100.00	12.50
C67	AP3	9p purple & red brn	6.75	60
C68	AP3	10p blk & dull red brn	18.00	1.00
C69	AP3	11p green & bister	10.00	50
C70	AP3	12p orange & gray	62.50	4.00
C71	AP3	13p dk grn & yel grn	16.00	1.00
C72	AP3	14p dk blue & org	18.00	1.65
C73	AP3	15p blue & bis brn	12.00	80
C74	AP3	16p black & ultra	18.00	3.00
C75	AP3	17p bister & sepia	15.00	1.50
C76	AP3	18p dk bl & yel grn	18.00	2.50
C77	AP3	19p carmine & org	18.00	1.00
C78	AP3	20p brn & brt grn	200.00	14.00
C79	AP3	23p olive & bister	25.00	3.00
C80	AP3	24p dk blue & blk	30.00	3.00
C83	AP3	31p car rose & rose red	750.00	
C84	AP3	33p red & dull pur	12.00	50
C85	AP3	50p emer & ind	650.00	200.00
C86	AP3	100p gray & dk brn	850.00	300.00
C87	AP3	200p dk vio & blk	1,000.	200.00

The existence of 26p and 27p denominations has been reported.
The status of the 31p has been questioned. If it exists it may not have been issued.
Issue years: 1968, 4p, 33p. 1969, 7p. 1970, 8p, 9p, 20p. 1971, 13p, 16p. 1974, 50p, 200p. 1975, 12p, 14p, 15p, 17p, 19p, 24p, 1976, 18p. 1978, 31p, 100p. Others, 1966.

1968-71   Wmk. 361   Litho.   Perf. 14

C88	AP3	1p lilac & green	8.25	20
C89	AP3	2p green & lilac	8.25	20
C90	AP3	3p rose lil & dull bl	37.50	2.00
C91	AP3	4p blue & dull pur	13.00	1.25
C92	AP3	7p rose & gray	13.00	1.65
C93	AP3	8p red & gray ol	42.50	6.50
C94	AP3	9p pur & red brn	57.50	8.00
C95	AP3	10p blk & dull red brn	40.00	4.00

Issue years: 1969, 3p, 10p. 1970, 4p. 1971, 7p-9p. Others, 1968.

Falcon — AP4

1968-71   Perf. 13½x14   Litho.   Wmk. 361

C96	AP4	1p green & red brn	6.50	15
C97	AP4	4p dk red & red brn	92.50	12.00
C98	AP4	10p blue & red brn	20.00	3.00
C99	AP4	20p green & red brn ('71)	35.00	6.00

Nine other denominations were printed but are not known to have been issued.

HEJAZ POSTAGE DUE STAMPS

From Old Door at El Ashraf Barsbai in Shari el Ashrafiya, Cairo — D1

Serrate Roulette 13

1917, June 27   Typo.   Unwmk.

LJ1	D1	20pa red	3.00	2.25
LJ2	D1	1pi blue	3.00	2.25
LJ3	D1	2pi magenta	3.00	2.25

For overprints see Nos. LJ4-LJ10, LJ17-LJ25, J9.

a   b

Nos. LJ1-LJ3 Overprinted Type "a" in Black or Red

1921, Dec.

LJ4	D1	20pa red	20.00	3.00
	a.	Double overprint, one at left	150.00	
	b.	Overprint at left	32.50	22.50
LJ5	D1	1pi blue (R)	6.00	4.00
LJ6	D1	1pi bl, ovpt. at left	30.00	20.00
	a.	Overprint at right	30.00	35.00
LJ7	D1	2pi magenta	11.00	8.00
	a.	Double overprint, one at left	70.00	
	b.	Overprint at left	30.00	

Nos. LJ1-LJ3 Overprinted Type "b" in Black

1922, Jan.

LJ8	D1	20pa red	25.00	30.00
	a.	Overprint at left	40.00	
LJ9	D1	1pi blue	3.50	3.50
	a.	Overprint at left	50.00	
LJ10	D1	2pi magenta	3.50	3.50
	a.	Overprint at left	35.00	

Regular issue of 1922 Overprinted

Black Overprint

1923   Perf. 11½

LJ11	A7	½pi red	4.00	1.50
LJ12	A7	1pi dark blue	6.00	1.50
LJ13	A7	2pi orange	4.00	2.00

1924

Blue Overprint

LJ14	A7	½pi red	17.50	3.00
LJ15	A7	1pi dark blue	40.00	3.00
LJ16	A7	2pi orange	30.00	5.00

This overprint reads "Mustahaq" (Due).

Jedda Issues

Nos. LJ1-LJ3 Overprinted in Red or Blue (Overprint reads up in illustration)

Jedda issues were also used in Medina and Yambo. Used values for #L51-L186 and LJ17-LJ39 are for genuine cancels. Privately applied cancels read "Mekke" (bilingual or all Arabic), often with wrong dates as early as 1916. These are worth half the used values.

1925, Jan.   Serrate Roulette 13

LJ17	D1	20pa red (R)	400.00	400.00
LJ19	D1	1pi blue (R)	20.00	20.00
LJ20	D1	1pi blue (Bl)	27.50	27.50
LJ21	D1	2pi magenta (Bl)	16.00	16.00

Overprint Reading Down

LJ17a	D1	20pa	600.00	600.00
LJ18	D1	20pa red (Bl)	500.00	
LJ19a	D1	20pa	20.00	20.00
LJ20a	D1	1pi	75.00	90.00
LJ21a	D1	2pi	60.00	60.00

Nos. LJ1-LJ3 Overprinted in Blue or Red

1925

LJ22	D1	20pa red (Bl)	475.00	475.00
	a.	Inverted overprint	350.00	350.00
LJ24	D1	1pi blue (R)	25.00	30.00
	a.	Inverted overprint	35.00	35.00
LJ25	D1	2pi magenta (Bl)	20.00	20.00
	a.	Inverted overprint	40.00	50.00
	b.	Double overprint	400.00	

No. LJ2 with this overprint in blue is bogus.

Regular Issues of 1922-24 Overprinted

a

and Handstamped

b

1925   Perf. 11½

LJ26	A7	⅛pi red brown	20.00	20.00
LJ27	A7	½pi red	27.50	27.50
LJ28	A7	1pi dark blue	20.00	20.00
LJ29	A7	1½pi violet	20.00	20.00
LJ30	A7	2pi orange	22.50	22.50
LJ31	A7	3pi olive brown	22.50	22.50
LJ32	A7	3pi dull red	50.00	50.00
LJ33	A7	3pi olive green	22.50	22.50
LJ34	A7	10pi vio & dk brn	30.00	30.00
		Nos. LJ26-LJ34 (9)	235.00	235.00

The printed overprint (a), consisting of the three top lines of Arabic, was used alone for the first issue (Nos. LJ26a-LJ34a). The "postage due" box was so small and indistinct that its equivalent in larger characters was added by boxed handstamp (b) at bottom of each stamp for the second issue (Nos. LJ26-LJ34).
The handstamped overprint (b) is found double, inverted, etc.
Counterfeits exist of both overprint and handstamp.

Without Boxed Handstamp "b"

LJ26a	A7	⅛pi red brown	47.50
LJ27a	A7	½pi red	47.50
LJ28a	A7	1pi dark blue	47.50
LJ29a	A7	1½pi violet	47.50
LJ30a	A7	2pi orange	47.50
LJ31a	A7	3pi olive brown	47.50
LJ32a	A7	3pi dull red	47.50
LJ33a	A7	3pi olive green	60.00
LJ34a	A7	10pi vio & dk brn	60.00
		Nos. LJ26a-LJ34a (9)	452.50

Regular Issue of 1922 Overprinted

and Handstamped

LJ35	A7	½pi red	150.00	150.00
LJ36	A7	1½pi violet	150.00	150.00
	a.	Overprint in red, boxed handstamp violet	1,500.	
LJ37	A7	2pi orange	200.00	200.00
LJ38	A7	3pi olive brown	150.00	150.00
LJ39	A7	5pi olive green	150.00	150.00
		Nos. LJ35-LJ39 (5)	800.00	800.00

Counterfeits exist of Nos. LJ4-LJ39.

Arabic Numeral of Value
D2   D3

1925, May-June   Perf. 11½

LJ40	D2	½pi light blue	3.00
LJ41	D2	1pi orange	3.00
LJ42	D2	2pi lt brown	3.00
LJ43	D2	3pi pink	3.00

Nos. LJ40-LJ43 exist imperforate. Impressions in colors other than issued are trial color proofs.

Black Overprint

1925

LJ44	D3	½pi light blue	3.00
LJ45	D3	1pi orange	3.00
LJ46	D3	2pi light brown	3.00
LJ47	D3	3pi pink	4.00

Nos. LJ44-LJ47 exist with either Jedda or Cairo overprints and the tablets normally read upward. Values are for Cairo overprints; Jedda overprints sell for more.

Red Overprint

LJ48	D3	½pi light blue	4.00
LJ49	D3	1pi orange	4.00
LJ50	D3	2pi light brown	4.00
LJ51	D3	3pi pink	4.00

Blue Overprint

LJ52	D3	½pi light blue	4.00
LJ53	D3	1pi orange	4.00
LJ54	D3	2pi light brown	4.00
LJ55	D3	3pi pink	4.00
		Nos. LJ40-LJ55 (16)	57.00

Red and blue overprints are from Cairo. Nos. LJ44-LJ55 exist imperf.

NEJD POSTAGE DUE STAMPS

Handstamped in Blue, Red or Black

On Hejaz Postage Due Stamps Typographed or Handstamped in Black

1925, Apr.-June   Unwmk.   Perf. 11½

J1	A7	½pi red (Bl)	30.00	30.00
J2	A7	1pi lt blue (R)	60.00	60.00
	a.	1pi dark blue (R)	40.00	40.00
J3	A7	2pi yel buff (Bl)	60.00	60.00
	a.	2pi orange (Bl)	52.50	52.50

Same, with Postage Due Overprint in Blue

J4	A7	½pi red (Bl)	55.00	
J5	A7	1pi dk blue (R)	375.00	
J6	A7	2pi orange (Bl)	650.00	

On Hejaz Stamps of 1922-24

Handstamped in Blue

J7	A7	½pi red (Bl & Bl)	18.00	18.00
J8	A7	3pi brn red (Bl & Bl)	21.00	21.00

Handstamped in
Blue, Black or Violet

See note before No. 35.

On Hejaz No. LJ9
Serrate Roulette 13¹/₂

J9	D1	1pi blue (V)	65.00	30.00

Same Overprint on Hejaz Stamps of 1924
with additional Handstamp in Black, Blue
or Red

Perf. 11¹/₂

J10	A7	3pi brn red (Bl & Bk)	12.00	12.00
J11	A7	3pi brn red (Bk & Bl)	12.00	12.00

Same Handstamps on Hejaz Railway Tax Stamps

J12	R3	1pi blue (Bk & R)	13.00	13.00
J13	R3	2pi ocher (Bl & Bk)	13.00	13.00
J14	R3	5pi green (Bk & R)	22.50	22.50
J15	R3	5pi green (V & BK)	22.50	10.00

The second handstamp, which is struck on the lower part of the Postage Due Stamps, is the word Mustahaq (Due) in various forms.

No. J13 exists with second handstamp in blue.

Hejaz-Nejd

D1

1926		Typo.	*Perf. 11*	
J16	D1	¹/₂pi carmine	4.50	75
J17	D1	2pi orange	4.50	75
J18	D1	6pi light brown	4.50	75

Nos. J16-J18 exist with perf. 14, 14x11 and 11x14, and imperf. These sell for six times the values quoted.

Nos. J16-J18 in colors other than listed (both perf. and imperf.) are proofs.

Counterfeit note after No. 80 also applies to Nos. J16-J21.

Pan-Islamic Congress Issue
Postage Due Stamps of 1926 Handstamped like Regular Issue

J19	D1	¹/₂pi carmine	6.00	5.00
J20	D1	2pi orange	6.00	5.00
J21	D1	6pi light brown	6.00	5.00

D2

1927			*Perf. 11¹/₂*	
J22	D2	1pi slate	20.00	50
a.		Inscription reads "2 piastres" in upper right circle	200.00	110.00
J23	D2	2pi dark violet	6.25	50

Saudi Arabia

Saudi Arabia No. 161
Handstamped in
Black

1935

J24	A9	¹/₂g dark carmine	150.00

Two types of overprint.

D3

D4

1937-39			Unwmk.	
J25	D3	¹/₂g org brn ('39)	13.00	1.50
J26	D3	1g light blue	13.00	1.50
J27	D3	2g rose vio ('39)	19.00	3.00

Catalogue values for unused stamps in this section, from this point to the end of the section, are for Never Hinged items.

1961		Litho.	*Perf. 13x13¹/₂*	
J28	D4	1p purple	5.50	1.00
J29	D4	2p green	9.50	1.00
J30	D4	4p rose red	11.00	2.00

The use of Postage Due stamps ceased in 1963.

OFFICIAL STAMPS

Official stamps were normally used only on external correspondence.

O1

O2

1939		Unwmk.	Typo.	*Perf. 11¹/₂*	
O1	O1	3g deep ultra		3.25	1.50

Perf. 11, 11¹/₂

O2	O1	5g red violet	4.25	2.00

Perf. 11

O3	O1	20g brown	8.75	4.00
O4	O1	50g blue green	17.00	8.00
O5	O1	100g olive grn	70.00	35.00
O6	O1	200g purple	55.00	25.00
		Nos. O1-O6 (6)	158.25	75.50

Catalogue values for unused stamps in this section, from this point to the end of the section, are for Never Hinged items.

1961		Litho.	*Perf. 13x13¹/₂*	
		Size: 18x22¹/₂mm		
O7	O2	1p black	1.00	20
O8	O2	2p dark green	1.65	30
O9	O2	3p bister	2.00	40
O10	O2	4p dark blue	2.50	50
O11	O2	5p rose red	3.00	60
O12	O2	10p maroon	5.25	2.00
O13	O2	20p violet blue	9.25	3.50
O14	O2	50p dull brown	25.00	10.00
O15	O2	100g dull green	45.00	18.00
		Nos. O7-O15 (9)	94.65	35.50

Nos. O8, O10-O15 exist imperf., probably not regularly issued.

1964-65		Wmk. 337	*Perf. 13¹/₂x13*	
		Size: 21x26mm		
O16	O2	1p black	1.00	40
O17	O2	2p green ('65)	2.00	80
O18	O2	3p bister	7.00	2.75
O19	O2	4p dark blue	5.00	2.00
O20	O2	5p rose red	6.00	1.25
		Nos. O16-O20 (5)	21.00	7.20

1965-70		Wmk. 337 Typo.	*Perf. 11*	
O21	O2	1p dark brown	4.00	1.50
O22	O2	2p green	4.00	1.50
O23	O2	3p bister	4.00	1.50
O24	O2	4p dark blue	4.00	1.50
O25	O2	5p deep orange	7.50	2.00
O26	O2	6p red lilac	7.50	2.00
O27	O2	7p emerald	7.50	2.00
O28	O2	8p car rose	7.50	2.00
O29	O2	9p red	30.00	
O30	O2	10p red brown	30.00	2.00
O31	O2	11p pale green	60.00	
O32	O2	12p violet	300.00	
O33	O2	13p blue	10.00	3.00
O34	O2	14p purple	10.00	3.00
O35	O2	15p orange	100.00	1.00
O36	O2	16p black	100.00	
a.		"19" instead of "16"	500.00	
O37	O2	17p gray green	100.00	
O38	O2	18p yellow	100.00	
O39	O2	19p dp red lilac	100.00	
O39A	O2	20p lt blue green	100.00	
O40	O2	23p ultra	250.00	
O41	O2	24p yellow green	100.00	
O42	O2	26p bister	100.00	
O43	O2	27p pale lilac	100.00	
O44	O2	31p pale salmon	150.00	
O45	O2	33p yellow green	100.00	
O46	O2	50p olive bister	400.00	
O47	O2	100p ol gray ('70)	900.00	
		Nos. O21-O39,O40-O47 (27)	3,086.	

Nos. O21-O28, O30 and O33-O34 were released to the philatelic trade in 1964. Nos. O21-O47 were printed from new plates; lines of the design are heavier. The numerals have been enlarged and the P's are smaller. Head of "P" 2mm wide on 1964-65 issue, 1mm wide on 1965-70 issue.

O3

Wmk. 361, 337 (7p, 8p, 9p, 11p, 12p, 23p)					
1970-72		Litho.	*Perf. 13¹/₂x14*		
O48	O3	1p red brown	3.00	1.00
O49	O3	2p deep green	3.00	1.00
O50	O3	3p rose red	4.00	1.50
O51	O3	4p bright blue	5.00	2.00
O52	O3	5p brick red	5.00	2.00
O53	O3	6p orange	5.00	2.00
a.		Wmk. 337	200.00	50.00
O54	O3	7p deep salmon	200.00	
O55	O3	8p violet		
O56	O3	9p dk blue green		
O57	O3	10p blue	7.00	3.00
a.		Wmk. 337		
O58	O3	11p olive green		
O58A	O3	12p black brown		
O59	O3	20p gray violet	15.00	5.00
a.		Wmk. 337	200.00	100.00
O59B	O3	23p ocher ('72)	425.00	
O60	O3	31p deep plum	50.00	20.00
O61	O3	50p light brown		
O62	O3	100p green		

Use of official stamps ceased in 1974.

NEWSPAPER STAMPS

Nos. 8, 9 and 14 with
Additional Overprint in
Black

1925		Unwmk.	*Perf. 11¹/₂*	
P1	A7	¹/₈pi red brown (Bk)	2,000.	2,000.
P2	A7	¹/₈pi red brown (V)	1,500.	1,000.
P3	A7	¹/₂pi red (V)	3,000.	2,000.

Overprint reads: "Matbu'a" (Newspaper), but these stamps were normally used for regular postage. Counterfeits exist.

The status of this set in question. The government may have declared it to be unauthorized.

POSTAL TAX STAMPS

PT1

1934, June		Unwmk.	*Perf. 11¹/₂*	
RA1	PT1	¹/₂g scarlet	200.00	5.00

No. RA1 collected a "war tax" to aid wounded of the 1934 Saudi-Yemen war.

Nos. RA2-RA8 raised funds for the Medical Aid Society.

General
Hospital,
Mecca — PT2

1936, Oct.

		Size: 37x20mm		
RA2	PT2	¹/₈g scarlet	600.00	10.00

Type of 1936, Redrawn

1937-42

		Size: 30¹/₂x18mm		
RA3	PT2	¹/₈g scarlet	65.00	1.00
a.		¹/₈g rose ('39)	100.00	2.00
b.		¹/₈g rose car, perf. 11 ('42)	200.00	7.50

General Hospital,
Mecca — PT3

1943		Typo.	*Perf. 11¹/₂, 11*	
		Grayish Paper		
RA4	PT3	¹/₈g car rose	40.00	15
a.		¹/₈g scarlet	40.00	15

The 1g green and 5g indigo were not for postal use.

Type of 1943, Redrawn

1948-53		Litho.	*Perf. 10*	
RA5	PT3	¹/₈g rose brn ('53)	22.50	20
c.		Perf. 11x10	30.00	20

Catalogue values for unused stamps in this section, from this point to the end of the section, are for Never Hinged items.

1950			*Rouletted*	
RA6	PT3	¹/₈g red brown	6.00	15
a.		¹/₈g rose	8.00	20
b.		¹/₈g carmine	10.00	25

All lines in lithographed design considerably finer; some shading in center eliminated.

Type of 1943

1955-56		Photo.	*Perf. 11*	
RA7	PT3	¹/₈g rose car	8.75	15
RA8	PT3	¹/₄g car rose ('56)	5.25	15
		Set value		20

The tax on postal matter was discontinued in May, 1964.

Coat of Arms, Waves and View — PT4

Wmk. 361

1974, Oct.   Litho.   Perf. 14

RA9 PT4   1r blue & multi   125.00

Obligatory on all mailed entries in a government television contest during month of Ramadan in 1974 and 1975. The tax aided a benevolent society.

SCHLESWIG

LOCATION — In the northern part of the former Schleswig-Holstein Province, in northern Germany.

Schleswig was divided into North and South Schleswig after the Versailles Treaty, and plebiscites were held in 1920. North Schleswig (Zone 1) voted to join Denmark, South Schleswig to stay German.

100 Pfennig = 1 Mark
100 Ore = 1 Krone

Watermark

Wmk. 114- Multiple Crosses

Plebiscite Issue

Arms — A11   View of Schleswig — A12

Perf. 14x15

1920, Jan. 25   Typo.   Wmk. 114

1	A11	2½pf gray	15	24
2	A11	5pf green	15	24
3	A11	7½pf yellow brown	15	30
4	A11	10pf deep rose	15	35
5	A11	15pf red violet	15	24
6	A11	20pf deep blue	18	42
7	A11	25pf orange	30	70
8	A11	35pf brown	40	1.00
9	A11	40pf violet	24	60
10	A11	75pf greenish blue	40	1.00
11	A12	1m dark brown	40	1.00
12	A12	2m deep blue	55	1.50
13	A12	5m green	85	2.00
14	A12	10m red	1.50	3.50
		Nos. 1-14 (14)	5.57	

The colored portions of type A11 are white, and the white portions are colored, on Nos. 7-10.

Types of 1920 Overprinted in Blue **1. ZONE**

1920, May 20

15	A11	1o dark gray	15	65
16	A11	5o green	15	32
17	A11	7o yel brn	15	50
18	A11	10o rose red	15	65
19	A11	15o lilac rose	15	65
20	A11	20o dark blue	15	85
21	A11	25o orange	20	3.00
22	A11	35o brown	85	6.50
23	A11	40o violet	30	2.25
24	A11	75o greenish blue	40	4.00
25	A12	1k dk brn	55	4.00
26	A12	2k deep blue	4.00	22.50
27	A12	5k green	2.75	22.50
28	A12	10k red	6.00	45.00
		Nos. 15-28 (14)	15.95	

OFFICIAL STAMPS

Nos. 1-14 Overprinted **C·I·S**

1920   Wmk. 114   Perf. 14x15

O1	A11	2½pf gray	35.00	45.00
O2	A11	5pf green	35.00	47.50
O3	A11	7½pf yel brn	35.00	45.00

O4	A11	10pf dp rose	32.50	47.50
O5	A11	15pf red vio	22.50	25.00
O6	A11	20pf dp bl	32.50	32.50
O7	A11	25pf orange	70.00	70.00
a.		Inverted overprint	1,250.	
O8	A11	35pf brown	70.00	75.00
O9	A11	40pf violet	55.00	45.00
O10	A11	75pf grnsh bl	60.00	110.00
O11	A12	1m dk brn	60.00	110.00
O12	A12	2m dp bl	100.00	110.00
O13	A12	5m green	140.00	190.00
O14	A12	10m red	250.00	260.00
		Nos. O1-O14 (14)	997.50	1,212.

The letters "C.I.S." are the initials of "Commission Interalliée Slesvig," under whose auspices the plebiscites took place.
Counterfeit overprints exist.

SENEGAL

LOCATION — West coat of Africa, bordering on the Atlantic Ocean
GOVT. — Republic
AREA — 76,000 sq. mi.
POP. — 6,300,000 (est. 1984)
CAPITAL — Dakar

The former French colony of Senegal became part of French West Africa in 1943. The Republic of Senegal was established Nov. 25, 1958. From Apr. 4, 1959, to June 20, 1960, the Republic of Senegal and the Sudanese Republic together formed the Mali Federation. After its breakup, Senegal resumed issuing its own stamps in 1960.

100 Centimes = 1 Franc

> Catalogue values for unused stamps in this country are for Never Hinged items, beginning with Scott 195 in the regular postage section, Scott B16 in the the in the semi-postal section, Scott C26 in the airpost section, Scott CB2 in the airpost semi-postal section, Scott J32 in the postage due section, and Scott O1 in the official section.

French Colonies Nos. 48, 49, 51, 52, 55, Type A9, Surcharged:

a   b   c   d   e

1887   Unwmk.   Perf. 14x13½
Black Surcharge

1	(a)	5c on 20c red, grn	95.00	95.00
a.		Double surcharge		
2	(b)	5c on 20c red, grn	175.00	175.00
3	(c)	5c on 20c red, grn	600.00	600.00
4	(d)	5c on 20c red, grn	125.00	120.00
5	(e)	5c on 20c red, grn	225.00	225.00
6	(a)	5c on 30c brn, bis	175.00	175.00
7	(b)	5c on 30c brn, bis	700.00	700.00
8	(d)	5c on 30c brn, bis	250.00	250.00

See Madagascar #6-7 for stamps with surcharge like "d" on 10c and 25c stamps.

f   g   h   i

j   k   l   m

9	(f)	10c on 4c cl, lav	65.00	65.00
10	(g)	10c on 4c cl, lav	90.00	90.00
11	(h)	10c on 4c cl, lav	45.00	45.00
12	(i)	10c on 4c cl, lav	250.00	250.00
a.		"1" without top stroke		
13	(f)	10c on 20c red, grn	400.00	400.00
14	(g)	10c on 20c red, grn	400.00	400.00
15	(h)	10c on 20c red, grn	350.00	350.00
16	(i)	10c on 20c red, grn	2,250.	2,250.
17	(j)	10c on 20c red, grn	400.00	400.00
18	(k)	10c on 20c red, grn	400.00	400.00
19	(l)	10c on 20c red, grn	400.00	400.00
20	(m)	10c on 20c red, grn	400.00	400.00

n   o   p   q   r

s   t   u   v

15
w

21	(n)	15c on 20c red, grn	50.00	50.00
22	(o)	15c on 20c red, grn	40.00	40.00
23	(p)	15c on 20c red, grn	35.00	35.00
24	(q)	15c on 20c red, grn	62.50	62.50
25	(r)	15c on 20c red, grn	40.00	40.00
26	(s)	15c on 20c red, grn	40.00	40.00
27	(t)	15c on 20c red, grn	120.00	120.00
28	(u)	15c on 20c red, grn	35.00	32.50
29	(v)	15c on 20c red, grn	45.00	45.00
30	(w)	15c on 20c red, grn	200.00	200.00

Counterfeits exist of Nos. 1-34.

SÉNÉGAL 75   SENEGAL 1F

1892
Black Surcharge

31	A9	75c on 15c blue	275.	90.
32	A9	1fr on 5c grn, grnsh	275.	120.

"SENEGAL" in Red

33	A9	75c on 15c blue	6,500.	2,750.
34	A9	1fr on 5c grn, grnsh	3,250.	700.00

Navigation and Commerce — A24

1892-1900   Typo.   Perf. 14x13½
Name of Colony in Blue or Carmine

35	A24	1c blk, lil bl	30	30
36	A24	2c brn, buff	85	65
37	A24	4c claret, lav	72	50
38	A24	5c grn, grnsh	72	50
39	A24	5c yel grn ('00)	60	35
40	A24	10c blk, lav	3.25	2.50
41	A24	10c red ('00)	1.65	35
42	A24	15c bl, quadrille paper	3.25	60
43	A24	15c gray ('00)	1.50	80
44	A24	20c red, grn	4.75	2.50
45	A24	25c blk, rose	7.25	2.50
46	A24	25c blue ('00)	18.00	12.00
47	A24	30c brn, bis	7.25	2.50
48	A24	40c red, straw	11.00	8.00
49	A24	50c car, rose	18.00	11.00
50	A24	50c brn, az ('00)	21.00	16.00
51	A24	75c vio, org	8.50	6.25
52	A24	1fr brnz grn, straw	8.50	6.25
		Nos. 35-52 (18)	117.09	73.55

Perf. 13½x14 stamps are counterfeits.
For surcharges see Nos. 53-56, 73-78.

Stamps of 1892 Surcharged:

5   10

1903

53	A24	5c on 40c red, straw	6.50	6.50
54	A24	10c on 50c car, rose	9.25	9.25
55	A24	10c on 75c vio, org	9.25	9.25
56	A24	10c on 1fr brnz grn, straw	50.00	40.00

General Louis Faidherbe — A25   Oil Palms — A26

Dr. Noel Eugène Ballay — A27

1906   Typo.
"SÉNÉGAL" in Red or Blue

57	A25	1c slate	28	25
a.		"SENEGAL" omitted	40.00	40.00
58	A25	2c choc (R)	38	35
58A	A25	2c choc (Bl)	70	65
59	A25	4c choc, gray bl	55	50
60	A25	5c green	65	25
61	A25	10c car (Bl)	3.50	30
a.		"SENEGAL" omitted	150.00	150.00
62	A25	15c violet	2.75	1.60
63	A26	20c blk, az	3.25	1.60
64	A26	25c bl, pnksh	1.00	75
65	A26	30c choc, pnksh	2.75	2.00
66	A26	35c blk, yellow	10.50	90
67	A26	40c car, az (Bl)	5.00	3.00
67A	A26	45c choc, grnsh	12.00	9.00
68	A26	50c dp violet	4.50	3.00
69	A26	75c bl, org	4.00	1.60
70	A27	1fr blk, azure	15.00	9.00
71	A27	2fr blue, pink	20.00	12.50
72	A27	5fr car, straw (Bl)	40.00	25.00
		Nos. 57-72 (18)	126.81	72.25

Stamps of 1892-1900 Surcharged in Carmine or Black **05   10**

1912

73	A24	5c on 15c gray (C)	35	35
74	A24	5c on 20c red, grn	55	55
75	A24	5c on 30c brn, bis (C)	55	55
76	A24	10c on 40c red, straw	55	55
77	A24	10c on 50c car, rose	1.50	1.50
78	A24	10c on 75c vio, org	3.00	3.00
		Nos. 73-78 (6)	6.50	6.50

Two spacings between the surcharged numerals found on Nos. 73 to 78.

Senegalese Preparing Food — A28

1914-33   Typo.

79	A28	1c ol brn & vio	15	15
80	A28	2c black & blue	15	15
81	A28	4c gray & brn	15	15
82	A28	5c yel grn & bl grn	15	15
83	A28	5c blk & rose ('22)	15	15
84	A28	10c org red & rose	15	15
85	A28	10c yel grn & bl grn ('22)	18	16
86	A28	10c red brn & bl ('25)	15	15
87	A28	15c red org & brn vio ('17)	15	15
88	A28	20c choc & blk	15	15
89	A28	20c grn & bl grn ('26)	15	15
90	A28	20c db & lt bl ('27)	18	16
91	A28	25c ultra & bl	16	15
92	A28	25c red & blk ('22)	16	15
93	A28	30c black & rose	16	15
94	A28	30c red org & rose ('22)	18	16
95	A28	30c gray & bl ('25)	25	20
96	A28	30c dl grn & dp grn ('28)	32	15
97	A28	35c orange & vio	15	15
98	A28	40c violet & grn	55	15
99	A28	45c bl & ol brn	85	70
100	A28	45c rose & bl ('22)	25	20
101	A28	45c rose & ver ('25)	25	20
102	A28	45c ol brn & org ('28)	1.90	55
103	A28	50c vio brn & bl	55	15
104	A28	50c ultra & bl ('22)	1.10	85
105	A28	50c red org & grn ('26)	25	16
106	A28	60c vio, pnksh ('26)	25	20
107	A28	65c rose red & dp grn ('28)	80	65
108	A28	75c gray & rose	65	35
109	A28	75c dk bl & lt bl ('25)	38	20
110	A28	75c rose & gray bl ('26)	95	28
111	A28	90c brn red & rose ('30)	3.25	2.50
112	A28	1fr violet & blk	70	28
113	A28	1fr blue ('26)	38	20

114	A28	1fr blk & gray bl ('26)		80	20
115	A28	1.10fr bl grn & blk ('28)		2.00	1.65
116	A28	1.25fr dp grn & dp org ('33)		55	42
117	A28	1.50fr dk bl & bl ('30)		1.25	1.00
118	A28	1.75fr dk brn & Prus bl ('33)		4.75	48
119	A28	2fr carmine & bl		1.25	72
120	A28	2fr lt bl & brn ('22)		1.50	28
121	A28	3fr red vio ('30)		3.00	1.00
122	A28	5fr green & vio		3.00	52
		Nos. 79-122 (44)		34.39	16.84

Nos. 79, 82, 84 and 97 are on both ordinary and chalky paper.
For surcharges see Nos. 123-137, B1-B2.

No. 108 and Type of 1914 Surcharged:

1922-25

123	A28	60c on 75c vio, *pnksh*		48	48
124	A28	65c on 15c red org & dl vio ('25)		70	70
125	A28	85c on 15c red org & dl vio ('25)		70	70
126	A28	85c on 75c ('25)		80	80

No. 87 Surcharged in Various Colors

1922

127	A28	1c on 15c (Bk)		20	20
128	A28	2c on 15c (Bl)		20	20
129	A28	4c on 15c (G)		20	20
130	A28	5c on 15c (R)		20	20
		Nos. 123-130 (8)		3.48	3.48

Stamps and Type of 1914 Surcharged with New Value and Bars in Black or Red

1924-27

131	A28	25c on 5fr grn & vio		28	28
132	A28	90c on 75c brn red & cer ('27)		52	48
a.		Double surcharge		40.00	40.00
133	A28	1.25fr on 1fr bl & lt bl (R) ('26)		28	28
134	A28	1.50fr on 1fr bl & ultra ('27)		40	32
135	A28	3fr on 5fr mag & ol brn ('27)		1.00	48
136	A28	10fr on 5fr dk bl & red org ('27)		3.25	1.10
137	A28	20fr on 5fr vio & ol bis ('27)		4.75	3.00
		Nos. 131-137 (7)		10.48	5.94

Colonial Exposition Issue
Common Design Types
Name of Country Typographed in Black

1931		**Engr.**	**Perf. 12½**	
138	CD70	40c deep green	1.25	1.25
139	CD71	50c violet	1.25	1.25
140	CD72	90c red orange	1.25	1.25
a.		"SENEGAL" double	50.00	
141	CD73	1.50fr dull blue	1.25	1.25

Faidherbe Bridge, St. Louis — A29

Diourbel Mosque A30

1935-40

			Perf. 12½x12	
142	A29	1c violet blue	15	15
143	A29	2c brown	15	15
144	A29	3c violet ('40)	15	15
145	A29	4c gray blue	15	15
146	A29	5c orange red	15	15
147	A29	10c violet	15	15
148	A29	15c black	15	15
149	A29	20c dk carmine	15	15
150	A29	25c black brn	15	15
151	A29	30c green	15	15
152	A29	40c rose lake	15	15
153	A29	45c dk blue grn	15	15
154	A30	50c red orange	15	15
155	A30	60c violet ('40)	20	18

156	A30	65c dk violet		20	18
157	A30	70c red brn ('40)		35	30
158	A30	75c brown		40	35
159	A30	90c rose car		1.40	1.00
160	A30	1fr violet		5.75	1.25
161	A30	1.25fr redsh brn		65	36
162	A30	1.25fr rose car ('39)		60	52
163	A30	1.40fr dk bl grn ('40)		35	30
164	A30	1.50fr dk blue		20	18
165	A30	1.60fr pck bl ('40)		40	35
166	A30	1.75fr dk blue grn		20	18
167	A30	2fr blue		20	18
168	A30	3fr green		20	18
169	A30	5fr black brn		52	30
170	A30	10fr rose lake		65	45
171	A30	20fr grnsh slate		65	45
		Nos. 142-171 (30)		14.87	
		Set value			7.50

Nos. 143, 148 and 156 surcharged with new values are listed under French West Africa.
For surcharges see Nos. B9, B11-B12.

Paris International Exposition Issue
Common Design Types

			Perf. 13	
1937				
172	CD74	20c deep violet	48	48
173	CD75	30c dark green	48	48
174	CD76	40c car rose	48	48
175	CD77	50c dark brown	60	60
176	CD78	90c red	60	60
177	CD79	1.50fr ultra	90	90
		Nos. 172-177 (6)	3.54	3.54

> Common Design Types pictured in section at front of book

Colonial Arts Exhibition Issue
Souvenir Sheet
Common Design Type

			Imperf.	
1937		**Unwmk.**		
178	CD76	3fr rose violet	3.50	3.50

Senegalese Woman — A31

1938-40　　**Perf. 12x12½, 12½x12**

179	A31	35c green		45	28
180	A31	55c chocolate		45	35
181	A31	80c violet		70	28
182	A31	90c lt rose vio ('39)		24	24
183	A31	1fr car lake		1.40	75
184	A31	1fr cop brn ('40)		20	20
185	A31	1.75fr ultra		45	28
186	A31	2.25fr ultra ('39)		45	45
187	A31	2.50fr black ('40)		65	65
		Nos. 179-187 (9)		4.99	3.48

For surcharge see No. B10.

Caillié Issue
Common Design Type

		Engr.	**Perf. 12½x12**	
1939				
188	CD81	90c org brn & org	28	28
189	CD81	2fr brt vio	42	42
190	CD81	2.25fr ultra & dk bl	42	42

For No. 188 surcharged 20fr and 50fr, see French West Africa.

New York World's Fair Issue
Common Design Type

			Perf. 12½x12	
1939				
191	CD82	1.25fr car lake	30	30
192	CD82	2.25fr ultra	30	30

Diourbel Mosque and Marshal Pétain A32

			Engr.	
1941				
193	A32	1fr green	22	
194	A32	2.50fr blue	22	

Nos. 193-194 were issued by the Vichy government, but it is doubtful whether they were placed on sale in Senegal.

Stamps of types A29, A30 and A31, without "RF", were issued in 1943 by the Vichy Government, but were not placed on sale in the colony.

See French West Africa No. 69 for additional stamp inscribed "Senegal" and "Afrique Occidentale Francaise."

> Catalogue values for unused stamps in this section, from this point to the end of the section, are for Never Hinged items.

Republic

Roan Antelope — A33

Animals: 10fr, Savannah buffalo, horiz. 15fr, Wart hog. 20fr, Giant eland. 25fr, Bushbuck, horiz. 85fr, Defassa waterbuck.

1960		**Unwmk.**	**Engr.**	**Perf. 13**	
195	A33	5fr brn, grn & claret		15	15
196	A33	10fr grn & brn		16	15
197	A33	15fr blk, cl & org brn		20	15
198	A33	20fr brn, grn, ocher & sal		25	15
199	A33	25fr brn, lt grn & org		35	16
200	A33	85fr brn, grn, ol & bis		1.10	50
		Nos. 195-200 (6)		2.21	
		Set value			98

> **Imperforates**
> Most Senegal stamps from 1960 onward exist imperforate in issued and trial colors, and also in small presentation sheets in issued colors.

Allegory of Independent State — A34

1961, Apr. 4				
201	A34	25fr bl, choc & grn	22	15

Independence Day, Apr. 4.

Wrestling A35

Designs: 1fr, Pirogues racing. 2fr, Horse race. 30fr, Male tribal dance. 45fr, Lion game.

				Perf. 13	
1961, Sept. 30					
202	A35	50c ol, bl & choc		15	15
203	A35	1fr grn, bl & maroon		15	15
204	A35	2fr ultra, bis & sepia		15	15
205	A35	30fr carmine & claret		30	18
206	A35	45fr indigo & brn org		40	25
		Set value		80	55

UN Headquarters, New York and Flag — A36

			Engr.	**Perf. 13**	
1962, Jan. 6					
207	A36	10fr grn, ocher & car		15	15
208	A36	30fr grn, ocher & car		30	20
209	A36	85fr grn, ocher & car		70	42

1st anniv. of Senegal's admission to the United Nations, Sept. 28, 1960.

Map of Africa, ITU Emblem and Man with Telephone A37

1962, Jan. 22　Photo.　Perf. 12½x12				
210	A37	25fr blk, grn, red & ocher	25	20

Meeting of the Commission for the Africa Plan of the ITU, Dakar.

African and Malgache Union Issue
Common Design Type

				Unwmk.	
1962, Sept. 8					
211	CD110	30fr grn, bluish grn, red & gold		40	35

Boxing — A38

Charaxes Varanes — A40

UPU Monument, Bern — A39

Designs: 15fr, Diving, horiz. 20fr, High jump, horiz. 25fr, Soccer. 30fr, Basketball. 85fr, Running.

			Engr.	**Perf. 13**	
1963, Apr. 11					
Athletes in Dark Brown					
212	A38	10fr ver & emer		15	15
213	A38	15fr dk bl & bis		16	15
214	A38	20fr ver & dk bl		22	15
215	A38	25fr grn & dk bl		25	16
216	A38	30fr ver & grn		35	20
217	A38	85fr vio bl		90	60
		Nos. 212-217 (6)		2.03	1.41

Friendship Games, Dakar, Apr. 11-21.

			Unwmk.	**Perf. 13**	
1963, June 14					
218	A39	10fr grn & ver		16	15
219	A39	15fr dk bl & red brn		20	16
220	A39	30fr red brn & dk bl		35	22

2nd anniv. of Senegal's admission to the UPU.

1963, July 20　Photo.　Perf. 12½x13				

Butterflies: 45fr, Papilio nireus. 50fr, Colotis danae. 85fr, Epiphora bauhiniae. 100fr, Junonia hierta. 500fr, Danaus chrysippus.

Butterflies in Natural Colors

221	A40	30fr bl gray & blk		60	16
222	A40	45fr org & blk		80	22
223	A40	50fr brt yel & blk		90	30
224	A40	85fr red & blk		1.40	55
225	A40	100fr bl & blk		1.65	65
226	A40	500fr emer & blk		6.25	2.25
		Nos. 221-226 (6)		11.60	4.13

Prof. Gaston Berger (1896-1960), Philosopher, and Owl — A41

			Perf. 12½x12	
1963, Nov. 13				
227	A41	25fr multi	22	15

Scales, Globe, Flag and UNESCO Emblem A42

1963, Dec. 10
228 A42 60fr multi   55 30

15th anniv. of the Universal Declaration of Human Rights.

Flag, Mother and Child — A43

1963, Dec. 21   Perf. 12x12½
229 A43 25fr multi   30 22

Issued for the Senegalese Red Cross.

Dredging of Titanium-bearing Sand — A44

Designs: 10fr, Titanium extraction works. 15fr, Cement works at Rufisque. 20fr, Phosphate quarry at Pallo. 25fr, Extraction of phosphate ore at Taiba. 85fr, Mineral dock, Dakar.

1964, July 4   Engr.   Perf. 13
230 A44 5fr grnsh bl, car & dk brn   15 15
231 A44 10fr ocher, grn & ind   15 15
232 A44 15fr dk bl, brt grn & dk brn   15 15
233 A44 20fr ultra, ol & pur   16 15
234 A44 25fr dk bl, yel & blk   25 15
235 A44 85fr bl, red & brn   80 42
      Nos. 230-235 (6)   1.66
      Set value   72

Cooperation Issue
Common Design Type

1964, Nov. 7   Engr.   Perf. 13
236 CD119 100fr dk grn, dk brn & car   90 60

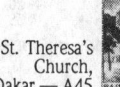
St. Theresa's Church, Dakar — A45

Designs: 10fr, Mosque, Touba. 15fr, Mosque, Dakar, vert.

1964, Nov. 28   Unwmk.   Perf. 13
237 A45 5fr bl, grn & red brn   15 15
238 A45 10fr dk bl, ocher & blk   15 15
239 A45 15fr brn, bl & sl grn   16 15
      Set value   35 26

Leprosy Examination A46

Leprosarium, Peycouk Village — A47

1965, Jan. 30   Engr.   Perf. 13
240 A46 20fr brn red, grn & blk   22 20
241 A47 65fr org, dk bl & grn   65 40

Issued to publicize the fight against leprosy.

Upper Casamance Region — A48

Views: 30fr, Sangalkam. 45fr, Forest along Senegal River.

1965, Feb. 27   Unwmk.   Perf. 13
242 A48 25fr red brn, sl bl & grn   22 15
243 A48 30fr indigo & lt brn   25 15
244 A48 45fr yel grn, red brn & dk grn 40 22

      See No. C41.

Abdoulaye Seck A49

Berthon-Ader Telephone A51

General Post Office, Dakar — A50

1965, Apr. 24   Unwmk.   Perf. 13
245 A49 10fr dk brn & blk   15 15
246 A50 15fr brn & dk sl grn   16 15
      Set value   16

1965, May 17   Engr.

Designs: 60fr, Cable laying ship "Alsace." 85fr, Picard's cable relay for submarine telegraph.

247 A51 50fr bl grn & org brn   50 30
248 A51 60fr mag & dk bl   60 38
249 A51 85fr ver, bl & red brn   90 50

      ITU, centenary.

Plowing with Ox Team — A52

Designs: 60fr, Harvesting millet, vert. 85fr, Men working in rice field.

1965, July 3   Unwmk.   Perf. 13
250 A52 25fr dk ol grn, brn & pur   25 15
251 A52 60fr ind, sl grn & dk brn   55 22
252 A52 85fr dp car, sl grn & brt grn 80 38

Gorée Sailboat A53

Cashew A54

Designs: 20fr, Large Seumbediou canoe. 30fr, Fadiouth one-man canoe. 45fr, One-man canoe on Senegal River.

1965, Aug. 7   Photo.   Perf. 12½x13
253 A53 10fr multi   15 15
254 A53 20fr multi   16 15
255 A53 30fr multi   30 16
256 A53 45fr multi   42 25
      Set value   58

1965   Photo.   Perf. 12½
257 A54 10fr shown   15 15
258 A54 15fr Papaya   16 15
259 A54 20fr Mango   20 15
260 A54 30fr Peanuts   30 15
      Set value   36

Issued: 10fr, 15fr, 20fr, Nov. 6. 30fr, Dec. 18.

"Elegant Man" — A55

Drummer and Map of Africa — A56

Dolls of Gorée: 2fr, "Elegant Woman." 3fr, Woman peddling fruit. 4fr, Woman pounding grain.

1966, Jan. 22   Engr.   Perf. 13
261 A55 1fr brn, rose car & ultra   15 15
262 A55 2fr brn, bl & org   15 15
263 A55 3fr brn, red & bl   15 15
264 A55 4fr brn, lil & emer   15 15
      Set value   22 22

1966

Designs: 15fr, Sculpture; mother and child. No. 267, Music; stringed instrument. 75fr, Dance; carved antelope headpiece (Bambara). 90fr, Ideogram.

265 A56 15fr dk red brn, bl & ocher   15 15
266 A56 30fr brn, red & grn   30 18
267 A56 30fr dk red brn, bl & yel   30 18
268 A56 75fr dk red brn, bl & blk   70 42
269 A56 90fr dk red brn, org & sl
             grn   90 55
  a. Souv. sheet of 4, #265, 267-269 2.50 2.50
      Nos. 265-269 (5)   2.35 1.48

Intl. Negro Arts Festival, Dakar, Apr. 1-24.
Issued: No. 266, Feb. 5. Others, Apr. 2. See No. 364.

Fish — A57

1966, Feb. 26   Photo.   Perf. 12½x13
270 A57 20fr Tuna   22 15
271 A57 30fr Merou   35 16
272 A57 50fr Girella   55 30
273 A57 100fr Parrot fish   1.10 50

Arms of Senegal — A58

Flowers — A59

1966, July 2   Litho.   Perf. 13x12½
274 A58 30fr multi   25 15

1966, Nov. 19   Photo.   Perf. 11½
275 A59 45fr Mexican poppy   42 18
276 A59 55fr Mimosa   50 20
277 A59 60fr Haemanthus   60 22
278 A59 90fr Baobab   80 38

Harbor, Gorée Island — A60

Designs: 25fr, S.S. France in roadstead, Dakar and seagulls. 30fr, Hotel and tourist village, N'Gor. 50fr, Hotel and bay, N'Gor.

1966, Dec. 25   Engr.   Perf. 13
279 A60 20fr mar & vio bl   20 15
280 A60 25fr red, grn & blk   22 15
281 A60 35fr dk red & dp bl   25 16
282 A60 50fr brn, sl grn & emer   45 20

Laying Urban Water Pipes — A61

Symbolic Water Cycle — A62

Designs: 20fr, Cattle at water trough. 50fr, Village well.

1967, Mar. 25   Engr.   Perf. 13
283 A61 10fr org brn, grn & dk bl   15 15
284 A61 20fr grn, brt bl & org brn   25 20

                     Typo.
              Perf. 13x14
285 A62 30fr sky bl, blk & org   35 15

                     Engr.
               Perf. 13
286 A62 50fr brn red, brt bl & bis   55 20
      Set value   60

Intl. Hydrological Decade (UNESCO), 1965-74.

Lions Emblem A63

1967, May 27 Photo. Perf. 12½x13
287 A63 30fr lt ultra & multi   30 16

50th anniversary of Lions International.

Blaise Diagne A64

1967, June 10   Engr.   Perf. 13
288 A64 30fr ocher, sl grn & dk red brn 30 20

Blaise Diagne (1872-1934), member of French Chamber of Deputies and Colonial Minister. For surcharge see No. 380.

City Hall and Arms, Dakar — A65

1967, June 10
289 A65 90fr bl, dk grn & blk   80 38

Eagle and Antelope
Carvings — A66

Design: 150fr, Flags, maple leaf and EXPO '67
emblem.

1967, Sept. 2 Photo.   Perf. 13x12¹/₂
290 A66 90fr red & blk   60 30
291 A66 150fr red & multi   1.00 50
EXPO '67 Intl. Exhib., Montreal, Apr. 28-Oct. 27.

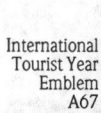

International
Tourist Year
Emblem
A67

Tourist Photographing Hippopotamus and
Siminti Hotel — A68

1967, Oct. 7 Typo.   Perf. 14x13
292 A67 50fr blk & bl   55 38
Perf. 13
Engr.
293 A68 100fr blk, sl grn & ocher   1.10 50
International Tourist Year.

Monetary Union Issue
Common Design Type
1967, Nov. 4 Engr.   Perf. 13
294 CD125 30fr multi   25 15
5th anniv. of the West African Monetary Union.

Lyre-shaped
Megalith,
Kaffrine
A69

Design: 70fr, Ancient covered bowl, Bandiala.

1967, Dec. 2 Engr.   Perf. 13
295 A69 30fr grn, grnsh bl & red brn   25 15
296 A69 70fr red brn, ocher & brt bl   60 25

Nurse Feeding
Child — A70

Human Rights
Flame — A71

1967, Dec. 23
297 A70 50fr bl grn, red & red brn   45 22
Issued for the Senegalese Red Cross.

1968, Jan. 20 Photo.   Perf. 13x12¹/₂
298 A71 30fr brt grn & gold   30 15
International Human Rights Year.

Parliament,
Dakar — A72

1968, Apr. 16 Photo.   Perf. 12¹/₂x13
299 A72 30fr car rose   25 15
Inter-Parliamentary Union Meeting, Dakar.

Pied Kingfisher
A73

Goose Barnacles
A74

Designs: 10fr, Green lobster. 15fr, African
jacana. 20fr, Sea cicada. 35fr, Shrimp. 70fr, African
anhinga.

1968-69 Photo.   Perf. 11¹/₂
Dated "1968" or (70fr) "1969"
Granite Paper
300 A73 5fr brn & multi   15 15
301 A74 10fr red & multi   15 15
302 A73 15fr yel & multi   16 15
303 A74 20fr ultra & multi   20 15
304 A74 35fr car rose & ol grn   30 20
305 A73 70fr Prus bl & multi   65 35
306 A74 100fr yel grn & multi   90 50
  Nos. 300-306 (7)   2.51
  Set value   1.35

Dates of issue: 5fr, July 13, 1968; 15fr, Dec. 21,
1968; 70fr, Apr. 26, 1969, others May 18, 1968.
See Nos. C53-C57.

Steer and
Hypodermic
Syringe
A75

1968, Aug. 17 Engr.   Perf. 13
307 A75 30fr dk grn, dp bl & brn red   22 16
Campaign against cattle plague.

Boy and WHO
Emblem — A76

Bambara
Antelope
Symbol — A77

1968, Nov. 16 Engr.   Perf. 13
308 A76 30fr blk, grn & car   25 15
309 A76 45fr red brn, grn & blk   40 20
WHO, 20th anniversary.

1969, Jan. 13 Engr.   Perf. 13
Design: 30fr, School of Medicine and Pharma-
cology, Dakar, horiz.
310 A77 30fr emer, brt bl & ind   25 16
311 A77 50fr red, gray ol & bl grn   40 20
6th Medical Meeting, Dakar, Jan. 13-18.

Panet, Camels and
Mogador-St. Louis
Route — A78

1969, Feb. 15 Engr.   Perf. 13
312 A78 75fr ultra, Prus bl & brn   60 25
Leopold Panet (1819-1859), first explorer of the
Mauritanian Sahara.

ILO Emblem
A79

1969, May 3 Photo.   Perf. 12¹/₂x13
313 A79 30fr blk & grnsh bl   22 15
314 A79 45fr blk & dp car   40 18
ILO, 50th anniversary.

Arms of
Casamance
A80

Mahatma
Gandhi
A81

Design: 20fr, Arms of Gorée Island.

1969, July 26 Litho.   Perf. 13¹/₂
315 A80 15fr rose & multi   15 15
316 A80 20fr bl & multi   15 15
  Set value   24 15

Development Bank Issue
Common Design Type
1969, Sept. 10 Engr.   Perf. 13
317 CD130 30fr gray, grn & ocher   25 16
318 CD130 45fr brn, grn & ocher   40 20

1969, Oct. 2 Engr.   Perf. 13
319 A81 50fr multi   52 52
  a. Miniature sheet of 4   2.25 2.25
Mohandas K. Gandhi (1869-1948), leader in
India's fight for independence.

Rotary
Emblem and
Symbolic
Ship — A82

1969, Nov. 29 Photo.   Perf. 12¹/₂x13
320 A82 30fr ultra, yel & blk   35 20
Dakar Rotary Club, 30th anniversary.

ASECNA Issue
Common Design Type
1969, Dec. 12 Engr.   Perf. 13
321 CD132 100fr dk gray   65 35

Niokolo-Koba
Campsite
A83

Tourism: 20fr, Cape Skiring, Casamance. 35fr,
Elephants at Niokolo-Koba National Park. 45fr, Millet granaries, pigs and boats, Fadiouth Island.

1969, Dec. 27
322 A83 20fr bl, red brn & ol   16 15
323 A83 30fr bl, red brn & ocher   30 16
324 A83 35fr grnsh bl, blk & ocher   30 16
325 A83 45fr vio bl & hn brn   35 16
  Set value   52

Bottle-nosed
Dolphins
A84

Lenin (1870-1924)
A85

1970, Feb. 21 Photo.   Perf. 12x12¹/₂
326 A84 50fr dl bl, blk & red   40 20

1970, Apr. 22 Photo.   Perf. 11¹/₂
327 A85 30fr brn, buff & ver   22 16
  a. A85 50fr Souv. sheet, perf. 12x11¹/₂ 40 40
No. 327a contains one 32x48mm stamp.

UPU Headquarters Issue
Common Design Type
1970, May 20 Engr.   Perf. 13
328 CD133 30fr dk red, ind & dp cl   22 15
329 CD133 45fr dl brn, dk car & bl grn 40 18

Textile Plant, Thies — A86

Design: 45fr, Fertilizer plant, Dakar.

1970, Nov. 21 Engr.   Perf. 13
330 A86 30fr grn, brt bl & brn red   25 15
331 A86 45fr brn red & brt bl   40 18
Industrialization of Senegal.

Boy
Scouts — A87

Three Heads and
Sun — A88

Design: 100fr, Lord Baden-Powell, map of Africa
with Dakar, and fleur-de-lis.

1970, Dec. 11 Photo.   Perf. 11¹/₂
332 A87 30fr multi   22 15
333 A87 100fr multi   80 38
1st African Boy Scout Conf., Dakar, Dec. 11-14.

1970, Dec. 19   Engr.   Perf. 13

Design: 40fr, African man and woman, globe with map of Africa.

334	A88	25fr ultra, org & vio brn	25 15
335	A88	40fr brn ol, dk brn & org	45 20

International Education Year.

Senegal
Arms — A89

Refugees and UN
Emblem — A90

1970-76   Photo.   Perf. 12

336	A89	30fr yel grn & multi	20 15
336A	A89	35fr brt pink & multi ('71)	22 15
b.		Bkt. pane of 10 ('72)	2.50
336C	A89	50fr bl & multi ('75)	25 15
336D	A89	65fr lil rose & multi ('76)	35 15
		Set value	40

The booklet pane has a control number in the margin.
See No. 654.

1971, Jan. 16   Perf. 12½x12

337	A90	40fr ver, blk, yel & grn	35 16

High Commissioner for Refugees, 20th anniversary. See No. C94.

Mare "Mbayang"
A91

Horses: 25fr, Mare Madjiguene. 100fr, Stallion Pass. 125fr, Stallion Pepe.

1971   Photo.   Perf. 11½

338	A91	25fr multi	20 15
339	A91	40fr multi	35 16
340	A91	100fr multi	70 40
341	A91	125fr multi	90 40

Improvements in horse breeding.
For surcharge see No. 392.

UN Emblem, Black
and White Children
A92

Globe and
Telephone
A94

UN Emblem,
Four
Races — A93

Perf. 13x12½, 12½x11

1971, Mar. 21   Litho.

342	A92	30fr multi	22 15
343	A93	50fr multi	40 20

Intl. Year against Racial Discrimination.

1971, May 17   Engr.   Perf. 13

Design: 40fr, Radar, satellite, orbits.

344	A94	30fr pur, grn & brn	22 15
345	A94	40fr Prus bl, dk brn & red brn	30 15

3rd World Telecommunications Day.

Drummer (Hayashida) — A95

Jamboree Emblem and: 50fr, Dwarf Japanese quince and grape hyacinth. 65fr, Judo. 75fr, Mt. Fuji.

1971, Aug. 7   Photo.   Perf. 13½

346	A95	35fr lt ultra & multi	32 15
347	A95	50fr yel & multi	52 20
348	A95	65fr dp org & multi	65 22
349	A95	75fr grn & multi	80 35

13th Boy Scout World Jamboree, Asagiri Plain, Japan, Aug. 2-10.

Map of West
Africa with
Senegal,
UNICEF
Emblem — A97

Design: 100fr, Nurse, children and UNICEF emblem.

1971, Oct. 30   Perf. 12½

352	A97	35fr dl bl, org & blk	25 15
353	A97	100fr multi	80 38

UNICEF, 25th anniv.

Basketball and Games'
Emblem — A98

Designs: 40fr, Basketball and emblem. 75fr, Games' emblem.

1971, Dec. 24   Photo.   Perf. 13½x13

354	A98	35fr lt vio & multi	30 16
355	A98	40fr emer & multi	35 18
356	A98	75fr ocher & multi	65 38

6th African Basketball Championships, Dakar, Dec. 25, 1971-Jan. 2, 1972.

"The Exile of Albouri" — A99

Design: 40fr, "The Merchant of Venice."

1972, Mar. 25   Perf. 13x12½

357	A99	35fr dk red & multi	30 16
358	A99	40fr dk red & multi	38 20

Intl. Theater Day. See No. C112.

WHO
Emblem and
Heart
A100

Design: 40fr, Physician with patient, WHO emblem and electrocardiogram.

1972, Apr. 7   Engr.   Perf. 13

359	A100	35fr brt bl & red brn	25 15
360	A100	40fr sl grn & brn	30 16

"Your heart is your health," World Health Month.

Containment of the Desert, Environment
Emblem — A101

1972, June 3   Photo.   Perf. 13x12½

361	A101	35fr multi	30 16

UN Conference on Human Environment, Stockholm, June 5-16. See No. C113.

Tartarin Shooting the Lion — A102

Design: 100fr, Alphonse Daudet.

1972, June 24   Engr.   Perf. 13

362	A102	40fr brt grn, rose car & brn	35 15
363	A102	100fr Prus bl, bl & brn	80 35

Alphonse Daudet (1840-1897), French novelist, and centenary of the publication of his "Tartarin de Tarascon."

Souvenir Sheet

Stringed Instrument — A103

1972, July 1   Engr.   Perf. 11½

364	A103	150fr rose red	1.25 1.00

Belgica 72, Intl. Phil. Exhib., Brussels, June 24-July 9. No. 364 contains one stamp in design similar to No. 267.

Wrestling, Olympic
Rings — A104

1972, July 22   Photo.   Perf. 14x13½

365	A104	15fr shown	15 15
366	A104	20fr 100-meter dash	16 15
367	A104	100fr Basketball	65 35
368	A104	125fr Judo	80 40
		Set value	92

Souvenir Sheet
Perf. 13½x14½

369	A104	240fr Torchbearer and Munich	1.90 1.60

20th Olympic Games, Munich, Aug. 26-Sept. 11.

Book Year Emblem,
Children Reading
A105

Senegalese
Fashion
A106

1972, Sept. 16   Photo.   Perf. 13

370	A105	50fr gray & multi	38 16

International Book Year.

1972-76   Engr.

371	A106	25fr black	16 15
a.		Booklet pane of 5	1.60
b.		Booklet pane of 10	3.50
372	A106	40fr brt ultra	25 15
a.		Booklet pane of 5	2.50
b.		Booklet pane of 10	5.50
372C	A106	60fr brt grn ('76)	35 15
372D	A106	75fr lil rose	50 20
		Set value	35

See Nos. 563-569.

Aleksander
Pushkin — A107

Amphicrasphedum
Murrayanum — A108

1972, Oct. 28   Photo.   Perf. 11½

373	A107	100fr sal & pur	80 40

Aleksander Pushkin (1799-1837), Russian writer.

West African Monetary Union Issue
Common Design Type

Design: 40fr, African couple, city, village and commemorative coin.

1972, Nov. 2   Engr.   Perf. 13

374	CD136	40fr ol brn, bl & gray	30 16

1972-73   Photo.   Perf. 11½

Marine Life: 10fr, Pterocanium tricolpum. 15fr, Ceratospyris polygona. 20fr, Cortiniscus typicus. 30fr, Theopera cortina.

375	A108	5fr multi	15 15
376	A108	10fr multi	15 15
377	A108	15fr multi	15 15
378	A108	20fr multi	15 15
379	A108	30fr multi	16 15
		Nos. 375-379,C115-C118 (9)	2.86
		Set value	1.30

Issue dates: Nos. 375-377, Nov. 25, 1972. Nos. 378-379, July 28, 1973.

1872-1972

100ᶠ

No. 288 Surcharged
in Vermilion

=

1972, Dec. 9   Engr.   Perf. 13

380	A64	100fr on 30fr multi	60 30

Blaise Diagne (1872-1934).

Melchior — A109

Black and White Men Carrying Emblem — A110

1972, Dec. 23   Photo.   *Perf. 13x13½*
381 A109   10fr shown   15   15
382 A109   15fr Caspar   15   15
383 A109   40fr Balthasar   22   15
384 A109   60fr Joseph   30   20
385 A109   100fr Virgin and Child   50   32
   Nos. 381-385 (5)   1.32
      Set value   72

Christmas. Nos. 381-385 printed se-tenant with continuous design, showing traditional Gorée dolls.

Europafrica Issue
1973, Jan. 20   Engr.   *Perf. 13*
386 A110   65fr blk & grn   42   22

Radar Station, Gandoul A111

1973, May 17   Engr.   *Perf. 13*
387 A111   40fr multi   25   16

Phases of Solar Eclipse A112

Designs: 65fr, Moon between earth and sun casting shadow on earth. 150fr, Diagram of areas of partial and total eclipse, satellite in space.

1973, June 30   Photo.   *Perf. 13x14*
388 A112   35fr dk bl & multi   22   15
389 A112   65fr dk bl & multi   38   25
390 A112   150fr dk bl & multi   90   60

Total solar eclipse over Africa, June 30.

Men Holding Torch over Africa — A113

1973, July 7   *Perf. 12½x13*
391 A113   75fr multi   42   30

Org. for African Unity, 10th anniv.

No. 338 Surcharged with New Value, 2 Bars, and Overprinted in Ultramarine: "SECHERESSE / SOLIDARITE AFRICAINE"

1973, July 21   Photo.   *Perf. 11½*
392 A91   100fr on 25fr multi   60   40

African solidarity in drought emergency.

African Postal Union Issue
Common Design Type
1973, Sept. 12   Engr.   *Perf. 13*
393 CD137   100fr dk grn, vio & dk red   60   30

Child, Map of Senegal, WMO Emblem A114

1973, Sept. 22
394 A114   50fr multi   30   15

Intl. meteorological cooperation, cent.

INTERPOL Headquarters, Paris — A115

1973, Oct. 6   Engr.   *Perf. 13*
395 A115   75fr ultra, bis & sl grn   42   25

50th anniv. of Intl. Criminal Police Org.

Souvenir Sheet

JOHN F. KENNEDY
1917
1963
150 F

REPUBLIQUE DU SENEGAL

John F. Kennedy (1917-1963) A116

1973, Nov. 22   Engr.   *Perf. 13*
396 A116   150fr ultra   1.00   1.00

Amilcar Cabral — A117

Victorious Athletes and Flag — A118

1973, Dec. 15   Photo.   *Perf. 12½x13*
397 A117   75fr multi   42   35

Cabral (1924-1973), leader of anti-Portuguese guerrilla movement in Portuguese Guinea.

1974, Apr. 6   Photo.   *Perf. 12½x13*
Design: 40fr, Folk theater.
398 A118   35fr multi   22   15
399 A118   40fr multi   30   20

National Youth Week.

Soccer Cup, Yugoslavia-Brazil Game, Our Lady's Church, Munich — A119

Soccer Cup and Games: 40fr, Australia-Germany (Fed. Rep.) and Belltower, Hamburg. 65fr, Netherlands-Uruguay and Tower, Hanover. 70fr, Zaire-Italy and Church, Stuttgart.

1974, June 29   Photo.   *Perf. 13x14*
400 A119   25fr car & multi   16   15
401 A119   40fr car & multi   25   16
402 A119   65fr car & multi   40   16
403 A119   70fr car & multi   42   18

World Cup Soccer Championship, Munich, June 13-July 7.
For surcharge see No. 406.

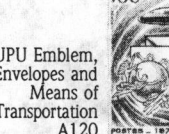

UPU Emblem, Envelopes and Means of Transportation A120

1974, Oct. 9   Engr.   *Perf. 13*
404 A120   100fr multi   60   40

Centenary of Universal Postal Union.

Fair Emblem — A121

1974, Nov. 28   Engr.   *Perf. 12½x13*
405 A121   100fr bl, org & dk brn   55   35

Dakar International Fair.

No. 401 Surcharged in Black on Gold

1975, Feb. 1   Photo.   *Perf. 13x14*
406 A119   200fr on 40fr multi   1.10   65

World Cup Soccer Championships, 1974, victory of German Federal Republic.

Pres. Senghor and King Baudouin A122

1975, Feb. 28   Photo.   *Perf. 13x13½*
407 A122   65fr lil & dk bl   35   20
408 A122   100fr org & grn   55   35

Visit of King Baudouin of Belgium.

ILO Emblem — A123

1975, Apr. 30   Photo.   *Perf. 13½x13*
409 A123   125fr multi   65   38

International Labor Festival.

Globe, Stamp, Letters, España 75 Emblem — A124

1975, June 6   Engr.   *Perf. 13*
410 A124   55fr indigo, grn & red   30   20

Espana 75 Intl. Phil. Exhib., Madrid, Apr. 4-13.

Apollo of Belvedere, Arphila 75 Emblem, Stamps — A125

1975, June 6
411 A125   95fr dk brn, brn & bis   50   35

Arphila 75 International Philatelic Exhibition, Paris, June 6-16.

Professional Instruction — A126

1975, June 28   Engr.   *Perf. 13*
412 A126   85fr multi   45   25

Dr. Albert Schweitzer (1875-1965), Medical Missionary, Lambarene Hospital — A127

1975, July 5
413 A127   85fr grn & vio brn   45   25

Senegalese Soldier, Batallion Flag, Map of Sinai — A128

1975, July 10   Litho.   *Perf. 12½*
414 A128   100fr multi   75   35

Senegalese Battalion of the United Nations' Sinai Service, 1973-1974.

The values of stamps in very fine to superb condition are greater than catalogue value.

Women and
Child — A129

Design: 55fr, Women pounding grain, IWY
emblem, vert.

1975, Oct. 18   Photo.   Perf. 13½
415 A129 55fr silver & multi   30 15
416 A129 75fr silver & multi   40 20

International Women's Year.

Staff of Aesculapius
and African
Mask — A130

1975, Dec. 1   Photo.   Perf. 12½x13
417 A130 50fr multi   25 15

40th French Medical Cong., Dakar, Dec. 1-3.

Map of Africa
with Senegal
and Namibia,
UN Emblem
A131

1976, Jan. 5   Photo.   Perf. 13
418 A131 125fr vio bl & multi   65 35

International Human Rights and Namibia Conference, Dakar, Jan. 5-8.

Sailfish
Fishing
A132

Design: 200fr, Racing yachts and Oceanexpo 75
emblem.

1976, Jan. 28   Photo.   Perf. 13½x13
419 A132 140fr multi   70 38
420 A132 200fr multi   1.10 55

Oceanexpo 75, 1st Intl. Oceanographic Exhib.,
Okinawa, July 20, 1975-Jan. 1976.

Servals — A133

Designs: 3fr, Black-tailed godwits. 4fr, River
hogs. 5fr, African fish eagles. No. 425, Okapis. No.
426, Sitatungas.

1976, Feb. 26   Photo.   Perf. 13
421 A133 2fr gold & multi   15 15
422 A133 3fr gold & multi   15 15
423 A133 4fr gold & multi   15 15
424 A133 5fr gold & multi   15 15
425 A133 250fr gold & multi   1.40 65
426 A133 250fr gold & multi   1.40 65
  a. Strip of 2, #425-426 + label 3.00
      Set value   3.00 1.50

Basse Casamance National Park.
See Nos. 473-478.

A. G. Bell, Telephone, ITU
Emblem — A134

1976, Mar. 31   Litho.   Perf. 12½x13
427 A134 175fr multi   90 42

Centenary of first telephone call by Alexander
Graham Bell, Mar. 10, 1876.

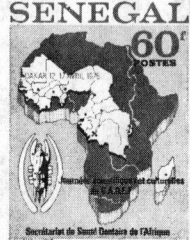

Map of African
French-speaking
Countries
A135

1976, Apr. 12   Litho.   Perf. 13½
428 A135 60fr yel grn & multi   35 20

Scientific and Cultural Meeting of the African
Dental Association, Dakar, Apr. 12-17.

Family and
Graph
A136

1976, Apr. 26
429 A136 65fr multi   35 20

1st population census in Senegal, Apr. 1976.

Thomas Jefferson and 13-star Flag — A137

1976, June 19   Engr.   Perf. 13
430 A137 50fr bl, red & blk   25 15

American Bicentennial.

Planting Seedlings — A138

1976, Aug. 21   Litho.   Perf. 12
431 A138 60fr yel & multi   35 16

Reclamation of Sahel region.

Campfire
A139

Jamboree Emblem,
Map of
Africa — A140

1976, Aug. 30   Litho.   Perf. 12½
432 A139 80fr multi   42 35
433 A140 100fr multi   55 40

1st All Africa Scout Jamboree, Sherehills, Jos,
Nigeria, Apr. 2-8, 1977.

A140a

1976 Summer Olympics,
Montreal — A140b

1976, Sept. 11   Litho.   Perf. 13½
433A A140a 5fr Swimming
433B A140a 10fr Weightlifting
433C A140a 15fr Hurdles, horiz.
433D A140a 20fr Equestrian, horiz.
433E A140a 25fr Steeplechase, horiz.
433F A140a 50fr Wrestling
433G A140a 60fr Field hockey
433H A140a 65fr Track
433I A140a 70fr Women's gymnastics
433J A140a 100fr Cycling, horiz.
433K A140a 400fr Boxing
433L A140a 500fr Judo
            Litho. & Embossed
433M A140b 1000fr Basketball
              Souvenir Sheet
433Q A140b 1000fr Boxers, city skyline

Nos. 433K-433Q are airmail.

Mechanized
Tomato
Harvest
A141

1976, Oct. 23   Photo.   Perf. 13
434 A141 180fr multi   1.00 42

Map of Dakar
and Gorée
A142

Designs: 60fr, Star over Africa. 70fr, Students in
laboratory and library. 200fr, Handshake over
world map, Pres. Senghor.

1976, Oct. 9   Litho.   Perf. 13½x14
435 A142 40fr multi   15 15
436 A142 60fr multi   20 16
437 A142 70fr multi   20 20
438 A142 200fr multi   58 55

70th birthday of Pres. Leopold Sedar Senghor.

Scroll with Map of
Africa, Senegalese
People — A143

1977, Jan. 8   Perf. 12½
439 A143 60fr multi   35 16

Day of the Black People.

Joe Frazier
and
Muhammad
Ali — A144

Design: 60fr, Ali and Frazier in ring, vert.

1977, Jan. 7   Photo.   Perf. 13x13½
440 A144 60fr blue & blk   65 16
441 A144 150fr emerald & blk   1.20 40

World boxing champion Muhammad Ali.

Dancer and
Musician
A145

Festival Emblem and: 75fr, Wood carving and
masks. 100fr, Dancers and ancestor statuette.

1977, Feb. 10   Litho.   Perf. 12½
442 A145 50fr yellow & multi   25 15
443 A145 75fr green & multi   40 20
444 A145 100fr rose & multi   55 25

2nd World Black and African Festival, Lagos,
Nigeria, Jan. 15-Feb. 12.

Cogwheels and Symbols of
Industry — A146

1977, Mar. 28   Engr.   Perf. 13
445 A146 70fr yel grn & ocher   38 18

Dakar Industrial Zone, 1st anniversary.

Burning Match and
Burnt Trees — A147

Design: 60fr, Burnt trees and house, fire-truck,
horiz.

1977, Apr. 30   Litho.   Perf. 12½
446 A147 40fr green & multi   20   15
447 A147 60fr slate & multi   35   16

Prevention of forest fires.

Drummer, Telephone, Agriculture and
Industry — A148

Electronic Tree and
ITU Emblem — A149

1977, May 17   Litho.   Perf. 13
448 A148 80fr multi   35   22
449 A149 100fr multi   40   25

World Telecommunications Day.

Symbol of Language
Studies — A150

Sassenage Castle, Grenoble — A151

Perf. 12x12½, 12½
1977, May 21   Litho.
450 A150 65fr multi   22   18
451 A151 250fr multi   1.00 65

10th anniv. of Intl. French Language Council.

Woman in
Boat,
Wooden Shoe
A152

Design: 125fr, Senegalese woman, symbolic tulip
and stamp, vert.

1977, June 4   Perf. 13½x14, 14x13½
452 A152 50fr blue grn & multi   25   15
453 A152 125fr ocher & multi   65   35

Amphilex '77 International Philatelic Exhibition,
Amsterdam, May 26-June 5.

Adult Reading
Class — A153

Design: 65fr, Man learning to read.

1977, Sept. 10   Litho.   Perf. 12½
454 A153 60fr multi   35   16
455 A153 65fr multi   38   16

National Literacy Week, Sept. 8-14.

A154   A155

Paintings: 20fr, Mercury, by Rubens. 25fr, Daniel
in the Lions' Den, by Peter Paul Rubens (1577-
1640). 40fr, The Empress, by Titian (1477-1576).
60fr, Flora, by Titian. 65fr, Jo, the Beautiful Irish
Woman, by Gustave Courbet (1819-1877). 100fr,
The Painter's Studio, by Courbet.

1977, Nov.   Photo.   Perf. 13x13½
456 A154 20fr multi   15   15
457 A154 25fr multi   15   15
458 A154 40fr multi   20   15
459 A154 60fr multi   30   16
460 A154 65fr multi   35   18
461 A154 100fr multi   55   25
          Nos. 456-461 (6)   1.70
          Set value   80

1977, Dec. 22   Litho.   Perf. 12½
Christmas: 20fr, Adoration by People of Various
Races. 25fr, Decorated arch and procession. 40fr,
Christmas tree, mother and child. 100fr, Adoration
of the Kings, horiz.
462 A155 20fr multi   15   15
463 A155 25fr multi   15   15
464 A155 40fr multi   20   15
465 A155 100fr multi   55   25
          Set value   46

Regatta at
Soumbedioun
A156

Tourism: 10fr, Senegalese wrestlers. 65fr,
Regatta at Soumbedioun, horiz. 100fr, Dancers,
horiz.

1978, Jan. 7   Litho.   Perf. 12½
466 A156 10fr multi   15   15
467 A156 30fr multi   16   15
468 A156 65fr multi   35   18
469 A156 100fr multi   55   25
          Set value   55

Acropolis,
Athens, and
African
Buildings
A157

1978, Jan. 30
470 A157 75fr multi   40   20

UNESCO campaign to save world's cultural
heritage.

Solar-powered Pump, Field and
Sheep — A158

Energy in Senegal: 95fr, Pylon bringing electricity to villages and factories.

1978, Feb. 25
471 A158 50fr multi   25   15
472 A158 95fr multi   50   25

Park Type of 1976

Designs: 5fr, Caspian terns in flight, royal terns
on ground. 10fr, Pink-backed pelicans. 15fr, Wart
hog and gray heron. 20fr, Greater flamingoes, nests,
eggs and young. No. 477, Gray heron and royal
terns. No. 478, Abyssinian ground hornbill and
wart hog.

1978, Apr. 22   Photo.   Perf. 13
473 A133 5fr gold & multi   15   15
474 A133 10fr gold & multi   15   15
475 A133 15fr gold & multi   15   15
476 A133 20fr gold & multi   15   15
477 A133 150fr gold & multi   1.00 65
478 A133 150fr gold & multi   1.00 65
a.   Strip of 2, #477-478 + label   2.00
     Nos. 473-478 (6)   2.60
     Set value   1.50

Salum Delta National Park. Nos. 477-478
printed se-tenant.

Dome of the Rock,
Jerusalem — A159

1978, May 15   Litho.   Perf. 12½
479 A159 60fr multi   40   15

Palestinian fighters and their families.

Vaccination,
Dr. Jenner,
WHO
Emblem
A160

1978, June 3
480 A160 60fr multi   40   15

Eradication of smallpox.

Soccer, Flags:
Argentina, Hungary,
France,
Italy — A161

Mahatma
Gandhi — A162

Soccer, Cup, Argentina '78 Emblem and Flags of:
40fr, No. 486a, Poland, German Democratic Rep.,
Tunisia, Mexico. 65fr, 125fr, Austria, Spain, Sweden, Brazil. 75fr, No. 484, Netherlands, Iran, Peru,
Scotland. 150fr, like 25fr.

1978, June 24   Photo.   Perf. 13
481 A161 25fr multi   15   15
482 A161 40fr multi   20   15
483 A161 65fr multi   32   15
484 A161 100fr multi   50   22
          Set value   48

Souvenir Sheets
485   Sheet of 2   1.10
a.   A161 75fr multi   38
b.   A161 125fr multi   65
486   Sheet of 2   1.40
a.   A161 100fr multi   50
b.   A161 150fr multi   75

11th World Cup Soccer Championship, Argentina, June 1-25.

1978, June 27   Perf. 12
Design: 150fr, No. 489a, Martin Luther King.
No. 489b, like 125fr.
487 A162 125fr multi   95   35
488 A162 150fr multi   1.25 40

Souvenir Sheet
489   Sheet of 2   3.50
a.   A162 200fr multi   1.65
b.   A162 200fr multi   1.65

Mahatma Gandhi and Martin Luther King, advocates of non-violence.

Homes and Industry — A163

1978, Aug. 5   Litho.   Perf. 12½
490 A163 110fr multi   70   30

3rd Intl. Fair, Dakar, Nov. 28-Dec. 10.

Wright Brothers and Flyer — A164

Designs: 150fr, like 75fr. 100fr, 250fr, Yuri
Gagarin and spacecraft. 200fr, 300fr, US astronauts
Frank Borman, William Anders, James Lovell Jr.
and spacecraft.

1978, Sept. 25   Litho.   Perf. 13½x14
491 A164 75fr multi   50   20
492 A164 100fr multi   65   28
493 A164 200fr multi   1.40 55

Souvenir Sheet
494   Sheet of 3   4.00
a.   A164 150fr multi   60
b.   A164 250fr multi   1.40
c.   A164 300fr multi   2.00

75th anniv. of 1st powered flight; 10th anniv. of
the death of Yuri Gagarin, first man in space; 10th
anniv. of Apollo 8 flight around moon.

Henri Dunant (1828-1910), Founder of Red Cross, and Patients A165

Design: 20fr, Henri Dunant, First Aid station, Red Cross flag.

1978, Oct. 28   Photo.   Perf. 11½
495 A165 5fr brt blue & red   15   15
496 A165 20fr multi   15   15
          Set value   18   15

Bedside Lecture and Emblem — A166

Design: 100fr, Pollution, fish and mercury bottles.

1979, Jan. 15   Litho.   Perf. 13½x13
497 A166 50fr multi   35   15
498 A166 100fr multi   65   25

9th Medical Days, Dakar, Jan. 15-20.

Map of Senegal with Shortwave Stations A167

Designs: 60fr, Children on vacation, ambulance, soccer player. 65fr, Rural mobile post office.

1978, Dec. 27   Litho.   Perf. 13½x13
499 A167 50fr multi   35   15
500 A167 60fr multi   40   16
501 A167 65fr multi   42   18

Achievements of postal service.

Farmer A168

Design: 150fr, Factories, communication, transportation, fish, physician and worker.

1979, Feb. 17   Litho.   Perf. 12½
502 A168 30fr multi   20   15
503 A168 150fr multi   1.00   40

Pride in workmanship.

Children's Village and Children — A169

Design: 60fr, Different view of village.

1979, Mar. 30   Perf. 12x12½
504 A169 40fr multi   25   15
505 A169 60fr multi   40   16

Children's SOS villages.

Infant, Physician Vaccinating Child, IYC Emblem — A170

Design: 65fr, Boys with book and globe, IYC emblem.

1979, Apr. 24   Litho.   Perf. 13½x13
506 A170 60fr multi   40   16
507 A170 65fr multi   42   18

International Year of the Child.

Drum, Carrier Pigeon, Satellite A171

Design: 60fr, Baobab tree and flower, Independence monument with lion, vert.

1979, June 8   Perf. 12½x13
Size: 36x48mm
508 A171 60fr multi   40   16
Perf. 12½
Size: 36x36mm
509 A171 150fr multi   1.00   40

Philexafrique II, Libreville, Gabon, June 8-17. Nos. 508, 509 each printed with labels showing UAPT '79 emblem.

People Walking through Open Book — A172

1979, Sept. 15   Photo.   Perf. 11½x12
510 A172 250fr multi   1.90   65

Intl. Bureau of Education, Geneva, 50th anniv.

Sir Rowland Hill (1795-1879), Originator of Penny Postage, Type AP3 with Exhibition Cancel — A173

1979, Oct. 9   Perf. 11½
511 A173 500fr multi   3.50 1.40

Black Trees, by Hundertwasser A174

Perf. 13½x14
1979, Dec. 10   Litho. & Engr.
512 A174 60fr shown   40   16
a.   Souvenir sheet of 4   1.90   80

513 A174 100fr Head of a man   65   25
a.   Souvenir sheet of 4   3.00 1.20
514 A174 200fr Rainbow windows   1.40   55
a.   Souvenir sheet of 4   5.75 2.25

Paintings by Friedensreich Hundertwasser, pseudonym of Friedrich Stowasser (b. 1928).

Running, Championship Emblem — A175

1980, Jan. 14   Litho.   Perf. 13
515 A175 20fr shown   15   15
516 A175 25fr Javelin   16   15
517 A175 50fr Relay race   35   15
518 A175 100fr Discus   80   25
          Set value   50

1st African Athletic Championships.

Mudra Afrique Arts Festival A176

1980, Mar. 22   Photo.   Perf. 14
519 A176 50fr Musicians   35   15
520 A176 100fr Dancers, festival build-
                ing   65   25
521 A176 200fr Drummer, dancers 1.40   55

Lions Emblem, Map of Dakar Harbor A177

1980, May 17   Litho.   Perf. 13
522 A177 100fr multi   80   25

22nd Congress, Lions Intl. District 403, Dakar.

Chimpanzees — A178

1980, June 2   Photo.   Perf. 13½
523 A178 40fr shown   25   15
524 A178 60fr Elephants   40   16
525 A178 65fr Derby's elands   42   18
526 A178 100fr Hyenas   65   25
527   Pair   2.50 1.10
a.   A178 200fr Herd   1.25   55
b.   A178 200fr Guest house 1.25   55
          Nos. 523-527 (5)   4.22 1.84

Souvenir Sheet
528   Sheet of 4   4.00 1.40
a.   A178 125fr like #523   1.00   35
b.   A178 125fr like #524   1.00   35
c.   A178 125fr like #525   1.00   35
d.   A178 125fr like #526   1.00   35

Niokolo Koba National Park. No. 527 printed in continuous design with label showing location of park.

Tree Planting Year — A179

1980, June 27   Litho.   Perf. 13
529 A179 60fr multi   40   16
530 A179 65fr multi   42   18

Rural Women Workers — A180

Designs: Rural women workers. 50fr, 200fr, horiz.

1980, July 19
531 A180 50fr multi   35   15
532 A180 100fr multi   65   25
533 A180 200fr multi   1.40   55

Wrestling, Moscow '80 Emblem — A181

1980, Aug. 21   Perf. 14½
534 A181 60fr shown   40   16
535 A181 65fr Running   42   18
536 A181 70fr Sports, map showing
                Moscow   45   20
537 A181 100fr Judo   80   25
538 A181 200fr Basketball   1.60   55
          Nos. 534-538 (5)   3.67 1.34

Souvenir Sheet
539   Sheet of 2   1.50
a.   A181 75fr like #534   50   22
b.   A181 125fr like #535   80   35
540   Sheet of 2   1.50
a.   A181 75fr like #527   50   22
b.   A181 125fr like #538   80   35

22nd Summer Olympic Games, Moscow, July 19-Aug. 3.

Caspian Tern and Sea Gulls, Kalissaye Bird Sanctuary A182

National Park Wildlife: 70fr, Laughing gulls and Hansel's tern, Barbarie Spit. 85fr, Turtle and crab, Madeleine Islands. 150fr, Cormorant, Madeleine Islands.

1981, Jan. 31   Litho.   Perf. 14½x14
541 A182 50fr multi   50   15
542 A182 70fr multi   65   20
543 A182 85fr multi   75   25
544 A182 150fr multi   1.20   40

Souvenir Sheet
545   Sheet of 4   4.00 1.40
a.   A182 125fr like #541   1.00   35
b.   A182 125fr like #542   1.00   35
c.   A182 125fr like #543   1.00   35
d.   A182 125fr like #544   1.00   35

Anti-Tobacco
Campaign — A183

1981, June 20   Litho.   Perf. 13
546 A183 75fr Healthy people   50 20
547 A183 80fr shown   55 22

4th Intl.
Dakar Fair,
Nov. 25-
Dec. 7
A184

1981, Sept. 19   Litho.   Perf. 12½
548 A184 80fr multi   55 22

Natl. Hero
Lat Dior
A185

1982, Jan. 11   Photo.   Perf. 14
549 A185 80fr Portrait, vert.   55 22
550 A185 500fr Battle   3.50 1.40

Local
Flora — A186

1982, Feb. 1   Perf. 11½
551 A186 50fr Nymphaea lotus   35 15
552 A186 75fr Strophanthus sar-
    mentosus   50 20
553 A186 200fr Crinum moorei   1.40 55
554 A186 225fr Cochlospermum
    tinctorium   1.50 60

Inscribed 1981.

Euryphrene
Senegalensis
A187

1982, Feb. 27   Litho.   Perf. 14
555 A187 45fr shown   30 15
556 A187 55fr Hypolimnas salmacis   38 15
557 A187 75fr Cymothoe caenis   50 20
558 A187 80fr Precis cebrene   55 22

Souvenir Sheet
Perf. 14½
559   Sheet of 4   6.00 2.00
 a.   A187 100fr like 45fr   65 25
 b.   A187 150fr like 55fr   1.00 40
 c.   A187 200fr like 75fr   1.40 55
 d.   A187 250fr like 80fr   1.60 65

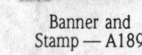

Destructive
Insects — A188

Banner and
Stamp — A189

Various insects. 80fr, 100fr horiz.

1982, Apr. 7   Litho.   Perf. 14
560 A188 75fr multi   50 20
561 A188 80fr multi   55 22
562 A188 100fr multi   65 25

Fashion Type of 1972

1982-93   Engr.   Perf. 13
563 A106 5fr Prus blue   15 15
564 A106 10fr dull red   15 15
565 A106 15fr orange   15 15
566 A106 20fr dk purple   15 15
567 A106 30fr henna brn   20 15
567A A106 45fr orange yellow   35 18
567B A106 75fr bright magenta   38 20
568 A106 90fr brt carmine   25 15
568A A106 125fr ultramarine   95 48
569 A106 180fr gray blue   1.40 70
    Nos. 563-569 (10)   4.13
    Set value   1.10

Issued: 5, 10, 15, 20, 30fr, Apr. 30; 90fr, Dec.,
1984; 180fr, 1991; 45, 50, 125fr, 1993.
This is an expanding set. Numbers will change.

1982, Dec. 30   Photo.   Perf. 13
575 A189 100fr shown   50 25
576 A189 500fr Stamp, arrows   3.00 1.40

PHILEXFRANCE Intl. Stamp Exhibition, Paris,
June 11-21.

Senegambia Confederation, Feb. 1 — A190

1982, Nov. 15   Litho.   Perf. 12½
577 A190 225fr Map, flags   1.00 65
578 A190 350fr Arms   1.60 1.00

Local
Birds — A191

1982 World
Cup — A192

1982, Dec. 1   Photo.   Perf. 11½
Granite Paper
579 A191 45fr Godwit   30 15
580 A191 75fr Jabiru   50 20
581 A191 80fr Francolin   55 22
582 A191 500fr Eagle   3.50 1.40

1982, Dec. 11   Litho.   Perf. 12½x13
583 A192 30fr Player   20 15
584 A192 50fr Player, diff.   35 15
585 A192 75fr Ball   50 20
586 A192 80fr Cup   55 22

Souvenir Sheets
Perf. 12½
587 A192 75fr like 30fr   50 25
588 A192 100fr like 50fr   65 35
589 A192 150fr like 75fr   1.00 50
590 A192 200fr like 80fr   1.40 65

A193

A194

Designs: 60fr, Exhibition poster, viewers, horiz.
70fr, Simulated butterfly stamps. 90fr, Simulated
stamps under magnifying glass. 95fr, Coat of Arms
over Exhibition Building.

1983, Aug. 6   Litho.   Perf. 12½
591 A193 60fr multi   20 15
592 A193 70fr multi   22 15
593 A193 90fr multi   30 15
594 A193 95fr multi   32 16
    Set value   52

Dakar '82 Stamp Exhibition.

1983, Oct. 25   Litho.   Perf. 12½x13
595 A194 90fr Electricity   30 15
596 A194 95fr Gasoline   32 16
597 A194 260fr Coal, wood   90 42

Energy conservation.

Namibia
Day — A195

1983, Nov. 14   Litho.   Perf. 13½x13
598 A195 90fr Torch   30 15
599 A195 95fr Chain, fist   32 16
600 A195 260fr Woman bearing torch   90 42

West African
Monetary Union,
20th
Anniv. — A196

Dakar Alizes
Rotary Club, First
Anniv. — A197

Designs: 60fr, Mask emblem, Ziguinchor Agency
building, Dakar, horiz. 65fr, Monetary Union headquarters, emblem.

Perf. 13½x13, 13x13½
1983, Nov. 28
601 A196 60fr multi   20 15
602 A196 65fr multi   20 15
    Set value   22

1983, Dec. 5   Perf. 13x13½
603 A197 70fr green & multi   22 15
604 A197 500fr blue & multi   1.60 80

Customs
Cooperation
Council, 30th
Anniv. — A198

Economic Comm.
for Africa, 25th
Anniv. — A199

1983, Dec. 23   Perf. 12½x13
605 A198 90fr multi   30 15
606 A198 300fr multi   1.00 50

1984, Jan. 10   Perf. 12½
607 A199 90fr multi   30 15
608 A199 95fr multi   32 16

SOS Children's
Village — A200

Perf. 13½x13, 13x13½
1984, Mar. 29
609 A200 90fr Village   30 15
610 A200 95fr Mother & child, vert.   32 16
611 A200 115fr Brothers & sisters   40 20
612 A200 260fr House, vert.   90 42

Scouting
Year — A201

1984, May 28   Litho.   Perf. 13
613 A201 60fr Sign   20 15
614 A201 70fr Emblem   22 15
615 A201 90fr Scouts   30 15
616 A201 95fr Baden-Powell   32 16

1984 Olympic
Games — A202

1984, July 28   Litho.   Perf. 13
617 A202 90fr Javelin   30 15
618 A202 95fr Hurdles   35 16
619 A202 165fr Soccer   55 30

Souvenir Sheet
Perf. 13x12½
620   Sheet of 3   1.90 1.00
 a.   A202 125fr like 90fr   40 20
 b.   A202 175fr like 95fr   60 30
 c.   A202 250fr like 165fr   80 45

World Food
Day — A203

Perf. 13x12½, 12½x12½
1984, Dec. 16   Litho.
621 A203 65fr Food production   18 15
622 A203 70fr Cooking, vert.   18 15
623 A203 225fr Dining   60 30
    Set value   50

No. 612 Overprinted "AIDE AU SAHEL
84"

1984, Dec.   Perf. 13x13½
624 A200 260fr multi   70 35

Drought relief.

UNESCO World
Heritage
Campaign — A204

Water
Emergency
Plan — A205

1984, Dec. 6   Litho.   Perf. 13½
625 A204 90fr William Ponty
    School   25 15
626 A204 95fr Island map, horiz.   25 15
627 A204 115fr History Museum   65 35
628 A204 500fr Slave Prison, horiz.   1.40 65

Souvenir Sheet
Perf. 13x12½, 12½x13

629		Sheet of 4	3.50	1.90
a.	A204	125fr like No. 625	30	16
b.	A204	150fr like No. 626	40	20
c.	A204	325fr like No. 627	90	40
d.	A204	675fr like No. 628	1.90	90

Restoration of historic sites, Goree Island.

Perf. 13x12½, 12½x13
1985, Mar. 28

630	A205	40fr Well and pump	15	15
631	A205	50fr Spigot and crops	15	15
632	A205	90fr Water tanks, livestock	25	15
633	A205	250fr Women at well	65	35
		Set value		60

Nos. 631-633 horiz.

World Communications Year — A206

Designs: 95fr, Maps of Africa and Senegal, transmission tower. 350fr, Globe, pigeon with letter.

1985, Apr. 13   **Litho.**   *Perf. 13*

634	A206	90fr multi	25	15
635	A206	95fr multi	25	15
636	A206	350fr multi	90	45

Traditional Musical Instruments
A207

Designs: 50fr, Gourd fiddle and bamboo flute. 85fr, Drums and stringed instrument. 125fr, Musician playing balaphone, drums. 250fr, Rabab, shawm and single-string fiddles.

1985, May 4   *Perf. 12½x13, 13x12½*

637	A207	50fr multi	15	15
638	A207	85fr multi	22	15
639	A207	125fr multi	35	16
640	A207	250fr multi	65	35
		Set value		70

Nos. 638-640 vert. For surcharge see No. 676.

PHILEXAFRICA '85, Lome, Togo, Nov. 16-24 — A208

1985, Oct. 21   *Perf. 13*

641	A208	100fr Political and civic education	35	16
642	A208	125fr Vocational training	42	20
643	A208	150fr Culture, space exploration	55	25
644	A208	175fr Self-sufficiency in food production	60	30

Intl. Youth Year
A209

1985, Nov. 30   *Perf. 14*

645	A209	40fr Vocational training	15	15
646	A209	50fr Communications	16	15
647	A209	90fr World peace	30	15
648	A209	125fr Cultural exchange	42	20
		Set value		50

Senegal Arms Type of 1970

1985, Dec.   **Litho.**   *Perf. 13*
Background Color

654	A89	95fr bright orange	35	16

Fishing at Kayar
A210

1986, Jan. 28   **Litho.**   *Perf. 14*

659	A210	40fr Hauling boat	20	15
660	A210	50fr Women on beach	25	15
661	A210	90fr Fisherman, catch	52	25
662	A210	125fr Women buying fish	68	35
663	A210	150fr Unloading fish	80	40
		Nos. 659-663 (5)	2.45	1.30

Nos. 661-662 vert.

Folk Costumes — A211

1985, Dec. 28   **Litho.**   *Perf. 13½*

664	A211	40fr multi	15	15
665	A211	95fr multi, vert., diff.	35	16
666	A211	100fr multi, vert., diff.	38	18
667	A211	150fr multi, vert., diff.	55	28

Coiffures
A212

1986 Africa Soccer Cup, Cairo
A213

1986, Mar. 3   *Perf. 13*

668	A212	90fr Perruque, Ceeli	50	25
669	A212	125fr Ndungu, Kearly, Rasta	68	35
670	A212	250fr Jamono Kura, Kooraa	1.35	68
671	A212	300fr Mbaram, Jeere	1.65	82

1986, Mar. 7   *Perf. 13½*

672	A213	115fr Soccer ball, flags	62	32
673	A213	125fr Athlete, map	68	35
674	A213	135fr Pyramid, heraldic lion	75	38
675	A213	165fr Flag, lions, map	90	45

No. 638 Surcharged with Lions Intl. Emblem, Two Bars, and "Ve CONVENTION / MULTI-DISTRICT / 403 / 8-10 / MAI / 1986" in Dark Ultramarine

1986, May 8   **Litho.**   *Perf. 13x12½*

676	A207	165fr on 85fr multi	1.00	50

World Wildlife Fund — A214

Ndama gazelles.

1986, June 30   *Perf. 13*

677	A214	15fr multi	15	15
678	A214	45fr multi	25	15
679	A214	85fr multi	48	24
680	A214	125fr multi	70	35
		Set value		75

UN Child Survival Campaign — A215

1986, Sept. 5   **Litho.**   *Perf. 14*

681	A215	50fr Immunization	32	16
682	A215	85fr Nutrition	50	25

1986 World Cup Soccer Championships, Mexico — A216

Various plays, world cup and artifacts: 125fr, Ceremonial vase. 135fr, Mayan mask, Palenque. 165fr, Gold breastplate. 340fr, Porcelain mask, Teofihuacan, 7th cent. B.C.

1986, Nov. 17   *Perf. 12½x12*

683	A216	125fr multi	80	40
684	A216	135fr multi	85	42
685	A216	165fr multi	1.10	55
686	A216	340fr multi	2.25	1.10

Nos. 683-686 Overprinted "ARGENTINE 3 / R.F.A. 2" in Scarlet

1986, Nov. 17

687	A216	125fr multi	80	40
688	A216	135fr multi	85	42
689	A216	165fr multi	1.10	55
690	A216	340fr multi	2.25	1.10

Guembeul Nature Reserve
A217

1986, Dec. 4   **Litho.**   *Perf. 13½*

691	A217	50fr Ostriches	28	15
692	A217	65fr Kob antelopes	38	20
693	A217	85fr Giraffes	48	24
694	A217	100fr Ostrich, buffalo, kob, giraffe	55	28
695	A217	150fr Buffaloes	85	42
		Nos. 691-695 (5)	2.54	1.29

Christmas
A218

1986, Dec. 22   **Litho.**   *Perf. 14*

696	A218	70fr Puppet, vert.	40	20
697	A218	85fr Folk musicians	48	24
698	A218	150fr Outdoor celebration, vert.	82	40
699	A218	250fr Boy praying, creche	1.40	70

Inscribed 1985.

Statue of Liberty, Cent. — A219

1986, Dec. 30   **Litho.**   *Perf. 12½*

700	A219	225fr multi	1.30	65

Marine Life
A220

1987, Jan. 2   *Perf. 14*

701	A220	50fr Jellyfish, coral	28	15
702	A220	85fr Sea urchin, starfish	48	24
703	A220	100fr Spiny lobster	55	28
704	A220	150fr Dolphin	85	42
705	A220	200fr Octopus	1.15	58
		Nos. 701-705 (5)	3.31	1.67

Senegal Stamp Cent. — A221

1987, Apr. 8   *Perf. 13*

706	A221	100fr Intl. express mail	55	28
707	A221	130fr #37	75	38
708	A221	140fr Similar to #201	80	40
709	A221	145fr #151, similar to #154	82	40
710	A221	320fr #27	1.80	90
		Nos. 706-710 (5)	4.72	2.36

Designs of Nos. 37, 151 and 27 same as originally released but perfs simulated.
For overprint see No. 784.

Paris-Dakar Rally
A222

1987, Jan. 22   *Perf. 14*

711	A222	115fr Motorcycle, truck, vert.	65	32
712	A222	125fr Official, race	72	35
713	A222	135fr Sabine, truck	78	40
714	A222	340fr Eiffel Tower, Dakar huts, vert.	1.95	95

Homage to Thierry Sabine. Inscribed 1986.

Ferlo Nature Reserve — A223

1987, Feb. 5   *Perf. 13½*

715	A223	55fr Antelope	30	15
716	A223	70fr Ostrich	40	20
717	A223	85fr Warthog	48	24
718	A223	90fr Elephant	52	25

Inscribed 1986.

Agena-Gemini 8 Link-up in Outer Space, 20th Anniv. — A224

1987, Feb. 27   Litho.   *Perf. 13*
719 A224 320fr multi   1.75   90

Souvenir Sheet
Perf. 12½
720 A224 500fr multi   2.75 1.40

Nos. 719-720 inscribed 1986 and have erroneous "10e Anniversaire" inscription.

Solidarity Against South African Apartheid — A225

1987, July 31   Litho.   *Perf. 13*
721 A225 130fr shown   85 42
722 A225 140fr Mandela, hand, broken chain, vert.   92 45
723 A225 145fr Mandela, dove, death   95 48

Inscribed 1986.

Intelsat, 20th Anniv. A226

1987, Aug. 31   *Perf. 14*
724 A226 50fr Emblem   32 16
725 A226 125fr Satellite   85 42
726 A226 150fr Emblem, globe   1.00 50
727 A226 200fr Earth, satellite in space 1.35 68

Inscribed 1985. Nos. 726-727 vert.

West African Union, 10th Anniv. — A227   Dakar Rotary Club, 45th Anniv. — A228

1987, Sept. 7
728 A227 40fr shown   30 15
729 A227 125fr Emblem, handshake   90 45

Inscribed 1985.

1987, Sept. 29   *Perf. 13*
730 A228 500fr multi   3.60 1.80

Inscribed 1985.

United Nations, 40th Anniv. — A229

1987, Oct. 8   *Perf. 14*
731 A229 85fr Emblem, New York office   62 30
732 A229 95fr Emblem   70 35
733 A229 150fr Hands, emblem   1.10 55

Inscribed 1985.

Cathedral of African Memory, 50th Anniv. A230

Designs: 130fr, Statue of saint, Fr. Daniel Brottier, vert.

Perf. 12½x13, 13x12½
1987, Oct. 16
734 A230 130fr multi   95 48
735 A230 140fr multi   1.00 50

Inscribed 1986.

Lat Dior, King of Cayor (d. 1887) A231

1987, Oct. 27   Litho.   *Perf. 14*
736 A231 130fr Battle of Dekhele   95 48
737 A231 160fr Lat Dior   1.20 60

World Food Day — A232

1987, Oct. 30   Litho.   *Perf. 12½*
738 A232 130fr Earth storing grain, vert.   90 45
739 A232 140fr shown   98 48
740 A232 145fr Emblem, vert.   1.00 50

Inscribed 1986.

Fauna, Bassa Casamance Natl. Park — A234

1987, Nov. 9   *Perf. 13*
741 A233 115fr Felis servaline   82 40
742 A233 135fr Galagoides demidovii   95 48
743 A233 150fr Potamochoerus porcus   1.10 55
744 A233 250fr Panthera pardus   1.80 90
745 A234 300fr Aigrette   2.15 1.10
746 A234 300fr Guepier   2.15 1.10
   Nos. 741-746 (6)   8.97 4.53

Inscribed 1986. Nos. 745-746 printed se-tenant in continuous design with corner label picturing map of Senegal with park highlighted.

Traditional Wrestling — A235   Birds in Djoudj Natl. Park — A236

Various moves.

1987, Nov. 30   Litho.   *Perf. 14*
747 A235 115fr multi, horiz.   82 40
748 A235 125fr multi, diff., horiz.   90 45
749 A235 135fr multi, diff.   95 48
750 A235 165fr multi, diff.   1.20 60

1987, Dec. 4
751 A236 115fr Stork   82 40
752 A236 125fr Pink flamingos, horiz.   90 45
753 A236 135fr White pelicans, horiz.   95 48
754 A236 300fr Pelicans in water   2.15 1.10
755 A236 350fr like 125fr, horiz.   2.50 1.25
756 A236 350fr like 135fr, horiz.   2.50 1.25
   Nos. 751-756 (6)   9.82 4.93

Nos. 755-756 printed se-tenant with center label picturing map of Senegal with park highlighted.

Christmas
A237

Designs: 145fr, Youth dreaming of presents. 150fr, Madonna and child. 180fr, Holy Family, congregation praying. 200fr, Holy Family, candle and Christmas tree.

1987, Dec. 24   *Perf. 12½x13*
757 A237 145fr multi   1.05 52
758 A237 150fr multi   1.10 55
759 A237 180fr multi   1.30 65
760 A237 200fr multi   1.45 72

Dakar Intl. Fair, 10th Anniv. (in 1985) — A238

1988, Feb. 27   Litho.   *Perf. 13*
761 A238 125fr multi   90 45

Inscribed 1985.

Fish
A239

1988, Feb. 29   Litho.   *Perf. 13*
762 A239 5fr Amelurus nebulosus   15 15
763 A239 100fr Heniochus acuminatus   72 35
764 A239 145fr Anthias anthias   1.05 52
765 A239 180fr Cyprinus carpio   1.30 65

World Meteorology Day — A240

1988, Mar. 15   *Perf. 13½*
766 A240 145fr multi   1.05 52

Paris-Dakar Rally, 10th Anniv. (in 1987) — A241

Various motorcycle and automobile entries in desert settings.

1988   *Perf. 13*
767 A241 145fr Motorcycle   1.05 52
768 A241 180fr Race car   1.30 65
769 A241 200fr Race car, truck   1.45 72
770 A241 410fr Thierry Sabine   2.90 1.45

Inscribed 1987. For surcharge see No. 1051.

Mollusks
A242

1988, Apr. 20   *Perf. 12½*
771 A242 10fr Squid   15 15
772 A242 20fr Donax trunculus   15 15
773 A242 145fr Achatina fulica, vert.   1.05 52
774 A242 165fr Helix nemoralis   1.20 60
   Set value   1.25

1988 African Soccer Cup Championships, Rabat — A243

1988, May 10   Litho.   *Perf. 13*
775 A243 80fr Cameroun (winner)   55 28
776 A243 100fr Kick, CAF emblem   70 35
777 A243 145fr Map, players, final score   1.00 50
778 A243 180fr Trophy   1.25 62

Nos. 776-778 vert.

US Peace Corps in Senegal, 25th Anniv. — A244

1988, May 11   Litho.   Perf. 13
779 A244 190fr multi   1.25   62

Marine Flora — A245

1988, June 13   Litho.   Perf. 12½
780 A245 10fr Dictyota atomaria   15   15
781 A245 65fr Agarum gmelini   45   22
782 A245 145fr Saccorrhiza bulbosa   95   48
783 A245 180fr Rhodymenia palmetta   1.20   60

Inscribed 1987.

No. 710 Overprinted

RICCIONE 88   27-29-08-89

1988, Aug. 27   Litho.   Perf. 13
784 A221 320fr multi   2.20 1.10

Stamp Fair, Riccione, Aug. 27-29, 1988. Stamp incorrectly overprinted "89," instead of "88."

ENDA — A246

1988   Litho.   Perf. 13
785 A246 125fr Thierno Saidou Nourou Tall Center   80   40

1988 Summer Olympics, Seoul — A247

1988, Sept. 17   Litho.   Perf. 13
786 A247   5fr shown   15   15
787 A247 75fr Running, swimming, soccer   50   25

Industries — A248   Indigenous Flowers — A250

788 A247 300fr Character trademark, torch   2.00 1.00
789 A247 410fr Emblems, running   2.75 1.40

Postcards, c. 1900 — A249

1988, Nov. 7   Litho.   Perf. 13
790 A248   5fr Phosphate, Thies   15   15
791 A248 20fr I.C.S.   15   15
792 A248 145fr Seib Mill, Diourbel   92   45
793 A248 410fr Mbao refinery   2.60 1.30

1988, Nov. 26

Designs: 20fr, Boys, Government Palace. 145fr, Wrestlers, St. Louis Great Mosque. 180fr, Dakar Depot, young woman in folk costume. 200fr, Governor's Residence, housewife using mortar and pestle.

794 A249 20fr red brn & blk   15   15
795 A249 145fr red brn & blk   92   45
796 A249 180fr red brn & blk   1.15   58
797 A249 200fr red brn & blk   1.30   65

1988, Dec. 4   Perf. 13x12½
798 A250 20fr Packia biglobosa   15   15
799 A250 60fr Eurphorbia pulcherrima   38   20
800 A250 65fr Cyrtosperma senegalense 42   20
801 A250 410fr Bombax costatum   2.60 1.30

11th Paris-Dakar Rally — A251

1989, Jan. 13   Litho.   Perf. 13½
802 A251 10fr Mask, vehicle, Eiffel Tower   15   15
803 A251 145fr Helmet, desert scene   95   48
804 A251 180fr Turban, rallyist in desert   1.20   60
805 A251 220fr Thierry Sabine   1.45   72

For surcharge see No. 1050.

Tourism — A252

1989, Feb. 15   Perf. 13
806 A252 10fr Teranga   15   15
807 A252 80fr Campement   52   25
808 A252 100fr Saly   65   32
809 A252 350fr Dior   2.25 1.15

Inscribed 1988.

Tourism — A253

1989, Mar. 11
810 A253 130fr Natl. tourism emblem, vert.   85   42
811 A253 140fr Visiting rural community   92   45
812 A253 145fr Sport fishing   95   48
813 A253 180fr Water skiing, polo   1.20   60

Inscribed 1987.

French Revolution, Bicent. — A254

Designs: 180fr, Governor's Palace, St. Louis. 220fr, Declaration of Human Rights and Citizenship, vert. 300fr, Flag, revolutionaries.

1989, May 24   Litho.   Perf. 13
814 A254 180fr shown   1.10   55
815 A254 220fr multi   1.30   65
816 A254 300fr multi   1.80   90

PHILEXFRANCE '89 — A255

1989, July 7   Litho.   Perf. 13x12½
817 A255 10fr shown   15   15
818 A255 25fr Simulated stamp, map of France   15   15
819 A255 75fr Exhibit   45   22
820 A255 145fr Affixing stamp   85   42
        Set value   75

Antoine de Saint-Exupery (1900-1944), French Aviator and Writer — A256

Scenes from novels: 180fr, *Southern Courier*, 1929. 220fr, *Night flier*, 1931. 410fr, *Bomber pilot*, 1942.

1989, Aug. 30   Litho.   Perf. 13
821 A256 180fr multi   1.15   58
822 A256 220fr multi   1.40   70
823 A256 410fr multi   2.65 1.35

No. 785 Surcharged in Bright Green

1989   Litho.   Perf. 13
824 A246 555fr on 125fr multi   4.00 2.00

3rd Francophone Summit on the Arts and Culture — A257

Designs: 5fr, Palette, quill pen in ink pot, dancer, vert. 30fr, Children reading. 100fr, Architecture, women, Earth. 200fr, Artist sketching, easel, gear wheels, chemist, computer operator.

1989   Perf. 13x13½, 13½x13
825 A257   5fr multicolored   15   15
826 A257 30fr multicolored   22   15
827 A257 100fr multicolored   70   35
828 A257 200fr multicolored   1.40   70

Pottery — A258

1989, Nov. 1   Perf. 13
829 A258 15fr shown   15   15
830 A258 30fr Potter, three-handled urn   22   15
831 A258 75fr Vases   52   15
832 A258 145fr Woman carrying pottery 1.05   52
        Set value   90

"30," Dakar Cancel — A259   Natl. Archives, 75th Anniv. — A260

Designs: 30fr, Telephone handset, map. 180fr, Map, simulated stamp, phone handset. 220fr, Telecommunications satellite, globe, map.

1989, Oct. 9   Perf. 13½
833 A259 25fr multicolored   18   15
834 A259 30fr multicolored   22   15
835 A259 180fr multicolored   1.25   62
836 A259 220fr multicolored   1.55   78

Conference of Postal and Telecommunication Administrations of West African Nations (CAPTEAO), 30th anniv.

1989, Oct. 23   Perf. 11½

Designs: 15fr, Stacks, postal card of 1922. 40fr, Document, 1825. 145fr, Document, Archives building. 180fr, Tome.

837 A260 15fr multicolored   15   15
838 A260 40fr multicolored   28   15
839 A260 145fr multicolored   1.05   52
840 A260 180fr multicolored   1.25   62

Jawarharlal Nehru, 1st Prime Minister of Independent India — A261

1989, Nov. 14   *Perf. 13*
841 A261 220fr Portrait, vert.   1.55   78
842 A261 410fr shown   2.90 1.45

Marine
Life
A262

1989, Nov. 27
843 A262 10fr *Grapsus grapsus*   15   15
844 A262 60fr *Hippocampus guttu-*
        latus   45   22
845 A262 145fr *Lepas anatifera*   1.00   50
846 A262 220fr Beach flea   1.55   78

Children's March to
the
Sanctuary — A263

1989, Dec. 9   Litho.   *Perf. 13½*
847 A263 145fr shown   1.05   52
848 A263 180fr Church   1.25   62

Pilgrimage to Notre Dame de Popenguine, cent.

Birds
A263a

Designs: 10fr, *Phalacrocovax carbolucidus, Anhinga rufa.* 45fr, *Lavius cirrocephalus.* 100fr, Dwarf bee-eater, *Lophogetus occipitalis.* 180fr, *Egretta gularis.*

1989, Dec. 11   *Perf. 13*
849 A263a 10fr multicolored   15   15
850 A263a 45fr multicolored   32   16
851 A263a 100fr multicolored   72   35
852 A263a 180fr multicolored   1.30   65

Natl. parks: Djoudj (10fr), Langue de Barbarie (45fr), Basse Casamance (100fr) and Saloum (180fr).

Christmas
A264

Joan of Arc
Institute, 50th
Anniv.
A265

1989, Dec. 22   Litho.   *Perf. 13*
853 A264 10fr shown   15   15
854 A264 25fr Teddy bear   18   15
855 A264 30fr Manger   22   15
856 A264 200fr Mother and child   1.40   70
       Set value   95

1989, Dec. 26   *Perf. 13½*
857 A265 20fr shown   15   15
858 A265 500fr Institute   3.50 3.50

Flight of the 1st Seaplane, Mar. 28,
1910 — A266

    Perf. 13x12½, 12½x13
1989, Dec. 30   Litho.
859 A266 125fr shown   90   45
860 A266 130fr Seaplane, Fabre   92   46
861 A266 475fr Fabre, schematic of
        aircraft, vert.   3.40 1.70
     Souvenir Sheet
862 A266 700fr like 475fr, vert.   5.00 2.50

Henri Fabre (1882-1984), aviator.

1992 Summer Olympics,
Barcelona — A267

Various athletes and monuments or architecture.

1990, Jan. 8   *Perf. 12½*
863 A267 10fr Basketball   15   15
804 A267 130fr High jump   92   45
865 A267 180fr Discus   1.25   62
866 A267 190fr Running   1.35   68
867 A267 315fr Tennis   2.25 1.10
868 A267 475fr Equestrian   3.35 1.65
     Nos. 863-868 (6)   9.27 4.65
     Souvenir Sheet
869 A267 600fr Soccer   4.25 2.10

Fight AIDS
Worldwide — A268

1989, Dec. 1   Litho.   *Perf. 13½*
870 A268 5fr shown   15   15
871 A268 100fr Umbrella   72   35
872 A268 145fr Fist crushing virus   1.05   52
873 A268 180fr Hammering away at
        virus   1.30   65

12th Paris-
Dakar
Rally — A269

1990, Jan. 16   *Perf. 13*
874 A269 20fr shown   15   15
875 A269 25fr Motorcycle   18   15
876 A269 180fr Trophy winner,
        crowd   1.25   62
877 A269 200fr Thierry Sabine   1.40   70

1990 World Cup Soccer Championships,
Italy — A270

Various athletes and: 45fr, Trophy, the Piazza Della Signoria, Florence. 140fr, Piazza Navona, Rome. 180fr, *The Virgin with St. Anne and the Infant Jesus,* by Leonardo da Vinci. 220fr, Portrait of Giuseppe Garibaldi (1807-1882), Risorgimento Museum, Turin. 300fr, *The Sistine Madonna,* by Raphael. 415fr, *The Virgin and Child,* by Daniele da Volterra. 700fr, Columbus Monument, Milan.

1990, Jan. 31   Litho.   *Perf. 13x12½*
878 A270 45fr multicolored   32   16
870 A270 140fr multicolored   1.00   50
880 A270 180fr multicolored   1.30   65
881 A270 220fr multicolored   1.60   80
882 A270 300fr multicolored   2.15 1.10
883 A270 415fr multicolored   3.00 1.50
     Souvenir Sheet
884 A270 700fr multicolored   5.00 2.50

1990 African Soccer Cup
Championships,
Algeria — A271

1990, Mar. 2   Litho.   *Perf. 13*
885 A271 20f shown   15   15
886 A271 60f Goalie   45   22
887 A271 100f Exchange of flags   75   38
888 A271 500f Ball, trophy   3.75 1.90

Postal Services
A272

1990, Apr. 30   Litho.   *Perf. 13*
889 A272 5fr Facsimile transmis-
        sion   15   15
890 A272 15fr Electronic mail   15   15
891 A272 100fr Postal money orders   75   38
892 A272 180fr CNE   1.30   65
       Set value   1.10

Multinational Postal
School, 20th
Anniv. — A273

1990, May 31   *Perf. 13½*
893 A273 145fr multicolored   1.00   50
894 A273 180fr Hand, wreath, envel-
        ope   1.30   65

S.O.S. Children's
Village Appeal for
Aid — A274

1990, May 31
895 A274 5fr multicolored   15   15
896 A274 500fr Family   3.75 1.50

Boy Scouts
A275

Scouting emblems and: 30fr, Camping. 100fr, Hiking at lakeshore. 145fr, Following trail. 200fr, Scout, vert.

1990, Nov. 5   Litho.   *Perf. 11½*
897 A275 30fr multicolored   25   15
898 A275 100fr multicolored   90   45
899 A275 145fr multicolored   1.25   65
900 A275 200fr multicolored   1.75   85

Medicinal
Plants — A276

1990, Nov. 30   *Perf. 13x13½*
901 A276 95fr Cassia tora   85   42
902 A276 105fr Tamarindus indica   95   45
903 A276 125fr Cassia occidentalis   1.10   55
904 A276 175fr Leptadenia hastata   1.50   75

A277   A278

1990, Dec. 24   Litho.   *Perf. 13½*
905 A277 25fr shown   20   15
906 A277 145fr Angel, stars, people   1.25   65
907 A277 180fr Adoration of the Ma-
        gi   1.60   80
908 A277 200fr Animals, baby in
        manger   1.75   85

     Christmas.

1991, Jan. 2   Litho.   *Perf. 13x12½*
909 A278 180fr multicolored   1.55   80

Intl. Red Cross, 125th Anniv., Senegalese Red Cross, 25th anniv. No. 909 inscribed 1988.

Paris-Dakar
Rally — A279

1991, Jan. 17

910	A279	15fr shown	15	15
911	A279	125fr Car, motorcycle	1.10	55
912	A279	180fr Car racing in water	1.55	80
913	A279	220fr Two motorcycles, beach	1.90	95

Reptiles
A280

LE PYTHON DE SEBA   Python sebae

1991, Jan. 31   Perf. 13½x13

914	A280	15fr Python sebae	15	15
915	A280	60fr Chelonia mydas	55	28
916	A280	100fr Crocolylus niloticus	90	45
917	A280	180fr Chameleo senegalensis	1.55	80

Inscribed 1990.

African Film
Festival — A281

Designs: 30fr, Sphinx, slave house, cave paintings, tomb of Mohammed. 60fr, Dogon mask, mosque of Dioulasso, drawing of Osiris, man on camel. 100fr, Ruins, drum, statue of scribe, camels. 180fr, mask, mosque of Djenne, pyramids, Moroccan architecture.

1991, Feb. 23   Perf. 11½

918	A281	30fr org & multi	25	15
919	A281	60fr org & multi	50	25
920	A281	100fr org & multi	90	45
921	A281	180fr org & multi	1.55	80

Alfred Nobel
(1833-1896),
Industrialist
A282

Designs: 145fr, Drawing of Nobel.

1991, Mar. 29   Litho.   Die Cut
Self-adhesive

922	A282	145fr multi, vert.	1.10	55
923	A282	180fr shown	1.35	65

Antelope
A283

1991, Apr. 24   Litho.   Perf. 13½x13

924	A283	5fr Ouerbia ourebi	15	15
925	A283	10fr Gazella dorcas	15	15
926	A283	180fr Kobos kob kob	1.35	70
927	A283	555fr Alcelaphus buce-laphus major	4.10	2.05

Trees
A284

Perf. 13½x13, 13x13½
1991, May 30

928	A284	90fr Ancardium occidentalus	65	35
929	A284	100fr Mangifera indica	75	38
930	A284	125fr Borassus flabellifer, vert.	95	48
931	A284	145fr Elaeis guineensis, vert.	1.10	55

Christopher Columbus — A285

Designs: 100fr, Meeting Haitian natives. 145fr, Columbus' personal coat of arms, vert. 180fr, Santa Maria, Columbus. 200fr, 220fr, Columbus, ships. 500fr, Details of voyages. 625fr, Columbus at chart table.

1991, July 8   Litho.   Perf. 13

932	A285	100fr multicolored	75	38
a.		Sheet of 1, perf. 12½	75	38
933	A285	145fr multicolored	1.10	55
a.		Sheet of 1, perf. 12½	1.10	55
934	A285	180fr multicolored	1.35	65
a.		Sheet of 1, perf. 12½	1.35	65
935	A285	200fr multicolored	1.50	75
a.		Sheet of 1, perf. 12½	1.50	75
936	A285	220fr multicolored	1.65	80
a.		Sheet of 1, perf. 12½	1.65	80
937	A285	500fr multicolored	3.70	1.85
a.		Sheet of 1, perf. 12½	3.70	1.85
938	A285	625fr multicolored	4.65	2.30
a.		Sheet of 1, perf. 12½	4.65	2.30
		Nos. 932-938 (7)	14.70	7.28

Tourism
A286

Designs: 10fr, Canoe excursion, Basse-Casamance. 25fr, Shore at Boufflers Hotel, Goree Island. 30fr, Huts built on stilts, Fadiouth Island. 40fr, Salt collecting on lake.

1991, July 30   Litho.   Perf. 13

939	A286	10fr multicolored	15	15
940	A286	25fr multicolored	18	15
941	A286	30fr multicolored	22	15
942	A286	40fr multicolored	30	15

Dated 1989.

Louis
Armstrong,
Jazz
Musician,
20th Death
Anniv.
A287

1991, Oct. 7   Perf. 13½

943	A287	10fr shown	15	15
944	A287	145fr Singing	1.20	60
945	A287	180fr With trumpets	1.50	75
946	A287	220fr Playing trumpet	1.80	90

Yuri Gagarin, First Man in Space, 30th
Anniv. — A288

Various portraits of Gagarin with Vostok I in Earth orbit.

1991, Nov. 25   Litho.   Perf. 13½

947	A288	15fr multicolored	15	15
948	A288	145fr multicolored	1.20	60
949	A288	180fr multicolored	1.50	75
950	A288	220fr multicolored	1.80	90

Rural Water Supply   6th Islamic
Project — A289   Summit — A290

1991, Dec. 2   Litho.   Perf. 13½

951	A289	30fr Bowl of water	25	15
952	A289	145fr Water faucet, huts	1.25	65
953	A289	180fr Dripping faucet, flags	1.60	80
954	A289	220fr Water tower, huts	1.90	95

1991, Dec. 9

955	A290	15fr shown	15	15
956	A290	145fr Upraised hands	1.25	65
957	A290	180fr Congress Center, Dakar	1.60	80
958	A290	220fr Grand Mosque, Dakar	1.90	95

A291   A292

Basketball, Cent.: 145fr, Player dribbling ball. 180fr, Couple holding trophy. 220fr, Lion, basketball, trophies.

1991, Dec. 21   Litho.   Perf. 13½

959	A291	125fr multicolored	1.00	50
960	A291	145fr multicolored	1.20	60
961	A291	180fr multicolored	1.50	75
962	A291	220fr multicolored	1.80	90

1991, Dec. 24   Litho.   Perf. 13½

963	A292	5fr Jesus	15	15
964	A292	145fr Madonna and Child	1.25	62
965	A292	160fr Angels	1.40	70
966	A292	220fr Christ Child, animals	1.90	95

Christmas. For surcharge see No. 975.

A293   A294

Musical score and: 5fr, Bust of Mozart. 150fr, Mozart conducting. 180fr, Mozart at piano. 220fr, Portrait.

1991, Dec. 31

967	A293	5fr multicolored	15	15
968	A293	150fr multicolored	1.30	65
969	A293	180fr multicolored	1.60	80
970	A293	220fr multicolored	1.90	95

Wolfgang Amadeus Mozart, death bicent.

1992, Jan. 12   Litho.   Perf. 13½

971	A294	10fr shown	15	15
972	A294	145fr Map, soccer balls	1.20	60
973	A294	200fr Lion, trophy	1.65	82
974	A294	220fr Players	1.80	90

18th African Soccer Cup Championships.

VISITE DU
PAPE JEAN PAUL II
AU SENEGAL
19 - 23 / 02 / 92

No. 965 Ovptd.
and Surcharged

180F

1992, Feb. 19   Litho.   Perf. 13½

975	A292	180fr on 160fr	1.50	75

Natl.
Parks
A295

1992, Mar. 20   Perf. 13½x13

976	A295	10fr Delta Du Saloum	15	15
977	A295	125fr Djoudj	1.05	50
978	A295	145fr Niokolo-Koba	1.20	60
979	A295	220fr Basse Casamance	1.80	90

Senegal's
Participation in Gulf
War — A296

Designs: 30fr, Oil wells, flag and missiles. 145fr, Oil wells, soldier. 180fr, Holy Ka'aba, soldier with gun. 220fr, Peace dove with flag, map.

1992, Apr. 4   Perf. 13½

980	A296	30fr multicolored	25	15
981	A296	145fr multicolored	1.20	60
982	A296	180fr multicolored	1.50	75
983	A296	220fr multicolored	1.80	90

Fish Industry
A297

Stylized designs: 5fr, Catching fish. 60fr, Retail outlets. 100fr, Processing plant. 150fr, Packaging.

1992, Apr. 6   Litho.   Perf. 13½

984	A297	5fr multicolored	15	15
985	A297	60fr multicolored	55	28
986	A297	100fr multicolored	90	45
987	A297	150fr multicolored	1.30	65

Tourism — A298

1992, May 5   Perf. 13½x13

988	A298	5fr Niokolo complex	15	15
989	A298	10fr Casamance River	15	15
990	A298	150fr Dakar region	1.30	65
991	A298	200fr Saint-Louis excursion	1.75	90

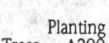

Planting
Trees — A299

Various designs showing children planting trees.

Perf. 13¹/₂x13, 13x13¹/₂
1992, May 29
992	A299	145fr multi	1.25	65
993	A299	180fr multi	1.60	80
994	A299	200fr multi	1.75	90
995	A299	220fr multi, vert.	1.90	95

Public Works
Projects
A300

Various scenes of people cleaning and repairing public walkways.

Perf. 13¹/₂x13, 13x13¹/₂
1992, June 1 Litho.
996	A300	25fr multi	22	15
997	A300	145fr multi	1.25	65
998	A300	180fr multi, vert.	1.60	80
999	A300	220fr multi, vert.	1.95	1.00

Children's Rights — A301

1992, June 12 *Perf. 13*
1000	A301	20fr Education	18	15
1001	A301	45fr Guidance	40	20
1002	A301	165fr Instruction	1.45	70
1003	A301	180fr Health care	1.60	80

African
Integration
A302

1992, June 29 Litho. *Perf. 13*
1004	A302	10fr Free trade	15	15
1005	A302	30fr Youth activities	25	15
1006	A302	145fr Communications	1.25	65
1007	A302	220fr Women's movements	1.95	1.00

1992 Summer
Olympics,
Barcelona — A303

Blue Train — A304

1992, July 25 Litho. *Perf. 13¹/₂*
1008	A303	145fr Map, horiz.	1.10	55
1009	A303	180fr Runner	1.40	70
1010	A303	200fr Sprinter, horiz.	1.50	75
1011	A303	300fr Torch bearer	2.25	1.15

1992, Aug. 3
1012	A304	70fr shown	55	28
1013	A304	145fr Train yard	1.10	55
1014	A304	200fr Train, passengers	1.50	75
1015	A304	220fr Station	1.65	85

Intl. Maritime
Heritage Year — A305

Designs: 25fr, Map of Antarctica, horiz. 100fr, Ocean, sea life. 180fr, Man addressing UN. 220fr, Hands holding globe, flags, ship, fish.

1992, Sept. 4
1016	A305	25fr multicolored	18	15
1017	A305	100fr multicolored	75	38
1018	A305	180fr multicolored	1.40	70
1019	A305	220fr multicolored	1.65	85

Corals
A306

Various coral formations.

Perf. 13¹/₂x13, 13x13¹/₂
1992, Sept. 18 Litho.
1020	A306	50fr multicolored	42	20
1021	A306	100fr multicolored	85	42
1022	A306	145fr multi, vert.	1.20	60
1023	A306	220fr multicolored	1.80	90

Konrad Adenauer (1876-1967) — A307

Designs: 5fr, Portrait, vert. 145fr, Schaumburg Palace, Bonn. 180fr, Hands clasped. 220fr, Map of West Germany.

Perf. 13x13¹/₂, 13¹/₂x13
1992, Sept. 30 Litho.
1024	A307	5fr multicolored	15	15
1025	A307	145fr multicolored	1.20	60
1026	A307	180fr multicolored	1.50	75
1027	A307	220fr multicolored	1.80	90

Shellfish — A308

1992, Oct. 1 Litho. *Perf. 13¹/₂*
1028	A308	20fr Crab	15	15
1029	A308	30fr Spider crab	22	15
1030	A308	180fr Lobster	1.40	70
1031	A308	200fr Shrimp	1.50	75

Fruit-bearing
Plants — A309

1992, Oct. 16 Litho. *Perf. 13x13¹/₂*
1032	A309	10fr Parkia biglobosa	15	15
1033	A309	50fr Balanites aegyptiaca	42	20
1034	A309	200fr Parinari macrophylla	1.60	80
1035	A309	220fr Opuntiatuna	1.80	90

John Glenn's Orbital
Flight, 30th
Anniv. — A310

Designs: 15fr, Astronaut in spacesuit, flag, map, spacecraft, horiz. 145fr, American flag, Glenn, horiz. 180fr, Flag, lift-off of rocket, Glenn in spacesuit, horiz. 200fr, Astronaut in spacesuit, spacecraft.

1992, Nov. 30 Litho. *Perf. 13¹/₂*
1036	A310	15fr multicolored	15	15
1037	A310	145fr multicolored	1.15	58
1038	A310	180fr multicolored	1.40	70
1039	A310	200fr multicolored	1.60	80

Maps Featuring Bakari II — A311

Designs: 100fr, Map from Spanish Atlas, 1375. 145fr, Stone head, Vera Cruz, Mexico, world map, 1413.

1992, Dec. 2 *Perf. 13*
1040	A311	100fr multicolored	82	40
1041	A311	145fr multicolored	1.20	60

No. 1041 issued only with black bar obliterating "Mecades."

Biennial of
Dakar — A312

Christmas — A313

Designs: 20fr, Picture frame. 50fr, Puppet head, stage. 145fr, Open book. 220fr, Musical instrument.

1992, Dec. 14 *Perf. 13¹/₂*
1042	A312	20fr multicolored	15	15
1043	A312	50fr multicolored	40	20
1044	A312	145fr multicolored	1.15	58
1045	A312	220fr multicolored	1.75	88

1992, Dec. 24 *Perf. 13¹/₂*

Designs: 15fr, Children dancing around large ornament, horiz. 145fr, Christmas tree. 180fr, Jesus Christ. 200fr, Santa Claus.
1046	A313	15fr multicolored	15	15
1047	A313	145fr multicolored	1.15	58
1048	A313	180fr multicolored	1.40	70
1049	A313	200fr multicolored	1.60	80

Nos. 770, 804 Surcharged in Red

145 F

Dakar le 17-01-93

15e

1993, Jan. 17 Litho. *Perf. 13¹/₂*
1050	A251	145fr on 180fr #804	1.15	58

Perf. 13
1051	A241	220fr on 410fr #770	1.75	88

Size and location of surcharge varies.

Environmental Protection — A314

Accident
Prevention
A315

Designs: 20fr, Medical clinic. 25fr, Preventing industrial accidents. 145fr, Preventing chemical spills. 200fr, Red Cross helicopter, airline crash.

Perf. 13 (#1052, 1055), 13¹/₂
1993, Mar. 22 Litho.
1052	A314	20fr multicolored	16	15
1053	A315	25fr multicolored	20	15
1054	A315	145fr multicolored	1.15	58
1055	A314	200fr multicolored	1.60	80

Abdoulaye Seck Marie
Parsine (1873-1931),
PTT Director — A316

1993, Apr. 21 Litho. *Perf. 13¹/₂*
1056	A316	220fr multicolored	1.75	88

Wild Animals
A317

Designs: 30fr, Crocuta crocuta. 50fr, Panthera leo. 70fr, Panthera pardus. 150fr, Giraffa camelopardalis peratta, vert. 180fr, Cervus.

1993, Nov. 26 Litho. *Perf. 13¹/₂*
1057	A317	30fr multicolored	15	15
1058	A317	50fr multicolored	20	15
1059	A317	70fr multicolored	25	15

1060	A317	150fr multicolored	55 28
1061	A317	180fr multicolored	70 35
Nos. 1057-1061 (5)			1.85 1.08

Christmas
A318

Designs: 80fr, Two children seated by Christmas tree. 145fr, Santa holding presents, three children. 150fr, Girl, Santa with present.

1993, Dec. 24   Litho.   *Perf. 13x13½*
1062	A318	5fr multicolored	15 15
1063	A318	80fr multicolored	32 16
1064	A318	145fr multicolored	55 28
1065	A318	150fr multicolored	60 30

Paris-Dakar Rally, 16th Anniv. A319

Designs: 145fr, Truck, car, motorcycle racing by tree. 180fr, Racing through desert, men with camel. 220fr, Car, truck, village.

1994, Jan. 5   *Perf. 13½*
1066	A319	145fr multicolored	55 28
1067	A319	180fr multicolored	70 35
1068	A319	220fr multicolored	90 45

Assassination of John F. Kennedy, 30th Anniv. — A320

1993, Dec. 31   Litho.   *Perf. 13*
1069	A320	80fr shown	32 16
1070	A320	555fr Kennedy, White House	2.25 1.10

Fishing Industry
A321

Designs: 5fr, Drying eels. 90fr, Sifting for shellfish. 100fr, Salting fish. 200fr, Cooking fish.

1994, Feb. 28
1071	A321	5fr multicolored	15 15
1072	A321	90fr multicolored	35 18
1073	A321	100fr multicolored	40 20
1074	A321	200fr multicolored	80 40

Conservation of the Seashore — A322

Stylized designs: 5fr, Halting removal of sand. 75fr, Fight against drifting sand dunes. 100fr, Dams, dikes against beach erosion. 200fr, Healthy, aesthetic environment.

1994, Mar. 7
1075	A322	5fr multicolored	15 15
1076	A322	75fr multicolored	30 15
1077	A322	100fr multicolored	40 20
1078	A322	200fr multicolored	80 40

Save the Elephant A323

1994, Apr. 18
1079	A323	30fr shown	15 15
1080	A323	60fr Elephant in "SOS"	25 15
1081	A323	90fr Elephants forming "SOS"	35 18
1082	A323	145fr Elephant, tusks	60 30

Arrival of Portuguese in Senegal, 550th Anniv. A324

1994   Litho.   *Perf. 12*
1083	A324	175fr multicolored	80 40

See Portugal No. 2036.

 A325   A326

Shells: 20fr, Murex saxatilis, horiz. 45fr, Nerita senegalensis. 75fr, Polymita picea, horiz. 175fr, Scalaria pretiosa. 215fr, Conus gloria maris.

1994, Oct. 3   Litho.   *Perf. 13½*
1084	A325	20fr multicolored	15 15
1085	A325	45fr multicolored	20 15
1086	A325	75fr multicolored	32 16
1087	A325	175fr multicolored	75 38
1088	A325	215fr multicolored	95 48
Nos. 1084-1088 (5)			2.37 1.32

1994
1089	A326	175fr multi, horiz.	75 38
1090	A326	215fr multi, horiz.	95 48
1091	A326	275fr multicolored	1.25 60
1092	A326	290fr multi, diff.	1.25 65
Nos. 1089-1092 (4)			4.20 2.11

Intl. Olympic Committee, Cent.

Wild Animals A327

1994   Litho.   *Perf. 13½*
1093	A327	60fr Canis aureus	28 15
1094	A327	70fr Aonyx capensis	30 15
1095	A327	100fr Herpestes ichneumon	45 22
1096	A327	175fr Manis gigantea	75 38
1097	A327	215fr Varanus niloticus	95 48
Nos. 1093-1097 (5)			2.73 1.38

African Children's Day — A329

UNICEF emblem and: 175fr, Children playing. 215fr, Family, huts.

1994, June 16   Litho.   *Perf. 13½*
1102	A329	175fr multicolored	80 40
1103	A329	215fr multicolored	1.00 50

1994 World Cup Soccer Championships, US — A330

Designs: 45fr, Flags of participants, soccer ball, vert. 175fr, Top of globe, bottom of soccer ball, vert. 215fr, Player. 665fr, Two players.

1994, June 17
1104	A330	45fr multicolored	20 15
1105	A330	175fr multicolored	80 40
1106	A330	215fr multicolored	1.00 50
1107	A330	665fr multicolored	3.00 1.50
Nos. 1104-1107 (4)			5.00 2.55

Intl. Year of the Family A333

UN emblem and: 5fr, People of different races, national flags, peace dove, globe, sun. 175fr, Globe, flags, people. 215fr, Globe, mother & child. 290fr, Buildings, family, dove, sun, globe.

1994, Sept. 9   *Perf. 13½x13*
1113	A333	5fr multicolored	15 15
1114	A333	175fr multicolored	80 40
1115	A333	215fr multicolored	1.00 50
1116	A333	290fr multicolored	1.40 70
Nos. 1113-1116 (4)			3.35 1.75

10th Toulouse to Saint-Louis Air Rally — A334

1994   *Perf. 13½*
1117	A334	100fr Breguet 14	45 22
1118	A334	145fr Guillaumet	65 32
1119	A334	180fr Jean Mermoz	85 42
1120	A334	220fr Saint-Exupery	1.00 50
Nos. 1117-1120 (4)			2.95 1.46

Dated 1993.

Christmas A335

Designs: 175fr, Santa Claus, Christ, children, presents, vert. 215fr, Christmas trees, religious scenes, vert. 275fr, Magi, Christ Child. 290fr, Madonna and Child, vert.

1994   *Perf. 13x13½, 13½x13*
1121	A335	175fr multicolored	80 40
1122	A335	215fr multicolored	1.00 50
1123	A335	275fr multicolored	1.25 65
1124	A335	290fr multicolored	1.40 70
Nos. 1121-1124 (4)			4.45 2.25

SEMI-POSTAL STAMPS

No. 84 Surcharged in Red +5c

1915   Unwmk.   *Perf. 14x13½*
B1	A28	10c + 5c org red & rose	35 35

No. B1 is on both ordinary and chalky paper.

Same Surcharge on No. 87

1918
B2	A28	15c + 5c red org & brn vio	38 38

Curie Issue
Common Design Type

1938   Engr.   *Perf. 13*
B3	CD80	1.75fr + 50c brt ultra	5.50 5.50

French Revolution Issue
Common Design Type

Photo., Name & Value Typo. in Black
1939
B4	CD83	45c + 25c grn	3.50 3.50
B5	CD83	70c + 30c brn	3.50 3.50
B6	CD83	90c + 35c red org	3.50 3.50
B7	CD83	1.25fr + 1fr rose pink	3.50 3.50
B8	CD83	2.25fr + 2fr bl	3.50 3.50
Nos. B4-B8 (5)			17.50 17.50

Stamps of 1935-38 Surcharged in Red or Black   SECOURS +1 fr. NATIONAL

1941   *Perf. 12x12½, 12*
B9	A30	50c + 1fr red org	45
B10	A31	80c + 2fr vio (R)	1.75
B11	A30	1.50fr + 2fr dk bl	2.50
B12	A30	2fr + 3fr blue	2.50

Common Design Type and

Bambara Sharpshooter SP1

Colonial Soldier SP2

1941   Photo.   *Perf. 13½*
B13	SP1	1fr + 1fr red	50
B14	CD86	1.50fr + 3fr maroon	50
B15	SP2	2.50fr + 1fr blue	50

The surtax was for the defense of the colonies. Nos. B13-B15 were issued by the Vichy government, but it is doubtful whether they were placed in use in Senegal.

Stamps of type A32 surcharged "OEUVRES COLONIALES" and new values were issued in 1944 by the Vichy Government, but were not placed on sale in the colony.

> Catalogue values for unused stamps in this section, from this point to the end of the section, are for Never Hinged items.

Republic
Anti-Malaria Issue
Common Design Type
Perf. 12½x12
1962, Apr. 7   Engr.   Unwmk.
B16	CD108	25fr + 5fr brt grn	40 40

Freedom from Hunger Issue
Common Design Type
1963, Mar. 21   *Perf. 13*
B17 CD112 25fr + 5fr dp vio, grn & brn   35   35

AIR POST STAMPS

Landscape
AP1

Caravan
AP2

Perf. 12¹/₂x12, 12x12¹/₂

		1935 Engr.	Unwmk.	
C1	AP1	25c dk brown	15	15
C2	AP1	50c red orange	35	25
C3	AP1	1fr rose lilac	15	15
C4	AP1	1.25fr yellow grn	15	15
C5	AP1	2fr blue	15	15
C6	AP1	3fr olive grn	15	15
C7	AP2	3.50fr violet	15	15
C8	AP2	4.75fr orange	35	28
C9	AP2	6.50fr dk blue	55	45
C10	AP2	8fr black	80	60
C11	AP2	15fr rose lake	55	42
		Nos. C1-C11 (11)	3.50	2.90

No. C8 surcharged "ENTR' AIDE FRANCAIS + 95f 25" in green, red violet or blue, was never issued in this colony.

Common Design Type
		1940 Engr.	*Perf. 12¹/₂x12*	
C12	CD85	1.90fr ultra	20	20
C13	CD85	2.90fr dk red	20	20
C14	CD85	4.50fr dk gray grn	28	28
C15	CD85	4.90fr yellow bis	35	35
C16	CD85	6.90fr dp orange	35	35
		Nos. C12-C16 (5)	1.38	1.38

Common Design Types
		1942		
C17	CD88	50c car & bl		15
C18	CD88	1fr brn & blk		20
C19	CD88	2fr dk grn & red brn		20
C20	CD88	3fr dk bl & scar		40
C21	CD88	5fr vio & brn red		22

Frame Engr., Center Typo.
C22	CD89	10fr ultra, ind & hn		22
C23	CD89	20fr rose car, mag & choc		25
C24	CD89	50fr yel grn, dl grn & yel	55	70

Engr. & Photo.
Size: 47x26mm
C25	CD88	100fr dk red & bl	1.00	1.00
		Nos. C17-C25 (9)	3.19	

There is doubt whether Nos. C17 to C23 were officially placed in use.

> Catalogue values for unused stamps in this section, from this point to the end of the section, are for Never Hinged items.

Republic

Abyssinian Roller — AP3

Designs: 50fr, Carmine bee-eater, vert. 200fr, Violet touraco, vert. 250fr, Red bishop, vert. 500fr, Fish eagle, vert.

1960-63   Photo.   Unwmk.
Birds in Natural Colors
C26	AP3	50fr blk & gray bl ('61)	65	20
C27	AP3	100fr blk, yel & lil	1.40	45
C28	AP3	200fr blk, grn & bl ('61)	2.50	1.50
C29	AP3	250fr blk & pale grn ('63)	3.50	1.90
C30	AP3	500fr blk & bl	8.50	2.50
		Nos. C26-C30 (5)	16.55	6.55

Air Afrique Issue
Common Design Type
1962, Feb. 17   Engr.   *Perf. 13*
C31 CD107 25fr vio brn, sl grn & ocher   30   16

African Postal Union Issue
Common Design Type
1963, Sept. 8   Photo.   *Perf. 12¹/₂*
C32 CD114 85fr choc, ocher & red   65   42

Air Afrique Issue, 1963
Common Design Type
1963, Nov. 19   Unwmk.   *Perf. 13x12*
C33 CD115 50fr multicolored   70   50

Independence Monument — AP4

1964, Apr. 4   Photo.   *Perf. 12x13*
C34 AP4 300fr ultra, tan, ocher & grn   2.00   1.00

Symbolic European and African Cities — AP5

1964, Apr. 18   Engr.   *Perf. 13*
C35 AP5 150fr grn, brn red & blk   1.60   1.00

Congress of the Intl. Federation of Twin Cities, Dakar.

Europafrica Issue, 1964

Peanuts, Globe, Factory, Figures of "Africa," and "Europe" — AP6

1964, July 20   Photo.   *Perf. 13x12*
C36 AP6 50fr multicolored   65   50

See note after Madagascar No. 357.

Basketball — AP7   Launching of Syncom 2 — AP8

1964, Aug. 22   Engr.   *Perf. 13*
C37	AP7	85fr shown	65	42
C38	AP7	100fr Pole vault	90	50

18th Olympic Games, Tokyo, Oct. 10-25.

1964, Oct. 24   Unwmk.   *Perf. 13*
C39 AP8 150fr grn, red brn & ultra   1.10   55

Communication through space.

Pres. John F. Kennedy (1917-1963) AP9   Mother and Child, Globe and Emblems AP10

1964, Dec. 5   Photo.   *Perf. 13*
C40	AP9	100fr brt yel, dk grn & brn red	90	75
a.		Souvenir sheet of 4	4.00	4.00

Scenic Type of Regular Issue, 1965
View: 100fr, Shore of Gambia River in Eastern Senegal.

1965, Feb. 27   Engr.   *Perf. 13*
Size: 48x27mm
C41 A48 100fr brn blk, grn & bis   1.00   42

1965, Sept. 25   Unwmk.   *Perf. 13*
C42 AP10 50fr choc, brt bl & grn   45   25

International Cooperation Year.

A-1 Satellite and Earth — AP11

Designs: No. C44, Diamant rocket. 90fr, Scout rocket and FR-1 satellite.

1966, Feb. 19   Engr.   *Perf. 13*
C43	AP11	50fr yel brn, dk grn & blk	38	20
C44	AP11	50fr Prus bl, lt red brn & car rose	38	20
C45	AP11	90fr dk red brn, dk gray & Prus bl	80	42

French achievements in space.

D-1 Satellite over Globe — AP12

1966, June 11   Engr.   *Perf. 13*
C46 AP12 100fr dk car, sl & vio   1.00   55

Launching of the D-1 satellite at Hammaguir, Algeria, Feb. 17, 1966.

Air Afrique Issue, 1966
Common Design Type
1966, Aug. 31   Photo.   *Perf. 13*
C47 CD123 30fr red brn, blk & lem   30   15

Mermoz Plane "Arc-en-Ciel" — AP13

Jean Mermoz — AP14

Designs: 35fr, Latecoére 300 "Croix du Sud." 100fr, Map showing last flight from Dakar to Brazil.

1966, Dec. 7   Engr.   *Perf. 13*
C48	AP13	20fr bl, rose lil & ind	22	16
C49	AP13	35fr sl, brn & grn	38	20
C50	AP13	100fr grn, lt grn & mar	1.00	42
C51	AP14	150fr blk, ultra & mar	1.50	70

Jean Mermoz (1901-36), French aviator, on the 30th anniv. of his last flight.

Dakar-Yoff Airport — AP15

1967, Apr. 22   Engr.   *Perf. 13*
C52 AP15 200fr red brn, ind & brt bl   1.10   38

Knob-billed Goose — AP16

Flowers and Birds: 100fr, Mimosa. 150fr, Flowering cactus. 250fr, Village weaver. 500fr, Bateleur.

1967-69   Photo.   *Perf. 11¹/₂*
Granite Paper
Dated "1967"
C53	AP16	100fr gray, yel & grn	1.10	45
C54	AP16	150fr multicolored	1.60	65

Dated "1969"
C55	AP16	250fr gray & multi	2.00	1.00

Dated "1968"

C56 AP16 300fr brt bl & multi 3.00 1.25
C57 AP16 500fr orange & multi 4.25 1.90
Nos. C53-C57 (5) 11.95 5.25

Issue dates: 100fr, 150fr, June 24, 1967; 500fr, July 13, 1968; 300fr, Dec. 21, 1968; 250fr, Apr. 26, 1969.

The Girls from Avignon, by Picasso — AP17

1967, July 22   *Perf. 12x13*
C59 AP17 100fr multicolored 1.20 80

African Postal Union Issue, 1967
Common Design Type

1967, Sept. 9 **Engr.** *Perf. 13*
C60 CD124 100fr brt grn, vio & car lake 90 45

Konrad Adenauer — AP18

Weather Balloon, Vegetation and WMO Emblem — AP19

1968, Feb. 17 **Photo.** *Perf. 12½*
C61 AP18 100fr dk red, ol & blk 1.10 55
  a. Souvenir sheet of 4 4.50 4.50

Konrad Adenauer (1876-1967), chancellor of West Germany (1949-63).

1968, Mar. 23 **Engr.** *Perf. 13*
C62 AP19 50fr blk, ultra & bl grn 45 22

8th World Meteorological Day, Mar. 23.

19th Olympic Games, Mexico City, Oct. 12-27 — AP20

1968, Oct. 12 **Engr.** *Perf. 13*
C63 AP20 20fr Hurdling 20 15
C64 AP20 30fr Javelin 22 16
C65 AP20 50fr Judo 42 18
C66 AP20 75fr Basketball 60 22

PHILEXAFRIQUE Issue

Young Woman Reading Letter, by Jean Raoux — AP21

1968, Oct. 26 **Photo.** *Perf. 12½*
C67 AP21 100fr buff & multi 1.10 1.00

PHILEXAFRIQUE, Phil. Exhib. in Abidjan, Feb. 14-23, 1969. Printed with alternating buff label.

2nd PHILEXAFRIQUE Issue
Common Design Type

Design: 50fr, Senegal No. 160 and Boulevard, Dakar.

1969, Feb. 14 **Engr.** *Perf. 13*
C68 CD128 50fr grn, gray & pur 60 50

Tourist Emblem with Map of Africa and Dove — AP22

1969   **Photo.** *Perf. 13*
C69 AP22 100fr red, lt grn & lt bl 70 35

Year of African Tourism, 1969.

Pres. Lamine Gueye (1891-1968) — AP23

Design: 45fr, Pres. Gueye wearing fez.

1969, June 10 **Photo.** *Perf. 12½*
C70 AP23 30fr brn, org & blk 22 15
C71 AP23 45fr brn, lt grnsh bl & blk 35 16
  a. Min. sheet of 4, 2 #C70, 2 #C71 1.25 1.25

"Transmission of Thought" Tapestry by Ousmane Faye — AP24

Fari, Tapestry by Allaye N'Diaye — AP25

1969, Oct. 25 **Photo.** *Perf. 12½*
C72 AP24 25fr multicolored 22 15
    Perf. 12x12½
C73 AP25 50fr multicolored 45 22

Europafrica Issue

Baila Bridge — AP26

1969, Nov. 15 **Photo.** *Perf. 13x12*
C74 AP26 100fr multicolored 70 38

Emile Lécrivain, Plane and Toulouse-Dakar Route — AP27

1970, Jan. 31 **Engr.** *Perf. 13*
C75 AP27 50fr grn, sl & rose brn 40 22

40th anniv. of the disappearance of the aviator Emile Lécrivain (1897-1929).

René Maran, Martinique — AP28

Portraits: 45fr, Marcus Garvey, Jamaica. 50fr, Dr. Price Mars, Haiti.

1970, Mar. 21 **Photo.** *Perf. 12½*
C76 AP28 30fr red brn, lt grn & blk 25 15
C77 AP28 45fr blue, pink & blk 42 16
C78 AP28 50fr grn, buff & blk 48 16

Issued to honor prominent Negro leaders.

"One People, One Purpose, One Faith" — AP29

1970, Apr. 3 **Photo.** *Perf. 11½*
C79 AP29 500fr gold & multi 4.00 1.90
  a. Souvenir sheet 4.50 4.50

10th anniv. of independence. No. C79 sold for 600fr.

Bay of Naples and Dakar Post Office — AP30

1970, May 2 **Photo.** *Perf. 13x12½*
C80 AP30 100fr multicolored 80 55

10th Europa Phil. Exhib., Naples, May 2-10.

Blue Cock, by Mamadou Niang — AP31

Tapestries: 45fr, Fairy. 75fr, "Lunaris," by Jean Lurçat.

1970, June 20 **Photo.** *Perf. 12½x12*
C81 AP31 30fr black & multi 20 15
C82 AP31 45fr dk red brn & multi 35 15
C83 AP31 75fr yellow & multi 50 30

Head of the Courtesan Nagakawa, by Chobunsai Yeishi, and Mt. Fuji, by Hokusai — AP32

EXPO Emblem and: 25fr, Woman Playing Guitar, by Hokusai, and Sun Tower, vert. 150fr, "One of the Present-day Beauties of Nanboku" by Katsukawa Shuncho, vert.

1970, July 18 **Engr.** *Perf. 13*
C84 AP32 25fr red & green 20 15
C85 AP32 75fr yel grn, dk bl & red brn 55 22
C86 AP32 150fr bl, red brn & ocher 1.10 55

EXPO '70 Intl. Exhib., Osaka, Japan, Mar. 15-Sept. 13.

Tuna, Processing Plant and Ship — AP33

Urban Development in Dakar — AP34

1970, Aug. 22 Engr. Perf. 13
C87 AP33 30fr dl red, blk & brt bl 22 15
C88 AP34 100fr choc & grn 70 40
Progress in industrialization and urbanization in Dakar.

Beethoven; Napoleon and Allegory of Eroica Symphony — AP35

Design: 100fr, Beethoven holding quill.

1970, Sept. 26 Engr. Perf. 13
C89 AP35 50fr ol, brn & ocher 52 22
C90 AP35 100fr Prus grn & dp cl 1.00 50
Ludwig van Beethoven (1770-1827), composer.

Globe, Scales and Women of Four Races — AP36

1970, Oct. 24 Engr. Perf. 13
C91 AP36 100fr grn, ocher & red 90 55
25th anniversary of United Nations.

De Gaulle, Map of Africa, Symbols — AP37
Phillis Wheatley, American Poet — AP39

"A Roof for Every Refugee" — AP38

Design: 100fr, Charles de Gaulle and map of Senegal.

1970, Dec. 31 Photo. Perf. 12½
C92 AP37 50fr multicolored 45 35
C93 AP37 100fr blue & multi 1.00 65
Honoring Pres. Charles de Gaulle as liberator of the colonies.

1971, Jan. 16
C94 AP38 100fr multicolored 80 42
High Commissioner for Refugees, 20th anniv.

1971, Apr. 10 Photo. Perf. 12½
Prominent Blacks: 40fr, James E. K. Aggrey, Methodist missionary, Ghana. 60fr, Alain Le Roy

Locke, American educator. 100fr, Booker T. Washington, American educator.
C95 AP39 25fr multicolored 16 15
C96 AP39 40fr blk, bl & bis 30 16
C97 AP39 60fr blk, bl & emer 45 18
C98 AP39 100fr blk, bl & red 70 38

Napoleon as First Consul, by Ingres — AP40

Designs: 25fr, Napoleon in 1809, by Robert Lefevre. 35fr, Napoleon on his death bed, by Georges Rouget. 50fr, Awakening into Immortality, sculpture by Francois Rude.

1971, June 19 Photo. Perf. 13
C99 AP40 15fr gold & multi 25 20
C100 AP40 25fr gold & multi 40 25
C101 AP40 35fr gold & multi 45 35
C102 AP40 50fr gold & multi 65 60
Napoleon Bonaparte (1769-1821).

Gamal Abdel Nasser — AP41
Alfred Nobel — AP41a

1971, July 17 Perf. 12½
C103 AP41 50fr multicolored 40 20
Nasser (1918-1970), President of Egypt.

1971, Sept. 25 Photo. Perf. 13½x13
C103A AP41a 100fr multicolored 80 45
Alfred Nobel (1833-1896), inventor of dynamite who established the Nobel Prizes.

Iranian Flag and Senegal Coat of Arms — AP42

1971, Oct. 15 Perf. 13x12½
C104 AP42 200fr multicolored 1.50 65
2500th anniversary of the founding of the Persian empire by Cyrus the Great.

African Postal Union Issue, 1971
Common Design Type

Design: 100fr, Arms of Senegal and UAMPT Building, Brazzaville, Congo.

1971, Nov. 13 Perf. 13x13½
C105 CD135 100fr blue & multi 70 30

Louis Armstrong (1900-1971), American Jazz Musician AP43

1971, Nov. 27 Photo. Perf. 12½
C106 AP43 150fr gold & dk brn 1.20 80

Sapporo Olympic Emblem and Speed Skating — AP44

Sapporo '72 Emblem and: 10fr, Bobsledding. 125fr, Skiing.

1972, Jan. 22 Perf. 13
C107 AP44 5fr multicolored 15 15
C108 AP44 10fr multicolored 15 15
C109 AP44 125fr multicolored 90 40
Set value 1.00 50
11th Winter Olympic Games, Sapporo, Japan, Feb. 3-13.

Fonteghetto della Farina, by Canaletto — AP45

Design: 100fr, San Giorgio Maggiore, by Giovanni Antonio Guardi, vert.

1972, Feb. 26
C110 AP45 50fr gold & multi 40 20
C111 AP45 100fr gold & multi 80 40
UNESCO campaign to save Venice.

Theater Type of Regular Issue
Design: 150fr, Daniel Sorano as Shylock, vert.

1972, Mar. 25 Photo. Perf. 12½x13
C112 A99 150fr multicolored 1.40 70

Environment Type of Regular Issue
Design: 100fr, Protection of the ocean (oil slick).

1972, June 3 Photo. Perf. 13x12½
C113 A101 100fr multicolored 80 45

Emperor Haile Selassie, Ethiopian and Senegalese Flags — AP46

1972, July 23 Photo. Perf. 13½x13
C114 AP46 100fr gold & multi 80 40
80th birthday of Emperor Haile Selassie of Ethiopia.

Swordfish — AP47

Designs: 65fr, Killer whale. 75fr, Rhincodon. 125fr, Common rorqual (whale).

1972-73 Photo. Perf. 11½
C115 AP47 50fr multi 35 15
C116 AP47 65fr multi 40 18
C117 AP47 75fr multi 45 22
C118 AP47 125fr multi 90 55
Issued: #C115, C118, 11/25/72; #C116-C117, 7/28/73.

Palace of the Republic — AP48

1973, Apr. 3 Photo. Perf. 13
C119 AP48 100fr multi 60 35

Hotel Teranga, Dakar — AP49

1973, May 26 Photo. Perf. 13
C120 AP49 100fr multi 60 35

Emblem of African Lions Club AP50

1973, June 2
C121 AP50 150fr multi 1.00 65
15th Congress of Lions Intl., District 403, Dakar, June 1-2.

"Couple with Mimosa," by Marc Chagall AP51

1973, Aug. 11 Photo. Perf. 13
C122 AP51 200fr multi 1.90 90

The lack of a value for a listed item does not necessarily indicate rarity.

Map of Italy with
Riccione — AP52

Human Rights
Flame and
People — AP54

Raoul Follereau and World Map — AP53

1973, Aug. 25　　　　Engr.
C123 AP52 100fr dk grn, red & pur　　60　38

　　Intl. Phil. Exhib., Riccione 1973.

1973, Dec. 22　　Engr.　　Perf. 13

Design: 100fr, Dr. Armauer G. Hansen and leprosy bacilli.

C124 AP53　40fr sl grn, pur & red brn　25　15
C125 AP53 100fr sl grn, mag & plum　65　40

　　Centenary of the discovery of the Hansen bacillus, the cause of leprosy.

1973, Dec. 15　　Photo.　　Perf. 13½

Design: 65fr, Human Rights flame and
drummer.

C126 AP54　35fr grn & multi　　　　20　15
C127 AP54　65fr org & multi　　　　25　22

　　25th anniv. of the Universal Declaration of
Human Rights.

Men of Four Races, Arms of Dakar,
Congress Emblem — AP55

Design: 50fr, Key joining twin cities and
emblem, vert.

1973, Dec. 26　　　　　Photo.
C128 AP55　50fr org & multi　　　　35　20
C129 AP55 125fr red & multi　　　　80　45

　　8th Congress of the World Federation of Twin
Cities, Dakar, Dec. 26-29.

Finfoots — AP56

1974, Feb. 9　　Photo.　　Perf. 13
C130 AP56　1fr shown　　　　　　15　15
C131 AP56　2fr Spoonbills　　　　15　15
C132 AP56　3fr Crested cranes　　15　15
C133 AP56　4fr Egrets　　　　　　15　15
C134 AP56 250fr Flamingos　　　1.40　90
C135 AP56 250fr Flamingos　　　1.40　90
　a.　　Strip of 2 + label　　　　3.00
　　　　　　　Set value　　　　　3.00　2.00

　　Djoudj Park bird sanctuary. Denomination in
gold on No. C134, in black on No. C135.

Tiger Attacking Wild Horse, by
Delacroix — AP57

　Design: 200fr, Tiger Hunt, by Eugéne Delacroix
(1798-1863).

1974, Mar. 23　　Photo.　　Perf. 13
C136 AP57 150fr gold & multi　　90　60
C137 AP57 200fr gold & multi　1.20　65

Intl. Fair, Dakar — AP57a

1974, Nov. 28　Embossed　Perf. 10½
C137A AP57a　350fr silver
C137B AP57a 1500fr gold

Soyuz and Apollo, Space Docking
Emblem — AP58

1975, May 23　　Engr.　　Perf. 13
C138 AP58 125fr multi　　　　50　35
　　　　US-USSR space cooperation.
　　　For overprint see No. C140.

Senegal Type
D6, Tuscany
Type A1, Map
of Italy — AP59

1975, Aug. 23　　Engr.　　Perf. 13
C139 AP59 125fr org, vio & dk red　65　35

　　Intl. Phil. Exhib., Riccione 1975.

No. C138 Overprinted: "JONCTION / 17
Juil. 1975"

1975, Oct. 21　　Engr.　　Perf. 13
C140 AP58 125fr multi　　　　50　35

　Apollo-Soyuz link-up in space, July 17, 1975.

Boston Massacre — AP60

Design: 500fr, Lafayette, Washington, Rochambeau and Battle of Yorktown.

1975, Dec. 20　　　　Engr.　　Perf. 13
C141 AP60 250fr ultra, red & brn　1.40　65
C142 AP60 500fr bl & ver　　　　2.50　1.40

　　　　American Bicentennial.

Concorde and Map — AP61

1976, Jan. 21　　Litho.　　Perf. 13
C143 AP61 300fr multi　　　　1.60　80

　　First commercial flight of supersonic jet Concorde, Paris to Rio de Janeiro, Jan. 21.
　　For overprint see No. C145.

2nd Intl. Fair, Dakar — AP61a

1976, Dec. 3　Embossed　Perf. 10½
C143A AP61a　500fr silver
C143B AP61a 1500fr gold

Spaceship and Control
Room — AP62

1977, June 25　　Litho.　　Perf. 12½
C144 AP62 300fr multi　　　　1.60　80

　　Viking space mission to Mars.

No. C143 Overprinted in Red: "22.11.77
/ PARIS NEW-YORK"

1977, Nov. 22　　　　　　Perf. 13
C145 AP61 300fr multi　　　　1.60　80

Concorde, 1st commercial flight, Paris-New York.

Philexafrique II-Essen Issue
Common Design Types

　Designs: No. C146, Lion & Senegal #C28. No.
C147, Capercaillie & Schleswig-Holstein #1.

1978, Nov. 1　　Litho.　　Perf. 12½
C146 CD138 100fr multi　　　　65　28
C147 CD139 100fr multi　　　　65　28
　a.　　Pair, #C146-C147　　　1.30　60

J. Dabry, L. Gimie, and J. Mermoz,
Airplane, Map of Route (St. Louis-
Natal) — AP63

1980, Dec.　　Photo.　　Perf. 13
C148 AP63 300fr multi　　　　2.25　80

　1st airmail crossing of South Atlantic, 50th
anniversary.

1st Transatlantic Commercial Airmail
Flight, 55th Anniv. — AP64

1985, May 12　　Litho.　　Perf. 13
C149 AP64 250fr multi　　　　65　35

Clement Ader (1841-1926), Engineer and
Aviation Pioneer — AP65

　Ader and: 145fr, Automobile, microphone.
180fr, 615fr, 940fr, Bat-winged steam powered
airplane.

1991, June 7　　Litho.　　Perf. 13
C150 AP65 145fr multicolored　1.10　55
C151 AP65 180fr multicolored　1.35　65
C152 AP65 615fr multi, vert.　4.50　2.25

　　　　Souvenir Sheet

C153 AP65 940fr multi, vert.　7.00　3.50

AIR POST SEMI-POSTAL STAMPS

French Revolution Issue
Common Design Type

1939　　Unwmk.　　Photo.　　Perf. 13
Name and Value Typo. in Orange
CB1 CD83 4.75 + 4fr brn blk　　5.50　5.50

　Surtax used for the defense of the colonies.

Stamps of types of Dahomey V1,
V2, V3, and V4 inscribed "Sénégal"
were issued in 1942 by the Vichy
Government, but were not placed on
sale in the colony.

Catalogue values for unused
stamps in this section, from this
point to the end of the section, are
for Never Hinged items.

Republic

Nile Gods Uniting Upper and Lower Egypt
(Abu Simbel) — SPAP1

1964, Mar. 7   Engr.   Perf. 13

CB2 SPAP1 25fr + 5fr Prus bl, red brn
    & sl grn   80   60

UNESCO campaign to save historic monuments in Nubia.

POSTAGE DUE STAMPS

Postage Due Stamps of French Colonies Surcharged

10

1903   Unwmk.   Imperf.

J1 D1 10c on 50c lilac   50.00 50.00
J2 D1 10c on 60c brn, *buff*   50.00 50.00
J3 D1 10c on 1fr rose, *buff*   225.00 225.00

D2

D3

1906   Typo.   Perf. 14x13½

J4 D2 5c grn, *grnsh*   2.75   2.75
J5 D2 10c red brn   3.25   3.25
J6 D2 15c dark blue   3.50   3.50
J7 D2 20c blk, *yellow*   4.25   4.25
J8 D2 30c red, *straw*   4.50   4.25
J9 D2 50c violet   4.50   4.25
J10 D2 60c blk, *buff*   6.00   6.00
J11 D2 1fr blk, *pinkish*   10.50 10.00
    Nos. J4-J11 (8)   39.25 38.25

1914

J12 D3 5c green   16   16
J13 D3 10c rose   26   26
J14 D3 15c gray   26   26
J15 D3 20c brown   40   26
J16 D3 30c blue   65   55
J17 D3 50c black   80   57
J18 D3 60c orange   1.10   90
J19 D3 1fr violet   1.10   90
    Nos. J12-J19 (8)   4.73   4.09

Type of 1914 Issue Surcharged   **2F.**

1927

J20 D3 2fr on 1fr lil rose   3.00   2.50
J21 D3 3fr on 1fr org brn   3.00   2.50

D4

1935   Engr.   Perf. 12½x12

J22 D4 5c yellow green   15   15
J23 D4 10c red orange   15   15
J24 D4 15c violet   15   15
J25 D4 20c olive green   15   15
J26 D4 30c reddish brown   15   15
J27 D4 50c rose lilac   40   40
J28 D4 60c orange   65   65
J29 D4 1fr black   45   45
J30 D4 2fr dark blue   45   45
J31 D4 3fr dark carmine   55   55
    Set value   2.75   2.75

> Catalogue values for unused stamps in this section, from this point to the end of the section, are for Never Hinged items.

Republic

D5

Lion — D6

1961, Feb. 20   Typo.   Perf. 14x13½

J32 D5 1fr orange & red   15   15
J33 D5 2fr ultra & red   15   15
J34 D5 5fr brown & red   15   15
J35 D5 20fr green & red   50   50
J36 D5 25fr red lilac & red   55   55
    Set value   1.30   1.30

1966-83   Typo.   Perf. 14x13
Lion in Gold

J37 D6 1fr red & black   15   15
J38 D6 2fr yel brn & blk   15   15
J39 D6 5fr red lil & blk   15   15
J40 D6 10fr brt bl & blk   20   20
J41 D6 20fr emer & blk   32   32
J42 D6 30fr gray & blk   55   55
J43 D6 60fr blue & blk   28   28
J44 D6 90fr rose & blk   42   42
    Set value   1.95   1.95

Issued: 1fr-30fr, Dec. 1, 1966; others, Oct. 1983.

OFFICIAL STAMPS

> Catalogue values for unused stamps in this section are for Never Hinged items.

Arms — O1

Baobab Tree — O2

Perf. 14x13½
1961, Sept. 18   Typo.   Unwmk.
Denominations in Black

O1 O1 1fr sepia & bl   15   15
O2 O1 2fr dk bl & org   15   15
O3 O1 5fr maroon & grn   15   15
O4 O1 10fr ver & bl   15   15
O5 O1 25fr vio bl & ver   35   15
O6 O1 50fr ver & gray   65   35
O7 O1 85fr lilac & org   1.20   62
O8 O1 100fr ver & yel grn   1.60   90
    Nos. O1-O8 (8)   4.40   2.62

1966-77   Typo.   Perf. 14x13

O9 O2 1fr yel & blk   15   15
O10 O2 5fr org & blk   15   15
O11 O2 10fr red & blk   15   15
O12 O2 20fr dp red lil & blk   15   15
O13 O2 25fr dp lil & blk ('75)   15   15
O14 O2 30fr bl & blk   28   15
O15 O2 35fr bl & blk ('73)   40   15
O16 O2 40fr grnsh bl & blk ('75) 25   15
O17 O2 55fr emer & blk   65   45
O18 O2 60fr emer & blk ('77)   32   15
O19 O2 90fr dk bl grn & blk   1.00   22
O20 O2 100fr brn & blk   1.20   22
    Nos. O9-O20 (12)   4.85
    Set value   1.55

See Nos. O22-O25.

No. O17 Surcharged with New Value and Two Bars

1969

O21 O2 60fr on 55fr emer & blk   1.00   15

Type of 1966

1983, Oct.   Typo.   Perf. 14x13

O22 O2 90fr dk grn & blk   42   15

"90F" is shorter and wider than on Nos. O9-O22.

Baobab Tree Type of 1966

1991   Litho.   Perf. 13

O23 O2 50fr red & blk   40   20
O24 O2 145fr brt grn & blk   1.25   62
O25 O2 180fr org yel & blk   1.50   75

This is an expanding set. Numbers will change if necessary.

SENEGAMBIA & NIGER

A French Administrative unit for the Senegal and Niger possessions in Africa during the period when the French possessions in Africa were being definitely divided into colonies and protectorates. The name was dropped in 1904 when this territory was

consolidated with part of French Sudan, under the name Upper Senegal and Niger.

100 Centimes = 1 Franc

Navigation and Commerce — A1

1903   Unwmk.   Typo.   Perf. 14x13½
Name of Colony in Blue or Carmine

1 A1 1c black, *lil bl*   85   85
2 A1 2c brown, *buff*   1.00   1.00
3 A1 4c claret, *lav*   1.90   1.90
4 A1 5c yel grn   2.50   2.50
5 A1 10c red   2.50   2.50
6 A1 15c gray   5.00   5.00
7 A1 20c red, *green*   5.00   5.00
8 A1 25c blue   7.00   7.00
9 A1 30c brn, *bister*   7.00   7.00
10 A1 40c red, *straw*   10.00 10.00
11 A1 50c brn, *azure*   20.00 20.00
12 A1 75c deep vio, *org*   22.50 22.50
13 A1 1fr brnz grn, *straw*   30.00 30.00
    Nos. 1-13 (13)   115.25 115.25

Perf. 13½x14 stamps are counterfeits.

SERBIA

LOCATION — In southeastern Europe, bounded by Romania and Bulgaria on the east, the former Austro-Hungarian Empire on the north, Greece on the south, and Albania and Montenegro on the west
GOVT. — A former Kingdom
AREA — 18,650 sq. mi.
POP. — 2,911,701 (1910)
CAPITAL — Belgrade

Following World War I, Serbia united with Montenegro, Bosnia and Herzegovina, Croatia, Dalmatia and Slovenia to form the kingdom (later republic) of Yugoslavia.

100 Paras = 1 Dinar

Coat of Arms — A1

Prince Michael (Obrenovich III) — A2

1866   Unwmk.   Typo.   Imperf.
Paper colored Through

1 A1 1p dk grn, *dk vio rose*   45.00

Surface Colored Paper, Thin or Thick

2 A1 1p dk grn, *lil rose*   50.00
a. 1p olive green, *rose*   50.00
b. 1p yel grn, *pale rose* (thick paper) 300.00
3 A1 2p red brn, *lil*   60.00
a. 2p red brn, *lil gray* (thick paper) 250.00
b. 2p dl grn, *lil gray* (thick paper) 800.00

Vienna Printing
Perf. 12

4 A2 10p orange   750.00 500.00
5 A2 20p brown   425.00 17.50
6 A2 40p blue   475.00 125.00
a. Half used as 20p on cover

Belgrade Printing
Perf. 9½

7 A2 1p green   15.00
8 A2 2p bister brn   22.50
9 A2 20p rose   15.00 11.50
a. Pair, imperf. between
10 A2 40p ultra   150.00 150.00
a. Half used as 20p on cover

Pelure Paper

11 A2 10p orange   65.00 70.00
12 A2 20p rose   60.00   8.75
a. Pair, imperf. between
13 A2 40p ultra   35.00 20.00
b. Half used as 20p on cover

Nos. 1-3, 7-8, 14-16, 25-26 were used only as newspaper tax stamps.

1868-69   Ordinary Paper   Imperf.

14 A2 1p green   35.00
a. 1p olive green ('69)   2,000.
15 A2 2p brown   50.00
a. 2p bister brown ('69)   150.00

Counterfeits of type A2 are common.

Prince Milan (Obrenovich IV)
A3   A4

Perf. 9½, 12 and Compound
1869-78

16 A3 1p yellow   2.25   95.00
17 A3 10p red brown   7.50   3.75
a. 10p yellow brown   350.00 35.00
18 A3 10p orange ('78)   1.25   3.25
19 A3 15p orange   85.00   15.00
20 A3 20p gray blue   1.50   2.50
b. 20p ultramarine   3.25   2.00
21 A3 25p rose   1.50   5.75
22 A3 35p lt green   2.75   3.50
23 A3 40p violet   1.40   2.75
a. Half used as 20p on cover
24 A3 50p blue green   3.25   3.50
    Nos. 16-24 (9)   106.40 135.00

The first setting, which included all values except No. 18, had the stamps 2-2½mm apart. A new setting, introduced in 1878, had the stamps 3-4mm apart, providing wider margins. Only Nos. 17, 18, 20 and 21 exist in this new setting, which differs also in shades from the earlier setting. The narrow-spaced Nos. 17, 20 and 21 are rarer, especially unused, as are the early shades of Nos. 23 and 24. All values except Nos. 19 and 24 are known in various partly perforated varieties.
Counterfeits exist.
See No. 25.

1872-79   Imperf.

25 A3 1p yellow   3.50   7.75
a. Tête bêche pair
26 A4 2p blk, thin paper ('79)   35   35
a. Thick paper ('73)   1.50   4.00

Used value of No. 26 is for canceled-to-order.

King Milan I — A5

King Alexander (Obrenovich V) — A6

1880   Perf. 13x13½

27 A5 5p green   40   15
a. 5p olive green   475.00   1.50
28 A5 10p rose   60   15
29 A5 20p orange   42   20
a. 20p yellow   2.75   1.10
30 A5 25p ultra   60   25
a. 25p blue   1.75   70
31 A5 50p brown   42   1.65
a. 50p brown violet   60.00   2.00
32 A5 1d violet   5.25   5.25
    Nos. 27-32 (6)   7.69   7.65

1890

33 A6 5p green   15   15
34 A6 10p rose red   35   15
35 A6 15p red violet   35   15
36 A6 20p orange   28   15
37 A6 25p blue   42   15
38 A6 50p brown   1.75   1.40
39 A6 1d dull lilac   9.00   7.75
    Nos. 33-39 (7)   12.30   9.90

King Alexander — A7

1894-96   Perf. 13x13½
Granite Paper

40 A7 5p green   3.75   15
41 A7 10p car rose   3.50   15
b. Perf. 11½   37.50   75

42	A7	15p violet	4.50	15
43	A7	20p orange	52.50	30
a.		Half used as 10p on cover		375.00
44	A7	25p blue	10.50	22
45	A7	50p brown	11.00	45
46	A7	1d dk green	1.50	2.50
47	A7	1d red brn, *bl* ('96)	11.00	3.75
		Nos. 40-47 (8)	98.25	7.67

1898-1900   *Perf. 13x13½, 11½*
Ordinary Paper

48	A7	1p dull red	15	25
49	A7	5p green	1.00	15
50	A7	10p rose	42.50	20
51	A7	15p violet	7.00	20
52	A7	20p orange	6.25	25
53	A7	25p dp bl	7.00	28
54	A7	50p brown	12.50	3.00
		Nos. 48-54 (7)	76.40	4.38

Nos. 49-54 exist imperf.
Nos. 49-51, 53 and 56-57 exist with perf.
13x13½x11½x13½.

Type of 1900 Stamp Surcharged   **10 ПАРА**

1900

56	A7	10p on 20p rose	1.25	15

Same, Surcharged   **10 ПАРА**

1901

57	A7	10p on 20p rose	1.75	15
58	A7	15p on 1d red brn, *bl*	3.75	1.00
a.		Inverted surcharge	100.00	110.00

King Alexander (Obrenovich V)
A8   A9

1901-03   Typo.   *Perf. 11½*

59	A8	5p green	15	15
60	A8	10p rose	15	15
61	A8	15p red violet	15	15
62	A8	20p orange	15	15
63	A8	25p ultra	15	15
64	A8	50p bister	15	15
65	A9	1d brown	55	60
66	A9	3d brt rose	6.75	5.75
67	A9	5d deep violet	5.25	5.75
		Nos. 59-67 (9)	13.45	13.00

Counterfeits of Nos. 66-67 exist. Nos. 59-67
imperf. value of set of pairs, $100.

Arms of Serbia on Head
of King Alexander — A10

Two Types of the Overprint

Type I - Overprint 12mm wide. Bottom of mantle
defined by a single line. Wide crown above shield.
Type II - Overprint 10mm wide. Double line at
bottom of mantle. Smaller crown above shield.

Arms Overprinted in Blue, Black, Red and
Red Brown

1903-04   **Type I**   *Perf. 13½*

68	A10	1p red lil & blk (Bl)	35	38
a.		Inverted overprint		6.75
69	A10	5p yel grn & blk (Bl)	20	15
70	A10	10p car & blk (Bk)	15	15
a.		Double overprint		8.25
71	A10	15p ol gray & blk (Bk)	15	15
a.		Double overprint		8.25
72	A10	20p org & blk (Bk)	20	15
73	A10	25p bl & blk (Bk)	20	15
a.		Double overprint		9.25
74	A10	50p gray & blk (Bk)	1.25	65

There were two printings of the type I overprint
on Nos. 68-74, one typographed and one
lithographed.

Type II

75	A10	1d bl grn & blk (Bk)	5.00	1.50

#68-75 with overprint omitted, value, set $75.

Perf. 11½
Type I

75A	A10	5p (Bl)	15	25
75B	A10	50p (R)	40	1.00
75C	A10	1d (Bk)	75	1.75

Type II

76	A10	3d vio & blk (R Br)	85	85
a.		Perf. 13½	100.00	100.00
77	A10	5d lt brn & blk (Bl)	85	85

Type I With Additional
Surcharge   **1 ПАРА 1**

78	A10	1p on 5d (R)	75	2.75
a.		Perf. 13½	265.00	265.00
		Nos. 68-78 (14)	11.25	10.73

Karageorge and
Peter I — A11

Insurgents,
1804 — A12

1904   Typo.

79	A11	5p yellow grn	15	15
80	A11	10p rose red	15	15
81	A11	15p red violet	15	15
82	A11	25p blue	15	15
83	A11	50p gray brn	22	22
84	A11	1d bister	90	1.10
85	A12	3d blue green	90	1.25
86	A12	5d violet	1.50	1.65
		Nos. 79-86 (8)	4.12	4.82

Centenary of the Karageorgevich dynasty and the
coronation of King Peter. Counterfeits of Nos. 79-
86 exist.

King Peter I Karageorgevich
A13   A14

Perf. 11½, 12x11½
1905   Wove Paper

87	A13	1p gray & blk	15	15
88	A13	5p yel grn & blk	24	15
89	A13	10p red & blk	85	15
90	A13	15p red lil & blk	1.00	15
91	A13	20p yel & blk	1.65	15
92	A13	25p ultra & blk	2.50	15
93	A13	30p sl grn & blk	1.65	15
94	A13	50p dk brn & blk	2.50	20
95	A13	1d bister & blk	32	25
96	A13	3d bl grn & blk	32	50
97	A13	5d violet & blk	1.25	85
		Nos. 87-97 (11)	12.43	
		Set value		2.35

Counterfeits of Nos. 87-97 abound.
The stamps of this issue may be found on both
thick and thin paper.

1908   Laid Paper

98	A13	1p gray & blk	28	15
99	A13	5p yel grn & blk	2.25	15
100	A13	10p red & blk	6.75	15
101	A13	15p red lil & blk	6.75	20
102	A13	20p yellow w blk	7.25	20
103	A13	25p ultra & blk	6.75	20
104	A13	30p gray grn & blk	10.00	20
105	A13	50p dk brn & blk	13.00	60
		Nos. 98-105 (8)	53.03	1.85

Nos. 90, 98-100, 102-104 are known imperforate but are not believed to have been issued in this
condition.
Values of Nos. 98-105 are for horizontally laid
paper. Four values also exist on vertically laid
paper (1p, 5p, 10p, 30p).

1911-14
Thick Wove Paper

108	A14	1p slate grn	15	15
109	A14	2p dk violet	15	15
110	A14	5p green	15	15
111	A14	5p pale yel grn ('14)	15	15

112	A14	10p carmine	15	15
113	A14	10p red ('14)	15	15
114	A14	15p red violet	15	15
115	A14	15p slate blk ('14)	15	15
a.		15p red (error)		
116	A14	20p yellow	20	15
117	A14	20p brown ('14)	35	20
118	A14	25p deep blue	30	15
119	A14	25p indigo ('14)	15	15
120	A14	30p blue green	15	15
121	A14	30p olive grn ('14)	15	15
122	A14	50p dk brown	16	15
123	A14	50p brn red ('14)	15	15
124	A14	1d orange	14.00	25.00
125	A14	1d slate ('14)	2.00	2.75
126	A14	3d lake	27.50	77.50
127	A14	3d olive yel ('14)	77.50	475.00
128	A14	5d violet	27.50	42.50
129	A14	5d dk violet ('14)	2.00	14.00
		Nos. 108-129 (22)	153.31	

Counterfeits exist.

King Peter and
Military
Staff — A15

1915   *Perf. 11½*

132	A15	5p yellow grn	15	1.00
133	A15	10p scarlet	15	1.00
134	A15	15p slate	1.50	
135	A15	20p brown	45	
136	A15	25p blue	3.25	
137	A15	30p olive grn	2.00	
138	A15	50p orange brn	16.00	
		Nos. 132-138 (7)	23.50	

Nos. 134-138 were prepared but not issued for
postal use. Instead they were permitted to be used
as wartime emergency currency. Some are known
imperf. The 15p also exists in blue; value $250.

POSTES SERBES

Stamps of France, 1900-1907, with
this handstamped control were issued in
1916-1918 by the Serbian Postal
Bureau, in the Island of Corfu, during a
temporary shortage of Serbian stamps.
On the 1c to 35c, the handstamp covers
2 or 3 stamps. It was applied after the
stamps were on the cover, and frequently no further cancellation was used.

King Peter and Prince
Alexander — A16

1918-20   Typo.   *Perf. 11, 11½*

155	A16	1p black	15	15
156	A16	2p olive brn	15	15
157	A16	5p apple grn	15	15
158	A16	10p red	15	15
159	A16	15p black brn	15	15
160	A16	20p red brn	15	15
161	A16	20p violet ('20)	3.00	1.50
162	A16	25p deep blue	15	15
163	A16	30p olive grn	15	15
164	A16	50p violet	15	15
165	A16	1d violet brn	22	15
166	A16	3d slate grn	70	60
167	A16	5d red brown	1.10	65
		Set value	5.65	3.45

#157-160, 164 exist imperf. Value each $6.

1920   Pelure Paper   *Perf. 11½*

169	A16	1p black	15	15
170	A16	2p olive brown	15	15
		Set value	20	

POSTAGE DUE STAMPS

Coat of Arms
D1   D2

1895   Unwmk.   Typo.   *Perf. 13x13½*
Granite Paper

J1	D1	5p red lilac	1.40	60
J2	D1	10p blue	1.40	42
J3	D1	20p orange brown	42.50	2.75
J4	D1	30p green	20	35
J5	D1	50p rose	28	42
a.		Cliché of 5p in plate of 50p	75.00	95.00

No. J1 exists imperf. Value $35.

1898-1904

Ordinary Paper

J6	D1	5p magenta ('04)	70	70
J7	D1	20p brown	3.00	70
a.		Tête bêche pair	150.00	150.00
J8	D1	20p dp brn ('04)	3.00	70

1906   Granite Paper   *Perf. 11½*

J9	D1	5p magenta	5.25	1.00

1909   Laid Paper

J10	D1	5p magenta	65	65
J11	D1	10p pale blue	2.25	1.65
J12	D1	20p pale brown	40	40

1914   White Wove Paper

J13	D1	5p rose	25	32
J14	D1	10p deep blue	1.50	2.25

1918-20   *Perf. 11*

J15	D2	5p red	40	85
J16	D2	5p red brown ('20)	40	85
J17	D2	10p yellow green	40	85
J18	D2	20p olive brown	40	85
J19	D2	30p slate green	40	85
J20	D2	50p chocolate	80	1.25
		Nos. J15-J20 (6)	2.80	5.50

NEWSPAPER STAMPS

N1

Overprinted with Crown-topped Shield in
Black

1911   Unwmk.   Typo.   *Perf. 11½*

P1	N1	1p gray	45	45
P2	N1	5p green	45	45
P3	N1	10p orange	45	45
a.		Cliché of 1p in plate of 10p		200.00
P4	N1	15p violet	45	45
P5	N1	20p yellow	45	45
a.		Cliché of 50p in plate of 20p	75.00	125.00
P6	N1	25p blue	45	45
P7	N1	30p slate	5.25	5.25
P8	N1	50p brown	4.50	4.50
P9	N1	1d bister	4.50	4.50
P10	N1	3d rose red	4.50	4.50
P11	N1	5d gray vio	4.50	4.50
		Nos. P1-P11 (11)	25.95	25.95

ISSUED UNDER AUSTRIAN
OCCUPATION

100 Heller = 1 Krone

Stamps of Bosnia, 1912-
14, Overprinted

SERBIEN

1916   Unwmk.   *Perf. 12½*

1N1	A23	1h olive grn	1.50	2.00
1N2	A23	2h brt blue	1.50	2.00
1N3	A23	3h claret	1.50	2.00

1N4	A23	5h green	35	55
1N5	A23	6h dk gray	70	1.10
1N6	A23	10h rose car	35	65
1N7	A23	12h dp ol grn	70	1.10
1N8	A23	20h org brn	42	70
1N9	A23	25h ultra	42	70
1N10	A23	30h org red	42	70
1N11	A24	35h myrtle grn	42	70
1N12	A24	40h dk vio	42	70
1N13	A24	45h olive brn	42	70
1N14	A24	50h slate bl	42	70
1N15	A24	60h brn vio	42	70
1N16	A24	72h dk bl	42	70
1N17	A25	1k brn vio, *straw*	65	90
1N18	A25	2k dk gray, *bl*	65	90
1N19	A24	3k car	65	90
1N20	A26	5k dk vio, *gray*	65	90
1N21	A25	10k dk ultra, *gray*	9.25	14.00
		Nos. 1N1-1N21 (21)	22.23	33.30

Stamps of Bosnia, 1912-14, Overprinted "SERBIEN" Horizontally at Bottom

1916

1N22	A23	1h olive grn	4.50	5.25
1N23	A23	2h brt blue	4.50	5.25
1N24	A23	3h claret	4.50	5.25
1N25	A23	5h gray	45	45
1N26	A23	6h dk gray	4.50	5.25
1N27	A23	10h rose car	45	45
1N28	A23	12h dp ol grn	4.50	5.25
1N29	A23	20h org brn	4.50	5.25
1N30	A23	25h ultra	4.50	5.25
1N31	A23	30h org red	4.50	5.25
1N32	A24	35h myrtle grn	4.50	5.25
1N33	A24	40h dk vio	4.50	5.25
1N34	A24	45h olive brn	4.50	5.25
1N35	A24	50h slate bl	4.50	5.25
1N36	A24	60h brn vio	4.50	5.25
1N37	A24	72h dk blue	4.50	5.25
1N38	A25	1k brn vio, *straw*	11.00	13.00
1N39	A25	2k dk gray, *bl*	11.00	13.00
1N40	A26	3k car, *grn*	11.00	13.00
1N41	A26	5k dk vio, *gray*	19.00	21.00
1N42	A25	10k dk ultra, *gray*	27.50	30.00
		Nos. 1N22-1N42 (21)	143.40	164.40

Nos. 1N22-1N42 were prepared in 1914, at the time of the 1st Austrian occupation of Serbia. They were not issued at that time because of the retreat. The stamps were put on sale in 1916, at the same time as Nos. 1N1-1N21.

ISSUED UNDER GERMAN OCCUPATION

In occupied Serbia, authority was ostensibly in the hands of a government created by the former Yugoslav General, Milan Nedich, supported by the Chetniks, a nationalist organization which turned fascist. Actually the German military ran the country.

Types of Yugoslavia, 1939-40, Overprinted in Black SERBIEN

1941 Unwmk. Typo. Perf. 12½
Paper with colored network

2N1	A16	25p blk *(lt grn)*	15	1.25
2N2	A16	50p orange *(pink)*	15	25
2N3	A16	1d yel grn *(lt grn)*	15	25
2N4	A16	1.50d red *(pink)*	15	25
2N5	A16	2d dp mag *(pink)*	15	25
2N6	A16	3d dl red brn *(pink)*	90	5.00
2N7	A16	4d ultra *(lt grn)*	15	75
2N8	A16	5d dk bl *(lt grn)*	50	2.00
2N9	A16	5.50d dk vio brn *(pink)*	50	2.00
2N10	A16	6d sl bl *(pink)*	50	2.00
2N11	A16	8d sep *(lt grn)*	70	3.00
2N12	A16	12d brt vio *(lt grn)*	70	3.00
2N13	A16	16d dl vio *(pink)*	1.10	10.00
2N14	A16	20d bl *(lt grn)*	1.10	12.50
2N15	A16	30d brt pink *(lt grn)*	5.75	75.00
		Nos. 2N1-2N15 (15)	12.65	

Double overprints exist on 50p, 1d, 5d, 5.50d and 12d. Value, each $125 to $250.

Stamps of Yugoslavia, 1939-40, Overprinted in Black SERBIEN

Paper with colored network

2N16	A16	25p blk *(lt grn)*	15	3.75
2N17	A16	50p org *(pink)*	15	75
2N18	A16	1d yel grn *(lt grn)*	15	50
2N19	A16	1.50d red *(pink)*	15	75
2N20	A16	2d dp mag *(pink)*	15	50
2N21	A16	3d dl red brn	32	3.00
2N22	A16	4d ultra *(lt grn)*	22	50
2N23	A16	5d dk bl *(lt grn)*	22	1.25
2N24	A16	5.50d dk vio brn *(pink)*	42	3.00
2N25	A16	6d sl bl *(pink)*	42	3.00
2N26	A16	8d sep *(lt grn)*	65	3.75
2N27	A16	12d brt vio *(lt grn)*	1.10	3.75
2N28	A16	16d dl vio *(pink)*	1.10	12.50
2N29	A16	20d bl *(lt grn)*	1.10	50.00
2N30	A16	30d brt pink *(lt grn)*	5.75	65.00
		Nos. 2N16-2N30 (15)	12.05	

Lazaritza Monastery — OS1

Ruins of Manassia Monastery OS4

Designs: 1d, Kalenica Monastery. 1.50d, Ravanica Monastery. 3d, Ljubostinja Monastery. 4d, Sopocane Monastery. 7d, Tsitsa Monastery. 12d, Goriak Monastery. 16d, Studenica Monastery.

1942-43 Typo. Perf. 11½

2N31	OS1	50p brt violet	15	15
2N32	OS1	1d red	15	15
2N33	OS1	1.50d red brn	75	2.00
2N34	OS1	1.50d green ('43)	15	20
2N35	OS4	2d dl rose violet	15	15
2N36	OS4	3d brt blue	75	2.00
2N37	OS4	3d rose pink ('43)	15	15
2N38	OS4	4d ultra	15	18
2N39	OS4	7d dk slate grn	15	18
2N40	OS1	12d lake	18	1.25
2N41	OS1	16d grnsh blk	1.00	1.50
		Set value	3.25	

For surcharges see Nos. 2NB29-2NB37.

Post Rider — OS10   Post Wagon — OS11

Designs: 9d, Mail train. 30d, Mail truck. 50d, Mail plane.

1943, Oct. 15 Photo. Perf. 12½

2N42	OS10	3d copper red & gray lilac	40	1.00
2N43	OS11	8d vio rose & gray	40	1.00
2N44	OS10	9d dk bl grn & sep	40	1.00
2N45	OS10	30d chnt & sl grn	40	1.00
2N46	OS10	50d dp bl & red brn	40	1.00
		Nos. 2N42-2N46 (5)	2.00	

Centenary of postal service in Serbia. Printed in sheets of 24 containing 4 of each stamp and 4 labels.

OCCUPATION SEMI-POSTAL STAMPS

Smederevo Fortress on the Danube OSP1   OSP5

Refugees OSP2

Perf. 11½x12½
1941, Sept. 22 Typo. Unwmk.

2NB1	OSP1	50p + 1d dk brn	32	65
2NB2	OSP2	1d + 2d dk gray grn	32	85
2NB3	OSP2	1.50d + 3d dp cl	65	1.50
a.		Perf. 12½	3.75	6.25
2NB4	OSP1	2d + 4d dk bl	95	2.00

Souvenir Sheets

2NB5		Sheet of 2	37.50	100.00
a.	OSP2	1d + 49d rose lake	6.75	17.50
b.	OSP1	2d + 48d gray	6.75	17.50

Imperf

2NB6		Sheet of 2	37.50	100.00
a.	OSP1	1d + 49d gray	6.75	17.50
b.	OSP1	2d + 48d rose lake	6.75	17.50

The surtax aided the victims of an explosion at Smederevo and was used for the reconstruction of the town.

Christ and Virgin Mary — OSP4

a   b

1941, Dec. 5 Photo. Perf. 11½
With Rose Burelage

2NB7	OSP4	50p + 1.50d brn red	35	3.75
2NB8	OSP4	1d + 3d sl grn	35	3.75
2NB9	OSP4	2d + 6d dp red	35	3.75
2NB10	OSP4	4d + 12d dp bl	35	3.75

With Symbol "a" Outlined in Cerise

2NB7a	OSP4	50p	8.75	37.50
2NB8a	OSP4	1d	8.75	37.50
2NB9a	OSP4	2d	8.75	37.50
2NB10a	OSP4	4d	8.75	37.50

With Symbol "b" Outlined in Cerise

2NB7b	OSP4	50p	8.75	37.50
2NB8b	OSP4	1d	8.75	37.50
2NB9b	OSP4	2d	8.75	37.50
2NB10b	OSP4	4d	8.75	37.50

Without Burelage

2NB7c	OSP4	50p	1.50	12.00
2NB8c	OSP4	1d	1.50	12.00
2NB9c	OSP4	2d	1.50	12.00
2NB10c	OSP4	4d	1.50	12.00

These stamps were printed in sheets of 50, in 2 panes of 25. In the panes, #8, 12, 13, 14, 18, forming a cross, are without burelage. #7, 17 are type "a," #9, 19 type "b." 16 of the 25 stamps have overall burelage.

Surtax aided prisoners of war.

1942, Mar. 26
Thicker Paper, Without Burelage

2NB11	OSP4	50p + 1.50d brn	60	2.75
2NB12	OSP4	1d + 3d bl grn	60	2.75
2NB13	OSP4	2d + 6d mag	60	2.75
2NB14	OSP4	4d + 12d ultra	60	3.00

OSP6

OSP7   OSP8

Designs: Anti-Masonic symbolisms.

1942, Jan. 1

2NB15	OSP5	50p + 50p yel brn	25	65
2NB16	OSP6	1d + 1d dk grn	25	65
2NB17	OSP7	2d + 2d rose car	45	1.25
2NB18	OSP8	4d + 4d indigo	45	1.25

Anti-Masonic Exposition of Oct. 22, 1941. The surtax was used for anti-Masonic propaganda.

Mother and Children — OSP9

1942

2NB19	OSP9	2d + 6d brt pur	1.10	2.50
2NB20	OSP9	4d + 8d dp bl	1.10	2.50
2NB21	OSP9	7d + 13d dk bl grn	1.10	2.50
2NB22	OSP9	20d + 40d dp rose lake	1.10	2.50

Nos. 2NB19-2NB22 were issued in sheets of 16 consisting of a block of four of each denomination. The surtax aided war orphans.

Broken Sword — OSP10

Wounded Flag-bearer OSP11

Designs: 1.50d+48.50d, Broken sword. 3d+5d, 2d+48d, Wounded soldier. 3d+47d, Wounded flag-bearer. 4d+10d, 4d+46d, Tending casualty.

1943

2NB23	OSP10	1.50d + 1.50d dk brn	55	1.25
2NB24	OSP11	2d + 3d dk bl grn	55	1.25
2NB25	OSP11	3d + 5d dp rose vio	80	2.00
2NB26	OSP10	4d + 10d dp bl	1.25	3.00

Souvenir Sheets
Thick Paper

2NB27		Sheet of 2	27.50	550.00
a.	OSP10	1.50d + 48.50d dk brn	10.00	225.00
b.	OSP10	4d + 46d dp bl	10.00	225.00
2NB28		Sheet of 2	27.50	550.00
a.	OSP11	2d + 48d dk bl grn	10.00	225.00
b.	OSP11	3d + 47d dp rose vio	10.00	225.00

The sheets measure 150x110mm. The surtax aided war victims.

Stamps of 1942-43 Surcharged in Black

За пострадале
од англо-американког
терор. бомбардовања
Ниша — 20-X-1943

+ 9

1943, Dec. 11
Pale Green Burelage

2NB29	OS1	50p + 2d brt vio	15	2.50
2NB30	OS1	1d + 3d red	15	2.50
2NB31	OS1	1.50d + 4d dp grn	15	2.50
2NB32	OS4	2d + 5d dl rose vio	18	2.50
2NB33	OS4	3d + 7d rose pink	18	2.50
2NB34	OS4	4d + 9d ultra	18	2.50
2NB35	OS4	7d + 15d dk sl grn	55	2.50
2NB36	OS1	12d + 25d lake	55	12.50
2NB37	OS1	16d + 33d grnsh blk	95	12.50
		Nos. 2NB29-2NB37 (9)	3.04	

The surtax aided victims of the bombing of Nisch.

OCCUPATION AIR POST STAMPS

Types of Yugoslavia, 1937-40, Overprinted in Carmine or Maroon

Nos. 2NC1-2NC3, 2NC5-2NC7, 2NC9

Nos. 2NC4, 2NC8, 2NC10

1941   **Unwmk.**   **Perf. 12½**
Paper with colored network

2NC1	AP6	50p brown	3.00	25.00
2NC2	AP7	1d brown vio	3.00	25.00
2NC3	AP8	2d blue gray	3.00	25.00
2NC4	AP9	2.50d rose red (M)	3.00	25.00
2NC5	AP6	5d brown vio	3.00	25.00
2NC6	AP7	10d brown lake (M)	3.00	25.00
2NC7	AP8	20d dk green	3.00	25.00
2NC8	AP9	30d ultra	3.00	25.00
2NC9	AP10	40d Prus grn & pale grn (C)	6.75	125.00
2NC10	AP11	50d sl bl & gray bl (C)	8.50	190.00
		Nos. 2NC1-2NC10 (10)	39.25	

Nos. 2NC1-2NC2 exist without network.

Same Surcharged in Maroon or Carmine with New Values and Bars
Without colored network

2NC11	AP7	1d on 10d brn lake (M)	2.25	15.00
2NC12	AP8	3d on 20d dk grn	2.25	15.00
2NC13	AP9	6d on 30d ultra	2.25	15.00
2NC14	AP10	8d on 40d Prus grn & pale grn	2.50	30.00
2NC15	AP11	12d on 50d sl bl & gray bl	5.00	75.00
		Nos. 2NC11-2NC15 (5)	14.25	

Regular Issue of Yugoslavia, 1939-40, Surcharged in Black

1942
Green Network

2NC16	A16	2d on 2d dp mag	16	1.25
2NC17	A16	4d on 4d ultra	16	1.25
2NC18	A16	10d on 12d brt vio	16	2.00
2NC19	A16	14d on 20d blue	16	2.00
2NC20	A16	20d on 30d brt pink	42	10.00
		Nos. 2NC16-2NC20 (5)	1.06	

OCCUPATION POSTAGE DUE STAMPS

Types of Yugoslavia Similar to OD3-OD4 Overprinted

1941   **Unwmk.**   **Typo.**   **Perf. 12½**

2NJ1	OD3	50p violet	65	3.75
2NJ2	OD3	1d lake	65	3.75
2NJ3	OD3	2d dk blue	65	3.75
2NJ4	OD3	3d red	95	5.00
2NJ5	OD4	4d lt blue	1.25	12.50
2NJ6	OD4	5d orange	1.25	12.50
2NJ7	OD4	10d violet	2.75	25.00
2NJ8	OD4	20d green	8.00	75.00
		Nos. 2NJ1-2NJ8 (8)	16.15	

OD3   OD4

1942   **Perf. 12½**

2NJ9	OD3	1d maroon & grn	30	1.25
2NJ10	OD3	2d dk bl & red	30	1.25
2NJ11	OD3	3d ver & bl	55	2.50
2NJ12	OD4	4d blue & red	55	2.50
2NJ13	OD4	5d orange & bl	60	3.00
2NJ14	OD4	10d violet & red	70	7.50
2NJ15	OD4	20d green & red	3.00	22.50
		Nos. 2NJ9-2NJ15 (7)	6.00	

OD5

2NJ16	OD5	50p black	20	1.25
2NJ17	OD5	3d violet	20	1.25
2NJ18	OD5	4d blue	20	1.25
2NJ19	OD5	5d dk sl grn	20	1.25
2NJ20	OD5	6d orange	35	3.75
2NJ21	OD5	10d red	60	6.25
2NJ22	OD5	20d ultra	1.75	15.00
		Nos. 2NJ16-2NJ22 (7)	3.50	

OCCUPATION OFFICIAL STAMP

OOS1

1943   **Unwmk.**   **Typo.**   **Perf. 12½**

2NO1	OOS1	3d red lilac	1.00	1.25

SHANGHAI

LOCATION — A city on the Whangpoo River, Kiangsu Province, China
POP. — 3,489,998

A British settlement was founded there in 1843 and by agreement with China settlements were established by France and the United States. Special areas were set aside for the foreign settlements and a postal system independent of China was organized which was continued until 1898.

16 Cash = 1 Candareen
100 Candareens = 1 Tael
100 Cents = 1 Dollar (1890)

Values for Nos. 1-71 are for fine stamps without gum. Stamps of higher grade are worth more.

Watermark

Wmk. 175- Kung Pu (Municipal Council)

 Dragon — A1

1865-66   **Unwmk.**   **Typo.**   *Imperf.*
Antique Numerals
Roman "I" in "I6"
"Candareens" in the Plural
Wove Paper

1	A1	2ca black	150.
a.		Pelure paper	200.
2	A1	4ca yellow	125.
a.		Pelure paper	375.
b.		Double impression	
3	A1	8ca green	150.
a.		8ca yellow green	175.
4	A1	16ca scarlet	200.
a.		16ca vermilion	200.
b.		Pelure paper	250.

No. 1: top character of three in left panel as illustrated. No. 5: top character is two horiz. lines.
Nos. 2, 3: center character of three in left panel as illustrated. Nos. 6, 7: center character much more complex.

Antique Numerals
"Candareens" in the Plural
Pelure Paper

5	A1	2ca black	200.
a.		Wove paper	150.
6	A1	4ca yellow	175.
7	A1	8ca deep green	150.

Antique Numerals
"Candareen" in the Singular
Laid Paper

8	A1	1ca blue	150.
9	A1	2ca black	1,500.
10	A1	4ca yellow	425.

Wove Paper

11	A1	1ca blue	250.
12	A1	2ca black	250.
13	A1	4ca yellow	200.
14	A1	8ca olive green	150.
15	A1	16ca vermilion	150.
a.		"1" of "16" omitted	

Only one copy of No. 15a is known.

Antique Numerals
Roman "I"
"Candareens" in the Plural Except on 1ca
Wove Paper

16	A1	1ca blue	400.
17	A1	12ca fawn	200.
18	A1	12ca chocolate	175.

Antique Numerals
"Candareens" in the Plural Except on 1ca
Wove Paper

19	A1	1ca indigo, pelure paper	125.
20	A1	3ca orange brown	150.
a.		Pelure paper	200.
21	A1	6ca red brown	100.
22	A1	6ca fawn	350.

23	A1	6ca vermilion	150.
24	A1	12ca orange brown	100.
25	A1	6ca vermilion	125.
a.		"1" of "16" omitted	250.

Antique Numerals
Roman "I"
"Candareens" in the Plural Except on 1ca
Laid Paper

26	A1	1ca blue	*11,000.*
27	A1	2ca black	1,500.
28	A1	3ca red brown	*7,000.*

Modern Numerals
"Candareen" in the Singular

29	A1	1ca dark blue	80.00
a.		1ca slate blue	80.00
30	A1	3ca red brown	90.00

"Candareens" in the Plural Except the 1c

31	A1	2ca black	65.00
32	A1	3ca red brown	85.00

Coarse Porous Wove Paper

33a	A1	1ca blue	85.00
34a	A1	2ca black	125.00
b.		Grayish paper	150.00
35a	A1	3ca red brown	65.00
36a	A1	4ca yellow	65.00
37a	A1	6ca olive green	75.00
38a	A1	8ca emerald	65.00
39a	A1	12ca orange vermilion	65.00
40a	A1	16ca red	75.00
41a	A1	16ca red brown	65.00

Chinese characters change on same denomination stamps.
Nos. 1, 2, 11 and 32 exist on thicker paper, usually toned. Most authorities consider these four stamps and Nos. 33a-41a to be official reprints made to present sample sets to other post offices. The tone in this paper is an acquired characteristic, due to various causes. Many shades and minor varieties exist of Nos. 1-41a.

A2   A3

A4   A5

1866   **Litho.**   **Perf. 12**

42	A2	2c rose	8.00	10.00
43	A3	4c lilac	17.50	20.00
44	A4	8c gray blue	17.50	20.00
45	A5	16c green	45.00	60.00

Nos. 42-45 imperf. are proofs. See No. 50. For surcharges see Nos. 51-61, 67.

A6   A7

A8   A9

1866   **Perf. 15**

46	A6	1ca brown	4.00	5.00
a.		"CANDS"	40.00	45.00
47	A7	3ca orange	20.00	25.00
48	A8	6ca slate	20.00	25.00
49	A9	12ca olive gray	40.00	50.00

See Nos. 69-77. For surcharges see Nos. 62-66, 68, 78-83.

1872

50	A2	2c rose	60.00	80.00

Handstamp Surcharged in Blue, Red or Black

a

1873   *Perf. 12*
51	A2	1ca on 2c rose	20.00 25.00
52	A3	1ca on 4c lil	12.50 15.00
53	A3	1ca on 4c lil (R)	1,250. 1,250.
54	A3	1ca on 4c lil (Bk)	15.00 20.00
55	A4	1ca on 8c gray bl	15.00 20.00
56	A4	1ca on 8c gray bl (R)	3,000. 3,000.
57	A5	1ca on 16c grn	2,000. 2,000.
58	A5	1ca on 16c grn (R)	3,000. 3,000.

Perf. 15
59	A2	1ca on 2c rose	25.00 30.00

1875   *Perf. 12*
60	A2	3ca on 2c rose	50. 50.
61	A5	3ca on 16c grn	1,000. 1,000.

Perf. 15
62	A7	1ca on 3ca org	3,000. 3,000.
63	A8	1ca on 6ca sl	200. 200.
64	A8	1ca on 6ca sl (R)	2,000. 2,000.
65	A9	1ca on 12ca ol gray	175. 175.
66	A9	1ca on 12ca ol gray (R)	2,000. 2,000.
67	A2	3ca on 2c rose	175. 175.
68	A9	3ca on 12ca ol gray	5,000. 5,000.

Counterfeits exist of Nos. 51-68.

Types of 1866

1875   *Perf. 15*
69	A6	1ca yel, *yel*	18.00 20.00
70	A7	3ca rose, *rose*	18.00 20.00

Perf. 11½
71	A6	1ca yel, *yel*	200.00 225.00

1876   *Perf. 15*
72	A6	1ca yellow	5.00 6.00
73	A7	3ca rose	30.00 35.00
74	A8	6ca green	55.00 55.00
75	A9	9ca blue	65.00 65.00
76	A9	12ca light brown	90.00 90.00

1877   Engr.   *Perf. 12½*
77	A6	1ca rose	700.00 750.00

Stamps of 1875-76 Surcharged type "a" in Blue or Red

1877   Litho.   *Perf. 15*
78	A7	1ca on 3ca rose, *rose*	165. 165.
79	A7	1ca on 3ca rose	35. 35.
80	A8	1ca on 6ca green	45. 45.
81	A9	1ca on 9ca blue	150. 150.
82	A9	1ca on 12ca lt brn	750. 750.
83	A9	1ca on 12ca lt brn (R)	2,500. 2,500.

Counterfeits exist of Nos. 78-83.

A11

A12

A13

A14

1877   *Perf. 15*
84	A11	20 cash violet	5.00 6.00
a.		20 cash blue violet	4.50 4.50
85	A12	40 cash rose	6.00 6.00
86	A13	60 cash green	9.00 10.00
87	A14	80 cash blue	15.00 15.00
88	A14	100 cash brown	14.00 20.00

Handstamp Surcharged in Blue

b

1879   *Perf. 15*
89	A12	20 cash on 40c rose	15.00 15.00
90	A14	60 cash on 80c blue	20.00 25.00
91	A14	60 cash on 100c brn	20.00 25.00

Types of 1877

1880   *Perf. 11½*
92	A11	20 cash violet	4.50 5.00
93	A12	40 cash rose	5.00 6.00
94	A13	60 cash green	2.50 2.50
95	A14	80 cash blue	6.00 7.50
96	A14	100 cash brown	7.50 9.00

Perf. 15x11½
97	A11	20 cash lilac	25.00 25.00

Surcharged type "b" in Blue

1884   *Perf. 11½*
98	A12	20 cash on 40c rose	6.00 7.50
99	A14	60 cash on 80c blue	12.00 15.00
100	A14	60 cash on 100c brn	15.00 15.00

Types of 1877

1884
101	A11	20 cash green	4.50 5.00

1885   *Perf. 15*
102	A11	20 cash green	2.25 2.50
103	A12	40 cash brown	3.00 3.00
104	A13	60 cash violet	6.00 7.00
a.		60 cash red violet	10.00 15.00
105	A14	80 cash buff	5.00 5.50
106	A14	100 cash brown	6.00 7.00

Perf. 11½x15
107	A11	20 cash green	3.00 5.00
108	A13	60 cash red vio	5.50 6.00

Surcharged type "b" in Blue

1886   *Perf. 15*
109	A14	40 cash on 80c buff	3.00 3.50
110	A14	60 cash on 100c yel	4.00 4.50

Types of 1877

1888   *Perf. 15*
111	A11	20 cash gray	3.00 3.00
112	A12	40 cash black	3.00 4.00
113	A13	60 cash rose	3.50 4.00
a.		Third character at left lacks dot at top	5.75 6.25
114	A14	80 cash green	4.00 4.50
115	A14	100 cash lt blue	5.25 6.00

Handstamp Surcharged in Blue or Red Type "b" or:

c   d

1888   *Perf. 15*
116	A14(b)	40 cash on 100c yel	3.50 5.00
117	A14(b)	40 cash on 100c yel (R)	4.00 5.00
118	A12(c)	20 cash on 40c brn	9.00 9.00
119	A14(c)	20 cash on 80c buff	2.00 2.00
120	A12(d)	20 cash on 80c brn	9.00 9.00

Inverted surcharges exist on Nos. 116-120; double on Nos. 116, 119, 120; omitted surcharges paired with normal stamp on Nos. 116, 119.

Handstamp Surcharged in Black and Red (100 cash) or Red (20 cash)

e

1889   Unwmk.
121	A14(e)	100 cash on 20c on 100c yel	25.00 25.00
a.		Without the surcharge "100 cash"	250.00
b.		Blue & red surcharge	
122	A14(c)	20 cash on 80c grn	4.00 5.00
123	A14(c)	20 cash on 100c bl	4.00 5.00

Counterfeits exist of Nos. 116-123.

1889   Wmk. 175   *Perf. 15*
124	A11	20 cash gray	1.25 1.25
125	A12	40 cash black	2.50 2.50
126	A13	60 cash rose	2.75 3.00
a.		Third character at left lacks dot at top	5.50 6.00

Perf. 12
127	A14	80 cash green	3.00 3.50
128	A14	100 cash dk bl	6.50 7.50

Nos. 124-126 are sometimes found without watermark. This is caused by the sheet being misplaced in the printing press, so that the stamps are printed on the unwatermarked margin of the sheet.

Shield with Dragon Supporters — A20

1890   Unwmk.   Litho.   *Perf. 15*
129	A20	2c brown	1.50 2.00
130	A20	5c rose	3.50 3.50
131	A20	15c blue	4.00 4.00

Nos. 129-131 imperforate are proofs.

   Wmk. 175
132	A20	10c black	5.00 5.00
133	A20	15c blue	10.00 10.00
134	A20	20c violet	4.00 4.00

See Nos. 135-141. For surcharges and overprints see Nos. 142-152, J1-J13.

1891   *Perf. 12*
135	A20	2c brown	1.50 1.50
136	A20	5c rose	3.00 3.00

1892
137	A20	2c green	1.00 1.00
138	A20	5c red	2.50 2.50
139	A20	10c orange	7.50 8.00
140	A20	15c violet	4.50 5.00
141	A20	20c brown	5.00 5.00

No. 130 Handstamp Surcharged in Blue

f

1892   Unwmk.   *Perf. 15*
142	A20	2c on 5c rose	30.00 20.00

Counterfeits exist of Nos. 142-152.

Stamps of 1892 Handstamp Surcharged in Blue:

銀分半   銀分壹

HALF CENT.   ONE CENT.

g   h

1893   Wmk. 175   *Perf. 12*
143	A20	½c on 15c violet	4.50 4.50
144	A20	1c on 20c brown	4.50 4.50
a.		½c on 20c brown (error)	3,500.

Surcharged in Blue or Red on Halves of Stamps:

½Ct.   ½Ct.   ½Ct.   1Ct.

i   j   k   m

145	A20(i)	½c on half of 5c rose	4.50 3.00
146	A20(j)	½c on half of 5c rose	6.00 4.50
147	A20(k)	½c on half of 5c rose	60.00 50.00
148	A20(i)	½c on half of 5c red	4.50 3.00
149	A20(j)	½c on half of 5c red	6.00 4.50
150	A20(k)	½c on half of 5c red	60.00 50.00

151	A20(m)	1c on half of 2c brn	1.50 1.50
c.		Dbl. surch., one in green	300.00
d.		Dbl. surch., one in black	300.00
152	A20(m)	1c on half of 2c grn (R)	9.00 9.00

The ½c surcharge setting of 20 (2x10) covers a vertical strip of 10 unsevered stamps, with horizontal gutter midway. This setting has 11 of type "i," 8 of type "j" and 1 of type "k." Nos. 145-152 are perforated vertically down the middle.

Inverted surcharges exist on Nos. 145-151. Double surcharges, one inverted, are also found in this issue.

Handstamped provisionals somewhat similar to Nos. 145-152 were issued in Foochow by the Shanghai Agency.

Coat of Arms — A24   Mercury — A26

1893   Litho.   *Perf. 13½x14*
Frame Inscriptions in Black
153	A24	½c orange, typo.	25 25
a.		½c orange, litho.	4.00 4.00
154	A24	1c brown, typo.	25 25
a.		1c brown, litho.	4.00 4.00
155	A24	2c vermilion	5.00 5.00
a.		Imperf.	
156	A24	5c blue	25 25
a.		Black inscriptions inverted	600.00
157	A24	10c grn, typo. & litho.	2.00 3.00
a.		10c green, litho.	4.00 4.00
158	A24	15c yellow	40 40
159	A24	20c lil, typo. & litho.	1.50 2.00
a.		20c lilac, litho.	3.00 3.00
		Nos. 153-159 (7)	9.65 11.15

On Nos. 157 and 159, frame inscriptions are lithographed, rest of design typographed.

See Nos. 170-172. For overprints and surcharges see Nos. 160-166, 168-169.

Stamps of 1893 Overprinted in Black

1843 Jubilee 1893

1893, Dec. 14
160	A24	½c orange & blk	25 25
161	A24	1c brown & blk	30 30
a.		Double overprint	20.00 20.00
162	A24	2c vermilion & blk	65 65
a.		Inverted overprint	50.00
163	A24	5c blue & black	2.25 2.50
a.		Inverted overprint	100.00
164	A24	10c green & blk	3.50 4.00
165	A24	15c yellow & blk	3.25 3.25
166	A24	20c lilac & blk	5.50 6.00
		Nos. 160-166 (7)	15.70 16.95

50th anniv. of the first foreign settlement in Shanghai.

1893, Nov. 11   Litho.   *Perf. 13½*
167	A26	2c vermilion & black	35 50

Nos. 158 and 159 Handstamp Surcharged in Black

FOUR CENTS. 分 四

1896   *Perf. 13½x14*
168	A24	4c on 15c yellow & blk	5.00 5.00
169	A24	6c on 20c lilac & blk	5.00 5.00

Surcharge occurs inverted or double on Nos. 168-169.

Arms Type of 1893

1896
170	A24	2c scarlet & blk	25 1.00
a.		Black inscriptions inverted	125.00
171	A24	4c orange & blk, *yel*	1.50 2.50
172	A24	6c car & blk, *rose*	1.00 3.00

POSTAGE DUE STAMPS

Postage Stamps of 1890-92 Handstamped in Black, Red or Blue

1892   **Unwmk.**   *Perf. 15*
J1	A20	2c brown (Bk)	175.00	250.00
J2	A20	5c rose (Bk)	3.00	4.00
J3	A20	15c blue (Bk)	17.50	17.50

     Wmk. 175
J4	A20	10c black (R)	6.00	6.00
J5	A20	15c blue (Bk)	7.00	9.00
J6	A20	20c violet (Bk)	3.00	4.00

1892-93   *Perf. 12*
J7	A20	2c brown (Bk)	1.50	1.50
J8	A20	2c brown (Bl)	1.00	1.50
J9	A20	5c rose (Bl)	2.00	2.50
J10	A20	10c orange (Bk)	60.00	60.00
J11	A20	10c orange (Bl)	3.00	3.00
J12	A20	15c violet (R)	9.00	9.00
J13	A20	20c brown (R)	8.00	8.00

D2

1893   **Litho.**   *Perf. 13½*
J14	D2	½c orange & blk	30	30

     Perf. 14x13½
J15	D2	1c brown & black	30	30
J16	D2	2c vermilion & black	30	30
J17	D2	5c blue & black	50	50
J18	D2	10c green & black	75	75
J19	D2	15c yellow & black	75	75
J20	D2	20c violet & black	75	75
		Nos. J14-J20 (7)	3.65	3.65

Stamps of Shanghai were discontinued in 1898.

SHARJAH & DEPENDENCIES

LOCATION — Oman Peninsula, Arabia, on Persian Gulf

GOVT. — Sheikdom under British protection

POP. — 5,000 (estimated)

CAPITAL — Sharjah

The dependencies on the Gulf of Oman are Dhiba, Khor Fakkan, and Kalba.

Sharjah is one of six Persian Gulf sheikdoms to join the United Arab Emirates which proclaimed independence Dec. 2, 1971. See United Arab Emirates.

100 Naye Paise = 1 Rupee

Catalogue values for all unused stamps in this country are for Never Hinged items.

Sheik Saqr bin Sultan al Qasimi, Flag and Map — A1

Malaria Eradication Emblem — A2

Perf. 14½x14

1963, July 10   **Photo.**   **Unwmk.**
Black Portrait and Inscriptions; Lilac Rose Flag
1	A1	1np lt bl grn & red	15	15
2	A1	2np grnsh bl & sal	15	15
3	A1	3np vio & yel	15	15
4	A1	4np emer & gray	15	15
5	A1	5np aqua & lt grn	15	15
6	A1	6np dl grn & brt yel	15	15
7	A1	8np Prus bl & bis	15	15
8	A1	10np aqua & tan	15	15
9	A1	16np ultra & bis	15	15
10	A1	20np lt vio & lem	15	15
11	A1	30np rose lil & brt yel grn	25	25
12	A1	40np dk bl & yel grn	30	30
13	A1	50np grn & fawn	42	42
14	A1	75np ultra & fawn	60	60
15	A1	100np ol bis & rose	75	75
		Set value	3.10	3.10

1963, Aug. 8
16	A2	1np grnsh bl	15	15
17	A2	2np dull blue	15	15
18	A2	3np lt blue	15	15
19	A2	4np emerald	15	15
20	A2	90np yel brn	50	50
		Set value	78	70

     Miniature Sheet
     Imperf
21	A2	100np brt blue	80	80

WHO drive to eradicate malaria. No. 21 contains one 39x67mm stamp.

See Nos. C1-C6. For surcharge and overprints see Nos. 35, C7-C12, O1-O9.

Red Crescent and Sheik — A3

1963, Aug. 25   *Perf. 14x14½*
22	A3	1np pur & red	15	15
23	A3	2np brt grn & red	15	15
24	A3	3np dk bl & red	15	15
25	A3	4np dk grn & red	15	15
26	A3	5np dk brn & red	15	15
27	A3	85np grn & red	40	40
		Set value	65	65

     Miniature Sheet
     Imperf
28	A3	100np plum & red	1.00	1.00

Cent. of the Intl. Red Cross. Imperfs. exist. No. 28 contains one 67x39m stamp.

Nos. 36-40 and No. 20 Surcharged

Nos. 29-34

No. 35

1963, Oct. 6   **Photo.**   *Perf. 14½x14*
29	A4	10np on 1np brt grn	15	15
30	A4	20np on 2np red brn	30	30
31	A4	30np on 3np ol grn	45	45
32	A4	40np on 4np dp ultra	60	60
33	A4	75np on 90np car	1.00	1.00
34	A4	80np on 90np car	1.25	1.25
35	A2	1r on 90np yel brn	1.65	1.65
		Nos. 29-35 (7)	5.40	5.40

Due to a stamp shortage the surcharged set appeared before the commemorative issue.

Wheat Emblem and Hands with Broken Chains — A4

1963, Oct. 15   *Perf. 14½x14*
36	A4	1np brt green	15	15
37	A4	2np red brown	15	15
38	A4	3np olive green	15	15
39	A4	4np deep ultra	15	15
40	A4	90np carmine	40	40
		Set value	60	60

     Miniature Sheet
     Imperf
41	A4	100np purple	50	50

"Freedom from Hunger" campaign of the FAO. Imperfs. exist. No. 41 contains one 39x67mm stamp.

For surcharges see Nos. 29-34.

Orbiting Astronomical Observatory — A5

Satellites: 2np, Nimbus weather satellite. 3np, Pioneer V space probe. 4np, Explorer XIII. 5np, Explorer XII. 35np, Relay satellite. 50np, Orbiting Solar Observatory.

1964, Feb. 5   **Photo.**   *Perf. 14*
42	A5	1np blue	15	15
43	A5	2np red brn & yel grn	15	15
44	A5	3np blk & grnsh bl	15	15
45	A5	4np lem & blk	15	15
46	A5	5np brt pur & lem	15	15
47	A5	35np grnsh bl & pur	50	50
48	A5	50np ol grn & redsh brn	70	70
		Set value	1.50	1.50

Issued to publicize space research. A 100np imperf. souvenir sheet shows various satellites, the Earth and stars. Colors: dark blus, gold, green & pink. Size: 112x80mm.

Runner — A6

1964, Mar. 3   **Unwmk.**
49	A6	1np shown	15	15
50	A6	2np Discus	15	15
51	A6	3np Hurdler	15	15
52	A6	4np Shot put	15	15
53	A6	20np High jump	15	15
54	A6	30np Weight lifting	20	20
55	A6	40np Javelin	28	28
56	A6	1r Diving	65	65
		Set value	1.45	1.45

18th Olympic Games, Tokyo, Oct. 10-25, 1964. An imperf. souvenir sheet contains one 1r stamp

---

similar to No. 56. Size of stamp: 67x67mm, size of sheet: 102x102mm.

Girl Scouts A7

1964, June 30   *Perf. 14x14½*
57	A7	1np grnsh gray	15	15
58	A7	2np emerald	15	15
59	A7	3np brt bl	15	15
60	A7	4np brt vio	15	15
61	A7	5np car rose	15	15
62	A7	2r dk red brn	2.00	2.00
		Set value	2.25	2.25

Issued to honor the Girl Scouts. An imperf. souvenir sheet contains one 2r bright red stamp. Size of stamp: 67x40mm. Size of sheet: 102½x76mm.

Sharjah Boy Scout — A8

Marching Scouts With Drummers — A9

Designs: 3np, 2r, Boy Scout portrait.

Perf. 14½x14, 14x14½

1964, June 30   **Photo.**   **Unwmk.**
63	A8	1np gray grn	15	15
64	A9	2np emerald	15	15
65	A8	3np brt bl	15	15
66	A8	4np brt vio	15	15
67	A9	5np brt car rose	15	15
68	A8	2r dk red brn	2.00	2.00
		Nos. 63-68 (6)	2.75	2.75

Issued to honor the Sharjah Boy Scouts. An imperf. souvenir sheet exists with one 2r bright red stamp in design of No. 68. Size of stamp: 39½x67mm. Size of sheet: 77x103mm.

Olympic Torch and Rings — A10

1964, Oct. 15   **Litho.**   *Perf. 14*
69	A10	1np ol grn	15	15
70	A10	2np ultra	15	15
71	A10	3np org brn	15	15
72	A10	4np bl grn	15	15
73	A10	5np dk vio	15	15
74	A10	40np brt bl	35	35
75	A10	50np dk red brn	40	40
76	A10	2r bister	1.60	1.60
		Set value	2.50	2.50

18th Olympic Games, Tokyo, Oct. 10-25. An imperf. souvenir sheet exists with one 2r yellow green stamp. Size of stamp: 82mm at base. Size of sheet: 107x76mm.

Early Telephone — A11

Designs: No. 78, Modern telewriter. No. 79, 1895 car. No. 80, American automobile, 1964. No. 81, Early X-ray. No. 82, Modern X-ray. No. 83, Mail coach. No. 84, Telstar and Delta rocket. No. 85, Sailing vessel. No. 86, Nuclear ship "Savannah." No. 88, Early astronomers. No. 88, Jodrell Bank telescope. No. 89, Greek messengers. No. 90, Relay satellite, Delta rocket and globe. No. 91, Early flying machine. No. 92, Caravelle plane. No. 93, Persian water wheel. No. 94, Hydroelectric dam. No. 95, Old steam locomotive. No. 96, Diesel locomotive.

Unwmk.

			Perf. 14
1965, Apr. 23		**Litho.**	
77	A11	1np rose red & blk	15 15
78	A11	1np rose red & blk	15 15
79	A11	2np org & indigo	15 15
80	A11	2np org & indigo	15 15
81	A11	3np dk brn & emer	15 15
82	A11	3np emer & dk brn	15 15
83	A11	4np yel grn & dk vio	15 15
84	A11	4np dk vio & yel grn	15 15
85	A11	5np bl grn & brn	15 15
86	A11	5np bl grn & brn	15 15
87	A11	30np gray & bl	20 15
88	A11	30np bl & gray	20 15
89	A11	40np vio bl & yel	30 15
90	A11	40np vio bl & yel	30 15
91	A11	50np blue & sepia	42 20
92	A11	50np blue & sepia	42 20
93	A11	75np brt grn & dk brn	60 30
94	A11	75np brt grn & dk brn	60 30
95	A11	1r yel & vio bl	75 38
96	A11	1r yel & vio bl	75 38
		Nos. 77-96 (20)	6.04
		Set value	3.20

Issued to show progress in science, transport and communications. Each two stamps of same denomination are printed se tenant. Two imperf. souvenir sheets exist. One contains one each of Nos. 89-90 and the other, of Nos. 95-96. Size: 102x75mm.

Stamps of Sharjah & Dependencies were replaced in 1972 by those of United Arab Emirates.

AIR POST STAMPS

Type of Regular Issue, 1963 with Flying Hawk and "Air Mail" in English and Arabic Added

Perf. 14¹/₂x14

1963, July 10	**Photo.**		**Unwmk.**
Black Portrait and Inscriptions; Lilac Rose Flag			
C1	A1	1r ultra & fawn	40 40
C2	A1	2r lt vio & lemon	70 70
C3	A1	3r drl grn & brt yel	1.00 1.00
C4	A1	4r grnsh bl & sal	1.40 1.40
C5	A1	5r emerald & gray	1.60 1.60
C6	A1	10r ol bis & rose	3.50 3.50
		Nos. C1-C6 (6)	8.60 8.60

ذكرى جون ف. كنيدى ۱۹۱۷-۱۹۶۳

In Memoriam

Nos. C1-C6 Overprinted

❧ John F Kennedy 1917-1963 ❧

1964, Apr. 7		
Black Portrait and Inscriptions; Lilac Rose Flag		
C7	A1	1r ultra & fawn
C8	A1	2r lt vio & lem
C9	A1	3r dl grn & brt yel
C10	A1	4r grnsh bl & sal
C11	A1	5r emer & gray
C12	A1	10r ol bis & rose
		Nos. C7-C12	35.00 27.50

Pres. John F. Kennedy (1917-63).

World Map and Flame AP1

1964, Apr. 15			*Perf. 14x14¹/₂*
C13	AP1	50np red brn	20 20
C14	AP1	1r purple	40 40
C15	AP1	150np Prus grn	60 60

Issued for Human Rights Day. An imperf. souvenir sheet contains one 3r carmine rose stamp. Size of stamp: 67x40mm. Size of sheet: 89x64mm.

View of Khor Fakkan AP2

Designs: 20np, Beni Qatab Bedouin camp near Dhaid. 30np, Oasis of Dhaid. 40np, Kalba Castle. 75np, Sharjah street with wind tower. 100np, Sharjah Fortress.

1964, Aug. 13		**Photo.**	**Unwmk.**
C16	AP2	10np multi	15 15
C17	AP2	20np multi	15 15
C18	AP2	30np multi	15 15
C19	AP2	40np multi	15 15
C20	AP2	75np multi	28 18
C21	AP2	100np multi	40 22
		Set value	1.05 65

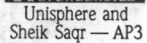

Unisphere and Sheik Saqr — AP3

J. F. Kennedy, Statue of Liberty — AP4

Designs: 20np, Offshore oil rig. 1r, New York skyline, horiz.

Perf. 14¹/₂x14

1964, Sept. 5		**Photo.**	**Unwmk.**
		Size: 26x45mm	
C22	AP3	20np yel, blk & brt bl	15 15
C23	AP3	40np blk, bl & yel	15 15
		Size: 86x45mm	
C24	AP3	1r brt bl & multi	40 40
a.		Strip of 3, Nos. C22-C24	60 60

Issued for the New York World's Fair, 1964-65. Nos. C22-C24 were printed setenant in the same sheet.

An imperf. souvenir sheet exists with one 40np stamp in AP3 design. Size of stamp: 40x68mm. Size of sheet: 76x108mm.

1964, Nov. 22			*Perf. 14x13¹/₂*
C25	AP4	40np multicolored	75 75
C26	AP4	60np multicolored	1.25 1.25
C27	AP4	100np multicolored	2.00 2.00

Pres. John F. Kennedy. A souvenir sheet contains one each of Nos. C25-C27, imperf. Size: 107x76mm.

Rock Dove AP5

Birds: 40np, 2r, Red jungle fowl. 75np, 3r, Hoopoe.

Perf. 14x14¹/₂

1965, Feb. 20		**Photo.**	**Unwmk.**
C28	AP5	30np gray & multi	15 15
C29	AP5	40np multi	15 15
C30	AP5	75np brt bl & multi	28 15
C31	AP5	150np blue & multi	60 20
C32	AP5	2r multi	65 28
C33	AP5	3r red & multi	1.00 40
		Nos. C28-C33 (6)	2.83
		Set value	1.10

OFFICIAL STAMPS

ON STATE SERVICE

Nos. 7-15 Overprinted

Perf. 14¹/₂x14

1965, Jan. 13		**Photo.**	**Unwmk.**
O1	A1	8np multi	15 15
O2	A1	10np multi	15 15
O3	A1	16np multi	15 15
O4	A1	20np multi	15 15
O5	A1	30np multi	16 16
O6	A1	40np multi	20 20
O7	A1	50np multi	22 22
O8	A1	75np multi	35 35
O9	A1	100np multi	50 50
		Set value	1.75 1.75

SIBERIA

LOCATION — A vast territory of Russia lying between the Ural Mountains and the Pacific Ocean.

The anti-Bolshevist provisional government set up at Omsk by Adm. Aleksandr V. Kolchak issued Nos. 1-10 in 1919. The monarchist, anti-Soviet government in Priamur province issued Nos. 51-118 in 1921-22.

(Stamps of the Czechoslovak Legion are listed under Czechoslovakia.)

100 Kopecks = 1 Ruble

Russian Stamps of 1909-18 Surcharged

35   **1**
a   **рубль**
          b

On Stamps of 1909-12

1919	**Unwmk.**		*Perf. 14x14¹/₂*
	Wove Paper		
	Lozenges of Varnish on Face		
1	A14(a)	35k on 2k dul! grn	45 1.10
a.		Inverted surcharge	27.50
2	A14(a)	50k on 3k carmine	45 1.25
a.		Inverted surcharge	35.00
3	A14(a)	70k on 1k dl org yel	90 3.00
a.		Inverted surcharge	27.50
4	A15(b)	1r on 4k carmine	90 1.75
		Dbl. surch., one inverted	45.00
		Inverted surcharge	50.00
5	A14(b)	3r on 7k blue	1.50 3.50
a.		Double surcharge	22.50
b.		Inverted surcharge	20.00
6	A11(b)	5r on 14k dk bl & car	2.50 5.50
a.		Double surcharge	22.50
b.		Inverted surcharge	22.50

On Stamps of 1917

Imperf

7	A14(a)	35k on 2k gray grn	90 1.75
8	A14(a)	50k on 3k red	90 1.75
a.		Inverted surcharge	100.00
9	A14(a)	70k on 1k orange	75 1.65
a.		Inverted surcharge	25.00
10	A15(b)	1r on 4k carmine	4.50 7.75
		Nos. 1-10 (10)	13.75 29.00

Nos. 1-10, were first issued in Omsk during the regime of Admiral Kolchak. Later they were used along the line of the Trans-Siberian railway to Vladivostok.

Some experts question the postal use of most offcover canceled copies of Nos. 1-10.

25 P 1-

Similar surcharges, handstamped as above are bogus.

Priamur Government Issues
Nikolaevsk Issue

A5   A6

A7

Russian Stamps Handstamp Surcharged or Overprinted
On Stamps of 1909-17

1921	**Unwmk.**	*Perf. 14x14¹/₂, 13¹/₂*	
51	A5	10k on 4k carmine	
52	A5	10k on 10k dark blue	
53	A6	15k on 14k dk blue & car	
54	A6	15k on 15k red brn & dp bl	
55	A6	15k on 35k red brn & grn	
56	A6	15k on 50k brn vio & grn	
57	A6	15k on 70k brn & red org	
58	A6	15k on 1r brn & orange	
59	A5	on 20k dl bl & dk car	
60	A5	on 20k on 14k dk bl & car (No. 118)	
a.		15k on 20k on 14k dk bl & car (error)	
61	A7	20k on 3¹/₂r mar & lt grn	
62	A7	20k on 5r ind, grn & lt bl	
63	A7	20k on 7r dk grn & pink	

Nos. 59-60 are overprinted with initials but original denominations remain.

A 10k on 5k claret (Russia No. 77) and a 15k on 20k blue & carmine (Russia No. 82a) were not officially issued. Some authorities consider them bogus.

Any postmark except the Vladivostok arrival cancel is bogus.

Reprints exist.

On Semi-Postal Stamp of 1914
64	SP6	20k on 3k mar & gray grn, *pink*	

On Stamps of 1917
Imperf

65	A5	10k on 1k orange	
66	A5	10k on 2k gray green	
67	A5	10k on 3k red	
68	A5	10k on 5k claret	
69	A6	15k on 1r pale brn, brn & red org	
70	A7	20k on 1r pale brn, brn & red org	
71	A7	20k on 3¹/₂r mar & lt grn	
72	A7	20k on 7r dk grn & pink	

The letters of the overprint are the initials of the Russian words for "Nikolaevsk on Amur Priamur Provisional Government".

As the surcharges on Nos. 51-72 are handstamped, a number exist inverted or double.

A 20k blue & carmine (Russia No. 126) with Priamur overprint and a 15k on 20k (Russia No. 126) were not officially issued. Some authorities consider them bogus.

Stamps of Far Eastern Republic Overprinted

1922			
78	A2	2k gray green	25.00 25.00
a.		Inverted overprint	125.00
79	A2a	4k rose	25.00 25.00
a.		Inverted overprint	*115.00*
80	A2	5k claret	25.00 25.00
81	A2a	10k blue	25.00 25.00

Anniv. of the overthrow of the Bolshevik power in the Priamur district.

The letters of the overprint are the initials of "Vremeno Priamurski Pravitel'stvo" i.e. Provisional Priamur Government, 26th May.

Russian Stamps of 1909-21 Overprinted in Dark Blue or Vermilion

Приам.
Земскій
Край

On Stamps of 1909-18

1922   *Perf. 14x14½*

85	A14	1k dull org yel	45.00	50.00
86	A14	2k dull green	80.00	65.00
87	A14	3k carmine	25.00	30.00
88	A15	4k carmine	12.50	15.00
89	A14	5k dk claret	25.00	27.50
90	A14	7k blue (V)	25.00	27.50
91	A15	10k dark blue (V)	35.00	40.00
92	A11	14k dk bl & car	45.00	55.00
93	A11	15k red brn & dp bl	12.50	15.00
94	A8	20k dl bl & dk car	12.50	15.00
95	A11	20k on 14k dk bl & car	100.00	100.00
96	A11	25k dl grn & dk vio (V)	25.00	30.00
97	A11	35k red brn & grn	7.50	10.00
a.		Inverted overprint	80.00	
98	A8	50k brn vio & grn	12.50	15.00
99	A11	70k brn & red org	25.00	30.00

On Stamps of 1917
Imperf

100	A14	1k orange	4.25	5.00
a.		Inverted overprint	65.00	85.00
101	A14	2k gray green	9.00	9.00
102	A14	3k red	12.00	12.00
103	A15	4k carmine	65.00	65.00
104	A14	5k claret	19.00	15.00
105	A11	15k red brn & dp bl	110.00	100.00
106	A8	20k blue & car	47.50	40.00
107	A9	1r pale brn, brn & red org	14.00	15.00

On Stamps of Siberia, 1919
Perf. 14½x15

108	A14	35k on 2k green	47.50	40.00

Imperf

109	A14	70k on 1k orange	65.00	60.00

On Stamps of Far Eastern Republic, 1921

110	A2	2k gray green	6.00	5.50
111	A2a	4k rose	6.00	5.50
112	A2	5k claret	6.00	5.50
a.		Inverted overprint	100.00	
113	A2a	10k blue (R)	4.00	3.50

Same, Surcharged with New Values

114	A2	1k on 2k gray grn	4.00	3.50
115	A2a	3k on 4k rose	4.00	3.50

The overprint is in a rectangular frame on stamps of 1k to 10k and 1r; on the other values the frame is omitted. It is larger on the 1 ruble than on the smaller stamps.

The overprint reads "Priamurski Zemski Krai," Priamur Rural Province.

Far Eastern Republic Nos. 30-32 Overprinted in Blue

П.З.К.

Perf. 14½x15

116	A14	35k on 2k green	5.00	6.50

Imperf

117	A14	35k on 2k green	60.00	85.00
118	A14	70k on 1k orange	8.25	11.50

Counterfeits of Nos. 51-118 abound.

SLOVAKIA

LOCATION — Central Europe
GOVT. — Independent republic
AREA — 18,932 sq. mi.
POP. — 5,296,768 (est. 1992)
CAPITAL — Bratislava

Formerly a province of Czechoslovakia, Slovakia declared its independence in Mar., 1939. A treaty was immediately concluded with Germany guaranteeing Slovakian independence but providing for German "protection" for 25 years.

In 1945 the republic ended and Slovakia again became a part of Czechoslovakia.

On January 1, 1993, Czechoslovakia split into the Czech Republic and Slovakia.

100 Halierov = 1 Koruna

Catalogue values for unused stamps in this country are for never hinged items, beginning with Scott 26 in the regular postage section, Scott B1 in the semi-postal section, Scott C1 in the airmail section, Scott EX1 in the personal delivery section, Scott J1 in the postage due section, and Scott P10 in the newspaper section.

Stamps of Czechoslovakia, 1928-39, Overprinted in Red or Blue

Slovenský štát 1939

1939   *Perf. 10, 12½, 12x12½*

2	A29	5h dk ultra	48	90
3	A29	10h brown	15	15
4	A29	20h red (Bl)	15	15
5	A29	25h green	95	1.75
6	A29	30h red violet (Bl)	15	15
7	A61a	40h dark blue	15	18
8	A73	50h deep green	15	15
9	A63	50h deep green	15	15
10	A63	60h dull violet	15	15
11	A63	60h dull blue	5.75	8.75
12	A60	1k rose lake (Bl) (On No. 212)	15	15

Overprinted Diagonally

13	A64	1.20k rose lilac (Bl)	18	32
14	A65	1.50k carmine (Bl)	18	32
15	A79	1.60k olive grn (Bl)	1.75	2.50
16	A66	2k dk blue green	1.75	2.50
17	A67	2.50k dark blue	28	52
18	A68	3k brown	38	65
19	A69	3.50k dk violet	17.50	26.00
20	A69	3.50k dk violet (Bl)	20.00	30.00
21	A70	4k dk violet	8.75	12.50
22	A71	5k green	9.50	14.00
23	A72	10k blue	70.00	100.00
		Nos. 2-23 (22)	*138.65*	*201.94*

Excellent counterfeit overprints exist.

Andrej Hlinka
A1   A2

Overprinted in Red or Blue

Perf. 12½

1939, Apr.   **Unwmk.**   **Photo.**

24	A1	50h dark green (R)	1.00	75
a.		Perf. 10½	1.00	95
b.		Perf. 10½x12½	2.75	3.00
25	A1	1k dk car rose (Bl)	95	75
a.		Perf. 10½	45.00	72.50
b.		Perf. 10½x12½	4.50	6.50

Catalogue values for unused stamps in this section, from this point to the end of the section, are for Never Hinged items.

1939   **Unwmk.**   *Perf. 12½*

26	A2	5h brt ultra	45	55
27	A2	10h olive green	70	85
a.		Perf. 10½x12½	20.00	30.00
b.		Perf. 10½	17.00	14.00
28	A2	20h orange red	70	85
a.		Imperf.	75	80
29	A2	30h dp violet	70	85
a.		Imperf.	1.00	1.25
b.		Perf. 10½x12½	5.00	6.25
c.		Perf. 10½	7.50	7.00
30	A2	50h dk green	70	85
31	A2	1k dk carmine rose	90	85
32	A2	2.50k brt blue	90	38
33	A2	3k black brown	2.75	38
		Nos. 26-33 (8)	*7.80*	*5.56*

On Nos. 32 and 33 a pearl frame surrounds the medallion. See Nos. 55-57, 69.

General Stefánik and Memorial Tomb — A3   Rev. Josef Murgas and Radio Towers — A4

1939, May   *Perf. 12½*
Size: 25x20mm

34	A3	40h dark blue		75
35	A3	60h slate green		75
36	A3	1k gray violet		75

Size: 30x23¾mm

37	A3	2k bl vio & sepia		75

20th anniv. of the death of Gen. Milan Stefánik, but not issued.

1939   **Unwmk.**

38	A4	60h purple	25	30
39	A4	1.20k slate black	50	20

10th anniv. of the death of Rev. Josef Murgas. See No. 65.

Girl Embroidering — A5   Woodcutter — A6

Girl at Spring — A7

1939-44   **Wmk. 263**   *Perf. 12½*

40	A5	2k dk blue green	6.25	48
41	A6	4k copper brown	1.40	95
42	A7	5k orange red	1.00	52
a.		Perf. 10 ('44)	1.65	1.25

Dr. Josef Tiso — A8   Presidential Residence — A9

1939-44   **Wmk. 263**   *Perf. 12½*

43	A8	50h slate green	30	30
43A	A8	70h dk red brn ('42)	20	20
b.		Perf. 10½ ('44)	50	35

See No. 88.

1940, Mar. 14

44	A9	10k deep blue	1.00	75

Tatra Mountains — A10   Krivan Peak — A11

Edelweiss in the Tatra Mountains A12   Chamois A13

Church at Javorina — A14

1940-43   **Wmk. 263**   *Perf. 12½*
Size: 17x21mm

45	A10	5h dk olive grn	18	20
46	A11	10h deep brown	15	15
47	A12	20h blue black	15	15
48	A13	25h olive brown	75	40
49	A14	30h chestnut brown	35	35
a.		Perf. 10½ ('43)	2.50	1.00
		Nos. 45-49 (5)	*1.58*	*1.25*

See Nos. 84-87, 103-107.

Hlinka Type of 1939

1940-42   **Wmk. 263**   *Perf. 12½*

55	A1	1k dk car rose	80	60
56	A2	2.50k brt blue ('42)	1.00	75
a.		Perf. 10½		75
57	A2	3k black brn ('41)	2.00	1.00
a.		Perf. 10½	1.75	90

On Nos. 56 and 57 a pearl frame surrounds the medallion.

Stiavnica A15   Lietava A16

Spissky Hrad — A17   Bojnice — A18

1941   *Perf. 12½*

58	A15	1.20k rose lake	18	22
59	A16	1.50k rose pink	18	22
60	A17	1.60k royal blue	24	15
61	A18	2k dk gray green	18	15
		Set value		*59*

Slovakian Castles.

S. M. Daxner and Stefan Moyses — A19   Andrej Hlinka — A20

1941, May 26   **Photo.**   **Wmk. 263**

62	A19	50h olive green	2.00	1.75
63	A19	1k slate blue	8.00	6.50
64	A19	2k black	8.00	6.50

80th anniv. of the Memorandum of the Slovak Nation.

Murgas Type of 1939

1941   **Wmk. 263**

65	A4	60h purple		50	25

1942

69	A20	1.30k dark purple		25	20

Post Horn and
Miniature
Stamp — A21

Philatelist — A22

Philatelist — A23

1942, May 23

70	A21	30h dark green	1.10	1.25
71	A22	70h dk car rose	1.10	1.25
72	A23	80h purple	1.10	1.25
73	A21	1.30k dark brown	1.10	1.25

Natl. Philatelic Exhibition at Bratislava.
On No. 70 the miniature stamp bears the coat-of-arms of Bratislava; on No. 73 it shows the National arms of Slovakia.

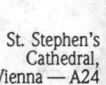

St. Stephen's
Cathedral,
Vienna — A24

1942, Oct. 12   **Perf. 14**

74	A24	70h blue green	75	1.10
75	A24	1.30k olive green	75	1.10
76	A24	2k sapphire	1.50	3.00

European Postal Congress held in Vienna.

Slovakian Educational Society — A25

1942, Dec. 14

77	A25	70h black	15	20
78	A25	1k rose red	24	35
79	A25	1.30k sapphire	15	26
80	A25	2k chestnut brown	24	35
81	A25	3k dark green	38	60
82	A25	4k dull purple	38	75
		Nos. 77-82 (6)	1.54	2.51

Slovakian Educational Soc., 150th anniv.

Andrej Hlinka — A26

1943   **Wmk. 263**

| 83 | A26 | 1.30k brt ultra | 25 | 20 |

See Nos. 93-94A.

Types of 1939-40

1943   **Unwmk.**   **Perf. 12½**

84	A11	10h deep brown	26	20
85	A12	20h blue black	70	48
86	A13	25h olive brown	70	48
87	A14	30h chestnut brown	45	38
88	A8	70h dk red brown	85	95
		Nos. 84-88 (5)	2.96	2.49

Presov Church
A27

Locomotive
A28

Railway
Tunnel — A29

Viaduct — A30

1943, Sept. 5   **Perf. 14**

89	A27	70h dk rose violet	35	42
90	A28	80h sapphire	35	42
91	A29	1.30k black	35	42
92	A30	2k dk violet brn	48	70

Inauguration of the new railroad line between Presov and Strazske.

Hlinka Type of 1943 and

Ludovit
Stur — A31

Martin Razus — A32

1944   **Unwmk.**

93	A31	80h slate green	15	15
94	A32	1k brown red	15	18
94A	A26	1.30k brt ultra	70	70

Prince Pribina — A33

Designs: 70h, Prince Mojmir. 80h, Prince Ratislav. 1.30k, Prince Kocel. 2k, Prince Kocel. 3k, Prince Mojmir II. 5k, Prince Svatopluk II. 10k, Prince Braslav.

1944, Mar. 14

95	A33	50h dark green	15	15
96	A33	70h lilac rose	15	15
97	A33	80h red brown	15	15
98	A33	1.30k brt ultra	16	15
99	A33	2k Prus blue	16	20
100	A33	3k dark brown	45	30
101	A33	5k violet	95	70
102	A33	10k black	2.50	2.00
		Nos. 95-102 (8)	4.67	3.80

Scenic Types of 1940

1944, Apr. 1   **Perf. 14**
Size: 18x23mm

103	A11	10h bright carmine	15	30
104	A12	20h bright blue	15	30
105	A13	25h brown red	15	30
106	A14	30h red violet	15	30
107	A10	50h deep green	15	30
		Nos. 103-107 (5)	75	1.50

5th anniv. of Slovakia's independence.

Symbolic of National
Protection — A41

President Josef
Tiso — A42

1944, Oct. 6   **Wmk. 263**

| 108 | A41 | 2k green | 38 | 60 |
| 109 | A41 | 3.80k red violet | 38 | 90 |

1945   **Unwmk.**

110	A42	1k orange	1.10	90
111	A42	1.50k brown	30	22
112	A42	2k green	38	22
113	A42	4k rose red	1.10	90
114	A42	5k sapphire	1.10	90

Wmk. 263

| 115 | A42 | 10k red violet | 75 | 45 |
| | | Nos. 110-115 (6) | 4.73 | 3.59 |

6th anniv. of the Republic of Slovakia's declaration of independence, Mar. 14, 1939.

Natl. Arms — A50

1993   **Photo. & Engr.**   **Perf. 11½**

| 150 | A50 | 3k multicolored | 30 |

Engr.
Perf. 12
Size: 30x44mm

| 151 | A50 | 8k multicolored | 1.20 |

Issue dates: 3k, Jan. 2. 8k, Jan. 1. No. 151 does not have black frameline.

Nitra — A51

Banska
Bystrica — A52

Ruzomberok
A53

Kosice
A54

Zvolen — A55

Bratislava — A56

No. 152-155 are churches, Nos. 156-157 are castles.

Perf. 11½x12, 12x11½

1993-95   **Photo. & Engr.**

152	A51	2k multicolored	15
153	A52	3k multicolored	28
154	A53	5k multicolored	40
155	A54	10k multicolored	80
156	A55	30k multicolored	2.50
157	A56	50k multicolored	6.50
		Nos. 152-157 (6)	10.63

Issued: 5k, 10k, 1993; 30k, 9/12/93; 50k, 12/31/93; 3k, 11/15/94; 2k, 3/15/95.

St. John
Nepomuk,
600th
Death
Anniv.
A57

1993   **Photo. & Engr.**   **Perf. 12x11½**

| 158 | A57 | 8k multicolored | 72 |

See Czech Republic #2880; Germany #1776.

A58

A59

President Michal Kovac

1993   **Engr.**   **Perf. 12x11½**

| 159 | A58 | 2k dark gray blue | 16 |
| 159A | A58 | 3k red brown & red | 25 |

Issued: 2k, 3/2/93; 3k, 11/3/93.

Photo. & Engr.
1993, May 14   **Perf. 11½**

Trees.

160	A59	3k Quercus robur	25
161	A59	4k Carpinus betulus	35
162	A59	10k Pinus silvestris	85

A60

A61

Famous Men: 5k, Jan Levoslav Bella (1843-1936), composer. 8k, Alexander Dubcek (1921-92), politician. 20k, Jan Kollar (1793-1852), writer.

Photo. & Engr.
1993, May 20   **Perf. 12x11½**

163	A60	5k red brown & blue	75
164	A60	8k brown & lilac red	1.20
165	A60	20k gray blue & orange	3.00

1993, May 31   **Engr.**   **Perf. 12**

Woman with Pitcher, by Marian Cunderlik.

| 166 | A61 | 14k multicolored | 1.50 |

Europa.

Literary
Slovak
Language,
150th
Anniv.
A62

Design: 8k, Arrival of St. Cyril and St. Methodius, 1130th Anniv.

Photo. & Engr.
1993, June 22   **Perf. 12x11½**

| 167 | A62 | 2k multicolored | 20 |
| 168 | A62 | 8k multicolored | 75 |

See Czech Republic No. 2886.

A63

A64

Arms of Dubnica nad Vahom.

Photo. & Engr.
1993, July 8   **Perf. 12x11½**

| 169 | A63 | 1k multicolored | 15 |

Photo. & Engr.

1993, Sept. 2   *Perf. 11½*

The Big Pets, by Lane Smith.

170 A64 5k multicolored   45

Bratislava Biennial of Illustrators.

Gavcikovo Dam — A65

Photo. & Engr.

1993, Nov. 12   *Perf. 11½*

172 A65 10k multicolored   1.25

No. 172 issued se-tenant with label.

Madonna and Child,
by J. B. Klemens
(1817-83) — A66

Photo. & Engr.

1993, Dec. 1   *Perf. 11½*

173 A66 2k multicolored   28

Christmas.

Souvenir Sheet

Monument to Gen. Milan Stefanik — A67

1993, Dec. 17   Engr.   *Perf. 11½x12*

174 A67 16k multicolored   2.00

Art from
Bratislava
Natl.
Gallery
A68

Sculpture: 9k, Plough of Springtime, by Josef
Kostka.

1993, Dec. 31

175 A68 9k multicolored   1.00

See Nos. 199-200.

A69   A70

Photo. & Engr.

1994, Jan. 26   *Perf. 11x11½*

176 A69 2k multicolored   22

1994 Winter Olympics, Lillehammer.

Photo. & Engr.

1994, Apr. 29   *Perf. 11x11½*

177 A70 3k multicolored   25

Intl. Year of the Family.

Jan Andrej Segner
(1704-77),
Physicist — A71

Design: 9k, Antoine de Saint-Exupery (1900-44),
aviator, author.

Photo. & Engr.

1994, May 25   *Perf. 11½x11*

178 A71 8k red brown & blue   80
179 A71 9k black, blue & pink   90

See Nos. 196-198.

Josef Murgas (1864-
1929), Inventor of
Radio
Transmitters — A72

1994, May 27   Engr.   *Perf. 11½*

180 A72 28k multicolored   2.25

Europa.

A73   A74

Photo. & Engr.

1994, May 31   *Perf. 11½x11*

181 A73 3k multicolored   25

Intl. Stop Smoking Day.

Photo. & Engr.

1994, June 10   *Perf. 11½*

182 A74 2k blue, black & green   15

1994 World Cup Soccer Championships, US.

*Slovakia stamps can be mounted
in either the Scott Czechoslovakia
part 1 or Germany part 2 albums.*

Raptors — A76

Photo. & Engr.

1994, July 4   *Perf. 11½x12*

184 A76 4k Aquila chrysaetos   38
185 A76 5k Falco peregrinus   48
186 A76 7k Bubo bubo   70
        Nos. 184-186 (3)   1.56

Prince Svatopluk of Moravia (870-
894) — A77

1994, July 20   Engr.   *Perf. 12*

187 A77 12k red brown, buff & black 1.25

UPU, 120th
Anniv. — A78

Photo. & Engr.

1994, Aug. 1   *Perf. 11½x12*

188 A78 8k multicolored   55

Slovak
Uprising,
50th
Anniv.
A79

Design: 6k, Gen. Rudolf Viest, Gen. Jan. Golian.
8k, French Volunteers' Memorial, Strecno hill.

Photo. & Engr.

1994, Aug. 27   *Perf. 12x11½*

189 A79 6k multicolored   1.40
190 A79 8k multicolored   75

Nos. 189-190 printed with se-tenant label.

Souvenir Sheet

Janko
Matuska,
Lyricist,
150th
Death
Anniv.
A80

Design: 34k, Matuska, woman with pitcher,
verse of "A Well She Dug."

Photo. & Engr.

1994, Sept. 1   *Perf. 12x11½*

191 A80 34k multicolored   3.25

Comenius University,
75th Anniv. — A81

Photo. & Engr.

1994, Oct. 18   *Perf. 11½x12*

192 A81 12k multicolored   1.25

Mojmirovce Horse Race, 180th
Anniv. — A82

1994, Oct. 25   *Perf. 12x11½*

193 A82 2k multicolored   20

St. George's
Church,
Kostotany pod
Tribecom
A83

1994, Nov. 8   *Perf. 11*

194 A83 20k multicolored   1.90

Christmas — A84

1994, Nov. 29   *Perf. 11½*

195 A84 2k multicolored   20

Personalities Type of 1994

Designs: 5k, Chatam Sofer (1762-1839), rabbi.
6k, Wolfgang Kempelen (1734-1804),
polytechnician. 10k, Stefan Banic (1870-1941),
inventor of aviation parachute.

1994, Dec. 12   *Perf. 11½x11*

196 A71 5k multicolored   48
197 A71 6k multicolored   60
198 A71 10k multicolored   1.00
        Nos. 196-198 (3)   2.08

Bratislava Art Type of 1993

Designs: 7k, Girls, by Janko Alexy, horiz. 14k,
The Bulls, by Vincent Hloznik.

Perf. 12x11½, 11½x12

1994, Dec. 15   Engr.

199 A68 7k multicolored   70
200 A68 14k multicolored   1.40

Ships
A85

Designs: 5k, Cargo ship, NL EMS. 8k, Cargo
ship, Ryn. 10k, 400-passenger cruise ship.

Photo. & Engr.
1994, Dec. 30   *Perf. 12x11½*
201	A85	5k multicolored	48	
202	A85	8k multicolored	75	
203	A85	10k multicolored	1.00	
	Nos. 201-203 (3)	2.23		

Samuel Jurkovic, Founder of Landlords Assoc., 1845 — A86

Photo. & Engr.
1995, Feb. 8   *Perf. 11½*
204 A86 9k multicolored   65

European Nature Conservation Year — A87

Protected plants: 2k, Ciminalis clusii. 3k, Pulsatilla slavica. 8k, Onosma tornense.

1995, Feb. 28
205	A87	2k multicolored	15
206	A87	3k multicolored	20
207	A87	8k multicolored	55
	Nos. 205-207 (3)	90	

Slovak Natl. Theatre, 75th Anniv. A88

1995, Feb. 28   *Perf. 12x11½*
208 A88 10k multicolored   70

1995 Group B World Cup Ice Hockey Championships, Bratislava — A89

1995, Mar. 29   *Perf. 11½*
209 A89 5k blue & yellow   35

SEMI-POSTAL STAMPS

Catalogue values for unused stamps in this section are for Never Hinged items.

Josef Tiso — SP1

Perf. 12½
1939, Nov. 6   Photo.   Wmk. 263
B1 SP1 2.50k + 2.50k royal blue   3.25 3.50

The surtax was used for Child Welfare.

Medical Corpsman and Wounded Soldier — SP2

1941, Nov. 10
B2	SP2	50h + 50h dull green	55	60
B3	SP2	1k + 1k rose lake	80	80
B4	SP2	2k + 1k brt blue	2.00	2.00

Mother and Child — SP3   Soldier and Hlinka Youth — SP4

1941, Dec. 10
B5	SP3	50h + 50h dull green	95	95
B6	SP3	1k + 1k brown	95	95
B7	SP3	2k + 1k violet	95	95

Surtax for the benefit of child welfare.

1942, Mar. 14
B8	SP4	70h + 1k brown org	50	48
B9	SP4	1.30k + 1k brt blue	70	60
B10	SP4	2k + 1k rose red	1.40	1.40

The surtax aided the Hlinka Youth Society "Hlinkova Mladez."

National Costumes
SP5   SP6   SP7

1943   *Perf. 14*
B11	SP5	50h + 50h dk slate grn	25	35
B12	SP6	70h + 1k dp carmine	25	35
B13	SP7	80h + 2k dark blue	25	35

The surtax was for the benefit of children, the Red Cross and winter relief of the Slovakian popular party.

Infantrymen — SP8

Aviator — SP9

Tank and Gun Crew SP10

1943, July 28
B14	SP8	70h + 2k rose brown	75	75
B15	SP9	1.30k + 2k sapphire	75	75
B16	SP10	2k + 2k olive green	85	95

The surtax was for soldiers' welfare.

"The Slovak Language Is Our Life" - L. Stur — SP11   Slovakian National Museum — SP12

Slovakian Foundation — SP13   Slovakian Peasant — SP14

1943, Oct. 16
B17	SP11	30h + 1k brown red	35	35
B18	SP12	70h + 1k slate green	45	55
B19	SP13	80h + 2k slate blue	35	35
B20	SP14	1.30k + 2k dull brown	35	35

The surtax was for the benefit of Slovakian cultural institutions.

Soccer Player — SP15   Skier — SP16

Diver — SP17   Relay Race — SP18

1944, Apr. 30   Unwmk.
B21	SP15	70h + 70h slate grn	60	1.00
B22	SP16	1k + 1k violet	75	1.25
B23	SP17	1.30k + 1.30k Prus bl	75	1.25
B24	SP18	2k + 2k chnt brn	90	1.65

Symbolic of National Protection SP19   Children SP20

1944, Oct. 6   Wmk. 263
B25	SP19	70h + 4h sapphire	1.00	1.75
B26	SP19	1.30k + 4k red brown	1.00	1.75

The surtax was for the benefit of social institutions.

1944, Dec. 18
B27	SP20	2k + 4k light blue	4.00	4.25
a.		Sheet of 8 + Label	50.00	62.50

The surtax was to aid social work for Slovak youth.

Red Cross — SP21

Photo. & Engr.
1993, Nov. 15   *Perf. 11x11½*
B28 SP21 3k + 1k red & gray blue   32

AIR POST STAMPS

Catalogue values for unused stamps in this section are for Never Hinged items.

Planes over Tatra Mountains
AP1   AP2

Perf. 12½
1939, Nov. 20   Photo.   Unwmk.
C1	AP1	30h violet	35	50
C2	AP1	50h dark green	35	50
C3	AP1	1k vermilion	40	50
C4	AP2	2k grnsh black	60	75
C5	AP2	3k dark brown	1.00	1.50
C6	AP2	4k slate blue	2.00	2.75
	Nos. C1-C6 (6)	4.70	6.50	

See No. C10.

Plane in Flight — AP3

1940, Nov. 30   Wmk. 263   *Perf. 12½*
C7	AP3	5k dk violet brn	90	1.40
C8	AP3	10k gray black	1.25	1.65
C9	AP3	20k myrtle green	1.40	2.00

Type of 1939
1944, Sept. 15   Wmk. 263
C10 AP1 1k vermilion   1.00 1.00

PERSONAL DELIVERY STAMPS

Catalogue values for unused stamps in this section are for Never Hinged items.

PD1

1940   Wmk. 263   Photo.   *Imperf.*
EX1	PD1	50h indigo & blue	90	1.90
EX2	PD1	50h carmine & rose	90	1.90

POSTAGE DUE STAMPS

Catalogue values for unused stamps in this section are for Never Hinged items.

D1   Letter, Post
                      Horn — D2

1939 Unwmk. Photo. Perf. 12½

J1	D1	5h bright blue	32	55
J2	D1	10h bright blue	32	55
J3	D1	20h bright blue	32	55
J4	D1	30h bright blue	1.40	95
J5	D1	40h bright blue	65	75
J6	D1	50h bright blue	1.65	80
J7	D1	60h bright blue	1.40	80
J8	D1	1k dark carmine	14.00	8.25
J9	D1	2k dark carmine	14.00	2.50
J10	D1	5k dark carmine	4.50	2.50
J11	D1	10k dark carmine	37.50	7.50
J12	D1	20k dark carmine	15.00	9.25
		Nos. J1-J12 (12)	91.06	34.95

1940-41   Wmk. 263

J13	D1	5h bright blue ('41)	75	55
J14	D1	10h bright blue ('41)	30	28
J15	D1	20h bright blue ('41)	48	28
J16	D1	30h bright blue ('41)	6.00	4.50
J17	D1	40h bright blue ('41)	60	75
J18	D1	50h bright blue ('41)	75	95
J19	D1	60h bright blue	90	95
J20	D1	1k dark carmine ('41)	90	1.10
J21	D1	2k dark carmine ('41)	9.00	7.50
J22	D1	5k dark carmine ('41)	2.50	2.75
J23	D1	10k dark carmine ('41)	3.00	3.25
		Nos. J13-J23 (11)	25.18	22.66

1942 Unwmk. Perf. 14

J24	D2	10h deep brown	15	15
J25	D2	20h deep brown	15	20
J26	D2	40h deep brown	15	20
J27	D2	50h deep brown	1.00	60
J28	D2	60h deep brown	20	20
J29	D2	80h deep brown	30	20
J30	D2	1k rose red	35	20
J31	D2	1.10k rose red	70	60
J32	D2	1.30k rose red	40	20
J33	D2	1.60k rose red	50	20
J34	D2	2k rose red	70	20
J35	D2	2.60k rose red	1.25	1.00
J36	D2	3.50k rose red	7.75	6.50
J37	D2	3k rose red	3.00	2.25
J38	D2	10k rose red	3.25	2.75
		Nos. J24-J38 (15)	19.85	15.45

NEWSPAPER STAMPS

Newspaper Stamps of
Czechoslovakia, 1937,
Overprinted in Red or Blue

1939, Apr. Unwmk. Imperf.

P1	N2	2h bister brn (Bl)	28	38
P2	N2	5h dull blue (R)	28	38
P3	N2	7h red org (Bl)	28	38
P4	N2	9h emerald (R)	28	38
P5	N2	10h henna brn (Bl)	28	38
P6	N2	12h ultra (R)	28	38
P7	N2	20h dk green (R)	60	85
P8	N2	50h dk brown (Bl)	2.00	2.50
P9	N2	1k grnsh gray (R)	6.75	10.50
		Nos. P1-P9 (9)	11.03	16.13

Excellent counterfeits exist of Nos. P1-P9.

Catalogue values for unused
stamps in this section, from this
point to the end of the section, are
for Never Hinged items.

Arms of   Type Block "N" (for
Slovakia   "Noviny" - Newspaper)
N1   N2

1939 Typo.

P10	N1	2h ocher	15	18
P11	N1	5h ultra	22	38
P12	N1	7h red orange	18	28
P13	N1	9h emerald	18	28
P14	N1	10h henna brown	95	1.10
P15	N1	12h dk ultra	18	32

P16	N1	20h dark green	95	1.10
P17	N1	50h red brown	1.10	1.25
P18	N1	1k grnsh gray	1.10	1.10
		Nos. P10-P18 (9)	5.01	5.99

1940-41   Wmk. 263

P20	N1	5h ultra	15	15
P23	N1	10h henna brown	15	15
P24	N1	15h brt purple ('41)	18	15
P25	N1	20h dark green	35	38
P26	N1	25h lt blue ('41)	35	38
P27	N1	40h red org ('41)	35	38
P28	N1	50h chocolate	60	55
P29	N1	1k grnsh gray ('41)	60	55
P30	N1	2k emerald ('41)	1.25	1.40
		Nos. P20-P30 (9)	3.98	4.09

1943 Photo. Unwmk.

P31	N2	10h green	15	22
P32	N2	15h dark brown	15	22
P33	N2	20h ultra	26	22
P34	N2	50h rose red	32	32
P35	N2	1k slate green	65	50
P36	N2	2k intense blue	1.10	1.00
		Nos. P31-P36 (6)	2.63	2.48

SLOVENIA

LOCATION — Southeastern Europe.
GOVT. — Independent state.
AREA — 7,819 sq. mi.
POP. — 1,725,088 (1971)
CAPITAL — Ljubljana

A constitutent republic of Yugoslavia
since 1945, Slovenia declared its independence on June 25, 1991.

100 Paras = 1 Dinar
Tolar (Oct. 10, 1991)

Catalogue values for unused
stamps in this country are for Never
Hinged items, beginning with Scott
100 in the regular postage section
and Scott RA1 in the postal tax
section.

Declaration of
Independence
A18

1991, June 26 Litho. Perf. 10½

100	A18	5d Parliament building	75

National Arms
A19   A20

1991-92 Perf. 14
Background Color

101	A19	1t brown	15
102	A20	1t brown	15
103	A20	2t lilac rose	15
105	A19	4t green	22
106	A20	4t green	22
107	A19	5t salmon	28
109	A20	6t yellow	32
114	A19	11t orange	60
115	A20	11t orange	60
119	A20	15t blue	82
123	A20	20t purple	1.10
126	A20	50t dark green	2.75
131	A20	100t gray	5.50
		Nos. 101-131 (13)	12.86

Issue dates: Nos. 101, 105, 107, 114, Dec. 26,
1991. Nos. 102, 6t, 20t, 50 and 100t, Feb. 12,
1992. 2t, 15t, Nos. 106, 115, Mar. 16, 1992.
This is an expanding set. Numbers may change.

1992 Winter Olympics, Albertville — A21

Designs: a, 30t, Ski jumper. b, 50t, Alpine skier.

1992, Feb. 8

134	A21	Pair, #a.-b., + 1 or 2 labels	4.25

Rhomboid stamps issued in sheets of 3 #134 plus
4 labels. See No. 143.

Ljubljana
Opera
House,
Cent.
A22

1992, Mar. 31

135	A22	20t multicolored	1.05

Giuseppe Tartini
(1692-1770), Italian
Violinist and
Composer — A23

1992, Apr. 8

136	A23	27t multicolored	1.40

Discovery of
America,
500th
Anniv.
A24

Designs: a, 27t, Map of northwestern Mexico
and Gulf of California, Marko Anton Kappus
preaching to natives. b, 47t, Map of parts of North
and South America, sailing ship.

1992, Apr. 21

137	A24	Pair, #a.-b.	2.50

Issued in sheets containing 6 No. 137.

Intl.
Conference
of Interior
Designers,
Ljubljana
A25

1992, May 17

138	A25	41t multicolored	1.60

A. M. Slomsek   Mountain Rescue
(1800-1862),   Service, 80th
Bishop of   Anniv. — A27
Maribor — A26

1992, May 29

139	A26	6t multicolored	25

1992, June 12

140	A27	41t multicolored	1.60

A28   A29

1992, June 20

141	A28	6t multicolored	25

Ljubljana Boatmen's Competition, 900th anniv.

1992, June 25

142	A29	41t multicolored	1.60

Independence, 1st anniv.

Olympic Type of 1992

Designs: a, 40t, Leon Stukelj, triple medalist in
1924, 1928. b, 46t, Olympic rings, three heads of
Apollo.

1992, July 25

143	A21	Pair, #a.-b. +1 or 2 labels	2.50

1992 Summer Olympics, Barcelona. Rhomboid
stamps issued in sheets of 3 #143 plus 4 labels.

World
Championship of
Registered Dogs,
Ljubljana — A30

1992, Sept. 4

144	A30	40t Slovenian sheep dog	1.00

Get free stamps every month!
A subscription to the
"Scott Stamp Monthly" entitles
you to write in for each month's
free offer. The value of the
free stamps more than
offsets the subscription cost.
For more information,
please call 1-800-488-5351.

Marij Kogoj (1892-1956), Composer — A31

Self-Portrait, by Matevz Langus (1792-1855), Painter — A32

1992, Sept. 30
145 A31 40t multicolored   1.00

1992, Oct. 30
146 A32 40t multicolored   1.00

Christmas A33

Designs: 6t, 7t, Nativity Scene, Ljubljana. 41t, Stained glass window of Madonna and Child, St. Mary's Church, Bovec, vert.

1992
147 A33   6t multicolored   15
147A A33   7t multicolored   20
148 A33 41t multicolored   1.00

Issued: 6t, 41t, Nov. 20. 7t, Dec. 15.

Herman Potocnik, Theoretician of Geosynchronous Satellite Orbit, Birth Cent. — A34

1992, Nov. 27   Litho.   Perf. 14
149 A34 46t multicolored   1.05

Prezihov Voranc (1893-1950), Writer — A35

1993, Jan. 22   Litho.   Perf. 14
150 A35 7t multicolored   20

Rihard Jakopic (1869-1943), Painter — A36

1993, Jan. 22
151 A36 44t multicolored   1.00

Jozef Stefan (1835-93), Physicist A37

1993, Jan. 22
152 A37 51t multicolored   1.20

A38

Designs: 1t, Early cake. 2t, Pan pipes. 5t, Lonceni bajs. 6t, Early building. 7t, Zither. 8t, Water mill. 9t, Sled. 10t, Drum. 11t, Kraski kos. 12t, Statue of boy on horseback, Ribnica. 20t, Cross-section of house. 44t, Stone building. 50t, Wind-powered pump. 100t, Potica.

1993-94
153 A38   1t multicolored   15
154 A38   2t multicolored   15
155 A38   5t multicolored   15
156 A38   6t multicolored   15
157 A38   7t multicolored   15
158 A38   8t multicolored   16
159 A38   9t multicolored   18
160 A38   10t multicolored   20
160A A38 11t multicolored   20
160B A38 12t multicolored   24
161 A38 20t multicolored   40
162 A38 44t multicolored   1.00
163 A38 50t multicolored   1.00
164 A38 100t multicolored   2.00
    Nos. 153-164 (14)   6.13

Issued: 1t, 6t, 7t, 44t, 2/18/93; 2t, 5t, 10t, 20t, 50t, 5/14/93; 8t, 9t, 8/25/93; 11t, 12t, 7/8/94. See Nos. 212, 214.

Mountain Climbers A39

1993, Feb. 27
165 A39   7t shown   15
166 A39 44t Route map, mountain   1.00

Slovenian Alpine Club, centennial (#165). Joza Cop (1893-1975), mountain climber (#166).

A40   A41

1993, Mar. 19
167 A40 7t multicolored   22

Slovenian Post Office, 75th anniv.

1993, Apr. 9   Litho.   Perf. 14

Designs: 7t, Altarpiece, by Tintoretto. 44t, Coat of arms.

168 A41   7t multicolored   15
169 A41 44t multicolored   1.00

Collegiate Church of Novo Mesto, 500th anniv.

Contemporary Art — A42

Schwagerina Carniolica — A43

Europa: 44t, Round Table of Pompeii, by Marij Pregelj (1913-1967). 159t, Little Girl at Play, by Gabrijel Stupica (1913-1990).

1993, Apr. 29   Litho.   Perf. 14
170 A42   44t multicolored   95
171 A42 159t multicolored   3.25
    a.   Pair, #170-171   4.20

1993, May 7
172 A43 44t multicolored   95

Admission of Slovenia to UN, 1st Anniv. A44

1993, May 21   Litho.   Perf. 14
173 A44 62t multicolored   1.30

Mediterranean Youth Games, Agde, France — A45

1993, June 8
174 A45 36t multicolored   72

Battle of Sisak, 400th Anniv. — A46

1993, June 22   Litho.   Perf. 14
175 A46 49t multicolored   1.00

Aphaenopidius Kamnikensis — A47

Designs: 7t, Monolistra spinosissima. 55t, Proteus anguinus. 65t, Zospeum spelaeum.

1993, July 12   Litho.   Perf. 14
176 A47   7t multicolored   15
177 A47 40t multicolored   78
178 A47 55t multicolored   1.10
179 A47 65t multicolored   1.25

A48   A49

1993, July 30
180 A48 65t multicolored   1.25

World dressage competition.

1993, Oct. 29   Litho.   Perf. 14

Coats of Arms: 9t, Janez Vajkard Valvasor. 65t, Citizen's Academy of Ljubljana.

181 A49   9t multicolored   16
182 A49 65t multicolored   1.25

Christmas A50

Designs: 9t, Slovenian Family Viewing Nativity, by Maxim Gaspari (1883-1980). 65t, Archbishop Joze Pogacnik (1902-80), writer.

1993, Nov. 15
183 A50   9t multicolored   16
184 A50 65t multicolored   1.25

Famous People — A51

Love — A52

Works by: 8t, Josip Jurcic (1844-81), writer. 9t, Simon Gregorcic (1844-1906), poet. 55t, Stanislav Skrabec (1844-1918), linguist. 65t, Jernej Kopitar (1780-1844), linguist.

1994, Jan. 14   Litho.   Perf. 14
185 A51   8t multicolored   15
186 A51   9t multicolored   15
187 A51 55t multicolored   1.00
188 A51 65t multicolored   1.10

1994, Jan. 25
189 A52 9t multicolored   30

1994 Winter Olympics, Lillehammer A53

1994, Feb. 4
190 A53 9t Cross-country skiing   15
191 A53 65t Slalom skiing   1.10
    a.   Pair, #190-191   1.25

World Ski Jumping
Championships,
Planica — A54

1994, Mar. 11   Litho.   *Perf. 14*
192 A54 70t multicolored   *1.25*

City of
Ljubljana,
850th Anniv.
A55

1994, Mar. 25   Litho.   *Perf. 14*
193 A55 9t multicolored   *20*

Europa
A56

Designs: 70t, Janez Puhar, camera. 215t, Moon,
Jurij Vega.

1994, Apr. 22
194 A56   70t multicolored   *1.25*
195 A56 215t multicolored   *3.50*
   a.   Pair, #194-195   *4.75*

Miniature Sheet

Flowers of
Slovenia
A57

Designs: a, 9t, Primula carniolica. b, 44t,
Hladnikia pastinacifolia. c, 60t, Daphne blagayana.
d, 70t, Campanula zoysii.

1994, May 20   Litho.   *Perf. 14*
196 A57   Sheet of 4 + 2 labels   *3.25*

1994 World Cup
Soccer
Championships,
US — A58

1994, June 10
197 A58 44t multicolored   *80*

Intl. Olympic
Committee,
Cent. — A59

1994, June 10
198 A59 100t multicolored   *1.75*

Mt.   Max Pletersnik,
Ojstrica — A60   Professors — A61

1994, July 1   Litho.   *Perf. 14*
199 A60 12t multicolored   *24*

1994, July 22
200 A61 70t multicolored   *1.25*

First Slovenian-German dictionary published by
Max Pletersnik (1840-1932), cent.

Battle of the
Frigidus,
1600th
Anniv.
A62

1994, Sept. 1   Litho.   *Perf. 14*
201 A62 60t multicolored   *1.10*

Maribor Post
Office,
Cent. — A63

1994, Sept. 23   Litho.   *Perf. 14*
202 A63 70t multicolored   *1.25*

Ljubljana-Novo Mesto Railway,
Cent. — A64

1994, Sept. 24   Litho.   *Perf. 14*
203 A64 70t Locomotive 5722, 1893 *1.25*

Philharmonic
Assoc.,
Bicent.
A65

Designs: 12t, Building, Ljubljana. 70t, Beethoven, Brahms, Dvorak, Haydn, Paganini.

1994, Oct. 20
204 A65 12t multicolored   *20*
205 A65 70t multicolored   *1.25*

Black Madonna of
Loreto, 700th
Anniv. — A66

1994, Nov. 18
206 A66 70t multicolored   *1.25*

Christmas — A67   Intl. Year of the
               Family — A68

1994, Nov. 18
207 A67 12t multicolored   *20*

1994, Nov. 18
208 A68 70t multicolored   *1.25*

Type of 1993

Designs: 300t, Slamnati doznjek. 400t, Wine
press.

1994   Litho.   *Perf. 14*
212 A38 300t brown   *4.50*
214 A38 400t brown & lake   *6.00*

Issued: 300t, 400t, 11/7/94.
This is an expanding set. Numbers may change.

Ljubljana
University,
75th
Anniv. — A69

Design: 70t, Provincial palace buildings, founders, I. Hribar, M. Rostohar, D. Majaron.

1994, Dec. 3   Litho.   *Perf. 14*
221 A69 70t multicolored   *1.10*

Postal Service
Emblem — A70

1995, Jan. 27
222 A70 13t multicolored   *22*

Love — A71   Famous
            People — A72

1995, Feb. 7
223 A71 20t multicolored   *32*

1995, Feb. 7

Works by: 20t, Anton Tomaz Linhart (1756-95),
playwrite, horiz. No. 225, Ivan Vurnik (1884-
1971), architect. No. 226, Lili Novy (1885-1958),
poet, horiz.

224 A72 20t multicolored   *32*
225 A72 70t multicolored   *1.10*
226 A72 70t multicolored   *1.10*
   Nos. 224-226 (3)   *2.52*

A73   A74

1995, Mar. 29   Litho.   *Perf. 14*
227 A73 13t multicolored   *22*

End of World War II, 50th anniv.

1995, Mar. 29
228 A74 70t Karavankina schellwieni *1.25*

Liberation of the Concentration Camps,
50th Anniv. — A75

Europa: 60t, Skeleton of Death lying on bride.
70t, Nike going from dark to light.

1995, Mar. 29
229 A75 60t multicolored   *1.10*
230 A75 70t multicolored   *1.25*

Nos. 229-230 were issued in sheets of 4 each.

European Nature Conservation
Year — A76

1995, Mar. 29
231 A76 70t Triglav Natl. Park   *1.25*

POSTAL TAX STAMPS

Catalogue values for unused
stamps in this section are for Never
Hinged items.

Red Cross — PT1

1992, May 8   Litho.   *Perf. 14*
RA1 PT1 3t blue, black & red   *16*

PT2 PT3

1992, June 2   *Perf. 14¹/₂x14*
RA2 PT2 3t multicolored   16
Red Cross, Solidarity.

1992, Sept. 14   **Litho.**   *Perf. 14*
RA3 PT3 3t multicolored   15
Stop Smoking Week, Sept. 14-21.

Red Cross — PT4   Rescue Team — PT5

1993, May 8   **Litho.**   *Perf. 14*
RA4 PT4 3.50t blue, black & red   15

1993, June 1
RA5 PT5 3.50t multicolored   15

Anti-Smoking Campaign — PT6

1993, Sept. 14   **Litho.**   *Perf. 14*
RA6 PT6 4.50t multicolored   15

PT7

1994, May 8   **Litho.**   *Perf. 14*
RA7 PT7 4.50t multicolored   15
Obligatory on mail May 8-15.

Red Cross Worker, Child — PT8

1994, June 1
RA8 PT8 4.50t multicolored   15
Obligatory on mail June 1-7.

SOMALIA
(Somali Democratic Republic)
(Italian Somaliland)
(Benadir)

LOCATION — Eastern Africa, bordering on the Indian Ocean and the Gulf of Aden
GOVT. — Republic
AREA — 246,201 sq. mi.
POP. — 3,862,000 (est. 1982)
CAPITAL — Mogadiscio

The former Italian colony which included the territory west of the Juba River became

known as Oltre Giuba (Trans-Juba), was absorbed into Italian East Africa in 1936. It was under British military administration from 1941-49. Italian trusteeship took effect in 1950, with a UN Advisory Council helping the administrator. On July 1, 1960, the former Italian colony merged with Somaliland Protectorate (British) to form the independent Republic of Somalia.

4 Besas = 1 Anna
16 Annas = 1 Rupee
100 Besas = 1 Rupee (1922)
100 Centesimi = 1 Lira (1905, 1925)
100 Centesimi = 1 Somalo (1950)
100 Centesimi = 1 Somali Shilling (1961)

Catalogue values for unused stamps in this country are for Never Hinged items, beginning with Scott 170 in the regular postage section, Scott B52 in the semi-postal section, Scott C17 in the airpost section, Scott CB11 in the airpost semi-postal section, Scott CE1 in the airpost special delivery section, Scott E8 in the special delivery section, Scott J55 in the postage due section, and Scott Q56 in the parcel post section.

Used values in italics are for postaly used Italian Somalia stamps. CTO's or stamps with fake cancels sell for about the same as unused, hinged stamps.

Watermark

Wmk. 140 - Crown

Italian Somaliland

Elephant — A1   Lion — A2

1903, Oct.   **Typo.**   **Wmk. 140**
                    Perf. 14

1	A1	1b brown	20.00	3.00
2	A1	2b blue green	1.25	1.00
3	A2	1a claret	1.25	1.75
4	A2	2a orange brown	2.50	7.25
5	A2	2¹/₂a blue	1.25	2.50
6	A2	5a orange	2.50	8.50
7	A2	10a lilac	2.50	8.50
		Nos. 1-7 (7)	31.25	32.50

For surcharges see Nos. 8-27, 40-50, 70-77.

Surcharged   **Centesimi 15**

1905, Dec. 29
8	A2	15c on 5a orange	*1,100.*	175.00
9	A2	40c on 10a lilac	175.00	65.00

Surcharged   **C. 2**

1906-07
10	A1	2c on 1b brown	4.50	7.25
11	A1	5c on 2b blue grn	4.50	5.00

Surcharged   **C. ~ 10**

12	A2	10c on 1a claret	4.50	3.50
13	A2	15c on 2a brn org ('06)	4.50	4.00
14	A2	25c on 2¹/₂a blue	7.00	4.00
15	A2	50c on 5a yellow	12.50	8.50

Surcharged   **1 LIRA 1**

16	A2	1 l on 10a lilac	12.50	12.00
		Nos. 10-16 (7)	50.00	44.25

Nos. 15 and 16 with bars over former Surcharge and   **C. 5**

1916, May
18	A2	5c on 50c on 5a yel	12.00	8.50
19	A2	20c on 1 l on 10a dl lil	5.75	6.00

No. 4 Surcharged   **C. ~ 20**

20	A2	20c on 2a org brn	7.25	1.50

Nos. 11-16 Surcharged:

3   **3 6 BESA 6**
a   b

1922, Feb. 1
22	A1(a)	3b on 5c on 2b	5.00	8.50
23	A2(b)	6c on 10c on 1a	5.00	7.25
24	A2(b)	9b on 15c on 2a	5.00	6.00
25	A2(b)	15b on 25c on 2¹/₂a	5.50	7.25
26	A2(b)	30b on 50c on 5a	7.75	12.50
27	A2(b)	60b on 1 l on 10a	9.00	20.00
		Nos. 22-27 (6)	37.25	61.50

Victory Issue

Italy Nos. 136-139   **SOMALIA ITALIANA**
Surcharged   **BESA 3**

1922, Apr.
28	A64	3b on 5c olive grn	35	2.00
29	A64	6b on 10c red	35	2.00
30	A64	9b on 15c slate grn	60	3.00
31	A64	15b on 25c ultra	60	3.00

Nos. 10-16 Surcharged with Bars and

2   **2 5 BESA 5**
c   d

1923, July 1
40	A1	1b brown	3.75	7.25
41	A1(c)	2b on 2c on 1b	3.75	7.25
42	A1(c)	3b on 2c on 1b	3.75	7.25
43	A2(d)	5b on 50c on 5a	3.75	6.00
44	A1(c)	6b on 5c on 2b	5.75	3.50
45	A2(d)	18b on 10c on 1a	5.75	3.50
46	A2(d)	20b on 15c on 2a	6.75	5.00
47	A2(d)	25b on 15c on 2a	6.75	5.00
48	A2(d)	30b on 25c on 2¹/₂a	8.75	6.75
49	A2(d)	60b on 1 l on 10a	10.50	14.00
50	A2(d)	1r on 1 l on 10a	12.50	20.00
		Nos. 40-50 (11)	71.75	85.50

No. 40 is No. 10 with bars over the 1907 surcharge.

Propagation of the Faith Issue
Italy Nos. 143-146 Surcharged

SOMALIA ITALIANA
besa 6

1923, Oct. 24   **Wmk. 140**
51	A68	6b on 20c ol grn & brn org	1.25	5.50
52	A68	13b on 30c cl & brn org	1.25	5.50
53	A68	20b on 50c vio & brn org	1.00	4.50
54	A68	30b on 1 l bl & brn org	1.00	4.50

Fascisti Issue

Italy Nos. 159-164   **SOMALIA ITALIANA**
Surcharged in Red or Black   **BESA 30**

1923, Oct. 29   **Unwmk.**   *Perf. 14*
55	A69	3b on 10c dk grn (R)	1.65	5.00
56	A69	13b on 30c dk vio (R)	1.65	5.00
57	A69	20b on 50c brn car	1.65	5.00

Wmk. 140
58	A70	30b on 1 l blue	1.65	5.00
59	A70	1r on 2 l brown	1.65	5.00
60	A71	3r on 5 l blk & bl (R)	2.75	10.00
		Nos. 55-60 (6)	11.00	35.00

Manzoni Issue
Italy Nos. 165-170 Surcharged in Red

SOMALIA ITALIANA
besa 9

1924, Apr. 1
61	A72	6b on 10c brn red & blk	70	5.00
62	A72	9b on 15c bl grn & blk	70	5.00
63	A72	13b on 30c blk & sl	70	5.00
64	A72	20b on 50c org brn & blk	70	5.00

Surcharged

SOMALIA ITALIANA   **rupie 3**

65	A72	30b on 1 l bl & blk	8.75	55.50
66	A72	3r on 5 l vio & blk	200.00	750.00
		Nos. 61-66 (6)	211.55	825.50

Victor Emmanuel Issue

Italy Nos. 175-177   **SOMALIA**
Overprinted   **ITALIANA**

1925-26   **Unwmk.**   *Perf. 13¹/₂*
67	A78	60c brown carmine	25	2.00
a.		Perf. 11	8.50	35.00
68	A78	1 l dk bl, perf. 11	40	2.00
a.		Perf. 13¹/₂	1.75	14.00
69	A78	1.25 l dk blue ('26)	35	6.00
a.		Perf. 11	85.00	200.00

Stamps of 1907-16 with Bars over Original Values

1926, Mar. 1   **Wmk. 140**   *Perf. 14*
70	A1	2c on 1b brown	10.00	17.00
71	A1	5c on 2b blue grn	9.00	12.50
72	A2	10c on 1a rose red	4.00	2.75
73	A2	15c on 2a org brn	4.00	3.50
74	A2	20c on 2a org brn	5.00	4.00
75	A2	25c on 2¹/₂a blue	5.00	5.00
76	A2	50c on 5a yellow	6.00	10.00
77	A2	1 l on 10a dull lil	6.50	12.50
		Nos. 70-77 (8)	49.50	67.25

Saint Francis of Assisi Issue

Italy Nos. 178-180   **SOMALIA ITALIAN/**
Overprinted

1926, Apr. 12   *Perf. 14*
78	A79	20c gray green	90	3.00
79	A80	40c dark violet	90	3.00
80	A81	60c red brown	90	3.00

Italy No. 182 and Type of 1926 Overprinted in Red   **Somalia**

		Unwmk.		*Perf. 11*
81	A82	1.25 l dark blue	90	3.00
				Perf. 14
82	A83	5 l + 2.50 l ol grn	2.25	5.50
		Nos. 78-82 (5)	5.85	17.50

Italian Stamps of 1901-26   **SOMALIA**
Overprinted   **ITALIANA**

1926-30   **Wmk. 140**
83	A43	2c orange brown	1.40	1.50
84	A48	5c green	1.65	1.50
85	A48	10c claret	55	30
86	A49	20c violet brown	80	42
87	A49	25c grn & pale grn	50	24
88	A49	30c gray ('30)	3.50	4.00
89	A49	60c brown orange	80	70
90	A46	75c dk red & rose	26.00	3.50
91	A46	1 l brown & green	1.00	35
92	A46	1.25 l blue & ultra	2.25	85
93	A46	2 l dk green & org	3.50	1.50
94	A46	2.50 l dk green & org	4.00	2.00

95	A46	5 l blue & rose	18.00	7.25
96	A51	10 l gray grn & red	18.00	8.50
		Nos. 83-96 (14)	81.95	32.61

Volta Issue
Type of Italy, 1927, Overprinted   **Somalia Italiana**

1927, Oct. 10

97	A84	20c purple	2.75	7.25
98	A84	50c deep orange	3.50	5.00
a.		Double overprint	12.50	
99	A84	1.25 l brt blue	4.00	7.25

Italian Stamps of 1927-28   **SOMALIA ITALIANA**
Overprinted in Black or Red

1928-30

100	A86	7½c lt brown	7.25	12.50
a.		Double overprint	85.00	
101	A85	50c brn & sl (R)	5.00	3.50
102	A86	50c brt violet ('30)	12.50	12.50

Perf. 11
Unwmk.

103	A85	1.75 l deep brown	12.50	6.00

Monte Cassino Issue
Types of Monte Cassino Issue of Italy Overprinted in Red or Blue   **SOMALIA ITALIANA**

1929, Oct. 14   Wmk. 140   Perf. 14

104	A96	20c dk green (R)	1.90	5.00
105	A96	25c red org (Bl)	1.90	5.00
106	A98	50c + 10c crim (Bl)	1.90	7.25
107	A98	75c + 15c ol brn (R)	1.90	7.25
108	A96	1.25 l + 25c dk vio (R)	3.25	7.25
109	A98	5 l + 1 l saph (R)	3.25	7.25

Overprinted in Red   **Somalia Italiana**

Unwmk.

110	A100	10 l + 2 l gray brn	2.75	10.00
		Nos. 104-110 (7)	16.85	49.00

Royal Wedding Issue
Type of Italian Royal Wedding Stamps of 1930 Overprinted   **SOMALIA ITALIANA**

1930, Mar. 17   Wmk. 140

111	A101	20c yellow green	50	2.00
112	A101	50c + 10c dp org	35	2.50
113	A101	1.25 l + 25c rose red	35	3.00

Ferrucci Issue
Types of Italian Stamps of 1930 Overprinted in Red or Blue   **SOMALIA ITALIANA**

1930, July 26

114	A102	20c violet (R)	35	1.50
115	A103	25c dark green (R)	35	1.50
116	A103	50c black (R)	35	1.50
117	A103	1.25 l deep blue (R)	35	1.50
118	A104	5 l + 2 l dp car (bl)	1.50	3.00
		Nos. 114-118 (5)	2.90	9.00

Virgil Issue
Types of Italian Stamps of 1930 Overprinted in Red or Blue

SOMALIA

1930, Dec. 4   Photo.   Wmk. 140

119	A106	15c violet blue	35	1.50
120	A106	20c orange brown	35	1.50
121	A106	25c dark green	35	1.25
122	A106	30c lt brown	35	1.50
123	A106	50c dull violet	35	1.25
124	A106	75c rose red	35	1.50
125	A106	1.25 l gray blue	35	1.50

Engr.
Unwmk.

126	A106	5 l + 1.50 l dk vio	1.65	6.00
127	A106	10 l + 2.50 l ol brn	1.65	6.00
		Nos. 119-127 (9)	5.75	

Saint Anthony of Padua Issue
Types of Italian Stamps of 1931
Overprinted in Blue or Red

SOMALIA

1931, May 7   Photo.   Wmk. 140

129	A116	20c brown (Bl)	70	2.00
130	A116	25c green (R)	70	2.00
131	A118	30c gray brn (Bl)	70	2.00
132	A118	50c dull vio (Bl)	70	1.50
133	A120	1.25 l slate bl (R)	70	2.00

Overprinted in Red or Black   **Somalia**

Engr.   Unwmk.

134	A121	75c black (R)	70	2.00
135	A122	5 l + 2.50 l dk brn (Bk)	2.00	7.25
		Nos. 129-135 (7)	6.20	

Italy Nos. 218, 221   **SOMALIA ITALIANA**
Overprinted in Red

1931   Wmk. 140

136	A94	25c dk green (R)	2.50	2.50
137	A95	50c purple (R)	4.50	1.00

Lighthouse at Cape Guardafui — A3

Tower at Mnara Ciromo — A4

Governor's Palace at Mogadishu — A5

Termite Nest — A6

Ostrich — A7

Hippopotamus — A8

Greater Kudu — A9

Lion — A10

1932   Wmk. 140   Photo.   Perf. 12

138	A3	5c deep brown	1.25	60
139	A3	7½c violet	1.50	3.50
140	A3	10c gray black	2.00	30
141	A3	15c olive green	70	30
142	A4	20c carmine	18.00	20
143	A4	25c deep green	70	15
144	A4	30c dark brown	2.50	30
145	A5	35c dark blue	2.00	1.65
146	A5	50c violet	27.50	15
147	A5	75c carmine	85	42
148	A6	1.25 l dark blue	85	42
149	A6	1.75 l red orange	1.25	35
150	A6	2 l carmine	70	42
151	A7	2.55 l indigo	25	14.00
152	A7	5 l carmine	3.00	1.10
153	A8	10 l violet	7.25	5.00
154	A9	20 l dark green	17.00	17.00
155	A10	25 l dark blue	25.00	25.00
		Nos. 138-155 (18)	119.30	70.79

1934-37   Perf. 14

138a	A3	5c deep brown	15	15
139a	A3	7½c violet	1	1.00
140a	A3	10c gray black	15	15
141a	A3	15c olive green	15	24

142a	A4	20c carmine	15	15
143a	A4	25c deep green	15	15
144a	A4	30c dark brown	24	24
145a	A5	35c dark blue	50	1.25
146a	A5	50c violet	2.50	15
147a	A5	75c carmine	85	20
148a	A6	1.25 l dark blue	6.00	30
149a	A6	1.75 l red orange	20.00	24
150a	A6	2 l carmine	7.25	30
151a	A7	2.55 l indigo	100.00	85.00
152a	A7	5 l carmine	1.50	85
153a	A8	10 l violet	35.00	12.50
154a	A9	20 l dark green	4,000.	275.00
155a	A10	25 l dark blue	100.00	100.00
		Nos. 138a-153a,155a (17)	274.74	202.87

Eleven denominations in the foregoing series exist perf. 12x14 or 14x12.

Types of 1932 Issue Overprinted in Black or Red   **ONORANZE AL DUCA DEGLI ABRUZZI**

1934, May   Perf. 14

156	A3	10c brown (Bk)	2.00	4.50
157	A4	25c green	2.00	4.50
158	A5	50c dull vio (Bk)	2.00	4.50
159	A6	1.25 l blue	2.00	4.50
160	A7	5 l brown black	3.00	5.00
161	A8	10 l car rose (Bk)	3.00	5.00
162	A9	20 l dull blue	3.00	5.00
163	A10	25 l dark green	3.00	5.00
		Nos. 156-163 (8)	20.00	38.00

Duke of the Abruzzi (Luigi Amadeo, 1873-1933).

Mother and Child — A11

1934, Oct.

164	A11	5c ol grn & brn	1.00	4.00
165	A11	10c yellow brn & blk	1.00	4.00
166	A11	20c scarlet & blk	1.00	4.00
167	A11	50c dk violet & brn	1.00	4.00
168	A11	60c org brn & blk	1.00	4.00
169	A11	1.25 l dk blue & grn	1.00	4.00
		Nos. 164-169 (6)	6.00	24.00

Second Colonial Arts Exhibition, Naples.

> Catalogue values for unused stamps in this section, from this point to the end of the section, are for Never Hinged items.

Somalia

Tower at Mnara Ciromo — A12

Governor's Palace, Mogadishu — A13

Design: 5c, 20c, 60c, Ostrich.

Wmk. 277

1950, Mar. 24   Photo.   Perf. 14

170	A12	1c gray black	15	15
171	A12	5c carmine rose	15	15
172	A13	6c violet	15	15
173	A12	8c Prus green	15	15
174	A13	10c dark green	15	15
175	A12	20c blue green	15	15
176	A13	35c red	20	20
177	A13	55c brt blue	25	15
178	A12	60c purple	32	15
179	A13	65c brown	42	15
180	A13	1s deep orange	65	15
		Nos. 170-180,E8-E9 (13)	4.39	
		Set value		3.00

Council in Session A14

1951, Oct. 4

181	A14	20c dk green & brn	1.65	24
182	A14	55c brown & violet	3.25	3.00

Meeting of First Territorial Council. See Nos. C27A-C27B.

Somali Tiger, Palm Tree and Minaret — A16

Mother and Child — A17

1952, Sept. 14   Wmk. 277   Perf. 14

185	A16	25c red & dk brown	1.25	1.75
186	A16	55c blue & dk brown	1.25	1.75

1st Somali Fair, Mogadishu, Sept. 14-28. See No. C28.

1953, May 27

Center in Dark Brown

187	A17	5c rose violet	15	15
188	A17	25c rose	15	15
189	A17	50c blue	50	70

Anti-tuberculosis campaign. See No. C29.

Laborer at Fair Entrance A18

1953, Sept. 28   Unwmk.   Perf. 11½

190	A18	25c dk green & gray	15	24
191	A18	60c blue & gray	32	50

2nd Somali Fair, Mogadishu, Sept. 28-Oct. 12. See Nos. C30-C31.

Map and Stamps of 1903 A19

Perf. 13x13½

1953, Dec. 16   Engr.   Wmk. 277
"Stamps" in Brown and Rose Carmine

192	A19	25c deep magenta	15	24
193	A19	35c dark green	15	24
194	A19	60c orange	15	24
		Nos. 192-194,C32-C33 (5)	1.09	1.72

50th anniv. of the 1st Somali postage stamps.

Somalia Brushwood — A20

Perf. 12½x13½

1954, June 1   Photo.   Unwmk.

195	A20	25c dp blue & dk gray	20	30
196	A20	60c orange brn & brown	20	32

Convention of Nov. 11, 1953, with the Sovereign Military Order of Malta, providing for the care of lepers. See Nos. C37-C38.

Somali Flag
A21

Adenium
Somalense
A22

Perf. 13¹/₂x13

1954, Oct. 12   Litho.   Wmk. 277
197 A21 25c blk, grn, bl, red & yel   20 30

Adoption of a Somali flag. See No. C39.

1955, Feb.   Photo.   Perf. 13

Flowers: 5c, Haemanthus multiflorus martyn.
10c, Grinum scabrum. 25c, Poinciana elata. 60c,
Calatropis procera. 1s, Pancratium. 1.20s,
Sesamothamnus bussernus.

198 A22	1c bl, dp rose & dk ol brn		15	15
199 A22	5c bl, rose lil & grn		15	15
200 A22	10c lilac & green		20	15
201 A22	25c vio brn, yel & grn		32	18
202 A22	60c blk, car & grn		15	18
203 A22	1s red brn & grn		15	22
204 A22	1.20s dk brn, yel & grn		15	22
	Set value		1.00	1.15

See Nos. 216-220, E10-E11. For overprint see
No. 242.

Weaver at
Loom — A23

Design: 30c, Cattle fording stream.

Perf. 13¹/₂x14
1955, Sept. 24   Wmk. 303
205 A23 25c dark brown   20 30
206 A23 30c dark green   20 30

3rd Somali Fair, Mogadishu, Sept. 1955. See
Nos. C46-C47.

Casting
Ballots — A24

Arms of
Somalia — A25

1956, Apr. 30   Perf. 14
207 A24 5c brown & gray grn   15 15
208 A24 10c brown & ol bis   15 15
209 A24 25c brown & brn red   15 15
         Set value, #207-209,
         C48-C49   48 70

Opening of the territory's first democratically
elected Legislative Assembly.

1957, May 6   Wmk. 303   Perf. 13¹/₂
**Coat of Arms in Dull Yellow, Blue and
Black**

210 A25 5c lt red brown   15 15
211 A25 25c carmine   15 18
212 A25 60c bluish violet   15 18
         Set value, #210-212,
         C50-C51   58 88

Issued in honor of the new coat of arms.

Dam at
Falcheiro
A26

Designs: 10c, Juba River Bridge. 25c, Silos at
Margherita.

1957, Sept. 28   Photo.   Perf. 14
213 A26 5c brown & purple   15 15
214 A26 10c bister & bl grn   15 15
215 A26 25c carmine & blue   15 15
         Set value, #213-215,
         C52-C53   62 88

Fourth Somali Fair and Film Festival.

Flower Type of 1955

Flowers: 1c, Adenium Somalense. 10c, Grinum
scabrum. 15c, Adansonia digitata. 25c, Poinciana
elata. 50c, Gloriosa virescens.

1956-59   Wmk. 303   Photo.   Perf. 13
216 A22 1c bl, dp rose & dk ol brn   15 15
217 A22 10c lil, grn & yel ('59)   15 15
218 A22 15c red, grn & yel ('58)   15 20
219 A22 25c dull lil, grn & yel ('59)   15 15
220 A22 50c bl, grn, red & yel ('58)   20 30
         Set value   60

Runner — A27

Soccer
Player — A28

Designs: 5c, Discus thrower. 6c, Motorcyclist.
8c, Fencer. 10c, Archer. 25c, Boxers.

1958, Apr. 28   Wmk. 303   Perf. 14
221 A27 2c violet   15 15
222 A28 4c green   15 15
223 A27 5c vermilion   15 15
224 A28 6c gray   15 15
225 A27 8c violet blue   15 15
226 A28 10c orange   15 15
227 A28 25c dark green   15 15
         Set value, #221-227,
         C54-C56   80 1.05

Book and Assembly
Palace — A29

White Stork — A30

1959, June 19
228 A29 5c green & ultra   15 15
229 A29 25c ocher & ultra   15 15
         Set value   20

Opening of Somalia's Constituent Assembly.
See Nos. C59-C60 and souvenir sheet No. C60a.

1959, Sept. 4   Photo.   Perf. 14

Birds: 10c, Saddle-billed stork. 15c, Sacred ibis.
25c, Pink-backed pelican.

230 A30 5c yellow, blk & red   15 15
231 A30 10c brown, red & yel   15 15
232 A30 15c orange & black   15 15
233 A30 25c dk car, blk & org   15 15
         Set value, #230-233,
         C61-C62   66 98

Incense
Bush — A31

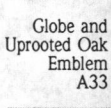

Arms of University
Institute — A32

Design: 60c, Girl burning incense.

1959, Sept. 28   Wmk. 303
234 A31 20c orange & black   15 15
235 A31 60c blk, org & dk red   15 22
         Set value   24

5th Somali Fair, Mogadishu. See Nos. C63-C64.

1960, Jan. 14   Photo.   Perf. 14

Designs: 50c, Map of Africa and arms, horiz.
80c, Arms of University Institute.

236 A32 5c brown & salmon   15 15
237 A32 50c lt vio bl, brn & blk   15 15
238 A32 80c brt red & blk   24 24
         Nos. 236-238,C65-C66 (5)   1.13 1.13

Opening of the University Institute of Somalia.

Globe and
Uprooted Oak
Emblem
A33

Palm — A34

Design: 60c, Like 10c but with inscription and
emblem rearranged.

1960, Apr. 7   Perf. 14
239 A33 10c yel brn, grn & blk   15 15
240 A33 60c dp bister & blk   15 15
241 A34 80c pink, grn & blk   15 15
         Set value   24 28

World Refugee Year, July 1, 1959-June 30, 1960.
See No. C67.

Republic

Somaliland

No. 217 Overprinted **Independence**
26 June 1960

Wmk. 303
1960, June 26   Photo.   Perf. 13
242 A22 10c lilac, grn & yel   6.00 6.50

Independence of British Somaliland, which
became part of the Republic of Somalia. See Nos.
C68-C69

Gazelle and Map of
Africa — A36

Design: 25c, New York skyline, UN Building and
UN flag.

1960, July 1   Perf. 14
243 A36 5c lilac & brown   15 15
244 A36 25c blue   15 15
         Set value   20

Somalia independence. See Nos. C70-C71.

Boy Drawing
Giraffe — A37

1960, Nov. 24
245 A37 10c shown   15 15
246 A37 15c Zebra   15 15
247 A37 25c Black rhinoceros   15 15
         Set value   24 18

See No. C72.

Olympic Torch,
Somalia Flag — A38

Girl Harvesting
Papaya — A39

Designs: 10c, Runners, flag and Olympic rings.

1960   Wmk. 303   Perf. 14
248 A38 5c green & blue   15 15
249 A38 10c yellow & blue   15 15
         Set value   16 15

17th Olympic Games, Rome, Aug. 25-Sept. 11.
See Nos. C73-C74.

1961, July 5   Photo.

Girl harvesting: 10c, Durrah (sorghum). 20c,
Cotton. 25c, Sesame. 40c, Sugar cane. 50c,
Bananas. 75c, Peanuts, horiz. 80c, Grapefruit,
horiz.

250 A39 5c multicolored   15 15
251 A39 10c multicolored   15 15
252 A39 20c multicolored   15 15
253 A39 25c multicolored   15 15
254 A39 40c multicolored   15 15
255 A39 50c multicolored   15 15
256 A39 75c multicolored   20 15
257 A39 80c multicolored   32 15
         Set value   1.00 55

Shield, Bow and
Quiver
A40

Pomacanthus
Semicirculatus
A41

Design: 45c, Pottery and incense jug.

1961, Sept. 28
258 A40 25c blk, car & ocher   15 15
259 A40 45c blk, bl grn & ocher   15 15
         Set value   20 16

6th Somali Fair, Mogadishu. See Nos. C82-C83.

1962, Apr. 26   Photo.

Fish: 15c, Girl embroidering fish on cloth. 40c,
Novaculichthys taeniorus.

260 A41 15c brown, blk & pink   15 15
261 A41 25c orange, blk & ultra   15 15
262 A41 40c green, blk & rose   28 15
         Set value   48 30

See No. C84.

Mosquito
Trapped by
Sprays — A42

Design: 25c, Man with spray gun and malaria eradication emblem, vert.

1962, Oct. 25   Wmk. 303   Perf. 14
263 A42 10c orange red & grn   15 15
264 A42 25c rose lilac, brn & blk   15 15
        Set value   20 16

WHO drive to eradicate malaria. See Nos. C85-C86.

Police
Auxiliary
Woman
A43

Designs: 10c, Army auxiliary woman. 25c, Radio police car. 75c, First aid army auxiliary, vert.

1963, May 15   Wmk. 303   Perf. 14
265 A43 5c multicolored   15 15
266 A43 10c black & orange   15 15
267 A43 25c multicolored   15 15
268 A43 75c multicolored   24 15
        Set value, #265-268,
        C87-C88   1.40 65

Women's auxiliary forces.

Carved Fork
and Spoon and
Wheat
Emblem
A44

1963, June 25   Photo.
269 A44 75c green & red brown   20 15

FAO "Freedom from Hunger" campaign. See No. C89.

Pres. Aden Abdulla
Osman — A45

1963, Sept. 15   Wmk. 303   Perf. 14
270 A45 25c bl, dk brn, org & lt bl   20 15

3rd anniv. of independence. See Nos. C90-C91.

Dunes
Theater
A46

Design: 55c, African Merchants' and Artisans' Exhibit.

1963, Sept. 28   Photo.
271 A46 25c blue green   15 15
272 A46 55c carmine rose   15 15
        Set value   20

7th Somali Fair, Mogadishu. See No. C92.

Somali Credit
Bank Building
A47

1964, May 16   Wmk. 303   Perf. 14
273 A47 60c indigo, red lil & yel   28 15

10th anniv. of the Somali Credit Bank. See Nos. C93-C94.

Running — A48   ITU Emblem and
                       Map of
                       Africa — A50

DC-3 — A49

1964, Oct. 10   Wmk. 303   Perf. 14
274 A48 10c shown   15 15
275 A48 25c High jump   15 15
        Set value   20 16

18th Olympic Games, Tokyo, Oct. 10-25. See Nos. C95-C96.

1964, Nov. 8   Photo.   Perf. 14

Design: 20c, Passengers leaving DC-3.

276 A49 5c dk blue & lil rose   15 15
277 A49 20c blue & orange   32 15
        Set value   40 15

Establishment of Somali Air Lines. See Nos. C97-C98.

1965, May 17   Wmk. 303   Perf. 14
278 A50 25c dp blue & dp org   20 15

ITU, centenary. See Nos. C99-C100.

Tanning
Industry
A51

Designs: 25c, Meat industry; cannery and cattle. 35c, Fishing industry; cannery and fishing boats.

1965, Sept. 28   Photo.   Perf. 14
279 A51 10c sepia & buff   15 15
280 A51 25c sepia & pink   15 15
281 A51 35c sepia & lt blue   15 15
        Nos. 279-281,C101-C102 (5)   1.60
        Set value   60

8th Somali Fair, Mogadishu.

Hottentot Fig
and Gazelle
A52

Designs: 60c, African tulip and giraffes. 1sh, Ninfea and flamingos. 1.30sh, Pervincia and ostriches. 1.80sh, Bignonia and zebras.

1965, Nov. 1   Wmk. 303   Perf. 14
Flowers in Natural Colors
282 A52 20c blk & brt bl   15 15
283 A52 60c blk & dk gray   15 15
284 A52 1sh blk, sl grn & ol grn   24 15
285 A52 1.30sh blk & dp grn   50 15
286 A52 1.80sh blk & brt bl   70 24
        Nos. 282-286 (5)   1.74
        Set value   64

Narina's
Trogon
A53

Birds: 35c, Bateleur eagle, vert. 50c, Vulture. 1.30sh, European roller. 2sh, Vulturine guinea fowl, vert.

1966, June 1   Photo.   Wmk. 303
287 A53 25c multicolored   15 15
288 A53 35c brt blue & multi   15 15
289 A53 50c multicolored   15 15
290 A53 1.30sh multicolored   32 20
291 A53 2sh multicolored   50 24
        Set value   1.10 66

Globe and UN
Emblem — A54

UN emblem and: 1sh, Map of Africa. 1.50sh, Map of Somalia.

1966, Oct. 24   Litho.   Perf. 13x12 1/2
292 A54 35c bl, pur & brt bl   15 15
293 A54 1sh brn, yel & brick red   15 15
294 A54 1.50sh grn, blk, bl & yel   28 28
        Set value   50 50

21st anniversary of United Nations.

Woman
Sitting on
Crocodile
A55

Paintings: 1sh, Woman and warrior. 1.50sh, Boy leading camel. 2sh, Women pounding grain.

Wmk. 303
1966, Dec. 1   Photo.   Perf. 14
295 A55 25c multicolored   15 15
296 A55 1sh multicolored   15 15
297 A55 1.50sh multicolored   20 15
298 A55 2sh multicolored   24 20
        Set value   64 52

Somali art, exhibited in the Garesa Museum, Mogadishu.

UNESCO
Emblem
A56

1966, Dec. 20   Wmk. 303   Perf. 14
299 A56 35c blk, dk red & gray   15 15
300 A56 1sh blk, emer & yel   15 15
301 A56 1.80sh blk, ultra & red   28 24
        Set value   48 44

UNESCO, 20th anniv.

Haggard's   Dancers — A58
Oribi — A57

Gazelles: 60c, Long-snouted dik-dik. 1sh, Gerenuk. 1.80sh, Soemmering's gazelle.

1967, Feb. 20   Photo.   Perf. 14
302 A57 35c blk, ultra & bis   15 15
303 A57 60c blk, org & brn   15 15
304 A57 1sh blk, red & brn   15 15
305 A57 1.80sh blk, yel grn & brn   28 24
        Set value   55 52

Unwmk.
1967, July 15   Litho.   Perf. 13

Designs: Various Folk Dances.

306 A58 25c multicolored   15 15
307 A58 50c multicolored   15 15
308 A58 1.30sh multicolored   20 20
309 A58 2sh multicolored   24 24
        Set value   60 60

Boy Scout Giving
Sign — A59

Designs: 50c, Boy Scouts with flags. 1sh, Boy Scout cooking and tent. 1.80sh, Jamboree emblem.

1967, Aug. 15
310 A59 35c multicolored   15 15
311 A59 50c multicolored   15 15
312 A59 1sh multicolored   24 15
313 A59 1.80sh multicolored   52 32
        Set value   92 60

12th Boy Scout World Jamboree, Farragut State Park, Idaho, Aug. 1-9.

Pres.
Abdirascid Ali
Scermarche
and King
Faisal — A60

Designs: 1sh, Clasped hands, flags of Somalia and Saudi Arabia.

Wmk. 303
1967, Sept. 21   Photo.   Perf. 14
314 A60 50c black & lt blue   15 15
315 A60 1sh multicolored   15 15
        Set value   22 20

Visit of King Faisal of Saudi Arabia. See No. C103.

Gaterin
Gaterinus — A61

Tropical Fish: 50c, Chaetodon semilar-vatus. 1sh, Priacanthus hamrur. 1.80sh, Epinephelus summana.

1967, Nov. 15   Litho.   Perf. 14
316 A61 35c dk bl, yel & blk   15 15
317 A61 50c brt bl, ocher & blk   15 15
318 A61 1sh emer, org, brn & blk   24 15
319 A61 1.80sh pur, yel & blk   50 42
                                       90 72

Physician Treating Infant — A62

Waterbuck — A64

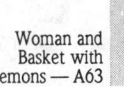

Woman and Basket with Lemons — A63

WHO, 20th anniv.: 1sh, Physician examining boy, and nurse. 1.80sh, Physician and nurse treating patient.

Wmk. 303

1968, Mar. 20   Photo.   Perf. 14

320	A62	35c blk, scar, bl & brn	15	15
321	A62	1sh blk, grn & brn	15	15
322	A62	1.80sh blk, org & brn	32	24
		Set value	52	44

1968   Litho.   Perf. 11½

Designs: 10c, Oranges. 25c, Coconuts. 35c, Papayas. 40c, Limes. 50c, Grapefruit. 1sh, Bananas. 1.30sh, Cotton bolls. 1.80sh, Speke's gazelle. 2sh, Lesser kudu. 5sh, Hunter's hartebeest. 10sh, Clark's gazelle (dibatag).

323	A63	5c lt blue & multi	15	15
324	A63	10c yellow & multi	15	15
325	A63	25c lt lilac & multi	15	15
326	A63	35c salmon & multi	15	15
327	A63	40c buff & multi	15	15
328	A63	50c multicolored	15	15
329	A63	1sh lt blue & multi	15	15
330	A63	1.30sh gray & multi	24	24
331	A64	1.80sh lt blue & multi	20	15
332	A64	1.80sh multicolored	28	24
333	A64	2sh pink & multi	32	24
334	A64	5sh multicolored	1.00	80
335	A64	10sh multicolored	2.75	1.25
		Nos. 323-335 (13)	5.84	
		Set value		3.40

Issue dates: Nos. 323-330, Apr. 25; Nos. 331-335, May 10.

Javelin A65

Statuette A66

Wmk. 303

1968, Oct. 12   Photo.   Perf. 14

336	A65	35c shown	15	15
337	A65	50c Running	15	15
338	A65	80c High jump	15	15
339	A65	1.50sh Basketball	24	15
a.		Souvenir sheet of 4, #336-339	70	60
		Set value	52	38

19th Olympic Games, Mexico City, Oct. 12-27. No. 339a sold for 3.65sh.

Perf. 11½x12

1968, Dec. 1   Litho.   Unwmk.

Statuettes: 25c, Woman grinding grain. 35c, Woman potter. 2.80sh, Woman mat maker.

340	A66	25c rose lil, blk & brn	15	15
341	A66	35c brick red, blk & brn	15	15
342	A66	2.80sh green, blk & brn	52	35
		Set value	68	48

Cornflower and Rhinoceros — A67

Flowers: 80c, Sunflower and elephant. 1sh, Oleander and antelopes. 1.80sh, Chrysanthemums and storks.

Perf. 13x12½

1969, Mar. 25   Litho.   Unwmk.

343	A67	40c red & multi	15	15
344	A67	80c violet & multi	15	15
345	A67	1sh blue & multi	15	15
346	A67	1.80sh yellow & multi	28	24
		Set value	62	52

ILO Emblem and Blacksmiths A68

Designs: 1sh, Oxdrawn plow. 1.80sh, Drawing water from well.

Wmk. 303

1969, May 10   Photo.   Perf. 14

347	A68	25c dk red, dp bis & blk	15	15
348	A68	1sh car rose, brn & blk	15	15
349	A68	1.80sh multicolored	28	24
		Set value	50	40

ILO, 50th anniversary.

GANDHI CENTENARY
1869   1969

Mahatma Gandhi — A69

Designs: 1.50sh, Gandhi, globe and hands releasing dove, horiz. 1.80sh, Gandhi seated.

Unwmk.

1969, Oct. 2   Photo.   Perf. 13
Size: 25x35½mm

350	A69	35c brown violet	15	15

Perf. 14½x14
Size: 37½x20mm

351	A69	1.50sh bister brn	20	20

Perf. 13
Size: 25x35½mm

352	A69	1.80sh olive gray	24	24

Mohandas K. Gandhi (1869-1948), leader in India's fight for independence.

1970

US Space Explorations. Set of seven. 60, 80c, 1, 1.50, 1.80, 2, 2.80sh. Souv. sheet, 14sh, issued Feb. 14. Nos. 7001-7008.

Nivprale Vevanes A70

Butterflies: 50c, Leschenault. 1.50sh, Papilio (ornytoptera) aeacus. 2sh, Urania riphaeus.

Perf. 12½x13

1970, Mar. 25   Litho.   Unwmk.

353	A70	25c multicolored	15	15
354	A70	50c multicolored	15	15
355	A70	1.50sh orange & multi	20	20
356	A70	2sh yellow & multi	28	28
		Set value	64	64

Somali Democratic Republic

Lenin Addressing Crowd — A71

Designs: 25c, Lenin walking with children. 1.80sh, Lenin in his study, horiz.

Perf. 12x12½, 12½x12

1970, Apr. 22   Litho.   Unwmk.

357	A71	25c multicolored	15	15
358	A71	1sh multicolored	20	15
359	A71	1.80sh multicolored	22	18
		Set value	50	36

Lenin (1870-1924), Russian communist leader.

Bird Feeding Young — A72

Designs: 35c, Monument and Battle of Dagahtur. 1sh, Arms of Somalia and UN emblem, vert. 2.80sh, Boy milking camel, and star, vert.

Perf. 14x13½, 13½x14

1970, July 28   Photo.   Wmk. 303

360	A72	25c blue & multi	15	15
361	A72	35c slate & multi	15	15
362	A72	1sh violet & multi	20	20
363	A72	2.80sh blue & multi	65	50
		Set value	1.00	85

10th anniversary of independence.

"Agriculture" A73

Designs: 40c, Soldier and flag. 1sh, Hand on open book. 1.80sh, Grain, scales of justice and dove.

Perf. 14x13½

1970, Oct. 21   Photo.   Wmk. 303

364	A73	35c green & multi	15	15
365	A73	40c ultra & blk	15	15
366	A73	1sh red brown & blk	20	15
367	A73	1.80sh multicolored	42	22
		Set value	78	50

First anniversary of Oct. 21st Revolution.

Snake Strangling Black Man, Map of South Africa — A74

Design: 1.80sh, Concentration camp and symbols of justice holding scales.

Perf. 14x13½

1971, June 20   Photo.   Wmk. 303

368	A74	1.30sh multicolored	30	20
369	A74	1.80sh gray, red & blk	45	32

Against racial discrimination in South Africa.

Waves A75

Design: 2.80sh, Waves and globe.

1971, June 30

370	A75	25c black & blue	15	15
371	A75	2.80sh blk, grn & bl	60	42
		Set value		48

3rd World Telecommunications Day, May 17.

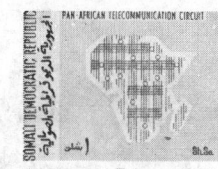

Map of Africa and Telecommunications System — A76

Design: 1.50sh, Map of Africa and telecommunications system (different design).

1971, July 25

372	A76	1sh blk, lt bl & grn	20	15
373	A76	1.50sh black & yellow	32	25

Pan-African Telecommunications system.

White Rhinoceros A77

Wild Animals: 1sh, Cheetahs. 1.30sh, Zebras. 1.80sh, Lion attacking camel.

1971, Aug. 25

374	A77	35c ocher & multi	15	15
375	A77	1sh violet & multi	22	15
376	A77	1.30sh violet & multi	42	18
377	A77	1.80sh multicolored	52	25

Headquarters, Mogadishu, Flag, Map of Africa — A78

Design: 1.30sh, Desert Fort.

1971, Oct. 18

378	A78	1.30sh blk & red org	22	22
379	A78	1.50sh blk, blue & yel	30	25

East and Central African Summit Conf.

Revolution Monument A79

Designs: 1sh, Field workers. 1.35sh, Building workers.

1971, Oct. 21
380	A79	10c black & blue	15	15
381	A79	1sh blk, yel brn & grn	18	18
382	A79	1.35sh blk, dp brn & yel	35	20
		Set value	58	42

2nd anniversary of 1969 revolution.

Vaccination of Cow — A80

Design: 1.80sh, Veterinarian vaccinating cow.

Perf. 14x13¹/₂

1971, Nov. 28   Photo.   Wmk. 303
383	A80	40c blk, red & bl	40	15
384	A80	1.80sh lt green & multi	45	35
		Set value		42

Rinderpest campaign.

Postal Union Emblem, Dove and Letter — A81

1972, Jan. 25   Unwmk.
385	A81	1.50sh multicolored	52	45

10th anniv. of APU. See No. C108.

Children and UNICEF Emblem A82

Design: 50c, Mother and child, vert.

1972, Mar. 30   *Perf. 13x14, 14x13*
386	A82	50c blk, bis brn & dk brn	15	15
387	A82	2.80sh lt blue & multi	70	52

UNICEF, 25th anniv. (in 1971).

Camel — A83

Designs: 10c, Cattle and cargo ship. 20c, Bull. 40c, Sheep. 1.70sh, Goat.

1972, Apr. 10   *Perf. 14x13*
388	A83	5c green & multi	15	15
389	A83	10c multicolored	15	15
390	A83	20c multicolored	15	15
391	A83	40c orange red & blk	15	15
392	A83	1.70sh dull grn & blk	85	45
		Set value	1.20	70

Hands Holding Infant — A84

Designs: 1sh, Youth Corps emblem, marchers with flags. 1.50sh, Woman, man, tent and tractor.

1972, Oct. 21   Photo.   *Perf. 14x13¹/₂*
393	A84	70c yellow & multi	18	15
394	A84	1sh red & multi	22	18
395	A84	1.50sh lt blue & multi	35	30

3rd anniversary of October 21 Revolution.

Folk Dance — A85

Folk Dances: 40c, Man and woman, vert. 1sh, Group dance, vert. 2sh, Two men and a woman.

1973   Photo.   *Perf. 14x13¹/₂, 13¹/₂x14*
396	A85	5c dull blue & multi	15	15
397	A85	40c brown & multi	15	15
398	A85	1sh yellow & multi	22	15
399	A85	2sh brick red & multi	45	30
		Set value	80	58

Hand Writing Somali Script — A86

Designs: 40c, Flame and "FAR SOMALI" inscription, vert. 1sh, Woman and sunburst with Somali script.

Perf. 13¹/₂x14, 14x13¹/₂

1973, Oct. 21   Photo.
400	A86	40c red & multi	15	15
401	A86	1sh blue & multi	20	15
402	A86	2sh yellow & multi	45	30
		Set value		52

Publicity for use of Somali script.

Map of Africa and Emblem — A87   Map of Africa with Target on Somalia — A88

1974, June 12   *Perf. 13¹/₂x14*
403	A87	40c multicolored	15	15
404	A88	2sh multicolored	52	30
		Set value		35

OAU Meeting, Mogadishu.

Hurdler A89

Designs: 1sh, Runners. 1.40sh, Netball, vert.

1974, Aug. 1   *Perf. 14x13, 13x14*
405	A89	50c black & orange	15	15
406	A89	1sh black & green	22	18
407	A89	1.40sh black & olive	35	22

Victory Pioneers — A90   Pioneers Helping Woman — A91

1974, Aug. 25   Photo.   *Perf. 13x14*
408	A90	40c multicolored	15	15
409	A91	2sh multicolored	40	30
		Set value		38

Victory Pioneers, founded Aug. 24, 1972, to defend Socialist Revolution.

Map of Arab Countries A92

Flags of Arab Countries A93

1974, Sept. 1   *Perf. 14x13*
410	A92	1.50sh multicolored	35	20
411	A93	1.70sh multicolored	42	22

Somalia's admission to the Arab League, Feb. 14, 1974.

Tank Tracks in Desert A94

Somalis Reading Books — A95

Perf. 14x13¹/₂, 13¹/₂x14

1974, Oct. 21   Litho.
412	A94	40c multicolored	15	15
413	A95	2sh multicolored	52	30
		Set value		38

5th anniversary of the Oct. 21st Revolution.

Carrier Pigeons A96

Design: 3sh, Postrider.

1975, Feb. 15   Litho.   *Perf. 14x13¹/₂*
414	A96	50c blue & multi	22	15
415	A96	3sh multicolored	1.25	45

UPU centenary (in 1974).

Africa — A97   AFRICAN POSTAL UNION

Design: 1.50sh, Carrier pigeons.

1975, Apr. 10
416	A97	1sh multicolored	30	15
417	A97	1.50sh multicolored	50	22

African Postal Union.

Somali Warrior — A98

Designs: Traditional costumes of Somali men (1sh, 10sh) and women (40c, 50c, 5sh).

1975, Oct. 27   Photo.   *Perf. 13¹/₂*
418	A98	10c yellow & multi	15	15
419	A98	40c lt blue & multi	15	15
420	A98	50c multicolored	15	15
421	A98	1sh green & multi	22	15
422	A98	5sh claret & multi	1.25	65
423	A98	10sh rose & multi	2.50	1.75
		Nos. 418-423 (6)	4.42	3.00

Monument — A99

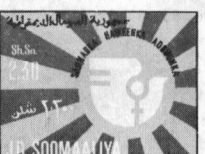

IWY Emblem A100

1975, Dec. 10   Litho.   *Perf. 13¹/₂x14*
424	A99	50c blk & red org	15	15
425	A100	2.30sh blk, pink & mag	50	40

International Women's Year.

Abdulla Hassan Monument A101

Abdulla Hassan with Warriors — A102

Designs: 1.50sh, Abdulla Hassan speaking to his men. 2.30sh, Attacking horsemen, horiz.

Perf. 14x13½, 13½x14
1976, Nov. 30 Photo.
426	A101	50c multicolored	15	15
427	A102	60c multicolored	15	15
428	A102	1.50sh multicolored	30	22
429	A102	2.30sh multicolored	50	35
		Set value		72

Sayid Mohammed Abdulla Hassan (1864-1920), poet and military leader.

Cypraea Gracilis A103

Sea Shells: 75c, Charonia bardayi. 1sh, Chlamys townsendi. 2sh, Cymatium ranzanii. 2.75sh, Conus argillaceus. 2.90sh, Strombus oldi.

1976, Dec. 15 Photo. *Perf. 14x13½*
430	A103	50c blue & multi	15	15
431	A103	75c blue & multi	18	15
432	A103	1sh blue & multi	25	15
433	A103	2sh blue & multi	50	32
434	A103	2.75sh blue & multi	75	45
435	A103	2.90sh blue & multi	85	45
a.		Souvenir sheet of 6, #430-435	4.00	4.00
		Nos. 430-435 (6)	2.68	1.67

No. 435a sold for 11sh.

Benin Head and Hunters — A104

Benin Head and: 75c, Handicrafts. 2sh, Dancers. 2.90sh, Musicians.

1977, Aug. 30 Photo. *Perf. 14x13½*
436	A104	50c multicolored	15	15
437	A104	75c multicolored	15	15
438	A104	2sh multicolored	45	32
439	A104	2.90sh multicolored	60	42

2nd World Black and African Festival, FESTAC '77, Lagos, Nigeria, Jan. 15-Feb. 12.

Arms of Somalia A105

Designs: 75c, Somali flags, vert. 1.50sh, Pres. Mohammed Siad Barre and globe. 2sh, Arms over rising sun and flags, vert.

Perf. 13½x14, 14x13½
1977, Sept. 30 Photo.
440	A105	75c multicolored	18	15
441	A105	1sh multicolored	20	15
442	A105	1.50sh multicolored	25	20
443	A105	2sh multicolored	45	35

Somali Socialist Revolutionary Party, established July 1, 1976.

Licaon Pictus A106

Protected Animals: 75c, Bush baby. 1sh, Somali ass. 1.50sh, Aardwolf. 2sh, Greater kudu. 3sh, Giraffe.

1977, Nov. 25 Photo. *Perf. 14x13½*
444	A106	50c multicolored	15	15
445	A106	75c multicolored	15	15
446	A106	1sh multicolored	22	18
447	A106	1.50sh multicolored	35	25
448	A106	2sh multicolored	50	35
449	A106	3sh multicolored	70	60
a.		Souvenir sheet of 6, #444-449	2.50	2.50
		Nos. 444-449 (6)	2.07	1.68

Leonardo da Vinci's Flying Machine A107

ICAO Emblem and: 1.50sh, Montgolfier's balloon. 2sh, Wright brothers' plane. 2.90sh, Somali Airlines' turbojet.

1977, Dec. 23 Photo. *Perf. 14x13½*
450	A107	1sh multicolored	22	18
451	A107	1.50sh multicolored	35	22
452	A107	2sh multicolored	45	40
453	A107	2.90sh multicolored	70	45
a.		Souvenir sheet of 4, #450-453	2.25	2.25

ICAO, 30th anniv. No. 453a sold for 10sh.

Dome of the Rock — A108

Lithographed and Engraved
1978, Apr. 30 *Perf. 13x14*
| 454 | A108 | 75c multicolored | 18 | 15 |
| 455 | A108 | 2sh multicolored | 45 | 35 |

Palestinian fighters and their families.

Stadium and Soccer Player — A109

Designs: 4.90sh, Stadium and goalkeeper. 5.50sh, Stadium and player.

1978, Aug. 5 Litho. *Perf. 14x13½*
456	A109	1.50sh multicolored	38	22
457	A109	4.90sh multicolored	1.25	90
458	A109	5.50sh multicolored	1.40	1.10
a.		Souvenir sheet of 3, #456-458	3.75	3.75

11th World Cup Soccer Championship, Argentina, June 1-25. No. 458a sold for 14sh.

Acacia Tortilis A110

Trees: 50c, Ficus sycomorus, vert. 75c, Terminalia catapa, vert. 2.90sh, Baobab.

1978, Sept. 5 Photo. *Perf. 14*
459	A110	40c multicolored	15	15
460	A110	50c multicolored	15	15
461	A110	75c multicolored	20	15
462	A110	2.90sh multicolored	45	35
		Set value		68

Forest conservation.

Hibiscus — A111

Flowers of Somalia: 1sh, Cassia baccarinii. 1.50sh, Kigelia somalensis. 2.30sh, Dichrostachys glomerata.

1978, Dec. 15 Photo. *Perf. 13½x14*
463	A111	50c multicolored	15	15
464	A111	1sh multicolored	22	18
465	A111	1.50sh multicolored	30	25
466	A111	2.30sh multicolored	52	35
a.		Souv. sheet of 4, #463-466, perf. 14	2.50	2.50

Huri and Siganus Rivulatus A112

Fishery Development: 80c, Sail huri, gaterin gaterinus. 2.30sh, Fishing boats, hypacanthus amia. 2.50sh, Motorized fishing boat, mackerel.

1979, Sept. 1 Photo. *Perf. 14x13½*
467	A112	75c multicolored	15	15
468	A112	80c multicolored	15	15
469	A112	2.30sh multicolored	42	42
470	A112	2.50sh multicolored	45	45

Sailing, IYC Emblem — A113

IYC Emblem, Children's Drawings: 50c, 90c, Schoolboy. 1.50sh, 2.50sh, Houses. 3sh, 4sh, Bird and flower. 1sh, as 75c.

1979, Sept. 10 Photo. *Perf. 13½x14*
471	A113	50c multicolored	15	15
472	A113	75c multicolored	15	15
473	A113	1.50sh multicolored	25	25
474	A113	3sh multicolored	52	52

Souvenir Sheet
| 474A | A113 | Sheet of 4, #b.-e. | 1.75 | 1.75 |

International Year of the Child. No. 474A contains 90c, 1sh, 2.50sh, 4sh stamps and sold for 10sh.

University Students, Outdoor Classrooms — A114

Flower and: 50c, Housing construction. 75c, Children's recreation. 1sh, Doctor examining child, woman and man carrying grain and fish. 2.40sh, Woman and children carrying produce over bridge. 3sh, Dish antenna.

1979, Nov. 30 Litho. *Perf. 14x13½*
475	A114	20c multicolored	15	15
476	A114	50c multicolored	15	15
477	A114	75c multicolored	18	15
478	A114	1sh multicolored	25	15
479	A114	2.40sh multicolored	60	25
480	A114	3sh multicolored	65	32
		Nos. 475-480 (6)	1.98	
		Set value		90

Oct. 21 revolution, 10th anniversary.

Barbopsis Devecchii A115

Freshwater Fish: 90c, Phreatichthys andruzzii. 1sh, Uegitglanis zammaranoi. 2.50sh, Pardi's catfish.

1979, Dec. 12
481	A115	50c multicolored	25	15
482	A115	90c multicolored	30	15
483	A115	1sh multicolored	35	15
484	A115	2.50sh multicolored	1.00	32
a.		Souvenir sheet of 4, #481-484	3.00	3.00
		Set value		64

No. 484a sold for 10sh.

Taleh Fortress, Congress Emblem — A116

1980, June 1 Photo. *Perf. 14x13½*
| 485 | A116 | 2.25sh multicolored | 60 | 35 |
| 486 | A116 | 3.50sh multicolored | 90 | 55 |

1st International Congress of Somalian Studies, Mogadishu, July 6-13.

View of Marka — A117

1980, July 1 Litho. *Perf. 14*
487	A117	75c shown	20	15
488	A117	1sh Gandershe	25	15
489	A117	2.30sh Afgooye	65	35
490	A117	3.50sh Muqdisho	1.00	55

Nos. 487-490 each se-tenant with label showing regional map. See Nos. 502-505, 527-530.

A118   A119

1980, July 30 Photo. *Perf. 13½x14*
491	A118	1sh Batis perkeo	32	15
492	A118	2.25sh Rynchostruthus socotranus louisae	32	35
493	A118	5sh Lanarius ruficeps	1.90	80
a.		Souvenir sheet of 3, #491-493	2.75	1.25

Perf. 13½x14, 14x13½
1981, Oct. 16 Litho.
494	A119	75c Globe, grain	18	15
495	A119	3.25sh Emblem, horiz.	75	52
496	A119	5.50sh like No. 494	1.50	90

World Food Day.

13th World
Telecommunications
Day — A120

1981, Oct. 10   *Perf. 13¹/₂x14*
497	A120	1sh Shepherdess, sheep, dish antenna	32	15
498	A120	3sh Emblems	1.10	50
499	A120	4.60sh like No. 498	1.10	52

Hegira, 1500th
Anniv. — A121

1982 World
Cup — A122

1981, Oct.   **Photo.**   *Perf. 13¹/₂x14*
500	A121	1.50sh multicolored	30	20
501	A121	3.80sh multicolored	85	65

View Type of 1980

1982, May 31   **Litho.**   *Perf. 13¹/₂x14*
502	A117	2.25sh Balcad	65	35
503	A117	4sh Jowhar	1.25	15
504	A117	5.50sh Golaleey	1.65	90
505	A117	8.30sh Muqdisho	2.25	1.25

Nos. 502-505 each se-tenant with label showing
regional map.

1982, June 13

Designs: Various soccer players.
506	A122	1sh multicolored	35	15
507	A122	1.50sh multicolored	55	22
508	A122	3.25sh multicolored	1.25	52
a.		Souvenir sheet of 3, #506-508	2.25	1.00

ITU Plenipotentiaries Conference, Nairobi,
Sept. — A123

1982, Oct. 15   **Photo.**   *Perf. 14x13¹/₂*
509	A123	75c green & multi	20	15
510	A123	3.25sh orange & multi	85	52
511	A123	5.50sh blue & multi	1.50	90

Local
Snakes
A124

Designs: 2.80sh, Bitis arietans. 3.20sh, Psammophis
punctulatus. 4.60sh, Rhamphiophis
oxyrhynchus. 8.60sh, Sphalerosophis
josephscorteccii.

1982, Dec. 20   **Photo.**   *Perf. 14*
512	A124	2.80sh multicolored	80	42
513	A124	3.20sh multicolored	85	50
514	A124	4.60sh multicolored	1.40	65

Souvenir Sheet
515	A124	8.60sh multicolored	4.00	2.25

Somali
Woman — A125

A126

1982, Dec. 30   *Perf. 14x13¹/₂*
516	A125	1sh yellow & multi	15	15
517	A125	5.20sh lilac & multi	90	85
518	A125	5.80sh orange & multi	1.00	90
519	A125	6.40sh blue & multi	1.10	1.00
520	A125	9.40sh lt brn & multi	1.65	1.50
521	A125	25sh green & multi	4.25	4.00
		Nos. 516-521 (6)	9.05	8.40

1983, July 20   *Perf. 13¹/₂x14*
522	A126	5.20sh multicolored	95	65
523	A126	6.40sh multicolored	1.00	85

World Communications Year.

2nd Intl.
Congress
of Somali
Studies,
Hamburg
A127

Various views of Hamburg.

1983, Aug. 1   *Perf. 14*
524	A127	5.20sh multicolored	85	65
525	A127	6.40sh multicolored	1.00	85

Military
Uniforms — A128

Designs: a, Air Force. b, Women's Auxiliary
Corps. c, Border Police. d, People's Militia. e, Army
Infantry. f, Custodial Corps. g, Police. h, Navy.

1983, Oct. 21   **Litho.**   *Perf. 13¹/₂x14*
526		Strip of 8	2.00	
a.-h.		A128 3.20sh, any single	25	20

View Type of 1980

1983
527	A117	2.80sh Barawe	32	15
528	A117	3.20sh Bur Hakaba	40	20
529	A117	5.50sh Baydhabo	65	32
530	A117	8.60sh Dooy Nuunaay	1.10	50

Sea Shells
A129

1984, Feb. 15   **Litho.**   *Perf. 14x13¹/₂*
531	A129	2.80sh Volutocorbis rosavittoriae	22	15
532	A129	3.20sh Phalium bi-tuberculosum	25	20
533	A129	5.50sh Conus milneedwarsi	42	32

Souvenir Sheet
Perf. 14
534	A129	15sh Cypraea broderipi	1.25	90

Olympics   Riccione
1984 — A130   Fair — A131

1984, Sept.   **Litho.**   *Perf. 13¹/₂x14*
535	A130	1.50sh Runners	15	15
536	A130	3sh Discus	24	15
537	A130	8sh Pole vaulting	65	45
a.		Souvenir sheet of 3, #535-537	1.25	90

No. 537a sold for 15sh.

1984, Sept.   **Litho.**   *Perf. 13¹/₂x14*
538	A131	5.20sh multicolored	42	30
539	A131	6.40sh multicolored	52	40

Animals
A132

1984, Sept.   **Litho.**   *Perf. 14x13¹/₂*
540	A132	1sh Hystrix cristata	15	15
541	A132	1.50sh Ichneumia albicauda	15	15
542	A132	2sh Mungos mungo	15	15
543	A132	4sh Mellivora capensis	35	22
a.		Souvenir sheet of 4, #540-543	90	60
		Set value		50

No. 543a sold for 10sh.

Intl.
Civil
Aviation
Org.,
40th
Anniv.
A133

1984, Nov. 20   **Litho.**   *Perf. 14*
544	A133	3sh multicolored	15	15
545	A133	6.40sh multicolored	22	15
		Set value		22

Souvenir Sheet
546		Sheet of 2	35	35
a.		A133 3sh like No. 544	15	15
b.		A133 6.40sh like No. 545	24	24

No. 546 contains 2 49¹/₂x46mm stamps. Sold
for 10sh.

Dove — A134

Constellations from the Book of Fixed Stars, by
Abd al-Rahman al-Sufi.

1985, Aug. 10   **Litho.**   *Perf. 13¹/₂x14*
547	A134	4.30sh shown	45	30
548	A134	11sh Bull	1.10	75
549	A134	12.50sh Rams	1.25	90
550	A134	13.80sh Archer	1.50	1.00

Architecture — A135

1985, Sept.   **Litho.**   *Perf. 13¹/₂x14*
551	A135	2sh Ras Kiambone	20	15
552	A135	6.60sh Hannassa	60	42
553	A135	10sh Mnarani	1.50	1.10
554	A135	18.60sh as #551, diff.	2.75	1.75

Nos. 551-554 each printed se-tenant with decorative
label. See Nos. 572-575.

Lady Somalia
Seated in
Posthorn
A136

1985, Oct.   *Perf. 14x14¹/₂*
555	A136	2sh multicolored	20	15
556	A136	20sh multicolored	2.00	1.50
a.		Souvenir sheet of 2, #555-556, perf. 13¹/₂	3.25	3.25

ITALIA '85, Rome. No. 556a sold for 30sh.

Bats — A137

1985, Dec. 25   **Litho.**   *Perf. 14x13¹/₂*
557	A137	2.50sh Triaenops persicus	15	15
558	A137	4.50sh Cardioderma cor	15	15
559	A137	16sh Tadarida condylura	55	40
560	A137	18sh Coleura afra	65	45

Souvenir Sheet
561		Sheet of 4	1.75	1.75
a.		A137 2.50sh like #552	15	15
b.		A137 4.50sh like #553	20	20
c.		A137 16sh like #554	70	70
d.		A137 18sh like #555	80	80

Nos. 561a-561d printed in continuous design.
No. 561 sold for 50sh.

Economic Trade Agreement with
Kenya — A138

Design: Presidents Arap Moi and Barre, satellite
communications.

1986, Feb. 15   *Perf. 14*
562	A138	9sh multi	32	22
563	A138	14.50sh multi	52	35

EUROFLORA
Flower Exhibition,
Genoa — A139

3rd Intl. Congress
on Somali
Studies — A140

1986, Apr. 25   Perf. 13¹/₂x14
564 A139   10sh Flower arrangement   35   24
565 A139   15sh Arrangement, diff.   52   38
a.   Souvenir sheet of 2, #564-565   1.25 1.25

No. 565a sold for 30sh.

1986, May 26
566 A140   11.35sh multi   40   30
567 A140   20sh multi   70   50

1986 World Cup Soccer Championships,
Mexico — A141

Various soccer plays.

1986, June   Perf. 14x13¹/₂
568 A141   3.60sh multi   15   15
569 A141   4.80sh multi   18   15
570 A141   6.80sh multi   24   18
571 A141   22.60sh multi   85   55
a.   Souvenir sheet of 4, #568-571   1.75 1.75

No. 571a sold for 50sh.

Architecture Type of 1985

1986   Litho.   Perf. 13¹/₂x14
572 A135   10sh Bulaxaar   35   30
573 A135   15sh Saylac   52   40
574 A135   20sh Saylac, diff.   70   55
575 A135   31sh Jasiiradaha Jawaay   1.10 85

Nos. 572-575 each printed se-tenant with decorative label.

Red Crescent -
Red Cross
Rehabilitation
Center,
Mogadishu
A143

1987, May 8   Litho.   Perf. 13¹/₂x13
576 A143   56sh multi   2.00 1.65

Souvenir Sheet
577 A143   56sh multi, diff.   2.25 2.25

No. 577 sold for 60sh. See Norway No. 908.

A144   A145

1987, Sept. 27   Litho.   Perf. 13¹/₂x14
578 A144   20sh Running   90   70
579 A144   48sh Javelin   2.00 1.65
a.   Souvenir sheet of 2, #578-579   3.50 3.50

OLYMPHILEX '87, Rome. No. 579a sold for 75sh.

1987, Oct. 5   Photo.   Perf. 13¹/₂x14¹/₂
580 A145   53sh multicolored   1.40 1.10
581 A145   72sh multicolored   1.90 1.40

Intl. Year of Shelter for the Homeless.

GEOSOM
'87 — A146   A147

Maps: 10sh, 160,000,000 years ago. 20sh,
60,000,000 years ago. 40sh, 15,000,000 years
ago. 50sh, Today.

1987, Nov. 24   Litho.   Perf. 13¹/₂x14
582 A146   10sh multi   25   20
583 A146   20sh multi, diff.   52   40
584 A146   40sh multi, diff.   1.00 75
585 A146   50sh multi, diff.   1.25 1.00
a.   Souv. sheet of 2, #583, 585   5.50 4.10

Symposium on the Geology of Somalia, Mogadishu, Nov. 24-Dec. 1. No. 585a sold for 130sh.

1988, Dec. 31   Litho.   Perf. 13¹/₂x14
586 A147   50sh multicolored   48   38
587 A147   168sh multicolored   1.60 1.20

World Health Organization, 40th anniv.

Wildlife
A148

1989   Litho.   Perf. 13¹/₂x14, 14x13¹/₂
588 A148   75sh Lepus somaliensis   35   28
589 A148   198sh Syncerus caffer   92   70
590 A148   200sh Papio hamadryas   95   72
591 A148   216sh Hippopotamus
               amphibius   1.00 75
a.   Souvenir sheet of 2, #590-591   3.25 3.25

No. 591a contains 2 labels like #588-589. Sold
for 700sh.

Somali Revolution, 20th Anniv. — A149

Flowers, children's games: 70sh, Kick ball.
100sh, Swinging. 150sh, Teeter-totter. 300sh,
Jumping rope, stick and hoop.

1989, Dec. 12   Litho.   Perf. 14x13¹/₂
592 A149   70sh multicolored   1.40 1.12
593 A149   100sh multicolored   2.00 1.60
594 A149   150sh multicolored   3.00 2.40
595 A149   300sh multicolored   6.00 4.80

A150   A151

Liberation: Nos. 599-600, Dove breaking chains,
horiz.

1991   Litho.   Perf. 13¹/₂x14, 14x13¹/₂
596 A150   70sh lilac & multi   65   48
597 A150   100sh grn bl & multi   90   70
598 A150   150sh brt blue & multi   1.35 1.00
599 A150   150sh yellow & multi   1.35 1.00
600 A150   300sh yel grn & multi   2.75 2.00
601 A150   300sh yel grn & multi   2.75 2.00
       Nos. 596-601 (6)   9.75 7.18

Issued: Nos. 599-600, July 2; others, July 4.

No. 599 Ovptd. in Blue

1991   Litho.   Perf. 14x13¹/₂
602 A150   150sh yellow & multi   1.35 1.00

1991   Litho.   Perf. 14

Various minarets.

603 A151   30sh multicolored   35   28
604 A151   40sh multicolored   45   35
605 A151   50sh multicolored   55   40
606 A151   150sh multicolored   1.70 1.25

Relief efforts have recently demon-
strated the breakdown of government
services in Somalia. It is unclear which
faction has control of the Postal Service,
if any is operating. The status of Scott
Nos. 607-638 will be reviewed once
more information is available.

Gazelles
A152

1992   Perf. 14x13¹/₂
Inscribed in Black
607 A152   500sh Two Speke's   2.25 1.80
608 A152   700sh One Speke's   3.20 2.50
609 A152   800sh One Soemmering's   3.75 2.75
610 A152   1000sh Two Soemmering's   4.50 3.25

World Wildlife Fund.

Without WWF Emblem
Inscribed in red lilac
611 A152   100sh like #607   55   40
612 A152   200sh like #608   1.10 80
613 A152   300sh like #609   1.65 1.25
614 A152   400sh like #610   2.25 1.65

Inscribed in black
615 A152   1500sh Baboons   8.25 6.25
616 A152   2500sh Hippopotamus   13.50 10.00
617 A152   3000sh Giraffes   16.50 12.00
618 A152   5000sh Leopard   27.00 20.00
       Nos. 607-618 (12)   84.50 62.65

Nos. 607-618 are part of an expanding set. Numbers may change.
For overprints see No. 629-632.

Nos. 607-610 Ovptd. "PARTICIPANT /
RIO 1992" in Orange

1992   Litho.   Perf. 14x13¹/₂
629 A152   500sh on #607   2.75 2.00
630 A152   700sh on #608   3.80 2.85
631 A152   800sh on #609   4.50 3.25
632 A152   1000sh on #610   5.50 4.00

Discovery of
America,
500th Anniv.
A153

Designs: 100sh, Sighting land from crow's nest.
200sh, Three men pointing from ship. 300sh,
Columbus in his cabin. 400sh, Claiming land.
2000sh, Building fort in New World.
No. 638a, 800sh, like No. 634. b, 900sh, like
No. 635. c, 1300sh, like No. 633.

1992
633 A153   100sh multicolored   55   40
634 A153   200sh multicolored   1.10 80
635 A153   300sh multicolored   1.65 1.25
636 A153   400sh multicolored   2.20 1.65
637 A153   2000sh multicolored   11.00 8.00
       Nos. 633-637 (5)   16.50 12.10

Souvenir Sheet
638 A153   Sheet of 3, #a.-c.   16.50 16.50

Nos. 638a-638c do not have white border. No.
638 exists imperf.

SEMI-POSTAL STAMPS

Italy Nos. B1-B4   SOMALIA
Overprinted

1916   Wmk. 140   Perf. 14
B1   SP1   10c + 5c rose   2.50 3.00
B2   SP2   15c + 5c slate   6.75 8.50
B3   SP2   20c + 5c orange   2.50 4.00
B4   SP2   20c on 15c + 5c slate   6.75 8.50

Holy Year Issue
Italy Nos. B20-B25 Surcharged in Black or
Red

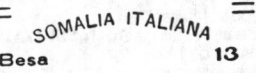

1925, June 1   Perf. 12
B5   SP4   6b + 3b on 20c + 10c   95   3.00
B6   SP4   13b + 6b on 30c + 15c   95   3.00
B7   SP4   15b + 8b on 50c + 25c   95   3.00
B8   SP4   18b + 9b on 60c + 30c   95   3.00
B9   SP8   30b + 15b on 1 l +50c (R)   95   3.00
B10 SP8   1r + 50b on 5 l +2.50 l
               (R)   95   3.00
       Nos. B5-B10 (6)   5.70

Colonial Institute Issue

"Peace" Substituting
Spade for
Sword — SP10

1926, June 1   Typo.   Perf. 14
B11 SP10   5c + 5c brown   25   1.65
B12 SP10   10c + 5c olive grn   25   1.65
B13 SP10   20c + 5c blue grn   25   1.65
B14 SP10   40c + 5c brown red   25   1.65
B15 SP10   60c + 5c orange   25   1.65
B16 SP10   1 l + 5c blue   25   1.65
       Nos. B11-B16 (6)   1.50

The surtax of 5c on each stamp was for the
Italian Colonial Institute.

Types of Italian Semi-   SOMALIA
Postal Stamps of 1926   ITALIANA
Overprinted

1927, Apr. 21   Unwmk.   Perf. 11¹/₂
B17 SP10   40c + 20c dk brn & blk   80   3.50
B18 SP10   60c + 30c brn red & ol
               brn   80   3.50
B19 SP10   1.25 l + 60c dp bl & blk   80   3.50
B20 SP10   5 l + 2.50 l dk grn &
               blk   1.25 4.50

The surtax was for the charitable work of the
Voluntary Militia for Italian National Defense.

Allegory of Fascism and Victory — SP11

1928, Oct. 15   Wmk. 140   Perf. 14

B21	SP11	20c + 5c blue grn	50	2.50
B22	SP11	30c + 5c red	50	2.50
B23	SP11	50c + 10c purple	50	2.50
B24	SP11	1.25 l + 20c dk blue	50	2.50

46th anniv. of the Societa Africana d'Italia. The surtax aided that society.

Types of Italian Semi-Postal Stamps of 1928   **SOMALIA ITALIANA**
Overprinted

1929, Mar. 4   Unwmk.   Perf. 11

B25	SP10	30c + 10c red & blk	1.40	3.50
B26	SP10	50c + 20c vio & blk	1.40	3.50
B27	SP10	1.25 l + 50c brn & bl	1.75	5.00
B28	SP10	5 l + 2 l ol grn & blk	1.75	5.00

The surtax was for the charitable work of the Voluntary Militia for Italian National Defense.

Types of Italian Semi-Postal Stamps of 1926   **SOMALIA ITALIANA**
Overprinted in Black or Red

1930, Oct. 20   Perf. 14

B29	SP10	30c + 10c dk grn & bl grn (Bk)	4.00	10.00
B30	SP10	50c + 10c dk grn & vio (R)	4.00	10.00
B31	SP10	1.25 l + 30c ol brn & red brn (R)	4.00	10.00
B32	SP10	5 l + 1.50 l ind & grn (R)	13.00	32.50

The surtax was for the charitable work of the Voluntary Militia for Italian National Defense.

Irrigation Canal SP14

1930, Nov. 27   Photo.   Wmk. 140

B33	SP14	50c + 20c olive brn	1.00	4.00
B34	SP14	1.25 l + 20c dp blue	1.00	4.00
B35	SP14	1.75 l + 20c green	1.00	4.00
B36	SP14	2.55 l + 50c purple	1.75	4.00
B37	SP14	5 l + 1 l dp carmine	1.75	4.00
		Nos. B33-B37 (5)	6.50	

25th anniv. of the Italian Colonial Agricultural Institute. The surtax was for the aid of that institution.

SP15

King Victor Emmanuel III — SP16

1935, Jan. 1

B38	SP15	5c + 5c blk brn	80	2.50
B39	SP15	7½c + 7½c vio	80	2.50
B40	SP15	15c + 10c ol blk	80	2.50
B41	SP15	20c + 10c rose red	80	2.50
B42	SP15	25c + 10c dp grn	80	2.50

B43	SP15	30c + 10c brn	80	2.50
B44	SP15	20c + 10c pur	80	2.50
B45	SP15	75c + 15c rose car	80	2.50
B46	SP15	1.25 l + 15c dp bl	80	2.50
B47	SP15	1.75 l + 25c red org	80	2.50
B48	SP15	2.75 l + 25c gray	8.00	25.00
B49	SP15	5 l + 1 l dp cl	8.00	25.00
B50	SP15	10 l + 1.80 l red brn	8.00	25.00
B51	SP16	25 l + 2.75 l brn & red	52.50	70.00
		Nos. B38-B51 (14)	84.50	

Visit of King Victor Emmanuel III.

> Catalogue values for unused stamps in this section, from this point to the end of the section, are for Never Hinged items.

Somalia

Nurse Holding Infant — SP17

1957, Nov. 30   Wmk. 303   Perf. 14

B52	SP17	10c + 10c red & brn	15	20
B53	SP17	25c + 10c grn & brn	15	20
		Set value	24	

The surtax was for the fight against tuberculosis. See Nos. CB11-CB12.

Republic

Refugees SP18

1964, Dec. 12   Photo.   Perf. 14

B54	SP18	25c + 10c vio bl & red	24	15

The surtax was to help refugees. See Nos. CB13-CB14.

Red Cross Nurse Feeding Child — SP19

Refugees — SP20

Famine Relief: 80c+20c, Nomad in parched land, horiz. 2.40sh+10c, Family with fish and produce. 2.90sh+10c, Physician and Aid Society emblem, horiz.

1976, Dec. 10   Perf. 13x14, 14x13

B55	SP19	75c + 25c multi	25	25
B56	SP19	80c + 20c multi	25	25
B57	SP19	2.40sh + 10c multi	52	52
B58	SP19	2.90sh + 10c multi	70	70

1981, Dec. 15   Photo.   Perf. 13½x14

B59	SP20	2sh + 50c multi	70	40
B60	SP20	6.80sh + 10c multi	2.00	60
	a.	Souvenir sheet of 2, #B59-B60	4.00	1.65

TB Bacillus Centenary — SP31

1982, Dec. 30   Photo.   Perf. 14

B61	SP31	4.60sh + 60c multi	2.00	85
B62	SP31	5.80sh + 60c multi	2.00	1.00

AIR POST STAMPS

View of Coast — AP1

Cheetahs AP2

1934, Oct.   Photo.   Wmk. 140   Perf. 14

C1	AP1	25c sl bl & red org	1.00	5.00
C2	AP1	50c dk grn & blk	1.00	5.00
C3	AP1	75c brn & red org	1.00	5.00
	a.	Imperf.		
C4	AP2	80c org brn & blk	1.00	5.00
C5	AP2	1 l scar & blk	1.00	5.00
C6	AP2	2 l dk bl & brn	1.00	5.00
		Nos. C1-C6 (6)	6.00	

2nd Colonial Arts Exhibition, Naples.
For overprint see No. CO1.

Banana Tree and Airplane AP3

Designs: 25c, 1.50 l, Banana tree and plane. 50c, 2 l, Plane over cotton field. 60c, 5 l, Plane over orchard. 75c, 10 l, Plane over field workers. 1 l, 3 l, Small girl watching plane.

1936   Photo.

C7	AP3	25c slate green	95	1.65
C8	AP3	50c brown	32	20
C9	AP3	60c red orange	1.50	3.50
C10	AP3	75c orange brn	80	70
C11	AP3	1 l deep blue	15	15
C12	AP3	1.50 l purple	80	30
C13	AP3	2 l slate blue	1.75	70
C14	AP3	3 l copper red	6.00	1.65
C15	AP3	5 l yellow green	6.00	2.00
C16	AP3	10 l dp rose red	6.00	6.75
		Nos. C7-C16 (10)	24.27	17.60

> Catalogue values for unused stamps in this section, from this point to the end of the section, are for Never Hinged items.

Somalia

AP8

1950-51   Wmk. 277

C17	AP8	30c yellow brn	15	30
C18	AP8	45c dk carmine	15	30
C19	AP8	65c dk blue vio	15	30
C20	AP8	70c dull blue	15	30
C21	AP8	90c olive brn	15	30
C22	AP8	1s lilac rose	18	30
C23	AP8	1.35s violet	25	70
C24	AP8	1.50s blue green	35	60
C25	AP8	3s blue	2.50	2.50
C26	AP8	5s chocolate	3.00	3.00
C27	AP8	10s red org ('51)	3.25	2.50
		Nos. C17-C27 (11)	10.28	11.10

Scene in Mogadishu — AP8a

1951, Oct. 4

C27A	AP8a	1s vio & Prus bl	85	1.00
C27B	AP8a	1.50s ol grn & chnt brn	1.65	3.00

First Territorial Council meeting.

Plane, Palm Tree and Minaret — AP9

Mother and Child — AP10

1952, Sept. 14

C28	AP9	1.20s ol bis & dp bl	1.00	2.00

1st Somali Fair, Mogadishu, Sept. 14-28.

1953, May 27

C29	AP10	1.20s dk grn & dk brn	60	85

Somali anti-tuberculosis campaign.

Fair Entrance AP11

1953, Sept. 28   Unwmk.   Perf. 11½

C30	AP11	1.20s brn car & pink	32	50
C31	AP11	1.50s yel brn & buff	32	50

2nd Somali Fair, Mogadishu, Sept. 28-Oct. 12, 1953.

Plane over Map and Stamps of 1903 AP12

Perf. 13x13½
1953, Dec. 16   Engr.   Wmk. 277
Early Stamps in Brown and Rose Carmine

C32	AP12	60c orange brown	32	50
C33	AP12	1s greenish black	32	50

50th anniv. of the first Somali postage stamps.

"UPU" among Constellations — AP13

Perf. 11½

1953, Dec. 16   Photo.   Unwmk.
C34 AP13 1.20s red & cream   24 35
C35 AP13 1.50s brown & cream   32 50
C36 AP13 2s green & lt blue   32 50

UPU, 75th anniv. (in 1949).

Alexander Island Juba River — AP14

Somali Flag — AP15

1954, June 1   Perf. 13½x12½
C37 AP14 1.20s dk grn & brn   35 50
C38 AP14 2s dk carmine & pur   42 60

See note after No. 196.

Perf. 13½x13
1954, Oct. 12   Litho.   Wmk. 277
C39 AP15 1.20s multicolored   20 30

Adoption of Somali flag.

Haggard's Oribi — AP16

Designs: 45c, Phillip's dik-dik. 50c, Speke's gazelle. 75c, Gerenuk. 1.20s, Soemmering's gazelle. 1.50s, Waterbuck.

Perf. 13½
1955, Apr. 12   Wmk. 277   Photo.
Antelopes in Natural Colors
Size: 22x33mm
C40 AP16 35c gray grn & blk   15 20
C41 AP16 45c lilac & blk   42 35
C42 AP16 50c rose lil & blk   15 20
C43 AP16 75c red   24 24
C44 AP16 1.20s dk gray grn   24 24
C45 AP16 1.50s bright blue   42 50
    Nos. C40-C45 (6)   1.62 1.73

See Nos. C57-C58.

Caravan at Water Hole — AP17

Design: 1.20s, Village well.

Perf. 13½x14
1955, Sept. 24   Wmk. 303
C46 AP17 45c brown & orange   20 30
C47 AP17 1.20s sapphire & pink   25 40

3rd Somali Fair, Mogadishu, Sept. 1955.

Ballot Type of Regular Issue

1956, Apr. 30   Photo.   Perf. 14
C48 A24 60c brown & ultra   15 15
C49 A24 1.20s brown & org   15 20
    Set value   24

Opening of the territory's first democratically elected Legislative Assembly.

Arms Type of Regular Issue

1957, May 6   Wmk. 303   Perf. 13½
Coat of Arms in Dull Yellow, Blue and Black
C50 A25 45c blue   15 20
C51 A25 1.20s bluish green   15 24

Issued in honor of the new coat of arms.

Type of Regular Issue, 1957 and

Oil Well — AP18

Design: 60c, Irrigation canal construction.

1957, Sept. 28   Perf. 14
C52 A26 60c blue & brown   18 28
C53 AP18 1.20s black & ver   18 28

Fourth Somali Fair and Film Festival.

Sport Type of Regular Issue

Designs: 60c, Runner. 1.20s, Bicyclist. 1.50s, Basketball player.

1958, Apr. 28   Wmk. 303   Perf. 14
C54 A27 60c brown   15 15
C55 A27 1.20s blue   15 18
C56 A27 1.50s rose carmine   15 18
    Set value   34

Animal Type of 1955

Designs: 3s, Lesser kudu. 5s, Hunter's hartebeest.

1958-59   Photo.
Size: 20½x36½mm
C57 AP16 3s ocher & sepia   60 85
C58 AP16 5s gray, blk & yel ('59) 60 85

See No. CE1.

Police Bugler AP19

1959, June 19   Photo.
C59 AP19 1.20s ocher & ultra   20 30
C60 AP19 1.50s olive grn & ultra 20 30
  a. Souv. sheet of 4, #228-229, C59-C60 2.50 2.50

Opening of the Constituent Assembly of Somalia.

Marabou AP20

1959, Sept. 4   Wmk. 303
C61 AP20 1.20s shown   18 28
C62 AP20 2s Great egret   20 30

Incense Shipment, 15th Century B.C. — AP21

Design: 2s, Incense burner and view of Mogadishu harbor.

1959, Sept. 28   Perf. 14
C63 AP21 1.20s red & blk   20 30
C64 AP21 2s blue, blk & org   30 45

5th Somali Fair, Mogadishu.

University Institute and Arms — AP22

Design: 1.20s, Front view of Institute.

1960, Jan. 14
C65 AP22 45c grn, blk & org brn   24 24
C66 AP22 1.20s blue, ultra & blk 35 35

Opening of the University Institute of Somalia.

Stork and Uprooted Oak Emblem — AP23

1960, Apr. 7   Wmk. 303   Perf. 14
C67 AP23 1.50s lt grn, bl & red   24 24

World Refugee Year, July 1, 1959-June 30, 1960.

Republic
#C42, C44 Overprinted Like #242
Perf. 13½
1960, June 26   Wmk. 277   Photo.
Antelopes in Natural Colors
C68 AP16 50c rose lil & blk   6.00 5.75
C69 AP16 1.20s dk gray grn   10.50 5.75

See note after No. 242.

Parliament and Italian Flag — AP25

Design: 1.80s, Somali flag and assembly building.

1960, July 1   Wmk. 303   Perf. 14
C70 AP25 1s org red, grn & red   28 15
C71 AP25 1.80s red org, ultra & blk 60 32

Somalia's independence.

Animal Type of Regular Issue
1960, Nov. 24
C72 A37 3s Leopard   60 50

Olympic Games Type of Regular Issue

Designs: 45c, Runner, flag and Olympic rings. 1.80s, Long distance runner, flag & Olympic rings.

1960, Nov. 24
C73 A38 45c lilac & blue   15 15
C74 A38 1.80s org ver & bl   30 30

17th Olympic Games, Rome, Aug. 25-Sept. 11.

Amauris Fenestrata and Jet Plane — AP26

Various Butterflies.

1961, Sept. 9
C75 AP26 60c blue, brn & yel   15 15
C76 AP26 90c yellow, blk & grn   15 15
C77 AP26 1s multicolored   1.65 15
C78 AP26 1.80s org, blk & red   40 24
C79 AP26 3s multicolored   52 40
C80 AP26 5s ver, blk & brt bl   1.25 70
C81 AP26 10s multicolored   2.50 1.25
    Nos. C75-C81 (7)   6.62 3.04

Wooden Headrest, Comb and Cap — AP27

Design: 1.80sh, Camel, metal sculpture.

1961, Sept. 28   Wmk. 303   Perf. 14
C82 AP27 1sh blk, ultra & ocher   24 15
C83 AP27 1.80sh blk, yel & brn   40 28

6th Somali Fair, Mogadishu.

Fish Type of Regular Issue
Fish: 2.70sh, Lutianus sebae.

1962, Apr. 26
C84 A41 2.70sh ultra, brn & rose brn 90 60

Mosquitoes and Malaria Eradication Emblem — AP28

Police Auxiliary Women — AP29

Wmk. 303
1962, Oct. 25   Photo.   Perf. 14
C85 AP28 1sh bis brn & blk   28 15
C86 AP28 1.80sh lt green & blk   60 28

WHO drive to eradicate malaria.

1963, May 15   Wmk. 303   Perf. 14

Women's Auxiliary Forces: 1.80sh, Army auxiliary women with flag.

C87 AP29 1sh dk bl, yel & org   32 15
C88 AP29 1.80sh multicolored   60 20

Freedom from Hunger Type of Regular Issue

Design: 1sh, Sower and wheat.

1963, June 25
C89 A44 1sh dk brn, yel & bl   42 20

President Osman Type of Regular Issue, 1963

1963, Sept. 15   Wmk. 303   Perf. 14
C90 A45 1sh multicolored   55 20
C91 A45 1.80sh multicolored   52 28

Somali Fair Type of Regular Issue, 1963

Design: 1.80sh, Government Pavilion.

1963, Sept. 28   Photo.
C92 A46 1.80sh blue   85 40

Map of
Somalia,
Animals and
Globe
AP30

Design: 1.80sh, Somali Credit Bank emblem.

1964, May 16   Wmk. 303   Perf. 14
C93 AP30 1sh multicolored   32 15
C94 AP30 1.80sh blk, bl & yel   70 32

10th anniversary of Somali Credit Bank.

Olympic Type of Regular Issue, 1964

1964, Oct. 10   Photo.
C95 A48 90c Diving   38 20
C96 A48 1.80sh Soccer   60 32

Elephants
and DC-3
AP31

Design: 1.80sh, Plane over Mogadishu.

1964, Nov. 8   Photo.   Perf. 14
C97 AP31 1sh brown & green   60 24
C98 AP31 1.80sh black & blue   1.25 40

Establishment of Somali Air Lines.

ITU Type of Regular Issue

1965, May 17   Wmk. 303   Perf. 14
C99 A50 1sh dp grn & blk   40 15
C100 A50 1.80sh rose lil & brn   80 40

Somali Fair Type of Regular Issue, 1965

Designs: 1.50sh, Sugar industry; harvesting sugar
cane and refinery. 2sh, Dairy industry; bottling
plant and milk cow.

1965, Sept. 28   Photo.   Perf. 14
C101 A51 1.50sh sep & pale bl   40 15
C102 A51 2sh sepia & rose   75 24

Faisal Type of Regular Issue

Design: 1.80sh, Ka'aba, Mecca, Pres. Abdirascid
Ali Scermarche and King Faisal.

1967, Sept. 21   Wmk. 303   Perf. 14
C103 A60 1.80sh blk, dp rose & org 28 20

Egret — AP32

Birds: 1sh, Southern carmine bee-eater. 1.30sh,
Bruce's green pigeon. 1.80sh, Broad-tailed paradise
whydah.

Perf. 11½
1968, Nov. 1   Unwmk.   Litho.
C104 AP32 35c blue & multi   15 15
C105 AP32 1sh green & multi   20 15
C106 AP32 1.30sh vio bl & multi   24 20
C107 AP32 1.80sh yellow & multi   28 24
          Set value   64

Somali Democratic Republic
Postal Union Type of Regular Issue

Design: 1.30sh, Postal Union emblem and letter.

Perf. 14x13½
1972, Jan. 25   Photo.   Unwmk.
C108 A81 1.30sh multicolored   42 35

AIR POST SEMI-POSTAL STAMPS

King Victor
Emmanuel
III — SPAP1

Wmk. 140
1934, Nov. 5   Photo.   Perf. 14
CB1 SPAP1 25c + 10c gray grn   1.75   4.00
CB2 SPAP1 50c + 10c brn   1.75   4.00
CB3 SPAP1 75c + 15c rose red   1.75   4.00
CB4 SPAP1 80c + 15c blk brn   1.75   4.00
CB5 SPAP1 1 l + 20c red brn   1.75   4.00
CB6 SPAP1 2 l + 20c brt bl   1.75   4.00
CB7 SPAP1 3 l + 25c pur   15.00 32.50
CB8 SPAP1 5 l + 25c org   15.00 32.50
CB9 SPAP1 10 l + 30c rose vio 15.00 32.50
CB10 SPAP1 25 l + 2 l dp grn 15.00 32.50
    Nos. CB1-CB10 (10)   70.50 154.00

65th birthday of King Victor Emmanuel III; non-
stop flight from Rome to Mogadishu.
For overprint see No. CBO1.

> Catalogue values for unused
> stamps in this section, from this
> point to the end of the section, are
> for Never Hinged items.

Somalia
Type of Semi-Postal Stamps, 1957

1957, Nov. 30   Wmk. 303   Perf. 14
CB11 SP17 55c + 20c dk bl & brn   15 24
CB12 SP17 1.20s + 20c vio & brn   22 32

The surtax was for the fight against tuberculosis.

Type of Semi-Postal Issue, 1964

Designs: 75c+20c, Destroyed Somali village.
1.80sh+50c, Soldier aiding children, and map of
Somalia, vert.

1964, Dec. 12   Photo.   Perf. 14
CB13 SP18 75c + 20c blk, org red
                        & brn   40 15
CB14 SP18 1.80sh + 50c blk, ol bis &
                        slate   90 32

AIR POST SPECIAL DELIVERY STAMP

> Catalogue value for the stamp in
> this section is for a Never Hinged
> item.

Antelopes
APSD1

Wmk. 303
1958, Oct. 4   Photo.   Perf. 14
CE1 APSD1 1.70s org ver & blk   60 85

AIR POST OFFICIAL STAMP

No. C1 Overprinted

11 NOV. 1934-XIII
SERVIZIO AEREO
SPECIALE

Wmk. 140
1934, Nov. 11   Photo.   Perf. 14
CO1 AP1 25c si bl & red org 700.00 1,050.

Forgeries of this overprint exist.

AIR POST SEMI-POSTAL OFFICIAL
STAMP

Type of Air Post Semi-Postal Stamps,
1934 Overprinted Crown and "SERVIZIO
DI STATO" in Black

1934, Nov. 5   Wmk. 140   Perf. 14
CBO1 SPAP1 25 l + 2 l cop red 1,050. 2,250.

SPECIAL DELIVERY STAMPS

Italy No. E3 Surcharged

BESA 30 Somalia Italiana

1923, July 16   Wmk. 140   Perf. 14
E1 SD1 30b on 60c dl red   12.50 12.50

Italy, Type of 1908 Special Delivery Stamp
Surcharged

60 BESA 60   SOMALIA ITALIANA

E2 SD2 60b on 1.20 l bl & red 18.00 18.00

"Italia"
SD3

1924, June   Engr.   Unwmk.
E3 SD3 30b dk red & brn   6.00 4.00
E4 SD3 60b dk blue & red   7.75 5.00

Nos. E3-E4 Surcharged in Black or Red
with Bars and

**CENT
70**

تينيتال

٧٠

1926, Oct.
E5 SD3 70c on 30b (Bk)   6.00 4.00
E6 SD3 2.50 l on 60b (R)   7.75 5.00
  a. Imperf., pair   150.00

Same Surcharge on No. E3

1927   Perf. 11
E7 SD3 1.25 l on 30b   6.00 6.00
  a. Perf. 14   100.00 175.00
  b. Imperf., pair   150.00

> Catalogue values for unused
> stamps in this section, from this
> point to the end of the section, are
> for Never Hinged items.

Somalia

Bananas,
Grant's
Gazelles
SD4

Wmk. 277
1950, Apr. 24   Photo.   Perf. 14
E8 SD4 40c blue green   65 60
E9 SD4 80c violet   1.00 1.25

Gardenias
SD5

Design: 1s, Eryrhina melanocantha.

1955, Feb.   Perf. 13
E10 SD5 50c lilac & green   20 30
E11 SD5 1s bl, rose brn & grn 42 60

AUTHORIZED DELIVERY STAMP

Italy No. EY2 Overprinted in **SOMALIA ITALIANA**
Black

1941   Wmk. 140   Perf. 14
EY1 AD2 10c dark brown   15

No. EY1 was prepared but not issued.

POSTAGE DUE STAMPS

Somalia Italiana

Postage Due Stamps
of Italy Overprinted   **Meridionale**

1906-08   Wmk. 140   Perf. 14
J1 D3 5c buff & mag   2.00 10.00
J2 D3 10c buff & mag   13.00 14.00
J3 D3 20c org & mag   8.50 14.00
J4 D3 30c buff & mag   6.00 14.00
J5 D3 40c buff & mag   8.50 14.00
J6 D3 50c buff & mag   8.50 14.00
J7 D3 60c buff & mag ('08) 10.50 17.00
J8 D3 1 l blue & mag   165.00 60.00
J9 D3 2 l blue & mag   150.00 65.00
J10 D3 5 l blue & mag   150.00 65.00
J11 D3 10 l blue & mag   35.00 85.00
   Nos. J1-J11 (11)   557.00 372.00

Postage Due Stamps
of Italy Overprinted at **Somalia Italiana**
Top of Stamps

1909-19
J12 D3 5c buff & mag   2.75   3.00
J13 D3 10c buff & mag   2.75   3.00
J14 D3 20c buff & mag   4.50   6.00
J15 D3 30c buff & mag   9.00   8.50
J16 D3 40c buff & mag   9.00   8.50
J17 D3 50c buff & mag   9.00   8.50
J18 D3 60c buff & mag ('19) 9.00   8.50
J19 D3 1 l blue & mag   22.50 10.00
J20 D3 2 l blue & mag   35.00 32.50
J21 D3 5 l blue & mag   45.00 45.00
J22 D3 10 l blue & mag   6.25 14.00
   Nos. J12-J22 (11)   154.75 147.50

Same with Overprint at Bottom of Stamps

1920
J12a D3 5c buff & magenta   25.00 21.00
J13a D3 10c buff & magenta 25.00 21.00
J14a D3 20c buff & magenta 27.50 21.00
J15a D3 30c buff & magenta 20.00 21.00
J16a D3 40c buff & magenta 20.00 21.00
J17a D3 50c buff & magenta 20.00 21.00
J18a D3 60c buff & magenta 25.00 21.00
J19a D3 1 l blue & magenta 27.50 21.00
J20a D3 2 l blue & magenta 27.50 21.00
J21a D3 5 l blue & magenta 32.50 21.00
   Nos. J12a-J21a (10)   250.00 210.00

D4

D5

1923, July 1
J23 D4 1b buff & black   75 1.25
J24 D4 2b buff & black   75 1.25
  a. Inverted numeral and ovpt. 62.50
J25 D4 3b buff & black   75 1.25
J26 D4 5b buff & black   85 1.25
J27 D4 10b buff & black   85 1.25
J28 D4 20b buff & black   85 1.25
J29 D4 40b buff & black   85 1.25
J30 D4 1r blue & black   1.75 2.00
   Nos. J23-J30 (8)   7.40 10.75

Type of Postage Due
Stamps of Italy   **Somalia Italiana**
Overprinted

1926, Mar. 1
J31 D3 5c buff & black   8.25 3.00
J32 D3 10c buff & black   6.50 3.00
J33 D3 20c buff & black   6.50 3.00
J34 D3 30c buff & black   6.50 3.00
J35 D3 40c buff & black   6.50 3.00

J36	D3	50c buff & black	12.00	3.00
J37	D3	60c buff & black	12.00	3.00
J38	D3	1 l blue & black	16.00	4.00
J39	D3	2 l blue & black	22.50	4.00
J40	D3	5 l blue & black	22.50	4.00
J41	D3	10 l blue & black	22.50	4.00
		Nos. J31-J41 (11)	141.75	37.00

Numerals and Ovpt. Invtd.

J32a	D3	10c	20.00
J33a	D3	20c	110.00
J34a	D3	30c	20.00
J35a	D3	40c	20.00
J36a	D3	50c	20.00
J37a	D3	60c	20.00

Postage Due Stamps of Italy, 1934, Overprinted in Black **SOMALIA ITALIANA**

1934, May 12

J42	D6	5c brown	75	1.50
J43	D6	10c blue	75	1.50
J44	D6	20c rose red	2.00	2.00
J45	D6	25c green	2.00	2.00
J46	D6	30c red org	3.75	4.00
J47	D6	40c blk brn	3.75	5.00
J48	D6	50c violet	4.25	1.50
J49	D6	60c black	7.50	10.00
J50	D7	1 l red org	10.50	3.50
J51	D7	2 l green	15.00	14.00
J52	D7	5 l violet	17.50	25.00
J53	D7	10 l blue	17.50	27.50
J54	D7	20 l carmine	19.00	30.00
		Nos. J42-J54 (13)	104.25	127.50

> Catalogue values for unused stamps in this section, from this point to the end of the section, are for Never Hinged items.

Somalia

1950		Wmk. 277 Photo.	**Perf. 14**	
J55	D5	1c dk gray vio	15	24
J56	D5	2c deep blue	15	24
J57	D5	5c blue green	15	24
J58	D5	10c rose lilac	15	24
J59	D5	40c violet	65	1.00
J60	D5	1s dark brown	1.10	1.65
		Nos. J55-J60 (6)	2.35	3.61

PARCEL POST STAMPS

These stamps were used by affixing them to the way bill so that one half remained on it following the parcel, the other half staying on the receipt given the sender. Most used halves are right halves. Complete stamps were and are obtainable canceled, probably to order. Both unused and used values are for complete stamps.

Parcel Post Stamps of Italy, 1914-17, Overprinted **SOMALIA ITALIANA**

1917-19 Wmk. 140 Perf. 13½

Q1	PP2	5c brown	1.75	2.50
a.		Double overprint	70.00	
Q2	PP2	10c blue	1.75	2.50
Q3	PP2	20c black ('19)	45.00	40.00
Q4	PP2	25c red	4.50	6.00
a.		Double overprint	150.00	
Q5	PP2	50c orange	32.50	20.00
Q6	PP2	1 l lilac	17.00	14.00
Q7	PP2	2 l green	18.00	15.00
Q8	PP2	3 l bister	24.00	20.00
Q9	PP2	4 l slate	25.00	25.00
		Nos. Q1-Q9 (9)	169.50	145.00

Halves Used

Q1, Q4	15
Q2	15
Q3, Q5	2.75
Q6-Q7	32
Q8	52
Q9	1.25

Nos. Q5-Q9 were overprinted in 1922 with a slightly different type in which the final "A" of SOMALIA is directly over the final "A" of ITALIANA. They were not regularly issued. Value for set, $400.

Parcel Post Stamps of Italy, 1914-17, Overprinted **SOMALIA**

1923

Q10	PP2	25c red	22.50	25.00
Q11	PP2	50c orange	21.00	25.00
Q12	PP2	1 l violet	21.00	25.00
Q13	PP2	2 l green	21.00	25.00
Q14	PP2	3 l bister	25.00	25.00
Q15	PP2	4 l slate	32.50	25.00
		Nos. Q10-Q15 (6)	143.00	150.00

Halves Used

Q10	1.10
Q11, Q12	32
Q13	40
Q14	85
Q15	1.65

Parcel Post Stamps of Italy, 1914-17, Surcharged

BESA SOMALIA ITALIANA — SOMALIA ITALIANA BESA 5

1923

Q16	PP2	3b on 5c brn	3.50	2.50
Q17	PP2	5b on 5c brn	3.50	2.50
Q18	PP2	10b on 10c blue	4.50	3.25
Q19	PP2	25b on 25c red	5.25	4.00
Q20	PP2	50b on 50c org	10.50	7.25
Q21	PP2	1r on 1 l lilac	12.00	10.00
Q22	PP2	2r on 2 l green	17.50	14.00
Q23	PP2	3r on 3 l bister	19.00	20.00
Q24	PP2	4r on 4 l slate	22.50	25.00
		Nos. Q16-Q24 (9)	98.25	88.50

Halves Used

Q16-Q17	15
Q18-Q19	20
Q20-Q21	32
Q22	60
Q23	1.10
Q24	1.65

No. Q16 has the numeral "3" at the left also.

Parcel Post Stamps of Italy, **SOMALIA** 1914-22 Overprinted **ITALIANA**

1926-31 Red Overprint

Q25	PP2	5c brown	8.75	10.00
Q26	PP2	10c blue	8.75	10.00
Q27	PP2	20c black	15.00	14.00
Q28	PP2	25c red	15.00	14.00
Q29	PP2	50c orange	15.00	14.00
Q30	PP2	1 l violet	15.00	14.00
Q31	PP2	2 l green	21.00	14.00
Q32	PP2	3 l yellow	7.00	14.00
Q33	PP2	4 l slate	7.00	10.00
Q34	PP2	10 l vio brn ('30)	8.75	14.00
Q35	PP2	12 l red brn ('31)	8.75	14.00
Q36	PP2	15 l olive ('30)	8.75	14.00
Q37	PP2	20 l dl vio ('31)	8.75	14.00
		Nos. Q25-Q37 (13)	147.50	166.00

Halves Used

Q25-Q26	32
Q27-Q28, Q33	70
Q29, Q34	90
Q30-Q31	52
Q32	40
Q35-Q36	1.10
Q37	1.25

Nos. Q25-Q31 come with two types of overprint: I - The first "I" and last "A" of ITALIANA extend slightly at both sides of SOMALIA. II - Only the "I" extends. These seven stamps with type I overprint were not regularly issued, and Nos. Q27-Q31 (type I) sell for less than with type II overprint.

Black Overprint

Q38	PP2	10 l violet brown	25.00	7.25
Q39	PP2	12 l red brown	16.00	7.25
Q40	PP2	15 l olive	16.00	7.25
Q41	PP2	20 l dull violet	16.00	7.25

Halves Used

Q38	45
Q39-Q41	30

Same Overprint on Parcel Post Stamps of Italy, 1927-38

1928-39 Black Overprint

Q42	PP3	25c red ('31)	17.50	25.00
Q43	PP3	30c ultra	24	1.50
Q43A	PP3	50c orange	7,500.	3,000.
Q44	PP3	60c red	24	1.50
Q45	PP3	1 l lilac ('31)	8.50	17.50
Q46	PP3	2 l green ('31)	8.50	17.50
Q47	PP3	3 l bister	30	2.50
Q48	PP3	4 l gray blk	35	3.00
Q49	PP3	10 l rose lilac ('34)	100.00	150.00
Q50	PP3	20 l lilac brn ('34)	100.00	150.00
		Nos. Q42-Q43,Q44-Q50 (9)	235.63	368.50

Halves Used

Q42, Q50	1.00
Q43, Q44	20
Q43A	40.00
Q45-Q48	32
Q49	1.25

The 25c, 1 l and 2 l come with both types of overprint (see note below No. Q37). Both types were regularly issued. Values are for type I on 25c, type II on 1 l and 2 l.

Red Overprint

Q51	PP3	5c brown ('39)	13.00	
Q52	PP3	3 l bister ('30)	10.00	14.00
		Half stamp		32
Q53	PP3	4 l gray blk ('30)	10.00	14.00
		Half stamp		32

Same Overprint in Black on Italy Nos. Q24-Q25

1940			**Perf. 13**	
Q54	PP3	5c brown	70	2.50
		Half stamp		15
Q55	PP3	10c deep blue	1.00	3.00
		Half stamp		15

> Catalogue values for unused stamps in this section, from this point to the end of the section, are for Never Hinged items.

Somalia

PP1

1950		Wmk. 277 Photo.	**Perf. 14**	
Q56	PP1	1c cerise	20	50
Q57	PP1	2c dk gray vio	20	50
Q58	PP1	5c rose lilac	20	50
Q59	PP1	10c red orange	20	50
Q60	PP1	20c dark brown	20	50
Q61	PP1	50c blue green	30	50
Q62	PP1	1 violet	1.25	3.00
Q63	PP1	2s brown	1.65	4.00
Q64	PP1	3s blue	1.75	4.50
		Nos. Q56-Q64 (9)	5.95	14.70

Halves Used

Q56-Q58	15
Q59-Q60	15
Q61	15
Q62	15
Q63	30
Q64	50

SOMALI COAST
(Djibouti)

LOCATION — Eastern Africa, bordering on the Gulf of Aden
GOVT. — French Overseas Territory
AREA — 8,500 sq. mi.
POP. — 86,000 (est. 1963)
CAPITAL — Djibouti (Jibuti)

The port of Obock, which issued postage stamps in 1892-1894, was included in the territory and began to use stamps of Somali Coast in 1902. See Obock in Vol. 4.

On Mar. 19, 1967, the territory changed its name to the French Territory of the Afars and Issas. The Republic of Djibouti was proclaimed June 27, 1977.

100 Centimes = 1 Franc

> Catalogue values for unused stamps in this country are for Never Hinged items, beginning with Scott 224 in the regular postage section, Scott B13 in the semi-postal section, Scott C1 in the airpost section, Scott CB1 in the airpost semipostal section, and Scott J39 in the postage due section.

Navigation and Commerce
A1   A2

A3

Camel and Rider A4

Obock Nos. 32-33, 35, 45 with Overprint or Surcharge Handstamped in Black, Blue or Red

1894		Unwmk.	**Perf. 14x13½**	
1	A1	5c grn & red, grnsh (with bar)	75.00	50.00
a.		Without bar	700.00	400.00
2	A2	25c on 2c brn & bl, buff (Bl & Bk)	200.00	100.00
a.		"25" omitted	600.00	450.00
b.		"DJIBOUTI" omitted	600.00	450.00
c.		"DJIBOUTI" inverted	625.00	600.00
3	A3	50c on 1c blk & red, bl (R & Bl)	225.00	160.00
a.		"5" instead of "50"	700.00	525.00
b.		"0" instead of "50"	700.00	525.00
c.		"DJIBOUTI" omitted	700.00	525.00
			Imperf	
4	A4	1fr on 5fr car	350.00	300.00
5	A4	5fr carmine	900.00	800.00

The overprint on No. 1 includes a bar to obliterate "OBOCK."
"DJIBOUTI" is in blue on No. 2, in red on No. 3.
Counterfeits exist of Nos. 4-5.

View of Djibouti, Somali Warriors — A5

French Gunboat A7

Crossing Desert (Size: 66mm. wide, including simulated perfs.) — A8

Designs: 15c, 25c, 30c, 40c, 50c, 75c, Different views of Djibouti. 1fr, 2fr, Djibouti quay.

Imperf. (Simulated Perforations in Frame Color)

1894-1902				**Typo.**
		Quadrille Lines Printed on Paper		
6	A5	1c blk & claret	1.50	1.50
7	A5	2c claret & blk	1.50	1.50
8	A5	4c vio brn & bl	5.00	3.75
9	A5	5c bl grn & red	5.00	3.75
10	A5	5c grn & yel grn ('02)	4.50	4.50
11	A5	10c brn & grn	7.00	3.75
a.		Half used as 5c on cover		65.00
12	A5	15c vio & grn	7.00	3.75
13	A5	25c rose & blue	11.00	6.00
14	A5	30c gray brn & rose	9.00	6.00
a.		Half used as 15c on cover		250.00
15	A5	40c org & bl ('00)	35.00	25.00
16	A5	50c blue & rose	11.00	9.00
a.		Half used as 25c on cover		800.00
17	A5	75c vio & org	20.00	17.50
18	A5	1fr ol grn & blk	12.00	9.00
19	A5	2fr gray brn & rose	50.00	40.00
20	A7	5fr rose & blue	110.00	60.00
21	A8	25fr rose & blue	625.00	625.00
22	A8	50fr blue & rose	500.00	500.00

High values are found with the overprint "S" (Specimen) erased and, usually, a cancellation added.
For surcharges see Nos. 24-27B.

A9

1899

Black Surcharge

23	A9	40c on 4c brn & bl	2,250.	10.00
a.		Double surcharge	4,000.	700.00

Nos. 17-20 Surcharged **0·05**

1902

			Blue Surcharge	
24	A5	0.05c on 75c	32.50	20.00
a.		Inverted surcharge	375.00	325.00
25	A5	0.10c on 1fr	42.50	35.00
a.		Inverted surcharge	300.00	225.00
26	A5	0.40c on 2fr	225.00	150.00

			Black Surcharge	
27	A7	0.75c on 5fr	300.00	250.00
a.		Double surcharge	1,750.	1,500.

Obock No. 57 Surcharged in Blue

27B	A7	0.05c on 75c gray lil & org	1,000.	700.00

A10

Nos. 15-16 Surcharged in Black

28	A10	5c on 40c	2.50	2.00
a.		Double surcharge	55.00	55.00
29	A10	10c on 50c	11.00	11.00
a.		Inverted surcharge	300.00	300.00

Surcharged on Stamps of Obock

Group of Warriors — A11

Black Surcharge

30	A11	5c on 30c bis & yel grn	5.00	3.75
a.		Inverted surcharge	140.00	110.00
b.		Double surcharge	120.00	110.00
c.		Triple surcharge		

A12

Red Surcharge

31	A12	10c on 25c blk & bl	6.25	5.00
a.		Inverted surcharge	150.00	140.00
b.		Double surcharge	150.00	125.00
c.		Triple surcharge	900.00	900.00

A13

Black Surcharge

32	A13	10c on 10fr org & red vio	16.00	14.00
a.		Double surcharge	140.00	120.00
b.		Triple surch., one invtd.	500.00	500.00

A14

Black Surcharge

33	A14	10c on 2fr dl vio & org	32.50	27.50
a.		"DJIBOUTI" inverted	160.00	140.00
b.		Large "0" in "10"	65.00	60.00
c.		Double surcharge	250.00	225.00

Same Surcharge on Obock No. 53 in Red

33D	A7	10c on 25c blk & bl	25,000.	14,500.

A14a

Black Surcharge on Obock Nos. 63-64

33E	A14a	5c on 25fr brn & bl	30.00	25.00
33F	A14a	10c on 50fr red vio & grn	35.00	27.50
g.		"01" instead of "10"	125.00	110.00
h.		"CENTIMES" inverted	1,750.	1,750.
i.		Double surcharge	1,000.	1,600.

Tadjoura Mosque A15

Somalis on Camel A16

Warriors — A17

1902   Engr.   Perf. 11½

34	A15	1c brn vio & org	50	42
35	A15	2c yel brn & yel grn	50	42
36	A15	4c bl & carmine	1.40	80
37	A15	5c bl grn & yel grn	1.00	70
38	A15	10c car & red org	3.75	2.00
39	A15	15c brn org & bl	3.50	2.00
40	A16	20c vio & green	5.00	4.25
41	A16	25c blue	9.00	7.50
a.		25c indigo & blue ('03)	12.50	10.00
42	A16	30c red & blk	3.25	2.50
43	A16	40c org & blue	7.50	5.00
44	A16	50c grn & red org	25.00	24.00
45	A16	75c org & vio	2.50	2.00
46	A17	1fr red org & vio	9.00	7.50
47	A17	2fr yel grn & car	18.00	15.00
a.		Without names of designer and engraver at bottom	82.50	82.50
48	A17	5fr org & blue	12.50	7.75
		Nos. 34-48 (15)	102.40	81.84

1903

49	A15	1c brn vio & blk	40	40
50	A15	2c yel brn & blk	55	55
51	A15	4c lake & blk	65	55
a.		4c red & black	70	60
52	A15	5c bl grn & blk	1.40	1.10
53	A15	10c car & blk	3.50	1.25
54	A15	15c org brn & blk	7.00	4.00
55	A16	20c dl vio & blk	9.00	8.00
56	A16	25c ultra & blk	4.00	3.50
58	A16	40c org & blk	4.00	3.50
59	A16	50c grn & blk	7.00	6.00
60	A16	75c buff & blk	5.00	4.25
a.		75c brown orange & black	40.00	35.00
61	A17	1fr org & blk	7.00	6.00
62	A17	2fr yel grn & blk	3.50	3.00
a.		Without names of designer and engraver at bottom	25.00	25.00

63	A17	5fr red org & blk	7.00	6.00
a.		5fr ocher & black	7.25	7.25
		Nos. 49-63 (14)	60.00	48.10

Imperforates, transposed colors and inverted centers exist in the 1902 and 1903 issues. Most of these were issued from Paris and some are said to have been fraudulently printed.

Tadjoura Mosque — A18

Somalis on Camel — A19

Warriors — A20

1909   Typo.   Perf. 14x13½

64	A18	1c maroon & brn	48	40
65	A18	2c vio & ol gray	48	40
66	A18	4c ol gray & bl	60	52
67	A18	5c grn & gray grn	75	40
68	A18	10c car & ver	1.90	95
69	A18	20c blk & red brn	3.50	3.25
70	A19	25c bl & pale bl	2.50	2.00
71	A19	30c red & scar	3.25	2.75
72	A19	35c vio & grn	3.50	3.00
73	A19	40c rose & vio	4.75	2.75
74	A19	45c brn & bl grn	4.75	3.25
75	A19	50c maroon & brn	4.75	4.00
76	A19	75c scarlet & grn	8.25	6.75
77	A20	1fr vio & brn	12.00	11.00
78	A20	2fr brn & rose	20.00	19.00
79	A20	5fr vio brn & bl grn	32.50	27.50
		Nos. 64-79 (16)	103.96	87.72

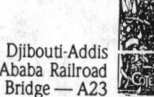

Drummer A21

Somali Girl A22

Djibouti-Addis Ababa Railroad Bridge — A23

1915-33   Perf. 13½x14
Chalky Paper

80	A21	1c brt vio & red brn	15	15
81	A21	2c ocher & ind	15	15
82	A21	4c dk brn & red	15	15
83	A21	5c yel grn & grn	28	25
84	A21	5c org & dl red ('22)	28	28
85	A22	10c car & dk red	35	32
86	A22	10c ap grn & grn ('22)	40	40
87	A22	10c ver & grn ('25)	15	15
88	A22	15c brn vio & car	22	22
89	A22	20c org & blk brn	15	15
90	A22	20c dp grn & bl grn ('25)	15	15
91	A22	20c dk grn & red ('27)	20	15
92	A22	25c ultra & dl bl	25	22
93	A22	25c blk & bl grn ('22)	40	40
94	A22	30c blk & bl grn	55	45
95	A22	30c rose & red brn ('22)	40	40
96	A22	30c vio & ol grn ('25)	15	15
97	A22	30c grn & dl grn ('25)	15	15
98	A22	35c lt grn & dl rose	28	25
99	A22	40c bl & brn vio	28	25
100	A22	45c red brn & dk bl	40	32
101	A22	50c car rose & blk	4.00	2.50
102	A22	50c ultra & ind ('24)	55	55
103	A22	50c dk brn & red vio ('25)	15	15
104	A22	60c ol grn & red vio ('25)	60	38
105	A22	65c car rose & ol grn ('25)	20	15
106	A22	75c dl vio & choc	40	28
107	A22	75c ind & ultra ('25)	15	15
108	A22	75c brt vio & ol brn ('27)	70	45
109	A22	85c vio brn & bl grn ('25)	60	38
110	A22	90c brn red & brt red ('30)	3.25	2.25
111	A23	1fr bis brn & red	80	38
112	A23	1.10fr lt brn & ultra ('28)	2.00	2.00

113	A23	1.25fr dk bl & blk brn ('33)	3.75	3.25
114	A23	1.50fr lt bl & dk bl ('30)	60	45
115	A23	1.75fr gray grn & lt red ('33)	2.50	2.00
116	A23	2fr bl vio & blk	1.25	80
117	A23	3fr red vio ('30)	4.00	2.50
118	A23	5fr rose red & blk	2.50	1.10
		Nos. 80-118 (39)	33.04	24.60

No. 99 is on ordinary paper.
For surcharges and overprints see Nos. 119-134, 183-193.

Nos. 83, 92 Surcharged in Green or Blue

1922
0ᶠ50

1922

119	A21	10c on 5c (G)	28	28
a.		Double surcharge	40.00	40.00
120	A22	50c on 25c (Bl)	28	28

Type of 1915 Surcharged in **0,01** Various Colors

1922

121	A22	0,01c on 15c vio & rose (Bk)	15	15
122	A22	0,02c on 15c vio & rose (Bl)	15	15
123	A22	0,04c on 15c vio & rose (G)	15	15
124	A22	0,05c on 15c vio & rose (R)	15	15

Nos. 88, 99 and Type of 1915 **60** Surcharged

1923-27

125	A22	60c on 75c ol grn & vio	15	15
126	A22	65c on 15c ('25)	40	40
127	A22	85c on 40c ('25)	50	50
128	A22	90c on 75c brn red & red ('27)	2.25	2.25

No. 118 and Type of 1915-17 Surcharged with New Value and Bars in Black or Red

1924-27

129	A23	25c on 5fr	40	40
130	A23	1.25fr on 1fr dk bl & ultra (R) ('26)	40	40
131	A23	1.50fr on 1fr lt bl & dk bl ('27)	55	55
132	A23	3fr on 5fr ver & red vio ('27)	1.50	1.50
133	A23	10fr on 5fr brn red & ol brn ('27)	4.00	4.00
134	A23	20fr on 5fr gray grn & lil rose ('27)	6.25	6.25
		Nos. 129-134 (6)	13.10	13.10

Colonial Exposition Issue
Common Design Types
Engr., Name of Country Typo. in Black

1931   Perf. 12½

135	CD70	40c dp grn	2.50	2.50
136	CD71	50c violet	2.50	2.50
137	CD72	90c red org	2.50	2.50
138	CD73	1.50fr dull blue	2.50	2.50

Paris International Exposition Issue
Common Design Types

1937   Engr.   Perf. 13

139	CD74	20c dp vio	55	55
140	CD75	30c dk grn	60	60
141	CD76	40c car rose	55	55
142	CD77	50c dk brn & bl	60	60
143	CD78	90c red	90	90
144	CD79	1.50fr ultra	90	90
		Nos. 139-144 (6)	4.10	4.10

Colonial Arts Exhibition Issue
Souvenir Sheet
Common Design Type

1937   Imperf.

145	CD75	3fr dull violet	2.50	2.50

Mosque of Djibouti — A24

Somali Warriors — A25

Governor Léonce Lagarde — A26

View of Djibouti — A27

1938-40   *Perf. 12x12½, 12½*

146	A24	2c dl red vio	15	15
147	A24	3c slate grn	15	15
148	A24	4c dl red brn	15	15
149	A24	5c carmine	15	15
150	A24	10c blue gray	15	15
151	A24	15c slate blk	15	15
152	A24	20c dk org	15	15
153	A25	25c dk brn	20	15
154	A25	30c dk blue	15	15
155	A25	35c olive grn	35	28
156	A24	40c org brn ('40)	15	15
157	A24	45c dl grn ('40)	15	15
158	A25	50c red	15	15
159	A25	55c dl red vio	40	35
160	A25	60c black ('40)	35	35
161	A25	65c org brn	28	28
162	A25	70c lt vio ('40)	55	55
163	A26	80c gray blk	65	55
164	A25	90c rose vio ('39)	65	65
165	A26	1fr carmine	80	55
166	A26	1fr black ('40)	22	22
167	A26	1.25fr magenta ('39)	40	40
168	A26	1.40fr pck bl ('40)	40	40
169	A26	1.50fr dull green	42	35
170	A26	1.60fr brn car ('40)	40	40
171	A26	1.75fr ultra	42	35
172	A26	2fr dk org	42	35
173	A26	2.25fr ultra ('39)	60	60
174	A26	2.50fr org brn ('40)	80	80
175	A26	3fr dl vio	42	35
176	A27	5fr brn & pale cl	80	65
177	A27	10fr ind & pale bl	80	65
178	A27	20fr car lake & gray	1.10	1.10
		Nos. 146-178 (33)	13.08	11.98

For overprints and surcharge see Nos. 194-223.

New York World's Fair Issue
Common Design Type

1939   **Engr.**   *Perf. 12½x12*

179	CD82	1.25fr car lake	60	60
180	CD82	2.25fr ultra	60	60

Mosque of Djibouti and Marshal Pétain — A28

1941   **Engr.**   *Perf. 12x12½*

181	A28	1fr yellow brown	30
182	A28	2.50fr blue	30

Nos. 181-182 were issued by the Vichy government, but it is doubtful whether they were placed in use in Somali Coast.

Stamps of types A24, A25 and A26, without "RF", were issued in 1944 by the Vichy Government, but were not placed on sale in the colony.

Nos. 80-82, 84, 88, 91, 97, 103, 105, 114-115
Overprinted in Black or Red

FRANCE LIBRE

Perf. 13½x14, 14x13½

1943   Unwmk.

183	A21	1c	40	40
184	A21	2c	55	55
185	A21	4c	11.00	11.00
186	A21	5c	55	55
187	A22	15c	2.50	2.50
188	A22	20c	55	55
189	A22	30c	55	55
190	A22	50c	50	50
191	A22	65c	65	65
192	A23	1.50fr (R)	65	65
193	A23	1.75fr	3.00	3.00
		Nos. 183-193 (11)	20.90	20.90

Stamps of 1938-40 Overprinted in Black or Red

FRANCE

France
Libre
On A24

LIBRE
On A25

France
Libre
On A26

FRANCE LIBRE
On A27

1943   *Perf. 12x12½, 12½*

194	A24	2c dl red vio	80	80
195	A24	3c sl grn (R)	80	80
196	A24	4c dl red brn	80	80
197	A24	5c carmine	80	80
198	A24	10c bl gray (R)	40	40
199	A24	15c sl blk (R)	80	80
200	A24	20c dk org	80	80
201	A25	25c dk brn (R)	1.00	1.00
202	A25	30c dk bl (R)	35	35
203	A25	35c olive (R)	1.00	1.00
204	A25	40c brn org	35	35
205	A24	45c dl grn	80	80
206	A25	55c dl red vio (R)	80	80
207	A25	60c blk (R)	40	40
208	A25	70c lt vio (R)	35	35
a.		Inverted overprint	90.00	90.00
209	A25	80c gray blk (R)	42	42
210	A25	90c rose vio (R)	35	35
211	A26	1.25fr magenta	42	42
212	A26	1.40fr pck bl (R)	35	35
213	A26	1.50fr dl grn	42	42
214	A26	1.60fr brn car	45	45
215	A26	1.75fr ultra (R)	3.75	3.75
216	A26	2fr dk org	35	35
217	A26	2.25fr ultra (R)	55	55
218	A26	2.50fr chestnut	55	55
219	A26	3fr dl vio (R)	80	80
220	A27	5fr brn & pale cl	3.50	3.50
221	A27	10fr ind & pale bl	80.00	80.00
222	A27	20fr car lake & gray	3.00	3.00

The space between overprint on Nos. 206 and 208 measures 10½mm.

FRANCE LIBRE

No. 161
Surcharged in
Black

50 c.

=

223	A25	50c on 65c org brn	35	35
		Nos. 194-223 (30)	105.51	105.51

> Catalogue values for unused stamps in this section, from this point to the end of the section, are for Never Hinged items.

Locomotive and Palms A29

1943 Unwmk. Photo.   *Perf. 14½x14*

224	A29	5c royal blue	15	15
225	A29	10c pink	15	15
226	A29	25c emerald	15	15

227	A29	30c gray blk	15	15
228	A29	40c violet	15	15
229	A29	80c red brn	15	15
230	A29	1fr aqua	20	20
231	A29	1.50fr scarlet	15	15
232	A29	2fr brown	22	22
233	A29	2.50fr ultra	28	28
234	A29	4fr brt org	35	35
235	A29	5fr dp rose lil	35	35
236	A29	10fr lt ultra	55	55
237	A29	20fr green	60	60
		Nos. 224-237 (14)	3.60	3.60

For surcharges see Nos. 240-247.

Eboue Issue
Common Design Type

1945   **Engr.**   *Perf. 13*

238	CD91	2fr black	28	28
239	CD91	25fr Prus grn	65	65

Nos. 238 and 239 exist imperforate.

Nos. 224, 226 and 233 Surcharged with New Values and Bars in Carmine or Black

1945   *Perf. 14½x14*

240	A29	50c on 5c (C)	28	28
241	A29	60c on 5c (C)	15	15
242	A29	70c on 5c (C)	15	15
a.		Inverted surcharge	65.00	
243	A29	1.20fr on 5c (C)	35	35
244	A29	2.40fr on 25c	40	40
a.		Inverted surcharge	60.00	
245	A29	2fr on 25c	28	28
246	A29	4.50fr on 25c	40	40
a.		Inverted surcharge	60.00	
247	A29	15fr on 2.50fr (C)	60	60
		Nos. 240-247 (8)	2.61	2.61

Danakil Tent — A30

Khor-Angar Outpost A31

Obock-Tadjouran Road — A32

Somali Woman A33

Somali Village — A34

Djibouti Mosque A35

1947   **Unwmk.**   **Photo.**   *Perf. 13*

248	A30	10c vio bl & org	15	15
249	A30	30c ol brn & org	15	15
250	A30	40c dp plum & org	15	15
251	A31	50c bl grn & org	15	15
252	A31	60c choc & dp yel	15	15
253	A31	80c bl & org	15	15
254	A32	1fr bl & choc	15	15
255	A32	1.20fr bl grn & ol grn	42	42
256	A32	1.50fr org & vio bl	15	15
257	A33	2fr red lil & bl gray	35	28
258	A33	3fr dp bl & brn org	45	40
259	A33	3.60fr car rose & cop red	80	70
260	A33	4fr choc & bl gray	70	50
261	A34	5fr org & choc	40	28
262	A34	6fr gray bl & int bl	55	35
263	A34	10fr gray bl & red lil	55	38
264	A35	15fr choc, gray bl & pink	70	45

265	A35	20fr dk bl, gray bl & org	80	55
266	A35	25fr vio brn, lil rose & gray bl	1.40	1.35
		Nos. 248-266 (19)	8.32	6.86

Military Medal Issue
Common Design Type

1952   **Engraved and Typographed**

267	CD101	15fr blk, grn, yel & dk pur	2.00	2.00

> **Imperforates**
> Most stamps of Somali Coast from 1956 onward exist imperforate in issued and trial colors, and also in small presentation sheets in issued colors.

FIDES Issue
Common Design Type and

Lighthouse, Ras-Bir — A36

Design: 15fr, Loading ship and map, Djibouti.

1956   **Unwmk.**   **Engr.**   *Perf. 13*

268	CD103	15fr purple	70	38
269	A36	40fr dp ultra & gray	1.50	1.00

Flower Issue
Common Design Type

Design: 10fr, Haemanthus, horiz.

1958   **Photo.**   *Perf. 12½x12*

270	CD104	10fr grn, red & yel	1.40	65

Wart Hog — A37

Designs: 40c, Cheetah. 50c, Gerenuk, vert.

1958   **Engr.**   *Perf. 13*

271	A37	30c red brn & sepia	15	15
272	A37	40c brn & olive	15	15
273	A37	50c brn, grn & gray	25	20
		Set value		40

See No. C21.

Human Rights Issue
Common Design Type

1958   Unwmk.

274	CD105	20fr brt pur & dk bl	85	85

Universal Declaration of Human Rights, 10th anniv.

Parrotfish A38

Designs: Various Tropical Fish.

1959   **Engr.**   *Perf. 13*

275	A38	1fr brt bl, brn & red org	16	16
276	A38	2fr blk, lt bl, yel & grn	18	16
277	A38	3fr vio & blk brn	18	16
278	A38	4fr brt grnsh bl, org & lt brn	40	30
279	A38	5fr brt grnsh bl & blk	42	28
280	A38	10fr bl, dl red brn & rose	90	70
281	A38	25fr red, grn & ultra	1.50	1.00
282	A38	60fr bl & dk grn	3.50	1.60
		Nos. 275-282 (8)	7.24	4.36

No. 276 is vertical.

Flamingo — A39

Birds: 15fr, Bee-eater, horiz. 30fr, Sacred ibis,
horiz. 75fr, Pink-backed pelican.

1960		**Unwmk.**		**Perf. 13**
283	A39	10fr bluish grn, bis & cl	35	25
284	A39	15fr rose lil, grn & yel	50	30
285	A39	30fr bl, blk, org & brn	1.25	90
286	A39	75fr grn, sl grn & yel	3.00	1.75

Dragon
Tree — A40

Klipspringer
A41

Meleagrina
Margaritifera
A42

Designs: 4fr, Cony. 6fr, Large flatfish. 25fr,
Fennecs. 40fr, Griffon vulture.

1962, Mar. 24		**Engr.**		**Perf. 13**
287	A40	2fr grn, yel, org & brn	50	25
288	A40	4fr ocher & choc	50	25
289	A40	6fr brn, mar, grn & yel	85	50
290	A40	25fr red brn, ocher & grn	1.25	1.00
291	A40	40fr dk bl, brn & gray	2.00	1.50
292	A41	50fr bis, bl & lil	3.00	2.00
		Nos. 287-292 (6)	8.10	5.50

1962, Nov. 24			**Photo.**

Sea Shells: 10fr, Tridacna squamosa, horiz. 25fr,
Strombus tricornis, horiz. 30fr, Trochus dentatus.

Shells in Natural Colors

293	A42	8fr red & blk	40	30
294	A42	10fr car rose & blk	40	30
295	A42	25fr dp bl & brn	1.40	65
296	A42	30fr rose lil & brn	1.10	60

See Nos. C28-C29.

Red Cross Centenary Issue
Common Design Type

1963, Sept. 2		**Engr.**		**Perf. 13**
297	CD113	50fr org brn, gray & car	2.50	2.50

Astraea Coral — A43

Design: 6fr, Organ-pipe coral.

1963, Nov. 30		**Photo.**		**Perf. 13x13¹⁄₂**
298	A43	5fr multi	40	35
299	A43	6fr multi	40	35

See Nos. C26-C27, C30.

Human Rights Issue
Common Design Type

1963, Dec. 20		**Engr.**		**Perf. 13**
300	CD117	70fr dk brn & ultra	3.50	3.50

Philatec Issue
Common Design Type

1964, Apr. 7		**Unwmk.**		**Perf. 13**
301	CD118	80fr dp lil rose, grn & brn	3.50	3.50

Houri (Somali
Sailboats)
A44

Design: 25fr, Sambouk (Somali sailboats).

1964, June 9				**Engr.**
302	A44	15fr multi	50	42
303	A44	25fr multi	90	70

View of
Dadwayya
and Map of
Somali
Coast — A45

Design: 20fr, View of Tadjourah and map of
Somali Coast.

1965, Oct. 20		**Engr.**		**Perf. 13**
304	A45	6fr ultra, sl grn & red brn	40	30
305	A45	20fr ultra, org brn & brt grn	40	35

Senna — A46

1966		**Engr.**		**Perf. 13**
306	A46	5fr shown	40	30
307	A46	8fr Poinciana	40	30
308	A46	25fr Aloe	60	50

See No. C41.

Desert
Monitor
A47

1967, May 8		**Engr.**		**Perf. 13**
309	A47	20fr red brn, ocher & sepia	1.00	70

Stamps of Somali Coast were replaced in 1967 by
those of the French Territory of the Afars and Issas.

SEMI-POSTAL STAMPS

Somali Girl — SP1

		Perf. 13¹⁄₂x14		
1915		**Unwmk.**		**Chalky Paper**
B1	SP1	10c + 5c car & dk red	4.00	4.00

Curie Issue
Common Design Type

1938		**Engr.**		**Perf. 13**
B2	CD80	1.75fr + 50c brt ultra	3.00	3.00

French Revolution Issue
Common Design Type
Photo., Name and Value Typo. in Black

1939				
B3	CD83	45c + 25c grn	3.50	3.50
B4	CD83	70c + 30c brn	3.50	3.50
B5	CD83	90c + 35c red org	3.50	3.50
B6	CD83	1.25fr + 1fr rose pink	3.75	3.75
B7	CD83	2.25fr + 2fr blue	4.25	4.25
		Nos. B3-B7 (5)	18.50	18.50

Common Design Type and

Somali Guard — SP2   Local
Police — SP3

1941		**Photo.**		**Perf. 13¹⁄₂**
B8	SP2	1fr + 1fr red		62
B9	CD86	1.50fr + 3fr maroon		62
B10	SP3	2.50fr + 1fr blue		62

Nos. B8-B10 were issued by the Vichy govern-
ment, but were not placed in use in the colony.
Nos. 181-182 surcharged "OEUVRES COLONI-
ALES" and surtax were issued in 1944 by the Vichy
Government, but were not placed on sale in the
colony.

> Catalogue values for unused
> stamps in this section, from this
> point to the end of the section, are
> for Never Hinged items.

Red Cross Issue
Common Design Type
Inscribed "Djibouti"

1944				**Perf. 14¹⁄₂x14**
B13	CD90	5fr + 20fr emerald	80	80

The surtax was for the French Red Cross and
national relief.

Tropical Medicine Issue
Common Design Type

1950		**Engr.**		**Perf. 13**
B14	CD100	10fr + 2fr red brn & red	2.00	2.00

The surtax was for charitable work.

Anti-Malaria Issue
Common Design Type

1962, Apr. 7		**Unwmk.**		**Perf. 13**
B15	CD108	25fr + 5fr aqua	3.25	3.25

Infant, Sun,
Chest and
Skulls — SP4

1965, Dec. 10		**Engr.**		**Perf. 13**
B16	SP4	25fr + 5fr ocher, sl & brt grn	1.20	1.20

Campaign against tuberculosis.

AIR POST STAMPS

> Catalogue values for unused
> stamps in this section are for Never
> Hinged items.

V1

Stamps of the design shown above
were issued in 1943 by the Vichy Government, but were not placed on sale in
the colony.

Common Design Type
Inscribed "Djibouti"

1944 Unwmk. Photo.				**Perf. 14¹⁄₂x14**
C1	CD87	1fr dk orange	35	35
C2	CD87	1.50fr brt red	35	35
C3	CD87	5fr brown red	50	50
C4	CD87	10fr black	55	55
C5	CD87	25fr ultra	90	90
C6	CD87	50fr dark green	80	80
C7	CD87	100fr plum	1.40	1.40
		Nos. C1-C7 (7)	4.85	4.85

Victory Issue
Common Design Type

1946		**Engr.**		**Perf. 12¹⁄₂**
C8	CD92	8fr deep blue	50	50

Chad to Rhine Issue
Common Design Types

1946				
C9	CD93	5fr gray black	45	45
C10	CD94	10fr dp orange	40	40
C11	CD95	15fr violet brn	40	40
C12	CD96	20fr brt violet	40	40
C13	CD97	25fr blue green	70	70
C14	CD98	50fr lt ultra	1.00	1.00
		Nos. C9-C14 (6)	3.35	3.35

Somali Gazing
Skyward — AP1

Frontier Post, Loyada — AP2

Governor's Mansion, Djibouti — AP3

	Perf. 12¹⁄₂x13, 13x12¹⁄₂			
1947		**Photo.**		**Unwmk.**
C15	AP1	50fr gray bl & choc	1.75	75
C16	AP2	100fr ol grn, org yel & gray bl	2.00	1.00
C17	AP3	200fr gray bl, org yel & ol grn	3.25	1.75

UPU Issue
Common Design Type

1949		**Engr.**		**Perf. 13**
C18	CD99	30fr bl, dp bl, brn red & grn	2.75	2.75

Liberation Issue
Common Design Type
1954, June 6
C19 CD102 15fr indigo & purple   2.50 2.50

Somali Woman and Map of
Djibouti — AP4

1956, Feb. 20   **Unwmk.**
C20 AP4 500fr dk vio & rose vio   25.00 15.00

Mountain Reedbucks — AP5

1958, July 7   **Engr.**   **Perf. 13**
C21 AP5 100fr ultra, lt grn & dk red
                      brn   1.60 1.25

Albert Bernard, Flag and Troops — AP6

1960, Jan. 18
C22 AP6 55fr ultra, sepia & car   80 55

25th death anniv. of Administrator Bernard at Moraito.

Great Bustard — AP7

1960, Oct. 24   **Unwmk.**   **Perf. 13**
C23 AP7 200fr brn, org & slate   4.25 2.50

Salt Dealers' Caravan at Assal Lake — AP8

1962, Jan. 6   **Engr.**   **Perf. 13**
C24 AP8 500fr dk bl, red brn, pink
              & blk   5.00 3.00

Obock — AP9

1962, Mar. 11   **Unwmk.**   **Perf. 13**
C25 AP9 100fr blue & org brn   1.50 1.00

Centenary of the founding of Obock.

Rostellaria Magna — AP10

Designs: 40fr, Millepore coral. 55fr, Brain coral. 100fr, Lambis bryonia (seashell). 200fr, Branch coral.

1962-63   **Photo.**   **Perf. 13¹/₂x12¹/₂**
C26 AP10 40fr multi ('63)   65   40
C27 AP10 55fr multi ('63)   1.20   60
C28 AP10 60fr multi   1.20   60
C29 AP10 100fr multi   1.50 1.00
C30 AP10 200fr multi ('63)   2.50 1.50
      Nos. C26-C30 (5)   7.05 4.10

Telstar Issue
Common Design Type
1963, Feb. 9   **Engr.**   **Perf. 13**
C31 CD111 20fr dp claret & dk grn 40   40

Zaroug (Somali Sailboats) — AP11

Designs: 50fr, Sambouk (boat) building. 300fr, Zeima sailboat.

1964-65   **Engr.**   **Perf. 13**
C32 AP11 50fr blue, ocher & choc 1.10 65
C33 AP11 85fr dk Prus grn, dk brn
                 & mag   1.40 1.10
C34 AP11 300fr ultra, lt brn & bl grn
                 ('65)   4.50 2.50

Discus
Thrower — AP12

1964, Oct. 10   **Engr.**
C35 AP12 90fr rose lil, red brn & blk 3.50 2.75

18th Olympic Games, Tokyo, Oct. 10-25.

ITU Issue
Common Design Type
1965, May 17
C36 CD120 95fr lil rose, brt bl & lt
              brn   5.00 3.50

Camels in Ghoubet Kharab and Map of
Somali Coast — AP13

1965   **Engr.**   **Perf. 13**
C37 AP13 45fr Abbe Lake   90   45
C38 AP13 65fr shown   1.00 70

Issue dates: 45fr, Oct. 20; 65fr, July 16.

French Satellite A-1 Issue
Common Design Type

Designs: 25fr, Diamant rocket and launching installations. 30fr, A-1 satellite.

1966, Jan. 28   **Engr.**   **Perf. 13**
C39 CD121 25fr redsh brn, ol brn &
              dl red   90   90
C40 CD121 30fr ol brn, dl red &
              redsh brn   90   90
  a.   Strip of 2, #C39-C40 + label 1.90 1.90

Each sheet contains 16 triptychs (2x8).

Stapelia — AP14

1966   **Engr.**   **Perf. 13**
C41 AP14 55fr sl grn, dl mag & emer 1.20 70

Feather Starfish and
Coral — AP15

Fish: 25fr, Regal angelfish. 40fr, Pomocanthops filamentosus. 50fr, Amphiprion ephippium. 70fr, Squirrelfish. 80fr, Surgeonfish. 100fr, Pterois lunulatus.

1966   **Photo.**   **Perf. 13**
C42 AP15   8fr multicolored   40   40
C43 AP15 25fr multicolored   80   80
C44 AP15 40fr multicolored   1.20 1.20
C45 AP15 50fr multicolored   1.90 1.90
C46 AP15 70fr multicolored   2.25 2.25
C47 AP15 80fr multicolored   2.50 2.50
C48 AP15 100fr multicolored   3.00 3.00
      Nos. C42-C48 (7)   12.05 12.05

French Satellite D-1 Issue
Common Design Type
1966, June 10   **Engr.**   **Perf. 13**
C49 CD122 48fr dk brn, brt bl & grn 1.20 80

AIR POST SEMI-POSTAL STAMPS

Catalogue values for unused stamps in this section are for Never Hinged items.

V2

Stamps of the design shown above and stamp of Cameroun type V10 inscribed "Côte Frcs. des Somalis" were issued in 1942 by the Vichy Government, but were not placed on sale in the colony.

Pharaoh Sacrificing before Horus and
Hathor — SPAP1

1964, Aug. 28   **Unwmk.**   **Perf. 13**
CB1 SPAP1 25fr + 5fr multi   3.25 3.25

UNESCO world campaign to save historic monuments in Nubia.

POSTAGE DUE STAMPS

D1   D2

Perf. 14x13¹/₂
1915 **Unwmk.** **Typo.** **Chalky Paper**
J1 D1 5c deep ultra   15   15
J2 D1 10c brown red   18   18
J3 D1 15c black   18   18
J4 D1 20c purple   35   35
J5 D1 30c orange   45   45
J6 D1 50c maroon   1.00 1.00
J7 D1 60c green   1.75 1.75
J8 D1 1fr dark blue   2.25 2.25
    Nos. J1-J8 (8)   6.31 6.31

See Nos. J11-J20.

Type of 1915 Issue Surcharged **2ᶠ·**

1927
J9 D1 2fr on 1fr light red   3.50 3.50
J10 D1 3fr on 1fr lilac rose   3.50 3.50

                 Type of 1915
1938   **Engr.**   **Perf. 12¹/₂x13**
J11 D1 5c light ultra   15   15
J12 D1 10c dark carmine   15   15
J13 D1 15c brown black   15   15
J14 D1 20c violet   15   15
J15 D1 30c orange yellow   35   35
J16 D1 50c brown   25   25
J17 D1 60c emerald   50   50
J18 D1 1fr indigo   1.10 1.10
J19 D1 2fr red   28   28
J20 D1 3fr dark brown   50   50
     Set value   3.20 3.20

Nos. J11 to J20 are inscribed "Inst de Grav" below design.

FRANCE

Postage Due Stamps of
1915 Overprinted in Red or
Black   LIBRE

1943   **Unwmk.**   *Perf. 14x13½*

J21	D1	5c ultra (R)	45	45
J22	D1	10c brown red	45	45
J23	D1	15c black (R)	45	45
J24	D1	20c purple	45	45
J25	D1	30c orange	45	45
J26	D1	50c maroon	45	45
J27	D1	60c green	45	45
J28	D1	1fr dark blue (R)	2.75	2.75
		Nos. J21-J28 (8)	5.90	5.90

France
Libre

Postage Due Stamps of
1938 Overprinted in Red
or Black

1943   *Perf. 12½x13*

J29	D1	5c lt ultra (R)	38	38
J30	D1	10c dark car	38	38
J31	D1	15c brn blk (R)	38	38
J32	D1	20c violet	38	38
J33	D1	30c org yel	38	38
J34	D1	50c brown	38	38
J35	D1	60c emerald	38	38
J36	D1	1fr indigo (R)	38	38
J37	D1	2fr red	3.00	3.00
J38	D1	3fr dk brn (R)	3.75	3.75
		Nos. J29-J38 (10)	9.79	9.79

In 1944 the Vichy Government issued five stamps of type D1, but without "RF," which were not placed on sale in the colony. The stamps were engraved, with the value numerals typographed, some in different color inks. Denominations: 30c, 50c, 60c, 2fr, 3fr.

> Catalogue values for unused stamps in this section, from this point to the end of the section, are for Never Hinged items.

1947   **Photo.**   *Perf. 13½x13*

J39	D2	10c purple	15	15
J40	D2	30c brown	15	15
J41	D2	50c green	15	15
J42	D2	1fr deep orange	15	15
J43	D2	2fr lilac rose	15	15
J44	D2	3fr dk org brn	15	15
J45	D2	4fr blue	25	25
J46	D2	5fr orange red	25	25
J47	D2	10fr olive green	30	30
J48	D2	20fr blue violet	50	50
		Set value	1.80	1.80

SOUTH KASAI

This part of a Congo province declared itself an autonomous state and in 1961 issued several series of stamps, some of which were overprints on Congo (ex-Belgian) stamps. Established nations did not recognize South Kasai as an independent state.

SOUTH MOLUCCAS

(Republik Maluku Selatan)

On the basis of information received from the Republic of Indonesia, it appears that stamps of the so-called republic of South Moluccas were privately issued and had no postal use. Accordingly, they are not recognized as postage stamps.

SOUTH RUSSIA

LOCATION — An area in southern Russia bordering on the Caspian and Black Seas.

A provisional government set up and maintained by General Denikin in opposition to the Bolshevik forces in Russia following the downfall of the Empire. The stamps were used in the field postal service established for carrying on communication between the various armies united in the revolt. These armies included the Don Cossacks, the Kuban Cossacks, and also the neighboring southern Russian people in

favor of the counter-revolution against the Bolsheviks.

100 Kopecks = 1 Ruble

> Values for used stamps are for canceled to order copies. Postally used specimens sell for considerably more.

Watermark

Wmk. 171-
Diamonds

Don Government
(Novocherkassk)
Rostov Issue

Russian Stamps of 1909-17
Surcharged **25**

1918   **Unwmk.**   *Perf. 14x14½*

1	A14	25k on 1k dl org yel	1.25	1.45
a.		Inverted surcharge	20.00	40.00
2	A14	25k on 2k dl grn	45	60
a.		Inverted surcharge	16.00	35.00
3	A14	25k on 3k car	45	75
a.		Double surcharge	30.00	55.00
4	A15	25k on 4k car	1.75	2.50
a.		Inverted surcharge	16.00	35.00
5	A14	50k on 7k blue	3.00	5.00

Imperf

6	A14	25k on 1k orange	45	1.00
a.		Inverted surcharge	16.00	40.00
7	A14	25k on 2k gray grn	4.75	10.00
8	A14	25k on 3k red	1.40	2.50
		Nos. 1-8 (8)	13.50	23.80

Counterfeits exist of Nos. 1-8.

Ermak, Cossack
Leader — A1

Inscription on Back

1919   *Perf. 11½*

10	A1	20k green	32.50	85.00

This stamp was available for both postage and currency.

Novocherkassk Issue

25   **1 P.**   **1 P.**

Russian stamps with these surcharges are bogus.

Kuban Government
Ekaterinodar Issues

Russian Stamps of 1909-17 Surcharged:

—25   —70 к.   —1 р.
d   e   f

1 р.   —3—   10
g   h   i

рубля   рублей
h   i

1918-20   **Unwmk.**   *Perf. 14x14½*

20	A14(d)	25k on 1k dl org yel	50	65
a.		Inverted surcharge	20.00	27.50
b.		Dbl. surch., one inverted	16.00	27.50
21	A14(d)	50k on 2k dl grn	5.00	6.00
a.		Inverted surcharge	16.00	22.50
b.		Double surcharge	10.50	13.00
c.		Double surcharge inverted	10.50	13.00
22	A14(e)	70k on 5k dk cl	75	1.50
23	A14(f)	1r on 3k car	1.50	2.00
a.		Inverted surcharge	11.50	16.00
b.		Double surcharge	5.25	10.00
c.		Pair, one without surcharge	5.25	10.00

24	A14(g)	1r on 3k car	65	1.00
a.		Inverted surcharge	8.00	13.00
b.		Double surcharge	8.00	13.00
c.		Pair, one without surcharge	11.50	13.00
25	A15(h)	3r on 4k rose	10.00	11.00
a.		Inverted surcharge	27.50	50.00
b.		Double surcharge	30.00	52.50
d.		Double surcharge inverted	30.00	52.50
26	A15(i)	10r on 4k rose	3.25	4.00
a.		10r on 4k carmine	8.00	13.00
b.		Inverted surcharge	32.50	50.00
27	A11(i)	10r on 15k red brn & dp bl	1.10	1.50
a.		Surchd. on face and back	13.00	13.00
b.		Dbl. surch., one inverted	30.00	60.00
28	A14(i)	25r on 3k car	2.25	1.65
a.		Inverted surcharge	4.50	10.00
29	A14(i)	25r on 7k bl	25.00	27.50
a.		Inverted surcharge	50.00	52.50
30	A11(i)	25r on 14k bl & car	50.00	65.00
a.		Inverted surcharge	52.50	70.00
31	A11(i)	25r on 25k dl grn & dk vio	30.00	42.50
a.		Inverted surcharge	52.50	70.00

Imperf

35	A14(d)	25d on 1k org	1.10	2.00
36	A14(d)	50k on 2k gray grn	24	32
a.		Inverted surcharge	20.00	22.50
b.		Double surcharge	20.00	22.50
c.		Pair, one without surcharge	20.00	27.50
37	A14(e)	70k on 5k claret	2.25	3.25
38	A14(f)	1r on 3k red	1.50	2.00
a.		Inverted surcharge	13.00	16.00
b.		Double surcharge	7.25	11.50
c.		Pair, one without surcharge	4.00	8.00
39	A14(g)	1r on 3k red	50	65
a.		Double surcharge	7.25	16.00
b.		Pair, one without surcharge	7.25	16.00
c.		As "a," inverted	21.00	40.00
40	A11(i)	10r on 15k red brn & dp bl	2.25	3.25
41	A14(i)	25r on 3k red	5.25	3.25
a.		Inverted surcharge	42.50	

Russian Stamps of 1909-17
Surcharged **70 коп.**

1919   *Perf. 14, 14½x15*

45	A14	70k on 1k dl org yel	1.00	1.00

Imperf

46	A14	70k on 1k orange	1.00	1.00
a.		Inverted surcharge	10.50	14.00
b.		Double surch., one inverted	14.00	14.00

The 1k postal savings stamp with this surcharge inverted is a proof.
Counterfeits exist of Nos. 20-46.

Postal Savings Stamps Surcharged for
Postal Use

A2

1919   **Wmk. 171**   *Perf. 14½x15*

47	A2	10r on 1k red, *buff*	15.00	21.00
a.		Inverted surcharge	70.00	
48	A2	10r on 5k grn, *buff*	32.50	40.00
a.		Double surcharge	250.00	
49	A2	10r on 10k brn, *buff*	100.00	100.00

Counterfeits exist of Nos. 47-49.

Crimea

Russian Stamp of 1917
Surcharged **35 коп.**

1919   **Unwmk.**   *Imperf.*

51	A14	35k on 1k orange	32	1.00
a.		Comma, instead of period in surcharge	85	

A3

Paper with Buff Network
Inscription on Back

1919   *Imperf.*

52	A3	50k brown	32.50	65.00

Available for both postage and currency.

Russia Nos. 77, 82, 123, 73, 119
Surcharged

5   ЮГЪ
           РОССІИ.

пять   100
рублей.   рублей.

Nos. 53-57   Nos. 58-59

1920   *Perf. 14x14½*

53	A14	5r on 5k dk claret	1.50	2.75
a.		Inverted surcharge	35.00	
b.		Double surcharge	42.50	
54	A8	5r on 20k dl bl & dk car	1.50	2.75
a.		Inverted surcharge	15.00	
b.		Double surcharge	35.00	
c.		"5" omitted	14.00	

Imperf

55	A14	5r on 5k claret	1.50	2.75
a.		Double surcharge	15.00	

**Same Surcharge on Stamp of Denikin
Issue, No. 64**

57	A5	5r on 35k lt bl	9.25	13.00
a.		Double surcharge	75.00	

1920   *Perf. 14x14½*

58	A14	100r on 1k dl org yel	3.25	
a.		"10" in place of "100"	50.00	
b.		Inverted surcharge	22.50	
c.		Double surcharge	50.00	

Imperf

59	A14	100r on 1k orange	2.75	

Nos. 53-57 were issued at Sevastopol during the occupation by General Wrangel's army. Nos. 58-59 were prepared but not used.

Denikin Issue

A5   St. George — A6

1919   **Unwmk.**   *Imperf.*

61	A5	5k orange	15	24
62	A5	10k green	15	24
63	A5	15k red	18	35
64	A5	35k light blue	15	24
65	A5	70k dark blue	15	35
a.		Tête bêche pair	65.00	
66	A6	1r brown & red	35	50
67	A6	2r gray vio & yellow	35	75
68	A6	3r dl rose & green	35	75
69	A6	5r slate & violet	75	1.10
70	A6	7r gray grn & rose	1.10	2.75
71	A6	10r red & gray	75	2.00
		Nos. 61-71 (11)	4.43	9.27

Perf. 11½

68a	A6	3r dull rose & green	1.25	1.25
69a	A6	5r slate & violet	1.75	1.75
71a	A6	10r red & gray	1.40	1.75

Nos. 61-71 were issued at Ekaterinodar and used in all parts of South Russia that were occupied by the People's Volunteer Army under Gen. Anton Ivanovich Denikin. The inscription on the stamps reads "United Russia."

Stamps of type A6 with rosettes instead of numerals in the small circles at the sides are private and fraudulent. So are perforated copies of Nos. 61-67 and 70.

For surcharges see Russia, Offices in Turkish Empire Nos. 303-319.

SPAIN

LOCATION — Southwestern Europe, Iberian Peninsula
GOVT. — Monarchy
AREA — 194,884 sq. mi.
POP. — 38,219,534 (est. 1983)
CAPITAL — Madrid

Spain was a monarchy until about 1931, when a republic was established. After the Civil War (1936-39), the Spanish State of Gen. Francisco Franco was recognized. The monarchy was restored in 1975.

32 Maravedis = 8 Cuartos = 1 Real
1000 Milesimas = 100 Centimos = 1 Escudo (1866)
100 Milesimas = 1 Real
4 Reales = 1 Peseta
100 Centimos = 1 Peseta (1872)

Catalogue values for unused stamps in this country are for Never Hinged items, beginning with Scott 909 in the regular postage section, Scott B139 in the semi-postal section, Scott C159 in the airpost section, and Scott E21 in the special delivery section.

Watermarks

Wmk. 104- Loops

Wmk. 105-
Crossed Lines

Wmk. 116- Crosses
and Circles

Wmk. 178- Castle

Values of early Spanish stamps vary according to condition. Quotations for Nos. 1-73 are for fine copies. Very fine to superb specimens sell at much higher prices, and inferior or poor copies sell at reduced prices, depending on the condition of the individual specimen.

Stamps punched with a small round hole have done telegraph service. In this condition they sell for 15 cents to $10 apiece.

Stamps of 1854 to 1882 canceled with three parallel horizontal bars are remainders. Most of these are valued through No. 101.

Kingdom

Queen Isabella II
A1   A2

6 CUARTOS:
Type I - "T" and "O" of CUARTOS separated.
Type II - "T" and "O" joined.

1850, Jan. 1 Unwmk. Litho. *Imperf.*

1	A1	6c blk, thin paper (II)	200.00	7.50
a.		Thick paper (II)	200.00	10.50
b.		Thick paper (I)	225.00	9.50
c.		Thin paper (I)	250.00	13.00
2	A2	12c lilac	2,000.	135.00
a.		Thin paper	2,750.	150.00
3	A2	5r red	1,500.	125.00
4	A2	6r blue	2,750.	275.00
5	A2	10r green	2,000.	1,500.

Stamps of types A2, A3, A4, A6, A7a and A8 are inscribed "FRANCO" on the cuarto values and "CERTIFICADO," "CERTIFO" or "CERT DO" on the reales values.

A3   A4

1851, Jan. 1 Typo.
Thin Paper

6	A3	6c black	125.00	1.50
a.		Thick paper	225.00	6.00
7	A3	12c lilac	2,750.	100.00
8	A3	2r red	12,500.	5,500.
9	A3	5r rose	2,400.	70.00
a.		5r red brown (error)	15,000.	7,000.
10	A3	6r blue	3,000.	300.00
a.		Cliché of 2r in plate of 6r		110,000.
11	A3	10r green	2,000.	200.00

1852, Jan. 1
Thick Paper

12	A4	6c rose	200.00	1.00
a.		Thin paper	225.00	1.50
13	A4	12c lilac	1,350.	70.00
a.		12c gray lilac	1,750.	90.00
14	A4	2r pale red	11,000.	3,500.
15	A4	5r green	1,350.	70.00
16	A4	6r grnsh blue	2,500.	275.00
a.		6r blue	3,250.	360.00

Arms of   Isabella
Madrid — A5   II — A6

1853, Jan. 1
Thin Paper

17	A5	1c bronze	2,000.	225.00
18	A5	3c bronze	11,000.	4,500.
19	A6	6c carmine rose	250.00	1.00
a.		Thick paper	275.00	5.50
b.		Thick bluish paper	400.00	6.75
20	A6	12c red violet	1,350.	60.00
21	A6	2r vermilion	7,000.	1,500.
22	A6	5r lt green	2,000.	70.00
23	A6	6r dp blue	2,000.	240.00

Nos. 17-18 were issued for use on Madrid city mail only. *They were reprinted on this white paper in duller colors.*

Coat of Arms of Spain
A7   A7a   A8

1854
Thin White Paper

24	A7	2c green	1,500.	200.00
25	A7a	4c carmine	165.00	1.00
a.		Thick paper	190.00	3.25
		Bar cancellation		3.75
26	A8	6c carmine	190.00	75
a.		Thick paper	400.00	10.00
		Bar cancellation		1.40
27	A7a	1r indigo	2,000.	150.00
		Bar cancellation		7.00
28	A8	2r scarlet	900.00	55.00
a.		2r ver	1,250.	70.00
		Bar cancellation		3.50
29	A8	5r green	1,000.	70.00
		Bar cancellation		6.00
30	A8	6r blue	1,500.	130.00
		Bar cancellation		10.00

See boxed note on bar cancellation below country heading.

Thick Bluish Paper

31	A7	2c green	12,500.	1,000.
32	A7a	4c carmine	190.00	3.25
33	A7a	1r pale blue		7,000.
		Bar cancellation		110.00
34	A8	2r dull red	4,500.	415.00

The 2c on paper watermarked loops is a proof.

Isabella II — A9

1855, Apr. 1 Wmk. 104
Blue Paper

36	A9	2c green	2,250.	60.00
a.		2c yellow green	2,750.	100.00
		Bar cancellation		4.00
37	A9	4c brown red	125.00	35
a.		4c carmine	135.00	40
b.		4c lake	135.00	95
		Bar cancellation		80
38	A9	1r green blue	550.00	8.00
a.		1r blue	900.00	10.00
b.		Cliché of 2r in plate of 1r	15,000.	1,600.
		Bar cancellation		2.25
39	A9	2r brown violet	375.00	7.00
a.		2r red violet	450.00	7.75
		Bar cancellation		2.25

1856, Jan. 1 Wmk. 105
Rough Yellowish Paper

40	A9	2c green	2,000.	100.00
		Bar cancellation		6.75
41	A9	4c rose	5.50	1.00
		Bar cancellation		70
42	A9	1r grnsh blue	2,500.	90.00
a.		1r dull blue	3,250.	90.00
		Bar cancellation		4.00
43	A9	2r brown violet	300.00	13.00
a.		2r reddish violet	275.00	25.00
		Bar cancellation		3.25

1856, Apr. 11 Unwmk.
White Smooth Paper

44	A9	2c blue green	200.00	16.00
a.		2c yellow green	250.00	25.00
		Bar cancellation		3.25
45	A9	4c rose	1.90	28
a.		4c carmine	30.00	14.00
46	A9	1r blue	11.00	6.00
a.		1r greenish blue	16.00	10.50
		Bar cancellation		1.65
47	A9	2r brown lilac	32.50	9.75
a.		2r dull lilac	45.00	12.00
		Bar cancellation		2.25

Three types of No. 45.

1859

48	A9	12c orange		92.50
		Bar cancellation		15.00

No. 48 was never put in use. *Reprints exist.*

A10   A11

1860-61
Tinted Paper

49	A10	2c green, *grn*	150.00	9.00
		Bar cancellation		1.10
50	A10	4c orange, *grn*	22.50	60
51	A10	12c car, *buff*	150.00	6.00
		Bar cancellation		2.25
52	A10	19c brn, buff ('61)	2,000.	800.00
53	A10	1r blue, *grn*	100.00	5.00
		Bar cancellation		1.90
54	A10	2r lilac, *lil*	135.00	5.00
		Bar cancellation		1.90

1862, July 16

55	A11	2c dp bl, *yel*	19.00	5.50
56	A11	4c dk brn, *redsh buff*	1.00	28
a.		4c brown, *white*	12.50	3.25
57	A11	12c blue, *pnksh*	25.00	4.50
		Bar cancellation		1.75
58	A11	19c car, *lil*	85.00	85.00
		19c carmine, *white*	150.00	110.00
59	A11	1r brown, *yel*	25.00	10.00
		Bar cancellation		1.90
60	A11	2r green, *pnksh*	16.00	6.00
		Bar cancellation		1.65

A12   A13

1864, Jan. 1

61	A12	2c dk bl, *lil*	19.00	9.50
62	A12	4c rose, *redsh buff*	95	28
a.		4c carmine, *reddish buff*	10.00	
63	A12	12c green, *pnksh*	25.00	8.25
64	A12	19c violet, *pnksh*	95.00	95.00
65	A12	1r brown, *grn*	80.00	35.00
		Bar cancellation		2.75
66	A12	2r dp bl, *pnksh*	22.50	6.00
		Bar cancellation		2.25

1865, Jan. 1 Litho. *Imperf.*

67	A13	2c rose	175.00	115.00
68	A13	4c blue	2,500.	
69	A13	12c blue & rose	200.00	11.00
a.		Frame inverted	10,000.	900.00
		Bar cancellation		2.75
70	A13	19c brown & rose	1,000.	325.00
		Bar cancellation		40.00
71	A13	1r yellow grn	175.00	27.50
		Bar cancellation		5.50
72	A13	2r red lilac	200.00	16.00
		Bar cancellation		4.00
73	A13	2r rose	250.00	25.00
a.		2r salmon	225.00	30.00
		Bar cancellation		6.75

No. 68 may not have been regularly issued.

1865, Jan. 1 Perf. 14

74	A13	2c rose red	400.00	47.50
		Bar cancellation		6.00
75	A13	4c blue	24.00	60
76	A13	12c blue & rose	275.00	24.00
		Bar cancellation		4.50
a.		Frame inverted	15,000.	2,250.
		As "a," bar cancel		425.00
77	A13	19c brown & rose	3,000.	1,500.
78	A13	1r yellow grn	1,250.	200.00
		Bar cancellation		12.00
79	A13	2r violet	900.00	125.00
		Bar cancellation		9.00
80	A13	2r rose	1,000.	150.00
a.		2r salmon	1,000.	150.00
b.		2r dull orange	1,000.	150.00
		Bar cancellation		15.00

Values for Nos. 74-80 are for fine centered copies.

SPAIN & COLONIES

RARE AND CLASSIC STAMPS, POSTAL HISTORY, PROOFS.
BUYING, SELLING, APPRAISALS.

For the Best Services in Classic Stamps and Postal History contact the RECOGNIZED LEADERS IN THE FIELD. Excellent stock of classic material for most countries of the World also available.

THE CLASSIC COLLECTOR
LIANE & SERGIO SISMONDO

Ph. 315-422-2331, Fax 315-422-2956
10035 Carousel Center Drive
Syracuse, NY 13290-0001

CANADIAN OFFICE: P.O. Box 6277, Station J, Ottawa, Canada K2A 1T4. Ph. 613-722-1621, Fax: 613-728-7305

A14

A14a

1866, Jan. 1

81	A14	2c rose	135.00	10.50
		Bar cancellation		2.50
82	A14	4c blue	20.00	45
83	A14	12c orange	125.00	7.25
a.		12c orange yellow	165.00	12.00
84	A14	19c brown	350.00	140.00
		Bar cancellation		21.00

1866

85	A14	10c green	150.00	11.00
		Bar cancellation		1.40
86	A14	20c lilac	105.00	10.00
		Bar cancellation		1.40
87	A14a	20c dull lilac	425.00	27.50
		Bar cancellation		1.65

A15

A15a

A15b

A15c

1867-68

88	A15	2c yellow brown	195.00	18.00
89	A15a	4c blue	13.00	45
90	A15b	12c orange yellow	115.00	3.25
a.		12c dark orange	150.00	6.00
b.		12c red orange ('68)	550.00	42.50
91	A15c	19c rose	1,000.	200.00
		Bar cancellation		21.00

See Nos. 100-102. For overprints see Nos. 114a-115a, 124-128, 124a-128a, 124c-124c, 124e-126e.

A15d

A15e

92	A15d	10c blue green	135.00	12.00
		Bar cancellation		1.25
93	A15e	20c lilac	60.00	4.75
		Bar cancellation		1.25

For overprints see Nos. 116-117, 116a-117a, 116c-117c, 117d, 117e, 117f.

A16

A17

A18

A19

94	A16	5m green	24.00	7.25
		Bar cancellation		1.25
95	A17	10m brown	24.00	6.00
a.		Tête bêche pair	15,000.	5,000.
96	A18	25m blue & rose	135.00	11.00
a.		Frame inverted		12,500.
		Bar cancellation		3.00
97	A18	50m bister brown	12.00	30

See No. 98. For overprints see Nos. 118-122, 118a-122a, 120c-122c, 122d, 120e, 122e, 119f, 122f.

1868-69

98	A18	25m blue	150.00	8.25
		Bar cancellation		1.75
99	A19	50m violet	12.00	35
100	A15b	100m brown	235.00	35.00
		Bar cancellation		1.25
101	A15c	200m green	90.00	5.00
		Bar cancellation		90
102	A15c	19c brown	1,600.	275.00

For overprints see Nos. 123, 123a, 123c, 123e.

Provisional Government

Excellent counterfeits exist of the provisional and provincial overprints.

Regular Issues Handstamped in Black

HABILITADO POR LA NACION.

1868-69

116	A15d	10c green	24.00	13.00
117	A15e	20c lilac	18.00	6.00
118	A16	5m green	12.00	4.50
119	A17	10m brown	10.50	4.50
120	A18	25m blue & rose	30.00	12.00
121	A18	25m blue	24.00	7.50
122	A18	50m bister brown	6.00	3.50
123	A19	50m violet	6.00	3.00
124	A15b	100m brown	75.00	24.00
125	A15c	200m green	24.00	7.50
126	A15b	12c orange	27.50	6.00
127	A15c	19c rose	240.00	90.00
128	A15c	19c brown	450.00	125.00

Nos. 116-128 exist with handstamp in blue, a few in red. These sell for more.

For Andalusian Provinces

Regular Issues Handstamped Vertically in Blue

HABILITADO POR LA NACION.

114a	A15	2c brown	60.00	24.00
115a	A15a	4c blue	22.50	20.00
116a	A15d	10c green	30.00	12.00
117a	A15e	20c lilac	21.00	10.00
118a	A16	5m green	15.00	6.50
119a	A17	10m brown	10.50	4.50
120a	A18	25m blue & rose	35.00	12.00
b.		Frame inverted		
121a	A18	25m blue	20.00	10.00
122a	A18	50m bister brown	7.50	4.50
123a	A19	50m violet	7.50	3.00
124a	A15b	100m brown	75.00	27.50
125a	A15c	200m green	25.00	10.00
126a	A15b	12c orange	30.00	7.50
127a	A15c	19c rose	275.00	135.00
128a	A15c	19c brown	550.00	175.00

For Valladolid Province

Regular Issues Handstamped in Black

HABILITADO POR LA NACION.

(Two types of overprint)

116c	A15d	10c green	32.50	15.00
117c	A15e	20c lilac	24.00	10.50
120c	A18	25m blue & rose	45.00	12.00
121c	A18	25m blue	35.00	12.00
122c	A18	50m bister brown	12.00	7.50
123c	A19	50m violet	12.00	6.00
124c	A15b	100m brown	90.00	36.00
125c	A15c	200m green	30.00	12.00
126c	A15b	12c orange	32.50	10.50
127c	A15c	19c rose	300.00	150.00
128c	A15c	19c brown	850.00	210.00

For Asturias Province

Regular Issues Handstamped in Black

Habilitado por la Junta Revolucionaria

117d	A15e	20c lilac	150.00	105.00
122d	A18	50m bister brown	165.00	105.00

For Teruel Province

Regular Issues Handstamped in Black

117e	A15e	20c lilac	60.00	45.00
120e	A18	25m blue & rose	75.00	45.00
122e	A18	50m bister brown	55.00	27.50
123e	A19	50m violet	55.00	27.50
124e	A15b	100m brown	125.00	60.00
125e	A15c	200m green	90.00	35.00
126e	A15b	12c orange	75.00	45.00

For Salamanca Province

Regular Issues Handstamped in Blue

117f	A15e	20c lilac	60.00	45.00
119f	A17	10m brown	55.00	35.00
122f	A18	50m bister brown	60.00	35.00

Duke de la Torre Regency

"España" — A20

1870, Jan. 1   **Typo.**

159	A20	1m brn lil, *buff*	5.50	4.25
b.		1m brn lil, *pnksh buff*	6.00	4.75
161	A20	2m blk, *pinkish*	6.00	4.75
a.		2m black, *buff*	6.50	5.50
163	A20	4m bister brn	10.50	9.00
164	A20	10m rose	12.00	4.50
a.		10m carmine	15.00	5.00
165	A20	25m gray lilac	30.00	6.00
a.		25m lilac	30.00	6.00
b.		25m aniline violet	45.00	7.50
166	A20	50m ultra	7.50	30
a.		50m dull blue	90.00	4.50
167	A20	100m red brown	15.00	4.50
a.		100m claret	21.00	6.50
b.		100m orange brown	21.00	6.50
168	A20	200m pale brown	18.00	4.50
169	A20	400m green	180.00	15.00
170	A20	1e600m dull lilac	1,000.	300.00
171	A20	2e blue	900.00	175.00
172	A20	12c red brown	135.00	6.00
173	A20	19c yellow green	175.00	125.00

The 12c pink was not regularly issued.

Kingdom

A21

A22

King Amadeo
A23   A24

1872, Oct. 1   **Imperf.**

174	A21	1/4c ultra	2.00	2.00
a.		Complete 1c (block of 4 1/4c)	35.00	40.00

See No. 221A.

1872-73   **Perf. 14**

176	A22	2c gray lilac	15.00	6.00
a.		2c violet	21.00	10.00
b.		Imperf.		50.00
177	A22	5c green	75.00	30.00
		Imperf., pair	225.00	
178	A23	5c rose ('73)	15.00	3.50
179	A23	6c blue	75.00	12.00
180	A23	10c brown lilac	165.00	60.00
181	A23	10c ultra ('73)	4.50	45
182	A23	12c gray lilac	10.00	90
183	A23	20c gray vio ('73)	75.00	24.00
184	A23	25c brown	25.00	6.00
185	A23	40c pale red brn	40.00	6.00
186	A23	50c deep green	60.00	6.00
187	A24	1p lilac	60.00	18.00
188	A24	4p red brown	300.00	200.00
189	A24	10p deep green	1,250.	1,000.

First Republic

Mural Crown
A25

"España"
A26

1873, July 1   **Imperf.**

190	A25	1/4c green	90	60
a.		Complete 1c (block of 4 1/4c)	24.00	12.00

1873, July 1   **Perf. 14**

191	A26	2c orange	9.00	4.50
192	A26	5c claret	21.00	4.50
193	A26	10c green	6.00	30
		Tête bêche pair		24,000.
194	A26	20c black	45.00	15.00
195	A26	25c deep brown	21.00	5.50
196	A26	40c brown vio	22.50	5.50
197	A26	50c ultra	10.00	5.50
198	A26	1p gray lilac	30.00	12.00
199	A26	4p red brown	240.00	210.00
200	A26	10p violet brn	1,250.	1,100.

"Justice"
A27

Coat of Arms
A28

1874, July 1

201	A27	2c yellow	15.00	5.50
202	A27	5c violet	21.00	5.50
a.		5c red violet	21.00	7.50
203	A27	10c ultra	7.50	30
a.		Imperf., pair	24.00	
204	A27	20c dark green	90.00	21.00
205	A27	25c red brown	21.00	5.50
a.		25c lilac (error)	300.00	325.00
b.		Imperf., pair		80.00
206	A27	40c violet	210.00	5.50
a.		40c brown (error)	150.00	
b.		Imperf., pair	275.00	
207	A27	50c yellow	60.00	4.75
a.		Imperf., pair	150.00	
208	A27	1p yellow green	45.00	12.00
a.		1p emerald	55.00	20.00
b.		Imperf., pair	175.00	
209	A27	4p rose	350.00	200.00
a.		4p carmine	450.00	250.00
210	A27	10p black	1,900.	1,100.

1874, Oct. 1

211	A28	10c red brown	12.00	60
a.		10c brown	12.00	60
b.		Imperf., pair	175.00	

Kingdom

King Alfonso XII — A29

1875, Aug. 1
Blue Framed Numbers on Back, 1-100 on Each Sheet

212	A29	2c orange brown	12.00	4.50
a.		2c chocolate brown	15.00	8.50
b.		Imperf., pair	90.00	90.00
213	A29	5c lilac	35.00	7.50
a.		Imperf., pair	125.00	125.00
214	A29	10c blue	3.00	30
a.		Imperf., pair	30.00	30.00
215	A29	20c brown orange	150.00	45.00
216	A29	25c rose	30.00	3.50
217	A29	40c deep brown	60.00	18.00
a.		Imperf., pair	240.00	240.00
218	A29	50c gray lilac	90.00	15.00
219	A29	1p black	105.00	30.00
220	A29	4p dark green	175.00	150.00
221	A29	10p ultra	1,000.	900.00

1876, June 1   **Imperf.**

221A	A21	1/4c green	22	15
b.		Complete 1c (block 4 1/4c)	1.00	35
c.		As "b," two 1/4c sideways	110.00	110.00
d.		As "b," both upper 1/4c invtd.	110.00	110.00
e.		As "b," upper left 1/4c invtd.	1,000.	350.00

King Alfonso XII
A30   A31

ONE PESETA:
Type I - Thin figures of value and "PESETA" in thick letters.
Type II - Thick figures of value and "PESETA" in thin letters.

Wmk. 178

1876, June 1	Engr.		*Perf. 14*
222 A30	5c yellow brown	6.00	1.50
223 A30	10c blue	3.00	30
224 A30	20c dark green	8.50	6.00
225 A30	25c brown	6.00	2.00
226 A30	40c black brown	40.00	21.00
227 A30	50c green	10.00	3.25
228 A30	1p dp blue, I	12.00	6.00
a.	1p ultra, II	16.00	6.50
229 A30	4p brown violet	30.00	21.00
230 A30	10p vermilion	75.00	75.00

		Imperf
222a A30	5c	10.00
223a A30	10c	4.50
224a A30	25c	10.00
227a A30	50c	12.00
228b A30	1p	18.00
229a A30	4p	60.00
230a A30	10p	150.00

Two plates each were used for the 5c, 10c, 25c, 50c, 1p and 10p. The 1p plates are most easily distinguished.

1878, July 1 Unwmk. Typo.		*Perf. 14*
232 A31	2c lilac	15.00	4.50
a.	Imperf.	40.00	
233 A31	5c orange	24.00	4.50
234 A31	10c brown	6.00	10
235 A31	20c black	105.00	45.00
a.	Imperf.	160.00	
236 A31	25c olive bis	15.00	1.75
237 A31	40c red brown	90.00	60.00
238 A31	50c blue green	45.00	6.00
239 A31	1p gray	40.00	12.00
240 A31	4p violet	105.00	60.00
241 A31	10p blue	180.00	180.00
a.	Imperf.	250.00	

A32   A33

1879, May 1			
242 A32	2c black	6.00	45
243 A32	5c gray green	7.50	45
244 A32	10c rose	6.50	30
245 A32	20c red brown	70.00	7.50
246 A32	25c bluish gray	7.50	30
247 A32	40c brown	15.00	2.50
248 A32	50c dull buff	60.00	2.50
a.	50c yellow	85.00	5.00
249 A32	1p brt rose	60.00	1.25
250 A32	4p lilac gray	275.00	15.00
251 A32	10p olive bis	1,250.	135.00

1882, Jan. 1			
252 A33	15c salmon	5.50	30
a.	15c orange	15.00	60
253 A33	30c red lilac	135.00	2.00
254 A33	75c gray lilac	135.00	2.00
a.	Imperf.	210.00	

King Alfonso XIII
A34   A35

1889-99			
255 A34	2c blue green	2.50	30
256 A34	2c black ('99)	13.00	2.00
257 A34	5c blue	4.50	15
258 A34	5c blue grn ('99)	42.50	60
259 A34	10c red brown	6.50	15
260 A34	10c red ('99)	85.00	1.75
261 A34	15c violet brown	1.75	15
262 A34	20c yellow green	16.00	1.75
263 A34	25c blue	5.75	15
264 A34	30c olive gray	22.50	1.25
265 A34	40c brown	22.50	90
266 A34	50c rose	22.50	60

---

267 A34	75c orange	65.00	1.40
268 A34	1p dark violet	18.00	30
269 A34	4p car rose	325.00	13.00
270 A34	10p orange red	550.00	32.50

The 15c yellow, type A34 is an official stamp listed as No. O9.
Several values exist imperf.

Control Number on Back

1900-05	Engr.		Unwmk.
272 A35	2c bister brown	1.90	15
273 A35	5c dark green	4.00	15
274 A35	10c rose red	5.50	15
275 A35	15c blue black	11.00	15
276 A35	15c dull lil ('02)	5.50	15
277 A35	15c purple ('05)	4.00	15
278 A35	20c grnsh black	19.00	60
279 A35	25c blue	3.25	15
b.	25c green (error)	3,200.	
280 A35	30c blue green	17.50	22
a.	30c deep green	20.00	22
281 A35	40c olive bister	67.50	2.00
282 A35	40c rose ('05)	135.00	80
283 A35	50c slate blue	22.50	22
b.	50c blue green (error)	2,000.	1,000.
284 A35	1p lake	22.50	22
285 A35	4p dk violet	135.00	8.25
286 A35	10p brown orange	135.00	32.50
Nos. 272-286 (15)		589.15	45.86

			Imperf
272a A35	2c	11.00	
273a A35	5c	14.00	
274a A35	10c	16.00	
275a A35	15c	37.50	
276a A35	15c	14.00	
277a A35	15c	11.00	
278a A35	20c	40.00	
279a A35	25c	11.00	
280b A35	30c	32.50	
281a A35	40c	135.00	
282a A35	40c	250.00	
283a A35	50c	55.00	
284a A35	1p	35.00	
285a A35	4p	225.00	
286a A35	10p	200.00	

Don Quixote Starts Forth — A36

Designs: 10c, Don Quixote attacks windmill. 15c, Meets country girls. 25c, Sancho Panza tossed in blanket. 30c, Don Quixote knighted. 40c, Tilting at sheep. 50c, On Wooden horse. 1p, Adventure with lions. 4p, In bullock cart, 10p, The Enchanted Lady.

Control Number on Back

1905, May 1			Typo.
287 A36	5c dark green	1.50	90
a.	Imperf.	32.50	
288 A36	10c orange red	2.25	90
289 A36	15c violet	2.25	90
a.	Imperf.	32.50	
290 A36	25c dark blue	5.75	1.25
291 A36	30c dk blue green	27.50	4.50
292 A36	40c bright rose	57.50	12.00
293 A36	50c slate	11.00	2.50
294 A36	1p rose red	165.00	32.50
295 A36	4p dk violet	60.00	35.00
296 A36	10p brown orange	110.00	70.00
Nos. 287-296 (10)		442.75	160.45

300th anniversary of the publication of Cervantes' "Don Quixote."
Counterfeits exist of Nos. 287-296.
For surcharges see Nos. 586-588, C91.

Six stamps picturing King Alfonso XIII and Queen Victoria Eugenia were issued Oct. 1, 1907, at the Madrid Industrial Exhibition. They were not valid for postage.

Alfonso XIII — A46   A47

Blue Control Number on Back

Perf. 13x12½, 13, 13½x13, 14

1909-22			Engr.
297 A46	2c dark brown	60	15
a.	No control number	60	30
298 A46	5c green	1.25	15
299 A46	10c carmine	1.25	15
300 A46	15c violet	6.00	15

---

301 A46	20c olive green	30.00	30
302 A46	25c deep blue	3.00	15
303 A46	30c blue green	6.00	15
304 A46	40c rose	9.00	30
305 A46	50c slate blue	7.50	30
a.	50c blue ('22)	9.00	30
306 A46	1p lake	21.00	15
307 A46	4p deep violet	60.00	4.50
308 A46	10p orange	65.00	10.50
Nos. 297-309 (12)		210.60	16.95

Nos. 297-309 exist imperforate.
The 5c exists in carmine (value $300); the 15c in blue (value $450); the 4p in lake (value $1,000). The 4p lake is known only with perfin "B.H.A." (Banco Hispano-Americano).
See Nos. 310-311, 315-317. For overprints see Nos. C1-C5, C58-C61.

Control Number on Back in Red or Orange

1917			
310 A46	15c yellow ocher	3.00	24
a.	Control number in blue	10.50	85

Control Number on Back in Blue

1918			
313 A46	40c light red	90.00	4.50

1920	Typo.	*Imperf.*
314 A47	1c blue green	30 15

Perf. 13x12½, 14
Litho.

1920			
315 A46	2c bister	3.50	15
316 A46	20c violet	35.00	15
Set value, #314-316			30

Nos. 314-315 have no control number on back.
For overprints and surcharge see Nos. 358, 449, 457, 468, 10L1, 11LB1.

1921		Engr.
317 A46	20c violet	24.00 15

Madrid Post Office — A48

1920, Oct. 1	Typo.	*Perf. 13½*
Center and Portrait in Black		
318 A48	1c blue green	28	24
319 A48	2c olive bister	28	24

Control Number on Back

320 A48	5c green	60	60
321 A48	10c red	60	48
322 A48	15c yellow	90	75
323 A48	20c violet	1.25	60
324 A48	25c gray blue	1.25	1.25
325 A48	30c dark green	3.75	2.50
326 A48	40c rose	16.00	3.50
327 A48	50c brt blue	20.00	10.50
328 A48	1p brown red	22.50	9.00
329 A48	4p brown violet	57.50	37.50
330 A48	10p orange	125.00	75.00
Nos. 318-330 (13)		249.91	142.16

Universal Postal Union Congress, Madrid, Oct. 10-Nov. 30.
Nos. 318-330 exist imperforate. Values: 5 times those of perforated stamps.

King Alfonso XIII
A49   A49a

FIFTEEN CENTIMOS:
Die I - Narrow "5."
Die II - Wide "5."

TWENTY FIVE CENTIMOS:
Die I - "25" is 2¾mm high. Vertical stroke of "5" is 1mm long.
Die II - "25" is 3mm high. Vertical stroke of "5" is 1½mm long.

Perf. 11 to 14, Compound

1922-26	Engr.		Unwmk.
331 A49	2c olive green	24	15
a.	2c deep orange (error)	75.00	90.00

Control Number on Back

332 A49	5c red violet	2.50	15
333 A49	5c claret	1.25	15
334 A49	10c carmine	1.25	90
335 A49	10c yellow green	1.65	15
a.	10c blue green ('23)	1.90	15
336 A49	15c slate bl (I)	4.00	15
a.	15c black green (II)	16.00	1.65
337 A49	20c violet	2.50	15
338 A49	25c carmine (I)	2.50	15
a.	25c rose red (II)	3.25	15
b.	25c lilac rose (error)	60.00	75.00
339 A49	30c black brn ('26)	6.50	18
340 A49	40c deep blue	2.75	15
341 A49	50c orange	11.00	15
a.	50c orange red	20.00	1.50
342 A49a	1p blue black	13.00	15
343 A49a	4p lake	45.00	3.00
344 A49a	10p brown	21.00	6.50
Nos. 331-344 (14)		115.14	12.08

Nos. 331, 334, 336-344 exist imperf.
The 5c exists in vermilion (value $120); the 25c in dark blue (value $180). The 50c exists in red brown, the 4p in brown and 10p in lake; value, each $125. These five were not regularly issued.
For overprints see Nos. 359-370, 467.

"Santa Maria" and View of Seville — A50

Herald of Barcelona — A51   Exposition Buildings — A52

King Alfonso XIII and View of Barcelona
A53

1929, Feb. 15			*Perf. 11*
345 A50	1c grnsh blue	25	30
346 A51	2c pale yel grn	25	30
347 A52	5c rose lake	52	60

Control Number on Back

348 A53	10c green	75	60
349 A53	15c Prus blue	52	30
350 A51	20c purple	75	60
351 A50	25c brt rose	75	60
352 A53	30c black brn	3.75	2.50
353 A53	40c dark blue	5.00	2.50
354 A51	50c deep orange	2.50	1.75
355 A52	1p blue black	7.50	4.50
356 A53	4p deep rose	20.00	12.00
357 A53	10p brown	42.50	27.50
Nos. 345-357,E2 (14)		96.04	62.30

			Perf. 14
345a A50	1c greenish blue	60	60
348a A53	10c green	21.00	21.00
350a A51	20c purple	21.00	21.00
351a A50	25c bright rose	21.00	21.00
352a A53	30c black brown	42.50	42.50
353a A53	40c dark blue	21.00	21.00
354a A51	50c deep orange	21.00	21.00
355a A52	1p blue black	21.00	21.00
356a A53	4p deep rose	21.00	21.00
357a A53	10p brown	75.00	75.00
Nos. 345a-357a,E2a (11)		285.10	285.10

Seville and Barcelona Exhibitions.
Nos. 345-357 exist imperf. Values about 6 times those of perf. stamps. See note after No. 432.

Nos. 314, 331, 333, 335-344 Overprinted in Red or Blue

Sociedad
de las Naciones
LV reunión
del Consejo
Madrid.

1929, June 10   *Imperf.*

358 A47   1c blue green   70   75

Perf. 13½x12½

359 A49   2c olive green   70   75
360 A49   5c claret (Bl)   70   75
361 A49   10c yellow green   70   75
362 A49   15c slate blue   70   75
363 A49   20c violet   70   75
364 A49   25c carmine (Bl)   45   40
365 A49   30c black brown   2.25 2.00
366 A49   40c deep blue   2.25 2.00
367 A49   50c orange (Bl)   2.25 2.00
368 A49a 1p blue black   7.25 7.75
369 A49a 4p lake (Bl)   9.50 9.50
370 A49a 10p brown (Bl)   30.00 40.00
    Nos. 358-370,E4 (14)   70.15 80.15

55th assembly of League of Nations at Madrid June 10-16. The stamps were available for postal use only on those days.

Nos. 359-370 values are for off-center copies.

Exposition Building — A54

1930   Litho.   *Perf. 11*

371 A54   5c dk blue & salmon   4.25 3.50
372 A54   5c dk violet & blue   4.25 3.50

Barcelona Philatelic Congress and Exhibition. "C. F. y E. F." are the initials of "Congreso Filatelico y Exposicion Filatelica." For each admission ticket, costing 2.75 pesetas, the holder was allowed to buy one of each of these stamps.

Locomotives
A55   A56

1930, May 10   *Perf. 14*

373 A55   1c light blue   26   50
374 A55   2c apple green   26   50

Control Number on Back

375 A55   5c lake   26   50
376 A55   10c yellow green   26   50
377 A55   15c bluish gray   26   50
378 A55   20c purple   26   50
379 A55   25c brt rose   15   24
380 A55   30c olive gray   1.00   65
381 A55   40c dark blue   85   65
382 A55   50c dk orange   2.00 2.25
383 A56   1p dark gray   2.50 2.75
384 A56   4p deep rose   27.50 25.00
385 A56   10p bister brn   175.00 140.00
    Nos. 373-385,C12-C17,E6 (20)   301.06 247.54

11th Intl. Railway Congress, Madrid, 1930.
These stamps were on sale May 10-21, 1930, exclusively at the Palace of the Senate in Madrid and at the Barcelona and Seville expositions.

Francisco de Goya at Age 80 ("1746 1828") ("1828 1928")
A57   A59

"La Maja Desnuda" — A58

1930, June 15   Litho.   *Perf. 12½*
Inscribed "Correos Espana"

386 A57   1c yellow   15   15
387 A57   2c bister brn   15   15
388 A57   5c lilac rose   15   15
389 A57   10c green   15   20

Engr.

390 A57   15c lt blue   15   15
391 A57   20c brown violet   15   15
392 A57   25c red   22   20
393 A57   30c brown   3.50 4.00
394 A57   40c dark blue   3.50 4.00
395 A57   50c vermilion   3.50 4.00
396 A57   1p black   4.50 5.00
397 A58   1p dark violet   65 1.00
398 A58   4p slate gray   45   65
399 A58   40p red brown   8.50 10.00

Inscribed "1828 Goya 1928"
Litho.

400 A59   2c olive green   15   15
401 A59   5c gray violet   15   15

Engr.

402 A59   25c rose carmine   22   20
    Nos. 386-402,C18-C30,CE1,E7 (32)   38.19 43.35

To commemorate the death of Francisco de Goya y Lucientes, painter and engraver.

Nos. 386-399 were issued in connection with the Spanish-American Exposition at Seville.

Nos. 386-402 exist imperf. Values about 6 times those of perf. stamps.

See note after No. 432.

King Alfonso XIII — A61

Two types of the 40c:

Type I   Type II

1930   *Perf. 11½, 12x11½*

406 A61   2c red brown   15   15

Control Number on Back

407 A61   5c black brown   45   15
408 A61   10c green   2.25   15
409 A61   15c slate green   7.00   15
410 A61   20c dark violet   3.00   50
411 A61   25c carmine   45   15
412 A61   30c brown lake   8.00 1.00
413 A61   40c dk blue (I)   12.00   65
  a.   Type II   16.00   65
414 A61   50c orange   12.00 1.25
    Nos. 406-414 (9)   45.30
    Set value   3.65

Nos. 406-414 exist imperf. Value for set, $325.
For overprints see #450-455, 458-466, 469-487.

Bow of "Santa Maria" — A63

Stern of "Santa Maria" — A64

"Santa Maria," "Niña," "Pinta" — A65

Columbus Leaving Palos — A66

Columbus Arriving in America — A67

1930, Sept. 29   Litho.   *Perf. 12½*

418 A63   1c olive gray   15   15
419 A64   2c olive green   15   15
420 A63   2c olive green   15   15
421 A64   5c red brown   15   15
422 A64   5c red brown   15   15
423 A64   10c blue green   52   50
424 A63   15c ultra   52   65
425 A64   20c violet   75   65

Engr.

426 A65   25c dark red   75   75
427 A66   30c bis brn, bl & blk brn   3.25 3.00
428 A65   40c ultra   2.75 2.50
429 A65   50c dk vio, bl & vio brn   3.25 3.00
430 A65   1p black   3.25 3.00
431 A67   4p blk & dk blue   3.50 3.50
432 A67   10p red brn & dk brn   15.00 15.00
    Nos. 418-432,E8 (16)   35.04 34.05

Christopher Columbus tribute.
Nos. 418 to 432 were privately produced. Their promoters presented a certain quantity of these labels to the Spanish Postal Authorities, who placed them on sale and allowed them to be used for three days, retaining the money obtained from the sale.

This note will also apply to Nos. 345-357, 386-402, 433-448, 557-571, B1-B105, C18-C57, C73-C87, CB1-CB5, CE1, E2, E7-E9, E15 and EB1.

Many so-called "errors" of color and perforation are known.

Nos. 418-432 exist imperf. Values about 5 times those of perf. stamps.

See Nos. 2671, B194.

Arms of Spain, Bolivia, Paraguay A68

Pavilion and Map of Central America — A69

Exhibition Pavilion of Ecuador — A70

Colombia Pavilion — A71

Dominican Republic Pavilion A72

Uruguay Pavilion A73

Argentina Pavilion A74

Chile Pavilion A75

Brazil Pavilion A76

Mexico Pavilion A77

Cuba Pavilion A78

Peru Pavilion A79

U.S. Pavilion A80

Exhibition Pavilion of Portugal — A81

King Alfonso XIII and Queen Victoria — A82

Unwmk.

1930, Oct. 10   **Photo.**   **Perf. 14**

433	A68	1c blue green	15	25
434	A69	2c bister brown	15	25
435	A70	5c olive brown	15	25
436	A71	10c dark green	25	25
437	A72	15c indigo	25	25
438	A73	20c violet	25	25
439	A74	25c car rose	25	25
440	A75	25c car rose	25	25
441	A76	30c rose lilac	75	1.40
442	A77	40c slate blue	42	75
443	A78	40c slate blue	42	75
444	A79	50c brown org	75	1.40
445	A80	1p ultra	1.40	1.75
446	A81	4p brown violet	6.00	7.50
447	A82	10p brown	75	1.40

Engr.   **Perf. 11, 14**

448	A82	10p orange brown	18.00	15.00
		Nos. 433-448,E9 (17)	30.44	32.20

Spanish-American Union Exhibition, Seville. See Nos. C50-C57.

The note after No. 432 will also apply to Nos. 433 to 448. All values exist imperforate.

Reprints of Nos. 433-448 have blurred colors, yellowish paper and an inferior, almost invisible gum. They sell for about $1 per set.

Revolutionary Issues
Madrid Issue

Regular Issues of 1920-30 Overprinted in Black, Green or Red

 REPUBLICA

On No. 314

1931   *Imperf.*

449	A47	1c blue green	15	15

On Nos. 406-411
Perf. 11½

450	A61	2c red brown (G)	35	22
451	A61	5c black brn (R)	35	22
452	A61	10c green	70	42
453	A61	15c slate grn (R)	1.75	1.10
454	A61	20c dk violet (R)	1.75	1.10
455	A61	25c carmine (G)	2.25	1.25
		Nos. 449-455 (7)	7.30	4.46

First Barcelona Issue

Regular Issues of 1920-30 Overprinted in Black or Red

REPUBLICA

On No. 314

1931   *Imperf.*

457	A47	1c blue green	15	15

On Nos. 406-414
Perf. 11½

458	A61	2c red brown	15	15
459	A61	5c black brown	15	15
460	A61	10c green	32	40
461	A61	15c slate grn (R)	35	45
462	A61	20c dk violet (R)	35	45
463	A61	25c carmine	35	45
464	A61	30c brown lake	2.50	3.00
465	A61	40c dk blue (R)	85	1.10
466	A61	50c orange	85	1.10

On Stamp of 1922-26

467	A49a	1p blue blk (R)	4.75	6.00
		Nos. 457-467 (11)	10.77	13.40

Nos. 457 to 467 are known both with and without accent over "U."

Second Barcelona Issue

Regular Issues of 1920-30 Overprinted in Black or Red

 REPUBLICA

On No. 314
Imperf.

468	A47	1c blue green	15	15

On Nos. 406-414
Perf. 11½

469	A61	2c red brown	15	15
470	A61	5c black brown (R)	18	22
471	A61	10c green	18	22
472	A61	15c slate grn (R)	90	1.10
473	A61	20c dark violet (R)	25	32
474	A61	25c carmine	25	32
475	A61	30c brown lake	4.00	5.00
476	A61	40c dark blue (R)	90	1.10
477	A61	50c orange	3.00	4.00
		Nos. 468-477 (10)	9.96	12.58

General Issue of the Republic

Nos. 406-414, 342 Overprinted in Blue or Red

República Española.

1931, May 27

478	A61	2c red brown	16	15
479	A61	5c black brn (R)	25	15
480	A61	10c green (R)	25	15
481	A61	15c slate grn (R)	2.25	24
482	A61	20c dk violet (R)	1.25	60
483	A61	25c carmine	16	15
484	A61	30c brown lake	3.50	60
485	A61	40c dk blue (R)	3.50	30
486	A61	50c orange	5.75	30
487	A49a	1p blue blk (R)	32.50	60
		Nos. 478-487 (10)	49.57	
		Set value		2.85

The setting contained 18 repetitions of "Republica Espanola" for each vertical row of 10 stamps. According to its sheet position, a stamp received different parts of the overprinted words.

Overprint position varieties include: reading down on 25c, 30c, 40c and 50c; double on 1p; double, both reading down, on 25c, 40c and 50c.

"Republica Espanola"
Stamps of various Spanish colonies overprinted "Republica Espanola" are listed with the colonies.

Fountain of Lions, The Alhambra, Granada A84

Interior of Mosque, Córdoba — A85

Alcántara Bridge and Alcazar, Toledo A86

Francisco García y Santos A87

Puerta del Sol, Madrid, on April 14, 1931 as Republic Was Proclaimed A88

Perf. 12½

1931, Oct. 10   **Unwmk.**   **Engr.**

491	A84	5c violet brown	18	30
492	A85	10c blue green	28	30
493	A86	15c dark violet	28	30
494	A85	25c deep red	35	30
495	A87	30c olive green	35	30
496	A84	40c indigo	65	60
497	A85	50c orange red	65	60
498	A81	1p black	1.10	1.25
499	A88	4p red violet	4.25	5.50
500	A88	10p red brown	15.00	13.00
		Nos. 491-500 (10)	23.09	22.45

Third Pan-American Postal Union Congress, Madrid. See Nos. C62-C67, CO1-CO6.

Nos. 491-500 exist imperforate. Values about 5 times those of perforated stamps.

For overprints see Nos. O20-O29.

Symbolical of Montserrat Cut With a Saw — A89

Abbott Oliva and Monastery Workman — A90

"Black Virgin"
A91   A92

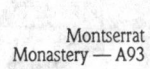
Montserrat Monastery — A93

1931, Dec. 9   **Perf. 11, 14**

501	A89	1c myrtle green	2.00	1.50
a.		Perf. 14	16.00	21.00
502	A89	2c red brown	1.25	90
a.		Perf. 14	12.50	15.00

Control Number on Back

503	A89	5c black brown	1.65	1.25
a.		Perf. 14	12.50	15.00
504	A89	10c yellow green	1.65	1.25
a.		Perf. 14	12.50	15.00
505	A90	15c myrtle green	1.90	1.50
a.		Perf. 14	16.00	21.00
506	A91	20c dark violet	3.25	2.00
a.		Perf. 14	105.00	125.00
507	A92	25c lake	4.75	3.00
a.		Perf. 14	5.00	6.00
508	A91	30c deep red	37.50	30.00
a.		Perf. 14	40.00	55.00
509	A93	40c dull blue	26.00	15.00
a.		Perf. 11	150.00	150.00
510	A90	50c dark orange	50.00	35.00
a.		Perf. 14	55.00	65.00
511	A92	1p gray black	50.00	35.00
a.		Perf. 11	80.00	90.00
512	A91	4p lilac rose	375.00	275.00
a.		Perf. 14	550.00	900.00
513	A92	10p deep brown	300.00	225.00
a.		Perf. 14	550.00	900.00
		Nos. 501-513,E13 (14)	870.95	647.40

Commemorative of the building of the old Monastery at Montserrat, started in 1031, and of

---

the image of the Black Virgin (said to have been carved by St. Luke) which was crowned by Pope Leo XIII in 1881.

Nos. 501-513 exist imperforate. Values about 3 times those of perforated stamps.

See Nos. C68-C72. For surcharges see Nos. 589, C92-C96.

Francisco Pi y Margall A95

Joaquín Costa A96

Nicolás Salmerón A97

Pablo Iglesias A99

Emilio Castelar — A100

1931-32   **Perf. 11½**
Control Number on Back

516	A95	5c brnsh black	1.90	30
517	A96	10c yellow green	4.50	30
518	A97	15c slate green	3.25	15
520	A99	25c lake	15.50	60
b.		Imperf.	45.00	
521	A99	30c car rose	4.75	15
c.		Imperf.	45.00	
522	A100	40c dark blue	27.50	2.75
523	A97	50c orange	35.00	4.50
		Nos. 516-523 (7)	92.40	8.75

Without Control Number

516a	A95	5c brownish blk ('32)	3.50	15
517a	A96	10c yellow green ('32)	3.25	15
518a	A97	15c slate green ('32)	55	15
520a	A99	25c lake	25.00	15
521a	A99	30c carmine rose	1.65	15
522a	A100	40c dark blue ('32)	15	15
523a	A97	50c orange ('32)	25.00	45
		Nos. 516a-523a (7)	59.10	

Without Control Number, Imperf.

516b	A95	5c	7.25
517b	A96	10c	9.50
518b	A97	15c	5.75
520c	A99	25c	6.00
521b	A99	30c	5.75
522b	A100	40c	10.50
523b	A97	50c	70.00

See Nos. 532, 538, 550, 579, 579a.
For overprints and surcharges see Nos. 7LC12-7LC13, 7LC15-7LC16, 7LC18, 7LE4, 8LB6, 8LB9-8LB10, 9LC17-9LC18, 10L7, 10L10-10L12, 10L16-10L18, 10L22-10L23, 11L7, 11L10-11L12, 11LB8, 12L4, 12L8, 12L11-12L12, 13L8, 14L6, 14L10-14L12, 14L18, 14L22-14L24.

Blasco Ibáñez A103

Manuel Ruiz-Zorrilla A104

Without Control Number

1931-34   **Perf. 11½**

526	A103	2c red brown ('32)	15	15
528	A103	5c chocolate ('34)	15	15
532	A95	20c dark violet	28	15
534	A104	25c lake ('34)	45	15
538	A100	60c apple green ('32)	15	15

Imperf

526a	A103	2c	9.50
528a	A103	5c	2.50
532a	A95	20c	5.75
534a	A104	25c	2.00
538a	A100	60c	5.75

For overprints and surcharges see Nos. 8LB3,8LB7, 9LC3, 9LC8-9LC9, 9LC14, 10L6, 10L13, 11L4, 11L8, 11LB5, 11LB9, 12L5, 12L9, 13L5, 13L7, 14L3, 14L7, 14L15, 14L19.

Cliff Houses,
Cuenca — A105

Alcázar of
Segovia — A106

Gate of the Sun at
Toledo — A107

1932-38   *Perf. 10*

539	A105	1p gray black ('38)	15	15
540	A106	4p magenta ('38)	32	25
541	A107	10p deep brown ('38)	50	55

Imperf

539a	A105	1p	1.75	2.50
540a	A106	4p	4.50	6.00
541b	A107	10p	2.75	5.50

Perf. 11½

539b	A105	1p	16	15
540b	A106	4p	65	60
541a	A107	10p	1.50	1.75

For overprints and surcharge see Nos. 9LC19, 10L19, 13L9, 14L25, 14L27-14L28.

Numeral
A108

Santiago Ramón y Cajal
A109

1933   **Unwmk.**   **Typo.**   *Imperf.*
542 A108 1c blue green   15 15

Perf. 11½
543 A108 2c buff   24 15
    a. Perf. 13½x13   45 15
    Set value   32 16

See Nos. 592-597. For surcharges and overprints see Nos. 590-590A, 634A-634D, 8LB1-8LB2, 9LC1-9LC2, 9LC4-9LC7, 9LC11-9LC12, 9LC20, 9LC26, 10L2-10L4, 11L1-11L2, 11LB2-11LB3, 12L1-12L2, 13L1-13L3, 14L1, 14L13.

1934   **Engr.**   *Perf. 11½x11*
545 A109 30c black brown   7.50 1.00
    a. Perf. 14   18.00 27.50
    b. Imperf.   35.00

Type of 1931 and

Mariana
Pineda
A110

Concepción
Arenal
A111

Gumersindo
de Azcarate
A112

Gaspar
Melchor de
Jovellanos
A113

1935

546	A110	10c green	15	15
547	A111	15c green	20	15
548	A112	30c car rose	6.50	15
549	A113	30c rose red	15	15
550	A97	50c dark blue	75	30
		Nos. 546-550 (5)	7.75	
		Set value		68

Imperf

546a	A110	10c	2.75
547a	A111	15c	2.75
548a	A112	30c	21.00
549a	A113	30c	3.00
550a	A97	50c	22.50

Shades exist.
For overprints and surcharges see Nos. 7LE3, 8LB4-8LB5, 8LB8, 10L8-10L9, 10L14, 10L20-10L21, 11L5-11L6, 11L9, 11LB6-11LB7, 11LB10, 12L6-12L7, 12L10, 13L6, 14L4-14L5, 14L8, 14L16-14L17, 14L20.

Lope's
Bookplate
A116

Lope de Vega
A117

Alcántara and
Alcázar, Toledo
A118

Perf. 11½x11, 11x11½
1935, Oct. 12

552	A116	15c myrtle green	4.75	30
553	A117	30c rose red	1.75	30
554	A117	50c dark blue	9.50	1.75
555	A118	1p blue black	16.00	1.25

Imperf

552a	A116	15c	140.00
553a	A117	30c	7.50
554a	A117	50c	40.00
555a	A118	1p	30.00

Perf. 14

553b	A117	30c	9.00	10.00
554b	A117	50c	20.00	27.50
555b	A118	1p	22.50	30.00

300th anniversary of the death of Lope Felix de Vega Carpio (1562-1635), Spanish dramatist and poet.
For surcharge see No. 11LB11.

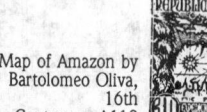

Map of Amazon by
Bartolomeo Oliva,
16th
Century — A119

1935, Oct. 12   *Perf. 11½*
556 A119 30c rose red   1.75 60
    a. Perf. 14   15.00 15.00
    b. Imperf.   24.00

Issued in commemoration of the proposed Iglesias Amazon Expedition.

Miguel
Moya — A120

Torcuato Luca
de Tena — A121

José Francos
Rodríguez
A122

Alejandro
Lerroux
A123

Nazareth School and Rotary Press — A124

1936, Feb. 14   **Photo.**   *Perf. 12½*
     Size: 22x26mm

557	A120	1c crimson	15	15
558	A121	2c orange brown	15	15
559	A122	5c black brown	15	15
560	A123	10c emerald	15	15

     Size: 24x28½mm

561	A120	15c blue green	15	15
562	A121	20c violet	15	15
563	A122	25c red violet	15	15
564	A123	30c crimson	15	15

     Size: 25½x30½mm

565	A120	40c orange	45	35
566	A121	50c ultra	24	15
567	A122	60c olive green	45	35
568	A123	1p gray black	65	35
569	A124	2p lt blue	5.50	2.50
570	A124	4p lilac rose	6.50	4.25
571	A124	10p red brown	10.50	7.00
		Nos. 557-571 (16)	25.79	16.47

Madrid Press Association, 40th anniversary.
Nos. 557-571 exist imperf. Values about 7 times those of perf. stamps.
See note after No. 432. See Nos. C73-C87.

Arms of
Madrid — A125

1936, Apr. 2   **Engr.**   *Imperf.*
572 A125 10c brown black   27.50 27.50
573 A125 15c dark green   27.50 27.50

1st National Philatelic Exhibition which opened in Madrid, Apr. 2, 1936.
For overprints see Nos. C88-C89.

"Republica
Espanola"
A126

Gregorio
Fernández
A127

1936   **Litho.**   *Perf. 11½, 13½x13*
574 A126 2c orange brown   15 15

For surcharges and overprints see Nos. 591, 9LC24, 10L5, 11L3, 11LB4, 12L3, 13L4, 14L2, 14L14.

1936, Mar. 10   **Engr.**   *Perf. 11½*
576 A127 30c carmine   1.00 65
    a. Perf. 14   10.00 10.00
    b. Imperf.   14.00

Tercentenary of the death of Gregorio Fernandez, sculptor.
For overprints see Nos. 7LC20-7LC21.

Type of 1931 and

Pablo Iglesias
A128   A129

Velázquez
A130

Fermín
Salvoechea
A131

1936-38   *Perf. 11, 11½, 11½x11*

577	A128	30c rose red	15	15
578	A129	30c car rose	1.00	30
579	A100	40c car rose ('37)	1.00	30
580	A129	45c car ('37)	15	15
581	A130	50c dark blue	15	15
582	A131	60c indigo ('37)	65	60
583	A131	60c dp org ('38)	4.25	3.50
		Nos. 577-583 (7)	7.35	5.15

Perf. 14

577a	A128	30c rose red	6.00
578a	A129	30c carmine rose	6.50
579a	A100	40c carmine rose	6.00
580a	A129	45c carmine	4.75
582a	A131	60c indigo	5.75
583a	A131	60c deep orange	10.50
		Nos. 577a-583a (6)	39.50

Nos. 577-583 exist imperf. Value, set $70.
For overprints see Nos. C90, 7LC17, 7LC22-7LC23, 10L15, 14L21.

Statue of
Liberty,
Spanish
and US
Flags
A132

1938, June 1   **Photo.**   *Perf. 11½*
585 A132 1p multicolored   9.00 9.00
    a. Imperf., pair   57.50 57.50
    b. Horiz. pair, imperf. vert.   67.50 67.50
    c. Souvenir sheet of 1   18.00 20.00
    d. As "c," imperf.   200.00 200.00

150th anniv. of the US Constitution
For surcharge see No. C97.

No. 289 Surcharged in Black

14 ABRIL 1938
VII Aniversario
de la República
45 cts.

1938   *Perf. 14*
586 A36 45c on 15c violet   8.00 8.00

7th anniversary of the Republic.

No. 289 Surcharged in Black:

Fiesta del Trabajo
1 MAYO
1938
1 Peseta
    b

1938, May 1
587 A36 45c on 15c violet   2.50 3.00
588 A36 1p on 15c violet   3.50 4.50

Issued to commemorate Labor Day.

No. 507 Surcharged in Black

2'50 PTAS.

1938, Nov. 10 *Perf. 11½*
589	A92 2.50p on 25c lake	15	15
b.	Perf. 14	1.90	3.50

Types of 1933-36
Surcharged in Blue or
Red

45
céntimos.

1938 *Perf. 10, 11, 13½x13, 13x14*
590	A108 45c on 1c grn (R)	30	18
b.	Imperf.	4.50	4.50
590A	A108 45c on 2c buff (Bl)	24.00	16.00
591	A126 45c on 2c org brn (Bl)	15	15

Numeral Type of 1933
1938-39 Litho. *Perf. 11½, 13*
White or Gray Paper
592	A108 5c gray brown	15	15
593	A108 10c yellow green	15	15
594	A108 15c slate green	15	15
595	A108 20c vio, gray paper	15	15
596	A108 25c red violet	15	15
597	A108 30c scarlet	15	15
	Set value	60	36

"Republic" — A133

1938 *Perf. 11½*
598	A133 40c rose red	15	15
599	A133 45c car rose	15	15
a.	Printed on both sides	10.00	10.00
600	A133 50c ultra	15	15
601	A133 60c dp ultra	40	60
	Set value	70	75

Nos. 598-601 exist imperf. Value for set $16.50.

Machine
Gunners
A134

Infantry — A135

Perf. 11½x11, 11x11½, Imperf.
1938, Sept. 1 Photo.
602	A134 25c dark green	5.00	8.25
603	A135 45c red brown	5.00	8.25

Issued in commemoration of the 43rd Division of the Republican Army. Sold only at the Philatelic Agency and for foreign exchange.

Blast Furnace
A136

Steel Mill and
Sculpture,
"Defenders of
Numantia"
A137

1938, Aug. 9 *Perf. 16*
604	A136 45c black	15	15
605	A137 1.25p dark blue	15	15

Issued in honor of the workers of Sagunto.

"Correo Submarino"

A set of six stamps and souvenir sheet inscribed "Correo Submarino" was issued Aug. 11, 1938. It was sold at double face value and only at the Philatelic Agency. The stamps and sheet were used on 300 agency-prepared covers carried on a single submarine voyage from Barcelona to Mahon, Minorca. Value for set of six, perf. $475, imperf. $525; souvenir sheet, $400.

Riflemen
A138

Machine
Gunners
A139

Bomb
Throwing — A140

1938, Nov. 25 Engr. *Perf. 10*
606	A138 5c sepia	2.25	3.00
607	A138 10c dp violet	2.25	3.00
608	A138 25c blue green	2.25	3.00
609	A139 45c rose red	1.75	2.50
610	A139 60c dark blue	3.75	4.00
611	A139 1.20p black	87.50	87.50
612	A140 2p orange	27.50	30.00
613	A140 5p dark brown	150.00	125.00
614	A140 10p dk blue grn	32.50	27.50
	Nos. 606-614 (9)	309.75	285.50

Issued in honor of the Militia. Sold only at the Philatelic Agency and for foreign exchange. Exist imperf.

Spanish State

Arms of Spain — A141

1936 Litho. *Imperf.*
Thin Transparent Paper
615	A141 30c blue	130.00
616	A141 30c pale green	130.00

Perf. 11
Thick Wove Paper
617	A141 30c dark blue	550.00	75.00

Issued in Granada during siege. After the city was liberated, these stamps were used throughout the province of Granada.

A143

Cathedral of
Burgos
A145

University of
Salamanca
A146

Cathedral del Pilar,
Zaragoza — A147

"La Giralda,"
Seville — A148

Xavier Castle,
Navarre — A149

Court of Lions,
Alhambra at
Granada — A150

Mosque,
Córdoba — A151

Alcántara Bridge
and Alcázar,
Toledo — A152

Soldier
Carrying
Flag — A153

Troops Landing at
Algeciras — A154

Two types of 30c:
Type I - Imprint 12mm long; "3" does not touch frame.
Type II - Imprint 8mm long; "3" touches frame.

1936 Unwmk. Litho. *Imperf.*
623	A143 1c green	3.25	3.00

Perf. 11½
624	A143 2c orange brown	60	45
625	A145 5c gray brown	65	60
626	A146 10c green	50	30
627	A147 15c dull green	50	30
628	A148 25c rose lake	85	30
629	A149 30c carmine (I)	85	45
a.	Type II	1.10	60
630	A150 50c deep blue	10.00	7.50
631	A151 60c yellow green	1.00	60
632	A152 1p black	4.00	2.50
633	A153 4p rose vio, red & yel	35.00	21.00
634	A154 10p light brown	42.50	18.00
	Nos. 623-634 (12)	99.70	55.00

Nos. 624-634 exist imperf. Value, set $275.
Nos. 625-631, 633-634 were privately overprinted "VIA AEREA" and plane, supposedly for use in Ifni.
For surcharges see Nos. 9LC21, 9LC23.

Nos. 542-543 Surcharged "Habilitado 0'05 ptas." in Two Lines
1936 *Imperf., Perf. 11½*
634A	A108 5c on 1c bl grn	2.75	2.75
634B	A108 5c on 2c buff	2.75	2.75
634C	A108 10c on 1c bl grn	2.75	2.75
634D	A108 15c on 2c buff	2.75	2.75

Issued in the Balearic Islands to meet a shortage of these values. Nos. 634A and 634C are imperf., Nos. 634B and 634D are perf. 11½.

St. James of
Compostela — A155

St. James
Cathedral
A156

Pórtico de la
Gloria
A157

Two types of 30c:
I - No dots in "1937."
II - Dot before and after "1937."

1937 *Perf. 11½, 11x11½*
635	A155 15c violet brown	1.25	1.10
636	A156 30c rose red (I)	4.00	50
a.	Type II	12.00	12.50
637	A157 1p blue & orange	12.50	3.00
a.	Center inverted	475.00	225.00

Holy Year of Compostela. Nos. 635-637 exist imperf. Value for set $140.

"Estado Espanol"
A159   A160

"El
Cid" — A161

Isabella I — A162

Two types of 5c, 30c and 10p:
5 Centimos: Type I Imprint 9½mm long. Type II Imprint 14mm long.
30 Centimos: Type I Imprint, "Hija De B. Fournier Burgos." Type II Imprint, "Fournier Burgos".
10 Pesetas: Type I "10" 2½mm high. Type II "10" 3mm high.

With Imprint
1936-40 *Imperf.*
638	A159 1c green	15	15

Perf. 11
640	A160 2c brown	15	15

Perf. 11, 11½, 11½x11, 11½x10½
641	A161 5c brown (I)	45	15
642	A161 5c brown (II)	15	15
643	A161 10c green	15	15

Perf. 11, 11x11½
644	A162 15c gray black	15	15
645	A162 20c dark violet	30	15
646	A162 25c brown lake	15	15
647	A162 30c rose (I)	40	15
648	A162 30c rose (II)	12.50	1.25
649	A162 40c orange	1.00	15

650	A162	50c dark blue	1.00	15
651	A162	60c yellow	25	15
652	A162	1p blue	10.50	32
653	A162	4p magenta	15.00	3.00
654	A161	10p dk bl (I) ('37)	50.00	30.00
655	A161	10p dp bl (II) ('40)	25.00	10.00
		Nos. 638-655 (17)	117.30	46.37

No. 638 was privately perforated. See Nos. 662-667. For overprint and surcharges see Nos. E18, 9LC10, 9LC13, 9LC15-9LC16, 9LC22, 9LC25, 9LC27-9LC30, 9LC34-9LC53.

Ferdinand the
Catholic
A163

Emblem of the
Falange
A164

1938   *Perf. 10½, 11½x11*

Imprint: "Lit Fournier Vitoria"

656	A163	15c deep green	2.00	15
657	A163	30c deep red	4.00	15

Imprint: "Fournier Vitoria"

Perf. 10

658	A163	15c deep green	1.25	15
659	A163	20c purple	8.25	1.10
660	A163	25c brown car	65	15
661	A163	30c deep red	4.00	15
		Nos. 656-661 (6)	20.15	
		Set value		1.40

Nos. 656-661 exist imperf.; value for set, $60. Part-perf. varieties exist.
For overprints see Nos. C98-C99.

Without Imprint

1938-48   *Perf. 11, 13½*

Two types of the 15 Centimos:
Type I - Medieval style numerals with diagonal line through "5."
Type II - Modern numerals. Narrower "5" without diagonal line.

662	A159	1c green, imperf.	15	15
663	A160	2c brn (18½x22mm; '40)	15	15
a.		2c bis brn (17½x21mm; '48)	15	15
664	A161	5c gray brn ('39)	20	15
665	A161	10c dk carmine	30	15
a.		10c rose	70	
666	A161	15c dk green (I)	1.00	15
666A	A161	15c dk green (II)	1.00	15
667	A162	70c dk blue ('39)	60	15
		Nos. 662-667 (7)	3.40	
		Set value		60

1938, July 17   *Perf. 10*

668	A164	15c bl grn & lt grn	3.75	4.00
669	A164	25c rose red & rose	3.75	4.00
670	A164	30c bl & lt bl	1.75	2.00
671	A164	1p brown & yellow	60.00	50.00

Second anniversary of the Civil War.

Isabella
I — A165

Gen. Francisco
Franco — A166

1938-39   *Litho.*   *Perf. 10*

672	A165	20c brt violet ('39)	42	15
673	A165	25c brown carmine	5.50	52
674	A165	30c rose red	28	15
675	A165	40c dull violet	28	15
676	A165	50c indigo ('39)	22.50	2.00
677	A165	1p deep blue	7.75	70
		Nos. 672-677 (6)	36.73	3.67

Imprint: "Sanchez Toda"

1939-40   *Litho.*   *Perf. 10*

678	A166	20c brt violet	20	15
679	A166	25c rose lake	20	15
680	A166	30c rose carmine	15	15
681	A166	40c slate green	15	15
682	A166	45c vermilion ('40)	1.10	1.50
683	A166	50c indigo	15	15
684	A166	60c orange	1.65	2.00
685	A166	70c blue	20	15
686	A166	1p black	6.50	15

687	A166	2p dark brown	10.00	1.00
688	A166	4p dark violet	50.00	10.00
689	A166	10p light brown	22.50	22.50
		Nos. 678-689 (12)	92.80	38.05

Nos. 686 to 689 have value and "Pta." on one line while Nos. 702 to 705 have value and "Pta." on two lines.

Without Imprint

Perf. 9½x10½, 12½x13

1939-51   **Litho.**   **Unwmk.**

690	A166	5c dull brn vio ('40)	50	15
691	A166	10c brown orange	1.65	60
692	A166	15c lt green	50	15
693	A166	20c brt violet	50	15
694	A166	25c dp claret	50	15
695	A166	30c blue	50	15
696	A166	35c aqua ('51)	40	15
697	A166	40c Prus grn ('40)	65	15
a.		40c greenish black	50	15
698	A166	45c ultra ('41)	50	15
699	A166	50c indigo ('40)	32	15
a.		Perf. 11½ ('47)	6.00	3.00
700	A166	60c dull org ('40)	42	20
701	A166	70c blue ('40)	50	15
702	A166	1p gray blk ('40)	4.00	15
703	A166	2p dull brn ('40)	6.00	20
704	A166	4p dull rose ('40)	15.00	20
705	A166	10p lt brown ('40)	115.00	2.50
		Nos. 690-705 (16)	146.94	
		Set value		4.60

The 40c exists in three types, with variations in the value tablet: I. "CTS" does not touch bottom line. II. Light background in tablet. "CTS" touches bottom line. III. As type I, but with well defined lines of white and color around rectangle.
The 60c exists in two types: I. Top and left side of value tablet touch rest of design. II. Tablet separated from rest of design by white lines.
Five values exist with perf. 10: 5c, 10c, 45c, 4p and 10p.
The imperforate 10c dull claret, type A166, without imprint, is a postal tax stamp, RA14.

1944   **Redrawn**

706	A166	1p gray	40.00	60

"PTS" instead of "PTA" as No. 702.
Nos. 690-706 exist imperforate.

The value reads "PTAS" instead of "PTS"

1944   **Unwmk.**   *Perf. 9½x10½, 13*

709	A166	10p brown	12.00	30

General
Franco — A167

St. John of the
Cross — A168

1942-48   **Engr.**   *Perf. 12½x13*

712	A167	40c chestnut	32	15
713	A167	75c dk bl, perf. 9½x10½ ('46)	2.00	30
714	A167	90c dk green ('48)	20	15
a.		Perf. 9½x10½ ('47)	85	15
715	A167	1.35p purple ('48)	20	15
a.		Perf. 9½x10½ ('46)	65	30
		Set value		58

1942   **Litho.**   *Perf. 9½x10½*

721	A168	20c violet	42	15
722	A168	40c salmon	1.25	60
723	A168	75c ultra	1.25	1.25

St. John of the Cross (1542-1591).
Nos. 721-723 exist imperforate.

Holy Year Issues

Statue in St. James
Cathedral
A169

St. James of
Compostela
A170

Incense
Burner — A171

Carvings in St. James Cathedral
A172   A174

St. James — A173

St. James'
Casket — A175

East Portal of
Cathedral
A176

St. James
Cathedral
A177

Perf. 9½x10½

1943, Oct.   **Litho.**   **Unwmk.**

724	A169	20c deep blue	18	15
725	A170	40c dk red brown	45	20
726	A171	75c deep blue	1.90	1.50

1943-44   *Perf. 9½x10½, 10½x9½*

727	A172	20c rose red ('44)	18	15
728	A173	40c dull green	40	20
729	A174	75c dk blue ('44)	2.50	1.90

1944

730	A175	20c red violet	18	15
731	A176	40c dull brown	50	20
732	A177	75c bright blue	22.50	21.00
		Nos. 724-734 (11)	31.47	26.05

Millenium of Castile Issues

Arms of
Soria — A178

Arms of
Castile — A179

Arms of
Avila — A180

Fortress — A181

Arms of
Segovia — A182

Arms of Fernan
González — A183

Arms of
Burgos — A185

Arms of
Santander — A186

1944   **Litho.**   *Perf. 9½x10½*

733	A178	20c violet	18	15
734	A179	40c dull brown	2.50	45
735	A180	75c blue	2.50	2.50

1944

736	A181	20c rose violet	18	15
737	A182	40c dull brown	2.50	28
738	A183	75c dull blue	2.25	2.50

1944

739	A180	20c red violet	18	15
740	A185	40c dull brown	1.90	28
741	A186	75c blue	3.00	3.00
		Nos. 733-741 (9)	15.19	9.46

Francisco Gomez de
Quevedo y Villegas (1580-
1645), Writer — A187

1945, Sept. 8   **Engr.**   *Perf. 10*

742	A187	40c dark brown	65	52

Type of Semi-Postal Stamp, 1940, Without Imprint at Lower Left and Right

1946, Jan. 1   **Litho.**   *Perf. 11*

743	SP20	50c (40c + 10c) sl grn & rose vio	1.50	20

No. 743 was used as an ordinary postage stamp of 50c denomination.

Elio Antonio de
Nebrija — A188

University of Salamanca
and Signature of
Francisco de
Vitoria — A189

1946, Oct. 12   **Engr.**   *Perf. 9½x10*

744	A188	50c deep plum	30	30
745	A189	75c deep blue	40	45

Issued in connection with Stamp Day and the Day of the Race, Oct. 12, 1946. See No. C121.

Francisco de
Goya — A190

Benito Jeronimo Feijoo y
Montenegro — A191

1946, Oct 26

746	A190	25c deep plum	15	15
747	A190	50c green	15	15
748	A190	75c dark blue	35	35
		Set value	48	48

Bicentenary of the birth of Francisco de Goya.

1947, June 1   **Unwmk.**

749	A191	50c deep green	40	30

Don Quixote
Reading — A192

"Don Quixote" by
Zuloaga — A193

1947, Oct. 9   **Engr.**   *Perf. 9½x10½*

750	A192	50c sepia	24	18
751	A193	75c dark blue	48	38

Stamp Day and the 400th anniv. of the birth of Miguel de Cervantes Saavedra. See No. C122.

General Franco
A194   A195

1948   Litho.   Perf. 12¹/₂x13
752 A194 15c green   15 15
753 A195 50c rose violet   1.00 15
        Set value   20

See Nos. 760-768, 780, 801-803. For surcharges see Nos. B137-B138.

Hernando   Mateo Aleman
Cortez   A197
A196

1948, June 15   Engr.   Perf. 12¹/₂x13
754 A196 35c black   24 15

Perf. 9¹/₂x10¹/₂
755 A197 70c dk violet brn   1.75 1.75
  a.   Perf. 12¹/₂x13   22.50 27.50

Ferdinand III   Grandson of
(The Saint)   Adm. Ramon de
A198   Bonifaz
                              A199

1948, Sept. 20 Litho.   Perf. 12¹/₂x13
756 A198 25c rose violet   20 15
757 A199 30c scarlet   16 15
        Set value   20

700th anniversary of the Spanish navy and of the capture of Seville by Ferdinand the Saint.

José de   Train Crossing
Salamanca y   Pancorbo
Mayol — A200   Viaduct — A201

Perf. 12¹/₂x13, 13x12¹/₂
1948, Oct. 9   Unwmk.
758 A200 50c brown   42 15
759 A201 5p deep green   1.25 15

Centenary of Spanish railroads. See No. C125.

Franco Types of 1948
1948-49   Litho.   Perf. 12¹/₂x13
760 A194 5c brown   15 15
761 A195 25c vermilion   15 15
762 A195 35c blue green   15 15
763 A195 40c red brown   40 15
764 A195 45c car rose ('49)   28 15
765 A194 50c bister   18 15
766 A195 70c purple ('49)   1.25 22
767 A195 75c dk vio blue   1.25 22
768 A195 1p rose pink   3.25 15
        Nos. 760-768 (9)   7.06
        Set value   90

No. 761 exists imperforate.

Symbols of
UPU — A202

1949, Oct. 9
769 A202 50c red brown   40 15
770 A202 75c violet blue   40 40

75th anniv. of the UPU. See No. C126.

St. John of   Pedro Calderon
God — A203   de la
                          Barca — A204

1950, Mar. 8   Engr.   Unwmk.
771 A203 1p dark violet   9.25 2.75

400th anniversary of the death of St. John of God, humanitarian.

1950-53   Photo.   Perf. 12¹/₂

Designs: 10c Lope de Vega. 15c, Tirso de Molina. 20c, Juan Ruiz de Alarcon, dramatist. 50c, St. Antonio Maria Claret y Clara.

772 A204 5c brown ('51)   15 15
773 A204 10c dp rose brn ('51) 15 15
773A A204 15c dk sl grn ('53)   20 15
774 A204 20c violet   22 15

Engr.   Perf. 12¹/₂x13
775 A204 50c dk blue ('51)   3.50 1.50
        Nos. 772-775 (5)   4.22
        Set value   1.80

Stamp of   Queen Isabella
1850 — A205   I — A206

1950, Oct. 12   Engr.   Imperf.
776 A205 50c purple   10.00 8.50
777 A205 75c ultra   10.00 8.50
778 A205 10p dk slate grn   135.00 125.00
779 A205 15p red   135.00 125.00
        Nos. 776-779,C127-C130 (8) 451.00 448.00

Centenary of Spain's stamps.

Franco Type of 1948
1950   Litho.   Perf. 12¹/₂x13
780 A195 45c red   75 15

1951, Apr. 22   Photo.   Perf. 12¹/₂
781 A206 50c brown   42 40
782 A206 75c blue   1.00 40
783 A206 90c rose brown   55 42
784 A206 1.50p orange   12.00 8.00
785 A206 2.80p olive grn   21.00 21.00
        Nos. 781-785 (5)   34.97 30.22

500th anniversary of the birth of Queen Isabella I. See No. C132-C136.

Ferdinand, the   Maria Michaela
Catholic   Dermaisiéres
A210   A211

1952, May 10   Photo.   Perf. 13
787 A210 50c green   85 70
788 A210 75c indigo   5.00 2.50
789 A210 90c rose brown   55 50
790 A210 1.50p orange   10.50 9.25
791 A210 2.80p brown   19.00 17.00
        Nos. 787-791 (5)   35.90 29.95

500th anniversary of the birth of Ferdinand the Catholic of Spain. See Nos. C139-C143.

1952, May 26   Perf. 12¹/₂x13
792 A211 90c claret   20 15

35th International Eucharistic Congress, Barcelona, 1952. See No. C137.

Dr. Santiago Ramon y
Cajal — A212

Portrait: 4.50p, Dr. Jaime Ferran y Clua.

1952, July 8   Photo.
793 A212 2p bright blue   22.00 50
794 A212 4.50p red brown   75 80

Centenary of the births of Dr. Santiago Ramon y Cajal and Dr. Jaime Ferran y Clua.

University   Luis de
Seal — A213   Leon — A214

Cathedral of
Salamanca
A215

Perf. 12¹/₂x13, 13x12¹/₂
1953, Oct. 12
795 A213 50c dp magenta   50 28
796 A214 90c dk olive gray   2.00 2.00
797 A215 2p brown   14.00 3.25

Issued in connection with Stamp Day, Oct. 12, 1953, to commemorate the 700th anniversary of the founding of the University of Salamanca.

The Magdalene — A216

1954, Jan. 10   Perf. 12¹/₂x13
798 A216 1.25p deep magenta   15 15

300th anniversary of the death of José de Ribera, painter.

St. James of   St. James
Compostela   Cathedral
A217   A218

1954, Mar. 1
799 A217 50c dark brown   15 15
800 A218 3p blue   40.00 2.50
        Set, never hinged   70.00

Holy year of Compostela, 1954.

Franco Types of 1948
1954   Litho.   Perf. 12¹/₂
801 A194 5c olive gray   15 15
802 A195 30c deep green   15 15
803 A194 80c dull car rose   2.00 15
        Set value   32
        Set, never hinged   6.25

Virgin by Alonso   Marcelino
Cano — A219   Menendez y
                              Pelayo — A220

Virgins: 15c, Begoña. 25c, Of the Abandoned. 30c, Black. 50c, Of the Pillar. 60c, Covadonga. 80c, Kings'. 1p, Almudena. 2p, Africa. 3p, Guadalupe.

1954, July 18   Photo.   Perf. 12¹/₂x13
804 A219 10c dk car rose   15 15
805 A219 15c olive green   15 15
806 A219 25c purple   16 15
807 A219 30c brown   18 15
808 A219 50c brn olive   60 15
809 A219 60c gray   18 15
810 A219 80c grnsh gray   2.72 15
811 A219 1p lilac gray   2.75 15
812 A219 2p red brown   85 15
813 A219 3p bright blue   75 75
        Nos. 804-813 (10)   8.49
        Set value   1.35
        Set, never hinged   16.00

Issued to publicize the Marian Year.

1954, Oct. 12
814 A220 80c dk gray grn   7.00 40
        Never hinged   15.00

Issued to publicize Stamp Day, October 12, 1954.

Gen. Franco — A221

Imprint: "F.N.M.T."
1954-56   Perf. 12¹/₂x13
815 A221 10c dk car lake   15 15
816 A221 15c bister   15 15
817 A221 20c dk ol grn ('55)   15 15
818 A221 25c blue violet   15 15
819 A221 30c brown   15 15
820 A221 40c rose vio ('55)   15 15
821 A221 50c dk brn olive   15 15
822 A221 60c dk vio brown   15 15
823 A221 70c dk green   15 15
824 A221 80c dk blue grn   15 15
825 A221 1p dp orange   15 15
826 A221 1.40p lil rose ('56)   15 15
827 A221 1.50p lt bl grn ('56)   15 15
828 A221 1.80p emerald ('56)   15 15
829 A221 2p red   17.50 80
830 A221 2p red lilac ('56)   15 15
831 A221 3p Prus blue   15 15
832 A221 5p dk red brn   22 15
833 A221 6p dk gray ('55)   22 15
834 A221 8p brt vio ('56)   35 15
835 A221 10p yel grn ('55)   35 15
        Nos. 815-835 (21)   20.84
        Set value   2.00
        Set, never hinged   40.00

Coils: The 1.50p, No. 830, the 3p and the 6p were issued in coils in brighter tones (the 3p in 1974, others in 1973). Every fifth stamp has a black control number on the back.
See Nos. 937-938, 1852-1855.

St. Ignatius of
Loyola — A222

St. Ignatius
and Loyola
Palace
A223

Perf. 13x12½, 12½x13

1955, Oct. 12   Photo.   Unwmk.
836 A222 25c dull purple   15   15
837 A223 60c bister   65   45
838 A222 80c Prus green   2.75   25
      Set, never hinged   7.00

4th centenary of the death of St. Ignatius of
Loyola, founder of the Jesuit Order and to publicize
the Day of the Stamp, 1955.

Symbols of
Telegraph and
Radio
Communi-
cation
A224

St. Vincent
Ferrer
A225

1955, Dec. 8   Perf. 13x12½
839 A224 15c dk olive bis   40   15
840 A224 80c Prus green   6.50   25
841 A224 3p bright blue   12.50 1.25
      Set, never hinged   40.00

Spanish telegraph system centenary.

1955, Dec. 20   Perf. 13
842 A225 15c olive bister   40   25
      Never hinged   85

Canonization of St. Vincent Ferrer, fifth
centenary.

"Holy Family"
by El
Greco — A226

Marching
Soldiers and
Dove — A227

1955, Dec. 24   Perf. 13x12½
843 A226 80c dark green   5.50   95
      Never hinged   9.50

1956, July 17   Unwmk.
844 A227 15c olive bis & brn   15   15
845 A227 50c lt ol grn & ol   60   28
846 A227 80c mag & grnsh blk   5.00   22
847 A227 3p ultra & dp blue   5.00 1.40
      Set, never hinged   22.50

20th anniversary of Civil War.

Ciudad de
Toledo
A228

1956, Aug. 3   Perf. 12½x13
848 A228 3p blue   5.00 2.00
      Never hinged   10.00

Issued to publicize the voyage of the S. S. Ciudad
de Toledo to Central and South America carrying
the First Floating (Industrial) Exposition.

Black Virgin of
Montserrat
A229

Archangel
Gabriel by Fra
Angelico
A230

Design: 60c, Monastery of Montserrat, mountains and crucifix.

1956, Sept. 11   Perf. 13x12½
849 A229 15c bister   15   15
850 A229 60c violet black   15   20
851 A229 80c blue green   35   42
      Set, never hinged   85

75th anniv. of the coronation of the Black Virgin
of Montserrat.

1956, Oct. 12   Engr.
852 A230 80c dull green   90   45
      Never hinged   1.25

Stamp Day, Oct. 12.

Statistical
Chart
A231

1956, Nov. 3   Perf. 12½x13
853 A231 15c dk olive bis   50   45
854 A231 80c green   5.25   90
855 A231 1p red orange   5.25   90
      Set, never hinged   15.00

Centenary of Spanish Statistics.

Hermitage
and
Monument
A232

1956, Dec. 4
856 A232 80c dull blue grn   3.00   25
      Never hinged   8.00

20th anniversary of the nomination of Gen.
Franco as chief of state and commander in chief of
the army.

Hungarian
Children
A233

St. Marguerite
Alacoque's
Vision of Jesus
A234

1956, Dec. 17   Perf. 13x12½
857 A233 10c brown lake   15   15
858 A233 15c dk bister   15   15
859 A233 50c olive gray   45   15
860 A233 80c dk blue grn   3.25   15
861 A233 1p red orange   3.50   15
862 A233 3p brt blue   9.50 2.50
      Nos. 857-862 (6)   17.00
      Set value   2.90
      Set, never hinged   32.50

Issued in sympathy to the children of Hungary.

1957, Oct. 12   Photo.   Unwmk.
863 A234 15c dk olive bis   15   15
864 A234 60c violet blk   25   15
865 A234 80c dk blue grn   28   15
      Set, never hinged   1.00

Centenary of the feast of the Sacred Heart of
Jesus and for Stamp Day 1957.

Gonzalo de
Cordoba — A235

1958, Feb. 28   Engr.   Perf. 13x12½
866 A235 1.80p yellow green   22   15
      Never hinged   25

Issued in honor of El Gran Capitan, 15th century
military leader.

"The Parasol," by
Goya — A236

"Wife of the
Bookseller of
Carretas
Street" — A237

Goya Paintings: 50c, Duke of Fernan-Nunez.
60c, The Crockery Seller. 70c, Isabel Cobos de
Porcel. 80c, Goya by Vicente Lopez. 1p, "El Pelele"
(Carnival Doll). 1.80p, Goya's grandson Marianito.
2p, The Vintage. 3p, The Drinker.

1958, Mar. 24   Photo.   Perf. 13
Gold Frame
867 A236 15c bister   15   15
868 A237 40c plum   15   15
869 A237 50c olive gray   15   15
870 A237 60c violet gray   15   15
871 A237 70c dp yellow grn   15   15
872 A237 80c dk slate grn   15   15
873 A237 1p orange red   15   15
874 A237 1.80p brt green   15   15
875 A237 2p red lilac   40   45
876 A236 3p brt blue   65   85
      Set value   1.75 1.80
      Set, never hinged   2.75

Issued to honor Francisco Jose de Goya and for
the "Day of the Stamp," Mar. 24.
   See Nos. 1111-1114. For other art types see
A240a, A246a, A257, A272, A285a, A300, A310,
A324, A340-A341, A360, A371 and footnote fol-
lowing No. 1606.

Exhibition Emblem and
Globe — A238

1958, June 7   Perf. 13x12½
877 A238 80c car, dk brn & gray 18   15
  a. Souvenir sheet, imperf. 22.50 22.50
878 A238 3p car, vio blk & bl   85   75
  a. Souvenir sheet, imperf. 22.50 22.50
      Set, never hinged   2.00
      #877a-878a never
        hinged   65.00

No. 877a sold for 2p, No. 878a for 5p.
Issued for the Universal and International Exposition at Brussels.

Charles V
A239

Various Portraits of Charles V: 50c, 1.80p, with
helmet. 70c, 2p, facing left. 80c, 3p, with beret.

1958, July 30   Photo.   Perf. 13
879 A239 15c buff & brown   15   15
880 A239 50c lt grn & ol brn   15   15
881 A239 70c gray, grn & blk   28   15
882 A239 80c pale brn & Prus grn 25   15
883 A239 1p bis & brick red   28   15
884 A239 1.80p pale grn & brt grn 25 15
885 A239 2p gray & lilac   65   80
886 A239 3p pale brn & brt bl 1.90 1.65
      Nos. 879-886 (8)   3.91
      Set value   2.95
      Set, never hinged   4.50

400th anniv. of the death of Charles V (Carlos I
of Spain.)

Escorial and
Streamlined
Train
A240

Designs: 60c, 2p, Railroad bridge at Despeñaper-
ros, vert. 80c, 3p, Train and Castle de La Mota.

1958, Sept. 29   Perf. 12½x13
887 A240 15c dk olive bis   15   15
888 A240 60c dk purple   15   15
889 A240 80c dk blue grn   15   15
890 A240 1p red orange   35   15
891 A240 2p red lilac   35   15
892 A240 3p blue   1.65   65
      Nos. 887-892 (6)   2.80
      Set value   1.00
      Set, never hinged   6.00

International Railroad Congress, Madrid, Sept.
28-Oct. 7.

Velazquez Self-
portrait — A240a

Velazquez Paintings: 15c, The Drinkers, horiz.
40c, The Spinners. 50c, Surrender of Breda. 60c,
The Little Princesses. 70c, Prince Balthazar. 1p,
The Coronation of Our Lady. 1.80p, Aesop. 2p,
Vulcan's Forge. 3p, Menippus.

1959, Mar. 24   Photo.   Perf. 13
Gold Frame

893	A240a	15c dk brown	15	15
894	A240a	40c rose violet	15	15
895	A240a	50c olive	15	15
896	A240a	60c black brown	15	15
897	A240a	70c dp yellow grn	15	15
898	A240a	80c dk slate grn	15	15
899	A240a	1p orange red	15	15
900	A240a	1.80p emerald	15	15
901	A240a	2p red lilac	15	15
902	A240a	3p brt blue	32	42
		Set value	1.10	1.10
		Set, never hinged	2.75	

Issued to honor Diego de Silva Velazquez (1599-1660) and for Stamp Day, Mar. 24.
For other art types see A236-A237, A246a, A257, A272, A285a, A300, A310, A324, A340-A341, A360, A371 and footnote following No. 1606.

Civil War Memorial
A241

1959, Apr. 1.   Litho.   Unwmk.

903	A241	80c yel grn & dk sl grn	15	15
		Never hinged	30	

Issued to commemorate the inauguration of the war memorial at the monastery of the Holy Cross in the Valley of the Fallen.

Louis XIV and Philip II — A242

1959, Oct. 24   Photo.   Perf. 13x12½

904	A242	1p gold & rose brn	15	15
		Never hinged	30	

300th anniv. of the signing of the Treaty of the Pyrenees. Design shows the French-Spanish meeting at Isle des Faisans in 1659, as pictured in the Lebrun Tapestry, Versailles.

Monastery of Guadalupe
A243

Designs: 80c, Monastery, different view. 1p, Portals.

1959, Nov. 16   Engr.   Perf. 12½x13

905	A243	15c lt red brown	15	15
906	A243	80c slate	15	15
907	A243	1p rose red	15	15
		Set value	38	30
		Set, never hinged	60	

50th anniversary of the entrance of the Franciscan Brothers into Guadalupe monastery.

Holy Family, by Goya — A244

1959, Dec. 10   Photo.   Perf. 13x12½

908	A244	1p orange brown	18	15
		Never hinged	40	

> Catalogue values for unused stamps in this section, from this point to the end of the section, are for Never Hinged items.

Lidian Bull — A245

Bullfighter, 19th Century — A246

Designs: 20c, Rounding up bulls. 25c, Running with the bulls, Pamplona. 30c, Bull entering arena. 50c, Bullfighting with cape. 70c, Bullfighting with banderillas. 80c, 1p, 1.40p, 1.50p, Fighting with muleta, various poses. 1.80p, Mounted bullfighter placing banderillas.

Perf. 12½x13, 13x12½

1960, Feb. 29   Engr.   Unwmk.

909	A245	15c sepia & bis	15	15
910	A245	20c vio & bl vio	15	15
911	A246	25c gray	15	15
912	A246	30c sepia & bister	15	15
913	A246	50c dull vio & sep	18	15
914	A246	70c sepia & sl grn	18	15
915	A246	80c blue grn & grn	15	15
916	A246	1p red & brn	30	15
917	A246	1.40p brown & lake	15	15
918	A246	1.50p grnsh bl & grn	15	15
919	A245	1.80p grn & dk grn	15	15
920	A246	5p brn & brn car	65	45
		Nos. 909-920,C159-C162 (16)	3.76	
		Set value		2.20

Murillo Self-portrait
A246a

Christ of Lepanto
A247

Murillo Paintings: 25c, The Good Shepherd. 40c, Rebecca and Eliezer. 50c, Virgin of the Rosary. 70c, Immaculate Conception. 80c, Children with Shell. 1.50p, Holy Family with Bird, horiz. 2.50p, Children Playing Dice. 3p, Children Eating. 5p, Children counting Money.

1960, Mar. 24   Photo.   Perf. 13
Gold Frame

921	A246a	25c dull violet	15	15
922	A246a	40c plum	15	15
923	A246a	50c olive gray	15	15
924	A246a	70c dp yel grn	15	15
925	A246a	80c deep green	15	15
926	A246a	1p violet brown	15	15
927	A246a	1.50p blue green	15	15
928	A246a	2.50p rose car	22	15
929	A246a	3p brt blue	1.50	80
930	A246a	5p deep red brn	65	20
		Nos. 921-930 (10)	3.42	
		Set value		1.80

Issued to honor Bartolome Esteban Murillo (1617-1682) and for Stamp Day, Mar. 24.
For other art types see A236-A237, A240a, A257, A272, A285a, A300, A310, A324, A340-A341, A360, A371 and footnote following No. 1606.

1960, Mar. 27   Perf. 13x12½

Designs: 80c, 2.50p, 10p, Holy Family Church, Barcelona.

931	A247	70c brn car & grn	2.25	1.75
932	A247	80c blk & ol grn	2.25	1.75
933	A247	1p claret & brt red	2.25	1.75
934	A247	2.50p brt vio & gray vio	2.25	1.75
935	A247	5p sepia & bister	2.25	1.75
936	A247	10p sepia & bister	2.25	1.75
		Nos. 931-936,C163-C166 (10)	34.50	25.50

First International Congress of Philately, Barcelona, March 26-Apr. 5. Nos. 931-936 could be bought at the exhibition upon presentation of 5p entrance ticket.

Franco Type of 1954-56
Imprint: "F.N.M.T.-B"

1960, Mar. 31   Photo.   Perf. 13

937	A221	1p deep orange	2.50	1.00
938	A221	5p dark red brown	2.50	1.00

Printed and issued at the International Congress of Philately in Barcelona.

St. Juan de Ribera — A248

St. Vincent de Paul — A249

1960, Aug. 16   Photo.   Perf. 13

939	A248	1p orange red	40	15
940	A248	2.50p lilac rose	15	15

Canonization of St. Juan de Ribera.

Europa Issue, 1960
Common Design Type

1960, Sept. 19   Perf. 12½x13
Size: 38½x21½mm

941	CD3	1p sl grn & ol bis	1.50	20
942	CD3	5p choc & salmon	1.50	60

1960, Sept. 27   Unwmk.   Perf. 13

943	A249	25c violet	15	15
944	A249	1p orange red	38	15
		Set value		20

3rd centenary of the death of St. Vincent de Paul.

Pedro Menendez de Aviles — A250

Runner — A251

Portraits: 70c, 2.50p, Hernando de Soto. 80c, 3p, Ponce de Leon. 1p, 5p, Alvar Nunez Cabeza de Vaca.

1960, Oct. 12   Perf. 13x12½

945	A250	25c vio bl, bl	15	15
946	A250	70c slate grn, pink	15	15
947	A250	80c dk grn, pale brn	15	15
948	A250	1p org brn, yel	16	15
949	A250	2p dk car rose, pink	30	15
950	A250	2.50p lil rose, buff	60	15
951	A250	3p dk blue, grnsh	2.75	50
952	A250	5p dk brown, cit	2.25	85
		Nos. 945-952 (8)	6.51	
		Set value		1.75

4th centenary of Florida's discovery and colonization.

Perf. 13x12½, 12½x13
1960, Oct. 31   Photo.

Sports: 40c, 2p, Bicycling, horiz. 70c, 2.50p, Soccer, horiz. 80c, 3p, Athlete with rings. 1p, 5p, Hockey on roller skates, horiz.

953	A251	25c dk vio, brn & blk	15	15
954	A251	40c purple, org & blk	15	15
955	A251	70c brt green & red	30	15
956	A251	80c dp grn, car & blk	22	15
957	A251	1p red org, brt grn & blk	55	15
958	A251	1.50p Prus grn, brn & blk	38	15
959	A251	2p red lil, emer & blk	1.10	15
960	A251	2.50p lil rose & green	38	15
961	A251	3p ultra, red & blk	75	15
962	A251	5p red brn, bl & blk	75	35
		Nos. 953-962,C167-C170 (14)	7.53	
		Set value		2.30

Isaac Albeniz — A252

1960, Nov. 7   Perf. 13

963	A252	25c dark gray	15	15
964	A252	1p orange red	40	15
		Set value		16

Centenary of the birth of Isaac Albeniz, composer.

Courtyard of Samos Monastery
A253

Designs: 1p, Fountain, vert. 5p, Facade, vert.

Perf. 12½x13, 13x12½
1960, Nov. 21   Engr.

965	A253	80c bl grn & Prus grn	15	15
966	A253	1p org brn & car rose	1.65	15
967	A253	5p sepia & ocher	1.65	45
		Set value		60

Issued in honor of the reconstructed Benedictine monastery at Samos, Lugo.

Adoration, by Velazquez — A254

1960, Dec. 1   Photo.   Perf. 13x12½

968	A254	1p orange red	50	15

Flight into Egypt by Francisco Bayeu
A255

1961, Jan. 23   Perf. 12½x13

969	A255	1p copper red	38	15
970	A255	5p dull red brown	80	15

World Refugee Year.

Leandro F. de Moratin, by Goya — A256

St. Peter by El Greco — A257

1961, Feb. 13　　　　　　*Perf. 13*

971	A256	1p henna brown	28	15
972	A256	1.50p dk blue green	15	15
		Set value		18

200th anniversary of the birth of Leandro Fernandez de Moratin (1760-1828), poet and dramatist.

1961, Mar. 24　　　　　　*Perf. 13*

El Greco Paintings: 40c, Virgin Mary. 70c, Head of Christ. 80c, Knight with Hand on Chest. 1p, Self-portrait. 1.50p, Baptism of Christ. 2.50p, Holy Trinity. 3p, Burial of Count Orgaz. 5p, Christ Stripped of His Garments. 10p, St. Mauritius and the Theban Legion.

Gold Frame

973	A257	25c violet black	20	15
974	A257	40c lilac	20	15
975	A257	70c green	25	20
976	A257	80c Prus green	25	15
977	A257	1p chocolate	2.00	15
978	A257	1.50p grnsh blue	25	15
970	A257	2.50p dk car rose	38	15
980	A257	3p bright blue	1.00	45
981	A257	5p black brown	3.00	1.40
982	A257	10p purple	50	28
		Nos. 973-982 (10)	8.03	3.23

Issued in honor of El Greco and for Stamp Day, March 24.

For other art types see A236-A237, A240a, A246a, A272, A285a, A300, A310, A324, A340-A341, A360, A371 and footnote following No. 1606.

Diego Velazquez — A258

Canceled Stamp — A259

Velazquez Paintings: 1p, Duke de Olivares. 2.50p, Infanta Margarita. 10p, Detail from The Spinners, horiz.

Unwmk.

1961, Apr. 17　　Engr.　　*Perf. 13*

983	A258	80c dk blue & sl grn	1.90	75
a.		Souvenir sheet	7.00	5.50
984	A258	1p brn red & choc	5.50	75
a.		Souvenir sheet	7.00	5.50
985	A258	2.50p vio bl & bl	1.40	95
a.		Souvenir sheet	7.00	5.50
986	A258	10p grn & yel grn	6.25	2.50
a.		Souvenir sheet	7.00	5.50

300th anniversary (in 1960) of the death of Velazquez, painter.

Each souvenir sheet contains one imperf. stamp. The colors of the stamps have been changed: 80c, red brown & slate; 1p, blue & violet; 2.50p, green & blue; 10p, slate blue & greenish blue. The sheets were sold at a premium.

1961, May 6　Photo.　*Perf. 13x12½*

987	A259	25c gray & red	16	15
988	A259	1p orange & blk	1.40	15
989	A259	10p olive grn & brn	1.40	65

Issued for International Stamp Day.

Juan Vazquez de Mella — A260

Flag, Angel and Peace Doves — A261

1961, June 8　Unwmk.　*Perf. 13*

990	A260	1p henna brown	85	15
991	A260	2.30p red lilac	15	15
		Set value		22

Birth centenary of Juan Vazquez de Mella y Fanjul, politician and writer.

1961, July 10

Designs: 80c, Ships and Strait of Gibraltar. 1p, Alcazar and horseman. 1.50p, Ruins and triumphal arch. 2p, Horseman over Ebro. 2.30p, Victory parade. 2.50p, Ship building. 3p, Steel industry. 5p, Map of Spanish irrigation dams and statue, horiz. 6p, Dama de Elche statue and power station. 8p, Mining development. 10p, General Franco.

992	A261	70c multicolored	15	15
993	A261	80c multicolored	15	15
994	A261	1p multicolored	20	15
995	A261	1.50p gold, pink & brn	15	15
996	A261	2p gold, gray & bl	15	15
997	A261	2.30p multicolored	16	15
998	A261	2.50p multicolored	16	15
999	A261	3p gold, red & dk gray	40	24
1000	A261	5p bl grn, ol gray & pink	2.50	1.10
1001	A261	6p multicolored	1.25	75
1002	A261	8p gold, ol & sep	80	55
1003	A261	10p gold, gray & grn	80	55
		Nos. 992-1003 (12)	6.87	
		Set value		3.60

25th anniversary of national uprising.

Christ, San Clemente, Tahull A262

Luis de Argote y Gongora A263

Designs: 25c, Bas-relief, Compostela Cathedral. 1p, Cloister of Silos. 2p, Virgin of Irache.

1961, July 24　Unwmk.　*Perf. 13*
Gold Frame

1004	A262	25c blue violet	38	15
1005	A262	1p orange brown	55	15
1006	A262	2p deep plum	75	15
1007	A262	3p grnsh bl, sal & blk	95	40
		Set value		70

Issued to publicize the Seventh Exposition of the Council of Europe dedicated to Romanesque art, Barcelona-Santiago de Compostela, July 10-Oct. 10, 1961.

1961, Aug. 10　Photo.　*Perf. 13*

1008	A263	25c violet black	15	15
1009	A263	1p henna brown	50	15
		Set value		22

400th anniversary of the birth of Luis de Argote y Gongora, poet.

Europa Issue, 1961
Common Design Type

1961, Sept. 18　　　*Perf. 12½x13*
Size: 37½x21½mm

1010	CD4	1p brt vermilion	15	15
1011	CD4	5p brown	52	30
		Set value		36

Cathedral at Burgos A264

Sebastian de Belalcazar A265

1961, Oct. 1　　　　　　*Perf. 13*

1012	A264	1p gold & ol grn	18	15

25th anniversary of the nomination of Gen. Francisco Franco as Head of State.

Builders of the New World

Portraits: 70c, 2.50p, Blas de Lezo. 80c, 3p, Rodrigo de Bastidas. 1p, 5p, Nuflo de Chaves.

1961, Oct. 12　Photo.　*Perf. 13x12½*

1013	A265	25c indigo, *grn*	22	15
1014	A265	70c grn, *cream*	22	15
1015	A265	80c sl grn, *pnksh*	22	15
1016	A265	1p dk blue, *sal*	80	15
1017	A265	2p dk car, *bluish*	5.25	15
1018	A265	2.50p lil, *pale lil*	1.25	45
1019	A265	3p blue, *grysh*	2.50	80
1020	A265	5p brown, *yel*	2.75	90
		Nos. 1013-1020 (8)	13.21	2.90

Issued to honor the discoverers and conquerors of Colombia and Bolivia.

See Nos. 1131-1138, 1187-1194, 1271-1278, 1316-1323, 1377-1384, 1489-1496, 1548, 1550, 1587-1594, 1632-1633.

Patio of the Kings, Escorial — A266

Views of Escorial: 80c, Patio. 1p, Garden of the Monks and Escorial, horiz. 2.50p, Staircase. 5p, General view of Escorial, horiz. 6p, Main altar.

Perf. 13x12½, 12½x13

1961, Oct. 31　Engr.　Unwmk.

1021	A266	70c bl grn & ol grn	20	15
1022	A266	80c Prus grn & ind	20	15
1023	A266	1p ocher & dk red	70	15
1024	A266	2.50p cl & dull vio	70	15
1025	A266	5p bister & dk brn	2.00	85
1026	A266	6p sl bl & dull pur	2.75	1.90
		Nos. 1021-1026 (6)	6.55	3.35

Alfonso XII Monument, Retiro Park — A267

Church of St. Mary, Naranco — A268

Designs: 1p, King Philip II. 2p, Town hall, horiz. 2.50p, Cibeles fountain, horiz. 3p, Alcala gate, horiz. 5p, Cervantes memorial, Plaza de España.

Photogravure (25c, 2p, 5p) Engraved (1p, 2.50p, 3p)

1961, Nov. 13　Unwmk.　*Perf. 13*

1027	A267	25c gray & dull pur	16	15
1028	A267	1p bis brn & gray	42	15
1029	A267	2p claret & gray	42	15
1030	A267	2.50p black & lilac	35	15
1031	A267	3p slate & ind	85	42
1032	A267	5p Prus grn & beige	1.65	75
		Nos. 1027-1032 (6)	3.85	1.77

400th anniversary of Madrid as capital of Spain.

1961, Nov. 27

Designs: 1p, King Fruela I, founder of Oviedo. 2p, Cross of the Angels. 2.50p, King Alfonso II. 3p, King Alfonso III. 5p, Apostles from Oviedo Cathedral (sculpture).

1033	A268	25c purple & gray grn	18	15
1034	A268	1p bis brn & brn	45	15
1035	A268	2p dk brn & pale pur	90	15
1036	A268	2.50p claret & ind	45	15
1037	A268	3p slate & indigo	90	65
1038	A268	5p ol & ol grn	1.65	75
		Nos. 1033-1038 (6)	4.53	2.00

1200th anniversary of the founding of Oviedo, capital of Asturia.

Nativity Sculptured by José Gines — A269

"La Cierva" Autogiro — A270

1961, Dec. 1　Photo.　*Perf. 13x12½*

1039	A269	1p dull purple	38	15

1961, Dec. 11　Unwmk.　*Perf. 13*

Designs: 2p, Hydroplane "Plus Ultra," horiz. 3p, "Jesus del Gran Poder," plane of Madrid-Manila flight, horiz. 5p, Bustard hunt by plane. 10p, Madonna of Loretto, patron saint of Spanish airmen.

1040	A270	1p indigo & blue	16	15
1041	A270	2p grn, dl pur & blk	16	15
1042	A270	3p blk & ol grn	2.00	35
1043	A270	5p dl pur, gray bl & blk	4.25	90
1044	A270	10p blk, lt bl & ol gray	2.25	60
		Nos. 1040-1044 (5)	8.82	2.15

50th anniversary of Spanish aviation.

Provincial Arms Issue

Alava — A271

Arms of Spain — A271a

1962　　　Photo.　　*Perf. 13*

1045	A271	5p Alava	20	15
1046	A271	5p Albacete	20	15
1047	A271	5p Alicante	35	40
1048	A271	5p Almeria	35	40
1049	A271	5p Avila	35	40
1050	A271	5p Badajoz	20	15
1051	A271	5p Baleares	30	15
1052	A271	5p Barcelona	20	15
1053	A271	5p Burgos	1.00	40
1054	A271	5p Caceres	55	25
1055	A271	5p Cadiz	70	35
1056	A271	5p Castellon de la Plana	5.50	1.50
		Nos. 1045-1056 (12)	9.90	4.45

1963

1057	A271	5p Ciudad Real	70	35
1058	A271	5p Cordoba	5.25	1.25
1059	A271	5p Coruña	90	35
1060	A271	5p Cuenca	90	35
1061	A271	5p Fernando Po	1.25	75
1062	A271	5p Gerona	16	15
1063	A271	5p Gran Canaria	16	15
1064	A271	5p Granada	35	25
1065	A271	5p Guadalajara	90	35
1066	A271	5p Guipuzcoa	25	15
1067	A271	5p Huelva	16	15
1068	A271	5p Huesca	16	15
		Nos. 1057-1068 (12)	11.14	4.40

1964

1069	A271	5p Ifni	15	15
1070	A271	5p Jaen	15	15
1071	A271	5p Leon	15	15
1072	A271	5p Lerida	15	15
1073	A271	5p Logrono	15	15
1074	A271	5p Lugo	15	15
1075	A271	5p Madrid	15	15
1076	A271	5p Malaga	15	15
1077	A271	5p Murcia	15	15
1078	A271	5p Navarra	20	15
1079	A271	5p Orense	20	15
1080	A271	5p Oviedo	20	15
		Nos. 1069-1080 (12)	1.95	1.80

1965

1081	A271	5p Palencia	20	15
1082	A271	5p Pontevedra	20	15
1083	A271	5p Rio Muni	20	15
1084	A271	5p Sahara	20	15
1085	A271	5p Salamanca	20	15
1086	A271	5p Santander	20	15
1087	A271	5p Segovia	20	15
1088	A271	5p Seville	20	15
1089	A271	5p Soria	15	15

1090	A271	5p Tarragona	20	15
1091	A271	5p Tenerife	15	15
1092	A271	5p Teruel	15	15
		Nos. 1081-1092 (12)	2.25	1.80

1966

1093	A271	5p Toledo	15	15
1094	A271	5p Valencia	15	15
1094A	A271	5p Valladolid	15	15
1094B	A271	5p Vizcaya	15	15
1094C	A271	5p Zamora	15	15
1094D	A271	5p Zaragoza	15	15
1094E	A271	5p Ceuta	15	15
1094F	A271	5p Melilla	15	15
1094G	A271a	10p black	25	15
		Set value, #1093-1094G	1.25	1.10
		Nos. 1045-1094G (57)	26.69	13.80

Zurbaran Self-
portrait — A272

Zurbaran Paintings: 25c, Martyr, horiz. 40c, Burial of St. Catherine. 70c, St. Casilda. 80c, Jesus crowning St. Joseph. 1.50p, St. Jerome. 2.50p, Virgin of Grace. 3p, The Apotheosis of St. Thomas Aquinas. 5p, The Virgin as a child. 10p, The Immaculate Virgin.

Unwmk.
1962, Mar. 24   Photo.   Perf. 13
Gold Frame

1095	A272	25c olive gray	40	15
1096	A272	40c purple	40	15
1097	A272	70c green	55	15
1098	A272	80c Prus green	40	15
1099	A272	1p chocolate	8.25	15
1100	A272	1.50p brt blue grn	95	15
1101	A272	2.50p dk car rose	95	15'
1102	A272	3p bright blue	1.10	38
1103	A272	5p deep brown	2.75	75
1104	A272	10p olive green	2.75	75
		Nos. 1095-1104 (10)	18.50	
		Set value		2.35

Issued to honor Francisco de Zurbaran (1598-1664) and for Stamp Day, March 24.

For other art types see A236-A237, A240a, A246a, A257, A285a, A300, A310, A324, A340-A341, A360, A371 and footnote following No. 1606.

San Jose
Convent,
Avila — A272a

St. Theresa (by
Velázquez?) — A273

Mercury — A274

Design: 1p, St. Theresa by Bernini.

1962, Apr. 10   Perf. 13

1105	A272a	25c bluish blk	15	15
1106	A272a	1p brown	16	15

Perf. 13x12½

1107	A273	3p bright blue	1.65	28
		Set value		48

4th centenary of St. Theresa's reform of the Carmelite order.

1962, May 7

1108	A274	25c vio, rose & mag	15	15
1109	A274	1p brn, org & lt brn	32	15
1110	A274	10p dp grn, ol grn & brt grn	2.75	80
		Set value		95

International Stamp Day, May 7.

Painting Type of 1958

Rubens Paintings: 25c, Ferdinand of Austria. 1p, Self-portrait. 3p, Philip II. 10p, Duke of Lerma on horseback.

1962, May 28   Perf. 13
Gold Frame
Size: 25x30mm

1111	A237	25c violet blk	75	30
1112	A237	1p chocolate	6.50	28
1113	A237	3p blue	6.00	2.00

Perf. 13x12½
Size: 26x38mm

1114	A237	10p slate green	4.50	2.75

St. Benedict
A275

El Cid, Statue by
Cristobal
A276

Berruguete Sculptures: 80c, Apostle. 1p, St. Peter. 2p, St. Christopher carrying Christ Child. 3p, Ecce Homo (Christ). 10p, St. Sebastian.

1962, July 9   Perf. 13x12½

1115	A275	25c lt blue & plum	16	15
1116	A275	80c salmon & ol gray	40	15
1117	A275	1p gray & red	60	15
1118	A275	2p gray & magenta	4.75	15
1119	A275	3p brn pink & dk bl	1.75	1.25
1120	A275	10p rose & brown	1.75	70
		Nos. 1115-1120 (6)	9.41	2.55

400th anniv. of the death of Alonso Berruguete (1486-1561), architect, sculptor and painter.

Perf. 13x12½, 12½x13
1962, July 30   Engr.

Designs: 2p, Equestrian statue by Anna Huntington. 3p, El Cid's treasure chest, horiz. 10p, Oath-taking ceremony at Santa Gadea, horiz.

1121	A276	1p lt green & gray	24	15
1122	A276	2p brown & choc	1.50	15
1123	A276	3p blue & sl grn	4.75	1.10
1124	A276	10p sl grn & sl grn	3.00	60

Issued to commemorate El Cid Campeador (Rodrigo Diaz de Vivar, 1040-99), Spain's national hero.

Europa Issue, 1962

Bee and
Honeycomb
A277

1962, Sept. 13   Photo.   Perf. 12½x13

1125	A277	1p deep rose	50	15
1126	A277	5p dull green	1.75	45

Discus
Thrower — A278

UPAE
Emblem — A279

Sports: 80c, Runner. 1p, Hurdler. 3p, Sprinter at start.

1962, Oct. 7   Perf. 13x12½

1127	A278	25c pale pink & vio blk	15	15
1128	A278	80c pale yel & dk grn	30	15
1129	A278	1p pale rose grn	20	15
1130	A278	3p pale bl & dk bl	40	20
		Set value		44

Second Spanish-American Games, Madrid, Oct. 7-12.

Builders of the New World
Portrait Type of 1961

Portraits: 25c, 2p, Alonso de Mendoza. 70c, 2.50p, Jiménez de Quesada. 80c, 3p, Juan de Garay. 1p, 5p, Pedro de la Gasca.

1962, Oct. 12   Unwmk.

1131	A265	25c rose lil, gray	20	15
1132	A265	70c grn, pale pink	1.50	15
1133	A265	80c dk grn, pale yel	1.00	15
1134	A265	1p red brn, gray	2.00	15
1135	A265	2p car, lt bl	4.50	15
1136	A265	2.50p dk vio, pnksh	1.00	25
1137	A265	3p dp bl, pale pink	10.00	1.40
1138	A265	5p brn, pale yel	5.00	1.65
		Nos. 1131-1138 (8)	25.20	4.05

1962, Oct. 20   Engr.   Perf. 13

1139	A279	1p sepia & green	20	15

50th anniv. of the founding of the Postal Union of the Americas and Spain, UPAE.

The Annunciation,
by Murillo — A280

Holy Family by
Pedro de
Mena — A281

Mysteries of the Rosary: 70c, The Visitation, Correa. 80c, Nativity, Murillo. 1p, The Presentation, Pedro de Campaña. 1.50p, The Finding in the Temple, (unknown painter). 2p, The Agony in the Garden, Gianquinto. 2.50p, The Scourging at the Pillar, Alonso Cano. 3p, The Crowning with Thorns, Tiepolo. 5p, Carrying of the Cross, El Greco. 8p, The Crucifixion, Murillo. 10p, The Resurrection, Murillo.

1962, Oct. 26

1140	A280	25c lilac & brown	15	15
1141	A280	70c grn & dk bl grn	15	15
1142	A280	80c ol & dk bl grn	15	15
1143	A280	1p green & gray	4.25	65
1144	A280	1.50p green & dk bl	1.25	52
1145	A280	2p brown & violet		
1146	A280	2.50p dk brn & rose claret	38	15
1147	A280	3p lilac & gray	38	15
1148	A280	5p brown & dk car	60	35
1149	A280	8p vio brn & blk	60	25
1150	A280	10p green & yel grn	95	25
		Nos. 1140-1150,C171-C174 (15)	11.73	4.00

1962, Dec. 6   Photo.   Perf. 13x12½

1151	A281	1p olive gray	58	15

Malaria
Eradication
Emblem
A282

1962, Dec. 21   Perf. 12½x13

1152	A282	1p blk, yel grn & yel	32	15

WHO drive to eradicate malaria.

Pope John
XXIII and St.
Peter's,
Rome
A283

1962, Dec. 29   Engr.

1153	A283	1p dp plum & blk	42	20

Vatican II, the 21st Ecumenical Council of the Roman Catholic Church. See No. 1199.

St. Paul, by El
Greco
A284

Courtyard,
Poblet
Monastery
A285

1963, Jan. 25   Perf. 13

1154	A284	1p brn, blk & olive	60	15

1,900th anniversary of St. Paul's visit to Spain.

Perf. 12½x13, 13x12½
1963, Feb. 25   Unwmk.

Designs: 1p, Royal sepulcher. 3p, View of monastery, horiz. 5p, Gothic arch.

1155	A285	25c choc & slate grn	15	15
1156	A285	1p org ver & rose car	50	15
1157	A285	3p vio bl & dk bl	1.50	15
1158	A285	5p brown & ocher	3.00	90

Issued in honor of the Cistercian monastery of Santa Maria de Poblet.

José de Ribera,
Self-portrait
A285a

Coach
A286

Ribera Paintings: 25c, Archimedes. 40c, Jacob's Flock. 70c, Triumph of Bacchus. 80c, St. Christopher. 1.50p, St. Andrew. 2.50p, St. John the Baptist. 3p, St. Onofre. 5p, St. Peter. 10p, The Immaculate Virgin.

Unwmk.
1963, Mar. 24   Photo.   Perf. 13
Gold Frame

1159	A285a	25c violet	40	15
1160	A285a	40c red lilac	45	15
1161	A285a	70c green	1.10	15
1162	A285a	80c dark green	1.10	15
1163	A285a	1p brown	1.10	15
1164	A285a	1.50p blue green	1.10	15
1165	A285a	2.50p car rose	3.25	15
1166	A285a	3p dark blue	3.50	50
1167	A285a	5p olive	12.00	2.25
1168	A285a	10p dull red brn	4.50	1.40
		Nos. 1159-1168 (10)	28.50	5.20

Issued to honor José de Ribera (1588-1652) and for Stamp Day, Mar. 24.

For other art types see A236-A237, A240a, A246a, A257, A272, A300, A310, A324, A340-A341, A360, A371 and footnote following No. 1606.

1963, May 3   Perf. 13x12½

1169	A286	1p multicolored	15	15

First Intl. Postal Conference, Paris, 1863.

Globe
A287

1963, May 8   *Perf. 12¹/₂x13*

1170	A287	25c multicolored	15	15
1171	A287	1p multicolored	20	15
1172	A287	10p multicolored	1.40	40
		Set value		52

Issued for International Stamp Day, 1963.

"Give us this
Day our
Daily
Bread..."
A288

1963, June 1   **Unwmk.**

1173	A288	1p multicolored	15	15

FAO "Freedom from Hunger" campaign.

"Pillars of Hercules" and Globes — A289   Seal of Council of San Sebastian — A290

Designs: 80c, Fleet of Columbus. 1p, Columbus and compass rose.

1963, June 4   *Perf. 13*

1174	A289	25c multicolored	15	15
1175	A289	80c brn, lt grn & gold	15	15
1176	A289	1p sl grn, sepia & gold	25	15
		Set value		30

Issued to publicize the Congress of Institutions of Spanish Culture, June 5-15.

1963, June 27   **Photo.**

Designs: 80c, Burning of city, 1813. 1p, View, 1836.

1177	A290	25c vio, grn & blk	15	15
1178	A290	80c dk brn, gray & red	15	15
1179	A290	1p dk grn, grn & ol	30	15
		Set value		30

Rebuilding of San Sebastian, 150th anniv.

Europa Issue, 1963

Our Lady of Europe — A291

1963, Sept. 16   **Engr.**   *Perf. 13x12¹/₂*

1180	A291	1p bis brn & choc	24	15
1181	A291	5p bluish grn & blk	1.10	45

Arms of Order of Mercy — A292   King James I — A293

Designs: 1p, Our Lady of Mercy. 1.50p, St. Pedro Nolasco. 3p, St. Raimundo de Penafort.

1963, Sept. 24   **Photo.**   *Perf. 13*

1182	A292	25c blk, car rose & gold	15	15

Engr.

1183	A293	80c sepia & green	15	15
1184	A293	1p gray vio & brn vio	15	15
1185	A293	1.50p dull bl & blk	15	15
1186	A293	3p gray & black	25	20
		Nos. 1182-1186 (5)	85	
		Set value		60

75th anniversary of the coronation of Our Lady of Mercy.

Builders of the New World
Portrait Type of 1961

Portraits: 25c, 2p, Father Junipero Serra. 70c, 2.50p, Vasco Nuñez de Balboa. 80c, 3p, José de Galvez. 1p, 5p, Diego Garcia de Paredes.

1963, Oct. 12   *Perf. 13x12¹/₂*

1187	A265	25c vio bl, *bl*	18	15
1188	A265	70c grn, *pale rose*	18	15
1189	A265	80c dk grn, *yel*	55	15
1190	A265	1p dk bl, *pale rose*	70	15
1191	A265	2p magenta, *lt bl*	2.00	15
1192	A265	2.50p vio blk, *dl rose*	1.25	15
1193	A265	3p brt bl, *pink*	2.75	45
1194	A265	5p brown, *yel*	3.50	1.75
		Nos. 1187-1194 (8)	11.11	3.10

The Good Samaritan — A294

1963, Oct. 28   **Unwmk.**

1195	A294	1p gold, pur & brt car	18	15

Centenary of International Red Cross.

Holy Family by Alonso Berruguete (1486-1561) A295   Father Raymond Lully A296

1963, Dec. 2   **Photo.**   *Perf. 13x12¹/₂*

1196	A295	1p dark green	18	15

Christmas 1963. See No. 1279.

1963, Dec. 5   **Engr.**

Portrait: 1.50p, Cardinal Luis Antonio de Belluga (1662-1743).

1197	A296	1p dk violet & blk	28	15
1198	A296	1.50p sepia & dull vio	18	15
		Set value		15

See Nos. C175-C176.

Papal Type of 1962

Design: 1p, Pope Paul VI and St. Peter's, Rome.

1963, Dec. 30   *Perf. 12¹/₂x13*

1199	A283	1p dk green & blk	18	15

Issued to commemorate the second session of Vatican II, the 21st Ecumenical Council of the Roman Catholic Church.

Alcazar, Segovia — A297   Dragon Caves, Majorca — A298

Tourism: 40c, Potes, Santander. 50c, Leon Cathedral. No. 1202, Crypt of San Isidro at Leon. No. 1203, Costa Brava. 80c, Christ of the Lanterns, Cordova. No. 1206, Court of Lions, Alhambra, Granada. No. 1208, Interior of La Mezquita, Cordova. 1.50p, View of Gerona.

1964   **Engr.**   *Perf. 13*

1200	A297	40c sepia & blue	15	15
1201	A297	50c gray & sepia	15	15
1202	A297	70c ind & dk bl grn	16	15
1203	A298	70c violet & brown	15	15
1204	A298	80c dp ultra & blk	16	15
1205	A297	1p vio bl & pur	16	15
1206	A297	1p rose red & dl pur	20	15
1207	A298	1p dk green & blk	15	15
1208	A298	1p brn vio & rose	15	15
1209	A297	1.50p gray grn, brn & blk	16	15
		Set value	1.25	80

See Nos. 1280-1289.

Santa Maria de Huerta Monastery A299   Joaquin Sorolla, Self-portrait A300

Designs: 1p, Great Hall. 5p, View of monastery with apse, horiz.

1964, Feb. 24   *Perf. 13x12¹/₂, 12¹/₂x13*

1212	A299	1p gray grn & grn	15	15
1213	A299	2p grnsh blue & sepia	28	15
1214	A299	5p dark blue	2.00	45
		Set value		65

8th century of Santa Maria Monastery, Huerta.

1964, Mar. 24   **Photo.**   *Perf. 13*

Sorolla Paintings: 25c, The Jug (woman and child). 40c, Oxen and Driver, horiz. 70c, Man and Woman from La Mancha. 80c, Fisher Woman of Valencia. 1p, Self-portrait. 1.50p, Round up, horiz. 2.50p, Fishermen, horiz. 3p, Children at the Beach, horiz. 5p, Unloading the Boat. 10p, Man and Woman on Horseback, Valencia.

Gold Frame

1215	A300	25c violet	15	15
1216	A300	40c purple	15	15
1217	A300	70c dp yellow grn	15	15
1218	A300	80c bluish grn	15	15
1219	A300	1p brown	15	15
1220	A300	1.50p Prus blue	15	15
1221	A300	2.50p dk car rose	20	15
1222	A300	3p violet blue	65	25
1223	A300	5p chocolate	1.25	75
1224	A300	10p deep green	75	25
		Nos. 1215-1224 (10)	3.75	
		Set value		1.95

Issued to honor Joaquin Sorolla y Bastida (1863-1923) and for Stamp Day, March 24.

For other art types see A236-A237, A240a, A246a, A257, A272, A285a, A310, A324, A340-A341, A360, A371 and footnote following No. 1606.

"Peace" — A301   "Sport" — A302

Designs: 40c, Radio and television. 50c, New apartments. 70c, Agriculture. 80c, Reforestation. 1p, Economic development. 1.50p, Modern architecture. 2p, Transportation. 2.50p, Hydroelectric development. 3p, Electrification. 5p, Scientific achievements. 6p, Buildings, tourism. 10p, Generalissimo Franco.

1964, Apr. 1

1225	A301	25c blk, emer & gold	15	15
1226	A302	30c blk, bl & sal pink	15	15
1227	A301	40c gold & blk	15	15
1228	A302	50c multicolored	15	15
1229	A301	70c multicolored	15	15
1230	A302	80c multicolored	15	15
1231	A302	1p multicolored	24	15
1232	A301	1.50p multicolored	16	15
1233	A301	2p multicolored	16	15
1234	A302	2.50p multicolored	16	15
1235	A301	3p gold, blk & red	1.00	65
1236	A302	5p gold, grn & red	30	24
1237	A301	6p multicolored	65	48
1238	A302	10p multicolored	65	48
		Set value	3.75	2.65

Issued to commemorate 25 years of peace.

Bullfight and Unisphere A303   Stamp of 1850 and Modern Stamps A304

Designs: 1p, Spanish pavilion, horiz. 2.50p, La Mota castle, Medina de Campo. 5p, Spanish dancer. 50p, Jai alai.

Perf. 12¹/₂x13, 13x12¹/₂

1964, Apr. 23   **Engr.**

1239	A303	1p bl grn & yel grn	30	15
1240	A303	1.50p carmine & brn	15	15
1241	A303	2.50p dk bl & sl grn	20	15
1242	A303	5p car & dk car rose	40	30
1243	A303	50p vio bl & dk bl	1.40	40
		Nos. 1239-1243 (5)	2.45	
		Set value		90

New York World's Fair, 1964-65.

1964, May 6   *Perf. 13x12¹/₂*

1244	A304	25c dk car rose & dl pur	15	15
1245	A304	1p yel grn & dk bl	28	15
1246	A304	10p orange & rose red	85	35
		Set value		55

Issued for International Stamp Day, 1964.

Virgin of Hope — A305   Santa Maria — A306

1964, May 31   **Photo.**   *Perf. 13x12¹/₂*

1247	A305	1p dark green	18	15

Canonical coronation of the Virgin of Hope (La Macarena) in St. Gil's Church, Seville, May 31.

1964, July 16   *Perf. 13*

Designs (ships): 15c, 13th cent. ship of King Alfonso X, from medieval manuscript, vert. 25c, Carrack, from 15th cent. engraving, vert. 50c, Galley. 70c, Galleon. 80c, Xebec. 1p, Warship, Santisima Trinidad, vert. 1.50p, 18th cent. corvette, Atrevida, vert. 2p, Steamer, Isabel II. 2.50p, Frigate, Numancia, Spain's 1st armored ship. 3p, Destroyer. 5p, Submarine of Isaac Peral. 6p, Cruiser, Baleares. 10p, Training ship, Juan Sebastian Elcano.

1248	A306	15c dp rose & vio blk	15	15
1249	A306	25c org yel & gray grn	15	15
1250	A306	40c ultra & dk bl	15	15
1251	A306	50c sl grn & dk bl	15	15

1252	A306	70c vio & dk bl	15	15
1253	A306	80c dl bl grn & ultra	15	15
1254	A306	1p org & vio brn	15	15
1255	A306	1.50p car & sepia	15	15
1256	A306	2p blk & sl grn	1.10	15
1257	A306	2.50p rose car & dl vio	25	15
1258	A306	3p sepia & indigo	25	15
1259	A306	5p dk bl, lt grn & vio	1.25	45
1260	A306	6p lt green & vio	60	40
1261	A306	10p org yel & rose red	50	20
		Nos. 1248-1261 (14)	5.15	
		Set value		2.10

Issued to honor the Spanish Navy.

Europa Issue, 1964
Common Design Type

1964, Sept. 14 Photo. Perf. 12¹/₂x13
Size: 21¹/₂x39mm

1262	CD7	1p bis, red & grn	40	15
1263	CD7	5p brt bl, mag & grn	1.65	45

Madonna of Alcazar — A307   Shot Put — A308

1964, Oct. 9 Photo. Perf. 13

1264	A307	25c bister & brn	15	15
1265	A307	1p gray & indigo	15	15
		Set value		15

700th anniversary of the reconquest of Jerez de la Frontera.

1964, Oct. 10
Gold Olympic Rings

1266	A308	25c shown	15	15
1267	A308	80c Broad jump	15	15
1268	A308	1p Slalom	15	15
1269	A308	3p Judo	25	15
1270	A308	5p Discus	30	18
		Set value	85	62

1964 Olympic Games.

Builders of the New World
Portrait Type of 1961

Portraits: 25c, 2p, Diego de Almagro. 70c. 2.50p, Francisco de Toledo. 80c, 3p, Archbishop Toribio de Mogrovejo. 1p, 5p, Francisco Pizarro.

1964, Oct. 12 Perf. 13x12¹/₂

1271	A265	25c pale grn & vio	15	15
1272	A265	70c pink & ol gray	15	15
1273	A265	80c buff & Prus grn	45	15
1274	A265	1p buff & gray vio	45	15
1275	A265	2p pale bl & ol gray	45	15
1276	A265	2.50p pale grn & cl	35	22
1277	A265	3p gray & dk bl	3.00	45
1278	A265	5p yellow & brown	1.75	80
		Nos. 1271-1278 (8)	6.75	2.42

Christmas Type of 1963

Design: Nativity by Francisco de Zurbaran (1598-1664).

1964, Dec. 4 Photo.

1279	A295	1p olive black	20	15

Tourism Types of 1964

Designs: 25c, Columbus monument, Barcelona. 30s, Facade of Santa Maria, Burgos. 50c, Santa Maria la Blanca (medieval synagogue), Toledo. 70c, Bridge, Zamora. 80c, La Giralda (tower) and Cathedral of Seville. 1p, Boat and nets in Cudillero harbor. No. 1286, Cathedral of Burgos, interior. No. 1287, View of Mogrovejo, Santander. 3p, Bridge, Cambados, Pontevedra. 6p, Silk merchants' hall (Lonja), Valencia, interior.

1965 Engr. Perf. 13

1280	A298	25c dk blue & blk	15	15
1281	A298	30c dull grn & sep	18	15
1282	A298	50c claret & rose car	15	15
1283	A297	70c vio bl & ind	15	15
1284	A298	80c rose cl & dk pur	15	15
1285	A298	1p dp cl, car & blk	15	15
1286	A298	2.50p brn vio & bis	15	15
1287	A297	2.50p dull bl & gray	15	15
1288	A298	3p rose car & dk brn	18	15
1289	A298	6p slate & black	22	15
		Nos. 1280-1289 (10)	1.63	
		Set value		52

Alfonso X, the Wise (1232-84) A309   Julio Romero de Torres, Self-portrait A310

Portraits: 25c, Juan Donoso-Cortes (1809-53). 2.50p, Gaspar M. Jovellanos (1744-1810). 5p, St. Dominic de Guzman (1170-1221).

1965, Feb. 25 Engr. Perf. 13x12¹/₂

1292	A309	25c slate bl & blk	15	15
1293	A309	70c blue & indigo	16	15
1294	A309	2.50p slate grn & sep	24	15
1295	A309	5p dull grn & sl grn	40	18
		Set value		44

1965, Mar. 24 Photo. Perf. 13
De Torres Paintings: 25c, Girl with Jar. 40c, "The Song" (girl with guitar). 70c, Madonna of the Lanterns. 80c, Girl with guitar. 1.50p, "The Poem of Cordova" (pensive woman). 2.50p, Martha and Mary. 3p, "The Poem of Cordova" (two women holding statue of angel). 5p, Girl with the Charcoal. 10p, Back of woman's head.

Gold Frame

1296	A310	25c dull purple	15	15
1297	A310	40c purple	15	15
1298	A310	70c olive green	15	15
1299	A310	80c slate green	15	15
1300	A310	1p dk red brn	15	15
1301	A310	1.50p blue green	15	15
1302	A310	2.50p lilac rose	20	15
1303	A310	3p dark blue	25	15
1304	A310	5p brown	38	15
1305	A310	10p slate green	60	20
		Nos. 1296-1305 (10)	2.33	
		Set value		1.15

Issued to honor Julio Romero de Torres (1880-1930) and for Stamp Day, March 24.
For other art types see A236-A237, A240a, A246a, A257, A272, A285a, A300, A324, A340-A341, A360, A371 and footnote following No. 1606.

Bull and Symbolic Stamps — A311

1965, May 6 Perf. 13x12¹/₂

1306	A311	25c multicolored	15	15
1307	A311	1p orange & multi	18	15
1308	A311	10p multicolored	75	25
		Set value		45

Issued to honor Julio Romero de Torres (1880-1930) and for Stamp Day, March 24. Issued for International Stamp Day, 1965.

ITU Emblem, Old and New Communication Equipment — A312

1965, May 17 Perf. 12¹/₂x13

1309	A312	1p salmon, blk & red	15	15

Centenary of the International Telecommunication Union.

Pilgrim — A313   Explorer, Royal Flag of Spain and Ships — A314

Design: 2p, Pilgrim (profile).

1965, July 25 Photo. Perf. 13

1310	A313	1p multicolored	15	15
1311	A313	2p multicolored	20	15
		Set value		15

Issued to commemorate the Holy Year of St. James of Compostela, patron saint of Spain.

1965, Aug. 28 Perf. 13x12¹/₂

1312	A314	3p red, blk & yel	15	15

400th anniv. of the settlement of Florida, and the 1st permanent European settlement in the continental US, St. Augustine, Fla. See US No. 1271.

St. Benedict A315   Sports Palace, Madrid A316

Europa Issue, 1965
1965, Sept. 27 Engr. Perf. 13x12¹/₂

1313	A315	1p yel grn & sl grn	20	15
1314	A315	5p lilac & violet	70	18

1965, Oct. 9 Photo. Perf. 13

1315	A316	1p gray, gold & dk brn	15	15

Issued to commemorate the meeting of the International Olympic Committee in Madrid.

Builders of the New World
Portrait Type of 1961

Portraits: 25c, 2p, Don Fadrique de Toledo. 70c, 2.50p, Father José de Anchieta. 80c, 3p, Francisco de Orellana. 1p, 5p, St. Luis Beltran.

1965, Oct. 12 Photo. Perf. 13x12¹/₂

1316	A265	25c pale grn & dp pur	15	15
1317	A265	70c pink & brown	15	15
1318	A265	80c cream & Prus grn	15	15
1319	A265	1p buff & dk vio	15	15
1320	A265	2p lt bl & dk ol grn	15	15
1321	A265	2.50p lt blue & pur	15	15
1322	A265	3p gray & dk bl	1.25	40
1323	A265	5p yellow & brn	1.50	45
		Nos. 1316-1323 (8)	3.65	
		Set value		1.00

Chamber of Charles V, Yuste Monastery — A317   Stamp of 1865 (No. 78) — A318

Yuste Monastery: 1p, Courtyard, horiz. 5p, View of monastery, horiz.

Perf. 12¹/₂x13, 13x12¹/₂
1965, Nov. 15 Engr.

1324	A317	1p bl gray & blk	15	15
1325	A317	2p red brn & brn blk	25	15
1326	A317	5p grayish bl & grn	40	20
		Set value		40

Monastery of Yuste, Estremadura.

1965, Nov. 22 Perf. 13x12¹/₂
Designs: 1p, Stamp of 1865 (No. 77). 5p, Stamp of 1865 (No. 80).

1327	A318	80c blk & yel grn	15	15
1328	A318	1p plum, brn & rose	15	15
1329	A318	5p sepia & org brn	15	15
		Set value	30	22

Centenary of the first Spanish perforated postage stamps.

Nativity A319

1965, Dec. 1 Photo. Perf. 12¹/₂x13

1330	A319	1p bright green	15	15

Virgin of Peace, Antipolo A320   Globe and Four Beasts of Apocalypse A321

Design: 3p, Father Andres de Urdaneta.

1965, Dec. 3 Perf. 13x12¹/₂

1331	A320	1p pale sal & ol brn	15	15
1332	A320	3p gray & dp blue	18	15
		Set value	25	16

Christianization of the Philippines, 400th anniv.

1965, Dec. 29 Photo. Perf. 13x12¹/₂

1333	A321	1p grnsh bl, yel & brn	18	15

Issued to commemorate Vatican II, the 21st Ecumenical Council of the Roman Catholic Church, Oct. 11, 1962-Dec. 8, 1965.

Adm. Alvaro de Bazan (1526-88) — A322   Exhibition Emblem; Type Block "P" — A323

Portrait: 2p, Daza de Valdes, scientist (17th century).

1966, Feb. 26 Engr. Perf. 13x12¹/₂

1334	A322	25c dull blue & gray	16	15
1335	A322	2p magenta & violet	25	15
		Set value		15

See Nos. C177-C178.

1966, Mar. 4 Photo. Perf. 13

1336	A323	1p red, grn & vio bl	15	15

Issued to publicize the Graphic Arts and Advertising Packaging Exhibition "Graphispack," Barcelona, March 4-13.

José Maria Sert,
Self-portrait
A324

Santa Maria
Church, Guernica
A325

Sert Paintings: 25c, The Magic Ball. 40c, Evocation of Toledo, horiz. 70c, Christ on the Cross. 80c, Parachutists. 1.50p, "Audacity." 2.50p, "Justice." 3p, Jacob Wrestling with the Angel. 5p, "The Five Continents." 10p, Sts. Peter and Paul.

1966, Mar. 24
Gold Frame
1337	A324	25c dk purple	15	15
1338	A324	40c dp magenta	15	15
1339	A324	70c green	15	15
1340	A324	80c dk ol grn	15	15
1341	A324	1p claret brn	15	15
1342	A324	1.50p dull blue	15	15
1343	A324	2.50p dk red	15	15
1344	A324	3p deep blue	15	15
1345	A324	5p sepia	15	15
1346	A324	10p grnsh blk	15	15
		Set value	75	55

Issued to honor José Maria Sert (1876-1945) and for Stamp Day, Mar. 24.
For other art types see A236-A237, A240a, A246a, A257, A272, A285a, A300, A310, A340-A341, A360, A371 and footnote following No. 1606.

1966, Apr. 28   Photo.   Perf. 13
Designs: 1p, Arms of Guernica and Luno. 3p, Tree of Guernica.
1347	A325	80c bl, sepia & grn	15	15
1348	A325	1p yellow grn & multi	15	15
1349	A325	3p bl, grn & vio brn	15	15
		Set value	24	22

6th centenary of the founding of Guernica and Luno.

Cover with
Stamp of
1850 (No.
1) — A326

Designs (covers): 1p, 5r (#3). 10p, 10r (#5).

1966, May 6   Perf. 12½x13
1350	A326	25c rose vio, blk & red	15	15
1351	A326	1p red brn, org & blk	15	15
1352	A326	10p ol grn, grn & org	25	15
		Set value	36	20

Issued for International Stamp Day, 1966.

Bohi
Valley — A327

Torla,
Huesca — A328

Tourism: 40c, Portal of Sigena Monastery, Huesca. 50c, Santo Domingo Church, Soria. 80c, Torre del Oro, Seville. 1p, Palm and view, Pico de Teyde, Santa Cruz de Tenerife. 1.50p, Monastery of Guadalupe, Caceres. 2p, Alcala de Henares University. 3p, Seo Cathedral, Lerida. 10p, Courtyard of St. Gregorio, Valladolid.

1966   Engr.   Perf. 13
1353	A327	10c gray grn & bl grn	15	15
1354	A328	15c gray grn & brn	15	15
1355	A327	40c bis brn & brn	15	15
1356	A327	50c car rose & dp cl	15	15
1357	A327	80c lilac & rose vio	15	15
1358	A327	1p vio bl & bl grn	15	15
1359	A328	1.50p dk bl & blk	15	15
1360	A328	2p sl bl & sepia	15	15
1361	A328	3p ultra & blk	15	15
1362	A327	10p brt bl & grnsh bl	15	15
		Set value	60	40

Tree and
Globe
A329

1966, June 6   Photo.   Perf. 12½x13
1363	A329	1p brn & dk grn	15	15

6th International Forestry Congress, Madrid, June 6-18.

Navy
Emblem — A330

1966, July 1   Photo.   Perf. 13
1364	A330	1p gray & dk bl	15	15

Naval Week, Barcelona, July 1-8.

Guadamur
Castle — A331

Castles: 25c, Alcazar, Segovia. 40c, La Mota. 50c, Olite. 70c, Monteagudo. 80c, Butron, vert. 1p, Manzanares. 3p, Almansa, vert.

1966, Aug. 13   Engr.   Perf. 13
1365	A331	10c grysh bl & sep	15	15
1366	A331	25c violet & purple	15	15
1367	A331	40c grnsh bl & bl grn	15	15
1368	A331	50c grnsh bl & ultra	15	15
1369	A331	70c vio bl & ind	15	15
1370	A331	80c vio & sl grn	15	15
1371	A331	1p ol bis & gray	15	15
1372	A331	3p rose & red lil	15	15
		Set value	45	40

Don
Quixote,
Dulcinea
and
Aldonza
Lorenzo
A332

1966, Sept. 5   Photo.   Perf. 13
1373	A332	1.50p sal, lt grn & blk	15	15

4th World Congress of Psychiatry, Madrid.

Europa Issue, 1966

The Rape of
Europa
A333

1966, Sept. 28   Photo.   Perf. 12½x13
1374	A333	1p multicolored	15	15
1375	A333	5p multicolored	30	20

Don Quixote
and Sancho
Panza on
Clavileno
A334

Title Page of
"Dotrina
Christiana"
A335

1966, Oct. 9   Perf. 13x12½
1376	A334	1.50p sl bl, red brn & dk brn	15	15

17th Congress of the International Astronautical Federation.

Builders of the New World
Types of 1961 and A335

Designs: 30c, Antonio de Mendoza. 1p, José A. Manso de Velasco. 1.20p, Coins of Lima, 1699. 1.50p, Manuel de Castro y Padilla. 3p, Portal of Oruro Convent, Bolivia. 3.50p, Manuel de Amat. 6p, Inca courier, El Chasqui.

1966, Oct. 12
1377	A265	30c pale pink & brn	15	15
1378	A335	50c pale bis & brn	15	15
1379	A265	1p gray & vio	15	15
1380	A335	1.20p gray & black	15	15
1381	A335	1.50p pale grn & dp grn	15	15
1382	A335	3p pale gray & dp bl	15	15
1383	A335	3.50p pale lil & pur	15	15
1384	A265	6p buff & sepia	15	15
		Set value	92	52

Ramon del Valle
Inclan — A336

Portraits: 3p, Carlos Arniches. 6p, Jacinto Benavente y Martinez.

1966, Nov. 7   Photo.   Perf. 13
1385	A336	1.50p blk & green	15	15
1386	A336	3p blk & gray vio	15	15
1387	A336	6p blk & slate	15	15
		Set value	30	28

Issued to honor Spanish writers.
See design A355.

Carthusian
Monastery,
Jerez
A337

St. Mary Carthusian Monastery: 1p, Portal, vert. 5p, Entrance gate.

Perf. 13x12½, 12½x13
1966, Nov. 24   Engr.
1388	A337	1p grnsh bl & sl bl	15	15
1389	A337	3p green & yel grn	15	15
1390	A337	5p lilac & claret	20	15
		Set value	40	28

Nativity,
Sculpture by
Pedro Duque
Cornejo
A338

1966, Dec. 5   Photo.   Perf. 12½x13
1391	A338	1.50p multicolored	15	15

Regional Costumes Issue

Woman from
Alava — A339

1967   Photo.   Perf. 13
1392	A339	6p shown	15	15
1393	A339	6p Albacete	15	15
1394	A339	6p Alicante	15	15
1395	A339	6p Almeria	15	15
1396	A339	6p Avila	15	15
1397	A339	6p Badajoz	15	15
1398	A339	6p Baleares	15	15
1399	A339	6p Barcelona	15	15
1400	A339	6p Burgos	15	15
1401	A339	6p Caceres	15	15
1402	A339	6p Cadiz	15	15
1403	A339	6p Castellon de la Plana	15	15
		Set value	1.20	1.20

1968
1404	A339	6p Ciudad Real	15	15
1405	A339	6p Cordoba	15	15
1406	A339	6p Coruna	15	15
1407	A339	6p Cuenca	15	15
1408	A339	6p Fernando Po	15	15
1409	A339	6p Gerona	15	15
1410	A339	6p Gran Canaria, Las Palmas	15	15
1411	A339	6p Granada	15	15
1412	A339	6p Guadalajara	15	15
1413	A339	6p Guipuzcoa	15	15
1414	A339	6p Huelva	15	15
1415	A339	6p Huesca	15	15
		Set value	1.40	1.20

1969
1416	A339	6p Ifni	15	15
1417	A339	6p Jaen	15	15
1418	A339	6p Leon	15	15
1419	A339	6p Lerida	15	15
1420	A339	6p Logroño	15	15
1421	A339	6p Lugo	15	15
1422	A339	6p Madrid	15	15
1423	A339	6p Malaga	15	15
1424	A339	6p Murcia	15	15
1425	A339	6p Navarra	15	15
1426	A339	6p Orense	15	15
1427	A339	6p Oviedo	15	15
		Set value	1.40	1.20

1970
1428	A339	6p Palencia	15	15
1429	A339	6p Pontevedra	15	15
1430	A339	6p Sahara	15	15
1431	A339	6p Salamanca	15	15
1432	A339	6p Santa Cruz de Tenerife	15	15
1433	A339	6p Santander	15	15
1434	A339	6p Segovia	15	15
1435	A339	6p Seville	15	15
1436	A339	6p Soria	15	15
1437	A339	6p Tarragona	15	15
1438	A339	6p Teruel	15	15
1439	A339	6p Toledo	15	15
		Set value	1.50	1.25

1971
1440	A339	6p Valencia	25	15
1441	A339	8p Valladolid	30	15
1442	A339	8p Vizcaya	30	15
1443	A339	8p Zamora	30	15
1444	A339	8p Zaragoza	30	15
	Nos. 1440-1444 (5)		1.45	
		Set value		60
	Set value, #1392-1444		7.00	5.50

Archers — A340   Ornament — A341

Designs: 50c, Boar hunt. 1.20p, Bison. 1.50p, Hands. 2p, Warrior. 2.50p, Deer. 3.50p, Archers. 4p, Hunters and gazelle. 6p, Hunters and deer herd.

1967, Mar. 27 **Photo.** *Perf. 13*
Gold Frame

1449	A340	40c ocher & car rose	15	15
1450	A340	50c gray & dk red	15	15
1451	A341	1p ocher & org ver	15	15
1452	A340	1.20p gray & rose brn	15	15
1453	A340	1.50p gray & red	15	15
1454	A341	2p lt brn & dk car rose	15	15
1455	A341	2.50p sky bl & rose brn	15	15
1456	A340	3.50p yellow & blk	15	15
1457	A341	4p citron & red	15	15
1458	A341	6p olive & red	15	15
		Set value	85	80

Issued for Stamp Day, 1967. The designs are from paleolithic and mesolithic wall paintings found in Spanish caves.

For other art types see A236-A237, A240a, A246a, A257, A272, A285a, A300, A310, A324, A360, A371 and footnote following No. 1606.

Palma Cathedral and Conference Emblem — A342

1967, Mar. 28

1459	A342	1.50p brt blue grn	15	15

Issued to publicize the Congress of the Interparliamentary Union, Palma de Mallorca.

W. K. Röntgen, X-ray Tube and Atom — A343

1967, Apr. 3 **Photo.** *Perf. 13*

1460	A343	1.50p green	15	15

Issued to publicize the 7th Congress of Latin Radiologists and the 1st Congress of European Radiologists, Barcelona, Apr. 2-8.

Averroes (1120-1198), Physician and Philosopher — A344

Portraits: 3.50p, Joséde Acosta (1539-1600), Jesuit, historian, poet. 4p, Moses ben Maimonides (1135-1204), Jewish philosopher and physician. 25p, Andres Laguna, 16th century physician.

1967, Apr. 6 **Engr.** *Perf. 13x12½*

1461	A344	1.20p lil & dl vio	15	15
1462	A344	3.50p mag & dl pur	15	15
1463	A344	4p brn & sep	15	15
1464	A344	25p dl bl & blk	35	15
		Set value		30

Europa Issue, 1967
Common Design Type

1967, May 2 **Photo.** *Perf. 13*
Size: 25x31mm

1465	CD10	1.50p sl grn, red brn & dl red	15	15
1466	CD10	6p vio, brt bl & brn	35	20

Exhibition Building and Fountain, Valencia — A345

1967, May 3

1467	A345	1.50p gray grn	15	15

International Fair at Valencia, 50th anniv.

Numeral Postmark No. 3 of 1850 — A346

Guardian Angel Over Indigent Sleeper — A347

Designs: 1.50p, No. 2, 12c stamp of 1850 with crowned M postmark of Madrid. 6p, No. 4, 6r stamp of 1850 with 1r postmark.

1967, May 6

1468	A346	40c brn org, dl bl & blk	15	15
1469	A346	1.50p brn, grn & blk	15	15
1470	A346	6p bl, red & blk	15	15
		Set value	24	20

Intl. Stamp Day, 1967. See #1527-1528.

1967, May 16 *Perf. 13*

1471	A347	1.50p bl, blk, brn & red	15	15

Issued for National Caritas Day to honor Caritas, Catholic welfare organization.

Betanzos Church, Coruña — A348

International Tourist Year Emblem — A349

Tourism: 1p, Tower of St. Miguel Church, Palencia. 1.50p, Human pyramid (Castellers). 2.50p, Columbus monument, Huelva. 5p, The Enchanted City, Cuenca. 6p, Church of Our Lady, Sanlucar, Cadiz.

1967, July 26 **Engr.** *Perf. 13*

1472	A348	10c ultra & blk	15	15
1473	A348	1p dl bl & blk	15	15
1474	A348	1.50p lt brn & blk	15	15
1475	A348	2.50p grnsh bl & dk bl	15	15
1476	A349	3.50p dl pur & dk bl	15	15
1477	A348	5p yel grn & dk grn	15	15
1478	A348	6p red lil & dl lil	15	15
		Set value	60	42

Balsareny Castle — A350

Castles: 1p, Jarandilla. 1.50p, Almodovar. 2p, Ponferrada, vert. 2.50p, Peniscola. 5p, Coca. 6p, Loarre. 10p, Belmonte.

1967, Aug. 11 **Engr.**

1479	A350	50c gray & lt brn	15	15
1480	A350	1p bl gray & dl pur	15	15
1481	A350	1.50p bl gray & sage grn	15	15
1482	A350	2p brick red & bis brn	15	15
1483	A350	2.50p grnsh bl & sep	15	15
1484	A350	5p rose vio & vio bl	15	15
1485	A350	6p bis brn & gray brn	15	15
1486	A350	10p aqua & sl	16	15
		Set value	80	68

Globe, Snowflake and Thermometer A351

Galleon, Map of Americas, Spain and Philippines A352

1967, Aug. 30 **Photo.**

1487	A351	1.50p brt bl	15	15

Issued to publicize the 12th International Refrigeration Congress, Madrid, Sept. 4-8.

1967, Oct. 10 **Photo.** *Perf. 13*

1488	A352	1.50p red lilac	15	15

Issued to commemorate the 4th Congress of Spanish, Portuguese, American and Philippine Municipalities, Barcelona, Oct. 6-12.

Builders of the New World
Type of 1961 and

Nootka Settlement A353

Designs: 40c, Francisco de la Bodega. 50c, Old map of Nootka coast, vert. 1p, Francisco Antonio Mourelle. 1.50p, Esteban José Martinez. 3p, Old maps of coast of Northern California. 3.50p, Cayetano Valdes. 6p, Ships, San Elias, Alaska.

1967, Oct. 12

1489	A265	40c pink & grnsh gray	15	15
1490	A353	50c dk brn	15	15
1491	A265	1p pale bl & red lil	15	15
1492	A353	1.20p dk ol grn	15	15
1493	A265	1.50p pale pink & bl grn	15	15
1494	A353	3p buff & vio blk	15	15
1495	A265	3.50p pale pink & bl	15	15
1496	A353	6p red brn, *bluish*	15	15
		Set value	72	50

Issued to honor the explorers of the Northwest coast of North America.

Roman Statue and Gate A354

José Bethencourt A355

Designs: 3.50p, Ancient plower with ox team, horiz. 6p, Roman coins of Caceres.

1967, Oct. 31 **Photo.** *Perf. 13*

1497	A354	1.50p multi	15	15
1498	A354	3.50p multi	15	15
1499	A354	6p multi	18	15
		Set value	38	32

Founding of Caceres by the Romans, 2000th anniv.

1967, Nov. 15

Portraits: 1.50p, Enrique Granados (composer). 3.50p, Ruben Dario (poet). 6p, St. Ildefonso.

1500	A355	1.20p gray & red brn	15	15
1501	A355	1.50p blk & grn	15	15
1502	A355	3.50p brn & pur	15	15
1503	A355	6p blk & slate	15	15
		Set value	32	26

Issued to honor famous Spanish men. See design A336.

Santa Maria de Veruela Monastery A356

St. José Receiving Last Unction, by Goya A357

Designs: 3.50p, Aerial view of monastery, horiz. 6p, Inside view, horiz.

1967, Nov. 24 **Engr.** *Perf. 13*

1504	A356	1.50p ultra & ind	15	15
1505	A356	3.50p grn & blk	15	15
1506	A356	6p rose vio & bis brn	22	15
		Set value	42	32

1967, Nov. 27 **Photo.**

1507	A357	1.50p multi	15	15

200th anniversary of the canonization of St. José de Calasanz (1556-1648), founder of the first Christian Schools in Rome.

Nativity, by Francisco Salzillo — A358

1967, Dec. 5

1508	A358	1.50p multi	15	15

Christmas, 1967.

Slalom A359

Designs: 3.50p, Bobsled, vert. 6p, Ice hockey.

1968, Feb. 6 **Photo.** *Perf. 13*

1509	A359	1.50p multi	15	15
1510	A359	3.50p multi	15	15
1511	A359	6p multi	16	15
		Set value	38	30

Issued to commemorate the 10th Winter Olympic Games, Grenoble, France, Feb. 6-18.

Mariano Fortuny, Self-portrait — A360

Fortuny Paintings: 40c, The Vicariate, horiz. 50c, "Fantasy" (pianist). 1p, "Idyll" (piper and sheep). 1.20p, The Print Collector, horiz. 2p, Old Man in the Sun. 2.50p, Calabrian Man. 3.50p, Lady with Fan. 4p, Battle of Tetuan, 1860. 6p, Queen Christina in Carriage, horiz.

1968, Mar. 25   Photo.   Perf. 13
Gold Frame

1512	A360	40c dp red lil	15	15
1513	A360	50c dk red grn	15	15
1514	A360	1p brown	15	15
1515	A360	1.20p dp vio	15	15
1516	A360	1.50p dp grn	15	15
1517	A360	2p org brn	15	15
1518	A360	2.50p car rose	15	15
1519	A360	3.50p dk red brn	16	15
1520	A360	4p dk ol	15	15
1521	A360	6p brt bl	15	15
		Set value	84	60

Issued to honor Mariano Fortuny y Carbo (1838-74), and for Stamp Day.
For other art types see A236-A237, A240a, A246a, A257, A272, A285a, A300, A310, A324, A340-A341, A371 and footnote following No. 1606.

Beatriz Galindo A361

Famous Women: 1.50p, Agustina de Aragon. 3.50p, Maria Pacheco. 6p, Rosalia de Castro.

1968, Apr. 8   Engr.   Perf. 12¹/₂x13

1522	A361	1.20p yel brn & blk brn	15	15
1523	A361	1.50p bl grn & dk bl	15	15
1524	A361	3.50p lt vio & dk vio	15	15
1525	A361	6p gray bl & blk	18	15
		Set value	50	36

Europa Issue, 1968
Common Design Type

1968, Apr. 29   Photo.   Perf. 13
Size: 38x22mm

1526	CD11	3.50p brt bl, gold & brn	22	15

Spain No. 1 with Galicia Puebla Postmark — A362

Map of León and Seal — A363

Stamp Day: 3.50p, Spain No. 4 with Serena postmark.

1968, May 6   Photo.   Perf. 13

1527	A362	1.50p blk, bl & ocher	15	15
1528	A362	3.50p bl, dk grn & blk	15	15
		Set value	20	20

See Nos. 1568-1569, 1608, 1677, 1754.

Perf. 13x12¹/₂, 12¹/₂x13

1968, June 15   Photo.

Designs: 1.50p, Roman legionary. 3.50p, Emperor Galba coin, horiz.

Size: 25x38¹/₂mm

1529	A363	1p lil, red brn & yel	15	15

Size: 25x47¹/₂mm

1530	A363	1.50p brn, dk brn & buff	15	15

Size: 37¹/₂x26mm

1531	A363	3.50p ocher & sl grn	30	15
		Set value	50	26

1900th anniversary of the founding of León by the Roman Legion VII Gemina.

Spain stamps can be mounted in the annually supplemented Scott Spain and Spanish Andorra album.

Human Rights Emblem — A364

Benavente Palace, Baeza — A365

1968, June 25   Photo.   Perf. 13x12¹/₂

1532	A364	3.50p bl, red & grn	15	15

International Human Rights Year, 1968.

1968, July 15   Engr.   Perf. 13

Tourism: 1.20p, View of Salamanca with Tormes River Bridge, horiz. 1.50p, Statuary group from St. Vincent's Church, Avila (The Adoration of the Magi). 2p, Tomb of Martin Vazquez de Arce, Cathedral of Sigüenza, horiz. 3.50p, Portal of St. Mary's Church, Sangüesa, Navarre.

1533	A365	50c dp rose & brn	15	15
1534	A365	1.20p emer & sl grn	15	15
1535	A365	1.50p dp grn & ind	15	15
1536	A365	2p lil rose & blk	16	15
1537	A365	3.50p brt lil & rose lil	15	15
		Set value	52	30

Escalona Castle, Toledo — A366

Castles: 1.20p, Fuensaldaña, Valladolid. 1.50p, Peñafiel, Valladolid. 2.50p, Villasobroso, Pontevedra. 6p, Frias, Burgos, vert.

1968, July 29   Engr.   Perf. 13

1538	A366	40c dk bl & sepia	15	15
1539	A366	1.20p vio brn & vio blk	15	15
1540	A366	1.50p ol & blk	15	15
1541	A366	2.50p ol grn & blk	15	15
1542	A366	6p vio bl & bl grn	25	15
		Set value	60	35

Rifle Shooting A367

Designs: 1.50p, Horse jumping. 3.50p, Bicycling. 6p, Sailing, vert.

Perf. 12¹/₂x13, 13x12¹/₂

1968, Sept. 24   Photo.

1543	A367	1p multi	15	15
1544	A367	1.50p multi	15	15
1545	A367	3.50p multi	20	15
1546	A367	6p multi	15	15
		Set value	52	34

Issued to publicize the 19th Olympic Games, Mexico City, Oct. 12-27.

Builders of the New World
Type of 1961 and

Map of Capuchin Missions along Orinoco River, 1732 — A368

Designs: 1p, Diego de Losada. 1.50p, Losada family coat of arms. 3.50p, Diego de Henares. 6p, Map of Caracas, drawn by Diego de Henares, 1578, horiz.

1968, Oct. 12   Photo.   Perf. 13

1547	A368	40c grnsh bl, bluish	15	15
1548	A368	1p red lil, gray	15	15
1549	A368	1.50p sl, pale rose	15	15
1550	A265	3.50p dk bl, pnksh	20	15
1551	A368	6p dk ol bis	28	16
		Set value	72	48

Issued to commemorate the Christianization of Venezuela and the founding of Caracas.

St. Maria del Parral Monastery, Segovia — A369

Designs: 3.50p, Monastery, inside view. 6p, Madonna and Child, statue from main altar.

1968, Nov. 25   Engr.   Perf. 13

1552	A369	1.50p gray bl & rose vio	18	15
1553	A369	3.50p brn & red brn	25	18
1554	A369	6p rose cl & brn	25	15
		Set value		36

Nativity, by Federico Fiori da Urbino — A370

Alonso Cano by Velázquez — A371

1968, Dec. 2   Photo.   Perf. 13x12¹/₂

1555	A370	1.50p gold & multi	15	15

Christmas, 1968.

1969, Mar. 24   Photo.   Perf. 13

Cano Paintings: 40c, St. Agnes. 50c, St. John. 1p, Jesus and Angel. 2p, Holy Family. 2.50p, Circumcision of Jesus. 3p, Jesus and the Samaritan Woman. 3.50p, Madonna and Child. 4p, Sts. John Capistrano and Bernardino, horiz. 6p, Vision of St. John the Baptist.

Gold Frame

1556	A371	40c deep plum	15	15
1557	A371	50c green	15	15
1558	A371	1p sepia	15	15
1559	A371	1.50p slate grn	15	15
1560	A371	2p red brown	15	15
1561	A371	2.50p dp red lil	15	15
1562	A371	3p ultra	15	15
1563	A371	3.50p dk rose brn	15	15
1564	A371	4p dull lilac	15	15
1565	A371	6p slate blue	15	15
		Set value	1.00	1.00

Issued to honor Alonso Cano (1601-1667), and for Stamp Day.
For other art types see A236-A237, A240a, A246a, A257, A272, A285a, A300, A310, A324, A340-A341, A360 and footnote following No. 1606.

DNA (Genetic Code) Molecule and Chart A372

1969, Apr. 7   Photo.   Perf. 13

1566	A372	1.50p gray & multi	15	15

Issued to publicize the 6th European Congress of Biochemistry, Madrid, Apr. 7-11.

Europa Issue, 1969
Common Design Type

1969, Apr. 28
Size: 38x22mm

1567	CD12	3.50p multi	35	15

Stamp Day Type of 1968

Design: 1.50p, Spain No. 6 with crowned M postmark. 3.50p, Spain No. 11 with Corvera postmark.

1969, May 6   Photo.   Perf. 13

1568	A362	1.50p blk, red & grn	15	15
1569	A362	3.50p grn, bl & red	15	15
		Set value	22	20

Issued for Stamp Day, 1969.

Spectrum A373

1969, May 26

1570	A373	1.50p blk & multi	15	15

Issued to publicize the 15th International Spectroscopy Colloquium, Madrid, May 26-30.

World Map, Red Crescent, Cross, Lion and Sun Emblems A374

1969, May 30

1571	A374	1.50p multi	15	15

Issued to commemorate the 50th anniversary of the League of Red Cross Societies.

Last Supper, Finial from Lugo Cathedral — A375

1969, June 4

1572	A375	1.50p grn, brn & blk	15	15

300th anniversary of the dedication of Galicia Province to the reign of Jesus.

Turegano Castle, Segovia — A376

Father Junipero Serra — A377

Castles: 1.50p, Villalonso, Zamora. 2.50p, Velez Blanco, Almeria. 3.50p, Castilnovo, Segovia. 6p, Torrelobaton, Valladolid.

1969, June 24   Engr.   Perf. 13

1573	A376	1p dl grn & sl	15	15
1574	A376	1.50p bluish lil & dk bl	22	15
1575	A376	2.50p bl vio & bluish lil	15	15
1576	A376	3.50p red brn & ol grn	25	15
1577	A376	6p gray grn & dl brn	16	15
		Nos. 1573-1577 (5)	93	
		Set value		62

1969, July 16   Photo.   Perf. 13

1578	A377	1.50p multi	15	15

Bicentenary of San Diego, Calif.

Rock of Gibraltar — A378

Dama de Elche — A379

Design: 2p, View of Gibraltar across the Bay of Algeciras.

1969, July 18

1579	A378	1.50p bl grn	16	15
1580	A378	2p brt rose lil	15	15
		Set value		20

1969, July 23   Engr.   Perf. 13

Tourism: 1.50p, Alcañiz Castle, Teruel, horiz. 3p, Murcia Cathedral. 6p, St. Maria de la Redonda, Logrono.

1581	A379	1.50p dl grn & blk	18	15
1582	A379	3p yel grn & bl grn	15	15
1583	A379	3.50p gray bl & dk bl	18	15
1584	A379	6p yel grn & vio blk	28	15
		Set value		40

Builders of the New World
Type of 1961 and

Santo Domingo Church, Santiago, Chile — A380

Designs: 1.50p, Casa de Moneda de Chile, horiz. 2p, Ambrosio O'Higgins. 3.50p, Pedro de Valdivia. 6p, First large bridge over Mapocho River, horiz.

1969, Oct. 12   Photo.   Perf. 13

1585	A380	40c lt bl & dk red brn	15	15
1586	A380	1.50p pale rose & dk vio	15	15
1587	A265	2p pale pink & ol	25	15
1588	A265	3.50p pale yel & dk Prus grn	30	18
1589	A380	6p pale yel & blk brn	35	15
		Nos. 1585-1589 (5)	1.20	
		Set value		62

Exploration and development of Chile. See Nos. 1630-1631, 1634.

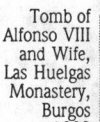

Adoration of the Magi, by Juan Bautista Mayno — A381

Christmas: 2p, Nativity, bas-relief from altar of Cathedral of Gerona.

1969, Nov. 3

1590	A381	1.50p multi	15	15
1591	A381	2p multi	15	15
		Set value	22	18

Tomb of Alfonso VIII and Wife, Las Huelgas Monastery, Burgos A382

Designs: 1.50p, Las Huelgas Monastery. 6p, Inside view, vert.

1969, Nov. 22   Engr.

1592	A382	1.50p lt bl grn & ind	25	15
1593	A382	3.50p ultra & vio bl	25	16
1594	A382	6p ol & yel grn	38	16

See Nos. 1639-1641.

St. Juan de Avila, by El Greco — A383

St. Stephen, by Luis de Morales — A384

Design: 50p, Bishop Rodrigo Ximenez de Rada, Juan de Borgona mural.

1970, Feb. 25   Engr.   Perf. 13

1595	A383	25p pale pur & ind	4.00	15
1596	A383	50p brn org & brn	3.25	40

1970, Mar. 24   Photo.   Perf. 13

Morales Paintings: 1p, Annunciation. 1.50p, Madonna and Child with St. John. 3.50p, Madonna and Child. 3p, Presentation at the Temple. 3.50p, St. Jerome. 4p, St. John de Ribera. 5p, Ecce Homo. 6p, Pieta. 10p, St. Francis of Assisi.

1597	A384	50c gold & multi	15	15
1598	A384	1p gold & multi	15	15
1599	A384	1.50p gold & multi	30	15
1600	A384	2p gold & multi	30	15
1601	A384	3p gold & multi	15	15
1602	A384	3.50p gold & multi	15	15
1603	A384	4p gold & multi	16	15
1604	A384	5p gold & multi	15	15
1605	A384	6p gold & multi	15	15
1606	A384	10p gold & multi	25	20
		Nos. 1597-1606 (10)	1.91	
		Set value		1.00

Issued to honor Luis de Morales, "El Divino" (1509-1586), and for Stamp Day.
For other art types see A397, A410, A431, A448, A473, A501, A522, A538, A558 and footnote following No. 876.

Europa Issue, 1970
Common Design Type

1970, May 4   Photo.   Perf. 13x12½
Size: 37½x22mm

1607	CD13	3.50p brt bl & gold	25	15

Stamp Day Type of 1968

Stamp Day: 2p, Spain No. 51 with "Ferro Carril de Langreo" postmark.

1970, May 4   Perf. 13x12½

1608	A362	2p dl red, grn & blk	15	15

Barcelona Fair Building A385

1970, May 27   Perf. 13

1609	A385	15p multi	40	15

Barcelona Trade Fair, 50th anniversary.

Miguel Primo de Rivera — A386

1970, June 6   Photo.   Perf. 13

1610	A386	2p buff, brn & ol grn	20	15

Issued to commemorate the centenary of the birth of Gen. Miguel Primo de Rivera (1870-1930), Spanish dictator, 1923-1930.

Valencia de Don Juan Castle — A387

Castles: 1.20p, Monterrey. 3.50p, Mombeltran. 6p, Sadaba. 10p, Bellver.

1970, June 24   Engr.

1611	A387	1p blk & dl bl	55	15
1612	A387	1.20p lt grnsh bl & vio	15	15
1613	A387	3.50p pale grn & brn	22	15
1614	A387	6p sep & dl pur	38	15
1615	A387	10p fawn & sepia	1.25	22
		Nos. 1611-1615 (5)	2.55	
		Set value		66

Alcazaba Castle, Almeria — A388

Tourism: 1p, Malaga Cathedral. 1.50p, St. Mary of the Assumption, Lequeitio, vert. 2p, Cloister of St. Francis of Orense. 3.50p, Market (Lonja), Zaragoza, vert. 5p, The Gate of Vitoria, vert.

1970, July 23   Engr.   Perf. 13

1616	A388	50c bluish gray & dl pur	15	15
1617	A388	1p red brn & ocher	22	15
1618	A388	1.50p bluish gray & sl grn	22	15
1619	A388	2p sl & dk bl	65	15
1620	A388	3.50p pur & vio bl	32	15
1621	A388	5p gray grn & red brn	1.40	20
		Nos. 1616-1621 (6)	2.96	
		Set value		66

Tailor, from Book Published in Madrid, 1589 A389

1970, Aug. 18   Photo.   Perf. 13

1622	A389	2p mag, brn & dl vio	15	15

Issued to publicize the 14th International Tailoring Congress, Madrid.

Diver and Map of Europe A390

1970, Aug. 25

1623	A390	2p grn & brt bl	15	15

Issued to publicize the 12th European Championships in Swimming, Diving and Water Polo, Barcelona.

Concha Espina — A391

Portraits: 1p, Guillen de Castro. 1.50p, Juan Ramon Jimenez. 2p, Gustavo Adolfo Becquer. 2.50p, Miguel de Unamuno. 3.50p, José M. Gabriel y Galan.

1970, Sept. 21   Photo.   Perf. 13x12½

1624	A391	50c brn, vio bl & pale rose	15	15
1625	A391	1p sl grn, dp rose lil & gray	15	15
1626	A391	1.50p dk bl, brt grn & gray	15	15
1627	A391	2p grn, dk ol & buff	30	15
1628	A391	2.50p pur, rose lake & buff	15	15
1629	A391	3.50p brn, dk red & gray	20	15
		Set value	90	55

Issued to honor Spanish writers.

Builders of the New World
Portrait Type of 1961 and Building Type of 1969

Designs: 40c, Ecala House, Queretaro, Mexico. 1.50p, Mexico Cathedral, horiz. 2p, Vasco de Quiroga. 3.50p, Brother Juan de Zumarraga. 6p, Cathedral Towers, Morelia, Mexico.

1970, Oct. 12   Photo.   Perf. 13

1630	A380	40c lt bl & ol gray	15	15
1631	A380	1.50p lt bl & brn	20	15
1632	A265	2p buff & dk vio	52	15
1633	A265	3.50p pale grn & dk grn	20	15
1634	A380	6p pale pink & Prus bl	40	15
		Nos. 1630-1634 (5)	1.47	
		Set value		54

Exploration and development of Mexico.

Map of Western Mediterranean — A392

1970, Oct. 20   Photo.   Perf. 13

1635	A392	2p multi	15	15

Issued to commemorate the centenary of the Geographical and Statistical Institute.

Adoration of the Shepherds, by El Greco — A393

Christmas: 2p, Adoration of the Shepherds, by Murillo.

1970, Oct. 30

1636	A393	1.50p multi	15	15
1637	A393	2p multi	15	15
		Set value	20	16

UN Emblem and Headquarters — A394

1970, Nov. 3

1638	A394	8p multi	25	15

25th anniversary of the United Nations.

Monastery Type of 1969

Ripoll Monastery: 2p, Portal. 3.50p, View of monastery. 5p, Inside court.

1970, Nov. 12   Engr.

1639	A382	2p vio & pur	1.10	15
1640	A382	3.50p org & mar	42	15
1641	A382	5p Prus grn & yel grn	1.65	15

Map with Main
European Pilgrimage
Routes — A395

Cathedral of
St. David,
Wales
A396

Designs: No. 1643, Map of main pilgrimage routes. No. 1644, St. Bridget statue, Vadstena, Sweden. No. 1645, Santiago Cathedral. No. 1646, Tower of St. Jacques, Paris. No. 1647, Pilgrim before entering Santiago de Compostela. No. 1648, St. James statue, Pistoia, Italy. No. 1649, Lugo Cathedral. 2.50p, Villafranca del Bierzo church. No. 1652, Astorga Cathedral. 3.50p, San Marcos de León. No. 1654, Charlemagne, bas-relief, Aachen Cathedral, Germany. No. 1655, San Tirso de Sahagun. 5p, San Martín de Fromista. 6p, Bas-relief, King's Hospital, Burgos. 7p, Portal of Santo Domingo de la Calzada. 7.50p, Cloister, Najera. 8p, Puente de la Reina (Christ on the Cross and portal). 9p, Santa Maria de Eunate. 10p, Cross of Roncesvalles.

1971		Engr.	Perf. 13	
1642	A395	50c grnsh bl & sep	15	15
1643	A396	50c bl & dl vio	15	15
1644	A395	1p brn & sl grn	16	15
1645	A395	1p grn & sl grn	15	15
1646	A395	1.50p dl grn & dp plum	32	15
1647	A395	1.50p vio bl & lil	16	15
1648	A395	2p dk pur & blk	25	15
1649	A395	2p sl grn & dk bl	1.00	16
1650	A396	2.50p vio brn & dl vio	20	15
1651	A396	3p ultra & dk bl	42	15
1652	A396	3p dl red & rose lil	55	15
1653	A396	3.50p dp org & gray grn	32	16
1654	A396	4p ol grn	55	16
1655	A396	4p grnsh bl & brn	32	15
1656	A395	5p lt grn & blk	85	15
1657	A395	6p lt ultra	32	15
1658	A395	7p lil & dl vio	30	25
1659	A396	7.50p car lake & dl vio	30	15
1660	A395	8p grn & vio blk	30	16
1661	A396	9p grn & vio	30	20
1662	A395	10p grn & brn	42	16
	Nos. 1642-1662 (21)		7.39	
	Set value			2.65

Holy Year of Compostela, 1971.

Ignacio Zuloaga,
Self-portrait
A397

Amadeo Vives,
Composer
A398

Zuloaga Paintings: 50c, "My Uncle Daniel." 1p, View of Segovia, horiz. 1.50p, Countess of Alba. 3p, Juan Belmonte. 4p, Countess of Noailles. 5p, Pablo Uranga. 8p, Cobblers' Houses at Lerma, horiz.

1971, Mar. 24		Photo.	Perf. 13	
1663	A397	50c gold & multi	15	15
1664	A397	1p gold & multi	15	15
1665	A397	1.50p gold & multi	15	15
1666	A397	2p gold & multi	28	15
1667	A397	3p gold & multi	28	15
1668	A397	4p gold & multi	15	15
1669	A397	5p gold & multi	28	15
1670	A397	8p gold & multi	52	25
	Nos. 1663-1670 (8)		1.96	
	Set value			94

Ignacio Zuloaga (1870-1945). Stamp Day.
For other art types see A384, A410, A431, A448, A473, A501, A522, A538, A558 and footnote following No. 876.

1971, Apr. 20

Portraits: 2p, St. Teresa of Avila. 8p, Benito Perez Galdos, writer. 15p, Ramon Menendez Pidal, writer.

1671	A398	1p multicolored	28	15
1672	A398	2p multicolored	28	15
1673	A398	8p multicolored	35	18
1674	A398	15p multicolored	45	18
	Set value			52

Europa Issue, 1971
Common Design Type

1971, Apr. 29   Photo.   Perf. 13
Size: 37x26mm

1675	CD14	2p lt grn & vio bl	1.10	15
1676	CD14	8p lt grn, dk brn & dk grn	60	25

Stamp Day Type of 1968

Stamp Day: 2p, Spain No. 1 with blue "A" cancellation.

1971, May 6
| 1677 | A362 | 2p black, bl & olive | 18 | 15 |

Gymnast
A399

Design: 2p, Gymnast on bar.

1971, May 14
1678	A399	1p ocher & multi	20	15
1679	A399	2p lt blue & multi	20	15
	Set value			20

9th European Gymnastic Championships for Men, Madrid, May 14-15.

Great
Bustard
A400

Designs: 2p, Pardine lynx. 3p, Brown bear. 5p, Red-legged partridge, vert. 8p, Spanish ibex, vert.

1971, May 24
1680	A400	1p multicolored	20	15
1681	A400	2p multicolored	28	15
1682	A400	3p multicolored	35	15
1683	A400	5p multicolored	70	25
1684	A400	8p multicolored	90	35
	Nos. 1680-1684 (5)		2.43	
	Set value			90

Legionnaires — A401

Designs: 2p, Legionnaires on dress parade. 5p, Memorial service. 8p, Desert fighter and tank column.

1971, June 21   Photo.   Perf. 13
1685	A401	1p multicolored	22	15
1686	A401	2p multicolored	45	15
1687	A401	5p multicolored	45	15
1688	A401	8p multicolored	45	32
	Set value			62

50th anniversary of the Legion, a voluntary military organization.

UNICEF Emblem,
Children of Various
Races — A402

1971, Sept. 10
| 1689 | A402 | 8p multicolored | 20 | 15 |

25th anniv. of UNICEF.

Don Juan of
Austria, Fleet
Commander
A403

Hockey Players,
Hockey League and
Games Emblems
A404

Designs: 5p, Battle of Lepanto, horiz. 8p, Holy League banner in Cathedral.

1971, Oct. 7   Engr.   Perf. 13
1690	A403	2p sepia & slate grn	1.10	15
1691	A403	5p chocolate	1.25	15
1692	A403	8p rose car & vio bl	1.25	35

400th anniversary of the Battle of Lepanto against the Turks.

1971, Oct. 15   Photo.
| 1693 | A404 | 5p multicolored | 1.00 | 18 |

First World Hockey Cup, Barcelona, Oct. 15-24.

De Havilland
DH-9 over
Seville
A405

Design: 15p, Boeing 747 over Plaza de la Cibeles, Madrid.

1971, Oct. 25
| 1694 | A405 | 2p multicolored | 52 | 15 |
| 1695 | A405 | 15p multicolored | 60 | 22 |

50th anniversary of Spanish air mail service.

Nativity, Avia
Altarpiece — A406

Emilia Pardo
Bazan — A407

Christmas: 8p, Nativity, Sagas altarpiece.

1971, Nov. 4   Perf. 12½x13
1696	A406	2p multicolored	15	15
1697	A406	8p multicolored	30	15
	Set value			22

1972, Jan. 27   Engr.   Perf. 13

Portraits: 25p, José de Espronceda. 50p, King Fernan Gonzalez.

1698	A407	15p brown & slate grn	40	15
1699	A407	25p lt grn & slate grn	40	15
1700	A407	50p claret & dp brn	70	35

Honoring Emilia Pardo Bazan (1852-1921), novelist (15p); José de Espronceda (1808-1842), poet (25p); Fernan Gonzalez (910-970), first King of Castile (50p).

Figure
Skating — A408

Don Quixote
Title Page,
1605 — A409

Design: 2p, Ski jump and Sapporo Olympic emblem, horiz.

1972, Feb. 10   Photo.
1701	A408	2p gray & multi	38	15
1702	A408	15p blue & multi	55	22
	Set value			30

11th Winter Olympic Games, Sapporo, Japan, Feb. 3-13.

1972, Feb. 24   Engr.   Perf. 13x12½
| 1703 | A409 | 2p brown & claret | 15 | 15 |

International Book Year 1972.

A410

A411

Gutierrez Solana Paintings: 1p, Clowns, horiz. 2p, José Gutierrez Solana with wife and child. 3p, Balladier. 4p, Fisherman. 5p, Mask makers. 7p, The book collector. 10p, Merchant marine captain. 15p, Afterdinner speaker, horiz.

1972, Mar. 24   Photo.   Perf. 13
1704	A410	1p gold & multi	52	25
1705	A410	2p gold & multi	52	15
1706	A410	3p gold & multi	52	15
1707	A410	4p gold & multi	52	15
1708	A410	5p gold & multi	1.75	18
1709	A410	7p gold & multi	1.10	18
1710	A410	10p gold & multi	1.10	30
1711	A410	15p gold & multi	75	25
	Nos. 1704-1711 (8)		6.78	1.61

José Gutierrez Solana (1886-1945). Stamp Day 1972.
For other art types see A384, A397, A431, A448, A473, A501, A522, A538, A558 and footnote following No. 876.

1972, Apr. 21
1712	A411	1p Fir	50	15
1713	A411	2p Strawberry tree	50	15
1714	A411	3p Cluster pine	50	15
1715	A411	5p Evergreen oak	50	18
1716	A411	8p Juniper	50	22
	Nos. 1712-1716 (5)		2.50	
	Set value			74

Europeans Interlocking A412 | Pre-stamp Cordoba Postmark (1824-42) A413

Europa, 1972
Common Design Type and Type A412

1972, May 2
1717 A412 2p dull grn & ocher 2.75 15
Size: 25x38mm
1718 CD15 8p multicolored 1.10 25

1972, May 6 *Perf. 12¹/₂x13*
1719 A413 2p dull yel, blk & car 15 15

Stamp Day 1972.

Santa Catalina Castle, Jaen — A414

Castles: 1p, Sajazarra, Rioja, vert. 3p, Biar, Alicante. 5p, San Servando, Toledo. 10p, Pedraza, Segovia.

1972, June 22 **Engr.** *Perf. 13*
1720 A414 1p dull bl grn & brn 60 18
1721 A414 2p gray olive & grn 1.00 15
1722 A414 3p rose car & red brn 1.00 15
1723 A414 5p vio bl & dull grn 1.00 20
1724 A414 10p slate & lilac 3.00 20
    Nos. 1720-1724 (5) 6.60 88

Weight Lifting, Olympic Emblems — A415

1972, Aug. 26 **Photo.** *Perf. 13*
1725 A415 1p Olympic emblems, fencing, horiz. 18 15
1726 A415 2p shown 38 15
1727 A415 5p Sculling 28 20
1728 A415 8p Pole vaulting 28 25
    Set value 65

20th Olympic Games, Munich, Aug. 26-Sept. 11.

Egyptian Mongoose A416

1972, Sept. 14
1729 A416 1p Aquatic mole, vert. 20 15
1730 A416 2p Chamois 50 15
1731 A416 3p Wolf 70 15
1732 A416 5p shown 70 20
1733 A416 7p Spotted genet 70 20
    Nos. 1729-1733 (5) 2.80 85

Brigadier M.A. de Ustariz — A417

San Juan, 1870 A418

1972, Oct. 12 **Photo.** *Perf. 13*
1734 A417 1p shown 35 15
1735 A418 2p shown 45 15
1736 A418 5p San Juan, 1625 45 15
1737 A418 8p Map of Plaza and Bay, 1792 45 40

450th anniversary of San Juan.

St. Tomas Monastery, Avila — A419

Designs: 8p, Inside view. 15p, Cloister, horiz.

1972, Oct. 26 **Engr.**
1738 A419 2p Prus bl & gray grn 1.25 15
1739 A419 8p gray & claret 1.25 25
1740 A419 15p violet & red lil 1.10 25

Teatro del Liceo, Barcelona A420

1972, Nov. 7 *Perf. 12¹/₂x13*
1741 A420 8p ultra & sepia 55 20

125th anniversary of the Gran Teatro del Liceo in Barcelona.

Annunciation A421

Christmas: 8p, Angel and shepherds. Designs are from Romanesque murals in the Collegiate Basilica of San Isidro, Leon.

1972, Nov. 14 **Photo.** *Perf. 13*
1742 A421 2p gold & multi 25 15
1743 A421 8p gold & multi 15 15
    Set value 16

Juan de Herrera and Escorial A422

Great Spanish Architects: 10p, Juan de Villanueva and Prado. 15p, Ventura Rodriguez and Apollo Fountain.

1973, Jan. 29 **Engr.** *Perf. 12¹/₂x13*
1744 A422 8p sepia & slate grn 85 15
1745 A422 10p blk brn & bluish blk 1.65 25
1746 A422 15p brt green & indigo 85 15

Myrica Faya — A423

Europa, Roman Mosaic — A424

Designs: Flora of Canary Islands.

1973, Mar. 21 **Photo.** *Perf. 13*
1747 A423 1p Apollonias canariensis, horiz. 30 15
1748 A423 2p shown 75 15
1749 A423 4p Palms 30 15
1750 A423 5p Holly 75 15
1751 A423 15p Dracaena draco 80 22
    Nos. 1747-1751 (5) 2.90
    Set value 62

Europa Issue
Common Design Type and A424

1973, Apr. 30 **Photo.** *Perf. 13*
1752 A424 2p multicolored 1.00 20
Size: 37x26mm
1753 CD16 8p lt blue, blk & red 80 25

Stamp Day Type of 1968

Stamp Day: 2p, Spain No. 23 with red Madrid, 1853, cancellation.

1973, May 5
1754 A362 2p black, blue & red 15 15

Iznajar Dam on Genil River — A425

1973, June 9 **Photo.** *Perf. 12¹/₂x13*
1755 A425 8p multicolored 20 15

11th Congress of the International Commission on High Dams, Madrid, June 11-15.

Oñate University, Guipuzcoa A426

Designs: 2p, Plaza del Campo and fountain, Lugo. 3p, Plaza de Llerena and fountain, Badajoz, vert. 5p, House of Columbus, Las Palmas. 8p, Windmills, La Mancha.

1973, June 11 **Engr.** *Perf. 13*
1756 A426 1p gray & sepia 42 15
1757 A426 2p brt grn & sl grn 75 15
1758 A426 3p dk brn & org brn 75 15
1759 A426 5p dk gray & vio blk 1.75 15
1760 A426 8p dk gray & car 1.10 35
    Nos. 1756-1760 (5) 4.77
    Set value 80

15-Cent Minimum Value
The minimum value for a single stamp is 15 cents. This value reflects the costs of handling inexpensive stamps.

Azure-winged Magpie — A427

Knight, Holy Fraternity of Castile, 1488 — A428

Birds: 1p, Black-bellied sand grouse, horiz. 2p, Black stork, horiz. 7p, Imperial eagle, horiz. 15p, Red-crested pochard.

1973, July 3 **Photo.** *Perf. 13*
1761 A427 1p multicolored 26 15
1762 A427 2p multicolored 50 15
1763 A427 5p multicolored 70 15
1764 A427 7p multicolored 90 15
1765 A427 15p multicolored 65 30
    Nos. 1761-1765 (5) 3.01
    Set value 62

1973, July 17

Uniforms: 2p, Knight, Castile, 1493, horiz. 3p, Harquebusier, 1534. 7p, Mounted rifleman, 1560. 8p, Infantry sergeants, 1567.
1766 A428 1p multicolored 32 15
1767 A428 2p multicolored 65 15
1768 A428 3p multicolored 85 15
1769 A428 7p multicolored 50 15
1770 A428 8p multicolored 65 20
    Nos. 1766-1770 (5) 2.97
    Set value 58

See Nos. 1794-1798, 1824-1828, 1869-1873, 1902-1906, 1989-1993, 2020-2024, 2051-2055, 2078-2082.

Fish in Net — A429

1973, Sept. 12 **Photo.** *Perf. 13*
1771 A429 2p multicolored 15 15

6th International Fishing Exhibition, Vigo, Sept. 12-19.

Conference Hall — A430

1973, Sept. 14
1772 A430 8p multicolored 16 15

Plenipotentiary Conference of the International Telecommunications Union, Torremolinos, Sept. 1973.

Vicente López, Self-portrait — A431

Paintings by Vicente López: 1p, King Ferdinand VII. 3p, Señora de Carvallo. 4p, Marshal Castelldosrrius. 5p, Queen Isabella II. 7p, Francisco Goya. 10p, Maria Amalia de Sajonia. 15p, The organist Felix López.

SPAIN

418

1973, Sept. 29   Photo.   Perf. 13

1773	A431	1p gold & multi	20 15
1774	A431	2p gold & multi	30 15
1775	A431	3p gold & multi	30 15
1776	A431	4p gold & multi	20 15
1777	A431	7p gold & multi	20 15
1778	A431	10p gold & multi	30 15
1779	A431	10p gold & multi	30 15
1780	A431	15p gold & multi	40 20
	Nos. 1773-1780 (8)		2.10
	Set value		85

Vicente Lopez y Portana (1772-1850), painter. Stamp Day 1973.

For other art types see A384, A397, A410, A448, A473, A501, A522, A538, A558 and footnote following No. 876.

Leon Cathedral, Nicaragua A432

Designs: 2p, Subtiava Church. 5p, Portal of Governor's House, vert. 8p, Rio San Juan Castle.

1973, Oct. 12

1781	A432	1p multicolored	22 15
1782	A432	2p multicolored	35 15
1783	A432	5p multicolored	45 15
1784	A432	8p multicolored	45 15
	Set value		38

Hispanic-American buildings in Nicaragua.

Pope Gregory XI and Pedro Fernandez Pecha — A433

1973, Oct. 26

1785	A433	2p multicolored	15 15

600th anniversary of the founding of the Order of the Hermites of St. Jerome by Pedro Fernandez Pecha.

St. Domingo de Silos Monastery A434

Nativity, Column Capital, Silos Church A435

Designs: 8p, Cloister walk, horiz. 15p, Three saints, sculpture.

Perf. 13x12½, 12½x13
Engr.

1786	A434	2p brown & rose mag	48 15
1787	A434	8p dk blue & purple	38 15
1788	A434	15p Prus grn & indigo	55 15
	Set value		38

St. Domingo de Silos Monastery, Burgos.

1973, Nov. 6   Photo.   Perf. 13

Christmas: 8p, Adoration of the Kings, Butrera Church, horiz.

1789	A435	2p multicolored	20 15
1790	A435	8p multicolored	20 15
	Set value		22

Map of Spain and Americas with Dates of First Printings A436

500 years of Spanish Printing: 7p, Teacher and Pupils, woodcut from "Libros de los Suenos," Valencia, 1474, vert. 15p, Title page from "Los Sinodales," Segovia, 1472.

1973, Dec. 11   Engr.   Perf. 13

1791	A436	1p indigo & slate grn	52 15
1792	A436	7p violet bl & purple	30 15
1793	A436	15p purple & black	60 25
	Set value		45

Uniform Type of 1973

Uniforms: 1p, Harquebusier on horseback, 1603. 2p, Harquebusiers, 1632. 3p, Cuirassier, 1635. 5p, Mounted drummer of the Dragoons, 1677. 9p, Two Musketeers, 1694.

1974, Jan. 5   Photo.   Perf. 13

1794	A428	1p multicolored	32 15
1795	A428	2p multicolored	65 15
1796	A428	3p multicolored	80 15
1797	A428	5p multicolored	1.25 16
1798	A428	9p multicolored	1.00 20
	Nos. 1794-1798 (5)		4.02
	Set value		60

Nautical Chart of Western Europe and North Africa — A437

1974, Jan. 26

1799	A437	2p multicolored	15 15

50th anniversary of the Superior Geographical Council of Spain. The chart is from a 14th century Catalan atlas.

M. Biada and Steam Engine A438

1974, Apr. 2   Photo.   Perf. 13

1800	A438	2p multicolored	15 15

125th anniversary of Barcelona-Mataro Railroad.

Young Collector, Album, Magnifier A439

Exhibition Emblem — A440

Design: 8p, Emblem, globe and arrows.

1974, Apr. 4   Perf. 13

1801	A439	2p lilac rose & multi	25 15

Perf. 12½

1802	A440	5p buff, blk & dull bl	50 15
1803	A440	8p dull green & multi	40 18

Espana 75, International Philatelic Exhibition, Madrid, Apr. 4-13, 1975.

Woman with Offering — A441

Europa: 8p, Woman from Baza, painted sculpture.

1974, Apr. 29   Photo.   Perf. 13

1804	A441	2p multicolored	1.00 15
1805	A441	8p multicolored	38 35

No. 28 and 1854 Seville Cancel A442

1974, May 6

1806	A442	2p black, blue & red	15 15

World Stamp Day.

Father Jaime Balmes A443

Designs: 10p, Father Pedro Poveda. 15p, Jorge Juan y Santacilla.

1974, May 28   Engr.   Perf. 13

1807	A443	8p blue gray & sepia	28 20
1808	A443	10p red brn & dk brn	80 15
1809	A443	15p brown & slate	38 15

Famous Spaniards: Jaime Balmes (1810-1848), mathematician; death centenary of Pedro Poveda, pedagogue; Don Jorge Juan (1712-1773), explorer and writer.

Templeto, by Bramante, Rome — A444

1974, June 4   Photo.

1810	A444	5p multicolored	30 15

Centenary of the Spanish Academy of Fine Arts, Rome.

Aqueduct, Segovia A445

Designs: 2p, Tajo Bridge, Alcantara. 3p, Marcus Valerius Martial lecturing. 4p, Triumphal Arch, Tarragona, vert. 5p, Theater, Merida. 7p, Bishop Ossius of Cordoba preaching. 8p, Tribunal Arch, Talavera Forum, vert. 9p, Emperor Trajan, vert.

1974, June 25   Engr.

1811	A445	1p brown & black	15 15
1812	A445	2p gray grn & sepia	40 15
1813	A445	3p lt & dk brown	15 15
1814	A445	4p green & indigo	15 15
1815	A445	5p gray bl & choc	18 15
1816	A445	7p gray grn & lilac	18 15
1817	A445	8p dk brown & green	18 16
1818	A445	9p brt red lil & cl	18 16
	Nos. 1811-1818 (8)		1.57
	Set value		80

Roman architecture and history in Spain.

Greek Tortoise A446

Reptiles: 2p, Common chameleon. 5p, Wall gecko. 7p, Emerald lizard. 15p, Blunt-nosed viper.

1974, July 3   Photo.

1819	A446	1p multicolored	32 15
1820	A446	2p multicolored	42 15
1821	A446	5p multicolored	55 25
1822	A446	7p multicolored	42 22
1823	A446	15p multicolored	42 20
	Nos. 1819-1823 (5)		2.13 97

Uniform Type of 1973

Uniforms: 1p, Hussar and horse, 1705. 2p, Artillery officers, 1710. 3p, Piper and drummer, Granada Regiment, 1734. 7p, Mounted standard-bearer, Numancia Dragoons, 1737. 8p, Standard-bearer and soldier, Zamora Regiment, 1739.

1974, July 17

1824	A428	1p multicolored	18 15
1825	A428	2p multicolored	55 15
1826	A428	3p multicolored	65 15
1827	A428	7p multicolored	55 18
1828	A428	8p multicolored	75 20
	Nos. 1824-1828 (5)		2.68
	Set value		65

Life Saving A447

1974, Sept. 5   Photo.   Perf. 13

1829	A447	2p multicolored	22 15

18th World Life Saving Championships, Barcelona, Sept. 1974.

Eduardo Rosales, by Federico Madrazo — A448

Eduardo Rosales Paintings: 1p, Tobias and the Angel. 3p, The Last Will of Isabella the Catholic, horiz. 4p, Nena (little girl). 5p, Presentation of John of Austria to Charles I, horiz. 7p, The First Step, horiz. 10p, St. John the Evangelist. 15p, St. Matthew.

1974, Sept. 29   Photo.   Perf. 13

1830	A448	1p gold & multi	15 15
1831	A448	2p gold & multi	15 15
1832	A448	3p gold & multi	15 15
1833	A448	4p gold & multi	18 15
1834	A448	5p gold & multi	22 15
1835	A448	7p gold & multi	22 15
1836	A448	10p gold & multi	40 15
1837	A448	15p gold & multi	40 22
	Nos. 1830-1837 (8)		1.87
	Set value		90

Eduardo Rosales (1836-1873). Stamp Day 1974.

For other art types see A384, A397, A410, A431, A473, A501, A522, A538, A558 and footnote following No. 876.

"International Mail" — A449

UPU Monument, Bern — A450

1974, Oct. 9
1838 A449 2p dark blue & multi   28 15
1839 A450 8p red & multi   22 20

Centenary of Universal Postal Union.

Sobremonte House, Cordoba, Argentina A451

Ruins of San Ignacio de Mini, 18th Century — A452

The Gaucho Martin Fierro — A453

Design: 2p, Municipal Council Building, Buenos Aires, 1829.

1974, Oct. 12
1840 A451 1p multicolored   20 15
1841 A451 2p multicolored   40 15
1842 A452 5p multicolored   40 15
1843 A453 10p multicolored   40 18
      Set value   42

Cultural ties with Latin America.

Nativity, Valdavia Church A454

Adoration of the Kings, Valcobero Church — A455

1974   Photo.   Perf. 13
1844 A454 2p multicolored   15 15
1845 A455 3p lt blue & multi   20 15
1846 A455 8p olive & multi   20 15
      Set value   26

Christmas 1974.
Issue dates: 2p, 8p, Nov. 4; 3p, Dec. 2.

Teucriun Lanigerum — A456

Flowers: 2p, Hypericum ericoides. 4p, Thymus longiflorus. 5p, Anthyllis onobrychioides. 8p, Helianthemun paniculatum.

1974, Nov. 8
1847 A456 1p multicolored   20 15
1848 A456 2p multicolored   30 15
1849 A456 4p multicolored   20 15
1850 A456 5p multicolored   30 15
1851 A456 8p multicolored   40 15
    Nos. 1847-1851 (5)   1.40
      Set value   35

Franco Type of 1954-56
Imprint: "F.N.M.T."

1974-75   Photo.   Perf. 12½x13
1852 A221   4p rose car ('75)   15 15
1853 A221   7p brt ultra   18 15
1854 A221   12p blue green   22 15
1855 A221   20p rose carmine   55 15
      Set value   26

Leyre Monastery A457

Designs: 8p, Column and bas-relief, vert. 15p, Crypt.

1974, Dec. 10   Engr.   Perf. 12½x13
1862 A457 2p slate   55 15
1863 A457 8p carmine   32 15
1864 A457 15p grnsh black   55 15
      Set value   35

Leyre Monastery, Navarre.

Spain Nos. 1 and 1802 — A458

Mail Coach, 1850 A459

Designs: 8p, Mail ship of Indian Service. 10p, Chapel of St. Mark.

    Perf. 12½x13, 13x12½
1975, Jan. 2   Engr.
1865 A458 2p slate blue   35 15
1866 A459 3p olive & brown   90 25
1867 A459 8p lilac & slate bl   90 28
1868 A458 10p brown & slate grn   90 35

125th anniversary of Spanish postage stamps.

Uniform Type of 1973

Uniforms: 1p, Sergeant and grenadier, Toledo Regiment, 1750. 2p, Royal Artillery, 1762. 3p, Queen's Regiment, 1763. 5p, Fusiliers, Vitoria Regiment, 1766. 10p, Dragoon, Sagunto Regiment, 1775.

1975, Jan. 7   Photo.   Perf. 13
1869 A428 1p multicolored   60 15
1870 A428 2p multicolored   60 15
1871 A428 3p multicolored   1.75 15

1872 A428 5p multicolored   75 15
1873 A428 10p multicolored   1.75 15
    Nos. 1869-1873 (5)   5.45
      Set value   58

Antonio Gaudi A460

Designs: 10p, Antonio Palacios and Casa Guell, Barcelona. 15p, Secundino Zuazo.

1975, Feb. 25   Engr.   Perf. 13
1874 A460 8p green & black   30 18
1875 A460 10p carmine & dp claret   60 15
1876 A460 15p brown & black   40 15

Contemporary Spanish architects.

Souvenir Sheets

Spanish Goldsmiths' Works — A461

Designs: 2p, Agate box, 9th cent. 3p, Votive crown of Recesvinto. 8p, Cover of Evangelistary, Roncesvalles Collegiate Church, 12th cent. 10p, Chalice of Infanta Donna Urraca, 11th cent. 12p, Processional monstrance, St. Domingo de Silos, 16th cent. 15p, Sword of Boabdil, 15th cent. 25p, Sword and head of Charles V (Carlos I of Spain). 50p, Earring and bracelet from Aliseda, 6th-4th centuries B.C. 3p, 10p, 12p, 25p vertical (No. 1878).

1975, Apr. 4   Engr.   Perf. 13
1877 A461   Sheet of 4   14.00 14.00
   a.   2p gray & Prussian blue   1.50 1.00
   b.   8p brown & Prus blue   2.50 2.00
   c.   15p gray & dark carmine   2.50 2.00
   d.   50p dark carmine & gray   7.00 6.00
1878 A461   Sheet of 4   14.00 14.00
   a.   3p slate green & gray   1.50 1.00
   b.   10p sepia & slate   2.50 2.00
   c.   12p gray & bluish black   2.50 2.00
   d.   25p sepia & bluish black   4.75 4.25

Espana 75 Intl. Phil. Exhib., Madrid, Apr. 4-13.

Pomegranates A462

Woman Gathering Honey, Arana Cave A463

1975, Apr. 21   Photo.
1879 A462 1p Almonds, nuts and blossoms, horiz.   18 15
1880 A462 2p shown   35 15
1881 A462 3p Oranges   35 15
1882 A462 4p Chestnuts   30 15
1883 A462 5p Apples   30 15
    Nos. 1879-1883 (5)   1.48
      Set value   35

1975, Apr. 28   Photo.   Perf. 13
Europa: 12p, Horse, wall painting from Tito Bustillo Cave, horiz.

1884 A463   3p brown & multi   1.00 15
1885 A463 12p brown & multi   75 20

Pre-stamp León Cancellation A464

1975, May 6   Perf. 12½x13
1886 A464 3p multicolored   15 15

World Stamp Day.

World Tourism Organization Emblem A465

1975, May 12   Photo.   Perf. 13
1887 A465 3p dark blue   15 15

First General Assembly of the World Tourism Organization, Madrid, May 1975.

Fair Emblem, Agricultural Symbols — A466

1975, May 14
1888 A466 3p multicolored   15 15

25th Agricultural Fair.

Equality Between Men and Women A467

1975, June 3
1889 A467 3p multicolored   15 15

International Women's Year.

Virgin of Cabeza Sanctuary A468

1975, June 18   Photo.   Perf. 13
1890 A468 3p multicolored   15 15

Virgin of Cabeza Sanctuary, site of siege during Civil War, 1937.

Cervantes' Prison Cell, Argamasilla de Alba — A469

Tourism: 2p, Bridge of St. Martin, Toledo. 3p, Church of St. Peter, Tarrasa. 4p, Arch, Alhambra, Granada, vert. 5p, Street, Mijas, Malaga, vert. 7p, Church of St. Mary, Tarrasa, vert.

1975, June 25   Engr.   Perf. 13

1891	A469	1p purple & black	15	15
1892	A469	2p red brn & brn	15	15
1893	A469	3p slate & sepia	15	15
1894	A469	4p orange & claret	15	15
1895	A469	5p slate grn & indigo	20	15
1896	A469	7p violet bl & indigo	75	15
		Nos. 1891-1896 (6)	1.55	
		Set value		56

Salamander
A470

1975, July 9   Photo.   Perf. 13

1897	A470	1p shown	25	15
1898	A470	2p Newt	38	15
1899	A470	3p Tree toad	38	15
1900	A470	6p Midwife toad	25	15
1901	A470	7p Leaf frog	25	15
		Nos. 1897-1901 (5)	1.51	
		Set value		54

Uniform Type of 1973

Uniforms: 1p, Cavalry officer, 1788. 2p, Fusilier, Asturias Regiment, 1789. 3p, Infantry Colonel, 1802. 4p, Artillery standard-bearer, 1803. 7p, Sapper, 1809.

1975, July 17

1902	A428	1p multicolored	22	15
1903	A428	2p multicolored	60	15
1904	A428	3p multicolored	22	15
1905	A428	4p multicolored	22	15
1906	A428	7p multicolored	60	15
		Nos. 1902-1906 (5)	1.86	
		Set value		48

Infant and Children Playing
A471

1975, Sept. 9   Photo.   Perf. 13

1907	A471	3p multicolored	15	15

"Defend Life."

Scroll and Emblem
A472

1975, Sept. 25

1908	A472	3p multicolored	15	15

13th International Congress of Latin Notaries, Barcelona, Sept. 26-Oct. 4.

Blessing of the Birds
A473

Designs (Scenes from Apocalypse): 2p, Angel at River of Life. 3p, Angel Guarding Gate of Paradise. 4p, Fox carrying cock. 6p, Daniel with wild bulls. 7p, The Last Judgment. 10p, Four horsemen of the Apocalypse. 12p, Bird holding snake. 2p, 3p, 7p, 10p, 12p are vertical.

1975, Sept. 29

1909	A473	1p gold & multi	15	15
1910	A473	2p gold & multi	20	15
1911	A473	3p gold & multi	20	15
1912	A473	4p gold & multi	15	15
1913	A473	6p gold & multi	15	15
1914	A473	7p gold & multi	24	15
1915	A473	10p gold & multi	28	15
1916	A473	12p gold & multi	32	18
		Nos. 1909-1916 (8)	1.69	
		Set value		82

Millenium Gerona Cathedral.

For other art types see A384, A397, A410, A431, A448, A501, AS22, A538, A558 and footnote following No. 876.

Symbols of Industry
A474

1975, Oct. 7   Engr.   Perf. 13

1917	A474	3p violet & lilac	15	15

Spanish industrialization.

Pioneers' Covered Wagon
A475

Designs: 1p, El Cabildo, meeting house of 1st Uruguayan Government. 3p, Fort St. Theresa over River Plate. 8p, Montevideo Cathedral, vert.

1975, Oct. 12   Photo.

1918	A475	1p multicolored	15	15
1919	A475	2p multicolored	22	15
1920	A475	3p multicolored	22	15
1921	A475	8p multicolored	18	15
		Set value		32

Cultural ties with Latin America; sesquicentennial of Uruguay's independence.

Ruined Columns, San Juan de la Peña — A476

Madonna, Mosaic, Navarra Cathedral — A477

Designs: 3p, Monastery, horiz. 8p, Cloister, horiz.

Perf. 13x12½, 12½x13

1975, Oct. 28   Engr.

1922	A476	3p slate grn & brn	30	15
1923	A476	8p violet & brt lil	25	15
1924	A476	10p dp magenta & car	42	18
		Set value		34

San Juan de la Pena Monastery.

1975, Nov. 4   Photo.   Perf. 13

Christmas: 12p, Flight into Egypt, carved capital, Navarra Cathedral, horiz.

1925	A477	3p multicolored	20	15
1926	A477	12p multicolored	20	15
		Set value		20

King Juan Carlos I — A478

Queen Sofia and King — A479

Designs: No. 1928, Queen Sofia.

1975, Dec. 29   Photo.   Perf. 13x12½

1927	A478	3p multicolored	15	15
1928	A478	3p multicolored	15	15

Perf. 12½

1929	A479	3p multicolored	15	15
1930	A479	12p multicolored	30	15
		Set value		26

King Juan Carlos I, accession to the throne.

Pilgrim Virgin, Pontevedra
A480

Mountains and Center Emblem
A481

1976, Jan. 2   Engr.   Perf. 13

1931	A480	3p rose & brown	15	15

Holy Year of St. James of Compostela, patron saint of Spain.

1976, Feb. 10   Photo.

1932	A481	6p multicolored	15	15

Catalunya Excursion Center, centenary.

Cosme Damian Churruca — A482

Navigators: 12p, Luis de Requesens. 50p, Juan Sebastian Elcano, horiz.

1976, Mar. 1   Engr.   Perf. 13

1933	A482	7p vio brn & grnsh blk	2.25	15
1934	A482	12p lt blue & violet	40	15
1935	A482	50p dp brown & gray ol	90	25

A. G. Bell, Radar and Telephone
A483

1976, Mar. 10   Photo.

1936	A483	3p multicolored	15	15

Centenary of first telephone call by Alexander Graham Bell, March 10, 1876.

"Watch at Street Crossings"
A484

Road Safety: 3p, "Don't pass when in doubt," vert. 5p, "Wear seat belts."

1976, Apr. 6   Photo.   Perf. 13

1937	A484	1p orange & multi	16	15
1938	A484	3p gray & multi	50	15
1939	A484	5p lilac & multi	35	15
		Set value		22

St. George, Alcoy Cathedral
A485

1976, Apr. 23

1940	A485	3p multicolored	18	15

7th centenary of the apparition of St. George in Alcoy.

Talavera Pottery
A486

Europa: 12p, Lace making.

1976, May 3   Photo.   Perf. 13

1941	A486	3p multicolored	1.00	15
1942	A486	12p multicolored	1.50	20

17th Conference of European Postal and Telecommunications Administrations.

6r Stamp of 1851 with Coruna Cancel — A487

1976, May 6

1943	A487	3p blue, org & blk	20	15

World Stamp Day.

Coin of Caesar Augustus
A488

Designs: 7p, Map of Roman camp on banks of Ebro, and coin. 25p, Orpheus, mosaic from Roman era, vert.

1976, May 26   Engr.   Perf. 13

1944	A488	3p dk brown & maroon	3.00	15
1945	A488	7p dk brown & blue	1.65	15
1946	A488	25p brown & black	1.25	18

2000th anniversary of the founding of Saragossa.

Spanish-made Rifle, 1757 — A489

Designs (Bicentennial Emblem and): 3p, Bernardo de Galvez, Spanish governor. 5p, Dollar bank note, Richmond, 1861. 12p, Spanish capture of Pensacola from English.

1976, May 29

1947	A489	1p dk brn & vio bl	24	15
1948	A489	3p sl grn & dk brn	1.25	15
1949	A489	5p dk brn & sl grn	55	15
1950	A489	12p sl grn & dk brn	95	18
		Set value		50

American Bicentennial.

Old Customs House, Cadiz
A490

1976, June 9

1951	A490	1p black & maroon	24	15
1952	A490	3p sepia & green	85	15
1953	A490	7p red brn & vio brn	1.25	15
		Set value	32	

Customs Houses: 3p, Madrid. 7p, Barcelona.

Postal Savings Box with Symbols — A491

Railroad Post Office — A492

Rural Mailman in Winter A493

Postal Service: 10p, Automatic letter sorting machine.

1976, June 16   Photo.

1954	A491	1p multicolored	18	15
1955	A492	3p multicolored	55	15
1956	A493	6p multicolored	28	15
1957	A493	10p multicolored	48	15
		Set value	40	

King and Queen, Map of Americas A494

1976, June 25

1958	A494	12p multicolored	35	15

Visit of King Juan Carlos I and Queen Sofia to the Americas, June 1976.

San Marcos, León A495

Greco-Roman Wrestling A496

Tourism (Famous Hotels): 2p, Las Cañadas, Tenerife. 3p, Portal of R. R. Catolicos, Santiago, vert. 4p, Cruz de Tejeda, Las Palmas. 7p, Gredos, Avila. 12p, La Arruzafa, Cordoba.

1976, June 30   Engr.   *Perf. 13*

1959	A495	1p slate & sepia	22	15
1960	A495	2p green & indigo	75	15
1961	A495	3p brn & red brn	50	15
1962	A495	4p sepia & slate	50	15
1963	A495	7p slate & sepia	1.00	15
1964	A495	12p rose brn & pur	1.75	15
		Nos. 1959-1964 (6)	4.72	
		Set value	52	

1976, July 9   Photo.

Designs (Montreal Olympic Emblem and): 1p, Men's rowing, horiz. 2p, Boxing, horiz. 12p, Basketball.

1965	A496	1p multicolored	18	15
1966	A496	2p lilac & multi	38	15
1967	A496	3p multicolored	28	15
1968	A496	12p multicolored	28	18
		Set value	42	

21st Olympic Games, Montreal, Canada, July 17-Aug. 1.

King Juan Carlos I — A497

1976-77   Photo.   *Perf. 13*

1969	A497	10c orange ('77)	15	15
1970	A497	25c apple grn ('77)	15	15
1971	A497	30c dp blue ('77)	15	15
1972	A497	50c purple ('77)	15	15
1973	A497	1p emerald ('77)	15	15
1974	A497	1.50p scarlet	15	15
1975	A497	2p dp blue	15	15
1976	A497	3p dp green	15	15
1977	A497	4p blue grn ('77)	15	15
1978	A497	5p dp car rose	15	15
1979	A497	6p brt green ('77)	15	15
1980	A497	7p olive	15	15
1982	A497	8p brt blue ('77)	18	15
1983	A497	10p lilac rose ('77)	20	15
1984	A497	12p golden brown	20	15
1985	A497	15p vio blue ('77)	28	15
1986	A497	20p brt red lil ('77)	35	15
		Set value	1.90	75

See Nos. 2185-2194.

Uniform Type of 1973

Uniforms: 1p, Trumpeter, Alcantara Regiment, 1815. 2p, Sapper, 1821. 3p, Engineer in dress uniform, 1825. 7p, Artillery infantry, 1828. 25p, Infantry riflemen, 1830.

1976, July 17

1989	A428	1p multicolored	18	15
1990	A428	2p multicolored	95	15
1991	A428	3p multicolored	28	15
1992	A428	7p multicolored	28	15
1993	A428	38p multicolored	38	25
		Nos. 1989-1993 (5)	2.07	
		Set value	60	

Blood Donors A498

Mosaic, Batitales A499

1976, Sept. 7   Engr.   *Perf. 13*

1994	A498	3p carmine & black	15	15

Give blood, save a life!

1976, Sept. 22

Designs: 3p, Lugo city wall. 7p, Obverse and reverse of Roman 1st Legion coin.

1995	A499	1p black & purple	15	15
1996	A499	3p black & dp brn	30	15
1997	A499	7p green & magenta	55	15
		Set value	32	

2000th anniversary of Lugo City.

Parliament, Madrid A500

1976, Sept. 23

1998	A500	12p green & sepia	20	15

63rd Conference of Inter-parliamentary Union, Madrid.

Still Life, by L. E. Menendez — A501

St. Christopher Carrying Christ Child — A502

Luis Eugenio Menendez Paintings: 2p, Peaches and jar. 3p, Pears, melon and barrel. 4p, Brace of pigeons and basket. 6p, Sea bream and oranges, horiz. 7p, Water melon and bread, horiz. 10p, Figs, bread and jug, horiz. 12p, Various fruits, horiz.

1976, Sept. 29   Photo.   *Perf. 13*

1999	A501	1p gold & multi	15	15
2000	A501	2p gold & multi	15	15
2001	A501	3p gold & multi	15	15
2002	A501	4p gold & multi	15	15
2003	A501	6p gold & multi	15	15
2004	A501	7p gold & multi	15	15
2005	A501	10p gold & multi	28	15
2006	A501	12p gold & multi	28	15
		Nos. 1999-2006 (8)	1.46	
		Set value	55	

Luis Eugenio Menendez (1716-1780). Stamp Day 1976.

For other art types see A384, A397, A410, A431, A448, A473, A522, A538, A558 and footnote following No. 876.

1976, Oct. 8

Christmas: 3p, Nativity, horiz. Both designs after painted wood carvings.

2007	A502	3p multicolored	1.60	15
2008	A502	12p multicolored	2.75	15
		Set value	16	

Nicoya Church, Costa Rica — A503

Juan Vazquez de Coronado — A504

Designs: 3p, Orosi Mission, Costa Rica, horiz. 12p, Tomas de Acosta.

1976, Oct. 12

2009	A503	1p multicolored	15	15
2010	A504	2p multicolored	15	15
2011	A503	3p multicolored	20	15
2012	A504	12p multicolored	32	15
		Set value	34	

Spain's link with Costa Rica.

Map of South and Central America, Santa Maria, King and Queen A505

1976, Oct. 12

2013	A505	12p multicolored	30	15

Visit of King Juan Carlos I and Queen Sofia to Latin America.

St. Peter of Alcantara Monastery A506

Tomb of Peter of Alcantara A507

St. Peter of Alcantara A508

1976, Oct. 29   Engr.   *Perf. 13*

2014	A506	3p dp brown & sepia	28	15
2015	A507	7p dk purple & blk	28	18
2016	A508	20p brown & dk brown	50	22

St. Peter of Alcantara (1499-1562), Franciscan reformer.

Hand Releasing Doves A509

1976, Nov. 23   Litho.   *Perf. 13*

2017	A509	3p multicolored	15	15

11th Philatelic Exhibition of the National Association of the Handicapped.

Casals and Cello A510

Design: 5p, Manuel de Falla and Fire Dance from El Amor Brujo.

1976, Dec. 29   Engr.   *Perf. 13*

2018	A510	3p black & vio bl	15	15
2019	A510	5p slate grn & car	15	15
		Set value	20	

Birth centenaries of Pablo Casals (1876-1973), cellist and composer, and of Manuel de Falla (1876-1946), composer.

Uniform Type of 1973

Uniforms: 1p, Outrider, Calatrava Lancers, 1844. 2p, Sapper, 1850. 3p, Corporal, Light Infantry, 1861. 4p, Drum Major, 1861. 20p, Artillery Captain, Mounted, 1862.

1977, Jan. 5   Photo.   *Perf. 13*

2020	A428	1p multicolored	18	15
2021	A428	2p multicolored	32	15
2022	A428	3p multicolored	18	15
2023	A428	4p multicolored	24	15
2024	A428	20p multicolored	32	15
		Nos. 2020-2024 (5)	1.24	
		Set value	38	

King
James I
A511

1977, Feb. 10   Engr.   Perf. 13
2025 A511 4p purple & ocher   15 15

James I, El Conquistador (1208-1276), King of
Aragon, 700th death anniversary.

Jacinto
Verdaguer — A512

Portraits: 7p, Miguel Servet. 12p, Pablo Sarasate.
50p, Francisco Tarrega.

1977, Feb. 22
2026 A512 5p purple & dk red   25 15
2027 A512 7p olive & slate grn   22 15
2028 A512 12p dk blue & bl grn   25 15
2029 A512 50p lt green & brown   75 25
          Set value   46

Honoring Jacinto Verdaguer (1845-1902), Catalan poet; Miguel Servet (1511-1553), physician and
theologian; Pablo Sarasate (1844-1908), violinist
and composer; Francisco Tarrega (1854-1909), creator of modern Spanish guitar music.

Marquis de
Penaflorida
A513

1977, Feb. 24   Engr.   Perf. 13
2030 A513 4p dull green & brn   15 15

Bicentenary of the Economic Society of the
Friends of the Land (agricultural improvements).

Trout
A514

1977, Mar. 8   Photo.
2031 A514 1p Salmon, vert.   15 15
2032 A514 2p shown   15 15
2033 A514 3p Eel   16 15
2034 A514 4p Carp   15 15
2035 A514 6p Barbel   22 15
      Nos. 2031-2035 (5)   83
          Set value   35

Slalom
A515

1977, Mar. 24   Engr.   Perf. 13
2036 A515 5p multicolored   15 15

World Ski Championships, Granada, Sierra
Nevada, Mar. 24-27.

La Cuadra,
1900
A516

Spanish Pioneer Automobiles: 4p, Hispano Suiza,
1916. 5p, Elizalde, 1915. 7p, Abadal, 1914.

1977, Apr. 23   Photo.   Perf. 13
2037 A516 2p multicolored   15 15
2038 A516 4p multicolored   15 15
2039 A516 5p multicolored   15 15
2040 A516 7p multicolored   16 15
          Set value   48 34

Ordesa
National
Park
A517

Europa: 3p, Tree in Doñana National Park.

1977, May 2   Litho.
2041 A517 3p multicolored   22 15
2042 A517 12p multicolored   25 15
          Set value   16

Plaza Mayor,
Spanish
Stamps,
Tongs
A518

1977, May 7   Engr.   Perf. 13
2043 A518 3p multicolored   15 15

50th anniversary of Philatelic Market on Plaza
Mayor, Madrid.

Enrique de
Osso, St.
Theresa and
Book
A519

1977, June 7   Photo.   Perf. 13
2044 A519 8p multicolored   16 15

Centenary of the founding by Enrique de Osso of
the Society of St. Theresa of Jesus.

Toledo Gate,
Ciudad
Real — A520

Tourism: 2p, Roman aqueduct, Almuñecar. 3p,
Cathedral, Jaen, vert. 4p, Ronda Gorge, Malaga,
vert. 7p, Ampudia Castle, Palencia. 12p, Bisagra
Gate, Toledo.

1977, June 24   Engr.   Perf. 13
2045 A520 1p orange & brown   15 15
2046 A520 2p sepia & slate   15 15
2047 A520 3p violet & purple   15 15
2048 A520 4p brt & dk green   15 15
2049 A520 7p brown & black   15 15
2050 A520 12p vio & org brn   15 15
          Set value   62 40

Uniform Type of 1973

Uniforms: 1p, Military Administration official,
1875. 2p, Cavalry lancers, 1883. 3p, General Staff
Commander, 1884. 7p, Trumpeter, Divisional Artillery, 1887. 25p, Medical Corps official, 1895.

1977, July 16   Photo.
2051 A428 1p multicolored   15 15
2052 A428 2p multicolored   18 15
2053 A428 3p multicolored   18 15
2054 A428 7p multicolored   18 15
2055 A428 25p multicolored   22 15
      Nos. 2051-2055 (5)   91
          Set value   38

A521   A522

St. Emilian Cuculatus and earliest known Catalan manuscript.

1977, Sept. 9   Engr.   Perf. 13
2056 A521 5p violet, grn & brn   15 15

Millennium of Catalan language.

1977, Sept. 29   Photo.   Perf. 13

Federico Madrazo (1815-94) Portraits: 1p, The
Boy Florez. 2p, Duke of San Miguel. 3p, Senora
Coronado. 4p, Campoamor. 6p, Marquesa de
Montelo. 7p, Rivadeneyra. 10p, Countess de
Vilches. 15p, Senora Gomez de Avellaneda.

2057 A522 1p gold & multi   15 15
2058 A522 2p gold & multi   15 15
2059 A522 3p gold & multi   15 15
2060 A522 4p gold & multi   15 15
2061 A522 6p gold & multi   15 15
2062 A522 7p gold & multi   15 15
2063 A522 10p gold & multi   16 15
2064 A522 15p gold & multi   16 15
          Set value   92 72

For other art types see A384, A397, A410,
A431, A448, A473, A501, A538, A558 and footnote following No. 876.

Sailing Ship and Mail Routes, 18th
Century — A523

1977, Oct. 7   Engr.
2065 A523 15p black, brn & grn   50 35

ESPAMER '77 Philatelic Exhibition, Barcelona,
Oct. 7-13, and for the Bicentenary for regular mail
routes to the Indies (Central and South America).

No. 2065 issued in sheets of 8 stamps and 8 labels
showing exhibition emblem.

Church of St.
Francis,
Guatemala
City
A524

Designs (Guatemala City): 3p, Modern buildings.
7p, Government Palace. 12p, Columbus Square and
monument.

1977, Oct. 12   Photo.   Perf. 13
2066 A524 1p multicolored   15 15
2067 A524 3p multicolored   15 15
2068 A524 7p multicolored   15 15
2069 A524 12p multicolored   15 15
          Set value   40 28

Spain's link with Guatemala.

San Pedro
Monastery,
Cardeña
A525

Designs: 7p, Cloister. 20p, Tomb of El Cid and
Dona Gimena.

1977, Oct. 28   Engr.
2070 A525 3p vio blue & slate   15 15
2071 A525 7p brown & maroon   15 15
2072 A525 20p green & slate   35 18
          Set value   55 30

San Pedro Monastery, Cardena, Bugos.

Adoration of
the Kings
A526

Christmas: 12p, Flight into Egypt, vert. Designs
from Romanesque paintings in Jaca Cathedral
Museum.

1977, Nov. 3   Photo.
2073 A526 5p multicolored   15 15
2074 A526 12p multicolored   18 15
          Set value   15

Old and New
Iberia Planes
A527

1977, Nov. 3
2075 A527 12p multicolored   20 15

IBERIA, Spanish Airlines, 50th anniversary.

Felipe de Borbon, Prince of Asturias — A528

Judo, Games Emblem — A529

1977, Dec. 22   Photo.   *Perf. 13*
2076 A528 5p multicolored   15 15

Felipe de Borbon, Spanish crown prince.

1977, Dec. 29
2077 A529 3p multicolored   15 15

10th World Judo Championships, Taiwan.

Uniform Type of 1973

Uniforms: 1p, Flag bearer, 1908. 2p, Lieutenant Colonel, Hussar, 1909. 3p, Mounted artillery lieutenant, 1912. 5p, Engineers' captain, 1921. 12p, Captain General, 1925.

1978, Jan. 5
2078 A428 1p multicolored   15 15
2079 A428 2p multicolored   15 15
2080 A428 3p multicolored   15 15
2081 A428 5p multicolored   16 15
2082 A428 12p multicolored   16 15
    Set value   60 34

Hilarión Eslava and Score A530

Designs: 8p, José Clara and sculpture. 25p, Pio Baroja and farm. 50p, Antonio Machado Ruiz and castle.

1978, Feb. 20   Engr.   *Perf. 13*
2083 A530 5p black & dk pur   15 15
2084 A530 8p blue grn & blk   20 15
2085 A530 25p yel grn & blk   48 15
2086 A530 50p dk pur & dk brn   75 25
    Set value   50

Miguel Hilarión Eslava (1807-1878), composer; José Clara, sculptor; Pio Baroja (1872-1956), author and physician; Antonio Machado Ruiz (1875-1939), poet and playwright.

Burial of Christ, by de Juni — A531

Detail from Burial of Christ — A532

Designs: No. 2089, Juan de Juni. No. 2090, Rape of Sabine Women, by Rubens. No. 2091, Rape (detail) and Rubens portrait. No. 2092, Rubens signature and palette. No. 2093, Judgment of Paris, by Titian. No. 2094, Judgment and Titian portrait. No. 2095, Initial "TF" and palette.

1978, Mar. 28   Engr.   *Perf. 12¹/₂x13*
2087 A532 3p multicolored   15 15
2088 A531 3p multicolored   15 15
2089 A532 3p multicolored   15 15
    a.   Strip of 3, #2087-2089   18 18
2090 A532 5p multicolored   15 15
2091 A531 5p multicolored   15 15
2092 A532 5p multicolored   15 15
    a.   Strip of 3, #2090-2092   30 30

2093 A532 8p multicolored   15 15
2094 A531 8p multicolored   15 15
2095 A532 8p multicolored   15 15
    a.   Strip of 3, #2093-2095   48 48
    Set value   95 50

Juan de Juni (1507-77), sculptor, (3p); Peter Paul Rubens (1577-1640), painter, (5p); Titian (1477-1576), painter, (8p).

Edelweiss in Pyrenees — A533

Designs: 5p, Fish and duck, wetlands. 7p, Forest, and forest destroyed by fire. 12p, Waves, oil rig, tanker and city. 20p, Sea gulls and seals, wet.

1978, Apr. 4   Photo.   *Perf. 13*
2096 A533 3p multicolored   15 15
2097 A533 5p multicolored   15 15
2098 A533 7p multicolored   15 15
2099 A533 12p multicolored   20 15
2100 A533 20p multicolored   32 15
    Set value   84 38

Protection of the environment.

Palace of Charles V, Granada A534

Europa: 12p, The Lonja, Seville.

1978, May 2   Engr.   *Perf. 13*
2101 A534 5p dull grn & sl grn   15 15
2102 A534 12p dull grn & car rose   20 15
    Set value   16

"España" — A535

1978, May 5   Photo.   *Perf. 12¹/₂*
2103 A535 12p multicolored   18 15

Spain's admission to the Council of Europe.

Symbols and Emblems of Postal Service A536

1978, June 27   Engr.   *Perf. 13*
2104 A536 5p slate green   15 15

Stamp Day.

Map of Las Palmas, 16th Century A537

Designs: 5p, Hermitage of Columbus Church, vert. 12p, View of Las Palmas, 16th century.

1978, June 23   Photo.
2105 A537 3p multicolored   15 15
2106 A537 5p multicolored   15 15
2107 A537 12p multicolored   15 15
    Set value   32 18

500th anniversary of the founding of Las Palmas.

Pablo Picasso, Self-portrait — A538

Picasso Paintings: 3p, Señora Canals. 8p, Jaime Sabartes. 10p, End of the Act (actress). 12p, Science and Charity (woman patient, doctor, nurse and child), horiz. 15p, "Las Mennas" (blue period), horiz. 20p, The Sparrows. 25p, The Painter and his Model, horiz.

1978, Sept. 29   Photo.   *Perf. 13*
2108 A538 3p gold & multi   15 15
2109 A538 5p gold & multi   15 15
2110 A538 8p gold & multi   15 15
2111 A538 10p gold & multi   15 15
2112 A538 12p gold & multi   20 15
2113 A538 15p gold & multi   25 15
2114 A538 20p gold & multi   25 15
2115 A538 25p gold & multi   35 15
    Nos. 2108-2115 (8)   1.65
    Set value   70

Pablo Picasso (1881-1973). Stamp Day 1978. A 7p stamp like No. 2111 was not issued.
For other art types see A384, A397, A410, A431, A448, A473, A501, A522, A558 and footnote following No. 876.

José de San Martin A539

Design: 12p, Simon Bolivar.

1978, Oct. 12   Engr.   *Perf. 13*
2116 A539 7p sepia & car   15 15
2117 A539 12p violet & car   18 15
    Set value   16

José de San Martin (1778-1850) and Simon Bolivar (1783-1830), South American liberators.

Flight into Egypt, Capital from St. Mary de Nieva A540

Christmas: 12p, Annunciation, capital from St. Mary de Nieva.

1978, Nov. 3   Photo.   *Perf. 13*
2118 A540 5p multicolored   15 15
2119 A540 12p multicolored   18 15
    Set value   16

Mexican Calendar Stone A541

Designs (King Juan Carlos I, Queen Sofia and): No. 2121, Machu Picchu. No. 2122, Calchaqui jars from Tucuman and Angalgala.

1978
2120 A541 5p multicolored   15 15
2121 A541 5p multicolored   15 15
2122 A541 5p multicolored   15 15
    Set value   30 18

Royal visits to Mexico, Peru and Argentina. Issued: #2120 (Mexico), Nov. 17; #2121 (Peru), Nov. 22; #2122 (Argentina), Nov. 26.

King Philip V — A542

Rulers of Spain: No. 2124, Louis I. 8p, Ferdinand VI. 10p, Carlos III. 12p, Carlos IV. 15p, Ferdinand VII. 20p, Isabella II. 25p, Alfonso XII. 50p, Alfonso XIII. 100p, Juan Carlos I.

1978, Nov. 22   Engr.   *Perf. 13*
2123 A542 5p dk blue & rose red   15 15
2124 A542 5p olive & dull grn   15 15
2125 A542 8p vio bl & red brn   15 15
2126 A542 10p blue grn & blk   16 15
2127 A542 12p brown & maroon   24 15
2128 A542 15p black & indigo   24 15
2129 A542 20p olive & indigo   35 15
2130 A542 25p ultra & vio brn   35 15
2131 A542 50p vermilion & brn   70 20
2132 A542 100p ultra & vio blk   1.50 55
    Nos. 2123-2132 (10)   3.99
    Set value   1.45

Spanish Flag, Preamble to Constitution, Parliament A543

1978, Dec.   Photo.   *Perf. 13*
2133 A543 5p multicolored   15 15

Proclamation of New Constitution.

Illuminated Pages from Bible and Codex — A544

1978, Dec. 27
2134 A544 5p multicolored   15 15

Millennium of the consecration of the Basilica of Santa Maria de Ripoll.

Car and Drop of Oil — A545

Designs: 8p, Insulated house and thermometer. 10p, Hand pulling plug.

1979, Jan. 24   Photo.   *Perf. 13*
2135 A545 5p multicolored   15 15
2136 A545 8p multicolored   15 15
2137 A545 10p multicolored   15 15
    Set value   32 18

Energy conservation.

De La Salle, Students
A546

1979, Feb. 14   Photo.   Perf. 13
2138 A546 5p multicolored   15 15

Institute of Christian Brothers, founded by Jean-Baptiste de la Salle, centenary.

Jorge Manrique — A547

Portraits: 8p, Fernan Caballero (pen name of Cecilia Böhl de Faber). 10p, Francisco Villaespesa. 20p, Gregorio Marañón.

1979, Feb. 28   Engr.
2139 A547 5p green & brown   15 15
2140 A547 8p dark red & blue   15 15
2141 A547 10p brown & purple   16 15
2142 A547 20p green & olive   24 15
        Set value   60 32

Jorge Manrique, poet, 500th death anniversary; Fernan Caballero, Francisco Villaespesa, and Gregorio Marañón, writers, birth centenaries.

Running and Jumping
A548

Sport for All: 8p, Children kicking ball and skipping rope, jogging and bicycling. 10p, Family jogging, and dog.

1979, Mar. 14   Photo.   Perf. 13
2143 A548 5p multicolored   15 15
2144 A548 8p multicolored   15 15
2145 A548 10p multicolored   15 15
        Set value   32 18

Children in Library
A549

1979, Apr. 27   Photo.   Perf. 13
2146 A549 5p multicolored   15 15

International Year of the Child.

Manuel Ysasi (1810-1855) Postal Reformer — A550

Europa: 5p, Mounted messenger and postilion, 1761 engraving, vert.

1979, Apr. 30   Engr.
2147 A550 5p brown & sepia   15 15
2148 A550 12p red brn & sl grn   20 15
        Set value   15

Radar and Satellite
A551

Design: 5p, Symbolic people and cables, vert.

1979, May 17   Photo.   Perf. 13
2149 A551 5p multicolored   15 15
2150 A551 8p multicolored   15 15
        Set value   22 15

World Telecommunications Day, May 17.

Bulgaria No. 1, Sofia Opera House, Housing Development — A552

1979, May 18
2151 A552 12p multicolored   20 15

Philaserdica '79, International Philatelic Exhibition, Sofia, Bulgaria, May 18-27.

Tank, Jet and Destroyer
A553

1979, May 25
2152 A553 5p multicolored   15 15

Armed Forces Day.

Messenger Handing Letter to King — A554

1979, June 15   Litho. & Engr.
2153 A554 5p multicolored   15 15

Stamp Day 1979.

Daroca Gate, Zaragoza — A555

Architecture: 8p, Gerona Cathedral. 10p, Interior, Carthusian Monastery Church, Granada. 20p, Portal, Palace of the Marques de Dos Aguas, Valencia.

1979, June 27   Engr.
2154 A555 5p vio bl & lilac brn   15 15
2155 A555 8p dk blue & sepia   15 15
2156 A555 10p black & green   15 15
2157 A555 20p brown & sepia   28 15
        Set value   34

Turkey Sponge
A556

Fauna: 7p, Crayfish. 8p, Scorpion. 20p, Starfish. 25p, Sea anemone.

1979, July 11   Photo.   Perf. 13
2158 A556 5p multicolored   15 15
2159 A556 7p multicolored   15 15
2160 A556 8p multicolored   15 15
2161 A556 20p multicolored   20 15
2162 A556 25p multicolored   20 15
        Nos. 2158-2162 (5)   85
        Set value   42

Gen. Antonio Gutierrez and Battle
A557

1979, Aug.   Engr.
2163 A557 5p multicolored   15 15

Naval defense of Tenerife, 18th century.

A558   A559

Juan de Juanes Paintings: 8p, Immaculate Conception. 10p, Holy Family. 15p, Ecce Homo. 20p, St. Stephen in the Synagogue. 25p, The Last Supper, horiz. 50p, Adoration of the Mystic Lamb, horiz.

1979, Sept. 28   Photo.   Perf. 13x13½
2164 A558 8p multicolored   15 15
2165 A558 10p multicolored   15 15
2166 A558 15p multicolored   25 15
2167 A558 20p multicolored   38 15
2168 A558 25p multicolored   38 15
2169 A558 50p multicolored   75 22
        Nos. 2164-2169 (6)   2.06
        Set value   75

For other art types see A384, A397, A410, A431, A448, A473, A501, A522, A538 and footnote following No. 876.

1979, Oct. 3   Photo.   Perf. 13x13½

Zaragoza Cathedral, Mother and Child statue.

2170 A559 5p multicolored   15 15

8th Mariology and 15th International Marianist Congresses, Zaragoza, Oct. 3-12.

Felipe de Borbon, Hospital
A560

1979, Oct.   Perf. 13½x13
2171 A560 5p multicolored   15 15

Hospital of the Child Jesus, centenary.

St. Bartholomew College, Bogota — A561

Hispanidad 79: 12p, University of St. Mark, Lima, coat of arms.

1979, Oct. 12   Engr.   Perf. 13
2172 A561 7p multicolored   15 15
2173 A561 12p multicolored   20 15
        Set value   18

Clasped Hands, Badge, Governor's Palace
A562

Design: No. 2175, Statute book, vert.

Lithographed and Engraved
1979, Oct. 27   Perf. 13
2174 A562 8p multicolored   15 15
2175 A562 8p multicolored   15 15
        Set value   20 15

Catalonian and Basque autonomy statute.

Type A54, Barcelona Coat of Arms
A563

Photogravure and Engraved
1979, Nov. 6   Perf. 13½x13
2176 A563 5p multicolored   15 15

Barcelona Philatelic Congress and Exhibition, 50th anniversary.

Nativity, Capital from St. Peter the Elder
A564

Christmas 1979: 19p, Flight into Egypt, column from St. Peter the Elder, Huesca.

1979, Nov. 14   Photo.
2177 A564 8p multicolored   15 15
2178 A564 19p multicolored   24 15
        Set value   18

Carlos I, Coat of Arms
A565

Kings of the House of Austria (Hapsburg Dynasty): 20p, Philip II. 25p, Philip III. 50c, Philip IV. 100p, Carlos II.

1979, Nov. 22   Engr.   Perf. 13
2179 A565 15p sl grn & dk bl   20 15
2180 A565 20p dk blue & mag   28 15
2181 A565 25p violet & yel bis   52 15
2182 A565 50p brown & sl grn   55 18
2183 A565 100p magenta & brn   1.25 45
        Nos. 2179-2183 (5)   2.80
        Set value   90

2nd International Olive Oil Year A566

1979, Dec. 4　Photo.　Perf. 13½x13
2184 A566 8p multicolored　15　15

King Juan Carlos I Type of 1976

1980-84　Photo.　Perf. 13
2185	A497	13p dk red brn ('81)	30	15
2186	A497	14p red orange ('82)	25	15
2187	A497	16p sepia	30	15
2188	A497	17p bluish gray ('84)	30	15
2189	A497	19p orange	50	15
2190	A497	30p dk green ('81)	55	15
2191	A497	50p org ver ('81)	75	15
2192	A497	60p blue ('81)	1.00	15
2193	A497	75p brt yel grn ('81)	1.00	15
2194	A497	85p gray ('81)	1.50	15
	Nos. 2185-2194 (10)		6.45	
	Set value			68

Train and People A567

1980, Feb. 20　Engr.　Perf. 13½
2200	A567	3p shown	15	15
2201	A567	4p Bus	15	15
2202	A567	5p Subway	15	15
	Set value		30	16

Public transportation.

Steel Export A568

1980, Mar. 15　Photo.　Perf. 13½x13
2203	A568	5p shown	15	15
2204	A568	8p Ships	15	15
2205	A568	13p Shoes	20	15
2206	A568	19p Machinery	20	15
2207	A568	25p Technology	30	22
	Nos. 2203-2207 (5)		1.00	
	Set value			50

Federico Garcia Lorca (1899-1936) — A569

Europa: 19p, José Ortega y Gasset (1883-1955), philosopher and statesman.

1980, Apr. 28　Engr.　Perf. 13½
2208	A569	8p violet & ol grn	15	15
2209	A569	19p brown & dk grn	25	15
	Set value			18

Armed Forces Day — A570

1980, May 24　Photo.　Perf. 13½x13
2210 A570 8p multicolored　20　15

Soccer Players A571

1980, May 23
2211	A571	8p shown	16	15
2212	A571	19p Soccer ball, flags	24	15
	Set value			20

World Soccer Cup 1982.

Bourbon Arms, Ministry of Finance A572

1980, June 9　Engr.　Perf. 13½
2213 A572 8p dark brown　20　15

Public Finances in Bourbon Spain Exhibition.

Helen Keller, Sign Language A573

1980, June 27
2214 A573 19p dk yel grn & rose lake　28　15

Helen Keller (1880-1968), deaf mute writer and lecturer.

Mounted Postman, 12th Century Panel, Barcelona — A574

Lithographed and Engraved
1980, June 28　Perf. 13x12½
2215 A574 8p multicolored　20　15

Stamp Day.

King Alfonso and Count of Maceda at 1930 National Exhibition A575

1980, July 1　Photo.　Perf. 13½
2216 A575 8p multicolored　20　15

1st Natl. Stamp Exhibition, Barcelona, 50th anniv.

A576

A577

Altar of the Virgin, La Palma Cathedral.

1980, July 12　Engr.　Perf. 13
2217 A576 8p black & brown　20　15

Appearance of the Virgin of the Snow at La Palma, 300th anniversary.

1980, Aug. 9　Engr.　Perf. 13
2218 A577 100p slate & sepia　1.40　25

Ramon Perez de Ayala (1881-1962), novelist and diplomat.

Souvenir Sheet

La Atlantida Ruins, Mexican Bonampak Musicians — A578

Designs: b, Sun Gate, Tiahuanaco; Roman arch, Medinaceli. c, Alonso de Ercilla, Garcilaso de la Vega; title pages from La Arauca and Commentario Reales. d, Virgin of Quito, Virgin of Seafarers.

1980, Oct. 3　Engr.　Perf. 13
2219	Sheet of 4 + 2 labels	3.50	3.50
a.	A578 25p multicolored	38	38
b.	A578 25p multicolored	38	38
c.	A578 50p multicolored	55	55
d.	A578 100p multicolored	1.25	1.25

ESPAMER '80 Stamp Exhib., Madrid, Oct. 3-12.

400th Anniversary of Buenos Aires — A579

1980, Oct. 24
2220 A579 19p multicolored　30　15

Miniature Sheet

The Creation, Tapestry, Gerona Cathedral — A580

1980, Nov.　Litho.　Perf. 13½x13
2221	A580	Sheet of 6	4.50	3.25
a.-c.		25p, any single	40	25
d.-f.		50p, any single	60	35

Conference Building, Flags of Participants A581

Holy Family Church of Santa Maria, Cuina A582

1980, Nov. 11　Photo.　Perf. 13½
2222 A581 22p multicolored　32　15

1980, Nov. 12

Christmas 1980, 22p, Adoration of the Kings, portal, Church of Santa Maria, Cuina, horiz.

2223	A582	10p multicolored	15	15
2224	A582	22p multicolored	25	15
	Set value			15

Pedro Vives and His Airplane A583

Designs: Aviation pioneers.

1980, Dec. 10
2225	A583	5p shown	15	15
2226	A583	10p Benito Loygorri	15	15
2227	A583	15p Alfonso De Orleans	25	15
2228	A583	22p Alfredo Kindelan	38	15
	Set value			34

Winter University Games A584

1981, Mar. 4　Perf. 13½x13
2229 A584 30p multicolored　50　15

Picasso's Birth Centenary Emblem, by Joan Miro — A585

1981, Mar. 27　Perf. 13
2230 A585 100p multicolored　1.75　30

Pablo Picasso (1881-1973).

Galician Autonomy — A586

1981, Mar. 27　Photo. Engr.　Perf. 13
2231 A586 12p multicolored　25　15

Homage to the Press A587

1981, Aug. 8　Photo.　Perf. 13½x13
2232 A587 12p multicolored　30　15

International Year of the Disabled — A588

1981, Apr. 29   **Litho.**
2233 A588 30p multicolored   50 15

Soccer Players A589

1981, May 2   **Photo.**
2234 A589 12p Soccer players, diff., vert.   25 15
2235 A589 30p shown   50 15
      Set value   20

1982 World Cup Soccer.

Europa Issue 1981

La Jota Folkdance A590

1981, May 4   **Engr.**
2236 A590 12p shown   22 15
2237 A590 30p Virgin of Rocio procession   48 15
      Set value   18

Armed Forces Day — A591

Gabriel Miro (1879-1930), Writer — A592

1981, May 29   Photo.   Perf. 13x13½
2238 A591 12p multicolored   25 15

1981, June 17   **Engr.**
Famous Men: 12p, Francisco de Quevedo (1580-1645), writer. 30p, St. Benedict (480-543), patron saint of Europe.

2239 A592 6p purple & dk grn   18 15
2240 A592 12p brown & purple   25 15
2241 A592 30p dk green & brown   35 15
      Set value   22

Mail Messenger, 14th Cent., Woodcut — A593

Photogravure and Engraved
1981, June 19   **Perf. 12½x13**
2242 A593 12p multicolored   25 15
      Stamp Day.

Map of Balearic Islands, Diego Homem's Atlas, 1563 — A594

1981, July 8   Photo.   Perf. 13x12½
2243 A594 7p shown   15 15
2244 A594 12p Canary Islds., Prunes map, 1563   25 15
      Set value   15

Kings Alfonso XII and Juan Carlos, Advocates Arms A595

1981, July 27   Engr.   Perf. 13½x13
2245 A595 50p multicolored   65 15
Chamber of Advocates of State (Public Prosecutor) centenary.

King Sancius VI of Navarre with City Charter, 12th Cent. Miniature A596

1981, Aug. 5   Photo.   Perf. 12½x13
2246 A596 12p multicolored   25 15
      Vitoria, 800th anniv.

Exports A597

1981, Sept. 30   Photo.   Perf. 13½x13
2247 A597 6p Fruit   15 15
2248 A597 12p Wine   25 15
2249 A597 30p Vehicles   38 15
      Set value   25

Congress Palace, Buenos Aires A598

1981, Oct. 12   Engr.   Perf. 13½x13
2250 A598 12p dk bl & car rose   20 15
ESPAMER '81 Intl. Stamp Exhibition, Buenos Aires, Nov. 13-22.

World Food Day — A599

1981, Oct. 16
2251 A599 30p multicolored   52 15

Souvenir Sheet

Guernica, by Pablo Picasso (1881-1973) — A600

1981, Oct. 25   **Photo.**
2252 A600 200p multicolored   3.75 3.75
Control number comes in two types.

Adoration of the Kings, Cervera de Pisuerga, Palencia — A601

1981, Nov. 18   **Litho.**   **Perf. 13**
2253 A601 12p shown   25 15
2254 A601 30p Nativity, Paredes de Nava   50 15
      Set value   20
      Christmas 1981.

King Juan Carlos I — A602

1981, Oct. 21   Engr.   Perf. 13x12½
2268 A602 100p brown   1.50 15
2269 A602 200p dark green   3.50 25
2270 A602 500p dark blue   8.50 90

Postal Museum, Madrid — A603

1981, Nov. 30   **Engr.**   **Perf. 13**
2273 A603 7p Telegrapher   18 15
2274 A603 12p Coach   25 15
      Set value   15
Souvenir Sheet
2275   Sheet of 4   3.00 3.00
  c.   A603 50p Emblem   75 48
  d.   A603 100p Cap, posthorn, pouch   1.50 80
No. 2275 also contains Nos. 2273, 2274.

Royal Mint Building, Seville A604

1981, Dec. 4   **Engr.**   **Perf. 13**
2276 A604 12p black & brown   28 15
Spanish Administration of the Bourbons in the Indies.

A605   A606

Designs: 12p, Iparraguirre (1820-1881). 30p, Juan Ramon Jimenez (1881-1958), writer. 50p, Pedro Calderon (1600-1681), playwright.

1981-82
2277 A605 12p black & dk bl   25 15
2278 A605 30p dk bl & dk grn   60 15
2279 A605 50p black & violet   1.00 15
      Set value   28
Issued: 12p, Dec. 16. 30p, 50p, Mar. 10, 1982.

1982, Feb. 24   **Photo.**
2280 A606 14p Poster by Joan Miro   25 15
2281 A606 33p Cup, emblem   60 15
      Set value   20
Espana '82 World Cup Soccer.

A607   A608

1982, Mar. 10   **Engr.**
2282 A607 30p grn & dk grn   60 15
Andres Bello (1782-1865), writer.

1982, Mar. 31   Photo.   Perf. 13
2283 A608 14p St. John of Compostelo   30 15
Holy Year of Compostelo.

Manuel Fernandez Caballero (1835-1906) and Scene from his Gigantes and Cabezudos

A609   A610

Designs: Operetta composers and scenes from their works. Stamps of same denomination setenant.

Lithographed and Engraved
1982, Apr. 28   **Perf. 13**
2284 A609 3p shown   15 15
2285 A610 3p shown   15 15
2286 A609 6p Amadeo Vives Roig (1871-1932)   15 15
2287 A610 6p Dona Franciscuita   15 15

2288	A609	8p	Tomas Breton Hernandez (1850-1923)	18 15
2289	A610	8p	Verbena of Paloma	18 15
			Set value	75 34

See Nos. 2319-2324, 2378-2383.

Europa 1982 — A611

1982, May 3   Engr.   *Perf. 12½*

2290	A611	14p	Unification, 1512	28 15
2291	A611	33p	Discovery of New World, 1492	65 15
			Set value	16

Armed Forces Day — A612

1982, May 28   Photo.   *Perf. 13*

2292	A612	14p	multicolored	30 15

1982 World Cup A613

Designs: Soccer players.

1982, June 13   *Perf. 13*

2293	A613	14p	multicolored	30 15
2294	A613	33p	multicolored	60 15
			Set value	20

Souvenir Sheets

2295		Sheets of 4, #2293-2294, 9p, 100p	5.00 5.00
	a.	A613 9p Captains' handshake	35 20
	b.	A613 100p Player holding cup	3.25 3.00

No. 2295 has two types of margin, each showing seven arms of the 14 host cities. One sheet has 3 blue coats of arms, the other has 2.

Stamp Day — A614

        Perf. 12½

1982, July 16   Litho.   Engr.

2296	A614	14p	Map, postal code	30 15

Organ Transplants — A615

1982, July 28   Photo.   *Perf. 13*

2297	A615	14p	Symbolic organs	30 15

Storks and Express Train A616

Locomotive, 1850 A617

       Perf. 12½, 13 (A617)

1982, Sept. 27   Photo.

2298	A616	9p	shown	15 15
2299	A617	14p	shown	25 15
2300	A617	33p	Santa Fe locomotive	60 15
			Set value	28

23rd Intl. Railways Congress, Malaga.

ESPAMER '82 Intl. Stamp Exhibition, San Juan, Oct. 12-17 A618

1982, Oct. 12   Engr.   *Perf. 13½x13*

2301	A618	33p	dk blue & pur	60 15

St. Teresa of Avila (1515-1582) — A619

1982, Oct. 15

2302	A619	33p	Statue by Gregorio Hernandez	60 15

Visit of Pope John Paul II, Oct. 31-Nov. 9 A620

1982, Oct. 31   Engr.   *Perf. 12½*

2303	A620	14p	multicolored	30 15

Water Wheel, Alcantarilla — A621

Landscapes and Monuments: 6p, Bank of Spain, 19th cent., horiz. 9p, Crucifixion. 14p, St. Martin's Tower, Teruel. 33p, St. Andrew's Gate, Zamora.

1982, Nov. 5   *Perf. 13x12½, 12½x13*

2304	A621	4p	gray & dk blue	15 15
2305	A621	6p	dk blue & gray	15 15
2306	A621	9p	brt blue & vio	20 15
2307	A621	14p	brt blue & vio	30 15
2308	A621	33p	claret & brown	55 15
		Nos. 2304-2308 (5)		1.35
			Set value	40

Christmas 1982 A622

1982, Nov. 17   Photo.   *Perf. 13½*

2309	A622	14p	Nativity, wood carving, by Gil de Siloe	25 15
2310	A622	33p	Flight into Egypt	55 15
				15

Pablo Gargallo, Sculptor, Birth Centenary A623

Salesian Fathers in Spain, Centenary A624

1982, Dec. 9   Engr.   *Perf. 13*

2311	A623	14p	blue & dk grn	30 15

1982, Dec. 16   Photo.   *Perf. 12½x13*

2312	A624	14p	multicolored	30 15

Arms of King Juan Carlos I A625

1983, Feb. 9   Photo.   *Perf. 12½*

2313	A625	14p	multicolored	30 15

Andalusia Autonomy Statute A626

1983   Litho.   Engr.   *Perf. 13½*

2314	A626	14p	shown	25 15
2315	A626	14p	Cantabria	25 15
			Set value	16

Issued: No. 2314, Feb. 28; No. 2315, Mar. 15.

State Security Forces A627

1983, Mar. 23   Photo.

2316	A627	9p	Natl. Police Force	18 15
2317	A627	14p	Civil Guard	25 15
2318	A627	33p	Superior Police Corps	55 15
			Set value	32

Operetta Type of 1982

Designs: 4p, Francisco Alonso Lopez (1887-1948), La Parranda. 6p, Jacinto Guerrero y Torres (1895-1951), La Rosa del Azafran. 9p, Jesus de Guridi Bidaola (1886-1961), El Caserio.

Lithographed and Engraved

1983, Apr. 22   *Perf. 13*

2319	A610	4p	multicolored	15 15
2320	A609	4p	multicolored	15 15
2321	A609	6p	multicolored	15 15
2322	A610	6p	multicolored	15 15
2323	A609	9p	multicolored	18 15
2324	A610	9p	multicolored	18 15
			Set value	72 44

Europa 1983 A628

Designs: 16p, Scene from Don Quixote, by Miguel Cervantes. 38p, L. Torres Quevaedo's Niagara Spanish aerocar.

1983, May 5   Engr.   *Perf. 13x12½*
         Granite Paper

2325	A628	16p	dk grn & brn red	30 15
2326	A628	38p	brown	75 18
			Set value	24

Francisco Salzillo Alvarez (1707-83), Painter — A629

World Communications Year — A630

Designs: 38p, Antonio Soler Ramos (1729-1783), composer. 50p, Joaquin Turina Perez (1882-1949), composer. 100p, St. Isidro Labrador (1082-1170), patron saint of Madrid.

1983, May 14   *Perf. 13*

2327	A629	16p	purple & dk grn	30 15
2328	A629	38p	blue & brown	75 15
2329	A629	50p	bl grn & dk brn	1.00 22
2330	A629	100p	red brn & pur	1.75 30
			Set value	70

1983, May 17   Photo.   *Perf. 13*

2331	A630	38p	multicolored	65 18

Rioja Autonomous Region A631

Lithographed and Engraved
1983, May 25   *Perf. 13*
2332 A631 16p multicolored   30 15

Armed Forces Day — A632

1983, May 26   Photo.
2333 A632 16p multicolored   30 15

Intl. Canine Exhibition, Madrid, June 1984 A633

Lithographed and Engraved
1983, June 8   *Perf. 13½*
2334 A633 10p Pointer   25 15
2335 A633 16p Mastiff   38 15
2336 A633 26p Iberian hound   50 18
2337 A633 38p Navarro pointer   75 30
     Set value   65

Discovery of Tungsten Bicentenary A634

Scouting Year — A635

400th Anniv. of University of Zaragoza A636

1983, June 22   Photo.   *Perf. 13*
2338 A634 16p Elhuyar brothers   32 15
2339 A635 38p multicolored   70 32
2340 A636 50p multicolored   95 50

Murcia Autonomous Region A637

Photogravure and Engraved
1983, July 8   *Perf. 13½*
2341 A637 16p Arms   35 15

Asturias Autonomous Region A638

Lithographed and Engraved
1983, Sept. 8   *Perf. 13*
2342 A638 14p Victory Cross, Covadonga Basilica   35 15

Intl. Institute of Statistics, 44th Congress, Madrid, Sept. 12-22 A639

1983, Sept. 12   Photo.   *Perf. 13*
2343 A639 38p Institute building   85 18

Stamp Day — A640

Lithographed and Engraved
1983, Oct. 8   *Perf. 13x12½*
2344 A640 16p Roman mail cart   75 50

No. 2344 se-tenant with label publicizing ESPANA '84 Philatelic Exhibition, April 27-May 6, 1984.

Valencia Automony Statute, 1st Anniv. A641

1983, Oct. 10   *Perf. 13*
2345 A641 16p multicolored   38 15

View of Seville, 16th cent. — A642

1983, Oct. 12   Engr.   *Perf. 12½x13*
2346 A642 38p multicolored   70 18

Spanish-American trade in 17th century.

Stained-glass Windows — A643

Designs: 10p King, Leon Cathedral. 16p, Epiphany, Gerona Cathedral. 38p, Apostle Santiago, Royal Hospital Chapel, Santiago.

Lithographed and Engraved
1983, Oct. 28   *Perf. 12½x13*
2347 A643 10p multicolored   18 15
2348 A643 16p multicolored   28 15
2349 A643 38p multicolored   65 18

Church at Llivia, Gerona — A644

Designs: 6p, Temple, Santa Maria del Mar, Barcelona. 16p, Cathedral, Ceuta. 38p, Gate of the Santiago Bridge, Melilla. 50p, Charity Hospital, Seville.

1983, Nov. 9   Engr.   *Perf. 13x12½*
2350 A644 3p dk bl gray & grn   15 15
2351 A644 6p dark blue gray   15 15
2352 A644 16p red brn & dull vio   28 15
2353 A644 38p bis brn & rose car   65 15
2354 A644 50p brown & org red   85 22
     Nos. 2350-2354 (5)   2.08
     Set value   50

Christmas 1983 — A645

Indalecio Prieto (1883-1962), Patriot — A646

1983, Nov. 23   Photo.   *Perf. 13x13½*
2355 A645 16p The Nativity, Tortosa   28 15
2356 A645 38p The Adoration, Vich   65 15
     Set value   18

1983, Dec. 14   Engr.   *Perf. 13*
2357 A646 16p red brn & blk   38 15

Industrial Accident Prevention A647

1984, Jan. 25   Photo.   *Perf. 13½*
2358 A647 7p Construction worker   15 15
2359 A647 10p Fire   18 15
2360 A647 16p Electrical plug, pliers   30 15
     Set value   22

Extremadura Statute of Autonomy, First Anniv. — A648

Lithographed and Engraved
1984, Feb. 25   *Perf. 13*
2361 A648 16p multicolored   30 15

1500th Anniv. of City of Burgos A649

1984, Mar. 1   Engr.
2362 A649 16p multicolored   30 15

Carnivals A650

1984   Photo.   *Perf. 13½x13*
2363 A650 16p Santa Cruz de Tenerife   30 15
2364 A650 16p Valencia Fallas   30 15
     Set value   15

Issued: No. 2363, Mar. 5; No. 2364, Mar. 16.

Man and the Biosphere A651

1984, Apr. 11
2365 A651 38p da Vinci's Study of Man   70 15

Aragon Statute of Autonomy, 2nd Anniv. A652

Lithographed and Engraved
1984, Apr. 23   *Perf. 13x13½*
2366 A652 16p Map   30 15

Juan Carlos — A653   Congress Emblem — A654

Souvenir Sheet

Espana '84 (Spanish Royal Family): b, Sofia of Greece. c, Cristina de Borbon. d, Prince of Asturias Felipe de Borbon. e, Elene de Borbon.

1984, Apr. 27   *Perf. 12½x13*
2367   Sheet of 5   5.00 5.00
a.-e. A653 38p, any single   85 85

1984, May 3   Engr.   *Perf. 13x13½*
2368 A654 38p purple & red   70 15

World Philatelic Federation, 53rd Congress, Madrid, May 7-9.

Europa (1959-84) A655

1984, May 5
2369 A655 16p orange   28 15
2370 A655 38p dark blue   65 22
     Set value   28

Armed Forces Day A656

Design: 17p, Monument to Hunters Regiment of Caceres, by Mariano Benlliure.

1984, May 19   Photo.   *Perf. 13½x13*
2371 A656 17p multicolored   30 15

Canary Islds. Statute of Autonomy — A657

Castilla-La Mancha Statute of Autonomy — A658

Lithographed and Engraved
1984, May 29   *Perf. 13*
2372 A657 16p Arms, map   30 15

1984, May 31   *Perf. 13*
2373 A658 17p Arms   30 15

King Alfonso X (1252-84) A659

Design: 38p, Ignacio Barroquer (1884-1965), ophthalmologist

1984, June 20   Engr.   *Perf. 13*
2374 A659 16p multicolored   30 15
2375 A659 38p multicolored   65 15
     Set value   18

Balearic Islands Statute of Autonomy — A660

1984, June 29   Litho. & Engr.
2376 A660 17p multicolored   30 15

Feast of San Fermin of Pamplona A661

1984, July 5   Photo.
2377 A661 17p Bull runners   30 15

Operetta Type of 1982

Designs: No. 2378, El Nino Judio. No. 2379, Pablo Luna (1880-1942). No. 2380, La Revoltosa. No. 2381, Ruperto Chapi (1851-1909). No. 2382, La Reina Mora. No. 2383, Jose Serrano (1873-1941).

Lithographed and Engraved
1984, July 20   *Perf. 13*
2378 A610 6p multicolored   15 15
2379 A609 6p multicolored   15 15
2380 A610 7p multicolored   15 15
2381 A609 7p multicolored   15 15
2382 A610 10p multicolored   18 15
2383 A609 10p multicolored   18 15
     Set value   80 30

1984 Summer Olympics A662

Greek or Roman sculptures.

1984, July 27   Photo.
2384 A662 1p Chariot race   15 15
2385 A662 2p Diving, vert.   15 15
2386 A662 5p Wrestling   15 15
2387 A662 8p Discus, vert.   15 15
     Set value   35 20

Navarra Statute of Autonomy A663

Lithographed and Engraved
1984, Aug. 16   *Perf. 13*
2388 A663 17p multicolored   30 15

Intl. Bicycling Championship, Barcelona, Aug. 27-Sept. 2 — A664

1984, Aug. 27   Photo.
2389 A664 17p multicolored   30 15

Castilla and Leon Statute of Autonomy A665

1984, Sept. 5   Litho. & Engr.
2390 A665 17p multicolored   30 15

Jerez Vintage Feast — A666

1984, Sept. 20   Photo.   *Perf. 13*
2391 A666 17p Women picking grapes   30 15

Journey to the Holy Land by Sister Egeria, 1600th Anniv. — A667

1984, Sept. 26
2392 A667 40p Map, Sister Egeria   70 15

Stamp Day A668

1984, Oct. 5   Litho. & Engr.
2393 A668 17p Arab postrider   30 15

Father Junipero Serra (1713-84), Mission Founder in California A669

1984, Oct. 12   Engr.   *Perf. 13*
2394 A669 40p Map, Serra, mission   85 15

Christmas 1984 A670

1984, Nov. 21   Photo.
2395 A670 17p Nativity   30 15
2396 A670 40p Adoration of the Kings, vert.   70 15
     Set value   15

Madrid Autonomy Statute A671

1984, Nov. 28   Litho. & Engr.
2397 A671 17p Arms, buildings   30 15

Andean Pact, 15th Anniv. A672

Condor, Flags of Bolivia, Colombia, Ecuador, Peru and Venezuela.

1985, Jan. 16   Photo.   *Perf. 13*
2398 A672 17p multicolored   30 15

The Virgin of Louvain, by Jan Gossaert (c. 1478-1536) A673

Santa Cruz College, Valladolid University, 500th Anniv. A674

1985, Jan. 21   *Perf. 13½*
2399 A673 40p multicolored   55 15

EUROPALIA '85. See Belgium No. 1185.

1985, Feb. 20   Litho. & Engr.
2400 A674 17p Main gateway   30 15

OLYMPHILEX '85, Lausanne, Switz. — A675

1985, Mar. 18   Photo.
2401 A675 40p multicolored   75 15

1985, Mar. 20
2402 A676 40p Cathedral, Havana

Fairs A677

Perf. 13½, 13½x14 (#2405)
1985   Photo.
2403 A677 17p Seville   35 15
2404 A677 17p Alcoy   35 15
2405 A677 17p Arriondas-Ribadesella   35 15
2406 A677 18p Toledo, vert.   38 15
     Set value   24

Issue dates: No. 2403, Apr. 16. No. 2404, Apr. 22. No. 2405, Aug. 2. No. 2406, June 6.

Intl. Youth Year — A678

1985, Apr. 17   Engr.   *Perf. 13½*
2407 A678 17p blk, hn brn & dk grn   35 15

Europa '85 — A680

Designs: 18p, Antonio de Cabezon (1510-1566), organist and composer, court Musician to Felipe II. 45p, Natl. Youth Orchestra.

1985, May 3   Engr.
2408 A680 18p dk bl, dk red & blk, *buff*   25 15
2409 A680 45p ol grn, dk red & blk, *buff*   60 15
     Set value   20

Armed Forces Day — A681

1985, May 24   Photo.
2410 A681 18p multicolored   30 15

Natl. Flag Bicent. — A682

Designs: No. 2411, Arms of King Carlos III, text of 1785 Decree, sailing ship Santisima Trinidad. No. 2412, Natl. arms, Article No. 4 from 1978 Constitution, lion ornament from Chamber of Deputies Building.

...ed and Engraved
Perf. 13x13½

	multicolored	30 15
	...p multicolored	30 15
	#2411-2412	60 22
	Set value	15

Intl. Environment Day — A683

1985, June 5   **Photo.**
2413 A683 17p multicolored   35 15

Juan Carlos I — A684

1985-92   **Photo.**   *Perf. 14*
2414	A684	10c indigo	15 15
2415	A684	50c lt blue green	15 15
2416	A684	1p brt blue	15 15
2417	A684	2p dark green	15 15
2418	A684	3p chestnut brn	15 15
2419	A684	4p olive green	15 15
2420	A684	5p brt rose lilac	15 15
2421	A684	6p brown black	15 15
2422	A684	7p brt violet	15 15
2423	A684	7p apple grn	15 15
2424	A684	8p gray black	15 15
2425	A684	10p lake	15 15
2426	A684	12p red	15 15
2427	A684	13p Prus blue	20 15
2428	A684	15p emerald	24 15
2429	A684	17p yellow bis	22 15
2430	A684	18p brt grnsh bl	24 15
2431	A684	19p violet brn	30 15
a.		Booklet pane of 6	1.80
2432	A684	20p brt pink	32 15
2433	A684	25p olive green	50 15
2434	A684	27p deep rose lil	55 15
2435	A684	30p ultra	48 15
2436	A684	45p brt green	58 15
2437	A684	50p violet blue	82 20
2438	A684	55p black brown	1.10 20
2439	A684	60p dark orange	98 25
2440	A684	75p deep rose lilac	1.20 30
		Set value	8.00 2.10

Issue dates: 1p, 5p, 8p, 12p, 18p, 45p, June 12. No. 2422, 17p, July 16. No. 2423, 17p, Jan. 1986. 2p, 3p, 4p, 10p, Apr. 3, 1986. 19p, Sept. 27, 1986. 6p, 20p, 30p, Jan. 26, 1987. 50p, 60p, 75p, Apr. 24, 1989. 10c, 50c, 13p, 15p, May 16, 1989. 25p, 55p, Dec. 14, 1990. 27p, Feb. 1992.

Astrophysical Observatory Opening, La Palma, Canary Islands A685

1985, June 25   **Photo.**   *Perf. 14*
2441 A685 45p multicolored   80 15

European Music Year — A686

Designs: 12p, Ataulfo Argenta, conductor. 17p, Tomas Luis de Victoria, composer. 45p, Fernando Sor, composer.

Litho. & Engr.
1985, June 26   *Perf. 13*
2442	A686	12p multicolored	16 15
2443	A686	17p multicolored	25 15
2444	A686	45p multicolored	60 15
		Set value	20

Bernal Diaz del Castillo (1492-1585), Historian — A687

Famous men: 12p, Esteban Terradas (1883-1950), mathematician. 17p, Vicente Aleixandre (1898-1984), 1977 Nobel laureate in literature. 45p, Leon Felipe Camino (1884-1968), poet.

1985, July 24   **Engr.**   *Perf. 13½*
2445	A687	7p dk red, blk & dk grn, *buff*	15 15
2446	A687	12p brt ver, dk bl & blk, *buff*	18 15
2447	A687	17p blk, dk grn & dk red, *buff*	28 15
2448	A687	45p bis, blk & dk grn, *buff*	70 15
		Set value	30

Monastic Mail Delivery, 1122 — A688

Lithographed and Engraved
1985, Sept. 27   *Perf. 13*
2449 A688 17p multicolored   35 15

Stamp Day 1985.

12th Rhythmic Gymnastics World Championships, Valladolid — A689

1985, Oct. 9   **Photo.**   *Perf. 13x13½*
2450	A689	17p Ribbon exercise	28 15
2451	A689	45p Hoop exercise	75 15
		Set value	20

Souvenir Sheet

Prado Museum, La Alcachofa Fountain — A690

Lithographed and Engraved
1985, Oct. 18   *Perf. 13*
2452 A690 17p multicolored   60 15

EXFILNA '85, Madrid, Oct. 18-27.

Virgin and Child, Seville Cathedral — A691

Stained glass windows: 12p, Monk, by Peter Boniface, Toledo Cathedral. 17p, King Henry II of Castile, Alcazar of Segovia.

1985, Oct. 24   *Perf. 12½x13*
2453	A691	7p multicolored	15 15
2454	A691	12p multicolored	20 15
2455	A691	17p multicolored	32 15
		Set value	16

Christmas 1985 A692

14th-15th century paintings in the Episcopal Museum, Vich: 17p, Nativity, Guimera Altarpiece retable, 14th cent., by Ramon de Mur. 45p, Epiphany, from an embroidered frontal, 15th cent.

1985, Nov. 27   **Photo.**   *Perf. 13½*
2456	A692	17p multicolored	28 15
2457	A692	45p multicolored	75 15
		Set value	20

Birds — A693

1985, Dec. 4   **Litho. & Engr.**
2458	A693	6p Sylvia cantillans	15 15
2459	A693	7p Monticola saxatilis	18 15
2460	A693	12p Sturnus unicolor	30 15
2461	A693	17p Panurus biarmicus	45 15
		Set value	20

Wildlife conservation.

Count of Penaflorida (1729-1785) A694

1985, Dec. 11   **Engr.**   *Perf. 13½*
2462 A694 17p dark blue   30 15

Francisco Javier de Munibe e Idiaguez, founded Natl. Economic Society of Friends in 1765.

Government Palace, Madrid, and Accession Agreement Text A695

Designs: 17p, Map and flags of EEC countries. 30p, Hall of Columns, Royal Palace. 45p, Member flags.

1986, Jan. 7.   **Litho.**   *Perf. 13½x13*
2463	A695	7p multicolored	15 15
2464	A695	17p multicolored	28 15
2465	A695	30p multicolored	48 15
2466	A695	45p multicolored	70 16
a.		Bklt. pane of 4, #2463-2466	3.50
		Set value	36

Admission of Spain and Portugal to European Economic Community. See Portugal Nos. 1661-1662.

Tourism — A696

Historic sites: 12p, Inner courtyard, La Lupiana Monastery, Guadalajara. 35p, Balcony of Europe, Nerja.

1986, Jan. 20   **Engr.**   *Perf. 13x12½*
2467	A696	12p dk rose, brn & gray brn	20 15
2468	A696	35p brt blue & sep	52 15
		Set value	16

2nd World Conference on Merino Sheep A697

1986, Jan. 27   **Photo.**   *Perf. 13½*
2469 A697 45p multicolored   80 16

Masquerade, 19th Cent., by F. Hohenleiter A698

1986, Feb. 5
2470 A698 17p multicolored   30 15

Cadiz Carnival.

Intl. Peace Year — A699

Lithographed and Engraved
1986, Feb. 12   *Perf. 13x13½*
2471 A699 45p multicolored   65 16

Festival of Religious Music, Cuenca A700

1986, Mar. 26   **Photo.**   *Perf. 13½*
2472 A700 17p multicolored   30 15

Chamber of Commerce, Cent. A701

Painting detail: Swearing in of the Regent, Queen Maria Christina, Before the Spanish Parliament, 1886, by Francisco Jover and Joaquin Sorolla y Bastida, Senate Palace, Madrid.

1986, Apr. 9   Engr.   *Perf. 13¹/₂*
2473 A701 17p sage grn & grnsh blk   30 15

Emigration of Spaniards — A702

1986, Apr. 22   Photo.
2474 A702 45p multicolored   65 16

Europa 1986 — A703

Lithographed and Engraved
1986, May 5   *Perf. 13x13¹/₂*
2475 A703 17p Youth feeding birds   30 15
2476 A703 45p Girl watering tree   75 16
    Set value   22

Our Lady of the Dew Festival, Almonte A704

1986, May 14   Photo.   *Perf. 13¹/₂x13*
2477 A704 17p multicolored   30 15

Army Day — A705

Design: Captains-General Building, Canary Islands.

1986, May 16   Engr.   *Perf. 13¹/₂*
2478 A705 17p pale yel brn, sep & red   30 15

Rodrigo City Cathedral A706

Design: 35p, Calella Lighthouse.

1986, June 16   *Perf. 12¹/₂x13¹/₂*
2479 A706 12p blue & black   25 15
2480 A706 35p multicolored   65 16
    Set value   16

10th World Basketball Championships, July 5-20 — A707

1986, July 4   Photo.   *Perf. 12¹/₂*
2481 A707 45p multicolored   90 16

Famous Men — A708

Mystery of the Virgin's Death Festival Elche — A709

Designs: 7p, Francisco Loscos Bernal (1823-1886), botanist. 11p, Salvador Espriu (1913-1985), author. 17p, Jose Martinez Ruiz (Azorin, 1873-1967), artist. 45p, Jose Vitoriano Gonzalez (Juan Gris, 1887-1927), painter.

1986, July 16   Engr.   *Perf. 13*
2482 A708 7p olive grn & bl   15 15
2483 A708 11p brt rose & blk   18 15
2484 A708 17p dk brn vio & blk   25 15
2485 A708 45p org, red vio & blk   68 18
    Set value   34

1986, Aug. 11   Photo.   *Perf. 13x13¹/₂*
2486 A709 17p Angels carrying soul   30 15

5th World Swimming, Water Polo, Diving and Synchronized Swimming Championships — A710

1986, Aug. 13   Engr.   *Perf. 13¹/₂*
2487 A710 45p multicolored   70 18

10th World Pelota Championships — A711

1986, Sept. 12
2488 A711 17p multicolored   30 15

Stamp Day — A712

Design: Messenger, The Husband's Return, Song 63, TI1 Codex, 1979 edition, Spanish Royal Academy.

1986, Sept. 27   Litho.   *Perf. 13x12¹/₂*
2480 A712 17p multicolored   30 15

Souvenir Sheet

EXFILNA '86, Cordova, Oct. 9-18 — A713

1986, Oct. 7   Litho. & Engr.
2490 A713 17p Man, Cordova "Mosque" 60 60

Discovery of America, 500th Anniv. (in 1992) — A714

Men and text: 7p, Aristotle, text from De Cielo et Mundo. 12p, Seneca, text from Medea. 17p, San Isidoro, text from Etimologias. 30p, Pedro de Ailly, text from Imago Mundi. 35p, Mayan, prophesy from Libros de Chilam Balam. 45p, European, prophesy from Libros de Chilam Balam.

Lithographed and Engraved
1986, Oct. 15   *Perf. 13x13¹/₂*
2491 A714 7p multicolored   15 15
2492 A714 12p multicolored   20 15
2493 A714 17p multicolored   28 15
2494 A714 30p multicolored   48 15
2495 A714 35p multicolored   55 15
2496 A714 45p multicolored   75 22
  a. Bklt. pane of 6, #2491-2496   2.35
    Nos. 2491-2496 (6)   2.41
    Set value   60

Caspar de Portola y Rovira (1717-1786), Pioneer of California — A715

1986, Nov. 6   *Perf. 13¹/₂*
2497 A715 22p multicolored   45 15

Christmas A716

Wood carving details: 19p, The Holy Family, by Diego de Siloe (c. 1495-1563), Natl. Sculpture Museum, Valladolid, vert. 48p, Nativity, Toledo Cathedral altarpiece, by Felipe de Borgona (c. 1475-1543).

1986, Nov. 19   Photo.   *Perf. 13¹/₂*
2498 A716 19p multicolored   30 15
2499 A716 48p multicolored   75 18
    Set value   26

Spanish-Islamic Cultural Heritage — A717

Famous men: 7p, Abd Al Rahman II (792-852), 4th independent emir of Cordoba. 12p, Ibn Hazm (994-1064), scholar. 17p, Al-Zarqali (1061-1100), astronomer. 45p, Alfonso VII, scholar, Toledo School of Translators.

1986, Dec. 3   Engr.
2500 A717 7p org red & dk red brn   15 15
2501 A717 12p brn blk & red org   22 15
2502 A717 17p black & dk blue   32 15
2503 A717 45p green & black   80 18
    Set value   36

Alfonso R. Castelao (1886-1950), Artist, Writer — A718

Lithographed and Engraved
1986, Dec. 11   *Perf. 13x13¹/₂*
2504 A718 32p El Buen Cura, 1917   60 15

Globe, Chateau de la Muette A719

1987, Jan. 14   *Perf. 14*
2505 A719 48p multicolored   75 18

Organization for Economic Cooperation and Development, OECD, 25th anniv.

EXPO '92, Seville A720

1987, Jan. 21   Photo.
2506 A720 19p Geometric shapes   30 15
2507 A720 48p Earth, Moon's surface   75 18
    Set value   26

See Nos. 2540-2541, 2550-2551.

Portrait of Vitoria, by Vera Fajardo A721

1987, Feb. 11   Engr.
2508 A721 48p dark rose brown   75 18

Francisco de Vitoria (c. 1486-1546), theologian, teacher and a founder of intl. law.

Marine Corps, 450th Anniv. A722

Design: 18th Cent. 74-gun man-of-war, period standard bearer, corps insignia.

1987, Feb. 25
2509 A722 19p multicolored — 30 15

Deusto University, Cent. — A723

1987, Feb. 26 Engr. Perf. 14x13½
2510 A723 19p blk, hn brn & dk grn — 30 15

UN Child Survival Campaign A724

1987, Mar. 4 Perf. 13½x14
2511 A724 19p red brown & blk — 30 15

Constitution of Cadiz, 175th Anniv. — A725

Nos. 2512a-2512c in a continuous design: The Promulgation of 1812, by Salvador Viniegra. No. 2512d, Anniv. emblem.

1987, Mar. 18 Litho. Perf. 13½
2512   Strip of 4 — 1.60 40
 a.-d. A725 25p, any single — 40 15

Ceramicware A726

Designs: 7p, Pharmaceutical jar, 15th cent., Manises of Valencia. 14p, Abstract figurine, 20th cent., Sargadelos of Galicia. 19p, Neo-classical lidded urn, 18th cent., Buen Retiro of Madrid. 32p, Water jar, 20th cent., Salvatierra of Extremadura. 40p, Pitcher, 18th cent., Talavera of Toledo. 48p, Pitcher, 18th-19th cent., Granada of Andalucia.

Lithographed and Engraved
1987, Mar. 20 Perf. 12½x13
2513   Block of 6 + 3 labels — 2.60 68
 a. A726 7p multicolored — 15 15
 b. A726 14p multicolored — 22 15
 c. A726 19p multicolored — 30 15
 d. A726 32p multicolored — 52 15
 e. A726 40p multicolored — 65 16
 f. A726 48p multicolored — 78 20

See No. 2552.

Passion Week in Zamora and Seville A727

Paintings: 19p, The Amanecer Procession, by Gallego Marquina, vert. 48p, Jesus Carrying the Cross, by Martinez Montanes, and the Gate of Forgiveness, Seville Cathedral.

1987, Apr. 13 Photo. Perf. 14x13½
2514 A727 19p multicolored — 32 15
2515 A727 48p multicolored — 80 20
    Set value — 28

Tourism — A728

Designs: 14p, Rock of Ifach, Calpe. 19p, Nave of Santa Marina d'Ozo Church, Pontevedra, before restoration. 40p, Sonanes Palace, Villacarriedo. 48p, Monastery of St. Joan de les Abadesses, Gerona, vert.

1987 Engr. Perf. 12½x13
2515A A728 14p dp bl & sage grn — 24 15
2516 A728 19p dp grn & grnsh blk — 32 15
2516A A728 40p dp claret — 68 18
2517 A728 48p black — 80 20
    Set value — 52

Issued: 19p, 48p, Apr. 21. 14p, 40p, June 10.

Europa 1987 A729

Modern architecture: 19p, Bilbao Bank, Madrid, designed by Saenz de Oiza, vert. 48p, Natl. Museum of Roman Art, Merida, designed by Rafael Moneo.

Lithographed and Engraved
1987, May 4 Perf. 14x13½
2518 A729 19p multicolored — 32 15
2519 A729 48p multicolored — 80 20
    Set value — 28

Horse Fair, Jerez de La Frontera A730

1987, May 6 Photo. Perf. 13½x14
2520 A730 19p multicolored — 32 15

Ramon Carande (1887-1986), Historian — A731

1987, May 29 Engr.
2521 A731 40p blk & dk vio brn — 68 18

Postal Code Inauguration — A732

1987, June 1 Litho. Perf. 14
2522 A732 19p multicolored — 32 15

Eibar Weaponry School, 75th Anniv. A733

1987, July 2 Litho. Perf. 14
2523 A733 20p multicolored — 32 15

1992 Summer Olympics, Barcelona A734

1987, July 15 Photo.
2524 A734 32p Casa de Battlo masonry — 52 15
2525 A734 65p Athletes — 1.05 28

25th Folk Festival of the Pyrenees, Jaca — A735

1987, July 22
2526 A735 50p multicolored — 80 20

Monturiol and Submarine Designs A736

1987, Sept. 9 Engr. Perf. 13½x14
2527 A736 20p black brown — 35 15

Narcis Monturiol (d. 1887), inventor of the submarine Ictineos.

Stamp Day — A737

Illuminated codex from *Constitutiones Jacobi II Regis Majoricum*, 14th cent., King Albert I Royal Library, Brussels.

1987, Sept. 16 Litho & Engr. Perf. 13
2528 A737 20p multicolored — 35 15

Postal service of Mallorca under James II.

ESPAMER '87 — A738

Designs: 8p, Handstamped letter that traveled from La Coruna to Havana, Cuba, 18th cent. 12p, La Coruna Harbor, 19th cent., engraving. 20p, Illustration of Havana harbor from *Viaje Alrededor da La Isla de Cuba*, by Francisco Mialche, 18th cent. 50p, West Indies packets.

1987, Oct. 2 Litho. & Engr. Perf. 13
2529   Sheet of 4 — 3.25 3.25
 a. A738 8p blk, brt blue & red — 28 28
 b. A738 12p brt blue, red & blk — 42 42
 c. A738 20p blk, brt blue & red — 75 75
 d. A738 50p blk, brt blue & red — 1.80 1.80

No. 2529 printed se-tenant (rouletted between) with ESPAMER entrance ticket. Sold for 180p. Size: 150x83mm (including ticket).

Souvenir Sheet

EXFILNA '87, Gerona, Oct. 24-Nov. 1 — A739

Design: Greek statue, Emporion, Olympic torchbearer.

1987, Oct. 24 Photo. Perf. 13x12½
2530 A739 20p multicolored — 35 35

Discovery of America, 500th Anniv. (in 1992) — A740

Ships and: 14p, Amerigo Vespucci (1454-1512), Italian navigator. 20p, Ferdinand and Isabella. 32p, Friar Juan Perez, Queen's confessor. 40p, Juan de la Cosa (c. 1460-1510), master of the Santa Maria, cartographer who made first map of the New World. 50p, Christopher Columbus. 65p, Vicente Yanez Pinzon (c. 1460-1523) and Martin Alonso Pinzon (c. 1441-1493), brothers, navigators and ship owners, accompanied Columbus on voyage.

1987, Oct. 30 Litho. & Engr. Perf. 13
2531 A740 14p multicolored — 25 15
2532 A740 20p multicolored — 35 15
2533 A740 32p multicolored — 58 15
2534 A740 40p multicolored — 72 18
2535 A740 50p multicolored — 90 22
2536 A740 65p multicolored — 1.20 30
 a. Bkt. pane of 6, #2531-2536 — 4.00
    Nos. 2531-2536 (6) — 4.00
    Set value — 98

Christmas A741

Self-portrait, Sculpture by Victorio Macho (1887-1966) A742

1987, Nov. 17 Photo. *Perf. 14x13¹/₂*
2537 A741 20p Ornaments 38 15
2538 A741 50p Zambomba, tambourine 92 24

1987, Dec. 23 Engr.
2539 A742 50p brown black 92 24

EXPO '92 Type of 1987

1987, Dec. 29 Photo. *Perf. 13¹/₂x14*
2540 A720 20p like No. 2506 38 15
2541 A720 50p like No. 2507 92 24

HRH Sofia and Juan Carlos, 50th Birth Anniv. — A743

1987, Jan. 5 *Perf. 13x13¹/₂*
2542 A743 20p Sofia 38 15
2543 A743 20p Juan Carlos 38 15
  Set value 20

Nos. 2542-2543 printed se-tenant with inscribed center.

Clara Campoamor (b. 1888), Suffragette A744

1988, Feb. 12 Photo. *Perf. 14*
2544 A744 20p multicolored 38 15

1988 Winter Olympics, Calgary — A745

Passion Week in Valladolid and Malaga — A746

1988, Feb. 15 *Perf. 14*
2545 A745 45p Speed skater 85 22

1988, Mar. 30 Photo. *Perf. 14*
Designs: 20p, Valladolid Cathedral and 17th cent. statue of Christ at the column by Gregorio Fernandez. 50p, Christ carrying the cross along Malaga procession route.

2546 A746 20p multicolored 38 15
2547 A746 50p multicolored 92 24

Tourism A747

1988, Apr. 7
2548 A747 18p Paella pan, ingredients 35 15
2549 A747 45p Covadonga Natl. Park 85 22
  Set value 30

EXPO '92 Type of 1987

Era of Discoveries: 8p, Road to globe, rays of light, vert. 45p, Compass rose, globe.

1988, Apr. 12
2550 A720 8p multicolored 15 15
2551 A720 45p multicolored 85 22
  Set value 26

Art Type of 1987

Glassware: a, Chalice, Valencia, 18th cent. b, Cadalso de los Vidrios, Madrid, 18th cent. c, Candy

dish, La Granja de San Ildefonso, 18th cent. d, Castril double-handled jar, Andalucia, 18th cent. e, Jug, Catalina, 17th cent. f, Bottle, Baleares, 20th cent.

Perf. 12¹/₂x13
1988, Apr. 13 Litho. & Engr.
2552 Block of 6 + 6 labels 2.30 60
a.-f. A726 20p any single 38 15

Stamp Day 1988 — A748

Francis of Taxis, postmaster by royal appointment (1505) in charge of establishing communications between Spain, France, Germany, Rome, Naples.

1988, Apr. 29 Engr. *Perf. 12¹/₂x13*
2553 A748 20p dk violet & dk brn 38 15

General Workers' Union (UGT), Cent. A749

Emblem and Pablo Iglesias, union pioneer.

1988, May 1 Photo. *Perf. 14*
2554 A749 20p multicolored 38 15

Europa 1988 — A750

Transport and communication: 20p, Locomotive made in Spain and operated in Cuba, 1837. 50p, Spanish telegraph in the Philippines linking Plaza de Manila and Bagumbayan Camp, 1818.

1988, May 5 Engr. *Perf. 13*
2555 A750 20p black & dk red 38 15
2556 A750 50p black & dk grn 95 24

Jean Monnet (1888-1979), Economist — A751

1988, May 9 *Perf. 14x13¹/₂*
2557 A751 45p blue black 85 22

Universal Exposition, Barcelona, Cent. A752

1988, May 31 Photo. *Perf. 13¹/₂x14*
2558 A752 50p multicolored 88 22

Intl. Music and Dance Festival, Granada — A753

1988, June 1 *Perf. 14x13¹/₂*
2559 A753 50p multicolored 88 22

World Expo '88, Brisbane, Australia A754

1988, June 14 *Perf. 13¹/₂x14*
2560 A754 50p Bull 88 22

Coronation of the Virgin of Hope — A755

1988, June 18 *Perf. 14x13¹/₂*
2561 A755 20p multicolored 35 15

Holy Week in Malaga.

Souvenir Sheet

EXFILNA '88, June 25-July 3, Madrid — A756

1988, June 25 *Perf. 13x12¹/₂*
2562 A756 20p Ciudadela Fortress floor plan 35 35

Tourism A757

1988, July 11 Engr. *Perf. 13¹/₂x14*
2563 A757 18p Cantabrian Coast storehouse 32 15
2564 A757 45p Dulzaina (wind instrument) 78 20
  Set value 28

28th World Roller Hockey Championships, La Coruna — A758

1988, Sept. 7 Photo. *Perf. 13¹/₂x14*
2565 A758 20p multicolored 35 15

1st World Cong. of Spanish Regional Shelters — A759

1988 Summer Olympics, Seoul — A760

1988, Sept. 9 *Perf. 14*
2566 A759 20p multicolored 35 15

1988, Sept. 10 Litho.
2567 A760 50p Yachting 85 22

Catalonia Millennium — A761

1988, Sept. 21 Photo. *Perf. 12¹/₂*
2568 A761 20p multicolored 35 15

1st Call to Session of the Leon Court, 800th Anniv. — A762

Design: Illumination and seal of Alfonso IX, King of Leon.

1988, Sept. 26 Photo. *Perf. 12¹/₂x13*
2569 A762 20p multicolored 35 15

Federation of Spanish Philatelic Societies, 25th Anniv. A763

1988, Sept. 27 *Perf. 14x13¹/₂*
2570 A763 20p multicolored 35 15

1992
Summer
Olympics,
Barcelona
A764

1988, Oct. 3   Photo.   *Perf. 14*
2571 A764 8p multicolored   15   15

See Nos. B139-B141.

A765   A766

Design: Castle in Valencia and royal seal of James
I, 13th cent.

1988, Oct. 7   *Perf. 14x13¹/₂*
2572 A765 20p multicolored   35   15

Reconquest of Valencia by King James I, 750th
anniv.

1988, Oct. 10   *Perf. 13x13¹/₂*
2573 A766 20p multicolored   35   15

Civil Law, cent.

Discovery of America (in 1992), 500th
Anniv. — A767

Conquerors, explorers and symbols: No. 2574,
Hernando Cortez, conqueror of Mexico, and
serpent Quetzalcoatl. No. 2575, Vasco Nunez de
Balboa, discoverer of the Pacific Ocean, and sun
setting over sea. No. 2576, Francisco Pizarro, conqueror of Peru, and llama. No. 2577, Portuguese
navigator Ferdinand Magellan, Juan de Elcano (c.
1476-1526) and globe symbolizing circumnavigation of the world. No. 2578, Alvar Nunez Cabeza
de Vaca (c. 1490-1560), explorer, and sunrise. No.
2579, Andres de Urdaneta (1498-1568), and symbol of the west-to-east route between the Philippines and America that he discovered.

1988, Oct. 13   Engr.   *Perf. 13x13¹/₂*
2574 A767 10p multicolored   18   15
2575 A767 10p multicolored   18   15
2576 A767 20p multicolored   35   15
2577 A767 20p multicolored   35   15
2578 A767 50p multicolored   88   22
2579 A767 50p multicolored   88   22
    a.   Bklt. pane of 6, #2574-2579   3.00
         Nos. 2574-2579 (6)   2.82
         Set value   70

Henry III of Castile, 1st Prince of
Asturias — A768

1988, Oct. 26   Photo.   *Perf. 13*
2580 A768 20p multicolored   35   15

1st Bestowal of the title Prince of Asturias, 600th
anniv., guaranteeing that the throne would continue to be inherited according to primogeniture.

Christmas
A769

1988, Nov. 24   Photo.   *Perf. 14*
2581 A769 20p Snowflakes   38   15
2582 A769 50p Shepherd, vert.   92   22

Sites and Cities Appearing on the
UNESCO World Heritage List — A770

1988, Dec. 1   Engr.   *Perf. 12¹/₂x13*
2583 A770 18p Mosque de Cordoba,
              vert.   35   15
2584 A770 20p Burgos Cathedral,
              vert.   38   15
2585 A770 45p El Escorial Monas-
              tery   82   20
2586 A770 50p The Alhambra, Gra-
              nada   92   22
         Set value   60

Natl. Constitution, 10th Anniv. — A771

1988, Dec. 7   Photo.   *Perf. 14*
2587 A771 20p multicolored   38   15

Souvenir Sheet

Charles III (1759-1788) and the
Enlightenment — A772

1988, Dec. 14   Engr.   *Perf. 13x12¹/₂*
2588 A772 45p black & dk grn   80   80

Natl. Organization for the Blind, 50th
Anniv. — A773

1988, Dec. 27   Photo.   *Perf. 14*
2589 A773 20p multicolored   38   15

Fr. Luis de Granada
(1504-1588)
A774

1988, Dec. 31
2590 A774 20p multicolored   38   15

1992
Summer
Olympics,
Barcelona
A775

Stamp
Collecting — A776

1989, Jan. 3
2591 A775 20p multicolored   38   15
2592 A776 20p multicolored   38   15
         Set value   20

French
Revolution,
Bicent. — A777

1989, Jan. 24   Photo.   *Perf. 13*
2593 A777 45p multicolored   78   20

Maria de
Maeztu (b.
1882),
Educator
A778

1989, Feb. 7   Photo.   *Perf. 14x13¹/₂*
2594 A778 20p multicolored   35   15

Postal
Service,
Cent.
A779

Perf. 13¹/₂x14
1989, Mar. 11   Litho. & Engr.
2595 A779 20p Uniform, 1889   35   15

Stamp
Day — A780

Design: Intl. postal treaty negotiated with France
and Italy by Franz von Taxis, 1601.

1989, Apr. 4   Engr.   *Perf. 13*
2596 A780 20p black   35   15

A781   A782

1989, Apr. 22   *Perf. 14x13¹/₂*
2597 A781 20p black   35   15

Casa del Cordon, Burgos.

1989, May 5   Photo.   *Perf. 13x13¹/₂*

Europa: Children's toys.

2598 A782 40p shown   70   15
2599 A782 50p Top   88   18

Spain's
Presidency
of the
European
Economic
Community
A783

1989, May 9   *Perf. 13¹/₂x14*
2600 A783 45p multicolored   80   16

Souvenir Sheet

Holy Family with St. Anne, by El
Greco — A784

1989, May 20   Litho.   *Perf. 14x13¹/₂*
2601 A784 20p multicolored   35   35

EXFILNA '89. Exists imperf in different colors.

Gabriela Mistral
(1889-1957), Chilean
Poet Awarded 1945
Nobel Prize for
Literature — A785

Perf. 14x13½
1989, June 1   **Litho. & Engr.**
2602 A785 50p multicolored   78   15

European Parliament 3rd
Elections — A786

1989, June 12   **Photo.**   *Perf. 13x13½*
2603 A786 45p multicolored   70   15

Lace — A787

Lace produced in: a, Catalonia. b, Andalusia. c, Extremadura. d, Canary Isls. e, Castile-La Mancha. f, Galicia.

Perf. 13x12½
1989, June 20   **Litho. & Engr.**
2604   Block of 6 + 3 labels   1.95   36
a.-f. A787 20p any single   32   15

Three center labels printed in a continuous design and picture lace-making.

Pope John Paul II at the Intl. Catholic
Youth Forum, Santiago — A788

1989, Aug. 19   **Engr.**   *Perf. 13x12½*
2605 A788 50p myrtle grn, dk red   brn & blk   80   16

Athletics
World Cup,
Barcelona
A789

1989, Sept. 1   **Photo.**   *Perf. 13½x14*
2606 A789 50p multicolored   80   16

A790   Type A34 — A791

Perf. 14x13½
1989, Sept. 19   **Litho. & Engr.**
2607 A790 50p multicolored   80   16

Charlie Chaplin (1889-1977), English comedian and actor.

1989, Oct. 2   **Photo.**   *Perf. 14x13½*
2608 A791 50p gray, ver & blk   85   18

Cent. of the 1st Alfonso XIII issue.

A792   A793

Fr. Andres Manjon (d. 1923), teacher.

1989, Oct. 13
2609 A792 20p multicolored   35   15

Founding of the Ave Maria Schools by Fr. Manjon, cent.

1989, Nov. 7   **Litho. & Engr.**
UPAE emblem and "Irrigating Corn Field in November, 17th Cent.," an illustration from the *New Chronicle and Good Government,* by Guaman Poma de Ayala.
2610 A793 50p multicolored   85   18

America issue.

Christmas
A794

Perf. 14x13½, 13½x14
1989, Nov. 29   **Photo.**
2611 A794 20p Star, "NAVIdAd 89," vert.   35   15
2612 A794 45p shown   80   16
    Set value   22

Sites on the UNESCO World Heritage
List — A795

Perf. 13x12½
1989, Dec. 5   **Litho. & Engr.**
2613 A795 20p Altamira Caverns   35   15
2614 A795 20p Santiago de Compostela   35   15
2615 A795 20p Roman aqueduct, Segovia   35   15
2616 A795 20p Guell Park and palace, Mila House   35   15
    Set value   28

Souvenir Sheet

Sites on the World Heritage List — A796

Royal palaces: a, El Escorial. b, Aranjuez. c, Summer palace, La Granja, San Ildefonso. e, Madrid.

1989, Dec. 20   **Engr.**   *Perf. 13x13½*
2617   Sheet of 4   3.25   3.25
a.-d. A796 45p any single   80   80

Illustration by Daniel
Garcia Perez, Winner
of the 2nd Youth
Stamp Design
Contest — A797

1990, Jan. 29   **Photo.**   *Perf. 14x13½*
2618 A797 20p multicolored   38   15

1992 Summer Olympics, Barcelona.

A798   A799

1990, Feb. 2
2619 A798 20p multicolored   38   15

World Cycle Cross Championship, Getzu.

1990, Feb. 12   **Engr.**
2620 A799 20p dark purple   38   15

Victoria Kent (1897-1987), prisons directer, reformer.

Honorary Postman Rafael Alvarez Sereix
and Cancel — A800

1990, Apr. 18   **Litho. & Engr.**   *Perf. 13*
2621 A800 20p sepia, buff & dull grn   38   15

Stamp Day.

Europa 1990
A801

Post offices.

Perf. 13½x14, 14x13½
1990, May 4   **Photo.**
2622 A801 20p Vitoria   38   15
2623 A801 50p Malaga, vert.   95   20
    Set value   28

Intl. Telecommunications Union, 125th
Anniv. — A802

1990, May 17   *Perf. 13½x14*
2624 A802 8p multicolored   15   15

Wrought
Iron — A803

Designs: a, 15th Cent. door knocker. b, 16th cent. lyre-shaped door knocker. c, 17th Cent. pistol. d, 17th-18th Cent. door knocker. e, 19th Cent. lock. f, Fire iron.

         Litho. & Engr.
1990, May 18   *Perf. 12½*
2625   Block of 6 + 3 labels   2.25   2.25
a.-f. A803 20p any single   38   15

Nos. 2625a-2625f printed se-tenant in a continuous design. Three labels continue the design and contain text or picture a forge.

Souvenir Sheet

Patio de La Infanta, Zaporta Palace,
Zaragoza — A804

Illustration reduced.

1990, May 25   **Engr.**   *Perf. 14x13½*
2626 A804 20p red brown   38   38

EXFILNA '90.

Charity, by Lopez
Alonso — A805

1990, June 19   **Litho.**   *Perf. 13½x13*
2627 A805 8p multicolored   17   15

Daughters of Charity in Spain, bicentennial.

Jose Padilla, Composer, Birth Centenary — A806

1990, June 19   Photo.   *Perf. 13x12½*
2628 A806 20p multicolored   38   15

Town of Estella, 900th Anniv. — A807

1990, June 19   Litho. & Engr.
2629 A807 45p multicolored   85   18

Novel, "Tirant lo Blanch," 500th Anniv. — A808

1990, June 19   *Perf. 12½x13*
2630 A808 50p multicolored   95   20

Souvenir Sheet

Crypt, Palencia Cathedral — A809

Illustration reduced.

1990, June 22   Engr.   *Perf. 13½x14*
2631 A809 20p red brown   38   38

Topical philatelic exposition.

A810   A811

1990, Aug. 27   Photo.   *Perf. 14x13½*
2632 A810 50p multicolored   95   20

17th Intl. Congress of Historical Sciences.

Litho. & Engr.
1990, Nov. 14   *Perf. 14*
America Issue: UPAE emblem and Carribean fauna.
2633 A811 50p multicolored   1.00   20

A812   A813

Christmas: Scenes from the film "Cosmic Poem" by Jose Antonio Sistiaga.

1990, Nov. 22   Photo.
2634 A812 25p multicolored   50   15
2635 A812 45p multi, horiz.   90   18

Litho. & Engr.
1990, Nov. 28   *Perf. 13*
Tapestries in Monastary of San Lorenzo: a, The Crucifixion by Jan van Roome and Bernard van Orley. b, Flamenco Soldiers by Philip Wouvermans. c, Shipwreck of the Telemac by Miguel Angel Houasse. d, Flowers by Francisco Goya.
2636   Sheet of 4   1.60 1.60
  a.-d. A813 20p any single   40   40

European Tourism Year — A814

1990, Dec. 1   Photo.   *Perf. 14*
2637 A814 45p multicolored   90   18

World Heritage List — A815

Designs: No. 2638, Church of San Vicente, Avila. No. 2639, Tower of San Pedro, Teruel, vert. No. 2640, Church of San Miguel de Lillo, Oviedo, vert. No. 2641, Tower of Bujaco, Caceres.

1990, Dec. 10   Litho. & Engr.   *Perf. 13*
2638 A815 20p multicolored   40   15
2639 A815 20p multicolored   40   15
2640 A815 20p multicolored   40   15
2641 A815 20p multicolored   40   15
              Set value   32

Natl. Orchestra of Spain A816

1990, Dec. 20   Photo.   *Perf. 13½x14*
2642 A816 25p grn, yel grn & blk   50   15

Maria Moliner (1900-1981), Spanish Linguist — A817

1991, Jan. 21   Photo.   *Perf. 14x13½*
2643 A817 25p multicolored   50   15

Souvenir Sheet

Santa Fe, 500th Anniv. — A818

Illustration reduced.

Perf. 13½x14
1991, Apr. 19   Litho. & Engr.
2644 A818 25p brown & pur   50   50

World Philatelic Exhibition, Granada '92.

Child's Drawing — A819

1991, Apr. 12   Photo.   *Perf. 14x13½*
2645 A819 25p Olympic rings, sailboats   50   15

Juan de Tassis y Peralta (1582-1622), Postal Reformer — A820

1991, Apr. 26   Engr.   *Perf. 12½*
2646 A820 25p black   50   15

Stamp Day.

Souvenir Sheet

Porcelain and Ceramics — A821

Designs: a, Apothecary jar, 17th cent. b, Figurine, 18th cent. c, Vase, 19th cent. d, Plate, 19th cent.

1991, May 3   Litho. & Engr.   *Perf. 13*
2647 A821 25p Sheet of 4, #a.-d.   1.85 1.85
              See No. 2692.

Europa A822

1991, May 28   Litho.   *Perf. 13½x14*
2648 A822 25p INTA-NASA ground
                station   50   15
2649 A822 45p Olympus I satellite   90   18
              Set value   28

St. John of the Cross (1651-1695), Mystic — A823

Anniversaries: No. 2651, Fr. Luis de Leon (1527-1591), Augustinian writer, vert. No. 2652, Abd Al Rahman III (891-961), Moslem caliph, vert. No. 2653, St. Ignatius of Loyola (1451-1556), founder of Society of Jesus, vert.

Perf. 13½x14, 14x13½
1991, June 6   Litho.
2650 A823 15p multicolored   30   15
2651 A823 15p multicolored   30   15
2652 A823 25p multicolored   50   15
2653 A823 25p multicolored   50   15
              Set value   32

Antique Furniture A824

Designs: a, Wedge top armoire, 18th cent. b, Hutch cabinet, c. 19th cent. c, Ladder-back cane chair, c. 19th cent. d, Baby cradle, 19th cent. e, Round-top trunk, c. 19th cent. f, Ornate chest, c. 18th cent.

Perf. 12½x13
1991, Sept. 9   Litho. & Engr.
2654   Block of 6 + 3 labels   3.00 3.00
  a.-f. A824 25p any single   50   50

Orfeo Catala (Catalan Choral Society), Cent. — A825

Intl. Fishing Exposition, Vigo — A826

1991, Sept. 6   Litho.   Perf. 14x13½
2655 A825 25p multicolored   50   15

1991, Sept. 10
2656 A826 55p multicolored   1.10   55

America Issue — A827

Christmas — A828

Perf. 14x13½
1991, Nov. 4   Litho. & Engr.
2657 A827 55p Nocturlabe   1.10   55

1991, Nov. 22   Photo.   Perf. 14x13½
Designs: 25p, The Nativity, illustration from 17th cent. book. 45p, The Birth of Christ, 16th century icon.

2658 A828 25p multicolored   50   15
2659 A828 45p multicolored   90   18
      Set value   28

Souvenir Sheet

The Meadowlands of St. Isidro by Goya — A829

Perf. 13½x14
1991, Dec. 12   Litho. & Engr.
2660 A829 25p multicolored   50   15

EXFILNA '91, Madrid.

Sites on UNESCO World Heritage List — A830

Designs: No. 2661, Giralda bell tower, Seville Cathedral. No. 2662, Alcantara Gate, Toledo, vert. No. 2663, Casa de las Conchas, Salamanca, vert. No. 2664, Garajonay Natl. Park, Gomera, Canary Islands.

Perf. 12½x13, 13x12½
1991, Dec. 16   Engr.
2661 A830 25p brown & blue   50   15
2662 A830 25p red brn & brn   50   15
2663 A830 25p red brn & blk   50   15
2664 A830 25p violet & dk grn   50   15
                See No. 2756.

Carlos Ibanez de Ibero (1825-1891), Cartographer A831

Antarctic Treaty, Research Ship A52 A832

1991, Dec. 27   Litho.   Perf. 14x13½
2665 A831 25p multicolored   50   15
2666 A832 55p multicolored   1.10   20

Margarita Xirgu (1889-1969), Actress A833

1992, Jan. 20   Perf. 14
2667 A833 25p lake & gold   50   15

Child's Drawing A834

1992, Feb. 14   Perf. 13½x14
2668 A834 25p multicolored   50   15

EXPO 92.

Pedro Rodriguez Campomanes (1723-1802), Historian, Postal Administrator — A835

1992, Feb. 21   Perf. 13x12½
2669 A835 27p multicolored   55   15

Expo '92, Seville A836

1992, Feb. 28   Perf. 13½x14
2670 A836 27p gray, blk & brn   55   15

Columbus Types of 1930
Souvenir Sheet
1992, Apr. 24   Engr.   Perf. 14
2671   Sheet of 2   10.00 10.00
  a.   A65 250p black   5.00   5.00
  b.   A67 250p brown   5.00   5.00

Intl. Philatelic Exhibition, Granada '92.

Miniature Sheets

Expo '92, Seville A837

Designs: No. 2672a, Expo '92 World Trade Center. b, Aerial tram. c, Avenue 4. d, Barqueta Gate. e, Nature pavilion. f, Biosphere. g, Alamillo Bridge. h, Press center. i, 15th Century pavilion. j, Expo harbor. k, Tourist train. l, One day entrance ticket.
No. 2673a, Cartuja Monastery. b, Arena. c, Monorail train. d, Europe Avenue. e, Discovery pavilion. f, Auditorium. g, Avenue 1. h, Plaza of the Future. i, Gate to Italy's exhibit. j, Terminal. k, Expo theater. l, Expo Mascot, Curro.

1992, Apr. 21   Litho.   Perf. 13½x14
2672 A837 Sheet of 12 + 4 labels   4.00   4.00
  a.-l.   17p any single   32   32
2673 A837 Sheet of 12 + 4 labels   6.25   6.25
  a.-l.   27p any single   55   55
                See No. B195.

1992 Paralympics, Barcelona A838

1992, Apr. 22   Photo.   Perf. 14
2674 A838 27p multicolored   55   15

Discovery of America, 500th Anniv. A839

Europa: 17p, Preparation Before Departing from Palos, by R. Espejo. 45p, Globe, ships, and buildings at La Rabida.

1992, May 5   Photo.   Perf. 14
2675 A839 17p multicolored   35   15
2676 A839 45p multicolored   95   18

Souvenir Sheets

Voyages of Columbus — A840

Designs: No. 2677, Columbus in sight of land. No. 2678, Landing of Columbus. No. 2679, Columbus soliciting aid from Isabella. No. 2680, Columbus welcomed at Barcelona. No. 2681, Columbus presenting natives. No. 2682, Columbus.
Borders on Nos. 2677-2682 are lithographed. Nos. 2677-2682 are similar in design to US Nos. 230-231, 234-235, 237, 245.

1992, May 22   Litho. & Engr.   Perf. 14
2677 A840 60c blue   1.20   1.20
2678 A840 60c brown violet   1.20   1.20
2679 A840 60c chocolate   1.20   1.20
2680 A840 60c purple   1.20   1.20
2681 A840 60c black brown   1.20   1.20
2682 A840 60c black   1.20   1.20

See US Nos. 2624-2629, Italy Nos. 1883-1888 and Portugal Nos. 1918-1923.

1992 Winter & Summer Olympics, Albertville & Barcelona A841

1992, June 19   Photo.   Perf. 14
2683 A841 45p multicolored   90   18

A842

A843

1992, June 5   Photo.   Perf. 14x13½
2684 A842 27p blue & yellow   58   15

World Environment Day.

1992, Oct. 29   Litho.   Perf. 14x13½
2685 A843 17p multicolored   35   15

Juan Luis Vives (1492-1540),pPhilosopher.

Pamplona Choir, Cent. A844

1992, Oct. 29   Perf. 13½x14
2686 A844 27p multicolored   58   15

Unified Europe — A845

1992, Nov. 4   Photo.   Perf. 14x13½
2687 A845 45p multicolored   95   18

Christmas A846

1992, Nov. 5   Perf. 13½x14
2688 A846 27p multicolored   58   15

1992 Special Olympics, Madrid A847

1992, Sept. 7   Photo.   Perf. 13½x14
2689 A847 27p brown & blue   48   15

Souvenir Sheet

St. Paul's Church, Valladolid — A848

Perf. 14x13¹/₂
1992, Oct. 9   Litho. & Engr.
2690 A848 27p multicolored   48   15

Exfilna '92, Natl. Philatelic Exhibition, Valladolid.

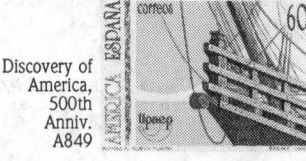

Discovery of
America,
500th
Anniv.
A849

1992, Oct. 15   Perf. 13¹/₂x14
2691 A849 60p dk brn, lt brn & bis   1.05   20

Natl. Heritage Type of 1991
Miniature Sheet

Codices: a, Veitia, 18th cent. b, Trujillo of Peru, 18th cent. c, The Chess Book, 13th cent. d, General History of New Spain, 16th cent.

1992, Dec. 10   Litho. & Engr.   Perf. 13
2692 A821 27p Sheet of 4, #a.-d.   95   95

Road Safety   Environmental Protection
A850   A851

Health and
Sanitation — A852

1993   Photo.   Perf. 14x13¹/₂
2693 A850 17p green & red   30   15
2694 A851 28p green & blue   48   15
2695 A852 65p blue & green   1.15   25

Issued: 17p, Apr. 20. 28p, Jan. 4. 65p, Feb. 12.

Maria
Zambrano
(1904-1991),
Writer
A854

1993, Jan. 18   Photo.   Perf. 14
2697 A854 45p buff, lil rose & brown   80   16

Andres Segovia (1893-
1987),
Guitarist — A855

1993, Feb. 19   Engr.   Perf. 14x13¹/₂
2698 A855 65p black & brown   1.15   25

1908
Mailbox,
Madrid Postal
Museum
A856

Perf. 13¹/₂x14
1993, Mar. 12   Litho. & Engr.
2699 A856 28p multicolored   48   15

Stamp Day.

Mushrooms
A857

1993, Mar. 18   Photo.   Perf. 14
2700 A857 17p Amanita caesarea   32   15
2701 A857 17p Lepiota procera   32   15
2702 A857 28p Lactarius sanguifluus   48   15
2703 A857 28p Russula cyanoxantha   48   15
              Set value   32

See Nos. 2759-2762.

Souvenir Sheet

Holy Week Celebration — A858

1993, Apr. 2   Litho.   Perf. 14x13¹/₂
2704 A858 100p multicolored   1.75   35

Exfilna '93, Alcaniz. Margin of No. 2704 is Litho. & Engr.

Fusees, by
Joan Miro
A859

Europa: 65p, La Bague d'Aurore, by Miro, vert.

Perf. 13¹/₂x14, 14x13¹/₂
1993, May 5   Litho.
2705 A859 45p blue & black   78   15
              Litho. & Engr.
2706 A859 65p multicolored   1.10   22

Year of St.
James
A860

Designs: 17p, Transfer of St. James' body by boat. 28p, Discovery of tomb of St. James. 45p, St. James on horseback.

1993, May 13   Photo.   Perf. 13¹/₂x14
2707 A860 17p multicolored   30   15
2708 A860 28p multicolored   48   15
2709 A860 45p multicolored   78   15
              Set value   30

World Telecommunications Day — A861

1993, May 17
2710 A861 28p multicolored   48   15

Compostela
'93 — A862

Stylized designs: 28p, Pilgrims paying homage to Saint James. 100p, Pilgrim under star tree while on way to Santiago de Compostela, vert.

1993, May 18   Photo.   Perf. 13¹/₂x14
2711 A862 28p multicolored   48   15
              Souvenir Sheet
              Perf. 14x13¹/₂
2712 A862 100p multicolored   1.75   1.75

World Environment
Day — A863

1993, June 4   Litho.   Perf. 14x13¹/₂
2713 A863 28p multicolored   48   15

Juan Carlos I — A864

1993-94   Photo.   Perf. 14x13¹/₂
2715 A864 1p gold & Prussian blue   15   15
2716 A864 17p gold & yellow orange   28   15
2717 A864 18p gold & green blue   28   15
2718 A864 19p gold & brown   30   15
2721 A864 28p gold & violet brown   48   15
2722 A864 29p gold & olive   45   15
2723 A864 30p gold & ultramarine   45   15
2725 A864 45p gold & bluish green   75   15
2727 A864 55p gold & sepia   85   16
  a.   Block of 4, #2715, 2717, 2722,
           2727 + 2 labels   1.65   32
2729 A864 65p gold & red orange   1.05   20
  a.   Block of 4, #2716, 2721, 2725,
           2729 + 2 labels   2.60   1.30
           Nos. 2715-2729 (10)   5.04
           Set value   1.75

Issued: 17p, 28p, 45p, 65p, 5/21/93; 1p, 18p, 29p, 1/31/94; 19p, 30p, 1994.
This is an expanding set. Numbers may change.

Don Juan de Borbon
(1913-1993), Count of
Barcelona — A865

1993, June 20   Photo.   Perf. 14x13¹/₂
2744 A865 28p multicolored   48   15

Igualada-Martorell Railway, Cent. — A866

1993, July 4   Engr.   Perf. 13¹/₂x14
2745 A866 45p black & green   78   15

Natl. Mint
(F.N.M.T.),
Cent.
A867

1993, Sept. 13
2746 A867 65p dark blue   1.10   22

Explorers
A868

Designs: 45p, Alejandro Malaspina (1754-1809), Italian explorer of South America. 65p, Jose Celestino Mutis (1732-1808), Spanish naturalist in the Americas, vert.

Perf. 13¹/₂x14, 14x13¹/₂
1993, Sept 20   Litho.
2747 A868 45p multicolored   78   15
2748 A868 65p multicolored   1.10   22

Ciconia Nigra
A869

Endangered birds: No. 2750, Gypaetus barbatus (Quebrantahuesos).

Perf. 13¹/₂x14
1993, Oct. 11   Litho. & Engr.
2749 A869 65p pink & black   1.10   22
2750 A869 65p orange & black   1.10   22

Child's
Painting — A870

1993, Oct. 2   Litho.   Perf. 14x13¹/₂
2751 A870 45p multicolored   70   15

European
Year of the
Elderly
A871

1993, Oct. 29   Photo.   *Perf. 14*
2752 A871 45p multicolored   70   15

A872

Christmas — A873

Perf. 13¹/₂x14, 14x13¹/₂
1993, Nov. 23   Photo.
2753 A872 17p multicolored   28   15
Litho., Photo. & Engr.
2754 A873 28p multicolored   48   15
Set value   16

Jorge Guillen (1893-
1984), Poet — A874

1993, Nov. 29   Engr.   *Perf. 14x13¹/₂*
2755 A874 28p green   48   15

UNESCO World Heritage Type of 1991

Design: 50p, Monastery of Santa Maria of Poblet,
Tarragona.

1993, Dec. 3   Engr.   *Perf. 13x12¹/₂*
2756 A830 50p multicolored   70   15

Spanish Film
Industry
A875

Designs: 29p, Luis Bunuel (1900-83), director.
55p, Segundo de Chomon (1871-1929), film
pioneer.

1994, Jan. 28   Photo.   *Perf. 14*
2757 A875 29p multicolored   40   15
2758 A875 55p multicolored   80   16
Set value   24

Mushroom Type of 1993

1994, Feb. 18   Photo.   *Perf. 14*
2759 A857 18p Boletus satanas   25   15
2760 A857 18p Boletus edulis   25   15
2761 A857 29p Amanita phalloides   40   15
2762 A857 29p Lactarius deliciosus 40   15
Set Value   26

Minerals
A876

Designs: a, Cinnabar. b, Sphalerite. c, Pyrite. d,
Galena.

1994, Feb. 25
2763 A876 29p Block of 4, #a.-d., +
            2 labels   1.65   32

Barrister's
Mailbox
A877

Perf. 13¹/₂x14
1994, Mar. 9   Litho. & Engr.
2764 A877 29p light brn & dark brn 42   15

Stamp Day.

ILO, 75th
Anniv.
A878

1994, Apr. 7   Photo.   *Perf. 13¹/₂x14*
2765 A878 65p multicolored   95   20

Art of
Salvador Dali
(1904-89)
A879

Paintings: No. 2766, Retrato de Gala. No. 2767,
Poesia de America, vert. No. 2768, El Gran Mas-
turbador. No. 2769, Port Alguer, vert. No. 2770,
Self portrait, vert. No. 2771, Cesta del Pan, vert.
No. 2172, El Enigma Sin Fin. No. 2173, Galatea de
las Esferas, vert.

Perf. 13¹/₂x14, 14x13¹/₂
1994, Apr. 22
2766 A879 18p multicolored   25   15
2767 A879 18p multicolored   25   15
2768 A879 29p multicolored   42   15
2769 A879 29p multicolored   42   15
2770 A879 55p multicolored   80   16
2771 A879 55p multicolored   80   16
2772 A879 65p multicolored   95   18
2773 A879 65p multicolored   95   18
      Nos. 2766-2773 (8)   4.84
            Set value   94

Josep Pla
(1897-1981),
Writer
A880

1994, Apr. 23   Engr.   *Perf. 13¹/₂x14*
2774 A880 65p dark green & lake   95   18

A881

A882

A883

Painting: 55p, Martyrdom of St. Andrew, by
Rubens.

1994, Apr. 29   Photo.   *Perf. 14*
2775 A881 55p multicolored   80   16

Carlos de Amberes Foundation, 400th anniv.

1994, May 3   Photo.
2776 A882 18p multicolored   25   15
Litho., Photo. & Engr.
2777 A883 29p multicolored   42   15

Santa Cruz de Tenerife, 400th anniv. (#2776).
Complutense University of Madrid, 700th Anniv.
(#2777).

Europa
A884

Designs: 55p, Severo Ochoa (1905-93), 1959
Nobel Laureate in Medicine. 65p, Miguel Angel
Catalan (1894-1957), physicist.

1994, May 5   Litho. & Engr.
2778 A884 55p multicolored   80   16
2779 A884 65p multicolored   95   20

Spanish
Literature
A885

Novels by Camilo Jose Cela: 18p, The Family of
Pascual Duarte. 29p, Journey to Alcarria.

1994, May 11   Photo.
2780 A885 18p multicolored   25   15
2781 A885 29p multicolored   42   15

King Sancho Ramirez,
900th Death
Anniv. — A886

Treaty of
Tordesillas,
500th Anniv.
A887

Design: 55p, Natl. Archives, Simancas.

1994, June 7   Litho. & Engr.   *Perf. 14*
2782 A886 18p multicolored   25   15
2783 A887 29p multicolored   42   15
2784 A887 55p multicolored   80   16

Souvenir Sheet

Cathedral of St. Anne, Las Palmas, Grand
Canary Island — A888

Illustration reduced.

1994, July 1   *Perf. 13¹/₂x14*
2785 A888 100p multicolored   1.50   30

Exfilna '94, Natl. Philatelic Exhibition, Grand
Canary Island.

Yachts — A889

1994, July 15   Photo.   *Perf. 14x13¹/₂*
2786 A889 16p Giralda   25   15
2787 A889 29p Saltillo   42   15

Roman City of Augusta Emerita (Merida),
Badajoz — A890

1994, Sept. 8   Litho. & Engr.   *Perf. 13*
2788 A890 55p lake, brown & buff   80   16

UNESCO World Heritage list.

Museum of Cards,
Alava — A891

Antique cards: 18p, Horse of Spades. 29p, Jack of
Diamonds. 55p, King of Hearts. 65p, War god,
Mars, of Diamonds.

1994, Sept. 20   Photo.   *Perf. 14x13¹/₂*
2789 A891 18p multicolored   25   15
2790 A891 29p multicolored   42   15
2791 A891 55p multicolored   80   16
2792 A891 65p multicolored   1.00   20

Postal Transportation — A892

1994, Oct. 11   Litho.   Perf. 13¹/₂
2793 A892 65p DC-8   1.00   20

Public Transit
A893

Civil Guard
A894

1994, Oct. 17   Photo.   Perf. 14x13¹/₂
2794 A893 18p multicolored   28   15
Perf. 13¹/₂x14
2795 A894 29p multicolored   45   15

Western European Union
A895

1994, Oct. 21   Perf. 13¹/₂x14
2796 A895 55p multicolored   85   16

SPAIN

BUYING AND SELLING,
QUALITY STAMPS OF
SPAIN MINT NH.

EUROPE

From Andorre to Turkey,
Europe (CEPT) and
The English Area,
Mint NH Sets.
Whether you're buying or selling,
my prices are very reasonable. The
list contains well over 12,000 sets,
with all kinds of topicals, where
you will find my selling prices,
and the price I pay for each set that
I need.

The Italian Area

Including San Marino, Vatican
City, Trieste A & B, Mint NH, LH
or Used, and some singles.

**SEND A #10 55¢ SASE
TODAY FOR YOUR FREE
COPY OF OUR PRICE LIST!
You will be glad you did.**

F. COPPOLA

P.O. Box 181022
Utica, MI 48318-1022

Intl. Olympic Committee, Cent.
A896

Symbols of Olympic venues: a, Track. b, Skiing.
c, Equestrian. d, Wrestling. e, Archery. f, Cycling. g,
Soccer. h, Field hockey. i, Swimming. j, Sailing.

1994, Oct. 27
2797   Block of 10 + 10 labels   4.75 4.75
a.-j. A896 29p any single   45   45

Spanish Motion Pictures
A898

Christmas — A897

1994, Nov. 18   Perf. 14x13¹/₂
2798 A897 29p multicolored   45   15

Designs: 30p, Belle Epoque, by Fernando Trueba.
60p Volver A Empezar (Begin the Beguine), by Jose
Luis Garci.

1995, Jan. 20   Photo.   Perf. 14
2799 A898 30p multicolored   48   15
2800 A898 60p multicolored   95   20

City of Logrono, 900th Anniv.
A899

1995, Jan. 25
2801 A899 30p multicolored   48   15

Souvenir Sheet

SIERRA NEVADA '95, Granada — A900

Illustration reduced.

1995, Jan. 30
2802 A900 130p White star flower   1.90 1.90

World Alpine Skiing Championships.

Mushrooms
A901

1995, Feb. 9   Photo.   Perf. 13¹/₂x14
2803 A901 19p Coprinus comatus   30   15
2804 A901 30p Dermocybe cin-
            namomea   45   15

Minerals
A902

Designs: a, Dolomite. b, Technical School for
Mining Engineers, Madrid. c, Aragonite.

1995, Feb. 24
2805   Strip of 3   1.35   28
a.-c. A902 30p any single   45   15

Stamp Day — A903

1995, Mar. 9   Engr.
2806 A903 30p Bronze lion's head   45   15

Alejandro Goicoechea Omar, TALGO Train
A904

Design: 60p, Young Omar, early train.

1995, Mar. 17   Photo.   Perf. 14
2807 A904 30p multicolored   45   15
2808 A904 95p multicolored   95   20

A905   A906

1995, Apr. 6
2809 A905 60p multicolored   95   20

Nature conservation in Europe.

1995, Apr. 7   Litho. & Engr.   Perf. 14
18th Century Sailing Ships: 19p, San Juan
Nepomuceno. 30p, San Telmo.
2810 A906 19p multicolored   30   15
2811 A906 30p multicolored   45   15
Nos. 2810-2811 printed in miniature sheets of 4.

Lebaniego Celebration Year
A907

Design: 60p, Mountains, St. Toribio Monastery.

1995, Apr. 21   Photo.   Perf. 12¹/₂
2812 A907 30p multicolored   48   15
2813 A907 60p multicolored   95   20

Spanish Literature
A908

Designs: 19p, El Nino Yuntero, by Miguel Hernandez (1910-42). 30p, Juanita la Larga, by Juan
Valera (1824-1905), vert.

1995, Apr. 27   Litho. & Engr.   Perf. 14
2814 A908 19p multicolored   30   15
Engr.
2815 A908 30p green & blue   48   15

Jose Marti (1853-95), Cuban Writer
A909

1995, Apr. 28   Photo.
2816 A909 60p multicolored   95   20

Spanish Cartoon Characters
A910

1995, May 4   Photo.   Perf. 14
2817 A910 30p Captain Trueno   50   15
2818 A910 60p Carpanta, vert.   1.00   20

Europa
A911

1995, May 5
2819 A911 60p multicolored   1.00   20

Motion Pictures, Cent.
A912

Designs: 19p, Auguste and Louis Lumiere, early
camera.

1995, May 12   Engr.   Perf. 14
2820 A912 19p brownish black   32   15

Press Assoc. of Madrid, Cent.
A913

1995, May 12   Litho.
2821 A913 30p multicolored   50   15

SEMI-POSTAL STAMPS
Red Cross Issue

Princesses María Cristina and Beatrice — SP1

Queen as a Nurse — SP2

Queen Victoria Eugénia — SP3

Prince of Asturias — SP4

King Alfonso XIII — SP5

Perf. 12½

1926, Sept. 15   Unwmk.   Engr.

B1	SP1	1c black	1.65	1.10
B2	SP2	2c ultra	1.65	1.10
B3	SP3	5c violet brn	3.25	2.25
B4	SP4	10c green	2.75	2.25
B5	SP1	15c indigo	1.10	90
B6	SP4	20c dull violet	1.10	1.10
a.		20c violet brown (error)	190.00	
B7	SP5	25c rose red	35	52
B8	SP1	30c blue green	22.50	22.50
B9	SP3	40c dark blue	14.00	10.50
B10	SP2	50c red orange	12.00	9.50
B11	SP4	1p slate	80	80
B12	SP3	4p magenta	35	35
B13	SP5	10p brown	52	52
	Nos. B1-B13,EB1 (14)		68.02	59.39

The 20c was printed in violet brown for use in the colonies (Cape Juby, Spanish Guinea, Spanish Morocco and Spanish Sahara). No. B6a, the missing overprint error, is listed here because it is not known to which colony it belongs.
For overprints see Nos. B19-B46.

Airplane and Map of Madrid-Manila Flight — SP6

1926, Sept. 15

B14	SP6	15c dp ultra & org	20	30
B15	SP6	20c car & yel grn	20	30
B16	SP6	30c dk brn & ultra	20	30
B17	SP6	40c dk grn & brn org	20	30
B18	SP6	4p magenta & yel	47.50	45.00
	Nos. B14-B18 (5)		48.30	46.20

Madrid to Manila flight of Captains Eduardo G. Gallarza and Joaquin Loriga y Taboada.
Nos. B1-B18, CB1-CB5 and EB1 were used for regular postage on Sept. 15, 16, 17, 1926. Subsequently the unsold stamps were given to the Spanish Red Cross Society, by which they were sold uncanceled but they then had no franking power.
For overprints see Nos. B47-B53.

Coronation Silver Jubilee Issue
Red Cross Stamps of 1926 Overprinted "ALFONSO XIII," Dates and Ornaments in Various Colors

1927, May 27

B19	SP1	1c black (R)	3.25	3.50
B20	SP2	2c ultra (Bl)	4.75	6.00
B21	SP3	5c vio brn (R)	1.25	1.50
a.		Double overprint	32.50	
B22	SP4	10c green (Bl)	27.50	30.00
B23	SP1	15c indigo (R)	1.00	1.25
B24	SP4	20c dull vio (Bl)	1.90	2.00
B25	SP5	25c rose red (Bl)	32	60
B26	SP1	30c blue grn (Bl)	65	90

B27	SP3	40c dk blue (R)	65	90
B28	SP2	50c red org (Bl)	65	90
B29	SP4	1p slate (R)	1.00	1.50
B30	SP3	4p magenta (Bl)	5.50	6.00
B31	SP5	10p brown (Bl)	19.00	24.00
	Nos. B19-B31 (13)		67.42	79.05

Same with Additional Surcharges of New Values

B32	SP2	3c on 2c (G)	8.50	7.50
B33	SP2	4c on 2c (Bk)	8.50	7.50
B34	SP5	10c on 25c (Bk)	42	30
B35	SP5	25c on 25c (Bl)	42	45
B36	SP2	55c on 2c (R)	90	90
B37	SP4	55c on 10c (Bk)	42.50	30.00
B38	SP4	55c on 20c (Bk)	42.50	30.00
B39	SP1	75c on 15c (R)	65	60
B40	SP1	75c on 30c (R)	125.00	105.00
B41	SP3	80c on 5c (R)	37.50	30.00
B42	SP3	2p on 40c (R)	90	90
B43	SP4	2p on 1p (R)	90	90
B44	SP2	5p on 50c (R)	1.75	1.75
B45	SP3	5p on 4p (Bk)	2.00	2.50
B46	SP5	10p on 10p (G)	16.00	15.00
	Nos. B32-B46 (15)		288.44	233.30

Nos. B14-B18 Overprinted

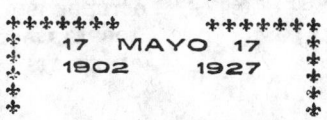

✚✚✚✚✚✚   ✚✚✚✚✚✚
✠   **17   MAYO   17**   ✠
✠   **1902   1927**   ✠
                                        ✠
ALFONSO XIII.

B47	SP6	15c (Br)	20	32
a.		Double overprint	22.50	
B48	SP6	20c (Bl)	20	32
a.		Brown overprint (error)	52.50	
b.		Inverted overprint	22.50	
B50	SP6	30c (R)	20	32
a.		Blue overprint (error)	52.50	
b.		Double overprint	22.50	
B52	SP6	40c (R)	20	32
a.		Inverted overprint	22.50	
b.		Double ovpt. (Bl + Br)	82.50	
B53	SP6	4p (Bl)	52.50	40.00
a.		Inverted overprint	150.00	

Semi-Postal Special Delivery Stamp of 1926 Overprinted "ALFONSO XIII," Dates and Ornaments in Violet

B54	SPSD1	20c red vio & vio brn	3.50	4.00
	Nos. B47-B54 (6)		56.80	45.28

Nos. CB1-CB5 Overprinted in Various Colors

17-V-1902 17-V-1927

A   **A**
XIII   XIII

B55	SPAP1	5c (R)	1.25	1.10
a.		Inverted overprint	22.50	
B56	SPAP1	10c (R)	1.25	1.25
a.		Inverted overprint	22.50	
B57	SPAP1	25c (Bl)	15	28
B58	SPAP1	50c (Bl)	15	28
a.		Double ovpt., one invtd.	65.00	
B59	SPAP1	1p (R)	1.25	1.25
a.		Inverted overprint	85.00	

Same with Additional Surcharges of New Values

B60	SPAP1	75c on 5c (R)	3.50	2.75
a.		Inverted surcharge	22.50	
B61	SPAP1	75c on 10c (R)	13.00	10.00
a.		Inverted surcharge	22.50	
B62	SPAP1	75c on 25c (Bl)	24.00	20.00
a.		Double surcharge	30.00	
B63	SPAP1	75c on 50c (Bl)	12.00	10.00
	Nos. B55-B63 (9)		56.55	46.91

Nos. B54-B63 were available for ordinary postage.

Stamps of Spanish Offices in Morocco and Spanish Colonies, 1926 (Spain Types SP3, SP5) Surcharged in Various Colors with New Values and

ALFONSO XIII   ALFONSO XIII

17-V-1902   17-V-1927

On Spanish Morocco

B64	SP3	55c on 4p bis (Bl)	5.50	6.00
B65	SP5	80c on 10c vio (Bl)	5.50	6.00

On Spanish Tangier

B66	SP5	1p on 10p vio (Br)	17.50	24.00
B67	SP3	4p bis (G)	8.75	9.00

On Cape Juby

B68	SP3	5p on 4p bis (R)	13.00	15.00
B69	SP5	10p on 10p vio (R)	8.75	9.00

On Spanish Guinea

B70	SP5	1p on 10p vio (Bl)	5.50	6.00
B71	SP3	2p on 4p bis (G)	5.50	6.00

On Spanish Sahara

B72	SP5	80c on 10p vio (R)	7.75	9.00
B73	SP3	2p on 4p bis (R)	5.50	6.00
	Nos. B64-B73 (10)		83.25	96.00

Nos. B64-B73 were available for postage in Spain only.
Nos. B19-B73 were for the 25th year of the reign of King Alfonso XIII.
Counterfeits of Nos. B64-B73 exist.

Catacombs Restoration Issues

Pope Pius XI and King Alfonso XIII SP7

1928, Dec. 23   Engr.   Perf. 12½
Santiago Issue

B74	SP7	2c vio & blk	28	30
B75	SP7	2c lake & blk	35	60
B76	SP7	3c bl blk & vio	28	30
B77	SP7	3c dl bl & vio	35	60
B78	SP7	5c ol grn & vio	75	90
B79	SP7	10c yel grn & blk	1.10	1.25
B80	SP7	15c bl grn & vio	3.25	3.50
B81	SP7	25c dp rose & vio	3.25	3.50
B82	SP7	40c ultra & blk	18	30
B83	SP7	55c ol brn & vio	18	30
B84	SP7	80c red & blk	18	30
B85	SP7	1p gray blk & vio	18	30
B86	SP7	2p red brn & blk	3.50	4.50
B87	SP7	3p pale rose & vio	3.50	4.50
B88	SP7	4p vio brn & blk	3.50	4.50
B89	SP7	5p grnsh blk & vio	3.50	4.50

Toledo Issue

B90	SP7	2c bl blk & car	28	30
B91	SP7	2c ultra & car	35	60
B92	SP7	3c bis brn & ultra	28	30
B93	SP7	3c ol grn & ultra	35	55
B94	SP7	5c red vio & car	75	90
B95	SP7	10c yel grn & car	1.10	1.25
B96	SP7	15c slate bl & car	3.25	3.50
B97	SP7	25c red brn & ultra	3.25	3.50
B98	SP7	40c ultra & car	18	30
B99	SP7	55c dk brn & ultra	18	30
B100	SP7	80c blk & car	18	30
B101	SP7	1p yel & car	18	30
B102	SP7	2p dk gray & ultra	3.50	4.50
B103	SP7	3p vio & car	3.50	4.50
B104	SP7	4p vio brn & car	3.50	4.50
B105	SP7	5p bis & ultra	3.50	4.50
	Nos. B74-B105 (32)		48.66	60.25

Nos. B74-B105 replaced regular stamps from Dec. 23, 1928 to Jan. 6, 1929. The proceeds from their sale were given to a fund to restore the catacombs of Saint Damasus and Saint Praetextatus at Rome.

Issues of the Republic

SP13

1938, Apr. 15   Perf. 11½

B106	SP13	45c + 2p bl & grnsh		
		bl	45	60
a.		Imperf., pair	9.00	9.00
b.		Souv. sheet of 1	15.00	18.00
c.		Souv. sheet of 1, imperf.	100.00	180.00

Surtax for the defenders of Madrid.
For overprint and surcharge see Nos. B108, CB6.

Nurse and Orderly Carrying Wounded Soldier — SP14

1938, June 1   Engr.   Perf. 10

B107	SP14	45c + 5p copper red	45	60
a.		Imperf., pair	30.00	

For surcharge see No. CB7.

No. B106 Overprinted in Black

SEGUNDO ANIVERSARIO DE LA
7 NOV. 1938·
HEROICA DEFENSA DE MADRID

1938, Nov. 7   Perf. 11½

B108	SP13	45c + 2p	2.50	4.00

Defense of Madrid, 2nd anniversary.
A similar but larger overprint was applied to cover blocks of four. Value $17.50.

Values for souvenir sheets of 1937-38 are for copies with some faults. Undamaged sheets are very hard to find.

Spanish State
Souvenir Sheets

Alcazar, Toledo SP15

Design: No. B108C, A patio of Alcazar after Civil War fighting.

1937   Unwmk.   Photo.   Perf. 11½
Control Numbers on Back

B108A	SP15	2p org brn	14.00	15.00
b.		Imperf.	200.00	200.00
B108C	SP15	2p dk grn	14.00	15.00
d.		Imperf.	200.00	200.00

Nos. B108A-B108C sold for 4p each.

SP16

Designs: 20c, Covadonga Cathedral. 30c, Palma Cathedral, Majorca. 50c, Alcazar of Segovia. 1p, Leon Cathedral.

1938   Unwmk.   Engr.   Perf. 12½
Control Numbers on Back

B108E	SP16	Sheet of 4	32.50	32.50
f.		20c dull violet	4.50	5.00
g.		30c rose red	4.50	5.00
h.		50c bright blue	4.50	5.00
i.		1p greenish gray	4.50	5.00
j.		Imperf. sheet	65.00	65.00

Each sheet sold for 4p.

SP17

Designs, alternating in sheet: Flag bearer. Battleship "Admiral Cervera." Soldiers in trenches. Moorish guard.

1938, July 1   Unwmk.   Perf. 13
Control Numbers on Back

B108K	SP17	Sheet of 20	16.00 22.50
i.		Imperf. sheet	120.00 130.00

Sheet measures 175x132mm. Consists of five vertical rows of four 2c violet, 3c deep blue, 5c olive gray, 10c deep green and 30c red orange, with each denomination appearing in two different designs. Marginal inscription: "Homenaje al Ejercito y a la Marina" (Honoring the Army and Navy). Sold for 4p, or double face value.

Souvenir Sheets

Don Juan of Austria — SP18

Battle of Lepanto SP19

Perf. 12½
1938, Dec. 15   Unwmk.   Engr.
Control Numbers on Back

B108M	SP18	30c dk car	7.50 9.00
B108N	SP19	50c bl blk	7.50 9.00

Imperf

B108O	SP18	30c blk vio	250.00 250.00
B108P	SP19	50c dk sl grn	250.00 250.00

Issued to commemorate the victory over the Turks in the Battle of Lepanto, 1571. Nos. B108M-B108P contain one stamp. The dates "1571-1938" appear in the lower sheet margin. Size: 89x74mm. Sold for 10p a pair.

LOCAL CHARITY STAMPS

Hundreds of different charity stamps were issued by local organizations and cities during the Civil War, 1936-39. Some had limited franking value, but most were simply charity labels. They are of three kinds: 1. Local semipostals. 2. Obligatory surtax stamps. 3. Propaganda or charity labels.

Ruins of Belchite SP20

Miracle of Calanda — SP21

Designs: 10c+5c, 70c+20c, Ruins of Belchite. 15c+10c, 80c+20c, The Rosary. 20c+10c, 1.50p+50c, El Pilar Cathedral. 25c+10c, 1p+30c, Mother Raffols praying. 40c+10c, 2.50p+50c, The Little Chamber. 45c+15c, 1.40p+40c, Oath of the Besieged. 10p+4p, The Apparition.

Perf. 10½, 11½x10½, 11½
1940, Jan. 29   Litho.   Unwmk.

B109	SP20	10c + 5c dp bl & vio brn	15 15
B110	SP20	15c + 10c rose vio & dk grn	18 18
B111	SP20	20c + 10c vio & dp bl	18 18
B112	SP20	25c + 10c dp rose & vio brn	18 18
B113	SP20	40c + 10c sl grn & rose vio	15 15
B114	SP20	45c + 15c vio & dp rose	35 30
B115	SP20	70c + 20c multi	35 30

B116	SP20	80c + 20c dp rose & vio	35 30
B117	SP20	1p + 30c dk sl grn & pur	35 30
B118	SP20	1.40p + 40c pur & gray blk	17.50 17.50
B119	SP20	1.50p + 50c lt bl & brn vio	65 65
B120	SP20	2.50p + 50c choc & bl	65 65
B121	SP21	4p + 1p rose lil & sl grn	10.00 10.00
B122	SP21	10p + 4p ultra & chnt	82.50 80.00
		Nos. B109-B122,EB2 (15)	113.89 111.16

19th centenary of the Virgin of the Pillar. The surtax was used to help restore the Cathedral at Zaragoza, damaged during the Civil War. No. B121 exists in violet & slate green, No. B122 in ultramarine & brown violet. Value, $37.50 each. Nos. B109-B122 exist imperf. Value, 1½ times that of perf. set.
See No. 743, CB8-CB17.

General Franco — SP23

Knight and Lorraine Cross — SP24

1940, Dec. 23   Unwmk.   Perf. 10

B123	SP23	20c + 5c dk grn & red	30 45
B124	SP23	40c + 10c dk bl & red	55 30

The surtax was for the tuberculosis fund. See Nos. RA15, RAC1.

Stamps of 10c denomination, types SP23 to SP28, are postal tax issues.

1941, Dec. 23

B125	SP24	20c + 5c bl vio & red	35 30
B126	SP24	40c + 10c sl grn & red	35 30

The surtax was used to fight tuberculosis. See Nos. RA16, RAC2.

Cross of Lorraine
SP25   SP26

1942, Dec. 23   Litho.

B127	SP25	20c + 5c pale brn & rose red	90 1.25
B128	SP25	40c + 10c lt bluish grn & rose red	85 32

The surtax was used to fight tuberculosis. See Nos. RA17, RAC3.

1943, Dec. 23   Photo.   Perf. 11½

B129	SP26	20c + 5c dl sl grn & dl red	3.25 1.25
B130	SP26	40c + 10c brt bl & dl red	2.00 1.00

The surtax was used to fight tuberculosis. See Nos. RA18, RAC4.

Dragon Slaying SP27   St. George Slaying the Dragon SP28

Perf. 9½x10
1944, Dec. 23   Litho.   Unwmk.

B131	SP27	20c + 5c sl grn & red	30 20
B132	SP27	40c + 10c dl vio & red	65 15
B133	SP27	80c + 10c ultra & rose	6.50 7.25

The surtax was used to fight tuberculosis. See Nos. RA19, RAC5.

1945, Dec. 23
Lorraine Cross in Red

B134	SP28	20c + 5c dl gray grn	18 15
B135	SP28	40c + 10c vio	35 22
B136	SP28	80c + 10c ultra	7.25 7.50

The surtax was used to fight tuberculosis. See Nos. RA20, RAC6.

VISITA DEL CAUDILLO A CANARIAS OCTUBRE 1950 SOBRETASA: DIEZ CTS

Nos. 753 and 768 Surcharged in Blue

1950, Oct. 23

B137	A195	50c + 10c	35.00 30.00
a.		"Caudillo" 14¾/4mm wide	90.00 80.00
B138	A195	1p + 10c	35.00 30.00
a.		"Caudillo" 14¾/4mm wide	70.00 60.00

Visit of General Franco to Canary Islands. First printing, brighter colors and pale blue surcharge, was issued in Canary Islands. Second printing was issued in Madrid Feb. 22, 1951. See No. CB18.

Catalogue values for unused stamps in this section, from this point to the end of the section, are for Never Hinged items.

1992 Summer Olympics, Barcelona SP29

1988, Oct. 3   Photo.   Perf. 14

B139	SP29	20p +5p Track and field	45 22
B140	SP29	45p +5p Badminton	88 45
B141	SP29	50p +5p Basketball	95 48

See Nos. B146-B152, B163-B168, B177-B179, B184-B186, B191-B193.

EXPO '92, Seville — SP30

Globes and sites of previous exhibitions: No. B142, Crystal Palace, London, 1851. No. B143, Eiffel Tower, Paris, 1889. No. B144, "The Atom," Brussels, 1958. No. B145, Monument, Osaka, 1970.

1989, Feb. 9   Photo.   Perf. 14x13½

B142	SP30	8p +5p multi	24 15
B143	SP30	8p +5p multi	24 15
B144	SP30	20p +5p multi	45 22
B145	SP30	20p +5p multi	45 22

1992 Summer Olympics Type of 1988
1989, Mar. 7   Photo.   Perf. 14

B146	SP29	18p +5p Handball	24 15
B147	SP29	18p +5p Boxing	42 20
B148	SP29	20p +5p Cycling	45 22
B149	SP29	45p +5p Equestrian	90 45

1989, Oct. 3   Photo.   Perf. 13½x14

B150	SP29	18p +5p Fencing	48 25
B151	SP29	20p +5p Soccer	52 25
B152	SP29	45p +5p Pommel horse	1.10 52

500th Anniv. Emblem and Produce or Fauna Indigenous to the Americas — SP31

1989, Oct. 16   Litho.   Perf. 13x13½

B153	SP31	8p +5p Cocoa	38 20
B154	SP31	8p +5p Corn	38 20
B155	SP31	20p +5p Tomato	42 20
B156	SP31	20p +5p Horse	42 20
B157	SP31	50p +5p Potato	92 45
B158	SP31	50p +5p Turkey	92 45
a.		Bkt. pane of 6, #B153-B158	3.45
		Nos. B153-B158 (6)	3.44 1.70

Discovery of America, 500th anniv.

EXPO '92, Seville SP32

Curro, the character trademark, and symbols of development in Spain.

1990, Feb. 22   Photo.   Perf. 14

B159	SP32	8p +5p multi	28 15
B160	SP32	8p +5p multi, diff.	52 28
B161	SP32	45p +5p multi	1.00 52
B162	SP32	50p +5p multi, diff.	1.25 58

1992 Summer Olympics Type of 1988
1990, Mar. 7   Photo.   Perf. 13½x14

B163	SP29	18p +5p Weight lifting	48 22
B164	SP29	20p +5p Field hockey	50 25
B165	SP29	45p +5p Judo	1.00 50

1990, Oct. 3   Photo.   Perf. 13½x14

B166	SP29	8p +5p Wrestling	15 15
B167	SP29	18p +5p Swimming	42 20
B168	SP29	20p +5p Baseball	45 22
		Set value		48

Discovery of America, 500th Anniv. (in 1992) — SP33

Drawings of sailing ships.

1990, Oct. 15   Litho.   Perf. 13

B169	SP33	8p +5p "Viajes-A"	25 15
B170	SP33	8p +5p "Viajes-B"	25 15
B171	SP33	20p +5p "Viajes-C"	50 25
B172	SP33	20p +5p "Viajes-D"	50 25
a.		Bkt. pane of 4, #B169-B172	1.80 90

Expo '92, Seville SP34

Designs: 15p+5p, La Cartuja, Monastery of Santa Maria de las Cuevas. 25p+5p, Amphitheater. 45p+5p, La Cartuja Bridge. 55p+5p, La Bargueta Bridge.

1991, Feb. 12   Litho. & Engr.   Perf. 14

B173	SP34	15p +5p multi	40 20
B174	SP34	25p +5p multi	60 30
B175	SP34	45p +5p multi	1.00 50
B176	SP34	55p +5p multi	1.20 60

Summer Olympics Type of 1988

1991, Mar. 7   Litho.   Perf. 13½x14

B177	SP29	15p + 5p Five athletes	40	20
B178	SP29	25p + 5p Kayaking	60	30
B179	SP29	45p + 5p Rowing	1.00	50

Madrid, European City of Culture, 1992 SP35

Designs: 15p+5p, Fountain of Apollo. 25p+5p, Statue of Alvaro de Bazan. 45p+5p, Bank of Spain. 55p+5p, St. Isidore's Institute.

1991, July 29   Photo.   Perf. 13½x14

B180	SP35	15p + 5p multi	40	20
B181	SP35	25p + 5p multi	60	30
B182	SP35	45p + 5p multi	1.00	50
B183	SP35	55p + 5p multi	1.20	60

1992 Summer Olympics Type of 1988

1991, Oct. 3   Litho.   Perf. 14

B184	SP29	15p +5p Tennis	40	20
B185	SP29	25p +5p Table tennis	60	30
B186	SP29	55p +5p Shooting	1.20	60

Discovery of America, 500th Anniv., 1992 — SP36

Designs: 15p+5p, Garcilaso Gomez Suarez de Figueroa, the Inca, poet. 25p+5p, Pope Alexander VI. 45p+5p, Luis de Santangel, banker. 55p+5p, Friar Toribio de Paredes, monk.

1991, Oct. 15   Photo.   Perf. 13x13½

B187	SP36	15p +5p multi	40	20
B188	SP36	25p +5p multi	60	30
B189	SP36	45p +5p multi	1.00	50
B190	SP36	55p +5p multi	1.20	60
a.		Bklt. pane of 4, #B187-B190	3.25	

1992 Summer Olympics Type of 1988

1992, Mar. 6   Photo.   Perf. 13½x14

B191	SP29	15p +5p Archery	40	20
B192	SP29	25p +5p Sailing	60	30
B193	SP29	55p +5p Volleyball	1.20	60

Columbus Type of 1930 Souvenir Sheet

1992, Mar. 31   Engr.   Perf. 14

B194		Sheet of 3	1.35	1.35
a.		A65 17p +5p dark red	45	45
b.		A65 17p +5p ultramarine	45	45
c.		A65 17p +5p black	45	45

Discovery of America, 500th anniv.

Expo '92 Type

Design: No. B195, Seville, 16th cent.

1992, Apr. 21   Litho.   Perf. 13½x14
Souvenir Sheet

B195	A837	17p +5p multi	45	45

1992 Summer Olympics, Barcelona — SP37

Perf. 14x13½, 13½x14

1992, July 16   Photo.

B196	SP37	17p +5p Mascot COBI	48	24
B197	SP37	17p +5p Hand holding torch, horiz.	48	24
B198	SP37	17p +5p "25 Jul"	48	24

1992 Summer Olympics, Barcelona SP38

Designs: a, Olympic Stadium. b, San Jordi Sports Palace. c, INEF Sports University.

1992, July 25   Perf. 13½x14

B199	SP38	27p +5p Triptych, #a.-c.	1.70	85

1992 Summer Olympics, Barcelona
SP39   SP40

Designs: No. B200, Olympic mascot as stamp collector. No. B201, Sagrada Family Church, Barcelona.

1992, July 29   Photo.   Perf. 14x13½

B200	SP39	17p +5p multi	48	24
B201	SP40	17p +5p multi	48	24

Olymphilex '92 (#B201).

Madrid, European City of Culture — SP41

Designs: No. B202, Municipal Museum. No. B203, Royal Theater. No. B204, The Prado Museum. No. B205, Queen Sofia Natl. Center for the Arts.

1992, Nov. 24   Photo.   Perf. 14x13½

B202	SP41	17p +5p multi	45	22
B203	SP41	17p +5p multi	45	22
B204	SP41	17p +5p multi	45	22
B205	SP41	17p +5p multi	45	22

AIR POST STAMPS

Regular Issue of 1909-10 Overprinted in Red or Black   **CORREO AEREO**

Perf. 13x12½, 14

1920, Apr. 4   Unwmk.

C1	A46	5c green (R)	55	65
a.		Imperf., pair	70.00	70.00
b.		Double overprint	25.00	25.00
c.		Inverted overprint	52.50	65.00
d.		Double ovpt., one invtd.	18.00	21.00
e.		Triple overprint	18.00	21.00
C2	A46	10c car (Bk)	90	65
a.		Imperf., pair	70.00	70.00
b.		Double overprint	21.00	25.00
d.		Double ovpt., one invtd.	18.00	21.00
C3	A46	25c dp blue (R)	1.50	90
a.		Inverted overprint	65.00	85.00
b.		Double overprint	25.00	25.00
C4	A46	50c sl blue (R)	5.00	3.50
a.		Imperf., pair	70.00	90.00
C5	A46	1p lake (Bk)	17.50	11.00
a.		Imperf., pair	225.00	225.00
		Nos. C1-C5 (5)	25.45	16.70

The overprint and its varieties have been counterfeited.
A 30c green was authorized, but not issued.
For overprints see Nos. C58-C61.

"Spirit of St. Louis" over Coast of Europe — AP1   Plane and Congress Seal — AP2

Seville-Barcelona Exposition Issue
Control Numbers on Back

1929, Feb. 15   Engr.   Perf. 11

C6	AP1	5c brown	4.25	4.00
C7	AP1	10c rose	4.25	4.50
C8	AP1	25c dark blue	5.00	5.00
C9	AP1	50c purple	6.50	6.50
C10	AP1	1p green	30.00	22.50
C11	AP1	4p black	35.00	16.00
		Nos. C6-C11 (6)	85.00	58.50

Nos. C6 to C11 exist imperforate. Values about six times those of perforated stamps.

The so-called errors of color of Nos. C10, C18-C21, C23-C24, C28-C31, C37, C40, C42, C44, C46, C48, C50, C52, C55, C62-C67 are believed to have been irregularly produced.

Railway Congress Issue
Control Numbers on Back

1930, May 10   Litho.   Perf. 14

C12	AP2	5c bister brn	4.50	3.50
a.		Imperf., pair	85.00	
C13	AP2	10c rose	4.50	3.50
C14	AP2	25c dark blue	4.50	3.50
C15	AP2	50c purple	9.00	7.50
a.		Vert. pair, imperf. between	210.00	
C16	AP2	1p yellow green	17.00	14.00
C17	AP2	4p black	21.00	17.00
		Nos. C12-C17 (6)	60.50	49.00

The note after No. 385 will apply here also. Dangerous counterfeits exist.

Goya Issue

Fantasy of Flight — AP3

Asmodeus and Cleofas — AP4

Fantasy of Flight — AP5

Fantasy of Flight — AP6

1930, June 15   Engr.   Perf. 12½

C18	AP3	5c brn red & yel	15	15
C19	AP3	15c blk & red org	15	15
C20	AP3	25c brn car & dp red	15	15
C21	AP4	5c ol grn & grnsh bl	15	15
C22	AP4	10c sl grn & yel grn	15	15
C23	AP4	20c ultra & rose red	15	15
C24	AP4	40c vio bl & lt bl	35	40
C25	AP5	30c brn & vio	35	40
C26	AP5	50c ver & grn	35	40
C27	AP5	4p brn car & blk	1.50	1.65
C28	AP6	1p vio brn & vio	35	40
C29	AP6	4p bl blk & sl grn	1.50	1.65
C30	AP6	10p blk brn & bis brn	6.25	6.75
		Nos. C18-C30,CE1 (14)	11.75	12.75

Nos. C18-C30 exist imperf. Value for set, $250.

Christopher Columbus Issue

La Rábida Monastery — AP7

Martín Alonso Pinzón — AP8   Vicente Yanez Pinzón — AP9

Columbus in His Cabin — AP10

1930, Sept. 29   Litho.

C31	AP7	5c lt red brn	20	15
C32	AP7	5c olive bister	20	15
C33	AP7	10c blue green	20	15
C34	AP7	15c dark violet	20	15
C35	AP7	20c ultra	20	15

Engr.

C36	AP8	25c car rose	20	15
C37	AP9	30c dp red brn	1.25	1.65
C38	AP9	40c indigo	1.25	1.65
C39	AP9	50c orange	1.25	1.65
C40	AP8	1p dull violet	1.25	1.65
C41	AP10	4p olive green	1.25	1.65
C42	AP10	10p light brown	6.00	8.25
		Nos. C31-C42 (12)	13.45	17.40

Nos. C31-C42 exist imperf. Value for set, $175.

Spanish-American Issue

AP11

Columbus — AP12

Columbus and Pinzón Brothers AP13

1930, Sept. 29   *Litho.*

C43	AP11	5c lt red	20	18
C44	AP11	10c dull green	20	18

Engr.

C45	AP12	25c scarlet	20	18
C46	AP12	50c slate gray	1.40	1.50
C47	AP12	1p fawn	1.65	1.50
C48	AP13	4p slate blue	1.65	1.50
C49	AP13	10p brown violet	7.25	6.00
		Nos. C43-C49 (7)	12.55	11.04

Nos. C43-C49 exist imperf. Value for set, $175.

Spanish-American Exhibition Issue

Santos-Dumont and First Flight of His Airplane — AP14

Teodoro Fels and His Airplane AP15

Dagoberto Godoy and Pass over Andes AP16

Sacadura Cabral and Gago Coutinho and Their Airplane AP17

Sidar of Mexico and Map of South America — AP18

Ignacio Jiménez and Francisco Iglesias — AP19

Charles A. Lindbergh, Statue of Liberty, Spirit of St. Louis and Cat — AP20

Santa Maria, Plane and Torre del Oro, Seville AP21

1930, Oct. 10   *Photo.*   *Perf. 14*

C50	AP14	5c gray black	30	30
C51	AP15	10c dk olive grn	30	30
C52	AP16	25c ultra	30	30
C53	AP17	50c blue gray	60	60
C54	AP18	50c black	60	60
C55	AP19	1p car lake	1.25	90
a.		1p brown violet	30.00	30.00
C56	AP20	1p deep green	1.25	90
C57	AP21	4p slate blue	3.25	3.25
		Nos. C50-C57 (8)	7.85	7.15

Exist imperf. Value, set $100.
Note after No. 432 also applies to Nos. C31-C57.
Reprints of Nos. C50-C57 have blurred impressions, yellowish paper. Value: one-tenth of originals.

Nos. C1-C4 Overprinted in Red or Black

REPUBLICA

1931   *Perf. 13x12½*

C58	A46	5c green (R)	6.00	7.50
C59	A46	10c carmine (Bk)	6.00	7.50
C60	A46	25c deep blue (R)	7.50	9.00
C61	A46	50c slate blue (R)	16.00	21.00

Counterfeits of overprint exist.

Plane and Royal Palace, Madrid AP22

Madrid Post Office and Cibeles Fountain AP23

Plane over Calle de Alcalá, Madrid AP24

1931, Oct. 10   *Engr.*   *Perf. 12*

C62	AP22	5c brown violet	30	30
C63	AP22	10c deep green	30	30
C64	AP22	25c dull red	30	30
C65	AP23	50c deep blue	40	40
C66	AP23	1p deep violet	50	50
C67	AP24	4p black	4.50	4.50
		Nos. C62-C67 (6)	6.30	6.30

Issued to commemorate the 3rd Pan-American Postal Union Congress, Madrid.
Exist imperf. Value, set $40.
For overprints see Nos. CO1-CO6.

Montserrat Issue

Plane over Montserrat Pass — AP25

1931, Dec. 9   *Perf. 11½*
Control Number on Back

C68	AP25	5c black brown	1.40	1.25
C69	AP25	10c yellow green	2.25	2.25
C70	AP25	25c deep rose	7.25	9.50
C71	AP25	50c orange	24.00	26.00
C72	AP25	1p gray black	16.00	19.00
		Nos. C68-C72 (5)	50.90	58.00

Perf. 14

C68a	AP25	5c	7.50	15.00
C69a	AP25	10c	32.50	37.50
C70a	AP25	25c	47.50	70.00
C71a	AP25	50c	47.50	70.00
C72f	AP25	1p	47.50	70.00

900th anniv. of Montserrat Monastery.
Nos. C68-C72 exist imperf. Values about 10 times those quoted for perf. 11½ stamps.

Autogiro over Seville — AP26

1935-39   *Perf. 11½*

C72A	AP26	2p gray blue	16.00	3.00
g.		Imperf., pair	165.00	

Re-engraved

C72B	AP26	2p dk blue ('38)	20	20
c.		Imperf., pair	18.00	
d.		Perf. 10 ('39)	1.00	1.00
e.		Perf. 14	6.50	6.50

The sky has heavy horizontal lines of shading. Entire design is more heavily shaded than No. C72A.
For overprints see Nos. 7LC14, 7LC19, 14L26.

Eagle and Newspapers — AP27

Press Building, Madrid — AP28

Don Quixote and Sancho Panza Flying on the Wooden Horse AP29

Design: 15c, 30c, 50c, 1p, Autogiro over House of Nazareth.

1936, Mar. 11   *Photo.*   *Perf. 12½*

C73	AP27	1c rose car	15	15
C74	AP28	2c dark brown	15	15
C75	AP27	5c black brown	15	15
C76	AP28	10c dk yellow grn	15	15
C77	AP28	15c Prus blue	15	15
C78	AP27	20c violet	15	15
C79	AP28	25c magenta	15	15
C80	AP28	30c red orange	15	15
C81	AP27	40c orange	35	15
C82	AP28	50c light blue	18	15
C83	AP28	60c olive green	52	32
C84	AP28	1p brnsh black	52	50
C85	AP29	2p brt ultra	2.75	2.25
C86	AP29	4p lilac rose	3.00	2.75
C87	AP29	10p violet brown	7.25	6.50
		Nos. C73-C87 (15)	15.77	13.82

Madrid Press Association, 40th anniv.
Exist imperf. Value, set $400.
See note after No. 432.

CORREO AEREO

Types of Regular Postage of 1936 Overprinted in Blue or Red

1936   *Imperf.*

C88	A125	10c dk red (Bl)	85.00	85.00
C89	A125	15c dk blue (R)	85.00	85.00

Issued in commemoration of the first National Philatelic Exhibition which opened in Madrid, April 2nd, 1936.

VUELO :-:-:
:-: MANILA
MADRID :-:
1936
ARNAIZ -:-:
:-:-: CALVO

No. 577 Overprinted in Black

1936, Aug. 1   *Perf. 11½*

C90	A128	30c rose red	3.50	3.00
a.		Perf. 14	42.50	42.50
b.		Imperf., pair	110.00	

Issued in commemoration of the flight of aviators Antonio Arnaiz and Juan Calvo from Manila to Spain.

No. 288 Surcharged in Black

CORREO AÉREO
14 Abril 1938
VII Aniversario
de la República
2'50 pts.

1938, Apr. 13   *Perf. 14*

C91	A36	2.50p on 10c	75.00	85.00

7th anniversary of the Republic.

No. 507 Surcharged in Various Colors

CORREO AEREO   50 CTS.   CORREO AEREO

1938, Aug.   *Perf. 11½*

C92	A92	50c on 25c (Bk)	18.00	16.00
C93	A92	1p on 25c (G)	1.10	1.25
C94	A92	1.25p on 25c (R)	1.10	1.25
C95	A92	1.50p on 25c (Bl)	1.10	1.25
C96	A92	2p on 25c (Bk & R)	18.00	16.00
		Nos. C92-C96 (5)	39.30	35.75

No. 585 Surcharged   AEREO + 5 Pts.

1938, June 1   *Perf. 11*

C97	A132	5p on 1p multi	150.	150.
a.		Imperf., pair	400.	475.
b.		Inverted surcharge	200.	200.
c.		Souvenir sheet	600.	600.
d.		Souvenir sheet, imperf.	3,000.	3,500.
e.		Double surcharge	275.	300.

Surcharge differs from above illustration.

Type of 1938-39 Overprinted in Red or Carmine

correo
aereo

1938, May   *Perf. 10, 10½*

C98	A163	50c indigo (R)	65	40
C99	A163	1p dk blue (C)	2.00	40

Exist imperf. Value, each $80.

Copies without overprint are proofs.

Juan de la Cierva and his Autogiro over Madrid AP30

1939, Jan.   Unwmk.   Litho.   *Perf. 11*

C100	AP30 20c red orange	35	20
C101	AP30 25c dk carmine	24	15
C102	AP30 35c brt violet	35	20
C103	AP30 50c dk brown	35	15
C105	AP30 1p blue	35	15
C107	AP30 2p green	1.65	90
C108	AP30 4p dull blue	2.75	1.65
	Nos. C100-C108 (7)	6.04	3.40

Exist imperf. Value, set $600.

1941-47   *Perf. 10*

C109	AP30 20c dk red orange	15	15
C110	AP30 25c redsh brown	15	15
C111	AP30 35c lilac rose	1.10	42
C112	AP30 50c brown	24	15
C113	AP30 1p chalky blue	90	15
C114	AP30 2p lt gray grn	1.10	15
C115	AP30 4p gray blue	2.25	30
C116	AP30 10p brt purple ('47)	2.00	60
	Nos. C109-C116 (8)	7.89	
	Set value		1.65

Issued in honor of Juan de la Cierva (1895-1936), inventor of the autogiro.
Nos. C109-C115 exist imperf. Value, set $75.
The overprint "EXPOSICION NACIONAL DE FILATELIA 1948 SAN SEBASTIAN" multiple, in parallel horizontal lines, on Nos. C109 to C113 and other airmail stamps, was privately applied.

Correo Aéreo   **Correo Aéreo**

Nos. 625-634, 660, 676 and 677 with either of these overprints have not been established as issues of the Spanish government.

Mariano Pardo de Figueroa (Dr. Thebussem) AP31

1944, Oct. 12   Engr.   *Perf. 10*

C117	AP31 5p brt ultra	12.00 11.00

"Stamp Day" and "Day of the Race," Oct. 12, 1944. Valid for franking air mail correspondence one day only.

Mail Coach, Plane and Count of St. Louis — AP32

1945, Oct. 12   Unwmk.

C118	AP32 10p yellow green	12.00 11.00

"Stamp Day" and "Day of the Race," Oct. 12, 1945, and to honor Luis José Sartorius, Count of St. Louis, who issued the decree for Spain's 1st postage stamps. No. C118 was valid for franking air mail correspondence one day only.

Maj. Joaquin Garcia Morato AP33

1945, Nov. 27

C119	AP33 10p deep claret	12.00 4.75

Capt. Carlos Haya Gonzalez AP34   Bartolomé de las Casas AP35

1945, Dec. 14

C120	AP34 4p red	6.75 4.00

1946, Oct. 12   *Perf. 11¹/₂x11*

C121	AP35 5.50p green	1.75 2.25

Stamp Day and Day of the Race. Exists imperf. Value $15.

Don Quixote and Sancho Panza Astride Clavileno — AP36

1947, Oct. 9   *Perf. 10*

C122	AP36 5.50p purple	3.25 3.00

Stamp Day and the 400th anniversary of the birth of Miguel de Cervantes Saavedra.

Manuel de Falla AP37   Ignacio Zuloaga AP38

1947, Dec. 1   *Perf. 9¹/₂x10¹/₂*
Control Number on Back

C123	AP37 25p dk vio & brn	24.00 15.00
C124	AP38 50p dk carmine	95.00 24.00
	Set, never hinged	200.00

For overprint see No. CB18.

Train and Plane — AP39

1948, Oct. 9   Litho.   *Perf. 13x12¹/₂*

C125	AP39 2p scarlet	1.75 1.25

Centenary of Spanish railroads and Stamp Day.

UPU Type of Regular Issue with Pedestal and Propeller Added

1949, Oct. 9   *Perf. 12¹/₂x13*

C126	A202 4p dk olive green	30 40

Stamp Day and the 75th anniv. of the UPU.

Stamp of 1850 — AP40   Map of Western Hemisphere — AP41

1950, Oct. 12   Engr.   *Imperf.*

C127	AP40 1p rose brown	5.50	5.50
C128	AP40 2.50p brown org	5.50	5.50
C129	AP40 20p dark blue	75.00	85.00
C130	AP40 25p green	75.00	85.00

Centenary of Spanish postage stamps.

1951, Apr. 16   Photo.   *Perf. 12¹/₂*

C131	AP41 1p blue	3.50 1.50

6th Congress of the Postal Union of the Americas and Spain.

Isabella I AP42

1951, Oct. 12   Engr.   *Perf. 13*

C132	AP42 60c dk gray grn	5.00	40
C133	AP42 90c orange	50	55
C134	AP42 1.30p sepia	4.00	4.00
C135	AP42 1.90p sepia	3.75	4.00
C136	AP42 2.30p dk blue	2.25	2.75
	Nos. C132-C136 (5)	15.50	11.70

Stamp Day and 500th anniv. of the birth of Queen Isabella I.

"The Eucharist" by Tiepolo — AP43   St. Francis Xavier — AP44

1952, May 26   Photo.   *Perf. 12¹/₂x13*

C137	AP43 1p gray green	3.50 60

35th International Encharistic Congress, Barcelona, 1952.

1952, July 3   Engr.

C138	AP44 2p deep blue	24.00 14.00

400th anniv. of the death of St. Francis Xavier.

Ferdinand the Catholic and Columbus Presenting Natives AP45

1952, Oct. 12

C139	AP45 60c dull green	18	18
C140	AP45 90c orange	18	18
C141	AP45 1.30p plum	35	30
C142	AP45 1.90p sepia	1.50	2.00
C143	AP45 2.30p deep blue	7.50	9.50
	Nos. C139-C143 (5)	9.71	12.16

500th anniversary of the birth of Ferdinand the Catholic and to publicize Stamp Day.

Joaquin Sorolla y Bastida — AP46   Miguel Lopez de Legazpi — AP47

1953, Oct. 9   *Perf. 13x12¹/₂*

C144	AP46 50p dk violet	300.00 20.00

Issued to honor Joaquin Sorolla y Bastida (1863-1923), impressionist painter.

1953, Nov. 5

C145	AP47 25p gray black	90.00 20.00

Spanish-Philippine Postal Convention of 1951.

Leonardo Torres Quevedo (1852-1939), Mathematician and Inventor — AP48

**   *Perf. 13x12¹/₂***
1955, Sept. 6   Engr.   Unwmk.

C146	AP48 50p bluish gray & blk	6.00 90
	Never hinged	15.00

Plane and Caravel AP49

1955-56   Photo.   *Perf. 12¹/₂x13*

C147	AP49 20c gray grn ('56)	15	15
C148	AP49 25c gray violet	15	15
C149	AP49 50c ol gray ('56)	15	15
C150	AP49 1p red orange	15	15
C151	AP49 1.10p emer ('56)	15	15
C152	AP49 1.40p rose car	15	15
C153	AP49 3p brt blue ('56)	15	15
C154	AP49 4.80p yellow	16	15
C155	AP49 5p redsh brown	1.25	15
C156	AP49 7p lilac ('56)	35	15
C157	AP49 10p lt ol grn ('56)	40	22
	Set value	2.85	1.15
	Set, never hinged	7.00	

Mariano Fortuny y Carbo (1838-1874), Painter — AP50

1956, Jan. 10   Engr.   *Perf. 13x12¹/₂*

C158	AP50 25p grnsh black	16.00 80
	Set, never hinged	32.50

Catalogue values for unused stamps in this section, from this point to the end of the section, are for Never Hinged items.

Bullfight Type of Regular Issue

Designs: 25c, Small town arena. 50c, Fighting with cape. 1p, Dedication of the bull. 5p, Bull ring.

Perf. 13x12¹/₂, 12¹/₂x13

1960, Feb. 29	Engr.	Unwmk.		
C159	A246	25c brn car & dl lil	15	15
C160	A245	50c blue	15	15
C161	A246	1p red & dull red	30	15
C162	A245	5p red lilac & vio	65	35
		Set value		65

Jai Alai — AP51

1960, Mar. 27	Photo.	Perf. 12¹/₂x13		
C163	AP51	1p brt red & dk brn	5.25	3.75
C164	AP51	5p dull brn & mag	5.25	3.75
C165	AP51	6p vio blk & mag	5.25	3.75
C166	AP51	10p grn, mag & dk brn	5.25	3.75

1st Intl. Cong. of Philately, Barcelona, Mar. 26-Apr. 5. Nos. C163-C166 could be bought at the exhibition upon presentation of 5p entrance ticket.

Sport Type of Regular Issue, 1960

Sports: 1.25p, 6p, Steeplechase, horiz. 1.50p, 10p, Basque ball game.

Perf. 12¹/₂x13, 13x12¹/₂

1960, Oct. 31		Unwmk.		
C167	A251	1.25p choc & car	30	15
C168	A251	1.50p pur, brn & blk	30	15
C169	A254	6p vio blk & car	95	55
C170	A251	10p ol grn, red & blk	1.25	55

Rosary Type of Regular Issue, 1962

Mysteries of the Rosary: 25c, The Ascension, Bayeu. 1p, The Descent of the Holy Ghost, El Greco. 5p, The Assumption, Mateo Cerezo. 10p, The Coronation of the Virgin Mary, El Greco.

1962, Oct. 26		Perf. 13		
C171	A280	25c vio & dl gray vio	24	15
C172	A280	1p olive & brown	38	16
C173	A280	5p brn & rose cl	60	25
C174	A280	10p bluish grn & yel grn	1.50	52

Recaredo I, Visigothic King, 586-601 — AP52

Portrait: 50p, Francisco Cardinal Jimenez de Cis-neros (1436-1517).

1963, Dec. 5	Engr.	Perf. 13x12¹/₂		
C175	AP52	25p dull purple	1.50	28
C176	AP52	50p green & black	2.00	65

1966, Feb. 26

Portraits: 25p, Seneca (4 B.C.-65 A.D.). 50p, Pope St. Damasus I (304?-384).

C177	AP52	25p yel grn & dk grn	1.65	18
C178	AP52	50p sky bl & gray bl	2.50	50

Plaza de Espana, Seville AP53

1981, Nov. 26	Engr.	Perf. 13		
C179	AP53	13p shown	25	15
C180	AP53	20p Rande River Bridge, Pontevedra	45	15
		Set value		15

St. Thomas, by El Greco — AP54

1982, July 7	Photo.	Perf. 13		
C181	AP54	13p Sts. Andrew and Francis	25	15
C182	AP54	20p shown	35	15
		Set value		16

Bowling AP55

1983, Apr. 13	Photo.	Perf. 13		
C183	AP55	13p Bicycling, vert.	25	15
C184	AP55	20p shown	50	15
		Set value		18

AIR POST SEMI-POSTAL STAMPS

Red Cross Issue

Ramon Franco's Plane Plus Ultra — SPAP1

Perf. 12¹/₂, 13

1926, Sept. 15	Engr.	Unwmk.		
CB1	SPAP1	5c black & vio	1.00	90
CB2	SPAP1	10c ultra & blk	1.00	90
CB3	SPAP1	25c carmine & blk	15	22
CB4	SPAP1	50c red org & blk	15	22
CB5	SPAP1	1p black & green	1.50	1.40
		Nos. CB1-CB5 (5)	3.80	3.64

For overprints and surcharges see Nos. B55-B63.

No. B106 | AEREO + 5 Pts.
Surcharged in Black

1938, Apr. 15		Perf. 11¹/₂		
CB6	SP13	45c + 2p + 5p	125.	125.
a.		imperf., pair	600.	600.
b.		Souvenir sheet of 1	3,750.	4,250.
c.		Souvenir sheet, imperf.	3,250.	4,000.
d.		Souv. sheet, surch. invtd.	3,250.	4,000.

The surtax was used to benefit the defenders of Madrid.

No. B107
Surcharged

1938, June 1		Perf. 10		
CB7	SP14	45c + 5p + 3p	6.00	6.00

Monument SPAP2

Caravel Santa Maria SPAP3

Dome Fresco by Goya, Cathedral of Zaragoza SPAP6

Designs: SPAP4, The Ascension. SPAP5, The Coronation, SPAP7, Bombardment of Cathedral of Zaragoza.

Perf. 10¹/₂, 11¹/₂x10¹/₂, 11¹/₂

1940, Jan. 29	Litho.	Unwmk.		
		Bicolored		
CB8	SPAP2	25c + 5c	18	18
CB9	SPAP3	50c + 5c	18	18
CB10	SPAP4	65c + 15c	18	18
CB11	SPAP2	70c + 15c	18	18
CB12	SPAP4	90c + 20c	18	18
CB13	SPAP5	1.20p + 30c	18	18
CB14	SPAP3	1.40p + 40c	35	30
CB15	SPAP5	2p + 50c	35	30
CB16	SPAP6	4p + 1p sl grn & rose lil	6.50	8.25
CB17	SPAP7	10p + 4p chnt & ultra	110.00	130.00
		Nos. CB8-CB17 (10)	118.28	139.93

19th centenary of the Pillar Virgin. The surtax was used to help restore the Cathedral at Zaragoza, damaged during the Civil War.

No. CB16 exists in slate green & violet, No. CB17 in red violet & ultramarine. Value, $32.50 each.

Nos. CB8-CB17 exist imperf. Value, set $450.

No. C123
Surcharged in Black

Correspondencia por avión
VISITA DEL CAUDILLO A CANARIAS OCTUBRE 1950
Sobretasa:
DIEZ CTS

1950-51		Perf. 9¹/₂x10¹/₂		
		Control Number on Back		
CB18	AP37	25p + 10c	275.	150.
		Never hinged	500.	
a.		Without control number	2,000.	250.
		Without control number, never hinged	3,000.	

Visit of Gen. Franco to the Canary Islands, Oct., 1950.

No. CB18 was issued Feb. 22, 1951. No. CB18a is from the 1st printing of the surcharge issued Oct. 23, 1950. The control number was printed on the gum, and regummed copies of No. CB18 are frequently offered as No. CB18a.

Counterfeit surcharges exist.

AIR POST SPECIAL DELIVERY STAMP

Goya Commemorative Issue

Type of Air Post Stamp of 1930 Overprinted

URGENTE

1930		Unwmk.	Perf. 12¹/₂	
CE1	AP4	20c bl blk & lt brn (Bk)	20	20
a.		Blue overprint	9.00	10.00
b.		Overprint omitted	14.00	15.00

See note after No. 432.

AIR POST OFFICIAL STAMPS

Pan-American Postal Union Congress Issue

Types of Air Post Stamps of 1931 Overprinted in Red or Blue

OFICIAL

1931		Unwmk.	Perf. 12	
CO1	AP22	5c red brown (R)	15	15
CO2	AP22	10c blue grn (Bl)	15	15
CO3	AP22	25c rose (Bl)	15	15
CO4	AP23	50c lt blue (R)	15	15
CO5	AP23	1p violet (R)	15	15
CO6	AP24	4p gray blk (R)	2.75	3.00
		Nos. CO1-CO6 (6)	3.50	3.75

Shades exist.

SPECIAL DELIVERY STAMPS

Pegasus and Coat of Arms SD1

1905-25	Unwmk.	Typo.	Perf. 14	
		Control Number on Back		
E1	SD1	20c deep red	24.00	30
a.		20c rose red, litho. ('25)	26.50	30
b.		Imperf., pair	125.00	
c.		As "a," imperf., pair	100.00	

Gazelle SD2

Pegasus SD3

1929	Engr.		Perf. 11	
		Control Number on Back		
E2	SD2	20c dull red	11.00	8.25
a.		Perf. 14	20.00	20.00

Seville and Barcelona Exhibitions. See note after No. 432.

1929-32		Perf. 13¹/₂x12¹/₂, 11¹/₂		
		Control Number on Back		
E3	SD3	20c red	9.00	60
a.		Imperf., pair	60.00	
b.		Without control number, perf. 11¹/₂ ('32)	48.00	90
c.		As "b," imperf., pair	500.00	

No. E3 Overprinted like Nos. 358-370

E4	SD3	20c red (Bl)	12.00	12.00

League of Nations 55th assembly.
For overprints see Nos. E5, E10-E12.

No. E3 Overprinted in **URGENCIA** Blue

1930		Perf. 13¹/₂x12¹/₂, 11¹/₂		
E5	SD3	20c red	9.00	60

Railway Congress Issue

Electric Locomotive SD4

1930, May 10	Litho.	Perf. 14		
		Control Number on Back		
E6	SD4	20c brown orange	30.00	24.00

The note after No. 385 will apply here also.

Goya Issue

Type of Regular Issue of **URGENTE** 1930 Overprinted

1930		Perf. 12¹/₂		
E7	A57	20c lilac rose	20	30

Christopher Columbus Issue

Type of Regular Issue of 1930 Overprinted **URGENTE**

1930 Sept. 29
E8 A64 20c brn vio   75 75

Spanish-American Exhibition Issue

View of Seville Exhibition — SD5

1930, Oct. 10   Photo.   Perf. 14
E9 SD5 20c orange   25 25

The note after No. 432 will apply to Nos. E8 and E9, also to No. E15.

Madrid Issue

No. E5 Overprinted in Green **REPUBLICA**

1931   Perf. 11½
E10 SD3 20c red   2.00 2.50

Barcelona Issue

No. E3 Overprinted **REPUBLICA**

E11 SD3 20c red   2.75 3.00

No. E11 also exists with accent over "U."

No. E3 Overprinted in Blue **República Española.**

E12 SD3 20c red   6.00   90

Montserrat Issue

Pegasus — SD6

1931   Engr.   Perf. 11
Control Number on Back
E13 SD6 20c vermilion   16.00 21.00
a.   Perf. 14   40.00 45.00

SD7

1934   Perf. 10
E14 SD7 20c vermilion   20 15
a.   Imperf., pair   4.25

For overprints see Nos. 10LE1, 11LE1-11LE4, 14LE1.

Newsboy — SD8   Pegasus — SD9

1936   Photo.   Perf. 12½
E15 SD8 20c rose car   30 32

Issued in commemoration of the 40th anniversary of the Madrid Press Association. See note after No. 432.

Spanish State

1937-38 Unwmk. Litho. Perf. 11
With imprint "Hija. deB Fournier-Burgos"
E16 SD9 20c vio brn   5.00 2.25
a.   Imperf., pair   50.00

Without Imprint
E17 SD9 20c dk vio brn ('38)   1.00   22
a.   Imperf., pair   32.50

No. 645 Overprinted in Black **CORRESPONDENCIA URGENTE**

1937
E18 A162 20c dk vio   7.25 7.25

Pegasus — SD10

1939-42   Perf. 10½
Imprint: "SANCHEZ TODA"
E19 SD10 25c carmine   3.25   65
a.   Imperf., pair   30.00

Without Imprint
Perf. 10
E20 SD10 25c car ('42)   20   15
a.   Imperf., pair   5.75

> Catalogue values for unused stamps in this section, from this point to the end of the section, are for Never Hinged items.

"Flight" SD11

Centaur — SD12

Perf. 12½x13, 13x12½
1956, Feb. 12   Photo.   Unwmk.
E21 SD11 2p scarlet   15   15
E22 SD12 4p blk & magenta   20   15

1965-66
E23 SD11 3p dp car   25   15
E24 SD11 5p dp org ('66)   15   15
E25 SD12 6.50p dk vio & rose brn ('66) 20 15
Nos. E21-E25 (5)   95
Set value   52

Chariot SD13

Mail Circling Globe — SD14

1971, June 1   Photo.   Perf. 13
E26 SD13 10p red & yel grn   20   15
E27 SD14 15p red, bl & blk   30   15
Set value   22

Communications — SD15

1993, Apr. 20 Photo. Perf. 14x13½
E28 SD15 180p red & yellow   3.10   60

SEMI-POSTAL SPECIAL DELIVERY STAMPS

Red Cross Issue

Royal Family Group — SPSD1

1926 Unwmk. Engr. Perf. 12½, 13
EB1 SPSD1 20c red vio & vio brn 6.00 6.00

See notes after Nos. 432 and B18.
For overprint see No. B54.

Motorcyclist and Zaragoza Cathedral SPSD2

1940   Litho.   Perf. 11½
EB2 SPSD2 25c + 5c rose red & buff 35 32

19th cent. of the Pillar Virgin. The surtax was used to help restore the Cathedral at Zaragoza, damaged during the Civil War.

DELIVERY TAX STAMPS

D1

1931 Unwmk. Litho. Perf. 11½
ER1 D1 5c black   5.00   20

For overprints see Nos. ER2-ER3, 7LE5-7LE6.

No. ER1 Overprinted in Red **REPUBLICA**

1931
ER2 D1 5c black   1.10 1.25

No. ER2 also exists with accent over "U."

No. ER1 Overprinted in Red **REPUBLICA**

ER3 D1 5c black   2.75 2.75

These stamps were originally issued for Postage Due purpose but were later used as regular postage stamps.

WAR TAX STAMPS

These stamps did not pay postage but represented a fiscal tax on mail matter in addition to the postal fees. Their use was obligatory.

Coat of Arms
WT1   WT2

1874, Jan. 1 Unwmk. Typo. Perf. 14
MR1 WT1 5c black   5.50   52
a.   Imperf. pair   12.00
MR2 WT1 10c pale bl   7.50 1.75
a.   Imperf., pair   52.50

1875, Jan. 1
MR3 WT2 5c green   3.75   55
a.   Imperf., pair   25.00
MR4 WT2 10c lilac   8.25 1.65
a.   Imperf., pair   50.00

King Alfonso XII
WT3   WT4

1876, June 1
MR5 WT3 5c pale grn   1.40   45
MR6 WT3 10c blue   1.40   45
a.   Cliche of 5c in plate of 10c 11.00 9.75
MR7 WT3 25c black   16.00 5.50
MR8 WT3 1p lilac   180.00 32.50
MR9 WT3 5p rose   225.00 100.00

Nos. MR5-MR9 exist imperforate.

1877, Sept. 1
MR10 WT4 15c claret   6.75   40
a.   Imperf., pair   67.50
MR11 WT4 50c yellow   225.00 30.00

WT5   WT6

1879
MR12 WT5 5c blue   27.50
MR13 WT5 10c rose   16.00
MR14 WT5 15c violet   9.75
MR15 WT5 25c brown   16.00
MR16 WT5 50c ol grn   11.00
MR17 WT5 1p bister   16.00
MR18 WT5 5p gray   65.50

Nos. MR12-MR18 were never placed in use.

Inscribed "1897 A 1898"

1897　　　　　　　　　　**Perf. 14**

MR19	WT6	5c green	2.75 80
MR20	WT6	10c green	2.75 80
MR21	WT6	15c green	325.00 100.00
MR22	WT6	20c green	6.75 2.50

Nos. MR19-MR22 exist imperf. Value for set $600.

Inscribed "1898-99"

1898

MR23	WT6	5c black	1.10 55
MR24	WT6	10c black	1.40 55
MR25	WT6	15c black	32.50 8.25
MR26	WT6	20c black	2.75 1.40

Nos. MR23-MR26 exist imperf. Value about $150 a pair.

King Alfonso XIII — WT7

1898

MR27	WT7	5c black	5.50 30
a.		Imperf., pair	55.00

OFFICIAL STAMPS

Coat of Arms
O1　O2

1854, July 1　Unwmk.　Typo.　Imperf.

O1	O1	½o blk, yellow	1.50 60
O2	O1	1o blk, rose	2.50 90
a.		1o black, blue	24.00
O3	O1	4o blk, green	6.00 1.50
O4	O1	1 l blk, blue	40.00 30.00

1855-63

O5	O2	½o blk, yellow	1.25 60
a.		½o black, straw ('63)	1.50 75
O6	O2	1o blk, rose	1.25 60
a.		1o black, salmon rose	3.00 1.75
O7	O2	4o blk, green	3.00 1.25
a.		4o black, yellow green	3.50 1.50
O8	O2	1 l blk, gray blue	10.50 6.00

The "value indication" on Nos. O1-O8 actually is the weight of the mail in onzas (ounces, "o") and libras (pounds, "l") for which they were valid.

Type of Regular Issue of 1889

1895　　　　　　　　　　**Perf. 14**

O9	A34	15c yellow	6.00 75
a.		Imperf., pair	6.00

Coat of Arms — O5

1896-98

O10	O5	rose	4.50 75
a.		Imperf., pair	50.00
O11	O5	dk bl ('98)	13.00 3.50

Cervantes Issue

Chamber of Deputies — O6

Statue of Cervantes — O7　　　Cervantes — O9

National Library — O8

1916, Apr. 22　Engr.　Perf. 12

For the Senate

O12	O6	grn & blk	90 75
O13	O7	brn & blk	90 75
O14	O8	car & blk	90 75
O15	O9	brn & blk	90 75

For the Chamber of Deputies

O16	O6	vio & blk	90 75
O17	O7	car & blk	90 75
O18	O8	grn & blk	90 75
O19	O9	vio & blk	90 75
		Nos. O12-O19 (8)	7.20 6.00

Exist imperf. Value set of pairs, $100.
Exist with centers inverted. Value for set, $80.

Pan-American Postal Union Congress Issue

Types of Regular Issue of 1931 Overprinted in Red or Blue　**Oficial.**

1931　　　　　　　　　　**Perf. 12½**

O20	A84	5c dk brn (R)	15 15
O21	A85	10c brt grn (Bl)	15 15
O22	A86	15c dl vio (R)	15 15
O23	A85	25c dp rose (Bl)	15 15
O24	A87	30c ol grn (Bl)	15 15
O25	A84	40c ultra (R)	22 25
O26	A85	50c dp org (Bl)	22 25
O27	A86	1p bl blk (R)	22 25
O28	A88	4p magenta (Bl)	3.75 3.75
O29	A88	10p lt brn (R)	10.00 10.00
		Nos. O20-O29 (10)	15.16 15.25

Nos. O22-O29 exist imperf. Values about 3 times those quoted.

POSTAL TAX STAMPS

PT5　　　　　PT6

Perf. 10½ x 11½

1937, Dec. 23　　　Litho.

RA11	PT5	10c blk, pale bl & red	3.50 2.00
a.		Imperf. pair	60.00

The tax was for the tuberculosis fund.

1938, Dec. 23　　　Perf. 11½

RA12	PT6	10c multi	3.00 1.50
a.		Imperf. pair	40.00

The tax was for the tuberculosis fund.

"Spain" Holding Wreath of Peace over Marching Soldiers PT7

1939, July 18　　　　　　**Perf. 11**

RA13	PT7	10c blue	25 20
a.		Imperf. pair	72.50

Type of Regular Issue, 1939
Without Imprint
Unwmk.

1939, Dec. 23　Litho.　Imperf.

RA14	A166	10c dull claret	25 20

Tuberculosis Fund Issues

Types of Corresponding Semi-Postal Stamps

1940, Dec. 23　　　　　　**Perf. 10**

RA15	SP23	10c vio & red	20 20

1941, Dec. 23

RA16	SP24	10c blk & red	20 18

1942, Dec. 23

RA17	SP25	10c dl sal & rose red	30 18

1943, Dec. 23　Photo.　Perf. 11

RA18	SP26	10c pur & dl red	55 50

Perf. 9½x10

1944, Dec. 23　Litho.　Unwmk.

RA19	SP27	10c salmon & rose	30 15

1945, Dec. 23

RA20	SP28	10c salmon & car	30 15

Mother and Child — PT8

1946, Dec. 22　Litho.　Perf. 9½x10½

RA21	PT8	5c vio & red	20 15
RA22	PT8	10c grn & red	20 15

See No. RAC7.

Lorraine Cross PT9　　　Tuberculosis Sanatorium PT10

Perf. 9½x10½

1947, Dec. 22　　　　　　**Unwmk.**

RA23	PT9	5c dk brn & red	15 15
RA24	PT10	10c vio bl & red	18 15
		Set value	24

See No. RAC8.

Aesculapius PT11　　　"El Cid" PT11a

Photogravure; Cross Engraved

1948, Dec. 22　Unwmk.　Perf. 12½

RA25	PT11	5c brn & car	18 15
RA26	PT11	10c dp grn & car	18 15
		Set value	24

The tax on Nos. RA15-RA26 was used to fight tuberculosis. See Nos. RAB1, RAC9.

1949, Feb. 1　Litho.　Perf. 10½x9½

RA27	PT11a	5c violet	32 15

The tax aided displaced children. Valid for ordinary postage after Dec. 24, 1949.

Tuberculosis Fund Issues

Galleon and Lorraine Cross — PT12　　　Pine Branch and Candle — PT13

Photogravure; Cross Engraved

1949, Dec. 22　　　　　**Perf. 12½**

RA28	PT12	5c vio & red	15 15
RA29	PT12	10c yel grn & red	15 15
		Set value	18 18

See Nos. RAB2, RAC10.

1950, Dec. 22

Cross in Carmine

RA30	PT13	5c rose violet	15 15
RA31	PT13	10c deep green	15 15
		Set value	24 16

See Nos. RAB3, RAC11.

Children at Seashore — PT14　　　Nurse and Baby — PT15

1951, Oct. 1

Cross in Carmine

RA32	PT14	5c rose brown	18 15
RA33	PT14	10c dull green	50 18

See No. RAC12.

1953, Oct. 1

Cross in Carmine

RA34	PT15	5c carmine lake	60 15
RA35	PT15	10c gray blue	85 18

The tax on RA28-RA35 was used to fight tuberculosis. See No. RAC13.

POSTAL TAX SEMI-POSTAL STAMPS

Types of Corresponding Postal Tax Stamps
Photogravure; Cross Engraved

1948　　Unwmk.　　Perf. 12½

RAB1	PT11	50c + 10c red brn & car	1.25 1.50

1949

RAB2	PT12	50c + 10c dk ol bis & red	1.00 50

1950

RAB3	PT13	50c + 10c brn & car	3.75 2.00

The surtax on Nos. RAB1-RAB3 was used to fight tuberculosis. Combines domestic letter rate and tax obligatory Dec. 22-Jan. 3.

POSTAL TAX AIR POST STAMPS

Tuberculosis Fund Issues

General Franco — PTAP1　　　Knight and Lorraine Cross — PTAP2

Unwmk.
1940, Dec. 23   **Litho.**   *Perf. 10*
RAC1 PTAP1 10c brt pink & red   40   30

1941, Dec. 23
RAC2 PTAP2 10c blue & red   40   30

Lorraine Cross
and
Doves — PTAP3

1942, Dec. 23
RAC3 PTAP3 10c dl sal & rose   1.00   60

Cross of   Tuberculosis
Lorraine   Sanatorium
PTAP4   PTAP5

1943, Dec. 23   **Photo.**   *Perf. 11*
RAC4 PTAP4 10c vio & dl red   1.00 1.25

1944, Dec. 23   **Litho.**   *Perf. 10x9½*
RAC5 PTAP5 25c salmon & rose   5.00 5.00

Lorraine Cross and
Eagle — PTAP6

1945, Dec. 23   *Perf. 10*
RAC6 PTAP6 25c red & car   1.65 1.50

Eagle — PTAP7

1946, Dec. 22
RAC7 PTAP7 25c red & car   40   25

Tuberculosis   Plane over
Sanatorium   Sanatorium
PTAP8   PTAP9

1947, Dec. 22   *Perf. 11½*
RAC8 PTAP8 25c red vio   25   20

Photogravure; Cross Engraved
1948, Dec. 22   *Perf. 12½*
RAC9 PTAP9 25c ultra & car   25   30

Bell and   Dove and
Lorraine Cross   Flowers
PTAP10   PTAP11

1949, Dec. 22
RAC10 PTAP10 25c maroon & red   22   30

1950, Dec. 22
RAC11 PTAP11 25c dk bl & car   1.00   50

Mother and   Tobias and
Child   Archangel
PTAP12   PTAP13

1951, Oct. 1
RAC12 PTAP12 25c brn & car   1.00   20

1953, Oct. 1
RAC13 PTAP13 25c brn & car   4.00 3.00

FRANCHISE STAMPS

F1   F2

1869   **Unwmk.**   **Litho.**   *Imperf.*
S1 F1   blue   42.50 32.50
a. Tête bêche pair   90.00 90.00

The franchise of No. S1 was granted to Diego
Castell to use in distributing his publications on
Spanish postal history.

1881
S2 F2   black, *buff*   30.00 12.00

The franchise of No. S2 was granted to Antonio
Fernandez Duro for his book, "Resena histórico-
descriptiva de los sellos correos de Espana."
*Reprints of No. S2 have been made on carmine,
blue, gray, fawn and yellow paper.*

CARLIST STAMPS

From the beginning of the Civil War
(April 21, 1872) until separate stamps were
issued on July 1, 1873, stamps of France
were used on all mail from the provinces
under Carlist rule.

King Carlos   Tilde on N — A1a
VII — A1

1873, July 1 Unwmk. Litho. Imperf.
X1 A1 1r blue   425.00 425.00
X2 A1a 1r blue   225.00 225.00

*These stamps were reprinted three times in
1881 and once in 1887. The originals have 23
white lines and dots in the lower right spandrel.
They are thin and of even width and spacing. The*

first reprint has 17 to 20 lines in the spandrel,
most of them thick and of irregular width and
length. The second and third reprints have 21
very thin lines, the second from the bottom being
almost invisible. In the fourth reprint the lower
right spandrel is an almost solid spot of color.
Originals of type A1 have the curved line above
"ESPANA" broken at the left of the "E." All
reprints of this type have the curved line
continuous.
The reprints exist in various shades of blue,
rose, red, violet and black.

King Carlos VII
A2   A3

A4   A5

1874
X3 A2 1r violet   150.00 165.00
X4 A3 16m rose   4.25 60.00
X5 A4 ½r rose   47.50 47.50

Nos. X3 and X6-X7 were for use in the Basque
Provinces and Navarra; No. X4 in Catalonia, and
No. X5 in Valencia.
Two types of No. X5, alternating in each sheet.
No. X4 with favor cancellation (lozenge of dots)
sells for same price as unused.

1875
White Paper
X6 A5 50c green   4.75 45.00
a.   50c blue green   21.00 82.50
b.   Bluish paper   35.00
X7 A5 1r brown   4.75 45.00
a.   Bluish paper   35.00

Fake cancellations exist on Nos. X1-X7.

REVOLUTIONARY OVERPRINTS

Issued by the Nationalist (Revolutionary) Forces

Many districts or cities made use of
the stamps of the Republic overprinted
in various forms. Most such overprinting
was authorized by military or postal officials but some were without official
sanction. These overprints were applied
in patriotic celebration and partly as a
protection from the use of unoverprinted
stamps seized or stolen by soldiers.

BURGOS AIR POST STAMPS

RAP1

Revenue Stamps Overprinted in Red, Blue
or Black

1936, Dec. 1   Unwmk.   *Perf. 11½*
Control Number on Face of Stamp
7LC1 RAP1   25c gray grn & blk
        (R)   16.00 16.00
a.   Blue overprint   22.50 22.50
7LC2 RAP1 1.50p bl & blk (R)   3.25 3.25
7LC3 RAP1   3p rose & blk (Bl) 3.25 3.25

RAP2   RAP4

Perf. 13½
Blue Control Number on Back
7LC4 RAP2 15c grn (R)   2.25 2.25
7LC5 RAP2 25c blue (R)   20.00 20.00
Perf. 11½
Without Control Number
Overprint in Black
7LC6 RAP4 1.50p dk bl   4.00 4.00
7LC7 RAP4 3p carmine   4.00 4.00

RAP5   RAP6

Overprint in Black
Perf. 13½, 11½
7LC8 RAP5 1.20p green   16.00 16.00
Perf. 14
Control Number on Back
7LC9 RAP6 1.20p green   16.00 16.00
7LC10 RAP6 2.40p green   16.00 16.00

No. 7LC9 is inscribed "CLASE 8a."

RAP7

1937   **Unwmk.**   *Perf. 11½*
Control Number on Back
7LC11 RAP7 25c ultra (R)   180.00 180.00

¡VIVA ESPAÑA!

Stamps of Spain,
1931-36, Overprinted   **Correo**
in Red
                        Aéreo

Perf. 11, 11½, 11x11½
1937, Apr. 1   Unwmk.
Overprint 15mm high
7LC12 A100 40c blue   65   65
7LC13 A97 50c dark blue   65   65
7LC14 AP26 2p gray blue   16.00 16.00

1937, May 1
Overprint 13mm high
7LC15 A100 40c dk bl   65   65
7LC16 A97 50c dk bl   1.00 1.00
7LC17 A130 50c dk bl   1.00 1.00
7LC18 A100 60c ap grn   1.25 1.25
7LC19 AP26 2p gray bl   20.00 20.00

¡VIVA ESPAÑA!

Spain No. 576   **CORREO**
Overprinted in
Black or Blue   **AÉREO**

1937, May   *Perf. 11½x11*
7LC20 A127 30c car (Bk)   1.25 1.25
7LC21 A127 30c car (Bl)   65   65

Spain No. 578 Overprinted in Black or Blue

¡VIVA ESPAÑA!
CORREO AÉREO

Perf. 11x11½

7LC22	A129	30c car rose (Bk)	1.25	1.25
7LC23	A129	30c car rose (Bl)	65	65

BURGOS ISSUE SPECIAL DELIVERY STAMPS

Pair of Spain No. 546 Overprinted in Black

Correspondencia
URGENTE

1936	**Unwmk.**	**Perf. 11½x11**		
7LE3	A110	20c (10c+10c) emer	3.00	3.00
a.	Overprint inverted		10.00	

CORRESPONDENCIA

Type of Regular Stamp of 1931 Overprinted in Red **URGENTE**

7LE4	A95	20c dk vio	7.25	7.25

HABILITA DO PARA LA CORRESPONDENCIA URGENTE

Type of Delivery Tax Stamp of 1931 Overprinted in Red on four 5c stamps

Perf. 11½

7LE5	D1	20c black	7.25	7.25

Same Overprinted in Red on four 5c stamps

Habilitado para la correspond urgente

7LE6	D1	20c black	14.00	14.00

SD1

1936	**Unwmk.**	**Perf. 11½**		
7LE7	SD1	20c grn & blk	5.00	5.00
7LE8	SD1	20c grn & red	5.00	5.00

Nos. 7LE7-7LE8 exist with control number on back. Value $37.50 each.

CADIZ ISSUE SEMI-POSTAL STAMPS

Stamps of Spain, 1931-36, Surcharged in Black or Red

1936		**Unwmk.**	**Imperf.**	
8LB1	A108	1c + 5c bl grn	15	15
		Perf. 11½x11, 11½		
8LB2	A108	2c + 5c org brn	15	15
8LB3	A103	2c + 5c choc (R)	32	32
8LB4	A110	10c + 5c grn	32	32
8LB5	A111	15c + 5c Prus grn (R)	2.00	2.00
8LB6	A95	20c + 5c dk vio (R)	2.00	3.50
8LB7	A104	25c + 5c lake	2.00	2.00
8LB8	A113	30c + 5c rose red	50	50
8LB9	A100	40c + 5c dk bl (R)	2.25	2.25
8LB10	A97	50c + 5c dk bl (R)	5.00	5.00
		Nos. 8LB1-8LB10 (10)	14.69	16.19

CANARY ISLANDS AIR POST STAMPS

Issued for Use via the Lufthansa Service

Stamps of Spain, 1932-34, Surcharged in Blue

VIVA ESPAÑA
18 JULIO 1936
HABILITADO
AVIÓN
Pts. 0'50

1936, Oct. 27		**Unwmk.**	**Imperf.**	
9LC1	A108	50c on 1c bl grn	13.00	6.50
		Perf. 11½x11		
9LC2	A108	80c on 2c buff	6.50	2.75
9LC3	A103	1.25p on 5c choc	18.00	11.50

The date July 18, 1936, in the overprints of Nos. 9LC1-9LC22 marks the beginning of the Franco insurrection.

Spain Nos. 542, 543, 528 and 641 Surcharged in Black, Red or Green

VIVA ESPAÑA
18 JULIO 1936
HABILITADO
AVIÓN
CANARIAS
50 Cts.

1936-37			**Imperf.**	
9LC4	A108	50c on 1c ol grn	2.75	2.00
9LC5	A108	50c on 1c bl grn (R) ('37)	3.25	2.00
		Perf. 11, 11½x11		
9LC6	A108	80c on 2c buff	1.10	1.00
9LC7	A108	80c on 2c buff (G) ('37)	2.75	1.25
9LC8	A103	1.25 Pts on 5c choc (R)	3.25	2.75
9LC9	A103	Pts 1.25 on 5c choc (R) ('37)	8.25	4.50
9LC10	A161	1.25p on 5c brn (G) ('37)	2.75	1.25
		Nos. 9LC4-9LC10 (7)	24.10	14.75

CANARIAS
∧
FRANCO
18 JULIO 1936
AVION
50 Cts.

Spain Nos. 542, 543 and 641 Surcharged in Blue

1937, Mar. 31			**Imperf.**	
9LC11	A108	50c on 1c bl grn	2.75	1.65
		Perf. 11		
9LC12	A108	80c on 2c buff	2.00	1.25
9LC13	A161	1.25p on 5c brn	2.25	1.25

Stamps of Spain, 1931-1936, Surcharged in Blue or Red

VIVA ESPAÑA
18 JULIO 1936
AVIÓN
CANARIAS
✈ 80

1937				
9LC14	A104	25c + 50c lake	22.50	11.50
9LC15	A162	30c + 80c rose	6.50	5.25
9LC16	A162	30c + 1.25p rose	10.00	6.50
9LC17	A97	50c + 1.25p dp bl (R)	16.00	11.50
9LC18	A100	60c + 80c ap grn (R)	10.00	7.25
9LC19	A105	1p + 1.25p bl blk (R)	27.50	14.00
		Nos. 9LC14-9LC19 (6)	92.50	56.00

The surcharge represents the airmail rate and the basic stamp the postage rate.

Spain Nos. 542, 624 and 641 Surcharged in Black

ARRIBA ESPAÑA
18 JULIO 1936
CANARIAS
AVION
50 Cts.

1937, May 25		**Unwmk.**	**Imperf.**	
9LC20	A108	50c on 1c bl grn	3.25	1.50
		Perf. 11½, 11½x11		
9LC21	A143	80c on 2c org brn	2.25	1.10
9LC22	A161	1.25p on 5c gray brn	2.25	1.10

Stamps and Type of Spain, 1933-36, Surcharged in Black

CANARIAS
CORREO AÉREO
50 Cts.

1937, July		**Perf. 13½x13, 11, 11½**		
9LC23	A143	50c on 2c org brn	65	42
9LC24	A126	80c on 2c org brn	200.00	110.00
9LC25	A161	80c on 5c gray brn	1.10	65
9LC26	A108	1.25p on 1c bl grn	1.50	65
9LC27	A161	2.50p on 10c grn	6.50	4.00

Spain Nos. 647, 650 and 652 Surcharged in Black or Red

CANARIAS
CORREO AÉREO
✈ 80

		Perf. 11		
9LC28	A162	30c + 80c rose	65	42
9LC29	A162	50c + 1.25p dk bl (R)	4.00	2.00
9LC30	A162	1p + 1.25p bl (R)	8.25	4.00

See note after No. 9LC19.

AP1

		Perf. 14x13½		
1937, July 16		**Wmk. 116**		
		Surcharge in Various Colors		
9LC31	AP1	50c on 5c ultra (Br)	2.25	2.75
9LC32	AP1	80c on 5c ultra (G)	1.25	1.65
9LC33	AP1	1.25p on 5c ultra (V)	1.65	2.00

Spain Nos. 641, 643 and 640 Surcharged in Green or Orange

50 Cts.
CORREO AEREO
CANARIAS

1937, Oct. 29		**Unwmk.**	**Perf. 11**	
9LC34	A161	50c on 5c (G)	8.50	3.25
9LC35	A161	80c on 10c (O)	2.75	1.65
9LC36	A160	1.25p on 2c (G)	10.00	5.00

CANARIAS
50 Cts.
Correo Aéreo

Spain Nos. 638, 640 and 643 Surcharged in Red, Blue or Violet

1937, Dec. 23			**Imperf.**	
9LC37	A159	50c on 1c (R)	6.50	3.25
		Perf. 11, 11x11½		
9LC38	A160	80c on 2c (Bl)	2.00	1.65
9LC39	A161	1.25p on 10c (V)	6.50	3.25

CANARIAS
Correo Aereo
✈ 30 C

Spain Nos. 647, 650 to 652 Surcharged in Black, Green or Brown

1937, Dec. 29				
9LC40	A162	30c + 30c rose	1.25	1.25
9LC41	A162	50c + 2.50p dk bl (G)	21.00	14.00
9LC42	A162	60c + 2.30p yel (G)	21.00	14.00
9LC43	A162	1p + 5p bl (Br)	21.00	14.00

See note after No. 9LC19.

CANARIAS
Vía Aérea
50 C

Stamps of Spain, 1936, Surcharged in Black, Green, Blue or Red

1938, Feb. 2		**Perf. 11, 11½, 11x11½**		
9LC44	A160	50c on 2c brn	2.00	1.00
9LC45	A161	80c on 5c brn (G)	2.00	1.00
9LC46	A162	80c on 30c rose (Bl)	1.65	85
9LC47	A161	1.25p on 10c grn (Bl)	2.00	1.00
9LC48	A161	1.25p on 50c dk bl (R)	2.25	1.00
		Nos. 9LC44-9LC48 (5)	9.90	4.85

Vía Aerea
CANARIAS
2'50 Pts.

Spain Nos. 645, 646 and 649 Surcharged in Brown, Green or Violet

1938, Feb. 14				
9LC51	A162	2.50p on 20c (Br)	30.00	20.00
9LC52	A162	5p on 25c (G)	30.00	20.00
9LC53	A162	10p on 40c (V)	30.00	20.00

MALAGA ISSUE

¡Arriba España!
Málaga Liberada
8-2-1937

Stamps of 1920-36 Overprinted in Black or Red

1937		**Unwmk.**	**Imperf.**	
10L1	A47	1c bl grn	15	15
10L2	A108	1c bl grn	15	15
10L3	A108	1c lt grn (R)	15	15
		Perf. 13½, 13½x13, 11, 11½x11		
10L4	A108	2c org brn	5.00	5.00
10L5	A126	2c org brn	15	15
10L6	A103	5c choc (R)	15	15
10L7	A96	10c yel grn	10.00	10.00
10L8	A110	10c emer	15	15
10L9	A111	15c Prus grn (R)	32	32
10L10	A97	15c bl grn (R)	32	32
10L11	A95	20c dk vio (R)	20	20
10L12	A99	25c lake	1.00	1.00
10L13	A104	25c lake	20	20
10L14	A113	30c car	15	15
10L15	A129	30c car rose	85	85
10L16	A100	40c blue (R)	15	15
10L17	A97	50c dk bl (R)	1.00	1.00
10L18	A100	60c ap grn (R)	65	65
10L19	A105	1p blk (R)	1.00	1.00
		Nos. 10L1-10L19 (19)	21.74	21.74

Stamps of 1932-35 Overprinted in Red or Black in panes of 25, reading down. "8.2.37" and "¡Arriba Espana!" form the lower half of all overprints. The upper half varies.

1st and 2nd rows: "MALAGA AGRADECIDA A TRANQUILLO-BIANCHI"
3rd row: "MALAGA A SU SALVADOR QUEIPO DE LLANO"
4th and 5th rows: "MALAGA A SU CAUDILLO FRANCO"

1937			*Perf. 11½*	
10L20	A111	15c Prus grn (R)	1.00	1.00
10L21	A113	30c rose red (Bk)	1.00	1.00
10L22	A97	50c dk bl (R)	1.75	1.75
10L23	A100	60c ap grn (Bk)	1.75	1.75

SPECIAL DELIVERY STAMP

Overprinted like Nos. 10L1-10L19 on Type of Special Delivery Stamp of 1934

1937			*Perf. 10*	
10LE1	SD7	20c rose red (Bk)		40 40

ORENSE ISSUE

¡ VIVA
Stamps of 1931-36
Overprinted in Red, Blue or   ESPAÑA!
Black

1936			*Imperf.*	
11L1	A108	1c bl grn (Bl)	40	40
Perf. 11½, 13½x13				
11L2	A108	2c org brn (Bk)	2.50	2.50
11L3	A126	2c org brn (Bk)	40	40
11L4	A103	5c brn (R)	85	85
11L5	A110	10c lt grn (Bl)	1.65	1.65
11L6	A111	15c Prus grn (R)	1.65	1.65
11L7	A95	20c vio (R)	1.65	1.65
11L8	A104	25c lake (Bk)	2.50	2.50
11L9	A113	30c rose red (Bl)	1.90	1.90
11L10	A100	40c bl (R)	2.75	2.75
a.		Imperf., pair	8.00	8.00
11L11	A97	50c dk bl (R)	4.50	4.50
11L12	A100	60c ap grn (R)	3.75	3.75
a.		Imperf., pair	6.75	6.50
Nos. 11L1-11L12 (12)			24.50	24.50

SEMI-POSTAL STAMPS

¡VIVA
Stamps of Spain, 1931-36, Surcharged in Blue   ESPAÑA!
on front and on back of stamp
+ 5 cts.

1936-37		Unwmk.	*Imperf.*	
11LB1	A47	1c + 5c bl grn	65	65
11LB2	A108	1c + 5c grn	32	32
Perf. 13½x13, 11½, 11½x11				
11LB3	A108	2c + 5c org brn	40	40
11LB4	A126	2c + 5c red brn	40	40
11LB5	A103	5c + 5c choc	60	60
11LB6	A110	10c + 5c emer	60	60
11LB7	A111	15c + 5c Prus grn	85	85
11LB8	A95	20c + 5c vio	60	60
11LB9	A104	25c + 5c lake	85	85
11LB10	A113	30c + 5c rose red	2.00	2.00
11LB11	A117	30c + 5c rose red	30.00	30.00
Nos. 11LB1-11LB11 (11)			37.27	37.27

SPECIAL DELIVERY STAMPS

Type of Special Delivery Stamp of 1934 Overprinted "¡VIVA ESPAÑA!" in Blue or Black

1936			*Perf. 10*	
11LE1	SD7	20c rose red (Bl)	1.75	1.75
11LE2	SD7	20c rose red (Bk)	3.75	3.75
Same with Surcharge "+ 5 cts."				
11LE3	SD7	20c + 5c rose red	90	90

Same Surcharge, Overprint Repeated at Right

11LE4	SD7	20c + 5c rose red	1.00	1.00

SAN SEBASTIAN ISSUE

For Use in Province of Guipuzcoa

Stamps of 1931-36 Overprinted in Red or Blue

¡¡ARRIBA
ESPAÑA!!
1936

1937		Unwmk.	*Imperf.*	
12L1	A108	1c bl grn (R)	42	42
Perf. 11, 13½				
12L2	A108	2c buff (Bl)	65	65
12L3	A126	2c org brn (R)	65	65
12L4	A95	5c choc (R)	4.00	4.00
12L5	A103	5c choc (R)	65	65
12L6	A110	10c emer (R)	1.00	1.00
12L7	A111	15c Prus grn (R)	1.10	1.10
12L8	A95	20c dk vio (R)	1.50	1.50
12L9	A104	25c car lake (Bl)	1.50	1.50
12L10	A113	30c rose red (Bl)	1.00	1.00
12L11	A100	40c blue (R)	3.00	3.00
12L12	A97	50c dk bl (R)	3.00	3.00
Nos. 12L1-12L12 (12)			18.47	18.47

SANTA CRUZ DE TENERIFE ISSUE

Stamps of Spain, 1931-36 Overprinted in Black or Red

Viva España
18 Julio
1936

1936		Unwmk.	*Imperf.*	
13L1	A108	1c bl grn (R)	70	70
13L2	A108	1c bl grn (Bk)	2.00	2.00
Perf. 11, 13½				
13L3	A108	2c buff (Bk)	5.00	5.00
13L4	A126	2c org brn (Bk)	70	70
13L5	A103	5c choc (R)	2.75	2.75
13L6	A110	10c grn (R)	2.50	2.50
13L7	A104	25c lake (Bk)	5.00	5.00
13L8	A100	40c dk bl (R)	2.00	2.00
13L9	A107	10p dp brn (Bk)	200.00	200.00
Nos. 13L1-13L9 (9)			220.65	220.65

SEVILLE ISSUE

Sevilla
Stamps of Spain, 1931-36, Overprinted in Black or Red
"VIVA ESPAÑA"
Julio-1936

1936			*Imperf.*	
14L1	A108	1c bl grn (Bk)	20	20
Perf. 13½x13, 11, 11½x11				
14L2	A126	2c org brn (R)	20	20
14L3	A103	5c choc (R)	32	32
14L4	A110	10c emer (Bk)	42	42
14L5	A111	15c Prus grn (R)	85	85
14L6	A95	20c vio (R)	85	85
14L7	A104	25c lake (Bk)	85	85
14L8	A113	30c car (Bk)	85	85
14L9	A128	30c rose red (Bk)	6.75	6.75
14L10	A100	40c bl (R)	4.50	4.50
14L11	A97	50c dk bl (R)	4.50	4.50
14L12	A100	60c ap grn (Bk)	5.50	5.50
Nos. 14L1-14L12 (12)			25.79	25.79

Stamps of Spain, 1931-36, Handstamped in Black

SEVILLA
"VIVA ESPAÑA"
JULIO-1936

			Imperf	
14L13	A108	1c bl grn	20	20
Perf. 13½x13, 11, 11x11½, 11½x11				
14L14	A126	2c org brn	32	32
14L15	A103	5c chocolate	32	32
14L16	A110	10c emerald	32	32
14L17	A111	15c Prus grn	42	42
14L18	A95	20c violet	32	32
14L19	A104	25c lake	32	32
14L20	A113	30c carmine	32	32
14L21	A128	30c rose red	2.00	2.00
14L22	A100	40c blue	70	70
14L23	A97	50c dk bl	2.00	2.00
14L24	A100	60c ap grn	70	70
14L25	A105	1p black	2.00	2.00

14L26	AP26	2p gray bl	11.00	11.00
14L27	A106	4p magenta	4.00	4.00
14L28	A107	10p dp brn	8.25	8.25
Nos. 14L13-14L28,14LE1 (17)			33.59	33.59

The date "Julio-1936" in the overprints of Nos. 14L1-14L14 and 14LE1 marks the beginning of the Franco insurrection.

SPECIAL DELIVERY STAMP

Overprinted like Nos. 14L13-14L25 on Type of Special Delivery Stamp of 1934

1936			*Perf. 10*	
14LE1	SD7	20c rose red	1.40	1.40

SPANISH GUINEA

LOCATION — In western Africa, bordering on the Gulf of Guinea
GOVT. — Spanish Colony
AREA — 10,852 sq. mi.
POP. — 212,000 (est. 1957)
CAPITAL — Santa Isabel

Spanish Guinea Nos. 1-84 were issued for and used only in the continental area later called Rio Muni. From 1909 to 1960, Spanish Guinea also included Fernando Po, Elobey, Annobon and Corisco.

Fernando Po and Rio Muni united in 1968 to become the Republic of Equatorial Guinea.

100 Centimos = 1 Peseta

Catalogue values for unused stamps in this country are for Never Hinged items, beginning with Scott 319 in the regular postage section, Scott B13 in the semi-postal section, and Scott C13 in the airpost section.

King Alfonso XIII
A1   A2

1902		Unwmk. Typo.	*Perf. 14*	
Blue Control Numbers on Back				
1	A1	5c dark green	5.50	1.00
2	A1	10c indigo	5.50	1.00
3	A1	25c claret	37.50	8.25
4	A1	50c deep brown	37.50	6.50
5	A1	75c violet	37.50	6.50
6	A1	1p carmine rose	65.00	6.50
7	A1	2p olive green	70.00	11.50
8	A1	5p dull red	110.00	35.00
Nos. 1-8 (8)			368.50	76.25

Revenue Stamps Surcharged

HABILITADO
PARA
CORREOS
10 cen de peseta

1903			*Imperf.*	
Blue or Black Control Numbers on Back				
8A		10c on 25c blk (R)	425.00	175.00
8B		10c on 50c org (Bl)	110.00	32.50
8D		10c on 1p 25c car (Bk)	500.00	300.00
8F		10c on 2p cl (Bk)	750.00	450.00
g.		Blue surcharge	1,250.	65.00
8H		10c on 2p 50c red brn (Bl)	1,110.	550.00
8I		10c on 2p 50c red brn (Bl)	1,110.	550.00
8J		10c on 5p ol blk (R)	1,110.	375.00

Nos. 8A-8J are surcharged on stamps inscribed "Posesiones Espanolas de Africa Occidental" and "1903," with arms at left.

This surcharge was also applied to revenue stamps of 10, 15, 25, 50, 75 and 100 pesetas and in other colors.
See Nos. 98-101C.

1903		Typo.	*Perf. 14*	
Blue Control Numbers on Back				
9	A2	¼c black	70	15
10	A2	½c blue green	70	15
11	A2	1c claret	70	15
12	A2	2c dark olive	70	15
13	A2	3c dark brown	70	15
14	A2	4c vermilion	70	15
15	A2	5c black brown	70	15
16	A2	10c red brown	1.10	15
17	A2	15c dark blue	3.75	1.00
18	A2	25c orange buff	3.75	1.50
19	A2	50c carmine lake	7.00	2.25
20	A2	75c violet	10.00	2.25
21	A2	1p blue green	12.50	3.50
22	A2	2p dark green	12.50	3.50
23	A2	3p scarlet	32.50	4.00
24	A2	4p dull blue	45.00	7.50
25	A2	5p dark violet	70.00	11.50
26	A2	10p carmine rose	125.00	14.00
Nos. 9-26 (18)			328.00	52.20

1905				
Same, Dated "1905"				
Blue Control Numbers on Back				
27	A2	1c black	15	15
28	A2	2c blue grn	15	15
29	A2	3c claret	15	15
30	A2	4c bronze grn	15	15
31	A2	5c dark brn	15	15
32	A2	10c red	65	50
33	A2	15c blk brn	2.25	1.50
34	A2	25c chocolate	2.25	1.50
35	A2	50c dark blue	4.75	3.25
36	A2	75c org buff	5.25	3.25
37	A2	1p car rose	5.25	3.25
38	A2	2p violet	11.50	5.00
39	A2	3p blue grn	27.50	10.00
40	A2	4p dark grn	27.50	12.50
40A	A2	5p vermilion	47.50	12.50
41	A2	10p dull blue	72.50	40.00
Nos. 27-41 (16)			207.65	94.00

Stamps of Elobey, 1905, Overprinted in Violet or Blue

1906				
42	A1	1c rose	3.25	1.50
43	A1	2c deep vio	3.25	1.50
44	A1	3c black	3.25	1.50
45	A1	4c org red	3.25	1.50
46	A1	5c deep grn	3.25	1.50
47	A1	10c blue grn	7.25	4.00
48	A1	15c violet	13.00	6.50
49	A1	25c rose lake	13.00	6.50
50	A1	50c org buff	18.00	8.50
51	A1	75c dark blue	22.50	10.50
52	A1	1p red brn	42.50	18.00
53	A1	2p blk brn	62.50	13.00
54	A1	3p vermilion	90.00	30.00
55	A1	4p dark brn	325.00	105.00
56	A1	5p bronze grn	325.00	105.00
57	A1	10p claret	2,000.	750.00
Nos. 42-54 (13)			285.00	104.50

King Alfonso XIII
A3   A4

1907			Typo.	
Blue Control Numbers on Back				
58	A3	1c dark grn	40	15
59	A3	2c dull blue	40	15
60	A3	3c violet	40	15
61	A3	4c yel grn	40	15
62	A3	5c car lake	40	15
63	A3	10c orange	2.00	42
64	A3	15c brown	1.10	25
65	A3	25c dark blue	1.10	25
66	A3	50c blk brn	1.10	25
67	A3	75c blue grn	1.10	30
68	A3	1p red	2.50	50
69	A3	2p dark brn	4.00	1.65
70	A3	3p olive gray	4.00	1.65
71	A3	4p maroon	5.00	1.65
72	A3	5p green	5.75	2.75
73	A3	10p red vio	8.25	3.00
Nos. 58-73 (16)			37.90	13.42

King Alfonso XIII and
Queen Victoria — A13

Issue of 1907
Surcharged in Black or Red

HABILITADO
PARA
O5CTMS

1908-09

74	A3	05c on 1c dk grn (R)	1.75	1.25
75	A3	05c on 2c blue (R)	1.75	1.25
76	A3	05c on 3c violet	1.75	1.25
77	A3	05c on 4c yel grn	1.75	1.25
78	A3	05c on 10c orange	2.25	1.25
a.		Red surcharge	6.00	2.75
84	A3	15c on 10c orange	10.00	5.75
		Nos. 74-84 (6)	19.25	12.00

Many stamps of this issue are found with the surcharge inverted, sideways, double and in both black and red. Other stamps of the 1907 issue are known with this surcharge but are not believed to have been put in use. Value, each $15.

1909   Typo.   Perf. 14½
Blue Control Numbers on Back

85	A4	1c org brn	15	15
86	A4	2c rose	15	15
87	A4	5c dark grn	75	15
88	A4	10c vermilion	25	15
89	A4	15c dark brn	25	15
90	A4	20c violet	40	18
91	A4	25c dull blue	45	18
92	A4	30c chocolate	48	15
93	A4	40c lake	30	15
94	A4	50c dark vio	30	15
95	A4	1p blue grn	7.75	2.75
96	A4	4p orange	1.90	1.50
97	A4	10p red	1.90	1.50
		Nos. 85-97 (13)	15.03	7.31

For overprints see Nos. 102-114.

Revenue Stamps Surcharged like Nos. 8A-8J in Black

1909   Imperf.
With or Without Control Numbers on Back

98		10c on 50c bl grn	72.50	50.00
a.		Red or violet surcharge	90.00	65.00
99		10c on 1p 25c violet	90.00	60.00
100		10c on 2p dk brn	550.00	350.00
100A		10c on 5p dk vio	550.00	350.00
101		10c on 25p red brn	1,000.	675.00
101A		10c on 50p brn lil	2,250.	1,800.
101B		10c on 75p carmine	2,250.	1,800.
101C		10c on 100p orange	2,250.	1,800.

Nos. 98-101C are surcharged on undated stamps, arms centered. Stamps inscribed: "Territorios Espanoles del Africa Occidental." Basic revenue stamps similar to Rio de Oro type A3.

Stamps of 1909 Overprinted with Handstamp in Black, Blue, Green or Red

GUINEA 1911

1911

102	A4	1c org brn (Bl)	20	15
103	A4	2c rose (G)	20	15
104	A4	5c dk grn (R)	65	15
105	A4	10c vermilion	52	20
106	A4	15c dk brn (R)	65	32
107	A4	20c violet	1.00	45
108	A4	25c dull bl (R)	1.10	85
109	A4	30c choc (Bl)	1.50	1.00
110	A4	40c lake (Bl)	1.65	1.10
111	A4	50c dark vio	2.25	2.00
112	A4	1p bl grn (R)	22.50	5.00
113	A4	4p orange (R)	10.50	4.50
114	A4	10p red (G)	14.00	7.25
		Nos. 102-114 (13)	56.72	23.12

The date "1911" is missing from the overprint on the first stamp in each row, or ten times in each sheet of 100 stamps. This variety occurs on all stamps of the series.

King Alfonso XIII
A5   A6

1912   Typo.   Perf. 13½
Blue Control Numbers on Back

115	A5	1c black	15	15
116	A5	2c dark brn	15	15
117	A5	5c deep grn	15	15
118	A5	10c red	18	15
119	A5	15c claret	22	15
120	A5	20c red	35	15
121	A5	25c dull blue	22	15
122	A5	30c lake	2.00	85
123	A5	40c car rose	95	50
124	A5	50c brn org	80	20
125	A5	1p dark vio	1.25	52
126	A5	4p lilac	1.90	1.10
127	A5	10p blue grn	6.50	3.25
		Nos. 115-127 (13)	14.82	7.47

For overprints and surcharges see Nos. 141-157.

1914   Perf. 13
Blue Control Numbers on Back

128	A6	1c dull vio	15	15
129	A6	2c car rose	15	15
130	A6	5c deep grn	15	15
131	A6	10c vermilion	15	15
132	A6	15c dark vio	15	15
133	A6	20c dark brn	50	20
134	A6	25c dark blue	22	16
135	A6	30c brn org	85	24
136	A6	40c blue grn	85	24
137	A6	50c dp claret	30	16
138	A6	1p vermilion	85	75
139	A6	4p maroon	3.50	1.75
140	A6	10p olive blk	4.00	2.75
		Nos. 128-140 (13)	11.82	7.00

GUINEA CORREOS 1914   GUINEA CORREOS 1914

Stamps with these or similar overprints are unauthorized and fraudulent.

Stamps of 1912 Overprinted 1917

1917   Perf. 13½

141	A5	1c black	42.50	10.50
142	A5	2c dark brn	42.50	10.50
143	A5	5c deep grn	38	15
144	A5	10c red	38	15
145	A5	15c claret	38	15
146	A5	20c red	38	15
147	A5	25c dull blue	15	15
148	A5	30c lake	38	15
149	A5	40c car rose	52	24
150	A5	50c brn org	30	15
151	A5	1p dark vio	52	24
152	A5	4p lilac	4.50	2.00
153	A5	10p blue grn	6.00	2.00
		Nos. 141-153 (13)	98.89	26.53

Nos. 143-153 exist with overprint double, inverted, in dark blue, reading "9117" and in pairs one without overprint.

HTADO
15 Cents.

Stamps of 1917 Surcharged

1918

154	A5	5c on 40c car rose	20.00	6.50
155	A5	10c on 4p lilac	21.00	6.50
156	A5	15c on 20c red	40.00	11.50
157	A5	25c on 10p bl grn	40.00	11.50
a.		"52" for "25"	265.00	225.00

The varieties "Gents" and "Censt" occur on Nos. 154-157. Values 50 percent more.

King Alfonso XIII
A7   A8

1919   Typo.   Perf. 13
Blue Control Numbers on Back

158	A7	1c lilac	65	15
159	A7	2c rose	65	15
160	A7	5c vermilion	65	15
161	A7	10c violet	1.00	15
162	A7	15c brown	1.00	20
163	A7	20c blue	1.00	32
164	A7	25c green	1.00	32
a.		25c blue (error)	50.00	
165	A7	30c orange	1.00	32
166	A7	40c orange	2.75	32
167	A7	50c red	2.75	32
168	A7	1p light green	2.75	65
169	A7	4p claret	6.00	2.75
170	A7	10p brown	10.50	4.00
		Nos. 158-170 (13)	31.70	9.80

1920
Blue Control Numbers on Back

171	A8	1c brown	15	15
172	A8	2c dull rose	15	15
173	A8	5c gray green	15	15
174	A8	10c dull rose	15	15
175	A8	15c orange	15	15
176	A8	20c yellow	15	15
177	A8	25c dull blue	40	15
178	A8	30c greenish bl	21.00	6.25
179	A8	40c light brn	32	15
180	A8	50c lilac	1.00	15
181	A8	1p light red	1.00	15
182	A8	4p bright rose	3.25	1.65
183	A8	10p gray lilac	4.50	3.00
		Nos. 171-183 (13)	32.37	12.40

A9

Nipa House — A10

1922
Blue Control Numbers on Back

184	A9	1c dark brn	32	15
185	A9	2c claret	32	15
186	A9	5c blue grn	32	15
187	A9	10c pale red	2.00	30
188	A9	15c orange	32	15
189	A9	20c lilac	1.25	28
190	A9	25c dark blue	2.25	30
191	A9	30c violet	2.00	35
192	A9	40c turq bl	1.10	18
193	A9	50c deep rose	1.10	18
194	A9	1p myrtle grn	1.10	20
195	A9	4p red brown	4.50	2.75
196	A9	10p yellow	12.00	4.75
		Nos. 184-196 (13)	28.58	9.89

1924
Blue Control Numbers on Back

197	A10	5c choc & bl	20	15
198	A10	10c gray grn & bl	20	15
199	A10	15c rose & blk	24	25
200	A10	20c vio & blk	20	15
201	A10	25c org red & blk	40	35
202	A10	30c org & blk	40	25
203	A10	40c dl bl & blk	40	25
204	A10	50c cl & blk	40	25
205	A10	60c brn & blk	40	25
206	A10	1p dk vio & blk	1.25	25
a.		Center inverted	225.00	100.00
207	A10	4p brt bl & blk	4.00	2.00
208	A10	10p bl grn & blk	7.25	4.75
		Nos. 197-208 (12)	15.34	9.05

Seville-Barcelona Exhibition Issue
Seville-Barcelona Issue of Spain, 1929, Overprinted in Red or Blue

GUINEA

1929   Perf. 11

209	A52	5c rose lake	15	15
210	A53	10c green (R)	15	15
211	A50	15c Prus bl (R)	15	15
212	A51	20c purple (R)	15	15
213	A50	25c brt rose	15	15
214	A52	30c black brn	15	15
215	A53	40c dk bl (R)	15	15
216	A51	50c dp orange	15	15
217	A52	1p bl blk (R)	1.40	85
218	A53	4p deep rose	3.25	1.75
219	A53	10p brown	4.75	2.75
		Nos. 209-219 (11)	10.60	6.55

Porter
A11

Drummers
A12

1931   Engr.   Perf. 14

220	A11	1c blue grn	15	15
221	A11	2c red brn	15	15

Blue Control Numbers on Back

222	A11	5c brn blk	15	15
223	A11	10c light grn	15	15
224	A11	15c dark grn	16	15
225	A11	20c deep vio	16	15
226	A12	25c carmine	15	15
227	A12	30c lake	20	15
228	A12	40c dark blue	52	35
229	A12	50c red org	1.25	40
230	A13	80c blue vio	2.00	1.10
231	A13	1p black	3.50	2.75
232	A13	4p vio rose	25.00	10.50
233	A13	5p dark brn	10.50	8.00
		Nos. 220-233 (14)	44.05	24.30

Exist imperf. Value for set, $300.
See Nos. 262-271. For overprints and surcharges see Nos. 234-277, 282-283, 298.

REPUBLICA
ESPAÑOLA

Stamps of 1931 Overprinted

1931

234	A11	1c blue grn	15	15
235	A11	2c red brn	15	15
236	A11	5c brn blk	15	15
237	A11	10c light grn	15	15
238	A11	15c dark grn	15	15
239	A11	20c deep vio	15	15
240	A12	25c carmine	15	15
241	A12	30c lake	38	16
242	A12	40c dark blue	1.10	35
243	A12	50c red org	6.75	3.75
244	A13	80c blue vio	2.25	1.00
245	A13	1p black	7.50	2.25
246	A13	4p vio rose	13.00	6.75
247	A13	5p dark brn	13.00	6.75
		Nos. 234-247 (14)	45.03	22.06

República
Española

Stamps of 1931 Overprinted in Red or Blue

1933

248	A11	1c bl grn (R)	15	15
249	A11	2c red brn (Bl)	15	15
250	A11	5c brn blk (R)	15	15
251	A11	10c lt grn (Bl)	15	15
252	A11	15c dk grn (R)	15	15
253	A11	20c dp vio (R)	35	15
254	A12	25c carmine (Bl)	28	16
255	A12	30c lake (Bl)	28	15
256	A12	40c dk blue (R)	2.00	50
257	A12	50c red org (R)	7.00	2.50
258	A13	80c bl vio (R)	3.75	2.25
259	A13	1p black (R)	8.00	2.25
260	A13	4p vio rose (Bl)	27.50	7.75
261	A13	5p dk brn (Bl)	27.50	10.50
		Nos. 248-261 (14)	77.41	26.97

Types of 1931
Without Control Number

1934-35   Engr.   Perf. 10

262	A11	1c blue grn ('35)	6.00	15
263	A11	2c red brn ('35)	6.00	15
264	A11	5c blk brn	1.00	15
265	A11	10c light grn	1.00	15
266	A11	15c dark grn	2.00	15
267	A12	30c rose red	2.50	15
268	A12	50c indigo ('35)	6.00	52
		Nos. 262-268 (7)	24.50	
		Set value		1.05

Types of 1931

1941   Litho.   Unwmk.

269	A11	5c olive gray	1.25	15
270	A11	20c violet	1.25	15
271	A12	40c gray green	55	15
		Set value		36

Stamps of 1931-33 Surcharged in Black

Habilitado

1

30 Cts. **peseta.**
a   b

1936-37   *Perf. 10, 14*
272 A12 30c on 40c (#228)   2.50 1.50
273 A12 30c on 40c (#242)   10.00 2.25
274 A12 30c on 40c (#256)   37.50 10.50

The surcharge on Nos. 272-274 exists in two types, differing in the "3" which is scarcer in italic.

No. 268 Surcharged Type "b" in Red
275 A12 1p on 50c indigo   14.00
276 A12 4p on 50c indigo   52.50
277 A12 5p on 50c indigo   27.50

Stamps of Spain, 1936,   *Territorios*
Overprinted in Black or   *Españoles del*
Carmine   *Golfo de Guinea*

1938   *Perf. 11*
278 A161 10c gray green   1.25 32
279 A162 15c gray blk (C)   1.25 32
280 A162 20c dark vio   2.75 90
281 A162 25c brown lake   2.75 90

Stamps of 1931-33,   **Habilitado**
Surcharged in Black   **40 cts.**

1939
282 A13 40c on 80c (#244)   8.00 4.00
283 A13 40c on 80c (#258)   8.00 2.50

A14   A15

Revenue Stamps Surcharged in Black
1940-41   *Perf. 11½*
284 A14   5c on 35c pale grn   5.25 1.75
285 A14 25c on 60c org brn   5.25 2.00
286 A14 50c on 75c blk brn   7.25 2.25

Red Surcharge
287 A15 10c on 75c blk brn   7.25 2.25
288 A15 15c on 1.50p lt vio   5.25 2.00
289 A15 25c on 60c org brn   9.00 3.00

A16   A17

Black or Carmine Surcharge
Perf. 11
290 A16 1p on 17p deep red   40.00 12.00
291 A17 1p on 40p yel grn (C) 10.00 3.25

See No. C1.

A18   A19

Black Surcharge
Perf. 11, 13x12½
292 A18 5c carmine   5.00 1.25
293 A19 1p yellow   80.00 30.00

A20   General Francisco
            Franco — A21

Black Surcharge
294 A20 1p on 15c gray grn   10.50 3.50

1940   *Perf. 11½, 13½*
295 A21   5c olive brown   2.00   32
296 A21 40c blue   3.00   32
297 A21 50c green   3.50   32
  a.   50c greenish gray   13.00 5.75

Nos. 295-297 exist imperf. Values twice those quoted.

Habilitado
No. 270 Surcharged in   **3 Pesetas**
Black

1942
298 A11 3p on 20c vio   8.25 1.10

Spain, Nos. 702 and 704   **Golfo**
Overprinted in Carmine or **de Guinea.**
Black

1942   *Perf. 9½x10½*
299 A166 1p gray blk (C)   35   15
300 A166 4p dl rose (Bk)   4.00 55

The overprint on No. 299 exists in two types: Spacing between lines of 2mm, and spacing of 3mm. The 3mm spacing sells for about twice as much.
For surcharges and overprint see #302-303, C3.

Spain, No. 703   **Territorios**
Overprinted in Carmine **españoles**
                        del
                        Golfo
                        de Guinea.

1943
301 A166 2p dull brown   85   15

Nos. 299 and 301   **Habilitado**
Surcharged in Green **para quince**
                     cts.

1949   **Unwmk.**   *Perf. 9½x10½*
302 A166   5c (cinco) on 1p gray blk   15   15
303 A166 15c on 2p dl brn   15   15
          Set value   15

The two types of No. 299, described in footnote, also exist on No. 302.

Men Poling
Canoe
A22

**1949, Oct. 9   Litho.   *Perf. 12½x13*
304 A22 4p dk vio   1.25   70

UPU, 75th anniversary.

San Carlos
Bay — A23

Designs: Various Views

1949-50   *Perf. 12½x13*
305 A23   2c brown   15   15
306 A23   5c rose vio   15   15
307 A23 10c Prussian bl   15   15
308 A23 15c dp ol gray   20   15
309 A23 25c red brown   20   15
309A A23 30c brt yel ('50)   15   15
310 A23 40c olive gray   15   15
311 A23 45c rose lake   15   15
312 A23 50c brn orange   15   15
312A A23 75c ultra ('50)   15   15
313 A23 90c dl bl grn   20   15
314 A23   1p gray   1.25   18
315 A23 1.35p violet   5.25   90
316 A23   2p sepia   12.50 1.25
317 A23   5p lilac rose   18.00 3.25
318 A23 10p light brn   50.00 15.00
  Nos. 305-318 (16)   88.80 22.23

Catalogue values for unused stamps in this section, from this point to the end of the section, are for Never Hinged items.

Surveyor
A24

1951, Dec. 5
319 A24 50c orange   40   15
320 A24   5p indigo   8.00 1.75

Intl. Conference of West Africans, 1951.

Drummer
A25

1952, Mar. 10
321 A25   5c red brown   15   15
322 A25 50c olive gray   15   15
323 A25   5p violet   2.50   15
          Set value   16

Musician
A26

Design: 60c, Musician facing right.

1953, July 1   **Photo.**
324 A26 15c sepia   15   15
325 A26 60c brown   15   15
          Set value   16   15

See Nos. B25-B26.

Woman and   Drummer
Dove   A28
A27

1953, Sept. 5   *Perf. 13x12½*
326 A27   5c orange   15   15
327 A27 10c brt lilac rose   15   15
328 A27 60c brown   15   15
329 A27   1p dull purple   1.00   15
330 A28 1.90p greenish blk   2.75   40
  Nos. 326-330 (5)   4.20
          Set value   60

Tragocephala
Nobilis — A29

Butterfly: 60c, Papilio antimachus.

1953, Nov. 23
331 A29 15c dark green   32   20
332 A29 60c brown   32   20

Colonial Stamp Day. See Nos. B27-B28.

Hunter
A30

Design: 60c, Hunter and elephant.

1954, June 10   *Perf. 12½x13*
333 A30 15c dark gray green   15   15
334 A30 60c dark brown   28   15
          Set value   34   18

See Nos. B29-B30.

Swimming
Turtle — A31

1954, Nov. 23
335 A31 15c shown   15   15
336 A31 60c Shark   28   15
          Set value   34   18

Colonial Stamp Day. See Nos. B31-B32.

Manuel
Iradier y
Bulfy, Birth
Cent. (in
1954)
A32

1955, Jan. 18
337 A32 60c orange brown   15   15
338 A32   1p dark violet   3.50   32
          Set value   40

Priest Saying
Mass — A33

**1955, June 1   Photo.   *Perf. 13x12½*
339 A33 50c olive gray   20   15

Centenary of the establishment of an Apostolic Prefecture at Fernando Po. See Nos. B33-B34.

Palace of
Pardo
A34

1955, July 18   *Perf. 12¹/₂x13*

340	A34	5c ol brn	15	15
341	A34	15c brn lake	15	15
342	A34	80c Prus grn	15	15
		Set value	25	15

Treaty of Pardo, 1778.

Red-eared   Orchid
Guenons   A36
A35

1955, Nov. 23   *Perf. 13x12¹/₂*

343	A35	70c gray grn & bl	24	20

Colonial Stamp Day. See Nos. B35-B36.

1956, June 1   Unwmk.

Flower: 50c, Strophantus Kombe.

344	A36	20c bluish green	16	15
345	A36	50c brown	16	15
		Set value	24	16

See Nos. 360-361, B37-B38, B53-B54.

Arms of Santa   African Gray
Isabel — A37   Parrot — A38

1956, Nov. 23   *Perf. 13x12¹/₂*

346	A37	70c light olive green	15	15

Colonial Stamp Day. See Nos. B39-B40.

1957, June 1   Photo.

347	A38	70c olive green	20	15

See Nos. B41-B42.

Elephants
A39

Design: 70c, Elephant, vert.

Perf. 12¹/₂x13, 13x12¹/₂
1957, Nov. 23

348	A39	20c blue green	15	15
349	A39	70c emerald	16	15
		Set value	24	18

Colonial Stamp Day. See Nos. B43-B44.

Boxing
A40

Basketball   Preaching
A41   Missionary
            A42

Various Sports: 15c, 2.30p, Jumping. 80c, 3p, Runner at finish line.

1958, Apr. 10   Photo.   Unwmk.

350	A40	5c violet brn	15	15
351	A41	10c orange brn	15	15
352	A40	15c brown	15	15
353	A41	80c green	15	15
354	A40	1p orange red	15	15
355	A41	2p rose lilac	28	15
356	A40	2.30p dl violet	50	15
357	A41	3p brt blue	50	15
		Set value	1.50	40

1958, June 1   *Perf. 13x12¹/₂*

Design: 70c, Crucifix and missal.

358	A42	20c blue green	15	15
359	A42	70c green	15	15
		Set value	20	15

75th anniversary of Catholic missions in Spanish Guinea. See Nos. B48-B49.

Type of 1956 Inscribed: "Pro-Infancia 1959"

1959, June 1   *Perf. 13x12¹/₂*

360	A36	20c Castor bean	15	15
361	A36	70c Digitalis	15	15
			16	15

Issued to promote child welfare. See Nos. B53-B54.

Stamps of Spanish Guinea were succeeded by those of Fernando Po and Rio Muni in 1960.

SEMI-POSTAL STAMPS

Red Cross Issue
Types of Semi-Postal Stamps of Spain, 1926, Overprinted in Black or Blue

CUINEA ESPAÑOLA

1926   Unwmk.   *Perf. 12¹/₂, 13*

B1	SP3	5c black brown	2.25	1.50
B2	SP4	10c dark green	2.25	1.50
B3	SP1	15c dark vio (Bl)	75	55
B4	SP4	20c vio brown	75	55
B5	SP5	25c dp carmine	75	55
B6	SP1	30c olive green	75	55
B7	SP3	40c ultra	15	15
B8	SP2	50c red brown	15	15
B9	SP5	60c myrtle green	15	15
B10	SP4	1p vermilion	15	15
B11	SP3	4p bister	60	42
B12	SP5	10p light violet	1.10	90
		Nos. B1-B12 (12)	9.80	7.12

See Spain No. B6a for No. B4 without overprint.

> Catalogue values for unused stamps in this section, from this point to the end of the section, are for Never Hinged items.

Allegory — SP1   Leopard — SP2

1950, Dec. 1   Photo.   *Perf. 13x12¹/₂*

B13	SP1	50c + 10c ultra	40	25
B14	SP1	1p + 25c dk grn	12.50	5.75
B15	SP1	6.50p + 1.65p dp org	3.00	2.50

The surtax was to help the native population.

1951, Nov. 23

B16	SP2	5c + 5c brown	15	15
B17	SP2	10c + 5c red orange	15	15
B18	SP2	60c + 15c olive brn	40	25
		Set value	52	36

Colonial Stamp Day, Nov. 23.

Love Lily — SP3   Brown-cheeked
               Hornbill — SP4

1952, June 1

B19	SP3	5c + 5c brown	15	15
B20	SP3	50c + 10c gray	15	15
B21	SP3	2p + 30c blue	1.50	1.10
		Set value		1.20

The surtax was to help the native population.

1952, Nov. 23   *Perf. 12¹/₂*

B22	SP4	5c + 5c brown	15	15
B23	SP4	10c + 5c brown car	20	15
B24	SP4	60c + 15c dk brown	45	30
		Set value		48

Colonial Stamp Day, Nov. 23.

Music Type of Regular Issue
1953, July 1   *Perf. 12¹/₂x13*

B25	A26	5c + 5c like #324	15	15
B26	A26	10c + 5c like #325	15	15
		Set value	15	15

The surtax was to help the native population.

Insect Type of Regular Issue
1953, Nov. 23   *Perf. 13x12¹/₂*

B27	A29	5c + 5c like #331	15	15
B28	A29	10c + 5c like #3332	15	15
		Set value	15	15

Hunter Type of Regular Issue
1954, June 10   *Perf. 12¹/₂x13*

B29	A30	5c + 5c like #333	15	15
B30	A30	10c + 5c like #334	15	15
		Set value	15	15

The surtax was to help the native population.

Type of Regular Issue
1954, Nov. 23

B31	A31	5c + 5c like #335	15	15
B32	A31	10c + 5c like #336	15	15
		Set value	15	15

Type of Regular Issue and

Baptism — SP5

Perf. 13x12¹/₂
1955, June 1   Photo.   Unwmk.

B33	A33	10c + 5c shown	15	15
B34	SP5	25c + 10c like #339	15	15
		Set value	15	15

Centenary of the establishment of an Apostolic Prefecture at Fernando Po.

Type of Regular Issue and

Red-eared
Guenons
SP6

Perf. 13x12¹/₂, 12¹/₂x13
1955, Nov. 23

B35	A35	5c + 5c like #343	20	15
B36	SP6	15c + 5c shown	20	15

Colonial Stamp Day.

Flower Type of Regular Issue
1956, June 1   *Perf. 13x12¹/₂*

B37	A36	5c + 5c like #344	15	15
B38	A36	15c + 5c like #345	15	15

The tax was for native welfare work.

Type of Regular Issue and

Drummers
and Arms of
Bata — SP7

Perf. 13x12¹/₂, 12¹/₂x13
1956, Nov. 23

B39	A37	5c + 5c like #346	15	15
B40	SP7	15c + 5c shown	15	15
		Set value	20	15

Colonial Stamp Day.

Type of Regular Issue and

African Gray
Parrot
SP8

Perf. 13x12¹/₂, 12¹/₂x13
1957, June 1   Photo.   Unwmk.

B41	A38	5c + 5c like #347	15	15
B42	SP8	15c + 5c shown	15	15
		Set value	15	15

The surtax was for child welfare.

Type of Regular Issue, 1957
Perf. 12¹/₂x13, 13x12¹/₂
1957, Nov. 23

B43	A39	10c + 5c like #348	15	15
B44	A39	15c + 5c like #349	15	15
		Set value	15	15

Pigeons and
Arms of
Valencia
and Santa
Isabel
SP9

1958, Mar. 6   *Perf. 12¹/₂x13*

B45	SP9	10c + 5c org brn	15	15
B46	SP9	15c + 10c bister	15	15
B47	SP9	50c + 10c ol gray	15	15
		Set value	26	22

The surtax was to aid the victims of the Valencia flood, Oct., 1957.

Type of Regular Issue, 1958
1958, June 1   Photo.   *Perf. 13x12¹/₂*

B48	A42	10c + 5c like #358	15	15
B49	A42	15c + 5c like #359	15	15
		Set value	15	15

The surtax was to help the native population.

Butterflies SP10 | Early Bicycle SP11

Stamp Day: Various butterflies.

1958, Nov. 23   **Unwmk.**

B50	SP10	10c + 5c brown red	15	15
B51	SP10	25c + 10c brt pur	15	15
B52	SP10	50c + 10c gray olive	15	15
		Set value	26	16

Type of Regular Issue 1956 Inscribed: "Pro-Infancia 1959"

1959, June 1   **Photo.**   *Perf. 13x12¹/₂*

B53	A36	10c + 5c like #361	15	15
B54	A36	15c + 5c like #360	15	15
		Set value	15	15

The surtax was for child welfare.

1959, Nov. 23

Designs: 20c+5c, Bicycle race. 50c+20c, Bicyclist winning race.

B55	SP11	10c + 5c lt rose brn	15	15
B56	SP11	20c + 5c turq blue	15	15
B57	SP11	50c + 20c olive gray	15	15
		Set value	25	16

Stamp Day.

AIR POST STAMPS

AP1

Revenue Stamp Surcharged "Habilitado para / Correo Aéreo / Intercolonial / Una Peseta"

Type I - "Correo Aereo," 20¹/₂mm.
Type II - "Correo Aereo," 22mm.

1941   **Unwmk.**   *Perf. 11*

C1	AP1	1p on 17p dp red, I	30.00	6.50
a.		Type II	40.00	9.25

Spain No. C113 Overprinted in Red   **Golfo de Guinea.**

1942, June 23

C2	AP30	1p chalky blue	1.50	25

No. 300 Overprinted in Green   **Correo Aéreo** / Viaje Ministerial / 10-19 Enero 1948

1948, Jan. 15   *Perf. 10¹/₂x9¹/₂*

C3	A166	4p dull rose	7.25	2.00

The overprint exists in two types: I - The numeral 1's are lower case L's. II - The numeral 1's are actual ones.

Count of Argelejo and Frigate Catalina at Fernando Po, 1778 — AP2

1949, Nov. 23   **Photo.**   *Perf. 12¹/₂x13*

C4	AP2	5p dark slate green	1.50	75

Stamp Day, Nov. 23, 1949.

Manuel Iradier and Native Products — AP3 | Woman Holding Dove — AP5

Benito Rapids — AP4

1950, Nov. 23   **Unwmk.**   *Perf. 12¹/₂*

C5	AP3	5p dk brn	2.50	75

Stamp Day, Nov. 23, 1950.

1951, Mar. 1   **Litho.**   *Perf. 12¹/₂x13*

Various views.

C6	AP4	25c ocher	15	15
C7	AP4	50c lilac rose	15	15
C8	AP4	1p green	15	15
C9	AP4	2p bright blue	22	15
C10	AP4	3.25p rose lilac	70	15
C11	AP4	5p gray brown	3.25	1.65
C12	AP4	10p rose red	20.00	4.50
		Nos. C6-C12 (7)	24.62	6.90

> Catalogue values for unused stamps in this section, from this point to the end of the section, are for Never Hinged items.

1951, Apr. 22   **Engr.**   *Perf. 10*

C13	AP5	5p dark blue	17.50	2.50

500th birth anniv. of Queen Isabella I.

Ferdinand the Catholic — AP6 | Soccer Players — AP7

1952, July 18   **Photo.**   *Perf. 13x12¹/₂*

C14	AP6	5p red brown	25.00	6.00

500th birth anniv. of Ferdinand the Catholic of Spain.

1955-56   **Unwmk.**

C15	AP7	25c bl vio ('56)	15	15
C16	AP7	50c olive ('56)	15	15
C17	AP7	1.50p brown ('56)	85	15
C18	AP7	4p rose car ('56)	2.75	35
C19	AP7	10p yel grn	1.50	35
		Nos. C15-C19 (5)	5.40	
		Set value		88

Planes and Arm Holding Spear — AP8

1957, Sept. 19   *Perf. 13x12¹/₂*

C20	AP8	25p bister & sepia	6.75	75

30th anniv. of the Atlantida Squadron flight to Spanish Guinea.

SPECIAL DELIVERY STAMP

View of Fernando Po — SD1

Perf. 12¹/₂x13

1951, Mar. 1   **Litho.**   **Unwmk.**

E1	SD1	25c rose carmine	30	20

SPANISH MOROCCO

LOCATION — Northwest coast of Africa
GOVT. — Former Spanish Protectorate
AREA — 17,398 sq. mi. (approx.)
POP. — 1,010,117 (1950)
CAPITAL — Tetuán

Spanish Morocco was a Spanish Protectorate until 1956 when it, along with the French and Tangier zones of Morocco, became the independent country, Morocco.

100 Centimos = 1 Peseta

> Catalogue values for unused stamps in this country are for Never Hinged items, beginning with Scott 280 in the regular postage section, Scott B27 in the semi-postal section, Scott C24 in the airpost section, and Scott E11 in special delivery section.

Spanish Offices in Morocco

Spain No. 221A Overprinted in Carmine   CORREO ESPAÑOL / MARRUECOS

1903-09   **Unwmk.**   *Imperf.*

1	A21	¹/₄c blue green	30	15

See Nos. 26, 39, 52, Tetuan 1, 7.

Stamps of Spain Overprinted in Carmine or Blue

a   CORREO ESPAÑOL / MARRUECOS

On Stamps of 1900

Perf. 14

2	A35	2c bis brn	60	40
3	A35	5c green	75	20
4	A35	10c rose red (Bl)	85	15
5	A35	15c brt vio	1.10	22
6	A35	20c grnsh blk	3.50	90
7	A35	25c blue	42	22
8	A35	30c bl grn	1.75	90
9	A35	40c rose (Bl)	4.25	1.00
10	A35	50c slate grn	2.50	1.00
11	A35	1p lake (Bl)	3.50	2.00
12	A35	4p dull vio	12.00	3.50
13	A35	10p brn org (Bl)	12.00	6.50
		Nos. 1-13 (13)	43.52	17.14

Many varieties of overprint exist. Nos. 7-13 exist imperf.
See Tetuan Nos. 2-6, 8-15.

On Stamps of 1909-10

1909-10   *Perf. 13x12¹/₂, 14*

14	A46	2c dark brn	28	15
15	A46	5c green	1.10	15
16	A46	10c car (Bl)	1.40	15
17	A46	15c violet	3.25	15
18	A46	20c olive grn	6.50	22
19	A46	25c deep bl	67.50	
20	A46	30c blue grn	2.50	15
21	A46	40c rose (Bl)	2.50	15
22	A46	50c slate bl	4.50	1.75
23	A46	1p lake (Bl)	9.00	3.75
24	A46	4p deep vio	67.50	
25	A46	10p org (Bl)	67.50	
		Nos. 14-18,20-23 (9)	31.03	6.62

The stamps overprinted "Correo Espanol Marruecos" were used in all Morocco until the year 1914. After the issue of special stamps for the Protectorate the "Correo Espanol" stamps were continued in use solely in the city of Tangier.
Many varieties of overprint exist.
Nos. 19, 24 and 25 were not regularly issued.
See Nos. 27-38, 40-51, 53-67, 75-76, 78.

Spanish Morocco

Spain No. 221A Overprinted in Carmine   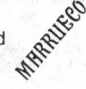 MARRUECOS

1914   *Imperf.*

26	A21	¹/₄c green	15	15

Stamps of Spain 1909-10 Overprinted in Carmine or Blue   MARRUECOS

Perf. 13x12¹/₂, 14

27	A46	2c dk brn (C)	15	15
28	A46	5c green (C)	15	15
29	A46	10c carmine (Bl)	15	15
30	A46	15c violet (C)	60	45
31	A46	20c ol grn (C)	90	65
32	A46	25c dp bl (C)	90	45
33	A46	30c bl grn (C)	2.00	90
34	A46	40c rose (Bl)	4.50	1.40
35	A46	50c slate bl (C)	2.50	90
36	A46	1p lake (Bl)	2.50	1.40
37	A46	4p dp vio (C)	11.50	7.75
38	A46	10p org (Bl)	13.00	9.00
		Nos. 26-38,E1 (14)	41.00	24.50

Many varieties of overprint exist, including inverted.
#27-38 exist imperf. Value for set, $475.

Stamps of Spain 1876 and 1909-10 Overprinted in Red or Blue   PROTECTORADO ESPAÑOL EN MARRUECOS

1915   *Imperf.*

39	A21	¹/₄c bl grn (R)	18	15

Perf. 13x12¹/₂, 14

40	A46	2c dk brn (R)	15	15
41	A46	5c green (R)	20	15
42	A46	10c carmine (Bl)	20	15
43	A46	15c violet (R)	24	15
44	A46	20c ol grn (R)	60	15
45	A46	25c deep bl (R)	60	15
46	A46	30c bl grn (R)	75	22
47	A46	40c rose (Bl)	1.10	22
48	A46	50c slate bl (R)	1.90	15
49	A46	1p lake (Bl)	1.90	22
50	A46	4p dp vio (R)	11.00	8.75
51	A46	10p org (Bl)	17.50	10.50
		Nos. 39-51,E2 (14)	37.82	21.86

One stamp in the setting on Nos. 39-51 has the first "R" of "PROTECTORADO" inverted. Many other varieties of overprint exist, including double and inverted.
Nos. 40-51 exist imperf. Value, set $700.

Stamps of Spain 1877 and 1909-10 Overprinted in Red or Blue

ZONA DE PROTECTORADO ESPAÑOL EN MARRUECOS

b

1916-18   Imperf.

52	A21	¼c bl grn (R)	60 15

Perf. 13x12½, 14

53	A46	2c dk brn (R)	60 15
54	A46	5c green (R)	2.25 15
55	A46	10c carmine (Bl)	3.00 15
56	A46	15c violet (R)	125.00
57	A46	20c ol grn (R)	125.00
58	A46	25c dp bl (R)	6.50 65
59	A46	30c bl grn (R)	12.00 5.25
60	A46	40c rose (Bl)	14.00 32
61	A46	50c slate bl (R)	6.00 15
62	A46	1p lake (Bl)	14.00 65
63	A46	4p dp vio (R)	25.00 10.00
64	A46	10p orange (Bl)	52.50 27.50
		Nos. 52-55,58-64 (11)	136.45 45.12

Nos. 56-57 were not regularly issued.
Varieties of overprint, including double and inverted, exist for several denominations.
The 5c exists in olive brown. Value $475.

Same Overprint on Spain No. 310

1920

65	A46	15c ocher (Bl)	3.50 15

Exists imperf.; also with overprint inverted.

Nos. 44, 46 Perforated through the middle and each half Surcharged "10 céntimos" in Red

1920

66	A46	10c on half of 20c	3.50 2.00
67	A46	15c on half of 30c	8.00 6.00

No. E2 Divided and Surcharged in Black

68	SD1	10c on half of 20c	10.00 8.00
a.		"10/cts." surcharge added	50.00 18.00

Values of Nos. 66-68 are for pairs, both halves of the stamp. Varieties were probably made deliberately.

"Justice" — A1

Revenue Stamps Perforated through the Middle and each half Surcharged with New Value in Red or Green

1920   Perf. 11½

69	A1	5c on 5p lt bl	8.00 2.25
70	A1	5c on 10p green	25 15
71	A1	10c on 25p dk grn	25 15
a.		Inverted surcharge	10.00 9.00
72	A1	10c on 50p indigo	50 40
73	A1	10c on 100p red (G)	50 40
74	A1	15c on 500p cl (G)	11.00 6.75
		Nos. 69-74 (6)	20.50 10.10

Values of Nos. 69-74 are for pairs, both halves of the stamp.

Stamps of Spain 1917-20 Overprinted Type "a" in Blue or Red

1921-24   Perf. 13

75	A46	15c ocher (Bl)	1.10 15
76	A46	20c violet (R)	1.75 15
		Set value	20

Stamps of Spain 1920-21 Overprinted Type "b" in Red

Imperf

77	A47	1c blue green	90 15

Engr.

Perf. 13

78	A46	20c violet	6.00 15
		Set value	20

See No. 92.

Stamps of Spain, 1922 Overprinted Type "a" in Red or Blue

1923-28   Perf. 13½ x 12½

79	A49	2c ol grn (R)	2.00 15
80	A49	5c red vio (Bl)	2.00 15
81	A49	10c yel grn (R)	2.25 15
82	A49	20c viol (R)	3.50 60
		Set value	90

Same Overprinted Type "b"

1923-25

83	A49	2c ol grn (R)	35 15
84	A49	5c red vio (Bl)	35 15
85	A49	10c yel grn (R)	1.40 15
86	A49	15c blue (R)	1.40 15
87	A49	20c violet (R)	2.75 15
88	A49	25c car (Bl)	4.75 45
89	A49	40c dp blue (R)	6.00 1.40
90	A49	50c org (Bl)	14.00 1.65
91	A49a	1p bl blk (R)	19.00 1.40
		Nos. 83-91 (9)	50.00 5.65

Spain No. 314 Overprinted Type "a" in Red

1927   Imperf.

92	A47	1c blue grn	15 15

Mosque of Alcazarquivir A2   Moorish Gateway at Larache A3

Well at Alhucemas A4

View of Xauen — A5

View of Tetuan — A6

1928-32   Engr.   Perf. 14, 14½

93	A2	1c red ("Cs")	15 15
94	A2	1c car rose ("Ct") ('32)	20 15
95	A2	2c dk vio	15 15
96	A2	5c dp blue	15 15
97	A2	10c dk grn	15 15
98	A2	15c org brn	24 15
99	A3	20c olive grn	24 15
100	A3	25c copper red	24 15
102	A3	30c blk brn	85 15
103	A3	40c dull blue	1.10 15
104	A3	50c brn vio	2.00 15
105	A4	1p yel grn	3.25 15
106	A5	2.50p red vio	10.50 2.25
107	A6	4p ultra	7.25 1.65
		Nos. 93-107, E4 (15)	28.47
		Set value	6.00

For surcharges see Nos. 164-167.

Seville-Barcelona Issue of Spain, 1929, Overprinted in Red or Blue

PROTECTORADO MARRUECOS

1929   Perf. 11, 14

108	A50	1c greenish bl	15 15
109	A51	2c pale yel grn	15 15
110	A52	5c rose lake (Bl)	15 15
111	A53	10c green	15 15
112	A50	15c Prussian bl	15 15
113	A51	20c purple	15 15
114	A50	25c brt rose (Bl)	15 15
115	A52	30c blk brn (bl)	22 20
116	A53	40c dark blue	22 20
117	A51	50c dp org (Bl)	22 20
118	A52	1p blue blk	1.65 1.25

119	A53	4p dp rose (Bl)	4.00 3.25
120	A53	10p brn (Bl)	6.50 4.50
		Nos. 108-120 (13)	13.86 10.65

See Nos. L1-L11.

Stamps of Spain, 1922-31, Overprinted Type "a" in Black, Blue or Red

1929-34   Perf. 11½, 13x12½

121	A49	5c claret (Bk)	1.75 15
122	A61	10c green (Bl)	1.90 15
123	A61	15c slate grn (R)	57.50 48
124	A61	20c vio (R)	2.00 20
125	A61	30c brn lake (Bl)	2.25 45
126	A61	40c dk bl (R)	8.50 1.50
127	A49	50c orange (Bl)	13.00 1.25
128	A49a	1p brown (Bl)	2.00 2.00
		Nos. 121-128 (8)	88.90 6.18

Stamps of Spain, 1922-26, overprinted diagonally as above, and with no control number, or with "A000,000" on back, were not issued but were presented to the delegates at the 1929 UPU Congress in London.

Stamps of Spain 1931-32, Overprinted in Black   **MARRUECOS**

1933-34   Imperf.

130	A108	1c bl grn	15 15

Perf. 11½

131	A108	2c buff	15 15
132	A95	5c brnsh blk	15 15
133	A96	10c yel grn	15 15
134	A97	15c slate grn	15 15
135	A95	20c dk vio	15 15
136	A104	25c lake	15 15
137	A99	30c car rose	27.50 1.90
138	A100	40c dk blue	30 15
139	A97	50c orange	70 15
140	A100	60c apple grn	70 15
141	A105	1p blue blk	70 15
142	A106	4p magenta	1.90 1.10
143	A107	10p deep brn	2.50 1.90
		Nos. 130-143, E7 (15)	36.45
		Set value	5.85

Street Scene in Tangier — A7

View of Xauen — A8

Gate in Town Wall, Arzila — A9

Street Scene in Tangier A10   Mosque of Alcazarquivir A11

Caliph and His Guard — A12

View of Tangier — A13

Green Control Numbers Printed on Gum

1933-35   Photo.   Perf. 14, 13½

144	A7	1c brt rose	15 15
145	A8	2c green ('35)	15 15
146	A9	5c magenta ('35)	15 15
147	A10	10c dark green	15 15
148	A11	15c yellow ('35)	85 15
149	A7	20c slate grn	32 15
150	A12	25c crimson ('35)	8.50 15
151	A10	30c red brown	2.50 15
152	A13	40c deep blue	5.25 15
153	A13	50c red org	14.00 1.75
154	A8	1p sl blk ('35)	6.00 15
155	A9	2.50p brown ('35)	10.00 1.75
156	A11	4p yel grn ('35)	10.00 1.75
157	A12	5p black ('35)	13.00 1.75
		Nos. 144-157,E5 (15)	71.87 8.65

For surcharge see No. CB1.

Mosque A14   Landscape A15

Green Control Numbers Printed on Gum

1935

158	A14	25c violet	44 15
159	A13	30c crimson	5.50 15
160	A14	40c orange	3.25 15
161	A15	50c bright bl	3.25 15
162	A14	60c dk bl grn	3.25 15
163	A15	2p brn lake	15.00 2.25
		Nos. 158-163 (6)	30.69 3.00

See No. 174.

Regular Issue and Special Delivery Stamp of 1928, Surcharged in Blue, Green or Red with New Values and Ornaments

1936

164	A6	1c on 4p ultra (Bl)	15 15
165	A5	2c on 2.50p red vio (G)	15 15
166	A3	5c on 25c cop red (R)	15 15
167	A4	10c on 1p yel grn (G)	4.00 2.25
168	SD2	15c on 20c blk (Bl)	3.25 1.10
		Nos. 164-168 (5)	7.70 3.80

Caliph and Viziers — A16   View of Bokoia — A17

View of Alcazarquivir A18

Sidi Saida Mosque A19   Caliph and Procession A20

Without Control Numbers

1937   Photo.   Perf. 13½

169	A16	1c green	15 15
170	A17	2c red vio	15 15
171	A18	5c orange	15 15
172	A16	15c violet	15 15
173	A19	30c red	32 15
a.		Souv. sheet of 4, #170-173	10.00 6.25

174	A14	1p ultra	2.75	15
a.		Souv. sheet of 4, #169-171, 174	10.00	6.25
175	A20	10p brown	27.50	8.50
		Nos. 169-175 (7)	31.17	9.40

Nos. 173a, 174a for 1st year of the Spanish Civil War.

Nos. 173a, 174a were privately overprinted "TANGER" in black on each stamp in the sheet for "use" in the International City of Tangier, and "GUINEA" for "use" in Spanish Guinea.

Harkeno Rifleman A21

Troops Marching A22

Designs: 2c, Legionnaires. 5c, Cavalryman leading his mount. 10c, Moroccan phalanx. 15c, Legion flag-bearer. 20c, Colonial soldier. 25c, Ifni sharpshooters. 30c, Mounted trumpeters. 40c, Cape Juby Dromedary Corps. 50c, Regular infantry. 60c, Caliphate guards. 1p, Orderly on guard. 2p, Sentry. 2.50p, Regular cavalry. 4p, Orderly.

1937 *Perf. 13½*

176	A21	1c dull blue	15	15
177	A21	2c org brn	15	15
178	A21	5c cerise	15	15
179	A21	10c emerald	15	15
180	A21	15c brt blue	15	15
181	A21	20c red brn	15	15
182	A21	25c magenta	15	15
183	A21	30c red org	15	15
184	A21	40c orange	15	15
185	A21	50c ultra	15	15
186	A21	60c yel grn	15	15
187	A21	1p blue vio	15	15
188	A21	2p Prus blue	3.75	3.00
189	A21	2.50p gray blk	3.75	3.00
190	A21	4p dark brn	3.75	3.00
191	A22	10p black	3.75	3.00
		Nos. 176-191,E6 (17)	16.95	13.95

First Year of Spanish Civil War. For overprints see Nos. 214-229.

Spanish Quarter — A25

Designs: 10c, Moroccan quarter. 15c, Street scene, Larache. 20c, Tetuan.

1939 Unwmk. Photo. *Perf. 13½*

194	A25	5c orange	15	15
195	A25	10c brt blue grn	15	15
196	A25	15c golden brn	35	15
197	A25	20c brt ultra	35	15
		Set value		24

Postman A26

Mail Box A27

Landscape A28

Street Scene, Alcazarquivir A29

View of Xauen — A30

The Chieftain A32

Scene in Alcazarquivir A36

Spanish War Veterans A38

Cavalry — A40

Sentry Guarding Palace at Sat — A31

Market Place, Larache A33

Tetuán — A34

Post Office A37

Victory Flag Bearers A39

Day of Court — A41

1940 Unwmk. Photo. *Perf. 11½x11*

198	A26	1c dark brown	15	15
199	A27	2c olive grn	15	15
200	A28	5c dk blue	15	15
201	A29	10c dk red lil	15	15
202	A30	15c dk green	15	15
203	A31	20c purple	15	15
204	A32	25c black brn	15	15
205	A33	30c brt green	15	15
206	A34	40c slate grn	1.10	15
207	A35	45c org ver	45	15
208	A36	50c brn org	45	15
209	A37	70c sapphire	45	15
210	A38	1p ind & brn	1.25	15
211	A39	2.50p choc & dk grn	6.50	1.75
212	A40	5p dk cer & sep	1.25	15
213	A41	10p dk ol grn & brn org	12.00	3.00
		Nos. 198-213,E8 (17)	24.90	
		Set value		5.75

"ZONA" printed in black on back.

Stamps of 1937 Overprinted in Various Colors

1940 Unwmk. *Perf. 13½*

214	A21	1c dull bl (Bk)	45	45
215	A21	2c orange brn (Bk)	45	45
216	A21	5c cerise (Bk)	45	45
217	A21	10c emerald (Bk)	45	45
218	A21	15c brt blue (Bk)	45	45
219	A21	20c red brn (Bk)	45	45
220	A21	25c magenta (Bk)	45	45
221	A21	30c red org (V)	45	45
222	A21	40c orange (V)	75	75
223	A21	50c ultra (Bk)	75	75
224	A21	60c yel grn (Bk)	75	75
225	A21	1p bl vio (V)	75	75
226	A21	2p Prus bl (Bl)	21.00	21.00
227	A21	2.50p gray blk (V)	21.00	21.00
228	A21	4p dk brn (Bl)	21.00	21.00
229	A22	10p black (R)	21.00	21.00
		Nos. 214-229,E10 (17)	97.10	97.10

4th anniversary of Spanish Civil War.

Larache A42

Alcazarquivir A43

Market Place, Larache — A44

Tangier
A45 A46

1941 Unwmk. Photo. *Perf. 10½*

230	A42	5c dk brn & brn	15	15
231	A43	10c dp rose & ver	15	15
232	A44	15c sl grn & yel grn	15	15
233	A45	20c vio bl & dp bl	30	15
234	A46	40c dp plum & claret	85	15
		Nos. 230-234 (5)	1.60	
		Set value		30

1943 *Perf. 12x12½*

234A	A43	5c dark blue	15	15
235	A44	40c dl vio brn	13.00	15
		Set value		16

Plowing — A47

Harvesting A48

Returning from Work — A49

Transporting Wheat — A50

Vegetable Garden — A51

Picking Oranges — A52

Goat Herd — A53

1944 Unwmk. Photo. *Perf. 12½*

236	A47	1c choc & lt bl	15	15
237	A48	2c sl grn & lt grn	15	15
238	A49	5c choc & grnsh blk	15	15
239	A50	10c brt ultra & red org	15	15
240	A51	15c sl grn & lt grn	15	15
241	A52	20c dp cl & blk	15	15
242	A53	25c lt bl & choc	15	15
243	A47	30c yel grn & brt ultra	15	15
244	A48	40c choc & red vio	15	15
245	A49	50c brt ultra & red brn	25	15
246	A50	75c yel grn & brt ultra	30	15
247	A51	1p brt ultra & choc	30	15
248	A52	2.50p blk & brt ultra	2.50	1.25
249	A53	10p sal & gray blk	5.50	2.50
		Nos. 236-249 (14)	10.20	
		Set value		4.45

Potters A54

Dyers — A55

Blacksmiths
A56

Cobblers
A57

Weavers
A58

Metal
Workers
A59

1946 Unwmk. Litho. Perf. 10½x10
250	A54	1c pur & brn	15	15
251	A54	2c dk Prus grn & vio blk	15	15
252	A54	10c dp org & vio bl	15	15
253	A55	15c dk bl & bl grn	15	15
254	A54	25c yel grn & ultra	15	15
255	A56	40c dk bl & brn, perf.		
		12½	15	15
256	A55	45c blk & rose	40	15
257	A57	1p dk Prus grn & dp bl	50	15
258	A58	2.50p dp org & gray	1.50	50
259	A59	10p dk bl & gray	2.50	1.25
		Nos. 250-259 (10)	5.80	
		Set value		2.15

Control letter "Z" in circle in black on back.

A60   Sanitorium — A61

1946, Sept. 1 Perf. 11½x10½, 10½
260	A60	10c crim & bl grn	15	15
261	A61	25c crim & brn	15	15
		Set value, #260-261,		
		B14-B16	1.00	54

Issued to aid anti-tuberculosis work.

A62   A63

1947 Perf. 10
262	A62	10c car & blue	15	15
263	A63	25c red & chocolate	15	15
		Set value, #262-263,		
		B17-B19	98	80

Issued to aid anti-tuberculosis work.

Commerce by
Railroad
A64

Commerce by
Truck — A65

Urban
Market — A66

Country
Market — A67

Caravan
A68

Maritime
Commerce
A69

1948 Litho. Perf. 10, 10x10½
264	A64	2c pur & brn	15	15
265	A65	5c dp cl & vio	15	15
266	A66	15c brt ultra & bl grn	15	15
267	A67	25c blk & Prus grn	15	15
268	A65	35c brt ultra & gray blk	15	15
269	A68	50c red & vio	15	15
270	A67	70c dk gray grn & ultra	15	15
271	A67	90c cer & dk gray grn	15	15
272	A68	1p brt ultra & vio	55	15
273	A64	2.50p vio brn & sl grn	1.40	40
274	A69	10p blk & dp ultra	2.50	1.10
		Set value	5.00	2.00

Emblem of Tuberculosis
Association
A70   A71

Design: 25c, Plane over sanatorium.

1948, Oct. 1 Perf. 10
275	A70	10c car & green	15	15
276	A70	25c car & grnsh gray	1.25	60
		Nos. 275-276,B20-B23 (6)	19.95	7.50

See No. B39.

1949

Designs: 10c, Road of Health. 25c, Minaret and Palm.

Black Control Number on Back
277	A71	5c car & green	15	15
278	A71	10c car & dk vio	15	15
279	A71	25c car & black	55	24
		Nos. 277-279,B25-B26 (5)	2.20	
		Set value		68

> Catalogue values for unused
> stamps in this section, from this
> point to the end of the section, are
> for Never Hinged items.

Mail Transport,
1890 — A72   Herald — A73

Designs: 5c, 50c, 90c, Mail transport, 1890. 10c, 45c, 1p, Mail transport, 1906. 15c, 1.50p, Mail transport, 1913. 35c, 75c, 5p, Mail transport, 1914. 10p, Mail transport, 1918.

1950 Litho. Perf. 10½
280	A72	5c choc & vio bl	15	15
281	A72	10c deep bl & sep	15	15
282	A72	15c grnsh blk & emer	15	15
283	A72	35c pur & gray blk	15	15
284	A72	45c dp car & rose lil	15	15
285	A72	50c emer & dk brn	15	15
286	A72	75c dk vio bl & bl	15	15
287	A72	90c grnsh blk & rose		
		car	15	15
288	A72	1p blk brn & gray	15	15
289	A72	1.50p car & blue	30	15
290	A72	5p blk & vio brn	60	15
291	A72	10p pur & blue	12.00	9.00
		Nos. 280-291,E11 (13)	26.25	19.65

UPU, 75th anniv. (in 1949).
Nos. 280-291 exist imperf. Value $350.

1950 Unwmk. Perf. 10
Frame and Device in Carmine
Black Control Number on Back
292	A73	5c gray blk	15	15
293	A73	10c Old fort	15	15
294	A73	25c Sanatorium	60	30
		Nos. 292-294,B27-B28 (5)	1.72	
		Set value		75

Boar
Hunt — A74

Designs: 10c and 1p, Hunters and hounds. 50c, Boar hunt. 5p, Fishermen. 10p, Moorish fishing boat.

1950, Dec. 30 Perf. 10½x10
Black Control Number on Back
295	A74	5c dk brn & rose vio	15	15
296	A74	10c car & gray	15	15
297	A74	50c grn & sepia	15	15
298	A74	1p bl vio & claret	35	15
299	A74	5p dp cl & bl vio	60	15
300	A74	10p grnsh blk & dp cl	1.75	30
		Nos. 295-300 (6)	3.15	
		Set value		55

Emblem — A75   Worship — A77

Armed
Attack — A76

Designs: 10c, Patients expressing gratitude. 25c, Plane in the Clouds.

Dated "1951"
1951 Litho. Perf. 12
Frame and Device in Carmine
Black Control Number on Back
301	A75	5c green	15	15
302	A75	10c blue vio	15	15
303	A75	25c gray blk	55	30
		Nos. 301-303,B29-B32 (7)	7.99	4.80

Issued to aid anti-tuberculosis work.

1952 Perf. 11

Designs: 10c, Horses on parade. 15c, Holiday procession. 20c, Road to market. 25c, "Brotherhoods." 35c, "Offering." 45c, Soldiers. 50c, On the rooftop. 75c, Teahouse. 90c, Wedding. 1p, Pilgrimage. 5p, Storyteller. 10p, Market corner.

Black Control Number on Back
304	A76	5c dk bl & brn	15	15
305	A76	10c dk brn & lil rose	15	15
306	A76	15c black & emer	15	15
307	A76	20c ol grn & red vio	15	15
308	A76	25c red & lt bl	15	15
309	A76	35c olive & org	15	15
310	A76	45c red & rose red	15	15
311	A76	50c rose car & gray grn	15	15
312	A76	75c pur & ultra	15	15
313	A76	90c dk bl & rose vio	15	15
314	A76	1p dk bl & red brn	15	15
315	A76	5p red & blue	1.40	25
316	A76	10p dk grn & gray blk	2.00	40
		Set value, #304-316,		
		E12	4.10	1.35

1952, Oct. 1 Dated "1952"

Designs: 10c, Distributing alms. 25c, Prickly pear.

Black Control Number on Back
317	A77	5c car & dk ol grn	15	15
318	A77	10c car & dk brn	15	15
319	A77	25c car & deep bl	32	20
		Nos. 317-319,B33-B37 (8)	6.37	3.64

Semi-Postal Types of 1948-49 Dated "1953"

1953 Litho. Perf. 10
Black Control Number on Back
320	SP7	5c shown	15	15
321	SP9	10c like #B26	15	15
322	SP7	25c like #B23	48	32
		Nos. 320-322,B38-B42 (8)	8.00	5.16

Issued to aid anti-tuberculosis work.

A78

1953, Nov. 15
Black Control Number on Back
323	A78	5c red	15	15
324	A78	10c gray green	15	15
		Set value		15

Mountain
Women — A79   Zauia — A80

Designs: 50c and 2.50p, Water carrier. 90c and 2p, Mountaineers and donkey. 1p and 4.50p, Moorish women and child. 10p, Mounted dignitary.

1953, Dec. 15 Photo.
Black Control Number on Back
334	A79	35c grn & rose vio	15	15
335	A79	50c red & green	15	15
336	A79	90c dk bl & org	15	15
337	A79	1p dk brn & grn	15	15
338	A79	1.25p dk grn & car rose	15	15
339	A79	2p dk rose vio & bl	18	18
340	A79	2.50p blk & org	42	20

341 A79 4.50p brt car rose & dk grn 1.75 30
342 A79 10p grn & blk 2.25 55
    Nos. 334-342,E13 (10) 5.50
      Set value 1.65

25th anniv. of Spanish Morocco's first definitive postage stamps.

1954, Nov. 1   Dated "1954"

Designs: 10c, "The Family." 25c, Plane and Spanish coast.

Black Control Number on Back

343 A80 5c car & bl grn 15 15
344 A80 10c car & dk brn 15 15
345 A80 25c car & blue 15 15
    Nos. 343-345,B43-B45 (6) 5.35 4.20

Queen's
Gate — A81

Honor
Guard — A82

1955   Litho.   Perf. 11
Black Control Number on Back
Frames in Black

346 A81 15c shown 15 15
347 A81 25c Saida 15 15
348 A81 80c like #346 15 15
349 A81 1p like #347 15 15
350 A81 15p Ceuta 2.50 65
    Nos. 346-350,E14 (6) 3.30
      Set value 1.00

Perf. 13x12¹/₂
1955, Nov. 8   Photo.   Unwmk.

Designs: 25c, 80c, 3p, Caliph Moulay Hassan ben el-Medi. 30c, 1p, 5p, Caliph and procession. 15p, Coat of arms.

351 A82 15c ol brn & ol 15 15
352 A82 25c lil & dp rose 15 15
353 A82 30c brn blk & Prus grn 15 15
354 A82 70c Prus grn & yel grn 15 15
355 A82 80c ol & ol brn 15 15
356 A82 1p dk bl & redsh brn 15 15
357 A82 1.80p blk & bl vio 18 15
358 A82 3p blue & gray 18 15
359 A82 5p dk grn & brn 1.25 45
Engr.
360 A82 15p red brn & yel grn 2.75 1.65
    Nos. 351-360 (10) 5.26
      Set value 2.55

30th anniv. of accession to throne by Caliph Moulay Hassan ben el-Medi ben Ismail.
Succeeding issues, released under the Kingdom, are listed under Morocco.

SEMI-POSTAL STAMPS

Types of Semi-Postal Stamps of Spain, 1926, Overprinted in Black or Blue

ZONA PROTECTORADO
ESPAÑOL

1926   Unwmk.   Perf. 12¹/₂, 13

B1 SP1 1c orange 2.25 1.65
B2 SP2 2c rose 3.00 1.90
B3 SP3 5c black brn 1.40 75
B4 SP4 10c dark grn 1.40 75
B5 SP1 15c dk vio (Bl) 35 30
B6 SP4 20c vio brn 35 30
B7 SP5 25c deep car 35 30
B8 SP1 30c olive grn 35 30
B9 SP3 40c ultra 15 15
B10 SP2 50c red brn 15 15
B11 SP4 1p vermilion 15 15
B12 SP3 4p bister 35 30
B13 SP1 10p light violet 85 60
    Nos. B1-B13,EB1 (14) 11.85 8.20

See Spain No. B6a for No. B6 without overprint.

Tuberculosis Fund Issues

SP1

SP2

SP3

Perf. 10¹/₂, 11¹/₂x10¹/₂
1946, Sept. 1   Litho.   Unwmk.

B14 SP1 25c + 5c crim & rose vio 15 15
B15 SP2 50c + 10c crimson & blue 24 15
B16 SP3 90c + 10c crim & gray brn 60 24
      Set value 42

Medical Center
SP4

Nurse and
Children
SP5

"Protection"
SP6

Herald
SP7

1947   Perf. 10
B17 SP4 25c + 5c red & violet 15 15
B18 SP5 50c + 10c red & blue 22 15
B19 SP6 90c + 10c red & sepia 55 45

1948, Oct. 1

Designs: No. B21, Protection. No. B22, Sun bath. No. B23, Plane over Ben Karrich.

B20 SP7 50c + 10c car & dk vio 15 15
B21 SP7 90c + 10c car & dk gray 90 35
B22 SP7 2.50p + 50c car & brn 7.00 2.50
B23 SP7 5p + 1p car & vio bl 10.50 3.75

See Nos. 320, 322.

Moulay Hassan ben
el-Medi ben
Ismail — SP8

Flag — SP9

1949, May 15
B24 SP8 50c + 10c lilac rose 22 18
Wedding of the Caliph at Tetuan, June 5.

Tuberculosis Fund Issues

Design: No. B26, Fight with dragon.

1949
Black Control Numbers on Back

B25 SP9 50c + 10 car & brown 35 15
B26 SP9 90c + 10 car & grnsh gray 1.00 24
      Set value 32

See No. 321.

Catalogue values for unused stamps in this section, from this point to the end of the section, are for Never Hinged items.

Crowd at
Fountain of
Life
SP10

Warrior
SP11

Design: 90c+10c, Mohammedan hermit's tomb.

1950, Oct. 1   Litho.   Perf. 10
Black Control Numbers on Back
Frame and Cross in Carmine

B27 SP10 50 + 10c dk brown 22 15
B28 SP10 90 + 10c dk green 60 30
      Set value 36

1951   Unwmk.   Perf. 12

Designs: 90c+10c, Fort. 1p+5p, Port of Salvation. 1.10p+25c, Road to market.

Black Control Numbers on Back

B29 SP11 50c + 10c car & brn 15 15
B30 SP11 90c + 10c car & bl 24 15
B31 SP11 1p + 5p car & gray 4.25 2.50
B32 SP11 1.10p + 25p car & gray 2.50 1.40

See No. B40.

Pilgrimage
SP12

Armed
Horseman in
Action
SP13

Designs: 60c+25c, Palmettos. 90c+10c, Fort. 1.10p+25c, Agave. 5p+2p, Warrior.

1952   Perf. 11
Black Control Numbers on Back

B33 SP12 50 + 10c car & gray 15 15
B34 SP12 60 + 25c car & dk grn 55 32
B35 SP12 90 + 10c car & vio brn 55 32
B36 SP12 1.10p + 25c car & pur 1.25 70
B37 SP12 5p + 2p car & gray 3.25 1.65
    Nos. B33-B37 (5) 5.75 3.14

1953   Perf. 10

Designs: 60c+25c, As No. 276. 1.10p+25c, Plane and clouds.

Black Control Numbers on Back

B38 SP13 50c + 10c car & vio 15 15
B39 A70 60c + 25c car & brn 1.10 65
B40 SP11 90c + 10c car & blk 32 24
B41 SP13 1.10p + 25c car & vio
      brn 1.65 1.00
B42 A73 5p + 2p car & bl 4.00 2.50
    Nos. B38-B42 (5) 7.22 4.54

Stork — SP14

Designs: 50c+10c, Father & Child. 5p+2p, Tomb.

1954   Photo.
Black Control Numbers on Back

B43 SP14 5c + 5c car & rose vio 15 15
B44 SP14 50c + 10c car & gray grn 50 35
B45 SP14 5p + 2p car & gray 4.25 3.25

AIR POST STAMPS

Mosque de Baja
and
Plane — AP1

View of Tetuán and
Plane — AP2

Designs: 10c, Stork of Alcazar. 25c, Shore scene and plane. 40c, Desert tribesmen watching plane. 75c, View of shoreline at Larache. 1p, Arab mailman and plane above. 1.50p, Arab farmers and stork. 2p, Plane at twilight. 3p, Shadow of plane over city.

1938   Unwmk.   Photo.   Perf. 13¹/₂

C1 AP1 5c red brn 15 15
C2 AP1 10c emerald 15 15
C3 AP1 25c crimson 15 15
C4 AP1 40c dull blue 1.50 45
C5 AP2 50c cerise 15 15
C6 AP2 75c ultra 15 15
C7 AP1 1p dark brown 15 15
C8 AP1 1.50p purple 50 30
C9 AP1 2p brown lake 32 15
C10 AP1 3p gray black 1.25 22
    Nos. C1-C10 (10) 4.47
      Set value 1.35

Nos. C1-C10 exist imperf. Value of set, $275. For surcharge see No. C32.

Landscape,
Ketama — AP3

Mosque,
Tangier — AP4

Velez — AP5

Sanjurjo — AP6

The Scott editorial staff regrettably cannot accept requests to identify, authenticate, or appraise stamps and postal markings.

Strait of Gibraltar
AP7   AP8

1942   *Perf. 12½*
C11 AP3   5c deep blue   15   15
C12 AP4   10c org brn   15   15
C13 AP5   15c grnsh blk   15   15
C14 AP6   90c dark rose   15   15
C15 AP7   5p black   1.00   70
       Set value   1.20   94

Nos. C11-C15 exist imperf. Value of set, $90.

1949   Litho.   *Perf. 10*

Designs: 5c, 1.75p, Strait of Gibraltar. 10c, 20c, 3p, Market day. 30c, 4p, Kebira Fortress. 6.50p, Airmail arrival. 8p, Horseman.

C16 AP8   5c vio brn & brt grn   15   15
C17 AP8   10c blk & rose lil   15   15
C18 AP8   30c dk vio bl & grnsh
          gray   15   15
C19 AP8   1.75c car & bl vio   15   15
C20 AP8   3p dk bl & gray   15   15
C21 AP8   4p grnsh blk & car rose   30   18
C22 AP8   6.50p brt grn & brn   1.00   22
C23 AP8   8p rose lil & bl vio   1.75   38
       Set value   3.45   1.05

Nos. C16-C23 exist imperf. Value of set, $150.

> Catalogue values for unused stamps in this section, from this point to the end of the section, are for Never Hinged items.

Road to
Tetuan
AP9

Designs: 4p, Arrival of mail from Spain. 8p, Greeting plane. 16p, Shadow of plane.

1952   *Perf. 11*
Black Frames and Inscriptions
Black Control Numbers on Back
C24 AP9   2p brt bl   15   15
C25 AP9   4p scarlet   25   15
C26 AP9   8p dk ol grn   40   22
C27 AP9   16p vio brn   2.00   85

Part of the proceeds was used toward the establishment of a postal museum at Tetuan.

Plane over Boat — AP10

Designs: 60c, Mosques, Sidi Saidi. 1.10p, Plowing. 4.50p, Fortress, Xauen.

1953   *Perf. 10*
C28 AP10   35c dp bl & car rose   15   15
C29 AP10   60c dk car & sl grn   15   15
C30 AP10   1.10p dp bl & blk   22   15
C31 AP10   4.50p dk car & dk brn   85   30
       Set value   52

Nos. C28-C31 exist imperf. Value of set, $75.

No. C6 Surcharged with New Value in Black

50   **50**
Type I   Type II

1953   *Perf. 13½*
C32 AP2 50c on 75c ultra (I)   45   15
 a.   50c on 75c ultra (II)   45   15
 b.   Vert. gutter pair, types I and II   2.50

Sheets of 2 panes, 25 stamps each, with gutter between. Upper pane surcharged type I, lower type II.

AIR POST SEMI-POSTAL STAMPS

No. 150 Surcharged in Black

18-7-36

= 0'25 + 2'00 =

1936   Unwmk.   *Perf. 14*
CB1 A12 25c + 2p on 25c   9.00   4.00
 a.   Bars at right omitted   30.00   30.00
 b.   Blue surcharge   21.00   10.50

25c was for postage, 2p for air post.

Nos. C1-C10 surcharged "Lucha Antituberculosa," a Lorraine cross and surtax are stated to be bogus.

Crowd at
Palace — SPAP1

1949, May 15   Unwmk.   *Perf. 10*
CB2 SPAP1 1p + 10c gray black   65   30
Wedding of the Caliph at Tetuan, June 5.

SPECIAL DELIVERY STAMPS

Special Delivery Stamp of Spain Overprinted in Blue

MARRUECOS

1914   Unwmk.   *Perf. 14*
E1   SD1 20c red   2.00   1.00

Special Delivery Stamp of Spain Overprinted in Blue

PROTECTORADO ESPAÑOL EN MARRUECOS

1915
E2   SD1 20c red   1.50   75
For bisected surcharge see No. 68.

Special Delivery Stamp of Spain Overprinted in Blue

ZONA DE PROTECTORADO ESPAÑOL EN MARRUECOS

1923
E3   SD1 20c red   6.00   2.75

Mounted
Courier — SD2

1928   Engr.   *Perf. 14, 14½*
E4   SD2 20c black   2.00   1.10
For surcharge see No. 168.

Moorish   Mounted
Postman — SD3   Courier — SD4

1935   Photo.   *Perf. 14*
Green Control Number on Back
E5   SD3 20c vermilion   85   15
See No. E9.

1937   *Perf. 13½*
E6   SD4 20c bright carmine   15   15
1st Year of the Spanish Civil War.
For surcharge see No. E10.

Spain No. E14 Overprinted in Black

MARRUECOS

1938   *Perf. 10*
E7   SD7 20c vermilion   1.10   20

Arab Postman   Airmail 1935
SD5   SD6

1940   Photo.   *Perf. 11½x11*
E8   SD5 25c scarlet   25   15
"ZONA" printed on back in black.

Type of 1935
1940   Litho.   *Perf. 10*
E9   SD3 20c black brown   1.25
No. E9 was prepared but not issued.

No. E6 Surcharged with New Value, Bars and

1940   *Perf. 13½*
E10   SD4 25c on 20c brt car   6.50   6.50
4th anniversary of Spanish Civil War.

> Catalogue values for unused stamps in this section, from this point to the end of the section, are for Never Hinged items.

1950   Unwmk. Litho.   *Perf. 10½*
E11   SD6 25c carmine & gray   12.00   9.00
UPU, 75th anniv. (in 1949).

Moorish
Postrider
SD7

1952   *Perf. 11*
Black Control Number on Back
E12   SD7 25c car & rose car   15   15

Rider with   Gate of
Special   Tangier
Delivery Mail   SD9
SD8

1953   Photo.   *Perf. 10*
Black Control Number on Back
E13   SD8 25c dk bl & car rose   15   15
25th anniv. of Spanish Morocco's first definitive postage stamps.

1955   Litho.   *Perf. 11*
Black Control Number on Back
E14   SD9 2p violet & black   20   15

SEMI-POSTAL SPECIAL DELIVERY STAMP

Type of Semi-Postal Special Delivery Stamp of Spain, 1926, Overprinted like #B1-B13
1926   Unwmk.   *Perf. 12½, 13*
EB1 SPSD1 20c ultra & black   75   60

POSTAL TAX STAMPS

General Francisco Franco
PT1   PT3

Soldiers
PT2

1937-39 Unwmk. Photo.   *Perf. 12½*
RA1 PT1 10c sepia   32   15
 a.   Sheet of 4, imperf.   1.75   1.25
RA2 PT1 10c copper brn ('38)   32   15
 a.   Sheet of 4, imperf.   1.75   1.25
RA3 PT1 10c blue ('39)   32   15
 a.   Sheet of 4, imperf.   1.75   1.25
       Set value   20

The tax was used for the disabled soldiers in North Africa.

1941   Litho.   *Perf. 13½*
RA4 PT2 10c brt grn   1.50   15
RA5 PT2 10c rose pink   1.50   15
RA6 PT2 10c henna brn   1.50   15
RA7 PT2 10c ultra   1.50   15

The tax was used for the disabled soldiers in North Africa.

1943 Photo. Perf. 10

RA8	PT3	10c chalky blue	2.50	15
RA9	PT3	10c slate blue	2.50	15
RA10	PT3	10c dl gray brn	2.50	15
RA11	PT3	10c blue violet	2.50	15
		Set value		42

1944 Perf. 12

RA12	PT3	10c dp mag & brn	2.50	15
RA13	PT3	10c dp org & dk grn	2.50	15
		Set value		24

1946 Litho.

RA14	PT3	10c ultra & brown	2.50	15
RA15	PT3	10c gray blk & rose lil	2.50	15
		Set value		24

TANGIER

For the International City of Tangier
Seville-Barcelona Issue of Spain, 1929,
Overprinted in Blue or Red

TANGER

1929 Perf. 11

L1	A52	5c rose lake	15	15
L2	A53	10c green (R)	15	15
L3	A53	15c Prus blue (R)	15	15
L4	A51	20c purple (R)	15	15
L5	A52	25c brt rose	15	15
L6	A52	30c black brn	15	15
L7	A53	40c dk blue (R)	20	18
L8	A51	50c deep org	20	18
L9	A52	1p blue blk (R)	2.00	1.25
L10	A53	4p deep rose	4.75	3.25
L11	A53	10p brown	7.00	4.25
		Nos. L1-L11 (11)	15.05	10.01

Overprints of 1937-39
The following overprints on stamps of Spain exist in black or in red:
"TANGER" vertically on Nos. 517-518, 522-523, 528, 532, 534, 539-543, 549.
"Correo Espanol Tanger" horizontally or vertically in three lines on Nos. 540, 592-597 (gray paper), 598-601.
"Tanger" horizontally on Nos. 539-541, 592-601.
"Correo Tanger" horizontally in two lines on five consular stamps.

Woman — A1

Palm Tree — A2

Man — A3

Old Map of Tangier — A4

Tangier Street — A5

Moroccan Women — A6

Head of Moor — A7

Perf. 9½x10½, 12½x13 (1c, 2c, 10c, 20c)

1948-51 Photo. Unwmk.

L12	A1	1c blue grn ('51)	15	15
L13	A1	2c red org ('51)	15	15
		Engr.		
L14	A2	5c vio brn ('49)	15	15
L15	A3	10c deep blue ('51)	15	15
L16	A3	20c gray ('51)	15	15
L17	A2	25c green ('51)	15	15
L18	A4	30c dk slate grn	24	15
L19	A5	45c car rose	24	15
L20	A6	50c dp claret	24	15
L21	A7	75c deep blue	48	15
L22	A7	90c green	35	15
L23	A4	1.35p org ver	1.50	18
L24	A6	2p purple	2.75	18
L25	A5	10p dk grnsh bl ('49)	3.25	35
		Nos. L12-L25,LE1 (15)	10.55	
		Set value		1.50

Nos. L18-L25, LE1 exist imperf. Value, set $250.

TANGIER SEMI-POSTAL STAMPS

Types of Semi-Postal Stamps of Spain, 1926, Overprinted

CORREO ESPAÑOL TANGER

1926 Perf. 12½, 13

LB1	SP1	1c orange	1.50	1.40
LB2	SP2	2c rose	1.50	1.40
LB3	SP3	5c black brn	75	65
LB4	SP4	10c dk green	75	65
LB5	SP1	15c dk violet	35	35
LB6	SP2	20c violet brn	35	35
LB7	SP5	25c dp carmine	35	35
LB8	SP3	30c olive grn	35	35
LB9	SP3	40c ultra	15	15
LB10	SP5	50c red brn	15	15
LB11	SP4	1p vermilion	18	18
LB12	SP3	4p bister	18	18
LB13	SP5	10p lt violet	75	65
		Nos. LB1-LB13,LE1 (14)	8.06	7.46

TANGIER AIR POST STAMPS

Overprints of 1939
The following overprints on stamps of Spain exist in black or in red:
"Correo Aereo Tanger" in two lines on Nos. 539-541, 596 (gray paper), 600, C72B.
"Via Aerea Tanger" in three lines on Nos. 539-540, 592-597 (gray paper), 599, 601, E14.
"Correo Aereo Tanger" in three lines on four consular stamps.
"Correo Espanol Tanger" in three lines on No. C72B.
"Tanger" on No. C72B.

Plane over Shore — AP1

Twin-Engine Plane — AP2

Passenger Plane in Flight — AP3

Perf. 11x11½, 11½

1949-50 Engr. Unwmk.

LC1	AP1	20c violet brn ('50)	24	15
LC2	AP2	25c bright red	24	15
LC3	AP3	35c dull green	24	15
LC4	AP1	1p violet ('50)	75	15
LC5	AP2	2p deep blue	1.40	22
LC6	AP3	10p brown violet	2.50	75
		Nos. LC1-LC6 (6)	5.37	
		Set value		1.20

Nos. LC1, LC4-LC6 exist imperf. Value $50 each.

TANGIER SPECIAL DELIVERY STAMP

Arab Postrider — SD1

1949 Unwmk. Engr. Perf. 13

LE1	SD1	25c red	60	20

TANGIER SEMI-POSTAL SPECIAL DELIVERY STAMP

Types of Semi-Postal Special Delivery Stamp of Spain, 1926, Overprinted like #LB1-LB13

1926 Unwmk. Perf. 12½, 13

LEB1	SPSD1	20c ultra & black	75	65

TETUAN

Stamps of Spanish Offices in Morocco, 1903-09, Handstamped in Black, Blue or Violet

1908 Unwmk. Imperf.

1	A21	¼c bl grn	8.25	5.25
		Perf. 14		
2	A35	2c bister brn	90.00	50.00
3	A35	5c green	65.00	22.50
4	A35	10c rose red	85.00	22.50
5	A35	20c grnsh blk	200.00	90.00
6	A35	25c blue	75.00	27.50
		Nos. 1-6 (6)	523.25	217.75

Same Handstamp On Stamps of Spain, 1877 and 1900-05, in Black, Blue or Violet

1908 Imperf.

7	A21	¼c dp grn	6.00	2.75
		Perf. 14		
8	A35	2c bister brn	22.50	8.00
9	A35	5c dk grn	27.50	13.00
10	A35	10c rose red	27.50	13.00
11	A35	15c purple	35.00	18.00
12	A35	20c grnsh blk	115.00	90.00
13	A35	25c blue	42.00	22.50
14	A35	30c blue grn	125.00	52.50
15	A35	40c olive bister	125.00	90.00
		Nos. 7-15 (9)	525.50	309.75

Counterfeits of this overprint are plentiful.

SPANISH SAHARA
(Spanish Western Sahara)

LOCATION — Northwest Africa, bordering on the Atlantic
GOVT. — Former Spanish possession.
AREA — 102,703 sq. mi.
POP. — 76,425 (1970)
CAPITAL — Aaiún.

Spanish Sahara is a subdivision of Spanish West Africa. It includes the colony of Rio de Oro and the territory of Saguiet el Hamra. Spanish Sahara was formerly known as Spanish Western Sahara, which superseded the older title of Rio de Oro.

In 1976, Spanish Sahara was divided between Morocco and Mauritania.

100 Centimos = 1 Peseta

Catalogue values for unused stamps in this country are for Never Hinged items, beginning with Scott 105 in the regular postage section, Scott B58 in the semi-postal section, Scott C17 in the airpost section, and Scott E2 in the special delivery section.

Tuareg and Camel — A1

1924 Unwmk. Typo. Perf. 13
Control Number on Back

1	A1	5c blue grn	1.25	30
2	A1	10c gray grn	1.25	30
3	A1	15c turq bl	1.25	30
4	A1	20c dark vio	1.25	38
5	A1	25c red	1.25	38
6	A1	30c red brn	1.25	38
7	A1	40c dark bl	1.25	38
8	A1	50c orange	1.25	38
9	A1	60c violet	1.25	38
10	A1	1p rose	5.75	1.65
11	A1	4p chocolate	27.50	9.00
12	A1	10p claret	57.50	24.00
		Nos. 1-12 (12)	102.00	37.83

Nos. 1-12 were for use in La Aguera and Rio de Oro.
A set of 10, similar to Nos. 3-12, exists with perf. 10 and no control number except on 50c.
For overprints see Nos. 24-35.

Seville-Barcelona Issue of Spain, 1929 Overprinted in Blue or Red

SAHARA

1929 Perf. 11

13	A52	5c rose lake	15	15
14	A53	10c green (R)	15	15
15	A53	15c Prus bl (R)	15	15
16	A51	20c purple (R)	15	15
17	A50	25c brt rose	15	15
18	A52	30c blk brn	15	15
19	A53	40c dk blue (R)	16	15
20	A51	50c dp org	16	15
21	A52	1p blk (R)	90	55
22	A53	4p dp rose	5.50	4.25
23	A53	10p brown	11.00	7.50
		Nos. 13-23 (11)	18.62	13.50

Stamps of 1924 Overprinted in Red or Blue

República Española

1931 Perf. 13

24	A1	5c bl grn (R)	32	20
25	A1	10c gray grn (R)	32	20
26	A1	15c turq bl (R)	32	20
27	A1	20c dk vio (R)	32	20
28	A1	25c red	40	20
29	A1	30c red brn	40	20
30	A1	40c dk bl (R)	1.65	32
31	A1	50c orange	1.65	65
32	A1	60c violet	1.65	65
33	A1	1p rose	1.65	65
34	A1	4p chocolate	18.00	6.00
35	A1	10p claret	32.50	10.00
		Nos. 24-35 (12)	59.18	19.47

The stamps of the 1931 issue exist with the overprint reading upward, downward or horizontally.

Stamps of Spain, 1936-40, Overprinted in Carmine or Blue

SAHARA ESPAÑOL

1941-46 Unwmk. Imperf.

36	A159	1c green	1.10	1.00
		Perf. 10 to 11		
37	A160	2c org brn (Bl)	1.10	1.00
38	A161	5c gray brn	35	35
39	A161	10c dk car (Bl)	1.10	1.00

40	A161	15c dk grn	35	35
41	A166	20c brt vio	35	35
42	A166	25c dp claret	70	52
43	A166	30c lt blue	70	75
44	A166	40c Prus grn	35	35
45	A166	50c indigo	3.50	75
46	A166	70c blue	2.50	1.25
47	A166	1p gray blk	11.00	1.75
48	A166	2p dl brn	60.00	37.50
49	A166	4p dl rose (Bl)	130.00	70.00
50	A166	10p lt brn	350.00	130.00
	Nos. 36-50 (15)		563.10	246.92

Counterfeit overprints exist.

Dorcas Gazelles — A2

Designs: 2c, 20c, 45c, 3p, Caravan. 5c, 75c, 10p, Camel troops.

1943   Unwmk.   Perf. 12½

51	A2	1c brn & lil rose	15	15
52	A2	2c yel brn & sl bl	15	15
53	A2	5c magenta & vio	15	15
54	A2	15c sl grn & grn	15	15
55	A2	20c vio & red brn	15	15
56	A2	40c rose vio & vio	15	15
57	A2	45c brn vio & red	15	15
58	A2	75c indigo & bl	15	15
59	A2	1p red & brn	65	65
60	A2	3p bl vio & sl grn	1.25	1.25
61	A2	10p blk brn & blk	16.00	14.00
	Nos. 51-61,E1 (12)		19.75	17.75

Nos. 51-61, E1 exist imperf. Value for set, $100.

Gen. Franco and Desert Scene — A5

1951   Photo.   Perf. 12½x13

62	A5	50c deep orange	15	15
63	A5	1p chocolate	35	28
64	A5	5p blue green	30.00	12.50

Visit of Gen. Francisco Franco, 1950.

Allegorical Figure and Globe — A6

Woman Musician — A7

1953, Mar. 2   Perf. 13x12½

65	A6	5c red orange	15	15
66	A6	35c dk slate grn	15	15
67	A6	60c brown	25	15
		Set value	36	22

75th anniv. of the founding of the Royal Geographical Society.

1953, June 1

Design: 60c, Man musician.

68	A7	15c olive gray	15	15
69	A7	60c brown	20	15
		Set value	26	15

See Nos. B25-B26.

Orange Scorpionfish A8

Fish: 60c, Banded sargo.

1953, Nov. 23   Perf. 12½x13

70	A8	15c dk olive grn	15	15
71	A8	60c orange	25	15
		Set value		20

Colonial Stamp Day. See Nos. B27-B28.

Hurdlers A9

Runner — A10

1954, June 1   Perf. 12½x13, 13x12½

72	A9	15c gray green	15	15
73	A10	60c brown	15	15
		Set value		15

See Nos. B29-B30.

Atlantic Flyingfish A11

1954, Nov. 23   Perf. 12½x13

74	A11	15c shown	15	15
75	A11	60c Gilthead	25	15
		Set value		15

Colonial Stamp Day. See Nos. B31-B32.

Emilio Bonelli A12

1955, June 1   Photo.   Unwmk.

76	A12	50c olive gray	15	15

Birth cent. of Emilio Bonelli, explorer. See Nos. B33-B34.

Scimitar-horned Oryx — A13

1955, Nov. 23

77	A13	70c green	25	15

Colonial Stamp Day. See Nos. B35-B36.

Antirrhinum Romosissimum — A14

Design: 50c, Sesiviun portulacastrum.

Arms of Aaiun and Camel Rider — A15

1956, June 1

78	A14	20c bluish green	15	15
79	A14	50c brown		15

See Nos. B37-B38.

1956, Nov. 23   Perf. 12½x13

80	A15	70c olive grn & sepia	15	15

Colonial Stamp Day. See Nos. B39-B40.

Dromedaries A16

Golden Eagle A17

Designs: 15c, 80c, Ostrich. 50c, 1.80p, Mountain gazelle.

1957, Apr. 10   Perf. 13x12½

81	A16	5c purple	15	15
82	A16	15c bister	15	15
83	A16	50c dk olive	15	15
84	A16	70c yel green	95	15
85	A16	80c blue green	95	15
86	A16	1.80p lilac rose	95	22
	Nos. 81-86 (6)		3.30	
		Set value		60

1957, June 1   Photo.   Unwmk.

87	A17	70c dark green	25	15

See Nos. B41-B42.

Striped Hyena — A18

Design: 70c, Striped Hyena, horiz.

Perf. 13x12½, 12½x13
1957, Nov. 23

88	A18	20c slate green	15	15
89	A18	70c yellowish green	20	15
		Set value	26	15

Stamp Day. See Nos. B43-B44.

Don Quixote and the Lion — A19

Cervantes A20

Gray Heron A21

1958, June 1   Perf. 12½x13, 13x12½

90	A19	20c bis brn & grn	15	15
91	A20	70c dk grn & yel grn	15	15
		Set value	20	15

See Nos. B48-B49.

Cervantes Type of 1958

Designs: 20c, Actor as "Peribanez," by Lope de Vega. 70c, Lope de Vega.

1959, June   Photo.   Perf. 13x12½

92	A20	20c lt grn & brn	15	15
93	A20	70c yel grn & sl grn	15	15
		Set value	20	15

Issued to promote child welfare. See Nos. B53-B54.

1959, Oct. 15   Perf. 13x12½

Birds: 50c, 1.50p, 5p, Sparrowhawk. 75c, 2p, 10p, Sea gull.

94	A21	25c dl vio	15	15
95	A21	50c dk olive	15	15
96	A21	75c dk brown	15	15
97	A21	1p red org	15	15
98	A21	1.50p brt grn	15	15
99	A21	2p brt red lil	75	15
100	A21	3p blue	75	15
101	A21	5p red brn	1.40	15
102	A21	10p olive grn	6.50	3.00
	Nos. 94-102 (9)		10.15	
		Set value		3.50

Scene from "The Pilferer Don Pablos" by Quevedo — A22

Francisco Gomez de Quevedo A23

1960, June   Perf. 13x12½, 12½x13

103	A22	35c slate green	15	15
104	A23	80c Prussian green	15	15
		Set value	24	15

Francisco Gomez de Quevedo, writer. See Nos. B58-B59.

> Catalogue values for unused stamps in this section, from this point to the end of the section, are for Never Hinged items.

Houbara Bustard — A24

Map of Spanish Sahara — A25

Gen. Franco and Camel Rider — A26

Design: 50c, 1p, 2p, 5p, Doves.

1961, Apr. 18   Photo.   Perf. 13x12½

105	A24	25c blue vio	15	15
106	A24	50c olive gray	15	15
107	A24	75c brn vio	15	15
108	A24	1p org ver	15	15
109	A24	1.50p blue grn	15	15
110	A24	2p magenta	90	15
111	A24	3p dark blue	1.00	15

112	A24	5p red brn	1.25	35
113	A24	10p olive	3.00	1.10

Nos. 105-113 (9)   6.90
Set value   1.80

1961, Oct. 1   *Perf. 13x12½, 12½x13*

Design: 70c, Chapel of Aaiun.

114	A25	25c gray vio	15	15
115	A26	50c ol brn	15	15
116	A25	70c brt grn	15	15
117	A26	1p red org	15	15

Set value   45   20

25th anniv. of the nomination of Gen. Francisco Franco as Chief of State.

Neurada
Procumbres
A27

Clock Fish
A28

Designs: 50c, 1.50p, 10p, Anabasis articulata, flower. 70c, 2p, Euphorbia resinifera, cactus.

1962, Feb. 26   *Perf. 13x12½*

118	A27	25c blk vio	15	15
119	A27	50c dark brn	15	15
120	A27	70c brt green	15	15
121	A27	1p org ver	15	15
122	A27	1.50p blue grn	32	15
123	A27	2p red lilac	1.10	15
124	A27	3p slate	1.75	28
125	A27	10p olive	4.00	95

Nos. 118-125 (8)   7.77
Set value   1.50

Perf. 13x12½, 12½x13

1962, July 10   Photo.

Design: 50c, Avia fish, horiz.

126	A28	25c vio black	15	15
127	A28	50c dk green	15	15
128	A28	1p org brown	20	15

Set value   30   16

Goats — A29

Stamp Day: 35c, Sheep.

1962, Nov. 23   *Perf. 12½x13*

129	A29	15c yel green	15	15
130	A29	35c magenta	15	15
131	A29	1p org brown	20	15

Set value   30   15

Seville Cathedral
Tower — A30

1963, Jan. 29   *Perf. 13x12½*

132	A30	50c olive	15	15
133	A30	1p brown org	15	15

Set value   15

Issued to help Seville flood victims.

Camel
Riders — A31

Hands Releasing
Dove and
Arms — A32

Design: 50c, Tuareg and camel.

1963, June 1   Unwmk.

134	A31	25c deep vio	15	15
135	A31	50c gray	15	15
136	A31	1p orange red	15	15

Set value   35   20

Issued for child welfare.

1963, July 12

137	A32	50c Prussian grn	15	15
138	A32	1p orange brn	15	15

Set value   20   15

Issued for Barcelona flood relief.

John
Dory — A33

Fish: 50c, Plain bonito, vert.

Perf. 12½x13, 13x12½

1964, Mar. 6   Photo.

139	A33	25c purple	15	15
140	A33	50c ol grn	15	15
141	A33	1p brn red	15	15

Set value   25   15

Issued for Stamp Day 1963.

Moth and
Flowers
A34

Design: 50c, Two moths, vert.

Perf. 12½x13, 13x12½

1964, June 1   Unwmk.

142	A34	25c dull vio	15	15
143	A34	50c brn blk	15	15
144	A34	1p org red	15	15

Set value   35   15

Issued for child welfare.

Camel Rider
and
Microphone
A35

Squirrel
A36

Designs: 50c, 1.50p, 3p, Boy with flute and camels. 70c, 2p, 10p, Woman with drum.

1964, Sept.   Photo.   *Perf. 13x12½*

145	A35	25c dull pur	15	15
146	A35	50c olive	15	15
147	A35	70c green	15	15
148	A35	1p dl red brn	15	15
149	A35	1.50p brt grn	15	15
150	A35	2p Prus grn	15	15

151	A35	3p dark blue	28	15
152	A35	10p car lake	1.75	90

Set value   2.45   1.40

1964, Nov. 23   Unwmk.

Stamp Day: 1p, Squirrel's head, horiz.

153	A36	50c ol gray	15	15
154	A36	1p brn car	15	15
155	A36	1.50p green	15	15

Set value   35   16

Tuareg
Girl — A37

Wellhead and
Camel
Rider — A38

25 Years of Peace: 1p, Physician examining patient, horiz.

Perf. 13x12½, 12½x13

1965, Feb. 22   Photo.

156	A37	50c blk brn	15	15
157	A38	1p dk red	15	15
158	A38	1.50p dp bl	15	15

Set value   35   16

Anthia
Sexmaculata
A39

Design: 1p, 3p, Blepharopsis mendica, vert.

Perf. 12½x13, 13x12½

1965, June 1   Photo.   Unwmk.

159	A39	50c slate blue	15	15
160	A39	1p blue grn	15	15
161	A39	1.50p brown	15	15
162	A39	3p dark blue	1.25	70

Set value   1.40   86

Issued for child welfare.

Basketball
A40

Arms and
Camels
A41

1965, Nov. 23   *Perf. 13x12½*

163	A40	50c rose claret	15	15
164	A41	1p deep magenta	15	15
165	A40	1.50p slate blue	15	15

Set value   35   16

Issued for Stamp Day.

Ship "Rio de
Oro" — A42

Design: 1.50p, S.S. Fuerte Ventura.

1966, June 1   Photo.   *Perf. 12½x13*

166	A42	50c olive	15	15
167	A42	1p dk red brn	15	15
168	A42	1.50p blue grn	15	15

Set value   35   16

Issued for child welfare.

Ocean
Sunfish — A43

A44

Designs: 10c, 1.50p, Bigeye tuna, horiz.

1966, Nov. 23   Photo.   *Perf. 13*

169	A43	10c bl gray & cit	15	15
170	A43	40c slate & pink	15	15
171	A43	1.50p brn & olive	15	15
172	A43	4p rose vio & gray	25	15

Set value   40   30

Issued for Stamp Day.

1967, June 1   Photo.   *Perf. 13*

Designs: 40c, 4p, Flower and leaves.

173	A44	10c blk, ocher & gray grn	15	15
174	A44	40c emer & lilac	15	15
175	A44	1.50p dk grn & yel grn	15	15
176	A44	4p brt bl & org	25	15

Set value   40   30

Issued for child welfare.

Aaiun Harbor
A45

Design: 4p, Villa Cisneros Harbor.

1967, Sept. 28   Photo.   *Perf. 12½x13*

177	A45	1.50p brt bl & red brn	15	15
178	A45	4p brt bl & bis brn	20	15

Set value   26   16

Modernization of harbor installations.

Ruddy
Sheldrake — A46

Stamp Day: 1.50p, Flamingo, vert. 3.50p, Rufous bush robin.

1967, Nov. 23   Photo.   *Perf. 13*

179	A46	1p bis brn & grn	15	15
180	A46	1.50p brt rose & gray	15	15
181	A46	3.50p brn red & sep	30	20

Set value   42   32

Scorpio — A47

Mailman — A48

Zodiac Issue

Signs of the Zodiac: 1.50p, Aries. 2.50p, Virgo.

1968, Apr. 25   Photo.   *Perf. 13*

182	A47	1p brt mag, *lt yel*	15	15
183	A47	1.50p brn, *pink*	15	15
184	A47	2.50p dk vio, *yel*	30	20

Set value   42   32

Issued for child welfare.

1968, Nov. Photo. *Perf. 13x12½*

Stamp Day: 1p, Post horn, pigeon, letter and Spain No. 1. 1.50p, Letter, canceller and various stamps of Spain and Ifni.

185 A48	1p dp lil rose & dk bl	15	15
186 A48	1.50p green & sl grn	15	15
187 A48	2.50p dp org & dk bl	25	15
	Set value	36	26

Dorcas Gazelle A49

Designs: 1.50p, Doe and fawn. 2.50p, Gazelle and camel. 6p, Leaping gazelle.

1969, June 1 Photo. *Perf. 13*

188 A49	1p gldn brn & blk	15	15
189 A49	1.50p gldn brn & blk	15	15
190 A49	2.50p gldn brn & blk	15	15
191 A49	6p gldn brn & blk	40	30
	Set value	65	46

Child welfare. See Nos. 196-199, 209-212.

Woman Playing Drum — A50

Stamp Day: 1.50p, Man with flute. 2p, Drum and camel rider, horiz. 25p, Flute, horiz.

1969, Nov. 23 Photo. *Perf. 13*

192 A50	50c brn red & lt ol	15	15
193 A50	1.50p dk bl grn & grnsh gray	15	15
194 A50	2p ind & bis brn	15	15
195 A50	25p brn & lt bl grn	1.40	45
	Set value	1.55	62

Animal Type of 1969

Fennec: 50c, Sitting. 2p, Running. 2.50p, Head. 6p, Vixen and pups.

1970, June 1 Photo. *Perf. 13*

196 A49	50c dp bis & blk	15	15
197 A49	2p org brn & blk	15	15
198 A49	2.50p dp bis & blk	20	15
199 A49	6p dp bis & blk	32	15
	Set value	65	32

Issued for child welfare.

Grammodes Boisdeffrei — A51

Designs: 1p, like 50c. 2p, 5p, Danaus chrysippus. 8p, Celerio euphorbiae.

1970, Nov. 23 Photo. *Perf. 12½*

200 A51	50c red & multi	15	15
201 A51	1p car & multi	15	15
202 A51	2p grn & multi	15	15
203 A51	5p Prus bl & multi	30	15
204 A51	8p dk bl & multi	45	20
	Set value	90	45

Issued for Stamp Day. See Nos. 233-234.

Gazelle, Arms of Aaiun — A52   Smara Mosque — A53

Designs: 2p, Inn, horiz. 5p, Assembly building, Aaiun, horiz.

Perf. 12½x13, 13x12½

1971, June 1 Photo.

205 A52	1p multi	15	15
206 A53	2p gray grn & ol	15	15
207 A53	5p lt bl & lt red brn	15	15
208 A53	25p lt bl & grnsh gray	85	18
	Set value	1.08	35

Issued for child welfare.

Animal Type of 1969

Birds: 1.50p, 2p, Trumpeter bullfinch. 5p, Cream-colored courser. 10p, Lanner (falcon).

1971, Nov. 23 Photo. *Perf. 12½*

209 A49	1.50p blk & multi	15	15
210 A49	2p bl & multi	15	15
211 A49	5p grn & multi	15	15
212 A49	24p blk & multi	85	20
	Set value	1.10	38

Stamp Day.

Saharan Woman — A55   Tuareg Woman — A56

Designs: 1.50p, 2p, Saharan man. 5p, as 1p. 8p, 10p, Man's head. 12p, Woman. 15p, Soldier. 24p, Dancer.

1972, Feb. 18 Photo. *Perf. 13*

213 A55	1p bl, pink & brn	15	15
214 A55	1.50p brn, lil & blk	15	15
215 A55	2p grn, buff & sep	15	15
216 A55	5p grn, pur & vio brn	15	15
217 A55	8p blk, lt grn & vio	22	15
218 A55	10p blk, gray & Prus bl	35	15
219 A55	12p multi	42	20
220 A55	15p multi	52	24
221 A55	24p multi	1.10	40
	Nos. 213-221 (9)	3.21	
	Set value		1.25

1972, June 1 Photo. *Perf. 13*

222 A56	8p shown	32	15
223 A56	12p Tuareg man	48	20
	Set value		28

Child welfare.

Mother and Child — A57

1972, Nov. 23 Photo. *Perf. 13*

224 A57	4p shown	24	15
225 A57	15p Saharan man	55	24
	Set value		30

Stamp Day. See No. 229.

Dunes A58

Design: 7p, Old Market and Gate, Aaiun.

1973, June 1 Photo. *Perf. 13*

226 A58	2p multi	15	15
227 A58	7p multi	30	15
	Set value	36	20

Child welfare.

Type of 1972 and

View of Villa Cisneros A59

1973, Nov. 23 Photo. *Perf. 13*

228 A59	2p shown	15	15
229 A57	7p Tuareg man	30	15
	Set value	36	20

Stamp Day.

UPU Monument, Bern — A60   Gate, Smara Mosque — A61

1974, May Photo. *Perf. 13*

230 A60	15p multi	65	20

Centenary of the Universal Postal Union.

1974, May

Design: 2p, Court and Minaret, Villa Cisneros Mosque.

231 A61	1p multi	15	15
232 A61	2p multi	15	15
	Set value		20

Child welfare.

Animal Type of 1970

1974, Nov. Photo. *Perf. 13*

233 A51	2p Desert eagle owl	15	15
234 A51	5p Lappet-faced vulture	20	15
	Set value		20

Stamp Day.

Espana 75 Emblem, Spain No. 1084 — A63   Old Man — A65

Children A64

1975, Apr. 4 Photo. *Perf. 13*

235 A63	8p olive, blk & bl	25	15

Espana 75 Intl. Phil. Exhib., Madrid, Apr. 4-13.

1975 Photo. *Perf. 13*

236 A64	1.50p shown	15	15
237 A64	3p Children's village	15	15
	Set value	20	15

Child welfare.

1975, Nov. 7 Photo. *Perf. 13*

238 A65	3p blk, lt grn & mar	20	15

SEMI-POSTAL STAMPS

Red Cross Issue
Types of Semi-Postal Stamps of Spain, 1926, Overprinted

SAHARA ESPAÑOL

1926 Unwmk. *Perf. 12½, 13*

B1	SP3	5c black brn	2.00	1.65
B2	SP4	10c dark grn	2.00	1.65
B3	SP1	15c dark vio	90	70
B4	SP4	20c vio brn	90	70
B5	SP5	25c deep car	90	70
B6	SP1	30c olive grn	90	70
B7	SP3	40c ultra	15	15
B8	SP2	50c red brown	15	15
B9	SP5	60c myrtle grn	15	15
B10	SP4	1p vermilion	15	15
B11	SP3	4p bister	65	60
B12	SP5	10p light vio	1.65	1.10
		Nos. B1-B12 (12)	10.50	8.40

See Spain No. B6a for No. B4 without overprint.

Shepherd and Lamb — SP1   Dromedary and Calf — SP2

1950, Oct. 20 Photo. *Perf. 13x12½*

B13	SP1	50c + 10c brown	20	15
B14	SP1	1p + 25c rose brn	9.25	4.75
B15	SP1	6.50p + 1.65p dk gray grn	4.50	1.65

The surtax was for child welfare.

1951, Nov. 23

B16	SP2	5c + 5c brown	15	15
B17	SP2	10c + 5 red org	15	15
B18	SP2	60c + 15c olive brn	24	15
		Set value	36	20

Colonial Stamp Day, Nov. 23.

Child and Protector SP3   Ostrich SP4

1952, June 1
B19	SP3	5c + 5c brown	15	15
B20	SP3	50c + 10c gray	15	15
B21	SP3	2p + 30c blue	1.50	75

The surtax was for child welfare.

1952, Nov. 23   *Perf. 12½*
B22	SP4	5c + 5c brn	15	15
B23	SP4	10c + 5c brn car	15	15
B24	SP4	60c + 15c dk grn	30	15
		Set value	50	35

Colonial Stamp Day, Nov. 23.

Musician Type of Regular Issue
1953, June 1   *Perf. 13x12½*
B25	A7	5c + 5c like #68	15	15
B26	A7	10c + 5c like #69	15	15
		Set value	15	15

The surtax was for child welfare.

Fish Type of Regular Issue
1953, Nov. 23   *Perf. 12½x13*
B27	A8	5c + 5c like #70	15	15
B28	A8	10c + 5c like #71	15	15
		Set value	20	20

Athlete Types of Regular Issue
1954, June 1   *Perf. 12½x13, 13x12½*
B29	A9	5c + 5c brn org	15	15
B30	A10	10c + 5c purple	15	15
		Set value	20	15

The surtax was to help the native population.

Fish Type of Regular Issue
1954, Nov. 23   *Perf. 12½x13*
B31	A11	5c + 5c like #74	15	15
B32	A11	10c + 5c like #75	15	15
		Set value	15	15

Type of Regular Issue and

Emilio Bonelli SP5

1955, June 1   Photo.   Unwmk.
B33	A12	10c + 5c red vio	15	15
B34	SP5	25c + 10c violet	15	15
		Set value	15	15

Birth cent. of Emilio Bonelli, explorer. The surtax was for child welfare.

Antelope Type of Regular Issue
Design: 15c+5c, Head of scimitar-horned oryx.

1955, Nov. 23   *Perf. 12½x13*
B35	A13	5c + 5c org brn	15	15
B36	A13	15c + 5c ol bis	15	15
		Set value	15	15

Flower Type of Regular Issue
1956, June 1   *Perf. 13x12½*
B37	A14	5c + 5c like #78	15	15
B38	A14	15c + 5c like #79	15	15
		Set value	20	15

The tax was for the children.

Aaiun Type of Regular Issue and

Arms of Villa Cisneros and Man — SP6

Perf. 12½x13, 13x12½
1956, Nov. 23   Unwmk.
B39	A15	5c + 5c pur & blk	15	15
B40	SP6	15c + 5c bis & grn	15	15
		Set value	20	15

Eagle Type of Regular Issue
Design: 15c+5c, Lesser spotted eagle in flight.

1957, June 1   *Perf. 13x12½*
B41	A17	5c + 5c red brown	15	15
B42	A17	15c + 5c golden brn	15	15
		Set value	15	15

The surtax was for child welfare.

Hyena Type of Regular Issue
Perf. 13x12½, 12½x13
1957, Nov. 23
B43	A18	10c + 5c like #88	15	15
B44	A18	15c + 5c like #89	15	15
		Set value	15	15

Stork and Arms of Valencia and Aaiun SP7

1958, Mar. 6   Photo.   *Perf. 12½x13*
B45	SP7	10c + 5c org brn	15	15
B46	SP7	15c + 10c bister	15	15
B47	SP7	50c + 10c brn olive	26	18

The surtax was to aid the victims of the Valencia flood, Oct. 1957.

Cervantes Type of Regular Issue
Designs: 15c+5c, Don Quixote and Sancho Panza.

1958, June 1   *Perf. 13x12½*
B48	A20	10c + 5c hn brn & chnt brn	15	15
B49	A20	15c + 5c dp org & sl grn	15	15
		Set value	15	15

The surtax was for child welfare.

Hoopoe Lark — SP8   Mailman — SP9

Designs: 25c+10c, Hoopoe larks, horiz. 50c+10c, Bird.

Perf. 13x12½, 12½x13
1958, Nov. 23   Photo.   Unwmk.
B50	SP8	10c + 5c brn red	15	15
B51	SP8	25c + 10c brt pur	15	15
B52	SP8	50c + 10c olive	15	15
		Set value	35	18

Cervantes Type of Regular Issue, 1958
Designs: 10c+5c, Lope de Vega. 15c+5c, Actress from "Star of Seville," by Lope de Vega.

1959, June   *Perf. 13x12½*
B53	A20	10c + 5c org brn & ol gray	15	15
B54	A20	15c + 5c dp ocher & choc	15	15
		Set value	20	15

The surtax was for child welfare.

1959, Nov. 23   Photo.
Stamp Day: 20c+5c, Mailman. 50c+20c, Mailman on camel.
B55	SP9	10c + 5c rose & brn	15	15
B56	SP9	20c + 5c lt grn & brn	15	15
B57	SP9	50c + 20c ol gray & slate	15	15
		Set value	28	20

Catalogue values for unused stamps in this section, from this point to the end of the section, are for Never Hinged items.

Quevedo Type of Regular Issue
Designs: 10c+5c, Francisco Gomez de Quevedo. 15c+5c, Winged wheel and hour-glass, symbolic of "Hora de Todas."

1960, June 1   *Perf. 12½x13, 13x12½*
B58	A23	10c + 5c maroon	15	15
B59	A22	15c + 5c bis brn	15	15
		Set value	24	15

The surtax was for child welfare.

Leopard — SP10   Alonso Fernandez de Lugo — SP11

Stamp Day: 20c+5c, Desert fox. 30c+10c, Eagle and leopard. 50c+20c, Sand fox.

1960, Nov. 23   Photo.   *Perf. 13x12½*
B60	SP10	10c + 5c rose lilac	15	15
B61	SP10	20c + 5c dk slate grn	15	15
B62	SP10	30c + 10c chocolate	15	15
B63	SP10	50c + 20c olive gray	20	15
		Set value	36	20

Animal Type of 1961 inscribed: "Pro-Infancia 1961"
Designs: Various Mountain Gazelles.

1961, June 21   Unwmk.
B64	SP10	10c + 5c rose brn	15	15
B65	SP10	25c + 10c gray vio	15	15
B66	SP10	80c + 20c dk grn	15	15
		Set value	25	15

The surtax was for child welfare.

1961, Nov. 23   *Perf. 13x12½*
Stamp Day: 25c+10c, 1p+10c, Diego de Herrera.
B67	SP11	10c + 5c org red	15	15
B68	SP11	25c + 10c dk pur	15	15
B69	SP11	30c + 10c dk red brn	15	15
B70	SP11	1p + 10c red org	15	15
		Set value	45	24

AIR POST STAMPS

In 1942, seven air post stamps of Spain, Nos. C100 to C108, were overprinted "SAHARA ESPANOL", but satisfactory information regarding their status is not available.

Ostriches — AP1   Desert Scene — AP2

1943   Unwmk.   Litho.   *Perf. 12½*
C8	AP1	5c cer & vio brn	15	15
C9	AP2	25c yel grn & ol grn	15	15
C10	AP1	50c ind & turq grn	15	15
C11	AP1	1p pur & grnsh bl	15	15
C12	AP1	1.40p gray grn & bl	15	15
C13	AP2	2p mag & org brn	85	85
C14	AP1	5p brn & pur	1.10	1.00
C15	AP2	6p brt bl & gray grn	18.00	14.00
		Nos. C8-C15 (8)	20.70	16.60

Nos. C8-C15 exist imperf. Value of set $125.

Diego Garcia de Herrera AP3

1950, Nov. 23   Photo.
| C16 | AP3 | 5p rose violet | 3.00 | 80 |

Stamp Day.

Catalogue values for unused stamps in this section, from this point to the end of the section, are for Never Hinged items.

Woman Holding Dove — AP4

1951, Apr. 22   Engr.   *Perf. 10*
| C17 | AP4 | 5p deep green | 17.50 | 5.00 |

500th birth anniv. of Queen Isabella I. No. C17 is valued in the grade of fine.

Helmet and Trappings AP5   Plane and Camel Rider AP6

1952, July 18   Photo.   *Perf. 13x12½*
| C18 | AP5 | 5p brown | 24.00 | 4.00 |

500th birth anniv. of Ferdinand the Catholic, of Spain.

1961, May 16   Unwmk.
| C19 | AP6 | 25p gray brown | 2.75 | 85 |

SPECIAL DELIVERY STAMPS

Type A2 Inscribed "URGENTE"
1943   Unwmk.   *Perf. 12½*
| E1 | A2 | 25c Camel troops | 65 | 65 |

Catalogue value for the unused stamp in this section, from this point to the end of the section, is for Never Hinged items.

Messenger on Motorcycle — SD1

     Unwmk.
1971, Sept. 6   Photo.   *Perf. 13*
| E2 | SD1 | 10p bright rose & olive | 40 | 22 |

SPANISH WEST AFRICA

LOCATION — Northwest Africa bordering on the Atlantic Ocean
GOVT. — Spanish administration
AREA — 117,000 sq. mi.
POP. — 95,000 (1950)
CAPITAL — Sidi Ifni

Spanish West Africa was the major political division of Spanish areas in northwest Africa. It included Spanish Sahara (Rio de Oro and Saguiet el Hamra) Ifni and, for administrative purposes, Southern Morocco. Separate stamp issues have been used for Rio de Oro, Ifni and La Aguera.

Catalogue values for all unused stamps in this country are for Never Hinged items.

Native — A1

Perf. 13x12½
1949, Oct.   Litho.   Unwmk.

1	A1	4p dark gray green	1.90	90

UPU, 75th anniversary.

Nomad Camp — A2

Designs: 5c, 30c, 75c, 2p, Tinzgarrentz Oasis. 10c, 40c, 90c, 5p, Desert well. 15c, 45c, 1p, Caravan.

1950, June 5   Perf. 12½x13

2	A2	2c brown	15	15
3	A2	5c rose violet	15	15
4	A2	10c Prussian bl	15	15
5	A2	15c dp ol gray	15	15
6	A2	25c red brown	15	15
7	A2	30c brt yellow	15	15
8	A2	40c olive gray	15	15
9	A2	45c rose lake	15	15
10	A2	50c brn orange	15	15
11	A2	75c ultra	15	15
12	A2	90c dl bl grn	15	15
13	A2	1p gray	15	15
14	A2	1.35p violet	60	32
15	A2	2p sepia	1.10	65
16	A2	5p lilac rose	9.25	2.00
17	A2	10p light brown	18.00	12.50
		Nos. 2-17 (16)	30.75	17.27

AIR POST STAMPS

Isabella the Catholic, Queen of Castile — AP1

Perf. 13x12½
1949, Nov. 23   Photo.   Unwmk.

C1	AP1	5p yellow brown	1.50	80

Stamp Day, Nov. 23, 1949.

Desert Camp — AP2

Designs: Various Desert Scenes.

1951, Mar. 1   Litho.   Perf. 12½x13

C2	AP2	25c ocher	15	15
C3	AP2	50c lilac rose	15	15
C4	AP2	1p green	20	15
C5	AP2	2p bright blue	52	15
C6	AP2	3.25p rose lilac	1.10	40
C7	AP2	5p gray brown	8.25	50
C8	AP2	10p rose red	20.00	11.50
		Nos. C2-C8 (7)	30.37	13.00

SPECIAL DELIVERY STAMP

Tilimenzo Pass and Franco — SD1

Perf. 12½x13
1951, Mar. 1   Litho.   Unwmk.

E1	SD1	25c rose carmine	32	20

SURINAM
(Dutch Guiana)

LOCATION — On the northeast coast of South America, bordering on the Atlantic Ocean
GOVT. — Republic
AREA — 70,087 sq. mi.
POP. — 370,000 (est. 1984)
CAPITAL — Paramaribo

The Dutch colony of Surinam became an integral part of the Kingdom of the Netherlands under the Constitution of 1954. It became an independent state November 25, 1975.

100 Cents = 1 Gulden (Florin)

Catalogue values for unused stamps in this country are for Never Hinged items, beginning with Scott 168 in the regular postage section, Scott B34 in the semi-postal section, Scott C23 in the airpost section, Scott CB1 in the airpost semi-postal section, and Scott J33 in the postage due section.

Watermark

Wmk. 202- Circles

King William III — A1

Numeral of Value — A2

1873-89   Typo.   Unwmk.
Perf. 11½, 11½x12, 12½x12, 13½, 14
Without Gum

1	A1	1c lilac gray ('85)	1.50	1.50
2	A1	2c yellow ('85)	55	55
3	A1	2½c rose	50	35
4	A1	3c green	13.00	11.00
5	A1	5c dull violet	14.00	4.50
6	A1	10c bister	2.50	1.75
7	A1	12½c slate bl ('85)	12.50	4.25
8	A1	15c gray ('89)	15.00	4.50
9	A1	20c green ('89)	27.50	20.00
10	A1	25c grnish blue	60.00	3.50
11	A1	25c ultra	14.00	14.00
12	A1	30c red brn ('88)	27.50	25.00
13	A1	40c dk brown ('89)	22.50	20.00
14	A1	50c brown orange	25.00	15.00
15	A1	1g brn & gray ('89)	40.00	35.00
16	A1	2.50g grn & org ('79)	60.00	55.00

Perf. 14, Small Holes

3b	A1	2½c rose	9.00	11.00
4b	A1	3c green	14.00	17.50
5b	A1	5c dull violet	17.50	14.00
6b	A1	10c bister	14.00	17.50
11b	A1	25c ultra	200.00	50.00
14b	A1	50c brown orange	42.50	40.00

The paper of Nos. 3-6, 11 and 14 sometimes has an accidental bluish tinge of varying strength. During its manufacture a chemical whitener (bluing agent) was added in varying quantities. No particular printing was made on bluish paper.

"Small hole" varieties have the spaces between the holes wider than the diameter of the holes. For surcharges, see Nos. 23, 31-35, 39-42.

1890   Perf. 11½x11, 12½

17	A2	1c gray	55	60
18	A2	2c yellow brn	1.25	1.10
19	A2	2½c carmine	1.65	95
20	A2	3c green	3.75	3.00
21	A2	5c ultra	20.00	1.40

For surcharges, see Nos. 63-64.

A3

1892, Aug. 11   Perf. 10½

22	A3	2½c black & org	85	55
a.		First and fifth vertical words have fancy "F"	24.00	16.00
b.		Imperf.	1.25	
c.		As "a," imperf.	25.00	

No. 22 was issued without gum.

2½ CENT.

No. 14 Surcharged in Black

1892, Aug. 1   Perf. 14

23	A1	2½c on 50c	250.00	10.00
a.		Perf. 12½x12	250.00	10.00
b.		Perf. 11½x12	325.00	11.50
c.		Double surcharge	300.00	275.00
d.		Perf. 14, small holes	275.00	15.00

Nos. 23-23c were issued without gum.

Queen Wilhelmina — A5

1892-93   Typo.   Perf. 12½

25	A5	10c bister	27.50	1.75
26	A5	12½c rose lilac	32.50	3.50
27	A5	15c gray	1.25	75
28	A5	20c green	1.75	1.25
29	A5	25c blue	7.25	3.25
30	A5	30c red brown	2.00	1.40

Nos. 25-30 were issued without gum.
For surcharges, see Nos. 65-66.

Nos. 7-12 Surcharged

1898   Perf. 11½x12, 12½x12, 13½

31	A1	10c on 12½c sl bl	22.50	2.50
32	A1	10c on 15c gray	55.00	47.50
33	A1	10c on 20c green	2.50	2.25
34	A1	10c on 25c grnsh bl	5.75	4.00
c.		Perf. 11½x12	10.00	10.00
34A	A1	10c on 25c ultra	500.00	475.00
b.		Perf. 11½x12	575.00	525.00
35	A1	10c on 30c red brn	2.50	2.25
a.		Double surcharge	275.00	

Nos. 31-35 were issued without gum.
Dangerous counterfeits exist.

Netherlands Nos. 80, 83-84 Surcharged

50 C^T.   2.50   2.50

SURINAME   SURINAME
No. 36   Nos. 37-38

1900, Jan. 8   Perf. 12½

36	A11	50c on 50c	21.00	6.00

Engr.
Perf. 11½x11

37	A12	1g on 1g dk grn	17.50	11.00
38	A12	2.50g on 2½g brn lil	12.50	9.00

Nos. 36-38 were issued without gum. For surcharge, see No. 67.

Nos. 13-16 Surcharged **25 cent**

1900   Perf. 11½, 11½x12, 12½x12, 14   Typo.

39	A1	25c on 40c	1.75	2.75
40	A1	25c on 50c	1.50	1.25
a.		Perf. 14, small holes	115.00	115.00
b.		Perf. 11½x12	3.50	4.00
41	A1	50c on 1g	21.00	21.00
42	A1	50c on 2.50g	125.00	140.00

Nos. 39-42 were issued without gum.
Counterfeits of No. 42 exist.

A9

Queen Wilhelmina
A10   A11

1902-08   Typo.   Perf. 12½

44	A9	½c violet	55	55
45	A9	1c olive grn	90	75
46	A9	2c yellow brn	6.50	2.50
47	A9	2½c blue grn	2.00	22
48	A9	3c orange	3.00	2.50
49	A9	5c red	4.00	22
50	A9	7½c gray ('08)	10.50	6.25
51	A10	10c slate	7.25	75
52	A10	12½c deep blue	1.00	15
53	A10	15c dp brown	18.00	7.00
54	A10	20c olive grn	18.00	4.00
55	A10	22½c brn & ol grn	13.00	9.00
56	A10	25c violet	14.00	1.10
57	A10	30c orange brn	27.50	11.00
58	A10	50c lake brown	18.00	5.50

Engr.
Perf. 11

59	A11	1g violet	40.00	9.50
60	A11	2½g slate blue	37.50	37.50
		Nos. 44-60 (17)	221.70	98.49

Nos. 44-58, and possibly 59-60, were partially issued without gum.

A12

1909   Typeset   Serrate Roulette 13½

61	A12	5c red	10.00	9.00
a.		Tête bêche pair	125.00	110.00

Perf. 11½x10½

62	A12	5c red	10.50	10.50
a.		Tête bêche pair	95.00	65.00

Nos. 61-62 were issued without gum.

Nos. 17-18, 29-30, 38 Surcharged in Red

½ cent
Nos. 63-64

15 cent.
Nos. 65-66

No. 67

30 cent

1911, July 15   Typo.   Perf. 12½

63	A2	½c on 1c	65	65
64	A2	½c on 2c	5.75	6.50
65	A5	15c on 25c	52.50	50.00
66	A5	20c on 30c	5.75	6.00

Engr.
Perf. 11½x11

67	A12	30c on 2.50g on 2½g	100.00	100.00
		Nos. 63-67 (5)	164.65	163.15

Nos. 63-67 were issued without gum.

A13

1912, July   Typeset   Perf. 11½

70	A13	½c lilac	55	55
a.		Horiz. pair, imperf. btwn.	150.00	
71	A13	2½c dk green	65	65
72	A13	5c pale red	6.25	6.25
a.		Vert. pair, imperf. btwn.	200.00	
73	A13	12½c deep blue	8.50	8.50

Nos. 70-73 were issued without gum.

Numeral of Value — A14

Queen Wilhelmina
A15   A16

1913-31   Typo.   Perf. 12½

74	A14	½c violet	20	24
75	A14	1c olive green	20	15
76	A14	1½c blue, perf 11½ ('21)	20	15
a.		Perf. 12½ ('32)	1.00	75
77	A14	2c yellow brn	85	1.00
78	A14	2½c green	40	15
79	A14	3c yellow	50	40
80	A14	3c green ('26)	2.00	2.00
81	A14	4c chlky bl ('26)	6.50	3.50
82	A14	5c rose	90	15
83	A14	5c green ('22)	90	70
84	A14	5c lilac ('26)	90	15
85	A14	6c bister ('26)	2.00	2.00
86	A14	6c red orange ('31)	1.65	20
87	A14	7½c drab	65	15
a.		Perf. 11x11½	75	25
88	A14	7½c orange ('27)	90	30
89	A14	7½c yellow ('31)	2.25	7.25
90	A14	10c violet ('22)	2.75	2.75
91	A14	10c rose ('26)	2.50	30
92	A15	10c car rose	1.10	50
93	A15	12½c blue	1.25	40
94	A15	12½c red ('22)	1.25	1.65
95	A15	15c olive grn	40	40
96	A15	15c lt blue ('26)	5.00	3.75
97	A15	20c green	2.75	2.75
98	A15	20c blue ('22)	2.00	1.25
99	A15	20c olive grn ('26)	2.25	1.75
100	A15	22½c orange	1.65	2.00
101	A15	25c red violet	2.75	30
102	A15	30c slate	3.75	90
103	A15	32½c vio & org ('22)	12.00	14.00
104	A15	35c sl & red ('26)	3.75	3.50

Perf. 11, 11½, 11½x11, 12½
Engr.

105	A16	50c green	2.50	40
a.		Perf. 12½ ('32)	10.50	1.00
106	A16	1g brown	3.25	30
a.		Perf. 12½ ('32)	11.50	40
107	A16	1½g dp vio ('26)	27.50	27.50
108	A16	2½g carmine	20.00	20.00
a.		Perf. 11½x11	27.50	27.50
		Nos. 74-108 (35)	119.40	102.89

All stamps issued before 1919 were without gum. Early printings of Nos. 74-104 had water soluble ink.

For surcharges, see Nos. 116-120, 139.

Queen Wilhelmina — A17

1923, Oct. 5   Perf. 11, 11x11½, 11½

109	A17	5c green	50	60
110	A17	10c car rose	70	1.40
111	A17	20c indigo	1.65	2.50
112	A17	50c brown org	10.50	17.50
113	A17	1g brown vio	16.00	12.50
114	A17	2½g gray blk	50.00	190.00
115	A17	5g brown	65.00	225.00
		Nos. 109-115 (7)	144.35	449.50

25th anniv. of the assumption of the government of the Netherlands by Queen Wilhelmina, at age 18.

Values for Nos. 114-115 used are for copies clearly dated before July 15, 1924.

Nos. 83, 93-94, 98 Surcharged in Black or Red:

j   k

10 CENT

= 15

m

= CENT

1925, Dec. 19   Typo.   Perf. 12½

116	A14	3c on 5c green	70	90
117	A15	10c on 12½c red	1.50	1.50
118	A15	15c on 12½c blue (R)	1.25	1.25
119	A15	15c on 20c blue	1.25	1.25

12½ ct.

No. 100 Surcharged in Blue

1926, Jan. 1

120	A15	12½c on 22½c org	22.50	24.00

Postage Due Stamps Nos. J14 and J29 Surcharged in Blue or Black:

Frankeerzegel
12½ Cent
SURINAME
o

Frankeerzegel
12½
CENT
SURINAME
p

121	D2(o)	12½c on 40c (Bl)	1.75	1.90
122	D2(p)	12½c on 40c (Bk)	24.00	25.00

No. 121 issued without gum.

Queen Wilhelmina — A21

1927-30   Engr.   Perf. 11½

123	A21	10c carmine	65	30
124	A21	12½c red orange	1.25	1.50
125	A21	15c dark blue	1.65	50
126	A21	20c indigo	1.65	40
127	A21	21c dk brown ('30)	13.00	13.00
128	A21	22½c brown ('28)	7.25	8.25
129	A21	25c dk violet	2.25	55
130	A21	30c dk green	2.25	90
131	A21	35c black brown	2.50	2.50
		Nos. 123-131 (9)	32.45	27.90

FRANKEER = ZEGEL =
10 CENT

Types of Netherlands Marine Insurance Stamps Inscribed "SURINAME" and Surcharged

1927, Oct. 26

132	MI1	3c on 15c dk grn	15	18
133	MI1	10c on 60c car rose	15	20
134	MI1	12½c on 75c gray brn	20	20
135	MI2	15c on 1.50 dk blue	1.75	1.75
136	MI2	25c on 2.25g org brn	4.00	4.00
137	MI3	30c on 4½g black	9.25	9.25
138	MI3	50c on 7½g red	4.00	4.00
		Nos. 132-138 (7)	19.50	19.58

Nos. 135-137 have "FRANKEERZEGEL" in small capitals in one line. Nos. 135 and 136 have a heavy bar across the top of the stamp.

No. 88 Surcharged

1930, Mar. 1   Typo.   Perf. 12½

139	A14	6c on 7½c orange	1.75	1.00

Surinam stamps can be mounted in the annually supplemented Scott Netherlands album.

Prince William I (Portrait by Van Key) — A22

1933, Apr. 24   Photo.

141	A22	6c deep orange	5.50	1.75

400th birth anniv. of Prince William I, Count of Nassau and Prince of Orange, frequently referred to as William the Silent.

Van Walbeeck's Ship A23 | Queen Wilhelmina A24

1936-41   Litho.   Perf. 13½x12½

142	A23	½c yellow brn	15	20
143	A23	1c lt yellow grn	25	15
144	A23	1½c brt blue	40	32
145	A23	2c black brown	50	20
146	A23	2½c green	15	15
a.		Perf. 13 ('41)	12.00	4.50
147	A23	3c dark ultra	42	32
148	A23	4c orange	50	55
149	A23	5c gray	50	15
150	A23	6c red	2.00	1.50
151	A23	7½c red violet	15	15
a.		7½c plum, perf. 13 ('41)	4.00	40

Engr.
Perf. 14, 12½
Size: 20x30mm

152	A24	10c vermilion	65	15
a.		Perf. 12½ ('39)	42.50	8.25
153	A24	12½c dull green	2.75	1.00
154	A24	15c dark blue	1.00	55
155	A24	20c yellow org	1.65	50
156	A24	21c dk gray	2.50	2.50
a.		Perf. 12½ ('39)	2.50	2.50
157	A24	25c brown lake	1.75	85
158	A24	30c brown vio	2.75	70
159	A24	35c olive brown	3.25	3.00

Perf. 12½x14
Size: 22x33mm

160	A24	50c dull yel grn	3.25	1.50
161	A24	1g dull blue	5.75	1.75
162	A24	1.50g black brown	16.00	13.00
163	A24	2.50g rose lake	10.00	6.50
		Nos. 142-163 (22)	56.32	35.64

For surcharges, see Nos. 181-183, B37-B40.

Queen Wilhelmina — A25

Perf. 12½x12
1938, Aug. 30   Photo.   Wmk. 202

164	A25	2c dull purple	50	45
165	A25	7½c red orange	1.00	90
166	A25	15c royal blue	3.00	2.75

Reign of Queen Wilhelmina, 40th anniv.

Catalogue values for unused stamps in this section, from this point to the end of the section, are for Never Hinged items.

Van
Walbeeck's
Ship
A26

Queen
Wilhelmina
A27

1941   Unwmk.   Typo.   Perf. 12
168 A26 1c lt yellow grn   60   15
169 A26 2c black brown   1.40 1.40

Type A26 is similar to type A23 except for the white side frame lines which extend to the base. For surcharges, see No. 180.

1941-46   Photo.   Perf. 13½x12½
Size: 18x22½mm
174 A27 12½c royal blue ('46)   24   15
Perf. 12½
175 A27 15c ultra   17.50 6.50

Royal Family — A28

1943, Nov. 2   Engr.   Perf. 13½x13
176 A28 2½c deep orange   26   26
177 A28 7½c red   26   26
178 A28 15c black   1.90 1.90
179 A28 40c deep blue   2.50 2.50

Birth of Princess Margriet Francisca of the Netherlands.

Nos. 168, 151, 152 Surcharged with New Values and Bars in Black

1945   Unwmk.   Perf. 13, 14, 12
180 A26 ½c on 1c   15   15
181 A23 2½c on 7½c   1.65 1.75
182 A24 5c on 10c   55   40
183 A24 7½c on 10c   65   40
  a. Double surcharge   225.00 225.00

Bauxite
Mine,
Moengo
A29

Queen Wilhelmina
A30   A31

Designs: 1½c, Bush Negroes on Cottica River near Moengo. 2c, Waterfall in interior. 2½c, Road scene, Coronie District. 3c, Surinam River near Berg en Dahl Plantation. 4c, Government Square, Paramaribo. 5c, Mining gold. 6c, Street in Paramaribo. 7½c, Sugar cane train.

1945, Nov. 5   Engr.   Perf. 12
184 A29 1c rose carmine   30   28
185 A29 1½c rose lake   1.10 1.10
186 A29 2c violet   48   35
187 A29 2½c olive brn   48   35
188 A29 3c dull green   1.10 60
189 A29 4c brown   1.10 60
190 A29 5c blue   1.10 30
191 A29 6c olive   2.00 1.25
192 A29 7½c deep orange   65   28
193 A30 10c blue   1.25 15
194 A30 15c brown   1.25 24
195 A30 20c dull green   2.50 15
196 A30 22½c gray   2.75 80
197 A30 25c carmine   7.75 3.50
198 A30 30c olive green   6.25 48
199 A30 35c brt bl grn   14.00 7.25

200 A30 40c rose lake   6.25 26
201 A30 50c red orange   6.25 24
202 A30 60c violet   6.25 65
203 A31 1g red brown   5.50 28
204 A31 1.50g lilac   5.75 65
205 A31 2.50g olive brn   12.00 75
206 A31 5g rose carmine   27.50 10.00
207 A31 10g red orange   42.50 15.00
  Nos. 184-207 (24)   156.06 45.51

For surcharges, see Nos. 240, CB2-CB3. For types surcharged, see Nos. B41-B46.

Nos. 151 and 152 Surcharged with New Value and Bar in Blue or Black

1947   Perf. 13½x12½, 14
209 A23 1½(c) on 7½c (Bl)   15   15
  a. Double surcharge   200.00
210 A24 2½c on 10c (Bk)   90   30

Numeral
A32

Queen
Wilhelmina
A33

Perf. 12½x13½
1948, July 21   Unwmk.   Photo.
211 A32 1c dark red   15   15
212 A32 1½c plum   15   15
213 A32 2c purple   20   15
214 A32 2½c olive grn   1.10 15
215 A32 3c dark green   15   15
216 A32 4c red brown   15   15
Perf. 13½x12½
217 A33 5c deep blue   32   15
218 A33 6c dark olive   85   70
219 A33 7½c scarlet   32   20
220 A33 10c blue   50   15
221 A33 12½c dark blue   1.10 1.10
222 A33 15c henna brown   1.25 35
223 A33 17½c dk vio brn   1.50 1.50
224 A33 20c dk blue grn   1.10 15
225 A33 22½c slate blue   1.10 70
226 A33 25c crimson   1.10 28
227 A33 27½c car lake   1.10 20
228 A33 30c olive green   1.50 20
229 A33 37½c olive brn   2.25 2.00
230 A33 40c lilac rose   1.65 28
231 A33 50c red orange   1.65 28
232 A33 60c purple   1.75 42
233 A33 70c black   2.00 55
  Nos. 211-233 (23)   22.94 10.11

See Nos. 241-242.

Wilhelmina - Juliana
A34   A35

1948, Aug. 30   Engr.   Perf. 12½x14
234 A34 7½c vermilion   65   65
235 A34 12½c deep blue   65   65

Reign of Queen Wilhelmina, 50th anniv.

Perf. 14x13
1948, Sept. 10   Wmk. 202   Photo.
236 A35 7½c deep orange   2.75 2.75
237 A35 12½c ultra   2.75 2.75

Investiture of Queen Juliana, Sept. 6, 1948. For surcharges, see Nos. B53-B54.

Post Horns
Entwined — A36

1949, Oct. 1   Unwmk.   Perf. 11½x12
238 A36 7½c brown red   4.75 3.00
239 A36 27½c dull blue   4.00 2.25

UPU, 75th anniversary.

No. 192 Surcharged with New Value, Square and Bar in Black

1950, Aug. 9   Perf. 12
240 A29 1c on 7½c dp org   55   55

Numeral Type of 1948
1951, Apr. 5   Perf. 12½x13½
241 A32 5c deep blue   1.75 15
242 A32 7½c deep orange   3.75 1.50

Queen Juliana
A37   A38

1951, Apr. 5   Perf. 13½x13
243 A37 10c blue   32   15
244 A37 15c henna brn   85   20
245 A37 20c dk blue grn   2.00 15
246 A37 25c crimson   1.25 32
247 A37 27½c carmine lake   1.25 15
248 A37 30c olive green   1.25 30
249 A37 35c olive brown   1.50 1.25
250 A37 40c lilac rose   1.65 32
251 A37 50c red orange   2.00 32
Engr.
Perf. 12½x12
252 A38 1g red brown   21.00 25
  Nos. 243-252 (10)   33.07 3.41

For surcharge, see No. 271.

Shooting Fish
A39

Plowing with
Water Buffalo
A40

Designs: 2½c, Fisherman. 5c, Bauxite mining. 6c, Log raft. 10c, Woman picking fruit. 12½c, Armored catfish. 15c, Macaw. 17½c, Armadillo. 20c, Poling canoe. 25c, Common iguana.

1953-55   Photo.   Perf. 14x13, 13x14
253 A39 2c olive green   15   15
254 A40 2½c blue green   26   15
255 A40 5c gray   30   15
256 A40 6c bright blue   1.50 1.00
257 A40 7½c purple   15   15
258 A40 10c bright red   18   15
259 A40 12½c dk gray blue   1.75 1.10
260 A40 15c crimson   60   20
261 A40 17½c red brown   2.75 1.65
262 A40 20c Prus green   50   15
263 A40 25c olive green   2.50 65
  a. Min. sheet of 4, #259-261, 263 32.50 32.50
  Nos. 253-263 (11)   10.64 5.50

Issue dates: 2c, 7½c, 10c, 230c, May 9, 1953. No. 263a, Feb. 14, 1955. Others, Dec. 1, 1954.

Queen
Juliana — A41

Harvesting
Bananas — A46

1954, Dec. 15   Perf. 13½
264 A41 7½c dark red brown   65   65

Charter of the Kingdom, adopted Dec. 15, 1954.

1955, May 12   Perf. 14x13
Designs: 7½c, Pounding rice. 10c, Preparing cassava. 15c, Fishing.
265 A46 2c dark green   1.25 1.25
266 A46 7½c dull yellow   2.25 2.00
267 A46 10c orange brown   2.25 2.00
268 A46 15c ultra   2.25 2.00

4th anniv. of the establishment of the Caribbean Tourist Assoc.

Globe and
Mercury's
Rod — A47

Flags and Map of
Caribbean — A48

1955, Sept. 19   Unwmk.   Perf. 13x12
269 A47 5c bright ultra   32   28

Paramaribo Trade Fair, Oct. 1955.

1956, Dec. 6   Litho.   Perf. 13x14
270 A48 10c lt blue & red   30   28

10th anniv. of Caribbean Commission.

No. 247 Surcharged   8 — C

1958, Nov. 11   Photo.   Perf. 13½x13
271 A37 8c on 27½c car lake   15   15

Queen
Juliana — A49

Symbolic
Flowers — A50

Perf. 12½x12
1959, Oct. 15   Unwmk.   Litho.
272 A49 1g magenta   1.25 15
273 A49 1.50g olive bister   2.00 50
274 A49 2.50g dk carmine   2.75 30
275 A49 5g dull blue   5.75 30

1959, Dec. 15   Photo.   Perf. 12½x13
276 A50 20c multicolored   2.50 1.50

5th anniv. of the constitution. Flowers in design symbolize Netherlands, Surinam and Netherlands Antilles.

Charles
Lindbergh's
Plane — A51

Designs: 10c, De Snip plane. 15c, Cessna 170B. 20c, Super Constellation. 40c, Boeing 707 Jet.

1960, Mar. 12   Perf. 12½
277 A51 8c chalky blue   90   1.00
278 A51 10c bright green   1.25 1.50
279 A51 15c rose red   1.25 1.50
280 A51 20c pale violet   1.50 1.75
281 A51 40c light brown   2.25 2.50
  Nos. 277-281 (5)   7.15 8.25

Inauguration of Zanderij Airport, Mar. 12. Nos. 277-281 show 25 years of Surinam's civil aviation.

Flag of Surinam and Map — A52   Arms of Surinam — A53

1960, July 1   Litho.   Perf. 12½x13
282 A52 10c multicolored 50 50
Perf. 13x12½
283 A53 15c multicolored 50 50

Day of Freedom, July 1.

Bananas — A54   Finance Building — A55

1961, Mar. 1   Litho.   Perf. 13½
284 A54 1c shown 15 15
285 A54 2c Citrus fruit 15 15
286 A54 3c Cacao 15 15
287 A54 4c Sugar cane 15 15
288 A54 5c Coffee 15 15
289 A54 6c Coconuts 15 15
290 A54 8c Rice 15 15
  Set value 65 65

1961   Perf. 13½x14, 14x13½
Buildings: 15c, Court of Justice. 20c, Concordia Lodge (Masons). 25c, Neve Shalom Synagogue, Paramaribo, horiz. 30c, Old Dutch lock in New Amsterdam. 35c, Government office, horiz. 40c, Governor's palace, horiz. 50c, Legislative Council, horiz. 60c, Old Dutch Reformed Church, horiz. 70c, Zeelandia Fortress, horiz.

201 A55 10c multi 15 15
202 A55 15c multi 15 15
203 A55 20c multi 24 24
204 A55 25c multi 50 50
205 A55 30c multi 1.25 1.25
206 A55 35c multi 1.25 1.25
297 A55 40c multi 65 65
298 A55 50c multi 65 65
299 A55 60c multi 70 70
300 A55 70c multi 90 90
  Nos. 291-300 (10) 6.44 6.44

Issue dates: 10c, 20c, 25c, 50c, 70c, Apr. 1; others, May 15.

Dag Hammarskjold (1905-1961) — A56

1962, Jan. 2   Litho.   Perf. 11½, 12½
301 A56 10c brt blue & blk 15 15
302 A56 20c lilac & blk 20 20

Dag Hammarskjold, Secretary General of the United Nations, 1953-61.
Sheets of both perfs. exist either with or without extension of perforations through the margins.

A56a   A57

1962, Feb. 1   Photo.   Perf. 14x13
303 A56a 20c olive green 24 24

Silver wedding anniversary of Queen Juliana and Prince Bernhard.

1962, May 2   Litho.   Perf. 13x14
Malaria eradication emblem.
304 A57 8c bright red 15 15
305 A57 10c blue 20 20

WHO drive to eradicate malaria.

Stoelmans Guesthouse A58

Design: 15c, Torarica Hotel.

1962, July 4   Perf. 14x13½
306 A58 10c multicolored 32 32
307 A58 15c multicolored 32 32

Opening of the Torarica Hotel in Paramaribo and Stoelmans Guesthouse on Stoelman Island.

Deaconess Residence and Recreation Area — A59

Design: 20c, Deaconess Hospital.

1962, Nov. 30
308 A59 10c multicolored 32 32
309 A59 20c multicolored 32 32

Hands Holding Wheat Emblem — A60

Design: 20c, Farmer harvesting and wheat emblem, vert.

Perf. 14x13, 13x14
1963, Mar. 21   Photo.
310 A60 10c deep carmine 15 15
311 A60 20c dark blue 15 15
  Set value 24 24

FAO "Freedom from Hunger" campaign.

Broken Chain — A61

1963, June 28   Litho.   Perf. 14x13
312 A61 10c red & blk 15 15
313 A61 20c green & blk 15 15
  Set value 24 24

Centenary of emancipation of the slaves.

Prince William of Orange Landing at Scheveningen A61a   Faja Lobbi Wreath A62

1963, Nov. 21   Photo.   Perf. 13½x14
Size: 26x26mm
314 A61a 10c dull bl, blk & brn 15 15

Founding of the Kingdom of the Netherlands, 150th anniv.

1964, Dec. 15   Litho.   Perf. 12½x13
315 A62 25c multicolored 22 22

Charter of the Kingdom of the Netherlands, 10th anniv.

Abraham Lincoln (1809-1865) — A63

1965, Apr. 14   Litho.   Perf. 12½x13
316 A63 25c olive bis & brn 15 15

ICY Emblem — A64

1965, May 26   Perf. 13x12½
317 A64 10c orange & blue 15 15
318 A64 15c red & violet bl 15 15
  Set value 16 16

International Cooperation Year.

Bauxite Mine, Moengo A65   Red-breasted Blackbird A66

Designs: 15c, Alum Pottery Works, Paranam. 20c, Hydroelectric plant, Afobaka. 25c, Aluminum smeltery, Paranam.

1965, Oct. 9   Photo.   Unwmk.
319 A65 10c ocher 15 15
320 A65 15c dark green 15 15
321 A65 20c dark blue 15 15
322 A65 25c carmine 15 15
  Set value 35 35

Opening of the Brokopondo Power Station.

1966, Feb. 16   Litho.   Perf. 13x14
Birds: 2c, Great kiskadee. 3c, Silver-beaked tanager. 4c, Ruddy ground dove. 5c, Blue-gray tanager. 6c, Glittering-throated emerald (hummingbird). 8c, Turquoise tanager. 10c, Pale-breasted robin.

323 A66 1c brt grn, blk & red 15 15
324 A66 2c lt ultra, yel & brn 15 15
325 A66 3c multi 15 15
326 A66 4c lt ol grn, red brn & blk 15 15
327 A66 5c org, ultra & blk 15 15
328 A66 6c multi 15 15
329 A66 8c gray, vio bl & blk 15 15
330 A66 10c multi 15 15
  Set value 80 80

Central Hospital — A67

Design: 15c, Hospital, side view.

1966, Mar. 9   Litho.   Perf. 13x12½
331 A67 10c multi 15 15
332 A67 15c multi 15 15
  Set value 22 22

Opening of Central Hospital, Paramaribo.

Father Petrus Donders — A68

Designs: 10c, Church and parsonage, Batavia. 15c, Msgr. Joannes B. Swinkels. 25c, Cathedral, Paramaribo.

1966, Mar. 26   Photo.   Perf. 12½x13
333 A68 4c org brn & blk 15 15
334 A68 10c rose brn & blk 15 15
335 A68 15c yel brn & blk 15 15
336 A68 25c lt vio & blk 15 15
  Set value 35 35

Centenary of the Redemptorist Mission in Surinam (Congregation of the Most Holy Redeemer).

100-Year-Old Tree — A69

1966, May 9   Litho.   Perf. 13x12½
337 A69 25c grn, dp org & blk 15 15
338 A69 30c red org, grn & blk 15 15
  Set value 25 25

Centenary of the Surinam Parliament.

Television Transmitter, Eye and Globe — A70

1966, Oct. 20   Litho.   Perf. 12½x13
339 A70 25c dk bl & ver 15 15
340 A70 30c brn & ver 15 15
  Set value 25 25

Inauguration of television service.

Bauxite Industry, 1916 — A71

Design: 25c, Bauxite industry, 1966.

1966, Dec. 19   Litho.   Perf. 13x12½
341 A71 20c yel, org & blk 15 15
342 A71 25c org, bl & blk 15 15
  Set value 25 25

50th anniversary of bauxite industry.

Central Bank, Paramaribo
A72

Design: 25c, Central Bank, different view.

1967, Apr. 1   Litho.   *Perf. 13x12½*
343 A72 10c dp yel & blk   15   15
344 A72 25c lil & blk   15   15
   Set value   25   25

Central Bank of Surinam, 10th anniv.

Amelia Earhart, Lockheed Electra and Paramaribo
A73

1967, June 3   Photo.   *Perf. 13x12½*
345 A73 20c yel & dk car   15   15
346 A73 25c yel & grn   15   15
   Set value   25   25

30th anniv. of Amelia Earhart's visit to Surinam, June 3-4, 1937.

Siva Nataraja, God of Dance, and Ballerina's Foot — A74

Design: 25c, Drummer's mask "Bashi Lele," and scroll of violin.

1967, June 21   Litho.   *Perf. 12½x13*
347 A74 10c yel grn & bl   15   15
348 A74 25c yel grn & brn   15   15
   Set value   25   25

20th anniv. of the Surinam Cultural Center Foundation.

New Amsterdam, 1660 (New York City)
A75

Designs after 17th Century Engravings: 10c, Fort Zeelandia, Paramaribo, 1670. 25c, Breda Castle, Netherlands, 1667.

1967, July 31   Litho.   *Perf. 13½x12½*
349 A75 10c yel, blk & bl   15   15
350 A75 20c red brn, yel & blk   15   15
351 A75 25c bl grn, yel & blk   15   15

300th anniv. of the Treaty of Breda between Britain, France and the Netherlands.

WHO Emblem
A76

1968, Apr. 7   Litho.   *Perf. 13x12½*
352 A76 10c mag & dk bl   16   16
353 A76 25c bl & dk pur   28   28

WHO, 20th anniversary.

Chandelier and Christian Symbols — A77

Design: 15c, like 10c, reversed. Brass chandelier from the Reformed Church, Paramaribo.

1968, May 29   Litho.   *Perf. 13x12½*
354 A77 10c dk bl   16   16
355 A77 25c dp yel grn   28   28

300th anniv. of the Reformed Church of Paramaribo.

Missionary Store, 1768 — A78

Designs: 25c, Main Church and store, Paramaribo, 1868. 30c, C. Kersten & Co., 1968.

1968, June 29   Litho.   *Perf. 13x12½*
356 A78 10c yel & blk   18   18
357 A78 25c lt grnsh bl & blk   18   18
358 A78 30c lil rose & blk   18   18

200th anniv. of C. Kersten & Co., which is partially owned by the Evangelical Brotherhood Missionary Society.

Joden Savanne Synagogue — A79

Mahatma Gandhi — A81

Spectacled Caiman — A80

Designs: 20c, Map of Joden Savanne and Surinam River. 30c, Gravestone, 1733. The Hebrew inscriptions are quotations from the Bible: 20c, Joshua 24:2; 25c, Isaiah 56:7; 30c, Genesis 31:52.

1968, Aug. 28   *Perf. 12½x13*
359 A79 20c multi   32   32
360 A79 25c multi   32   32
361 A79 30c multi   32   32

Founding of the first synagogue in the Western Hemisphere in 1685 in Joden Savanne, Surinam.

Perf. 13x12½, 12½x13
1969, Aug. 20   Litho.

Designs: 20c, Squirrel monkey, vert. 25c, Armadillo.

362 A80 10c grn & multi   50   40
363 A80 20c bl gray & multi   50   40
364 A80 25c vio & multi   50   40

1969, Oct. 2   Litho.   *Perf. 12½x13*
365 A81 25c red & blk   26   26

Mohandas K. Gandhi (1869-1948), leader in India's fight for independence.

ILO Emblem — A82

1969, Oct. 29   Litho.   *Perf. 13x12½*
366 A82 10c brt bl grn & blk   15   15
367 A82 25c red & blk   24   24

ILO, 50th anniversary.

Queen Juliana and Rising Sun — A82a

1969, Dec. 15   Photo.   *Perf. 14x13*
368 A82a 25c blue & multi   28   28

15th anniv. of the Charter of the Kingdom of the Netherlands. Phosphorescent paper.

"1950-1970"
A83

1970, Apr. 3   Litho.   *Perf. 13x12½*
369 A83 10c brn, grn & org   15   15
370 A83 25c emer, dk bl & org   22   22

20th anniv. of secondary education in Surinam.

Inauguration of UPU Headquarters, Bern — A84

Design: 25c, UPU Headquarters, sideview and UPU emblem.

1970, May 20   Litho.   *Perf. 13x12½*
371 A84 10c sky bl & dk pur   16   16
372 A84 25c red & blk   28   28

"UNO"
A85

Plane over Paramaribo
A86

1970, June 26   Litho.   *Perf. 12½x13*
373 A85 10c ocher & yel   16   16
374 A85 25c dp bl & ultra   28   28

25th anniversary of the United Nations.

1970, July 15

Designs: 20c, Plane over map of Totness. 25c, Plane over Nieuw-Nickerie.

375 A86 10c bl, vio bl & gray   26   26
376 A86 20c red, vio & gray   26   26
377 A86 25c pink, dk red & gray   26   26

40th anniv. of domestic airmail service.

Plan of Soccer Field and Ball — A87

Morse Key — A89

Cocoi Heron — A88

Designs: Plan of soccer field with ball in different positions.

1970, Oct. 1
378 A87 4c yel, red brn & blk   15   15
379 A87 10c pale lem, red brn & blk 18   18
380 A87 15c lt yel grn, red brn & blk 18   18
381 A87 25c lt grn, red brn & blk 30   30

50th anniv. of the Soccer Assoc. of Surinam.

1971, Feb. 14   Litho.   *Perf. 13x12½*

Birds in Flight: 20c, Flamingo. 25c, Scarlet macaw.

382 A88 15c gray & multi   65   40
383 A88 20c ultra & multi   65   40
384 A88 25c pale grn & multi   65   40

25th anniversary of regular air service between the Netherlands, Surinam and Netherlands Antilles.

1971, May 17   Photo.   *Perf. 12½x13*

Designs: 20c, Telephone. 25c, Lunar landing module, telescope.

385 A89 15c lt grn & multi   35   32
386 A89 20c bl & multi   42   40
387 A89 25c lil & multi   50   45

3rd World Telecommunications Day.

Prince Bernhard, Fokker F27, Boeing 747B — A89a

Map of Surinam, Population Chart — A90

1971, June 29   Photo.   *Perf. 13x14*
388 A89a 25c multi   28   30

60th birthday of Prince Bernhard.

1971, July 31   Litho.   *Perf. 12½x13*

Design: 30c, Map of Surinam and individual representing population.

389 A90 15c gray bl, blk & ver   15   15
390 A90 30c ver, gray bl & blk   24   24

50th anniv. of the first census; introduction of civil registration in Surinam.

William Mogge's Map of Surinam — A91

1971, Oct. 27   *Perf. 11½x11*
391 A91 30c dl yel & dk brn   45   50

300th anniv. of the first map of Surinam.

Map of Albina — A92

August
Kappler — A93

Drop of
Water — A94

Design: 20c, View of Albina from Maroni River.

Perf. 13x12½, 12½x13
1971, Dec. 13
392 A92 15c saph & blk 32 32
393 A92 20c brt grn & blk 32 32
394 A93 25c yel & blk 32 32

125th anniv. of the founding of Albina by August
Kappler (1815-1887).

1972, Feb. 2   **Perf. 12½x13**
Design: 30c, Faucet and water tower.

395 A94 15c vio & blk 30 30
396 A94 30c bl & blk 40 40

Surinam water works, 40th anniversary.

Air Mail
Envelope
A95

1972, Aug. 2   **Litho.**   **Perf. 13x12½**
397 A95 15c red & bl 15 15
398 A95 30c bl & red 24 24

50th anniversary of the arrival of the first airmail
in Surinam, carried by Capt. Dutertre from French
Guiana.

Giant
Tree — A96

Hindu Woman in Rice
Field — A97

Designs: 20c, Wood transport by air lift. 30c,
Hands tending seedling.

1972, Dec. 20   **Photo.**   **Perf. 12½x13**
399 A96 15c yel & dk brn 20 20
400 A96 20c bl & dp brn 20 20
401 A96 30c brt grn & dp brn .. 42 42

Surinam Forestry Commission, 25th anniv.

1973, June 5   **Litho.**   **Perf. 13½x14**
Designs: 25c, J. F. A. Cateau van Rosevelt with
map of Surinam and ship "Lalla Rookh." 30c, Symbolic flower, sun, flag and factories.

402 A97 15c purple & yel 24 24
403 A97 25c maroon & gray 24 20
404 A97 30c yel & light blue ... 32 32

1st immigrants from India, cent.

Queen
Juliana,
Surinam and
House of
Orange
Colors
A97a

1973, Sept. 4   **Perf. 12½x12**
405 A97a 30c sil, blk & org 55 55

25th anniversary of reign of Queen Juliana.

INTERPOL
Emblem
A98

Mailman
A99

Design: 30c, INTERPOL emblem, Surinam visa
handstamp.

1973, Nov. 7   **Litho.**   **Perf. 14x14½**
406 A98 15c vio bl & multi 20 20
407 A98 30c lt bl, lil & blk 32 32

50th anniv. of Intl. Criminal Police Org.

1973, Dec. 12   **Litho.**   **Perf. 12½x13**
Designs: 15c, Pigeons carrying Letters. 30c, Map
of Surinam, plane, ship, train and truck.

408 A99 15c lt yel grn & bl 15 15
409 A99 25c sal, blk & bl 24 24
410 A99 30c ver & multi 40 40

Centenary of stamps of Surinam.

Patient and
Blood
Transfusion
A100

Design: 30c, Cross section of tissue and
oscilloscope.

1974, June 1   **Litho.**   **Perf. 14½x14**
411 A100 15c red brn & multi ... 15 15
412 A100 30c lem & multi 24 24

75th anniversary of the Medical College.

Crop Dusting
A101

1974, July 17   **Litho.**   **Perf. 13½**
413 A101 15c shown 15 15
414 A101 30c Fertilizer plant ... 24 24

Foundation for Development of Mechanical Agriculture in Surinam, 25th anniv.

Old Title Page — A102

1974, July 31   **Perf. 14x14½**
415 A102 15c multi 15 15
416 A102 30c multi 24 24

Bicentenary of the "Weekly Wednesday Surinam
Newspaper." First editor was Beeldsnijder
Matroos.

Paramaribo
Main Post
Office — A103

Design: 30c, Post Office, different view.

1974, Sept. 11   **Litho.**   **Perf. 14½x14**
417 A103 15c brn & blk 20 20
418 A103 30c bl & blk 32 32

Centenary of Universal Postal Union.

Gold Panner
A104

Design: 30c, Modern excavator.

1975, Feb. 5   **Litho.**   **Perf. 13x12½**
419 A104 15c brn & ol bis 15 15
420 A104 30c ver & mar 24 24

Centenary of prospecting policy granting conces-
sions for winning of raw materials.

Symbolic
Design — A105

1975, June 25   **Litho.**   **Perf. 13x12½**
421 A105 15c grn & multi 32 32
422 A105 25c bl & multi 32 32
423 A105 30c red & multi 32 32

Cent. of Intl. Meter Convention, Paris, 1875.

Hands Holding
Saw — A106

Designs: 50c, Book with notes and letter "a."
75c, Hands holding ball.

1975, Nov. 25   **Litho.**   **Perf. 13x14**
424 A106 25c yel, red & brn 32 32
425 A106 50c yel, red & pur 65 65
426 A106 75c dk bl, org & emer 1.00 1.00

Independence. Sheets of 10 (5x2) with ornamental margins.

Oncidium
Lanceanum
A107

Central Bank,
Paramaribo
A109

Orchids: 2c, Epidendrum stenopetalum. 3c,
Brassia lanceana. 4c, Epidendrum ibaguense. 5c,
Epidendrum fragrans.

1975-76   **Litho.**   **Perf. 14½x13½**
427 A107 1c multi 15 15
428 A107 2c multi 15 15
429 A107 3c multi 15 15
430 A107 4c multi 15 15
431 A107 5c multi 15 15

Perf. 13½x13
436 A109 1g rose lil & blk 90 18
437 A109 1½g brn, dp org & blk 1.25 18
438 A109 2½g red brn, org red &
     blk 2.75 22
439 A109 5g grn, yel grn & blk . 5.00 35
440 A109 10g dk vio bl & blk .. 10.00 70
   Nos. 427-431, 436-440 (10) 20.65
   Set value 1.85

Issue dates: Nos. 436-439, Nov. 25, 1975. Nos.
427-431, Feb. 18, 1976. No. 440, May 6, 1976.
For surcharges see Nos. 772-774, 810.

Flag of
Surinam — A110

Design: 35c, Coat of Arms.

1976, Mar. 3   **Perf. 14x13**
445 A110 25c emer & multi 32 32
446 A110 35c red org & multi ... 50 50

Sheets of 12 (6x2) with ornamental margins.

Pomacanthus
Semicirculatus
A111

Fish: 2c, Adioryx diadema. 3c, Pogonoculius
zebra. 4c, Balistes vetula. 5c, Myripristis jacobus.

1976, June 2   **Litho.**   **Perf. 12½x13**
447 A111 1c multi 15 15
448 A111 2c multi 15 15
449 A111 3c multi 15 15
450 A111 4c multi 15 15
451 A111 5c multi 24 15
   Nos. 427-431, C55-C57 (8) 5.65 3.20

See #471-475, 504-508, C72-C74, C85-C87.

19th Century Switchboard and
Telephone — A112

Design: 35c, Satellite, globe and 1976
telephone.

1976, Aug. 5   **Litho.**   **Perf. 13x13½**
452 A112 20c yel & multi 20 20
453 A112 35c ultra & multi 40 40

Centenary of first telephone call by Alexander
Graham Bell, Mar. 10, 1876.

The Story of Anansi Tori, by A.
Baag — A113

Designs: 30c, "Surinam Now" (young people),
by R. Chang. 35c, Lamentation, by Nola Hat-
terman, vert. 50c, Chess Players, by Q. Jan Telting.

Perf. 13x13½, 13½x13
1976, Sept. 29   Photo.
454 A113 20c multi   30 26
455 A113 30c multi   42 40
456 A113 35c multi   55 50
457 A113 50c multi   75 70

Paintings by Surinam artists.

Franklin's Divided Snake Poster, 1754 — A114

1976, Nov. 10   Litho.   Perf. 13x13½
458 A114 20c green & blk   30 30
459 A114 60c orange & blk   1.00 1.00

American Bicentennial.

Ionopsis Utricularioides A115

Surinam Costume A116

Orchids: 30c, Rodiguezia secunda. 35c, Oncidium pusillum. 55c, Sobralia sessilis. 60c, Octomeria surinamensis.

1977, Jan. 19   Litho.   Perf. 14½x13
460 A115 20c ver & multi   26 22
461 A115 30c ultra & multi   40 32
462 A115 35c mag & multi   50 40
463 A115 55c yel & multi   75 60
464 A115 60c grn & multi   80 65
    Nos. 460-464 (5)   2.71 2.19

1977, Mar. 2   Photo.   Perf. 14x13½
Designs: Various Surinamese women's costumes.

465 A116 10c brt bl & multi   15 15
466 A116 15c grn & multi   15 15
467 A116 35c vio & multi   35 35
468 A116 60c org & multi   65 65
469 A116 75c ultra & multi   80 80
470 A116 1g yel & multi   1.10 1.10
    Nos. 465-470 (6)   3.20 3.20

Fish Type of 1976
Tropical Fish: 1c, Liopropoma carmabi. 2c, Holacanthus ciliaris. 3c, Opistognathus aurifrons. 4c, Anisotremus virginicus. 5c, Gramma loreto.

1977, June 8   Litho.   Perf. 12½x13
471 A111 1c multi   15 15
472 A111 2c multi   15 15
473 A111 3c multi   15 15
474 A111 4c multi   15 15
475 A111 5c multi   16 15
    Nos. 471-475,C72-C74 (8)   6.66
    Set value   3.00

Edison's Phonograph, 1877 — A117

Design: 60c, Modern turntable.

1977, Aug. 24   Litho.   Perf. 13½x14
476 A117 20c multi   15 15
477 A117 60c multi   50 50

Invention of the phonograph, cent.

Packet Curacao, 1827 — A118

Designs: 15c, Hellevoetsluis Harbor and postmark, 1827. 30c, Sea chart and technical details of packet Curacao. 35c, Logbook and compass rose. 60c, Map of Paramaribo harbor and 1852 postmark. 95c, Modern liner Stuyvesant.

1977, Sept. 28   Litho.   Perf. 14x13½
478 A118 5c grnsh bl & dk bl   15 15
479 A118 15c org & mar   15 15
480 A118 30c lt brn & blk   16 16
481 A118 35c olive & blk   20 20
482 A118 60c lilac & blk   32 32
483 A118 95c yel grn & dk grn   55 55
    Nos. 478-483 (6)   1.53 1.53

Regular steamer connection between the Netherlands and Surinam, 150th anniversary.

Passiflora Quadrangularis A119

Javanese Costume A120

Flowers: 30c, Centropogon surinamensis. 55c, Gloxinia perennis. 60c, Hydrocleis nymphoides. 75c, Clusia grandiflora.

1978, Feb. 8   Litho.   Perf. 13x14
484 A119 20c multi   15 15
485 A119 30c multi   22 20
486 A119 55c multi   42 40
487 A119 60c multi   45 42
488 A119 75c multi   55 50
    Nos. 484-488 (5)   1.79 1.67

1978, Mar. 1   Photo.   Perf. 14x13
People of Surinam, Costumes: 20c, Forest black. 35c, Chinese. 60c, Creole. 75c, Aborigine Indian. 1g, Hindustani.

480 A120 10c multi   15 15
490 A120 15c multi   15 15
491 A120 35c multi   24 24
492 A120 60c multi   45 45
493 A120 75c multi   55 55
494 A120 1g multi   85 85
    Nos. 489-494 (6)   2.39 2.39

Air Post Stamps of 1972 Surcharged   **10**

1978   Litho.   Perf. 13x13½
495 AP6 1c on 25c #C44   15 15
496 AP6 4c on 15c #C42   18 15
497 AP6 4c on 30c #C45   18 15
498 AP6 4c on 40c #C47   24 16
499 AP6 10c on 75c #C54   30 20
    Nos. 495-499 (5)   1.05 81

"Luchtpost" obliterated with 2 bars.

Old Municipal Church — A121

Johannes King — A122

Designs: 55c, New Municipal Church. 60c, Johannes Raillard.

1978, May 31   Litho.   Perf. 14x13
500 A121 10c bl, blk & gray   15 15
501 A122 20c gray & blk   16 16
502 A121 55c rose lil & blk   38 38
503 A122 60c org & blk   42 42

Evangelical Brothers Community Church, Paramaribo, bicentenary.

Tropical Fish Type of 1976
Tropical Fish: 1c, Nannacara Anomala. 2c, Leporinus fasciatus. 3c, Pristella riddlei. 4c, Nannostomus beckfordi. 5c, Rivulus agilae.

1978, June 21   Perf. 12½x13
504 A111 1c multi   15 15
505 A111 2c multi   15 15
506 A111 3c multi   15 15
507 A111 4c multi   15 15
508 A111 5c multi   15 15
    Nos. 504-508,C85-C87 (8)   6.75
    Set value   3.20

Souvenir Sheet

Commewijne River Development A124

Development: 60c, Map of Surinam and dam. 95c, Planes and world map.

1978, Oct. 18   Litho.   Perf. 13½x14
509   Sheet of 3   1.10 1.10
a.   A124 20c multi   15 15
b.   A124 60c multi   35 35
c.   A124 95c multi   50 50

Coconuts A125

Wright Brothers' Flyer 1 A126

1978-85   Photo.   Perf. 13½x12½
510 A125 5c shown   15 15
a.   Bklt. pane of 12 (4 #510, 3 #511, 5 #515) ('80)   2.50
511 A125 10c Oranges   15 15
512 A125 15c Papayas   15 15
a.   Bklt. pane of 11 + label (5 #512, 6 #514) ('79)   2.50
513 A125 20c Bananas   15 15
514 A125 25c Soursop   20 20
514A A125 30c Cocoa beans ('85)   55 55
b.   Bklt. pane of 7 + label (5 #514A, 1 #513) ('85)   4.00 4.00
515 A125 35c Watermelon   28 28
    Nos. 510-515 (7)   1.63 1.63

Perf. 13x14, 14x13
1978, Dec. 13   Litho.
Designs: 20c, Daedalus and Icarus, vert. 95c, DC 8. 125c, Concorde.

516 A126 20c multi   15 15
517 A126 60c multi   50 50
518 A126 95c multi   75 75
519 A126 125c multi   1.00 1.00

75th anniversary of 1st powered flight.

Rodriguezia Candida A127

Javanese Dancer A128

Flowers: 20c, Stanhopea grandiflora. 35c, Scuticaria steelei. 60c, Bollea violacea.

1979, Feb. 7   Photo.   Perf. 12½x14
520 A127 10c multi   15 15
521 A127 20c multi   20 15
522 A127 35c multi   35 28
523 A127 60c multi   65 50

1979, Feb. 28
Dancing Costumes: 10c, Forest Negro. 15c, Chinese. 20c, Creole. 25c, Aborigine Indian. 35c, Hindustani.

524 A128 5c multi   15 15
525 A128 10c multi   15 15
526 A128 15c multi   15 15
527 A128 20c multi   16 15
528 A128 25c multi   22 20
529 A128 35c multi   32 28
    Set value   1.00 90

Equetus Pulchellus A129

Tropical Fish: 2c, Apogon binotatus. 3c, Anisotremus virginicus. 5c, Bodianus rufus. 35c, Microspathodon chrysurus.

1979, May 30   Photo.   Perf. 14x13
530 A129 1c multi   15 15
531 A129 2c multi   15 15
532 A129 3c multi   15 15
533 A129 5c multi   15 15
534 A129 35c multi   55 28
    Nos. 530-534,C89-C91 (8)   5.50
    Set value   2.65

See Nos. 557-561, C92-C94.

Javanese Wooden Head — A130

Folkart: 35c, Head ornament, Indian. 60c, Horse's head, Javanese.

1979, Aug. 29   Litho.   Perf. 14x13
535 A130 20c multi   15 15
536 A130 35c multi   28 28
537 A130 60c multi   50 50

Sir Rowland Hill A131

Javanese Girl's Costume A133

SOS Emblem, House — A132

YEAR OF THE CHILD

1979, Oct. 3   Litho.   Perf. 13x14
538 A131 1g yel & olive   75 85

Sir Rowland Hill (1795-1879), originator of penny postage.

1979, Oct. 3   Perf. 14x13
Design: 60c, SOS emblem and buildings.

539 A132 20c multi   15 15
540 A132 60c multi   50 50

Intl. Year of the Child; SOS Children's Villages, 30th anniv.

1980, Feb. 6   Photo.   Perf. 13x14
541 A133 10c shown   15 15
542 A133 15c Forest Black boy   15 15
543 A133 25c Chinese girl   24 20
544 A133 60c Creole girl   60 50
545 A133 90c Indian girl   85 70
546 A133 1g Hindustani boy   95 80
    Nos. 541-546 (6)   2.94 2.50

Rotary Intl.,
75th
Anniversary
A134

Design: 20c, Handshake, Rotary emblem, vert.

Perf. 13x14, 14x13

1980, Feb. 23 Litho.
547 A134 20c ultra & yel 15 15
548 A134 60c ultra & yel 60 60

Rowland
Hill — A135

Weight
Lifting — A136

1980, May 6 Litho. **Perf. 13x14**
549 A135 50c Mailcoach 35 35
550 A135 1g shown 70 70
a. Souvenir sheet 80 80
551 A135 2g People mailing letters 1.40 1.40

London 1980 Intl. Stamp Exhibition, May 6-14.
No. 550a contains No. 550 in changed colors. Blue
and black margin shows designs of Nos. 549, 551,
London 1980 emblem. (No. 550 in lilac rose and
multicolored; stamps of No. 550a in light green and
multicolored).

1980, June 17
552 A136 20c shown 15 15
553 A136 30c Diving 24 24
554 A136 50c Gymnast 40 40
555 A136 75c Basketball 60 60
556 A136 150c Running 1.25 1.25
a. Souvenir sheet of 3, #554-556 2.25 2.25
Nos. 552-556 (5) 2.64 2.64

22nd Summer Olympic Games, Moscow, July
19-Aug. 3.

Fish Type of 1979

Tropical Fish: 10c, Osteoglossum bicirrhosum.
15c, Colossoma species. 25c, Hemigrammus
pulcher. 30c, Petitella georgiae. 45c, Copeina
guttata.

1980, Sept. 10 Photo. **Perf. 14x13**
557 A129 10c multi 16 15
558 A129 15c multi 24 15
559 A129 25c multi 40 20
560 A129 30c multi 48 24
561 A129 45c multi 70 35
Nos. 557-561,C92-C94 (8) 5.53 2.84

Open Hands
(Reflection)
A137

Passiflora Laurifolia
A138

Souvenir Sheet
1980, Nov. 19 Litho. **Perf. 13x14**
562 Sheet of 3 2.75 2.75
a. A137 50c shown 35 35
b. A137 1g Shaking hands (cooperation) 65 65
c. A137 2g Victory sign 1.50 1.50

5th anniv. of independence.

1981, Jan. 14 Litho. **Perf. 13x14**
Designs: Flower paintings by Maria Sibylle Merian (1647-1717).

563 A138 20c shown 15 15
564 A138 30c Aphelandra pectinata 24 24
565 A138 60c Caesalpinia pulcherrima 50 50
566 A138 75c Hibiscus mutabilis 60 60

567 A138 1.25g Hippeastrum puniceum 1.10 1.10
Nos. 563-567 (5) 2.59 2.59

Renovation of the
Economic
Order — A139

1981, Feb. 25 **Perf. 14x13**
568 A139 30c shown 16 16
569 A139 60c Educational Order 35 35
570 A139 75c Social Order 40 40
571 A139 1g Political Order 55 55
a. Souvenir sheet of 2, #569, 571 1.40 1.40

Government renovation.

Miniature Sheet

Youths — A140

1981, Apr. 29 Litho. **Perf. 13½**
572 Sheet of 2 1.75 1.75
a. A140 1g shown 75 75
b. A140 1.50g Youths, diff. 75 75

Youth and its future. Entire sheet in continuous
design.

Souvenir Sheet

No. 424,
Exhibition
Hall — A141

1981, May 22 Litho. **Perf. 13½x14**
573 Sheet of 3 2.50 2.50
a. A141 50c shown 35 38
b. A141 1g Penny Black 70 75
c. A141 2g Austria #5 1.40 1.50

WIPA '81 Intl. Philatelic Exhibition, Vienna, May
22-31.

Leptodactylus
Pentadactylus
A142

1981, June 24 Photo. **Perf. 14x13**
574 A142 40c Phyllomedusa hy-
pochondrialis 60 32
575 A142 50c shown 75 40
576 A142 60c Hyla boans 90 50
Nos. 574-576,C95-C97 (6) 6.60 3.62

Child Wearing
Earphones
A143

1981, Sept. 16 Litho. **Perf. 14x13**
580 A143 50c shown 40 40
581 A143 100c Child reading Braille 80 80
582 A143 150c Woman in wheelchair 1.25 1.25

Intl. Year of the Disabled.

Planter's House
on Parakreek
River — A144

Designs: Illustrations from Voyage to Surinam,
by P.I. Benoit.

1981, Oct. 21 Photo. **Perf. 14x13**
583 A144 20c shown 15 15
584 A144 30c Sarameca St., Paramaribo 22 22
585 A144 75c Negro Hamlet, Paramaribo 60 60
586 A144 1g Fish Market, Paramaribo 80 80
a. Miniature sheet of 1 1.25 1.10
587 A144 1.25g Blaauwe Berg Cascade 1.00 1.00
Nos. 583-587 (5) 2.77 2.77

Research and
Peaceful Uses
of
Space — A145

1982, Jan. 13 Litho.
588 A145 35c Satellites 32 32
589 A145 65c Columbia space shuttle 65 65
590 A145 1g Apollo-Soyuz 1.00 1.00

Caretta
Caretta — A146

1982, Feb. 17 Photo. **Perf. 14x13**
591 A146 5c shown 15 15
592 A146 10c Chelonia mydas 16 15
593 A146 20c Dermochelys coriacea 30 20
594 A146 25c Eretmochelys imbricata 40 28
595 A146 35c Lepidochelys olivacea 50 32
Nos. 591-595,C98-C100 (8) 5.76 3.95

SURINAME

25th Anniv. of
Lions Intl. in
Surinam
A147

1982, May 7 Litho.
596 A147 35c multi 38 38
597 A147 70c multi 75 75

A148 A149

1982, May 18 Litho. **Perf. 13x14**
598 A148 35c Helping the sick 50 50
599 A148 65c Birthplace, map 1.00 1.00
a. Souvenir sheet 1.00 1.00

Beatification of Father Petrus Donders, May 23.

1982, June 9 Litho. **Perf. 13x14**
600 A149 50c Stamp designing 40 40
601 A149 100c Printing 85 85
602 A149 150c Collecting 1.25 1.25
a. Souvenir sheet of 3, #600-602 2.50 2.50

PHILEXFRANCE '82 Stamp Exhibition, Paris,
June 11-21. Nos. 600-602 in continuous design.

TB Bacillus
Centenary
A150

1982, Sept. 15 Litho. **Perf. 14x13**
603 A150 35c Text 38 35
604 A150 65c Microscope 75 70
605 A150 150c Bacillus 1.90 1.90

Marienburg
Sugar Co.
Centenary
A151

1982, Oct. 20
606 A151 35c Mill 30 30
607 A151 65c Gathering cane 60 60
608 A151 100c Rail transport 95 95
609 A151 150c Gears 1.50 1.50

A152

Inga
Edulis — A153

EBG Missionaries, 250th Anniv. in Caribbean:
35c, Municipal Church, horiz. 65c, St. Thomas
Monastery, horiz. 150c, Johan Leonhardt Dober
(1706-1766).

Perf. 14x13, 13x14
1982, Dec. 13 Litho.
610 A152 35c multi 28 28
611 A152 65c multi 55 55
612 A152 150c multi 1.50 1.50

1983, Jan. 12
Flower Paintings by Maria Sibylle Merian (1647-
1717). Nos. 613-618 horiz.

613 A153 1c Erythrina fusca 15 15
614 A153 2c Ipomoea acuminata 15 15
615 A153 3c Heliconia psittacorum 15 15
616 A153 5c Ipomoea 16 15
617 A153 10c Herba non denominata 22 20
618 A153 15c Anacardium occidentale 32 30
619 A153 20c shown 40 38
620 A153 25c Abelmoschus mos-
chatus 55 50
621 A153 30c Argemone mexicana 70 65
622 A153 35c Costus arabicus 80 75
623 A153 45c Muellera frutescens 1.00 90
624 A153 65c Punica granatum 1.50 1.40
Nos. 613-624 (12) 6.10 5.68

Scouting
Year — A154

500th Birth Anniv.
of Raphael — A155

1983, Feb. 22 Litho. **Perf. 13x14**
625 A154 40c Anniv. emblem 65 65
626 A154 65c Baden-Powell 1.00 1.00
627 A154 70c Tent, campfire 1.10 1.10
628 A154 80c Ax in log 1.25 1.25

1983, Apr. 13 Photo.

Crayon sketches.

629 A155 5c multi 15 15
630 A155 10c multi 15 15
631 A155 40c multi 48 48
632 A155 65c multi 75 75
633 A155 70c multi 80 80
634 A155 80c multi 1.00 1.00
Nos. 629-634 (6) 3.33 3.33

1982 Coins and
Banknotes
A156

1983, June 1   Litho.   *Perf. 14x13*

635	A156	5c	1-cent coin	15 15
636	A156	10c	5-cent coin	15 15
637	A156	40c	10-cent coin	48 48
638	A156	65c	25-cent coin	75 75
639	A156	70c	1g note	80 80
640	A156	80c	2.50g note	1.00 1.00
		Nos. 635-640 (6)		3.33 3.33

For surcharge, see No. 751. For overprints see Nos. J59-J60.

25th Anniv. of
Dept. of
Construction
A157

Manned
Ballooning, 200th
Anniv.
A159

Local Butterflies
A158

1983, June 15   Litho.   *Perf. 13x14*

641	A157	25c	Map	30 30
642	A157	50c	Map, bulldozers	60 60

Perf. 13x14, 14x13
1983, Sept. 14   Litho.

Drawings by Maria Sibylle Merian (1647-1717). Nos. 643-648 vert.

643	A158	1c	Papile anchisiades esper	15 15
644	A158	2c	Urania leilus	15 15
645	A158	3c	Morpho deidamia	15 15
646	A158	5c	Thysania aguippina	18 15
647	A158	10c	Oncidium papilio	24 16
648	A158	15c	Metamorpha dido	35 25
649	A158	20c	Morpho menelaus	45 30
650	A158	25c	Manduca rustica	60 40
651	A158	30c	Rothschildia sp.	75 50
652	A158	35c	Catopsilia ebule	90 60
653	A158	45c	Pailio androgeos	1.25 80
654	A148	65c	Eumorpha vitis	1.75 1.25
		Nos. 643-654 (12)		6.92 4.86

1983, Oct. 19   Litho.   *Perf. 13x14*

Designs: 5c, 1783, sheep, cock and duck. 10c, first manned flight, d'Arlandes and Pilatre de Rozier. 40c, first hydrogen balloon, Jacques Charles. 65c, 1870, Paris flight, minister Gambetta. 70c, Double Eagle II, transatlantic flight. 80c, Intl. Balloon Festival, Albuquerque.

655	A159	5c	multi	15 15
656	A159	10c	multi	16 16
657	A159	40c	multi	65 65
658	A159	65c	multi	1.00 1.00
659	A159	70c	multi	1.10 1.10
660	A159	80c	multi	1.25 1.25
		Nos. 655-660 (6)		4.31 4.31

Martin Luther, 500th
Birth Anniv. — A160

1983, Dec. 7   Litho.

661	A160	25c	Portrait	30 25
662	A160	50c	Engraving	60 55

Local
Flowers — A161

Local
Seashells — A162

1984, Jan. 11   Litho.

663	A161	5c	Catasetum discolor	15 15
664	A161	10c	Menadenium labiosum	16 15
665	A161	40c	Comparettia falcata	65 60
666	A161	50c	Rodriquezia decora	1.00 90
667	A161	70c	Oncidium papilio	1.10 1.00
668	A161	75c	Epidendrum porpax	1.25 1.10
		Nos. 663-668 (6)		4.31 3.90

1984, Feb. 22   Litho.

669	A162	40c	Arca zebra	95 65
670	A162	65c	Trachycardium egmontianum	1.65 1.10
671	A162	70c	Tellina radiata	1.65 1.10
672	A162	80c	Vermicularia knorrii	2.00 1.25

Intl. Civil
Aviation Org.,
40th
Anniv. — A163

1984, May 16   Litho.   *Perf. 14x13*

673	A163	35c	Sea plane	42 42
674	A163	65c	Surinam Airways jet	90 90

A164

A165

Greek Art and Artifacts: Ancient Games.

1984, June 13   *Perf. 13x14*

675	A164	2c	Running	15 15
676	A164	3c	Javelin, discus, long jump	15 15
677	A164	5c	Massage	15 15
678	A164	10c	Ointment massage	15 15
679	A164	15c	Wrestling	16 16
680	A164	20c	Boxing	20 20
681	A164	30c	Horse racing	35 35
682	A164	35c	Chariot racing	40 40
683	A164	50c	Temple of Olympia	50 50
684	A164	50c	Crypt entrance	60 60
685	A164	65c	Olympia Stadium	80 80
686	A164	75c	Zeus (bust)	85 85
a.		Min. sheet of 3, #675, 682, 686		1.50 1.50
		Nos. 675-686 (12)		4.46 4.46

1984 Summer Olympics.

1984, Sept. 18   Litho.   *Perf. 13x14*

687	A165	50c	Ball, net	80 75
688	A165	90c	Ball in net	1.40 1.25

Intl. Council of Military Sports basketball championship.

World Chess
Championship,
Moscow
A166

1984, Oct. 10   Litho.   *Perf. 14x13*

689	A166	10c	Red Square	15 15
690	A166	15c	Knight, king, pawn	18 18
691	A166	30c	Kasparov	35 35
692	A166	50c	Board	60 60
693	A166	75c	Karpov	1.00 1.00
a.		Souv. sheet of 3 (30c, 50c, 75c)		2.00 2.00
694	A166	90c	Game	1.10 1.10
		Nos. 689-694 (6)		3.38 3.38

For overprints, see Nos. 742, 796.

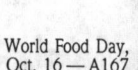
World Food Day,
Oct. 16 — A167

1984, Oct. 10

695	A167	50c	Children receiving milk	60 60
696	A167	90c	Food	1.00 1.00

Cacti — A168

Independence,
5th
Anniv. — A169

1985, Jan. 9   Litho.   *Perf. 13x14*

697	A168	5c	Leaf	15 15
698	A168	10c	Melon	15 15
699	A168	30c	Pillar	45 45
700	A168	50c	Fig	70 70
701	A168	75c	Nightqueen	1.10 1.10
702	A168	90c	Segment	1.25 1.25
		Nos. 697-702 (6)		3.80 3.80

1985, Feb. 22   Litho.   *Perf. 12½x14*

Designs, 5c, Star, red stripe from national flag. 30c, Unified labor. 50c, Perpetual flowering plant. 75c, Growth of agriculture. 90c, Peace dove and plant.

703	A169	5c	multi	15 15
704	A169	30c	multi	40 40
705	A169	50c	multi	65 65
a.		Min. sheet of 3, 2 #703, #705		85
706	A169	75c	multi	1.00 1.00
707	A169	90c	multi	1.25 1.25
		Nos. 703-707 (5)		3.45 3.45

Chamber of Commerce
and Industry, 75th
Anniv. — A170

UN Emblem,
Natl. Coat of
Arms — A171

1985, Apr. 17   Litho.   *Perf. 14x12½*

708	A170	50c	Chamber emblem	50 50
709	A170	90c	Chamber, factories	90 90

1985, Apr. 29   Litho.   *Perf. 13x14*

710	A171	50c	multi	50 50
711	A171	90c	multi	90 90

UN, 40th anniv.

Trains — A172

1985, June 5   Litho.   *Perf. 13½*

712	A172	5c	No. 192	15 15
713	A172	5c	Monaco, No. J50	15 15
714	A172	10c	Locomotive "Dam"	16 16
715	A172	10c	Diesel locomotive	16 16
716	A172	20c	Steam locomotive "No. 3737"	24 24
717	A172	20c	Netherlands locomotive "IC III"	24 24
718	A172	30c	Stephenson's locomotive "Rocket"	40 40
719	A172	30c	French Railways high-speed TGV	40 40
720	A172	50c	Stephenson's locomotive "Adler"	65 65
721	A172	50c	French Railways commuter train	65 65
722	A172	75c	Locomotive "General"	1.00 1.00
723	A172	75c	Japanese bullet train "Shinkansen"	1.00 1.00
		Nos. 712-723 (12)		5.20 5.20

Stamps of the same denomination se-tenant. For surcharges see Nos. 749-750, 808-809, 928-929.

Birds — A173

1985-93   Litho.   *Perf. 14x13*

725	A173	10c	Toucan	15 15
729	A173	1g	American purple fowl	90 90
a.		Miniature sheet of 1		1.90 1.90
730	A173	1.50g	Tiger bird	1.50 1.50
732	A173	2.50g	Red ibis	2.50 2.50
734	A173	5g	Guyana red cockerel	4.50 4.50
735	A173	10g	Harpy eagle	9.00 9.00
735A	A173	15g	Parrot	18.00 18.00
735B	A173	25g	Owl	28.00 28.00
735C	A173	1300f	Rose lepelaar	47.50 47.50
		Nos. 725-735C (9)		112.05 112.05

Nos. 725, 735A inscribed 1990.
Issued: 1g, 1.50g, 2.50g, 8/21; 5g, 1/2/86; 10g, 10/1/86; 10c, 15g, 1/30/91; 25g, 1/20/93; 1300f, 3/31/94.
For surcharge and overprint see Nos. 964, J63.
This is an expanding set. Numbers will change if necessary.

Mailboxes
A174

Natl.
Independence,
10th Anniv.
A175

1985, Oct. 2   Litho.   *Perf. 13x14*

736	A174	15c	Germany, 1900	15 15
737	A174	30c	France, 1900	30 30
738	A174	50c	England, 1932	48 48
739	A174	90c	Netherlands, 1850	90 90

1985, Nov. 22

740	A175	50c	Agriculture	48 48
741	A175	90c	Industry	90 90
a.		Miniature sheet of 2, #740-741		1.40 1.40

КАСПАРОВ
Wereldkampioen
9 nov. 1985

No. 691 Ovptd. in Red

1985, Nov. 22   Litho.   *Perf. 14x13*

742	A166	30c	multi	1.50 1.50

World Wildlife
Fund — A177

Orchids.

1986, Feb. 19   Litho.   *Perf. 14x13*

743	A177	5c	Epidendrum ciliare	16 16
744	A177	15c	Cycnoches chlorochilon	50 50
745	A177	30c	Epidendrum anceps	1.00 1.00
746	A177	50c	Epidendrum vespa	1.65 1.65

Halley's
Comet — A178

Designs: 50c, The Bayeux Tapestry, c. 1092, France. 110c, Halley's Comet.

1986, Mar. 5 Litho. Perf. 14x12½
747	A178	50c multi	48	48
748	A178	110c multi	1.00	1.00

Nos. 720-721 Surcharged in Red

1986, May 28 Litho. Perf. 13½
749	A172	15c on 50c #720	50	50
750	A172	15c on 50c #721	50	50

30c

No. 639
Surcharged

150 jaar FINANCIËNGEBOUW

1986, June 25 Litho. Perf. 14x13
751	A156	30c on 70c multi	1.00	1.00

Finance Building, Paramaribo, 150th anniv.

Surinam
Shipping Co.,
50th
Anniv. — A179

1986, Sept. 1 Litho. Perf. 14x13
752	A179	50c Emblem	50	50
753	A179	110c Freighter Saramacca	1.10	1.10

Monkeys
A180

1987, Jan. 7 Litho.
755	A180	35c Alouatta	38	38
756	A180	60c Aotus	65	65
757	A180	110c Saimiri	1.25	1.25
758	A180	120c Cacajao	1.40	1.40

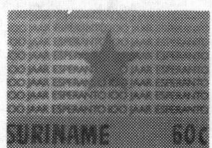

Esperanto,
Cent. — A181

1987, Feb. 4 Litho.
759	A181	60c shown	60	60
760	A181	110 World map, doves	1.25	1.25
761	A181	120c L.L. Zamenhof	1.40	1.40

10th Pan-American
Games, Indianapolis,
July 23 — A182

Forestry
Commission, 40th
Anniv. — A183

1987, June 3 Litho. Perf. 13x14
763	A182	90c Soccer	85	85
764	A182	110c Swimming	1.10	1.10
765	A182	150c Basketball	1.40	1.40

1987, July 21 Litho. Perf. 13x14
766	A183	90c Emblem	1.00	1.00
767	A183	120c Logging	1.25	1.25
768	A183	150c Parrot in virgin forest	1.65	1.65

Intl. Year of
Shelter for the
Homeless
A184

1987, Sept. 2 Litho. Perf. 14x13
769	A184	90c Distressed boy, en-		
		campment	85	85
770	A184	120c Man, ghetto	1.25	1.25

Founders
Catherine and
William Booth
A185

1987, Sept. 2 Perf. 14x13
771	A185	150c multi	1.40	1.40

Salvation Army in the Caribbean, cent.

Nos. 436-438
Surcharged **35 ct**

1987, Mar. Litho. Perf. 13½x13
772	A109	35c on 1g	1.50	1.50
773	A109	50c on 1.50g	2.25	2.25
774	A109	60c on 2.50g	2.75	2.75

Fruits — A186

Perf. 12½x13½

1987, Oct. 14 Litho.
775	A186	10c Bananas	15	15
776	A186	15c Cacao	16	16
777	A186	20c Pineapple	20	20
778	A186	25c Papaya	28	28
779	A186	35c Oranges	40	40
		Nos. 775-779 (5)	1.19	1.19

Aircraft and Aircraft on Stamps — A187

1987, Oct. 14 Litho. Perf. 13½
784	A187	25c Degen, 1808	25	25
785	A187	25c Ultra Light	25	25
786	A187	35c J.C.H. Ellehammer,		
		1906	35	35
787	A187	35c Concorde jet	35	35
788	A187	60c Fokker F7, 1924	60	60
789	A187	60c Fokker F28 jet	60	60
790	A187	90c Spin Fokker, 1910	85	85
791	A187	90c DC-10	85	85
792	A187	110c Orion, 1932	1.10	1.10
793	A187	110c Boeing 747	1.10	1.00
794	A187	120c No. 346	1.25	1.25
795	A187	120c No. 518	1.25	1.25
		Nos. 784-795 (12)	8.80	8.70

Stamps of the same denominaion printed se-
tenant.

No. 693a Overprinted "3e match sevilla
1987" on Stamps in 3 or 4 Lines and with
Bar and "sevilla 1987" in Sheet Margin

1987, Nov. 2 Litho. Perf. 14x13
Souvenir Sheet
796		Sheet of 3	19.00	
a.		A166 30c Kasparov	3.50	
b.		A166 50c Board	6.00	
c.		A166 75c Karpov	9.00	

Alligators and
Crocodiles
A188

1988, Jan. 20 Litho. Perf. 14x13
797	A188	50c Gavialis gangeticus	50	50
798	A188	60c Crocodylus niloticus	65	65
799	A188	90c Melanosuchus niger	95	95
800	A188	110c Mississippi alligator	1.25	1.25

Traditional Wedding
Costumes — A189

1988, Feb. 24 Litho. Perf. 13x14
801	A189	35c Javanese	35	35
802	A189	60c Bushman	60	60
803	A189	80c Chinese	80	80
804	A189	110c Creole	1.10	1.10
805	A189	120c Indian	1.25	1.25
806	A189	130c Hindustan	1.40	1.40
		Nos. 801-806 (6)	5.50	5.50

Nos. 722-723 and 440 Surcharged in
Black or Silver

 60c **125 c**

Perf. 13½x13, 13½

1988, Mar. 23 Litho.
808	A172	60c on 75c #722	3.50	
809	A172	60c on 75c #723	3.50	
a.		Pair, #808-809	7.00	
810	A109	125c on 10g #440 (S)	7.50	

1988 Summer
Olympics,
Seoul — A190

Abolition of
Slavery, 125th
Anniv. — A191

1988, May 4 Litho. Perf. 13x14
812	A190	90c Relay	85	85
813	A190	110c Soccer	1.10	1.10
814	A190	120c Pole vault	1.25	1.25
a.		Souvenir sheet of 3, #812-814	3.25	3.25
815	A190	250c Women's tennis	2.50	2.50

1988, June 29 Litho.
816	A191	50c Abaisa Monument	58	58
817	A191	110c Kwakoe Monument	1.25	1.25
818	A191	120c Home of Anton de		
		Kom	1.35	1.35

See Netherlands Antilles Nos. 597-598.

Intl. Fund for
Agricultural
Development
(IFAD), 10th
Anniv.
A192

1988, Sept. 21 Perf. 14x13
819	A192	105c Crop harvest	1.20	1.20
820	A192	110c Net fishing	1.25	1.25
821	A192	125c Agricultural research	1.40	1.40

FILACEPT '88, The
Netherlands, Oct. 18-
23 — A193

1988, Oct. 18 Litho. Perf. 13
822	A193	120c Egypt #49	1.15	1.15
823	A193	150c Netherlands #334	1.40	1.40
824	A193	250c Surinam #238	2.35	2.35

Souvenir Sheet
**Same Types, Colors Changed (120c,
150c)**
825		Sheet of 3	5.00	5.00
a.		A193 120c Egypt Type A23 (4m green)	1.15	1.15
b.		A193 150c Netherlands Type A81 (10c red brown)	1.40	1.40
c.		A193 250c Surinam No. 239	2.35	2.35

Stylized
Butterfly
Stroke — A194

1988, Nov. 1 Litho. Perf. 14x13
826	A194	110c multi	1.25	1.25

Anthony Nesty, swimmer and 1st Olympic gold
medalist from Surinam.

Otters — A195

1989, Jan. 18 Litho. Perf. 14x13
827	A195	10c Otter	15	15
828	A195	20c Two on land	22	22
829	A195	25c Two crossing log	28	28
830	A195	30c Fishing	35	35
		Nos. 827-830,C107 (5)	3.05	3.05

Classic and Modern Automobiles — A196

1989, June 7 Litho. Perf. 13½
831	A196	25c 1930 Mercedes Tourenwagen	25	25
832	A196	25c 1985 Mercedes-Benz 300E	25	25
833	A196	60c 1897 Daimler	60	60
834	A196	60c 1986 Jaguar Sovereign	60	60
835	A196	90c 1898 Renault Voiturette	90	90
836	A196	90c 1989 Renault 25TX	90	90
837	A196	105c 1927 Volvo Jacob	1.05	1.05
838	A196	105c 1989 Volvo 440	1.05	1.05
839	A196	110c Left half of Monaco #484	1.10	1.10
840	A196	110c Right half of Monaco #484	1.10	1.10
841	A196	120c 1936 Toyota AA	1.20	1.20
842	A196	120c 1988 Toyota Corolla sedan	1.20	1.20
		Nos. 831-842 (12)	10.20	10.20

Stamps of the same denomination printed se-
tenant.

No. 686a Ovptd. "PHILEXFRANCE 7t/m
17 juli 1989" on Margin, with Exhibition
Emblem on Stamps in Gold

1989, July 7 Litho. Perf. 13x14
Miniature Sheet
843		Sheet of 3	1.50	1.50
a.		A164 2c on No. 675	15	15
b.		A164 35c on No. 682	42	42
c.		A164 75c on No. 686	95	95

PHILEXFRANCE '89.

Photography, 150th Anniv. — A197

1989, Sept. 6   Litho.   Perf. 14x13
844 A197 60c Joseph Niepce   68   68
845 A197 110c Daguerreotype camera 1.25 1.25
846 A197 120c Louis Daguerre   1.35 1.35

America Issue — A198

UPAE emblem and pre-Columbian amulets.

1989, Oct. 12   Litho.   Perf. 13x14
847 A198 60c Amazon or Jade Stones 68   68
848 A198 110c Bisque fertility statue 1.25 1.25

The White House, Washington, DC, and Stamps on Stamps — A199

Perf. 13x14, 14x13
1989, Nov. 17   Litho.
849 A199 110c No. 445, vert.   1.25 1.25
850 A199 150c US No. 990   1.70 1.70
851 A199 250c No. 459   2.80 2.80
  a. Souvenir sheet of 3, #849-851 5.75 5.75

World Stamp Expo '89 and 20th UPU Congress, Washington, DC.

UNESCO Intl. Literacy Year — A200

Arya Dewaker Temple, 60th Anniv. — A201

1990, Jan. 19   Photo.   Perf. 13x14
852 A200 60c shown   68   68
853 A200 110c Emblems   1.25 1.25
854 A200 120c Emblems, youth reading 1.35 1.35

1990, Feb. 14   Litho.
855 A201 60c dk red brn, blk & red 68   68
856 A201 110c vio blue & blk   1.25 1.25
857 A201 200c emer grn & blk   2.25 2.25

A202   A203

1990, May 4
858 A202 110c Surinam #C1   1.25 1.25
859 A202 200c Great Britain #1 2.25 2.25
860 A202 250c Great Britain #208 2.75 2.75
  a. Souvenir sheet of 3, #858-860 6.75 6.75

Penny Black, 150th anniv. Stamps World London '90.

1990, Aug. 9
861 A203 60c Couple carrying baskets 70   70
862 A203 110c Woman carrying bundle 1.25 1.25
863 A203 120c Man carrying baskets 1.40 1.40

Javanese Immigration, cent.

Flowers A204

1990, Sept. 5   Perf. 13½
864 A204 25c Punica granatum   28   28
865 A204 25c Passiflora laurifolia 28   28
866 A204 35c Hippeastrum puniceum 40   40
867 A204 35c Ipomaea batatas   40   40
868 A204 60c Hibiscus syriacus 68   68
869 A204 60c Jasminum officinale 68   68
870 A204 105c Musa serapionis 1.20 1.20
871 A204 105c Hibiscus mutabilis 1.20 1.20
872 A204 110c Plumiria rubra   1.25 1.25
873 A204 110c Hibiscus diversifolius 1.25 1.25
874 A204 120c Bixa orellana   1.35 1.35
875 A204 120c Ceasalpinia pulcherima 1.35 1.35
  Nos. 864-875 (12)   10.32 10.32

Stamps of the same denomination printed setenant.

America Issue — A205

1990, Oct. 10   Litho.   Perf. 14x13
876 A205 60c bluish green & blk 68   68
877 A205 110c brn & blk   1.25 1.25

Organization of American States, Cent. — A206

1990, Oct. 10
878 A206 110c multicolored   1.25 1.25

Independence, 15th Anniv. — A207

1990, Nov. 21   Litho.   Perf. 13x14
879 A207 10c shown   15   15
880 A207 60c Passion flower   72   72
881 A207 110c Dove with olive branch 1.30 1.30

Architecture A208

Buildings: 35c, Waterfront warehouse. 60c, Upper class residence. 75c, Labor inspection building. 105c, Plantation supervisor's residence. 110c, Ministry of Labor. 200c, Small residences.

1991, May 15   Litho.   Perf. 14x13
882 A208 35c multicolored   42   42
883 A208 60c multicolored   75   75
884 A208 75c multicolored   90   90
885 A208 105c multicolored   1.25 1.25
886 A208 110c multicolored   1.35 1.35
887 A208 200c multicolored   2.45 2.45
  Nos. 882-887 (6)   7.12 7.12

Puma Concolor A209

Various pictures of pumas.

Perf. 13x14, 14x13
1991, Sept. 12   Litho.
892 A209 10c multi, vert.   15   15
893 A209 20c multi, vert.   22   22
894 A209 25c multi, vert.   28   28
895 A209 30c multi, vert.   35   35
896 A209 125c multi   1.40 1.40
897 A209 500c multi   5.60 5.60
  Nos. 892-897 (6)   8.00 8.00

Nos. 896-897 are airmail.

Discovery of America, 500th Anniv. (in 1991) — A210

Diagram showing Columbus' route: 60c, Western Atlantic and Caribbean Sea. 110c, Eastern Atlantic.

1991, Oct. 11   Perf. 13x14
898 A210 60c lt bl, red & blk 70   70
899 A210 110c lt bl, red & blk 1.25 1.25
  a. Pair, #898-899   2.00 2.00

UPAEP. No. 899a has continous design.

Snakes — A211

Designs: No. 900, Corallus enydris. No. 901, Corallus caninus. No. 902, Lachesis muta. No. 903, Boa constrictor. No. 904, Micrurus surinamensis. No. 905, Crotalus durissus. No. 906, Eunectes murinus. No. 907, Clelia cloelia. No. 908, Epicrates cenchris. No. 909, Chironius carinatus. No. 910, Oxybelis argenteus. No. 911, Spilotes pullatus.

1991, Nov. 14   Perf. 13½
900 A211 25c multicolored   28   28
901 A211 25c multicolored   28   28
  a. Pair, #900-901   56   56
902 A211 35c multicolored   40   40
903 A211 35c multicolored   40   40
  a. Pair, #902-903   80   80
904 A211 60c multicolored   70   70
905 A211 60c multicolored   70   70
  a. Pair, #904-905   1.40 1.40
906 A211 75c multicolored   85   85
907 A211 75c multicolored   85   85
  a. Pair, #906-907   1.70 1.70
908 A211 110c multicolored   1.25 1.25
909 A211 110c multicolored   1.25 1.25
  a. Pair, #908-909   2.50 2.50
910 A211 200c multicolored   2.25 2.25
911 A211 200c multicolored   2.25 2.25
  a. Pair, #910-911   4.50 4.50
  Nos. 900-911 (12)   11.46 11.46

Orchids — A212   A213

Designs: 50c, Cycnoches haagii. 60c, Lycaste cristata. 75c, Galeandra dives, horiz. 125c, Vanilla mexicana. 150c, Cyrtopodium glutiniferum. 250c, Gongora quinquenervis.

1992, Feb. 12   Perf. 13x14, 14x13
912 A212 50c multicolored   58   58
913 A212 60c multicolored   70   70
914 A212 75c multicolored   85   85
915 A212 125c multicolored   1.40 1.40
916 A212 150c multicolored   1.70 1.70
917 A212 250c multicolored   2.80 2.80
  Nos. 912-917 (6)   8.03 8.03

Souvenir Sheet

Designs: a, 75c, #847. b, 125c, #848. c, 150c, #898. d. 250c, #899.

1992, Mar. 24   Litho.   Perf. 13x13½
918 A213 Sheet of 4, #a.-d.   7.00 7.00

Granada '92, Intl. Philatelic Exibition.

1992 Summer Olympics, Barcelona — A214

1992, Apr. 8   Litho.   Perf. 13x14
919 A214 35c Basketball   40   40
920 A214 60c Volleyball   70   70
921 A214 75c Running   85   85
922 A214 125c Soccer   1.40 1.40
923 A214 150c Cycling   1.70 1.70
924 A214 250c Swimming   2.80 2.80
  a. Souvenir sheet of 3, #921, 922, 924, perf 13x13½ 5.00 5.00
  Nos. 919-924 (6)   7.85 7.85

YWCA, 50th Anniv. — A215

1992, June 12   Litho.   Perf. 14x13
925 A215 60c red brown & multi 68   68
926 A215 250c purple & multi 2.80 2.80

Expulsion of Jews from Spain, 500th Anniv. — A216

1992, Aug. 17
927 A216 250c multicolored   2.80 2.80

Nos. 712-713 Surcharged ≡ **1c**

1992, Aug. 17   Perf. 13½
928 A172 1c on 5c multi   15   15
929 A172 1c on 5c multi   15   15
  Set value   15   15

A217   A218

1992, Sept. 15   *Perf. 13x14*
930 A217 60c green & multi   68 68
931 A217 250c pink & multi   2.80 2.80

Jan E. Matzeliger (1852-1889), inventor of shoe lasting machine.

1992, Oct. 12
932 A218 60c blue green & multi   68 68
933 A218 250c deep orange & multi   2.80 2.80

Discovery of America, 500th anniv.

Christmas — A219

Various abstract designs.

1992, Nov. 15
934 A219 10c multicolored   15 15
935 A219 60c multicolored   68 68
936 A219 250c multicolored   2.80 2.80
937 A219 400c multicolored   4.50 4.50

Medicinal Plants — A220

Designs: 50c, Costus arabicus, vert. 75c, Quassia amara, vert. 125c, Combretum rotundifolium. 500c, Bixa orellana.

Perf. 13x14, 14x13
1993, Feb. 3   *Litho.*
938 A220 50c multicolored   45 45
939 A220 75c multicolored   65 65
940 A220 125c multicolored   1.10 1.10
941 A220 500c multicolored   4.25 4.25

Beetles and Grasshoppers — A221

Designs: No. 942, Macrodontia cervicornis. No. 943, Acrididae, diff. No. 944, Curculionidae. No. 945, Acrididae, diff. No. 946, Euchroma gigantea. No. 947, Tettigonidae. No. 948, Tettigonidae. No. 949, Phanaeus festivus. No. 950, Gryllidae. No. 951, Phanaeus lancifer. No. 952, Tettigonidae. No. 953, Batus barbicornis.

1993, June 30   *Litho.*   *Perf. 13½*
942 A221 25c multicolored   28 28
943 A221 25c multicolored   28 28
  a.   Pair, #942-943   55 55
944 A221 35c multicolored   40 40
945 A221 35c multicolored   40 40
  a.   Pair, #944-945   80 80
946 A221 50c multicolored   55 55
947 A221 50c multicolored   55 55
  a.   Pair, #946-947   1.10 1.10
948 A221 100c multicolored   1.10 1.10
949 A221 100c multicolored   1.10 1.10
  a.   Pair, #948-949   2.25 2.25
950 A221 175c multicolored   2.00 2.00
951 A221 175c multicolored   2.00 2.00
  a.   Pair, #950-951   4.00 4.00

952 A221 220c multicolored   2.50 2.50
953 A221 220c multicolored   2.50 2.50
  a.   Pair, #952-953   5.00 5.00
    Nos. 942-953 (12)   13.66 13.66

A222   A223

Designs: #956b, 250c, like #955. #956c, 500c, like #956.

1993, July 30   *Perf. 13x14*
954 A222 50c Brazil No. 3   55 55
955 A222 250c Brazil No. 2   2.75 2.75
956 A222 500c Brazil No. 1   5.75 5.75
Souvenir Sheet
956A A222 Sheet of 2, #b.-c.   8.50 8.50

1st Brazilian postage stamps, 150th Anniv. Brasiliana '93 (#956A). Nos. 956b-956c have purple border.

1993, Oct. 12   *Perf. 14x13*
America issue: Paleosuchus palpebrosus.
957 A223 50f brown & multi
958 A223 100f green & multi

Christmas Angels — A224

Designs: 25c, African angel with drum. 45c, Asian angel holding lamp. 50c, Oriental angel holding lantern. 150c, American Indian angel holding wand.

1993, Nov. 15   *Litho.*   *Perf. 13x14*
959 A224 25c multicolored   40 40
960 A224 45c multicolored   75 75
961 A224 50c multicolored   80 80
962 A224 150c multicolored   2.50 2.50

The foreign exchange rate of the Surinam florin was allowed to float freely against foreign currencies on Oct. 19, 1994. The florin's value against the dollar has fluctuated dramatically. Stamps may sell for values significantly different from those quoted in the Scott listings.

No. 735A Surcharged

f 5.-

1993, Dec. 28   *Litho.*   *Perf. 14x13*
964 A173 5f on 15g Parrot   4.50 4.50

Traditional Musical Instruments — A225

1994, Feb. 16   *Litho.*   *Perf. 13x14*
965 A225 25g Indian drum   1.25 1.25
966 A225 50g Bosland Creooise drum   2.25 2.25
967 A225 75g Tambourine   3.50 3.50
968 A225 100g Hindu drum   4.75 4.75

Environmental Protection A226

1994, June 8   *Litho.*   *Perf. 14x13*
969 A226 50f Smoke stacks   1.75 1.75
970 A226 350f Dying fish   12.50 12.50

Intl. Olympic Committee, Cent. — A227

1994, July 4   *Litho.*   *Perf. 14x13*
971 A227 250f multicolored   7.75 7.75

1994 World Cup Soccer Championships, US — A228

1994, June 15   *Perf. 13x14*
972 A228 100f Goalkeeper's hands   3.00 3.00
973 A228 250f Soccer shoe   7.75 7.75
974 A228 300f Goal   9.00 9.00
    Nos. 972-974 (3)   19.75 19.75

A number has been reserved for a souvenir sheet with this set.

SEMI-POSTAL STAMPS

Green Cross
SP1   SP2   SP3

Perf. 12½
1927, Aug. 1   *Unwmk.*   *Photo.*
B1 SP1 2c (+ 2c) bl blk & grn   90 90
B2 SP2 5c (+ 3c) vio & grn   90 90
B3 SP3 10c (+ 3c) ver & grn   1.50 1.50

Surtax was given to the Green Cross Society, which promotes public health services.

Nurse and Patient SP4   Good Samaritan SP5

1928, Dec. 1   *Perf. 11½*
B4 SP4 1½c (+ 1½c) ultra   4.00 4.00
B5 SP4 2c (+ 2c) bl grn   4.00 4.00
B6 SP4 5c (+ 3c) vio   4.00 4.00
B7 SP4 7½c (+ 2½c) ver   4.00 4.00

The surtax on these stamps was for a fund to combat indigenous diseases.

1929, Dec. 1   *Perf. 12½*
B8 SP5 1½c (+ 1½c) grn   5.50 5.50
B9 SP5 2c (+ 2c) scar   5.50 5.50
B10 SP5 5c (+ 3c) ultra   5.50 5.50
B11 SP5 6c (+ 4c) blk   5.50 5.50

The surtax on these stamps was for the benefit of the Green Cross Society.

Surinam Mother and Child — SP6

1931, Dec. 14
B12 SP6 1½c (+ 1½c) blk   4.00 4.00
B13 SP6 2c (+ 2c) car rose   4.00 4.00
B14 SP6 5c (+ 3c) ultra   4.00 4.00
B15 SP6 6c (+ 4c) dp grn   4.00 4.00

The surtax was for Child Welfare Societies.

Designs Symbolical of the Creed of the Moravians
SP7   SP8

1935, Aug. 1   *Perf. 13x14*
B16 SP7 1c (+ ½c) dk brn   2.00 2.00
B17 SP7 2c (+ 1c) dp ultra   2.25 2.25
B18 SP8 3c (+ 1½c) grn   2.75 2.75
B19 SP8 4c (+ 2c) red org   2.75 2.75
B20 SP8 5c (+ 2½c) blk brn   2.75 3.00
B21 SP7 10c (+ 5c) car   2.75 3.00
    Nos. B16-B21 (6)   15.25 15.75

200th anniv. of the founding of the Moravian Mission in Surinam.

Surinam Child — SP9

1936, Dec. 14   *Perf. 12½*
B22 SP9 2c (+ 1c) dk grn   2.75 2.75
B23 SP9 3c (+ 1½c) dk bl   2.75 2.75
B24 SP9 5c (+ 2½c) brn blk   3.25 3.25
B25 SP9 10c (+ 5c) lake   3.25 3.25

Surtax for baby food and the Green Cross Society.

"Emancipation" SP10   Surinam Girl SP11

1938, June 1   *Litho.*   *Perf. 12½x12*
B26 SP10 2½c (+ 2c) dk bl grn   1.75 1.75
Photo.
B27 SP11 3c (+ 2c) vio blk   1.75 1.75
B28 SP11 5c (+ 3c) dk brn   1.75 1.75
B29 SP11 7½c (+ 5c) indigo   1.75 1.75

75th anniv. of the abolition of slavery in Surinam. Surtax to Slavery Remembrance Committee.

Creole Woman — SP12   Javanese Woman — SP13

Hindustani
Woman — SP14

American Indian
Woman — SP15

1940, Jan. 8   Engr.   *Perf. 13x14*

B30 SP12	2½c (+ 2c) dk grn	2.25	2.25
B31 SP13	3c (+ 2c) red org	2.25	2.25
B32 SP14	5c (+ 3c) dp bl	2.25	2.25
B33 SP15	7½c (+ 5c) henna brn	2.25	2.25

Surtax to lepra care and baby food.

> Catalogue values for unused stamps in this section, from this point to the end of the section, are for Never Hinged items.

Netherlands Coat of Arms and Inscription, "Netherlands Shall Rise Again" — SP16

1941, Aug. 30   Litho.   *Perf. 12½*

B34 SP16	7½c + 7½c dp org, ultra & blk	2.50	2.50
B35 SP16	15c + 15c scar, ultra & blk	3.25	3.25
B36 SP16	1g + 1g gray & ultra	21.00	21.00

The surtax was used to buy fighters for Dutch pilots in the Royal Air Force of Great Britain.

Nos. 145, 169, 146, 151 Surcharged in Red:

I   II

III   IV   V

1942, Jan. 2

B37 A23	2c + 2c blk brn, I	2.25	1.90
a.	Type II	2.25	1.90
B38 A26	2c + 2c blk brn, I	52.50	42.50
a.	Type II	52.50	42.50
B39 A23	2½c + 2c green, I	2.25	1.90
a.	Type II	2.25	1.90
B40 A23	7½c + 5c red vio, III	2.25	1.90
a.	Type IV	8.00	7.25
b.	Type V	20.00	18.00

The surtax was for the Red Cross.
In type III, the "c" may be "large," as illustrated, or "small," as in type II. Value is the same.
The distinctive feature of type IV is the pointed ending of the lower part of the "5."

Types of Regular Issue of 1945 Surcharged in Black

5 CENT VOOR HET NATIONAL STEUNFONDS

Unwmk.

1945, July 23   Engr.   *Perf. 12*

B41 A29	7½c + 5c dp org	3.50	2.00
B42 A30	15c + 10c brn	2.50	2.00
B43 A30	20c + 15c dl grn	2.50	2.00
B44 A30	22½c + 20c gray	2.50	2.00
B45 A30	40c + 35c rose lake	2.50	2.00
B46 A30	60c + 50c vio	2.50	2.00
Nos. B41-B46 (6)		16.00	12.00

Surtax for the National Welfare Fund.

Star — SP17

Marie Curie — SP18

1947, Dec. 16   Photo.   *Perf. 13½x13*

B47 SP17	7½c + 12½c red org	2.50	2.50
B48 SP17	12½c + 37½c blue	2.50	2.50

The surtax was used to combat leprosy. See Nos. CB4-CB5.

1950, May 15   *Perf. 14x13*

Designs: 7½c+22½c, 27½c+12½c, William Roentgen.

B49 SP18	7½c + 7½c	12.50	8.00
B50 SP18	7½c + 22½c	12.50	8.00
B51 SP18	27½c + 12½c	12.50	8.00
B52 SP18	27½c + 97½c	12.50	8.00

The surtax was used to combat cancer.

12½c + 7½c

Nos. 236-237 Surcharged in Black (#B53) or Red (#B54)

STORMRAMP NEDERLAND 1953

1953, Feb. 18   Wmk. 202

B53 A35	12½c + 7½c on 7½c	2.75	2.75
B54 A35	20c + 10c on 12½c	2.75	2.75

The surtax was for flood relief in the Netherlands.

Stadium, Paramaribo — SP19

1953, Aug. 29   Unwmk.   *Perf. 13½*

B55 SP19	10c + 5c claret	10.00	7.50
B56 SP19	15c + 5c bl & grn	10.00	7.50
B57 SP19	30c + 15c dk grn	10.00	7.50

Opening of the new stadium.

Surinam Children — SP20

Doves — SP21

1954, Nov. 1   *Perf. 13x14*

B58 SP20	7½c + 3c sepia	7.00	5.50
B59 SP20	10c + 5c bl grn	7.00	5.50
B60 SP20	15c + 7½c red brn	7.00	5.50
B61 SP20	30c + 15c blue	7.00	5.50

The surtax was for the youth center of the Moravian Church.

1955, May 5   *Perf. 14x13*

B62 SP21	7½c + 3½c brt red	2.75	3.00
B63 SP21	15c + 8c ultra	2.75	3.00

The Netherlands' liberation, 10th anniv.

Queen Juliana and Prince Bernhard SP22

1955, Oct. 27   Unwmk.

B64 SP22	7½c + 2½c dk olive	55	55

Royal visit to Surinam, 1955. Surtax for the Royal present.

Theater, 1837 — SP23

Designs: 10c+5c, Theater and car, circa 1920. 15c+7½c, Theater and car, circa 1958. 20c+10c, Theater interior.

1958, Feb. 15   Litho.   *Perf. 13x12½*

B65 SP23	7½c + 3c lt bl & blk	45	45
B66 SP23	10c + 5c rose lil & blk	45	45
B67 SP23	15c + 7½c lt grn & blk	45	45
B68 SP23	20c + 10c org & blk	45	45

120th anniv. of the "Thalia" theatrical society.

Carved Eating Utensils and Map of South America — SP24

Native Art (Map of So. America and): 10c+5c, Feather headgear. 15c+7c, Clay pottery. 20c+10c, Carved wooden stool.

1960, Jan. 15

B69 SP24	8c + 4c multi	90	90
B70 SP24	10c + 5c sal, red & bl	90	90
B71 SP24	15c + 7c red org, grn & sep	90	90
B72 SP24	20c + 10c lt bl, ultra & bis	90	90

SP25

SP26

Design: Uprooted Oak emblem of WRY.

1960, Apr. 7   *Perf. 13x14*

B73 SP25	8c + 4c choc & grn	18	18
B74 SP25	10c + 5c vio bl & ol grn	18	18

World Refugee Year, July 1, 1959-June 30, 1960. The surtax was for aid to refugees.

1960, Aug. 10   Litho.   *Perf. 14x13*

B75 SP26	8c + 4c Shot put	55	55
B76 SP26	10c + 5c Basketball	55	55
B77 SP26	15c + 7c Runner	85	85
B78 SP26	20c + 10c Swimmer	85	85
B79 SP26	40c + 20c Soccer	85	85
Nos. B75-B79 (5)		3.65	3.65

17th Olympic Games, Rome, Aug. 25-Sept. 11. Surtax for Olympic Committee.

Girl Scout Signaling SP27

Designs: 10c+3c, Scout Saluting, vert. 15c+4c, Brownies around toadstool. 20c+5c, Scouts around campfire, vert. 25c+6c, Scouts cooking outdoors.

Perf. 14x13, 13x14

1961, Aug. 19   Litho.

Multicolored Designs

B80 SP27	8c + 2c blue	32	32
B81 SP27	10c + 3c lilac	32	32
B82 SP27	15c + 4c yellow	32	32
B83 SP27	20c + 5c brn red	40	40
B84 SP27	25c + 6c aqua	40	40
Nos. B80-B84 (5)		1.76	1.76

Caribbean Girl Scout Jamborette. Surtax for various charities.

Hibiscus SP28

Flowers: 10c+5c, Caesalpinia pulcherrima. 15c+6c, Heliconia psittacorum. 20c+10c, Lochnera rosea. 25c+12c, Ixora macrothyrsa.

1962, Mar. 7   Photo.   *Perf. 14x13*

Cross in Red

B85 SP28	8c + 4c dk ol & scar	32	30
B86 SP28	10c + 5c dk bl & org	32	30
B87 SP28	15c + 6c multi	32	30
B88 SP28	20c + 10c multi	32	30
B89 SP28	25c + 12c dk bl grn, red & yel	32	30
Nos. B85-B89 (5)		1.60	1.50

The surtax was for the Red Cross.

Hands Protecting Duck — SP29

American Indian Girl — SP30

1962, Dec. 15   Litho.   *Perf. 13x14*

B90 SP29	2c + 1c shown	15	15
B91 SP29	8c + 2c Dog	15	15
B92 SP29	10c + 3c Donkey	15	15
B93 SP29	15c + 4c Horse	24	24

The surtax was for the Organization for Animal Protection.

1963, Oct. 30   Photo.   Unwmk.

Girls: 10c+4c, Negro. 15c+10c, East Indian. 20c+10c, Indonesian. 40c+20c, Caucasian.

B94 SP30	8c + 3c Prus grn	15	15
B95 SP30	10c + 4c red brn	15	15
a.	Min. sheet, 2 each #B94-B95	1.25	1.25
B96 SP30	15c + 10c dp bl	24	24
B97 SP30	20c + 10c brn red	24	24
B98 SP30	40c + 20c red vio	32	32
Set value		95	95

The surtax was for Child Welfare.

X-15 — SP31

Designs: 8c+4c, Flag of the Aeronautical and Astronautical Foundation. 10c+5c, 20c+10c, Agena B Ranger rocket.

1964, Apr. 15   *Perf. 13x12½*

B99 SP31	3c + 2c blk & rose lake	18	18
B100 SP31	8c + 4c blk, ultra & lt ultra	18	18
B101 SP31	10c + 5c blk & grn	18	18
B102 SP31	15c + 7c blk & yel brn	18	18
B103 SP31	20c + 10c blk & vio	18	18
Nos. B99-B103 (5)		90	90

Surtax for the Aeronautical and Astronautical Foundation of Surinam.

Stylized Campfire amid Trees — SP32

Girls Skipping Rope — SP33

1964, July 29 Litho. Perf. 13x14
B104 SP32 3c + 1c brn ol, yel bis & lem 15 15
B105 SP32 8c + 4c bluish blk, vio bl & yel bis 15 15
B106 SP32 10c + 5c dk red, red & yel bis 18 18
B107 SP32 20c + 10c grnsh blk, ol grn & yel bis 18 18
　　Set value 55 55

Jamborette at Paramaribo, Aug. 20-30, marking the 40th anniv. of the Surinam Boy Scout Association.

1964, Nov. 30 Photo. Perf. 14x13
Designs: 10c+4c, Children on swings. 15c+9c, Girl on scooter. 20c+10c, Boy rolling hoop.
B108 SP33 8c + 3c dk bl 15 15
B109 SP33 10c + 4c red 15 15
　　a. Min. sheet, 2 each #B108-B109 55 55
B110 SP33 15c + 9c ol grn 15 15
B111 SP33 20c + 10c mag 18 18
　　Set value 50 50

Issued for Child Welfare.

Mother and Child — SP34

Designs: 4c+2c, Pregnant woman. 15c+7c, Child. 25c+12c, Old man.

1965, Feb. 27 Photo. Perf. 13x14
B112 SP34 4c + 2c green 15 15
B113 SP34 10c + 5c brn & grn 15 15
B114 SP34 15c + 7c Prus bl & grn 15 15
B115 SP34 25c + 12c brt pur & grn 16 16
　　Set value 40 40

50th anniv. of the Green Cross Assoc. which promotes public health services.

Girl with Leopard and Spider — SP35

Designs: 10c+5c, Boy with monkey and spider. 15c+7c, Girl with tortoise and spider. 25c+10c, Boy with rabbit and spider.

**　　　　Perf. 13x12½**
1965, Nov. 26 Litho. Unwmk.
B116 SP35 4c + 4c lt grn & blk 15 15
B117 SP35 10c + 5c ocher & blk 15 15
B118 SP35 15c + 7c dp org & blk 18 18
　　a. Min. sheet, 2 each #B116, B118 55 55
B119 SP35 25c + 10c lt ultra & blk 15 15
　　Set value 45 45

Issued for Child Welfare.

"Help them to a safe haven" — SP35a

1966, Jan. 31 Photo. Perf. 14x13
B120 SP35a 10c + 5c blk & grn 15 15
B121 SP35a 25c + 10c blk & rose brn 15 15
　　a. Min. sheet of 3, 2 #B120, B121 45 45
　　Set value 22 22

The surtax was for the Intergovernmental Committee for European Migration (ICEM). The message on the stamps was given and signed by Queen Juliana.

Mary Magdalene, Disciples and "Round Table" Emblem — SP36

"New Year's Eve" Boys with Bamboo Gun — SP37

Mary Magdalene (John 20:18), and Service Club Emblems: 15c+8c, Toastmasters Intl. 20c+10c, Junior Chamber, Surinam. 25c+12c, Rotary Intl. 30c+15c, Lions Intl.

1966, Apr. 13 Photo. Perf. 12½x13
B122 SP36 10c + 5c dp crim, blk & gold 18 18
B123 SP36 15c + 8c dp vio, blk & bl 18 18
B124 SP36 20c + 10c yel org, blk & ultra 18 18
B125 SP36 25c + 12c grn, blk & gold 18 18
B126 SP36 30c + 15c ultra, blk & gold 18 18
　　Nos. B122-B126 (5) 90 90

Easter charities.

1966, Nov. 25 Litho. Perf. 12½x13
Designs: 15c+8c, "The End of Lent," boys pouring paint over each other. 20c+10c, "Liberation Day," parading children. 25c+12c, "Queen's Birthday," children on hobbyhorses. 30c+15c, "Christmas," Children decorating room with star.
B127 SP37 10c + 5c multi 15 15
B128 SP37 15c + 8c multi 15 15
B129 SP37 20c + 10c multi 15 15
　　a. Min. sheet of 3, 2 #B127, B129 35 35
B130 SP37 25c + 12c multi 15 15
B131 SP37 30c + 15c multi 15 15
　　Set value 60 60

Child welfare.

Good Samaritan Giving His Coat SP38

Children Stilt-walking SP39

The Good Samaritan: 15c+8c, Dressing the wounds. 20c+10c, Feeding the poor man. 25c+12c, Poor man riding Samaritan's horse. 30c+15c, Samaritan taking poor man to the inn.

1967, Mar. 22
B132 SP38 10c + 5c yel & blk 15 15
B133 SP38 15c + 8c lt bl & blk 16 16
B134 SP38 20c + 10c buff & blk 15 15
B135 SP38 25c + 12c pale rose & blk 15 15
B136 SP38 30c + 15c grn & blk 15 15
　　Nos. B132-B136 (5) 76 76

Easter charities.

1967, Nov. 21 Litho. Perf. 12½x13
Children's Games: 15c+8c, Boys playing with marbles. 20c+10c, Girl playing dibs (five stones). 25c+12c, Boy making kite. 30c+15c, Girls play-cooking.
B137 SP39 10c + 5c multi 15 15
B138 SP39 15c + 8c multi 16 16
B139 SP39 20c + 10c multi 16 16
　　a. Min. sheet, #B139, 2 #B137 45 45
B140 SP39 25c + 12c multi 16 16
B141 SP39 30c + 15c multi 16 16
　　Nos. B137-B141 (5) 79 79

Child welfare.

Cross, Ash Wednesday SP40

Hopscotch SP41

Easter Symbols: 15c+8c, Palms, Palm Sunday. 20c+10c, Bread and Wine, Maundy Thursday. 25c+12c, Cross, Good Friday. 30c+15c, Chrismon, Easter Sunday.

1968, Mar. 27 Litho. Perf. 12½x13
B142 SP40 10c + 5c lil & gray 15 15
B143 SP40 15c + 8c brick red & grn 18 18
B144 SP40 20c + 10c yel & dk grn 18 18
B145 SP40 25c + 12c gray & blk 18 18
B146 SP40 30c + 15c brt yel & brn 18 18
　　Nos. B142-B146 (5) 87 87

Easter charities.

1968, Nov. 22 Litho. Perf. 12½x13
Designs: 15c+8c, Balancing pyramid. 20c+10c, Handball. 25c+12c, Handicraft. 30c+15c, Tug-of-war.
B147 SP41 10c + 5c fawn & blk 15 15
B148 SP41 15c + 8c lt ultra & blk 15 15
B149 SP41 20c + 10c pink & blk 15 15
　　a. Min. sheet, #B149, 2 #B147 50 50
B150 SP41 25c + 12c yel grn & blk 24 24
B151 SP41 30c + 15c bluish lil & blk 32 32
　　Nos. B147-B151 (5) 1.01 1.01

Child welfare.

Globe with Map of South America — SP42

Pillow Fight — SP43

1969, Apr. 2 Litho. Perf. 12½x13
B152 SP42 10c + 5c bl & lt bl 25 25
B153 SP42 15c + 8c sl grn & yel 25 25
B154 SP42 20c + 10c sl grn & gray grn 25 25
B155 SP42 25c + 12c brn & bis 25 25
B156 SP42 30c + 15c vio & gray 25 25
　　Nos. B152-B156 (5) 1.25 1.25

Easter charities.

1969, Nov. 21 Litho. Perf. 12½x13
Designs: 15c+8c, Eating contest. 20c+10c, Pole climbing. 25c+12c, Sack race. 30c+15c, Obstacle race.
B157 SP43 10c + 5c lt ultra & mag 15 15
B158 SP43 15c + 8c yel & brn 24 24
B159 SP43 20c + 10c gray & dp bl 15 15
　　a. Min. sheet, #B159, 2 B157 80 80
B160 SP43 25c + 12c pink & brt bl 24 24
B161 SP43 30c + 15c emer & brn 24 24
　　Nos. B157-B161 (5) 1.02 1.02

Child welfare.

Flower — SP44

Ludwig van Beethoven, 1786 — SP45

Designs: 15c+8c, Butterfly. 20c+10c, Flying bird. 25c+12c, Sun. 30c+15c, Star.

1970, Mar. 25 Litho. Perf. 12½x13
B162 SP44 10c + 5c multi 52 52
B163 SP44 15c + 8c multi 52 52
B164 SP44 20c + 10c multi 52 52
B165 SP44 25c + 12c multi 52 52
B166 SP44 30c + 15c multi 52 52
　　Nos. B162-B166 (5) 2.60 2.60

Easter.

1970, Nov. 25 Litho. Perf. 12½x13
Various Portraits of Beethoven: 15c+8c, In 1804. 20c+10c, In 1812. 25c+12c, In 1814. 30c+15c, In 1827 (death mask).

Portrait and Inscription in Gray and Ocher
B167 SP45 10c + 5c grn 52 52
B168 SP45 15c + 8c scar 52 52
B169 SP45 20c + 10c bl 52 52
　　a. Min. sheet, #B169, 2 #B167 1.65 1.65
B170 SP45 25c + 12c red org 52 52
B171 SP45 30c + 15c pur 52 52
　　Nos. B167-B171 (5) 2.60 2.60

Ludwig van Beethoven (1770-1827), composer. The surtax was for child welfare.

Donkey and Palm — SP46

Leapfrog, by Peter Brueghel — SP47

Easter: 15c+8c, Cock. 20c+10c, Lamb of God. 25c+12c, Cross and Crown of Thorns. 30c+15c, Sun.

1971, Apr. 7 Litho. Perf. 12½x13
B172 SP46 10c + 5c multi 52 52
B173 SP46 15c + 8c bl & multi 52 52
B174 SP46 20c + 10c multi 52 52
B175 SP46 25c + 12c multi 52 52
B176 SP46 30c + 15c multi 52 52
　　Nos. B172-B176 (5) 2.60 2.60

Easter charities.

1971, Nov. 24 Photo. Perf. 13x14
Children's Games, by Peter Brueghel: 15c+8c, Girl strewing flowers. 20c+10c, Spinning the hoop. 25c+12c, Ball players. 30c+15c, Stilt walker.
B177 SP47 10c + 5c multi 60 60
B178 SP47 15c + 8c multi 60 60
B179 SP47 20c + 10c multi 60 60
　　a. Min. sheet, #B179, 2 #B177 1.90 1.90
B180 SP47 25c + 12c multi 60 60
B181 SP47 30c + 15c multi 60 60
　　Nos. B177-B181 (5) 3.00 3.00

Child welfare.

Easter Candle SP48

Toys SP49

Easter: 15c+8c, Christ teaching Apostles, and crosses. 20c+10c, Cup and folded hands. 25c+12c, Fish in net. 30c+15c, Judas' bag of silver.

1972, Mar. 29 Litho. Perf. 12½x13
B182 SP48 10c + 5c multi 45 45
B183 SP48 15c + 8c multi 45 45
B184 SP48 20c + 10c multi 45 45
B185 SP48 25c + 12c multi 45 45
B186 SP48 30c + 15c multi 45 45
　　Nos. B182-B186 (5) 2.25 2.25

Easter charities.

1972, Nov. 29 Litho. *Perf. 12½x13*

Designs: 15c+8c, Abacus and clock. 20c+10c, Pythagorean theorem. 25c+12c, Model of molecule. 30c+15c, Monkey wrench and drill. Each design represents a different stage of education.

B187	SP49	10c + 5c multi	45	45
B188	SP49	15c + 8c multi	45	45
B189	SP49	20c + 10c multi	45	45
a.	Min. sheet, #B189, 2 #B187		1.40	1.40
B190	SP49	25c + 12c multi	45	45
B191	SP49	30c + 15c multi	45	45
	Nos. B187-B191 (5)		2.25	2.25

Child welfare.

Jesus Calming the Waves — SP50

Easter: 15c+8c, The washing of the feet. 20c+10c, Jesus carrying Cross. 25c+12c, Cross and "ELI, ELI, LAMA SABACHTHANI?" 30c+15c, on the road to Emmaus.

1973, Apr. 4 Litho. *Perf. 12½x13*

B192	SP50	10c + 5c multi	38	38
B193	SP50	15c + 8c multi	38	38
B194	SP50	20c + 10c multi	38	38
B195	SP50	25c + 12c multi	38	38
B196	SP50	30c + 15c multi	38	38
	Nos. B192-B196 (5)		1.90	1.90

Easter charities.

Red Cross and Florence Nightingale SP51

1973, Oct. 3 Litho. *Perf. 14½x14*

B197	SP51	30c + 10c multi	90	90

30th anniversary of Surinam Red Cross.

Flower SP52

Bitterwood SP53

1973, Nov. 28 Litho. *Perf. 14x14½*

B198	SP52	10c + 5c shown	24	24
B199	SP52	15c + 8c Tree	40	40
B200	SP52	20c + 10c Dog	32	32
a.	Min. sheet, #B200, 2 #B198		1.10	1.10
B201	SP52	25c + 12c House	50	50
B202	SP52	30c + 15c Girl	50	50
	Nos. B198-B202 (5)		1.96	1.96

Child welfare.

1974, Apr. 3 Litho. *Perf. 14x14½*

Tropical Flowers: 15c+8c, Passion flower. 20c+10c, Wild angelica. 25c+12c, Candlestick senna. 30c+15c, Blood flower.

B203	SP53	10c + 5c multi	45	45
B204	SP53	15c + 8c multi	45	45
B205	SP53	20c + 10c multi	45	45
B206	SP53	25c + 12c multi	45	45
B207	SP53	30c + 15c multi	45	45
	Nos. B203-B207 (5)		2.25	2.25

Easter charities.

Boy Scout, Tent and Trees — SP54

Designs: 15c+8c, 5th Caribbean Jamboree emblem. 20c+10c, Scouts and emblem.

1974, Aug. 21 Litho. *Perf. 14x14½*

B208	SP54	10c + 5c multi	38	38
B209	SP54	10c + 8c multi	38	38
B210	SP54	20c + 10c multi	38	38

50th anniversary of Surinam Boy Scouts.

Fruit — SP55

Designs: 15c+8c, Children, birds and nest (security). 20c+10c, Flower, mother and child (protection). 25c+12c, Child and corn (good food). 30c+15c, Dancing children (child care).

1974, Nov. 27 Litho. *Perf. 14½x14*

B211	SP55	10c + 5c multi	24	24
B212	SP55	15c + 8c multi	32	32
B213	SP55	20c + 10c multi	32	32
a.	Min.sheet of 3, 2 #B211, B213		90	90
B214	SP55	25c + 12c multi	50	50
B215	SP55	30c + 15c multi	55	55
	Nos. B211-B215 (5)		1.93	1.93

Child welfare.

The Good Shepherd SP56

Woman and IWY Emblem SP57

Designs: 20c+10c, Peter's denial. 30c+ 15c, The Women at the Tomb. 35c+20c, Jesus showing His wounds to Thomas.

1975, Mar. 26 Litho. *Perf. 12½x13*

B216	SP56	15c + 5c yel grn & grn	45	45
B217	SP56	20c + 10c org & dk bl	60	60
B218	SP56	30c + 15c yel & red	60	60
B219	SP56	35c + 20c bl & pur	60	60

Easter charities.

1975, May 14 Litho. *Perf. 12½x13*

B220	SP57	15c + 5c multi	65	65
B221	SP57	30c + 15c multi	65	65

International Women's Year.

Carib Indian Water Jug — SP58

Feeding the Hungry — SP59

Designs: 20c+10c, 35c+20c, Indian arrow head, diff. 30c+15c, Wayana board with animal figures.

1975, Nov. 12 Litho. *Perf. 12½x13*

B222	SP58	15c + 5c multi	15	15
B223	SP58	20c + 10c multi	50	50
a.	Min. sheet, #B223, 2 #B222		1.50	1.50
B224	SP58	30c + 15c multi	80	80
B225	SP58	35c + 20c multi	80	80

Child welfare.

1976, Apr. 14 Photo. *Perf. 14x13*

Paintings: 25c+15c, Visiting the Sick. 30c+15c, Clothing the Naked. 35c+15c, Burying the Dead. 50c+25c, Giving Water to the Thirsty. Designs after panels in Alkmaar Church, 1504.

B226	SP59	20c + 10c multi	40	40
B227	SP59	25c + 15c multi	50	50
B228	SP59	30c + 15c multi	65	65
a.	Souv. sheet, #B228, 2 #B226		2.00	2.00
B229	SP59	35c + 15c multi	65	65
B230	SP59	50c + 25c multi	1.00	1.00
	Nos. B226-B230 (5)		3.20	3.20

Easter.

Pekingese and Boy's Head — SP60

Child's Head and: 25c+10c, German shepherd. 30c+15c, Dachshund. 35c+15c, Retriever. 50c+25c, Terrier.

1976 Litho. *Perf. 13½*

B231	SP60	20c + 10c multi	75	50
B232	SP60	25c + 10c multi	1.00	70
B233	SP60	30c + 15c multi	1.25	80
a.	Min. sheet, #B233, 2 #B231		2.50	2.00
B234	SP60	35c + 15c multi	1.25	85
B235	SP60	50c + 25c multi	2.00	1.25
	Nos. B231-B235 (5)		6.25	4.10

Surtax was for child welfare.

St. Veronica's Veil — SP61

Descent from the Cross — SP62

Easter: Religious scenes, side panels, front and back, from triptych by Jan Mostaert (1473-1555).

1977, Apr. 6 Litho. *Perf. 13½x14*

B236	SP61	20c + 10c multi	22	22
B237	SP61	25c + 15c multi	30	30
B238	SP61	30c + 15c multi	35	35
B239	SP62	35c + 15c multi	38	38
B240	SP61	50c + 25c multi	55	55
	Nos. B236-B240 (5)		1.80	1.80

Dog and Girl's Head — SP63

Crosses, Luke 23:43 — SP64

Child's Head and: 25c+15c, Monkey. 30c+15c, Rabbit. 35c+15c, Cat. 50c+25c, Parrot.

1977, Nov. 23 Litho. *Perf. 13x14*

B241	SP63	20c + 10c multi	22	22
B242	SP63	25c + 15c multi	30	30
B243	SP63	35c + 15c multi	35	35
a.	Min. sheet, #B243, 2 #B241		90	90
B244	SP63	35c + 15c multi	38	38
B245	SP63	50c + 25c multi	55	55
	Nos. B241-B245 (5)		1.80	1.80

Surtax was for child welfare.

1978, Mar. 22 Litho. *Perf. 12½x14*

Easter: 25c+15c, Serpent and Cross, John 3:14. 30c+15c, Lamb and blood, Exodus 12:13. 35c+15c, Passover plate, chalice and bread. 60c+30c, Cross and solar eclipse.

B246	SP64	20c + 10c multi	24	24
B247	SP64	25c + 15c multi	30	30
B248	SP64	35c + 15c multi	35	35
B249	SP64	35c + 15c multi	38	38
B250	SP64	60c + 30c multi	75	75
	Nos. B246-B250 (5)		2.02	2.02

Child's Head and White Cat — SP65

Church, Cross and Chalice — SP66

Designs: Child's head and cats in various positions.

1978, Nov. 22 Litho. *Perf. 14x13*

B251	SP65	20c + 10c multi	25	22
B252	SP65	25c + 15c multi	40	32
B253	SP65	30c + 15c multi	45	35
a.	Min. sheet, #B253, 2 #B251		90	90
B254	SP65	35c + 15c multi	50	40
B255	SP65	60c + 30c multi	85	70
	Nos. B251-B255 (5)		2.45	1.99

Surtax was for child welfare.

1979, Apr. 11 Litho. *Perf. 13x14*

Easter: Cross, chalice and various churches.

B256	SP66	20c + 10c multi	22	22
B257	SP66	30c + 15c multi	32	32
B258	SP66	35c + 15c multi	38	38
B259	SP66	40c + 20c multi	42	42
B260	SP66	60c + 30c multi	65	65
	Nos. B256-B260 (5)		1.99	1.99

Boy, Bird, Red Cross, Blood Transfusion Bottle — SP67

1979, Nov. 21 Litho. *Perf. 13x14*

B261	SP67	20c + 10c multi	22	22
B262	SP67	30c + 15c multi	32	32
B263	SP67	35c + 15c multi	38	38
a.	Min. sheet, #B263, 2 #B261		1.25	1.25
B264	SP67	40c + 20c multi	42	42
B265	SP67	60c + 30c multi	65	65
	Nos. B261-B265 (5)		1.99	1.99

Surtax was for child welfare.

Cross — SP68

Anansi — SP69

Easter: Various symbols.

1980, Mar. 26   Litho.   Perf. 13x14
B266	SP68	20c + 10c multi	22	22
B267	SP68	30c + 15c multi	35	35
B268	SP68	40c + 20c multi	45	45
B269	SP68	50c + 25c multi	55	55
B270	SP68	60c + 30c multi	65	65
		Nos. B266-B270 (5)	2.22	2.22

1980, Nov. 5   Litho.   Perf. 13x14

Designs: Characters from Anansi and His Creditors.

B271	SP69	20c + 10c shown	25	25
B272	SP69	25c + 15c Ba Tigri	32	32
B273	SP69	30c + 15c Kakafowroe	40	40
B274	SP69	35c + 15c Ontiman	45	45
B275	SP69	60c + 30c Mat Kalaka	80	80
a.		Min. sheet, #B275, 2 #B271	1.40	1.40
		Nos. B271-B275 (5)	2.22	2.22

Surtax was for child welfare.

Woman Reading — SP70

1980, Dec. 10   Perf. 14x13
B276	SP70	25c + 10c shown	30	30
B277	SP70	50c + 15c Gardening	55	55
B278	SP70	75c + 20c With grandchildren	80	80

Surtax was for the elderly.

Crucifixion — SP71   Indian Girl — SP72

Easter: Scenes from the Passion of Christ.

1981, Apr. 8   Litho.   Perf. 13x14
B279	SP71	20c + 10c multi	25	25
B280	SP71	30c + 15c multi	40	40
B281	SP71	50c + 25c multi	70	70
B282	SP71	60c + 30c multi	75	75
B283	SP71	75c + 35c multi	90	90
		Nos. B279-B283 (5)	3.00	3.00

Surtax was for the elderly.

1981, Nov. 26   Litho.
B284	SP72	20c + 10c shown	26	26
B285	SP72	30c + 15c Black	45	45
B286	SP72	50c + 25c Hindustani	75	75
B287	SP72	60c + 30c Javanese	80	80
B288	SP72	75c + 35c Chinese	90	90
a.		Souv. sheet, #B288, 2 #B285	2.50	2.50
		Nos. B284-B288 (5)	3.16	3.16

Surtax was for child welfare.

Easter SP73   Man Pushing Wheelbarrow SP74

Designs: Stained-glass windows, Sts. Peter and Paul Church, Paramaribo.

1982, Apr. 7   Litho.   Perf. 13x14
B289	SP73	20c + 10c multi	28	28
B290	SP73	35c + 15c multi	52	52
B291	SP73	65c + 30c multi	80	80
B292	SP73	65c + 30c multi	85	85
B293	SP73	75c + 35c multi	1.00	1.00
		Nos. B289-B293 (5)	3.45	3.45

1982, Nov. 17   Litho.

Children's Drawings of City Cleaning Activities.

B294	SP74	20c + 10c multi	28	28
B295	SP74	35c + 15c multi	52	52
B296	SP74	50c + 25c multi	80	80
B297	SP74	65c + 30c multi	85	85
B298	SP74	75c + 35c multi	1.00	1.00
a.		Souv. sheet, #B298, 2 #B295	2.25	2.25
		Nos. B294-B298 (5)	3.45	3.45

Surtax was for child welfare.

Easter — SP75   Pitcher — SP76

Mosaic Symbols.

1983, Mar. 23   Litho.   Perf. 13x14
B299	SP75	10c + 5c Dove	18	18
B300	SP75	15c + 5c Bread	20	20
B301	SP75	25c + 10c Fish	38	38
B302	SP75	50c + 25c Eye	90	90
B303	SP75	65c + 30c Wine cup	1.00	1.00
		Nos. B299-B303 (5)	2.66	2.66

1983, Nov. 16   Litho.   Perf. 13x14
B304	SP76	10c + 5c shown	18	18
B305	SP76	15c + 5c Headdress	20	20
B306	SP76	25c + 10c Medicine rattle	38	38
B307	SP76	50c + 25c Sieve	90	90
B308	SP76	65c + 30c Basket	1.00	1.00
a.		Min. sheet, #B305, B306, B308	1.75	1.75
		Nos. B304-B308 (5)	2.66	2.66

Easter — SP77   SP78

1984, Apr. 4   Litho.   Perf. 13x14
B309	SP77	10c + 5c Cross, rose	18	18
B310	SP77	15c + 15c Cemetery	20	20
B311	SP77	25c + 10c Candles	38	38
B312	SP77	50c + 25c Cross, crown of thorns	90	90
B313	SP77	65c + 30c Candle	1.00	1.00
		Nos. B309-B313 (5)	2.66	2.66

1984, Aug. 15   Litho.   Perf. 13x14

Boy Scouts in Surinam, 60th Anniv.: 30c+10c, 8th Caribbean Jamboree emblem. 35c+10c, Salute. 50c+10c, Gardening. 90c+10c, Campfire in map of Surinam. Surtax was for Boy Scouts.

B314	SP78	30c + 10c multi	45	45
B315	SP78	35c + 10c multi	52	52
B316	SP78	50c + 10c multi	65	65
B317	SP78	90c + 10c multi	1.10	1.10

Children's Games — SP79   Easter — SP80

1984, Nov. 14   Litho.   Perf. 13x14
B318	SP79	5c + 5c Kites	15	15
B319	SP79	10c + 5c Kites, diff.	18	18
B320	SP79	30c + 10c Pingi-pingi-kasi	45	45
B321	SP79	50c + 25c Cricket	90	90
a.		Souv. sheet of 3, #B319-B321	1.65	1.65
B322	SP79	90c + 30c Peroen, peroen	1.40	1.40
		Nos. B318-B322 (5)	3.08	3.08

Surtax was for child welfare.

1985, Mar. 27   Litho.   Perf. 12½x14
B323	SP80	5c + 5c multi	15	15
B324	SP80	10c + 5c multi	15	15
B325	SP80	30c + 15c multi	45	45
B326	SP80	50c + 25c multi	75	75
B327	SP80	90c + 30c multi	1.25	1.25
		Nos. B323-B327 (5)	2.75	2.75

Surtax for child welfare.

Map, Emblem SP81   Literacy SP82

1985, Oct. 22   Litho.   Perf. 13x14
B328	SP81	30c + 10c shown	38	38
B329	SP81	50c + 10c Crucifix, missionaries	60	60
B330	SP81	90c + 20c Scroll	1.00	1.00

Evangelical Brotherhood Mission in Surinam, 250th anniv. Surtax for mission medical and social work.

1985, Nov. 6
B331	SP82	5c + 5c Boy reading	15	15
B332	SP82	10c + 5c Learning alphabet	15	15
B333	SP82	30c + 10c Writing	38	38
B334	SP82	50c + 25c Girl reading	75	75
a.		Min. sheet of 3, #B332-B334	1.40	1.40
B335	SP82	90c + 30c Studying	1.25	1.25
		Nos. B331-B335 (5)	2.68	2.68

Surtax was for child welfare.

Easter — SP83   Sts. Peter and Paul Cathedral, Cent. — SP84

1986, Mar. 19   Litho.
B336	SP83	5c + 5c multi	15	15
B337	SP83	10c + 5c multi	15	15
B338	SP83	30c + 15c multi	45	45
B339	SP83	50c + 25c multi	75	75
B340	SP83	90c + 30c multi	1.10	1.10
		Nos. B336-B340 (5)	2.60	2.60

1986, May 28   Litho.
B341	SP84	30c + 10c Exterior	45	45
B342	SP84	50c + 10c Saints, bas-relief	65	65
B343	SP84	110c + 30c Baptismal font	1.65	1.65

Ancient Order of Foresters Court Charity, Cent. — SP85

1986, July 29   Litho.   Perf. 14x13
B344	SP85	50c + 20c Foresters emblem	75	75
B345	SP85	110c + 30c Court building	1.65	1.65

Youth Activities SP86

Easter — SP87   Natl. Girl Guides Movement, 40th Anniv. — SP88

1986, Nov. 5   Litho.   Perf. 14x13
B346	SP86	5c + 5c Hopscotch	15	15
B347	SP86	10c + 5c Ballet	16	16
B348	SP86	30c + 10c Mobile library	40	40
B349	SP86	50c + 25c Crafts	70	70
a.		Min. sheet of 3, #B347-B349	1.40	1.40
B350	SP86	110c + 30c Education	1.50	1.50
		Nos. B346-B350 (5)	2.91	2.91

Surtax for Children's Charities.

Stations of the cross.

1987, Apr. 9   Litho.   Perf. 13x14
B351	SP87	5c + 5c Crucifixion	15	15
B352	SP87	10c + 5c Christ on cross	16	16
B353	SP87	35c + 15c Descent from cross	50	50
B354	SP87	60c + 30c Funeral procession	85	85
B355	SP87	110c + 50c Entombment	1.50	1.50
		Nos. B351-B355 (5)	3.16	3.16

Surtax for annual Easter Charity programs.

1987, May 7   Litho.

Designs: 15c+10c, Mushroom, Brownie's emblem. 60c+10c, Clover, Guides' emblem. 110c+10c, Campfire, Rangers' emblem. 120c+10c, Ivy, Captain's emblem.

B356	SP88	15c + 10c multi	30	30
B357	SP88	60c + 10c multi	75	75
B358	SP88	110c + 10c multi	1.40	1.40
B359	SP88	120c + 10c multi	1.50	1.50

Surtax for the Surinam Girl Guides.

Caribbean Manari — SP89   Easter — SP90

1987, Nov. 4   Litho.   Perf. 13x14
B360	SP89	50c + 25c Herring bone	80	80
B361	SP89	60c + 30c Tortoise-back	90	90
B362	SP89	110c + 50c Whirlpool (squares)	1.65	1.65
a.		Min. sheet of 2, #B360, B362	2.50	2.50

Surtax to benefit child welfare organizations.

1988, Mar. 23   Perf. 13x13½
B363	SP90	50c + 25c multi	65	65
B364	SP90	60c + 30c multi	85	85
B365	SP90	110c + 50c multi	1.65	1.65

Surtax for annual Easter Charity programs.

Intl. Red Cross and Red Crescent Organizations, 125th Anniv. — SP91

Design: #B367, Anniv. and blood donation emblems.

1988, Oct. 26   Litho.   Perf. 13x14
B366 SP91 60c + 30c multi   1.00 1.00
B367 SP91 120c + 60c multi   2.00 2.00

Children's
Drawings
SP92

1988, Dec. 5   Litho.   Perf. 14x13
B368 SP92 50c + 25c Man and
              animal   70   70
B369 SP92 60c + 30c Children and
              nature   85   85
B370 SP92 110c + 50c Stop drugs   1.50 1.50
  a.   Souv. sheet of 3, #B368-B370   3.25 3.25

Surtax to benefit children's charities.

Easter 1989 — SP93

Details from Hungarian altarpieces: 60c+30c,
Scenes of the Passion, by M.S., 1506. 105c+50c,
Crucifixion, by Tamas of Koszvar, 1427. 110c+55c,
Miracles, by Tamas of Koszvar, 1427.

1989, Mar. 21   Litho.   Perf. 13¹/2
Size: No. B372, 28¹/2x36¹/2mm
B371 SP93 60c + 30c multi   1.00 1.00
B372 SP93 105c + 50c multi   1.75 1.75
B373 SP93 110c + 55c multi   1.85 1.85

Surtax for annual East Charity programs.

Children's
Drawings
SP94

Designs: No. B374, Helping each other. No.
B375, Child and nature. No. B376, In the school
bus.

1989, Dec. 6   Litho.   Perf. 14x13
B374 SP94 60c +30c multi   1.00 1.00
B375 SP94 105c +50c multi   1.75 1.75
B376 SP94 110c +55c multi   1.85 1.85
  a.   Souv. sheet of 2, #B374, B376 2.85 2.85

Surtax for children's charities.

Easter — SP95

Designs: No. B377, Mother holding Christ child.
No. B378, Christ, follower. No. B379, Mary holding martyred Christ.

1990, Mar. 28   Litho.   Perf. 13x14
B377 SP95 60c +30c multi   1.00 1.00
B378 SP95 105c +50c multi   1.75 1.75
B379 SP95 110c +55c multi   1.85 1.85

Children's
Drawings
SP96

1990, Dec. 4   Litho.   Perf. 14x13
B380 SP96 60c +30c Children,
                  hammock   1.20 1.20
B381 SP96 105c +50c Child, animal,
                  palm tree   2.00 2.00
B382 SP96 110c +55c Child, bird in
                  tree   2.15 2.15
  a.   Souv. sheet of 2, #B380, B382,
          perf. 13¹/2x13   3.00 3.00

SP97   SP98

Easter: 60c+30c, Christ carrying cross.
105c+50c, The Crucifixion. 110c+55c, Woman
cradling Christ's body.

1991, Mar. 20   Litho.   Perf. 13x14
B383 SP97 60c +30c multi   1.10 1.10
B384 SP97 105c +50c multi   1.30 1.30
B385 SP97 110c +55c multi   2.00 2.00
  a.   Souv. sheet of 2, #B383, B385 3.10 3.10

1991, Dec. 4   Litho.   Perf. 13x14
Children's Drawings: 60c+30c, Child in wheel-
chair. 105c+50c, Child beside trees. 110c+55c,
Children playing outdoors.

B386 SP98 60c +30c multi   1.00 1.00
B387 SP98 105c +50c multi   1.75 1.75
B388 SP98 110c +55c multi   1.85 1.85
  a.   Souv. sheet of 2, #B386, B388 2.85 2.85

SP99   SP100

Easter: 60c+30c, Crucifixion. 105c+50c, Taking
away body of Christ. 110c+55c, Resurrection.

1992, Mar. 18
B389 SP99 60c +30c multi   1.00 1.00
B390 SP99 105c +50c multi   1.75 1.75
B391 SP99 110c +55c multi   1.85 1.85

1992, Dec. 3   Litho.   Perf. 13x14
Children's Drawings: 60c + 30c, Child as tree.
105c + 50c, Face as tree. 110c + 55c, Boy and girl
hanging from tree.

B392 SP100 60c +30c multi   1.00 1.00
B393 SP100 105c +50c multi   1.75 1.75
B394 SP100 110c +55c multi   1.85 1.85
  a.   Souv. sheet of 2, #B392, B394 2.85 2.85

Surtax for Child Welfare.

SP101   SP102

Easter: 60c + 30c, Message from Christ. 110c +
50c, Crucifixion. 125c + 60c, Resurrection.

1993, Mar. 31   Litho.   Perf. 13x14
B395 SP101 60c +30c multi   1.05 1.05
B396 SP101 110c +50c multi   1.80 1.80
B397 SP101 125c +60c multi   2.10 2.10

1993, Dec. 3   Litho.   Perf. 12¹/2x13¹/2
Children Playing Hopscotch: 25c+10c, 2 children. 35c+10c, 3 children. 50c+25c, 8 children.
75c+25c, 7 children.

B398 SP102 25c +10c green & multi   80   80
B399 SP102 35c +10c blue & multi   80   80
B400 SP102 50c +25c green & multi   1.75 1.75
  a.   Souvenir sheet of 2, #B399-B400 3.75 3.75
B401 SP102 75c +25c blue & multi   2.25 2.25

Surtax for Child Welfare.

———

AIR POST STAMPS

 Allegory of Flight — AP1

Perf. 12¹/2
1930, Sept. 3   Unwmk.   Engr.
C1 AP1 10c dull red   3.00   40
C2 AP1 15c ultra   3.00   55
C3 AP1 20c dull green   15   15
C4 AP1 40c orange   15   28
C5 AP1 60c brown vio   40   32
C6 AP1 1g gray black   1.10 1.25
C7 AP1 1¹/2g deep brn   1.25 1.50
   Nos. C1-C7 (7)   9.05 4.45

Nos. C1-C7
Overprinted in Black
or Red

Drucht
Do. X
1931

1931, Aug. 8
C8 AP1 10c red (Bk)   15.00 13.00
  a.   Double overprint   300.00
C9 AP1 15c ultra (Bk)   15.00 13.00
C10 AP1 20c dl grn (Bk)   15.00 13.00
C11 AP1 40c org (Bk)   22.50 17.50
  a.   Double overprint   300.00
C12 AP1 60c brn vio (R)   45.00 45.00
C13 AP1 1g gray blk (R)   55.00 52.50
C14 AP1 1¹/2g dp brn (Bk)   55.00 55.00
   Nos. C8-C14 (7)   222.50 209.00

The variety with period omitted after "Do"
occurs twice on each sheet.
Warning: The red overprint may dissolve in
water.

Type of 1930
Thick Paper
1941, Sept. 25   Litho.   Perf. 13
C15 AP1 20c lt grn   1.40   75
C16 AP1 40c lt org   6.75 4.25
C17 AP1 2¹/2g yellow   8.50 8.50
C18 AP1 5g bl grn   180.00 225.00
C19 AP1 10g lt bister   20.00 35.00
   Nos. C15-C19 (5)   216.65 273.50

The lines of shading on Nos. C15 and C16 are
not as heavy as on Nos. C3 and C4. For surcharges,
see Nos. C24-C25.

Type of 1930
Redrawn
1941   Engr.   Perf. 12
C20 AP1 10c light red   1.50   32
C21 AP1 60c dl brn vio   1.00   42
C22 AP1 1g black   20.00 19.00

Redrawn stamps have three horizontal lines
through post horn and many minor variations. For
surcharges, see Nos. C23, CB1.

> Catalogue values for unused
> stamps in this section, from this
> point to the end of the section, are
> for Never Hinged items.

Nos. C21, C17, C19 Surcharged with
New Values and Bars in Carmine
1945, Mar. 12   Perf. 13, 12
C23 AP1 22¹/2c on 60c   40   60
  a.   Inverted surcharge   250.00 250.00
C24 AP1 1g on 2¹/2g   10.50 13.00
C25 AP1 5g on 10g   17.50 20.00

Women of   Globe and
Netherlands and   Winged Post
Surinam — AP2   Horn — AP3

Perf. 12x12¹/2
1949, May 10   Photo.   Unwmk.
C26 AP2 27¹/2c henna brown   5.00 3.00

Valid only on first flight of Paramaribo-Amster-
dam service.

1954, Sept. 25   Perf. 13¹/2x12¹/2
C27 AP3 15c dp ultra & ultra   1.10 1.00

Establishment of airmail service in Surinam, 25th
anniv.

Redstone
Mercury Rocket
and Comdr.
Alan B.
Shepard,
Jr. — AP4

Design: 15c, Cosmonaut Gagarin in capsule and
globe.

1961, July 3   Litho.   Perf. 12
C28 AP4 15c multi   85   85
C29 AP4 20c multi   85   85

"Man in Space," Major Yuri A. Gagarin, USSR,
and Comdr. Alan B. Shepard, Jr., US.
Printed in sheets of 12 (4x3) with ornamental
borders and inscriptions. Two printings differ in
shades and selvage perforations.

Water   Eucyane
Tower — AP5   Bicolor — AP6

Designs: 15c, 65c, Brewery. 20c, Boat on lake.
25c, 75c, Wood industry. 30c, Bauxite mine. 35c,
50c, Poelepantje bridge. 40c, Ship in harbor. 45c,
Wharf.

1965, July 31   Photo.   Perf. 14x13¹/2
Size: 25x18mm
C30 AP5 10c olive grn   15   15
C31 AP5 15c ocher   15   15
C32 AP5 20c slate grn   15   15
C33 AP5 25c vio blue   15   15
C34 AP5 30c bl green   15   15
C35 AP5 35c red org   24   24
C36 AP5 40c orange   24   24
C37 AP5 45c dk car   24   24
C38 AP5 50c vermilion   24   24
C39 AP5 55c emerald   24   24
C40 AP5 65c bister   32   32
C41 AP5 75c blue   32   32
   Nos. C30-C41 (12)   2.59
   Set value   2.00

See Nos. C75-C82.

1972, July 26   Litho.   Perf. 13x13¹/2
C42 AP6 15c shown   18   18
C43 AP6 20c Helicopis cupido   22   18
C44 AP6 25c Papilio thoas thoas   25   18
C45 AP6 30c Urania leilus   30   15
C46 AP6 35c Stalachtis calliope   30   42
C47 AP6 40c Stalachtis phlegia   35   30
C48 AP6 45c Victorina steneles   42   15
C49 AP6 50c Papilio neophilus   52   15
C50 AP6 55c Anartia amathea   60   62
C51 AP6 60c Adelpha cytherea   65   95
C52 AP6 65c Heliconius doris
              metharmina   65   65
C53 AP6 70c Nessaea obrinus   75   75
C54 AP6 75c Ageronia feronia   75   60
   Nos. C42-C54 (13)   5.94 5.28

Surinam butterflies. Valid for regular postage
also. For surcharges, see Nos. 495-499.
Nos. C42, C45 exist perf 14 with redrawn
design.

Fish Type of 1976

Fish: 35c, Chaetodon unimaculatus. 60c, Centropyge loriculus. 95c, Caetodon collare.

1976, June 2   Litho.   Perf. 12½x13

C55	A111	35c multi	90 45
C56	A111	60c multi	1.50 75
C57	A111	95c multi	2.50 1.25

Black-headed Sugarbird — AP7

Birds of Surinam: 20c, Leistes militaris. 30c, Paradise tangara. 40c, Whippoorwill. 45c, Hemitraupis flavicollis. 50c, White-tailed gold-throated hummingbird. 55c, Saberwing. 60c, Blackcap parrot, vert. 65c, Toucan, vert. 70c, Manakin, vert. 75c, Collared parrot, vert. 80c, Cayenne cotinga, vert. 85c, Trogon, vert. 95c, Black-striped tropical tree owl, vert.

1977   Litho.   Perf. 14x12½, 12½x14

C58	AP7	20c multi	25 15
C59	AP7	25c multi	30 18
C60	AP7	35c multi	35 20
a.	Min. sheet of 4, 2 each #C59-C60, perf. 13½		2.50 1.50
C61	AP7	40c multi	52 32
C62	AP7	45c multi	55 35
C63	AP7	50c multi	65 40
C64	AP7	55c multi	75 45
C65	AP7	60c multi	80 50
C66	AP7	65c multi	85 55
C67	AP7	70c multi	95 55
C68	AP7	75c multi	1.00 65
C69	AP7	80c multi	1.00 65
C70	AP7	85c multi	1.10 75
C71	AP7	95c multi	1.40 90
	Nos. C58-C71 (14)		10.47 6.60

A souv. sheet of 4 with same stamps and perf. as No. C60a has marginal inscription "Amphilex 77" with magnifier over No. 424. Sold in folder at phil. exhib. in Amsterdam May 26-June 5, 1977.
Issue dates: 25c, 30c, 50c, 60c, 75c, 80c, 95c, Apr. 27. No. C60a, May 26. Others, Aug. 24.
See Nos. C88, C101. For surcharges and overprints see Nos. C102-C105, C108, J58, J62.

Fish Type of 1976

Tropical Fish: 60c, Chaetodon striatus. 90c, Bodianus pulchellus. 120c, Centropyge argi.

1977, June 8   Litho.   Perf. 12½x13

C72	A111	60c multi	1.25 60
C73	A111	90c multi	1.90 95
C74	A111	120c multi	2.75 1.25

Type of 1965 Redrawn

Designs: 5c, Brewery. 10c, Water tower. 20c, Boat on lake. 25c, Wood industry. 30c, Bauxite mine. 35c, Poelepantje bridge. 40c, Ship in harbor. 60c, Wharf.

1977-78   Photo.   Perf. 12½x13½
Size: 22x18mm

C75	AP5	5c ocher ('78)	15 15
a.	Bklt. pane, 4 #C75, 3 #C82 + label		2.50
C76	AP5	10c olive green	55 55
a.	Bklt. pane, 1 #C76, 4 #C80 + label		2.75
C77	AP5	20c slate green	15 15
a.	Bklt. pane, 2 #C77, 2 #C78, 2 #C79		2.75
b.	Bklt. pane, 6 #C77, 2 #C81 ('78)		2.50
C78	AP5	25c vio bl	55 55
C79	AP5	30c bl grn	65 65
C80	AP5	35c red org	55 55
C81	AP5	40c org ('78)	90 90
C82	AP5	60c dk car ('78)	75 75
	Nos. C75-C82 (8)		4.25 4.25

Nos. C75-C82 issued in booklets only. Nos. C75a and C77b have inscribed selvage the size of 4 stamps; Nos. C76a and C77a the size of 6 stamps.

Fish Type of 1976

Tropical Fish: 60c, Astyanax species. 90c, Corydoras wotroi. 120c, Gasteropelecus sternicla.

1978, June 21   Litho.   Perf. 12½x13

C85	A111	60c multi	1.25 65
C86	A111	90c multi	2.25 1.10
C87	A111	120c multi	2.50 1.25

Bird Type of 1977

Design: 5g, Crested curassow, vert.

1979, Jan. 10   Engr.   Perf. 13x13½

C88	AP7	5g violet	6.00 3.00

Fish Type of 1979

Tropical Fish: 60c, Cantherinus macrocerus. 90c, Holocenthrus rufus. 120c, Holacanthus tricolor.

1979, May 30   Photo.   Perf. 14x13

C89	A129	60c multi	95 48
C90	A129	90c multi	1.40 70
C91	A129	120c multi	2.00 1.00

Fish Type of 1979

Tropical Fish: 60c, Symphysodon discus. 75c, Aeqidens curviceps. 90c, Catoprion mento.

1980, Sept. 10   Photo.   Perf. 14x13

C92	A129	60c multi	90 45
C93	A129	75c multi	1.25 60
C94	A129	90c multi	1.40 70

Frog Type of 1981

1981, June 24   Perf. 13x14

C95	A142	75c Phyllomedusa burmeisteri, vert.	1.10 60
C96	A142	1g Dendrobates tinctorius, vert.	1.50 80
C97	A142	1.25g Bufo guttatus, vert.	1.75 1.00

Turtle Type of 1982

1982, Feb. 17   Photo.   Perf. 14x13

C98	A146	65c Platemys platycephala	1.00 65
C99	A146	75c Phrynops gibba	1.25 80
C100	A146	125c Rhinoclemys punctularia	2.00 1.40

Bird Type of 1977

1985, Jan. 9   Litho.   Perf. 13x14

C101	AP7	90c Venezuelan Amazon, vert.	2.50 2.50

For overprint, see No. J61.

No. C60 Surcharged

1986, Oct. 1   Litho.   Perf. 14x13

C102	AP7	15c on 30c multi	2.50 2.50

Nos. C70-C71 and C67 Surcharged

 10 ct

1987, Mar.   Litho.   Perf. 12½x14

C103	AP7	10c on 85c No. C70	1.50 1.50
C104	AP7	10c on 95c No. C71	1.50 1.50
C105	AP7	25c on 70c No. C67	4.00 4.00

Otter Type of 1989

1989, Jan. 18   Litho.   Perf. 13x14

C107	A195	185c Otters, vert.	2.05 2.05

No. C63 Surcharged

35ct

1993, Jan. 20   Litho.   Perf. 14x12½

C108	AP7	35c on 50c multi	40 40

AIR POST SEMI-POSTAL STAMPS

Catalogue values for unused stamps in this section are for Never Hinged items.

No. C20 Surchd. in Red like No. B40

1942, Jan. 2   Engr.   Unwmk.   Perf. 12

CB1	AP1	10c + 5c lt red, III	4.00 4.00
a.	Type IV		10.00 10.00
b.	Type V		18.00 21.00

The surtax was for the Red Cross.
See note on types III and IV below No. B40.

Nos. 193 and 194 Surcharged in Carmine

1946, Feb. 24   Perf. 12

CB2	A30	10c + 40c blue	1.00 1.00
CB3	A30	15c + 60c brown	1.00 1.00

The surtax was used for the prevention of tuberculosis.

Star — SPAP1

Perf. 13½x12½

1947, Dec. 16   Photo.

CB4	SPAP1	22½c + 27½c gray	2.25 2.00
CB5	SPAP1	27½c + 47½c grn	2.25 2.00

The surtax was used to combat leprosy.

POSTAGE DUE STAMPS

D1

D2

Type I - 34 loops. "T" of "BETALEN" over center of loop; top branch of "E" of "TE" shorter than lower branch.
Type II - 33 loops. "T" of "BETALEN" over space between two loops.
Type III - 32 loops. "T" of "BETALEN" slightly to the left of center of loop; top branch of first "E" of "BETALEN" shorter than lower branch.
Type IV - 37 loops and letters of "PORT" larger than in the other three types.

Value in Black
Perf. 12½x12

1886-88   Typo.   Unwmk.
Type III

J1	D1	2½c lilac	3.00 3.00
J2	D1	5c lilac	9.00 9.00
J3	D1	10c lilac	100.00 65.00
J4	D1	20c lilac	9.00 9.00
J5	D1	25c lilac	12.50 12.50
J6	D1	30c lilac ('88)	2.50 2.50
J7	D1	40c lilac	6.00 6.00
J8	D1	50c lilac ('88)	3.00 3.00
		Type I	
J1a	D1	2½c	6.00 6.00
J2a	D1	5c	11.00 11.00
J3a	D1	10c	125.00 90.00
J4a	D1	20c	22.50 22.50
J5a	D1	25c	19.00 19.00
J6a	D1	30c	22.50 22.50
J7a	D1	40c	12.50 12.50
J8a	D1	50c	4.00 4.00
		Type II	
J1b	D1	2½c	5.00 5.00
J2b	D1	5c	10.00 10.00
J3b	D1	10c	1,250. 1,250.
J4b	D1	20c	9.00 9.00
J5b	D1	25c	300.00 300.00
J6b	D1	30c	75.00 75.00
J7b	D1	40c	350.00 350.00
J8b	D1	50c	5.00 5.00
		Type IV	
J3c	D1	10c	350.00 250.00
J5c	D1	25c	165.00 150.00
J7c	D1	40c	150.00 150.00

Nos. J1-J16 were issued without gum. For surcharges, see Nos. J15-J16.

1892-96   Value in Black   Perf. 12½
Type III

J9	D2	2½c lilac	40 40
J10	D2	5c lilac	1.25 1.00
J11	D2	10c lilac	24.00 22.50
J12	D2	20c lilac	2.50 2.25
J13	D2	25c lilac	10.00 10.00
		Type I	
J9a	D2	2½c	40 40
J10a	D2	5c	2.00 2.00
J11a	D2	10c	24.00 20.00
J12a	D2	20c	5.00 5.00
J13a	D2	25c	13.00 12.50
J14	D2	40c ('96)	3.25 4.50
		Type II	
J9b	D2	2½c	80 80
J10b	D2	5c	3.00 3.00
J11b	D2	10c	40.00 42.50
J12b	D2	20c	90.00 90.00
J13b	D2	25c	100.00 100.00

For surcharges, see Nos. 121-122.

Stamps of 1888 Surcharged in Red

10 cent

1911, July 15

J15	D1	10c on 30c lil (III)	80.00 80.00
a.	10c on 30c lilac (I)		200.00 225.00
b.	10c on 30c lilac (II)		1,800. 1,800.
J16	D1	10c on 50c lil (III)	110.00 110.00
a.	10c on 50c lilac (I)		115.00 115.00
b.	10c on 50c lilac (II)		115.00 115.00

D3

D4

Type I
Value in Color of Stamp

1913-31   Perf. 12½, 13½x12½

J17	D2	½c lilac ('30)	16 16
J18	D2	1c lilac ('31)	16 24
J19	D2	2c lilac ('31)	28 28
J20	D2	2½c lilac	16 16
J21	D2	5c lilac	16 16
J22	D2	10c lilac	24 20
J23	D2	12c lilac ('31)	24 28
J24	D2	12½c lilac ('22)	24 16
J25	D2	15c lilac ('26)	40 40
J26	D2	20c lilac	80 40
J27	D2	25c lilac	30 16
J28	D2	30c lilac ('26)	30 60
J29	D2	40c lilac	16.00 16.00
J30	D2	50c lilac ('26)	1.25 1.10
J31	D2	75c lilac ('26)	1.40 1.40
J32	D3	1g lilac ('26)	1.75 1.40
	Nos. J17-J32 (16)		23.84 23.10

Catalogue values for unused stamps in this section, from this point to the end of the section, are for Never Hinged items.

1945   Litho.   Perf. 12

J33	D4	1c light brown violet	16 30
J34	D4	5c light brown violet	3.00 2.50
J35	D4	25c light brown violet	7.00 50

D5

D6

Perf. 13½x12½

1950   Unwmk.   Photo.

J36	D5	1c purple	1.75 1.50
J37	D5	2c purple	2.75 1.40
J38	D5	2½c purple	2.25 1.50
J39	D5	5c purple	3.25 32
J40	D5	10c purple	1.75 32
J41	D5	15c purple	4.50 2.00
J42	D5	20c purple	1.50 2.75
J43	D5	25c purple	9.00 20
J44	D5	50c purple	15.00 1.10
J45	D5	75c purple	37.50 30.00
J46	D5	1g purple	14.00 5.50
	Nos. J36-J46 (11)		93.25 46.59

1956

J47	D6	1c purple	15 15
J48	D6	2c purple	32 28
J49	D6	2½c purple	32 28
J50	D6	5c purple	32 28
J51	D6	10c purple	32 28
J52	D6	15c purple	50 50
J53	D6	20c purple	50 50
J54	D6	25c purple	55 28
J55	D6	50c purple	1.50 35
J56	D6	75c purple	2.00 1.10
J57	D6	1g purple	2.75 90
	Nos. J47-J57 (11)		9.23 4.90

Stamps of 1977-1985 Overprinted "TE BETALEN"

1987, July   Litho.   Perf. 13x14, 14x13

J58	AP7	65c No. C66	2.00 2.00
J59	A156	65c No. 638	2.00 2.00
J60	A156	80c No. 640	2.50 2.50
J61	AP7	90c No. C101	2.75 2.75
J62	AP7	95c No. C71	3.00 3.00
J63	A173	1g No. 729	3.25 3.25
	Nos. J58-J63 (6)		15.50 15.50

SCANDINAVIA and SWEDEN

"Exclusively since 1975"

*For SWEDEN YEAR SET and PACKET Price List
see our ad in the Iceland section of the Scott 1996 Volume 3 catalogue, page 736

FREE PRICE LISTS
ALL SCANDINAVIAN COUNTRIES!

- Early Bird Discounts
- Want Lists Filled
- Major Buyers
- Public Auctions

CALL TOLL FREE
1-800-950-0058

NORTHLAND CO.

Box 34
Verona, NJ 07044

ASDA

Port Payé
Post Suède

SWEDEN
and other
NORDIC
COUNTRIES

You are welcome to try
filling your wants from
Scandinavia's
biggest
stamp stock
• • •
Satisfaction
Guaranteed!

Rolf Gummesson AB
(Since 1939)
Kungsgatan 55
111 22 Stockholm, Sweden

We accept VISA, MasterCard, Euro Card
and American Express

ASDA member since 1948.
BUY NOW AND TAKE ADVANTAGE OF THE
LOW VALUE OF THE SWEDISH CURRENCY!

SWEDEN

LOCATION — Northern Europe, occupying the eastern half of the Scandinavian Peninsula
GOVT. — Constitutional Monarchy
AREA — 173,341 sq. mi.
POP. — 8,330,577 (est. 1983)
CAPITAL — Stockholm

48 skilling banco = 1 rixdaler banco (until 1858)

100 öre = 1 rixdaler (1858 to 1874)

100 öre = 1 krona (since 1874)

Catalogue values for unused stamps in this country are for Never Hinged items, beginning with Scott 358 in the regular postage section, and Scott B37 in the semi-postal section.

Watermarks

Wmk. 180- Crown   Wmk. 307- Crown and 1955

Wmk. 181- Wavy Lines

Coat of Arms
A1   A2

			Typo.	Perf. 14
1855		**Unwmk.**		
1	A1	3s blue green	5,000.	3,000.
a.		3s orange (error)		
2	A1	4s lt blue	1,000.	55.
a.		4s gray blue	6,000.	200.
3	A1	6s gray	6,250.	675.
a.		6s gray brown	7,250.	700.
b.		Imperf.		8,000.
4	A1	8s orange	3,500.	400.
a.		8s yellow orange	4,000.	425.
b.		8s lemon yellow	4,250.	875.
c.		Imperf.		
5	A1	24s dull red	5,250.	1,750.

Nos. 1-5 were reprinted two or three times perf. 14, once perf. 13. Value of the lowest cost perf. 14 reprints, $275 each. Perf. 13, $225 each.
The reprints were made after Nos. 1-5 were withdrawn, but before being demonetized. Used copies are known.

				Perf. 14
1858-61				
6	A2	5o green	140.00	16.00
a.		5o deep green	275.00	110.00
7	A2	9o violet	325.00	175.00
a.		9o lilac	375.00	200.00
8	A2	12o blue	140.00	2.50
9	A2	12o ultra ('61)	275.00	9.00
10	A2	24o orange	210.00	20.00
a.		24o yellow	300.00	32.50
11	A2	30o brown	275.00	22.50
a.		30o red brown	275.00	25.00
12	A2	50o rose	250.00	65.00
a.		50o carmine	400.00	67.50

Nos. 6 and 8 exist with double impressions. No. 8 is known printed on both sides. No. 11 exists imperf.
Nos. 6-8, 10-12 were reprinted in 1885, perf. 13. Value $80 each. Also reprinted in 1963, perf. 13½, with lines in stamp color crossing denominations, and affixed to book page. Value $12.50 each.

Lion and Arms
A3   A4

1862-69				
13	A3	3o bister brown	75.00	14.00
a.		Printed on both sides		1,500.
14	A4	17o red violet ('66)	400.00	125.00
15	A4	17o gray ('69)	575.00	600.00
16	A4	20o vermilion ('66)	150.00	13.00

Nos. 13, 15-16 were reprinted in 1885, perf. 13. Value $80 each.

Numeral of Value — A5   Coat of Arms — A6

1872-77				Perf. 14
17	A5	3o bister brown	32.50	5.50
18	A5	4o gray ('76)	350.00	95.00
19	A5	5o blue green	200.00	3.00
a.		5o emerald	200.00	12.00
20	A5	6o violet	250.00	21.00
a.		6o dark violet	250.00	21.00
21	A5	6o gray ('74)	600.00	40.00
22	A5	12o blue	80.00	90
23	A5	20o vermilion	550.00	4.50
a.		20o dull org yel ('75)	1,750.	18.00
b.		Double impression, dull yel & ('76)		
24	A5	24o orange	500.00	20.00
a.		24o yellow	500.00	20.00
25	A5	30o pale brown	250.00	5.50
a.		30o black brown	250.00	6.00
26	A5	50o rose	475.00	25.00
a.		50o carmine	500.00	25.00
27	A6	1rd bister & blue	600.00	45.00
a.		1rd bister & ultra	600.00	45.00

1877-79				Perf. 13
28	A5	3o yellow brown	35.00	2.50
29	A5	4o gray ('79)	125.00	2.00
30	A5	5o dark green	95.00	75
31	A5	6o lilac	100.00	3.75
a.		6o red lilac	100.00	5.50
32	A5	12o blue	17.50	48
33	A5	20o vermilion	165.00	75
a.		"TRETIO" instead of "TJUGO" ('79)	6,750.	6,000.
34	A5	24o orange ('78)	37.50	13.00
a.		24o yellow	45.00	13.00
35	A5	30o pale brown	225.00	1.10
a.		30o black brown	225.00	1.10
36	A5	50o carmine ('78)	195.00	4.00
37	A6	1rd bister & blue	1,400.	300.00
38	A6	1k bister & bl ('78)	450.00	10.00

Imperf., Pairs				
28a	A5	3o		675.00
29a	A5	4o		675.00
30a	A5	5o		675.00
31b	A5	6o		675.00
32a	A5	12o		675.00
33b	A5	20o		675.00
34b	A5	24o		675.00
35b	A5	30o		675.00
36a	A5	50o		675.00
38a	A6	1k		675.00

See Nos. 40-44, 46-49. For surcharges see Nos. B1-B10, B22-B31.
No. 37 has been reprinted in yellow brown and dark blue; perforated 13. Value, $150.

King Oscar II — A7

1885			Typo.	
39	A7	10o dull rose	130.00	50
a.		Imperf., pair	1,750.	

Numeral Type with Post Horn on Back

1886-91				
40	A5	2o orange ('91)	3.00	3.00
b.		Period before "FRIMARKE"	5.00	5.50
a.		Imperf., pair	525.00	
41	A5	3o yellow brn ('87)	9.00	9.75
42	A5	4o gray	22.50	75
43	A5	5o green	42.50	45
44	A5	6o red lilac ('88)	24.00	20.00
a.		6o violet	27.50	20.00
45	A7	10o pink	52.50	15
a.		10o rose	52.50	15
b.		Imperf.		2,250.

46	A5	20o vermilion	85.00	45
47	A5	30o pale brown	125.00	85
48	A5	50o rose	100.00	3.25
49	A6	1k bister & dk bl	60.00	1.65
a.		Imperf., pair	525.00	

Nos. 32, 34 with Blue Surcharge

TIO ÖRE

1889, Oct. 1				
50	A5	10o on 12o blue	3.00	3.00
51	A5	10o on 24o orange	12.00	25.00

A9   A10

King Oscar II — A11

		Wmk. 180		
1891-1904		**Typo.**		**Perf. 13**
52	A9	1o brown & ultra ('92)	1.25	15
53	A9	2o blue & yellow org	4.75	15
54	A9	3o brown & orange ('92)	80	1.00
55	A9	4o carmine & ultra ('92)	8.00	15
		Engr.		
56	A10	5o yellow green	2.75	15
a.		5o blue green	6.00	15
d.		5o brown (error)	6,250.	
e.		Booklet pane of 6	45.00	
57	A10	8o red violet ('03)	4.00	85
58	A10	10o carmine	4.75	15
c.		Booklet pane of 6	52.50	
59	A10	15o red brown ('96)	19.00	15
60	A10	20o blue	20.00	15
61	A10	25o red orange ('96)	24.00	22
62	A10	30o brown	35.00	18
63	A10	50o slate	55.00	35
64	A10	50o olive gray ('04)	55.00	28
65	A11	1k car & sl ('00)	90.00	1.25
		Nos. 52-65 (14)	324.30	5.28

		Imperf., Pairs		
52a	A9	1o		75.00
53a	A9	2o		210.00
54a	A9	3o		225.00
55a	A9	4o		200.00
56b	A10	5o No. 56		265.00
c.		No. 56a		265.00
57a	A10	8o		265.00
58a	A10	10o		35.00
59a	A10	15o		265.00
60a	A10	20o		100.00
61a	A10	25o		315.00
62a	A10	30o		315.00
63a	A10	50o		315.00
64a	A10	50o		250.00
65a	A11	1k		400.00

See Nos. 75-76.

Stockholm Post Office — A12

1903, Oct. 26				
66	A12	5k blue	200.00	24.00
a.		Imperf., pair	1,500.	

Opening of the new General Post Office at Stockholm.
For surcharge see No. B11.

Arms — A13

Gustaf
V — A14

Arms — A15

Heraldic Lion Supporting
Arms of Sweden — A16

Perf. 13, 13x13½

			Wmk. 180
1910-14	**Typo.**		
67	A13	1o black ('11)	90	1.00
68	A13	2o orange	2.25	2.00
69	A13	4o violet	3.00	1.00

Engr.

70	A14	5o green ('11)	11.00	24.00
71	A14	10o carmine	12.50	35
72	A14	1k black, *yel* ('11)	90.00	30
73	A14	5k claret, *yel* ('14)	2.75	2.00
	Nos. 67-73 (7)		122.40	30.65

See #77-98. For surcharges see #99-104, Q1-Q2.

1911			**Unwmk.**
75	A10	20o blue	15.00	9.00
76	A10	25o red orange	18.00	2.50

1910-19

77	A14	5o green ('11)	2.25	15
a.	Booklet pane of 10		200.00	
b.	Booklet pane of 4		105.00	
78	A14	7o gray grn ('18)	25	15
a.	Booklet pane of 10		8.00	
79	A14	8o magenta ('12)	25	24
80	A14	10o carmine ('10)	3.50	15
a.	Booklet pane of 10		200.00	
b.	Booklet pane of 4		105.00	
81	A14	12o rose lake ('18)	25	15
a.	Booklet pane of 10		8.00	
82	A14	15o red brown ('11)	7.00	15
a.	Booklet pane of 10		300.00	
83	A14	20o deep blue ('11)	12.00	15
a.	Booklet pane of 10		315.00	
84	A14	25o orange red ('11)	25	15
85	A14	27o pale blue ('18)	40	70
86	A14	30o claret brn ('11)	19.00	15
87	A14	35o dk violet ('11)	17.50	15
88	A14	40o olive green ('17)	30.00	15
89	A14	50o gray ('12)	35.00	15
90	A14	55o pale blue ('18)	1,000.	3,150.
91	A14	65o pale ol grn ('18)	75	1.50
92	A14	80o black ('18)	1,000.	3,150.
93	A14	90o gray green ('18)	75	42
94	A14	1k black, *yel* ('19)	80.00	28
	Nos. 77-89,91,93-94 (16)		209.15	
	Set value			4.20

Excellent forgeries of Nos. 90 and 92 exist.

1911-19	**Typo.**	**Wmk. 181**	**Perf. 13**
95	A13	1o black	15	15
96	A13	2o orange	15	15
97	A13	3o pale brown ('19)	15	15
98	A13	4o pale violet	15	15

Remainders of Nos. 95-98 received various private overprints, mostly as publicity for stamp exhibitions. They were not postally valid.

Unwatermarked Stamps with Watermarks

Stamps of these and later issues through the UPU Congress issue of 1924, are frequently found with watermark showing parts of the words "Kungl Postverket" in double-lined capitals. This watermark is normally located in the margins of the sheets of unwatermarked paper or paper watermarked wavy lines or crown.

Nos. 80, 84, 91, 90, 92 Surcharge:

7 **7** **12** **12**
a b

1918			**Unwmk.**
99	A14(a)	7o on 10o	38	22
100	A14(b)	12o on 25o	2.75	30
a.	Inverted surcharge		150.00	250.00
101	A14(a)	12o on 65o	1.75	90
102	A14(a)	27o on 55o	90	1.45
103	A14(a)	27o on 65o	1.90	2.50
104	A14(a)	27o on 80o	80	1.25
	Nos. 99-104 (6)		8.48	6.62

Two types each of 5o green, 5o copper red and 10o violet, type A16.

Perf. 10 Vertically

1920-25		**Engr.**	**Unwmk.**
115	A15	3o copper red	25	20
116	A16	5o green	3.50	15
117	A16	5o copper red ('21)	5.75	15
118	A16	10o green ('21)	16.00	15
a.	Tête bêche pair		1,000.	1,250.
119	A16	10o violet ('25)	3.50	15
120	A16	25o orange ('21)	17.50	25
121	A16	30o brown	50	20

Wmk. 181

122	A16	5o green	1.40	15
123	A16	5o copper red ('22)	7.50	42
124	A16	10o violet ('22)	2.00	30
125	A16	30o brown	4.25	6.50
	Nos. 115-125 (11)		62.15	8.62

Coil Stamps

Unless part of a booklet pane any stamp perforated only horizontally or vertically is a coil stamp.

1920-26		**Unwmk.**	**Perf. 10**
126	A16	5o green	4.00	42
a.	Booklet pane of 10		50.00	
127	A16	10o green ('21)	9.50	2.00
a.	Booklet pane of 10		105.00	
128	A16	10o violet ('25)	5.00	28
a.	Booklet pane of 10		55.00	
129	A16	30o brown	24.00	3.00

Wmk. 181

130	A16	5o green	9.50	11.00
131	A16	10o green ('21)	21.00	27.50
a.	Booklet pane of 10		300.00	

Perf. 13 Vertically

Unwmk.

132	A16	5o green ('25)	4.00	80
133	A16	5o copper red ('21)	200.00	100.00
134	A16	10o violet ('26)	12.00	17.50

Wmk. 181

135	A16	5o green ('25)	1.75	1.75
136	A16	5o copper red ('22)	1.75	1.90
137	A16	10o green ('24)	6.00	12.50
138	A16	10o violet ('25)	4.00	7.50
	Nos. 126-138 (13)		302.50	186.15

The paper used for the earlier printings of types A16, A17, A18, A18a and A20 is usually tinted by the color of the stamp. Printings of 1934 and later are on white paper in slightly different shades.

King Gustaf V — A17

1920-21		**Unwmk.**	**Perf. 10 Vertically**
139	A17	10o rose	17.50	20
140	A17	15o claret	30	18
141	A17	20o blue	25.00	20

Perf. 10

142	A17	10o rose	10.50	3.75
143	A17	20o blue ('21)	21.00	4.50
a.	Booklet pane of 10		300.00	
	Nos. 139-143 (5)		74.30	8.83

Wmk. 181

| 144 | A17 | 20o blue | 2,250. | |

Crown and Post Horn
A18   A18a

See note after No. 138 regarding paper. There are 2 types of the 35, 40, 45 and 60o.

1920-34		**Unwmk.**	**Perf. 10 Vert.**
145	A18	35o yellow ('22)	25.00	32
146	A18	40o olive green	25.00	40
147	A18	45o brown ('22)	1.10	40

148	A18	60o claret	17.50	15
149	A18	70o red brown ('22)	80	1.25
150	A18	80o deep green	70	20
151	A18	85o myrtle grn ('29)	2.75	32
152	A18	90o lt blue ('25)	40.00	15
153	A18a	1kr dp orange ('21)	6.00	15
154	A18	110o ultra	70	15
155	A18	115o red brown ('29)	7.00	30
156	A18	120o gray black ('25)	47.50	40
157	A18	120o lilac rose ('33)	6.00	52
158	A18	140o gray black	95	30
159	A18	145o brt green ('30)	5.75	52

Wmk. 181

160	A18	35o yellow ('23)	35.00	2.50
161	A18	60o red violet	47.50	45.00
162	A18	80o blue green	4.00	3.00
163	A18	110o ultra	2.75	1.75
	Nos. 145-163 (19)		276.00	57.78

Gustavus
Adolphus
A19

King Gustaf
V
A20

Perf. 10 Vertically

1920, July 28			**Unwmk.**
164	A19	20o deep blue	3.00	40

Wmk. 181

| 165 | A19 | 20o blue | 70.00 | 10.00 |

Unwmk.			**Perf. 10**
166	A19	20o blue	6.00	1.50
a.	Booklet pane of 10		75.00	

Tercentenary of Swedish post which first ran between Stockholm and Hamburg.

1921-36		**Unwmk.**	**Perf. 10 Vert.**

See note after No. 138 regarding paper. There are two types each of the 15o rose and 40o olive green.

167	A20	15o violet ('22)	13.00	15
168	A20	15o rose ('25)	6.50	15
169	A20	15o brown ('36)	4.75	15
170	A20	20o violet	28	15
171	A20	20o rose ('22)	15.00	28
172	A20	20o orange ('25)	28	35
174	A20	25o rose red ('22)	45	90
175	A20	25o dk blue ('25)	15.00	20
176	A20	25o dk ultra ('34)	15.00	20
177	A20	25o yel org ('36)	25.00	15
178	A20	30o blue ('23)	15.00	20
179	A20	30o brown ('25)	25.00	15
180	A20	30o lt ultra ('36)	5.50	20
181	A20	35o red violet ('30)	10.50	15
182	A20	40o blue	40	55
183	A20	40o olive grn ('29)	25.00	60
184	A20	45o brown ('29)	3.50	28
185	A20	50o gray	1.75	15
186	A20	85o myrtle grn ('25)	9.00	1.25
187	A20	115o brown red ('25)	10.00	1.25
188	A20	145o apple grn ('25)	6.25	1.25
	Nos. 167-188 (21)		207.16	8.66

Wmk. 181

| 189 | A20 | 15o violet ('22) | 1,600. | 450.00 |
| 189A | A20 | 20o violet | | 2,500. |

1922-36		**Unwmk.**	**Perf. 10**
190	A20	15o violet	18.00	40
a.	Booklet pane of 10		300.00	
191	A20	25o rose red ('25)	20.00	30
a.	Booklet pane of 10		315.00	

192	A20	15o brown ('36)	4.50	20
a.	Booklet pane of 10		72.50	
193	A20	20o violet ('22)	45	1.00
a.	Booklet pane of 10		7.25	

Gustavus Vasa — A21

1921, June			**Perf. 10 Vertically**
194	A21	20o violet	8.25	14.00
195	A21	110o ultra	50.00	15.00
196	A21	140o gray black	27.50	3.50

400th anniversary of Gustavus Vasa's war of independence from the Danes.

Universal Postal Union Congress

Composite View of Stockholm's Skyline — A22

King Gustaf V — A23

1924, July 4		**Unwmk.**	**Perf. 10**
197	A22	5o red brown	1.50	1.75
198	A22	10o green	1.50	1.75
199	A22	15o dk violet	1.50	1.50
200	A22	20o rose red	8.00	8.50
201	A22	25o dp orange	12.50	12.00
202	A22	30o deep blue	12.00	12.00
a.	30o greenish blue		75.00	75.00
203	A22	35o black	15.00	17.00
204	A22	40o olive green	17.00	20.00
205	A22	45o deep brown	22.50	22.50
206	A22	50o gray	20.00	21.00
207	A22	60o violet brn	37.50	40.00
208	A22	80o myrtle grn	30.00	25.00
209	A23	1k green	55.00	80.00
210	A23	2k rose red	125.00	175.00
211	A23	5k deep blue	225.00	350.00

Wmk. 181

212	A22	10o green	11.00	22.50
	Nos. 197-212 (16)		595.00	810.50
	Set, never hinged		1,050.	

Postrider Watching Airplane — A24

Sweden and Scandinavia
• Free Catalog • Stamps
• Postal History • Literature
• Want Lists Filled • Albums
• New Issue Service

Jay Smith
P.O. Box 650-X666
Snow Camp, NC 27349
(Formerly of Madison, Wisconsin)

CALL TOLL FREE
1-800-447-8267
(U.S. and CANADA)
or 910-376-9991
FAX 910-376-6750

• The Scandinavia Specialist Since 1973 •

Carrier Pigeon and Globe — A25

1924, Aug. 16   Engr.   Unwmk.
213	A24	5o red brown	2.00	2.25
214	A24	10o green	2.50	2.25
215	A24	15o dk violet	2.25	2.00
216	A24	20o rose red	11.00	14.00
217	A24	25o deep orange	14.00	11.00
218	A24	30o deep blue	14.00	12.00
a.		30o greenish blue	75.00	32.50
219	A24	35o black	15.00	19.00
220	A24	40o olive green	17.50	19.00
221	A24	45o deep brown	24.00	20.00
222	A24	50o gray	26.00	32.50
223	A24	60o violet brown	35.00	42.50
224	A24	80o myrtle green	35.00	22.50
225	A25	1k green	57.50	80.00
226	A25	2k rose red	110.00	57.50
227	A25	5k deep blue	225.00	165.00

Wmk. 181
228	A24	10o green	16.00	22.50
		Nos. 213-228 (16)	606.75	524.00
		Set, never hinged	1,200.	

Universal Postal Union issue.

Royal Palace at Stockholm — A26   Death of Gustavus Adolphus — A27

1931, Nov. 26   Unwmk.   Perf. 10
229	A26	5k dark green	97.50	7.00
		Never hinged	275.00	
		Booklet pane of 10	1,750.	

1932, Nov. 1
230	A27	10o dark violet	2.00	1.75
a.		Booklet pane of 10	27.50	
231	A27	15o dark red	3.00	1.00
a.		Booklet pane of 10	52.50	

Perf. 10 Vertically
232	A27	10o dark violet	2.00	18
233	A27	15o dark red	2.00	18
234	A27	20o dark blue	5.75	60
235	A27	90o dark green	18.00	1.65
		Nos. 230-235 (6)	32.75	5.36
		Set, never hinged	80.00	

300th anniv. of the death of King Gustavus Adolphus II who was killed on the battlefield of Lützen, Nov. 6, 1632.

Catching Sunlight in Bowl — A28

1933, Dec. 6   Perf. 10
236	A28	5o green	2.75	60
a.		Booklet pane of 10	37.50	

There are two types of No. 236.

Perf. 10 Vertically
237	A28	5o green	2.75	15

Perf. 13 Vertically
238	A28	5o green	3.50	3.00
		Set, never hinged	20.00	

50th anniv. of the Swedish Postal Savings Bank.

The Old Law Courts — A29   The "Four Estates" and Arms of Engelbrekt — A34

Designs: 10o, Stock exchange. 15o, Parish church (Storkyrkan). 25o, House of the Nobility. 35o, House of Parliament.

1935, Jan. 10   Perf. 10
239	A29	5o green	2.50	50
a.		Booklet pane of 10	45.00	
240	A29	10o dull violet	2.50	2.25
a.		Booklet pane of 10	45.00	
241	A29	15o carmine	3.50	1.10
a.		Booklet pane of 10	67.50	

Perf. 10 Vertically
242	A29	5o green	1.25	15
243	A29	10o dull violet	4.75	15
244	A29	15o carmine	1.90	15
245	A29	25o ultra	9.00	50
246	A29	35o deep claret	14.00	1.40
247	A34	60o deep claret	18.00	1.40
		Nos. 239-247 (9)	57.40	7.60
		Set, never hinged	130.00	

500th anniv. of the Swedish Parliament.

Chancellor Axel Oxenstierna A35   Post Runner A36

Mounted Courier — A37   Old Sailing Packet — A38

Mail Paddle Steamship — A39   Mail Coach — A40

1855 Stamp Model — A41   Mail Train — A42

Postmaster General A. W. Roos — A43   Mail Truck and Trailer — A44

Modern Swedish Liner — A45   Junkers Plane with Pontoons — A46

1936, Feb. 20   Engr.   Perf. 10
248	A35	5o green	1.70	35
a.		Booklet pane of 18	95.00	
249	A36	10o dk violet	1.80	1.40
a.		Booklet pane of 18	110.00	
250	A37	15o dk carmine	3.25	35
a.		Booklet pane of 18	225.00	

Perf. 10 Vertically
251	A35	5o green	1.70	18
252	A36	10o dk violet	1.70	18
253	A37	15o dk carmine	1.70	18
254	A38	20o lt blue	8.00	2.25
255	A39	25o lt ultra	5.25	35
256	A40	30o yellow brn	20.00	1.65
257	A41	35o plum	6.00	1.10
258	A42	40o olive grn	5.50	1.40
259	A43	45o myrtle grn	8.25	1.65
260	A44	50o gray	21.50	1.65

261	A45	60o maroon	27.50	48
262	A46	1k deep blue	8.25	4.00
		Nos. 248-262 (15)	122.10	17.17
		Set, never hinged	265.00	

300th anniv. of the Swedish Postal Service. See Nos. 946-950, B55-B56.

Airplane over Bromma Airport A47   Emanuel Swedenborg A48

1936, May 23   Perf. 10 Vert.
263	A47	50o ultra	6.00	6.25
		Never hinged	11.00	

Opening of Bromma Airport near Stockholm.

Swedish Booklets
Before 1940, booklets were hand-made and usually held two panes of 10 stamps (2x5). About every third booklet contained one row of stamps with straight edges at right or left side. Se-tenant pairs may be obtained with one stamp perforated on 4 sides and one perforated on 3 sides.
Starting in 1940, booklet stamps have one or more straight edges.

1938, Jan. 29   Perf. 12½
264	A48	10o violet	90	15
a.		Perf. on 3 sides	12.00	2.00
		Never hinged	17.50	
b.		Booklet pane of 10	20.00	

Perf. 12½ Vertically
266	A48	10o violet	90	15
267	A48	100o green	6.00	75
		Set, never hinged	14.00	

250th anniv. of the birth of Emanuel Swedenborg, scientist, philosopher and religious writer.

Johann Printz and Indian Chief — A49   "Kalmar Nyckel" Sailing from Gothenburg — A50

Symbolizing the Settlement of New Sweden — A51   Holy Trinity Church, Wilmington, Del. — A52

Queen Christina — A53

1938, Apr. 8   Perf. 12½ Vert.
268	A49	5o green	60	15
269	A50	15o brown	60	15
270	A51	20o red	3.00	40
271	A52	30o ultra	6.50	60
272	A53	60o brown lake	9.75	15

Perf. 12½
273	A49	5o green	95	48
a.		Perf. on 3 sides	11.00	3.50
		Never hinged	13.00	
b.		Booklet pane of 18	57.50	

274	A50	15o brown	1.65	40
a.		Perf. on 3 sides	16.00	3.25
		Never hinged	20.00	
b.		Booklet pane of 18	90.00	
		Nos. 268-274 (7)	23.05	2.33
		Set, never hinged	37.50	

Tercentenary of the Swedish settlement at Wilmington, Del. See No. B54.

King Gustaf V — A54

1938, June 16   Perf. 12½ Vert.
275	A54	5o green	60	15
276	A54	15(o) brown	60	15
277	A54	30(o) ultra	16.00	55

Perf. 12½
278	A54	5o green	95	25
a.		Perf. on 3 sides	20.00	2.50
		Never hinged	22.50	
b.		Booklet pane of 10	22.50	
279	A54	15(o) brown	1.25	18
a.		Perf. on 3 sides	27.50	80
		Never hinged	32.50	
b.		Booklet pane of 10	27.50	
		Nos. 275-279 (5)	19.40	
		Set value		1.10
		Set, never hinged	32.50	

80th birthday of King Gustaf V.

King Gustaf V — A55   Three Crowns — A56

1939   Perf. 12½ Vertically
280	A55	10o violet	1.00	15
281	A55	20o carmine	1.75	25
282	A56	60o lake	3.25	15
283	A56	85o dk green	1.00	15
284	A56	90o peacock blue	2.25	15
285	A56	1k orange	75	15
286	A56	1.15k henna brn	90	15
287	A56	1.20k brt rose vio	3.25	15
288	A56	1.45k lt yel grn	4.25	40

Perf. 12½
289	A55	10o violet	2.00	1.75
a.		Perf. on 3 sides	45.00	60.00
		Never hinged	75.00	
b.		Bkt. pane of 10, perf. on 4 sides	21.00	
		Nos. 280-289 (10)	20.40	
		Set value		2.90
		Set, never hinged	27.50	

See Nos. 394-398, 416-417, 425-426, 431, 439-441, 473, 588-591, 656-664.

Per Henrik Ling — A57

1939, Feb. 25   Perf. 12½ Vert.
290	A57	5o green	15	15
291	A57	25(o) brown	1.00	20

Perf. 12½
292	A57	5o green	85	32
a.		Perf. on 3 sides	16.00	2.00
		Never hinged	26.00	
b.		Booklet pane of 10	13.00	
		Set value		56
		Set, never hinged	3.00	

Centenary of the death of P. H. Ling, father of Swedish gymnastics.

J. J. Berzelius A58   Carl von Linné A59

Perf. 12½ Vertically
1939, June 2   Engr.

293	A58	10o violet	1.75	15
294	A59	15o fawn	42	15
295	A58	30o ultra	12.50	25
296	A59	50o gray	11.00	60

Perf. 12½

297	A58	10o violet	1.75	48
a.		Perf. on 3 sides	70.00	15.00
		Never hinged	92.50	
b.		Booklet pane of 10	30.00	
298	A58	15o fawn	2.75	15
a.		Perf. on 3 sides	16.00	15
		Never hinged	19.00	
c.		As "a," bklt. pane of 20	550.00	
		Nos. 293-298 (6)	30.17	1.78
		Set, never hinged	60.00	

200th anniv. of the founding of the Royal Academy of Science at Stockholm.

King Gustaf V — A60

Type A55 Re-engraved
1939-46   Perf. 12½

299	A60	5o dp green ('46)	20	15
a.		Bklt. pane of 20, perf. on 4 sides	400.00	
b.		Perf. on 3 sides ('41)	35	15
		Never hinged	42	
c.		As "b," bklt. pane of 20	11.00	
300	A60	10o(o) violet ('46)	20	15
a.		Bklt. pane of 10, on 4 sides	32.50	
b.		Bklt. pane of 20, perf. on 4 sides	500.00	
		Never hinged	2.00	
c.		Perf. on 3 sides	1.00	15
i.		As "c," booklet pane of 20	55.00	
300D	A60	15(o) chestnut ('46)	20	15
e.		Bklt. pane of 20	60.00	
f.		Perf. on 3 sides ('45)	50	20
		Never hinged	60	
g.		As "f," booklet pane of 20	10.00	
300G	A60	20(o) red ('42)	30	15
h.		Booklet pane of 20	8.00	
		Set value		35
		Set, never hinged		1.25

No. 300 differs slightly from the original due to deeper engraving. No. 300G was issued only in booklets; all copies have one straight edge.

1940-42   Perf. 12½ Vertically

301	A60	5o dp green ('41)	18	15
302	A60	10(o) violet	18	15
302A	A60	15(o) chestnut ('42)	22	15
303	A60	20(o) red	18	15
304	A60	25(o) orange	1.10	15
305	A60	30(o) ultra	52	15
306	A60	35(o) red vio ('41)	95	15
307	A60	40(o) olive grn	95	15
308	A60	45(o) dk brown	95	15
309	A60	50(o) gray blk ('41)	3.50	15
		Nos. 301-309 (10)	8.73	
		Set value		60
		Set, never hinged	11.00	

Numerals measure 4½mm high. Less shading around head gives a lighter effect. Horizontal lines only as background for "SVERIGE."
See Nos. 391-393, 399.

Carl Michael
Bellman
A61

Tobias Sergel
A62

1940, Feb. 4   Engr.   Perf. 12½ Vert.

310	A61	5o green	15	15
311	A61	35(o) rose red	75	25

Perf. 12½

312	A61	5o green	1.00	35
a.		Perf. on 3 sides	9.00	50
		Never hinged	19.00	
b.		Booklet pane of 10	21.00	
c.		As "a," bklt. pane of 20	425.00	
		Set, never hinged	3.25	

Bellman (1740-95), lyric poet.

1940, Sept. 5   Perf. 12½ on 3 Sides

313	A62	15o lt brown	5.00	25
a.		Booklet pane of 20	275.00	

Perf. 12½ Vertically

314	A62	15o lt brown	2.00	15
315	A62	50o gray black	18.00	65
		Set, never hinged	42.50	

Bicentenary of birth of Johan Tobias von Sergel (1740-1814), sculptor.

Reformers Presenting
Bible to Gustavus
Vasa
A63

View of
Skansen
A64

1941, May 11   Perf. 12½ on 3 Sides

316	A63	15o brown	1.90	45
a.		Booklet pane of 18	100.00	

Perf. 12½ Vertically

317	A63	15o brown	25	15
318	A63	90o ultra	16.00	65
		Set, never hinged	37.50	

400th anniv. of the 1st authorized version of the Bible in Swedish.

1941, June 18   Perf. 12½ on 3 Sides

319	A64	10o violet	2.00	55
a.		Booklet pane of 20	70.00	

Perf. 12½ Vertically

320	A64	10o violet	1.25	15
321	A64	60o red lilac	11.50	45
		Set, never hinged	20.00	

50th anniv. of Skansen, an open air extension of the Nordic Museum.

Royal Palace at
Stockholm
A65

Artur
Hazelius
A66

1941   Perf. 12½ on 3 Sides

322	A65	5k blue	2.00	30
		Never hinged	4.00	
a.		Perf. on 4 sides	30.00	1.00
		Never hinged	55.00	
b.		Bklt. pane of 20, perf. 3 sides	50.00	
c.		Bklt. pane of 10, perf. 4 sides	575.00	

For coil stamp see No. 537.

1941, Aug. 30   Perf. 12½ on 3 Sides

323	A66	5o lt green	2.50	55
a.		Booklet pane of 20	110.00	

Perf. 12½ Vertically

324	A66	5o lt green	18	15
325	A66	1k lt orange	10.00	2.25
		Set, never hinged	16.00	

Issued to honor Artur Hazelius, founder of Skansen, Nordic museum.

St. Bridget of
Sweden — A67

Perf. 12½ on 3 Sides
1941, Oct. 7   Engr.

326	A67	15o deep brown	1.65	28
a.		Booklet pane of 18	60.00	

Perf. 12½ Horiz.

327	A67	15o deep brown	35	15
328	A67	1.20k red vio	32.50	8.25
		Set, never hinged	52.50	

King Gustavus
III
A68

K. G. Tessin,
Architect
A69

1942, June 29   Perf. 12½ on 3 Sides

329	A68	20o red	1.25	35
a.		Booklet pane of 20	45.00	

Perf. 12½ Vertically

330	A68	20o red	60	15
331	A69	40o olive green	22.50	1.00
		Set, never hinged	30.00	

Sesquicentennial of the Swedish National Museum, Stockholm.

Torsten Rudenschold and Nils
Mansson — A70

1942, July 1   Perf. 12½ Horiz.

332	A70	10o magenta	45	25
a.		Booklet pane of 10	4.50	

Perf. 12½ Vertically

333	A70	10o magenta	40	25
334	A70	90o light blue	4.00	4.00
		Set, never hinged	6.25	

100th anniversary of the Swedish Public School System.

Carl Wilhelm
Scheele — A71

King Gustaf
V — A72

1942, Dec. 9   Perf. 12½ on 3 Sides

335	A71	5o green	1.40	50
a.		Booklet pane of 20	55.00	

Perf. 12½ Vertically

336	A71	5o green	15	15
337	A71	60o deep magenta	10.00	1.00
		Set, never hinged	18.00	

200th anniv. of the birth of Carl Wilhelm Scheele, chemist.

Perf. 12½ Horizontally
1943, June 16

338	A72	20o red	60	25
339	A72	30o ultra	1.40	2.50
340	A72	60o brt red vio	2.25	3.75

Perf. 12½ on 3 Sides

341	A72	20o red	6.50	65
a.		Booklet pane of 20	275.00	
		Set, never hinged	16.00	

85th birthday of King Gustaf V, June 16.

Rifle
Federation
Emblem
A73

Oscar
Montelius
A74

1943, July 22   Perf. 12½ Vert.

342	A73	10o rose violet	18	15
343	A73	90o dp ultra	5.00	30

Perf. 12½ on 3 Sides

344	A73	10o rose violet	42	42
a.		Booklet pane of 20	10.00	
		Set, never hinged	8.00	

50th anniversary of the Swedish Voluntary Rifle Associations.

1943, Sept. 9   Engr.   Perf. 12½ Vert.

345	A74	5o green	15	15
346	A74	1.20k brt red vio	10.00	1.65

Perf. 12½ on 3 Sides

347	A74	5o green	55	28
a.		Booklet pane of 20	19.00	
		Set, never hinged	13.00	

Birth centenary of Oscar Montelius (1843-1921), archaeologist.

Johan Mansson's Chart of
Baltic, 1644 — A75

1944, Apr. 15   Engr.   Unwmk.

348	A75	5o green	95	50
a.		Booklet pane of 20	30.00	

Perf. 12½ Vertically

349	A75	5o green	15	15
350	A75	60o lake	6.50	30
		Set, never hinged	15.00	

Tercentenary of the first Swedish Marine Chart.

"The Lion of
Smaland"
A76

Clas Fleming
A77

Designs: 30o, "Kung Karl." 40o, "Gustaf V." 90o, Stern of "Amphion," Flagship of Gustavus III.

1944, Oct. 13   Perf. 12½ Vert.

351	A76	10o purple	30	18
352	A77	20o red	45	15
353	A76	30o blue	60	40
354	A76	40o olive green	75	55
355	A76	90o gray black	9.75	1.00

Perf. 12½ on 3 Sides

356	A76	10o purple	75	55
a.		Booklet pane of 20	19.00	
357	A77	20o red	2.50	25
a.		Booklet pane of 20	90.00	
		Nos. 351-357 (7)	15.10	3.08
		Set, never hinged	15.00	

Issued to honor the Swedish Fleet and mark the tercentenary of the Swedish naval victory at Femern, 1644.
See Nos. B53, B57-B58.

> Catalogue values for unused stamps in this section, from this point to the end of the section, are for Never Hinged items.

Red
Cross — A81

Torch and
Quill
Pen — A82

1945, Feb. 27   Perf. 12½ Vert.

358	A81	20o red	85	15

Perf. 12½ on 3 Sides

359	A81	20o red	2.75	50
a.		Booklet pane of 20	92.50	

80th anniversary of the Swedish Red Cross Society.

1945, May 29   Perf. 12½ Vert.

360	A82	5o green	20	15

361 A82 60o carmine rose 7.50 28
Perf. 12¹/₂ on 3 Sides
362 A82 5o green 38 35
  a. Booklet pane of 20 7.75
  Tercentenary of Swedish press.

Rydberg
A83

Oak Tree
A84

1945, Sept. 21 **Perf. 12¹/₂ Vert.**
363 A83 20o red 32 15
364 A83 90o blue 8.50 25
Perf. 12¹/₂ on 3 Sides
365 A83 20o red 1.40 25
  a. Booklet pane of 20 57.50
  Set value 65
  Viktor Rydberg (1828-95), author.

1945, Oct. 27 **Perf. 12¹/₂ Vert.**
366 A84 10o violet 32 25
367 A84 40o olive 1.65 95
Perf. 12¹/₂ on 3 Sides
368 A84 10o violet 50 50
  a. Booklet pane of 20 10.00
  125th anniv. of the Savings Bank movement.

Angel and Lund
Cathedral — A85

View of Lund
Cathedral — A86

Perf. 12¹/₂ Vertically
1946, May 28 **Unwmk.**
369 A85 15o orange brn 80 24
370 A86 20o red 25 15
371 A86 90o ultra 10.00 60
Perf. 12¹/₂ on 3 Sides
372 A85 15o orange brn 1.10 85
  a. Booklet pane of 20 25.00
373 A86 20o red 2.00 25
  a. Booklet pane of 20 45.00
  Nos. 369-373 (5) 14.15 2.09
  Lund Cathedral, 800th anniversary.

Mare and
Colt — A87

Esaias
Tegner — A88

1946, June 8 **Perf. 12¹/₂ Vert.**
374 A87 5o green 18 15
375 A87 60o carmine rose 7.00 25
Perf. 12¹/₂ on 3 Sides
376 A87 5o green 30 30
  a. Booklet pane of 20 6.50
  Centenary of Swedish agricultural shows.

Perf. 12¹/₂ Vertically
1946, Nov. 2 **Engr.** **Unwmk.**
377 A88 10o deep violet 18 15
378 A88 40o dk olive grn 2.00 55
Perf. 12¹/₂ on 3 Sides
379 A88 10o dp violet 30 32
  a. Booklet pane of 20 6.00
  Death centenary of Esaias Tegner (1782-1846), poet.

Sweden stamps can be mounted in the annually supplemented Scott Scandinavia and Finland album.

Nobel — A89

Geijer — A90

1946, Dec. 10 **Perf. 12¹/₂ Vert.**
380 A89 20o red 70 15
381 A89 30o ultra 2.50 45
Perf. 12¹/₂ on 3 Sides
382 A89 20o red 1.90 25
  a. Booklet pane of 20 40.00
  50th anniversary of the death of Alfred Nobel, inventor and philanthropist.

1947, Apr. 23 **Perf. 12¹/₂ Vert.**
383 A90 5o dk yellow grn 15 15
384 A90 90o ultra 3.75 15
Perf. 12¹/₂ on 3 Sides
385 A90 5o dk yellow grn 20 35
  a. Booklet pane of 20 7.00
  Centenary of the death of Erik Gustaf Geijer, historian, philosopher and poet.

King Gustaf V — A91

1947, Dec. 8 **Engr.** **Perf. 12¹/₂ Horiz.**
386 A91 10o deep violet 15 15
387 A91 20o red 20 18
388 A91 60o red violet 1.50 1.25
Perf. 12¹/₂ on 3 Sides
389 A91 10o deep violet 15 18
  a. Booklet pane of 20 3.00
390 A91 20o red 35 28
  a. Booklet pane of 20 7.50
  Nos. 386-390 (5) 2.35 2.04
  40th anniv. of the reign of King Gustaf V.

King and 3-Crown Types of 1939
1948 **Unwmk.** **Perf. 12¹/₂ Vertically**
391 A60 5o orange 25 15
392 A60 10o green 30 15
393 A60 25o violet 1.00 15
394 A60 55o orange brown 4.50 15
395 A56 80o olive green 1.50 15
396 A56 1.10k violet 11.00 15
397 A56 1.40k dk blue green 1.50 15
398 A56 1.75k brt grnsh blue 35.00 6.50
Perf. 12¹/₂ on 3 Sides
399 A60 10o green 25 15
  a. Booklet pane of 20 6.00
  Nos. 391-399 (9) 55.30 7.70

Plowman, Early and
Modern Buildings
A92

August
Strindberg
A93

1948, Apr. 26 **Perf. 12¹/₂ Vert.**
400 A92 15o orange brown 22 15
401 A92 30o ultra 80 32
402 A92 1k orange 2.25 55
Perf. 12¹/₂ on 3 Sides
403 A92 15o orange brown 32 30
  a. Booklet pane of 20 8.50
  Centenary of the Swedish pioneers' settlement in the United States.

1949, Jan. 22 **Perf. 12¹/₂ Vert.**
404 A93 20o red 45 15
405 A93 30o blue 1.00 45
406 A93 80o olive green 2.75 35
Perf. 12¹/₂ on 3 Sides
407 A93 20o red 80 18
  a. Booklet pane of 20 16.00
  Birth centenary of August Strindberg (1849-1912), author and playwright.

Girl and Boy
Gymnasts — A94

Perf. 12¹/₂ Horiz.
1949, July 27 **Engr.**
408 A94 5o ultra 20 16
409 A94 15o brown 24 16
Perf. 12¹/₂ on 3 Sides
410 A94 15o brown 45 55
  a. Booklet pane of 20 9.00
  Issued to publicize the second Lingiad or World Gymnastics Festival, Stockholm, July-August 1949.

A95

Symbols of
UPU — A96

1949, Oct. 9 **Perf. 12¹/₂ Vert.**
411 A95 10o green 20 15
412 A95 20o red 25 15
Perf. 12¹/₂ Horizontally
413 A96 30o lt blue 60 32
Perf. 12¹/₂ on 3 Sides
414 A95 10o green 16 15
  a. Booklet pane of 20 3.50
415 A95 20o red 20 15
  a. Booklet pane of 20 4.00
  Nos. 411-415 (5) 1.41 92
  75th anniv. of the formation of the UPU.

Three-Crown Type of 1939
Perf. 12¹/₂ Vertically
1949, Nov. 11 **Unwmk.**
416 A56 65o lt yellow grn 1.00 15
417 A56 70o peacock blue 6.25 95

Gustaf VI Adolf (Letters in
color)
A97

Christopher
Polhem
A98

1951, June 6 **Perf. 12¹/₂ Vert.**
Without Imprint
418 A97 10o dull green 24 15
419 A97 15o chestnut brown 35 15
420 A97 20o carmine rose 35 15
421 A97 25o gray 80 15
422 A97 30o ultra 48 15
Perf. 12¹/₂ on 3 sides
423 A97 10o dull green 24 15
  a. Booklet pane of 20 5.50
424 A97 25o gray 48 15
  a. Booklet pane of 20 15.00
  Nos. 418-424 (7) 2.94
  Set value 80
  See Nos. 435-438, 442-443, 456-461, 502, 505-509, 515-517.

Three-Crown Type of 1939
1951, June 1 **Perf. 12¹/₂ Vert.**
425 A56 85o orange brown 9.00 1.25
426 A56 1.70k red 1.65 15

1951, Aug. 30 **Perf. 12¹/₂ Vert.**
427 A98 25o gray 70 15
428 A98 45o brown 55 35
Perf. 12¹/₂ on 3 sides
429 A98 25o gray 45 30
  a. Booklet pane of 20 9.00
  200th anniversary of the death of Christopher Polhem, engineer and technician.

Numeral
(Lettering in
color)
A99

Olaus Petri
Preaching
A100

Type A99 and 3-Crown Type of 1939
1951, Nov. **Engr.** **Perf. 12¹/₂ Vert.**
430 A99 5o rose carmine 24 15
431 A56 1.50k red violet 2.25 1.10
  For other stamps similar to type A99, see type A115a, Nos. 503-504, 513-514, 570, 580, 666-667.

1952, Apr. 19 **Perf. 12¹/₂ Horiz.**
432 A100 25o gray black 30 15
433 A100 1.40k brown 4.00 45
Perf. 12¹/₂ on 3 sides
434 A100 25o gray black 1.90 2.25
  a. Booklet pane of 20 50.00
  400th anniversary of death of Olaus Petri (1493-1552), Lutheran clergyman, historian and Bible translator.

King and 3-Crown Types of 1951 and 1939
1952 **Perf. 12¹/₂ Vertically**
Without Imprint
435 A97 20o gray 35 15
436 A97 25o car rose 2.50 15
437 A97 30o dk brown 45 30
438 A97 40o blue 90 25
439 A56 50o gray 10.00 15
440 A56 75o orange brown 5.50 45
441 A56 2k red violet 1.40 15
Perf. 12¹/₂ on 3 sides
442 A97 20o gray 70 35
  a. Booklet pane of 20 15.00
443 A97 25o carmine rose 90 15
  a. Booklet pane of 20 22.50
  Nos. 435-443 (9) 22.70
  Set value 1.40

Ski Jump
A101

Ice Hockey
A102

Designs: 40o, Woman throwing slingball. 1.40kr, Wrestlers.

Perf. 12¹/₂ Vert. (V), Horiz. (H)
1953, May 27
444 A101 10o green (V) 55 22
445 A102 15o brown (H) 90 40
446 A102 40o deep blue (H) 1.40 95
447 A101 1.40k red violet (V) 4.00 80
Perf. 12¹/₂ on 3 sides
448 A101 10o green (V) 85 70
  a. Booklet pane of 20 17.50
  Nos. 444-448 (5) 7.70 3.07
  50th anniv. of Swedish Athletic Association.

Old
Stockholm — A103

Original and Present
Seals of
Stockholm — A104

1953, June 17 **Perf. 12¹/₂ Vert.**
449 A103 25o blue 30 15
450 A104 1.70k red 4.25 45
Perf. 12¹/₂ on 3 sides
451 A103 25o blue 85 22
  a. Booklet pane of 20 17.50
  700th anniv. of the founding of Stockholm.

"Telephone" — A105

1953, Nov. 2   *Perf. 12¹/₂ Horiz.*
452 A105 25o shown   30   15
453 A105 40o "Radio"   1.25   85
454 A105 60o "Telegraph"   1.75 1.25
          Perf. 12¹/₂ on 3 sides
455 A105 25o shown   80   18
a.   Booklet pane of 20   20.00

Centenary of the foundation of the Swedish Telegraph Service.

King Type of 1951
1954   *Perf. 12¹/₂ Vertically*
          Without Imprint
456 A97 10o dark brown   15   15
457 A97 25o ultra   25   15
458 A97 30o red   25.00   15
459 A97 40o olive green   85   15
          Perf. 12¹/₂ on 3 sides
460 A97 10o dark brown   22   15
a.   Booklet pane of 10   9.00
b.   Booklet pane of 20   7.50
461 A97 25o ultra   22   15
a.   Booklet pane of 4   14.00
b.   Booklet pane of 8   125.00
c.   Booklet pane of 20   10.00
          Nos. 456-461 (6)   26.69
          Set value   60

The booklet pane of 4 contains two copies of No. 461 which are perforated on two adjoining sides.

Skier
A106

Anna Maria
Lenngren
A107

1954, Feb. 13   *Perf. 12¹/₂ Vert.*
462 A106 20o shown   60   24
463 A106 1k Girl skier   13.00   90
          Perf. 12¹/₂ on 3 sides
464 A106 20o shown   2.00 1.25
a.   Booklet pane of 20   40.00

Issued to publicize the World Ski Championship Matches, 1954.

1954, June 18   *Perf. 12¹/₂ Horiz.*
465 A107 20o gray   35   15
466 A107 65o dark brown   9.00 1.65
          Perf. 12¹/₂ on 3 sides
467 A107 20o gray   2.00 1.00
a.   Booklet pane of 20   40.00

200th anniversary of the birth of Anna Maria Lenngren, author.

Rock
Carvings
A108

Coat of Arms
A109

1954, Nov. 8   *Perf. 12¹/₂ Vert.*
468 A108 50o gray   28   15
469 A108 60o dp carmine   28   15
470 A108 65o dk olive grn   1.40   20
471 A108 75o dk brown   2.25   20
472 A108 90o dk blue   70   15
          Nos. 468-472 (5)   4.91
          Set value   58

See Nos. 510-512, 655.

Three-Crown Type of 1939
1954, Dec. 10   *Perf. 12¹/₂ Vert.*
473 A56 2.10k dp ultra   15.00   15

1955, May 16   *Perf. 12¹/₂ Vert.*
474 A109 25o blue   15   15
475 A109 40o green   1.65   25
          Perf. 12¹/₂ on 3 sides
476 A109 25o blue   15   15
a.   Booklet pane of 4   9.00
b.   Booklet pane of 20   4.00
          Set value   40

Centenary of Sweden's 1st postage stamps. The booklet pane of 4 contains two copies of No. 476 which are perforated on two adjoining sides.

Crown and Flag — A110   A111

          Perf. 12¹/₂
1955, June 6   Unwmk.   Litho.
477 A110 10o green, bl & yel   20   15
478 A110 15o lake, bl & yel   24   15

National Flag Day.

          Wmk. 307
1955, July 1   Typo.   *Perf. 13*
479 A111 3o yellow green   2.75 3.50
480 A111 4o blue   2.75 3.50
481 A111 6o gray   2.75 3.50
482 A111 8o orange yellow   2.75 3.50
483 A111 24o salmon   2.75 3.50
          Nos. 479-483 (5)   13.75 17.50

Cent. of the 1st Swedish postage stamps. Nos. 479-483 were printed in sheets of nine. They were sold in complete sets at the Stockholmia Philatelic Exhibition, July 1-10, 1955. A set cost 45 ore (face value) plus 2k (entrance fee).

Per Atterbom
A112

Greek Horseman
A113

          Perf. 12¹/₂ Horizontally
1955, July 21   Engr.   Unwmk.
484 A112 20o dark blue   32   20
485 A112 1.40k sepia   4.50   55
          Perf. 12¹/₂ on 3 sides
486 A112 20o dark blue   1.65 1.00
a.   Booklet pane of 20   35.00

Cent. of the death of Per Daniel Amadeus Atterbom, poet.

1956, Apr. 16   *Perf. 12¹/₂ Vert.*
487 A113 20o carmine   20   15
488 A113 25o ultra   20   15
489 A113 40o gray green   1.75 1.00
          Perf. 12¹/₂ on 3 sides
490 A113 20o carmine   42   30
a.   Booklet pane of 20   8.75
491 A113 25o ultra   42   18
a.   Booklet pane of 20   8.75
          Nos. 487-491 (5)   2.99 1.78

Issued to publicize the Olympic Equestrian Competitions, Stockholm, June 10-17, 1956.

Northern Countries Issue

Whooper
Swans — A113a

          Perf. 12¹/₂ Vertically
1956, Oct. 30   Engr.   Unwmk.
492 A113a 25o rose red   60   15
493 A113a 40o ultra   2.25   48

See footnote after Norway No. 354.

Railroad
Builders — A114

Ship in Distress and
Lifeboat — A115

Designs: 25o, First Swedish locomotive and passenger car. 40o, Express train crossing Arsta bridge.

1956, Dec. 1   *Perf. 12¹/₂ Vert.*
494 A114 10o olive green   48   15
495 A114 25o ultra   32   15
496 A114 40o orange   2.25 2.00
          Perf. 12¹/₂ on 3 sides
497 A114 10o olive green   48   35
a.   Booklet pane of 20   15.00
498 A114 25o ultra   60   45
a.   Booklet pane of 20   14.00
          Nos. 494-498 (5)   4.13 3.10

Centenary of Swedish railroads.

          Perf. 12¹/₂ Vertically
1957, June 1   Engr.   Unwmk.
499 A115 30o blue   4.75   15
500 A115 1.40k deep rose   6.00   75
          Perf. 12¹/₂ on 3 sides
501 A115 30o blue   1.50   75
a.   Booklet pane of 20   50.00

Swedish Life Saving Society, 50th anniv.

King Type of 1951
1957, June 1   *Perf. 12¹/₂ Vert.*
          Without Imprint
502 A97 25o dark brown   1.65 1.65

Re-engraved Types of 1951 and 1954 with Imprint, and

Numeral (Letters in
white) — A115a

1957-64   *Perf. 12¹/₂ Vertically*
503 A115a 5o red ('61)   15   15
a.   5o dark red   15   15
504 A115a 10o blue ('61)   15   15
a.   10o dark blue   30   15
505 A97 15o dark red   32   15
506 A97 20o gray   32   15
507 A97 25o brown   1.10   15
508 A97 30o blue   60   15
509 A97 40o olive green   1.40   15
510 A108 55o vermilion   1.50   18
511 A108 70o orange   1.10   15
512 A108 80o yellow green   1.10   15
          Perf. 12¹/₂ on 3 sides
513 A115a 5o red ('61)   15   15
a.   Bklt. pane of 20 ('64)   2.00
b.   5o dark red   5.00   25
c.   Bklt. pane, 5 #513b, 5 #515 47.50
514 A115a 10o blue ('61)   15   15
a.   10o dark blue   20.00 2.00
b.   Bklt. pane, #514a, 3 #517   37.50
515 A97 15o dark red   60   15
a.   Bklt. pane of 20   12.00
516 A97 20o gray   1.10   32
a.   Bklt. pane of 20   30.00
517 A97 30o blue   1.40   15
a.   Bklt. pane of 20   35.00
          Nos. 503-517 (15)   11.14
          Set value   1.35

In the redrawn Numeral type A99, "Sverige, ore" and the "g" tail flourishes are white instead of in color.
Booklet pane including #513 is listed as #581b.
The booklet pane of 4, No. 514b, contains two copies of No. 517 which are imperf. on two adjoining sides. No. 514a was issued only in booklet pane No. 514b.
See Nos. 570, 580, 580a, 581b, 584b, 586b-586c, 666-667, 668a, 669b-669c.

Helicopter Mail
Service — A116

Modern and 17th
Century
Vessels — A117

          Perf. 12¹/₂ Vertically
1958, Feb. 10   Engr.   Unwmk.
518 A116 30o blue   20   15
519 A116 1.40k brown   7.25   70
          Perf. 12¹/₂ on 3 sides
520 A116 30o blue   1.00   30
a.   Booklet pane of 20   20.00

10th anniversary of helicopter mail service to the Stockholm archipelago, Feb. 10.

1958, Feb. 10   *Perf. 12¹/₂ Vert.*
521 A117 15o dark red   35   25
522 A117 40o gray olive   6.00 2.75
          Perf. 12¹/₂ on 3 sides
523 A117 15o dark red   60   60
a.   Booklet pane of 20   12.00

3 centuries of transatlantic mail service.

Soccer
Player — A118

1958, May 8   *Perf. 12¹/₂ Vert.*
524 A118 15o vermilion   30   25
525 A118 20o yellow green   35   25
526 A118 1.20k dark blue   1.50   85
          Perf. 12¹/₂ on 3 sides
527 A118 15o vermilion   45   45
a.   Booklet pane of 20   9.00
528 A118 20o yellow green   45   45
a.   Booklet pane of 20   9.50
          Nos. 524-528 (5)   3.05 2.25

Issued to publicize the 6th World Soccer Championships, Stockholm, June 8-29.

Bessemer
Converter
A119

Selma Lagerlof
A120

          Perf. 12¹/₂ Horizontally
1958, June 18   Engr.   Unwmk.
529 A119 30o gray blue   30   15
530 A119 1.70k dull red brown   4.00   75
          Perf. 12¹/₂ on 3 sides
531 A119 30o gray blue   75   38
a.   Booklet pane of 20   15.00

Centenary of the first successful Bessemer blow in Sweden, July 18, 1858.

1958, Nov. 20   *Perf. 12¹/₂ Horiz.*
532 A120 20o dark red   20   20
533 A120 30o blue   20   15
534 A120 80o gray olive   1.00   75
          Perf. 12¹/₂ on 3 Sides
535 A120 20o dark red   55   55
a.   Booklet pane of 20   12.00
536 A120 30o blue   55   45
a.   Booklet pane of 20   16.00
          Nos. 532-536 (5)   2.50 2.10

Selma Lagerlof, writer, birth cent.

Palace Type of 1941
1958, Sept. 17   *Perf. 12¹/₂ Vert.*
537 A65 5k blue   3.00   18

Electric Power
Line — A121

Hydroelectric Plant
and Dam — A122

     Perf. 12¹/₂ Horiz. (H), Vert. (V)
1959, Jan. 20   Unwmk.
538 A121 30o ultra (H)   50   15
539 A122 90o carmine rose (V)   4.00 1.90

Perf. 12½ on 3 sides
540 A121 30o ultra 65 32
a. Booklet pane of 20 14.00

50th anniv. of the establishment of the State Power Board.

Verner von Heidenstam A123 / Forest A124

Perf. 12½ Horizontally
1959, July 6 Engr. Unwmk.
541 A123 15o rose carmine 85 15
542 A123 1k slate 5.50 55
Perf. 12½ on 3 Sides
543 A123 15o rose carmine 75 52
a. Booklet pane of 20 18.00

Verner von Heidenstam, poet, birth cent.

1959, Sept. 4 Perf. 12½ Horiz.
Design: 1.40k, Felling tree.
544 A124 30o green 1.50 20
545 A124 1.40k brown red 5.00 45
Perf. 12½ on 3 sides
546 A124 30o green 1.00 1.00
a. Booklet pane of 20 22.50

Administration of crown lands and forests, cent.

Svante Arrhenius A125 / Anders Zorn A126

Perf. 12½ Horizontally
1959, Dec. 10 Engr. Unwmk.
547 A125 15o dull red brown 35 15
548 A125 1.70k dark blue 4.50 35
Perf. 12½ on 3 sides
549 A125 15o dull red brown 50 30
a. Booklet pane of 20 10.00

Arrhenius (1859-1927), chemist and physicist.

1960, Feb. 18 Perf. 12½ Horiz.
550 A126 30o gray 28 15
551 A126 80o sepia 3.50 1.10
Perf. 12½ on 3 sides
552 A126 30o gray 1.65 30
a. Booklet pane of 20 35.00

Zorn (1860-1920), painter and sculptor.

Uprooted Oak Emblem — A127 / People of Various Races, WRY Emblem — A128

Perf. 12½ Vert. (V), Horiz. (H)
1960, Apr. 7 Engr. Unwmk.
553 A127 20o red brown (V) 15 15
554 A128 40o purple (H) 45 22
Perf. 12½ on 3 sides
555 A127 20o red brown 45 38
a. Booklet pane of 20 9.50

World Refugee Year, July 1, 1959-June 30, 1960.

Target Shooting A129 / Gustaf Froding A130

Design: 90o, Parade of riflemen.

1960, June 30 Perf. 12½ Vert.
556 A129 15o rose carmine 28 15
557 A129 90o grnsh blue 3.00 1.25
Perf. 12½ on 3 sides
558 A129 15o rose carmine 45 30
a. Booklet pane of 20 8.50

Centenary of the founding of the Voluntary Shooting Organization.

1960, Aug. 22 Perf. 12½ Horiz.
559 A130 30o red brown 25 15
560 A130 1.40k slate green 3.50 32
Perf. 12½ on 3 sides
561 A130 30o red brown 40 25
a. Booklet pane of 20 9.50

Gustaf Froding (1860-1911), poet.

Europa Issue, 1960
Common Design Type
1960, Sept. 19 Perf. 12½ Vert.
Size: 27x21mm
562 CD3 40o blue 20 16
563 CD3 1k red 48 30

Hjalmar Branting (1860-1925), Labor Party Leader and Prime Minister — A131

Perf. 12½ Horiz.
1960, Nov. 23 Engr.
564 A131 15o rose carmine 16 15
565 A131 1.70k slate blue 5.00 35
Perf. 12½ on 3 sides
566 A131 15o rose carmine 30 20
a. Booklet pane of 20 6.00

SAS Issue

DC-8 Airliner — A131a

Perf. 12½ Vertically
1961, Feb. 24 Unwmk.
567 A131a 40o blue 28 15
Perf. 12½ on 3 sides
568 A131a 40o blue 1.00 75
a. Booklet pane of 10 10.00

Scandinavian Airlines System, SAS, 10th anniv.

Numeral Type of 1957, Three-Crown Type of 1939 and

Gustaf VI Adolf (Letters, numerals in white) A132 / Rune Stone, Oland, 11th Century A133

1961-65 Perf. 12½ Vert.
570 A115a 15o green ('62) 28 15
571 A132 15o red 32 15
572 A132 20o gray 32 15
573 A132 25o brown 32 15

574 A132 30o ultra 1.50 15
575 A132 30o lilac ('62) 55 15
576 A132 35o lilac 55 15
577 A132 35o ultra ('62) 1.10 15
578 A132 40o emerald 1.00 15
579 A132 50o gray grn ('62) 65 15
Perf. 12½ on 3 sides
580 A115a 15o grn ('65) 28 15
   Bkt. pane, 2 each #514, 580, 583 2.25
581 A132 15o red 22 15
   Bkt. pane of 20 5.00
   b. Bkt. pane, 5 #513, 5 #581 2.50
582 A132 20o gray 90 75
   Bkt. pane of 20 17.50
583 A132 25o brown ('62) 32 15
   Bkt. pane of 20 15.00
   b. Bkt. pane of 4 2.25
584 A132 30o ultra 65 20
   Bkt. pane of 20 15.00
   b. Bkt. pane, #514 + 3 #584 4.00
585 A132 30o lilac ('64) 65 35
   Bkt. pane of 20 14.00
586 A132 35o ultra ('62) 55 15
   Bkt. pane of 20 12.50
   b. Bkt. pane, 3 #514, 2 #586 + blank label 5.00
   c. As "b," inscribed label 3.50

Perf. 12½ Vertically
588 A56 1.05k Prus grn ('62) 2.00 25
589 A56 1.50k brown ('62) 1.50 25
590 A56 2.15k dk sl grn ('62) 7.00 25
591 A56 2.50k emerald 1.40 15
Perf. 12½ on 3 sides
592 A133 10k dl red brn 16.00 75
   a. Bkt. pane of 10 ('68) 190.00
   b. Bkt. pane of 20 475.00
   Nos. 570-592 (22) 38.06
   Set value 5.10

Booklet panes of 4, 5 or 6 (Nos. 580a, 583b, 584b, 586b, 586c) contain two stamps which are imperf. on two adjoining sides.
Combination panes (Nos. 580a, 581b, 584b, 586b, 586c) come in different arrangements of the denominations.
The label of No. 586c is inscribed "ett brev / betyder / sa / mycket" ("a letter means so much").
The label inscription "nord 63 / 5-13 oktober / GÖTEBORG" was privately applied to No. 586b by the Gothenburg Philatelic Society to raise funds for Nord 63 Philatelic Exhibition in Gothenburg. The pane was sold for the equivalent of $1 US, 5 times face value.
See Nos. 648-654A, 666a, 668-672F.

K.-G. Pilo, Self-portrait A134 / Jonas Alstromer A135

1961, Apr. 17 Perf. 12½ Horiz.
594 A134 30o brown 22 15
595 A134 1.40k Prus blue 4.25 80
Perf. 12½ on 3 sides
596 A134 30o brown 1.10 30
a. Booklet pane of 20 30.00

Karl-Gustaf Pilo (1711-1793), painter. Self-portrait from "The Coronation of Gustavus III."

1961, June 2 Perf. 12½ Vert.
597 A135 15o dull claret 18 15
598 A135 90o grnsh blue 1.50 1.10
Perf. 12½ on 3 sides
599 A135 15o dull claret 35 25
a. Booklet pane of 20 7.00

200th anniversary of the birth of Jonas Alstromer, pioneer of agriculture and industry.

17th Century Printer and Student in Library — A136 / Roentgen, Prudhomme, von Behring, van't Hoff — A137

1961, Sept. 22 Engr. Perf. 12½ Vert.
600 A136 20o dark red 16 15
601 A136 1k blue 10.50 75

Perf. 12½ on 3 sides
602 A136 20o dark red 26 26
a. Booklet pane of 20 7.25

300th anniversary of the regulation requiring copies of all Swedish printed works to be deposited in the Royal Library.

1961, Dec. 9 Perf. 12½ Vertically
603 A137 20o vermilion 18 15
604 A137 40o blue 18 15
605 A137 50o green 28 15
Perf. 12½ on 3 sides
606 A137 20o vermilion 30 24
a. Booklet pane of 20 6.00

Winners of the 1901 Nobel Prize; Wilhelm K. Roentgen, Rene Sully Prudhomme, Emil von Behring, Jacob van't Hoff.
See Nos. 617-619, 673-676, 689-692, 710-713, 769-772, 804-807.

A138 / A139

Footsteps and postmen's badges.

1962, Jan. 29 Engr. Perf. 12½ Vert.
607 A138 30o lilac 24 15
608 A138 1.70k rose red 3.50 25
Perf. 12½ on 3 sides
609 A138 30o lilac 35 35
a. Booklet pane of 20 9.50

Local mail delivery service in Sweden, cent.

1962, Mar. 21 Perf. 12½ Horiz.
Voting Tool (Budkavle), Codex of Law and Gavel
610 A139 30o dark blue 32 15
611 A139 2k red 4.75 25
Perf. 12½ on 3 sides
612 A139 30o dark blue 45 42
a. Booklet pane of 20 9.50

Centenary of the municipal reform laws.

St. George, Great Church, Stockholm — A140 / Skokloster Castle — A141

Perf. 12½ Horiz. (H), Vert. (V)
1962, Sept. 24
613 A140 20o rose lake (H) 28 15
614 A141 50o dk slate grn (V) 45 20
Perf. 12½ on 3 sides
615 A140 20o rose lake 28 18
a. Booklet pane of 20 6.00
616 A141 50o dk slate grn 90 1.00
a. Booklet pane of 10 9.00

Nobel Prize Winners Type of 1961

Designs: 25o, Theodor Mommsen and Sir Ronald Ross. 50o, Hermann Emil Fischer, Pieter Zeeman and Hendrik Antoon Lorentz.

1962, Dec. 10 Perf. 12½ Vert.
617 A137 25o dark red 38 22
618 A137 50o blue 38 15
Perf. 12½ on 3 sides
619 A142 25o dark red 60 65
a. Booklet pane of 20 12.50

Winners of the 1902 Nobel Prize.

Ice Hockey — A143

1963, Feb. 15   *Perf. 12½ Horiz.*
620	A143	25o green	20	15
621	A143	1.70k violet bl	3.50	45

Perf. 12½ on 3 sides
622	A143	25o green	35	45
a.		Booklet pane of 20	7.00	

1963 Ice Hockey World Championships.

Wheat Emblem and Stylized Hands — A144

Engineering and Industry Symbols — A145

1963, Mar. 21   *Perf. 12½ Vertically*
623	A144	35o lilac rose	20	15
624	A144	50o violet	32	24

Perf. 12½ on 3 sides
625	A144	35o lilac rose	30	24
a.		Booklet pane of 20	6.00	

FAO "Freedom from Hunger" campaign.

1963, May 27   *Perf. 12½ Vertically*
626	A145	50o gray	40	20
627	A145	1.05k orange	3.50	2.50

Perf. 12½ on 3 sides
628	A145	50o gray	2.75	2.75
a.		Booklet pane of 10	27.50	

Gregoire François Du Reitz — A146

Hammarby, Home of Carl von Linné (Linnaeus) — A147

1963, Sept. 16   *Perf. 12½ Vertically*
    Engr.   Unwmk.
629	A146	25o brown	35	30
630	A146	35o dark blue	20	15
631	A146	2k dark red	4.25	48

Perf. 12½ on 3 sides
632	A146	25o brown	75	70
a.		Booklet pane of 20	16.00	
633	A146	35o dark blue	40	20
a.		Booklet pane of 20	9.00	
		Nos. 629-633 (5)	5.95	1.83

300th anniversary of the Swedish Board of Health. Dr. Du Rietz (1607-1682) was first president of the "Collegium Medicorum," forerunner of the Board of Health.

1963, Oct. 25   *Perf. 12½ Vert.*
634	A147	20o orange red	18	15
635	A147	50o yellow grn	30	15

Perf. 12½ on 3 sides
636	A147	20o orange red	30	35
a.		Booklet pane of 20	5.50	

Nobel Prize Winners Type of 1961

Designs: 25o, Svante Arrhenius, Niels Finsen, Bjornstjerne Bjornson. 50o, Antoine Henri Becquerel, Pierre and Marie Curie.

1963, Dec. 10   Engr.   Unwmk.
Perf. 12½ Vertically
637	A137	25o gray olive	50	42
638	A137	50o chocolate	50	24

Perf. 12½ on 3 sides
639	A137	25o gray olive	75	90
a.		Booklet pane of 20	16.00	

Winners of the 1903 Nobel Prize.

A149

A150

"The Assumption of Elijah."

1964, Feb. 3   *Perf. 12½ Horiz.*
640	A149	35o lt ultra	55	15
641	A149	1.05k dull red	5.25	3.50

Perf. 12½ on 3 sides
642	A149	35o lt ultra	32	20
a.		Booklet pane of 20	9.00	

Erik Axel Karlfeldt (1864-1931), poet.

1964, June 12   *Perf. 12½ Horiz.*

Seal of Archbishop Stephen.
643	A150	40o slate green	20	15
644	A150	60o orange brown	32	24

Perf. 12½ Vertically
645	A150	40o slate green	20	15
a.		Booklet pane of 10	2.25	
646	A150	60o orange brown	32	24
a.		Booklet pane of 10	3.25	

800th anniv. of the Archbishopric of Uppsala.

Types of Regular Issues, 1939-61, and

Post Horns A151

Ship Grave, Skane (Bronze Age) A152

1964-71   Engr.   *Perf. 12½ Vert.*
647	A151	20o sl bl & org yel ('65)	15	15
648	A132	35o gray	60	22
649	A132	40o ultra	80	15
650	A132	45o orange	80	15
651	A132	45o violet bl ('67)	80	15
652	A132	50o green ('68)	52	15
652A	A132	55o dark red ('69)	52	15
653	A132	60o rose car	1.10	75
653A	A132	65o dull grn ('71)	1.25	15
654	A132	70o lilac rose ('67)	60	22
654A	A132	85o dp claret ('71)	1.25	40
655	A108	95o violet	7.75	3.75
656	A56	1.20k lt blue	9.50	2.50
657	A56	1.80k dk blue ('67)	3.50	45
658	A56	1.85k blue ('67)	10.50	90
659	A56	2k dp car ('69)	70	15
660	A56	2.30k choc ('65)	30.00	25
661	A56	2.55k red	8.75	2.50
662	A56	2.80k red ('67)	5.50	18
663	A56	2.85k orange ('65)	7.00	3.75
664	A56	3k brt ultra	2.50	15
665	A152	3.50k grnsh gray ('66)	1.75	18

Perf. 12½ on 3 Sides
666	A115a	10o brown	20	22
a.		Bklt. pane, 2 each #666, 667, 583	3.00	
667	A115a	15o brown	45	42
668	A132	30o rose red ('66)	1.10	35
a.		Bklt. pane, 2 each #513, 580, 668	3.00	
b.		Perf. on 3 sides	1.10	1.10

No. 668 is perf. on 2 adjoining sides.
669	A132	40o ultra	42	15
a.		Bklt. pane of 20	15.00	
b.		Bklt. pane, 2 each #514, 669	5.75	
c.		Bklt. pane, 2 each #513-514, 580, 668b-669	14.00	
670	A132	45o org ('67)	42	15
a.		Bklt. pane of 20	19.00	
671	A132	45o vio bl ('67)	52	15
a.		Bklt. pane of 20	19.00	
672	A132	50o green ('69)	55	45
a.		Bklt. pane of 20	7.25	
672B	A132	55o dk red ('69)	55	15
a.		Bklt. pane of 20	7.25	
672D	A132	65o dull grn ('71)	90	60
a.		Bklt. pane of 20	11.00	
672F	A132	85o dp claret ('71)	1.10	1.00
a.		Bklt. pane of 20	14.00	
		Nos. 647-672F (32)	102.05	21.04

Some combination booklet panes of 4, 6 or 10 contain two stamps which are imperf. on two adjoining sides. Combination panes come in different arrangements of the denominations.

Fluorescent Paper

Starting in 1967, fluorescent paper was used in printing both definitive and commemorative issues. Its use was gradually eliminated starting in 1976. Numerous definitives and a few commemoratives were printed on both ordinary and fluorescent paper.

Nobel Prize Winners Type of 1961

Designs: 30o, José Echegaray y Eizaguirre, Frédéric Mistral and John William Strutt, Lord Rayleigh. 40o, Sir William Ramsey and Ivan Petrovich Pavlov.

1964, Dec. 10   *Perf. 12½ Vertically*   Engr.
673	A137	30o blue	50	35
674	A137	40o red	55	15

Perf. 12½ on 3 Sides
675	A137	30o blue	60	50
a.		Booklet pane of 20	12.00	
676	A137	40o red	80	15
a.		Booklet pane of 20	16.00	

Winners of the 1904 Nobel Prize.

Visby Town Wall — A154

Antenna — A155

1965, Apr. 5   *Perf. 12½ Horiz.*
677	A154	30o dk car rose	18	15
678	A154	2k brt ultra	4.00	20

Perf. 12½ on 3 Sides
679	A154	30o dk car rose	35	45
a.		Booklet pane of 20	7.00	

Prince Eugen — A156

1965, May 17   *Perf. 12½ Horiz.*
680	A155	60o lilac	38	20
681	A155	1.40k bluish blk	3.75	70

Perf. 12½ on 3 Sides
682	A155	60o lilac	80	1.00
a.		Booklet pane of 10	9.50	

Centenary of the ITU.

1965, July 5   *Perf. 12½ Horiz.*
683	A156	40o black	22	15
684	A156	1k brown	2.50	30

Perf. 12½ on 3 Sides
685	A156	40o black	35	15
a.		Booklet pane of 20	7.00	
		Set value		48

Prince Eugen (1865-1947), painter and patron of the arts.

Fredrika Bremer (1801-65), Novelist — A157

1965, Oct. 25   *Perf. 12½ Vertically*   Engr.
686	A157	25o violet	15	15
687	A157	3k gray grn	6.75	35

Perf. 12½ on 3 Sides
688	A157	25o violet	18	18
a.		Booklet pane of 20	4.00	
		Set value		58

Nobel Prize Winners Type of 1961

Designs: 30o, Philipp von Lenard and Adolf von Baeyer. 40o, Robert Koch and Henryk Sienkiewicz.

1965, Dec. 10   *Perf. 12½ Vertically*   Unwmk.
689	A137	30o ultra	50	15
690	A137	40o dark red	40	15

Perf. 12½ on 3 Sides
691	A137	30o ultra	55	42
a.		Booklet pane of 20	11.00	
692	A137	40o dark red	75	15
a.		Booklet pane of 20	16.00	
		Set value		80

Winners of the 1905 Nobel Prize.

Nathan Soderblom A158

Speed Skater A159

1966, Jan. 15   *Perf. 12½ Horiz.*
693	A158	60o brown	40	20
694	A158	80o green	1.00	15

Perf. 12½ on 3 Sides
695	A158	60o brown	60	50
a.		Booklet pane of 10	6.50	

Nathan Soderblom (1866-1931), Protestant theologian, who worked for the union of Christian churches and received 1930 Nobel Peace Prize.

1966, Feb. 18   *Perf. 12½ on 3 Sides*   Engr.
696	A159	5o rose red	15	15
697	A159	25o slate green	15	18
698	A159	55o red	55	50
a.		Bklt. pane, 4 #696, 4 #697, 2 #698	2.25	

World Speed Skating Championships for Men, Gothenburg, Feb. 18-20, and 75th anniversary of World Skating Championships.

National Museum, Staircase, 1866 — A160

Baron Louis Gerhard De Geer — A161

1966, Mar. 26   *Perf. 12½ Vert.*
699	A160	30o violet	15	15
a.		Booklet pane of 10	1.40	
700	A160	2.30k olive green	90	1.00
a.		Booklet pane of 10	9.00	

National Gallery, Blasieholmen, Stockholm, cent. The design is from an 1866 woodcut showing the inauguration of the Museum.

1966, May 12   *Perf. 12½ Vertically*
701	A161	40o dark blue	48	20
702	A161	3k brown carmine	6.50	55

Perf. 12½ on 3 Sides
703	A161	40o dark blue	40	25
a.		Booklet pane of 20	8.00	

Cent. of the reform of the Representative Assembly under the leadership of Minister of Justice (1858-70) Baron Louis Gerhard De Geer (1818-96).

Stage, Drottningholm Court Theater — A162

Almqvist and Wild Rose — A163

Perf. 12½ on 3 Sides

1966, June 15   Engr.

Salmon Paper

704	A162	5o vermilion	15 15
705	A162	25o olive bister	15 15
706	A162	40o dark purple	55 55
a.		Bklt. pane, 4 #704, 4 #705, 2 #706	2.00

Drottningholm Court Theater, 200th anniv.

Perf. 12½ Horizontally

1966, Sept. 26   Engr.

707	A163	25o magenta	30 15
708	A163	1k green	3.50 20

Perf. 12½ on 3 Sides

709	A163	25o magenta	26 20
a.		Booklet pane of 20	5.50

Carl Jonas Love Almqvist (1793-1866), writer and poet.

Nobel Prize Winner Type of 1961

Designs: 30o, Joseph John Thomson and Giosue Carducci. 40o, Henri Moissan, Camillo Golgi and Santiago Ramon y Cajal.

Perf. 12½ Vertically

1966, Dec. 10   Engr.

710	A137	30o rose lake	60 20
711	A137	40o dark green	40 15

Perf. 12½ on 3 Sides

712	A137	30o rose lake	45 45
a.		Booklet pane of 20	9.00
713	A137	40o dark green	45 25
a.		Booklet pane of 20	9.50

Winners of the 1906 Nobel Prize.

Field Ball Player — A164   EFTA Emblem — A165

1967, Jan. 12   **Perf. 12½ Horiz.**

714	A164	45o dk violet blue	20 16
715	A164	2.70k dp rose lilac	3.50 1.40

Perf. 12½ on 3 Sides

716	A164	45o dk violet blue	30 20
a.		Booklet pane of 20	6.00

World Field Ball Championships, Jan. 12-21.

1967, Feb. 15   **Perf. 12½ Horiz.**

717	A165	70o orange	48 25

Perf. 12½ on 3 Sides

718	A165	70o orange	1.25 1.10
a.		Booklet pane of 10	12.50

European Free Trade Association. Tariffs were abolished Dec. 31, 1966, among EFTA members: Austria, Denmark, Finland, Great Britain, Norway, Portugal, Sweden, Switzerland.

"The Fjeld," by Sixten Lundbohm A166

Lion Fortress, Gothenburg A167

Uppsala Cathedral A168   Gripsholm Castle A169

1967   Engr.   **Perf. 12½ Vert.**

719	A166	35o dl bl & blk brn	18 15

Perf. 12½ Horiz.

720	A167	3.70k violet	2.50 15
721	A168	4.50k dull red	2.25 15

Perf. 12½ Vert.

722	A169	7k vio bl & rose red	4.75 30

Perf. 12½ on 3 Sides

723	A166	35o dl bl & blk brn	22 15
a.		Booklet pane of 10	2.50
		Nos. 719-723 (5)	9.90
		Set value	65

Issue Dates: Nos. 719, 721, 723, Mar. 15; No. 720, Feb. 15; No. 722, Apr. 11.

Table Tennis — A170

1967, Apr. 11   **Perf. 12½ Horiz.**

724	A170	35o bright magenta	20 15
725	A170	90o greenish blue	1.00 50

Perf. 12½ on 3 Sides

726	A170	35o bright magenta	30 24
a.		Booklet pane of 20	6.00

World Table Tennis Championships, Stockholm.

Man with Axe and Fettered Beast — A171   Double Mortise Corner — A172

Designs: 15o, Man fighting two bears. 30o, Warrior disguised as wolf pursuing enemy. 35o, Two warriors with swords and lances. The designs are taken from 6th century bronze plates (1¾in. x 2½in.) used to decorate helmets; now in Swedish Museum of National Antiquities.

Perf. 12½ on 3 Sides

1967, May 17   Engr.

727	A171	10o brown & dp bl	15 15
728	A171	15o dp blue & dk brn	20 15
729	A171	30o brt pink & dk brn	22 15
730	A171	35o dk brown & brt pink	22 15
a.		Bklt. pane, 4 #727, 2 each #728-730	1.75
		Set value	38

Lithographed and Photogravure

1967, June 16   **Perf. 12½**

731	A172	10o olive & multi	15 15
732	A172	35o dk blue multi	20 15
a.		Bklt. pane, 6 #731, 4 #732	1.75
		Set value	24

Issued to honor generations of Finnish settlers in Sweden.

Right-hand Driving as Seen Through Windshield — A173

1967, Sept. 2   Engr.   **Perf. 12½ Vert.**

733	A173	35o dp bl, ocher & blk	15 25
734	A173	45o yel grn, ocher & blk	15 15

Perf. 12½ Horiz.

735	A173	35o dp bl, ocher & blk	24 25
a.		Booklet pane of 10	2.50
736	A173	45o yel grn, ocher & blk	24 15
a.		Booklet pane of 10	2.50

Issued to publicize the introduction of right-hand driving in Sweden, Sept. 3, 1967.

1967-72   **Perf. 12½ Horiz. or Vert.**

737	A174	5o red & blk	15 15
738	A174	10o blue & blk	15 15
739	A177d	15o sl grn, grnsh ('71)	16 15
740	A174a	20o sep, buff ('70)	16 15
741	A174a	25o bister & blk ('71)	20 15
742	A174a	25o black & bis ('71)	20 15
a.		Pair, #741-742	40 40
743	A175	30o ultra & ver	16 15
744	A176	40o blk, dk grn & ultra ('68)	16 15
745	A177	45o bl & brn blk ('70)	20 15
746	A176a	55o bl & vio, perf. 12½ vert. ('71)	32 15
747	A176	60o black brn ('71)	25 15

Postrider A174   Griffin A174a

Rocky Isles in Bloom, by Harald Lindberg A175   Dalsland Canal A176

Gothenburg Harbor — A176a

Nils Holgersson Riding Wild Goose — A176b   Elk — A177

Mail Coach, by Eigil Schwab A177a

Illustration from Lapponia, by Johannes Schefferus A177b

Blood-money Coins and Old Map of Sweden A177c   Great Seal, 1439 (St. Erik with Banner and Shield) A177d

Designs: 10o, Merchant vessel in Oresund, 1661. 15o, The Prodigal Son, 13th cent., Rada Church. 20o, St. Stephen as a boy tending horses, medallion from Dädesjo Church. No. 742, Lion, from Grodinge tapestry, 15th cent. 45o, Log roller. 60o, Horse-drawn timber sled. 75o, Windmills, Öland Island. 80o, Steamer Storskär and Royal Palace, Stockholm. 95o, Roe deer. 1k, Dancing cranes. 2.55k, Seal of Magnus Ladulas, 1285 (King Magnus Birgersson on throne with lily scepter and orb). 3k, Seal of Duke Erik Magnusson, 1306 (Duke on horseback with standard of Folkunga dynasty). 6k, Gustavus Vasa's silver daler.

747A	A176b	65o brt blue ('71)	28 15
748	A177	75o slate grn ('71)	40 15
749	A176	80o blue & blk ('71)	32 15
750	A177	90o sep & bl gray	35 15
750A	A175	95o sepia ('72)	40 15
751	A177	1k slate grn ('68)	40 15
751A	A177a	1.20k multi ('71)	50 15
751B	A177b	1.40k lt bl & red ('72)	60 18
752	A177d	2.55k brt blue ('70)	1.65 55
753	A177d	3k dk gray bl ('70)	1.00 15
754	A177c	4k black ('71)	1.65 15
755	A177d	5k Prus grn ('70)	2.00 15
755A	A177c	6k indigo ('72)	2.00 15

Perf. 12½ on 3 Sides

756	A174	5o red & blk	15 15
a.		Booklet pane of 20	1.20
757	A174	10o bl & blk ('69)	15 15
a.		Booklet pane of 20	1.40
758	A175	30o ultra & ver	20 15
a.		Booklet pane of 10	3.00
759	A176	40o blk, dk grn & ultra ('68)	32 25
a.		Booklet pane of 10	3.50
760	A176	45o bl & brn blk ('70)	32 15
a.		Booklet pane of 10	3.50
761	A176a	55o bl & vio, perf. 12½ horiz. ('71)	32 15
a.		Booklet pane of 10	3.50
762	A176b	65o brt blue ('71)	32 15
a.		Booklet pane of 10	3.50
763	A177	75o slate grn ('72)	1.10 15
a.		Booklet pane of 10	11.00
764	A177	90o sepia & bl gray	1.10 75
a.		Booklet pane of 10	11.00
		Nos. 737-764 (33)	17.64
		Set value	4.70

King Gustaf VI Adolf — A178

1967, Nov. 11   Engr.

765	A178	45o lt ultra	22 15
766	A178	70o green	30 15

Perf. 12½ on 3 Sides

767	A178	45o lt ultra	22 22
a.		Booklet pane of 20	4.50
768	A178	70o green	65 65
a.		Booklet pane of 10	6.50

85th birthday of King Gustaf VI Adolf.

Nobel Prize Winners Type of 1961

Designs: 35o, Eduard Buchner (Chemistry) & Albert A. Michelson (Physics). 45o, Charles L. A. Laveran (Medicine) & Rudyard Kipling (Literature).

1967, Dec. 9   **Perf. 12½ Vert.**

769	A137	35o vermilion	65 45
770	A137	45o dark blue	35 15

Perf. 12½ on 3 Sides

771	A142	35o vermilion	65 75
a.		Booklet pane of 10	6.50
772	A142	45o dark blue	55 40
a.		Booklet pane of 10	5.50

Winners of the 1907 Nobel Prize.

Franz Berwald, Violin and His Music — A179   National Bank Seal — A180

1968, Apr. 3   **Perf. 12½ Horiz.**

773	A179	35o black & red	22 25
774	A179	2k blk, vio bl & org yel	3.50 65

Perf. 12½ on 3 Sides

775	A179	35o black & red	40 40
a.		Booklet pane of 10	4.00

Franz Berwald (1796-1868), composer. Design includes opening bar of overture to his opera, "The Queen of Golconda."

Perf. 12½ Vertically

1968, May 15   Engr.

776	A180	45o dull blue	25 15
777	A180	70o black, *pink*	40 15

Perf. 12½ on 3 Sides

778	A180	45o dull blue	40	30
a.		Booklet pane of 10	4.00	
779	A180	70o black, *pink*	60	50
a.		Booklet pane of 10	6.00	

300th anniv. of the National Bank of Sweden. Nos. 777, 779 are on non-fluorescent paper.

Seal of Lund University A181

Butterfly Orchid A182

1968, June 4   Perf. 12½ on 3 sides

780	A181	10o deep blue	15	15
781	A181	35o red	40	40
a.		Bkt. pane, 6 #780, 4 #781	2.25	

300th anniversary of University of Lund.

1968, June 4

Nordic Wild Flowers: No. 783, Wood anemone. No. 784, Dog rose. No. 785, Prune Cherry. No. 786, Lily of the valley.

782	A182	45o slate green	70	40
783	A182	45o gray green	70	40
784	A182	45o sl grn & rose car	70	40
785	A182	45o gray green	70	40
786	A182	45o slate green	70	40
a.		Bkt. pane, 2 each #782-786	8.00	
		Nos. 782-786 (5)	3.50	2.00

World Council of Churches' Emblem — A183

Electron Orbits — A184

1968, July 4   Perf. 12½ Horiz.

787	A183	70o plum	35	30
788	A183	90o Prus green	1.00	18

Perf. 12½ on 3 Sides

789	A183	70o plum	60	50
a.		Booklet pane of 10	5.00	

4th General Assembly of the World Council of Churches, Uppsala, July 4-19.

Perf. 12½ Horizontally

				Engr.
1968, Aug. 9				
790	A184	45o rose carmine	32	15
791	A184	2k dark blue	3.00	25

Perf. 12½ on 3 Sides

792	A184	45o rose carmine	25	40
a.		Booklet pane of 10	2.50	

Establishment of the 1st 3 People's Colleges, cent.

"Orienteer" Finding Way through Forest — A185

"Fingerkrok" by Axel Petersson — A186

Perf. 12½ Horizontally

				Engr.
1968, Sept. 5				
793	A185	40o violet & red brn	32	18
794	A185	2.80k green & violet	3.00	2.50

Perf. 12½ on 3 Sides

795	A185	40o violet & red brn	50	42
a.		Booklet pane of 10	5.00	

Issued to publicize the World Championships in Orienteering, Linkoping, Sept. 28-29.

Perf. 12½ on 3 Sides

1968, Oct. 28				Engr.
796	A186	5o green	15	15
797	A186	25o sepia	1.00	90
798	A186	45o blk brn & red brn	22	15
a.		Bkt. pane, 3 #796, 2 #797, 3 #798	3.00	

Axel Petersson, called "Doderhultarn" (1868-1925), sculptor.

Black-backed Gull — A187

Designs: No. 799, Varying hare. No. 801, Red fox. No. 802, Hooded crows harassing golden eagle. No. 803, Weasel.

Perf. 12½ on 3 Sides

1968, Nov. 9				Engr.
799	A187	30o blue	60	70
800	A187	30o black	60	70
801	A187	30o dark brown	60	70
802	A187	30o black	60	70
803	A187	30o blue	60	70
a.		Bkt. pane, 2 each #799-803	6.00	
		Nos. 799-803 (5)	3.00	3.50

See Nos. 873-877.

Nobel Prize Winners Type of 1961

Designs: 35o, Elie Metchnikoff, Paul Ehrlich and Ernest Rutherford. 45o, Gabriel Lippmann and Rudolf Eucken.

1968, Dec. 10   Perf. 12½ Vertically

804	A137	35o maroon	45	32
805	A137	45o dark green	35	15

Perf. 12½ on 3 Sides

806	A137	35o maroon	60	70
a.		Booklet pane of 10	6.00	
807	A137	45o dark green	45	35
a.		Booklet pane of 10	4.50	

Nordic Cooperation Issue

Five Ancient Ships — A187a

1969, Feb. 28   Engr.   Perf. 12½ Vert.

808	A187a	45o dark gray	48	20
809	A187a	70o blue	60	55

Perf. 12½ on 3 Sides

810	A187a	45o dark gray	1.10	1.20
a.		Booklet pane of 10	11.00	

See footnote after Norway No. 524.

Worker, by Albin Amelin — A188

1969, Mar. 31   Engr.

811	A188	55o dk carmine rose	25	15
812	A188	70o dk blue	75	35

Perf. 12½ on 3 Sides

813	A188	55o dk carmine rose	40	15
a.		Booklet pane of 10	4.00	

50th anniv. of the ILO.

Europa Issue, 1969
Common Design Type

1969, Apr. 28   Photo.   Perf. 14 Vert.
Size: 27x22mm

814	CD12	70o orange & multi	60	40
815	CD12	1k vio blue & multi	60	16

Perf. 14 on 3 Sides

816	CD12	70o orange & multi	1.50	1.50
a.		Booklet pane of 10	18.00	

Not fluorescent.

Albert Engstrom with Owl, Self-portrait — A189

1969, May 12   Engr.   Perf. 12½ Vert.

817	A189	35o black brown	30	25
818	A189	55o blue gray	30	15

Perf. 12½ on 3 Sides

819	A189	35o black brown	35	35
a.		Booklet pane of 10	3.50	
820	A189	55o blue gray	30	20
a.		Booklet pane of 10	3.00	

Albert Engstrom (1869-1940), cartoonist.

Souvenir Sheet

Paintings by Ivan Agueli — A190

1969, June 6   Litho.   Perf. 13½

821	A190	Sheet of 6	2.25	3.25
a.		45o Landscape	35	42
b.		45o Still life	35	42
c.		45o Near East town	35	42
d.		55o Young woman	35	42
e.		55o Sunny landscape	35	42
f.		55o Street at night	35	42

Ivan Agueli (1869-1917), painter. Size: #821a-821c, 35x28mm. #821d-821e, 28x44mm. #821f, 48x44mm. Not fluorescent.

Tjorn Bridges A191

Designs: 15o, 30o, Various bridges.

Perf. 12½ on 3 Sides

1969, Sept. 3				Engr.
		Size: 20x19mm		
		Bluish Paper		
822	A191	15o deep blue	3.00	50
823	A191	30o dk grn & blk	3.00	50
		Size: 41x19mm		
824	A191	55o blk & dp bl	3.50	60
a.		Bkt. pane, 2 each #822-824	22.50	

Issued to publicize the Tjorn highway bridges connecting the Islands of Orust and Tjorn in the Gothenburg Archipelago with the mainland.

Man's Head, Woodcarving — A192

Warship Wasa, 1628 A193

Designs: No. 826, Crowned lion. No. 827, Great Swedish coat of arms. No. 828, Lion, front view. No. 829, Man's head (different from No. 825).

1969, Sept. 3   Perf. 12½ on 3 Sides

825	A192	55o dark red	35	15
826	A192	55o brown	35	15
827	A192	55o dark blue	35	25
828	A192	55o brown	35	15
829	A192	55o dark red	35	15
830	A193	55o dark blue	35	25
a.		Bkt. pane, #827, #830, 2 each #825-826, 828-829	3.50	
		Nos. 825-830 (6)	2.10	1.10

Salvaging in 1961 of the warship Wasa, sunk on her maiden voyage, Aug. 10, 1628.

Soderberg A194

Bo Bergman A195

1969, Oct. 13   Engr.   Perf. 12½ Horiz.

831	A194	45o brown, *buff*	24	15

Perf. 12½ Vert.

832	A195	55o green, grnsh	24	15

Perf. 12½ on 3 Sides

833	A194	45o brown, *buff*	40	35
a.		Booklet pane of 10	4.00	
834	A195	55o green, grnsh	40	20
a.		Booklet pane of 10	4.00	

Hjalmar Soderberg (1869-1941), writer; Bo Bergman (1869-1967), poet.

Lever Light, Lightship, Landsort and Svenska Lighthouses — A196

Perf. 12½ Vert.

1969, Nov. 17				Photo.
835	A196	30o gray, blk & pink	24	20
836	A196	55o lt bl, blk & brn	24	15

300th anniversary of Swedish lighthouses.

Pelle's New Suit — A197

The Adventures of Nils — A198

Swedish Fairy Tales: No. 839, Pippi Longstocking (little girl, horse and monkey). No. 840, Vill-Vallareman (boy blowing horn). No. 841, Kattresan (child riding on back of cat).

Perf. 12½ on 3 Sides

1969, Nov. 17				Engr.
837	A197	35o org, red & dk brn	1.75	1.65
838	A198	35o dark brown	1.75	1.65
839	A197	35o org, red & dk brn	1.75	1.65
840	A198	35o dark brown	1.75	1.65
841	A197	35o org, red & dk brn	1.75	1.65
a.		Bkt. pane, 2 each #837-841	17.50	
		Nos. 837-841 (5)	8.75	8.25

Issued for use in Christmas cards.

Dr. Emil T. Kocher and Wilhelm Ostwald — A199

Designs: 55o, Selma Lagerlof and open book. 70o, Guglielmo Marconi and Carl Ferdinand Braun.

1969, Dec. 10   Perf. 12½ Vert.

842	A199	45o dull green	75	30
843	A199	55o blk, pale sal	60	15
844	A199	70o black	70	50

Perf. 12½ on 3 Sides

845	A199	45o dull green	60	50
a.		Booklet pane of 10	6.00	
846	A199	50o blk, *pale sal*	50	35
a.		Booklet pane of 10	5.00	
		Nos. 842-846 (5)	3.15	1.80

Winners of the 1909 Nobel Prize.

5 SVERIGE
Weather Vane, Soderala Church — A200

SVERIGE 55
Door with Iron Fittings, Bjorksta Church, Vastmanland — A201

Swedish Art Forgings: 10o, like 5o, facing right. 30o, Memorial cross, Ekshärad churchyard, Varmland.

Perf. 12½ on 3 sides

1970, Feb. 9   Engr.

847	A200	5o slate grn & brn	55	15
848	A200	10o slate grn & brn	55	15
849	A200	30o blk & slate grn	55	20

Perf. 12½ Vert.

850	A201	55o brn & slate grn	55	15
a.		Bklt. pane, 2 each #847-850	5.00	

Ljusman River Rapids A202

1970, May 11   Engr.   Perf. 12½ Vert.

851	A202	55o black & multi	55	15
852	A202	70o black & multi	1.00	55

European Nature Conservation Year, 1970.

Skiing — A203

"Around the Arctic Circle": No. 853, View of Kiruna. No. 855, Boat on mountain lake in Stora Sjöfellet National Park. No. 856, Reindeer herd and herdsman. No. 857, Rocket probe under northern lights.

1970, June 5   Engr.   Perf. 12½ Horiz.

853	A203	45o sepia	45	55
854	A203	45o violet blue	45	55
855	A203	45o dull green	45	55
856	A203	45o sepia	45	55
857	A203	45o violet blue	45	55
a.		Bklt. pane, 2 each #853-857	4.50	
		Nos. 853-857 (5)	2.25	2.75

China Palace, Drottningholm Park, 1769 — A204

Perf. 12½ Vert.

1970, Aug. 28   Photo.

858	A204	2k yel, grn & pink	2.00	15

Glimmingehus, Skane Province, 15th Century — A205

Perf. 12½ Horiz.

1970, Aug. 28

859	A205	55o gray green	30	15

Perf. 12½ on 3 Sides

860	A205	55o gray green	35	25
a.		Booklet pane of 10	3.50	

Timber Industry — A206

Miner — A208

Shipping Industry — A207

Designs: No. 863, Heavy industry (propeller). No. 864, Hydroelectric power (dam and diesel). No. 865, Mining (freight train and mine). No. 866, Technical research.

Perf. 12½ on 3 sides

1970, Sept. 28   Engr.

861	A206	70o indigo & lt brn	4.00	3.00
862	A207	70o ind, lt brn & dp plum	4.00	3.00
863	A206	70o indigo & dp plum	4.00	3.00
864	A206	70o indigo & dp plum	4.00	3.00
865	A207	70o indigo & dp plum	4.00	3.00
866	A206	70o dp plum & lt brn	4.00	3.00
a.		Booklet pane of 6, #861-866	25.00	
867	A208	1k black, *buff*	40	15
a.		Booklet pane of 10	4.00	

Perf. 12½ Vertically

868	A208	1k black, *buff*	65	15
		Nos. 861-868 (8)	25.05	18.30

Swedish trade and industry.

"Love, Not War" A209

Design: 70o, Four-leaf clovers symbolizing efforts for equality and brotherhood.

Engraved and Lithographed

1970, Oct. 24   Perf. 12½ Horiz.

869	A209	55o rose red, yel & blk	50	15
a.		Booklet pane of 4	2.25	
870	A209	70o emerald, yel & blk	70	30
a.		Booklet pane of 4	3.25	

Perf. 12½ Vert.

871	A209	55o rose red, yel & blk	25	15
872	A209	70o emerald, yel & blk	52	25

25th anniversary of the United Nations.

Bird Type of 1968

Birds: No. 873, Blackbird. No. 874, Great titmouse. No. 875, Bullfinch. No. 876, Greenfinch. No. 877, Blue titmouse.

Perf. 12½ on 3 Sides

1970, Nov. 20   Photo.

873	A187	30o blue grn & multi	85	80
874	A187	30o bister & multi	85	80
875	A187	30o blue & multi	85	80
876	A187	30o pink & multi	85	80
877	A187	30o orange yel & multi	85	80
a.		Bklt. pane, 2 each #873-877	9.00	
		Nos. 873-877 (5)	4.25	4.00

Paul Johann Ludwig Heyse A210

Kerstin Hesselgren A211

Designs: 55o, Otto Wallach and Johannes Diderik van der Waals. 70o, Albrecht Kossel.

Perf. 12½ Horiz.

1970, Dec. 10   Engr.

878	A210	45o violet	90	55
879	A210	55o slate blue	70	15
880	A210	70o gray	1.25	65

Perf. 12½ on 3 Sides

881	A210	45o violet	90	85
a.		Booklet pane of 10	9.00	
882	A210	55o slate blue	95	35
a.		Booklet pane of 10	9.50	
		Nos. 878-882 (5)	4.70	2.55

Winners of the 1910 Nobel Prize.

Perf. 12½ Horiz.

1971, Feb. 19   Engr.

883	A211	45o dp claret, *gray*	32	20
884	A211	1k dp brn, *buff*	75	15

Perf. 12½ on 3 Sides

885	A211	45o dp claret, *gray*	50	35

50th anniv. of woman suffrage; Kerstin Hesselgren, was 1st woman member of Swedish Upper House.

Terns in Flight — A212

Abstract Music, by Ingvar Lidholm — A213

1971, Mar. 26   Perf. 13½ Vert.

886	A212	40o dark red	42	18
887	A212	55o violet blue	95	15

Perf. 12½ on 3 Sides

888	A212	55o violet blue	1.00	18
a.		Booklet pane of 10	10.00	

Joint northern campaign for the benefit of refugees.

Perf. 12½ Horiz.

1971, Aug. 27   Engr.

889	A213	55o deep lilac	35	15
890	A213	85o green	55	25

Perf. 12½ on 3 Sides

891	A213	55o deep lilac	25	20
a.		Booklet pane of 10	2.50	

The Three Kings, Grotlingbo Church — A214

Flight into Egypt, Stanga Church A215

Designs: 10o, Adam and Eve, Gammelgarn Church. 55o, Saint on horseback and Samson with the lion, Hogrän Church.

Perf. 12½ on 3 Sides

1971, Sept. 28   Engr.

892	A214	5o violet & brn	60	40
893	A214	10o violet & sl grn	60	40

Perf. 12½ Horiz.

894	A215	55o slate grn & brn	80	20
895	A215	65o brown & vio blk	35	15
a.		Bklt. pane of 5 (#892-894, 2 #895)	3.00	

Art of medieval stonemasons in Gotland.

35 SVERIGE
Toddler and Automobile Wheel — A216

1971, Oct. 20   Perf. 12½ Vert.

896	A216	35o black & red	24	16
897	A216	65o dp blue & multi	35	16

Perf. 12½ on 3 Sides

898	A216	65o dp blue & multi	80	32
a.		Booklet pane of 10	8.00	

Publicity for road safety.

King Gustavus Vasa's Sword, c. 1500 — A217   SVERIGE 65

Swedish Crown Regalia: No. 900, Scepter. No. 901, Crown. No. 902, Orb (Scepter, crown and orb were made in 1561 for Erik XIV). No. 903, Karl IX's anointing horn, 1606.

Perf. 12½ on 3 Sides

1971, Oct. 20   Engr.

899	A217	65o lt blue & multi	50	45
900	A217	65o lt ol grn & multi	50	45
901	A217	65o dk blue & multi	50	45
902	A217	65o lt ol grn & multi	50	45
903	A217	65o lt blue & multi	50	45
a.		Bklt. pane, 2 each #899-903	5.00	
		Nos. 899-903 (5)	2.50	2.25

Christmas Elf and Goat Bringing Gifts — A218

Christmas Customs (Old Prints): No. 905, Christmas market. No. 906, Dancing children and father playing fiddle. No. 907, Ice-skating on frozen waterways in Stockholm. No. 908, Sleigh ride to church.

1971, Nov. 10

904	A218	35o deep carmine	1.25	1.10
905	A218	35o violet blue	1.25	1.10
906	A218	35o violet brown	1.25	1.10
907	A218	35o violet blue	1.25	1.10
908	A218	35o slate green	1.25	1.10
a.		Bklt. pane, 2 each #904-908	12.50	
		Nos. 904-908 (5)	6.25	5.50

Maurice Maeterlinck A219

Women Athletes A220

Designs: 65o, Wilhelm Wien and Allvar Gullstrand. 85o, Marie Sklodovska Curie.

1971, Dec. 10   Perf. 12½ Horiz.

909	A219	55o orange	55	90
910	A219	65o green	55	20
911	A219	85o dk carmine	1.00	55

Perf. 12½ on 3 Sides

912	A219	55o orange	75	90
a.		Booklet pane of 10	9.00	
913	A219	65o green	75	40
a.		Booklet pane of 10	8.00	
		Nos. 909-913 (5)	3.60	2.35

Winners of the 1911 Nobel Prize.

1972, Feb. 23   Perf. 12½ on 3 Sides

914	A220	55o	Figure skating	60	70
915	A220	55o	Tennis	60	70
916	A220	55o	Gymnastics	60	70
917	A220	55o	Diving	60	70
918	A220	55o	Fencing	60	70
a.			Bklt. pane, 2 each #914-918	6.00	
			Nos. 914-918 (5)	3.00	3.50

Lars Johan
Hierta, by
Christian
Eriksson — A221

Frans Michael
Franzen, by
Soderberg and
Hultstrom — A222

Hugo Alfven, by
Carl Milles
A223

Georg
Stiernhielm, by
David K.
Ehrenstrahl
A224

**Photo., Perf 12½ Horiz. (35, 85o);
Engr., Perf. 12½ Vert. (50, 65o)**

1972 Feb. 23

919	A221	35o	multicolored	25	20
920	A222	50o	violet	30	15
921	A223	65o	bluish black	45	15
922	A224	85o	multicolored	40	20
			Set value		55

Hierta (1801-72), journalist. Franzen (1772-1847), poet. Alfven (1872-1960), composer. Stiernhielm (1598-1672), poet, writer, scientist.

Glass
Blower
A225

Swedish Glassmaking: No. 923, Lifting molten glass. No. 925, Decorating vase. No. 926, Annealing vase. No. 927, Polishing jug.

Perf. 12½ Horiz.

1972, Mar. 22   Engr.

923	A225	65o	black	1.10	60
924	A225	65o	violet blue	1.10	60
925	A225	65o	carmine	1.10	60
926	A225	65o	black	1.10	60
927	A225	65o	violet blue	1.10	60
a.			Bklt. pane, 2 each #923-927	11.00	
			Nos. 923-927 (5)	5.50	3.00

Horses and
Ruin of
Borgholm
Castle
A226

Designs: No. 929, Oland Island Bridge. No. 930, Kalmar Castle. No. 931, Salmon fishing. No. 932, Schooner Falken, Karlskrona.

1972, May 8   Perf. 12½ Horiz.

928	A226	55o	chocolate	40	45
929	A226	55o	dk violet blue	40	45
930	A226	55o	chocolate	40	45
931	A226	55o	blue green	40	45
932	A226	55o	dk violet blue	40	45
a.			Bklt. pane, 2 each #928-932	4.00	
			Nos. 928-932 (5)	2.00	2.25

Tourist attractions in Southeast Sweden.

"Only one Earth" Environment
Emblem — A227

"Spring," Bror
Hjorth — A228

1972, June 5   Engr.   Perf. 12½ Vert.

933	A227	65o	blue & carmine	35	15

Perf. 12½ Horiz.

934	A227	65o	blue & carmine	35	15
a.			Booklet pane of 10	3.50	

Perf. 12½ Vert.

935	A228	85o	brown & multi	75	45
a.			Booklet pane of 4	3.00	

UN Conference on Human Environment, Stockholm, June 5-16.

Junkers
JU52
A229

Historic Planes: 5o, Junkers F13. 25o, Friedrichshafen FF49. 75o, Douglas DC-3.

1972, Sept. 8   Perf. 12½ on 3 Sides

Size: 20x19mm

936	A229	5o	lilac	18	15

Size: 44x19mm

937	A229	15o	blue	35	15
938	A229	25o	blue	35	15
939	A229	75o	gray green	65	15
a.			Bklt. pane, #937-938, 2 #936, 2 #939	2.50	
			Set value		50

Lady with Veil, by
Alexander
Roslin — A230

Amphion
Figurehead, by Per
Ljung — A231

Stockholm from the South, by Johan
Fredrik Martin — A232

Designs: No. 941, (Queen) Sofia Magdalena, by Carl Gustaf Pilo. No. 943, Quadriga, by Johan Tobias von Sergel. No. 945, Anchor Forge, by Pehr Hillestrom.

**Perf. 12½ on 2 Sides, or on 3 Sides
(#942-943)**

1972, Oct. 7   Engr.

940	A230	75o	dk brn, blk & dk car	50	30
941	A230	75o	dk brn, blk & dk car	50	30
942	A231	75o	dk carmine	50	30
943	A231	75o	dk carmine	50	30
944	A232	75o	dk brown	50	30
945	A232	75o	greenish blk	50	30
a.			Booklet pane of 6, #940-945	3.00	
			Nos. 940-945 (6)	3.00	1.80

18th century Swedish art.

Types of 1936
Imprint: "1972"

1972, Oct. 7   Perf. 12½ on 3 Sides

946	A36	10o	dk carmine	32	40
947	A37	15o	yellow green	32	40
948	A42	40o	deep blue	32	40
949	A44	50o	deep claret	32	40
950	A45	60o	deep blue	32	40
a.			Bklt. pane, 2 each #946-950	3.25	
			Nos. 946-950 (5)	1.60	2.00

Centenary of the birth of Olle Hjortzberg (1872-1959), stamp designer. Value of booklet was 5k of which 1.50k was for "Stockholmia 74," International Philatelic Exhibition, Sept. 21-29, 1973.

Santa Claus — A233

St. Lucia
Singers
A234

Perf. 14 on 3 Sides

1972, Nov. 6   Photo.

951	A233	45o	Candles	35	20
952	A233	45o	shown	35	20
a.			Bklt. pane, 5 each #951-952	3.50	

Perf. 12½ Vert.

953	A234	75o	gray & multi	55	15

Christmas 1972 (children's drawings).

Horse — A235

Viking
Ship — A236

Willows,
by Peter A.
Persson
A237

Trosa, by
Reinhold
Ljunggren
A238

Spring Birches, by
Oskar Bergman
A239

King Gustaf VI
Adolf — A240

Perf. 12½ Horiz. or Vert.

1972-73   Engr.

954	A235	5o	maroon ('73)	15	15
955	A236	10o	dk blue ('73)	15	15
956	A237	40o	sepia ('73)	20	15
957	A238	50o	blk & brn ('73)	40	15
958	A239	55o	yel grn ('73)	40	15
959	A240	75o	indigo	50	15
960	A240	1k	dp carmine	75	15

1973   Perf. 12½ on 3 Sides

961	A235	5o	maroon	15	15
a.			Booklet pane of 20	75	
962	A236	10o	dark blue	15	15
a.			Booklet pane of 20	75	
963	A240	75o	indigo	35	15
a.			Booklet pane of 10	3.50	
			Nos. 954-963 (10)	3.20	
			Set value		78

King Gustaf VI
Adolf — A245

Chinese
Objects — A246

Designs: No. 983, King opening Parliament. No. 984, Etruscan vase and dish. No. 985, King with flowers.

1972, Nov. 11   Perf. 12½ Vert.

981	A245	75o	violet blue	2.50	2.75
982	A246	75o	slate green	2.50	2.75
983	A245	75o	maroon	2.50	2.75
984	A246	75o	violet blue	2.50	2.75
985	A245	75o	slate green	2.50	2.75
a.			Bklt. pane of 5, #981-985	12.50	
			Nos. 981-985 (5)	12.50	13.75

90th birthday of King Gustaf VI Adolf. Booklet sold for 4.75k of which 1k was for the King Gustaf VI Adolf Foundation for Swedish Cultural Activities.

Paul Sabatier and
Victor Grignard
A247

Dr. Alexis
Carrel
A248

Designs: 75o, Nils Gustaf Dalen. 1k, Gerhart Hauptmann.

1972, Dec. 8   Engr.   Perf. 12½ Vert.

986	A247	60o	olive bister	65	30

Perf. 12½ Horiz.

987	A248	65o	dark blue	80	30
988	A248	75o	violet	1.10	15
989	A248	1k	redsh brown	1.40	15

Winners of the 1912 Nobel Prize.

Mail Coach,
1923 — A249

Design: 70o, Postal autobus, 1972.

1973, Jan. 18   Perf. 12½ on 3 Sides

					Engr.
990	A249	60o	black, yellow	25	18
a.			Booklet pane of 10	2.50	

Perf. 12½ Vert.

991	A249	70o	blue, orange & grn	38	15

Tintomara, by Lars Johan
Werle — A250

Orpheus
and
Eurydice,
by
Christoph
W. Gluck
A251

1973, Jan. 18   Perf. 12½ Horiz.

992	A250	75o	green	32	15

Booklet Stamp

993 A251	1k red lilac	50	20
a.	Booklet pane of 5	2.50	
	Set value		28

Bicentenary of the Royal Theater in Stockholm. The 75o shows a stage setting by Bo-Ruben Hedwall for Tintomara, a new opera, performed for the bicentenary celebration. The 1k shows painting by Pehr Hillestrom of Orpheus and Eurydice, which was first opera performed in Royal Theater.

Vaasa Ski Race, Dalecarlia A252

Designs: No. 995, "Going to Church in Mora" (church boats), by Anders Zorn. No. 996, Church stables, Rättvig. No. 997, Falun copper mine. No. 998, Midsummer Dance, by Bengt Nordenberg.

1973, Mar. 2   Perf. 12½ Horiz.

994 A252	65o slate green	35	30
995 A252	65o slate green	35	30
996 A252	65o black	35	30
997 A252	65o slate green	35	30
998 A252	65o claret	35	30
a.	Bklt. pane, 2 each #994-998	3.50	
	Nos. 994-998 (5)	1.75	1.50

Tourist attractions in Dalecarlia.

Worker, Confederation Emblem A253

Observer Reading Temperature A254

1973, Apr. 26   Perf. 12½ Vert.

999 A253	75o dark carmine	45	15
1000 A253	1.40k slate blue	80	15
	Set value		20

75th anniversary of the Swedish Confederation of Trade Unions (LO).

1973, May 24   Engr.   Perf. 12½ Vert.

Design: No. 1002, Clouds, photographed by US weather satellite.

1001 A254	65o slate green	1.50	35
1002 A254	65o black & ultra	1.50	35
a.	Pair, #1001-1002	3.00	2.50

Cent. of the Swedish Weather Organization and of Intl. Meteorological Cooperation.

Nordic Cooperation Issue 1973

Nordic House, Reykjavik A254a

1973, June 26   Perf. 12½ Vert.

1003 A254a	75o multicolored	55	15
1004 A254a	1k multicolored	85	20

A century of postal cooperation among Denmark, Finland, Iceland, Norway and Sweden and in connection with the Nordic Postal Conference, Reykjavik, Iceland.

Carl Peter Thunberg (1743-1828) — A255

Swedish Explorers: No. 1006, Anders Sparrman (1748-1820) and Polynesian double canoe. No. 1007, Nils Adolf Erik Nordenskjold (1832-1901) and ship in pack ice. No. 1008, Salomon August

---

Andrée (1854-1897) and balloon on snow field. No. 1009, Sven Hedin (1865-1952) and camel riders.

1973, Sept. 22   Perf. 12½ Horiz.

1005 A255	1k sl grn, bl & brn	1.40	1.50
1006 A255	1k bl, sl grn & brn	1.40	1.50
1007 A255	1k bl, sl grn & brn	1.40	1.50
1008 A255	1k black & multi	1.40	1.50
1009 A255	1k black & multi	1.40	1.50
a.	Bklt. pane of 5, #1005-1009	7.00	
	Nos. 1005-1009 (5)	7.00	7.50

Plower with Ox Team A256

Designs: No. 1011, Woman working flax brake. No. 1012, Farm couple planting potatoes. No. 1013, Women baking bread. No. 1014, Man with horse-drawn sower.

1973, Oct. 24   Perf. 12½ Horiz.

1010 A256	75o grnsh black	2.25	30
1011 A256	75o red brown	2.25	30
1012 A256	75o grnsh black	2.25	30
1013 A256	75o plum	2.25	30
1014 A256	75o red brown	2.25	30
a.	Bklt. pane, 2 each #1010-1014	22.50	
	Nos. 1010-1014 (5)	11.25	1.50

Centenary of Nordic Museum, Stockholm.

Gray Seal — A257

King Gustaf VI Adolf — A258

Protected Animals: 20o, Peregrine falcon. 25o, Lynx. 55o, Otter. 65o, Wolf. 75o, White-tailed sea eagle.

1973, Oct. 24   Perf. 12½ on 3 Sides

1015 A257	10o slate green	15	15
1016 A257	20o violet	15	15
1017 A257	25o Prus green	15	15
1018 A257	55o Prus green	24	25
1019 A257	65o violet	28	30
1020 A257	75o slate green	35	35
a.	Bklt. pane, 2 each #1015-1020	1.65	
	Set value	1.20	1.10

1973, Oct. 24   Perf. 12½ Vert.

1021 A258	75o dk violet blue	32	15
1022 A258	1k purple	50	15

King Gustaf VI Adolf (1882-1973).

The Three Kings A259

Charles XIV John A260

The Goosegirl, by Josephson A261

Designs: No. 1024, Merry country dance. No. 1026, Basket with stylized Dalecarlian gourd plant.

1973, Nov. 12   Photo.   Perf. 14 Horiz.

1023 A259	45o multicolored	55	15
1024 A259	45o multicolored	55	15
a.	Bklt. pane, 5 each #1023-1024	5.50	

Coil Stamps

1025 A260	45o multicolored	2.50	15
1026 A260	75o multicolored	2.50	15
a.	Pair, #1025-1026	4.50	4.50

Christmas 1973. Designs are from Swedish peasant paintings.

Perf. 12½ Horiz.

Alfred Werner and Heike Kamerlingh-Onnes A262

Charles Robert Richet A263

1027 A261	10k multicolored	3.75	30

Ernst Josephson (1851-1906), painter.

Design: 1.40k, Rabindranath Tagore.

1973, Dec. 10   Engr.   Perf. 12½ Vert.

1028 A262	75o dark violet	45	15

Perf. 12½ Horiz.

1029 A263	1k dark brown	75	15
1030 A263	1.40k green	1.00	15
	Set value		38

Winners of 1913 Nobel Prize.

Ski Jump A264

Skiing: No. 1032, Cross-country race. No. 1033, Relay race. No. 1034, Slalom. No. 1035, Women's cross-country race.

1974, Jan. 23   Engr.

1031 A264	65o slate green	55	55
1032 A264	65o violet blue	55	55
1033 A264	65o slate green	55	55
1034 A264	65o dk carmine	55	55
1035 A264	65o violet blue	55	55
a.	Bklt. pane, 2 each #1031-1035	5.50	
	Nos. 1031-1035 (5)	2.75	2.75

Drawing of First Industrial Digester A265

Hans Järta and Quotation from 1809 A266

Samuel Owen and 19th Century Factory A267

1974, Mar. 5   Engr.   Perf. 12½ Vert.

1036 A265	45o sepia	30	15
1037 A266	60o green	30	20
1038 A267	75o dull red	38	15
	Set value		42

Centenary of sulphite pulp process (45o); Hans Järta (1774-1847), statesman responsible for the Instrument of Government Act of 1809 (60o); Samuel Owen (1774-1854), English-born industrialist who introduced new production methods (75o).

Perf. 12½ Horiz.

Stora Sjofallet (Great Falls) — A268

Street in Ystad — A269

1974, Apr. 2   Perf. 12½ Horiz.

1039 A268	35o blue grn & blk	25	15

Perf. 12½ on 3 Sides

1040 A269	75o dull claret	30	15
a.	Booklet pane of 10	3.00	
	Set value		20

UPU Type of 1924 A270

1974   Engr.   Perf. 12½ on 3 Sides

1041 A270	20o green	18	25
1042 A270	25o ultra	18	25
1043 A270	30o dark brown	18	25
1044 A270	35o dark red	18	25
a.	Bklt. pane, 2 each #1041-1044	1.50	

Miniature Sheets

Perf. 12½

1045	Sheet of 4	1.90	1.90
a.	A270 20o ocher, single stamp	45	45
1046	Sheet of 4	1.90	1.90
a.	A270 25o dk vio, single stamp	45	45
1047	Sheet of 4	1.90	1.90
a.	A270 30o dk red, single stamp	45	45
1048	Sheet of 4	1.90	1.90
a.	A270 35o yel grn, single stamp	45	45

Stockholmia 74 philatelic exhibition, Stockholm, Sept. 21-29. Booklet sold for 3k with surtax going toward financing the exhibition.
Nos. 1045-1048 sold during exhibition in folder with 5k entrance ticket.
Issue dates: Nos. 1041-1044, Apr. 2. Nos. 1045-1048, Sept. 21.

"Man in Storm," by Bror Marklund — A271

Europa: 1k, Sculpture by Picasso, Lake Vanern, Kristinehamm.

Perf. 12½ Horiz.

1974, Apr. 29   Engr.

1049 A271	75o violet brown	95	20
1050 A271	1k slate green	1.00	15

King Carl XVI Gustaf — A272

1974-78   Engr.   Perf. 12½ Vert.

1068 A272	75o slate grn	60	15
1069 A272	90o brt blue ('75)	75	15
1070 A272	1k maroon	38	15
1071 A272	1.10k rose red ('75)	40	15
1072 A272	1.30k green ('76)	48	15
1073 A272	1.40k violet bl ('77)	60	22
1074 A272	1.50k red lilac ('80)	45	15
1075 A272	1.70k orange ('78)	65	18
1076 A272	2k dk brown ('80)	75	15

Perf. 12½ on 3 Sides

1077 A272	75o slate green	60	15
a.	Booklet pane of 10	6.00	
1078 A272	90o brt blue ('75)	60	15
a.	Booklet pane of 10	6.00	
1079 A272	1k maroon ('76)	60	15
a.	Booklet pane of 10	6.00	
1080 A272	1.10k rose red ('77)	40	15
a.	Booklet pane of 10	4.00	
1081 A272	1.30k green ('78)	48	15
a.	Booklet pane of 10	5.00	

1082 A272 1.50k red lilac ('80)   45   15
  a. Booklet pane of 10   4.50
    Nos. 1068-1082 (15)   8.19
    Set value   1.25

Central Post Office, Stockholm
A273   A274

Mailman, Northernmost Rural Delivery
Route — A275

Perf. 12¹/₂ on 3 Sides
1974, June 7   **Engr.**
1084 A273 75o violet brown   1.50 25
1085 A274 75o violet brown   1.50 25
  a. Bklt. pane, 5 each #1084-1085   15.00

Perf. 12¹/₂ Vert.
1086 A275 1k slate green   75 15

Centenary of Universal Postal Union.

Regatta
A276

Scenes from Sweden's West Coast: No. 1088,
Vinga Lighthouse. No. 1089, Varberg Fortress. No.
1090, Seine fishing. No. 1091, Fishing village
Mollosund.

1974, June 7   **Perf. 12¹/₂ Horiz.**
1087 A276 65o crimson   38 35
1088 A276 65o blue   38 35
1089 A276 65o dk olive green   38 35
1090 A276 65o slate green   38 35
1091 A276 65o brown   38 35
  a. Bklt. pane, 2 each #1087-1091   4.00
    Nos. 1087-1091 (5)   1.90 1.75

Mr. Simmons,   Thread and
by Axel   Spool — A278
Fridell — A277

Perf. 12¹/₂ on 3 Sides
1974, Aug. 28   **Engr.**
1092 A277 45o black   30 20
  a. Booklet pane of 10   3.00
Perf. 12¹/₂ Horiz.
1093 A277 1.40k deep claret   60 15

Swedish Publicists' Club, centenary.

1974, Aug. 28   **Perf. 12¹/₂ Horiz.**
Design: #1094, Sewing machines (abstract).

1094 A278 85o deep violet   38 30
1095 A278 85o black & org   38 30
  a. Pair, #1094-1095   80 70

Swedish textile and clothing industries.

Tugs in Stockholm Harbor — A279

Designs: No. 1097, Skane Train Ferry, Trel-
leborg-Sassnitz. No. 1098, Ice breakers Tor and
Atle. No. 1099, Liner "Snow Storm." No. 1100,
Tanker.

1974, Nov. 16   **Perf. 12¹/₂ Horiz.**
1096 A279 1k dark blue   1.00 60
1097 A279 1k dark blue   1.00 60
1098 A279 1k dark blue   1.00 60
1099 A279 1k dark blue   1.00 60
1100 A279 1k dark blue   1.00 60
  a. Bklt. pane of 5, #1096-1100   5.00
    Nos. 1096-1100 (5)   5.00 3.00

Swedish shipping industry.

Miniature Sheet

Quilt from Skepptuna Church — A280

Sverige 75 Deer, Quilt from Hog
Church — A281

Designs are from woolen quilts, 15th-16th centuries. Motifs shown on No. 1101 are stylized deer,
griffins, lions, unicorn and horses.

1974, Nov. 16   **Photo.**   **Perf. 14**
1101 A280 Sheet of 10   11.00 12.50
  a.-j. 45o, single stamp   1.10 1.10
Perf. 13 Horiz.
1102 A281 75o bl blk, red & yel   35 15

Max von
Laue — A282

Designs: 70o, Theodore William Richards. 1k,
Robert Bárány.

1974, Dec. 10 Engr. Perf. 12¹/₂ Vert.
1103 A282 65o rose red   60 25
1104 A282 70o slate   60 25
1105 A282 1k indigo   60 15

Winners of 1914 Nobel Prize.

Sven Jerring's   Televising
Children's   Parliamentary
Program — A283   Debate — A284

1974, Dec. 10   **Perf. 12¹/₂ Vert.**
1106 A283 75o dk blue & brn   90 18
1107 A284 75o brown & dk bl   90 18
  a. Pair, #1106-1107   2.00 2.25

Swedish Broadcasting Corp., 50th anniv.

Account
Holder's
Envelope
A285

Photogravure and Engraved
1975, Jan. 21   **Perf. 14 Vert.**
1108 A285 1.40k ocher & blk   60 15

Swedish Postal Giro Office, 50th anniv.

Male and Female   Jenny Lind
Architects, New   (1820-87), by
Parliament   J. O.
A286   Sodermark
                       A287

1975, Mar. 25 Engr. Perf. 12¹/₂ Vert.
1109 A286 75o slate green   28 15
Perf. 12¹/₂ Horiz.
1110 A287 1k claret   55 15
Perf. 12¹/₂ on 3 Sides
1111 A286 75o slate green   30 18
  a. Booklet pane of 10   3.00
    Set value   38

International Women's Year 1975.

Horseman,   "Gold Men"
Helmet   A289
Decoration
A288

Designs: 15o, Scabbard and hilt. 20o, Shield
buckle. 55o, Iron helmet.

1975, Mar. 25   **Perf. 12¹/₂ Vert.**
1112 A288 10o dull red   15 15
1113 A288 15o slate green   15 15
1114 A288 20o violet   15 15
1115 A288 55o violet brown   27 15
  a. Bklt. pane, 2 each #1112-1115   1.00
Perf. 12¹/₂ Horiz.
1116 A289 25o deep yellow   18 15
    Set value   68 55

Treasures from tombs of the Vendel period (550-
800 A.D.), and "gold men" (25o) from Eketorp II
excavations (400-700 A.D.).

Europa Issue 1975

New
Year's Eve
at
Skansen,
by Eric
Hallstrom
A290

1¹⁰ Inferno, by August
SVERIGE Strindberg — A291

Perf. 12¹/₂ Vert.
1975, Apr. 28   **Photo.**
1117 A290 90o multi   48 20
Perf. 12¹/₂ Horiz.
1118 A291 1.10k multi   65 25

Capercaillie   Rok Stone, 9th
A292   Century
                       A293

1975, May 20 Engr. Perf. 12¹/₂ Vert.
1119 A292 170o indigo   70 15
Perf. 12¹/₂ Horiz.
1120 A293 2k deep claret   70 15
    Set value   24

Metric Tape   Folke Filbyter
Measure — A294   Statue, by
                       Milles — A296

Hernqvist
by Per
Krafft the
Younger
A295

1975, May 20   **Perf. 12¹/₂ Vert.**
1121 A294 55o deep blue   30 25
1122 A295 70o yel brn & dk brn   30 15
Perf. 12¹/₂ Horiz.
1123 A296 75o violet   30 30

Cent. of Intl. Meter Convention, Paris, 1875;
bicent. of Swedish veterinary medicine, founded by
Peter Hernqvist (1726-1808); Carl Milles (1875-
1955), sculptor.

Officers' Mess, Rommehed, 1798 — A297

Designs: No. 1125, Falun Mine pithead gear,
1852. No. 1126, Gunpowder Tower, Visby. No.
1127, Foundry and furnace, Engelsberg, 18th century. No. 1128, Skelleftea Church Village, 17th
century.

1975, June 13   **Perf. 12¹/₂ Horiz.**
1124 A297 75o violet blue   30 30
1125 A297 75o dk carmine   30 30
1126 A297 75o black   30 30
1127 A297 75o dk carmine   30 30
1128 A297 75o black   30 30
  a. Bklt. pane, 2 each #1124-1128   3.00
    Nos. 1124-1128 (5)   1.50 1.50

European Architectural Heritage Year 1975.

Rescue at
Sea:
Helicopter
over Ice-
covered
Tanker
A298

Designs: No. 1129, Fire fighters: firemen fighting fire. No. 1130, Customs narcotics service:
trained dogs checking cargo. No. 1131, Police:
Officer talking to boy on bridge. No. 1132, Hospital
Service: patient arriving by ambulance.

1975, Aug. 27   **Perf. 12¹/₂ Horiz.**
1129 A298 90o dk car rose   45 25
1130 A298 90o dk bl   45 25
1131 A298 90o dk car rose   45 25
1132 A298 90o dk bl   45 25

498 SWEDEN

1133	A298 90o green	45	25
a.	Bklt. pane, 2 each #1129-1133	4.50	
	Nos. 1129-1133 (5)	2.25	1.25

Public service organizations watching, guarding, helping.

SVERIGE 5   SVERIGE 5

"Fryckstad" A299   "Gotland" A300

Design: 90o, "Prins August."

1975, Aug. 27   Perf. 12½ on 3 Sides
Size: 20x19mm

1134	A299 5o green	16	15
1135	A300 5o dark blue	16	15

Size: 45x19mm

1136	A299 90o slate green	80	15
a.	Bklt. pane, 2 each #1134-1136	2.50	
	Set value		35

Scouts Around Campfire — A301   Scouts in Canoes — A302

1975, Oct. 11   Photo.   Perf. 14 Vert.

1137	A301 90o multi	1.00	20
1138	A302 90o multi	1.00	20
a.	Pair, #1137-1138		1.90

Nordjamb 75, 14th World Boy Scout Jamboree, Lillehammer, Norway, July 29-Aug. 7.

Hedgehog — A303

Old Man Playing Key Fiddle — A304   Romeo and Juliet Ballet — A305

1975, Oct. 11   Engr.   Perf. 12½ Vert.

1139	A303 55o black	30	15
1140	A304 75o dk red	32	15

Perf. 12½ Horiz.

1141	A305 7k blue green	2.25	20

Perf. 12½ on 3 Sides

1142	A303 55o black	35	20
a.	Booklet pane of 10	3.50	

Virgin Mary, 12th Cent. Statue A306   Chariot of the Sun, from 12th Cent. Altar A307

Mourning Mary, c. 1280 — A308   Jesse at Foot of Genealogical Tree, c. 1510 — A309

Christmas: No. 1145, Nativity, from 12th century gilt-copper altar. No. 1148, like No. 1147.

1975, Nov. 11   Photo.   Perf. 14 Horiz.

1143	A306 55o multi	25	15

Perf. 12½ on 3 Sides

1144	A307 55o gold & multi	38	20
1145	A307 55o gold & multi	35	20
a.	Bklt. pane, 5 each #1144-1145	4.00	

Perf. 12½ Horiz.
Engr.

1146	A308 90o brown	42	15

Perf. 12½ on 3 Sides

1147	A309 90o red	1.00	20
1148	A309 90o blue	1.00	20
a.	Bklt. pane, 5 each #1147-1148	10.00	
	Nos. 1143-1148 (6)	3.40	1.10

No. 1145a was issued with top row of 5 either No. 1144 or No. 1145.

William H. and William L. Bragg — A310

Designs: 90o, Richard Willstätter. 1.10k, Romain Rolland.

1975, Dec. 10   Engr.   Perf. 12½ Vert.

1149	A310 75o claret	30	18
1150	A310 90o violet blue	45	15
1151	A310 1.10k slate green	52	20

Winners of 1915 Nobel Prize.

Cave of the Winds, by Eric Grate — A311

1976, Jan. 27   Perf. 12½ Vert.

1152	A311 1.90k slate green	65	15

The sculpture by Eric Grate (b. 1896) stands in front of the Town Hall of Vasteras.

Razor-billed Auks and Black Guillemot A312   Bobbin Lace Maker from Vadstena A313

1976, Mar. 10   Engr.   Perf. 12½ Vert.

1153	A312 85o dark blue	42	15

Perf. 12½ Horiz.

1154	A313 1k claret brn	40	15

Perf. 12½ on 3 Sides

1155	A312 85o dk bl	25	30
a.	Booklet pane of 10	2.50	
1156	A313 1k claret brn	25	15
a.	Booklet pane of 10	2.50	
	Set value		54

Old and New Telephones, Relays — A314

1976, Mar. 10   Perf. 12½ Vert.

1157	A314 1.30k brt violet	48	25
1158	A314 3.40k red	1.25	50

Centenary of first telephone call by Alexander Graham Bell, March 10, 1876.

Europa Issue 1976

Lapp Elk Horn Spoon — A315   Tile Stove — A316

Perf. 14½ Horiz.

1976, May 3   Photo.

1159	A315 1k multi	60	15
1160	A316 1.30k multi	60	35

Wheat and Cornflower Seeds — A317   Viable and Nonviable Seedlings — A318

1976, May 3   Engr.   Perf. 12½ Vert.

1161	A317 65o brown	38	20
1162	A318 65o choc & grn	38	20
a.	Pair, #1161-1162	80	50

Swedish seed testing centenary.

King Carl XVI Gustaf and Queen Silvia — A319

1976, June 19   Engr.   Perf. 12½ Vert.

1163	A319 1k rose car	38	15
1164	A319 1.30k slate grn	52	25

Perf. 12½ on 3 Sides

1165	A319 1k rose car	35	15
a.	Booklet pane of 10	3.50	

Wedding of King Carl XVI Gustaf and Silvia Sommerlath.

View from Ringkallen, by Helmer Osslund A320

Views in Angermanland Province: No. 1167, Tugboat pulling timber. No. 1168, Hay-drying racks. No. 1169, Granvagsnipan slope, Angerman River. No. 1170, Seine fishing.

1976, June 19   Perf. 12½ Horiz.

1166	A320 85o slate grn	32	30
1167	A320 85o vio bl	32	30
1168	A320 85o dp brn	32	30
1169	A320 85o vio bl	32	30
1170	A320 85o brn red	32	30
a.	Bklt. pane, 2 each #1166-1170	3.25	
	Nos. 1166-1170 (5)	1.60	1.50

Roman Cross and Ship's Wheel — A321

1976, June 19   Perf. 12½ Horiz.

1171	A321 85o brt bl & bl	40	25

Swedish Seamen's Church, centenary.

Torgny Segerstedt and 1917 Page of Gothenburg Journal — A322

1976, June 19   Perf. 12½ Vert.

1172	A322 1.90k brn & blk	85	20

Torgny Segerstedt (1876-1945), editor in chief of the Gothenburg Journal of Commerce and Shipping, birth centenary.

Coiled Snake, Bronze Buckle — A323   Pilgrim's Badge, Adoration of the Magi — A324

Drinking Horn, 14th Century — A325   Chimney Sweep — A326

Girl's Head, by Bror Hjorth, 1922 — A327

Perf. 12½ Horiz., Vert. (30o)

1976, Sept. 8   Engr.

1173	A323 15o bister	15	15
1174	A324 20o green	15	15
1175	A325 30o dk rose brn	15	15
1176	A326 90o indigo	35	15
1177	A327 9k yel grn & sl grn	2.75	25
	Nos. 1173-1177 (5)	3.55	
	Set value		56

John Ericsson, Ship Propeller and "Monitor" — A328

Designs: No. 1179, Helge Palmcrantz (1842-1880) and reaper. No. 1180, Lars Magnus Ericsson (1846-1926) and switchboard. No. 1181, Sven Wingquist (1876-1953) and ball bearing. No. 1182, Gustaf de Laval (1845-1913) and milk separator.

1976, Oct. 9   Engr.   Perf. 12½ Horiz.

1178	A328 1.30k multi	80	85
1179	A328 1.30k multi	80	85
1180	A328 1.30k multi	80	85
1181	A328 1.30k multi	80	85

1182 A328 1.30k multi	80	85	
a. Bklt. pane of 5, #1178-1182	4.50		
Nos. 1178-1182 (5)	4.00	4.25	

Swedish inventors and their technological inventions.

Hands and Cogwheels — A329

Verner von Heidenstam, Lake Vattern — A330

1976, Oct. 9 — *Perf. 12½ Vert.*
1183 A329 85o org & dk vio	42	22
1184 A329 1k yel grn & brn	42	15

Industrial safety.

1976, Nov. 17 — *Perf. 12½ Vert.*
1185 A330 1k yellow green	60	20
1186 A330 1.30k blue	75	30

Verner von Heidenstam (1859-1940), Swedish poet, 1916 Nobel Prize winner.

Archangel Michael A331

Virgin Mary Visiting St. Elizabeth A332

Christmas: No. 1189, like No. 1187. No. 1190, St. Nicholas saving 3 children. No. 1191, like No. 1188. No. 1192, Illuminated page, prayer to Virgin Mary. 65o stamps are from Flemish prayer book, c. 1500. 1k stamps are from Austrian prayer book, late 15th century.

Perf. 12½ Horiz. — Photo.
1187 A331 65o blue & multi	25	20
1188 A332 1k gold & multi	40	15

Perf. 12½ on 3 Sides
1189 A331 65o blue & multi	25	20
1190 A331 65o blue & multi	25	20
a. Bklt. pane, 5 each #1189-1190	2.50	

Perf. 12½ Vert.
1191 A332 1k gold & multi	35	15
1192 A332 1k gold & multi	35	15
a. Bklt. pane, 5 each #1191-1192	3.50	
Nos. 1187-1192 (6)	1.85	
Set value		75

Five Water Lilies — A333

Tailor — A334

Photogravure and Engraved
1977, Feb. 2 — *Perf. 12½ Horiz.*
1193 A333 1k brt grn & multi	52	15
1194 A333 1.30k ultra & multi	42	40

Nordic countries cooperation for protection of the environment and 25th Session of Nordic Council, Helsinki, Feb. 19.

1977, Feb. 24 — *Perf. 12½ Vert.*
1195 A334 2.10k red brn	70	15

Longdistance Skating A335

Perf. 12½ Horiz.
1977, Mar. 24 — Engr.
1196 A335 95o shown	30	30
1197 A335 95o Swimming	30	30
1198 A335 95o Bicycling	30	30
1199 A335 95o Jogging	30	30
1200 A335 95o Badminton	30	30
a. Bklt. pane, 2 each #1196-1200	3.00	
Nos. 1196-1200 (5)	1.50	1.50

Physical fitness.

Politeness, by "OA," 1905 — A336

1977, Mar. 24 — *Perf. 12½ on 3 Sides*
1201 A336 75o black	25	20
a. Booklet pane of 10	2.50	

Perf. 12½ Horiz.
1202 A336 3.80k red	1.50	45

Oskar Andersson (1877-1906), cartoonist.

Calle Schewen — A337

Designs: No. 1204, Seagull. No. 1205, Dancers and accordionist. No. 1206, Fishermen in boat. No. 1207, Tree on shore at sunset. Designs are illustrations for poem The Calle Schewen Waltz, by Evert Taube, and include bars of music of this song.

1977, May 2 Engr. *Perf. 12½ Horiz.*
1203 A337 95o slate grn	30	30
1204 A337 95o vio bl	30	30
1205 A337 95o grn & blk	30	30
1206 A337 95o dark blue	30	30
1207 A337 95o red	30	30
a. Bklt. pane, 2 each #1203-1207	3.00	
Nos. 1203-1207 (5)	1.50	1.50

Tourist publicity for Roslagen (archipelago) and to honor Evert Taube (1890-1976), poet.

Gustavianum, Uppsala University — A338

1977, May 2 Photo. *Perf. 12½ Vert.*
1208 A338 1.10k multi	30	15

Perf. 12½ on 3 Sides
1209 A338 1.10k multi	30	20
a. Booklet pane of 10	3.00	
Set value		24

Uppsala University, 500th anniversary.

Europa Issue 1977

Forest in Snow A339

Rapadalen Valley A340

1977, May 2 — *Perf. 12½ Vert.*
1210 A339 1.10k multi	55	15
1211 A340 1.40k multi	80	55

Owl A341

Cast-iron Stove Decoration A342

Gotland Ponies A343

1977, Sept. 8 Engr. *Perf. 12½ Vert.*
1212 A341 45o dk slate grn	30	20

Perf. 12½ Horiz.
1213 A342 70o dk vio bl	30	20

Booklet Stamp
1214 A343 1.40k brown	40	35
a. Booklet pane of 5	2.00	

Wild Berries — A344

Perf. 14 on 3 Sides
1977, Sept. 8 — Photo.
1215 A344 75o Blackberry	35	35
1216 A344 75o Cranberry	35	35
1217 A344 75o Raspberry	35	35
1218 A344 75o Whortleberry	35	35
1219 A344 75o Alpine strawberry	35	35
a. Bklt. pane, 2 each #1215-1219	4.00	
Nos. 1215-1219 (5)	1.75	1.75

Horse-drawn Trolley A345

Designs: Public transportation.

1977, Oct. 8 Engr. *Perf. 12½ Horiz.*
1220 A345 1.10k shown	40	30
1221 A345 1.10k Electric trolley	40	30
1222 A345 1.10k Ferry	40	30
1223 A345 1.10k Tandem bus	40	30
1224 A345 1.10k Subway	40	30
a. Bklt. pane of 5, #1220-1224	2.00	
Nos. 1220-1224 (5)	2.00	1.50

Putting up Sheaf for the Birds — A346

Preparing Dried Soaked Fish — A347

Traditional Christmas Preparations: No. 1227, Children baking ginger snaps. No. 1228, Bringing in Yule tree. No. 1229, Making straw goat. No. 1230, Candle dipping.

Perf. 12½ Horiz.
1977, Nov. 17 — Engr.
1225 A346 75o violet	25	20
1226 A347 1.10k yel grn	45	15

Perf. 12½ on 3 Sides
1227 A346 75o ocher	25	30
1228 A346 75o slate grn	25	30
a. Bklt. pane, 5 each #1227-1228	2.50	
1229 A347 1.10k dk red	35	15
1230 A347 1.10k dk bl	35	15
a. Bklt. pane, 5 each #1229-1230	3.50	
Nos. 1225-1230 (6)	1.90	1.25

Christmas 1977.

Henrik Pontoppidan, Karl Adolph Gjellerup — A348

Design: 1.40k, Charles Glover Barkla.

1977, Nov. 17 — *Perf. 12½ Vert.*
1231 A348 1.10k red brn	50	30
1232 A348 1.40k yel grn	70	70

1917 Nobel Prize winners: Henrik Pontoppidan (1857-1943) and Karl Adolph Gjellerup (1857-1919), Danish writers; Charles Glover Barkla (1877-1944), English X-ray pioneer.

Space Without Affiliation, by Arne Jones — A349

Brown Bear — A350

1978, Jan. 25 — *Perf. 12½ Horiz.*
1233 A349 2.50k vio bl	90	15

1978, Apr. 11 — *Perf. 12½ Horiz.*
1234 A350 1.15k dk brn	50	15

Europa Issue 1978

Örebro Castle — A351

Arch and Stairs — A352

1978, Apr. 11 — *Perf. 12½ Vert.*
1235 A351 1.30k slate green	65	15

Perf. 12½ Horiz.
1236 A352 1.70k dull red	80	60

Pentecostal Preacher and Congregation A353

Free Churches: No. 1238, Swedish Missionary Society. No. 1239, Evangelical National Missionary Society. No. 1240, Baptist Society. No. 1241, Salvation Army.

1978, Apr. 11 — *Perf. 12½ on 3 sides*
1237 A353 90o purple	35	40
1238 A353 90o slate	35	40
1239 A353 90o violet	35	40
1240 A353 90o slate	35	40

1241	A353	90o purple	35	40
a.		Bklt. pane, 2 each #1237-1241	3.50	
		Nos. 1237-1241 (5)	1.75	2.00

Independent Christian Associations.

Brosarp Hills — A354

Grindstone Production — A355   Red Limestone Cliff — A356

Designs: No. 1243, Avocets. No. 1245, Linnaea borealis (Linné's favorite flower.) No. 1247, Linné with Lapp drum, wearing Lapp clothes and Dutch doctor's hat.

Perf. 12¹/₂ Horiz.

1978, May 23			Engr.	
1242	A354	1.30k gray green	40	35
1243	A354	1.30k violet blue	40	35

Perf. 12¹/₂ on 3 Sides

1244	A355	1.30k violet brown	40	35
1245	A355	1.30k brown red	40	35
1246	A356	1.30k violet blue	40	35
1247	A356	1.30k violet brown	40	35
a.		Bklt. pane of 6, #1242-1247	2.50	
		Nos. 1242-1247 (6)	2.40	2.10

Travels of Carl von Linné (1707-1778), botanist.

Cranes, Lake Hornborgasjon — A357

Designs: No. 1248, Gliding School, Alleberg. No. 1250, Skara Church, Lacko Island. No. 1251, Ancient rock tomb, Luttra. No. 1252, Cloth merchants, sculpture by Nils Sjogren.

1978, May 23			**Perf. 12¹/₂ Horiz.**	
1248	A357	1.15k dull green	40	35
1249	A357	1.15k maroon	40	35
1250	A357	1.15k violet blue	40	35
1251	A357	1.15k dk gray grn	40	35
1252	A357	1.15k brn & gray grn	40	35
a.		Bklt. pane, 2 each #1284-1252	4.00	
		Nos. 1248-1252 (5)	2.00	1.75

Tourist publicity for Vastergotland.

Laurel and Scroll — A358

1978, May 23			**Perf. 12¹/₂ Vert.**	
1253	A358	2.50k gray & slate green	1.10	40

Stockholm University, centenary.

Homecoming, by Carl Kylberg A359

Nude, by Karl Isakson — A360   Self-portrait, by Ivar Arosenius — A361

1978, Sept. 5			Engr.	**Perf. 12¹/₂ Vert.**	
1254	A359	90o multicolored		48	20

Perf. 12¹/₂ Horiz.

1255	A360	1.15k multi	48	20
1256	A361	4.50k multi	1.90	50

Swedish painters: Carl Kylberg (1878-1952); Karl Isakson (1878-1922); Ivar Arosenius (1878-1909).

North Arrow (Compass Rose), Map, 1769 — A362

1978, Sept. 5			**Perf. 12¹/₂ Horiz.**	
1257	A362	10k lilac		3.00	15

Coronation Coach, 1699 — A363

1978, Oct. 7			Engr.	**Perf. 12¹/₂ Horiz.**	
1258	A363	1.70k dk red, yel		60	60
a.		Booklet pane of 5		3.00	

Orange Russula — A364

Designs: Edible mushrooms.

1978, Oct. 7			**Perf. 12¹/₂ on 3 Sides**	
1259	A364	1.15k shown	38	35
1260	A364	1.15k Lycoperdon perlatum	38	35
1261	A364	1.15k Macrolepiota procera	38	35
1262	A364	1.15k Cantharellus cibarius	38	35
1263	A364	1.15k Boletus edulis	38	35
1264	A364	1.15k Ramaria botrytis	38	35
a.		Bklt. pane of 6, #1259-1264	2.50	
		Nos. 1259-1264 (6)	2.28	2.10

Toy Ferris Wheel — A365   Rider Drawing Water Cart — A366

Toys: No. 1266, Teddy bear. No. 1267, Dalecarlian wooden horse. No. 1268, Doll. No. 1270, Spinning tops.

Perf. 12¹/₂ Horiz.

1978, Nov. 14			Engr.	
1265	A365	90o dk red & grn	30	15
1266	A365	1.30k brt ultra	35	15

Perf. 12¹/₂ on 3 Sides
Photo.

1267	A365	90o multicolored	30	25
1268	A365	90o multicolored	30	25
a.		Bklt. pane, 5 each #1267-1268	3.00	
1269	A366	1.30k multicolored	35	15
1270	A366	1.30k multicolored	35	15
a.		Bklt. pane, 5 each #1269-1270	3.50	
		Nos. 1265-1270 (6)	1.95	1.10

Christmas 1978.

Fritz Haber — A367

Design: 1.70k, Max Planck.

1978, Nov. 14			Engr.	**Perf. 12¹/₂ Vert.**	
1271	A367	1.30k dark brown		60	20
1272	A367	1.70k dark violet bl		80	75

1918 Nobel Prize winners: Fritz Haber (1868-1934), German chemist; Max Planck (1858-1947), German physicist.
See #1310-1312, 1341-1344, 1387-1389.

Bandy — A368

1979, Jan. 25			Engr.	**Perf. 12¹/₂ Vert.**	
1273	A368	1.05k violet blue		45	20
1274	A368	2.50k orange		85	22

Child Wearing Gas Mask in Heavy Traffic — A369

1979, Mar. 13			**Perf. 12¹/₂ Vert.**	
1275	A369	1.70k dark blue		75	70

International Year of the Child.

Drill-weave Tapestry, c. 1855-1860 A370   Carrier Pigeon, Hand with Quill A371

1979, Mar. 13			**Perf. 12¹/₂ Horiz.**	
1276	A370	4k gray & red		1.10	15

Perf. 14x14¹/₂ on 3 Sides

1979, Apr. 2			Photo.	
1277	A371	(1k) ultra & yel	35	15
a.		Booklet pane of 20	7.50	

Every Swedish household received during Apr., 1979, 2 coupons for the purchase of 2 discount booklets. The stamps were for use on post cards and letters within Sweden. Price of booklet 20k.

Mail Service by Boat, Grisslehamn to Echero — A372

Europa: 1.70k, Hand on telegraph.

1979, May 7			Engr.	**Perf. 12¹/₂ Vert.**	
1278	A372	1.30k slate grn & blk		65	15
1279	A372	1.70k ocher & blk		80	75

Woodcutter, Winter — A373

Designs: No. 1281, Sowing, spring. No. 1282, Grazing cattle, summer. No. 1283, Harvester, summer. No. 1284, Plowing, autumn.

1979, May 7			**Perf. 12¹/₂ Horiz.**	
1280	A373	1.30k multicolored	45	18
1281	A373	1.30k sl grn & dk brn	45	18
1282	A373	1.30k dk brn & sl grn	45	18
1283	A373	1.30k sl grn & ocher	45	18
1284	A373	1.30k multicolored	45	18
a.		Bklt. pane, 2 each #1280-1284	4.50	
		Nos. 1280-1284 (5)	2.25	
		Set value		75

Tourist Steamer Juno — A374

Roller Bridge, Hajstorp — A375   Sailing Ship — A376

Gota Canal: No. 1286, Borenshult Lock. No. 1288, Hand-drawn gate. No. 1290, Rowboat in Forsvik lock.

1979, May 7			**Perf. 12¹/₂ Horiz.**	
1285	A374	1.15k violet blue	45	45
1286	A374	1.15k slate green	45	45

Perf. 12¹/₂ on 3 Sides

1287	A375	1.15k dull purple	45	45
1288	A375	1.15k carmine	45	45

Perf. 12¹/₂ on 2 Sides

1289	A376	1.15k violet blue	45	45
1290	A376	1.15k slate green	45	45
a.		Bklt. pane of 6, #1285-1290	2.75	
		Nos. 1285-1290 (6)	2.70	2.70

Strikers and Sawmill A377

Temperance Movement Banner — A378

Jons Jacob Berzelius — A379

Johan Olof Wallin — A380

1979, Sept. 6   Engr.   Perf. 12½ Vert.
1291 A377 90o car & dp brn   38 25

Perf. 12½ Horiz.
Litho.
1292 A378 1.30k multi   50 20

Engr.
1293 A379 1.70k brown & grn   70 65
1294 A380 4.50k slate blue   1.90 60

Centenaries of Sundsvall strike and Swedish Temperance Movement; birth bicentennials of Jons Jacob Berzelius (1779-1848), physician and chemist; Johan Olof Wallin (1779-1839), Archbishop and poet.

Dragonfly A381

Green Spotted Toad A383

Pike A382

1979, Sept. 6   Perf. 12½ Horiz.
1295 A381 60o violet   55 22
Perf. 12½ Vert.
1296 A382 65o gray   55 20
1297 A383 80o olive green   55 28

Potpourri Pot — A384

Portrait, by Johan Henrik Scheffel — A385

Designs: 1.30k, Silver coffeepot. 1.70k, Bust of Carl Johan Cronstedt.

Souvenir Sheet
Engraved and Photogravure
1979, Oct. 6   Perf. 12x12½
1298   Sheet of 4   2.75 3.00
a.   A384 90o multi   65 70
b.   A385 1.15k multi   65 70
c.   A384 1.30k multi   65 70
d.   A385 1.70k multi   65 70

Swedish Rococo. No. 1298 sold for 6k; surtax was for philately.

Herrings, Age Determination — A386

Sea Research: No. 1300, Acoustic survey of sea bottom. No. 1301, Water bloom of algae in Baltic Sea. No. 1302, Computer map of herring distribution in South Baltic Sea. No. 1303, Research ship Argos.

1979, Oct. 6   Engr.   Perf. 12½ Horiz.
1299 A386 1.70k multicolored   60 65
1300 A386 1.70k sepia   60 65
1301 A386 1.70k multicolored   60 65
1302 A386 1.70k sepia   60 65
1303 A386 1.70k multicolored   60 65
a.   Bkt. pane of 5, #1299-1303   3.00
     Nos. 1299-1303 (5)   3.00 3.25

Brooch from Jamtland A387

Ljusdal Costume A388

Christmas 1979 (Costumes and Jewelry from): No. 1305, Pendant, Smaland. No. 1307, Osteraker. No. 1308, Goinge. No. 1309, Mora.

Perf. 12½ Horiz.
1979, Nov. 15   Engr.
1304 A387 90o dk Prus blue   25 15
1305 A387 1.30k dull red   45 15
Perf. 12½ on 3 Sides
Photo.
Size: 22x27mm
1306 A388 90o multicolored   25 18
1307 A388 90o multicolored   25 18
a.   Bkt. pane, 5 each #1306-1307   2.50
Perf. 12½ Vert.
Size: 26x44mm
1308 A388 1.30k multicolored   35 15
1309 A388 1.30k multicolored   35 15
a.   Bkt. pane, 5 each #1308-1309   3.50
     Nos. 1304-1309 (6)   1.90
     Set value   80

Nobel Prize Winner Type of 1978

1919 Nobel Prize Winners: 1.30k, Jules Bordet (1870-1961), Belgian bacteriologist. 1.70k, Johannes Stark (1874-1957), German physicist. 2.50k, Carl Spitteler (1845-1924), Swiss poet.

1979, Nov. 15   Engr.   Perf. 12½ Vert.
1310 A367 1.30k lilac   55 15
1311 A367 1.70k ultra   70 85
1312 A367 2.50k olive green   1.10 20

Wind Power — A389

Renewable Energy Sources: No. 1314, Biodegradable material. No. 1315, Solar energy. No. 1316, Geothermal energy. No. 1317, Hydro power.

1980, Jan. 29   Perf. 12½ on 3 sides
1313 A389 1.15k dark blue   35 45
1314 A389 1.15k dk grn & bis   35 45
1315 A389 1.15k yellow orange   35 45
1316 A389 1.15k dark green   35 45
1317 A389 1.15k dk bl & dk grn   35 45
a.   Bkt. pane, 2 each #1313-1317   3.50
     Nos. 1313-1317 (5)   1.75 2.25

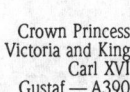

Crown Princess Victoria and King Carl XVI Gustaf — A390

1980, Feb. 26   Perf. 12½ on 3 sides
1318 A390 1.30k brt blue   32 15
a.   Booklet pane of 10   3.25
Perf. 12½ Vert.
1319 A390 1.30k brt blue   52 15
1320 A390 1.70k carmine rose   70 60

Child Holding Adult's Hand — A391

Hand Holding Cane — A392

1980, Apr. 22   Perf. 12½ Horiz.
1321 A391 1.40k red brown   55 15
1322 A392 1.60k slate green   55 25

Parents' insurance system; care for the elderly.

SVERIGE Squirrel — A393

Perf. 15 on 3 Sides
1980, May 12   Photo.
1323 A393 (1k) ultra & yellow   45 15
a.   Booklet pane of 20   9.00

See note after No. 1277.

Elise Ottesen-Jensen (1886-1973), Journalist — A394

Europa: 1.70k, Joe Hill (1879-1915), member of American Workers' Movement and poet.

1980, June 4   Engr.   Perf. 12½ Vert.
1324 A394 1.30k green   65 15
1325 A394 1.70k red   85 80

Banga Farm, Alfta, Halsingland Province A395

Tourism (Halsingland Province): No. 1327, Iron Works, Iggesund. No. 1328, Blaxas Ridge, Forsa. No. 1329, Tybling farm, Tyby. No. 1330, Sunds Canal, Hudiksvall.

1980, June 4   Perf. 12½ Horiz.
1326 A395 1.15k red   40 40
1327 A395 1.15k dark blue   40 40
1328 A395 1.15k dark green   40 40
1329 A395 1.15k chocolate   40 40
1330 A395 1.15k dark blue   40 40
a.   Bkt. pane, 2 each #1326-1330   4.00
     Nos. 1326-1330 (5)   2.00 2.00

Chair, Scania, 1831 — A396

Cradle, North Bothnia, 19th Century — A397

Perf. 12½ Horiz.
1980, Sept. 9   Engr.
1331 A396 1.50k grnsh blue   65 15
Perf. 12½ Vert.
1332 A397 2k dk red brown   85 45

Norden 80.

Scene from "Diagonal Symphony," 1924 — A398

1980, Sept. 9   Perf. 12½ Horiz.
1333 A398 3k dark blue   1.10 15

Viking Eggeling (1880-1925), artist and film maker.

Souvenir Sheet

Gustaf Erikson's Carriage — A399

Vabis, 1909 A400

Swedish Automobile History: 1.30k, Thulin, 1923. 1.40k, Scania, 1903. 1.50k, Tidaholm, 1917. 1.70k, Volvo, 1927.

Photogravure and Engraved
1980, Oct. 11   Perf. 12½
1334   Sheet of 6   3.25 3.25
a.   A399 90o lt blue & dk brn   45 50
b.   A400 1.15k cream & dk brn   45 50
c.   A399 1.30k lt blue & dk brn   45 50
d.   A400 1.40k lt blue & dk brn   45 50
e.   A400 1.50k cream & dk brn   45 50
f.   A399 1.70k lt blue & dk brn   45 50

No. 1334 sold for 9k.

Bamse the Bear — A401

Farmer Kronblom A402

Christmas 1980 (Comic Strip Characters): No. 1336, Mandel Karlsson, vert. No. 1337, Adamson, vert.

1980, Oct. 11   Engr.   Perf. 12½ Vert.
1335 A401 1.15k multicolored   45 15
Perf. 12½ on 3 sides
Photo.
1336 A401 1.15k multicolored   30 25
a.   Booklet pane of 10   3.00
Perf. 12½ Horiz.
Engr.
1337 A401 1.50k black   65 15
Photo.
1338 A402 1.50k multicolored   40 20
a.   Booklet pane of 10   4.00

Angel Blowing Horn — A403

Necken, by Ernst Josephson — A404

1980, Nov. 18 Engr. *Perf. on 3 Sides*
1339 A403 1.25k multicolored   40 20
  a. Booklet pane of 12   5.00

Christmas 1980.

1980, Nov. 18   *Perf. 12½ Horiz.*
1340 A404 8k multicolored   2.25 15

Nobel Prize Winner Type of 1978

1920 Nobel Prize Winners: No. 1341, Knut Hamsun (1859-1953), Norwegian writer. No. 1342, August Krogh (1874-1949), Danish Physiologist, No. 1343, Charles-Edouard Guillaume (1861-1938), French chemist. No. 1344, Walther Nernst (1864-1941), German physicist.

1980, Nov. 18   *Perf. 13 on 3 Sides*
1341 A367 1.40k dk blue gray   40 35
1342 A367 1.40k red   40 35
  a. Bklt. pane, 5 each #1341-1342   4.00
1343 A367 2k green   50 45
1344 A367 2k brown   50 45
  a. Bklt. pane, 5 each #1343-1344   5.00

Ernst Wigforss (1881-1977), Politician & Writer A405

Freya (Fertility Goddess) A406

1981, Jan. 29 Engr.   *Perf. 12½ Vert.*
1345 A405 5k rose carmine   1.90 40

1981, Jan. 29   *Perf. 12½ on 3 Sides*

Norse Mythological Characters: 10o, Thor (thunder god). 15o, Heimdall (rainbow god). 50o, Frey (god of peace, fertility, weather). 1k, Odin.

1346 A406 10o blue black   15 15
1347 A406 15o dk carmine   15 15
1348 A406 50o blue green   20 15
1349 A406 75o deep green   30 15
1350 A406 1k blue black   40 18
  a. Bklt. pane, 2 each #1346-1350   2.00
     Set value   1.00 45

Gyrfalcon — A407

1981, Feb. 26 Engr.   *Perf. 12½ Vert.*
1351 A407 50k multicolored   13.50 1.10
  a. Booklet pane of 4   55.00

Troll Chasing Boy — A408

Intl. Year of the Disabled — A409

Europa: 2k, Lady of the Woods.

1981, Apr. 28   Engr.
1352 A408 1.50k dk blue & red   60 15
1353 A408 2k dk green & red   80 25

1981, Apr. 28
1354 A409 1.50k dk green   55 15
1355 A409 3.50k purple   1.25 30

Arms of Oster-gotland Province A410

Sail Boat, Bohuslan A411

Perf. 14½ on 3 Sides
1981, May 18   Photo.
1356 A410 1.40k shown   40 15
1357 A410 1.40k Jamtland   40 15
1358 A410 1.40k Dalarna   40 15
1359 A410 1.40k Bohuslan   40 15
  a. Bklt. pane, 5 each #1356-1359   8.00
     Set value   48

See note after No. 1277. See Nos. 1403-1406, 1456-1459, 1492-1495, 1534-1537, 1592-1595.

Perf. 12½ on 3 Sides
1981, May 26   Engr.
1360 A411 1.65k shown   50 32
1361 A411 1.65k Blekinge   50 32
1362 A411 1.65k Norrbotten   50 32
1363 A411 1.65k Halsingland   50 32
1364 A411 1.65k Gotland   50 32
1365 A411 1.65k Skane   50 32
  a. Bklt. pane of 6, #1360-1365   3.00
     Nos. 1360-1365 (6)   3.00 1.92

King Carl XVI Gustaf A412

Queen Silvia A413

1981-84   *Perf. 12½ Vert.*
1366 A412 1.65k dark green   45 15
1367 A413 1.75k dark blue   90 25
1368 A412 1.80k dark blue   60 15
1369 A412 1.90k red ('84)   60 15
1370 A412 2.40k violet brn   75 20
1371 A412 2.40k grnsh black ('84)   75 45
1372 A412 2.70k brt lilac   75 25
1373 A413 3.20k red   90 30
     Nos. 1366-1373 (8)   5.70 1.90

Day and Night A414

Scene from Par Lagerkvist's Autobiography Guest of Reality A415

Perf. 12½ on 3 Sides
1981, Sept. 9   Engr.
1376 A414 1.65k dark blue   50 15
  a. Booklet pane of 10   5.00

1981, Sept. 9
1377 A415 1.50k dark green   42 15

Conductor Sixten Ehrling and Opera Singer Birgit Nilsson A416

Bjorn Borg, Tennis Player — A417

Baker's Sign — A418

Designs: No. 1378, Electric locomotive. No. 1379, Trucks. No. 1381, Oil rig. No. 1383, Ingemar Stenmark, skier.

1981, Sept. 9
1378 A416 2.40k rose carmine   65 60
1379 A416 2.40k red   65 60
1380 A416 2.40k rose lilac   65 60
1381 A416 2.40k deep violet   65 60
1382 A417 2.40k dark blue   65 65
1383 A417 2.40k dark blue   65 65
  a. Bklt. pane of 6, #1378-1383   4.00
     Nos. 1378-1383 (6)   3.90 3.70

1981, Sept. 9   *Perf. 12½ Vert.*
1384 A418 2.30k shown   75 15
1385 A418 2.30k Pewter shop sign   75 15
  a. Pair, #1384-1385   1.50 35

Ingrid Bergman and Gosta Ekman in Intermezzo A419

Kari Sylwan and Harriet Andersson in Cries and Whispers — A420

Swedish Films: a, Olof Ahs in The Coachman. c, Greta Garbo in The Gosta Berling Saga, d, Stig Jarrel and Alf Kjellin in Persecution.

Photogravure and Engraved
1981, Oct. 10   *Perf. 13½*
1386   Sheet of 5   3.50 3.50
  a. A419 1.50k multi   70 65
  b. A419 1.50k multi   70 65
  c. A419 1.65k multi   70 65
  d. A419 1.65k multi   70 65
  e. A420 2.40k multi   70 70

No. 1386 sold for 10k.

Nobel Prize Winner Type of 1978

1921 Winners: 1.35k, Albert Einstein (1879-1955), German physicist 1.65k, Anatole France (1844-1924), French writer. Frederick Soddy (1877-1956), British chemist.

1981, Nov. 24 Engr.   *Perf. 12½ Vert.*
1387 A367 1.35k red   55 30
1388 A367 1.65k green   55 15
1389 A367 2.70k blue   85 75

Christmas 1981 — A421

Designs: Wooden birds.

1981, Nov. 24   *Perf. 12½ on 3 Sides*
1390 A421 1.40k red   40 25
1391 A421 1.40k green   40 25
  a. Bklt. pane, 5 each #1390-1391   4.00

Knight on Horseback, by John Bauer — A422

John Bauer (1882-1918), Fairytale Illustrator: No. 1393, "What a Miserable Little Paleface, said the Troll Mother." No. 1394, Marsh Princess. No. 1395, Now the Dusk of the Night is already Upon Us.

Perf. 12x12½ on 3 sides
1982, Feb. 16   Engr.
1392 A422 1.65k multicolored   50 40
1393 A422 1.65k multicolored   50 40
1394 A422 1.65k multicolored   50 40
1395 A422 1.65k multicolored   50 40
  a. Bklt. pane of 4, #1392-1395   2.00

Impossible Figures — A423 SVERIGE 25

Designs: Geometric figures.

1982, Feb. 16   *Perf. 12½ Horiz.*
1396 A423 25o violet brown   16 15
1397 A423 50o brown olive   16 15
1398 A423 75o dark blue   25 15
     Set value   30

Newspaper Distributor, by Svenolov Ehren — A424

Graziella, by Carl Larsson — A425

1982, Feb. 16
1399 A424 1.35k deep violet   50 18
1400 A425 5k violet brown   1.50 15

Europa Issue 1982

Land Reform, 19th Cent. A426

Anders Celsius (1701-1744), Inventor of Temperature Scale — A427

1982, Apr. 26 Engr.   *Perf. 12½ Vert.*
1401 A426 1.65k dk olive grn   90 20
Perf. 12½ on 3 Sides
1402 A427 2.40k dark green   75 65
  a. Booklet pane of 6   4.50

Provincial Arms Type of 1981
Perf. 14 on 3 Sides
1982, Apr. 26   Photo.
1403 A410 1.40k Dalsland   35 15
1404 A410 1.40k Halsingland   35 15
1405 A410 1.40k Vastmandland   35 15
1406 A410 1.40k Oland   35 15
  a. Bklt. pane, 5 each #1403-1406   7.50
     Set value   32

See note after No. 1277.

Elin Wagner (1882-1949), Writer — A428

1982, June 3 Engr. Perf. 12¹/₂ Horiz.
1407 A428 1.35k Sketch by Siri Derkert 50 35

Burgher House — A429

Embroidered Lace Ribbon, 19th Cent. — A430

1982, June 3 Perf. 12¹/₂ Vert.
1408 A429 1.65k brown 55 15
Perf. 12¹/₂ Horiz.
1409 A430 2.70k bister 90 60

Cent. of Museum of Cultural History, Lund.

1982 Intl. Buoyage System A431

Designs: Various buoy signals.

1982, June 3 Perf. 13 Horiz.
1410 A431 1.65k shown 60 20
1411 A431 1.65k Ferry 60 20
1412 A431 1.65k Six sailboats 60 20
1413 A431 1.65k One-globed buoy 60 20
1414 A431 1.65k Two-globed buoy 60 20
  a. Bklt. pane, 2 each #1410-1414 6.00
    Nos. 1410-1414 (5) 3.00 1.00

Vietnamese Workers in Sweden — A432

Living Together: Swedish emigration and immigration.

1982, Aug. 26 Engr. Perf. 13 Horiz.
1415 A432 1.65k Leaving Sweden, 1880 50 25
1416 A432 1.65k shown 50 25
1417 A432 1.65k Local voting right 50 25
1418 A432 1.65k Girls 50 25
  a. Bklt. pane, 2 each #1415-1418 4.00

Early Purple Orchid — A433

Photogravure and Engraved
1982, Oct. 9 Perf. 12x13
1419   Sheet of 4 4.50 4.50
  a. A433 1.65k shown 1.10 1.00
  b. A433 1.65k Lady's-slipper 1.10 1.00
  c. A433 2.40k Marsh helleborine 1.10 1.00
  d. A433 2.70k Elder-flowered orchid 1.10 1.00

Wild orchids. Sold for 10k for benefit of stamp collecting.

Christmas 1982 — A434

Stained-glass Windows, Church at Lye, Gotland, 14th cent.

Perf. 13 on 3 Sides
1982, Nov. 24 Photo.
1420 A434 1.40k Angel 45 40
1421 A434 1.40k Child in the Temple 45 40
1422 A434 1.40k Adoration of the Kings 45 40
1423 A434 1.40k Tidings to the Shepherds 45 40
1424 A434 1.40k Birth of Christ 45 40
  a. Bklt. pane, 2 each #1420-1424 4.50
    Nos. 1420-1424 (5) 2.25 2.00

Signature, Atomic Model A435

Nobel Prizewinners in Physics (Quantum Mechanics). Various Atomic Models: No. 1425, Niels Bohr, Denmark, 1922. No. 1426, Erwin Schrodinger, Austria, 1933. No. 1427, Louis de Broglie, France, 1929. No. 1428, Paul Dirac, England, 1933. No. 1429, Werner Heisenberg, Germany, 1932.

1982, Nov. 24 Engr. Perf. 13 Horiz.
1425 A435 2.40k multi 80 65
1426 A435 2.40k multi 80 65
1427 A435 2.40k multi 80 65
1428 A435 2.40k multi 80 65
1429 A435 2.40k multi 80 65
  a. Bklt. pane of 5, #1425-1429 4.00
    Nos. 1425-1429 (5) 4.00 3.25

Fruit A436

Games A436a

Crown and Posthorn A436b

King Carl XVI Gustaf A436c

Queen Silvia A436d

Games A436e

1983-85 Engr. Perf. 12¹/₂ Vert.
1430 A436 5o Horse chestnut 15 15
1431 A436 10o Norway maple 15 15
1432 A436 15o Dogrose 15 15
1433 A436 20o Sloe 15 15
1434 A436a 50o Fox and cheese 18 15
1435 A436a 60o Dominoes 20 15
1436 A436a 70o Ludo 24 15
1437 A436a 80o Chinese checkers 28 15
1438 A436a 90o Backgammon 30 15
1439 A436b 1.60k deep blue 45 15
1440 A436b 2k black 60 15
1441 A436b 2.50k bister 75 15
1442 A436c 2.70k dl red brn 80 35
Perf. 12¹/₂ Horiz.
1443 A436e 3k Chess 90 15

Perf. 12¹/₂ Vert.
1444 A436d 3.20k brt blue 1.00 45
1445 A436b 4k dp car 1.25 20
    Nos. 1430-1445 (16) 7.55
    Set value 1.35

Issue dates: Nos. 1430-1433, Feb. 10, 1983. Nos. 1434-1438, 1443, Oct. 12, 1985. Nos. 1439-1442, 1444-1445, Jan. 24, 1985.
See Nos. 1567-1580, 1783.

Peace Movement Centenary — A437

1983, Feb. 10
1446 A437 1.35k blue 50 40

Nils Ferlin (1898-1961), Poet — A438

1983, Feb. 10
1447 A438 6k dk grn 1.65 25

500th Anniv. of Printing in Sweden A439

1983, Feb. 10 Perf. 13 Horiz.
1448 A439 1.65k Lead type 45 25
1449 A439 1.65k Dialogus Creaturarum, 1483 45 25
1450 A439 1.65k Carolus XII Bible, 1793 45 25
1451 A439 1.65k ABC Books, 1760s 45 25
1452 A439 1.65k Laser photo composition 45 25
  a. Bklt. pane, 2 each #1448-1452 4.50
    Nos. 1448-1452 (5) 2.25 1.25

Sweden-US Relations Bicentenary — A440

1983, Mar. 24
1453 A440 2.70k Ben Franklin, Swedish Arms 80 65
  a. Booklet pane of 5 4.00

See US No. 2036.

Nordic Cooperation Issue — A441

Perf. 12¹/₂ Horiz.
1983, Mar. 24 Engr.
Size: 21x27mm
1454 A441 1.65k Bicycling 60 15
Perf. 13 Vert.
1455 A441 2.40k Sailing 90 65

Provincial Arms Type of 1981
1983, Apr. 25 Photo. Perf. 14¹/₂x14
1456 A410 1.60k Gotland 45 15
1457 A410 1.60k Gastrikland 45 15
1458 A410 1.60k Medelpad 45 15

1459 A410 1.60k Vastergotland 45 15
  a. Bklt. pane, 5 each #1456-1459 9.00
    Set value 32

See note after No. 1277.

Europa — A442   A443

1983, Apr. 25 Perf. 12¹/₂ Horiz.
Engr.
1460 A442 1.65k Swedish Ballet Co. 90 20
1461 A442 2.70k Sliding-jaw spanner 1.25 75

1983, May 25 Perf. 12¹/₂

Designs: 1k, 3k, 10-ore King Oscar II definitive essays, 1884. 2k, No. 39. 4k, No. 58.

1462 A443 1k blue 25 35
1463 A443 2k red 55 55
1464 A443 3k blue 95 85
1465 A443 4k green 1.25 1.00
  a. Bklt. pane of 4, #1462-1465 3.00

STOCKHOLMIA Intl. Stamp Exhibition, Aug. 28-Sept. 7, 1986.

Red Cross — A444

Greater Karlso — A445

1983, Aug. 24 Perf. 12¹/₂ Horiz.
1466 A444 1.50k red 55 20
1467 A445 1.60k dk blue 55 15

Planorbis Snail — A446

Arctic Fox — A447

1983, Aug. 24 Perf. 12¹/₂ on 3 Sides
1468 A446 1.80k green 50 15
  a. Booklet pane of 10 5.00
Perf. 12¹/₂ Horiz.
1469 A447 2.10k grnsh blk 65 15

See Nos. 1488-1489, 1526-1527, 1623-1626, 1678-1680, 1762-1763.

Hjalmar Bergman (1883-1931), Writer — A448

1983, Aug. 24 Perf. 13 Horiz.
1470 A448 1.80k Portrait 70 15
1471 A448 1.80k Jac the Clown illustration by Nisse Skoog 70 15
  a. Pair, #1470-1471 1.50 65
    Set value 24

View of Helgeandsholmen, Stockholm, by Franz Hogenberg, 1580 — A449

1983, Aug. 24   *Perf. 12½ Vert.*
1472 A449 2.70k dl pur & dk bl   95 50

Wilhelm Stenhammar Composer and Pianist — A450

Hins-Anders, Violinist — A451

Photogravure and Engraved
1983, Oct. 1   *Perf. 13½*
1473   Sheet of 5   4.50 4.00
  a.   A450 1.80k shown   75 60
  b.   A450 1.80k Aniara (opera)   75 60
  c.   A450 1.80k Lars Gullin jazz saxo-
      phonist   75 60
  d.   A450 1.80k ABBA pop music group   75 60
  e.   A451 2.70k shown   1.25 1.00
    Sold for 11.50k.

Christmas 1983 — A452

Postcard designs: No. 1474, Christmas Gnomes around the tree. No. 1475, on straw goats. No. 1476, Folk children, Christmas porridge and gingerbread. No. 1477, Gnomes carrying Christmas gifts on a pole.

Perf. 12½ on 3 sides
1983, Nov. 22   Photo.
1474 A452 1.60k multi   45 30
1475 A452 1.60k multi   45 30
1476 A452 1.60k multi   45 30
1477 A452 1.60k multi   45 30
  a.   Bklt. pane, 3 each #1474-1477   5.50

Chemistry, Nobel Prize Winners A453

Designs: No. 1478, Arne Tiselius (1902-1971), Electrophoresis Studies. No. 1479, George De Hevsy (1885-1966), Radioactive isotope tracers. No. 1480 Svante Arrhenius (1859-1927), Theory of Electrolytic Dissociation. No. 1481, Theodor Svedberg (1884-1971), Colloid Studies. No. 1482, Hans Von Euler-Chelpin (1873-1964). Enzyme and Vitamin Structures.

Photogravure and Engraved
1983, Nov. 22   *Perf. 12½ Horiz.*
1478 A453 2.70k slate   80 60
1479 A453 2.70k dp bl vio   80 60
1480 A453 2.70k red lilac   80 60
1481 A453 2.70k blue blk   80 60
1482 A453 2.70k grnsh blk   80 60
  a.   Bklt. pane of 5, #1478-1482   4.00
    Nos. 1478-1482 (5)   4.00 3.00

Postal Savings Centenary — A454

Design: 100o, Three crowns.

1984, Feb. 9   Engr.   *Perf. 12½ Vert.*
1483 A454 100o orange   35 15
1484 A454 1.60k purple   55 30
1485 A454 1.80k pink   65 15

Europa 1984 A455

Design: Symbolic bridge of communications exchange.

1984, Feb. 9   *Perf. 12½ Horiz.*
1486 A455 1.80k red   55 15
  a.   Booklet pane of 10   5.50

Perf. 13 Vert.
1487 A455 2.70k dp ultra   1.10 65

Conservation Type of 1983 and

Angelica — A457

1984, Mar. 27   *Perf. 12½ on 3 Sides*
1488 A447 1.90k Lemmings   60 15
1489 A447 1.90k Musk ox   60 15
  a.   Bklt. pane, 5 each #1488-1489   6.00

Perf. 12½ Horiz.
1490 A457   2k shown   70 15
1491 A457 2.25k Alpine birch   80 50

Provincial Arms Type of 1981

1984, Apr. 24   Photo.   *Perf. 14½x14*
1492 A410 1.60k Skane   50 15
1493 A410 1.60k Blekinge   50 15
1494 A410 1.60k Sodermanland   50 15
1495 A410 1.60k Vasterbotten   50 15
  a.   Bklt. pane, 5 each #1492-1495   10.00
    Set value   32

See note after No. 1277.

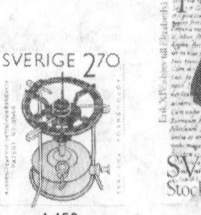

A458   A459

Swedish Patent System Centenary: No. 1496, Paraffin stove, F.W. Lindquist, 1892. No. 1497, Industrial robot ASEA-IRB 6. No. 1498, Fan suction vacuum cleaner, Axel Wennergren, 1912. No. 1499, Inboard-outboard motor, AQ-200, No. 1500, SLIC integrated electronic circuit. No. 1501, Tetrahedron container, 1948, 1951.

Perf. 12½ on 3 Sides
1984, June 6   Engr.
1496 A458 2.70k red   80 70
1497 A458 2.70k sepia   80 70
1498 A458 2.70k green   80 70
1499 A458 2.70k green   80 70
1500 A458 2.70k sepia   80 70
1501 A458 2.70k blue   80 70
  a.   Bklt. pane of 6, #1496-1501   5.00
    Nos. 1496-1501 (6)   4.80 4.20

Lithographed and Engraved
1984, June 6   *Perf. 12½*
Stockholmia '86 (Famous Letters): 1k, Erik XIV's marriage proposal to Queen Elizabeth I, 1561. 2k, Erik Dahlbergh to Sten Bielke, 1684. 3k, Feather letter, 1834. 4k, August Strindberg to Harriet Bosse, 1905.
1502 A459 1k multi   28 28
1503 A459 2k multi   55 55
1504 A459 3k multi   80 80
1505 A459 4k multi   1.10 1.10
  a.   Bklt. pane of 4, #1502-1505   3.00

Fredrika Bremer Assn. (Women's Rights) Centenary — A460

1984, Aug. 28   Engr.   *Perf. 12½ Vert.*
1506 A460 1.50k pink   60 15
1507 A460 6.50k red   2.25 60

Medieval Towns A461

Engravings by E. Dahlbergh or M. Karl.

1984, Aug. 28   *Perf. 12½x13*
1508 A461 1.90k Jonkoping   50 35
1509 A461 1.90k Karlstad   50 35
1510 A461 1.90k Gavle   50 35
1511 A461 1.90k Sigtuna   50 35
1512 A461 1.90k Norrkoping   50 35
1513 A461 1.90k Vadstena   50 35
  a.   Bklt. pane of 6, #1508-1513   3.25
    Nos. 1508-1513 (6)   3.00 2.10

Viking Satellite, 1985 A462

1984, Oct. 13   *Perf. 12½ Vert.*
1514 A462 1.90k Satellite   60 30
1515 A462 3.20k Receiving station   1.00 75

Souvenir Sheet

Thulin D Two-Seater, 1915 — A463

Carl Nyberg's Flugan, 1900 — A464

Swedish Aviation History: b. SAAB-90 Scandia, 1946. c. Carl Gustaf Cederstrom (1867-1918, "The Flying Baron"), Bleriot, 1910. d. Tomten, 1927. Sold for 12k.

1984, Oct. 13   *Perf. 12½*
1516   Sheet of 5   4.50 4.00
  a.-d.   A463 1.90k, any single   85 75
  e.   A464 2.70k, multi   1.10 1.00

Christmas 1984 — A465

Birds.

Lithographed and Engraved
1984, Nov. 29   *Perf. 12½ on 3 Sides*
1517 A465 1.60k Coccothraustes coc-
      cothraustes   45 35
1518 A465 1.60k Bombycilla garrulus   45 35
1519 A465 1.60k Dendrocopos major   45 35
1520 A465 1.60k Sitta europaea   45 35
  a.   Bklt. pane, 3 each #1517-1520   5.50

Inner Ear A466

Nobel Prize Winners in Physiology or Medicine: No. 1521, Georg von Bekesy, 1961, hearing. No. 1522, John Eccles, Alan Hodgkin & Andrew Huxley, 1963, Nerve cell activation. No. 1523, Julius Axelrod, Bernard Katz & Ulf von Euler, 1970, nerve cell storage and release. No. 1524, Roger Sperry, Hubel, Wiesel, 1981, brain functions. No. 1525, David Hubel, Torsten Wiesel, 1981, Visual information processing.

Perf. 12½ Horiz.
1984, Nov. 29   Engr.
1521 A466 2.70k shown   1.00 65
1522 A466 2.70k Nerve, arrows   1.00 65
1523 A466 2.70k Nerve (front, side)   1.00 65
1524 A466 2.70k Brain halves   1.00 65
1525 A466 2.70k Eye   1.00 65
  a.   Bklt. pane of 5, #1521-1525   5.00
    Nos. 1521-1525 (5)   5.00 3.25

Conservation Type of 1983 and

A467

Perf. 13 on 3 Sides
1985, Mar. 14   Engr.
1526 A447 2k Muscardinus avellanari-
      us   55 15
1527 A447 2k Salvelinus salvelinus   55 15
  a.   Bklt. pane, 5 each #1526-1527   5.50

World Wildlife Fund.

Perf. 12½ Horiz.
1528 A467 2.20k Nigritella nigra   60 20
1529 A467 3.50k Nymphaea alba   1.10 20
    Set value   56

World Table Tennis Championships A468

1985, Mar. 14   *Perf. 12½ Vert.*
1530 A468 2.70k Jan-Ove Waldner,
      Sweden   1.00 35
1531 A468 3.20k Cai Zhenhua, China   1.25 55

Clavichord — A469

Key Harp — A470

1985, Apr. 24 — *Perf. 13 Vert.*
1532 A469 2k bluish blk, *buff*   70 20

Perf. 13 on 3 Sides
1533 A470 2.70k dl red brn, *buff*   80 55
  a.   Booklet pane of 6   5.00

Europa 1985.

Provincial Arms Type of 1981
Perf. 14¹/₂x14 on 3 Sides
1985, Apr. 24 — *Photo.*
1534 A410 1.80k Narke   52 15
1535 A410 1.80k Angermanland   52 15
1536 A410 1.80k Varmland   52 15
1537 A410 1.80k Smaland   52 15
  a.   Bklt. pane, 5 each #1534-1537   10.50
      Set value   32

See note after No. 1277.

St. Cnut's Land
Grant to Lund
Cathedral, 900th
Anniv. — A471

Seal of St. Cnut and: No. 1538, Lund Cathedral.
No. 1539, City of Helsingdorg.

Perf. 12¹/₂ on 3 Sides
1985, May 21 — *Engr.*
1538 A471 2k bluish blk & blk   60 15
1539 A471 2k blk & dk red   60 15
  a.   Bklt. pane, 5 each, #1538-1539   6.00
      Set value   25

See Denmark Nos. 777-778.

Stockholmia
'86 — A472

Paintings of old Stockholm: No. 1540, A View of
Slussen, by Sigrid Hjerten (1919). No. 1541,
Skeppsholmen, Winter, by Gosta Adrian-Nilsson
(1919). No. 1542, A Summer's Night by the Rid-
darholmen, by Hilding Linnquist (1945). No.
1543, Klara Church Tower, by Otte Skold (1927).

Lithographed and Engraved
1985, May 21 — *Perf. 12¹/₂*
1540 A472 2k multi   55 45
1541 A472 2k multi   55 45
1542 A472 3k multi   90 85
1543 A472 4k multi   1.25 1.00
  a.   Bklt. pane of 4, #1540-1543   3.50

Swedish Touring Club Cent. — A473

Designs: No. 1544, Af Chapman Hostel, Stockholm. No. 1545, Touring Club Syl Station (c.
1920).

1985, May 21 Engr. *Perf. 12¹/₂ Vert.*
1544 A473 2k blk & dp bl   65 15
      Size: 58x23m
1545 A473 2k dp bl & blk   65 15
  a.   Pair, #1544-1545   1.30 80

Trade Signs — A474

Perf. 12¹/₂ on 3 Sides
1985, Aug. 28 — *Engr.*
1546 A474 10o Music Shop, Slott-
      sgatan   15 15
1547 A474 20o Furrier, Stockholm   15 15
1548 A474 20o Coppersmith, Land-
      skrona   15 15
1549 A474 50o Haberdasher, Stock-
      holm   18 15
1550 A474 2k Shoemaker, Norrko-
      ping   70 20
  a.   Bklt. pane, #1546-1549, 2 #1550   1.75
      Set value   1.00 60

The Dying Spartan Hero, Otryades, 1779,
by Johan Tobias Sergel
A475

Baron Carl Frederik
Adelcrantz, Academy
Pres., 1754, by Alexander
Roslin (1718-
1793) — A476

1985, Aug. 28 — *Perf. 12¹/₂ Vert.*
1551 A475 2k slate blue   70 30
Perf. 12¹/₂ Horiz.
1552 A476 7k dk red brn   2.50 45

Royal Academy of Fine Arts, 250th anniv.

Intl. Youth
Year — A477

Children's drawings: 2k, Participation, by
Marina Karlsson. 2.70k, Development, by Madeleine Andersson. 3.20k, Peace, by Charlotta Ankar.

Lithographed and Engraved
1985, Oct. 12 — *Perf. 12¹/₂x13*
1553   Sheet of 3   3.00 3.25
  a.   A477 2k multi   90 1.00
  b.   A477 2.70k multi   90 1.00
  c.   A477 3.20k multi   90 1.00
      Sold for 10k.

Prime Minister Per Albin Hansson (1885-
1946) — A478

Birger Sjoberg (1885-
1929), Journalist,
Novelist, Poet — A479

1985, Oct. 12 Engr. *Perf. 12¹/₂ Vert.*
1556 A478 1.60k black & red   55 35
Perf. 12¹/₂ Horiz.
1557 A479 4k dk blue grn   1.25 35

Christmas 1985 — A480

15th cent. religious paintings by Albertus Pictor.

Perf. 13x12¹/₂ on 3 Sides
1985, Nov. 21 — *Engr.*
1558 A480 1.80k Annunciation   52 35
1559 A480 1.80k Birth of Christ   52 35
1560 A480 1.80k Adoration of the Ma-
      gi   52 35
1561 A480 1.80k Mary as the Apoca-
      lyptic Virgin   52 35
  a.   Bklt. pane, 3 each #1558-1561   6.50

Nobel
Laureates in
Literature
A481

Authors: No. 1562, William Faulkner (1897-
1962), 1949, Southern United States. No. 1563,
Halldor Kiljan Laxness (b.1902), 1955, Iceland.
No. 1564, Miguel Angel Asturias (1899-1974),
1967, Guatemala. No. 1565, Yasunari Kawabata
(1899-1972), 1968, Japan. No. 1566, Patrick
White (b. 1912), 1973, Australia.

Lithographed and Engraved
1985, Nov. 21 — *Perf. 13 Horiz.*
1562 A481 2.70k myr grn   80 60
1563 A481 2.70k dp brn, chlky bl &
      myr grn   80 60
1564 A481 2.70k myr grn & tan   80 60
1565 A481 2.70k chlky bl & myr grn   80 60
1566 A481 2.70k chlky bl & ocher   80 60
  a.   Bklt. pane of 5, #1562-1566   4.00
      Nos. 1562-1566 (5)   4.00 3.00

Types of 1983-85
Engr., Litho. (1.80k, 3.20k, 6k)
1986-89 — *Perf. 12¹/₂ Vert.*
1567 A436b 1.70k dk violet   52 15
1568 A436b 1.80k brt violet   48 15
1569 A436c 2.10k dk blue   55 15
1570 A436c 2.20k int blue   65 15
1571 A436c 2.30k dk ol grn   78 15
1572 A436c 2.80k emerald   75 35
1573 A436c 2.90k dk green   80 30
1574 A436c 3.10k dk brown   90 30
1575 A436b 3.20k yellow brn   90 40
1576 A436c 3.30k dk rose brn   1.10 42
1577 A436d 3.40k dk red   90 45
1578 A436d 3.60k green   1.00 60
1579 A436d 3.90k violet blue   1.65 65
1580 A436b 6k blue green   2.00 25
      Nos. 1567-1580 (14)   12.98 4.47

Issue dates: 2.10, 2.90, 3.40k, Jan. 23. 1.70,
2.80k, Feb. 20. 1.80, 3.10, 3.20, 3.60, 6k, Jan. 27,
1987. 2.20k, Jan. 29, 1988. 2.30, 3.30, 3.90k,
Apr. 20, 1989.
See No. 1796.

Waterbirds — A484   A485

Perf. 13 on 2 or 3 Sides
1986, Jan. 23 — *Engr.*
1582 A484 2.10k Eider   55 15
1583 A484 2.10k Smaspov   55 15
  a.   Bklt. pane, 5 each #1582-1583   5.50
1584 A484 2.30k Storlom   75 15

Lithographed and Engraved
1986, Jan. 23 — *Perf. 13*
1585 A485 2k #33a, cancel   55 55
1586 A485 2k Stamp engraver   55 55
1587 A485 3k #268, 271, US #836   90 90
1588 A485 4k Boy soaking stamps   1.10 1.10
  a.   Bklt. pane of 4, #1585-1588   3.25

STOCKHOLMIA '86. See US Nos. 2198-2201a.

Swedish PO, 350th   Sundial — A487
Anniv. — A486

Lithographed and Engraved
1986, Feb. 20 — *Perf. 13x12¹/₂*
1589 A486 2.10k org yel & dk bl   70 15
  a.   Bklt pane of 8   5.75

1986, Feb. 20 Engr. *Perf. 13 Horiz.*
Design: No. 1591, Motto of the Swedish
Academy.
1590 A487 1.70k dk bl & lake, *gray*   55 35
1591 A487 1.70k grn & dk red, *gray*   55 35
  a.   Pair, #1590-1591   1.25 1.10

Royal Swedish Academy of Letters, History and
Antiquities, and Swedish Academy, bicents.

Provincial Arms Type of 1981
Perf. 15x14¹/₂ on 3 Sides
1986, Apr. 23 — *Photo.*
1592 A410 1.90k Harjedalen   50 15
1593 A410 1.90k Uppland   50 15
1594 A410 1.90k Halland   50 15
1595 A410 1.90k Lapland   50 15
  a.   Bklt. pane, 5 each #1592-1595   10.00

See note after No. 1277.

King Carl XVI   Royal
Gustaf — A488   Cipher — A489

40th birthday: No. 1598, King presenting Nobel
Prize for literature to Czeslaw Milosz, 1980. No.
1600, Royal family at Soldien palace

Lithographed and Engraved
1986, Apr. 23 — *Perf. 12 on 3 Sides*
1596 A488 2.10k grnsh pale grn   60 30
1597 A489 2.10k dk bl, pink & gold   60 30
1598 A488 2.10k dk bl & pale bl   60 30
1599 A489 2.10k dk bl, pale grn & gold   60 30
1600 A488 2.10k blk & pale pink   60 30
  a.   Bklt. pane, 2 each #1596-1600   6.00

Olof Palme (1927-
1986), Prime
Minister — A490

Perf. 13 on 3 Sides
1986, Apr. 11 — *Engr.*
1601 A490 2.10k dk lilac rose   85 70
1602 A490 2.90k grnsh black   1.10 85
  a.   Bklt. pane, 5 each #1601-1602   10.00

Nordic Cooperation   Europa
Issue — A491   1986 — A492

Sister towns.

1986, May 27 Engr. Perf. 13 Vert.
1603 A491 2.10k Uppsala 70 15
1604 A491 2.90k Eskilstuna 1.00 65

1986, May 27 Perf. 13 Horiz.
1605 A492 2.10k Automotive pollutants 70 20

Perf. 13 on 3 Sides
1606 A492 2.90k Industrial pollutants 1.00 70
a. Booklet pane of 6 6.00

STOCKHOLMIA '86 — A493

Designs: No. 1607, Mail handling terminal, Tomteboda, 1986. No. 1608, Railroad mail car, 19th cent. No. 1609, Post Office, 18th cent. No. 1610, Postman, 17th cent.

Lithographed and Engraved
1986, Aug. 29 Perf. 13
1607 A493 2.10k multi 5.00 5.00
1608 A493 2.10k multi 5.00 5.00
1609 A493 2.90k multi 5.00 5.00
1610 A493 2.90k multi 5.00 5.00
a. Bklt. pane of 4, #1607-1610 20.00

Bklt. sold for 40k, including 30k ticket to STOCKHOLMIA '86.

Souvenir Sheet

World Class Athletes in Track and Field — A494

Designs: a, Ann-Louise Skoglund, 400-meter hurdle, 1982. b, Dag Wennlund, 1986, and Eric Lemming, c. 1900, javelin. c, Standing high jumper and Patrik Sjoberg, high jump, 1985. d, Anders Garderud, 300-meter steeplechase record-holder.

1986, Oct. 18 Engr. Perf. 12½
1611 Sheet of 4 3.75 3.75
a.-d. A494 2.10k, any single 85 85

No. 1611 sold for 11k to benefit philatelic organizations.

Intl. Peace Year — A495   Amnesty Intl., 25th Anniv. — A496

1986, Oct. 18 Perf. 13 Vert.
1612 A495 3.40k bluish blk & emer grn 1.10 75
1613 A496 3.40k dk red & bluish blk 1.10 75
a. Pair, #1612-1613 2.50 2.25

Keep up to date with all new stamp issues by subscribing to the "Scott Stamp Monthly". Please call 1-800-488-5351 for more information.

Christmas — A497

Winter village scenes.

Perf. 13x12½ on 3 Sides
1986, Nov. 25 Litho. & Engr.
1614 1.90k Postal van 65 38
1615 1.90k Postman on bicycle 65 38
1616 1.90k Children, sled 65 38
1617 1.90k Child mailing letter 65 38
a. A497 Block of 4, #1614-1617 2.75 1.90
b. Bklt. pane of 12, 3 #1617a 8.50

Nobel Peace Prize Laureates — A498

Designs: No. 1618, Bertha von Suttner, 1905. No. 1619, Carl von Ossietzky, 1935. No. 1620, Albert Luthuli, 1960. No. 1621, Martin Luther King, Jr., 1964. No. 1622, Mother Teresa, 1979.

1986, Nov. 25 Engr. Perf. 13 Horiz.
1618 A498 2.90k brt bl, blk & hn brn 80 70
1619 A498 2.90k blk & hn brn 80 70
1620 A498 2.90k brt bl, blk & brn blk 80 70
1621 A498 2.90k brn blk & hn brn 80 70
1622 A498 2.90k blk, brt bl & hn brn 80 70
a. Bklt pane of 5, #1618-1622 4.00

Conservation Type of 1983
Perf. 13 on 3 Sides
1987, Mar. 10 Engr.
1623 A446 2.10k Parnassius mnemosyne 60 20
1624 A446 2.10k Gentianella campestris 60 20
a. Booklet pane, 5 each #1623-1624 6.00

Perf. 13 Horiz.
1625 A446 2.50k Osmoderma eremita 85 15
1626 A446 4.20k Arnica montana 1.40 25

Swedish Aviation Industry A500

1987, Mar. 10 Perf. 13 Vert.
1627 A500 25k Saab SF340 6.75 60

Europa 1987 — A501

Designs: Nos. 1628-1629, City Library, Asplund. No. 1630, Lewerentz Marcus Church.

1987, May 14 Engr. Perf. 13 Vert.
1628 A501 2.10k int blk & grn 68 25

Perf. 13 on 3 Sides
1629 A501 3.10k emer grn & red brn 80 70
1630 A501 3.10k emer grn & sep 80 70
a. Bklt. pane, 3 each #1629-1630 5.00

Illustrations from Children's Novels by Astrid Lindgren (b. 1907) — A502

Perf. 13x12½ on 3 Sides
1987, May 14 Litho. & Engr.
1631 A502 1.90k Karlsson Pa Taket 50 25
1632 A502 1.90k Barnen and Bullerbyn 50 25
1633 A502 1.90k Madicken 50 25
1634 A502 1.90k Mio, Min Mio 50 25
1635 A502 1.90k Nils Karlsson-Pyssling 50 25
1636 A502 1.90k Emil and Lonneberga 50 25
1637 A502 1.90k Ronja Rovardotter 50 25
1638 A502 1.90k Pippi Longstocking 50 25
1639 A502 1.90k Broderna Lejonhjarta 50 25
1640 A502 1.90k Lotta Pa Brakmakargatan 50 25
a. Bklt. pane, 2 each #1631-1640 10.00
Nos. 1631-1640 (10) 5.00 2.50

Medieval Towns — A503

Designs: No. 1641, Hans Brask, Bishop of Linkoping, 16th cent. No. 1642, Nykopingshus Castle.

1987, May 14 Engr. Perf. 12½ Vert.
1641 A503 2.10k blk, dk vio & yel bis 68 25
1642 A503 2.10k dk vio, blk & yel bis 68 25
a. Pair, #1641-1642 1.40 1.00

Swedes in the Service of Mankind A504

Designs: No. 1643, Raoul Wallenberg, Swedish diplomat in Budapest during World War II. No. 1644, Dag Hammarskjold (1905-1961), UN secretary-general. No. 1645, Folke Bernadotte af Wisborg (1895-1948), organizer of the Red Cross operation that saved thousands from Nazi death camps.

Perf. 12½ Horiz.
1987, Aug. 10 Engr.
1643 A504 3.10k blue 80 75
1644 A504 3.10k green 80 75
1645 A504 3.10k brown violet 80 75
a. Bklt. pane, 2 each #1643-1645 5.00

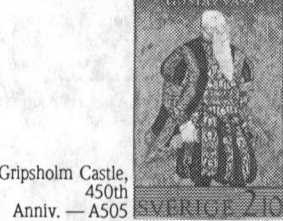

Gripsholm Castle, 450th Anniv. — A505

Paintings from the Royal Castle Collection, Gripsholm: No. 1646, King Gustav I Vasa (d. 1560), artist unknown. No. 1647, Blue Tiger, 1673, favorite horse of King Charles XI, by D.K. Ehrenstrahl. No. 1648, Hedvig Charlotta Nordenflycht (1718-1763), poet, by Kopia J.H. Scheffel. No. 1649, Gripsholm Castle Outer Courtyard, 17th Cent., 19th cent. lithograph by C.J. Billmark.

1987, Aug. 10 Perf. 13 Vert.
1646 A505 2.10k multi 42 30
1647 A505 2.10k multi 42 30
1648 A505 2.10k multi 42 30
1649 A505 2.10k multi 42 30
a. Bklt. pane of 8, 2 strips of #1646-1649 with gutter btwn. 4.50

Botanical Gardens — A506

Designs: No. 1650, Victoria cruziana (water lily), Victoria House, Bergian Garden, c. 1790, Stockholm University. No. 1651, Layout of baroque palace garden, by Carl Harleman (1700-1753), Uppsala University. No. 1652, White anemones, rock garden, Gothenberg Botanical Gardens, 1923. No. 1653, Tulip tree blossoms, Academy Garden, c. 1860, Lund University.

1987, Oct. 10 Engr. Perf. 13 Vert.
1650 A506 2.10k multi 42 30
1651 A506 2.10k multi 42 30
1652 A506 2.10k multi 42 30
1653 A506 2.10k multi 42 30
a. Bklt. pane, 2 each #1650-1653 with gutter between 4.50

The Circus in Sweden, Bicent. — A507

Litho. & Engr.
1987, Oct. 10 Perf. 13
1654 A507 2.10k Juggler, clown 85 65
1655 A507 2.10k High wire 85 65
1656 A507 2.10k Equestrian 85 65
a. Bklt. pane of 3, #1654-1656 2.55

Stamp Day. Sold for 8k.

Christmas — A508

Customs: No. 1657, Putting porridge in the stable for the gray Christmas elf. No. 1658, Watering horses at a north-running stream on Boxing Day. No. 1659, Sled-race home from church on Christmas Day. No. 1660, Hanging out sheaves of wheat to foretell a good harvest.

Perf. 13 on 3 Sides
1987, Nov. 25 Litho.
1657 A508 2k multi 52 30
1658 A508 2k multi 52 30
1659 A508 2k multi 52 30
1660 A508 2k multi 52 30
a. Bklt. pane, 3 each #1657-1660 6.50

Nobel Prize Winners in Physics A509

Space and diagram or formula: No. 1661, Antony Hewish, Great Britain, 1974. No. 1662, Subrahmanyan Chandrasekhar, US, 1983. No. 1663, William Fowler, US, 1983. No. 1664, Arno Penzias and Robert Wilson, US, 1978. No. 1665, Martin Ryle, Great Britain, 1974.

1987, Nov. 25 Engr. Perf. 13
1661 A509 2.90k dark blue 85 65
1662 A509 2.90k blk 85 65
1663 A509 2.90k dark blue 85 65

1664	A509 2.90k dark blue	85	65
1665	A509 2.90k blk	85	65
a.	Bklt. pane of 5, #1661-1665	4.25	

Inland Boats — A510

1988, Jan. 29   **Engr.**   *Perf. 13*

1666	A510 3.10k Skiff, Lake Hjalmaren	80	70
1667	A510 3.10k Village boat, Lake Vattern	80	70
1668	A510 3.10k Rowboat, Byske	80	70
1669	A510 3.10k Flat-bottomed rowboat, Asnen	80	70
1670	A510 3.10k Ice boat, Lake Vanern	80	70
1671	A510 3.10k Church boat, Lake Locknesjon	80	70
a.	Bklt. pane of 6, #1666-1671	5.00	

A511

A512

Settling of New Sweden, 350th Anniv. — A513

Designs: No. 1672, 17th Cent. European settlers negotiating with American Indians, map of New Sweden, the Swedish ships *Kalmar Nyckel* and *Fogel Grip*, based on an 18th cent. illustration from a Swedish book about the American Colonies. No. 1673, Bishop Hill and painter Olof Krans. No. 1674, Carl Sandburg (1878-1967), author, and Jenny Lind (1820-1867), opera singer known as the "Swedish Nightingale." No. 1675, Charles Lindbergh (1902-1974), and *The Spirit of St. Louis.* No. 1676, American astronaut with Swedish Hasselblad camera on the Moon. No. 1677, Swedish players in National Hockey League.

Litho. & Engr., Engr. (#1674-1675)
Perf. 13x12¹/₂ on 2 or 3 Sides
1988, Mar. 29

1672	A511 3.60k multi	1.00	85
1673	A511 3.60k multi	1.00	85
1674	A512 3.60k brn	1.00	85
1675	A512 3.60k dk bl & brn	1.00	85
1676	A513 3.60k dk bl & yel	1.00	85
1677	A513 3.60k dk red, dk bl & blk	1.00	85
a.	Bklt. pane of 6, #1672-1677	6.00	
	Nos. 1672-1677 (6)	6.00	5.10

See US No. C117 and Finland No. 768.

Conservation Type of 1983

Species Inhabiting Coastal Waters

Perf. 13 on 3 Sides
1988, Mar. 29   **Engr.**

1678	A446 2.20k Haliaetus albicilla	55	20
1679	A446 2.20k Halichoerus grypus	55	20
a.	Bklt. pane, 5 #1678, 5 #1679	5.50	

Perf. 13 Horiz.

1680	A446 4.40k Anguilla anguilla	1.45	25

Midsummer Celebration — A515   Skara Township Millennium — A516

Perf. 12¹/₂ on 3 Sides
1988, May 17   **Litho. & Engr.**

1681	A515 2k Wildflowers in meadow	55	20
1682	A515 2k Rowing	55	20
1683	A515 2k Children making wreaths	55	20
1684	A515 2k Raising maypole	55	20
1685	A515 2k Fiddlers	55	20
1686	A515 2k Ferry	55	20
1687	A515 2k Dancing	55	20
1688	A515 2k Accordion player	55	20
1689	A515 2k Maypole, residence	55	20
1690	A515 2k Bouquet of flowers	55	20
a.	Bklt. pane, 2 each #1681-1690	11.00	
	Nos. 1681-1690 (10)	5.50	2.00

1988, May 17   *Perf. 13 Horiz.*

Design: Detail from Creation, a Skara Cathedral stained-glass window by Bo Beskow, 20th cent.

1691	A516 2.20k multi	78	40

Stora Mining Co., 700th Anniv. — A517   Royal Dramatic Theater, Stockholm, Founded by King Gustav III in 1788 — A518

1988, May 17   **Engr.**

1692	A517 4.40k Mine, 18th cent.	1.60	30

1988, May 17

Design: Scene from *The Queen's Diamond Ornament,* about the murder of King Gustav III at the Royal Opera in 1792.

1693	A518 8k grn, red & blk	2.80	45

Self-portrait, 1923, by Nils Dardel (1888-1943) — A519

Paintings: No. 1695, *Old Age Home in Autumn,* c. 1930, by Vera Nilsson (1888-1979). No. 1696, *Self-portrait,* 1912, by Isaac Grunewald (1899-1979). No. 1697, *Visit of an Eccentric Lady,* 1921, by Dardel. No. 1698, *Soap Bubbles,* 1927, by Nilsson. No. 1699, *The Fair,* 1915, by Grunewald.

Perf. 13 on 3 Sides
1988, Aug. 25   **Litho. & Engr.**
Size: 33x35mm (Nos. 1695, 1698)

1694	A519 2.20k shown	72	45
1695	A519 2.20k multi	72	45
1696	A519 2.20k multi	72	45
1697	A519 2.20k multi	72	45
1698	A519 2.20k multi	72	45
1699	A519 2.20k multi	72	45
a.	Bklt. pane of 6, #1694-1699	4.50	
	Nos. 1694-1699 (6)	4.32	2.70

Europa — A520   Common Swift — A521

Transport and communication.

1988, Aug. 25   **Engr.**   *Perf. 13 Vert.*

1700	A520 2.20k like No. 1701	72	35

Perf. 13 on 3 Sides

1701	A520 3.10k X2 high-speed train	1.00	75
1702	A520 3.10k Steam locomotive, 1887	1.00	75
a.	Bklt. pane, 3 each #1701-1702	6.00	

1988, Aug. 25   *Perf. 12¹/₂ Vert.*

1703	A521 20k brt vio & dk vio	6.50	60

Dan Andersson (1888-1920), Poet, and Manuscript — A522

Forest and Pond, Finnmarken — A523

1988, Oct. 8   **Engr.**   *Perf. 13 Vert.*

1704	A522 2.20k vio, dk bl & dk bl grn	70	35
1705	A523 2.20k vio, dk bl & dk bl grn	70	35
a.	Pair, #1704-1705	1.40	1.00

Soccer — A524

Match scenes: No. 1706, Dribble (Torbjorn Nilsson representing local club matches). No. 1707, Heading the ball (Ralf Edstrom of the national league). No. 1708, Kick (Pia Sundhage, women's soccer).

1988, Oct. 8   **Litho. & Engr.**   *Perf. 13*

1706	A524 2.20k multi	1.20	75
1707	A524 2.20k multi	1.20	75
1708	A524 2.20k multi	1.20	75
a.	Bklt. pane of 3, #1706-1708	3.60	

No. 1708a sold for 8.50k; surtax benefited stamp collecting.

Nobel Laureates in Chemistry A525   Christmas A526

Designs: No. 1709, Willard F. Libby, US, 1960, carbon-14 method of dating artifacts. No. 1710, Karl Ziegler, West Germany, and Guilio Natta, Italy, 1963, catalysts. No. 1711, Aaron Klug, South

Africa, 1982, electron microscopy. No. 1712, Ilya Prigogine, Belgium, 1977, proof that molecular order can occur spontaneously out of chaos.

1988, Nov. 29   *Perf. 12¹/₂ Vert.*

1709	A525 3.10k multi	1.05	70
1710	A525 3.10k multi	1.05	70
1711	A525 3.10k multi	1.05	70
1712	A525 3.10k multi	1.05	70
a.	Bklt. pane, 2 each #1709-1712	8.50	

Perf. 12¹/₂x13 on 3 Sides
1988, Nov. 29

Story of Christ's birth according to Luke (2:7-20): No. 1713, Angels appear to inform shepherds of Christ's birth. No. 1714, Star of Bethlehem, angel, horse. No. 1715, Birds singing. No. 1716, Magi offering gifts. No. 1717, Holy family. No. 1718, Shepherds with palm offering.

1713	A526 2k multi	65	32
1714	A526 2k multi	65	32
1715	A526 2k multi	65	32
1716	A526 2k multi	65	32
1717	A526 2k multi	65	32
1718	A526 2k multi	65	32
a.	Bklt. pane, 2 each #1713-1718	7.80	
	Nos. 1713-1718 (6)	3.90	1.92

Nos. 1713 and 1716, 1714 and 1717, 1715 and 1718 have continuous designs.

Lighthouses A527   Endangered Species A528

Designs: 1.90k, Twin masonry lighthouses, 1832, and concrete lighthouse, 1946, Nidingen, Kattegat Is. 2.70k, Soderarm, Uppland, 1839. 3.80k, Sydostbrotten, Gulf of Bothnia, 1963. 3.90k, Sandhammaren, Skane, c. 1860.

1989, Jan. 31   **Engr.**   *Perf. 13 Vert.*

1719	A527 1.90k multi	65	32
1720	A527 2.70k multi	90	30
1721	A527 3.80k multi	1.25	45
1722	A527 3.90k multi	1.30	75

1989, Jan. 31   *Perf. 13 on 3 Sides*

1723	A528 2.30k Gulo gulo	75	25
1724	A528 2.30k Strix uralensis	75	25
a.	Bklt. pane, 5 each #1723-1724	7.50	

Perf. 13 Horiz.

1725	A528 2.40k Dendrocopos minor	80	15
1726	A528 2.60k Calidris alpina schinzii	88	65
1727	A528 3.30k Hyla arborea	1.10	55
1728	A528 4.60k Ficedula parva	1.55	40
	Nos. 1723-1728 (6)	5.83	2.25

Opening of The Globe Arena, Stockholm A529

Perf. 13 Horiz.
1989, Apr. 14   **Litho. & Engr.**

1729	A529 2.30k Exterior	75	38
1730	A529 2.30k Ice hockey	75	38
1731	A529 2.30k Gymnastics	75	38
1732	A529 2.30k Concert	75	38
a.	Bklt. pane of 4, #1729-1732	3.00	

Nordic Cooperation Issue — A530

Folk costumes.

Perf. 13 Horiz.

1989, Apr. 20		**Litho. & Engr.**
1733 A530 2.30k Woman's wool		
waist	75	30
1734 A530 3.30k Belt pouch	1.10	65

Natl. Labor Movement, Cent. — A531

Europa 1989 — A532

1989, May 17 Engr.	**Perf. 13 Horiz.**	
1735 A531 2.30k dk red & blk	75	25

1989, May 17		**Perf. 13 Vert.**

Children's games: 2.30k, No. 1738, Sailing toy boats. No. 1737, Kick-sledding.

1736 A532 2.30k car lake	75	30

Perf. 13

1737 A532 3.30k greenish blue	1.10	75
1738 A532 3.30k lilac	1.10	75
a. Bklt. pane, 3 #1737, 3 #1738	6.60	

Summer — A533

Perf. 13 on 3 Sides

1989, May 17		**Litho.**
1739 A533 2.10k Sailing	68	35
1740 A533 2.10k Beach ball	68	35
1741 A533 2.10k Cycling	68	35
1742 A533 2.10k Canoeing	68	35
1743 A533 2.10k Angling	68	35
1744 A533 2.10k Camping	68	35
1745 A533 2.10k Croquet	68	35
1746 A533 2.10k Badminton	68	35
1747 A533 2.10k Gardening	68	35
1748 A533 2.10k Sand sculpture	68	35
a. Bklt. pane, 2 each #1739-1748	13.00	
Nos. 1739-1748 (10)	6.80	3.50

Polar Exploration — A534

Swedish polar techniques used in the Arctic (Nos. 1749-1751) and Antarctic: No. 1749, Aircraft, temperature experiment. No. 1750, Settlement, Arctic pass. No. 1751, Icebreaker, experiment. No. 1752, Penguins, tall ship and longboat. No. 1753, Antarctic transports, helicopter. No. 1754, Surveying, albatross.

Perf. 13 on 3 Sides

1989, Aug. 22		**Litho. & Engr.**
Size: 40x43mm (Nos. 1750, 1753)		
1749 A534 3.30k multi	98	75
1750 A534 3.30k multi	98	75
1751 A534 3.30k multi	98	75
1752 A534 3.30k multi	98	75
1753 A534 3.30k multi	98	75
1754 A534 3.30k multi	98	75
a. Bklt. pane of 6, #1749-1754	5.90	
Nos. 1749-1754 (6)	5.88	4.50

Smaland Businesses A535

Perf. 12½x12 on 3 Sides

1989, Aug. 22		**Engr.**
1755 A535 2.30k Furniture	68	55
1756 A535 2.30k Assembly equipment	68	55
1757 A535 2.30k Sewing machines	68	55
1758 A535 2.30k Glassware	68	55
1759 A535 2.30k Metal springs	68	55
1760 A535 2.30k Matchsticks	68	55
a. Bklt. pane of 6, #1755-1760	4.10	
Nos. 1755-1760 (6)	4.08	3.30

Eagle Owl, Bubo bubo A536

1989, Aug. 22		**Perf. 13 Vert.**
1761 A536 30k vio, blk & grn blk	9.00	1.25

Conservation Type of 1983 and

Birds and Coastline, Bla Jungfrun Natl. Park — A537

Perf. 13x12½ on 3 Sides

1989, Sept. 12		**Engr.**
1762 A447 2.40k Rhododendron lapponicum	75	25
1763 A447 2.40k Calypso bulbosa	75	25
a. Bklt. pane, 5 each #1762-1763	7.50	

Perf. 12½ Vert.

1764 A537 4.30k dark blue, blk & brn vio	1.35	80

See Nos. 1776-1780.

Swedish Kennel Club, Cent. — A538

Designs: a, Large spitz. b, Fox hound. c, Small spitz.

1989, Oct. 7 Litho.	**Perf. 13x12½**	
1765 A538 Bklt. pane of 3	3.00	3.00
a.-c. 2.40k any single	1.00	1.00

Sold for 9.50k.

Christmas — A539

Holiday symbols: No. 1766, Top of Christmas tree, wreath. No. 1767, Candelabrum, foods. No. 1768, Star, poinsettia plant, pot rot. No. 1769, Bottom of tree, straw goat, gifts. No. 1770, Gifts, television, girl. No. 1771, Boy, grandfather, girl opening gift.

Perf. 12½x13 on 3 Sides

1989, Nov. 24		**Litho.**
1766 A539 2.10k multi	65	32
1767 A539 2.10k multi	65	32
1768 A539 2.10k multi	65	32
1769 A539 2.10k multi	65	32
1770 A539 2.10k multi	65	32
1771 A539 2.10k multi	65	32
a. Bklt. pane, 2 each #1766-1771	7.80	
Nos. 1766-1771 (6)	3.90	1.92

Nobel Laureates in Physiology — A540

Genetics: No. 1772, Thomas Morgan (1866-1945), US, 1933, chromosomal study of fruit flies to determine laws and mechanism of heredity. No. 1773, James Watson, US, and Francis Crick with Maurice Wilkins, Great Britain, 1962, molecular structure of DNA. No. 1774, Werner Arber, Switzerland, Daniel Nathans and Hamilton Smith, US, 1978, enzymatic cutting of nucleotides to create gene hybrids. No. 1775, Barbara McClintock, botanist, US, 1983, corn color studies that led to theory of gene jumping.

Perf. 12½ Vert.

1989, Nov. 24		**Litho. & Engr.**
1772 A540 3.60k multi	1.15	75
1773 A540 3.60k multi	1.15	75
1774 A540 3.60k multi	1.15	75
1775 A540 3.60k multi	1.15	75
a. Bklt. pane, 2 each #1772-1775	9.20	

Natl. Parks Type of 1989

Designs: No. 1776, Campground, sailboat on lake, Angso Park. No. 1777, Hiking, Pieljekaise Park. 3.70k, Three whooper swans over wetlands, Muddus Park. 4.10k, Deer, lake, Padjelanta Park. 4.80k, Bears, forest, Sanfjallet Park.

Perf. 13 on 3 Sides

1990, Jan. 26		**Engr.**
1776 A537 2.50k multicolored	82	20
1777 A537 2.50k multicolored	82	20
a. Bklt. pane, 5 each #1776-1777	8.25	

Perf. 13 Vert.

1778 A537 3.70k multicolored	1.20	70
1779 A537 4.10k multicolored	1.35	85
1780 A537 4.80k multicolored	1.55	90
Nos. 1776-1780 (5)	5.74	2.85

King and Queen Types of 1985-86 and

Queen Silvia — A541

King Carl XVI Gustaf — A542

King Carl XVI Gustav — A543

Queen Silvia — A544

Perf. 12½ Vert., Horiz. (A541, A542)

1990-95		**Engr.**
1783 A436c 2.50k deep claret	82	15
1785 A542 2.80k dk blue	95	15
1786 A542 2.90k deep green	75	20
1789 A542 3.20k violet	80	20
1792 A542 3.70k dark red brown	1.00	20
1796 A436d 4.60k bright orange	1.50	35
1797 A541 5k deep rose vio	1.80	20
1798 A541 6k deep claret	1.50	1.00
1798A A544 6k dark green	1.50	50
1799 A541 6.50k purple	1.60	50
Nos. 1783-1799 (10)	12.22	3.50

Issued: 2.50k, 4.60k, 1/26; 5k, 3/20/91; 2.80k, 11/20/91; 2.90k, #1798, 1/2/93; 3.20k, 1/17/94; 6.50k, 3/18/94; 3.70k, #1798A, 1/2/95.

This is an expanding set. Numbers will change if necessary.

Viking Heritage A546

Designs: No. 1801, Viking head of carved bone, dragon carving from a molding found in Birka. No. 1802, Three viking longships. No. 1803, Viking town. No. 1804, Bronze statue of pagan fertility god, silver filigree cross. No. 1805, Bishop's crosier, southern Russian carved statue of a deer. No. 1806, Viking longship (stern). No. 1807, Viking longship (bow), horsemen, woman, warrior, wolf. No. 1808, Sword hilts.

Perf. 12x13 on 3 Sides

1990, Mar. 28		**Litho. & Engr.**
1801 A546 2.50k multicolored	82	55
1802 A546 2.50k multicolored	82	55
1803 A546 2.50k multicolored	82	55
1804 A546 2.50k multicolored	82	55
1805 A546 2.50k multicolored	82	55
1806 A546 2.50k multicolored	82	55
1807 A546 2.50k multicolored	82	55
1808 A546 2.50k multicolored	82	55
a. Bklt. pane of 8, #1801-1808	6.60	
Nos. 1801-1808 (8)	6.56	4.40

Nos. 1802-1803, 1806-1807 printed in a continuous design.

Swedish Industrial Safety, Cent. — A547

1990, Mar. 28 Engr.	**Perf. 13 Horiz.**	
1809 A547 2.50k Lumberjack	80	25

Europa 1990 — A548

Post offices.

1990, Mar. 28		**Perf. 13 Vert.**
1810 A548 2.50k Postal Museum, 1720	80	30

Perf. 13 on 3 Sides

1811 A548 3.80k Sollebrunn, 1985	1.20	85
1812 A548 3.80k Vasteras, 1956	1.20	85
a. Bklt. pane, 3 each #1811-1812	7.25	

World Equestrian Games, Stockholm A549

Perf. 12½x13

1990, May 15		**Litho. & Engr.**
1813 A549 3.80k Endurance riding	1.25	90
1814 A549 3.80k Jumping tests	1.25	90
1815 A549 3.80k Show jumping	1.25	90
1816 A549 3.80k Dressage	1.25	90
1817 A549 3.80k Volting	1.25	90
1818 A549 3.80k Four-in-hand	1.25	90
a. Bklt. pane of 6, #1813-1818	7.50	
Nos. 1813-1818 (6)	7.50	5.40

Apiculture — A550

Designs: No. 1819, Worker bee collecting nectar. No. 1820, Bee, bilberry flower. No. 1821, Worker bee. No. 1822, Apiary hive. No. 1823, Two bees in honeycomb. No. 1824, Drone, 7 cells, blue green panel. No. 1825, Queen bee, 7 cells, yellow panel. No. 1826, Hive hanging from tree. No. 1827, Bee-keeper. No. 1828, Honey.

1990, May 15   Litho.
1819 A550	2.30k multicolored	75	38
1820 A550	2.30k multicolored	75	38
1821 A550	2.30k multicolored	75	38
1822 A550	2.30k multicolored	75	38
1823 A550	2.30k multicolored	75	38
1824 A550	2.30k multicolored	75	38
1825 A550	2.30k multicolored	75	38
1826 A550	2.30k multicolored	75	38
1827 A550	2.30k multicolored	75	38
1828 A550	2.30k multicolored	75	38
a.	Bklt. pane, 2 each #1819-1828	15.00	
	Nos. 1819-1828 (10)	7.50	3.80

Wasa Nautical Museum — A551

Man-of-war *Wasa*: 2.50k, Bow. 4.60k, Stern.

1990, May 15   Engr.   Perf. 13 Vert.
1829 A551	2.50k org & blk	82	30
1830 A551	4.60k dk bl & org	1.50	85

Dearest Brothers, Sisters and Friends — A552

Proud City A553

Allusions to poetry verses of Carl Michael Bellman (No. 1833) and Evert Taube: No. 1833, Fredmen in the gutter. No. 1834, Happy baker in San Remo. No. 1835, At sea. No. 1836, Violava.

Perf. 13 on 3 Sides
1990, Aug. 8   Litho. & Engr.
1831 A552	2.50k multicolored	82	55
1832 A553	2.50k multicolored	82	55
1833 A552	2.50k multicolored	82	55
1834 A553	2.50k multicolored	82	55
1835 A553	2.50k multicolored	82	55
1836 A553	2.50k multicolored	82	55
a.	Bklt. pane of 6, #1831-1836	4.95	
	Nos. 1831-1836 (6)	4.92	3.30

Paper Production — A554

Designs: No. 1837, Paper production c. 1600. No. 1838, Watermark. No. 1839, Newspaper mastheads. No. 1840, Modern paper production.

1990, Aug. 8   Perf. 12½ Vert.
1837 A554	2.50k multicolored	82	40
1838 A554	2.50k multicolored	82	40
1839 A554	2.50k multicolored	82	40
1840 A554	2.50k multicolored	82	40
a.	Bklt. pane, 2 each #1837-1840	6.60	

Ovedskloster Palace — A555

1990, Aug. 8   Engr.   Perf. 13 Vert.
1841 A555	40k multicolored	13.00	50

See No. 1877.

Photography A556

Litho. & Engr.
1990, Oct. 6   Perf. 12½
1842 A556	2.50k Bellows camera	1.10	1.00
1843 A556	2.50k August Strindberg	1.10	1.00
1844 A556	2.50k 35mm camera	1.10	1.00
a.	Bklt. pane of 3, #1842-1844	3.30	

Stamp Day. Booklet of two panes sold for 20k. Surtax benefited stamp collecting.

Clouds — A557

A558

1990, Oct. 6   Engr.   Perf. 12½ Horiz.
1845 A557	4.50k Cumulus	1.50	45
1846 A557	4.70k Cumulonimbus	1.55	95
1847 A557	4.90k Cirrus	1.60	95
1848 A557	5.20k Alto cumulus	1.75	1.00

1990, Oct. 6   Perf. 12½ Vert.
1849 A558	2.50k shown	82	25
1850 A558	2.50k Women bathing	82	25
a.	Pair, #1849-1850	1.65	1.00

Moa Martinson (1890-1964), author.

Nobel Laureates in Literature — A559

Perf. 13 on 2 Sides
1990, Nov. 27   Engr.
1851 A559	3.80k Par Lagerkvist, 1951	1.30	85
1852 A559	3.80k Ernest Hemingway, 1954	1.30	85
1853 A559	3.80k Albert Camus, 1957	1.30	85
1854 A559	3.80k Boris Pasternak, 1958	1.30	85
a.	Bklt. pane, 2 each #1851-1854	10.40	

See Nos. 1914-1917.

Christmas — A560

Flowers.
Perf. 13 on 3 Sides
1990, Nov. 27   Litho.
1855 A560	2.30k Schlumbergera x buckleyi	80	38
1856 A560	2.30k Helleborus niger	80	38
1857 A560	2.30k Rhododendron simsii	80	38
1858 A560	2.30k Hippeastrum x hortorum	80	38
1859 A560	2.30k Hyacinthus orientalis	80	38
1860 A560	2.30k Euphorbia pulcherrima	80	38
a.	Bklt. pane, 2 each #1855-1860	9.60	
	Nos. 1855-1860 (6)	4.80	2.28

Carta Marina by Olaus Magnus, 1572 — A561

Scandanavia by A. Bureas and J. Blaeus, 1662 — A562

Maps: No. 1863, Celestial globe by Anders Akerman, 1759. No. 1864, Contour map, 1938. No. 1865, Stockholm, 1989. No. 1866, Bedrock Map, Geological Survey, 1984.

Perf. 13 on 3 Sides
1991, Jan. 30   Litho. & Engr.
1861 A561	5k multicolored	1.80	95
1862 A562	5k multicolored	1.80	95
1863 A561	5k multicolored	1.80	95
1864 A561	5k multicolored	1.80	95
1865 A562	5k multicolored	1.80	95
1866 A561	5k multicolored	1.80	95
a.	Bklt. pane of 6, #1861-1866	10.80	
	Nos. 1861-1866 (6)	10.80	5.70

Fish — A563

A564

Perf. 13 on 3 Sides
1991, Jan. 30   Engr.
1867 A563	2.50k shown	90	25
1868 A563	2.50k Siluris glanis, diff.	90	25
b.	Bklt. pane, 5 each #1867-1868	9.00	

Perf. 13 Vert.
1869 A563	5k Cobitis taenia	1.80	20
1870 A563	5.40k Gobio gobio	1.90	1.40
1871 A563	5.50k Noemacheilus barbatulus	1.95	25
1872 A563	5.60k Leucaspius delineatus	2.00	1.00
	Nos. 1867-1872 (6)	9.45	3.35

Palace Type of 1990

Design: 10k, Stromsholm Castle. 20k, Karlberg Castle. 25k, Drottningholm Palace.

1991-92   Engr.   Perf. 13 Vert.
1874 A555	10k blk & olive brn	3.20	35
1876 A555	20k multicolored	7.00	1.10

Size: 58x23mm
1877 A555	25k multicolored	9.00	2.25

Issued: 10k, Aug. 27; 25k, Mar. 20; 20k, May 21, 1992.

This is an expanding set. Numbers will change if necessary.

Perf. 12½x13 on 3 Sides
1991, May 15   Litho.
1883 A564	2.40k Seglora church	80	25
1884 A564	2.40k Flag above park	80	25
1885 A564	2.40k Wedding	80	25
1886 A564	2.40k Animals	80	25
b.	Bklt. pane, 5 each #1883-1886	17.50	

Skansen Park, Stockholm, 100th anniv. Complete booklet of 20 stamps sold for 46k.

A565

A566

Kolmarden Zoological Park, Ostergotland.

Perf. 12½ Horiz.
1991, May 15   Engr.
1887 A565	2.50k Polar bears	90	25
1888 A565	4k Dolphin show	1.45	65

Norden '91.

1991, May 15   Perf. 13 Vert.

Public Parks, Cent.: No. 1890, Dancing in park.
1889 A566	2.50k dark blue	90	25
1890 A566	2.50k dark blue	90	25
a.	Pair, #1889-1890	1.80	1.00

Europa — A567

1991, May 15   Litho. & Engr.   Perf. 13
1891 A567	4k Hermes space plane	1.45	65
1892 A567	4k Freja satellite	1.45	65
1893 A567	4k Tele-X satellite	1.45	65
a.	Bklt. pane of 3, #1891-1893	4.35	

Olympic Champions A568

Designs: No. 1894, Magda Julin, figure skating, Antwerp, 1920. No. 1895, Toini Gustaffson, cross country skiing, Grenoble, 1968. No. 1896, Agneta Andersson, Anna Olsson, two-person kayak, Los Angeles, 1984. No. 1897, Ulrika Knape, diving, Munich, 1972.

Perf. 12x13 on 3 Sides
1991, Aug. 27   Litho. & Engr.
1894 A568	2.50k multicolored	90	40
1895 A568	2.50k multicolored	90	40
1896 A568	2.50k multicolored	90	40
1897 A568	2.50k multicolored	90	40
a.	Bklt. pane, 2 each #1894-1897	7.25	

See Nos. 1937-1940, 1953-1956.

Iron Mining — A569

Designs: No. 1898, Spetal Mine, Norberg. No. 1899, Forsmark Mill. No. 1900, Ironworks forge. No. 1901, Forge welding. No. 1902, Dannemora Mine. No. 1903, Blast furnace, Pershyttan.

Perf. 13 on 2 or 3 Sides
1991, Aug. 27   Engr.

1898	A569 2.50k multicolored	90	40
1899	A569 2.50k multicolored	90	40

Size: 31x26mm

1900	A569 2.50k multicolored	90	40
1901	A569 2.50k multicolored	90	40

Size: 31x40mm

1902	A569 2.50k multicolored	90	40
1903	A569 2.50k multicolored	90	40
a.	Bklt. pane of 6, #1898-1903	5.40	
	Nos. 1898-1903 (6)	5.40	2.40

A570   A571

Details from painting, Coronation of King Gustavus III, by Carl Gustaf Pilo: No. 1904, King Gustavus III. No. 1905, Gustavus with crown held above head. No. 1906, Chancellor Arvid Horn, Archbishop Mattias Beronius holding crown above Gustavus III.

1991, Oct. 5   Engr.   Perf. 13

1904	A570 10k blue	3.75	2.00
1905	A570 10k violet	3.75	2.00

Size: 76x44mm

1906	A570 10k greenish black	3.75	2.50
a.	Bklt. pane of 3, #1904-1906	11.25	

Czeslaw Slania, engraver, 70th birthday. No. 1906a sold for 35k to benefit stamp collecting.

1991, Oct. 5   Litho. & Engr.

Rock musicians.

1907	A571 2.50k Lena Philipsson	90	40
1908	A571 2.50k Roxette	90	40
1909	A571 2.50k Jerry Williams	90	40
a.	Bklt. pane of 3, #1907-1909	2.75	

A572   A573

Christmas: No. 1910, Boy with star, girl with snacks. No. 1911, Family dancing around Christmas tree. No. 1912, Cat beside tree. No. 1913, Child beside bed.

Perf. 12¹/₂x13 on 3 Sides
1991, Nov. 20   Litho.

1910	A572 2.30k multicolored	85	35
1911	A572 2.30k multicolored	85	35
1912	A572 2.30k multicolored	85	35
1913	A572 2.30k multicolored	85	35
b.	Bklt. pane, 3 each #1910-1913	10.25	

Nobel Laureates Type of 1990

Nobel Peace Prize Winners: No. 1914, Jean Henri Dunant, founder of Red Cross. No. 1915, Albert Schweitzer, physician and theologian. No. 1916, Alva Myrdal, disarmament negotiator. No. 1917, Andrei Sakharov, physicist.

1991, Nov. 20   Engr.   Perf. 13 Horiz.

1914	A559 4k carmine	1.50	90
1915	A559 4k dk green	1.50	90
1916	A559 4k dk ultra	1.50	90
1917	A559 4k dk violet	1.50	90
a.	Bklt. pane, 2 each #1914-1917	12.00	

1992, Jan. 30   Engr.   Perf. 13 Horiz.

1918	A573 2.30k red, grn & blk	85	25

Outdoor Life Assoc., cent.

Wild Animals
A574   A575

1992-93   Engr.   Perf. 13 on 3 Sides

1923	A574 2.80k Capreolus capreolus	95	20
1924	A574 2.80k Capreolus capreolus (with fawn)	95	20
b.	Bklt. pane, 5 each #1923-1924	9.50	
1925	A574 2.90k Ursus arctos (2 cubs)	75	25
1926	A574 2.90k Ursus arctos (adult)	75	25
b.	Bklt. pane, 5 each #1925-1926	7.50	

Perf. 13 Vert.

1930	A574 2.80k like #1924	95	15
1931	A574 2.90k like #1925	75	15
1932	A575 3k Mustela putorius, horiz.	78	40
1932A	A575 5.80k Canis lupus, horiz.	1.50	20

Perf. 13 Horiz.

1933	A575 6k Sciurus vulgaris	2.20	65
1934	A575 7k Alces alces	2.60	75
1936	A575 12k Lynx lynx	3.10	85
	Nos. 1923-1936 (11)	15.28	4.05

Issued: Nos. 1923-1924, 1930, 6k, 7k, Jan. 30. #1925-1926, 1931-1932A, 1936, Jan. 28, 1993. This is an expanding set. Numbers will change if necessary.

Olympic Champions Type of 1991

Designs: No. 1937, Gunde Svan, cross-country skiing, Sarajevo, 1984. No. 1938, Thomas Wassberg, cross-country skiing, Lake Placid, 1980. No. 1939, Tomas Gustafson, speed skating, Sarajevo, 1984. No. 1940, Ingemar Stenmark, slalom skiing, Lake Placid, 1980.

Perf. 12x13 on 3 Sides
1992, Jan. 30   Litho. & Engr.

1937	A568 2.80k multicolored	95	48
1938	A568 2.80k multicolored	95	48
1939	A568 2.80k multicolored	95	48
1940	A568 2.80k multicolored	95	48
a.	Bklt. pane, 2 each #1937-1940	7.75	

European Soccer
Championships,
Sweden — A576

1992, Mar. 26   Engr.   Perf. 13 Vert.

1941	A576 2.80k shown	95	25
1942	A576 2.80k Two players	95	25
a.	Pair, #1941-1942	1.90	95

Sweden
No. 1a
A577

Litho. & Engr.
1992, Mar. 26   Perf. 13

1943	A577 2.80k No. 1	1.10	1.00
1944	A577 4.50k No. 1	2.00	1.75
1945	A577 5.50k shown	2.50	1.25
a.	Bklt. pane, #1943-1944, 2 #1945	9.00	

No. 1945a sold for 25k. Surtax benefited stamp collecting.

Sailing
Ships — A578

1992, Mar. 26

1946	A578 4.50k Sprengtporten, 1785	1.50	75
1947	A578 4.50k Superb, 1855	1.50	75
1948	A578 4.50k Big T	1.50	75
		4.50	2.75

Europa. Discovery Race, Spain-Florida (No. 1948).

Children's
Drawings — A579

Perf. 13x12¹/₂ on 3 Sides
1992, May 21   Litho.

1949	A579 2.50k Rabbit	85	25
1950	A579 2.50k Horses	85	25
1951	A579 2.50k Cat	85	25
1952	A579 2.50k Elephant	85	25
a.	Bklt. pane, 5 each #1949-1952	18.00	

Olympic Champions Type of 1991

Designs: No. 1953, Gunnar Larsson, swimming, 1972. No. 1954, Bernt Johansson, cycling, 1976. No. 1955, Anders Garderud, steeplechase, 1976. No. 1956, Gert Fredriksson, kayaking, 1948-1956.

Perf. 12x13 on 3 Sides
1992, May 21   Litho. & Engr.

1953	A568 5.50k multicolored	1.85	92
1954	A568 5.50k multicolored	1.85	92
1955	A568 5.50k multicolored	1.85	92
1956	A568 5.50k multicolored	1.85	92
a.	Bklt. pane, 2 each #1953-1956	16.00	

Greetings
Stamps — A580

Perf. 13x12 on 3 Sides
1992, Aug. 14   Litho.

1957	A580 2.80k Hand with flower	1.10	35
1958	A580 2.80k Cheese	1.10	35
1959	A580 2.80k Baby	1.10	35
1960	A580 2.80k Hand holding pen	1.10	35
b.	Bklt. pane, 2 each #1957-1960	9.00	

88th Inter-Parliamentary Union
Conference, Stockholm — A581

Swedish Patent and
Registration Office,
Cent. — A582

Designs: No. 1961, Riksdag building. No. 1962, First automatic lighthouse, Gustaf Dalen's sun valve.

1992, Aug. 27   Engr.   Perf. 12¹/₂ Vert.

1961	A581 2.80k violet, tan	1.10	25

Perf. 13 Horiz.

1962	A582 2.80k blue & black	1.10	25

Kitchen Maid, by
Rembrandt — A583

The
Triumph of
Venus, by
Francois
Boucher
A584

Paintings: No. 1965, Portrait of a Girl, by Albrecht Durer. No. 1966, Rorstrand Vase, by Erik Wahlberg. No. 1967, Motif from the Seine/The Tree and the River Bend III, by Carl Fredrik Hill. No. 1968, Sergel in his Studio, by Carl Larsson.

Perf. 12¹/₂ on 3 Sides
1992, Aug. 27   Litho. & Engr.

1963	A583 5.50k multicolored	2.00	1.00
1964	A584 5.50k multicolored	2.00	1.00
1965	A583 5.50k multicolored	2.00	1.00
1966	A583 5.50k multicolored	2.00	1.00
1967	A583 5.50k multicolored	2.00	1.00
1968	A583 5.50k multicolored	2.00	1.00
a.	Bklt. pane of 6, #1963-1968	12.00	
	Nos. 1963-1968 (6)	12.00	6.00

National Museum of Fine Arts, 200th anniv.

Prehistoric Animals   1950 Automobiles
A585   A586

Perf. 13x12¹/₂ on 3 Sides
1992, Oct. 3   Litho. & Engr.

1969	A585 2.80k Plateosaurus	1.30	75
1970	A585 2.80k Thoraco- saurus scanicus	1.30	75
1971	A585 2.80k Coelodonta antiquitatis	1.30	75
1972	A585 2.80k Mammuthus primigenius	1.30	75
a.	Bklt. pane, 2 each #1969-1972	10.40	

No. 1972a sold for 27k to benefit stamp collecting.

1992, Oct. 3   Engr.   Perf. 12¹/₂ Vert.

1973	A586 4k Saab 92	1.50	75
1974	A586 4k Volvo P 831	1.50	75
a.	Pair, #1973-1974	3.00	2.25

Birds of the Baltic
Shores — A587

1992, Oct. 3   Litho. & Engr.   Perf. 13

1975	A587 4.50k Pandion haliaetus	1.75	85
1976	A587 4.50k Limosa limosa	1.75	85
1977	A587 4.50k Mergus merganser	1.75	85
1978	A587 4.50k Tadorna tadorna	1.75	85
a.	Bklt. pane of 4, #1975-1978	7.00	

A588   A589

A590   A591

Christmas

Icons: No. 1979, Joachim and Anna, 16th cent. No. 1980, Madonna and Child, 14th cent. No. 1981, Archangel Gabriel, 12th cent. No. 1982, St. Nicholas, 16th cent.

Perf. 12¹/₂x13 on 3 Sides

1992, Nov. 27			Litho. & Engr.	
1979	A588	2.30k multicolored	82	30
1980	A589	2.30k multicolored	82	30
1981	A590	2.30k multicolored	82	30
1982	A591	2.30k multicolored	82	30
a.		Bkt. pane, 3 each #1979-1982	10.00	

See Russia Nos. 6103-6106.

Derek Walcott, Nobel Laureate in Literature, 1992 — A592

1992, Nov. 27   Engr.   Perf. 12¹/₂ Vert.

1983	A592	5.50k Text	1.60	70
1984	A592	5.50k Portrait	1.60	70
a.		Pair, #1983-1984	3.25	2.25

1993 Sports Championships — A593

Perf. 12¹/₂x13 on 3 Sides

1993, Jan. 28			Litho. & Engr.	
1985	A593	6k Gliding	1.55	1.00
1986	A593	6k Wrestling	1.55	1.00
1987	A593	6k Table tennis	1.55	1.00
1988	A593	6k Bowling	1.55	1.00
1989	A593	6k Team handball	1.55	1.00
1990	A593	6k Cross-country skiing	1.55	1.00
a.		Booklet pane of 1985-1990	9.50	
		Nos. 1985-1990 (6)	9.30	6.00

World Gliding Championships, Borlange (#1985). World Wrestling Championships, Stockholm (#1986). World Table Tennis Championships, Gothenburg (#1987). European Bowling Championships, Malmo (#1988). World Team Handball Championships, Gothenburg (#1989). World Cross-Country Skiing Championships, Falun (#1990).

Uppsala Convocation, 400th Anniversary A594

Litho. & Engr.

1993, Mar. 25			Perf. 13 Vert.	
1991	A594	2.90k Stone carving	75	25
1992	A594	2.90k Uppsala Cathedral	75	25
a.		Pair, #1991-1992	1.50	75

A595

Fruit — A596

Fruit — A596a

Tourist Attractions in Gothenburg: No. 1993, Roller coaster Liseberg Loop, Liseburg Amusement Park. No. 1994, Fountain of Poseidon, by Carl Milles.

1993, Mar. 25

1993	A595	3.50k multicolored	90	55
1994	A595	3.50k multicolored	90	55
a.		Pair, #1993-1994	1.80	1.25

1993-94   Engr.   Perf. 12¹/₂ on 3 Sides

1995	A596	2.40k Ribes uva crispa	62	30
1996	A596	2.40k Pyrus communis	62	30
b.		Booklet pane, 5 each #1996-1996	6.25	
1997	A596	2.80k Victoria plum	70	30
1998	A596	2.80k Opal plum	70	30
b.		Booklet pane, 5 each #1997-1998	7.00	
2001	A596a	3.35k Ribes nigrum	90	35
2002	A596a	3.35k Rubus idaeus	90	35
a.		Booklet pane, 5 each #2001-2002	9.00	
		Complete booklet, #2002a	9.00	

Perf. 12¹/₂ Vert.

2004	A596	2.40k Prunus avium	62	30
2005	A596	2.80k James Grieve apple	70	20
2008	A596a	3.35k Fragaria ananassa	90	35
		Nos. 1995-2008 (9)	6.66	2.75

Issued: #1995-1996, 2004, 3/25/93; #1997-1998, 2005, 1/17/94; 3.35k, 1/2/95.
This is an expanding set. Numbers may change.

Oxe-eye Daisy — A597

Poppy — A598

Buttercup A599

Bluebell A600

Perf. 12¹/₂x13 on 3 Sides

1993, May 21			Litho.	
2013	A597	2.60k multicolored	72	35
2014	A598	2.60k multicolored	72	35
2015	A599	2.60k multicolored	72	35
2016	A600	2.60k multicolored	72	35
b.		Booklet pane, 5 each #2013-2016	14.50	

Contemporary Art — A601

Europa: No. 2017, Oguasark, by Olle Baertling (1911-81). No. 2018, Ade-Lidic-Nander II, by

---

Oyvind Fahlstrom (1928-76), horiz. No. 2019, The Cubist Chair, by Otto G. Carlsund (1897-1948).

1993, May 21   Litho. & Engr.   Perf. 13

2017	A601	5k multicolored	1.30	60
2018	A601	5k multicolored	1.30	60
2019	A601	5k multicolored	1.30	60
a.		Booklet pane of 3, #2017-2019	4.00	

Butterflies A602

1993, May 21   Perf. 12¹/₂ Horiz.

2020	A602	6k Papilio machaon	1.75	85
2021	A602	6k Nymphalis antiopa	1.75	85
2022	A602	6k Colias palaeno	1.75	85
2023	A602	6k Euphydryas maturna	1.75	85
a.		Booklet pane, 2 each #2020-2023	14.00	

A603   A604

A605   A606

Greetings

Perf. 13 on 3 Sides

1993, Aug. 6			Litho.	
2024	A603	2.90k multicolored	75	25
2025	A604	2.90k multicolored	75	30
2026	A605	2.90k multicolored	75	30
2027	A606	2.90k multicolored	75	30
b.		Booklet pane, 3 each #2024, 2026, 2 each #2025, 2027	7.50	

Sea Birds A607

Perf. 12¹/₂ Horiz.

1993, Aug. 26			Engr.	
2028	A607	5k Mergus serrator	1.30	75
2029	A607	5k Melanitta fusca	1.30	75
2030	A607	5k Aythya fuligula	1.30	75
2031	A607	5k Somateria mollissima	1.30	75
a.		Booklet pane, 2 each #2028-2031	10.40	

A608

A609

1993, Oct. 2   Engr.   Perf. 13 Vert.

2032	A608	2.90k Modern echo sounding	75	25
2033	A608	2.90k 1643 Method	75	25
a.		Pair, #2032-2033	1.50	65

Hydrographic survey.

1993, Oct. 2   Engr.   Perf. 13

2034	A609	8k King holding flag	2.00	1.65
2035	A609	10k King	2.50	1.90

2036	A609	10k Queen Silvia	2.50	1.90

Size: 75x43mm

2037	A609	12k Royal family	3.00	2.50
a.		Booklet pane, #2034-2037	10.00	

Reign of King Carl XVI Gustaf, 20th anniv.

Christmas — A610   A611

Perf. 12¹/₂ on 3 Sides

1993, Nov. 25			Engr.	
2038	A610	2.40k Plaited heart	60	25
2039	A610	2.40k Straw goat	60	25
b.		Booklet pane, 5 each #2038-2039	6.25	

1993, Nov. 25   Engr.   Perf. 12¹/₂ Vert.

Designs: No. 2040, Toni Morrison, Nobel laureate in literature, 1993. No. 2041, Stockholm City Hall.

2040	A611	6k red brown & brown	1.60	1.00
2041	A611	6k multicolored	1.60	1.00
a.		Pair, #2040-2041	3.25	2.50

A612   A613

1994, Jan. 17   Perf. 12¹/₂ Vert.

2042	A612	5k Mother Svea	1.25	50

European Economic Assoc. agreement.

1994   Engr.   Perf. 13 on 3 Sides

Domestic Animals: No. 2047, North Sweden horse, vert. No. 2048, Two horses, vert. No. 2049, Red polled cattle, vert. No. 2050, Goat, vert. 3.10k, Swedish dwarf poultry. No. 2055, Gotland sheep. 6.40k, Mountain cow. 7.40k, Scanian goose. 7.50k, Yellow duck.

2047	A613	3.20k multicolored	80	25
2048	A613	3.20k multicolored	80	25
a.		Booklet pane, 5 each #2047-2048	8.00	
2049	A613	3.70k multicolored	1.00	30
2050	A613	3.70k multicolored	1.00	30
a.		Booklet pane, 5 each #2049-2050	10.00	
		Complete booklet, #2050a	10.00	

Perf. 13 Vert.

2054	A613	3.10k multicolored	80	40
2055	A613	3.20k multicolored	80	20
2059	A613	6.40k multicolored	1.50	40
2060	A613	7.40k multicolored	2.00	1.00
2060A	A613	7.50k multicolored	2.00	1.00
		Nos. 2047-2060A (9)	10.70	4.10

Issued: #2047-2048, 2055, 2059, 1/17/94; #2049-2050, 3.10k, 1/2/95; 7.40k, 7.50k, 3/17/95.
This is an expanding set. Numbers may change.

Cats — A614

Litho. & Engr.

1994, Mar. 18			Perf. 13	
2061	A614	4.50k Siamese	1.10	65
2062	A614	4.50k Persian	1.10	65
2063	A614	4.50k European	1.10	65
2064	A614	4.50k Abyssinian	1.10	65
a.		Booklet pane of 4, #2061-2064	4.50	

Roman De La
Rose — A615

Swedish,
French
Flags
A616

Swedish-French cultural relations: No. 2067,
House of the Nobility, designed by Simon and Jean
de la Vallee. No. 2068, Household Chores, by Hil-
lestrom. No. 2069, Banquet for Gustavus III at the
Trianon, 1784, by Lafrensen. No. 2070, Charles
XIV John, by Gerard.

Litho. & Engr., Litho. (#2066)
1994, Mar. 18   Perf. 13 on 3 Sides

2065	A615	5k multicolored	1.25	1.00
2066	A616	5k multicolored	1.25	1.00
2067	A615	5k multicolored	1.25	1.00
2068	A616	5k multicolored	1.25	1.00
2069	A616	5k multicolored	1.25	1.00
2070	A615	5k multicolored	1.25	1.00
a.		Booklet pane of 6, #2065-2070	7.50	

See France Nos. 2410-2415.

SWEDEN

BUYING AND SELLING,
QUALITY STAMPS OF
SWEDEN MINT NH.

EUROPE

From Andorre to Turkey,
Europe (CEPT) and
The English Area,
Mint NH Sets.
Whether you're buying or selling,
my prices are very reasonable. The
list contains well over 12,000 sets,
with all kinds of topicals, where
you will find my selling prices,
and the price I pay for each set that
I need.

The Italian Area

Including San Marino, Vatican
City, Trieste A & B, Mint NH, LH
or Used, and some singles.

SEND A #10 55¢ SASE
TODAY FOR YOUR FREE
COPY OF OUR PRICE LIST!
You will be glad you did.

F. COPPOLA

P.O. Box 181022
Utica, MI 48318-1022

Roses — A617

Perf. 12¹/₂x13 on 3 Sides
1994, May 11   Litho.

2071	A617	3.20k Nyponros rosa dumalis	85	25
2072	A617	3.20k Rosa alba maxima	85	25
2073	A617	3.20k Tuscany superb	85	25
2074	A617	3.20k Peace	85	25
2075	A617	3.20k Quatre saisons	85	25
a.		Booklet pane, 2 each #2071-2075	8.50	

Swedish
Design — A618

Designs: No. 2076, Vase with Irises, by Gunnar
Wennerberg, 1897. No. 2077, Table and Chair, by
Carl Malmsten; Wallpaper, by Uno Ahren, 1917.
No. 2078, Cabinet, 1940s, and textile, 1920s, by
Josef Franck. No. 2079, Fireworks Bowl, by
Edward Hald, 1921. No. 2080, Silver water jug, by
Wiwen Nilsson, 1941. No. 2081, Towel, by Astrid
Sampe; Plate, by Stig Lindberg; Fork and Spoon, by
Sigurd Persson, 1955.

Perf. 12¹/₂ on 3 Sides
1994, May 11   Litho. & Engr.

2076	A618	6.50k multicolored	1.75	1.25
2077	A618	6.50k multicolored	1.75	1.25
2078	A618	6.50k multicolored	1.75	1.25
2079	A618	6.50k multicolored	1.75	1.25
2080	A618	6.50k multicolored	1.75	1.25
2081	A618	6.50k multicolored	1.75	1.25
a.		Booklet pane of 6, #2076-2081	10.50	

1994 World Cup Soccer Championships,
US — A619

1994, May 11   Engr.   Perf. 12¹/₂ Vert.

2082	A619	3.20k red & blue	85	25

First
Manned
Moon
Landing,
25th
Anniv.
A620

1994, May 11

2083	A620	6.50k multicolored	1.75	85

Greetings — A621

Perf. 12¹/₂ on 3 Sides
1994, Aug. 5   Litho.

2084	A621	3.20k Cat	80	25
2085	A621	3.20k Snail	80	25
2086	A621	3.20k Frog	85	30
2087	A621	3.20k Dog	85	30
a.		Booklet pane, 3 each #2084-2085, 2 each #2086-2087	8.25	

Swedish
Explorers — A622

Europa: No. 2088, Erland Nordenskiold (1877-
1932), explored South America. No. 2089, Eric
Von Rosen (1879-1948), explored Africa. No. 2090,
Sten Bergman (1895-1975), explored Asia and the
Pacific.

Litho. & Engr.
1994, Aug. 26   Perf. 12¹/₂

2088	A622	5.50k multicolored	1.50	1.00
2089	A622	5.50k multicolored	1.50	1.00
2090	A622	5.50k multicolored	1.50	1.00
a.		Booklet pane of 3, #2088-2090	4.50	

Finland-Sweden Track
and Field
Meet — A623

Designs: No. 2091, Seppo Raty, Finland, javelin.
No. 2092, Patrick Sjoberg, Sweden, high jump.

1994, Aug. 26   Perf. 12¹/₂ on 3 Sides

2091	A623	4.50k multicolored	1.25	90
2092	A623	4.50k multicolored	1.25	90
a.		Booklet pane, 2 each #2091-2092	5.00	

See Finland Nos. 942-943.

Johan Helmich
Roman (1694-1758),
Composer — A624

Design: No. 2094, Opera House, Gothenburg.

1994, Aug. 26   Engr.   Perf. 12¹/₂ Vert.

2093	A624	3.20k multicolored	80	25
2094	A624	3.20k multicolored	80	25

Yes & No
Stamps — A625

1994, Oct. 1   Litho.   Perf. 12¹/₂ Vert.

2095	A625	3.20k Ja	85	35
2096	A625	3.20k Nej	85	35

See Nos. 2107-2108.

World Wildlife
Fund — A626

Designs: No. 2097, Sterna caspia. No. 2098,
Haliaeetus albicilla. No. 2099, Dendrocopos
leucotos. No. 2100, Anser erythropus.

Litho. & Engr.
1994, Oct. 1   Perf. 12¹/₂

2097	A626	5.50k multicolored	1.50	1.00
2098	A626	5.50k multicolored	1.50	1.00
2099	A626	5.50k multicolored	1.50	1.00
2100	A626	5.50k multicolored	1.50	1.00
a.		Booklet pane of 4, #2097-2100	6.00	
		Nos. 2097-2100 (4)	6.00	4.00

Frans G. Bengtsson (1894-1954),
Writer — A627

1994, Oct. 1   Engr.   Perf. 12¹/₂ Vert.

2101	A627	6.40k multicolored	1.75	65

Nobel Laureates in
Literature
A628

Christmas
A629

Designs: 4.50k, Erik Axel Karlfeldt (1864-1931).
5.50k, Eyvind Johnson (1900-76). 6.50k, Harry
Martinson (1904-78).

1994, Nov. 11

2102	A628	4.50k multicolored	1.25	90
2103	A628	5.50k multicolored	1.50	1.00
2104	A628	6.50k multicolored	1.75	1.25
		Nos. 2102-2104 (3)	4.50	3.15

Perf. 12¹/₂x13 on 3 Sides
1994, Nov. 11   Litho. & Engr.

Scenes from medieval altar pieces: No. 2105,
Annunciation. No. 2106, Flight to Egypt.

2105	A629	2.80k multicolored	75	35
2106	A629	2.80k multicolored	75	35
a.		Booklet pane, 5 each #2105-2106	7.50	

Yes & No Type of 1994
1995, Jan. 2   Litho.   Perf. 12¹/₂ Vert.

2107	A625	3.70k Ja	1.00	30
2108	A625	3.70k Nej	1.00	30

Houses
A630

Designs: No. 2109, Country cottage. No. 2110,
Soldier's log house. No. 2111, Farmhouse court-
yard. No. 2112, Timbered farmhouse. No. 2113,
Manor house.

Perf. 14 Horiz.
1995, Mar. 17   Litho. & Engr.

2109	A630	3.70k multicolored	1.00	50
2110	A630	3.70k multicolored	1.00	50
2111	A630	3.70k multicolored	1.00	50
2112	A630	3.70k multicolored	1.00	50
2113	A630	3.70k multicolored	1.00	50
a.		Booklet pane, #2109-2113	5.00	
		Complete booklet, #2113a	5.00	

1995 Ice Hockey World
Championships — A631

1995 World Track &
Field Championships
A632

Litho. & Engr.
1995, Mar. 17   **Perf. 13 Vert.**
2114 A631 3.70k multicolored   1.00   50

Perf. 13 Horiz.
2115 A632 3.70k multicolored   1.00   50

Wood Sculptures, by Bror Hjorth
A633   A634

Europa: Nos. 2116, 2118, Walt Whitman, Christ, Socrates. Nos. 2117, 2119, Patrice Lumumba, Albert Schweitzer, children dancing.

1995, Mar. 17   Litho.   **Perf. 13**
2116 A633 5k multicolored   1.40   70
2117 A634 5k multicolored   1.40   70
2118 A633 6k multicolored   1.65   82
2119 A634 6k multicolored   1.65   82
   a. Booklet pane, #2116-2119   6.25
   Complete booklet, 2 #2119a   12.50
   Nos. 2116-2119 (4)   6.10 3.04

Swedish Membership in European Union — A635

1995, Mar. 17   **Perf. 13 Vert.**
2120 A635 6k multicolored   1.65   82

Rock Speedwell   Cloudberry
A636   A637

Mountain Heath — A638   Alpine Arnica — A639

Perf. 13 on 3 Sides
1995, May 12   Litho.
2121 A636 3.70k multicolored   1.00   45
2122 A637 3.70k multicolored   1.10   55
2123 A638 3.70k multicolored   1.00   45
2124 A639 3.70k multicolored   1.10   55
   a. Booklet pane, 3 each #2121, 2123, 2 each #2122, 2124   10.50
   Complete booklet, #2124a   10.50
   Nos. 2121-2124 (4)   4.20 2.00

Tourist Attractions — A640

Designs: No. 2125, Canal boat Wilhelm Tham on Gota Canal. No. 2126, Sail boat anchored on Lake Vattern.

1995, May 12   Engr.
2125 A640 5k dark green   1.40 1.10
2126 A640 5k dark violet   1.40 1.10
   a. Booklet pane, 2 each #2125-2126   5.75
   Complete booklet, #2126a   5.75

Trams A641

Designs: No. 2127, Gothenburg, c. 1900. No. 2128, Norrkoping, 1905. No. 2129, Helsingborg, 1921. No. 2130, Kiruna, 1958. No. 2131, Stockholm, 1967.

1995, May 12   **Perf. 13 Horiz.**
2127 A641 7.50k rose claret   2.00 1.75
2128 A641 7.50k dp brown violet   2.00 1.75
2129 A641 7.50k dk green   2.00 1.75
2130 A641 7.50k dk gray violet   2.00 1.75
2131 A641 7.50k dk violet blue   2.00 1.75
   a. Booklet pane, #2127-2131   10.00
   Complete booklet, #2131a   10.00

SEMI-POSTAL STAMPS

Type of 1872-91 Issues Surcharged in Dark Blue

Perf. 13x13½
1916, Dec. 21   **Wmk. 181**
B1 A5 5o + 5o on 2o org   4.50 5.50
B2 A5 5o + 5o on 3o yel brn   4.50 5.50
B3 A5 5o + 5o on 4o gray   4.50 5.50
B4 A5 5o + 5o on 5o grn   4.50 5.50
B5 A5 5o + 5o on 6o lilac   4.50 5.50
B6 A5 10o + 10o on 12o pale bl   4.50 5.50
B7 A5 10o + 10o on 20o red org   4.50 5.50
B8 A5 10o + 10o on 24o yel   4.50 5.50
B9 A5 10o + 10o on 30o brn   4.50 5.50
B10 A5 10o + 10o on 50o rose red   4.50 5.50
   Nos. B1-B10 (10)   45.00 55.00

The surtax on Nos. B1-B31 was for the militia. See note after No. B21.
For surcharges see Nos. B22-B31.

No. 66 Surcharged in Dark Blue

1916, Dec. 21   **Wmk. 180**   **Perf. 13**
B11 A12 10o + 4.90k on 5k   125.00 250.00

Nos. J12-J22 Surcharged in Dark Blue

1916, Dec. 21   Unwmk.   **Perf. 13**
B12 D1 5o + 5o on 1o   5.50 7.00
B13 D1 5o + 5o on 3o   2.25 3.75
B14 D1 5o + 5o on 5o   2.25 3.75
B15 D1 5o + 10o on 6o   3.00 4.75
B16 D1 5o + 15o on 12o   27.50 17.00
B17 D1 10o + 20o on 20o   9.00 18.00
B18 D1 10o + 40o on 24o   40.00 62.50
B19 D1 10o + 20o on 30o   3.00 4.75
B20 D1 10o + 40o on 50o   20.00 27.50
B21 D1 10o + 90o on 1kr   105.00 290.00
   Nos. B12-B21 (10)   217.50 439.00

The surtax on Nos. B12-B21 is indicated not in figures, but in words at bottom of surcharge: Fem, 5; Tio, 10; Femton, 15; Tjugo, 20; Fyrtio, 40; Nittio, 90.

Nos. B1-B10 Surcharged

1918, Dec. 18   **Wmk. 181**
B22 A5 7o + 3o on #B1   6.50 6.50
B23 A5 7o + 3o on #B2   1.90 1.40
B24 A5 7o + 3o on #B3   1.90 1.40
B25 A5 7o + 3o on #B4   1.90 1.40
B26 A5 7o + 3o on #B5   1.90 1.40
B27 A5 12o + 8o on #B7   1.90 1.40
B28 A5 12o + 8o on #B7   1.90 1.40
B29 A5 12o + 8o on #B8   1.90 1.40
B30 A5 12o + 8o on #B9   2.00 1.40
B31 A5 12o + 8o on #B10   2.00 1.40
   Nos. B22-B31 (10)   23.80 19.10

The 12o+8o surcharge exists on Nos. B1-B5 and the 7o+3o surcharge exists on Nos. B6-B10. Value, each $65.
Nos. B24, B26, B28 and B30 exist with surcharge inverted. Value unused, each $125.

King Gustaf V
SP1   SP2

Unwmk.
1928, June 16   Engr.   **Perf. 10**
B32 SP1 5o (+ 5o) yel grn   3.00 4.50
   a. Booklet pane of 8   115.00
B33 SP1 10o (+ 50) dk vio   3.00 4.50
   a. Booklet pane of 8   115.00
B34 SP1 15o (+ 50) car   3.00 4.50
   a. Booklet pane of 8   115.00
B35 SP1 20o (+ 50) org   4.75 2.00
B36 SP1 25o (+ 50) dk bl   4.75 2.00
   Nos. B32-B36 (5)   18.50 17.50
   Set, never hinged   27.50

70th birthday of King Gustaf V. The surtax was used for anti-cancer work.

> Catalogue values for unused stamps in this section, from this point to the end of the section, are for Never Hinged items.

King Gustaf VI Adolf — SP3   Henri Dunant — SP4

1948, June 16   **Perf. 12½ Vertically**
B37 SP2 10o + 10o green   55 60
B38 SP2 20o + 10o red   80 75
B39 SP2 30o + 10o ultra   55 60

Perf. 12½ on 3 Sides
B40 SP2 10o + 10o green   65 70
   a. Booklet pane of 20   13.00
B41 SP2 20o + 10o red   80 65
   a. Booklet pane of 20   16.00
   Nos. B37-B41 (5)   3.35 3.30

90th anniv. of the birth of King Gustaf V. The surtax provided aid for Swedish youth.

1952, Nov. 11   **Perf. 12½ Horiz.**
B42 SP3 10o + 10o green   25 25
B43 SP3 25o + 10o car rose   32 32
B44 SP3 40o + 10o ultra   45 45

Perf. 12½ on 3 Sides
B45 SP3 10o + 10o green   25 32
   a. Booklet pane of 20   5.00
B46 SP3 25o + 10o car rose   32 32
   a. Booklet pane of 20   6.50
   Nos. B42-B46 (5)   1.59 1.66

70th birthday of King Gustaf VI Adolf. The surtax was used to promote Swedish culture.

1959, May 8   **Perf. 12½ Horizontally**
B47 SP4 30o + 10o red   80 90

Perf. 12½ on 3 Sides
B48 SP4 30o + 10o red   1.00 1.10
   a. Booklet pane of 20   20.00

Centenary of the Red Cross idea. The surtax went to the Swedish Red Cross.

King Gustav VI Adolf — SP5

Perf. 12½ Vertically
1962, Nov. 10   Engr.   Unwmk.
   Size: 58x24mm
B49 SP5 20o + 10o brown   15 20
B50 SP5 35o + 10o blue   15 20

Perf. 12½ Horizontally
B51 SP5 20o + 10o brown   28 30
   a. Booklet pane of 10   2.75
B52 SP5 35o + 10o blue   28 30
   a. Booklet pane of 10   2.75

80th birthday of King Gustav VI Adolf. The surtax went to the King Gustav VI Adolf 80th anniv. Foundation for Swedish Cultural Activities.

Ship Types of Regular Issues, 1936-44
Imprint: "1966"

Designs (Ships): 10o, "The Lion of Smaland." 15o, "Kalmar Nyckel." 20o, Old Sailing Packet. 25o, Mail Paddle Steamship. 30o, "Kung Karl." 40o, Stern of "Amphion."

1966, Nov. 15   **Perf. 12½ on 3 Sides**
B53 A76 10o vermilion   30 35
B54 A50 15o vermilion   30 35
B55 A38 20o slate grn   30 35
B56 A39 25o ultra   20 15
B57 A76 30o vermilion   30 40
B58 A76 40o vermilion   30 40
   a. Bklt. pane of 10 (#B53-B54, B57-B58, 2 #B55, 4 #B56)   2.75
   Nos. B53-B58 (6)   1.70 2.00

The booklet sold for 3.50k and the surtax of 1.15k went to the National Cancer Fund.

AIR POST STAMPS

Official Stamps Surcharged in Dark Blue

1920, Sept. 17   **Wmk. 181**   **Perf. 13**
C1 O3 10o on 3o brn   2.75 5.50
   a. Inverted surcharge   100.00 250.00
C2 O3 20o on 2o org   4.50 8.50
   a. Inverted surcharge   100.00 250.00
C3 O3 50o on 4o vio   18.00 21.00
   a. Inverted surcharge   100.00 250.00

Wmk. 180
C4 O3 20o on 2o org   1,700.
C5 O3 50o on 4o vio   125.00 210.00

Airplane over Stockholm — AP2   Flying Swans — AP3

Perf. 10 Vertically
1930, May 9   Engr.   Unwmk.
C6 AP2 10o deep blue   30 65
C7 AP2 50o dark violet   70 1.00
   Set, never hinged   1.50

1942-53   **Perf. 12½ on 3 Sides**
C8 AP3 20k brt ultra ('53)   5.00 65
   Never hinged   7.00
   a. Bklt. pane of 20 ('53)   600.00
   b. Bklt. pane of 10 ('68)   50.00

c.	Perf. on 4 sides		65.00	9.00
	Never hinged		110.00	
d.	As "c," bklt. pane of 10		1,200.	

Issued: No. C8c, May 4, 1942. No. C8, July 7.

POSTAGE DUE STAMPS

D1

1874   Unwmk.   Typo.   Perf. 14

J1	D1	1o black	22.50	20.00
J2	D1	3o rose	22.50	22.50
J3	D1	5o brown	22.50	20.00
J4	D1	6o yellow	50.00	45.00
J5	D1	12o pale red	4.50	4.00
J6	D1	20o blue	30.00	22.50
J7	D1	24o violet	175.00	125.00
J8	D1	24o gray	22.50	27.50
J9	D1	30o dk grn	22.50	22.50
J10	D1	50o brown	57.50	27.50
J11	D1	1k bl & bis	95.00	35.00

1877-86   Perf. 13

J12	D1	1o blk ('80)	2.00	2.50
J13	D1	3o rose	3.50	4.00
J14	D1	5o brown	3.50	3.50
J15	D1	6o yellow	3.50	3.50
a.		Printed on both sides	600.00	
J16	D1	12o pale red ('82)	7.00	8.00
J17	D1	20o pale bl ('78)	3.75	3.00
J18	D1	24o red lil ('86)	12.00	14.00
a.		24o violet ('84)	12.00	15.00
J19	D1	24o gray lil ('82)	70.00	67.50
J20	D1	30o yel grn	3.25	3.00
J21	D1	50o yel brn	5.75	4.00
J22	D1	1k bl & bis	25.00	15.00

Nos. J12-J17, J19-J22 exist imperf. Value, pairs, each $300.

For surcharges see Nos. B12-B21.

STAMPS FOR CITY POSTAGE

S1

Perf. 14x13¹/₂

1856-62   Typo.   Unwmk.

LX1	S1	(1sk or 3o) blk	425.00 250.00
LX2	S1	(3o) bis brn ('62)	225.00 300.00

From 1856 to 1858 No. LX1 was sold at 1sk, from 1858 to 1862 at 3o. The paper of the 1sk black is thin while the paper of the 3o black is medium thick.

No. LX1 was reprinted three times with perf. 14, once with perf. 13. No. LX2 was reprinted once with each perforation. Value of lowest-cost Perf. 14 reprints, $135 each. Perf. 13, $110 each.

OFFICIAL STAMPS

O1   O3

1874-77   Unwmk.   Typo.   Perf. 14

O1	O1	3o bister	35.00	20.00
O2	O1	4o gray ('77)	115.00	30.00
O3	O1	5o yel green	115.00	17.50
O4	O1	6o lilac	175.00	20.00
O5	O1	6o gray	300.00	95.00
O6	O1	12o blue	85.00	1.75
O7	O1	20o pale red	375.00	50.00
O8	O1	24o yellow	375.00	14.00
a.		24o orange	375.00	14.00
O9	O1	30o pale brn	225.00	17.50
O10	O1	50o rose	325.00	60.00
O11	O1	1k bl & bis	1,100.	30.00

Imperf., Pairs

O1a	O1	3o	350.
O2a	O1	4o	350.
O3a	O1	5o	500.
O4a	O1	6o	500.
O6a	O1	12o	350.
O7a	O1	20o	1,000.
O8b	O1	24o	1,000.
O9a	O1	30o	600.
O10a	O1	50o	800.
O11a	O1	1k	1,500.

1881-93   Perf. 13

O12	O1	2o org ('91)	1.25	1.25
O13	O1	3o bis brn	1.25	2.00
O14	O1	4o gray blk ('93)	1.50	30
a.		4o gray ('82)	6.25	1.10
O15	O1	5o grn ('84)	2.00	20
O16	O1	6o red lil ('82)	20.00	30.00
a.		6o lilac ('81)	20.00	30.00
O17	O1	10o car ('85)	2.50	15
b.		10o rose	20.00	85
O18	O1	12o blue	35.00	11.50
O19	O1	20o ver ('82)	110.00	1.50
O20	O1	20o dk bl ('91)	2.50	25
O21	O1	24o yellow	40.00	9.00
a.		24o orange	40.00	9.00
O22	O1	30o brown	14.00	40
O23	O1	50o pale rose	100.00	12.00
O24	O1	50o pale gray ('93)	12.00	1.50
O25	O1	1k dk bl & yel bis	7.50	1.50

Imperf., Pairs

O12a	O1	2o	150.00
O17a	O1	10o No. O17	150.00
c.		No. O17b	180.00
O20a	O1	20o	32.50
O24a	O1	50o	150.00

Surcharged in Dark Blue

1889

O26	O1	10o on 12o blue	10.50	11.00
a.		Inverted surcharge	300.00	850.00
b.		Perf. 14	2,750.	1,800.
O27	O1	10o on 24o yel	13.00	13.00
a.		Inverted surcharge	900.00	800.00
b.		Perf. 14	1,800.	1,800.

1910-12   Wmk. 180   Typo.

O28	O3	1o black	20	22
O29	O3	2o orange	1.45	2.25
O30	O3	4o pale violet	2.50	3.25
O31	O3	5o green	65	80
O32	O3	8o claret	65	80
O33	O3	10o red	13.00	65
O34	O3	15o red brown	85	80
O35	O3	20o deep blue	7.25	80
O36	O3	25o red orange	7.25	1.50
O37	O3	30o chocolate	9.25	2.00
O38	O3	50o gray	9.25	2.00
O39	O3	1k black, yellow	11.50	6.50
O40	O3	5k claret, yellow	10.00	4.50
		Nos. O28-O40 (13)	73.80	26.07

1910-19   Wmk. Wavy Lines (181)

O41	O3	1o black	2.00	2.00
O42	O3	2o orange	20	15
O43	O3	3o pale brown	32	32
O44	O3	4o pale violet	20	20
O45	O3	5o green	15	15
O46	O3	7o gray green	65	65
O47	O3	8o rose	14.00	14.00
O48	O3	10o red	15	15
O49	O3	12o rose red	15	15
O50	O3	15o org brown	15	15
O51	O3	20o deep blue	15	15
O52	O3	25o orange	1.00	40
O53	O3	30o chocolate	40	40
O54	O3	35o dark violet	85	40
O55	O3	50o gray	2.00	85
		Nos. O41-O55 (15)	22.37	20.12

For surcharges see Nos. C1-C5.

Use of official stamps ceased on July 1, 1920.

PARCEL POST STAMPS

Regular Issue of 1914   **Kr. 1.98** Surcharged

1917   Wmk. 180   Perf. 13

Q1	A14	1.98k on 5k claret, yel	2.00	3.75
Q2	A14	2.12k on 5k claret, yel	2.00	3.75

SWITZERLAND
(Helvetia)

LOCATION — Central Europe, between France, Germany and Italy
GOVT. — Republic
AREA — 15,943 sq. mi.
POP. — 6,423,100 (est. 1983)
CAPITAL — Bern

100 Rappen or Centimes = 1 Franc

> Catalogue values for unused stamps in this country are for Never Hinged items, beginning with Scott 365 in the regular postage section, Scott B272 in the semi-postal section, Scott C46 in the airpost section, Scott CB1 in the airpost semi-postal section, and for the various official stamps, and Scott 3094 for the International Labor Bureau.
> Also, Scott 4040 for the Intl. Bureau of Education, Scott 5O26 for the WHO, Scott 7O31 for the UN European Office, Scott 9O1 for the World Meteorological Organization, Scott 9O1 for the Intl. Bureau of the UPU, Scott 10O1 for the ITU, and Scott 11O1 for the World Intellectual Property Organization.

> Unused values of Nos. 1L1-3L1 are for stamps without gum.
> Counterfeit and repaired copies of Nos. 1L1-3L1 abound.

Watermarks

Wmk. 182- Cross in Oval   Wmk. 183- Swiss Cross

Watermark 182 is not a true watermark, having been impressed after the paper was manufactured. There are two types: 1- width just under 9mm. 2- width just under 8¹/₂mm. There are many other differences of ¹/₁₀mm to ¹/₃mm.

CANTONAL ADMINISTRATION
Zurich

Numerals of Value
A1   A2

1843   Unwmk.   Litho.   Imperf.
Red Vertical Lines

1L1	A1	4r black	13,500. 13,000.
1L2	A2	6r black	5,000. 1,500.

1846   Red Horizontal Lines

1L3	A1	4r black	12,000. 14,000.
1L4	A2	6r black	1,500. 1,400.

Five varieties of each value.

Reprints of the Zurich stamps show signs of wear and lack the red lines. Values 4r, $3,250; 6r, $1,100.

Coat of Arms — A3

1850   Unwmk.   Imperf.

1L5	A3	2¹/₂r black & red	4,500. 3,500.

Geneva

Coat of Arms — A1

1843   Unwmk.   Litho.   Imperf.

2L1	A1	10c blk, yel grn	40,000. 30,000.
a.		Either half	15,000. 7,000.
b.		Stamp composed of right half at left & left half at right	60,000. 50,000.

A2   A3

1845-48

2L2	A2	5c blk, yel grn	1,900. 1,500.
2L3	A3	5c blk, yel grn ('47)	1,250. 1,500.
2L4	A3	5c blk, dk grn ('48)	2,750. 2,100.

Coat of Arms
A4   A5

1849-50

2L5	A4	4c black & red	24,000. 15,000.
2L6	A4	5c blk & red ('50)	1,600. 1,250.

1850

2L7	A5	5c black & red	6,500. 2,400.

ENVELOPE STAMP USED AS ADHESIVE

E1

1849   Unwmk.   Imperf.

2LU1	E1	5c yel grn	15,000.

Value is for cut-out stamp used on folded letters. Value of unused envelope (1846) or cut-out, $300. Value of used cut-out off cover, $3,000.

Basel

Dove of Basel — A1

Typo. & Embossed
1845 Unwmk. Imperf.

3L1 A1 2½r blk, crim & bl — 8,500. 8,250.

Proofs are black, vermilion and green. Value, $3,000.

FEDERAL ADMINISTRATION

 A10 A11

1850 Unwmk. Litho. Imperf.
Full Black Frame Around Cross

1	A10	2½r black & red	1,600.	1,250.
2	A11	2½r black & red	1,250.	950.

Without Frame Around Cross

3	A10	2½r black & red	3,300.	1,700.
4	A11	2½r blk & red	32,500.	17,000.

Forty types of each.

 A12 A13

1850
Full Black Frame Around Cross

5	A12	5r blk & red, *dk bl*	3,500.	800.
a.		5r blk & red, *dk grayish bl*	3,250.	1,000.
6	A13	10r blk & red, *yel*		55,000.

No. 6 used, with only parts of frame around cross showing, value $120 to $450.
Beware of copies of Nos. 7-8 with faked frame added.

Without Frame Around Cross

7	A12	5r blk & red, *lt bl*	1,150.	400.
a.		5r blk & red, *dp bl*	1,350.	500.
b.		5r blk & red, *pur bl*	4,500.	1,750.
c.		5r blk & red, *grnsh bl*	1,000.	350.
8	A13	10r blk & red, *yel*	850.	80.
a.		10r blk & red, *buff*	600.	80.
b.		10r blk & red, *org yel*	850.	150.
c.		Half used as 5r on cover		4,000.

1851
Full Blue Frame Around Cross

9	A12	5r lt blue & red		67,500.

No. 9 used, with only parts of frame around cross showing, value $120 to $3,000.
Beware of copies of No. 10 with faked frame added.

Without Frame Around Cross

10	A12	5r lt blue & red	375.	80.

Forty types of each.

 A14 A15 A16

1852
Vermilion Frame Around Cross

11	A14	15r vermilion	5,500.	450.
12	A15	15r vermilion	1,400.	85.
13	A16	15c vermilion	8,000.	675.

Ten types of each.

On October 1st, 1854, all stamps of the preceding issues were declared obsolete.

Values of Nos. 14-40 are for copies which show three full frame lines and not cut into design. Those with fewer sell for half price or less. Copies with complete frame and white margin all around bring double the catalogue value or more. Beware of thinned down papers.

 Helvetia — A17

1854 Embossed. Unwmk.
Thin Paper, Fine Impressions
Emerald Silk Threads

14	A17	5r orange brn	3,750.	1,100.
15	A17	5r red brown	275.00	70.00
16	A17	10r blue	375.00	15.00
17	A17	15r carmine rose	600.00	90.00
a.		15r pale rose	600.00	90.00
18	A17	40r pale yel grn	52.50	800.00
19	A17	40r yellow grn	550.00	150.00

1854-55
Emerald Silk Threads
Medium Thick Paper
Fine Impressions

20	A17	5r pale yel brn	375.00	70.00
a.		5r blue	6,000.	5,000.
21	A17	10r blue	825.00	60.00
22	A17	15r rose	550.00	40.00
23	A17	20r pale orange	850.00	80.00

Some authorities question whether No. 20a is an essay or an error.

1855-57
Colored ( ) Silk Threads
Medium Thick Paper
Fine to Rough Impressions

24	A17	5r yel brn (yel)	275.00	50.00
25	A17	5r dk brown (blk)	185.00	13.00
26	A17	10r mlky bl (red)	350.00	60.00
27	A17	10r blue (car)	175.00	13.00
a.		Thin paper	2,500.	250.00
28	A17	15r rose (bl)	300.00	30.00
29	A17	40r yel grn (mar)	425.00	35.00
30	A17	1fr lav (blk)	575.00	350.00
31	A17	1fr lav (yel)	725.00	350.00
a.		Thin paper		4,500.

1857
Thin (Emergency) Paper
Rough Impressions
Green Silk Threads

32	A17	5r pale gray brn	2,300.	750.
33	A17	5r pale dl rose	1,750.	175.
34	A17	20r pale dl org	1,750.	100.

1858-62
Thick Ordinary Paper
Rough Impressions
Green Silk Threads

35	A17	2r gray	125.00	250.00
a.		One and one-half used as 3r on newspaper or wrapper		8,000.
36	A17	5r brown	80.00	5.00
a.		5r black brown	125.00	20.00
37	A17	10r dark blue	90.00	4.00
38	A17	15r dark rose	200.00	20.00
39	A17	20r dark orange	190.00	27.50
40	A17	40r dk yellow grn	190.00	25.00

 Helvetia — A18

Double embossing errors, Nos. 43a, 44a, 55b, 60a, 61a, 67b, have the design impressed twice. These do not refer to the "embossed" watermark.

Perf. 11½
1862-63 Embossed Wmk. 182
White Wove Paper

41	A18	2c gray	40.00	1.25
42	A18	3c black	6.25	47.50
43	A18	5c dark brown	1.50	15
a.		5c bister brown	62.50	20.00
b.		5c gray brown	40.00	5.00
c.		Dbl. embossing, one invtd.	3,000.	350.00
d.		Double impression of lower left "5"		1,000.
44	A18	10c blue	150.00	50
a.		Dbl. embossing, one invtd.		7,500.
45	A18	20c orange	1.00	1.00
a.		20c yellow orange	4.00	1.00
46	A18	30c vermilion	700.00	10.00
47	A18	40c green	400.00	22.50
48	A18	60c bronze	425.00	70.00
50	A18	1fr gold	11.00	30.00
a.		1fr bronze	700.00	150.00

1867-78

52	A18	2c bister brown	1.00	30
a.		2c red brown	450.00	130.00
53	A18	10c carmine	3.50	15
54	A18	15c lemon	2.50	14.00
55	A18	25c blue green	1.00	1.00
a.		25c yellow green	7.50	3.50
b.		Dbl. embossing, one invtd.		550.00
56	A18	30c ultra	150.00	2.00
a.		30c blue	1,100.	160.00
58	A18	40c gray	90	32.50
59	A18	50c violet	40.00	20.00

1881
Granite Paper

60	A18	2c bister	20	7.50
a.		Dbl. embossing, one invtd.	300.00	
61	A18	5c brown	15	1.65
a.		Dbl. embossing, one invtd.	17.50	275.00
b.		Double impression of lower left "5"		700.00
62	A18	10c rose	1.75	1.40
63	A18	15c lemon	3.75	250.00
64	A18	20c orange	20	60.00
65	A18	25c green	15	45.00
66	A18	40c gray	20	1,800.
67	A18	50c deep violet	9.50	275.00
b.		Dbl. embossing, one invtd.	200.00	2,500.
68	A18	1fr gold	9.00	600.00

The granite paper contains fragments of blue and red silk threads.
Forged or backdated cancellations are found frequently on Nos. 42, 50, 54, 58 and 60-68.
All stamps of the preceding issues were declared obsolete on October 1st, 1883. Some of the remainders of Nos. 41-68 were overprinted "AUSSER KURS" (Obsolete) diagonally in black.

 Numeral — A19

1882-99 Typo. Perf. 11½
Granite Paper

69	A19	2c bister	75	20
70	A19	3c gray brown	90	1.90
a.		3c gray	14.00	14.00
71	A19	5c maroon	12.50	15
		Tête bêche pair		
72	A19	5c deep grn ('99)	7.00	15
73	A19	10c red	2.00	15
a.		10c carmine	6.00	15
b.		10c light rose	175.00	2.00
74	A19	12c ultra	3.50	15
a.		12c chalky blue	8.00	40
b.		12c greenish blue	450.00	
75	A19	15c yellow	125.00	7.00
a.		15c orange		
		Tête bêche pair		
76	A19	15c violet ('89)	27.50	50

1882
White Paper

77	A19	2c bister	325.00	275.00
78	A19	5c maroon	600.00	55.00
79	A19	10c rose	2,000.	45.00
80	A19	12c chalky blue	125.00	15.00
81	A19	15c yellow	200.00	150.00

See Nos. 113-118.

 Helvetia (Large numerals) — A20 Helvetia (Small numerals) — A21

1882-1904 Engr. Perf. 11½

82	A20	20c orange	92.50	1.40
83	A20	25c green	45.00	75
84	A20	40c gray	65.00	12.00
85	A21	40c gray ('04)	22.50	4.00

A. KOCHER & FILS
MAGASINS DE L'ANCRE
CONFECTIONS NOUVEAUTÉS
HELVETIA
LA CHAUX-DE-FONDS
VEVEY

Switzerland
Comprehensive stock of top quality material, 1843-Date. Year Units, Sets, Singles and Specialized Material. Want lists invited for all singles, 19th century, Cantonals, Covers, FDC's, Diplomatic Presentation Books and Specialized Material.

Free Price List
Complete sets, NH, Hinged and Used - includes Official and Back-of-the-Book. Also ask for our free Liechtenstein price list and Special Offers lists. **Want lists invited! Prompt Service!**

We Buy
We buy all Switzerland including quantity material. Also wanted - Covers and Specialized Material. Especially needed pre-1962 FDC's. Sell to the specialists! All U.S. & Worldwide stamps bought at top prices!

For buying or selling Switzerland and all other U.S. & Worldwide call

1-800-9-4-STAMPS
(1-800-947-8267)

Henry Gitner Philatelists, Inc.
P.O. Box 3077-S
Middletown, NY 10940
Tel: 914-343-5151 Fax: 914-343-0068 1-800-947-8267

Philately – The Quiet Excitement!

No.	Type	Description	Unused	Used
86	A20	50c blue	85.00	5.50
87	A20	1fr claret	175.00	1.65
88	A20	3fr yellow brn ('91)	150.00	6.25

1888　　Perf. 9½

No.	Type	Description	Unused	Used
89	A20	20c orange	350.00	30.00
90	A20	25c yellow grn	85.00	2.00
91	A20	40c gray	525.00	325.00
92	A20	50c blue	1,200.	150.00
93	A20	1fr claret	800.00	30.00

1891-99　　Perf. 11½x11

No.	Type	Description	Unused	Used
82a	A20	20c orange	17.50	60
83a	A20	25c green	7.00	40
94	A20	25c blue ('99)	6.00	50
95	A20	30c red brn ('92)	35.00	75
84a	A20	40c gray	30.00	1.50
86a	A20	50c blue	42.50	4.50
96	A20	50c green ('99)	30.00	4.00
87a	A20	1fr claret	42.50	75
97	A20	1fr carmine	65.00	2.75
88a	A20	3fr yellow brown	140.00	11.50

1901-03　　Perf. 11½x12

No.	Type	Description	Unused	Used
82b	A20	20c orange	15.00	55
94a	A20	25c blue	6.00	35
95a	A20	30c red brown	22.50	70
84b	A20	40c gray	70.00	9.00
96a	A20	50c green	27.50	2.00
87b	A20	1fr claret	2,000.	125.00
97a	A20	1fr carmine ('03)	400.00	11.50
88b	A20	3fr yellow brown	150.00	7.50

Numerous retouches and plate flaws exist on all values of this issue.

Nos. 82-88 have wmk. type 1 and are ½mm taller (paper size) than Nos. 82b-88b, which have wmk. type 2.

See Nos. 105-112, 119-125.

UPU Allegory — A22

We are the world's leading auction house and specialists in first-class stamp auctions since 1925.

We are pleased to accept suitable rarities and collections at any time for our forthcoming auctions. Confidentiality is guaranteed.

CORINPHILA AUCTIONS Ltd.

Bellerivestrasse 34
CH-8034 Zurich/Switzerland
Phone +41-1-383 10 60
Fax +41-1-383 09 14

1900　　Perf. 11½

No.	Type	Description	Unused	Used
98	A22	5c gray green	18.00	35
99	A22	10c carmine rose	7.75	32
100	A22	25c blue	12.00	6.75

Re-engraved

No.	Type	Description	Unused	Used
101	A22	5c gray green	2.75	45
102	A22	10c carmine rose	37.50	13.00
103	A22	25c blue	950.00	11,500.

Universal Postal Union, 25th anniv.

The impression of the re-engraved stamps is much clearer, especially the horizontally lined background. The figures of value are lined instead of being solid.

Helvetia Types of 1882-1904
1905　Wmk. 183　Perf. 11½x11
White Paper

No.	Type	Description	Unused	Used
105	A20	20c orange	4.50	1.00
106	A20	25c blue	6.50	3.75
107	A20	30c brown	6.00	1.00
108a	A21	40c gray	130.00	70.00
109	A20	50c green	35.00	2.00
110	A20	1fr carmine	75.00	1.05
111	A20	3fr yellow brn	225.00	42.50

Some clichés in the plates of the 20c, 25c, 30c, 50c and 3fr have been retouched.

1906　Re-engraved　Perf. 11½x11

No.	Type	Description	Unused	Used
112	A20	25c pale blue	3.25	60

In the re-engraved stamp the stars are larger and the background below "FRANCO" is of horiz. or horiz. and vert. crossed lines, instead of horiz. and curved lines.

1906　　Perf. 11½

No.	Type	Description	Unused	Used
112a	A20	25c pale blue	50.00	1.75
108	A21	40c gray	25.00	3.00

1907　　Perf. 11½x12

No.	Type	Description	Unused	Used
105a	A20	20c orange	6.50	2.50
109a	A20	50c green	32.50	3.00
110a	A20	1fr carmine	110.00	2.50
111a	A20	3fr yellow brown	310.00	77.50

Numeral Type of 1882-99
1905　Typo.　Perf. 11½
Granite Paper

No.	Type	Description	Unused	Used
113	A19	2c dull bister	2.50	60
114	A19	3c gray brown	2.25	22.50
115	A19	5c green	3.00	15
116	A19	10c scarlet	2.75	15
117	A19	12c ultra	2.50	40
118	A19	15c brown vio	50.00	3.75
Nos. 113-118 (6)			63.00	27.55

Helvetia Types of 1882-1904
Perf. 11½x12
1907　Engr.　Granite Paper

No.	Type	Description	Unused	Used
119	A20	20c orange	1.50	1.00
120	A20	25c blue	10.00	2.25
121	A20	30c red brown	6.00	2.75
122	A21	40c gray	22.50	8.50
a.		Helvetia without diadem	325.00	900.00
123	A20	50c gray green	5.00	1.75
124	A20	1fr carmine	24.00	1.00
125a	A20	3fr yel brn		10,000.

There are retouches and plate flaws on all values.

Perf. 11½x11

No.	Type	Description	Unused	Used
120a	A20	25c deep blue	12.50	1.75
121a	A20	30c red brown	160.00	225.00
122b	A21	40c gray		16,000.
124a	A20	1fr carmine		4,500.
125	A20	3fr yel brn	165.00	7.50

William Tell's Son — A23

Helvetia
A24　　A25

1907-25　Typo.　Perf. 11½
Granite Paper

No.	Type	Description	Unused	Used
126	A23	2c pale bister	35	15
127	A23	3c lilac brn	15	4.25
128	A23	5c yellow grn	3.50	15
129	A24	10c rose red	3.00	25
130	A24	12c ocher	35	1.40
131	A24	15c red vio	4.25	5.00
132	A25	20c red & yel ('08)	1.65	15
133	A25	25c dp blue ('08)	1.40	15
a.		Tête bêche pair	15.00	50.00
134	A25	30c yel brn & pale grn ('08)	1.75	15
135	A25	35c yel grn & yel ('08)	1.75	15
136	A25	40c red vio & yel ('08)	11.00	15
a.		Designer's name in full on the rock ('08)	10.00	20.00
137	A25	40c dp blue ('22)	2.00	15
a.		40c light blue ('21)	5.75	30
138	A25	40c red vio & grn ('25)	14.00	15
139	A25	50c dp grn & pale grn ('08)	5.25	30
140	A25	60c brn org & buff ('18)	6.50	15
141	A25	70c dk brn & buff ('08)	90.00	6.00
142	A25	70c vio & buff ('24)	13.00	50
143	A25	80c slate & buff ('15)	8.25	25
144	A25	1fr dp cl & pale grn ('08)	7.00	20
145	A25	3fr bis & yel ('08)	200.00	60
Nos. 126-145 (20)			375.15	20.40

No. 136 has two leaves and "CL" below sword hilt. No. 136a has three leaves and designer's full name below hilt.

For surcharges and overprints see Nos. 189, 199, O10-O13, O15, 106-108, 1014-1016, 2018-2026, 3014-3022.

1933
With Grilled Gum

No.	Type	Description	Unused	Used
135a	A25	35c yel grn & yel	2.50	3.25
138a	A25	40c red vio & grn	42.50	30
139a	A25	50c dp grn & pale grn	14.00	30
140a	A25	60c brn org & buff	9.00	25
142a	A25	70c vio & buff	15.00	1.40
143a	A25	80c slate & buff	9.00	1.00
144a	A25	1fr dp cl & pale grn	17.50	1.75
Nos. 135a-144a (7)			109.50	8.25

"Grilled" Gum

In 1930-44 many Swiss stamps were treated with a light grilling process, applied with the gumming to counteract the tendency to curl. It resembles a faint grill of vertical and horizontal ribs covering the entire back of the stamp, and can be seen after the gum has been removed. Listings of the grilled gum varieties begin with No. 135a.

William Tell's Son — A26

Bow-string in front of stock

1909　　Perf. 11½, 12
Granite Paper

No.	Type	Description	Unused	Used
146	A26	2c bister	42	30
a.		Tête bêche pair	3.00	16.00
147	A26	3c dark violet	25	4.00
148	A26	5c green	1.40	15
a.		Tête bêche pair	45.00	

See Nos. 149-163. For surcharges and overprints see Nos. 186, 193-195, 207-208, 101-103, 109-1011, 201-207, 301-305.

First Redrawing

Bow-string behind stock. Thin loop above crossbow. Letters of "HELVETIA" without serifs.

1910-17
Granite Paper

No.	Type	Description	Unused	Used
149	A26	2c bister ('10)	11.00	1.40
150	A26	3c dk violet ('10)	20	15
a.		Tête bêche pair	2.50	1.50
b.		Booklet pane of 6	11.50	
151	A26	3c brown org ('17)	15	15
a.		Tête bêche pair	7.50	10.00
152	A26	5c green ('10)	25.00	1.50
a.		Tête bêche pair	85.00	165.00

Second Redrawing

Bow-string behind stock. Thick loop above crossbow. Letters of "HELVETIA" have serifs.

7½ CENTIMES:
Type I - Top of "7" is ½mm thick. The "1" of "½" has only traces of serifs. The two base plates of the statue are of even thickness.

Type II - Top of "7" is 1mm thick. The "1" of "½" has distinct serifs. The upper base plate is thinner than the lower.

1911-30
Granite Paper

No.	Type	Description	Unused	Used
153	A26	2c bister ('11)	15	15
a.		Tête bêche pair	3.00	1.50
154	A26	2½c claret ('18)	15	45
155	A26	2½c ol, buff ('28)	50	90
156	A26	3c ultra, buff ('30)	3.00	3.75
157	A26	5c green ('11)	2.00	15
a.		Tête bêche pair	5.00	9.00
158	A26	5c org, buff ('21)	15	15
a.		Bklt. pane of 6 (5 #158, 168)	12.50	42.50
159	A26	5c gray vio, buff ('24)	15	15
a.		Bklt. pane of 6 (5 #159, 168)	6.00	17.50
160	A26	5c red vio, buff ('27)	15	15
a.		Bklt. pane of 6 (5 #160, 168)	27.50	70.00
161	A26	5c dk grn, buff ('30)	30	30
a.		Bklt. pane of 6 (5 #161, 169)	25.00	62.50
162	A26	7½c gray (I) ('18)	2.25	15
c.		7½c slate (II)	12.00	40.00
163	A26	7½c dp grn, buff (I) ('28)	4.00	55
			35	1.75
Nos. 153-163 (11)			9.15	8.05

1933
With Grilled Gum

No.	Type	Description	Unused	Used
156a	A26	3c ultra, buff	3.75	4.50
161b	A26	5c dark green, buff	50	50

Helvetia — A27

William Tell — A28

1909
Granite Paper

No.	Type	Description	Unused	Used
164	A27	10c carmine	1.00	15
a.		Tête bêche pair	2.00	5.50
165	A27	12c bister brn	1.65	15
166	A27	15c red violet	22.50	45
		Set value		65

For surcharge see No. 187.

1914-30　Granite Paper　Perf. 11½

TEN CENTIMES:
Type I - Bust 16½mm high. "HELVETIA" 15½mm wide. Cross bar of "H" at middle of the letter.

Type II - Bust 15mm high. "HELVETIA" 15mm wide. Cross bar of "H" above middle of the letter.

No.	Type	Description	Unused	Used
167	A28	10c red, buff (type II)	90	15
a.		10c red, buff (type I)	3.25	24.00
b.		Tête bêche pair (II)	3.00	3.75
d.		Bklt. pane 6 (5 #167, 172)	45.00	150.00
168	A28	10c grn, buff (type II) ('21)	15	15
a.		Tête bêche pair	1.00	1.25
168C	A28	10c bl grn, buff (type II) ('28)	15	15
d.		Tête bêche pair	2.25	2.25
169	A28	10c vio, buff (type II) ('30)	2.75	15
a.		Tête bêche pair	9.50	1.25
170	A28	12c brn, buff	20	1.25
171	A28	13c ol grn, buff ('15)	1.25	15
172	A28	15c vio, buff	4.00	15
b.		15c dk vio, buff	30.00	1.50
c.		Tête bêche pair	80.00	100.00
173	A28	15c brn red, buff ('28)	2.75	75
174	A28	20c red vio, buff ('21)	3.75	15
a.		Tête bêche pair	6.00	6.75
175	A28	20c ver, buff ('24)	1.25	15
a.		Tête bêche pair	5.25	8.50
176	A28	20c car, buff ('25)	25	15
a.		Tête bêche pair	2.25	50
177	A28	25c ver, buff ('21)	2.50	75
178	A28	25c car, buff ('22)	1.40	65
179	A28	25c brn, buff ('25)	3.75	90
180	A28	30c dp bl, buff ('24)	7.50	15
Nos. 167-180 (15)			32.55	
		Set value		5.10

1932-33　With Grilled Gum

No.	Type	Description	Unused	Used
169c	A28	10c violet, buff	2.75	30
173a	A28	15c brn red, buff ('33)	55.00	11.00
176c	A28	20c carmine, buff	12.00	75
179a	A28	25c brown, buff ('33)	125.00	15.00
180a	A28	30c deep blue, buff	50.00	75

For surcharges and overprints see Nos. 188, 196-198, 104-105, 1012-1013, O208-2017, 306-3013.

The Mythen — A29

The Rütli — A30

The Jungfrau
A31

1914-30　Engr.　Granite Paper

181	A29	3fr dk green	775.00　2.50
182	A29	3fr red ('18)	110.00　38
183	A30	5fr dp ultra	30.00　1.10
184	A31	10fr dull violet	110.00　1.25
185	A31	10fr gray grn ('30)	200.00　19.00
		Nos. 181-185 (5)	1,225.　24.23

See No. 206. For overprints see Nos. 2027-2030, 3023-3026.

Stamps of 1909-14 Surcharged

a　　b　　c

1915

186	A26(a)	1c on 2c bister	15　15
187	A27(b)	13c on 12c bis grn	20　3.00
188	A28(c)	13c on 12c brn, buff	38　65

No. 141 Surcharged

189	A25　80c on 70c	30.00　4.75

Significant of
Peace — A32

"Peace"
A33

"Dawn of
Peace"
A34

Perf. 11½
1919, Aug. 1　Typo.　Unwmk.

190	A32	7½c olive drab & blk	75　1.10
191	A33	10c red & yel	1.00　2.25
192	A34	15c violet & yel	2.00　1.10

Commemorating Peace after World War I.

Nos. 151, 149, 162, 171-172, 133
Surcharged in Black, Red or Dark Blue

A26　　A28　　A25

1921　　　　Wmk. 183

193	A26	2½c on 3c (Bl)	15　15
a.		Tête bêche pair	1.00　3.00
b.		Inverted surcharge	700.00　1,300.
c.		Double surcharge	425.00　675.00
194	A26	5c on 2c (R)	15　1.00
a.		Double surcharge	300.00　500.00
195	A26	5c on 7½c (R)	15　22
a.		Tête bêche pair	6.00　16.00
b.		Double surcharge	350.00　575.00
c.		5c on 7½c slate (II)	2,750.　3,750.

196	A28	10c on 13c (R)	20　1.40
a.		Double surcharge	350.00　575.00
197	A28	20c on 15c (Bk)	1.00　1.25
a.		Tête bêche pair	2.25　50.00
b.		Double surcharge	600.00　1,000.
198	A28	20c on 15c (Bl)	3.50　1.50
b.		Double surcharge	600.00　1,000.
199	A25	20c on 25c dp bl (R)	15　28
a.		Tête bêche pair	1.40　4.00
		Nos. 193-199 (7)	5.30　5.80

A36

1924　Typo.　Perf. 11½
Granite Paper, Surface Colored

200	A36	90c grn & red, grn	10.50　30
201	A36	1.20fr brn rose & red, rose	5.25　85
202	A36	1.50fr bl & red, bl	12.00　85
203	A36	2fr gray blk & red, gray	55.00　85

1933　　　With Grilled Gum

200a	A36	90c grn & red, grn	14.00　50
201a	A36	1.20fr brn rose & red, rose	42.50　1.00
202a	A36	1.50fr blue & red, blue	19.00　1.00
203a	A36	2fr gray blk & red, gray	40.00　1.00

For overprints see Nos. O16-O18, 2031-2034, 3027-3030.

Building in Bern, Location of 1st
UPU Congress, 1874
A37　　　　　A38

1924, Oct. 9　Engr.　Wmk. 183
Granite Paper

204	A37	20c vermilion	42　40
205	A38	30c dull blue	1.10　2.50
		Set, never hinged	2.25

50th anniv. of the UPU.

The
Rütli — A39

Type of 1914 Issue

1928　Re-engraved　Perf. 11½

206	A39	5fr blue	125.00　1.75
		Never hinged	350.00
a.		Imperf., pair	15,000.

In the re-engraved stamp the picture is clearer and lighter than on No. 183. "HELVETIA" is in smaller letters. The names at foot of the stamp are "Grasset-J. Sprenger" instead of "E. GRASSET-A. BURKHARD."
For overprints see Nos. 2035, 3031.

Nos. 155 and 163 Surcharged　

1930, June　　　　Perf. 11½

207	A26	3c on 2½c ol grn, buff	15　80
208	A26	5c on 7½c dp grn, buff	18　4.50
		Set value	26
		Set, never hinged	50

The Mythen
A40

1931　Engr.　Granite Paper

209	A40	3fr orange brown	60.00　1.40
		Never hinged	140.00

For overprints see Nos. 2056, 3047.

Dove on
Broken
Sword — A41　　"Peace" — A42

1932, Feb. 2　Typo.　Perf. 11½
Granite Paper

210	A41	5c peacock blue	15　15
211	A41	10c orange	15　15
212	A41	20c cerise	20　15
213	A41	30c ultra	1.75　30
214	A41	60c olive brown	17.00　80

Unwmk.　Photo.

215	A42	1fr olive gray & bl	20.00　3.75
		Nos. 210-215 (6)	39.25　5.30
		Set, never hinged	85.00

Intl. Disarmament Conf., Geneva, Feb. 1932.
For overprints see #2036-2041, 3032-3037.

Louis
Favre — A43　　Alfred
Escher — A44

Design: 30c, Emil Welti.

Perf. 11½
1932, May 31　Engr.　Wmk. 183
Granite Paper

216	A43	10c red brown	15　15
217	A44	20c vermilion	15　15
218	A44	30c deep ultra	25　70
		Set, never hinged	1.00

Completion of the St. Gotthard tunnel, 50th anniv.
Nos. 216-218 exist imperforate.

Staubbach
Falls — A46　　Mt. Pilatus — A47

Chillon
Castle — A48　　Rhone
Glacier — A49

St. Gotthard
Railroad — A50　　Via Mala
Gorge — A51

Rhine Falls — A52

1934, July 2　Typo.　Perf. 11½
Granite Paper

219	A46	3c olive	15　1.10
220	A47	5c emerald	15　15
221	A48	10c brt violet	20　15
222	A49	15c orange	30　75
223	A50	20c red	35　15
224	A51	25c brown	7.00　2.75
225	A52	30c ultra	24.00　40
		Nos. 219-225 (7)	32.15　5.45
		Set, never hinged	90.00

Tête bêche Pairs

220a	A47	5c	1.50　1.50
221a	A48	10c	1.35　75
222a	A49	15c	1.65　2.75
223a	A50	20c	3.25　2.00

Souvenir Sheet
1934, Sept. 29

226	Sheet of 4	450.00　625.00
	Never hinged	825.00

No. 226 was issued in connection with the Swiss National Philatelic Exhibition at Zurich, Sept. 29 to Oct. 7, 1934. It contains one each of Nos. 220-223. Size: 62x72mm.
For overprints see Nos. 2042-2046, 3048.

Staubbach
Falls — A53　　Mt. Pilatus — A54

Chillon
Castle — A55　　Rhone
Glacier — A56

St. Gotthard
Railroad — A57　　Via Mala
Gorge — A58

Rhine Falls — A59　　Balsthal Pass — A60

Alpine Lake of
Säntis — A61

Two types of 10c red violet:
I - Shading inside "0" of 10 has only vertical lines.
II - Shading in "0" includes two diagonal lines.

1936-42　Unwmk.　Engr.　Perf. 11½

227	A53	3c olive	18　25
228	A54	5c blue green	18　15
229	A55	10c red vio (II)	40　15
b.		Type I	1.65　20
230	A55	10c dk red brn ('39)	15　15
230B	A55	10c org brn ('42)	15　15
231	A56	15c orange	50　60
232	A57	20c carmine	6.50　15
233	A58	25c lt brown	75　42
234	A59	30c ultra	1.25　15
235	A60	35c yellow grn	1.25　15
236	A61	40c gray	9.00　15
		Nos. 227-236 (11)	20.31
		Set value	2.55
		Set, never hinged	35.00

Two types of the 20c. See Nos. 316-321.
For overprints see Nos. O1-O4, O6-O9, O19-O19-O22, O24-O27, 2047-2055, 2068-2068A, 2070-2073, 2075-2078, 3038-3046, 3060-3060A, 3062-3065, 3067-3070, 401-404, 406-409, 4023-4024, 4027-4028, 501-502, 505.

Tête bêche Pairs

228a	A54	5c blue green	40　32
229a	A55	10c red violet (II)	4.00　5.00
230a	A55	10c dark red brown	1.65　1.00
230d	A55	10c orange brown	45　55
232a	A57	20c carmine	22.50　32.50

1936-40 — With Grilled Gum

227a	A53	3c olive	75	2.50
228d	A54	5c blue green	18	15
229d	A55	10c red violet (I)	60	15
e.		Type II	70	15
230e	A55	10c dark red brown ('40)	2.50	18.00
231a	A56	15c orange	60	20
232c	A57	20c carmine	8.00	15
233a	A58	25c light brown	1.00	1.50
234a	A59	30c ultra	1.10	18
235a	A60	35c yellow green	1.10	1.10
236a	A61	40c gray	6.00	18
		Nos. 227a-236a (10)	21.83	24.11
		Set, never hinged	37.50	

Mobile Post Office — A62

1937, Sept. 5 — Photo. — Granite Paper

237	A62	10c black & yellow	38	25
		Never hinged	50	

No. 237 was sold exclusively by the traveling post office. It exists on two kinds of granite paper, black and red fibers or blue and red fibers. See No. 307 for type A62 redrawn.

View of Labor Building from Lake Geneva A63

Palace of League of Nations A64

Main Building, Palace of League of Nations A65

Labor Building and Albert Thomas Monument A66

1938, May 2 — Perf. 11½ — Granite Paper

238	A63	20c red & buff	16	15
239	A64	30c blue & lt blue	35	15
240	A65	60c brown & buff	1.75	42
241	A66	1fr black & buff	8.00	7.50
		Set, never hinged	22.50	

Opening of Assembly Hall of the Palace of the League of Nations.
For overprints see #O2O57-2064, 3049-3056.

Souvenir Sheet

A67

Switzerland stamps can be mounted in the annually supplemented Scott Switzerland album.

Engraved and Typographed
1938, Sept. 17 — Unwmk. — Perf. 11½ — Granite Paper

242	A67	Sheet of 3	40.00	32.50
		Never hinged	65.00	
a.		AP4 10c on 65c gray bl & dp bl	30.00	25.00
b.		A68 20c red	3.00	2.25

Natl. Phil. Exhib. at Aarau, Sept. 17-25, and 25th anniv. of Swiss air mail. No. 242 contains 2 No. 243, but on granite paper, and a 10c on 65c similar to No. C22 but redrawn, with wing tips 1½mm from side frame lines; overall size 37x20½mm; no watermark. On No. C22, wing tips touch frame lines; size is 36x21½mm; Wmk. 183.

Lake Lugano — A68

First Federal Pact, 1291 — A69

Diet of Stans, 1481 — A70

Citizens Voting A71

1938, Sept. 17 — Engr. — Perf. 11½

243	A68	20c red	18	15
a.		Tête bêche pair	75	45
c.		Grilled gum	32	15
d.		As "c," tête bêche pair	2.00	7.50

Granite Paper

244	A69	3fr brn car, grnsh	11.00	1.90
245	A70	5fr slate bl, grnsh	11.00	1.65
246	A71	10fr grn, grnsh	42.50	11.50
		Set, never hinged	150.00	

No. 243 is printed on ordinary paper. Nos. 244-246 are on granite surface-colored paper. The greenish surface coating has faded on most copies.
For type A68 in orange brown, see No. 318.
See Nos. 242b, 284-286. For overprints see Nos. O5, O23, 2065-2067, 2069, 2074, 2088-2090, 3057-3059, 3061, 3066, 3080-3082, 4O5, 4019-4021, O4O25, 5O3, 5023-5025, 7018-7020.

Deputation of Trades and Professions A72

Swiss Family A73

Alpine Scenery A74

Engr., Photo. (30c)
1939, Feb. 1 — Perf. 11½
Inscribed in French

247	A72	10c dl pur & red	22	15
248	A73	20c lake & red	45	15
249	A74	30c dp blue & red	2.25	2.50

Inscribed in German

250	A72	10c dl pur & red	22	15
251	A73	20c lake & red	45	15
252	A74	30c dp blue & red	2.25	1.00

Inscribed in Italian

253	A72	10c dl pur & red	22	15
254	A73	20c lake & red	95	15
255	A74	30c dp blue & red	2.50	3.00
		Nos. 247-255 (9)	9.51	7.40
		Set, never hinged	21.00	

National Exposition of 1939, Zurich.

Tree and Crossbow — A75

1939, May 6 — Photo. — Perf. 11½ — Granite Paper
Inscribed in French

256	A75	5c deep green	48	1.75
257	A75	10c gray brn	80	1.50
258	A75	20c brt carmine	1.40	15.00
259	A75	30c violet blue	2.00	5.50

Inscribed in German

260	A75	5c deep green	48	1.75
261	A75	10c gray brn	40	1.10
262	A75	20c brt car	1.40	15.00
263	A75	30c violet bl	2.00	4.75

Inscribed in Italian

264	A75	5c deep green	48	1.75
265	A75	10c gray brn	80	1.50
266	A75	20c brt carmine	1.40	15.00
267	A75	30c violet bl	2.25	5.50
		Nos. 256-267 (12)	13.89	70.10
		Set, never hinged	27.50	

National Exposition of 1939.
The 5c, 10c and 20c stamps in the three languages exist se-tenant in coils.

1939 — With Grilled Gum

256a	A75	5c deep green	70	1.00
257a	A75	10c gray brown	70	80
258a	A75	20c bright carmine	1.40	80
260a	A75	5c deep green	70	80
262a	A75	20c bright carmine	1.40	90
264a	A75	5c deep green	70	1.40
265a	A75	10c gray brown	70	1.00
266a	A75	20c bright carmine	1.40	1.25
		Nos. 256a-266a (8)	7.70	7.95

View of Geneva A76

1939, Aug. 22 — Perf. 11½ — Photo. — Unwmk. — Granite Paper

268	A76	20c red, car & buff	25	15
269	A76	30c blue, car & gray	50	60
		Set, never hinged	1.00	

75th anniv. of the founding of the Intl. Red Cross Society.

"The Three Swiss" — A77

William Tell — A78

Fighting Soldier — A79

Dying Warrior — A80

Standard Bearer — A81

Ludwig Pfyffer — A82

Jürg Jenatsch A83

Francois de Reynold A84

Joachim Forrer — A85

1941-59 — Engr. — Perf. 11½ — Granite Paper

270	A77	50c dp pur, grnsh	5.25	15
271	A78	60c red brn, buff	6.25	15
272	A79	70c rose vio, pale lil	4.25	60
273	A80	80c blk, pale gray	1.00	15
a.		80c black, pale lilac ('58)	1.25	30
274	A81	90c dk red, pale rose	1.10	15
a.		90c dark red, buff ('59)	1.40	32
275	A82	1fr dk grn, grnsh	1.25	15
276	A83	1.20fr red vio, pale gray	1.40	15
a.		1.20fr red vio, pale lil ('58)	1.65	30
277	A84	1.50fr dk bl, buff	1.65	25
278	A85	2fr mar, pale rose	2.50	15
a.		2fr maroon, buff ('59)	3.25	30
		Nos. 270-278 (9)	24.65	
		Set value		1.40
		Set, never hinged	42.50	

For overprints see Nos. O28-O36, 2079-2087, 3071-3079, 4010-4018, 5017-5022, 606-608, 7012-7017.

Farmer Plowing A86

1941, Mar. 21 — Photo. — Granite Paper

279	A86	10c brn & buff	15	15
		Never hinged	20	

Issued to publicize the National Agriculture Development Plan of 1941.

Masons, Knight and Bern Coat of Arms — A87

1941, Sept. 6 — Granite Paper

280	A87	10c multi	15	18
		Never hinged	20	

750th anniversary of Bern.

"In order to Endure, Reclaim Used Materials" Inscribed in French A88

1942, Mar. 21   Unwmk.   Perf. 11½

281	A88	10c shown	52	30
282	A88	10c German	15	15
283	A88	10c Italian	8.75	1.10
		Set, never hinged	14.00	
		Sheet of 25	90.00	550.00

Printed in sheets of 25, containing 8 No. 281, 12 No. 282 and 5 No. 283.

Types of 1938

1955   Engr.
Cream-surfaced Granite Paper

284	A69	3fr brown car	9.00	18
285	A70	5fr slate blue	5.00	28
286	A71	10fr green	9.00	90
		Set, never hinged	27.50	

1942   Cream paper

284a	A69	3fr	32.50	16
285a	A70	5fr	22.50	16
286a	A71	10fr	32.50	32
		Set, never hinged	120.00	

The 1955 set is on cream-surfaced granite paper with white back, and blue and red fibers. The 1942 set is on colored-through cream paper with black and red fibers.

Zurich Stamps of 1843 — A91

1943, Feb. 26

287	A91	10c blk & salmon	15	15
		Never hinged	16	

Centenary of postage stamps of Switzerland. See Nos. B130-B131.

Apollo Statue — A94

1944, Mar. 21   Photo.
Granite Paper

290	A94	10c org yel & gray blk	15	75
291	A94	20c cer & gray blk	30	75
292	A94	30c lt bl & gray blk	75	4.00
		Set, never hinged	1.75	

Olympic Jubilee.

Numeral of Value — A95

Olive Branch — A96

Designs: 60c, Keys of peace. 80c, Horn of plenty. 1fr, Dove of peace. 2fr, Plowing. 3fr, Field of crocus. 5fr, Clasped hands. 10fr, Aged couple.

1945, May 9   Unwmk.   Perf. 12
Granite Paper

293	A95	5c gray & grn	15	20
294	A95	10c gray & brn	16	20
295	A95	20c gray & car rose	38	15
296	A95	30c gray & ultra	65	1.50
297	A95	40c gray & org	1.65	6.75
298	A96	50c dk red	2.50	11.00
299	A96	60c dl gray	2.25	4.00
300	A96	80c slate gray	5.50	42.50
301	A96	1fr blue	8.00	47.50
302	A96	2fr red brn	24.00	80.00

Engr.

303	A96	3fr dk sl grn, buff	30.00	35.00
304	A96	5fr brn lake, buff	110.00	200.00
305	A96	10fr rose vio, buff	125.00	80.00
		Nos. 293-305,B145 (14)	310.66	509.40
		Set, never hinged	500.00	

End of war in Europe.

Johann Heinrich Pestalozzi — A104

1946, Jan. 12   Engr.   Perf. 11½

306	A104	10c rose vio	15	15
		Never hinged	16	

200th anniversary of the birth of J. H. Pestalozzi, educational reformer.

For overprint see No. 4022.

Mobile P.O. Type of 1937
Redrawn

1946, July 6   Photo.
Granite Paper

307	A62	10c blk & yel	1.75	15
		Never hinged	2.50	

The designer's and printer's names are larger on the redrawn stamp. There are many minor differences in the two designs. Sizes: 1937, 37½x21mm. 1946, 38x22½mm.

First Swiss Steam Locomotive A105

Modern Steam Locomotive A106

Electric Gotthard Express A107

Electric Trains Passing on Bridge A108

1947, Aug. 6   Photo.   Perf. 11½
Granite Paper

308	A105	5c dk grn, blk & yel	15	20
309	A106	10c dk brn, gray & blk	18	15
310	A107	20c dk red & red	20	15
311	A108	30c dk bl & bl gray	90	1.00
		Set, never hinged	2.00	

Centenary of the opening of the first Swiss railroad, between Zurich and Baden.

Johann Rudolf Wettstein A109

Castle at Neuchatel A110

"Helvetia" A111

Symbol of Swiss Federal State A112

1948, Feb. 27   Granite Paper

312	A109	5c dp grn	15	18
313	A110	10c gray blk	15	15
314	A111	20c dk red	15	15
315	A112	30c dk bl & red	35	75
		Set value	65	
		Set, never hinged	1.00	

Tercentenary of the acknowledgment of independence of the Swiss Confederation, and the centenaries of the Neuchatel Revolution and the Swiss Federal State.

See Nos. B178a and B178b for 10c and 20c denominations, type A109.

Types of 1936-42 and

Grisons National Park — A113

1948, Mar. 1   Engr.

316	A54	5c chocolate	15	15
a.		Tête bêche pair	1.25	1.25
317	A55	10c green	15	15
a.		Tête bêche pair	1.25	1.50
318	A68	20c org brn	30	15
a.		Tête bêche pair	1.65	2.25
319	A113	25c carmine	1.75	85
320	A59	30c grnsh bl	7.50	1.00
321	A61	40c ultra	13.00	25
		Nos. 316-321 (6)	22.85	2.55
		Set, never hinged	45.00	

For overprints see Nos. 4026, 504.

Figures Encircling Globe A114

Designs: 25c, Globe and inscribed ribbon. 40c, Globe and pigeons.

Perf. 11½

1949, May 16   Photo.   Unwmk.

322	A114	10c green	15	15
323	A114	25c dk red	42	5.00
324	A114	40c brt bl	60	2.00
		Set, never hinged	1.75	

75th anniv. of the UPU.

Post Horn A115

Horse Drawn Mail Coach A116

Design: 30c, Post bus with trailer.

1949, May 16

325	A115	5c gray, yel & pink	15	28
326	A116	20c pur, gray & yel	24	28
327	A116	30c dk org brn, gray & yel	45	4.50
		Set, never hinged	1.10	

Centenary of the establishment of the Federal Post in Switzerland.

High Tension Conductors A117 | Viaducts A118

Mountain Railway — A119 | Rotary Snow Plow — A120

Reservoir, Grimsel — A121 | Lake Dam — A122

Dam and Power Station — A123 | Alpine Postal Road — A124

Harbor of the Rhine — A125 | Suspension Railway — A126

Railway Viaduct — A127 | Triangulation Point — A128

Two types of 20c:
I- Three lines above curved rock.
II- Two lines above rock.

Perf. 12x11½

1949, Aug. 1   Engr.   Unwmk.

328	A117	3c gray	1.90	3.25
329	A118	5c orange	18	15
a.		Tête bêche pair	90	15
330	A119	10c yel grn	15	15
a.		Tête bêche pair	60	15
331	A120	15c aqua	18	15
332	A121	20c brn car (II)	30	15
a.		Tête bêche pair	1.75	75
c.		Type I	2,500.	67.50
c.		Never hinged	3,500.	
333	A122	25c red	32	15
334	A123	30c olive	40	15
335	A124	35c red brn	50	30
336	A125	40c deep blue	1.50	15
337	A126	50c slate gray	1.50	15
338	A127	60c bl grn	2.75	15
339	A128	70c purple	1.25	30
		Nos. 328-339 (12)	10.93	
		Set value		4.30
		Set, never hinged	16.00	

For use in vending machines, some printings of the 5c, 10c, 20c (II), 25c, 30c and 40c carry a control number on the back of every fifth stamp. The number was applied on top of the gum.

For overprints see Nos. O37-O47, 3083-3093, 4029-4039, 506-5016, 601-605, 701-7011.

Symbolical of the Telegraph — A129

Symbolical Designs: 10c, Telephone. 20c, Radio. 40c, Television.

1952, Feb. 1   Photo.   Perf. 11½

340	A129	5c org & yel	25	30
341	A129	10c brt grn & pink	32	15
342	A129	20c dp red lil & gray bl	48	15
343	A129	40c dp bl & lt bl	1.90	3.25
		Set, never hinged	5.25	

"A century of telecommunications."

Zurich Airport and Tail of Plane
A130

1953, Aug. 29

344	A130	40c bl red & gray	2.75	6.00
		Never hinged	5.00	

Opening of Zurich-Kloten airport.

Alpine Post Bus, Winter Background
A131

Design: 20c, Same, summer background.

1953, Oct. 8

345	A131	10c dk grn, grn & yel	15	15
346	A131	20c dk red, red brn & yel	18	15
		Set value	26	15
		Set, never hinged	35	

Sold only on Swiss alpine post buses.

Symbols of Agriculture, Forestry and Horticulture
A132

Map and Nautical Emblems — A133

Alphorn Blower — A135

Lausanne Cathedral
A134

Designs: 20c, Winged spoon. 40c, Football and map.

1954, Mar. 15   Perf. 14

347	A132	10c multi	15	15
348	A132	20c multi	15	15
349	A133	25c red, dk ol grn & gray	1.00	2.00
350	A132	40c bl, yel & brn	1.50	1.50
		Set, never hinged	5.50	

Nos. 347-348 were issued to publicize exhibitions at Lucerne and Bern; No. 349, fifty years of navigation on the Rhine; No. 350, the 1954 World Soccer Championships in Switzerland.

1955, Feb. 15   Perf. 11½

Designs: 10c, Vaud costume hat. 40c, Automobile steering wheel.

351	A134	5c multi	20	15
352	A134	10c grn, yel & red	25	15
a.		Souvenir sheet of 2	60.00	87.50
		Never hinged	85.00	

353	A135	20c red & sepia	60	15
354	A134	40c bl, pink & gray	1.50	1.40
		Set value		1.64
		Set, never hinged		4.00

No. 352a contains 10c and 20c multicolored, imperf. stamps of Cathedral type A134. Size: 104x52mm.

National Philatelic Exhibition (5c, #352a), Winegrowers' Festival (10c), Alpine Herdsman and Costume Festival (20c) and 25th Intl. Automobile Show (40c).

First Swiss Post Bus — A136

Designs: 10c, North Gate of Simplon Tunnel and Stockalper Palace. 20c, Children crossing street and road signs. 40c, Planes and emblem of Swissair, vert.

1956, Mar. 1   Granite Paper   Photo.

355	A136	5c ol gray, blk & yel	20	16
356	A136	10c brt grn, gray & red	25	15
357	A136	20c multi	50	15
358	A136	40c blue & red	1.25	85
		Set, never hinged	3.75	

50th anniv. of the Swiss Motor Coach Service (#355); 50th anniv. of the opening of Simplon Tunnel (#356); Accident prevention (#357); 25th anniv. of the founding of Swissair (#358).

Inking Device, Printing Machine — A137

Designs: 10c, Train on southern ramp of Gotthard Railroad. 20c, Shield of civil defense and coat of arms. 40c, Munatius Plancus and view of Basel.

Two types of 10c:
I- "Black" bottom line on train.
II- Brown bottom line.

1957, Feb. 27   Perf. 11½

Granite Paper

359	A137	5c multi	15	15
360	A137	10c lt bl grn, dk grn & red brn (I)	1.40	15
a.		Type II	1.00	18
		Never hinged	1.75	
361	A137	20c red org & gray	35	15
362	A137	40c multi	1.00	85
		Set value		1.10
		Set, never hinged	4.25	

Intl. Exhibition for Graphic Arts, Lausanne, June 1-16, 1957 (#359). 75th anniv. of St. Gotthard railroad (#360). Civil defense (#361). 2000th anniv. of Basel (#362).

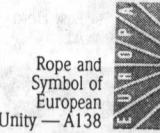

Rope and Symbol of European Unity — A138

1957, July 15   Engr.   Perf. 11½

363	A138	25c lt red	45	18
364	A138	40c blue	2.25	15
		Set, never hinged	3.75	

Issued to emphasize European unity.

> Catalogue values for unused stamps in this section, from this point to the end of the section, are for Never Hinged items.

Nyon Castle and Corinthian Capital — A139

Designs: 10c, Woman's head and ribbons in Swiss colors. 20c, Crossbow emblem. 40c, Salvation Army hat.

1958, Mar. 5   Photo.   Unwmk.

Granite Paper

365	A139	5c ol bis & dl pur	15	15
366	A139	10c grn, dk grn & red	15	15
367	A139	20c ver, lil & car	35	15
368	A139	40c multi	1.75	80
		Set value		1.05

2000th anniv. of Nyon (#365). Saffa Exhibition, Zurich, July 17-Sept. 15 (#366). 25th anniv. of Swiss manufacturing emblem (#367). 75th anniv. of the Salvation Army in Switzerland (#368).

Symbol of Nuclear Fission — A140

1958, Aug. 25   Perf. 11½

Granite Paper

369	A140	40c bl, yel & red	42	40

2nd UN Atomic Conf. for peaceful uses of atomic power, Geneva, Sept. 1958.

"Transportation"
A141

Designs: 10c, Fasces and post horn. 20c, Owl, rabbit and fish. 50c, Jean Calvin, Theodore de Beze and University of Geneva.

1959, Mar. 9   Photo.   Unwmk.

Granite Paper

370	A141	5c multi	20	15
371	A141	10c emer, yel & lt gray	30	15
a.		Souvenir sheet of 2, imperf.	14.00	16.00
372	A141	20c multi	75	15
373	A141	50c multi	1.40	75
		Set value		1.00

Opening of the Swiss House of Transport and Communications (5c). Natl. Phil. Exhib., St. Gall, Aug. 21-30 (10c and #371a). Protection of animals (20c). 400th anniv. of the University of Geneva (50c).

No. 371a contains a 10c green, gold and light gray and a 20c deep carmine. Sold for 2fr; the money went for the St. Gall Phil. Exhib.

Chain Symbolizing European Unity — A142

1959, June 22   Engr.   Perf. 11½

374	A142	30c brick red	70	15
375	A142	50c lt ultra	85	15
		Set value		22

Issued to emphasize European Unity.

Overprinted "REUNION DES PTT D'EUROPE 1959" in Ultramarine or Red

1959, June 22

376	A142	30c brick red	8.25	6.25
377	A142	50c lt ultra	8.25	6.25

European Conference of PTT Administrations, Montreux, June 22-July 31. Nos. 376-377 were on sale only during the conference at a special P. O. in Montreux.

"Cancer Control" — A143

Designs: 20c, Founding charter and scepter of University of Basel. 50c, Uprooted Oak Emblem. 75c, Swissair Jet DC-8.

1960, Apr. 7   Photo.   Perf. 11½

Granite Paper

378	A143	10c brt grn & red	30	15
379	A143	20c car rose, gray blk & yel	90	15
380	A143	50c ultra & yel	70	75
381	A143	75c lt bl, gray & red	1.65	2.25

50th anniv. of the Swiss League for Cancer control (10c). 500th anniv. of the University of Basel (20c). World Refugee Year, July 1, 1959-June 30, 1960 (50c). Swissair's entry into the jet age (75c).

Messenger, Fribourg
A144

Cathedral, Lausanne
A145

Designs: 10c, Messenger, Schwyz. 15c, Messenger and pack animal. 20c, Postilion on horseback. 30c, Grossmünster (church), Zürich. 35c, 13th. Woodcutters' Guildhall, Biel. 40c, Cathedral, Geneva. 50c, Spalen Gate, Basel. 60c, Clock Tower, Berne. 70c, 2.80fr, Sts. Peter and Stephen Church, Bellinzona (tower omitted on 2.80fr). 75c, Bridge and water tower, Lucerne. 80c, Cathedral, St. Gallen. 90c, Munot tower, Schaffhausen. 1fr, Townhall, Fribourg. 1.20fr, Basel gate, Solothurn. 1.50fr, Reding house, Schwyz. 1.70fr, 2fr, 2.20fr, Church, Einsiedeln.

Two types of 5c, 10c, 20c, 50c:
5 Centimes:
Type I - Four lines on pike at left of hand.
Type II - Three lines.
10 Centimes:
Type I - Dot on pike below head.
Type II - No dot.
20 Centimes:
Type I - Ten dots on horiz. harness strip.
Type II - Nine dots.
50 Centimes:
Type I - 3 shading lines at right above arch.
Type II - 2 shading lines.

1960-63   Engr.   Perf. 11½
1.30fr, 1.70fr, 2.20fr, 2.80fr on Granite Paper, Red and Blue Fibers

382	A144	5c lt ultra (I)	15	15
c.		Tête bêche pair	15	15
383	A144	10c blue grn (I)	15	15
c.		Tête bêche pair	35	20
384	A144	15c lt red brn	16	15
385	A144	20c rose pink (I)	20	15
c.		Tête bêche pair	60	45
386	A145	25c emerald	28	15
387	A145	30c vermilion	32	15
388	A145	35c orange red	40	30
389	A145	40c lilac	52	15
390	A145	50c lt vio bl (I)	52	15
c.		Tête bêche pair	2.50	2.50
391	A145	60c rose red	55	15
392	A145	70c orange	60	42
393	A145	75c lt blue	48	18
394	A145	80c dp claret	80	15
395	A145	90c olive green	80	15
396	A144	1fr dull orange	90	15
397	A144	1.20fr dull red	1.00	30
397A	A144	1.30fr red brn, pink ('63)	1.25	15
398	A144	1.50fr brt green	1.40	28
398A	A144	1.70fr rose lil, pink ('63)	1.50	15
399	A144	2fr brt blue	8.50	85
399A	A144	2.20fr bl grn, grn ('63)	2.00	32
399B	A145	2.80fr org, buff ('63)	2.75	28
		Nos. 382-399B (22)	25.23	
		Set value		3.75

See Nos. 440-455.

1963-76
Violet Fibers, Fluorescent Paper

382d	A144	5c lt ultra (I)	15	15
g.		Tête bêche pair ('68)	20	20
383d	A144	10c bl grn (I)	15	15
e.		Bklt. pane of 2 + 2 labels ('68)	65	65
g.		Tête bêche pair ('68)	30	20
384a	A144	15c lt red brn	48	30
385d	A144	20c rose pink (I)	24	15
g.		Tête bêche pair ('68)	60	15
386a	A145	25c emerald	28	15
387a	A145	30c vermilion	35	15
e.		Tête bêche pair ('68)	90	65
389a	A145	40c lilac ('67)	48	15
e.		Tête bêche pair ('76)	1.25	1.00
390d	A145	50c lt vio bl (I)	70	15
391a	A145	60c rose red ('67)	60	15
393a	A145	75c lt bl ('68)	80	38
394a	A145	80c dp claret	1.00	15
395a	A145	90c ol grn ('67)	1.00	15
396a	A144	1fr lt org ('67)	1.75	15
397b	A144	1.20fr dl red ('68)	2.50	1.50
398b	A144	1.50fr brn grn ('68)	2.75	1.50
		Nos. 382a-398b (15)	13.23	
		Set value		4.40

Coil Stamps

1960   **White Paper**

382b	A144	5c lt ultra (II)	90	90
383b	A144	10c bl grn (II)	75	75
385b	A144	20c rose pink (II)	1.00	1.00
390b	A145	50c lt vio bl (II)	3.25	3.25

The coil stamps were printed in sheets (available to collectors) and pasted into coils. Every fifth stamp has a control number on the back.
Other denominations issued in coils on white paper are: 40c, 60c, 90c, 1fr, 1.30fr, 1.70fr, 2.20fr and 2.80fr.
Denominations issued in coils on granite paper (red & blue fibers) are: 1.30fr, 1.70fr, 2.20fr and 2.80fr.

Coil Stamps

1965-68
Violet Fibers, Fluorescent Paper

382e	A144	5c lt ultra (II)	90	90
383e	A144	10c bl grn (II)	40	15
385e	A144	20c rose pink (II)	40	25
390e	A145	50c lt vio bl (II)	3.00	3.00

Other denominations issued in coils on violet-fiber paper are: 40c, 60c, 90c and 1fr.

Europa Issue, 1960
Common Design Type

1960, Sept. 19   **Unwmk.**   **Perf. 11½**
Size: 33x23mm

400	CD3	30c vermilion	35	15
401	CD3	50c ultra	45	15

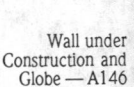

Wall under Construction and Globe — A146

Designs: 10c, Symbolic sun (HYSPA Emblem). 20c, Ice hockey stick and puck. 50c, Wiring diagram on map of Switzerland.

1961, Feb. 20   **Photo.**   **Perf. 11½**
Granite Paper

402	A146	5c gray, brick red & grnsh bl	38	15
403	A146	10c aqua & yel	38	15
404	A146	20c multi	95	15
405	A146	50c ultra, gray & car rose	1.65	1.25
		Set value		1.45

Development aid to new nations (5c). HYSPA 1961, Health and Sports Exhibition, Bern, May 18-July 17 (10c). Intl. Ice Hockey Championships, Lausanne and Geneva, Mar. 2-12 (20c). Fully automatic Swiss telephone service (50c).

MATTHAEUS
St. Matthew and Angel — A147

Evangelists: 5fr, St. Mark and winged lion. 10fr, St. Luke and winged ox. 20fr, St. John and eagle.

Perf. 11½

1961, Sept. 18   **Unwmk.**   **Engr.**
Granite Paper

406	A147	3fr rose car	4.75	15
407	A147	5fr dk bl	3.75	18
408	A147	10fr dk brn	8.25	45
409	A147	20fr red	15.00	1.75

Designs are after 15th century wood carvings from St. Oswald's church, Zug.

Europa Issue, 1961
Common Design Type

1961, Sept. 18
Size: 26x21mm

410	CD4	30c vermilion	32	15
411	CD4	50c blue	38	18

Trans-Europe Express — A148

Designs: 10c, Rower. 20c, Jungfrau railroad station and Mönch. 50c, W.H.O. Anti-malaria emblem.

1962, Mar. 19   **Photo.**   **Perf. 11½**

412	A148	5c multi	52	15
413	A148	10c brt grn, lem & lil	52	15
414	A148	20c rose lil, pale bl & bis	70	15
415	A148	50c ultra, lt grn & rose lil	1.25	85
		Set value		1.00

Introduction of Swiss electric TEE trains (5c). Rowing world championship, Lucerne, Sept. 6-9 (10c). 50th anniv. of the railroad station on the Jungfrau mountain (20c). WHO Anti-Malaria campaign (50c).

Europa Issue, 1962
Common Design Type

1962, Sept. 17   **Unwmk.**   **Perf. 11½**
Size: 33x23mm

416	CD5	30c org, yel & brn	38	25
417	CD5	50c ultra, lt grn & brn	75	50

Boy Scout — A149

Designs: 10c, Swiss Alpine Club emblem. 20c, Luegelkinn viaduct. 30c, Wheat Emblem. No. 426, 428a, Red Cross Jubilee Emblem. No. 427, Post Office Building, Paris, 1863.

1963, Mar. 21   **Photo.**

422	A149	5c gray, dk red & brn	60	15
423	A149	10c dk grn, gray & red	35	15
424	A149	20c dk car, brn & gray	1.10	15
425	A149	30c yel grn, yel & org	1.50	1.25
426	A149	50c bl, sil & red	65	65
427	A149	50c ultra, pink, yel & gray	65	65
		Nos. 422-427 (6)	4.85	3.00

Souvenir Sheet
Imperf

428		Sheet of 4	8.00	5.75
a.		A149 50c bl, lt bl, sil & red	2.00	1.00

50 years of Swiss Boy Scouts (5c). Cent. of Swiss Alpine Club (10c). 50 years Lötschberg Railroad (20c). FAO "Freedom from Hunger" campaign (30c). Red Cross Cent. (#426, 428). 1st Intl. Postal Conf., Paris 1863 (#427).
No. 428 sold for 3fr.

Common Design Types pictured in section at front of book.

Europa Issue, 1963
Common Design Type

1963, Sept. 16   **Unwmk.**   **Perf. 11½**
Granite Paper
Size: 26x21mm

429	CD6	50c ultra & ocher	60	28

EXPO Emblem — A150

Designs: 50c, EXPO emblem on globe and moon ("Outlook"). 75c, EXPO emblem on globe ("Insight").

1963, Sept. 16   **Unwmk.**   **Perf. 11½**
Granite Paper

430	A150	10c brt grn & dk grn	30	15
431	A150	20c red & mar	35	15
432	A150	50c ultra & red	42	40
433	A150	75c pur & red	60	45
		Set value		95

Issued to publicize the Swiss National Exhibition, Lausanne, Apr. 30-Oct. 25, 1964.

Road Tunnel Through Great St. Bernard — A151

Designs: 10c, Symbolic water god and waves. 20c, Soldiers of 1864 and 1964. 50c, Standards of Swiss Confederation and Geneva.

1964, Mar. 9   **Photo.**
Granite Paper

434	A151	5c ol, ultra & red	18	15
435	A151	10c Prus bl & grn	18	15
436	A151	20c red, ultra, blk & sal	38	15
437	A151	50c ultra, red, yel & blk	95	65
		Set value		85

1st Trans-Alpine Automobile route from Switzerland to Italy (5c). "Pro Aqua" water conservation campaign (10c). Centenary of the Swiss Noncommissioned Officers' Association (20c). Sesquicentennial of union of Geneva with Swiss Confederation (50c).

Europa Issue, 1964
Common Design Type

1964, Sept. 14   **Engr.**   **Perf. 11½**
Size: 21x26mm
Violet Fibers, Fluorescent Paper

438	CD7	20c vermilion	30	15
439	CD7	50c ultra	65	20
		Set value		26

Type of Regular Issue, 1960-63

Designs: 5c, Lenzburg. 10c, Freuler Mansion, Näfels. 15c, St. Mauritius Church, Appenzell. 20c, Planta House, Samedan. 30c, Gabled houses, Gais. 50c, Castle and Abbey Church, Neuchâtel. 70c, Lussy House, Wolfenschiessen. 1fr, Santa Croce Church, Riva San Vitale. 1.20fr, Abbey Church, Payerne. 1.30fr, Church of St. Pierre de Clages. 1.50fr, La Porte de France, Porrentruy. 1.70fr, Frauenfeld Castle. 2fr, A Pro Castle, Seedorf. 2.20fr, Thomas Tower and Gate. Liestal. 2.50fr, St. Oswald's Church, Zug. 3.50fr, Benedictine Abbey, Engelberg.

1964-68   **Engr.**   **Perf. 11½**
Violet Fibers, Fluorescent Paper

440	A144	5c car rose ('68)	15	15
441	A144	10c vio bl ('68)	15	15
b.		Tête bêche pair	25	15
c.		Booklet pane of 2 + 2 labels	70	
442	A144	15c brn red ('68)	15	15
b.		Tête bêche pair	35	35
443	A144	20c bl grn ('68)	18	15
b.		Tête bêche pair	50	35
444	A144	30c ver ('68)	30	15
b.		Tête bêche pair	90	80
445	A144	50c ultra ('68)	48	15
446	A145	70c brown ('67)	65	15
447	A145	1fr dk green ('68)	95	15
448	A145	1.20fr brn red ('68)	1.10	15
449	A145	1.30fr vio bl ('66)	1.50	24
450	A145	1.50fr green ('68)	1.50	15
451	A145	1.70fr brn org ('66)	1.50	24
452	A145	2fr orange ('67)	1.90	24
453	A145	2.20fr green	3.25	42
454	A145	2.50fr Prus grn ('67)	2.25	30
455	A145	3.50fr purple ('67)	2.75	35
		Nos. 440-455 (16)	18.76	
		Set value		2.40

The 15c was issued in coils in 1972 (?) with control number on the back of every fifth stamp.

Nurse and Patient — A152

Seated Helvetia, 1854 — A153

Women's Army Auxiliary — A154

Intercontinental Communications Map — A155

1965, Mar. 8   **Photo.**   **Perf. 11½**
Violet Fibers, Fluorescent Paper

462	A152	5c lt ultra & red	15	15
463	A153	10c emer, brn & blk	20	15
464	A154	20c red & multi	35	15

Granite Paper, Red and Blue Fibers

465	A155	50c dl bl grn & mar	60	35
		Set value		56

Nursing and auxiliary medical professions (5c). Natl. Postage Stamp Exhibition, NABRA, Bern, Aug. 27-Sept. 5, 1965 (10c). 20th anniv. of Women's Army Auxiliary Corps (20c). Cent. of ITU (50c).
See No. B344.

Swiss Arms, Cantonal Emblems of Valais, Neuchatel, Geneva
A156

1965, June 1   **Unwmk.**   **Perf. 11½**
Granite Paper, Red and Blue Fibers

466	A156	20c multicolored	22	15

150th anniversary of the entry of the cantons of Valais, Neuchatel and Geneva in the Swiss Confederation.

Matterhorn A157

Design: 30c, like 10c but inscribed in French "Cervin."

1965, June 1   **Photo.**
Granite Paper, Red and Blue Fibers

467	A157	10c grn, slate & dk red	15	15

Violet Fibers, Fluorescent Paper

468	A157	30c dk red, grn & slate	35	40

Year of the Alps; the cent. of the 1st wintertime visitors to the Alps and cent. of the 1st ascent of the Matterhorn. Nos. 467-468 on sale only at Swiss Alpine post buses.

Europa Issue, 1965
Common Design Type

1965, Sept. 14   **Unwmk.**   **Perf. 11½**
Violet Fibers, Fluorescent Paper

469	CD8	50c bl, dk bl & grn	48	28

Figure Skating — A159

1965, Sept. 14   **Photo.**
Violet Fibers, Fluorescent Paper

470	A159	5c grn, dl bl & blk	15	15

Issued to publicize the World Figure Skating Championships, Davos, Feb. 22-27, 1966.

ITU Emblem and Atom Diagram A160

Cent. of the ITU: 30c, Symbol of communications, waves.

1965, Sept. 14
Violet Fibers, Fluorescent Paper
471 A160 10c ultra & multi   15 15

Granite Paper, Red and Blue Fibers
472 A160 30c org, red & gray   35 35

Violet Fibers, Fluorescent Paper
Paper from No. 473 onward is fluorescent and has violet fibers, unless otherwise noted.

European
Kingfisher
A161

Mercury's
Helmet and
Laurel — A162

Flags of 13
Member Nations
and Nuclear
Fission — A163

1966, Feb. 21   **Photo.**
473 A161 10c emer & multi   15 15
474 A162 20c dp mag, red & brt grn   18 15
475 A163 50c slate blue & multi   48 38
       Set value   50

Intl. Cong. for Conservation "Pro Natura," Lucerne (10c). 50th anniv. of Swiss Trade Fair, Basel, Apr. 16-26 (20c). European Organization for Nuclear Research, CERN (50c).

Emblem of
Society of
Swiss Abroad
A164

Finsteraarhorn
A165

1966, June 1   Photo.   Perf. 11½
476 A164 20c ultra & ver   18 15

50th anniv. of the Society of Swiss Abroad.

Europa Issue, 1966
Common Design Type
1966, Sept. 26   Engr.   Perf. 11½
Size: 21x26mm
477 CD9 20c vermilion   20 15
478 CD9 50c ultra   50 15
       Set value   20

1966, Sept. 26   **Photo.**
479 A165 10c lt grnsh bl, dk bl & dk red 15 15

Automobile
Wheels and
White
Cane — A166

Flags of EFTA
Members
A167

1967, Mar. 13   Photo.   Perf. 11½
480 A166 10c bl grn, blk & yel   15 15
481 A167 20c multicolored   18 15
       Set value   26 15

No. 480 issued to publicize the white cane as a distinguishing mark for blind pedestrians. No. 481 publicizes the European Free Trade Association, EFTA. See note after Norway No. 501.

Europa Issue, 1967
Common Design Type
1967, Mar. 13
482 CD10 30c blue gray   30 15

Cogwheel and
Swiss
Emblem — A169

Hourglass and
Sun — A170

San Bernardino,
from
North — A171

Railroad
Wheel — A172

1967, Sept. 18   Photo.   Perf. 11½
483 A169 10c multicolored   15 15
484 A170 20c red, yel & blk   15 15
485 A171 30c multicolored   35 15
486 A172 50c multicolored   50 32
       Set value   52

50th anniv. of Swiss Week (10c). 50th anniv. of the Foundation for the Aged (20c). Opening of the San Bernardino Road Tunnel (30c). 75th anniv. of the Central Office for Intl. Railroad Transportation (50c).

Mountains and
Club's
Emblem — A173

Golden Key with
CEPT
Emblem — A174

Rook and
Chessboard
A175

Aircraft Tail and
Satellites
A176

1968, Mar. 14   Photo.   Perf. 11½
487 A173 10c grn, lt ultra & red   15 15
488 A174 20c Prus bl, yel & brn   20 15
489 A175 30c dk ol bis & vio bl   28 15
490 A176 50c dk blue & red   48 35
       Set value   55

50th anniv. of the Swiss Women's Alpine Club (10c). A unified Europe through postal cooperation

---

(20c). 18th Chess Olympics, Lugano, Oct. 17-Nov. 6 (30c). Inauguration of the new Geneva-Cointrin Air Terminal (50c).

Worker's
Protective
Helmet — A177

Double Geneva
and Zurich
Stamps of
1843 — A178

Map Showing
Systematic
Planning
A179

Flag of Rhine
Navigation
Committee
A180

1968, Sept. 12   Photo.   Perf. 11½
491 A177 10c bl grn & yel   15 15
492 A178 20c dp car, blk & yel grn   16 15
493 A179 30c multicolored   25 15
494 A180 50c bl, yel & blk   55 35
       Set value   52

50th anniv. of the Swiss Accident Insurance comp., SUVA (10c). 125th anniv. of 1st Swiss postage stamps (20c). 25th anniv. of the Swiss Society for Territorial Planning (30c). Cent. of the Rhine Navigation Act (50c).

Swiss Girl Scouts'
Emblem and
Camp — A181

Pegasus
Constellation
A182

Comptoir Suisse
Emblem and
Beaulieu
Building,
Lausanne
A183

Gymnaestrada
Emblem (Man in
Circle) — A184

Swissair DC-8 and
DH-3 — A185

1969, Feb. 12   Photo.   Perf. 11½
495 A181 10c multicolored   15 15
496 A182 20c dark blue   25 15
497 A183 30c red, ocher, grn & gray   25 15
498 A184 50c vio bl, bl, red, grn &
              sil   45 40
499 A185 2fr bl, dk bl & red   1.90 1.65
       Nos. 495-499 (5)   3.00 2.50

50th anniv. of Swiss Girl Scouts (10c). Opening of 1st Swiss Planetarium, Lucerne, July 1 (20c). 50th anniv. of the Comptoir Suisse (trade fair, 30c).

5th Gymnaestrada (gymnastic meet), Basel, July 1-5 (50c). 50th anniv. of Swiss airmail service (2fr).

Europa Issue, 1969
Common Design Type
1969, Apr. 28
Size: 32½x23mm
500 CD12 30c brn org & multi   24 15
501 CD12 50c chlky bl & multi   48 45

Huldreich Zwingli
(1484-1531) — A186

Famous Swiss: 20c, Gen. Henri Guisan (1874-1960). 30c, Francesco Borromini, architect (1599-1667). 50c, Othmar Schoeck, musician (1886-1957). 80c, Germaine de Stael, writer (1766-1817).

1969, Sept. 18   Engr.   Perf. 11½
502 A186 10c brt purple   15 15
503 A186 20c green   15 15
504 A186 30c deep carmine   30 15
505 A186 50c deep blue   52 50
506 A186 80c red brown   75 70
       Nos. 502-506 (5)   1.87
       Set value   1.35

Kreuzberge,
Alpstein
Mountains
A187

Children
Crossing
Street — A188

Steelworker
A189

1969, Sept. 18   **Photo.**
507 A187 20c blue & multi   24 15
508 A188 30c car & multi   24 15
509 A189 50c violet & multi   48 35
       Set value   45

No. 508 publicizes the traffic safety campaign; No. 509 for 50th anniv. of the ILO.

Telex
Tape — A190

Fireman
Rescuing
Child — A191

Pro Infirmis
Emblem
A192

United Nations
Emblem
A193

New UPU
Headquarters
A194

1970, Feb. 26   Photo.   Perf. 11½

510	A190	20c dk grn, yel & blk	15	15
511	A191	30c dk car & multi	24	15
512	A192	30c red & multi	24	15
513	A193	50c dk bl, lt grnsh bl & sil	40	35
514	A194	80c dk pur, sep & tan	80	70
		Nos. 510-514 (5)	1.83	
		Set value		1.25

75th anniv. of the Swiss Telegraph Agency (20c). Cent. of the Swiss Firemen's Assoc. (No. 511). 50th anniv. of the Pro Infirmis Foundation (No. 512). UN, 5th anniv. (50c). New Headquarters of the UPU in Bern (80c).

Europa Issue, 1970
Common Design Type

1970, May 4   Engr.   Perf. 11½
Size: 21x26mm

515	CD13	30c vermilion	25	15
516	CD13	50c brt blue	55	32
		Set value		40

Soccer — A195

Census
Form — A196

Piz Palu,
Grisons — A197

"Nature Conservation"
A198

Numeral
A199

1970, Sept. 17   Photo.   Perf. 11½

517	A195	10c green & multi	15	15
518	A196	20c dk grn & multi	15	15
519	A197	30c sl bl & multi	38	15
520	A198	50c dk bl & multi	45	32
		Set value		52

75th anniv. of Swiss Soccer Association (10c). Federal Census of 1970 (20c). Swiss Alps (30c). Nature Conservation Year (50c).

Coil Stamps

1970, Sept. 17   Engr.   Perf. 11½

521	A199	10c brown lake	15	15
522	A199	20c olive grn	22	15
523	A199	50c ultra	55	45
		Set value		55

Control number in stamp's color on back of every fifth stamp. Nos. 521-523 were regularly issued only in coils, but exist in sheets of 50.

Gymnastic
Trio — A200

Rose — A201

Switzerland No.
8 — A202

Rising
Spiral — A203

Intelsat 4
Satellite
A204

Adaptation of 1850 Design — A205

Design: No. 525, Runners (men).

1971, Mar. 11   Photo.   Perf. 11½

524	A200	10c ol, brn & bl	18	15
525	A200	10c gray, brn & yel	18	15
	a.	Pair, #524-525	40	30
526	A201	20c dk grn & multi	15	15
527	A202	30c dp car & multi	22	15
528	A203	50c dk bl & bls	40	45
529	A204	80c multicolored	65	75
		Nos. 524-529 (6)	1.78	
		Set value		1.45

Souvenir Sheet
Typo.
Imperf

530	A205	2fr blue & multi	3.00	3.00

New article on gymnastics and sports in Swiss Constitution (10c); Intl. Child Welfare Org. (20c); NABA Natl. Postage Stamp Exhibition, Basel, June 4-13 (30c, 2fr); 2nd decade of development aid (50c); Intl. Space Communications Conf., Geneva, June-July, 1971 (80c).
#525a printed checkerwise. #530 sold for 3fr.

Europa Issue, 1971
Common Design Type

1971, May 3   Engr.   Perf. 11½
Size: 26x21mm

531	CD14	30c rose car & org	28	15
532	CD14	50c blue & org	52	40

Les Diablerets,
Vaud — A206

Telecommunications Symbols — A207

1971, Sept. 23   Photo.   Perf. 11½

533	A206	30c rose lil & bl gray	35	15
534	A207	40c ultra, yel & brt pink	45	45

No. 534 for the 50th anniv. of Radio-Suisse, which is also in charge of air traffic control.

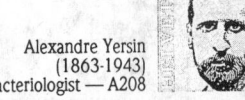
Alexandre Yersin
(1863-1943)
Bacteriologist — A208

Physicians: 20c, Auguste Forel (1848-1931), psychiatrist. 30c, Jules Gonin (1870-1935), ophthalmologist. 40c, Robert Koch (1843-1910), German bacteriologist. 80c, Frederick G. Banting (1891-1941), Canadian physiologist.

1971, Sept. 23   Engr.

535	A208	10c gray olive	15	15
536	A208	20c bluish grn	16	15
537	A208	30c car rose	20	15
538	A208	40c dk blue	60	52
539	A208	80c brt purple	80	70
		Nos. 535-539 (5)	1.91	1.67

Wrench, Road
Sign, Club
Emblems
A209

Electronic Switch
Panel — A210

Boy's Head and
Radio
Waves — A211

Symbolic
Tree — A212

1972, Feb. 17   Photo.   Perf. 11½

540	A209	10c multicolored	15	15
541	A210	20c olive & multi	15	15
542	A211	30c orange & mar	22	15
543	A212	40c bl, grn & pur	48	48
		Set value		74

75th anniv. of the touring and automobile clubs of Switzerland (10c). 125th anniv. of Swiss railroads (20c). 50th anniv. of Swiss radio (30c). 50th annual congress of Swiss citizens living abroad, Bern, Aug. 25-27 (40c).

Europa Issue 1972
Common Design Type

1972, May 2
Size: 21x26mm

544	CD15	30c multicolored	25	15
545	CD15	40c multicolored	40	30

Alberto Giacometti
(1901-66), Painter and
Sculptor — A213

Portraits and Signatures: 20c, Charles Ferdinand Ramuz (1878-1947), writer. 30c, Le Corbusier (Charles Edouard Jeanneret; 1887-1965) architect. 40c, Albert Einstein (1879-1955), physicist. 80c, Arthur Honegger (1892-1955), composer.

Engraved & Photogravure

1972, Sept. 21   Perf. 11½

546	A213	10c ocher & blk	15	15
547	A213	20c lt olive & blk	15	15
548	A213	30c pink & blk	18	15
549	A213	40c lt blue & blk	60	50
550	A213	80c lil rose & blk	80	65
		Nos. 546-550 (5)	1.88	1.60

Civil Defense
Emblem — A214

Spannörter
A215

Red Cross
Rescue
Helicopter
A216

Clean Air, Fire, Earth and Water — A217

1972, Sept. 21   Photo.

551	A214	10c org, bl & yel	15	15
552	A215	20c bl grn & multi	15	15
553	A216	30c lilac, red & ind	22	15
554	A217	40c lt blue & multi	45	32
		Set value		52

Issued to publicize Civil Defense (10c); Swiss Alps (20c); Air Rescue Service (30c); Nature and environment protection (40c).

Earth Satellite
Station, Leuk,
World
Map — A218

Quill Pen and
Arrows in
Circle — A219

INTERPOL
Emblem — A220

1973, Feb. 15   Photo.   Perf. 11½

555	A218	15c gray, yel & bl	15	15
556	A219	30c multicolored	25	15
557	A220	40c dp bl, lt bl & gray	60	32
		Set value		52

Opening of the satellite station at Leuk; Swiss Association of Commercial Employees, cent. (30c); International Criminal Police Organization (INTERPOL), 59th anniv.

Sottoceneri
A221

Sign of Inn "Zur Sonne,"
Toggenburg
A222

Villages: 10c, Graubunden. 15c, Central Switzerland. 25c, Jura. 30c, Simme Valley. 35c, Central Switzerland (2 buildings). 40c, Vaud. 50c, Valais. 60c, Engadine. 70c, Sopraceneri. 80c, Eastern Switzerland.

Designs: 1fr, Rose window, Lausanne Cathedral. 1.10fr, Gallus Portal, Basel Cathedral. 1.20fr, Romanesque capital (eagle), St. Jean Baptiste Church, Grandson. 1.50fr, Ceiling medallion (pelican feeding nestlings), Stein am Rhein Convent. 1.70fr, Romanesque capital (St. George and dragon), St. Jean Baptiste, Grandson. 1.80fr, Gargoyle, Bern Cathedral. 2fr, Bay window, Schaffhausen. 2.50fr, Cock weather vane, St. Ursus Cathedral, Solothurn. 3fr, Font, St. Maurice Church, Saanen. 3.50fr, Astronomical clock, Bern clock tower.

1973-80   Engr.   *Perf. 11½*
Fluorescent, No Violet Fibers

558	A221	5c dl yel & dk bl	15	15
559	A221	10c rose lil & ol grn	15	15
560	A221	15c org & vio bl	15	15
561	A221	25c emer & vio bl	22	15
562	A221	30c brick red & dk bl	25	15
563	A221	35c red org & brt vio ('75)	35	15
564	A221	40c brt bl & blk	38	15
565	A221	50c ol grn & org	45	15
566	A221	60c yel brn & gray	52	15
567	A221	70c sep & dk grn	60	18
568	A221	80c brt grn & brick red	75	18

Violet Fibers, Fluorescent Paper

569	A222	1fr pur ('74)	95	15
a.		Without fibers, fluorescent paper ('78)	95	15
570	A222	1.10fr Prus bl ('75)	1.10	15
571	A222	1.20fr rose red ('74)	1.10	75
572	A222	1.30fr ocher	2.50	60
573	A222	1.50fr grn ('74)	1.40	15
574	A222	1.70fr gray	1.25	42
575	A222	1.80fr dp org	1.25	20
576	A222	2fr ultra ('74)	1.90	30
a.		Without fibers, fluorescent paper ('78)	1.90	30
577	A222	2.50fr gldn brn ('75)	2.00	35
578	A222	3fr dk car ('79)	2.50	35
579	A222	3.50fr ol grn ('80)	2.75	90
		Nos. 558-579 (22)	22.67	
		Set value		5.40

No. 577 exists without tagging. Value, $60 unused, $30 used.

Europa Issue 1973
Common Design Type
1973, Apr. 30   Engr. and Photo.
Size: 38x28mm

580	CD16	25c brown & yel	28	15
581	CD16	40c ultra & yel	55	35

"Man and Time" — A223

Skier and Championship Emblem — A224

Child — A225

1973, Aug. 30   Photo.   *Perf. 11½*

582	A223	15c multicolored	15	15
583	A224	30c pink & multi	24	15
584	A225	40c blue vio & blk	45	35
		Set value		50

Opening of the Intl. Clock Museum, La Chaux-de-Fonds, 1974 (15c); Intl. Alpine Skiing Championships, St. Moritz, Feb. 2-10, 1974 (30c); "Terre des hommes" children's aid program (40c).

Souvenir Sheet

Medieval Postal Couriers — A226

1974, Jan. 29   Photo.   *Perf. 11½*

585	A226	Sheet of 4	6.00	6.00
a.		30c Basel (with staff)	1.40	1.40
b.		30c Zug (without staff)	1.40	1.40
c.		60c Uri	1.40	1.40
d.		80c Schwyz	1.40	1.40

Cent. of UPU and for INTERNABA 74 Intl. Phil. Exhib., Basel, June 7-16. No. 585 sold for 3fr.

Pine and Cabin on Globe — A227

Gymnast and Hurdlers — A228

Target and Pistol — A229

1974, Jan. 29

586	A227	15c lt green & multi	15	15
587	A228	30c red & multi	25	15
588	A229	40c blue & multi	45	30
		Set value		50

50th anniv. of Swiss Youth Hostels (15c); Cent. of Swiss Workers' Gymnast and Sports Association (SATUS) (30c); World Marksmanship Championships, Thun and Bern, Sept. 1974 (40c).

Old Houses, Parliament RR Station, Bern — A230

Eugéne Borel — A231

Designs: No. 590, Castle, Town Hall, Chauderon Center, Lausanne. 40c, Heinrich von Stephan. 80c, Montgomery Blair.

1974, Mar. 28   Photo.   *Perf. 11½*

589	A230	30c orange & multi	30	20
590	A230	30c scarlet & multi	30	20

Engr.

591	A231	30c rose & blk	18	15
592	A231	40c gray & blk	28	22
593	A231	80c lt yel grn & blk	75	45

Cent. of the UPU. Nos. 589-590 publicize the Cent. Cong., Lausanne, May 22-July 5; Nos. 591-593 honor the founders of the UPU.

"Continuity," by Max Bill — A232

Europa: 40c, "Amazon," bronze sculpture by Carl Burckhardt.

1974, Mar. 28   Photo.

594	A232	30c red & black	35	15
595	A232	40c ultra & sepia	95	42

Oath of Allegiance, by Werner Witschi — A233

Sports Foundation Emblem — A234

Conveyor Belts, Paths of Mail Transport and Delivery — A235

1974, Sept. 19   Photo.   *Perf. 11½*

596	A233	15c lil, ol & dk ol	15	15
597	A234	30c silver & multi	28	15
598	A235	30c plum & multi	28	15
		Set value		30

Centenary of Swiss Constitution (15c); Swiss Sports Foundation (No. 597); 125th anniversary of Swiss Federal Post (No. 598).

Standard Meter, Krypton Spectrum A236

Women of Four Races — A237

Red Cross Flag, Barbed Wire — A238

"Ville de Lucerne" Dirigible A239

1975, Feb. 13   Photo.   *Perf. 11½*

599	A236	15c grn, org & ultra	15	20
600	A237	30c brown & multi	28	15
601	A238	60c ultra, blk & red	52	75
602	A239	90c blue & multi	90	60

Cent. of Intl. Meter Convention, Paris, 1875 (15c); Intl. Women's Year 1975 (30c); 2nd Session of Diplomatic Conf. on Humanitarian Intl. Law, Geneva, Feb. 1975 (60c); Aviation and Space Travel exhibition in Museum of Transport and Communications, Lucerne (90c).

Mönch, by Ferdinand Hodler — A240

Vineyard Worker, by Maurice Barraud — A241

Europa: 50c, Still Life with Guitar, by René Auberjonois.

1975, Apr. 28   Photo.   *Perf. 12x11½*

603	A240	30c gray & multi	28	15
604	A241	50c multicolored	48	45
605	A241	60c bl gray & multi	65	52

Man Pulling Wheel Chair Upstairs A242

"The Helping Hand" — A243

Architectural Heritage Year Emblem — A244

Beat Fischer von Reichenbach A245

1975, Sept. 11   Photo.

606	A242	15c lilac, blk & grn	20	15
607	A243	30c red, blk & car	24	15
608	A244	50c yel brn & mar	42	38
609	A245	60c blue & multi	60	55

Special building features for the handicapped (15c); interdenominational telephone pastoral counseling (30c); European Architectural Heritage Year 1975 (50c); Fischer Post, Bern, tercentenary (60c).

Forest — A246

Fruits and Vegetables A247

Black Infant — A248

Telephones of 1876 and 1976 — A249

1976, Feb. 12   Photo.   *Perf. 11½*
Fluorescent, No Violet Fibers

610	A246	20c green & multi	15	15
611	A247	40c car & multi	35	15
612	A248	40c lil rose & multi	35	15

Engr.
Violet Fibers, Fluorescent Paper

| 613 | A249 | 80c lt bl & dk bl | 75 | 65 |

Centenary of Federal forest laws (20c); healthy nutrition to combat alcoholism (No. 611); fight against leprosy (No. 612); telephone centenary (80c).

Cotton and Gold Lace, St. Gall — A250

Pocket Watch, 18th Century — A251

1976, May 3   Engr.   *Perf. 11½*

| 614 | A250 | 40c red brn & multi | 50 | 20 |
| 615 | A251 | 80c black & multi | 1.00 | 50 |

Europa. Both 40c and 80c are on fluorescent paper, the 80c having violet fibers.

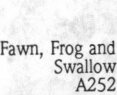
Fawn, Frog and Swallow A252

"Conserve Energy" — A253

St. Gotthard Mountains A254

Skater — A255

1976, Sept. 16   Photo.   *Perf. 11½*
Fluorescent, No Violet Fibers

616	A252	20c multicolored	16	15
617	A253	40c multicolored	35	15
618	A254	40c multicolored	42	15
619	A255	80c multicolored	70	70

Wildlife protection (20c); energy conservation (No. 617); Pizzo Lucendro to Pizzo Rotondo, seen from Altanca (No. 618); World Men's Skating Championships, Davos, Feb. 5-6, 1977 (80c).

Oskar Bider, Bleriot Monoplane A256

Swiss Aviation Pioneers: 80c, Eduard Spelterini and balloon gondola. 100c, Armand Dufaux and Dufaux plane. 150c, Walter Mittelholzer and Dornier hydroplane.

1977, Jan. 27   Engr.   *Perf. 11½*

620	A256	40c multicolored	45	18
621	A256	80c multicolored	95	95
622	A256	100c multicolored	95	95
623	A256	150c multicolored	1.65	1.50

Blue Cross — A257

Festival Emblem — A258

Balloons Carrying Letters — A259

1977, Jan. 27   Photo.

624	A257	20c gray, bl & blk	20	16
625	A258	40c red, gold & brn	40	15
626	A259	80c lt bl & multi	80	80

Blue Cross Society (care of alcoholics and fight against alcoholism), centenary (20c); Vintage Festival, Vevey, July 30-Aug. 14 (40c); JUPHILEX 77 Youth Philatelic Exhibition, Bern, Apr. 7-11 (80c).

Fluorescent Paper
From No. 624 onward the paper lacks violet fibers but is fluorescent, unless otherwise noted.

St. Ursanne on Doubs River — A260

Europa: 80c, Sils-Baselgia on Inn River.

1977, May 2   Engr.   *Perf. 11½*

| 627 | A260 | 40c multicolored | 55 | 16 |
| 628 | A260 | 80c multicolored | 1.10 | 60 |

Worker and Factories — A261

Ionic Column and Shield — A262

Swiss Cross, Arrow and Butterfly — A263

1977, Aug. 25   Photo.   *Perf. 11½*

629	A261	20c multicolored	16	15
630	A262	40c multicolored	35	18
631	A263	80c multicolored	85	60

Federal Factories Act, centenary (20c); protection of cultural monuments (40c); Swiss hiking trails (80c).

Star Singer, Bergün — A264

Folk Customs: 10c, Horse race, Zürich. 20c, New Year's Eve costumes, Herisau. 25c, Chesslete,

Solothurn. 30c, Rollelibutzen, Altstatten. 35c, Cutting off the goose, Sursee. 40c, Herald reading proclamation and men scaling wall, Geneva. 45c, Klausjagen, Kussnacht. 50c, Masked men, Laupen. 60c, Schnabelgeissen, Ottenbach. 70c, Procession (horse and masked men), Mendrisio. 80c, Griffins, Basel. 90c, Masked men, Lotschental.

1977-84   Engr.   *Perf. 11½*

632	A264	5c blue grn	15	15
	a.	Bkt. pane of 4 ('84)	24	
633	A264	10c dark red	15	15
	a.	Bkt. pane of 2 + 2 labels ('79)	45	
	b.	Bkt. pane of 4 ('84)	48	
634	A264	20c orange	20	15
	a.	Booklet pane of 4 ('79)	80	
635	A264	25c brown	24	20
636	A264	30c brt green	28	20
637	A264	35c olive	35	15
	a.	Bkt. pane of 4 ('84)	1.40	
638	A264	40c brown lake	40	15
	a.	Booklet pane of 4 ('79)	1.65	
	b.	Violet fibers, flourescent paper ('78)	35	15
639	A264	45c gray blue	40	32
640	A264	50c red brown	48	18
	a.	Bkt. pane of 2+2 labels ('84)	98	
	b.	Bkt. pane of 4 ('84)	1.95	
641	A264	60c gray brown	55	45
642	A264	70c purple	65	24
643	A264	80c steel blue	80	30
644	A264	90c deep brown	90	32
		Nos. 632-644 (13)	5.55	2.96

Issue dates: 30c, Nov. 25, 1982; 25c, 40c, 60c, Sept. 11, 1984; others, Aug. 25, 1977.

Arms of Vaud Canton — A265

Old Lucerne A266

Title Page of "Melusine" A267

Stylized Lens and Bellows A268

1978, Mar. 9   Photo.   *Perf. 11½*

652	A265	20c multicolored	18	15
653	A266	40c multicolored	38	15
654	A267	70c multicolored	65	60
655	A268	80c multicolored	75	65

Miniature Sheet

656	A269	Sheet of 8	9.00	9.00
	a.	20c La Suisse, 1910	38	38
	b.	20c Il Verbano, 1826	38	38
	c.	40c MS Gotthard, 1970	1.10	1.10
	d.	40c Ville de Neuchatel, 1972	1.10	1.10
	e.	40c MS Romanshorn, 1958	1.10	1.10
	f.	40c Le Winkelried, 1871	1.10	1.10
	g.	70c DS Loetschberg, 1914	1.25	1.25
	h.	80c DS Waedenswil, 1895	1.65	1.65

LEMANEX 78 Philatelic Exhibition, Lausanne, May 26-June 4 (#652); Founding of Lucerne, 800th anniv. (#653); printing in Geneva, 500th anniv. (#654); 2nd Intl. Triennial Photography Exhibition, Fribourg, June 17-Oct. 22 (#655).
Size of No. 656: 134x129mm. Sold for 5fr.

Stockalper Palace, Brig — A270

Europa: 80c, Diet Hall, Bern.

1978, May 2   Engr.   *Perf. 11½*

| 657 | A270 | 40c multicolored | 55 | 18 |
| 658 | A270 | 80c multicolored | 1.10 | 60 |

Machinist A271

Joseph Bovet (1879-1951), Composer A272

Designs: No. 660, Chemical worker (French inscription). No. 661, Construction worker (Italian inscription).

1978, Sept. 14   Photo.   *Perf. 11½*

659	A271	40c multicolored	40	28
660	A271	40c multicolored	40	28
661	A271	40c multicolored	40	28
	a.	Strip of 3, #659-661	1.25	1.00

Industrial safety.

1978, Sept. 14   Engr.

Portraits: 40c, Henri Dunant (1828-1910), founder of Red Cross. 70c, Carl Gustave Jung (1875-1961), psychologist. 80c, Auguste Piccard (1884-1962), physicist and balloonist.

662	A272	20c dull green	20	15
663	A272	40c rose lake	35	15
664	A272	70c gray	65	60
665	A272	80c blue gray	80	70

Arms of Switzerland and Jura — A273

1978, Sept. 25   Photo.   *Perf. 11½*

| 666 | A273 | 40c buff, red & blk | 38 | 15 |

Admission of Jura as 23rd Canton.

Rainer Maria Rilke (1875-1926), Poet, Muzot Castle — A274

Designs: 40c, Paul Klee (1879-1940), painter and "heroic roses." 70c, Hermann Hesse (1877-1962), writer, and vines. 80c, Thomas Mann (1875-1955), writer, and Lubeck buildings.

1979, Feb. 21   Engr.   *Perf. 11½*

667	A274	20c gray green	18	15
668	A274	40c red	35	15
669	A274	70c brown	65	65
670	A274	80c gray blue	80	75

O. H. Ammann, Verrazano-Narrows Bridge, NY — A275

Target Hit with Pole and Lucerne Flag — A276

Hot Air Balloon — A277

Airport, Swissair and Air France Jets — A278

1979, Feb. 21   Photo.
671 A275 20c multicolored   18   15
672 A276 40c multicolored   35   15
673 A277 70c multicolored   65   65
674 A278 80c multicolored   80   75

Othmar H. Ammann (1879-1965), engineer, bridge builder in US; 50th Federal Riflemen's Festival, Lucerne, July 7-22; World Esperanto Congress, Lucerne; new runway at Basel-Mulhouse Intl. Airport.

Letter Box, 1845, Spalentor, Basel — A279

Europa: 80c, Microwave radio relay station on Jungfraujoch.

1979, Apr. 30   Engr.   *Perf. 11½*
675 A279 40c multicolored   55   15
676 A279 80c multicolored   1.10   75

Helvetian Gold Quarter Stater, 2nd Century B.C. — A280

Child and Dove — A281

Morse Key and Satellite — A282

Three-stage Launcher Ariane — A283

1979, Sept. 6   Photo.
677 A280 20c multicolored   16   15
678 A281 40c multicolored   35   20
679 A282 70c multicolored   70   45
680 A283 80c multicolored   75   65

Centenary of Swiss Numismatic Society; International Year of the Child; Union of Swiss Radio Amateurs, 50th anniv.; European Space Agency (ESA).

Tree in Bloom A284

Hand Carved Milk Bucket A285

Winterthur Town Hall — A286

"Pic-Pic," 1930 — A287

1980, Feb. 21   Photo.
681 A284 20c multicolored   20   15
682 A285 40c multicolored   40   22
683 A286 65c multicolored   65   55
684 A287 80c multicolored   75   65

Green '80, Swiss Horticultural and Gardening Expo., Basel, Apr. 12-Oct. 12; Swiss Arts and Crafts Centers, 50th anniv.; Soc. for Swiss Art History, cent.; 50th Intl. Automobile Show, Geneva, Mar. 16.

Johann Konrad Kern (1808-1888), Politician — A288

Europa: 80c, Gustav Adolf Hasler (1830-1900), communications pioneer.

1980, Apr. 28   Lith. & Engr.
       Granite Paper
685 A288 40c multicolored   50   15
686 A288 80c multicolored   1.00   55

Postal Giro System — A289

Postal Bus System — A290

Security Printing Plant, 50th Anniversary A291

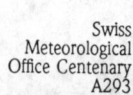

Swiss Telephone Service Centenary A292

Photo., Photo. & Engr. (70c)
1980, Sept. 5   *Perf. 12*
687 A289 20c multicolored   20   15
688 A290 40c multicolored   38   15
689 A291 70c multicolored   65   50
690 A292 80c multicolored   75   55

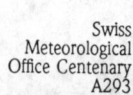

Swiss Meteorological Office Centenary A293

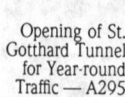

Swiss Trade Union Federation Centenary A294

Opening of St. Gotthard Tunnel for Year-round Traffic — A295

1980, Sept. 5   Photo.
691 A293 20c multicolored   18   15
692 A294 40c multicolored   38   15
693 A295 80c multicolored   75   55

Granary, Kiesen, 17th Century — A296

International Year of the Disabled — A297

The Parish Clerk, by Albert Anker — A298

Theodolite and Rod — A299

DC-9 (50th Anniversary of Swissair) A300

1981, Mar. 9   Photo.   *Perf. 11½*
694 A296 20c multicolored   22   15
695 A297 40c multicolored   40   18
696 A298 70c multicolored   70   50
697 A299 80c multicolored   80   55
698 A300 110c multicolored   1.10   85
   Nos. 694-698 (5)   3.22   2.23

Ballenberg Open-air Museum of Rural Architecture, Furnishing and Crafts; Albert Anker (1831-1910), artist (70c); 16th Congress of the International Federation of Surveyors, Montreux, Aug. (80c).

Europa Issue 1981

Couple Dancing in Native Costumes — A301

1981, May 4   Photo.   *Perf. 11½*
699 A301 40c shown   50   18
700 A301 80c Stone putting   1.00   48

Seal of Fribourg A302

1981, Sept. 3   Photo. & Engr.
701 A302 40c shown   40   25
702 A302 40c Seal of Solothurn   40   25
703 A302 80c Old Town Hall, Stans   80   52

500th anniv. of Diet of Stans and of entry of Fribourg and Solothurn into the Swiss Confederation.

Voltage Regulator A303

Crossbow Quality Emblem A304

Youths A305

Flower Mosaic, St. Peter's Cathedral, Geneva A306

1981, Sept. 3   Photo.
704 A303 20c multi   18   18
705 A304 40c multi   38   32
706 A305 70c multi   65   50
707 A306 1.10fr multi   1.10   80

Technorama Industrial Fair, Winterthur; Crossbow Quality Emblem, 50th anniv.; Swiss Youth Assoc., 50th anniv.; restoration of St. Peter's Cathedral.

Gotthard Railway Centenary A307

Designs: Locomotives. Nos. 708-709 se-tenant with label showing workers' monument.

1982, Feb. 18   Photo.
708 A307 40c Steam   50   18
709 A307 40c Electric   50   18

Swiss Hoteliers' Assoc. Centenary A308

Federal Gymnastic Society
Sesquicentennial — A309

Intl. Gas
Union, 50th
Anniv.
Convention,
Lausanne
A310

Bern Museum of Natural History
Sesquicentennial — A311

Society of
Chemical
Industries
Centenary
A312

1982, Feb. 18

710	A308	20c multicolored	15	15
711	A309	40c multicolored	35	32
712	A310	70c multicolored	60	50
713	A311	80c multicolored	70	58
714	A312	110c multicolored	1.00	80
		Nos. 710-714 (5)	2.80	2.35

Europa
1982 — A313

1982, May 3   Photo.   Perf. 11½

715	A313	40c Oath of Eternal Fealty	50	15
716	A313	80c Pact of 1291	1.00	55

Virgo, Schwarzee above
Zermatt — A314

Signs of the Zodiac and City Views.

Photogravure and Engraved
1982-86   Perf. 11½

717	A314	1fr Aquarius, Old Bern	1.10	25
718	A314	1.10fr Pisces, Nax near Sion	1.25	30
719	A314	1.20fr Aries, Graustock	1.40	32
719A	A314	1.40fr Gemini, Bischofszell	1.40	22
720	A314	1.50fr Taurus, Basel Cathedral	1.75	38
721	A314	1.60fr Gemini, Schonengrund	1.75	38
722	A314	1.70fr Cancer, Wetterhorn, Grindelwald	2.00	50
723	A314	1.80fr Leo, Areuse Gorge, Neuchatel	2.25	50
724	A314	2fr Virgo, Jungfrau Monch Eiger Mts.	2.50	65
725	A314	2fr shown	2.25	42
726	A314	2.50fr Libra, Fechy	2.00	15
727	A314	3fr Scorpio, Corippo	55	22
728	A314	4fr Sagittarius, Glarus	4.25	1.10
728A	A314	4.50fr Capricorn, Schuls	5.50	1.40
		Nos. 717-728A (14)	29.95	6.79

Issue dates: Nos. 717-719, 720-721, Aug. 23, 1982. No. 719A, Feb. 11, 1986. Nos. 722-724, Feb. 17, 1983. No. 725, Nov. 24, 1983. Nos. 726-727, Feb. 19, 1985. Nos. 728-728A, Feb. 21, 1984.

Zurich Tram
Centenary
A315

Centenary of
Salvation Army
in Switzerland
A316

World Dressage
Championship,
Lausanne, Aug.
25-29 — A317

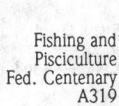

Intl. Water
Supply Assoc.,
14th World
Congress,
Zurich, Sept. 6-
10 — A318

1982, Aug. 23   Photo.

729	A315	20c multicolored	25	15
730	A316	40c multicolored	50	25
731	A317	70c multicolored	90	50
732	A318	80c multicolored	1.00	55

Fishing and
Pisciculture
Fed. Centenary
A319

Zurich University
Sesquicentennial — A320

Journalists' Fed.
Centenary
A321

Machine
Manufacturers'
Assoc.
Centenary
A322

1983, Feb. 17   Photo.
Granite Paper

733	A319	20c Perch	25	15
734	A320	40c multicolored	50	28
735	A321	70c Computer print outs	80	50
736	A322	80c Micrometer, cycloidal computer pattern	90	55

Europa 1983
A323

Basel Seal,
1832-1848
A324

Photogravure and Engraved
1983, May 3   Perf. 11½

737	A323	40c Celestial globe, 1594	55	25
738	A323	80c Cog railway, 1871	1.10	70

1983, May 26   Photo.

739	A324	40c multicolored	45	15

Basel Canton sesquicentennial (land division).

Octodurus
Martigny
Bimillenium
A325

Swiss Kennel
Club Centenary
A326

Bicycle and
Motorcycle
Federation
Centenary
A327

World
Communications
Year — A328

1983, Aug. 22   Photo.

740	A325	20c multicolored	25	15
741	A326	40c multicolored	42	25
742	A327	70c multicolored	75	50
743	A328	80c multicolored	85	55

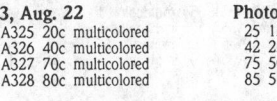

NABA-ZURI'84 Natl. Stamp Show, Zurich,
June 22-July 1 — A329

1100th Anniv.
of Saint
Imier — A330

Upper City,
Lausanne
A331

1984, Feb. 21   Photo.

744	A329	25c multicolored	25	15
745	A330	50c multicolored	55	22
746	A331	80c multicolored	90	38

Selection of Lausanne as permanent headquarters for the Intl. Olympic Committee (80c).

Europa (1959-1984)
A332

1984, May 2   Photo.   Perf. 11½

747	A332	50c lilac rose	65	20
748	A332	80c ultra	1.00	75

Souvenir Sheet

Panoramic View of
Zurich — A333

1984, May 24

749		Sheet of 4	4.25	4.25
a.-d.	A333	50c any single	90	90

NABA-ZURI '84 Stamp Show. Sold for 3fr.

Fire
Prevention
A334

1984, Sept. 11   Photo.

750	A334	50c Flames, match	55	15

Railway Staff
Association,
Cent. — A335

Rheto-Roman
Culture
Bimillennium
A336

Lake Geneva
Rescue Soc.,
Cent. — A337

Intl. Congress on
Large Dams,
Lausanne
A338

1985, Feb. 19   Photo.   Perf. 12x11½

751	A335	35c Conductor's hat, paraphernalia	40	15
752	A336	50c Engraved artifact, Chur	55	15
753	A337	70c Rescuing drowning victim	75	20
754	A338	80c Grande Dizence Dam, Canton Valais	90	24

Europa 1985 — A339

Designs: 50c, Ernest Ansermet (1883-1969), composer, conductor. 80c, Frank Martin (1890-1974), composer.

1985, May 7   Photo.   Perf. 11½x12
755 A339 50c multicolored   60 15
756 A339 80c multicolored   95 22

Swiss Master Bakers and Confectioners Federation, Bern, Cent. — A340

Swiss Radio Intl., 50th Anniv. — A341

HELVETIA 80
Postal, Telegraph & Telephone Intl. Congress, Sept. 16-21, Interlaken A342

1985, Sept. 10   Photo.   Perf. 12x11½
757 A340 50c Baker   55 15
758 A341 70c multi   75 20
759 A342 80c PTTI 75th anniv.   90 24

Swiss Worker's Relief Org., 50th Anniv. — A343

Battle of Sempach, 600th Anniv. — A344

Roman Chur Bimillennium A345

Vindonissa Bimillennium A346

Zurich Bimillennium A347

1986, Feb. 11   Photo.   Perf. 12
772 A343 35c Knot   38 15
773 A344 50c Military map, 1698   55 16
774 A345 80c Mercury statue   90 28
775 A346 90c Gallic head   1.00 30
776 A347 1.10fr Augustus coin   1.25 35
Nos. 772-776 (5)   4.08 1.24

Europa 1986 — A348   Mail Handling — A349

1986, Apr. 22   Photo.   Perf. 13½
777 A348 50c Woman   60 18
778 A348 90c Man   1.10 32

Photo. & Engr.
1986-89   Perf. 13½x13
779 A349 5c Franz mail van, 1911   15 15
780 A349 10c Parcel sorting   15 15
781 A349 20c Mule post   28 15
782 A349 25c Letter-facing, canceling   25 15
783 A349 30c Mail coach, 1735-1960   40 15
784 A349 35c Counter service   35 15
785 A349 45c Packet steamer, 1837-40   60 20
786 A349 50c Postman, 1986   65 22
 a.   Bklt. pane of 10 ('88)   6.50
787 A349 60c Loading airmail, 1986   80 28
788 A349 75c 17th Cent. courier   1.00 32
789 A349 80c Postman, ca. 1900   85 28
790 A349 90c Railroad mail car   95 32
Nos. 779-790 (12)   6.43
Set value   2.15

Issue dates: 5c, 10c, 25c, 35c, 80c, 90c, Sept. 9. 20c, 30c, 45c, 50c, 60c, Mar. 10, 1987. 75c, Mar. 7, 1989.

Intl. Peace Year — A351

Swiss Winter Relief Fund, 50th Anniv. — A352

Berne Convention for the Protection of Literary and Artistic Copyrights, Cent. — A353

25th Intl. Red Cross Conference, Geneva, Oct. 23-31 — A354

1986, Sept. 9   Photo.   Perf. 12x11½
799 A351 35c multicolored   38 15
800 A352 50c multicolored   55 18
801 A353 80c multicolored   95 30
802 A354 90c multicolored   1.10 35

Mobile P.O., 50th Anniv. — A355

Lausanne University, 450th Anniv. — A356

Swiss Engineers & Architects Assoc., Sesquicent. A357

Cointrin Airport-Geneva, Rail Link Opening, June 1, 1987 — A358

Baden Hot Springs, 2000th Anniv. — A359

1987, Mar. 10   Photo.
803 A355 35c multicolored   45 16
804 A356 50c multicolored   60 22
805 A357 80c multicolored   95 35
806 A358 90c multicolored   1.00 40
807 A359 1.10fr multicolored   1.25 48
Nos. 803-807 (5)   4.25 1.61

Europa 1987 — A360

Sculpture: 50fr, Scarabaeus, 1979, by Bernard Luginbuhl. 90fr, Carnival Fountain, 1977, by Jean Tinguely, Basel Theater.

1987, May 26   Photo.   Perf. 11½
808 A360 50c multicolored   70 24
809 A360 90c multicolored   1.25 42

Swiss Master Butchers' Federation, Cent. — A361

Stamp Day, 50th Anniv. — A362

Swiss Dairy Assoc., Cent. — A363

1987, Sept. 4   Photo.   Perf. 12x11½
810 A361 35c multicolored   48 16
811 A362 50c multicolored   68 22
812 A363 90c Cheesemaker   1.20 40

Tourism Industry, Bicent. — A364

Switzerland's four language regions: 50c, Clock Tower, Zug, German. 80c, Church of San Carlo, Blenio Valley, Italian. 90c, Witches' Tower, Sion Castle, French. 140c, Jorgenberg Castle ruins, Waltensburg/Vuorz, Surselva, Rhaeto-Romansh.

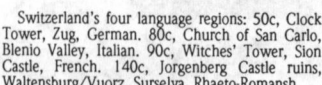

1987, Sept. 4   Perf. 11½
813 A364 50c multicolored   70 25
814 A364 80c multicolored   1.25 40
815 A364 90c multicolored   1.40 42
816 A364 140c multicolored   2.00 70
 a.   Souvenir sheet of 4, #813-816   5.00

Swiss Women's Benevolent Soc., Cent. — A365

Swiss Hairdressers Assoc., Cent. — A366

Battle of Naefels, 600th Anniv. — A367

European Campaign to Protect Undeveloped and Developing Lands — A368

Intl. Music Festival, Lucerne, 50th Anniv. — A369

1988, Mar. 8   Photo.   Perf. 12x11½
817 A365 25c multicolored   38 15
818 A366 35c multicolored   52 18
819 A367 50c Banner of St. Fridolin, medieval manuscript   75 25
820 A368 80c multicolored   1.20 40
821 A369 90c Girl playing a shawm   1.30 45
Nos. 817-821 (5)   4.15 1.43

Europa 1988 — A370

1988, May 24   Photo.   Perf. 11½
822 A370 50c Arrows (transport)   75 25
823 A370 90c Circuitry (communication)   1.35 45

Swiss Accident Prevention Office, 50th Anniv. — A371

Assoc. of Metalworkers and Watchmakers, Cent. — A372

Federal Topography Office, 150th Anniv. — A373

Intl. Red Cross Museum, Geneva — A374

1988, Sept. 13   Photo.   Perf. 12x11½
824 A371 35c multicolored   45 15
825 A372 50c multicolored   65 22
826 A373 80c Triangulation pyramid, theodolite, map   1.05 35
827 A374 90c multicolored   1.20 40

Metamecanique, by Jean Tinguely — A375

1988, Nov. 25 Photo. Perf. 13x12½
828 A375 90c multicolored 1.20 40

See France No. 2137.

Military Post, Cent. — A376

Delemont Municipal Charter, 700th Anniv. — A377

Public Transport Assoc., Cent. — A378

Rhaetian Railway, Cent. — A379

Great St. Bernard Pass Bimillennium A380

Designs: 25c, Army postman. 35c, Fontaine du Sauvage and the Porte au Loup, Delemont. 50c, Eye, modes of transportation. 80c, Train, viaduct. 90c, St. Bernard dog, statue of saint, hospice on summit.

1989, Mar. 2 Photo. Perf. 12x11½
829 A376 25c multicolored 32 15
830 A377 35c multicolored 45 15
831 A378 50c multicolored 65 22
832 A379 80c multicolored 1.05 35
833 A380 90c multicolored 1.20 40
   Nos. 829-833 (5) 3.67 1.27

Europa — A381   Industry — A382

Children's games: 50c, Hopscotch. 90c, Blindman's buff.

1989, May 23 Perf. 11½
834 A381 50c multicolored 65 22
835 A381 90c multicolored 1.20 40

Engr., Litho. & Eng. (2.80, 3, 3.60, 4, 5fr)
1989-95 Perf. 13x13½
842 A382 2.75fr Bricklayer 3.15 1.05
843 A382 2.80fr Cook 3.75 75
843A A382 3fr Cabinet maker 4.25 85
844 A382 3.60fr Pharmacist 4.90 1.00
845 A382 3.75fr Fisherman 5.00 1.00
846 A382 4fr Wine grower 5.50 1.10

847 A382 5fr Cheesemaker 6.75 1.40
848 A382 5.50fr Dressmaker 6.25 2.10
   Nos. 842-848 (8) 39.55 9.25

Issued: 2.75fr, 5.50fr, 8/29/89; 3.75fr, 3/6/90; 2.80fr, 3.60fr, 1/24/92; 5fr, 9/7/93; 4fr, 3/15/94; 3fr, 7/5/94.
This is an expanding set. Numbers will change if necessary.

Swiss Electricians' Assoc., Cent. — A383

Swiss Travel Fund, 50th Anniv. — A384

Fribourg University, Cent. — A385

Opening of the Natl. Sound-Recording Archives, 1st Anniv. — A386

Interparliamentary Union, Cent. — A387

1989, Aug. 25 Photo. Perf. 11½
851 A383 35c multicolored 40 15
852 A384 50c multicolored 58 20
853 A385 80c "Wisdom" and "Science" 92 30
854 A386 90c multicolored 1.05 35
855 A387 140c multicolored 1.60 52
   Nos. 851-855 (5) 4.55 1.52

Union of Swiss Philatelic Societies, Cent. — A388

Urban Railway System, Zurich — A389

Assistance for Mountain Communities, 50th Anniv. — A390

1990 World Ice Hockey Championships A391

1990, Mar. 6
856 A388 25c 5c maroon type A19, 50c stamp type A20 35 15
857 A389 35c Locomotives 48 16
858 A390 50c Mountain farmer 70 22
859 A391 90c Athletes 1.20 40

Europa 1990 — A393

Post offices.

Litho. & Engr.
1990, May 22 Perf. 13½
861 A393 50c Lucerne 70 22
862 A393 90c Geneva 1.20 40

Conrad Ferdinand Meyer (1825-1898), Writer — A394

Designs: 50c, Angelika Kaufmann (1741-1807), painter. 80c, Blaise Cendrars (1887-1961), journalist. 90c, Frank Buchser (1828-1890), artist.

1990, Sept. 5 Litho.
863 A394 35c green & blk 46 15
864 A394 50c blue & blk 65 22
865 A394 80c yellow & blk 1.05 35
866 A394 90c vermilion & blk 1.20 40

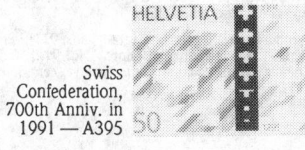

Swiss Confederation, 700th Anniv. in 1991 — A395

1990, Sept. 5 Photo. Perf. 11½
867 A395 50c shown 65 22
868 A395 90c multi, diff. 1.20 40

Natl. Census — A396

1990, Nov. 20
869 A396 50c multicolored 70 24

Animals — A397

1990-93 Litho. & Engr. Perf. 13
871 A397 10c Cow 15 15
877 A397 50c House cats 52 16
879 A397 70c Rabbit 80 16
880 A397 80c Barn owls 90 18
881 A397 100c Horses 95 35
882 A397 120c Dog 1.25 40
882A A397 150c Goats 2.25 42
883 A397 160c Turkey 1.65 35
883A A397 200c Chickens 2.75 55
   Nos. 871-883A (9) 11.22 2.72

Issued: 50c, 3/6/90; 70c, 80c, 1/15/91; 10c, 160c, 1/24/92; 100c, 120c, 3/16/93; 150c, 200c, 7/5/94.
This is an expanding set. Numbers will change if necessary.

Swiss Confederation, 700th Anniv. — A398

Swiss Parliament, US Capitol A399

1991, Feb. 22 Photo. Perf. 12
884 A398 50c "700 jahre" 80 25
885 A398 50c "700 onns" 80 25
886 A398 50c "700 ans" 80 25
887 A398 50c "700 anni" 80 25
   a. Block of 4, #884-887 3.20 1.00
888 A399 1.60fr multicolored 2.50 82
   Nos. 884-888 (5) 5.70 1.82

See US No. 2532.

Bern, 800th Anniv. — A400

1991, Feb. 22 Perf. 11½
889 A400 80c multicolored 1.25 40

Europa — A401

1991, May 14 Litho. Perf. 11½
890 A401 50c Ariane payload fairing 70 22
891 A401 90c Giotto probe 1.30 40

SWITZERLAND

BUYING AND SELLING, QUALITY STAMPS OF SWITZERLAND MINT NH.

EUROPE

From Andorre to Turkey, Europe (CEPT) and The English Area, Mint NH Sets. Whether you're buying or selling, my prices are very reasonable. The list contains well over 12,000 sets, with all kinds of topicals, where you will find my selling prices, and the price I pay for each set that I need.

The Italian Area

Including San Marino, Vatican City, Trieste A & B, Mint NH, LH or Used, and some singles.

SEND A #10 55¢ SASE TODAY FOR YOUR FREE COPY OF OUR PRICE LIST! You will be glad you did.

F. COPPOLA
P.O. Box 181022
Utica, MI 48318-1022

Union of Postal, Telephone and Telegraph Officials, Cent. — A402

1991, Sept. 10 Photo. Perf. 11½

| 892 A402 | 80c multicolored | 1.10 | 36 |

Bridges — A403

Designs: 50c, Stone bridge near Lavertezzo. 70c, Wooden "New Bridge" near Bremgarten. 80c, Railway bridge between Koblenz and Felsenau. 90c, Ganter Bridge, Simplon Pass.

1991, Sept. 10

893 A403	50c multicolored	68	22
894 A403	70c multicolored	95	32
895 A403	80c multicolored	1.10	36
896 A403	90c multicolored	1.20	40

Mountain Lakes — A404   A404a

Design: 60c, Lake de Tanay.

Litho., Litho. & Engr. (60c, #908)

1991-93 Perf. 13½x13

904 A404	50c blue & multi	68	15
905 A404	60c blue & multi	85	28
a.	Booklet pane of 10	8.50	
907 A404	80c red & multi, diff.	1.10	22
908 A404a	80c multicolored	1.15	38

Issued: 50c, #907, Dec. 16; 60c, #908, Jan. 19, 1993. This is an expanding set. Numbers will change if necessary.

Bird Over Rhine River — A405

Faces of Parents, Child — A406

Molecular Formula, Structure and Model — A407

1992, Mar. 24 Photo. Perf. 11½

911 A405	50c multicolored	68	22
912 A406	80c multicolored	1.10	36
913 A407	90c multicolored	1.20	40

Intl. Rhine Regulation, cent. (No. 911), Pro Familia Switzerland, 50th anniv. (No. 912), Intl. Chemical Nomenclature Conf., Geneva, cent. (No. 913).

A408   A409

Europa: 90c, Columbus, map of voyage.

1992, Mar. 24

| 914 A408 | 50c multicolored | 68 | 22 |
| 915 A408 | 90c multicolored | 1.20 | 40 |

Discovery of America, 500th anniv.

1992, May 22 Photo. Perf. 12

| 916 A409 | 90c multicolored | 1.20 | 40 |

Protect the Alps.

Comic Strips — A410

1992, May 22 Perf. 11½

917 A410	50c Cosey	68	22
918 A410	80c Zep	1.10	36
919 A410	90c Aloys	1.20	40

World of the Circus — A411

Designs: 50c, Clowns on trapeze. 70c, Sea lion, clown. 80c, Clown, elephant. 90c, Lipizzaner, harlequin.

1992, Aug. 25 Photo. Perf. 12x11½

920 A411	50c multicolored	80	28
921 A411	70c multicolored	1.15	38
922 A411	80c multicolored	1.30	42
923 A411	90c multicolored	1.45	48

Central Office for Intl. Carriage by Rail, Cent. (in 1993) — A412

1992, Nov. 24 Photo. Perf. 11½

| 924 A412 | 90c multicolored | 1.25 | 42 |

First Swiss Postage Stamps, 150th Anniv. — A413

Designs: 60c, Zurich Types A1, A2, Geneva Type A1. 80c, Stylized canceled stamp. 100c, Stylized stamps on album page.

1993, Mar. 16 Photo. Perf. 11½

925 A413	60c multicolored	80	28
926 A413	80c multicolored	1.05	35
927 A413	100c multicolored	1.30	45

Paracelsus (1493-1541), Physician A414   Opening of Olympic Museum, Lausanne A415

Intl. Metalworkers' Federation, Cent. — A416

1993, Mar. 16 Photo. Perf. 11½

928 A414	60c blue & sepia	80	25
929 A415	80c multicolored	1.05	35
930 A416	180c multicolored	2.40	80

Lake Constance Steamer Hohentwiel A417

1993, May 5 Photo. Perf. 11½x12

| 931 A417 | 60c multicolored | 85 | 28 |

See Austria No. 1598, Germany No. 1786.

Contemporary Architecture — A418

Europa: 60c, Media House, Villeurbanne, France. 80c, House, Breganzona, Switzerland.

Litho. & Engr.

1993, May 5 Perf. 13½

| 932 A418 | 60c multicolored | 85 | 28 |
| 933 A418 | 80c red & black | 1.15 | 38 |

Works of Art by Swiss Women A419

Designs: 60c, Work No. 095, by Emma Kunz. 80c, Grande Cantatrice Lilas Goergens, by Aloise Corbaz. 100c, Under the Rain Cloud, by Meret Oppenheim. 120c, Four Spaces in Horizontal Bands, by Sophie Taeuber-Arp.

1993, Sept. 7 Photo. Perf. 11½

| 934 A419 | 60c multicolored | 80 | 28 |

Size: 33x33½mm

935 A419	80c multicolored	1.10	38
936 A419	100c multicolored	1.40	45
937 A419	120c multicolored	1.65	55

Swiss Sports School, 50th Anniv. — A420

THE MATTERHORN MAIL

P.O. Box 1137 (Kelly Ave.), Pine Bush, NY 12566

Tel: 1-(914) 744-2950
Fax: 1-(914) 744-2246

FREE NET PRICE SALE CATALOGUE

• Special Offers on Switzerland and other European countries

• Extensively Photographed

Swiss Price List
Liechtenstein Price List

Finest Quality • Satisfaction Guaranteed

Jakob Bernoulli (1654-1705), Mathematician
A421

Swiss Telecom PTT Participation in Unisource
A422

ICAO, 50th Anniv. — A423

1994, Mar. 15   Photo.   Perf. 11½
938 A420 60c multicolored   85   28
939 A421 80c multicolored   1.10   35
940 A422 100c multicolored   1.40   45
941 A423 180c multicolored   2.50   80

Intl. Congress of Mathematicians, Zurich (#939).

"Books and the Press" Exhibition, Geneva — A424

1994, Mar. 15
942 A424 60c Early manuscripts   85   28
943 A424 80c Letterpress   1.10   35
944 A424 100c Electronic publishing 1.40 45

1994 World Cup Soccer Championships, US — A425

1994, Mar. 15
945 A425 80c multicolored   1.10   35

Research Vehicles of August & Jacques Piccard — A426

Europa: 60c, Stratospheric balloon. 100c, Bathyscaphe Trieste.

1994, May 17   Photo.   Perf. 12
946 A426 60c multicolored   85   28
947 A426 100c multicolored   1.40   45

Georges Simenon (1903-89), Writer A427

1994, Oct. 15 Litho. & Engr. Perf. 13
948 A427 100c multicolored   1.60   52

See Belgium No. 1567, France No. 2443.

A428   A429

1994, Oct. 15   Photo.   Perf. 11½
949 A428 60c multicolored   95   32

Campaign to stop AIDS.

1995, Mar. 7   Photo.   Perf. 11½
Endangered species.
950 A429 60c European beaver   95   32
951 A429 80c Map butterfly   1.25   40
952 A429 100c Green tree frog   1.65   55
953 A429 120c Litte owl   1.90   80
      Nos. 950-953 (4)   5.75 2.07

Swiss Wrestling Assoc., Cent. — A430

Swiss Assoc. of Producers & Distributors of Electricity, Cent. — A431

Swiss News Agency, Cent. — A432

UN, 50th Anniv.— A433

1995, Mar. 7
954 A430 60c blue & black   95   32
955 A431 60c multicolored   95   32
956 A432 80c multicolored   1.25   40
957 A433 180c multicolored   2.75   90
      Nos. 954-957 (4)   5.90 1.94

Peace & Freedom A434

Europa: 60c, Dove, faces. 100c, Zeus disguised as bull, abducting Europa, daughter of King of Phoenicia.

Litho., Engr. & Embossed
1995, May 16   Perf. 13
958 A434 60c lt blue & dk blue   1.10   38
959 A434 100c orange & brown   1.75   60

SEMI-POSTAL STAMPS

Nos. B1-B76, B81-B84 were sold at premiums of 2c for 3c stamps, 5c for 5c-20c stamps and 10c for 30c-40c stamps.

Helvetia and Matterhorn — SP2

Perf. 11½, 12
1913, Dec. 1   Typo.   Wmk. 183
Granite Paper
B1   SP2 5c green   2.50 3.50
       Never hinged   6.00

Boy (Appenzell) — SP3   Girl (Lucerne) — SP4

1915, Dec. 1   Perf. 11½
B2   SP3 5c green, buff   5.00 3.75
  a.   Tête bêche pair   75.00 800.00
B3   SP4 10c red, buff   100.00 55.00
       Set, never hinged   275.00

Girl (Fribourg) — SP5   Dairy Boy (Bern) — SP6

Girl (Vaud) — SP7

1916, Dec. 1
B4   SP5 3c vio, buff   5.00 18.00
B5   SP6 5c grn, buff   10.00 4.50
B6   SP7 10c brn red, buff   47.50 40.00
       Set, never hinged   175.00

Girl (Valais) SP8   Girl (Unter-walden) SP9

Girl (Ticino) — SP10

1917, Dec. 1
B7   SP8 3c vio, buff   5.50 27.50
B8   SP9 5c green, buff   7.25 3.25
B9   SP10 10c red, buff   21.00 16.00
       Set, never hinged   85.00

Uri — SP11   Geneva — SP12

1918, Dec. 1   Straw-Surfaced Paper
B10 SP11 10c red, org & blk   6.25 8.75
B11 SP12 15c vio, red, org & blk 8.25 5.00
       Set, never hinged   40.00

Nidwalden — SP13   Vaud — SP14

Obwalden — SP15

1919, Dec. 1   Cream-Surfaced Paper
B12 SP13 7½c gray, red & blk   2.50 10.00
B13 SP14 10c lake, grn & blk   2.50 10.00
B14 SP15 15c pur, red & blk   3.00 3.50
       Set, never hinged   18.00

Schwyz — SP16   Zürich — SP17

Ticino — SP18

1920, Dec. 1   Cream-Surfaced Paper
B15 SP16 7½c gray & red   2.75 6.00
B16 SP17 10c red & lt bl   5.50 5.50
B17 SP18 15c vio, red & bl   2.25 2.25
       Set, never hinged   24.00

Valais — SP19   Bern — SP20

Switzerland — SP21

1921, Dec. 1   Cream-Surfaced Paper
B18 SP19 10c grn, red & blk   90 1.25
B19 SP20 20c vio, red, org & blk 1.25 1.50
B20 SP21 40c blue & red   8.00 25.00
       Set, never hinged   19.00

Zug — SP22   Fribourg — SP23

Lucerne — SP24   Switzerland — SP25

1922, Dec. 1   Cream-Surfaced Paper
B21 SP22 5c org, pale bl & blk 55 2.00
B22 SP23 10c grn & blk   55 1.00
B23 SP24 20c vio, pale bl & blk 55 1.00
B24 SP25 40c bl & red   9.00 25.00
       Set, never hinged   20.00

Basel — SP26

Glarus (St. Fridolin) — SP27

Neuchâtel — SP28　　　Switzerland — SP29

1923, Dec. 1　Cream-Surfaced Paper

B25	SP26	5c org & blk	35	1.50
B26	SP27	10c multi	35	80
B27	SP28	20c multi	35	80
B28	SP29	40c dk bl & red	6.00	22.50
		Set, never hinged	16.00	

Appenzell — SP30　　　Solothurn — SP31

Schaffhausen SP32　　　Switzerland SP33

1924, Dec. 1　Cream-Surfaced Paper

B29	SP30	5c dk vio & blk	15	60
B30	SP31	10c grn, red & blk	15	50
B31	SP32	20c car, yel & blk	15	50
B32	SP33	30c bl, red & blk	1.40	4.00
		Set, never hinged	4.00	

St. Gallen (Canton) SP34

Appenzell-Ausser-Rhoden SP35

Grisons — SP36　　　Switzerland — SP37

1925, Dec. 1　Cream-Surfaced Paper

B33	SP34	5c vio, grn & blk	15	50
B34	SP35	10c grn & blk	16	38
B35	SP36	20c multi	20	50
B36	SP37	30c dk bl, red & blk	1.25	4.00
		Set, never hinged	3.50	

Thurgau — SP38　　　Basel — SP39

Aargau — SP40　　　Switzerland — SP41

1926, Dec. 1　Cream-Surfaced Paper

B37	SP38	5c vio, bis & grn	15	50
B38	SP39	10c gray grn, red & blk	20	50
B39	SP40	20c red, blk & bl	24	50
B40	SP41	30c dk bl & red	1.10	3.75
		Set, never hinged	3.50	

Orphan SP42

Orphan at Pestalozzi School SP43

J. H. Pestalozzi
SP44　　　SP45

1927, Dec. 1　Typo.　Wmk. 183
Granite Paper

B41	SP42	5c red vio & yel, *grysh*	15	60
B42	SP43	10c grn & fawn, *grnsh*	15	35

Engr.

B43	SP44	20c red	18	35

Unwmk.
Photo.

B44	SP45	30c gray bl & blk	1.00	3.50
		Set, never hinged	3.50	

Nos. B43-B44 for the centenary of the death of Johann Heinrich Pestalozzi, the Swiss educational reformer.

Lausanne — SP46　　　Winterthur — SP47

St. Gallen (City) — SP48

J. H. Dunant — SP49

1928, Dec. 1　Typo.　Wmk. 183
Cream-Surfaced Paper.

B45	SP46	5c dk vio, red & blk	22	75
B46	SP47	10c bl grn, org red & blk	25	70
B47	SP48	20c brn red, blk & yel	30	70

Unwmk.
Photo.
Thick White Paper

B48	SP49	30c dl bl & red	1.50	3.50
		Set, never hinged	3.25	

No. B48 for the centenary of the birth of Jean Henri Dunant, Swiss author, philanthropist and founder of the Red Cross Society.

Lake Lugano and Mt. Salvatore SP50

Lake Engstlen and Mt. Titlis — SP51

Mt. Lyskamm SP52

Nicholas von der Flüe — SP53

1929, Dec. 1　　Perf. 11x11½

B49	SP50	5c dk vio & red org	15	50
B50	SP51	10c ol brn & gray bl	20	32
B51	SP52	20c brn garnet & bl	22	32
B52	SP53	30c dk blue	1.10	4.75
		Set, never hinged	4.00	

No. B52 for Nicholas von der Flüe, the Swiss patriot. By his advice the Swiss Confederation was continued and Swiss independence was saved.

Fribourg — SP54　　　Altdorf — SP55

Schaffhausen — SP56

Jeremias Gotthelf SP57

Perf. 11½

1930, Dec. 1　Typo.　Wmk. 183
Cream-Surfaced Paper

B53	SP54	5c dp grn, dl bl & blk	15	52
B54	SP55	10c multicolored	20	52
B55	SP56	20c multicolored	24	52

Engr.
White Paper

B56	SP57	30c slate blue	1.40	3.50
		Set, never hinged	3.50	

No. B56 for Jeremias Gotthelf, pen name of Albrecht Bitzius, pastor and author.

Lakes Silvaplana and Sils — SP58

Wetterhorn SP59

Lake Geneva SP60

Alexandre Vinet — SP61

1931, Dec. 1　Photo.　Unwmk.
Granite Paper

B57	SP58	5c dp grn	25	52
B58	SP59	10c dk vio	25	32
B59	SP60	20c brn red	40	32

Wmk. 183
Engr.

B60	SP61	30c ultra	4.00	9.00
		Set, never hinged	10.50	

No. B60 for Alexandre Rudolph Vinet, critic and theologian.

Flag Swinger — SP62

Putting the Stone — SP63

Wrestling — SP64

Eugen Huber — SP65

1932, Dec. 1　Typo.　Unwmk.
Granite Paper

B61	SP62	5c dk grn & red	38	75
B62	SP63	10c org	55	75
B63	SP64	20c scar	55	75

Wmk. 183
Engr.

B64	SP65	30c ultra	2.25	3.75
		Set, never hinged	6.25	

No. B64 for Eugen Huber, jurist and author of the Swiss Civil Law Book.

Girl of Vaud — SP66

Girl of Bern — SP67

Girl of Ticino — SP68

Jean Baptiste Girard (Le Père Grégoire) — SP69

1933, Dec. 1　Photo.　Unwmk.
Granite Paper

B65	SP66	5c grn & buff	22	50
B66	SP67	10c vio & buff	30	30
B67	SP68	20c red & buff	40	38

Wmk. 183
Engr.

B68	SP69	30c ultra	2.00	3.50
		Set, never hinged	5.25	

Girl of Appenzell — SP70

Girl of Valais — SP71

Girl of Grisons — SP72

Albrecht von Haller — SP73

1934, Dec. 1　Photo.　Unwmk.

B69	SP70	5c grn & buff	20	50
B70	SP71	10c vio & buff	32	38
B71	SP72	20c red & buff	40	38

Wmk. 183
Engr.

B72 SP73	30c ultra	2.00	*4.00*
	Set, never hinged	5.00	

Girl of Basel — SP74

Girl of Lucerne — SP75

Girl of Geneva — SP76

Stefano Franscini — SP77

1935, Dec. 1   **Photo.**   **Unwmk.**
Granite Paper

B73 SP74	5c grn & buff	22	*45*
B74 SP75	10c vio & buff	38	*38*
B75 SP76	20c red & buff	38	*65*

Wmk. 183
Engr.

B76 SP77	30c ultra	2.25	*4.25*
	Set, never hinged	5.50	

No. B76 honors Stefano Franscini (1796-1857), political economist and educator.

Alpine Herdsman — SP78

Perf. 11½
1936, Oct. 1   **Photo.**   **Unwmk.**
Granite Paper

B77 SP78	10c + 5c vio	35	*42*
B78 SP78	20c + 10c dk red	65	*1.75*
B79 SP78	30c + 10c ultra	3.00	*10.00*
	Set, never hinged	8.00	

Souvenir Sheet

B80 SP78	Sheet of 3	35.00	*185.00*
	Never hinged	60.00	
a.	Block of 4 sheets	175.00	*775.00*
	Never hinged	250.00	

Swiss National Defense Fund Drive.
No. B80 contains stamps similar to Nos. B77-B79, but on grilled granite paper with blue and red fibers instead of black and red. Sold for 2fr. Size: 120x130mm.

Johann Georg Nägeli — SP79

Girl of Neuchâtel — SP80

Girl of Schwyz — SP81

Girl of Zurich — SP82

Perf. 11½
1936, Dec. 1   **Engr.**   **Wmk. 183**
Granite Paper

B81 SP79	5c green	18	*32*

Unwmk.
Photo.

B82 SP80	10c vio & buff	24	*32*
B83 SP81	20c red & buff	30	*48*
B84 SP82	30c ultra & buff	2.50	*8.00*
	Set, never hinged	7.75	

Gen. Henri Dufour SP83

Nicholas von der Flüe SP84

Boy — SP85

Girl SP86

Perf. 11½
1937, Dec. 1   **Unwmk.**   **Engr.**

B85 SP83	5c + 5c bl grn	15	*18*
B86 SP84	10c + 5c red vio	16	*22*

Photo.
Granite Paper

B87 SP85	20c + 5c red & silver	18	*22*
B88 SP86	30c + 10c ultra & sil	1.40	*3.25*
	Set, never hinged	3.00	

25th anniv. of the Pro Juventute (child welfare) stamps.

Souvenir Sheet
1937, Dec. 20   **Imperf.**

B89	Sheet of 2	3.50	*47.50*
a.	B85 20c + 5c red & silver	1.10	*15.00*
b.	B86 30c + 10c ultra & silver	1.10	*15.00*
	Never hinged	6.50	

Simulated perforation in silver. Sheet sold for 1fr.

Tell Chapel, Lake Lucerne SP87

1938, June 15   **Perf. 11½**
Granite Paper

B90 SP87	10c + 10c brt vio & yel	50	30
	Never hinged	70	
a.	Grilled gum	20.00	*75.00*
	Never hinged	27.50	

National Fête Day.

Salomon Gessner — SP88

Girl of St. Gallen — SP89

Girl of Uri — SP90

Girl of Aargau — SP91

1938, Dec. 1   **Engr.**   **Perf. 11½**

B91 SP88	5c + 5c dp bl grn	15	15

Photo.
Granite Paper

B92 SP89	10c + 5c pur & buff	15	20
B93 SP90	20c + 5c red & buff	15	20
B94 SP91	30c + 10c ultra	1.25	*3.00*
	Set, never hinged	4.00	

Castle at Laupen SP92

1939, June 15

B95 SP92	10c + 10c brn, gray & red	40	30
	Never hinged	50	

600th anniversary of the Battle of Laupen. The surtax was used to aid needy mothers.

Hans Herzog — SP93

Girl of Fribourg — SP94

Girl of Nidwalden — SP95

Girl of Basel — SP96

Perf. 11½
1939, Dec. 1   **Unwmk.**   **Engr.**

B96 SP93	5c + 5c dk grn	15	16

Photo.
Granite Paper

B97 SP94	10c + 5c rose vio & buff	18	16
B98 SP95	20c + 5c org red	30	18
B99 SP96	30c + 10c ultra & buff	1.65	*3.75*
	Set, never hinged	3.50	

Sempach, 1386 — SP97

Giornico, 1478 — SP98

Calven, 1499 — SP99

WWI Ranger — SP100

1940, Mar. 20   **Photo.**
Granite Paper

B100 SP97	5c + 5c emer, blk & red	38	*1.25*
B101 SP98	10c + 5c brn org, blk & car	38	40

B102 SP99	20c + 5c brn red, blk & car	1.90	85
B103 SP100	30c + 10c brt bl, brn blk & red	2.00	*6.00*

National Fête Day. The surtax was for the National Fund and the Red Cross.

Redrawn

B104 SP99	20c + 5c brn red, blk & car	12.00	4.75
	Nos. B100-B104 (5)	16.66	*13.25*
	Set, never hinged	26.00	

The base of statue has been heavily shaded "Calven 1499" moved nearer to bottom line of base. Top line of base removed.

Souvenir Sheet
Unwmk.
1940, July 16   **Photo.**   **Imperf.**
Granite Paper

B105	Sheet of 4	200.00	*650.00*
	Never hinged	400.00	
a.	SP97 5c+5c yel grn, blk & red	15.00	*30.00*
b.	SP98 10c+5c org yel, blk & red	50.00	*250.00*
c.	SP99 20c+5c brn red, blk & red (redrawn)	50.00	*250.00*
d.	SP100 30c+10c chlky bl, blk & red	15.00	*30.00*

National Fete Day. Sheets measure 125x65mm and sold for 5fr.

Gottfried Keller — SP102

Girl of Thurgau — SP103

Girl of Solothurn — SP104

Girl of Zug — SP105

1940, Dec. 1   **Engr.**   **Perf. 11½**

B106 SP102	5c + 5c dk bl grn	15	*20*

Photo.

B107 SP103	10c + 5c brn & buff	18	*20*
B108 SP104	20c + 5c org red & buff	24	22
B109 SP105	30c + 10c dp ultra & buff	1.65	*3.75*
	Set, never hinged	4.00	

Lake Lucerne, Arms of Cantons SP106

Tell Chapel at Chemin Creux SP107

1941, June 15

B110 SP106	10c + 10c multi	38	25
B111 SP107	20c + 10c org, red & lt buff	38	25
	Set, never hinged	1.00	

Natl. Fête Day and 650th anniv. of Swiss Independence.

Johann Lavater SP108

Girl of Schaffhausen SP109

Girl of
Obwalden
SP110

Daniel Jean
Richard
SP111

1941, Dec. 1   Engr.
B112 SP108 5c + 5c dk grn   18   15
B113 SP111 30c + 10c dp ultra   1.50   2.50

Photo.
B114 SP109 10c + 5c chnt & buff   28   20
B115 SP110 20c + 5c ver & buff   28   20
    Set, never hinged   3.75

Souvenir Sheet
Imperf
B116   Sheet of 2   45.00   300.00
a.   SP109 10c +5c chnt & buff   15.00   125.00
b.   SP110 20c +5c ver & buff   15.00   125.00
    Never hinged   90.00

Issued in sheets measuring 75x70mm and sold
for 2fr. The surtax was used for charity.

Ancient
Geneva
SP113

Soldiers'
Monument,
Forch
SP114

1942, June 15   Perf. 11½
B117 SP113 10c + 10c gray blk, red &
          yel   35   30
B118 SP114 20c + 10c cop red, red &
          buff   35   30
    Set, never hinged   1.00

National Fête Day, 1942. No. B117 for the
2000th anniv. of the City of Geneva.

Souvenir Sheet
Imperf
B119   Sheet of 2   45.00   225.00
a.   SP113 10c +10c gray black, red
      & yellow   15.00   70.00
b.   SP113 20c +10c copper red, red
      & buff   15.00   70.00
    Never hinged   82.50

Issued in sheets measuring 105x63mm in commemoration of National Fete and the 2000th anniv.
of the City of Geneva. Sold for 2fr. The surtax was
divided between the Swiss Alliance of Samaritans
and the National Community Chest.

Niklaus
Riggenbach
SP116

Girl of
Appenzell
SP117

Girl of Glarus
SP118

Konrad Escher
von der Linth
SP119

1942, Dec. 1   Engr.   Perf. 11½
B120 SP116 5c + 5c deep grn   15   30
B121 SP119 30c + 10c royal bl   1.65   3.25

Photo.
B122 SP117 10c + 5c dp brn & buff   18   32
B123 SP118 20c + 5c org red   24   32
    Set, never hinged   3.25

Intragna
SP120

Parliament
Buildings,
Bern
SP121

1943, June 15   Photo.   Perf. 11½
B124 SP120 10c + 10c blk brn, buff &
         dk red   30   45
B125 SP121 20c + 10c cop red, buff &
         dk red   35   65
    Set, never hinged   1.00

National Fête Day, 1943.

Emanuel von
Fellenberg
SP122

Silver Thistle
SP123

Designs: 20c+5c, Lady slipper. 30c+10c,
Gentian.

1943, Dec. 1   Engr.
B126 SP122 5c + 5c green   15   16

Photo.
B127 SP123 10c + 5c sl grn & ocher   15   25
B128 SP123 20c + 5c copper red &
         yel   15   28
B129 SP123 30c + 10c royal bl & lt
         bl   1.25   4.25
    Set, never hinged   3.25

Souvenir Sheets

SP126

1943   Engr.   Imperf.
B130 SP126   Sheet of 12   37.50   57.50
a.   10c black, single stamp   1.00   3.50
    Never hinged   65.00

Sold for 5fr. Size: 165x140mm.

SP127

Red Horizontal Lines
B131 SP127   Sheet of 2   37.50   60.00
a.   4c black & red   12.50   20.00
b.   6c black & red   12.50   20.00
    Never hinged   65.00

Sold for 3fr. Size: 70x75mm.

Arms of
Geneva
SP128

B132 SP128   Sheet of 2   32.50   40.00
a.   5c green & black   8.50   10.50
    Never hinged   55.00

Sold for 3fr. Size: 72x72mm. Centenary of
Swiss postage stamps. The surtax aided the Swiss
Red Cross.

Heiden
SP129

St. Jacob
SP130

Mesocco
SP131

Basel
SP132

Perf. 11½
1944, June 15   Photo.   Unwmk.
B133 SP129 5c + 5c dk bl grn,
         red & buff   20   1.25
B134 SP130 10c + 10c gray blk,
         red & buff   20   40
B135 SP131 20c + 10c hn, red &
         buff   20   70
B136 SP132 30c + 10c brt ultra &
         red   2.75   12.00
    Set, never hinged   5.25

National Fete Day.

Numa Droz
SP133

Edelweiss
SP134

Designs: 20c+5c, Lilium martagon. 30c+10c,
Aquilegia alpina.

1944, Dec. 1   Engr.
B137 SP133 5c + 5c green   15   22

Photo.
B138 SP134 10c + 5c dk sl grn, yel
         & gray   22   28
B139 SP134 20c + 5c red, yel & gray   38   28
B140 SP134 30c + 10c bl, gray & lt
         bl   1.50   4.50
    Set, never hinged   4.00

Symbol of Faith,
Hope and
Love — SP137

Lifeboat Making a
Rescue — SP138

1945, Feb. 20   Perf. 11½
B141 SP137 10c + 10c multi   40   55
B142 SP137 20c + 60c multi   1.65   5.00
    Set, never
    hinged   2.50

Imperf
Souvenir Sheet
B143 SP138 3fr + 7fr bl gray   135.00   275.00
    Never hinged   225.00

Issued in sheets measuring 70x110mm.
The surtax on Nos. B141-B143 was for the benefit of war victims.

Souvenir Sheet

Dove of
Basel
SP139

1945, Apr. 14   Typo.
B144 SP139   Sheet of 2   65.00   85.00
a.   10c gray, maroon & blk   21.00   30.00
    Never hinged   110.00

Cent. of the Basel Cantonal Stamp. The sheets
measure 71x63mm and sold for 3fr. The surtax
was for the Pro Juventute Foundation.

Numeral of Value and
Red Cross — SP140

1945   Photo.   Perf. 12
B145 SP140 5c + 10c grn & red   42   60
    Never hinged   75

Weaver
SP141

Farm of Jura
SP142

Farm of
Emmental
SP143

Frame
House,
Eastern
Switzerland
SP144

1945, June 15   Engr.   Perf. 11½

B146 SP141 5c + 5c bl grn & red   60   1.50

Photo.

B147 SP142 10c + 10c brn, gray
            bl & red   60   60
B148 SP143 20c + 10c hn brn,
            buff & red   90   60
B149 SP144 30c + 10c saph & red   9.00 30.00
            Set, never hinged   13.00

The surtax was for needy mothers.

Ludwig
Forrer — SP145

Susanna
Orelli — SP146

Alpine Dog-
Rose — SP147

Crocus — SP148

1945, Dec. 1   Engr.

B150 SP145 5c + 5c dk grn   15   18
B151 SP146 10c + 10c dk red brn   15   22

Photo.

B152 SP147 20c + 10c rose brn, rose
            & yel org   32   22
B153 SP148 30c + 10c dk bl, gray &
            lil   1.25 4.00
            Set, never hinged   3.75

Cheese
Making
SP149

Farm
Buildings and
Vineyards
SP150

House in
Appenzell
SP151

House in
Engadine
SP152

1946, June 15   Engr.

B154 SP149 5c + 5c bl grn & red   45   1.25

Photo.

B155 SP150 10c + 10c brn, buff &
            red   35   38
B156 SP151 20c + 10c henna, buff
            & red   45   38
B157 SP152 30c + 10c saph & red   3.50   6.50
            Set, never hinged   7.50

Rodolphe
Toepffer
SP153

Narcissus
SP154

Designs: 20c+10c, Mountain sengreen.
40c+10c, Blue thistle.

1946, Nov. 30   Engr.

B158 SP153 5c + 5c green   15   18

Photo.

B159 SP154 10c + 10c dk sl grn,
            gray & red org   20   22
B160 SP154 20c + 10c brn car, gray
            & yel   22   22
B161 SP154 30c + 10c dk bl, gray &
            pink   1.90   3.75
            Set, never hinged   3.50

Railroad
Laborers
SP157

Railroad
Station,
Rorschach
SP158

Lüen-Castiel
Station
SP159

Flüelen
Station
SP160

1947, June 14   Engr.   Unwmk.

B162 SP157 5c + 5c dk grn & red   35   1.10

Photo.

B163 SP158 10c + 10c gray blk,
            cream & red   35   45
B164 SP159 20c + 10c rose lil,
            cream & red   35   45
B165 SP160 30c + 10c bl, gray &
            red   3.25   5.00
            Set, never hinged   7.00

The surtax was for professional education of
invalids and for the fight against cancer.

Jakob
Burckhardt
SP161

Alpine
Primrose
SP162

Designs: 20c+10c, Red lily. 40c+10c,
Cyclamen.

1947, Dec. 1   Engr.

B166 SP161 5c + 5c dk grn   15   15

Photo.

B167 SP162 10c + 10c sl blk, gray &
            yel   15   22
B168 SP162 20c + 10c red brn, gray
            & cop red   20   22
B169 SP162 30c + 10c dk bl, gray &
            pink   1.25   3.75
            Set, never hinged   3.50

Sun and Olympic
Emblem — SP165

Snowflake and
Olympic
Emblem — SP166

Icehockey
Player — SP167

Ski-runner — SP168

1948, Jan. 15

B170 SP165 5c + 5c dk bl grn &
            yel   25   80
B171 SP166 10c + 10c choc & bl   25   80
B172 SP167 20c + 10c dp mag, gray
            & org yel   50   80
B173 SP168 30c + 10c dk bl, bl &
            gray blk   1.10   2.75
            Set, never hinged   5.00

Issued to publicize the 5th Olympic Winter
Games, St. Moritz, Jan. 30-Feb. 8, 1948.

Frontier
Guard
SP169

House of
Fribourg
SP170

House of
Valais
SP171

House of
Ticino
SP172

1948, June 15   Engr.

B174 SP169 5c + 5c dk grn & red   15   30

Photo.

B175 SP170 10c + 10c sl & gray   15   24
B176 SP171 20c + 10c brn red &
            pink   18   24
B177 SP172 30c + 10c bl & gray   2.00   3.25
            Set, never hinged   5.00

Johann R. Wettstein — SP173

1948, Aug. 21   Perf. 11x12½

B178 SP173   Sheet of 2   35.00 62.50
   a.   10c rose lilac   13.00 20.00
   b.   20c chalky blue   13.00 20.00
         Never hinged   77.50

Intl. Phil. Expo., Basel, Aug. 21-29, 1948. Sheet,
size 110x60mm, sold for 3fr, of which the surtax
was used for the exhibition and charitable purposes.

Gen. Ulrich
Wille
SP174

Foxglove
SP175

Designs: 20c+10c, Alpine rose. 40c+10c, Lily
of paradise.

1948, Dec. 1   Engr.   Perf. 11½

B179 SP174 5c + 5c dk vio brn   15   18

Photo.

B180 SP175 10c + 10c dk grn, yel
            grn & yel   25   22
B181 SP175 20c + 10c brn, crim &
            buff   32   22
B182 SP175 40c + 10c bl, gray & org   1.25   3.25
            Set, never hinged   3.75

Postman
SP176

Mountain
Farmhouse
SP177

House of
Lucerne
SP178

House of
Prattigau
SP179

Engraved and Photogravure
1949, June 15
Shield in Carmine

B183 SP176 5c + 5c rose vio   45   75

Photo.

B184 SP177 10c + 10c bl grn & car   35   50
B185 SP178 20c + 10c dk brn & cr   45   50
B186 SP179 40c + 10c bl & pale bl   3.50   5.50
            Set, never hinged   7.00

The surtax was for professional education of
Swiss youth.

Niklaus Wengi
SP180

Anemone
Sulphureous
SP181

Designs: 20c+10c, Alpine clematis. 40c+10c,
Superb pink.

1949, Dec. 1   Engr.   Perf. 11½

B187 SP180 5c + 5c vio brn   18   15

Photo.

B188 SP181 10c + 10c grn, gray &
            yel   24   24
B189 SP181 20c + 10c brn, bl & yel   30   32
B190 SP181 40c + 10c bl, lav & yel   1.65   4.00
            Set, never hinged   3.75

Adaptation of
1850 Design
SP182

Putting the
Stone
SP183

Designs: 20c+10c, Wrestlers. 30c+10c, Runners. 40c+10c, Target shooting.

1950, June 1   **Engr. & Photo.**
Shield in Red

B191	SP182	5c + 5c black	20	55

Photo.
Inscribed: "I. VIII. 1950"

B192	SP183	10c + 10c green	50	55
B193	SP183	20c + 20c brown ol	65	75
B194	SP183	30c + 10c rose lil	4.00	11.00
B195	SP183	40c + 10c dull bl	4.00	8.50
		Nos. B191-B195 (5)	9.35	21.35
		Set, never hinged	15.00	

The surtax was for the Red Cross and the Society of Swiss History of Art.

Theophil Sprecher von Bernegg
SP184

Admiral Butterfly
SP185

Designs: 20c+10c, Blue Underwing Butterfly. 30c+10c, Bee. 40c+10c, Sulphur Butterfly.

1950, Dec. 1   **Engr.**

B196	SP184	5c + 5c sepia	18	16

Photo.

B197	SP185	10c + 10c multi	32	28
B198	SP185	20c + 10c multi	45	38
B199	SP185	30c + 10c rose lil, gray & dk brn	3.50	10.00
B200	SP185	40c + 10c bl, dk brn & yel	3.50	7.00
		Nos. B196-B200 (5)	7.95	17.82
		Set, never hinged	11.00	

Arms of Switzerland and Zurich
SP186

Valaisan Polka
SP187

Designs: 20c+10c, 40c, Flag-swinging. 30c+10c, Hornussen (national game). 40c+10c, Blowing alphorn.

1951, June 1   **Engr.**
Shield in Red

B201	SP186	5c + 5c gray	15	30

Photo.
Inscribed: "1. VIII. 1951"
Shield in Red, Figure Shaded in Gray

B202	SP187	10c + 10c green	45	42
B203	SP187	20c + 10c ol bis	45	42
B204	SP187	30c + 10c red vio	3.50	8.00
B205	SP187	40c + 10c brt blue	3.75	8.00
		Nos. B201-B205 (5)	8.30	17.14
		Set, never hinged	17.50	

The surtax was used primarily for needy mothers.

Souvenir Sheet
1951, Sept. 29   **Imperf.**

B206	SP187	40c brt bl, sheet	175.00	175.00
		Never hinged	275.00	

No. B206 sold for 3fr, size: 74x56mm. Natl. Phil. Exhib., LUNABA, Sept. 29-Oct. 7, 1951, Lucerne. The net proceeds were used for Swiss schools abroad.

Johanna Spyri
SP189

Dragonfly
SP190

Butterflies: 20c+10c, Black-Veined. 30c+10c, Orange-Tip. 40c+10c, Saturnia pyri.

1951, Dec. 1   **Engr.**   **Perf. 11½**

B207	SP189	5c + 5c red brn	15	15

Photo.

B208	SP190	10c + 10c grn & dk bl	18	22
B209	SP190	20c + 10c rose lil, cr & blk	22	22
B210	SP190	30c + 10c ol grn, gray & org	2.75	5.50
B211	SP190	40c + 10c bl, dk brn & car	2.75	5.50
		Nos. B207-B211 (5)	6.05	11.59
		Set, never hinged	8.00	

Arms of Switzerland, Glarus and Zug
SP191

Doubs River — SP192

Designs: 20c+10c, Lake of St. Gotthard. 30c+10c, Moesa River. 40c+10c, Lake of Marjelen.

1952, May 31   **Engr. & Typo.**

B212	SP191	5c + 5c gray & red	28	45

Photo.

B213	SP192	10c + 10c blue green	32	30
B214	SP192	20c + 10c brown car	32	30
B215	SP192	30c + 10c brown	2.75	4.50
B216	SP192	40c + 10c blue	2.75	4.50
		Nos. B212-B216 (5)	6.42	10.05
		Set, never hinged	11.00	

The surtax was used primarily for historical research and popular culture.

See Nos. B222-B226, B233-B236, B243-B246, B253-B256.

Portrait of a Boy, by Albert Anker
SP193

Ladybug
SP194

Designs: 20c+10c, Barred-wing butterfly. 30c+10c, Argus butterfly. 40c+10c, Silkworm moth.

Perf. 11½
1952, Dec. 1   **Unwmk.**   **Engr.**

B217	SP193	5c + 5c brown car	15	15

Photo.

B218	SP194	10c + 10c bluish grn, blk & grd red	22	18
B219	SP194	20c + 10c rose lil, cr & blk	30	18
B220	SP194	30c + 10c brn, blk & gray bl	2.00	4.75
B221	SP194	40c + 10c pale vio, brn & buff	2.75	4.50
		Nos. B217-B221 (5)	5.42	9.76
		Set, never hinged	9.00	

See Nos. B227-B231, B238-B241.

Types Similar to 1952

Designs: 5c+5c, Arms of Switzerland and Bern. 10c+10c, Reuss River. 20c+10c, Sihl Lake. 30c+10c, Bisse River. 40c+10c, Lake of Geneva.

Engraved and Photogravure
1953, June 1

B222	SP191	5c + 5c gray & red	22	40

Photo.

B223	SP192	10c + 10c blue green	30	28
B224	SP192	20c + 10c brown car	38	28
B225	SP192	30c + 10c brown	2.00	4.00
B226	SP192	40c + 10c blue	2.00	4.00
		Nos. B222-B226 (5)	4.90	8.96
		Set, never hinged	10.50	

The surtax was used for Swiss nationals abroad and for disabled persons.

Booklet Panes
Panes consisting of blocks, strips or pairs removed from large sheets of regular issue and fastened or enclosed within a cover or folder, often by stapling or sewing in the sheet margin, are no longer being listed. Such panes contain no straight edges and can easily be made privately.

Types Similar to 1952, Dated "1953"

Designs: 5c+5c, Portrait of a girl, by Albert Anker. 10c+10c, Nun moth. 20c+10c, Camberwell beauty butterfly. 30c+10c, Purple longicorn beetle. 40c+10c, Self-portrait, Ferdinand Hodler, facing left.

1953, Dec. 1   **Engr.**   **Perf. 11½**

B227	SP193	5c + 5c rose brown	15	15

Photo.

B228	SP194	10c + 10c bl grn, brn & rose pink	16	15
B229	SP194	20c + 10c multi	22	15
a.		Sheet of 24	250.00	
		Never hinged	400.00	
b.		Bklt. pane, 4 #B229, 2 #B230	32.50	
B230	SP194	30c + 10c ol, blk & red	2.25	4.50

Engr.

B231	SP193	40c + 10c blue	3.00	4.50
		Nos. B227-B231 (5)	5.78	9.45
		Set, never hinged	10.00	

No. B229a consists of 16 No. B229 and 8 No. B230, arranged to include four se-tenant pairs and four pairs which are both se-tenant and tête bêche.

Opening Bars of "Swiss Hymn"
SP195

Jeremias Gotthelf
SP196

Types Similar to 1952, Dated "1954"

Views: 10c+10c, Neuchatel lake. 20c+10c, Maggia river. 30c+10c, Cascade, Taubenloch gorge. 40c+10c, Sils lake.

1954, June 1   **Engr.**   **Perf. 11½**

B232	SP195	5c + 5c dk bl grn	35	30

Photo.

B233	SP192	10c + 10c blue grn	35	25
B234	SP192	20c + 10c deep plum	35	25
B235	SP192	30c + 10c dk brown	2.50	4.25
B236	SP192	40c + 10c dp blue	2.50	4.25
		Nos. B232-B236 (5)	6.05	9.30
		Set, never hinged	10.00	

The surtax was used to aid vocational training and home nursing.

No. B232 commemorates the centenary of the death of Alberik Zwyssig, composer of the "Swiss Hymn."

Types Similar to 1952, Dated "1954"

Insects: 10c+10c, Garden tiger. 20c+10c, Bumble bee. 30c+10c, Ascalaphus. 40c+10c, Swallowtail.

1954, Dec. 1   **Engr.**

B237	SP196	5c + 5c dk red brn	15	28

Photo.

B238	SP194	10c + 10c multi	30	28
B239	SP194	20c + 10c multi	40	38
B240	SP194	30c + 10c rose vio, brn & yel	2.75	4.25
B241	SP194	40c + 10c multi	2.75	4.25
		Nos. B237-B241 (5)	6.35	9.44
		Set, never hinged	10.00	

Type Similar to 1952, Dated "1955," and

Federal Institute of Technology, Zurich — SP197

Views: 10c+10c, Saane river. 20c+10c, Lake of Aegeri. 30c+10c, Grappelen Lake. 40c+10c, Lake of Bienne.

1955, June 1   **Engr.**   **Perf. 11½**

B242	SP197	5c + 5c gray	25	40

Photo.

B243	SP192	10c + 10c dp green	32	34
B244	SP192	20c + 10c rose brn	32	38
B245	SP192	30c + 10c brown	2.25	3.50
B246	SP192	40c + 10c dp blue	2.25	3.50
		Nos. B242-B246 (5)	5.39	8.12
		Set, never hinged	10.00	

The surtax aided mountain dwellers.

No. B242 for the centenary of the Federal Institute of Technology in Zurich.

Charles Pictet de Rochemont
SP198

Peacock Butterfly
SP199

Insects: 20c+10c, Great Horntail. 30c+10c, Yellow Bear moth. 40c+10c, Apollo butterfly.

1955, Dec. 1   **Engr.**   **Unwmk.**

B247	SP198	5c + 5c brn car	15	15

Photo.
Insects in Natural Colors

B248	SP199	10c + 10c yel grn	18	16
B249	SP199	20c + 10c red	25	18
B250	SP199	30c + 10c dk ocher	1.90	3.25
B251	SP199	40c + 10c ultra	1.90	3.25
		Nos. B247-B251 (5)	4.38	6.99
		Set, never hinged	9.00	

Types Similar to 1952, Dated "1956", and

"Woman's Work" — SP200

Designs: 10c+10c, Rhone at St. Maurice. 20c+10c, Katzensee. 30c+10c, Rhine at Trin. 40c+10c, Lake Wallen.

1956, June 1   **Engr.**   **Perf. 11½**

B252	SP200	5c + 5c turq bl	20	30

Photo.

B253	SP192	10c + 10c green	32	30
B254	SP192	20c + 10c brn car	32	30
B255	SP192	30c + 10c brown	2.50	3.25
B256	SP192	40c + 10c ultra	2.50	3.25
		Nos. B252-B256 (5)	5.84	7.40
		Set, never hinged	9.50	

The surtax was for the National Day Collection, the National Library and Academy of Arts and Letters. No. B252 was issued in honor of Swiss women.

Carlo Maderno
SP201

Burnet Moth
SP202

Insects: 20c+10c, Purple Emperor. 30c+10c,
Blue ground beetle. 40c+10c, Cabbage butterfly.

1956, Dec. 1   Engr.   Perf. 11½
B257 SP201 5c + 5c brn car   15   15
Photo.
Granite Paper
B258 SP202 10c + 10c grn, dk grn
              & car rose   20   15
B259 SP202 20c + 10c multi   28   20
B260 SP202 30c + 10c yel & dp bl 1.40 2.75
B261 SP202 40c + 10c lt ultra, pale
              yel & sep   1.50 2.75
  Nos. B257-B261 (5)   3.53 6.00
  Set, never hinged   7.00

Red Cross and
Swiss
Emblems — SP203

"Charity" — SP204

Engraved and Photogravure
1957, June 1   Unwmk.   Perf. 11½
B262 SP203 5c + 5c gray & red   30   35
Photo.
Granite Paper
Cross in Deep Carmine
B263 SP204 10c + 10c brt grn &
              gray   30   28
B264 SP204 20c + 10c red & bl
              gray   40   28
B265 SP204 30c + 10c brn & vio
                                   2.00 3.00
B266 SP204 40c + 10c brt bl & bis 2.00 3.00
  Nos. B262-B266 (5)   5.00 6.91
  Set, never hinged   8.50

The surtax went to the Red Cross for the needs
of the sick and to combat cancer.

Leonhard Euler
SP205

Clouded
Yellow
SP206

Insects: 20c+10c, Magpie moth. 30c+10c, Rose
Chafer. 40c+10c, Red Underwing.

1957, Nov. 30   Engr.   Perf. 11½
B267 SP205 5c + 5c brn car   15   15
Photo.
Granite Paper
B268 SP206 10c + 10c multi   15   15
B269 SP206 20c + 10c lil rose, blk
              & yel   30   15
B270 SP206 30c + 10c rose brn,
              ind & brt grn   2.25 2.50
B271 SP206 40c + 10c multi   2.25 2.25
  Nos. B267-B271 (5)   5.10 5.20
  Set, never hinged   6.25

┌─────────────────────────────────────┐
│ Catalogue values for unused   │
│ stamps in this section, from this   │
│ point to the end of the section, are │
│ for Never Hinged items.   │
└─────────────────────────────────────┘

Mother and
Child — SP207

Fluorite — SP208

Designs: 20c+10c, Ammonite. 30c+10c, Garnet.
40c+10c, Rock Crystal.

Perf. 11½
1958, May 31   Unwmk.   Engr.
B272 SP207 5c + 5c brn car   35   35
Photo.
Granite Paper
B273 SP208 10c + 10c multi   52   50
B274 SP208 20c + 10c blk, red &
              ol bis   52   50
B275 SP208 30c + 10c blk, dl yel &
              mag   2.75 3.25
B276 SP208 40c + 10c blk, chlky bl
              & sl bl   2.75 3.00
  Nos. B272-B276 (5)   6.89 7.60

The surtax was for needy mothers.
See #B283-B286, B292-B295, B304-B307.

Albrecht von
Haller
SP209

Pansy
SP210

Flowers: 20c+10c, China aster. 30c+10c, Morning glory. 40c+10c, Christmas rose.

1958, Dec. 1   Engr.   Perf. 11½
B277 SP209 5c + 5c brn car   15   15
Photo.
Granite Paper
B278 SP210 10c + 10c grn, yel &
              brn   22   15
B279 SP210 20c + 10c multi   32   15
B280 SP210 30c + 10c multi   2.00 3.50
B281 SP210 40c + 10c dk bl, yel &
              grn   2.00 3.25
  Nos. B277-B281 (5)   4.69 7.20

See Nos. B287-B291.

Mineral Type of 1958 and

Globe and Swiss
Flags — SP211

Designs: 10c+10c, Agate. 20c+10c, Tourmaline.
30c+10c, Amethyst. 40c+10c, Fossil salamander
(andrias).

1959, June 1   Engr.   Perf. 11½
B282 SP211 5c + 5c dl grn & red   22   42
Photo.
Granite Paper
B283 SP208 10c + 10c gray, yel grn
              & ver   42   32
B284 SP208 20c + 10c blk, lil rose &
              bl grn   42   32
B285 SP208 30c + 10c blk, lt brn &
              vio   2.00 3.00
B286 SP208 40c + 10c blk, bl & gray 2.00 3.00
  Nos. B282-B286 (5)   5.06 7.06

Types of 1958
Designs: 5c+5c, Karl Hilty. 10c+10c, Marigold.
20c+10c, Poppy. 30c+10c, Nasturtium. 50c+10c,
Sweet pea.

1959, Dec. 1   Engr.   Perf. 11½
B287 SP209 5c +5c brn car   15   15
Photo.
Granite Paper
B288 SP210 10c + 10c dk grn, grn &
              yel   22   16
B289 SP210 20c + 10c mag, red &
              grn   45   22

B290 SP210 30c + 10c multi   1.75 2.75
B291 SP210 50c + 10c multi   1.90 2.75
  Nos. B287-B291 (5)   4.47 6.03

Mineral Type of 1958 and

Owl, T-Square and
Hammer — SP212

Designs: 5c+5c, Smoky quartz. 10c+10c, Feld-
spar. 20c+10c, Gryphaea, fossil. 30c+10c, Azurite.

1960, June 1   Photo.   Perf. 11½
Granite Paper
B292 SP208 5c + 5c blk, bl & ocher 50   35
B293 SP208 10c + 10c blk, yel grn &
              pink   80   25
B294 SP208 20c + 10c blk, lil rose &
              yel   80   25
B295 SP208 30c + 10c multi   3.00 2.50
Engr.
B296 SP212 50c + 10c bl & gold   3.00 2.50
  Nos. B292-B296 (5)   8.10 5.85
Souvenir Sheet
Imperf
Typo.
B297   Sheet of 4   40.00 18.00

No. B297 contains four 50c+10c stamps of type
SP212 in gold and blue. Size: 84x75mm. Sold for
3fr.

Alexandre
Calame
SP213

Dandelion
SP214

Flowers: 20c+10c, Phlox. 30c+10c, Larkspur.
50c+10c, Thorn apple.

1960, Dec. 1   Engr.   Unwmk.
B298 SP213 5c + 5c grnsh bl   22   15
Photo.
Granite Paper
B299 SP214 10c + 10c grn, yel &
              gray   30   15
B300 SP214 20c + 10c mag, grn &
              gray   45   15
B301 SP214 30c + 10c org brn, grn
              & bl   2.50 2.00
B302 SP214 50c + 10c ultra & grn 2.50 2.25
  Nos. B298-B302 (5)   5.97 4.70

See Nos. B308-B312, B329-B333, B339-B343.

Mineral Type of 1958 and

Book of History with
Symbols of Time and
Eternity — SP215

Designs: 10c+10c, Fluorite. 20c+10c, Petrified
fish. 30c+10c, Lazulite. 50c+10c, Petrified fern.

1961, June 1   Engr.   Perf. 11½
B303 SP215 5c + 5c lt blue   15   35
Photo.
Granite Paper
B304 SP208 10c + 10c gray, grn &
              pink   30   28
B305 SP208 20c + 10c gray & car
              rose   30   28
B306 SP208 30c + 10c gray, org &
              grnsh bl   1.50 2.50
B307 SP208 50c + 10c gray, mag, bl & bis 1.50 2.50
  Nos. B303-B307 (5)   3.75 5.91

Types of 1960
Designs: 5c+5c, Jonas Furrer. 10c+10c, Sunflower. 20c+10c, Lily of the valley. 30c+10c, Iris.
50c+10c, Silverweed.

1961, Dec. 1   Engr.   Perf. 11½
B308 SP213 5c + 5c dk blue   15   15
Photo.
Granite Paper
B309 SP214 10c + 10c grn, yel & org 15   15
B310 SP214 20c + 10c dk red, grn &
              gray   30   20
B311 SP214 30c + 10c multi   1.40 1.90
B312 SP214 50c + 10c dk bl, yel &
              grn   1.50 2.00
  Nos. B308-B312 (5)   3.50 4.40

Jean Jacques
Rousseau
SP216

Half-Thaler,
Obwalden,
1732
SP217

Coins: 20c+10c, Ducat, Schwyz, ca. 1653.
30c+10c, "Steer Head" Batzen, Uri, 1659.
50c+10c, Nidwalden Batzen.

Perf. 11½
1962, June 1   Unwmk.   Engr.
B313 SP216 5c + 5c dk blue   70   15
Photo.
Granite Paper
B314 SP217 10c + 10c grn & stl bl 20   22
B315 SP217 20c + 10c car rose & yel 20   22
B316 SP217 30c + 10c org & sl bl 1.10 1.00
B317 SP217 50c + 10c ultra & vio bl 1.10 1.00
  Nos. B313-B317 (5)   3.30 2.59

Apple
Blossoms — SP218

Mother and
Child — SP219

Designs: 10c+10c, Boy chasing duck. 30c+10c,
Girl and sunflowers. 50c+10c, Forsythia. 1fr+20c,
Mother and child, facing right.

1962, Dec. 1   Perf. 11½
Granite Paper
B318 SP218 5c + 5c bl gray, pink,
              grn & yel   15   15
B319 SP218 10c + 10c grn, pink &
              dk grn   15   15
B320 SP219 20c + 10c org red, brn,
              grn & pink   35   15
B321 SP218 30c + 10c org, red & yel 1.25 1.40
B322 SP218 50c + 10c dp bl, yel &
              brn   1.40 1.50
  Nos. B318-B322 (5)   3.30 3.35
Souvenir Sheet
Imperf
B323 SP219 1fr + 20c Sheet of 2 5.00 3.75

50th anniv. of the Pro Juventute (Youth Aid)
Foundation. No. B323 sold for 3fr.

Anna Heer,
M.D. — SP220

Bandage
Roll — SP221

Designs: 20c+10c, Gift parcel. 30c+10c, Plasma
bottles. 50c+10c, Red Cross armband.

1963, June 1   Engr.   Perf. 11½
B324 SP220 5c + 5c dk blue   15   15

Photo.
Granite Paper
Cross in Red

B325 SP221 10c + 10c lt & dk grn & gray — 18 18
B326 SP221 20c + 10c rose, gray & blk — 30 18
B327 SP221 30c + 10c multicolored — 1.10 1.25
B328 SP221 50c + 10c bl, gray & blk — 1.25 1.25
Nos. B324-B328 (5) — 2.98 3.01

Types of 1960

Designs: 5c+5c, Portrait of a Boy by Albert Anker. 10c+10c, Daisy. 20c+10c, Geranium. 30c+10c, Cornflower. 50c+10c, Carnation.

1963, Nov. 30   Engr.   Perf. 11½
B329 SP213 5c + 5c blue — 20 28
a.   Booklet pane of 4 — 3.00

Photo.
B330 SP214 10c + 10c grn, gray & yel — 24 42
a.   Booklet pane of 4 — 4.00
B331 SP214 20c + 10c multi — 80 42
a.   Booklet pane of 4 — 4.00
B332 SP214 30c + 10c multi — 1.40 1.25
B333 SP214 50c + 10c ultra, lil rose & grn — 1.40 1.25
Nos. B329-B333 (5) — 4.04 3.62

Nos. B329-B331 were printed on two kinds of paper: I. Fluorescent, with violet fibers. II. Nonfluorescent, the 10c+10c and 20c+10c with mixed red and blue fibers. Nos. B332-B333 exist only on violet-fibered, fluorescent paper. The booklet panes, Nos. B329a, B330a and B331a, exist only on nonfluorescent paper.

Johann Georg Bodmer
SP222

Copper Coin, Zurich
SP223

Coins: 20c+10c, Doppeldicken, Basel. 30c+10c, Silver taler, Geneva. 50c+10c, Gold half florin, Bern.

Violet Fibers, Fluorescent Paper

1964, June 1   Engr.   Perf. 11½
B334 SP222 5c + 5c blue — 15 15

Photo.
B335 SP223 10c + 10c grn, bis & blk — 15 15
B336 SP223 20c + 10c rose car, gray & blk — 30 25
B337 SP223 30c + 10c org, gray & blk — 55 50

Granite Paper, Red and Blue Fibers
B338 SP223 50c + 10c ultra, yel & brn — 80 65
Nos. B334-B338 (5) — 1.95 1.70

Fluorescent Paper
Paper of Nos. B334-B425, B427 and B429 is fluorescent and has violet fibers. Nos. B426, B428 and all semipostals from No. B430 onward are fluorescent but lack violet fibers, unless otherwise noted.

Types of 1960

Designs: 5c+5c, Portrait of a Girl by Albert Anker. 10c+10c, Daffodil. 20c+10c, Rose. 30c+10c, Clover. 50c+10c, Water lily.

1964, Dec. 1   Engr.   Perf. 11½
B339 SP213 5c + 5c grnsh bl — 15 15

Photo.
B340 SP214 10c + 10c dp grn, yel & org — 15 15
B341 SP214 20c + 10c dp car, rose & grn — 15 15
B342 SP214 30c + 10c brn, lil & grn — 60 55
B343 SP214 50c + 10c red, blk — 45 45
Nos. B339-B343 (5) — 1.50 1.45

Type of Regular Issue, 1965
Souvenir Sheet

Designs: 10c, 20r Seated Helvetia. 20c, 40r Seated Helvetia.

1965, Mar. 8   Photo.   Imperf.
Granite Paper, Nonfluorescent
B344 A153 Sheet of 2 — 1.50 1.00
a.   10c grn, pale org & blk — 75 50
b.   20c dk red, yel & blk — 75 50

Natl. Postage Stamp Exhib., NABRA, Bern, Aug. 27-Sept. 5, 1965. Sold for 3fr, the net proceeds were used to cover expenses of the exhibition and to promote philately.

Father Theodosius Florentini
SP224

The Temptation of Christ
SP225

Ceiling Paintings from Church of St. Martin at Zillis, 12th century: 10c+10c, Symbol of evil (goose with fishtail). 20c+10c, Magi on horseback. 30c+10c, Fishermen on Sea of Galilee.

Perf. 11½
1965, June 1   Unwmk.   Engr.
B345 SP224 5c + 5c blue — 15 15

Photo.
B346 SP225 10c + 10c ol grn, ocher & bl — 15 15
B347 SP225 20c + 10c dk brn, red & buff — 15 15
B348 SP225 30c + 10c dk brn, sep & bl — 40 32
B349 SP225 50c + 10c vio bl, bl & brn — 40 32
Set value — 92

See Nos. B355-B359, B365-B369.

Hedgehogs — SP226

Designs: 10c+10c, Alpine marmots. 20c+10c, Red deer. 30c+10c, European badgers. 50c+10c, Varying hares.

1965, Dec. 1   Photo.   Perf. 11½
B350 SP226 5c + 5c multi — 15 15
B351 SP226 10c + 10c multi — 15 15
B352 SP226 20c + 10c multi — 20 15
B353 SP226 30c + 10c multi — 28 22
B354 SP226 50c + 10c multi — 42 32
Nos. B350-B354 (5) — 1.20
Set value — 75

See Nos. B360-B364.

Types of 1965

Designs: 5c+5c, Heinrich Federer (1866-1928), writer. 10c+10c, Joseph's dream. 20c+10c, Joseph on his way. 30c+10c, Virgin and Child fleeing to Egypt. 50c+10c, Angel leading the way. Nos. B356-B359 from ceiling paintings, Church of St. Martin at Zillis.

1966, June 1   Engr.   Perf. 11½
B355 SP224 5c + 5c dp blue — 15 15

Photo.
B356 SP225 10c + 10c multi — 15 15
B357 SP225 20c + 10c multi — 18 15
B358 SP225 30c + 10c multi — 28 24
B359 SP225 50c + 10c multi — 50 35
Nos. B355-B359 (5) — 1.26 1.04

Animal Type of 1965

Designs: 5c+5c, Ermine. 10c+10c, Red squirrel. 20c+10c, Red fox. 30c+10c, Hares. 50c+10c, Two chamois.

1966, Dec. 1   Photo.
Animals in Natural Colors
B360 SP226 5c + 5c grnsh bl — 15 15
B361 SP226 10c + 10c emer — 15 15
B362 SP226 20c + 10c ver — 22 15
B363 SP226 30c + 10c brt lem — 30 22
B364 SP226 50c + 10c ultra — 45 35
Nos. B360-B364 (5) — 1.27 1.02

Types of 1965

Designs: 5c+5c, Dr. Theodor Kocher. 10c+10c, Annunciation to the Shepherds. 20c+10c, Jesus and the Samaritan Woman at the Well. 30c+10c, Adoration of the Magi. 50c+10c St. Joseph. (Ceiling paintings, St. Martin at Zillis).

Perf. 11½
1967, June 1   Unwmk.   Engr.
B365 SP224 5c + 5c blue — 15 15

Photo.
B366 SP225 10c + 10c multi — 15 15
B367 SP225 20c + 10c multi — 22 15
B368 SP225 30c + 10c multi — 30 22
B369 SP225 50c + 10c multi — 45 35
Nos. B365-B369 (5) — 1.27

Roe Deer — SP227

Hunter, Month of May — SP228

Designs: 20c+10c, Pine marten. 30c+10c, Alpine ibex. 50c+20c, Otter.

1967, Dec. 1   Photo.   Perf. 11½
Animals in Natural Colors
B370 SP227 10c + 10c yel grn — 15 15
B371 SP227 20c + 10c dp car — 30 18
B372 SP227 30c + 10c ol bis — 40 25
B373 SP227 50c + 10c ultra — 75 50

1968, May 30   Photo.   Perf. 11½
Designs from Rose Window, Lausanne Cathedral: 20c+10c, Leo. 30c+10c, Libra. 50c+20c, Pisces.

B374 SP228 10c + 10c multi — 15 15
B375 SP228 20c + 10c multi — 28 20
B376 SP228 30c + 10c multi — 40 30
B377 SP228 50c + 10c multi — 70 70

Capercaillie
SP229

St. Francis
SP230

Birds: 20c+10c, Bullfinch. 30c+10c, Woodchat shrike. 50c+20c, Firecrest.

1968, Nov. 28   Photo.   Perf. 11½
Birds in Natural Colors
B378 SP229 10c + 10c dull yel — 15 15
B379 SP229 20c + 10c olive grn — 25 15
B380 SP229 30c + 10c lilac rose — 35 20
B381 SP229 50c + 20c dp violet — 65 48

See Nos. B386-B389.

1969, May 29   Photo.   Perf. 11½
Designs: 10c+10c, St. Francis Preaching to the Birds, Königsfelden Convent Church. 20c+10c, Israelites Drinking from Spring of Moses, Berne Cathedral. 30c+10c, St. Christopher, Laufelfinger Church (now Basel Museum). 50c+20c, Virgin and Child, Chapel at Grapplang (now National Museum).

B382 SP230 10c + 10c multi — 15 15
B383 SP230 20c + 10c multi — 28 22
B384 SP230 30c + 10c multi — 38 25
B385 SP230 50c + 20c multi — 70 45

Bird Type of 1968

Birds: 10c+10c, European goldfinch. 20c+10c, Golden oriole. 30c+10c, Wall creeper. 50c+20c, Eurasian jay.

1969, Dec. 1   Photo.   Perf. 11½
Birds in Natural Colors
B386 SP229 10c + 10c gray — 15 15
B387 SP229 20c + 10c green — 18 16
B388 SP229 30c + 10c plum — 32 22
B389 SP229 50c + 20c ultra — 70 55

Sailor, by Gian Casty, Gellert Schoolhouse, Basel
SP231

Blue Titmice
SP232

Contemporary Stained Glass Windows: 20c+10c, Abstract composition, by Celestino Piatti. 30c+10c, Bull (Assyrian god Marduk), by Hans Stocker. 50c+20c, Man and Woman, by Max Hunziker and Karl Ganz.

1970, May 29   Photo.   Perf. 11½
B390 SP231 10c + 10c multi — 15 15
B391 SP231 20c + 10c multi — 18 16
B392 SP231 30c + 10c multi — 35 25
B393 SP231 50c + 20c multi — 65 50

See Nos. B398-B401.

1970, Dec. 1   Photo.   Perf. 11½
Birds: 20c+10c, Hoopoe. 30c+10c, Greater spotted woodpecker. 50c+20c, Crested grebes.

Birds in Natural Colors
B394 SP232 10c + 10c orange — 20 15
B395 SP232 20c + 10c emerald — 28 16
B396 SP232 30c + 10c brt rose — 40 22
B397 SP232 50c + 20c blue — 90 75

See Nos. B402-B405.

Art Type of 1970

Contemporary Stained Glass Windows: 10c+10c, "Composition," by Jean-François Comment. 20c+10c, Cock, by Jean Prahin. 30c+10c, Fox, by Kurt Volk. 50c+20c, "Composition," by Bernard Schorderet.

1971, May 27   Photo.   Perf. 11½
B398 SP231 10c + 10c multi — 16 15
B399 SP231 20c + 10c multi — 22 15
B400 SP231 30c + 10c multi — 30 22
B401 SP231 50c + 20c multi — 65 45

Bird Type of 1970

Birds: 10c+10c, European redstarts. 20c+10c, White-spotted bluethroats. 30c+ 10c, Peregrine falcon. 40c+20c, Mallards.

1971, Dec. 1
B402 SP232 10c + 10c multi — 15 15
B403 SP232 20c + 10c multi — 18 15
B404 SP232 30c + 10c multi — 30 15
B405 SP232 40c + 20c multi — 95 85

Harpoon Heads, Late Stone Age
SP233

McGredy's Sunset
SP234

Archaeological Treasures: 20c+10c, Bronze hydria, Hallstadt period. 30c+10c, Gold bust of Emperor Marcus Aurelius, Roman period. 40c+20c, Horseback rider (decorative disk), early Middle Ages.

1972, June 1
B406 SP233 10c + 10c multi — 15 15
B407 SP233 20c + 10c multi — 20 15
B408 SP233 30c + 10c multi — 25 16
B409 SP233 40c + 20c multi — 1.00 70
Set value — 1.10

1972, Dec. 1   Photo.   Perf. 11½
Famous Roses: 20c+10c, Miracle. 30c+10c, Papa Meilland. 40c+20c, Madame Dimitriu.

B410 SP234 10c + 10c multi — 28 18
B411 SP234 20c + 10c multi — 35 18
B412 SP234 30c + 10c multi — 30 18
B413 SP234 40c + 20c multi — 1.50 1.10

Rauraric (Gallic) Jug
SP235

Chestnut
SP236

Archeologic Finds: 30c+10c, Bronze head of a Gaul. 40c+20c, Alemannic dress fasteners (fish), 6th century. 60c+20c, Gold bowl, 6th century B.C.

1973, May 29   Photo.   Perf. 11½

B414	SP235	15c + 5c multi	18	16
B415	SP235	30c + 10c multi	18	18
B416	SP235	40c + 20c multi	65	60
B417	SP235	60c + 20c multi	90	85

See Nos. B422-B425.

1973, Nov. 29   Photo.   Perf. 11½

Fruits of the Forest: 30c+10c, Sweet cherries. 40c+20c, Blackberries. 60c+20c, Blueberries.

B418	SP236	15c + 5c multi	15	15
B419	SP236	30c + 10c multi	15	15
B420	SP236	40c + 20c multi	70	60
B421	SP236	60c + 20c multi	90	70

Archaeological Type of 1973

Archaeological Finds: 15c+5c, Polychrome glass bowl. 30c+10c, Bull's head. 40c+20c, Gold fibula. 60c+20c, Ceramic bird.

1974, May 30   Photo.   Perf. 11½

B422	SP235	15c + 5c multi	15	15
B423	SP235	30c + 10c multi	35	28
B424	SP235	40c + 20c multi	65	55
B425	SP235	60c + 20c multi	80	70

Laurel — SP237

Gold Fibula, 6th Century — SP238

Designs: 30c+20c, Belladonna. 50c+20c, Laburnum. 60c+25c, Mistletoe.

1974, Nov. 29   Photo.   Perf. 11½

B426	SP237	15c + 10c multi	15	15
B427	SP237	30c + 20c multi	22	15
B428	SP237	50c + 20c multi	65	60
B429	SP237	60c + 25c multi	90	85

1975, May 30   Photo.   Perf. 11½

Archaeological Treasures: 30c+20c, Bronze head of Bacchus, 2nd century. 50c+20c, Bronze daggers, 1800-1600 B.C. 60c+25c, Colored glass bottle, 1st century.

B430	SP238	15c + 10c multi	20	18
B431	SP238	30c + 20c multi	30	28
B432	SP238	50c + 20c multi	75	70
B433	SP238	60c + 25c multi	80	75

Mail Bucket
SP239

Hepatica
SP240

Forest Plants: 30c+20c, Mountain ash berries. 50c+20c, Yellow nettle. 60c+25c, Sycamore maple.

1975, Nov. 27   Photo.   Perf. 11½

B434	SP239	10c + 5c multi	18	18
B435	SP240	15c + 10c multi	20	18
B436	SP240	30c + 20c multi	35	30
B437	SP240	50c + 20c multi	80	65
B438	SP240	60c + 25c multi	85	75
	Nos. B434-B438 (5)		2.38	2.06

See Nos. B443-B446.

Castles — SP241

1976, May 28   Photo.   Perf. 11½

B439	SP241	20c + 10 Kyburg	28	22
B440	SP241	40c + 20 Grandson	35	30
B441	SP241	40c + 20 Murten	42	30
B442	SP241	80c + 40 Bellinzona	1.10	85

See #B447-B450, B455-B458, B463-B466.

Plant Type of 1975

Medicinal Forest Plants: 20c+10c, Barberry. No. B444, Black elder. No. B445, Linden. 80+40c, Pulmonaria.

1976, Nov. 29   Photo.   Perf. 11½

B443	SP240	20c + 10c multi	20	15
B444	SP240	40c + 20c lil & multi	32	15
B445	SP240	40c + 20c terra cotta & multi	32	15
B446	SP240	80c + 40c multi	1.10	80

Castle Type of 1976

1977, May 26   Photo.   Perf. 11½

B447	SP241	20c + 10c Aigle	25	22
B448	SP241	40c + 20c Pratteln	40	35
B449	SP241	70c + 30c Sargans	1.10	90
B450	SP241	80c + 40c Hallwil	1.25	1.00

Wild Rose
SP242

Communal Arms
SP243

Designs: Roses.

1977, Nov. 28   Photo.   Perf. 11½

B451	SP242	20c + 10c multi	22	15
B452	SP242	40c + 20c multi	45	15
B453	SP242	70c + 30c multi	1.00	80
B454	SP242	80c + 40c multi	1.25	1.00

See Nos. B492-B496.

Castle Type of 1976

1978, May 26   Photo.   Perf. 11½

B455	SP241	20c + 10c Hagenwil	25	22
B456	SP241	40c + 20c Burgdorf	48	48
B457	SP241	70c + 30c Tarasp	1.00	1.00
B458	SP241	80c + 40c Chillon	1.25	1.25

1978, Nov. 28   Photo.   Perf. 11½

B459	SP243	20c + 10c Aarburg	25	22
B460	SP243	40c + 20c Gruyeres	42	22
B461	SP243	70c + 30c Castasegna	75	70
B462	SP243	80c + 40c Wangen an der Aare	95	85

See #B467-B470, B475-B478, B484-B487.

Castle Type of 1976

1979, May 25   Photo.   Perf. 11½

B463	SP241	20c + 10c Oron	28	25
B464	SP241	40c + 20c Spiez	42	35
B465	SP241	70c + 30c Porrentruy	1.10	85
B466	SP241	80c + 40c Rapperswil	1.25	1.10

Arms Type of 1978

1979, Nov. 28   Photo.   Perf. 11

B467	SP243	20c + 10c Cadro	18	15
B468	SP243	40c + 20c Rute	40	22
B469	SP243	70c + 30c Schwamendingen	75	65
B470	SP243	80c + 40c Perroy	1.10	95

Masons' and Carpenters' Sign — SP244

1980, May 29   Photo.   Perf. 11½

B471	SP244	20c + 10c shown	32	32
B472	SP244	40c + 20c Barber	48	32
B473	SP244	70c + 30c Hat maker	1.00	1.00
B474	SP244	80c + 40c Baker	1.25	1.25

Arms Type of 1978

1980, Nov. 26   Photo.   Perf. 11½

B475	SP243	20c + 10c Cortaillod	20	15
B476	SP243	40c + 20c Sierre	48	25
B477	SP243	70c + 30c Scuol	1.00	90
B478	SP243	80c + 40c Wolfenschiessen	1.25	95

Icarus in Flight — SP245

1981, Mar. 9   Photo.

| B479 | SP245 | 2fr + 1fr multi | 3.00 | 3.00 |

Swissair, 50th Anniversary. Surtax was for Pro Aero Foundation Issued in sheet of 8.

Post Office Sign, Aarburg, 1685 — SP246

Post Office Signs (c. 1849).

1981, May 4   Photo.

B480	SP246	20c + 10c shown	30	30
B481	SP246	40c + 20c Fribourg	60	50
B482	SP246	70c + 30c Gordola	1.10	1.10
B483	SP246	80c + 40c Splugen	1.25	1.25

Arms Type of 1978

1981, Nov. 26   Photo.   Perf. 11½

B484	SP243	20c + 10c Uffikon	32	18
B485	SP243	40c + 20c Torre	60	32
B486	SP243	70c + 30c Benken	1.00	60
B487	SP243	80c + 40c Preverenges	1.10	75

Sonne Inn Sign, Willisau — SP247

1982, May 27   Photo.   Perf. 11½

B488	SP247	20c + 10c shown	30	18
B489	SP247	40c + 20c A L'Onde, St. Saphorin	55	32
B490	SP247	70c + 30c Three Kings, Rheinfelden	95	55
B491	SP247	80c + 40c Krone, Winterthur	1.25	70

See Nos. B497-B500.

Rose Type of 1977

Designs: 10c+10c, Letter balance. 20c+10c, La Belle Portugaise. 40c+20c, Hugh Dickson. 70c+30c, Mermaid. 80c+40c, Madame Caroline.

1982, Nov. 25   Photo.

B492	SP242	10c + 10c multi	25	15
B493	SP242	20c + 10c multi	40	15
B494	SP242	40c + 20c multi	75	28
B495	SP242	70c + 30c multi	1.25	80
B496	SP242	80c + 40c multi	1.40	1.10
	Nos. B492-B496 (5)		4.05	2.48

Inn Sign Type of 1982

1983, May 26   Photo.

B497	SP247	20c + 10c Lion Inn, Heimiswil, 1669	40	28
B498	SP247	40c + 20c Cross Hotel, Sachseln, 1489	75	48
B499	SP247	70c + 30c Tankard Inn, 1830	1.25	80
B500	SP247	80c + 40c Au Cavalier Inn, Vaud	1.40	1.00

Antique Toys — SP248

1983, Nov. 24

B501	SP248	20c + 10c Kitchen stove, 1850	35	18
B502	SP248	40c + 20c Rocking horse, 1826	70	35
B503	SP248	70c + 30c Doll, 1870	1.10	55
B504	SP248	80c + 40c Steam locomotive, 1900	1.40	70

Ceramic Tiled Stoves — SP249

Children's Stories — SP250

1984, May 24   Photo.   Perf. 11½

B505	SP249	35c + 15c 1566	55	38
B506	SP249	50c + 20c 1646	70	50
B507	SP249	70c + 30c 1768	1.00	70
B508	SP249	80c + 40c 18th cent.	1.25	90

1984, Nov. 26   Photo.

B509	SP250	35c + 15c Heidi	60	38
B510	SP250	50c + 20c Pinocchio	75	50
B511	SP250	70c + 30c Pippi Longstocking	1.10	70
B512	SP260	80c + 40c Max and Moritz	1.40	90

Musical Museum Exhibits — SP251

1985, May 28   Photo.   Perf. 11½

B513	SP251	25c + 10c Music box, 1895	30	15
B514	SP251	35c + 15c Rattle box, 18th cent.	50	15
B515	SP251	50c + 20c Emmenthal necked zither, 1828	70	20
B516	SP251	70c + 30c Drum, 1571	1.00	28
B517	SP251	80c + 40c Diatonic accordion, 20th cent.	1.25	32
	Nos. B513-B517 (5)		3.75	1.10

Surtax for Swiss cultural programs.

Hansel and Gretel — SP252

Fairy tales by Jakob (1785-1863) and Wilhelm (1786-1859) Grimm.

1985, Nov. 26   Photo.

B518	SP252	35c + 15c shown	52	15
B519	SP252	50c + 20c Snow White	75	20
B520	SP252	80c + 40c Little Red Riding Hood	1.25	35
B521	SP252	90c + 40c Cinderella	1.40	38

Surtax for Pro Juventute Foundation and youth welfare orgs.

Man, Vitality and
Movement
SP253

1986, Feb. 11   Photo.   Perf. 12
B522 SP253 50c + 20c multi   90 24

Surtax for Natl. Sports Federation and cultural
programs.

SP254   SP255

Paintings in Natl. Museums (Swiss art):
35c+15c, Bridge in the Sun, 1907, by Giovanni
Giacometti (1868-1933). 50c+20c, The Violet Hat,
1907, by Cuno Amiet (1868-1961). 80c+40c, After
the Funeral, 1905, by Max Buri (1868-1915).
90c+40c, Still Life, 1914, by Felix Vallotton (1865-
1925).

1986, Apr. 22   Photo.   Perf. 11½
B523 SP254 35c + 15c multi   52 18
B524 SP254 50c + 20c multi   72 24
B525 SP254 80c + 40c multi   1.25 42
B526 SP254 90c + 40c multi   1.40 45

Surtax for National Day Collection and monuments preservation, social and cultural
organizations.

1986, Nov. 25   Photo.

Children's toys.

B527 SP255 35c + 15c Teddy bear   62 22
B528 SP255 50c + 20c Top   88 30
B529 SP255 80c + 40c Steamroller 1.50 50
B530 SP255 90c + 40c Doll   1.60 55

Surtax was for youth welfare organizations and
the Pro Juventute Foundation.

Antique Furniture
SP256

Designs: 35c+15c, Saane Valley wall cabinet,
1764, Vieux Pays d'Enhaut Museum, Chateau
d'Oex. 50c+20c, Raised chest, 16th cent., Rhaetian
Museum, Chur. 80c+40c, Ticino canton cradle,
1782, Valmaggia Museum, Cevio. 90c+40c,
Appenzell region wardrobe, 1698, St. Gallen Historical Museum.

1987, May 26   Photo.
B531 SP256 35c + 15c multi   55 24
B532 SP256 50c + 20c multi   80 35
B533 SP256 80c + 40c multi   1.40 58
B534 SP256 90c + 40c multi   1.50 60

Surtax for Red Cross and patriotic funds.

No. 786 Surcharged with Clasped Hands
and "7.9.87" in Red
Photo. & Engr.
1987, Sept. 7   Perf. 13½x13
B535 A349 50c + 50c multi   1.30 45

Surtaxed to benefit flood victims.

Christmas   Child Development
SP257   SP258

1987, Nov. 24   Photo.   Perf. 11½
B536 SP257 25c +10c shown   48 16
B537 SP258 35c +15c shown   68 22
B538 SP258 50c +20c Boy, building
                       blocks   95 32
B539 SP258 80c +40c Boy, girl in
                       sandbox   1.65 55
B540 SP258 90c +40c Father, child 1.80 60
    Nos. B536-B540 (5)   5.56 1.85

Surtax for national youth welfare projects and
the Pro Juventute Foundation.
See Nos. B555-B558.

Junkers JU-52,
1939, and the
Matterhorn
SP259

1988, Mar. 8   Photo.
B541 SP259 140c +60c multi   2.65 88

Pro Aero Foundation, Zurich, 50th Anniv. Issued
in sheets of 8.

SP260   SP261

Minnesingers.

1988, May 24   Photo.
B542 SP260 35c +15c Count Rudolf of
                  Neuchatel   60 25
B543 SP260 50c +20c Rudolf von
                  Rotenburg   85 35
B544 SP260 80c +40c Master Johannes
                  Hadlaub   1.50 58
B545 SP260 90c +40c The Hardegger 1.65 65

700 Years of art and culture.

1988, Nov. 25   Perf. 11½
B546 SP261 35c +15c Reading   68 22
B547 SP261 50c +20c Music   95 32
B548 SP261 80c +40c Math   1.65 55
B549 SP261 90c +40c Art   1.75 58

Child development. Surtax for natl. youth welfare projects and the Pro Juventute Foundation.

700 Years of Art
and
Culture — SP262

Illuminations in Zurich Central, Bern Burgher
and Lucerne Central libraries: No. B550, King
Friedrich II presenting Bern municipal charter,
1218, Bendicht Tschachtlan Chronicle, 1470. No.
B551, Capt. Adrian von Bubenberg and troops passing through Murten town gate, 1476, Bern Chronicle, by Diebold Schilling, 1483. No. B552, Official
messenger of Schwyz before the Council of Zurich,
c. 1440, Gerold Edlibach Chronicle, 1485. No.
B553, Schilling presenting manuscript to the mayor
and councilmen in the council chamber, Lucerne,
c. 1500, Diebold Schilling's Lucerne Chronicle,
1513.

1989, May 23
B550 SP262 35c +15c multi   65 22
B551 SP262 50c +20c multi   90 30
B552 SP262 80c +40c multi   1.55 52
B553 SP262 90c +40c multi   1.70 55

Surtax to benefit women's and cultural
organizations.

Gymnastics
SP263

1989, Aug. 25   Photo.   Perf. 11½
B554 SP263 50c +20c multi   80 28

Surtax to benefit Swiss Natl. Sports Federation,
cultural and social work.

Child Development Type of 1987
1989, Nov. 24
B555 SP258 35c +15c Community
                  work   62 20
B556 SP258 50c +20c Friendship   85 28
B557 SP258 80c +40c Vocational
                  training   1.50 50
B558 SP258 90c +40c Higher educa-
                  tion and research 1.60 55

Surtax for natl. youth welfare projects and the
Pro Juventute Foundation.

700 Years of Art and
Culture — SP264

Street criers: No. B559, Fly swatter and starch-
sprinkler vendor. No. B560, Clock vendor. No.
B561, Knife grinder. No. B562, Pinewood sellers.

1990, May 22   Photo.
B559 SP264 35c +15c multi   70 24
B560 SP264 50c +20c multi   95 32
B561 SP264 80c +40c multi   1.60 55
B562 SP264 90c +40c multi   1.75 58

Souvenir Sheet

Natl. Philatelic
Exhibition,
Geneva
'90 — SP265

Designs: a, Brass badge worn by Geneva Cantonal post drivers before 1849. b, Place du Bourg-
de-Four and entrance to Rue Etienne-Dumont. c, Ile
Rousseau and Pont des Bergues. d, No. 2L1 on
cover.

1990, Sept. 5
B563   Sheet of 4   4.00 1.35
a.-d. SP265 50c +25c any single 1.00 35

Child
Development
SP266

1990, Nov. 20
B564 SP266 35c +15c Model making 70 24
B565 SP266 50c +20c Youth groups 1.00 32
B566 SP266 80c +40c Sports   1.70 55
B567 SP266 90c +40c Music   1.85 60

700 Years of Art
and
Culture — SP267

Contemporary paintings by: 50c+20c, Wolf
Barth. 70c+30c, Helmut Federle. 80c+40c, Matthias Bosshart. 90c+40c, Werner Otto Leuenberger.

1991, May 14   Photo.   Perf. 11½
B568 SP267 50c +20c multi   1.00 32
B569 SP267 70c +30c multi   1.40 45
B570 SP267 80c +40c multi   1.70 55
B571 SP267 90c +40c multi   1.80 60

SP268   SP269

Woodland Flowers: 50c+25c, Allium ursinum.
70c+30c, Geranium sylvaticum. 80c+40c, Campanula trachelium. 90c+40c, Hieracium murorum.

1991, Nov. 26
B572 SP268 50c +25c multi   1.05 40
B573 SP268 70c +30c multi   1.40 45
B574 SP268 80c +40c multi   1.65 55
B575 SP268 90c +40c multi   1.80 60

Surtax for youth and family welfare projects and
the Pro Juventute Foundation.

1992, May 22   Photo.   Perf. 11½

Swiss Folk Art: 50c + 20c, Earthenware plate,
Heimberg, 18th cent. 70c + 40c, Paper cutout by
Johann Jakob Hauswirth (1809-1871). 80c + 40c,
Cream spoon, Gruyeres. 90c + 40c, Embroidered
silk carnation, Grisons.

B576 SP269 50c +20c multi   95 30
B577 SP269 70c +30c multi   1.30 45
B578 SP269 80c +40c multi   1.60 52
B579 SP269 90c +40c multi   1.70 58

Surtax for preservation of cultural heritage.

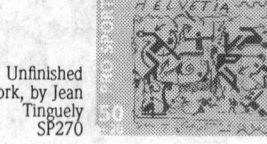

Unfinished
Work, by Jean
Tinguely
SP270

1992, Aug. 25   Photo.   Perf. 12
B580 SP270 50c +20c blue & black 1.15 38

Surtax for Natl. Sports Federation and sports-
related social and cultural activities.

Wood Puppet of
Melchior, 18th
Cent. — SP271

Trees — SP272

1992, Nov. 24   Photo.   Perf. 11½
B581 SP271 50c +25c multi   1.05 35
B582 SP272 50c +25c Copper beech 1.05 35
B583 SP272 70c +30c Norway maple 1.40 48
B584 SP272 80c +40c Common oak 1.65 55
B585 SP272 90c +40c Spruce   1.80 60
    Nos. B581-B585 (5)   6.95 2.33

Christmas. Surtax for youth and family welfare
projects and the Pro Juventute Foundation.

Swiss Folk
Art — SP273

Designs: No. B586, Appenzell dairyman's earring. No. B587, Fluhli glassware. 80c + 40c, Painting of cattle drive, by Sylvestre Pidoux. 100c + 40c, Straw hat ornament.

1993, May 5   Photo.   Perf. 11½

B586	SP273	60c +30c multi	1.25	42
B587	SP273	60c +30c multi	1.25	42
B588	SP273	80c +40c multi	1.15	38
B589	SP273	100c +40c multi	2.00	68

Architectural Heritage Type of 1960

Design: 80c+20c, Kapell Bridge and Water Tower, Lucerne.

1993, Sept. 7   Litho.   Perf. 13½x13

B590	A145	80c +20c orange & red	1.40	45

Surtax for reconstruction of Kapell Bridge with any excess for preservation of architectural heritage.

SP274   SP275

Woodland plants.

1993, Nov. 23   Photo.   Perf. 11½

B591	SP274	60c +30c Christmas wreath	1.25	40
B592	SP274	60c +30c Male fern	1.25	40
B593	SP274	80c +40c Guelder rose	1.65	55
B594	SP274	100c +50c Mnium punctatum	2.00	65

Christmas. Surtax for youth and family welfare projects and the Pro Juventute Foundation.

1994, May 17   Photo.   Perf. 11½

Swiss Folk Art: No. B595, Weight-driven Neuchatel clock. No. B598, Linen-embroidered pomegranate. 80c+40c, Biscuit mold for Krafli. 100c+40c, Paper bird mobile for child's cradle.

B595	SP275	60c +30c multi	1.25	42
B596	SP275	60c +30c multi	1.25	42
B597	SP275	80c +40c multi	1.65	55
B598	SP275	100c +40c multi	1.90	65

Christmas SP276

Mushrooms SP277

Designs: No. B600, Wood blewit. 80c+40c, Red boletus. 100c+50c, Shaggy pholiota.

1994, Nov. 28   Litho.   Perf. 11½

B599	SP276	60c +30c multi	1.40	45
B600	SP277	60c +30c multi	1.40	45
B601	SP277	80c +40c multi	1.90	60
B602	SP277	100c +50c multi	2.50	80
		Nos. B599-B602 (4)	7.20	2.30

Surtax for youth and family welfare projects and the Pro Juventute Foundation.

Swiss Folk Art — SP278

Designs: No. B603, Wooden cream pail. No. B604, Straw hat. 80c+40c, Chest lock, c. 1580. 100c+40c, Langnau pottery sugar bowl.

1995, May 16   Photo.   Perf. 11½

B603	SP278	60c +30c multi	1.65	52
B604	SP278	60c +30c multi	1.65	52
B605	SP278	80c +40c multi	2.25	70
		Complete booklet, 10 #B605	22.50	
B606	SP278	100c +40c multi	2.50	80
		Nos. B603-B606 (4)	8.05	2.54

Surtax for Swiss Pro Patria Foundation and special cultural, social projects.

Souvenir Sheet

Basler Taube '95 Philatelic Exhibition, Basel — SP279

Designs: a, 80c+30c, like Switzerland #3L1. Engraved panorama of Basel, by Matthaus Merian, 17th cent.: b, 60c+30c, Buildings, twin church steeples. c, 100c+50c, Buildings. d, 100c+50c, Buildings, bridge.

1995, May 16   Photo.   Perf. 13x14

B607	SP279	Sheet of 4	9.00	3.00
a.		80c +30c multi	1.90	60
b.		60c +30c black & blue	1.65	55
c.-d.		100c +50c any single	2.75	90

Nos. B607b-B607d are a continuous design.

AIR POST STAMPS

Nos. 134 and 139 Overprinted in Carmine

1919-20   Wmk. 183   Perf. 11½
Granite Paper

C1	A25	30c yel brn & pale grn ('20)	110.00	875.00
C2	A25	50c dp & pale grn	40.00	100.00
		Set, never hinged	425.00	

Counterfeits of overprint and fraudulent cancellations exist.

Airplane AP1

Pilot at Controls of Airplane AP2

Biplane against Sky — AP3

Allegorical Figure of Flight — AP4

Perf. 11½, 12 and Compound

1923-25				**Typo.**
C3	AP1	15c brn red & ap grn	1.25	3.00
C4	AP1	20c grn & lt grn ('25)	32	2.50
C5	AP1	25c dk bl & bl	4.00	9.00
C6	AP2	35c brn & buff	10.00	27.50
C7	AP2	40c vio & gray vio	10.00	27.50
C8	AP3	45c red & ind	1.00	3.00
C9	AP3	50c blk & red	8.00	9.50

		Perf. 11½		
C10	AP4	65c gray bl & dp bl ('24)	2.00	7.25
C11	AP4	75c org & brn red ('24)	10.00	30.00
C12	AP4	1fr vio & dp vio ('24)	30.00	18.00
		Nos. C3-C12 (10)	76.57	137.25
		Set, never hinged	250.00	

For surcharges see Nos. C19, C22, C26.

1933-37		**With Grilled Gum**		
C4a	AP1	20c grn & lt grn ('37)	40	32
C5a	AP1	25c dk bl & bl ('34)	5.00	45.00
C8a	AP3	45c red & ind ('37)	2.75	47.50
C9a	AP3	50c gray grn & scar ('35)	1.00	1.50
C10a	AP4	65c gray bl & dp bl ('37)	1.40	7.25
C11a	AP4	75c org & brn red ('36)	30.00	165.00
C12a	AP4	1fr vio & dp vio	2.75	2.25
		Nos. C4a-C12a (7)	43.30	268.82

See Grilled Gum note after No. 145.

Allegory of Air Mail — AP5

Bird Carrying Letter — AP6

1929-30		**Granite Paper**		
C13	AP5	35c red brn, bis & claret	20.00	22.50
C14	AP5	40c dl grn, yel grn & bl	45.00	55.00
C15	AP6	2fr blk brn & red brn, gray ('30)	75.00	37.50
		Set, never hinged	375.00	

1933-35		**With Grilled Gum**		
C13a	AP5	35c red brn, bis & cl	8.00	30.00
C14a	AP5	40c dk grn, yel grn & bl	35.00	35.00
C15a	AP6	2fr blk brn & red brn ('35)	8.50	5.25
		Set, never hinged	85.00	

Front View of Airplane AP7

1932, Feb. 2		**Granite Paper**		
C16	AP7	15c dp grn & lt grn	50	95
C17	AP7	20c dk red & buff	75	1.10
C18	AP7	90c dp bl & gray	8.50	22.50
		Set, never hinged	18.00	

Intl. Disarmament Conf., Geneva, Feb. 1932. For surcharges see Nos. C20, C23-C25.

Nos. C3, C10, C16-C18 Surcharged with New Values and Bars in Black or Red

1935-38				
C19	AP1	10c on 15c	5.25	25.00
C20	AP7	10c on 15c	55	42
a.		Inverted surcharge	6,000.	11,000.
C21	AP7	10c on 20c ('36)	85	1.65
C22	AP7	10c on 65c ('38)	20	18
C23	AP7	30c on 90c ('36)	4.00	10.00
C24	AP7	40c on 20c ('37)	4.75	11.50
C25	AP7	40c on 90c ('36) (R)	4.00	10.50
a.		Vermilion surcharge	77.50	725.00
		Nos. C19-C25 (7)	19.60	59.25
		Set, never hinged	35.00	

Stamp similar to No. C22, but from souvenir sheet, is listed as No. 242a.

Type of Air Post Stamp of 1923 Surcharged in Black

1938

«PRO AERO»

75   75

1938, May 22   Wmk. 183   Perf. 11½

C26	AP3	75c on 50c gray & scar	5.25

"Pro Aero" Meeting, May 21-22. No. C26 was not sold to the public in the ordinary way, but affixed to air mail letters by postal officials. It was not regularly obtainable unused.

Jungfrau — AP8

Designs: 40c, View of Valais. 50c, Lake Geneva. 60c, Alpstein. 70c, View of Ticino. 1fr, Lake Lucerne. 2fr, The Engadine. 3fr, Churfirsten.

Perf. 11½

1941, May 1   Unwmk.   Engr.
Tinted Granite Paper

C27	AP8	30c ultra	60	15
C28	AP8	40c gray blk	60	15
C29	AP8	50c slate grn	60	15
C30	AP8	60c chestnut	1.10	15
C31	AP8	70c plum	1.25	18
C32	AP8	1fr Prus grn	2.00	25
C33	AP8	2fr car lake	7.75	1.10
C34	AP8	5fr deep blue	25.00	4.75
		Nos. C27-C34 (8)	38.90	6.88
		Set, never hinged	70.00	

See Nos. C43-C44.

•PRO AERO•

Type of 1941 Overprinted in Red

20·V·1941

1941, May 12

C35	AP8	1fr blue green	6.00	16.00
		Never hinged	11.00	

Issued to commemorate special flights between Payerne and Buochs, May 28, 1941.

Parliament Buildings, Bern — AP16

1943, July 13   Photo.

C36	AP16	1fr cop red, buff & blk	2.00	8.00
		Never hinged	4.00	

30th anniv. of the 1st Alpine flight, by Oscar Bider, July 13, 1913.

DH-3 Haefeli AP17

Fokker AP18

Lockheed-Orion — AP19

1944, Sept. 1

C37	AP17	10c gray brn & pale grn	15	15
C38	AP18	20c rose car & buff	20	15
C39	AP19	30c ultra & pale gray	38	45
		Set, never hinged	1.25	

25th anniv. of the 1st regular air route in Switzerland.

Douglas DC-3 AP20

1944, Sept. 20   Granite Paper

C40	AP20	1.50fr multi	7.00	14.00
		Never hinged	13.00	

25th anniv. of the Zurich-Geneva air route.

Zoegling Training Glider AP21

1946, May 1   Granite Paper

C41	AP21	1.50fr henna brn & gray	15.00	20.00
		Never hinged	18.00	

Valid for use only on two special flights.

Douglas DC-4 Linking Geneva and New York AP22

1947, Mar. 17   Granite Paper

C42	AP22	2.50fr bl gray, dk bl & red	8.00	13.00
		Never hinged	12.00	

Valid only on the Geneva-New York flight of May 2, 1947.

Types of 1941

1948, Oct. 1   Engr.
Tinted Granite Paper

C43	AP8	30c dk slate bl	5.00	5.00
C44	AP8	40c deep ultra	27.50	1.75
		Set, never hinged	52.50	

Glider in Symbolized Aerodynamic Buoyancy AP23

1949, Apr. 11   Engr. & Typo.

C45	AP23	1.50fr dk vio & yel	16.00	22.50
		Never hinged	27.50	

Valid only on special flights, Apr. 27-29, 1949. Proceeds were for the advancement of national aviation.

> Catalogue values for unused stamps in this section, from this point to the end of the section, are for Never Hinged items.

Glider and Jets — AP24

1963, June 1   Photo.   *Perf. 11½*
Granite Paper

C46	AP24	2fr multicolored	5.00	4.75

50th anniversary of the first Alpine flight by Oscar Bider, July 13, 1913. Valid for postage on July 13, 1963, on flights from Bern to Locarno and Langenbruck to Bern. Proceeds went to the Pro Aero Foundation.

AIR POST SEMI-POSTAL STAMP

> Catalogue values for unused stamps in this section are for Never Hinged items.

Boeing 747 — SPAP1

1972, Feb. 17   Photo.   *Perf. 12½*
Violet Fibers, Fluorescent Paper

CB1	SPAP1	2fr + 1fr dp bl, red & gray	2.75	3.00

50th anniv. of 1st Swiss Intl. flight, Zurich to Nuremberg, and 25th anniv. of 1st Swissair trans-Atlantic flight, Zurich to NYC. Valid on all mail but obligatory on special flights from Geneva to NYC in May, and from Geneva to Nuremberg in June, 1972.

Surtax was for Pro Aero Foundation and the training of young airmen, and for the Swiss Air Rescue Service.

POSTAGE DUE STAMPS

D1   D2

Perf. 11½

1878-80   Typo.   Wmk. 182

J1	D1	1c ultra	1.00	60
J2	D2	2c ultra	1.00	60
J3	D2	3c ultra	9.00	9.00
J4	D2	5c ultra	11.00	5.00
J5	D2	10c ultra	160.00	5.00
J6	D2	20c ultra	190.00	3.00
J7	D2	50c ultra	350.00	15.00
J8	D2	100c ultra	450.00	6.00
J9	D2	500c ultra	400.00	4.00

A 5c in design D1 exists.

1882-83

Granite Paper

J10	D2	10c ultra	140.00	25.00
J11	D2	20c ultra	325.00	40.00
J12	D2	50c ultra	2,000.	400.00
J13	D2	100c ultra	625.00	275.00
J14	D2	500c ultra	12,000.	190.00

1883-84

Numerals in Red

J15	D2	5c blue green	30.00	25.00
J16	D2	10c blue green	50.00	10.00
J17	D2	20c blue green	100.00	10.00
J18	D2	50c blue green	110.00	35.00
J19	D2	100c blue green	325.00	275.00
J20	D2	500c blue green	600.00	125.00

1884-92

Numerals in Red

J21	D2	1c olive green	35	25
J22	D2	3c olive green	3.75	3.25
J23	D2	5c olive green	1.50	1.25
a.		5c yellow green	17.50	5.00
J24	D2	10c olive green	3.50	35
a.		10c yellow green	22.50	3.00
J25	D2	20c olive green	7.00	55
a.		20c yellow green	110.00	4.00
J26	D2	50c olive green	10.50	1.75
a.		50c yellow green	225.00	65.00
J27	D2	100c olive green	13.00	1.40
a.		100c yellow green	250.00	65.00
J28	D2	500c olive green	110.00	10.00
a.		500c yellow green	475.00	10.00

1908-09   Wmk. 183

Numerals in Red

J29	D2	1c olive green	25	50
J30	D2	5c olive green	80	80
J31	D2	10c olive green	2.50	1.75
J32	D2	20c olive green	5.00	5.00
J33	D2	50c olive green	25.00	80
J34	D2	100c olive green	45.00	1.00
		Nos. J29-J34 (6)	78.55	9.85

D3

1910   *Perf. 11½, 12*

Numerals in Red

J35	D3	1c blue green	15	18
J36	D3	3c blue green	15	18
J37	D3	5c blue green	15	18
J38	D3	10c blue green	50	18
J39	D3	15c blue green	40	50
J40	D3	20c blue green	13.00	15
J41	D3	25c blue green	1.00	30
J42	D3	30c blue green	1.00	25
J43	D3	50c blue green	1.75	50
		Nos. J35-J43 (9)	18.10	2.42

See Nos. S1-S12.

No. J36 Surcharged

1916

J44	D3	5c on 3c bl grn & red	15	35

Nos. J35-J36, J43 Surcharged

1924

J45	D3	10c on 1c	32	6.00
J46	D3	10c on 3c	28	1.25
J47	D3	20c on 50c	95	1.00

D4   D5

Perf. 11½

1924-26   Typo.   Wmk. 183
Granite Paper

J48	D4	5c ol grn & red	48	25
J49	D4	10c ol grn & red	1.90	15
J50	D4	15c ol grn & red ('26)	1.65	30
J51	D4	20c ol grn & red	4.50	15
J52	D4	25c ol grn & red	1.90	30
J53	D4	30c ol grn & red	1.90	65
J54	D4	40c ol grn & red ('26)	2.75	30
J55	D4	50c ol grn & red	2.75	60
		Nos. J48-J55 (8)	17.83	2.70

1924

With Grilled Gum

J48a	D4	5c olive green & red	75	60
J49a	D4	10c olive green & red	3.00	1.00
J51a	D4	20c olive green & red	5.25	1.00
J52a	D4	25c olive green & red	8.50	60.00

See Grilled Gum note after No. 145.

Nos. J50, J53 and J55 Surcharged with New Value in Black

1937

J56	D4	5c on 15c	1.00	3.75
J57	D4	10c on 15c	1.00	1.75
J58	D4	20c on 50c	2.00	5.00
J59	D4	40c on 50c	3.25	12.50

1938   Engr.   Unwmk.

J60	D5	5c scarlet	35	15
J61	D5	10c scarlet	50	15
J62	D5	15c scarlet	70	2.00
J63	D5	20c scarlet	90	15
J64	D5	25c scarlet	1.10	1.75
J65	D5	30c scarlet	1.25	80
J66	D5	40c scarlet	1.50	15
J67	D5	50c scarlet	1.75	1.75
		Nos. J60-J67 (8)	8.05	6.90

1938

With Grilled Gum

J60a	D5	5c scarlet	60	75
J61a	D5	10c scarlet	50	75
J62a	D5	15c scarlet	1.25	1.40
J63a	D5	20c scarlet	1.10	20
J64a	D5	25c scarlet	1.25	4.25
J65a	D5	30c scarlet	1.25	75
J66a	D5	40c scarlet	1.65	75
J67a	D5	50c scarlet	2.25	1.40
		Nos. J60a-J67a (8)	9.85	10.25

See Grilled Gum note after No. 145.

OFFICIAL STAMPS

For General Use

> **With Perforated Cross**
> In 1935 the government authorized the use of regular postage issues perforated with a nine-hole cross for all government departments. Twenty-seven different stamps were so perforated. These were succeeded in 1938 by the cross overprints.

> Values for canceled Official Stamps are for those canceled to order. Postally used stamps sell for considerably less. This note does not apply to Nos. 1O1-1O16, 2O27-2O30, 3O23-3O26.

Counterfeit overprints exist of most official stamps.

Official stamps without unused values were not made available to the public unused.

Regular Issues of 1908-36 Overprinted in Black

1938   Unwmk.   *Perf. 11½*

O1	A53	3c olive	15	20
O2	A54	5c bl green	15	18
O3	A55	10c red vio	85	30
O4	A56	15c orange	30	1.25
O5	A68	20c red	45	30
O6	A58	25c brown	45	85
O7	A59	30c ultra	60	75
O8	A60	35c yel grn	60	75
O9	A61	40c gray	60	75

Wmk. 183

With Grilled Gum

O10	A25	50c dp grn & pale grn	75	1.25
O11	A25	60c brn org & buff	1.40	1.75
O12	A25	70c vio & buff	1.40	2.50
O13	A25	80c sl & buff	1.75	2.50
O14	A36	90c grn & red, grn	1.90	2.75
O15	A25	1fr dp cl & pale grn	1.90	3.00
O16	A36	1.20fr brn rose & red, rose	2.00	3.50
O17	A36	1.50fr bl & red, bl	2.75	3.75
O18	A36	2fr gray blk & red, gray	3.25	5.00
		Nos. O1-O18 (18)	21.25	31.33

Nos. O14, O16, O17 and O18 are on surface-colored paper.

1938   Unwmk.   **With Grilled Gum**

O1a	A53	3c olive	5.00	38
O2a	A54	5c blue green	1.40	24
O3a	A55	10c red violet	1.90	38
O4a	A56	15c orange	3.25	1.10
O5a	A68	20c red	1.90	42
O6a	A58	25c brown	67.50	6.00
O7a	A59	30c ultra	2.75	90

O8a A60 35c yellow green 2.25 1.50
O9a A61 40c gray 2.50 90
Nos. O1a-O9a (9) 88.45 11.82

See Grilled Gum note after No. 145.

Postage Stamps of 1936-42 Overprinted in Black — *Officiel*

1942-45 Unwmk. Perf. 11½

O19 A53 3c olive 40 90
O20 A54 5c bl grn 40 15
O21 A55 10c dk red brn 52 35
O21A A55 10c org brn ('45) 10 15
O22 A56 17c orange 60 1.50
O23 A68 20c red 65 15
O24 A58 25c lt brn 80 1.75
O25 A59 30c ultra 1.00 60
O26 A60 35c yel grn 1.25 1.75
O27 A61 40c gray 1.40 60
O28 A77 50c dp pur, grnsh 3.50 2.50
O29 A78 60c red brn, buff 4.00 2.50
O30 A79 70c rose vio, pale lil 4.00 5.75
O31 A80 80c blk, pale gray 1.25 1.10
O32 A81 90c dk red, pale rose 1.40 1.50
O33 A82 1fr dk grn, grnsh 1.50 1.50
O34 A83 1.20fr red vio, pale gray 1.75 2.00
O35 A84 1.50fr dk bl, pale bl 2.00 3.00
O36 A85 2fr mar, pale rose 3.00 3.50
Nos. O19-O36 (19) 29.52 31.25

Same Overprint on Nos. 329-339

1950 Unwmk. Perf. 12x11½

O37 A118 5c orange 70 60
O38 A119 10c yel grn 1.10 90
O39 A120 15c aqua 5.75 7.75
O40 A121 20c brn car 2.75 60
O41 A122 25c red 4.00 5.50
O42 A123 30c olive 3.50 2.50
O43 A124 35c red brn 4.75 5.50
O44 A125 40c dp bl 5.00 2.50
O45 A126 50c slate gray 6.25 3.50
O46 A127 60c bl grn 8.00 4.00
O47 A128 70c purple 19.00 13.00
Nos. O37-O47 (11) 60.80 46.05

FOR THE WAR BOARD OF TRADE

Regular Issues of 1908-18 Overprinted — Industrielle Kriegswirtschaft

1918 Wmk. 183 Perf. 11½, 12

IO1 A26 3c brn org 75.00 125.00
IO2 A26 5c green 6.50 20.00
IO3 A26 7½c gray (I) 225.00 325.00
a. 7½c slate (II) 550.00 600.00
IO4 A28 10c red, buff 10.50 22.50
IO5 A28 15c vio, buff 10.50 27.50
IO6 A25 20c red & yel 90.00 180.00
IO7 A25 25c dp bl 90.00 180.00
IO8 A25 30c yel brn & pale grn 90.00 180.00
Nos. IO1-IO8 (8) 597.50 1,060.

Most unused copies of Nos. IO1-IO8 are reprints made using the original overprint forms. Counterfeits exist.

Overprinted — Industrielle Kriegswirtschaft

1918

IO9 A26 3c brn org 5.50 25.00
IO10 A26 5c green 17.50 50.00
IO11 A26 7½c gray 7.00 20.00
IO12 A28 10c red, buff 70.00 75.00
IO13 A28 15c vio, buff 110.00
IO14 A25 20c red & yel 12.50 50.00
IO15 A25 25c dp bl 12.50 50.00
IO16 A25 30c yel brn & pale grn 20.00 75.00
Nos. IO9-IO16 (8) 255.00

No. IO13 was never placed in use. Fraudulent cancellations are found on Nos. IO1-IO16.

FOR THE LEAGUE OF NATIONS

Regular Issues Overprinted — SOCIÉTÉ DES NATIONS

On 1908-30 Issues

1922-31 Wmk. 183 Perf. 11½, 12

2O1 A26 2½c ol, buff ('28) 18
2O2 A26 3c ultra, buff ('30) 6.00
2O3 A26 5c orange, buff 2.75
2O4 A26 5c gray vio, buff ('26) 2.50
2O5 A26 5c red vio, buff ('27) 1.75
2O6 A26 5c dk grn, buff ('31) 11.00
2O7 A26 7½c dp grn, buff ('28) 25
2O8 A28 10c green, buff 35
2O9 A28 10c bl grn, buff ('28) 50
2O10 A28 10c vio, buff ('31) 1.50
2O11 A28 15c brn red, buff ('28) 50
2O12 A28 20c red vio, buff 5.00
2O13 A28 20c car, buff ('26) 1.40
2O14 A28 25c ver, buff 5.75
2O15 A28 25c car, buff 70
2O16 A28 25c brn, buff ('27) 12.50
2O17 A28 30c dp bl, buff ('25) 3.50
2O18 A28 30c yel brn & pale grn 10.00
2O19 A25 35c yel grn & yel 5.00
2O20 A25 40c deep blue 1.25
2O21 A25 40c red vio & grn ('28) 4.25
2O22 A25 50c dp grn & pale grn 5.00
2O23 A25 60c brn org & buff 24.00 60
2O24 A25 70c vio & buff ('25) 7.50
2O25 A25 80c slate & buff 1.10
2O26 A25 1fr dp cl & pale grn 5.75
2O27 A29 3fr red 25.00
2O28 A30 5fr ultra 60.00
2O29 A31 10fr dull violet 125.00
2O30 A31 10fr gray grn ('30) 110.00
Nos. 2O1-2O30 (30) 416.58

1930-44 With Grilled Gum

2O2a A26 5c ultra, buff ('33) 8.50
2O6a A26 5c dk grn, buff ('33) 17.50
2O17a A28 30c dp bl, buff 375.00
2O22a A25 50c dp grn & pale grn ('35) 1.25 75
2O23a A25 60c brn org & buff ('44) 35.00 150.00
2O24a A25 70c violet & buff ('32) 1.50 2.50
2O25a A25 80c slate & buff ('42) 4.00 2.25
2O26a A25 1fr dp cl & pale grn ('42) 4.00

1935-36 With Grilled Gum

2O31 A36 90c grn & red, grn ('36) 2.50
2O32 A36 1.20fr brn rose & red, rose ('36) 2.50 4.00
b. Inverted overprint 3,750.
2O33 A36 1.50fr bl & red, bl 2.50 3.00
2O34 A36 2fr gray blk & red, gray ('36) 4.00 4.50

1922-25 Ordinary Gum

2O31a A36 90c 6.00
2O32a A36 1.20fr ('25) 3.50
2O33a A36 1.50fr ('25) 6.00
2O34a A36 2fr ('25) 6.00

1928

2O35 A39 5fr blue 75.00

On 1932 Issue

1932

2O36 A41 5c peacock bl 17.50
2O37 A41 10c orange 1.40
2O38 A41 20c cerise 1.00
2O39 A41 30c ultra 40.00
2O40 A41 60c olive brn 13.50

Unwmk.

2O41 A42 1fr ol gray & bl 13.50
Nos. 2O36-2O41 (6) 86.90

On 1934 Issue

1934-35 Wmk. 183

2O42 A46 3c olive 25
2O43 A47 5c emerald 38
2O44 A49 15c orange ('35) 1.10
2O45 A51 25c brown 10.00
2O46 A52 30c ultra 1.25
Nos. 2O42-2O46 (5) 12.98

On 1936 Issue

1937 Unwmk.

2O47 A53 3c olive 18 25
2O48 A54 5c blue green 25 25
2O49 A55 10c red violet 70
2O50 A56 15c orange 55 45
2O51 A57 20c carmine 1.50
2O52 A58 25c brown 70 1.00
2O53 A59 30c ultra 70 90
2O54 A60 35c yellow green 70 90
2O55 A61 40c gray 85 1.10
Nos. 2O47-2O55 (9) 7.05

1937 With Grilled Gum

2O47a A53 3c olive 35
2O48a A54 5c blue green 45
2O49a A55 10c red violet 5.25
2O50a A56 15c orange 50
2O51a A57 20c carmine 1.50
2O52a A58 25c brown 1.00
2O53a A59 30c ultra 1.00
2O54a A60 35c yellow green 3.00
2O55a A61 40c gray 2.25
Nos. 2O47a-2O55a (9) 15.30

On 1931 Issue

1937 Wmk. 183

2O56 A40 3fr orange brown 190.00

On 1938 Issue

1938 Unwmk. Perf. 11½
Granite Paper

2O57 A63 20c red & buff 1.25
2O58 A64 30c blue & lt blue 2.00
2O59 A65 60c brown & buff 4.00
2O60 A66 1fr black & buff 6.25

Regular Issue of 1938 Overprinted in Black or Red — SERVICE DE LA SOCIÉTÉ DES NATIONS

Granite Paper

2O61 A63 20c red & buff 1.65
2O62 A64 30c blue & lt blue 3.25
2O63 A65 60c brown & buff 5.50
2O64 A66 1fr black & buff (R) 11.50

Regular Issue of 1938 Overprinted in Black — SOCIÉTÉ DES NATIONS

1939

2O65 A69 3fr brn car, buff 3.00 10.00
2O66 A70 5fr slate bl, buff 5.50 12.50
2O67 A71 10fr green, buff 10.00 35.00

Same Overprint in Black on Regular Issues of 1939-42

1942-43

2O68 A55 10c dk red brown 85
2O68A A55 10c orange brn ('43) 60 85
2O69 A68 20c red 75 85

Stamps of 1936-42 Overprinted in Black — COURRIER DE LA SOCIÉTÉ DES NATIONS

1944

2O70 A53 3c olive 18 25
2O71 A54 5c blue green 18 25
2O72 A55 10c orange brown 35 38
2O73 A56 15c orange 35 40
2O74 A68 20c red 52 60
2O75 A58 25c lt brown 52 65
2O76 A59 30c ultra 75 90
2O77 A60 35c yellow green 90 90
2O78 A61 40c gray 90 1.25

Nos. 2O73-2O75 and 2O78 exist with grilled gum. Value each $2,000 unused, $2,250 used.

Stamps of 1941 Overprinted in Black — COURRIER DE LA SOCIÉTÉ DES NATIONS

2O79 A77 50c dp pur, grnsh 1.50 1.75
2O80 A78 60c red brn, buff 1.50 2.25
2O81 A79 70c rose vio, pale lil 1.90 2.50
2O82 A80 80c blk, pale gray 1.90 2.25
2O83 A81 90c dk red, pale rose 1.90 2.25
2O84 A82 1fr dk grn, grnsh 2.00 2.50
2O85 A83 1.20fr red vio, pale gray 2.25 3.00
2O86 A84 1.50fr dk bl, buff 2.25 3.50
2O87 A85 2fr mar, pale rose 4.00 4.50

Stamps of 1942 Overprinted in Black — COURRIER DE LA SOCIÉTÉ DES NATIONS

Unwmk. Perf. 11½

2O88 A69 3fr brn car, cr 6.75 10.00
2O89 A70 5fr slate bl, cr 9.25 14.00
2O90 A71 10fr green, cr 21.00 32.50
Nos. 2O70-2O90 (21) 60.85 86.58

FOR THE INTERNATIONAL LABOR BUREAU

Regular Issues Overprinted — S.d.N. Bureau international du Travail

On 1908-30 Issues

1923-30 Wmk. 183 Perf. 11½, 12

3O1 A26 2½c ol grn, buff ('28) 30
3O2 A26 3c ultra, buff ('30) 75
3O3 A26 5c org, buff 35
3O4 A26 5c red vio, buff ('28) 20
3O5 A26 7½c dp grn, buff ('28) 40
3O6 A28 10c grn, buff 20
3O7 A28 10c bl grn, buff ('28) 1.10
3O8 A28 15c brn red, buff ('28) 1.10
3O9 A28 20c red vio, buff 10.00
3O10 A28 20c car, buff ('27) 4.50
3O11 A28 25c car, buff 1.00
3O12 A28 25c brn, buff ('28) 2.75
3O13 A28 30c dp bl, buff ('25) 75
3O14 A25 30c yel brn & pale grn 50.00
3O15 A25 35c yel grn & yel 8.00
3O16 A25 40c dp bl 1.25
3O17 A25 40c red vio & grn ('28) 11.00
3O18 A25 50c dp grn & pale grn 1.50
3O19 A25 60c brn org & buff 1.25 2.25
3O20 A25 70c vio & buff ('24) 17.50
3O21 A25 80c sl & buff 12.50 1.00
3O22 A25 1fr dp cl & pale grn 2.25
3O23 A29 3fr red 30.00
3O24 A30 5fr ultra 45.00
3O25 A31 10fr dl vio 150.00
3O26 A31 10fr gray grn ('30) 140.00
Nos. 3O1-3O26 (26) 483.15

1937-44 With Grilled Gum

3O18a A25 50c dp grn & pale grn ('42) 1.75 1.90
3O20a A25 70c vio & buff 1.75 2.75
3O21a A25 80c slate & buff ('44) 25.00 110.00
3O22a A25 1fr dp cl & pale grn ('42) 3.00

1925-42 With Grilled Gum

3O27 A36 90c grn & red, grn ('37) 7.50
a. Ordinary gum 2.00
3O28 A36 1.20fr brn rose & red, rose ('42) 11.00 3.25
a. Ordinary gum 2.50
3O29 A36 1.50fr bl & red, bl ('37) 2.75 2.00
a. Ordinary gum 3.00
3O30 A36 2fr gray blk & red, gray ('36) 3.75 5.75
a. Ordinary gum 15.00

1928

3O31 A39 5fr blue 75.00

On 1932 Issue

1932

3O32 A41 5c pck bl 1.00
3O33 A41 10c orange 90
3O34 A41 20c cerise 1.25
3O35 A41 30c ultra 7.00
3O36 A41 60c olive brn 7.00

Unwmk.

3O37 A42 1fr ol gray & bl 9.00
Nos. 3O32-3O37 (6) 26.15

On 1936 Issue

1937

3O38 A53 3c olive 20 25
3O39 A54 5c bl grn 20 25
3O40 A55 10c red vio 1.75
3O41 A56 15c orange 40 50
3O42 A57 20c carmine 1.25
3O43 A58 25c brown 60 70
3O44 A59 30c ultra 65 80
3O45 A60 35c yel grn 65 1.10
3O46 A61 40c gray 1.00 1.25
Nos. 3O38-3O46 (9) 8.85

1937 With Grilled Gum

3O38a A53 3c olive 60
3O39a A54 5c blue green 40
3O40a A55 10c red violet 80
3O41a A56 15c orange 70
3O42a A57 20c carmine 80
3O43a A58 25c brown 1.10
3O44a A59 30c ultra 1.65
3O45a A60 35c yellow green 1.65
3O46a A61 40c gray 1.65
Nos. 3O38a-3O46a (9) 8.80

On 1931 Issue

1937 Wmk. 183

3O47 A40 3fr orange brown 190.00

On 1934 Issue

3O48 A46 3c olive 3.50

On 1938 Issue

1938   Unwmk.   Perf. 11½
Granite Paper

3049	A63	20c red & buff		1.00
3050	A64	30c bl & lt bl		2.25
3051	A65	60c brn & buff		4.00
3052	A66	1fr blk & buff		6.00

Regular Issue of 1938
Overprinted in Black or Red

3053	A63	20c red & buff (Bk)		2.25
3054	A64	30c bl & lt bl (Bk)		2.75
3055	A65	60c brn & buff (Bk)		5.50
3056	A66	1fr blk & buff (R)		6.25

Regular Issue of 1938
Overprinted in Black

S. a. N.
Bureau
international
du Travail

1939

3057	A69	3fr brn car, *buff*	3.50	6.00
3058	A70	5fr slate bl, *buff*	6.00	7.25
3059	A71	10fr grn, *buff*	10.00	15.00

Same Overprint in Black on Regular Issues
of 1939-42

1942-43

3060	A55	10c dk red brn		70
3060A	A55	10c org brn ('43)	45	70
3061	A68	20c red	55	70

Stamps of 1936-42
Overprinted in Black

COURRIER DU BUREAU
INTERNATIONAL
DU TRAVAIL

1944

3062	A53	3c olive	20	20
3063	A54	5c bl grn	20	20
3064	A55	10c org brn	30	30
3065	A56	15c orange	55	55
3066	A68	20c red	75	80
3067	A58	25c lt brn	85	90
3068	A59	30c ultra	1.10	1.25
3069	A60	35c yel grn	1.40	1.50
3070	A61	40c gray	1.65	1.75

Stamps of 1941
Overprinted

COURRIER DU BUREAU
INTERNATIONAL
DU TRAVAIL

3071	A77	50c dp pur, *grnsh*	2.25	9.50
3072	A78	60c red brn, *buff*	2.25	7.50
3073	A79	70c rose vio, *pale lil*	2.25	6.00
3074	A80	80c blk, *pale gray*	65	2.00
3075	A81	90c dk red, *pale rose*	80	2.00
3076	A82	1fr dk grn, *grnsh*	1.00	2.00
3077	A83	1.20fr red vio, *pale gray*	1.40	2.00
3078	A84	1.50fr dull bl, *buff*	1.65	2.00
3079	A85	2fr mar, *pale rose*	2.25	2.00

Stamps of 1942 Overprinted

COURRIER DU BUREAU
INTERNATIONAL DU TRAVAIL

3080	A69	3fr brn car, *cr*	4.00	3.50
3081	A70	5fr slate bl, *cr*	6.50	5.00
3082	A71	10fr grn, *cr*	15.00	12.50
		Nos. 3062-3082 (21)	47.00	63.45

Nos. 329 to 339
Overprinted in
Black

BUREAU
INTERNATIONAL
DU TRAVAIL

1950   Unwmk.   Perf. 12x11½

3083	A118	5c orange	1.10	2.00
3084	A119	10c yel grn	3.50	6.00
3085	A120	15c aqua	4.75	3.00
3086	A121	20c brn car	5.00	3.00
3087	A122	25c red	5.75	3.25
3088	A123	30c olive	6.25	8.00
3089	A124	35c red brn	6.75	3.75
3090	A125	40c dp bl	6.75	3.75
3091	A126	50c slate gray	7.75	4.00
3092	A127	60c bl grn	7.75	4.50
3093	A128	70c purple	15.00	8.00
		Nos. 3083-3093 (11)	70.35	49.25
		Set, never hinged	90.00	

Catalogue values for unused stamps in this section, from this point to the end of the section, are for Never Hinged items.

Miners — O1   Globe, Chimney and Wheel — O2

1956-60   Unwmk.   Engr.   Perf. 11½

3094	O1	5c dk gray	15	15
3095	O1	10c green	15	15
3096	O2	20c vermilion	1.65	1.25
3097	O2	20c car rose ('60)	16	16
3098	O2	30c org ver ('60)	24	24
3099	O1	40c blue	1.75	1.50
30100	O1	50c lt ultra ('60)	40	40
30101	O1	60c reddish brn	28	25
30102	O2	2fr rose vio	90	70
		Nos. 3094-30102 (9)	5.68	4.80

Type of 1960 Overprinted: "Visite du / Pape Paul VI / Genève / 10 juin 1969"

1969, June 10
Violet Fibers, Fluorescent Paper

30103	O2	30c org ver	15	15

Visit of Pope Paul VI to the Intl. Labor Bureau to celebrate its 50th anniv., Geneva, June 10.

ILO
Headquarters,
Geneva — O3

1974, May 30   Photo.   Perf. 11½
Violet Fibers, Fluorescent Paper

30104	O3	80c bl, yel & gray	65	65

Inauguration of the new International Labor Organization Building.

Young Man at
Lathe,
Cogwheels
O4

Designs: 60c, Woman at drilling machine. 90c, Welder and lab assistant using protective devices and clothing. 100c, Surveyor with theodolite and topographical map. 120c, Professional education for youth.

1975-88   Photo.   Perf. 11½

30105	O4	30c red brn & dk brn	25	25
30106	O4	60c ultra & blk	50	50
30107	O4	100c dk grn & blk	75	75
30108	O4	120c multi	1.25	1.25

Perf. 12x11½

30109	O4	90c multi	1.00	1.00
		Nos. 30105-30109 (5)	3.75	3.75

Issue dates: 30c-100c, Feb. 13, 1975. 120c, Aug. 22, 1983. 90c, Sept. 13, 1988.

ILO, 75th
Anniv. — O5

1994, May 17   Litho.   Perf. 13

30110	O5	180c multicolored	2.50	2.50

FOR THE INTERNATIONAL BUREAU OF EDUCATION

Regular Issues of 1936-42, Overprinted in Black

COURRIER DU
BUREAU INTERNATIONAU
D'ÉDUCATION

1944   Unwmk.   Perf. 11½

401	A53	3c olive	50	75
402	A54	5c bl grn	55	1.10
403	A55	10c org brn	65	1.25
404	A56	15c orange	70	1.50
405	A68	20c red	75	1.65
406	A58	25c lt brn	1.00	1.75
407	A59	30c ultra	1.10	2.25
408	A60	35c yel grn	1.10	2.25
409	A61	40c gray	1.25	2.50

Regular Issue of 1941, Overprinted in Black

COURRIER DU
BUREAU INTERNATIONAL
D'ÉDUCATION

4010	A77	50c dp pur, *grnsh*	4.50	8.25
4011	A78	60c red brn, *buff*	4.50	8.25
4012	A79	70c rose vio, *pale lil*	4.50	8.25
4013	A80	80c blk, *pale gray*	75	1.65
4014	A81	90c dk red, *pale rose*	1.00	1.75
4015	A82	1fr dk grn, *grnsh*	1.10	2.25
4016	A83	1.20fr red vio, *pale gray*	1.40	3.50
4017	A84	1.50fr bl bl, *buff*	1.65	3.50
4018	A85	2fr mar, *pale rose*	1.90	5.75

Regular Issue of 1942, Overprinted in Black

COURRIER DU BUREAU INTERNATIONAL
D'ÉDUCATION

4019	A69	3fr brn car, *cr*	6.75	16.00
4020	A70	5fr slate bl, *cr*	9.00	22.50
4021	A71	10fr grn, *cr*	17.50	40.00
		Nos. 401-4021 (21)	62.15	136.65
		Set, never hinged	95.00	

No. 306 Overprinted in Carmine   B / I / É

1946

4022	A104	10c rose vio	18	45
		Never hinged	20	

Nos. 316 to 321
Overprinted in Black

BUREAU
INTERNATIONAL
D'EDUCATION

1948   Unwmk.   Perf. 11½

4023	A54	5c chocolate	2.25	3.00
4024	A55	10c green	2.25	3.00
4025	A68	20c org brn	2.25	3.00
4026	A113	25c carmine	2.25	3.00
4027	A59	30c grnsh bl	2.25	3.00
4028	A61	40c ultra	2.25	3.00
		Nos. 4023-4028 (6)	13.50	18.00
		Set, never hinged	20.00	

Same Overprint on Nos. 329 to 339

1950   Perf. 12x11½
Overprint 18mm wide

4029	A118	5c orange	75	1.65
4030	A119	10c yel grn	1.00	1.65
4031	A120	15c aqua	1.50	3.50
4032	A121	20c brn car	4.00	3.50
4033	A122	25c red	5.25	5.75
4034	A123	30c olive	5.25	5.75
4035	A124	35c red brn	6.00	7.50
4036	A125	40c dp bl	6.00	7.50
4037	A126	50c slate gray	6.25	7.75
4038	A127	60c bl grn	6.25	9.00
4039	A128	70c purple	8.25	11.00
		Nos. 4029-4039 (11)	50.50	64.55
		Set, never hinged	60.00	

Catalogue values for unused stamps in this section, from this point to the end of the section, are for Never Hinged items.

Globe and Books — O1

Designs: 20c, 30c, 60c, 2fr, Pestalozzi Monument at Yverdon.

1958-60   Engr.   Perf. 11½

4040	O1	5c dark gray	15	15
4041	O1	10c green	15	15
4042	O1	20c vermilion	2.00	2.00
4043	O1	20c car rose ('60)	15	15
4044	O1	30c org ver ('60)	20	20
4045	O1	40c blue	2.25	2.25

4046	O1	50c lt ultra ('60)	32	32
4047	O1	60c reddish brn	32	32
4048	O1	2fr rose violet	1.00	1.00
		Nos. 4040-4048 (9)	6.54	6.54

FOR THE WORLD HEALTH ORGANIZATION

No. 316-319, 321
Overprinted in Black

ORGANISATION
MONDIALE DE LA
SANTÉ

1948   Unwmk.   Perf. 11½

501	A54	5c chocolate	1.50	3.75
502	A55	10c green	4.00	3.75
503	A68	20c org brn	4.00	3.75
504	A113	25c carmine	4.00	3.75
505	A61	40c ultra	4.00	3.75
		Nos. 501-505 (5)	17.50	18.75
		Set, never hinged	22.50	

Regular Issues of
1941, 1942 and
1949 Overprinted in
Black

ORGANISATION
MONDIALE DE LA
SANTÉ

1948-50

506	A118	5c orange	65	35
507	A119	10c yel grn	70	70
508	A120	15c aqua	70	90
509	A121	20c brn car	3.50	3.50
5010	A122	25c red	3.50	3.00
5011	A123	30c olive	1.00	1.65
5012	A124	35c red brn	3.50	2.50
5013	A125	40c dp bl	3.50	2.75
5014	A126	50c slate gray	3.75	2.75
5015	A127	60c bl grn	4.00	3.00
5016	A128	70c purple	5.25	3.50
5017	A80	80c blk, *pale gray* ('48)	1.00	2.75
5018	A81	90c dk red, *pale rose*	6.00	6.50
5019	A82	1fr dk grn, *grnsh* ('48)	1.10	2.75
5020	A83	1.20fr red vio, *pale gray*	7.50	9.25
5021	A84	1.50fr dk bl, *buff* ('48)	15.00	10.00
5022	A85	2fr mar, *pale rose* ('48)	2.00	5.00
5023	A69	3fr brn car, *cr*	35.00	32.50
5024	A70	5fr sl bl, *cr* ('48)	5.25	10.50
5025	A71	10fr grn, *cr*	70.00	60.00
		Nos. 506-5025 (20)	172.90	163.35
		Set, never hinged	250.00	

Catalogue values for unused stamps in this section, from this point to the end of the section, are for Never Hinged items.

WHO Emblem — O2

1957-60   Unwmk.   Engr.   Perf. 11½

5026	O2	5c gray	15	15
5027	O2	10c lt grn	15	15
5028	O2	20c vermilion	1.65	1.65
5029	O2	20c car rose ('60)	18	18
5030	O2	30c org ver ('60)	25	25
5031	O2	40c blue	1.75	1.90
5032	O2	50c lt ultra ('60)	45	45
5033	O2	60c red brn	28	30
5034	O2	2fr rose lilac	90	85
		Nos. 5026-5034 (9)	5.76	5.88

No. 5032 Overprinted: "ERADICATION DU PALUDISME"

1962, Apr. 7

5035	O2	50c lt ultra	28	28

WHO drive to eradicate malaria.

World Health Organization Emblem — O3

1975-86		Typo.	Perf. 11½	
5O36	O3	30c multi	25	25
5O37	O3	60c lt bl & multi	50	50
5O38	O3	90c lilac & multi	70	70
5O39	O3	100c org & multi	80	80

		Litho.	Perf. 12	
5O40	O3	140c lt grn, scar & grn	1.50	50

Issue dates: 140c, May 27, 1986. Others, Feb. 13, 1975.

FOR THE INTERNATIONAL ORGANIZATION FOR REFUGEES

Stamps of 1941 and 1949 Overprinted in Black	ORGANISATION INTERNATIONALE POUR LES RÉFUGIÉS

1950		Unwmk.	Perf. 12x11½, 11½	
6O1	A118	5c orange	12.00	12.50
6O2	A119	10c yel grn	12.00	12.50
6O3	A121	20c brn car	12.00	12.50
6O4	A122	25c red	12.00	12.50
6O5	A125	40c dp bl	12.00	12.50
6O6	A80	80c blk, *pale gray*	12.00	12.50
6O7	A82	1fr dk grn, *grnsh*	12.00	12.50
6O8	A85	2fr mar, *pale rose*	12.00	12.50
		Nos. 6O1-6O8 (8)	96.00	100.00
		Set, never hinged	150.00	

FOR THE UNITED NATIONS EUROPEAN OFFICE

See No. 510 for postage issue commemorating the United Nations.

Stamps of 1941-49 Overprinted in Black	NATIONS UNIES OFFICE EUROPÉEN

1950		Unwmk.	Perf. 12x11½, 11½	
7O1	A118	5c orange	20	1.00
7O2	A119	10c yel grn	60	1.00
7O3	A120	15c aqua	90	2.00
7O4	A121	20c brn car	1.25	2.50
7O5	A122	25c red	2.50	4.50
7O6	A123	30c olive	2.50	4.50
7O7	A124	35c red brn	2.50	7.50
7O8	A125	40c dp bl	4.00	4.50
7O9	A126	50c sl gray	6.00	7.00
7O10	A127	60c bl grn	6.00	8.00
7O11	A128	70c purple	7.75	8.00
7O12	A80	80c blk, *pale gray*	6.00	9.00
7O13	A81	90c dk red, *pale rose*	6.00	9.00
7O14	A82	1fr dk grn, *grnsh*	6.00	9.00
7O15	A83	1.20fr red vio, *pale gray*	6.75	12.00
7O16	A84	1.50fr dk bl, *buff*	6.75	12.00
7O17	A85	2fr mar, *pale rose*	6.75	12.00
7O18	A69	3fr brn car, cr	65.00	100.00
7O19	A70	5fr sl bl, cr	85.00	125.00
7O20	A71	10fr grn, cr	130.00	150.00
		Nos. 7O1-7O20 (20)	352.45	488.50
		Set, never hinged	600.00	

UN Emblem — O1

Statue from UN Building, Geneva — O2

1955-59		Engr.	Perf. 11½	
7O21	O1	5c dk vio brn	15	15
7O22	O1	10c green	15	15
7O23	O2	20c vermilion	5.00	*5.00*
7O24	O2	20c car rose ('59)	18	15
7O25	O2	30c org ver ('59)	20	15
7O26	O1	40c ultra	5.00	*3.00*
7O27	O1	50c ultra ('59)	32	30
7O28	O2	60c red brn	45	35
7O29	O2	2fr lilac	2.00	*1.25*
		Nos. 7O21-7O29 (9)	13.45	10.50
		Set, never hinged	15.00	

See Nos. 7O34-7O37. For overprints see Nos. 7O31-7O32.

United Nations Emblem — O3

1955, Oct. 24		Photo.	
7O30	O3	40c dk bl & bis	2.00	4.00
		Never hinged		3.25

10th anniv. of the UN, Oct. 24, 1955.

> **Catalogue values for unused stamps in this section, from this point to the end of the section, are for Never Hinged items.**

Nos. 7O24 and 7O27 Overprinted in Black or Red: "ANNÉE MONDIALE DU RÉFUGIÉ 1959 1960"

1960			
7O31	O2	20c car rose	15	15
7O32	O1	50c ultra (R)	25	28

Issued to publicize World Refugee Year, July 1, 1959-June 30, 1960.

Palace of Nations, Geneva O4

1960		Granite Paper	Perf. 11½	
7O33	O4	5fr blue	3.25	3.75

Types of 1955 Inscribed: "MUSÉE PHILATELIQUE" (O1) or "ONU MUSÉE PHILATELIQUE" (O2)

Engraved; Inscription Typographed

1962, Oct. 24		Unwmk.	Perf. 11½	
7O34	O1	10c grn & red	15	15
7O35	O2	30c org ver & ultra	18	18
7O36	O1	50c ultra & org	22	22
7O37	O2	60c red brn & emer	28	28

Opening of the Philatelic Museum, UN European Office, Geneva.

UNCSAT Emblem
O5   O6

1963, Feb. 4		Engr.	Perf. 11½	
7O38	O5	50c ultra & car rose	15	15
7O39	O6	2fr lilac & emer	1.00	1.10

UN Conf. on the Application of Science and Technology for the Benefit of the Less Developed Areas (UNCSAT), Geneva, Feb. 4-20.

Stamps issued, starting Oct. 4, 1969, by the UN in Swiss currency for use by UN staff members or the public are listed under "United Nations" in Vol. 1 of this catalogue and in Scott's U.S. Specialized Catalogue. These stamps are on sale in various UN post offices, but are valid only in the UN enclave in Geneva. They are not inscribed "Helvetia."

FOR THE WORLD METEOROLOGICAL ORGANIZATION

> **Catalogue values for unused stamps in this section are for Never Hinged items.**

Sun, Cloud, Rain and Snow — O1

Design: 20c, 30c, 60c, 2fr, Direction indicator and anemometer.

1956-60		Unwmk. Engr.	Perf. 11½	
8O1	O1	5c dark gray	15	15
8O2	O1	10c green	15	15
8O3	O1	20c vermilion	1.75	1.50
8O4	O1	20c car rose ('60)	20	20
8O5	O1	30c org ver ('60)	30	30
8O6	O1	40c blue	2.00	1.75
8O7	O1	50c lt ultra ('60)	40	40
8O8	O1	60c reddish brn	30	25
8O9	O1	2fr rose violet	90	75
		Nos. 8O1-8O9 (9)	6.15	5.45

WMO Emblem — O2

1973, Aug. 30		Engr.	Perf. 11½	
Violet Fibers, Fluorescent Paper				
8O10	O2	30c carmine	15	25
8O11	O2	40c blue	15	35
8O12	O2	1fr ocher	35	90

Type O2 Inscribed: "OMI / OMM / 1873 / 1973"

1973, Aug. 30		Photo.	Perf. 11½	
Violet Fibers, Fluorescent Paper				
8O13	O2	80c deep violet & gold	30	75

Centenary of intl. meteorological cooperation.

FOR THE INTERNATIONAL BUREAU OF THE UNIVERSAL POSTAL UNION

> **Catalogue values for unused stamps in this section are for Never Hinged items.**

See Nos. 98-103, 204-205, 514, 589-590 for postage issues commemorating the UPU.

UPU Monument, Bern — O1

Design: 10c, 20c, 30c, 60c, Pegasus.

1957-60		Unwmk.	Perf. 11½	
9O1	O1	5c gray	15	15
9O2	O1	10c lt grn	15	15
9O3	O1	20c vermilion	1.65	1.65
9O4	O1	20c car rose ('60)	15	15
9O5	O1	30c org ver ('60)	25	25
9O6	O1	40c blue	1.75	1.90
9O7	O1	50c lt ultra ('60)	45	45
9O8	O1	60c red brn	24	30
9O9	O1	2fr rose lilac	90	85
		Nos. 9O1-9O9 (9)	5.69	5.85

First Class Mail — O2

Parcel Post — O3

Money Orders — O4

Technical Cooperation O5

Intl. Reply and Notication Service — O6

Express Mail Service — O7

1976-89		Photo.	Perf. 11½	
Fluorescent Paper				
9O10	O2	40c multi	35	35
9O11	O3	80c multi	65	65
9O12	O4	90c multi	75	75
9O13	O5	100c multi	80	80
9O14	O6	120c multi	1.25	1.25
9O15	O7	140c multi	1.75	1.75
		Nos. 9O10-9O15 (6)	5.55	5.55

Issue dates: 120c, Aug. 22, 1983. 140c, Mar. 7, 1989; others, Sept. 16, 1976.

FOR THE INTERNATIONAL TELECOMMUNICATION UNION

> **Catalogue values for unused stamps in this section are for Never Hinged items.**

Transmitter — O1

ITU Headquarters, Geneva — O2

Designs: 20c, 30c, 60c, 2fr, Antenna.

1958-60		Unwmk. Engr.	Perf. 11½	
10O1	O1	5c dark gray	15	15
10O2	O1	10c green	15	15
10O3	O1	20c vermilion	2.00	1.65
10O4	O1	20c car rose ('60)	18	18
10O5	O1	30c org ver ('60)	28	28
10O6	O1	40c blue	2.25	1.90
10O7	O1	50c lt ultra ('60)	45	45
10O8	O1	60c redsh brn	35	30
10O9	O1	2fr rose vio	1.10	90
		Nos. 10O1-10O9 (9)	6.91	5.96

1973, Aug. 30		Photo.	Perf. 11½	
Violet Fibers, Fluorescent Paper				
10O10	O2	80c blue & black	65	65

Sound Waves, ITU Emblem — O3

Airplane, Ocean Liner — O4

Radio Waves, Face on TV, Microphone O5

Photogravure and Engraved
1976, Feb. 12   *Perf. 11½*
Violet Fibers, Fluorescent Paper

1OO11	O3	40c dp org & vio bl	25	25
1OO12	O4	90c bl, vio bl & yel	60	60
1OO13	O5	1fr grn & multi	90	90

ITU activities: world telecommunications, mobile radio and mass media.

Fiber Optic Communication Links — O6

1988, Sept. 13 Litho. Perf. 12x11½

1OO14	O6	1.40fr multi	1.40	1.40

Radio Waves, ITU Emblem — O7

1994, May 17 Litho. Perf. 13½

1OO15	O7	1.80fr multicolored	2.50	2.50

FOR THE WORLD INTELLECTUAL PROPERTY ORGANIZATION

Catalogue values for unused stamps in this section are for Never Hinged items.

WIPO Emblem — O1

1982, May 27 Photo. Perf. 12x11½

1IO1	O1	40c shown	32	32
1IO2	O1	80c Headquarters, Geneva	60	60
1IO3	O1	100c Industrial symbols	90	90
1IO4	O1	120c Educational and artistic symbols	1.10	1.10

1985, Sept. 10 Photo. Perf. 12x11½

1IO5	O1	50c Mind in action	55	55
		Nos. 1IO1-1IO5 (5)	3.47	3.47

This is an expanding set. Numbers will change if necessary.

FRANCHISE STAMPS

These stamps were distributed to many institutions and charitable societies for franking their correspondence.

F1

Control Figures Overprinted in Black   214

Perf. 11½, 12
1911-21   Typo.   Wmk. 183
Blue Granite Paper

S1	F1	2c ol grn & red	15	18
S2	F1	3c ol grn & red	2.50	25
S3	F1	5c ol grn & red	70	15
S4	F1	10c ol grn & red	1.25	15
S5	F1	15c ol grn & red	19.00	1.65
S6	F1	20c ol grn & red	4.25	40
		Nos. S1-S6 (6)	27.85	2.78

Without Control Figures

S1a	F1	2c olive green & red	45	17.50
S2a	F1	3c olive green & red	35	25.00
S3a	F1	5c olive green & red	3.75	30.00
S4a	F1	10c olive green & red	7.50	50.00
S5a	F1	15c olive green & red	4.50	100.00
S6a	F1	20c olive green & red	8.25	42.50
		Nos. S1a-S6a (6)	24.80	265.00

Control Figures Overprinted in Black   365

1926

S7	F1	5c ol grn & red	14.00	3.25
S8	F1	10c ol grn & red	8.75	2.25
S9	F1	20c ol grn & red	13.00	3.50

Control Figures Overprinted in Black   806

1927
White Granite Paper

S10	F1	5c green & red	4.25	30
S11	F1	10c green & red	2.00	20
b.		Grilled gum	300.00	600.00
S12	F1	20c green & red	4.00	20

Without Control Figures

S10a	F1	5c green & red	7.50	100.00
S11a	F1	10c green & red	22.50	100.00
c.		Grilled gum	175.00	500.00
S12a	F1	20c green & red	25.00	100.00

Nurse — F2

Nun — F3

J. H. Dunant — F4

Control Figures Overprinted in Black
1935   Perf. 11½

S13	F2	5c turq grn	2.00	2.50
b.		Grilled gum	5.00	25
S14	F3	10c lt vio	1.10	2.50
b.		Grilled gum	5.00	15
S15	F4	20c scarlet	2.00	2.50
b.		Grilled gum	6.50	18

Without Control Figures

S13a	F2	5c turquoise green	2.00	2.50
c.		Grilled gum	22.50	1.25
S14a	F3	10c light violet	2.00	2.50
c.		Grilled gum	22.50	1.25
S15a	F4	20c scarlet	1.10	3.50
c.		Grilled gum	22.50	2.50

SYRIA

LOCATION — Asia Minor, bordering on Turkey, Iraq, Lebanon, Israel and the Mediterranean Sea
GOVT. — Republic
AREA — 71,498 sq. mi.
POP. — 9,840,000 (est. 1983)
CAPITAL — Damascus

Syria was originally part of the Turkish province of Sourya conquered by British and Arab forces in late 1918 and later partitioned. The British assumed control of the Palestine and Transjordan regions; the French were permitted to occupy the sanjaks of Lebanon, Alaouites and Alexandretta; and the remaining territory, including the vilayets of Damascus and Aleppo, was established as an independent Arab kingdom, under which the first Syrian stamps were issued.

French forces from Beirut deposed King Faisal in July 1920, and two years of military occupation followed until Syria was mandated to France in July 1922. Syrian autonomy was substituted for the mandate in 1934, but full independence was not again achieved until 1946. In 1958, Syria and Egypt merged to form the United Arab Republic. Syria left this union in 1961, adopting the name Syrian Arab Republic. UAR issues for Syria are listed following Syria's 1919-20 Issues of the Arabian Government.

10 Milliemes = 1 Piaster
40 Paras = 1 Piaster (Arabian Govt.)
100 Centimes = 1 Piaster (1920)

Catalogue values for unused stamps in this country are for Never Hinged items, beginning with Scott 314 in the regular postage section, Scott B13 in the semi-postal section, Scott C124 in the airpost section, Scott CB5 in the airpost semipostal section, Scott J40 in the postage due section, and all of the items in the UAR sections.

Watermark

Wmk. 291- National Emblem Multiple

Issued under French Occupation
T. E. O.
Stamps of France, 1900-07, Surcharged
5 MILLIEMES

Perf. 14x13½
1919, Nov. 21   Unwmk.

1	A16	1m on 1c gray	82.50	82.50
2	A16	2m on 2c vio brn	225.00	225.00
3	A16	3m on 3c red org	95.00	95.00
4	A20	4m on 15c gray grn	12.50	12.50
5	A22	5m on 5c dp grn	7.50	7.50
6	A22	1p on 10c red	10.00	10.00
7	A22	2p on 25c bl	6.00	6.00
8	A18	5p on 40c red & pale bl	8.00	8.00
9	A18	9p on 50c bis brn & lav	19.00	19.00
10	A18	10p on 1fr cl & ol grn	30.00	30.00
		Nos. 1-10 (10)	495.50	495.50

The letters "T.E.O." are the initials of "Territoires Ennemis Occupés." There are two types of the numerals in the surcharges on Nos. 2, 3, 8 and 9.

T. E. O.
Stamps of French Offices in Turkey, 1902-03, Surcharged
2 MILLIEMES

1919

11	A2	1m on 1c gray	18	15
a.		Inverted surcharge	5.50	5.50
12	A2	2m on 2c vio brn	18	15
a.		Inverted surcharge	5.50	5.50
13	A2	3m on 3c red org	38	30
14	A3	4m on 15c pale red	18	18
a.		Inverted surcharge	5.50	5.50
15	A2	5m on 5c grn	18	15

Overprinted   **T. E. O.**

16	A5	1p on 25c blue	22	15
a.		Inverted overprint	5.50	5.50
17	A6	2p on 50c bis brn & lav	50	30
18	A6	4p on 1fr claret & ol grn	55	45
19	A6	8p on 2fr gray vio & yel	2.75	2.00
a.		"T.E.O." double	15.00	15.00
20	A6	20p on 5fr dk bl & buff	140.00	82.50
		Nos. 11-20 (10)	145.12	86.33

On Nos. 17-20 "T.E.O." reads vertically up.
Nos. 1-20 were issued in Beirut and mainly used in Lebanon. Nos. 16-20 were also used in Cilicia.

O. M. F. Syrie 1 MILLIEME
Stamps of France, 1900-07, Surcharged

1920

21	A16	1m on 1c gray	1.25	1.25
a.		Inverted surcharge	11.50	11.50
b.		Double surcharge		
22	A16	2m on 2c vio brn	1.50	1.50
a.		Double surcharge		
23	A22	3m on 5c grn	2.75	2.75
a.		Double surcharge		
24	A18	20p on 5fr dk bl & buff	240.00	240.00

The letters "O.M.F." are the initials of "Occupation Militaire Francaise."

O. M. F. Syrie 2 MILLIEMES
Stamps of France, 1900-07, Surcharged in Black or Red

1920

25	A16	1m on 1c gray	15	15
26	A16	2m on 2c vio brn	30	30
27	A22	3m on 5c grn	22	22
28	A22	5m on 10c red	15	15
a.		Inverted surcharge		
29	A18	20p on 5fr dk bl & buff	32.50	32.50
30	A18	20p on 5fr dk bl & buff (R)	140.00	140.00
		Nos. 25-30 (6)	173.32	173.32

Stamps of France, 1900-21, Surcharged in Black or Red:

O. M. F. Syrie 50 CENTIMES or **O. M. F. Syrie 3 PIASTRES**

1920-22

31	A16	25c on 1c gray	32	32
32	A16	50c on 2c vio brn	32	32
33	A16	75c on 3c red org	32	32
34	A22	1p on 5c grn (R)	16	16
35	A22	1p on 5c grn	15	15
36	A22	1p on 20c red brn ('21)	15	15
37	A22	1.25p on 25c bl ('22)	32	32
38	A22	1.50p on 30c org ('22)	20	16
39	A22	2p on 10c red	15	15
40	A22	2p on 25c bl (R)	15	15
41	A18	2p on 40c red & pale bl ('21)		15
42	A20	2.50p on 50c dl bl ('22)	32	20
a.		Final "S" of "Piastres" omitted	4.25	4.25
43	A22	3p on 25c bl (R)	25	25
44	A18	3p on 60c vio & ultra ('21)	32	25
45	A20	5p on 15c gray grn	38	38
46	A18	5p on 1fr cl & ol grn ('21)	65	50
47	A18	10p on 40c red & pale bl ('21)	50	40
48	A18	10p on 2fr org & pale bl ('21)	1.50	1.00
49	A18	25p on 50c bis brn & lav	65	55
50	A18	25p on 5fr dk bl & buff ('21)	55.00	50.00
51	A18	50p on 1fr cl & ol grn	1.25	1.10
a.		"PIASRTES"	700.00	700.00
52	A18	100p on 5fr dk bl & buff (R)	17.50	16.00

53 A18 100p on 5fr dk bl &
    buff (Bk) 140.00 125.00
    a. "PIASTRES" *1,100. 1,100.*
    Nos. 31-53 (23) 220.81 197.98

In first printing, space between "Syrie" and numeral is 2mm, second printing, 1mm.
Surcharge is found inverted on Nos. 32, 35-38, 42, 44-45. Value, each $2-$3.
Surcharge is found double on Nos. 31, 37, 40, 42. Value, each $2.
For overprints see Nos. C1-C9.

O. M. F.
Syrie
25
CENTIEMES

Surcharged in Black or Red

1920-23

54	A16	10c on 2c vio ('23)	15	15
55	A22	10c on 5c org (R) ('23)	15	15
56	A16	25c on 1c dk gray	15	15
a.		50c on 1c dk gray (error)	65	65
57	A22	25c on 5c grn ('21)	15	15
58	A22	25c on 5c org ('22)	15	15
a.		"CENTIEMES" omitted	6.50	6.50
59	A16	50c on 2c vio brn	15	15
60	A22	50c on 10c red ('21)	15	15
61	A22	50c on 10c grn ('22)	22	15
62	A16	75c on 3c red org	18	15
63	A20	75c on 15c sl grn ('21)	15	15
		Nos. 54-63 (10)	1.60	1.50

Surcharge is found inverted on Nos. 54-55, 58-59, 62-63; double on Nos. 60, 62. Value $1.50-$2.

Preceding Issues Overprinted

1920

Black Overprint

64	A16	25c on 1c sl gray	3.50	3.50
65	A16	50c on 2c vio brn	3.50	3.50
66	A22	1p on 5c green	3.00	2.50
67	A22	2p on 25c blue	5.00	5.00
68	A20	5p on 15c gray grn	15.00	15.00
69	A18	10p on 40c red & pale bl	22.50	22.50
70	A18	25p on 50c bis brn & lav	65.00	65.00
71	A18	50p on 1fr cl & ol grn	250.00	250.00
72	A18	100p on 5fr dk bl & buff	1,100.	1,100.
		Nos. 64-72 (9)	1,467.	1,467.

Red Overprint

73	A16	25c on 1c sl gray	3.00	3.00
74	A16	50c on 2c vio brn	1.90	1.90
75	A22	1p on 5c green	2.00	2.00
76	A22	2p on 25c blue	1.50	1.50
77	A20	5p on 15c gray grn	15.00	15.00
78	A18	10p on 40c red & pale bl	22.50	22.50
79	A18	25p on 50c bis brn & lav	100.00	100.00
80	A18	50p on 1fr cl & ol grn	125.00	125.00
81	A18	100p on 5fr dk bl & buff	700.00	700.00
		Nos. 73-81 (9)	970.90	970.90

Nos. 64-81 were used only in the vilayet of Aleppo where Egyptian gold currency was still in use.

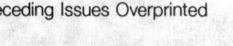

A1

Black or Red Surcharge

1921   *Perf. 11½*

82	A1	25c on ¹⁄₁₀p lt brn	30	22
a.		"25 Centiemes" omitted		
83	A1	50c on ²⁄₁₀p grn	38	22
84	A1	1p on ³⁄₁₀p yel	50	22
a.		"³⁄₁₀" for "³⁄₁₀"	3.75	3.75
85	A1	1p on 5m rose	65	45
86	A1	2p on 5m rose	65	55
a.		Tête bêche pair	37.50	37.50
87	A1	3p on 1p gray bl	75	42
88	A1	5p on 2p bl grn	1.90	1.50
89	A1	10p on 5p vio brn	3.00	1.90
90	A1	25p on 10p gray (R)	3.75	2.50
		Nos. 82-90 (9)	11.88	7.98

Nos. 82-90 are surcharged on stamps of the Arabian Government Nos. 85, 87-93 and have the designs and sizes of those stamps.
Surcharge is found inverted on Nos. 84-88, 90; double on No. 86.

Kilis Issue

A2

Sewing Machine Perf. 9
1921   **Handstamped**
Pelure Paper

91 A2 (1p) violet   37.50 25.00

Issued at Kilis to meet a shortage of the regular issue, caused by the sudden influx of a large number of Armenian refugees from Turkey. The Kilis area was restored to Turkey in Oct. 1923.

Stamps of France, Surcharged

O. M. F.
Syrie
3 PIASTRES

1921-22   *Perf. 14x13½*

92	A18	2p on 40c red & pale bl	15	15
93	A18	2.50p on 50c bis brn & lav ('22)	22	20
a.		2p on 50c bister brown & lavender (error)	15.00	11.50
94	A18	3p on 60c vio & ultra	30	22
95	A18	5p on 1fr cl & ol grn	2.00	1.90
96	A18	10p on 2fr org & pale bl	3.75	3.50
97	A18	25p on 5fr dk bl & buff	3.50	3.00
		Nos. 92-97 (6)	9.92	8.97

On No. 93 the surcharge reads: "2 PIASTRES 50."
Surcharge is found inverted on Nos. 92-95; double on No. 94. Value $2-$3.
For overprints see Nos. C10-C17.

French Mandate

French Stamps of 1900-23 Surcharged

Syrie
Grand Liban
25
CENTIEMES

1923

104	A16	10c on 2c vio brn	15	15
105	A22	25c on 5c org	15	15
106	A22	50c on 10c grn	15	15
a.		25c on 10c green (error)	50.00	
107	A20	75c on 15c sl grn	25	25
108	A22	1p on 20c red brn	15	15
109	A22	1.25p on 25c bl	70	15
110	A22	1.50p on 30c org	15	15
111	A22	1.50p on 30c red	15	15
112	A20	2.50p on 50c dl bl	15	15

On Pasteur Stamps of 1923

113	A23	50c on 10c grn	30	30
114	A23	1.50p on 30c red	30	30
115	A23	2.50p on 50c blue	30	30

Surcharge is found inverted on #104-108, 110, 115; double on #104, 106. Value $1.50-$2.

Syrie - Grand Liban
Surcharged
2 PIASTRES

116	A18	2p on 40c red & pale bl	15	15
a.		Inverted surcharge	5.50	
b.		Double surcharge	6.50	
c.		"Liabn"		
117	A18	3p on 60c vio & ultra	30	30
a.		"Liabn"		
118	A18	5p on 1fr cl & ol grn	50	50
a.		"Liabn"		
119	A18	10p on 2fr org & pale bl	2.50	2.50
a.		"Liabn"		
120	A18	25p on 5fr dk bl & buff	10.00	8.00
a.		Inverted surcharge	15.00	15.00
		Nos. 104-120 (17)	16.35	13.80

SYRIE

Stamps of France, 1900-21, Surcharged

50
CENTIEMES

1924   *Perf. 14x13½*

121	A16	10c on 2c vio brn	15	15
a.		Double surcharge		
122	A22	25c on 5c org	15	15
a.		"25" omitted	2.00	

123	A22	50c on 10c grn	15	15
124	A20	75c on 15c sl grn	38	38
125	A22	1p on 20c red brn	15	15
a.		"1 PIASTRES"	2.75	
126	A22	1.25p on 25c blue	22	22
127	A22	1.50p on 30c org	22	22
128	A22	1.50p on 30c red	22	22
129	A20	2.50p on 50c dl bl	22	20

Same on Pasteur Stamps of France, 1923
1924

130	A23	50c on 10c grn	15	15
131	A23	1.50p on 30c red	30	30
132	A23	2.50p on 50c grn	15	15
		Set value, #121-132	2.00	1.90

Olympic Games Issue

Stamps of France, 1924, Surcharged "SYRIE" and New Values
1924

133	A24	50c on 10c gray grn & yel grn	12.50	12.50
134	A25	1.25p on 25c rose & dk rose	12.50	12.50
135	A26	1.50p on 30c brn red & blk	12.50	12.50
136	A27	2.50p on 50c ultra & dk bl	12.50	12.50

See Nos. 166-169.

SYRIE

Stamps of France 1900-20 Surcharged
2 PIASTRES

137	A18	2p on 40c red & pale bl	15	15
138	A18	3p on 60c vio & ultra	25	22
139	A18	5p on 1fr cl & ol grn	80	80
140	A18	10p on 2fr org & pale bl	1.00	75
141	A18	25p on 5fr dk bl & buff	1.90	1.40

For overprints see Nos. C18-C21.

Syrie
0, P. 25
سوريا
١⁄٤ الغرش

Stamps of France 1900-21, Surcharged

Syrie
2 Piastres
or
سوريا
غرش ٢

1924-25

143	A16	10c on 2c vio brn	15	15
a.		Double surcharge	6.50	
b.		Inverted surcharge	5.50	
144	A22	25c on 5c org	15	15
a.		Double surcharge	6.50	
b.		Inverted surcharge	5.50	
145	A22	50c on 10c grn	15	15
a.		Double surcharge	6.50	
b.		Inverted surcharge	5.50	
146	A20	75c on 15c gray grn	15	15
a.		Double surcharge	6.50	
b.		Inverted surcharge	5.50	
147	A22	1p on 20c red brn	15	15
a.		Inverted surcharge	5.50	
148	A22	1.25p on 25c blue	15	15
a.		Inverted surcharge	5.50	
149	A22	1.50p on 30c red	15	15
a.		Inverted surcharge	5.50	
150	A22	1.50p on 30c org	15.00	15.00
151	A22	2p on 35c vio ('25)	15	15
152	A18	2p on 40c red & pale bl	15	15
a.		Arabic "Piastre" in singular	15	15
153	A18	2p on 45c grn & bl ('25)	1.75	1.75
154	A18	3p on 60c vio & ultra	30	30
155	A20	3p on 60c lt vio ('25)	45	45
156	A20	4p on 85c ver	15	15
157	A18	5p on 1fr cl & ol grn	30	30
158	A18	10p on 2fr org & pale bl	65	65
159	A18	25p on 5fr dk bl & buff	65	65
		Nos. 143-159 (17)	20.60	20.60

On No. 152a, the surcharge is as illustrated. The correct fourth line ("2 Piastres" plural), as it appears on Nos. 151, 152 and 153, has four characters, the third resembling "9."
For overprints see Nos. C22-C25.

Same Surcharge on Pasteur Stamps of France
1924-25

160	A23	50c on 10c grn	18	18
161	A23	75c on 15c grn ('25)	45	45
162	A23	1.50p on 30c red	38	38

163	A23	2p on 45c red ('25)	18	18
164	A23	2.50p on 50c blue	30	30
165	A23	4p on 75c blue	40	40
		Nos. 160-165 (6)	1.89	1.89

Olympic Games Issue

Stamps of France, 1924, Surcharged "Syrie" and New Values in French and Arabic
1924

Same Colors as #133-136

166	A24	50c on 10c	12.50	12.50
167	A25	1.25p on 25c	12.50	12.50
168	A26	1.50p on 30c	12.50	12.50
169	A27	2.50p on 50c	12.50	12.50

Ronsard Issue

Same Surcharge on France No. 219
1925

170 A28 4p on 75c bl, *bluish*   22 22

Mosque at Hama
A3

Mosque at Damascus
A5

View of Merkab — A4

Designs: 50c, View of Alexandretta. 75c, View of Hama. 1p, Omayyad Mosque, Damascus. 1.25p, Latakia Harbor. 1.50p, View of Damascus. 2p, View of Palmyra. 2.50p, View of Kalat Yamoun. 3p, Bridge of Daphne. 5p, View of Aleppo. 10p, View of Aleppo. 25p, Columns at Palmyra.

1925   *Perf. 12½, 13½*

			Litho.	Unwmk.
173	A3	10c dk vio	15	15
			Photo.	
174	A4	25c ol blk	38	38
175	A4	50c yel grn	15	15
176	A4	75c brn org	15	15
177	A5	1p magenta	15	15
178	A4	1.25p dp grn	65	42
179	A4	1.50p rose red	18	18
180	A4	2p dk brn	18	15
181	A4	2.50p peacock blue	38	25
182	A4	3p org brn	15	15
183	A4	5p violet	32	15
184	A4	10p vio brn	85	15
185	A4	25p ultra	1.00	38
		Nos. 173-185 (13)	4.69	
		Set value		2.15

For surcharges see Nos. 186-206, B1-B12, C26-C45, CB1-CB4.

Surcharged in Black or Red

═   ═
1P.   ١غ

1926-30

186	A4	1p on 3pi org brn ('30)	22	15
187	A4	2p on 1p25 dp grn (R) ('28)	20	15
a.		Double surcharge		
188	A4	3.50 on 75c org brn	18	15
a.		Double surcharge	2.75	2.75
189	A4	4p on 25c ol blk	30	15
190	A4	4p on 25c ol blk ('27)	40	32
191	A4	4p on 25c ol blk (R) ('28)	20	15
192	A4	4.50p on 75c brn org	18	15
193	A4	6p on 2p50 pck bl	22	15
194	A4	7.50p on 2p50 pck bl	18	15
195	A4	7.50p on 2p50 pck bl (R) ('28)	48	30
			1.25	
196	A4	12p on 1p25 dp grn	18	15
a.		Surcharge on face and back	17.50	17.50

197 A4	15p on 25p ultra	30	15
198 A4	20p on 1p25 dp grn	20	15
	Nos. 186-198 (13)	3.24	
	Set value		1.95

Size of numerals and arrangement of this surcharge varies on the different denominations.
No. 189 has slanting foot on "4."
No. 190, foot straight.

No. 173 Surcharged in Red

1928

199 A3	05c on 10c dk vio	15	15

Stamps of 1925 Issue Overprinted in Red or Blue

EXPOSITION INDUSTRIELLE
DAMAS 1929
معرض الصناعات الوطنية
دمشق ١٩٢٩

1929   *Perf. 13½*

200 A4	50c yel grn (R)	1.10	1.10
201 A5	1p magenta (Bl)	1.10	1.10
202 A4	1.50p rose red (Bl)	1.10	1.10
203 A4	3p org brn (R)	1.10	1.10
204 A4	5p vio (R)	1.10	1.10
205 A4	10p vio brn (Bl)	1.10	1.10
206 A4	25p ultra (R)	1.10	1.10
	Nos. 200-206 (7)	7.70	7.70

Industrial Exhibition, Damascus, Sept. 1929.

View of Hama — A6

View of Alexandretta — A9

Citadel at Aleppo — A10

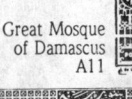

Great Mosque of Damascus A11

Ruins of Bosra — A13

Mosque at Homs — A15

View of Sednaya A16

Citadel at Aleppo A17

Ancient Bridge at Antioch A18

Mosque at Damascus A22

Designs: 20c, Great Mosque, Aleppo. 25c, Minaret, Hama. 2p, View of Antioch. 4p, Square at Damascus. 15p, Mosque at Hama. 25p, Monastery of St. Simeon the Stylite (ruins). 50p, Sun Temple (ruins), Palmyra.

Perf. 12x12½

1930-36   Litho.   Unwmk.

208 A6	10c red vio	15	15
209 A6	10c vio brn ('33)	15	15
209A A6	10c vio brn, redrawn ('35)	15	15
210 A6	20c dk bl	15	15
211 A6	20c brn org ('33)	15	15
212 A6	25c gray grn	15	15
213 A6	25c dk bl gray ('33)	15	15

Photo.

Perf. 13

214 A9	50c violet	15	15
215 A15	75c org red ('32)	15	15
216 A10	1p green	15	15
217 A10	1p bis brn ('36)	15	15
218 A11	1.50p bis brn	1.40	1.25
219 A11	1.50p dp grn ('33)	15	15
220 A9	2p dk vio	15	15
221 A13	3p yel grn	30	18
222 A10	4p yel org	15	15
223 A15	4.50p rose car	30	18
224 A16	6p grnsh blk	15	15
225 A17	7.50p dl blue	32	18
226 A18	10p dk brn	32	15
227 A10	15p dp grn	55	30
228 A18	25p vio brn	50	35
229 A15	50p ol brn	2.00	1.90
230 A22	100p red org	6.00	4.00
	Nos. 208-230 (24)	13.94	
	Set value		9.25

On No. 209A Arabic inscriptions, upper right, are entirely redrawn with lighter lines. Hyphen added in "Helio-Vaugirard" imprint. Lines in buildings and background more distinct.
On No. 215 the letters of "VAUGIRARD" in the imprint are reversed as in a mirror.
For overprints and surcharges see Nos. 253-268, 346, M1-M2.

Autonomous Republic

Parliament Building A23

abu-al-Ala al-Maarri — A24

President Ali Bek el Abed — A25

Saladin — A26

1934, Aug. 2   Engr.   *Perf. 12½*

232 A23	10c olive grn	42	42
233 A23	20c black	42	42
234 A23	25c red org	42	42
235 A23	50c ultra	42	42
236 A23	75c plum	42	42
237 A24	1p vermilion	1.40	1.40
238 A24	1.50p green	2.25	2.25
239 A24	2p red brn	2.25	2.25
240 A24	3p Prus blue	2.25	2.25
241 A24	4p brt vio	2.25	2.25
242 A24	4.50p carmine	2.25	2.25
243 A24	5p dk blue	2.25	2.25
244 A24	6p dk brn	2.25	2.25
245 A24	7.50p dk ultra	2.25	2.25

---

246 A25	10p dk brn	3.50	3.50
247 A25	15p dull bl	4.25	4.25
248 A25	25p rose red	9.00	9.00
249 A26	50p dk brn	13.00	13.00
250 A26	100p lake	19.00	19.00
	Nos. 232-250 (19)	70.25	70.25

Proclamation of the Republic. See Nos. C57-C66. For surcharge see No. M3.

Stamps of 1930-36 Overprinted in Red or Black

معرض دمشق
1936-١٩٣٦
FOIRE DE DAMAS

1936, Apr. 15

253 A9	50c violet (R)	90	90
254 A10	1p bis brn (Bk)	90	90
255 A9	2p dk vio (R)	90	90
256 A13	3p yel grn (Bk)	90	90
257 A10	4p yel org (Bk)	90	90
258 A15	4.50p rose car (Bk)	90	90
259 A16	6p grnsh blk (R)	90	90
260 A17	7.50p dull bl (R)	1.10	1.10
261 A18	10p dk brn (Bk)	1.40	1.40
	Nos. 253-261 (9)	8.80	8.80

Industrial Exhibition, Damascus, May 1936. See Nos. C67-C71.

Stamps of 1930 Surcharged in Black

1937-38   *Perf. 13½x13*

262 A10	2.50p on 4p yel org ('38)	15	15
263 A22	10p on 100p red org	32	32

Stamps of 1930-33 Surcharged in Red or Black

1938   *Perf. 13½*

264 A15	25c on 75c org red (Bk)	15	15
265 A11	50c on 1.50p dp grn (R)	15	15
266 A17	2p on 7.50p dl bl (R)	15	15
267 A17	5p on 7.50p dl bl (R)	25	15
268 A15	10p on 50p ol brn (Bk)	50	32
	Set value	95	65

President Hashem Bek el Atassi — A27

1938-43   Photo.   Unwmk.

268A A27	10p dp bl ('43)	18	18
269 A27	12.50p on 10p dp bl (R)	25	25
270 A27	20p dk brn	25	25

The 10pi and 20pi exist imperf.

Columns at Palmyra A28

1940   Litho.   *Perf. 11½*

271 A28	5p pale rose	18	15

Exists imperf.

Museum at Damascus — A29

Hotel at Bloudan A30

Kasr-el-Heir A31

1940   Typo.   *Perf. 13x14*

272 A29	10c bright rose	15	15
273 A29	20c light blue	15	15
274 A29	25c fawn	15	15
275 A29	50c ultra	15	15

Engr.

Perf. 13

276 A30	1p peacock blue	15	15
277 A30	1.50p chocolate	15	15
278 A30	2.50p dark green	15	15
279 A31	5p violet	18	15
280 A31	7.50p vermilion	32	22
281 A31	50p sepia	70	65
	Set value	1.55	1.25

For overprints see Nos. 298-299.

President Taj Eddin Hassani A32

1942, Apr. 6   Litho.   *Perf. 11½*

282 A32	50c sage green	1.65	1.65
283 A32	1.50p dull gray brn	1.65	1.65
284 A32	6p fawn	1.65	1.65
285 A32	15p light blue	1.65	1.65
	Nos. 282-285,C96-C97 (6)	13.85	13.10

Proclamation of independence by the Allies, Sept. 27, 1941.

President Taj Eddin Hassani — A33

President Hassani and Map of Syria — A34

1942   Photo.   Unwmk.

286 A33	6p rose lake & sal rose	95	95
287 A33	15p dl bl & bl	95	95

See No. C98. Nos. 286-287 exist imperf.

1943   Litho.

288 A34	1p light grn	95	95
289 A34	4p buff	95	95
290 A34	8p pale vio	95	95
291 A34	10p salmon	95	95
292 A34	20p dl chalky bl	95	95
	Nos. 288-292,C99-C102 (9)	8.55	8.55

Proclamation of a United Syria.

Stamps of 1943 Overprinted with Border in Black

1943

293 A34	1p light grn	95	95
294 A34	4p buff	95	95
295 A34	8p pale vio	95	95
296 A34	10p salmon	95	95
297 A34	20p dl chalky bl	95	95
	Nos. 293-297,C103-C106 (9)	8.55	8.55

Mourning for President Hassani. Nos. 288-297 exist imperf.

Nos. 278 and 280
Overprinted in
Carmine or Black

1944   Unwmk.   Perf. 13
298 A30 2.50p dk grn (C)   1.50 1.50
299 A31 7.50p ver (Bk)   1.50 1.50
  Nos. 298-299,C114-C116 (5) 13.20 13.20

1000th anniv. of the Arab poet and philosopher, abu-al-Ala al-Maarri.

President Shukri el
Kouatly — A35

1945, Mar. 15   Litho.   Perf. 11½
300 A35 4p pale lilac   18 18
301 A35 6p dull blue   18 18
302 A35 10p salmon   18 18
303 A35 15p dk brown   32 32
304 A35 20p slate green 40 40
305 A35 40p orange   70 70
  Nos. 300-305,C117-C123 (13) 8.75 5.29

Resumption of constitutional government.

A36   A37

A38   A39

Fiscal Stamps Overprinted or Surcharged in
Black

1945   Typo.   Perf. 11, 11½x11
306 A36 12½p on 15p yel grn 95 95
307 A37 25p buff   1.65 1.65
307A A38 25p on 25s lt vio brn 1.10 1.10
308 A39 50p on 75p brn org 2.25 2.25
309 A39 75p brn org   3.00 3.00
310 A37 100p yel grn   3.50 3.50
  Nos. 306-310 (6)   12.45 12.45

Type of 1945 and Nos. 308 and 310
Overprinted in Black

a   b

1945   Unwmk.   Perf. 11
311 A37(b) 50p magenta   1.10 1.10
312 A39(a) 50p on 75p brn org 75 75
313 A37(b) 100p yellow grn   1.25 1.25

Catalogue values for unused stamps in this section, from this point to the end of the section, are for Never Hinged items.

Independent Republic

A40

Fiscal Stamp Overprinted in Carmine
1946
314 A40 200p light blue   6.00 6.00

Sun and Ears
of Wheat
A41

President Shukri
el Kouatly
A42

1946   Litho.   Perf. 13x13½
315 A41 50c brn org   15 15
316 A41 1p violet   20 15
317 A41 2.50p bl gray 22 15
318 A41 5p lt bl grn 30 15

Photo.   Perf. 13½x13, 13x13½
319 A42 7.50p dk brown 15 15
320 A42 10p Prussian grn 15 15
321 A42 12.50p deep vio 40 15
  Nos. 315-321 (7)   1.57
    Set value   58

For overprints see Nos. 328-329, 335-336.

Arab Horse
A44

1946-47   Litho.
325 A44 50p olive brown 2.00 50
326 A44 100p dk bl grn ('47) 1.00 50
327 A44 200p rose vio ('47) 12.00 3.50

For overprints and surcharges see Nos. 330, 337, 356-357.

Nos. 320, 321 and 325
Overprinted in Black or
Green

1946, Apr. 17
328 A42 10p Prus grn   40 40
329 A42 12.50p dp vio   60 60
330 A44 50p olive brn (G) 1.50 1.50

Evacuation of British and French troops from Syria. See No. C135. For surcharge see No. 347.

President Shukri el
Kouatly — A45

1946 Unwmk. Litho.   Perf. 13½x13
331 A45 15p red   15 15
332 A45 20p violet 30 20
333 A45 25p ultra   42 20

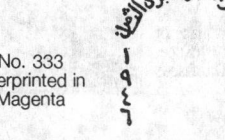

No. 333
Overprinted in
Magenta

1946, Aug. 28
334 A45 25p ultra   1.20 1.10

8th Arab Medical Congress, Aleppo, Aug. 28-Sept. 4. See Nos. C136-C138.

Nos. 328 to 330 With Additional
Overprint in Black

e

f

Perf. 13½x13, 13x13½
1947, June 10
335 A42(e) 10p Prus grn   40 15
336 A42(e) 12.50p deep vio 60 20
337 A44(f) 50p olive brn   1.50 50

1st anniv. of the evacuation of British and French troops from Syria. See No. C139.

Hercules and
the
Lion — A46

Mosaics from Omayyad
Mosque,
Damascus — A47

1947, Nov. 15   Litho.   Perf. 11½
338 A46 12.50p slate green 70 55
339 A47 25p gray blue   1.20 80

1st Arab Archaeological Congress, Damascus, Nov. See Nos. C140-C141, C141a.

Courtyard of
Azem
Palace — A48

Telephone
Building
A49

1947, Nov. 15
340 A48 12.50p deep claret 50 50
341 A49 25p brt blue   1.00 70

3rd Congress of Arab Engineers, Damascus, Nov. See Nos. C142-C143, C143a.

House of Parliament   Pres. Shukri el
A50   Kouatly A51

1948, June 23 Unwmk.   Perf. 10½
342 A50 12.50p blk & org   35 20
343 A51 25p dp rose   65 42

Reelection of Pres. Shukri el Kouatly. See Nos. C144-C145, C145a.

National   Syrian Flag and
Emblem — A52   Soldier — A53

1948, June 23   Litho.
344 A52 12.50p gray & choc 42 25
345 A53 25p multi   80 40

Inauguration of compulsory military training. See Nos. C146-C147, C147a.

Nos. 215 and 327 Surcharged with New
Value and Bars in Black

1948   Perf. 13, 13x13½
346 A15 50c on 75c org red 15 15
347 A44 25p on 200p rose vio 80 30
  Set value   35

Col. Husni   Palmyra
Zayim   A56
A54

Ain el
Arous — A55

1949, June 20   Litho.   Perf. 11½
348 A54 25p blue   60 42

Revolution of Mar. 30, 1949. See No. C153.
A souvenir sheet comprises Nos. 348 and C153, imperf. Value $80.

1949, June 20
349 A55 12.50p violet   1.50 1.50
350 A56 25p blue   2.25 2.25

UPU, 75th anniversary.
See #C154-C155 and note after #C155.

Pres. Husni
Zayim and
Map — A57

Perf. 11½

1949, Aug. 6   Litho.   Wmk. 291
351 A57 25p blue & brown   2.00 1.25

Election of President Husni Zayim. See Nos. C156, C156a.

Tel-Chehab Waterfall A58

Damascus Scene A59

1949
352 A58 5p gray   15 15
353 A58 7.50p olive gray 20 15
354 A59 12.50p violet brown 40 15
355 A59 25p blue   80 35
           Set value   65

See No. 376.

Nos. 327 and 326 Surcharged with New Value and Bars in Black

1950   Unwmk.   Perf. 13x13½
356 A44 2.50p on 200p rose vio 38 15
357 A44 10p on 100p dk bl grn   38 16

National Emblem A60

Road to Damascus A61

Postal Administration Building, Damascus A62

1950-51   Litho.   Perf. 11½
358 A60 50c org brn   15 15
359 A60 2.50p pink   15 15
360 A61 10p pur ('51)   25 16
361 A62 12.50p sage grn ('51) 50 35
362 A62 25p blue ('51)   90 22
363 A62 50p black ('51)   3.00 55
           Nos. 358-363 (6) 4.95 1.58

Nos. 358 to 363 exist imperforate.

Parliament Building, Damascus A63

1951, Apr. 14
364 A63 12.50p gray blk   22 20
365 A63 25p blue   50 35

New constitution adopted Sept. 5, 1950. See Nos. C162-C163.
Nos. 364-365 exist imperforate.

Water Wheel, Hama — A64

Palace of Justice, Damascus A65

Perf. 11½

1952, Apr. 22   Litho.   Unwmk.
366 A64 50c dk brn   15 15
367 A64 2.50p dk blue   15 15
368 A64 5p bl grn   15 15
369 A64 10p red   22 15
370 A65 12.50p gray blk   55 15
371 A65 15p lilac rose   70 22
372 A65 25p deep blue   1.50 35
373 A65 100p olive brn   5.00 1.50
           Nos. 366-373 (8) 8.42
           Set value   2.40

Nos. 366-373 exist imperforate.

Type of 1949 and

Crusaders' Fort — A66

Crusaders' Fort — A67

1953   Photo.
374 A67 50c rose red   15 15
375 A66 2.50p dk brown   15 15
376 A58 7.50p green   22 15
377 A67 12.50p deep blue 1.20 15
           Set value   35

Farm Workers A68   Family Group A69

Designs: 1pi, 5pi, Farm workers. 10pi, 12½p, Family group. 20pi, 25pi, 50pi, Factory and construction workers.

1954   Perf. 11½
378 A68 1p olive   15 15
379 A68 2½p brn red   15 15
380 A68 5p deep bl   15 15
381 A69 7½p violet   15 15
382 A69 10p black   20 15
383 A69 12½p violet   30 15
384 A69 20p dp plum   42 15
385 A69 25p violet   1.00 25
386 A69 50p dk grn   2.25 60
           Nos. 378-386 (9) 4.77
           Set value   1.25

For overprints see Nos. 387-388, UAR 20, 34.

Nos. 382 and 385 Overprinted in Carmine

1954, Oct. 9
387 A69 10p black   65 38
388 A69 25p violet   70 45

Issued to publicize the Cotton Festival, Aleppo, October 1954. See Nos. C185-C186.

Globe — A69a

Mother and Child — A70

Arab Postal Union Issue
1955   Photo.   Perf. 13½x13
389 A69a 12½p green   35 15
390 A69a 25p violet   60 25

Founding of the APU, July 1, 1954. Exist imperf. See No. C191. For overprints see Nos. 396-399, C203, C207.

1955, May 13   Litho.   Perf. 11½
391 A70 25p red   35 25

Mother's Day. See Nos. C194-C195.

United Nations Emblem A71

1955   Photo.
392 A71 7½p crimson   35 22
393 A71 12½p Prus grn   60 30

UN, 10th anniv., Oct. 24. See Nos. C200-C201. For overprints see Nos. 401-402.

Aqueduct at Aleppo A72

1955   Litho.   Unwmk.
394 A72 7.50p lilac   20 15
395 A72 12.50p carmine   30 15
           Set value   15

New aqueduct bringing water from the Euphrates to Northern Syria. Exist imperf. See No. C202.

Nos. 389-390 Overprinted in Ultramarine or Green

1955   Photo.   Perf. 13½x13
396 A69a 12½p green   35 18
397 A69a 25p vio (G)   1.00 40

APU Congress held at Cairo, Mar. 15. See No. C203.

Nos. 389-390 Overprinted in Black

1956
398 A69a 12½p green   50 28
399 A69a 25p violet   90 50

Visit of King Hussein of Jordan to Damascus, Apr. 1956. See No. C207.

Cotton — A73

1956   Unwmk.   Litho.   Perf. 11½
400 A73 2½p bluish green 30 15

Issued to publicize a Cotton Festival.

Nos. 392-393 Overprinted in Black

1956   Photo.   Perf. 11½
401 A71 7½p crimson   35 22
402 A71 12½p Prussian green 42 35

UN, 11th anniv. See Nos. C221-C222.

People's Army — A74

1957   Litho.   Perf. 11½
403 A74 5p lilac rose   15 15
404 A74 20p gray green   35 20

Formation of the Popular Resistance Movement. For overprints see Nos. 405-406, 413-414.

Nos. 403-404 Overprinted in Black or Red

1957
405 A74 5p lilac rose   20 15
406 A74 20p gray green (R) 35 25

Evacuation of Port Said by British and French troops, Dec. 22, 1956.

Azem Palace, Damascus A75

1957   Litho.   Perf. 11½
407 A75 12½p lilac   15 15
408 A75 15p gray   30 15
           Set value   15

For overprint see UAR No. 33.

Map of Near East, Scales and Damascus Skyline — A76

Cotton, Bale and Ship — A77

1957   Wmk. 291   Perf. 11½
409 A76 12½p brt grn   20 15

3rd Congress of the Union of Arab Lawyers, Damascus, Sept. 21-25. See Nos. C240-C241.

1957
410 A77 12½p lt bl grn & blk 30 20

Cotton Festival, Aleppo, Oct. 3-5. See Nos. C242-C243.

Column 9 (image captions)

Children — A78

1957, Oct. 7
411 A78 12½p olive   35 25

Intl. Children's Day, Oct. 7. See #C244-C245.
For overprint see UAR Nos. 13A, C10-C11.

Mailing
and
Receiving
Letter
A79

1957   **Unwmk.**
412 A79 5p magenta   35 16

Intl. Letter Writing Week, Oct. 6-12. See No.
C246.

أسبوع التحصين
٧-١ نوفمبر ت.ن ١٩٥٧

Nos. 403-404
Overprinted in
Black or Red

1957   **Perf. 11½**
413 A74 5p lilac rose   15 15
414 A74 20p gray green (R)   28 20
         Set value   25

Digging of fortifications along the Syrian-Israeli
frontier.

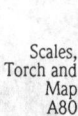

Scales,
Torch and
Map
A80

1957, Nov. 8   **Wmk. 291**
415 A80 20p olive gray   35 20

Congress of Afro-Asian Jurists, Damascus. See
Nos. C247-C248.

Glider
A81

1957, Nov. 8   **Litho.**   **Perf. 11½**
416 A81 25p red brown   60 30
417 A81 35p green   90 40
418 A81 40p ultra   2.00 55

Issued to commemorate a glider festival.

Khaled ibn el Walid
Mosque, Homs — A82

1957   **Unwmk.**   **Perf. 12**
419 A82 2½p dull brown   15 15

Scroll, Communications Building and
Telephone — A83

1958   **Wmk. 291**   **Perf. 11½**
420 A83 25p ultra   22 16

See Nos. C249-C250.

> Issues of 1958-61 released by
> the United Arab Republic are listed
> following the listings of Syria,
> Issues of the Arabian Government.

Syrian Arab Republic

Hall of Parliament,
Damascus — A83a

1961   **Unwmk.**   **Litho.**   **Perf. 12**
420A A83a 15p magenta   25 15
420B A83a 35p olive gray   65 18
         Set value   22

Establishment of Syrian Arab Republic.

Water Wheel,   Roman Arch of
Hama — A84   Triumph,
           Latakia — A85

Qalb Lozah
Church,
Aleppo
A86

Design: 7½p, 10p, Khaled ibn el Walid
Mosque, Homs.

       Perf. 11½x11
1961-62   **Unwmk.**   **Litho.**
421 A84 2½p rose red   15 15
422 A84 5p blue   15 15
423 A84 7½p bl grn ('62)   15 25
424 A84 10p org ('62)   22 15
         Perf. 12x11½
425 A85 12½p gray brn   32 15
426 A86 17½p ol gray ('62)   22 15
427 A86 25p dl red brn   45 15
428 A86 35p dl grn ('62)   30 15
     Nos. 421-428 (8)   1.96
         Set value   72

Types of 1961, Regular and Air Post

Designs: 2½p, 5p, 7½p, 10p, Arch, Jupiter
Temple. 12½p, 15p, 17½p, 22½p, "The Beauty
of Palmyra."

1962   ***Perf. 11½x11***
429 A84 2½p gray bl   15 15
430 A84 5p brn org   15 15
431 A84 7½p ol bis   18 15
432 A84 10p claret   15 15

       Perf. 12x11½
       Size: 26x38mm
433 AP68 12½p gray olive   25 15
434 AP68 15p ultra   30 15
435 AP68 17½p brown   30 15
436 AP68 22½p grnsh blue   32 15
     Nos. 429-436 (8)   1.80
         Set value   45

Martyrs'   Pres. Nazem el-
Memorial — A87   Kodsi — A88

1962, June 11   **Litho.**
440 A87 12½p tan & sepia   15 15
441 A87 35p grn & bl grn   25 18
         Set value   22

1925 Revolution.

1962, Dec. 14   **Perf. 12x11½**
442 A88 12½p sepia & lt bl   15 15

1st anniv. of the election of Pres. Nazem el-
Kodsi. See No. C278.

Queen Zenobia — A89

Central Bank
of
Syria — A90

Designs: 2½p, 5p, "The Beauty of Palmyra."
17½p, Hejaz Railway Station, Damascus. 22½p,
Mouassat Hospital, Damascus. 35p, P.T.T. Jalaa
Avenue Office, Damascus.

1963   **Unwmk.**   **Perf. 11½x11**
443 A89 2½p dk bl gray   15 15
444 A89 5p rose lil   15 15
445 A89 7½p dl bl   24 15
446 A89 10p ol gray   50 15
447 A89 12½p ultra   75 15
448 A89 15p vio brn   1.25 15
         Perf. 11½x12
449 A90 17½p dl vio   42 16
450 A90 22½p brt vio   20 15
451 A90 25p bis brn   20 15
452 A90 35p brt pink   25 20
     Nos. 443-452 (10)   4.11
         Set value   75

Wheat Emblem and   Boy Playing Ball
Globe — A91   and UN
            Emblem — A92

1963, Mar. 21   **Litho.**   **Perf. 12x11½**
453 A91 12½p ultra & blk   15 15

FAO "Freedom from Hunger" Campaign. See
No. C291 and souvenir sheet No. C291a.

Cotton Festival Type of Air Post Issue,
1962, Inscribed "1963"

1963, Sept. 26   **Perf. 12x11½**
455 AP75 17½p multi   15 15
456 AP75 22½p multi   25 15

The 1963 Cotton Festival, Aleppo.

1963, Oct. 24   **Perf. 12x11½**
457 A92 12½p emer & sl grn   15 15
458 A92 22½p rose red & dk grn   18 15
         Set value   26 18

Issued for International Children's Day.

Ugharit Princess — A93

1964   **Litho.**   **Perf. 11½x11**
459 A93 2½p gray   15 15
460 A93 5p brown   15 15
461 A93 7½p rose claret   15 15
462 A93 10p emerald   15 15
463 A93 12½p light vio   15 15
464 A93 17½p ultra   15 15
465 A93 20p rose car   38 15
466 A93 25p orange   65 22
         Set value   1.40 65

Map of
North Africa
and Middle
East, Flag of
Syria, and
Crowd
A94

1965, Mar. 8   **Litho.**   **Perf. 11½x12**
467 A94 12½p multi   15 15
468 A94 17½p multi   15 15
469 A94 20p multi   15 15
         Set value   32 15

Mar. 8 Revolution, 2nd anniv.

Weather Map
and
Anemometer
A95

1965, Mar. 23   **Litho.**   **Unwmk.**
470 A95 12½p dl lil & blk   15 15
471 A95 27½p lt bl & blk   18 15
         Set value   22 15

Fifth World Meteorological Day.

"Evacuation of Apr.   Peasants'
17, 1946"   Union Emblem
A96   A97

1965, Apr. 17   **Litho.**   **Perf. 12x11½**
472 A96 12½p bl & brt yel grn   15 15
473 A96 27½p rose red & lt lil   18 15
         Set value   22 15

19th anniv. of the evacuation of British and
French troops from Syria.

1965, Aug. Unwmk. *Perf. 11¹/₂x11*

474	A97	2¹/₂p blue green	15 15
475	A97	12¹/₂p purple	15 15
476	A97	15p maroon	15 15
		Set value	24 15

Issued to publicize the Peasants' Union.

Torch, Map of Arab Countries and Farmer, Soldier, Woman, Intellectual and Worker — A98

Workers, Factory and Emblem — A99

1965, Nov. 23   *Perf. 12x11¹/₂*

477	A98	12¹/₂p multi	15 15
478	A98	25p multi	18 15
		Set value	22 15

National Council of the Revolution, a legislative body working for a socialist and democratic society.

1966, Jan.   Litho.   *Perf. 11¹/₂x11*

479	A99	12¹/₂p blue	15 15
480	A99	15p carmine	15 15
481	A99	20p dl vio	15 15
482	A99	25p ol gray	15 15
		Set value	36 24

Establishment of the General Union of Trade Unions.

Roman Lamp A100

Islamic Vessel, 12th Century A101

1966   Litho.   *Perf. 11¹/₂x11*

483	A100	2¹/₂p slate grn	15 15
484	A100	5p magenta	15 15
485	A100	7¹/₂p brown	15 15
486	A101	10p brt rose lil	15 15
		Set value	42 25

"Evacuation of Troops" — A102

Bust of Core, Terra Cotta Vase — A103

1966, Apr. 17   Litho.   *Perf. 12x11¹/₂*

487	A102	12¹/₂p multi	15 15
488	A102	27¹/₂p multi	15 15
		Set value	20 15

20th anniv. of the evacuation of British and French troops from Syria.

1967   *Perf. 11¹/₂x11*

Design: 15p, 20p, 25p, 27¹/₂p, Bronze vase in form of seated African woman.

489	A103	2¹/₂p brt grn	15 15
490	A103	5p sal pink	15 15
491	A103	10p grnsh bl	15 15
492	A103	12¹/₂p dl brn	15 15
493	A103	15p brt pink	15 15
494	A103	20p brt bl	15 15
495	A103	25p green	15 15
496	A103	27¹/₂p vio bl	18 15
		Set value	70 50

Arab Revolution Monument, Damascus — A104

1968, Mar. 8   Litho.   *Perf. 12x12¹/₂*

497	A104	12¹/₂p blk, yel & brn	15 15
498	A104	25p blk, pink & car rose	15 15
499	A104	27¹/₂p blk, lt grn & grn	15 15
		Set value	35 18

Mar. 8 Revolution, 5th anniversary.

Map of Syria — A105

Hands Holding Wrench, Gun and Torch — A106

1968, Apr. 4   Litho.   *Perf. 12x12¹/₂*

500	A105	12¹/₂p pink & multi	15 15
501	A105	60p gray & multi	25 15
		Set value	30 20

Arab Baath Socialist Party, 21st anniv.

1968, Apr. 13

502	A106	12¹/₂p tan & multi	15 15
503	A106	17¹/₂p rose & multi	15 15
504	A106	25p yel & multi	15 15
		Set value	25 15

Issued to publicize the mobilization effort.

Rising Sun, Power Lines and Railroad Tracks A107

1968, Apr. 17   Litho.   *Perf. 12¹/₂x12*

505	A107	12¹/₂p multi	15 15
506	A107	27¹/₂p vio & multi	15 15
		Set value	20 15

22nd anniv. of the evacuation of British and French troops from Syria.

Oil Wells and Oil Pipe Line on Map — A108

1968, May 1

507	A108	12¹/₂p lt & dk grn & ultra	15 15
508	A108	17¹/₂p pink, brn & ultra	15 15
		Set value	22 15

Syrian oil exploitation; completion of the oil pipe line to Tartus.

Map of Palestine and Torch — A109

Citadel of Aleppo, Wheat and Cogwheel — A110

1968, May   Litho.   *Perf. 12x12¹/₂*

509	A109	12¹/₂p ultra, blk & red	15 15
510	A109	25p ol bis, blk & red	25 15
511	A109	27¹/₂p gray, blk & red	32 15
		Set value	32

Issued for Palestine Day.

1968, July 18   Litho.   *Perf. 12x12¹/₂*

512	A110	12¹/₂p multi	15 15
513	A110	27¹/₂p multi	15 15
		Set value	16 15

Industrial and Agricultural Fair, Aleppo.

Fair Emblem, Globe, Grain, Wheel and Horse — A111

Woman Carrying Cotton, and Castle of Aleppo — A112

Design: 27¹/₂p, Syrian flag, hand with torch, fair emblem, globe, grain and wheel.

Perf. 12x12¹/₂, 12¹/₂x12

1968, Aug. 25   Litho.

514	A111	12¹/₂p dp brn, blk & emer	15 15
515	A111	27¹/₂p multi	15 15
516	A111	60p bl gray, blk & dp org	22 18
		Set value	42 28

15th Intl. Damascus Fair, Aug. 25-Sept. 20.

1968, Oct. 3   Litho.   *Perf. 12x12¹/₂*

517	A112	12¹/₂p multi	15 15
518	A112	27¹/₂p multi	20 15
		Set value	15

13th Cotton Festival, Aleppo.

Al Jahez — A113

Oil Derrick and Pipe Line — A114

1968, Nov. 9   Litho.   *Perf. 12x12¹/₂*

519	A113	12¹/₂p blk & buff	15 15
520	A113	27¹/₂p blk & gray	38 15
		Set value	15

9th Science Week; Al Jahez Abu Uthman Amr ben Bahr (776-868).

1968   *Perf. 12x11*

521	A114	2¹/₂p grnsh bl & dk grn	15 15
522	A114	5p grn & vio bl	15 15
523	A114	7¹/₂p lt yel grn & bl	15 15
524	A114	10p brt yel & grn	15 15
525	A114	12¹/₂p yel & ver	15 15
526	A114	15p ol bis & dk brn	15 15
527	A114	27¹/₂p dl org & dk red brn	18 15
		Set value	55 35

Broken Chains and Sun — A115

1969, Mar. 8   Litho.   *Perf. 12¹/₂x12*
Sun in Yellow and Red

528	A115	12¹/₂p vio bl & blk	15 15
529	A115	25p gray & blk	15 15
530	A115	27¹/₂p dl grn & blk	15 15
		Set value	35 15

March 8 Revolution, 6th anniversary.

"Sun of Freedom, Young Man and Woman" A116

Liberation through Knowledge and Construction A117

1969, Mar. 29   *Perf. 12x12¹/₂*

531	A116	12¹/₂p multi	15 15
532	A116	25p multi	15 15
		Set value	16 15

Youth Week; 5th Youth Festival, Homs, Apr. 18-24.

1969, Apr. 17   Litho.   *Perf. 12x12¹/₂*

533	A117	12¹/₂p yel & multi	15 15
534	A117	27¹/₂p gray & multi	15 15
		Set value	16 15

23rd anniv. of the evacuation of British and French troops from Syria.

Mahatma Gandhi — A118

Cotton — A119

1969, Oct. 7   Litho.   *Perf. 12x12¹/₂*

535	A118	12¹/₂p brn & dl yel	15 15
536	A118	27¹/₂p grn & yel	15 15
		Set value	20 15

Mohandas K. Gandhi (1869-1948), leader in India's fight for independence.

1969, Oct. 10

537	A119	12¹/₂p multi	15 15
538	A119	17¹/₂p multi	15 15
539	A119	25p multi	15 15
		Set value	28 18

14th Cotton Festival, Aleppo.

Map of Arab Countries A120

Designs: 25p, Arab Academy. 27¹/₂p, Damascus University.

1969, Nov. 2   Litho.   Perf. 12¹/₂x12
540 A120 12¹/₂p ultra & lt grn   15 15
541 A120   25p dk pur & dp pink   15 15
542 A120 27¹/₂p dp bis & yel grn   15 15
           Set value   32 26

10th Science Week, and 6th Arab Scientific Conf. No. 541 also for 50th anniv. of the Arab Academy and No. 542, the 50th anniv. of the Medical School of the Damascus University.

Symbols of Progress A121

1970, Mar. 8   Litho.   Perf. 12¹/₂x12
543 A121 12¹/₂p brt blk & bis brn   15 15
544 A121   25p red, blk & dp bl   15 15
545 A121 27¹/₂p lt grn, blk & tan   15 15
           Set value   32 25

March 8 Revolution, 7th anniversary.

Map of Arab League Countries, Flag and Emblem A122

1970, Mar. 22
546 A122 12¹/₂p multi   15 15
547 A122   25p gray & multi   15 15
548 A122 27¹/₂p multi   15 15
           Set value   32 22

25th anniversary of the Arab League.

Sultan Saladin and Battle of Hattin, 1187, between Saracens and Crusaders — A123

1970, Apr. 17   Litho.   Perf. 12¹/₂x12
549 A123 15p brn & buff   15 15
550 A123 35p lil & buff   25 15
           Set value   16

24th anniv. of the evacuation of British and French troops from Syria.

Development of Agriculture and Industry — A124

1970-71   Litho.   Perf. 11x11¹/₂
551 A124   2¹/₂p brn & red ('71)   15 15
552 A124   5p orange & bl   15 15
553 A124   7¹/₂p lil & gray ('71)   15 15
554 A124   10p lt & dk brn   15 15
555 A124 12¹/₂p blue & org ('71)   15 15
556 A124   15p grn & red lil   15 15
557 A124   20p vio & red brn   15 15
558 A124 22¹/₂p red brn & blk ('71) 15 15
559 A124   25p gray & vio bl ('71)   18 15
560 A124 27¹/₂p brt grn & dk brn
                  ('71)   20 15
561 A124   35p rose red & emer
                  ('71)   25 15
           Set value   1.20 65

Young Man and Woman, Map of Arab Countries A125

1970, May 7   Unwmk.   Perf. 12¹/₂x12
569 A125 15p green & ocher   15 15
570 A125 25p brown & ocher   15 15
           Set value   16 15

First Youth Week, Latakia, Apr. 23-29. Inscribed "Youth's First Weak" (sic.).

Refugee Family A126

1970, May 15
571 A126 15p multicolored   15 15
572 A126 25p gray & multi   15 15
573 A126 35p green & multi   15 15
           Set value   35 25

Issued for Arab Refugee Week.

Cotton — A127

Designs: 10p, Tomatoes. 15p, Tobacco. 20p, Beets. 35p, Wheat.

1970, Aug. 18   Litho.   Perf. 12¹/₂
574 A127   5p multicolored   15 15
575 A127 10p yellow & multi   15 15
576 A127 15p multicolored   15 15
577 A127 20p yel grn & multi   25 15
578 A127 35p lilac & multi   45 25
    a.   Strip of 5, #574-578   1.00 75
           Set value   95 60

Industrial and Agricultural Fair, Aleppo.

Boy Scout, Tent, Emblem and Map of Arab Countries A128

1970, Aug. 25   Perf. 12¹/₂x12
579 A128 15p gray green   25 15

9th Pan-Arab Boy Scout Jamboree, Damascus.

Olive Tree and Emblem A129

1970, Sept. 28   Litho.   Perf. 11¹/₂x12
580 A129 15p gray grn, yel & blk   15 15
581 A129 25p red brn, yel & blk   35 15
           Set value   15

Issued to publicize World Olive Year.

Protection of Industry, Agriculture, Arts and Commerce A130

1971, Mar. 8   Litho.   Perf. 12¹/₂x12
582 A130 15p olive, yel & bl   15 15
583 A130 22¹/₂p red brn, yel & ol   15 15
584 A130 27¹/₂p bl, yel & red brn   15 15
           Set value   28 18

March 8 Revolution, 8th anniversary.

Workers Memorial, Hands with Wrench and Olive Branch A131

1971, May 1   Litho.   Perf. 12¹/₂x12
585 A131 15p brn vio, yel & bl   15 15
586 A131 25p dk bl, bl & yel   15 15
           Set value   22 15

Labor Day.

Child and Traffic Lights A132

World Traffic Day: 25p, Road signs, traffic lights, children, vert.

1971, May 4   Perf. 11¹/₂x12, 12x11¹/₂
587 A132 15p black, red & bl   15 15
588 A132 25p gray & multi   15 15
589 A132 45p black, red & yel   22 18
           Set value   38 30

Factories, Cogwheel and Cotton A133

1971, July 15   Litho.   Perf. 12¹/₂x12
590 A133 15p lt grn, bl & blk   15 15
591 A133 30p red & black   15 15
           Set value   20 16

11th Industrial and Agricultural Fair, Aleppo.

Arab Postal Union Emblem — A134

Flag, Map of Syria, Egypt and Libya — A135

1971, Aug. 13   Perf. 12x12¹/₂
592 A134 15p claret & multi   15 15
593 A134 20p vio bl & multi   15 15
           Set value   20 15

25th anniv. of the Conference of Sofar, Lebanon, establishing the APU.

1971, Aug. 13   Perf. 12x11¹/₂
594 A135 15p car, dl grn & blk   15 15

Confederation of the Arab states of Syria, Libya and Egypt.

Red Pepper and Chemical Factory (Fertilizer Industry) — A136

18th Intl. Damascus Fair: 15p, Electronics industry (TV, telephone, computer). 35p, Glass industry (old map and glass manufacture). 50p, Carpet industry (carpet and looms).

1971, Aug. 25   Perf. 12¹/₂
595 A136   5p violet & multi   15 15
596 A136 15p dull grn & multi   15 15
597 A136 35p multicolored   32 15
598 A136 50p yel grn & multi   38 15
           Set value   82 34

Pres. Hafez al Assad and Crowd — A137

UNESCO Emblem, Radar, Spacecraft, Telephone — A138

1971, Nov.   Litho.   Perf. 12x12¹/₂
599 A137 15p vio bl, blk & car   15 15
600 A137 20p dk & lt grn, car & blk 15 15
           Set value   16 15

1st anniv. of Correctionist Movement of Nov. 16, 1970.

1971, Dec. 8
601 A138 15p vio bl & multi   15 15
602 A138 50p green & multi   25 15
           Set value   30 22

25th anniv. of UNESCO.

UNICEF Emblem and Playing Children — A139

1971, Dec. 21
603 A139 15p ultra, dk bl & dp car   15 15
604 A139 25p grnsh bl, ocher & dk bl 15 15
           Set value   22 15

UNICEF, 25th anniv.

Conference Emblem A140

1971, Dec.   Perf. 12¹/₂x12
605 A140 15p blk, grnsh bl & org   15 15

Scholars' Conference.

Book Year Emblem A141

1972, Jan. 2
606 A141 15p tan, lt bl & vio   15 15
607 A141 20p brn, lt grn & grn   15 15
           Set value   20 15

International Book Year.

Wheel, "8" and Scales of Justice — A142

Baath Party Emblem — A143

1972, Mar. 8   Litho.   Perf. 12x12½
608 A142 15p blue grn & vio   15 15
609 A142 20p olive bis & car   15 15
Set value   15 15

March 8 Revolution, 9th anniversary.

1972, Mar. 7
610 A143 15p dk blue & multi   15 15
611 A143 20p violet & multi   15 15
Set value   15 15

Arab Baath Socialist Party, 25th anniv.

Eagle, Chimneys, Grain and Oil Rigs — A144

1972, Apr. 17   Perf. 12½x12
612 A144 15p gold, blk & car   15 15

Federation of Arab Republics, 1st anniv.

Symbolic Flower, Broken Chain — A145

Hand Holding Wrench and Spade — A146

1972, Apr. 17   Perf. 12x11½
613 A145 15p rose red & gray   15 15
614 A145 50p pale bl grn & gray   22 18
Set value   26 22

26th anniv. of the evacuation of British and French troops from Syria.

1972, May 1
615 A146 15p ol grn, bl & blk   15 15
616 A146 50p vio bl, brn & blk   22 18
Set value   26 22

Labor Day.

Environment Emblem, Crystals, Microscope A147

Dove over Factory A148

1972, June 5
617 A147 15p multicolored   15 15
618 A147 50p blue & multi   25 18
Set value   30 22

UN Conference on Human Environment, Stockholm, June 5-16.

1972, July 17   Litho.   Perf. 12x11½
619 A148 15p yellow & multi   15 15
620 A148 20p yellow & multi   15 15
Set value   15 15

Agricultural and Industrial Fair, Aleppo.

Folk Dance A149

1972, Aug. 25   Litho.   Perf. 12x12½
621 A149 15p shown   15 15
622 A149 20p Women and tambourine player   15 15
623 A149 50p Men and drummer   30 18
Set value   50 28

19th International Damascus Fair.

Olympic Rings, Discus, Soccer, Swimming — A150

Warriors on Horseback, Olympic Emblems — A151

Design: 60p, Olympic rings, running, gymnastics, fencing.

1972   Litho.   Perf. 12½x12
624 A150 15p ol bis, blk & vio   15 15
625 A150 60p dull bl, blk & org   30 22
Set value   38 26

Souvenir Sheet
Imperf
626 A151 75p lt grn, bl & blk   65 65

20th Olympic Games, Munich, Aug. 26-Sept. 11, 1972.

Emblem of Revolution and Prancing Horse A152

1973, Mar. 8   Litho.   Perf. 11½x12
627 A152 15p brt grn, blk & red   15 15
628 A152 20p dull org, blk & red   15 15
629 A152 25p blue, blk & red   15 15
Set value   26 15

March 8 Revolution, 10th anniversary.

Heart and WHO Emblem A153

1973, Mar. 21
630 A153 15p gray & multi   15 15
631 A153 50p lt brown & multi   25 15
Set value   32 20

WHO, 25th anniversary.

Cogwheel and Grain Emblem — A154

1973, Apr. 17   Perf. 12x12½
632 A154 15p blue & multi   15 15
633 A154 20p multicolored   15 15
Set value   15 15

27th anniv. of the evacuation of British and French troops from Syria.

Workers and Globe A155

1973, May 1   Perf. 11½x12
634 A155 15p rose & multi   15 15
635 A155 50p blue & multi   22 15
Set value   30 16

Labor Day.

UN, FAO Emblems, People and Symbols — A156

Stock — A157

1973, May 7   Perf. 12x11½
636 A156 15p lt grn & red brn   15 15
637 A156 50p lilac & blue   22 15
Set value   30 16

World food program, 10th anniv.

1973, May 15
638 A157 5p shown   15 15
639 A157 10p Gardenia   15 15
640 A157 15p Jasmine   15 15
641 A157 20p Rose   15 15
642 A157 25p Narcissus   18 15
a.   Strip of 5, #638-642   60 40
Set value   55 26

Intl. Flower Show, Damascus.

Children and Flame — A158

Children's Day: 3 children's heads and flame in different arrangements; 25p, 35p, 70p, vertical.

Perf. 11½x12, 12x11½
1973-74   Litho.
643 A158 2½p lt olive grn   15 15
644 A158 5p orange   15 15
645 A158 7½p dk brown   15 15
646 A158 10p crimson   15 15
647 A158 15p ultra   15 15
648 A158 25p gray   15 15
649 A158 35p brt blue   15 15
650 A158 55p green   18 15
651 A158 70p rose lilac   25 15
Set value   90 60

Issue dates: 15p, 55p, 70p, May, 1973. Others, Mar. 1974.

Fair Emblem A159

1973, June 17   Perf. 11½x12
652 A159 15p multicolored   15 15

13th Agricultural and Industrial Fair, Aleppo.

Euphrates Dam and Power Plant — A160

1973, July 5   Perf. 12½x12
653 A160 15p green & multi   15 15
654 A160 50p brown & multi   20 15
Set value   28 16

Euphrates River diversion and dam project.

Woman from Deir Ezzor — A161

Map of Palestine, Barbed Wire, Human Rights Emblem — A162

Women's Costumes from: 10p, Hassaké. 20p, As Sahel. 25p, Zakié. 50p, Sarakeb.

1973, July 25   Perf. 12
655 A161 5p multicolored   15 15
656 A161 10p multicolored   15 15
657 A161 20p multicolored   15 15
658 A161 25p multicolored   15 15
659 A161 50p multicolored   22 15
a.   Strip of 5, #655-659   60 40
Set value   52 32

20th International Damascus Fair.

1973, Aug. 20   Perf. 12x11½
660 A162 15p lt green & multi   15 15
661 A162 50p lt blue & multi   30 20
Set value   26

25th anniversary of the Universal Declaration of Human Rights.

Citadel of Ja'abar A163

Designs: 15p, Minaret of Meskeneh, vert. 25p, Statue of Psyche at Anab al Safinah, vert.

Perf. 11½x12, 12x11½
1973, Sept. 5   Litho.
662 A163 10p black, org & blue   15 15
663 A163 15p black, org & blue   15 15
664 A163 25p black, org & blue   18 15
Set value   18 15

Salvage of monuments threatened by Euphrates Dam.

WMO
Emblem
A164

1973, Sept. 12   *Perf. 11½x12*
665 A164 70p yellow & multi   30 15

Intl. meteorological cooperation, cent.

Maalula
A165

Design: 50p, Ruins of Afamia.

1973, Oct. 22   Litho.   *Perf. 11½x12*
666 A165 15p gray blue & blk   15 15
667 A165 50p brown & blk   15 15
    Set value   20 15

Arab Emigrants' Congress, Buenos Aires.

Workers and
Soldiers
A166

1973, Nov. 16   Litho.   *Perf. 12½x12*
668 A166 15p ultra & yellow   15 15
669 A166 25p purple & red brn   15 15
    Set value   15 15

3rd anniv. of Correctionist Movement of Nov. 16, 1970.

Nicolaus
Copernicus
A167

UPU Emblem
A169

Arms of Syria
and Emblems
A168

Design: 25p, Abu-al-Rayhan al-Biruni.

1973, Dec. 15   *Perf. 12x11½*
670 A167 15p gold & black   15 15
671 A167 25p gold & black   15 15
    Set value   16 15

14th Science Week.

1974, Mar. 8   *Perf. 11x12*
672 A168 20p gray & blue   15 15
673 A168 25p lt green & vio   15 15
    Set value   15 15

11th anniversary of March 8th Revolution.

Perf. 12x11½, 11½x12
1974, Mar. 15

Designs: 20p, Air mail letter and UPU emblem, horiz. 70p, like 15p.

674 A169 15p gray & multi   15 15
675 A169 20p multicolored   15 15
676 A169 70p gray & multi   30 18
    Set value   44 28

Centenary of Universal Postal Union.

Arab Postal
Institute
A170

1974, Apr. 10   *Perf. 11½x12*
677 A170 15p multicolored   15 15

Inauguration of the Higher Arab Postal Institute, Damascus, Apr. 10.

Sun and
Monument
A171

1974, Apr. 10
678 A171 15p emerald, blk & org   15 15
679 A171 20p dp org, blk & org   15 15
    Set value   15 15

28th anniversary of the evacuation of British and French troops from Syria.

Machine Shop
Worker
A172

Abulfeda
A173

1974, May 1   *Perf. 12x12½*
680 A172 15p black, yel & bl   15 15
681 A172 50p black, buff & bl   15 15
    Set value   20 16

Labor Day.

1974   Litho.   *Perf. 11½x11*

Design: 200p, al-Farabi.

682 A173 100p pale green   38 22
683 A173 200p lt brown   75 45

Damascus Fair
Emblem — A174

Figs — A175

Design: 25p, Cog wheel and sun.

1974, July 25   *Perf. 11½x11*
684 A174 15p multicolored   15 15
685 A174 25p blue, blk & yel   15 15
    Set value   15 15

21st International Damascus Fair.

1974, Aug. 21   *Perf. 12x12½*

Fruits: 15p, Grapes. 20p, Pomegranates. 25p, Cherries. 35p, Rose hips.

686 A175 5p gray & multi   15 15
687 A175 15p gray & multi   15 15
688 A175 20p gray & multi   15 15
689 A175 25p gray & multi   15 15
690 A175 35p gray & multi   18 15
  a.   Strip of 5, #686-690   50 35
    Set value   48 25

Agricultural and Industrial Fair, Aleppo.

Burning Fuse and
Flowers — A176

Rook and
Knight — A177

Design: 20p, Bomb and star-shaped holes in target.

1974, Oct. 6   Litho.   *Perf. 12x12½*
691 A176 15p multicolored   50 15
692 A176 20p multicolored   65 18

First anniv. of October Liberation War (Yom Kippur War).

1974, Nov. 23

Design: 50p, Knight and chess board.

693 A177 15p blue & black   38 15
694 A177 50p orange, blk & bl   50 38

Chess Federation, 50th anniversary.

WPY
Emblem — A178

Ishtup,
Ilum — A179

1974, Dec. 4   Litho.   *Perf. 12x12½*
695 A178 50p black, slate & red   18 15

World Population Year.

1975   *Perf. 12x11½*

Ancient Statuettes: 55p, Woman holding pitcher. 70p, Ur-Nina.

696 A179 20p brt green   15 15
697 A179 55p brown   18 15
698 A179 70p gray blue   30 15
    Set value   26

"A," People and
Sun — A180

Postal Savings
Bank Emblem,
Family — A181

1975, Mar. 8   Litho.   *Perf. 12x11½*
699 A180 15p gray & multi   15 15

12th anniversary, March 8th Revolution.

1975, Mar. 17

Design: 20p, Family depositing money, and stamped envelope.

700 A181 15p brt green & multi   15 15
701 A181 20p orange & black   15 15

Publicity for Savings Certificates and Postal Savings Bank.

"Sun" and
Dove — A182

1975, Apr. 17   Litho.   *Perf. 12x11½*
702 A182 15p bister, red & blk   15 15
703 A182 25p bister, grn & blk   15 15
    Set value   15 15

29th anniversary of the evacuation of British and French troops from Syria.

"Worker and
Industry"
A183

Camomile
A184

1975, May 1   Litho.   *Perf. 12x11½*
704 A183 15p blue grn & blk   15 15
705 A183 25p brown, yel & blk   15 15
    Set value   15 15

Labor Day.

1975, May 17

Flowers: 10p, Chincherinchi. 15p, Carnation. 20p, Poppy. 25p, Honeysuckle.

706 A184 5p ultra & multi   15 15
707 A184 10p lilac & multi   15 15
708 A184 15p blue & multi   25 15
709 A184 20p gray grn & multi   32 18
710 A184 25p vio bl & multi   50 25
  a.   Strip of 5, #706-710   1.50 1.00
   Nos. 706-710 (5)   1.37
    Set value   70

International Flower Show, Damascus.

Kuneitra Destroyed and Rebuilt — A185

1975, June 5   *Perf. 12½*
711 A185 50p black & multi   28 15

Re-occupation of Kuneitra by Syria.

Apples — A186

1975, July 7

712	A186	5p shown	15	15
713	A186	10p Quince	15	15
714	A186	15p Apricots	22	15
715	A186	20p Grapes	30	15
716	A186	25p Figs	38	15
a.		Strip of 5, #712-716	1.25	75
		Nos. 712-716 (5)	1.20	
		Set value		42

Agricultural and Industrial Fair, Aleppo.

22nd Intl. Damascus Fair — A187

Farm Woman — A189

Pres. Hafez al Assad A188

1975, July 25   Litho.   Perf. 12x11½

717	A187	15p olive grn & multi	15	15
718	A187	35p brown & multi	18	15
		Set value	26	15

1975, Nov. 29   Litho.   Perf. 11½x12

719	A188	15p green & multi	15	15
720	A188	50p blue & multi	18	15
		Set value	22	16

5th anniv. of Correctionist Movement of Nov. 16, 1970.

1975, Nov. 29   Perf. 12x11½

IWY Emblem and: 15p, Mother. 25p, Student. 50p, Laboratory technician.

721	A189	10p buff & multi	15	15
722	A189	15p rose & black	15	15
723	A189	25p dull green & blk	25	15
724	A189	50p orange & blk	35	15
		Set value		30

International Women's Year.

Horse-shaped Bronze Lamp A190

Man's Head Inkstand A191

Designs: 10p, 25p, like 20p. 35p, like 30p. 50p, 60p, Nike. 75p, Hera. 100p, Imdugug-Mari (winged animal). 500p, Palmyrene coin of Vasalathus. 1000p, Abraxas coin.

1976   Perf. 11½x12, 12x11½

725	A190	10p brt bluish grn	15	15
726	A190	20p lilac rose	15	15
727	A190	25p violet rose	15	15
728	A191	30p brown	15	15
729	A191	35p olive	15	15
730	A191	50p brt blue	20	15
731	A191	60p violet	22	15

732	A191	75p orange	25	18
733	A191	100p lilac rose	38	18
734	A191	500p grnsh gray	1.75	1.75
735	A191	1000p dk green	3.50	2.25
		Nos. 725-735 (11)	7.05	5.41

See Nos. 798-803.

National Theater, Damascus and Pres. al Assad A192

1976, Mar. 8   Litho.   Perf. 11½x12

736	A192	25p brt grn, sil & blk	15	15
737	A192	35p olive, sil & blk	15	15
		Set value	20	15

13th anniversary of March 8 Revolution.

Syria, Arabian Government #85 — A193

1976, Apr. 12   Perf. 12x12½

738	A193	25p brt green & multi	15	15
739	A193	35p blue & multi	18	15
		Set value		16

Post's Day.

Nurse and Emblem — A194

Eagle and Stars — A195

1976, Apr. 8   Perf. 12x11½

740	A194	25p blue, blk & red	15	15
741	A194	100p violet, blk & red	38	30
		Set value		35

Arab Red Cross and Red Crescent Societies, 8th Conference, Damascus.

1976, Apr. 17

742	A195	25p blk, red & brt grn	15	15
743	A195	35p blk, red & brt grn	15	15
		Set value		15

30th anniversary of the evacuation of British and French troops from Syria.

Hand Holding Wrench — A196

Cotton and Factory — A197

May Day: 60p, Hand holding globe.

1976, May 1

744	A196	25p blue & black	15	15
745	A196	60p citron & multi	25	18
		Set value		22

1976, July 1

746	A197	25p vio & multi	15	15
747	A197	35p bl & multi	18	15
		Set value		15

Agricultural and Industrial Fair, Aleppo.

Tulips — A198

1976, July 26

748	A198	5p shown	15	15
749	A198	15p Yellow daisies	15	15
750	A198	20p Turk's-cap lilies	18	15
751	A198	25p Irises	35	15
752	A198	35p Freesia	50	15
a.		Strip of 5, #748-752	1.50	75
		Nos. 748-752 (5)	1.33	
		Set value		30

Intl. Flower Show, Damascus.

People, Globe and Olive Branch A199

Design: 60p, Symbolic arrow piercing darkness.

1976, Sept. 2   Perf. 11½x12

753	A199	40p yel & multi	15	15
754	A199	60p multi	22	15

5th Summit Conference of Non-aligned Countries, Colombo, Sri Lanka, Aug. 9-19.

Soccer, Pan Arab Games Emblem — A200

1976, Oct. 6   Litho.   Perf. 12½

755	A200	5p shown	15	15
756	A200	10p Swimming	15	15
757	A200	25p Running	15	15
758	A200	35p Basketball	18	15
759	A200	50p Javelin	22	15
a.		Strip of 5, #755-759	75	50
		Set value	62	40

Souvenir Sheet
Imperf

760	A200	100p Steeplechase	75	75

5th Pan Arab Sports Tournament.
Size of stamp of No. 760: 55x35mm.

"Development" A201

The Fox and the Crow A202

1976, Nov. 16   Perf. 12½x12½

761	A201	35p multi	15	15

6th anniv. of Correctionist Movement of Nov. 16, 1970.

1976, Dec. 7   Perf. 12x12½, 12½x12

Fairy Tales: 15p, The Hare and the Tortoise, horiz. 20p, Little Red Riding Hood. 25p, The Lamb and the Wolf, horiz. 35p, The Lamb and the Wolf.

762	A202	10p multi	15	15
763	A202	15p multi	15	15
764	A202	20p multi	15	15
765	A202	25p multi	15	15
766	A202	35p multi	15	15
		Set value	38	30

Children's literature.

Syrian Airlines Boeing 747 — A203

1977, Feb.   Litho.   Perf. 12½x12

767	A203	35p multi	18	15

Civil Aviation Day.

Muhammad Kurd-Ali (1876-1953), Philosopher, Birth Cent. — A204

1977, Feb.   Perf. 12x12½

768	A204	25p lt grn & multi	15	15

Woman Holding Syrian Flag — A205

APU Emblem — A207

Warrior on Horseback — A206

1977, Mar. 8   Litho.   Perf. 12x12½

769	A205	35p multi	15	15

14th anniversary of March 8 Revolution.

1977, Apr. 10   Litho.   Perf. 12½

770	A206	100p multi	20	30

31st anniversary of the evacuation of British and French troops from Syria.

1977, Apr. 12   Litho.   Perf. 12x12½

771	A207	35p sil & multi	15	15

Arab Postal Union, 25th anniversary.

Tools and Factories A208

1977, May 1   *Perf. 12½x12*
772 A208 60p multi   22 15

Labor Day.

ICAO Emblem, Plane and Globe A209

1977, May 11
773 A209 100p multi   38 25

Intl. Civil Aviation Org., 30th anniv.

Pioneers — A210   Citrus Fruit — A211

1977, Aug. 15   Litho.   *Perf. 12x12½*
774 A210 35p multi   18 15

Al Baath Pioneer Organization.

1977, Aug. 1
775 A211 10p Lemon   15 15
776 A211 20p Lime   15 15
777 A211 25p Grapefruit   15 15
778 A211 35p Oranges   18 15
779 A211 60p Tangerines   25 15
a.   Strip of 5, #775-779   75 50
   Set value   65 35

Agricultural and Industrial Fair, Aleppo.

Mallow — A212

Flowers: 20p, Coxcomb. 25p, Morning glories. 35p, Almond blossoms. 60p, Lilacs.

1977, Aug. 6   Litho.   *Perf. 12½x12*
780 A212 10p sil & multi   15 15
781 A212 20p sil & multi   15 15
782 A212 25p sil & multi   15 15
783 A212 35p sil & multi   18 15
784 A212 60p sil & multi   22 18
a.   Strip of 5, #780-784   75 50
   Set value   65 45

Intl. Flower Show, Damascus.

Coffeepot and Ornament — A213

1977, Sept. 10   *Perf. 12x12½*
785 A213 25p blk, bl & red   15 15
786 A213 60p blk, grn & brn   22 15
   Set value   30 20

24th Intl. Damascus Fair.

Blind Man, Globe and Eye — A214   Globe and Measures — A215

1977, Nov. 17   Litho.   *Perf. 12x12½*
787 A214 55p multi   15 15
788 A214 70p multi   18 15
   Set value   20

World Blind Week.

1977, Nov. 5
789 A215 15p grn & multi   15 15

World Standards Day, Oct. 14.

Microscope, Book, Harp, UNESCO Emblem A216

1977, Nov. 5   *Perf. 12½x12*
790 A216 25p multi   15 15

30th anniversary of UNESCO.

Archbishop Capucci, Map of Palestine, Bars — A217   Fight Cancer Shield, Crab and Surgeon — A218

1977, Nov. 17   *Perf. 12x12½*
791 A217 60p multi   25 15

Palestinian Archbishop Hilarion Capucci, jailed by Israel in 1974.

1977, Nov. 17
792 A218 100p multi   32 18

Fight Cancer Week.

Dome of the Rock, Jerusalem A219

1977, Dec. 6   *Perf. 12*
793 A219 5p multi   25 15
794 A219 10p multi   38 15
   Set value   20

Palestinian fighters and their families.

Mural A220   Pres. Hafez al Assad A221

Designs: 10p, 15p, Murals from Dura-Europos, in National Museum, Damascus (15p horiz.).

1978, Jan. 22   Litho.   *Perf. 12x11½*
795 A220 5p gray grn   15 15
796 A220 10p vio bl   15 15
797 A220 15p brown   15 15
   Set value   15 15

Types of 1976

Designs: 40p, Man's head inkstand. 55p, Nike. 70p, 80p, Hera. 200p, Arab-Islamic astrolabe. 300p, Palmyrene (Herod) coin.

1978   Litho.   *Perf. 12x11½, 11½x12*
798 A191 40p pale org   15 15
799 A191 55p brt rose   15 15
800 A191 70p vermilion   25 15
801 A191 80p green   25 15
802 A191 200p lt ultra   70 30
803 A190 300p rose lil   1.00 50
   Nos. 798-803 (6)   2.50
   Set value   1.05

1978   *Perf. 12x11½*
805 A221 50p multi   15 15

Anniversary of "Correction Movement."

Blood Circulation, WHO Emblem — A222   Factory — A223

1978, Apr. 7   Litho.   *Perf. 12x11½*
806 A222 100p multi   32 18

World Health Day, fight against hypertension.

1978, Apr. 17
807 A223 35p multi   15 15

32nd anniversary of the evacuation of British and French troops from Syria.

Rosette — A224   Map of Arab Countries, Police, Flag and Eye — A225

1978, Apr. 21
808 A224 25p blk & grn   15 15

14th Arab Engineering Conference, Damascus, Apr. 21-26.

1978, May
809 A225 35p multi   15 15

6th Conf. of Arab Police Commanders.

European Goldfinch A226

Birds: 20p, Peregrine falcon. 25p, Rock dove. 35p, Eurasian hoopoe. 60p, Old World quail.

1978   *Perf. 11½x12*
810 A226 10p multi   15 15
811 A226 20p multi   15 15
812 A226 25p multi   16 15
813 A226 35p multi   25 15
814 A226 60p multi   32 16
a.   Strip of 5, #810-814   1.10 60
   Nos. 810-814 (5)   1.03
   Set value   48

Trout — A227

Designs: Various fish.

1978, July   Litho.   *Perf. 11½x12*
815 A227 10p multi   15 15
816 A227 20p multi   15 15
817 A227 25p multi   18 15
818 A227 35p multi   25 15
819 A227 60p multi   35 25
a.   Strip of 5, #815-819   1.10 75
   Nos. 815-819 (5)   1.08
   Set value   70

Pres. Assad Type of Air Post, 1978
Miniature Sheet

1978, Sept.   Litho.   *Imperf.*
820 AP161 100p gold & multi   42 42

Reelection of President Assad. Size of stamp: 58x80mm.

Flowering Cactus — A228   Fair Emblem — A229

Designs: Flowering cacti.

1978	**Litho.**	**Perf. 12½**	
821 A228	25p multi	15	15
822 A228	30p multi	15	15
823 A228	35p multi	15	15
824 A228	50p multi	18	15
825 A228	60p multi	20	15
a.	Strip of 5, #821-825	70	45
	Set value	62	38

International Flower Show, Damascus.

1978	**Litho.**	**Perf. 12x12½**	
826 A229	25p sil & multi	15	15
827 A229	35p sil & multi	15	15
	Set value	20	15

Miniature Sheet
Imperf

828 A229	100p sil & multi	42	42

25th Intl. Damascus Fair. No. 828 shows different ornament, size of stamp: 40x46mm.

Euphrates Dam and Pres. Assad — A230

1978, Dec.	**Litho.**	**Perf. 12½x12**	
829 A230	60p multi	22	15

Inauguration of Euphrates Dam.

Pres. Hafez al Assad — A231

1978, Nov. 16	**Litho.**	**Perf. 12x12½**	
830 A231	60p multi	18	15

Nov. 16 Movement.

Racial Equality Emblem — A232

1978, Mar.	**Litho.**	**Perf. 12½**	
831 A232	35p multi	15	15

International Year to Combat Racism.

Averroes — A233

Human Rights Flame and Globe — A234

1979, Mar.

832 A233	100p multi	50	22

Averroes (1126-1198), Spanish-Arabian philosopher and physician.

1978, Dec.   **Perf. 12x12½**

833 A234	60p multi	18	15

30th anniversary of Universal Declaration of Human Rights (in 1978).

Symbolic Design A235

Princess, 2nd Century Shield A236

1979, Mar.

834 A235	100p multi	42	15

16th anniversary of March 8 Revolution.

1979   **Litho.**   **Perf. 11½**

Designs: 20p, Helmet of Homs. 35p, Ishtar.

836 A236	20p green	15	15
837 A236	25p rose car	15	15
838 A236	35p sepia	15	15
	Set value	22	15

Molar, Emblem with Mosque — A237

Flame Emblem — A238

1979   **Litho.**   **Perf. 12x11½**

846 A237	35p multi	15	15

Intl. Middle East Dental Congress.

1979

847 A238	35p multi	15	15

33rd anniversary of evacuation.

Ibn Assaker, 900th Anniv. A239

1979   **Perf. 11½x12**

848 A239	75p multi	20	15

Telephone Lineman — A240

Girl with IYC Emblem — A242

Wright Brothers' Plane A241

1979, May 1   **Litho.**   **Perf. 12x11½**

849 A240	50p multi	18	15
850 A240	75p multi	20	15
	Set value		18

May Day.

1979   **Perf. 11½x12**

Designs: 75p, Bleriot's plane crossing English Channel. 100p, Spirit of St. Louis.

851 A241	50p multi	15	15
852 A241	75p multi	22	15
853 A241	100p multi	38	22

75th anniversary of 1st powered flight.

1979   **Perf. 12x11½**

Design: 15p, Boy, globe, IYC emblem.

854 A242	10p multi	18	15
855 A242	15p multi	25	15
	Set value		16

International Year of the Child.

Power Plant — A243

Flags and Pavilion — A244

1979   **Perf. 11x11½**

856 A243	5p blue	15	15
857 A243	10p lil rose	15	15
858 A243	15p gray grn	15	15
	Set value		18

1979   **Photo.**   **Perf. 12x11½**

Design: 75p, Lamppost and flags.

859 A244	60p multi	18	15
860 A244	75p multi	22	15
	Set value		20

26th International Damascus Fair.

Correction Movement, 9th Anniversary A245

1979   **Photo.**   **Perf. 11½x12**

861 A245	100p multi	38	15

Games Emblem, Running A246

1979, Nov.

862 A246	25p shown	15	15
863 A246	35p Diving	15	15
864 A246	50p Soccer	15	15
	Set value	34	18

8th Mediterranean Games, Split, Yugoslavia, Sept. 15-29.

Butterfly — A247

Damascus Intl. Flower Show — A248

Designs: Various butterflies.

1979, Dec.   **Litho.**   **Perf. 12x11½**

865 A247	20p multi	15	15
866 A247	25p multi	15	15
867 A247	30p multi	15	15
868 A247	35p multi	15	15
869 A247	50p multi	20	15
	Set value	62	35

1980, Jan. 9   **Litho.**   **Perf. 12½**

Design: Roses.

870 A248	5p multi	15	15
871 A248	10p multi	15	15
872 A248	15p multi	15	15
873 A248	50p multi	15	15
874 A248	75p multi	22	15
875 A248	100p multi	42	18
	Set value	90	45

March 8 Revolution, 17th Anniv. — A249

Astrolabe — A250

1980, Mar. 25   **Litho.**   **Perf. 12x11½**

876 A249	40p multi	20	15

1980, May 2   **Perf. 12½**

877 A250	50p violet	15	15
878 A250	100p sepia	32	18
879 A250	1000p gray grn	3.00	1.25

2nd International History of Arabic Sciences Symposium, Apr. 5.

Lit Cigarette, Skull A251

Evacuation, 34th Anniversary A252

1980, June 25   **Photo.**   **Perf. 12x11½**

880 A251	60p Smoker	45	24
881 A251	100p shown	65	30

World Health Day; anti-smoking campaign.

1980, June 25   **Litho.**

882 A252	40p multi	18	15
883 A252	60p multi	22	15
	Set value		16

Moscow '80 Emblem and Wrestling A253

1980, July   Litho.   Perf. 11½x12

884	A253	15p shown	15 15
885	A253	25p Fencing	18 15
886	A253	35p Weight lifting	25 15
887	A253	50p Judo	35 15
888	A253	75p Boxing	60 25
a.		Strip of 5, #884-888	1.60 80
		Nos. 884-888 (5)	1.53
		Set value	52

Souvenir Sheet
Imperf

888A A253 300p Discus, running   4.25 4.25

22nd Summer Olympic Games, Moscow, July 19-Aug. 3.

Sinbad the Sailor A254

1980   Litho.   Perf. 11½x12

889	A254	15p shown	15 15
890	A254	25p Scheherezade and Shahrayar	18 15
891	A254	35p Ali Baba and the Forty Thieves	24 15
892	A254	50p Hassan the Clever	35 15
893	A254	100p Aladdin's Lamp	65 30
a.		Strip of 5, #889-893	1.75 1.00
		Nos. 889-893 (5)	1.57
		Set value	60

Popular stories.

Savings Certificates A255

1980
894 A255 25p multi   18 15

Hegira, 1500th Anniv. — A256

1980   Perf. 12½x12
895 A256 35p multi   25 15

Intl. Flower Show, Damascus — A257

1980   Perf. 12x11½

896	A257	20p Daffodils	15 15
897	A257	30p Chrysanthemums	18 15
898	A257	40p Clematis	22 15
899	A257	60p Yellow roses	32 15
900	A257	100p Chrysanthemums, diff.	50 22
a.		Strip of 5, #896-900	1.50 75
		Nos. 896-900 (5)	1.37
		Set value	54

May Day — A258

Children's Day — A259

1980, May
901 A258 35p multi   30 15

1980
902 A259 25p multi   28 15

November 16th Movement, 10th Anniv. A260

1980   Perf. 11½x12
903 A260 100p multi   70 25

Steam-powered Passenger Wagon — A261

1980

904	A261	25p shown	25 15
905	A261	35p Benz, 1899	32 16
906	A261	40p Rolls-Royce, 1903	45 16
907	A261	50p Mercedes, 1906	50 25
908	A261	60p Austin, 1915	65 30
a.		Strip of 5, #904-908	2.25 1.25
		Nos. 904-908 (5)	2.17 1.02

Mother's Day — A262

1980   Perf. 12x11½

909	A262	40p shown	38 15
910	A262	100p Mother and child	75 18
		Set value	26

27th International Damascus Fair — A263

1981, Jan. 24   Perf. 11½x12

911	A263	50p multi	45 15
912	A263	100p multi	80 22

Army Day — A264

1981, Jan. 24   Perf. 12½x12
913 A264 50p multi   45 15

A265

A266

1981, Mar. 8   Litho.   Perf. 12x11½
914 A265 50p multi   35 15

18th anniv. of March 8th revolution.

1981, Apr. 17   Litho.   Perf. 12x11½
915 A266 50p multi   35 15

35th anniversary of evacuation.

World Conference on History of Arab and Islamic Civilization, Damascus — A267

1981, May 30   Photo.   Perf. 12½x12
916 A267 100p multi   60 20

Intl. Workers' Solidarity Day — A268

Housing and Population Census — A269

1981, May 30   Litho.   Perf. 12x11½
917 A268 100p multi   60 18

1981, June 1
918 A269 50p multi   35 15

Umayyad Window A270

Abdul Malik Gold Coin A270a

Designs: 10p, figurine. 15p, Rakkla's cavalier, Abbcid ceramic. 160p, like 5p. 500p, Umar B. Abdul Aziz gold coin.

1981   Perf. 12x11½, 11½x12

919	A270	5p crim rose	15 15
920	A270	10p brt grn	15 15
921	A270	15p dp rose lil	15 15
922	A270a	75p blue	38 16
923	A270	160p dk grn	70 38
924	A270a	500p dk brn	2.50 1.10
		Nos. 919-924 (6)	4.03
		Set value	1.75

Olives — A270b

Harbor — A270c

1982   Perf. 12x11½

925	A270b	50p ol grn	38 18
926	A270b	60p bl gray	42 18
929	A270c	100p lilac	55 28
930	A270c	180p red	1.10 55

Saving Certificates Plan — A271

Avicenna (980-1037), Philosopher and Physician — A272

1981, June 22
931 A271 50p gldn brn & blk   35 15

1981, Aug.
932 A272 100p multi   60 20

Syria-P.L.O. Solidarity, Intl. Conference — A273

1981, June 22
933 A273 160p multi   3.50 90

Grand Mosque, Damascus — A274

1981   Perf. 12½

934	A274	50p Glass lamp, 13th cent.	32 15
935	A274	180p shown	1.40 40
936	A274	180p Hunter	1.40 40

Youth Festival A275

1981   Perf. 12½
937 A275 60p multi   40 16

28th Intl.
Damascus
Fair — A276

Intl. Palestinian
Solidarity
Day — A277

1981   *Perf. 12x11 1/2*
938 A276   50p Ornament   32   16
939 A276 160p Emblem   1.00   45

1981
940 A277 100p multi   75   15

1300th Anniv.
of Bulgaria
A278

1981   *Perf. 11 1/2x12*
941 A278 380p multi   2.25   1.00

Intl.
Children's
Day
A279

1981
942 A279 180p multi   1.10   45

World Food
Day,
Oct. 16
A280

1981
943 A280 180p multi   1.10   45

9th Intl. Flower
Show,
Damascus — A281

Designs: Flowers.

1981   *Perf. 12x11 1/2*
944 A281   25p multi   25   15
945 A281   40p multi   38   25
946 A281   50p multi   50   28
947 A281   60p multi   75   32
948 A281 100p multi   1.10   50
   a. Strip of 5, #944-948   3.00   2.00
   Nos. 944-948 (5)   2.98   1.50

*Keep up to date with all new
stamp issues by subscribing to
the "Scott Stamp Monthly".
Please call 1-800-488-5351
for more information.*

Souvenir Sheet

Koran Competition — A282

1981   **Litho.**   *Imperf.*
949 A282 500p multi   5.00   5.00

11th Anniv. of
Correction
Movement — A283

1981, Nov.   *Perf. 12x11 1/2*
950 A283 60p multi   45   30

TB Bacillus
Centenary
A284

1982   **Litho.**   *Perf. 11 1/2x12*
951 A284 180p multi   1.25   65

Mothers'
Day — A285

Mar. 8th
Revolution, 19th
Anniv. — A286

1982   *Perf. 11 1/2*
952 A285 40p green   22   15
953 A285 75p brown   52   25

1982, Mar.   *Perf. 12x11 1/2*
954 A286 50p multi   32   18

Intl. Year of the
Disabled
(1981) — A287

Pres. Hafez al
Assad — A288

1982   *Perf. 12x11 1/2*
955 A287 90p multi   75   32

1982   *Perf. 11 1/2*
956 A288 150p ultra   90   50

36th Anniv. of
Evacuation
A289

World Traffic Day
A290

1982   *Perf. 12x11 1/2*
957 A289 70p multi   50   25

1982
958 A290 180p multi   1.25   65

Intl. Workers'
Solidarity Day — A291

1982
959 A291 180p multi   1.25   65

World Telecommunication Day,
May 17 — A292

1982
960 A292 180p multi   1.25   65

Soldier Holding
Rifles — A293

Arab Postal Union,
30th
Anniv. — A294

1982   **Photo.**   *Perf. 12x11 1/2*
961 A293 50p multi   30   20

1982
962 A294 60p multi   45   22

1982
World
Cup
A295

Various soccer players. 300p, Ball.

1982, July   *Perf. 12 1/2*
963 A295   40p multi   28   16
964 A295   60p multi   40   20
965 A295 100p multi   65   40

Size: 75x55mm
Imperf
966 A295 300p multi   10.00   10.00

10th Intl. Flower
Show,
Damascus — A297

1982   *Perf. 12x11 1/2*
967 A297 50p Honeysuckle   45   22
968 A297 60p Geraniums   60   30

Scouting
Year — A298

1982, Nov. 4   *Perf. 11 1/2x12*
969 A298 160p green   1.40   75

Ladybug
A299

1982   *Perf. 12x12 1/2*
970   Strip of 5   75   40
   a. A299   5p Dragonfly   15   15
   b. A299 10p Stag Beetle   15   15
   c. A299 20p shown   15   15
   d. A299 40p Grasshopper   22   15
   e. A299 50p Honeybee   30   15

ITU Plenipotentiaries Conference, Nairobi,
Sept — A300

1982   *Perf. 11 1/2x12*
971 A300   50p Map   30   22
972 A300 180p Dish antenna   1.40   75

12th Anniv.
of
Correction
Movement
A301

1982, Nov.
973 A301 50p dk bl & sil   35   22

A302

Factory — A302a

Designs: 70p, Walled arch. 200p, Ruins.

1982-83   **Litho.**   *Perf. 11 1/2*
974 A302   30p brown   15   15
975 A302a 50p dark green   22   15
976 A302   70p green   35   20
977 A302 200p red   1.00   55

Issue dates: 50p, Nov. 16, 1983. Others, Nov. 4,
1982.

Dove and
Satellite — A303

Intl. Palestinian
Solidarity
Day — A304

1982   **Litho.**   *Perf. 12x11½*
978 A303 50p multi   50 32
2nd UN Conference on Peaceful Uses of Outer
Space, Vienna, Aug. 9-21.

1982
979 A304 50p multi   90 22

20th Anniv. of March 8th
Revolution — A305

1983   *Perf. 12½x12*
980 A305 60p multi   1.00 50

World Communications Year — A305a

1983
981 A305a 180p multi   1.25 65

9th Anniv. of
Liberation of Al-
Kuneitra — A306

25th Anniv. of Intl.
Maritime
Org. — A308

Arab
Pharmacists'
Day, Apr. 2
A307

1983, June 26   **Litho.**   *Perf. 11½*
982 A306 50p View   1.50 50
983 A306 100p View, diff.   3.00 65

1983, Apr. 2   *Perf. 11½x12*
984 A307 100p multi   75 32

1983, June   *Perf. 12x11½*
985 A308 180p multi   1.40 75

Namibia
Day, Aug.
26 — A309

1983, Aug. 26
986 A309 180p multi   1.40 75

Eibla
Sculpture,
3rd Cent.
BC — A310

1983
987 A310 380p ol & brn   2.50 1.35

World Standards
Day — A311

11th Intl. Flower
Show,
Damascus — A312

1983, Oct. 14   **Photo.**   *Perf. 11½*
988 A311   50p Factory, emblem   40 20
989 A311 100p Measuring equipment   80 40

1983, Oct. 14   **Litho.**   *Perf. 11½*
990 A312 50p multi   40 20
991 A312 60p multi, diff.   50 25

World Heritage
Day — A313

1983, Oct. 14   **Photo.**   *Perf. 11½*
992 A313 60p dk brn   50 25

World Food
Day
A313a

1983, Oct. 16   **Litho.**   *Perf. 11½x12*
992A A313a 180p multi   1.50 75

Waterwheels of
Hama — A314

Perf. 11x11½, 11½x11

1982-84   **Litho.**
993 A314   5p sepia   15 15
994 A314 10p violet   15 15
995 A314 20p red   25 15
997 A314 50p dk grn   60 30
     Set value   52
Issue dates: 50p, Nov. 25, 1982. Others, Jan. 15,
1984.
On No. 997 "50" is in outlined numbers.

Statue — A316

View of
Aleppo — A317

1983   *Perf. 12*
1003 A316 225p brown   2.00 1.00
Issue dates: 50p, Nov. 25, 1982. Others, Jan. 15,
1984. Intl. Symposium on History and Archaeology
of Deir Ez-zor.

1983   *Perf. 12½x12½*
1004 A317 245p multi   2.25 1.10
Intl. Symposium on Conservation of Old City of
Aleppo, Sept. 26-30.

Mar. 8th
Revolution,
21st Anniv.
A318

1984, Mar. 8   *Perf. 12½x12*
1005 A318 60p Alassad Library   75 35

Massacre at
Sabra and
Shatilla
A319

1983   **Litho.**   *Perf. 11½x12*
1006 A319 225p Victims, mother &
child   2.00 50

Mothers'
Day — A320

12th Intl. Flower
Show,
Damascus — A321

1984, Mar. 21   *Perf. 12x11½*
1007 A320 245p Mother & child   2.50 1.25

1984, May 25
Various flowers.
1008 A321 245p multi   2.50 1.25
1009 A321 285p multi   2.75 1.40

1984 Summer
Olympics — A322

Aleppo Agricultural
& Industrial
Fair — A324

9th
Regional
Pioneers'
Festival
A323

1984   **Litho.**   *Perf. 12x11½*
1010   Strip of 5   3.00 1.50
  a.   A322 30p Swimming   30 15
  b.   A322 50p Wrestling   48 24
  c.   A322 60p Running   60 30
  d.   A322 70p Boxing   65 35
  e.   A322 90p Soccer   90 45
     Souvenir Sheet
     Imperf
1011 A322 200p Soccer, diff.   3.50 3.50

1984   *Perf. 11½x12*
1012 A323 50p Pioneers   48 24
1013 A323 60p Pioneers, diff.   60 30

1984, June 12   **Litho.**   *Perf. 12x12½*
1014 A324 150p Peppers, Aleppo Cas-
tle   1.25 50

Supreme
Council of
Science,
25th Anniv.
A325

Aleppo
University,
25th Anniv.
A326

1985, Feb. 23   *Perf. 12½x12*
1015 A325 65p multi   40 15

1985, Feb. 23
1016 A326 45p multi   25 15

Syrian Arab
Army, 39th
Anniv.
A327

1985, Feb. 23
1017 A327 65p brn & gldn brn   40 15

Pres. Assad,
Soldier
Saluting,
Troops
A328

1984, Aug. 1   *Perf. 11½x12*
1018 A328 60p multi   60 30
4th General Revolutionary Youth Conference.

*The index in each volume of the
Scott Catalogue contains many listings that help identify stamps.*

ITU Emblem,
Satellite Dish,
Telephone
A329

1984, Oct. 2   *Perf. 12¹/₂*
1019 A329 245p multi   1.75 90

Intl. Telecommunications Day.

APU Emblem and Administration Building,
Damascus — A330

1984, Oct. 9
1020 A330 60p multi   60 30

Arab Postal Union Day.

Gearwheel,   Gold
Arabesque   Necklace — A332
Pattern — A331

     Perf. 12x12¹/₂, 12x11¹/₂
1984, Oct. 27
1021 A331 45p multi   45 20
1022 A332 100p multi   1.00 45

Intl. Fair, Damascus.

Intl. Civil
Aviation
Org., 40th
Anniv.
A333

1984, Oct. 27   *Perf. 11¹/₂x12*
1023 A333 45p brt bl & lt bl   25 15
1024 A333 245p brt ultra, brt bl & lt
     bl   1.25 60

14th Anniv.
of 11-16-70
Movement
A334

1984, Dec. 3   *Perf. 12¹/₂x12*
1025 A334 65p red brn, blk & org   65 35

Pres. Assad, Text
on
Scroll — A335

1984, Nov. 29   *Perf. 12¹/₂*
1026 A335 50p grn, brn org & sep   50 25

Vow of Dedication taken by Youth of the
Revolution.

Agricultural
Exhibition
A336

1984, June 12   *Perf. 12¹/₂x12*
1027 A336 65p multi   65 35

Al-Kuneitra
Memorial,
Rose
A337

1984
1028 A337 70p multi   1.25 35

Roman Arch and Colonnades,
Palmyra — A338

1984, Dec. 3
1029 A338 100p multi   1.00 50

Intl. Tourism Day.

Woodland
Conservation
A339

1984
1030 A339 45p multi   25 15

March 8   UPU Emblem,
Revolution, 22nd   Postal
Anniv. — A340   Headquarters,
     Damascus — A341

1985, Apr. 27
1031 A340 60p multi   40 20

1985, Apr. 27
1032 A341 285p multi   3.00 1.50

World Post Day.

APU Building, Damascus — A342

1985, Apr. 27   *Perf. 12¹/₂*
1033 A342 245p multi   2.50 1.25

Arab Parliamentary Union, 10th Anniv.

Natl. Flag,
Map of
Arab
Countries
A343

1985   *Perf. 12¹/₂x12*
1034 A343 50p multi   50 25

Arab League.

Re-election of
President
Assad — A344

1985, Mar. 12   *Perf. 12¹/₂*
1035 A344 200p multi   1.25 70
1036 A344 300p multi   2.00 1.00
1037 A344 500p multi   3.25 1.75
     a.   Souvenir sheet of 3, #1035-1037,
        imperf.   7.00 3.50

Arab Postal Union,
12th Congress,
Damascus — A345

1985, Aug. 12   *Perf. 12x12¹/₂*
1038 A345 60p multi   60 30

Labor
Day — A346

1985, Aug. 12   *Perf. 12¹/₂*
1039 A346 60p Order of Labor   60 30

32nd Intl. Fair,
Damascus
A347

1986, Feb. 1   Litho.   *Perf. 12¹/₂*
1040 A347 60p multi   50 25

2nd Scientific Symposium — A348

1985, Nov. 16   *Perf. 12¹/₂*
1041 A348 60p Locomotives   60 30

UN Child
Survival
Campaign
A349

1985, Nov. 16   *Perf. 12¹/₂x12*
1042 A349 60p Malnourished child   50 25

UN, 40th
Anniv. — A350

1985, Nov. 16   *Perf. 12x12¹/₂*
1043 A350 245p multi   2.25 1.10

November 16th Movement, 15th
Anniv. — A351

1985, Nov. 16   *Perf. 12¹/₂*
1044 A351 60p Pres. Assad, highway   50 25

Abdul Rahman Dakhei in Andalusia, 1200th Anniv. A352

1986, Feb. 1   *Perf. 12¹/₂x12*
1045 A352 60p beige & brn   60 30

Tulips — A353   World Traffic Day — A355

Dental Congress, Damascus A354

1986, Feb. 1   *Perf. 12¹/₂*
1046 A353 30p multi   30 15
1047 A353 60p multi, diff.   60 30

Intl. Flower Show, Damascus.

1986   *Perf. 12¹/₂x12*
1048 A354 110p yel, grysh grn & bl   1.10 55

1986   *Perf. 12x12¹/₂*
1049 A355 330p multi   3.00 1.50

Syrian Investment Certificates, 15th Anniv. — A357   Day of Internal Security Forces — A359

Liberation of Al-Kuneitra, 12th Anniv. A358

1986   *Litho.*   *Perf. 12x11¹/₂*
1055 A357 100p multi   1.00 50

1986   *Litho.*   *Perf. 11¹/₂x12*
1056 A358 110p Government Building   75 40

1986   *Perf. 12x11¹/₂*
1057 A359 110p multi   75 40

Labor Day — A360   1986 World Cup Soccer Championships, Mexico — A361

1986, Aug. 12
1058 A360 330p multi   1.25 60

1986, July 7
1059 A361 330p multi   3.25 1.75
1060 A361 370p multi   3.50 1.90

Booklet Stamp
Size: 105x80mm
Imperf
1061 A361 500p Hemispheres, ball   5.00 2.50

Pres. Hafez al Assad — A362

1986-90   *Litho.*   *Perf. 12x11¹/₂*
1068 A362 10p rose   15 15
1069 A362 30p dl ultra   20 15
1070 A362 50p claret   38 15
1071 A362 100p brt lt bl   65 32
1072 A362 150p brn vio   1.40 65
1073 A362 175p violet   1.65 80
1074 A362 200p pale red brn   1.40 65
1075 A362 300p brt rose lil   2.00 1.00
1076 A362 500p orange   3.25 1.65
1077 A362 550p pink   5.00 2.50
1078 A362 600p dull grn   5.25 2.75
1079 A362 1000p brt pink   6.50 3.25
1080 A362 2000p pale grn   13.00 6.50
    Nos. 1068-1080 (13)   40.83 20.52

Issue dates: 150p, 175p, 550p, 600p, 1988. 50p, Oct. 30, 1990.

Intl. Day for Solidarity with the Palestinian People — A363   Mothers' Day — A364

1986, Aug. 7   *Litho.*
1081 A363 110p multi   1.10 55

1986, Aug. 7
1082 A364 100p multi   1.00 50

March 8 Revolution, 23rd Anniv. A365

1986, Aug. 7   *Perf. 11¹/₂x12*
1083 A365 110p multi   1.10 55

Arab Post Day — A366

1986, Aug. 7
1084 A366 110p multi   1.10 55

A367

33rd Intl. Damascus Fair — A368

1986, Dec. 9   *Litho.*   *Perf. 11¹/₂x12*
1085 A367 110p multi   90 45
1086 A368 330p multi   2.50 60

14th Intl. Flower Show, Damascus — A369

Various flowers.

1986, Oct. 11   *Perf. 12¹/₂*
1087   Strip of 5   6.50 3.50
  a. A369 10p multi   15 15
  b. A369 50p multi   52 28
  c. A369 100p multi   1.00 50
  d. A369 100p multi   1.10 60
  e. A369 330p multi   3.50 1.75

Syria-Soviet Joint Space Project — A370   World Children's Day — A371

1986, Nov. 16   *Litho.*   *Perf. 12¹/₂*
1088 A370 330p multi   3.50 1.75

1986   *Perf. 12x12¹/₂, 12¹/₂x12*
1089 A371 330p shown   1.75 90
1090 A371 330p Youth art exhibi-   1.75 90
    tion, horiz.

World Post Day — A372

1986, Jan. 28   *Perf. 12¹/₂x12*
1091 A372 330p multi   1.75 90

Intl. Tourism Day — A373

Women wearing folk costumes, landmarks.

1986
1092 A373 330p multi   1.75 90
1093 A373 370p multi   2.00 1.00

Pres. Assad, Tishreen Palace — A374

1986, Nov. 16   *Litho.*   *Perf. 12¹/₂*
1094 A374 110p multi   1.25 60

Nov. 16 Corrective Movement.

March 8th Revolution, 24th Anniv. — A375

1987, Mar. 6
1095 A375 100p multi   60 32

Intl. Peace Year — A376

1987, Mar. 8   *Perf. 12x11¹/₂*
1096 A376 370p multi   2.25 1.20

Arab Baath Socialist Party, 40th Anniv. — A377

1987, Apr. 7   *Litho.*   *Perf. 12¹/₂*
1097 A377 100p multi   60 32

Arab Post Day, 35th Anniv. A378

1987, May 1 *Perf. 11¹/₂x12*
1098 A378 110p multi 72 35

Evacuation, Day, 41st Anniv. A379

1987, Apr. 17 *Perf. 12¹/₂x12*
1099 A379 100p multi 60 32

Labor Day — A380   Al-Kuneitra Monument — A382

Hitteen's Battle, 800th Anniv. — A381

1987, May 1 *Perf. 12x11¹/₂*
1100 A380 330p multi 2.00 1.00

1987, June 25 Litho. *Perf. 12¹/₂*
1101 A381 110p multi 1.00 45

1987, June 25 *Perf. 12x11¹/₂*
1102 A382 100p multi 65 32

Child Vaccination Campaign A383

1987, June 25 *Perf. 11¹/₂x12*
1103 A383 100p multi 50 32
1104 A383 330p multi 2.00 1.10

A384

A385

Syrian-Soviet Joint Space Flight, July 22-30 — A386

Designs: No. 1105, Launch, July 22. No. 1106, Docking at space station, July 24. No. 1107, Landing, July 30, vert. No. 1108a, Lift-off. No. 1108b, Parachute landing. No. 1108c, Docked at space station. No. 1108d, Cosmonauts.

Perf. 12¹/₂, 11¹/₂x12, 12x11¹/₂
1987 Litho.
1105 A384 330p multi 2.00 1.00
1106 A385 330p multi 2.00 1.00
1107 A385 330p multi 2.00 1.00

Souvenir Sheet
Imperf
1108 Sheet of 4 10.00 10.00
a.-d. A386 300p, any single 2.25 2.25

6th Conference of Arab Ministers of Culture — A387

1987, Apr. 21 Litho. *Perf. 12¹/₂*
1109 A387 330p dull blue grn & blk 3.00 1.50

President Assad Conversing with Syrian Cosmonaut — A388

1987
1110 A388 500p multi 3.50 1.75

10th Mediterranean Games, Latakia — A389

Designs: 100p, Gymnastic rings, weight lifting, vert. 330p, Phoenician sailing ship. 370p, Flags spelling "SYRIA." No. 1115a, Emblem, gymnastics. No. 1115b, Emblem, weight lifting. No. 1115c, Emblem, tennis. No. 1115d, Emblem, soccer.

Perf. 12x11¹/₂, 11¹/₂x12
1987, Sept. 10
1111 A389 100p brt rose lil & blk 68 35
1112 A389 110p shown 75 38
Size: 58x28mm
Perf. 12¹/₂
1113 A389 330p multi 2.25 1.15
1114 A389 370p multi 2.50 1.25
Souvenir Sheet
Imperf
1115 Sheet of 4 7.75 7.75
a.-d. A389 300p any single 1.90 1.90

34th Intl. Damascus Fair — A390   Arbor Day — A392

Intl. Flower Show, Damascus A391

1987 *Perf. 12x11¹/₂*
1116 A390 330p multi 2.00 1.00

1987, Oct. 20 *Perf. 11¹/₂x12*
1117 A391 330p Poppies 1.90 1.00
1118 A391 370p Gentian 2.00 1.00

1987, Oct. 20 *Perf. 12x11¹/₂*
1119 A392 330p multi 2.00 1.00

Army Day — A393   Intl. Palestine Day — A394

1987, Oct. 20 Litho. *Perf. 12x11¹/₂*
1120 A393 100p multi 60 30

1987, Nov. 16
1121 A394 500p multi 3.50 1.75

Corrective Movement, 17th Anniv. — A395

1987, Nov. 16 *Perf. 12¹/₂*
1122 A395 150p Assad waving to crowd 1.00 50

World Post Day — A396

1988, Mar. 8 Litho. *Perf. 12¹/₂x12*
1123 A396 500p multi 3.00 1.50

Intl. Tourism Day — A397

Women wearing folk costumes and: No. 1124, Palmyra Ruins. No. 1125, Reconstructed Roman amphitheater, Busra.

1988, Feb. 25 Litho. *Perf. 11¹/₂x12*
1124 A397 500p multi 3.00 1.50
1125 A397 500p multi 3.00 1.50

See Nos. 1147-1148, 1178-1179.

Intl. Children's Day — A398

1988, Feb. 27 *Perf. 12¹/₂*
1126 A398 500p multi 3.00 1.50

March 8th Revolution, 25th Anniv. — A399   Mothers' Day — A400

1988, Mar. 15 Litho. *Perf. 12x11¹/₂*
1127 A399 150p multi 98 50
Size: 110x81mm
Imperf
1128 A399 500p multi, diff. 4.75 4.75

No. 1128 pictures vignette like 150p without denomination, in diff. colors, and Arab Revolt flag, text, outline map; denomination at LR in sheet.

1988, Apr. 12 Litho. *Perf. 12x12¹/₂*
1129 A400 500p multi 3.00 1.50

Arab Post Day — A401

1988, Apr. 17 *Perf. 12¹/₂x12*
1130 A401 150p multi 98 50

1946 Evacuation A402   Labor Day A403

1988, Apr. 17 *Perf. 12x12¹/₂*
1131 A402 150p multi 98 50

1988, May 1
1132 A403 550p multi 3.00 1.50

Intl. Flower Show, Damascus — A404

Arab Engineers' Union — A405

1988, May 25 — *Perf. 12x11 1/2*
1133 A404 550p Tiger Lily — 3.25 1.65
1134 A404 600p Carnations — 3.75 1.90

1988, May 25
1135 A405 150p multi — 98 50

A406   A407

1988, Aug. 28 — *Litho. Perf. 12x11 1/2*
1136 A406 600p blk, grn & olive — 3.50 1.75
Intl. Children's Day.

1988, Aug. 28 — *Perf. 12 1/2*
1137 A407 550p multi — 3.00 1.50
Restoration of San'a, Yemen Arab Republic.

Ebla Intl. Symposium on Archaeology of Idlib — A408

1988, Aug. 28
1138 A408 175p Hieroglyphic tablet — 1.00 50
1139 A408 550p Bas-relief (votive basin) — 3.00 1.50
1140 A408 600p Gold statue, 3000 B.C. — 3.50 1.75

1988 Summer Olympics, Seoul A409

1988, Sept. 17 — *Perf. 11 1/2x12*
1141 A409 550p Cycling — 3.25 1.65
1142 A409 600p Soccer — 3.50 1.75

Size: 81x61mm
Imperf
1143 A409 1200p Emblem, character trademark — 12.50 12.50

35th Intl. Fair, Damascus — A410

WHO, 40th Anniv. — A411

1988, Aug. 28 — *Perf. 12x11 1/2*
1144 A410 600p multi — 3.50 1.75

1988, Aug. 28 — *Litho. Perf. 12x11 1/2*
1145 A411 600p multi — 3.25 1.65

Arab Scouting Movement, 50th Anniv. — A412

1988, Sept. 17 — *Perf. 12 1/2x12*
1146 A412 150p multi — 1.50 75

Tourism Type of 1988

Women wearing folk costumes on: 550p, Euphrates Bridge, Deir-ez-Zor, 600p, The Tetrapylon, Latakia.

1988, Oct. 18
1147 A397 550p multi — 3.20 1.60
1148 A397 600p multi — 3.50 1.75

World Post Day — A413

Arbor Day — A414

1988, Dec. 7 — *Litho. Perf. 12x12 1/2*
1149 A413 600p multi — 3.50 1.80

1988, Nov. 16
1150 A414 600p multi — 3.50 1.80

Shelter for the Homeless — A415

1988-89 — *Perf. 12 1/2x12*
1151 A415 150p Arab Housing Day — 68 35
1151A A415 175p Intl. Year of Shelter for the Homeless — 1.20 60
1152 A415 550p World Housing Day — 2.45 1.20
1153 A415 600p as No. 1151A — 2.70 1.35

The IYSH emblem is pictured on the 175p, 550p and 600p.

Issue dates: 175p, Feb 6, 1989. Others, Oct. 18, 1988.

Al-Assad University Hospital — A416

1988, Nov. 16 — *Litho. Perf. 12 1/2*
1154 A416 150p multi — 90 45
Corrective Movement, 18th anniv.

World Food Day — A417

1988, Oct. 18 — *Perf. 12x12 1/2*
1155 A417 550p multi — 2.75 1.40

Birds A418

1989, Mar. 21 — *Litho. Perf. 11 1/2x12*
1156 A418 600p Goldfinch — 1.50 75
1157 A418 600p Turtledove — 1.50 75
1158 A418 600p Bee eater — 1.50 75

Jawaharlal Nehru, 1st Prime Minister of Independent India — A419

1989, Mar. 8 — *Perf. 12 1/2*
1159 A419 550p brn & chest — 1.15 58

Mothers' Day — A420

1989, Mar. 21
1160 A420 550p multi — 1.15 58

Teacher's Day — A421

1989, Mar. 8 — *Litho. Perf. 11 1/2x12*
1161 A421 175p multi — 68 35

5th General Congress of the Union of Women — A422

1989, Mar. 8 — *Perf. 12 1/2*
1162 A422 150p multi — 32 16

March 8th Revolution, 26th Anniv. A423

1989, Mar. 8 — *Perf. 11 1/2x12*
1163 A423 150p multi — 32 16

Arab Board for Medical Specializations, 10th Anniv. — A424

1989, Feb. 6 — *Perf. 12 1/2*
1164 A424 175p multi — 60 30

1946 Evacuation of British and French Troops A425

1989, Apr. 17 — *Litho. Perf. 11 1/2x12*
1165 A425 150p multi — 38 20

Intl. Flower Show, Damascus A426

1989, June 3 — *Perf. 12 1/2*
1166 Strip of 5 — 5.15 2.55
a. A426 150p Snapdragon — 30 15
b. A426 150p Canaria — 30 15
c. A426 450p Compositae — 92 45
d. A426 850p Clematis sackmani — 1.75 88
e. A426 900p Gesneriaceae — 1.85 92

N·E·W
Scott Supplement Pages for
Syria
are now available

A427   A428

1989, May 1   *Perf. 12x11½*
1167 A427 850p blue grn & blk   1.75   88

Labor Day.

1989, June 6   Litho.   *Perf. 12x11½*
1168 A428 175p multi   50   25

13th General Congress of the Arab Teachers' Union.

Arab Post Day — A429   Liberation of Al-Kuneitra, 15th Anniv. — A430

1989, June 6
1169 A429 175p multi   50   25

1989, June 26
1170 A430 450p multi   1.20   60

17th Congress of the Arab Advocates Union A431

1989, June 19   *Perf. 11½x12*
1171 A431 175p multi   50   25

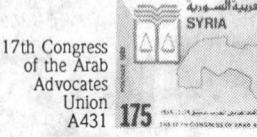

World Post Day — A432

1989, June 26
1172 A432 550p multi   1.50   75

World Telecommunications Day — A433

1989, June 6
1173 A433 550p multi   1.50   75

Interparliamentary Union, Cent. — A434

1989, July 12   *Perf. 12½*
1174 A434 900p multi   2.50   1.25

Butterflies A435

1989, June 6
1175 A435 550p Small white   1.50   75
1176 A435 550p Clouded yellow   1.50   75
1177 A435 550p Painted Lady   1.50   75

Intl. Tourism Day Type of 1988

Women wearing folk costumes and: 550p, Jaabar Castle, Rakka. 600p, Temple of the Bell, Palmyra.

1989, Oct. 16   Litho.   *Perf. 11½x12*
1178 A397 550p multicolored   3.75   1.85
1179 A397 600p multicolored   4.10   2.05

36th Intl. Fair, Damascus — A436

1989, Oct. 16   *Perf. 12x11½*
1180 A436 450p multicolored   3.10   1.55

Fish — A437

1989, Oct. 24   *Perf. 11½x12*
1181 A437 550p Carp   3.75   1.85
1182 A437 600p Trout   4.10   2.05

2nd Anniv. of the Palestinian Uprising — A438

1989, Oct. 24   *Perf. 12x11½*
1183 A438 550p Child's drawing   3.75   1.85

Corrective Movement, 19th Anniv. — A439

1989, Nov. 16   Litho.   *Perf. 12½x12*
1184 A439 150p multicolored   1.05   52

A440   A441

1990, Feb. 13   Litho.   *Perf. 12x11½*
1185 A440 850p multicolored   1.00   50

World Children's Day.

1990
1186 A441 600p multicolored   70   35

March 8th Revolution, 27th anniv.

Revolutionary Youth Union — A442

1990   *Perf. 12½*
1187 A442 150p multicolored   18   15

World Food Day — A443

1990, Feb. 13   Litho.   *Perf. 11½x12*
1188 A443 850p multicolored   1.00   50

Dated 1989.

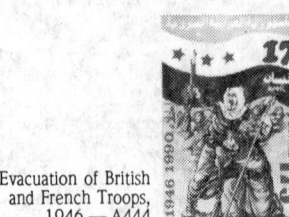

Evacuation of British and French Troops, 1946 — A444

1990, Apr. 17   *Perf. 12x11½*
1189 A444 175p multicolored   20   15

Mother's Day — A445

1990, Apr. 17   *Perf. 12½*
1190 A445 550p multicolored   65   32

Labor Day — A446

1990, May 1   Litho.   *Perf. 12x12½*
1191 A446 550p multicolored   75   38

World Cup Soccer Championships, Italy — A447

Perf. 11½x12, 12x11½
1990, June 8   Litho.
1192 A447 550p shown   42   20
1193 A447 550p Denomination at right   42   20
1194 A447 600p Map, soccer ball, vert.   45   22

Miniature Sheet
Imperf
1195 A447 1300p Stadium   3.60   1.80

Intl. Flower Show, Damascus — A448

1990, May 27   *Perf. 12x11½*
1196 A448 600p Lily   45   22
1197 A448 600p Pastelkleurig   45   22
1198 A448 600p Marigold   45   22
1199 A448 600p Viburnum opulus   45   22
1200 A448 600p Swan river daisy   45   22
   Nos. 1196-1200 (5)   2.25   1.10

World Health Day — A449

1990, May 1   Litho.   *Perf. 12½*
1201 A449 600p multicolored   2.40   1.20

Liberation of Al-Kuneitra, 16th Anniv. — A450

Intl. Literacy Year — A451

1990, June 26   *Perf. 12x11½*
1202 A450 550p multicolored   2.60 1.30

1990, June 26   *Perf. 12x11½*
1203 A451 550p multicolored   2.25 1.10

UN Conference on Least Developed Countries A452

1990, July 10   *Perf. 11½x12*
1204 A452 600p multicolored   2.40 1.20

37th Damascus Intl. Fair — A453

Arbor Day — A455

World Meteorology Day — A454

1990, Aug. 28   *Perf. 12x11½*
1205 A453 550p multicolored   2.25 1.10

1990, Aug. 28   *Perf. 11½x12*
1206 A454 450p multicolored   1.90 95

1990, Oct. 30   *Perf. 12x11½*
1207 A455 550p multicolored   2.25 1.10

World Food Day — A456

1990, Oct. 30   *Perf. 12½*
1208 A456 850p multicolored   3.40 1.70

Al Maqdisi, Cartographer -— A457

1990, Nov. 6   *Perf. 12x11½*
1209 A457 550p multicolored   2.25 1.10

A458   A459

Pres. Hafez al Assad A460

1990, Nov. 16   Litho.   *Perf. 11½*
1210 A458 50p claret   20 15
1211 A458 70p gray   28 15
1212 A458 100p blue   40 20
1213 A458 150p brown   60 30
    Perf. 12x11½
1214 A459 175p multicolored   70 35
1215 A459 300p multicolored   1.20 60
1216 A459 550p multicolored   2.25 1.10
1217 A459 600p multicolored   2.40 1.20
    Perf. 11½x12
1219 A460 1000p multicolored   4.00 2.00
1220 A460 1500p multicolored   6.00 3.00
1222 A460 2000p multicolored   8.00 4.00
1224 A460 2500p multicolored   10.00 5.00
   Nos. 1210-1224 (12)   36.03 18.05

This may be an expanding set. Numbers will change if necessary.

1992, May 19   Litho.   *Perf. 11½*
    Without Date at Right
1225 A458 150p brown   60 30
1225A A458 300p violet   1.20 60
1225B A458 350p gray   1.40 70
1225C A458 400p red   1.60 80

Souvenir Sheet

Corrective Movement, 20th Anniv. — A461

Designs: a, Pres. Assad with children. b, Assad addressing crowd. c, Assad, memorial. d, Assad, dam.

1990, Nov. 16   *Imperf.*
1227 A461 550p Sheet of 4, #a.-d.   9.00 9.00

UN Development Program, 40th Anniv. A462

1990, Dec. 11   *Perf. 11½x12*
1228 A462 550p multicolored   2.25 1.10

Arab Civil Aviation Day — A463

1990, Dec. 11
1229 A463 175p multicolored   1.00 50

World Post Day — A464   Intl. Children's Day — A465

1990, Dec. 11   *Perf. 12x11½*
1230 A464 550p multicolored   2.25 1.10

1990, Dec. 11
1231 A465 550p multicolored   2.25 1.10

Arab-Spanish Cultural Symposium A466   World AIDS Day A467

1990, Dec. 24
1232 A466 550p multicolored   2.25 1.10

1990, Dec. 24
1233 A467 550p multicolored   2.25 1.10

March 8th Revolution, 28th Anniv. A468

1991, Mar. 8   Litho.   *Perf. 11½x12*
1234 A468 150p multicolored   60 30

Butterflies — A469

1991, Mar. 17   *Perf. 12½*
1235 A469 550p Small tortoiseshell   2.25 1.10
1236 A469 550p Changeful great mars   2.25 1.10
1237 A469 550p Papilion machaon   2.25 1.10

Birds — A470   Mother's Day — A471

1991, Mar. 17   *Perf. 12x11½*
1238 A470 600p Golden oriole   2.40 1.20
1239 A470 600p European roller   2.40 1.20
1240 A470 600p House sparrow   2.40 1.20

1991, Mar. 21
1241 A471 550p multicolored   2.25 1.10

1946 Evacuation of British and French Troops A472

1991, Apr. 17   *Perf. 11½x12*
1242 A472 150p multicolored   60 30

Labor Day — A473

1991, May 1
1243 A473 550p multicolored   2.25 1.10

Intl. Flower Show, Damascus — A474

1991, July 8   *Perf. 12x12½*
1244 A474 550p Narcissus   2.25 1.10
1245 A474 600p Monarda didyma   2.40 1.20

Liberation of Kuneitra, 17th Anniv. A475

1991, July 22   *Perf. 11½x12*
1246 A475 550p multicolored   2.25 1.10

11th Mediterranean Games, Athens — A476

1991, July 22
1247 A476 550p Running   2.25 1.10
1248 A476 550p Soccer   2.25 1.10
1249 A476 600p Equestrian   2.40 1.20
Size: 80x64mm
Imperf
1250 A476 1300p Dolphins playing
         water polo   5.30 5.30

38th Damascus Intl. Fair — A477

1991, Aug. 28   *Perf. 12x12½*
1251 A477 550p multicolored   2.25 1.10

Intl. Tourism Day — A478

Designs: 450p, Woman at Khan Asaad Pasha El Azem. 550p, Woman at Castle of Arwad Island.

1991, Sept. 27   *Perf. 11½x12*
1252 A478 450p multicolored   1.90 95
1253 A478 550p multicolored   2.25 1.10

Housing Day — A479   Intl. Children's Day — A480

1991, Oct. 7   *Perf. 12x11½*
1254 A479 175p multicolored   1.00 50

1991, Oct. 16
1255 A480 600p multicolored   2.40 1.20

Physician Abu Bakr Al Razi (Rhazes), Patient A481

1991, Nov. 2   Litho.   *Perf. 12½x12*
1256 A481 550p multicolored   2.25 1.10
    31st Science Week.

World Post Day — A482

1991, Nov. 12
1257 A482 550p multicolored   2.25 1.10

World Food Day — A483

1991, Nov. 12
1258 A483 550p multicolored   2.25 1.10

Tomb of Unknown Soldier, Damascus A484

1991, Nov. 16   *Perf. 12½*
1259 A484 600p multicolored   2.40 1.20
Size: 65x80mm
Imperf
1260 A484 1000p multicolored   4.00 2.00

Corrective Movement, 21st Anniv. — A485

Illustration reduced.

1991, Nov. 16   *Imperf.*
1261 A485 2500p multicolored   10.00 5.00

Protect the Environment A486

1991, Nov. 20   *Perf. 12½x12*
1262 A486 175p multicolored   70 35

World Telecommunications Fair — A487

1991, Nov. 20   *Perf. 12x12½*
1263 A487 600p multicolored   2.40 1.20

March 8th Revolution, 29th Anniv. — A488

1992, Mar. 8   Litho.   *Perf. 12½*
1264 A488 600p multicolored   2.40 1.20

1992   POSTAGE   5000

Re-election of Pres. Assad — A489

1992, Mar. 12   Litho.   *Imperf.*
1265 A489 5000p shown   20.00 10.00
Size: 100x85mm
1266 A489 5000p inscription at
         right   20.00 10.00
Nos. 1265-1266 incorporate designs of #1036, C496 & C506.

Baath Party, 45th Anniv. A490

1992, Apr. 7   *Perf. 12½x12*
1267 A490 850p multicolored   3.40 1.70

Labor Day — A491   Mother's Day — A492

1992, May 1   *Perf. 12x12½*
1268 A491 900p multicolored   3.60 1.80

1992, May 19
1269 A492 900p multicolored   3.60 1.80

Evacuation of British and French Troops, 46th Anniv. A493

1992, May 19   *Perf. 12½x12*
1270 A493 900p multicolored   3.60 1.80

Traffic Safety Day — A494   Intl. Flower Show, Damascus — A495

1992, May 19   *Perf. 12x12½*
1271 A494 850p multicolored   3.40 1.70

    Perf. 11½x12, 12x11½
1992, July 5   Litho.
Designs: 300p, Linum mucronatum, horiz. 800p, Yucca filamentosa. 900p, Zinnia elegans.

1272 A495 300p multicolored   1.20 60
1273 A495 800p blue & multi   3.20 1.60
1274 A495 900p multicolored   3.60 1.80

1992 Summer Olympics, Barcelona — A496

Designs: No. 1275a, 150p, Team handball. b, 150p, Running. c, 450p, Swimming. d, 750p, Wrestling. 5000p, Incorporates designs of Nos. 1275a-1275d.

1992, July 25   Litho.   *Perf. 12x11½*
1275 A496   Strip of 4, #a.-d.   6.00 3.00
         Imperf
    Size: 80x124mm
1276 A496 5000p multicolored   20.00 10.00

Anti-Smoking Campaign — A497

39th Intl. Damascus Fair — A498

1992, Aug. 28   *Perf. 12x12¹/₂*
1277 A497 750p multicolored   3.00 1.50

1992, Aug. 28
1278 A498 900p multicolored   3.60 1.80

7th Arab Games, Damascus — A499

Designs: a, 750p, Soccer. b, 850p, Pommel horse. c, 900p, Pole vault.

1992, Sept. 4   *Perf. 12¹/₂*
1279 A499   Strip of 3, #a.-c.   10.00 5.00

World Post Day — A500

World Children's Day — A501

1992, Oct. 9   *Perf. 12x12¹/₂*
1280 A500 600p multicolored   2.40 1.20

1992, Nov. 7   *Perf. 12x11¹/₂*
1281 A501 850p multicolored   3.40 1.70

Sebtt El Mardini (826-912) — A502

1992, Nov. 7   Litho.   *Perf. 12x11¹/₂*
1282 A502 850p multicolored   3.40 1.70

1992 Special Olympics, Madrid — A503

1992, Nov. 7   *Perf. 12¹/₂*
1283 A503 850p multicolored   3.40 1.70

Corrective Movement, 22nd Anniv. A504

1992, Nov. 16   *Perf. 11¹/₂x12*
1284 A504 450p multicolored   1.80 90

Arbor Day — A505

1992, Dec. 31   *Perf. 12x12¹/₂*
1285 A505 600p multicolored   2.40 1.20

2nd Intl. Conference of PACO A506

Design: 1150p, Eye surrounded by scenes of day and night, rainbow.

1993, May 12   Litho.   *Perf. 12*
1286 A506 1100p multicolored   1.00 50
Size: 35¹/₂x24mm
    Perf. 11¹/₂x12
1287 A506 1150p multicolored   1.10 55
Syrian Ophthamological Society, 25th anniv. (#1287).

March 8th Revolution, 30th Anniv. A507

1993, Mar. 8   Litho.   *Perf. 11¹/₂x12*
1288 A507 1100p multicolored   80 40

Butterflies A508

Designs: a, 1000p, Common blue. b, 1500p, Silver-washed fritillary. c, 2500p, Precis orithya.

1993, Mar. 13
1289 A508   Strip of 3, #a.-c.   4.80 2.40

Mother's Day — A509

1993, Apr. 17   *Perf. 12x11¹/₂*
1290 A509 1100p multicolored   80 40

Evacuation of British and French Troops, 47th Anniv. A510

1993, Apr. 17   *Perf. 11¹/₂x12*
1291 A510 1100p multicolored   80 40

A511

1993, Apr. 17   Litho.   *Perf. 11¹/₂x12*
1292 A511 2500p multicolored   1.75 85

Agricultural Reform, 25th Anniv. A512

1993, Apr. 20   Litho.   *Perf. 11¹/₂x12*
1293 A512 1150p multicolored   92 46

A513   A514

1993, May 1   *Perf. 12x11¹/₂*
1294 A513 1100p multicolored   80 40
Labor day.

1993, June 17   Litho.   *Perf. 12x11¹/₂*
Intl. Flower Show, Damascus: a, 1000p, Alcea setosa. b, 1100p, Primulaceae. c, 1150p, Gesneriaceae.
1295 A514   Strip of 3, #a.-c.   2.25 2.25

Tourism A515

1993, Sept. 27   *Perf. 11¹/₂x12*
1296 A515 1000p Woman, prism tomb   1.00 50

World Post Day — A516

1993, Oct. 9   *Perf. 12¹/₂x12*
1297 A516 1000p multicolored   1.00 50

World Child Day — A517

1993, Nov. 6   *Perf. 11¹/₂x12*
1298 A517 1150p multicolored   1.10 55

Ibn El Bittar, Chemist — A518

1993, Nov. 6   *Perf. 12x11¹/₂*
1299 A518 1150p multicolored   1.10 55

Corrective Movement, 23rd Anniv. A519

Illustration reduced.

1993, Nov. 16   Litho.   *Imperf.*
1300 A519 2500p multicolored   2.50 1.25

Arabian Horses — A520

1994, Jan.   Litho.   *Perf. 12¹/₂*
1301 A520 1000p shown   60 30
1302 A520 1000p White horse   60 30
1303 A520 1500p Tan horse   90 45
1304 A520 1500p Black horse   90 45
   a.   Strip of 4, #1301-1304   3.00 1.50

Arbor Day — A521

1994, Jan.   Litho.   *Perf. 12¹/₂x12*
1305 A521 1100p multicolored   1.75 85

40th Intl. Damascus Fair — A522

1994, Jan.
1306 A522 1100p multicolored   1.75 85

Basel Al Assad (1962-94) — A523

1994, Mar. 1   *Perf. 12x12½*
1307 A523 2500p multicolored   4.00 2.00

March 8th Revolution, 31st Anniv. A524

Designs: a, Oranges. b, Mandarin oranges. c, Lemons.

1994, Mar. 8   *Perf. 12½x12*
1308 A524 1500p Strip of 3, #a.-c.   7.50 3.75

Evacuation of British and French Troops, 48th Anniv. A525

1994, Apr. 17
1309 A525 1800p multicolored   2.75 1.40

Mother's Day — A526

1994, May 1   *Litho.*   *Perf. 12½x12*
1310 A526 1800p multicolored   2.75 1.40

Labor Day — A527

1994, May 1
1311 A527 1700p multicolored   2.75 1.40

ILO, 75th Anniv. A528

1994, June 1
1312 A528 1700p multicolored   2.75 1.40

1994 World Cup Soccer Championships, US — A529

Various soccer plays.

1994, June 17   *Perf. 12½*
1313 A529 1700p Pair, #a.-b.   5.75 2.75
Size: 80x80mm
Imperf
1314 A529 4000p multicolored   6.75 3.25

41st Intl. Fair, Damascus — A530   Intl. Flower Show, Damascus — A531

1994, Aug. 3   *Litho.*   *Perf. 12x12½*
1315 A530 1800p multicolored   1.65 80

1994, Aug. 3   *Perf. 12x11½*
Designs: a, Daisies. b, Red flowers. c, Yellow flowers.
1316 A531 1800p Strip of 3, #a.-c.   4.50 2.25

Intl. Olympic Committee, Cent. A532

1994, Aug. 3   *Perf. 11½x12*
1317 A532 1700p multicolored   1.50 75

SEMI-POSTAL STAMPS

Nos. 174-185 Surcharged in Red or Black

اعانات للاجئين
Aff¹   الاجرة
0ᴾ·25   ¼ غ

1926	Unwmk.	Perf. 12½, 13½		
B1	A4	25c + 25c ol blk (R)	75	75
B2	A4	50c + 25c yel grn	75	75
B3	A4	75c + 25c brn org	75	75
B4	A5	1p + 50c magenta	75	75
B5	A4	1.25p + 50c dp grn (R)	75	75
B6	A4	1.50p + 50c rose red	75	75
B7	A4	2p + 75c dk brn (R)	75	75
B8	A4	2.50p + 75c pck bl (R)	75	75
B9	A4	3p + 1p org brn (R)	75	75
B10	A4	5p + 1p violet	75	75
B11	A4	10p + 2p vio brn	75	75
B12	A4	25p + 5p ultra (R)	75	75
		Nos. B1-B12 (12)	9.00	9.00

On No. B4 the surcharge is set in six lines to fit the shape of the stamp.
The surcharge was a contribution to the relief of refugees from the Djebel Druze War. See Nos. CB1-CB4.

> Catalogue values for unused stamps in this section, from this point to the end of the section, are for Never Hinged items.

Syrian Arab Republic

Jordanian Flags on Map of Israel, and Arabs — SP1

1965, June 12   *Litho.*   *Perf. 12x11½*
B13 SP1 12½p + 5p multi   15 15
B14 SP1 25p + 5p multi   15 15
    Set value   20 20

Issued for Palestine Week.

Father with Children and Red Crescent — SP2

1968, May   *Litho.*   *Perf. 12½x12*
B15 SP2 12½p + 2½p multi   25 25
B16 SP2 27½p + 7½p multi   25 25

The surtax was for refugees.

AIR POST STAMPS

POSTE PAR AVION
a

Nos. 35, 45, 47 Handstamped Type "a" in Violet

1920, Dec.	Unwmk.	Perf. 13½		
C1	A22	1p on 5c	72.50	16.50
C2	A20	5p on 15c	140.00	16.00
C3	A18	10p on 40c	225.00	35.00

Nos. 36, 46, 48 Overprinted Type "a" in Violet

1921, June 12
C4 A22 1p on 20c   30.00 16.00
C5 A18 5p on 1fr   175.00 65.00
C6 A18 10p on 2fr   175.00 65.00

Excellent counterfeits exist of Nos. C1-C6.

Nos. 36, 46, 48 Overprinted Type "b"

1921, Oct. 5
C7 A22 1p on 20c   27.50 7.50
C8 A18 5p on 1fr   60.00 12.50
C9 A18 10p on 2fr   90.00 20.00
  a.   Double overprint   165.00 150.00

Nos. 92, 94-96 Overprinted

c   **Poste par Avion**

1922, May 28
C10 A18 2p on 40c   7.50 7.50
  a.   Inverted overprint
C11 A18 3p on 60c   7.50 7.50
C12 A18 5p on 1fr   7.50 7.50
C13 A18 10p on 2fr   7.50 7.50

Nos. 116-119 Overprinted Type "c"

1923, Nov. 22
C14 A18 2p on 40c   11.50 11.50
  b.   Inverted surcharge
C15 A18 3p on 60c   11.50 11.50
C16 A18 5p on 1fr   11.50 11.50
C17 A18 10p on 2fr   11.50 11.50
  b.   Double overprint

Overprinted "Liabn"
C14a A18 2p on 40c   165.00 165.00
C15a A18 3p on 60c   165.00 165.00
C16a A18 5p on 1fr   165.00 165.00
C17a A18 10p on 2fr   165.00 165.00

Nos. 137-140 Overprinted Type "c"

1924, Jan. 13
C18 A18 2p on 40c   95 95
  a.   Double overprint
C19 A18 3p on 60c   95 95
  a.   Inverted overprint   12.50

C20 A18 5p on 1fr   95 95
  a.   Double overprint
C21 A18 10p on 2fr   95 95

Nos. 152, 154, 157-158 Overprinted
طيارة

Avion

1924, July 17
C22 A18 2p on 40c   1.50 1.50
  a.   Inverted overprint   12.50
C23 A18 3p on 60c   1.50 1.50
  a.   Inverted overprint   12.50
  b.   Double overprint   12.50
C24 A18 5p on 1fr   1.50 1.50
C25 A18 10p on 2fr   1.50 1.50
  a.   Inverted overprint   12.50

A V I O N
طيارة

Regular Issue of 1925 Overprinted in Green

1925, Mar. 1
C26 A4 2p dk brn   70 70
C27 A4 3p org brn   70 70
C28 A4 5p violet   70 70
C29 A4 10p vio brn   70 70

Regular Issue of 1925 Overprinted in Red

f

1926
C30 A4 2p dk brn   32 32
  a.   Inverted overprint   12.50
C31 A4 3p org brn   40 40
  a.   Inverted overprint   12.50
C32 A4 5p violet   50 95
  a.   Inverted overprint   12.50
  b.   Double overprint
C33 A4 10p vio brn   50 50
  a.   Inverted overprint   12.50
  b.   Double overprint

Nos. C30-C33 received their first airmail use June 16, 1929, at the opening of the Beirut-Marseille line.
For surcharges see Nos. CB1-CB4.

Regular Issue of 1925 Overprinted Type "f" in Red or Black

1929
C34 A4 50c yel grn (R)   22 22
  b.   Inverted overprint   11.50
  c.   Overprinted on face and back
  d.   Double overprint   11.50
  e.   Double overprint, one inverted   16.00
    Pair, one without overprint
C35 A5 1p magenta (Bk)   30 30
  a.   Reversed overprint
  b.   Red overprint
C36 A4 25p ultra (R)   1.25 1.25
  a.   Inverted overprint   22.50
  b.   Pair, one without overprint

On No. C35, the overprint is vertical, with plane nose down.

No. 197 Overprinted Type "f" in Red

1929, July 9
C37 A4 15p on 25p ultra   75 75
  a.   Inverted overprint

Air Post Stamps of 1926-29 Overprinted in Various Colors

1929, Sept. 5
C38 A4 50c yel grn (R)   90 90
C39 A5 1p mag (Bl)   90 90
C40 A4 2p dk brn (V)   90 90
C41 A4 3p org brn (Bl)   90 90
  a.   Inverted overprint
C42 A4 5p vio (R)   90 90
C43 A4 10p vio brn (Bl)   90 90
C44 A4 25p ultra (R)   90 90
    Nos. C38-C44 (7)   6.30 6.30

Damascus Industrial Exhibition.

AP1

Red Surcharge

1930, Jan. 30
C45 AP1	2p on 1.25p dp grn		45	45
a.	Inverted surcharge			
b.	Double surcharge		16.00	

Plane over Homs — AP2

Designs: 1pi, City Wall, Damascus. 2pi, Euphrates River. 3pi, Temple Ruins, Palmyra. 5pi, Deir-el-Zor. 10pi, Damascus. 15pi, Aleppo, Citadel. 25pi, Hama. 50pi, Zebdani. 100pi, Telebisse.

1931-33   Photo.   Unwmk.
C46 AP2	50c ocher		15	15
C47 AP2	50c blk brn ('33)		28	25
C48 AP2	1p chnt brn		28	22
C49 AP2	2p Prus bl		85	65
C50 AP2	3p bl grn		28	18
C51 AP2	5p red vio		28	18
C52 AP2	10p slate grn		28	18
C53 AP2	15p org red		65	50
C54 AP2	25p org brn		70	65
C55 AP2	50p black		85	75
C56 AP2	100p magenta		90	90
	Nos. C46-C56 (11)		5.50	4.61

Nos. C46 to C56 exist imperforate.
For overprints see Nos. C67-C71, C110-C112, C114-C115, MC1-MC4.

Village of Bloudan AP12

1934, Aug. 2   Engr.   Perf. 12½
C57 AP12	50c yel brn		75	75
C58 AP12	1p green		75	75
C59 AP12	2p pck bl		75	75
C60 AP12	3p red		75	75
C61 AP12	5p plum		75	75
C62 AP12	10p brt vio		9.00	9.00
C63 AP12	15p org brn		9.00	9.00
C64 AP12	25p dk ultra		11.50	11.50
C65 AP12	50p black		19.00	19.00
C66 AP12	100p red brn		37.50	37.50
	Nos. C57-C66 (10)		89.75	89.75

Proclamation of the Republic. Exist imperf.

Air Post Stamps of 1931-33 Overprinted in Red or Black

1936, Apr. 15   Perf. 13½x13, 13½
C67 AP2	50c blk brn		1.50	1.50
C68 AP2	1p chnt brn (Bk)		1.50	1.50
C69 AP2	2p Prus bl		1.50	1.50
C70 AP2	3p bl grn		1.50	1.50
C71 AP2	5p red vio (Bk)		1.50	1.50
	Nos. C67-C71 (5)		7.50	7.50

Industrial Exhibition, Damascus, May 1936.

Syrian Pavilion at Paris Exposition AP13

1937, July 1   Photo.   Perf. 13½
C72 AP13	½p yel grn		70	70
C73 AP13	1p green		70	70
C74 AP13	2p lt brn		70	70
C75 AP13	3p rose red		70	70
C76 AP13	5p brn org		85	85
C77 AP13	10p grnsh blk		1.40	1.40

C78 AP13	15p blue		1.65	1.65
C79 AP13	25p dk vio		1.65	1.65
	Nos. C72-C79 (8)		8.35	8.35

Paris International Exposition. Exist imperf.

Ancient Citadel at Aleppo AP14

Omayyad Mosque and Minaret of Jesus at Damascus AP15

1937   Engr.   Perf. 13
C80 AP14	½ dk vio		15	15
C81 AP15	1p black		15	15
C82 AP14	2p dp grn		15	15
C83 AP15	3p dp ultra		15	15
C84 AP14	5p rose lake		45	45
C85 AP14	10p red brn		38	38
C86 AP14	15p lake brn		1.25	1.25
C87 AP15	25p dk bl		1.65	1.65
	Nos. C80-C87 (8)		4.33	4.33

No. C80 to C87 exist imperforate.
For overprint see No. C109.

Maurice Noguès and Route of France-Syria Flight — AP16

1938, July   Photo.   Perf. 11
C88 AP16	10p dark green		1.10	1.10
a.	Souv. sheet of 4, perf. 13½		11.00	11.00
b.	Perf. 13½		1.90	1.90

10th anniversary of first Marseille-Beirut flight, by Maurice Noguès.
No. C88a exists imperf.; value $200.

Bridge at Deir-el-Zor AP17

1940   Engr.   Perf. 13
C89 AP17	25c brn blk		15	15
C90 AP17	50c peacock bl		15	15
C91 AP17	1p dp ultra		15	15
C92 AP17	2p dk org brn		15	15
C93 AP17	5p green		22	22
C94 AP17	10p rose car		30	30
C95 AP17	50p dk vio		1.00	1.00
	Set value		1.80	1.80

No. C89 to C95 exist imperforate.

President Taj Eddin Hassani AP18

1942   Litho.   Perf. 11½
C96 AP18	10p blue gray		1.25	1.25
C97 AP18	50p gray lilac		1.25	1.25

Proclamation of Independence by the Allies, Sept. 27, 1941.

President Taj Eddin Hassani — AP19

President Hassani and Map of Syria — AP20

1942   Photo.
C98 AP19	10p sl grn & yel grn		1.90	1.90

No. C98 exists imperforate.

1943   Litho.
C99 AP20	2p dull brown		95	95
C100 AP20	10p red violet		95	95
C101 AP20	20p aqua		95	95
C102 AP20	50p rose pink		95	95

Proclamation of United Syria.

Same, Overprinted with Black Border

1943, May 5
C103 AP20	2p dull brown		95	95
C104 AP20	10p red violet		95	95
C105 AP20	20p aqua		95	95
C106 AP20	50p rose pink		95	95

Mourning for President Hassani.
Nos. C99-C106 exist imperf.

President Shukri el Kouatly — AP21

1944
C107 AP21	200p sepia		3.75	3.75
C108 AP21	500p dl bl		6.50	6.50

For overprints see Nos. C113, C116.

Stamps of 1931-44 Overprinted in Black, Blue or Carmine

1944   Perf. 13, 13½, 11½
C109 AP15	10p red brn (Bk)		1.10	1.10
C110 AP2	15p org red		1.10	1.10
C111 AP2	25p org brn		1.10	1.10
C112 AP2	100p magenta		3.50	3.50
C113 AP21	200p brown (C)		4.50	4.50
	Nos. C109-C113 (5)		11.30	11.30

1st congress of Arab lawyers held in Damascus, Sept. 1944.

Nos. C53-C54, C108 Overprinted in Black or Orange

1944
C114 AP2	15p org red		1.10	1.10
C115 AP2	25p org brn		1.10	1.10
C116 AP21	500p dl bl (O)		8.00	8.00

See note after No. 299.

President Shukri el Kouatly AP22

1945, Mar. 15   Litho.   Perf. 11½
C117 AP22	5p pale grn		15	20
C118 AP22	10p dl red		18	20
C119 AP22	15p orange		18	20
C120 AP22	25p lt bl		38	20
C121 AP22	50p lt vio		65	28
C122 AP22	100p dp brn		1.50	50
C123 AP22	200p fawn		3.75	1.75
	Nos. C117-C123 (7)		6.79	3.33

Resumption of constitutional government.

> Catalogue values for unused stamps in this section, from this point to the end of the section, are for Never Hinged items.

Plane and Flock of Sheep AP23

Kattineh Dam AP24

Kanawat, Djebel Druze AP25

Sultan Ibrahim Mosque AP26

1946-47   Perf. 13x13½
C124 AP23	3p rose brn		50	15
C125 AP23	5p lt bl grn ('47)		50	15
C126 AP23	6p dp org ('47)		50	15
C127 AP24	10p sl gray ('47)		16	15
C128 AP24	15p scar ('47)		16	15
C129 AP24	25p blue		22	15
C130 AP25	50p violet		40	20
C131 AP25	100p bl grn		1.50	38
C132 AP25	200p brn ('47)		2.50	80
C133 AP26	300p red brn ('47)		4.50	1.50
C134 AP26	500p ol gray ('47)		9.00	3.00
	Nos. C124-C134 (11)		19.94	6.78

For overprints and surcharges see Nos. C135-C139, C148-C152, C157, C172.

No. C129 Overprinted in Red

1946, Apr. 17
C135 AP24	25p blue		1.00	70

Evacuation of British and French troops from Syria.

Nos. C129-C131 Overprinted in Magenta

1946, Aug. 28
C136 AP24	25p blue		1.00	60
C137 AP25	50p violet		1.60	90
C138 AP25	100p bl grn		3.00	90

See note after No. 334.

No. C135 with Additional Overprint in Black

1947, June 10   **Perf. 13x13½**
C139 AP24 25p blue   1.00 60

1st anniv. of the evacuation of British and French troops from Syria.

Window at Kasr El-Heir El-Gharbi AP27

Ram-headed Sphinxes Carved in Ivory, from King Hazael's Bed — AP28

1947, Nov. 15 Litho. Perf. 11½
C140 AP27 12.50p dk vio   1.00 55
C141 AP28 50p brown   3.00 1.60
  a. Souv. sheet of 4, #338-339,
      C140-C141   26.00 26.00

1st Arab Archaeological Cong., Damascus, Nov., 1947.
No. C141a sold for 125 plasters.

Kasr El-Heir El-Charqui AP29   Congress Emblem AP30

1947, Nov. 15
C142 AP29 12.50p ol blk   70 40
C143 AP30 50p dl vio   2.00 1.25
  a. Souv. sheet of 4, #340, 341,
      C142, C143   25.00 25.00

3rd Congress of Arab Engineers, Damascus, Nov. 1947.
No. C143a sold for 125 plasters.

Kouatly Types of Regular Issue
1948, June 22 Litho. Perf. 10½
C144 A50 12.50p dp bl & vio brn   35 15
C145 A51 50p vio brn & grn   1.60 65
  a. Souv. sheet of 4, #342, 343,
      C144, C145, imperf.   100.00 100.00

Reelection of Pres. Shukri el Kouatly.

Military Training Types of Regular Issue
1948, June 22
C146 A52 12.50p bl & dk bl   50 20
C147 A53 50p grn car & blk   1.60 60
  a. Souv. sheet of 4, #344, 345,
      C146, C147, imperf.   100.00 100.00

Inauguration of compulsory military training.

Nos. C124, C126 and C132 to C134 Surcharged with New Value and Bars in Black or Carmine
1948, Oct. 18   Perf. 13x13½
C148 AP23 2.50p on 3p   15 15
C149 AP23 2.50p on 6p   15 15
C150 AP25 25p on 200p (C)   35 15
C151 AP26 50p on 300p   1.00 40
C152 AP26 50p on 500p   1.00 40
  Nos. C148-C152 (5)   2.65
  Set value   1.00

Husni Zayim Type of Regular Issue
1949, June 20 Litho. Perf. 11½
C153 A54 50p brown   2.25 1.50
Revolution of March 30, 1949.

Pigeons and Globe AP36

Husni Zayim and View of Damascus AP37

1949, June 20   Unwmk.
C154 AP36 12.50p claret   4.50 4.50
C155 AP37 50p gray blk   12.50 9.00

UPU, 75th anniv. A souvenir sheet contains one each of Nos. 349, 350, C154 and C155. Value $125.

Election Type of Regular Issue
Perf. 11½
1949, Aug. 6 Wmk. 291 Litho.
C156 A57 50p car rose & dk grnsh bl 2.25 1.50
  a. Souv. sheet of 2, #351, C156,
      imperf.   100.00 100.00

Election of Pres. Husni Zayim.

No. C131 Surcharged with New Value and Bars in Black
1950 Unwmk. Perf. 13x13½
C157 AP25 2.50p on 100p bl grn   15 15

Port of Latakia AP38

1950, Dec. 25   Perf. 11½
C158 AP38 2.50p dull lilac   35 15
C159 AP38 10p grnsh bl   60 15
C160 AP38 15p org brn   1.50 15
C161 AP38 25p brt bl   3.50 20
  Set value   48

Exist imperf. See No. C173. For overprint see No. C169.

Symbolical of Constitution AP39

1951, Apr. 14   Unwmk.
C162 AP39 12.50p crim rose   22 15
C163 AP39 50p brn vio   70 00

New constitution adopted Sept. 5, 1950. Both values exist imperforate.

Ruins, Palmyra AP40

Citadel at Aleppo AP41

1952, Apr. 22 Litho. Perf. 11½
C164 AP40 2.50p vermilion   15 15
C165 AP40 5p green   22 15
C166 AP40 15p violet   30 15

C167 AP41 25p dp bl   50 22
C168 AP41 100p lil rose   3.00 60
  Nos. C164-C168 (5)   4.17
  Set value   1.05

Nos. C164-C168 exist imperforate.
For overprints see Nos. C170-C171, C186.

Stamps of 1946-52 Overprinted in Black

U.N.S.W.S. Damascus 8-20 Dec. 1952

1953, Feb. 16 Perf. 13x13½, 11½
C169 AP38 10p grnsh bl   1.25 70
C170 AP40 15p violet   1.25 70
C171 AP41 25p dp bl   2.00 1.25
C172 AP41 50p violet   5.50 1.60

UN Social Welfare Seminar, Damascus, Dec. 8-20, 1952.

Type of 1950 and

Post Office, Aleppo AP42

1953, Oct. Photo. Perf. 11½
C173 AP38 10p vio bl   35 15
C174 AP42 50p red brn   1.00 20
  Set value   26

For overprint see No. C185.

Building at Hama and PTT Emblem AP43   University of Syria, Damascus AP44

1954
C175 AP43 5p violet   15 15
C176 AP43 10p brown   20 15
C177 AP43 15p dl grn   20 15
C178 AP44 30p dk brn   40 15
C179 AP44 35p blue   60 15
C180 AP44 40p orange   70 30
C181 AP44 50p deep plum   1.00 40
C182 AP44 70p purple   1.60 50
  Nos. C175-C182 (8)   4.85
  Set value   1.65

For overprints see UAR Nos. C27-C28.

Monument, Damascus Square — AP45   Mosque and Syrian Flag — AP46

1954, Sept. 2
C183 AP45 40p car rose   60 35
C184 AP46 50p green   70 40

Damascus Fair, Sept., 1954.
Nos. C183-C184 exist imperforate.

Nos. C174 and C168 Overprinted in Blue or Black

FESTIVAL du COTON Alep. oct. 1954

1954, Oct. 9
C185 AP42 50p red brn (Bl)   60 50
C186 AP41 100p lil rose   1.50 1.00

Cotton Festival, Aleppo, October 1954.

Virgin of Sednaya Concent AP47   Omayyad Mosque AP48

1955, Mar. 27 Photo. Perf. 11½
C187 AP47 25p dp pur   35 20
C188 AP47 75p dp bl grn   1.25 70

50th anniv. of the founding of Rotary Intl. Exist imperforate.

1955, Mar. 26
C189 AP48 35p cerise   50 30
C190 AP48 65p dp grn   1.00 60

1955 Regional Congress of Rotary Intl., Damascus.

Arab Postal Union Type of Regular Issue
For overprints see Nos. C203, C207.
1955, Jan. 1   Perf. 13½x13
C191 A69a 5p yel brn   20 15

Founding of the APU, July 1, 1954.

Young Couple and View of Damascus AP49

Design: 60p, Tank and planes leading advancing troops.

1955, Apr. 16 Litho. Perf. 11½
C192 AP49 40p dk rose lake   40 30
C193 AP49 60p ultra   60 35

9th anniv. of the evacuation of British and French troops from Syria.

Mother's Day Type of Regular Issue
1955, May 13   Unwmk.
C194 A70 35p violet   60 35
C195 A70 40p black   1.00 40

Issued to publicize Mother's Day.

Emigrants under Syrian Flag — AP51   Mother and Child — AP52

Design: 15p, Airplane over globe and fountain.

1955, July 26   *Perf. 11½*
C196 AP51 5p magenta   35 15
C197 AP51 15p light blue   40 22

Emigrants' Congress. Exist imperf.

1955, Oct. 3   Photo.
C198 AP52 25p dp bl   42 22
C199 AP52 50p plum   80 40

International Children's Day.

Globe, Scales and Dove AP53

1955, Oct. 30
C200 AP53 15p ultra   42 20
C201 AP53 35p brn blk   80 40

10th anniv. of the UN, Oct. 24, 1955.
For overprints see Nos. C221-C222.

Aqueduct Type of Regular Issue
1955, Nov. 21 Litho.   Unwmk.
C202 A72 30p dk bl   1.50 70

No. C191 Overprinted in Ultramarine

1955, Dec. 29 Photo. Perf. 13½x13
C203 A69a 5p yel brn   30 15

APU Congress, Cairo, Mar. 15, 1955.

Liberation Monument — AP54

Designs: 65p, Winged figure with shield and sword. 75p, President Shukri el Kouatly.

1956, Apr. 17 Litho.   Perf. 11½
C204 AP54 35p blk brn   50 35
C205 AP54 65p rose red   65 50
C206 AP54 75p dk slate grn   1.00 70

10th anniv. of the evacuation of British and French troops from Syria.

No. C191 Overprinted in Black

1956, Apr. 11 Photo. Perf. 13½x13
C207 A69a 5p yel brn   30 15

Visit of King Hussein of Jordan to Damascus, Apr. 1956.

President Shukri el Kouatly AP55

Gate of Kasr el Heir, Palmyra AP56

1956, July 7 Litho.   Perf. 11½
C208 AP55 100p black   1.00 70
C209 AP55 200p violet   2.00 1.00
C210 AP55 300p dl rose   5.50 2.00
C211 AP55 500p dk bl grn   5.00 3.50

Nos. CB5-CB8 Overprinted with 3 Bars Obliterating Surtax
1956
C212 SPAP1 25p gray blk   42 18
C213 SPAP2 35p ultra   50 25
C214 SPAP2 40p rose lil   90 38
C215 SPAP1 70p Prus grn   1.25 90

1956, Sept. 1   Unwmk.

Designs: 20p, Hand loom and modern mill. 30p, Ox-drawn plow and tractor. 35p, Cogwheels and galley. 50p, Textiles and vase.

C216 AP56 15p gray   22 22
C217 AP56 20p brt ultra   30 30
C218 AP56 30p bl grn   42 42
C219 AP56 35p blue   55 55
C220 AP56 50p rose lilac   60 60
  Nos. C216-C220 (5)   2.09 2.09

3rd International Fair, Damascus.

#C200-C201 Overprinted in Red or Green

1956, Oct. 30 Photo. Perf. 11½
C221 AP53 15p ultra (R)   70 30
C222 AP53 35p brn blk (G)   1.50 70

United Nations, 11th anniversary.

Clay Tablet with First Alphabet AP57

Helmet of Syrian Legionary and Ornament AP58

Design: 50p, Lintel from Temple of the Sun, Palmyra.

1956, Oct. 8   Typo.
C223 AP57 20p gray   50 30
C224 AP58 30p magenta   70 40
C225 AP57 50p gray brn   1.25 80

Intl. Museum Week (UNESCO), Oct. 8-14.

Trees and Mosque AP59

1956, Dec. 27 Litho.   Perf. 11½
C226 AP59 10p olive bister   20 15
C227 AP59 40p slate green   40 40

Day of the Tree, Dec. 27, 1956.
See UAR No. 36. For overprint see UAR No. 49.

Mother and Child AP60

Sword and Shields AP61

Design: 60p, Mother holding infant.

1957, Mar. 21   Unwmk.
C228 AP60 40p ultra   50 42
C229 AP60 60p vermilion   85 60

Mother's Day, 1957.

1957, Apr. 20   Wmk. 291

Designs: 15p, 35p, Map and "Syria" holding torch. 25p, Pres. Kouatly.

C230 AP61 10p redsh brn   15 15
C231 AP61 15p bl grn   20 15
C232 AP61 25p violet   30 15
C233 AP61 35p cerise   42 30
C234 AP61 40p gray   65 40
  Nos. C230-C234 (5)   1.72
        Set value   98

11th anniv. of the British-French troop evacuation.

Ship Loading — AP62

Sugar Production AP63

Desidn: 30p, 40p, Harvesting grain and cotton.

1975, Sept. 1 Unwmk.   Perf. 11½
C235 AP62 25p magenta   25 24
C236 AP62 30p lt red brn   35 24
C237 AP63 35p lt bl   60 35
C238 AP62 40p bl grn   70 42
C239 AP62 70p ol bis   95 50
  Nos. C235-C239 (5)   2.85 1.75

4th International Fair, Damascus.

Arab Lawyers Type of Regular Issue, 1957
1957, Sept. 21 Litho.   Wmk. 291
C240 A76 17½p red   30 20
C241 A76 40p black   55 35

Cotton Festival Type of Regular Issue, 1957
1957, Oct. 17
C242 A77 17½p org & blk   42 24
C243 A77 40p lt bl & blk   75 35

Children's Day Type of Regular Issue, 1957
1957, Oct. 3
C244 A78 17½p ultra   80 35
C245 A78 20p red brn   80 35

International Children's Day, Oct. 7.
For overprints see UAR Nos. C10-C11.

Family Writing and Reading Letters AP64

1957, Oct. 18 Litho.   Unwmk.
C246 AP64 5p brt grn   30 15

Intl. Letter Writing Week Oct. 6-12.
For overprint see No. C26.

Afro-Asian Jurists Type of Regular Issue, 1957
1957, Nov.   Wmk. 291   Perf. 11½
C247 A80 30p lt bl grn   30 22
C248 A80 50p lt vio   42 35

Type of Regular Issue and

Radio, Telegraph and Telephone — AP65

1958, Feb. 12   *Perf. 11½*
C249 A83 10p brt grn   20 15
C250 AP65 15p brown   22 14
        Set value   20

Syrian Arab Republic

Syrian Flag — AP67

Souvenir Sheet
1961 Unwmk. Litho.   Imperf.
C253 AP67 50p multi   1.90 1.90

Establishment of Syrian Arab Republic.

"The Beauty of Palmyra" — AP68

Archway, Palmyra — AP69

Design: 200p, 300p, 500p, 1000p, Niche, King Zahir Bibar's tomb.

1961-63   Litho.   Perf. 12x11½
C255 AP68 45p citron   30 18
C256 AP68 50p red org   38 25
C257 AP69 85p sepia   65 30
C258 AP69 100p lilac   85 32
C259 AP69 200p sl grn ('62)   1.25 65
C260 AP69 300p dk bl ('62)   1.65 70
C261 AP69 500p lilac ('63)   2.25 1.50
C262 AP69 1000p dk gray ('63) 7.50 2.75
  Nos. C255-C262 (8)   14.83 6.65

See Nos. 433-436.

Arab League Building, Cairo, and Emblem — AP70

Malaria Eradication Emblem — AP71

1962, Apr. 1   *Perf. 12x11¹/₂*
C264 AP70 17¹/₂p Prus grn & yel grn   15 15
C265 AP70 22¹/₂p dk & lt bl   18 15
C266 AP70 50p dk brn & dl org   38 18
    Set value   38

Arab League Week, Mar. 22-28.

1962, Apr. 7
C267 AP71 12¹/₂p ol, lt bl & pur   15 15
C268 AP71 50p brn, yel & grn   30 25
    Set value   34

WHO drive to eradicate malaria.

Prancing Horse — AP72   Gen. Yusef al-Azmeh — AP73

1962, Apr. 17
C269 AP72 45p vio & org   25 15
C270 AP73 55p vio bl & lt bl   38 18

Evacuation Day, 1962.

Martyrs' Square Memorial, Globe and Handshake AP74   Cotton and Cogwheel AP75

Design: 40p, 45p, Eastern Gate at Fair.

1962, Aug. 25   Litho.   *Perf. 12x11¹/₂*
C271 AP74 17¹/₂p rose cl & brn   15 15
C272 AP74 22¹/₂p ver & mag   15 15
C273 AP74 40p vio brn & lt brn   18 15
C274 AP74 45p grnsh bl & lt grn   32 18
    Set value   42

9th International Damascus Fair.

1962, Sept. 20   *Perf. 12x11¹/₂*
C275 AP75 12¹/₂p multi   15 15
C276 AP75 50p multi   30 22
    Set value   30

Cotton Festival, Aleppo. See Nos. 455-456.

President Type of Regular Issue
1962, Dec. 14   Unwmk.
C278 A88 50p bl gray & tan   30 18

1st anniv. of the election of Pres. Nazem el-Kodsi.

Queen Zenobia of Palmyra — AP76   Saad Allah El Jabri — AP77

1962, Dec. 28   *Perf. 12x11¹/₂*
C279 AP76 45p violet   32 15
C280 AP76 50p rose red   42 15
C281 AP76 85p blue green   45 22
C282 AP76 100p rose claret   1.00 32

1962, Dec. 30   Litho.
C283 AP77 50p dull blue   25 15

Saad Allah El Jabri (1894-1947), a leader in Syria's struggle for independence.

Woman from Moharde — AP78   Eagle in Flight — AP79

Regional Costumes: 40p, Marje Sultan. 45p, Kalamoun. 55p, Jabal-Al-Arab. 60p, Afrine. 65p, Hauran.

1963   *Perf. 12*
Costumes in Original Colors
C285 AP78 40p pale lil & blk   18 15
C286 AP78 45p pink & blk   20 15
C287 AP78 50p lt grn & blk   30 18
C288 AP78 55p lt bl & blk   32 22
C289 AP78 60p tan & blk   38 22
C290 AP78 65p pale grn & blk   50 25
    Nos. C285-C290 (6)   1.88 1.17

Hunger Type of Regular Issue

Design: 50p, Wheat emblem and bird feeding nestlings.

    Perf. 12x11¹/₂
1963, Mar. 21   Unwmk.
C291 A91 50p ver & blk   25 15
  a.   Souv. sheet of 2, #453, C291, imperf.   1.10 1.10

FAO "Freedom from Hunger" campaign.

1963, Apr. 18   Litho.
C292 AP79 12¹/₂p brt grn   15 15
C293 AP79 50p lilac rose   25 18
    Set value   30 22

Revolution of Mar. 8, 1963.

Faris el Khouri — AP80   Arms and Wreath — AP81

1963, Apr. 27   *Perf. 12x11¹/₂*
C294 AP80 17¹/₂p gray   15 15
C295 AP81 22¹/₂p bl grn & blk   15 15
    Set value   16

Evacuation Day, 1963.

abu-al-Ala al-Maarri — AP82   Copper Pitcher, Arch and Fair — AP83

1963, Aug. 19   *Perf. 12x11¹/₂*
C296 AP82 50p vio bl   30 22

abu-al-Ala al-Maarri (973-1057), poet and philosopher.

1963, Aug. 25
C297 AP83 37¹/₂p ultra, yel & brn   25 15
C298 AP83 50p brt bl, yel & brn   32 18

10th International Damascus Fair.

Centenary Emblem — AP84   Abou Feras al Hamadani — AP85

Design: 50p, Centenary emblem and globe.

1963, Sept. 19   Litho.
C299 AP84 15p chlky bl, red & blk   25 15
C300 AP84 50p yel grn, blk & red   28 22

Centenary of the International Red Cross.

1963, Nov. 13   *Perf. 12x11¹/₂*
C301 AP85 50p yel ol & dk brn   30 22

Abou Feras (932-968), poet.

Heads of Three Races and Flame — AP86

1964, Jan. 6   Unwmk.
C302 AP86 17¹/₂p multi   15 15
C303 AP86 22¹/₂p grn, blk & red   15 15
C304 AP86 50p vio, blk & red   25 15
  a.   Souv. sheet of 3   90 90
    Set value   28

15th anniv. of the Universal Declaration of Human Rights. No. C304a contains 3 imperf. stamps similar to Nos. C302-C304 with simulated perforations.

Flag, Torch and Map of Arab Countries AP87

1964, Mar. 8   Unwmk.   *Perf. 11¹/₂*
C305 AP87 15p multi   15 15
C306 AP87 17¹/₂p multi   15 15
C307 AP87 22¹/₂p multi   18 15
    Set value   36 20

Revolution of Mar. 8, 1963, 1st anniv.

Kaaba, Mecca, and Mosque, Damascus AP88

1964, Mar. 14   Litho.   *Perf. 11¹/₂x12*
C308 AP88 12¹/₂p bl & blk   15 15
C309 AP88 22¹/₂p rose lil & blk   15 15
C310 AP88 50p lt grn & blk   25 15
    Set value   46 28

First Arab Conference of Moslem Wakf Ministers, Damascus.

Young Couple and View of Damascus AP89

1964, Apr. 17   Unwmk.
C311 AP89 20p blue   15 15
C312 AP89 25p rose car   15 15
C313 AP89 60p emerald   25 15
    Set value   28

Evacuation Day, Apr. 17, 1964.

Abul Kasim (Albucasis) — AP90

1964, Apr. 21   *Perf. 12x11¹/₂*
C314 AP90 60p brown   30 22

4th Arab Congress of Dental and Oral Surgery, Damascus.

Mosaic, Chahba, Thalassa AP91

1964, June-July   Litho.   *Perf. 11¹/₂x12*
C315 AP91 27¹/₂p car rose   15 15
C316 AP91 45p gray   22 15
C317 AP91 50p brt grn   30 15
C318 AP91 55p slate grn   30 18
C319 AP91 60p ultra   40 18
    Nos. C315-C319 (5)   1.37
    Set value   62

Hanging Lamp, Fair Emblem — AP92   Globe and Fair Emblem — AP93

1964, Aug. 28   *Perf. 12x11¹/₂*
C320 AP92 20p multi   18 15
C321 AP93 25p multi   22 15
    Set value   15

11th International Damascus Fair.

Industrial and Agricultural Symbols — AP94

1964, Sept. 22   Litho.   Unwmk.
C322 AP94 25p muld   15 15
Same Overprinted with two Red Lines in Arabic
C323 AP94 25p multi   15 15
    Set value   16

Cotton Festival, Aleppo. Overprint on No. C323 translates: "Market for Industrial and Agricultural Products."

Arms of Syria and Aero Club Emblem AP95

1964, Oct. 8   Litho.   Perf. 11½x12
C324 AP95 12½p emer & blk   15 15
C325 AP95 17½p crim & blk   15 15
C326 AP95 20p brt bl & blk   30 15
    Set value   22

10th anniversary of Syrian Aero Club.

Arab Postal Union Emblem — AP96

Grain and Hands Holding Book — AP97

1964, Nov. 12   Litho.   Perf. 12x11½
C327 AP96 12½p org & blk   15 15
C328 AP96 20p emer & blk   15 15
C329 AP96 25p dp lil rose & blk   15 15
    Set value   32 18

10th anniv. of the permanent office of the APU.

1964, Nov. 30   Unwmk.
C330 AP97 12½p emer & blk   15 15
C331 AP97 17½p mar & blk   15 15
C332 AP97 20p dp bl & blk   15 15
    Set value   32 18

Burning of the library of Algiers, June 7, 1962.

Tennis Player — AP98 SYRIAN ARAB REPUBLIC

Designs: 17½p, Wrestlers and drummer. 20p, Weight lifter. 100p, Wrestlers and drummer, horiz.

1965, Feb. 7   Perf. 12x11½
C333 AP98 12½p multi   15 15
C334 AP98 17½p multi   15 15
C335 AP98 20p multi   18 15

    Set value   38 18
Souvenir Sheet
C336 AP98 100p multi   1.25 1.25

18th Olympic Games, Tokyo, Oct. 10-25, 1964. No. C336 contains one stamp 45x33mm.

Ramses Battling the Hittites AP99

Design: 50p, Two statues of Ramses II.

1965, Mar. 21   Litho.   Perf. 11x12
C337 AP99 22½p emer, ultra & blk   15 15
C338 AP99 50p ultra, emer & blk   25 15
    Set value   22

UNESCO world campaign to save historic monuments in Nubia.

Al-Sharif Al-Radi — AP100

Dagger in Map of Palestine — AP102

Hippocrates and Avicenna — AP101

1965, Apr. 3   Litho.   Perf. 12x11½
C339 AP100 50p gray brn   30 18

5th Poetry Festival held in Latakia; Al-Sharif Al-Radi (970-1015), poet.

1965, Apr. 19   Perf. 11½
C340 AP101 60p dl bl grn & blk   38 30

"Medical Days of the Near and Middle East," a convention held at Damascus Apr. 19-25.

1965, May 15
C341 AP102 12½p multi   15 15
C342 AP102 60p multi   25 18
    Set value   22

Deir Yassin massacre, Apr. 9, 1948.

ITU Emblem, Old and New Communication Equipment — AP103

Perf. 11½x12
1965, May 24   Litho.   Unwmk.
C343 AP103 12½p multi   15 15
C344 AP103 27½p multi   18 15
C345 AP103 60p multi   32 25
    Set value   38

ITU, centenary.

Syrian Welcoming AP104

Bridge and Gate AP105

1965, Aug.   Unwmk.   Perf. 12x11½
C346 AP104 25p pur & multi   15 15
C347 AP104 100p blk & multi   45 22
    Set value   26

Issued to welcome Arab immigrants.

1965, Aug. 28   Litho.
Designs: 27½p, Fair emblem. 60p, Jug and ornaments.
C348 AP105 12½p blk, brt ultra & brn   15 15
C349 AP105 27½p multi   15 15
C350 AP105 60p multi   25 18
    Set value   45 28

12th International Damascus Fair.

Fair Emblem and Cotton Pickers — AP106

1965, Sept. 30   Perf. 12x11½
C351 AP106 25p ol & multi   15 15

10th Cotton Festival, Aleppo.

Same with Red Overprint

1965, Sept. 30
C352 AP106 25p ol & multi   15 15

Industrial and Agricultural Fair, Aleppo.

View of Damascus and ICY Emblem AP107

1965, Oct. 24   Perf. 11½x12
C353 AP107 25p multi   15 15

International Cooperation Year.

Radio Transmitter, Globe, Syrian Flag and View of Damascus AP108

Hand (shaped like a dove) Holding Flower AP109

1966, Feb. 16   Litho.   Perf. 12x11½
C354 AP108 25p multi   15 15
C355 AP108 60p multi   25 15
    Set value   20

3rd Conference of Arab Information Ministers, Damascus, Feb. 14-18.

1966, Mar. 8   Perf. 12x11½, 11½x12
Design: 17½p, Stylized people, horiz.
C356 AP109 12½p multi   15 15
C357 AP109 17½p multi   15 15
C358 AP109 50p multi   45 15
    Set value   58 25

March 8 Revolution, 3rd anniversary.

Statues of Ramses II from Abu Simbel — AP110

1966, Mar. 15   Perf. 12x11½
C359 AP110 25p dk bl   15 15
C360 AP110 60p dk sl grn   25 15
    Set value   20

Arab "Save the Nubian Monument Week."

UN Headquarters Building and Emblem — AP111

Design: 100p, UN Flag.

1966, Apr. 11   Litho.   Perf. 11½x12
C361 AP111 25p blk & gray   15 15
C362 AP111 50p blk & pale grn   22 15
    Set value   30 20
Souvenir Sheet
Imperf
C363 AP111 100p yel, brt bl & blk   90 90

20th anniv. (in 1965) of the UN. No. C363 contains one stamp 42x36mm.

Marching Workers AP112

1966, May 1   Litho.   Perf. 11½x12
C364 AP112 60p multi   25 15

Issued for May Day.

Inauguration of WHO Headquarters,
Geneva — AP113

1966, May 3
C365 AP113 60p blk, bl & yel   25 15

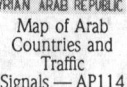

Map of Arab
Countries and
Traffic
Signals — AP114

Astarte & Tyche, 1st
cent. Basrelief,
Palmyra — AP115

1966, May 4   *Perf. 12x11¹/₂*
C366 AP114 25p gray & multi   15 15

Issued to publicize Traffic Day.

1966, July 26 Litho. *Perf. 12x11¹/₂*
C367 AP115 50p pale brn   22 15
C368 AP115 60p slate   32 18

Symbolic Flag,
Wheat, Globe and
Fair
Emblem — AP116

Shuttle and
Symbols of
Agriculture,
Industry and
Cotton — AP117

1966, Aug. 25 Litho. *Perf. 12x11¹/₂*
C369 AP116 12¹/₂p multi   15 15
C370 AP116 60p multi   25 18
        Set value   30 22

13th Intl. Damascus Fair, Aug. 25-Sept. 20.

1966, Sept. 9 Litho. *Perf. 12x11¹/₂*
C371 AP117 50p sil, blk & plum   25 15

11th Cotton Festival, Aleppo.

Symbolic Water
Cycle — AP118

Abd-el
Kader — AP119

1966, Oct. 24 Litho. *Perf. 12x11¹/₂*
C372 AP118 12¹/₂p emer, blk & org   15 15
C373 AP118 60p ultra, blk & org   25 18
        Set value   30 22

Hydrological Decade (UNESCO), 1965-74.

1966, Nov. 7
C374 AP119 12¹/₂p brt grn & blk   15 15
C375 AP119 50p brt grn & red brn   22 18
        Set value   22

Transfer from Damascus to Algiers of the ashes of
Abd-el Kader (1807?-1883), Emir of Mascara.

Clasped Hands over
Map of South
Arabia — AP120

Pipelines and
Pigeons — AP121

1967, Feb. 8 Litho. *Perf. 12x11¹/₂*
C376 AP120 20p pink & multi   15 15
C377 AP120 25p multi   15 15
        Set value   24 15

3rd Congress of Solidarity with the Workers and
People of Aden, Damascus, Jan. 15-18.

1967, Mar. 8 Litho. *Perf. 12x11¹/₂*
C378 AP121 17¹/₂p multi   15 15
C379 AP121 25p multi   15 15
C380 AP121 27¹/₂p multi   15 15
        Set value   38 18

4th anniversary of March 8 Revolution.

Soldier, Woman
and Man Holding
Flag
AP122

Workers'
Monument,
Damascus
AP123

1967, Apr. 17 Litho. *Perf. 12x11¹/₂*
C381 AP122 17¹/₂p green   15 15
C382 AP122 25p dp claret   15 15
C383 AP122 27¹/₂p vio blue   18 15
        Set value   24

21st anniv. of the evacuation of British and
French troops from Syria.

1967, May 1
C384 AP123 12¹/₂p bl grn   15 15
C385 AP123 50p brt pink   25 15
        Set value   30 20

Issued for Labor Day, May 1.

Fair Emblem and
Gate, Minaret,
Omayyad
Mosque — AP124

1967, Aug. 25 Litho. *Perf. 12x12¹/₂*
C386 AP124 12¹/₂p multi   15 15
C387 AP124 60p multi   25 18
        Set value   30 22

14th Intl. Damascus Fair, Aug. 25-Sept. 20.

Statue of Ur-Nina
and ITY Emblem
AP125

1967, Sept. 2   *Perf. 12¹/₂x12*
C388 AP125 12¹/₂p lt bl, brt rose lil &
                blk   15 15
C389 AP125 25p bl bl, ver & blk   15 15
C390 AP125 27¹/₂p lt bl, dk bl & blk 18 15
        Set value   35 20

Souvenir Sheet
Imperf
C391 AP125 60p lt bl & vio bl   50 50

Intl. Tourist Year.

Cotton Boll and
Cogwheel
Segment — AP126

Head of Young
Man, Amrith, 4th-
5th Century
B.C. — AP127

1967, Sept. 28 Litho. *Perf. 12x12¹/₂*
C392 AP126 12¹/₂p ocher, brn & blk   15 15
C393 AP126 60p ap grn, brn & blk   25 15
        Set value   30 20

12th Cotton Festival, Aleppo.

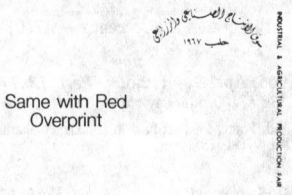

Same with Red
Overprint

1967, Sept. 28
C394 AP126 12¹/₂p multi   15 15
C395 AP126 60p multi   25 15
        Set value   30 20

Industrial and Agricultural Production Fair,
Aleppo.

1967, Oct. 7

Design: 100p, 500p, Bronze bust of a Princess,
2nd century.

C396 AP127 45p orange   18 15
C397 AP127 50p brt pink   25 15
C398 AP127 60p grnsh bl   30 22
C399 AP127 100p green   38 30
C400 AP127 500p brn red   1.90 1.50
        Nos. C396-C400 (5)   3.01 2.32

Ibn el-
Naphis — AP128

1967, Dec. 28 Litho. *Perf. 12x12¹/₂*
C401 AP128 12¹/₂p grn & org   15 15
C402 AP128 27¹/₂p dk bl & lil rose   18 15
        Set value   22 15

700th death anniv. of Ibn el-Naphis (1210-
1288), Arab physician.

Human
Rights Flame
and People
AP129

Design: 100p, Heads of various races and
Human Rights flame.

1968, Feb. 21 Litho. *Perf. 12¹/₂x12*
C403 AP129 12¹/₂p lt grnsh bl, bl &
                blk   15 15
C404 AP129 60p pink, blk & dl
                red   25 18
        Set value   30 22

Souvenir Sheet
Imperf
C405 AP129 100p multi   65 65

20th anniv. of the Declaration of Human Rights;
Intl. Human Rights Year.

Old Man and Woman
Reading — AP130

Design: 17¹/₂p, 45p, Torch and book.

1968, Mar. 3   *Perf. 12x12¹/₂*
C406 AP130 12¹/₂p rose car, blk & org 15 15
C407 AP130 17¹/₂p multi   15 15
C408 AP130 25p grn, blk & org   15 15
C409 AP130 45p bl & multi   15 15
        Set value   42 26

Issued to publicize the literacy campaign.

Euphrates Dam Project — AP131

1968, Apr. 11 Litho. *Perf. 12¹/₂x12*
C410 AP131 12¹/₂p multi   15 15
C411 AP131 17¹/₂p multi   15 15
C412 AP131 25p multi   20 15
        Set value   32 18

Proposed dam across Euphrates River.

WHO
Emblem and
Avenzoar
(1091-1162)
AP132

Designs (WHO Emblem and): 25p, Rhazes (Razi,
850-923). 60p, Geber (Jabir 721-776).

1968, June 10 Litho. *Perf. 12¹/₂x12*
C413 AP132 12¹/₂p brn, grn & sal   15 15
C414 AP132 25p brn, gray & sal   15 15
C415 AP132 60p brn, gray bl & sal   25 15
        Set value   42 25

WHO, 20th anniv.

Monastery of
St. Simeon
the Stylite
AP133

Designs: 17½p, El Tekkieh Mosque, Damascus, vert. 22½p, Columns, Palmyra, vert. 45p, Chapel of St. Paul, Bab Kisan. 50p, Theater of Bosra.

1968, Oct. 10 *Perf. 12½x12, 12x12½* **Litho.**
C416 AP133 15p pale grn & rose brn 15 15
C417 AP133 17½p redsh brn & dk red brn 15 15
C418 AP133 22½p grn gray & dk red 15 15
C419 AP133 45p yel & dk red brn 20 15
C420 AP133 50p lt bl & dk red brn 22 18
Set value 65 50

Hammer Throw — AP134

Designs: 25p, Discus. 27½p, Running. 60p, Basketball. 50p, Polo, horiz.

1968, Dec. 19 Litho. *Perf. 12x12½*
C421 AP134 12½p brt pink, blk & grn 15 15
C422 AP134 25p red, grn & blk 15 15
C423 AP134 27½p blk, gray & grn 15 15
C424 AP134 60p multi 22 15
Set value 54 32

Souvenir Sheet
Imperf
C425 AP134 50p multi 45 45

19th Olympic Games, Mexico City, Oct. 12-27. No. C425 contains one horizontal stamp 52x80mm.

Construction of Damascus Intl. Airport — AP135

1969, Jan. 20 Litho. *Perf. 12½x12*
C426 AP135 12½p yel, brt bl & grn 15 15
C427 AP135 17½p org, pur & lt grn 15 15
C428 AP135 60p car, blk & yel 25 15
Set value 38 25

Baal Shamin Temple, Palmyra AP136

Designs: 45p, Interior of Omayyad Mosque, Damascus, vert. 50p, Amphitheater, Palmyra. 60p, Khaled ibn al-Walid Mosque, Homs, vert. 100p, Ruins of St. Simeon, Djebel Samaan.

1969, Jan. 20 Photo. *Perf. 12x11½*
C429 AP136 25p multi 15 15
C430 AP136 45p bl & multi 15 15
C431 AP136 50p multi 18 15
C432 AP136 60p multi 22 15
C433 AP136 100p vio & multi 38 22
Nos. C429-C433 (5) 1.08
Set value 55

Workers, ILO Emblem, Cogwheel AP137

Designs: 60p, ILO emblem.

1969, May 1 Litho. *Perf. 12½x12*
C434 AP137 12½p multi 15 15
C435 AP137 27½p multi 15 15

Set value 22 15
Miniature Sheet
Imperf
C436 AP137 60p multi 30 22

ILO, 50th anniv. No. C436 contains one stamp 53½x47mm.

Ballet Dancers AP138

Designs: 12½p, Russian dancers. 45p, Lebanese singer and dancers. 55p, Egyptian dancer and musicians. 60p, Bulgarian dancers.

1969, Aug. 25 Litho. *Perf. 12½x12*
C437 AP138 12½p multi 15 15
C438 AP138 27½p bl & multi 15 15
C439 AP138 45p multi 18 15
C440 AP138 55p multi 22 15
C441 AP138 60p multi 25 18
a. Strip of 5, #C437-C441 1.10 75
Nos. C437-C441 (5) 95
Set value 55

16th Intl. Fair, Damascus, Aug. 25-Sept. 20.

Children Playing — AP139   Fortuna — AP140

1969, Oct. 6 Litho. *Perf. 12x12½*
C442 AP139 12½p aqua, dk bl & emer 15 15
C443 AP139 25p brn red, dk bl & lt vio 15 15
C444 AP139 27½p ultra, dk bl & gray 15 15
Set value 32 18

Issued for Children's Day.

1969, Oct. 10
Designs: 25p, Seated woman from Palmyra. 60p, Motherhood. All sculptures from Greco-Roman period.
C445 AP140 17½p blk, yel grn & grn 15 15
C446 AP140 25p dk brn, red brn & lt grn 15 15
C447 AP140 60p blk, lt gray & bl gray 25 15
Set value 45 28

9th Intl. Congress for Classical Archaeology, Oct. 11-20.

Damascus Agricultural Museum — AP141

1969, Dec. 24 Litho. *Perf. 12½x12*
C448 AP141 12p Cock 15 15
C449 AP141 17½p Cow 15 15
C450 AP141 20p Corn 15 15
C451 AP141 50p Olives 18 15
a. Strip of 4, #C448-C451 + label 50 30
Set value 42 26

Weather Satellite Tracking and UN Emblem AP142

1970, Mar. 23 Litho. *Perf. 12½x12*
C452 AP142 25p blk, sl grn & yel 15 15
C453 AP142 60p blk, dk bl & yel 25 18
Set value 26

10th World Meteorological Day.

Lenin (1870-1924) AP143

1970, Apr. 15 Litho. *Perf. 12x12½*
C454 AP143 15p red & dk brn 15 15
C455 AP143 60p red & grn 25 18
Set value 32 22

Workers' Syndicate Emblem AP144

1970, May 1 Litho. *Perf. 12½x12*
C456 AP144 15p dk brn & brt grn 15 15
C457 AP144 60p dk brn & org 25 18
Set value 30 22

Issued for Labor Day.

Radar and Open Book AP145

1970, May 17
C458 AP145 15p brt pink & blk 15 15
C459 AP145 60p bl & blk 25 18
Set value 30 22

International Telecommunications Day.

Opening of UPU Headquarters, Bern — AP146

1970, May 30
C460 AP146 15p multi 15 15
C461 AP146 60p multi 25 18
Set value 30 22

"Zahier Piebers and Maarouf" — AP147

Folk Tales: 10p, Two warriors on horseback. 15p, Two warriors on white horses. 20p, Lady and warrior on horseback. 60p, Warriors, woman and lion.

1970, Aug. 12 Litho. *Perf. 12½*
C462 AP147 5p lt bl & multi 15 15
C463 AP147 10p lt bl & multi 15 15
C464 AP147 15p lt bl & multi 15 15
C465 AP147 20p lt bl & multi 15 15
C466 AP147 60p lt bl & multi 38 18
a. Strip of 5, #C462-C466 75 50
Set value 65 40

Al Aqsa Mosque on Fire — AP148

1970, Aug. 21 *Perf. 12½x12*
C467 AP148 15p multi 15 15
C468 AP148 60p multi 25 18
Set value 30 22

1st anniv. of the burning of Al Aqsa Mosque, Jerusalem.

Wood Carving — AP149

Handicrafts: 20p, Jewelry. 25p, Glass making. 30p, Copper engraving. 60p, Shellwork.

1970, Aug. 25 *Perf. 12½*
C469 AP149 15p vio & multi 15 15
C470 AP149 20p ol & multi 15 15
C471 AP149 25p multi 15 15
C472 AP149 30p multi 18 15
C473 AP149 60p multi 32 18
a. Strip of 5, #C469-C473 85 60
Set value 75 45

17th Intl. Fair, Damascus.

Education Year Emblem — AP150

1970, Nov. 2 Litho. *Perf. 12*
C474 AP150 15p dl grn & dk brn 15 15
C475 AP150 60p vio bl & dk brn 25 18
Set value 30 22

International Education Year.

UN Emblem, Symbols of Progress, Justice and Peace AP151

1970, Nov. 3
C476 AP151 15p lt ultra, red & blk 15 15
C477 AP151 60p bl, yel & blk 25 18
Set value 30 22

United Nations, 25th anniversary.

Khaled ibn-al-Walid
AP152

Woman with
Garland
AP153

1970-71   *Perf. 12x11½, 12½x12½*

C478	AP152	45p brt pink	22	15
C479	AP152	50p green	25	15
C480	AP152	60p vio brn	32	18
C481	AP152	100p dk bl	45	18
C482	AP152	200p grnsh gray ('71)	95	50
C483	AP152	300p lil ('71)	1.25	95
C484	AP152	500p gray ('71)	2.00	1.65
		Nos. C478-C484 (7)	5.44	3.76

1971, Apr. 17   **Litho.**   *Perf. 12*

C485	AP153	15p dl red, blk & grn	25	15
C486	AP153	60p grn, blk & dk red	25	18
		Set value	30	22

25th anniv. of the evacuation of British and French troops from Syria.

People Dancing Around Globe
AP154

1971, Apr. 28   **Litho.**   *Perf. 12½x12*

C487	AP154	15p vio & multi	15	15
C488	AP154	60p grn & multi	22	15
		Set value	26	20

Intl. Year against Racial Discrimination.

Pres. Hafez al Assad and Council Chamber — AP155

1971, Sept. 30   **Litho.**   *Perf. 12½x12*

C489	AP155	15p grn & multi	15	15
C490	AP155	65p bl & multi	30	15
		Set value	35	20

People's Council and presidential election.

Gamal Abdel Nasser (1918-1970), President of Egypt — AP156

1971, Oct. 17   *Perf. 12x12½*

C491	AP156	15p lt ol grn & brn	15	15
C492	AP156	20p gray & brn	15	15
		Set value	16	15

Globe and Arrows
AP157

1972, May 17   **Litho.**   *Perf. 11½*

C493	AP157	15p bl, vio bl & pink	15	15
C494	AP157	50p org, yel & sep	22	15
		Set value	26	20

4th World Telecommunications Day.

Pres. Hafez al Assad
AP158

Airline Emblem, Eastern Hemisphere
AP159

1972, July   **Litho.**   *Perf. 12x11½*

C495	AP158	100p dk grn	45	25
C496	AP158	500p dk brn	2.25	1.10

1972, Sept. 16   **Litho.**   *Perf. 12x11½*

C497	AP159	15p blk, lt bl & Prus bl	15	15
C498	AP159	50p blk, gray & Prus bl	22	15
		Set value	30	20

Syrianair, Syrian airline, 25th anniversary.

Pottery — AP160

Handicraft Industries: 25p, Rugs. 30p, Metal (weapons). 35p, Straw (baskets, mats). 100p, Wood carving.

1976, July   **Litho.**   *Perf. 12x12½*

C499	AP160	10p multi	15	15
C500	AP160	25p multi	15	15
C501	AP160	30p multi	15	15
C502	AP160	35p multi	15	15
C503	AP160	100p multi	40	32
a.		Strip of 5, #C499-C503	90	60
		Set value	80	50

23rd Intl. Damascus Fair.

Pres. Hafez al Assad
AP161

1978, Sept.   **Litho.**   *Perf. 12½x12*

C504	AP161	25p sil & multi	18	15
C505	AP161	35p grn & multi	28	15
C506	AP161	60p gold & multi	35	15
		Set value		18

Reelection of Pres. Assad. See No. 820.

AIR POST SEMI-POSTAL STAMPS

Nos. C30-C33 Surcharged Like Nos. B1-B12 in Black and Red

1926, Apr. 1   **Unwmk.**   *Perf. 13½*

CB1	A4	2p + 1p dk brn	95	95
CB2	A4	3p + 2p org brn	95	95
CB3	A4	5p + 3p vio	95	95
CB4	A4	10p + 5p vio brn	95	95

The new value is in red and rest of the surcharge in black on Nos. CB1-CB3. The entire surcharge is black on No. CB4.
See note following Nos. B1-B12.

> Catalogue values for unused stamps in this section, from this point to the end of the section, are for Never Hinged items.

Fair Entrance
SPAP1

Industry, Handicraft and Farming
SPAP2

Design: 70p+10p, Fairgrounds.

1955   *Perf. 11½, Imperf.*

		Litho.	**Unwmk.**	
CB5	SPAP1	25p + 5p gray blk	40	40
CB6	SPAP2	35p + 5p ultra	42	42
CB7	SPAP2	40p + 10p rose lil	60	60
CB8	SPAP1	70p + 10p Prus grn	1.10	1.10

Intl. Fair, Damascus, Sept. 1955.
For overprint see Nos. C212-C215.

United Nations Refugee Emblem
SPAP3

1966, Dec. 12   **Litho.**   *Perf. 11½x12*

CB9	SPAP3	12½p + 2½p ultra & blk	25	15
CB10	SPAP3	50p + 5p grn & blk	50	25
		Set value		32

21st anniv. of UN Day; Refugee Week, Oct. 24-31.

POSTAGE DUE STAMPS

Under French Occupation

Stamps of French Offices in the Turkish Empire, 1902-03, Surcharged

O. M. F Syrie Ch. taxe 1 PIASTRE

1920   **Unwmk.**   *Perf. 14x13½*

J1	A3	1p on 10c rose red	85.00	85.00
J2	A3	2p on 20c brn vio	85.00	85.00
J3	A3	3p on 30c lil	85.00	85.00
J4	A4	4p on 40c red & pale bl	85.00	85.00

Postage Due Stamps of France, 1893-1920, Surcharged in Black or Red

O. M. F. Syrie 2 PIASTRES

1920

J5	D2	1p on 10c brn	70	70
J6	D2	2p on 20c ol grn (R)	70	70
a.		"PIASTRE"	190.00	190.00

J7	D2	3p on 30c red	70	70
a.		"PIASTRE"		
J8	D2	4p on 50c brn vio	2.00	2.00
a.		3p in setting of 4p	190.00	190.00

1921-22

J9	D2	50c on 10c brn	30	30
a.		"75" instead of "50"	19.00	
b.		"CENTIEMES" instead of "CEN-TIEMES"	2.75	
J10	D2	1p on 20c ol grn	30	30
J11	D2	2p on 30c red	1.00	1.00
J12	D2	3p on 50c brn vio	1.25	1.25
J13	D2	5p on 1fr red brn, *straw*	2.50	2.50
		Nos. J9-J13 (5)	5.35	5.35

D3   D4

1921   *Perf. 11½*

Red Surcharge

J14	D3	50c on 1p black	3.75	3.75
J15	D3	1p on 1p black	2.50	2.50

1922

J16	D4	2p on 5m rose	5.50	5.50
a.		"AX" of "TAXE" inverted	55.00	55.00
J17	D4	3p on 1p gray bl	11.00	11.00

French Mandate

Postage Due Stamps of France, 1893-1920, Surcharged

Syrie Grand Liban 2 PIASTRES

1923

J18	D2	50c on 10c brown	70	42
J19	D2	1p on 20c ol grn	1.00	70
J20	D2	2p on 30c red	90	50
J21	D2	3p on 50c vio brn	90	50
J22	D2	5p on 1fr red brn, *straw*	1.75	1.75
		Nos. J18-J22 (5)	5.25	3.87

Postage Due Stamps of France, 1893-1920, Surcharged

SYRIE 1 PIASTRE

1924

J23	D2	50c on 10c brown	28	28
J24	D2	1p on 20c ol grn	32	32
J25	D2	2p on 30c red	45	45
J26	D2	3p on 50c vio brn	62	45
J27	D2	5p on 1fr red brn, *straw*	55	55
		Nos. J23-J27 (5)	2.22	2.05

Postage Due Stamps of France, 1893-1920, Surcharged

Syrie 2 Piastres سوريا غروش ٢

1924

J28	D2	50c on 10c brown	28	28
J29	D2	1p on 20c ol grn	32	32
J30	D2	2p on 30c red	38	38
J31	D2	3p on 50c vio brn	48	48
J32	D2	5p on 1fr red brn, *straw*	75	75
		Nos. J28-J32 (5)	2.21	2.21

Water Wheel at Hama — D5

Bridge at Antioch — D6

Designs: 2p, The Tartous. 3p, View of Banias. 5p, Chevaliers' Castle.

1925 Photo. Perf. 13½

J33	D5	50c brown, yel	15 15
J34	D6	1p violet, rose	15 15
J35	D5	2p black, blue	15 15
J36	D5	3p black, red org	32 32
J37	D5	5p black, bl grn	1.40 50
		Nos. J33-J37 (5)	2.17 1.27

D7

Lion — D8

1931

J38	D7	8p black, gray blue	1.25 1.25
J39	D8	15p black, dull rose	2.00 2.00

Catalogue values for unused stamps in this section, from this point to the end of the section, are for Never Hinged items.

Syrian Arab Republic

D9

1965 Unwmk. Litho. Perf. 11½x11

J40	D9	2½p violet blue	15 15
J41	D9	5p black brown	15 15
J42	D9	10p green	15 15
J43	D9	17½p carmine rose	16 16
J44	D9	25p blue	22 22
		Set value	54 54

MILITARY STAMPS

Free French Administration
Syria No. 222 Surcharged in Black

FORCES FRANÇAISES LIBRES
LEVANT
50c

1942 Unwmk. Perf. 13

M1	A10	50c on 4p yel org	2.50 2.50

Lebanon Nos. 155 and 142A Surcharged in Carmine

FORCES FRANÇAISES LIBRES
LEVANT
1f.

FORCES FRANÇAISES LIBRES
LEVANT
2 f.50

M2	A13	1fr on 5p grnsh bl	2.50 2.50
M3	A25	2.50fr on 12½p dp ultra	2.50 2.50

Camel Corps, Palmyra
M1

1942 Unwmk. Litho. Perf. 11½

M4	M1	1fr deep rose	22 22
M5	M1	1.50fr bright violet	22 22
M6	M1	2fr orange	22 22
M7	M1	2.50fr brown gray	22 22
M8	M1	3fr Prussian blue	32 32
M9	M1	4fr deep green	50 50
M10	M1	5fr deep claret	50 50
		Nos. M4-M10 (7)	2.20 2.20

Nos. M4 to M10 exist imperforate.
For surcharges see Nos. MB1-MB2, MC10.

MILITARY SEMI-POSTAL STAMPS

Free French Administration

RÉSISTANCE

Military Stamps of 1942 Surcharged in Black

+9F

1943 Unwmk. Perf. 11½

MB1	M1	1fr + 9fr deep rose	1.65 1.65
MB2	M1	5fr + 20fr deep claret	1.65 1.65

MILITARY AIR POST STAMPS

Free French Administration
Syria Nos. C55-C56 Surcharged in Black, Carmine or Orange

LIGNES
AERIENNES
F.A.F.L.
✈ 10f.

1942 Unwmk. Perf. 13

MC1	AP2	4fr on 50p blk (C)	1.90 1.90
MC2	AP2	6.50fr on 50p blk (C)	1.90 1.90
MC3	AP2	8fr on 50p blk (O)	1.90 1.90
MC4	AP2	10fr on 100p mag	1.90 1.90

Winged Shields and Cross of Lorraine
MAP1

1942 Litho. Perf. 11½

MC5	MAP1	6.50fr pale pink & rose car	40 40
MC6	MAP1	10fr lt bl & dl vio	40 40

Nos. MC5 and MC6 exist imperforate.
See Nos. MC7-MC8. For surcharges see Nos. MC9, MCB1-MCB2.

Souvenir Sheets

1942 Without Gum Perf. 11

MC7		Sheet of 2	8.25 8.25
a.	MAP1	6.50fr pale pink & rose carmine	2.00 2.00
b.	MAP1	10fr lt bl & dl violet	2.00 2.00

Imperf

MC8		Sheet of 2	8.25 8.25
a.	MAP1	6.50fr pale pink & rose carmine	2.00 2.00
b.	MAP1	10fr lt bl & dl violet	2.00 2.00

No. MC5 Surcharged in Rose Carmine With New Value and Bars
Perf. 11½

MC9	MAP1	4fr on 6.50fr	60 50

Military Stamp of 1942 Surcharged in Black

4F

1943

MC10	M1	4fr on 3fr Prus blue	60 50

MILITARY AIR POST SEMI-POSTAL STAMPS

Free French Administration
Military Air Post Stamps of 1942 Surcharged in Black

+48F50

RÉSISTANCE

1943 Unwmk. Perf. 11½

MCB1	MAP1	6.50fr + 48.50fr	8.50 8.50
MCB2	MAP1	10fr + 100fr	8.50 8.50

POSTAL TAX STAMPS

Revenue Stamps Overprinted in Red or Black

R1

طابع الجيش
السوري
a

طابع
لجيش السوري
b

1945 Unwmk. Perf. 10½x11½

RA1	R1(a)	5p dark blue (R)	62.50 22.50

On Stamps Overprinted

RA2	R1(a)	5p dk bl (Bk+Bk)	75.00 26.00
RA3	R1(a)	5p dk bl (Bk+R)	75.00 26.00
RA4	R1(a)	5p dk bl (R+R)	75.00 26.00
RA5	R1(b)	5p dk bl (R+R)	82.50 22.50

On Stamps Overprinted

RA6	R1(a)	5p dk bl (Bk+Bk)	75.00 26.00
RA7	R1(a)	5p dk bl (Bk+R)	75.00 26.00
RA8	R1(a)	5p dk bl (R+R)	75.00 26.00
RA9	R1(b)	5p dk bl (R+R)	90.00 26.00
		Nos. RA1-RA9 (9)	685.00 227.00

The tax was for national defense.

طابع
الجيش السوري
٥ ت ن .

≡

c. 25

R2

Revenue Stamp Surcharged in Black

1945 Unwmk. Perf. 11

RA10	R2	5p on 25c on 40c rose red	60.00 1.75

The surcharge reads "Tax (postal) for Syrian Army."

طابع الجيش
السوري
٥ ت ن .

٢٥

c. 25

Revenue Stamp Surcharged in Black

1945

RA11	R2	5p on 25c on 40c rose red	60.00 1.75

No. RA11 Overprinted in Black

RA12	R2	5p on 25c on 40c	67.50

The tax on Nos. RA11 and RA12 was for the army.
This overprint exists on No. RA10.

ISSUES OF THE ARABIAN GOVERNMENT

The following issues replaced the British Military Occupation (E.E.F.) stamps (Palestine Nos. 2-14) which were used in central and eastern Syria from Nov. 1918 until Jan. 1920.

Turkish Stamps of 1913-18 Handstamped in Various Colors

Also Handstamp Surcharged with New Values as:

1 millieme

1 Egyptian piaster

The Seal reads: "Hakuma al Arabie" (The Arabian Government)

Perf. 11½, 12, 12½, 13½

1919-20 Unwmk.

1	A24	1m on 2pa red lil (254)	55	55
2	A25	1m on 3pa dk brn (255)	55	55
3	A26	2m on 5pa vio brn (256)	85	85
4	A15	2m on 5pa on 10pa gray grn (291)	55	55
5	A18	2m on 5pa ocher (304)	16.00	14.00
6	A41	2m on 5pa grn (345)	200.00	150.00
7	A18	2m on 5pa ocher (378)	40.00	40.00
8	A28	4m on 10pa grn (258)	4.50	4.50
9	A28	4m on 10pa grn (271)	55	55
10	A22	4m on 10pa bl grn (329)	1.10	1.10
11	A41	4m on 10pa car (346)	19.00	19.00
12	A23	4m on 10pa grn (415)	4.50	4.50
13	A44	4m on 10pa grn (424)	80	80
14	A11	4m on 10pa on 20pa vio brn (B38)	80	80
15	A41	4m on 10pa car (B42)	55	55
16	SP1	4m on 10pa red vio (B46)	80	80
17	SP1	4m on 10pa on 20pa car rose (B47)	80	80

19	A21	5pa ocher (317)		
21	A21	20pa car rose (153)	50.00	100.00
22	A29	20pa red (259)	80	80
23	A29	20pa red (272)	200.00	200.00
24	A17	20pa car (299)	1.65	1.65
25	A21	20pa car rose (318)	1.65	1.65
26	A22	20pa car rose (330)	8.50	8.50
27	A21	20pa car rose (342)	4.50	4.50
28	A41	20pa ultra (347)	1.50	1.50
29	A16	20pa mag (363)	6.50	6.50
30	A17	20pa car (371)		
31	A18	20pa car (379)	4.50	4.50
32	A45	20pa dp rose (425)	2.25	2.25
33	A21	20pa car rose (B8)	1.40	1.40
34	A22	20pa car rose (B33)	1.65	1.65
35	A22	20pa car rose (B36)	8.75	8.75
36	A41	20pa ultra (B43)	28	28
37	A16	20pa mag (P140)	2.25	2.25
38	A17	20pa car (P144)	200.00	200.00
39	A30	1pi bl (260)	1.65	1.65
40	A31	1pi on 1½pi car & blk (261)	250.00	250.00
41	A30	1pi bl (273)	40.00	40.00
42	A30	1pi on 1pi bl (273)	60.00	60.00
43	A17	1pi blue (300)	2.75	2.75
44	A18	1pi blue (307)	50.00	50.00
45	A22	1pi ultra (331)	4.50	4.50
46	A21	1pi ultra (343)	8.50	8.50
47	A41	1pi vio & blk (348)	85	85
48	A18	1pi brt bl (389)	4.50	4.50
49	A16	1pi dl vio (426)	1.50	1.50
50	A47	1pi on 50pa ultra (428)	55	55
51	A21	1pi ultra (B9)	55	55
52	A22	1pi ultra (B15)	8.75	8.75
53	A18	1pi brt bl (B21)	5.50	5.50
54	A18	1pi blue (B23)	14.00	14.00
55	A22	1pi ultra (B34)	11.50	11.50
56	A41	1pi vio & blk (B44)	1.50	1.50
57	A33	2pi grn & blk (263)	40.00	35.00
58	A13	2pi brn org (289)	1.10	1.10
59	A18	2pi slate (308)	14.00	14.00
60	A18	2pi slate (314)	14.00	14.00
61	A21	2pi bl blk (320)	2.75	2.75
62	A17	2pi org (373)	2.75	2.75
63	A18	2pi brn (310)	6.50	6.50
64	A22	5pi dl vio (333)	14.00	14.00
65	A41	5pi yel brn & blk (349)	2.25	2.25
66	A41	5pi yel brn & blk (418)	2.25	2.25
67	A53	5pi on 2pa Prus bl (547)	1.65	1.65
68	A21	5pi dk grn (B10)	175.00	175.00
69	A17	5pi lil rose (B20)	30.00	30.00
70	A41	5pi yel brn & blk (B45)	2.75	2.75
72	A50	10pi dk grn (431)	60.00	60.00
73	A50	10pi dk vio (432)	55.00	55.00
74	A50	10pi dk brn (433)	350.00	
75	A18	10pi org brn (B2)	150.00	150.00
76	A37	25pi ol grn (267)	200.00	200.00
77	A40	25pi on 200pi grn & blk (287)	250.00	250.00
78	A17	25pi brn (303)	200.00	200.00
79	A51	25pi car, straw (434)	50.00	50.00
81	A52	50pi ind (438)	125.00	125.00

The variety "surcharge omitted" exists on Nos. 1-5, 12-13, 16, 32, 49-50, 67.

A few copies of No. 377 (50pi) and No. 269 (100pi) were overprinted but not regularly issued.

Overprinted

The Inscription reads "Hakum Soria Arabie" (Syrian-Arabian Government)

On Stamp of 1913

83	A26	2m on 5pa vio brn (256)	3.50	3.50

On Stamp of 1916-18

84	A45	20pa dp rose (425)	50	50

A1

		Litho.	**Perf. 11½**	
85	A1	5m rose	50	50
a.		Tête bêche pair	10.00	7.50
b.		Imperf.		

Independence Issue

Arabic Overprint in Green:
"Souvenir of Syrian Independence March 8, 1920"

86	A1	5m rose	40.00	35.00
a.		Tête bêche pair	100.00	75.00
b.		Inverted overprint		

A2

Litho.
Size: 22x18mm

87	A2	½₁₀pi lt brn	15	15

Size: 28x22mm

88	A2	²⁄₁₀pi yel grn	25	18
a.		²⁄₁₀pi yellow (error)	6.25	4.00
89	A2	³⁄₁₀pi yellow	15	15
90	A2	1pi gray blue	15	15
91	A2	2pi blue grn	1.00	38

Size: 31x25mm

92	A2	5pi vio brn	1.50	75
93	A2	10pi gray	1.50	1.00
		Nos. 86-93 (8)	44.70	37.76

Nos. 86-93 exist imperf.
For overprint see No. J5.

PF1   PF2

Revenue Stamps Surcharged as on Postage Stamps, for Postal Use

1920		**Unwmk.**	**Perf. 11½**	
94	PF1	5m on 5pa red	25	25
95	PF2	1m on 5pa red	18	15
96	PF2	2m on 5pa red	25	15
97	PF2	1pi on 5pa red	50	38

Surcharged in Syrian Piasters

98	PF2	2pi on 5pa red	18	18
99	PF2	3pi on 5pa red	18	18
		Nos. 94-99 (6)	1.54	1.29

ISSUES OF THE ARABIAN GOVERNMENT POSTAGE DUE STAMPS

Postage Due Stamps of Turkey, 1914, Handstamped and Surcharged with New Value

1920		**Unwmk.**	**Perf. 12**	
J1	D1	2m on 5pa claret	4.00	4.00
J2	D2	20pa red	4.00	4.00
J3	D3	1pi dark blue	4.00	4.00
J4	D4	2pi slate	4.00	4.00

Type of Regular Issue
Perf. 11½
Litho.

J5	A2	1pi black	75	75

UNITED ARAB REPUBLIC

Catalogue values for unused stamps in this section are for Never Hinged items.

See Egypt for stamps of types A1, A4, A7, A8, A14, A17, A19, A20, A24 with denomination in "M" (milliemes).

Issues for Syria

Linked Maps of Egypt and Syria — A1

1958		**Unwmk.**	**Litho.**	**Perf. 11½**
1	A1	12½p yellow & green		20 15

Establishment of United Arab Republic. See No. C1.

Freedom Monument — A2

1958, May				
2	A2	5p yel & vio	40	16
3	A2	15p yel grn & brn red	60	35

12th anniv. of the British-French troop evacuation. See Nos. C2-C3.

Bronze Rattle — A3   Hand Holding Torch, Broken Chain and Flag — A4

Antique Art: 15p, Goddess. 20p, Lamgi Mari. 30p, Mithras fighting bull. 40p, Aspasia. 60p, Minerva. 75p, Flask. 100p, Enameled Vase. 150p, Mosaic from Omayyad Mosque, Damascus.

1958, Sept. 14		**Litho.**	**Perf. 12**	
4	A3	10p lt ol grn	15	15
5	A3	15p brn org	15	15
6	A3	20p rose lilac	15	15
7	A3	30p lt brn	15	15
8	A3	40p gray	30	15
9	A3	60p green	50	20
10	A3	75p blue	80	30
11	A3	100p brn car	1.20	40
12	A3	150p dull pur	2.25	60
		Nos. 4-12 (9)	5.65	
		Set value		1.95

Archaeological collections and museums.

1958, Oct. 14			**Perf. 11½**	
13	A4	12.50p car rose		20 15

Establishment of Republic of Iraq.

Syria No. 411 Overprinted

RAU

1958, Oct. 6		**Wmk. 291**	**Perf. 11½**	
13A	A78	12½p olive	37.50	35.00

Intl. Children's Day, 1958. See #C10-C11.

View of Damascus — A5

1958, Dec. 10			**Unwmk.**	
14	A5	12½p green		22 15

4th Near East Regional Conference, Damascus, Dec. 10-20. See No. C14.

Secondary School, Damascus — A6

1959, Feb. 26		**Litho.**	**Perf. 12**	
15	A6	12½p dull green		15 15

See No. 26.

Flags of UAR and Yemen A7

Perf. 13x13½

1959, Mar. 8		**Photo.**	**Wmk. 318**	
16	A7	12½p grn, red & blk		20 15

1st anniversary of United Arab States.

Arms of UAR — A8   Mother and Children — A9

Perf. 12x11½

1959, Feb. 22		**Litho.**	**Wmk. 291**	
17	A8	12½p grn, blk & red		20 15

United Arab Republic, 1st anniv.

1959, Mar. 21			**Perf. 11½**	
18	A9	15p car rose	20	15
19	A9	25p dk slate grn	30	22

Arab Mother's Day, Mar. 21. For overprints see Nos. 41-42.

Syria No. 378 Surcharged "U.A.R." in Arabic and English, and New Value in Red

1959, Apr. 6		**Photo.**	**Unwmk.**	
20	A68	2½p on 1p olive		15 15

Type of 1959 and

A10   Boys' School, Damascus — A11

Designs: 5p, 7½p, 10p, Various arabesques. 12½p, St. Simeon's Monastery. 17½p, Hittin school. 35p, Normal School for Girls, Damascus.

1959-61		Unwmk.	Litho.	Perf. 11½	
21	A10	2½p violet		15	15
22	A10	5p olive bister		15	15
23	A10	7½p ultra		15	15
24	A10	10p bl grn		15	15
25	A11	12½p lt bl ('61)		16	15
26	A6	17½p brt lilac ('60)		22	15
27	A11	25p brt grnsh bl		30	15
28	A11	35p brown ('60)		40	16
		Set value		1.35	65

Male Profile and Fair Emblem — A12

Fair Emblem and Globe — A13

1959, Aug. 30		Unwmk.	Perf. 11½	
30	A12	35p gray, grn & vio	42	20

Souvenir Sheet
Imperf

31	A13	30p dl yel & grn	1.50	1.50

6th International Damascus Fair.

Shield and Cogwheel — A14

1959, Oct. 20			Wmk. 328	Perf. 13½x13
32	A14	50p sepia	60	35

Issued for Army Day, 1959.

Syria Nos. 408 and 386 with Red Overprint Similar to

Similar to

1959		Unwmk.	Litho.	Perf. 11½	
33	A75	15p gray		22	15
			Photo.		
34	A69	50p dk grn		60	42

The overprints differ in size and lettering: No. 33 is 28x8½/2mm; No. 34 is 21x6mm. A period follows "R" on Nos. 33-34. The Arabic overprint means "United Arab Republic."

Cogwheel, Wheat and Cotton — A15 A. R. Kawakbi — A16

1959, Oct. 30			Litho.
35	A15	35p gray, bl & ocher	42 20

Industrial and Agricultural Production Fair, Aleppo. For overprint see No. 46.

Type of Syria Air Post, 1956, Inscribed "U.A.R."

1959, Dec. 31		Unwmk.	Perf. 13½
36	AP59	12½p gray ol & bister	20 15

Day of the Tree. For overprint see No. 49.

1960, Jan. 11			Perf. 12x11½
37	A16	15p dark green	20 15

50th death anniv. of A. R. Kawakbi, Arabic writer.

Arms and Flag — A17

1960, Feb. 22		Photo.	Wmk. 328	Perf. 13½x13
38	A17	12½p red & dk sl grn		20 15

United Arab Republic, 2nd anniversary.

Diesel Train and Old Town — A18

1960, Mar. 15		Litho.	Unwmk.	Perf. 11½x11
39	A18	12½p brn & brt bl		35 20

Construction of the Latakia-Aleppo railroad.

Arab League Center, Cairo, and Arms of UAR A19

1960, Mar. 22		Photo.	Wmk. 328	Perf. 13x13½
40	A19	12½p dl grn & blk		20 15

Opening of the Arab League Center and the Arab Postal Museum in Cairo.

Nos. 18-19 Overprinted in Black or Magenta

1960, Apr. 3		Wmk. 291	Litho.	Perf. 11½
41	A9	15p car rose		22 15
42	A9	25p dk slate grn (M)		35 16

Issued for Arab Mother's Day.

Refugees Pointing to Map of Palestine A20

1960, Apr. 7		Photo.	Wmk. 328	Perf. 13x13½
43	A20	12½p car rose		40 15
44	A20	50p green		70 30

World Refugee Year, July 1, 1959-June 30, 1960.

A21

1960, May 12		Unwmk.	Litho.	Perf. 11½
45	A21	12½p vio, rose & pale grn		22 15

Evacuation Day, 1960.

No. 35 Overprinted in Red

1960			
46	A15	35p gray, bl & ocher	30 20

1960 Industrial and Agricultural Production Fair, Aleppo.

Souvenir Sheet

Flags in Symbolic Design — A22

1960		Unwmk.	Imperf.
47	A22	100p gray, brn & lt bl	1.50 1.50

7th Intl. Damascus Fair.

Child — A23

1960		Litho.	Perf. 11½
48	A23	35p dk grn & fawn	42 22

Issued for Children's Day.

No. 36 Overprinted in Carmine

1960		Unwmk.	Perf. 11½
49	AP59	12½p gray ol & bis	22 15

Issued to publicize the Day of the Tree.

Coat of Arms and Victory Wreath — A24 Cogwheel, Retort and Ear of Wheat — A25

1961, Feb. 22		Photo.	Wmk. 328	Perf. 13½x13
50	A24	12½p lt vio		15 15

United Arab Republic, 3rd anniversary.

1961, June 8		Unwmk.	Litho.	Perf. 11½
51	A25	12½p multi		15 15

Industrial and Agricultural Fair, Aleppo.

SEMI-POSTAL STAMP

Catalogue values for unused stamp in this section is for a Never Hinged item.

Postal Emblem — SP1

1959, Jan. 2		Photo.	Wmk. 318	Perf. 13½x13
B1	SP1	20p + 10p grn, red & blk		42 42

Issued for Post Day. The surtax went to the social fund for postal employees.
See Egypt No. B18 for similar stamp with denomination in "M" (milliemes).

AIR POST STAMPS

Catalogue values for unused stamps in this section are for Never Hinged items.

Map Type of Regular Issue

1958, Apr. 3		Unwmk.	Litho.	Perf. 11½
C1	A1	17½p ultra & brn		35 20

Broken Chain, Dove and Olive Branch AP1

1958, May 17
C2 AP1 35p rose & blk   70 35
C3 AP1 45p bl & brn   1.25 42

12th anniv. of the British-French troop evacuation.

Scout Putting up Tent — AP2

1958, Aug. 31   **Perf. 12**
C4 AP2 35p dk brn   1.50 1.50
C5 AP2 40p ultra   2.00 2.00

3rd Pan-Arab Boy Scout Jamboree.

View of Damascus Fair AP3

UAR Flag and Fair Emblem — AP4

Designs: 30p, Minaret, vase and emblem, vert. 45p, Mosque, chimneys and wheel, vert.

1958, Sept. 1   Litho.   Perf. 11½
C6 AP3 25p vermilion   70 60
C7 AP3 30p brt bl grn   1.00 62
C8 AP3 45p violet   80 55

Souvenir Sheet
Imperf
C9 AP4 100p brt grn, car & blk   50.00 50.00

Fifth Damascus International Fair.

Syria Nos. C244-C245
Overprinted   RAU

1958, Oct. 6   Wmk. 291   Perf. 11½
C10 A78 17½p ultra   25.00 25.00
C11 A78 20p red brn   25.00 25.00

International Children's Day.

Cotton and Cotton Material — AP5

1958, Oct. 10   Unwmk.   Perf. 12
C12 AP5 25p brn & yel   42 40
C13 AP5 35p brn & brick red   70 50

Cotton Festival, Aleppo, Oct. 9-11.

Type of Regular Issue, 1958
1958, Dec. 10
C14 A5 17½p brt vio   22 15

Children and Glider — AP6

1958, Dec. 1   Litho.   Perf. 12
C15 AP6 7½p gray green   50 30
C16 AP6 12½p olive   2.00 1.20

1958 glider festival.

UN Emblem — AP7

1958, Dec. 10
C17 AP7 25p dl pur   22 16
C18 AP7 35p light blue   35 22
C19 AP7 40p brn red   50 30

10th anniv. of the signing of the Universal Declaration of Human Rights.

Globe, Radio and Telegraph — AP8

1959, Mar. 1   Perf. 12
C20 AP8 40p grn & blk   50 35

Arab Union of Telecommunications.
See Egypt No. 464 for similar stamp with denomination in "M" (milliemes).

Same Overprinted in Red

2nd CONFERANCE
DAMASCUS 1-3-1959

1959, Mar. 1
C21 AP8 40p grn & blk   40 20

2nd Conference of the Arab Union of Telecommunications, Damascus.

Laurel and Map of Syria — AP9

Design: 35p, Torch and broken chain.

1959, Apr. 17   Perf. 12x11½
C22 AP9 15p ocher & green   20 15
C23 AP9 35p gray & carmine   40 22

13th anniv. of the British-French troop evacuation.

"Emigration" — AP10

1959, Aug. 4 Unwmk. Perf. 11½x12
C24 AP10 80p brt grn, blk & red   70 42

Convention of the Assoc. of Arab Emigrants in the US.

Refinery AP11

1959, Aug. 12   Litho.
C25 AP11 50p bl, blk & car   90 40

Opening of first oil refinery in Syria.

Syria Nos. C246 and C181-C182
Overprinted like Nos. 33-34
1959   Perf. 11½
C26 AP64 5p brt grn   15 15
C27 AP44 35p dp plum   42 22
C28 AP44 70p purple   70 30
          Set value   56

The overprints differ in size and lettering: #C26 is 25½x9½mm; #C27-C28 are 27x8mm. A period follows "R" on #C27-C28.

Cotton Boll and Thread — AP12   Boy and Building Blocks — AP13

1959, Oct. 1   Litho.   Perf. 11½
C29 AP12 45p gray blue   42 16
C30 AP12 50p claret   42 30

Cotton Festival, Aleppo.
For overprints see Nos. C33-C34.

1959, Oct. 5
C31 AP13 25p dl lil, red & dk bl   22 15

Issued for Children's Day.

Crane and Compass AP14

1960   Unwmk.   Perf. 11½
C32 AP14 50p lt brn, crim & blk   42 30

7th Damascus International Fair.

١٩٦٠

Nos. C29-C30
Overprinted in Claret or Gray Blue

1960   Litho.   Perf. 11½
C33 AP12 45p gray blue (C)   40 16
C34 AP12 50p claret (GB)   42 30

1960 Cotton Festival, Aleppo.

17th Olympic Games, Rome — AP15   Globe, Laurel and "UN" — AP16

1960, Dec. 27   Unwmk.   Perf. 12
C35 AP15 15p Basketball   22 15
C36 AP15 20p Swimmer   35 15
C37 AP15 25p Fencing   35 15
C38 AP15 40p Horsemanship   60 30
            Set value   64

1960, Dec. 31
C39 AP16 35p multi   35 15
C40 AP16 50p bl, red & yel   42 22

United Nations, 15th anniversary.

Ibrahim Hanano — AP17   Soldier with Flag — AP18

1961   Litho.   Perf. 12x11½
C41 AP17 50p buff & slate grn   32 18

Hanano, leader of liberation movement.

1961, Apr. 17 Wmk. 291 Perf. 11½
C42 AP18 40p gray green   32 18

Issued for Evacuation Day, 1961.

Stamps of Tadjikistan can be mounted in the annual Scott Russia and Commonwealth of Independent States supplement.

Arab and Map of
Palestine
AP19

Abu-Tammam
AP20

1961, May 15   *Perf. 12*
C43 AP19 50p ultra & blk   50 25

Issued for Palestine Day.

1961, July 20   Unwmk.   Perf. 11½
C44 AP20 50p brown   38 18

Abu-Tammam (807-845?), Arabian poet.

Discus
Thrower and
Lyre — AP21

1961, Aug. 23   Litho.   Perf. 11½
C45 AP21 15p crimson & blk   18 15
C46 AP21 35p bl grn & vio   50 18
     Set value   22

5th University Youth Festival.
A souvenir sheet contains one each of Nos. C45-
C46 imperf.

Fair
Emblem — AP22

UAR
Pavilion — AP23

1961, Aug. 25
C47 AP22 17½p vio & grn   15 15
C48 AP23 50p brt lil & blk   32 18
  a.   Black omitted
     Set value   26

8th International Damascus Fair.

St. Simeon's
Monastery — AP24

1961, Oct.   Litho.   Perf. 12
C49 AP24 200p violet blue   1.50 90

No. C49 was issued by the Syrian Arab Republic
after dissolution of the UAR.

AIR POST SEMI-POSTAL STAMP

Catalogue value for the unused
stamp in this section is for a Never
Hinged item.

Eye, Hand and UN
Emblem — SPAP1

Perf. 12x11½
1961, Apr. 29   Litho.   Wmk. 291
CB1 SPAP1 40p + 10p sl grn & blk   30 30

UN welfare program for the blind.

TADJIKISTAN

(Tadzikistan)

LOCATION — Asia, bounded by Uzbeki-
stan, Kyrgyzstan, People's Republic of
China and Afghanistan
GOVT. — Independent republic, member
of the Commonwealth of Independent
States
AREA — 54,019 sq. mi.
POP. — 5,100,000 (1989)
CAPITAL — Dushanbe

With the breakup of the Soviet Union on
Dec. 26, 1991, Tadjikistan and ten former
Soviet republics established the Common-
wealth of Independent States.

100 Kopecks = 1 Ruble

Catalogue values for all unused
stamps in this country are for Never
Hinged items.

Gold Statue of Man
on Horse — A1

1992, May 20   Litho.   Perf. 12x12½
1 A1 50k multicolored   65

For surcharge see No. 12.

Sheik
Muslihiddin
Mosque — A2

1992, May 25   Photo.   Perf. 11½
2 A2 50k multicolored   38

Musical Instruments of Tadjikistan — A3

Photo. & Engr.
1992, Aug. 15   Perf. 12x11½
3 A3 35k multicolored   25

For surcharges see Nos. 5-7.

Ram — A4

1992, Aug. 21   Photo.   Perf. 12x12½
4 A4 30k multicolored   24

15.00

No. 3 Surcharged in Black or
Blue

Photo. & Engr.
1992, Nov. 12   Perf. 12x11½
5 A3 15r on 35k   1.30
6 A3 15r on 35k (Bl)   1.30
7 A3 50r on 35k   4.50

3.00

Russia No. 5838
Surcharged

1992
Тадж.

1992, Jan. 4   Litho.   Perf. 12x12½
8 A2765   3r on 1k   15
9 A2765 100r on 1k   2.25

No. 1 Surcharged in Black and Russia No.
5984 Surcharged in Violet Blue or Green

Точикистон

10.00   00   '09

1992, May 7   Litho.   Perf. 12x12½
10 A2765 10r on 2k (VB)   i5
11 A2765 15r on 2k (Gr)   18
12 A1   60r on 50k   70

Location and size of lettering on Nos. 10-11
varies.

Wild
Animals — A5

Designs: 3r, Ursus arctos. 10r, Cervas elaphus.
15r, Capra falconeri. 25r, Hystrix leucura. 100r,
Uncia uncia.

1993, June 8   Litho.   Perf. 13½
15 A5   3r multicolored   15
16 A5 10r multicolored   50
17 A5 15r multicolored   75
18 A5 25r multicolored   1.25
19 A5 100r multicolored   5.00
   Nos. 15-19 (5)   7.65

Fortress, 19th
Cent. — A6

Designs: 1r, Statue of Rudaki, poet, vert. 5r,
Mountains, river. 10r, Statue with oriental inscription, vert. 15r, Mausoleum of Aini, poet, vert. 20r,

---

Map, flag. 35r, Post office. 50r, Aini Opera House.
No. 29, Theater. No. 30, Flag, map, diff. No. 31,
Observatory. No. 32, Academy.

1993-94
20 A6   1r multicolored   15
22 A6   5r multicolored   15
23 A6 10r multicolored   15
24 A6 15r multicolored   48
25 A6 20r green & multi   65
26 A6 25r multicolored   75
27 A6 35r multicolored   15
28 A6 50r multicolored   1.50
29 A6 100r multicolored   35
30 A6 100r blue & multi   3.25
31 A6 160r multicolored   55
32 A6 160r multicolored   55
   Nos. 20-32 (12)   8.68

Issued: 1r, 5r, 15r, 20r, 25r, 50r, No. 30,
6/8/93, others, 1994.
This is an expanding set. Numbers will change if
necessary.

Souvenir Sheet

1992 Summer Olympics, Barcelona — A7

1993, June 8
33 A7 50r multicolored   6.75

Epic Poem
"Book of
Kings", by
Ferdowsi,
1000th
Anniv. — A8

Designs: 5r, Combat with swords. 20r, Two men
on horseback fighting with spears. 30r, Men in
combat stopped by guide on giant bird, vert. 50r,
Ferdowsi (c. 935-c. 1020), vert.

1993, June 8   Litho.   Perf. 13½
34 A8   5r multicolored   52
35 A8 20r multicolored   2.00
36 A8 30r multicolored   3.00
     Souvenir Sheet
37 A8 50r multicolored   5.25

No. 37 contains one 30x45mm stamp.

Ali Hamadani (1314-
85), Persian
Mystic — A9

1994   Litho.   Perf. 13½
38 A9 1000r multicolored   3.25
39 A9 1000r multicolored   3.25

Name in latin letters on No. 38 and in cyrillic
letters on No. 39.

Natl. Arms — A10

1994

40	A10	10r black brown & multi	15	
41	A10	15r purple & multi	15	
43	A10	35r olive & multi	15	
44	A10	50r red & multi	16	
46	A10	100r green & multi	32	
47	A10	160r blue & multi	50	

Size: 23x36mm

50	A10	500r blue & multi	1.65	
52	A10	1000r brown & multi	3.25	
		Nos. 40-52 (8)	6.33	

This is an expanding set. Numbers will change if necessary.

Prehistoric Animals A11

Designs: No. 53, Diatryma. No. 54, Triceratops. No. 55, Anatosaurus. No. 56, Tyrannosaurus. No. 57, Parasaurolophus. No. 58, Tyrannosaurus, with horns. No. 59, Spinosaurus. No. 60, Stegosaurus.

1994		Litho.		Perf. 13½
53-60	A11	500r Set of 8		10.00

TAHITI

LOCATION — An island in the South Pacific Ocean, one of the Society group
GOVT. — A part of the French Oceania Colony
AREA — 600 sq. mi.
POP. — 19,029
CAPITAL — Papeete

The stamps of Tahiti were replaced by those of French Oceania (see French Polynesia in Vol. 3).

100 Centimes = 1 Franc

Counterfeits exist of surcharges and overprints on Nos. 1-31.

Stamps of French Colonies Surcharged in Black:

TAHITI

Handstamped in Black

1893

Perf. 14x13½

5	A9	1c blk, lil bl	400.	250.
6	A9	2c brown, buff	2,000.	1,500.
7	A9	4c claret, lav	800.	650.
8	A9	5c green, grnsh	15.	15.
9	A9	10c black, lav	15.	15.
10	A9	15c blue	15.	15.
11	A9	20c red, green	15.	15.
12	A9	25c yel, straw	4,000.	3,750.
13	A9	25c blk, rose	15.	15.
14	A9	35c violet, org	1,250.	1,250.
15	A9	75c carmine, rose	24.	24.
16	A9	1fr bmz grn, straw	26.	26.

Nearly all values of this set are known with overprint inverted, sloping up, sloping down and horizontal. Some occur double. Values the same as for the listed stamps.

1893

Overprinted in Black   **TAHITI**

1893

17	A9	1c blk, lil bl	400.00	375.00
a.		Inverted overprint	550.00	
18	A9	2c brn, buff	2,250.	1,750.
a.		Inverted overprint	2,750.	
19	A9	4c claret, lav	1,000.	900.00
a.		Inverted overprint	1,200.	
20	A9	5c grn, grnsh	550.00	450.00
a.		Inverted overprint	700.00	700.00
21	A9	10c black, lav	160.00	160.00
a.		Inverted overprint	350.00	350.00
22	A9	15c blue	15.00	15.00
a.		Inverted overprint	62.50	62.50
23	A9	20c red, grn	15.00	15.00
a.		Inverted overprint	82.50	82.50
24	A9	25c yel, straw	22,500.	18,500.
25	A9	25c black, rose	15.00	15.00
a.		Inverted overprint	82.50	82.50
26	A9	35c violet, org	1,500.	1,400.
a.		Inverted overprint	1,600.	
27	A9	75c carmine, rose	15.00	15.00
a.		Inverted overprint	82.50	82.50
b.		Double overprint	120.00	120.00
28	A9	1fr brmz grn, straw	15.00	15.00
a.		Inverted overprint	82.50	82.50

Stamps of French Polynesia Surcharged in Black or Carmine:

TAHITI	TAHITI
10	**10**
CENTIMES	centimes
g	h

1903

29	A1 (g)	10c on 15c bl (Bk)	3.25	3.25
a.		Double surcharge	17.50	17.50
b.		Inverted surcharge	17.50	17.50
30	A1 (h)	10c on 25c blk, rose (C)	3.25	3.25
a.		Double surcharge	17.50	17.50
b.		Inverted surcharge	17.50	17.50
31	A1 (h)	10c on 40c red, straw (Bk)	3.50	3.50
a.		Double surcharge	17.50	17.50
b.		Inverted surcharge	17.50	17.50

In the surcharges on Nos. 29-31 there are two varieties of the "1" in "10," i. e. with long and short serif.

SEMI-POSTAL STAMPS

Stamps of French Polynesia Overprinted in Red

1915		Unwmk.		Perf. 14x13½
B1	A1	15c blue	80.00	80.00
a.		Inverted overprint	250.00	250.00
B2	A1	15c gray	10.00	10.00
a.		Inverted overprint	100.00	100.00

Counterfeits exist.

TAHITI (surcharge types)

25c	25c
a	b

TAHITI 5c	TAHITI 10c
c	d

1882		Unwmk.		Imperf.
1	A8(a)	25c on 35c dk vio, org	150.	115.
1A	A8(b)	25c on 35c dk vio, org	2,750.	2,750.
1B	A8(a)	25c on 40c ver, straw	2,400.	2,400.

Inverted and vertical surcharges on Nos. 1 and 1A are about the same value as upright surcharges. Value for No. 1B is for inverted surcharge. Value for upright surcharge, $5,500.

1884				Perf. 14x13½
2	A9(c)	5c on 20c red, grn	110.	80.
3	A9(d)	10c on 20c red, grn	150.	125.

Imperf

| 4 | A8(b) | 25c on 1fr brnz grn, straw | 350. | 200. |

Inverted and vertical surcharges on Nos. 2-4 are same value as normally placed surcharges.

POSTAGE DUE STAMPS

Counterfeits exist of overprints on Nos. J1-J26.

Postage Due Stamps of French Colonies Handstamped in Black like Nos. 5-16

1893		Unwmk.		Imperf.
J1	D1	1c black	150.	150.
J2	D1	2c black	150.	150.
J3	D1	3c black	175.	175.
J4	D1	4c black	175.	175.
J5	D1	5c black	175.	175.
J6	D1	10c black	200.	200.
J7	D1	15c black	200.	200.
J8	D1	20c black	150.	150.
J9	D1	30c black	175.	175.
J10	D1	40c black	175.	175.
J11	D1	60c black	175.	175.
J12	D1	1fr brown	450.	450.
J13	D1	2fr brown	450.	450.

Many values exist with inverted or double overprint.

Overprinted in Black like Nos. 17-28

1893

J14	D1	1c black	1,100.	1,100.
a.		Inverted overprint	1,600.	1,600.
J15	D1	2c black	275.	275.
J16	D1	3c black	275.	275.
J17	D1	4c black	275.	275.
J18	D1	5c black	275.	275.
J19	D1	10c black	275.	275.
J20	D1	15c black	275.	275.
J21	D1	20c black	275.	275.
J22	D1	30c black	275.	275.
J23	D1	40c black	275.	275.
J24	D1	60c black	275.	275.
J25	D1	1fr brown	275.	275.
J26	D1	2fr brown	275.	275.

Nos. J15-J20, J22-J26 exist with overprint inverted, double or both. Value, each $600.

TANNU TUVA

(Tuva Autonomous Region.)

LOCATION — In the Tannu Mountains on the Siberian border in northwestern Mongolia
GOVT. — A former republic closely identified with Soviet Russia in Asia
AREA — 64,000 sq. mi. (approx.)
POP. — 65,000 (approx.)
CAPITAL — Kyzyl

The status of this country which has been under both Chinese and Russian rule at various times, was settled in 1926 by a Mixed Claims Commission. As a republic, its independence was maintained under Soviet protection. Later it became part of the Soviet Union as the Tuva Autonomous Soviet Socialist Republic.

100 Kopecks = 1 Ruble

Watermark

Wmk. 204- Stars and Diamonds

Wheel of Life — A1

1926		Typo.	Wmk. 204		Perf. 13½
		Size: 20x26mm			
1	A1	1k red		80	80
2	A1	2k light blue		80	80
3	A1	5k orange		80	80
4	A1	8k yel green		80	80
5	A1	10k violet		80	80

6	A1	30k dark brown	80	80
7	A1	50k gray black	1.65	1.65

Size: 22½x30mm
Perf. 10½

8	A1	1r blue green	4.50	4.50
9	A1	3r red brown	6.50	6.50
10	A1	5r dark ultra	10.00	10.00
		Nos. 1-10 (10)	27.45	27.45

Nos. 7-10 Surcharged in Red or Black — A2

1927			Perf. 13½, 11
11	A2	8k on 50k	10.50	10.00
12	A2	14k on 1r	13.00	12.00
13	A2	18k on 3r (Bk)	20.00	16.00
14	A2	28k on 5r (Bk)	22.50	20.00

Nos. 11-14 exist with surcharge inverted and No. 14 with surcharge double. Value $32.50 each. Reprints exist of Nos. 1-14.

Mongol Woman — A3	Map of Tannu Tuva — A8

Sheep Herding — A11

Fording a Stream — A13

Mongols Riding Reindeer — A16

Designs: 2k, Stag. 3k, Mountain goat. 4k, Mongol and tent. 5k, Mongol man. 10k, Bow-and-arrow hunters. 14k, Camel caravan. 28k, Landscape. 50k, Weaving. 70k, Mongol on horseback.

1927		Typo.	Perf. 12½, 12½x12
15	A3	1k blk, lt brn & red	50	25
16	A3	2k pur, dp brn & grn	65	50
17	A3	3k blk, bl grn & yel	65	50
18	A3	4k vio bl & choc	65	25
19	A3	5k org, blk & dk bl	50	25
20	A8	8k ol brn, pale bl & red brn	1.00	1.00
21	A8	10k blk, grn & brn red	3.50	1.00
22	A8	14k vio bl & red org	9.50	6.50

Perf. 10, 10½

23	A11	18k dk bl & red brn	9.50	5.50
24	A11	28k emer & blk brn	5.00	1.50
25	A13	40k rose & bl grn	3.50	1.50
26	A13	50k blk, grn & red brn	3.50	1.65
27	A13	70k dl red & bis	4.50	3.00
28	A16	1r yel brn & vio	10.00	5.50
		Nos. 15-28 (14)	52.95	28.90

Nos. 25-27, 20-22 Surcharged "Tuva", "Posta" and New Values in Various Colors

1932

29	A13	1k on 40k (Bk)	6.50	6.50
30	A13	2k on 50k (Br)	6.50	6.50
31	A13	3k on 70k (Bl)	6.50	6.50
a.		Inverted surcharge	140.00	

32	A8	5k on 8k (Bk)	8.50	8.50
33	A8	10k (Bk)	8.50	8.50
34	A8	15k on 14k (Bk)	8.50	8.50
		Nos. 29-34 (6)	45.00	45.00

Issued in connection with the Romanization of the alphabet.

#23-24 Surcharged in Black

No. 35

No. 36

1933			**Wmk. 204**	
35	A11	35k on 18k	110.00	110.00
36	A11	35k on 28k	110.00	110.00

A19

Revenue Stamps Surcharged "Posta" and New Values

1933			**Perf. 12x12½**	
37	A19	15k on 6k orange	200.00	175.00
38	A19	35k on 15k brn	700.00	700.00

Various pictorial sets, perf. and imperf., of triangular, diamond, square and oblong shapes, inscribed, "Postage," "Air-Mail" and "Registered," appeared in 1934 and 1935. The editors do not consider them to have been issued primarily for postal purposes.

TETE

LOCATION — In southeastern Africa between Nyasaland and Southern Rhodesia.
GOVT. — A district of the Portuguese East Africa Colony.
AREA — 46,600 sq. mi. (approx.)
POP. — 367,000 (approx.)
CAPITAL — Tete

This district was formerly a part of Zambezia. Stamps of Mozambique replaced those of Tete. See Mozambique.

100 Centavos = 1 Escudo

Vasco da Gama Issue of Various Portuguese Colonies Surcharged as

REPUBLICA
TETE
¼   C.

1913			**Unwmk.**	**Perf. 12½, 16**
		On Stamps of Macao		
1	CD20	¼c on ½a bl grn	3.50	6.00
2	CD21	½c on 1a red	2.00	3.00
3	CD22	1c on 2a red vio	2.00	3.00
4	CD23	2½c on 4a yel grn	2.00	3.00
5	CD24	5c on 8a dk blue	2.00	3.00

6	CD25	7½c on 12a vio brn	3.00	4.75
7	CD26	10c on 16a bis brn	2.00	3.00
8	CD27	15c on 24a bister	2.00	3.00
		Nos. 1-8 (8)	18.50	28.75
		On Stamps of Portuguese Africa		
9	CD20	¼c on 2½r bl grn	2.00	3.00
10	CD21	½c on 5r red	2.00	3.00
11	CD22	1c on 10r red vio	2.00	3.00
12	CD23	2½c on 25r yel grn	2.00	3.00
13	CD24	5c on 50r dk blue	2.00	3.00
14	CD25	7½c on 75r vio brn	3.00	4.75
15	CD26	10c on 100r bis brn	2.00	3.00
16	CD27	15c on 150r bister	2.00	3.00
		Nos. 9-16 (8)	17.00	25.75
		On Stamps of Timor		
17	CD20	¼c on ½a bl grn	2.00	3.00
18	CD21	½c on 1a red	2.00	3.00
19	CD22	1c on 2a red vio	2.00	3.00
a.		Inverted overprint	37.50	37.50
20	CD23	2½c on 4a yel grn	2.00	3.00
21	CD24	5c on 8a dk blue	2.00	3.00
22	CD25	7½c on 12a vio brn	3.00	4.75
23	CD26	10c on 16a bis brn	2.00	3.00
24	CD27	15c on 24a bister	2.00	3.00
		Nos. 17-24 (8)	17.00	25.75
		Nos. 1-24 (24)	52.50	80.25

Common Design Types pictured in section at front of book.

Ceres — A1

1914		**Typo.**	**Perf. 15x14**	
		Name and Value in Black		
25	A1	¼c olive brn	1.00	2.50
26	A1	½c black	1.00	2.50
27	A1	1c blue grn	60	1.10
28	A1	1½c lilac brn	1.00	2.50
29	A1	2c carmine	1.00	2.50
30	A1	2½c light vio	65	1.25
31	A1	5c deep blue	1.10	2.50
32	A1	7½c yel brn	2.00	3.75
33	A1	8c slate	2.25	4.25
34	A1	10c org brn	2.25	4.25
35	A1	15c plum	4.50	10.00
36	A1	20c yel green	3.00	8.75
37	A1	30c brn, green	5.25	9.25
38	A1	40c brn, pink	5.25	9.50
39	A1	50c org, salmon	5.25	11.00
40	A1	1e grn, blue	5.75	12.00
		Nos. 25-40 (16)	41.85	87.60

THAILAND

(Siam)

LOCATION — Western part of the Malay peninsula in southeastern Asia
GOVT. — Republic
AREA — 198,250 sq. mi.
POP. — 50,000,000 (est. 1984)
CAPITAL — Bangkok

32 Solot = 16 Atts = 8 Sio = 4 Sik = 2 Fuang = 1 Salung
4 Salungs = 1 Tical
100 Satangs (1909) = 1 Tical = 1 Baht (1912)

Catalogue values for unused stamps in this country are for Never Hinged items, beginning with Scott 260 in the regular postage section, Scott B34 in the semi-postal section, Scott C20 in the airpost section, and Scott O1 in the official section.

Watermarks

Wmk. 176- Chakra

Wmk. 233- Harrison & Sons, London in Script Letters

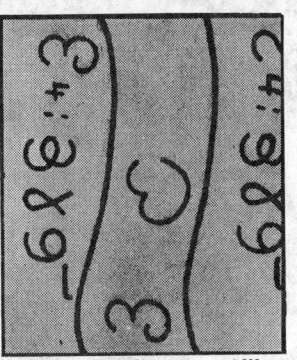

Wmk. 299- Thai Characters and Wavy Lines

Wmk. 329- Zigzag Lines

Wmk. 334- Rectangles

Wmk. 356-
POSTAGE

Wmk. 368- JEZ Multiple

Wmk. 371- Wavy Lines

Wmk. 374-
Circles and
Crosses

Wmk. 375- Letters

Wmk. 385 -
CARTOR

Wmk. 387- Squares and Rectangles

King Chulalongkorn
A1   A2

A4

		Perf. 14½, 15		
1883, Aug. 4		**Unwmk.**	**Engr.**	
1	A1	1sol blue	7.25	10.00
b.		Imperf., pair		
2	A1	1att carmine	8.50	8.50
3	A1	1sio vermilion	32.50	20.00
4	A2	1sik yellow	10.00	15.00
5	A4	1sa orange	45.00	45.00
a.		1sa ocher	50.00	50.00

There are three types of No. 1, differing mainly in the background of the small oval at the top.
A 1 fuang red, of similar design to the foregoing, was prepared but not placed in use.
For surcharges see Nos. 6-8, 19.

THAILAND

RARE AND CLASSIC STAMPS, POSTAL HISTORY, PROOFS. BUYING, SELLING, APPRAISALS.

For the Best Services in Classic Stamps and Postal History contact the RECOGNIZED LEADERS IN THE FIELD.
Excellent stock of classic material for most countries of the World also available.

THE CLASSIC COLLECTOR
LIANE & SERGIO SISMONDO

Ph. 315-422-2331, Fax 315-422-2956
10035 Carousel Center Drive
Syracuse, NY 13290-0001

CANADIAN OFFICE: P.O. Box 6277, Station J, Ottawa, Canada K2A 1T4. Ph. 613-722-1621, Fax: 613-728-7305

King Chulalongkorn — A7

1887-91   Typo.   Wmk. 176   Perf. 14

11	A7	1a green ('91)	2.00	1.00
12	A7	2a green & car	2.75	1.00
13	A7	3a grn & blue	9.25	3.00
14	A7	4a grn & org brn	7.00	3.00
15	A7	8a green & yel	7.00	3.00
16	A7	12a lilac & car	19.00	1.50
17	A7	24a lilac & blue	21.00	1.50
18	A7	64a lil & org brn	92.50	24.00
		Nos. 11-18 (8)	160.50	38.00

The design of No. 11 has been redrawn and differs from the illustration in many minor details.
Issue dates: #12-18, Apr. 1; #11, Feb.
For surcharges see Nos. 20-69, 109, 111, 126.

No. 3 Handstamp Surcharged **อัฐ**

1889, Aug.   Unwmk.   Perf. 15

19	A1	1a on 1sio	9.00	12.00

Three different handstamps were used.
Doubles, etc. exist.

Nos. 12 and 13
Handstamp Surcharged **๑ อัฐ 1**

1889-90   Wmk. 176   Perf. 14

20	A7	1a on 2a	2.75	2.00
a.		"1" omitted	250.00	250.00
c.		1st Siamese character invtd.		
d.		First Siamese character omitted	300.00	300.00
21	A7	1a on 3a ('90)	7.50	7.25
a.		Inverted "1"	150.00	150.00

For surcharge see No. 29.

No. 1 Handstamp Surcharged in Red:

1 TICAL
a

1 Tical   **1 Tical**
b   *c*

1 Tical   **1 Tical**
d   *e*

1885, July 1

6	A1 (a)	1t on 1sol blue	450.	450.
7	A1 (b)	1t on 1sol blue	350.	350.
c.		"1" inverted	1,200.	1,200.
8	A1 (c)	1t on 1sol blue	450.	450.

Surcharges of Nos. 6-8 have been counterfeited.
Types "d" and "e" are typeset *official reprints*.
As is usual with handstamps, double impressions, etc., exist.

๑ อัฐ 1

22	A7	1a on 2a grn & car	400.00	450.00

๑ อัฐ 1

24	A7	1a on 2a grn & car	175.00	125.00

๑ อัฐ 1

25	A7	1a on 2a grn & car	1,000.	1,000.

Buying & Selling Stamps and Covers of...
Thailand ★ Vietnam ★ Laos
All China ★ Hong Kong
Japan ★ Korea ★ Cambodia
• WANT LISTS SERVICED •
Buying Worldwide! Write, Call or Send Insured For Our Top Offer!
PACIFIC MIDWEST CO.
(Our 29th year)
P.O. Box 1696, Daly City, CA 94014
Ph. 415-994-1117 • FAX 415-994-7439
• We accept Visa, MasterCard, Diner's Card, Carte Blanche •
China Stamp Soc.   Soc. Thai. Philately

๑ อัฐ 1

26	A7	1a on 3a grn & bl		

Some authorities consider No. 26 a forgery.
Doubles, etc., exist in this issue.
Issue dates: Nov. 1889. Sept. 1890.

No. 13 Handstamp Surcharged **๒ อัฐ 2**

1891

27	A7	2a on 3a grn & bl	50.00	40.00

๒ อัฐ 2

28	A7	2a on 3a grn & bl	45.00	40.00
a.		Double surcharge	250.00	250.00
b.		"2" omitted	250.00	

No. 21 with Additional 2 Att Surcharge

๒ อัฐ 2

29	A7	2a on 1a on 3a grn & bl	1,500.	1,500.

On No. 29 the 2a surcharge consists of Siamese numeral like No. 27 and English numeral like No. 28.
Most examples of No. 29 show attempts to remove the "1" of the first surcharge.

๒ อัฐ 2

Typeset Surcharge

30	A7	2a on 3a grn & bl	37.50	30.00

There are 7 types of this surcharge in the setting.
Issue dates: Nos. 27-28, Jan.; No. 29, Feb.; No. 30, Mar.

No. 17 Handstamp Surcharged:

f   *g*

1892, Oct.

33	A7 (f)	4a on 24a lil & bl	47.50	45.00
34	A7 (g)	4a on 24a lil & bl	30.00	30.00

Surcharges exist double on Nos. 33-34 and inverted on No. 33.

Nos. 33-34 Handstamp Surcharged in English
4 atts

1892, Nov.

35	A7	4a on 24a lil & bl	7.50	5.00
c.		Inverted "s"	40.00	40.00

4 atts.

36	A7	4a on 24a lil & bl	12.00	5.00
a.		Inverted "s"	40.00	40.00

4 atts

37	A7	4a on 24a lil & bl	11.00	10.00

4 atts.

38	A7	4a on 24a lil & bl	12.00	10.00

Numerous inverts., doubles, etc., exist.

Nos. 18 and 17 Typeset Surcharged in English (Shown) and Siamese

1   Atts

1894

39	A7	1a on 64a lil & org brn	3.00	2.50
a.		Inverted "s"	40.00	40.00
b.		Inverted surcharge	900.00	900.00
d.		Italic "s"	50.00	50.00
e.		Italic "1"	50.00	50.00

1   Att.

40	A7	1a on 64a lil & org brn	1.50	1.50
a.		Inverted capital "S" added to the surcharge	175.00	200.00

2   Atts.   2   Atts.
h   *i*

2   Atts.   2   Atts.
j   *k*

2.   Atts.   2   Atts.
l   *m*

41	A7 (h)	2a on 64a	20.00	20.00
a.		Inverted "s"	40.00	40.00
b.		Double surcharge	100.00	100.00
42	A7 (i)	2a on 64a	3,000.	3,000.
43	A7 (j)	2a on 64a	55.00	55.00
44	A7 (k)	2a on 64a	30.00	30.00
45	A7 (l)	2a on 64a	50.00	50.00
46	A7 (m)	2a on 64a	1.65	1.50
a.		"Att.s"	40.00	40.00

1 Att.

1894, Oct. 12

47	A7	1a on 64a	2.00	1.90
a.		Surcharged on face and back	150.00	
b.		Surcharge on back inverted	200.00	
c.		Double surcharge	400.00	
d.		Inverted surcharge	500.00	
e.		Siamese surcharge omitted	400.00	

2 Atts.

48	A7	2a on 64a	2.50	2.00
a.		"Att"	35.00	30.00
b.		Inverted surcharge	300.00	300.00
c.		Surcharged on face and back	400.00	400.00
d.		Surcharge on back inverted	400.00	400.00
e.		Double surcharge	300.00	300.00
f.		Double surcharge, one inverted	1,100.	1,100.
g.		Inverted "s"	40.00	40.00

10 Atts.

1895, July 23

49	A7	10a on 24a lil & bl	6.00	1.50
a.		Inverted "s"	40.00	25.00
b.		Surcharged on face and back	175.00	175.00
c.		Surcharge on back inverted	175.00	175.00

No. 16 Surcharged in English (Shown) and Siamese

4 Atts.

1896

50	A7	4a on 12a lil & car	10.00	3.75
a.		Inverted "s"	50.00	50.00
b.		Surcharged on face and back	175.00	175.00
c.		Double surcharge on back	175.00	175.00

Two types of surcharge.

Nos. 16-18 Surcharged in English (Shown) and Siamese
Antique Surcharges:

1 Atts.	1 Att.	2 Atts.
a	*b*	*c*

3 Atts.	4 Atts.	10 Atts
d	*e*	*f*

Atts.
Antique Letters

Atts.
Roman Letters

1898-99
51	A7 (a)	1a on 12a	325.00	325.00
52	A7 (b)	1a on 12a	15.00	5.00
53	A7 (c)	2a on 64a ('99)	11.00	4.50
54	A7 (d)	3a on 12a	8.50	2.75
a.		Double surcharge	350.00	350.00
55	A7 (e)	4a on 12a	8.00	3.25
a.		Double surcharge	350.00	350.00
56	A7 (e)	4a on 24a ('99)	15.00	5.50
57	A7 (f)	10a on 12a ('99)	1,100.	1,100.

Roman Surcharges:

1 Atts.	1 Att.	2 Atts.
g	*h*	*i*

3 Atts.	4 Atts.	10 Atts.
j	*k*	*l*

58	A7 (g)	1a on 12a	75.00	75.00
59	A7 (h)	1a on 12a	27.50	7.00
60	A7 (i)	2a on 64a ('99)	22.50	6.00
61	A7 (j)	3a on 12a	8.00	7.00
62	A7 (k)	4a on 12a	4.50	3.00
a.		Double surcharge	175.00	175.00
b.		No period after "Atts."	30.00	30.00
63	A7 (k)	4a on 24a ('99)	9.00	5.50
64	A7 (l)	10a on 24a ('99)	250.00	250.00

In making the settings to surcharge Nos. 51 to 64 two fonts were mixed. Antique and Roman letters are frequently found on the same stamp.

Issue dates: Nos. 54-55, 61-62, Feb. 22. Nos. 51-52, 58-59, June 4. Nos. 56-57, 63-64, Oct. 3.

Nos. 16 and 18 Surcharged in English (Shown) and Siamese
Surcharged:

1 Att.	1 Att.
m	*n*

1 Att.	
o	

2 Atts.	2 Atts.
p	*r*

1894-99
65	A7 (m)	1a on 12a	20.00	2.25
66	A7 (n)	1a on 12a	18.00	6.00
a.		Inverted "I"	150.00	150.00
b.		Inverted 1st "t"	150.00	150.00
67	A7 (o)	1a on 64a	4.50	3.50
68	A7 (p)	2a on 64a	8.50	4.50
a.		" 1 Atts."	500.00	500.00
69	A7 (r)	2a on 64a	24.00	3.25

Issued: #67, 10/12/94; others, 2/14/99.

A13

A14

1899, Oct.
		Typo.	Unwmk.	
70	A13	1a dull green	250.00	100.
71	A13	2a dl grn & rose	350.00	125.
72	A13	3a carmine & blue	750.00	350.

73	A13	4a black & grn	1,400.	525.
74	A13	10a carmine & grn	2,100.	800.
		Nos. 70-74 (5)	4,850.	1,900.

The King rejected Nos. 70-74 in 1897, but some were released by mistake to three post offices in Oct. 1899. Used values are for copies canceled to order at Korat in Dec. 1899. Postally used examples sell for more.

1899-1904
75	A14	1a gray green	2.50	1.00
76	A14	2a yellow green	3.50	1.00
77	A14	2a scarlet & bl	4.00	1.40
78	A14	3a red & blue	11.00	2.75
79	A14	3a green	30.00	14.00
80	A14	4a dark rose	4.00	1.40
81	A14	4a vio brn & rose	13.00	2.75
82	A14	6a dk rose	40.00	15.00
83	A14	8a dk grn & org	9.50	1.40
84	A14	10a ultra	12.50	3.50
85	A14	12a brn vio & rose	55.00	2.75
86	A14	14a ultra	32.50	17.50
87	A14	24a brn vio & bl	225.00	17.50
88	A14	28a vio brn & bl	35.00	21.00
89	A14	64a brn vio & org brn	82.50	7.00
		Nos. 75-89 (15)	560.00	109.95

Two types of 1a differ in size and shape of Thai "1" are in drawing of spandrel ornaments.
Issue dates: 6a, 14a, 28a, Nos. 77, 79, 81, Jan. 1, 1904; others, Sept. 1899.
For surcharges see Nos. 90-91, 112, 125, 127.

Nos. 78 and 85 With Typewritten Surcharge of 6 or 7 Siamese Characters (1 line) in Violet

1902
78a	A14	2a on 3a	1,900.	2,250.
85a	A14	10a on 12a	1,900.	2,250.

Nos. 78a and 85a were authorized provisionals, surcharged and issued by the Battambang postmaster.

1 Att.

Nos. 86 and 88 Surcharged in Black

๑ อ๊

1905, Feb.
90	A14	1a on 14a	9.50	7.00
a.		No period after "Att"	35.00	35.00
91	A14	2a on 28a	11.00	8.50
a.		Double surcharge	110.00	110.00

King Chulalongkorn
A15   A16

1905-08   Engr.
92	A15	1a orange & green	1.25	50
93	A15	2a violet & slate	2.50	95
94	A15	2a green ('08)	7.50	3.75
95	A15	3a green	3.50	1.50
96	A15	3a vio & sl ('08)	11.00	5.00
97	A15	4a gray & red	3.50	1.00
98	A15	4a car & rose ('08)	6.25	1.00
99	A15	5a carmine & rose	6.75	2.50
100	A15	8a blk & ol bis	6.25	95
101	A15	9a blue ('08)	21.00	7.50
102	A15	12a blue	16.00	2.75
103	A15	18a red brn ('08)	60.00	15.00
104	A15	24a red brown	27.50	5.00
105	A15	1t dp bl & brn org	47.50	7.50
		Nos. 92-105 (14)	220.50	54.90

Issue dates: Dec. 1905, Apr. 1, 1908.
For surcharges and overprints see Nos. 110, 113-117, 128-138, 161-162, B15, B21.

1907, Apr. 24
Black Surcharge
106	A16	10t gray green	650.	140.
107	A16	20t gray green	1,300.	400.
108	A16	40t gray green	3,750.	775.

Counterfeits of Nos. 106-108 exist. In the genuine, the surcharged figures correspond to the Siamese value inscriptions on the basic revenue stamps.

No. 17 Surcharged

1907, Dec. 16
109	A7	1a on 24a lil & bl	1.25	80
a.		Double surcharge	125.00	125.00

No. 99 Surcharged   4

1908, Sept.
110	A15	4a on 5a car & rose	8.00	3.25

The No. 110 surcharge is found in two spacings of the numerals: normally 15mm apart, and a narrow, scarcer spacing of 13½mm.

Nos. 17 and 84 Surcharged in Black:

๒ อ๊   ๔ อ๊

2 Atts   9 Atts

111	A7	2a on 24a lil & bl	1.50	80
a.		Inverted surcharge	675.00	675.00
112	A14	9a on 10a ultra	12.00	5.00
a.		Inverted surcharge	675.00	450.00

THAILAND/SIAM/BANGKOK
★ BUYING AND SELLING ★
RARE AND CLASSIC STAMPS, POSTAL HISTORY, COINS AND BANKNOTES.
WANTED: SPECIALIZED THAI COLLECTIONS OR FINE STOCK OF STAMPS AND COVERS. IF YOU HAVE, PLEASE CONTACT:
LENG STAMPS COMPANY
717/2 SRIPHRAYA ROAD, BANGKOK, THAILAND 10500
Postal Address: G.P.O. BOX 1214, BANGKOK, THAILAND 10501
Phone + 662-233-3178 • FAX + 662-267-0938

Jubilee Issue

รัชมังคลา
ภิเศก
๘๓–๑๒๓๗.

Nos. 92, 95, 110, 100 and 103 Overprinted in Black or Red

Jubilee
1868-1908

1908, Nov. 11
113	A15	1a	2.25	1.10
a.		Siamese date "137" instead of "127"	900.00	900.00
b.		Pair, one without ovpt.		
114	A15	3a	3.25	2.50
115	A15	4a on 5a	5.25	3.50
a.		Horiz. pair, imperf. btwn.	500.00	
116	A15	8a (R)	17.50	17.50
117	A15	18a	25.00	20.00
		Nos. 113-117 (5)	53.25	44.60

40th year of the reign of King Chulalongkorn.
Nos. 113 to 117 exist with a small "i" in "Jubilee."

Statue of King Chulalongkorn
A19

1908, Nov. 11   Engr.   Perf. 13½
118	A19	1t green & vio	37.50	3.00
119	A19	2t red vio & org	80.00	12.00
120	A19	3t pale ol & bl	92.50	15.00
121	A19	5t dl vio & dk grn	140.00	24.00
122	A19	10t bister & car	950.00	75.00

HOW TO SELL FOR THE HIGHEST PRICE
Everyone says they pay the highest price but as Thailand/Asia can be complicated, going far beyond Scott & buylists, not everyone knows the material. Buylists are fine for modern sets.

Consider our references: Asia specialist since 1982 filling over 4,000 mail orders yearly to collectors in over 60 countries; conducts 2-3 Asia Public Auctions yearly; extensive Asia specialist writings published in USA (Linn's), Australasia, Europe, Japan etc.; publisher of many Asia/China handbooks/monographs; quoted in Forbes; member of over 32 professional and collector societies.

THREE WAYS TO SELL
1. No nonsense buy lists (sent for 52¢ long SASE)
2. Send material not appropriate for buylists for fair, immediate offer. Include your phone number.
3. Consign to our Asia Public Auction. Reserved at half the estimated cash value, no chance your material is given away. Over 3,000 erudite, well illustrated catalogues sent to proven buyers. We charge the seller simply 10% commission. Minimum consignment $500.

MICHAEL ROGERS, INC.

199 E. Welbourne Avenue, Winter Park, Florida 32789
1-800-843-3751 • (407) 645-4434 Fax

123 A19 20t gray & red brn 275.00 67.50
124 A19 40t sl bl & blk brn 475.00 150.00
Nos. 118-124 (7) 2,050. 346.50

The inscription at the foot of the stamps reads: "Coronation Commemoration-Forty-first year of the reign-1908."

๖ สตางค์

Stamps of 1887-1904 Surcharged

6 Satang

1909 Perf. 14
125 A14 6s on 6a dk rose 2.25 1.50
126 A7 14s on 12a lil & car 90.00 85.00
127 A14 14s on 14a ultra 17.00 13.00

Nos. 92-102 Surcharged with Bar and ๒ สตางค์

2 Satang

1909, Aug. 15
128 A15 2s on 1a #92 85 35
129 A15 2s on 2a #93 85.00 80.00
130 A15 2s on 2a #94 85 50
a. "2" omitted 100.00
131 A15 3s on 3a #95 1.75 1.75
132 A15 3s on 3a #96 1.25 40
133 A15 6s on 4a #97 60.00 47.50
134 A15 6s on 4a #98 2.25 75
135 A15 6s on 4a #99 2.00 1.75
136 A15 12s on 8a #100 3.50 75
137 A15 14s on 9a #101 4.00 1.25
138 A15 14s on 12a #102 20.00 18.00
Nos. 128-138 (11) 181.45 153.00

King Chulalongkorn — A20

1910 Engr. Perf. 14x14½
139 A20 2s org & green 1.10 45
140 A20 3s green 1.90 45
141 A20 6s carmine 3.00 45
142 A20 12s blk & ol brn 5.75 75
143 A20 14s blue 17.50 1.25
144 A20 28s red brown 40.00 7.00
Nos. 139-144 (6) 69.25 10.35

Issue dates: 12s, June 5. Others, May 5.
For surcharges see Nos. 163, 223-224.

King Vajiravudh
A21 A22

Printed at the Imperial Printing Works, Vienna

1912 Perf. 14½
145 A21 2s brown orange 95 18
a. Vert. pair, imperf. btwn. 500.00 500.00
b. Horiz. pair, imperf. btwn. 500.00 500.00
146 A21 3s yellow green 95 18
a. Horiz. pair, imperf. btwn. 500.00 500.00
147 A21 6s carmine rose 1.75 52
148 A21 12s gray blk & brn 2.50 55
149 A21 14s ultramarine 4.00 70
150 A21 28s chocolate 14.00 6.50
151 A22 1b blue & blk 14.00 1.25
a. Pair, imperf. btwn. 1,000. 1,000.
152 A22 2b car rose & ol brn 18.00 2.25
153 A22 3b yel grn & bl blk 24.00 4.00
154 A22 5b vio & blk 32.50 4.00
155 A22 10b ol grn & vio brn 165.00 65.00
156 A22 20b sl bl & red brn 300.00 55.00
Nos. 145-156 (12) 577.65 140.13

See Nos. 164-175.
For surcharges and overprints see Nos. 157-160, 176-186, 206, B1-B14, B16-B20, B22, B31-B33.

Nos. 147-150 Surcharged in Red or Blue
๕ สตางค์ 5 Satang

1914-15
157 A21 2s on 14s (R) ('15) 1.00 30
a. Vert. pair, imperf. btwn. 900.00 900.00
b. Double surcharge 70.00 45.00
158 A21 5s on 6s (Bl) 1.90 30
a. Horiz. pair, imperf. btwn. 900.00 900.00
b. Double surcharge 70.00 70.00
159 A21 10s on 12s (R) 2.25 30
a. Double surcharge 75.00 60.00
160 A21 15s on 28s (Bl) 3.00 30

The several settings of the surcharges on Nos. 157 to 160 show variations in the figures and letters.

Nos. 92-93 Surcharged ๒ สตางค์ 2 Satang

1915, Apr. 3
161 A15 2s on 1a org & grn 3.50 3.00
a. Pair, one without surcharge 62.50 62.50
162 A15 2s on 2a vio & slate 3.50 3.00

No. 143 Surcharged in Red ๒ สตางค์ 2 Satang

1916, Oct.
163 A20 2s on 14s blue 2.00 75

Printed by Waterlow & Sons, London
Types of 1912 Re-engraved

1917, Jan. 1 Perf. 14
164 A21 2s orange brown 70 22
165 A21 3s emerald 45 18
166 A21 5s rose red 60 18
167 A21 10s black & olive 90 18
168 A21 15s blue 1.40 35
170 A22 1b bl & gray blk 32.50 75
171 A22 2b car rose & brn 42.50 6.00
172 A22 3b yellow grn & blk 125.00 125.00
173 A22 5b dp violet & blk 67.50 20.00
174 A22 10b ol gray & vio brn 300.00 20.00
a. Perf. 12½ 600.00 40.00
175 A22 20b sea green & brn 400.00 60.00
a. Perf. 12½ 700.00 80.00
Nos. 164-175 (11) 971.55 262.86

The re-engraved design of the satang stamps varies in numerous minute details from the 1912 issue. Four lines of the background appear between the vertical strokes of the "M" of "SIAM" in the 1912 issue and only three lines in the 1917 stamps.
The 1912 stamps with value in bahts are 37½mm high; those of 1917 are 39mm. In the latter the king's features, especially the eyes and mouth, are more distinct and the uniform and decorations are more sharply defined.
The 1912 stamps have seven pearls between the earpieces of the crown. On the 1917 stamps there are nine pearls in the same place. Nos. 174 and 175 exist imperforate.

Nos. 164-173 Overprinted in Red วันชัย VICTORY

1918, Dec. 2
176 A21 2s orange brown 1.50 55
a. Double overprint 50.00
177 A21 3s emerald 1.40 50
178 A21 5s rose red 85 70
a. Double overprint 50.00
179 A21 10s black & olive 4.00 1.10
180 A21 15s blue 4.75 1.35
181 A22 1b bl & gray blk 45.00 8.50
182 A22 2b car rose & brn 70.00 15.00
183 A22 3b yellow grn & blk 87.50 18.00
184 A22 5b dp vio & blk 250.00 50.00
Nos. 176-184 (9) 465.00 95.70

Counterfeits of this overprint exist.

Nos. 147-148 Surcharged in Green or Red
๕ 5 ๓๐ 10

1919-20
185 A21 5s on 6s (G) 90 20
186 A21 10s on 12s (R) ('20) 2.75 40
Issue dates: 5s, Nov. 11. 10s, Jan. 1.

King Vajiravudh A23   Throne Room A24

1920-26 Engr. Perf. 14-15, 12½
187 A23 2s brn, yel ('21) 1.90 38
188 A23 3s grn, grn ('21) 3.00 38
189 A23 3s chocolate ('24) 3.00 32
190 A23 5s rose, pale rose 3.50 38
191 A23 5s green ('22) 27.50 2.50
192 A23 5s dk vio, lil ('26) 6.75 38

193 A23 10s black & org ('21) 5.25 38
194 A23 15s bl, bluish ('21) 7.75 55
195 A23 15s carmine ('22) 37.50 2.25
196 A23 25s chocolate ('21) 19.00 1.65
197 A23 25s dk blue ('22) 22.50 1.25
198 A23 50s blk & blk ('21) 21.00 1.25
Nos. 187-198 (12) 158.65 11.67

For overprints see Nos. 205, B23-B30.

1926, Mar. 5 Perf. 12½
199 A24 1t gray vio & grn 9.25 1.75
200 A24 2t car & org red 27.50 5.50
201 A24 3t ol grn & bl 57.50 32.50
202 A24 5t dl vio & ol grn 37.50 11.00
203 A24 10t red & ol bis 325.00 20.00
204 A24 20t gray bl & brn 250.00 75.00
Nos. 199-204 (6) 706.75 145.75

This issue was intended to commemorate the fifteenth year of the reign of King Vajiravudh. Because of the King's death the stamps were issued as ordinary postage stamps.

Nos. 195 and 150 with Surcharge similar to 1914-15 Issue in Black or Red

1928, Jan.
205 A23 5s on 15s car 3.00 70
206 A21 5s on 28s choc (R) 3.00 85

King Prajadhipok
A25 A26

1928 Engr. Perf. 12½
207 A25 2s deep red brown 28 15
208 A25 3s deep green 38 15
209 A25 5s dark violet 38 15
210 A25 10s deep rose 38 15
211 A25 15s dark blue 52 40
212 A25 25s black & org 80 60
213 A25 50s brn org & blk 1.40 1.25
214 A25 80s blue & black 2.00 80
216 A26 1b dk blue & blk 2.25 1.25
217 A26 2b car rose & blk brn 4.75 2.00
218 A26 3b yellow grn & blk 8.00 2.75
219 A26 5b dp vio & gray blk 21.00 4.00
220 A26 10b ol grn & red vio 30.00 8.00
221 A26 20b Prus grn & brn 50.00 14.00
222 A26 40b dk grn & ol brn 110.00 45.00
Nos. 207-222 (15) 232.14 80.65

On the single colored stamps, type A25, the lines in the background are uniform; those of the bicolored values are shaded and do not extend to the frame.
Issue dates: 5s, 10s, 2b-40b, Apr. 15. 2s, 3s, 15s, 25s, 50s, May 1. 1b, June 1. 80s, Nov. 15.
For overprints & surcharge see Nos. 300-301, B34.

Nos. 142, 144 Surcharged in Red or Blue ๒๕ สตางค์ 25 SATANG

1930 Perf. 14
223 A20 10s on 12s blk & ol brn 1.50 75
224 A20 25s on 28s red brn (Bl) 5.00 1.25

King Prajadhipok and Chao P'ya Chakri
A27   A28

Statue of Chao P'ya Chakri — A29

1932, Apr. 1 Engr. Perf. 12½
225 A27 2s dark brown 1.75 22
226 A27 3s deep green 4.00 42
227 A27 5s dull violet 4.00 22
228 A28 10s red brn & blk 4.50 22
229 A28 15s dull blue & blk 11.00 90

PLAN NOW TO FEATURE YOUR ADVERTISING MESSAGE IN THE

S·C·O·T·T CATALOGUES

Call Scott advertising 513-498-0832 or write to us and we'll place your name on our prospect list to receive full information, as soon as it is available, on advertising rates and copy deadlines. If you are interested in specific positions, place your name on our reservation list as soon as possible.

Scott Publishing Company

FAX: 513-498-0807 • P.O. Box 828, Sidney, OH 45365 U.S.A.

230 A28	25s violet & black	15.00	1.40
231 A28	50s claret & black	27.50	3.25
232 A29	1b blue black	80.00	11.00
	Nos. 225-232 (8)	147.75	17.63

150th anniv. of the Chakri dynasty, the founding of Bangkok in 1782, and the opening of the memorial bridge across the Chao Phraya River.

Assembly Hall, Bangkok — A30

1939, June 24   Litho.   Perf. 11, 12

233 A30	2s dull red brown	3.75	45
234 A30	3s green	7.50	1.90
235 A30	5s dark violet	6.25	24
236 A30	10s carmine	12.00	24
237 A30	15s dark blue	30.00	1.10
	Nos. 233-237 (5)	59.50	3.93

7th anniv. of the Siamese Constitution.

Chakri Palace, Bangkok — A31

1940   Typo.   Perf. 12½

238 A31	2s dull brown	5.50	45
239 A31	3s dp yellow grn	7.50	1.90
a.	Cliché of 5s in plate of 3s	1,000.	800.00
240 A31	5s dark violet	10.00	22
241 A31	10s carmine	18.00	22
242 A31	15s dark blue	24.00	90
	Nos. 238-242 (5)	65.00	3.69

Issue dates: 2s, 3s, May 13. 5s, May 24. 15s, May, 28. 10s, May 30.

King Ananda Mahidol — A32   Plowing Rice Field — A33

Royal Pavilion at Bang-pa-in A34   King Ananda Mahidol A35

1941, Apr. 17   Engr.

243 A32	2s brown	45	24
244 A32	3s deep green	45	48
245 A32	5s violet	45	24
246 A32	10s dark red	45	24
247 A33	15s dp bl & gray blk	60	24
248 A33	25s slate & org	80	48
249 A33	50s red org & gray	95	48
250 A34	1b brt ultra & gray	8.50	95
251 A34	2b dk car rose & gray	16.00	2.00
252 A34	3b dp grn & gray	19.00	4.25
253 A34	5b blk & rose red	47.50	17.00
a.	Horiz. pair, imperf. btwn.		
254 A34	10b ol blk & yel	70.00	42.50
	Nos. 243-254 (12)	165.15	69.10

1943, May 1   Unwmk.   Perf. 11

255 A35	1b dark blue	5.00	1.50

See No. 274.

Indo-China War Monument A36   Bangkhaen Monument A37

1943   Engr.   Perf. 11, 12½

256 A36	3s dark green	5.50	1.10

Litho.   Perf. 12½x11

257 A36	3s dull green	1.40	1.25

Issue dates: #256, June 1. #257, Nov. 2.

1943, Nov. 25   Perf. 12½, 12½x11

Two types of 10s:
I - Size 19½x24mm.
II - Size 20¾x25¼mm.

258 A37	2s brown orange	1.75	1.65
259 A37	10s car rose (I)	1.50	40
a.	Type II	1.50	60

10th anniv. of the quelling of a counter-revolution led by a member of the royal family on Oct. 11, 1933.

Stamps of similar design, but with values in "cents", are listed in Volume 1 under Malaya, Occupation Stamps.

Catalogue values for unused stamps in this section, from this point to the end of the section, are for Never Hinged items.

King Bhumibol Adulyadej A38   A39

1947, Dec. 5   Pin-perf. 12½x11

260 A38	5s orange	3.75	80
261 A38	10s olive ('48)	3.75	80
a.	10s light brown	45.00	27.50
262 A38	20s blue	15.00	80
263 A38	50s blue green	2.00	2.50

Coming of age of King Bhumibol Adulyadej. Values for Nos. 260-263 arefor copies with gum.

1947-49   Unwmk.   Engr.   Perf. 12½
Size: 20x25mm

264 A39	5s violet	1.75	15
265 A39	10s red	1.75	15
266 A39	20s chocolate	2.50	16
267 A39	50s olive	5.75	16

Size: 22x27mm

268 A39	1b vio & dp bl	19.00	20
269 A39	2b ultra & green	37.50	1.25
270 A39	3b brn red & blk	52.50	3.00
271 A39	5b bl grn & brn red	110.00	4.00
272 A39	10b dk brn & pur	165.00	1.25
273 A39	20b blk & rose brn	325.00	4.00
	Nos. 264-273 (10)	720.75	14.82

Issued: 5s, 20s, 11/15/47; 10s, 50s, 1/3/49; 1b-20b, 11/1/48.

For surcharges see Nos. 302-303.

Type of 1943
Perf. 11½, 12½x11½
1948, Jan.   Litho.

274 A35	1b chalky blue	18.00	7.50
a.	Pair, imperf. btwn.	60.00	60.00

King Bhumibol Adulyadej and Palace
A40   A41

Perf. 12½
1950, May 5   Unwmk.   Engr.

275 A40	5s red violet	1.65	20
276 A40	10s red	1.65	20
277 A40	15s purple	2.25	1.25
278 A40	20s chocolate	3.25	20
279 A40	80s green	6.25	2.50
280 A40	1b deep blue	6.25	20
281 A40	2b orange yellow	17.00	8.25
282 A40	3b gray	50.00	3.25
	Nos. 275-282 (8)	88.30	16.05

Coronation of Bhumibol Adulyadej as Rama IX, May 5, 1950.

1951-60   Perf. 12½, 13x12½

283 A41	5s rose lilac	65	15
284 A41	10s deep green	65	15
285 A41	15s red brown	95	20
285A A41	20s chocolate	95	15
286 A41	25s carmine	75	15
287 A41	50s gray olive	1.10	15
288 A41	1b deep blue	2.25	20
289 A41	1.15b deep blue	4.75	50
290 A41	1.25b orange brn	5.50	35
291 A41	2b dull blue grn	6.00	35
292 A41	3b gray	10.50	50
293 A41	5b aqua & red	42.50	65
294 A41	10b black brn & vio	300.00	1.40
295 A41	20b gray & olive	225.00	11.00
	Nos. 283-295 (14)	601.55	15.90

Issue dates: 25s, Feb. 15. 5s, 10s, 1b, June 4. 2b, 3b, Dec. 1. 15s, Feb. 15, 1952. 1.15b, Sept. 1, 1953. 1.25b, Oct. 1, 1954. 5b, 10b, 20b, Feb. 1, 1955. 50s, Oct. 15, 1956. 20s, 1960.

United Nations Day — A42

1951, Oct. 24

296 A42	25s ultramarine	3.50	3.50

Overprinted "1952" in Carmine
1952, Oct.

297 A42	25s ultramarine	2.00	2.00

Overprinted "1953" in Carmine
1953, Oct.

298 A42	25s ultramarine	1.00	1.00

Overprinted "1954" in Carmine
1954, Oct. 24

299 A42	25s ultramarine	6.50	6.50

For more overprints see Nos. 315, 320.

Nos. 209 and 210 Overprinted in Black

ไทย THAILAND

King Naresuan (1555-1605), on War Elephant — A43   Tao Suranari — A44

1955, Jan. 4   Perf. 12½

300 A25	5s dark violet	2.25	2.25
301 A25	10s deep rose	2.25	3.50

No. 266 Surcharged with New Value in Black or Carmine

302 A39	5s on 20s choc	1.00	40
303 A39	10s on 20s choc (C)	1.00	40

THAILAND

BUYING

PAYING TOP DOLLAR

SHIP - WRITE - CALL - FAX
...what you have for sale with your best price or for our prompt offer.

We are always in need of good materials to supply our customers' needs.

We are also looking to buy other Asian Stamps - Japan, China, Indonesia, Singapore, Vietnam, etc. Please contact us.

SELLING

We maintain a comprehensive stock of Thailand Stamps from 1883 to date.

We carry a complete range of Stamps and Souvenir Sheets and many other specialty items for the collectors of this very popular country.

Please write for our Price List containing items which are currently in stock ... or, you may also send us your Want List and we will do our best to fill your needs.

We Attend Numerous Major Stamp Shows in the U.S. and Abroad. We Look Forward To Meeting You in Person.

QUALITY PHILATELICS

P.O. Box 2871, Newport Beach, CA 92663
PHONE: 714-642-7529
FAX: 714-963-5121

Perf. 13½
1955, Feb. 15 Unwmk. Engr.
304 A43 25s brt carmine 5.00 18
305 A43 80s rose violet 27.50 5.50
306 A43 1.25b dark olive grn 22.50 1.10
307 A43 2b deep blue 17.00 1.40
308 A43 3b henna brown 37.50 85
Nos. 304-308 (5) 109.50 9.03

1955, Apr. 15 Perf. 12x13½
309 A44 10s purple 3.00 35
310 A44 25s emerald 6.50 22
311 A44 1b brown 30.00 2.10

Lady Mo, called Tao Suranari (Brave Woman) for her role in stopping an 1826 rebellion.

King Taksin Statue at Thonburi A45

Don Jedi Monument A46

1955, May 1 Perf. 12½x12
312 A45 5s violet blue 3.00 35
313 A45 25s Prus green 4.75 22
314 A45 1.25b red 35.00 2.50

King Somdech P'ya Chao Taksin (1734-1782).

No. 296 Overprinted "1955" in Red
1955, Oct. 24 Perf. 12½
315 A42 25s ultramarine 3.00 3.00

United Nations Day, Oct. 24, 1955.

1956, Feb. 1 Perf. 13½x13
316 A46 10s emerald 1.40 70
317 A46 50s reddish brown 17.00 1.25
318 A46 75s violet 5.75 1.90
319 A46 1.50b brown orange 12.00 1.10

No. 296 Overprinted "1956" in Red Violet
1956, Oct. 24
320 A42 25s ultramarine 1.90 1.65

United Nations Day, Oct. 24, 1956.

Dharmachakra and Deer — A47

Designs: 20s, 25s, 50s, Hand of peace and Dharmachakra. 1b, 1.25b, 2b, Pagoda of Nakon Phatom.

Perf. 13½
1957, May 13 Photo. Wmk. 329
321 A47 5s dark brown 80 25
322 A47 10s rose lake 85 25
323 A47 15s brt green 1.50 1.00
324 A47 20s orange 1.50 1.25
325 A47 25s reddish brown 1.65 25
326 A47 50s magenta 3.75 38
327 A47 1b olive brown 5.75 50
328 A47 1.25b slate blue 15.00 4.50
329 A47 2b deep claret 9.50 75
Nos. 321-329 (9) 40.30 9.13

2500th anniversary of birth of Buddha.

UN Day — A48

Thai Archway — A49

1957, Oct. 24 Perf. 13½
330 A48 25s olive 95 35

1958, Oct. 24
331 A48 25s bright ocher 90 40

1959, Oct. 24
332 A48 25s indigo 1.00 35

1959, Oct. 15 Photo. Perf. 13½
Designs (inscribed "SEAP Games 1959"): 25s, Royal tiered umbrellas. 1.25b, Thai archer, ancient costume. 2b, Wat Arun pagoda and prow of royal barge.
333 A49 10s orange 42 15
334 A49 25s dk carmine rose 80 15
335 A49 1.25b bright green 1.75 1.00
336 A49 2b light blue 2.00 55

Issued to publicize the South-East Asia Peninsula Games, Bangkok, Dec. 12-17.

Wat Arun, WRY Emblem A50

Wat Arun, Bangkok A51

1960, Apr. 7
337 A50 50s chocolate 55 30
338 A50 2b yellow green 95 45

WRY, July 1, 1959-June 30, 1960.

1960, Aug. Wmk. 329 Perf. 13½
339 A51 50s carmine rose 90 15
340 A51 2b ultramarine 2.00 50

Anti-leprosy campaign.

Elephants in Teak Forest — A52

Globe and SEATO Emblem — A53

1960, Aug. 29 Photo. Perf. 13½
341 A52 25s emerald 70 20

5th World Forestry Cong., Seattle, WA, Aug. 29-Sept. 10.

1960, Sept. 8
342 A53 50s chocolate 80 18

SEATO Day, Sept. 8.

Siamese Child — A54

Hand with Pen and Globe — A55

1960, Oct. 3 Wmk. 329
343 A54 50s magenta 1.00 15
344 A54 1b orange 2.25 50

Children's Day, 1960.

1960, Oct. 3
345 A55 50s carmine rose 90 18
346 A55 2b blue 1.90 80

Intl. Letter Writing Week, Oct. 3-9.

UN Emblem and Globe A56

King Bhumibol Adulyadej A57

1960, Oct. 24 Perf. 13½
347 A56 50s purple 75 25

15th anniversary of the United Nations. See Nos. 369, 390.

Perf. 13½x13
1961-68 Engr. Wmk. 334
348 A57 5s rose claret ('62) 1.25 38
349 A57 10s green ('62) 1.25 15
350 A57 15s red brown ('62) 1.25 25
351 A57 20s brown ('62) 1.25 35
352 A57 25s carmine ('63) 1.25 15
353 A57 50s olive ('62) 1.25 15
354 A57 80s orange ('62) 1.50 75
355 A57 1b violet bl & brn 2.00 25
355A A57 1.25b red & citron ('65) 2.00 52
356 A57 1.50b dk vio & yel green 2.50 15
357 A57 2b red & violet 3.00 18
358 A57 3b brown & blue 4.75 38
358A A57 4b olive bis & blk ('68) 4.75 1.25
359 A57 5b blue & green 15.00 52
360 A57 10b red org & blk 70.00 65
361 A57 20b emerald & ultra 50.00 3.25
362 A57 25b green & blue 35.00 2.00
362A A57 40b yellow & blk ('65) 65.00 4.25
Nos. 348-362A (18) 263.00 15.58

For overprint see No. 588.

Children in Garden — A58

Pen and Envelope with Map — A59

Perf. 13½
1961, Oct. 2 Wmk. 329 Photo.
363 A58 20s indigo 75 22
364 A58 2b purple 2.25 70

Issued for Children's Day.

1961, Oct. 9
Design: 1b, 2b, Pen and letters circling globe.
365 A59 25s gray green 30 22
366 A59 50s rose lilac 52 22
367 A59 1b bright rose 75 40
368 A59 2b ultramarine 1.50 45

Intl. Letter Writing Week, Oct. 2-8.

UN Type of 1960
1961, Oct. 24 Wmk. 329 Perf. 13½
369 A56 50s maroon 60 25

Issued for United Nations Day, Oct. 24.

Scout Emblem — A60

Scouts Saluting and Tents — A61

Design: 2b, King Vajiravudh and Scouts.

1961, Nov. 1 Photo.
370 A60 50s carmine rose 45 28
371 A61 1b bright green 60 40
372 A61 2b bright blue 1.40 80

Thai Boy Scouts, 50th anniversary.

Malaria Eradication Emblem and Siamese Designs
A62 A63

1962, Apr. 7 Wmk. 329 Perf. 13
373 A62 5s orange brown 15 15
374 A62 10s sepia 15 15
375 A62 20s blue 24 15
376 A62 50s carmine rose 50 15
377 A63 1b green 1.10 20
378 A63 1.50b dk car rose 1.75 60
379 A63 2d dark blue 3.25 30
380 A63 3b violet 3.75 2.50
Nos. 373-380 (8) 10.89 4.20

WHO drive to eradicate malaria.

View of Bangkok and Seattle Fair Emblem A64

1962, Apr. 21 Wmk. 329 Perf. 13
381 A64 50s red lilac 1.10 16
382 A64 2b deep blue 3.25 75

"Century 21" Intl. Expo., Seattle, WA, Apr. 21-Oct. 12.

Mother and Child — A65

Globe, Letters, Carrier Pigeons — A66

Wmk. 329
1962, Oct. 1 Photo. Perf. 13
383 A65 25s lt blue green 90 15
384 A65 50s bister brown 1.10 70
385 A65 2b bright pink 4.50 30

Issued for Children's Day.

1962, Oct. 8
Design: 1b, 2b, Quill pen and scroll.
386 A66 25s violet 80 15
387 A66 50s red 1.10 70
388 A66 1b lemon 1.65 35
389 A66 2b lt bluish green 3.25 80

Intl. Letter Writing Week, Oct. 7-13.

UN Type of 1960
1962, Oct. 24 Perf. 13½
390 A56 50s carmine rose 55 25

United Nations Day, Oct. 24.

Exhibition
Emblem
A67

Temple Lion
A69

Woman
Harvesting
Rice
A68

1962, Nov. 1   Unwmk.
391 A67 50s olive bister   80 18

Students' Exhibition, Bangkok.

Wmk. 334
1963, Mar. 21   Engr.   *Perf. 14*
392 A68 20s green   65 35
393 A68 50s ocher   75 20

FAO "Freedom from Hunger" campaign.

1963, Apr. 1   Wmk. 329   *Perf. 13½*
394 A69 50s green & bister   70 15

1st anniv. of the formation of the Asian-Oceanic
Postal Union, AOPU.

New and Old Post and Telegraph
Buildings — A70

Wmk. 334
1963, Aug. 4   Engr.   *Perf. 14*
395 A70 50s org, bluish blk & grn   95 20
396 A70 3b grn, dk red & brn   5.00 1.65

80th anniv. of the Post and Telegraph Dept.

King Bhumibol
Adulyadej — A71

Child with
Dolls — A72

Perf. 13x13½
1963-71   Wmk. 329   Photo.
397 A71   5s dk carmine rose   32   15
398 A71   10s dark green   32   15
399 A71   15s red brown   32   15
400 A71   20s black brown   32   15
401 A71   25s carmine   32   15
402 A71   50s olive gray   45   15
402A A71   75s brt violet ('71)   70   20
403 A71   80s dull orange   1.75   45
404 A71   1b dk bl & dk brn   1.40   20
404A A71   1.25b org brn & ol
        ('65)   7.50   1.00
405 A71   1.50b vio bl & grn   1.40   20
406 A71   2b dk red & vio   1.40   18
407 A71   3b brown & dk bl   3.25   25
407A A71   4b dp bis & blk
        ('68)   3.75   35
408 A71   5b blue & green   10.50   40
409 A71   10b orange & blk   18.00   70
410 A71   20b brt green & ind   150.00   4.25
411 A71   25b dk green & blue   18.00   1.10
411A A71   40b yellow & blk
        ('65)   110.00   3.50
  Nos. 397-411A (19)   329.70 13.68

Nos. 397-403 were issued in 1963; Nos. 404,
405-407, 408-411 in 1964.
For overprint see No. 589.

1963, Oct. 7   Litho.   *Perf. 13½*
412 A72 50s rose red   1.50 16
413 A72 2b dull blue   5.00 65

Issued for Children's Day.

Garuda Carrying Letter — A73

Design: 2b, 3b, Thai women writing letters.

1963, Oct. 7   Wmk. 329
414 A73 50s lt blue & claret   2.00   15
415 A73 1b lt grn & vio brn   6.00   45
416 A73 2b yel brn & turq bl   11.00   1.25
417 A73 3b org brn & yel grn   20.00   1.75

Intl. Letter Writing Week, Oct. 6-12.

UN Emblem — A74

UNICEF
Emblem — A76

King Bhumibol Adulyadej — A75

1963, Oct. 24   Wmk. 329   *Perf. 13½*
418 A74 50s bright blue   55 15

United Nations Day, Oct. 24.

1963, Dec. 5   Photo.   *Perf. 13½*
419 A75 1.50b blue, orange & ind   3.25 35
420 A75 5b brt lil rose, org & blk   8.75 2.00

King Bhumibol's 36th birthday.

1964, Jan. 13   Litho.
421 A76 50s blue   1.10 15
422 A76 2b olive green   2.75 45

17th anniv. of UNICEF.

Hand
(flags),
Pigeon
and
Globe
A77

Designs: 1b, Girls and world map. 2b, Pen, pencil and unfolded world map. 3b, Globe and hand
holding quill.

1964, Oct. 5   Wmk. 329   *Perf. 13½*
423 A77 50s lilac & lt grn   1.10   18
424 A77 1b red brown & grn   2.75   30
425 A77 2b yellow & vio bl   5.75   35
426 A77 3b blue & dk brown   9.25   1.50

Intl. Letter Writing Week, Oct. 5-11.

UN Emblem
and
Globe — A78

King and
Queen — A79

1964, Oct. 24   Photo.   *Perf. 13½*
427 A78 50s gray   1.00 15

United Nations Day, Oct. 24.

1965, Apr. 28   Wmk. 329   *Perf. 13½*
428 A79 2b brown & multi   7.75   30
429 A79 5b violet & multi   16.00   2.00

15th wedding anniversary of King Bhumibol
Adulyadej and Queen Sirikit.

ITU Emblem, Old and New
Communications Equipment — A80

1965, May 17   Photo.
430 A80 1b bright green   3.00 50

Cent. of the ITU.

World
Map,
Letters
and
Goddess
A81

Designs: 2b, 3b, World map, letters and
handshake.

1965, Oct. 3   Wmk. 329   *Perf. 13½*
431 A81 50s dp plum, gray & sal   1.25   15
432 A81 1b dk vio bl, lt vio & yel   2.75   35
433 A81 2b dk gray, bis & dp org   8.25   50
434 A81 3b multicolored   12.50   2.50

Intl. Letter Writing Week, Oct. 3-9.

A82   A83

Gates of Royal Chapel of Emerald Buddha.

Perf. 13½x14
Engr. & Litho.
1965, Oct. 24   Wmk. 356
435 A82 50s sl grn, bl & ocher   1.50 15

International Cooperation Year, 1965.

Perf. 13½
1965, Nov. 1   Wmk. 329   Litho.

Map of Thailand and UPU monument, Bern.

436 A83 20s dk blue & lilac   42   15
437 A83 50s gray & blue   1.50   15
438 A83 1b orange brn & vio bl   4.25   35
439 A83 3b green & bister   10.50   1.75

80th anniv. of Thailand's admission to the UPU.

Lotus
Blossom
and
Child
A84

Design: 1b, Boy with book walking up steps.

1966, Jan. 8   Wmk. 334   *Perf. 13½*
440 A84 50s henna brn & blk   1.00 15
441 A84 1b green & black   1.65 60

Issued for Children's Day, 1966.

Bicycling — A85

1966, Aug. 4   Photo.   Wmk. 329
442 A85   20s shown   1.00   20
443 A85   25s Tennis   1.00   20
444 A85   50s Running   1.10   22
445 A85   1b Weight lifting   4.00   45
446 A85   1.25b Boxing   5.25   2.50
447 A85   2b Swimming   10.50   45
448 A85   3b Netball   15.00   3.50
449 A85   5b Soccer   30.00   12.50
  Nos. 442-449 (8)   67.85 20.02

5th Asian Games, Bangkok.

Trade Fair Emblem and
Temple of Dawn — A86

1966, Sept. 1   Litho.   *Perf. 13½*
450 A86 50s lilac   95 25
451 A86 1b brown red   2.00 75

1st Intl. Asian Trade Fair, Bangkok.

Letter
Writer
A87

Design: 50s, 1b, Letters, maps and pen.

1966, Oct. 3   Photo.   Wmk. 329
452 A87 50s scarlet   80   15
453 A87 1b orange brown   1.90   20
454 A87 2b brt violet   4.00   35
455 A87 3b brt blue grn   6.75   2.25

Intl. Letter Writing Week, Oct. 6-12.

UN Emblem
A88

Pra Buddha Bata
Monastery, UNESCO
Emblem
A90

Rice
Field
A89

Perf. 13½
1966, Oct. 24   Wmk. 334   Litho.
456 A88 50s ultramarine   65 15

United Nations Day, Oct. 24.

1966, Nov. 1   Engr.   Wmk. 329
457 A89 50s dp bl & grnsh bl   2.50 40
458 A89 3b plum & pink   7.50 3.00

Intl. Rice Year under sponsorship of the FAO.

1966, Nov. 4   Photo.   Wmk. 329
459 A90 50s black & yel grn   55 15

20th anniv. of UNESCO.

Thai Boxing A91

Designs: 1b, Takraw (three men playing ball). 2b, Kite fighting. 3b, Cudgel play.

1966, Dec. 9   Wmk. 329   Perf. 13½
460 A91 50s black, brn & red   1.25 25
461 A91 1b black, brn & red   6.50 2.75
462 A91 2b black, brn & red   14.00 4.00
463 A91 3b black, brn & red   24.00 9.00

5th Asian Games.

Snakehead — A92

Pigmy Mackerel — A93

Fish: 3b, Barb. 5b, Siamese fighting fish.

1967, Jan. 1   Photo.
464 A92 1b brt blue & multi   3.25 1.25
465 A93 2b multicolored   10.00 1.25
466 A93 3b yel grn & multi   14.00 6.25
467 A92 5b pale grn & multi   25.00 7.25

Dharmachakra, Globe and Temples — A94

Perf. 13½
1967, Jan. 15   Wmk. 329   Litho.
468 A94 2b black & yellow   2.50 70

Establishment of the headquarters of the World Fellowship of Buddhists in Thailand.

Great Hornbill A95   Ascocentrum Curvifolium A96

Birds: 25s, Hill myna. 50s, White-rumped shama. 1b, Diard's fireback pheasant. 1.50b, Spotted dove. 2b, Sarus crane. 3b, White-breasted kingfisher. 5b, Asiatic open-bill (stork).

1967, Feb. 1   Photo.
469 A95 20s tan & multi   22 22
470 A95 25s lt gray & multi   25 25
471 A95 50s yel grn & multi   55 32
472 A95 1b olive & multi   3.75 1.25
473 A95 1.50b dull yel & multi   5.00 1.25
474 A95 2b pale salmon & multi   15.00 1.90
475 A95 3b gray & multi   13.00 7.00
476 A95 5b multicolored   32.50 9.25
   Nos. 469-476 (8)   70.27 21.44

1967, Apr. 1   Wmk. 329   Perf. 13½
Orchids: 20s, Vandopsis parishii. 80s, Rhynchostylis retusa. 1b, Rhynchostylus gigantea. 1.50b, Dendrobium falconeri. 2b, Paphiopedilum callosum. 3b, Dendrobium formosum. 5b, Dendrobium primulinum.

477 A96 20s black & multi   45 30
478 A96 50s brt blue & multi   45 30
479 A96 80s black & multi   3.75 1.65
480 A96 1b blue & multi   4.00 1.25
481 A96 1.50b black & multi   5.75 1.25
482 A96 2b ver & multi   18.00 1.25
483 A96 3b brown & multi   13.00 6.25
484 A96 5b multicolored   24.00 9.50
   Nos. 477-484 (8)   69.40 21.75

Thai Architecture — A97

1967, Apr. 6   Engr.
485 A97 50s Mansion   1.10 32
486 A97 1.50b Pagodas   6.00 1.25
487 A97 2b Bell tower   9.50 1.65
488 A97 3b Temple   14.00 8.75

Grand Palace and Royal Barge on Chao Phraya River A98

1967, Sept. 15   Wmk. 329   Perf. 13½
489 A98 2b ultra & sepia   2.50 60

International Tourist Year, 1967.

Globe, Dove, People and Letters A99

Design: 2b, 3b, Clasped hands, globe and doves.

1967, Oct. 8   Photo.
490 A99 50s dk blue & multi   65 15
491 A99 1b multicolored   1.50 32
492 A99 2b brt yel grn & blk   3.75 50
493 A99 3b brown & blk   5.25 2.50

Intl. Letter Writing Week, Oct. 6-12.

UN Emblem — A100

1967, Oct. 24   Wmk. 329   Perf. 13½
494 A100 50s multicolored   60 15

Issued for United Nations Day, Oct. 24.

Flag and Map of Thailand — A101

1967, Dec. 5   Photo.   Perf. 13½
495 A101 50s greenish blue, red & vio bl   50 20
496 A101 2b ol gray, red & vio bl   3.50 1.25

50th anniversary of the flag.

Elephant Carrying Teakwood — A102

1968, Mar. 1   Engr.   Wmk. 329
497 A102 2b rose claret & gray ol   2.25 35

See Nos. 537, 566.

Syncom Satellite over Thai Tracking Station — A103

1968, Apr. 1   Photo.   Perf. 13
498 A103 50s multicolored   38 15
499 A103 3b multicolored   2.75 1.25

Earth Goddess — A104

1968, May 1   Wmk. 329   Perf. 13
500 A104 50s blk, gold, red & bl grn   55 15

Hydrological Decade (UNESCO), 1965-74.

Snake-skinned Gourami — A105

Fish: 20s, Red-tailed black "shark." 25s, Tor tambroides. 50s, Pangasius sanitwongsei. 80s, Bagrid catfish. 1.25b, Vaimosa rambaiae. 1.50b, Catlocarpio siamensis. 4b, Featherback.

1968, June 1   Photo.   Perf. 13
501 A105 10s multicolored   52 15
502 A105 20s multicolored   52 15
503 A105 25s multicolored   52 15
504 A105 50s multicolored   65 15
505 A105 80s multicolored   3.50 16
506 A105 1.25b multicolored   6.25 1.25
507 A105 1.50b multicolored   17.50 4.00
508 A105 4b multicolored   35.00 9.50
   Nos. 501-508 (8)   64.46 15.51

Arcturus Butterfly — A106

Various butterflies.

1968, July 1   Wmk. 329   Perf. 13
509 A106 50s lt blue & multi   5.50 15
510 A106 1b multicolored   8.75 65
511 A106 3b multicolored   17.00 2.50
512 A106 4b buff & multi   26.00 6.75

Queen Sirikit — A107

Designs: Various portraits of Queen Sirikit.

Photogravure and Engraved
Perf. 13½x14
1968, Aug. 12   Wmk. 334
513 A107 50s gold & multi   45 15
514 A107 2b gold & multi   1.75 55
515 A107 3b gold & multi   2.50 1.90
516 A107 5b gold & multi   8.75 2.00

Queen Sirikit's 36th birthday, or third 12-year "cycle."

WHO Emblem and Medical Apparatus — A108

1968, Sept. 1   Photo.   Perf. 12½
517 A108 50s olive, blk & gray   60 15

20th anniv. of the WHO.

Globe, Pen and Envelope — A109

Design: 1b, 3b, Pen nib, envelope and globe.

1968, Oct. 6   Wmk. 329   Perf. 13½
518 A109 50s brown & multi   70 15
519 A109 1b pale brown & multi   1.65 20
520 A109 2b multicolored   1.90 30
521 A109 3b violet & multi   3.75 1.40

Intl. Letter Writing Week, Oct. 7-13.

UN Emblem and Flags — A110   King Rama II — A112

Human Rights Flame and Bas-relief — A111

1968, Oct. 24
522 A110 50s multicolored 55 15

Issued for United Nations Day.

1968, Dec. 10 Photo. Perf. 13½
523 A111 50s sl grn, red & vio 75 15

International Human Rights Year.

1968, Dec. 30 Engr. Wmk. 329
524 A112 50s sepia & bister 40 15

Rama II (1768-1824), who reigned 1809-24.

National Assembly Building — A113

Photogravure and Engraved
1969, Feb. 10 Wmk. 329 Perf. 13½
525 A113 50s multicolored 60 15
526 A113 2b multicolored 2.25 60

First constitutional election day.

ILO Emblem and Cogwheels — A114

1969, May 1 Photo. Perf. 13½
527 A114 50s rose vio & dk bl 40 15

50th anniv. of the ILO.

Ramwong Dance — A115

Designs: 1b, Candle dance. 2b, Krathop Mai dance. 3b, Nohra dance.

1969, July 15 Wmk. 329 Perf. 13
528 A115 50s multicolored 35 15
529 A115 1b multicolored 85 25
530 A115 2b multicolored 1.40 35
531 A115 3b multicolored 2.00 1.75

Posting and Receiving Letters — A116

Design: 2b, 3b, Writing and posting letters.

1969, Oct. 5 Photo. Wmk. 334
532 A116 50s multicolored 32 15
533 A116 1b multicolored 70 26
534 A116 2b multicolored 1.40 38
535 A116 3b multicolored 2.25 1.10

International Letter Writing Week.

Hand Holding Globe — A117

1969, Oct. 24 Wmk. 329 Perf. 13
536 A117 50s multicolored 40 15

Issued for United Nations Day.

Teakwood Type of 1968
1969, Nov. 18 Engr. Perf. 13½
537 A102 2b Tin mine 2.25 30

Issued to publicize tin export, and the 2nd Technical Conf. of the Intl. Tin Council, Bangkok.

Loy Krathong Festival — A118

Designs: 1b, Marriage ceremony. 2b, Khwan ceremony. 5b, Songkran festival.

1969, Nov. 23 Photo. Wmk. 329
538 A118 50s gray & multi 28 15
539 A118 1b multicolored 70 25
540 A118 2b multicolored 1.25 35
541 A118 5b multicolored 3.50 1.25

Biplane, Mailmen and Map of First Thai Airmail Flight, 1919 — A119

1969, Dec. 10 Engr. Perf. 13½
542 A119 1b multicolored 85 20

50th anniversary of Thai airmail service.

Shadow Play — A120

Photogravure and Engraved
1969, Dec. 18 Wmk. 329
543 A120 50s Phra Rama 24 15
544 A120 2b Ramasura 1.00 30
545 A120 3b Mekhala 1.90 1.00
546 A120 5b Ongkhot 3.00 90

Symbols of Agriculture, Industry and Shipping — A121

1970, Jan. 1 Photo.
547 A121 50s multicolored 40 15

Productivity Year 1970.

World Map, Thai Temples and Emblem — A122

1970, Jan. 31 Litho.
548 A122 50s brt blue & blk 50 15

19th triennial meeting of the Intl. Council of Women, Bangkok.

Earth Station Radar and Satellite — A123

Perf. 14½x15
1970, Apr. 1 Litho. Wmk. 356
549 A123 50s multicolored 40 15

Communication by satellite.

Household and Population Statistics — A124

Perf. 13x13½
1970, Apr. 1 Photo. Wmk. 329
550 A124 1b multicolored 40 15

Issued to publicize the 1970 census.

Inauguration of New UPU Headquarters, Bern — A125

Lithographed and Engraved
1970, June 15 Wmk. 334 Perf. 13½
551 A125 50s lt bl, lt grn & grn 40 15

Khun Ram Kamhang Teaching (Mural) — A126

1970, July 1 Litho.
552 A126 50s black & multi 40 15

Issued for International Education Year.

Swimming Stadium — A127

Designs: 1.50b, Velodrome. 3b, Subhajalasaya Stadium. 5b, Kittikachorn Indoor Stadium.

Lithographed and Engraved
1970, Sept. 1 Wmk. 329 Perf. 13½
553 A127 50s yellow, red & pur 25 25
554 A127 1.50b ultra, grn & dk red 60 40
555 A127 3b gold, black & dk red 1.40 52
556 A127 5b brt grn, ultra & dk red 2.75 95

6th Asian Games, Bangkok.

Children Writing Letters — A128

Designs: 1b, Woman writing letter. 2b, Two women reading letters. 3b, Man reading letter.

1970, Oct. 4 Photo. Perf. 13½
557 A128 50s black & multi 42 15
558 A128 1b black & multi 80 20
559 A128 2b black & multi 1.25 30
560 A128 3b black & multi 2.00 80

Intl. Letter Writing Week, Oct. 6-12.

Royal Palace, Bangkok, and UN Emblem — A129

1970, Oct. 24 Photo. Perf. 13½
561 A129 50s multicolored 70 15

25th anniversary of the United Nations.

Heroes of Bangrachan — A130

Designs: 1b, Monument to Thao Thepkrasatri and Thao Srisunthorn. 2b, Queen Suriyothai riding elephant. 3b, Phraya Phichaidaphak and battle scene.

1970, Oct. 25 Engr. Perf. 13½

562	A130	50s pink & violet	45 15
563	A130	1b violet & maroon	75 28
564	A130	2b rose & brown	1.25 52
565	A130	3b blue & green	2.00 1.25

Heroes from Thai history.

Teakwood Type of 1968

1970, Nov. 1 Engr.

566	A102	2b Rubber plantation	1.90 30

Issued to publicize rubber export.

King Bhumibol Lighting Flame — A131

1970, Dec. 9 Photo. Wmk. 329

567	A131	1b multicolored	40 15

Opening of 6th Asian Games, Bangkok.

Woman Playing So Sam Sai A132

Women Playing Classical Thai Musical Instruments: 2b, Khlui Phiang-O. 3b, Krachappi. 5b, Thon Rammana.

1970, Dec. 20

568	A132	50s multicolored	16 15
569	A132	2b multicolored	1.10 30
570	A132	3b multicolored	1.65 40
571	A132	5b multicolored	2.25 80

Chocolate Point Siamese Cats — A133

Siamese Cats: 1b, Blue point. 2b, Seal point. 3b, Pure white cat and kittens.

1971, Mar. 15 Litho. Wmk. 356 Perf. 13½x14

572	A133	50s multicolored	75 15
573	A133	1b multicolored	1.40 40
574	A133	2b multicolored	2.75 30
575	A133	3b multicolored	4.25 1.65

Muang Nakhon Temple — A134

Temples: 1b, Phanom. 3b, Pathom Chedi. 4b, Doi Suthep.

Lithographed and Engraved

1971, Mar. 30 Wmk. 329 Perf. 13½

576	A134	50s rose, black & brn	40 15
577	A134	1b emerald, bis & pur	65 20
578	A134	3b orange, brn & dk brn	1.65 30
579	A134	4b ultra, ocher & brn	2.25 1.75

Corn and Tractor in Field A135

1971, Apr. 20 Engr. Wmk. 329

580	A135	2b multicolored	1.50 20

Export promotion.

Buddha's Birthplace, Lumbini, Nepal — A136

Designs (Buddha's): 1b, Place of Enlightenment, Bihar. 2b, Place of first sermon, Benares. 3b, Place of death, Kusinara.

1971, May 9 Engr. Perf. 13½

581	A136	50s violet blue & blk	32 15
582	A136	1b green & black	42 25
583	A136	2b dull yellow & blk	85 40
584	A136	3b red & black	1.65 80

20th anniv. of World Fellowship of Buddhists.

King Bhumibol and Subjects — A137

Floating Market — A138

Perf. 13½

1971, June 9 Unwmk. Litho.

585	A137	50s silver & multi	65 15

King Bhumibol's Silver Jubilee.

1971, June 20 Photo. Wmk. 329

586	A138	4b gold & multi	1.65 40

Visit Asia Year.

Boy Scouts Saluting A139

1971, July 1 Litho.

587	A139	50s orange & multi	35 15

60th anniversary of Thai Boy Scouts.

Blocks of four of Nos. 354 and 403 Overprinted in Dark Blue

a

b

Perf. 13½x13

1971, Aug. Wmk. 334 Engr.

588	A57 (a)	Block of 4	2.75 2.75
a.		80s orange, single stamp	45 45

Perf. 13x13½

Photo. Wmk. 329

589	A71 (b)	Block of 4	2.75 2.75
a.		80s dull orange, single stamp	45 45

THAILANDPEX '71, Philatelic Exhib., Aug. 4-8.

Woman Writing Letter A140

Designs: 1b, Women reading mail. 2b, Woman sitting on porch. 3b, Man handing letter to woman.

Perf. 13½

1971, Oct. 3 Wmk. 334 Litho.

590	A140	50s gray & multi	48 15
591	A140	1b red brown & multi	65 15
592	A140	2b ultra & multi	1.40 35
593	A140	3b lt gray & multi	2.00 80

Intl. Letter Writing Week, Oct. 6-12.

Wat Benchamabopit (Marble Temple), Bangkok — A141

Perf. 13½x14

1971, Oct. 24 Litho. Unwmk.

594	A141	50s multicolored	40 15

United Nations Day, Oct. 24.

Duck Raising A142

Rural occupations: 1b, Raising tobacco. 2b, Fishermen. 3b, Rice winnowing.

Perf. 12½

1971, Nov. 15 Wmk. 329 Photo.

595	A142	50s lt blue & multi	32 15
596	A142	1b multicolored	45 20
597	A142	2b blue & multi	90 30
598	A142	3b buff & multi	1.40 75

UNICEF Emblem, Mother and Child — A143

1971, Dec. 11 Wmk. 334 Perf. 13½

599	A143	50s blue & multi	40 15

25th anniv. of UNICEF.

Thai Costumes, 17th Century — A144

Thai Costumes: 1b, 13th to 14th centuries. 1.50b, 14th to 17th centuries. 2b, 18th to 19th centuries.

Perf. 13½x14

1972, Jan. 12 Litho. Unwmk.

600	A144	50s multicolored	35 15
601	A144	1b multicolored	70 20
602	A144	1.50b multicolored	1.40 35
603	A144	2b blue & multi	2.00 55

Globe A145

Perf. 13x13½

1972, Apr. 1 Photo. Wmk. 334

604	A145	75s violet blue	40 15

Asian-Oceanic Postal Union, 10th anniv.

King Bhumibol Adulyadej — A146

Perf. 13½x13

1972-77 Litho. Wmk. 329

Size: 21x26mm

605	A146	10s yellow green	35 15
606	A146	20s blue	35 15
607	A146	25s rose red	35 15
608	A146	75s lilac	35 15

Engr.

609	A146	1.25b yel grn & pink	1.40 20
610	A146	2.75b red brn & blue grn	65 20
611	A146	3b brn & dk blue ('74)	2.75 25
612	A146	4b blue & org red ('73)	1.40 20
613	A146	5b dk vio & red brown	1.40 30
614	A146	6b green & violet	2.75 40
615	A146	10b ver & black	2.25 60
616	A146	20b orange & yel grn	4.50 1.00
617	A146	40b dp bis & lilac ('74)	35.00 3.00
618	A146	50b pur & brt grn ('77)	27.50 2.50
619	A146	100b dp org & dk bl ('77)	55.00 5.00
	Nos. 605-619 (15)		136.00 14.25

See Nos. 835-838, 907-908.

Iko Women A147

Hill Tribes: 2b, Musoe musician. 4b, Yao weaver. 5b, Maeo farm woman.

Perf. 13½

1972, May 11   Photo.   Wmk. 334
620	A147	50s multicolored	55	15
621	A147	2b dark gray & multi	2.00	20
622	A147	4b multicolored	4.25	2.50
623	A147	5b multicolored	5.00	70

Ruby A148

Precious Stones: 2b, Yellow sapphire. 4b, Zircon. 6b, Star sapphire.

1972, June 7   Litho.
624	A148	75s gray & multi	65	15
625	A148	2b multicolored	3.50	30
626	A148	4b multicolored	7.75	2.50
627	A148	6b crimson & multi	13.00	2.00

Prince Vajiralongkorn A149

Thai Costume A150

Perf. 13½x13

1972, July 28   Photo.   Wmk. 329
628	A149	75s tan & multi	40	15

20th birthday of Prince Vajiralongkorn, heir apparent.

Perf. 14x13½

1972, Aug. 12   Litho.   Wmk. 356

Designs: Costumes of Thai women.

629	A150	75s tan & multi	42	15
630	A150	2b multicolored	1.40	20
631	A150	4b yellow & multi	2.25	1.65
632	A150	5b gray & multi	4.00	75
a.		Souvenir sheet of 4, #629-632	30.00	8.00

Rambutan — A151

Fruits: 1b, Mangosteen. 3b, Durian. 5b, Mango.

1972, Sept. 7   Wmk. 334   Perf. 13½
633	A151	75s multicolored	55	15
634	A151	1b multicolored	1.25	30
635	A151	3b pink & multi	3.00	60
636	A151	5b lt ultra & multi	5.25	1.75

Lod Cave, Phangnga — A152

Designs: 1.25b, Kang Krachara Reservoir. 2.75b, Erawan Waterfalls, Kanchanaburi. 3b, Nok-Kaw Cliff, Loei.

1972, Nov. 15   Litho.   Wmk. 334
637	A152	75s multicolored	55	15
638	A152	1.25b multicolored	95	15
639	A152	2.75b multicolored	2.50	35
640	A152	3b multicolored	3.00	1.00

Intl. Letter Writing Week, Oct. 9-15.

Princess Mother Visiting Old People A153

1972, Oct. 21   Photo.   Wmk. 329
641	A153	75s dk green & ocher	40	15

Princess Mother Sisangwan, 72nd birthday.

UN Emblem and Globe — A154

Wmk. 334
1972, Nov. 15   Litho.   Perf. 14
642	A154	75s blue & multi	40	15

25th anniversary of the Economic Commission for Asia and the Far East (ECAFE).

Educational Center and Book Year Emblem — A155

1972, Dec. 8   Perf. 13½
643	A155	75s multicolored	40	15

International Book Year 1972.

Crown Prince Vajiralongkorn A156

1972, Dec. 28   Photo.   Wmk. 329
644	A156	2b brt blue & multi	75	15

Investiture of Prince Vajiralongkorn Salayacheevin as Crown Prince.

Flag, Soldiers and Civilians — A157

1973, Feb. 3   Wmk. 334   Perf. 13½
645	A157	75s multicolored	40	15

25th anniversary of Veterans Day.

Savings Bank, Emblem and Coin — A158

1973, Apr. 1   Wmk. 329
646	A158	75s emerald & multi	40	15

60th anniv. of Government Savings Bank.

WHO Emblem and Deity A159

1973, Apr. 1   Wmk. 329
647	A159	75s brt green & multi	40	15

25th World Health Organization Day.

Water Lily A160

Designs: Various water lilies (Thai lotus).

Perf. 11x13
1973, May 15   Litho.   Wmk. 356
648	A160	75s violet & multi	75	22
649	A160	1.50b brown & multi	1.25	32
650	A160	2b dull green & multi	2.00	65
651	A160	4b black & multi	3.00	1.25

King Bhumibol Adulyadej — A161

Perf. 14x13½
1973-81   Photo.   Wmk. 334
652	A161	5s purple	42	15
653	A161	20s blue	45	15
a.		Perf. 14½, wmk. 233	45	15
654	A161	25s rose carmine	55	15

Wmk. 233   Perf. 14½
655	A161	25s brown red ('81)	55	18
656	A161	50s dk olive grn ('79)	1.10	15
657	A161	75s violet	1.10	15
a.		Perf. 14x13½, wmk. 334	1.10	15

Wmk. 334
Engr.   Perf. 13
658	A161	5b violet & brown	3.25	60
659	A161	6b green & violet	3.25	55
660	A161	10b red & black	6.00	75
661	A161	20b org & yel grn ('75)	60.00	3.25
		Nos. 652-661 (10)	76.67	6.08

For surcharges see Nos. 1168A, 1548.

Silversmiths — A162

1973, June 15   Litho.   Perf. 13½
662	A162	75s shown	55	15
663	A162	2.75b Lacquerware	2.25	30
664	A162	4b Pottery	3.25	1.50
665	A162	5b Paper umbrellas	4.50	50

Thai handicrafts.

Fresco from Temple of the Emerald Buddha — A163

Designs: Frescoes illustrating Ramayana in Temple of the Emerald Buddha.

1973, July 17   Photo.   Wmk. 329
666	A163	25s multicolored	15	15
667	A163	75s multicolored	32	15
668	A163	1.50b multicolored	1.90	18
669	A163	2b multicolored	2.50	80
670	A163	2.75b multicolored	2.25	30
671	A163	3b multicolored	7.50	1.25
672	A163	5b multicolored	11.00	2.75
673	A163	6b multicolored	4.00	1.25
		Nos. 666-673 (8)	29.62	6.83

Development of Postal Service — A164

Design: 2b, Telecommunications development.

1973, Aug. 4   Perf. 13½
674	A164	75s multicolored	45	15
675	A164	2b multicolored	95	50

90th anniv. of Post and Telegraph Dept.

No. 1 and Other Stamps A165

Various Stamps and: 1.25b, No. 147. 1.50b, No. 209. 2b, No. 244.

1973, Aug. 4   Photo. & Engr.
676	A165	75s dp rose & dk blue	90	20
677	A165	1.25b blue & dp rose	1.25	30
678	A165	1.50b olive & vio blk	1.50	55
679	A165	2b orange & sl grn	2.75	55
a.		Souvenir sheet of 4	16.00	2.50

2nd Natl. Phil. Exhib., THAIPEX '73, Aug. 4-8. No. 679a contains 4 stamps with simulated perforations similar to Nos. 676-679.

INTERPOL Emblem — A166

1973, Sept. 3   **Photo.**
680 A166 75s gray & multi   40   15

50th anniv. of Intl. Criminal Police Organization.

"Lilid Pralaw" A167

Designs: Scenes from Thai literature.

Perf. 11x13
1973, Oct. 7   Litho.   Wmk. 368
681 A167 75s green & multi   60   15
682 A167 1.50b blue & multi   1.25   30
683 A167 2b multicolored   2.25   60
684 A167 5b blue & multi   4.75 1.00
 a. Souvenir sheet of 4, #681-684, perf.   25.00 8.00
      13x14

Intl. Letter Writing Week, Oct. 7-13.

Wat Suan Dok, Chiangmai; UN Emblem — A168

1973, Oct. 24   Perf. 13x11
685 A168 75s blue & multi   40   35

United Nations Day.

Schomburgk's Deer — A169

Perf. 13 1/2
1973, Nov. 14   Wmk. 329   Photo.
686 A169 20s shown   24   15
687 A169 25s Kouprey   35   20
688 A169 75s Gorals   55   20
689 A169 1.25b Water buffalos   1.75   15
690 A169 1.50b Javan rhinoceros   2.75   15
691 A169 2b Eld's deer   4.00 1.25
692 A169 2.75b Asiatic 2-horned
               rhinoceros   6.75   40
693 A169 4b Serows   10.00 2.25
        Nos. 686-693 (8)   26.39 4.75

Protected animals.

Human Rights Flame A170

Perf. 12 1/2
1973, Dec. 10   Litho.   Wmk. 371
694 A170 75s multicolored   75   15

25th anniversary of the Universal Declaration of Human Rights.

Children and Flowers — A171

1974, Jan. 12   Litho.   Perf. 13
695 A171 75s multicolored   55   15

Children's Day.

Siriraj Hospital and Statue of Prince Nakarin — A172

Perf. 13x13 1/2
1974, Mar. 17   Photo.   Wmk. 368
696 A172 75s multicolored   40   15

84th anniversary of Siriraj Hospital, oldest medical school in Thailand.

Phala Piang Lai — A173

Classical Thai Dances: 2.75b, Phra Lux Phlaeng Rit. 4b, Chin Sao Sai. 5b, Charot Phra Sumen.

Wmk. 334
1974, June 25   Litho.   Perf. 14
697 A173 75s pink & multi   70   15
698 A173 2.75b gray bl & multi   1.90   25
699 A173 4b gray & multi   3.00 1.50
700 A173 5b yellow & multi   3.50   50

Large Teak Tree in Uttaradit Province — A174

1974, July 5   Wmk. 329   Perf. 12 1/2
701 A174 75s multicolored   40   15

15th Arbor Day.

People and WPY Emblem — A175

Perf. 10 1/2x13
1974, Aug. 19   Litho.   Wmk. 368
702 A175 75s multicolored   35   15

World Population Year, 1974.

Ban Chiang Painted Vase A176

Designs: 75s, Royal chariot. 2.75b, Avalokitesavara Bodhisattva. 3b, King Mongkut, Rama IV.

1974, Sept. 19 Wmk. 262   Perf. 12 1/2
703 A176 75s blue & multi   45   15
704 A176 2b black, brn & bis   1.10   40
705 A176 2.75b black, brn & tan   1.25   30
706 A176 3b black & multi   1.90   60

Centenary of National Museum. Inscribed "BATH" in error.

Purging Cassia A177

1974, Oct. 6   Wmk. 368   Perf. 11x13
707 A177 75s shown   45   15
708 A177 2.75b Butea   1.90   25
709 A177 3b Jasmine   2.00   30
710 A177 4b Lagerstroemia   2.50   75
 a. Souvenir sheet of 4, #707-710,   30.00 10.00
      perf. 13 1/2x14

Intl. Letter Writing Week, Oct. 6-12.

"UPU" and UPU Emblem A178

1974, Oct. 9   Wmk. 371   Perf. 12 1/2
711 A178 75s dk green & multi   40   15

Centenary of Universal Postal Union.

Wat Suthat Thepvararam — A179

Wmk. 329
1974, Oct. 24   Photo.   Perf. 13
712 A179 75s multicolored   40   15

United Nations Day.

Elephant Roundup — A180

Perf. 12 1/2
1974, Nov. 16   Engr.   Wmk. 371
713 A180 4b multicolored   2.00   80

Tourist publicity.

Vanda Coerulea — A181

Orchids: 2.75b, Dendrobium aggregatum. 3b, Dendrobium scabrilingue. 4b, Aerides falcata.

Perf. 11x13
1974, Dec. 5   Photo.   Wmk. 368
714 A181 75s red & multi   65   15
715 A181 2.75b multicolored   1.50   25
716 A181 3b olive & multi   2.25   50
717 A181 4b green & multi   2.75   80
 a. Souvenir sheet of 4, #714-717,   37.50 11.00
      perf. 13 1/2x14

See Nos. 745-748.

Boy — A182

Perf. 14x13 1/2
1975, Jan. 11   Wmk. 374
718 A182 75s vermilion & multi   55   15

Children's Day.

Democracy Monument — A183

Designs: 2b, Mother with children and animals, bas-relief from Democracy Monument. 2.75b, Workers, bas-relief from Democracy Monument. 5b, Top of Democracy Monument and quotation from speech of King Rama VII.

Perf. 14x14 1/2
1975, Jan. 26   Wmk. 233
719 A183 75s dull grn & multi   30   15
720 A183 2b multicolored   1.00   20
721 A183 2.75b blue & multi   1.25   25
722 A183 5b multicolored   2.50   70

Movement of Oct. 14, 1973, to re-establish democratic institutions.

Marbled Tiger Cat A184

1975, Mar. 5   Wmk. 334   Perf. 13 1/2
723 A184 20s shown   35   15
724 A184 75s Gaurs   1.40   15
725 A184 2.75b Asiatic elephant   4.00   55
726 A184 3b Clouded tiger   5.00   80

Protected animals.

White-eyed River Martin — A185

Birds: 2b, Paradise flycatchers. 2.75b, Long-tailed broadbills. 5b, Sultan tit.

Perf. 12½
1975, Apr. 2   Litho.   Wmk. 371
727	A185	75s ocher & multi	55	15
728	A185	2b lt blue & multi	1.40	15
729	A185	2.75b lt violet & multi	2.25	30
730	A185	5b rose & multi	4.25	1.25

King Bhumibol Adulyadej and Queen Sirikit — A186

Design: 3b, King and Queen, different background design.

Perf. 10½x13
1975, Apr. 28   Photo.   Wmk. 368
731	A186	75s violet bl & multi	24	15
732	A186	3b multicolored	95	30

25th wedding anniversary of King Bhumibol Adulyadej and Queen Sirikit.

Round-house Kick — A187

Thai Boxing: 2.75b, Reverse elbow. 3b, Flying knee. 5b, Ritual homage.

Perf. 12½
1975, May 20   Litho.   Wmk. 371
733	A187	75s green & multi	60	15
734	A187	2.75b blue & multi	2.25	30
735	A187	3b orange & multi	3.50	80
736	A187	5b orange & multi	4.75	1.65

Tosakanth Mask — A188

Masks: 2b, Kumbhakarn. 3b, Rama. 4b, Hanuman.

1975, June 10   Litho.   Wmk. 371
737	A188	75s dark gray & multi	70	15
738	A188	2b dull vio & multi	2.00	20
739	A188	3b purple & multi	3.75	50
740	A188	4b multicolored	7.50	2.50

Thai art and literature.

THAIPEX 75 Emblem — A189

THAIPEX 75 Emblem and: 2.75b, Stamp designer. 4b, Stamp printing plant. 5b, Stamp collector.

1975, Aug. 4   Wmk. 371   Perf. 12½
741	A189	75s yellow & multi	22	15
742	A189	2.75b orange & multi	95	30
743	A189	4b lt blue & multi	1.50	1.00
744	A189	5b carmine & multi	1.75	40

THAIPEX 75, Third National Philatelic Exhibition, Aug. 4-10.

Orchid Type of 1974

Orchids: 75s, Dendrobium cruentum. 2b, Dendrobium parishii. 2.75b, Vanda teres. 5b, Vanda denisoniana.

Perf. 11x13
1975, Aug. 12   Photo.   Wmk. 368
745	A181	75s olive & multi	65	15
746	A181	2b multicolored	1.50	30
747	A181	2.75b scarlet & multi	2.25	30
748	A181	5b ultra & multi	3.50	75
a.		Souvenir sheet of 4, #745-748, perf. 13½	30.00	9.00

Mytilus Smaragdinus — A190

Sea Shells: 1b, Turbo marmoratus. 2.75b, Oliva mustelina. 5b, Cypraea moneta.

Perf. 14x14½
1975, Sept. 5   Litho.   Wmk. 375
749	A190	75s yellow & multi	85	40
750	A190	1b ver & multi	1.40	15
751	A190	2.75b blue & multi	4.00	30
752	A190	5b green & multi	12.00	2.00

Yachting and Games Emblem — A191

Designs: 1.25b, Badminton. 1.50b, Volleyball. 2b, Target shooting.

Perf. 11x13
1975, Sept. 20   Litho.   Wmk. 368
753	A191	75s ultra & black	28	15
754	A191	1.25b brt rose & blk	80	25
755	A191	1.50b red & black	1.40	65
756	A191	2b ap grn & blk	2.00	60
a.		Souvenir sheet of 4, #753-756, perf. 13½	25.00	8.00

8th SEAP Games, Bangkok, Sept. 1975.

Pataya Beach — A192

Views: 2b, Samila Beach. 3b, Prachuap Bay. 5b, Laem Singha Bay.

1975, Oct. 5   Wmk. 371   Perf. 12½
757	A192	75s orange & multi	60	15
758	A192	2b orange & multi	1.10	30
759	A192	3b orange & multi	1.40	40
760	A192	5b orange & multi	4.00	80

Intl. Letter Writing Week, Oct. 6-12.

"u n," UN Emblem, Food and Education for Children — A193

1975, Oct. 24   Litho.   Wmk. 371
761	A193	75s ultra & multi	40	20

United Nations Day.

Morse Telegraph — A194

Design: 2.75b, Teleprinter and radar.

Perf. 14x14½
1975, Nov. 4   Litho.   Wmk. 334
762	A194	75s multicolored	50	20
763	A194	2.75b blue & multi	1.50	30

Centenary of telegraph system.

Sukhrip Khrong Mueang Barge — A195

Thai ceremonial barges: 1b, Royal escort barge Anekchat Phuchong. 2b, Royal barge Anantanakarat. 2.75b, Krabi Ran Ron Rap barge. 3b, Asura Wayuphak barge. 4b, Asura paksi barge. 5b, Royal barge Sri Suphanahong, 6b, Phali Rang Thawip barge.

Perf. 12½
1975, Nov. 18   Litho.   Wmk. 371
764	A195	75s multicolored	52	15
765	A195	1b multicolored	65	30
766	A195	2b lilac & multi	2.50	40
767	A195	2.75b multicolored	3.25	45
768	A195	3b yellow & multi	4.25	45
769	A195	4b multicolored	5.00	1.25
770	A195	5b gray & multi	10.00	2.50
771	A195	6b blue & multi	6.00	1.75
		Nos. 764-771 (8)	32.17	7.25

Thai Flag, Arms of Chakri Royal Family — A196 · King Bhumibol Adulyadej — A197

Perf. 15x14
1975, Dec. 5   Litho.   Wmk. 375
772	A196	75s multicolored	24	15
773	A197	5b multicolored	1.25	45
		Set value		50

King Bhumibol's 48th birthday.

Shot Put and SEAP Emblem — A198

Designs: 2b, Table tennis. 3b, Bicycling. 4b, Relay race.

1975, Dec. 9   Wmk. 368   Perf. 11x13
774	A198	1b orange & black	42	15
775	A198	2b brt green & blk	90	60
776	A198	3b ocher & blk	1.40	35
777	A198	4b violet & blk	1.75	60
a.		Souvenir sheet of 4, #774-777, perf. 13½	25.00	8.00

8th SEAP Games, Bangkok, Dec. 9-20.

IWY Emblem and Globe — A199

Perf. 14x14½
1975, Dec. 20   Wmk. 375
778	A199	75s blk, org & vio bl	40	15

International Women's Year.

Children Writing on Slate — A200

Perf. 13x14
1976, Jan. 10   Litho.   Wmk. 368
779	A200	75s lt green & multi	40	15

Children's Day.

Macrobrachium Rosenbergii — A201

Designs: 2b, Penaeus merguiensis. 2.75b, Panulirus ornatus. 5b, Penaeus monodon.

1976, Feb. 18   Perf. 11x13
780	A201	75s multicolored	1.40	15
781	A201	2b multicolored	3.00	70
782	A201	2.75b multicolored	4.25	20
783	A201	5b multicolored	6.50	1.40

Shrimp and lobster exports.

Golden-backed Three-toed Woodpecker A202 · Ban Chiang Vase A203

Birds: 1.50b, Greater green-billed malcoha. 3b, Pomatorhinus hypoleucos. 4b, Green magple.

1976, Apr. 2   Litho.   Wmk. 371

784	A202	1b multicolored	55	15
785	A202	1.50b multicolored	1.00	20
786	A202	3b yellow & multi	2.00	55
787	A202	4b rose & multi	2.25	55

Perf. 14¹/₂x14

1976, May 5   Litho.   Wmk. 375

Designs: Ban Chiang painted pottery, various vessels, Bronze Age.

788	A203	1b olive & multi	75	15
789	A203	2b dp blue & multi	1.25	15
790	A203	3b green & multi	2.50	35
791	A203	4b org red & multi	3.25	1.75

Mailman, 1883 — A204

Designs: 3b, Mailman, 1935. 4b, Mailman, 1950. 5b, Mailman, 1974.

Perf. 12¹/₂

1976, Aug. 4   Litho.   Wmk. 377

792	A204	1b multicolored	55	15
793	A204	3b multicolored	2.00	45
794	A204	4b multicolored	3.00	65
795	A204	5b multicolored	3.50	80

Development of mailmen's uniforms.

Kinnari A205

Thai Mythology: 2b, Suphan-mat-cha. 4b, Garuda. 5b, Naga.

1976, Oct. 3   Wmk. 368   Perf. 11x13

796	A205	1b green & multi	90	20
797	A205	2b ultra & multi	42	20
798	A205	4b gray & multi	3.00	45
799	A205	5b slate & multi	3.50	50

International Letter Writing Week.

UN Emblem, Drug Addicts, Alcohol, Cigarettes, Drugs — A206

Perf. 13¹/₂

1976, Oct. 24   Photo.   Wmk. 329

800	A206	1b ultra & multi	40	15

United Nations Day.

Old and New Telephones — A207

Perf. 14x14¹/₂

1976, Nov. 10   Litho.   Wmk. 375

801	A207	1b multicolored	40	15

Centenary of first telephone call by Alexander Graham Bell, Mar. 10, 1876.

Sivalaya-Mahaprasad Hall — A208

Royal Houses: 2b, Cakri-Mahaprasad. 4b, Mahisra-Prasad. 5b, Dusit-Mahaprasad.

Perf. 14x15

1976, Dec. 5   Wmk. 375   Litho.

802	A208	1b multicolored	95	15
803	A208	2b multicolored	1.50	50
804	A208	4b multicolored	4.75	75
805	A208	5b multicolored	5.25	80

Banteng A209

Protected animals: 2b, Tapir and young. 4b, Sambar deer and fawn. 5b, Hog deer family.

Wmk. 334

1976, Dec. 26   Litho.   Perf. 11

806	A209	1b multicolored	75	15
807	A209	2b multicolored	1.10	20

Wmk. 368

808	A209	4b multicolored	3.00	40
809	A209	5b multicolored	3.75	65

Child Casting Shadow of Man — A210

Perf. 13¹/₂

1977, Jan. 8   Photo.   Wmk. 329

810	A210	1b multicolored	40	15

National Children's Day.

Alsthom's Electric Engine — A211

Locomotives: 2b, Davenport's electric engine. 4b, Pacific's steam engine. 5b, George Egestoff's steam engine.

Perf. 11x13

1977, Mar. 26   Litho.   Wmk. 368

811	A211	1b multicolored	2.00	15
812	A211	2b multicolored	3.75	35
813	A211	4b multicolored	9.50	2.00
814	A211	5b multicolored	12.50	80

80th anniv. of State Railroad of Thailand.

Chulalongkorn University Auditorium — A212

1977, Mar. 26   Photo.

815	A212	1b multicolored	60	15

Chulalongkorn University, 60th anniversary.

Flags of AOPU Members — A213

Perf. 12¹/₂

1977, Apr. 1   Wmk. 371   Litho.

816	A213	1b multicolored	55	15

Asian-Oceanic Postal Union (AOPU), 15th anniv.

Invalid in Wheelchair and Soldiers — A214

Perf. 13¹/₂

1977, Apr. 2   Wmk. 329   Photo.

817	A214	5b multicolored	1.10	45

Sai-Jai-Thai Day, to publicize Sai-Jai-Thai Foundation which helps wounded soldiers.

Phra Aphai Mani and Phisua Samut A215

Puppets: 3b, Rusi and Sutsakhon. 4b, Nang Vali and Usren. 5b, Phra Aphai Mani and Nang Laweng's portrait.

Perf. 11x13

1977, June 16   Wmk. 368

818	A215	2b multicolored	45	20
819	A215	3b multicolored	65	25
820	A215	4b multicolored	1.25	45
821	A215	5b multicolored	1.50	55

Thai plays and literature.

Drum Dance — A216

Designs: 3b, Dance of dip nets. 4b, Harvest dance. 5b, Kan dance.

1977, July 14   Photo.   Perf. 13x11

822	A216	2b rose & multi	60	15
823	A216	3b lt green & multi	70	20
824	A216	4b yellow & multi	1.10	38
825	A216	5b lt violet & multi	1.40	40

Thailand No. 609, Various Stamps and Thaipex Emblem — A217

Perf. 12¹/₂

1977, Aug. 4   Litho.   Wmk. 377

826	A217	75s multicolored	60	15

THAIPEX 77, 4th National Philatelic Exhibition, Aug. 4-12.

Scenes from Thai Literature — A218

Perf. 11x13

1977, Oct. 5   Photo.   Wmk. 368

827	A218	75s multicolored	55	15
828	A218	2b multi, diff.	90	20
829	A218	5b multi, diff.	2.25	40
830	A218	6b multi, diff.	3.00	65

Intl. Letter Writing Week, Oct. 6-12.

Old and New Buildings, UN Emblem — A219

1977, Oct. 5   Litho.   Perf. 11x13

831	A219	75s multicolored	75	15

United Nations Day.

King Bhumibol as Scout Leader, Camp and Emblem — A220

1977, Nov. 21   Photo.   Wmk. 368

832	A220	75s multicolored	1.10	45

9th National Jamboree, Nov. 21-27.

Diseased Hand and Elbow — A221

1977, Dec. 20   Perf. 11x13

833	A221	75s multicolored	60	15

World Rheumatism Year.

Map of South East Asia and ASEAN Emblem A222

Perf. 12½
1977, Dec. 1   Litho.   Wmk. 377
834 A222 5b multicolored   1.50 30

ASEAN, 10th anniv.

King Type of 1972-74 Redrawn
1976   Perf. 12½x13
Size: 21x27mm
835 A146 20s blue   80 15
836 A146 75s lilac   80 15

Engr.
837 A146 10b vermilion & blk   8.50 1.00
838 A146 40b bister & lilac   20.00 2.25

Numerals are taller and thinner and leaves in background have been redrawn.

Children Carrying Flag of Thailand A223

Perf. 13½
1978, Jan. 9   Photo.   Wmk. 329
839 A223 75s multicolored   75 15

Children's Day.

Dendrobium Heterocarpum — A224

Orchids: 1b, Dendrobium pulchellum. 1.50b, Doritis pulcherrima. 2b, Dendrobium hercoglossum. 2.75b, Aerides odorata. 3b, Trichoglottis fasciata. 5b, Dendrobium wardianum. 6b, Dendrobium senile.

1978, Jan. 18   Wmk. 368   Perf. 11x14
840 A224 75s multicolored   15 15
841 A224 1b multicolored   22 15
842 A224 1.50b multicolored   35 20
843 A224 2b multicolored   65 60
844 A224 2.75b multicolored   2.50 30
845 A224 3b multicolored   95 30
846 A224 5b multicolored   1.40 50
847 A224 6b multicolored   3.75 60
      Nos. 840-847 (8)   9.97 2.70

9th World Orchid Conference.

Census Chart, Symbols of Agriculture — A225

Perf. 12½
1978, Mar. 1   Litho.   Wmk. 377
848 A225 75s multicolored   30 15

Agricultural census, Apr. 1978.

Anabas Testudineus — A226

Fish: 2b, Datnioides microlepis. 3b, Kryptopterus apogon. 4b, Probarbus Jullieni.

Perf. 11x13
1978, Apr. 13   Photo.   Wmk. 368
849 A226 1b multicolored   26 15
850 A226 2b multicolored   65 20
851 A226 3b multicolored   1.25 32
852 A226 4b multicolored   1.75 55

Birth of Prince Siddhartha — A227

Murals: 3b, Prince Siddhartha cuts his hair. 5b, Buddha descending from Tavatimsa Heaven. 6b, Buddha entering Nirvana.

Perf. 13½
1978, June 15   Photo.   Wmk. 329
853 A227 2b multicolored   1.40 24
854 A227 3b multicolored   2.00 48
855 A227 5b multicolored   6.25 80
856 A227 6b multicolored   4.50 1.10

Story of Gautama Buddha, murals in Puthi Savan Hall, National Museum, Bangkok.

Bhumibol Dam — A228

Dams and Reservoirs: 2b, Sirikit dam. 2.75b, Vajiralongkorn dam. 6b, Ubol Ratana dam.

Perf. 14x14½
1978, July 28   Litho.   Wmk. 233
857 A228 75s multicolored   80 15
858 A228 2b multicolored   1.00 20
859 A228 2.75b multicolored   1.50 20
860 A228 6b multicolored   2.75 90

Idea Lynceus — A229

Butterflies: 3b, Sephisa chandra. 5b, Charaxes durnfordi. 6b, Cethosia penthesilea methypsia.

Perf. 11x13
1978, Aug. 25   Litho.   Wmk. 368
861 A229 2b lilac, blk & red   1.00 20
862 A229 3b multicolored   1.25 30
863 A229 5b multicolored   2.00 48
864 A229 6b multicolored   3.25 1.00

Chedi Chai Mongkhon Temple — A230

Mother and Children, UN Emblem — A231

Temples: 2b, That Hariphunchai. 2.75b, Borom That Chaiya. 5b, That Choeng Chum.

1978, Oct. 8   Perf. 13x11
865 A230 75s multicolored   65 15
866 A230 2b multicolored   1.10 15
867 A230 2.75b multicolored   1.50 20
868 A230 5b multicolored   2.25 80

Intl. Letter Writing Week, Oct. 6-12.

Perf. 14½x14
1978, Oct. 24   Litho.   Wmk. 375
869 A231 75s multicolored   40 15

United Nations Day.

Boxing, Soccer, Pole Vault — A232

Designs: 2b, Javelin, weight lifting, running. 3b, Ball games and sailing. 5b, Basketball, hockey stick and boxing gloves.

Perf. 14x14½
1978, Oct.   Wmk. 233   Litho.
870 A232 75s multicolored   30 15
871 A232 2b multicolored   80 20
872 A232 3b multicolored   1.25 25
873 A232 6b multicolored   1.65 80

8th Asian Games, Bangkok.

Five Races and World Map A233

1978, Nov.
874 A233 75s multicolored   35 15

Anti-Apartheid Year.

Children Painting Thai Flag A234

Children and Children's SOS Village, Tambol Bangpu — A235

1979, Jan. 17   Perf. 14x14½
875 A234 75s multicolored   60 15
876 A235 75s multicolored   60 15

International Year of the Child.

Matuta Lunaris A236

Crabs: 2.75b, Matuta planipes fabricius. 3b, Portunus pelagicus. 5b, Scylla serrata.

Perf. 12½
1979, Mar. 22   Wmk. 377   Litho.
877 A236 2b multicolored   80 15
878 A236 2.75b multicolored   1.25 20
879 A236 3b multicolored   1.50 25
880 A236 5b multicolored   2.25 70

A237   A238

1979, June 25
881 A237 1b Sweetsop   48 15
882 A237 2b Pineapple   75 15
883 A237 5b Bananas   1.75 45
884 A237 6b Longans (litchi) 2.25 1.25

See Nos. 1145-1148.

Perf. 13x11
1979, July 10   Litho.   Wmk. 368
Young man and woman planting tree.
885 A238 75s multicolored   40 15

20th Arbor Day.

Pencil, Pen, Thaipex '79 Emblem A239

Thaipex '79 Emblem and: 2b, Envelopes. 2.75b, Stamp album. 5b, Magnifying glass and tongs.

1979, Aug. 4   Perf. 11x13
886 A239 75s multicolored   28 15
887 A239 2b multicolored   75 15
888 A239 2.75b multicolored   1.10 15
889 A239 5b multicolored   1.90 30
      Set value   62

Thaipex '79, 5th National Philatelic Exhibition, Bangkok, Aug. 4-12.

Floral Arrangement A240

UN Day A241

Designs: Decorative arrangements.

Perf. 14½x14

1979, Oct. 7   Litho.   Wmk. 233

890	A240	75s multicolored	42	15
891	A240	2b multicolored	75	15
892	A240	2.75b multicolored	1.10	20
893	A240	5b multicolored	1.75	60

Intl. Letter Writing Week, Oct. 8-14.

1979, Oct. 24   Litho.   Perf. 14½x14

894	A241	50s multicolored	40	15

Frigate Makut Rajakumarn — A242

Thai Naval Ships: 3b, Frigate Tapi. 5b, Fast strike craft, Prabparapak. 6b, Patrol boat T-91.

Perf. 13½

1979, Nov. 20   Photo.   Wmk. 329

895	A242	2b multicolored	1.25	16
896	A242	2b multicolored	1.90	25
897	A242	5b multicolored	3.25	70
898	A242	6b multicolored	3.75	1.00

Rajamitrabhorn Order
A243   A244

Thai Royal Orders (Medallions and Ribbons): Nos. 901-902, House of Chakri. Nos. 903-904, The nine gems. Nos. 905-906, Chula Chom Klao. Stamps of same denomination printed se-tenant.

Perf. 13x11

1979, Dec. 5   Litho.   Wmk. 368

899	A243	1b multicolored	35	25
900	A244	1b multicolored	35	25
901	A243	2b multicolored	70	15
902	A244	2b multicolored	70	15
903	A243	5b multicolored	1.75	40
904	A244	5b multicolored	1.75	40
905	A243	6b multicolored	2.25	60
906	A244	6b multicolored	2.25	60
		Nos. 899-906 (8)	10.10	2.80

See Nos. 1278-1285.

King Type of 1972-77

Perf. 13½x13

1979, Dec. 23   Litho.   Wmk. 329
Size: 21x26mm

907	A146	50s olive green	40	15

Engr.

908	A146	2b org red & lilac	55	15
		Set value		22

Rice Planting — A245

Children's Day: No. 910, Family in rice field.

Perf. 13x11

1980, Jan. 12   Litho.   Wmk. 368

909	A245	75s multicolored	48	15
910	A245	75s multicolored	48	15
		Set value		25

Family, House, Map of Thailand —A246

Gold-fronted Leafbird — A247

Perf. 15x14

1980, Feb. 1   Litho.   Wmk. 233

911	A246	75s multicolored	30	15

Natl. Population & Housing Census, Apr.

1980, Feb. 26   Wmk. 368   Perf. 13x11

912	A247	75s shown	25	15
913	A247	2b Yellow-cheeked tit	70	15
914	A247	3b Chestnut-tailed siva	95	30
915	A247	5b Scarlet minivet	1.65	45

Intl. Commission for Bird Preservation, 9th Conf. of Asian Section, Chieng-mai, Feb. 26-29.

Smokers and Lungs, WHO Emblem — A248

1980, Apr. 7   Wmk. 329   Perf. 13½

916	A248	75s multicolored	25	15

World Health Day; fight against cigarette smoking.

Garuda and Rotary Emblem — A249

1980, May 6   Wmk. 368   Perf. 13x11

917	A249	5b multicolored	95	35

Rotary International, 75th anniversary.

Sai Yok Falls, Kanchanaburi — A250

Perf. 14x15

1980, July 1   Litho.   Wmk. 233

918	A250	1b shown	30	15
919	A250	2b Punyaban Falls, Ranong	55	20
920	A250	5b Heo Suwat Falls, Nakhon Ratchasima	1.25	45
921	A250	6b Siriphum Falls, Chiang Mai	1.50	60

Queen Sirikit — A251

Family with Cattle, Ceres Medal (Reverse) — A252

Design: No. 524, Ceres medal (obverse), potters.

Perf. 13½, 11x13 (5b)

1980, Aug. 12   Wmk. 329, 368 (5b)   Litho.

922	A251	75s multicolored	28	15
923	A252	5b multicolored	1.10	38
924	A252	5b multicolored	1.10	45

Queen Sirikit's 48th birthday.

Khao Phanomrung Temple, Buri Ram — A253

International Letter Writing Week, Oct. 6-12 (Temples): 2b, Prang Ku, Chaiiyaphum. 2.75b, Phimai, Nakhon Ratchasima. 5b, Sikhoraphum, Surin.

Perf. 11x13

1980, Oct. 5   Litho.   Wmk. 368

925	A253	75s multicolored	42	15
926	A253	2b multicolored	55	16
927	A253	2.75b multicolored	75	25
928	A253	5b multicolored	1.25	50

Princess Mother — A254

Golden Mount, Bangkok — A255

Perf. 15x14

1980, Oct. 21   Litho.   Wmk. 233

929	A254	75s multicolored	30	15

Princess Mother, 80th birthday.

1980, Oct. 24

930	A255	75s multicolored	30	15

United Nations Day.

King Bhumibol Adulyadej — A256

Perf. 11x13

1980-84(?)   Litho.   Wmk. 368

933	A256	25s salmon	2.50	15
933A	A256	50s olive green	15	15
	b.	Wmk. 233, perf. 14x15	2.00	15
	c.	Wmk. 387, perf. 11x13	20	15
934	A256	75s lilac	60	15
936	A256	1.25b yellow green	60	15
	a.	Wmk. 387, perf. 11x13	75	20
	b.	Wmk. 233, perf. 14x15		

Perf. 13½x13
Engr.   **Wmk. 329**

939	A256	3b brown & dk bl	5.75	20
941	A256	5b purple & brn	9.00	30
942	A256	6b dk green & pur	12.00	35
944	A256	8.50b green & brn org	2.50	50
945	A256	9.50b olive & dk grn	3.00	55
		Nos. 933-945 (9)	36.10	2.50

Issued: 50s, 1.25b, 1981. 3b-9.50b, 1983. See Nos. 1079-1097. For surcharges see Nos. 1226-1226A.

This is an expanding set. Numbers will change if necessary.

King Rama VII Monument Inauguration — A257

Perf. 15x14

1980, Dec. 10   Wmk. 233

946	A257	75s multicolored	25	15

Bencharongware Bowl — A258

Perf. 11x13

1980, Dec. 15   Wmk. 368

947	A258	2b shown	50	20
948	A258	2.75b Covered bowls	70	28
949	A258	3b Covered jar	75	32
950	A258	5b Stem plates	1.25	55

King Vajiravudh Birth Centenary — A259

Children's Day — A260

1981, Jan. 1   Wmk. 233   Perf. 15x14

951	A259	75s multicolored	30	15

1981, Jan. 16   Wmk. 368   Perf. 13x11

952	A260	75s multicolored	35	15

Hegira, 1500th Anniv. A261

Perf. 12½
1981, Jan. 18   Litho.   Wmk. 377
953 A261 5b multicolored   1.90 35

Dolls in Native Costumes — A262

Perf. 13½
1981, Feb. 6   Litho.   Wmk. 368
954 A262 75s Palm-leaf fish mobile   28 15
955 A262 75s Teak elephants   28 15
956 A262 2.75b shown   85 25
957 A262 2.75b Baskets   85 25
            Set value   70
CONEX '81 International Crafts Exhibition.

Scout Leader and
Boy on
Crutches — A263

1981, Feb. 28   *Perf. 13x11*
958 A263 75s shown   24 15
959 A263 5b Diamond cutter in wheel-
            chair   75 32
International Year of the Disabled.

Dindaeng-Tarua Expressway
Opening — A264

1981, Oct. 29   *Perf. 13½*
960 A264 1b Klongtoey   28 15
961 A264 5b Vipavadee Rangsit High-
            way   1.25 40

Ongkhot, Khon
Mask — A265

Designs: Various Khon masks.

1981, July 1   Litho.   *Perf. 13x11*
962 A265 75s shown   16 15
963 A265 2b Maiyarab   45 18
964 A265 3b Sukrip   85 28
965 A265 5b Indrajit   1.10 45

Exhibition Emblem, No. 83 — A266

Wmk. 370
1981, Aug. 4   Litho.   *Perf. 12*
966 A266 75s shown   30 15
967 A266 75s No. 144   30 15
968 A266 2.75b No. 198   95 25
969 A266 2.75b No. 226   95 25
            Set value   60

ประเทศไทย THAILAND   75 ST.

A267   A268

Perf. 15x14
1981, Aug. 26   Wmk. 233
970 A267 1.25b multicolored   40 15
Luang Praditphairo, courtmMusician, birth centenary. THAIPEX '81 Intl. Stamp Exhibition.

1981, Oct. 4   Wmk. 329
Designs: Dwarfed trees.
971 A268 75s Mai hok-hian   48 15
972 A268 2b Mai kam-ma-lo   65 16
973 A268 2.75b Mai khen   85 16
974 A268 5b Mai khabuan   1.50 60
25th Intl. Letter Writing Week, Oct. 6-12.

World
Food
Day
A269

Wmk. 370
1981, Oct. 16   Litho.   *Perf. 12*
975 A269 75s multicolored   35 15

United
Nations
Day
A270

1981, Oct. 24   Wmk. 368   *Perf. 13½*
976 A270 1.25b Samran Mukhamat Pa-
            vilion   40 15

King
Cobra
A271

1981, Dec. 1   Wmk. 329   *Perf. 13½*
977 A271 75s shown   40 15
978 A271 2b Banded krait   70 30
979 A271 2.75b Thai cobra   85 20
980 A271 5b Malayan pit viper   1.40 45

Children's   Scouting
Day — A272   Year — A273

1982, Jan. 9   Wmk. 370   *Perf. 12*
981 A272 1.25b multicolored   40 15

1982, Feb. 22
982 A273 1.25b multicolored   35 15

Bicentenary of
Bangkok (Thai
Capital) — A274

Chakri Dynasty kings. (Rama I-Rama IX).

1982, Apr. 4   Litho.   *Perf. 12*
983 A274 1b Buddha Yod-Fa
            (1736-1809)   55 15
984 A274 1.25b shown   70 15
985 A274 2b Buddha Lert La
            Naphalai (1767-
            1824)   1.10 20
986 A274 3b Nang Klao (1787-
            1851)   1.50 30
987 A274 4b Mongkut (1804-
            1868)   2.00 40
988 A274 5b Chulalongkorn
            (1853-1910)   2.50 50
989 A274 6b Vajiravudh (1880-
            1925)   3.25 60
990 A274 7b Prachathipok
            (1893-1941)   3.75 65
991 A274 8b Ananda Mahidol
            (1925-1946)   4.25 75
992 A274 9b Bhumibol Aduly-
            adej (b. 1927)   4.50 85
a. Souv. sheet of 9, 205x142mm   32.50
b. Souv. sheet of 9, 195x180mm   42.50
    Nos. 983-992 (10)   24.10 4.55
Nos. 992a-992b each contain Nos. 983, 985-
992. No. 992a sold for 60b, No. 992b for 70b.

TB Bacillus Centenary — A275

Perf. 13½
1982, Apr. 7   Litho.   Wmk. 368
993 A275 1.25b multicolored   30 15

Local
Flowers
A276

Perf. 14x14½
1982, June 30   Wmk. 233
994 A276 1.25b Quisqualis indica   25 15
995 A276 1.50b Murraya aniculata   30 15
996 A276 6.50b Mesua ferrea   1.40 65
997 A276 7b Desmos chinensis   1.50 70

Buddhist Temples in Bangkok — A277

1982, Aug. 4   Wmk. 368   *Perf. 13½*
998 A277 1.25b shown   24 15
999 A277 4.25b Wat Pho   80 38
1000 A277 6.50b Mahathat
             Yuwarat Rang-
             sarit   1.10 55
1001 A277 7b Phra Sri Rattana
             Satsadaram   1.25 60
a. Souv. sheet of 4, #998-1001, perf.
     12½   50.00
BANGKOK '83 Intl. Stamp Exhibition, Aug. 4-
13, 1983. No. 1001a sold for 30b.
See Nos. 1025-1026.

LANDSAT
Satellite — A278

1982, Aug. 9   Wmk. 370   *Perf. 12*
1002 A278 1.25b multicolored   30 15
2nd UN Conference on Peaceful Uses of Outer
Space, Vienna, Aug. 9-21.

Prince Purachatra of
Kambaengbejra
(1882-1936)
A279

1982, Sept. 14   Wmk. 233   *Perf. 14*
1003 A279 1.25b multicolored   28 15

26th Intl. Letter Writing Week, Oct. 6-
12 — A280

Sangalok Pottery.

1982, Oct. 3   Wmk. 329   *Perf. 13½*
1004 A280 1.25b Covered glazed jar   28 15
1005 A280 3b Glazed jar   70 24
1006 A280 4.25b Glazed plate   95 34
1007 A280 7b Painted plate   1.50 55

*New issue listings, plus
the most interesting read in
the hobby, characterize the
"Scott Stamp Monthly".
For more information,
please call 1-800-488-5351.*

UN Day — A281

1982, Oct. 24
1008 A281 1.25b Loha Prasat Tower   30 15

Musical Instruments — A282

1982, Nov. 30   Wmk. 370   Perf. 12
1009 A282 50s Chap, ching   15   15
1010 A282   1b Pi nai, pi nok   20   15
1011 A282 1.25b Klong that, taphon 26   15
1012 A282 1.50b Khong mong, krap   32   15
1013 A282   6b Khong wong yai   1.40 60
1014 A282   7b Khong wong lek   1.50 65
1015 A282   8b Ranat ek   1.75 80
1016 A282   9b Ranat thum   2.00 90
       Nos. 1009-1016 (8)   7.58 3.55

Pileated   ASEAN Members'
Gibbon — A283   Flags — A284

1982, Dec. 26
1017 A283 1.25b shown   30   15
1018 A283   3b Pig-tailed macaque 60   20
1019 A283   5b Slow loris   1.10 32
1020 A283   7b Silvered leaf monkey 1.65 65

1982, Dec. 26   Wmk. 233
1021 A284 6.50b multicolored   1.10 65
15th Anniv. of Assoc. of Southeast Asian Nations.

Children's
Day — A285

Perf. 14¹/₂x14
1983, Jan. 8   Litho.   Wmk. 233
1022 A285 1.25b multicolored   30   15

First
Anniv.
of
Postal
Code
A286

1983, Feb. 25   Wmk. 329   Perf. 13¹/₂
1023 A286 1.25b Codes   35   20
1024 A286 1.25b Code on envelope   35   15

BANGKOK '83 Type of 1982
Design: Old General Post Office.

1983, Feb. 25   Wmk. 368   Photo.
1025 A277 7b multicolored   1.10 38
1026 A277 10b multicolored   1.75 70
  a.   Souv. sheet of 2, #1025-1026,
       perf. 12¹/₂   15.00 4.50

25th Anniv. of Intl. Maritime
Org. — A287

Perf. 14x14¹/₂
1983, Mar. 17   Litho.   Wmk. 233
1029 A287 1.25b Chinese junks   30   15

Civil Servants' Day   Prince Sithiporn
A288   Kridakara (1883-
                         1971)
                         A289

1983, Apr. 1   Wmk. 370   Perf. 12
1030 A288 1.25b multicolored   30   15

Perf. 14¹/₂x14
1983, Apr. 11   Wmk. 233
1031 A289 1.25b multicolored   30   15

Domestic Satellite Communications System
Inauguration — A290

Perf. 13¹/₂
1983, Aug. 4   Litho.   Wmk. 368
1032 A290 2b Map, dish antenna, satel-
               lite   40   15

BANGKOK '83 Intl. Stamp Show, Aug. 4-
13 — A291

1983, Aug. 4   Wmk. 370   Perf. 12
1033 A291 1.25b Mail collection   16   15
1034 A291 7.50b Posting letters   1.00 65
1035 A291 8.50b Mail transport   1.10 80
1036 A291 9.50b Mail delivery   1.25 95
  a.   Souv. sheet of 4, #1033-1036 20.00 3.75

No. 1036a exist imperf, sold for 50b.

A292   A293

Prince Bhanurangsi memorial statue.

Perf. 15x14
1983, Aug. 4   Litho.   Wmk. 233
1037 A292 1.25b multicolored   35   15

Wmk. 370
1983, Sept. 27   Litho.   Perf. 12
1038 A293 1.25b multicolored   18   38
1039 A293   7b multicolored   1.10 50
Malaysia/ Thailand/ Singapore submarine cable
inauguration.

Intl.
Letter
Writing
Week
A294

1983, Oct. 6   Wmk. 329   Perf. 13¹/₂
1040 A294 2b Acropora asper   48   18
1041 A294 3b Platygyra lamellina 65   25
1042 A294 4b Fungia   90   38
1043 A294 7b Pectinia lactuca   1.50 60

Prince Mahidol of
Songkhla — A295

Wmk. 370
1983, Oct. 10   Litho.   Perf. 12
1044 A295 9.50b multicolored   1.10 55

Siriraj Hospital Faculty of Medicine and Rockefel-
ler Foundation, 60th Anniv. of cooperation.

World Communications Year — A296

Design: 3b, Telecommunications equipment,
diff.

Perf. 14x14¹/₂
1983, Oct. 24   Litho.   Wmk. 233
1045 A296 2b multicolored   25   20
1046 A296 3b multicolored   40   30

United
Nations
Day
A297

1983, Oct. 24
1047 A297 1.25b multicolored   40   15

Thai Alphabet, 700th Anniv. — A298

Designs: 3b, Painted pottery, Sukothai period.
7b, Thai characters, reign of King Ramkamhaeng.
8b, Buddha, Sukothai period. 9b, Mahathat Temple,
Sukothai province.

1983, Nov. 17   Wmk. 370   Perf. 12
1048 A298 3b multicolored   40   25
1049 A298 7b multicolored   95   60
1050 A298 8b multi, vert.   1.10 75
1051 A298 9b multi, vert.   1.25 80

National Development Program — A299

Designs: No. 1052, King and Queen initiating
Royal Projects. No. 1053, Technical aid. No. 1054,
Terrace farming, Irrigation dam. No. 1055, Gathering grain. No. 1056, Receiving the peoples'
gratitude.

1984, May 5
1052 A299 1.25b multicolored   32   16
1053 A299 1.25b multicolored   32   16
1054 A299 1.25b multicolored   32   16
1055 A299 1.25b multicolored   32   16
1056 A299 1.25b multicolored   32   16
       Nos. 1052-1056 (5)   1.60 80

1052-1056 se-tenant.

Children's Day — A300

1984, Jan. 14   Wmk. 329   Perf. 13¹/₂
1057 A300 1.25b multicolored   30   15

17th
Natl.
Games,
Jan. 22-
28
A301

1984, Jan. 22
1058 A301 1.25b Running   22   15
1059 A301   3b Soccer   52   20

5th Rheumatology Congress, Jan. 22-27 — A302

1984, Jan. 22 Wmk. 233 Perf. 14x15
1060 A302 1.25b Rheumatic joints 30 15

Armed Forces Day — A303

50th Anniv. of Royal Institute — A304

1984, Jan. 25 Perf. 15x14
1061 A303 1.25b King Naresuan, tanks, jet, ship 40 15

1984, Mar. 31
1062 A304 1.25b multicolored 30 15

Thammasat University, 50th Anniv. — A305

1984, June 27 Perf. 14x15
1063 A305 1.25b Dome Building 30 15

Asia-Pacific Broadcasting Union, 20th Anniv. — A306

1984, July 1 Wmk. 387 Perf. 12
1064 A306 4b Map, emblem 75 20

Seated Buddha, Chiang Saen Style — A307

Intl. Letter Writing Week — A308

Seated Buddhas in various styles.

Perf. 14¹/₂x14
1984, July 12 Wmk. 233
1065 A307 1.25b shown 15 15
1066 A307 7b Sukhothai 95 50
1067 A307 8.50b U-Thong 1.10 75
1068 A307 9.50b Ayutthaya 1.25 85

Perf. 13¹/₂
1984, Oct. 7 Litho. Wmk. 385
Medicinal Succulents.

1069 A308 1.50b Taro 28 15
1070 A308 2b Star cactus 40 25
1071 A308 4b Gynura pseudochina DC 75 25
1072 A308 10b Oyster plant 2.00 65

Princess Mother (b. 1900) — A309

UN Day — A310

1984, Oct. 21 Wmk. 233 Perf. 15x14
1073 A309 1.50b Portrait 25 15

1984, Oct. 24 Wmk. 233
1074 A310 1.50b Woman in rice paddy 25 15

Local Butterflies — A311

Perf. 13¹/₂
1984, Nov. 27 Photo. Wmk. 329
1075 A311 2b Bhutanitis lidderdalei 42 18
1076 A311 3b Stichophthalma louisa 60 28
1077 A311 5b Parthenos sylvia 1.00 45
1078 A311 7b Stichophthalma godfreyi 1.40 70

King Type of 1980
Perf. 13¹/₂x13, 14x15 (1.50b, 2b)
Wmk. 329, 233 (1.50b, 2b)
1984-87 Litho.
1079 A256 1b Prus blue 20 15
1081 A256 1.50b brt yel org ('85) 30 15
1082 A256 2b dk carmine ('85) 40 16
a. Wmk. 387, perf. 11x13¹/₂ ('86?) 1.10 16
b. Wmk. 387, perf. 14¹/₂x14 ('87) 65 16

Engr.
1083 A256 2b hn brn & gray vio 38 16
1084 A256 4b turq bl & hn brn 65 24
1085 A256 6.50b dk yel grn & ol brn 85 35
1086 A256 7b dl red brn & sep 1.10 42
1087 A256 7.50b dk org & saph ('85) 1.10 48
1088 A256 8b brn vio & ol grn ('85) 1.25 52
1089 A256 9b int bl & dk ol bis ('85) 1.40 58
1090 A256 10b hn brn & sl grn 1.65 62
1091 A256 20b dk orange & grn 6.25 1.25
1093 A256 50b dp violet & grn 7.50 3.00
1097 A256 100b dp org & dk bl 15.00 6.00
Nos. 1079-1097 (14) 38.03 14.08

This is an expanding set. Numbers will change if necessary.
For surcharge see No. 1212.

Children's Day — A313

Children's drawings.

Perf. 13¹/₂
1985, Jan. 12 Litho. Wmk. 385
1101 A313 1.50b Pedestrians, overpass 25 20
1102 A313 1.50b Climbing overpass, vert. 25 20

Bangkok Mail Center Opening — A314

1985, Feb. 25
1103 A314 1.50b multicolored 30 20

Phuket Province Heroes Bicent. — A315

Perf. 15x14
1985, Mar. 13 Litho. Wmk. 233
1104 A315 2b multicolored 30 25
Tao-Thep-Krasattri, Tao-Sri-Sundhorn Monument.

Government Savings Bank, 72nd Anniv. — A316

1985, Apr. 1 Perf. 14x15
1105 A316 1.50b King Rama VI, headquarters 30 15

Intl. Telecommunications Satellite Org., 20th Anniv. — A317

1985, Apr. 6 Wmk. 387 Perf. 12
1106 A317 2b multicolored 38 20

Thai Airways Intl., 25th Anniv. — A318

Wmk. 385
1985, May 1 Litho. Perf. 13
1107 A318 2b DC-6 38 30
1108 A318 7.50b DC-10 1.40 1.00
1109 A318 8.50b Airbus A-300 1.50 1.25
1110 A318 9.50b Boeing 747 1.50 1.25

Natl. Flag and UPU Emblem — A319

1985, July 1 Wmk. 387 Perf. 12
1111 A319 2b shown 22 18
Perf. 13¹/₂
Wmk. 385
1112 A319 10b Flag and ITU emblem 1.10 90

Thai membership to UPU and Intl. Telecommunications Union, cent.

Natl. Communications Day, Aug. 5 — A320

1985, Aug. 4 Wmk. 329 Perf. 13¹/₂
1113 A320 2b multicolored 25 15

THAIPEX '85, Aug. 4-13 — A321

1985, Aug. 4 Wmk. 385
1114 A321 2b Aisvarya Pavilion, vert. 28 15
1115 A321 3b Varopas Piman Pavilion 42 25
1116 A321 7b Vehas Camrun Pavilion 90 60
1117 A321 10b Vitoon Tassana Tower, vert. 1.40 80
a. Souv. sheet of 4, #1114-1117 47.50 2.75

No. 1117a exists imperf, sold for 40b.

Natl. Science Day, Aug. 18 A322

1985, Aug. 18 Wmk. 387 Perf. 12
1118 A322 2b King Rama IV, solar eclipse 25 15

1885 Seal, Modern Map and Crest A323

Perf. 14¹/₂x15
1985, Sept. 3 Wmk. 233
1119 A323 2b multicolored 25 15
Royal Thai Survey Department, Cent.

13th SEA Games, Bangkok, Dec. 8-17 — A324

Designs: a, Boxing. b, Shot put. c, Badminton. d, Javelin. e, Weight lifting.

1985, Oct. 1 Wmk. 387 Perf. 12
1120		Strip of 5		1.50	80
a.-e.	A324	2b, any single		30	15
f.		Souv. sheet of 5, #a.-e. + label		20.00	2.40

No. 1120f sold for 20b.

Climbing Plants — A325   UN Child Survival Campaign — A326

1985, Oct. 6 Wmk. 385 Perf. 13½
1121	A325	2b Allemanda cathartica	25	15
1122	A325	3b Jasminum auriculatum	38	25
1123	A325	7b Passiflora laurifolia	80	55
1124	A325	10b Antigonon leptopus	1.25	80

International Letter Writing Week.

1985, Oct. 24
1125	A326	2b multicolored	25	15

UN Day.

Prince Kromamun Bidyalabh Bridhyakorn (1885-1974), Govt. Minister — A327   Rangsit (1885-1951), Prince of Jainad — A328

1985, Nov. 7
1126	A327	2b multi	15	15
1126A	A327	2b multi, diff.	2.25	15
b.		Pair, #1126-1126A	30.00	
		Set value		24

No. 1126A has flower design framing portrait reversed.

Perf. 15x14½
1985, Nov. 12 Wmk. 233
1127	A328	1.50b multicolored	25	15

Asian-Pacific Postal Union, 5th Congress, Nov. 25-Dec. 4 — A329

1985, Nov. 25 Wmk. 385 Perf. 13½
1128	A329	2b multicolored	16	15
1129	A329	10b multicolored	85	62

Intl. Youth Year A330

Perf. 14x15
1985, Nov. 26 Wmk. 233
1130	A330	2b multicolored	30	15

12th Asian-Pacific Dental Congress, Bangkok, Dec. 5-10 — A331

1985, Dec. 5
1131	A331	2b multicolored	30	15

13th SEA Games — A332   French Envoys — A333

1985, Dec. 8 Wmk. 387 Perf. 12
1132	A332	1b Volleyball	16	15
1133	A332	2b Sepak-takraw	32	15
1134	A332	3b Women's gymnastics	48	15
1135	A332	4b Bowling	65	38
a.		Souv. sheet of 4, #1132-1135 + label	18.00	1.10

No. 1135a sold for 20b.

1985, Dec. 12 Wmk. 385 Perf. 13½
1136	A333	2b shown	20	15
1137	A333	8.50b Thai envoys	80	65

Diplomatic relations with France, 300th anniv.

Domestic Express Mail Service Inauguration — A334

1986, Jan. 1
1138	A334	2b multicolored	25	15

Intl. Express Mail Service, EMS, 3rd anniv.

Wildlife Conservation — A335

Marine turtles.

1986, Jan. 8 Wmk. 329
1139	A335	1.50b Chelonia mydas	28	15
1140	A335	3b Eretmochelys imbricata	55	20
1141	A335	5b Dermochelys coriacea	90	30
1142	A335	10b Lepidochelys olivacea	1.75	62

Natl. Children's Day — A336   Statue of Sunthon Phu, Poet — A337

Design: Children picking lotus, by Areeya Makarabhundhu, age 12.

1986, Jan. 11 Wmk. 385
1143	A336	2b multicolored	25	15

1986, June 26
1144	A337	2b multicolored	25	15

Fruit Type of 1979

1986, June 26 Wmk. 385
1145	A237	2b Watermelon	45	15
1146	A237	2b Malay apple	45	15
1147	A237	6b Pomelo	1.40	35
1148	A237	6b Papaya	1.40	35

Nos. 1145-1148 horiz.

Natl. Year of the Trees A338

1986, July 21
1149	A338	2b multicolored	25	15

Communications Day — A339

1986, Aug. 4
1150	A339	2b multicolored	25	15

Bamboo Baskets — A340

1986, Oct. 5
1151	A340	2b Chalom	28	15
1152	A340	2b Krabung	28	15
1153	A340	6b Kratib	85	42
1154	A340	6b Kaleb	85	42

Intl. Letter Writing Week.

Intl. Peace Year A341

1986, Oct. 24
1155	A341	2b multicolored	22	15

Productivity Year — A342

1986, Oct. 24 Wmk. 329
1156	A342	2b multicolored	22	15

6th ASEAN Orchid Congress — A343

1986, Nov. 7 Wmk. 385
1157	A343	2b Vanda varavuth, vert.	35	15
1158	A343	3b Ascocenda emma, vert.	55	22
1159	A343	4b Dendrobium sri-siam	70	28
1160	A343	5b Dendrobium ekapol panda	90	35
a.		Souv. sheet of 4, #1157-1160	50.00	2.25

No. 1160a sold for 25b.

Fungi A344

Perf. 13x13½
1986, Nov. 26 Wmk. 329 Photo.
1161	A344	2b Volvariella volvacea	35	15
1162	A344	2b Pleurotus ostreatus	35	15
1163	A344	6b Auricularia polytricha	1.10	42
1164	A344	6b Pleurotus cystidiosus	1.10	42

Fisheries Dept., 60th Anniv. — A345

Perf. 13½
1986, Dec. 16 Wmk. 385 Litho.
1165	A345	2b Morulius chrysophekadion	25	15
1166	A345	2b Notopterus blanci	25	15
1167	A345	7b Scleropages formosus	85	48
1168	A345	7b Pangasianodon gigas	85	48

No. 653 Surcharged in Dark Olive Green =1บาท BAHT=

Perf. 14x13½
1986, Dec. Photo. Wmk. 233
1168A	A161	1b on 20s blue	45	15

Children's
Day — A346

Child's drawing.

Perf. 14¹/₂x15

1987, Jan. 10		Litho.		Wmk. 387
1169 A346	2b	School, playground	20	15
1170 A346	2b	Pool	20	15
a.		Pair, #1169-1170	45	45

No. 1170a has continuous design.

F-16 &
F-5
Fighter
Planes,
Pilot
A347

1987, Mar. 27	Wmk. 385	*Perf. 13¹/₂*
1171 A347	2b multicolored	25 15

Royal Thai Air Force, 72nd anniv.

King Rama III (Nang Klao, 1787-
1851) — A348

1987, Mar. 31	Wmk. 387	*Perf. 15*
1172 A348	2b multicolored	25 15

Ministry of Communications, 75th
Anniv. — A349

1987, Apr. 1		*Perf. 15x14¹/₂*
1173 A349	2b multicolored	25 15

Forestry
Year
A350

1987, July 11	Wmk. 385	*Perf. 13¹/₂*
1174 A350	2b multicolored	25 15

THAIPEX '87 — A351

Gold artifacts.

1987, Aug. 4			Wmk. 385
1175 A351	2b	Peacock, vert.	40 18
1176 A351	2b	Hand mirrors, vert.	40 18
1177 A351	6b	Water urn, finger bowls	1.10 55
1178 A351	6b	Swan vase	1.10 55
a.		Souv. sheet of 4, #1175-1178	45.00 4.00

No. 1178a exists imperf.

ASEAN,
20th
Anniv.
A352

1987, Aug. 20		
1179 A352	2b multicolored	25 16
1180 A352	3b multicolored	35 24
1181 A352	4b multicolored	52 35
1182 A352	5b multicolored	65 42

Natl. Communications Day — A353

1987, Aug. 4		
1183 A353	2b multicolored	25 18

Chulachamklao Royal Military Academy,
Cent. — A354

Design: School crest, King Rama V, and King
Rama IX conferring sword on graduating officer.

1987, Aug. 5		
1184 A354	2b multicolored	25 18

Intl. Literacy   Tourism
Day — A355   Year — A356

1987, Sept. 8		
1185 A355	2b multicolored	25 18

1987, Sept. 18

Designs: 2b, Flower-offering ceremony, Saraburi
province. 3b, Duan Sib Festival, Nakhon Si Tham-
marat province. 5b, Bang Fai Festival, Yasothon
province. 7b, Loi Krathong Festival, Sukhothai
province.

1186 A356	2b multicolored	24 15
1187 A356	3b multicolored	35 22
1188 A356	5b multicolored	60 35
1189 A356	7b multicolored	80 48

Auditor General's Office, 72nd
Anniv. — A357

1987, Sept. 18		
1190 A357	2b multicolored	25 18

Diplomatic Relations Between Thailand
and Japan, Cent. — A358

1987, Sept. 26		Wmk. 329
1191 A358	2b multicolored	25 18

Intl. Letter Writing
Week — A359

Floral garlands.

1987, Oct. 4			Wmk. 385
1192 A359	2b	Floral tassel	22 15
1193 A359	3b	Tasselled garland	35 22
1194 A359	5b	Wrist garland	60 35
1195 A359	7b	Double-ended garland	80 50

Thai
Pavilion
A360

1987, Oct. 9	Wmk. 387	*Perf. 15*
1196 A360	2b multicolored	25 15

Social Education and Cultural Center
inauguration.

A361

A362

King Bhumibol Adulyadej, 60th
Birthday — A363

Royal ciphers and: No. 1197, Adulyadej as a
child. No. 1198, King and Queen, wedding portrait,
1950. No. 1199, King taking the Oath of Accession,
1950. No. 1200, King dressed as a monk, collecting
alms. No. 1201, Greeting 100 year-old woman. No.
1202, In military uniform holding pen and with hill
tribes. No. 1203, Royal couple visiting wounded
servicemen. No. 1204, Visiting farm. No. 1205,
Royal family. No. 1206, King, Queen Sirikit. No.
1207, Princess Mother Somdej Phra Sri Nakarindra
Boromrajjonnani, emblem of Medical Volunteer
Assoc. No. 1208, Crown Prince Maha
Vajiralongkorn, crown prince's royal standard. No.
1209, Princess Maha Chakri Sirindhorn, emblem of
Sai Jai Thai Foundation. No. 1210, Princess Chulabhorn, Albert Einstein gold medal awarded by
UNESCO.

1987, Dec. 5	Photo.	Wmk. 329	*Perf. 13¹/₂*
1197 A361	2b shown	32	15
1198 A361	2b multicolored	32	15
1199 A361	2b multicolored	32	15
1200 A361	2b multicolored	32	15
1201 A361	2b multicolored	32	15
1202 A361	2b multicolored	32	15
1203 A361	2b multicolored	32	15
1204 A361	2b multicolored	32	15
a.	Souv. sheet of 8, #1197-1204	12.00	4.00

Litho.
Wmk. 385

1205 A362	2b multicolored	32	15
1206 A362	2b multicolored	32	15
1207 A362	2b multicolored	32	15
1208 A362	2b multicolored	32	15
1209 A362	2b multicolored	32	15
1210 A362	2b multicolored	32	15

Litho. & Embossed

1211 A363	100b vio blue & gold	50.00	8.25
	Nos. 1197-1211 (15)	54.48	10.35

Size of Nos. 1206-1210: 45x27mm. No. 1211
printed in sheets of 10. No. 1204a sold for 40b.

No. 1081
Surcharged

2 บาท BAHT

1987	Litho.	Wmk. 233	*Perf. 14x15*
1212 A256	2b on 1.50b brt yel org	45 15

Children's   Thai Agricultural
Day — A364   Cooperatives, 72nd
                Anniv. — A365

Perf. 14x14¹/₂

1988, Jan. 9	Litho.	Wmk. 387
1213 A364	2b multicolored	22 15

1988, Feb. 26		Wmk. 387
1214 A365	2b	Prince Bridhyalongkorn, founder	25 15

Royal Siam Soc., 84th Anniv. A366

1988, Mar. 10   *Perf. 14¹/₂x14*
1215 A366 2b multicolored   25 15

Cultural Heritage Preservation — A367

Ruins in Sukhothai Historic Park.

1988, Apr. 2   *Perf. 14¹/₂x14*
1216 A367 2b Wat Phra Phai Luang   32 15
1217 A367 3b Wat Traphang Thonglang   42 18
1218 A367 4b Wat Maha That   65 28
1219 A367 6b Thewalai Maha Kaset   85 38

Red Cross Fair A368

1988, Apr.   **Wmk. 387**   *Perf. 14*
1220 A368 2b Prevention of rabies   25 15

King Rama V, Founder — A369   Intl. Council of Women, Cent. — A371

Pheasants — A370

1988, Apr. 26   *Perf. 14x14¹/₂*   **Wmk. 387**
1221 A369 5b multicolored   70 32

Siriraj Hospital, cent.

1988, June 15   *Perf. 13¹/₂*   **Photo.**   **Wmk. 329**
1222 A370 2b Crested fireback   32 15
1223 A370 3b Kalij   42 18
1224 A370 6b Silver pheasant   85 38
1225 A370 7b Hume's pheasant   1.00 42

No. 936a Surcharged

=   = = =   =

1 บาท **BAHT**   **1** บาท **BAHT**
a   b

1988-92   *Perf. 11x13*   **Litho.**   **Wmk. 387**
1226 A256(a) 1b on 1.25b yel green   25 15
1226A A256(b) 1b on 1.25b yel green   45 15
   b.   Wmk. 368   45 15

Issued: #1226, 1988; #1226A, Dec. 5, 1992.

1988, June 26   **Wmk. 385**   *Perf. 13¹/₂*
1227 A371 2b multicolored   25 16

King Bhumibol Adulyadej
A372   A372a

1988-93   *Perf. 13¹/₂x13*   **Litho.**   **Wmk. 387**
1228 A372 25s brown   15 15

Perf. 14x14¹/₂
1229 A372 50s olive   15 15
1230 A372 1b brt blue   15 15
   a.   Photo, wmk. 233   18 15
1233 A372 2b scarlet   25 16
   a.   Wmk. 329, perf. 13¹/₂x13   25 15

Issued: 25s, Aug. 12, 1992; 1b-2b, July 2, 1988; 50s, July 28, 1993; No. 1230a, 1990; No. 1233a, 1992.

1988-90   *Perf. 14¹/₂*   **Engr.**   **Wmk. 233**
1236 A372a 1b bright blue   15 15

Wmk. 329   *Perf. 13¹/₂x13*
1242 A372a 3b brn & bluish gray   32 25
1242A A372a 4b brt bl & red brn   45 32
1243 A372a 5b violet & brn   40 30
1244 A372a 6b green & vio   48 35
1244A A372a 7b red brn & dk brn   78 58
1245 A372a 8b red brn & gray ol   65 48
1245A A372a 9b dk blue & brn   72 55
1246 A372a 10b henna brn & blk   1.10 80
1248 A372a 20b brn org & sage grn   2.20 1.65
1248A A372a 25b olive grn & dark blue   2.00 1.50
1249 A372a 50b violet & grn   5.50 4.00
1251 A372a 100b brn org & bluish blk   11.00 8.00
   Nos. 1228-1251 (17)   26.45 19.54

Issue dates: 3b, 10b, 50b, 100b, Dec. 5, 1988. 5b, 6b, 8b, 9b, July 1, 1989. 4b, 7b, 20b, Dec. 5, 1989. 25b, Jan. 9, 1990. 1b, 1990.
This is an expanding set, Numbers will change if necessary.

A373   A375

King Bhumibol's Reign (since 1950) — A374

Designs: No. 1253, King Bhumibol. Regalia: No. 1254, Great Crown of Victory. No. 1255, Sword of Victory and matching scabbard. No. 1256, Scepter. No. 1257, Fan and feather fly swatter. No. 1258, Royal slippers.
Canopied thrones in the Grand Palace: No. 1259, Queen's round ottoman on 1-tier dais in front of decorative screen. No. 1260, King's throne on 1-tier dais in front of decorative screen. No. 1261, 3-Tier throne with 3 gilded trees. No. 1262, 3-Canopy throne on high gold dais. No. 1263, 3-Tier throne with 4 gilded trees, altar in background. No. 1264, 3-Canopy throne on 5-stair dais, in front of arch flanked by columns.

1988, July 2   *Perf. 13¹/₂*   **Litho.**   **Wmk. 385**
1253 A373 2b shown   32 16

Photo.   **Wmk. 329**
1254 A374 2b multi, vert.   32 16
1255 A374 2b multicolored   32 16
1256 A374 2b multicolored   32 16
1257 A374 2b multicolored   32 16
1258 A374 2b multicolored   32 16

Litho.   *Perf. 14x14¹/₂*   **Wmk. 387**
1259 A375 2b multicolored   32 16
1260 A375 2b multicolored   32 16
1261 A375 2b multicolored   32 16
1262 A375 2b multicolored   32 16
1263 A375 2b multicolored   32 16
1264 A375 2b multicolored   32 16
   a.   Souv. sheet of 6, #1259-1264   30.00 3.25
   Nos. 1253-1264 (12)   3.84 1.92

No. 1264a sold for 25b.

Arbor Year A376

1988, July 29   *Perf. 14¹/₂x14*   **Litho.**   **Wmk. 387**
1265 A376 2b multicolored   25 16

Natl. Communications Day — A377

Wmk. Alternating Interlaced Wavy Lines (340)

1988, Aug. 4   *Perf. 13¹/₂*
1266 A377 2b multicolored   25 16

Intl. Letter Writing Week A378

Designs: Coconut leaf sculptures.

1988, Oct. 9   *Perf. 14¹/₂x14*   **Wmk. 387**
1267 A378 2b Grasshopper   25 16
1268 A378 2b Fish   25 16
1269 A378 6b Bird   75 50
1270 A378 6b Takro (box)   75 50

Housing Development — A379

1988, Oct. 24   **Wmk. 233**   **Litho.**   *Perf. 14*
1271 A379 2b multicolored   25 16

Traffic Safety — A380   King's Bodyguard, 120th Anniv. — A381

1988, Nov. 11   **Wmk. 329**   *Perf. 13¹/₂*
1272 A380 2b multicolored   25 16

1988, Nov. 11   **Wmk. 385**
1273 A381 2b Chulalongkorn   25 16

New Year — A382

Flowers.

1988, Dec. 1   **Wmk. 387**
1274 A382 1b Crotalaria sessiliflora   38 15
1275 A382 1b Uvaria grandiflora   38 15
1276 A382 1b Reinwardtia trigyna   38 15
1277 A382 1b Impatiens griffithii   38 15
   Set value   35

Thai Royal Orders Type of 1979

Designs: Nos. 1278-1279, Knight Grand Commander, Order of Rama, 1918. Nos. 1280-1281, Knight Grand Cordon, Order of the White Elephant, 1861. Nos. 1282-1283, Knight Grand Cordon, Order of the Crown of Thailand, 1869. Nos. 1284-1285, Ratana Varabhorn Order of Merit, 1911. Printed se-tenant in continuous designs.

1988, Dec. 5   **Wmk. 385**
1278 A243 2b multicolored   25 16
1279 A243 2b multicolored   25 16
1280 A243 3b multicolored   35 25
1281 A244 3b multicolored   35 25
1282 A243 5b multicolored   65 40
1283 A244 5b multicolored   65 40
1284 A243 7b multicolored   85 55
1285 A244 7b multicolored   85 55
   Nos. 1278-1285 (8)   4.20 2.72

A383

Buddha Monthon
Celebrations, Tambol
Salaya — A384

Perf. 14x15, 15x14

1988, Dec. 5   **Wmk. 233**
1286 A383 2b Birthplace   30   16
1287 A383 3b Enlightenment place   42   25
1288 A383 4b Location of 1st ser-
     mon   60   32
1289 A383 5b Place Buddha
     achieved nirvana   75   40
1290 A384 6b Statue   90   48
     Nos. 1286-1290 (5)   2.97   1.61

Souvenir Sheet
Perf. 14¹/₂x14
1291 A384 6b like No. 1290   15.00   1.65

No. 1291 sold for 15b.

Children's Day — A385

"Touch" paintings by blind youth: No. 1292,
Floating Market, by Thongbai Siyam. No. 1293,
Flying Bird, by Kwanchai Kerd-Daeng. No. 1294,
Little Mermaid, by Chalermpol Jiengmai. No. 1295,
Golden Fish, by Natetip Korsantirak.

Perf. 13¹/₂
1989, Jan. 14   **Litho.**   **Wmk. 387**
1292 A385 2b multicolored   25   16
1293 A385 2b multicolored   25   16
1294 A385 2b multicolored   25   16
1295 A385 2b multicolored   25   16

Communications Authority of Thailand,
12th Anniv. — A386

1989, Feb. 25   **Perf. 14¹/₂x14**
1296 A386 2b multicolored   25   16

Chulalongkorn University, 72nd
Anniv. — A387

Design: 2b, Statue of Chulalongkorn and King
Vajiravudh in front of university auditorium.

1989, Mar. 26
1297 A387 2b multicolored   25   16

A388   A389

Perf. 15x14
1989, Mar. 31   **Litho.**   **Wmk. 233**
1298 A388 2b shown   22   16
       Wmk. 387
       Perf. 13¹/₂
1299 A388 10b Emblem   1.10   82

Thai Red Cross Society, 96th anniv. (2b); Intl.
Red Cross and Red Crescent organizations, 125th
annivs. (10b).

Perf. 14x14¹/₂
1989, Apr. 2   **Wmk. 387**

Phra Nakhon Khiri Historical Park: 2b, Wat Phra
Kaeo. 3b, Chatchawan Wiangchai Observatory. 5b,
Phra That Chom Phet Stupa. 6b, Wetchayan
Wichian Phrasat Throne Hall.

1300 A389 2b multicolored   32   16
1301 A389 3b multicolored   45   24
1302 A389 5b multicolored   80   42
1303 A389 6b multicolored   95   50

Natl. Lottery Office, 50th Anniv. — A390

1989, Apr. 5   **Perf. 13¹/₂**
1304 A390 2b multicolored   25   16

Seashells — A391

1989, June 28   **Wmk. 329**   **Perf. 13¹/₂**
1305 A391 2b Conus thailandis   30   16
1306 A391 3b Spondylus princeps   42   24
1307 A391 6b Cyprea guttata   85   50
1308 A391 10b Nautilus pompilius   1.50   82

Arts and
Crafts
Year
A392

1989, June 28   **Litho.**   **Wmk. 387**
1309 A392 2b Ceramic figurines   28   16
1310 A392 2b Gold niello ginger jar,
     chicken   28   16
1311 A392 6b Textiles   85   50
1312 A392 6b Gemstone flower or-
     nament   85   50

Asia-Pacific Telecommunications
Organization, 10th Anniv. — A393

Design: APT emblem, map of submarine cable
network and satellites of member nations.

1989, July 1   **Wmk. 329**   **Perf. 13¹/₂**
1313 A393 9b multicolored   1.00   75

Phya Anuman   9th Natl. Phil.
Rajadhon (1888-   Exhib., Aug. 4-
1969),   13 — A395
Ethnologist — A394

1989, July 1   **Wmk. 387**   **Perf. 13¹/₂**
1314 A394 2b multicolored   25   16

1989, Aug. 4   **Wmk. 233**   **Perf. 15x14**

Various mailboxes.

1315 A395 2b multicolored   28   16
1316 A395 3b multi, diff.   42   24
1317 A395 4b multi, diff.   55   32
1318 A395 5b multi, diff.   70   40
1319 A395 6b multi, diff.   85   50
   a.   Souvenir sheet of 5, #1315-1319,
       perf. 14   25.00   3.25
     Nos. 1315-1319 (5)   2.80   1.62

No. 1319a sold for 30b.

A396   A398

A397

Perf. 13¹/₂
1989, June 26   **Litho.**   **Wmk. 387**
1320 A396 2b multicolored   25   16

Intl. Anti-drug Day.

1989, Aug. 4   **Wmk. 233**   **Perf. 14x15**
1321 A397 2b multicolored   25   16

Post and Telecommunications School, cent.

1989, Aug. 4   **Wmk. 387**   **Perf. 13¹/₂**
1322 A398 2b multicolored   25   16

Natl. Communications Day.

Dragonflies — A399

Perf. 13¹/₂
1989, Oct. 8   **Photo.**   **Wmk. 329**
1323 A399 2b shown   24   16
1324 A399 5b multi, diff.   60   42
1325 A399 6b multi, diff.   70   48
1326 A399 10b Damselfly   1.25   82
   a.   Souv. sheet of 4, #1323-1326   25.00   3.50

Intl. Letter Writing Week. #1326a sold for 40b.

Transport and Communications Decade for
Asia and the Pacific — A400

Perf. 14¹/₂x14
1989, Oct. 24   **Litho.**   **Wmk. 387**
1327 A400 2b multicolored   25   16

Mental Health Care,   New Year
Cent. — A401   1990 — A402

1989, Nov. 1   **Wmk. 233**   **Perf. 15x14**
1328 A401 2b multicolored   25   16

Perf. 14x14¹/₂
1989, Nov. 15   **Wmk. 387**

Flowering plants.

1329 A402 1b Hypericum uralum   25   15
1330 A402 1b Uraria rufescens   25   15
1331 A402 1b Manglietia garrettii   25   15
1332 A402 1b Aeschynanthus
     macranthus   25   15
   a.   Souv. sheet of 4, #1329-1332   3.00   1.50
     Set value   40

No. 1332a sold for 14b.

Insects
A403

Perf. 13¹/₂
1989, Nov. 15   **Photo.**   **Wmk. 329**
1333 A403 2b Catacanthus in-
     carnatus   25   16
1334 A403 3b Aristobia approxi-
     mator   35   24
1335 A403 6b Chrysochroa chinen-
     sis   70   48
1336 A403 10b Enoplotrupes sharpi   1.25   82

Population and Housing Census of
1990 — A404

Perf. 13¹/₂
1990, Jan. 1　　Litho.　　Wmk. 387
1337 A404 2b multicolored　　　　25　16

Children's Day　　　　Emblems
A405　　　　　　　　A406

1990, Jan. 13　Wmk. 233　*Perf. 15x14*
1338 A405 2b Jumping rope, horiz.　25　15
1339 A405 2b Sports　　　　　　　25　15

1990, Mar. 29　Wmk. 387　*Perf. 13¹/₂*
1340 A406 2b multicolored　　　　25　16
WHO Fight AIDS Worldwide campaign and the
Natl. Red Cross Soc.

Thai Heritage Conservation Day — A407

Prize-winning inlaid mother-of-pearl containers:
No. 1341, Tiap (footed bowl with lid), vert. No.
1342, Phan waenfa (two-tiered vessel), vert. No.
1343, Lung (lidded bowl). No. 1344, Chiat klom
(spade-shaped lidded container signifying noble
rank).

1990, Apr. 2　　Photo.　　Wmk. 329
1341 A407 2b multicolored　　　　25　15
1342 A407 2b multicolored　　　　25　15
1343 A407 8b multicolored　　　　1.00　54
1344 A407 8b multicolored　　　　1.00　54

A408　　　　　　　　A409

Minerals.

Perf. 14x14¹/₂
1990, June 29　　Litho.　　Wmk. 387
1345 A408 2b Tin　　　　　　　25　15
1346 A408 3b Zinc　　　　　　38　18
1347 A408 5b Lead　　　　　　60　30
1348 A408 6b Fluorite　　　　　75　35
　a.　Souv. sheet of 4, #1345-1348　6.00　3.25

No. 1348a sold for 30b, exists imperf.

1990, May 16
1349 A409 2b multicolored　　　　25　20
Faculty of Dentistry, Chulalongkorn Univ., 50th
anniv.

Communications Day — A410

1990, Aug. 4　　　　*Perf. 14¹/₂x14*
1350 A410 2b multicolored　　　　25　20

Asian-Pacific Postal Training Center, 20th
Anniv. — A411

1990, Sept. 10
1351 A411 2b multicolored　　　　25　20
1352 A411 8b multicolored　　　　1.10　82

Rotary Intl. in Thailand, 60th
Anniv. — A412

1990, Sept. 16　　　　*Perf. 13¹/₂*
1353 A412 2b Health care　　　　32　20
1354 A412 3b Immunizations　　　48　30
1355 A412 6b Literacy project　　95　60
1356 A412 1.25b Thai museum project　1.25　82

Intl. Letter Writing Week, 1990 — A413

Illustration reduced.

1990, Oct. 7　　　　　　*Perf. 14*
1357 A413 2b multicolored　　　　30　20
1358 A413 3b multi, diff.　　　　45　30
1359 A413 5b multi, diff.　　　　75　50
1360 A413 6b multi, diff.　　　　90　60
　a.　Souv. sheet of 4, #1357-1360　6.75　4.30

No. 1360a sold for 30b, exists imperf.

Dept. of Comptroller-General,
Cent. — A414

1990, Oct. 7　　　　*Perf. 14¹/₂x14*
1361 A414 2b multicolored　　　　25　20

A415　　　　　　　　A416

1990, Oct. 21　　　*Perf. 14x14¹/₂*
1362 A415 2b multicolored　　　　25　20
Princess Mother, 90th birthday.

1990, Nov. 15　Wmk. 233　*Perf. 14¹/₂*
Flowers: No. 1363, Cyrtandromoea grandiflora.
No. 1364, Rhododendron arboreum. No. 1365,
Merremia vitifolia. No. 1366, Afgekia mahidolae.
1363 A416 1b multicolored　　　　22　15
1364 A416 1b multicolored　　　　22　15
1365 A416 1b multicolored　　　　22　15
1366 A416 1b multicolored　　　　22　15
　a.　Sheet of 4, #1363-1366　3.00　1.20
　　Set value　　　　　　　　40

New Year 1991. No. 1366a sold for 10b, exists
imperf.
See Nos. 1417-1420.

Wiman
Mek
Royal
Hall
A417

Royal Throne Rooms in the Dusit Palace: 3b,
Ratcharit Rungrot Royal House. 4b, Aphisek Dusit
Royal Hall. 5b, Amphon Sathan Palace. 6b, Udon
Phak Royal Hall. 8b, Anantasamakhom Throne
Hall.

Perf. 13¹/₂
1990, Dec. 5　　Photo.　　Wmk. 329
1367 A417 2b multicolored　　　　28　22
1368 A417 3b multicolored　　　　42　35
1369 A417 4b multicolored　　　　55　45
1370 A417 5b multicolored　　　　70　55
1371 A417 6b multicolored　　　　85　65
1372 A417 8b multicolored　　　　1.25　90
　Nos. 1367-1372 (6)　　　　　4.05　3.12

Somdet Phra Maha Samanachao Kromphra
Paramanuchitchinorot (1790-1853),
Supreme Patriarch — A418

1990, Dec. 11　Wmk. 387　*Perf. 13¹/₂*
1373 A418 2b multicolored　　　　25　20

Petroleum Authority, 12th Anniv. — A419

Perf. 14¹/₂x14
1990, Dec. 29　　Litho.　　Wmk. 387
1374 A419 2b multicolored　　　　25　20

Locomotives — A420

Designs: 2b, No. 6, Krauss & Co., Germany,
1908. 3b, No. 32, Kyosan Kogyo, Japan, 1949. 5b,
No. 715, C56, Japan, 1946. 6b, No. 953, Mikado,
Japan, 1949-1951.

Perf. 14¹/₂x14
1990, Dec. 29　　Litho.　　Wmk. 387
1375 A420 2b multicolored　　　　30　20
1376 A420 3b multicolored　　　　42　25
1377 A420 5b multicolored　　　　65　45
1378 A420 6b multicolored　　　　80　55
　a.　Souv. sheet of 4, #1375-1378　6.00　2.75

No. 1378a sold for 25b, exists imperf.

Children's Day — A421

Children's games: 2b, Tops. 5b, Race. 6b, Blind-
man's buff.

1991, Jan. 12
1379 A421 2b multicolored　　　　25　20
1380 A421 3b shown　　　　　　38　30
1381 A421 5b multicolored　　　　62　50
1382 A421 6b multicolored　　　　75　60

A422　　　　　　　　A423

1991, Feb. 17　　　　*Perf. 14x14¹/₂*
1383 A422 2b multicolored　　　　25　20
Land titling project.

Perf. 14x14¹/₂
1991, Mar. 30　　Litho.　　Wmk. 387
1384 A423 2b Princess Maha　　30　20
　a.　Souvenir sheet of 1　　　3.00　1.00

Red Cross. No. 1384a sold for 8b, exists imperf.

Cultural Heritage A424

Floral decorations: 2b, Indra's heavenly abode. 3b, Celestial couch. 4b, Crystal ladder. 5b, Crocodile.

Perf. 13¹/₂

1991, Apr. 2	Photo.	Wmk. 329	
1385	A424	2b multicolored	25	20
1386	A424	3b multicolored	38	30
1387	A424	4b multicolored	50	40
1388	A424	5b multicolored	62	50
a.		Souvenir sheet of 4, #1385-1388	6.00	3.75

No. 1388a sold for 30b, exists imperf.

Year of the Sheep — A425

Perf. 14x14¹/₂

1991, Apr. 13	Wmk. 387	Litho.	
1389	A425	2b multicolored	2.25	20
a.		Souvenir sheet of 1	10.00	1.00

No. 1389a sold for 8b, exists imperf.

Prince Narisranuvattivongs (1863-1947) — A426

1991, Apr. 28		Perf. 14¹/₂x14	
1390	A426	2b brown & yellow	25	20

Mosaics — A427

Various lotus flowers.

1991, May 28		Perf. 13¹/₂	
1391	A427	2b multi, vert.	28	20
1392	A427	3b multi, vert.	35	25
1393	A427	5b multi	60	45
1394	A427	6b multi	75	52

Natl. Communications Day — A428

1991, Aug. 4		Perf. 13¹/₂	
	Litho.	Wmk. 387	
1395	A428	2b multicolored	25	20

Thaipex '91, Natl. Philatelic Exhibition — A429

Various fabric designs.

1991, Aug. 4		Perf. 14x14¹/₂	
1396	A429	2b multicolored	20	15
1397	A429	4b multicolored	42	32
1398	A429	6b multicolored	65	50
1399	A429	8b multicolored	85	65
a.		Souv. sheet of 4, #1396-1399	6.00	3.25

No. 1399a sold for 30b. No. 1399a overprinted with Philanippon emblem in lower left corner of margin sold for 200b.

Intl. Productivity Congress — A430

Perf. 14¹/₂x14

1991, Sept. 3	Litho.	Wmk. 387	
1400	A430	2b multicolored	20	15

26th Intl. Council of Women Triennial — A431

Perf. 13¹/₂

1991, Sept. 23	Litho.	Wmk. 387	
1401	A431	2b multicolored	25	15

Bantam Chickens — A432

Perf. 13¹/₂

1991, Oct. 6	Photo.	Wmk. 329	
1402	A432	2b Black bantams	25	15
1403	A432	3b Black-tailed buff bantams	38	22
1404	A432	6b Fancy bantams	75	45
1405	A432	8b White bantams	1.00	60
a.		Souv. sheet of 4, #1402-1405	7.00	4.00

No. 1405a sold for 35b, exists imperf. Intl. Letter Writing Week.

World Bank/Intl. Monetary Fund Annual Meetings — A433

Temples, meeting emblem and: 2b, Silver coin of King Rama IV. 4b, Pod Duang money. 8b, Chieng and Hoi money. 10b, Funan, Dvaravati and Srivijaya money.

Perf. 14¹/₂x14

1991, Oct. 15	Litho.	Wmk. 387	
1406	A433	2b multicolored	20	15
1407	A433	4b multicolored	40	30
1408	A433	8b multicolored	80	60
1409	A433	10b multicolored	1.00	75
a.		Souv. sheet of 4, #1406-1409	7.00	4.00

No. 1409a sold for 35b, exists imperf.

1993 World Philatelic Exhibition, Bangkok — A434

1991, Oct. 23		Perf. 14x14¹/₂	
1410	A434	2b No. 118	20	15
1411	A434	3b No. 119	30	22
1412	A434	4b No. 120	40	30
1413	A434	5b No. 121	50	38
1414	A434	6b No. 122	60	45
1415	A434	7b No. 123	70	52
1416	A434	8b No. 124	80	60
a.		Souvenir sheet of 1	3.50	1.75
		Nos. 1410-1416 (7)	3.50	2.62

No. 1416a sold for 15b, exists imperf.

Flower Type of 1990

Perf. 13¹/₂

1991, Nov. 5			
1417	A416	1b Dillenia obovata	16	15
1418	A416	1b Melastoma sanguine-um	16	15
1419	A416	1b Commelina diffusa	16	15
1420	A416	1b Plumbago indica	16	15
a.		Souv. sheet of 4, #1417-1420	3.00	1.50
		Set value		30

No. 1420a sold for 10b, exists imperf.

Asian Elephants — A435

Perf. 13¹/₂

1991, Nov. 5	Photo.	Wmk. 329	
1421	A435	2b shown	25	15
1422	A435	4b Pulling logs	50	32
1423	A435	6b Lying down	75	45
1424	A435	8b In river	1.00	60
a.		Souvenir sheet of 1, litho.	10.00	2.20

No. 1424a sold for 22b and stamp does not have border. No. 1424a exists imperf.

Wild Animals — A436

Perf. 14¹/₂x14

1991, Dec. 26	Wmk. 387	Litho.	
1425	A436	2b Viverra zibetha	20	15
1426	A436	3b Prionodon linsang	32	24
1427	A436	6b Felis temmincki	65	48
1428	A436	8b Ratufa bicolor	85	65
a.		Sheet of 4, #1425-1428	6.00	3.25

No. 1428a sold for 30b.

Prince Mahidol of Songkla (1891-1929), Medical Pioneer — A437

1992, Jan. 1		Perf. 14x14¹/₂	
1429	A437	2b multicolored	30	22

Department of Mineral Resources, Cent. — A438

Designs: No. 1430, Locating fossils. No. 1431, Mining excavation. No. 1432, Drilling for natural gas and petroleum. No. 1433, Digging artesian wells.

Perf. 14¹/₂x14

1992, Jan. 1	Litho.	Wmk. 387	
1430	A438	2b multicolored	25	18
1431	A438	2b multicolored	25	18
1432	A438	2b multicolored	25	18
1433	A438	2b multicolored	25	18

Children's Day — A439

Children's drawings on "World Under the Sea": 2b, Divers, fish. 3b, Fish, sea grass. 5b, Mermaid, vert.

1992, Jan. 11	Wmk. 329	Perf. 13¹/₂	
1434	A439	2b multicolored	25	18
1435	A439	3b multicolored	38	28
1436	A439	5b multicolored	60	42

Duel on Elephants, 400th Anniv. — A440

Perf. 14¹/₂x14

1992, Jan. 18	Litho.	Wmk. 387	
1437	A440	2b multicolored	25	18

Orchids (Paphiopedilum) — A441

1992, Jan. 20			
1438	A441	2b Bellatulum	24	18
1439	A441	2b Exul	24	18
1440	A441	3b Concolor	36	28
1441	A441	3b Godefroyae	36	28
1442	A441	6b Niveum	72	55
1443	A441	6b Villosum	72	55
1444	A441	10b Parishii	1.20	90
a.		Souv. sheet of 4, #1438, 1440, 1442, 1444	4.75	3.60

1445 A441 10b Sukhakulii 1.20 90
  a.   Souv. sheet of 4, #1439, 1441, 1443, 1445   4.75 3.60
  Nos. 1438-1445 (8) 5.04 3.82

Fourth Asia Pacific Orchid Conference. Nos. 1444a-1445a each sold for 30b.

21st Intl. Society of Sugar Cane Technologists Conf. — A442

1992, Mar. 5   *Perf. 14x14¹/₂*
1446 A442 2b multicolored 30 22

Intl. Red Cross A443

Perf. 14¹/₂x14
1992, Mar.   **Litho.**   **Wmk. 387**
1447 A443 2b multicolored 25 18

Ministry of Justice, Cent. — A444

Designs: 3b, Prince Rabi Badhanasakdi of Ratchaburi, founder of Thailand's School of Law. 5b, King Rama V, reformer of court system.

1992, Mar. 25   *Perf. 13¹/₂*
1448 A444 3b multicolored 35 28
1449 A444 5b multicolored 55 42

Ministry of Agriculture and Cooperatives, Cent. — A445

1992, Apr. 1   *Perf. 14¹/₂x14*
1450 A445 2b gray & multi 24 18
1451 A445 3b lil & multi 35 28
1452 A445 4b pink & multi 42 32
1453 A445 5b gray bl & multi 55 40

A446   A447

Ministry of Interior, Cent.: No. 1454, Prince Damrong Rajanubharb, first Minister of the Interior. No. 1455, People voting. No. 1456, Police and fire protection. No. 1457, Water and electricity provided to remote areas.

1992, Apr. 1   *Perf. 14x14¹/₂*
1454 A446 2b multicolored 24 18
1455 A446 2b multicolored 24 18
1456 A446 2b multicolored 24 18
1457 A446 2b multicolored 24 18

1992, Apr. 1
1458 A447 2b Ships, truck 24 18
1459 A447 3b Truck, bus, train 35 28
1460 A447 5b Airplanes 55 42
1461 A447 6b Truck, satellites 65 48

Ministry of Transport and Communications, 80th anniv.

Ministry of Education, Cent. — A448

Perf. 14x14¹/₂
1992, Apr. 1   **Litho.**   **Wmk. 387**
1462 A448 2b multicolored 25 18

Carts A449

1992, Apr. 2   *Perf. 14¹/₂x14*
1463 A449 2b West 24 18
1464 A449 3b North 35 28
1465 A449 5b Northeast 55 42
1466 A449 10b East 1.15 90
  a.   Souvenir sheet of 4, #1463-1466 5.00 1.75

Heritage Conservation Day. No. 1466a sold for 30b and exists imperf. without sheet price in margin.

Songkran Day — A450

1992, Apr. 13   *Perf. 14x14¹/₂*
1467 A450 2b Demon on monkey, zodiac 30 18
  a.   Souvenir sheet of 1 4.00 2.10

No. 1467a sold for 8b and exists imperf. with sale price in different colors.
See Nos. 1530, 1566.

Department of Livestock Development, 50th Anniv. — A451

Perf. 14¹/₂x14
1992, May 5   **Litho.**   **Wmk. 387**
1468 A451 2b multicolored 25 18

Wisakhabucha Day — A452

Scenes from Buddha's life: 2b, Birth. 3b, Enlightenment. 5b, Death.

Perf. 14¹/₂
1992, May 16   **Litho.**   **Wmk. 387**
1469 A452 2b multicolored 28 18
1470 A452 3b multicolored 35 25
1471 A452 5b multicolored 60 42

Meteorological Department, 50th Anniv. — A453

1992, June 23   *Perf. 14x14¹/₂*
1472 A453 2b multicolored 25 18

1993 World Philatelic Exhibition, Bangkok — A454   Visit ASEAN Year — A455

Perf. 14x14¹/₂
1992, July 1   **Litho.**   **Wmk. 387**
1473 A454 2b No. 18 22 16
1474 A454 3b No. 156 32 24
1475 A454 5b No. 222 52 40
1476 A454 7b No. 255 75 55
1477 A454 8b No. 273 85 65
  a.   Souv. sheet of 5, #1473-1477 + label 4.00 3.75
  Nos. 1473-1477 (5) 2.66 2.00

No. 1477a sold for 35b, exists imperf. with price in blue.

1992, July 1

Designs: 2b, Bua Tong field, Mae Hong Son Province. 3b, Klong Larn Waterfall, Kamphaeng Phet Province. 4b, Coral, Chumphon Province. 5b, Khao Ta-Poo, Phangnga Province.

1478 A455 2b multicolored 22 16
1479 A455 3b multicolored 32 24
1480 A455 4b multicolored 42 32
1481 A455 5b multicolored 52 40

N·E·W

Scott Specialty Album Pages for

Thailand

are now available

Prince Chudadhuj Dharadilok of Bejraburna (1892-1923) A456

Perf. 13¹/₂
1992, July 5   **Litho.**   **Wmk. 368**
1482 A456 2b multicolored 25 16

Natl. Communications Day — A457

Perf. 14¹/₂x14
1992, Aug. 4   **Litho.**   **Wmk. 387**
1483 A457 2b multicolored 25 18

ASEAN, 25th Anniv. — A458

Flags and: 2b, Cultures and sports. 3b, Tourist attractions. 5b, Transportation, communications. 7b, Agriculture.

1992, Aug. 8   **Wmk. 368**   *Perf. 13¹/₂*
1484 A458 2b multicolored 22 16
1485 A458 3b multicolored 32 24
1486 A458 5b multicolored 52 40
1487 A458 7b multicolored 75 55

Queen Sirikit, 60th Birthday A459

Designs: No. 1488, Wedding, with King, Queen being anointed. No. 1489, Coronation, King and Queen on throne. No. 1490, Being crowned, Queen with crown, being anointed. No. 1491, Formal portrait, Queen seated. No. 1492, Visiting wounded. No. 1493, Visiting public.

Perf. 13¹/₂
1992, Aug. 12   **Photo.**   **Wmk. 329**
1488 A459 2b multicolored 24 18
1489 A459 2b multicolored 24 18
1490 A459 2b multicolored 24 18
1491 A459 2b multicolored 24 18
1492 A459 2b multicolored 24 18
1493 A459 2b multicolored 24 18
  a.   Souvenir sheet of 6, #1488-1493 3.75 3.75
  Nos. 1488-1493 (6) 1.44 1.08

No. 1493a sold for 30b and exists imperf. with sale price in different colors.

Royal Regalia of Queen Sirikit — A460

Designs: No. 1494, Tray. No. 1495, Kettle. No. 1496, Bowl. No. 1497, Box. No. 1498, Covered dish.

1992, Aug. 12
Background Colors
1494	A460	2b dark blue	24	18
1495	A460	2b violet	24	18
1496	A460	2b yellow green	24	18
1497	A460	2b Prussian blue	24	18
1498	A460	2b dark green	24	18
	Nos. 1494-1498 (5)	1.20	90

Opening of Sirikit Medical Center — A461

Perf. 14¹/₂x14
1992, Aug. 12   Litho.   Wmk. 387
1499 A461 2b multicolored   25   16

Queen Sirikit, 60th Birthday — A462

Litho. & Embossed
1992, Aug. 12   Perf. 13¹/₂
1500 A462 100b blue & gold   12.00 9.00

A463   A464

Perf. 13¹/₂
1992, Aug. 25   Litho.   Wmk. 387
1501 A463 2b multicolored   22   16

Prince Wan Waithayakon Krommun Naradhip Bongsprabandh (1891-1976).

1992, Sept. 15   Perf. 14x14¹/₂
1502 A464 2b multicolored   25   18

Professor Silpa Bhirasri, Sculptor, cent. of birth.

Coral
A465

Perf. 14¹/₂x14
1992, Oct. 4   Litho.   Wmk. 387
1503	A465	2b Catalaphyllia jardinei	22	16
1504	A465	3b Porites lutea	32	24
1505	A465	6b Tubastraea coccinea	65	50
1506	A465	8b Favia pallida	90	70
a.		Souv. sheet of 4, #1503-1506	5.00	3.75

Intl. Letter Writing Week. No. 1506a sold for for 30b.

New Year
1993 — A466

Flowers: No. 1507, Rhododendron simsii. No. 1508, Cynoglossum lanceolatum. No. 1509, Tithonia diversifolia. No. 1510, Agapetes parishii.

Perf. 14x13¹/₂
1992, Nov. 15   Wmk. 368   Litho.
1507	A466	1b multicolored	15	15
1508	A466	1b multicolored	15	15
1509	A466	1b multicolored	15	15
1510	A466	1b multicolored	15	15
a.		Souvenir sheet of 4, #1507-1510	3.00	1.30
	Set value			35

Nos. 1510a sold for 10b. Exists imperf. with sheet price in green.

1st Asian Congress of Allergies and Immunology — A467

1992, Nov. 22   Perf. 13¹/₂
1511 A467 2b black, red & yellow   28 22

Natl. Assembly, 60th Anniv. — A468

Perf. 13¹/₂
1992, Dec. 10   Litho.   Wmk. 387
1512 A468 2b multicolored   25   18

Bank of Thailand, 50th Anniv. — A469

1992, Dec. 10   Perf. 14¹/₂x14
1513 A469 2b multicolored   25   18

Children's Day — A470

Children's drawings: No. 1514, River scene. No. 1515, Wild animals, forest. No. 1516, Trains, planes, monorail.

1993, Jan. 9   Wmk. 368   Perf. 13¹/₂
1514	A470	2b multicolored	24	18
1515	A470	2b multicolored	24	18
1516	A470	2b multicolored	24	18

Pottery
A471

Designs: 3b, Jug with bird's neck spout, two bottles. 6b, Pear-shaped vase, two jars. 7b, Three bowls. 8b, Three jars.

1993, Jan. 9   Photo.   Wmk. 329
1517	A471	3b multicolored	32	24
1518	A471	6b multicolored	65	48
1519	A471	7b multicolored	75	55
1520	A471	8b multicolored	85	75
a.		Souvenir sheet of 4, #1517-1520	4.00	4.00

1993 World Philatelic Exhibition, Bangkok. No. 1520a sold for 35b.

Thai Teachers' Training Institute, Cent. — A472

Perf. 13¹/₂x14
1993, Jan. 16   Litho.   Wmk. 368
1521 A472 2b multicolored   28   22

Kasetsart University, 50th Anniv. — A473

1993, Feb. 2   Wmk. 329   Perf. 13¹/₂
1522 A473 2b multicolored   28   22

Maghapuja
Day — A474

Perf. 14¹/₂
1993, Mar. 7   Litho.   Wmk. 387
1523 A474 2b multicolored   25   18

Queen Sri Bajarindra — A475

1993, Mar. 27   Perf. 14x14¹/₂
1524 A475 2b multicolored   25   18

Thai Red Cross, cent.

Office of Attorney General, Cent. — A476

1993, Apr. 1   Wmk. 368   Perf. 12¹/₂
1525 A476 2b multicolored   25   18

Heritage Conservation Day — A477

Historical landmarks, Si Satchanalai Park: 3b, Wat Chedi Chet Thaeo. 4b, Wat Chang Lom. 6b, Wat Phra Si Rattanamahathat (Chaliang). 7b, Wat Suan Kaeo Utthayan Noi.

Perf. 13¹/₂
1993, Apr. 2   Litho.   Wmk. 368
1526	A477	3b multicolored	32	25
1527	A477	4b multicolored	42	32
1528	A477	6b multicolored	65	48
1529	A477	7b multicolored	75	55
a.		Souvenir sheet of 4, #1526-1529	3.75	3.00

No. 1529a sold for 25b.
See Nos. 1561-1564.

Songkran Day Type of 1992
Perf. 14x14¹/₂
1993   Litho.   Wmk. 387
1530	A450	2b Demon on rooster's back, zodiac	38	18
a.		Souvenir sheet of 1	2.40	2.40
b.		#1530a ovptd. in gold	7.75	7.75

No. 1530b overprinted on sheet margin in both Thai and Chinese for Chinpex '93.
Nos. 1530a-1530b sold for 8b and exist imperf. with sale price in different colors.
Issued: #1530, 1530a, Apr. 13.

Mushrooms — A478

Perf. 13¹/₂
1993, July 1   Litho.   Wmk. 368
1531	A478	2b Marasmius	22	15
1532	A478	4b Coprinus	45	30
1533	A478	6b Mycena	65	45
1534	A478	8b Cyathus	85	58
a.		Souvenir sheet of 4, #1531-1534	4.25	4.25

No. 1534a sold for 30b.

Natl. Communications Day — A479

1993, Aug. 4 Wmk. 387 *Perf. 13¹/₂*
1535 A479 2b multicolored   25 18

Post and Telegraph Department, 110th Anniv. — A480

Perf. 13¹/₂
1993, Aug. 4 Litho. Wmk. 387
1536 A480 2b multicolored   25 18

Queen Suriyothai's Monument — A481

1993, Aug. 12
1537 A481 2b multicolored   28 22

Fruit — A482

Perf. 13¹/₂
1993, Oct. 1 Photo. Wmk. 368
1538 A482 2b Citrus reticulata   20 15
1539 A482 3b Musa sp.   30 22
1540 A482 6b Phyllanthus distichus   60 45
1541 A482 8b Bouea burmanica   80 60

Thai Ridgeback Dogs — A483

Various dogs.
1993, Oct. 1
1542 A483 2b multicolored   20 15
1543 A483 3b multicolored   30 22
1544 A483 5b multicolored   50 38
1545 A483 10b multicolored   1.00 75
  a.   Souvenir sheet of 4, #1542-1545   3.75 2.25

Intl. Letter Writing Week. No. 1545a sold for 30b.

5th Conference & Exhibition of ASEAN Council on Petroleum (ASCOPE) — A484

Perf. 13¹/₂
1993, Nov. 2 Litho. Wmk. 387
1546 A484 2b multicolored   25 15

King Rama VII (1893-1941) — A485

1993, Nov. 8 *Perf. 14x14¹/₂*
1547 A485 2b multicolored   25 15

No. 655 Surcharged ≡ 1บาท BAHT ≡

1993 Photo. Wmk. 233 *Perf. 14¹/₂*
1548 A161 1b on 25s brown red   50 15

Bencharong and Lai Nam Thong Wares — A486

Designs: 3b, Bencharong cosmetic jar, divinity design. 5b, Bencharong cosmetic jar, gold knob. 6b, Lai Nam Thong cosmetic jar, floral design. 7b, Lai Nam Thong cosmetic jar, floral design, diff.

Perf. 13¹/₂
1993, Oct. 1 Photo. Wmk. 368
1549 A486 3b multicolored   30 22
1550 A486 5b multicolored   50 38
1551 A486 6b multicolored   60 45
1552 A486 7b multicolored   70 52
  a.   Souvenir sheet of 4, #1549-1552   4.00 2.25

Bangkok '93. No. 1552a sold for 30b.

New Year 1994 — A487

Perf. 14¹/₂x14
1993, Nov. 15 Litho. Wmk. 387
1553 A487 1b Ipomoea cairica   15 15
1554 A487 1b Decaschistia parviflora   15 15
1555 A487 1b Hibiscus tiliaceus   15 15
1556 A487 1b Passiflora foetida   15 15
  a.   Souvenir sheet of 4, #1553-1556   1.25 1.10
      Set value   42 32

No. 1556a sold for 10b.

THAICOM, Natl. Satellite Project — A488

1993, Dec. 1 *Perf. 14x14¹/₂*
1557 A488 2b multicolored   25 16

Children's Day — A489

1994, Jan. 8 *Perf. 14¹/₂x14*
1558 A489 2b Play land   25 16

Administrative Building, Chulalongkorn Hospital, 80th Anniv. — A490

Perf. 14¹/₂x14
1994, Mar. 30 Litho. Wmk. 387
1559 A490 2b multicolored   22 16

Thai Red Cross.

Royal Institute, 60th Anniv. — A491

1994, Mar. 31 *Perf. 14x14¹/₂*
1560 A491 2b multicolored   22 16

Heritage Conservation Day Type of 1993

Historical landmarks, Phra Nakhon Si Ayutthaya Park: 2b, Wat Ratchaburana. 3b, Wat Maha That. 6b, Wat Maheyong. 9b, Wat Phra Si Samphet.

1994, Apr. 2 *Perf. 14¹/₂x14*
1561 A477 2b multicolored   22 16
1562 A477 3b multicolored   32 25
1563 A477 6b multicolored   65 52
1564 A477 9b multicolored   1.25 95
  a.   Souvenir sheet of 4, #1561-1564   2.50 2.50

No. 1564a sold for 25b.

Opening of Friendship Bridge, Thailand-Laos — A492

1994, Apr. 8
1565 A492 9b multicolored   1.00 75

Songkran Day Type of 1992

1994, Apr. 13 Litho.
1566 A450 2b Demon on dog's back, zodiac   22 16
  a.   Souvenir sheet of 1   1.00 1.00

No. 1566 sold for 8b and exists imperf. with frame around stamp and sale price in different color.

Intl. Olympic Committee, Cent. — A493

Wmk. 387
1994, June 23 Litho. *Perf. 14*
1567 A493 2b Soccer   20 15
1568 A493 3b Running   30 22
1569 A493 5b Swimming   50 38
1570 A493 6b Weight lifting   60 45
1571 A493 9b Boxing   90 70
    Nos. 1567-1571 (5)   2.50 1.90

Thammasat University, 60th Anniv. — A494

Wmk. 387
1994, June 27 Litho. *Perf. 14*
1572 A494 2b multicolored   20 15

THAILAND/SIAM
• BUYING AND SELLING •

FROM CLASSICS TO NEW ISSUES...
SEND FOR OUR SPECIAL OFFERS/PRICE LISTS!
WANT LISTS SERVICED!

Top Prices Paid For Singles, Sets, Collections, Dealer Stocks. Write, Ship or Fax for our Prompt Offer!

BE-LINE COMPANY
P.O. Box 40C
Oakwood, TX 75855
FAX 903-322-5054

Asalhapuja Day — A495

1994, July 22   Wmk. 329   Perf. 13½
1573 A495 2b multicolored   20   15

Natl. Communications Day — A496

1994, Aug. 4   Wmk. 368
1574 A496 2b multicolored   20   15

Crabs
A497

Designs: 3b, Phricotelphusa limula. 5b, Thaipotamon chulabhorn. 6b, Phricotelphusa sirindhorn. 10b, Thaiphusa sirikit.

Wmk. Alternating Interlaced Wavy Lines (340)
1994, Aug. 12   Photo.   Perf. 13½x13
1575 A497 3b multicolored   30   22
1576 A497 5b multicolored   50   38
1577 A497 6b multicolored   60   45
1578 A497 10b multicolored   1.00   75
a.   Souvenir sheet of 4, #1575-1578   3.00   3.00
b.   As "a," inscribed in margin   3.00   3.00

No. 1578b has PHILAKOREA '94 Exhibition emblem added to sheet margin.

Intl. Letter Writing Week A498

Winning paintings in design contest: 2b, Gold niello bowls, octagonal footed tray. 6b, Pumpkin shaped bowls. 8b, Silver niello betel-nut set. 9b, Covered square bowl with gold finial, small lotus-shaped footed tray.

Perf. 13½
1994, Oct. 9   Photo.   Wmk. 368
1579 A498 2b multicolored   16   15
Booklet, 5 #1579   80
1580 A498 6b multicolored   48   35
1581 A498 8b multicolored   65   48
1582 A498 9b multicolored   75   55
a.   Souvenir sheet of 4, #1579-1582   2.50   1.75
Nos. 1579-1582 (4)   2.04   1.53

No. 1582a sold for 30b.

ILO, 75th Anniv. A499

Perf. 15x14
1994, Oct. 29   Litho.   Wmk. 387
1583 A499 2b multicolored   16   15
Booklet, 5 #1583   80

New Year 1995 — A500

Herbs: No. 1584, Utricularia delphinioides. No. 1585, Utricularia minutissima. No. 1586, Eriocaulon odoratum. No. 1587, Utricularia bifida.

1994, Nov. 15   Perf. 14x14½
1584 A500 1b multicolored   15   15
1585 A500 1b multicolored   15   15
1586 A500 1b multicolored   15   15
1587 A500 1b multicolored   15   15
a.   Souvenir sheet of 4, #1584-1587   1.00   1.00
Set value   38   25

No. 1587a sold for 10b.

SEMI-POSTAL STAMPS

Nos. 164-175 Overprinted in Red

1918, Jan. 11   Unwmk.   Perf. 14
B1 A21   2s orange brown   1.90   80
B2 A21   3s emerald   1.90   80
B3 A21   5s rose red   4.00   1.65
B4 A21   10s black & olive   5.75   2.50
B5 A21   15s blue   5.75   2.50
B6 A22   1b blue & gray blk   30.00   12.00
B7 A22   2b car rose & brn   52.50   20.00
B8 A22   3b yel grn & blk   75.00   32.50
B9 A22   5b dp vio & blk   190.00   50.00
a.   Double overprint   775.00   400.00
B10 A22 10b ol grn & vio brn   475.00   125.00
B11 A22 20b sea grn & brn   1,600.   450.00
Nos. B1-B11 (11)   2,441.   697.75

Excellent counterfeit overprints are known.
These stamps were sold at an advance over face value, the excess being given to the Siamese Red Cross Society.

Stamps of 1905-19
Handstamp Overprinted

1920, Feb.
On Nos. 164, 146, 168
B12 A21   2s (+ 3s) org brn   40.00   40.00
B13 A21   3s (+ 2s) green   40.00   40.00
B14 A21   15s (+ 5s) blue   45.00   45.00
On No. 105
B15 A15   1t (+ 25s)   200.00   200.00
On Nos. 185-186
B16 A21   5s on 6s (+ 20s)   100.00   100.00
a.   Overprint inverted
B17 A21   10s on 12s (+ 5s)   40.00   40.00
Nos. B12-B17 (6)   465.00   465.00

Stamps of 1905-20
Handstamp Overprinted

On Nos. 164, 146, 168
B18 A21   2s (+ 3s) org brn   26.00   26.00
B19 A21   3s (+ 2s) green   26.00   26.00
a.   Pair, one without ovpt.
B20 A21   15s (+ 5s) blue   62.50   62.50
On No. 105
B21 A15   1t (+ 25s)   140.00   140.00
On No. 186
B22 A21   10s on 12s (+ 5s)   32.50   32.50
On No. 190
B23 A23   5s (+ 20s)   32.50   32.50
Nos. B18-B23 (6)   319.50   319.50

Nos. 187-188, 190, 193-194, 196, 198 Overprinted in Blue or Red

1920, Dec. 21
B24 A23   2s brown, yel   18.00   19.00
B25 A23   3s grn, grn (R)   18.00   19.00
B26 A23   5s rose, pale rose   18.00   19.00
B27 A23   10s blk & org (R)   18.00   19.00
B28 A23   15s bl, bluish (R)   30.00   32.50
B29 A23   25s chocolate   72.50   75.00
B30 A23   50s ocher & blk (R)   140.00   150.00
Nos. B24-B30 (7)   314.50   333.50

Nos. B12 to B30 were sold at an advance over face value, the excess being for the benefit of the Wild Tiger Corps. Counterfeits exist.

Nos. 170-172
Surcharged in Red

1939, Apr. 6   Unwmk.   Perf. 14
B31 A22   5s + 5s on 1b   13.00   13.00
B32 A22   10s + 5s on 2b   16.00   17.50
B33 A22   15s + 5s on 3b   16.00   17.50

Founding of the Intl. Red Cross Soc., 75th anniv. Bottom line of overprint is different on Nos. B32-B33.

Catalogue values for unused stamps in this section, from this point to the end of the section, are for Never Hinged items.

No. 214 Surcharged in Carmine

1952   Unwmk.   Perf. 12½
B34 A25   80s + 20s blue & blk   20.00   10.00
New constitution.

Red Cross and Dancer — SP1

Lithographed, Cross Typographed
1953, Apr. 6   Wmk. 299   Perf. 11
Cross in Red, Dancer Dark Blue
B35 SP1   25s + 25s yellow grn   8.50   2.50
B36 SP1   50s + 50s brt rose   16.00   4.00
B37 SP1   1b + 1b lt blue   21.00   5.50

60th anniv. of the founding of the Siamese Red Cross Society.

Nos. B35-B37 Overprinted with Year Date "24 98," in Black
1955, Apr. 3
Cross in Red, Dancer Dark Blue
B38 SP1   25s + 25s yellow grn   40.00   12.00
B39 SP1   50s + 50s brt rose   80.00   22.50
B40 SP1   1b + 1b lt blue   100.00   32.50

Counterfeits exist.

Red Cross Cent. Emblem
SP2   SP3

1963   Wmk. 334   Litho.   Perf. 13½
B41 SP2 50s + 10s gray & red   50   15
B42 SP3 50s + 10s gray & red   50   15
a.   Pair, #B41-B42   1.00

Cent. of the Intl. Red Cross.

75+25
สต. ST.

Nos. B41-B42
Surcharged

1973, Feb. 15
B43 SP2 75s + 25s on 50s + 10s   75   75
B44 SP3 75s + 25s on 50s + 10s   75   75
a.   Pair, #B43-B44   1.50

Red Cross Fair, Feb. 15-19.

75+25

Nos. B41-B42
Surcharged   1973

1974, Feb. 2
B45 SP2 75s + 25s on 50s + 10s   40   30
B46 SP3 75s + 25s on 50s + 10s   40   30
a.   Pair, #B45-B46   1.00

Red Cross Fair, Feb. 1974. Position of surcharge reversed on No. B46.

75+25

Nos. B41-B42   1974
Surcharged   2517

1975, Feb 11
B47 SP2 75s + 25s on 50s + 10s   48   30
B48 SP3 75s + 25s on 50s + 10s   48   30
a.   Pair, #B47-B48   1.00

Red Cross Fair, Feb. 1975. Position of surcharge reversed on No. B48.

75+25

Nos. B41-B42   2518
Surcharged
1975

1976, Feb. 26
B49 SP2 75s + 25s on 50s + 10s   38   38
B50 SP3 75s + 25s on 50s + 10s   38   38
a.   Pair, #B49-B50   76

Red Cross Fair, Feb. 16-Mar. 1. Position of surcharge reversed on #B50.

75+25

Nos. B41-B42 Surcharged   2520-1977

1977, Apr. 6   Wmk. 334   Perf. 13½
B51 SP3 75s + 25s on 50s + 10s   45   32
B52 SP3 75s + 25s on 50s + 10s   45   32
a.   Pair, #B51-B52   90

Red Cross Fair 1977.

Red Cross Blood
Collection
SP4

Eye and Blind
People
SP5

Wmk. 329
1978, Apr. 6	**Photo.**	*Perf. 13*
B53 SP4 2.75b + 25s multi	1.00 25

"Give blood, save life."
For surcharge see No. B58.

Perf. 14x13¹/₂
1979, Apr. 6	**Litho.**	**Wmk. 368**
B54 SP5 75s + 25s multi	55 18

"Give an eye, save new life." Red Cross Fair.
Surtax was for Thai Red Cross.
For surcharge see No. B59.

Extracting Snake Venom, Red Cross — SP6

1980, Apr.	*Perf. 11x13*
B55 SP6 75s + 25s multi	55 20

Red Cross Fair. Surtax was for Thai Red Cross.
For surcharge see No. B60.

Nurse
Helping
Victim
SP7

1981, Apr. 6	**Wmk. 377**	*Perf. 12¹/₂*
B56 SP7 75 + 25s red & gray grn	1.00 20

Red Cross Fair (canceled). Surtax was for Thai
Red Cross.
For surcharge see No. B65.

Red
Cross
Fair
SP8

Perf. 13x13¹/₂
1983, Apr. 6	**Litho.**	**Wmk. 329**
B57 SP8 1.25b + 25s multi	70 15

Surtax was for Thai Red Cross.

บำรุงกาชาด
๒๕๒๗

No. B53 Surcharged

3.25+0.25

1984, Apr.	**Photo.**	*Perf. 13*
B58 SP4 3.25b + 25s on 2.75b + 25s	1.50 25

Red Cross Fair. Surtax was for Thai Red Cross.
Overprint translates: Red Cross Donation.

No. B54
Surcharged

2+.25 บาท BAHT

Wmk. 368
1985, Mar. 30	**Litho.**	*Perf. 13*
B59 SP5 2b + 25c on 75s + 25s	1.00 35

Surtax for the Thai Red Cross.

บำรุงกาชาด
๒๕๒๙	1986

No. B55
Overprinted and
Surcharged

2+.25 บาท BAHT

1986, Apr. 6	**Wmk. 368**	*Perf. 11x13*
B60 SP6 2b + 25s on 75s + 25s	1.00 15

Natl. Children's Day. Surtax for Natl. Red Cross
Society. Overprint translates "Red Cross Donation."

Natl. Scouting Movement, 75th Anniv.,
15th Asia-Pacific Conference,
Thailand — SP9

Designs: No. B61, Scouts, saluting, community
service. No. B62, Scout activities. No. B63, King
and queen at ceremony. No. B64, 15th Asia-Pacific
conference.

1986, Nov. 7	**Wmk. 385**	*Perf. 13¹/₂*
B61 SP9 2b + 50s multi	30 18
B62 SP9 2b + 50s multi	30 18
B63 SP9 2b + 50s multi	30 18
B64 SP9 2b + 50s multi	30 18

Surtax for the Natl. Scouting Fund.

No. B56 Surcharged
1987, Apr.	**Wmk. 377**	*Perf. 12¹/₂*
B65 SP7 2b + 50s on 75s + 25s	95 18

Sports
SP10	SP11

Designs: No. B66, Hurdles, medal winners. No.
B67, Race, nurse treating injured cyclist. No. B68,
Boxers training. No. B69, Soccer.

1989, Dec. 16	**Wmk. 387**	*Perf. 13¹/₂*
B66 SP10 2b + 1b multi	38 25
B67 SP10 2b + 1b multi	38 25
B68 SP10 2b + 1b multi	38 25
B69 SP10 2b + 1b multi	38 25

Surtax for sports welfare organizations.

1990, Dec. 16
B70 SP11 2b + 1b Judo	38 25
B71 SP11 2b + 1b Archery	38 25
B72 SP11 2b + 1b High jump	38 25
B73 SP11 2b + 1b Windsurfing	38 25

Surtax for sports welfare organization.

Sports — SP12

Perf. 13¹/₂
1991, Dec. 16	**Wmk. 387**	**Litho.**
B74 SP12 2b + 1b Jogging	30 22
B75 SP12 2b + 1b Cycling	30 22
B76 SP12 2b + 1b Soccer, jumping
	rope	30 22
B77 SP12 2b + 1b Swimming	30 22

Surtax for sports welfare organizations.

AIR POST STAMPS

Garuda — AP1

**1925 Unwmk.	Engr.	*Perf. 14, 14¹/₂***
C1 AP1 2s brown, *yel*	1.90 22
C2 AP1 3s dark brown	2.00 22
C3 AP1 5s green	6.00 45
C4 AP1 10s black & org	15.00 45
C5 AP1 15s carmine	4.50 90
C6 AP1 25s dark blue	4.00 90
C7 AP1 50s brown org & blk	32.50 6.75
C8 AP1 1b blue & brown	30.00 8.25
	Nos. C1-C8 (8)	95.90 18.14

Issue dates: 2s, 50s, Apr. 21. Others, Jan. 3.

Nos. C1-C8 received this overprint
("Government Museum 2468") in 1925,
but were never issued. The death of King
Vajiravudh caused cancellation of the fair
at which this set was to have been
released.
They were used during 1928 only in
the interdepartmental service for
accounting purposes of the money-
order sections of various Bangkok post
offices, and were never sold to the public. Value for canceled set, $20.

1930-37	*Perf. 12¹/₂*
C9 AP1 2s brown, *yel*	6.25 80
C10 AP1 5s green	1.65 20
C11 AP1 10s black & org	3.25 20
C12 AP1 15s carmine	32.50 4.75
C13 AP1 25s dark blue ('37)	1.90 80
	a. Vert. pair, imperf. btwn.	275.00
C14 AP1 50s brn org & blk ('37)	3.50 1.25
	Nos. C9-C14 (6)	49.05 8.00

Monument of
Democracy,
Bangkok — AP2

1942-43	**Engr.**	*Perf. 11*
C15 AP2 2s dk org brn ('43)	1.90 80
C16 AP2 3s dark green ('43)	20.00 19.00
C17 AP2 5s deep claret	2.25 25
	a. Horiz. pair, imperf. btwn.	37.50
	b. Vert. pair, imperf. btwn.	45.00
C18 AP2 10s carmine ('43)	2.25 60
	a. Vert. pair, imperf. btwn.	45.00 45.00
C19 AP2 15s dark blue	3.00 1.65
	Nos. C15-C19 (5)	29.40 22.30

Catalogue values for unused
stamps in this section, from this
point to the end of the section, are
for Never Hinged items.

Garuda and
Bangkok
Skyline — AP3

1952-53	*Perf. 13x12¹/₂*
C20 AP3 1.50b red violet ('53)	4.50 20
C21 AP3 2b dark blue	11.00 2.00
C22 AP3 3b gray ('53)	16.00 80

Issue dates: June 15, 1952. Sept. 15, 1953.

OFFICIAL STAMPS

Catalogue values for unused
stamps in this section are for Never
Hinged items.

O1

Perf. 10¹/₂ Rough
1963, Oct. 1	**Typo.**	**Unwmk.**
Without Gum
O1 O1 10s pink & dp car	15 15
O2 O1 20s brt grn & car rose	20 15
O3 O1 25s blue & dp car	30 35
O4 O1 50s deep carmine	85 1.10
O5 O1 1b silver & car rose	1.00 1.50
O6 O1 2b bronze & car rose	1.75 1.50
	Nos. O1-O6 (6)	4.25 4.75

Issued as an official test from Oct. 1, 1963, to
Jan. 31, 1964, to determine the amount of mail
sent out by various government departments.

1964	**Without Gum**
O7 O1 20s green	35 28
O8 O1 25s blue	35 40
O9 O1 1b silver	65 65
O10 O1 2b bister	1.90 2.25

Others values exist printed in one color.

THRACE

LOCATION — In southeastern Europe
between the Black and Aegean Seas
GOVT. — Former Turkish Province
AREA — 89,361 sq. mi. (approx.)

Thrace underwent many political changes
during the Balkan Wars and World War I. It
was finally divided among Turkey, Greece
and Bulgaria.

100 Lepta = 1 Drachma
40 Paras = 1 Piaster
100 Stotinki = 1 Leva (1919)

Giumulzina District Issue

ΕΛΛ. ΔΙΟΙΚ.
ΓΚΙΟΥΜΟΥ
ΛΤΖΙΝΑΣ
ΛΕΠΤΑ 25

Turkish Stamps of
1909 Surcharged in
Blue or Red

1913	**Unwmk.**	*Perf. 12, 13¹/₂*
1 A21 10 l on 20pa rose (Bl)	30.00 25.00
2 A21 25 l on 10pa bl grn	35.00 32.50
3 A21 25 l on 20pa rose (Bl)	35.00 32.50
4 A21 25 l on 1pi ultra	35.00 32.50

Counterfeits exist of Nos. 1-4.

Turkish Inscriptions
A1	A2

1913	**Litho.**	*Imperf.*
Laid Paper
Control Mark in Rose
5 A1 1pi blue	3.00 3.00
6 A1 2pi violet	4.50 4.50

Wove Paper

7	A2	10pa vermilion	3.75	3.75
8	A2	20pa blue	3.75	3.75
9	A2	1pi violet	3.75	3.75
		Nos. 5-9 (5)	18.75	18.75

Turkish Stamps of 1908-13 Surcharged in Red or Black

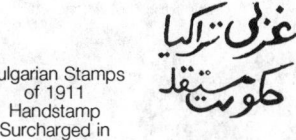

1913   *Perf. 12*

10	A22	1pi on 2pa ol grn (R)	6.75	6.75
10A	A22	1pi on 2pa ol grn	6.00	6.00
11	A22	1pi on 5pa ocher	9.00	8.25
11A	A22	1pi on 5pa ocher (R)	9.75	9.00
12	A22	1pi on 20pa rose	15.00	15.00
13	A21	1pi on 5pi dk vio (R)	62.50	52.50
13A	A21	1pi on 5pi dk vio	62.50	52.50
14	A21	1pi on 10pi dl red	125.00	110.00
15	A19	1pi on 25pi dk grn	185.00	165.00
		Nos. 10-15 (9)	481.50	425.00

On Nos. 13-15 the surcharge is vertical, reading up. No. 15 exists with double surcharge, one black, one red.
Nos. 10-15 exist with forged surcharges.

Bulgarian Stamps of 1911 Handstamp Surcharged in Red or Blue

1913

16	A20	10pa on 1s myr grn (R)	2.25	1.10
17	A21	20pa on 2s car & blk	4.50	2.25
18	A23	1pi on 5s grn & blk (R)	7.50	3.25
19	A22	2pi on 3s lake & blk	10.00	5.75
20	A24	2½pi on 10s dp red & blk	7.50	7.50
21	A25	5pi on 15s brn bis	18.00	15.00
		Nos. 16-21 (6)	57.25	34.85

Same Surcharges on Greek Stamps
On Issue of 1911

1913   *Serrate Roulette 13½*

22	A24	10pa on 1 l grn (R)	15.00	15.00
23	A24	10pa on 1 l grn	15.00	15.00
25	A25	10pa on 2 l ultra (R)	18.00	18.00
26	A25	20pa on 2 l car rose	11.00	11.00
27	A24	1pi on 3 l ver	11.00	11.00
28	A26	2pi on 5 l green	22.50	22.50
29	A24	2½pi on 10 l car rose	25.00	25.00
30	A25	5pi on 40 l dp bl (R)	37.50	30.00
		Nos. 22-30 (8)	155.00	147.50

On Occupation Stamps of 1912

31	O1	10pa on 1 l brn	6.00	6.00
32	O1	20pa on 1 l brn	6.00	6.00
33	O1	1pi on 1 l brn	6.00	6.00

These surcharges were made with handstamps, two of which were required for each surcharge. One or both parts may be found inverted, double or omitted.
Nos. 16-33 exist with forged surcharges.

OCCUPATION STAMPS

Issued under Allied Occupation

Bulgarian Stamps of 1915-19 Handstamped in Violet Blue

Perf. 11½, 11½x12, 14

1919   Unwmk.

N1	A43	1s black	40	40
N2	A43	2s olive green	40	40
N3	A44	5s green	22	22
N4	A44	10s rose	22	22
N5	A44	15s violet	32	32
N6	A26	25s indigo & black	32	32
		Nos. N1-N6 (6)	1.88	1.88

The overprint on Nos. N1-N6 is frequently inverted and known in other positions.

Bulgarian Stamps of 1911-19 Handstamp Overprinted in Red or Black   THRACE INTERALLIÉE

1919

N7	A43	1s black (R)	15	15
N8	A43	2s olive green	15	15
N9	A44	5s green	15	15
N10	A44	10s rose	15	15
N11	A44	15s violet	15	15
N12	A26	25s indigo & black	15	15
N13	A29	1 l chocolate	2.25	1.50
N14	A37a	2 l brown orange	3.75	2.25
N15	A38	3 l claret	5.75	4.50
		Nos. N7-N15 (9)	12.65	9.15

Overprint is vertical, reading up, on Nos. N9-N13.
The following varieties are found in the setting of "INTERALLIEE": Inverted "V" for "A," second "L" inverted, "F" instead of final "E."

Bulgarian Stamps of 1919 Overprinted   Thrace Interalliée

1920

N16	A44	5s green	15	15
N17	A44	10s rose	15	15
N18	A44	15s violet	15	15
N19	A44	50s yellow brown	25	30
		Set value	40	45

The varieties: "Irteraliiee" and final "e" inverted are found on all stamps.

Bulgarian Stamps of 1919 Overprinted   THRACE OCCIDENTALE

1920   *Perf. 12x11½*

N20	A44	5s green	15	15
a.		Inverted overprint	75	
N21	A44	10s rose	15	15
a.		Inverted overprint	75	
N22	A44	15s violet	15	15
N23	A44	25s deep blue	15	15
N24	A44	50s ocher	15	15

Imperf

N25	A44	30s chocolate	18	22
		Set value	45	48

No. N25 is not known without overprint.

ISSUED UNDER GREEK OCCUPATION

For Use in Western Thrace
Greek Stamps of 1911-19 Overprinted   Διοίκησις Δυτικῆς Θράκης

Serrate Roulette 13½

1920   Litho.   Unwmk.

N26	A24	1 l green	15	15
a.		Inverted overprint	8.00	
N27	A25	2 l rose	15	15
N28	A24	3 l vermilion	15	15
N29	A26	5 l green	15	15
N30	A24	10 l rose	15	15
N31	A25	15 l dull blue	15	15
a.		Inverted overprint	10.00	10.00
b.		Dbl. ovpt. one inverted	12.00	12.00
N32	A25	25 l blue	40	80
N33	A26	30 l rose	25.00	40.00
N34	A25	40 l indigo	1.65	4.00
N35	A26	50 l violet brn	2.00	5.75
N36	A27	1d ultra	5.75	14.00
N37	A27	2d vermilion	13.00	27.50

Engr.

N38	A25	2 l car rose	60	60
N39	A24	3 l vermilion	60	60
N40	A27	1d ultra	24.00	40.00
N41	A27	2d vermilion	6.75	6.75
N42	A27	3d car rose	24.00	40.00
N43	A27	5d ultra	12.00	15.00
N44	A27	10d deep blue	8.00	12.00
		Nos. N26-N44 (19)	124.65	207.90

Nos. N42-N44 are overprinted on the reissues of Greece Nos. 210-212. See footnote below Greece No. 213. Counterfeits exist of Nos. N26-N84.

Overprinted   ΔΙΟΙΚΗΣΙΣ ΔΥΤΙΚΗΣ ΘΡΑΚΗΣ

N45	A28	25d deep blue	25.00	50.00

This overprint reads: "Administration Western Thrace."

With Additional Overprint

Litho.

N46	A24	1 l green	15	40
N47	A25	2 l rose	15	40
a.		Inverted overprint		
N48	A24	10 l rose	40	40
N49	A25	20 l slate	80	1.50
N50	A26	30 l rose	80	2.00

Engr.

N51	A27	2d vermilion	14.00	25.00
N52	A27	3d car rose	5.50	20.00
N53	A27	5d ultra	20.00	30.00
N54	A27	10d deep blue	14.00	25.00
a.		Double overprint		
		Nos. N46-N54 (9)	55.80	104.70

For Use in Eastern and Western Thrace
Greek Stamps of 1911-19 Overprinted   Διοίκησις Θράκης

1920   Litho.

N55	A24	1 l green	15	15
a.		Pair, one without ovpt.	5.00	
N56	A24	2 l rose	15	15
N57	A24	3 l vermilion	15	15
a.		Double overprint	3.00	
N58	A26	5 l green	15	15
a.		Pair, one without ovpt.	3.00	
N59	A24	10 l rose	60	1.25
a.		Double overprint	4.00	
N60	A25	20 l slate	60	1.25
a.		Inverted overprint	5.00	
N61	A25	25 l blue	1.25	2.00
N62	A25	40 l indigo	2.25	6.00
N63	A26	50 l violet brn	2.50	8.00
N64	A27	1d ultra	10.50	20.00
N65	A27	2d vermilion	20.00	35.00

Engr.

N66	A24	3 l vermilion	2.00	3.50
N67	A25	20 l gray lilac	6.00	18.00
N68	A28	25d deep blue	45.00	85.00
		Nos. N55-N68 (14)	91.30	180.60

This overprint reads "Administration Thrace."

With Additional Overprint as Nos. N46-N54

Litho.

N69	A25	2 l car rose	40	80
N70	A26	5 l green	2.00	3.00
N71	A25	20 l slate	60	1.25
N72	A26	30 l rose	60	1.25

Engr.

N73	A27	3d car rose	5.50	8.00
N74	A27	5d ultra	8.00	25.00
N75	A27	10d deep blue	27.50	55.00
		Nos. N69-N75 (7)	44.60	94.30

Turkish Stamps of 1916-20 Surcharged in Blue, Black or Red
Υπάτη Αρμοστεία Θρακης   5 Λεπτὰ 5

1920   *Perf. 11½, 12½*

N76	A43	1 l on 5pa org (Bl)	40	40
N77	A43	1 l on 1pi bl grn	40	40
N78	A30	20 l on 1pi bl grn	40	40
N79	A53	25 l on 5pi on 2pa Prus bl (R)	60	60
N80	A44	50 l on 5pi bl & blk (R)	3.50	3.50
N81	A45	1d on 20pa dp rose (Bl)	1.00	1.00
N82	A22	2d on 10pa on 2pa ol grn (R)	1.50	1.50
N83	A57	3d on 1pi dp bl (R)	8.00	8.00
N84	A23	5d on 20pa rose	8.00	8.00
		Nos. N76-N84 (9)	23.80	23.80

Nos. N77, N78 and N84 are on the 1920 issue with designs modified. Nos. N81, N82 and N83 are on stamps with the 1919 overprints.
Varieties found on some values of this issue include: inverted surcharge, double surcharge with one inverted, and surcharge on both face and back.

POSTAGE DUE STAMPS

Issued under Allied Occupation
Bulgarian Postage Due Stamps of 1919 Handstamp Overprinted like Nos. N7-N15 Reading Vertically Up

1919   Unwmk.   *Perf. 12x11½*

NJ1	D6	5s emerald	20	20
NJ2	D6	10s purple	28	28
NJ3	D6	50s blue	42	42

Type of Bulgarian Postage Due Stamps of 1919-22 Overprinted

1920   *Imperf.*

NJ4	D6	5s emerald	15	15
NJ5	D6	10s deep violet	52	50
NJ6	D6	20s salmon	15	15
NJ7	D6	50s blue	42	35

Perf. 12x11½

NJ8	D6	10s deep blue	35	25
		Nos. NJ4-NJ8 (5)	1.59	1.40

TIBET

LOCATION — A high tableland in Central Asia
GOVT. — A semi-independent state, nominally under control of China (under Communist China since 1950-51).
AREA — 463,200 sq. mi.
POP. — 1,500,000 (approx.)
CAPITAL — Lhasa

Tibet's postage stamps were valid only within its borders.
In 1965 Tibet became an autonomous region of the People's Republic of China.

6 2/3 Trangka = 1 Sang

Excellent counterfeits of Nos. 1-18 exist. Numerous shades of all values.
All stamps issued without gum
Small bits of foreign matter (inclusions) are to be expected in Native Paper. These do not reduce the value of the stamp unless they have caused serious damage to the design or paper.

Lion
A1   A2

1912-50   Unwmk.   Typo.   *Imperf.*
Native Paper

1	A1	⅛t green	25.00	30.00
2	A1	⅓t blue	30.00	40.00
a.		⅓t ultramarine	35.00	50.00
3	A1	½t violet	30.00	40.00
4	A1	⅔t carmine	35.00	45.00
a.		"POTSAGE"	125.00	140.00
5	A1	1t vermilion	40.00	40.00
6	A1	1s sage green ('50)	90.00	100.00
		Nos. 1-6 (6)	250.00	305.00

The "POTSAGE" error is found on all shades of the ⅓t (positions 6 and 7).
Pin-perf. copies of Nos. 1 and 3 exist.
Issued in sheets of 12.
Nos. 1-5 were "reprinted" in the US around 1986. Sheets of 12 bear "J. Crow Co." imprint. The set of 5 sheets was sold for $5.

TIBET

STAMPS AND POSTAL HISTORY

We specialize in the Stamps and Postal History of Tibet. Maintaining one of the World's largest and most comprehensive stocks of this Mysterious Land.

SELLING?
We are always interested in Better Individual Items or Collections.

GEOFFREY FLACK
P.O. Box 65987
Station F, Vancouver, B.C.
Canada V5N 5L4
Phone (604) 986-3898
FAX: (604) 986-4777

TIBET NEPAL BHUTAN

PUBLIC AUCTIONS
Rare stamps, errors, and postal history with a minimum net value of $150.

MAIL SALES
Scarce stamps, errors, and postal history in the $50-$150 range.

Please send $1 for each catalog desired.

DIRECT SALES
We maintain an exceptional stock of these countries. Please let us know your requirements.

We are keen buyers of all better material.

George Alevizos

2800 28th St.
Suite 323
Santa Monica, CA 90405
Telephone: 310-450-2543
FAX 310-450-6919

Printed Using Shiny Enamel Paint

1920
1a	A1	¼t green	50.00	20.00
2b	A1	⅓t blue	400.00	400.00
3d	A1	½t purple	90.00	100.00
4h	A1	⅔t dark blue	90.00	100.00
i.		"POTSAGE"	200.00	225.00
5c	A1	1t carmine	300.00	300.00

In some 1920-30 printings, European enamel paint was used instead of ink. It has a glossy surface.

1914
7	A2	4t blue	600.	650.
8	A2	8t carmine	150.	150.

Printed Using Shiny Enamel Paint

1920
7b	A2	4t blue	1,000.	1,000.
8b	A2	8t carmine	800.	800.

See note following No. 5c.

 A3

Thin White Native Paper

1933 　　　　　　　　　　*Pin-perf.*
9	A3	½t orange	75.00	75.00
10	A3	⅔t dark blue	75.00	90.00
11	A3	1t rose carmine	75.00	90.00
12	A3	2t scarlet	75.00	90.00
13	A3	4t emerald	75.00	90.00
		Nos. 9-13 (5)	375.00	435.00

Exist imperf.

Heavy Toned Native Paper

1934 　　　　　　　　　　*Imperf.*
14	A3	½t yellow	10.00	12.00
a.		½t orange		
15	A3	⅔t blue	7.00	9.00
16	A3	1t orange ver	6.00	6.00
a.		1t carmine	9.00	9.00
17	A3	2t red	6.00	6.00
a.		2t orange vermilion	6.00	6.00
18	A3	4t green	6.00	6.00
a.		25x25mm instead of 24x24mm	30.00	45.00
		Nos. 14-18 (5)	35.00	39.00

Nos. 14-18 are also known with a private pin-perf.
The ½t and 1t exist printed on both sides.

"Stamps" produced by the "Tibetan Government in Exile" have no postal value.

OFFICIAL STAMPS

O1

O2

Various Designs and Sizes Inscribed "STAMP"

Sizes: No. O1, 32½x32½mm. No. O2, 38x28½mm. No. O3, 34x33mm. No. O4, 44x44mm. No. O5, 66x66mm.

1945　　Unwmk.　Typo.　*Imperf.*
Native Paper
O1	O1	⅓t bronze green		
O2	O2	⅓t slate black		
O3	O3	⅔t reddish brown		
O4	O1	1⅓t olive green		
O5	O5	1s dark gray blue		

The status of Nos. O1-O5 is in question. Other values exist.

TIMOR

LOCATION — The eastern part of Timor island, Malay archipelago
GOVT. — Portuguese Overseas Territory
AREA — 7,330 sq. mi.
POP. — 660,000 (est. 1974)
CAPITAL — Dili

The Portuguese territory of Timor was annexed by Indonesia May 3, 1976.

1000 Reis = 1 Milreis
78 Avos = 1 Rupee (1895)
100 Avos = 1 Pataca
100 Centavos = 1 Escudo (1960)

Catalogue values for unused stamps in this country are for Never Hinged items, beginning with Scott 256 in the regular postage section, Scott J31 in the postage due section, and Scott RA11 in the postal tax section.

Watermark

Wmk. 232 -
Maltese Cross

Stamps of Macao
Overprinted in Black or
Carmine　　　**TIMOR**

1885　　Unwmk.　　*Perf. 12½, 13½*
1	A1	5r black (C)	2.00	1.50
a.		Double overprint	22.50	22.50
b.		Triple overprint		
2	A1	10r green	2.50	1.90
a.		Overprint on Mozambique stamp	20.00	12.50
b.		Overprinted on Portuguese India stamp	190.00	140.00
3	A1	20r rose	6.75	4.50
a.		Double overprint		
b.		Perf. 13½	5.50	4.00
4	A1	25r violet	1.10	75
a.		Perf. 13½	17.50	10.00
5	A1	40r yellow	3.75	2.75
a.		Double overprint		
b.		Inverted overprint	16.00	16.00
c.		Perf. 13½	12.50	10.00
6	A1	50r blue	1.75	1.10
a.		Perf. 13½	10.50	8.50
7	A1	80r slate	5.00	2.50
8	A1	100r lilac	3.00	1.25
a.		Double overprint		
b.		Perf. 13½	7.00	3.00
9	A1	200r orange	3.75	3.00
a.		Perf. 12½	10.00	3.00
10	A1	300r brown	3.75	2.75
		Nos. 1-10 (10)	33.35	22.00

The 20r brown, 25r rose and 50r green were prepared for use but not issued.
The reprints are printed on a smooth white chalky paper, ungummed, with rough perforation 13½, and on thin white paper with shiny white gum and clean-cut perforation 13½.

King Luiz — A2

King Carlos — A3

1887　　Embossed　　*Perf. 12½*
11	A2	5r black	1.75	1.50
12	A2	10r green	3.00	2.75
13	A2	20r bright rose	3.00	2.75
14	A2	25r violet	6.00	3.00
15	A2	40r chocolate	10.00	4.00
16	A2	50r blue	12.00	5.00
17	A2	80r gray	12.00	6.75
18	A2	100r yellow brown	17.50	8.00
19	A2	200r gray lilac	22.50	15.00
20	A2	300r orange	22.50	15.00
		Nos. 11-20 (10)	110.25	63.75

Reprints of Nos. 11, 16, 18 and 19 have clean-cut perforation 13½.
For surcharges see Nos. 34-43, 83-91, .

TIMOR

Macao No. 44
Surcharged in Black

30　　30

1892　　Without Gum　　*Perf. 12½, 13*
21	A7	30r on 300r orange	5.00	5.00

For surcharge see No. 44.

1894　　Typo.　　*Perf. 11½*
22	A3	5r yellow	85	60
23	A3	10r red violet	1.00	60
24	A3	15r chocolate	1.25	85
25	A3	20r lavender	1.65	95
26	A3	25r green	1.90	70
27	A3	50r light blue	3.25	3.00
a.		Perf. 13½	125.00	110.00
28	A3	75r rose	4.00	2.50
29	A3	80r light green	4.50	3.75
30	A3	100r brown, *buff*	3.00	2.50
31	A3	150r car, *rose*	10.50	6.00
32	A3	200r dk bl, *lt bl*	10.50	7.25
33	A3	300r dk bl, *salmon*	13.00	9.50
		Nos. 22-33 (12)	55.40	38.20

For surcharges and overprints see Nos. 92-102, 120-122, 124-128, 131-133, 183-193, 199.

1 avo

Stamps of 1887
Surcharged in Red,
Green or Black

PROVISORIO

仙壹

1895　　Without Gum　　*Perf. 12½*
34	A2	1a on 5r black (R)	90	75
35	A2	2a on 10r green	1.10	75
a.		Double surcharge		
36	A2	3a on 20r brt rose (G)	2.50	1.65
37	A2	4a on 25r violet	2.50	1.00
38	A2	6a on 40r choc	4.00	2.25
39	A2	8a on 50r blue (R)	3.50	2.00
40	A2	13a on 80r gray	12.00	8.00
41	A2	16a on 100r yellow brn	13.00	6.00
42	A2	31a on 200r gray lilac	25.00	16.00
43	A2	47a on 300r orange (G)	25.00	17.50
		Nos. 34-43 (10)	89.50	55.90

5 avos

No. 21 Surcharged

PROVISORIO

—仙伍—

1895　　Without Gum　　*Perf. 12½, 13*
44	A7	5a on 30r on 300r org	5.00	4.50

Vasco da Gama Issue
Common Design Types

1898　　Engr.　　*Perf. 14 to 15*
45	CD20	½a blue green	95	85
46	CD21	1a red	95	85
47	CD22	2a red violet	95	85
48	CD23	4a yellow green	95	85
49	CD24	8a dark blue	1.50	1.25
50	CD25	12a violet brown	1.90	1.40
51	CD26	16a bister brown	2.00	1.90
52	CD27	24a bister	3.50	2.50
		Nos. 45-52 (8)	12.70	10.45

400th anniversary of Vasco da Gama's discovery of the route to India.

King Carlos
A5   A6

1898-1903   Typo.   Perf. 11½
Name & Value in Black Except #79

53	A5	½a gray	35	30
a.		Perf. 12½	2.50	1.75
54	A5	1a orange	35	30
a.		Perf. 12½	2.50	1.75
55	A5	2a light green	35	30
56	A5	2½a brown	1.25	1.10
57	A5	3a gray violet	1.25	1.10
58	A5	3a gray green ('03)	1.50	1.00
59	A5	4a sea green	1.65	1.00
60	A5	5a rose ('03)	1.50	1.00
61	A5	6a pale yel brn ('03)	1.50	1.00
62	A5	8a blue	2.00	1.10
63	A5	9a red brown ('03)	1.50	1.00
64	A5	10a slate blue ('00)	2.00	1.10
65	A5	10a gray brown ('03)	1.50	1.00
66	A5	12a rose	3.50	3.00
67	A5	12a dull blue ('03)	10.00	8.50
68	A5	13a violet	3.50	3.00
69	A5	13a red lilac ('03)	2.25	1.75
70	A5	15a gray lilac ('03)	5.25	3.75
71	A5	16a dark bl, bl	4.25	3.50
72	A5	20a brn, yelsh ('00)	4.50	3.00
73	A5	22a brn org, pink ('03)	3.50	3.50
74	A5	24a brown, buff	3.50	3.00
75	A5	31a red lil, pinkish	3.50	3.00
76	A5	31a brn, straw ('03)	4.25	2.50
77	A5	47a dk blue, rose	6.00	4.25
78	A5	47a red vio, pink ('03)	5.25	3.25
79	A5	78a blk & red, bl ('00)	10.50	6.00
80	A5	78a dl bl, straw ('03)	12.50	8.00
		Nos. 53-80 (28)	98.95	71.55

Most of Nos. 53-80 were issued without gum.
For surcharges and overprints see Nos. 81-82, 104-119, 129-130, 134-147, 195-196.

1899
Black Surcharge

81	A6	10a on 16a dk bl, bl	2.50	2.50
82	A6	20a on 31a red lil, pnksh	2.50	2.50

Common Design Types
pictured in section at front of book.

Surcharged in Black

1902
On Issue of 1887

83	A2	5a on 25r violet	2.00	1.75
84	A2	5a on 200r gray lil	3.00	2.00
85	A2	6a on 10r blue grn	65.00	40.00
86	A2	6a on 300r orange	2.50	2.25
87	A2	9a on 40r choc	3.00	2.50
88	A2	9a on 100r yel brn	3.00	2.50
89	A2	15a on 20r blue	3.50	2.75
90	A2	15a on 50r blue	65.00	40.00
91	A2	22a on 80r gray	7.50	5.00

Reprints of Nos. 83-88, 90-91, 104A have clean-cut perf. 13½.

On Issue of 1894

92	A3	5a on 5r yellow	1.25	1.00
a.		Inverted surcharge	30.00	30.00
93	A3	5a on 25r green	1.65	1.00
94	A3	5a on 50r lt blue	1.40	1.10
95	A3	6a on 20r lavender	1.40	1.10
96	A3	9a on 15r choc	1.40	1.10
97	A3	9a on 75r rose	1.40	1.10
98	A3	15a on 10r red vio	1.75	1.50
99	A3	15a on 100r brn, buff	1.75	1.50
100	A3	15a on 300r bl, sal	1.75	1.50
101	A3	22a on 80r lt green	4.25	3.50
102	A3	22a on 200r bl, blue	5.00	3.50

On Newspaper Stamp of 1893

103	N2	6a on 2½r brn	75	60
a.		Inverted surcharge	27.50	27.50
		Nos. 92-103 (12)	23.75	18.50

Nos. 93-97, 99-102 issued without gum.

Stamps of 1898
Overprinted in Black

104	A5	3a gray violet	1.75	1.25
104A	A5	12a rose	4.00	3.50

Reprint noted after No. 91.

1905

105	A5	10a on 12a dull blue	2.50	2.00

Stamps of 1898-1903
Overprinted in
Carmine or Green

1911

106	A5	½a gray	30	30
a.		Inverted overprint	11.00	11.00
107	A5	1a orange	30	30
a.		Perf. 12½	9.00	9.00
108	A5	2a light green	40	35
109	A5	3a gray green	40	35
110	A5	5a rose (G)	40	35
111	A5	6a yel brown	40	35
112	A5	9a red brown	50	45
113	A5	10a gray brown	50	45
114	A5	13a red lilac	60	50
115	A5	15a gray lilac	1.25	1.25
116	A5	22a brn org, pink	1.25	1.25
117	A5	31a brown, straw	1.25	1.25
118	A5	47a red vio, pink	2.75	2.50
119	A5	78a dl bl, straw	4.50	3.50
		Nos. 106-119 (14)	14.80	13.15

Preceding Issues
Overprinted in Red

1913
Without Gum
On Provisional Issue of 1902

120	A3	5a on 5r green	1.50	2.25
121	A3	5a on 25r green	1.50	2.25
122	A3	5a on 50r lt bl	3.50	6.75
123	N2	6a on 2½r brn	3.00	5.50
124	A3	6a on 20r lavender	1.50	3.00
125	A3	9a on 15r choc	1.50	3.50
126	A3	15a on 100r brn, buff	2.50	5.25
127	A3	22a on 80r lt grn	4.50	6.75
128	A3	22a on 200r bl, bl	3.50	7.25

On Issue of 1903

129	A5	3a gray green	3.00	7.25

On Issue of 1905

130	A5	10a on 12a dull bl	2.00	3.75
		Nos. 120-130 (11)	28.00	53.50

Overprinted in Green or
Red

1913
On Provisional Issue of 1902

131	A3	9a on 75r rose (G)	2.25	2.25
132	A3	15a on 10r red vio (G)	2.25	2.25
a.		Inverted overprint	27.50	27.50
133	A3	15a on 300r bl, sal (R)	4.75	4.75
a.		"REUBPLICA"	19.00	19.00
b.		"REPBLICAU"	19.00	19.00

On Issue of 1903

134	A5	5a rose (G)	2.50	2.50

Stamps of 1898-1903
Overprinted in Red

1913

135	A5	6a yellow brown	1.65	1.25
136	A5	9a red brown	1.25	1.25
137	A5	10a gray brown	1.25	1.25
138	A5	13a violet	1.65	1.65
a.		Inverted overprint	27.50	27.50
139	A5	13a red lilac	1.50	1.50
140	A5	15a gray lilac	2.25	2.00
141	A5	22a brn org, pnksh	2.75	2.50
142	A5	31a red lil, pnksh	2.75	2.50
143	A5	31a brown, straw	4.00	4.00
144	A5	47a blue, pink	5.00	4.25
145	A5	47a red vio, pink	5.00	6.75
146	A5	78a dl bl, straw	4.50	4.00

No. 79 Overprinted in
Red

147	A5	78a blk & red, bl	5.00	7.50
		Nos. 135-147 (13)	38.55	40.40

Vasco da Gama Issue of 1898 Overprinted
or Surcharged in Black:

REPUBLICA

REPUBLICA   10   A.

1913

148	CD20	½a blue green	65	60
149	CD21	1a red	65	60
150	CD22	2a red violet	65	60
151	CD23	4a yellow green	65	60
152	CD24	8a dark blue	1.25	1.10
153	CD25	10a on 12a vio brn	2.00	2.00
154	CD26	16a bister brown	2.00	1.75
155	CD27	24a bister	2.00	2.00
		Nos. 148-155 (8)	9.85	9.25

Ceres — A7

1914-23   Typo.   Perf. 15x14, 12x11½
Name and Value in Black

156	A7	½a olive brown	20	15
157	A7	1a black	20	15
158	A7	1½a yel grn ('23)	60	1.10
159	A7	2a blue green	25	25
160	A7	3a lilac brown	1.00	75
161	A7	4a carmine	1.00	75
162	A7	6a light violet	1.00	75
163	A7	7a lt green ('23)	1.75	1.75
164	A7	7½a ultra ('23)	2.50	3.50
165	A7	9a blue ('23)	3.25	6.75
166	A7	10a deep blue	1.25	75
167	A7	11a gray ('23)	2.75	6.75
168	A7	12a yellow brown	1.50	1.25
169	A7	15a lilac ('23)	6.00	7.25
170	A7	16a slate	2.00	3.75
171	A7	18a dp blue ('23)	8.00	6.25
172	A7	19a gray green ('23)	8.00	5.50
173	A7	20a org brown	15.00	6.00
174	A7	36a turq blue ('23)	6.00	4.25
175	A7	40a plum	6.00	4.50
176	A7	54a choc ('23)	8.00	6.25
177	A7	58a brown, grn	7.00	5.00
178	A7	72a brt rose ('23)	16.00	16.00
179	A7	76a brown, rose	7.50	6.50
180	A7	1p org, salmon	16.00	11.00
181	A7	3p green, blue	30.00	25.00
182	A7	5p car rose ('23)	65.00	52.50
		Nos. 156-182 (27)	217.75	184.40

For surcharges see Nos. 200-201, MR1.

Preceding Issues
Overprinted in
Carmine

1915   Perf. 11½
On Provisional Issue of 1902

183	A3	5a on 5r yellow	60	35
184	A3	5a on 25r green	60	35
185	A3	5a on 50r lt blue	60	35
186	A3	6a on 20r lavender	45	35
187	A3	9a on 15r lavender	45	35
188	A3	9a on 75r rose	75	50
189	A3	15a on 10r red vio	75	1.50
190	A3	15a on 100r brn, buff	50	1.50
191	A3	15a on 300r bl, sal	50	3.00
192	A3	22a on 80r lt grn	2.00	2.75
193	A3	22a on 200r bl, bl	3.00	5.00

On No. 103

194	N2	6a on 2½r, perf. 13½	35	30
a.		Perf. 12½	1.90	1.25
b.		Perf. 11½	3.75	1.75

On No. 104

195	A5	3a gray violet	35	30

On No. 105

196	A5	10a on 12a dull bl	50	40
		Nos. 183-196 (14)	11.40	17.00

Type of 1915 with
Additional Surcharge in
Black

199	A3	½a on 5a on 50r lt bl	6.50	5.75
a.		Perf. 11½	16.00	12.50

Nos. 178 and 169
Surcharged

1932   Perf. 12x11½

200	A7	6a on 72a brt rose	1.00	85
201	A7	12a on 15a lilac	1.00	85

"Portugal" and Vasco da
Gama's Flagship "San
Gabriel" — A8

1935   Typo.   Perf. 11½x12   Wmk. 232

202	A8	½a bister	15	15
203	A8	1a olive brown	15	15
204	A8	2a blue green	22	15
205	A8	3a red violet	55	30
206	A8	4a black	55	55
207	A8	5a gray	65	45
208	A8	6a brown	75	60
209	A8	7a bright rose	90	90
210	A8	8a bright blue	1.00	1.00
211	A8	10a red orange	1.40	1.10
212	A8	12a dark blue	1.90	1.90
213	A8	14a olive green	1.90	1.90
214	A8	15a maroon	2.50	2.50
215	A8	20a orange	2.50	2.50
216	A8	30a apple green	2.50	2.50
217	A8	40a violet	5.25	3.50
218	A8	50a olive bister	5.25	4.00
219	A8	1p light blue	16.00	10.50
220	A8	2p brn orange	30.00	20.00
221	A8	3p emerald	40.00	30.00
222	A8	5p dark violet	67.50	40.00
		Nos. 202-222 (21)	181.62	124.75

Common Design Types

1938   Unwmk.   Engr.   Perf. 13½x13
Name and Value in Black

223	CD34	1a gray green	18	22
224	CD34	2a orange brown	18	28
225	CD34	3a dk violet brn	18	28
226	CD34	4a brt green	18	60
227	CD35	5a dk carmine	18	1.50
228	CD35	6a slate	28	20
229	CD35	8a rose violet	28	1.10
230	CD37	10a brt red violet	28	1.50
231	CD37	12a red	55	2.25
232	CD37	15a orange	90	2.25
233	CD36	20a blue	90	70
234	CD36	40a gray black	2.50	1.10
235	CD36	50a brown	2.00	1.10
236	CD38	1p brown carmine	6.25	5.00
237	CD38	2p olive green	12.50	4.50
238	CD38	3p blue violet	15.00	9.50
239	CD38	5p red brown	30.00	13.00
		Nos. 223-239 (17)	72.34	45.08

For overprints see Nos. 245A-245K.

Mozambique Nos. 273, 276, 278, 280, 282 and 283 Surcharged in Black

TIMOR 12 AVOS

≋ ≈≈≈ ≋

1946			Perf. 13¹/₂x13	
240	CD34	1a on 15c dk vio brn	5.25	4.50
241	CD35	4a on 35c brt grn	5.25	4.50
242	CD35	8a on 50c brt red vio	5.25	4.50
243	CD36	10a on 70c brn vio	5.25	4.50
244	CD36	12a on 1e red	5.25	4.50
245	CD37	20a on 1.75e blue	5.25	4.50
		Nos. 240-245 (6)	31.50	27.00

Nos. 223-227 and 229-234 Overprinted "Libertacao"

1947				
245A	CD34	1a gray green	16.00	10.50
245B	CD34	2a org brown	25.00	19.00
245C	CD34	3a dk vio brn	10.00	6.00
245D	CD34	4a brt green	10.00	8.00
245E	CD35	5a dark carmine	4.50	2.00
245F	CD35	8a rose violet	2.25	1.50
245G	CD37	10a brt red vio	6.25	3.25
245H	CD37	12a red	6.50	2.50
245I	CD37	15a orange	5.00	2.50
245J	CD36	20a blue	55.00	35.00
m.		Inverted overprint	70.00	70.00
245K	CD36	40a gray black	12.00	8.25
		Nos. 245A-245K (11)	152.50	98.50

Timor Woman — A9

UPU Symbols — A10

Designs: 3a, Gong ringer. 4a, Girl with basket. 8a, Aleixo de Ainaro. 10a, 1p, 3p, Heads of various chieftains. 20a, Warrior and horse.

1948		Litho.		Perf. 14	
246	A9	1a aqua & dk brn	50	50
247	A9	3a gray & dk brn	1.00	60
248	A9	4a pink & dk grn	1.00	60
249	A9	8a red & blue blk	50	35
250	A9	10a blue grn & org	75	45
251	A9	20a ultra, aqua & bl	70	45
252	A9	1p org, bl & ultra	18.00	9.00
253	A9	3p vio & dk brn	15.00	9.00
a.		Sheet of 8, #246-253	50.00	50.00
		Nos. 246-253 (8)	37.45	20.95

No. 253a sold for 5p.

Lady of Fatima Issue
Common Design Type

1948, Oct.
254 CD40 8a slate gray   4.50   4.50

UPU Issue

1949   Unwmk.   Perf. 14.
255 A10 16a brown & buff   4.25   6.50

UPU, 75th anniversary.

Catalogue values for unused stamps in this section, from this point to the end of the section, are for Never Hinged items.

Craftsman A11

Timor Woman A12

1950			Perf. 14¹/₂	
256	A11	20a dull vio blue	1.10	70
257	A12	50a dull brown	2.25	1.25

Holy Year Issue
Common Design Types

1950, May			Perf. 13x13¹/₂	
258	CD41	40a green	1.50	1.25
259	CD42	70a black brown	2.25	2.00

Blackberry Lily — A13

Designs: Various flowers.

1950		Unwmk. Litho.	Perf. 14¹/₂	
260	A13	1a multicolored	24	24
261	A13	3a multicolored	1.25	1.00
262	A13	10a multicolored	1.25	1.00
263	A13	16a multicolored	3.25	1.75
264	A13	20a multicolored	2.50	1.65
265	A13	30a multicolored	1.25	1.10
266	A13	70a multicolored	1.65	1.25
267	A13	1p multicolored	4.00	2.75
268	A13	3p multicolored	5.50	3.75
269	A13	5p multicolored	9.00	6.50
		Nos. 260-269 (10)	29.89	20.99

Holy Year Extension Issue
Common Design Type

1951   Perf. 14
270 CD43 86a bl & pale bl   2.00 1.75

Medical Congress Issue
Common Design Type

Design: Weighing baby.

1952   Litho.   Perf. 13¹/₂
271 CD44 10a ol blk & brn   90 85

St. Francis Xavier Issue

Statue of St. Francis Xavier — A14

Designs: 16a, Miraculous Arm of St. Francis. 1p, Tomb of St. Francis.

1952, Oct. 25			Perf. 14	
272	A14	1a black	15	15
273	A14	16a blk brn & brn	90	85
274	A14	1p dk car & gray	3.50	2.00

400th death anniv. of St. Francis Xavier.

Madonna and Child — A15

Stamp of Portugal and Arms of Colonies — A16

1953			Perf. 13x13¹/₂	
275	A15	3a dk brn & dull gray	15	15
276	A15	16a dk brown & cream	80	60
277	A15	50a dk bl & dull gray	1.75	1.35

Exhibition of Sacred Missionary Art, Lisbon, 1951.

Stamp Centenary Issue

1953   Photo.   Perf. 13
278 A16 10a multicolored   1.10 1.00

Sao Paulo Issue
Common Design Type

1954   Litho.   Perf. 13¹/₂
279 CD46 16a dk brn red, bl & blk   85 70

Map of Timor — A17

1956	Unwmk.		Perf. 14x12¹/₂	
Inscription and design in brown, red, green, ultramarine & yellow
280	A17	1a pale salmon	15	15
281	A17	3a pale gray blue	15	15
282	A17	8a buff	25	15
283	A17	24a pale green	25	15
284	A17	32a lemon	35	15
285	A17	40a pale gray	55	30
286	A17	1p yellow	1.65	1.10
287	A17	3p pale blue	3.75	1.50
		Nos. 280-287 (8)	7.10	3.65

For surcharges see Nos. 291-300.

Brussels Fair Issue

Exhibition Emblems and View — A18

1958   Perf. 14¹/₂
288 A18 40a multicolored   50 40

Tropical Medicine Congress Issue
Common Design Type

Design: Calophyllum inophyllum.

1958   Perf. 13¹/₂
289 CD47 32a multicolored   3.00 2.75

Symbolical Globe — A19

Carved Elephant Jar — A20

1960   Unwmk. Litho.   Perf. 13¹/₂
290 A19 4.50e multicolored   50 35

500th death anniv. of Prince Henry the Navigator.

Nos. 280-287 Surcharged with New Value and Bars

1960	Unwmk.		Perf. 14x12¹/₂	
Inscription and design in brown, red, green, ultramarine & yellow
291	A17	5c on 1a pale salmon	15	15
292	A17	10c on 3a pale gray bl	15	15
293	A17	20c on 8a buff	15	15
294	A17	30c on 24a pale grn	15	15
295	A17	50c on 32a lemon	15	15
296	A17	1e on 40a pale gray	35	15
297	A17	2e on 40a pale gray	40	20
298	A17	5e on 1p yellow	60	35
299	A17	10e on 3p pale blue	1.65	1.50
300	A17	15e on 3p pale blue	2.00	1.40
		Nos. 291-300 (10)	5.75	4.35

1961   Litho.   Perf. 11¹/₂x12

Native Art: 10c, House on stilts. 20c, Madonna and Child. 30c, Silver rosary. 50c, Two men in boat, horiz. 1e, Silver box in shape of temple. 2.50e, Archer. 4.50e, Elephant. 5e, Man climbing tree. 10e, Woman carrying pot on head. 20e, Cockfight. 50e, House on stilts and animals.

Multicolored Designs

301	A20	5c pale violet	15	32
302	A20	10c pale green	15	32
a.		Value & legend inverted	72.50	72.50
303	A20	20c pale blue	16	32
304	A20	30c rose	24	15
305	A20	50c pale grnsh bl	16	15
306	A20	1e bister	70	15
307	A20	2.50e pale ol bis	48	16
308	A20	4.50e lt salmon	48	16
309	A20	5e lt gray	60	16
310	A20	10e gray	1.40	32
311	A20	20e yellow	2.75	1.00
312	A20	50e lt bluish gray	9.25	2.50
		Nos. 301-312 (12)	16.52	5.71

Sports Issue
Common Design Type

Sports: 50c, Duck hunting. 1e, Horseback riding. 1.50e, Swimming. 2e, Gymnastics. 2.50e, Soccer. 15e, Big game hunting.

1962, Mar. 22	Unwmk.		Perf. 13¹/₂	
Multicolored Designs
313	CD48	50c gray & bis	15	15
314	CD48	1e olive bister	45	30
315	CD48	1.50e gray & bl grn	55	38
316	CD48	2e buff	45	35
317	CD48	2.50e gray	55	48
318	CD48	15e salmon	2.25	1.90
		Nos. 313-318 (6)	4.40	3.56

Anti-Malaria Issue
Common Design Type

Design: Anopheles sundaicus.

1962   Litho.   Perf. 13¹/₂
319 CD49 2.50e multicolored   75 60

National Overseas Bank Issue
Common Design Type

Design: 2.50e, Manuel Pinheiro Chagas.

1964, May 16   Unwmk.   Perf. 13¹/₂
320 CD51 2.50e grn, gray, yel, lt bl & blk   75 60

ITU Issue
Common Design Type

1965, May 17   Litho.   Perf. 14¹/₂
321 CD52 1.50e multicolored   1.50 90

National Revolution Issue
Common Design Type

Design: 4.50e, Dr. Vieira Machado Academy and Dili Health Center.

1966, May 28   Litho.   Perf. 11¹/₂
322 CD53 4.50e multicolored   1.50 90

Navy Club Issue
Common Design Type

Designs: 10c, Capt. Gago Coutinho and gunboat Patria. 4.50e, Capt. Sacadura Cabral and seaplane Lusitania.

1967, Jan. 31		Litho.	Perf. 13	
323	CD54	10c multicolored	2.00	1.00
324	CD54	4.50e multicolored	2.00	1.00

Sepoy Officer, 1792 — A21

Our Lady of Fatima — A22

Designs: 1e, Officer, 1815. 1.50e, Infantry soldier, 1879. 2e, Infantry soldier, 1890. 2.50e, Infantry officer, 1903. 3e, Sapper, 1918. 4.50e, Special forces soldier, 1964. 10e, Paratrooper, 1964.

1967, Feb. 12		Photo.	Perf. 13¹/₂	
325	A21	35c multicolored	25	32
326	A21	1e multicolored	1.50	1.00
327	A21	1.50e multicolored	35	32
328	A21	2e multicolored	35	20
329	A21	2.50e multicolored	35	25
330	A21	3e multicolored	50	35
331	A21	4.50e multicolored	70	42
332	A21	10e multicolored	1.25	65
		Nos. 325-332 (8)	5.25	3.51

1967, May 13   Litho.   Perf. 12¹/₂x13
333 A22 3e multicolored   60 30

50th anniversary of the apparition of the Virgin Mary to three shepherd children at Fatima, Portugal.

Cabral Issue

Map of Brazil, by Lopo Homem-Reinéis, 1519 — A23

1968, Apr. 22   Litho.   Perf. 14
334 A23 4.50e multicolored   80 50

See note after Macao No. 416.

Admiral Coutinho Issue
Common Design Type

Design: 4.50e, Adm. Coutinho and frigate Adm. Gago Coutinho.

1969, Feb. 17   Litho.   Perf. 14
335 CD55 4.50e multicolored   1.10 85

View of Dili, 1834 — A24

1969, July 25   Litho.   Perf. 14
336 A24 1e multicolored   30 20

Bicentenary of Dili as capital of Timor.

da Gama Medal in St. Jerome's Convent — A25

Emblem of King Manuel, St. Jerome's Convent — A26

Vasco da Gama Issue
1969, Aug. 29   Litho.   Perf. 14
337 A25 5e multicolored   40 30

Vasco da Gama (1469-1524), navigator.

Administration Reform Issue
Common Design Type
1969, Sept. 25   Litho.   Perf. 14
338 CD56 5e multicolored   40 25

King Manuel I Issue
1969, Dec. 1   Litho.   Perf. 14
339 A26 4e multicolored   40 25

King Manuel I, 500th birth anniv.

Capt. Ross Smith, Arms of Great Britain, Portugal and Australia, and Map of Timor A27

1969, Dec. 9
340 A27 2e multicolored   50 40

50th anniv. of the first England to Australia flight of Capt. Ross Smith and Lt. Keith Smith.

Marshal Carmona Issue
Common Design Type

Design: 1.50e, Antonio Oscar Carmona in civilian clothes.

1970, Nov. 15   Litho.   Perf. 14
341 CD57 1.50e multicolored   20 15

Lusiads Issue

Sailing Ship and Monks Preaching to Islanders — A28

1972, May 25   Litho.   Perf. 13
342 A28 1e brown & multi   20 35

4th centenary of publication of The Lusiads by Luiz Camoens.

Olympic Games Issue
Common Design Type

Design: 4.50e, Soccer, Olympic emblem.

1972, June 20   Perf. 14x13 1/2
343 CD59 4.50e multicolored   50 50

Lisbon-Rio de Janeiro Flight Issue
Common Design Type

Design: 1e, Sacadura Cabral and Gago Coutinho in cockpit of "Lusitania."

1972, Sept. 20   Litho.   Perf. 13 1/2
344 CD60 1e multicolored   25 40

WMO Centenary Issue
Common Design Type

1973, Dec. 15   Litho.   Perf. 13
345 CD61 20e multicolored   1.75 2.00

AIR POST STAMPS

Common Design Type
1938   Unwmk.   Engr.   Perf. 13 1/2x13
Name and Value in Black

C1	CD39	1a scarlet	60	50
C2	CD39	2a purple	60	55
C3	CD39	3a orange	70	60
C4	CD39	5a ultra	75	65
C5	CD39	10a lilac brown	1.65	1.10
C6	CD39	20a dark green	2.50	1.40
C7	CD39	50a red brown	6.00	2.75
C8	CD39	70a rose carmine	6.50	4.25
C9	CD39	1p magenta	11.00	4.25
		Nos. C1-C9 (9)	30.30	16.05

No. C7 exists with overprint "Exposicao Internacional de Nova York, 1939-1940" and Trylon and Perisphere.
For overprints see Nos. C15-C23.

TIMOR 12 AVOS

Mozambique Nos. C3, C4, C6, C7 and C9 Surcharged in Black

1946   Unwmk.   Perf. 13 1/2x13

C10	CD39	8a on 50c orange	5.00	2.50
C11	CD39	12a on 1e ultra	5.00	2.50
C12	CD39	40a on 3e dk green	5.00	2.50
C13	CD39	50a on 5e red brown	5.00	2.50
C14	CD39	1p on 10e magenta	5.00	2.50
		Nos. C10-C14 (5)	25.00	12.50

Nos. C1-C9 Overprinted "Libertacao"
1947

C15	CD39	1a scarlet	17.50	13.00
C16	CD39	2a purple	17.50	13.00
C17	CD39	3a orange	17.50	13.00
C18	CD39	5a ultra	17.50	13.00
C19	CD39	10a lilac brown	5.00	3.25
C20	CD39	20a dark green	5.00	3.75
C21	CD39	50a red brown	6.00	3.25
C22	CD39	70a rose carmine	20.00	8.00
C23	CD39	1p magenta	7.00	3.25
		Nos. C15-C23 (9)	113.00	73.50

POSTAGE DUE STAMPS

D1

1904   Unwmk.   Typo.   Perf. 12
Without Gum
Name and Value in Black

J1	D1	1a yellow green	50	50
J2	D1	2a slate	50	50
J3	D1	5a yellow brown	2.25	1.50
J4	D1	6a red orange	2.25	2.25
J5	D1	10a gray brown	2.50	2.00
J6	D1	15a red brown	3.50	2.75
J7	D1	24a dull blue	6.00	5.50
J8	D1	40a carmine	6.00	5.50
J9	D1	50a orange	9.50	7.50
J10	D1	1p dull violet	16.00	13.00
		Nos. J1-J10 (10)	49.00	41.00

Overprinted in Carmine or Green

REPUBLICA

1911   **Without Gum**

J11	D1	1a yellow green	25	25
J12	D1	2a slate	25	25
a.		Inverted overprint		
J13	D1	5a yellow brown	25	25
J14	D1	6a deep orange	35	35
J15	D1	10a gray brown	75	60
J16	D1	15a brown	1.25	1.10
J17	D1	24a dull blue	2.25	2.00
J18	D1	40a carmine (G)	2.50	2.50
J19	D1	50a orange	2.50	2.50
J20	D1	1p dull violet	7.50	7.00
		Nos. J11-J20 (10)	17.85	16.80

tEPUBLICA

Nos. J1-J10 Overprinted in Red or Green

1913   **Without Gum**

J21	D1	1a yellow green	6.00	9.00
J22	D1	2a slate	6.00	9.00
J23	D1	5a yellow brown	4.00	4.50
J24	D1	6a deep orange	3.00	4.50
a.		Inverted surcharge		
J25	D1	10a gray brown	4.00	6.00
J26	D1	15a red brown	4.00	6.00
J27	D1	24a dull blue	4.00	6.00
J28	D1	40a carmine (G)	4.00	6.00
J29	D1	50a orange	8.00	12.00
J30	D1	1p gray violet	8.00	12.00
		Nos. J21-J30 (10)	51.00	75.00

> Catalogue values for unused stamps in this section, from this point to the end of the section, are for Never Hinged items.

Common Design Type
1952   Photo. & Typo.   Perf. 14
Numeral in Red, Frame Multicolored

J31	CD45	1a chocolate	20	20
J32	CD45	3a brown	20	20
J33	CD45	5a dark green	20	20
J34	CD45	10a green	20	20
J35	CD45	30a purple	40	40
J36	CD45	1p brown carmine	85	85
		Nos. J31-J36 (6)	2.05	2.05

WAR TAX STAMP

2 AVOS

Regular Issue of 1914 Surcharged in Red

TAXA DE GUERRA

1919   Unwmk.   Perf. 15x14
Without Gum
MR1 A7 2a on 1/2a ol brn   17.50 15.00

See note after Macao No. MR2.

NEWSPAPER STAMPS

King Luiz — N1

Stamps of Macao Surcharged in Black
1892   Unwmk.   Perf. 12 1/2
Without Gum

P1	N1	2 1/2r on 20r brt rose	2.00	75
a.		"TIMOR" inverted		
P2	N1	2 1/2r on 40r chocolate	2.00	75
a.		"TIMOR" inverted		
b.		Perf. 13 1/2	4.50	3.00
c.		As "a," perf. 13 1/2		
P3	N1	2 1/2r on 80r gray	2.00	75
a.		"TIMOR" inverted		
b.		Perf. 13 1/2	12.50	8.00

N2   N3

1893-95   Typo.   Perf. 11 1/2, 13 1/2
P4	N2	2 1/2r brown	40	35
a.		Perf. 12 1/2	2.00	1.50
P5	N3	1/2a on 2 1/2r brn ('95)	45	30

For surcharges see Nos. 103, 123, 194.

POSTAL TAX STAMPS

Pombal Issue
Common Design Types
1925   Unwmk.   Perf. 12 1/2
RA1	CD28	2a lake & black	30	30
RA2	CD29	2a lake & black	30	30
RA3	CD30	2a lake & black	30	30

Type of War Tax Stamp of Portuguese India Overprinted in Red

Instrução

D. L. n.º 7 de 3 2-1934

1934-35   Perf. 12
RA4	WT1	2a green & blk	6.50	8.00
RA5	WT1	5a green & blk	8.00	8.00

Surcharged in Black
RA6 WT1 7a on 1/2a rose & blk ('35) 9.00 7.50

The tax was for local education.

Type of War Tax Stamp of Portuguese
India Overprinted in Black

Assistência
D. L. n.º 72

1936   *Perf. 12x11½*
RA7 WT1 10a rose & black   7.00 9.00

1937   *Perf. 11½*
RA8 WT1 10a green & blk   5.50 8.25

PT1	PT2
REPÚBLICA PORTUGUESA, 10 avos TIMOR, Assistência	REPÚBLICA PORTUGUESA, $70 TIMOR, ASSISTÊNCIA

1948 **Unwmk.** **Typo.** *Perf. 11½*
Without Gum
RA9 PT1 10a dark blue   3.00 2.00
RA10 PT1 20a green   3.50 3.00

The 20a bears a different emblem.

> Catalogue values for unused stamps in this section, from this point to the end of the section, are for Never Hinged items.

1960 **Without Gum** *Perf. 11½*
RA11 PT2 70c dark blue   1.50 1.25
RA12 PT2 1.30e green   2.25 2.25

See Nos. RA13-RA16. For surcharges see Nos. RA20-RA25.

Type of 1960 Redrawn

1967 **Typo.** *Perf. 10½*
Without Gum
RA13 PT2 70c deep blue   3.00 1.90
RA14 PT2 1.30e emerald   3.00 2.50

The denominations of Nos. RA13-RA14 are 2mm high. They are 2½mm high on Nos. RA11-RA12. Other differences exist. The printed area of No. RA13 measures 18x31mm; "Republica" 16mm.

Type of 1960
Serif Type Face

1967
RA14A PT2 70c deep blue   12.00 10.00

Type of 1960, 2nd Redrawing

1967-68 **Typo.** *Perf. 10½*
Without Gum
RA15 PT2 70c violet blue   60 60
RA16 PT2 1.30e bluish grn ('68)   1.25 1.25

The printed area measures 13x30mm on Nos. RA15-RA16; "Republica" measures 10½mm.

Woman and Star — PT3

1969-70 **Litho.** *Perf. 13½*
RA17 PT3 30c vio bl & lt bl ('70)   15 15
RA18 PT3 50c dl org & maroon   15 15
RA19 PT3 1e yellow & brown   20 20
    Set value   40 40

The 2.50e and 10e in design PT3 were revenue stamps.

Nos. RA15-RA16 Surcharged in Red or Carmine

1970 **Typo.** *Perf. 10½*
Without Gum
RA20 PT2 30c on 70c   7.00 6.00
RA21 PT2 30c on 1.30e   6.00 6.00
RA22 PT2 50c on 70c   85.00 85.00
RA23 PT2 50c on 1.30e   6.00 6.00
RA24 PT2 1e on 70c (C)   125.00 125.00
RA25 PT2 1e on 1.30e   8.00 7.25

POSTAL TAX DUE STAMPS

Pombal Issue
Common Design Types

1925 **Unwmk.** *Perf. 12½*
RAJ1 CD31 4a lake & black   40 1.00
RAJ2 CD32 4a lake & black   40 1.00
RAJ3 CD33 4a lake & black   40 1.00

TOGO

LOCATION — Western Africa, bordering on the Gulf of Guinea
GOVT. — Republic
AREA — 20,400 sq. mi.
POP. — 2,890,000 (est. 1984)
CAPITAL — Lome

The German Protectorate of Togo was occupied by Great Britain and France in World War I, and later mandated to them. The British area became part of Ghana. The French area was granted internal autonomy in 1956 and achieved independence in 1958. See Togo in Vol. 1 for British issues.

100 Pfennig = 1 Mark
12 Pence = 1 Shilling
100 Centimes = 1 Franc

> Catalogue values for unused stamps in this country are for Never Hinged items, beginning with Scott 309 in the regular postage section, Scott B11 in the semi-postal section, Scott C14 in the airpost section, and Scott J32 in the postage due section.

Watermark

Wmk. 125-
Lozenges

German Protectorate

AREA - 34,934 sq. mi.
POP. - 1,000,368 (1913)

A1	A2

Stamps of Germany Overprinted in Black

1897 **Unwmk.** *Perf. 13½x14½*
1 A1 3pf dark brn   3.75 6.50
  a. 3pf yellow brown   5.50 16.00
  b. 3pf reddish brown   14.00 40.00
2 A1 5pf green   3.50 2.00
3 A2 10pf carmine   3.50 2.25
4 A2 20pf ultra   4.50 13.50
5 A2 25pf orange   30.00 55.00
6 A2 50pf red brown   30.00 55.00

Kaiser's Yacht, the "Hohenzollern"
A3   A4

1900 **Typo.** *Perf. 14*
7 A3 3pf brown   65 65
8 A3 5pf green   11.00 65
9 A3 10pf carmine   25.00 65
10 A3 20pf ultra   90 1.40
11 A3 25pf org & blk, *yel*   90 8.25
12 A3 30pf org & blk, *sal*   1.10 8.25
13 A3 40pf lake & blk   1.00 8.25
14 A3 50pf pur & blk, *sal*   1.10 8.25
15 A3 80pf lake & blk, *rose*   2.00 16.50

Engr.
Perf. 14½x14
16 A4 1m carmine   3.00 45.00
17 A4 2m blue   4.25 80.00
18 A4 3m black vio   5.00 135.00
19 A4 5m slate & car   80.00 300.00
  Nos. 7-19 (13)   135.90 612.85

Counterfeit cancellations are found on Nos. 10-19 and 22.

1909-19 **Wmk. 125** **Typo.** *Perf. 14*
20 A3 3pf brown ('19)   65
21 A3 5pf green   1.00 1.40
22 A3 10pf carmine ('14)   1.00 90.00

Engr.
Perf. 14½x14
23 A4 5m slate & car ('15)   12.00

Nos. 20 and 23 were never placed in use.

Issued under French Occupation
Stamps of German Togo Surcharged:

TOGO
Occupation
c   franco-anglaise

05 05 05
d e f

10 10 10
g h i

Wmk. Lozenges (5pf and 10pf) (125), Unwmk. (other values)
1914   *Perf. 14, 14½*
151 A3(c+d) 5c on 3pf brown   27.50 27.50
152 A3(c+e) 5c on 3pf brown   27.50 27.50
153 A3(c+f) 5c on 3pf brown   27.50 27.50
154 A3(c+g) 10c on 5pf green   16.50 20.00
  a. Double surcharge   625.00 625.00
155 A3(c+h) 10c on 5pf green   19.00 22.50
156 A3(c+i) 10c on 5pf green   25.00 26.50
158 A3(c) 20pf ultra   26.50 30.00
  a. 3½mm between "TOGO" and "Occupation"   1,500.
159 A3(c) 25pf org & blk, *yel*   30.00 35.00
160 A3(c) 30pf org & blk, *sal*   82.50 90.00
161 A3(c) 40pf lake & black   375.00 400.00
162 A3(c) 80pf lake & blk, *rose*   375.00 425.00
  Nos. 151-162 (11)   1,032. 1,131.

Surcharged or Overprinted in Sans-Serif Type:

TOGO
Occupation
franco anglaise
05

TOGO
Occupation
franco anglaise

1915
164 A3 5c on 3pf brown   2,800.
165 A3 5c on 3pf brown   575. 350.
166 A3 10pf carmine   700. 350.
  a. Inverted overprint   15,000.
167 A3 20pf ultra   900. 650.
168 A3 25pf org & blk, *yel*   4,800. 6,000.
169 A3 30pf org & blk, *sal*   4,800. 6,000.
170 A3 40pf lake & blk   4,500. 6,000.
171 A3 50pf pur & blk, *sal*   13,000. 13,000.
172 A4 1m carmine
173 A4 2m blue   13,000.
174 A4 3m black vio   13,000.
175 A4 5m slate & car

TOGO

Stamps of Dahomey, 1913-17, Overprinted

Occupation franco-anglaise

1916-17 **Unwmk.** *Perf. 13½x14*
176 A5 1c violet & blk   15 15
177 A5 2c choc & rose   15 15
178 A5 4c black & brn   15 15
  a. Double overprint   160.00 160.00
179 A5 5c yel grn & bl grn   35 35
180 A5 10c org red & rose   22 22
181 A5 15c brn org & dk vio   55 55
182 A5 20c gray & choc   35 35
183 A5 25c ultra & dp bl   35 35
184 A5 30c choc & vio   35 35
185 A5 35c brown & blk   55 55
186 A5 40c blk & red org   50 50
187 A5 45c gray & ultra   35 35
188 A5 50c choc & brn   35 35
189 A5 75c blue & vio   2.25 2.25
190 A5 1fr bl grn & blk   3.50 3.50
191 A5 2fr buff & choc   4.50 4.50
192 A5 5fr vio & do bl   6.25 6.25
  Nos. 176-192 (17)   20.87 20.87

All values of the 1916-17 issue exist on chalky paper and all but the 15c, 25c and 35c on ordinary paper.

French Mandate

AREA - 21,893 sq. mi.
POP. - 780,497 (1938)

Type of Dahomey, 1913-39, Overprinted **TOGO**

1921
193 A5 1c gray & yel grn   15 15
  a. Overprint omitted   60.00
194 A5 2c blue & org   15 15
195 A5 4c ol grn & org   15 15
196 A5 5c dull red & blk   15 15
  a. Overprint omitted   275.00
197 A5 10c bl grn & yel grn   15 15
198 A5 15c brown & car   42 42
199 A5 20c bl grn & org   55 55
200 A5 25c slate & org   35 35
201 A5 30c dp rose & ver   42 42
202 A5 35c red brn & yel grn   55 55
203 A5 40c bl grn & ol   80 80
204 A5 45c red brn & ol   80 80
205 A5 50c deep blue   45 45
206 A5 75c dl red & ultra   80 80
207 A5 1fr gray & ultra   85 85
208 A5 2fr ol grn & rose   2.75 2.75
209 A5 5fr orange & blk   3.50 3.50
  Nos. 193-209 (17)   12.99 12.99

Stamps and Type of 1921 Surcharged

1922-25
210 A5 25c on 15c ol brn & rose red   15 15
211 A5 25c on 2fr ol grn & rose   22 22
212 A5 25c on 5fr org & blk   22 22
213 A5 60c on 75c vio, *pnksh*   45 45
  a. "60" omitted   90.00 90.00
214 A5 65c on 45c red brn & ol   70 70
  a. "TOGO" omitted   70.00
215 A5 85c on 75c dl red & ultra   80 80
  Nos. 210-215 (6)   2.54 2.54

Issue years: #213, 1922; #211-212, 1924; others, 1925.

Coconut Grove — A6

Cacao Trees — A7

Oil Palms — A8

1924-38 — Typo.

216 A6	1c yellow & blk	15	15
217 A6	2c dp rose & blk	15	15
218 A6	4c dk blue & blk	15	15
219 A6	5c dp org & blk	15	15
220 A6	10c red vio & blk	15	15
221 A6	15c green & blk	15	15
222 A7	20c gray & blk	15	15
223 A7	25c grn & blk, yel	25	25
224 A7	30c gray grn & blk	15	15
225 A7	30c dl grn & lt grn ('27)	15	15
226 A7	35c lt brown & blk	35	35
227 A7	35c dp bl grn & grn ('38)	15	15
228 A7	40c red org & blk	15	15
229 A7	45c carmine & blk	15	15
230 A7	50c ocher & blk, bluish	15	15
231 A7	55c vio bl & car rose ('38)	35	35
232 A7	60c vio brn & blk, pnksh	15	15
233 A7	60c dp red ('26)	15	15
234 A7	65c gray lil & brn	15	15
235 A7	75c blue & black	28	18
236 A7	80c ind & dl vio ('38)	45	35
237 A7	85c brn org & brn	40	40
238 A7	90c brn red & cer ('27)	50	50
239 A8	1fr red brn & blk, bluish	42	42
240 A8	1fr blue ('26)	15	15
241 A8	1fr gray lil & grn ('28)	1.25	1.20
242 A8	1fr dk red & red org ('38)	15	15
243 A8	1.10fr vio & dk brn ('28)	2.65	2.00
244 A8	1.25fr mag & rose ('33)	45	38
245 A8	1.50fr bl & lt bl ('27)	15	15
246 A8	1.75fr bis & pink ('33)	4.50	1.20
247 A8	1.75fr vio bl & ultra ('38)	45	35
248 A8	2fr bl blk & blk, bluish	55	55
249 A8	3fr bl grn & red org ('27)	65	65
250 A8	5fr red org & blk, bluish	1.00	1.00
251 A8	10fr ol brn & rose ('26)	1.00	1.00
252 A8	20fr brn red & blk, yel ('26)	1.20	1.20
	Nos. 216-252 (37)	19.55	15.28

For surcharges see Nos. 253, 301-302, B8-B9.

No. 240 Surcharged with New Value and Bars in Red

1926
253 A8	1.25fr on 1fr lt bl	20	20

Colonial Exposition Issue
Common Design Types
Engr., "TOGO" Typo. in Black
1931, Apr. 13 — Perf. 12½

254 CD70	40c deep green	2.75	2.75
255 CD71	50c violet	2.75	2.75
256 CD72	90c red orange	2.75	2.75
257 CD73	1.50fr dull blue	2.75	2.75

Paris International Exposition Issue
Common Design Types
1937 — Perf. 13

258 CD74	20c deep violet	1.00	1.00
259 CD75	30c dark green	1.00	1.00
260 CD76	40c carmine rose	1.00	1.00
261 CD77	50c dark brown	1.00	1.00
262 CD78	90c red	1.00	1.00
263 CD79	1.50fr ultra	1.00	1.00
	Nos. 258-263 (6)	6.00	6.00

Common Design Types pictured in section at front of book.

Colonial Arts Exhibition Issue
Souvenir Sheet
Common Design Type
1937 — Imperf.

264 CD77	3fr Prus bl & blk	2.65	2.65

Caillié Issue
Common Design Type
1939, Apr. 5 — Perf. 12½x12

265 CD81	90c org brn & org	35	35
266 CD81	2fr brt violet	35	35
267 CD81	2.25fr ultra & dk bl	35	35

New York World's Fair Issue
Common Design Type
1939, May 10

268 CD82	1.25fr carmine lake	35	35
269 CD82	2.25fr ultra	35	35

Togolese Women
A9   A12

Mono River Bank — A10

Hunters A11

1941 — Engr. — Perf. 12½

270 A9	2c brown vio	15	15
271 A9	3c yellow grn	15	15
272 A9	4c brown blk	15	15
273 A9	5c lilac rose	15	15
274 A9	10c light blue	15	15
275 A9	15c chestnut	15	15
276 A10	20c plum	15	15
277 A10	25c violet blue	15	15
278 A10	30c brown blk	15	15
279 A10	40c dk carmine	15	15
280 A10	45c dk green	15	15
281 A10	50c chestnut	15	15
282 A10	60c red violet	15	15
283 A11	70c black	38	38
284 A11	90c lt violet	50	50
285 A11	1fr yellow grn	25	25
286 A11	1.25fr cerise	50	50
287 A11	1.40fr orange brn	25	25
288 A11	1.60fr orange	38	38
289 A11	2fr lt ultra	38	38
290 A12	2.25fr ultra	62	62
291 A12	2.50fr lilac rose	50	50
292 A12	3fr brown vio	42	42
293 A12	5fr vermilion	45	45
294 A12	10fr rose violet	68	68
295 A12	20fr brown blk	1.25	1.25
	Set value	7.25	7.25

For surcharges see Nos. 303-308, B7, B10.

Mono River Bank and Marshal Pétain A12a

1941 — Engr. — Perf. 12½x12

296 A12a	1fr green	22	
297 A12a	2.50fr blue	22	

Nos. 296-297 were issued by the Vichy government, and were not placed on sale in Togo. This is also true of nine stamps of types A9-A12 without "RF," issued in 1942-44.

Nos. 231, 238, 284 Surcharged with New Values in Various Colors

a   **1 fr. 50**   —

b   **4 fr.**

Perf. 14x13½, 12½
1943-44 — Unwmk.

301 A7(a)	1.50fr on 55c (Bk)	40	40
302 A7(a)	1.50fr on 90c (Bk)	40	40
303 A11(b)	3.50fr on 90c (Bk)	35	35
304 A11(b)	4fr on 90c (Bk)	35	35
305 A11(b)	5fr on 90c (Bl)	65	65
306 A11(b)	5.50fr on 90c (Br)	80	80

307 A11(b)	10fr on 90c (G) ('44)	80	80
308 A11(b)	20fr on 90c (R)	1.10	1.10
	Nos. 301-308 (8)	4.85	4.85

Catalogue values for unused stamps in this section, from this point to the end of the section, are for Never Hinged items.

Extracting Palm Oil — A13

Hunter — A14

Cotton Spinners — A15

Village of Atakpamé A16

Red-fronted Gazelles A17

Houses of the Cabrais A18

1947, Oct. 6 — Engr. — Perf. 12½

309 A13	10c dark red	15	15
310 A13	30c brt ultra	15	15
311 A13	50c bluish green	15	15
312 A14	60c lilac rose	15	15
313 A14	1fr chocolate	15	15
314 A15	1.20fr yellow grn	15	15
315 A15	1.50fr brown org	25	25
316 A15	2fr olive	25	24
317 A15	2.50fr gray blk	60	50
318 A16	3fr slate	25	24
319 A16	3.60fr rose car	42	35
320 A16	4fr Prus green	25	24
321 A17	5fr black brn	75	15
322 A17	6fr ultra	75	65
323 A17	10fr orange red	85	15
324 A18	15fr dp yel grn	95	42
325 A18	20fr grnsh black	95	60
326 A18	25fr lilac rose	95	60
	Nos. 309-326 (18)	8.12	
	Set value		4.75

Military Medal Issue
Common Design Type
1952, Dec. 1 — Engr. & Typo. — Perf. 13

327 CD101	15fr multicolored	2.00	2.00

Gathering Palm Nuts — A19

1954, Nov. 29 — Engr.

328 A19	8fr vio & vio brn	55	45
329 A19	15fr ind & dk brn	65	35

Goliath Beetle — A20

1955, May 2

330 A20	8fr black & green	1.20	90

Intl. Exhibition for Wildlife Protection, Paris, May 1955.

FIDES Issue
Common Design Type
Design: 15fr, Teacher and children planting tree.

1956 — Unwmk. — Perf. 13x12½

331 CD103	15fr dk vio brn & org brn	3.25	1.40

Republic

Woman Holding Flag — A21

1957, June 8 — Engr. — Perf. 13

332 A21	15fr dk bl grn, sep & red	28	15

Konkomba Helmet — A22

Teak Forest — A23

Design: 4fr, 5fr, 6fr, 8fr, 10fr, Buffon's kob.

1957, Oct. — Unwmk.

333 A22	30c violet & claret	15	15
334 A22	50c indigo & blue	15	15
335 A22	1fr pur & lil rose	15	15
336 A22	2fr dk brn & olive	15	15
337 A22	3fr black & green	15	15
338 A22	4fr blue & gray	22	15
339 A22	5fr bluish gray & mag	22	15
340 A22	6fr crim rose & bl gray	22	15
341 A22	8fr bluish gray & vio	22	15
342 A22	10fr grn & red brn	22	15
343 A23	15fr multicolored	15	15
344 A23	20fr violet, mar & org	15	15
345 A23	25fr indigo & bis brn	16	15
346 A23	40fr brn, ol & dk grn	26	15
	Set value	2.00	1.00

See Nos. 350-363.

Flags, Dove and UN Emblem — A24

1958, Dec. 10 — Engr. — Perf. 13

347 A24	20fr dk grn & rose red	15	15

Universal Declaration of Human Rights, 10th anniversary.

Flower Issue
Common Design Type

Designs: 5fr, Flower of Bombax tree (kapok).
20fr, Tectona grandis (teakwood) flower, horiz.

Perf. 12x12¹/₂, 12¹/₂x12

1959, Jan. 15		Photo.	Unwmk.	
348 CD104	5fr dp bl, rose & grn		15	15
349 CD104	20fr black, yel & grn		15	15
	Set value		24	15

Types of 1957 Inscribed: "Republique du Togo"

1959, Jan. 15		Engr.	Perf. 13	
Designs as Before				
350 A22	30c ultra & gray		15	15
351 A22	50c org & brt grn		15	15
352 A22	1fr red lil & lt ol grn		15	15
353 A22	2fr olive & bl grn		15	15
354 A22	3fr vio & rose car		15	15
355 A22	4fr lil rose & pale pur		15	15
356 A22	5fr green & brown		15	15
357 A22	6fr ultra & gray bl		15	15
358 A22	8fr sl grn & bis		15	15
359 A22	10fr vio & lt brn		15	15
360 A23	15fr dk brn, bis & cl		15	15
361 A23	20fr blk, bl grn & brn		15	15
362 A23	25fr sep, red brn, ol & vio		22	15
363 A23	40fr dk grn, org brn & bl		22	15
	Set value		1.60	1.00

"Five Continents,"
Ceiling Painting, Palais
des Nations,
Geneva — A25

1959, Oct. 24		Engr.	Perf. 12¹/₂	
Centers in Dark Ultramarine				
364 A25	15fr brown		15	15
365 A25	20fr purple		15	15
366 A25	25fr dark orange		20	18
367 A25	40fr dark green		28	25
368 A25	60fr carmine rose		35	32
	Nos. 364-368 (5)		1.13	1.05

Issued for United Nations Day, Oct. 24.

Skier — A26

Bicyclist
A27

Sports: 50c, Ice Hockey. 1fr, Tobogganing. 15fr, Discus thrower, vert. 20fr, Boxing, vert. 25fr, Runner.

1960		Unwmk.	Perf. 13	
369 A26	30c sl grn, car & bl grn		15	15
370 A26	50c red & black		15	15
371 A26	1fr red, blk & emer		15	15
372 A27	10fr brown, ultra & sl		15	15
373 A27	15fr dk red brn & grn		15	15
374 A27	20fr dk grn, gldn brn & brn		22	15
375 A27	25fr orange, mag & brn		30	15
	Set value		1.00	50

8th Winter Olympic Games, Squaw Valley, Calif. (Nos. 369-371); 17th Olympic Games, Rome (Nos. 372-375).

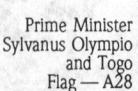

Prime Minister
Sylvanus Olympio
and Togo
Flag — A28

1960, Apr. 27			Litho.	
Center in Green, Red, Yellow & Brown				
376 A28	30c black & buff		15	15
377 A28	50c brown & buff		15	15
378 A28	1fr lilac & buff		15	15
379 A28	10fr blue & buff		15	15

380 A28	20fr red & buff		15	15
381 A28	25fr green & buff		15	15
	Set value		35	30

Proclamation of Togo's full independence, Apr. 27, 1960.
See Nos. C31-C33.

Flags of "Big
Four," and
British
Flag — A29

1960, May 21			Perf. 14x14¹/₂	
382 A29	50c shown		15	15
383 A29	1fr USSR		15	15
384 A29	20fr France		16	15
385 A29	25fr US		20	15
	Set value		46	36

Summit Conference of France, Great Britain, United States and Russia, Paris, May 16.

Flag of Togo
and UN
Emblem
A30

1961, Jan. 6			Perf. 14¹/₂x15	
Flag in red, olive green & yellow				
386 A30	30c red		15	15
387 A30	50c brown		15	15
388 A30	1fr ultramarine		15	15
389 A30	10fr maroon		15	15
390 A30	25fr black		20	15
391 A30	30fr violet		50	38
	Set value		50	38

Togo's admission to United Nations.

Crowned
Cranes over
Map — A31

Augustino de
Souza — A32

1961, Apr. 1			Perf. 14¹/₂x15	
392 A31	1fr multicolored		15	15
393 A31	10fr multicolored		15	15
394 A31	25fr multicolored		25	15
395 A31	30fr multicolored		32	20
			70	40

1961, Apr. 27		Litho.	Perf. 15	
396 A32	50c yellow, red & blk		15	15
397 A32	1fr emerald, brn & blk		15	15
398 A32	10fr grnsh bl, vio & blk		15	15
399 A32	25fr salmon, grn & blk		15	15
400 A32	30fr rose lil, bl & blk		20	15
	Set value		50	25

1st anniv. of independence; "Papa" Augustino de Souza, leader of the independence movement.

Daniel C.
Beard
A33

Designs: 1fr, Lord Baden-Powell. 10fr, Togolese Scout and emblems. 25fr, Togolese Scout and flag, vert. 30fr, Symbolic tents and fire, vert. 100fr, Three hands of different races giving Scout sign.

1961, Oct. 7		Photo.	Perf. 13	
401 A33	50c brt rose & grn		15	15
402 A33	1fr dp violet & car		15	15
403 A33	10fr dk gray & brn		15	15
404 A33	25fr multicolored		15	15

405 A33	30fr grn, red & org brn		22	15
406 A33	100fr rose car & bl		60	22
	Set value		1.10	45

Togolese Boy Scouts; 20th anniv. of the deaths of Daniel C. Beard and Lord Baden-Powell.
Four imperf. souvenir sheets each contain the six stamps, Nos. 401-406. Two sheets have a solid background of bright yellow, two a background of pale grayish brown. One yellow and one brown sheet have simulated perforations around the stamps. Size: 120x145mm. "REPUBLIQUE DU TOGO" is inscribed in white on bottom sheet margin. Value, each $3.

Plane, Ship and
Part of Map of
Africa — A34

Part of Map of Africa and: 25fr, Electric train and power mast. 30fr, Tractor and oil derricks. 85fr, Microscope and atomic symbol.

1961, Oct. 24			Litho.	
Black Inscriptions; Map in Ocher				
407 A34	20fr vio bl, org & yel		15	15
408 A34	25fr gray, org & yel		18	15
409 A34	30fr dk red, yel & org		24	15
410 A34	85fr blue, yel & org		48	18
a.	Souvenir sheet of 4		1.65	1.40
	Set value			34

UN Economic Commission for Africa. No. 410a contains one each of Nos. 407-410, imperf., printed without separating margin between the individual stamps to show a complete map of Africa.

Children Dancing
around
Globe — A35

Cmdr. Alan B.
Shepard — A36

Design: UNICEF Emblem, children and globe.

1961, Dec. 9		Unwmk.	Perf. 13¹/₂	
Black Inscription; Multicolored Design				
411 A35	1fr ultra		15	15
412 A35	10fr red brown		15	15
413 A35	20fr lilac		15	15
414 A35	25fr gray		15	15
415 A35	30fr bright blue		25	15
416 A35	85fr deep lilac		48	24
	Set value		1.00	50

UNICEF, 15th anniv.
Nos. 411-416 assembled in two rows show the globe and children of various races dancing around it.

1962, Feb. 24			Perf. 15x14	
Design: 1fr, 30fr, Yuri A. Gagarin.				
417 A36	50c green		15	15
418 A36	1fr carmine rose		15	15
419 A36	25fr blue		15	15
420 A36	30fr purple		20	15
	Set value		46	32

Astronauts of 1961.
Issued in sheets of 50 and in miniature sheets of 12 stamps plus four central labels showing photographs of Alan B. Shepard (US), Virgil I. Grissom (US), Yuri A. Gagarin (USSR), Gherman S. Titov (USSR).

No. 417 Surcharged: "100F COL. JOHN H. GLENN USA VOL ORBITAL 20 FEVRIER 1962" and Bars in Black

1962, Mar.				
421 A36	100fr on 50c green		75	50
a.	Carmine surcharge		75	50

Orbital flight of Lt. Col. John H. Glenn, Jr., US, Feb. 20, 1962.

Independence
Monument,
Lomé — A37

Woman Carrying
Fruit Basket — A38

1962, Apr. 27		Litho.	Perf. 13¹/₂x14	
422 A37	50c multicolored		15	15
423 A38	1fr green & pink		15	15
424 A37	5fr multicolored		15	15
425 A38	20fr purple & yel		15	15
426 A37	25fr multicolored		15	15
427 A38	30fr red & yellow		15	15
a.	Souv. sheet of 3, #424-425, 427, imperf.		35	35
	Set value		50	30

2nd anniversary of Togo's independence.

Malaria
Eradication
Emblem
A39

1962, June 2			Perf. 13¹/₂x13	
Multicolored Design				
428 A39	1fr yellow green		15	15
429 A39	25fr pale lilac		15	15
430 A39	30fr ocher		18	15
431 A39	85fr light blue		42	16
	Set value			34

WHO drive to eradicate malaria.

Capitol, Pres. John F. Kennedy and Pres.
Sylvanus Olympio
A40

1962, July 4		Unwmk.	Perf. 13	
Inscription and Portraits in Slate Green				
432 A40	50c yellow		15	15
433 A40	1fr blue		15	15
434 A40	2fr vermilion		15	15
435 A40	5fr lilac		15	15
436 A40	25fr pale violet		45	15
437 A40	100fr brt green		1.75	80
a.	Souvenir sheet, imperf.		5.75	5.75
	Nos. 432-437 (6)		2.80	
	Set value			1.10

Visit of Pres. Sylvanus Olympio of Togo to the US, Mar. 1962.

Mail Coach and Stamps of 1897
A41

Designs: 50c, Mail ship and stamps of 1900. 1fr, Mail train and stamps of 1915. 10fr, Motorcycle truck and stamp of 1924. 25fr, Mail truck and stamp of 1941. 30fr, DC-3 and stamp of 1947.

1963, Jan. 12		Photo.	Perf. 13	
438 A41	30c multicolored		15	15
439 A41	50c multicolored		15	15
440 A41	1fr multicolored		15	15
441 A41	10fr vio, dp org & blk		15	15
442 A41	25fr dk red brn, blk & yel grn		15	15
443 A41	30fr ol brn & lil rose		16	15
	Set value, #438-443,			
	C34		1.05	95

65th anniv. of Togolese mail service.
For souvenir sheet see No. C34a.

Hands Reaching for FAO Emblem A42

1963, Mar. 21 — *Perf. 14*
444 A42 50c bl, org & dk brn   15 15
445 A42 1fr ol grn, org & dk brn   15 15
446 A42 25fr brn, dk brn & org   16 15
447 A42 30fr vio, dk brn & org   24 15
  Set value   50 28

FAO "Freedom from Hunger" campaign.

Togolese Flag and Lomé Harbor A43

1963, Apr. 27 Litho. *Perf. 13x12½*
Flag in Red, Green and Yellow
448 A43 50c red brn & blk   15 15
449 A43 1fr dk car rose & blk   15 15
450 A43 25fr dull bl & blk   15 15
451 A43 50fr bister & blk   25 15
  Set value   50 30

3rd anniversary of independence.

Centenary Emblem — A44

1963, June 1 Photo. *Perf. 14*
Flag in Red, Olive Green, Yellow
452 A44 25fr blue, blk & red   15 15
453 A44 30fr dull grn, blk & red   22 15
  Set value   24

International Red Cross centenary.

Lincoln, Broken Fetters, Maps of Africa and US. — A45

1963, Oct. Unwmk. *Perf. 13x14*
454 A45 50c multicolored   15 15
455 A45 1fr multicolored   15 15
456 A45 25fr multicolored   16 15
  Set value   26 16

Centenary of the emancipation of the American slaves. See No. C35 and souvenir sheet No. C35a. For overprints see Nos. 473-475, C41.

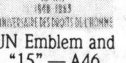

UN Emblem and "15" — A46

Hibiscus — A47

1963, Dec. 10 Photo. *Perf. 14x13*
457 A46 50c ultra, dk bl & rose red   15 15
458 A46 1fr yel grn, dk bl & rose red   15 15
459 A46 25fr lil, dk bl & rose red   18 15
460 A46 85fr gold, dk bl & rose red   65 25
  Set value   90 42

15th anniv. of the Universal Declaration of Human Rights.

1964 *Perf. 14*
Designs: 50c, Orchid. 2fr, Butterfly. 5fr, Hinged tortoise. 8fr, Ball python. 10fr, Bunea alcinoe (moth). 20fr, Octopus. 25fr, John Dory (fish). 30fr, French angelfish. 40fr, Hippopotamus. 60fr, Bohor reedbuck. 85fr, Anubius baboon.

Size: 22½x31mm
461 A47 50c multicolored   15 15
462 A47 1fr yellow, car & grn   15 15
463 A47 2fr lilac, yel & blk   15 15
464 A47 5fr gray & multi   15 15
465 A47 8fr cit, red brn & blk   15 15
466 A47 10fr multicolored   15 15
467 A47 20fr dl bl, yel & brn   15 15
468 A47 25fr dl bl, grn & yel   18 15
469 A47 30fr multicolored   22 15
470 A47 40fr grn, red brn & blk   30 15
471 A47 60fr grnsh bl & red brn   45 15
472 A47 85fr lt grn, brn & org   65 25
  Set value   2.25 95

See Nos. 511-515, C36-C40, J56-J63.

Nos. 454-456 Overprinted Diagonally: "En Mémoire de / JOHN F. KENNEDY / 1917-1963"

1964, Feb. *Perf. 13x14*
473 A45 50c multicolored   15 15
474 A45 1fr multicolored   15 15
475 A45 25fr multicolored   15 15
  Set value   24 15

Issued in memory of John F. Kennedy. See No. C41 and note on souvenir sheets following it.

Isis of Kalabsha A48

Designs: 25fr, Head of Ramses II. 30fr, Colonnade of Birth House at Philae.

1964, Mar. 8 Litho. *Perf. 14*
476 A48 20fr black, pale grn & red   15 15
477 A48 25fr black & lil rose   18 15
478 A48 30fr black & citron   22 15
  a. Souvenir sheet of 3   65 65
  Set value   24

UNESCO world campaign to save historic monuments in Nubia. No. 478a contains three imperf. stamps similar to Nos. 476-478 with simulated perforations.

Phosphate Mine, Kpeme A49

Designs: 25fr, Phosphate plant, Kpeme. 60fr, Phosphate train. 85fr, Loading ship with phosphate.

1964, Apr. 27 Unwmk. *Perf. 14*
479 A49 5fr brown & bis brn   15 15
480 A49 25fr dk pur & brn car   18 15
481 A49 60fr dk green & olive   45 18
482 A49 85fr vio blk & Prus bl   65 22
  Set value   55

Fourth anniversary of independence.

African Breaking Slavery Chain, and Map — A50

1964, May 25 Photo. *Perf. 14x13*
483 A50 5fr dp orange & brn   15 15
484 A50 25fr olive grn & brn   15 15
485 A50 85fr rose car & brn   52 15
  Set value   70 20

1st anniv. of the meeting of African heads of state at Addis Ababa. See No. C42.

Pres. Nicolas Grunitzky and Butterfly A51

1964, Aug. 18 Litho. *Perf. 14*
486 A51 1fr shown   15 15
487 A51 5fr Dove   15 15
488 A51 25fr Flower   20 15
489 A51 45fr as 1fr   35 15
490 A51 85fr Flower   65 25
  Set value   1.30 55

National Union and Reconciliation.

Soccer A52

1964, Oct. Photo. *Perf. 14*
491 A52 1fr shown   15 15
492 A52 5fr Runner   15 15
493 A52 25fr Discus   15 15
494 A52 45fr as 1fr   24 15
  Set value, #491-494, C43   1.20 60

18th Olympic Games, Tokyo, Oct. 10-25. For souvenir sheet see No. C43a.

Cooperation Issue
Common Design Type

1964, Nov. 7 Engr. *Perf. 13*
495 CD119 25fr mag, dk brn & ol bis   20 15

Dirigible and Balloons — A53

Designs: 25fr, 45fr, Otto Lilienthal's glider, 1894; Wright Brothers' plane, 1903; Boeing 707.

1964, Dec. 5 Photo. *Perf. 14x13*
496 A53 5fr org lil & grn   15 15
497 A53 10fr brt grn, dl bl & dk red   15 15
498 A53 25fr bl, vio bl & org   15 15
499 A53 45fr brt pink, vio bl & grn   26 15
  a. Souv. sheet of 4   1.25 1.25
  Set value, #496-499, C44   1.30 55

Inauguration of the national airline, Air Togo. No. 499a contains four imperf. stamps similar to Nos. 497-499 and No. C44 with simulated perforations.

Orbiting Geophysical Observatory and Mariner — A54

Space Satellites: 15fr, 25fr, Tiros, Telstar and Orbiting Solar Observatory. 20fr, 50fr, Nimbus, Syncom and Relay.

1964, Dec. 12 Litho. *Perf. 14*
500 A54 10fr dp rose, bl & yel   15 15
501 A54 15fr multi   15 15
502 A54 20fr yel, grn & vio   15 15
503 A54 25fr multi   18 15
504 A54 45fr brt grn, dk bl & yel   32 15

505 A54 50fr yel, grn & org   38 15
  a. Souvenir sheet of 4, #502-505, imperf.   1.00 1.00
  Nos. 500-505 (6)   1.33
  Set value   35

Intl. Quiet Sun Year.

Togo Olympic Stamps Printed in Israel — A55

Arms of Israel and Togo A56

Pres. Nicolas Grunitzky of Togo and: 20fr, Church of the Mount of Beatitudes. 45fr, Ruins of Synagogue at Capernaum.

Perf. 13½x14½, 14x13½
1964, Dec. 26 Photo.
506 A55 5fr rose violet   15 15
507 A56 20fr grnsh bl, grn & dl pur   15 15
508 A56 25fr red & bluish grn   18 15
509 A56 45fr dl yel, ol & dl pur   45 25
510 A56 85fr mag & bluish grn   38 15
  a. Souv. sheet of 4, imperf.   2.50 2.50
  Nos. 506-510 (5)   1.31
  Set value   55

Israel-Togo friendship.

Type of Regular Issue, 1964

1965, June Unwmk. *Perf. 14*
Designs: 3fr, Morpho aega butterfly. 4fr, Scorpion. 6fr, Bird-of-paradise flower. 15fr, Flapnecked chameleon. 45fr, Ring-tailed palm civet.

Size: 23x31mm
511 A47 3fr bister & multi   15 15
512 A47 4fr org & bluish blk   15 15
513 A47 6fr multi   15 15
514 A47 15fr brt pink, yel & brn   15 15
515 A47 45fr dl grn, org & brn   32 15
  Set value   55 30

Syncom Satellite, Radar Station and ITU Emblem — A57

1965, June *Perf. 13x14*
516 A57 10fr Prus blue   15 15
517 A57 20fr olive bister   15 15
518 A57 25fr bright blue   20 15
519 A57 45fr crimson   32 16
520 A57 50fr green   38 18
  Nos. 516-520 (5)   1.20
  Set value   52

ITU, centenary.

Get free stamps every month! A subscription to the "Scott Stamp Monthly" entitles you to write in for each month's free offer. The value of the free stamps more than offsets the subscription cost. For more information, please call 1-800-488-5351.

Abraham Lincoln — A58

Discus Thrower, Flags of Togo and Congo — A59

1965, June 26   Photo.   Perf. 13x14
521 A58   1fr magenta   15   15
522 A58   5fr dull green   15   15
523 A58   20fr brown   15   15
524 A58   25fr slate   15   15
      Set value, #521-524,
      C45   1.25 50

Death cent. of Abraham Lincoln. For souvenir sheet see No. C45a.

1965, July   Unwmk.   Perf. 14x13

Flags and: 10fr, Javelin thrower. 15fr, Handball player. 25fr, Runner.

Flags in Red, Yellow and Green
525 A59   5fr deep magenta   15   15
526 A59   10fr dark blue   15   15
527 A59   15fr brown   15   15
528 A59   25fr dark purple   16   15
      Set value, #525-528,
      C46   1.15 52

1st African Games, Brazzaville, July 18-25.

Winston Churchill and "V" — A60

Stalin, Roosevelt and Churchill at Yalta — A61

Perf. 13½x14, 14x13½
1965, Aug. 7   Photo.
529 A60   5fr dull green   15   15
530 A61   10fr brt vio & gray   15   15
531 A60   20fr brown   15   15
532 A61   45fr Prus bl & gray   32   15
      Set value, #529-532,
      C47   1.35 60

Sir Winston Spencer Churchill (1874-1965), British statesman and World War II leader.

Unisphere and New York Skyline — A62

Designs: 10fr, Togolese dancers and drummer, Unisphere. 50fr, Michelangelo's Pieta and Unisphere.

1965, Aug. 28   Photo.   Perf. 14
533 A62   5fr grnsh bl & vio blk   15   15
534 A62   10fr yel grn & dk brn   15   15
535 A62   25fr brn org & dk grn   18   15
536 A62   50fr vio & sl grn   32   18
537 A62   85fr rose red & brn   65   30
   a.   Souvenir sheet of 2   1.00 1.00
      Set value   1.25 65

New York World's Fair, 1964-65. No. 537a contains two imperf. stamps similar to Nos. 536-537 with simulated perforations.

"Constructive Cooperation" and Olive Branch — A63

Designs: 25fr, 40fr, Hands of various races holding globe and olive branch. 85fr, Handclasp, olive branch and globe.

1965, Sept. 25   Unwmk.   Perf. 14
538 A63   5fr violet, lt bl & org   15   15
539 A63   15fr brn, org & gray   15   15
540 A63   25fr blue & orange   18   15
541 A63   40fr dp car, gray & org   28   15
542 A63   85fr green & org   60   30
      Set value   1.20 60

International Cooperation Year.

Major White and Gemini 4 — A64

Design: 25fr, Lt. Col. Alexei Leonov and Voskhod 2.

1965, Nov. 25   Photo.   Perf. 13½x14
543 A64   25fr dp bl & brt car rose   18   15
544 A64   50fr green & brown   38   15
      Set value   22

"Walks in Space" of Lt. Col. Alexei Leonov (USSR), and Major Edward H. White (US). Printed in sheets of 12 with ornamental borders. For overprints and surcharges see Nos. 563-566.

Adlai E. Stevenson and UN Headquarters — A65

Designs: 5fr, "ONU" and doves. 10fr, UN emblem and headquarters. 20fr, "ONU" and orchids.

1965, Dec. 15   Perf. 14x13½
545 A65   5fr dk brn, yel & lt bl   15   15
546 A65   10fr org, dk bl & grn   15   15
547 A65   20fr dk grn, yel grn & org
            brn   15   15
548 A65   25fr brt yel, dk bl & bluish
            grn   20   15
      Nos. 545-548,C48 (5)
      Set value   1.65
                                     65

UN, 20th anniv.; Adlai E. Stevenson (1900-1965), US ambassador to the UN.

Pope Paul VI, Plane and UN Emblem — A66

Designs: 15fr, 30fr, Pope addressing UN General Assembly and UN emblem, vert. 20fr, Pope and New York skyline with UN Headquarters.

1966, Mar. 5   Litho.   Perf. 12
549 A66   5fr blue & multi   15   15
550 A66   15fr lt violet & multi 15   15
551 A66   20fr bister & multi   15   15
552 A66   30fr lt ultra & multi   16   15
      Set value, #549,552
      C49-C50   1.40 50

Visit of Pope Paul VI to the UN, New York City, Oct. 4, 1965.

Surgical Operation and Togolese Flag — A67

Togolese Flag and: 10fr, 30fr, Blood transfusion. 45fr, Profiles of African man and woman.

1966, May 7   Litho.   Perf. 12
553 A67   5fr multicolored   15   15
554 A67   10fr multicolored   15   15
555 A67   15fr multicolored   18   15
556 A67   30fr multicolored   18   15
557 A67   45fr multicolored   30   15
      Set value, #553-557,
      C51   1.55 60

Togolese Red Cross, 7th anniversary.

Talisman Roses and WHO Headquarters, Geneva — A68

Designs: Various flowers and WHO Headquarters.

1966, May   Litho.   Perf. 12
558 A68   5fr lt yel grn & multi   15   15
559 A68   10fr pale pink & multi   15   15
560 A68   15fr dull yel & multi   15   15
561 A68   20fr pale gray & multi   15   15
562 A68   30fr tan & multi   18   15
      Set value, #558-562,
      C52-C53   1.60 50

Inauguration of WHO Headquarters, Geneva.

Nos. 543-544 Overprinted or Surcharged in Red

1966, July 11   Photo.   Perf. 13½x14
563 A64   50fr Envolée Surveyor 1   32   15
564 A64   50fr Envolée Gemini 9   32   15
565 A64   100fr on 25fr Envolée Luna 9 75   15
566 A64   100fr on 25fr Envolée Venus
            3   75   15
      Set value   35

US and USSR achievements in Space. Sheets of 12 of Nos. 543-544 received two different overprints each, creating 6 se-tenant pairs of Nos. 563-564 and of Nos. 565-566 each.

Wood Carver — A69

Togolese Dancer — A70

Arts and Crafts: 10fr, Basket maker. 15fr, Woman weaver. 30fr, Woman potter.

1966, Sept.   Photo.   Perf. 13x14
567 A69   5fr blue, yel & dk brn   15   15
568 A69   10fr emer, org & dk brn   15   15
569 A69   15fr ver, yel & dk brn   15   15
570 A69   30fr lilac, dk brn & yel 16   15
      Set value, #567-570,
      C55-C56   1.50 50

1966, Nov.   Photo.   Perf. 13x14

Designs: 5fr, Togolese man. 20fr, Woman dancer from North Togo holding branches. 25fr, Male dancer. 30fr, Male dancer from North Togo with horned helmet. 45fr, Drummer.

571 A70   5fr emerald & multi   15   15
572 A70   10fr dl yel & multi   15   15
573 A70   20fr lt ultra & multi   15   15
574 A70   25fr dp orange & multi   15   15
575 A70   30fr red violet & multi 18   15
576 A70   45fr blue & multi   25   15
      Set value, #571-576,
      C57-C58   1.70 70

Soccer Players and Jules Rimet
Cup — A71

Various Soccer Scenes.

1966, Dec. 14   Photo.   Perf. 14x13
577	A71	5fr blue, brn & red	15	15
578	A71	10fr brick red & multi	15	15
579	A71	20fr ol, brn & dk grn	15	15
580	A71	25fr vio, brn & org	15	15
581	A71	30fr ocher & multi	18	15
582	A71	45fr emerald, brn & mag	26	15
		Set value, #577-582,		
		C59-C60	1.70	65

England's victory in the World Soccer Cup
Championship, Wembley, July 30. For souvenir
sheet see No. C60a.

African Mouthbreeder and Sailboat — A72

Designs: 10fr, Yellow jack and trawler. 15fr,
Banded distichodus and seiner. 25fr, Jewelfish and
galley. 30fr, like 5fr.

1967, Jan. 14   Photo.   Perf. 14
Fish in Natural Colors
583	A72	5fr lt ultra & blk	15	15
584	A72	10fr brn org & brn	15	15
585	A72	15fr brt rose & dk bl	15	15
586	A72	25fr olive & blk	18	15
587	A72	30fr grnsh bl & blk	22	15
		Nos. 583-587,C61-C62 (7)	2.17	
		Set value		80

African Boy and Greyhound — A73

UNICEF Emblem and: 10fr, Boy and Irish setter.
20fr, Girl and doberman.

1967, Feb. 11   Photo.   Perf. 14x13½
588	A73	5fr orange, plum & blk	15	15
589	A73	10fr yel grn, red brn & dk grn	15	15
590	A73	15fr brt rose, brn & blk	15	15
591	A73	20fr bl, vio bl & blk	16	15
592	A73	30fr ol, sl grn & blk	18	15
		Set value, #588-592,		
		C63-C64	1.60	60

UNICEF, 20th anniv. (in 1966).

French A-1 Satellite — A74

Designs: 5fr, Diamant rocket, vert. 15fr, Fr-1
satellite, vert. 20fr, 40fr, D-1 satellite. 25fr, A-1
satellite.

Perf. 14x13½, 13½x14
1967, Mar. 18   Photo.
593	A74	5fr multi	15	15
594	A74	10fr multi	15	15
595	A74	15fr multi	15	15
596	A74	20fr multi	15	15
597	A74	25fr multi	16	15
598	A74	40fr multi	26	15
		Set value, #593-598		
		C65-C66	1.95	70

French achievements in space.

Duke Ellington, Saxophone, Trumpet,
Drums — A75

UNESCO Emblem and: 5fr, Johann Sebastian
Bach and organ. 10fr, Ludwig van Beethoven, violin and clarinet. 20fr, Claude A. Debussy, piano and
harp. 30fr, like 15fr.

1967, Apr. 15   Photo.   Perf. 14x13½
599	A75	5fr org & multi	15	15
600	A75	10fr multi	15	15
601	A75	15fr multi	15	15
602	A75	20fr lt bl & multi	15	15
603	A75	30fr lil & multi	18	15
		Set value, #599-603,		
		C67-C68	1.60	55

20th anniv. (in 1966) of UNESCO.

EXPO Emblem, British Pavilion and Day
Lilies — A76

Designs: 10fr, French pavilion and roses. 30fr,
African village and bird-of-paradise flower.

1967, May 30   Photo.   Perf. 14
604	A76	5fr brt pink & multi	15	15
605	A76	10fr dull org & multi	15	15
606	A76	30fr blue & multi	18	15
		Nos. 604-606,C69-C72 (7)	2.60	
		Set value		95

EXPO '67 Intl. Exhibition, Montreal, Apr. 28-
Oct. 27.
For overprints see Nos. 628-630, C86-C89.

REPUBLIQUE TOGOLAISE

Lions Emblem — A77

Designs: 20fr, 45fr, Lions emblem and flowers.

1967, July 29   Photo.   Perf. 13x14
607	A77	10fr yellow & multi	15	15
608	A77	20fr multicolored	15	15
609	A77	30fr green & multi	22	15
610	A77	45fr blue & multi	38	15
		Set value		28

50th anniversary of Lions International.

Montagu's Harriers — A78

Designs: 5fr, Bohor reedbucks. 15fr, Zebras.
20fr, 30fr, Marsh harriers. 25fr, Leopard.

1967, Aug. 19   Photo.   Perf. 14x13½
611	A78	5fr lilac & org brn	15	15
612	A78	10fr dk red, yel & dl bl	15	15
613	A78	15fr grn, blk & lil	15	15
614	A78	20fr dk brn, yel & dl bl	15	15
615	A78	25fr brn, ol & yel	18	15
616	A78	30fr vio, yel & dl bl	22	15
		Set value, #611-616,		
		C79-C80	1.80	70

Stamp Auction and Togo Nos. 16 and
C42 — A79

Designs: 10fr, 45fr, Exhibition and Nos. 67 (British) and 520. 15fr, 30fr, Stamp store and No. 230.
20fr, Stamp packet vending machine and No. 545.

1967, Oct. 14   Photo.   Perf. 14x13
Stamps on Stamps in Original Colors
617	A79	5fr purple	15	15
618	A79	10fr dk brown	15	15
619	A79	15fr deep blue	20	15
620	A79	20fr slate green	25	15
621	A79	30fr red brown	38	15
622	A79	45fr Prus blue	50	16
		Nos. 617-622,C82-C83 (8)	3.93	
		Set value		1.10

70th anniv. of the 1st Togolese stamps. For
souvenir sheet see No. C82a.
See Nos. 853-855, C205.

Monetary Union Issue
Common Design Type
1967, Nov. 4   Engr.   Perf. 13
623	CD125	30fr dk bl, vio bl & brt grn	22	15

Broad Jump, Summer Olympics Emblem
and View of Mexico City — A80

Designs: 15fr, Ski jump, Winter Olympics
emblem and ski lift. 30fr, Runners, Summer Olympics emblem and view of Mexico City. 45fr, Bobsledding, Winter Olympics emblem and ski lift.

1967, Dec. 2   Photo.   Perf. 13x14
624	A80	5fr orange & multi	15	15
625	A80	15fr multicolored	15	15
626	A80	30fr multicolored	18	15
627	A80	45fr multicolored	25	15
		Nos. 624-627,C84-C85 (6)	1.96	
		Set value		70

1968 Olympic Games. For souvenir sheet see
No. C85a.

Nos. 604-606 Overprinted: "JOURNÉE
NATIONALE / DU TOGO / 29
SEPTEMBRE 1967"
1967, Dec.   Perf. 14
628	A76	5fr multicolored	15	15
629	A76	10fr multicolored	15	15
630	A76	30fr blue & multi	25	15
		Nos. 628-630,C86-C89 (7)	3.47	
		Set value		1.05

National Day, Sept. 29, 1967.

The Gleaners, by François Millet and
Phosphate Works, Benin — A81

Industrialization of Togo: 20fr, 45fr, 90fr, The
Weaver at the Loom, by Vincent van Gogh, and
textile plant, Dadia.

1968, Jan.   Photo.   Perf. 14
631	A81	10fr olive & multi	15	15
632	A81	20fr multicolored	15	15
633	A81	30fr brown & multi	22	15
634	A81	45fr multicolored	32	15
635	A81	60fr dk blue & multi	45	15
636	A81	90fr multicolored	70	25
		Nos. 631-636 (6)	1.99	
		Set value		65

Togolese Women Brewing Beer — A82

The Beer Drinkers,
by Edouard
Manet — A83

Design: 45fr, Modern beer bottling plant.

1968, Mar. 26   Litho.   Perf. 14
637	A82	20fr emerald & multi	15	15
638	A83	30fr dk car & multi	22	15
639	A82	45fr orange & multi	32	15
		Set value		26

Publicity for local beer industry.

Symbolic Water Cycle,
Flower and
Cogwheels — A84

1968, Apr. 6
640	A84	30fr multicolored	16	15

Hydrological Decade (UNESCO), 1965-74. See
No. C90.

Viking Ship and Portuguese
Brigantine — A85

Designs: 10fr, Fulton's steamship and modern steamship. 20fr, Harbor activities and map of Africa.

1968, Apr. 26   Photo.   Perf. 14x13½
641 A85 5fr brt green & multi   15   15
642 A85 10fr dp orange & multi   15   15
643 A85 20fr green & multi   15   15
644 A85 30fr yel grn & multi   18   15
       Set value, #641-644,
         C91-C92   1.50   50

Inauguration of Lomé Harbor.

Adenauer and 1968
Europa Emblem — A86

1968, May 25   Photo.   Perf. 14
645 A86 90fr ol grn & brn org   60   18

Konrad Adenauer (1876-1967), chancellor of West Germany (1949-63).

Adam and Eve Expelled from Paradise, by
Michelangelo — A87

Paintings: 20fr, The Anatomy Lesson of Dr. Tulp, by Rembrandt. 30fr, The Anatomy Lesson, by Rembrandt (detail). 45fr, Jesus Healing the Sick, by Raphael.

1968, June 22   Photo.   Perf. 14
646 A87 15fr crimson & multi   15   15
647 A87 20fr multicolored   15   15
648 A87 30fr green & multi   18   15
649 A87 45fr multicolored   25   15
       Nos. 646-649,C93-C94 (6)   1.96
       Set value   60

WHO, 20th anniv.

Olympic Monument, San Salvador Island,
Bahamas — A88

1968, July 27   Perf. 14x13½
650 A88 15fr Wrestling   15   15
651 A88 20fr Boxing   15   15
652 A88 30fr Judo   18   15
653 A88 45fr Running   25   15
       Nos. 650-653,C95-C96 (6)   1.96
       Set value   60

19th Olympic Games, Mexico City, Oct. 12-27.

Chick Holding
Lottery
Ticket — A89

Scout Before
Tent — A90

Design: 45fr, Lottery ticket, horseshoe and four-leaf clover.

1968, Oct. 5   Litho.   Perf. 14
654 A89 30fr dk green & multi   22   15
655 A89 45fr multicolored   32   15
       Set value   20

2nd anniversary of National Lottery.

1968, Nov. 23

Designs: 10fr, 45fr, Scout leader training cub scouts, horiz. 20fr, First aid practice, horiz. 30fr, Scout game.
656 A90 5fr dp org & multi   15   15
657 A90 10fr emerald & multi   15   15
658 A90 20fr multicolored   15   15
659 A90 30fr multicolored   22   15
660 A90 45fr blue & multi   32   15
       Nos. 656-660,C97-C98 (7)   2.49
       Set value   95

Issued to honor the Togolese Boy Scouts.

Adoration of the Shepherds, by
Giorgione — A91

Paintings: 20f, Adoration of the Magi, by Pieter Brueghel. 30fr, Adoration of the Magi, by Botticelli. 45fr, Adoration of the Magi, by Durer.

1968, Dec. 28   Litho.   Perf. 14
661 A91 15fr green & multi   15   15
662 A91 20fr multicolored   15   15
663 A91 30fr multicolored   22   15
664 A91 45fr multicolored   32   15
       Nos. 661-664,C100-C101 (6)   2.34
       Set value   80

Christmas.

Martin Luther King,
Jr. — A92

Portraits and Human Rights Flame: 20fr, Professor René Cassin (author of Declaration of Human Rights). 45fr, Pope John XXIII.

1969, Feb. 1   Photo.   Perf. 13½x14
665 A92 15fr brn org & sl grn   15   15
666 A92 20fr grnsh bl & vio   15   15
667 A92 30fr ver & sl bl   15   15
668 A92 45fr ol & car rose   25   15
       Nos. 665-668,C102-C103 (6)   1.65
       Set value   80

International Human Rights Year.

For overprints see Nos. 683-686, C110-C111.

Omnisport Stadium and Soccer — A93

Stadium and: 15fr, Handball. 20fr, Volleyball. 30fr, Basketball. 45fr, Tennis.

1969, Apr. 26   Photo.   Perf. 14x13½
669 A93 10fr emer, dp car & dk brn   15   15
670 A93 15fr org, ultra & dk brn   15   15
671 A93 20fr yel, ol & dk brn   15   15
672 A93 30fr dl grn, bl & dk brn   15   15
673 A93 45fr org, lil & dk brn   22   15
       Set value, #669-673,
         C105-C106   1.60   65

Opening of Omnisport Stadium, Lomé.

Lunar Module
Eagle Landing
on
Moon — A94

Designs: 20fr, 45fr, Astronaut and Eagle on moon, earth and stars in sky.

1969, July 21   Litho.   Perf. 14
674 A94 1fr green & multi   15   15
675 A94 20fr brown & multi   15   15
676 A94 30fr scarlet & multi   20   15
677 A94 45fr ultra & multi   35   15
       Nos. 674-677,C107-C108 (6)   1.90
       Set value   90

Man's first landing on the moon, July 20, 1969. US astronauts Neil A. Armstrong and Col. Edwin E. Aldrin, Jr., with Lieut. Col. Michael Collins piloting Apollo 11.
For overprints see Nos. 710-712, C120-C121.

Christ at
Emmaus, by
Velazquez
A95

Paintings: 5fr, The Last Supper, by Tintoretto. 20fr, Pentecost, by El Greco. 30fr, The Annunciation, by Botticelli. 45fr, Like 10fr.

1969, Aug. 16   Litho.   Perf. 14
678 A95 5fr red, gold & multi   15   15
679 A95 10fr multicolored   15   15
680 A95 20fr grn, gold & multi   15   15
681 A95 30fr multicolored   20   15
682 A95 45fr pur, gold & multi   30   15
       Set value, #678-682,
         C109   1.65   75

Nos. 665-668
Overprinted

EN MEMOIRE
DWIGHT D. EISENHOWER
1890-1969

1969, Sept. 1   Photo.   Perf. 13½x14
683 A92 15fr brn org & sl grn   15   15
684 A92 20fr grnsh bl & vio   15   15
685 A92 30fr ver & slate bl   18   15
686 A92 45fr olive & car rose   25   15
       Nos. 683-686,C110-C111 (6)   1.73
       Set value   70

Gen. Dwight D. Eisenhower (1890-1969), 34th President of the US.

African Development
Bank and
Emblem — A96

Designs: 45fr, Bank emblem and hand holding railroad bridge and engine.

1969, Sept. 10   Photo.   Perf. 13x14
687 A96 30fr ultra, blk gold & grn   20   15
688 A96 45fr grn, dk bl, gold & dk red 32 15
       Set value   18

5th anniv. of the African Development Bank. See No. C112.

Louis Pasteur and Help for 1968 Flood
Victims — A97

Designs: 15fr, Henri Dunant and Red Cross workers meeting Biafra refugees at airport. 30fr, Alexander Fleming and help for flood victims. 45fr, Wilhelm C. Roentgen and Red Cross workers with children in front of Headquarters.

1969, Sept. 27   Litho.   Perf. 14
689 A97 15fr red & multi   15   15
690 A97 20fr emerald & multi   15   15
691 A97 30fr purple & multi   18   15
692 A97 45fr brt blue & multi   32   15
       Nos. 689-692,C113-C114 (6)   1.90
       Set value   90

50th anniv. of the League of Red Cross Societies.

Glidji
Agricultural
Center — A98

Designs (Emblem of Young Pioneer and Agricultural Organization and): 1fr, Corn harvest. 3fr, Founding meeting of Agricultural Pioneer Youths, Mar. 7, 1967. 4fr, Class at Glidji Agricultural School. 5fr, Boys forming human pyramid. 7fr, Farm students threshing. 8fr, Instruction in gardening. 10fr, 50fr, Cooperative village. 15fr, Gardening School. 20fr, Cattle breeding. 25fr, Chicken farm. 30fr, Independence parade. 40fr, Boys riding high wire. 45fr, Tractor and trailer. 60fr, Instruction in tractor driving.

1969-70   Litho.   Perf. 14
693	A98	1fr multi ('70)	15	15
694	A98	2fr multi	15	15
695	A98	3fr multi ('70)	15	15
696	A98	4fr multi ('70)	15	15
697	A98	5fr ultra & multi	15	15
698	A98	7fr multi ('70)	15	15
699	A98	8fr red & multi	15	15
700	A98	10fr bl & multi ('70)	15	15
701	A98	15fr red & multi ('70)	15	15
702	A98	20fr lilac & multi	15	15
703	A98	25fr multi ('70)	15	15
704	A98	30fr brt bl & multi	15	15
705	A98	40fr brt yel & multi	20	15
706	A98	45fr rose lil & multi	22	15
707	A98	50fr blue & multi	24	15
708	A98	60fr orange & multi	25	15
		Nos. 693-708,C115-C119 (21)	9.86	
		Set value		2.75

Books and Map of Africa — A99

1969, Nov. 27   Litho.   Perf. 14
709	A99	30fr lt blue & multi	20	15

12th anniv. of the Intl. Assoc. for the Development of Libraries in Africa.

Christmas Issue
Nos. 674-675, 677 Overprinted "JOYEUX NOEL"

1969, Dec.   Litho.   Perf. 14
710	A94	1fr green & multi	20	15
711	A94	20fr brown & multi	70	35
712	A94	45fr ultra & multi	1.20	65
		Nos. 710-712,C120-C121 (5)	5.35	2.15

George Washington — A100

Portraits: 20fr, Albert Luthuli. 30fr, Mahatma Gandhi. 45fr, Simon Bolivar.

1969, Dec. 27   Photo.   Perf. 14x13½
713	A100	15fr dk brn, emer & buff	15	15
714	A100	20fr dk brn, org & buff	15	15
715	A100	30fr dk brn, grnsh bl & ocher	15	15
716	A100	45fr dk brn, sl grn & dl yel	18	15
		Nos. 713-716,C122-C123 (6)	1.65	
		Set value		78

Issued to honor leaders for world peace. For overprint and surcharges see Nos. 764-766, C143.

Plower, by M.K. Klodt and ILO Emblem A101

Paintings and ILO Emblem: 10fr, Gardening, by Camille Pissarro. 20fr, Fruit Harvest, by Diego Rivera. 30fr, Spring Sowing, by Vincent van Gogh. 45fr, Workers, by Rivera.

1970, Jan. 24   Litho.   Perf. 12½x13
717	A101	5fr gold & multi	15	15
718	A101	10fr gold & multi	15	15
719	A101	20fr gold & multi	15	15
720	A101	30fr gold & multi	24	15
721	A101	45fr gold & multi	35	15
		Nos. 717-721,C124-C125 (7)	2.04	
		Set value		65

ILO, 50th anniversary.

Togolese Hair Styles — A102

Designs: Various hair styles. 20fr, 30fr, vertical.

Perf. 13x12½, 12½x13
1970, Feb. 21
722	A102	5fr multicolored	15	15
723	A102	10fr ver & multi	15	15
724	A102	20fr purple & multi	18	15
725	A102	30fr yellow grn & multi	25	18
		Nos. 722-725,C126-C127 (6)	1.49	
		Set value		80

Togo No. C127 and Independence Monument, Lomé — A103

Designs: 30fr, Pres. Etienne G. Eyadéma, Presidential Palace and Independence Monument. 50fr, Map of Togo, dove and Independence Monument, vert.

Perf. 13x12½, 12½x13
1970, Apr. 27   Litho.
726	A103	20fr multicolored	15	15
727	A103	30fr multicolored	20	15
728	A103	50fr multicolored	38	15
		Set value		28

10th anniv. of independence. See No. C128.

Inauguration of UPU Headquarters, Bern — A104

1970, May 30   Photo.   Perf. 14x13½
729	A104	30fr orange & pur	22	15

See No. C129.

Soccer, Jules Rimet Cup and Flags of Italy and Uruguay — A105

Designs (Various Scenes from Soccer, Rimet Cup and Flags of): 10fr, Great Britain and Brazil. 15fr, USSR and Mexico. 20fr, Germany and Morocco. 30fr, Romania and Czechoslovakia.

1970, June 27   Litho.   Perf. 13x14
730	A105	5fr olive & multi	15	15
731	A105	10fr pink & multi	15	15
732	A105	15fr yellow & multi	16	15
733	A105	20fr multicolored	20	15
734	A105	30fr emerald	30	15
		Nos. 730-734,C130-C132 (8)	2.17	
		Set value		1.00

Soccer Championships for the Jules Rimet Cup, Mexico City, May 30-June 21, 1970.

Lenin and UNESCO Emblem A106

1970, July 25   Litho.   Perf. 12½
735	A106	30fr fawn & multi	22	15

Lenin (1870-1924), Russian communist leader. See No. C133.
For surcharge see No. C179.

EXPO '70 Emblem and View of US Pavilion — A107

Designs: 2fr, Paper carp flying over Sanyo pavilion. 30fr, Russian pavilion. 50fr, Tower of the Sun pavilion. 60fr, French and Japanese pavilions.

1970, Aug. 8   Litho.   Perf. 13
Size: 56½x35mm
736	A107	2fr gray & multi	15	15

Size: 50x33mm
737	A107	20fr blue & multi	15	15
738	A107	30fr blue & multi	15	15
739	A107	50fr blue & multi	24	15
740	A107	60fr blue & multi	30	15
		Set value	80	35

EXPO '70 Intl. Exhibition, Osaka, Japan, Mar. 15-Sept. 13. Nos. 737-740 printed se-tenant in sheet with continuous view of EXPO. See No. C134.

Neil A. Armstrong, Michael Collins and Edwin E. Aldrin, Jr. — A108

Designs: 2fr, US flag, moon rocks and Apollo 11 emblem. 20fr, Astronaut checking Surveyor 3 on moon, and Apollo 12 emblem. 30fr, Charles Conrad, Jr., Richard F. Gordon, Jr., Alan L. Bean and Apollo 12 emblem. 50fr, US flag, moon rocks and Apollo 12 emblem.

1970, Sept. 26
741	A108	1fr multi	15	15
742	A108	2fr multi	15	15
743	A108	20fr multi	16	15
744	A108	30fr multi	22	15
745	A108	50fr multi	45	16
		Nos. 741-745,C135 (6)	2.08	
		Set value		95

Moon landings of Apollo 11 and 12.
For overprints see Nos. 746=750, C136.

Nos. 741-745 Inscribed: "FELICITATIONS / BON RETOUR APOLLO XIII"

1970, Sept. 26
746	A108	1fr multi	15	15
747	A108	2fr multi	15	15
748	A108	20fr multi	16	15
749	A108	30fr multi	22	15
750	A108	50fr multi	45	16
		Nos. 746-750,C136 (6)	2.13	
		Set value		95

Safe return of the crew of Apollo 13.

Forge of Vulcan, by Velazquez, and ILO Emblem — A109

Paintings and Emblems of UN Agencies: 15fr, Still Life, by Delacroix, and FAO emblem. 20fr, Portrait of Nicholas Kratzer, by Holbein, and UNESCO emblem. 30fr, UN Headquarters, New York, and UN emblem. 50fr, Portrait of a Little Girl, by Renoir, and UNICEF emblem.

1970, Oct. 24   Litho.   Perf. 13x12½
751	A109	1fr car, gold & dk brn	15	15
752	A109	15fr ultra, gold & blk	15	15
753	A109	20fr grnsh bl, gold & dk grn	15	15
754	A109	30fr lil & multi	22	15
755	A109	50fr org brn, gold & sepia	42	20
		Nos. 751-755,C137-C138 (7)	1.99	
		Set value		90

United Nations, 25th anniversary.

Euchloron Megaera — A110

Butterflies and Moths: 2fr, Cymothoe chrysippus. 30fr, Danaus chrysippus. 50fr, Morpho.

1970, Nov. 21   Litho.   Perf. 13x14
756	A110	1fr yellow & multi	15	15
757	A110	2fr lt vio & multi	15	15
758	A110	30fr multicolored	20	15
759	A110	50fr orange & multi	40	15
		Nos. 756-759,C139-C140 (6)	2.00	
		Set value		60

For surcharge see No. 859.

Nativity, by Botticelli — A111

Paintings: 20fr, Adoration of the Shepherds, by Veronese. 30fr, Adoration of the Shepherds, by El Greco. 50fr, Adoration of the Kings, by Fra Angelico.

1970, Dec. 26   Litho.   Perf. 12½x13
760	A111	15fr gold & multi	15	15
761	A111	20fr gold & multi	15	15
762	A111	30fr gold & multi	20	15
763	A111	50fr gold & multi	38	16
		Nos. 760-763,C141-C142 (6)	2.03	
		Set value		85

Christmas.

Nos. 715, C123, 714 Surcharged and Overprinted: "EN MEMOIRE / Charles De Gaulle / 1890-1970"

1971, Jan. 9   Photo.   Perf. 14x13½

764	A100	30fr multicolored	22 15
765	A100	30fr on 90fr multi	22 15
766	A100	150fr on 20fr multi	1.10 36
		Set value	52

"Aerienne" obliterated with heavy bar on No. 765. See No. C143.

De Gaulle and Churchill
A112

De Gaulle and: 30fr, Dwight D. Eisenhower. 40fr, John F. Kennedy. 50fr, Konrad Adenauer.

1971, Feb. 20   Photo.   Perf. 13x14

767	A112	20fr blk & brt blue	15 15
768	A112	30fr blk & crimson	16 15
769	A112	40fr blk & dp green	32 15
770	A112	50fr blk & brown	35 15
		Nos. 767-770,C144-C145 (6)	2.18
		Set value	80

Nos. 764-770 issued in memory of Charles de Gaulle (1890-1970), President of France.

Resurrection, by Raphael
A113

Easter: 30fr, Resurrection, by Master of Trebon. 40fr, like 1fr.

Perf. 10½x11½

1971, Apr. 10   Litho.

771	A113	1fr gold & multi	15 15
772	A113	30fr gold & multi	16 15
773	A113	40fr gold & multi	20 15
		Nos. 771-773,C146-C148 (6)	1.99
		Set value	88

Cmdr. Alan B. Shepard, Jr. — A114

Designs: 10fr, Edgar D. Mitchell and astronaut on moon. 30fr, Stuart A. Roosa, module on moon. 40fr, Take-off from moon, and spaceship.

1971, May   Litho.   Perf. 12½

774	A114	1fr blue & multi	15 15
775	A114	10fr green & multi	15 15
776	A114	30fr dull red & multi	20 15
777	A114	40fr dk green & multi	25 15
		Nos. 774-777,C149-C151 (7)	3.15
		Set value	1.45

Apollo 14 moon landing, Jan. 31-Feb. 9. For overprints see Nos. 788, C162-C164.

Cacao Tree and Pods — A115

Designs: 40fr, Sorting and separating beans and pods. 50fr, Drying cacao beans.

1971, June 6   Litho.   Perf. 14

778	A115	30fr multicolored	30 15
779	A115	40fr ultra & multi	35 15
780	A115	50fr multicolored	35 16
		Nos. 778-780,C152-C154 (6)	2.70 1.31

International Cacao Day, June 6.

Napoleon, Death Sesquicentennial — A115a

Die Cut Perf. 12

1971, June 11   Embossed

780A	A115a	1000fr gold	
	b.	Sheet of 1, imperf.	

No. 780b contains one 48x69mm stamp.

Control Tower and Plane — A116

1971, June 26   Litho.   Perf. 14

781	A116	30fr multicolored	22 15

10th anniv. of the Agency for the Security of Aerial Navigation in Africa and Madagascar (ASECNA). See No. C155.

Great Market, Lomé — A117

Tourist publicity: 30fr, Bird-of-paradise flower and sculpture of a man. 40fr, Aledjo Gorge and anubius baboon.

1971, July 17

782	A117	20fr multicolored	15 15
783	A117	30fr multicolored	20 15
784	A117	40fr multicolored	25 15
		Nos. 782-784,C156-C158 (6)	2.00
		Set value	1.00

For surcharge and overprint see Nos. 804, C172.

Great Fetish of Gbatchoume — A118

Religions of Togo: 30fr, Chief Priest in front of Atta Sakuma Temple. 40fr, Annual ceremony of the sacred stone.

1971, July 31   Litho.   Perf. 14½

785	A118	20fr multicolored	15 15
786	A118	30fr multicolored	20 15
787	A118	40fr multicolored	25 15
		Nos. 785-787,C159-C161 (6)	1.85
		Set value	88

No. 777 Overprinted in Silver: "EN MEMOIRE / DOBROVOLSKY - VOLKOV - PATSAYEV / SOYUZ 11"

1971, Aug.   Perf. 12½

788	A114	40fr multicolored	25 15

In memory of the Russian astronauts Lt. Col. Georgi T. Dobrovolsky, Vladislav N. Volkov and Victor I. Patsayev, who died during the Soyuz 11 space mission, June 6-30, 1971. See Nos. C162-C164.

Sapporo '72 Emblem and Speed Skating — A119

Sapporo '72 Emblem and: 10fr, Slalom skiing. 20fr, Figure skating, pairs. 30fr, Bobsledding. 50fr, Ice hockey.

1971, Oct. 30   Perf. 14

789	A119	1fr multicolored	15 15
790	A119	10fr multicolored	15 15
791	A119	20fr multicolored	15 15
792	A119	30fr multicolored	20 15
793	A119	50fr multicolored	35 16
		Nos. 789-793,C165 (6)	2.40
		Set value	92

11th Winter Olympic Games, Sapporo, Japan, Feb. 3-13, 1972.

Toy Crocodile and UNICEF Emblem — A120

Toys and UNICEF Emblem: 30fr, Fawn and butterfly. 40fr, Monkey. 50fr, Elephants.

1971, Nov. 27

794	A120	20fr multicolored	15 15
795	A120	30fr violet & multi	20 15
796	A120	40fr green & multi	25 15
797	A120	50fr bister & multi	35 16
		Nos. 794-797,C167-C168 (6)	1.95
		Set value	86

UNICEF, 25th anniv. For overprints see Nos. 918, C263-C264.

Virgin and Child, by Botticelli
A121

Virgin and Child by: 30fr, Master of the Life of Mary. 40fr, Dürer. 50fr, Veronese.

1971, Dec. 24   Perf. 14x13

798	A121	10fr purple & multi	15 15
799	A121	30fr green & multi	20 15
800	A121	40fr brown & multi	30 15
801	A121	50fr dk blue & multi	40 16
		Nos. 798-801,C169-C170 (6)	2.15
		Set value	1.10

Christmas.

St. Mark's Basilica — A122

Design: 40fr, Rialto Bridge.

1972, Feb. 26   Litho.   Perf. 14

802	A122	30fr multicolored	20 15
803	A122	40fr multicolored	25 15
		Set value	24

UNESCO campaign to save Venice. See No. C171.

No. 784 Surcharged with New Value, Two Bars and "VISITE DU PRESIDENT / NIXON EN CHINE / FEVRIER 1972"

1972, Mar.   Litho.   Perf. 14

804	A117	300fr on 40fr multi	2.00 1.20

Visit of Pres. Richard M. Nixon to the People's Republic of China, Feb. 20-27. See No. C172.

Crucifixion, by Master MS — A123

Easter (Paintings): 30fr, Pietà, by Botticelli.

1972, Mar. 31

805	A123	25fr gold & multi	16 15
806	A123	30fr gold & multi	20 15
807	A123	40fr gold & multi	25 15
		Nos. 805-807,C173-C174 (5)	1.71
		Set value	70

Market value for a particular scarce stamp may remain relatively low if few collectors want it.

Heart, Smith, WHO
Emblem — A124

Video
Telephone — A125

Org. of African and Malagasy Union
Conf. — A124a

Heart, WHO Emblem and: 40fr, Typist. 60fr,
Athlete with javelin.

1972, Apr. 4
808	A124	30fr multicolored	20	15
809	A124	40fr multicolored	22	15
810	A124	60fr multicolored	40	20

"Your heart is your health," World Health Day.
See No. C175.

Die Cut Perf. 12x12½
1972, Apr. 24   Litho. & Embossed
Self-adhesive
810A	A124a	1000fr gold, red &	
		green	

On No. 810A embossing may cut through stamp
and embossed backing paper may not adhere well
to the unused stamps.
For overprint see No. 893A.

1972, June 24   Litho.   Perf. 14
811	A125	40fr violet & multi	25	15

4th World Telecommunications Day. See No.
C176.
For overprints see Nos. 880, C229.

Grating
Cassava — A126

Basketball — A127

Designs: 25fr, Cassava collection by truck, horiz.

1972, June 30
812	A126	25fr yellow & multi	16	15
813	A126	40fr multicolored	25	15
		Set value		22

Cassava production. See Nos. C177-C178.
For overprint and surcharge see Nos. 866-867.

1972, Aug. 26   Litho.   Perf. 14
814	A127	30fr shown	20	15
815	A127	40fr Running	25	15
816	A127	50fr Discus	35	15
	Nos. 814-816,C180-C181 (5)		2.95	1.46

20th Olympic Games, Munich, Aug. 26-Sept. 11.
For overprints see Nos. C234-C235.

Pin-tailed
Whydah — A128

Paul P. Harris,
Rotary
Emblem — A129

Birds: 30fr, Broad-tailed widowbird. 40fr, Yellow-
shouldered widowbird. 60fr, Yellow-tailed
widowbird.

1972, Sept. 9
817	A128	25fr citron & multi	16	15
818	A128	30fr lt blue & multi	22	15
819	A128	40fr multicolored	25	15
820	A128	60fr lt green & multi	40	20
	Nos. 817-820,C182 (5)		1.68	
	Set value			85

1972, Oct. 7   Litho.   Perf. 14

Design: 50fr, Flags of Togo and Rotary Club.

821	A129	40fr green & multi	22	15
822	A129	50fr multicolored	35	16
a.	Souvenir sheet of 2		65	65
	Nos. 821-822,C183-C185 (5)		2.02	1.20

Rotary International, Lomé. No. 822a contains 2
stamps with simulated perforations similar to Nos.
821-822.
For overprints see Nos. 862, 898, C212-C213,
C244-C235.

Mona Lisa, by
Leonardo da
Vinci — A130   25fr REPUBLIQUE TOGOLAISE

Design: 40fr, Virgin and Child, by Giovanni
Bellini.

1972, Oct. 21
823	A130	25fr gold & multi	20	15
824	A130	40fr gold & multi	25	15
	Nos. 823-824,C186-C188 (5)		2.10	1.15

West African Monetary Union Issue
Common Design Type

Design: 40fr, African couple, city, village and
commemorative coin.

1972, Nov. 2   Engr.   Perf. 13
825	CD136	40fr red brn, rose red & gray	22	15

Presidents Pompidou and Eyadema, Party
Headquarters — A131

1972, Nov. 23   Litho.   Perf. 14
826	A131	40fr purple & multi	30	15

Visit of Pres. Georges Pompidou of France to
Togo, Nov. 1972. See No. C189.

Anunciation,
Painter
Unknown
A132

Paintings: 30fr, Nativity, Master of Vyshchibrod.
40fr, Like 25fr.

1972, Dec. 23
827	A132	25fr gold & multi	16	15
828	A132	30fr gold & multi	20	15
829	A132	40fr gold & multi	25	15
	Nos. 827-829,C191-C193 (6)		2.46	1.35

Christmas.

Raoul Follereau and Lepers — A133

1973, Jan. 23   Photo.   Perf. 14x13½
830	A133	40fr violet & green	25	15

World Leprosy Day and 20th anniv. of the Raoul
Follereau Foundation. See No. C194.

WHO Emblem
A134

Christ on the Cross
A135

1973, Apr. 7   Photo.   Perf. 14x13
831	A134	30fr blue & multi	20	15
832	A134	40fr dp yellow & multi	25	15
	Set value			24

WHO, 25th anniv.

1973, Apr. 21   Litho.   Perf. 14
833	A135	25fr shown	16	15
834	A135	30fr Pietá	20	15
835	A135	40fr Ascension	25	15
	Set value			32

Easter. See No. C195.

Eugene Cernan, Ronald Evans, Harrison
Schmitt, Apollo 17 Badge — A136

Design: 40fr, Lunar rover on moon.

1973, June 2   Litho.   Perf. 14
836	A136	30fr multicolored	20	15
837	A136	40fr multicolored	25	15
	Set value			24

Apollo 17 moon mission, Dec. 7-19, 1972. See
Nos. C196-C197.

Scouts Pitching
Tent — A137

Nicolaus
Copernicus — A138

Designs: 20fr, Campfire, horiz. 30fr, Rope climbing. 40fr, Like 10fr.

1973, June 30
838	A137	10fr multicolored	15	15
839	A137	20fr multicolored	15	15
840	A137	30fr violet & multi	20	15
841	A137	40fr ocher & multi	25	15
	Nos. 838-841,C198-C199 (6)		2.95	
	Set value			1.40

24th Boy Scout World Conference (1st in Africa),
Nairobi, Kenya, July 16-21.
For overprints see Nos. C265-C266.

1973, July 18

Designs: 10fr, Heliocentric system. 30fr, Seated
figure of Astronomy and spacecrafts around earth
and moon. 40fr, Astrolabe.

842	A138	10fr multicolored	15	15
843	A138	15fr multicolored	15	15
844	A138	30fr multicolored	20	15
845	A138	40fr lilac & multi	25	15
	Nos. 842-845,C200-C201 (6)		2.05	
	Set value			1.05

Copernicus (1473-1543), Polish astronomer.

Red Cross
Ambulance
Crew — A139

1973, Aug. 4
846	A139	40fr multicolored	25	15

Togolese Red Cross. See No. C202.
For overprints see Nos. 846, C294.

Teacher and Students — A140

Designs: 40fr, Hut and man reading under tree,
vert.

1973, Aug. 18   Litho.   Perf. 14
847	A140	30fr multicolored	20	15
848	A140	40fr multicolored	25	15
	Set value			24

Literacy campaign. See No. C203.

African Postal Union Issue
Common Design Type
1973, Sept. 12   Engr.   Perf. 13
849	CD137	100fr yel, red & claret	70	35

INTERPOL Emblem
and Headquarters
A141

Weather Vane
and WMO
Emblem
A142

1973, Sept. 29 Photo. Perf. 13½x14
850 A141 30fr yel, brn & gray grn   20 15
851 A141 40fr yel grn, bl & mag   25 15
    Set value   24

50th anniv. of Intl. Criminal Police Org.

1973, Oct. 4   Perf. 14x13
852 A142 40fr yel, dp brn & grn   25 15

Intl. meteorological cooperation, cent. See No.
C204.

Type of 1967

Designs: 25fr, Old and new locomotives, No.
795. 30fr, Mail coach and bus, No. 613. 90fr,
Mail boat and ship, Nos. C61 and 469.

1973, Oct. 20 Photo. Perf. 14x13
853 A79 25fr multicolored   20 15
854 A79 30fr purple & green   25 15
855 A79 90fr dk blue & multi   65 30
    Set value   48

75th anniv. of Togolese postal service. See No.
C205.

Republique
TOGOLAISE
John F.
Kennedy and
Adolf
Schaerf — A143

Virgin and Child,
Italy, 15th
Century — A144

Designs: 30fr, Kennedy and Harold MacMillan.
40fr, Kennedy and Konrad Adenauer.

1973, Nov. 22 Litho. Perf. 14
856 A143 20fr blk, gray & vio   15 15
857 A143 30fr blk, rose & brn   20 15
858 A143 40fr blk, lt grn & grn   25 18
    Nos. 856-858,C206-C208 (6)   3.30 1.81

John F. Kennedy (1917-1963).

No. 758 Surcharged with New Value, 2
Bars and Overprinted in Ultramarine:
"SECHERESSE SOLIDARITE AFRICAINE"
1973, Dec.   Perf. 13x14
859 A110 100fr on 30fr multi   70 50

African solidarity in drought emergency.

1973, Dec. 22 Litho. Perf. 14
Design: 30fr, Adoration of the Kings, Italy, 15th
century.

860 A144 25fr gold & multi   16 15
861 A144 30fr gold & multi   22 15

Christmas. See Nos. C210-C211.

No. 821 Overprinted: "PREMIERE
CONVENTION / 210eme DISTRICT /
FEVRIER 1974 / LOME"
1974, Feb. 21 Litho. Perf. 14
862 A129 40fr green & multi   25 18

First convention of Rotary Intl., District 210,
Lomé, Feb. 22-24. See Nos. C212-C213.

Soccer and
Games'
Cup — A145

Designs: Various soccer scenes and games' cup.

1974, Mar. 2 Litho. Perf. 14
863 A145 20fr lt blue & multi   16 15
864 A145 30fr yellow & multi   26 15
865 A145 40fr lilac & multi   30 15
    Nos. 863-865,C214-C216 (6)   3.94 1.94

World Soccer Championships, Munich, Germany, June 13-July 7.

Nos. 812-813 Overprinted and Surcharged:
"10e ANNIVERSAIRE DU P.A.M."
1974, Mar. 25 Litho. Perf. 14
866 A126 40fr multicolored   35 18
867 A126 100fr on 25fr multi   75 50

10th anniv. of World Food Program. Overprint
on No. 866 is in one line; 2 lines on No. 867 and 2
bars through old denomination.

Girl Before Mirror, by
Picasso — A146

Mailman, UPU
Emblem — A148

Kpeme
Village and
Wharf
A147

Paintings by Picasso: 30fr, The Turkish Shawl.
40fr, Mandolin and Guitar.

1974, Apr. 6
868 A146 20fr vio blue & multi   15 15
869 A146 30fr maroon & multi   22 15
870 A146 40fr multicolored   30 15
    Nos. 868-870,C217-C219 (6)   3.37 1.75

Pablo Picasso (1881-1973), Spanish painter.

1974, Apr. 20
Design: 40fr, Tropicana tourist village.

871 A147 30fr multicolored   22 15
872 A147 40fr multicolored   25 15

See Nos. C220-C221.

1974, May 10 Litho. Perf. 14
Design: 40fr, Mailman, different uniform.

873 A148 30fr salmon & multi   22 15
874 A148 40fr multicolored   30 15

UPU, centenary. See Nos. C222-C223.

Map and Flags
of Members
A148a

1974, May 29 Litho. Perf. 13x12½
875 A148a 40fr blue & multi   30 22

15th anniversary of the Council of Accord.

Fisherman
with
Net — A149

Design: 40fr, Fisherman casting net from canoe.

1974, June 22 Litho. Perf. 14
876 A149 30fr multicolored   25 15
877 A149 40fr multicolored   30 15
    Nos. 876-877,C224-C226 (5)   2.70 1.45

Lagoon fishing.

Pioneer Communicating with
Earth — A150

Design: 30fr, Radar station and satellite, vert.

1974, July 6   Perf. 14
878 A150 30fr multicolored   22 15
879 A150 40fr multicolored   30 15

US Jupiter space probe. See #C227-C228.

No. 811 Overprinted with INTERNABA
Emblem in Silver Similar to No. C229
1974, July
880 A125 40fr multicolored   1.10 55

INTERNABA 1974 Intl. Philatelic Exhibition,
Basel, June 7-16. See No. C229.

Tympanotomus
Radula — A151

Designs: Seashells.

1974, July 13 Litho. Perf. 14
881 A151 10fr shown   15 15
882 A151 20fr Tonna galea   18 15
883 A151 30fr Conus mercator   25 15
884 A151 40fr Cardium costatum   38 15
    Nos. 881-884,C230-C231 (6)   2.01
    Set value   1.00

Groom with
Horses
A152

Design: 40fr, Trotting horses.

1974, Aug. 3 Litho. Perf. 14
885 A152 30fr multicolored   22 15
886 A152 40fr multicolored   30 15

Horse racing. See Nos. C232-C233.

Leopard
A153

1974, Sept. 7 Litho. Perf. 14
887 A153 20fr shown   15 15
888 A153 30fr Giraffes   18 15
889 A153 40fr Elephants   25 15
    Nos. 887-889,C236-C237 (5)   1.73 1.10

Wild animals of West Africa.

1974, Oct. 14
890 A153 30fr Herding cattle   18 15
891 A153 40fr Milking cow   25 15
    Set value   24

Domestic animals. See Nos. C238-C239.

Churchill
and Frigate
F390
A154

Design: 40fr, Churchill and fighter planes.

1974, Nov. 1 Photo. Perf. 13x13½
892 A154 30fr multicolored   22 15
893 A154 40fr multicolored   30 15
    Set value   24

Winston Churchill (1874-1965). See Nos. C240-
C241.

No. 810A Ovptd. "Inauguration de l'hotel
de la Paix 9-1-75"
Litho. & Embossed
1975, Jan. 9   Perf. 12½
Self-adhesive
893A A124a 1000fr gold, red & grn

On No. 893A embossing may cut through stamp
and embossed backing paper may not adhere well
to the unused stamps.

Chlamydocarya Macrocarpa — A155

Flowers of Togo: 25fr, Strelitzia reginae, vert.
30fr, Storphanthus sarmentosus, vert. 60fr, Clerodendrum scandens.

1975, Feb. 15 Litho. Perf. 14
894 A155 25fr multicolored   15 15
895 A155 30fr multicolored   18 15
896 A155 40fr multicolored   25 16
897 A155 60fr multicolored   38 18
    Nos. 894-897,C242-C243 (6)   2.61 1.39

No. 821 Overprinted: "70e
ANNIVERSAIRE / 23 FEVRIER 1975"
1975, Feb. 23 Litho. Perf. 14
898 A129 40fr green & multi   32 15

Rotary Intl., 70th anniv. See Nos. C244-C245.

Radio Station,
Kamina
A156

Designs: 30fr, Benedictine Monastery, Zogbe-
gan. 40fr, Causeway, Atchinedji. 60fr, Ayome
Waterfalls.

1975, Mar. 1   Photo.   Perf. 13x14
899	A156	25fr multicolored	15	15
900	A156	40fr multicolored	18	15
901	A156	50fr multicolored	25	16
902	A156	60fr multicolored	38	22
		Set value		58

Jesus Mocked, by El Greco — A157

Paintings: 30fr, Crucifixion, by Master Janoslet. 40fr, Descent from the Cross, by Bellini. 90fr, Pietà, painter unknown.

1975, Apr. 19   Litho.   Perf. 14
903	A157	25fr black & multi	18	15
904	A157	30fr black & multi	22	15
905	A157	40fr black & multi	30	15
906	A157	90fr black & multi	55	32
		Nos. 903-906,C246-C247 (6)	2.90	1.57

Easter.

Stilt Walking, Togolese Flag — A158

Design: 30fr, Flag and dancers.

1975, Apr. 26   Litho.   Perf. 14
907	A158	25fr multicolored	18	15
908	A158	30fr multicolored	22	15
		Set value		22

15th anniv. of independence. See Nos. C248-C249.

Rabbit Hunter with Club A159

Design: 40fr, Beaver hunter with bow and arrow.

1975, May 24   Photo.   Perf. 13x13½
909	A159	30fr multicolored	18	15
910	A159	40fr multicolored	25	16
		Set value		25

See Nos. C250-C251.

Pounding Palm Nuts — A160

Design: 40fr, Man extracting palm oil, vert.

1975, June 28   Litho.   Perf. 14
911	A160	30fr multicolored	22	15
912	A160	40fr multicolored	25	15

Palm oil production. See Nos. C252-C253.

Apollo-Soyuz Link-up — A161

1975, July 15
913	A161	30fr multicolored	18	15
		Nos. 913,C254-C258 (6)	2.88	1.50

Apollo Soyuz space test project (Russo-American cooperation), launching July 15; link-up July 17.

Women's Heads, IWY Emblem — A162

1975, July 26   Litho.   Perf. 12½
914	A162	30fr blue & multi	18	15
915	A162	40fr multicolored	25	16
		Set value		25

International Women's Year.

Dr. Schweitzer and Children — A163

1975, Aug. 23   Litho.   Perf. 14x13½
916	A163	40fr multicolored	25	18

Dr. Albert Schweitzer (1875-1965), medical missionary and musician. See #C259-C261.

Merchant Writing Letter, by Vittore Carpaccio — A164

Virgin and Child, by Mantegna — A165

1975, Oct. 9   Litho.   Perf. 14
917	A164	40fr multicolored	25	18

Intl. Letter Writing Week. See No. C262.

No. 797 Overprinted: "30ème Anniversaire / des Nations-Unies"

1975, Oct. 24   Litho.   Perf. 14
918	A120	50fr multi	32	22

UN, 30th anniv. See Nos. C263-C264.

1975, Dec. 20   Litho.   Perf. 14

Paintings of the Virgin and Child: 30fr, El Greco. 40fr, Barend van Orley.
919	A165	20fr red & multi	15	15
920	A165	30fr bl & multi	22	15
921	A165	40fr red & multi	30	15
		Nos. 919-921,C267-C269 (6)	2.82	1.42

Christmas.

Crashed Plane and Pres. Eyadema A166

1976, Jan. 24   Photo.   Perf. 13
922	A166	50fr multi	55	38
923	A166	60fr multi	75	45

Airplane crash at Sara-kawa, Jan. 24, 1974, in which Pres. Eyadema escaped injury.

1976 Summer Olympics, Montreal A166a

Litho. & Embossed
1976, Feb. 24   Perf. 11
923A	A166a	1000fr Diving	
923B	A166a	1000fr Track	
923C	A166a	1000fr Pole vault	
923D	A166a	1000fr Equestrian	
923E	A166a	1000fr Cycling	

Exist imperf.

Frigates on the Hudson — A167

American Bicentennial: 50fr, George Washington, by Gilbert Stuart, and Bicentennial emblem, vert.

1976, Mar. 3   Litho.   Perf. 14
924	A167	35fr multicolored	22	15
925	A167	50fr multicolored	30	22
		Nos. 924-925,C270-C273 (6)	2.90	1.53

For overprints see Nos. C280-C283.

ACP and CEE Emblems A168

Design: 50fr, Map of Africa, Europe and Asia.

1976, Apr. 24   Photo.   Perf. 13x14
926	A168	10fr orange & multi	15	15
927	A168	50fr pink & multi	30	22
		Set value		26

First anniv. of signing of treaty between Togo and European Common Market, Lomé, Feb. 28, 1975. See Nos. C274-C275.

Cable-laying Ship — A169

Design: 30fr, Telephone, tape recorder, speaker.

1976, Mar. 10   Photo.   Perf. 13x14
928	A169	25fr ultra & multi	15	15
929	A169	30fr pink & multi	18	15

Centenary of first telephone call by Alexander Graham Bell, Mar. 10, 1876. See Nos. C276-C277.

Blind Man and Insect — A170

Marine Exhibition Hall — A171

1976, Apr. 8   Perf. 14x13
930	A170	50fr brt grn & multi	30	18

World Health Day: "Foresight prevents blindness." See No. C278.

Air Post Type, 1976, and Type A171

Design: 10fr, Pylon, flags of Ghana, Togo and Dahomey.

1976   Litho.   Perf. 14
931	A171	5fr multicolored	15	15
932	AP19	10fr multicolored	15	15
933	A171	50fr multicolored	30	22
		Set value		42	32

Marine Exhibition, 10th anniv. (5fr, 50fr). Ghana-Togo-Dahomey electric power grid, 1st anniversary (10fr). See No. C279.
Issue dates: 50fr, May 8; 5fr, 10fr, August.

Running — A172

Montreal Olympic Emblem and: 30fr, Kayak. 50fr, High jump.

1976, June 15   Photo.   Perf. 14x13
934	A172	25fr multicolored	18	15
935	A172	30fr multicolored	20	15
936	A172	50fr multicolored	38	20
		Nos. 934-936,C284-C286 (6)	3.11	1.82

21st Olympic Games, Montreal, Canada, July 17-Aug. 1.
For overprints see Nos. 947, C298-C299.

Titan 3 and Viking Emblem — A173

Design: 50fr, Viking trajectory, Earth to Mars.

1976, July 15   Litho.   Perf. 14
937	A173	30fr blue & multi	18	15
938	A173	50fr rose & multi	30	18
		Nos. 937-938,C287-C290 (6)	2.86	1.61

US Viking Mars missions.

Young Routy at Celeyran, by Toulouse-Lautrec A174

Mohammed Ali Jinnah, Flags of Togo and Pakistan A176

Adoration of the Shepherds, by Pontormo — A175

Paintings by Toulouse-Lautrec: 20fr, Model in Studio. 35fr, Louis Pascal, portrait.

1976, Aug. 7   Litho.   Perf. 14
939 A174 10fr black & multi   15   15
940 A174 20fr black & multi   15   15
941 A174 35fr black & multi   22   15
    Nos. 939-941,C291-C293 (6)   2.35
    Set value   1.20

Henri Toulouse-Lautrec (1864-1901), French painter, 75th death anniversary.

No. 846 Overprinted: "Journée / Internationale / de l'Enfance"
1976, Nov. 27   Litho.   Perf. 14
942 A139 40fr multi   22   15

Intl. Children's Day. See No. C294.

1976, Dec. 18
Paintings: 30fr, Nativity, by Carlo Crivelli. 50fr, Virgin and Child, by Jacopo da Pontormo.

943 A175 25fr multi   15   15
944 A175 30fr multi   18   15
945 A175 50fr multi   30   18
    Nos. 943-945,C295-C297 (6)   2.66   1.58

Christmas.

1976, Dec. 24   Litho.   Perf. 13
946 A176 50fr multi   30   18

Jinnah (1876-1948), first Governor General of Pakistan.

No. 936 Overprinted: "CHAMPIONS OLYMPIQUES / SAUT EN HAUTEUR / POLOGNE"
1976, Dec.   Photo.   Perf. 14x13
947 A172 50fr multi   32   18

Olympic winners. See Nos. C298-C299.

Queen Elizabeth II, Silver Jubilee A176a

Designs: No. 947A, Portrait. No. 947B, Wearing coronation regalia.

Litho. & Embossed
1977, Jan. 10   Perf. 11
947A A176a 1000fr silver & multi
Souvenir Sheet
947B A176a 1000fr silver & multi
        Exist imperf.

Kpeme Phosphate Mine, Sara-kawa Crash A177

1977, Jan. 13   Photo.   Perf. 13x14
948 A177 50fr multi   30   18

10th anniv. of presidency of Etienne Eyadema. See Nos. C300-C301.

Gongophone A178

Musical Instruments: 10fr, Tamtam, vert. 25fr, Dondon.

1977, Feb. 7   Litho.   Perf. 14
949 A178 5fr multi   15   15
950 A178 10fr multi   15   15
951 A178 25fr multi   15   15
    Nos. 949-951,C302-C304 (6)   1.75
    Set value   75

Victor Hugo and his Home A179

1977, Feb. 26   Perf. 13x14
952 A179 50fr multi   30   18

Victor Hugo (1802-1885), French writer, 175th birth anniversary. See No. C305.
For overprints see Nos. 959, C316.

Beethoven and Birthplace, Bonn — A180

Design: 50fr, Bronze bust, 1812, and Heiligen-stadt home.

1977, Mar. 7   Perf. 14
953 A180 30fr multi   18   15
954 A180 50fr multi   30   18

Ludwig van Beethoven (1770-1827), composer. See Nos. C306-C307.

Benz, 1894, Germany — A181

Early Automobiles: 50fr, De Dion Bouton, 1903, France.

1977, Apr. 11   Litho.   Perf. 14
955 A181 35fr multi   22   15
956 A181 50fr multi   30   18
    Nos. 955-956,C308-C311 (6)   2.90   1.66

Lindbergh, Ground Crew and Spirit of St. Louis — A182

Design: 50fr, Lindbergh and Spirit of St. Louis.

1977, May 9
957 A182 25fr multi   18   15
958 A182 50fr multi   38   18
    Nos. 957-958,C312-C315 (6)   2.76   1.11

Charles A. Lindbergh's solo transatlantic flight from New York to Paris, 50th anniv.

No. 952 Overprinted: "10ème ANNIVERSAIRE DU / CONSEIL INTERNATIONAL / DE LA LANGUE FRANCAISE"
1977, May 17   Litho.   Perf. 14
959 A179 50fr multi   38   18

Intl. French Language Council, 10th anniv. See No. C316.

African Slender-snouted Crocodile — A183

Endangered wildlife: 15fr, Nile crocodile.

1977, June 13
960 A183 5fr multi   15   15
961 A183 15fr multi   15   15
    Nos. 960-961,C317-C320 (6)   3.35
    Set value   92

Agriculture School, Tove — A184

1977, July 11   Litho.   Perf. 14
962 A184 50fr multi   38   18

Agricultural development. See Nos. C321-C323.

Landscape with Cart, by Peter Paul Rubens (1577-1640) — A185

Rubens Painting: 35fr, Exchange of the Princesses at Hendaye, 1623.

1977, Aug. 8
963 A185 15fr multi   15   15
964 A185 35fr multi   25   15
    Set value   20

See Nos. C324-C325.

Orbiter 101 on Ground — A186

Designs: 30fr, Launching of Orbiter, vert. 50fr, Ejection of propellant tanks at take-off.

1977, Oct. 4   Litho.   Perf. 14
965 A186 20fr multi   15   15
966 A186 30fr multi   22   15
967 A186 50fr multi   38   18
    Nos. 965-967,C326-C328 (6)   3.35   1.17

Space shuttle trials in the US.

Lafayette Arriving in Montpelier, Vt. — A187

Design: 25fr, Lafayette, age 19, vert.

1977, Nov. 7   Perf. 14x13, 13x14
968 A187 25fr multi   18   15
969 A187 50fr multi   38   18
    Set value   26

Arrival of the Marquis de Lafayette in North America, 200th anniv. See Nos. C329-C330.

Lenin, Cruiser Aurora, Red Flag — A188

1977, Nov. 7   Litho.   Perf. 12
970 A188 50fr multi   38   18

Russian October Revolution, 60th anniv.

Virgin and Child, by Lorenzo Lotto — A189

Edward Jenner — A190

Virgin and Child by: 30fr, Carlo Bellini. 50fr, Cosimo Tura.

1977, Dec. 19   Perf. 14
971 A189 20fr multi   15   15
972 A189 30fr multi   22   15
973 A189 50fr multi   38   18
    Nos. 971-973,C331-C333 (6)   3.40   1.17

Christmas.

Perf. 14x13, 13x14
1978, Jan. 9   Litho.

Design: 20fr, Vaccination clinic, horiz.

974 A190 5fr multi   15   15
975 A190 50fr multi   15   15
    Set value   20   15

Worldwide eradication of smallpox. See Nos. C334-C335.

Orville and Wilbur Wright — A191

Design: 50fr, Wilbur Wright flying at Kill Devil Hill, 1902.

1978, Feb. 6   Litho.   Perf. 14
976	A191	35fr multi	25	15
977	A191	50fr multi	38	18

Nos. 976-977,C336-C339 (6)   4.88 1.61

75th anniversary of first motorized flight.

Anniversaries and Events — A192

Designs: No. 978, High jump. No. 979, Westminster Abbey. No. 980, Soccer players, World Cup. No. 981, Apollo 8. No. 982, Duke of Wellington, by Goya. No. 983, Hurdles. No. 984, Coronation coach. No. 985, Soccer players. No. 986, Apollo launch. No. 987, Dona Isabel Cobos de Porcel, by Goya.

1978, Mar. 13   Litho.   Perf. 11
978	A192	1000fr gold & multi	
979	A192	1000fr gold & multi	
980	A192	1000fr gold & multi	
981	A192	1000fr gold & multi	
982	A192	1000fr gold & multi	

Souvenir Sheets
983	A192	1000fr gold & multi
984	A192	1000fr gold & multi
985	A192	1000fr gold & multi
986	A192	1000fr gold & multi
987	A192	1000fr gold & multi

Nos. 978, 983, 1980 Summer Olympics, Moscow. Nos. 979, 984, Coronation of Queen Elizabeth II, 25th anniv. Nos. 980, 985, 1978 World Cup Soccer Championships, Argentina. Nos. 981, 986, 1st manned lunar orbit, 10th anniv. Nos. 982, 987, Death sesquicent. of Francisco Goya.

For overprints see Nos. 1056A-1056B, 1094A-1094B.

Exist imperf.

John, the Evangelist and Eagle — A197

Evangelists: 10fr, Luke and ox. 25fr, Mark and lion. 30fr, Matthew and angel.

1978, Mar. 20   Litho.   Perf. 13½x14
988	A197	5fr multi	15	15
989	A197	10fr multi	15	15
990	A197	25fr multi	18	15
991	A197	30fr multi	22	15
a.		Souvenir sheet of 4	60	60
		Set value	50	28

No. 991a contains one each of Nos. 988-991 with simulated perforations.

Anchor, Fishing Harbor, Lomé A199

1978, Apr. 26   Photo.   Perf. 13
997	A199	25fr multi	18 15

See Nos. C340-C342.

Venera I, USSR — A200   Soccer — A201

Designs: 30fr, Pioneer, US, horiz. 50fr, Venera, fuel base and antenna.

1978, May 8   Litho.   Perf. 14
998	A200	20fr multi	15	15
999	A200	30fr multi	22	15
1000	A200	50fr multi	38	18

Nos. 998-1000,C343-C345 (6)   3.40 1.21

US Pioneer and USSR Venera space missions.

1978, June 5   Perf. 14

Design: 50fr, Soccer players and Argentina '78 emblem.
1001	A201	30fr multi	22	15
1002	A201	50fr multi	38	18

Nos. 1001-1002,C346-C349 (6)   4.95 1.51

11th World Cup Soccer Championship, Argentina, June 1-25.

Celerifère, 1818 A202

History of the Bicycle: 50fr, First bicycle sidecar, c. 1870, vert.

Perf. 13x14, 14x13
1978, July 10   Photo.
1003	A202	25fr multi	18	15
1004	A202	50fr multi	38	18

Nos. 1003-1004,C350-C353 (6)   2.76 1.15

Thomas A. Edison, Sound Waves — A203   Dunant's Birthplace, Geneva — A204

Design: 50fr, Victor's His Master's Voice phonograph, 1905, and dancing couple.

1978, July 8   Photo.   Perf. 14x13
1005	A203	30fr multicolored	22	15
1006	A203	50fr multicolored	38	18

Nos. 1005-1006,C354-C357 (6)   4.90 1.53

Centenary of the phonograph, invented by Thomas Alva Edison.

1978, Sept. 4   Photo.   Perf. 14x13

Designs: 10fr, Henri Dunant and red cross. 25fr, Help on battlefield, 1864, and red cross.
1007	A204	5fr Prus bl & red	15	15
1008	A204	10fr red brn & red	15	15
1009	A204	25fr grn & red	18	15
		Set value	30	18

Henri Dunant (1828-1910), founder of Red Cross, birth sesquicentennial. See No. C358.

Threshing, by Raoul Dufy — A205

Painting: 50fr, Horsemen on Seashore, by Paul Gauguin.

1978, Nov. 6   Litho.   Perf. 14
1010	A205	25fr multi	18	15
1011	A205	50fr multi	38	18

Nos. 1010-1011,C359-C362 (6)   3.36 1.75

Eiffel Tower, Paris — A206   Virgin and Child, by Antonello da Messina — A207

1978, Nov. 27   Photo.   Perf. 14x13
1012	A206	50fr multi	38 18

Centenary of the Congress of Paris. See Nos. C365-C367.

1978, Dec. 18   Litho.   Perf. 14

Paintings (Virgin and Child): 30fr, by Carlo Crivelli. 50fr, by Cosimo Tura.
1013	A207	20fr multi	15	15
1014	A207	30fr multi	22	15
1015	A207	50fr multi	38	18

Nos. 1013-1015,C368-C370 (6)   3.35 1.78

Christmas.

Capt. Cook's Ship off New Zealand — A208   Entry into Jerusalem — A209

Design: 50fr, Endeavour in drydock, N.E. Coast of Australia, horiz.

1979, Feb. 12   Litho.   Perf. 14
1016	A208	25fr multi	18	15
1017	A208	50fr multi	38	18

Nos. 1016-1017,C371-C374 (6)   3.41 2.25

200th death anniv. of Capt. James Cook.

1979, Apr. 9

Easter: 40fr, The Last Supper, horiz. 50fr, Descent from the Cross, horiz.
1018	A209	30fr multi	22	15
1019	A209	40fr multi	30	15
1020	A209	50fr multi	38	18

Nos. 1018-1020,C375-C377 (6)   3.35 1.68

Einstein Observatory, Potsdam — A210

Design: 50fr, Einstein and James Ramsay MacDonald, Berlin, 1931.

1979, July 2   Photo.   Perf. 14x13
1021	A210	15fr multi	25	15
1022	A210	50fr multi	38	18

Nos. 1021-1022,C380-C383 (6)   3.68 1.81

Albert Einstein (1879-1955), theoretical physicist.

Children and Children's Village Emblem A211   Man Planting Tree A212

IYC: 10fr, Mother and children. 15fr, Map of Africa, Children's Village emblem, horiz. 20fr, Woman and children walking to Children's Village, horiz. 25fr, Children sitting under African fan palm. 30fr, Map of Togo with location of Children's Villages.

1979, July 30   Photo.   Perf. 14x13
1023	A211	5fr multi	15	15
1024	A211	10fr multi	15	15
1025	A211	15fr multi	15	15
1026	A211	20fr multi	15	15
1027	A211	25fr multi	18	15
1028	A211	30fr multi	22	15
a.		Souv. sheet of 2, #1027-1028	45	
		Set value	78	42

1979, Aug. 13   Perf. 14x13
1029	A212	50fr lil & grn	38 18

Second Arbor Day. See No. C384.

Sir Rowland Hill (1795-1879), Originator of Penny Postage — A213   Olympic Flame, Lake Placid 80 Emblem, Slalom — A215

Norris Locomotive, 1843 — A214

Designs: 30fr, French mail-sorting office, 18th century, horiz. 50fr, Mailbox, Paris, 1850.

1979, Aug. 27
1030 A213 20fr multi		15	15
1031 A213 30fr multi		22	15
1032 A213 50fr multi		38	18
Nos. 1030-1032,C385-C387 (6)		3.40	1.78

1979, Oct. 1   Litho.   Perf. 14

Design: 35fr, Stephenson's "Rocket," 1829, vert.

1033 A214 35fr multi		25	15
1034 A214 50fr multi		38	18
Nos. 1033-1034,C388-C391 (6)		3.63	1.81

1979, Oct. 18   Litho.   Perf. 13½

1980 Olympic Emblems, Olympic Flame and: 30fr, Yachting 50fr, Discus.

1035 A215 20fr multi		15	15
1036 A215 30fr multi		22	15
1037 A215 50fr multi		38	18
Nos. 1035-1037,C392-C394 (6)		3.40	1.78

13th Winter Olympic Games, Lake Placid, NY, Feb. 12-24, 1980. (90fr); 22nd Summer Olympic Games, Moscow, July 19-Aug. 3, 1980.

Catholic Priests A216

Design: 30fr, Native praying, vert.

1979, Oct. 29   Perf. 13x14
1038 A216 30fr multi		22	15
1039 A216 50fr multi		38	18

Religions in Togo. See Nos. C396-C397.

Astronaut Walking on Moon — A217

Design: 50fr, Space capsule orbiting moon.

1979, Nov. 5
1040 A217 35fr multi		25	15
1041 A217 50fr multi		38	18
Nos. 1040-1041,C398-C401 (6)		4.88	2.40

Apollo 11 moon landing, 10th anniversary.

Telecom 79 — A218

1979, Nov. 26   Photo.   Perf. 13x14
1042 A218 50fr multi		38	18

3rd World Telecommunications Exhibition, Geneva, Sept. 20-26. See No. C402.

Holy Family — A219   Rotary Emblem — A220

Christmas: 30fr, Virgin and Child. 50fr, Adoration of the Kings.

1979, Dec. 17   Litho.   Perf. 14
1043 A219 20fr multi		15	15
1044 A219 30fr multi		22	15
1045 A219 50fr multi		38	18
Nos. 1043-1045,C403-C405 (6)		3.35	1.78

1980, Jan. 14

Rotary Emblem and: 30fr, Anniversary emblem. 40fr, Paul P. Harris, Rotary founder.

1046 A220 25fr multi		18	15
1047 A220 30fr multi		22	15
1048 A220 40fr multi		30	15
Nos. 1046-1048,C406-C408 (6)		3.30	1.75

Rotary International, 75th anniversary.

Biathlon, Lake Placid '80 Emblem — A221

1980, Jan. 31   Litho.   Perf. 13½
1049 A221 50fr multi		38	18

13th Winter Olympic Games, Lake Placid, NY, Feb. 12-24. See Nos. C409-C412.

1980 Winter Olympics, Lake Placid — A221a

Gold medalist: No. 1049F, Hanni Wenzel, Liechtenstein, women's slalom. No. 1049G, Eric Heiden, US, men's speed skating. No. 1049H, Jouko Tormanen, Finland, 90-meter ski jumping. No. 1049I, Erich Schaerer, Josef Benz, Switzerland, 2-man bobsled. No. 1049J, US, ice hockey.

1980   Litho.   Perf. 11
Souvenir Sheets
1049F A221a 1000fr gold & multi			
1049G A221a 1000fr gold & multi			
1049H A221a 1000fr gold & multi			
1049I A221a 1000fr gold & multi			
1049J A221a 1000fr gold & multi			

Exist imperf.

Swimming, Moscow '80 Emblem — A222

1980, Feb. 29   Litho.   Perf. 13½
1050 A222 20fr shown		18	15
1051 A222 30fr Gymnastics		25	15
1052 A222 50fr Running		45	21
Nos. 1050-1052,C413-C415 (6)		5.83	2.98

22nd Summer Olympic Games, Moscow, July 19-Aug. 3.

Christ and the Angels, by Andrea Mantegna — A223

Easter 1980 (Paintings by): 40fr, Carlo Crivelli. 50fr, Jacopo Pontormo.

1980, Mar. 31   Perf. 14
1053 A223 30fr multi		22	15
1054 A223 40fr multi		30	15
1055 A223 50fr multi		38	18
Nos. 1053-1055,C416-C418 (6)		3.30	1.68

Jet over Map of Africa — A224

1980, Mar. 24   Litho.   Perf. 12½
1056 A224 50fr multi		38	18

ASECNA (Air Safety Board), 20th anniv. See No. C419.

Nos. 979, 984 Ovptd. "Londres / 1980"
Litho. & Embossed
1980, May 6   Perf. 11
1056A A192 1000fr gold & multi			

Souvenir Sheet
1056B A192 1000fr gold & multi			

12th World Telecommunications Day — A225

1980, May 17   Photo.   Perf. 14x13½
1057 A225 50fr multi		38	18

See No. C420.

Red Cross over Globe Showing Lomé, Togo — A226

1980, June 16   Photo.   Perf. 14x13
1058 A226 50fr multi		38	18

Togolese Red Cross. See No. C421.

Jules Verne (1828-1905), French Science Fiction Writer — A227

Baroness James de Rothschild, by Ingres — A228

Design: 50fr, Shark (20,000 Leagues Under the Sea).

1980, July 14   Litho.   Perf. 14
1059 A227 30fr multi		22	15
1060 A227 50fr multi		38	18
Nos. 1059-1060,C422-C425 (6)		3.55	1.78

1980, Aug. 29   Litho.   Perf. 14

Paintings by Jean Auguste Dominique Ingres (1780-1867): 30fr, Napoleon I on Imperial Throne. 40fr, Don Pedro of Toledo and Henri IV.

1061 A228 25fr multi		18	15
1062 A228 30fr multi		22	15
1063 A228 40fr multi		30	15
Nos. 1061-1063,C426-C428 (6)		3.30	1.75

Minnie Holding Mirror for Leopard A229

Disney Characters and Animals from Fazao Reserve: 2fr, Goofy (Dingo) cleaning teeth of hippopotamus. 3fr, Donald holding snout of crocodile. 4fr, Donald dangling over cliff from horn of rhinoceros. 5fr, Goofy riding water buffalo. 10fr, Monkey taking picture of Mickey. 100fr, Mickey as doctor examining giraffe with sore throat. 200fr, Pluto in party hat. No. 1071, Elephant giving shower to Goofy. No. 1072, Lion carrying Goofy by seat of his pants. No. 1072A, Pluto.

1980, Sept. 15   Perf. 11
1064 A229 1fr multi		15	15
1065 A229 2fr multi		15	15
1066 A229 3fr multi		15	15
1067 A229 4fr multi		15	15
1068 A229 5fr multi		15	15
1069 A229 10fr multi		15	15
1070 A229 100fr multi		75	38
1070A A229 200fr multi		1.50	75
1071 A229 300fr multi		2.25	1.10
Set value		5.25	2.50

Souvenir Sheets
1072 A229 300fr multi		2.25	1.10
1072A A229 300fr multi		2.25	1.10

50th anniv. of the Disney character Pluto.

Market Activities, Women Preparing Meat A230

1980-81   *Perf. 14*

1073	A230	1fr	Grinding savo	15 15
1074	A230	2fr	shown	15 15
1075	A230	3fr	Truck going to market	15 15
1076	A230	4fr	Unloading produce	15 15
1077	A230	5fr	Sugar cane vendor	15 15
1078	A230	6fr	Barber curling child's hair, vert.	15 15
1079	A230	7fr	Vegetable vendor	15 15
1080	A230	8fr	Sampling mangos, vert.	15 15
1081	A230	9fr	Grain vendor	15 15
1082	A230	10fr	Spiced fish vendor	15 15
1083	A230	15fr	Clay pot vendor	15 15
1084	A230	20fr	Straw baskets	15 15
1085	A230	25fr	Selling lemons and onions, vert.	18 15
1086	A230	30fr	Straw baskets, diff.	22 15
1087	A230	40fr	Shore market	30 15
1087A	A230	45fr	Vegatable stall	30 15
1088	A230	50fr	Women carrying produce, vert.	38 18
1088A	A230	60fr	Rice wine	40 20
			Set value	2.50 1.40

Issue dates: 45fr, 60fr, Mar 8, 1981. Others, Mar. 17, 1980.
Nos. 1087A, 1088A dated 1980.
See Nos. C440-C445, J68-J71. For overprints see Nos. C486-C487.

Commemorative Wreath — A231

Famous Men of the Decade: 40fr, Mao Tse-tung, vert.

1980, Feb. 11   *Perf. 14x13*

1089	A231	25fr	multi	25 15
1090	A231	40fr	emer grn & dk grn	40 20
		Nos. 1089-1090,C429-C431 (5)		3.25 1.65

World Tourism Conference, Manila, Sept. 27 — A232

1980, Sept. 15   Litho.   *Perf. 14*

1091	A232	50fr	Hotel tourism emblem, vert.	50 25
1092	A232	150fr	shown	1.50 75

Map of Australia and Human Rights Flame A233

1980, Oct. 13   Photo.   *Perf. 13x14*

1093	A233	30fr	shown	30 15
1094	A233	50fr	Europe and Asia map	50 25

Declaration of Human Rights, 30th anniversary.
See Nos. C432-C433.

#980, 985 Ovptd. in Gold & Black

COUPE DU MONDE DE FOOTBALL ESPAÑA 1982

Litho. & Embossed

1980, Nov. 24   *Perf. 11*
1094A A192 1000fr gold & multi
Souvenir Sheet
1094B A192 1000fr gold & multi

No. 1094B ovptd. with additional text and black bars in sheet margin.

Melk Monastery, Austria, 18th Century A234

Perf. 14½x13½

1980, Dec. 22   Litho.

1095	A234	20fr	shown	20 15
1096	A234	30fr	Tarragon Cathedral, Spain, 12th cent.	30 15
1097	A234	50fr	St. John the Baptist, Florence, 1964	50 25
		Nos. 1095-1097,C435-C437 (6)		4.00 2.05

Christmas.

African Postal Union, 5th Anniversary — A235

1980, Dec. 24   Photo.   *Perf. 13½*
1098 A235 100fr multi   75 38

February 2nd Hotel Opening A236

1981, Feb. 2   Litho.   *Perf. 12½x13*
1099 A236 50fr multi   50 25

See No. C437B.

West African Rice Development Assoc. — A236a

1981, Dec. 21   Litho.   *Perf. 12½*
1100 A236a 70fr lt grn & multi   70 35

See No. C461.

Rembrandt's Father — A237

Easter (Rembrandt Paintings): 40fr, Self-portrait. 50fr, Artist's father as an old man. 60fr, Rider on Horseback.

1981, Apr. 13   *Perf. 14½x13½*

1101	A237	30fr	multi	22 15
1102	A237	40fr	multi	30 15
1103	A237	50fr	multi	38 18
1104	A237	60fr	multi	45 22
		Nos. 1101-1104,C438-C439 (6)		3.35 1.70

Wedding of Prince Charles and Lady Diana Spencer — A237a

1981, July 29   Litho.   *Perf. 11*
1105 A237a 1000fr gold & multi
Souvenir Sheet
Litho. & Embossed
1106 A237a 1000fr Charles & Diana, diff.

No. 1105 printed with embossed se-tenant label. For overprints see Nos. 1143A-1143B.

Red-headed Rock Fowl — A238

1981, Aug. 10   *Perf. 13½x14½*

1107	A238	30fr	shown	20 15
1108	A238	40fr	Splendid sunbird	25 15
1109	A238	60fr	Violet-backed starling	40 20
1110	A238	90fr	Red-collared widowbird	60 30
		Nos. 1107-1110,C446-C447 (6)		2.45 1.31

1982 World Soccer Championships, Spain — A238a

Flags (Nos. 1110A-1110E) or Players (Nos. 1110F-1110J) and stadiums: Nos. 1110A, 1110F, Athletico de Madrid. Nos. 1110B, 1110G, Real Madrid C.F. Nos. 1110C, 1110H, R.C.D. Espanol. Nos. 1110D, 1110I, Real Zaragoza. Nos. 1110E, 1110J, Valencia.

Litho. & Embossed

1981, Aug. 17   *Perf. 11*
1110A-1110E A238a 1000fr Set of 5
Souvenir Sheets
1110F-1110J A238a 1000fr Set of 5

African Postal Union Ministers, 6th Council Meeting, July 28-20 — A239

1981, Aug. 31   Litho.   *Perf. 12½*

1111	A239	70fr	Dish antenna	50 25
1112	A239	90fr	Computer operator, vert.	70 35
1113	A239	105fr	Map	75 42

Intl. Year of the Disabled A240

1981, Aug. 31   *Perf. 14*
1114 A240 70fr Blind man   70 35

See Nos. C448-C449A.

Woman with Hat, by Picasso, 1961 — A241

Picasso Birth Centenary: Sculptures.

1981, Sept. 14   *Perf. 14½x13½*

1116	A241	25fr	shown	16 15
1117	A241	50fr	She-goat	35 16
1118	A241	60fr	Violin, 1915	40 20
		Nos. 1116-1118,C450-C452 (6)		3.51 1.81

Aix-la-Chapelle Cathedral, Germany — A242

World Heritage Year: 40fr, Geyser, Yellowstone Natl. Park. 50fr, Nahanni Natl. Park, Canada. 60fr, Stone crosses, Ethiopia.

1981, Sept. 28   *Perf. 13½x14½*

1119	A242	30fr	multi	22 15
1120	A242	40fr	multi	30 15
1121	A242	50fr	multi	38 18
1122	A242	60fr	multi	45 22
		Nos. 1119-1122,C453-C454 (6)		3.60 1.80

20th Anniv. of Alan Shepard's
Flight — A243

Space Anniversaries: 25fr, Yuri Gagarin's Vostok
I, 20th. 60fr, Lunar Orbiter I, 15th.

1981, Nov.   *Perf. 14*
1123	A243	25fr multi	18	15
1124	A243	50fr multi	38	18
1125	A243	60fr multi	45	22
	Nos. 1123-1125,C455-C456 (5)		2.46	1.28

Christmas
A244

Rubens Paintings: 20fr, Adoration of the Kings.
30fr, Adoration of the Shepherds. 50fr, St.
Catherine.

        Perf. 14¹/₂x13¹/₂
1981, Dec. 10   Litho.
1126	A244	20fr multi	15	15
1127	A244	30fr multi	20	15
1128	A244	50fr multi	35	16
	Nos. 1126-1128,C457-C459 (6)		4.75	2.46

15th Anniv. of Natl. Liberation — A245

1982, Jan. 13   Litho.   *Perf. 12¹/₂*
1129	A245	70fr Dove, flag	70	35
1130	A245	90fr Citizens, Pres. Eyadema, vert.	90	45

See Nos. C462-C463.

Scouting
Year — A246

1982, Feb. 25   Litho.   *Perf. 14*
1131	A246	70fr Pitching tent	45	22
	Nos. 1131,C464-C467 (5)		3.65	1.79

Easter — A247

Designs: The Ten Commandments.

1982, Mar. 15   *Perf. 14x14¹/₂*
1132	A247	10fr multi	15	15
1133	A247	25fr multi	16	15
1134	A247	30fr multi	20	15
1135	A247	45fr multi	30	15
1136	A247	35fr multi	35	16
1137	A247	70fr multi	45	22
1138	A247	90fr multi	60	30
	Nos. 1132-1138,C469-C470 (9)		3.71	
	Set value			1.80

Papilio
Dardanus
A248

1982, July 15   Litho.   *Perf. 14¹/₂x14*
1139	A248	15fr shown	15	15
1140	A248	20fr Belenois calypso	15	15
1141	A248	35fr Palla decius	16	15
	Nos. 1139-1141,C474-C475 (5)		1.76	
	Set value			85

1982 World
Cup — A249

Designs: Various soccer players.

1982, July 26   *Perf. 14x14¹/₂*
1142	A249	25fr multi	16	15
1143	A249	45fr multi	30	15
	Nos. 1142-1143,C477-C479 (5)		4.51	2.30

For overprints see Nos. 1150-1155.

Nos. 1105-1106 Ovptd. "BEBE ROYALE
21 JUIN 1982" on one or two lines

1982, Oct. 28   Litho.   *Perf. 11*
1143A	A237a	1000fr gold & multi	

Souvenir Sheet
Litho. & Embossed
1143B	A237a	1000fr gold & multi	

Christmas
A250

Design: Madonna of Baldacchino, by Raphael.
Nos. 1144-1148 show details; No. 1149 entire
painting.

1982, Dec. 24   Litho.   *Perf. 14¹/₂x14*
1144	A250	45fr multi	30	15
1145	A250	70fr multi	45	22
1146	A250	105fr multi	70	35
1147	A250	130fr multi	90	42
1148	A250	150fr multi	1.00	50
	Nos. 1144-1148 (5)		3.35	1.64

Souvenir Sheet
       Perf. 14x14¹/₂
1149	A250	500fr multi, vert.		3.50 1.60

Nos. 1142-1143, C477-C480 Overprinted:
VAINQUER / COUPE DU MONDE /
FOOTBALL 82 / "ITALIE"

1983, Jan. 31   Litho.   *Perf. 14x14¹/₂*
1150	A249	25fr multi	16	15
1151	A249	45fr multi	30	15
1152	A249	105fr multi	70	35
1153	A249	200fr multi	1.40	65
1154	A249	300fr multi	2.00	1.00
	Nos. 1150-1154 (5)		4.56	2.30

Souvenir Sheet
1155	A249	500fr multi		3.50 1.60

Italy's victory in 1982 World Cup. Nos. 1152-
1155 airmail.

20th Anniv. of West
African Monetary Union
(1982) — A251

1983, May   Litho.   *Perf. 12¹/₂x12*
1156	A251	70fr Map	45	22
1157	A251	90fr Emblem	60	30

Visit of Pres. Mitterand of France, Jan. 13-
15 — A252

1983, Jan. 13   Litho.   *Perf. 13*
1158	A252	35fr Sokode Regional Hospital	22	15
a.	Souvenir sheet, imperf.		22	15
1159	A252	45fr Citizens joining hands	30	15
a.	Souvenir sheet, imperf.		35	16
1160	A252	70fr Soldiers, vert.	45	22
a.	Souvenir sheet, imperf.		50	22
1161	A252	90fr Pres. Mitterand, vert.	60	30
a.	Souvenir sheet, imperf.		65	35
1162	A252	105fr Pres. Eyadema, Mitterand, vert.	70	35
a.	Souvenir sheet, imperf.		70	35
1163	A252	130fr Greeting crowd	90	42
a.	Souvenir sheet, imperf.		90	42
	Nos. 1158-1163 (6)		3.17	1.59

Nos. 1161-1163 airmail.

Easter
A253

Paintings: 35fr, Mourners at the Death of Christ,
by Bellini. 70fr, Crucifixion, by Raphael, vert. 90fr,
Descent from the Cross, by Carracci. 500fr Christ,
by Reni.

1983   Litho.   *Perf. 13¹/₂x14¹/₂*
1164	A253	35fr multi	15	15
1165	A253	70fr multi	22	15
1166	A253	90fr multi	30	15
	Set value			34

Souvenir Sheet
       Perf. 14¹/₂x13¹/₂
1167	A253	500fr multi		1.65 80

90fr, 500fr airmail.

Folkdances
A254

1983, Dec. 1   *Perf. 14¹/₂x14*
1168	A254	70fr Kondona	22	15
1169	A254	90fr Kondona, diff.	30	15
1170	A254	105fr Touboule	35	16
1171	A254	130fr Adjogbo	42	20

90fr, 105fr, 130fr airmail.

World
Communications
Year — A255

1983, June 20   Litho.   *Perf. 14x14¹/₂*
1172	A255	70fr Drummer	22	15
1173	A255	90fr Modern communication	30	15

90fr airmail.

Christmas — A256

1983, Dec.   *Perf. 13¹/₂x14¹/₂*
1174	A256	70fr Catholic Church, Kante	22	15
1175	A256	90fr Altar, Dapaong Cathedral	30	15
1176	A256	105fr Protestant Church, Dapaong	35	18

Souvenir Sheet
1177	A256	500fr Ecumenical Church, Pya	1.65	80

90fr, 105fr, 500fr airmail.

Sarakawa Presidential Assassination
Attempt, 10th Anniv. — A257

1984, Jan. 24   Litho.   *Perf. 13*
1178	A257	70fr Wrecked plane	22	15
1179	A257	90fr Plane, diff.	30	15
1180	A257	120fr Memorial Hall	40	20
1181	A257	270fr Pres. Eyadema statue, vert.	90	42

120fr, 270fr airmail.

N·E·W
Scott Supplement Pages for
Togo
will be available in
November

20th Anniv. of World Food Program (1983)
REPUBLIQUE TOGOLAISE A258

1984, May 2   Litho.   Perf. 13
1182	A258	35fr Orchard	15	15
1183	A258	70fr Fruit tree	22	15
1184	A258	90fr Rice paddy	30	15
		Set value		34

Souvenir Sheet
1185	A258	300fr Village, horiz.	1.00	50

25th Anniv. of Council of Unity — A259

Easter 1984 — A260

1984, May 29   Perf. 12
1186	A259	70fr multi	22	15
1187	A259	90fr multi	30	15

1984   Litho.   Perf. 14x14½
Various stained-glass windows.
1188	A260	70fr multi	22	15
1189	A260	90fr multi	30	15
1190	A260	120fr multi	40	20
1191	A260	270fr multi	90	45
1192	A260	300fr multi	1.00	50
		Nos. 1188-1192 (5)	2.82	1.45

Souvenir Sheet
1193	A260	500fr multi	1.65	80

Nos. 1189-1193 airmail.

Centenary of German-Togolese Friendship — A261

Designs: No. 1194, Degbenou Catholic Mission, 1893. No. 1195, Kara Bridge, 1911. No. 1196, Treaty Site, Baguida, 1884. No. 1197, Degbenou Students, 1893. No. 1198, Sansane Administrative Post, 1908. No. 1199, Adjido Official School.
No. 1200, Sokode Cotton Market, 1910. No. 1201, William Fountain, Atakpame, 1906. No. 1202, Lome Main Street, 1895, No. 19. No. 1203, Police, 1905. No. 1204, Lome Railroad Construction. No. 1205, Governor's Palace, Lome, 1905, No. 1206, No. 9, Commerce Street, Lome.
No. 1207, Nos. 10 and 17. No. 1208, Lome Wharf, 1903. No. 1209, G. Nachtigal. No. 1210, Wilhelm II. No. 1211, O.F. de Bismark. No. 1212, J. de Puttkamer. No. 1213, A. Koehler. No. 1214, W. Horn. No. 1215, J.G. de Zech. No. 1216, E. Bruckner. No. 1217, A.F. de Mecklenburg. No. 1218, H.G. de Doering. No. 1219, Land Development, 1908.
No. 1220, Postal Courier, No. 8. No. 1221, Treaty Signers, 1885. No. 1222, German & Togolese Children, Flags. No. 1223, Aneho Line Locomotive, 1905. No. 1224, Mallet Locomotive, 1907. No. 1225, German Ship "Mowe", 1884. No. 1226, "La Sophie", 1884. No. 1227, Pres. Eyadema, Helmut Kohl.

1984, July 5   Litho.   Perf. 13
1194	A261	35fr multi	15	15
1195	A261	35fr multi	15	15
1196	A261	35fr multi, vert.	15	15
1197	A261	35fr multi	15	15
1198	A261	35fr multi	15	15
1199	A261	35fr multi	15	15
1200	A261	35fr multi	15	15
1201	A261	45fr multi, vert.	15	15
1202	A261	45fr multi	15	15
1203	A261	45fr multi	15	15
1204	A261	45fr multi	15	15
1205	A261	45fr multi	15	15
1206	A261	45fr multi	15	15
1207	A261	70fr multi	22	15
1208	A261	70fr multi	22	15
1209	A261	90fr multi, vert.	30	15
1210	A261	90fr multi, vert.	30	15
1211	A261	90fr multi	30	15
1212	A261	90fr multi	30	15
1213	A261	90fr multi	30	15
1214	A261	90fr multi	30	15
1215	A261	90fr multi	30	15
1216	A261	90fr multi	30	15
1217	A261	90fr multi	30	15
1218	A261	90fr multi	30	15
1219	A261	90fr multi	30	15
1220	A261	120fr multi, vert.	40	20
1221	A261	120fr multi	40	20
1222	A261	150fr multi, vert.	50	25
1223	A261	270fr multi	90	45
1224	A261	270fr multi	90	45
1225	A261	270fr multi	90	45
1226	A261	270fr multi	90	45
1227	A261	300fr multi	1.00	50
		Nos. 1194-1227 (34)	11.59	
		Set value		5.75

Souvenir sheets of one exist for each design. Stamp size: 65x80mm.

Donald Duck, 50th Anniv. — A262

1984, Sept. 21   Litho.   Perf. 11
1230	A262	1fr Donald, Chip	15	15
1231	A262	2fr Donald, Chip and Dale	15	15
1232	A262	3fr Louie, Chip and Dale	15	15
1233	A262	5fr Donald, Chip	15	15
1234	A262	10fr Daisy Duck, Donald	15	15
1235	A262	15fr Goofy, Donald	15	15
1236	A262	105fr Huey, Dewey and Louie	30	15
1237	A262	500fr Nephews, Donald	1.40	70
1238	A262	1000fr Nephews, Donald	3.00	1.40
		Set value	5.00	2.50

Souvenir Sheets
Perf. 14
1239	A262	1000fr Surprised Donald	3.00	1.40
1240	A262	1000fr Perplexed Donald	3.00	1.40

Nos. 1236-1240 airmail.
For overprints see Nos. C551-C554.

Endangered Mammals A263

1984, Oct. 1   Litho.   Perf. 15x14½
1241	A263	45fr Manatee swimming	15	15
1242	A263	70fr Manatee eating	20	15
1243	A263	90fr Manatees floating	25	15
1244	A263	105fr Young manatee, mother	30	15
		Set value		45

Souvenir Sheets
Perf. 14x15, 15x14
1245	A263	1000fr Olive Colobus monkey, vert.	3.00	1.40
1246	A263	1000fr Galago (Bushbaby)	3.00	1.40

Nos. 1243-1246 airmail.   See #1444-1447.

Birth Centenary of Eleanor Roosevelt A264

1984, Oct. 10   Litho.   Perf. 13½
1247	A264	70fr shown	20	15
1248	A264	90fr Mrs. Roosevelt, Statue of Liberty	25	15
		Set value		24

No. 1248 airmail.

Classic Automobiles A265

1984, Nov. 15   Litho.   Perf. 15
1249	A265	1fr 1947 Bristol	15	15
1250	A265	2fr 1925 Frazer Nash	15	15
1251	A265	3fr 1950 Healey	15	15
1252	A265	4fr 1925 Kissell	15	15
1253	A265	50fr 1927 La Salle	15	15
1254	A265	90fr 1921 Minerva	25	15
1255	A265	500fr 1950 Morgan	1.40	70
1256	A265	1000fr 1921 Napier	3.00	1.40
		Nos. 1249-1256 (8)	5.40	
		Set value		2.40

Souvenir Sheets
1257	A265	1000fr 1941 Nash	3.00	1.40
1258	A265	1000fr 1903 Peugeot	3.00	1.40

Nos. 1254-1258 airmail.
For overprints see Nos. 1328-1331, C542-C544, C564-C565.

Christmas A266

Perf. 14½x13½
1984, Nov. 23   Litho.
1259	A266	70fr Connestable Madonna	20	15
1260	A266	290fr Cowper Madonna	80	40
1261	A266	300fr Alba Madonna	80	42
1262	A266	500fr Madonna of the Curtain	1.40	70

Souvenir Sheet
1263	A266	1000fr Madonna with Child	3.00	1.40

Nos. 1260-1263 airmail.

African Locomotives A267

1984, Nov. 30   Litho.   Perf. 15
1264	A267	1fr Decapod, Madeira	15	15
1265	A267	2fr 2-6-0, Egypt	15	15
1266	A267	3fr 4-8-2+2-8-4, Algeria	15	15
1267	A267	4fr Congo-Ocean diesel	15	15
1268	A267	50fr 0-4-0+0-4-0, Libya	15	15
1269	A267	90fr #49, Malawi	25	15
1270	A267	105fr 1907 Mallet, Togo	30	15
1271	A267	500fr 4-8-2, Rhodesia	1.40	70
1272	A267	1000fr Beyer-Garratt, East Africa	2.75	1.40
		Nos. 1264-1272 (9)	5.45	
		Set value		2.60

Souvenir Sheets
1273	A267	1000fr 2-8-2, Ghana	2.75	1.40
1274	A267	1000fr Locomotive, Senegal	2.75	1.40

Nos. 1269-1274 airmail.
For overprints see Nos. 1343-1346, 1356-1360, C541, C566.

Economic Convention, Lome — A268

1984, Dec. 8   Litho.   Perf. 12½
1275	A268	100fr Map of the Americas	28	15
1276	A268	130fr Map of Eurasia, Africa	38	18
1277	A268	270fr Map of Asia, Australia	75	38

Souvenir Sheet
1278	A268	500fr President Eyadema	1.40	70

Nos. 1275-1277 se-tenant.

Intl. Civil Aviation Org., 40th Anniv. A269

Map of Togo, ICAO emblem and: 70fr, Lockheed Constellation, 1944. 105fr, Boeing 707, 1954. 200fr, Doublas DC-8-61, 1966. 500fr, Bac/Sud Concorde, 1966. 1000fr, Icarus, by Hans Erni.

1984, Oct. 15   Litho.   Perf. 15x14
1279	A269	70fr multi	15	15
1280	A269	105fr multi	22	15
1281	A269	200fr multi	40	20
1282	A269	500fr multi	1.00	50
		Set value		88

Souvenir Sheet
1283	A269	500fr multi	2.00	1.00

Nos. 1280-1283 airmail.

Fresco of the 12 Apostles, Baptistry of the Aryans, Ravenna, Italy, — A270

Designs: 1fr, St. Paul. 2fr, St. Thomas. 3fr, St. Matthew. 4fr, St. James the Younger. 5fr, St. Simon. 70fr, St. Thaddeaus Judas. 90fr, St. Bartholomew. 105fr, St. Philip. 200fr, St. John. 270fr, St. James the Greater. 400fr, St. Andrew. 500fr, St. Peter. No. 1296, The Last Supper, by Andrea del Castagno, c. 1421-1457, horiz.. No. 1297, Coronation of the Virgin, by Raphael, 1483-1520, horiz..

1984, Dec. 14   Perf. 15
1284	A270	1fr multi	15	15
1285	A270	2fr multi	15	15
1286	A270	3fr multi	15	15
1287	A270	4fr multi	15	15
1288	A270	5fr multi	15	15
1289	A270	70fr multi	15	15
1290	A270	90fr multi	18	15
1291	A270	105fr multi	20	15
1292	A270	200fr multi	40	20
1293	A270	270fr multi	55	30
1294	A270	400fr multi	80	40
1295	A270	500fr multi	1.00	50

Set value 3.50 1.80

Souvenir Sheets

1296-1297 A270 1000fr each 2.00 1.00

Nos. 1290-1297 airmail.
For overprints see Nos. C545-C547.

Race Horses
A271

1985, Jan. 10

1298	A271	1fr Allez France	15	15
1299	A271	2fr Arkle, vert.	15	15
1300	A271	3fr Tingle Creek, vert.	15	15
1301	A271	4fr Interco	15	15
1302	A271	50fr Dawn Run	15	15
1303	A271	90fr Seattle Slew, vert.	18	15
1304	A271	500fr Nijinsky	1.00	50
1305	A271	1000fr Politician	2.00	1.00
		Set value	3.40	1.75

Souvenir Sheets

1306	A271	1000fr Shergar	2.00	1.00
1307	A271	1000fr Red Rum	2.00	1.00

Nos. 1303-1307 airmail.
For overprints see Nos. 1353-1355.

Easter 70f
A272

Paintings by Raphael (1483-1520).

Perf. 13¹/₂x14¹/₂, 14¹/₂x13¹/₂

1985, Mar. 7

1308	A272	70fr Christ and His Flock	15	15
1309	A272	90fr Christ and the Fishermen	18	15
1310	A272	135fr The Blessed Christ, vert.	25	15
1311	A272	150fr The Entombment, vert.	30	16
1312	A272	250fr The Resurrection, vert.	50	25
		Nos. 1308-1312 (5)	1.38	
		Set value		72

Souvenir Sheet

1313 A272 1000fr The Resurrection, diff. 2.00 1.00

Nos. 1309-1313 airmail.

Technical & Cultural Cooperation Agency,
15th Anniv. — A273

1985, Mar. 20 *Perf. 12¹/₂*

1314	A273	70fr multi	15	15
1315	A273	90fr multi	18	15
		Set value		18

Philexafrica '85, Lome — A274

1985, May 9 *Perf. 13*

1316	A274	200fr Woman carrying fruit basket	40	20
1317	A274	200fr Man plowing field	40	20

Nos. 1316-1317 printed se-tenant with central
label picturing UAPT emblem.

Scarification
Ritual — A275

1985, May 14 *Perf. 14x15*

1318	A275	25fr Kabye (Pya)	15	15
1319	A275	70fr Mollah (Kotokoli)	15	15
1320	A275	90fr Maba (Dapaong)	18	15
1321	A275	105fr Kabye (Pagouda)	22	15
1322	A275	270fr Peda	55	30
		Nos. 1318-1322 (5)	1.25	
		Set value		62

Nos. 1320-1322 airmail.

Seashells
A276

Designs: 70fr, Clavatula muricata. 90fr,
Marginella desjardini. 120fr, Clavatula nifat. 135fr,
Cypraea stercoraria. 270fr, Conus genuanus.
1000fr, Dancers wearing traditional shell
decorations.

1985, June 1 *Perf. 15x14*

1323	A276	70fr multi	15	15
1324	A276	90fr multi	18	15
1325	A276	120fr multi	25	15
1326	A276	135fr multi	25	15
1327	A276	270fr multi	55	30
		Nos. 1323-1327 (5)	1.38	
		Set value		70

Souvenir Sheet

1327A A276 1000fr multi 2.00 1.00

Nos. 1324-1327A airmail.

Nos. 1253, 1256-1258 Overprinted
"Exposition Mondiale 1985 / Tsukuba,
Japon"

1985, June *Perf. 15*

1328	A265	50fr #1253	15	15
1329	A265	1000fr #1256	2.00	1.00

Souvenir Sheets

1330	A265	1000fr #1257	2.00	1.00
1331	A265	1000fr #1258	2.00	1.00

EXPO '85.

Audubon Birth
Bicent. — A277

Illustrations by artist-naturalist J.J. Audubon
(1785-1851).

1985, Aug. 13 *Perf. 13*

1332	A277	90fr Larus bonapartii	18	15
1333	A277	120fr Pelecanus occidentalis	25	15
1334	A277	135fr Cassidix mexicanus	25	15
1335	A277	270fr Aquila chrysaetos	55	30
1336	A277	500fr Picus erythrocephalus	1.00	50
		Nos. 1332-1336 (5)	2.23	1.25

Souvenir Sheet

1337 A277 1000fr Dendroica petechia 2.00 1.00

Nos. 1332, 1334 and 1336-1337 airmail.

Dove, UN Emblem — A278

Kara Port Construction — A279

Design: 115fr, Hands, UN emblem. 250fr, Millet
crop, Atalote Research Facility. 500fr, UN, Togo
flags, statesmen.

1985, Oct. 24 *Litho.* *Perf. 13*

1338	A278	90fr multi	18	15
1339	A278	115fr multi	22	15
1340	A279	150fr multi	30	16
1341	A279	250fr multi	50	25
1342	A279	500fr multi	1.00	50
		Nos. 1338-1342 (5)	2.20	1.21

UN, 40th anniv. Nos. 1340-1342 are airmail.

Nos. 1267, 1270, 1272, 1273 Ovptd.
with Rotary Emblem and "80e
ANNIVERSAIRE DU / ROTARY
INTERNATIONAL"

1985 *Litho.* *Perf. 15*

1343	A267	4fr multi	15	15
1344	A267	105fr multi	20	15
1345	A267	1000fr multi	2.00	1.00

Souvenir Sheet

1346 A267 1000fr multi 2.00 1.00

Nos. 1344-1346 are airmail.

Christmas
A280

Religious paintings and statuary: 90fr, The Garden of Roses Madonna. 115fr, Madonna and
Child, Byzantine, 11th cent. 150fr, Rest During
the Flight to Egypt, by Gerard David (1450-1523).
160fr, African Madonna, 16th cent. 250fr, African
Madonna, c. 1900. 500fr, Mystic Madonna, by
Sandro Botticelli (1444-1510).

Perf. 14¹/₂x13¹/₂

1985, Dec. 10 *Litho.*

1347	A280	90fr multi	22	15
1348	A280	115fr multi	32	16
1349	A280	150fr multi	40	20
1350	A280	160fr multi	42	20
1351	A280	250fr multi	65	35
		Nos. 1347-1351 (5)	2.01	1.06

Souvenir Sheet

1352 A280 500fr multi 1.40 65

Nos. 1348-1352 air airmail. No. 1352 contains
one stamp 36x51mm.

Nos. 1302, 1305-1306 Ovptd. "75e
Anniversaire / du Scoutisme Feminin"

1986, Jan. *Perf. 15*

1353	A271	50fr multi	20	15
1354	A271	1000fr multi	4.00	2.00

Souvenir Sheet

1355 A271 1000fr multi 4.00 2.00

Nos. 1354-1355 airmail.

Nos. 1268-1269, 1271, 1273-1274 Ovptd.
"150e ANNIVERSAIRE / DE CHEMIN
FER 'LUDWIG'."

1985, Dec. 27 *Litho.* *Perf. 15*

1356	A267	50fr multi	28	15
1357	A267	90fr multi	50	25
1358	A267	500fr multi	2.75	1.40

Souvenir Sheets

1359	A267	1000fr No. 1273	5.50	2.75
1360	A267	1000fr No. 1274	5.50	2.75

Halley's Comet
A281

Designs: 70fr, Suisei space probe, comets. 90fr,
Vega-1 probe. 150fr, Space telescope. 200fr,
Giotto probe, comet over Togo. 1000fr, Edmond
Halley, Sir Isaac Newton.

1986, Mar. 27 *Perf. 13*

1361	A281	70fr multi	40	20
1362	A281	90fr multi	50	25
1363	A281	150fr multi	82	40
1364	A281	200fr multi	1.10	55

Souvenir Sheet

1365 A281 1000fr multi 5.50 2.75

Nos. 1362-1365 are airmail.
For overprints see Nos. 1405-1409.

Flowering and
Fruit-bearing
Plants — A282

1986, June *Perf. 14*

1366	A282	70fr Anacardium occidentale	40	20
1367	A282	90fr Ananas comosus	50	25
1368	A282	120fr Persea americana	65	32
1369	A282	135fr Carica papaya	75	38
1370	A282	290fr Mangifera indica, vert.	1.60	80
		Nos. 1366-1370 (5)	3.90	1.95

Nos. 1368-1370 airmail.

1986 World Cup Soccer Championships,
Mexico — A283

Various soccer plays.

1986, May 5 *Litho.* *Perf. 15x14*

1371	A283	70fr multi	38	20
1372	A283	90fr multi	50	25
1373	A283	130fr multi	70	35
1374	A283	300fr multi	1.60	80

Souvenir Sheet

1375 A283 1000fr multi 5.50 2.75

Nos. 1372-1375 are airmail.
For overprints see Nos. 1394-1397.

Mushrooms — A284

1986, June 9   *Perf. 13x12½*
1376	A284	70fr Ramaria moelleriana	38	20
1377	A284	90fr Hygrocybe firma	50	25
1378	A284	150fr Kalchbrennera coral-		
		locephala	82	40
1379	A284	200fr Cookeina tricholoma	1.10	55

Intl. Youth Year — A285

1986, June   *Perf. 13½x14½*
1380	A285	25fr shown	15	15
1381	A285	90fr Youths, doves	50	25
		Set value		32

Dated 1985.

Wrestling — A286   Wedding of Prince Andrew and Sarah Ferguson — A287

1986, July 16   *Perf. 14x15, 15x14*
1382	A286	15fr Single-leg takedown		
		move	15	15
1383	A286	20fr Completing takedown	15	15
1384	A286	70fr Pinning combination	38	20
1385	A286	90fr Riding	50	25
		Set value		55

Nos. 1384-1385 horiz. No. 1385 is airmail.

1986, July 23   *Perf. 14*
1386	A287	10fr Sarah Ferguson	15	15
1387	A287	1000fr Prince Andrew	5.50	2.75

Souvenir Sheet
1388	A287	1000fr Couple	5.50	2.75

Nos. 1387-1388 are airmail.

Easter A288

Paintings (details): 25fr, 1000fr, The Resurrection, by Andrea Mantegna (1431-1506), vert. 70fr, The Calvary, by Paolo Veronese (1528-1588), vert. 90fr, The Last Supper, by Jacopo Tintoretto (1518-1594). 200fr, Christ at the Tomb, by Alonso Berruguette (1486-1561).

Perf. 14x15, 15x14
1986, Mar. 24   *Litho.*
1389	A288	25fr multi	15	15
1390	A288	70fr multi	38	20
1391	A288	90fr multi	50	25

1392	A288	200fr multi	1.10	55

Souvenir Sheet
1393	A288	1000fr multi	5.50	2.75

Nos. 1391-1393 are airmail.

Nos. 1371-1374 Ovptd. or Inscribed "DEMI-FINALE / ARGENTINE 2 / BELGIQUE 0," "DEMI-FINALE / ALLEMAGNE / DE L'OUEST 2 / FRANCE 0," "3 eme et 4 eme PLACE / FRANCE 4 / BELGIQUE 2," & "FINALE / ARGENTINE 3 / ALLEMAGNE / DE L'OUEST 2"

1986, Aug. 4   *Litho.*   *Perf. 15x14*
1394	A283	70fr multi	38	20
1395	A283	90fr multi	50	25
1396	A283	100fr multi	70	35
1397	A283	300fr multi	1.60	80

Nos. 1395-1397 are airmail.

Hotels — A289

1986, Aug. 18   *Perf. 12½*
1398	A289	70fr Fazao	38	20
1399	A289	90fr Sarakawa	50	25
1400	A289	120fr Le Lac	65	32

Nos. 1399-1400 are airmail.

Keran Natl. Park A290

1986, Sept. 15   *Litho.*   *Perf. 14½*
1401	A290	70fr Wild ducks	40	20
1402	A290	90fr Antelope	50	25
1403	A290	100fr Elephant	55	28
1404	A290	130fr Waterbuck	70	35

Nos. 1402-1404 are airmail.

Nos. 1361-1365 Ovptd. with Halley's Comet Emblem in Silver

1986, Oct. 9   *Perf. 13*
1405	A281	40fr multi	40	20
1406	A281	90fr multi	50	25
1407	A281	150fr multi	82	40
1408	A281	200fr multi	1.10	55

Souvenir Sheet
1409	A281	1000fr multi	5.50	2.75

Nos. 1406-1409 are airmail.

Frescoes from Togoville Church — A291   Togoville Church — A292

1986, Dec. 22   *Litho.*   *Perf. 14½x15*
1410	A291	45fr Annunciation	25	15
1411	A291	120fr Nativity	65	32
1412	A291	130fr Adoration of the		
		Magi	70	35
1413	A291	200fr Flight into Egypt	1.10	55

Souvenir Sheet
1414	A292	1000fr multi	5.50	2.75

Christmas. Nos. 1411-1414 are airmail.

Phosphate Mining — A293

Natl. Liberation, 20th Anniv. — A294

1987, Jan. 13   *Litho.*   *Perf. 12½*
1415	A293	35fr shown	22	15
1416	A293	50fr Sugar refinery, Anie	30	15
1417	A293	70fr Nangbeto Dam	42	20
1418	A293	90fr Hotel, post office in		
		Lome	55	28
1419	A293	100fr Post office, Kara	60	30
1420	A293	100fr Peace monument	72	35
1421	A293	130fr Youth vaccination		
		campaign	78	40
	Nos. 1415-1421 (7)		3.59	1.83

Souvenir Sheet
Perf. 13
1422	A294	500fr shown	3.00	1.50

Nos. 1419-1422 are airmail.

Easter — A295   World Rugby Cup — A296

Paintings in Nadoba Church, Keran: 90fr, The Last Supper. 130fr, Christ on the Cross. 300fr, The Resurrection. 500fr, Evangelization in Tamberma, fresco, horiz.

1987, Apr. 13   *Litho.*   *Perf. 14½x15*
1423	A295	90fr multi	55	28
1424	A295	130fr multi	78	40
1425	A295	300fr multi	1.80	90

Souvenir Sheet
Perf. 15x14½
1426	A295	500fr multi	3.00	1.50

Nos. 1424-1426 are airmail.

1987, May 11   *Perf. 15x14½*
1427	A296	70fr Dive	42	20
1428	A296	130fr Running with the		
		ball	78	40
1429	A296	300fr Scrimmage	1.80	90

Souvenir Sheet
Perf. 14½x15
1430	A296	1000fr shown	6.00	3.00

Nos. 1427-1429 are horiz. Nos. 1428-1430 are airmail.

Indigenous Flowers A297

Fish — A298

1987, June 22   *Litho.*   *Perf. 13*
1431	A297	70fr Adenium obesum	38	20
1432	A297	90fr Amorphophallus abys-		
		sinicus, vert.	50	25
1433	A297	100fr Ipomoea mauritana	55	28
1434	A297	120fr Salacia togoica, vert.	68	35

Nos. 1432-1434 are airmail.

1987, Sept. 8   *Litho.*   *Perf. 13*
1435	A298	70fr Chaetodon hoefleri	48	25
1436	A298	90fr Tetraodon lineatus	60	30
1437	A298	120fr Chaetodipterus goreen-		
		sis	80	40
1438	A298	130fr Labeo parvus	88	45

1988 Summer Olympics, Seoul — A299

Buddha and athletes

1987, Sept. 14   *Perf. 12½*
1439	A299	70fr Long jump	48	25
1440	A299	90fr Relay	60	30
1441	A299	200fr Cycling	1.35	68
1442	A299	250fr Javelin	1.70	85

Souvenir Sheet
1443	A299	1000fr Tennis	6.75	3.40

Nos. 1440-1443 are airmail.

World Wildlife Fund Type of 1984

1987, Dec. 15   *Perf. 14*
Size: 32x24mm
1444	A263	60fr like 45fr	42	20
1445	A263	75fr like 70fr	52	25
1446	A263	80fr like 90fr	55	28
1447	A263	100fr like 105fr	72	35

No. 1447 is airmail.

Christmas A300   Eradication of Tuberculosis A301

Paintings: 40fr, Springtime in Paradise, horiz.. 45fr, Creation of Man, Sistine Chapel, by Michelangelo, horiz.. 105fr, Presentation in the Temple. 270fr, Original Sin. 500fr, Nativity, horiz.

Perf. 15x14, 14x15
1987, Dec. 15   *Litho.*
1448	A300	40fr multi	28	15
1449	A300	45fr multi	32	16
1450	A300	105fr multi	75	38
1451	A300	270fr multi	1.90	95

Souvenir Sheet
1452	A300	500fr multi	3.50	1.75

Nos. 1450-1452 are airmail.

Perf. 12½x13, 13x12½
1987, Dec. 28
1453	A301	80fr Inoculation, horiz.	58	30
1454	A301	90fr Family under umbrella	65	32
1455	A301	115fr Hospital, horiz.	80	40

Health for all by the year 2000. Nos. 1454-1455 are airmail.

Intl. Fund for
Agricultural
Development
(IFAD), 10th
Anniv.
A302

1988, Feb. 25   Litho.   Perf. 13½
1456 A302 90fr multi   65 32

Easter 1988 — A303

Stained-glass windows: 70fr, Jesus and the Disciples at Emmaus. 90fr, Mary at the Foot of the
Cross. 120fr, The Crucifixion. 200fr, St. Thomas
Touching the Resurrected Christ. 500fr, The Agony
of Jesus on the Mount of Olives.

1988, June 6   Litho.   Perf. 14x15
1457 A303 70fr multi   40 20
1458 A303 90fr multi   65 32
1459 A303 120fr multi   85 42
1460 A303 200fr multi   1.40 70
Souvenir Sheet
1461 A303 500fr multi   3.50 1.75

Nos. 1459-1461 are airmail.

Paintings by
Picasso
(1881-1973)
A304

Designs: 45fr, The Dance. 160fr, Portrait of a
Young Girl. No. 1464, Gueridon. No. 1465, Mandolin and Guitar.

1988, Apr. 25   Litho.   Perf. 12½x13
1462 A304 45fr multi   30 15
1463 A304 160fr multi   1.05 52
1464 A304 300fr multi   2.00 1.00
Souvenir Sheet
1465 A304 300fr multi   2.00 1.00

Nos. 1464-1465 are airmail.

A305   A306

1988, Aug. 30   Perf. 14x15
1466 A305 70fr Basketball   45 22
1467 A305 90fr Tennis   60 30
1468 A305 120fr Archery   80 40
1469 A305 200fr Discus   1.30 65
Souvenir Sheet
1470 A305 500fr Marathon   3.25 1.65

1988 Summer Olympics, Seoul. Nos. 1468-1470
are airmail.

1988, Oct. 28   Litho.   Perf. 13
1471 A306 80fr shown   55 28
1472 A306 125fr Emblems   85 42

WHO, 40th anniv.

Traditional
Costumes — A307

1988, July 25   Litho.   Perf. 13½
1473 A307 80fr Watchi chief   52 20
1474 A307 125fr Watchi woman   80 40
1475 A307 165fr Kotokoli   1.05 52
1476 A307 175fr Ewe   1.15 58
Souvenir Sheet
1477 A307 500fr Moba   3.25 1.65

PHILTOGO 3,
Aug. 11-
12 — A308

Children's drawings by: 10fr, B. Gossner. 35fr,
K. Ekoue-Kouvahey. 70fr, A. Abbey. 90fr, T.D.
Lawson. 120fr, A. Tazzar.

1988, Dec. 3
1478 A308 10fr multi   15 15
1479 A308 35fr multi   22 15
1480 A308 70fr multi   45 22
1481 A308 90fr multi   58 30
1482 A308 120fr multi   78 40
     Nos. 1478-1482 (5)   2.18
         Set value   1.08

Christmas — A309

Paintings: 80fr, Adoration of the Magi, by Brue-
ghel. 150fr, The Virgin, Infant Jesus, Sts. Jerome
and Dominic, by Lippi. 175fr, Madonna, Infant
Jesus, St. Joseph and Infant John the Baptist, by
Barocci. 195fr, Virgin and Child, by Bellini. 750fr,
The Holy Family and a Shepherd, by Titian.

1988, Dec. 15   Perf. 14½x15
1483 A309 80fr multi   50 25
1484 A309 150fr multi   92 45
1485 A309 175fr multi   1.10 55
1486 A309 195fr multi   1.20 60
Souvenir Sheet
1487 A309 750fr multi   3.60 1.80

Nos. 1484-1487 are airmail.

Natl.
Industries
A310

1988, May 28   Litho.   Perf. 13
1488 A310 125fr Cement factory   82 40
1489 A310 165fr Bottling plant   1.10 55
1490 A310 195fr Phosphate mine   1.30 65
1491 A310 200fr Plastics factory   1.35 68
1492 A310 300fr Manufacturing
               plant   2.00 1.00
     Nos. 1488-1492 (5)   6.57 3.28

John F.
Kennedy
A311

Designs: 125fr, Arrival in Paris, 1961. 155fr, At
Hotel de Ville, vert. 165fr, With De Gaulle at Elysee
Palace, vert. 180fr, Boarding Air Force One with
Jackie at Orly, France. 750fr, Kennedy and De
Gaulle, natl. colors, vert.

1988, July 30   Litho.   Perf. 14
1493 A311 125fr multi   82 40
1494 A311 155fr multi   1.05 52
1495 A311 165fr multi   1.10 55
1496 A311 180fr multi   1.20 60
Souvenir Sheet
Perf. 13½x13
1497 A311 750fr multi   5.00 2.50

Hairstyles
A312

1988, Nov. 20   Perf. 13
1498 A312 80fr shown   52 25
1499 A312 125fr multi, diff.   82 40
1500 A312 170fr multi   1.15 58
1501 A312 180fr multi, diff., vert.   1.20 60
Souvenir Sheet
Perf. 14
1502 A312 500fr multi, diff.   3.25 1.65

Sarakawa Plane
Crash, 15th
Anniv. — A313

Portrait and various views of the wreckage.

1989, Jan. 24   Perf. 13½
1503 A313 10fr multi   15 15
1504 A313 80fr multi, vert.   52 25
1505 A313 125fr multi   82 40
         Set value   70

1990 World
Cup Soccer
Championships,
Italy — A314

ITALIA '90 emblem, flag of Togo, athletes and
architecture: 80fr, Cathedral of St. Januarius,
Naples. 125fr, Milan Cathedral. 165fr, Bevilacqua
Palace, Verona. 175fr, Baptistery of San Giovanni,
Florence. 380fr, Madama Palace, Turin. 425fr,
Cathedral of San Lorenzo, Genoa. 650fr, The Colos-
seum, Rome.

1989, Jan. 10   Litho.   Perf. 13½
1506 A314 80fr multi   50 25
1507 A314 125fr multi   78 40
1508 A314 165fr multi   1.05 52
1509 A314 175fr multi   1.10 55
1510 A314 380fr multi   2.40 1.20
1511 A314 425fr multi   2.65 1.30
     Nos. 1506-1511 (6)   8.48 4.22
Souvenir Sheet
1512 A314 650fr multi   4.10 2.05

Nos. 1510-1512 are airmail.

Prince Emanuel Foundation of
Liechtenstein — A316

Flags of Liechtenstein, Togo, athletes, Pres.
Eyadema.

1989, May 25   Litho.   Perf. 13½
1520 A316 80fr Boxing   50 25
1521 A316 125fr Long jump   78 40
1522 A316 165fr Running   1.05 52

Federal
Republic of
Germany,
40th Anniv.
A317

1989, June 1
1523 A317 90fr Palace   58 25
1524 A317 125fr Statesmen, vert.   78 40
1525 A317 180fr Natl. flag, crest   1.05 52

Council for Rural Development, 30th
Anniv. — A318

1989, June 19   Perf. 15x14
1526 A318 75fr Flags, well, tractor,
              field   48 25

See Ivory Coast No. 874.

Intl. Red
Cross,
125th
Anniv.
A319

1989, June 30   Perf. 13½
1527 A319 90fr shown   58 30
1528 A319 125fr Geneva Conven-
               tion, 1864   78 40

French
Revolution,
Bicent.
A320

Designs: 90fr, Storming of the Bastille, vert.
125fr, Tennis Court Oath. 180fr, Abolition of privileges. 1000fr, Declaration of Human Rights and
Citizenship, vert.

1989, July 15
1529 A320 90fr multi   58 30
1530 A320 125fr multi   78 40
1531 A320 180fr multi   1.15 58
Souvenir Sheet
1532 A320 1000fr multi   6.25 3.10

Electric Corp. of Benin, 20th Anniv. A321

1989, July 15
1533	A321	80fr multi	50	25
1534	A321	125fr multi	78	40

PHILEXFRANCE '89, French Revolution Bicent. — A322

Figures and scenes from the revolution: 90fr, Jacques Necker (1732-1804), financier, statesman, and The Three Estates. 190fr, Guy Le Chapelier (1754-1794), politician, and abolition of feudalism (seigniorial privileges), Aug. 4, 1789. 425fr, Talleyrand-Perigord (1754-1838), statesman, and Lafayette's Oath at the Festival of Federation, July 14, 1790. 480fr, Paul Barras (1755-1829), revolutionary, and overthrowing of Robespierre during the Revolution of 9th Thermidor, July 27, 1794. 750fr, Georges Jacques Danton (1759-1794), revolutionary leader, and arrest of Louis XVI at Varennes, June 21, 1791, horiz. Nos. 1537-1539 are airmail.

1989, June 12   Litho.   Perf. 13½
1535	A322	90fr multicolored	65	32
1536	A322	190fr multicolored	1.35	68
1537	A322	425fr multicolored	3.00	1.50
1538	A322	480fr multicolored	3.40	1.70

Souvenir Sheet
1539	A322	750fr multicolored	5.25	2.65

Nos. 1535-1538 exist in souvenir sheets of 1.

Gen. Kpalime's Role in Natl. Unity and Peace Struggle, 20th Anniv. — A323

1989, Aug. 21
1540	A323	90fr shown	65	32
1541	A323	125fr Giving speech	88	45

A324   A325

Butterflies.

1990, Apr. 30   Litho.   Perf. 13½
1542	A324	5fr Danaus chrysippus	15	15
1543	A324	10fr Morpho aega	15	15
1544	A324	15fr Papilio demodocus	15	15
1545	A324	90fr Papilio dardanus	70	35

	Set value		52

Souvenir Sheet
1545A	A324	500fr Papilio zalmoxis	3.80	1.90

No. 1545A is airmail.

1989, Dec. 1   Litho.   Perf. 13½
1546	A325	40fr Apollo 11 liftoff	28	15
1547	A325	90fr Module transposition	65	32
1548	A325	150fr Eagle	1.05	52
1549	A325	250fr Splashdown	1.75	88

Souvenir Sheet
1550	A325	500fr Astronaut on Moon	3.50	1.75

1st Moon Landing, 20th anniv.

Lome IV Conference, Dec. 1989 — A326

1989, Dec. 15   Litho.   Perf. 13
1551	A326	100fr "Dec. 89"	70	35
1552	A326	100fr "15 Dec. 89"	70	35

Boy Scouts, Flora and Fauna — A327

1990, Jan. 8   Litho.   Perf. 13½
1553	A327	80fr Myrina silenus	58	30
1554	A327	90fr Phlebobus silvaticus	65	32
1555	A327	125fr Volvariella esculenta	90	45
1556	A327	165fr Hypolicaena antifaunus	1.15	58
1557	A327	380fr Termitomyces striatus	2.70	1.35
1558	A327	425fr Axiocerces harpax	3.00	1.50
		Nos. 1553-1558 (6)	8.98	4.50

Souvenir Sheet
1559	A327	750fr Cupidopsis jobates	5.25	2.60

No. 1557-1559 airmail.

People's Republic of Togo, 20th Anniv. — A328

1990, Jan. 8
1560	A328	45fr Government House, Kara	32	16
1561	A328	90fr Pres. Eyadema, House	65	32

Pan-African Postal Union, 10th Anniv. — A329

1990, Jan. 1   Perf. 13½
1562	A329	125fr bronze, blk & bl	90	45

US-Togo Relations A330

Design: 180fr, Pres. Bush and Pres. Eyadema, horiz.

1990, July 20   Litho.   Perf. 13½
1563	A330	125fr multicolored	95	48
1564	A330	180fr multicolored	1.40	70

Size: 90 x 75mm
1565	A330	125fr multicolored	1.00	50
1566	A330	180fr multicolored	1.40	70

Nos. 1565-1566 printed in sheets of 1.

Reptiles A331

1990, May 22
1567	A331	1fr Varanus niloticus	15	15
1568	A331	25fr Vipere bitis arietans	20	15
1569	A331	60fr Naja melaneuloca	50	25
1570	A331	90fr Python de sebae	70	35
		Set value		75

Cowrie Shell Ornaments A332

1990, July, 20   Litho.   Perf. 13½
1571	A332	90fr shown	70	35
1572	A332	125fr Shell necklace	1.00	50
1573	A332	180fr Shells on horned helmet	1.40	70

Stamp Day A333

1990, Aug. 23
1574	A333	90fr multicolored	70	35

Traditional Homes A334

1990, Sept. 9
1575	A334	90fr shown	70	35
1576	A334	125fr multi, diff.	1.00	50
1577	A334	190fr multi, diff.	1.50	75

Charles de Gaulle (1890-1970), Speech at Brazzaville, 1944 — A335

1990, Aug. 30   Litho.   Perf. 14
1578	A335	125fr multicolored	1.00	50

New Lome Airport A336

1990, Sept. 17   Perf. 13½
1579	A336	90fr multicolored	70	35

Children's Art — A337

1990, Sept. 28   Litho.   Perf. 13½
1580	A337	90fr multicolored	75	35

Forest Wildlife — A342

1991, June 5   Litho.   Perf. 13½x14
1593	A342	90fr Chimpanzee	65	32
1594	A342	1.70fr Green parrot	1.25	60
1595	A342	1.85fr White parrot	1.35	65

Python Regius A343

Various snakes emerging from eggs.

1992, Aug. 24   Litho.   Perf. 13½
1596	A343	90fr multicolored	70	35
1597	A343	125fr multicolored	1.00	50
1598	A343	190fr multicolored	1.50	75
1599	A343	300fr multicolored	2.35	1.20

Dated 1991.

Voodoo Dances A344

Various women dancing.

1992, Aug. 24

1600	A344	90fr multicolored	70	35
1601	A344	125fr multicolored	1.00	50
1602	A344	190fr multicolored	1.50	75

Dated 1991.

A345

1994 World Cup Soccer Championships, US — A346

Various soccer players in action: 5fr, 10fr, 25fr, 60fr, 90fr, 100fr, 200fr, 1000fr.
1500fr, Player in white & green uniform. 3000fr, Two players in air, horiz.

1994 Litho. Perf. 14

1603-1610	A345	Set of 8	5.75	3.00

Souvenir Sheets

1611	A346	1500fr multicolored	5.75	3.00
1612	A346	3000fr multicolored	11.50	5.75

UPU, 120th Anniv. — A347

Stamp Day — A348

1994, July 29 Perf. 13½

1613	A347	180fr multicolored	70	35

1994, Oct. 9

1614	A348	90fr pale blue & multi	35	18
1615	A348	125fr pale yellow & multi	48	25

Birds A349

Designs: 5fr, Secretary bird, vert. 10fr, Paradise flycatcher, vert. 25fr, African spoonbill. 60fr, Cordon bleu waxbill. 90fr, Orange-breasted sunbird, vert. 100fr, Yellow-billed hornbill, vert. 200fr, African hoopoe. 1000fr, Red-throated bee eater, vert.

1995, Jan. 23 Litho. Perf. 14

1616-1623	A349	Set of 8	5.75	2.75

Souvenir Sheet

1624	A349	1500fr Vulture	5.75	2.75

SEMI-POSTAL STAMPS

Curie Issue
Common Design Type

1938 Unwmk. Engr. Perf. 13

B1	CD80	1.75fr + 50c brt ultra	11.00	11.00

French Revolution Issue
Common Design Type
Photo., Name and Value Typo. in Black

1939

B2	CD83	45c + 25c grn	3.25	3.25
B3	CD83	70c + 30c brn	3.25	3.25
B4	CD83	90c + 35c red org	3.25	3.25
B5	CD83	1.25fr + 1fr rose pink	3.25	3.25
B6	CD83	2.25fr + 2fr blue	3.25	3.25
		Nos. B2-B6 (5)	16.25	16.25

French Revolution, 150th anniv. Surtax for defense of the colonies.

Nos. 281, 236, 245, 289 Surcharged in Red or Black

SECOURS + 1 fr. NATIONAL

1941 Perf. 14 x 13½, 12½

B7	A10	50c + 1fr	70	70
B8	A7	80c + 2fr	2.50	2.50
B9	A8	1.50fr + 2fr	2.50	2.50
B10	A11	2fr + 3fr (R)	2.50	2.50

Catalogue values for unused stamps in this section, from this point to the end of the section, are for Never Hinged items.

Common Design Type and

Togolese Militiaman SP1

Military Infirmary SP2

1941 Photo. Perf. 13½

B10A	SP1	1fr + 1fr red	40
B10B	CD86	1.50fr + 3fr maroon	40
B10C	SP2	2.50fr + 1fr blue	40

Nos. B10A-B10C were issued by the Vichy government, and were not placed on sale in Togo.
Nos. 296-297 were surcharged "OEUVRES COLONIALES" and surtax (including change of denomination of the 2.50fr to 50c). These were issued in 1944 by the Vichy government and were not placed on sale in Togo.

Tropical Medicine Issue
Common Design Type

1950 Engr. Perf. 13

B11	CD100	10fr + 2fr indigo & dk bl	2.00	2.00

The surtax was for charitable work.

Republic

Patient on Stretcher — SP3

Uprooted Oak Emblem — SP4

Designs: 30fr+5fr, Feeding infant. 50fr+10fr, Blood transfusion.

1959 Engr. Perf. 13

B12	SP3	20fr + 5fr multi	30	25
a.		Souvenir sheet of 4	1.50	1.50
B13	SP3	30fr + 5fr bl, car & brn	30	25
a.		Souvenir sheet of 4	1.50	1.50
B14	SP3	50fr + 10fr emer, brn & car	30	30
a.		Souvenir sheet of 4	1.50	1.50

Issued for the Red Cross.
Nos. B12a, B13a, B14a exist imperf.; same values.

1960 Unwmk. Perf. 13

Design: No. B16 similar to No. B15, with emblem on top.

B15	SP4	25fr + 5fr dk bl, brn & yel grn	20	20
B16	SP4	45fr + 5fr dk bl, brn & ol	35	35

World Refugee Year, July 1, 1959-June 30, 1960. The surtax was for aid to refugees.

AIR POST STAMPS

Common Design Type

1940 Unwmk. Engr. Perf. 12½x12

C1	CD85	1.90fr ultra	15	15
C2	CD85	2.90fr dk red	15	15
C3	CD85	4.50fr dk gray grn	22	15
C4	CD85	4.90fr yel bister	35	20
C5	CD85	6.90fr deep org	55	38
		Nos. C1-C5 (5)	1.42	
		Set value		90

Common Design Type
Inscribed "Togo" across top

1942

C6	CD88	50c car & bl	15
C7	CD88	1fr brn & blk	15
C8	CD88	2fr grn & red brn	15
C9	CD88	3fr dk bl & scar	15
C10	CD88	5fr vio & brn red	15

Frame Engraved, Center Typographed

C11	CD89	10fr ultra, ind & org	15
C12	CD89	20fr rose car, mag & gray blk	15
C13	CD89	50fr yel grn, dl grn & lt vio	55	65
		Set value	1.35

There is doubt whether Nos. C6-C12 were officially placed in use.

Catalogue values for unused stamps in this section, from this point to the end of the section, are for Never Hinged items.

Elephants — AP1

Plane — AP2

Plane — AP3

Post Runner and Plane — AP4

1947, Oct. 6 Engr. Perf. 12½

C14	AP1	40fr blue	2.50	1.50
C15	AP2	50fr lt ultra, & red vio	1.45	90
C16	AP3	100fr emer & dk brn	2.25	1.40
C17	AP4	200fr lilac rose	4.00	1.50

UPU Issue
Common Design Type

1949, July 4 Perf. 13

C18	CD99	25fr multi	3.00	3.00

Liberation Issue
Common Design Type

1954, June 6

C19	CD102	15fr indigo & pur	2.25	2.25

Freight Highway — AP5

1954, Nov. 29

C20	AP5	500fr ind & dk grn	15.00	14.00

Republic

Independence Allegory — AP6

1957, Oct. 29 Unwmk. Engr. Perf. 13

C21	AP6	25fr bl, ol bis & ver	38	30

1st anniv. of Togo's autonomy.

Flag and Torch AP7

Great White Egret AP8

1957, Oct. 29

C22	AP7	50fr multi	60	30
C23	AP7	100fr multi	1.10	45
C24	AP7	200fr multi	2.25	75
C25	AP8	500fr ind, lt bl & grn	7.00	3.00

Types of 1957 inscribed: "Republique du Togo" and

Flag, Plane and Map — AP9

1959, Jan. 15 Engr. Perf. 13

C26	AP9	25fr ultra, emer & vio brn	18	15
C27	AP7	50fr dk bl, dl grn & red	38	15
C28	AP7	100fr multi	1.10	38
C29	AP7	200fr dk grn, red & ultra	2.25	85

C30 AP8 500fr blk brn, rose lil &
    grm   6.25 1.90
    Nos. C26-C30 (5)   10.16 3.46

Hotel Le Benin — AP10

Eagle and Map of Togo — AP11

Perf. 14½x15, 15x14½
1960, Apr. 27 Litho. Unwmk.
C31 AP10 100fr crim, emer & yel 55 15
C32 AP10 200fr multi 1.40 20
C33 AP11 500fr grn & gldn brn 3.00 18

Proclamation of Togo's full independence, Apr. 27, 1960.

Type of Mail Service Issue, 1963
Design: 100fr, Boeing 707 and stamps of 1960.

1963, Jan. 12 Photo. Perf. 13
C34 A41 100fr multi 60 30
  a. 1.25 1.25

No. C34a contains 4 stamps similar to Nos. 441-443 and C34, with simulated perforations.

Type of Emancipation Issue, 1963
1963, Oct. Unwmk. Perf. 13x14
C35 A45 100fr multi 65 32
  a. Souv. sheet of 4, #454-456, C35, imperf. 90 75

For overprint see No. C41.

Type of 1964 Regular Issue
Designs: 50fr, Black-bellied seed-cracker. 100fr, Blue-billed mannikin. 200fr, Redheaded lovebird. 250fr, African gray parrot. 500fr, Yellow-breasted barbet.

1964-65 Photo. Perf. 14
Size: 22½x31mm
Birds in Natural Colors
C36 A47 50fr yel grn 40 22
C37 A47 100fr ocher 80 30
C38 A47 200fr dl bl grn 1.50 80
C39 A47 250fr dl rose ('65) 2.00 1.00
C40 A47 500fr violet 4.00 1.50
  Nos. C36-C40 (5) 8.70 3.82

No. C35 Overprinted Diagonally: "En Mémoire de / JOHN F. KENNEDY / 1917-1963"

1964, Feb. Perf. 13x14
C41 A45 100fr multi 60 32

Issued in memory of John F. Kennedy. Same overprint was applied to stamps of No. C35a, with black border and commemorative inscription added. Two sheets exist: with and without gray silhouetted head of Kennedy covering all four stamps.

Liberation Type of 1964
1964, May 25 Perf. 14x13
C42 A50 100fr dl bl grn & dk brn 65 32

Olympic Games Type of Regular Issue, 1964
1964, Oct. Photo. Perf. 14
C43 A52 100fr Tennis 75 30
  a. Souv. sheet of 3, #493-494, C43, imperf. 1.10 1.10

Flag of Togo and Jet AP12

1964, Dec. 5 Unwmk. Perf. 14x13
C44 AP12 100fr multi 80 32

Inauguration of the national airline "Air Togo." For souvenir sheet see No. 499a.

Lincoln Type of Regular Issue, 1965
1965, June Photo. Perf. 13½x14
C45 A58 100fr ol gray 90 30
  a. Souv. sheet of 2, #545, C45, imperf. 90 90

Sports Type of Regular Issue, 1965
Design: 100fr, Soccer player, flags of Togo and Congo.

1965, July Unwmk. Perf. 14x13
C46 A59 100fr multi 80 32

Churchill Type of Regular Issue
1965, Aug. 7 Photo. Perf. 13½x14
C47 A60 85fr car rose 80 30
  a. Souv. sheet of 2, #532, C47, imperf. 1.10 1.10

UN Type of Regular Issue, 1965
Design: 100fr, Apple, grapes, wheat and "ONU."

1965, Dec. 15 Perf. 14x13½
C48 A65 100fr dk bl & bis 1.00 40
  a. Souvenir sheet of 2 1.40 1.40

No. C48a contains two imperf. stamps similar to Nos. 548 and C48 with simulated perforations.

Pope Type of Regular Issue
Designs: 45fr, Pope speaking at UN rostrum, world map and UN emblem. 90fr, Pope, plane and UN emblem.

1966, Mar. 5 Litho. Perf. 12
C49 A66 45fr emer & multi 32 15
C50 A66 90fr gray & multi 70 16
  a. Souvenir sheet of 2, #C49-C50 1.25 1.00

Red Cross Type of Regular Issue
Design: 100fr, Jean Henri Dunant and Togolese Flag.

1966, May 7 Litho. Perf. 12
C51 A67 100fr multi 90 28

WHO Type of Regular Issue
Flowers: 50fr, Daisies and WHO Headquarters. 90fr, Talisman roses and WHO Headquarters.

1966, May Litho. Perf. 12
C52 A68 50fr lt bl & multi 40 15
C53 A68 90fr gray & multi 70 15
  a. Souvenir sheet of 2, #C52-C53 1.10 90
    Set value 20

Air Afrique Issue
Common Design Type
1966, Aug. 31 Photo. Perf. 13
C54 CD123 30fr brt grn, blk & lem 30 15

Arts and Crafts Type of Regular Issue
Designs: 60fr, Basket maker. 90fr, Wood carver.

1966, Sept. Perf. 13x14
C55 A69 60fr ultra, org & blk 45 15
C56 A69 90fr brt rose, yel & blk 70 15

Dancer Type of Regular Issue
Designs: 50fr, Woman from North Togo holding branches. 60fr, Man from North Togo with horned helmet.

1966, Nov. Photo. Perf. 13x14
C57 A70 50fr multi 40 16
C58 A70 60fr ol & multi 48 18

Soccer Type of Regular Issue
Designs: Different Soccer Scenes.

1966, Dec. 14 Photo. Perf. 14x13
C59 A71 50fr org, brn & pur 40 15
C60 A71 60fr ultra, brn & org 48 16
  a. Souv. sheet of 3, #582, C59-C60, imperf. 1.10 1.00

Fish Type of Regular Issue
Designs: 45fr, Yellow jack and trawler. 90fr, Banded distichodus and seiner.

1967, Jan. 14 Photo. Perf. 14
Fish in Natural Colors
C61 A72 45fr org & brn 42 16
C62 A72 90fr emer & dk bl 90 30

UNICEF Type of Regular Issue
UNICEF Emblem and: 45fr, Girl and miniature poodle. 90fr, African boy and greyhound.

1967, Feb. 11 Photo. Perf. 14x13½
C63 A73 45fr yel, red brn & blk 35 15
C64 A73 90fr ultra, dk grn & blk 70 25
  a. Souvenir sheet of 2 1.10 90

No. C64a contains 2 imperf., lithographed stamps with simulated perforations similar to Nos. C63-C64.

Satellite Type of Regular Issue
Designs: 50fr, Diamant rocket, vert. 90fr, Fr-1 satellite, vert.

1967, Mar. 18 Photo. Perf. 13½x14
C65 A74 50fr multi 45 15
C66 A74 90fr multi 80 24
  a. Souvenir sheet of 2 1.25 1.00

No. C66a contains 2 imperf. stamps similar to Nos. C65-C66 with simulated perforations.

Musician Type of Regular Issue
UNESCO Emblem and: 45fr, Johann Sebastian Bach and organ. 90fr, Ludwig van Beethoven, violin and clarinet.

1967, Apr. 15 Photo. Perf. 14x13½
C67 A75 45fr multi 35 15
C68 A75 90fr pink & multi 75 20
  a. Souvenir sheet of 2 1.10 85

No. C68a contains 2 imperf. stamps similar to Nos. C67-C68 with simulated perforations.

EXPO '67 Type of Regular Issue
EXPO '67 Emblem and: 45fr, French pavilion, roses. 60fr, British pavilion, day lilies. 90fr, African village, bird-of-paradise flower. 105fr, US pavilion, daisies.

1967, May 30 Photo. Perf. 14
C69 A76 45fr emer & multi 32 15
C70 A76 60fr multi 45 15
C71 A76 90fr yel & multi 60 26
  a. Souv. sheet of 3, #C69-C71, imperf. 1.50 1.50
C72 A76 105fr multi 75 30

For overprints see Nos. C86-C89.

Mural by José Vela Zanetti — AP13

The designs are from a mural in the lobby of the UN Conf. Building, NYC. The mural depicting mankind's struggle for a lasting peace is shown across 3 stamps twice in the set: on the 5fr, 15fr, 30fr and 45fr, 60fr, 90fr.

1967, July 15 Litho. Perf. 14
C73 AP13 5fr multi 15 15
C74 AP13 15fr org & multi 15 15
C75 AP13 30fr multi 25 15
C76 AP13 45fr multi 40 15
C77 AP13 60fr car & multi 60 16
C78 AP13 90fr ind & multi 90 22
  a. Souvenir sheet of 3, #C76-C78 1.90 1.50
  Nos. C73-C78 (6) 2.45
    Set value 65

Issued to publicize general disarmament.

Animal Type of Regular Issue, 1967
1967, Aug. 19 Photo. Perf. 14x13½
C79 A78 45fr Lion 42 16
C80 A78 60fr Elephant 60 20

African Postal Union Issue, 1967
Common Design Type
1967, Sept. 9 Engr. Perf. 13
C81 CD124 100fr bl, brt grn & ol brn 75 30

Stamp Anniversary Type of Regular Issue
Designs: 90fr, Stamp auction and Togo Nos. 16 and C42. 105fr, Father and son with stamp album and No. 474.

1967, Oct. 14 Photo. Perf. 14x13
Stamps on Stamps in Original Colors
C82 A79 90fr olive 90 25
  a. Souvenir sheet of 3 2.00 1.50
C83 A79 105fr dk car rose 1.40 38

No. C82a contains 3 imperf. stamps similar to Nos. 621-622 and C82 with simulated perforations.

Pre-Olympics Type of Regular Issue
Designs: 60fr, Runners, Summer Olympics emblem and view of Mexico City. 90fr, Broad jump, Summer Olympics emblem and view of Mexico City.

1967, Dec. 2 Perf. 13x14
C84 A80 60fr pink & multi 48 16
C85 A80 90fr multi 75 28
  a. Souv. sheet of 3, #627, C84-C85, imperf. 1.50 1.25

Nos. C69-C72 Overprinted: "JOURNÉE NATIONALE / DU TOGO / 29 SEPTEMBRE 1967"

1967, Dec. Photo. Perf. 14
C86 A76 45fr multi 42 15
C87 A76 60fr multi 60 15
C88 A76 90fr yel & multi 90 25
C89 A76 105fr multi 1.00 35

Issued for National Day, Sept. 29, 1967.

Hydrological Decade Type of Regular Issue
1968, Apr. 6 Litho. Perf. 14
C90 A84 60fr multi 45 15

Ship Type of Regular Issue
Designs: 45fr, Fulton's and modern steamships. 90fr, US atomic ship Savannah and atom symbol.

1968, Apr. 26 Photo. Perf. 14x14½
C91 A85 45fr yel & multi 35 15
C92 A85 90fr bl & multi 75 20
  a. Souvenir sheet of 2 1.10 90

No. C92a contains 2 imperf. stamps similar to Nos. C91-C92 with simulated perforations.

WHO Type of Regular Issue
Paintings: 60fr, The Anatomy Lesson, by Rembrandt (detail). 90fr, Jesus Healing the Sick, by Raphael.

1968, June 22 Photo. Perf. 14
C93 A87 60fr multi 48 15
C94 A87 90fr pur & multi 75 20
  a. Souvenir sheet of 2 1.10 90

No. C94a contains 2 imperf. stamps similar to Nos. C93-C94 with simulated perforations.

Olympic Games Type of Regular Issue
1968, July 27 Perf. 14x13½
C95 A88 60fr Wrestling 48 15
C96 A88 90fr Running 75 20
  a. Souvenir sheet of 2 1.10 90

No. C96a contains 2 imperf. stamps similar to Nos. C95-C96 with simulated perforations.

Boy Scout Type of Regular Issue
Designs: 60fr, First aid practice, horiz. 90fr, Scout game.

1968, Nov. 23 Litho. Perf. 14
C97 A90 60fr ol & multi 60 22
C98 A90 90fr org & multi 90 35
  a. Souvenir sheet of 2 1.50 1.25

No. C98a contains 2 imperf. stamps with simulated perforations similar to Nos. C97-C98.

Demand, as well as supply, determine a stamp's market value.

PHILEXAFRIQUE Issue

The Letter, by
Jean Auguste
Franquelin
AP14

1968, Nov. 9   Photo.   *Perf. 12¹/₂x12*
C99 AP14 100fr multi   1.00 80

PHILEXAFRIQUE Philatelic Exhibition in
Abidjan, Feb. 14-23. Printed with alternating light
ultramarine label.

Christmas Type of Regular Issue

Paintings: 60fr, Adoration of the Magi, by Pieter
Brueghel. 90fr, Adoration of the Magi, by Dürer.

1968, Dec. 28   Litho.   *Perf. 14*
C100 A91 60fr red & multi   60 20
C101 A91 90fr multi   90 30
  a.   Souvenir sheet   1.25 1.00

No. C101a contains 2 imperf. stamps similar to
Nos. C100-C101 with simulated perforations.

Human Rights Type of Regular Issue

Portraits and Human Rights Flame: 60fr, Robert
F. Kennedy. 90fr, Martin Luther King, Jr.

1969, Feb. 1   Photo.   *Perf. 13¹/₂x14*
C102 A92 60fr brt rose lil & vio bl   40 18
C103 A92 90fr emer & brn   55 28
  a.   Souvenir sheet   1.00 65

No. C103a contains 2 imperf. stamps similar to
Nos. C102-C103 with simulated perforations.
For overprints see Nos. C110-C111.

2nd PHILEXAFRIQUE Issue
Common Design Type

Design: 50fr, Togo #16 and Aledjo Fault.

1969, Feb. 14   Engr.   *Perf. 13*
C104 CD128 50fr red brn, grn & car
             rose   42 42

Sports Type of Regular Issue

Designs (Stadium and): 60fr, Boxing. 90fr,
Bicycling.

1969, Apr. 26   Photo.   *Perf. 14x13¹/₂*
C105 A93 60fr bl, red & dk brn   40 15
C106 A93 90fr ultra, brt pink & dk
             brn   70 22
  a.   Souvenir sheet   1.00 80

No. C106a contains 2 imperf. stamps similar to
Nos. C105-C106 with simulated perforations.

Lunar Type of Regular Issue

Designs: 60fr, Astronaut exploring moon surface. 100fr, Astronaut gathering rocks.

1969, July 21   Litho.   *Perf. 14*
C107 A94 60fr dk bl & multi   40 20
C108 A94 100fr multi   65 40
  a.   Souvenir sheet   4.00 3.50

No. C108a contains 4 imperf. stamps with simulated perforations similar to Nos. 676-677 and
C107-C108, magenta margin. No. C108a also
exists with colors of 30fr and 100fr stamps
changed, and margin in orange. Value $6.
For overprints see Nos. C120-C121.

Painting Type of Regular Issue

Painting: 90fr, Pentecost, by El Greco.

1969, Aug. 16   Litho.   *Perf. 14*
C109 A95 90fr multi   1.00 40
  a.   Souvenir sheet   1.00 75

No. C109a contains two imperf. stamps with
simulated perforations similar to Nos. 682 and
C109.

Nos. C102-C103 Overprinted Like Nos. 683-686

1969, Sept. 1   Photo.   *Perf. 13¹/₂x14*
C110 A92 60fr brt rose lil & vio bl   40 20
C111 A92 90fr emer & brn   60 25
  a.   Souv. sheet of 2   2.50 1.90

No. C111a is No. C103a with Eisenhower
overprint.

Bank Type of Regular Issue

Design: 100fr, Bank emblem and hand holding
cattle and farmer.

1969, Sept. 10   Photo.   *Perf. 13x14*
C112 A96 100fr multi   80 40

Red Cross Type of Regular Issue

Designs: 60fr, Wilhelm C. Roentgen and Red
Cross workers with children in front of Togo Headquarters. 90fr, Henri Dunant and Red Cross workers meeting Biafra refugees at airport.

1969, Sept. 27   Litho.   *Perf. 14*
C113 A97 60fr brn & multi   45 22
C114 A97 90fr ol & multi   65 35
  a.   Souv. sheet of 2   1.00 70

No. C114a contains 2 imperf. stamps with simulated perforations similar to Nos. C113-C114.

Type of Regular Issue, 1969

Emblem of Young Pioneer and Agricultural
Organization and: 90fr, Manioc harvest. 100fr,
Instruction in gardening. 200fr, Corn harvest.
250fr, Marching drum corps. 500fr, Parade of
Young Pioneers.

1969-70   Litho.   *Perf. 14*
C115 A98 90fr multi   55 18
C116 A98 100fr org & multi   60 22
C117 A98 200fr multi ('70)   1.25 38
C118 A98 250fr ol & multi   1.50 60
C119 A98 500fr multi ('70)   3.25 75
  Nos. C115-C119 (5)   7.15 2.13

Christmas Issue
Nos. C107-C108, C108a Overprinted: "JOYEUX NOEL"

1969, Dec.   Litho.   *Perf. 14*
C120 A94 60fr multi   1.35 40
C121 A94 100fr multi   1.90 60
  a.   Souvenir sheet of 4   6.00 6.00

Peace Leaders Type of Regular Issue

Portraits: 60fr, Friedrich Ebert. 90fr, Mahatma
Gandhi.

1969, Dec. 27   Litho.   *Perf. 14x13¹/₂*
C122 A100 60fr dk brn, dk red & yel   42 18
C123 A100 90fr dk brn, vio bl & ocher   60 30

ILO Type of Regular Issue

Paintings and ILO Emblem: 60fr, Spring Sowing,
by Vincent van Gogh. 90fr, Workers, by Diego de
Rivera.
For surcharges see Nos. 765, C143.

1970, Jan. 24   Litho.   *Perf. 12¹/₂x13*
C124 A101 60fr gold & multi   35 15
C125 A101 90fr gold & multi   65 18
  a.   Souvenir sheet of 2   1.00 75

No. C125a contains two stamps similar to Nos.
C124-C125, with simulated perforations.

Hair Styles Type of Regular Issue

Designs: Various hair styles (45fr, vertical. 90fr,
horizontal).

Perf. 12¹/₂x13, 13x12¹/₂
1970, Feb. 21
C126 A102 45fr car & multi   26 15
C127 A102 90fr multi   50 30

Independence Type of Regular Issue

Design: 60fr, Togo No. C33 and Independence
Monument, Lomé.

1970, Apr. 27   Litho.   *Perf. 13x12¹/₂*
C128 A103 60fr yel & multi   30 15

UPU Type of Regular Issue

1970, May 30   Photo.   *Perf. 14x13¹/₂*
C129 A104 50fr grnsh bl & dk car   28 15

Soccer Type of Regular Issue

Various Scenes from Soccer, Rimet Cup and Flags
of: 50fr, Sweden and Israel. 60fr, Bulgaria and
Peru. 90fr, Belgium and Salvador.

1970, June 27   Litho.   *Perf. 13x14*
C130 A105 50fr multi   28 15
C131 A105 60fr lil & multi   38 20
C132 A105 90fr multi   55 28
  a.   Souvenir sheet of 4   1.50 1.50

No. C132a contains 4 stamps similar to Nos.
734, C130-C132, but imperf. with simulated
perforations.

Lenin Type of Regular Issue

Design: 50fr, Lenin Meeting Peasant Delegation,
by V. A. Serov, and UNESCO emblem.

1970, July 25   Litho.   *Perf. 12¹/₂*
C133 A106 50fr multi   35 15

For overprint see No. C179.

EXPO '70 Type of Regular Issue
Souvenir Sheet

Design: 150fr, Mitsubishi pavilion and EXPO '70
emblem.

1970, Aug. 8   Litho.   *Perf. 13*
C134 A107 150fr yel & multi   1.00 35
  a.   Inscribed "AERINNE"

No. C134 contains one stamp 86x33mm.

Astronaut Type of Regular Issue

Design: 200fr, James A. Lovell, Fred W. Haise,
Jr. and Tom Mattingly (replaced by John L. Swigert,
Jr.) and Apollo 13 emblem.

1970, Sept. 26
C135 A108 200fr multi   95 55
  a.   Souv. sheet of 3   1.50 1.10

Space flight of Apollo 13. No. C135a contains 3
stamps similar to Nos. 741, 744 and C135, with
simulated perforations.
For overprint see No. C136.

Nos. C135, C135a Inscribed: "FELICITATIONS / BON RETOUR APOLLO XIII"

1970, Sept. 26
C136 A108 200fr multi   1.00 55
  a.   Souvenir sheet of 3   1.50 1.10

Safe return of the crew of Apollo 13.

UN Type of Regular Issue

Paintings and Emblems of UN Agencies: 60fr,
The Mailman Roulin, by van Gogh, and UPU
emblem. 90fr, The Birth of the Virgin, by Vittore
Carpaccio, and WHO emblem.

1970, Oct. 24   Litho.   *Perf. 13x12¹/₂*
C137 A109 60fr grn, gold & blk   35 16
C138 A109 90fr red org, gold & brn   55 28
  a.   Souvenir sheet of 4   1.50 1.10

No. C138a contains one each of Nos. 754-755
and C137-C138 with simulated perforations.

Moth Type of Regular Issue

Moths: 60fr, Euchloron megaera.   90fr,
Pseudocraea boisduvali.

1970, Nov. 21   Photo.   *Perf. 13x14*
C139 A110 60fr multi   55 15
C140 A110 90fr multi   55 16

Christmas Type of Regular Issue

Paintings: 60fr, Adoration of the Shepherds, by
Botticelli. 90fr, Adoration of the Kings, by Tiepolo.

1970, Dec. 26   Litho.   *Perf. 12¹/₂x13*
C141 A111 60fr gold & multi   45 20
C142 A111 90fr gold & multi   70 30
  a.   Souv. sheet of 2, #C141-C142   1.00 75

No. C122 Surcharged and Overprinted: "EN MEMOIRE / Charles De Gaulle / 1890-1970"

1971, Jan. 9   Photo.   *Perf. 14x13¹/₂*
C143 A100 200fr on 60fr   1.50 60

De Gaulle Type of Regular Issue

Designs: 60fr, De Gaulle and Pope Paul VI.
90fr, De Gaulle and satellite.

1971, Feb. 20   Photo.   *Perf. 13x14*
C144 A112 60fr blk & dp vio   48 16
C145 A112 90fr blk & bl grn   72 24
  a.   Souvenir sheet of 4   1.75 1.10

Nos. C143-C145 issued in memory of Charles
De Gaulle (1890-1970), President of France. No.
C145a contains 4 imperf. stamps similar to Nos.
769-770, C144-C145.

Easter Type of Regular Issue

Paintings: 50fr, Resurrection, by Matthias Grunewald. 60fr, Resurrection, by Master of Trebon.
90fr, Resurrection, by El Greco.

Perf. 10¹/₂x11¹/₂
1971, Apr. 10   Litho.
C146 A113 50fr gold & multi   35 15
C147 A113 60fr gold & multi   48 18
C148 A113 90fr gold & multi   65 32
  a.   Souvenir sheet of 4, #773, C146-
        C148   1.65 1.10

Apollo 14 Type of Regular Issue

Designs: 50fr, 200f, Apollo 14 badge 100fr,
Take-off from moon, and spaceship.

1971, May   Litho.   *Perf. 12¹/₂*
C149 A114 50fr grn & multi   35 15
C150 A114 100fr multi   65 35
C151 A114 200fr org & multi   1.40 65
  a.   Souv. sheet of 4   3.00 2.25

No. C151a contains 4 stamps similar to Nos. 777
and C149-C151 with simulated perforations.
For surcharge and overprints see Nos. C162-
C164.

Cacao Type of Regular Issue

Designs: 60fr, Ministry of Agriculture. 90fr,
Cacao tree and pods. 100fr, Sorting and separating
beans from pods.

1971, June 6   Litho.   *Perf. 14*
C152 A115 60fr multi   40 20
C153 A115 90fr multi   60 30
C154 A115 100fr multi   70 35

ASECNA Type of Regular Issue

1971, June 26
C155 A116 100fr multi   70 35

Tourist Type of Regular Issue

Designs: 50fr, Château Viale and antelope. 60fr,
Lake Togo and crocodile. 100fr, Old lime furnace,
Tokpli, and hippopotamus.

1971, July 17
C156 A117 50fr multi   35 15
C157 A117 60fr multi   40 20
C158 A117 100fr multi   65 35

For overprint see No. C172.

Religions Type of Regular Issue

Designs: 50fr, Mohammedans praying in front of
Lomé Mosque. 60fr, Protestant service. 90fr,
Catholic bishop and priests.

1971, July 31   Litho.   *Perf. 14¹/₂*
C159 A118 50fr multi   30 16
C160 A118 60fr multi   35 20
C161 A118 90fr multi   60 25
  a.   Souvenir sheet of 4, #787, C159-
        C161   1.65 1.40

Nos. C149-C151 Overprinted and Surcharged in Black or Silver: "EN MEMOIRE / DOBROVOLSKY - VOLKOV - PATSAYEV / SOYUZ 11"

C162 A114 90fr on 50fr multi   60 25
C163 A114 100fr multi (S)   65 30
C164 A114 200fr multi   1.40 50
  a.   Souvenir sheet of 4, #788, C162-
        C164   2.75 2.25

See note after No. 788.

Olympic Type of Regular Issue

Design: 200fr, Sapporo '72 emblem and Ski
jump.

1971, Oct. 30   Litho.   *Perf. 14*
C165 A119 200fr multi   1.40 50
  a.   Souvenir sheet of 4   2.00 1.90

No. C165 contains 4 stamps with simulated perforations similar to Nos. 791-793 and C165 printed
on glazed paper.

African Postal Union Issue, 1971
Common Design Type

Design: 100fr, Adjogbo dancers and UAMPT
Building, Brazzaville, Congo.

1971, Nov. 13   Photo.   *Perf. 13x13¹/₂*
C166 CD135 100fr bl & multi   70 40

Intl. Organization for the Protection of Children (U.I.P.E.) — AP14a

Die Cut Perf. 10½
1971, Nov. 13   **Embossed**
C166A AP14a 1500fr gold

UNICEF Type of Regular Issue

Toys and UNICEF Emblem: 60fr, Turtle. 90fr, Parrot.

1971, Nov. 27   **Litho.**   *Perf. 14*
C167 A120 60fr lt bl & multi   40   18
C168 A120 90fr multi   60   22
    a.   Souvenir sheet of 4   1.90 1.90

No. C168a contains 4 stamps with simulated perforations similar to Nos. 796-797 and C167-C168.
For overprints see Nos. C263-C264.

Christmas Type of Regular Issue

Virgin and Child by: 60fr, Giorgione. 100fr, Raphael.

1971, Dec. 24   *Perf. 14x13*
C169 A121 60fr ol & multi   40   25
C170 A121 100fr multi   70   40
    a.   Souvenir sheet of 4   2.00 1.65

No. C170a contains 4 stamps with simulated perforations similar to Nos. 800-801, C169-C170.

Venice Type of Regular Issue

Design: 100fr, Ca' d'Oro, Venice.

1972, Feb. 26   **Litho.**   *Perf. 14*
C171 A122 100fr multi   70   40
    a.   Souvenir sheet of 3   1.50 1.50

No. C171a contains 3 stamps similar to Nos. 802-803, C171 with simulated perforations.

No. C156 Overprinted "VISITE DU PRESIDENT / NIXON EN CHINE / FEVRIER 1972"

1972, Mar.   **Litho.**   *Perf. 14*
C172 A117 50fr multi   35   20

Visit of Pres. Richard M. Nixon to the People's Republic of China, Feb. 20-27.

Easter Type of Regular Issue

Paintings: 50fr, Resurrection, by Thomas de Coloswa. 100fr, Ascension by Andrea Mantegna.

1972, Mar. 31
C173 A123 50fr gold & multi   45   15
C174 A123 100fr gold & multi   65   35
    a.   Souvenir sheet of 4   2.00 1.90

No. C174a contains 4 stamps similar to Nos. 806-807, C173-C174 with simulated perforations.

Heart Type of Regular Issue

Design: 100fr, Heart, WHO emblem and smith.

1972, Apr. 4
C175 A124 100fr multi   65   40
    a.   Souvenir sheet of 2   1.25 1.20

No. C175a contains 2 stamps similar to Nos. 810 and C175 with simulated perforations.

Telecommunications Type of Regular Issue

Design: 100fr, Intelsat 4 over Africa.

1972, June 24   *Perf. 14*
C176 A125 100fr multi   70   30

       For overprint see No. C229.

Cassava Type of Regular Issue

Designs: 60fr, Truck and cassava processing factory, horiz. 80fr, Children, mother holding tapioca cake.

1972, June 30
C177 A126 60fr multi   45   22
C178 A126 80fr multi   55   25

No. C133 Surcharged in Deep Carmine: "VISITE DU PRESIDENT / NIXON EN RUSSIE / MAI 1972"

1972, July 15   **Litho.**   *Perf. 12½*
C179 A106 300fr on 50fr multi   2.50 1.40

President Nixon's visit to the USSR, May 1972. Old denomination obliterated with 6x5mm rectangle.

Olympic Type of Regular Issue

1972, Aug. 26   **Litho.**   *Perf. 14*
C180 A127 90fr Gymnastics   65   35
    a.   Souv. sheet of 2   1.25 1.10
C181 A127 200fr Basketball   1.50   65

No. C180a contains 2 stamps with simulated perforations similar to Nos. 816 and C180.
For overprints see Nos. C234-C235.

Bird Type of Regular Issue

Bird: 90fr, Rose-ringed parakeet.

1972, Sept. 9
C182 A128 90fr multi   65   35
    a.   Souvenir sheet of 4   1.90 1.50

No. C182a contains 4 stamps similar to Nos. 818-820, C182 with simulated perforations.

Rotary Type of Regular Issue

Rotary Emblem and: 60fr, Map of Togo, olive branch. 90fr, Flags of Togo and Rotary Club. 100fr, Paul P. Harris.

1972, Oct. 7   **Litho.**   *Perf. 14*
C183 A129 60fr brn & multi   35   16
C184 A129 90fr multi   50   35
C185 A129 100fr multi   60   38

For overprints see Nos. C212-C213, C244-C245.

Painting Type of Regular Issue, 1972

Designs: 60fr, Mystical Marriage of St. Catherine, by Assistant to the P. M. Master. 80fr, Self-portrait, by Leonardo da Vinci. 100fr, Sts. Mary and Agnes by Botticelli.

1972, Oct. 21
C186 A130 60fr gold & multi   40   20
C187 A130 80fr gold & multi   45   25
C188 A130 100fr gold & multi   80   40
    a.   Souvenir sheet of 4   2.25 1.50

No. C188a contains 4 stamps with simulated perforations similar to Nos. 824, C186-188.

Presidential Visit Type of Regular Issue

Design: 100fr, Pres. Pompidou and Col. Etienne Eyadema, front view of party headquarters.

1972, Nov. 23   **Litho.**   *Perf. 14*
C189 A131 100fr multi   80   40

Johann Wolfgang von Goethe (1749-1832), German Poet and Dramatist — AP15

1972, Dec. 2   **Photo.**   *Perf. 13x14*
C190 AP15 100fr grn & multi   80   40

Christmas Type of Regular Issue

Paintings: 60fr, Nativity, by Master Vyshchibrod. 80fr, Adoration of the Kings, anonymous. 100fr, Flight into Egypt, by Giotto.

1972, Dec. 23   **Litho.**   *Perf. 14*
C191 A132 60fr gold & multi   45   20
C192 A132 80fr gold & multi   60   30
C193 A132 100fr gold & multi   80   40
    a.   Souvenir sheet of 4   2.00 2.00

No. C193a contains 4 stamps with simulated perforations similar to Nos. 829, C191-C193.

Leprosy Day Type of Regular Issue

Design: 100fr, Dr. Armauer G. Hansen, apparatus, microscope and Petri dish.

1973, Jan. 23   **Photo.**   *Perf. 14x13½*
C194 A133 100fr rose car & bl   70   40

World Leprosy Day and centenary of the discovery of the Hansen bacillus, the cause of leprosy.

Miniature Sheets

1972 Summer Olympics, Munich — AP15a

Medalists: No. C194A, Mark Spitz, US, swimming. No. C194B, L. Linsenhoff, West Germany, equestrian. No. C194C, D. Morelon, France, cycling.

Litho. & Embossed
1973, Jan.   *Perf. 13½*
C194A- AP15a 1500fr multi
C194C

       Exist imperf.

Miniature Sheet

Apollo 17 Moon Landing — AP15b

1973, Jan.
C194D AP15b 1500fr gold & multi

       Exists imperf.

Easter Type of Regular Issue

1973, Apr. 21   *Perf. 14*
C195 A135 90fr Christ in Glory   60   35
    a.   Souvenir sheet of 2   1.00 1.00

No. C195a contains one each of Nos. 835 and C195 with simulated perforations.

Apollo 17 Type of Regular Issue

Designs: 100fr, Astronauts on moon and orange rock. 200fr, Rocket lift-off at Cape Kennedy and John F. Kennedy.

1973, June 2   **Litho.**   *Perf. 14*
C196 A136 100fr multi   70   38
C197 A136 200fr multi   1.50   60
    a.   Souvenir sheet of 2   2.25 2.00

No. C197a contains 2 stamps similar to Nos. C196-C197 with simulated perforations.

Boy Scout Type of Regular Issue

Designs: 100fr, Canoeing, horiz. 200fr, Campfire, horiz.

1973, June 30   **Litho.**   *Perf. 14*
C198 A137 100fr bl & multi   70   40
C199 A137 200fr bl & multi   1.50   65
    a.   Souvenir sheet of 2   2.25 2.00

No. C199a contains 2 stamps similar to Nos. C198-C199 with simulated perforations.
For overprints see Nos. C265-C266.

Copernicus Type of Regular Issue

Designs: 90fr, Heliocentric system. 100fr, Nicolaus Copernicus.

1973, July 18
C200 A138 90fr multi   60   30
C201 A138 100fr bls & multi   70   40
    a.   Souv. sheet of 2, #C200-C201   1.50 1.35

Red Cross Type of Regular Issue

Design: 100fr, Dove carrying Red Cross letter, sun, map of Togo.

1973, Aug. 4
C202 A139 100fr multi   65   35

       For overprint see No. C294.

Literacy Type of Regular Issue

Design: 90fr, Woman teacher in classroom.

1973, Aug. 18   **Litho.**   *Perf. 14*
C203 A140 90fr multi   60   35

WMO Type of Regular Issue

1973, Oct. 4   **Photo.**   *Perf. 14x13*
C204 A142 200fr dl bl, pur & brn   1.50   60

Type of Regular Issue 1967

Design: 100fr, Early and contemporary planes, Nos. 758 and C36.

1973, Oct. 20   **Photo.**   *Perf. 14x13*
C205 A79 100fr multi   80   35
    a.   Souvenir sheet of 2   1.60 1.40

75th anniversary of Togolese postal service. No. C205a contains 2 stamps similar to Nos. 855 and C205 with simulated perforations.

Kennedy Type of Regular Issue

Designs: 90fr, Kennedy and Charles De Gaulle. 100fr, Kennedy and Nikita Krushchev. 200fr, Kennedy and model of Apollo spacecraft.

1973, Nov. 22   **Litho.**   *Perf. 14*
C206 A143 90fr blk & pink   60   35
C207 A143 100fr blk, lt bl & bl   70   38
C208 A143 200fr blk, buff & brn   1.40   60
    a.   Souvenir sheet of 2   2.25 2.00

No. C208a contains 2 stamps similar to Nos. C207-208 with simulated perforations.

Human Rights Flame and People — AP16

1973, Dec. 8   **Photo.**   *Perf. 13x14*
C209 AP16 250fr lt bl & multi   1.90   80

25th anniversary of the Universal Declaration of Human Rights.

Christmas Type of Regular Issue

Paintings: 90fr, Virgin and Child. 100fr, Adoration of the Kings. Both after 15th century Italian paintings.

1973, Dec. 22   **Litho.**   *Perf. 14*
C210 A144 90fr gold & multi   60   25
C211 A144 100fr gold & multi   70   35
    a.   Souvenir sheet of 2   1.60 1.50

No. C211a contains 2 stamps with simulated perforations similar to Nos. C210-C211.

Nos. C183 and C185 Overprinted: "PREMIERE CONVENTION / 210eme DISTRICT / FEVRIER 1974 / LOME"

1974, Feb. 21   **Litho.**   *Perf. 14*
C212 A129 60fr brn & multi   40   20
C213 A129 100fr multi   60   35

First convention of Rotary International, District 210, Lomé, Feb. 22-24.

Soccer Type of Regular Issue

Designs: Various soccer scenes and games' cup.

1974, Mar. 2   Litho.   *Perf. 14*

C214	A145	90fr multi	72 35
C215	A145	100fr multi	85 42
C216	A145	200fr multi	1.65 72
a.		Souvenir sheet of 2	3.00 2.50

No. C216a contains 2 stamps with simulated perforations similar to Nos. C215-C216.

Picasso Type of 1974

Paintings: 90fr, The Muse. 100fr, Les Demoiselles d'Avignon. 200fr, Sitting Nude.

1974, Apr. 6   *Perf. 14*

C217	A146	90fr brn & multi	60 30
C218	A146	100fr pur & multi	70 35
C219	A146	200fr multi	1.40 65
a.		Souvenir sheet of 3	3.50 3.00

No. C219a contains 3 stamps similar to Nos. C217-C219 with simulated perforations.

Coastal Views Type of 1974

Designs: 90fr, Fishermen on Lake Togo. 100fr, Mouth of Anecho River.

1974, Apr. 20

C220	A147	90fr multi	60 22
C221	A147	100fr multi	65 30
a.		Souvenir sheet of 2	1.40 1.20

No. C221a contains 2 stamps similar to Nos. C220-C221 with simulated perforations.

UPU Type of 1974

Designs: Old mailmen's uniforms.

1974, May 10   Litho.   *Perf. 14*

C222	A148	50fr multi	40 16
C223	A148	100fr multi	70 35
a.		Souvenir sheet of 2	10.00 8.25

No. C223a contains 2 stamps similar to Nos. C222-C223, rouletted.

Fishing Type of 1974

Designs: 90fr, Fishermen bringing in net with catch. 100fr, Fishing with rod and line. 200fr, Fishing with basket, vert.

1974, June 22   Litho.   *Perf. 14*

C224	A149	90fr multi	50 25
C225	A149	100fr multi	55 25
C226	A149	200fr multi	1.10 65
a.		Souvenir sheet of 3	2.25 2.00

No. C226a contains 3 stamps with simulated perforations similar to Nos. C224-C226.

Jupiter Probe Type of 1974

Designs: 100fr, Rocket take-off, vert. 200fr, Satellite in space.

1974, July 6   *Perf. 14*

C227	A150	100fr multi	65 35
C228	A150	200fr multi	1.40 65
a.		Souvenir sheet of 2	5.00 3.75

No. C228a contains 2 stamps similar to Nos. C227-C228 with simulated perforations; imperf. or rouletted.

No. C176 Overprinted

1974, July   *Perf. 14*

C229 A125 100fr multi   1.60   65

INTERNABA 1974 Intl. Philatelic Exhibition, Basel, June 7-16.

Seashell Type of 1974

1974, July 13   Litho.   *Perf. 14*

C230	A151	90fr Alcithoe ponsonbyi	50 25
C231	A151	100fr Casmaria iredalei	55 35
a.		Souvenir sheet of 2	1.25 1.10

No. C231a contains 2 stamps similar to Nos. C230-C231 with simulated perforations.

Horse Racing Type of 1974

Designs: 90fr, Steeplechase. 100fr, Galloping horses.

1974, Aug. 3   Litho.   *Perf. 14*

C232	A152	90fr multi	60 25
C233	A152	100fr multi	70 35
a.		Souvenir sheet of 2	1.50 1.20

No. C233a contains one each of Nos. C232-C233 with simulated perforations.

Nos. C180, C180a and C181 Overprinted: "COUPE DU MONDE / DE FOOTBALL / VAINQUEURS / REPUBLIQUE FEDERALE / d'ALLEMAGNE"

1974, Aug. 19

C234	A127	90fr multi	60 25
a.		Souvenir sheet of 2	1.20 1.20
C235	A127	200fr multi	1.20 65

World Cup Soccer Championship, Munich, 1974, victory of German Federal Republic. For description of No. C234a see note after No. C181.

Animal Type of 1974

1974, Sept. 7   Litho.   *Perf. 14*

C236	A153	90fr Lions	55 30
C237	A153	100fr Rhinoceroses	60 35
a.		Souvenir sheet of 3	1.60 1.40

Wild animals of West Africa. No. C237a contains 3 stamps similar to Nos. 889, C236-C237 with simulated perforations.

1974, Oct. 14

C238	A153	90fr Herd at waterhole	50 25
C239	A153	100fr Village and cows	55 35
a.		Souvenir sheet of 2	1.50 1.20

Domestic animals. No. C239a contains 2 stamps with simulated perforations similar to Nos. C238-C239.

Churchill Type of 1974

Designs: 100fr, Churchill and frigate. 200fr, Churchill and fighter planes.

1974, Nov. 1   Photo.   *Perf. 13x13¹/₂*

C240	A154	100fr multi	60 30
C241	A154	200fr org & multi	1.20 60
a.		Souvenir sheet of 2	2.25 1.90

No. C241a contains 2 stamps similar to Nos. C240-C241; perf. or imperf.

Flower Type of 1975

Flowers of Togo: 100fr, Clerodendrum thosonae. 200fr, Gloriosa superba.

1975, Feb. 15   Litho.   *Perf. 14*

C242	A155	100fr multi	55 25
C243	A155	200fr multi	1.10 50
a.		Souvenir sheet of 2	3.25 2.50

No. C243a contains one each of Nos. C242-C243, perf. 13x14 or imperf.

Nos. C184-C185 Overprinted: "70e ANNIVERSAIRE / 23 FÉVRIER 1975"

1975, Feb. 23   Litho.   *Perf. 14*

C244	A129	90fr multi	50 25
C245	A129	100fr multi	55 35

Rotary International, 70th anniversary.

Easter Type of 1975

Paintings: 100fr, Christ Rising from the Tomb, by Master MS. 200fr, Holy Trinity (detail), by Dürer.

1975, Apr. 19   Litho.   *Perf. 14*

C246	A157	100fr multi	55 25
C247	A157	200fr multi	1.10 50
a.		Souvenir sheet of 2	1.65 1.40

No. C247a contains 2 stamps similar to Nos. C246-C247 with simulated perforations.

Independence Type of 1975

Designs: 50fr, National Day parade, flag and map of Togo, vert. 60fr, Warriors' dance and flag of Togo.

1975, Apr. 26   Litho.   *Perf. 14*

C248	A158	50fr multi	25 15
C249	A158	60fr multi	35 15
a.		Souvenir sheet of 2	90 50
		Set value	24

No. C249a contains 2 stamps similar to Nos. C248-C249 with simulated perforations.

Hunt Type of 1975

Designs: 90fr, Running deer. 100fr, Wild boar hunter with shotgun.

1975, May 24   Photo.   *Perf. 13x13¹/₂*

C250	A159	90fr multi	50 22
C251	A159	100fr multi	55 25

Palm Oil Type of 1975

Designs: 85fr, Selling palm oil in market, vert. 100fr, Oil processing plant, Alokoegbe.

1975, June 28   Litho.   *Perf. 14*

C252	A160	85fr multi	45 22
C253	A160	100fr multi	55 25

Apollo-Soyuz Type of 1975 and

Soyuz Spacecraft — AP17

Designs: 60fr, Donald K. Slayton, Vance D. Brand and Thomas P. Stafford. 90fr, Aleksei A. Leonov and Valery N. Kubasov. 100fr, Apollo-Soyuz link-up, American and Russian flags. 200fr, Apollo-Soyuz emblem and globe.

1975, July 15

C254	AP17	50fr yel & multi	25 15
C255	A161	60fr lil & multi	35 15
C256	A161	90fr bl & multi	45 22
C257	A161	100fr grn & multi	55 38
C258	A161	200fr yel & multi	1.10 45
a.		Souv. sheet of 4, #C255-C258	3.00 2.00
		Nos. C254-C258 (5)	2.70 1.35

See note after No. 913.

Schweitzer Type of 1975

Dr. Schweitzer: 80fr, playing organ, vert. 90fr, with pelican, vert. 100fr, and Lambarene Hospital.

1975, Aug. 23   Litho.   *Perf. 14x13¹/₂*

C259	A163	80fr multi	42 25
C260	A163	90fr multi	50 30
C261	A163	100fr multi	55 35

Letter Writing Type of 1975

Design: 80fr, Erasmus Writing Letter, by Hans Holbein.

1975, Oct. 9   Litho.   *Perf. 14*

C262 A164 80fr multi   42   25

Nos. C167-C168a Overprinted: "30ème Anniversaire / des Nations-Unies"

1975, Oct. 24   Litho.   *Perf. 14*

C263	A120	60fr multi	35 15
C264	A120	90fr multi	45 25
a.		Souvenir sheet of 4	1.40 1.10

UN, 30th anniv. #C264a contains Nos. 796 (with overprint), 918, C263-C264.

Nos. C198-C199 Overprinted: "14ème JAMBORÉE / MONDIAL / DES ÉCLAIREURS"

1975, Nov. 7

C265	A137	100fr multi	55 25
C266	A137	200fr multi	1.10 50
a.		Souvenir sheet of 2	1.65 1.50

14th World Boy Scout Jamboree, Lillehammer, Norway, July 29-Aug. 7. No. C266a contains one each of Nos. C265-C266 with simulated perforations.

Christmas Type of 1975

Paintings of the Virgin and Child: 90fr, Nativity, by Federico Barocci. 100fr, Bellini. 200fr, Correggio.

1975, Dec. 20   Litho.   *Perf. 14*

C267	A165	90fr bl & multi	50 22
C268	A165	100fr red & multi	55 25
C269	A165	200fr bl & multi	1.10 50
a.		Souv. sheet of 2, #C268-C269	1.90 1.50

Bicentennial Type of 1976

Paintings (and Bicentennial Emblem): 60fr, Surrender of Gen. Burgoyne, by John Trumbull. 70fr, Surrender at Trenton, by Trumbull, vert. 100fr, Signing of Declaration of Independence, by Trumbull. 200fr, Washington Crossing the Delaware, by Emanuel Leutze.

1976, Mar. 3   Litho.   *Perf. 14*

C270	A167	60fr multi	35 16
C271	A167	70fr multi	38 20
C272	A167	100fr multi	55 25
C273	A167	200fr multi	1.10 55
a.		Souv. sheet of 2, #C272-C273	1.65 1.65

No. C273a also exists imperf.; same value. For overprints see Nos. C280-C283.

Common Market Type of 1976

Designs: 60fr, ACP and CEE emblems. 70fr, Map of Africa, Europe and Asia.

1976, Apr. 24   Photo.   *Perf. 13x14*

C274	A168	60fr lt bl & multi	35 16
C275	A168	70fr yel & multi	38 20

Telephone Type of 1976

Designs: 70fr, Thomas A. Edison, old and new communications equipment. 105fr, Alexander Graham Bell, old and new telephones.

1976, Mar. 10   Photo.   *Perf. 13x14*

C276	A169	70fr multi	38 20
C277	A169	105fr multi	55 35
a.		Souv. sheet of 2, #C276-C277	1.00 90

No. C277a exists imperf.; same value.

Eye Examination   Pylon, Flags of
AP18   Ghana, Togo, Dahomey AP19

1976, Apr. 8   *Perf. 14x13*

C278 AP18 60fr dk red & multi   35   18

World Health Day: "Foresight prevents blindness."

1976, May 8   Litho.   *Perf. 14*

C279 AP19 60fr multi   35   18

Ghana-Togo-Dahomey electric power grid, 1st anniv. See No. 932.

Nos. C270-C273, C273a, Overprinted: "INTERPHIL / MAI 29-JUIN 6, 1976"

1976, May 29

C280	A167	60fr multi	35 16
C281	A167	70fr multi	38 20
C282	A167	100fr multi	55 25
C283	A167	200fr multi	1.10 55
a.		Souvenir sheet of 2	1.60 1.50

Interphil 76 Intl. Philatelic Exhibition, Philadelphia, Pa., May 29-June 6. Overprint on No. C281 in 3 lines; overprint on No. C283a applied to each stamp.

Olympic Games Type of 1976

Montreal Olympic Emblem and: 70fr, Yachting. 105fr, Motorcycling. 200fr, Fencing.

1976, June 15   Photo.   *Perf. 14x13*

C284	A172	70fr multi	45 25
C285	A172	105fr multi	65 42
C286	A172	200fr multi	1.25 65
a.		Souvenir sheet of 2, #C285-C286, perf. 14	2.50 2.25

For overprints see Nos. C298-C299.

Viking Type of 1976

Designs: 60fr, Viking landing on Mars. 70fr, Nodus Gordii (view on Mars). 105fr, Lander over Mare Tyrrhenum. 200fr, Landing on Mars.

1976, July 15   Litho.   *Perf. 14*

C287	A173	60fr bis & multi	35 18
C288	A173	70fr multi	38 20
C289	A173	105fr bl & multi	55 35
C290	A173	200fr multi	1.10 55
a.		Souv. sheet of 2, #C289-C290, perf. 14x13¹/₂	1.90 1.65

Toulouse-Lautrec Type, 1976

Paintings: 60fr, Carmen, portrait. 70fr, Maurice at the Somme. 200fr, "Messalina."

1976, Aug. 7   Litho.   Perf. 14

C291	A174	60fr blk & multi	35	18
C292	A174	70fr blk & multi	38	25
C293	A174	200fr blk & multi	1.10	55
a.		Souv. sheet of 2, #C292-C293, perf. 13½x14	1.60	1.50

No. C202 Overprinted: "Journeé / Internationale / de l'Enfance"

1976, Nov. 27   Litho.   Perf. 14

C294	A139	100fr multi	55	35

International Children's Day.

Christmas Type of 1976

Paintings: 70fr, Holy Family, by Lorenzo Lotto. 105fr, Virgin and Child with Saints, by Jacopo da Pontormo. 200fr, Virgin and Child with Saints, by Lotto.

1976, Dec. 18

C295	A175	70fr multi	38	20
C296	A175	105fr multi	55	35
C297	A175	200fr multi	1.10	55
a.		Souv. sheet of 2, #C296-C297	1.90	1.60

No. C284 Overprinted: "CHAMPIONS OLYMPIQUES / YACHTING - FLYING DUTCHMAN / REPUBLIQUE FEDERALE ALLEMAGNE"

No. C286 Overprinted: "CHAMPIONS OLYMPIQUES / ESCRIMEFLEURET PAR EQUIPES / REPUBLIQUE FEDERALE ALLEMAGNE"

1976, Dec.   Photo.   Perf. 14x13

C298	A172	70fr multi	38	20
C299	A172	200fr multi	1.10	60
a.		Souvenir sheet of 2	1.90	1.65

Olympic winners. No. C299a (on No. C286a) contains Nos. C285 and C299.

Eyadema Anniversary Type of 1977

Designs: 60fr, National Assembly Building. 100fr, Pres. Eyadema greeting people at Aug. 30th meeting.

1977, Jan. 13   Photo.   Perf. 13x14

C300	A177	60fr multi	35	15
C301	A177	100fr multi	55	30
a.		Souv. sheet of 2, #C300-C301	90	85

Musical Instrument Type of 1977

Musical Instruments: 60fr, Atopani. 80fr, African violin, vert. 105fr, African flutes, vert.

1977, Feb. 7   Litho.   Perf. 14

C302	A178	60fr multi	35	15
C303	A178	80fr multi	40	18
C304	A178	105fr multi	55	25
a.		Souv. sheet of 2, #C303-C304	1.20	1.00

Victor Hugo Type of 1977

Design: 60fr, Victor Hugo in exile on Guernsey Island.

1977, Feb. 26   Perf. 13x14

C305	A179	60fr multi	35	18
a.		Souvenir sheet of 2, #952, C305	65	60

For overprint see No. C316.

Beethoven Type of 1977

Designs: 100fr, Beethoven's piano and 1818 portrait. 200fr, Beethoven on his deathbed and Holy Trinity Church, Vienna.

1977, Mar. 7   Perf. 14

C306	A180	100fr multi	55	35
C307	A180	200fr multi	1.10	65
a.		Souv. sheet of 2, #C306-C307	1.65	1.65

Automobile Type of 1977

Early Automobiles: 60fr, Cannstatt-Daimler, 1899, Germany. 70fr, Sunbeam, 1904, England. 100fr, Renault, 1908, France. 200fr, Rolls Royce, 1909, England.

1977, Apr. 11   Litho.   Perf. 14

C308	A181	60fr multi	35	18
C309	A181	70fr multi	38	20
C310	A181	100fr multi	55	30
C311	A181	200fr multi	1.10	65
a.		Souv. sheet of 2, #C310-C311	1.65	1.65

Lindbergh Type of 1977

Designs: 60fr, Lindbergh and son Jon, birds in flight. 85fr, Lindbergh home in Kent, England. 90fr, Spirit of St. Louis over Atlantic Ocean. 100fr, Concorde over NYC.

1977, May 9

C312	A182	60fr multi	40	16
C313	A182	85fr multi	55	20
C314	A182	90fr multi	60	20
C315	A182	100fr multi	65	22
a.		Souv. sheet of 2, #C314-C315	1.40	85

No. C305 Overprinted: "10ème ANNIVERSAIRE DU / CONSEIL INTERNATIONAL / DE LA LANGUE FRANCAISE"

1977, May 17   Litho.   Perf. 14

C316	A179	60fr multi	40	20

10th anniv. of the French Language Council.

Wildlife Type of 1977

Designs: 60fr, Colobus monkeys. 90fr, Chimpanzee, vert. 100fr, Leopard. 200fr, West African manatee.

1977, June 13

C317	A183	60fr multi	40	15
C318	A183	90fr multi	60	16
C319	A183	100fr multi	65	18
C320	A183	200fr multi	1.40	35
a.		Souv. sheet of 2, #C319-C320	2.25	1.25

Agriculture Type of 1977

Designs: 60fr, Corn silo. 100fr, Hoeing and planting by hand. 200fr, Tractor on field.

1977, July 11   Litho.   Perf. 14

C321	A184	60fr multi	40	15
C322	A184	100fr multi	65	20
C323	A184	200fr multi	1.40	35
a.		Souv. sheet of 2, #C322-C323, perf. 13x14	2.25	1.25

Rubens Type of 1977

Paintings: 60fr, Heads of Black Men, 1620. 100fr, Anne of Austria, 1624.

1977, Aug. 8

C324	A185	60fr multi	40	15
C325	A185	100fr multi	65	18
a.		Souv. sheet of 2, #C324-C325, perf. 14x13	1.20	65

Orbiter Type of 1977

Designs: 90fr, Retrieval of unmanned satellite in space, vert. 100fr, Satellite's return to space after repairs. 200fr, Manned landing of Orbiter.

1977, Oct. 4   Litho.   Perf. 14

C326	A186	90fr multi	60	16
C327	A186	100fr multi	65	18
C328	A186	200fr multi	1.35	35
a.		Souv. sheet of 2, #C327-C328	2.25	1.25

Lafayette Type of 1977

Designs: 60fr, Lafayette landing in New York, 1824. 105fr, Lafayette and Washington at Valley Forge.

1977, Nov. 7   Perf. 13x14

C329	A187	60fr multi	40	15
C330	A187	105fr multi	70	18
a.		Souv. sheet of 2, #C329-C330	1.20	65

Christmas Type of 1977

Virgin and Child by: 90fr, 200fr, Carlo Crivelli (different). 100fr, Bellini.

1977, Dec. 19   Perf. 14

C331	A189	60fr multi	60	16
C332	A189	100fr multi	65	18
C333	A189	200fr multi	1.40	35
a.		Souv. sheet of 2, #C332-C333	2.25	1.25

Jenner Type of 1978

Designs: 50fr, Edward Jenner. 60fr, Smallpox vaccination clinic, horiz.

1978, Jan. 9   Perf. 14x13, 13x14

C334	A190	50fr multi	35	15
C335	A190	60fr multi	40	15
a.		Souv. sheet of 2	80	50

No. C335a contains 2 stamps with simulated perforations similar to Nos. C334-C335.

Wright Brothers Type of 1978

Designs: 60fr, Orville Wright's 7½-minute flight. 70fr, Orville Wright injured in first aircraft accident, 1908. 200fr, Wrights' bicycle shop, Dearborn, Mich. 300fr, First flight, 1903.

1978, Feb. 6   Litho.   Perf. 14

C336	A191	60fr multi	40	15
C337	A191	70fr multi	45	18
C338	A191	100fr multi	1.40	35
C339	A191	300fr multi	2.00	60
a.		Souvenir sheet of 2	3.50	2.00

No. C339a contains one each of Nos. C338-C339 with simulated perforations.

Port of Lomé Type, 1978

Anchor and: 60fr, Industrial harbor. 100fr, Merchant marine harbor. 200fr, Bird's-eye view of entire harbor.

1978, Apr. 26   Photo.   Perf. 13

C340	A199	60fr multi	40	15
C341	A199	100fr multi	65	20
C342	A199	200fr multi	1.40	35
a.		Souv. sheet of 2, #C341-C342	2.25	1.25

Space Type of 1978

Designs: 90fr, Module camera, horiz. 100fr, Module antenna. 200fr, Pioneer, US, in orbit.

1978, May 8   Litho.   Perf. 14

C343	A200	90fr multi	60	20
C344	A200	100fr multi	65	20
C345	A200	200fr multi	1.40	35
a.		Souv. sheet of 2, #C344-C345, perf. 13½x14	2.25	1.25

Soccer Type of 1978

Designs: Various soccer scenes and Argentina '78 emblem.

1978, June 5   Perf. 14

C346	A201	60fr multi	40	15
C347	A201	80fr multi	55	18
C348	A201	100fr multi	1.40	35
C349	A201	200fr multi	2.00	50
a.		Souvenir sheet of 2, #C348-C349, perf. 13½x14	3.75	2.25

Bicycle Type of 1978

History of Bicycle: 60fr, Bantam, 1896, vert. 85fr, Fold-up bicycle for military use, 1897. 90fr, Draisienne, 1816, vert. 100fr, Penny-farthing, 1884, vert.

Perf. 14x13, 13x14   Photo.

1978, July 10

C350	A202	60fr multi	40	15
C351	A202	85fr multi	55	20
C352	A202	90fr multi	60	22
C353	A202	100fr multi	65	25
a.		Souv. sheet of 2, #C352-C353	1.40	85

Phonograph Type of 1978

Designs: 60fr, Edison's original phonograph, horiz. 80fr, Emile Berliner's phonograph, 1888. 200fr, Berliner's improved phonograph, 1894, horiz. 300fr, His Master's Voice phonograph, 1900, horiz.

Perf. 13x14, 14x13

1978, July 8   Photo.

C354	A203	60fr multi	40	15
C355	A203	80fr multi	55	20
C356	A203	200fr multi	1.35	35
C357	A203	300fr multi	2.00	50
a.		Souv. sheet of 2, #C356-C357	3.50	2.00

Red Cross Type of 1978

Design: 60fr, Red Cross and other pavilions at Paris Exhibition, 1867.

1978, Sept. 4   Photo.   Perf. 14x13

C358	A204	60fr pur & red	40	20
a.		Souvenir sheet of 2, #1009, C358	65	40

Paintings Type of 1978

Paintings: 60fr, Langlois Bridge, by Vincent van Gogh. 70fr, Witches' Sabbath, by Francisco Goya. 90fr, Jesus among the Doctors, by Albrecht Dürer. 200fr, View of Arco, by Dürer.

1978, Nov. 6   Litho.   Perf. 14

C359	A205	60fr multi	40	20
C360	A205	70fr multi	45	22
C361	A205	90fr multi	60	35
C362	A205	200fr multi	1.35	65
a.		Souv. sheet of 2, #C361-C362	2.00	1.20

Birth and death anniversaries of famous painters.

Philexafrique II - Essen Issue
Common Design Types

Designs: No. C363, Warthog and Togo No. C36. No. C364, Firecrest and Thurn and Taxis No. 1.

1978, Nov. 1   Litho.   Perf. 13x12½

C363	CD138	100fr multi	65	35
C364	CD139	100fr multi	65	35

Nos. C363-C364 printed se-tenant.

Congress of Paris Type of 1978

Designs: 60fr, Mail ship "Slieve Roe" 1877, and post horn. 105fr, Congress of Paris medal. 200fr, Locomotive, 1870. All horizontal.

1978, Nov. 27   Photo.   Perf. 14x13

C365	A206	60fr multi	40	20
C366	A206	105fr multi	70	35
C367	A206	200fr multi	1.40	65
a.		Souv. sheet of 2, #C366-C367	2.25	1.25

Christmas Type of 1978

Paintings (Virgin and Child): 90fr, 200fr, by Carlo Crivelli, diff. 100fr, by Cosimo Tura.

1978, Dec. 18

C368	A207	90fr multi	60	30
C369	A207	100fr multi	65	35
C370	A207	200fr multi	1.35	65
a.		Souv. sheet of 2, #C369-C370	2.25	1.25

Capt. Cook Type of 1979

Designs: 60fr, "Freelove," Whitby Harbor, horiz. 70fr, Trip to Antarctica, 1773, horiz. 90fr, Capt. Cook. 200fr, Sails of Endeavour.

1979, Feb. 12   Litho.   Perf. 14

C371	A208	60fr multi	40	20
C372	A208	70fr multi	45	22
C373	A208	90fr multi	60	30
C374	A208	200fr multi	1.40	1.20
a.		Souv. sheet of 2, #C373-C374	2.00	1.75

Easter Type of 1979

Designs: 60fr, Resurrection. 100fr, Ascension. 200fr, Jesus appearing to Mary Magdalene.

1979, Apr. 9

C375	A209	60fr multi	40	20
C376	A209	100fr multi	65	35
C377	A209	200fr multi	1.40	65
a.		Souv. sheet of 2, #C376-C377	2.25	1.25

UPU Emblem, Drummer — AP20

Design: 100fr, UPU emblem, hands passing letter, satellites.

1979, June 8   Engr.   Perf. 13

C378	AP20	60fr multi	40	20
C379	AP20	100fr multi	65	35

Philexafrique II, Libreville, Gabon, June 8-17.

Einstein Type of 1979

Designs: 60fr, Sights and actuality diagram. 85fr, Einstein playing violin, vert. 100fr, Atom symbol and formula of relativity, vert. 200fr, Einstein portrait, vert.

Perf. 14x13, 13x14

1979, July 2   Photo.

C380	A210	60fr multi	40	15
C381	A210	85fr multi	60	28
C382	A210	100fr multi	65	35
C383	A210	200fr multi	1.40	65
a.		Souv. sheet of 2, #C382-C383	2.25	1.25

Tree Type of 1979

Design: 60fr, Man watering tree.

1979, Aug. 13   Perf. 14x13

C384	A212	60fr blk & brn	40	20

Rowland Hill Type of 1979

Designs: 90fr, Bellman, England, 1820. 100fr, "Centercycles" used for parcel delivery, 1883, horiz. 200fr, French P.O. railroad car, 1848, horiz.

1979, Aug. 27   Photo.

C385	A213	90fr multi	60	30
C386	A213	100fr multi	65	35
C387	A213	200fr multi	1.40	65
a.		Souv. sheet of 2, #C386-C387	2.25	2.25

Train Type of 1979

Historic Locomotives: 60fr, "Le General," 1862. 85fr, Stephenson's, 1843. 100fr, "De Witt Clinton," 1831. 200fr, Joy's "Jenny Lind," 1847.

1979, Oct. 1   Litho.   Perf. 14

C388	A214	60fr multi	40	20
C389	A214	85fr multi	55	28
C390	A214	100fr multi	65	35
C391	A214	200fr multi	1.40	65
a.		Souv. sheet of 2, #C390-C391	2.25	2.25

Olympic Type of 1979

1980 Olympic Emblems and: 90fr, Ski jump. No. C393, Doubles canoeing, Olympic flame. No. C394, Rings. No. C395a, Bobsledding, horiz. No. C395b, Gymnast, horiz.

1979, Oct. 18   Litho.   *Perf. 13½*

C392	A215	90fr multi	60	30
C393	A215	100fr multi	65	35
C394	A215	200fr multi	1.40	65
a.		Souvenir sheet of 2	2.25	2.25

Souvenir Sheet

C395		Sheet of 2	2.25	2.25
a.	A215	100fr multi	65	35
b.	A215	200fr multi	1.40	65

Religion Type of 1979

Designs: 60fr, Moslems praying. 70fr, Protestant ministers.

1979, Oct. 29   *Perf. 13x14*

C396	A216	60fr multi	40	20
C397	A216	70fr multi	45	22
a.		Souvenir sheet of 2, #C396-C397	1.00	1.00

Apollo 11 Type of 1979

Designs: 60fr, Astronaut leaving Apollo 11. 70fr, US flag. 200fr, Sun shield. 300fr, Lunar take-off.

1979, Nov. 5   *Perf. 13½*

C398	A217	60fr multi	40	20
C399	A217	70fr multi	45	22
C400	A217	200fr multi	1.40	65
C401	A217	300fr multi	2.00	1.00
a.		Souv. sheet of 2, #C400-C401	3.75	3.75

Telecom Type of 1979

Design: 60fr, Telecom 79, dish antenna.

1979, Nov. 26   Photo.   *Perf. 14x13*

C402	A218	60fr multi	40	20

Miniature Sheets

President Eyadema, 10th Anniv. of the People's Republic — AP21

Illustration reduced.

Litho. & Embossed
1979, Nov. 30   *Perf. 13½*

C402A	AP21	1000fr In uniform	

Imperf

C402B	AP21	1000fr In suit, vert.	

Exist imperf.

Christmas Type of 1979

Designs: 90fr, Adoration of the Kings. 100fr, Presentation of Infant Jesus. 200fr, Flight into Egypt.

1979, Dec. 17   Litho.   *Perf. 14*

C403	A219	90fr multi	60	30
C404	A219	100fr multi	65	35
C405	A219	200fr multi	1.35	65
a.		Souv. sheet of 2, #C404-C405	2.25	1.25

Rotary Type of 1980

3-H Emblem and: 90fr, Man reaching for sun. 100fr, Fish, grain. 200fr, Family, globe.

1980, Jan. 14

C406	A220	90fr multi	60	30
C407	A220	100fr multi	65	35
C408	A220	200fr multi	1.35	65
a.		Souv. sheet of 2, C407-C408	2.25	1.25

Rotary Intl., 75th anniv.; 3-H program (health, hunger, humanity).

Winter Olympic Type, 1980

1980, Jan. 31   Litho.   *Perf. 13½*

C409	A221	90fr Downhill skiing	40	20
C410	A221	100fr Speed skating	65	35
C411	A221	200fr Cross-country skiing	1.35	65

Souvenir Sheet

C412		Sheet of 2	2.00	1.00
a.	A221	100fr Ski jump, horiz.	65	35
b.	A221	200fr Hockey, horiz.	1.35	65

Olympic Type of 1980

1980, Feb. 29   Litho.   *Perf. 13½*

C413	A222	100fr Fencing	80	42
C414	A222	200fr Pole vault	1.65	80
C415	A222	300fr Hurdles	2.50	1.25
a.		Souv. sheet of 2, #C414-C415	4.75	2.50

Easter Type of 1980

Easter 1980 (Paintings by): 60fr, Lorenzo Lotto. 100fr, El Greco. 200fr, Carlo Crivelli.

1980, Mar. 31   *Perf. 14*

C416	A223	60fr multi	40	20
C417	A223	100fr multi	65	35
C418	A223	200fr multi	1.35	65
a.		Souv. sheet of 2, #C417-C418	2.00	1.00

ASECNA Type of 1980

1980, Mar. 24   Litho.   *Perf. 12½*

C419	A224	60fr multi	40	20

Telecommunications Type of 1980

1980, May 17   Photo.   *Perf. 13½x14*

C420	A225	60fr "17 MAI", vert.	40	20

Red Cross Type of 1980

1980, June 16   Photo.   *Perf. 14x13*

C421	A226	60fr Nurses, patient	40	20

Jules Verne Type of 1980

Designs: 60fr, Rocket (From Earth to Moon). 80fr, Around the World in 80 Days. 100fr, Rocket and moon (From Earth to Moon). 200fr, Octopus (20,000 Leagues Under the Sea).

1980, July 14   Litho.   *Perf. 14*

C422	A227	60fr multi	40	20
C423	A227	80fr multi	55	25
C424	A227	100fr multi	65	35
C425	A227	200fr multi	1.35	65
a.		Souv. sheet of 2, #C424-C425, perf. 13½x14	2.00	1.00

Ingres Type of 1980

Ingres Paintings: 90fr, Jupiter and Thetis. 100fr, Countess d'Hassonville. 200fr, "Tu Marcellus Eris."

1980, Aug. 29   Litho.   *Perf. 14*

C426	A228	90fr multi	60	30
C427	A228	100fr multi	65	35
C428	A228	200fr multi	1.35	65
a.		Souv. sheet of 2, C427-C428	2.00	1.00

Famous Men Type of 1980

Designs: 90fr, Salvador Allende, vert. 100fr, Pope Paul VI, vert. 200fr, Jomo Kenyatta, vert.

1980, Feb. 11   Litho.   *Perf. 14x13*

C429	A231	90fr ultra & lt bl grn	60	30
C430	A231	100fr pur & pink	65	35
C431	A231	200fr brn & yel bis	1.35	65
a.		Souv. sheet of 2, #C430-C431	2.00	1.00

Human Rights Type of 1980

1980, Oct. 13   *Perf. 13x14*

C432	A233	60fr Map of Americas	40	20
C433	A233	150fr Map of Africa	1.00	50
a.		Souv. sheet of 2, #C432-C433	1.50	65

American Order of Rosicrucians Emblem — AP22

1980, Nov. 17   Litho.   *Perf. 13*

C434	AP22	60fr multi	40	20

General Conclave of the American Order of Rosicrucians, meeting of French-speaking countries, Lome, Aug.

Christmas Type of 1980

Designs: 100fr, Cologne Cathedral, Germany, 13th cent. 150fr, Notre Dame, Paris, 12th cent. 200fr, Canterbury Cathedral, England, 11th cent.

1980, Dec. 22   *Perf. 14½x13½*

C435	A234	100fr multi	65	35
C436	A234	150fr multi	1.00	50
C437	A234	200fr multi	1.35	65
a.		Souv. sheet of 2, #C436-C437	2.25	1.25

Hotel Type of 1981

1981, Feb. 2   Litho.   *Perf. 12½x13*

C437B	A236	60fr multi	40	20

Easter Type of 1981

Rembrandt Paintings: 100fr, Artist's Mother. 200fr, Man in a Ruff.

Perf. 14½x13½

1981, Apr. 13   Litho.

C438	A237	100fr multi	65	35
C439	A237	200fr multi	1.35	65
a.		Souv. sheet of 2, #C438-C439	2.00	1.00

Market Type of 1980

1981, Mar. 8   Litho.   *Perf. 14*

C440	A230	90fr Fabric dealer	60	30
C441	A230	100fr Bananas	65	35
C442	A230	200fr Clay pottery	1.40	65
C443	A230	250fr Setting up	1.60	80
C444	A230	500fr Selling	3.50	1.60
C445	A230	1000fr Measuring grain	6.50	3.50
		Nos. C440-C445 (6)	14.25	7.20

For overprints see Nos. C486-C487.

Bird Type of 1981

Perf. 13½x14½

1981, Aug. 10   Litho.

C446	A238	50fr Violet-backed sunbird	35	16
C447	A238	100fr Red bishop	65	35
a.		Souvenir sheet of 2, #C446-C447	1.00	50

IYD Type of 1981

1981, Aug. 31   *Perf. 14*

C448	A240	90fr Carpenter	60	30
C449	A240	200fr Basketball players	1.35	65

Souvenir Sheet

C449A	A240	300fr Weaver	2.00	1.00

Picasso Type of 1981

1981, Sept. 14   *Perf. 14½x13½*

C450	A241	90fr Violin and Bottle on Table, 1916	60	30
C451	A241	100fr Baboon and Young	60	35
C452	A241	200fr Mandolin and Clarinet, 1914	1.40	65
a.		Souv. sheet of 2, #C451-C452	2.00	1.00

World Heritage Year Type of 1981

1981, Sept. 28   *Perf. 13½x14½*

C453	A242	100fr Cracow Museum, Poland	75	35
C454	A242	200fr Goree Isld., Senegal	1.50	75
a.		Souv. sheet of 2, #C453-C454	2.25	1.10

Space Type of 1981

1981, Nov.   *Perf. 14*

C455	A243	90fr multi	70	35
C456	A243	100fr multi	75	38

Souvenir Sheet
Perf. 13x14

C456A	A243	300fr multi, vert.	2.25	1.10

10th anniv. of Soyuz 10 (90fr) and Apollo 14 (100fr).

Christmas Type of 1981

Rubens Paintings: 100fr, Adoration of the Kings. 200fr, Virgin and Child. 300fr, Virgin giving Chasuble to St. Idefonse.

Perf. 14½x13½

1981, Dec. 10   Litho.

C457	A244	100fr multi	65	35
C458	A244	200fr multi	1.40	65
C459	A244	300fr multi	2.00	1.00
a.		Souv. sheet of 2, #C458-C459	3.75	1.90

West African Rice Development Assoc. Type of 1981

1981, Dec. 21   Litho.   *Perf. 12½*

C461	A236a	105fr yel & multi	70	35

Liberation Type of 1982

Designs: 105fr, Citizens holding hands, Pres. Eyadema, vert. 130fr, Hotel.

1982, Jan. 13   Litho.   *Perf. 12½*

C462	A245	105fr multi	70	35
C463	A245	130fr multi	90	42

Scouting Year Type of 1982

1982, Feb. 25   *Perf. 14*

C464	A246	90fr Semaphore	60	30
C465	A246	120fr Tower	80	40
C466	A246	130fr Scouts, canoe	90	42
C467	A246	135fr Scouts, tent	90	45

Souvenir Sheet
Perf. 13x14

C468	A246	500fr Baden-Powell	3.50	1.60

Easter Type of 1982

1982, Apr.   *Perf. 14x14½*

C469	A247	105fr multi	70	38
C470	A247	120fr multi	80	40

Souvenir Sheet

C471	A247	500fr multi	3.50	1.60

PHILEXFRANCE '82 Intl. Stamp Exhibition, Paris, June 11-21 — AP23

1982   Litho.   *Perf. 13*

C472	AP23	90fr shown	60	30
C473	AP23	105fr ROMOLYMPHIL '82, vert.	70	35

Issue dates: 90fr, June 11; 105fr, May 19.

Butterfly Type of 1982

1982, July 15   *Perf. 14½x14*

C474	A248	90fr Euxanthe eurionome	60	30
C475	A248	105fr Mylothris rhodope	70	35

Souvenir Sheet

C476	A248	500fr Papilio zalmoxis	3.50	1.65

World Cup Type of 1982

1982, July 26   *Perf. 14x14½*

C477	A249	105fr multi	70	35
C478	A249	130fr multi	1.35	65
C479	A249	300fr multi	2.00	1.00

Souvenir Sheet

C480	A249	500fr multi	3.50	1.65

For overprints see Nos. 1152-1155.

Pre-Olympics, 1984 Los Angeles — AP24

1983, Oct. 3   Photo.   *Perf. 12½*

C481	AP24	70fr Boxing	22	15
C482	AP24	90fr Hurdles	30	15
C483	AP24	105fr Pole vault	35	18
C484	AP24	130fr Runner	42	20

Souvenir Sheet

C485	AP24	500fr Runner, diff.	1.65	80

Nos. C443-C444 Overprinted: "19E CONGRES UPU HAMBOURG 1984"

1984, June   Litho.   *Perf. 14*

C486	A230	250fr multi	80	40
C487	A230	500fr multi	1.65	80

1984 Summer Olympics — AP25

1984, July 27   *Perf. 13*

C488	AP25	70fr Pole vault	22	15
C489	AP25	90fr Bicycling	30	15
C490	AP25	120fr Soccer	40	20

C491	AP25	250fr Boxing	80	40
C492	AP25	400fr Running	1.35	65
		Nos. C488-C492 (5)	3.07	1.55

Souvenir Sheet

C493	AP25	1000fr like 120fr, without flag	3.50	1.65

Nos. C488-C490, C493 vert.

Olympic Champions — AP26   Peace and Human Rights — AP28

1984, Nov. 15   Litho.   Perf. 15

C494	AP26	500fr Jim Thorpe, US	1.40	70
C495	AP26	500fr Jesse Owens, US	1.40	70
C496	AP26	500fr Muhammad Ali, US	1.40	70
C497	AP26	500fr Bob Beamon, US	1.40	70

Souvenir Sheets

C498	AP26	500fr Bill Steinkraus, US	1.40	70
C499	AP26	500fr New Zealand rowing team	1.40	70
C500	AP26	500fr Pakistani hockey team	1.40	70
C501	AP26	500fr Yukio Endo, Japan	1.40	70

West German Olympians

1984, Nov. 15

C502	AP26	500fr Dietmar Mogenburg	1.40	70
C503	AP26	500fr Fredy Schmidtke	1.40	70
C504	AP26	500fr Matthias Behr	1.40	70
C505	AP26	500fr Sabine Everts	1.40	70

Souvenir Sheets

C506	AP26	500fr Karl-Heinz Radschinsky	1.40	70
C507	AP26	500fr Pasquale Passarelli	1.40	70
C508	AP26	500fr Michale Gross	1.40	70
C509	AP26	500fr Jurgen Hingsen	1.40	70

For overprints see Nos. C521-C536, C563.

1985, Jan. 14   Litho.   Perf. 13½x14

Designs: 230fr, Map of Togo, globe, doves. 270fr, Palm tree, emblem. 500fr, Opencast mining operation. 1000fr, Human Rights Monument, UN, New York.

C510	AP28	230fr multi	45	22
C511	AP28	270fr multi	55	30
C512	AP28	500fr multi	1.00	50
C513	AP28	1000fr multi	2.00	1.00

Tribal Dances
AP29

1985, July   Perf. 15x14

C514	AP29	120fr Adifo, Adangbe	25	15
C515	AP29	135fr Fouet (whip), Kente	25	15
C516	AP29	290fr Idjombi, Pagouda	60	30
C517	AP29	500fr Moba, Dapaong	1.00	50

Visit of Pope John Paul II
AP30

Designs: 90fr, The Pope outside Lome Cathedral. 130fr, Blessing crowd in St. Peter's Square, vert. 500fr, Greeting Pres. Eyadema.

1985, Aug. 9   Perf. 13

C518	AP30	90fr multi	18	15
C519	AP30	130fr multi	25	15
C520	AP30	500fr multi	1.00	50

Nos. C495, C497, C499, C502, C505-C508 Overprinted with Winners Names, Country and Type of Olympic Medal

1985, Aug.   Perf. 15

C521	AP26	500fr Kirk Baptiste, US	1.00	50
C522	AP26	500fr Carl Lewis, US	1.00	50
C523	AP26	500fr Patrik Sjoborg, Sweden	1.00	50
C524	AP26	500fr Glynis Nunn, Australia	1.00	50

Souvenir Sheets

C525	AP26	500fr Rowing eights, Canada	2.00	1.00
C526	AP26	500fr Rolf Milser, W. Germany	2.00	1.00
C527	AP26	500fr Takashi Irie, Japan	2.00	1.00
C528	AP26	500fr Frederic Delcourt, France	2.00	1.00

Nos. C494, C496, C503-C504, C498, C500, C501, C509, with Winners Names, Country and Type of Olympic Medal

1985, Sept. 19   Litho.   Perf. 15

C529	AP26	500fr Italy	1.00	50
C530	AP26	500fr Kevin Barry	1.00	50
C531	AP26	500fr Rolf Golz	1.00	50
C532	AP26	500fr Philippe Boisse	1.00	50

Souvenir Sheets

C533	AP26	500fr Karen Stives	1.00	50
C534	AP26	500fr R.F.A. (West Germany)	1.00	50
C535	AP26	500fr Koji Gushiken	1.00	50
C536	AP26	500fr Daley Thompson	1.00	50

Traditional Instruments — AP31

Youth and Development — AP32

Designs: No. C537, Xylophone, Kante horn, tambour. No. C538, Bongo drums, castanets, bassar horn. No. C539, Communications. No. C540, Agriculture and industry.

1985   Litho.   Perf. 13

C537	AP31	100fr multi	20	15
C538	AP31	100fr multi	20	15
C539	AP32	200fr multi	40	20
C540	AP32	200fr multi	40	20

PHILEXAFRICA '85, Lome, Togo, Nov. 16-24. Stamps of same denomination printed se-tenant with center label picturing UAPT emblem. Issue dates: 100fr, Nov. 4. 200fr, Nov. 16.

No. 1274 Ovptd. with Organization Emblem and "80e Anniversaire du Rotary International."

1985, Nov. 15   Litho.   Perf. 15
Souvenir Sheet

C541	A267	1000fr multi	2.50	1.35

Nos. 1254-1255, 1258 Ovptd. "10e ANNIVERSAIRE DE APOLLO-SOYUZ" in 1 or 2 lines

1985, Dec. 27   Litho.   Perf. 15

C542	A265	90fr multi	35	15
C543	A265	500fr multi	1.90	90

Souvenir Sheet

C544	A265	1000fr multi	3.75	1.90

Nos. 1294-1295, 1297 Ovptd. "75e ANNIVERSAIRE DE LA MORT DE HENRI DUNANT FONDATEUR DE LA CROIX ROUGE" in 2 or 4 lines

1985, Dec. 27

C545	A270	400fr multi	1.50	70

C546	A270	500fr multi	1.90	90

Souvenir Sheet

C547	A270	1000fr multi	3.75	1.90

Statue of Liberty, Cent. — AP33

1986, Apr. 10   Perf. 13

C548	AP33	70fr Eiffel Tower	40	20
C549	AP33	90fr Statue of Liberty	50	25
C550	AP33	500fr Empire State Building	2.75	1.40

Nos. 1237-1240 Ovptd. with AMERIPEX '86 Emblem

1986, May 22   Perf. 11

C551	A262	500fr multi	2.75	1.40
C552	A262	1000fr multi	5.50	2.75

Souvenir Sheets
Perf. 14

C553	A262	1000fr No. 1239	5.50	2.75
C554	A262	1000fr No. 1240	5.50	2.75

Air Africa, 25th Anniv. AP34

1986, Dec. 29   Litho.   Perf. 12½x13

C555	AP34	90fr multi	50	25

Konrad Adenauer (1876-1967) West German Chancellor AP35

1987, July 15   Litho.   Perf. 12½x13

C556	AP35	120fr At podium	68	35
C557	AP35	500fr With Pres. Kennedy, 1962	2.75	1.40

Souvenir Sheet
Perf. 13x12½

C558	AP35	500fr Portrait, vert.	2.75	1.40

Berlin, 750th Anniv. AP36

Designs: 90fr, Wilhelm I (1781-1864) coin, Victory statue. 150fr, Frederick III (1831-1888) coin, Brandenburg Gate. 300fr, Wilhelm II (1882-1951) coin, Reichstag building. 750fr, Otto Leopold von Bismarck (1815-1898), first chancellor of the German empire, and Charlottenburg Palace.

1987, Aug. 31   Litho.   Perf. 13½

C559	AP36	90fr multi	60	30
C560	AP36	150fr multi	1.00	50
C561	AP36	300fr multi	2.00	1.00

Souvenir Sheet

C562	AP36	750fr multi	5.00	2.50

Nos. C506, 1258, 1273 and 1274 Overprinted in Black for Philatelic Exhibitions

a
OLYMPHILEX '88

---

b   INDEPENDENCE 40

c   FINLANDIA-88

d   Praga 88

1988, Apr. 25   Litho.   Perf. 15
Souvenir Sheets

C563	AP26 (a)	500fr #C506	3.25	1.60
C564	A265 (b)	1000fr #1258	7.00	3.50
C565	A265 (c)	1000fr #1273	7.00	3.50
C566	A267 (d)	1000fr #1274	6.50	3.25

AIR POST SEMI-POSTAL STAMPS

V4

Stamps of the design shown above and type of Cameroun V10 inscribed "Togo" were issued in 1942 by the Vichy Government, but were not placed on sale in the colony.

POSTAGE DUE STAMPS

Postage Due Stamps of Dahomey, 1914 Overprinted **TOGO**

1921   Unwmk.   Perf. 14x13½

J1	D2	5c green	45	45
J2	D2	10c rose	45	45
J3	D2	15c gray	80	80
J4	D2	20c brown	1.65	1.50
J5	D2	30c blue	1.65	1.50
J6	D2	50c black	1.00	80
J7	D2	60c orange	1.40	1.00
J8	D2	1fr violet	3.00	2.25
		Nos. J1-J8 (8)	10.40	8.75

Cotton Field — D3

1925   Typo.   Unwmk.

J9	D3	2c blue & blk	15	15
J10	D3	4c dl red & blk	15	15
J11	D3	5c ol grn & blk	15	15
J12	D3	10c cerise & blk	16	16
J13	D3	15c org & blk	20	20
J14	D3	20c red vio & blk	28	28
J15	D3	25c gray & blk	40	40
J16	D3	30c ocher & blk	20	20
J17	D3	50c brn & blk	30	30
J18	D3	60c grn & blk	40	40
J19	D3	1fr dk vio & blk	45	45
		Set value	2.50	2.50

Type of 1925 Issue Surcharged **2^f**

1927

J20	D3	2fr on 1fr rose red & vio	2.50	2.50
J21	D3	3fr on 1fr org brn, blk & ultra	2.50	2.50

Mask — D4

Carved Figures — D5

1941 **Engr.** *Perf. 13*

J22	D4	5c brn blk	15	15
J23	D4	10c yel grn	15	15
J24	D4	15c carmine	15	15
J25	D4	20c ultra	20	20
J26	D4	30c chestnut	20	20
J27	D4	50c olive grn	1.00	1.00
J28	D4	60c violet	20	20
J29	D4	1fr light blue	50	50
J30	D4	2fr org vermilion	28	28
J31	D4	3fr rose violet	55	55
		Nos. J22-J31 (10)	3.38	3.38

Stamps of type D4 without "RF" monogram were issued in 1942 to 1944 by the Vichy Government, but were not placed on sale in the colony.

Catalogue values for unused stamps in this section, from this point to the end of the section, are for Never Hinged items.

1947

J32	D5	10c brt ultra	15	15
J33	D5	30c red	15	15
J34	D5	50c dp yel grn	15	15
J35	D5	1fr chocolate	15	15
J36	D5	2fr carmine	20	20
J37	D5	3fr gray blk	20	20
J38	D5	4fr ultra	38	38
J39	D5	5fr sepia	42	42
J40	D5	10fr dp org	45	45
J41	D5	20fr dk bl vio	65	65
		Set value	2.50	2.50

Republic

Konkomba Helmet
D6   D7

1957 **Engr.** *Perf. 14x13*

J42	D6	1fr brt vio	15	15
J43	D6	2fr brt org	15	15
J44	D6	3fr dk gray	15	15
J45	D6	4fr brt red	15	15
J46	D6	5fr ultra	15	15
J47	D6	10fr dp grn	30	30
J48	D6	20fr dp claret	48	48
		Set value	1.20	1.20

1959 *Perf. 14x13*

J49	D7	1fr org brn	15	15
J50	D7	2fr lt bl grn	15	15
J51	D7	3fr orange	15	15
J52	D7	4fr blue	15	15
J53	D7	5fr lil rose	15	15
J54	D7	10fr vio blue	30	30
J55	D7	20fr black	52	52
		Set value	1.25	1.25

Type of Regular Issue, 1964

Shells: 1fr, Conus papilionaceus. 2fr, Marginella faba. 3fr, Cypraea stercoraria. 4fr, Strombus latus. 5fr, Costate cockle (sea shell). 10fr, Cancellaria cancellata. 15fr, Cymbium pepo. 20fr, Tympanotomus radula.

1964-65 **Unwmk.** **Photo.** *Perf. 14*
Size: 20x25½mm

J56	A47	1fr gray grn & red brn ('65)	15	15
J57	A47	2fr tan & ol grn ('65)	15	15
J58	A47	3fr gray, brn & yel ('65)	15	15
J59	A47	4fr tan & multi ('65)	15	15
J60	A47	5fr sep, org & grn	28	28
J61	A47	10fr sl bl, brn & bis	40	40
J62	A47	15fr grn & brn	1.00	1.00
J63	A47	20fr sl, dk brn & yel	1.25	1.25
		Nos. J56-J63 (8)	3.53	3.53

 Tomatoes — D8

1969-70 **Litho.** *Perf. 14*

J64	D8	5fr yellow & multi	15	15
J65	D8	10fr blue & multi	20	20
J66	D8	15fr multi ('70)	30	30
J67	D8	20fr multi ('70)	40	40

Market Type of 1980

1981, Mar. 8 **Litho.** *Perf. 14*
Size: 23x32mm, 32x23mm

J68	A230	5fr Millet, vert.	15	15
J69	A230	10fr Packaged goods	15	15
J70	A230	25fr Chickens	15	15
J71	A230	50fr Ivory vendor	25	15
		Set value	46	26

TRANSCAUCASIAN FEDERATED REPUBLICS

(Armenia, Georgia, Azerbaijan)

LOCATION — In southeastern Europe, south of the Caucasus Mountains between the Black and Caspian Seas
GOVT. — Former republic
AREA — 71,255 sq. mi.
POP. — 5,851,000 (approx.)
CAPITAL — Tiflis

The Transcaucasian Federation was made up of the former autonomies of Armenia, Georgia and Azerbaijan. Its stamps were replaced by those of Russia.

100 Kopecks = 1 Ruble

Russian Stamps of 1909-17 Overprinted in Black or Red

1923 **Unwmk.** *Perf. 14½x15*

1	A15	10k dark blue	3.00	5.00
2	A14	10k on 7k lt bl	3.00	5.00
3	A11	25k grn & gray vio	3.00	5.00
4	A11	35k red brn & grn (R)	3.00	5.00
a.		Double overprint	40.00	40.00
5	A8	50k brn red & grn	3.00	5.00
6	A9	1r pale brn, brn & org	7.50	10.00
7	A12	3½r mar & lt grn	18.00	

Imperf

8	A9	1r pale brn, brn & red org	3.00	5.00

No. 7 was prepared but not issued.

Overprinted on Stamps of Armenia Previously Handstamped:

a   c

Perf. 14½x15

9	A11(c)	25k grn & gray vio	125.00	200.00
10	A8(c)	50k vio & grn	75.00	125.00

Perf. 13½

11	A9(a)	1r pale brn, brn & org	32.50	32.50
12	A9(c)	1r pale, brn, brn & org	50.00	32.50

Imperf

13	A9(c)	1r pale brn, brn & red org	32.50	32.50

Counterfeit overprints exist.

Oil Fields — A1

Soviet Symbols — A2

1923 *Perf. 11½*

14	A1	40,000r red violet	1.10	2.25
15	A1	75,000r dark grn	1.10	2.25
16	A1	100,000r blk vio	1.10	2.25
17	A1	150,000r red	1.10	2.25
18	A2	200,000r dull grn	1.10	2.25
19	A2	300,000r blue	1.10	2.50

20	A2	350,000r dark brn	1.10	2.50
21	A2	500,000r rose	1.10	2.50
		Nos. 14-21 (8)	8.80	18.75

Nos. 14-15 Surcharged in Brown

700 000 РУБ.

1923

22	A1	700,000r on 40,000r	2.50	4.00
a.		Imperf., pair	13.00	
23	A1	700,000r on 75,000r	2.50	4.00
a.		Imperf., pair	13.00	

Types of Preceding Issue with Values in Gold Kopecks

1923, Oct. 24

25	A2	1k orange	1.00	2.50
26	A2	2k blue green	1.00	2.50
27	A2	3k rose	1.00	2.50
28	A2	4k gray brown	1.00	2.50
29	A1	5k dark violet	1.00	2.50
30	A1	9k deep blue	1.00	2.50
31	A1	18k slate	1.00	2.50
		Nos. 25-31 (7)	7.00	17.50

Nos. 14-21, 25-31 exist imperf. but are not known to have been issued in that condition. Value, $7.50 each.

TRIPOLITANIA

LOCATION — In northern Africa, bordering on Mediterranean Sea
GOVT. — A former Italian Colony
AREA — 350,000 sq. mi. (approx.)
POP. — 570,716 (1921)
CAPITAL — Tripoli

Formerly a Turkish province, Tripolitania became part of Italian Libya. See Libya.

100 Centesimi = 1 Lira

Used values in italics are for postally used stamps. CTO's or stamps with fake cancels sell for about the same as unused, hinged stamps.

Watermark

Wmk. 140-
Crowns

Propaganda of the Faith Issue

Italian Stamps of 1923 Overprinted   TRIPOLITANIA

1923, Oct. 24 **Wmk. 140** *Perf. 14*

1	A68	20c ol grn & brn org	1.25	5.50
2	A68	30c claret & brn org	1.25	5.50
3	A68	50c vio & brn org	.95	4.50
4	A68	1 l blue & brn org	.95	4.50

Fascisti Issue

Italian Stamps of 1923 Overprinted in Red or Black   TRIPOLITANIA

1923, Oct. 29 **Unwmk.**

5	A69	10c dk green (R)	1.40	4.50
6	A69	30c dk violet (R)	1.40	4.50
7	A69	50c brown car	1.40	4.50

Wmk. 140

8	A70	1 l brown	1.40	4.50
9	A70	2 l brown	1.40	4.50
10	A71	5 l blk & bl (R)	1.40	7.25
		Nos. 5-10 (6)	8.40	29.75

Manzoni Issue

Stamps of Italy, 1923,   **TRIPOLITANIA**
Overprinted in Red

1924, Apr. 1 **Wmk. 140** *Perf. 14*

11	A72	10c brown red & blk	.55	5.75
12	A72	15c blue grn & blk	.55	5.75
13	A72	30c black & slate	.55	5.75
14	A72	50c org brn & blk	.55	5.75
15	A72	1 l blue & blk	8.75	55.00
16	A72	5 l violet & blk	200.00	800.00
		Nos. 11-16 (6)	210.95	878.00

On Nos. 15 and 16 the overprint is placed vertically at the left side.

Victor Emmanuel Issue

Italy Nos. 175-177 **TRIPOLITANIA**
Overprinted

1925-26 **Unwmk.** *Perf. 11*

17	A78	60c brown carmine	.18	2.00
18	A78	1 l dark blue	.20	2.00
a.		Perf. 13½	.90	10.00

Perf. 13½

19	A78	1.25 l dk blue ('26)	.50	6.00
a.		Perf. 11	175.00	425.00

Saint Francis of Assisi Issue

Italy Nos. 178-180 TRIPOLITANIA
Overprinted

1926, Apr. 12 **Wmk. 140** *Perf. 14*

20	A79	20c gray green	1.00	3.00
21	A80	40c dark violet	1.00	3.00
22	A81	60c red brown	1.00	3.00

Italy No. 182 and Type of A83 Overprinted in **Tripolitania**
Red

Unwmk.

23	A82	1.25 l dark blue	1.00	3.00
24	A83	5 l + 2.50 l ol grn	2.50	5.50
		Nos. 20-24 (5)	6.50	17.50

Volta Issue

Type of Italy, 1927, **Tripolitania**
Overprinted

1927, Oct. 10 **Wmk. 140** *Perf. 14*

25	A84	20c purple	2.75	6.00
26	A84	50c deep orange	3.75	5.00
a.		Double overprint	13.00	
27	A84	1.25 l brt blue	4.50	7.25

Monte Cassino Issue

Types of Italy, 1929, Overprinted in Red or Blue   TRIPOLITANIA

1929, Oct. 14

28	A96	20c dk green (R)	2.00	5.00
29	A96	25c red org (Bl)	2.00	5.00
30	A98	50c + 10c crim (Bl)	2.00	7.50
31	A98	75c + 15c ol brn (R)	2.00	7.50
32	A96	1.25 l + 25c dk vio (R)	4.25	7.50
33	A98	5 l + 1 l sapphire (R)	4.25	7.50

Overprinted in Red **Tripolitania**

Unwmk.

34	A100	10 l + 2 l gray brn	3.50	10.00
		Nos. 28-34 (7)	20.00	50.00

Royal Wedding Issue

Type of Italy, 1930, Overprinted   TRIPOLITANIA

1930, Mar. 17 **Wmk. 140**

35	A101	20c yellow green	.50	2.00
36	A101	50c + 10c dp orange	.38	2.50
37	A101	1.25 l + 25c rose red	.38	3.00

Ferrucci Issue

Types of Italy, 1930, Overprinted in Red or Blue   TRIPOLITANIA

1930, July 26

38	A102	20c violet (R)	.38	1.50
39	A103	25c dk green (R)	.38	1.50
40	A103	50c black (R)	.38	1.50
41	A103	1.25 l deep blue (R)	.38	1.50
42	A104	5 l + 2 l dp car (Bl)	1.50	3.00
		Nos. 38-42 (5)	3.02	9.00

Virgil Issue

Types of Italy, 1930, Overprinted in Red or Blue

TRIPOLITANIA

1930, Dec. 4   Photo.

43	A106	15c violet black	.42	1.50
44	A106	20c orange brown	.42	1.50
45	A106	25c dark green	.42	1.25
46	A106	30c lt brown	.42	1.50
47	A106	50c dull violet	.42	1.25
48	A106	75c rose red	.42	1.50
49	A106	1.25 l gray blue	.42	1.50

Unwmk.
Engr.

50	A106	5 l + 1.50 l dk vio	2.00	6.00
51	A106	10 l + 2.50 l ol brn	2.00	6.00
		Nos. 43-51 (9)	6.94	22.00

Saint Anthony of Padua Issue

Types of Italy, 1931, Overprinted in Blue or Red   **TRIPOLITANIA**

1931, May 7   Photo.   Wmk. 140

52	A116	20c brown (Bl)	.75	2.25
53	A116	25c green (R)	.75	2.25
54	A118	30c gray brn (Bl)	.75	2.25
55	A118	50c dull vio (Bl)	.75	1.50
56	A120	1.25 l slate bl (R)	.75	2.25

Overprinted in Red or **Tripolitania** Black

Unwmk.   **Engr.**

57	A121	75c black (R)	.75	2.25
58	A122	5 l + 2.50 l dk brn (Bk)	2.25	7.50
		Nos. 52-58 (7)	6.75	20.25

Native Village Scene — A14

1934, Oct. 16   Wmk. 140

73	A14	5c ol grn & brn	1.40	4.25
74	A14	10c brown & black	1.40	4.25
75	A14	20c scar & indigo	1.40	4.25
76	A14	50c purple & brown	1.40	4.25
77	A14	60c org brn & ind	1.40	4.25
78	A14	1.25 l dk blue & green	1.40	4.25
		Nos. 73-78 (6)	8.40	25.50

2nd Colonial Arts Exhibition, Naples. See Nos. C43-C48.

SEMI-POSTAL STAMPS

Many issues of Italy and Italian Colonies include one or more semipostal denominations. To avoid splitting sets, these issues are generally listed as regular postage, airmail, etc., unless all values carry a surtax.

Holy Year Issue

Italian Stamps of 1924 Overprinted in Black or Red   **TRIPOLITANIA**

1925   Wmk. 140   Perf. 12

B1	SP4	20c + 10c dk grn & brn	1.10	3.00
B2	SP4	30c + 15c dk brn & brn	1.10	3.00
B3	SP4	50c + 25c vio & brn	1.10	3.00
B4	SP4	60c + 30c dp rose & brn	1.10	3.00
B5	SP8	1 l + 50c dp bl & vio (R)	1.10	3.00
B6	SP8	5 l + 2.50 l org brn & vio (R)	1.10	3.00
		Nos. B1-B6 (6)	6.60	18.00

Colonial Institute Issue

Peace Substituting Spade for Sword — SP1

1926, June 1   Typo.   Perf. 14

B7	SP1	5c + 5c brown	.22	1.65
B8	SP1	10c + 5c ol brn	.22	1.65
B9	SP1	20c + 5c bl grn	.22	1.65
B10	SP1	40c + 5c brn red	.22	1.65
B11	SP1	60c + 5c orange	.22	1.65
B12	SP1	1 l + 5c blue	.22	1.65
		Nos. B7-B12 (6)	1.32	9.90

The surtax was for the Italian Colonial Institute.

Fiera Campionaria Tripoli
See Libya for stamps with this inscription.

Types of Italian Semi-Postal Stamps of 1926 Overprinted like Nos. 17-19

1927, Apr. 21   Unwmk.   Perf. 11

B19	SP10	40c + 20c dk brn & blk	1.00	3.50
B20	SP10	60c + 30c brn red & ol brn	1.00	3.50
B21	SP10	1.25 l + 60c dp bl & blk	1.00	3.50
B22	SP10	5 l + 2.50 l dk grn & blk	1.50	4.50

The surtax was for the charitable work of the Voluntary Militia for Italian National Defense.

Allegory of Fascism and Victory — SP2

1928, Oct. 15   Wmk. 140

B29	SP2	20c + 5c bl grn	.90	2.50
B30	SP2	30c + 5c red	.90	2.50
B31	SP2	50c + 10c pur	.90	2.50
B32	SP2	1.25 l + 20c dk bl	.90	2.50

46th anniv. of the Societa Africana d'Italia. The surtax aided that society.

Types of Italian Semi-Postal Stamps of 1928 Overprinted

TRIPOLITANIA

1929, Mar. 4   Unwmk.   Perf. 11

B33	SP10	30c + 10c red & blk	1.40	3.75
B34	SP10	50c + 20c vio & blk	1.40	3.75
B35	SP10	1.25 l + 50c brn & bl	1.90	5.00
B36	SP10	5 l + 2 l ol grn & blk	1.90	5.00

The surtax on these stamps was for the charitable work of the Voluntary Militia for Italian National Defense.

Types of Italian Semi-Postal Stamps of 1926, Overprinted in Black or Red Like Nos. B33-B36

1930, Oct. 20

B50	SP10	30c + 10c dp grn & bl grn (Bk)	5.00	10.00
B51	SP10	50c + 10c dk grn & vio (R)	5.00	10.00
B52	SP10	1.25 l + 30c blk brn & red brn (R)	5.00	10.00
B53	SP10	5 l + 1.50 l ind & grn (R)	15.00	32.50

Ancient Arch — SP3

1930, Nov. 27   Photo.   Wmk. 140

B54	SP3	50c + 20c ol brn	1.10	4.00
B55	SP3	1.25 l + 20c dp bl	1.10	4.00
B56	SP3	1.75 l + 20c green	1.10	4.00
B57	SP3	2.55 l + 50c purple	1.75	4.00
B58	SP3	5 l + 1 l deep car	1.75	4.00
		Nos. B54-B58 (5)	6.80	20.00

25th anniv. of the Italian Colonial Agricultural Institute. The surtax was for the benefit of that institution.

AIR POST STAMPS

Ferrucci Issue

Type of Italian Air Post Stamps of 1930 Overprinted in Blue or Red like #38-42

1930, July 26   Wmk. 140   Perf. 14

C1	AP7	50c brown vio (Bl)	1.10	2.50
C2	AP7	1 l dk blue (R)	1.10	2.50
C3	AP7	5 l + 2 l dp car (Bl)	4.75	10.00

Virgil Issue

Types of Italian Air Post Stamps, 1930 Overprinted in Red or Blue like #43-51

1930, Dec. 4   Photo.

C4	AP8	50c deep green	1.00	2.50
C5	AP8	1 l rose red	1.00	2.50

Unwmk.
Engr.

C6	AP8	7.70 l + 1.30 l dk brn	2.50	7.50
C7	AP8	9 l + 2 l gray	2.50	7.50

Airplane over Columns of the Basilica, Leptis — AP1

Arab Horseman Pointing at Airplane AP2

1931-32   Photo.   Wmk. 140

C8	AP1	50c rose car	.80	.18
C9	AP1	60c red org	2.50	2.50
C10	AP1	75c dp bl ('32)	2.50	2.50
C11	AP1	80c dull violet	5.00	3.00
C12	AP2	1 l deep blue	.80	.15
C13	AP2	1.20 l dk brown	5.75	4.50
C14	AP2	1.50 l org red	5.75	3.25
C15	AP2	5 l green	6.50	4.00
		Nos. C8-C15 (8)	29.60	20.08

For surcharges and overprint see Nos. C29-C32.

Airplane over Ruins — AP3

1931, Dec. 7

C16	AP3	50c dp blue	1.40	5.00
C17	AP3	80c violet	1.40	5.00
C18	AP3	1 l gray black	1.40	5.00
C19	AP3	2 l deep green	1.90	7.50
C20	AP3	5 l + 2 l rose red	3.25	15.00
		Nos. C16-C20 (5)	9.35	37.50

Graf Zeppelin Issue

Mercury, by Giovanni da Bologna, and Zeppelin AP4

Designs: 3 l, 12 l, Mercury. 10 l, 20 l, Guido Reni's "Aurora." 5 l, 15 l, Arch of Marcus Aurelius.

1933, May 5

C21	AP4	3 l dark brown	4.00	37.50
C22	AP4	5 l purple	4.00	37.50
C23	AP4	10 l deep green	4.00	62.50
C24	AP4	12 l deep blue	4.00	85.00
C25	AP4	15 l carmine	4.00	75.00
C26	AP4	20 l gray black	4.00	100.00
		Nos. C21-C26 (6)	24.00	397.50

For overprints and surcharges see Nos. C38-C42.

North Atlantic Flight Issue

Airplane, Lion of St. Mark — AP7

1933, June 1

C27	AP7	19.75 l blk & ol brn	8.50	225.00
C28	AP7	44.75 l dk bl & lt grn	8.50	225.00

Type of 1931 Overprinted or Surcharged

1934-XII
PRIMO VOLO DIRETTO
ROMA = BUENOS-AYRES
TRIMOTORE "LOMBARDI-MAZZOTTI"

1934, Jan. 20

C29	AP2	2 l on 5 l org brn	1.25	27.50
C30	AP2	3 l on 5 l grn	1.25	27.50
C31	AP2	5 l ocher	1.25	27.50
C32	AP2	10 l on 5 l rose	1.25	27.50

For use on mail to be carried on a special flight from Rome to Buenos Aires.

Types of Libya 1934 Airmail Issue Overprinted in Black or Red   CIRCUITO DELLE OASI TRIPOLI MAGGIO 1934-XII

1934, May 1   Wmk. 140

C38	AP4	50c rose red	2.75	3.75
C39	AP4	75c lemon	2.75	3.75
C40	AP4	5 l + 1 l brn	2.75	3.75
C41	AP4	10 l + 2 l dk bl	125.00	150.00
C42	AP5	25 l + 3 l pur	125.00	150.00
		Nos. C38-C42 (5)	258.25	311.25

"Circuit of the Oases."

Plane Shadow on Desert AP11

Designs: 25c, 50c, 75c, Plane shadow on desert. 80c, 1 l, 2 l, Camel corps.

1934, Oct. 16   Photo.

C43	AP11	25c sl bl & org red	1.40	4.25
C44	AP11	50c dk grn & ind	1.40	4.25
C45	AP11	75c dk brn & org red	1.40	4.25
C46	AP11	80c org brn & ol grn	1.40	4.25
C47	AP11	1 l scar & ol grn	1.40	4.25
C48	AP11	2 l dk bl & brn	1.40	4.25
		Nos. C43-C48 (6)	8.40	25.50

Second Colonial Arts Exhibition, Naples.

AIR POST SEMI-POSTAL STAMPS

King Victor
Emmanuel
III — SPAP1

1934, Nov. 5	Wmk. 140		Perf. 14	
CB1	SPAP1	25c + 10c gray grn	1.65	5.00
CB2	SPAP1	50c + 10c brn	1.65	5.00
CB3	SPAP1	75c + 15c rose red	1.65	5.00
CB4	SPAP1	80c + 15c blk brn	1.65	5.00
CB5	SPAP1	1 l + 20c red brn	1.65	5.00
CB6	SPAP1	2 l + 20c brt bl	1.65	5.00
CB7	SPAP1	3 l + 25c pur	14.00	40.00
CB8	SPAP1	5 l + 25c org	14.00	40.00
CB9	SPAP1	10 l + 30c rose vio	14.00	40.00
CB10	SPAP1	25 l + 2 l dp grn	14.00	40.00
		Nos. CB1-CB10 (10)	65.90	190.00

65th birthday of King Victor Emmanuel III; non-stop flight from Rome to Mogadiscio.
For overprint see No. CBO1.

AIR POST SEMI-POSTAL OFFICIAL STAMP

Type of Air Post Semi-Postal Stamps, 1934
Overprinted Crown and "SERVIZIO DI STATO" in Black

1934	Wmk. 140		Perf. 14	
CBO1	SPAP1	25 l + 2 l cop red	950.00	1,700.

AIR POST SPECIAL DELIVERY STAMPS

Type of Libya 1934
Overprinted in Black

CIRCUITO DELLE OASI
TRIPOLI
MAGGIO 1934-XII

1934, May 1	Wmk. 140		Perf. 14	
CE1	APSD1	2.25 l red orange	4.00	5.00
CE2	APSD1	4.50 l + 1 l dp rose	4.00	5.00

"Circuit of the Oases."

AUTHORIZED DELIVERY STAMP

Authorized Delivery Stamp of Italy 1930,
Overprinted like Nos. 38-42

1931, Mar.	Wmk. 140		Perf. 14	
EY1	AD2	10c dark brown	5.00	2.50

TUNISIA

LOCATION — Northern Africa, bordering on the Mediterranean Sea
GOVT. — Republic
AREA — 63,362 sq. mi.
POP. — 6,966,173 (1984)
CAPITAL — Tunis

The former French protectorate became a sovereign state in 1956 and a republic in 1957.

100 Centimes = 1 Franc
1000 Millimes = 1 Dinar (1959)

Catalogue values for unused stamps in this country are for Never Hinged items, beginning with Scott 163 in the regular postage section, Scott B78 in the semi-postal section, Scott C13 in the airpost section, Scott CB1 in the airpost semi-postal section, and Scott J33 in the postage due section.

Coat of Arms — A1

Perf. 14x13½

1888, July 1		Typo.		Unwmk.	
1	A1	1c blk, *blue*		1.25	70
2	A1	2c pur brn, *buff*		1.25	70
3	A1	5c grn, *grnsh*		8.00	4.00
4	A1	15c bl, *grysh*		22.50	6.50
5	A1	25c blk, *rose*		40.00	22.50
6	A1	40c red, *straw*		35.00	22.50
7	A1	75c car, *rose*		40.00	22.50
8	A1	5fr gray vio, *grysh*		210.00	150.00

All values exist imperforate.

Reprints were made in 1893 and some values have been reprinted twice since then. The shades usually differ from those of the originals and some reprints have white gum instead of grayish. All values except the 15c and 40c have been reprinted from retouched designs, having a background of horizontal ruled lines.

A2   A3

1888-1902				
9	A2	1c blk, *lil bl*	80	28
10	A2	2c pur brn, *buff*	80	28
11	A2	5c grn, *grnsh*	3.25	40
12	A2	5c yel grn ('99)	3.25	40
13	A2	10c blk, *lav* ('93)	4.00	28
14	A2	10c red ('01)	3.00	32
15	A2	15c blue, *grysh*	30.00	40
16	A2	15c gray ('01)	5.00	52
17	A2	20c red, *grn* ('99)	8.00	1.40
18	A2	25c blk, *rose*	8.75	65
19	A2	25c blue ('01)	4.75	80
20	A2	35c brn ('02)	25.00	80
21	A2	40c red, *straw*	5.25	65
22	A2	75c car, *rose*	65.00	50.00
23	A2	75c dp vio, *org* ('93)	8.75	4.50
24	A3	1fr olive, *olive*	13.00	5.00
25	A3	2fr dl vio ('02)	75.00	60.00
26	A3	5fr rose lil, *lav*	72.50	50.00
		Bar cancellation		48

Quadrille Paper

| 27 | A2 | 15c bl, *grysh* ('93) | 18.00 | 28 |
| | | Nos. 9-27 (19) | 354.10 | 176.96 |

For surcharges see Nos. 28, 58-61.

25

No. 27 Surcharged in Red

≡

1902				
28	A2	25c on 15c blue	1.25	1.25

Mosque at
Kairouan
A4

Ruins of
Hadrian's
Aqueduct
A6

Carthaginian
Galley -- A7

Plowing
A5

Arab and Ruins of
Dougga — A9

1906-26				Typo.	
29	A4	1c blk, *yel*		15	15
30	A4	2c red brn, *straw*		15	15
31	A4	3c lt red ('19)		15	15
32	A4	5c grn, *grnsh*		15	15
33	A4	5c orange ('21)		15	15
34	A5	10c red		16	15
35	A5	10c green ('21)		15	15
36	A5	15c vio, *pnksh*		30	15
a.		Imperf., pair			
37	A5	15c brn, *org* ('23)		15	15
38	A5	20c brn, *pnksh*		15	15
39	A5	25c dp blue		65	15
a.		Imperf., pair			
40	A5	25c vio ('21)		15	15
41	A6	30c red brn & vio ('19)		42	22
42	A5	30c pale red ('21)		50	30
43	A6	35c ol grn & brn		5.00	40
44	A6	40c blk brn & red brn		3.00	15
45	A5	40c blk, *pnksh* ('23)		65	25
46	A5	40c gray grn ('26)		15	15
47	A5	50c blue ('21)		42	22
48	A6	60c ol grn & vio ('21)		40	16
49	A6	60c ver & rose ('25)		35	15
50	A6	75c red brn & red		42	15
51	A6	75c ver & dl red ('26)		16	15
52	A7	1fr red & dk brn		50	15
53	A7	1fr ind & ultra ('25)		16	15
54	A7	2fr brn & ol grn		2.50	80
55	A7	2fr grn & red, *pink* ('25)		40	20
56	A7	5fr vio & bl		5.00	3.00
57	A7	5fr gray vio & grn ('25)		40	15
		Nos. 29-57 (29)		22.89	
		Set value			7.00

For surcharges and overprints see Nos. 62-64, 70-73 115-116, B1-B23, B25-B27, B29-B30, B32-B36, C1-C6.

Stamps and Type of 1888-1902 Surcharged **10**

1908, Sept.				
58	A2	10c on 15c gray, *lt gray* (R)	90	90
59	A3	35c on 1fr ol, *ol* (R)	1.40	1.40
60	A3	40c on 2fr dl vio (Bl)	4.00	4.00
61	A3	75c on 5fr red lil, *lav* (Bl)	3.00	3.00

10

No. 36 Surcharged

≡

1911				
62	A5	10c on 15c vio, *pinkish*	70	20

15ª

No. 34 Surcharged

≡

1917, Mar. 16				
63	A5	15c on 10c red	40	15
a.		"15c" omitted	7.00	
b.		Double surcharge	20.00	

20ᶜ·

No. 36 Surcharged

≡

1921				
64	A5	20c on 15c vio, *pinkish*	40	15

1922-26		Typo.	Perf. 13½x14	
65	A9	10c green	15	15
66	A9	10c rose ('26)	15	15
67	A9	30c rose	45	45
68	A9	30c lilac ('26)	15	15
69	A9	50c blue	35	35
		Set value	95	95

For surcharges see Nos. 117, B24, B28, B31.

Stamps and Type of 1906 Surcharged in Red or Black

50

≡**10**
a   b

1923-25				
70	A4(a)	10c on 5c grn, *grnsh* (R)	18	15
a.		Double surcharge	20.00	
71	A5(b)	20c on 15c vio (Bk)	55	15
72	A5(b)	30c on 20c yel brn (Bk) ('25)	15	15
73	A5(b)	50c on 25c bl (R)	70	15
		Set value		26

Arab Woman
Carrying
Water — A10

Grand Mosque at
Tunis — A11

Mosque,
Tunis — A12

Roman Amphitheater, El
Djem (Thysdrus) — A13

1926-46		Typo.	Perf. 14x13½	
74	A10	1c lt red	15	15
75	A10	2c olive grn	15	15
76	A10	3c slate bl	15	15
77	A10	5c yel grn	15	15
78	A10	10c rose	15	15
78A	A12	10c brn ('46)	15	15
79	A11	15c gray lil	15	15
80	A11	20c dp red	15	15
81	A11	25c gray grn	15	15
82	A11	25c lt vio ('28)	25	15
83	A11	30c lt vio	15	15
84	A11	30c bl grn ('28)	15	15
84A	A12	30c dk ol grn ('46)	15	15
85	A11	40c deep brn	15	15
85A	A12	40c lil rose ('46)	15	15
86	A11	45c emer ('40)	50	35
87	A12	50c black	15	15
88	A12	50c ultra ('34)	22	15
88B	A12	50c emer ('40)	15	15
88C	A12	50c lt bl ('46)	15	15
89	A12	60c red org ('40)	15	15
89A	A12	60c ultra ('45)	15	15
90	A12	65c ultra ('38)	35	15
91	A12	70c dk red ('40)	15	15
92	A12	75c vermilion	15	15
93	A12	75c lil rose ('28)	40	15
94	A12	80c blue grn	60	16
94A	A12	80c blk brn ('40)	15	15
94B	A12	80c emer ('45)	15	15
95	A12	90c org red ('28)	15	15
96	A12	90c ultra ('39)	6.00	4.00
97	A12	1fr brn violet	25	15
97A	A12	1fr rose ('40)	15	15
98	A13	1.05fr dl bl & mag	15	15
98A	A12	1.20fr blk brn ('45)	15	15
99	A13	1.25fr gray bl & dk bl	22	15
100	A13	1.25fr car rose ('40)	70	42
100A	A13	1.30fr bl & vio bl ('42)	15	15
101	A13	1.40fr brt red vio ('40)	40	25
102	A13	1.50fr bl & dp bl ('28)	50	15
102A	A13	1.50fr rose red & red org ('42)	15	15
102B	A13	1.50fr rose lil ('46)	15	15
103	A13	2fr rose & ol brn	60	15
104	A13	2fr red org ('39)	15	15
104A	A12	2fr Prus grn ('45)	15	15
105	A13	2.25fr ultra ('39)	50	35
105A	A13	2.40fr red ('46)	15	15
106	A13	2.50fr green ('40)	50	15
107	A13	3fr dl bl & org	70	15
108	A13	3fr violet ('39)	15	15
108A	A13	3fr blk brn ('46)	15	15
108B	A13	4fr ultra ('45)	30	30
109	A13	5fr red & grn, *grnsh*	1.60	15
110	A13	5fr dp red brn ('40)	55	38
110A	A13	5fr dk grn ('46)	15	15
110B	A13	6fr dp ultra ('45)	15	15
111	A13	10fr brn red & blk, *bluish*	5.00	15
112	A13	10fr rose pink ('40)	45	30
112A	A13	10fr ver ('46)	15	15
112B	A13	10fr ultra ('45)	15	15
112C	A13	15fr rose lil ('45)	15	15
113	A13	20fr lil & red, *pnksh* ('28)	1.50	35
113A	A13	20fr dk grn ('45)	16	15
113B	A13	25fr violet ('45)	25	20

113C	A13	50fr car ('45)	55 20
113D	A13	100fr car rose ('45)	80 22
		Set value	26.00 11.50

See Nos. 152A-162, 185-189, 199-206.
For surcharges and overprints see Nos. 114, 118-121, 143-152, B74-B77, B87-B88, B91-B95, B98, C7-C12.

No. 99 Surcharged with New Value and Bars in Red

1927, Mar. 24

114	A13	1.50fr on 1.25fr	20 15

Stamps of 1921-26 Surcharged

≡ 3 c

1928, May 1

115	A4	3c on 5c orange	15 15
116	A5	10c on 15c brn, org	15 15
117	A9	25c on 30c lilac	16 15
118	A12	40c on 80c bl grn	22 20
119	A12	50c on 75c ver	30 15
		Set value	80 54

No. 83 Surcharged

≡ 10

1929

120	A11	10c on 30c lt vio	60 40

No. 120 exists precanceled only. The value in first column is for a stamp which has not been through the post and has original gum. The value in the second column is for a postally used, gumless stamp. See No. 199a.

No. 85 Surcharged with New Value and Bars

1930

121	A11	50c on 40c dp brn	2.00 15

A14

A15

A16

A17

Perf. 11, 12½, 12½x13

1931-34			**Engr.**
122	A14	1c deep blue	15 15
123	A14	2c yel brown	15 15
124	A14	3c black	15 15
125	A14	5c yel green	15 15
126	A14	10c red	15 15
127	A15	15c dull vio	24 15
128	A15	20c dl brown	15 15
129	A15	25c rose red	15 15
130	A15	30c dp green	15 15
131	A15	40c red org	15 15
132	A16	50c ultra	15 15
133	A16	75c yellow	1.00 1.00
134	A16	90c red	24 30
135	A16	1fr olive blk	15 15
136	A16	1fr dk brn ('34)	15 15
137	A17	1.50fr brt ultra	24 24
138	A17	2fr dp brown	24 15
139	A17	3fr bl green	4.00 4.00
140	A17	5fr car rose	8.25 5.50
a.		Perf. 12½	12.50 6.50
141	A17	10fr black	20.00 14.00
142	A17	20fr dk brown	30.00 17.50
		Nos. 122-142 (21)	66.01 44.64

For surcharges see Nos. B54-B73.

Nos. 88, 102 Surcharged in Red or Black:

1 f 75

■ 0,65 ≡

1937 — Perf. 14x13½

143	A12	65c on 50c (R)	45 15
b.		Double surcharge	30.00 25.00
144	A12	1.75fr on 1.50fr (R)	3.00 1.00
a.		Double surcharge	25.00 25.00

1 f 75

≡ 65 ≡

1938

145	A12	65c on 50c (Bk)	50 15
146	A13	1.75fr on 1.50fr (R)	4.00 3.50

Stamps of 1938-39 Surcharged in Red or Carmine:

25 c.   1 FR.

≡   ≡

1940

147	A12	25c on 65c ultra (C)	16 15
148	A12	1fr on 90c ultra (R)	35 16

Stamps of 1938-40 Surcharged in Red or Black:

25 c.   1 F.

≡   ≡

1941

149	A12	25c on 65c ultra (R)	15 16
150	A13	1fr on 1.25fr car rose	15 15
151	A13	1fr on 1.40fr brt red vio	15 15
152	A13	1fr on 2.25fr ultra (R)	15 15
		Set value	25 46

Types of 1926 Without RF

1941-45		**Typo.**	**Perf. 14x13½**
152A	A11	30c carmine ('45)	15 15
152B	A12	1.20fr int blue ('45)	15 15
153	A12	1.50fr brn red ('42)	16 16
154	A13	2.40fr car & brt pink ('42)	15 15
155	A13	2.50fr dk bl & lt bl	15 15
156	A13	3fr lt violet ('42)	15 15
157	A13	4fr blk & bl vio ('42)	15 15
158	A13	4.50fr ol grn & brn ('42)	15 15
159	A13	5fr brown blk ('42)	15 15
160	A13	10fr lil & dull vio	16 15
161	A13	15fr henna brn ('42)	1.90 1.60
162	A13	20fr lt vio & car	1.60 40
		Set value	4.00 2.50

Catalogue values for unused stamps in this section, from this point to the end of the section, are for Never Hinged items.

One Aim Alone - Victory A18

Mosque and Olive Tree A19

1943 — Litho. — Perf. 12

163	A18	1.50fr rose	15 15

1944-45 — Unwmk. — Perf. 11½
Size: 15½x19mm

165	A19	30c yellow ('45)	15 15
166	A19	40c org brn ('45)	15 15
168	A19	60c red org ('45)	15 15
169	A19	70c rose pink ('45)	15 15
170	A19	80c Prus grn ('45)	15 15
171	A19	90c violet ('45)	15 15
172	A19	1fr red ('45)	15 15
173	A19	1.50fr dp bl ('45)	15 15

Size: 21¼x26½mm

175	A19	2.40fr red	15 15
176	A19	2.50fr red brn	15 15
177	A19	3fr lt vio	15 15
178	A19	4fr brt bl vio	15 15
179	A19	4.50fr apple grn	15 15
180	A19	5fr gray	15 15
181	A19	6fr choc ('45)	20 20
182	A19	10fr brn lake ('45)	20 20
183	A19	15fr copper brn	20 20
184	A19	20fr lilac	30 30
		Set value	1.50 1.50

For surcharge see No. B79.

Types of 1926

1946-47		**Typo.**	**Perf. 14x13½**
185	A12	2fr emerald ('47)	15 15
186	A12	3fr rose pink	15 15
187	A12	4fr violet ('47)	15 15
188	A13	4fr violet ('47)	15 15
189	A12	6fr carmine ('47)	15 15
		Set value	30 30

Neptune, Bardo Museum A20

1947-49 — Engr. — Perf. 13

190	A20	5fr dk grn & bluish blk	35 35
191	A20	10fr blk brn & bluish blk	15 15
192	A20	18fr dk bl gray & Prus bl ('48)	50 30
193	A20	25fr dk bl & bl grn ('49)	62 30

For surcharge see No. B108.

Detail from Great Mosque at Kairouan — A21

1948-49

194	A21	3fr dk bl grn & bl grn	35 30
195	A21	4fr dk red vio & red vio	20 15
196	A21	6fr red brn & red	15 15
197	A21	10fr purple ('49)	15 15
198	A21	12fr henna brn	35 20
198A	A21	12fr dk brn & org brn ('49)	22 15
198B	A21	15fr dk red ('49)	22 15
		Nos. 194-198B (7)	1.64
		Set value	95

See No. 225. For surcharge see No. B103.

Types of 1926

1947-49		**Typo.**	**Perf. 14x13½**
199	A12	2.50fr brown orange	15 15
a.		2.50fr brown	30 15
200	A12	4fr brn org ('49)	22 18
201	A12	4.50fr lt ultra	15 15
202	A13	5fr blue ('48)	20 20
203	A12	5fr lt bl grn ('49)	20 15
204	A13	6fr rose red	15 15
205	A12	15fr rose red	20 20
206	A13	25fr red org	38 25
		Set value	1.40 1.05

No. 199a is known only precanceled. See note after No. 120.

Dam on the Oued Mellegue A22

1949, Sept. 1 — Engr. — Perf. 13

207	A22	15fr grnsh blk	80 20

UPU Symbols and Tunisian Post Rider A23

Berber Hermes at Carthage A24

1949, Oct. 28 — Bluish Paper

208	A23	5fr dk grn	50 50
209	A23	15fr red brn	50 50

UPU, 75th anniversary.
Nos. 208-209 exist imperf. See No. C13.

1950-51

210	A24	15fr red brn	35 30
211	A24	25fr indigo ('51)	35 30
212	A24	50fr dk grn ('51)	1.10 45

Horse, Carthage Museum — A25

1950, Dec. 26 — Typo. — Perf. 13½x14
Size: 21½x17½mm

213	A25	10c aquamarine	15 15
214	A25	50c brown	15 15
215	A25	1fr rose lilac	15 15
216	A25	2fr gray	15 15
217	A25	4fr vermilion	15 15
218	A25	5fr blue grn	15 15
219	A25	8fr deep blue	16 15
220	A25	12fr red	50 15
221	A25	15fr car rose ('50)	16 15
		Set value	1.20 60

See Nos. 222-224, 226-228.

1951-53 — Engr. — Perf. 13x14
Size: 22x18mm

222	A25	15fr car rose	35 20
223	A25	15fr ultra ('53)	35 20
224	A25	30fr dp ultra	70 20

Type of 1948-49

1951, Aug. 1			**Perf. 13**
225	A21	30fr dark blue	42 22

Horse Type of 1950

1952		**Typo.**	**Perf. 13½x14**
226	A25	3fr brn org	15 15
227	A25	12fr car rose	50 15
228	A25	15fr ultra	20 15
		Set value	20

Charles Nicolle — A26

Flags, Pennants and Minaret — A27

1952, Aug. 4 — Engr. — Perf. 13

229	A26	15fr blk brn	50 35
230	A26	30fr dp blue	50 35

Founding of the Society of Medical Sciences of Tunisia, 50th anniv.

1953, Oct. 18

231	A27	8fr blk brn & choc	40 40
232	A27	12fr dk grn & emer	40 40
233	A27	15fr indigo & ultra	40 40
234	A27	18fr dk pur & pur	40 40
235	A27	30fr dk car & car	40 40
		Nos. 231-235 (5)	2.00 2.00

First International Fair of Tunis.

Courtyard at Sousse
A28

Sidi Bou Maklouf Mosque
A29

Designs: 1fr, Courtyard at Sousse. 2fr, 4fr, Citadel, Takrouna. 5fr, 8fr, View of Tatahouine. 10fr, 12fr, Ruins at Matmata. 15fr, Street Corner, Sidi Bou Said. 20fr, 25fr, Genoese fort, Tabarka. 30fr, 40fr, Bab-El-Khadra gate. 50fr, 75fr, Four-story building, Medenine.

Perf. 13½x13 (A28), 13
1954, May 29

236	A28	50c emerald	15	15
237	A28	1fr car rose	15	15
238	A28	2fr vio brn	15	15
239	A28	4fr turq bl	15	15
240	A28	5fr violet	15	15
241	A28	8fr blk brn	15	15
242	A28	10fr dk bl grn	15	15
243	A28	12fr rose brn	22	15
244	A28	15fr dp ultra	1.60	15
245	A29	18fr chocolate	90	42
246	A29	20fr dp ultra	65	15
247	A29	25fr indigo	50	15
248	A29	30fr dp claret	40	15
249	A29	40fr dk Prus grn	50	22
250	A29	50fr dk vio	1.60	15
251	A29	75fr car rose	1.60	1.10

Typo.
Perf. 14x13½

252	A28	15fr ultra	50	15
		Nos. 236-252 (17)	9.52	
		Set value		2.50

Imperforates exist. See Nos. 271-287. For surcharge see No. B125.

Mohammed al-Amin, Bey of Tunis — A30

1954, Oct.   *Perf. 13*

253	A30	8fr bl & dk bl	25	25
254	A30	12fr lil gray & indigo	25	25
255	A30	15fr dp car & brn lake	25	25
256	A30	18fr red brn & blk brn	25	25
257	A30	30fr bl grn & dk bl grn	45	45
		Nos. 253-257 (5)	1.45	1.45

Theater Drapes, Dove and Sun — A31

1955

258	A31	15fr dk red brn, bl & org	30	30

Essor, Tunisian amateur theatrical society.

Rotary Emblem, Map and Symbols of Punic, Roman, Arab and French Civilizations
A32

1955, May 14   *Unwmk.*

259	A32	12fr vio brn & blk brn	32	32
260	A32	15fr vio gray & dk brn	32	32
261	A32	18fr rose vio & dk pur	32	32
262	A32	25fr bl & dp ultra	32	32
263	A32	30fr dk Prus grn & ind	60	60
		Nos. 259-263 (5)	1.88	1.88

Rotary International, 50th anniv.

Bey of Tunis
A33

Embroiderers
A34

1955   *Engr.*   *Perf. 13½x13*

264	A33	15fr dark blue	22	15

1955, July 25   *Perf. 13*

Designs: 15fr, 18fr, Potters. 20fr, 30fr, Florists.

265	A34	5fr rose brn	35	35
266	A34	12fr ultra	35	35
267	A34	15fr Prussian grn	40	40
268	A34	18fr red	40	40
269	A34	20fr dark vio	50	50
270	A34	30fr vio brn	50	50
		Nos. 265-270 (6)	2.50	2.50

For surcharge see No. B126.

Independent Kingdom
Types of 1954 Redrawn with "RF" Omitted

1956, Mar. 1   *Perf. 13½x13, 13 (A29)*

271	A28	50c emerald	15	15
272	A28	1fr car rose	15	15
273	A28	2fr vio brn	15	15
274	A28	4fr turquoise bl	15	15
275	A28	5fr violet	15	15
276	A28	8fr blk brn	15	15
277	A28	10fr dk blue grn	15	15
278	A28	12fr rose brn	15	15
279	A28	15fr dp ultra	55	15
280	A29	18fr chocolate	20	15
281	A29	20fr dp ultra	16	15
282	A29	25fr indigo	15	15
283	A29	30fr dp claret	70	15
284	A29	40fr dk Prus grn	65	15
285	A29	50fr dk vio	50	15
286	A29	75fr car rose	65	55

Perf. 14x13
Typo.

287	A28	15fr ultra	15	15
		Set value	4.00	1.50

Mohammed al-Amin Bey of Tunis — A35

Farhat Hached — A36

Designs: 12fr, 18fr, 30fr, Woman and Dove. 5fr, 20fr, Bey of Tunis.

1956   *Unwmk.*   *Engr.*   *Perf. 13*

288	A35	5fr deep blue	16	15
289	A35	12fr brn vio	20	15
290	A35	15fr red	22	20
291	A35	18fr dk bl gray	35	20
292	A35	25fr dark grn	35	15
293	A35	30fr copper brown	60	22
		Nos. 288-293 (6)	1.88	1.07

Issued to commemorate Tunisian autonomy.

1956, May 1

294	A36	15fr rose brown	20	20
295	A36	30fr indigo	25	25

Farhat Hached (1914-1952), nationalist leader.

Grapes — A37

Fruit Market — A38

Designs: 15fr, Hand holding olive branch. 18fr, Wheat harvest. 20fr, Man carrying food basket ("Gifts for the wedding").

1956-57   *Unwmk.*   *Engr.*   *Perf. 13*

296	A37	12fr lil, vio & vio brn	35	15
297	A37	15fr ind, dk ol grn & red brn	35	15
298	A37	18fr brt vio bl	60	20
299	A37	20fr brn org	60	20
300	A38	25fr chocolate	70	40
301	A38	30fr dp ultra	80	40
		Nos. 296-301 (6)	3.40	1.50

Habib Bourguiba A39

Farmers and Workers A40

Perf. 14 (A39), 11½x11 (A40)
1957, Mar. 20

302	A39	5fr dark blue	15	15
303	A40	12fr magenta	15	15
304	A39	20fr ultra	18	15
305	A40	25fr green	18	15
306	A39	30fr chocolate	22	18
307	A40	50fr crim rose	38	25
		Nos. 302-307 (6)	1.26	
		Set value		75

First anniversary of independence.

Dove and Handclasp A41

Labor Bourse, Tunis — A42

1957, July 5   *Engr.*   *Perf. 13*

308	A41	18fr dk red vio	22	22
309	A42	20fr crimson	25	25
310	A41	25fr green	25	25
311	A42	30fr dark blue	30	30

5th World Congress of the Intl. Federation of Trade Unions, Tunis, July 5-13.

Republic

Officer and Soldier — A43

1957, Aug. 8   *Typo.*   *Perf. 11*

312	A43	20fr rose pink	7.00	7.00
313	A43	25fr light vio	7.00	7.00
314	A43	30fr brn org	7.00	7.00

Proclamation of the Republic.

Bourguiba in Exile, Ile de la Galité — A44

1958, Jan. 18   *Engr.*   *Perf. 13*

315	A44	20fr bl & dk brn	25	20
316	A44	25fr lt bl & vio	30	20

6th anniv. of Bourguiba's deportation.

Map of Tunisia — A45

Designs: 25fr, Woman and child. 30fr, Hand holding flag.

1958, Mar. 20   *Perf. 13*

317	A45	20fr dk brn & emer	20	15
318	A45	25fr blue & sepia	20	15
319	A45	30fr red brn & red	25	15
		Set value		36

2nd anniv. of independence. See No. 321.

Andreas Vesalius and Abderrahman ibn Khaldoun A46

1958, Apr. 17   *Unwmk.*

320	A46	30fr bister & slate grn	30	15

World's Fair, Brussels, Apr. 17-Oct. 19.

Redrawn Type of 1958
1958, June 1   *Engr.*   *Perf. 13*

321	A45	20fr brt bl & ocher	25	16

Date has been changed to "1 Juin 1955-1958." 3rd anniv. of the return of Pres. Habib Bourguiba.

Gardener — A47

A48

1958, May 1

322	A47	20fr multi	30	30

Labor Day, May 1.

1958, July 25   *Unwmk.*   *Perf. 13*
Blue Paper

323	A48	5fr dk vio brn & ol	32	15
324	A48	10fr dk grn & yel grn	32	15
325	A48	15fr org red & brn lake	32	15
326	A48	20fr vio, ol grn & yel	32	15
327	A48	25fr red lilac	32	15
		Nos. 323-327 (5)	1.60	
		Set value		45

First anniversary of the Republic.

Pres. Habib Bourguiba A49

Fishermen Casting Net A50

1958, Aug. 3   Unwmk.   Perf. 13
328 A49 20fr vio & brn lake   20 15
Pres. Bourguiba's 55th birthday.

1958, Oct. 18   Engr.   Perf. 13
329 A50 25fr dk brn, grn & red   30 20
6th International Fair, Tunis.

UNESCO Building, Paris — A51

1958, Nov. 3
330 A51 25fr grnsh blk   30 20
Opening of UNESCO Headquarters, Nov. 3.

Woman Opening Veil — A52

Hand Planting Symbolic Tree — A53

Habib Bourguiba at Borj le Boeuf — A54

1959, Jan. 1   Engr.   Perf. 13
331 A52 20m greenish blue   25 16
Emancipation of Tunisian women.

1959, Mar. 2   Unwmk.   Perf. 13
Designs: 10m, Shield with flag and people holding torch. 20m, Habib Bourguiba at Borj le Boeuf, Sahara.
332 A53 5m vio brn, car & sal   15 15
333 A53 10m multi   16 15
334 A53 20m blue   20 16
335 A54 30m grnsh bl, ind & org brn   38 35
25th anniv. of the founding of the Neo-Destour Party at Kasr Helal, Mar. 2, 1934.

"Independence" — A55

1959, Mar. 20
336 A55 50m ol, blk & red   40 25
3rd anniversary of independence.

Map of Africa and Drawings — A56

1959, Apr. 15   Litho.   Perf. 13
337 A56 40m lt bl & red brn   42 30
Africa Freedom Day, Apr. 15.

Camel Camp and Mosque, Kairouan A57

Horseback Rider — A58

Olive Picker — A59

Open Window A58a

Designs: ½m, Woodcock in Ain-Draham forest. 2m, Camel rider. 3m, Saddler's shop. 4m, Old houses of Medenine, gazelle and youth. 6m, Weavers. 8m, Woman of Gafsa. 10m, Unveiled woman holding fruit. 12m, Ivory craftsman. 15m, Skanes Beach, Monastir, and mermaid. 16m, Minaret of Ez-Zitouna University, Tunis. 20m, Oasis of Gabès. 25m, Oil, flowers and fish of Sfax. 30m, Modern and Roman aqueducts. 40m, Festival at Kairouan (drummer and camel). 45m, Octagonal minaret, Bizerte (boatman). 50m, Three women of Djerba island. 60m, Date palms, Djerid. 70m, Tapestry weaver. 75m, Pottery of Nabeul. 90m, Le Kef (man on horse). 100m, Road to Sidi-bou-Said. 200m, Old port of Sfax. ½d, Roman temple, Sbeitla. 1d, Farmer plowing with oxen, Beja.

1959-61   Unwmk.   Engr.   Perf. 13
338 A58 ½m emer, brn & bl grn ('60)   15 15
339 A57 1m lt bl & ocher   15 15
340 A58 2m multicolored   15 15
341 A58 3m slate green   15 15
342 A57 4m red brn ('60)   15 15
343 A58 5m gray green   15 15
344 A58 6m rose violet   15 15
345 A58 8m vio brn ('60)   45 15
346 A58 10m ol, dk grn & car   15 15
347 A58 12m vio bl & ol bis ('61)   38 15
348 A57 15m brt bl ('60)   18 15
349 A57 16m grnsh blk ('60)   18 15
350 A58a 20m grnsh blue   60 15
351 A58 20m grnsh blk, ol & mar ('60)   1.25 15
352 A57 25m multi ('60)   18 15
353 A58a 30m brn, grnsh bl & ol   26 15
354 A59 40m dp green ('60)   60 15
355 A58a 45m brt green ('60)   40 18
356 A58a 50m Prus grn, dk bl & rose ('60)   55 15
357 A58a 60m grn & red brn ('60)   55 19
358 A59 70m multi ('60)   80 25
359 A59 75m ol gray ('60)   60 32
360 A58a 90m brt grn, ultra & choc ('60)   80 30
361 A59 95m multicolored   90 50
362 A59 100m dk bl, ol & brn   1.10 50
363 A58a 200m brt bl, bis & car   2.75 1.25
363A A59 ½d lt brn ('60)   6.75 3.50
363B A58a 1d sl grn & bis ('60)   12.50 7.00
Nos. 338-363B (28)   32.98 16.69

UN Emblem and Clasped Hands — A60

Dancer and Coin — A61

1959, Oct. 24
364 A60 80m org brn, brn & ultra   60 40
UN Day, Oct. 24.

1959, Nov. 4
365 A61 50m grnsh bl & blk   42 42
Central Bank of Tunisia, first anniversary.

Uprooted Oak Emblem — A62

Doves and WRY Emblem A63

1960, Apr. 7   Engr.   Perf. 13
366 A62 20m blue black   35 20
367 A63 40m red lil & dk grn   42 30
Issued to publicize World Refugee Year, July 1, 1959-June 30, 1960.

Girl, Boy and Scout Badge — A64

Cyclist — A65

Designs: 25m, Hand giving Scout sign. 30m, Bugler and tent. 40m, Peacock and Scout emblem. 60m, Scout and campfire.

1960, Aug. 9
368 A64 10m lt bl grn   15 15
369 A64 25m grn, red & brn   18 15
370 A64 30m vio bl, grn & mar   25 18
371 A64 40m blk, car & bl   30 22
372 A64 60m dk brn, vio blk & lake   65 32
Nos. 368-372 (5)   1.53 1.02
4th Arab Boy Scout Jamboree, Tunis, Aug.

1960, Aug. 25
Designs: 10m, Olympic rings forming flower. 15m, Girl tennis player and minaret. 25m, Runner and minaret. 50m, Handball player and minaret.
373 A65 5m dk brn & olive   20 20
374 A65 10m sl, red vio & emer   22 22
375 A65 15m rose red & rose car   22 22
376 A65 25m grnsh bl & gray bl   35 35
377 A65 50m brt grn & ultra   65 60
Nos. 373-377 (5)   1.64 1.59
17th Olympic Games, Rome, Aug. 25-Sept. 11.

Symbolic Forest Design — A66

National Fair Emblems — A67

Designs: 15m, Man working in forest. 25m, Tree superimposed on leaf. 50m, Symbolic tree and bird.

1960, Aug. 29
378 A66 8m multi   15 15
379 A66 15m dk grn   20 15
380 A66 25m dk pur, crim & brt grn   30 18
381 A66 50m Prus grn, yel grn & rose lake   42 30
5th World Forestry Congress, Seattle, Wash., Aug. 29-Sept. 10.

1960, June 1
382 A67 100m blk & grn   55 35
5th Natl. Fair, Sousse, May 27-June 12.

Pres. Bourguiba Signing Constitution — A68

Pres. Bourguiba — A69

1960, June 1
383 A68 20m choc, red & emer   22 15
384 A69 20m grayish blk   15 15
385 A69 30m bl, dl red & blk   22 15
386 A69 40m grn, dl red & blk   25 15
Set value   36
Promulgation of the Constitution (No. 383).

UN Emblem and Arms — A70

Dove and "Liberated Tunisia" — A71

1960, Oct. 24   Engr.   Perf. 13
387 A70 40m mag, ultra & gray grn   45 35
15th anniversary of the United Nations.

1961, Mar. 20   Perf. 13
Design: 75m, Globe and arms.
388 A71 20m maroon, bis & bl   16 15
389 A71 30m bl, vio & brn   20 16
390 A71 40m yel grn & ultra   40 35
391 A71 75m bis, red lil & Prus bl   50 40
5th anniversary of independence.

Map of Africa,
Woman and
Animals — A72

Mother and
Child with
Flags — A73

Map of Africa: 60m, Negro woman and Arab.
100m, Arabic inscription and Guinea masque.
200m, Hands of Negro and Arab.

1961, Apr. 15   Engr.   Unwmk.
392	A72	40m bis brn, red brn & dk grn	
393	A72	60m brn, blk & org brn	20 15
394	A72	100m sl grn, emer & vio	38 20
395	A72	200m dk brn & org brn	75 65

Africa Freedom Day, Apr. 15.

1961, June 1   Unwmk.   Perf. 13

Designs: 50m, Tunisians. 95m, Girl with wings
and half-moon.
396	A73	25m pale vio, red & brn	22 15
397	A73	50m bl grn, sep & brn	35 16
398	A73	95m pale vio, rose lil & ocher	42 30

National Feast Day, June 1.

Dag
Hammarskjold
A74

Arms of
Tunisia
A75

1961, Oct. 24   Photo.   Perf. 14
399 A74 40m ultramarine   30 20

UN Day; Dag Hammarskjold (1905-1961), Secretary General of the UN, 1953-61.

1962, Jan. 18   Perf. 11½

Arms in Original Colors
400	A75	1m blk & yel	15 15
401	A75	2m blk & pink	15 15
402	A75	3m blk & lt bl	15 15
403	A75	6m blk & gray	15 15
		Set value	30 25

Tunisia's campaign for independence, 10th anniv.

Mosquito in Spider Web
and WHO
Emblem — A76

Designs: 30m, Symbolic horseback rider spearing
mosquito. 40m, Hands crushing mosquito, horiz.

1962, Apr. 7   Engr.   Perf. 13
404	A76	20m chocolate	42 20
405	A76	30m red brn & sl grn	35 20
406	A76	40m dk brn, mar & grn	48 25

WHO drive to eradicate malaria.

Boy and Map
of Africa
A77

African Holding
"Africa"
A78

1962, Apr. 15   Photo.   Perf. 14
407	A77	50m brn & org	35 22
408	A78	100m bl, blk & org	50 25

Africa Freedom Day, Apr. 15.

Farm
Worker — A79

Industrial
Worker — A80

1962, May 1   Unwmk.
409	A79	40m multi	30 16
410	A80	60m dk red brn	38 22

Labor Day.

"Liberated
Tunisia" — A81

Woman of
Gabès — A82

1962, June 1   Typo.   Perf. 13½x14
411 A81 20m salmon & blk   20 15

National Feast Day, June 1.

1962-63   Photo.   Perf. 11½

Women in costume of various localities: 10m,
30m, Mahdia. 15m, Kairouan. 20m, 40m, Ham-
mamet. 25m, Djerba. 55m, Ksar Hellal. 60m,
Tunis.
412	A82	5m multi	25 15
413	A82	10m multi	32 18
414	A82	15m multi ('63)	38 25
415	A82	20m multi	50 30
416	A82	25m multi ('63)	50 30
417	A82	30m multi	65 38
418	A82	40m multi	70 38
419	A82	50m multi	70 45
420	A82	55m multi ('63)	85 55
421	A82	60m multi ('63)	1.25 85
		Nos. 412-421 (10)	6.10 3.79

6 stamps issued July 25, 1962 (July 25) for the
6th anniv. of Tunisia's independence. 4 issued June
1, 1963 for Natl. Feast Day. See Nos. 470-471.

UN Emblem,
Flag and
Dove -— A83

Aboul-Qasim
Chabbi — A84

Designs: 30m, Leaves and globe, horiz. 40m,
Dove and globe.

1962, Oct. 24   Unwmk.
422	A83	20m gray, blk & scar	25 20
423	A83	30m multi	30 20
424	A83	40m claret brn, blk & bl	55 30

Issued for United Nations Day, Oct. 24.

1962, Nov. 20   Engr.   Perf. 13
425 A84 15m purple   20 15

Aboul-Qasim Chabbi (1904-34), Arab poet.

Pres. Habib
Bourguiba
A85

Hached
Telephone
Exchange
A86

Perf. 12½x13½

1962, Dec. 7   Photo.
426	A85	20m bright blue	15 15
427	A85	30m rose claret	15 15
428	A85	40m green	15 15
		Set value	28 20

1962, Dec. 7   Litho.

Designs: 10m, Carthage Exchange. 15m, Sfax
telecommunications center. 50m, Telephone operators. 100m, Symbol of automatization. 200m, Belvedere Central Exchange.
429	A86	5m multi	20 15
430	A86	10m multi	20 15
431	A86	15m multi	32 15
432	A86	50m multi	52 25
433	A86	100m multi	1.40 55
434	A86	200m multi	1.90 90
		Nos. 429-434 (6)	4.54 2.15

1st Afro-Asian Philatelic Exhibition; automation
of the telephone system.

Dove over
Globe
A87

"Hunger"
A88

1963, Mar. 21   Engr.   Perf. 13
435	A87	20m brt bl & brn	20 16
436	A88	40m bis brn & dk brn	30 20

FAO "Freedom from Hunger" campaign.

Runner and
Walker — A89

Centenary
Emblem — A90

1963, Feb. 17   Litho.   Perf. 13
437 A89 30m brn, blk & grn   30 20

Army Sports Day; 13th C.I.S.M. cross country
championships.

1963, May 8   Engr.   Perf. 13
438 A90 20m brn, gray & red   20 15

Centenary of International Red Cross.

"Human
Rights" — A91

Hand Raising Gateway
of Great Temple of
Philae — A92

1963, Dec. 10   Unwmk.   Perf. 13
439 A91 30m grn & dk brn   20 15

15th anniv. of the Universal Declaration of
Human Rights.

1964, Mar. 8   Engr.
440 A92 50m red brn, bis & bluish blk   35 25

UNESCO world campaign to save historic monuments in Nubia.

Sunshine, Rain and
Barometer — A93

Mohammed
Ali — A94

1964, Mar. 8   Unwmk.   Perf. 13
441 A93 40m brn, red lil & slate   30 20

4th World Meteorological Day, Mar. 23.

1964, May 15   Engr.
442 A94 50m sepia   25 16

Mohammed Ali (1894-1928), labor leader.

Map of Africa
and Symbolic
Flower — A95

Pres. Habib
Bourguiba — A96

1964, May 25   Photo.   Perf. 13x14
443 A95 60m multi   35 22

1st anniv. of the Addis Ababa charter on African
Unity.

1964, June 1   Engr.   Perf. 12½x13½
444	A96	20m vio bl	15 15
445	A96	30m black	15 15
		Set value	22 15

"Ship and Torch" — A97

1964, Oct. 19   Photo.   Perf. 11½x11
446 A97 50m blk & grn   22 15

Neo-Destour Congress, Bizerte. "Bizerte" in
Arabic forms the ship and "Neo-Destour Congress
1964" the torch of the design.

Communication Equipment and ITU
Emblem — A98

1965, May 17   Engr.   *Perf. 13*
447 A98 55m gray & blue   35 15

ITU, centenary.

Carthaginian   Girl with
Coin — A99   Book — A100

Perf. 12¹/₂x14
1965, July 9   Photo.   Unwmk.
448 A99   5m grn & blk brn   15 15
449 A99 10m bis & blk brn   20 15
450 A99 75m bl & blk brn   50 20
          Set value   40

Festival of Popular Arts, Carthage.

1965, Oct. 1   Engr.   *Perf. 13*
451 A100 25m brt bl, blk & red   18 15
452 A100 40m blk, bl & red   25 15
453 A100 50m red, bl & blk   28 15
     a.   Souvenir sheet of 3, #451-453 3.00 3.00
          Set value   32

Girl Students' Center; education for women. No.
453a sold for 200m. Issued perf. and imperf.; same
value.

Links and ICY   Man Pouring
Emblem — A101   Water — A102

1965, Oct. 24
454 A101 40m blk, brt bl & rose lil   30 15

International Cooperation Year.

1966, Jan. 18   Photo.   *Perf. 13x14*

Symbolic Designs: 10m, Woman and pool. 30m,
Woman pouring water. 100m, Mountain and
branches.

Inscribed "Eaux Minerales"

455 A102 10m gray, ocher & dk red   15 15
456 A102 20m multi   20 15
457 A102 30m yel, bl & red   25 16
458 A102 100m ol, bl & yel   65 38

Mineral waters of Tunisia.

President
Bourguiba and
Hands
A103

"Promotion of
Culture" — A104

Designs: 5m, like 10m. 25m, "Independence"
(arms raised), flag and doves. 40m, "Development,"
horiz.

1966, June 1   Engr.   *Perf. 13*
459 A103   5m dl pur & vio   15 15
460 A103 10m gray grn & sl grn   15 15
          Perf. 11¹/₂
          Photo.
461 A104 25m multi   15 15
462 A104 40m multi   35 16
463 A104 60m multi   50 16
          Nos. 459-463 (5)   1.30
          Set value   62

10th anniversary of independence.

Map of Africa through
View Finder, Plane and
UN Emblem — A105

1966, Sept. 12   Engr.   *Perf. 13*
464 A105 15m lilac & multi   15 15
465 A105 35m blue & multi   15 15
466 A105 40m multi   25 15
     a.   Souvenir sheet of 3, #464-466 7.50 7.50
          Set value   32

2nd UN Regional Cartographic Conference for
Africa, held in Tunisia, Sept. 12-24.
     No. 466a sold for 150m. Issued perf. and
imperf.; same value.

UNESCO
Emblem and
Nine Muses
A106

1966, Oct. 24   *Perf. 13*
467 A106 100m blk & brn   60 25

UNESCO, 20th anniv.

Runners and
Mediterranean
Map — A107

1967, March 20   Engr.   *Perf. 13*
468 A107 20m dk red, brn ol & bl   15 15
469 A107 30m brt bl & blk   22 15
          Set value   22

Mediterranean Games, Sept. 8-17.

Types of 1962-63 and 1965-66 with EXPO
'67 Emblem and Inscription and

Symbols of Various
Activities — A108

Designs: 50m, Woman of Djerba. 75m, Woman
of Gabes. 155m, Pink flamingoes.

Perf. 11¹/₂, 13 (A108)
1967, Apr. 28   Photo.; Engr. (A108)
470 A82   50m multi   25 15
471 A82   75m multi   32 24
472 A108 100m dk grn, sl bl & blk   42 24
473 A108 110m dk brn, ultra & red   55 30
474 AP6   155m multi   90 32
          Nos. 470-474 (5)   2.44 1.25

EXPO '67, Intl. Exhibition, Montreal, Apr. 28-
Oct. 27.

Tunisian Pavilion, Pres. Bourguiba and
Map of Tunisia — A109

Designs: 105m, 200m, Tunisian Pavilion and
bust of Pres. Bourguiba.

1967, June 13   Engr.   *Perf. 13*
475 A109   65m red lil & dp org   22 15
476 A109 105m multi   30 18
477 A109 120m brt bl   38 25
478 A109 200m red, lil & blk   65 32

Tunisia Day at EXPO '67.

"Tunisia"
Holding 4-leaf
Clovers
A110

Woman Freeing
Doves — A111

1967, July 25   Litho.   *Perf. 13¹/₂*
479 A110 25m multi   16 15
480 A111 40m multi   20 15

10th anniversary of the Republic.

Tennis Courts, Players and Games'
Emblem — A112

Designs: 10m, Games' emblem and sports
emblems, vert. 15m, Swimming pool and swimmers. 35m, Sports Palace and athletes. 75m, Stadium and athletes.

1967, Sept. 8   Engr.   *Perf. 13*
481 A112   5m sl grn & hn brn   15 15
482 A112 10m brn red & multi   15 15
483 A112 15m black   20 15
484 A112 35m dk brn & Prus bl   30 15
485 A112 75m dk car rose, vio & bl
              grn   55 35
          Nos. 481-485 (5)   1.35
          Set value   82

Mediterranean Games, Tunis, Sept. 8-17.

Bird, Punic   "Mankind" and
Period — A113   Human Rights
                     Flame — A114

History of Tunisia: 20m, Sea horse, medallion
from Kerkouane. 25m, Hannibal, bronze bust,
Volubilis. 30m, Stele, Carthage. 40m, Hamilcar,
coin. 60m, Mask, funereal pendant.

1967, Dec. 1   Litho.   *Perf. 13¹/₂*
486 A113 15m gray grn, pink & blk   16 15
487 A113 20m dp bl, red & blk   16 15
488 A113 25m dk grn & org brn   22 15
489 A113 30m grnsh gray, pink &
              blk   22 15
490 A113 40m red brn, yel & blk   30 15
491 A113 60m multi   35 20
          Nos. 486-491 (6)   1.41
          Set value   75

1968, Jan. 18   Engr.   *Perf. 13*
492 A114 25m brick red   22 15
493 A114 60m deep blue   25 16

International Human Rights Year.

Computer
Fantasy
A115

1968, Mar. 20   Engr.   *Perf. 13*
494 A115 25m mag, bl vio & ol   22 15
495 A115 40m ol grn, red brn & brn   22 15
496 A115 60m ultra, sl & brn   30 15

Introduction of electronic equipment for postal
service.

Physician and   Arabian
Patient — A116   Jasmine — A117

1968, Apr. 7   Engr.   *Perf. 13*
497 A116 25m dp grn & brt grn   22 15
498 A116 60m magenta & car   30 15

WHO, 20th anniversary.

1968-69   Photo.   *Perf. 11¹/₂*

Flowers: 5m, Flax. 6m, Canna indica. 10m,
Pomegranate. 15m, Rhaponticum acaule. 20m,
Geranium. 25m, Madonna lily. 40m, Peach blos-
soms. 50m, Caper. 60m, Ariana rose. 100fr,
Jasmine.

Granite Paper
499 A117   5m multi   15 15
500 A117   6m multi   15 15
501 A117 10m multi   15 15
502 A117 12m multi   15 15
503 A117 15m multi   15 15
504 A117 20m multi   18 15
505 A117 25m multi   20 15

506 A117	40m multi	28	15
507 A117	50m multi	32	18
508 A117	60m multi	55	30
509 A117	100m multi	85	45
	Nos. 499-509 (11)	3.13	
	Set value		1.70

Issue dates: 12m, 50m, 60m, 100m, Apr. 9, 1968. Others, Mar. 20, 1969.

Flower with Red Crescent and Globe — A118

Flutist — A119

Design: 25m, Dove with Red Crescent and globe.

1968, May 8   Engr.   Perf. 13

510 A118	15m Prus bl, grn & red	20	15
511 A118	25m brt rose lil & red	25	16

Red Crescent Society.

1968, June 1   Litho.   Perf. 13

512 A119	20m vio & multi	20	15
513 A119	50m multi	25	15

Stamp Day.

Jackal — A120

Animals: 8m, Porcupine. 10m, Dromedary. 15m, Dorcas gazelle. 20m, Desert fox (fennec). 25m, Desert hedgehog. 40m, Arabian horse. 60m, Boar.

1968-69   Photo.   Perf. 11½

514 A120	5m dk brn, lt bl & bis	15	15
515 A120	8m dk vio brn & yel grn	16	15
516 A120	10m dk brn, lt bl & ocher	25	15
517 A120	15m dk brn, ocher & yel grn	25	16
518 A120	20m dl yel & dk brn	35	30
519 A120	25m blk, tan & brt grn	55	30
520 A120	40m blk, lil & pale grn	70	55
521 A120	60m dk brn, buff & yel grn	1.00	80
	Nos. 514-521 (8)	3.41	2.56

Issue dates: 5m, 8m, 20m, 60m, Sept. 15, 1968. Others, Jan. 18, 1969.

Worker and ILO Emblem — A121

Design: 60m, Young man and woman holding banner.

1969, May 1   Engr.   Perf. 13

522 A121	25m Prus bl, blk & bis	20	15
523 A121	60m rose car, bl & yel	30	15

ILO, 50th anniversary.

Veiled Women and Musicians with Flute and Drum A122

1969, June 20   Litho.   Perf. 14x13½

524 A122	100m dp yel grn & multi	50	30

Stamp Day.

Tunisian Coat of Arms A123

Symbols of Industry A124

1969, July 25   Photo.   Perf. 11½

525 A123	15m yel & multi	15	15
526 A123	25m pink & multi	16	15
527 A123	40m gray & multi	20	15
528 A123	60m lt bl & multi	22	15
	Set value		45

1969, Sept. 10   Perf. 13x12

529 A124	60m blk, red & yel	25	15

African Development Bank, 5th anniv.

Lute — A125

Nurse and Maghrib Flags — A126

Musical Instruments: 50m, Zither, horiz. 70m, Rebab (2-strings). 90m, Drums and flute, horiz.

1970, Mar. 20   Photo.   Perf. 11½
Granite Paper

530 A125	25m multi	22	16
531 A125	50m multi	35	22
532 A125	70m multi	55	22
533 A125	90m multi	60	35

1970, May 4   Photo.   Perf. 11½

534 A126	25m lil & multi	20	15

6th Medical Seminar of Maghrib Countries (Morocco, Algeria, Tunisia and Libya), Tunis, May 4-10.

UPU Headquarters Issue
Common Design Type
1970, May 20   Engr.   Perf. 13

535 CD133	25m dl red & dk ol bis	25	15

Common Design Types pictured in section at front of book.

Mail Service Symbol A127

Design: 35m, Mailmen of yesterday and today, vert.

1970, Oct. 15   Litho.   Perf. 12½x13
Size: 37x31½mm

536 A127	25m pink & multi	30	15

Size: 22x37½mm
Perf. 13x12½

537 A127	35m blk & multi	40	15
	Set value		22

United Nations, 25th anniversary.

Dove, Laurel and UN Emblem A128

1970, Oct. 24   Photo.   Perf. 13x12½

538 A128	40m multi	25	15

United Nations, 25th anniversary.

Jasmine Vendor and Veiled Woman — A129

Lenin, after N.N. Joukov — A130

Scenes from Tunisian Life: 25m, "The 3rd Day of the Wedding." 35m, Perfume vendor. 40m, Fish vendor. 85m, Waiter in coffeehouse.

1970, Nov. 9   Photo.   Perf. 14

539 A129	20m dk grn & multi	15	15
540 A129	25m multi	15	15
541 A129	35m multi	22	15
542 A129	40m dp car & multi	25	15
543 A129	85m brt bl & multi	38	20
a.	Souvenir sheet of 5, #539-543	3.50	3.50
	Nos. 539-543 (5)	1.15	
	Set value		60

No. 543a sold for 500m. Issued perf. and imperf.; same value.

1970, Dec. 28   Engr.   Perf. 13

544 A130	60m dk car rose	25	15

Lenin (1870-1924), Russian communist leader.

Radar, Flags and Carrier Pigeon — A131

UN Headquarters, Symbolic Flower — A132

1971, May 17   Litho.   Perf. 13x12½

545 A131	25m lt bl & multi	22	15

Coordinating Committee for Post and Telecommunications Administrations of Maghrib Countries.

1971, May 10   Photo.   Perf. 12½x13

546 A132	80m brt rose lil, blk & yel	30	22

Intl. year against racial discrimination.

"Telecommunications" — A133

1971, May 17   Perf. 13x12½

547 A133	70m sil, blk & lt grn	35	20

3rd World Telecommunications Day.

Earth, Moon, Satellites A134

Design: 90m, Abstract composition.

1971, June 21   Photo.   Perf. 13x12½

548 A134	15m brt bl & blk	20	15
549 A134	90m scar & blk	40	22

Conquest of space.

"Pottery Merchant" — A135

Life in Tunisia (stylized drawings): 30m, Esparto weaver selling hats and mats. 40m, Poultry man. 50m, Dyer.

1971, July 24   Photo.   Perf. 14x13½

550 A135	25m gold & multi	15	15
551 A135	30m gold & multi	15	15
552 A135	40m gold & multi	22	15
553 A135	50m gold & multi	25	15
a.	Sheet of 4, #550-553, perf. 13½	2.50	2.50
	Set value		34

No. 553a sold for 500m. Issued perf. and imperf.; same value.

Pres. Bourguiba Sick in 1938 A136

Designs: 25m, Bourguiba and "8," vert. 50m, Bourguiba carried in triumph, vert. 80m, Bourguiba and irrigation dam.

Perf. 13½x13, 13x13½
1971, Oct. 11

554 A136	25m multi	15	15
555 A136	30m multi	15	15
556 A136	50m multi	15	15
557 A136	80m blk, ultra & grn	25	15
	Set value	56	42

8th Congress of the Neo-Destour Party.

Shah Mohammed Riza Pahlavi and Stone Head 6th Century B.C. — A137

Designs: 50m, King Bahram-Gur hunting, 4th century. 100m, Coronation, from Persian miniature, 1614.

1971, Oct. 17   *Perf. 11½*
Granite Paper
558	A137	25m multi	15	15
559	A137	50m multi	20	15
560	A137	100m multi	40	22
a.		Souvenir sheet of 3, #558-560	2.25	2.25
		Set value		44

2500th anniv. of the founding of the Persian empire by Cyrus the Great. No. 560a sold for 500m. Issued perf. and imperf.; same value.

Pimento and Warrior A138

Designs: 2m, Mint and farmer. 5m, Pear and 2 men under pear tree. 25m, Oleander and girl. 60m, Pear and sheep. 100m, Grapefruit and fruit vendor.

1971, Nov. 15   Litho.   *Perf. 13*
561	A138	1m lt bl & multi	15	15
562	A138	2m gray & multi	15	15
563	A138	5m cit & multi	15	15
564	A138	25m lil & multi	22	15
565	A138	60m multi	40	15
566	A138	100m buff & multi	80	25
a.		Souvenir sheet of 6, #561-566	2.50	2.50
		Set value	1.60	70

Fruit, flowers and folklore. No. 566a sold for 500m. Exists imperf.; same value.

Dancer and Musician — A139

1971, Nov. 22   Photo.   *Perf. 11½*
567	A139	50m blue & multi	25	15

Stamp Day.

Map of Africa, Communica-tion Symbols A139a   UNICEF Emblem, Mother and Child A140

Perf. 13½x12½
1971, Nov. 30   Litho.
568	A139a	95m multi	35	20

Pan-African telecommunications system.

1971, Dec. 6   Photo.   *Perf. 11½*
569	A140	110m multi	35	20

UNICEF, 25th anniv.

Symbolic Olive Tree and Oil Vat — A141   Gondolier in Flood Waters — A142

1972, Jan. 9   Litho.   *Perf. 13½*
570	A141	60m multi	22	15

International Olive Year.

1972, Feb. 7   Photo.   *Perf. 11½*

Designs: 30m, Young man and Doge's Palace. 50m, Gondola's prow and flood. 80m, Rialto Bridge and hand holding gondolier's hat, horiz.
571	A142	25m lt bl & multi	15	15
572	A142	30m blk & multi	20	15
573	A142	50m yel grn, gray & blk	22	15
574	A142	80m bl & multi	40	20
		Set value		55

UNESCO campaign to save Venice.

Man Reading and Book Year Emblem A143   "Your Heart is Your Health" A144

1972, Mar. 27   Photo.   *Perf. 11½*
Granite Paper
575	A143	90m brn & multi	35	20

International Book Year.

1972, Apr. 7   *Perf. 13x13½*

World Health Day: 60m, Smiling man pointing to heart.
576	A144	25m grn & multi	22	15
577	A144	60m red & multi	25	16

"Only one Earth" Environment Emblem A145

1972, June 5   Engr.   *Perf. 13*
578	A145	60m lemon & slate grn	30	20

UN Conference on Human Environment, Stockholm, June 5-16.

Hurdler, Olympic Emblems A146

1972, Aug. 26   Photo.   *Perf. 11½*
579	A146	5m Volleyball	15	15
580	A146	15m shown	15	15
581	A146	20m Athletes	15	15
582	A146	25m Soccer	15	15
583	A146	60m Swimming, women's	22	15

584	A146	80m Running	35	20
a.		Souv. sheet of 6	2.25	2.25
		Nos. 579-584 (6)	1.17	
		Set value		74

20th Olympic Games, Munich, Aug. 26-Sept. 11. No. 584a contains 6 imperf. stamps similar to Nos. 579-584. Sold for 500m.

Chessboard and Pieces — A147   Fisherman — A148

1972, Sept. 25   Photo.   *Perf. 11½*
585	A147	60m grn & multi	1.00	50

20th Men's Chess Olympiad, Skopje, Yugoslavia, Sept.-Oct.

1972, Oct. 23   Litho.   *Perf. 13½*
586	A148	5m shown	15	15
587	A148	10m Basket maker	15	15
588	A148	25m Musician	20	15
589	A148	50m Married Berber woman	30	15
590	A148	60m Flower merchant	30	15
591	A148	80m Festival	42	16
a.		Souvenir sheet of 6, #586-591	2.25	2.25
		Nos. 586-591 (6)	1.52	
		Set value		74

Life in Tunisia. No. 591a sold for 500m; exists imperf.

Post Office, Tunis A149

1972, Dec. 8   Litho. & Engr.   *Perf. 13*
592	A149	25m ver, org & blk	16	15

Stamp Day.

Dome of the Rock, Jerusalem A150

1973, Jan. 22   Photo.   *Perf. 13½*
593	A150	25m multi	65	35

Globe, Pen and Quill — A151   Family — A152

Design: 60m, Lyre and minaret.

1973, Mar. 19   Photo.   *Perf. 14x13½*
594	A151	25m gold, brt mag & brn	15	15
595	A151	60m bl & multi	20	15

9th Congress of Arab Writers.

1973, Apr. 2   *Perf. 11½*

Family Planning: 25m, profiles and dove.
596	A152	20m grn & multi	15	15
597	A152	25m lil & multi	20	15
		Set value		20

"10" and Bird Feeding Young A153

Design: 60m, "10" made of grain and bread, and hand holding spoon.

1973, Apr. 26   Photo.   *Perf. 11½*
598	A153	25m multi	15	15
599	A153	60m multi	20	15
		Set value		20

World Food Program, 10th anniversary.

Roman Head and Ship — A154

Drawings of Tools and: 25m, Mosaic with ostriches and camel. 30m, Mosaic with 4 heads and 4 emblems. 40m, Punic stele to the sun, vert. 60m, Outstretched hand and arm of Christian preacher; symbols of 4 Evangelists. 75m, 17th century potsherd with Arabic inscription, vert.

1973, May 6
600	A154	5m multi	15	15
601	A154	25m multi	15	15
602	A154	30m multi	22	15
603	A154	40m multi	25	15
604	A154	60m multi	30	15
605	A154	75m multi	32	15
a.		Souvenir sheet of 6	2.75	2.75
		Nos. 600-605 (6)	1.39	
		Set value		74

UNESCO campaign to save Carthage. No. 605a contains 6 imperf. stamps similar to Nos. 600-605. Sold for 500m.

Overlapping Circles — A155   Map of Africa as Festival Emblem — A156

Design: 75m, Printed circuit board.

1973, May 17   Photo.   *Perf. 14x13½*
606	A155	60m yel & multi	20	15
607	A155	75m vio & multi	25	20

5th Intl. Telecommunications Day.

1973, July 15   Photo.   *Perf. 13½x13*

Design: 40m, African heads, festival emblem in eye.
608	A156	25m multi	20	15
609	A156	40m multi	25	20

Pan-African Youth Festival, Tunis.

Scout Emblem and Pennants — A157

1973, July 23   Litho.   Perf. 13¹/₂x13
610 A157 25m multi 20 15
International Boy Scout Organization.

Crescent-shaped Racing Cars — A158

1973, July 30   Perf. 13x13¹/₂
611 A158 60m multi 25 15
2nd Pan-Arab auto race.

Highway Cloverleaf A159

Traffic Lights and Signs — A160   Stylized Camel — A161

Perf. 12¹/₂x13, 13x12¹/₂
1973, Sept. 28   Litho.
612 A159 25m lt bl & multi 20 15
613 A160 30m multi 25 15
Highway safety campaign.

1973, Oct. 8   Photo.   Perf. 13¹/₂
Stamp Day: 10m, Stylized bird and philatelic symbols, horiz.
614 A161 10m multi 20 15
615 A161 65m multi 25 15

Copernicus A162   African Unity A163

Lithographed and Engraved
1973, Oct. 16   Perf. 13x12¹/₂
616 A162 60m blk & multi 25 15
500th anniversary of the birth of Nicolaus Copernicus (1473-1543), Polish astronomer.

1973, Nov. 4   Photo.   Perf. 14x13¹/₂
617 A163 25m blk & multi 25 15
10th anniv. of the OAU.

Handshake and Emblems — A164   Globe, Hand Holding Carnation — A165

1973, Nov. 15   Litho.   Perf. 14¹/₂x14
618 A164 65m yel & multi 30 15
25th anniv. of Intl. Criminal Police Org.

1973, Dec. 10   Photo.   Perf. 11¹/₂
619 A165 60m blk & multi 30 20
25th anniv. of Universal Declaration of Human Rights.

WMO Headquarters and Emblem — A166

Design: 60m, Globe and emblem.

1973, Dec. 24   Litho.   Perf. 14x14¹/₂
620 A166 25m multi 20 15
621 A166 60m multi 25 16
Intl. meteorological cooperation, cent.

Bourguiba in the Desert, 1945 — A167   Scientist with Microscope — A168

Portraits of Pres. Habib Bourguiba: 25m, Exile transfer from Galite Island to Ile de la Groix, France, 1954. 60m, Addressing crowd, 1974. 75m, In Victory Parade, 1955. 100m, In 1934.

1974, Mar. 2   Photo.   Perf. 11¹/₂
622 A167 15m plum & multi 15 15
623 A167 25m multi 15 15
624 A167 60m multi 20 15
625 A167 75m multi 30 20
626 A167 100m multi 35 25
a.   Souvenir sheet of 5, #622-626 .. 1.50 1.50
      Nos. 622-626 (5) 1.15 90
40th anniv. of the Neo-Destour Party. No. 626a sold for 500m. Issued perf. and imperf.; same value.

1974, Mar. 21   Perf. 14
627 A168 60m multi 40 20
6th African Congress of Micropaleontology, Mar. 21-Apr. 3.

Woman with Telephones and Globe — A169   Pres. Bourguiba and Sun Flower Emblem — A171

WPY Emblem and Symbolic Design A170

Design: 60m, Telephone dial, telephones, wires.

1974, July 1   Photo.   Perf. 11¹/₂
628 A169 15m multi 16 15
629 A169 60m multi 35 15
Introduction of international automatic telephone dialing system.

1974, Aug. 19   Photo.   Perf. 11¹/₂
630 A170 110m multi 40 20
World Population Year.

1974, Sept. 12   Photo.   Perf. 11¹/₂
Designs: 60m, Bourguiba and cactus flower, horiz. 200m, Bourguiba and verbena, horiz.
631 A171 25m blk, ultra & grnsh bl .. 15 15
632 A171 60m red, car & yel 20 15
633 A171 200m blk, brt lil & grn ... 65 40
a.   Souv. sheet of 3, #631-633, imperf. .. 1.50 1.50
Congress of the Socialist Destour Party.

Jets Flying over Old World Map A172

1974, Sept. 23   Litho.   Perf. 12¹/₂
634 A172 60m brn & multi 35 20
25th anniversary of Tunisian aviation.

Symbolic Carrier Pigeons — A173   Handshake, Letter, UPU Emblem — A174

1974, Oct. 9   Photo.   Perf. 13
635 A173 25m multi 20 15
636 A174 60m multi 30 15
Centenary of Universal Postal Union.

Le Bardo, National Assembly — A175   Pres. Bourguiba Ballot — A176

1974, Nov. 3   Photo.   Perf. 11¹/₂
637 A175 25m grn, bl & blk 20 20
638 A176 100m org & blk 35 20
Legislative (25m) and presidential elections (100m), Nov. 1974.

Mailman with Letters and Bird — A177   Water Carrier — A178

1974, Dec. 5   Litho.   Perf. 14¹/₂x14
639 A177 75m lt vio & multi 30 16
Stamp Day.

1975, Feb. 17   Photo.   Perf. 13¹/₂
640 A178 5m shown 15 15
641 A178 15m Perfume vendor 15 15
642 A178 25m Laundresses 15 15
643 A178 60m Potter 18 15
644 A178 110m Fruit vendor 40 15
a.   Souvenir sheet of 5, #640-644 .. 2.00 2.00
      Set value 82 40
Life in Tunisia. No. 644a sold for 500m. Issued perf. and imperf.; same value.

Steel Tower, Skyscraper — A179

Geometric Designs and Arrow A180

Perf. 14x13¹/₂, 13¹/₂x14
1975, Mar. 17   Photo.
645 A179 25m yel, org & blk 15 15
646 A180 65m ultra & multi 22 15
      Set value 22
Union of Arab Engineers, 13th Conference, Tunis, Mar. 17-21.

Brass Coffeepot and Plate A181

Designs: 15m, Horse and rider. 25m, Still life. 30m, Bird cage, vert. 40m, Woman with earrings, vert. 60m, Design patterns.

1975, Apr. 14   *Perf. 13x14, 14x13*
647 A181 10m blk & multi   15 15
648 A181 15m blk & multi   15 15
649 A181 25m blk & multi   16 15
650 A181 30m blk & multi   16 15
651 A181 40m blk & multi   20 15
652 A181 60m blk & multi   22 15
  Nos. 647-652 (6)   1.04
    Set value   68

Artisans and their works.

Communications and Weather Symbols — A182

1975, May 17   Photo.   *Perf. 11½*
653 A182 50m lt bl & multi   20 15

World Telecommunications Day (communications serving meteorology).

Youth and Hope — A183

Tunisian Woman, IWY Emblem — A184

Design: 65m, Bourguiba arriving at La Goulette, Tunis, horiz.

1975, June 1   Photo.   *Perf. 11½*
654 A183 25m multi   15 15
655 A183 65m multi   22 15

Victory (independence), 20th anniversary.

1975, June 19   Litho.   *Perf. 14x13½*
656 A184 110m multi   40 25

International Women's Year.

Children Crossing Street A185

1975, July 5   Photo.   *Perf. 13½x14*
657 A185 25m multi   15 15

Highway safety campaign, July 1-Sept. 30.

Djerbian Minaret, Hotel and Marina, Jerba A186

Old and new Tunisia: 15m, 17th century minaret and modern hotel, Tunis. 20m, Fortress, earring and hotel, Monastir. 65m, View of Sousse, hotel and pendant. 500m, Town wall, mosque and palms, Tozeur. 1d, Mosques and Arab ornaments, Kairouan.

1975, July 12   Litho.   *Perf. 14x14½*
658 A186 10m multi   15 15
659 A186 15m multi   15 15
660 A186 20m multi   15 15
661 A186 65m multi   22 15
662 A186 500m multi   1.75 75
663 A186 1d multi   3.00 1.40
  Nos. 658-663 (6)   5.42 2.75

Victors — A187

Symbolic Ship A188

1975, Aug. 23   Photo.   *Perf. 13½*
664 A187 25m ol & multi   15 15
665 A188 50m bl & multi   20 15
    Set value   22

7th Mediterranean Games, Algiers, 8/23-9/6.

Flowers in Vase, Birds Holding Letters — A189

1975, Sept. 29   Litho.   *Perf. 13½x13*
666 A189 100m bl & multi   30 15

Stamp Day.

Sadiki College, Young Bourguiba A190

Engr. & Litho.
1975, Nov. 17   *Perf. 13*
667 A190 25m sepia, org & olive 15 15

Sadiki College, centenary.

Duck — A191   Vergil — A192

Mosaics: 10m, Fish. 25m, Lioness, horiz. 60m, Head of Medusa, horiz. 75m, Circus spectators.

1976, Feb. 16   Photo.   *Perf. 13*
668 A191 5m multi   15 15
669 A191 10m multi   15 15
670 A192 25m multi   15 15
671 A192 60m multi   20 15
672 A192 75m multi   25 15
673 A192 100m multi   32 15
  a. Souvenir sheet of 6, #668-673 2.50 2.50
    Set value   1.08 52

Tunisian mosaics, 2nd-5th centuries. No. 673a sold for 500m. Issued perf. and imperf.; same value.

Telephone — A193

1976, Mar. 10   Litho.   *Perf. 14x13½*
674 A193 150m bl & multi   42 25

Centenary of first telephone call by Alexander Graham Bell, Mar. 10, 1876.

Pres. Bourguiba and "20" — A194

Pres. Bourguiba and: 100m, "20" and symbolic Tunisian flag. 150m, "Tunisia" rising from darkness, and 20 flowers.

1976, Mar. 20   Photo.   *Perf. 11½*
675 A194 40m multi   15 15
676 A194 100m multi   20 15
677 A194 150m multi   30 15
    Set value   32

Souvenir Sheets
Perf. 11½, Imperf.
678   Sheet of 3   1.50 1.50
  a. A194 50m like 40m   15 15
  b. A194 200m like 100m   35 15
  c. A194 250m like 150m   45 22

20th anniversary of independence.

Blind Man with Cane A195

Procession and Buildings A196

1976, Apr. 7   Engr.   *Perf. 13*
679 A195 100m blk & red   42 16

World Health Day: "Foresight prevents blindness."

1976, May 31   Photo.   *Perf. 12x11½*
680 A196 40m multi   20 15

Habitat, UN Conf. on Human Settlements, Vancouver, Canada, May 31-June 11.

Face and Hands Decorated with Henna — A197

Old and new Tunisia: 50m, Sponge fishing at Jerba. 65m, Textile industry. 110m, Pottery of Guellala.

1976, June 15   Photo.   *Perf. 13x13½*
681 A197 40m multi   15 15
682 A197 50m multi   15 15
683 A197 65m multi   20 15
684 A197 110m multi   38 15
    Set value   46

The Spirit of '76, by Archibald M. Willard A198

1976, July 4   *Perf. 13x14*
685 A198 200m multi   80 50

Souvenir Sheets
Perf. 13x14, Imperf.
686 A198 500m multi   2.00 2.00

American Bicentennial.

Running A199

Montreal Olympic Games Emblem and: 75m, Bicycling. 120m, Peace dove.

1976, July 17   Photo.   *Perf. 11½*
687 A199 50m gray, red & blk 15 15
688 A199 75m red, yel & blk   20 15
689 A199 120m org & multi   35 22
    Set value   44

21st Olympic Games, Montreal, Canada, July 17-Aug. 1.

Child Reading — A200

Heads and Bird — A201

1976, Aug. 23   Litho.   *Perf. 13*
690 A200 100m brn & multi   35 15

Books for children.

1976, Sept. 30   Litho.   *Perf. 13*
691 A201 150m org & multi   42 20

Non-aligned Countries, 15th anniv. of 1st Conference.

Mouradite Mausoleum, 17th Century — A202

Electronic Tree and ITU Emblem — A204

Globe and Emblem A203

Cultural Heritage: 100m, Minaret, Kairawan Great Mosque and psalmodist. 150m, Monastir Ribat monastery and Alboracq (sphinx). 200m, Barber's Mosque, Kairawan and man's bust.

1976, Oct. 25   Photo.   Perf. 14
692 A202 85m multi   22 15
693 A202 100m multi   25 15
694 A202 150m multi   40 20
695 A202 200m multi   60 30

1976, Dec. 24   Photo.   Perf. 13x14
696 A203 150m multi   50 25

25th anniv. of UN Postal Administration.

1977, May 17   Photo.   Perf. 14x13¹/₂
697 A204 150m multi   50 30

9th World Telecommunications Day.

"Communication," Sassenage Castle, Grenoble — A205

1977, May 19   Litho.   Perf. 13¹/₂x13
698 A205 100m multi   50 30

10th anniv. of Intl. French Language Council.

Soccer
A206

1977, June 27   Photo.   Perf. 13¹/₂
699 A206 150m multi   50 30

Junior World Soccer Tournament, Tunisia, June 27-July 10.

Gold Coin, 10th Century — A207

Cultural Heritage: 15m, Stele, Gorjani Cemetery, Tunis, 13th century. 20m, Floral design, 17th century illumination. 30m, Bird and flowers, glass painting, 1922. 40m, Antelope, from 11th century clay pot. 50m, Gate, Sidi Bou Said, 20th century.

1977, July 9   Photo.   Perf. 13
700 A207 10m multi   15 15
701 A207 15m multi   15 15
702 A207 20m multi   15 15
703 A207 30m multi   15 15
704 A207 40m multi   16 15
705 A207 50m multi   22 15
  a.   Miniature sheet of 6, #700-705   1.00 1.00
        Set value   70 45

"The Young Republic" and Bourguiba — A208

Diseased Knee, Gears and Globe — A210

Symbolic Cancellation, APU Emblem A209

Habib Bourguiba and: 100m, "The Confident Republic" and 20 doves. 150m, "The Determined Republic" and 20 roses.

1977, July 25   Photo.   Perf. 13x13¹/₂
706 A208 40m multi   22 15
707 A208 100m multi   40 15
708 A208 150m multi   65 20
  a.   Souvenir sheet of 3, #706-708   2.00 2.00

20th anniv. of the Republic. No. 708a sold for 500m. Exists imperf., same value.

1977, Aug. 16   Litho.   Perf. 13x12¹/₂
709 A209 40m multi   15 15

Arab Postal Union, 25th anniversary.

1977, Sept. 26   Photo.   Perf. 14x13¹/₂
710 A210 120m multi   40 20

World Rheumatism Year.

Farmer, Road, Water and Electricity — A211

1977, Dec. 15   Photo.   Perf. 13¹/₂
711 A211 40m multi   15 15

Rural development.

Factory Workers — A212

Pres. Bourguiba, Torch and "9" — A213

Designs: 20m, Bus driver and trains, horiz. 40m, Farmer driving tractor, horiz.

1978, Mar. 6   Perf. 13x14, 14x13
712 A212 20m rose red & multi   15 15
713 A212 40m blk & grn   15 15
714 A212 100m multi   30 15
        Set value   35

5th development plan, creation of new jobs.

1978, Apr. 9   Engr.   Perf. 13
Design: 60m, Pres. Bourguiba and "9."
715 A213 40m multi   15 15
716 A213 60m multi   16 15
        Set value   20

40th anniversary of first fight for independence, Apr. 9, 1938.

Policeman
A214

Tunisian Goalkeeper
A215

1978, May 2   Photo.   Perf. 13x13¹/₂
717 A214 150m multi   50 22

6th Regional African Interpol Conference, Tunis, May 2-5.

1978, June 1   Photo.   Perf. 13x14
Designs: 150m., Soccer player, maps of South America and Africa, flags.
718 A215 40m multi   15 15
719 A215 150m multi   50 30

11th World Cup Soccer Championship, Argentina, June 1-25.

Destruction of Apartheid, Map of South Africa A216

Fight Against Apartheid: 100m, White and black doves flying in unison.

1978, Aug. 30   Litho.   Perf. 13¹/₂x14
720 A216 50m multi   15 15
721 A216 100m multi   30 15

"Pollution is a Plague" A217

"Eradication of Smallpox" A218

Designs: 50m, "The Sea, mankind's patrimony." 120m, "Greening of the desert."

1978, Sept. 11   Photo.   Perf. 14x13
722 A217 10m multi   15 15
723 A217 50m multi   20 15
724 A217 120m multi   50 20
        Set value   35

Protection of the environment.

1978, Oct. 16   Litho.   Perf. 12¹/₂
725 A218 150m multi   42 25

Global eradication of smallpox.

Jerba Wedding A219

Designs: 5m, Horseman from Zlass (vert.). 75m, Women potters from the Mogods. 100m, Dove over Marabout Sidi Mahrez cupolas, Tunis. 500m, Plowing in Jenduba. 1d, Spring Festival in Tozeur (man on swing).

1978, Nov. 1   Photo.   Perf. 13
726 A219 5m multi   15 15
727 A219 60m multi   16 15
728 A219 75m multi   25 15
729 A219 100m multi   35 16
730 A219 500m multi   2.25 80
731 A219 1d multi   3.50 1.50
        Nos. 726-731 (6)   6.66 2.91

Traditional Arab calligraphy.

Lenin and Red Banner over Kremlin — A220

Farhat Hached, Union Emblem — A221

1978, Nov. 7   Perf. 13¹/₂
732 A220 150m multi   42 22

Russian October Revolution, 60th anniv.

1978, Dec. 5   Photo.   Perf. 14
733 A221 50m multi   16 15

Farhat Hached (1914-1952), founder of General Union of Tunisian Workers.

Family — A222

Sun with Man's Face — A223

1978, Dec. 15   Photo.   Perf. 13¹/₂
734 A222 50m multi   22 15

Tunisian Family Planning Assoc., 10th anniv.

1978, Dec. 25   Perf. 14
735 A223 100m multi   40 20

Sun as a source of light and energy.

Plane, Weather Map and Instruments A224

1978, Dec. 29
736 A224 50m multi   20 15

Tunisian civil aviation and meteorology, 20th anniv.

Habib Bourguiba and Constitution — A225

1979, May 31   Photo.   Perf. 14x13¹/₂
737 A225 50m multi   15 15

20th anniversary of Constitution.

El Kantaoui
Port — A226

1979, June 3   *Perf. 13¹/₂x14*
738 A226 150m multi   42 15

Development of El Kantaoui as a resort area.

Landscapes — A227

1979, July 14   *Perf. 12¹/₂x13¹/₂*
739 A227   50m Korbous   15 15
740 A227 100m Mides   22 15
    Set value   15

Bow Net
Weaving — A228

Pres. Bourguiba,
"10" and
Hands — A229

1979, Aug. 15   **Photo.**   *Perf. 11¹/₂*
741 A228 10m shown
742 A228 50m Beekeeping   16 15
    Set value   22 15

1979, Sept. 5
743 A229 50m multi   20 15

Socialist Destour Party, 10th Congress.

Modes of
Communication, ITU
Emblem — A230

1979, Sept. 20   **Litho.**   *Perf. 11¹/₂*
744 A230 150m multi   50 30

3rd World Telecommunications Exhibition,
Geneva, Sept. 20-26.

Arab
Achievements
A231

1979, Oct. 1   *Perf. 14¹/₂*
745 A231 50m multi   16 15

Children Crossing
Street, IYC
Emblem — A232

1979, Oct. 16   *Perf. 14x13¹/₂*
746 A232   50m shown   15 15
747 A232 100m Child and birds   35 20
    Set value   25

International Year of the Child.

Dove, Olive
Tree, Map of
Tunisia — A233

Woman Wearing
Crown — A234

1979, Nov. 1   **Litho.**   *Perf. 12*
748 A233 150m multi   50 30

2nd International Olive Oil Year.

1979, Nov. 3   *Perf. 14¹/₂*
749 A234 50m multi   15 15

Central Bank of Tunisia, 20th anniversary.

Children and
Jujube
Tree — A235

1979, Dec. 25   **Litho.**   *Perf. 15x14¹/₂*
750 A235 20m shown   15 15
751 A235 30m Peacocks   15 15
752 A235 70m Goats   25 15
753 A235 85m Girl, date palm   30 15
    Set value   30

Postal Code
Introduction
A236

1980, Mar. 20   **Photo.**   *Perf. 14*
754 A236 50m multi   15 15

Fight
Against
Cigarette
Smoking
A237

1980, Apr. 7
755 A237 150m multi   42 16

Pres. Bourguiba in
Flower, Open
Book — A238

1980, June 1   **Photo.**   *Perf. 11¹/₂*
756 A238   50m shown   22 15
757 A238 100m Dove, Bourguiba,
    mosque   45 20

Victory (independence), 25th anniversary.

Butterfly and
Gymnast
A239

1980, June 3   **Photo.**   *Perf. 12x11¹/₂*
    Granite Paper
758 A239 100m multi   45 20

Turin Gymnastic Games, June 1-7.

Artisans
A240   A241

1980, July 21   **Photo.**   *Perf. 13¹/₂*
759 A240 30m multi   15 15
760 A241 75m multi   28 15
    Set value   15

ibn-Khaldun (1332-
1406),
Historian — A242

Avicenna (Arab
Physician), Birth
Millenium — A243

1980, July 28   *Perf. 14*
761 A242 50m multi   20 15

1980, Aug. 18   **Engr.**   *Perf. 12¹/₂x13*
762 A243 100m redsh brn & sep   40 15

Arab
Achievements
A244

1980, Aug. 25   **Photo.**   *Perf. 13¹/₂x14*
763 A244 50m multi   20 15

Port Sidi
bou Said
A245

1980, Sept. 4   *Perf. 14*
764 A245 100m multi   48 16

World
Tourism
Conference,
Manila, Sept.
27 — A246

1980, Sept. 27   **Photo.**   *Perf. 14*
765 A246 150m multi   52 20

Wedding in Jerba, by Yahia (1903-
1969) — A247

1980, Oct. 1   *Perf. 12*
766 A247 50m multi   28 15

Tozeur-Nefta
International Airport
Opening — A248

1980, Oct. 13   **Photo.**   *Perf. 13x13¹/₂*
767 A248 85m multi   32 15

Eye and Text
A249

1980, Oct. 26   **Litho.**   *Perf. 13¹/₂x14*
768 A249 100m multi   45 20

7th Afro-Asian Ophthalmologic Congress.

Hegira,
1500th
Anniv.
A250

1980, Nov. 9
769 A250 50m Spiderweb   22 15
770 A250 80m City skyline   32 15
    Set value   22

Film Strip and
Woman's
Head — A251

1980, Nov. 15   **Photo.**   *Perf. 14x13¹/₂*
771 A251 100m multi   45 15

Carthage Film Festival.

Orchid
A252

1980, Nov. 17   *Perf. 13¹/₂x14*
772 A252 20m shown   15 15
773 A252 25m Wild cyclamen   15 15

Size: 39x27mm
Perf. 14
774 A252 50m Mouflon   15 15
775 A252 100m Golden eagle   25 15
       Set value   52 30

Campaign to
Save
Kairouan
Mosque
A253

1980, Dec. 29   Photo.   Perf. 12
Granite Paper
776 A253 85m multi   30 15

Heinrich von
Stephan (1831-
1897), Founder of
UPU — A254

Blood Donors'
Assoc., 20th
Anniv. — A255

1981, Jan. 7
777 A254 150m multi   55 30

1981, Mar. 5   Litho.   Perf. 14x13¹/₂
778 A255 75m multi   26 15

Pres. Bourguiba and
Flag — A256

1981, Mar. 20   Photo.   Perf. 12x11¹/₂
Granite Paper
779 A256 50m shown   18 15
780 A256 60m Dove, "25"   20 15
781 A256 85m Doves   28 15
782 A256 120m Victory on winged
             horse   42 16
 a.   Souvenir sheet of 4, #779-782 1.25 1.25
       Set value   48

25th anniversary of independence. No. 782 sold
for 500m. Exists imperf., same value.

Pres.
Bourguiba
and Flower
A257

1981, Apr. 10   Photo.   Perf. 12x11¹/₂
783 A257 50m shown   15 15
784 A257 75m Bourguiba, flower, diff. 20 15
       Set value   20

Destourien Socialist Party Congress.

Mosque
Entrance,
Mahdia
A258

1981, Apr. 20   Perf. 13¹/₂
785 A258 50m shown   22 15
786 A258 85m Tozeur Great Mosque,
             vert.   50 15
787 A258 100m Needle Rocks, Tabarka 55 15
       Set value   32

A259

Youth
Festival — A260

1981, May 17   Litho.   Perf. 14x15
788 A259 150m multi   42 25

13th World Telecommunications Day.

1981, June 2   Photo.   Perf. 11¹/₂
Granite Paper
789 A260 100m multi   40 20

A261   A262

1981, June 15   Photo.   Perf. 14
790 A261 150m multi   85 25

Kemal Ataturk (1881-1938), 1st president of
Turkey.

1981, July 15   Photo.   Perf. 11¹/₂x12
791 A262 150m Skifa, Mahdia   55 30

Mohammed
Tahar Ben
Achour
(1879-1973),
Scholar
A263

1981, Aug. 6   Perf. 13
792 A263 200m multi   1.10 35

25th Anniv.
of Personal
Status Code
(Women's
Liberation)
A264

1981, Aug. 13
793 A264 50m Woman   20 15
794 A264 100m shown   32 15
       Set value   22

Intl. Year of the
Disabled — A265

1981, Sept. 21   Photo.   Perf. 13¹/₂
795 A265 250m multi   85 50

Pilgrimage to
Mecca — A266

World Food
Day — A267

1981, Oct. 7   Photo.   Perf. 13¹/₂
796 A266 50m multi   20 15

1981, Oct. 16   Litho.   Perf. 12
Granite Paper
797 A267 200m multi   65 42

Traditional
Jewelry
A268

Designs: 150m, Mneguech silver earrings, vert.
180m Mahfdha (silver medallion worn by married
women). 200m, Essalta gold headdress, vert.

1981, Dec. 7   Photo.   Perf. 14
798 A268 150m multi   60 25
799 A268 180m multi   80 30
800 A268 200m multi   1.00 35

Bizerta Bridge
A269

Perf. 12x11¹/₂
1981, Dec. 14   Granite Paper   Litho.
801 A269 230m multi   90 35

A270   A271

Chemist compounding honey mixture, manuscript miniature, 1224.

1982, Apr. 3   Photo.   Perf. 13
802 A270 80m multi   38 15

Arab Chemists' Union, 16th anniv.

1982, May 12   Photo.   Perf. 13¹/₂
803 A271 150m multi   75 30

Oceanic Enterprise Symposium, Tunis, May 12-
14.

The Productive Family
Employment
Campaign — A272

1982, June 26   Perf. 12¹/₂
Granite Paper
804 A272 80m multi   32 15

25th Anniv. of
Republic — A273

Scouting
Year — A274

Pres. Bourguiba and Various Women.

1982, July 25   Litho.   Perf. 14x13¹/₂
805 A273 80m multi   30 15
806 A273 100m multi   45 15
807 A273 200m multi   75 30

Perf. 14¹/₂x14, 14x14¹/₂
1982, Aug. 23
808 A274 80m multi   30 15
809 A274 200m multi   60 20

75th anniv. of scouting and 50th anniv. of scouting in Tunisia (80m).

Tunisian
Fossils — A274a

30th Anniv. of
Arab Postal
Union — A275

Designs: 80m, Pseudophillipsia azzouzi, vert.
200m, Mediterraneotrigonia cherahilensis, vert.
280m, Numidiopleura enigmatica. 300m,
Micreschara tunisiensis, vert. 500m, Mantelliceras
pervinquieri, vert. 1000m, Elephas africanavus.

1982, Sept. 20   Photo.   Perf. 11¹/₂x12
809A A274a 80m multi   20 15
809B A274a 200m multi   20 15
809C A274a 280m multi   90 45
809D A274a 300m multi   1.00 50
809E A274a 500m multi   1.60 80
809F A274a 1000m multi   3.50 1.60
       Nos. 809A-809F (6)   7.40 3.65

1982, Sept. 29   Perf. 14x13¹/₂
810 A275 80m shown   22 15
       Size: 23x40mm
811 A275 200m Woman, buildings   50 22

ITU Plenipotentiaries
Conference,
Nairobi — A276

1982, Oct. 1   Photo.   Perf. 12
Granite Paper
812 A276 200m multi   50 35

World Food
Day — A277

Tahar Haddad
(1899-1935),
Social
Reformer — A278

1982, Oct. 16   Litho.   Perf. 13
813 A277 200m multi   50 22

1982, Oct. 25   Engr.
814 A278 200m dk brn   50 20

TB Bacillus
Centenary — A279

Folk Songs and
Stories — A280

1982, Nov. 16   Litho.   Perf. 13½
815 A279 100m multi   25 15

1982, Nov. 22   Photo.   Perf. 14
816 A280 20m Dancing in the Rain   15 15
817 A280 30m Woman Sweeping   15 15
818 A280 70m Fisherman and the
        Child   20 15
819 A280 80m Rooster and the Or-
        anges, horiz.   20 15
820 A280 100m Woman and the Mir-
        ror, horiz.   32 15
821 A280 120m The Two Girls, horiz. 40 15
        Nos. 816-821 (6)   1.42
        Set value   50

Intl.
Palestinian
Solidarity
Day
A281

1982, Nov. 30   Litho.   Perf. 13x12
822 A281 80m multi   20 15

Farhat Hached
(1914-1952)
A282

Bourguiba Dam
Opening
A283

1982, Dec. 6   Engr.   Perf. 13
823 A282 80m brn red   22 15

1982, Dec. 20   Litho.   Perf. 13½
824 A283 80m multicolored   20 15

Environmental Training
College Opening — A284

1982, Dec. 29   Photo.   Perf. 11½
        Granite Paper
825 A284 80m multicolored   20 15

World Communications Year — A285

1983, May 17   Litho.   Perf. 13½x14
826 A285 200m multicolored   42 22

20th Anniv. of
Org. of African
Unity — A286

Aly Ben Ayed
(1930-1972),
Actor — A288

30th Anniv.
of Customs
Cooperation
Council
A287

1983, May 25   Photo.   Perf. 12
        Granite Paper
827 A286 230m ultra & grnsh bl   55 35

1983, May 30   Litho.   Perf. 13½
828 A287 100m multicolored   25 15

1983, Aug. 15   Engr.   Perf. 13
829 A288 80m dk car, dl red & gray 20 15

Stone-carved Face, El-
Mekta — A289

Pre-historic artifacts: 20m, Neolithic necklace,
Kel el-Agab. 30m, Mill and grindstone, Redeyef.
40m, Orynx head rock carving, Gafsa. 80m, Dol-
men Mactar. 100m, Acheulian Bi-face flint, El-
Mekta.

1983, Aug. 20   Photo.   Perf. 11½x12
830 A289 15m multicolored   15 15
831 A289 20m multicolored   15 15
832 A289 30m multicolored   15 15
833 A289 40m multicolored   15 15
834 A289 80m multicolored   20 15
835 A289 100m multicolored   22 15
        Set value   70 35

Sports
for All
A290

1983, Sept. 27   Litho.   Perf. 12½
836 A290 40m multicolored   15 15

World
Fishing
Day
A291

1983, Oct. 17   Perf. 14½
837 A291 200m multicolored   42 16

Evacuation of French
Troops, 20th
Anniv. — A292

1983, Oct. 17   Litho.   Perf. 14x13½
838 A292 80m multicolored   20 15

Tapestry Weaver, by Hedi Khayachi (1882-
1948) — A293

1983, Nov. 22   Photo.   Perf. 11½
        Granite Paper
839 A293 80m multicolored   20 15

Natl. Allegiance
A294

Jet, Woman's Head,
Emblem
A295

1983, Nov. 30   Litho.   Perf. 14½
840 A294 100m Children, flag   25 15

1983, Dec. 21   Perf. 13½
841 A295 150m multicolored   35 15

Pres. Bourguiba
A296

4th Molecular
Biology
Symposium
A297

Destourien Socialist Party, 50th Anniv.: Portraits
of Bourguiba. 200m, 230m horiz.

Perf. 12½x12, 12x12½
1984, Mar. 2   Photo.
        Granite Paper
842 A296 40m multicolored   15 15
843 A296 70m multicolored   15 15
844 A296 80m multicolored   20 15
  a.   Pair, #843-844   35 30
845 A296 150m multicolored   35 20
  a.   Pair, #842, 845   50 30
846 A296 200m multicolored   42 22
847 A296 230m multicolored   55 35
  a.   Pair, #846-847   1.00 60
        Nos. 842-847 (6)   1.82
        Set value   1.05

Nos. 844a, 845a and 847a were printed checkerwise in sheets of ten.

1984, Apr. 3   Perf. 13½x13
848 A297 100m Map, diagram   25 15

Ibn El Jazzar,
Physician — A298

Economic
Development
Program, 20th
Anniv. — A299

1984, May 15   Photo.   Perf. 14x13
849 A298 80m multicolored   20 15

1984, June 15   Perf. 11½
        Granite Paper
850 A299 230m Merchant, worker   50 20

Coquette,
The
Sorceress and
the Fairy
Carabosse
A300

Perf. 13½x14, 14x13½
1984, Aug. 27   Photo.
851 A300 20m shown   15 15
852 A300 80m Counting with fingers 20 15
853 A300 100m Boy riding horse, vert. 25 15
        Set value   50 25

Legends and folk tales.

Family and
Education
Org., 20th
Anniv.
A301

1984, Sept. 4   Perf. 13x14
854 A301 80m Family looking into fu-
        ture   20 15

Natl. Heritage Protection A302

Aboul-Qasim Chabbi, Poet (1909-1934) A303

1984, Sept. 13   *Perf. 14*
855 A302 100m Medina Mosque Mina-
ret, hand   25 15

1984, Oct. 9   Engr.   *Perf. 12¹/₂x13*
856 A303 100m multicolored   25 15

40th Anniv., ICAO A304

1984, Oct. 25   Photo.   *Perf. 13*
857 A304 200m Aircraft tail, bird   50 25

Sahara Festival A305

1984, Dec. 3   Litho.   *Perf. 14¹/₂*
858 A305 20m Musicians   15 15

20th Anniv., Intelsat A306

Perf. 13¹/₂x14¹/₂
1984, Dec. 25   Photo.
859 A306 100m Tunisian Earth Station 25 15

Mediterranean Landscape, by Jilani Abdelwaheb (Abdul) — A307

1984, Dec. 31   Photo.   *Perf. 14¹/₂*
860 A307 100m multicolored   25 15

EXPO '85, Tsukuba, Japan — A308

1985, Mar. 20   Photo.   *Perf. 12*
861 A308 200m multicolored   35 16

Civil Protection Week — A309

1985, May 13   Litho.   *Perf. 14*
862 A309 100m Hands, water and fire   22 15

Pres. Habib Bourguiba, Crowded Pier — A310

Pres. Bourguiba: 75m, On horseback, vert.
200m, Wearing hat, vert. 230m, Waving to crowd.

1985, June 1   *Perf. 12¹/₂*
863 A310 75m multicolored   15 15
864 A310 100m multicolored   16 15
865 A310 200m multicolored   35 16
866 A310 230m multicolored   40 18
              Set value   48

Natl. independence, 30th anniv.

Head of a Statue, Carthage and Pres. Bourguiba A311

1985, June 4   *Perf. 14*
867 A311 250m multicolored   40 20

EXPO '85.

Intl. Amateur Film Festival, Kelibia — A312

Natl. Folk Tales — A313

1985, July 20   *Perf. 14¹/₂x13*
868 A312 250m multicolored   40 20

1985, July 29   *Perf. 14*
869 A313 25m Sun, Sun Shine Again,
                    horiz.   15 15
870 A313 50m I Met a Man With
                    Seven Wives   15 15
871 A313 100m Uncle Shisbene   16 15
              Set value   30 18

Intl. Youth Year — A314

1985, Sept. 30   *Perf. 14¹/₂x13¹/₂*
872 A314 250m multicolored   42 20

The Perfumers' Courtyard, 1912, by Hedi Larnaout — A315

1985, Oct. 4   *Perf. 14*
873 A315 100m multicolored   20 15

Regional Bridal Costumes A316

UN, 40th Anniv. A317

1985, Oct. 22   *Perf. 12*
874 A316 20m Matmata   15 15
875 A316 50m Moknine   15 15
876 A316 100m Tunis   25 15
              Set value   44 26

1985, Oct. 24   *Perf. 14x13¹/₂*
877 A317 250m multicolored   50 25

Self-Sufficiency in Food Production — A318

Perf. 13¹/₂x14¹/₂
1985, Nov. 26   Photo.
878 A318 100m Makhtar stele of feast   22 15

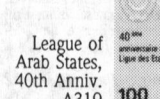

League of Arab States, 40th Anniv. A319

1985, Nov. 29   Litho.   *Perf. 13¹/₂x14*
879 A319 100m multicolored   22 15

Aziza Othmana (d. 1669) — A320

Land Law, Cent. — A321

1985, Dec. 16   Engr.   *Perf. 12¹/₂x13*
880 A320 100m dk grn, hn brn & brn   22 15

1985, Dec. 25   Litho.   *Perf. 13¹/₂*
881 A321 100m multicolored   22 15

Natl. Independence, 30th Anniv. — A322

Perf. 13x13¹/₂, 13¹/₂x13
1986, Mar. 20   Photo.
882 A322 100m Dove, vert.   28 15
883 A322 120m Rocket   32 16
884 A322 280m Horse and rider   75 38
885 A322 300m Balloons, vert.   82 40
a.   Souvenir sheet of 4, #882-885   2.20 1.10

No. 885a exists imperf.

3rd Mediterranean Rheumatology Day — A323

Intl. Geographical Ophtalmological Society Congress — A324

1986, Apr. 30   Litho.   *Perf. 14x13¹/₂*
886 A323 300m multicolored   85 42
887 A324 380m multicolored   1.05 52

Prof. Hulusi Behcet (1889-1948), discovered virus causing Behcet's Disease affecting eyes and joints.

12th Destourian Socialist Party Congress A325

1986, June 19   Photo.   *Perf. 12*
888 A325 120m shown   35 18
889 A325 300m Torchbearer   85 42

A326   A327

Regional bridal costumes.

1986, Aug. 25   Litho.   *Perf. 14*
890 A326 40m Homi-Souk   15 15
891 A326 280m Mahdia   78 40
892 A326 300m Nabeul   82 40

1986, Sept. 20   Engr.   *Perf. 13*
893 A327 160m dark red   45 22

Hassen Husni Abdul-Wahab (1883-1968), historian, archaeologist

Founding of Carthage, 2800th Anniv. — A328

1986, Oct. 18   Engr.   *Perf. 13*
894 A328 2d dark violet   8.00 4.00

Protohistoric Artifacts — A329   Bedouins, by Ammar Farhat — A330

Design: 10m, Flint arrowhead, El Borma, c. 3000 B.C. 20m, Rock cut-out dwelling, Sejnane, c. 1000 B.C. 50m, Lintel bas-relief from a cult site in Tunis, c. 1000 B.C., horiz. 120m, Base of a Neolithic vase, Kesra. 160m, Phoenician trireme, petroglyph, c. 800 B.C., horiz. 250m, Ceramic pot, c. 700 B.C., found at Sejnane, vert.

1986, Oct. 30   Litho.   *Perf. 13¹/₂*
895 A329 10m multicolored   15 15
896 A329 20m multicolored   15 15
897 A329 50m multicolored   22 15
898 A329 120m multicolored   52 25
899 A329 160m multicolored   68 35
900 A329 250m multicolored   1.05 52
    Nos. 895-900 (6)   2.77
    Set value   1.30

1986, Nov. 20   Photo.   *Perf. 13¹/₂*
901 A330 250m multicolored   70 35

Intl. Peace Year A331

1986, Nov. 24   *Perf. 13¹/₂x13*
902 A331 300m multicolored   85 42

FAO, 40th Anniv. A332   Computer Education Inauguration A333

1986, Nov. 27   *Perf. 13x13¹/₂*
903 A332 280m multicolored   78 40

1986, Dec. 8   *Perf. 13¹/₂*
904 A333 2d multicolored   5.50 2.75

Breast-feeding for Child Survival — A334   Wildlife, Natl. Parks — A335

1986, Dec. 22   Photo.   *Perf. 14*
905 A334 120m multicolored   48 24

1986, Dec. 29   *Perf. 12*
Designs: 60m, Mountain gazelle, Chambi Natl. Park. 120m, Addax, Bou. Hedma. 350m, Seal, Zembretta. 380m, Greylag goose, Ichkeul.

Granite Paper
906 A335 60m multicolored   15 15
907 A335 120m multicolored   48 24
908 A335 350m multicolored   1.40 70
909 A335 380m multicolored   1.50 75

City of Monastir, Cent. — A336

1987, Jan. 24   Litho.   *Perf. 12x11¹/₂*
Granite Paper
910 A336 120m Pres. Bourguiba, city arms   40 24

Invention of the Telegraph by Samuel F.B. Morse, 150th Anniv. A337

1987, June 15   Litho.   *Perf. 13¹/₂x14*
911 A337 500m multicolored   1.75 1.00

30th Anniv. of the Republic A338

Pres. Bourguiba and women of various sects.

1987, July 25   Photo.   *Perf. 13¹/₂*
912 A338 150m multi   60 30
913 A338 250m multi   1.00 50
914 A338 350m multi, diff.   1.40 70
915 A338 500m multi, diff.   2.00 1.00
  a. Souvenir sheet of 4, #912-915   6.00 3.00

No. 915a sold for 1.50d. Exists imperf.

UN Universal Vaccination by 1990 Campaign — A339

1987, Sept. 14   *Perf. 12*
Granite Paper
916 A339 250m multicolored   1.00 50

The Street, by Azouz ben Raiz (1902-1962) A340

1987, Sept. 22   Granite Paper
917 A340 250m multicolored   1.00 50

Arab Day for Shelter of the Homeless A341

1987, Oct. 5   Photo.   *Perf. 12x11¹/₂*
Granite Paper
918 A341 150m multicolored   48 25

Advisory Council for Postal Research, 30th Anniv. A342

1987, Oct. 9   *Perf. 14*
919 A342 150m Express mail   48 25
920 A342 350m Use postal code   1.15 58

The Arabs, by Ibn-Mandhour (1233-1312), Lexicographer — A343

1987, Oct. 26   Engr.   *Perf. 13*
921 A343 250m plum   1.00 50

Pasteur Institute, Tunis — A344

1987, Nov. 21   *Perf. 13x12¹/₂*
922 A344 250m blk, grn & rose lake   1.00 50

Pasteur Institute, Paris, cent.

Intl. Year of the Vine (Wine) — A345   6th Volleyball Championships of African Nations — A346

1987, Nov. 27   Photo.   *Perf. 14*
923 A345 250m multicolored   1.00 50

1987, Dec. 2   Litho.   *Perf. 14x13¹/₂*
924 A346 350m multicolored   1.40 70

African Basketball Championships A347   Folk Costumes A348

1987, Dec. 15
925 A347 350m multicolored   1.40 70

1987, Dec. 25   Photo.
926 A348 20m Midoun   15 15
927 A348 30m Tozeur   18 15
928 A348 150m Sfax   85 42
    Set value   58

Flowering Plants — A349

1987, Dec. 29   *Perf. 14¹/₂*
929 A349 30m Narcissus tazetta   15 15
930 A349 150m Gladiolus communis   62 30
931 A349 400m Iris xiphium   1.65 82
932 A349 500m Tulipa sylvestris   2.10 1.05

Declaration of Nov. 7, 1987 — A350

Cameo portrait of Pres. Zine el Abidine Ben Ali and: 150m, Scales of Justice. 200m, Girl with flowers (party badges) in her hair, vert. 350m, Mermaid, doves, natl. coat of arms. 370m, "CMA," emblem of the Maghreb states (Tunisia, Mauritania, Morocco, Algeria and Libya), vert.

1988, Mar. 21   Photo.   *Perf. 12*
Granite Paper
933 A350 150m multicolored   48 25
934 A350 200m multicolored   62 30
935 A350 350m multicolored   1.10 55
936 A350 370m multicolored   1.15 58

Youth and
Change — A351

1988, Mar. 22   Litho.   *Perf. 14x14¹/₂*
937 A351 75m shown   25 15
938 A351 150m Happy family   48 25

Martyr's Day,
50th Anniv.
A352

Perf. 13x13¹/₂, 13¹/₂x13
1988, Apr. 9   Photo.
939 A352 150m shown   45 22
940 A352 500m Monument, vert.   1.50 75

Opening Conference of the Constitutional
Democratic Assembly — A353

1988, July 30   *Perf. 12x11¹/₂*
Granite Paper
941 A353 150m Flag, Pres. Ben Ali   48 25

1988
Summer
Olympics,
Seoul
A354

1988, Sept. 20   Photo.   *Perf. 13¹/₂*
942 A354 150m shown   32 16
943 A354 430m Running, boxing, weight
                lifting, wrestling   92 45

A355   A356

1988, Sept. 21
944 A355 200m multicolored   42 20

Restoration of the City of San'a, Yemen.

1988, Nov. 7   Photo.   *Perf. 14*
945 A356 150m multicolored   72 35

Appointment of Pres. Zine El Abidine Ben Ali, 1st
anniv.

*Amilcar
Beach,
1942, by
A.
Debbeche
A357*

1988, Nov. 21   Photo.   *Perf. 13¹/₂x13*
946 A357 100m multicolored   22 15

Tunis Air,
40th Anniv.
A358

Perf. 12x11¹/₂
1988, Nov. 28   Photo.
Granite Paper
947 A358 500m multicolored   1.65 82

UN Declaration of
Human Rights, 40th
Anniv. — A359

1988, Dec. 10 Granite Paper *Perf. 12*
948 A359 370m black   1.20 62

Tunisian Postage Stamp Cent. — A360

1988, Dec. 16   *Perf. 12¹/₂*
Granite Paper
949 A360 150m multicolored   52 25

A361   A362

Decorative doorways.

1988, Dec. 26   *Perf. 14x13¹/₂*
950 A361 50m multi   15 15
951 A361 70m multi, diff.   15 15
952 A361 100m multi, diff.   22 15
953 A361 150m multi, diff.   32 16
954 A361 370m multi, diff.   78 40
955 A361 400m multi, diff.   85 42
          Nos. 950-955 (6)   2.47
          Set value   1.20

1989, Mar. 7   Engr.   *Perf. 13¹/₂x13*
956 A362 1000m dark blue   2.20 1.10

Ali Douagi (1909-49).

Natl. Day for the
Handicapped — A363

1989, May 30   Photo.   *Perf. 13¹/₂*
957 A363 150m multicolored   35 18

Education
A364

1989, July 10   *Perf. 14*
958 A364 180m multicolored   40 20

Family Planning
Assoc., 20th
Anniv. — A365

1989, Aug. 14   Litho.   *Perf. 14*
959 A365 150m multicolored   35 18

Family Care
A366

1989, Aug. 14   Litho.   *Perf. 14*
960 A366 150m multicolored   35 18

Fauna
A367

1989, Aug. 28   Photo.   *Perf. 13¹/₂x14*
961 A367 250m Tortoise   55 28
962 A367 350m Oryx   78 40

Intl. Fair, Tunis   Mohamed
A368   Beyram V (1840-
                            1889)
                          A369

1989, Oct. 16   Photo.   *Perf. 14*
963 A368 150m shown   35 18
964 A368 370m Pavilion, horiz.   85 42

1989, Oct. 28   Engr.   *Perf. 13*
965 A369 150m blk & dp rose lil   35 18

Theater, Carthage   Monument
A370   A371

1989, Nov. 3   Photo.   *Perf. 14*
966 A370 300m multicolored   70 35

Perf. 11¹/₂x12
1989, Nov. 7   Granite Paper
967 A371 150m multicolored   35 18

Appointment of Pres. Zine El Abidine Ben Ali,
2nd Anniv.

Nehru — A372   Flags — A373

1989, Nov. 29   Engr.   *Perf. 13*
968 A372 300m dark brown   70 35

Jawaharlal Nehru, 1st prime minister of independent India.

Perf. 12x11¹/₂
1990, Jan. 15   Photo.   Granite Paper
969 A373 200m multicolored   48 24

Maghreb Union summit, Tunis.

Museum of
Bardo, Cent.
A374

1990, Feb. 20   Litho.   *Perf. 13¹/₂*
970 A374 300m multicolored   65 32

Pottery
A375

1990, Mar. 22   *Perf. 14*
971 A375 75m multicolored   16 15
972 A375 100m multi, diff.   22 15
          Set value   18

Sheep Museum — A376

1990, Apr. 13   Litho.   Perf. 13½
973 A376 400m Sheep   1.00   50
974 A376 450m Ram's head   1.10   55
  a. Souvenir sheet of 2, #973-974   2.50   1.25

No. 974a sold for 1000m, exists imperf. Nos. 973-974 inscribed 1989.

Tunisian Olympic Movement — A377

1990, May 27
975 A377 150m multicolored   40   20

Child's Drawing A378

1990, June 5   Perf. 14
976 A378 150m multicolored   40   20

A379   A380

Traditional costumes.

1990, July 13   Photo.   Perf. 14x14½
977 A379 150m Sbiba   40   20
978 A379 500m Bou Omrane   1.30   65

1990, Aug. 1   Litho.   Perf. 14

Relic from Punic city of Dougga.
979 A380 300m multicolored   80   40

Intl. Literacy Year A381

1990, Sept. 8   Photo.   Perf. 12x11½
Granite Paper
980 A381 120m multicolored   30   15

A382

A383

1990, Oct. 15   Perf. 11½x12
Granite Paper
981 A382 150m multicolored   40   20
  Importance of water.

1990, Nov. 7
Granite Paper
982 A383 150m shown   40   20
983 A383 150m Clock tower   40   20

Appointment of Pres. Zine El Abidine Ben Ali, 3rd anniv.

A384

A385

1990, Nov. 16   Engr.   Perf. 13½x13
984 A384 150m green   40   20

Kheireddine Et-Tounsi (1822-1889), politician.

1990, Dec. 17   Photo.   Perf. 13½

Fauna and flora.
985 A385 150m Cervus elaphus
     barbarus   40   20
986 A385 200m Cynara cardenculus   50   25
987 A385 300m Bubalus bubalis   80   40
988 A385 600m Ophris lutea   1.55   80

Maghreb Arab Union, 2nd Anniv. — A386   Harbor of Tabarka — A387

1991, Jan. 21   Photo.   Perf. 13½
989 A386 180m multicolored   45   22

1991, Mar. 17
990 A387 450m multicolored   1.05   50

Fish — A388

1991, Sept. 10   Photo.   Perf. 14x13
991 A388 180m Pagre   45   22
992 A388 350m Rouget de roche   85   42
993 A388 450m Maquereau   1.10   55
994 A388 550m Pageot commun   1.35   65

Child Welfare — A389

1991, Sept. 29   Perf. 14
995 A389 450m multicolored   1.10   55

A390

1991, Oct. 9   Perf. 13½x14
996 A390 400m multicolored   1.00   50

A391

A392

Jewelry.

Perf. 14x13, 13x14
1991, Oct. 22   Litho.
997 A391 120m Ring, bracelets,
     horiz.   28   15
998 A391 180m Necklace   42   22
999 A391 220m Earrings   52   26
1000 A391 730m shown   1.75   88

1991, Nov. 7   Perf. 11½
1001 A392 180m multicolored

Appointment of Pres. Zine El Abidine Ben Ali, 4th anniv.

Tunis-Carthage Center — A393

1991, Nov. 22   Engr.   Perf. 13
1002 A393 80m red, blue & green

N·E·W
Scott Supplement
Pages for
Tunisia
will be available in
November

A394

A395

1991, Dec. 12   Photo.   Perf. 14
1003 A394 450m bright blue   1.10   55
  World Day of the Rights of Man.

1991, Dec. 26   Engr.   Perf. 12½x13
1004 A395 200m blue   50   25

Mahmoud Bayram Et Tounsi (1893-1960), poet.

Expo '92, Seville — A396   General Post Office, Tunis, Cent. — A397

1992, Apr. 20   Photo.   Perf. 13½
1005 A396 180m multicolored   35   18

Perf. 13x12½, 12½x13
1992, June 15   Engr.
1006 A397 180m red brown, horiz.   35   18
1007 A397 450m dark brown   90   45

"When the Subconscious Awakes," by Moncef ben Amor — A398

1992, July 21   Litho.   Perf. 13½
1008 A398 500m multicolored   1.00   50

1992 Summer Olympics, Barcelona A399

1992, Aug. 4
1009 A399 180m Running   35   18
1010 A399 450m Judo, vert.   90   45

Birds — A400   A401

1992, Sept. 22 Photo. Perf. 11½
Granite Paper
1011 A400 100m Merops apiaster 20 15
1012 A400 180m Carduelis carduelis 35 18
1013 A400 200m Serinus serinus 40 20
1014 A400 500m Carduelis chloris 1.00 50

1992, Oct. 21 Perf. 11½x12
Granite Paper
1015 A401 180m multicolored 35 18
UN Conference on Rights of the Child.

African Human Rights
Conference,
Tunis — A402

1992, Nov. 2 Photo. Perf. 11½
Granite Paper
1016 A402 480m multicolored 95 48

A403 A404

1992, Nov. 7
Granite Paper
1017 A403 180m multicolored 35 18
1018 A404 730m multicolored 1.45 75

Appointment of Pres. Zine El Abidine Ben Ali, 5th anniv.

Arbor
Day — A405

1992, Nov. 8 Perf. 11½x12
Granite Paper
1019 A405 180m Acacia tortilis 35 18

Intl. Conference on Nutrition,
Rome — A406

1992, Dec. 15 Litho. Perf. 13½
1020 A406 450m multicolored 90 45

Traditional
Costumes — A407

1992, Dec. 23
1021 A407 100m Chemesse 20 15
1022 A407 350m Hanifites 70 35
  Set value 45

Mosaics
A408

1992, Dec. 29
1023 A408 100m Goat 20 15
1024 A408 180m Duck 35 18
1025 A408 350m Horse 70 35
1026 A408 450m Gazelle 90 45

Arab-African Fair of
Tunisia — A410

1993, July 10 Litho. Perf. 13½x14
1028 A410 450m multicolored 90 45

Relaxation in the
Patio, by Ali
Guermassi
A411

Reassembly of
the Democratic
Congress
A412

1993, July 20 Litho. Perf. 13½
1029 A411 450m multicolored 90 45

1993, July 29 Litho. Perf. 13½
1030 A412 180m multicolored 35 18

A413 A414

1993 Perf. 13
1031 A413 20m Wolf 15 15
1032 A414 60m Hoya carnosa 15 15
  Set value 16 15

Appointment of Pres. Zine El
Abidine, 6th Anniv.
A414 A415

1993, Nov. 7 Perf. 13½
1033 A414 180m multicolored 35 18
1034 A415 450m multicolored 90 45

Kairouan
Tapestries — A416

Designs: Various ornate patterns.

1993, Dec. 13 Perf. 13½
1035 A416 100m multicolored 20 15
1036 A416 120m multicolored 25 15
1037 A416 180m multicolored 35 18
1038 A416 350m multicolored 70 35

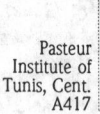

Pasteur
Institute of
Tunis, Cent.
A417

Design: 450m, Charles Nicolle (1866-1936), bacteriologist, 1928 Nobel medal.

1993, Oct. 12 Litho. Perf. 13½
1039 A417 450m multicolored 90 45

A418

School
Activities
A419

1993, Dec. 30 Litho. Perf. 13½
1040 A418 180m Music 35 18
1041 A419 180m Art, reading 35 18

19th African
Cup of
Nations Soccer
Tournament
A420

1994, Mar. 26
1042 A420 180m shown 35 18
1043 A420 350m Two players, diff. 70 35
1044 A420 450m Map, player 90 45

Presidential and
Legislative
Elections — A421

1994, Mar. 20
1045 A421 180m multicolored 35 18

Election of Pres.
Zine El Abidine
ben Ali — A422

1994 Photo. Perf. 11½
Granite Paper
1046 A422 180m multicolored 35 18
1047 A422 350m multicolored 70 35
  a. Souvenir sheet of 2, #1046-1047 1.10 55

No. 1047a exists imperf.

ILO, 75th
Anniv. — A423

1994 Perf. 13½x14
1048 A423 350m multicolored 70 35

SEMI-POSTAL STAMPS

No. 36 Overprinted in Red ✚

1915, Feb. Unwmk. Perf. 14x13½
B1 A5 15c vio, *pnksh* 60 30

✚

No. 32 Overprinted in Red

＝

1916, Feb. 15
B2 A4 5c grn, *grnsh* 75 50

Types of Regular Issue of
1906 in New Colors and
Surcharged ✚10c.

1916, Aug.
B3 A5 10c on 15c brn vio, *bl* 52 22
B4 A5 10c on 20c brn, *org* 30 30
B5 A5 10c on 25c bl, *grn* 1.25 1.25
B6 A6 10c on 35c ol grn & vio 2.75 2.75
B7 A6 10c on 40c bis & blk 1.25 1.25

B8	A6	10c on 75c vio brn & grn	3.00 3.00
B9	A7	10c on 1fr red & grn	1.25 1.25
B10	A7	10c on 2fr bis & bl	35.00 22.50
B11	A7	10c on 5fr vio & red	60.00 37.50
		Nos. B3-B11 (9)	105.32 70.02

Nos. B3 to B11 were sold at their face value but had a postal value of 10c only. The excess was applied to the relief of prisoners of war in Germany.

15c

Types of Regular Issue of 1906 in New Colors and Surcharged in Carmine

1918

B12	A5	15c on 20c blk, *grn*	50 50
B13	A6	15c on 25c dk bl, *buff*	50 50
B14	A6	15c on 35c gray grn & red	1.00 32
B15	A6	15c on 40c brn & lt bl	2.00 70
B16	A6	15c on 75c red brn & blk	2.50 2.50
B17	A7	15c on 1fr red & vio	8.00 8.00
B18	A7	15c on 2fr bis brn & red	40.00 15.00
B19	A7	15c on 5fr vio & blk	85.00 32.50
		Nos. B12-B19 (8)	139.50 60.02

The different parts of the surcharge are more widely spaced on the stamps of types A6 and A7. These stamps were sold at their face value but had a postal value of 15c only. The excess was intended for the relief of prisoners of war in Germany.

Types of 1906-22 Surcharged

AFFᵗ 0c

1923

B20	A4	0c on 1c blue	60 60
B21	A4	0c on 2c ol brn	60 60
B22	A4	1c on 3c grn	60 60
B23	A4	2c on 5c red vio	60 60
B24	A9	3c on 10c vio, *bluish*	60 60
B25	A5	5c on 15c ol grn	60 60
B26	A5	5c on 20c bl, *pink*	2.00 2.00
B27	A5	5c on 25c vio, *bluish*	2.00 2.00
B28	A5	5c on 30c org	2.00 2.00
B29	A6	5c on 35c bl & vio	2.50 2.50
B30	A6	5c on 40c bl & brn	2.50 2.50
B31	A9	10c on 50c blk, *bluish*	2.50 2.50
B32	A6	5c on 60c ol brn & bl	2.50 2.50
B33	A6	10c on 75c vio & lt grn	5.50 5.50
B34	A7	25c on 1fr mar & vio	5.50 5.00
B35	A7	25c on 2fr bl & rose	21.00 21.00
B36	A7	25c on 5fr grn & ol brn	100.00 100.00
		Nos. B20-B36 (17)	151.60 151.10

These stamps were sold at their original values but had postal franking values only to the amounts surcharged on them. The difference was intended to be used for the benefit of wounded soldiers. This issue was entirely speculative. Before the announced date of sale most of the stamps were taken by postal employees and practically none of them were offered to the public.

Mail Delivery — SP1

Type of Parcel Post Stamps, 1906, with Surcharge in Black

1925, June 7   Perf. 13¹/₂x14

B37	SP1	1c on 5c brn & red, *pink*	22 22
	a.	Surcharge omitted	40.00 40.00
B38	SP1	2c on 10c brn & bl, *yel*	22 22
B39	SP1	3c on 20c red vio & rose, *lav*	40 40
B40	SP1	5c on 25c sl grn & rose, *bluish*	40 40
B41	SP1	5c on 40c rose & grn, *yel*	40 40
B42	SP1	10c on 50c vio & bl, *lav*	90 90
B43	SP1	10c on 75c grn & ol, *grnsh*	65 65
B44	SP1	25c on 1fr bl & grn, *bluish*	65 65

B45	SP1	25c on 2fr rose & vio, *pnksh*	3.50 3.50
B46	SP1	25c on 5fr red & brn, *lem*	21.00 21.00
		Nos. B37-B46 (10)	28.34 28.34

These stamps were sold at their original values but paid postage only to the amount of the surcharged values. The difference was given to Child Welfare societies.

Tunis-Chad Motor Caravan — SP2

1928, Feb.   Engr.   Perf. 13¹/₂

B47	SP2	40c + 40c org brn	45 45
B48	SP2	50c + 50c dp vio	45 45
B49	SP2	75c + 75c dk bl	55 55
B50	SP2	1fr + 1fr carmine	55 55
B51	SP2	1.50fr + 1.50fr brt bl	55 55
B52	SP2	2fr + 2fr dk grn	65 65
B53	SP2	5fr + 5fr red brn	65 65
		Nos. B47-B53 (7)	3.85 3.85

The surtax on these stamps was for the benefit of Child Welfare societies.

Nos. 122-135, 137-142 Surcharged in Black

a   b

1938   Perf. 11, 12¹/₂, 12¹/₂x13

B54	A14(a)	1c + 1c	80 60
B55	A14(a)	2c + 2c	80 60
B56	A14(a)	3c + 3c	80 60
B57	A14(a)	5c + 5c	80 60
B58	A14(a)	10c + 10c	80 60
B59	A15(a)	15c + 15c	80 60
B60	A15(a)	20c + 20c	80 60
B61	A15(a)	25c + 25c	80 60
B62	A15(a)	30c + 30c	80 60
B63	A15(a)	40c + 40c	60 60
B64	A16(a)	50c + 50c	60 60
B65	A16(a)	75c + 75c	60 60
B66	A16(a)	90c + 90c	60 60
B67	A16(a)	1fr + 1fr	60 60
B68	A17(b)	1.50fr + 1fr	60 60
B69	A17(b)	2fr + 1.50fr	1.50 1.25
B70	A17(b)	3fr + 2fr	1.65 1.25
B71	A17(b)	5fr + 3fr	10.00 7.00
	a.	Perf. 12¹/₂	37.50 37.50
B72	A17(b)	10fr + 5fr	20.00 17.50
B73	A17(b)	20fr + 10fr	30.00 12.50
		Nos. B54-B73 (20)	73.95 63.50

50th anniversary of the post office.

Nos. 86, 100-101, 105 Surcharged in Black, Blue or Red

SECOURS NATIONAL

1941

1ᶠ.50

1941   Perf. 14x13¹/₂

B74	A11	1fr on 45c (Bk)	30 30
B75	A13	1.30fr on 1.25fr (Bl)	30 30
B76	A13	1.50fr on 1.40fr (Bk)	30 30
B77	A13	2fr on 2.25fr (R)	30 30

The surcharge measures 11x14mm on #B74.

> Catalogue values for unused stamps in this section, from this point to the end of the section, are for Never Hinged items.

British, French and American Soldiers — SP3

1943   Litho.   Perf. 12

B78	SP3	1.50fr + 8.50fr crimson	15 15

Liberation of Tunisia.

V1

Stamps of the design shown above were issued in 1944 by the Vichy Government, but were not placed on sale in the colony.

Native Scene — SP4

Surcharge in Black: "+ 48frcs / pour nos / Combattants"

1944   Perf. 11¹/₂

B79	SP4	2fr + 48fr red	35 35

The surtax was for soldiers.

Sidi Mahrez Mosque — SP5

Ramparts of Sfax — SP6

Fort Saint SP7

Sidi-bou-Said — SP8

1945   Unwmk.   Litho.   Perf. 11¹/₂

B80	SP5	1.50fr + 8.50fr choc & red	30 30
B81	SP6	3fr + 12fr dk bl grn & red	30 30
B82	SP7	4fr + 21fr brn org & red	30 30
B83	SP8	10fr + 40fr red & blk	30 30

The surtax was for soldiers.

France No. B193 Overprinted in Black

c   TUNISIE

1945   Perf. 14x13¹/₂

B84	SP147	2fr + 1fr red org	15 15

The surtax was for the aid of tuberculosis victims.

Same Overprint on Type of France, 1945

1945   Engr.   Perf. 13

B85	SP150	2fr + 3fr dk grn	22 22

Stamp Day.

Same Overprint on France No. B192

1945

B86	SP146	4fr + 6fr dk vio brn	35 15

The surtax was for war victims of the P.T.T.

Types of 1926 Surcharged in Carmine

4ᶠ+6ᶠ

1945   Typo.   Perf. 14x13¹/₂

B87	A10	4fr + 6fr on 10c ultra	45 22
B88	A12	10fr + 30fr on 80c dk grn	45 22

The design of type A12 is redrawn, omitting "RF." The surtax was for war veterans.

Tunisian Soldier — SP9

1946   Unwmk.   Engr.   Perf. 13

B89	SP9	20fr + 30fr grn, red & blk	60 60

The surtax aided Tunisian soldiers in Indo-China.

Type of France, 1946, Overprinted Type "c" in Carmine

1946

B90	SP160	3fr + 2fr dk bl	35 35

Stamp Day.

+ 1946

Stamps and Types of 1926-46 Surcharged in Carmine and Black

+50ᶜ

1946   Perf. 14x13¹/₂

B91	A12	80c + 50c emerald	30 30
B92	A12	1.50fr + 1.50fr rose lil	30 30
B93	A12	2fr + 2fr Prus grn	30 30
B94	A13	2.40fr + 2fr sal pink	30 30
B95	A13	4fr + 4fr ultra	30 30
		Nos. B91-B95 (5)	1.50 1.50

The two parts of the surcharge are more widely spaced on stamps of type A13.

Type of France, 1947, Overprinted Type "c" in Carmine

1947   Perf. 13

B96	SP172	4.50fr + 5.50fr sepia	35 35

On Type of France, 1946, Surcharged in Carmine with New Value and Bars

B97	SP158	10fr + 15fr on 2fr + 3fr brt ultra	35 35

SOLIDARITE 1947
Type of 1926
Surcharged in
Carmine

+40ᶠ

1947		Typo.	Perf. 14x13½
B98	A13 10fr + 40fr black		40 40

Feeding Young
Bird — SP10

1947		Engr.	Perf. 13
B99	SP10 4.50fr + 5.50fr dk bl grn		50 50
B100	SP10 6fr + 9fr brt ultra		50 50
B101	SP10 8fr + 17fr dp car		50 50
B102	SP10 10fr + 40fr dk pur		50 50

The surtax was for child welfare.

Type of Regular **AIDEZ LES**
Issue of 1948 **+10ᶠ**
Surcharged in
Blue **TUBERCULEUX**

1948			
B103	A21 4fr + 10fr ol grn & org		30 30

The surtax was for anti-tuberculosis work.

Arch of
Triumph,
Sbeitla
SP11

1948			
B104	SP11 10fr + 40fr ol grn & olive		50 50
B105	SP11 18fr + 42fr dk bl & indigo		50 50

Surtax for charitable works of the army.

Arago Type of France, 1948,
Overprinted in Carmine

1948			
B106	SP176 6fr + 4fr brt car		50 50

Stamp Day, Mar. 6-7.

Sleeping
Child — SP12

1949, June 1			
B107	SP12 25fr + 50fr dk grn		1.10 1.10

The surtax was for child welfare.

Neptune Type of 1947 Surcharged in
Black with Lorraine Cross and "FFL+15F"
1949, Dec. 8

B108	A20 10fr + 15fr dp ultra & car	42 42

The surtax was for the Tunisian section of the
Association of Free French.

Type of France, 1949, Overprinted in
Carmine

e **TUNISIE**

1949, Mar. 26		
B109	SP180 15fr + 5fr indigo	60 60

Stamp Days, Mar. 26-27.

Type of France, 1950, Ovptd. Like No.
B106 in Ultramarine

1950, Mar. 11	Unwmk.	Perf. 13
B110	SP183 12fr + 3fr dk grn	60 60

Stamp Days, Mar. 11-12.

Tunisian and
French Woman
Shaking
Hands — SP13

1950, June 5		
B111	SP13 15fr + 35fr red	60 60
B112	SP13 25fr + 45fr dp ultra	60 60

The surtax was for Franco-Tunisian Mutual
Assistance.

Arab Soldier — SP14

1950, Aug. 21		Engr.
B113	SP14 25fr + 25fr dp bl	80 80

The surtax was for old soldiers.

Type of France, 1951, Overprinted Type
"c" in Black

1951, Mar. 10		
B114	SP186 12fr + 3fr brnsh gray	50 40

Stamp Days, Mar. 10-11.

Mother
Carrying
Child — SP15

1951, June 19		Engr.	Perf. 13
B115	SP15 30fr + 15fr dp ultra		1.00 1.00

The surtax was for child welfare.

National
Cemetery of
Gammarth
SP16

1952, June 15		
B116	SP16 30fr + 10fr blue	1.00 1.00

Surtax aided orphans of the military services.

Type of France 1952 Overprinted Type "e"
in Lilac

1952, Mar. 8		Unwmk.
B117	SP190 12fr + 3fr purple	42 42

Stamp Day, Mar. 8.

Stucco Work,
Bardo
SP17

Boy Campers
SP18

1952, May 5		Engr.	Perf. 13
B118	SP17 15fr + 1fr ultra & indigo		50 50

Surtax for charitable works of the army.

1952, June 15		
B119	SP18 30fr + 10fr dk grn	80 80

The surtax was for the Educational League vacation camps.

Type of France, 1952, Surcharged Type
"c" and Surtax

1952, Oct. 15		
B120	A226 15fr + 5fr bl grn	80 80

Creation of the French Military Medal, cent.

Type of France, 1953, Overprinted Type
"c"

1953, Mar. 14		
B121	SP193 12fr + 3fr vermilion	42 42

"Day of the Stamp."

Type of France, 1954, Overprinted Type
"c"

1954, Mar. 20		
B122	SP196 12fr + 3fr indigo	42 42

Stamp Day.

Balloon Post,
1870 — SP19

1955, Mar. 19		
B123	SP19 12fr + 3fr red brown	50 50

Stamp Days, Mar. 19-20.

Independent Kingdom

Franz von
Taxis — SP20

1956, Mar. 17		
B124	SP20 12fr + 3fr dark green	42 42

Stamp Days, Mar. 17-18.

Republic

No. 246
Surcharged in +
Red 10ᶠ

1957, Aug. 8		Engr.
B125	A29 20fr + 10fr dp ultra	40 40

15th anniversary of the army.

Florist Type of 1955 with Added
Inscriptions, Surcharged in Red

1957, Oct. 19		Perf. 13
B126	A34 20fr + 10fr dk vio	35 35

No. B126 is inscribed "5e. Foire Internationale"
at bottom and lines of Arabic at either side.

Mailman
Delivering
Mail — SP21

Ornamental
Cock — SP22

1959, May 1		Engr.	Perf. 13
B127	SP21 20fr + 5fr dk brn & org brn		35 35

Day of the Stamp. The surtax was for the Post
Office Mutual Fund.

1959, Oct. 24		Litho.	Perf. 13
B128	SP22 10m + 5m yel, lt bl & red		22 22

Surtax for the Red Crescent Society.

Mailman on
Camel
Phoning — SP23

Dancer of
Kerkennah
Holding
Stamp — SP24

1960, Apr. 16		Engr.	Perf. 13
B129	SP23 60m + 5m ol, org & ultra		50 50

Day of the Stamp.

1961, May 6		Unwmk.	Perf. 13

Stamp Day: 15m+5m, Mail truck, horiz.
20m+6m, Hand holding magnifying glass and
stamps. 50m+5m, Running boy, symbols of mail.

B130	SP24 12m + 4m multi	32 32
B131	SP24 15m + 5m multi	38 38
B132	SP24 20m + 6m multi	42 42
B133	SP24 50m + 5m multi	52 52

Nos. B130-B133
Overprinted
1963
O.N.U

1963, Oct. 24		
B134	SP24 12m + 4m cl, vio & ol	22 22
B135	SP24 15m + 5m ol, cl & vio bl	28 28
B136	SP24 20m + 6m multi	38 38
B137	SP24 50m + 5m multi	60 60

United Nations Day.

Old Man, Red
Crescent
SP25

Nurse Holding
Bottle of Blood
SP26

Tunisian Red Crescent: 75m+10m, Mother,
child and Red Crescent.

1972, May 8		Engr.	Perf. 13
B138	SP25 10m + 10m pur & dk red		22 20
B139	SP25 75m + 10m bis brn & dl red		35 22

1973, May 10   Engr.   *Perf. 13*

Design: 60m+10m, Red Crescent and blood donors' arms, horiz.

B140	SP26	25m + 10m multi	22 20
B141	SP26	60m + 10m gray & car	35 20

Red Crescent appeal for blood donors.

Blood Donors — SP27

Man Holding Scales with Balanced Diet — SP28

Red Crescent Society: 75m+10m, Blood transfusion, symbolic design.

1974, May 8   Photo.   *Perf. 14x13*

B142	SP27	25m + 10m multi	35 20
B143	SP27	75m + 10m multi	50 30

1975, May 8   Photo.   *Perf. 11½*

B144	SP28	50m + 10m multi	22 22

Tunisian Red Crescent fighting malnutrition.

Blood Donation, Woman and Man — SP29

1976, May 8   Photo.   *Perf. 11½*

B145	SP29	40m + 10m multi	25 20

Tunisian Red Crescent Society.

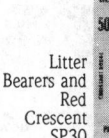
Litter Bearers and Red Crescent SP30

1977, May 8   Photo.   *Perf. 13½x14*

B146	SP30	50m + 10m multi	22 22

Tunisian Red Crescent Society.

Blood Donors — SP31

Hand and Red Crescent — SP32

1978, May 8   Photo.   *Perf. 13x14*

B147	SP31	50m + 10m multi	22 20

Blood drive of Tunisian Red Crescent Society.

1979, May 8   Photo.   *Perf. 13½*

B148	SP32	50m + 10m multi	40 22

Tunisian Red Crescent Society.

Red Crescent Society
SP33   SP34

1980, May 8   Photo.   *Perf. 13½*

B149	SP33	50m + 10m multi	22 20

1981, May 8   *Perf. 14½x13½*

B150	SP34	50m + 10m multi	35 15

Dome of the Rock, Jerusalem SP35

1981, Nov. 29   Photo.   *Perf. 13½*

B151	SP35	50m + 5m multi	35 15
B152	SP35	150m + 5m multi	60 30
B153	SP35	200m + 5m multi	1.00 42

Intl. Palestinian Solidarity Day.

Red Crescent Society SP36

1982, May 8   Photo.   *Perf. 13½*

B154	SP36	80m + 10m multi	22 20

Red Crescent Society — SP37

1983, May 8   Litho.   *Perf. 14x13½*

B155	SP37	80m + 10m multi	22 15

Sabra and Chatilla Massacre SP38

1983, Sept. 20   Photo.   *Perf. 13*

B156	SP38	80m + 5m multi	20 15

Red Crescent Society — SP39

1984, May 8   Litho.   *Perf. 12½*

B157	SP39	80m + 10m First aid	22 15

Red Crescent Society
SP40   SP41

1985, May 8   Litho.   *Perf. 14*

B158	SP40	100m + 10m multi	25 15

1986, May 9   Litho.   *Perf. 14½x13½*

B159	SP41	120m + 10m Map of Tunisia	52 25

Red Crescent Society SP42

1987, May 8   Litho.   *Perf. 13x13½*

B160	SP42	150m + 10m multi	65 32

Intl. Red Cross and Red Crescent Organizations, 125th Anniv. — SP43

1988, May 9   Photo.   *Perf. 14*

B161	SP43	150m + 10m multi	50 25

Red Crescent Society — SP44

**1989, May 8   Photo.   *Perf. 11½*
Granite Paper**

B162	SP44	150m + 10m multi	40 20

Red Crescent Society
SP45   SP46

1990, May 8   Litho.   *Perf. 14x13½*

B163	SP45	150m + 10m multi	35 18

1991, May 8   Litho.   *Perf. 13½*

B164	SP46	180m + 10m multi	45 22

Red Crescent Society — SP47

1993, Aug. 17   Litho.   *Perf. 14x13½*

B165	SP47	120m + 30m multi	30 15

AIR POST STAMPS

No. 43 Surcharged in Red

1919, Apr.   Unwmk.   *Perf. 14x13½*

C1	A6	30c on 35c ol grn & brn	65	65
a.		Inverted surcharge	40.00	40.00
b.		Double surcharge	40.00	40.00
c.		Double inverted surcharge	42.50	42.50
d.		Double surcharge, one inverted	40.00	40.00

Type A6, Overprinted in Rose

1920, Apr.

C2	A6	30c ol grn, bl & rose	32 32

Nos. 53 and 55 Overprinted in Red

Poste Aérienne

1927, Mar. 24

C3	A7	1fr indigo & ultra	40	40
C4	A7	2fr grn & red, *pink*	1.50	1.50

Nos. 51 and 57 Surcharged in Black or Red

1ᶠ75

Poste Aérienne

C5	A6	1.75fr on 75c (Bk)	45	26
C6	A7	1.75fr on 5fr (R)	1.25	95

Type A13 Ovptd. like #C3-C4 in Blue

1928, Feb.

C7	A13	1.30fr org & lt vio	1.50	85
C8	A13	1.80fr gray grn & red	2.00	50
C9	A13	2.55fr lil & ol brn	85	50

The only revenue stamps listed in this catalogue are those also authorized for prepayment of postage.

Type A13 Surcharged like #C5-C6 in Blue
1930, Aug.

C10	A13	1.50fr on 1.30fr org & lt vio	1.25 50
C11	A13	1.50fr on 1.80fr gray grn & red	2.00 32
C12	A13	1.50fr on 2.55fr lil & ol brn	4.00 1.00

> Catalogue values for unused stamps in this section, from this point to the end of the section, are for Never Hinged items.

UPU Type of Regular Issue
1949, Oct. 28   Engr.   Perf. 13

C13	A23	25fr dk bl, *bluish*	1.00 1.00

UPU, 75th anniv. Exists imperf.; value $35.

Bird from Antique Mosaic, Museum of Sousse — AP2

(Arabic on one line) — AP3

1949   Unwmk.

C14	AP2	200fr dk bl & indigo	2.50 75

1950-51

C15	AP3	100fr bl grn & brn	1.25 40
C16	AP3	200fr dk bl & ind ('51)	2.75 1.40

Monastir AP4

Coast at Korbous AP5

Design: 1000fr, Air view of Tozeur mosque.

1953-54

C17	AP4	100fr dk bl, ind & dk grn	1.25 45
C18	AP4	200fr cl, blk brn & red brn ('54)	2.25 85
C19	AP5	500fr dk brn & ultra	11.00 6.00
C20	AP5	1000fr dk green	17.50 13.00

Imperforates exist.

Independent Kingdom
Types of 1953-54 Redrawn with "RF" Omitted
1956, Mar. 1

C21	AP4	100fr slate bl, indigo & dk grn	70 25
C22	AP4	200fr multi	1.25 50
C23	AP5	500fr dk brn & ultra	4.00 2.00
C24	AP5	1000fr dk green	7.25 3.75

Republic

Desert Swallows — AP6

Birds: No. C26, Butcherbird. No. C27, Cream-colored courser. 100m, European chaffinch. 150m, Pink flamingos. 200m, Barbary partridges. 300m, European roller. 500m, Bustard.

1965-66   Photo.   Perf. 12½
Size: 23x31mm

C25	AP6	25m multi	55 25
C26	AP6	55m blk & lt bl	65 40
C27	AP6	55m multi ('66)	80 55

Size: 22½x33mm
Perf. 11½

C28	AP6	100m multi	1.00 60
C29	AP6	150m multi ('66)	3.75 1.65
C30	AP6	200m multi ('66)	4.00 1.90
C31	AP6	300m multi ('66)	6.00 3.50
C32	AP6	500m multi	6.50 4.00
		Nos. C25-C32 (8)	23.25 12.85

See No. 474.

AIR POST SEMI-POSTAL STAMP

> Catalogue value for the unused stamp in this section is for a Never Hinged item.

Window, Great Mosque of Kairouan — SPAP1

Unwmk.
1952, May 5   Engr.   Perf. 13

CB1	SPAP1	50fr + 10fr blk & gray grn	1.00 1.00

Surtax for charitable works of the army.

POSTAGE DUE STAMPS

Regular postage stamps perforated with holes in the form of a "T," the holes varying in size and number, were used as postage due stamps from 1888 to 1901.

D1   D2

Perf. 14x13½
1901-03   Unwmk.   Typo.

J1	D1	1c black	15 15
J2	D1	2c orange	15 15
J3	D1	5c blue	15 15
J4	D1	10c brown	16 15
J5	D1	20c blue green	2.25 28
J6	D1	30c carmine	1.00 32
J7	D1	50c brown violet	75 32
J8	D1	1fr olive green	65 32
J9	D1	2fr carmine, *grn*	2.25 60
J10	D1	5fr blk, *yellow*	27.50 16.00
		Nos. J1-J10 (10)	35.01 18.44

No. J10 Surcharged in Blue

2 FRANCS

1914, Nov.

J11	D1	2fr on 5fr blk, *yellow*	55 45

In Jan. 1917 regular 5c postage stamps were overprinted "T" in an inverted triangle and used as postage due stamps.

1922-49

J12	D2	1c black	15 15
J13	D2	2c black, *yellow*	15 15
J14	D2	5c violet brown	15 15
J15	D2	10c blue	15 15
J16	D2	10c yel green ('45)	15 15
J17	D2	20c orange, *yel*	15 15
J18	D2	30c brown ('23)	15 15
J19	D2	50c rose red	50 15
J20	D2	50c blue vio ('45)	15 15
J21	D2	60c violet ('28)	50 15
J22	D2	80c bister ('28)	15 15
J23	D2	90c orange red ('28)	75 30
J24	D2	1fr green	15 15
J25	D2	2fr olive grn, *straw*	42 15
J26	D2	2fr car rose ('45)	15 15
J27	D2	3fr vio, *pink* ('29)	15 15
J28	D2	4fr grnsh bl ('45)	15 15
J29	D2	5fr violet	42 22
J30	D2	10fr cerise ('49)	15 15
J31	D2	20fr olive gray ('49)	48 15
		Set value	4.10 1.80

Inscribed: "Timbre Taxe"
1950   Unwmk.   Perf. 14x13½

J32	D2	30fr blue	95 35

> Catalogue values for unused stamps in this section, from this point to the end of the section, are for Never Hinged items.

Independent Kingdom

Grain and Fruit — D3

1957, Apr. 1   Engr.   Perf. 14x13

J33	D3	1fr bright green	15 15
J34	D3	2fr orange brown	15 15
J35	D3	3fr bluish green	25 25
J36	D3	4fr indigo	28 28
J37	D3	5fr lilac	25 25
J38	D3	10fr carmine	25 25
J39	D3	20fr chocolate	80 80
J40	D3	30fr blue	1.00 1.00
		Nos. J33-J40 (8)	3.13 3.13

Republic
Inscribed "Republique Tunisienne"
1960-77

J41	D3	1m emerald	15 15
J42	D3	2m red brown	15 15
J43	D3	3m bluish green	15 15
J44	D3	4m indigo	15 15
J45	D3	5m lilac	15 15
J46	D3	10m carmine rose	22 22
J47	D3	20m violet brown	40 40
J48	D3	30m blue	50 50
J49	D3	40m lake ('77)	15 15
J50	D3	100m blue green ('77)	25 20
		Set value	1.80 1.75

PARCEL POST STAMPS

Mail Delivery — PP1

Gathering Dates — PP2

1906   Unwmk.   Typo.   Perf. 13½x14

Q1	PP1	5c grn & vio brn	15 15
Q2	PP1	10c org & red	42 15
Q3	PP1	20c dk brn & org	52 15
Q4	PP1	25c bl & brn	70 15
Q5	PP1	40c gray & rose	95 15
Q6	PP1	50c vio brn & vio	70 15
Q7	PP1	75c bis brn & bl	1.25 22
Q8	PP1	1fr red brn & red	95 15
Q9	PP1	2fr car & bl	2.75 22
Q10	PP1	5fr vio & vio brn	6.75 42
		Nos. Q1-Q10 (10)	15.14
		Set value	1.50

1926

Q11	PP2	5c pale brn & dk bl	15 15
Q12	PP2	10c rose & vio	15 15
Q13	PP2	20c yel grn & blk	15 15
Q14	PP2	25c org brn & blk	22 15
Q15	PP2	40c dp rose & dp grn	65 24
Q16	PP2	50c lt vio & blk	65 24
Q17	PP2	60c ol & brn red	70 38
Q18	PP2	75c gray vio & bl grn	70 15
Q19	PP2	80c ver & ol brn	65 15
Q20	PP2	1fr Prus bl & dp rose	65 15
Q21	PP2	2fr vio & mag	1.25 15
Q22	PP2	4fr red & blk	1.50 15
Q23	PP2	5fr brn red & dp rose	2.00 22
Q24	PP2	10fr dl red & grn, *grnsh*	4.25 28
Q25	PP2	20fr yel grn & dp vio, *lav*	7.50 50
		Nos. Q11-Q25 (15)	21.17
		Set value	2.75

Parcel post stamps were discontinued July 1, 1940.

TURKEY

LOCATION — Southeastern Europe and Asia Minor, between the Mediterranean and Black Seas
GOVT. — Republic
AREA — 300,947 sq. mi.
POP. — 48,000,000 (est. 1984)
CAPITAL — Ankara

The Ottoman Empire ceased to exist in 1922, and the Republic of Turkey was inaugurated in 1923.

40 Paras = 1 Piaster
40 Paras = 1 Ghurush (1926)
40 Paras = 1 Kurush (1926)
100 Kurush = 1 Lira

> Catalogue values for unused stamps in this country are for Never Hinged items, beginning with Scott 817 in the regular postage section, Scott B69 in the semi-postal section, Scott C1 in the airpost section, Scott J97 in the postage due section, Scott O1 in the official section, Scott P175 in the newspaper section, and Scott RA139 in the postal tax section.

Watermark

Wmk. 394- "PTT," Crescent and Star

Turkish Numerals

"Tughra," Monogram of Sultan Abdul-Aziz

A1   A2

A3   A4

1863 Unwmk. Litho. *Imperf.*
Red Band: 20pa, 1pi, 2pi
Blue Band: 5pi
Thin Paper

1	A1	20pa blk, *yellow*	27.50	17.50
a.		Tête bêche pair	125.00	125.00
b.		Without band	45.00	
c.		Green band		
2	A2	1pi blk, *dl vio*	30.00	20.00
a.		1pi black, *gray*	30.00	20.00
b.		Tête bêche pair	150.00	150.00
c.		Without band	42.50	
d.		Design reversed		175.00
e.		1pi blk, *yel* (error)	150.00	125.00
4	A3	2pi blk, *grnsh bl*	35.00	22.50
a.		2pi black, *ind*	35.00	22.50
b.		Tête bêche pair	150.00	150.00
c.		Without band	50.00	
5	A4	5pi blk, *rose*	55.00	27.50
a.		Tête bêche pair	250.00	250.00
b.		Without band	75.00	
c.		Green band	95.00	
d.		Red band	95.00	

Thick, Surface Colored Paper

6	A1	20pa blk, *yellow*	45.00	30.00
a.		Tête bêche pair	350.00	350.00
b.		Design reversed	275.00	275.00
c.		Without band	35.00	35.00
d.		Paper colored through	75.00	75.00
7	A2	1pi blk, *gray*	50.00	42.50
a.		Tête bêche pair	350.00	350.00
b.		Design reversed		
c.		Without band		
d.		Paper colored through	125.00	125.00

The 2pi and 5pi had two printings. In the common printing, the stamps are more widely spaced and alternate horizontal rows of 12 are inverted. In the first and rare printing, the stamps are more closely spaced and no rows are tête bêche.
See Nos. J1-J4.

Crescent and Star, Symbols of Turkish Caliphate — A5

Surcharged

The bottom characters of this and the following surcharges denote the denomination. The characters at top and sides translate, "Ottoman Empire Posts."

1865 Typo. *Perf. 12½*

8	A5	10pa deep green	3.00	5.50
c.		"1" instead of "10" in each corner	300.00	300.00
9	A5	20pa yellow	75	70
a.		Star without rays	70	65
10	A5	1pi lilac	3.50	2.00
a.		Star without rays	3.50	1.65
11	A5	2pi blue	1.00	1.00
12	A5	5pi carmine	65	1.75
d.		Inverted surcharge		375.00
13	A5	25pi red orange	115.00	110.00

Imperf., Pairs

8b	A5	10pa	125.00	125.00
9b	A5	20pa	125.00	125.00
10b	A5	1pi	90.00	90.00
11a	A5	2pi	90.00	90.00
12b	A5	5pi	110.00	110.00
13a	A5	25pi	700.00	700.00

See Nos. J6-J35. For overprints and surcharges see Nos. 14-52, 64-65, 446-461, 467-468, J71-J77.

Surcharged

1867

14	A5	10pa gray green		70
a.		Imperf., pair	50.00	
15	A5	20pa yellow		2.00
a.		Imperf., pair	70.00	
16	A5	1pi lilac		3.50
a.		Imperf., pair	95.00	
b.		Imperf., with surcharge of 5pi	15.00	
17	A5	2pi blue	65	1.00
a.		Imperf.		

18	A5	5pi rose	35	2.00
a.		Imperf.		
19	A5	25pi orange	375.00	

Nos. 14, 15, 16 and 19 were never placed in use.

Surcharged

1869 *Perf. 13½*

20	A5	10pa dull violet	12.50	75
a.		Printed on both sides	80.00	80.00
b.		Imperf., pair		
c.		Inverted surcharge		90.00
d.		Double surcharge		
e.		10pa yellow (error)		250.00
21	A5	20pa pale green	27.50	75
a.		Printed on both sides	90.00	90.00
22	A5	1pi yellow	32	20
c.		Inverted surcharge	80.00	80.00
d.		Double surcharge		
e.		Surcharged on both sides		
f.		Printed on both sides		
23	A5	2pi orange red	7.50	1.50
b.		Imperf., pair	130.00	130.00
c.		Printed on both sides		130.00
d.		Inverted surcharge	70.00	70.00
e.		Surcharged on both sides		140.00
24	A5	5pi blue	15	20
25	A5	5pi gray	5.00	4.50
26	A5	25pi dull rose	14.00	20.00

Pin-perf., Perf. 5 to 11 and Compound
1870-71

27	A5	10pa lilac	150.00	25.00
28	A5	10pa brown	30.00	2.50
29	A5	20pa gray green	9.00	50
a.		Printed on both sides		
30	A5	1pi yellow	22.50	40
a.		Inverted surcharge	100.00	80.00
b.		Without surcharge		
31	A5	2pi red	55	35
a.		Imperf.	20.00	20.00
b.		Printed on both sides		32.50
c.		Surcharged on both sides		
32	A5	5pi blue	20	60
a.		5pi greenish blue	2.75	2.75
33	A5	5pi slate	7.50	6.00
a.		Printed on both sides		
b.		Surcharged on both sides		32.50
34	A5	25pi dull rose	12.50	12.50

1873 *Perf. 12, 12½*

35	A5	10pa dark lilac	27.50	2.25
a.		Inverted surcharge		90.00
36	A5	10pa olive brown	35.00	4.00
a.		10pa bister	40.00	
37	A5	2pi vermilion	50	1.00
a.		Surcharged on both sides	22.50	22.50

Surcharged

1874-75 *Perf. 13½*

38	A5	10pa red violet	6.00	75
a.		Imperf., pair	70.00	50.00
39	A5	20pa yellow green	7.50	75
b.		Inverted surcharge	30.00	13.00
c.		Double surcharge		
40	A5	1pi yellow	12.50	1.00
a.		Imperf., pair	100.00	80.00

Perf. 12, 12½

41	A5	10pa red violet	21.00	7.50
a.		Inverted surcharge	45.00	60.00

Surcharged

1876, Apr. *Perf. 13½*

42	A5	10pa red lilac	15	15
a.		Inverted surcharge		70.00
b.		Imperf., pair	15.00	15.00
43	A5	20pa pale green	15	15
b.		Inverted surcharge		70.00
c.		Imperf., pair	15.00	15.00

44	A5	1pi yellow	15	15
a.		Imperf., pair	27.50	27.50
46	A5	5pi gray blue	250.00	
47	A5	25pi dull rose	250.00	

Nos. 46 and 47 were never placed in use.

Surcharged

1876, Jan.

48	A5	¼pi on 10pa violet	35	50
49	A5	½pi on 20pa yel grn	75	75
50	A5	1¼pi on 50pa rose	20	35
a.		Imperf., pair	60.00	
51	A5	2pi on 2pi redsh brn	6.50	2.25
52	A5	5pi on 5pi gray blue	1.00	2.00

The surcharge on Nos. 48-52 restates in French the value originally expressed in Turkish characters.

A7

1876, Sept. Typo. *Perf. 13½*

53	A7	10pa black & rose lil	15	16
54	A7	20pa red vio & grn	15.00	1.50
55	A7	50pa blue & yellow	20	25
56	A7	2pi black & redsh brn	15	25
57	A7	5pi red & blue	85	90
b.		Cliché of 25pi in plate of 5pi	400.00	375.00
58	A7	25pi claret & rose	7.00	7.50
a.		Imperf.	160.00	

Nos. 56-58 exist perf. 11½, but were not regularly issued.
See Nos. 59-63, 66-91, J36-J38. For overprints see Nos. 462-466, 469-476, J78-J79, P10-P14.

1880-84 *Perf. 13½*

59	A7	5pa black & ol ('81)	15	15
a.		Imperf.	30.00	
60	A7	10pa black & grn ('84)	15	15
61	A7	20pa black & rose	16	15
62	A7	1pi blk & bl (*piastres*)	15	15
a.		1pi black & gray blue	16	
b.		Imperf.	40.00	
63	A7	1pi blk & bl (*piastre*) ('81)	6.50	1.50

A cliché of No. 63 was inserted in a plate of the Eastern Rumelia 1pi (No. 13), but this "error" is found only in the remainders.
Nos. 60-61 and 63 exist perf. 11½, but were not regularly issued.

1881-82
Surcharged like Apr., 1876 Issue

64	A7	20pa gray	15	15
a.		Inverted surcharge	13.50	
b.		Imperf., pair	25.00	
65	A7	2pi pale salmon	15	15
a.		Inverted surcharge	22.50	
		Set value	20	20

1884-86 *Perf. 11½, 13½*

66	A7	5pa lil & pale lil ('86)	27.50	22.50
67	A7	10pa grn & pale grn	15	15
68	A7	20pa rose & pale rose	15	15
69	A7	1pi blue & lt blue	15	15

Perf. 11½

70	A7	2pi ocher & pale ocher	15	15
71	A7	5pi red brn & pale brn	20	40
c.		5pi ocher & pale ocher (error)	12.00	12.00

Perf. 11½, 13½

73	A7	25pi blk & pale gray ('86)	75.00	75.00

Imperf

66a	A7	5pa	60.00	
67a	A7	10pa	20.00	
68b	A7	20pa	20.00	
69b	A7	1pi	20.00	
73a	A7	25pi	150.00	

1886 *Perf. 13½*

74	A7	5pa black & pale gray	15	15
75	A7	2pi orange & lt bl	15	15
76	A7	5pi grn & pale grn	18	15
77	A7	25pi bis & pale bis	7.75	8.50

Imperf

74a	A7	5pa	20.00	
75b	A7	2pi	20.00	
76b	A7	5pi	20.00	
77a	A7	25pi	35.00	

Stamps of 1884-86, bisected and surcharged as above, 10pa, 20pa, 1pi and 2pi or surcharged "2" in red are stated to have been made privately and without authority. With the aid of employees of the post office, copies were passed through the mails.

1888 *Perf. 13½*

83	A7	5pa green & yellow	15	15
84	A7	2pi red lilac & bl	15	15
85	A7	5pi dk brown & gray	15	15
86	A7	25pi red & yellow	7.50	6.00

Imperf

83a	A7	5pa	20.00	
84a	A7	2pi	20.00	
85a	A7	5pi	20.00	
86a	A7	25pi	25.00	

Nos. 74-86 exist perf. 11½, but were not regularly issued.

1890 *Perf. 11½, 13½*

87	A7	10pa green & gray	15	15
88	A7	20pa rose & gray	15	15
89	A7	1pi blue & gray	15	15
90	A7	2pi yellow & gray	25	15
91	A7	5pi buff & gray	50	60
		Set value	1.00	88

Imperf

87a	A7	10pa	20.00	
88a	A7	20pa	20.00	
89a	A7	1pi	20.00	
90b	A7	2pi	25.00	
91a	A7	5pi	25.00	

TURKEY

RARE AND CLASSIC STAMPS, POSTAL HISTORY, PROOFS.
BUYING, SELLING, APPRAISALS.

For the Best Services in Classic Stamps and Postal History contact the RECOGNIZED LEADERS IN THE FIELD.
Excellent stock of classic material for most countries of the World also available.

THE CLASSIC COLLECTOR
LIANE & SERGIO SISMONDO

Ph. 315-422-2331, Fax 315-422-2956
10035 Carousel Center Drive
Syracuse, NY 13290-0001
Ph. 613-722-1621, Fax: 613-728-7305

CANADIAN OFFICE: P.O. Box 6277, Station J, Ottawa, Canada K2A 1T4.

Arms and Tughra of "El Gazi"
(The Conqueror) Sultan Abdul
Hamid

A10   A11

A12   A13

A14

5 ته 5
Cinq ته Paras
No. 100

1892-98		Typo.	Perf. 13½	
95	A10	10pa gray green	15	15
96	A11	20pa violet brn ('98)	15	15
		20pa dark pink	7.50	15
b.		20pa pink	4.00	20
97	A12	1pi pale blue	5.00	15
98	A13	2pi brown org	2.00	15
a.		Tête bêche pair	5.00	5.00
99	A14	5pi dull violet	5.00	55
a.		Turkish numeral in upper right corner reads "50" instead of "5"	12.50	12.50
		Set value		75

See Nos. J39-J42. For surcharges and overprints
see Nos. 100, 288-291, 350, 355-359, 477-478,
B38, B41, J80-J82, P25-P34, P36, P121-P122,
P134-P137, P153-P154.

Red Surcharge

1897

100	A10	5pa on 10pa gray grn	25	15
a.		"Cniq" instead of "Cinq"	10.00	10.00

Turkish stamps of types A11, A17-
A18, A21-A24, A26, A28-A39, A41 with
or without Turkish overprints and English
surcharges with "Baghdad" or "Iraq" are
listed under Mesopotamia in Vol. 1.

Turkish stamps of types A19 and A21
with Double-headed Eagle and
"Shqipenia" handstamp are listed under
Albania in Vol. 2.

A16   A17

1901		Typo.	Perf. 13½	
		For Foreign Postage		
102	A16	5pa bister	1.00	20
103	A16	10pa yellow green	1.00	15
104	A16	20pa magenta	1.00	15
a.		Perf. 12	1.25	15
105	A16	1pi violet blue	1.00	15
106	A16	2pi gray blue	1.50	20
107	A16	5pi ocher	2.00	40
108	A16	25pi dark green	12.00	7.50
109	A16	50pi yellow	30.00	20.00
		Nos. 102-109 (8)	49.50	28.75
		For Domestic Postage		
		Perf. 12, 13½		
110	A17	5pa purple	1.00	15
111	A17	10pa green	1.00	15
112	A17	20pa carmine	1.00	15
113	A17	1pi blue	75	15
a.		Imperf.	20.00	
114	A17	2pi orange	1.00	15
115	A17	5pi lilac rose	2.50	15
		Perf. 13½		
116	A17	25pi brown	3.00	65
a.		Perf. 12	20.00	1.25

117	A17	50pi yellow brown	7.50	1.50
a.		Perf. 12	20.00	3.00
		Nos. 110-117 (8)	17.75	
		Set value		2.45

Nos. 110-113 exist perf. 12x13½.
For overprints and surcharges see Nos. 165-180,
292-303, 340-341, 361-377, 479-493, B19-B20,
B37, J43-J46, P37-P48, P69-P80, P123-P126,
P138-P146, P155-P164.

A18   A19

1905		Perf. 12, 13½ and Compound		
118	A18	5pa ocher	15	15
119	A18	10pa dull green	15	15
a.		Imperf.	4.00	3.50
120	A18	20pa carmine	15	15
a.		Imperf.	4.00	3.50
121	A18	1pi blue	15	15
122	A18	2pi slate	1.00	15
123	A18	2½pi red violet	20	15
a.		Imperf.	11.00	9.00
124	A18	5pi brown	16	15
125	A18	10pi orange brn	1.00	15
126	A18	25pi olive green	2.50	1.00
127	A18	50pi deep violet	7.50	2.75

See Nos. J47-J48. For overprints and surcharges
see Nos. 128-131, 181-182, 304-314, 351-354,
378-389, 494-508, B1-B3, B21-B23, B39-B40, P49-
P54, P127-P129, P147-P150, P165-P171.

Overprinted in Carmine or
Blue   ب

1906

128	A18	10pa dull green (C)	15	15
129	A18	20pa carmine (Bl)	15	15
130	A18	1pi blue (C)	20	15
131	A18	2pi slate (C)	2.50	70
		Nos. 118-131 (14)	15.96	
		Set value		5.00

Stamps bearing this overprint were sold to
merchants at a discount from face value to
encourage the use of Turkish stamps on foreign
correspondence, instead of those of the various
European powers which maintained post offices in
Turkey. The overprint is the Arab "B," for "Béhié,"
meaning "discount."

1908

132	A19	5pa ocher	20	15
133	A19	10pa blue green	50	15
134	A19	20pa carmine	3.00	15
135	A19	1pi bright blue	5.00	15
a.		1pi ultramarine	15.00	2.25
136	A19	2pi blue black	7.50	15
137	A19	2½pi violet brown	1.00	15
138	A19	5pi dark violet	2.50	15
139	A19	10pi red	5.00	30
140	A19	25pi dark green	2.50	1.00
141	A19	50pi red brown	6.00	1.00

See Nos. J49-J50. For overprints and surcharges
see Nos. 142-145, 314B-316B, 390-396, 509-
516A, B4-B6, B17, B24-B27, P55-P60, P130-P131,
P151, P172, Thrace 15.

Overprinted in Carmine or Blue   ب

142	A19	10pa blue green (C)	65	20
143	A19	20pa carmine (Bl)	1.50	30
144	A19	1pi brt blue (C)	3.00	50
145	A19	2pi blue black (C)	5.00	90
		Nos. 132-145 (14)	43.35	
		Set value		4.50

 A20

		Perf. 12, 13½ & Compound		
1908, Dec. 17				
146	A20	5pa ocher	15	15
147	A20	10pa blue green	15	15
148	A20	20pa carmine	35	15
149	A20	1pi ultra	50	15
150	A20	2pi gray black	3.00	1.10
		Nos. 146-150 (5)	4.15	
		Set value		1.40
		Imperf		
146a	A20	5pa	1.75	1.75
147a	A20	10pa	2.00	2.00
148a	A20	20pa	2.75	2.75
149a	A20	1pi	1.75	1.75

Granting of a Constitution, the date of which is
inscribed on the banderol: "324 Temuz 10" (July
24, 1908).
For overprints see Nos. 397, 517.

Tughra and "Reshad" of
Sultan Mohammed V — A21

1909, Dec.

151	A21	5pa ocher	15	15
152	A21	10pa blue green	25	15
a.		Imperf.	1.75	1.75
153	A21	20pa carmine rose	15	15
154	A21	1pi ultra	15	15
a.		1pi bright blue	5.00	15
155	A21	2pi blue black	40	15
156	A21	2½pi dark brown	10.00	5.00
157	A21	5pi dark violet	5.00	15
158	A21	10pi dull red	3.50	35
159	A21	25pi dark green	60.00	22.50
160	A21	50pi red brown	17.50	12.50

The 2pa olive green, type A21, is a newspaper
stamp, No. P68.
Two types exist for the 10pa, 20pa and 1pi. In
the second type, the damaged crescent is restored.
See Nos. J51-J52. For overprints and surcharges
see Nos. 161-164, 317-327, 342-343, 398-406,
518-528, 567, B7-B14, B18, B28-B32, P61-P68,
P81, P132-P133, P152, P173, Turkey in Asia 67,
72, Thrace 1-4, 13, 13A, 14.

Overprinted in Carmine or Blue   ب

161	A21	10pa blue green (C)	50	15
a.		Imperf.		
162	A21	20pa carmine rose (Bl)	50	15
a.		Imperf.		
163	A21	1pi ultra (C)	50	15
a.		Imperf.	4.00	
b.		1pi bright blue	75	20
164	A21	2pi blue black (C)	10.00	2.00
a.		Imperf.		
		Nos. 151-164 (14)	108.60	43.70

Stamps of 1901-05
Overprinted in Carmine or
Blue

MONASTIR

The overprint was applied to 18 denominations
in four settings with change of city name, producing
individual sets for each city: "MONASTIR," "PRIS-
TINA," "SALONIKA" and "USKUB."

1911, June 26			Perf. 12, 13½	
165	A16	5pa bister	50	
166	A16	10pa yellow green	50	
167	A16	20pa magenta	2.50	
168	A16	1pi violet blue	2.50	
169	A16	2pi gray blue	2.50	
170	A16	5pi ocher	22.50	
171	A16	25pi dark green	30.00	
172	A16	50pi yellow	35.00	
173	A17	5pa purple	50	
174	A17	10pa green	50	
175	A17	20pa carmine	2.50	
176	A17	1pi blue	2.50	
177	A17	2pi orange	2.50	
178	A17	5pi lilac rose	22.50	
179	A17	25pi chocolate	35.00	
180	A17	50pi yellow brown	50.00	
181	A18	2½pi red violet	21.00	
182	A18	10pi orange brown	30.00	
		Nos. 165-182 (18)	263.00	

Sultan's visit to Macedonia. The Arabic overprint
reads: "Souvenir of the Sultan's Journey, 1329".
Value for Salonika and Uskub sets, each $325. See
Nos. P69-P81.

General Post Office,
Constantinople — A22

1913, Mar. 14			Perf. 12	
237	A22	2pa olive green	15	15
238	A22	5pa ocher	15	15
239	A22	10pa blue green	15	15
240	A22	20pa carmine rose	15	15
241	A22	1pi ultra	15	15
242	A22	2pi indigo	15	15
243	A22	5pi dull violet	20	15
244	A22	10pi dull red	2.00	40
245	A22	25pi gray green	2.50	1.50
246	A22	50pi orange brown	10.00	10.00

See Nos. J53-J58. For overprints and surcharges
see Nos. 247-250, 328-339, 344, 407-414, 529-
538, 568, B15-B16, B33-B36, Turkey in Asia 68,
Thrace 10, 10A, 11, 11A, 12, N82.

Overprinted in Carmine or Blue   ب

247	A22	10pa blue green (C)	15	15
248	A22	20pa car rose (Bl)	15	15
249	A22	1pi ultra (C)	25	15
250	A22	2pi indigo (C)	1.25	1.00
		Nos. 237-250 (14)	17.40	14.40

Mosque of
Selim,
Adrianople
A23

1913, Oct. 23			Engr.	
251	A23	10pa green	30	15
252	A23	20pa red	45	25
253	A23	40pa blue	80	50

Recapture of Adrianople (Edirne) by the Turks.
See Nos. 592, J59-J62. For overprints and
surcharge see Nos. 415-417, 539-540, J59-J62, J67-
J70, J83-J86, Thrace N84.

Obelisk of   Column of
Theodosius in   Constantine
the Hippodrome   A25
A24

Leander's Tower — A26   One of the
Seven
Towers — A27

Fener Bahçe
(Garden
Lighthouse)
A28

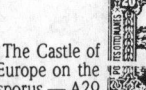

The Castle of
Europe on the
Bosporus — A29

Mosque of Sultan
Ahmed — A30

Monument to the Martyrs of Liberty — A31

Fountains of Suleiman A32

Cruiser "Hamidie" A33

View of Kandili on the Bosporus A34

War Ministry (Later Istanbul University) A35

Sweet Waters of Europe Park — A36

Mosque of Suleiman A37

The Bosporus A38

Sultan Ahmed's Fountain A39

Sultan Mohammed V — A40

Designs A24-A39: Views of Constantinople.

1914, Jan. 14   Litho.

254	A24	2pa red lilac	15	15
255	A25	4pa dark brown	15	15
256	A26	5pa violet brown	15	15
257	A27	6pa dark blue	15	15

Engr.

258	A28	10pa green	30	15
259	A29	20pa red	20	15
260	A30	1pi blue	30	15
b.		Booklet pane of 2+2 labels		
261	A31	1½pi carmine & blk	40	15
262	A32	1¾pi slate & red brn	20	15
263	A33	2pi green & blk	65	15
264	A34	2½pi orange & ol grn	50	15
265	A35	5pi dull violet	1.40	25
266	A36	10pi red brown	5.00	40
267	A37	25pi olive green	20.00	2.50
268	A38	50pi carmine	4.00	2.00
269	A39	100pi deep blue	32.50	12.50
		Cut cancellation		1.25

270	A40	200pi green & blk	250.00	125.00
		Cut cancellation		8.75
		Nos. 254-270 (17)	316.05	144.30

See Nos. 590-591, 593-598.
For overprints and surcharges see Nos. 271-287, 419, 541, 552-553, 574A, 601, 603-604, P174, Turkey in Asia 1-3, 5-9, 73-74, Thrace N77, N78.

Stamps of Preceding Issue Overprinted in Red or Blue ★

271	A28	10pa green (R)	20	15
272	A29	20pa red (Bl)	1.50	35
273	A30	1pi blue (R)	40	15
275	A32	1¾pi sl & red brn (Bl)	50	25
276	A33	2pi green & blk (R)	6.50	75
		Nos. 271-276 (5)	9.10	1.65

No. 261 Surcharged

1914, July 23

277	A31	1pi on 1½pi car & blk	35	20
a.		"1330" omitted	2.50	1.50
b.		Double surcharge		
c.		Triple surcharge	5.00	5.00

7th anniv. of the Constitution. The surcharge reads "10 July, 1330, National fête" and has also the numeral "1" at each side, over the original value of the stamp.

Stamps of 1914 Overprinted in Black or Red

278	A26	5pa violet brn (Bk)	40	15
279	A28	10pa green (R)	50	20
280	A29	20pa red (Bk)	1.00	35
281	A30	1pi blue (R)	3.00	50
282	A33	2pi green & blk (R)	1.75	30
283	A35	5pi dull violet (R)	15.00	2.00
284	A36	10pi red brown (R)	27.50	12.50
		Nos. 278-284 (7)	49.15	16.00

This overprint reads "Abolition of the Capitulations, 1330".

No. 269 Surcharged

1915

286	A39	10pi on 100pi	10.00	3.25
a.		Inverted surcharge	75.00	75.00

No. 270 Surcharged

287	A40	25pi on 200pi	6.00	2.25

Preceding Issues Overprinted in Carmine or Black

1915

On Stamps of 1892

288	A10	10pa gray green	25	15
a.		Inverted overprint	7.50	7.50
289	A13	2pi brown orange	25	15
a.		Inverted overprint	7.50	7.50
290	A14	5pi dull violet	2.50	25
a.		On No. 99a	16.50	16.50
		Set value		35

On Stamps of 1897

291	A15	5pa on 10pa gray grn	15	15
a.		Inverted overprint	5.00	5.00
b.		On No. 100a	10.00	10.00

On Stamps of 1901

292	A16	5pa bister	20	15
293	A16	1pi violet blue	25	15
294	A16	2pi gray blue	2.50	15

295	A16	5pi ocher	3.00	30
296	A16	25pi dark green	15.00	10.00
297	A17	5pa purple	15	15
298	A17	10pa green	15	15
299	A17	20pa carmine	20	15
a.		Inverted overprint	7.50	7.50
300	A17	1pi blue	20	15
a.		Inverted overprint	5.00	5.00
301	A17	2pi orange	25	15
a.		Inverted overprint	7.50	7.50
b.		Double ovpt. (R and Bk)	5.00	5.00
302	A17	5pi lilac rose	2.50	15
303	A17	25pi brown	3.50	1.10

On Stamps of 1905

304	A18	5pa ocher	15	15
305	A18	10pa dull green	15	15
a.		Inverted overprint	5.00	5.00
306	A18	20pa carmine	15	15
a.		Inverted overprint	5.00	5.00
307	A18	1pi brt blue	20	15
a.		Inverted overprint	5.00	5.00
308	A18	2pi slate	2.50	15
a.		Inverted overprint	10.00	10.00
309	A18	2½pi red violet	1.50	15
310	A18	5pi brown	2.00	15
a.		Inverted overprint	10.00	10.00
311	A18	10pi orange brown	3.50	15
312	A18	25pi olive green	12.50	3.50

On Stamps of 1906

313	A18	10pa dull green	15	15
314	A18	2pi slate	45	20
a.		Inverted overprint	5.00	5.00
		Set value, #313-314		25

On Stamps of 1908

314B	A19	2pi blue black	75.00	25.00
315	A19	2½pi violet brown	75	15
315A	A19	5pi dark violet	75.00	10.00
315B	A19	10pi red	10.00	7.50
316	A19	25pi dark green	10.00	5.00
a.		Inverted overprint	16.50	16.50

With Additional Overprint

316B	A19	2pi blue black	10.00	5.00

On Stamps of 1909

317	A21	5pa ocher	15	15
a.		Inverted overprint	10.00	10.00
b.		Double overprint	10.00	5.00
318	A21	20pa carmine rose	20	15
a.		Inverted overprint	5.00	5.00
319	A21	1pi ultra	35	15
a.		Inverted overprint	5.00	5.00
320	A21	2pi blue black	30	15
a.		Inverted overprint	5.00	5.00
321	A21	2½pi dark brown	27.50	12.50
322	A21	5pi dark violet	20	20
a.		Inverted overprint	6.50	6.50
323	A21	10pi dull red	3.25	25
324	A21	25pi dark green	400.00	250.00

With Additional Overprint

325	A21	20pa carmine rose	15	15
a.		Inverted overprint	5.00	5.00
326	A21	1pi ultra	15	15
327	A21	2pi blue black	25	15
		Set value, #325-327		20

On Stamps of 1913

328	A22	5pa ocher	15	15
a.		Inverted overprint	7.50	7.50
329	A22	10pa blue green	20	15
a.		Inverted overprint	10.00	10.00
330	A22	20pa carmine rose	15	15
a.		Inverted overprint	7.50	7.50
331	A22	1pi ultra	25	15
a.		Inverted overprint	5.00	5.00
332	A22	2pi indigo	1.50	15
a.		Inverted overprint	5.00	5.00
333	A22	5pi dull violet	1.50	15
334	A22	10pi dull red	3.00	35
a.		Inverted overprint	10.00	10.00
335	A22	25pi gray green	10.00	10.00

With Additional Overprint

336	A22	10pa blue green	25	15
337	A22	20pa carmine rose	15	20
338	A22	1pi ultra	25	15
339	A22	2pi indigo	2.50	55
a.		Inverted overprint	10.00	10.00

See Nos. P121-P133.

Stamps of 1901-13 Overprinted

1916

340	A17	5pa purple	15	15
a.		5pa purple, #P43	80.00	80.00
341	A17	10pa green	15	15
a.		Double overprint	6.50	6.50
b.		10pa yellow green, #103	80.00	80.00
342	A21	20pa car rose, #153	25	15
a.		20pa carmine rose, #162	110.00	110.00

343	A21	1pi ultra	50	15
344	A22	5pi dull violet	4.25	50
		Set value		80

Occupation of the Sinai Peninsula.

Old General Post Office of Constantinople — A41

Perf. 12½, 13½

1916, May 29   Litho.

345	A41	5pa green	25	20
346	A41	10pa carmine	25	20
347	A41	20pa ultra	25	20
348	A41	1pi violet & blk	60	75
349	A41	5pi yel brn & blk	12.50	40
		Nos. 345-349 (5)	13.85	1.75

Introduction of postage in Turkey, 50th anniv.
For overprints see Nos. 418, B42-B45.

Stamps of 1892-1905 Overprinted

1916

350	A10	10pa gray grn (R)	1.00	55
351	A18	20pa carmine (Bl)	75	45
352	A18	1pi blue (R)	2.50	45
353	A18	2pi slate (Bk)	2.50	45
354	A18	2½pi red violet (Bk)	2.50	45
		Nos. 350-354 (5)	9.25	2.35

National Fête Day. Overprint reads "10 Temuz 1332" (July 23, 1916).

Preceding Issues Overprinted or Surcharged in Red or Black:

a   b

1916

On Stamps of 1892-98

355	A10(a)	10pa gray green	20	20
355A	A11(a)	20pa violet brown	55	15
b.		Inverted overprint	10.00	10.00
356	A12(a)	1pi gray blue	25.00	15.00
357	A13(a)	2pi brown orange	1.75	55
358	A14(a)	5pi dull violet	9.00	7.50

On Stamp of 1897

359	A15(b)	5pa on 10pa gray grn	20	15

On Stamps of 1901

361	A16(a)	5pa bister	15	20
a.		Double overprint	7.50	7.50
362	A16(a)	10pa yellow green	15	20
363	A16(a)	20pa magenta	15	20
364	A16(a)	1pi violet blue	15	20
a.		Inverted overprint	7.50	7.50
365	A16(a)	2pi gray blue	10	35
366	A16(b)	5pi on 25pi dk grn	20.00	20.00
367	A16(b)	10pi on 25pi dk grn	20.00	20.00
368	A16(a)	25pi dark green	20.00	20.00
369	A17(a)	5pa purple	7.50	10.00
370	A17(a)	10pa green	25	25
371	A17(a)	20pa carmine	25	25
a.		Inverted overprint	7.50	7.50
372	A17(a)	1pi blue	25	25
a.		Inverted overprint	7.50	7.50
373	A17(a)	2pi orange	25	25
374	A17(b)	10pi on 25pi brown	3.00	50
375	A17(b)	10pi on 50pi yel brn	5.00	65
376	A17(a)	25pi brown	5.00	75
377	A17(a)	50pi yellow brown	5.00	1.00

On Stamps of 1905

378	A18(a)	5pa ocher	15	15
379	A18(a)	20pa carmine	15	15
a.		Inverted overprint	10.00	5.00
380	A18(a)	1pi brt blue	2.00	15
a.		Inverted overprint	10.00	5.00
381	A18(a)	2pi slate	35	15
382	A18(a)	2½pi red violet	45	15
383	A18(b)	10pi on 25pi ol grn	3.00	1.00
384	A18(b)	10pi on 50pi dp vio	3.00	60

385	A18(a)	25pi olive green	5.00	1.50
386	A18(a)	50pi deep violet	6.00	1.00

On Stamps of 1906

387	A18(a)	10pa dull green	18	25
388	A18(a)	20pa carmine	15	15
389	A18(a)	1pi brt blue	25	15

On Stamps of 1908

390	A19(a)	2½pi violet brown	10.00	5.00
391	A19(b)	10pi on 25pi dk grn	4.00	2.50
392	A19(b)	10pi on 50pi red brn	15.00	15.00
393	A19(b)	25pi on 50pi red brn	15.00	15.00
394	A19(a)	25pi dark green	12.50	2.50
395	A19(a)	50pi red brown	12.50	12.50

With Additional Overprint ب

396	A19(a)	2pi blue black	12.50	12.50

On Stamps of 1908-09

397	A20(a)	5pa ocher	12.50	12.50
398	A21(a)	5pa ocher	15	15
399	A21(a)	10pa blue green	15.00	12.50
400	A21(a)	20pa carmine rose	15.00	15.00
401	A21(a)	1pi ultra	50	15
402	A21(a)	2pi blue black	50	35
403	A21(a)	2½pi dark brown	20.00	17.50
404	A21(a)	5pi dark violet	20.00	17.50

With Additional Overprint ب

405	A21(a)	1pi ultra	15.00	12.50
406	A21(a)	2pi blue black	15.00	12.50

On Stamps of 1913

407	A22(a)	5pa ocher	15	15
408	A22(a)	20pa carmine rose	25	1.00
409	A22(a)	1pi ultra	1.00	15
410	A22(a)	2pi indigo	50	42
411	A22(b)	10pi on 50pi org brn	2.50	1.25
412	A22(a)	25pi gray green	2.50	1.00
413	A22(a)	50pi orange brown	1.25	1.25

With Additional Overprint ب

414	A22(a)	1pi ultra	50	15

On Commemorative Stamps of 1913

415	A23(a)	10pa green	15	15
416	A23(a)	20pa red	45	55
417	A23(a)	40pa blue	4.00	15
		Set value, #415-417		72

On Commemorative Stamp of 1916

418	A41(a)	5pi yel brn & blk	1.00	15

No. 277 Surcharged in Blue

419	A31	60pa on 1pi on 1½pi	1.25	20
a.		"1330" omitted	10.00	10.00

See Nos. P134-P152, J67-J70.

Turkish Artillery — A42

Mosque at Orta Köy, Constantinople A43

Turkey stamps can be mounted in the annually supplemented Scott Turkey album.

Lighthouse on Bosporus — A44

Monument to Martyrs of Liberty — A45

Map of the Dardanelles; Sultan Mohammed V — A46

Map of the Dardanelles A47

Istanbul Across the Golden Horn — A48

Pyramids of Egypt — A49

Dolma Bahçe Palace and Mohammed V — A50

Sentry and Shell — A51

Sultan Mohammed V — A52

1916-18 Typo. Perf. 11½, 12½

420	A42	2pa violet	15	15
421	A43	5pa orange	15	15
424	A44	10pa green	15	15

Engr.

425	A45	20pa deep rose	25	15
426	A46	1pi dull violet	35	15

Typo.

428	A47	50pi ultra	40	15
429	A48	2pi org brn & ind	35	15
430	A49	5pi pale blue & blk	6.00	1.25

Engr.

431	A50	10pi dark green	3.50	30
432	A50	10pi dark violet	3.50	30
433	A50	10pi dark brown	2.50	20
434	A51	25pi carmine, straw	50	35
437	A52	50pi carmine	1.00	55
438	A52	50pi indigo	1.00	55
439	A52	50pi green, straw	3.00	3.00
		Nos. 420-439 (15)	22.80	7.55

For overprints and surcharge see Nos. 541B-541E, 554-560, 565-566, 569-574, 575, 577-578, 579A-580, Turkey in Asia 4, 10, 64-66, Thrace N76, N80, N81.

Preceding Issues Overprinted or Surcharged in Red, Black or Blue:

d

e

f

g

1917

On Stamps of 1865

446	A5(d)	20pa yellow (R)	15.00	15.00
a.		Star without rays (R)	15.00	15.00
447	A5(d)	1pi pearl gray (R)	15.00	15.00
a.		Star without rays (R)	15.00	15.00
448	A5(d)	2pi blue (R)	15.00	15.00
449	A5(d)	5pi carmine (Bk)	25.00	25.00

On Stamp of 1867

450	A5(d)	5pi rose (Bk)	15.00	15.00

On Stamps of 1870-71

451	A5(d)	2pi red (Bl)	20.00	20.00
452	A5(d)	5pi blue (Bk)	20.00	20.00
453	A5(d)	25pi dull rose (Bl)	25.00	25.00

On Stamp of 1874-75

454	A5(d)	10pa red violet (Bl)	25.00	25.00

On Stamps of April, 1876

455	A5(d)	10pa red lilac (Bl)	12.50	15.00
a.		10pa red violet (Bl)	12.50	15.00
457	A5(d)	20pa pale green (R)	15.00	15.00
458	A5(d)	1pi yellow (Bl)	15.00	15.00

On Stamps of January, 1876

459	A5(d)	¼pi on 10pa rose lil (Bl)	15.00	12.50
460	A5(d)	½pi on 20pa yel grn (R)	15.00	12.50
461	A5(d)	1¼pi on 50pa rose (Bl)	14.00	13.00

On Stamps of September, 1876

462	A7(d)	50pa blue & yel (R)	12.50	15.00
463	A7(d)	2pi blk & redsh brn (R)	12.50	15.00
464	A7(d)	25pi claret & rose (Bk)	22.50	22.50

On Stamps of 1880-84

465	A7(d)	5pa black & ol (R)	12.50	12.50
466	A7(d)	10pa black & grn (R)	15.00	15.00

On Stamps of 1881-82

467	A5(d)	20pa gray (Bl)	14.00	12.50
468	A5(d)	2pi pale salmon (R)	14.00	12.50

On Stamps of 1884-86

469	A7(d)	10pa grn & pale grn (Bk)	15.00	15.00
470	A7(d)	2pi ocher & pale ocher (Bk)	15.00	15.00
471	A7(d)	5pi red brn & pale brn (Bk)	15.00	15.00

On Stamps of 1886

472	A7(d)	5pa blk & pale gray (R)	15	15
a.		Inverted overprint	20.00	20.00
473	A7(d)	2pi orange & bl (Bk)	35	40
a.		Inverted overprint	20.00	20.00
474	A7(d)	5pi grn & pale grn (R)	20.00	20.00
475	A7(d)	25pi bis & pale bis (Bk)	35.00	35.00

On Stamp of 1888

476	A7(d)	5pi dk brn & gray (Bk)	20.00	20.00

On Stamps of 1892-98

477	A11(d)	20pa violet brn (R)	1.25	1.25
478	A13(d)	2pi brown org (R)	1.25	1.25
a.		Tête bêche pair	13.50	13.50

On Stamps of 1901

479	A16(d)	5pa bister (R)	50	75
a.		Inverted overprint	20.00	20.00
480	A16(d)	20pa magenta (Bk)	15	25
a.		Inverted overprint	25.00	25.00
481	A16(d)	1pi violet blue (R)	40	65
a.		Inverted overprint	20.00	20.00
482	A16(d)	2pi gray blue (R)	1.00	80
483	A16(d)	5pi ocher (R)	25.00	20.00

484	A16(e)	10pi on 50pi yel (R)	25.00	20.00
485	A16(d)	25pi dark green (R)	17.50	15.00
486	A17(d)	5pa purple (Bk)	17.50	17.50
487	A17(d)	10pa green (R)	50	65
488	A17(d)	20pa carmine (Bk)	20	15
a.		Inverted overprint	20.00	20.00
489	A17(d)	1pi blue (R)	20	15
490	A17(d)	2pi orange (R)	65	65
a.		Inverted overprint	20.00	20.00
491	A17(d)	5pi lilac rose (R)	25.00	20.00
492	A17(e)	10pi on 50pi yel brn (R)	30.00	30.00
493	A17(d)	25pi brown (R)	65	65

On Stamps of 1905

494	A18(d)	5pa ocher (R)	15	15
a.		Inverted overprint	20.00	20.00
495	A18(d)	10pa dull green (R)	25.00	27.50
496	A18(d)	20pa carmine (Bk)	15	15
a.		Double ovpt., one invtd.	20.00	20.00
b.		Inverted overprint	20.00	20.00
497	A18(d)	1pi blue (R)	15	15
a.		Inverted overprint	20.00	20.00
498	A18(d)	2pi slate (R)	40	35
499	A18(d)	2½pi red violet (Bk)	55	65
a.		Inverted overprint	20.00	20.00
500	A18(d)	5pi brown (R)	20.00	20.00
501	A18(d)	10pi orange brn (R)	25.00	35.00
502	A18(e)	10pi on 50pi dp vio (R)	25.00	30.00
503	A18(d)	25pi olive grn (R)	22.50	30.00

On Nos. 128-131

504	A18(d)	10pa dull green (R)	15	15
a.		Inverted overprint	20.00	20.00
505	A18(d)	20pa carmine (Bk)	15	15
a.		Double ovpt., one invtd.	20.00	20.00
b.		Inverted overprint	20.00	20.00
506	A18(d)	1pi brt blue (Bk)	35	18
a.		Inverted overprint	20.00	20.00
507	A18(d)	1pi brt blue (R)	25	75
a.		Inverted overprint	20.00	20.00
508	A18(d)	2pi slate (Bk)	25.00	25.00
		Nos. 494-508 (15)	144.80	170.18

On Stamps of 1908

509	A19(d)	5pa ocher (R)	60	1.00
510	A19(d)	10pa blue green (R)	25	20
510A	A19(d)	1pi brt blue (R)	250.00	250.00
511	A19(d)	2pi blue black (R)	22.50	25.00
512	A19(d)	2½pi violet brn (Bk)	60	1.00
512A	A19(d)	10pi red (R)	250.00	250.00
513	A19(e)	10pi on 50pi red brn (R)	25.00	35.00
514	A19(d)	25pi dark green (R)	25.00	35.00

With Additional Overprint ب

514A	A19(d)	10pa blue green (Bk)	50.00	50.00
515	A19(d)	1pi brt blue (Bk)	35.00	50.00
516	A19(d)	2pi blue black (R)	65	1.00
516A	A19(d)	2pi blue black (Bk)	30.00	40.00

On Stamps of 1908-09

517	A20(d)	5pa ocher (R)	50	1.00
518	A21(d)	5pa ocher (R)	25	20
a.		Double overprint	20.00	20.00
b.		Dbl. ovpt., one inverted	20.00	20.00
519	A21(d)	10pa blue green (R)	25	20
520	A21(d)	20pa carmine rose (Bk)	25	20
a.		Double overprint	20.00	20.00
521	A21(d)	1pi ultra (R)	25	15
a.		1p bright blue (R)	30.00	30.00
522	A21(d)	2pi blue black (R)	75	1.00
523	A21(d)	2½pi dk brown (Bk)	35.00	35.00
524	A21(d)	5pi dk violet (R)	35.00	35.00
525	A21(d)	10pi dull red (R)	27.50	27.50

With Additional Overprint ت

525A	A21(d)	10pa blue green (Bk)	125.00	125.00
526	A21(d)	1pi ultra (Bk)	30.00	30.00
527	A21(d)	1pi ultra (R)	20	20
a.		1pi bright blue (R)	30.00	30.00
528	A21(d)	2pi blue blk (Bk)	17.50	17.50

On Stamps of 1913

529	A22(d)	5pa ocher (R)	50	50
530	A22(d)	10pa blue grn (R)	25.00	20.00
531	A22(d)	20pa carmine rose (Bk)	25	20
532	A22(d)	1pi ultra (R)	35	35
533	A22(d)	2pi indigo (R)	75	25
534	A22(d)	5pi dull violet (R)	30.00	30.00
535	A22(d)	10pi dull red (Bk)	35.00	35.00

With Additional Overprint ب

536	A22(d)	10pa blue green (Bk)	20	20
a.		Inverted overprint	20.00	20.00

537	A22(d)	1pi ultra (Bk)	75	75
a.		Inverted overprint	20.00	20.00
538	A22(d)	2pi indigo (Bk)	30.00	25.00

On Commemorative Stamps of 1913

539	A23(d)	10pa green (R)	1.00	1.00
a.		Inverted overprint	20.00	20.00
540	A23(d)	40pa blue (R)	1.00	1.00
a.		Inverted overprint	20.00	20.00

On No. 277, with Addition of New Value

541	A31	60pa on 1pi on 1 1/2pi (Bk)	2.00	1.50
a.		"1330" omitted	25.00	25.00

On Stamps of 1916-18

541B	A51(f)	25pi car, straw	3.50	50
541C	A52(g)	50pi carmine	10.00	5.00
541D	A52(g)	50pi indigo	12.50	10.00
541E	A52(g)	50pi green, straw	12.50	10.00

Ovptd. on Eastern Rumelia No. 12

542	A4(d)	20pa blk & rose (Bl)	12.50	12.50

Ovptd. in Black on Eastern Rumelia #15-17

543	A4(d)	5pa lilac & pale lilac	12.50	12.50
544	A4(d)	10pa green & pale green	12.50	12.50
545	A4(d)	20pa carmine & pale rose	12.50	12.50

Some experts question the status of Nos. 510A, 512A and 525A.

See Nos. J71-J86, P153-P172.

Soldiers in Trench — A52a

Surcharged ❂

1917

545A	A52a	5pa on 1pi red	15	15

It is stated that No. 545A was never issued without surcharge.

See Nos. 548f, 545A, 602.

Turkish Artillery — A53

1917   Typo.   Perf. 11 1/2, 12 1/2

546	A53	2pa Prussian blue	50.00	

In type A42 the Turkish inscription at the top is in one group, in type A53 it is in two groups. It is stated that No. 546 was never placed in use. Copies were distributed through the Universal Postal Union at Bern.

For surcharges see Nos. 547-548, Turkey in Asia 69-70.

Surcharged

(Arabic surcharge text)

Surcharged

5 Plastres (with Arabic surcharge text)

547	A53	5pi on 2pa Prus bl	40	15
a.		Inverted surcharge	9.00	9.00
b.		Turkish "5" omitted at lower left		

1918

548	A53	5pi on 2pa Prus blue	50	20
g.		Inverted surcharge	10.00	10.00

Top line of surcharge on Nos. 547-548 reads "Ottoman Posts."

For surcharge see Thrace No. N79.

No. 545A Surcharged

1918

548A	A52a	2pa on 5pa on 1pi red	15	15
b.		Double surcharge	10.00	10.00
c.		Inverted surcharge	10.00	10.00
d.		Double surcharge inverted	10.00	10.00
e.		Dbl. surch. one inverted	10.00	10.00
f.		In pair with No. 545A	17.50	17.50

Enver Pasha and Kaiser Wilhelm II on Battlefield A54

St. Sophia and Obelisk of the Hippodrome A55

1918   Typo.   Perf. 12, 12 1/2

549	A54	5pa brown red	75.00
550	A55	10pa gray green	75.00

The stamps, of which very few saw postal use, were converted into paper money by pasting on thick yellow paper and reperforating.

Values are for copies with original gum. Copies removed from the yellow paper are worth $7.50 each.

Armistice Issue

Overprinted in Black or Red

(Arabic overprint text)

1919, Nov. 30

On Stamps of 1913

552	A34	2 1/2pi org & ol grn	35.00	25.00
553	A38	50pi carmine	40.00	40.00

On Stamps of 1916-18

554	A46	1pi dull violet (R)	50	55
555	A47	50pa ultra (R)	35	35
556	A48	2pi org brn & ind	20	20
557	A49	5pi pale bl & blk (R)	20	15
558	A50	10pi dark green (R)	1.00	1.25
559	A51	25pi carmine, straw	1.00	1.25
560	A52	50pi grn, straw (R)	1.00	1.00

Fountain in Desert near Sinai — A56

Sentry at Beersheba — A57

Turkish Troops at Sinai — A58

Typo.

562	A56	20pa claret	20	15
563	A57	1pi blue (R)	40.00	40.00
564	A58	25pi slate blue (R)	40.00	40.00
		Nos. 552-564 (12)	159.45	149.90

The overprint reads: "Souvenir of the Armistice, 30th October 1334." Nos. 562 to 564 are not known to have been regularly issued without overprint.

See No. J87. For overprints and surcharges see Nos. 576, 579, 582, 583-584, 586, Turkey in Asia 71, Thrace N83.

Stamps of 1911-19 Overprinted in Turkish "Accession to the Throne of His Majesty, 3rd July 1334-1918," the Tughra of Sultan Mohammed VI and sometimes Ornaments and New Values

Dome of the Rock, Jerusalem A59

1919

565	A42	2pa violet	15	25
566	A43	5pa orange	15	15
567	A21	5pa on 2pa ol grn	15	15
a.		Inverted surcharge	10.00	10.00
568	A22	10pa on 2pa ol grn	15	15
569	A44	10pa green	25	50
a.		Inverted overprint	25.00	25.00
570	A45	20pa deep rose	20	15
a.		Inverted overprint	12.00	12.00
571	A46	1pi dull violet	20	15
572	A47	60pa on 50pa ultra	35	35
573	A48	60pa on 2pa orn & ind	15	15
574	A48	2pi orange brn & ind	20	15
574A	A34	2 1/2pi orange & ol grn	15.00	12.50
575	A49	5pi pale blue & blk	15	15
576	A56	20pa on 20pa claret	20	15
577	A50	10pi dark brown	60	75
578	A51	25pi carmine, straw	1.00	1.00
579	A57	35pi on 1pi blue	75	35
579A	A52	50pi carmine	20.00	20.00
580	A52	50pi green, straw	3.25	3.50
581	A59	100pi on 10pa green	3.25	3.25
582	A58	250pi on 25pi slate bl	3.25	3.25
		Nos. 565-582 (20)	49.40	47.15

See Nos. J88-J91.

For overprint and surcharge see Nos. 585, Thrace N82.

Surcharged with Ornaments, New Values and   1919-1335

Perf. 11 1/2, 12 1/2

583	A56	20pa claret	20	20
584	A57	1pi deep blue	20	15
585	A59	60pa on 10pa green	20	15
586	A58	25pi slate blue	2.50	2.50
a.		Inverted overprint	100.00	

#576, 579, 581, 582, 583-586 were prepared in anticipation of the invasion and conquest of Egypt by the Turks. They were not issued at that time but subsequently received various overprints in commemoration of Sultan Mehmet Sadi's accession to the throne (#565-582) and of the 1st anniv. of this event (#583-586).

For surcharge see Thrace No. N83.

Designs of 1913 Modified

1920		Litho.	Perf. 11, 12	
590	A26	5pa brown orange	15	15

			Engr.	
591	A28	10pa green	20	25
592	A23	20pa rose	15	15
593	A30	1pi blue green	45	15
594	A32	3pi blue	15	15
595	A34	5pi gray	3.50	25
596	A36	10pi gray violet	40	15
597	A37	25pi dull violet	65	65
598	A38	50pi brown	1.50	1.50
		Nos. 590-598 (9)	7.15	
		Set value		3.00

On most stamps of this issue the designs have been modified by removing the small Turkish word at right of the tughra of the Sultan. In the 3pi and 5pi the values have been altered, while for the 25pi the color has been changed.

For surcharges see Thrace Nos. N77, N78, N84.

30 PARAS		PARAS 60

Black Surcharge

1921-22

600	SP1	30pa on 10pa red vio	15	15
a.		Double surcharge	37.50	37.50
b.		Imperf.		
601	A28	60pa on 10pa green	20	15
a.		Double surcharge	22.50	22.50
602	A52a	4 1/2pi on 1pi red	40	25
a.		Inverted surcharge	20.00	20.00
603	A32	7 1/2pi on 3pi blue	3.50	30
604	A32	7 1/2pi on 3pi bl (R) ('22)	3.50	50
a.		Double surcharge	30.00	30.00
		Nos. 600-604 (5)	7.75	
		Set value		1.10

Issues of the Republic

Crescent and Star — A64

TWO PIASTERS:
Type I - "2" measures 3 1/4x1 3/4mm
Type II - "2" measures 2 3/4x1 1/2mm

FIVE PIASTERS:
Type I - "5" measures 3 1/2x2 1/4mm
Type II - "5" measures 3x1 3/4mm

Perf. 11, 12, 13 1/2, 13 1/2x12

1923-25			Litho.	
605	A64	10pa gray black	15	15
606	A64	20pa citron	20	15
607	A64	1pi deep violet	25	15
a.		Slanting numeral in lower left corner	48	25
608	A64	1 1/2pi emerald	15	15
609	A64	2pi bluish grn (I)	80	15
a.		2pi deep green (II)	4.00	15
610	A64	3pi yellow brown	1.00	20
611	A64	3 3/4pi lilac brown	1.00	20
612	A64	4 1/2pi carmine	1.25	20
613	A64	5pi purple (I)	1.75	15
a.		5pi violet (II)	7.50	25
614	A64	7 1/2pi blue	1.00	15
615	A64	10pi slate	2.25	15
a.		10pi blue	7.50	20
616	A64	11 1/4pi dull rose	75	20
617	A64	15pi brown	3.50	25
618	A64	18 3/4pi myrtle green	1.75	20
619	A64	22 1/2pi orange	2.00	25
620	A64	25pi black brown	6.00	20
621	A64	50pi gray	17.50	35
622	A64	100pi dark violet	35.00	45
624	A64	500pi deep green	175.00	75.00
		Cut cancellation		1.60
		Nos. 605-624 (19)	251.30	78.75

#605-610, 612-617 exist imperf. & part perf.

Bridge of Sakarya and Mustafa Kemal — A65

1924, Jan. 1   Perf. 12

625	A65	1 1/2pi emerald	20	20
626	A65	3pi purple	20	20
627	A65	4 1/2pi pale rose	80	80
628	A65	5pi yellow brown	20	20

629	A65	7½pi deep blue	25	25
630	A65	50pi orange	6.50	6.50
631	A65	100pi brown violet	16.50	16.50
632	A65	200pi olive brown	30.00	30.00
		Nos. 625-632 (8)	54.65	54.65

Signing of Treaty of Peace at Lausanne.

The Legendary Blacksmith and his Gray Wolf — A66

Sakarya Gorge — A67

Fortress of Ankara — A68

Mustafa Kemal Pasha — A69

1926 Engr.

634	A66	10pa slate	15	15
635	A66	20pa orange	15	15
636	A66	1g brt rose	15	15
637	A67	2g green	15	15
638	A67	2½g gray black	15	15
639	A67	3g copper red	20	15
640	A68	5g lilac gray	35	15
641	A68	6g red	50	15
642	A68	10g deep blue	45	15
643	A68	15g deep orange	2.00	15
644	A69	25g dk green & blk	3.50	15
645	A69	50g carmine & blk	5.25	15
646	A69	100g olive grn & blk	9.00	50
647	A69	200g brown & blk	22.50	1.00
		Nos. 634-647 (14)	44.50	
		Set value		2.00

Stamps of 1926 Overprinted in Black, Silver or Gold

اط.ا.ك ١١٢٧

1927, Sept. 9

648	A66	1g brt rose	15	15
649	A67	2g green	15	15
650	A67	2½g gray black	20	15
651	A67	3g copper red	30	16
652	A68	5g lilac gray	50	22
653	A68	6g red	20	15
654	A68	10g deep blue	1.90	65
655	A68	15g deep orange	1.90	65
656	A69	25g dk green & blk (S)	5.00	3.00
657	A69	50g carmine & blk (S)	10.00	5.00
658	A69	100g ol grn & blk (G)	28.00	22.50
		Nos. 648-658 (11)	48.30	32.78

Agricultural and industrial exhibition at Izmir, Sept. 9-20, 1927.

The overprint reads: "1927" and the initials of "Izmir Dokuz Eylul Sergisi" (Izmir Exhibition, September 9).

Second Izmir Exhibition Issue
Nos. 634-647 Overprinted in Red or Black

On A66-A68   On A69

1928, Sept. 9

659	A66	10pa slate (R)	15	15
660	A66	20pa orange	15	15
661	A66	1g brt rose	15	15
662	A67	2g green (R)	15	15
663	A67	2½g gray blk (R)	35	15
664	A67	3g copper red	25	15
665	A68	5g lilac gray (R)	55	42
666	A68	6g red	35	15
667	A68	10g deep blue	70	25
668	A68	15g deep orange	1.25	32
669	A69	25g dk grn & blk (R)	5.00	2.00

670	A69	50g car & blk	12.00	4.50
671	A69	100g ol grn & blk (R)	25.00	12.00
672	A69	200g brown & blk (R)	37.50	18.00
		Nos. 659-672 (14)	83.55	38.54

The overprint reads "Izmir, September 9, 1928."

Nos. 636, 652, 654
Surcharged in Black
(#673) or Red (#674-675)

2½ kuruşlur

1929

673	A66	20pa on 1g brt rose	25	15
a.		Inverted surcharge	3.50	3.50
674	A68	2½k on 5g lilac gray	42	15
a.		Inverted surcharge	7.50	7.50
675	A68	6k on 10g deep blue	5.50	25
		Set value		40

Railroad Bridge over Kizil Irmak — A70

A71

A72

A73

Latin Inscriptions
Without umlaut over first "U" of
"CUMHURIYETI"

1929 Engr.

676	A70	2k gray black	48	15
677	A70	2½k green	48	15
678	A70	3k violet brown	48	15
679	A71	6k dark violet	6.50	15
680	A72	12½k deep blue	10.00	55
681	A73	50k carmine & blk	17.50	40
		Nos. 676-681 (6)	35.44	
		Set value		1.10

See Nos. 682-691, 694-695, 697, 699. For surcharges & overprints see #705-714, 716-717, 719, 721, 727, 765-766, 770-771, 777, C2, C7.

Sakarya Gorge — A74

Mustafa Kemal Pasha — A75

With umlaut over first "U" of
"CUMHURIYETI"

1930

682	A71	10pa green	15	15
683	A70	20pa gray violet	15	15
684	A70	1k olive green	18	15
685	A71	1½k olive black	15	15
686	A70	2k dull violet	1.40	15
687	A70	2½k deep green	22	15
688	A70	3k brown orange	2.25	15
689	A71	4k deep rose	3.25	15
690	A72	5k rose lake	2.25	15
691	A71	6k indigo	2.50	15
692	A74	7½k red brown	18	15
694	A72	12½k deep ultra	52	15
695	A72	15k deep orange	55	15
696	A74	17½k dark gray	60	15
697	A72	20k black brown	15	30
698	A74	25k olive brown	1.10	15
699	A72	30k yellow brown	1.75	15
700	A74	40k red violet	1.10	15
701	A74	50k red & black	1.65	15
702	A75	100k olive grn & blk	3.25	15
703	A75	200k dk green & blk	3.75	45
704	A75	500k chocolate & blk	17.00	2.25
		Nos. 682-704 (22)	44.10	
		Set value		4.10

For surcharges and overprints see Nos. 715, 718, 720, 722-726, 767-769, 772-773, 775-776, 778-780, 823-828, 848-850, C1, C3-C6, C8-C11.

Nos. 682-704 Surcharged in Red or Black:

Sivas
D. Y.
30 ag. 930
1 K.
a

D. Y. Sivas
30 ag. 930
10 P.
b

Sivas

c

D.   Y.
30 ag. 930
40 K.

1930, Aug. 30

705	A71(a)	10pa on 10pa (R)	15	15
706	A70(b)	10pa on 20pa	15	15
707	A70(b)	20pa on 1ku	15	15
708	A71(a)	1k on 1½k (R)	15	15
709	A70(b)	1½k on 2k	20	15
710	A70(b)	2k on 2½k (R)	38	15
711	A70(b)	2½k on 3k	38	15
712	A71(a)	3k on 4k	50	15
713	A72(a)	4k on 5k	1.00	20
714	A71(a)	5k on 6k (R)	30	20
715	A74(a)	6k on 7½k	50	15
716	A72(a)	7½k on 12½k (R)	60	15
717	A72(a)	12½k on 15k	1.50	20
718	A74(a)	15k on 17½k (R)	1.50	50
719	A72(b)	17½k on 20k (R)	1.90	50
720	A74(b)	20k on 25k (R)	1.90	50
721	A72(b)	25k on 30k	1.90	50
722	A74(b)	30k on 40k	2.50	60
723	A75(c)	40k on 50k	2.50	50
724	A75(c)	50k on 100k (R)	25.00	8.00
725	A75(c)	100k on 200k (R)	28.00	12.00
726	A75(c)	250k on 500k (R)	30.00	8.00
		Nos. 705-726 (22)	101.16	33.20

Inauguration of the railroad between Ankara and Sivas.

There are numerous varieties in these settings as: "309," "390," "930" inverted, no period after "D," no period after "Y" and raised period before "Y."

No. 685 Surcharged in Red

1
Kuruş

1931, Apr. 1

727	A71	1k on 1½k olive blk	60	15

Olive Tree with Roots Extending to All Balkan Capitals — A76

1931, Oct. 20 Engr. Perf. 12

728	A76	2½k dark green	15	15
729	A76	4k carmine	15	15
730	A76	6k steel blue	18	15
731	A76	7½k dull red	18	15
732	A76	12k deep orange	25	15
733	A76	12½k dark blue	40	15
734	A76	30k dark violet	90	15
735	A76	50k dark brown	1.90	24
736	A76	100k brown violet	4.00	1.00
		Nos. 728-736 (9)	8.11	
		Set value		1.60

Second Balkan Conference.

A77

A78

Mustafa Kemal Pasha
(Kemal Atatürk) — A79

1931-42 Typo. Perf. 11½, 12

737	A77	10pa blue green	15	15
738	A77	20pa deep orange	15	15
739	A77	30pa brt violet ('38)	15	15
740	A78	1k dk slate green	15	15
740A	A77	1½k magenta ('42)	50	15
741	A78	2k dark violet	15	15
741A	A78	2k yellow green ('40)	15	15
742	A77	2½k green	15	15
743	A78	3k brown orange ('38)	15	15
744	A78	4k slate	15	15
745	A78	5k rose red	15	15
745A	A78	5k brown blk ('40)	35	15
746	A78	6k deep blue	22	15
746A	A78	6k rose ('40)	20	15
747	A77	7½k deep rose ('32)	15	15
747A	A78	8k brt blue ('38)	20	15
b.		8k dark blue ('36)	20	15
748	A77	10k black brn ('32)	3.00	15
748A	A77	10k deep blue ('40)	1.90	15
749	A77	12k bister ('32)	38	15
750	A79	12½k indigo ('32)	22	15
751	A77	15k orange yel ('32)	38	15
752	A77	20k olive grn ('32)	38	15
753	A77	25k Prus blue ('32)	38	15
754	A77	30k magenta ('32)	7.50	15
755	A79	100k maroon ('32)	10.00	15
756	A79	200k purple ('32)	12.50	15
757	A79	250k chocolate ('32)	35.00	38
		Nos. 737-757 (27)	74.76	
		Set value		1.75

See Nos. 1015-1033, 1117B-1126. For overprints see Nos. 811-816.

Symbolizing 10th Anniversary of Republic — A80

President Atatürk — A81

1933, Oct. 29 Perf. 10

758	A80	1½k blue green	50	16
759	A80	2k olive brown	50	20
760	A81	3k red brown	50	16
761	A81	6k deep blue	50	25
762	A80	12½k dark blue	1.50	1.35
763	A80	25k dark brown	3.00	2.50
764	A81	50k orange brown	6.50	6.00
		Nos. 758-764 (7)	13.00	10.62

10th year of the Turkish Republic. The stamps were in use for three days only.

Nos. 682, 685, 692, 694, 696-698, 702
Overprinted or Surcharged in Red:

İzmir
9 Eylûl 934
Sergisi

İzmir
9 Eylûl 934
Sergisi
2 Kurus

1934, Aug. 26 Perf. 12

765	A71	10pa green	16	15
766	A71	1k on 1½k	24	15
767	A74	2k on 25k	40	15
768	A74	5k on 7½k	1.10	28
769	A74	6k on 17½k	1.10	38
770	A72	12½k deep ultra	3.50	15
771	A72	15k on 20k	32.50	14.00
772	A74	20k on 25k	27.50	11.25
773	A75	50k on 100k	27.50	11.25
		Nos. 765-773 (9)	93.75	38.36

Izmir Fair, 1934.

Nos. 696, 698, 701-704 Surcharged in Black

20/7/1936
6   6

1936, Oct. 26

775 A74	4k on 17½k	80	38
776 A74	5k on 25k	80	38
777 A73	6k on 50k	80	38
778 A75	10k on 100k	1.25	50
779 A75	20k on 200k	4.50	1.40
780 A75	50k on 500k	8.00	2.25
	Nos. 775-780 (6)	16.15	5.29

"1926" in Overprint

775a A74	4k on 17½k	6.50	3.75
776a A74	5k on 25k	7.00	3.75
777a A73	6k on 50k	7.00	3.75
778a A75	10k on 100k	9.00	4.50
779a A75	20k on 200k	20.00	10.00
780a A75	50k on 500k	55.00	27.50

Re-militarization of the Dardanelles.

Hittite Bronze Stag — A82

Thorak's Bust of Kemal Atatürk — A83

1937, Sept. 20   Litho.   Perf. 12

781 A82	3k light violet	65	30
782 A83	6k blue	85	45
783 A82	7½k bright pink	1.65	1.00
784 A83	12½k indigo	3.00	1.50

2nd Turkish Historical Congress, Istanbul, Sept. 20-30.

Arms of Turkey, Greece, Romania and Yugoslavia — A84

1937, Oct. 29   Perf. 11½

785 A84	8k carmine	6.75	3.00
786 A84	12½k dark blue	15.00	3.75

The Balkan Entente.

Street in Izmir A85

Fig Tree — A87

Designs: 30pa, View of Fair Buildings. 3k, Tower, Government Square. 5k, Olive branch. 6k, Woman with grapes. 7½k, Woman picking grapes. 8k, Izmir Harbor through arch. 12k, Statue of President Atatürk. 12½k, President Atatürk.

1938, Aug. 20   Photo.   Perf. 11½
Inscribed: "Izmir Enternasyonal Fuari 1938"

789 A85	10pa dark brown	15	15
790 A85	30pa purple	15	15
791 A87	2½k brt green	48	15
792 A85	3k brown orange	22	15
793 A87	5k olive green	45	15
794 A85	6k brown	1.40	25
795 A87	7½k scarlet	1.40	45
796 A87	8k brown lake	80	30

797 A87	12k rose violet	1.10	65
798 A87	12½k deep blue	2.50	1.40
	Nos. 789-798 (10)	8.65	
	Set value		3.40

Izmir International Fair.

President Atatürk Teaching Reformed Turkish Alphabet A95

1938, Nov. 2

799 A95	2½k brt green	22	15
800 A95	3k orange	22	15
801 A95	6k rose violet	35	15
802 A95	7½k deep rose	35	35
803 A95	8k red brown	55	40
804 A95	12½k brt ultra	1.10	80
	Nos. 799-804 (6)	2.79	2.00

Reform of the Turkish alphabet, 10th anniv.

Army and Air Force A96

Atatürk Driving Tractor — A98

Designs: 3k, View of Kayseri. 7½k, Railway bridge. 8k, Scout buglers. 12½k, President Atatürk.

1938, Oct. 29
Inscribed: "Cumhuriyetin 15 inc yil donumu hatirasi"

805 A96	2½k dark green	20	15
806 A96	3k red brown	25	15
807 A98	6k bister	28	16
808 A96	7½k red	70	25
809 A96	8k rose violet	2.50	1.35
810 A98	12½k deep blue	1.75	80
	Nos. 805-810 (6)	5.68	2.86

15th anniversary of the Republic.

Stamps of 1931-38 Overprinted in Black   **21-11-1938**

1938, Nov. 21   Perf. 11½x12

811 A78	3k brown orange	20	16
812 A78	5k rose red	20	16
813 A78	6k deep blue	20	20
814 A77	7½k deep rose	38	25
815 A78	8k dark blue	45	38
a.	8k bright blue	12.00	10.00
816 A79	12½k indigo	70	65
	Nos. 811-816 (6)	2.13	1.80

President Kemal Atatürk (1881-1938). The date is that of his funeral.

Catalogue values for unused stamps in this section, from this point to the end of the section, are for Never Hinged items.

Turkish and American Flags — A102

Presidents Inönü and F. D. Roosevelt and Map of North America A103

Designs: 3k, 8k, Inonu and Roosevelt. 7½k, 12½k, Kemal Atatürk and Washington.

1939, July 15   Photo.   Perf. 14

817 A102	2½k ol grn, red & bl	24	16
818 A103	3k dk brn & Bl grn	24	16
819 A102	6k purple, red & bl	24	16
820 A103	7½k org ver & bl grn	30	38
821 A103	8k dp claret & bl grn	65	38
822 A103	12½k brt bl & bl grn	1.10	80
	Nos. 817-822 (6)	2.77	2.04

US constitution, 150th anniversary.

Anavatana

Nos. 698, 702-704 Surcharged in Black

Hatayın   Kavuşması

23/7/1939
3   3

1939, July 23   Unwmk.   Perf. 13

823 A74	3k on 25k	15	15
824 A75	6k on 200k	22	15
825 A74	7½k on 25k	32	16
826 A75	12k on 100k	35	20
827 A75	12½k on 200k	55	30
828 A75	17½k on 500k	1.00	60
	Nos. 823-828 (6)	2.59	1.56

Annexation of Hatay.

Railroad Bridge A105

Locomotive A106

Track Through Mountain Pass A107

Design: 12½k, Railroad tunnel, Atma Pass.

1939, Oct. 20   Typo.   Perf. 11½

829 A105	3k lt orange red	2.50	1.00
830 A106	6k chestnut	4.50	2.00
831 A107	7½k rose pink	5.50	2.25
832 A107	12½k dark blue	8.25	3.75

Completion of the Sivas to Erzerum link of the Ankara-Erzerum Railroad.

Atatürk Residence in Ankara — A109

Kemal Atatürk — A110

TÜRKİYE POSTALARI

KEMAL ATATÜRK 1880-1938

A111

Designs: 5k, 6k, 7½k, 8k, 12½k, 17½k, Various portraits of Atatürk, "1880-1938."

1939-40   Photo.

833 A109	2½k brt green	15	15
834 A110	3k dk blue gray	15	15
835 A110	5k chocolate	20	15
836 A110	6k chestnut	20	15
837 A110	7½k rose red	28	20
838 A110	8k gray green	24	20
839 A110	12½k brt blue	42	16
840 A110	17½k brt rose	1.25	80
	Nos. 833-840 (8)	2.89	
	Set value		1.70

Souvenir Sheet

841 A111 100k blue black   30.00 19.00

Death of Kemal Atatürk, first anniversary. Size of No. 841: 90x120mm.
Issue dates: 2½k, 6k, 12½k, Nov. 11, 1939. Others, Jan. 3, 1940.

Namik Kemal A118

Arms of Turkey, Greece, Romania and Yugoslavia A119

1940, Jan. 3

842 A118	6k chestnut	28	15
843 A118	8k dk olive grn	38	18
844 A118	12k brt rose red	1.10	30
845 A118	12½k brt blue	1.25	75

Birth cent. of Namik Kemal, poet and patriot.

1940, Jan. 1   Perf. 11½
Typo.   Unwmk.

846 A119	8k light blue	2.75	45
847 A119	10k deep blue	2.75	38

The Balkan Entente.

Nos. 703-704 Surcharged in Red or Black

IZMIR ENTERNASYONAL FUARI 1940
6 KURUS

1940, Aug. 20   Perf. 12

848 A75	6k on 200k dk grn & blk (R)	38	16
849 A75	10k on 200k dk grn & blk	55	32
850 A75	12k on 500k choc & blk	65	32

13th International Izmir Fair.

Map of Turkey and Census Figures A120

1940, Oct. 1 Typo. Perf. 11½

851	A120	10pa	dark blue green	16 15
852	A120	3k	orange	28 15
853	A120	6k	carmine rose	52 25
854	A120	10k	dark blue	1.40 50

Census of Oct. 20, 1940.

Runner — A121

Pole Vaulter — A122

Hurdler A123

Discus Thrower — A124

1940, Oct. 5

855	A121	3k	olive green	1.00 50
856	A122	6k	rose	3.75 1.65
857	A123	8k	chestnut brown	2.25 70
858	A124	10k	dark blue	3.75 2.00

11th Balkan Olympics.

Mail Carriers on Horseback A125

Postman of 1840 and 1940 — A126

Old Sailing Vessel and Modern Mailboat — A127

Design: 12k, Post Office, Istanbul.

1940, Dec. 31 Typo. Perf. 10

859	A125	3k	gray green	24 15
860	A126	6k	rose	32 16
861	A127	10k	dark blue	1.00 60
862	A127	12k	olive brown	1.00 50

Centenary of the Turkish post.

Harbor Scene A129

Statue of Atatürk — A132

Designs: 3k, 6k, 17½k, Various Izmir Fair buildings. 12k, Girl picking grapes.

1941, Aug. 20 Litho. Perf. 11½
Inscribed: "Izmir Enternasyonal Fuari 1941"

863	A129	30pa	dull green	15 15
864	A129	3k	olive gray	18 15
865	A129	6k	salmon rose	28 15
866	A129	10k	blue	48 15
867	A129	12k	dull brown vio	65 15
868	A129	17½k	dull brown	1.40 38
		Nos. 863-868 (6)		3.14
		Set value		75

Izmir International Fair, 1941.

Tomb of Barbarossa II — A135

Barbarossa II (Khair ed-Din) — A137

Barbarossa's Fleet in Battle A136

1941

869	A135	20pa	dark violet	15 15
870	A136	3k	light blue	15 15
871	A136	6k	rose red	25 16
872	A136	10k	deep ultra	42 15
873	A136	12k	dull brn & bis	1.10 35
874	A137	17½k	multicolored	2.25 1.50
		Nos. 869-874 (6)		4.32 2.46

400th death anniv. of Barbarossa II.

President Inönü
A138   A138a

1942-45 Perf. 11½x11, 11

875	A138	0.25k	yellow bis	15 15
876	A138	0.50k	lt yellow grn	15 15
877	A138	1k	gray green	15 15
877A	A138	1½k	brt vio ('45)	52 15
878	A138	2k	bluish green	15 15
879	A138	4k	fawn	15 15
880	A138	4½k	slate	15 15
881	A138	5k	light blue	15 15
882	A138	6k	salmon rose	15 15
883	A138	6¾k	ultra	16 15
884	A138	9k	blue violet	11.00 15
885	A138	10k	dark blue	15 15
886	A138	13½k	brt pink	15 15
887	A138	16k	Prus green	28 15
888	A138	17½k	rose lake	28 15
889	A138	20k	brown violet	60 15
890	A138	27½k	orange	35 15
891	A138	37k	buff	38 15
892	A138	50k	purple	1.00 15
893	A138	100k	olive bister	2.75 45
894	A138a	200k	brown	9.50 65
		Nos. 875-894 (21)		28.32
		Set value		2.00

Ankara — A139   Antioch — A141

Designs: 0.50k, Mohair goats. 1½k, Ankara Dam. 2k, Oranges. 4k, Merino sheep. 4½k, Train. 5k, Tile decorating. 6k, Atatürk statue, Ankara. 6¾k, 10k, President Ismet Inonu. 13½k, Grand National Assembly. 16k, Arnavutkoy, Istanbul. 17½k, Republic monument, Istanbul. 20k, Safety monument, Ankara. 27½k, Post Office, Istanbul. 37k, Monument at Afyon. 50k, "People's House," Ankara. 100k, Atatürk and Inonu. 200k, President Inonu.

1943, Apr. 1 Perf. 11

896	A139	0.25k	citron	15 15
897	A139	0.50k	brt green	30 15
898	A141	1k	yellow olive	15 15
899	A141	1½k	deep violet	15 15
900	A139	2k	brt blue green	35 15
901	A139	4k	copper red	65 15
902	A139	4½k	black	55 15
903	A141	5k	sapphire	40 15
904	A139	6k	carmine rose	15 15
905	A139	6¾k	brt ultra	15 15
906	A139	10k	dark blue	15 15
907	A141	13½k	brt red violet	20 15
908	A141	16k	myrtle green	1.00 15
909	A139	17½k	brown orange	40 15
910	A139	20k	sepia	50 15
911	A139	27½k	dk orange	1.00 22
912	A139	37k	lt yellow brn	50 15
913	A141	50k	purple	2.50 15
914	A139	100k	dk olive grn	4.25 20
915	A139	200k	dark brown	6.00 30
a.		Souvenir sheet		22.50 8.75
		Nos. 896-915 (20)		19.50
		Set value		1.75

No. 915a contains one stamp similar to No. 915, perf. 13½ and printed in sepia. Issued Apr. 20. For surcharge see No. 928.

Girl with Grapes — A158

Entrance to Izmir Fair — A159

Fair Building A160

1943, Aug. 20 Litho. Perf. 11½

916	A158	4½k	dull olive	25 15
917	A159	6k	carmine rose	22 15
918	A160	6¾k	blue	25 15
919	A159	10k	dark blue	28 15
920	A158	13½k	sepia	90 20
921	A160	27½k	dull gray	90 30
		Nos. 916-921 (6)		2.80
		Set value		85

Izmir International Fair.

Soccer Team on Parade A161

Turkish Flag and Soldier — A162

Designs: 6¾k, Bridge. 10k, Hospital. 13½k, View of Ankara. 27½k, President Inonu.

Perf. 11x11½, 11½x11
1943, Oct. 29
Inscribed: "Cumhuriyetin 20 nci Yildonomu Hatirasi"

922	A161	4½k	lt olive grn	65 30
923	A162	6k	rose red	18 15
924	A161	6¾k	ultra	15 15
925	A161	10k	violet blue	18 15
926	A161	13½k	olive	30 16
927	A162	27½k	lt brown	60 42
		Nos. 922-927 (6)		2.06
		Set value		1.10

20th anniversary of Republic. Nos. 922-927 exist imperf.

No. 905 Surcharged with New Value in Red

1945 Perf. 11

928	A139	4½k on 6¾k brt ultra		24 15

Recording Census Data — A167

President Ismet Inönü — A169

1945, Oct. 21 Litho. Perf. 11½

929	A167	4½k	olive black	45 22
930	A167	9k	violet	45 22
931	A167	10k	violet blue	45 22
932	A167	18k	dark red	90 50

Souvenir Sheet
Imperf

933	A167	1 1 chocolate		14.00 5.50

Census of 1945.

Perf. 11½ to 12½
1946, Apr. 1 Unwmk.

934	A169	0.25k	brown red	15 15
935	A169	1k	dk slate grn	15 15
936	A169	1½k	plum	15 15
937	A169	9k	purple	35 15
938	A169	10k	deep blue	1.10 15
939	A169	50k	chocolate	3.25 15
		Nos. 934-939 (6)		5.15
		Set value		32

U.S.S. Missouri A170

1946, Apr. 5 Perf. 11½

940	A170	9k	dark purple	18 15
941	A170	10k	dk chalky blue	18 15
942	A170	27½k	olive green	75 30
a.		Imperf., pair		15.00
		Set value		46

Visit of the U.S.S. Missouri to Istanbul, Apr. 5.

Sower
A171

Dove and Flag-
Decorated
Banderol
A172

1946, June 16   **Perf. 11½ to 12½**
943 A171	9k violet	15	15
944 A171	10k dark blue	15	15
945 A171	18k olive green	22	15
946 A171	27½k red orange	60	22
	Set value		42

Passing of legislation to distribute state lands to poor farmers.

1947, Aug. 20   **Photo.**   **Perf. 12**
947 A172	15k violet & dk bl	15	15
948 A172	20k blue & dk blue	15	15
949 A172	30k brown & gray blk	18	15
950 A172	1 l ol grn & dk grn	80	45
	Set value		62

Izmir International Fair.

Victory
Monument,
Afyon
Karahisar
A173

Ismet İnönü as
General
A174

Kemal Atatürk as
General — A175

1947, Aug. 30
951 A173	10k dk brn & pale brn	15	15
952 A174	15k brt violet & gray	15	15
953 A175	20k dp blue & gray	15	15
954 A173	30k grnsh blk & gray	18	15
955 A174	60k ol gray & pale brn	35	15
956 A175	1 l dk green & gray	1.10	30
	Nos. 951-956 (6)	2.08	
	Set value		60

25th anniv. of the Battle of Dumlupinar, Aug. 30, 1922.

Grapes and
Istanbul
Skyline
A176

1947, Sept. 22
957 A176	15k rose violet	15	15
958 A176	20k deep blue	18	15
959 A176	60k dark brown	65	40

International Vintners' Congress, Istanbul.

Approaching Train,
Istanbul Skyline and
Sirkeci
Terminus — A177

1947, Oct. 9
960 A177	15k rose violet	38	15
961 A177	20k brt blue	55	15
962 A177	60k olive green	1.00	65

International Railroad Congress, Istanbul.

President Ismet İnönü
A178   A179

1948   **Unwmk.**   **Engr.**   **Perf. 12, 14**
963 A178	0.25k dark red	15	15
964 A178	1k olive black	15	15
965 A178	2k brt rose lilac	15	15
966 A178	3k red orange	15	15
967 A178	4k dark green	15	15
968 A178	5k blue	15	15
969 A178	10k chocolate	15	15
970 A178	12k deep red	15	15
971 A178	15k violet	16	15
972 A178	20k deep blue	28	15
973 A178	30k brown	70	15
974 A178	60k black	1.25	15
975 A179	1 l olive green	3.00	35
976 A179	2 l dark brown	21.00	1.10
977 A179	5 l deep plum	14.00	2.25
	Nos. 963-977 (15)	41.59	
	Set value		4.25

For overprints see Nos. O13-O42.

President
Ismet İnönü
and Lausanne
Conference
A180

Conference
Building
A180a

1948, July 23   **Photo.**   **Perf. 11½**
978 A180	15k rose lilac	15	15
979 A180a	20k blue	20	15
980 A180a	40k gray green	30	15
981 A180	1 l brown	1.10	38
	Set value		62

25th anniversary of Lausanne Treaty.

Statue of Kemal Atatürk,
Ankara — A181

1948, Oct. 29
982 A181	15k violet	15	15
983 A181	20k blue	15	15
984 A181	40k gray green	25	18
985 A181	1 l brown	1.10	65
	Set value		92

25th anniv. of the proclamation of the republic.

A182   A183

A184

Wrestlers
A185

1949, June 3
986 A182	15k rose lilac	1.25	1.00
987 A183	20k blue	2.50	1.40
988 A184	30k brown	2.50	1.65
989 A185	60k green	3.50	2.75

5th European Wrestling Championships, Istanbul, June 3-5, 1949.

Ancient
Galley
A186

Galleon
Mahmudiye
A187

Monument to
Khizr Barbarossa
A188

Designs: 15k, Cruiser Hamidiye. 20k, Submarine Sakarya. 30k, Cruiser Yavuz.

1949, July 1
990 A186	5k violet	22	15
991 A187	10k brown	26	15
992 A186	15k lilac rose	30	15
993 A186	20k gray blue	35	15
994 A186	30k gray	65	28
995 A188	40k olive gray	95	55
	Nos. 990-995 (6)	2.73	
	Set value		1.15

Fleet Day, July 1, 1949.

A189

UPU
Monument,
Bern — A190

   Perf. 11½
1949, Oct. 9   **Unwmk.**   **Photo.**
996 A189	15k violet	15	15
997 A189	20k blue	20	20
998 A190	30k dull rose	30	30
999 A190	40k green	65	65

UPU, 75th anniversary.

Istanbul Fair
Building
A191

1949, Oct. 1   **Litho.**   **Perf. 10**
1000 A191	15k brown	15	15
1001 A191	20k blue	20	15
1002 A191	30k olive	65	25
	Set value		42

Istanbul Fair, Oct. 1-31.

Boy and Girl and
Globe — A192

Aged Woman
Casting
Ballot — A193

Kemal
Atatürk and
Map
A194

1950, Aug. 13   **Perf. 11½**
1003 A192	15k purple	15	15
1004 A192	20k deep blue	20	15
	Set value		22

2nd World Youth Council Meeting, 1950. No. 1004 exists imperf. Value $3.

1950, Aug. 30
1005 A193	15k dark brown	15	15
1006 A193	20k dark blue	20	15
1007 A194	30k dk blue & gray	32	15
	Set value		28

Election of May 14, 1950.

Hazel
Nuts — A195

Symbolical of
1950
Census — A196

Designs: 12k, Acorns. 15k, Cotton. 20k, Symbolical of the fair. 30k, Tobacco.

1950, Sept. 9
1008 A195	8k gray grn & buff	20	15
1009 A195	12k magenta	30	15
1010 A195	15k brn blk & lt brn	52	22
1011 A195	20k dk blue & aqua	90	40
1012 A195	30k brn blk & dull org	1.40	65
	Nos. 1008-1012 (5)	3.32	1.57

Izmir International Fair, Aug. 20-Sept. 20.

1950, Oct. 9   **Litho.**   **Perf. 11½**
1013 A196	15k dark brown	16	15
1014 A196	20k violet blue	30	16
	Set value		24

General census of 1950.

Atatürk Types of 1931-42
Perf. 10x11½, 11½x12
1950-51   **Typo.**
1015 A77	10p dull red brn	15	15
1016 A77	10p vermilion ('51)	15	15
1017 A77	20p blue green	15	15
1018 A78	1k olive green	15	15
1019 A78	2k plum	22	15

1020	A78	2k dp yellow ('51)	40	15
1021	A78	3k yellow orange	52	15
1022	A78	3k gray ('51)	30	15
1023	A78	4k green ('51)	30	15
1024	A78	5k blue	25	15
1025	A78	5k plum ('51)	2.00	15
1026	A77	10k brown orange	1.00	15
1027	A77	15k purple	1.20	15
1028	A77	15k brown carmine	11.00	15
1029	A77	20k dark blue	6.50	15
1030	A77	30k pink ('51)	10.50	15
1031	A79	100k red brown ('51)	1.25	20
1032	A79	200k dark brown	6.00	50
1033	A79	200k rose violet ('51)	5.00	65

Nos. 1015-1033 (19)   47.04
Set value   2.00

16th Century Flight of
Hezarfen Ahmet
Celebi — A197

Plane over
Istanbul
A198

Design: 40k, Biplane over Taurus Mountains.

1950, Oct. 17   Litho.   *Perf. 11*

1034	A197	20k dk green & blue	35	20
1035	A197	40k dk brown & blue	55	35
1036	A198	60k purple & blue	90	60

Regional meeting of the ICAO, Istanbul, Oct. 17.

Farabi
A199

1950, Dec. 1   Unwmk.   *Perf. 11½*
Multicolored Center

1037	A199	15k blue	50	22
1038	A199	20k blue violet	1.00	30
1039	A199	60k red brown	2.50	1.00
1040	A199	1 l gold & bl vio	2.25	2.50

Death millenary of Farabi, Arab philosopher.

Mithat Pasha and Security Bank
Building — A200

Design: 20k, Agricultural Bank.

1950, Dec. 21   Photo.

1041	A200	15k rose violet	35	20
1042	A200	20k blue	45	28

3rd Congress of Turkish Cooperatives, Istanbul,
Dec. 25, 1950.

Floating a
Ship — A201

Lighthouse — A202

1951, July 1

1043	A201	15k shown	28	16
1044	A201	20k Steamship	28	16
1045	A201	30k Diver rising	60	40
1046	A202	1 l shown	1.40	80

25th anniv. of the recognition of coastal rights in
Turkish waters to ships under the Turkish flag.

Mosque of
Sultan Ahmed
A203

Henry Carton de
Wiart — A204

Designs: 20k, Dolma Bahce Palace. 60k, Rumeli
Hisari Fortress.

1951, Aug. 31   Photo.   *Perf. 13½*

1047	A203	15k dark green	22	16
1048	A203	20k deep ultra	22	16
1049	A204	30k brown	32	25
1050	A203	60k purple brown	90	70

40th Interparliamentary Conf., Istanbul.

Allegory of
Food and
Agriculture
A205

Designs: 20k, Dam. 30k, United Nations Building. 60k, University, Ankara.

1952, Jan. 3   Unwmk.   *Perf. 14*
Inscribed: "Akdeniz Yetistirme
Merkezi. Ankara 1951."

1051	A205	15k green	50	15
1052	A205	20k blue violet	60	15
1053	A205	30k blue	90	35
1054	A205	60k red	2.25	1.40
a.		Souvenir sheet of 4	45.00	35.00

UN Mediterranean Economic Instruction Center.
No. 1054a contains one each of Nos. 1051-
1054, imperf., with inscriptions in dark blue gray.

Abdulhak Hamid
Tarhan, Poet, Birth
Cent. — A206

1952, Feb. 5   Photo.   *Perf. 13½*

1055	A206	15k dark purple	15	15
1056	A206	20k dark blue	16	15
1057	A206	30k brown	28	15
1058	A206	60k dark olive grn	70	40
		Set value		68

Ruins, Bergama
A207

Tarsus Cataract
A208

Designs: 2k, Ruins, Milas. 3k, Karatay Gate,
Konya. 4k, Kozak plateau. 5k, Urgup. 10k, 12k,
15k, 20k, Kemal Ataturk. 30k, Mosque, Bursa.
40k, Mosque, Istanbul. 75k, Rocks, Urgup. 1 l,
Palace, Istanbul. 2 l, Pavilion, Istanbul. 5 l,
Museum interior, Istanbul.

1952, Mar. 15   *Perf. 13½*

1059	A207	1k brown orange	15	15
1060	A207	2k olive green	15	15
1061	A207	3k rose brown	15	15
1062	A207	4k blue green	15	15
1063	A207	5k brown	15	15
1064	A207	10k dark brown	15	15
1065	A207	12k brt rose car	15	15
1066	A207	15k purple	15	15
1067	A207	20k chalky blue	60	15
1068	A207	30k grnsh gray	28	15
1069	A207	40k slate blue	60	15
1070	A208	50k olive	65	15
1071	A208	75k slate	70	22
1072	A208	1 l deep purple	85	20
1073	A208	2 l brt ultra	1.65	30
1074	A208	5 l sepia	13.00	3.00

Nos. 1059-1074 (16)   19.53
Set value   4.25

Imperfs, value, set $60.
For surcharge & overprint see #1075, 1255.

No. 1059 Surcharged with New Value in
Black

1952, June 1

1075	A207	0.50k on 1k brn org	22	15

Technical
Faculty
Building
A209

1952, Aug. 20   *Perf. 12x12½*

1076	A209	15k violet	25	15
1077	A209	20k blue	35	15
1078	A209	60k brown	1.00	75

8th Intl. Congress of Theoretic and Applied
Mechanics.

Turkish
Soldier — A210

Pigeons
Bandaging
Wounded
Hand — A212

Designs: 20k, Soldier with Turkish flag. 30k, Soldier and child with comic book. 60k, Raising Turkish flag.

1952, Sept. 25   *Perf. 14*

1079	A210	15k Prus blue	24	18
1080	A210	20k deep blue	24	20
1081	A210	30k brown	45	32
1082	A210	60k olive blk & car	90	75

Turkey's participation in the Korean war.

1952, Oct. 29   *Perf. 12½x12*

Design: 20k, Flag, rainbow and ruined homes.

Dated "1877-1952"

1085	A212	15k dk green & red	45	26
1086	A212	20k blue & red	1.00	45

Turkish Red Crescent Society, 75th anniv.

Relief From Panel of
Aziziye
Monument — A213

Aziziye
Monument
A214

Design: 40k, View of Erzerum.

1952, Nov. 9   *Perf. 11*

1087	A213	15k purple	25	16
1088	A214	20k blue	32	25
1089	A214	40k olive gray	55	52

75th anniv. of the Battle of Aziziye at Erzerum.

Rumeli Hisari
Fortress
A215

Troops Entering
Constan-
tinople — A216

Sultan Mohammed
II — A217

Designs: 8k, Soldiers moving cannon. 10k,
Mohammed II riding into sea, and Turkish armada.
12k, Landing of Turkish army. 15k, Ancient wall,
Constantinople. 30k, Mosque of Faith. 40k,
Presenting mace to Patriarch Yenadios. 60k, Map of
Constantinople, c. 1574. 1 l, Tomb of Mohammed
II. 2.50 l, Portrait of Mohammed II.

1953, May 29   Photo.   *Perf. 11½*
Inscribed: "Istanbulun Fethi 1453-
1953"

1090	A215	5k brt blue	15	15
1091	A215	8k gray	15	15
1092	A215	10k blue	15	15
1093	A215	12k rose lilac	15	15
1094	A215	15k brown	20	15
1095	A216	20k vermilion	26	15
1096	A216	30k dull green	65	15
1097	A216	40k violet blue	65	24
1098	A215	60k chocolate	65	35
1099	A215	1 l blue green	1.65	60

Perf. 12

1100	A217	2 l multi	3.75	2.50
1101	A217	2.50 l multi	5.25	3.00
a.		Souvenir sheet	55.00	35.00

Nos. 1090-1101 (12)   13.66   7.74

Conquest of Constantinople by Sultan Mohammed II, 500th anniv.

Ruins of the
Odeon,
Ephesus
A218

Designs: 15k, Church of St. John the Apostle. 20k, Shrine of Virgin Mary, Panaya Kapulu. 40k, Ruins of the Double Church. 60k, Shrine of the Seven Sleepers. 1 l, Restored house of the Virgin Mary.

1953, Aug. 16   Litho.   Perf. 13½
Multicolored Center

1102	A218	12k sage green	15	15
1103	A218	15k lilac	15	15
1104	A218	20k dk slate blue	15	15
1105	A218	40k light green	38	20
1106	A218	60k violet blue	50	38
1107	A218	1 l brown red	1.50	1.35
		Nos. 1102-1107 (6)	2.83	2.38

Pres. Celal Bayar, Mithat Pasha. Herman Schulze-Delitzsch and People's Bank — A219

Design: 20k, Pres. Bayar, Mithat Pasha and University of Ankara.

1953, Sept. 2   Photo.   Perf. 10½

1108	A219	15k orange brown	22	10
1109	A219	20k Prus green	50	40

5th Intl. People's Circuit Congress, Istanbul, Sept.

Combined Harvester A220

Kemal Atatürk — A221

Designs: 15k, Berdan dam. 20k, Military parade. 30k, Diesel train. 35k, Yesilkoy airport.

1953, Oct. 29   Perf. 14

1110	A220	10k olive bister	15	15
1111	A220	15k dark gray	15	15
1112	A220	20k rose red	20	15
1113	A220	30k olive green	40	20
1114	A220	35k dull blue	28	20
1115	A221	55k dull purple	90	60
		Nos. 1110-1115 (6)	2.08	
		Set value		1.25

Turkish Republic, 30th anniv.

Kemal Atatürk and Mausoleum at Ankara A222

1953, Nov. 10

1116	A222	15k gray black	28	25
1117	A222	20k violet brown	60	40

15th death anniv. of Kemal Ataturk.

Type of 1931-42
Without umlaut over first "U" of "CUMHURIYETI"
Perf. 11½x12, 10x11½

1953-56   Typo.   Unwmk.

1117B	A77	20p yellow	15	15
1118	A78	1k brown orange	15	15
1119	A78	2k rose pink ('53)	15	15
1120	A78	3k yellow brn ('53)	15	15
1120A	A78	4k slate ('56)	1.00	15
1121	A78	5k blue	25	20
1121A	A78	8k violet ('56)	15	15
1122	A77	10k dark olive ('53)	15	15

1123	A77	12k brt car rose ('53)	15	15
1124	A77	15k fawn	15	15
1125	A77	20k rose lilac	2.00	15
1126	A77	30k lt blue grn ('54)	75	15
		Set value	4.60	90

Compass and Map — A223

Designs: 20k, Globe, crescent and stars. 40k, Tree symbolical of 14 NATO members.

1954, Apr. 4   Photo.   Perf. 14

1127	A223	15k brown	1.50	1.10
1128	A223	20k violet blue	2.00	1.50
1129	A223	40k dark green	14.00	12.00

NATO, 5th anniv.

Industry, Engineering and Agriculture A224

Justice and Council of Europe Flag — A225

1954, Aug. 8   Litho.   Perf. 10½

1130	A224	10k brown	3.75	2.50
1131	A225	15k dark green	3.50	2.50
1132	A225	20k blue	3.75	2.50
1133	A224	30k brt violet	19.00	15.00

Council of Europe, 5th anniv.

Flag Signals to Plane — A226   Amaury de La Grange and Plane — A227

Design: 45k, Kemal Ataturk and air fleet.

1954, Sept. 20   Perf. 12½

1134	A226	20k black brown	15	15
1135	A227	35k dull violet	22	20
1136	A227	45k deep blue	45	30

47th congress of the Intl. Aeronautical Federation, Istanbul, 1954.

Souvenir Sheet

A228

1954, Oct. 18   Imperf.

1137	A228	Sheet of 3	11.00	5.50
a.		20k aquamarine	65	65
b.		30k violet blue	65	65
c.		1 l red violet	1.40	1.40

First anniv. of Law of Oct. 17, 1953, reorganizing the Department of Post, Telephone and Telegraph.

Ziya Gokalp — A229   Kemal Atatürk — A230

1954, Oct. 25   Perf. 11

1138	A229	15k rose lilac	15	15
1139	A229	20k dark green	16	15
1140	A229	30k crimson	35	22
		Set value		40

30th death anniv. of Ziya Gokalp, author and historian.

1955, Mar. 1   Perf. 12½

1141	A230	15k carmine rose	15	15
1142	A230	20k blue	18	15
1143	A230	40k dark gray	30	15
1144	A230	50k blue green	55	15
1145	A230	75k orange brown	65	15
		Nos. 1141-1145 (5)	1.83	
		Set value		30

Relief Map of Dardanelles A231

  Artillery Loaders — A232

Designs: 30k, Minelayer Nusrat. 60k, Colonel Kemal Ataturk.

1955, Mar. 18   Perf. 10½

1146	A231	15k green	15	15
1147	A232	20k orange brown	15	15
1148	A231	30k ultra	25	16
1149	A232	60k olive gray	80	45
		Set value		65

Battle of Gallipoli, 40th anniversary.

Aerial Map — A233

1955, Apr. 14   Perf. 11

1150	A233	15k gray	15	15
1151	A233	20k aquamarine	15	15
1152	A233	50k brown	25	16
1153	A233	1 l purple	70	30
		Set value		60

City Planning Congress, Ankara, 1955.

Carnation — A234

1955, May 19   Litho.   Perf. 10

1154	A234	10k shown	24	15
1155	A234	15k Tulip	16	15
1156	A234	20k Rose	22	15
1157	A234	50k Lily	1.65	1.00
		Set value		1.25

National Flower Show, Istanbul, May 20-Aug. 20.

Battle First Aid Station A235

Design: 30k, Gulhane Military Hospital, Ankara.

1955, Aug. 28   Unwmk.   Perf. 12

1158	A235	20k red, lake & gray	25	15
1159	A235	30k dp grn & yel grn	50	20

XVIII Intl. Congress of Military Medicine, Aug. 8-Sept. 1, Istanbul.

Soccer Game — A236   Emblem and Soccer Ball — A237

Design: 1 l, Emblem with oak and olive branches.

1955, Aug. 30   Perf. 10

1160	A236	15k light ultra	48	15
1161	A237	20k crimson rose	40	15
1162	A236	1 l light green	1.25	75

Intl. Military Soccer Championship games, Istanbul, Aug. 30.

Sureté Monument, Ankara A238

Designs: 20k, Dolma Bahce Palace. 30k, Police College, Ankara. 45k, Police Martyrs' Monument, Istanbul.

1955, Sept. 5   Perf. 10
Inscribed: "Enterpol Istanbul 1955"

1163	A238	15k blue green	15	15
1164	A238	20k brt violet	16	15
1165	A238	30k gray black	30	20
1166	A238	45k lt brown	70	45
		Set value		78

24th general assembly of the Intl. Criminal Police, Istanbul, Sept. 5-9.

Early Telegraph Transmitter A239

Modern
Transmitter — A240

Perf. 13½x14, 14x13½
1955, Sept. 10   **Photo.**
1167 A239 15k olive   15 15
1168 A240 20k crimson rose   15 15
1169 A239 45k fawn   40 16
1170 A240 60k ultra   40 38
          Set value   68

Centenary of telecommunication.

Academy of
Science,
Istanbul
A241

Designs: 20k, University. 60k, Hilton Hotel. 1 l,
Kiz Kulesi (Leander's Tower).

1955, Sept. 12   **Perf. 13½x14**
1171 A241 15k yellow orange   18 15
1172 A241 20k crimson rose   20 15
1173 A241 60k purple   30 15
1174 A241 1 l deep blue   55 38
          Set value   68

10th meeting of the governors of the Intl. Bank
of Reconstruction and Development and the Intl.
Monetary Fund, Istanbul, Sept. 12-16.

Surlari,
Istanbul
A242

Mosque of   Congress
Sultan Ahmed   Emblem
A243   A244

Designs: 30k, Haghia Sophia. 75k, Map of Constantinople, by Christoforo Buondel- monti, 1422.

1955, Sept. 15   Litho.   Perf. 11½
1175 A242 15k grnsh blk & Prus grn   35 20
1176 A243 20k vermilion & org   25 16
1177 A242 30k sepia & vio brn   25 16
1178 A243 75k ultramarine   70 50

10th Intl. Congress of Byzantine Research, Istanbul, Sept. 15-21, 1955.

1955, Sept. 26   Perf. 10½x11

Designs: 30k, Chalet in Istanbul. 55k, Bridges.

**Inscribed: "Beynelmiel X. Vol Kongresi
Istanbul 1955"**
1179 A244 20k red violet   15 15
1180 A244 30k dk grn & yel grn   18 15
1181 A244 55k dp bl & brt bl   75 40
          Set value   60

10th International Transportation Congress.

Map of
Turkey,
Showing
Population
Increase
A245

1955, Oct. 22   Unwmk.   Perf. 10
Map in Rose
1182 A245 15k lt & dk gray & red   30 15
1183 A245 20k lt & dk vio & red   18 15
1184 A245 30k lt & dk ultra & red   24 15
1185 A245 60k lt & dk bl grn & red   60 22
          Set value   50

Census of 1955.

Waterfall,
Antalya — A246

Alanya and
Seljukide
Dockyards
A247

Designs: 30k, Theater at Aspendos. 45k, Ruins at
Side. 50k, View of Antalya. 65k, St. Nicholas
Church at Myra (Demre) and St. Nicholas.

Perf. 14x13½, 13½x14
1955, Dec. 10   Photo.   Unwmk.
1186 A246 18k bl, ol grn & ultra   18 15
1187 A247 20k blue, ultra & brn   15 15
1188 A247 30k dl grn, ol bis & grn   22 15
1189 A246 45k yel grn & brn   1.00 45
1190 A246 50k Prus grn & ol bis   26 20
1191 A247 65k orange ver & blk   38 32
     Nos. 1186-1191 (6)   2.19
          Set value   1.20

Kemal Atatürk — A248

1955-56   Litho.   Perf. 12½
1192 A248 0.50k carmine   15 15
1193 A248 1k yellow orange   15 15
1194 A248 2k brt blue   15 15
1195 A248 3k scarlet   15 15
1196 A248 5k lt brown   15 15
1197 A248 6k lt blue grn   15 15
1198 A248 10k blue green   15 15
1199 A248 18k rose violet   18 15
1200 A248 20k lt violet bl   24 15
1201 A248 25k olive green   28 15
1202 A248 30k violet   32 15
1203 A248 40k fawn   45 15
1204 A248 75k slate blue   1.25 15
          Set value   3.25 60

Issue dates: 3k, 1955. Others, 1956.

Tomb at   Zubeyde
Nigde — A249   Hanum — A250

1956, Apr. 12   Perf. 10½
1205 A249 40k violet bl & bl   18 15

25th anniv. of the Turkish History Society. The
tomb of Hüdavent Hatun, a sultan's daughter,
exemplifies Seljukian architecture of the 14th
century.

1956, May 13   Perf. 11
1206 A250 20k pale brn & dk brn   15 15

Imperf
1207 A250 20k lt grn & dk grn   45 25
          Set value   32

Mother's Day; Zubeyde Hanum, mother of
Kemal Ataturk.

Shah and
Queen of
Iran
A251

1956, May 15   Unwmk.   Perf. 11
1208 A251 100k grn & pale grn   1.40 75
Imperf
1209 A251 100k red & pale grn   8.25 4.50

Visit of the Shah and Queen of Iran to Turkey,
May 15.

Erenkoy
Sanitarium
A252

1956, July 31   Perf. 11
1210 A252 50k dk bl grn & pink   40 20

Anti-Tuberculosis work among PTT employees.

Symbol of Izmir
Fair — A253

A254

1956, Aug. 20   Perf. 11
1211 A253 45k brt green   20 15
Souvenir Sheet
Imperf
1212 A254 Sheet of 2   1.40 80
  a. 50k rose red   26 22
  b. 50k bright ultramarine   26 22

25th Intl. Fair, Izmir, Aug. 20-Sept. 20. See No.
C28.

Hands Holding Bottled
Serpent — A255

1956, Sept. 10   Litho.   Perf. 10½
1213 A255 25k multicolored   18 15
  a. Tete beche pair   1.00

25th Intl. Anti-Alcoholism congress, Istanbul
Sept. 10-15.
Printed both in regular sheets and in sheets with
alternate vertical rows inverted.

Medical Center at   Sariyar
Kayseri — A256   Dam — A257

1956, Nov. 1   Perf. 12½x12
1214 A256 60k violet & yel   20 15

750th anniv. of the first medical school and clinic
in Anatolia.

1956, Dec. 2   Litho.   Perf. 10½
1215 A257 20k vermilion   16 15
1216 A257 20k bright blue   16 15
          Set value   15

Inauguration of Sariyar Dam.

Freestyle   Mehmet Akif
Wrestling — A258   Ersoy — A259

Design: 65k, Greco-Roman wrestling.

1956, Dec. 8   Unwmk.   Perf. 10½
1217 A258 40k brt yel grn & brn   35 22
1218 A258 65k lt bluish gray & dp car 48 25

16th Olympic Games, Melbourne, Nov. 22-Dec.
8, 1956.

1956, Dec. 26
1219 A259 20k brn & brt yel grn   16 15
1220 A259 20k rose car & lt gray   16 15
1221 A259 20k vio bl & brt pink   16 15
          Set value   15

20th death anniv. of Mehmet Akif Ersoy, author
of the Turkish National Anthem.
Each value bears a different verse of the anthem.

Theater in
Troy — A260

Trojan Vase — A261

Design: 30k, Trojan Horse.

Perf. 13½x14, 14x13½
1956, Dec. 31   Photo.   Unwmk.
1222 A260 15k green   80 50
1223 A261 20k red violet   80 50
1224 A260 30k chestnut   80 50

Excavations at Troy.

Mobile Chest X-Ray Unit
A262

Kemal Atatürk
A263

1957, Jan. 1   Litho.   Perf. 12
1225 A262 25k ol brn & red   18 15

Fight against tuberculsois.

1956-57   Perf. 12½
1226 A263 ½k blue green   15 15
1227 A263 1k yellow orange   15 15
1228 A263 3k gray olive   15 15
1229 A263 5k violet   15 15
1230 A263 6k rose car ('57)   15 15
1231 A263 10k rose violet   15 15
1232 A263 12k fawn ('57)   15 15
1233 A263 15k lt violet bl   15 15
1234 A263 18k carmine ('57)   15 15
1235 A263 20k lt brown   15 15
1236 A263 25k lt blue green   15 15
1237 A263 30k slate blue   15 15
1238 A263 40k olive ('57)   25 15
1239 A263 50k orange   35 15
1240 A263 60k brt blue ('57)   35 15
1241 A263 70k Prus green ('57) 1.10 15
1242 A263 75k brown   60 15
      Nos. 1226-1242 (17)   4.45
          Set value   80

Pres. Heuss of Germany — A264

1957, May 5   Unwmk.   Perf. 10½
1243 A264 40k yellow & brown   20 15

Visit of Pres. Theodor Heuss of Germany to Turkey, May 5. See No. C29.

View of Bergama and Ruin — A265

Design: 40k, Dancers in kermis at Bergama.

1957, May 24
1244 A265 30k brown   15 15
1245 A265 40k green   22 15
          Set value   15

20th anniv. of the kermis at Bergama (Pergamus).

Symbols of Industry and Flags — A266

1957, July 1   Photo.   Perf. 13½x14
1246 A266 25k violet   16 15
1247 A266 40k gray blue   20 15
          Set value   16

Turkish-American collaboration, 10th anniv.

Osman Hamdi Bey — A267

Hittite Sun Course from Alaca Höyük A268

1957, July 6   Perf. 10½
1248 A267 20k beige, pale brn & blk   18 15
1249 A268 30k Prussian green   22 15

75th anniv. of the Academy of Art. The 20k exists with "cancellation" omitted.

King of Afghanistan — A269

1957, Sept. 1   Litho.   Perf. 10½
1250 A269 45k car lake & pink   22 15

Visit of Mohammed Zahir Shah, King of Afghanistan, to Turkey. See No. C30.

Medical Center, Amasya A270

Design: 65k, Suleiman Medical Center.

1957, Sept. 29   Unwmk.   Perf. 10½
1251 A270 25k vermilion & yellow   15 15
1252 A270 65k brt grnsh bl & citron   28 15
          Set value   18

11th general meeting of the World Medical Assoc.

Mosque of Suleiman A271

Architect Mimar Koca Sinan (1489-1587) — A272

1957, Oct. 18   Perf. 11
1253 A271 20k gray green   15 15
1254 A272 100k brown   30 25
          Set value   32

400th anniv. of the opening of the Mosque of Suleiman, Istanbul.

No. 1073 Surcharged with New Value and "ISTANBUL Filatelik n. Sergisi 1957"

1957, Nov. 11   Photo.   Perf. 13½
1255 A208 50k on 2 l brt ultra   22 15

1957 Istanbul Philatelic Exhibition.

Forestation Map of Turkey A273

Design: 25k, Forest & hand planting tree, vert.

1957, Nov. 18   Litho.   Perf. 10½
1256 A273 20k green & brown   18 15
1257 A273 25k emerald & bl grn   18 15
          Set value   24

Centenary of forestry in Turkey. Nos. 1256-1257 each come with two different tabs attached (four tabs in all) bearing various quotations.

A274

A275

1957, Nov. 23
1258 A274 50k pink, vio, red & yel   32 20

400th death anniv. of Fuzuli (Mehmet Suleiman Ogiou), poet.

1957, Nov. 28   Photo.   Perf. 14x13½
1259 A275 65k dk Prus blue   20 15
1260 A275 65k rose violet   20 15
          Set value   24

Benjamin Franklin (1707-1790).

Green Dome, Tomb of Mevlana, at Konya — A276

Mevlana — A278

Konya Museum A277

Perf. 11x10½, 10½x11
1957, Dec. 17   Litho.   Unwmk.
1261 A276 50k green, bl & vio   15 15
1262 A277 100k dark blue   30 18
Miniature Sheet
Imperf
1263 A278 100k multicolored   1.10 1.00

Jalal-udin Mevlana (1207-1273), Persian poet and founder of the Mevlevie dervish order. No. 1263 contains one stamp 32x42mm.

Kemal Atatürk (Double Frame; Serifs) — A279

1957   Unwmk.   Perf. 11½
Size: 18x22mm
1264 A279 ½k lt brown   15 15
1265 A279 1k lt violet bl   15 15
1266 A279 2k black violet   15 15
1267 A279 3k orange   15 15
1268 A279 5k blue green   15 15
1269 A279 6k dk slate grn   15 15
1270 A279 10k violet   15 15
1271 A279 12k brt green   15 15
1272 A279 15k dk blue grn   15 15
1273 A279 18k rose carmine   15 15
1274 A279 20k brown   15 15
1275 A279 25k brown red   15 15
1276 A279 30k brt blue   15 15
1277 A279 40k slate blue   15 15
1278 A279 50k yellow orange   18 15
1279 A279 60k black   22 15
1280 A279 70k rose violet   22 15
1281 A279 75k gray olive   32 15
Size: 21x29mm
1282 A279 100k carmine   65 15
1283 A279 250k olive   2.00 22
      Nos. 1264-1283 (20)   5.69
          Set value   1.20

College Emblem A280

View of Adana A281

1958, Jan. 16   Litho.   Perf. 10½x11
1288 A280 20k bister, ind & org   15 15
1289 A280 25k dk blue, bis & org   18 15
          Set value   15

"Türkiye" on top of 25k. 75th anniv. of the College of Economics and Commerce, Istanbul.

1958   Photo.   Perf. 11½
Size: 26x20½mm
1290 A281 5k Adana   15 15
1291 A281 5k Adapazari   15 15
1292 A281 5k Adiyaman   15 15
1293 A281 5k Afyon   15 15
1294 A281 5k Amasya   15 15
1295 A281 5k Ankara   15 15
1296 A281 5k Antakya   15 15
1297 A281 5k Antalya   15 15
1298 A281 5k Artvin   15 15
1299 A281 5k Aydin   15 15
1300 A281 5k Balikesir   15 15
1301 A281 5k Bilecik   15 15
1302 A281 5k Bingol   15 15
1303 A281 5k Bitlis   15 15
1304 A281 5k Bolu   15 15
1305 A281 5k Burdur   15 15
1306 A281 5k Bursa   15 15
1307 A281 5k Canakkale   15 15
1308 A281 5k Cankiri   15 15
1309 A281 5k Corum   15 15
1310 A281 5k Denizli   15 15
1311 A281 5k Diyarbakir   15 15
Size: 32½x22mm
1312 A281 20k Adana   28 15
1313 A281 20k Adapazari   28 15
1314 A281 20k Adiyaman   28 15
1315 A281 20k Afyon   28 15
1316 A281 20k Amasya   28 15
1317 A281 20k Ankara   28 15
1318 A281 20k Antakya   28 15
1319 A281 20k Antalya   28 15
1320 A281 20k Artvin   28 15
1321 A281 20k Aydin   28 15
1322 A281 20k Balikesir   28 15
1323 A281 20k Bilecik   28 15
1324 A281 20k Bingol   28 15
1325 A281 20k Bitlis   28 15
1326 A281 20k Bolu   28 15
1327 A281 20k Burdur   28 15
1328 A281 20k Bursa   28 15
1329 A281 20k Canakkale   28 15
1330 A281 20k Cankiri   28 15
1331 A281 20k Corum   28 15
1332 A281 20k Denizli   28 15
1333 A281 20k Diyarbakir   28 15
          Set value   8.00 3.50

1959

Size: 26x20½mm

1334	A281	5k Edirne	15	15
1335	A281	5k Elazig	15	15
1336	A281	5k Erzincan	15	15
1337	A281	5k Erzurum	15	15
1338	A281	5k Eskisehir	15	15
1339	A281	5k Gaziantep	15	15
1340	A281	5k Giresun	15	15
1341	A281	5k Gumusane	15	15
1342	A281	5k Hakkari	15	15
1343	A281	5k Isparta	15	15
1344	A281	5k Istanbul	15	15
1345	A281	5k Izmir	15	15
1346	A281	5k Izmit	15	15
1347	A281	5k Karakose	15	15
1348	A281	5k Kars	15	15
1349	A281	5k Kastamonu	15	15
1350	A281	5k Kayseri	15	15
1351	A281	5k Kirklareli	15	15
1352	A281	5k Kirsehir	15	15
1353	A281	5k Konya	15	15
1354	A281	5k Kutahya	15	15
1355	A281	5k Malatya	15	15

Size: 32½x22mm

1356	A281	20k Edirne	28	15
1357	A281	20k Elazig	28	15
1358	A281	20k Erzincan	28	15
1359	A281	20k Erzurum	28	15
1360	A281	20k Eskisehir	28	15
1361	A281	20k Gaziantep	28	15
1362	A281	20k Giresun	28	15
1363	A281	20k Gumusane	28	15
1364	A281	20k Hakkari	28	15
1365	A281	20k Isparta	28	15
1366	A281	20k Istanbul	28	15
1367	A281	20k Izmir	28	15
1368	A281	20k Izmit	28	15
1369	A281	20k Karakose	28	15
1370	A281	20k Kars	28	15
1371	A281	20k Kastamonu	28	15
1372	A281	20k Kayseri	28	15
1373	A281	20k Kirklareli	28	15
1374	A281	20k Kirsehir	28	15
1375	A281	20k Konya	28	15
1376	A281	20k Kutahya	28	15
1377	A281	20k Malatya	28	15
		Set value	8.00	3.50

1960

Size: 26x20½mm

1378	A281	5k Manisa	15	15
1379	A281	5k Maras	15	15
1380	A281	5k Mardin	15	15
1381	A281	5k Mersin	15	15
1382	A281	5k Mugla	15	15
1383	A281	5k Mus	15	15
1384	A281	5k Nevsehir	15	15
1385	A281	5k Nigde	15	15
1386	A281	5k Ordu	15	15
1387	A281	5k Rize	15	15
1388	A281	5k Samsun	15	15
1389	A281	5k Siirt	15	15
1300	A281	5k Sinop	15	15
1391	A281	5k Sivas	15	15
1392	A281	5k Tekirdag	15	15
1393	A281	5k Tokat	15	15
1394	A281	5k Trabzon	15	15
1395	A281	5k Tunceli	15	15
1396	A281	5k Urfa	15	15
1397	A281	5k Usak	15	15
1398	A281	5k Van	15	15
1399	A281	5k Yozgat	15	15
1400	A281	5k Zonguldak	15	15

Size: 32½x22mm

1401	A281	20k Manisa	28	15
1402	A281	20k Maras	28	15
1403	A281	20k Mardin	28	15
1404	A281	20k Mersin	28	15
1405	A281	20k Mugla	28	15
1406	A281	20k Mus	28	15
1407	A281	20k Nevsehir	28	15
1408	A281	20k Nigde	28	15
1409	A281	20k Ordu	28	15
1410	A281	20k Rize	28	15
1411	A281	20k Samsun	28	15
1412	A281	20k Siirt	28	15
1413	A281	20k Sinop	28	15
1414	A281	20k Sivas	28	15
1415	A281	20k Tekirdag	28	15
1416	A281	20k Tokat	28	15
1417	A281	20k Trabzon	28	15
1418	A281	20k Tunceli	28	15
1419	A281	20k Urfa	28	15
1420	A281	20k Usak	28	15
1421	A281	20k Van	28	15
1422	A281	20k Yozgat	28	15
1423	A281	20k Zonguldak	28	15
		Set value	8.25	3.60
		Set value, #1290-1423	24.25	10.60

Ruins at Pamukkale A282

Designs: 25k, Travertines at Pamukkale.

1958, May 18   Litho.   Perf. 12

1424	A282	20k brown	15	15
1425	A282	25k blue	15	15
		Set value		15

"Industry" A283   Symbolizing New Europe A284

1958, Oct. 10   Unwmk.   Perf. 10½

1426	A283	40k slate blue	15	15

National Industry Exhibition.

Europa Issue
1958, Oct. 10

1427	A284	25k vio & dull pink	15	15
1428	A284	40k brt ultra	24	15
		Set value		22

Letters A285

1958, Oct. 5

1429	A285	20k orange & blk	15	15

Intl. Letter Writing Week, Oct. 5-11.

Flame and Mausoleum A286   Kemal Atatürk A287

1958, Nov. 10   Perf. 12

1430	A286	25k red	15	15
1431	A287	75k blue green	22	15
a.		Pair, #1430-1431	25	20
		Set value		15

20th death anniv. of Kemal Ataturk.

Emblem — A288

1959, Jan. 10   Litho.   Perf. 10

1432	A288	25k dk violet & yel	15	15

25th anniv. of the Agricultural Faculty of Ankara University.

Blackboard and School Emblem A289

1959, Jan. 15   Perf. 10½

1433	A289	75k black & yellow	20	15

75th anniv. of the establishment of a secondary boys' school in Istanbul.

State Theater, Ankara A290

Design: 25k, Portrait of Sinasi.

1959, Mar. 30   Unwmk.   Perf. 10½

1434	A290	20k red brn & emer	15	15
1435	A290	25k Prus grn & org	15	15
		Set value		15

Centenary of the Turkish theater; Sinasi, writer of the first Turkish play in 1859.

Globe and Stars — A291

1959, Apr. 4   Perf. 10

1436	A291	105k red	22	16
1437	A291	195k green	38	25

10th anniversary of NATO.

Aspendos Theater A292

1959, May 1   Litho.   Perf. 10½

1438	A292	20k bis brn & vio	15	15
1439	A292	20k grn & ol bis	18	15
		Set value		15

Aspendos (Belkins) Festival.

No. B70 Surcharged in Ultramarine

105   X YIL   AVRUPA KONSEYİ

1959, May 5

1440	SP25	105k on 15k + 5k org	35	20

Council of Europe, 10th anniversary.

Basketball — A293

1959, May 21   Perf. 10

1441	A293	25k red org & dk bl	18	15

11th European and Mediterranean Basketball Championship.

"Karadeniz" — A294

Telegraph Mast A295   Kemal Atatürk A296

Designs: 1k, Turkish Airlines' SES plane. 10k, Grain elevator, Ankara. 15k, Iron and Steel Works, Karabück. 20k, Euphrates Bridge, Birecik. 25k, Zonguldak Harbor. 30k, Gasoline refinery, Batman. 40k, Rumeli Hisari Fortress. 45k, Sugar factory, Konya. 55k, Coal mine, Zonguldak. 75k, Railway. 90k, Crane loading ships. 100k, Cement factory, Ankara. 120k, Highway. 150k, Harvester. 200k, Electric transformer.

Perf. 10½, 11, 11½, 12½, 13½

1959-60		Litho.	Unwmk.	
1442	A294	1k indigo	15	15
1443	A294	5k brt blue ('59)	15	15
1444	A294	10k blue	18	15
1445	A294	15k brown	15	15
1446	A294	20k slate green	15	15
1447	A294	25k violet	15	15
1448	A294	30k lilac	24	15
1449	A294	40k blue	18	15
1450	A294	45k dull violet	18	15
1451	A294	55k olive brown	26	15
1452	A295	60k green	65	15
1453	A295	75k gray olive	2.25	15
1454	A295	90k dark blue	3.25	15
1455	A295	100k gray	2.25	15
1456	A295	120k magenta	1.90	15
1457	A295	150k orange	3.25	15
1458	A295	200k yellow green	3.25	16
1459	A295	250k black brown	3.25	35
1460	A296	500k dark blue	6.75	45
		Nos. 1442-1460 (19)	28.59	
		Set value		1.75

Postage Due Stamps of 1936 Surcharged   **20═20**

1959, June 1   Perf. 11½

1461	D6	20k on 20pa brown	15	15
1462	D6	20k on 2k lt blue	15	15
1463	D6	20k on 3k brt vio	15	15
1464	D6	20k on 5k Prus bl	15	15
1465	D6	20k on 12k brt rose	15	15
		Nos. 1461-1465 (5)	75	
		Set value		25

Anchor Emblem — A297

Design: 40k, Sea Horse emblem.

1959, July 4   Perf. 11

1466	A297	30k multicolored	15	15
1467	A297	40k multicolored	24	15
		Set value		15

50th anniv. of the Merchant Marine College.

11th Century Warrior A298

1959, Aug. 26   Litho.   Perf. 11

1468	A298	2½ l rose lil & lt bl	70	50

Battle of Malazkirt, 888th anniversary.

Ornament
A299   A300

Design: 40k, Mosque.

1959, Oct. 19   Unwmk.   Perf. 12½
1469 A299 30k black & red   15 15
1470 A299 40k lt blue, blk & ocher   15 15
1471 A300 75k dp blue, yel & red   28 20
    Set value   35

Turkish Artists Congress, Ankara.

Kemal Atatürk — A301

Litho.; Center Embossed
1959, Nov. 10   Perf. 14
1472 A301 500k dark blue   1.25 65
   a.   Min. sheet of 1, red, imperf.   2.00 2.00

School of
Political
Science,
Ankara
A302

Emblem
A303   Crossed Swords
             Emblem
             A304

1959, Dec. 4   Photo.   Perf. 13½
1473 A302 40k green & brown   15 15
1474 A302 40k red brown & bl   15 15
1475 A303 1 l lt & dk vio & buff   32 15
    Set value   22

Political Science School, Ankara, cent.

Inscribed: "Kara Harbokulunum 125 Yili"

Design: 40k, Bayonet and flame.

1960, Feb. 28   Litho.   Perf. 10½
1476 A304 30k vermilion & org   15 15
1477 A304 40k brown, car & yel   20 15
    Set value   15

125th anniv. of the Territorial War College.

Window on World and   Spring Flower
WRY Emblem — A305   Festival — A306

Design: 150k, Symbolic shanties and uprooted oak emblem.

1960, Apr. 7
1478 A305 90k brt grnsh bl & blk   22 15
1479 A305 105k yellow & blk   28 18

World Refugee Year, July 1, 1959-June 30, 1960.

1960, June 4   Photo.   Perf. 11½
Granite Paper
1480 A306 30k Carnations   15 15
1481 A306 40k Jasmine   25 15
1482 A306 75k Rose   45 20
1483 A306 105k Tulip   65 28
    Set value   64

Atatürk
Square,
Nicosia
A307

Design: 105k, Map of Cyprus.

1960, Aug. 16   Litho.   Perf. 10½
1484 A307 40k blue & pink   15 15
1485 A307 105k blue & yellow   25 15
    Set value   18

Independence of the Republic of Cyprus.

Women and
Nest — A308

Design: 30k, Globe and emblem.

1960, Aug. 22   Photo.   Perf. 11½
1486 A308 30k lt vio & yel   15 15
1487 A308 75k grnsh bl & gray   28 15
    Set value   16

16th meeting of the Women's Intl. Council.

Soccer — A309

Sports: No. 1489, Basketball. No. 1490, Wrestling. No. 1491, Hurdling. No. 1492, Steeplechase.

1960, Aug. 25
1488 A309 30k yellow green   20 15
1489 A309 30k black   20 15
1490 A309 30k slate blue   20 15
1491 A309 30k purple   20 15
1492 A309 30k brown   20 15
   a.   Sheet of 25, #1488-1492   7.50 7.00
    Nos. 1488-1492 (5)   1.00
    Set value   50

17th Olympic Games, Rome, Aug. 25-Sept. 11. Printed in sheets of 25 (5x5) with every horizontal and every vertical row containing one of each design. Also printed in normal sheets of 100.

Europa Issue, 1960
Common Design Type
1960, Sept. 19
Size: 33x22mm
1493 CD3 75k green & bl grn   50 30
1494 CD3 105k dp bl & lt bl   1.00 45

Agah Efendi and Front   UN Emblem and
Page of Turcamani   Torch — A311
Ahval — A310

1960, Oct. 21   Photo.   Perf. 11½
1495 A310 40k brown blk & sl   15 15
1496 A310 60k brn blk & bis brn   20 15
    Set value   15

Centenary of Turkish journalism.

1960, Oct. 24   Unwmk.
Design: 105k, UN headquarters building and UN emblem forming "15," horiz.
1497 A311 90k brt bl & dk bl   20 15
1498 A311 105k lt bl grn & brn   24 18

15th anniversary of the United Nations.

Army
Emblem
A312

Tribunal
A313

Design: 195k, "Justice," vert.

1960, Oct. 14   Litho.   Perf. 13
1499 A312 40k violet & bister   15 15
1500 A313 105k red, gray & brn   24 15
1501 A313 195k grn, rose red & brn   42 20
    Set value   36

Trial of ex-President Celal Bayar and ex-Premier Adnan Menderes.

Revolutionaries and   Prancing Horse,
Statue — A314   Broken
            Chain — A315

Designs: 30k, Ataturk and hand holding torch. 105k, Youth, soldier and broken chain.

1960, Dec. 1   Photo.   Perf. 14½
1502 A314 10k gray & blk   15 15
1503 A314 30k purple   15 15
1504 A315 40k brt red & blk   15 15
1505 A314 105k blue blk & red   40 15
    Set value   30

Revolution of May 27, 1960.

Faculty
Building
A316

Sculptured Head of
Atatürk — A317

Designs: 40k, Map of Turkey and sun disk.

1961, Jan. 9   Litho.   Perf. 13
1506 A316 30k slate grn & gray   15 15
1507 A316 40k brn blk & bis brn   16 15
1508 A317 60k dk green & buff   24 15
    Set value   20

25th anniv. of the Faculty of Languages, History and Geography, University of Ankara.

Communication and
Transportation — A318

Designs: 40k, Highway construction, telephone and telegraph. 75k, New parliament building, Ankara.

1961, Apr. 27   Unwmk.   Perf. 13
1509 A318 30k dull vio & blk   15 15
1510 A318 40k green & black   20 15
1511 A318 75k dull blue & blk   35 15
    Set value   28

9th conference of ministers of the Central Treaty Org. (CENTO), Ankara.

Flag and   Legendary Wolf and
People — A319   Osman
           Warriors — A320

Design: 60k, "Progress" (Atatürk showing youth the way).

1961, May 27   Litho.
1512 A319 30k multicolored   15 15
1513 A320 40k sl grn & yel   18 15
1514 A319 60k grn, pink & dk red   28 15
    Set value   25

First anniversary of May 27 revolution.

Rockets
A321

Designs: 40k, Crescent and star emblem, "50" and Jet. 75k, Atatürk, eagle and jets, vert.

1961, June 1
1515 A321 30k brn, org yel & blk   15 15
1516 A321 40k violet & red   18 15
1517 A321 75k slate blk & bis   42 38

50th anniversary of Turkey's air force.

Europa Issue, 1961
Common Design Type
1961, Sept. 18   Perf. 13
Size: 32x22mm
1518 CD4 30k dk violet bl   85 70
1519 CD4 40k gray   85 70
1520 CD4 75k vermilion   95 75

Tulip and   Open Book and
Cogwheel — A322   Olive
            Branch — A324

Torch, Hand
and Cogwheel
A323

1961, Oct. 21   Unwmk.   Litho.
1521 A322 30k slate, pink & sil   15 15
1522 A323 75k ultra, org & blk   35 15
          Set value   16

Technical and professional schools, cent.

1961, Oct. 29
1523 A324 30k red, blk & olive   15 15
1524 A324 75k brt blue, blk & grn   28 15
          Set value   16

Inauguration of the new Parliament.

Kemal Atatürk
A325   A326

1961-62   Litho.   Perf. 10x10½
          Size: 20x25mm
1525 A325 1k brown org ('62)   15 15
1526 A325 5k blue   15 15
1527 A325 10k sepia   28 15
1528 A326 10k car rose   28 15
1529 A326 30k dull grn ('62)   1.90 15
          Size: 21½x31mm
1530 A325 10 l violet ('62)   6.25 75
          Nos. 1525-1530 (6)   9.01
          Set value   1.00

NATO Emblem   Scouts at
and   Campfire — A328
Dove — A327

Design: 105k, NATO emblem, horiz.

1962, Feb. 18   Unwmk.   Perf. 13
1545 A327 75k dl bl, blk & sil   20 15
1546 A327 105k crim, blk & sil   28 20

10th anniv. of Turkey's admission to NATO.

1962, July 22   Litho.
Designs: 60k, Scouts with flag. 105k, Scouts
saluting.

1547 A328 30k lt grn, blk & red   15 15
1548 A328 60k gray, blk & red   24 15
1549 A328 105k tan, blk & red   35 22
          Set value   38

Turkish Boy Scouts, 50th anniversary.

Soldier   Oxcart from Victory
Statue — A329   Monument,
                     Ankara — A330

Design: 75k, Atatürk.

1962, Aug. 30   Unwmk.   Perf. 13
1550 A329 30k slate green   15 15
1551 A330 40k gray & sepia   15 15
1552 A329 75k gray blk & lt gray   26 15
          Set value   28

40th anniv. of Battle of Dumlupinar.

Europa Issue, 1962
Common Design Type
1962, Sept. 17
          Size: 37x23mm
1553 CD5 75k emerald & blk   28 15
1554 CD5 105k blue & blk   40 22
1555 CD5 195k blue & blk   1.00 55

Brown imprint.

Virgin Mary's   20pa Stamp of
House, Ephesus   1863
A331   A332

Designs: 40k, Inside view after restoration, horiz.
75k, Outside view, horiz. 105k, Statue of Virgin
Mary.

1962, Dec. 8   Photo.   Perf. 13½
1556 A331 30k multicolored   16 15
1557 A331 40k multicolored   20 15
1558 A331 75k multicolored   25 15
1559 A331 105k multicolored   38 18
          Set value   42

1963, Jan. 13   Perf. 13x13½
Issue of 1863: 30k, 1pi. 40k, 2pi. 75k, 5pi.

1560 A332 10k yellow, brn & blk   15 15
1561 A332 30k rose, lil & blk   16 15
1562 A332 40k lt bl, bluish grn & blk 24 15
1563 A332 75k red brn, rose & blk   42 20
          Set value   40

Centenary of Turkish postage stamps. See No.
1601, souvenir sheet.

Starving
People
A333

Designs: 40k, Sowers. 75k, Hands protecting
Wheat Emblem, and globe.

1963, Mar. 21   Unwmk.   Perf. 13
1564 A333 30k dp bl & dk bl   15 15
1565 A333 40k brn org & brn   15 15
1566 A333 75k grn & dk grn   25 15
          Set value   30

FAO "Freedom from Hunger" campaign.

Julian's   Ethnographic
Column,   Museum — A335
Ankara — A334

Designs: 10k, Ankara Citadel. 30k, Gazi Institute
of Education. 50k, Atatürk's mausoleum. 60k, President's residence. 100k, Ataturk's home, Cankaya.
150k, Parliament building.

1963   Litho.   Perf. 13
1568 A334   1k sl grn & yel grn   15 15
1569 A334   1k purple   15 15
1570 A334   5k sepia & buff   15 15
1571 A335 10k lil rose & pale bl   24 15
1573 A335 30k black & violet   60 15
1574 A335 50k blue & yellow   1.50 15
1575 A335 60k dk blue gray   38 15
1576 A335 100k olive brown   90 15
1577 A335 150k dull green   4.50 15
          Nos. 1568-1577 (9)   8.57
          Set value   50

Map of Turkey
and Atom
50 Symbol
A336

Designs: 60k, Symbols of medicine, agriculture,
industry and atom. 100k, Emblem of Turkish
Atomic Energy Commission.

1963, May 27   Unwmk.   Perf. 13
1584 A336 50k red brn & blk   18 15
1585 A336 60k grn, dk grn, yel & red 24 15
1586 A336 100k violet bl & bl   50 30
          Set value   52

1st anniv. of the Turkish nuclear research center.

Meric Bridge   Sultan Murad I
A337   A338

Designs: 10k, Üçserefeli Mosque. 60k, Summer-
house, Edirne Palace.

1963, June 17
1587 A338 10k dp bl & yel grn   15 15
1588 A337 30k red org & ultra   15 15
1589 A337 60k dk bl, red & brn   18 15
1590 A338 100k multicolored   65 25
          Set value   45

600th anniv. of the conquest of Edirne
(Adrianople).

Soldier and
Rising
Sun — A339

1963, June 28
1591 A339 30k red, blk & gray   15 15
1592 A339 100k red, blk & ol   28 16
          Set value   22

600th anniversary of the Turkish army.

Plowing
A340

Mithat Pasha — A341

Design: 50k, Agriculture Bank, Ankara.

          Perf. 13x13½, 13½x13
1963, Aug. 27   Photo.   Unwmk.
1593 A340 30k brt yel grn, red brn &
                          grn   15 15
1594 A340 50k pale vio & Prus bl   16 15
1595 A341 60k gray & green   28 15
          Set value   25

Centenary of Agriculture Bank, Ankara.

Sports and
Exhibition
Palace,
Istanbul and
#5 — A342

Designs: 50k, Sultan Ahmed Mosque & Turkey in
Asia #22. 60k, View of Istanbul & Turkey in Asia
#87. 100k, Rumeli Hisari Fortress & #679. 130k,
Ankara Fortress & #C2.

1963, Sept. 7   Litho.   Perf. 13
1596 A342 10k black, yel & rose   15 15
  a.   Rose omitted
1597 A342 50k blk, grn & rose lil   32 15
1598 A342 60k dk brn, dk bl & blk   48 15
1599 A342 100k dk vio & lil rose   75 18
1600 A342 130k brn, tan & dp org   1.00 28
          Nos. 1596-1600 (5)   2.70
          Set value   62

"Istanbul 63" Intl. Stamp Exhibition.

Type of 1963 Inscribed: "F.I.P. GÜNÜ"
          Souvenir Sheet

Issues of 1863: 10k, 20pa. 50k, 1pi. 60k, 2pi.
130k, 5pi.

                     Unwmk.
1963, Sept. 13   Litho.   Imperf.
1601   Sheet of 4   1.25 1.25
  a.   A332 10k yel, brown & blk   15 15
  b.   A332 50k lilac, pink & blk   20 15
  c.   A332 60k bluish grn, lt bl & blk 30 15
  d.   A332 130k red brn, pink & blk 35 15

Intl. Philatelic Federation.

Europa Issue, 1963
Common Design Type
1963, Sept. 16
          Size: 32x24mm
1602 CD6 50k red & black   35 18
1603 CD6 130k bl grn, blk & bl   60 32

Atatürk and
First
Parliament
Building
A343

Atatürk and: 50k, Turkish flag. 60k, New Parliament building.

1963, Oct. 29   Photo.   Perf. 13½
1604 A343 30k blk, gold, yel & mar   18 15
1605 A343 50k dk grn, gold, yel & red 24 16
1606 A343 60k dk brn, gold & yel   28 20

40th anniversary of Turkish Republic.

Atatürk, 25th Death
Anniv. — A344

1963, Nov. 10
1607 A344 50k red, gold, grn & brn   18 15
1608 A344 60k red, gold, bl & brn   24 16

NATO, 15th
Anniv.
A346

Designs: 130k, NATO emblem and olive branch.

1964, Apr. 4   Litho.   Perf. 13
1610 A346 50k grnsh bl, vio bl & red 24 16
1611 A346 130k red & black   45 38

12 Stars and
Europa with
Torch
A347

Design: 130k, Torch and stars.

1964, May 5   Litho.   Perf. 12
1612	A347	50k red brn, yel & vio bl	32	16
1613	A347	130k vio bl, lt bl & org	60	38

15th anniversary of Council of Europe.

Recaizade Mahmut
Ekrem, Writer — A348

Portraits: 1k, Hüseyin Rahmi Gürpinar, novelist.
5k, Ismail Hakki Izmirli, scientist. 10k, Sevket Dag,
painter. 60k, Gazi Ahmet Muhtar Pasha, commander. 100k, Ahmet Rasim, writer. 130k, Salih
Zeki, mathematician.

1964   Litho.   Perf. 13½x13
1614	A348	1k red & blk	15	15
1615	A348	5k dull grn & blk	15	15
1616	A348	10k tan & blk	15	15
1617	A348	50k ultra & dk bl	45	15
1618	A348	60k gray & blk	50	15
1619	A348	100k grnsh bl & dk bl	52	15
1620	A348	130k brt grn & dk grn	2.25	15
		Nos. 1614-1620 (7)	4.17	
		Set value		45

Mosque of
Sultan Ahmed
A349

Kiz Kulesi,
Mersin — A350

Designs: No. 1622, Zeus Temple, Silifke. No.
1623, View of Amasra. No. 1625, Augustus' Gate
and minaret, Ankara.

1964, June 11   Unwmk.   Perf. 13
1621	A349	50k gray ol & yel grn	24	15
1622	A349	50k claret & car	28	15
1623	A349	50k dk bl & vio bl	28	15
1624	A350	60k sl grn & dk gray	35	15
1625	A350	60k dk brn & org brn	35	15
		Nos. 1621-1625 (5)	1.50	
		Set value		45

Kars   Alp Arslan,
Castle — A351   Conqueror of
                      Kars,
                      1064 — A352

1964, Aug. 16   Unwmk.   Perf. 13
1626	A351	50k blk & pale vio	15	15
1627	A352	130k blk, gold, sal & pale vio	35	20
		Set value		28

900th anniversary of conquest of Kars.

Europa Issue, 1964
Common Design Type

1964, Sept. 14   Litho.   Perf. 13
Size: 22x33mm
1628	CD7	50k orange, indigo & sil	32	25
1629	CD7	130k lt bl, mag & citron	65	50

Fuat, Resit and Ali Pashas — A353

Design: 60k, Mustafa Resit Pasha, vert.

1964, Nov. 3   Perf. 13
Sizes: 48x33mm (50k, 100k);
22x33mm (60k)
1630	A353	50k multicolored	20	15
1631	A353	60k multicolored	30	20
1632	A353	100k multicolored	50	30

125th anniversary of reform decrees.

Parachutist — A354

Designs: 90k, Glider, horiz. 130k, Ataturk
watching squadron in flight.

1965, Feb. 16   Litho.   Perf. 13
1633	A354	60k lt bl, blk, red & yel	16	15
1634	A354	90k bister & multi	32	15
1635	A354	130k lt blue & multi	50	22
		Set value		42

Turkish Aviation League, 40th anniv.

Emblem — A355

Designs: 50k, Radio mast and waves, vert. 75k,
Hand pressing button.

1965, Feb. 24   Unwmk.   Perf. 13
1636	A355	30k multicolored	15	15
1637	A355	50k multicolored	20	15
1638	A355	75k multicolored	32	20
		Set value		36

Telecommunications meeting of the Central
Treaty Org., CENTO.

Coast of
Ordu — A356

Designs: 50k, Manavgat Waterfall, Antalya. 60k,
Sultan Ahmed Mosque, Istanbul. 100k, Hali
Rahman Mosque, Urfa. 130k, Red Tower, Alanya.

1965, Apr. 5   Litho.
1639	A356	30k multicolored	15	15
1640	A356	50k multicolored	26	15
1641	A356	60k multicolored	26	15
1642	A356	100k multicolored	45	20
1643	A356	130k multicolored	65	25
		Nos. 1639-1643 (5)	1.77	
		Set value		70

ITU Emblem, Old and New
Communication Equipment — A357

1965, May 17   Perf. 13
1644	A357	50k multicolored	18	15
1645	A357	130k multicolored	55	25

ITU, centenary.

ICY
Emblem — A358

1965, June 26   Litho.   Unwmk.
1646	A358	100k red org, red brn & brt grn	30	15
1647	A358	130k gray, lil & ol grn	45	22

International Cooperation Year.

Hands Holding
Book
A358a

Map and
Flags of
Turkey, Iran
and Pakistan
A358b

1965, July 21   Unwmk.   Perf. 13
1648	A358a	50k org brn, yel & dk brn	28	15
1649	A358b	75k dl bl, red, grn blk & org	42	16

1st anniv. of the signing of the Regional Cooperation Development Pact by Turkey, Iran and
Pakistan.

Kemal Ataturk — A359

1965   Litho.   Perf. 12½
1650	A359	1k brt green	15	15
1651	A359	5k violet blue	15	15
1652	A359	10k blue	32	15
1653	A359	25k gray	75	15
1654	A359	30k magenta	60	15
1655	A359	50k brown	75	15
1656	A359	150k orange	1.65	15
		Nos. 1650-1656 (7)	4.37	
		Set value		42

Europa Issue, 1965
Common Design Type

1965, Sept. 27   Perf. 13
Size: 32x23mm
1665	CD8	50k gray, ultra & grn	65	50
1666	CD8	130k tan, blk & grn	1.00	75

Map of Turkey
and
People — A360

Designs: 50k, "1965." 100k, "1965," symbolic
eye and man, vert.

Unwmk.

1965, Oct. 24   Litho.   Perf. 13
1667	A360	10k multicolored	15	15
1668	A360	50k grn, blk & lt yel grn	15	15
1669	A360	100k orange, sl & blk	38	15
		Set value		28

Issued to publicize the 1965 census.

Plane over
Ankara Castle
A361

Designs: 30k, Archer and Ankara castle. 50k,
Horsemen with spears (ancient game). 100k, Three
stamps and medal. 150k, Hands holding book, vert.

1965, Oct. 25
1670	A361	10k brt vio, yel & red	15	15
1671	A361	30k multicolored	18	15
1672	A361	50k lt gray ol, ind & red	20	15
1673	A361	100k gray & multi	45	25
		Set value		50

Souvenir Sheet
Imperf
1674	A361	150k multicolored	1.10	1.00

1st Natl. Postage Stamp Exhibition "Ankara 65."

Resat Nuri Guntekin,
Novelist — A362

Portraits: 5k, Besim Omer Akalin, M.D. 10k,
Tevfik Fikret, poet. 25k, Tanburi Cemil, composer.
30k, Ahmet Vifik Pasha, playwright. 50k, Omer
Seyfettin, novelist. 60k, Kemalettin Mimaroglu,
architect. 150k, Halit Ziya Usakligil, novelist. 220k,
Yahya Kemal Beyatli, poet.

1965   Litho.   Perf. 13½x13
Black Portrait and Inscriptions
1675	A362	1k rose	15	15
1676	A362	5k blue	15	15
1677	A362	10k buff	15	15
1678	A362	25k dull red brn	32	15
1679	A362	30k gray	32	15
1680	A362	50k orange	80	15
1681	A362	60k red lilac	80	15
1682	A362	150k lt green	85	15
1683	A362	220k tan	1.25	15
		Nos. 1675-1683 (9)	4.79	
		Set value		50

Training Ship
Savarona
A363

Designs: 60k, Submarine "Piri Reis." 100k,
Cruiser "Alpaslan." 130k, Destroyer "Gelibolu."
220k, Destroyer "Gemlik."

1965, Dec. 6   Photo.   Perf. 11½
1684	A363	50k blue & brown	35	15
1685	A363	60k blue & black	48	15
1686	A363	100k blue & black	75	22
1687	A363	130k blue & vio blk	1.10	40
1688	A363	220k blue & indigo	1.75	65
		Nos. 1684-1688 (5)	4.43	1.57

First Congress of Turkish Naval Society.

Kemal   Halide Edip Adivar,
Ataturk — A364   Writer — A365

1965   Litho.   *Perf. 13¹/₂*
Imprint: "Apa Ofset Basimevi"
Black Portrait and Inscriptions

1689	A364	1k rose lilac	15	15
1690	A364	5k lt green	15	15
1691	A364	10k blue gray	18	15
1692	A364	50k olive bister	45	15
1693	A364	150k silver	1.25	15
		Nos. 1689-1693 (5)	2.18	
		Set value		30

See Nos. 1724-1728.

1966   Litho.   *Perf. 13¹/₂*

Portraits: 25k, Huseyin Sadettin Arel, writer and composer. 30k, Kamil Akdik, graphic artist. 60k, Abdurrahman Seref, historian. 130k, Naima, historian.

1694	A365	25k gray & brn blk	35	15
1695	A365	30k rose vio & blk brn	28	15
1696	A365	50k blue & black	42	15
1697	A365	60k lt grn & blk brn	42	15
1698	A365	130k lt vio bl & blk	80	15
		Nos. 1694-1698 (5)	2.27	
		Set value		28

Tiles, Green
Mausoleum,
Bursa — A366

Tiles: 60k, Spring flowers, Hurrem Sultan Mausoleum, Istanbul. 130k, Stylized flowers, 16th century.

1966, May 15   Litho.   *Perf. 13¹/₂x13*

1699	A366	50k multicolored	26	15
1700	A366	60k multicolored	48	30
1701	A366	130k multicolored	60	35

On No. 1700 the black ink was applied by a thermographic process and varnished, producing a shiny, raised effect to imitate the embossed tiles of the design source.

Volleyball
A367

View of Bodrum
A368

1966, May 20   *Perf. 13x13¹/₂*

1702	A367	50k tan & multi	38	16

4th Intl. Military Volleyball Championship.

Perf. 13x13¹/₂, 13¹/₂x13
1966, May 25

Views: 30k, Kusadasi. 50k, Anadolu Hisari, Istanbul, horiz. 90k, Marmaris. 100k, Izmir, horiz.

1703	A368	10k multicolored	15	15
1704	A368	30k multicolored	60	25
1705	A368	50k multicolored	18	15
1706	A368	90k multicolored	32	16
1707	A368	100k multicolored	38	20
		Nos. 1703-1707 (5)	1.63	
		Set value		70

Inauguration
of Keban
Dam
A369

Design: 60k, View of Keban Dam area.

1966, June 10   *Perf. 13¹/₂*

1708	A369	50k multicolored	15	15
1709	A369	60k multicolored	42	15
		Set value		16

Visit of King
Faisal of Saudi
Arabia — A370

1966, Aug. 29   Litho.   *Perf. 13¹/₂x13*

1710	A370	100k car rose & dk car	55	22

Symbolic
Postmark and
Stamp — A371

Designs: 60k, Flower made of stamps. 75k, Stamps forming display frames. 100k, Map of Balkan states, magnifying glass and stamp.

1966, Sept. 3   *Perf. 13¹/₂x13*

1711	A371	50k multicolored	15	15
1712	A371	60k multicolored	16	15
1713	A371	75k multicolored	40	15
		Set value		30

Souvenir Sheet
Imperf

1714	A371	100k multicolored	85	55

2nd "Balkanfila" stamp exhibition, Istanbul.

Sultan Suleiman
on Horseback
A372

Designs: 90k, Mausoleum, Istanbul. 130k, Sultan Suleiman.

1966, Sept. 6   *Perf. 13¹/₂x13*

1715	A372	60k multicolored	18	15
1716	A372	90k multicolored	45	28
1717	A372	130k multicolored	75	38

Sultan Suleiman the Magnificent (1496?-1566). On No. 1717 a gold frame was applied by raised thermographic process.

Europa Issue, 1966
Common Design Type
1966, Sept. 26   Litho.   *Perf. 13x13¹/₂*
Size: 22x33mm

1718	CD9	50k lt bl, vio bl & blk	75	40
a.		Black (inscriptions & imprint) omitted	65.00	
1719	CD9	130k lil, dk red lil & blk	90	50

Symbols of
Education,
Science and
Culture
A373

1966, Nov. 4   Litho.   *Perf. 13*

1720	A373	130k brn, bis brn & yel	48	22

UNESCO, 20th anniversary.

University of
Technology
A374

Designs: 100k, Atom symbol. 130k, design symbolizing sciences.

1966, Nov. 15

1721	A374	50k multicolored	18	15
1722	A374	100k multicolored	32	20
1723	A374	130k multicolored	55	30

10th anniv. of the Middle East University of Technology.

Ataturk Type of 1965
Imprint: "Kiral Matbaasi - Ist"

1966   Litho.   *Perf. 12¹/₂*
Black Portrait and Inscriptions

1724	A364	25k yellow	15	15
1725	A364	30k pink	24	15
1726	A364	50k rose lilac	1.10	15
1727	A364	90k pale brown	52	15
1728	A364	100k gray	70	15
		Nos. 1724-1728 (5)	2.71	
		Set value		26

Statue of Ataturk,
Ankara — A375

Equestrian Statues of Ataturk: No. 1729A, Statue in Izmir. No. 1729B, Statue in Samsun.

Without Imprint
1967   Litho.   *Perf. 13x12¹/₂*
Size: 23x16mm

1729	A375	10k black & yellow	30	15

Inscribed "1967"
Imprint: Kiral Matbaasi
Size: 22x15mm

1729A	A375	10k black & salmon	30	15
1729B	A375	10k black & lt grn	30	15
		Set value		15

Issued for use on greeting cards. See Nos. 1790-1791A, 1911.

Puppets Karagöz and Hacivat — A376

Intl. Tourist Year Emblem and: 60k, Sword and shield game. 90k, Traditional military band. 100k, raised effect.

Perf. 13x13¹/₂, 13¹/₂x13
1967, Mar. 30   Litho.

1730	A376	50k multicolored	28	15
1731	A376	60k multicolored	45	20
1732	A376	90k multicolored	55	22
1733	A376	100k multicolored	70	30

Intl. Tourist Year. On No. 1733 the black ink was applied by a thermographic process and varnished, producing a shiny, raised effect.

Woman Vaccinating
Child, Knife and
Lancet — A377

Fallow
Deer — A378

1967, Apr. 1   *Perf. 13x13¹/₂*

1734	A377	100k multicolored	60	22

250th anniv. of smallpox vaccination in Turkey. The gold was applied by a thermographic process and varnished, producing a shiny, raised effect.

1967, Apr. 23   Litho.   *Perf. 13x13¹/₂*

1735	A378	50k shown	16	15
1736	A378	60k Wild goat	28	15
1737	A378	100k Brown bear	48	18
1738	A378	130k Wild boar	70	25
		Set value		60

Soccer
Players and
Emblem
with Map
of Europe
A379

Design: 130k, Players at left, smaller emblem.

1967, May 1   *Perf. 13*

1739	A379	50k multicolored	22	15
1740	A379	130k yellow & multi	50	32

20th Intl. Youth Soccer Championships.

Sivas Hospital
A380

1967, July 1   Litho.   *Perf. 13*

1741	A380	50k multicolored	40	15

750th anniversary of Sivas Hospital.

Selim Sirri
Tarcan
A381

Design: 60k, Olympic Rings and Baron Pierre de Coubertin.

1967, July 20

1742	A381	50k lt blue & multi	30	18
1743	A381	60k lilac & multi	30	18
a.		Pair, #1742-1743	60	40

1st Turkish Olympic competitions.

Ahmed Mithat,
Writer — A382

Portraits: 5k, Admiral Turgut Reis. 50k, Sikullu Mehmet, statesman. 100k, Nedim, poet. 150k, Osman Hamdi, painter.

1967   Litho.   *Perf. 12¹/₂*

1744	A382	1k green & blk	15	15
1745	A382	5k dp bister & blk	15	15
1746	A382	50k brt violet & blk	38	15

1747	A382 100k citron & blk	65	15
1748	A382 150k yellow & blk	90	15
	Nos. 1744-1748 (5)	2.23	
	Set value		35

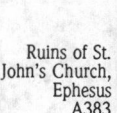

Ruins of St.
John's Church,
Ephesus
A383

Design: 130k, Inside view of Virgin Mary's House, Ephesus.

1967, July 26   *Perf. 13*

1749	A383 130k multicolored	28	20
1750	A383 220k multicolored	55	30

Visit of Pope Paul VI to the House of the Virgin Mary in Ephesus, July 26.

Plate on Firing
Grid and
Ornaments
A384

1967, Sept. 1

1751	A384 50k pale lil, blk, ind & bl	32	15

5th International Ceramics Exhibition.

View of Istanbul
and
Emblem — A385

1967, Sept. 4   Litho.   *Perf. 13*

1752	A385 130k dk blue & gray	32	20

9th Congress of the Intl. Commission of Large Dams.

Stamps, Ornament and   Kemal
Map of Turkey — A386   Ataturk — A387

Design: 60k, Grapes and stamps.

1967

1753	A386 50k multicolored	18	15
1754	A386 60k multicolored	26	15
a.	Souvenir sheet of 2, #1753-1754	75	75
	Set value		24

Intl. Trade Fair, Izmir.

1967   Litho.   *Perf. 11¹⁄₂x12*
Booklet Stamps

1755	A387 10k black & lt ol grn	20	15
a.	Booklet pane of 10	3.00	
b.	Booklet pane of 25	6.00	
1756	A387 50k black & pale rose	65	15
a.	Booklet pane of 2	1.75	
b.	Bklt. pane, 5 #1755, 4 #1756 + label	12.50	
	Set value		15

Symbolic Water
Cycle — A388

Human Rights
Flame — A390

Child and
Angora Cat,
Man with
Microscope
A389

1967, Dec. 1   Litho.   *Perf. 13*

1757	A388 90k lt grn, blk & org	22	18
1758	A388 130k lilac, blk & org	30	22

Hydrological Decade (UNESCO), 1965-74.

1967, Dec. 23   *Perf. 13*

Design: 60k, Horse and man with microscope.

1759	A389 50k multicolored	32	18
1760	A389 60k multicolored	45	22

125th anniv. of Turkish veterinary medicine.

1968, Jan. 1   *Perf. 13x13¹⁄₂*

1761	A390 50k rose lil, dk bl & org	15	15
1762	A390 130k lt bl, dk bl & red org	35	15
	Set value		22

International Human Rights Year.

Archer on Horseback — A391

Miniatures, 16th Century: 50k, Investiture. 60k, Sultan Suleiman the Magnificent receiving an ambassador, vert. 100k, Musicians.

Perf. 13x13¹⁄₂, 13¹⁄₂x13

1968, Mar. 1   Litho.

1763	A391 50k multicolored	18	15
1764	A391 60k multicolored	20	15
1765	A391 90k multicolored	40	20
1766	A391 100k multicolored	55	30

Kemal Ataturk — A392

1968   Litho.   *Perf. 12¹⁄₂*

1767	A392 1k dk & lt blue	15	15
1768	A392 5k dk & lt green	18	15
1769	A392 50k orange brn & yel	90	15
1770	A392 200k dk brown & pink	2.50	25
	Set value		42

Law Book
and Oak
Branch
A393

Mithat Pasha
and Scroll
A394

1968, Apr. 1   *Perf. 13*

1771	A393 50k multicolored	18	15
1772	A394 60k multicolored	26	16

Centenary of the Court of Appeal.

1968, Apr. 1

Designs: 50k, Scales of Justice. 60k, Ahmet Cevdet Pasha and scroll.

1773	A393 50k multicolored	18	15
1774	A394 60k multicolored	26	16

Centenary of the Supreme Court.

Europa Issue, 1968
Common Design Type

1968, May 6   Litho.   *Perf. 13*
     Size: 31¹⁄₂x23mm

1775	CD11 100k pck bl, yel & red	70	50
1776	CD11 130k green, yel & red	1.25	90

Yacht   "Fight Usury" — A396
Kismet — A395

1968, June 15   Litho.   *Perf. 13*

1777	A395 50k ultra & multi	35	15

Round-the-world trip of the yacht Kismet, Aug. 22, 1965-June 14, 1968.

1968, June 19

1778	A396 50k multicolored	25	15

Centenary of the Pawn Office, Istanbul.

Sakarya Battle and Independence
Medal — A397

Design: 130k, National anthem and reverse of medal.

1968, Aug. 30   *Perf. 13x13¹⁄₂*

1779	A397 50k gold & multi	15	15
1780	A397 130k gold & multi	35	20
	Set value		28

Turkish Independence medal. The gold on Nos. 1779-1780 was applied by a thermographic process and varnished, producing a shiny, raised effect.

Ataturk and Galatasaray High
School — A398

Designs: 50k, "100" and old and new school emblems. 60k, Portraits of Beyazit II and Gulbaba.

1968, Sept. 1   Litho.

1781	A398 50k gray & multi	20	15
1782	A398 60k tan & multi	28	15
1783	A398 100k lt blue & multi	52	25

Centenary of Galatasaray High School.

Charles de
Gaulle — A399

1968, Oct. 25   Litho.   *Perf. 13*

1784	A399 130k multicolored	70	38

Visit of President Charles de Gaulle of France to Turkey.

Kemal   Ataturk and his Speech
Ataturk — A400   to Youth — A401

Designs: 50k, Ataturk's tomb and Citadel of Ankara. 60k, Ataturk looking out a train window. 250k, Framed portrait of Ataturk in military uniform.

1968, Nov. 10

1785	A400 30k orange & blk	22	15
1786	A400 50k brt grn & sl grn	22	15
1787	A400 60k bl grn & blk	24	15
1788	A401 100k blk, gray & brt grn	55	16
1789	A401 250k multicolored	1.00	40
	Nos. 1785-1789 (5)	2.23	
	Set value		75

30th death anniv. of Kemal Ataturk.

Ataturk Statue Type of 1967

Equestrian Statues of Ataturk: No. 1790, Statue in Zonguldak. No. 1791, Statue in Antakya. No. 1791A, Statue in Bursa.

Imprint: Kiral Matbaasi 1968
1968-69   Litho.   *Perf. 13x12¹⁄₂*
     Size: 22x15mm

1790	A375 10k black & lt blue	20	15
1791	A375 10k blk & brt rose lil	20	15

     Perf. 13¹⁄₂
**Imprint: Tifdruk Matbaacilik Sanayii A.
S. 1969**
     Size: 21x16¹⁄₂mm

1791A	A375 10k dk grn & tan ('69)	30	15
	Set value		15

Ince Minare   ILO Emblem — A403
Mosque,
Konya — A402

Historic Buildings: 10k, Doner Kumbet (tomb), Kayseri. 50k, Karatay Medrese (University Gate), Konya. 100k, Ortakoy Mosque, Istanbul. 200k, Ulu Mosque, Divriki.

1968-69   Photo.   *Perf. 13x13¹⁄₂*

1792	A402 1k dk brn & buff ('69)	15	15
1793	A402 10k plum & dl rose ('69)	18	15
1794	A402 50k dk ol grn & gray	40	15

1795	A402	100k dk & lt grn ('69)	95	15
1796	A402	200k dp bl & lt bl ('69)	1.65	22
		Nos. 1792-1796 (5)	3.33	
		Set value		44

1969, Apr. 15   Litho.   Perf. 13
1797 A403 130k dk red & black   30   15

ILO, 50th anniv.

Sultana Hafsa,
Medical
Pioneer — A404

1969, Apr. 26   Litho.   Perf. 13¹/₂x13
1798 A404 60k multicolored   30   15

**Europa Issue, 1969
Common Design Type**
**1969, Apr. 28   Perf. 13
Size: 32x23mm**
1799 CD12 100k dull vio & multi   55   42
1800 CD12 130k gray grn & multi   75   55

Kemal
Ataturk — A405

Map of
Istanbul — A407

Ataturk and
S.S. Bandirma
A406

1969, May 19   Litho.   Perf. 13
1801 A405 50k multicolored   22   15
1802 A406 60k multicolored   26   15
    Set value   18

50th anniv. of the landing of Kemal Ataturk at Samsun.

1969, May 31
1803 A407 130k vio bl, lt bl, gold & red   35 20

22nd Congress of the Intl. Chamber of Commerce, Istanbul.

Educational
Progress — A408

Agricultural
Progress — A409

Designs: 90k, Pouring ladle and industrial symbols. 100k, Road sign (highway construction). 180k, Oil industry chart and symbols.

1969   Litho.   Perf. 13¹/₂x13
1804 A408   1k black & gray   15   15
1805 A408   1k black & bis brn   15   15
1806 A408   1k black & lt grn   15   15

1807	A408	1k black & lt vio	15	15
1808	A408	1k black & org red	15	15
1809	A409	50k brown & ocher	40	15
1810	A409	90k blk & grnsh gray	65	15
1811	A409	100k black & org red	90	15
1812	A408	180k violet & orange	1.65	15
		Nos. 1804-1812 (9)	4.35	
		Set value		50

Issue dates: 1k, 100k, Apr. 8; 50k, June 11; 90k, 180k, Aug. 15.

Sultan Suleiman
Receiving Sheik Abdul
Latif — A410

Kemal
Ataturk — A411

Designs: 80k, Lady Serving Wine, Safavi miniature, Iran. 130k, Lady on Balcony, Mogul miniature, Pakistan.

1969, July 21   Litho.   Perf. 13
1813 A410 50k yellow & multi   30   15
1814 A410 80k yellow & multi   50   18
1815 A410 130k yellow & multi   85   35

5th anniv. of the signing of the Regional Cooperation for Development Pact by Turkey, Iran and Pakistan.

1969, July 23
Design: 60k, Ataturk monument and bas-relief showing congress.
1816 A411 50k black & gray   18   15
1817 A411 60k black & grnsh gray   22   15
    Set value   20

50th anniversary, Congress of Erzerum.

Sivas
Congress
Delegates
A412

Design: 50k, Congress Hall.

1969, Sept. 4   Litho.   Perf. 13
1818 A412 50k dk brn & dp rose   20   15
1819 A412 60k olive blk & yel   24   15
    Set value   22

50th anniv. of the Congress of Sivas (preparation for the Turkish war of independence).

Bar Dance — A413

Folk Dances: 50k, Candle dance (çaydaçira). 60k, Scarf dance (halay). 100k, Sword dance (kiliç-kalkan). 130k, Two male dancers (zeybek), vert.

1969, Sept. 9
1820 A413 30k brown & multi   18   15
1821 A413 50k multicolored   32   15
1822 A413 60k multicolored   42   20
1823 A413 100k yellow & multi   60   20
1824 A413 130k multicolored   1.00   40
    Nos. 1820-1824 (5)   2.52 1.10

1914
Airplane
"Prince
Celaleddin"
A414

Design: 75k, First Turkish letter carried by air.

1969, Oct. 18   Litho.   Perf. 13
1825 A414 60k dk blue & blue   26   15
1826 A414 75k black & bister   35   18

55th anniv. of the first Turkish mail transported by air.

"Kutadgu
Bilig"
A415

1969, Nov. 20   Litho.   Perf. 13
1827 A415 130k ol bis, brn & gold   35   20

900th anniv. of "Kutadgu Bilig," a book about the function of the state, compiled by Jusuf of Balasagun in Tashkent, 1069.

Ataturk's Arrival in Ankara, after a
Painting — A416

Design: 60k, Ataturk and his coworkers in automobiles arriving in Ankara, after a photograph.

1969, Dec. 27   Litho.   Perf. 13
1828 A416 50k multicolored   20   15
1829 A416 60k multicolored   30   18

50th anniv. of Kemal Ataturk's arrival in Ankara, Dec. 27, 1919.

Bosporus Bridge, Map of Europe and
Asia — A417

Design: 60k, View of proposed Bosporus Bridge and shore lines.

1970, Feb. 20   Litho.   Perf. 13
1830 A417 60k gold & multi   90   30
1831 A417 130k gold & multi   1.75   65

Foundation ceremonies for the bridge across the Bosporus linking Europe and Asia.

Kemal Ataturk
and Signature
A418

Kemal Ataturk
A419

1970   Litho.   Perf. 13
1832 A418   1k dp orange & brn   15   15
1833 A419   5k silver & blk   15   15
1834 A419   30k citron & blk   15   15
1835 A418   50k lt olive & blk   40   15
1836 A419   50k pink & blk   28   15

1837	A419	75k lilac & blk	55	15
1838	A419	100k blue & blk	70	15
		Nos. 1832-1838 (7)	2.38	
		Set value		35

Education Year
Emblem — A420

Turkish EXPO '70
Emblem — A421

1970, Mar. 16
1839 A420 130k ultra, pink & rose lil   45   18

International Education Year.

1970, Mar. 27
Design: 100k, EXPO '70 emblem and Turkish pavilion.
1840 A421 50k gold & multi   15   15
1841 A421 100k gold & multi   25   15
    Set value   22

EXPO '70 International Exhibition, Osaka, Japan, Mar. 15-Sept. 13.

Opening of
Grand
National
Assembly
A422

Design: 60k, Session of First Grand National Assembly, 1920.

1970, Apr. 23
1842 A422 50k multicolored   15   15
1843 A422 60k multicolored   25   15
    Set value   18

Turkish Grand National Assembly, 50th anniv.

Emblem of
Cartographic
Service — A423

Map of Turkey and Gen. Mehmet Sevki
Pasha — A424

Designs: 60k, Plane and aerial mapping survey diagram. 100k, Triangulation point in mountainous landscape.

**Perf. 13¹/₂x13 (A423), 13x13¹/₂
(A424)**
1970, May 2   Litho.
1844 A423 50k blue & multi   15   15
1845 A424 60k blk, gray grn & brick
            red   20   15
1846 A423 100k multicolored   30   15
1847 A424 130k multicolored   50   30
    Set value   58

Turkish Cartographic Service, 75th anniv.

Europa Issue, 1970
Common Design Type
1970, May 4   *Perf. 13*
Size: 37x23mm
1848 CD13	100k ver, blk & org	38	38
1849 CD13	130k dk bl grn, blk & org	60	60

Inauguration of UPU Headquarters, Bern — A425

1970, May 20
1850 A425	60k blk & dull blue	22	15
1851 A425	130k blk & dl ol grn	42	18

Lady with Mimosa, by Osman Hamdi (1842-1910) A426

Paintings: No. 1853, Deer, by Seker Ahmet (1841-1907). No. 1854, Portrait of Fevzi Cakmak, by Avni Lifij (d. 1927). No. 1855, Sailboats, by Nazmi Ziya (1881-1937); horiz.

1970   **Litho.**   *Perf. 13*
Size: 29x49mm
1852 A426	250k multicolored	1.10	35
1853 A426	250k multicolored	1.10	35

Size: 32x49mm
1854 A426	250k multicolored	1.10	35

Size: 73½x33mm
1855 A426	250k multicolored	1.10	35

Issue dates: Nos. 1852-1853, June 15. Nos. 1854-1855, Dec. 15.

Turkish Folk Art — A427

1970, June 15
1856 A427	50k multicolored	30	15

3rd National Stamp Exhibition, ANKARA 70, Oct. 28-Nov. 4. Pane of 50, each stamp se-tenant with label. This 50k, in pane of 50 without labels, was re-issued Oct. 28 with Nos. 1867-1869.

View of Fethiye A428

Designs: 80k, Seeyo-Se-Pol Bridge, Esfahan, Iran. 130k, Saiful Malook Lake, Pakistan.

1970, July 21   **Litho.**   *Perf. 13*
1857 A428	60k multicolored	20	15
1858 A428	80k multicolored	22	15
1859 A428	130k multicolored	38	15
	Set value		32

6th anniv. of the signing of the Regional Cooperation for Development Pact by Turkey, Iran and Pakistan.

Sultan Balim's Tomb — A429   Haci Bektas Veli — A430

Designs: 30k, Tomb of Haci Bektas Veli, horiz.

1970, Aug. 16   **Litho.**   *Perf. 13*
1860 A429	30k multicolored	15	15
1861 A429	100k multicolored	28	15
1862 A430	180k multicolored	50	20
	Set value		35

700th death anniv. of Haci Bektas Veli, mystic.

Hittite Sun Disk and "ISO" — A431

1970, Sept. 15
1863 A431	110k car rose, gold & blk	20	15
1864 A431	150k ultra, gold & blk	30	20

8th General Council Meeting of the Intl. Standardization Org., Ankara.

UN Emblem, People and Globe — A432   Stamp "Flower" and Book — A433

Design: 100k, UN emblem and propeller, horiz.

1970, Oct. 24   **Litho.**   *Perf. 13*
1865 A432	100k gray & multi	26	15
1866 A432	220k multicolored	50	25

25th anniversary of the United Nations.

1970, Oct. 28

Designs: 60k, Ataturk monument and stamps, horiz. 130k, Abstract flower.

1867 A433	10k multicolored	15	15
1868 A433	60k blue & multi	20	15
	Set value		25	15

Souvenir Sheet
1869 A433	130k dk green & org	1.00	1.00

3rd National Stamp Exhibition, ANKARA 70, Oct. 28-Nov. 4. See note below No. 1856.

Inönü Battle Scene A434

Design: No. 1871, Second Battle of Inönü.

1971   **Litho.**   *Perf. 13*
1870 A434	100k multicolored	30	15
1871 A434	100k multicolored	30	15
	Set value		24

1st and 2nd Battles of Inönü, 50th anniv.

Issue dates: #1870, Jan. 10. #1871, Apr. 1.

Village on River Bank, by Ahmet Sekür — A435

Painting: No. 1872, Landscape, Yildiz Palace Garden, by Ahmet Ragip Bicakcilar.

1971, Mar. 15   **Litho.**   *Perf. 13*
1872 A435	250k multicolored	80	40
1873 A435	250k multicolored	80	40

See Nos. 1901-1902, 1909-1910, 1937-1938.

Campaign Against Discrimination A436

1971, Mar. 21   **Litho.**   *Perf. 13*
1874 A436	100k multicolored	16	15
1875 A436	250k gray & multi	45	25

Intl. Year against Racial Discrimination.

Europa Issue, 1971
Common Design Type
1971, May 3   **Litho.**   *Perf. 13*
Size: 31½x22½mm
1876 CD14	100k lt bl, cl & mag	70	70
1877 CD14	150k dp org, grn & red	80	80

Kemal Ataturk
A437   A438

1971
1878 A437	5k gray & ultra	15	15
1879 A437	25k gray & dk red	15	15
1880 A438	25k brown & pink	15	15
1881 A437	100k gray & violet	35	15
1882 A438	100k green & salmon	35	15
1883 A438	250k blue & gray	95	15
1884 A437	400k tan & olive grn	95	15
	Nos. 1878-1884 (7)	3.05	
	Set value		45

Pres. Kemal Gürsel — A439   Mosque of Selim, Edirne — A440

1971, May 27   **Litho.**   *Perf. 13*
1885 A439	100k multicolored	35	15

Revolution of May 27, 1960; Kemal Gürsel (1895-1966), president.

1971, July 21   **Litho.**   *Perf. 13*

Designs: 150k, Religious School, Chaharbagh, Iran. 200k, Badshahi Mosque, Pakistan, horiz.

1886 A440	100k multicolored	24	15
1887 A440	150k multicolored	32	15
1888 A440	200k multicolored	48	18
	Set value		40

Regional Cooperation by Turkey, Iran and Pakistan, 7th anniversary.

Alp Arslan and Battle of Malazkirt — A441

Design: 250k, Archers on horseback.

1971, Aug. 26   **Litho.**   *Perf. 13x13½*
1889 A441	100k multicolored	1.00	16
1890 A441	250k red, org & blk	1.50	38

900th anniversary of the Battle of Malazkirt, which established the Seljuk Dynasty in Asia Minor.

Battle of Sakarya — A442

1971, Sept. 13
1891 A442	100k violet & multi	35	15

50th anniversary of the victory of Sakarya.

Turkey-Bulgaria Railroad — A443

Designs: 110k, Ferry and map of Lake Van. 250k, Turkey-Iran railroad.

1971
1892 A443	100k multicolored	85	20
1893 A443	110k multicolored	85	20
1894 A443	250k yellow & multi	1.90	60

Turkish railroad connections with Bulgaria and Iran. Issued: 110k, 250k, Sept. 27; 100k, Sept. 30.

Netball and Map of Mediterranean A444

Designs: 200k, Runner and stadium, vert. 250k, Shot put and map of Mediterranean, vert.

1971, Oct. 6
1895 A444	100k dull vio & blk	30	15
1896 A444	200k brown, blk & emer	50	25

Souvenir Sheet
Imperf
1897 A444	250k ol bis & sl grn	85	85

Mediterranean Games, Izmir.

Tomb of Cyrus the Great A445

Designs: 100k, Harpist, Persian mosaic, vert. 150k, Ataturk and Riza Shah Pahlavi.

1971, Oct. 13

1898	A445	25k lt blue & multi	25	15
1899	A445	65k multicolored	65	15
1900	A445	150k dk brown & buff	1.10	22
		Set value		42

2500th anniversary of the founding of the Persian empire by Cyrus the Great.

Painting Type of 1971

Paintings: No. 1901, Sultan Mohammed I and his Staff. No. 1902, Palace with tiled walls.

1971, Nov. 15   Litho.   Perf. 13

1901	A435	250k multicolored	1.25	40
1902	A435	250k multicolored	1.25	40

Yunus Emre — A446

1971, Dec. 27   Litho.   Perf. 13

1903	A446	100k brown & multi	65	16

650th death anniv. of Yunus Emre, Turkish folk poet.

First Turkish World Map and Book Year Emblem — A447

1972, Jan. 3   Perf. 13

1904	A447	100k buff & multi	50	16

International Book Year.

Doves and NATO Emblem A448

Fisherman, by Cevat Dereli A449

1972, Feb. 18   Litho.   Perf. 13

1905	A448	100k dull grn, blk & gray	80	22
1906	A448	250k dull bl, blk & gray	1.00	60

Turkey's membership in NATO, 20th anniv.

Europa Issue 1972
Common Design Type

1972, May 2   Litho.   Perf. 13
Size: 22x33mm

1907	CD15	110k blue & multi	80	60
1908	CD15	250k brown & multi	1.10	80

Painting Type of 1971

Paintings: No. 1909, Forest, Seker Ahmet. No. 1910, View of Gebze, Anatolia, by Osman Hamdi.

1972, May 15   Litho.

1909	A435	250k multicolored	1.25	35
1910	A435	250k multicolored	1.25	35

Ataturk Statue Type of 1967

Design: 25k, Ataturk Statue in front of Ethnographic Museum, Ankara.

Imprint: Ajans - Turk/Ankara 1972

1972, June 12   Perf. 12½x11½   Litho.
Size: 22x15½mm

1911	A375	25k black & buff	15	15

1972, July 21   Litho.   Perf. 13

Paintings: 125k, Young Man, by Abdur Rehman Chughtai (Pakistan). 150k, Persian Woman, by Behzad.

1912	A449	100k gold & multi	60	20
1913	A449	125k gold & multi	90	25
1914	A449	150k gold & multi	1.00	35

Regional Cooperation for Development Pact among Turkey, Iran and Pakistan, 8th anniv.

Ataturk and Commanders at Mt. Koca — A450

Designs: No. 1916, Battle of the Commander-in-chief. No. 1917, Turkish army entering Izmir. 110k, Artillery and cavalry.

1972   Litho.   Perf. 13x13½

1915	A450	100k lt ultra & blk	30	15
1916	A450	100k pink & multi	35	15
1917	A450	100k yellow & multi	35	15
1918	A450	110k orange & multi	40	16

50th anniversary of fight for establishment of independent Turkish republic. Issue dates: Nos. 1915, 1918, Aug. 26; No. 1916, Aug. 30; No. 1917, Sept. 9.

"Cancer is Curable" A451

International Railroad Union Emblem A452

1972, Oct. 10   Litho.   Perf. 12½x13

1919	A451	100k blk, brt bl & red	35	15

Fight against cancer.

1972, Dec. 31   Litho.   Perf. 13

1920	A452	100k sl grn, ocher & red	32	15

Intl. Railroad Union, 50th anniv.

Kemal Ataturk — A453

1972-76   Litho.   Perf. 13½x13
Size: 21x26mm

1921	A453	5k gray & blue	15	15
1922	A453	25k orange ('75)	15	15
1923	A453	100k buff & red brn ('73)	48	15
1924	A453	100k lt gray & gray ('75)	22	15
1925	A453	110k lt bl & vio bl	60	15
1926	A453	125k dull green ('73)	70	15
1927	A453	150k tan & brown	75	15
1928	A453	150k lt grn & grn ('75)	28	15
1929	A453	175k yellow & lil ('73)	80	15
1930	A453	200k buff & red	80	15
1931	A453	250k pink & pur ('75)	60	15
1931A	A453	400k gray & Prus bl ('76)	1.00	15
1932	A453	500k pink & violet	2.00	18
1933	A453	500k gray & ultra ('75)	1.10	18

Size: 22x33mm
Perf. 13

1934	A453	10 l pink & car rose ('75)	2.00	30
		Nos. 1921-1934 (15)	11.63	
		Set value		1.40

See Nos. 2060-2061.

Europa Issue 1973
Common Design Type

1973, Apr. 4   Litho.   Perf. 13
Size: 32x23mm

1935	CD16	110k gray & multi	35	28
1936	CD16	250k multicolored	70	55

Painting Type of 1971

Paintings: No. 1937, Beyazit Almshouse, Istanbul, by Ahmet Ziya Akbulut. No. 1938, Flowers, by Suleyman Seyyit, vert.

1973, June 15   Litho.   Perf. 13

1937	A435	250k multicolored	85	35
1938	A435	250k multicolored	85	35

Helmet, Sword and Oak Leaves — A454

Mausoleum of Antiochus I — A455

Design: 100k, Helmet, sword and laurel.

1973, June 28   Perf. 13x12½

1939	A454	90k brown, gray & grn	25	15
1940	A454	100k brown, lem & grn	25	15

Army Day.

1973, July 21   Litho.   Perf. 13

Designs: 100k, Colossal heads, mausoleum of Antiochus I (69-34 B.C.), Commagene, Turkey. 150k, Statue, Shahdad Kerman, Persia, 3000 B.C. 200k, Street, Mohenjo-daro, Pakistan.

1941	A455	100k lt blue & multi	22	15
1942	A455	150k olive & multi	28	16
1943	A455	200k brown & multi	40	22

Regional Cooperation for Development Pact among Turkey, Iran and Pakistan, 9th anniv.

Minelayer Nusret — A456

Designs: 25k, Destroyer Istanbul. 100k, Speedboat Simsek and Naval College. 250k, Two-masted training ship Nuvid-i Futuh.

1973, Aug. 1
Size: 31½x22mm

1944	A456	5k Prus blue & multi	15	15
1945	A456	25k Prus blue & multi	15	15
1946	A456	100k Prus blue & multi	45	15

Size: 48x32mm

1947	A456	250k blue & multi	1.10	25
		Set value		45

---

abu-al-Rayhan al-Biruni A457

Emblem of Darussafaka Foundation A458

1973, Sept. 4   Litho.   Perf. 13x12½

1948	A457	250k multicolored	70	70

abu-al-Rayhan al-Biruni (973-1048), philosopher and mathematician.

1973, Sept. 15   Perf. 13

1949	A458	100k silver & multi	32	15

Centenary of the educational and philanthropic Darussafaka Foundation.

BALKANFILA IV Emblem — A459

Designs: 110k, Symbolic view and stamps. 250k, "Balkanfila 4."

1973   Litho.   Perf. 13

1950	A459	100k gray & multi	32	15
1951	A459	110k multicolored	16	15
1952	A459	250k multicolored	42	18
		Set value		38

BALKANFILA IV, Philatelic Exhibition of Balkan Countries, Izmir, Oct. 26-Nov. 5. Issued: 100k, Sept. 26; 110k, 250k, Oct. 26.

Sivas Shepherd A460

Kemal Ataturk A461

1973, Oct. 4

1953	A460	25k shown	20	15
1954	A460	100k Angora cat	60	15
		Set value		15

1973, Oct. 10   Litho.   Perf. 13

1955	A461	100k gold & blk brn	40	15

35th death anniv. of Kemal Ataturk.

Flower and "50" — A462

Ataturk — A463

Designs: 250k, Torch and "50." 475k, Grain and cogwheel.

1973, Oct. 29

1956	A462	100k purple, red & bl	15	15
1957	A462	250k multicolored	42	20

1958 A462 475k brt blue & org   65   35

Souvenir Sheet

Imperf

1959 A463 500k multicolored   1.00   90

50th anniversary of the Turkish Republic. No. 1959 contains one stamp with simulated perforations.

Bosporus Bridge A464

Design: 150k, Istanbul and Bosporus Bridge. 200k, Bosporus Bridge, children and UNICEF emblem, vert.

1973, Oct. 30   *Perf. 13*

1960 A464 100k multicolored   30   16
1961 A464 150k multicolored   48   30
1962 A464 200k multicolored   55   30

Inauguration of the Bosporus Bridge from Istanbul to Üsküdar, Oct. 30, 1973; UNICEF; children from East and West brought closer through Bosporus Bridge (No. 1962).

Mevlana's Tomb and Dancers A465   Jalal-udin Mevlana A466

1973, Dec. 1   *Perf. 13x12½*

1963 A465 100k blk, lt ultra & grn   28   15
1964 A466 250k blue & multi   52   25

Jalal-udin Mevlana (1207-1273), poet and founder of the Mevlevie dervish order.

Cotton and Ship — A467

Export Products: 90k, Grapes. 100k, Figs. 250k, Citrus fruits. 325k, Tobacco. 475k, Hazelnuts.

1973, Dec. 10   **Litho.**   *Perf. 13*

1965 A467 75k black, gray & bl   20   15
1966 A467 90k black, olive & bl   30   15
1967 A467 100k black, emer & bl   38   15
1968 A467 250k black, brt yel & bl   1.10   22
1969 A467 325k black, yellow & bl   1.10   25
1970 A467 475k black, org brn & bl   1.65   38
Nos. 1965-1970 (6)   4.73
Set value   1.10

Pres. Inönü — A468   Hittite King, 8th Century B.C. — A469

1973, Dec. 25   **Litho.**   *Perf. 13*

1971 A468 100k sepia & buff   30   16

Ismet Inönü, (1884-1973), first Prime Minister and second President of Turkey.

1974, Apr. 29   **Litho.**   *Perf. 13*

Europa: 250k, Statuette of a Boy, (2nd millenium B.C.).

1972 A469 110k multicolored   80   65
1973 A469 250k lt blue & multi   1.40   1.20

Silver and Gold Figure, 3000 B.C. — A470   Child Care — A471

Archaeological Finds: 175k, Painted jar, 5000 B.C., horiz. 200k, Vessels in bull form, 1700-1600 B.C., horiz. 250k, Pitcher, 700 B.C.

1974, May 24   **Litho.**   *Perf. 13*

1974 A470 125k multicolored   45   15
1975 A470 175k multicolored   70   15
1976 A470 200k multicolored   85   20
1977 A470 250k multicolored   1.25   35

1974, May 24

1978 A471 110k gray blue & blk   30   15

75th anniversary of the Sisli Children's Hospital, Istanbul.

Anatolian Rug, 15th Century — A472

Designs: 150k, Persian rug, late 16th century. 200k, Kashan rug, Lahore.

1974, July 21   **Litho.**   *Perf. 12½x13*

1979 A472 100k blue & multi   65   15
1980 A472 150k brown & multi   1.00   20
1981 A472 200k red & multi   2.00   25

10th anniversary of the Regional Cooperation for Development Pact among Turkey, Iran and Pakistan.

Dove with Turkish Flag over Cyprus — A473

1974, Aug. 26   **Litho.**   *Perf. 13*

1982 A473 250k multicolored   80   42

Cyprus Peace Operation.

Wrestling — A474   Arrows Circling Globe — A475

Designs: 90k, 250k, various wrestling holds, horiz.

1974, Aug. 29

1983 A474 90k multicolored   25   15
1984 A474 100k multicolored   38   15
1985 A474 250k multicolored   70   26

World Freestyle Wrestling Championships.

1974, Oct. 9   **Litho.**   *Perf. 13*

UPU Emblem and: 110k, "UPU" in form of dove. 200k, Dove.

1986 A475 110k bl, gold & dk bl   22   15
1987 A475 200k green & brown   32   16
1988 A475 250k multicolored   55   30

Centenary of Universal Postal Union.

"Law Reforms" A476

"National Economy" A477   "Education" A478

1974, Oct. 29

1989 A476 50k blue & black   15   15
1990 A477 150k red & multi   24   15
1991 A478 400k multicolored   65   30
Set value   45

Works and reforms of Kemal Ataturk.

Arrows Pointing Up — A479   Cogwheel and Map of Turkey — A480

1974, Nov. 29   **Litho.**   *Perf. 13*

1992 A479 25k brown & black   15   15
1993 A480 100k brown & gray   32   15
Set value   15

3rd 5-year Development Program (#1992), and industrialization progress (#1993).

Volleyball — A481

1974, Dec. 30

1994 A481 125k shown   35   15
1995 A481 175k Basketball   55   15
1996 A481 250k Soccer   90   20

Automatic Telex Network A482

Postal Check — A483

Radio Transmitter and Waves — A484

1975, Feb. 5   **Litho.**   *Perf. 13*

1997 A482 5k black & yellow   15   15
1998 A483 50k ol grn & org   15   15
1999 A484 100k blue & black   28   15
Set value   48   22

Post and telecommunications.

Child Entering Classroom A485

Children's paintings: 50k, View of village. 100k, Dancing children.

1975, Apr. 23   **Litho.**   *Perf. 13*

2000 A485 25k multicolored   15   15
2001 A485 50k multicolored   15   15
2002 A485 100k multicolored   28   15
Set value   20

Karacaoglan Monument in Mut, by Huseyin Gezer — A486

1975, Apr. 25

2003 A486 110k dk grn, bis & red   30   25

Karacaoglan (1606-1697), musician.

Orange Harvest in Hatay, by Cemal Tollu — A487

Europa: 250k, Yoruk Family on Plateau, by Turgut Zaim.

1975, Apr. 28

2004 A487 110k bister & multi   30   22
2005 A487 250k bister & multi   52   38

Porcelain Vase, Turkey — A488

Designs: 200k, Ceramic plate, Iran, horiz. 250k, Camel leather vase, Pakistan.

Perf. 13¹/₂x13, 13x13¹/₂

1975, July 21		Litho.	
2006	A488 110k multicolored	40	20
2007	A488 200k multicolored	65	25
2008	A488 250k ultra & multi	1.00	40

Regional Cooperation for Development Pact among Turkey, Iran and Pakistan.

Horon Folk Dance — A489

Regional Folk Dances: 125k, Kasik. 175k, Bengi. 250k, Kasap. 325k, Kafkas, vert.

1975, Aug. 30		Perf. 13	
2009	A489 100k blue & multi	26	15
2010	A489 125k green & multi	42	15
2011	A489 175k rose & multi	55	16
2012	A489 250k multicolored	85	25
2013	A489 325k orange & multi	1.10	35
	Nos. 2009-2013 (5)	3.18	
	Set value		92

Knight Slaying Dragon — A490

The Plunder of Salur Kazan's House — A491

Design: 175k, Two Wanderers, horiz.

1975, Oct. 15		Litho.	Perf. 13
2014	A490 90k multicolored	18	15
2015	A490 175k multicolored	32	25
2016	A491 200k multicolored	42	26
	Set value		56

Illustrations for tales by Dede Korkut.

Common Carp A492

1975, Nov. 27	Litho.	Perf. 12¹/₂x13	
2017	A492 75k Turbot	26	15
2018	A492 90k shown	35	15
2019	A492 175k Trout	70	18
2020	A492 250k Red mullet	85	28
2021	A492 475k Red bream	1.75	45
	Nos. 2017-2021 (5)	3.91	
	Set value		1.05

Women's Participation — A493

Insurance Nationalization — A494

Fine Arts — A495

1975, Dec. 5	Perf. 12¹/₂x13, 13x12¹/₂		
2022	A493 100k bis, blk & red	18	15
2023	A494 110k violet & multi	25	15
2024	A495 250k multicolored	38	22
	Set value		38

Works and reforms of Ataturk.

Ceramic Plate — A496

Europa: 400k, Decorated pitcher.

1976, May 3		Litho.	Perf. 13
2025	A496 200k purple & multi	55	50
2026	A496 400k multicolored	90	80

Sultan Ahmed Mosque — A497

1976, May 10

2027 A497 500k gray & multi   80 40

7th Islamic Conference, Istanbul.

Lunch in the Field A498

Children's Drawings: 200k, Boats on the Bosporus, vert. 400k, Winter landscape.

1976, May 19		Litho.	Perf. 13
2028	A498 50k multicolored	15	15
2029	A498 200k multicolored	25	15
2030	A498 400k multicolored	50	20
	Set value		80 35

Samsun 76, First National Junior Philatelic Exhibition, Samsun.

Storks, Sultan Marsh A499

Conservation Emblem and: 200k, Horses, Manyas Lake. 250k, Borabay Lake. 400k, Manavgat Waterfall.

1976, June 5

2031	A499 150k multicolored	2.00	62
2032	A499 200k multicolored	50	15
2033	A499 250k multicolored	80	20
2034	A499 400k multicolored	1.10	26

European Wetland Conservation Year.

Nasreddin Hodja Carrying Liver — A500

Montreal Olympic Emblem and Flame — A501

Turkish Folklore: 250k, Friend giving recipe for cooking liver. 600k, Hawk carrying off liver and Hodja telling hawk he cannot enjoy liver without recipe.

1976, July 5		Litho.	Perf. 13
2035	A500 150k multicolored	25	15
2036	A500 250k multicolored	38	16
2037	A500 600k multicolored	95	35

1976, July 17

Designs: 400k, "76," Montreal Olympic emblem, horiz. 600k, Montreal Olympic emblem and ribbons.

2038	A501 100k red & multi	15	15
2039	A501 400k red & multi	50	25
2040	A501 600k red & multi	90	40
	Set value		70

21st Olympic Games, Montreal, Canada, 7/17-8/1.

Kemal Ataturk A502

Designs: 200k, Riza Shah Pahlavi. 250k, Mohammed Ali Jinnah.

1976, July 21		Litho.	Perf. 13¹/₂
2041	A502 100k multicolored	15	15
2042	A502 200k multicolored	26	15
2043	A502 250k multicolored	35	15
	Set value		28

Regional Cooperation for Development Pact among Turkey, Pakistan and Iran, 12th anniversary.

"Ataturk's Army" A503

Ataturk's Speeches A504

"Peace at Home and in the World" — A505

1976, Oct. 29		Litho.	Perf. 13
2044	A503 100k black & red	18	15
2045	A504 200k gray grn & multi	24	15
2046	A505 400k blue & multi	48	25
	Set value		40

Works and reforms of Ataturk.

Hora A506

1977, Jan. 19		Litho.	Perf. 13
2047	A506 400k multicolored	70	25

MTA Sismik 1 "Hora" geophysical exploration ship.

Keyboard and Violin Sound Hole — A507

1977, Feb. 24		Litho.	Perf. 13x13¹/₂
2048	A507 200k multicolored	40	16

Turkish State Symphony Orchestra, sesquicentennial.

Ataturk and "100" — A508

Design: 400k, Hand holding ballot.

1977, Mar. 21		Litho.	Perf. 13
2049	A508 200k black & red	22	15
2050	A508 400k black & brown	52	25

Centenary of Turkish Parliament.

Hierapolis (Pamukkale) A509

Europa: 400k, Zelve (mountains and poppies).

1977, May 2		Litho.	Perf. 13¹/₂x13
2051	A509 200k multicolored	52	50
2052	A509 400k multicolored	1.00	90

Terra Cotta Pot, Turkey A510

Designs: 225k, Terra cotta jug, Iran. 675k, Terra cotta bullock cart, Pakistan.

1977, July 21		Litho.	Perf. 13
2053	A510 100k multicolored	15	15
2054	A510 225k multicolored	40	15
2055	A510 675k multicolored	95	35
a.	Souv. sheet of 3, #2053-2055	9.00	9.00
	Set value		54

Regional Cooperation for Development Pact among Turkey, Iran and Pakistan, 13th anniv.

Finn-class Yacht A511 | Kemal Ataturk A512

Designs: 200k, Three yachts. 250k, Symbolic yacht.

1977, July 28
2056 A511 150k lt bl, bl & blk 25 15
2057 A511 200k ultra & blue 40 15
2058 A511 250k ultra & black 55 20

European Finn Class Sailing Championships, Istanbul, July 28.

Ataturk Type of 1972
1977, June 13 Litho. Perf. 13¹/₂x13
2060 A453 100k olive 15 15
2061 A453 200k brown 25 15
Set value 15

Imprint: "GUZEL SANATLAR MATBAASI A.S. 1977"
1977, Sept. 23 Litho. Perf. 13
Size: 20¹/₂x22mm
2062 A512 200k blue 20 15
2063 A512 250k Prussian blue 25 15
Set value 15

Imprint: "TIFDRUK-ISTANBUL 1978"
1978, June 28 Photo. Perf. 13
Size: 20x25mm
2065 A512 10k brown 15 15
2066 A512 50k grnsh gray 15 15
2067 A512 1 l fawn 15 15
2068 A512 2¹/₂ l purple 30 15
2069 A512 5 l blue 55 15
2072 A512 25 l dl grn & lt bl 2.25 32
2073 A512 50 l dp org & tan 3.50 1.40
Nos. 2065-2073 (7) 7.05
Set value 2.00

No. 1832 Surcharged with New Value and Wavy Lines
1977, Aug. 17
2078 A418 10k on 1k dp org & brn 25 15

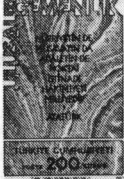

"Rationalism" A513 | "National Sovereignty" A514

"Liberation of Nations" — A515

1977, Oct. 29 Litho. Perf. 13
2079 A513 100k multicolored 15 15
2080 A514 200k multicolored 20 15
2081 A515 400k multicolored 40 20
Set value 35

Works and reforms of Ataturk.

Mohammad Allama Iqbal — A516 | Trees and Burning Match — A517

1977, Nov. 9 Perf. 13x12¹/₂
2082 A516 400k multicolored 45 15

Mohammad Allama Iqbal (1877-1938), Pakistani poet and philosopher.

1977, Dec. 15 Litho. Perf. 13
Design: 250k, Sign showing growing tree.
2083 A517 50k green, blk & red 15 15
2084 A517 250k gray, grn & blk 22 15
Set value 30 15

Forest conservation.
See type A542.

Wrecked Car — A518

Passing on Wrong Side — A519 | Traffic Sign, "Slow!" — A520

Two types of 50k:
I - Number on license plate.
II - No number on plate.

Traffic Safety: 250k, Tractor drawing overloaded farm cart. 800k, Accident caused by incorrect passing. 10 l, "Use striped crossings."

1977-78 Perf. 13¹/₂x13, 13x13¹/₂
2085 A518 50k ultra, blk & red, II 1.10 55
a. Type I 1.40 55
2086 A519 150k red, gray & blk 15 15
2087 A518 250k ocher, blk & red 38 15
2088 A520 500k gray, red & blk 32 16
2089 A520 800k multicolored 1.10 25
2090 A520 10 l dl grn, blk & brn 1.75 35
Nos. 2085-2090 (6) 4.80
Set value 94

Issued: 500k, 1977; others, 1978.

Ishak Palace, Dogubeyazit — A521

Europa: 5 l, Anamur Castle.

1978, May 2 Litho. Perf. 13
2091 A521 2¹/₂ l multicolored 45 45
2092 A521 5 l multicolored 75 75

Riza Shah Pahlavi — A522

1978, June 16 Litho. Perf. 13x13¹/₂
2093 A522 5 l multicolored 70 70

Riza Shah Pahlavi (1877-1944) of Iran, birth centenary.

Yellow Rose, Turkey A523

Designs: 3¹/₂ l, Pink roses, Iran. 8 l, Red roses, Pakistan.

1978, July 21 Litho. Perf. 13
2094 A523 2¹/₂ l multi 16 15
2095 A523 3¹/₂ l multi 25 15
2096 A523 8 l multi 65 25
Set value 38

Regional Cooperation for Development Pact among Turkey, Iran and Pakistan.

Anti-Apartheid Emblem A524

1978, Aug. 14 Litho. Perf. 13¹/₂x13
2097 A524 10 l multicolored 85 25

Anti-Apartheid Year.

View of Ankara — A525

Design: 5 l, View of Tripoli, horiz.

Perf. 13x12¹/₂, 12¹/₂x13
1978, Aug. 17
2098 A525 2¹/₂ l multi 25 15
2099 A525 5 l multi 70 16
Set value 25

Turkish-Libyan friendship.

Souvenir Sheet

Bridge and Mosque — A526

1978, Oct. 25 Imperf.
2100 A526 15 l multicolored 85 80

Edirne '78, 2nd Natl. Phil. Youth Exhib.

Independence Medal — A527 | Latin Alphabet — A529

Speech Reform — A528

Perf. 13x13¹/₂, 13¹/₂x13
1978, Oct. 29
2101 A527 2¹/₂ l multi 16 15
2102 A528 3¹/₂ l multi 18 15
2103 A529 5 l multi 30 15
Set value 26

Ataturk's works and reforms.

House on Bosporus, 1699 — A530

Turkish Houses: 2¹/₂ l, Izmit, 1774, vert. 3¹/₂ l, Kula, 17th cent., vert. 5 l, Milas, 18th-19th cent., vert. 8 l, Safranbolu, 18th-19th cent.

Perf. 13x12¹/₂, 12¹/₂x13
1978, Nov. 22
2104 A530 1 l multi 15 15
2105 A530 2¹/₂ l multi 18 15
2106 A530 3¹/₂ l multi 35 15
2107 A530 5 l multi 48 15
2108 A530 8 l multi 95 25
Nos. 2104-2108 (5) 2.11
Set value 56

Carrier Pigeon, Plane, Horseback Rider, Train A531

Europa: 5 l, Morse key, telegraph and Telex machine. 7¹/₂ l, Telephone dial and satellite.

1979, Apr. 30 Litho. Perf. 13
2109 A531 2¹/₂ l multicolored 16 16
2110 A531 5 l org brn & blk 30 30
2111 A531 7¹/₂ l brt blue & blk 42 42

Plowing, by Namik Ismail A532

Paintings: 7¹/₂ l, Potters, by Kamalel Molk, Iran. 10 l, At the Well, by Allah Baksh, Pakistan.

1979, Sept. 5 Litho. Perf. 13¹/₂x13
2112 A532 5 l multi 20 15
2113 A532 7¹/₂ l multi 35 15
2114 A532 10 l multi 55 22
Set value 44

Regional Cooperation for Development Pact among Turkey, Pakistan and Iran, 15th anniversary.

A533   A534

1979, Sept. 17   *Perf. 13*
2115	A533	5 l	Colemanite	35	15
2116	A533	7½ l	Chromite	60	16
2117	A533	10 l	Antimonite	1.00	20
2118	A533	15 l	Sulphur	1.25	32

10th World Mining Congress.

1979, Sept. 24

8-shaped road, train tunnel, plane and emblem.

2119	A534	5 l	multicolored	30	15

European Ministers of Communications, 8th Symposium.

Youth — A535   Secularization — A536

Design: 5 l, National oath.

Perf. 13x12½, 12½x13
1979, Oct. 29
2120	A535	2½ l	multi	15	15
2121	A536	3½ l	multi	20	15
2122	A535	5 l	black & orange	30	16
			Set value	28	

Ataturk's works and reforms.

Poppies — A537

1979, Nov. 26   **Litho.**   *Perf. 13x13½*
2123	A537	5 l	shown	25	15
2124	A537	7½ l	Oleander	42	15
2125	A537	10 l	Late spider orchid	60	16
2126	A537	15 l	Mandrake	1.25	22
			Set value	50	

See Nos. 2154-2157.

Kemal Ataturk
A538   A538a

Perf. 12½x11½, 13x12½(No. 2131)
1979-81   **Litho.**
2127	A538	50k	olive ('80)	15	15
2128	A538	1 l	grn & lt grn	15	15
2129	A538	2½ l	purple	25	15
2130	A538	2½ l	bl grn & lt bl ('80)	15	15
2131	A538	2½ l	orange ('81)	16	15
2132	A538	5 l	ultra & gray	50	15
a.			Sheet of 8	3.00	3.00
2133	A538	7½ l	brown	60	15
2134	A538	7½ l	red ('80)	52	15

2135	A538	10 l	rose carmine	90	20
2136	A538	20 l	gray ('80)	1.50	28
			Nos. 2127-2136 (10)	4.88	
			Set value		85

No. 2132a for Ankara '79 Philatelic Exhibition, Oct. 14-20.
For surcharge see No. 2261.

1980-82   **Photo.**   *Perf. 13½*
2137	A538a	7½ l	red brown	16	15
c.			Sheet of 4	70	32
2137A	A538a	10 l	brown	65	15
2138	A538a	20 l	lilac	55	15
2138A	A538a	30 l	gray	80	15
2139	A538a	50 l	orange red	1.40	15
2140	A538a	75 l	brt green	2.25	28
2141	A538a	100 l	blue	3.00	70
			Nos. 2137-2141 (7)	8.81	
			Set value		1.48

No. 2137c for ANTALYA '82 4th Natl. Junior Stamp Show. Issue dates: 7½ l, July 15, 1981; 7½ l sheet, Oct. 3, 1982; 30 l, Sept. 23, 1981. Others, Dec. 10, 1980.
See Nos. 2164-2169.

Turkish Printing, 250th Anniversary — A539

1979, Nov. 30   **Litho.**   *Perf. 13*
2142	A539	10 l	multicolored	45	45

2nd International Olive Oil Year — A540

Perf. 12½x13, 13x12½
1979, Dec. 20   **Litho.**
2143	A540	5 l	shown	15	15
2144	A540	10 l	Globe, oil drop, vert.	38	15
			Set value		15

Uskudarli Hoca Ali Riza Bey (1857-1930), Painter A541

Designs: 15 l, Ali Sami Boyar (1880-1967), painter. 20 l, Dr. Hulusi Behcet (1889-1948), physician, discovered Behcet skin disease.

1980, Apr. 28   *Perf. 13*
2145	A541	7½ l	multi	18	15
2146	A541	15 l	multi	32	25
2147	A541	20 l	multi	50	38

Forest Conservation A542   Earthquake Destruction A543

1980, July 3   *Perf. 13½x13*
2148	A542	50k	ol grn & red org	45	15

See type A517. For surcharge see No. 2262.

1980, Sept. 8   *Perf. 13*
2149	A543	7½ l	shown	50	15
2150	A543	20 l	Seismograph	1.00	50

7th World Conference on Earthquake Engineering, Istanbul.

Games' Emblem, Sports — A544   Hegira — A545

1980, Sept. 26   *Perf. 13x13½*
2151	A544	7½ l	shown	45	15
2152	A544	20 l	Emblem, sports, diff.	1.00	15
			Set value		18

First Islamic Games, Izmir.

1980, Nov. 9
2153	A545	20 l	multicolored	1.10	70

Plant Type of 1979

1980, Nov. 26   *Perf. 13*
2154	A537	2½ l	Manisa tulip	15	15
2155	A537	7½ l	Ephesian bellflower	48	15
2156	A537	15 l	Angora crocus	95	15
2157	A537	20 l	Anatolian orchid	1.50	15
			Set value		34

Avicenna Treating Patient A546

Avicenna (Arab Physician), Birth Millenium: 20 l, Portrait, vert.

1980, Dec. 15
2158	A546	7½ l	multi	32	15
2159	A546	20 l	multi	65	15
			Set value		18

Balkanfila VIII Stamp Exhibition, Ankara A547

1981, Jan. 1   **Litho.**   *Perf. 13*
2160	A547	10 l	red & black	50	15

Kemal Ataturk — A548

1981, Feb. 4   *Perf. 13*
2163	A548	10 l	lilac rose	30	15

Ataturk Type of 1980

1983-84   *Perf. 13x13½*
2164	A538a	15 l	grnsh blue	20	15
2165	A538a	20 l	orange ('84)	24	15
2167	A538a	65 l	bluish grn	80	16
2169	A538a	90 l	lilac rose	1.00	20
			Set value		50

Issue dates: Nos. 2164, 2167, 2169, Nov. 30. No. 2165, July 25.

Sultan Mehmet the Conqueror (1432-1481) — A549

1981, May 3   **Litho.**   *Perf. 13x12½*
2173	A549	10 l	multicolored	32	25
2174	A549	20 l	multicolored	65	50

Gaziantep (Folk Dance) A550

Antalya A551

1981, May 4   **Litho.**   *Perf. 13*
2175	A550	7½ l	shown	15	15
2176	A550	10 l	Balikesir	18	15
2177	A550	15 l	Kahramanmaras	25	15
2178	A551	35 l	shown	55	40
2179	A551	70 l	Burdur	1.00	70
			Nos. 2175-2179 (5)	2.13	
			Set value		1.35

Nos. 2178-2179 show CEPT (Europa) emblem.

Nos. C40, 1925, 1931A, 2089 Surcharged in Black with New Value and Wavy Lines

1981, June 3   *Perf. 13½x13*
2179A	AP7	10 l	on 60k	18	15
2180	A453	10 l	on 110k	18	15
2181	A453	10 l	on 400k	18	15
2182	A520	10 l	on 800k	18	15
			Set value		28

A552   Kemal Ataturk — A553

1981, June 22   *Perf. 13x12½*
2183	A552	7½ l	Rug, Bilecik	15	15
2184	A552	10 l	Embroidery	18	15
2185	A552	15 l	Drum, zurna players	30	15
2186	A552	20 l	Embroidered napkin	30	15
2187	A552	30 l	Rug, diff.	55	20
			Nos. 2183-2187 (5)	1.48	
			Set value		52

22nd Intl. Turkish Folklore Congress.

1981, May 19   **Litho.**   *Perf. 14x15*
2188	A553	2½ l	No. 1801	20	15
2189	A553	7½ l	No. 1816	20	15
2190	A553	10 l	No. 1604	15	15
2191	A553	20 l	No. 804	95	15
2192	A553	25 l	No. 777	1.25	15
2193	A553	35 l	No. 1959	1.65	18
			Nos. 2188-2193 (6)	4.40	
			Set value		58

Souvenir Sheet
2194			Sheet of 6	9.50	4.00
a.	A553	2½ l	like 2½ l	15	15
b.	A553	37½ l	like 7½ l	42	15
c.	A553	50 l	like 10 l	60	20
d.	A553	100 l	like 20 l	1.25	40
e.	A553	125 l	like 25 l	1.50	50
f.	A553	175 l	like 35 l	2.25	65

Souvenir Sheet

Balkanfila VIII Stamp Exhibition, Ankara — A554

1981, Aug. 8   **Litho.**   *Perf. 13*
2195			Sheet of 2	5.50	5.50
a.	A554	50 l	No. B68	2.50	2.50
b.	A554	50 l	No. 733	2.50	2.50

5th General
Congress of
European
Physics
Society
A555

1981, Sept. 7   *Perf. 12¹/₂x13*
2196 A555 10 l red & multi   15 15
2197 A555 30 l blue & multi   45 20
     Set value   26

World Food
Day
A556

1981, Oct. 16
2198 A556 10 l multicolored   15 15
2199 A556 30 l multicolored   45 20
     Set value   26

Constituent Assembly
Inauguration — A557

1981, Oct. 23   *Perf. 13*
2200 A557 10 l multicolored   18 15
2201 A557 30 l multicolored   55 18
     Set value   25

Ataturk — A558

Portraits of Ataturk.

1981-82   *Perf. 11¹/₂x12¹/₂, 13 (#2204)*
2202 A558   1 l green   15 15
2203 A558   2¹/₂ l purple   15 15
2204 A558   2¹/₂ l gray & org   50 16
2205 A558   5 l blue   15 15
2206 A558   10 l orange   18 15
2207 A558   35 l brown   65 15
     Set value   1.50 45

Issue dates: No. 2204, Dec. 10, 1981; others,
Jan. 27, 1982.

Literacy Campaign
A559

Energy
Conservation
A560

1981, Dec. 24   *Perf. 13¹/₂*
2217 A559 2¹/₂ l Procession   35 15

1982, Jan. 11   *Perf. 13*
2218 A560 10 l multicolored   35 15

Magnolias, by
Ibrahim Calli
(b. 1882)
A561

Sultanhan
Caravanserai
A562

Perf. 13x13¹/₂, 13¹/₂x13
1982, Mar. 17
2219 A561 10 l shown   15 15
2220 A561 20 l Fishermen, horiz.   25 15
2221 A551 30 l Sewing Woman   32 15
     Set value   20

Europa Issue
1982, Apr. 26   *Perf. 13x12¹/₂*
2222 A562 30 l shown   25   15
2223 A562 70 l Silk Route   60 20
   a.   Min. sheet, 2 each #2222-2223   2.50 65
   b.   Pair, #2222-2223   85 45
     Set value   26

1250th Anniv. of Kul-
Tigin Monument, Kosu
Saydam,
Mongolia — A563

1982, June 9   *Perf. 13*
2224 A563 10 l Monument   15 15
2225 A563 30 l Kul-Tigin (685-732),
     Gok-Turkish command-
     er   40 15
     Set value   15

Pendik
Shipyard
Opening
A564

1982, July 1   *Perf. 12¹/₂x13*
2226 A564 30 l Ship, emblem   38 15

Mountains of
Anatolia
A565

1982, July 17   *Perf. 13*
2227 A565 7¹/₂ l Agri Dagi, vert.   15 15
2228 A565 10 l Buzul Dagi   28 15
2229 A565 15 l Demirkazik, vert.   42 15
2230 A565 20 l Erciyes   65 15
2231 A565 30 l Kackar Dagi, vert.   70 15
2232 A565 35 l Uludag   95 15
     Nos. 2227-2232 (6)   3.15
     Set value   42

Beyazit
State
Library
Centenary
A566

1982, Sept. 27
2233 A566 30 l multicolored   45 25

Musical Instruments of Anatolia — A567

1982, Oct. 13
2234 A567 7¹/₂ l Davul   20 15
2235 A567 10 l Baglama   32 15
2236 A567 15 l shown   42 15
2237 A567 20 l Kemence   65 15
2238 A567 30 l Mey   85 15
     Nos. 2234-2238 (5)   2.44
     Set value   35

Roman
Temple
Columns,
Start
A568

1982, Nov. 3
2239 A568 30 l multi   40 40

Family
Planning and
Mother-Child
Health
A569

1983, Jan. 12   *Litho.*   *Perf. 13*
2240 A569 10 l Family on map   16 15
2241 A569 35 l Mother and child   48 15
     Set value   15

30th Anniv.
of Customs
Cooperation
Council
A570

1983, Jan. 26
2242 A570 45 l multi   55 15

1982
Constitution
A571

1983, Jan. 27
2243 A571 10 l Ballot box   15 15
2244 A571 30 l Open book, scale   35 15
     Set value   15

Manastirli
Bey
A572

1983, Mar. 16   *Litho.*
2245 A572 35 l multi   40 15

Manastirli Hamdi Bey (1890-1945), telegrapher
of news of Istanbul's occupation to Ataturk, 1920.

Europa Issue

Piri Reis,
Geographer
A573

1983, May 5   *Litho.*   *Perf. 12¹/₂x13*
2246 A573 50 l shown   60 15
2247 A573 100 l Ulug Bey (1394-
     1449), astronomer   1.25 25

Youth Week
A574

1983, May 16
2248 A574 15 l multi   25 15

World Communications Year — A575

1983, May 16   *Perf. 13*
2249 A575 15 l Carrier pigeon, vert.   16 15
2250 A575 50 l Phone lines   48 15
2251 A575 70 l Emblem, vert.   70 20
     Set value   36

50th Anniv.
of State Civil
Aviation
A576

1983, May 20   *Litho.*   *Perf. 13*
2252 A576 50 l Plane, jet   48 15
2253 A576 70 l Airport   68 20

18th Council
of Europe Art
Exhibition
A577

Designs: 15 l, Eros, 2nd cent. BC, vert. 35 l,
Two-headed duck, Hittite, 14th cent BC. 50 l, Zinc
jugs, plate, 16th cent., vert. 70 l, Marcus Aurelius
and his wife Faustina the Young, 2nd cent.

1983, May 22   *Perf. 13*
2254 A577 15 l multi   28 15
2255 A577 35 l multi   70 15
2256 A577 50 l multi   85 15
2257 A577 70 l multi   1.10 18
     Set value   42

Council of Europe's
"The Water's Edge"
Campaign — A578

Coastal Views.

1983, June 1   Litho.   Perf. 13x12¹/₂
2258 A578 10 l Olodeniz				15 15
2259 A578 25 l Olympus				35 15
2260 A578 35 l Kekova				50 15
			Set value			18

Nos. 2127, 2148 Surcharged
Perf. 12¹/₂x11¹/₂, 13¹/₂x13
1983, June 8
2261 A538 5 l on 50k olive				15 15
2262 A542 5 l on 50k ol grn & red
		org			15 15
		Set value			25 15

Kemal Ataturk
A579

Aga Khan Architecture
Award
A580

1983, June 22   Perf. 13
2263 A579 15 l bl grn & bl		18 15
 a. Sheet of 5 + label		1.00 25
2264 A579 50 l green & blue		65 15
2265 A579 100 l orange & blue		1.40 25
			Set value			42

For surcharge, see No. 2432.

1983, Sept. 4   Photo.   Perf. 11¹/₂
2266 A580 50 l View of Istanbul			55 15

60th Anniv. of
the Republic
A582

1983, Oct. 29   Perf. 13¹/₂x13
2268 A582 15 l multi				25 15
2269 A582 50 l multi				75 15
			Set value			16

Columns,
Aphrodisias
A583

1983, Nov. 2   Perf. 13
2270 A583 50 l multi				75 75

UNESCO Campaign for
Istanbul and
Goreme — A584

1984, Feb. 15   Litho.   Perf. 13
2271 A584 25 l St. Sophia Basilica		32 15
2272 A584 35 l Goreme			45 15
2273 A584 50 l Istanbul			60 15
			Set value			20

Natl. Police Org.
Emblem — A585

1984, Apr. 10   Litho.   Perf. 13
2274 A585 15 l multi				30 25

Europa (1959-84)
A586

1984, Apr. 30   Perf. 13¹/₂x13
2275 A586 50 l blue & multi		42 15
2276 A586 100 l gray & multi		95 15
			Set value			20

Mete Khan,
Hun Ruler,
204 BC,
Flag — A587

Sixteen States (Hun Rulers and Flags): 20 l, Panu, Western Hun empire (48-216). 50 l, Attila, 375-454. 70 l, Aksunvar, Ak Hun empire, 420-562.

1984, June 20   Litho.   Perf. 13
2277 A587 10 l multi				15 15
2278 A587 25 l multi				25 15
2279 A587 50 l multi				65 15
2280 A587 70 l multi				1.00 15
			Set value			26

See Nos. 2315-2318, 2349-2352, 2382-2385.

Occupation of
Cyprus, 10th
Anniv. — A588

1984, July 20   Litho.   Perf. 13
2281 A588 70 l Dove, olive branch	1.10 50

Wild
Flowers
A589

Armed Forces Day
A590

1984, Aug. 1   Perf. 11¹/₂x12¹/₂
2282 A589   10 l Marshmallow flow-
		er			15 15
2283 A589 20 l Red poppy		24 15
2284 A589 70 l Sowbread		85 15
2285 A589 200 l Snowdrop		2.50 28
2286 A589 300 l Tulip			4.00 42
		Nos. 2282-2286 (5)		7.74
			Set value			90

See Nos. 2301-2308. For surcharges see Nos. 2479-2480.

1984, Aug. 26   Perf. 13¹/₂x13
2287 A590 20 l Soldier, dove, flag		15 15
2288 A590 50 l Sword			38 15
2289 A590 70 l Arms, soldier, flag		55 15
2290 A590 90 l Map, soldier			65 15
			Set value			32

Trees and Wood
Products
A591

Pres. Ismet Inonu
(1884-1973),
A592

Seed, Tree and Product: 10 l, Liquidambar, liquidambar grease. 20 l, Oriental spruce, stringed instrument. 70 l, Oriental beech, chair. 90 l, Cedar of Lebanon, ship.

1984, Sept. 19   Litho.   Perf. 13x12¹/₂
2291 A591 10 l multi				15 15
2292 A591 20 l multi				16 15
2293 A591 70 l multi				72 15
2294 A591 90 l multi				85 15
			Set value			30

1984, Sept. 24   Perf. 13
2295 A592 20 l Portrait				30 15

First Intl. Turkish Carpet
Congress — A593

1984, Oct. 7   Perf. 13x13¹/₂
2296 A593 70 l Seljukian carpet, 13th
		cent.			45 15

Ruins of
Ancient City
of Harran
A594

1984, Nov. 7   Perf. 13¹/₂x13
2297 A594 70 l Columns, arch		85 15

Turkish Women's
Suffrage, 50th
Anniv. — A595

1984, Dec. 5   Litho.   Perf. 13
2298 A595 20 l Women voting		25 25

40th Anniv.,
ICAO — A596

1984, Dec. 7   Litho.   Perf. 13
2299 A596 100 l Icarus, ICAO em-
		blem			1.10 1.00

Souvenir Sheet

No. 1047
A597

1985, Jan. 13   Litho.   Imperf.
2300		Sheet of 4			2.50 2.50
a.-b. A597 70 l, any single		35 15

Istanbul '87. No. 2300b has denomination in lower right.

Flower Type of 1984

1985   Perf. 11¹/₂x12¹/₂
2301 A589 5 l Narcissus		15 15
		Perf. 12¹/₂x13
2308 A589 100 l Daisy			60 20
			Set value			65 25

Issue dates: #2301, Feb. 6. #2308, July 31.

Turkish
Aviation
League, 60th
Anniv.
A598

1985, Feb. 16   Perf. 13
2310 A598 10 l Parachutist, glider		16 15
2311 A598 20 l Hot air balloon, vert.	24 15
			Set value			15

INTELSAT, 20th
Anniv. — A599

1985, Apr. 3
2312 A599 100 l multi				45 15

Europa Issue

Ulvi Cemal
Erkin (1906-
1972) and
Kosekce
A600

Composers and music: 200 l, Mithat Fenmen (1916-1982) and Concertina.

1985, Apr. 29   Perf. 13¹/₂x13
2313 A600 100 l multi				48 15
2314 A600 200 l multi				90 16
			Set value			24

Turkish States Type of 1984

Sixteen States (Kagan rulers and flags): 10 l, Bilge, Gokturk Empire (552-743) and Orhon-Turkish alphabet. 20 l, Bayan, Avar Empire (565-803). 70 l, Hazar, Hazar Empire (651-983). 100 l, Kutlug Kul Bilge, Uygur State (774-1335).

1985, June 20
2315 A587 10 l multi				15 15
2316 A587 20 l multi				15 15
2317 A587 70 l multi				32 15
2318 A587 100 l multi				50 15
			Set value			25

Intl. Youth
Year — A601

1985, Aug. 8
2319 A601 100 l multi				38 15
2320 A601 120 l multi				48 15
			Set value			18

Postal Code
Inauguration — A602

1985, Sept. 4   Perf. 13
Background Color
2321 A602 10 l pale yel brn		15 15
2322 A602 16 l fawn			16 15
2323 A602 20 l gray green		16 15
2324 A602 20 l brt blue			16 15
2325 A602 70 l rose lilac		60 15
2326 A602 100 l gray			85 15
		Nos. 2321-2326 (6)		2.08
			Set value			35

Symposium
of Natl.
Palaces
A603

1985, Sept. 25   *Perf. 13¹/₂x13*
2327 A603   20 l Aynalikavak, c. 1703   15 15
2328 A603   100 l Beylerbeyi, 1865   55 15
     Set value   15

UN, 40th
Anniv.
A604

1985, Oct. 24
2329 A604   100 l multi   50 15

Alanya
Fortress and
City
A605

1985, Nov. 7
2330 A605   100 l multi   50 15

A606   A607

1985, Nov. 12   *Perf. 13x13¹/₂*
2331 A606   100 l multi   65 15

Turkish Meteorological Service, 60th anniv.

1985, Dec. 14
2332 A607   20 l multi   15 15

Isik Lyceum, Istanbul, cent.

Ataturk — A608

Perf. 11¹/₂x12¹/₂
1985, Dec. 18   **Litho.**
2334 A608   10 l pale bl & ultra   15 15
2336 A608   20 l beige & brn   15 15
2340 A608   100 l lt pink & claret   60 15
     Set value   20

For surcharges, see Nos. 2433-2434.
This is an expanding set. Numbers will change if
necessary.

7th Intl.
Children's
Festival,
Ankara
A609

Various children's drawings.

1986, Apr. 23   **Litho.**   *Perf. 12¹/₂x13*
2342 A609   20 l multi   15 15
2343 A609   100 l multi   60 15
2344 A609   120 l multi   75 15
     Set value   26

Europa Issue

Pollution
A610

1986, Apr. 28   *Perf. 13*
2345 A610   100 l shown   38 15
2346 A610   200 l Bandaged leaf   70 16
     Set value   24

1st Ataturk Intl.   Kirkpinar Wrestling
Peace   Matches,
Prize — A611   Edirne — A613

1st Turkish
Submarine,
Cent.
A612

1986, May 19   **Litho.**   *Perf. 13*
2347 A611   20 l gold & multi   15 15
2348 A611   100 l silver & multi   48 15
     Set value   16

States Type of 1984

Sixteen States (Devleti rulers and flags): 10 l,
Bilge Kul Kadir Khan, Kara Khanids State (840-
1212). 20 l, Alp-Tekin, Ghaznavids State (963-
1183). 100 l, Seldjuk Bey, Seldjuks State (1040-
1157). 120 l, Muhammed Harezmsah, Khwarizm-
Shahs State (1157-1231).

1986, June 20
2349 A587   10 l multi   15 15
2350 A587   20 l multi   15 15
2351 A587   100 l multi   70 15
2352 A587   120 l multi   80 15
     Set value   35

1986, June 16   **Litho.**   *Perf. 13*
2353 A612   20 l Torpedo sub Abdulhamid   25 15

1986, June 30
2354 A613   10 l Oiling bodies   15 15
2355 A613   20 l Five wrestlers   15 15
2356 A613   100 l Two wrestlers   55 15
     Set value   22

Organization for Economic Cooperation
and Development, 25th Anniv. — A614

1986, Sept. 30 Litho.   *Perf. 13¹/₂x13*
2357 A614   100 l multi   38 45

Automobile,
Cent.
A615

1986, Oct. 15
2358 A615   10 l Benz Velocipede,
        1886   15 15
2359 A615   20 l Rolls-Royce Silver
        Ghost, 1906   15 15

2360 A615   100 l Mercedes Touring
        Car, 1928   60 15
2361 A615   200 l Abstract speeding car   1.10 20
     Set value   40

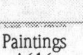

Paintings   Celal Bayar
A616   (1883-1986),
         3rd President
         A617

Designs: 100 l, Bouquet with Tulip, by
Feyhaman Duran (1886-1970). 120 l, Landscape
with Fountain, by H. Avni Lifij (1886-1927), horiz.

Perf. 13¹/₂x13, 13x13¹/₂
1986, Oct. 22
2362 A616   100 l multi   38 15
2363 A616   120 l multi   48 15
     Set value   22

1986, Oct. 27   *Perf. 13*
2364 A617   20 l shown   15 15
2365 A617   100 l Profile   40 15
     Set value   15

Kubad-Abad
Ruins,
Beysehir
Lake
A618

1986, Nov. 7   *Perf. 13¹/₂x13*
2366 A618   100 l multi   45 15

Mehmet Akif Ersoy (1873-1936),
Composer of the Turkish National Anthem
A619

1986, Dec. 27 Litho.   *Perf. 13¹/₂x13*
2367 A619   20 l multi   20 15

Road Safety   Intl. Year of
A620   Shelter for the
         Homeless
         A622

Butterflies
A621

1987, Feb. 4   **Litho.**   *Perf. 13x13¹/₂*
2368 A620   10 l Use seatbelts   15 15
2369 A620   20 l Don't drink alcohol
        and drive   15 15
2370 A620   150 l Observe speed limit   55 15
     Set value   70 22

For surcharges see Nos. 2477-2478.

1987, Feb. 25   *Perf. 13¹/₂x13*
2371 A621   10 l Celerio euphorbiae   15 15
2372 A621   20 l Vanessa atalanta   15 15
2373 A621   100 l Euplagia
        quadripunctaria   35 15
2374 A621   120 l Colias crocea   42 15
     Set value   90 28

1987, Mar. 18   **Litho.**   *Perf. 13x13¹/₂*
2375 A622   200 l multi   70 15

Karabuk Iron
and Steel
Works, 50th
Anniv.
A623

1987, Apr. 3   **Litho.**   *Perf. 13¹/₂x13*
2376 A623   50 l Interior   15 15
2377 A623   200 l Exterior   60 15
     Set value   20

Natl.
Sovereignty
A624

1987, Apr. 23   *Perf. 13¹/₂x13*
2378 A624   50 l multi   20 15

67th anniv. of the founding of the Turkish state.

Architecture
A625

Europa: 50 l, Turkish History Institute, 1951-67,
designed by Turgut Cansever with Ertur Yener.
200 l, Social Insurance Institute, 1963, designed by
Sedad Hakki Eldem.

1987, Apr. 28   *Perf. 13*
2379 A625   50 l multi   15 15
2380 A625   200 l multi   60 15
     Set value   20

92nd Session, Intl.
Olympic Committee,
Istanbul, May 9-
12 — A626

1987, May 9   **Litho.**   *Perf. 13x13¹/₂*
2381 A626   200 l multi   70 15

Turkish States Type of 1984

Sixteen states (Devleti and Imparatorlugu rulers
and flags): 10 l, Batu Khan, Golden Horde State
(1227-1502). 20 l, Kutlug Timur Khan, Great
Timur Empire (1368-1507). 50 l, Babur Shah,
Babur Empire (1526-1858). 200 l, Osman Bey
Gasi, Ottoman Empire (1299-1923).

1987, June 20   *Perf. 12¹/₂x13*
2382 A587   10 l multi   15 15
2383 A587   20 l multi   15 15
2384 A587   50 l multi   15 15
2385 A587   200 l multi   60 15
     Set value   85 30

Album of the Conqueror, Mehmet II, 15th
Cent., Topkapi Palace Museum — A627

Untitled paintings by Mehmet Siyah Kalem: 10 l,
Two warriors, vert. 20 l, Three men, donkey. 50 l,
Blackamoor whipping horse. 200 l, Demon, vert.

Perf. 13¹/₂x13, 13x13¹/₂

1987, July 1			Litho.	
2386 A627	10 l	multi	15	15
2387 A627	20 l	multi	15	15
2388 A627	50 l	multi	28	15
2389 A627	200 l	multi	1.10	15
		Set value		30

Natl.
Palaces
A628

1987, Sept. 25		**Perf. 13¹/₂x13**	
2390 A628	50 l Ihlamur, c. 1850	15	15
2391 A628	200 l Kucuksu Pavilion, 1857	60	15
	Set value		20

See Nos. 2425-2426.

"Tughra," Suleiman's Calligraphic
Signature — A629

Designs: 30 l, Portrait, vert. 200 l, Suleiman
Receiving a Foreign Minister, contemporary miniature, vert. 270 l, Bust, detail of bas-relief, The
Twenty-Three Law-Givers, entrance to the gallery of
the US House of Representatives.

Litho., Litho. & Engr. (270 l)

1987, Oct. 1		**Perf. 13¹/₂x13, 13x13¹/₂**	
2392 A629	30 l multi	15	15
2393 A629	50 l shown	15	15
2394 A629	200 l multi	60	15
2395 A629	270 l multi	80	16
	Set value		38

Suleiman the Magnificent (1494-1566), sultan of
the Turkish Empire (1520-1566). On No. 2395, the
gold ink was applied by a thermographic process
producing a shiny, raised effect.

A630   A631

Presidents: a, Cemal Gursel (1961-1966). b,
Cevdet Sunay (1966-1973). c, Fahri S. Koruturk
(1973-1980). d, Kenan Evren (1982-). e, Ismet
Inonu (1938-1950). f, Celal Bayar (1950-1960). g,
Mustafa Kemal Ataturk (1923-1938).

1987, Oct. 29	Litho.	*Imperf.*	
	Souvenir Sheet		
2396	Sheet of 7	1.10	40
a.-f.	A630 50 l any single	15	15
g.	A630 100 l multi, 26x37mm	24	15

1988, Apr. 9		Litho.	*Perf. 13*	
2397 A631	50 l shown		15	15
2398 A631	200 l	Mosque, architectural elements	40	15
		Set value		15

Joseph (Mimar) Sinan (1489-1588), architect.

Health — A632

1988, May 4			
2399 A632	50 l Immunization, horiz.	15	15
2400 A632	200 l Fight drug abuse	35	15
2401 A632	300 l Safe work conditions, horiz.	52	15
2402 A632	600 l Organ donation	1.05	28
	Set value		55

Europa Issue

Telecommunications — A633

Transport and communication: 200 l, Modes of
transportation, vert.

1988, May 2		Litho.	*Perf. 13, 12¹/₂*	
2403 A633	200 l multi		48	15
2404 A633	600 l multi		1.40	28
		Set value		36

Steam,
Electric and
Diesel
Locomotives
A634

Designs: 50 l, American Standard steam engine,
c. 1850. 100 l, Steam engine produced in Esslingen
for Turkish railways, 1913. 200 l, Henschel Krupp
steam engine, 1926. 300 l, E 43001 Toshiba electric engine produced in Japan, 1987. 600 l, MTE-
Tulomsas No. 24361 diesel-electric high-speed
engine, 1984.

1988, May 24		*Perf. 13*	
2405 A634	50 l buff, brn & blk	15	15
2406 A634	100 l buff, brn & blk	22	15
2407 A634	200 l buff, brn & blk	45	15
2408 A634	300 l buff, brn & blk	65	15
2409 A634	600 l buff, brn & blk	1.40	28
	Nos. 2405-2409 (5)	2.87	
	Set value		60

Court of
Cassation
(Supreme
Court),
120th
Anniv.
A635

1988, July 1		Litho.	*Perf. 13¹/₂x13*	
2410 A635	50 l multi		25	15

Bridge Openings — A636

Designs: 200 l, Fatih Sultan Mehmet Bridge,
Kavacik-Hisarustu. 300 l, Seto Ohashi (Friendship)
Bridges, the Minami and Kita.

1988, July 3		Litho.	*Perf. 13x13¹/₂*	
2411 A636	200 l multi		45	15
2412 A636	300 l multi		60	15
		Set value		20

Telephone
System — A637

1988, Aug. 24		Litho.	*Perf. 13¹/₂x13*	
2413 A637	100 l multi		30	15

1988
Summer
Olympics,
Seoul
A638

Perf. 12¹/₂x13, 13x12¹/₂

1988, Sept. 17		Litho.	
2414 A638	100 l Running	24	15
2415 A638	200 l Archery	50	15
2416 A638	400 l Weight lifting	1.00	24
2417 A638	600 l Gymnastics, vert.	1.50	35
	Set value		76

Naim Suleymanoglu,
1988 Olympic Gold
Medalist, Weight
Lifting — A639

1988, Oct. 5		Litho.	*Perf. 13x12¹/₂*	
2418 A639	1000 l multi		2.75	60

Aerospace
Industries
A640

Perf. 13¹/₂x13, 13x13¹/₂

1988, Oct. 28			
2419 A640	50 l Gear, aircraft, vert.	15	15
2420 A640	200 l shown	48	15
	Set value		15

Butterflies
A641

1988, Oct. 28		*Perf. 13¹/₂x13*	
2421 A641	100 l Gonepteryx rhamni	28	15
2422 A641	200 l Chazara briseis	52	15
2423 A641	400 l Allancastria cerisyi godart	1.00	22
2424 A641	600 l Nymphalis antiopa	1.50	35
a.	Souv. sheet of 4, #2421-2424	3.50	75
	Set value		75

ANTALYA '88.

Natl. Palaces Type of 1987

1988, Nov. 3		Litho.	*Perf. 13*	
2425 A628	100 l Maslak Royal Lodge, c. 1890		16	15
2426 A628	400 l Yildiz Sale Pavilion, 1889		65	15
		Set value		18

Souvenir Sheet

Kemal Ataturk — A642

1988, Nov. 10		*Perf. 13x13¹/₂*	
2427 A642	400 l multi	95	25

Medicinal
Plants of
Anatolia
A643

1988, Dec. 14		Litho.	*Perf. 13*	
2428 A643	150 l Tilia rubra		22	15
2429 A643	300 l Malva silvestris		42	15
2430 A643	600 l Hyoscyamus niger		85	18
2431 A643	900 l Atropa belladonna		1.25	28
		Set value		60

Stamps of 1983-85
Surcharged

Perf. 13, 11¹/₂x12¹/₂

1989, Feb. 8			Litho.	
2432 A579	50 l on 15 l No. 2263		15	15
2433 A608	75 l on 10 l No. 2334		15	15
2434 A608	150 l on 20 l No. 2336		20	15
	Set value		38	15

Surcharge on No. 2432 is slightly different.

Artifacts in
the Museum
of Anatolian
Civilizations,
Ankara
A644

Designs: 150 l, Seated Goddess with Child, neolithic bisque figurine, Hacilar, 6th millennium B.C.
300 l, Lead figurine, Alisar Huyuk, Assyrian Trading
Colonies Era, c. 19th cent. B.C. 600 l, Human-
shaped vase, Kultepe, Assyrian Trading Colonies
Era, 18th cent. B.C. 1000 l, Ivory mountain god,
Bogazkoy, Hittite Empire, 14th cent. B.C.

1989, Feb. 8		Litho.	*Perf. 13¹/₂x13*	
2435 A644	150 l multi		24	15
2436 A644	300 l multi		45	15
2437 A644	600 l multi		85	18
2438 A644	1000 l multi		1.40	30
		Set value		62

See Nos. 2458-2461, 2495-2498, 2520-2523,
2617-2620.

NATO, 40th
Anniv.
A645

1989, Apr. 4		*Perf. 13¹/₂* Litho.	Wmk. 394	
2439 A645	600 l multi		90	20

Europa Issue

Children's
Games — A646

Perf. 13x12½
1989, Apr. 23 **Wmk. 394**
2440 A646 600 l Leapfrog 80 20
2441 A646 1000 l Open the door,
Headbezirgan 1.35 35

Steamships
A647

Perf. 13½x13
1989, July 1 **Litho.** **Wmk. 394**
2442 A647 150 l Sahilbent 20 15
2443 A647 300 l Ragbet 40 15
2444 A647 600 l Tari 80 20
2445 A647 1000 l Guzelhisar 1.30 32
 Set value 66

French
Revolution,
Bicent. — A648

Kemal
Ataturk — A649

Wmk. 394
1989, July 14 **Litho.** **Perf. 14**
2446 A648 600 l multi 85 20

1989, Aug. 16 **Perf. 13x13½**
2447 A649 2000 l gray & bluish gray 2.00 50
2448 A649 5000 l gray & deep red
brn 5.00 1.25

See Nos. 2485-2486, 2537, 2539, 2541, 2544.

No. 2336 Surcharged in Bright Blue
Perf. 11½x12½
1989, Aug. 31 **Litho.** **Unwmk.**
2449 A608 500 l on 20 l 68 17

Photography,
150th Anniv.
A650

1989, Oct. 17 **Perf. 13½x13**
2450 A650 175 l Camera 20 15
2451 A650 700 l Shutter 82 20
 Set value 25

State
Exhibition of
Paintings
and
Sculpture
A651

Designs: 200 l, *Manzara*, by Hikmet Onat. 700 l,
Sari Saz, by Bedri Rahmi Eyuboglu. 1000 l, *Kadin*,
by Zuhtu Muridoglu.

Perf. 13½x13
1989, Oct. 30 **Litho.** **Wmk. 394**
2452 A651 200 l multicolored 22 15
2453 A651 700 l multicolored 80 20
2454 A651 1000 l multicolored 1.15 30
 Set value 55

Jawaharlal Nehru, 1st
Prime Minister of
Independent
India — A652

1989, Nov. 14 **Perf. 13½x12½**
2455 A652 700 l multicolored 80 20

Sea Turtles
A653

1989, Nov. 16 **Perf. 13½x13**
2456 A653 700 l Caretta caretta 80 20
2457 A653 1000 l Chelonia mydas 1.15 30
 a. Souv. sheet of 2, #2456-2457 2.00 1.00

Artifacts Type of 1989
Perf. 13x12½, 12½x13
1990, Feb. 8 **Litho.** **Wmk. 394**
2458 A644 100 l Ivory female deity 15 15
2459 A644 200 l Ceremonial vessel 25 15
2460 A644 500 l Seated goddess
pendant 65 15
2461 A644 700 l Carved lion 90 15
 Set value 35

Nos. 2458 and 2460 vert.

Wars of Dardanelles,
1915 — A654

1990, Mar. 18 **Perf. 13**
2462 A654 1000 l multicolored 85 21

EXPO '90 Intl. Garden and Greenery
Exposition, Osaka
A655 A656

Illustration reduced.

Perf. 12½x13
1990, Apr. 1 **Litho.** **Wmk. 394**
2463 A655 1000 l multicolored 1.00 25
2464 A656 1000 l multicolored 1.00 25
 a. Pair, #2463-2464 2.00 75

Nos. 2301, 2368 and 2284 Surcharged
1990, Apr. 4 **Litho.** **Perfs. as Before**
2465 A589 50 l on 5 l #2301 15 15
2466 A620 100 l on 10 l #2368 15 15
2467 A589 200 l on 70 l #2284 20 15
 Set value 35 15

Grand Natl.
Assembly, 70th
Anniv. — A657

Europa
1990 — A658

1990, Apr. 23 **Perf. 13**
2468 A657 300 l multicolored 30 15

1990, May 2
Post offices.
2469 A658 700 l Ulus, Ankara 70 18
2470 A658 1000 l Sirkeci, Istanbul,
horiz. 1.00 25

8th
European
Supreme
Courts Conf.
A659

1990, May 7 **Litho.** **Perf. 12½x13**
2471 A659 1000 l multicolored 1.00 25

Salamandra
Salamandra
A660

World Environment Day: No. 2473, Trituris vit-
tatus. No. 2474, Bombina bombina. No. 2475,
Hyla arborea, vert.

1990, June 5 **Perf. 13½x13**
2472 A660 300 l multicolored 25 15
2473 A660 500 l multicolored 42 20
2474 A660 1000 l multicolored 85 42
2475 A660 1500 l multicolored 1.25 62

Turkey-Japan
Relations,
Cent.
A661

1990, June 13 **Perf. 12½x13**
2476 A661 1000 l multicolored 1.00 50

Traffic Types of 1987 and Nos. 2283-2284
Surcharged
1990, June 20 **Perf. 14**
2477 A620 150 l on 10 l 15 15
2478 A620 300 l on 20 l 25 15
Perf. 11½x12½
2479 A589 300 l on 70 l #2284 25 15
2480 A589 1500 l on 20 l #2283 1.25 62
 Set value 92

Boats in Saintes Marines — A662

Paintings by Vincent Van Gogh (1853-1890): 300
l, Self-portrait, vert. 1000 l, Vase with Sunflowers,
vert. 1500 l, Road of Cypress and Stars.

Wmk. 394
1990, July 29 **Litho.** **Perf. 13**
2481 A662 300 l multicolored 25 15
2482 A662 700 l multicolored 55 28
2483 A662 1000 l multicolored 80 40
2484 A662 1500 l multicolored 1.20 65

Ataturk Type of 1989
1990, Aug. 1 **Unwmk.** **Perf. 14**
2485 A649 500 l gray & olive grn 42 20
2486 A649 1000 l gray & rose vio 85 42

A664 A665

Perf. 13x13½
1990, Aug. 22 **Wmk. 394**
2487 A664 300 l multicolored 25 15

Intl. Literacy Year.

1990, Oct. 17 **Litho.** **Perf. 13x13½**
State exhibition of paintings and sculpture by:
300 l, Nurullah Berk. 700 l, Cevat Dereli. 1000 l,
Nijad Sirel.
2488 A665 300 l multicolored 20 15
2489 A665 700 l multicolored 50 25
2490 A665 1000 l multicolored 72 35

PTT, 150th
Anniv. — A666

Past and present communication methods: 200 l,
Post rider, truck, train, airplane, ship. 250 l, Telegraph key, computer terminal. 400 l, Telephone
switchboard, computerized telephone exchange.
1500 l, Power lines, satellite.

1990, Oct. 23 **Perf. 14**
2491 A666 200 l multicolored 15 15
2492 A666 250 l multicolored 18 15
2493 A666 400 l multicolored 28 15
2494 A666 1500 l multicolored 1.10 55
 a. Souv. sheet of 4, #2491-2494 1.70 85
 Set value 82

Artifacts Type of 1989
Designs: 300 l, Figurine of a woman, c. 5000-
4500 BC. 500 l, Sistrum, c. 2100-2000 BC. 1000 l,
Spouted vessel with three-footed pedestal, c. 2000-
1750 BC. 1500 l, Ceremonial vessel, 1900-1700
BC.
1991, Feb. 8 **Litho.** **Perf. 13x12½**
2495 A644 300 l multi 20 15
2496 A644 500 l multi 38 18
2497 A644 1000 l multi 72 35
2498 A644 1500 l multi 1.10 55

Nos. 2495-2498 are vert.

Lakes of
Turkey
A667

Wmk. 394
1991, Apr. 24 **Litho.** **Perf. 13**
2499 A667 250 l Abant 18 15
2500 A667 500 l Egridir 38 18
2501 A667 1500 l Van 1.10 55

Europa — A668

Unwmk.

1991, May 6	Litho.	Perf. 13
2502 A668 1000 l multicolored		72 35
2503 A668 1500 l multi, diff.		1.10 55

Natl. Statistics Day — A669

1991, May 9		Perf. 13½x13
2504 A669 500 l multicolored		38 18

Eastern Mediterranean Fiber Optic Cable System — A670

1991, May 13		
2505 A670 500 l multicolored		38 18

European Conf. of Transportation Ministers — A671

1991, May 22		Perf. 13
2506 A671 500 l multicolored		38 18

Caricature Art A672

Designs: 500 l, "Amcabey" by Cemal Nadir Guler. 1000 l, "Abdulcanbaz" by Turhan Selcuk, vert.

Wmk. 394

1991, Sept. 11	Litho.	Perf. 13
2507 A672 500 l multicolored		40 20
2508 A672 1000 l multicolored		80 40

Ceramics A673

Wall facings: 500 l, 13th cent. Seljuk bird. 1500 l, 16th cent. Ottoman floral pattern.

1991, Sept. 23		Perf. 13½x13
2509 A673 500 l multicolored		40 20
2510 A673 1500 l multicolored		1.20 60

Symposium on Intl. Protection of Human Rights, Antalya — A674

1991, Oct. 4		Perf. 13x12½
2511 A674 500 l multicolored		40 20

Southeastern Anatolia Irrigation and Power Project — A675

1991, Oct. 6	Unwmk.	Perf. 13½x13
2512 A675 500 l multicolored		40 20

Turkish Fairy Tales — A676

Baldboy: 500 l, With genie. 1000 l, At party. 1500 l, Plowing field.

1991, Oct. 9		Perf. 13x13½
2513 A676 500 l multicolored		40 20
2514 A676 1000 l multicolored		80 40
2515 A676 1500 l multicolored		1.20 60

Snakes A677

	Perf. 12½x13	
1991, Oct. 23		**Wmk. 394**
2516 A677 250 l Eryx jaculus		20 15
2517 A677 500 l Elaphe quatuorlineata		40 20
2518 A677 1000 l Vipera xanthina		80 40
2519 A677 1500 l Vipera kaznakovi		1.20 60

World Environment Day.

Antiquities Type of 1989

Designs: 300 l, Statuette of Mother Goddess, Neolithic, 6000 B.C., vert. 500 l, Hasanoglan statuette, Early Bronze Age, 3000 B.C., vert. 1000 l, Inandik vase, Old Hittite, 18th cent. B.C., vert. 1500 l, Lion statuette, Urartian, 8th cent. B.C., vert.

Wmk. 394

1992, Feb. 12	Litho.	Perf. 13
2520 A644 300 l multicolored		25 15
2521 A644 500 l multicolored		40 20
2522 A644 1000 l multicolored		80 40
2523 A644 1500 l multicolored		1.20 60

Discovery of America, 500th Anniv. A678

Wmk. 394

1992, May 4	Litho.	Perf. 13
2524 A678 1500 l shown		56 28
2525 A678 2000 l Balloons, vert.		70 35

Europa.

Settlement of Jews in Turkey, 500th Anniv. A679

1992, May 15		Perf. 12½x13
2526 A679 1500 l multicolored		56 28

A681   A682

Wmk. 394

1992, June 1	Litho.	Perf. 13
2529 A681 500 l multicolored		22 15

Turkish Court of Accounts, 130th anniv.

1992, June 4		
2530 A682 1500 l multicolored		58 28

Economics Congress, Izmir.

World Environment Day — A683

1992, June 5	Litho.	Perf. 13
2531 A683 500 l Vanellus vanellus		15 15
2532 A683 1000 l Oriolus oriolus		35 18
2533 A683 1500 l Tadorna tadorna		56 28
2534 A683 2000 l Halcyon smyrnensis, vert.		70 35

Ataturk Type of 1989 and:

Kemal Ataturk — A649a

Design: 10,000 l, Full face.

	Perf. 13, 14 (#2539, 2541, 2543)	
1992-94	**Litho.**	**Unwmk.**
2537 A649	250 l gold, brn & org	15 15
2539 A649	5000 l gold & violet	80 40
2540 A649	10,000 l gold & blue	3.75 1.85
2541 A649	20,000 l gold & lilac rose	3.20 65
2543 A649a	50,000 l multicolored	3.50 1.75
Nos. 2537-2543 (5)		11.40 4.80

Issued: 250 l, 10,000 l, 5/28/92; 5000 l, 20,000 l, 9/29/93; 50,000 l, 11/10/94.
This is an expanding set. Numbers may change.

Black Sea Economic Cooperation Summit — A684

Wmk. 394

1992, June 25	Litho.	Perf. 13
2545 A684 1500 l multicolored		58 28

1992 Summer Olympics, Barcelona A685

1992, July 25		Wmk. 394
2546 A685 500 l Doves		15 15
2547 A685 1000 l Boxing		45 22
2548 A685 1500 l Weight lifting		58 28
2549 A685 2000 l Wrestling		90 45

Anatolian Folktales — A686

Scenes: 500 l, Woman carrying milk to soldiers. 1000 l, Pouring milk into trough. 1500 l, Soldiers dipping into trough.

	Perf. 13x12½	
1992, Sept. 23	**Litho.**	**Wmk. 394**
2550 A686 500 l multicolored		16 15
2551 A686 1000 l multicolored		32 16
2552 A686 1500 l multicolored		48 24

Turkish Handicrafts A687

Designs: 500 l, Embroidered flowers. 1000 l, Dolls in traditional costumes, vert. 3000 l, Saddlebags.

	Perf. 13½x13, 13x13½	
1992, Oct. 21		
2553 A687 500 l multicolored		16 15
2554 A687 1000 l multicolored		32 16
2555 A687 3000 l multicolored		95 48

See Nos. 2585-2588, 2611-2612.

Fruits — A688

Wmk. 394

1992, Nov. 25	Litho.	Perf. 13
2556 A688 500 l Cherries		15 15
2557 A688 1000 l Peaches		30 15
2558 A688 3000 l Grapes		90 45
2559 A688 5000 l Apples		1.50 75

See Nos. 2565-2568.

Famous Men — A689

Designs: No. 2560, Sait Faik Abasiyanik (1906-54), writer. No. 2561, Fikret Mualla Saygi (1904-67), artist. No. 2562, Cevat Sakir Kabaagacli (1886-

1973), author. No. 2563, Muhsin Ertugrul (1892-1979), actor and producer. No. 2564, Asik Veysel Satiroglu (1894-1973), composer.

Perf. 14, 13¹/₂x13 (#2561, 2564)

1992, Dec. 30			Litho.		
2560	A689	T	multicolored	15	15
2561	A689	T	multicolored	15	15
2562	A689	M	multicolored	30	15
2563	A689	M	multicolored	30	15
2564	A689	M	multicolored	30	15
	Nos. 2560-2564 (5)			1.20	
	Set value				60

Value on day of issue: Nos. 2560-2561, 500 l. Nos. 2562-2564, 1000 l. See Nos. 2577-2581.

Fruit Type of 1992
Wmk. 394

1993, Apr. 28		Litho.	*Perf. 13*	
2565	A688	500 l Bananas	15	15
2566	A688	1000 l Oranges	25	15
2567	A688	3000 l Pears	75	35
2568	A688	5000 l Pomegranates	1.25	65

Europa — A690

Sculptures by: 1000 l, Hadi Bara. 3000 l, Zuhtu Muridoglu.

1993, May 3			
2569	A690	1000 l multicolored	25	15
2570	A690	3000 l multicolored	75	35

A691   Houses — A692

Wmk. 394

1993, July 6		Litho.	*Perf. 13*	
2571	A691	2500 l lt bl, dk bl & gold	52	25

Economic Cooperation Organization Meeting, Istanbul.

1993, July 7

Various houses from Black Sea region.

2572	A692	1000 l multicolored	22	15
2573	A692	2500 l multi, horiz.	52	25
2574	A692	3000 l multicolored	65	32
2575	A692	5000 l multi, horiz.	1.00	52

See Nos. 2604-2607.

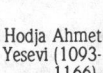

Hodja Ahmet Yesevi (1093-1166), Poet — A693

1993, July 28

2576	A693	3000 l lt bl, dk bl & gold	65	32

Famous Men Type of 1992

Designs: No. 2577, Haci Arif Bey (1831-84), composer. No. 2578, Neyzen Tevfik Kolayli (1878-1953), poet. No. 2579, Munir Nurettin Selcuk (1900-81), composer, musician. No. 2580, Cahit Sitki Taranci (1910-56), poet. No. 2581, Orhan Veli Kanik (1914-50), writer.

Perf. 14, 13¹/₂x13 (2578-2580)

1993, Aug. 4			Litho.	Unwmk.	
2577	A689	T	brown & red brown	15	15
2578	A689	T	brown & red brown	15	15
2579	A689	M	brown & red brown	22	15
2580	A689	M	brown & red brown	22	15
2581	A689	M	brown & red brown	22	15
	Nos. 2577-2581 (5)			96	75

Value on day of issue: Nos. 2577-2578, 500 l. Nos. 2579-2581, 1000 l.

Istanbul, Proposed Site for 2000 Olympics A694

1993, Aug. 11		*Perf. 12¹/₂x13*	
2582	A694	2500 l multicolored	52	25

Protection of Mediterranean Sea Against Pollution — A695

Unwmk.

1993, Oct. 12		Litho.	*Perf. 13*	
2583	A695	1000 l Amphora on sea floor	16	15
2584	A695	3000 l Dolphin jumping	48	25

Handicrafts Type of 1992
Perf. 12¹/₂x13, 13x12¹/₂

1993, Oct. 21			Wmk. 394	
2585	A687	1000 l Painted rug	16	15
2586	A687	2500 l Earrings	40	20
2587	A687	5000 l Money purse, vert.	80	40

Republic, 70th Anniv. — A696

1993, Oct. 29		Wmk. 394	*Perf. 13*	
2588	A696	1000 l multicolored	16	15

Civil Defence Organization A697

Perf. 12¹/₂x13

1993, Nov. 25		Unwmk.	
2589	A697	1000 l multicolored	16	15

Turksat Satellite — A698   Natl. Water Project — A699

Designs: 1500 l, Satellite, globe, map of Turkey. 5000 l, Satellite transmissions to areas in Europe and Asia.

Perf. 13x13¹/₂

1994, Jan. 21		Litho.	Wmk. 394	
2590	A698	1500 l multicolored	15	15
2591	A698	5000 l multicolored	40	20

1994, Feb. 28			*Perf. 13x12¹/₂*	
2592	A699	1500 l multicolored	15	15

Native Cuisine A700

Perf. 12¹/₂x13

1994, Mar. 23		Litho.	Wmk. 394	
2593	A700	1000 l Ezogel in corbasi	15	15
2594	A700	1500 l Mixed dolma	15	15
2595	A700	3500 l Shish kebabs	28	15
2596	A700	5000 l Baklava	40	20

Europa A701

Designs: 1500 l, Marie Curie (1867-1934), chemist, vert. 5000 l, Albert Einstein (1879-1955), physicist.

Unwmk.

1994, May 2		Litho.	*Perf. 13*	
2597	A701	1500 l multicolored	15	15
2598	A701	5000 l multicolored	40	20

World Environment Day — A703

Views of: 6000 l, Antalya. 8500 l, Mugla, vert.

Wmk. 394

1994, June 5		Litho.	*Perf. 13*	
2602	A703	6000 l multicolored	42	20
2603	A703	8500 l multicolored	60	30

Houses Type of 1993

Designs: 2500 l, Two-story housing complex. 3500 l, Three-story home with balconies. 6000 l, Tri-level country home. 8500 l, Two-story home.

1994, July 7

2604	A692	2500 l multi, horiz.	18	15
2605	A692	3500 l multi, horiz.	25	15
2606	A692	6000 l multi, horiz.	45	22
2607	A692	8500 l multi, horiz.	60	30

Tourism A704

Wmk. 394

1994, Aug. 3		Litho.	*Perf. 13*	
2608	A704	5000 l Hiking	35	18
2609	A704	10,000 l Rafting	70	35

Project of the Year 2001 A705

1994, Aug. 27

2610	A705	2500 l multicolored	18	15

Handicrafts Type of 1992

Designs: 7500 l, Kusak pattern used on 18th cent. clothing, vert. 12,000 l, Pacalik pattern used on 19th cent. clothing.

Wmk. 394

1994, Oct. 21		Litho.	*Perf. 13*	
2611	A687	7500 l multicolored	42	20
2612	A687	12,500 l multicolored	70	35

Mushrooms — A706

Wmk. 394

1994, Nov. 16		Litho.	*Perf. 13*	
2613	A706	2500 l Morchella conica	18	15
2614	A706	5000 l Agaricus bernardii	35	18
2615	A706	7500 l Lactarius deliciosus	52	25
2616	A706	12,500 l Macrolepiota procera	85	42
	Nos. 2613-2616 (4)		1.90	1.00

Antiquities Type of 1989

Lydian Treasures, 6th cent. B.C.: 2500 l, Silver pitcher, vert. 5000 l, Silver incense burner, vert. 7500 l, Gold, glass necklace. 12,500 l, Gold brooch.

Wmk. 394

1994, Dec. 7		Litho.	*Perf. 13*	
2617	A644	2500 l multicolored	18	15
2618	A644	5000 l multicolored	35	18
2619	A644	7500 l multicolored	52	25
2620	A644	12,500 l multicolored	85	42
	Nos. 2617-2620 (4)		1.90	1.00

Nevruz, New Day — A707

1995		Litho.	Wmk. 394	*Perf. 13*	
2621	A707	3500 l multicolored		20	15

SEMI-POSTAL STAMPS

Regular Issues Overprinted in Carmine or Black

Overprint reads: "For War Orphans"
Perf. 12, 13¹/₂ and Compound

1915			Unwmk.	
		On Stamps of 1905		
B1	A18	10pa dull grn (#119)	15	15
B2	A18	10pi org brn	2.75	25
		On Stamp of 1906		
B3	A18	10pa dull grn (#128)	6.50	7.50
		On Stamps of 1908		
B4	A19	10pa blue green	50	50
B5	A19	5pi dk violet	25.00	7.50

With Additional Overprint

B6	A19	10pa blue green	75.00	25.00
		On Stamps of 1909		
B7	A21	10pa blue green	15	15
a.		Inverted overprint	22.50	22.50
		Double overprint, one invtd.	30.00	30.00
B8	A21	20pa car rose	15	15
a.		Inverted overprint	27.50	27.50
B9	A21	1pi ultra	15	15
B10	A21	5pi dk violet	1.00	15
		Set value, #B7-B10	1.20	25

With Additional Overprint

B11 A21 10pa blue green ... 15 15
  b. Double overprint, one inverted ... 5.00 5.00
B12 A21 20pa carmine rose ... 15 15
B13 A21 1pi ultra ... 1.50 15
  Set value ... 28

On Stamps of 1913
B14 A22 10pa blue green ... 20 20
  a. Inverted overprint ... 22.50 22.50
B15 A22 1pi ultra ... 20 20
  a. Double overprint ... 5.00 5.00

With Additional Overprint

B16 A22 10pa blue green ... 20 20
  a. Inverted overprint ... 27.50 27.50

On Newspaper Stamp of 1908
B17 A19 10pa blue green ... 100.00 35.00

On Newspaper Stamp of 1909
B18 A21 10pa blue green ... 25 20

Regular Issues Overprinted in Carmine or Black

1916
On Stamps of 1901
B19 A17 1pi blue ... 20 20
B20 A17 5pi lilac rose ... 2.75 20
On Stamps of 1905
B21 A18 1pi brt blue ... 20 15
B22 A18 5pi brown ... 3.50 1.00
On Stamp of 1906
B23 A18 1pi brt blue ... 25 15
On Stamps of 1908
B24 A19 20pa carmine (Bk) ... 300.00
B25 A19 10pa red ... 60.00 45.00

With Additional Overprint
B26 A19 20pa carmine ... 15 15
B27 A19 1pi brt blue (C) ... 20.00 5.00
On Stamps of 1909
B28 A21 20pa carmine rose ... 70 15
B29 A21 1pi ultra ... 30 15
B30 A21 10pi dull red ... 27.50 27.50

With Additional Overprint
B31 A21 20pa carmine rose ... 15 20
B32 A21 1pi ultra ... 30 15
  Set value, #B31-B32 ... 27

On Stamps of 1913
B33 A22 20pa carmine rose ... 15 15
B34 A22 1pi ultra ... 1.00 15
  a. Inverted overprint ... 5.00 5.00
B35 A22 10pi dull red ... 10.00 10.00

With Additional Overprint
B36 A22 20pa carmine rose ... 15 15
On Newspaper Stamps of 1901
B37 A16 5pi ocher ... 3.00 3.00
  a. 5pa bister, No. P37 ... 150.00 150.00

Regular Issues Surcharged in Black

On Stamp of 1899
B38 A11 10pa on 20pa vio brn ... 15 15
On Stamp of 1905
B39 A18 10pa on 20pa car ... 15 15
On Stamp of 1906
B40 A18 10pa on 20pa car ... 20 20

On Newspaper Stamp of 1893-99
B41 A11 10pa on 20pa vio brn ... 15 15
  Set value, #B38-B41 ... 50 35

Nos. 346-349 Overprinted

B42 A41 10pa carmine ... 15 15
  a. Inverted overprint ... 6.75 6.75
B43 A41 20pa ultra ... 15 15
  a. Inverted overprint ... 6.75 6.75
B44 A41 1pi violet & blk ... 35 15
  a. Inverted overprint ... 6.75 6.75
B45 A41 5pi yel brn & blk ... 50 15
  a. Inverted overprint ... 11.00 11.00
  Set value ... 95 22

Nos. B42 to B45 formed part of the Postage Commemoration issue of 1916.

A Soldier's Farewell — SP1

1917, Feb. 20   Engr.   Perf. 12½
B46 SP1 10pa red violet ... 15 15
For surcharges see Nos. 600, B47.

Stamp of Same Design Surcharged

B47 SP1 10pa on 20pa car rose ... 15 15

Badge of the Society — SP9   School Teacher — SP10

Carrie Chapman Catt — SP16   Kemal Atatürk — SP23

Designs: 2k+2k, Woman farmer. 2½k+2½k, Typist. 4k+4k, Aviatrix and policewoman. 5k+5k, Women voters. 7½k+7½k, Yildiz Palace, Istanbul. 12½k+12½k, Jane Addams. 15k+15k, Grazia Deledda. 20k+20k, Selma Lagerlof. 25k+25k, Bertha von Suttner. 30k+30k, Sigrid Undset. 50k+50k, Marie Sklodowska Curie.

1935, Apr. 17   Photo.   Perf. 11½
Inscribed: "XII Congres Suffragiste International"
B54 SP9 20pa + 20pa brown ... 24 15
B55 SP10 1k + 1k rose car ... 28 15
B56 SP10 2k + 2k sl bl ... 28 15
B57 SP10 2½k + 2½k yel grn ... 28 15
B58 SP10 4k + 4k blue ... 35 20
B59 SP10 5k + 5k dull vio ... 60 24
B60 SP10 7½k + 7½k org red ... 95 52
B61 SP16 10k + 10k orange ... 1.75 80
B62 SP16 12½k + 12½k dk bl ... 4.75 2.25
B63 SP16 15k + 15k violet ... 4.75 2.25
B64 SP16 20k + 20k red org ... 8.75 3.75

B65 SP16 25k + 25k green ... 15.00 7.25
B66 SP16 30k + 30k ultra ... 35.00 35.00
B67 SP16 50k + 50k dk sl grn ... 60.00 60.00
B68 SP23 100k + 100k brn car ... 57.50 57.50
  Nos. B54-B68 (15) ... 190.48 170.36
12th Congress of the Women's Intl. Alliance.

> Catalogue values for unused stamps in this section, from this point to the end of the section, are for Never Hinged items.

Katip Chelebi — SP24

1958, Sept. 24   Litho.   Unwmk.
B69 SP24 50k + 10k gray ... 15 15
Mustafa ibn 'Abdallah Katip Chelebi Hajji Khalifa (1608-1657), Turkish author.

Road Building Machine SP25

Kemal Atatürk — SP26   Ruins, Göreme — SP27

Design: 25k+5k, Tanks and planes.

1958, Oct. 29
B70 SP25 15k + 5k orange ... 15 15
B71 SP26 20k + 5k lt red brn ... 15 15
B72 SP25 25k + 5k brt grn ... 16 15
  Set value ... 35 18

The surtax went to the Red Crescent Society and to the Society for the Protection of Children. For surcharge see No. 1440.

1959, July 8   Litho.   Perf. 10
B73 SP27 105k + 10k pur & buff ... 30 22
Issued for tourist publicity.

Istanbul — SP28

1959, Sept. 11
B74 SP28 105k + 10k lt bl & red ... 25 15
15th International Tuberculosis Congress.

Manisa Asylum SP29

Merkez Muslihiddin SP30

Kermis at Manisa: 90k+5k, Sultan Camil Mosque, Manisa, vert.

1960, Apr. 17   Unwmk.   Perf. 13
B75 SP29 40k + 5k grn & lt bl ... 15 15
B76 SP29 40k + 5k vio & rose lil ... 15 15
B77 SP29 90k + 5k dp cl & car rose ... 25 15
B78 SP30 105k + 10k multi ... 38 20
  Set value ... 42

Census Chart — SP31   Census Symbol — SP32

1960, Sept. 23   Photo.   Perf. 11½
Granite Paper
B79 SP31 30k + 5k bl & rose pink ... 15 15
B80 SP32 50k + 5k grn, dk bl & ultra ... 20 15
  Set value ... 15

Issued for the 1960 Census.

Old Observatory SP33   Fatin Gökmen SP34

Designs: 30k+5k, Observatory emblem. 75k+5k, Building housing telescope.

1961, July 1   Litho.   Perf. 13
B81 SP33 10k + 5k grnsh bl & grn ... 15 15
B82 SP33 30k + 5k vio & blk ... 15 15
B83 SP34 40k + 5k brown ... 18 15
B84 SP33 75k + 5k olive grn ... 32 18
  Set value ... 35

Kandill Observatory, 50th anniversary.

Anti-Malaria Work — SP35

UNICEF, 10th anniv.: 30k+5k, Mother and infant, horiz. 75k+5k, Woman distributing pasteurized milk.

1961, Dec. 11   Unwmk.   Perf. 13
B85 SP35 10k + 5k Prus green ... 15 15
B86 SP35 30k + 5k dull violet ... 18 15
B87 SP35 75k + 5k dk olive bis ... 32 15
  Set value ... 25

Malaria Eradication Emblem, Map and Mosquito SP36

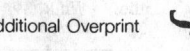

1962, Apr. 7 — Litho.
B88 SP36 30k + 5k dk & lt brn   15 15
B89 SP36 75k + 5k blk & lil   22 15
Set value   16

WHO drive to eradicate malaria.

Poinsettia
SP37

Wheat and
Census Chart
SP38

Flowers: 40k+10k, Bird of paradise flower. 75k+10k, Water lily.

1962, May 19 — Perf. 12½x13½
Flowers in Natural Colors
B90 SP37 30k + 10k lt bl & blk   15 15
B91 SP37 40k + 10k lt bl & blk   22 15
B92 SP37 75k + 10k lt bl & blk   55 30
Set value   50

Inscribed: "Umumi Ziraat Sayimi"

1963, Apr. 14 — Photo. Perf. 11½
Design: 60k+5k, Wheat and chart, horiz.
B93 SP38 40k + 5k gray grn & yel   15 15
B94 SP38 60k + 5k org yel & blk   18 15
Set value   20

1961 agricultural census. Two black bars obliterate "Kasim 1960" inscription.

Red Lion and
Sun, Red
Crescent, Red
Cross and
Globe — SP39

Designs: 60k+10k, Emblems in flowers, vert. 100k+10k, Emblems on flags.

1963, Aug. 1 — Perf. 13
B95 SP39 50k + 10k bl, lt brn, gray & red   20 15
B96 SP39 60k + 10k multi   25 16
B97 SP39 100k + 10k grn, gray & red   40 28

Centenary of International Red Cross.

Angora
Goat — SP40

Olympic Torch
Bearer — SP41

Animals: 10k+5k, Steppe cattle, horiz. 50k+5k. Arabian horses, horiz. 60k+5k, Three Angora goats. 100k+5k, Montofon cattle, horiz.

1964, Oct. 4 — Litho. Perf. 13
B98 SP40 10k + 5k multi   15 15
B99 SP40 30k + 5k multi   15 15
B100 SP40 50k + 5k multi   25 15
B101 SP40 60k + 5k multi   35 15
B102 SP40 100k + 5k multi   42 20
Nos. B98-B102 (5)   1.32
Set value   55

Issued for Animal Protection Day.

1964, Oct. 10 — Unwmk.
Designs: 10k+5k, Running, horiz. 60k+5k, Wrestling. 100k+5k, Discus.
B103 SP41 10k + 5k org brn, blk & red 15 15
B104 SP41 50k + 5k ol, blk & red   18 15
B105 SP41 60k + 5k bl, blk & red   30 18
B106 SP41 100k + 5k vio, blk, red & sil 42 30

18th Olympic Games, Tokyo, Oct. 10-25.

Map of
Dardanelles and
Laurel — SP42

Designs: 90k+10k, Soldiers and war memorial, Canakkale. 130k+10k, Turkish flag and arch, vert.

1965, Mar. 18 — Litho. Perf. 13
B107 SP42 50k + 10k vio, yel & gold   16 15
B108 SP42 90k + 10k vio bl, bl, yel & grn   25 20
B109 SP42 130k + 10k dk brn, red & yel 45 40

50th anniversary of Battle of Gallipoli.

Tobacco
Plant — SP43

Goddess, Basalt
Carving — SP44

Designs: 50k+5k, Tobacco leaves and Leander's tower, horiz. 100k+5k, Tobacco leaf.

1965, Sept. 16 — Unwmk. Perf. 13
B110 SP43 30k + 5k brn, lt brn & grn   20 15
B111 SP43 50k + 5k vio bl, ocher & pur   28 15
B112 SP43 100k + 5k blk, ol grn & ocher   52 25

Second International Tobacco Congress.

Perf. 13½x13, 13x13½
1966, June 6 — Litho.
Designs (from Archaeological Museum, Ankara): 30k+5k, Eagle and rabbit, ivory carving, horiz. 60k+5k, Bronze bull. 90k+5k, Gold pitcher.
B113 SP44 30k + 5k multi   20 15
B114 SP44 50k + 5k multi   30 20
B115 SP44 60k + 5k multi   45 25
B116 SP44 90k + 5k multi   60 40

Grand Hotel
Ephesus
SP45

Designs: 60k+5k, Konak Square, Izmir, vert. 130k+5k, Izmir Fair Grounds.

1966, Oct. 18 — Litho. Perf. 12
B117 SP45 50k + 5k multi   18 15
B118 SP45 60k + 5k multi   28 20
B119 SP45 130k + 5k multi   55 35

33rd Congress of the Intl. Fair Assoc.

Europa Issue, 1967
Common Design Type
1967, May 2 — Litho. Perf. 13x13½
Size: 22x33mm
B120 CD10 100k + 10k multi   45 45
   a. Dark blue ("Europa") omitted
B121 CD10 130k + 10k multi   60 60

Cloverleaf
Crossing, Map of
Turkey — SP46

Design: 130k+5k, Highway E5 and map of Turkey, vert.

1967, June 30 — Litho. Perf. 13
B122 SP46 60k + 5k multi   30 20
B123 SP46 130k + 5k multi   60 30

Inter-European Express Highway, E5.

WHO
Emblem — SP47

1968, Apr. 7 — Litho. Perf. 13
B124 SP47 130k + 10k lt ultra, blk & yel 35 18

WHO, 20th anniversary.

Efem Pasha, Dr. Marko Pasha and View of Istanbul — SP48

Designs: 60k+10k, Omer Pasha, Dr. Abdullah Bey and wounded soldiers. 100k+10k, Ataturk and Dr. Refik Say in front of Red Crescent headquarters, vert.

1968, June 11 — Litho. Perf. 13
B125 SP48 50k + 10k multi   25 20
B126 SP48 60k + 10k multi   35 25
B127 SP48 100k + 10k multi   60 40

Centenary of Turkish Red Crescent Society.

NATO
Emblem and
Dove
SP49

NATO, 20th anniv.: 130k+10k, NATO emblem and globe surrounded by 15 stars, symbols of the 15 NATO members.

1969, Apr. 4 — Litho. Perf. 13
B128 SP49 50k + 10k brt grn, blk & lt bl   22 15
B129 SP49 130k + 10k bluish blk, bl & gold   45 30

Red Cross,
Crescent, Lion
and Sun
Emblems
SP50

Design: 130k+10k, Conference emblem and Istanbul skyline.

1969, Aug. 29 — Litho. Perf. 13
B130 SP50 100k + 10k dk & lt bl & red   32 15
B131 SP50 130k + 10k red, lt bl & blk   45 25

21st Intl. Red Cross Conf., Istanbul.

Erosion
Control
SP51

Designs: 60k+10k, Protection of flora (dead tree). 130k+10k, Protection of wildlife (bird of prey).

1970, Feb. 9 — Litho. Perf. 13
B132 SP51 50k + 10k multi   22 22
B133 SP51 60k + 10k multi   42 42
B134 SP51 130k + 10k multi   95 95

1970 European Nature Conservation Year.

Globe and
Fencer — SP52

Design: 130k+10k, Globe, fencer and folk dancer with sword and shield.

1970, Sept. 13 — Litho. Perf. 13
B135 SP52 90k + 10k bl & blk   28 15
B136 SP52 130k + 10k ultra, lt bl, blk & org   40 20

International Fencing Championships.

"Children's
Protection"
SP53

Designs: 100k+15k, Hand supporting child, vert. 110k+15k, Mother and child.

1971, June 30 — Litho. Perf. 13
Star and Crescent Emblem in Red
B137 SP53 50k + 10k lil rose & blk   16 15
B138 SP53 100k + 15k brn, rose & blk   26 15
B139 SP53 110k + 15k org brn, bis & blk   32 20

50th anniv. of the Child Protection Assoc.

UNICEF, 25th
Anniv. — SP54

"Your Heart is
your
Health" — SP55

1971, Dec. 11
B140 SP54 100k + 10k multi   28 16
B141 SP54 250k + 15k multi   60 40

1972, Apr. 7 — Litho. Perf. 13
B142 SP55 250k + 25k gray, blk & red   55 40

World Health Day.

Olympic Emblems,
Runners — SP56

Designs: 100k+15k, Olympic rings and motion emblem. 250k+25k, Olympic rings and symbolic track ('72).

1972, Aug. 26
B143 SP56 100k + 15k multi   25 15
B144 SP56 110k + 25k multi   35 18
B145 SP56 250k + 25k multi   50 30

20th Olympic Games, Munich, Aug. 26-Sept. 11.

Emblem of
Istanbul Technical
University
SP57

1973, Apr. 21 — Litho. Perf. 13
B146 SP57 100k + 25k multi   35 15

Bicentenary of the Istanbul Technical University.

Dove and "50" — SP58

1973, July 24   Litho.   Perf. 12½x13
B147 SP58 100k + 25k multi   35   15

Peace Treaty of Lausanne, 50th anniversary.

World Population Year — SP59

1974, June 15   Litho.   Perf. 13
B148 SP59 250k + 25k multi   75   35

Guglielmo Marconi (1874-1937), Italian Electrical Engineer and Inventor — SP60

1974, Nov. 15   Litho.   Perf. 13½
B149 SP60 250k + 25k multi   75   35

Dr. Albert Schweitzer SP61

Africa with South-West Africa SP62

1975, Jan 14   Litho.   Perf. 13
B150 SP61 250k + 50k multi   90   45

Dr. Albert Schweitzer (1875-1965), medical missionary and music scholar.

1975, Aug. 26   Litho.   Perf. 13x12½
B151 SP62 250k + 50k multi   70   35

Namibia Day (independence for South-West Africa).

Ziya Gökalp SP63

Spoonbill SP64

1976, Mar. 23   Litho.   Perf. 13
B152 SP63 200k + 25k multi   35   15

Ziya Gökalp (1876-1924), philosopher.

1976, Nov. 19   Litho.   Perf. 13

Birds: 150k+25k, European roller. 200k+25k, Flamingo. 400k+25k, Hermit ibis, horiz.

B153 SP64 100k + 25k multi   38   15
B154 SP64 150k + 25k multi   42   16
B155 SP64 200k + 25k multi   85   25
B156 SP64 400k + 25k multi   1.25   40

Decree by Mehmet Bey, and Ongun Holy Bird — SP65

1977, May 13   Litho.   Perf. 13
B157 SP65 200k + 25k grn & blk   40   20

700th anniv. of Turkish as official language.

10th World Energy Conference SP66

Design: 600k+50k, Conference emblem and globe with circles.

1977, Sept. 19   Litho.   Perf. 12½
B158 SP66 100k + 25k multi   40   16
B159 SP66 600k + 50k multi   1.25   50

Running SP67

Designs: 2½ l+50k, Gymnastics. 5 l+ 50k, Table tennis. 8 l+50k, Swimming.

1978, July 18   Litho.   Perf. 13
B160 SP67   1 l + 50k multi   18   15
B161 SP67 2½ l + 50k multi   22   15
B162 SP67   5 l + 50k multi   60   15
B163 SP67   8 l + 50k multi   1.00   20
      Set value   48

GYMNASIADE '78, World School Games, Izmir.

Ribbon and Chain SP68

Design: 5 l+50k, Ribbon and flower, vert.

**   Perf. 12½x13, 13x12½**
1978, Sept. 3   Litho.
B164 SP68 2½ l + 50k multi   75   15
B165 SP68   5 l + 50k multi   1.00   20

European Declaration of Human Rights, 25th anniversary.

Children, Head of Ataturk — SP69

Black Francolin — SP70

IYC Emblem and: 5 l+50k, Children with globe as balloon. 8 l+50k, Kneeling person and child, globe.

1979, Apr. 23   Litho.   Perf. 13x13½
B166 SP69 2½ l + 50k multi   22   15
B167 SP69   5 l + 50k multi   40   15
B168 SP69   8 l + 50k multi   60   25
      Set value   46

International Year of the Child.

1979, Dec. 3   Litho.   Perf. 13x13½

Designs: No. B170, Great bustard. No. B171, Crane. No. B172, Gazelle. No. B173, Mouflon muffelwild.

B169 SP70 5 l + 1 l multi   80   16
B170 SP70 5 l + 1 l multi   80   16
B171 SP70 5 l + 1 l multi   80   16
B172 SP70 5 l + 1 l multi   80   16
B173 SP70 5 l + 1 l multi   80   16
  a. Strip of 5, #B169-B173   4.00 2.00
      Nos. B169-B173 (5)   4.00   80

European Wildlife Conservation Year. No. B173a has continuous design.

Flowers, Trees and Sun — SP71

Rodolia Cardinalis — SP72

Environment Protection: 7½ l+ 1 l Sun, water. 15 l+1 l, Industrial pollution, globe. 20 l+1 l, Flower in oil puddle.

1980, June 4   Litho.   Perf. 13
B174 SP71 2½ l + 1 l multi   15   15
B175 SP71 7½ l + 1 l multi   24   15
B176 SP71 15 l + 1 l multi   45   25
B177 SP71 20 l + 1 l multi   52   30
      Set value   74

1980, Dec. 3   Litho.   Perf. 13

Useful Insects: 7½ l+1 l, Bracon hebetor; 15 l+1 l, Calosoma sycophanta; 20 l+1 l, Deraeocoris rutilus.

B178 SP72 2½ l + 1 l multi   24   15
B179 SP72 7½ l + 1 l multi   45   15
B180 SP72 15 l + 1 l multi   80   15
B181 SP72 20 l + 1 l multi   1.00   18
      Set value   42

Intl. Year of the Disabled SP73

TB Bacillus Centenary SP75

Insects SP74

1981, Mar. 25   Litho.   Perf. 13
B182 SP73 10 l + 2½ l multi   30   15
B183 SP73 20 l + 2½ l multi   45   15
      Set value   24

1981, Dec. 16   Litho.   Perf. 13

Useful Insects: No. B184, Cicindela campestris. No. B185, Syrphus vitripennis. No. B186, Ascalaphus macaronius. No. B187, Empusa fasciata.

B184 SP74 10 l + 2½ l multi   30   15
B185 SP74 20 l + 2½ l multi   48   15
B186 SP74 30 l + 2½ l multi   75   25
B187 SP74 40 l + 2½ l multi   1.00   32

See Nos. B190-B194, B196-B200.

1982, Mar. 24   Perf. 13x12½

Portraits: #B188, Dr. Tevfik Saglam (1882-1963). #B189, Robert Koch.

B188 SP75 10 l + 2½ l multi   20   15
B189 SP75 30 l + 2½ l multi   55   20
      Set value   26

Insect Type of 1981

Useful Insects: 10 l+2½ l, Eurydema spectabile. 15 l+2½ l, Dacus oleae. 20 l+2½ l, Klapperichicen viridissima. 30 l+2½ l, Leptinotarsa decemlineata. 35 l+2½ l, Rhynchites auratus.

1982, Aug. 18   Litho.   Perf. 13
B190 SP74 10 l + 2½ l multi   25   15
B191 SP74 15 l + 2½ l multi   45   15
B192 SP74 20 l + 2½ l multi   45   15
B193 SP74 30 l + 2½ l multi   65   20
B194 SP74 35 l + 2½ l multi   70   20
      Nos. B190-B194 (5)   2.50
      Set value   68

Richard Wagner (1813-1883), Composer — SP76

1983, Feb. 13
B195 SP76 30 l + 5 l multi   1.10 1.00

Insect Type of 1981

Harmful Insects: 15 l+5 l, Eurygaster Intergriceps Put. 25 l+5 l, Phyllobius nigrofasciatus Pes. 35 l+5 l, Cercopis intermedia Kbm. 50 l+10 l, Graphosoma lineatum (L). 75 l+10 l, Capnodis miliaris (King).

1983, Sept. 14   Litho.   Perf. 13
B196 SP74 15 l + 5 l multi   45   15
B197 SP74 25 l + 5 l multi   65   15
B198 SP74 35 l + 5 l multi   85   18
B199 SP74 50 l + 10 l multi   1.25   25
B200 SP74 75 l + 10 l multi   1.75   40
      Nos. B196-B200 (5)   4.95 1.13

Topkapi Museum Artifacts SP77

1984 Summer Olympics SP78

1984, May 30   Litho.   Perf. 13
B201 SP77 20 l + 5 l Kaftan, 16th cent.   28   15
B202 SP77 70 l + 15 l Ewer   95   38
B203 SP77 90 l + 20 l Swords   1.25   45
B204 SP77 100 l + 25 l Lock, key 1.65   55

Surtax was for museum. See Nos. B208-B211, B213-B216, B218-B221.

1984, July 28

Designs: 20 l+5 l, Banners, horiz. 70 l+15 l, Medalist Oyunlari. 100 l+20 l, Running, horiz.

B205 SP78 20 l + 5 l multi   28   15
B206 SP78 70 l + 15 l multi   88   38
B207 SP78 100 l + 20 l multi   1.40   55

Artifacts Type of 1984

Ceramicware: 10 l+5 l, Iznik plate. 20 l+10 l, Iznik boza pitcher and mug, 16th cent. 100 l+15 l, Du Paquier ewer and basin, 1730. 120 l+20 l, Ching dynasty plate, 1522-1566.

1985, May 30   Litho.   Perf. 13
B208 SP77 10 l + 5 l multi   15   15
B209 SP77 20 l + 10 l multi   20   15
B210 SP77 100 l + 15 l multi   60   15
B211 SP77 120 l + 20 l multi   75   15
      Set value   32

Rabies Vaccine, Cent. — SP79

1985, July 16   *Perf. 13x13¹/₂*
B212 SP79 100 l + 15 l Pasteur   65 15

Artifacts Type of 1984

Designs: 20 l+5 l, Metal and ceramic incense burner, c. 17th cent. 100 l+10 l, Jade lidded mug decorated with precious gems, 16th cent. 120 l+15 l, Dagger designed by Mahmut I, 1714. 200 l+30 l, Willow buckler, defensive shield, undated.

1986, May 30 **Litho.**   *Perf. 13x12¹/₂*
B213 SP77 20 l + 5 l multi   15 15
B214 SP77 100 l + 10 l multi   65 15
B215 SP77 120 l + 15 l multi   80 18
B216 SP77 200 l + 30 l multi   1.40 28
       Set value   65

General Assembly of NATO SP80

1986, Nov. 13 **Litho.**   *Perf. 13¹/₂x13*
B217 SP80 100 l + 20 l multi   70 15

Artifacts Type of 1984

Designs: 20 l+5 l, Crystal and gold ewer, 16th cent., vert. 50 l+10 l, Emerald and gold pendant, 17th cent. 200 l+15 l, Sherbet jug, 19th cent., vert. 250 l+30 l, Crystal and gold pen box, 16th cent.

1987, May 30 **Litho.**   *Perf. 13*
B218 SP77 20 l + 5 l multi   15 15
B219 SP77 50 l + 10 l multi   22 15
B220 SP77 200 l + 15 l multi   80 16
B221 SP77 250 l + 30 l multi   1.10 22
       Set value   48

15th Intl. Chemotherapy Congress, Istanbul — SP81

1987, July 19 **Litho.**   *Perf. 13*
B222 SP81 200 l + 25 l multi   85 18

Intl. Road Transport Union (IRU) 21st World Congress SP82

1988, June 13 **Litho.**   *Perf. 12¹/₂x13*
B223 SP82 200 l + 25 l multi   55 15

European Environmental Campaign Balancing Nature and Development — SP83

Designs: 100 l+25 l, Hands, desert reclamation. 400 l+50 l, Eye, road, planted field.

1988, Oct. 19 **Litho.**   *Perf. 12¹/₂x13*
B224 SP83 100 l +25 l multi   35 15
B225 SP83 400 l +50 l multi   1.20 28
       Set value   36

Silkworm Industry SP84

      Perf. 13¹/₂x13
1989, Apr. 15 **Litho.**   **Wmk. 394**
B226 SP84 150 l +50 l Silkworm   32 15
B227 SP84 600 l +10 l Cocoon,
              strands   1.10 24
       Set value   30

Council of Europe, 40th Anniv. SP85

1989, May 5 **Litho.**   *Perf. 13*
B228 SP85 600 l +100 l multi   90 22

European Tourism Year — SP86

1990, Apr. 26   **Wmk. 394**
B229 SP86 300 l +50 l Antalya   35 15
B230 SP86 1000 l +100 l Istanbul   1.10 28
       Set value   36

Fight Against Addictions — SP87

Fight Against: No. B231, Smoking. No. B232, Drugs, horiz.

1990, June 26 **Litho.**   *Perf. 13*
B231 SP87 300 l +50 l multi   30 15
B232 SP87 1000 l +100 l multi   90 45

Yunus Emre (died c.1321), Poet
SP88   SP89

1991, June 26 **Litho.**   *Perf. 13*
B233 SP88 500 l +100 l multi   50 25
B234 SP89 1500 l +100 l multi   1.30 65

Wolfgang Amadeus Mozart (1756-1791), Composer SP90

1991, July 24
B235 SP90 1500 l +100 l multi   1.30 65

Turkish Supreme Court, 30th Anniv. SP91

1992, Apr. 25   **Wmk. 394**
             Litho.   *Perf. 13*
B236 SP91 500 l + 100 l multi   50 25

Scouts Planting Tree — SP92

Design: 1000 l + 200 l, Mountain climber on rope, vert.

1992, Dec. 18 **Litho.**   *Perf. 13*
B237 SP92 1000 l +200 l multi   30 15
B238 SP92 3000 l +200 l multi   80 40

Travertine, Pamukkale — SP93

Different views of rock formations.

Wmk. 394
1993, June 6 **Litho.**   *Perf. 13*
B239 SP93 1000 l +200 l multi   28 15
B240 SP93 3000 l +500 l multi   78 40

Intl. Day for Natural Disaster Reduction SP94

       Perf. 12¹/₂x13
1993, Oct. 13 **Litho.**   **Wmk. 394**
B241 SP94 3000 l + 500 l multi   60 30

Intl. Olympic Committee, Cent. — SP95

Wmk. 394
1994, Aug. 17 **Litho.**   *Perf. 13*
B242 SP95 12,500 l +500 l multi   90 45

Trees SP96

Designs: No. B243, Platanus orientalis. No. B244, Cupressus sempervirens, vert.

Wmk. 394
1994, Nov. 30 **Litho.**   *Perf. 13*
B243 SP96 7500 l +500 l multi   52 25
B244 SP96 12,500 l +500 l multi   85 42

AIR POST STAMPS

Catalogue values for unused stamps in this section are for Never Hinged items.

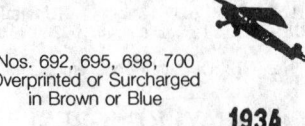

Nos. 692, 695, 698, 700 Overprinted or Surcharged in Brown or Blue

1934, July 15 **Unwmk.**   *Perf. 12*
C1 A74 7¹/₂k (Br)   20 15
C2 A72 12¹/₂k on 15k (Br)   28 15
C3 A74 20k on 25k (Br)   30 20
C4 A74 25k (Bl)   50 25
C5 A74 40k (Br)   95 60
      Nos. C1-C5 (5)   2.23 1.35

Regular Stamps of 1930 Surcharged in Brown

1937
C6 A74 4¹/₂k on 7¹/₂k red brn   1.00 65
C7 A72 9k on 15k dp org   27.50 19.00
C8 A74 35k on 40k red vio   5.00 3.50

Nos. 698, 703-704 Surcharged in Black

1941, Dec. 18
C9 A74 4¹/₂k on 25k   2.25 2.00
C10 A75 9k on 200k   13.00 11.00
C11 A75 35k on 500k   9.50 8.00

Plane over Izmir — AP1

Designs: 5k, 40k, Plane over Izmir. 20k, 50k, Plane over Ankara. 30k, 1 l, Plane over Istanbul.

1949, Jan. 1 Photo. Perf. 11½

C12	AP1	5k gray & vio	15	15
C13	AP1	20k bl gray & brn	32	15
C14	AP1	30k bl gray & ol brn	45	15
C15	AP1	40k bl & dp ultra	60	15
C16	AP1	50k gray vio & red brn	65	25
C17	AP1	1 l gray bl & dk grn	1.10	65
		Nos. C12-C17 (6)	3.27	
		Set value		1.30

For overprints see Nos. C19-C21.

Plane Over
Rumeli Hisari
Fortress
AP2

1950, May 19 Unwmk.

C18	AP2	2½ l gray bl & dk grn	22.50	10.00

Nos. C12, C14 and C16 Overprinted in
Red

SANAYÎ KONGRESİ

9-NİSAN-1951

1951, Apr. 9 Perf. 11½

C19	AP1	5k gray & vio	1.75	50
C20	AP1	30k bl gray & ol brn	2.25	15
C21	AP1	50k gray vio & red brn	2.75	70

Industrial Congress, Ankara, Apr. 9.

Yesilkoy
Airport and
Plane — AP3

Designs: 20k, 45k, Yesilkoy Airport and plane in
flight. 35k, 55k, Ankara Airport and plane. 40k, as
No. C22.

1954, Nov. 1 Perf. 14

C22	AP3	5k red brn & bl	25	15
C23	AP3	20k brn org & bl	15	15
C24	AP3	35k dk grn & bl	15	15
C25	AP3	40k dp car & bl	15	15
C26	AP3	45k violet & bl	25	15
C27	AP3	55k black & bl	45	20
		Nos. C22-C27 (6)	1.40	
		Set value		55

Symbol of Izmir
Fair — AP4

1956, Aug. 20 Litho. Perf. 10½

C28	AP4	25k reddish brown	18	15

25th Intl. Fair at Izmir, Aug. 20-Sept. 20.

Heuss Type of Regular Issue, 1957

1957, May 5

C29	A264	40k sal pink & magenta	15	15

Zahir Shah Type of Regular Issue, 1957

1957, Sept. 1

C30	A269	25k grn & lt grn	15	15

Hawk — AP5   Crane — AP6

Birds: 40k, 125k, Swallows. 65k, Cranes. 85k,
195k, Gulls. 245k, Hawk.

1959, Aug. 13 Litho. Perf. 10½

C31	AP5	40k bright lilac	16	15
C32	AP5	65k blue green	24	15
C33	AP5	85k bright blue	30	15
C34	AP5	105k yel & sepia	30	15
C35	AP6	125k brt violet	48	15
C36	AP6	155k yel green	70	20
C37	AP6	195k violet blue	70	25
C38	AP6	245k brn & brn org	1.50	45
		Nos. C31-C38 (8)	4.38	
		Set value		1.35

De Havilland Rapide
Biplane — AP7   Kestrel — AP8

Designs: 60k, Fokker Friendship transport plane.
130k, DC9-30. 220k, DC-3. 270k, Viscount 794.

1967, July 13 Litho. Perf. 13½x13

C39	AP7	10k pink & blk	30	15
C40	AP7	60k lt grn, red & blk	30	15
C41	AP7	130k bl, blk & red	65	15
C42	AP7	220k lt brn, blk & red	95	20
C43	AP7	270k org, blk & red	1.40	28
		Nos. C39-C43 (5)	3.60	
		Set value		65

1967, Oct. 10 Litho. Perf. 13

Birds: 60k, Golden eagle. 130k, Falcon. 220k,
Sparrow hawk. 270k, Buzzard.

C44	AP8	10k brown & salmon	35	15
C45	AP8	60k brown & yellow	45	15
C46	AP8	130k brown & lt bl	90	15
C47	AP8	220k brown & lt grn	1.50	20
C48	AP8	270k org brn & gray	2.00	30
		Nos. C44-C48 (5)	5.20	
		Set value		65

F-104 Jet Plane — AP9

Turkish Air
Force
Emblem and
Jets — AP10

Designs: 200k, Victory monument, Afyon, and
Jets. 325k, F-104 jets and pilot. 400k, Bleriot XI
plane with Turkish flag. 475k, Flight of Hezarfen
Ahmet Celebi from Galata Tower to Uskudar.

1971, June 1 Litho. Perf. 13

C49	AP9	110k multi	32	15
C50	AP9	200k multi	48	15
C51	AP10	250k multi	80	15
C52	AP9	325k multi	1.10	22
C53	AP10	400k multi	1.50	20
C54	AP10	475k multi	1.65	35
		Nos. C49-C54 (6)	5.85	
		Set value		1.05

The gold ink on No. C51 is applied by a thermographic process which gives a raised and shiny
effect.

F-28
Plane — AP11

1973, Dec. 11 Litho. Perf. 13

C55	AP11	110k shown	40	15
C56	AP11	250k DC-10	80	20

POSTAGE DUE STAMPS

Same Types as Regular Issues of
Corresponding Dates

1863 Unwmk. Imperf.
Blue Band

J1	A1	20pa blk, red brn	45.00	20.00
a.		Tête bêche pair	225.00	225.00
b.		Without band	25.00	
c.		Red band	62.50	30.00
J2	A2	1pi blk, red brn	55.00	25.00
a.		Tête bêche pair	225.00	225.00
b.		Without band	25.00	
J3	A3	2pi blk, red brn	140.00	50.00
a.		Tête bêche pair	650.00	450.00
J4	A4	5pi blk, red brn	90.00	45.00
a.		Tête bêche pair	425.00	425.00
b.		Without band	65.00	
c.		Red band	90.00	

1865 Perf. 12½

J6	A5	20pa brown	15	20
J7	A5	1pi brown	15	15
b.		Half used as 20pa on cover		
c.		Printed on both sides	16.50	
J8	A5	2pi brown	50	60
a.		Half used as 1pi on cover		
J9	A5	5pi brown	50	45
a.		Half used as 2½pi on cover		
J10	A5	25pi brown	7.00	8.00

The 10pa brown is an essay. Exist imperf. Values,
$60 to $100.

1867

J11	A5	20pa bister brn	1.40	7.50
J12	A5	1pi bister brn	1.00	
a.		With surcharge of 5pi	13.50	
b.		Imperf., pair	65.00	
J13	A5	2pi fawn	6.00	
J14	A5	5pi fawn	4.00	
J15	A5	25pi bis brn	3,000.	

Nos. J12-J15 were not placed in use.

1869 Perf. 13½

		With Red Brown Border		
J16	A5	20pa bister brn	2.50	75
a.		Without surcharge		
J17	A5	1pi bister brn	82.50	5.00
a.		Without surcharge		
J18	A5	2pi bister brn	120.00	4.00
J19	A5	5pi bister brn	30	1.50
b.		Without border		
c.		Printed on both sides	14.00	
J20	A5	8pi bister brn	8.00	10.00
		With Black Brown Border		
J21	A5	20pa bister brn	22.50	7.50
a.		Inverted surcharge		
b.		Without surcharge		
J22	A5	1pi bister brn	120.00	12.50
a.		Without surcharge		
J23	A5	2pi bister brn	190.00	16.50
b.		Inverted surcharge		
J24	A5	5pi bister brn	15	70
J25	A5	25pi bister brn	12.50	20.00

**Pin-perf., Perf. 5 to 11 and Compound
1871**

		With Red Brown Border		
J26	A5	20pa bister brn	60.00	12.50
J27	A5	1pi bister brn		400.00
J28	A5	2pi bister brn	10.00	5.00
J29	A5	5pi bister brn	50	1.65
		With Black Brown Border		
J31	A5	20pa bister brn	12.50	40
a.		Half used as 10pa on cover		
b.		Imperf., pair		16.50
c.		Printed on both sides	40.00	40.00
J32	A5	1pi bister brn	15.00	25
a.		Half used as 20pa on cover		
c.		Inverted surcharge	50.00	35.00
d.		Printed on both sides		
J33	A5	2pi bister brn	25	40
a.		Half used as 1pi on cover		
c.		Imperf., pair		16.50
J34	A5	5pi bister brn	15	2.50
a.		Half used as 2½pi on cover		
c.		Printed on both sides		
J35	A5	25pi bister brn	8.00	12.50
a.		Inverted surcharge		

1888 Perf. 11½ and 13½

J36	A7	20pa black	15	15
J37	A7	1pi black	15	15
J38	A7	2pi black	15	15
b.		Diagonal half used as 1pi		

		Set value	24	36
		Imperf		
J36a	A7	20pa	11.00	
J37a	A7	1pi	11.00	
J38a	A7	2pi	11.00	

1892 Perf. 13½

J39	A11	20pa black	75	30
J40	A12	1pi black	5.00	30
J41	A13	2pi black	75	30
		Printed on both sides		

1901

J42	A11	20pa black, *deep rose*	15	20

1901

J43	A17	10pa black, *deep rose*	50	20
J44	A17	20pa black, *deep rose*	50	20
J45	A17	1pi black, *deep rose*	20	25
J46	A17	2pi black, *deep rose*	20	25

1905 Perf. 12

J47	A18	1pi black, *deep rose*	35	35
J48	A18	2pi black, *deep rose*	40	40

1908, Perf. 12, 13½ and Compound

J49	A19	1pi black, *deep rose*	2.00	35
J50	A19	2pi black, *deep rose*	25	45

1909

J51	A21	1pi black, *deep rose*	75	75
J52	A21	2pi black, *deep rose*	20.00	20.00
a.		Imperf.	65.00	

1913 Perf. 12

J53	A22	2pi black, *deep rose*	15	15
J54	A22	5pa black, *deep rose*	15	15
J55	A22	10pa black, *deep rose*	15	15
J56	A22	20pa black, *deep rose*	15	15
J57	A22	1pi black, *deep rose*	50	50
J58	A22	2pi black, *deep rose*	1.25	1.25
		Set value	1.85	1.85

Adrianople Issue

Nos. 251-253
Surcharged in
Black, Blue or
Red

1913

J59	A23	2pa on 10pa green (Bk)	25	15
J60	A23	5pa on 20pa red (Bl)	35	20
J61	A23	10pa on 40pa blue (R)	60	40
J62	A23	20pa on 40pa blue (Bk)	2.00	80

For surcharges see Nos. J67-J70, J83-J86.

D1   D2

D3   D4

1914 Engr.

J63	D1	5pa claret	20	15
J64	D2	20pa red	20	15
J65	D3	1pi dark blue	35	20
J66	D4	2pi slate	75	50

For surcharges and overprints see Nos. J87-J91.

Nos. J59 to J62 Surcharged in Red or
Black

1916

J67	A23	10pa on 2pa on 10pa (R)	12.50	12.50
J68	A23	20pa on 5pa on 20pa	12.50	12.50
J69	A23	40pa on 10pa on 40pa	12.50	12.50
J70	A23	40pa on 20pa on 40pa (R)	17.50	12.50

Preceding Issues Overprinted in Red, Black or Blue

1917

On Stamps of 1865

J71	A5	20pa red brn (Bl)	15.00	15.00
J72	A5	1pi red brn (Bl)	15.00	15.00
J73	A5	2pi bis brn (Bl)	15.00	15.00
J74	A5	5pi bis brn (Bl)	15.00	15.00
J75	A5	25pi dk brn (Bl)	35.00	35.00

On Stamp of 1869

Red Brown Border

J76	A5	5pi bis brn (R)	20.00	20.00

On Stamp of 1871

Black Brown Border

J77	A5	5pi bis brn	40.00	40.00

On Stamps of 1888

J78	A7	1pi black (R)	12.50	12.50
J79	A7	2pi black (R)	12.50	12.50

On Stamps of 1892

J80	A11	20pa black (R)	1.25	1.50
J81	A12	1pi black (R)	1.25	1.50
J82	A13	2pi black (R)	1.25	50

Adrianople Issue

On Nos. J59 to J62 with Addition of New Value

J83	A23	10pa on 2pa on 10pa (R)	50	50
J84	A23	20pa on 5pa on 20pa (Bk)	50	50
J85	A23	40pa on 10pa on 40pa (Bk)	60	35
a.		"40pa" double		
J86	A23	40pa on 20pa on 40pa (R)	1.00	75

Nos. J71-J86 were used as regular postage stamps.

Armistice Issue

No. J65 Overprinted

J87	D3	1pi dark blue	30.00	30.00

1919, Nov. 30

Accession to the Throne Issue

Postage Due Stamps of 1914 Overprinted in Turkish "Accession to the Throne of His Majesty. 3rd July, 1334-1918"

1919

J88	D1	10pa on 5pa claret	10.00	10.00
J89	D2	20pa red	10.00	10.00
J90	D3	1pi dark blue	10.00	10.00
J91	D4	2pi slate	10.00	10.00

Railroad Bridge over Kizil Irmak — D5   Kemal Atatürk — D6

1926 Engr.

J92	D5	20pa ocher	35	35
J93	D5	1g red	42	42
J94	D5	2g blue green	55	55
J95	D5	3g lilac brown	55	55
J96	D5	5g lilac	90	90
		Nos. J92-J96 (5)	2.77	2.77

Catalogue values for unused stamps in this section, from this point to the end of the section, are for Never Hinged items.

1936 Litho. Perf. 11½

J97	D6	20pa brown	15	15
J98	D6	2k light blue	15	15
J99	D6	3k bright violet	15	15

J100	D6	5k Prussian blue	18	15
J101	D6	12k bright rose	42	25
		Set value	85	45

For surcharges see Nos. 1461-1465.

Local Issues

During the years 1869-82 Turkish stamps with the above overprints were used for local postage in Constantinople and Mount Athos.

MILITARY STAMPS

For the Army in Thessaly

Tughra and Bridge at Larissa — M1

1898, Apr. 21 Unwmk. Perf. 13

M1	M1	10pa yellow green	1.75	1.10
M2	M1	20pa rose	1.75	1.10
M3	M1	1pi dark blue	1.75	1.10
M4	M1	2pi orange	1.75	1.10
M5	M1	5pi violet	1.75	1.10
		Nos. M1-M5 (5)	8.75	5.50

Issued for Turkish occupation forces to use in Thessaly during the Greco-Turkish War of 1897-98. Forgeries of Nos. M1-M5 are perf. 11½.

OFFICIAL STAMPS

Catalogue values for unused stamps in this section are for Never Hinged items.

O1

Perf. 10 to 12 and Compound

1948 Typo. Unwmk.

O1	O1	10pa rose brown	15	15
O2	O1	1k gray green	15	15
O3	O1	2k rose violet	15	15
O4	O1	3k orange	15	15
O5	O1	5k blue	5.00	15
O6	O1	10k brown org	3.25	15
O7	O1	15k violet	1.00	15
O8	O1	20k dk blue	1.00	15
O9	O1	30k olive bister	1.40	15
O10	O1	50k black	1.25	15
O11	O1	1 l bluish grn	1.65	15
O12	O1	2 l lilac rose	3.00	15
		Nos. O1-O12 (12)	18.15	
		Set value		60

Regular Issue of 1948 Overprinted Type "a" in Black

a

1951

O13	A178	5k blue	20	15
O14	A178	10k chocolate	30	15
O15	A178	20k deep blue	60	15
O16	A178	30k brown	85	15
		Set value		34

Overprint "a" is 15½mm wide. Points of crescent do not touch star. The 0.25k (No. 963) exists with overprint "a" but its status is questionable.

b   c

Overprinted Type "b" in Dark Brown

1953

O17	A178	0.25k dk red	15	15
O18	A178	5k blue	20	15
O19	A178	10k chocolate	35	15
O20	A178	15k violet	60	15
O21	A178	20k deep blue	1.60	15
O22	A178	30k brown	70	15
O23	A178	60k black	1.40	16
		Nos. O17-O23 (7)	5.00	
		Set value		50

Overprint "b" is 14mm wide. Lettering thin with sharp, clean corners.

Overprinted Type "c" in Black or Green Black

1953-54

O23A	A178	0.25k dk red (G Bk) ('53)	15	15
f.		Black overprint	4.00	4.00
g.		Violet overprint ('53)	4.00	4.00
O23B	A178	10k chocolate	3.50	65
O23C	A178	15k violet	3.50	35
O23D	A178	30k brown	2.00	65
O23E	A178	60k black	3.00	65
		Nos. O23A-O23E (5)	12.15	2.45

Lettering of type "c" heavy with rounded corners.

Small Star — d   Large Star — e

Overprinted or Surcharged Type "d" in Black

1955-56

O24	A178	0.25k dark red	15	15
O25	A178	1k olive black	15	15
O26	A178	2k brt rose lil	15	15
O27	A178	3k red orange	15	15
O28	A178	4k dk green	15	15
O29	A178	5k on 15k vio	15	15
O31	A178	10k on 15k vio	15	15
O32	A178	15k violet	15	15
O33	A178	20k deep blue	24	15
O35	A179	40k on 1 l ol grn	40	15
O36	A179	75k on 2 l dk brn	95	38
O37	A179	75k on 5 l dp plum	4.75	2.50
		Nos. O24-O37 (12)	7.54	
		Set value		3.25

Type "d" is 15x16mm wide. Overprint on Nos. O35-O37 measures 19x22mm. Nos. O29, O31 and O35-O37 have two bars and new value added.

Overprinted or Surcharged Type "e" in Black

1955

O25a	A178	1k olive black	15	15
O29a	A178	5k on 15k violet	15	15
O30	A178	5k blue	55	15
O31a	A178	10k on 15k violet	2.65	2.00
c.		"10" without serif	15	15

O33a	A178	20k deep blue	45	15
O34	A178	30k brown	80	15
		Set value, #O25a-		
		O30, O31c-O34	2.00	30

Heavy crescent   Thin crescent
f   g

Overprinted or Surcharged Type "f" in Black

1957

O24b	A178	0.25k dark red	30	15
O38b	A178	½k on 1k ol blk	15	15
O25b	A178	1k olive black	15	15
O31b	A178	10k on 15k violet	70	35
O35b	A179	40k on 1 l olive grn	8.00	1.35
		Nos. O24b-O35b (5)	9.30	2.15

Type "f" crescent is larger and does not touch wavy line. The surcharged "10" on No. O31b exists only without serifs. The overprint on No. O35b measures 17x22½mm.

Overprinted or Surcharged Type "g" in Black

1957

O38	A178	½k on 1k ol blk	15	15
O39	A178	1k ol blk	15	15
O40	A178	2k on 4k dk grn	15	15
O41	A178	3k on 4k dk grn	15	15
O42	A178	10k on 12k dp red	60	25

The shape of crescent and star on type "g" varies on each value. Overprint measures 14x18mm. The surcharged stamps have two bars and new value added.

O2   O3   O4

1957 Litho. Perf. 10½

O43	O2	5k blue	15	15
O44	O2	10k orange brn	15	15
O45	O2	15k lt violet	15	15
O46	O2	20k red	15	15
O47	O2	30k gray olive	15	15
O48	O2	40k brown vio	15	15
O49	O2	50k grnsh blk	16	15
O50	O2	60k lt yel grn	20	15
O51	O2	75k yellow org	40	15
O52	O2	100k green	50	15
O53	O2	200k deep rose	90	25
		Set value	2.60	70

1959 Unwmk. Perf. 10

O54	O2	5k rose	15	15
O55	O2	10k rose lilac	15	15
O56	O2	15k car rose	15	15
O57	O2	20k lilac	15	15
O58	O2	40k blue	15	15
O59	O2	60k orange	24	15
O60	O2	75k gray	48	15
O61	O2	100k violet	65	16
O62	O2	200k red brn	1.10	40
		Set value	2.80	90

1960 Litho. Perf. 10½

O63	O3	1k orange	15	15
O64	O3	5k vermilion	15	15
O65	O3	10k gray grn	35	15
O67	O3	30k red brn	15	15
O70	O3	60k green	24	15
O71	O3	1 l rose lilac	30	15
O72	O3	1½ l brt ultra	95	15
O74	O3	2½ l violet	1.45	35
O75	O3	5 l blue	2.50	80
		Nos. O63-O75 (9)	6.24	
		Set value		1.50

For surcharge see No. O83.

1962 Typo. Perf. 13

O76	O4	1k olive bister	15	15
O77	O4	5k brt grn	15	15
O78	O4	10k red brn	15	15
O79	O4	15k dk bl	15	15
O80	O4	25k carmine	15	15
O81	O4	30k ultra	15	15
		Set value	75	30

For surcharge see No. O82.

Nos. O81 and O70 Surcharged
1963
O82 O4 50k on 30k ultra 35 15
Perf. 10½
Litho.
O83 O3 100k on 60k grn 50 15
Set value 15

O5 O6 O7

1963 **Litho.** **Perf. 12½**
O84 O5 1k gray 15 15
O85 O5 5k salmon 15 15
O86 O5 10k green 15 15
O87 O5 50k car rose 20 15
O88 O5 100k ultra 55 15
Set value 95 26

For surcharge see No. O139.

1964 **Unwmk.** **Perf. 12½**
O89 O6 1k gray 15 15
O90 O6 5k blue 15 15
O91 O6 10k yellow 15 15
O92 O6 30k red 15 15
O93 O6 50k lt green 18 15
O94 O6 60k brown 22 15
O95 O6 80k pale grnsh bl 32 15
O96 O6 130k indigo 70 15
O97 O6 200k lilac 90 15
Set value 2.50 50

For surcharge see No. O140.

1965 **Litho.** **Perf. 13**
O98 O7 1k emerald 15 15
O99 O7 10k ultra 15 15
O100 O7 50k orange 24 15
Set value 40 15

For surcharge see No. O141.

Usak Carpet Design — O8
Seljuk Tile, 13th Century — O9

Carpet designs: 50k, Bergama. 100k, Ladik. 150k, Seljuk. 200k, Nomad. 500k, Anatolia.

1966 **Litho.** **Perf. 13**
O101 O8 1k orange 15 15
O102 O8 50k green 15 15
O103 O8 100k brt pink 20 15
O104 O8 150k vio bl 32 15
O105 O8 200k olive bister 48 15
O106 O8 500k lilac 1.25 32
Nos. O101-O106 (6)
Set value 2.55 62

For surcharge see No. O142.

1967 **Litho.** **Perf. 11½x12**
O107 O9 1k dk bl & lt bl 15 15
O108 O9 50k org & dk bl 18 15
O109 O9 100k lil & dk bl 28 15
Set value 52 16

For surcharge see No. O143.

Leaf Design — O10

1968 **Litho.** **Perf. 13**
O110 O10 50k brn & lt grn 16 15
O111 O10 150k blk & dl yel 50 15
O112 O10 500k red brn & lt bl 1.65 15
Set value 25

O11 O12 O13

1969, Aug. 25 **Litho.** **Perf. 13**
O113 O11 1k lt grn & red 15 15
O114 O11 10k lt grn & bl 15 15
O115 O11 50k lt grn & brn 15 15
O116 O11 100k lt grn & red vio 35 15
Set value 65 25

1971, Mar. 1 **Litho.** **Perf. 11½x12**
O117 O12 5k brown & blue 15 15
O118 O12 10k vio bl & ver 15 15
O119 O12 30k org & vio bl 20 15
O120 O12 50k Prus bl & sepia 28 15
O121 O12 75k yellow & green 50 15
Set value 1.05 35

1971, Nov. 15 **Litho.** **Perf. 11½x12**
O122 O13 5k lt bl & gray 15 15
O123 O13 25k cit & lt brn 15 15
O124 O13 100k org & olive 20 15
O125 O13 200k dk brn & bis 42 15
O126 O13 250k rose lil & vio 60 15
O127 O13 500k dk bl & brt bl 95 45
Nos. O122-O127 (6)
Set value 2.47 70

O14 O15 O16

1972, Apr. 7 **Litho.** **Perf. 13**
O128 O14 5k buff & blue 15 15
O129 O14 100k buff & olive 25 15
O130 O14 200k buff & carmine 50 15
Set value 24

1973, Sept 20 **Litho.** **Perf. 13**
O131 O15 100k violet & buff 65 15

1974, June 17 **Litho.** **Perf. 13½x13**
O132 O16 10k sal pink & brn 15 15
O133 O16 25k blue & dk brn 15 15
O134 O16 50k brt pink & brn 15 15
O135 O16 100k blue & brn 40 15
O136 O16 250k rose & brn 65 15
O137 O16 500k yellow & brn 1.25 25
Nos. O132-O137 (6)
Set value 2.75 52

O17 O18 O19

1975, Nov. 5 **Litho.** **Perf. 12½x13**
O138 O17 100k lt blue & maroon 20 15

Nos. O84, O89, O98, O101, O107
Surcharged in Red or Black
Perf. 12½, 13, 11½x12
1977, Aug. 17 **Litho.**
O139 O5 5k on 1k gray 15 15
O140 O6 5k on 1k gray 15 15
O141 O7 5k on 1k emer 15 15
O142 O8 5k on 1k org (B) 15 15
O143 O9 5k on 1k dk & lt bl 15 15
Nos. O139-O143 (5)
Set value 75 25

1977, Dec. 29 **Litho.** **Perf. 13½x13**
O144 O18 250k lt bl & grn 35 15

1978 **Photo.** **Perf. 13½**
O145 O19 50k pink & rose 15 15
O146 O19 2½ l buff & grnsh blk 22 15
O147 O19 4½ l lil rose & sl grn 38 15
O148 O19 5 l lt blue & pur 42 15
O149 O19 10 l lt grn & grn 85 15
O150 O19 25 l yellow & red 2.25 20
Nos. O145-O150 (6)
Set value 4.27 58

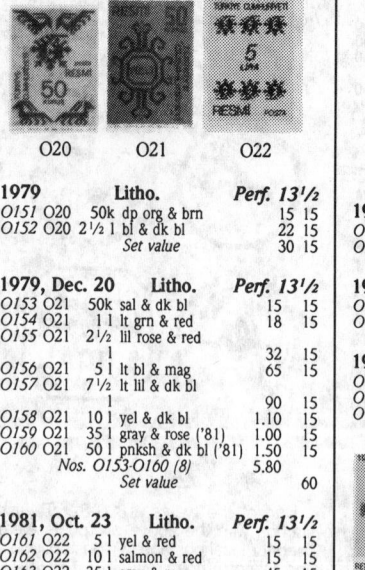
O20 O21 O22

1979 **Litho.** **Perf. 13½**
O151 O20 50k dp org & brn 15 15
O152 O20 2½ l bl & dk bl 22 15
Set value 30 15

1979, Dec. 20 **Litho.** **Perf. 13½**
O153 O21 50k sal & dk bl 15 15
O154 O21 1 l lt grn & red 18 15
O155 O21 2½ l lil rose & red
1 32 15
O156 O21 5 l lt bl & mag 65 15
O157 O21 7½ l lt lil & dk bl
1 90 15
O158 O21 10 l yel & dk bl 1.10 15
O159 O21 35 l gray & rose ('81) 1.00 15
O160 O21 50 l pnksh & dk bl ('81) 1.50 15
Nos. O153-O160 (8)
Set value 5.80 60

1981, Oct. 23 **Litho.** **Perf. 13½**
O161 O22 5 l yel & red 15 15
O162 O22 10 l salmon & red 15 15
O163 O22 35 l gray & rose 45 15
O164 O22 50 l pink & dk bl 65 15
O165 O22 75 l pale grn & grn 1.00 15
O166 O22 100 l lt bl & dk bl 1.25 16
Nos. O161-O166 (6)
Set value 3.65 55

O23 O24

1983-84 **Litho.** **Perf. 12½x13**
Background Color
O167 O23 5 l yellow 15 15
O168 O23 15 l yel bister 18 15
O169 O23 20 l gray ('84) 15 15
O170 O23 50 l sky blue 55 15
O171 O23 65 l pink 70 15
O172 O23 70 l pale rose ('84) 50 15
O173 O23 90 l bister brn 95 15
O174 O23 90 l bl gray ('84) 60 15
O175 O23 100 l green ('84) 70 15
O176 O23 125 l lt green 1.50 20
O177 O23 230 l pale sal ('84) 1.65 35
Nos. O167-O177 (11)
Set value 7.63 1.40

For surcharges see Nos. O184, O186-O190.

1986-87
O178 O24 5 l yel & vio 15 15
O179 O24 10 l org & vio 15 15
O180 O24 20 l gray & vio 15 15
O180A O24 50 l blk & pale lil rose ('87) 30 15
O181 O24 100 l lt yel grn & vio 75 15
O182 O24 300 l brt ultra & lt bl grn ('87) 1.90 15
Nos. O178-O182 (6)
Set value 3.40 38

For surcharges see Nos. O183, O185.

Nos. O179, O168, O180, O172, O173, O177 Surcharged in Dark Orange
1989
O183 O24 500 l on 10 l 52 15
O184 O23 500 l on 15 l 52 15
O185 O24 500 l on 20 l 52 15
O186 O23 1000 l on 70 l 1.05 26
O187 O23 1000 l on 90 l 1.05 26
O188 O23 1250 l on 230 l 1.30 32
Nos. O183-O188 (6)
Set value 4.96 1.29

Issue dates: Nos. O183, O185-O188, Aug. 9; No. O184, June 7.

Nos. O171 & O174
Surcharged in Black

1991, Mar. 27
O189 O23 100 l on 65 l 15 15
O190 O23 250 l on 90 l 18 15
Set value 15

O25 O26 O27

Perf. 11½x12½
1992, Mar. 24 **Litho.**
O191 O25 3000 l lt brn & dk brn 1.05 50
O192 O25 5000 l lt grn & dk grn 1.75 90

1992, Dec. 2 **Litho.** **Perf. 12½x13**
O193 O26 1000 l bl grn & vio bl 32 16
O194 O26 10,000 l vio bl & bl grn 3.10 1.50

1993, Sept. 27 **Litho.** **Perf. 12½x13**
O195 O27 1000 l brown & green 16 15
O196 O27 1500 l brown & green 25 15
O197 O27 5000 l green & claret 80 40

O28 O29

1994, May 9 **Litho.** **Perf. 11½x12**
O198 O28 2500 l pink & violet 20 15
O199 O28 25,000 l yellow & brown 2.00 1.00

1995 **Litho.** **Perf. 11½x12½**
O200 O29 3500 l violet & lt violet 16 15
O201 O29 17,500 l blue green & lt grn 90 45

NEWSPAPER STAMPS

N1

Black Overprint
1879 **Unwmk.** **Perf. 11½ and 13½**
P1 N1 10pa blk & rose lil 55.00 40.00
Other stamps found with this "IMPRIMES" overprint were prepared on private order and have no official status as newspaper stamps. Counterfeits exist of No. P1.

The 10pa surcharge, on half of 20pa rose and pale rose was made privately. See note after No. 77.

Regular Issue of 1890
Handstamped in Black

There are two types of this handstamp, varying slightly in size.

1891 **Perf. 13½, 11½**
P10 A7 10pa grn & gray 4.50 3.50
  a. Imperf. 22.50 12.50
P11 A7 20pa rose & gray 6.00 4.00
  a. Imperf. 22.50 14.00
P12 A7 1pi blue & gray 22.50 14.00
P13 A7 2pi yel & gray 100.00 40.00
P14 A7 5pi buff & gray 225.00 110.00

Blue Handstamp

P10b	A7	10pa green & gray	25.00	3.50
P11a	A7	20pa rose & gray	25.00	4.00
P12a	A7	1pi blue & gray	110.00	22.50

This overprint in red and on 2pi and 5pi in blue is considered bogus.

Same Handstamp on Regular Issue of 1892
1892   *Perf. 13½*

P25	A10	10pa gray green	25.00	4.50
P26	A11	20pa rose	42.50	20.00
P27	A12	1pi pale blue	12.50	7.50
P28	A13	2pi brown org	14.00	7.50
P29	A14	5pi pale violet	150.00	100.00
a.		On No. 99a		500.00

The handstamps on Nos. P10-P29 are found double, inverted and sideways. Counterfeit overprints are plentiful.

Regular Issues of 1892-98 Overprinted in Black

1893-98

P30	A10	10pa gray grn	20	15
P31	A11	20pa vio brn ('98)	25	15
a.		20pa dark pink	35	1.00
b.		20pa pink	15.00	2.00
P32	A12	1pi pale blue	50	15
P33	A13	2pi brown org	7.50	1.50
a.		Tete beche pair		22.50
P34	A14	5pi pale violet	25.00	7.50
a.		On No. 99a	135.00	65.00
		Nos. P30-P34 (5)	33.45	9.45

For surcharge and overprints see Nos. B41, P134-P136, P153-P154.

1897

P36	A10	5pa on 10pa gray grn	20	15
a.		"Cniq" instead of "Cinq"	7.50	7.50

For overprint see No. P137.

Nos. 102-107 Overprinted in Black

1901   *Perf. 12, 13½ and Compound*

P37	A16	5pa bister	15	20
a.		Inverted overprint		
P38	A16	10pa yellow grn	55	50
P39	A16	20pa magenta	1.25	1.00
P40	A16	1pi violet blue	2.50	1.25
P41	A16	2pi gray blue	20.00	10.00
P42	A16	5pi ocher	25.00	15.00
		Nos. P37-P42 (6)	49.45	27.95

For overprints see Nos. B37, P69-P74, P123, P138-P141, P155-P158.

Same Overprint on Nos. 110-115
1901

P43	A17	5pa purple	25	15
P44	A17	10pa green	2.00	15
P45	A17	20pa carmine	25	15
a.		Overprinted on back		
P46	A17	1pi blue	1.50	25
P47	A17	2pi orange	8.50	1.50
a.		Inverted overprint		
P48	A17	5pi lilac rose	25.00	7.50
		Nos. P43-P48 (6)	37.50	9.70

For overprints see Nos. P75-P80, P124-P126, P142-P146, P159-P164.

Same Overprint on Regular Issue of 1905
1905

P49	A18	5pa ocher	15	15
P50	A18	10pa dull green	2.25	50
P51	A18	20pa carmine	35	15
P52	A18	1pi pale blue	20	15
P53	A18	2pi slate	3.50	1.50
P54	A18	5pi brown	10.00	3.25
		Nos. P49-P54 (6)	16.45	5.70

For overprints see Nos. P127-P129, P147-P150, P165-P171.

Regular Issue of 1908 Overprinted in Carmine or Blue

1908

P55	A19	5pa ocher (Bl)	2.00	15
P56	A19	10pa blue grn (C)	1.50	15
P57	A19	20pa carmine (C)	2.50	65
P58	A19	1pi brt blue (C)	3.50	1.00
P59	A19	2pi blue blk (C)	13.50	2.25
P60	A19	5pi dk violet (C)	13.50	3.75
		Nos. P55-P60 (6)	36.50	7.95

For overprints see Nos. B17, P130-P131, P151, P172.

Same Overprint on Regular Issue of 1909
1909

P61	A21	5pa ocher (Bl)	65	15
a.		Imperf.		
P62	A21	10pa blue grn (C)	65	15
P63	A21	20pa car rose (Bl)	7.50	1.00
a.		Imperf.		
P64	A21	1pi brt blue (C)	12.50	3.25
P65	A21	2pi blue blk (C)	20.00	7.50
P66	A21	5pi dk violet (C)	22.50	12.50
		Nos. P61-P66 (6)	63.80	24.55

For surcharge and overprints see Nos. B18, P67-P68, P81, P132-P133, P152.

No. 151 Surcharged in Blue

1910   *Perf. 12, 13½ and Compound*

P67	A21	2pa on 5pa ocher	15	15

1911   *Perf. 12*

P68	A21	2pa olive green	15	15

Newspaper Stamps of 1901-11 Overprinted in Carmine or Blue

MONASTIR

The overprint was applied to 13 denominations in four settings with change of city name, producing individual sets for each city: "MONASTIR," "PRISTINA," "SALONIKA" and "USKUB."

1911   *Perf. 12, 13½*

P69	A16	5pa bister	1.75
P70	A16	10pa yellow grn	1.75
P71	A16	20pa magenta	1.75
P72	A16	1pi violet blue	1.75
P73	A16	2pi gray blue	2.75
P74	A16	5pi ocher	4.25
P75	A17	5pa purple	1.75
P76	A17	10pa green	1.75
P77	A17	20pa carmine	1.75
P78	A17	1pi blue	3.00
P79	A17	2pi orange	2.75
P80	A17	5pi lilac rose	4.75
P81	A21	5pi olive green	50
		Nos. P69-P81 (13)	30.25

Values for each of the 4 city sets of 13 are as printed.
The note after No. 182 will also apply to Nos. P69-P81.

Preceding Newspaper Issues with additional Overprint in Carmine or Black

1915

On Stamps of 1893-98

P121	A10	10pa gray green	20	15
a.		Inverted overprint	10.00	10.00
P122	A13	2pi yellow brn	1.50	1.00
a.		Inverted overprint	10.00	10.00

On Stamps of 1901

P123	A16	10pa yellow grn	20	15
P124	A17	5pa purple	15	15
P125	A17	20pa carmine	25	25
P126	A17	5pi lilac rose	6.00	1.65

On Stamps of 1905

P127	A18	5pa ocher	15	15
a.		Inverted overprint	7.50	7.50
P128	A18	2pi slate	2.00	1.50

P129	A18	5pi brown	1.00	25

On Stamps of 1908

P130	A19	2pi blue blk	250.00	75.00
P131	A19	5pi dk violet	7.50	1.00

On Stamps of 1909

P132	A21	5pa ocher	15	15
P133	A21	5pi dk violet	35.00	12.50
		Nos. P121-P129,P131-P133 (12)	54.10	18.90

Preceding Newspaper Issues with additional Overprint in Red or Black

1916

On Stamps of 1893-98

P134	A10	10pa gray green	15	15
P135	A11	20pa violet brn	15	15
P136	A14	5pi dull violet	11.00	11.00

On Stamp of 1897

P137	A10	5pa on 10pa gray grn	15	15

On Stamps of 1901

P138	A16	5pa bister	15	15
P139	A16	10pa yellow grn	15	15
P140	A16	20pa magenta	20	15
a.		Inverted overprint	10.00	10.00
P141	A16	1pi violet blue	40	40
P142	A17	5pa purple	20.00	15.00
P143	A17	10pa green	20.00	15.00
P144	A17	20pa carmine	15	15
P145	A17	1pi blue	35	15
P146	A17	2pi orange	20	15

On Stamps of 1905

P147	A18	5pa ocher	15	15
P148	A18	10pa dull green	12.50	12.50
P149	A18	20pa carmine	12.50	12.50
P150	A18	1pi pale blue	25	15

On Stamps of 1908

P151	A19	5pa ocher	6.50	6.50

On Stamp of 1909

P152	A21	5pa ocher	10.00	10.00
		Nos. P134-P152 (19)	94.95	84.55

Preceding Newspaper Issues with additional Overprint in Red or Black

1917

On Stamps of 1893-98

P153	A12	1pi gray (R)	2.00	1.50
P154	A11	20pa vio brn (R)	2.25	1.75

On Stamps of 1901

P155	A16	5pa bister (Bk)	65	60
a.		Inverted overprint	20.00	20.00
P156	A16	10pa yellow grn (R)	65	60
P157	A16	20pa magenta (Bk)	65	40
P158	A16	2pi gray blue (R)	40.00	30.00
P159	A17	5pa purple (Bk)	60	75
a.		Inverted overprint	20.00	20.00
b.		Double overprint	20.00	20.00
c.		Double ovpt., one inverted	25.00	25.00
P160	A17	10pa green (R)	15.00	15.00
P161	A17	20pa carmine (Bk)	20	20
P162	A17	1pi blue (R)	2.50	2.50
P163	A17	2pi orange (Bk)	50	50
P164	A17	5pi lilac rose (R)	20.00	20.00

On Stamps of 1905

P165	A18	5pa ocher (R)	15	15
a.		Inverted overprint	10.00	10.00
P166	A18	5pa ocher (Bk)	30	35
a.		Inverted overprint	10.00	10.00
P167	A18	10pa dull green (R)	50	60
P168	A18	20pa carmine (Bk)	15	20
a.		Double overprint	15.00	15.00
P169	A18	1pi blue (R)	15	20
a.		Inverted overprint	25.00	25.00
P170	A18	2pi slate (R)	30.00	30.00
P171	A18	5pi brown (R)	30.00	30.00

On Stamp of 1908

P172	A19	5pa ocher (R)	20.00	20.00

Nos. P153-P172 were used as regular postage stamps.

            ٥

ش پاره   يكصنه

٥   ٥   **5**

#P173   #P174

1919   **Blue Surcharge and Red Overprint**

P173	A21	5pa on 2pa ol grn	15	15
a.		Red overprint double	12.50	5.00
b.		Blue surcharge double	12.50	5.00

1920   **Red Surcharge**

P174	A25	5pa on 4pa brn	15	15

> Catalogue values for unused stamps in this section, from this point to the end of the section, are for Never Hinged items.

Dove and Citadel of Ankara — N6

1952-55   Litho.   *Perf. 12½*

P175	N6	0.50k grnsh gray	20	15
P176	N6	0.50k violet ('53)	20	15

                Perf. 10½, 10

P177	N6	0.50k red org ('54)	20	15
P178	N6	0.50k brown ('55)	20	15
		Set value		36

POSTAL TAX STAMPS

Map of Turkey and Red Crescent — PT1

1928   Unwmk.   Typo.   *Perf. 14*
Crescent in Red

RA1	PT1	½pi lt brn	15	15
RA2	PT1	1pi red vio	15	15
RA3	PT1	2½pi orange	16	15

Engr.
Various Frames

RA4	PT1	5pi dk brn	25	15
RA5	PT1	10pi yel grn	42	25
RA6	PT1	20pi slate	70	35
RA7	PT1	50pi dk vio	2.50	1.35
		Nos. RA1-RA7 (7)	4.33	
		Set value		2.10

The use of these stamps on letters, parcels, etc. in addition to the regular postage, was obligatory on certain days in each year.
For surcharges see Nos. RA16, RA21-RA22.

Cherubs Upholding Star — PT2

1932

RA8	PT2	1k ol bis & red	48	15
RA9	PT2	2½k dk brn & red	32	15
RA10	PT2	5k grn & red	75	20
RA11	PT2	25k blk & red	2.50	90
		Set value		1.20

For surcharges and overprints see Nos. RA12-RA15, RA28-RA29, RA36-RA38.

No. RA8 Surcharged **20 para**

RA12	PT2	20pa on 1k	15	15
RA13	PT2	3k on 1k	1.00	38
a.		3 "kruus"	2.50	2.50

By a law of Parliament the use of these stamps on letters and telegraph forms, in addition to the regular fees, was obligatory from Apr. 20-30 of each year. The inscription in the tablet at the bottom of the design states that the money derived from the sale of the stamps is devoted to child welfare work.

No. RA8 Surcharged **20 para**

1933

RA14	PT2	20pa on 1k ol bis & red	15	15
RA15	PT2	3k on 1k ol bis & red	42	22
		Set value		30

No. RA5 Surcharged **5 Beş Kuruş**

RA16	PT1	5k on 10pi yel grn & red	50	25

PT3   PT4

1933   *Perf. 11, 11½*

RA17	PT3	20pa gray vio & red	40	16
RA18	PT4	1k vio & red	25	15
RA19	PT4	5k dk brn & red	90	50
RA20	PT3	15k grn & red	1.10	50

Nos. RA17 and RA20 were issued in Ankara; Nos. RA18 and RA19 in Izmir. For overprint see No. RA27.

Nos. RA3, RA1 Surcharged in Black **5 Beş kuruş**

1933-34

RA21	PT1	1k on 2½pi org	20	15
RA22	PT1	5k on ½pi lt brn	40	25

Map of Turkey — PT5

1934-35   Crescent in Red   *Perf. 12*

RA23	PT5	½k blue ('35)	15	15
RA24	PT5	1k red brn	15	15
RA25	PT5	2½k brn ('35)	15	15
RA26	PT5	5k bl grn ('35)	35	15
		Set value	66	26

Frame differs on No. RA26. See Nos. RA30-RA35B. For surcharge see No. RA63.

Nos. RA17, RA8-RA9 Overprinted "P.Y.S." in Roman Capitals

1936   *Perf. 11, 14*

RA27	PT3	20pa gray vio & red	42	20
RA28	PT2	1k ol bis & red	42	15
RA29	PT2	3k on 2½k dk brn & red	75	30

Type of 1934-35, Inscribed "Türkiye Kizilay Cemiyeti"

1938-46   *Perf. 8½-11½*

Type I · Imprint, "Devlet Basimevi". Crescent red.
Type II · Imprint, "Alaeddin Kiral Basimevi". Crescent carmine.
Type III · Imprint, "Damga Matbaasi". Crescent red.

Crescent in Red or Carmine

RA30	PT5	½k blue (I)	15	15
a.		Type II	3.50	1.00
b.		Type III	22	15
RA31	PT5	1k red vio (I)	15	15
a.		Type II	6.50	2.00
b.		Type III	18	15
RA32	PT5	2½k orange (I)	15	15
a.		Type III	1.25	22
RA33	PT5	5k blue grn (I)	35	15
RA33A	PT5	5k choc (III) ('42)	1.00	18
RA34	PT5	10k pale grn (I)	95	30
a.		Type III	1.25	30
RA35	PT5	20k black (I)	1.40	45
RA35A	PT5	50k pur (III) ('46)	5.00	55
RA35B	PT5	1 l blue (III) ('44)	22.50	2.50
		Nos. RA30-RA35B (9)	31.65	4.58

No. RA9 Surcharged in Black **20 Para P. Y. S.**

1938   *Perf. 14*

RA36	PT2	20pa on 2½k	35	20
RA37	PT2	1k on 2½k	50	20

No. RA9 Surcharged in Black **P. Y. S. 20 Para**

1938   Unwmk.   *Perf. 14*

RA37A	PT2	20pa on 2½k	30	15
RA37B	PT2	1k on 2½k	40	20

No. RA9 Surcharged "1 Kurus" in Black

1939   *Perf. 14*

RA38	PT2	1k on 2½k dk brn & red	50	20

Child — PT6   Nurse with Child — PT7

1940   Typo.   *Perf. 12*
Star in Carmine

RA39	PT6	20pa bluish grn	15	15
RA40	PT6	1k violet	15	15
RA41	PT7	1k lt bl	15	15
RA42	PT7	2½k pale red lil	15	15
RA43	PT6	3k black	22	15
RA44	PT7	5k pale vio	22	15
RA45	PT7	10k bl grn	60	15
RA46	PT6	15k dk bl	40	15
RA47	PT7	25k olive bister	1.75	65
RA48	PT7	50k olive gray	4.00	1.25
		Nos. RA39-RA48 (10)	7.79	
		Set value		2.50

Soldier and Map of Turkey — PT8

1941-44   *Perf. 11½*

RA49	PT8	1k purple	25	15
RA50	PT8	2k light blue	1.10	15
RA51	PT8	3k chestnut	1.25	25
RA51A	PT8	4k mag ('44)	3.75	30
RA52	PT8	5k brt rose	4.00	1.25
RA53	PT8	10k dk blue	5.00	1.20
		Nos. RA49-RA53 (6)	15.35	3.30

The tax was used for national defense.

Baby — PT9   Nurse and Baby — PT13

Nurse and Children PT10

Nurse Feeding Child PT11

Nurse and Child PT12

Nurse and Child — PT14   President Inonu Holding Child — PT16

Children PT15

1942   Unwmk.   Typo.   *Perf. 11½*
Star in Red

RA54	PT9	20pa brt vio	15	15
RA55	PT9	20pa chocolate	15	15
RA56	PT10	1k dk sl grn	15	15
RA57	PT11	2½k yel grn	15	15
RA58	PT12	3k dk bl	15	15
RA59	PT13	5k brt pink	16	15
RA60	PT14	10k lt bl	35	25
RA61	PT15	15k dk red brn	60	42
RA62	PT16	25k brown	90	65
		Nos. RA54-RA62 (9)	2.76	
		Set value		1.95

See Nos. RA175, RA179-RA180.

No. RA32 Surcharged with New Value in Brown

1942   *Perf. 10*

RA63	PT5	1k on 2½k org & red (I)	15	15

Child Eating — PT17   Nurse and Child — PT18

Nurse and Child PT19

Child and Red Star — PT20   President Inönü and Child — PT21

Inscribed: "Sefcat Pullari 23 Nisan 1943 Cocuk Esirgeme Kurumu."

1943   Star in Red   *Perf. 11*

RA64	PT17	50pa lilac	15	15
RA65	PT17	50pa gray grn	15	15
RA66	PT18	1k lt ultra	15	15
RA67	PT19	3k dk red	15	15
RA68	PT20	15k cr & blk	55	40
RA69	PT21	100k brt vio bl	1.40	1.65
a.		Souvenir sheet, #RA64-RA69, imperf.	4.25	4.25
		Nos. RA64-RA69 (6)	2.55	
		Set value		2.25

Star and Crescent PT23   Hospital PT24

Nurse and Children PT25   Baby PT26

Nurse Bathing Baby — PT27   Nurse Feeding Child — PT28

Baby with Bottle — PT29   Child — PT30

Hospital — PT31

Perf. 10 to 12 and Compound
1943-44
Star in Red

RA71	PT23	20pa deep blue	15	15
RA72	PT24	1k gray gree	15	15
RA73	PT25	3k pale gray brn	15	15

RA74	PT26	5k yel org	28	18
RA75	PT26	5k vio brn	16	15
RA76	PT27	10k red	16	15
RA77	PT28	15k red vio	28	15
RA78	PT29	25k pale vio	45	25
RA79	PT30	50k lt blue	85	50
RA80	PT31	100k lt grn	2.25	1.00
	Nos. RA71-RA80 (10)		4.88	
		Set value		2.35

For surcharge see No. RA156.

Nurse Holding
Baby
PT32

Nurse
Feeding Child
PT33

Child — PT34

Star and
Crescent — PT35

1945-47 Unwmk. Litho. Perf. 11½
Star in Red

RA81	PT32	1k lil brn	15	15
a.		1k rose violet	15	15
RA82	PT33	5k yel grn	35	15
a.		5k green	35	15
RA83	PT34	10k red brn	24	15
RA84	PT35	250k gray blk	6.50	3.50
RA84A	PT35	500k dl vio ('47)	30.00	12.50
	Nos. RA81-RA84A (5)		37.24	16.45

Imprint on No. RA82: "Kagit ve Basim isleri A.S. ist." On No. RA82a: "Guzel Sanatlar Matbaasi - Ankara."

Nurse and
Wounded Soldier
PT36

President Inönü
and Victim of
Earthquake
PT37

Removing
Wounded from
Hospital
Ship — PT38

Nurse and
Soldier — PT39

Feeding the
Poor — PT40

Wounded
Soldiers on
Landing
Raft — PT41

Symbolical of
Red Crescent
Relief — PT42

1945 Perf. 12x10, 10x12
Crescent in Red

RA85	PT36	20pa dp bl & brn org	15	15
RA86	PT37	1k ol grn & ol bis	15	15
RA87	PT38	2½k dp bl & red	24	15
RA88	PT39	5k dp bl & red	75	15
RA89	PT40	10k dp bl & lt grn	75	22
RA90	PT41	50k blk & gray grn	2.00	55
RA91	PT42	1 l blk & yel	6.50	1.50
	Nos. RA85-RA91 (7)		10.54	
		Set value		2.50

See Nos. RA181-RA182.

Ankara
Sanatorium — PT43

1946 Perf. 12

RA92	PT43	20k red & lt bl	65	30

See No. RA210. For surcharge see No. RA186.

Covering Sleeping
Child — PT44

Designs: 1k, Mother and child. 2½k, Nurse at playground. 5k, Doctor examining infant. 15k, Feeding child. 25k, Bathing child. 50k, Weighing baby. 150k, Feeding baby.

1946 Litho. Perf. 12½
Inscribed: "25ci Yil Hatirasi 1946"
Star in Carmine

RA93	PT44	20pa brown	15	15
RA94	PT44	1k blue	15	15
RA95	PT44	2½k carmine	15	15
RA96	PT44	5k vio brn	20	15
RA97	PT44	15k violet	20	15
RA98	PT44	25k gray grn	32	20
RA99	PT44	50k bl grn	65	45
RA100	PT44	150k gray brn	2.00	1.25
	Nos. RA93-RA100 (8)		3.82	
		Set value		2.30

For surcharge see No. RA155.

Hospital
Ship — PT52

Ambulance
Plane — PT53

Hospital
Train — PT54

Ambulance — PT55

Boy Scout and
Red Crescent
Flag — PT56

Stretcher Bearers and
Wounded Soldier
PT57

Nurse and
Hospital
PT58

Sanatorium
PT59

1946 Perf. 11½

RA101	PT52	1k multi	1.00	1.00
RA102	PT53	4k multi	1.00	1.00
RA103	PT54	10k multi	3.00	3.00
RA104	PT55	25k multi	2.00	2.00
RA105	PT56	40k multi	3.50	3.50
RA106	PT57	70k multi	3.75	3.75
RA107	PT58	1 l multi	5.25	5.25
RA108	PT59	2½ l multi	12.50	12.50
	Nos. RA101-RA108 (8)		32.00	32.00

For overprints see Nos. RA139-RA146.

Souvenir Sheet

Pres. Inönü and
Child — PT60

1946 Unwmk. Typo. Imperf.

RA109	PT60	250k sl blk, pink & red	10.00	10.00

Turkish Society for the Prevention of Cruelty to Children, 25th anniv.

Nurse and
Wounded Soldier
PT61

Nurse and
Soldier — PT64

Symbolical of
Red Crescent
Relief — PT67

1946-47 Litho. Perf. 11½
Crescent in Red

RA113	PT61	20pa dk bl vio & ol ('47)	15	15
RA114	PT62	1k dk brn & yel	45	22
RA115	PT64	5k dp bl & red	38	25
RA116	PT67	1 l brn blk & yel	1.90	1.25

Pres. Inönü and
Victim of
Earthquake
PT62

Nurse and Wounded Soldier
PT68   PT69

Victory and
Soldier — PT70

1947 Crescent in Red

RA117	PT68	250k brn blk & grn	3.00	2.00
RA118	PT69	5 l sl gray & org	5.00	3.50

Booklet Pane of One
Perf. 11½ (top) x Imperf.

RA119	PT70	10 l deep blue	13.50	10.00

Black numerals above No. RA119 indicate position in booklet.

President Inönü
and Victim of
Earthquake
PT71

Nurse and Child
PT72

1947 Perf. 11½

RA120	PT71	1k dk brn, pale bl & red	16	15
RA121	PT72	2½k bl vio & car	20	15
		Set value		15

See Nos. RA221-RA223. For surcharge see No. RA154.

Nurse Offering
Encouragement
PT73

Plant with Broken
Stem
PT74

Perf. 8½, 11½x10, 11x10½
1948-49 Typo. Unwmk.
Crescent in Red

RA122	PT73	½k ultra ('49)	32	20
RA123	PT73	1k indigo	15	15
RA124	PT73	2k lilac rose	15	15
RA125	PT73	2½k orange ('49)	15	15
RA126	PT73	3k blue green	15	15
RA127	PT73	4k gray ('49)	20	15
RA128	PT73	5k blue	40	15
RA129	PT73	10k pink	70	15
RA130	PT73	25k chocolate	90	25

Perf. 10

RA130A	PT74	50k ultra & bl gray ('49)	1.25	75
RA130B	PT74	100k grn & pale grn ('49)	3.00	1.00
	Nos. RA122-RA130B (11)		7.37	
		Set value		2.60

For surcharges see Nos. RA151-RA153, RA187.

Nurse and
Children — PT75

Various Scenes with Children.

Inscribed: "1948 Cocuk Yili Hatirasi"

1948   Litho.   Perf. 11
Star in Red

RA131	PT75	20pa dp ultra	15	15
RA132	PT75	20pa rose lilac	15	15
RA133	PT75	1k dp Prus bl	15	15
RA134	PT75	3k dk brn vio	22	16
RA135	PT75	15k slate blk	70	50
RA136	PT75	30k orange	1.50	1.00
RA137	PT75	150k yel grn	2.50	2.00
RA138	PT75	300k brn red	3.50	3.00
		Nos. RA131-RA138 (8)	8.87	7.11

No. RA136 is arranged horizontally. For overprints and surcharges see Nos. RA199-RA206.

> Catalogue values for unused stamps in this section, from this point to the end of the section, are for Never Hinged items.

Nos. RA101 to RA108 **Şefkat pulu**
Overprinted in
Carmine

1949   Perf. 11½

RA139	PT52	1k multi	35	35
RA140	PT53	4k multi	60	60
RA141	PT54	10k multi	3.50	3.50
RA142	PT55	25k multi	1.75	1.75
RA143	PT56	40k multi	2.75	2.75
RA144	PT57	70k multi	4.50	4.50
RA145	PT58	1 1 multi	6.25	6.25
RA146	PT59	2½ 1 multi	27.50	27.50
		Nos. RA139-RA146 (8)	47.20	47.20

Ruins and Tent
PT76   "Protection"
PT77

Booklet Panes of One
1949   Perf. 10 (top) x Imperf.

RA149	PT76	5k gray, vio gray & red	25	16
RA150	PT76	10k red vio, sal & red	40	22

Black numerals above each stamp indicate its position in the booklet.

No. RA124 Surcharged in Black

1950   Unwmk.   Perf. 8½

RA151	PT73	20pa on 2k	15	15

Postal Tax Stamps of 1944-48 Surcharged with New Value in Black or Carmine
Perf. 8½ to 12½ and Compound
1952

RA152	PT73	20pa on 3k bl grn	15	15
RA153	PT73	20pa on 4k gray	15	15
RA154	PT72	1k on 2½k bl vio & car (C)	15	15
RA155	PT44	1k on 2½k car	15	15
RA156	PT75	1k on 3k pale gray brn	15	15
		Set value	62	44

Various Symbolical Designs Inscribed "75 iNCi" etc.

1952   Typo.   Perf. 10
Crescent in Carmine

RA157	PT77	5k bl grn & bl	60	50
RA158	PT77	15k yel grn, bl & cr	60	50
RA159	PT77	30k bl, grn & brn	60	50
RA160	PT77	1 1 blk, bl & cr	90	80
a.		Souvenir sheet, #RA157-RA160, imperf.	9.00	9.00

Printed in sheets of 20 containing one horizontal row of each value.

Nurse and
Children
PT78

Design: 1k, Nurse and baby.

1954   Litho.   Perf. 10½
Star in Red

RA161	PT78	20pa aqua	15	15
RA162	PT78	20pa yellow	15	15
RA163	PT78	1k deep blue	15	15
		Set value	24	15

Globe and Flag — PT79

Designs: 5k, Winged nurse in clouds. 10k, Protecting arm of Red Crescent.

1954

RA164	PT79	1k multi	15	15
RA165	PT79	5k multi	50	15
RA166	PT79	10k car, grn & gray	1.00	15
		Set value		18

See Nos. RA208, RA211-RA213. For surcharges see Nos. RA187A-RA187B.

Florence
Nightingale
PT80   Selimiye Barracks
PT81

Portrait: 30k, Florence Nightingale, full-face.

1954, Nov. 4
Crescent in Carmine

RA167	PT80	20k gray grn & dk brn	42	38
RA168	PT80	30k dl brn & blk	42	38
RA169	PT81	50k buff & blk	80	80

Arrival of Florence Nightingale at Scutari, cent.

Type of 1942 and

Children
Kissing — PT82   Nurse Holding
Baby — PT83

1955, Apr. 23
Star in Red

RA170	PT82	20pa chalky bl	15	15
RA171	PT82	20pa org brn	15	15
RA172	PT82	1k lilac	15	15
RA173	PT82	3k gray bis	15	15
RA174	PT82	5k orange	15	15
RA175	PT12	10k green	35	16
RA176	PT83	15k dk blue	18	15
RA177	PT83	25k brn car	48	20
RA178	PT83	50k dk gray grn	1.20	80
RA179	PT12	2½ 1 dl brn	30.00	20.00
RA180	PT12	10 1 rose lil	72.50	50.00
		Nos. RA170-RA180 (11)	105.46	72.06

Types of 1945
Inscribed: "Turkiye Kizilay Dernegi"
1955 Litho. Perf. 10½x11½, 10½
Crescent in Red

RA181	PT36	20pa vio brn & lem	15	15
RA182	PT41	1k blk & gray grn	15	15
		Set value	15	15

Nurse — PT85   Nurses on
Parade — PT86

Design: 100k, Two nurses under Red Cross and Red Crescent flags and UN emblem.

Perf. 10½
1955, Sept. 5 Unwmk. Litho.
Crescent and Cross in Red

RA183	PT85	10k blk & pale brn	75	40
RA184	PT86	15k dk grn & pale yel grn	75	40
RA185	PT85	100k lt ultra	1.90	65

Meeting of the board of directors of the Intl. Council of Nurses, Istanbul, Aug. 29-Sept. 5, 1955.

Nos. RA92 and RA130B Surcharged "20 Para"

1955

RA186	PT43	20p on 20k	40	15

Typo.

RA187	PT74	20p on 100k (surch. 11½x2mm)	60	15
c.		Surcharge 13½x2½mm	60	15
		Set value	15	15

No. RA164 Surcharged with New Value and Two Bars

1956   Litho.   Perf. 10½

RA187A	PT79	20p on 1k multi	15	15
RA187B	PT79	2.50k on 1k multi	15	15
		Set value	15	15

Woman and
Children — PT87

Designs: 10k, 25k, 50k, Flag and building. 250k, 5 1, 10 1, Mother nursing baby.

1956   Litho.   Perf. 10½
Star in Red

RA188	PT87	20pa red org	15	15
RA189	PT87	20pa gray grn	15	15
RA190	PT87	1k purple	15	15
RA191	PT87	1k grnsh bl	15	15
RA192	PT87	3k lt red brn	25	15
RA193	PT87	10k rose car	40	20
RA194	PT87	25k brt grn	1.00	50
RA195	PT87	50k brt ultra	1.65	90
RA196	PT87	250k red lilac	8.50	5.00
RA197	PT87	5 1 sepia	10.00	5.00
RA198	PT87	10 1 dk sl grn	14.00	7.50
		Nos. RA188-RA198 (11)	36.40	19.85

Nos. RA131-RA138 Overprinted and Surcharged in Black or Red: "IV. DUNYA Cocuk Gunu 1 Ekim 1956"

1956, Oct. 1   Unwmk.   Perf. 11

RA199	PT75	20pa (R)	4.25	4.25
RA200	PT75	20pa	4.25	4.25
RA201	PT75	1k (R)	4.25	4.25
RA202	PT75	3k (R)	4.25	4.25
RA203	PT75	15k (R)	4.75	4.75
RA204	PT75	25k on 30k	4.75	4.75
RA205	PT75	100k on 150k (R)	6.00	6.00
RA206	PT75	250k on 300k	7.75	7.75
		Nos. RA199-RA206 (8)	40.25	40.25

The tax was for child welfare. No. RA204 is horizontal.

Type of 1954, Redrawn Type of 1946, and

Flower
PT88   Children
PT89

1957   Unwmk.   Perf. 10½
Crescent in Red

RA207	PT88	½k lt gray & brn	15	15
RA208	PT79	1k ol bis, blk & grn	15	15
RA209	PT88	2½k yel grn & bl grn	15	15
RA210	PT43	20k red & lt bl	16	15
RA211	PT79	25k lt gray, blk & grn	42	30
RA212	PT79	50k bl, dk grn & grn	65	30
RA213	PT79	100k vio, blk & grn	1.00	55
		Set value	2.50	1.40

No. RA210 inscribed "Turkiye Kizilay Cemiyeti."
No. RA92 inscribed ". . . . Dernegi."

1957   Unwmk.   Perf. 10½

RA214	PT89	20pa car & red	15	15
RA215	PT89	20pa grn & red	15	15
RA216	PT89	1k ultra & car	15	15
RA217	PT89	3k red org & car	25	16
		Set value	42	30

"Blood Donor
and Recipient"
PT90   Child and
Butterfly
PT91

Designs: 75k, Figure showing blood circulation. 150k, Blood transfusion symbolism.

1957, May 22
Size: 24x40mm

RA218	PT90	25k gray, blk & red	25	15

Size: 22½x37½mm

RA219	PT90	75k grn, blk & red	40	30
RA220	PT90	150k yel grn & red	65	45

Redrawn Type of 1947
Inscribed: "V Dunya Cocuk Gunu"

1957   Star in Red   Perf. 10½

RA221	PT72	100k blk & bis brn	65	60
RA222	PT72	50k blk & yel grn	65	60
RA223	PT72	250k blk & vio	70	65

The tax was for child welfare.

1958   Litho.   Unwmk.

Designs: Various Butterflies. Nos. RA226-RA227 arranged horizontally.

RA224	PT91	20k gray & red	30	25
RA225	PT91	25k multi	30	25
RA226	PT91	50k multi	40	30
RA227	PT91	75k grn, yel & blk	50	40
RA228	PT91	150k multi	80	65
		Nos. RA224-RA228 (5)	2.30	1.85

Florence
Nightingale — PT92

1958

Crescent in Red

RA229	PT92	1 1 bluish green	40	25
RA230	PT92	1½ 1 gray	60	50
RA231	PT92	2½ 1 blue	80	60

Turkey stopped issuing postal tax stamps in June, 1958. Similar stamps of later date are private charity stamps issued by the Red Crescent Society and the Society for the Protection of Children.

POSTAL TAX AIR POST STAMPS

Air Fund Issues

These stamps were obligatory on all air mail for 21 days a year. Tax for the Turkish Aviation Society: 20pa for a postcard, 1k for a regular letter, 2 1/2k for a registered letter, 3k for a telegram, 5k-50k for a package, higher values for air freight. Postal tax air post stamps were withdrawn Aug. 21, 1934 and remainders destroyed later that year.

Biplane
PTAP1

Perf. 11, Pin Perf.

1926	Unwmk.		Litho.

Type PTAP1
Size: 35x25mm

RAC1	20pa brn & pale grn	1.00	30
RAC2	1g blue grn & buff	1.00	30

Size: 40x29mm

RAC3	5g vio & pale grn	2.25	60
RAC4	5g car lake & pale grn	16.50	4.00

PTAP2   PTAP3

1927-29

Type PTAP2

RAC5	20pa dl red & pale grn	42	16
RAC6	1k green & yel	35	15

Type PTAP3
Perf. 11½

RAC7	2k dp cl & yel grn	60	35
RAC8	2½k red & yel grn	4.50	1.65
RAC9	5k dk bl gray & org	45	45
RAC10	10k dk grn & rose	3.75	1.65
RAC11	15k green & yel	3.75	2.00
RAC12	20k ol brn & yel	3.75	1.50
RAC13	50k dk bl & cob bl	6.00	3.25
RAC14	100k car & lt bl	60.00	35.00
	Nos. RAC5-RAC14 (10)	83.57	46.16

#RAC1, RAC5, RAC7 and RAC11 Surcharged in Black (RAC15-RAC16, RAC18-RAC19) or Red (Others)

1930-31

RAC15	1k ("Bir kurus") on RAC1	60.00	55.00
RAC16	1k ("Bir Kurus") on RAC5	25	15
RAC17	100pa ("Yuz Para") on RAC7	35	20
RAC18	5k ("Bes Kurus") on RAC5	35	20
RAC19	5k ("5 Kurus") on RAC5	35	20
RAC20	10k ("On kurus") on RAC7	1.20	60
RAC21	50k ("Elli kurus") on RAC7	6.00	2.50
RAC22	1 l ("Bir lira") on RAC7	5.00	25.00
RAC23	5 l ("Bes lira") on RAC11	425.00	300.00
	Nos. RAC15-RAC23 (9)	498.50	383.85

PTAP4   PTAP5

1931-32	Litho.		Perf. 11½
RAC24	PTAP4 20pa black	15	15

Typo.

RAC25	PTAP5 1k brown car ('32)	25	15
RAC26	PTAP5 5k red ('32)	60	25
RAC27	PTAP5 10k green ('32)	1.50	50

PTAP6

1933

Type PTAP6

RAC28	10pa ("On Para") grn	30	15
RAC29	1k ("Bir Kurus") red	75	16
RAC30	5k ("Bes Kurus") lil	1.50	1.00

TURKEY IN ASIA

(Anatolia)

40 Paras = 1 Piaster

This designation, which includes all of Turkey in Asia Minor, came into existence during the uprising of 1919, led by Mustafa Kemal Pasha. Actually there was no separation of territory, the Sultan's sovereignty being almost immediately reduced to a small area surrounding Constantinople. The formation of the Turkish Republic and the expulsion of the Sultan followed in 1923. Subsequent issues of postage stamps are listed under Turkey (Republic).

Issues of the Nationalist Government.

Turkish Revenue Stamps Handstamped in Turkish "Osmanli Postalari, 1336" (Ottoman Post, 1920).

انتره

Turkish Stamps of 1913-18 Surcharged in Black or Red

٣ عروش

(The Surcharge reads "Angora 3 Piastres")

1920	Unwmk.		Perf. 12

On Stamps of 1913

1	A24 3pi on 2pa red lilac	1.00	75
2	A25 3pi on 4pa dk brn	7.50	7.50
3	A27 3pi on 6pa dk bl	20.00	20.00

On Stamp of 1916-18

4	A42 3pi on 2pa vio (Bk)	5.00	3.50

دَرس

خسردشن
٣

Turkish Stamps of 1913-18 Handstamped in Black or Red

(The Surch. reads "Post, Piastre 3")

1921			Perf. 12, 12½

On Stamps of 1913

5	A24 3pi on 2pa red lil	5.50	3.75
a.	On No. 1	12.50	12.50
6	A25 3pi on 4pa dk brn	7.50	5.00
a.	On No. 2	12.50	12.50
7	A25 3pi on 4pa dk brn (R)	18.00	18.00
a.	On No. 2	10.50	10.50
8	A27 3pi on 6pa dk bl	17.50	17.50
a.	On No. 3	32.50	32.50

9	A27 3pi on 6pa dk bl (R)	20.00	15.00
a.	On No. 3	16.00	14.00

On Stamps of 1916-18

10	A42 3pi on 2pa vio (R)	17.50	16.00
a.	On No. 4	13.00	13.00

A1

The overprint on Nos. 12-28 comes in 3 types, 20-24mm wide. All 3 types are found on Nos. 12, 14, 21; 2 on Nos. 13, 18, 25; 1 on the others.

12	A1 1pi green	125.00	60.00
13	A1 5pi ultra	1,700.	1,500.
14	A1 50pi gray grn	3.00	2.50
	Cut cancellation		50
15	A1 100pi buff	52.50	12.50
a.	100pi yellow	32.50	26.00
	Cut cancellation		2.50
16	A1 500pi orange	60.00	42.50
	Cut cancellation		5.00
17	A1 1000pi brown	1,000.	1,000.
	Cut cancellation		67.50

See Nos. 29-32.

A2

Black Overprint

18	A2 10pa green	67.50	60.00
19	A2 1pi ultra	1,600.	1,500.
20	A2 5pi rose	900.00	825.00
21	A2 50pi ocher	4.50	3.50
a.	50pi yellow	10.50	10.50
	Cut cancellation		50
22	A2 100pi brown	32.50	32.50
	Cut cancellation		2.25
23	A2 500pi slate	125.00	95.00
	Cut cancellation		5.50

See Nos. 24, 33-39.

A3

Red and Black Overprints

24	A3 50pi ocher	100.00	25.00
	Cut cancellation		5.00

A4   A5

Black Overprint

25	A4 2pi emerald		2,000.
26	A5 100pi yellow brn	200.00	67.50
	Cut cancellation		4.50

See Nos. 46-48.

A6   A7

27	A6 20pa black	1,400.	1,400.
28	A7 2pi blue black	1,500.	1,500.

See No. 45.

A8

Perf. 12

29	A8 10pa slate	6.50	5.25
a.	Handstamped overprint	8.00	8.00
b.	Double overprint		
30	A8 1pi green	6.50	6.00
a.	Inverted overprint	16.00	13.00
b.	Handstamped overprint		
31	A8 5pi ultra	4.50	4.00
a.	"1337" inverted	90.00	82.50
b.	Half used as 2½pi on cover		
c.	Handstamped overprint	15.00	15.00

Handstamped Overprint

32	A8 50pi green	825.00	600.00

IF YOU COLLECT...

TURKEY IN ASIA

(ANATOLIA)

WHY NOT BUY FROM THE MAN WHO WROTE THE BOOK...

ANATOLIA

and has the largest stock of genuine stamps of...

TURKEY IN ASIA

Free price lists

Menachim Max Mayo

P.O. Box 289 Ivy, VA 22945

A9

33 A9	10pa green	3.50 3.00
a.	Handstamped overprint	
34 A9	1pi ultra	5.25 5.00
a.	Handstamped overprint	22.50 22.50
35 A9	5pi red	3.25 3.00
a.	Inverted overprint	
b.	"1337" inverted	8.00 5.50
c.	Half used as 2½pi on cover	
d.	Handstamped overprint	
36 A9	50pi ocher	52.50 52.50
a.	Handstamped overprint	32.50 32.50

A10

With Additional Turkish Overprint in Red or Black

37 A10	10pa green (R)	26.00 26.00
a.	Black overprint inverted	60.00 60.00
38 A10	1pi ultra (R)	22.50 22.50
39 A10	5pi rose (Bk)	26.00 26.00
a.	"1337" inverted	82.50 82.50

A11   A12

40 A11	2pi blue black	20.00 20.00
a.	Handstamped overprint	

1921   *Perf. 12*

41 A12	5pi green	26.00 26.00
a.	Cut cancellation	2.00
a.	Handstamped overprint	

A13

42 A13	1pi ultra	140.00 140.00
a.	Handstamped overprint	1,000. 1,000.
43 A13	5pi deep green	135.00 135.00
a.	Handstamped overprint	1,000. 1,000.

Handstamped Overprint

44 A13	5pi dark vio	2,000. 2,000.

The overprint variety "337" for "1337" exists on Nos. 42-43.

Turkey in Asia Stamps can be mounted in the Scott Turkey album.

A14

Perf. 12, 12½

45 A14	20pa black	2.00 2.00
a.	Date 4½mm high	3.50 3.50
b.	"337" for "1337"	3.50 3.50

A15   A16

46 A15	10pa green	3.50 3.50
a.	Overprint 21mm long	
b.	"131" for "1337"	
47 A15	1pi ultra	6.50 5.75
a.	"13" for "1337"	22.50 22.50
b.	"131" for "1337"	22.50 22.50
c.	Inverted overprint	32.50 32.50
d.	Handstamped overprint	
48 A15	5pi red	12.50 12.50
a.	Inverted overprint	67.50 60.00
b.	"131" for "1337"	60.00 60.00
c.	Handstamped overprint	

Perf. 11½, 11½x11

49 A16	10pa pink	75 60
a.	Imperf.	
b.	Date "1237"	1.00 1.00
d.	Inverted overprint	
50 A16	1pi yellow	1.00 65
a.	Overprint 18mm long	1.00 80
b.	Date "1332"	5.50
c.	Date "1317"	
d.	Inverted overprint	1.65 1.65
51 A16	2pi yellow grn	1.00 75
a.	Date "1237"	5.50
b.	Date "1317"	
c.	Imperf.	
d.	Inverted overprint	3.25 3.25
52 A16	5pi red	2.50 75
a.	Horiz. pair, imperf. vert.	
b.	Inverted overprint	3.25 2.50
c.	Double overprint	4.50 3.25
d.	Date "1332"	5.50
e.	Half used as 2½pi on cover	
f.	Overprint 18mm long	2.75 2.25

Turkish Revenue Stamps Overprinted "Osmanli Postalari 1337"

A17

TURKISH INSCRIPTIONS:

20 Paras	1 Piaster
2 Piasters	5 Piasters

1921   *Perf. 11½*

Dark Red & Blue

53 A17	20pa on 1pi	14.00 12.50
54 A17	1pi on 1pi	1.00 75
55 A17	2pi on 1pi	1.00 75
a.	Inverted surcharge	
56 A17	5pi on 1pi	2.50 2.50

No. 55 is also surcharged with the Turkish numeral "2." See No. 57.

A18   A19

57 A18	1pi on 1pi dk red & bl	17.50 17.50
58 A19	1pi grn & brn red	1.00 75
a.	Double overprint	
b.	Handstamped overprint	

The errors "1307," "1331" and "2337" occur once in each sheet of Nos. 53-58.

Naval League Stamps Overprinted in Turkish "Osmanli Postalari, 1337" (Ottoman Post, 1921)

A20

1921   *Perf. 12x11½*

59 A20	1pa orange	50 50
a.	Date "1327"	1.10 1.10
60 A20	2pa indigo	1.00 1.00
61 A20	5pa green	2.25 2.25
62 A20	10pa brown	20.00 20.00
63 A20	40pa red brown	15.00 15.00
	Nos. 59-63 (5)	38.75 38.75

The error "2337" occurs on all values of this issue.

The Naval League stamps have pictures of three Turkish warships. They were sold for the benefit of sailors of the fleet but did not pay postage until they were surcharged in 1921.

Overprinted

On Stamps of 1916-18
Perf. 12

64 A44	10pa green	5.50 5.00
65 A45	20pa deep rose	5.50 5.00
a.	Inverted overprint	16.50 16.50
66 A51	25pi car, straw	20.00 20.00
a.	Double overprint	
b.	Inverted overprint	37.50 37.50

On Newspaper Stamp of 1909, Overprinted Crescent and Star in 1915

67 A21	5pa ocher	150.00 55.00

Turkish Stamps of 1915-20 Surcharged

1921

On Stamp of 1913, Overprinted Crescent and Star in 1915

68 A22	5pa ocher	70.00 50.00

On Stamps of 1917-18

69 A53	5pi on 2pa (#547)	3.75 3.75
70 A53	5pi on 2pa (#548)	4.00 4.00

On Stamp of 1919

71 A57	35pi on 1pi bl (Bk)	10.00 10.00
a.	Inverted surcharge	

On Newspaper Stamp of 1909, Overprinted Crescent and Star in 1915

72 A21	5pa ocher	200.00 200.00

On No. 72 the overprint is vertical, half reading up and half reading down.

On Stamps of 1920

73 A32	3pi blue	3.00 3.00
74 A36	10pi gray violet	3.00 3.00

The overprints on Nos. 64-74 read "Adana December 1st, 1921." This issue was to commemorate the withdrawal of the French from Cilicia. On No. 71 the lines of the overprint are further apart than on Nos. 68-70, and 73-74.

Postage Due Stamps of Turkey, 1914, Overprinted:

a   b

1921   **Unwmk.**   *Perf. 12*

75 D1 (a)	5pa claret	55.00 50.00
76 D2 (a)	20pa red	55.00 50.00
a.	Inverted overprint	
77 D3 (b)	1pi dark blue	55.00 50.00
a.	Inverted overprint	70.00 70.00

Withdrawal of the French from Cilicia. Forged overprints exist.

Pact of Revenge, Burning Village at Top — A21   Izmir Harbor — A22

Mosque of Selim, Adrianople — A23   Mosque of Selim, Konya — A24

Soldier — A25   Legendary Gray Wolf — A26

Snake Castle and Seyhan River, Adana — A27

Parliament Building at Sivas — A28

A29   Mosque at Urfa — A30

Map of Anatolia — A31   Declaration of Faith from the Koran — A32

1922 — Litho. — Perf. 11½

78	A21	10pa violet brn	20	50
79	A22	20pa blue grn	25	15
80	A23	1pi dp blue	45	15
81	A24	2pi red brown	1.00	15
82	A25	5pi dk blue	1.25	15
83	A26	10pi dk brown	5.50	20
84	A27	25pi rose	4.50	15
85	A28	50pi indigo	4.00	65
86	A29	50pi dk gray	4.00	5.00
87	A30	200pi violet	35.00	2.00
		Cut cancellation		50
88	A31	200pi slate	70.00	12.50
		Cut cancellation		50
89	A32	500pi green	65.00	7.50
		Cut cancellation		1.00
		Nos. 78-89 (12)	191.15	29.10

Imperf

79a	A22	20pa	2.50	2.50
80a	A23	1pi	5.00	5.00
82a	A25	5pi	5.00	5.00
84a	A27	25pi	32.50	32.50
85a	A28	50pi	8.25	8.25

املنه

Stamps of Type A23
Overprinted

٥ كانون ثانى ١٣٢٨

1922

90	A23	1pi deep blue	5.50	4.50
91	A23	5pi deep blue	5.50	4.50
92	A23	10pi brown	5.50	4.50
93	A23	25pi rose	5.50	4.50
94	A23	50pi slate	5.50	4.50
95	A23	100pi violet	5.50	4.50
96	A23	200pi black vio	5.50	4.50
97	A23	500pi blue grn	5.50	4.50
		Nos. 90-97 (8)	44.00	36.00

Withdrawal of the French from Cilicia and the return of the Kemalist Natl. army. The overprint reads: "Adana, Jan. 5, 1922."

No. 90-97 without overprint were presented to some high government officials.

First Parliament House, Ankara — A33

1922 — Litho.

98	A33	5pa violet	20	15
99	A33	10pa green	20	15
100	A33	20pa pale red	35	20
101	A33	1pi brown org	1.75	95
102	A33	2pi red brown	7.50	1.20
103	A33	3pi rose	1.75	25
a.		Arabic "13" in right corner	6.50	3.50
b.		Thin grayish paper	14.00	1.40
		Nos. 98-103 (6)	11.75	2.45

Nos. 98-103, 103b exist imperf. In 1923 several stamps of Turkey and Turkey in Asia were overprinted in Turkish for advertising purposes. The overprint reads: "Izmir Economic Congress, 17 Feb., 1339."

POSTAGE DUE STAMPS

D1

1922 — Litho. — Perf. 11½

J1	D1	20pa dull green	20	20
a.		Imperf.		
J2	D1	1pi gray green	25	25
J3	D1	2pi red brown	90	65
J4	D1	3pi rose	1.75	1.50
J5	D1	5pi dark blue	2.25	2.00
		Nos. J1-J5 (5)	5.35	4.60

ΕΛΛΗΝΙΚΗ
ΚΑΤΟΧΗ
ΛΕΠΤΑ∙50

Turkish Stamps of 1916-21 with Greek surcharge as above in blue or black are of private origin.

TURKISH REPUBLIC OF NORTHERN CYPRUS

LOCATION — Northern 40% of the Island of Cyprus in the Mediterranean Sea off the coast of Turkey.

Established following Turkish invasion of Cyprus in 1974. On Nov. 15, 1983 Turkey declared the Turkish Republic of Northern Cyprus to be independent. No other country has recognized this country.

1000 Milliemes = 1 Pound
100 Kurus = 1 Turkish Lira (1978)

Catalogue values for all unused stamps in this country are for Never Hinged items.

Letters bearing these stamps enter international mail via the Turkish Post Office.

Watermark

Wmk. 390

Republic of Turkey, 50th Anniv.
A1   A2

Designs: 3m, Woman sentry. 5m, Military parade. 10m, Flag bearers. 15m, Anniversary emblem. 20m, Ataturk statue. 50m, Painting, "The Fallen". 70m, Turkish flag, map of Cyprus.

Perf. 12x11½, 11½x12

1974, July 27 — Litho. — Unwmk.

1	A1	3m multicolored	85	85
2	A2	5m multicolored	1.40	1.40
3	A1	10m multicolored	2.75	2.75
4	A1	15m multicolored	4.25	4.25
5	A1	20m multicolored	5.75	5.75
6	A1	50m multicolored	14.00	14.00
7	A2	70m multicolored	20.00	20.00
		Nos. 1-7 (7)	49.00	49.00

KIBRIS
TÜRK
FEDERE
DEVLETİ
13.2.1975

Nos. 5, 3 Surcharged

30 M
—

Historical Sites and Landmarks
A3

1975, Mar. 3 — Perf. 12x11½

8	A1	30m on 20m, #5	20	20
9	A1	100m on 10m, #3	70	70

Surcharge appears in different positions.

Designs: 3m, Namik Kemal's bust, Famagusta. 5m, 30m, Kyrenia Harbor. 10m, Ataturk Statue, Nicosia. 15m, St. Hilarion Castle. 20m, Ataturk Square, Nicosia. 25m, Coastline, Famagusta. 50m, Lala Mustafa Pasha Mosque, Famagusta vert. 100m, Kyrenia Castle. 250m, Kyrenia Castle, exterior walls. 500m, Othello Tower, Famagusta vert.

1975-76 — Perf. 13

10	A3	3m pink & multi	15	15
11	A3	5m bl & multi	15	15
12	A3	10m pink & multi	15	15
13	A3	15m pink & multi	15	15
14	A3	15m bl & multi	15	15
15	A3	20m pink & multi	15	15
16	A3	20m bl & multi	15	15
17	A3	25m pink & multi	15	15
18	A3	30m pink & multi	16	16
19	A3	50m pink & multi	26	26
20	A3	100m pink & multi	52	52
21	A3	250m pink & multi	1.25	1.25
22	A3	500m pink & multi	2.50	2.50
		Set value	5.25	5.25

Issue dates: Nos. 10, 12-13, 15, 17-22, Apr. 21, 1975. Nos. 11, 14, 16, Aug. 2, 1976. Nos. 1, 14, 16 have different inscriptions and "1976." For surcharges see Nos. 28-29.

Peace in Cyprus — A4

Designs: 50m, Map, olive branch, severed chain. 150m, Map, globe, olive branch, vert.

Perf. 13½x13, 13x13½

1975, July 20

23	A4	30m multicolored	16	16
24	A4	50m multicolored	26	26
25	A4	150m multicolored	75	75

Europa — A5

Paintings: 90m, Pomegranates by I.V. Guney. 100m, Harvest Time by F. Direkoglu.

1975, Dec. 29 — Perf. 13

26	A5	90m multicolored	38	38
27	A5	100m multicolored	42	42

Nos. 19, 20 Surcharged

10 M
—

1976, Apr. 28 — Perf. 13

28	A3	10m on 50m, #19	45	45
29	A3	30m on 100m, #20	1.40	1.40

Europa — A6   Olympic Games, Montreal — A8

Fruits — A7

1976, May 3

30	A6	60m Expectation	35	35
31	A6	120m Man in Meditation	70	70

1976, June 28

32	A7	10m Ceratonia siliqua	15	15
33	A7	25m Citrus nobilis	15	15
34	A7	40m Fragaria vesca	20	20
35	A7	60m Citrus sinensis	30	30
36	A7	80m Citrus limon	40	40
		Nos. 32-36 (5)	1.20	1.20

For surcharges see Nos. 66-69.

1976, July 17

Design: 100m, Olympic rings, doves, horiz.

37	A8	60m multicolored	20	20
38	A8	100m multicolored	35	35

Liberation Monument — A9

1976, Nov. 1 — Perf. 13x13½

39	A9	30m multi	15	15
40	A9	150m multi, diff.	45	45

Europa — A10

1977, May 2 — Perf. 13

41	A10	80m Salamis Bay	50	50
42	A10	100m Kyrenia Port	65	65

Handicrafts
A11

1977, June 27

43	A11	15m Pottery	15	15
44	A11	30m Gourds, vert.	15	15
45	A11	125m Baskets	52	52
		Set value	72	72

Landmarks
A12

Designs: 20m, Arap Ahmet Pasha Mosque, Nicosia, vert. 40m, Paphos Castle. 70m, Bekir Pasha aqueduct, Larnaca. 80m, Sultan Mahmut library, Nicosia.

1977, Dec. 2 — Perf. 13x13½, 13½x13

46	A12	20m multicolored	15	15
47	A12	40m multicolored	15	15
48	A12	70m multicolored	26	26
49	A12	80m multicolored	30	30

Namik Kemal (1840-1888), Writer — A13

1977, Dec. 21 — Perf. 13

50	A13	30m Bust, home	15	15
51	A13	140m Portrait, vert.	55	55

Social
Security — A14

Europa — A15

Designs: 275k, Man with sling, crutch. 375k,
Woman with children.

1978, Apr. 17   *Perf. 13x13½*
52 A14 150k blk, bl & yel   15   15
53 A14 275k blk, grn & red org   18   18
54 A14 375k blk, red org & bl   24   24

1978, May 2   *Perf. 13x13½, 13½x13*

Designs: 225k, Oratory in Buyuk Han, Nicosia.
450k, Reservoir, Selimiye Mosque, Nicosia, horiz.

55 A15 225k multicolored   20   20
56 A15 450k multicolored   40   40

Transportation
A16

1978, July 10   *Perf. 13½x13*
57 A16   75k Roadway   15   15
58 A16 100k Hydrofoil   15   15
59 A16 650k Airplane   52   52
     Set value   65   65

National Oath — A17

Kemal
Ataturk — A18

1978, Sept. 13
60 A17 150k Dove, olive branch   15   15
61 A17 225k Stylized pen, vert.   15   15
62 A17 725k Stylized dove   40   40
     Set value   60   60

1978, Nov. 10
63 A18   75k bl grn & lt grn   15   15
64 A18 450k brn & buff   26   26
65 A18 650k Prus bl & lt bl   38   38

50 Krs.
Nos. 33-36 Surcharged   «×××»

1979, June 4
66 A7 50k on 25m   15   15
67 A7 1 l on 40m   15   15
68 A7 3 l on 60m   15   15
69 A7 5 l on 80m   16   16
     Set value   30   30

Souvenir Sheet

5th ANNIVERSARY OF THE TURKISH PEACE
OPERATION IN CYPRUS

Turkish Invasion of Cyprus, 5th
Anniv. — A19

Illustration reduced.

1979, July 2   *Imperf.*
70 A19 15 l multicolored   65   65

Europa
A20

Communications: 3 l, Stamps, building, map. 8 l,
Early and modern telephones, globe, satellite.

1979, Aug. 20   *Litho.*   *Perf. 13*
71 A20 2 l multicolored   15   15
72 A20 3 l multicolored   16   16
73 A20 8 l multicolored   42   42

Intl. Consultative Radio
Committee, 50th
Anniv. — A21

1979, Sept. 24
74 A21 2 l blue & multi   15   15
75 A21 5 l gray & multi   22   22
76 A21 6 l green & multi   26   28
     Set value   55   55

Intl. Year of
the
Child — A22

Childrens' drawings of children.

1979, Oct. 29
77 A22 1½ l multi, vert.   15   15
78 A22 4½ l multi, vert.   24   24
79 A22 6 l multi, vert.   32   32

Press reports in Jan. 1980 state that
the 1979 UPU Congress declared Turkish Cyprus stamps invalid for international mail.

A23   Europa — A24

Anniv. and events: 2½ l, Lala Mustafa Pasha
Mosque, Famagusta. 10 l, Arap Ahmet Pasha
Mosque, Lefkosa. 20 l, Holy Kaaba, Mosque.

1980, Mar. 23
80 A23 2½ l multicolored   15   15
81 A23 10 l multicolored   20   20
82 A23 20 l multicolored   42   42

1st Islamic Conference in Turkish Cyprus
(2½ l). General Assembly of World Islam Congress
(10 l). Moslem year 1400 AH (20 l).

1980, May 23
83 A24 5 l Ebu-Suud Efendi   15   15
84 A24 30 l Sultan Selim II   65   65

Historic
Landmarks
A25

Designs: 2½ l, Omer's Shrine, Kyrenia. 3½ l,
Entrance gate, Famagusta. 5 l, Funerary monuments, Famagusta. 10 l, Bella Paise Abbey, Kyrenia.
20 l, Selimiye Mosque, Nicosia.

1980, June 25
     Blue Paper
85 A25 2½ l buff & Prus bl   15   15
86 A25 3½ l pale pink & dk grn   15   15
87 A25 5 l pale bl grn & dk car   15   15
88 A25 10 l lt grn & red lil   18   18
89 A25 20 l buff & dk bl   35   35
     Set value   75   75

For overprints and surcharges see Nos. 198-200.

Cyprus
Postage
Stamps,
Cent.
A26

1980, Aug. 16
90 A26 7½ l No. 5, vert.   15   15
91 A26 15 l No. 199   28   28
92 A26 50 l Social welfare, vert.   95   95

Palestinian
Solidarity
A27

Design: 15 l, Dome of the Rock, entrance, vert.

1980, Mar. 24
93 A27 15 l multicolored   20   20
94 A27 35 l multicolored   50   50

World Muslim Congress
Statement — A28

1981, Mar. 24
95 A28 1 l In Turkish   15   15
96 A28 35 l In English   65   65
     Set value   68   68

Ataturk by Feyhamam Duran — A29

1981, May 19
97 A29 20 l multicolored   40   40

Printed with se-tenant label promoting Ataturk
Stamp Exhibition.

Europa
A30

Folk dances.

1981, June 29
98 A30 10 l multicolored   20   20
99 A30 30 l multi, diff.   60   60

Souvenir Sheet

Ataturk, Birth Cent. — A31

Illustration reduced.

1981, July 23   *Imperf.*
100 A31 150 l multicolored   1.40   1.40

No. 100 has simulated perfs.

Flowers
A32

Designs: 1 l, Convolvulus althaeoides, vert. 5 l,
Cyclamen persicum. 10 l, Mandragara officinarum.
25 l, Papaver rhoeas, vert. 30 l, Arum dioscoridis,
vert. 50 l, Chrysanthemum segetum. 100 l, Cistus
salyiaefolius, vert. 150 l, Ferula communis.

1981-82   *Perf. 13*
101 A32   1 l multicolored   15   15
102 A32   5 l multicolored   15   15
103 A32   10 l multicolored   15   15
104 A32   25 l multicolored   35   35
105 A32   30 l multicolored   42   42
106 A32   50 l multicolored   70   70
107 A32 100 l multicolored   1.40   1.40
108 A32 150 l multicolored   2.00   2.00
     Nos. 101-108 (8)   5.32   5.32

Issue dates: 1 l, 10 l, 25 l, 150 l, Sept. 28. 5 l,
30 l, 50 l, 100 l, Jan. 22, 1982.
For surcharge & overprints see #138-141, 201.

Intl. Year for
Disabled
Persons
A33

Fight Against
Apartheid — A34

World Food
Day — A35

1981, Oct. 16
109	A33	7½ l multicolored	15	15
110	A34	10 l multicolored	20	20
111	A35	20 l multicolored	38	38

Palestinian
Solidarity
A36

1981, Nov. 29
112	A36	10 l multicolored	24	24

Royal Wedding of Prince
Charles and Lady Diana
Spencer — A37

1981, Nov. 30
113	A37	50 l multicolored	70	70

Souvenir Sheet

Charter of Cyprus, 1865 — A38

Turkish Forces Landing in Tuzla — A39

1982, July 30
114		Sheet of 4	2.25	2.25
a.	A38	30 l multicolored	65	65
b.	A39	70 l multicolored	1.50	1.50

Europa. #114 contains 2 each #114a, 114b.

Buffavento Castle — A40

Windsurfing
A41

Kantara
Castle — A42

Tourism: 30 l, Shipwreck museum.

Perf. 12½x12, 12x12½
1982, Aug. 20
116	A40	5 l multicolored	15	15
117	A41	10 l multicolored	15	15
118	A42	15 l multicolored	18	18
119	A42	30 l multicolored	35	35

Art Treasures — A43

Designs: 30 l, The Wedding by Aylin Orek. 50 l,
Carob Pickers by Ozden Nazim, vert.

1982, Dec. 3   *Perf. 13x13½, 13½x13*
120	A43	30 l multicolored	42	42
121	A43	50 l multicolored	70	70

Robert Koch,
TB Bacillus
A44

World Cup Soccer Championships,
Spain — A45

Scouting, 75th
Anniv. — A46

1982, Dec. 15   *Perf. 12½*
122	A44	10 l multicolored	15	15
123	A45	30 l multicolored	42	42
124	A46	70 l multicolored	1.00	1.00

Paintings — A47

Designs: 30 l, Calloused Hands by Salih Oral.
35 l, Malya-Limassol Bus by Emin Cizenel.

1983, May 16   *Perf. 13½x13*
125	A47	30 l multicolored	42	42
126	A47	35 l multicolored	50	50

Miniature Sheet

Europa — A48

Designs: a, Map by Piri Reis. b, Cyprus seen from
Skylab.

1983, June 30   *Perf. 13*
127	A48	Sheet of 2	2.00	2.00
a.-b.		100 l any single	1.00	1.00

25th Anniv.
of Turkish
Resistance
A49

Designs: 15 l, No. 3. 20 l, Exploitation, Suppres-
sion & Resurrection by Aziz Hasan. 25 l, Resistance
by Guner Pir.

1983, Aug. 1   *Perf. 13*
129	A49	15 l multi, vert.	32	32
130	A49	20 l multi	42	42
131	A49	25 l multi, vert.	52	52

World Communications Year — A50

1983, Aug. 1
132	A50	30 l shown	60	60
133	A50	50 l Letters	1.00	1.00

Birds — A51

1983, Oct. 10
134	A51	10 l Merops apiaster	15	15
135	A51	15 l Carduelis carduelis	20	20
136	A51	50 l Erithacus rubecula	65	65
137	A51	85 l Oriolus oriolus	85	85
a.		Block of 4, #134-137	1.90	1.90

Kuzey Kıbrıs
Türk Cumhuriyeti
15.11.1983

**Kuzey Kıbrıs
Türk Cumhuriyeti
15.11.1983**   **15**

Nos. 103, 108 Ovptd.	Nos. 101, 104 Ovptd. or Surcharged

1983, Dec. 7
138	A32	10 l multicolored	15	15
139	A32	15 l on 1 l multi	20	20
140	A32	25 l multicolored	35	35
141	A32	150 l multicolored	2.00	2.00

Europa, 25th
Anniv.
A52

1984, May 30   *Perf. 12x12½*
142	A52	50 l blk, yel & brn	45	45
143	A52	100 l blk, bl & ultra	90	90
a.		Pair, #142-143	1.40	1.40

Olympics,
Los Angeles
A53

Perf. 12½x12, 12x12½
1984, June 19
144	A53	10 l Olympic flame, vert.	15	15
145	A53	20 l Olympic rings	18	18
146	A53	70 l Judo	65	65
		Set value	85	85

Ataturk
Cultural
Center — A54

Perf. 12x12½
1984, July 20   **Wmk. 390**
147	A54	120 l blk, yel & brn	90	90

Turkish
Invasion of
Cyprus, 10th
Anniv.
A55

1984, July 20
148	A55	20 l shown	16	16
149	A55	70 l Map, flag, olive branch	55	55

Forest Conservation — A56

1984, Aug. 20
150	A56	90 l multicolored	75	75

Paintings — A57

Designs: 20 l, Old Turkish Houses in Nicosia by
Cevdet Cagdas. 70 l, Scenery by Olga Rauf.

1984, Sept. 21   *Perf. 13*
151	A57	20 l multicolored	16	16
152	A57	70 l multicolored	55	55

Proclamation of Turkish
Republic of Northern
Cyprus — A58

Unanimous
Vote by
Legislative
Assembly
A59

Perf. 12½x12, 12x12½
1984, Nov. 15
153	A58	20 l multicolored	16	16
154	A59	70 l multicolored	55	55

Independence, 1st Anniv.

European Taekwondo Championship,
Kyrenia — A60

1984, Dec. 10
155	A60	10 l Competitors	15	15
156	A60	70 l Flags	55	55

Balance of the Spirit — A61

Paintings by Saulo Mercader: 20 l, The Look, vert.

Perf. 12¹/₂x13, 13x12¹/₂
1984, Dec. 10
157	A61	20 l multicolored	15	15
158	A61	70 l multicolored	50	50

Visit by Nuremburg Chamber Orchestra A62

1984, Dec. 10   *Perf. 12¹/₂*
159	A62	70 l multicolored	45	45

Dr. Fazil Kucuk (1906-1984), Politician — A63

Design: 70 l, Kucuk reading newspaper, c. 1970.

1985, Jan.
160	A63	20 l multicolored	15	15
161	A63	70 l multicolored	50	50

Domestic Animals A64

1985, May 29   *Perf. 12x12¹/₂*
162	A64	100 l Capra	55	55
163	A64	200 l Bos taurus	1.10	1.10
164	A64	300 l Ovis aries	1.65	1.65
165	A64	500 l Equus asinus	2.75	2.75

Europa — A65   Paintings — A66

Composers: No. 166, George Frideric Handel (1685-1759). No. 167, Domenico Scarlatti (1685-1757). No. 168, Johann Sebastian Bach (1685-1750). No. 169, Buhurizade Mustafa Itri (1640-1712).

1985, June 26   *Perf. 12¹/₂x12*
166	A65	20 l grn & multi	15	15
167	A65	20 l brn lake & multi	15	15
168	A65	100 l bl & multi	40	40
169	A65	100 l brn & multi	40	40
a.		Block of 4, #166-169	1.10	1.10

1985, Aug.   *Perf. 12¹/₂x13*
Paintings: 20 l, Pastoral Life by Ali Atakan. 50 l, Woman Carrying Water by Ismet V. Guney.
170	A66	20 l multicolored	15	15
171	A66	50 l multicolored	30	30

Intl. Youth Year — A67

Perf. 12¹/₂
1985, Oct. 29   Litho.   Wmk. 390
172	A67	20 l shown	15	15
173	A67	100 l Globe, dove	60	60

Northern Cyprus Air League — A68   Development of Rabies Vaccine, Cent. — A69

Ismet Inonu (1884-1973), Turkish Pres. — A70

UN, 40th Anniv. A71

Blood Donor Services A72

1985, Nov. 29
174	A68	20 l multicolored	15	15
175	A69	50 l Pasteur	30	30
176	A70	100 l brown	60	60
177	A71	100 l multicolored	60	60
178	A72	100 l multicolored	60	60
		Nos. 174-178 (5)	2.25	2.25

Paintings — A73

Designs: 20 l, House with Arches by Gonen Atakol. 100 l, Ataturk Square by Yalkin Muhtaroglu.

1986, June 20   *Perf. 13*
179	A73	20 l multicolored	15	15
180	A73	100 l multicolored	40	40

Miniature Sheet

Europa — A74

1986, June 20   *Perf. 12x12¹/₂*
181	A74	Sheet of 2	1.00	1.00
a.		100 l Gyps fulvus	32	32
b.		200 l Roadside litter	65	65

Karagoz Puppets — A75

1986, July 25   *Perf. 12¹/₂x13*
182	A75	100 l multicolored	40	40

Anatolian Artifacts A76

Designs: 10 l, Ring-shaped composite pottery, Kernos, Old Bronze Age (2300-1050 B.C.). 20 l, Bird-shaped lidded pot, Skuru Hill tomb, Morphou, late Bronze Age (1600-1500 B.C.), vert. 50 l, Earthenware jug, Vryse, Kyrenia, Neolithic Age (4000 B.C.). 100 l, Terra sigillata statue of Artemis, Sea of Salamis, Roman Period (200 B.C.), vert.

1986, Sept. 15   *Perf. 12¹/₂*
183	A76	10 l multicolored	15	15
184	A76	20 l multicolored	15	15
185	A76	50 l multicolored	25	25
186	A76	100 l multicolored	50	50

Defense Forces, 10th Anniv. — A77   World Food Day — A78

World Cup Soccer Championships, Mexico — A79

Halley's Comet A80

1986, Oct. 13
187	A77	20 l multicolored	16	16
188	A78	50 l multicolored	28	28
189	A79	100 l multicolored	36	36
190	A80	100 l multicolored	40	40

Development Projects — A81

1986, Nov. 17
191	A81	20 l Water resources	15	15
192	A81	50 l Housing	22	22
193	A81	100 l Airport	45	45

Royal Wedding of Prince Andrew and Sarah Ferguson — A82

Anniv. and events: No. 195, Queen Elizabeth II, 60th birthday.

Perf. 12¹/₂x13
1986, Nov. 20   **Wmk. 390**
194	A82	100 l multicolored	32	32
195	A82	100 l multicolored	32	32
a.		Pair, #194-195	65	65

Trakhoni Station, 1904 — A83

1986, Dec. 31
196	A83	50 l shown	15	15
197	A83	100 l Locomotive #1, 1904	30	30

Rail transport, 1904-1951.

Nos. 86, 88-89, 105 Overprinted or Surcharged

POSTA

15

Kuzey Kıbrıs Türk Cumhuriyeti
a
POSTA

Kuzey Kıbrıs Türk Cumhuriyeti
b

1987, May 18 Unwmk. Perf. 13
198 A25(a) 10 l on #89 15 15
199 A25(a) 15 l on 3½ l, #86 15 15
200 A25(a) 20 l on #88 15 15
201 A32(b) 30 l on #105 15 15
Set value 20 20

Paintings — A84
Folk Dancers — A86

Europa A85

Designs: 50 l, Shepherd by Feridun Isiman. 125 l, Pear Woman by Mehmet Uluhan.

1987, May 27 Perf. 12½x13 Wmk. 390
202 A84 50 l multicolored 15 15
203 A84 125 l multicolored 38 38

1987, June 30 Perf. 12½
Modern architecture: 50 l, Bauhaus-style house, designed by A. Vural Behaeddin, 1973. 200 l, House, designed by Necdet Turgay, 1979.
204 A85 50 l multicolored 16 16
205 A85 200 l multicolored 65 65
a. Bklt. pane, 2 each #204-205 6.00

1987, Aug. 20
206 A86 20 l multicolored 15 15
207 A86 50 l multi, diff. 15 15
208 A86 200 l multi, diff. 50 50
209 A86 1000 l multi, diff. 2.50 2.50

Infantry Regiment, 1st Anniv. — A87
5th Islamic Summit Conf., Kuwait — A88

Pharmaceutical Federation — A89

1987, Sept. 30
210 A87 50 l multicolored 15 15
211 A88 200 l multicolored 50 50
212 A89 200 l multicolored 50 50

Ahmet Belig Pasha (1851-1924), Egyptian Judge — A90
Mehmet Emin Pasha (1813-1871), Turkish Grand Vizier — A91

Famous men: 125 l, Mehmet Kamil Pasha (1832-1913), grand vizier.

1987, Oct. 22
213 A90 50 l brn & yel 15 15
214 A91 50 l multicolored 15 15
215 A91 125 l multicolored 32 32

Pres. Rauf Denktash, Turkish Prime Minister Turgut Ozal — A92

1987, Nov. 2
216 A92 50 l multi 16 16

New Kyrenia Harbor A93

1987, Nov. 20 Perf. 12½ Litho. Wmk. 390
217 A93 150 l shown 40 40
218 A93 200 l Eastern Mediterranean University 52 52

Chair Weaver, by Osman Guvenir — A94

Paintings: 20 l, Woman Making Pastry, by Ayhan Mentes, vert. 150 l, Woman Weaving a Rug, by Zekai Yesiladali, vert.

1988, May 2 Wmk. 390 Litho. Perf. 13
219 A94 20 l multi 15 15
220 A94 50 l multi 15 15
221 A94 150 l multi 35 35

Europa A95

1988, May 31 Perf. 12½
222 A95 200 l Tugboat Piyale Pasha 38 38
223 A95 500 l Satellite dish, broadcast tower, vert. 95 95

Bayrak Radio and Television Corporation, 25th anniv. (500 l).

Tourism A96

Photographs: 150 l, Nicosia, by Aysel Erduran. 200 l, Famagusta, by Sonia Halliday and Laura Lushington. 300 l, Kyrenia, by Halliday and Lushington.

1988, June 17
224 A96 150 l multi 25 25
225 A96 200 l multi 35 35
226 A96 300 l multi 50 50

Turkish Prime Ministers — A97

Portraits: No. 227, Bulent Ecevit, 1970's. No. 228, Bulent Ulusu, Sept. 21, 1980-Dec. 13, 1983. No. 229, Turgut Ozal, from Dec. 13, 1983.

1988, July 20
227 A97 50 l shown 15 15
228 A97 50 l multi 15 15
229 A97 50 l multi 15 15
Set value 35 35

Civil Defense A98

1988, Aug. 8 Perf. 12x12½
230 A98 150 l multicolored 35 35

Summer Olympics, Seoul — A99

1988, Sept. 17 Perf. 12½
231 A99 200 l shown 32 32
232 A99 250 l Women's running 40 40
233 A99 400 l Seoul 65 65

Sedat Simavi (1896-1953), Turkish Journalist — A100

Intl. Conferences, Kyrenia A101

North Cyprus Intl. Industrial Fair — A102
Intl. Red. Cross and Red Crescent Organizations, 125th Anniv. — A103

US-USSR Summit Meeting on Nuclear Arms Reduction A104

WHO, 40th Anniv. — A105

1988, Oct. 17 Perf. 12½x12, 12x12½
234 A100 50 l olive grn 15 15
235 A101 100 l multi 15 15
236 A102 300 l multi 42 42
237 A103 400 l multi 65 65
238 A104 400 l Gorbachev and Reagan 65 65
239 A105 600 l multi 85 85
Nos. 234-239 (6) 2.87 2.87

Miniature Sheet

Portraits and Photographs of Kemal Ataturk — A106

Designs: b, Holding canteen. c, In uniform. d, Facing left.

1988, Nov. 10 Perf. 12½
240 Sheet of 4 1.25 1.25
a.-d. A106 250 l any single 30 30

Souvenir Sheet

Turkish Republic of Northern Cyprus, 5th Anniv. — A107

1988, Nov. 15 Imperf.
241 A107 500 l multicolored 65 65

Dervis Pasha Mansion, 19th Cent., Nicosia — A108

Designs: 400 l, Gamblers' Inn, 17th cent., Asmaalti Meydani. 600 l, Camii Cedit Mosque, 1902, Paphos, vert.

1989, Apr. 28   *Perf. 13*
242	A108	150 l shown	30	30
243	A108	400 l multi	80	80
244	A108	600 l multi	1.25	1.25

Europa — A109

1989, May 31   *Perf. 12¹/₂x12*
245	A109	600 l Girl, doll	1.25	1.25
246	A109	1000 l Flying kite	2.00	2.00
a.		Bklt. pane, 2 each #245-246, perf. 12¹/₂	6.50	

Geneva Peace Summit, Aug. 24, 1988 A110

1989, June 30   *Perf. 12¹/₂*
247	A110	500 l blk & dark red	1.00	1.00

Wildlife A111

1989, July 31
248	A111	100 l Alectoris chukar	20	20
249	A111	200 l Lepus cyprius	40	40
250	A111	700 l Francolinus francolinus	1.40	1.40
251	A111	2000 l Vulpes vulpes	4.00	4.00

Natl. Development Projects A112

1989, Sept. 29   *Perf. 12¹/₂x12, 12x12¹/₂*
252	A112	100 l Road construction	20	20
253	A112	150 l Sanitary water supply	30	30
254	A112	200 l Afforestation	40	40
255	A112	450 l Telecommunications	90	90
256	A112	650 l Power station	1.25	1.25
257	A112	700 l Irrigation ponds	1.40	1.40
		Nos. 252-257 (6)	4.45	4.45

Nos. 253-256 vert.

Free Port, Famagusta, 15th Anniv. A113

Turkish Cypriot Post, 25th Anniv. — A114

Saded Newspaper, Cent. — A115

Intl. Marine Organization, 30th Anniv. A116

Erenkoy Uprising, 25th Anniv. A117

Perf. 12x12¹/₂, 12¹/₂x13 (450 l)
1989, Nov. 17
258	A113	100 l multicolored	20	20
259	A114	450 l multicolored	90	90
260	A115	500 l multicolored	1.00	1.00
261	A116	600 l multicolored	1.25	1.25
262	A117	1000 l multicolored	2.00	2.00
		Nos. 258-262 (5)	5.35	5.35

Erdal Inonu A118

Agriculture A119

1989, Dec. 15   *Perf. 12¹/₂x12*
263	A118	700 l multicolored	1.40	1.40

Visit of Inonu, Turkish politician, to northern Cyprus.

Perf. 12x12¹/₂, 12¹/₂x12
1989, Dec. 25
264	A119	150 l Mule plow	30	30
265	A119	450 l Ox plow	90	90
266	A119	550 l Millstone, olive press	1.10	1.10
		Nos. 264-265 horiz.		

World Health Day — A120

Perf. 12x12¹/₂
1990, Apr. 19   Litho.   Wmk. 390
267	A120	200 l shown	42	15
268	A120	700 l Cigarette, heart	1.50	38

Europa A121

Post offices.

Perf. 12x12¹/₂
1990, May 31   Litho.   Wmk. 390
269	A121	1000 l Yenierenkoy	2.10	2.10
270	A121	1500 l Ataturk Meydani	3.15	3.15
a.		Souv. sheet, 2 #269, 2 #270	10.50	10.50

World Cup Soccer Championships, Italy — A122

1990, June 8
271	A122	300 l Turkish Cypriot team	65	65
272	A122	1000 l Ball, emblem, globe	2.10	2.10

A123   A126

A125

World Environment Day: Birds.

1990, June 5   *Perf. 12*
273	A123	150 l Turdus philomelos	30	30
274	A123	300 l Sylvia atricapilla	65	65
275	A123	900 l Phoenicurus ochruros	1.90	1.90
276	A123	1000 l Phyllosopus collybita	2.10	2.10

For surcharge see No. 386.

Perf. 13x12¹/₂, 12¹/₂x13
1990, July 31

Designs: 300 l, Painting by Filiz Ankac. 1000 l, Sculpture by Sinasi Tekman, vert.

279	A125	300 l multicolored	65	65
280	A125	1000 l multicolored	2.10	2.10

Perf. 12¹/₂
1990, Aug. 24   Litho.   Wmk. 390
281	A126	150 l Amphitheater, Soli	32	32
282	A126	1000 l Mosaic, Soli	2.10	2.10

European Tourism Year.

Visit by Turkish President Kenan Evren A127

1990, Sept. 19
283	A127	500 l multicolored	1.05	1.05

Traffic Safety A128

1990, Sept. 21
284	A128	150 l Wear seat belts	32	32
285	A128	300 l Obey the speed limit	65	65
286	A128	1000 l Obey traffic signals	2.10	2.10

A129   Flowers — A130

1990, Oct. 1
287	A129	1000 l multicolored	2.10	2.10

Visit by Turkish Prime Minister Yildirim Akbulut.

Perf. 12¹/₂x12
1990, Oct. 31   Litho.   Wmk. 390
288	A130	150 l Rosularia cypria	32	15
289	A130	200 l Silene fraudratrix	42	15
290	A130	300 l Scutellaria sibthorpii	65	15
291	A130	600 l Sedum lampusae	1.30	30
292	A130	1000 l Onosma caespitosum	2.10	52
293	A130	1500 l Arabis cypria	3.15	80
		Nos. 288-293 (6)	7.94	2.07

For surcharge see No. 387.

Intl. Literacy Year — A131

1990, Nov. 24   *Perf. 12x12¹/₂*
294	A131	300 l Ataturk as teacher	65	15
295	A131	750 l A, b, c, books, map	1.60	40

Orchids — A132   A133

Wmk. 390
1991, July 8   Litho.   *Perf. 14*
296	A132	250 l Ophrys lapethica	55	55
297	A132	500 l Ophrys kotschyi	1.60	1.60

See Nos. 303-306.

Perf. 12¹/₂x12
1991, July 29   Litho.   Wmk. 390

Europa: a, Hermes space shuttle. b, Ulysses probe.

Miniature Sheet
298	A133	2000 l Sheet of 2, #a.-b.	8.40	8.40

Public Fountains A134

Wmk. 390
1991, Sept. 9   Litho.   *Perf. 12*
299	A134	250 l Kuchuk Medrese	18	18
300	A134	500 l Djafer Pasha	35	35
301	A134	1500 l Sarayonu Square	1.10	1.10
302	A134	5000 l Arabahmet Mosque	3.50	3.50

Orchid Type of 1991

1991, Oct. 10			*Perf. 14*	
303	A132	100 l	Serapias levantina	15 15
304	A132	500 l	Dactylorhiza romana	35 35
305	A132	2000 l	Orchis simia	1.40 1.40
306	A132	3000 l	Orchis sancta	2.10 2.10

Hindiler by Salih M. Cizel — A135

Painting: 500 l, Dusme by Asik Mene.

Wmk. 390

1991, Nov. 5		**Litho.**	*Perf. 13*	
307	A135	250 l	multicolored	15 15
308	A135	500 l	multicolored	25 25

See type A143. For surcharge see No. 381.

World Food Day — A136

Basbakan Mustafa Cagatay (1937-1989) — A137

Eastern Mediterranean University — A138

Wolfgang Amadeus Mozart, Death Bicent. A139

1991, Nov. 20			*Perf. 12*	
309	A136	250 l	multicolored	15 15
310	A137	500 l	multicolored	28 28
311	A138	500 l	multicolored	28 28
312	A139	1500 l	multicolored	85 85

For surcharge see No. 380.

World AIDS Day — A140

1991, Dec. 13			*Perf. 12*	
313	A140	1000 l	multicolored	55 55

Lighthouses A141

1991, Dec. 16			*Perf. 12x12½*	
314	A141	250 l	Canbulat Burcu, Famagusta	15 15
315	A141	500 l	Yat Limani, Kyrenia	28 28
316	A141	1500 l	Turizm Limani, Kyrenia	85 85

Tourism A142

Designs: 250 l, Elephant and hippopotamus fossils, Kyrenia. 500 l, Roman fish ponds, Lambusa (58 BC-398 AD). 1500 l, Roman tomb and church, Lambusa (58 BC-1192 AD).

1991, Dec. 27				
317	A142	250 l	multicolored	15 15
318	A142	500 l	multicolored	28 28
319	A142	1500 l	multicolored	85 85

Paintings — A143

Designs: 500 l, Ebru, by Arife Kandulu. 3500 l, Nicosia, by Ismet Tartar.

Wmk. 390

1992, Mar. 31		**Litho.**	*Perf. 14*	
320	A143	500 l	multicolored	25 25
321	A143	3500 l	multicolored	1.75 1.75

See type A135.

Tourism A144

Designs: No. 322, Ancient building, Famagusta. No. 323, Trap shooting range, Nicosia. 1000 l, Salamis Bay resort, Famagusta. 1500 l, Casino, Kyrenia, vert.

Perf. 13½x14, 14x13½				
1992, Apr. 21				
322	A144	500 l	multicolored	25 25
323	A144	500 l	multicolored	25 25
324	A144	1000 l	multicolored	50 50
325	A144	1500 l	multicolored	75 75

Souvenir Sheet

Discovery of America, 500th Anniv. A145

Designs: a, 1500 l, Santa Maria, Nina and Pinta. b, 3500 l, Columbus.

1992, May 29			*Perf. 13½x14*	
326	A145	Sheet of 2, #a.-b.		2.50 2.50

Europa.

Sea Turtles A146

Perf. 13½x14				
1992, June 30		**Litho.**	**Wmk. 390**	
327	A146	1000 l	Green turtle	50 50
328	A146	1500 l	Loggerhead turtle	75 75
a.		Souv. sheet, 2 #327, 2 #328		2.50 2.50

World Wildlife Fund.

1992 Summer Olympics, Barcelona A147

Designs: No. 329a, Women's gymnastics, vert. b, Tennis, vert. 1000 l, High jump. 1500 l, Cycling.

1992, July 25			*Perf. 14x13½*	
329	A147	500 l	Pair, #a.-b.	50 50
Perf. 13½x14				
330	A147	1000 l	multicolored	50 50
331	A147	1500 l	multicolored	75 75

Electric Power Plant, Kyrenia A148

Social Insurance, 15th Anniv. A149

Intl. Federation of Women Artists A150

Veterinary Services A151

Perf. 13½x14				
1992, Sept. 30		**Litho.**	**Wmk. 390**	
332	A148	500 l	multicolored	25 25
333	A149	500 l	multicolored	25 25
334	A150	1500 l	multicolored	75 75
335	A151	1500 l	multicolored	75 75

Civil Aviation Office, 17th Anniv. A152

Meteorology Office, 18th Anniv. A153

Mapping, 14th Anniv. A154

Perf. 13½x14				
1992, Nov. 20		**Litho.**	**Wmk. 390**	
336	A152	1000 l	multicolored	50 50
337	A153	1000 l	multicolored	50 50
338	A154	1200 l	multicolored	60 60

Native Cuisine A155

Food: 2000 l, Zulbiye (pastry). 2500 l, Cicek Dolmasi (stuffed squash flowers). 3000 l, Tatar Boregi (flaky pastry dish). 4000 l, Seftali kebab (meat dish).

1992, Dec. 14				
339	A155	2000 l	multicolored	1.00 1.00
340	A155	2500 l	multicolored	1.25 1.25
341	A155	3000 l	multicolored	1.50 1.50
342	A155	4000 l	multicolored	2.00 2.00

Intl. Conference on Nutrition, Rome.

Tourism A156

Designs: 500 l, Church and Monastery of St. Barnabas. 10,000 l, Bowl.

Perf. 13½x14				
1993, Apr. 1		**Litho.**	**Wmk. 390**	
343	A156	500 l	multi	25 25
344	A156	10,000 l	multi	5.00 5.00

Souvenir Sheet

Europa — A157

Contemporary paintings by: a, 2000 l, Turksal Ince. b, 3000 l, Ilkay Onsoy.

Perf. 14x13½				
1993, May 5			**Wmk. 390**	
345	A157	Sheet of 2, #a.-b.		2.50 2.50

Trees — A158

1993, June 11			*Perf. 14x13½*	
346	A158	500 l	Olea europea	25 15
347	A158	1000 l	Eucalyptus camaldulensis	50 50
348	A158	3000 l	Platanus orientalis	1.50 1.50
349	A158	4000 l	Pinus brutia tenore	2.00 2.00

Arabahmet Rehabilitation Project A159

Perf. 13½x14				
1993, Sept. 20		**Litho.**	**Wmk. 390**	
350	A159	1000 l	shown	16 16
351	A159	3000 l	Homes, diff.	48 48

Creation of
Turkish
Republic of
Northern
Cyprus, 10th
Anniv.
A160

Designs: No. 353, Flags changing to dove, vert.
1000 l, Dove flying from flag. 5000 l, Flowers forming "10," map.

Perf. 13¹/₂x14, 14x13¹/₂

		1993, Nov. 15	Litho.	Wmk. 390	
352	A160	500 l multicolored		15	15
353	A160	500 l multicolored		15	15
354	A160	1000 l multicolored		16	16
355	A160	5000 l multicolored		80	80

Ataturk, 55th Death
Anniv. — A161

State
Theaters,
30th Anniv.
A162

Turkish Resistance Organization, 35th
Anniv. — A163

Turkish
News
Agency,
20th Anniv.
A164

Tchaikovsky, Death Cent. — A165

Perf. 14x13¹/₂, 13¹/₂x14

		1993, Dec. 27	Litho.	Wmk. 390	
356	A161	500 l multicolored		15	15
357	A162	500 l multicolored		15	15
358	A163	1500 l multicolored		32	32

TURKISH REPUBLIC OF NORTHERN CYPRUS

Sell or collect our stamps and FDC's. Standing order accounts.

**Please write to us at
our address below:**
Philatelic Branch
Directorate of Posts,
Turkish Republic of
Northern Cyprus
Lefkosa, Mersin 10, TURKEY
Fax: 90-392-2288618 &
      90-392-2281503

Or to our agents in Europe
a) James Davis and Son Ltd.
   Rickmansworth WD3 1DG
   England
   Fax: 44-923-720226

b) F.a. Phileurope,
   D-55026 Mainz,
   Postfach 3645, Germany
   Fax: 49-6131-237342

359	A164	2000 l multicolored		42	42
360	A165	5000 l multicolored		1.10	1.10
		Nos. 356-360 (5)		2.14	2.14

Soyle Falci, by
Goral
Ozkan — A166

Design: 6500 l, Sculpture, IV Hareket, by Senol
Ozdevrim.

				Wmk. 390	
		1994, Mar. 31	Litho.	Perf. 14	
361	A166	1000 l multicolored		22	22
362	A166	6500 l multicolored		1.40	1.40

Fazil Kucuk (1906-84), Physician and
Political Leader — A167

1994, Apr. 1
363 A167 1500 l multicolored   32   32

Souvenir Sheet

Archaeological Discoveries — A168

Europa: a, Neolithic village, Ayios Epectitos Vrysi.
b, Neolithic man, early tools found in excavation.

Perf. 13¹/₂

		1994, May 16	Litho.	Wmk. 390	
364	A168	8500 l Sheet of 2, #a.-b.		1.40	1.40

1994 World Cup Soccer Championships,
US — A169

1994, June 30
365	A169	2500 l Trophy, vert.	20	20
366	A169	10,000 l US map	80	80

Turkish
Postal Service
in Northern
Cyprus, 30th
Anniv.
A170

1994, June 30
367 A170 50,000 l multicolored   4.00 4.00

A171

A172

Turkish Peace
Operation,
20th Anniv.
A173

				Wmk. 390	
		1994, July 20	Litho.	Perf. 14	
368	A171	2500 l shown		18	18
369	A172	5000 l Monument		38	38
370	A172	7000 l Monument, diff.		52	52
371	A173	8500 l shown		65	65

First Rural
Postal
Cancellations,
Cent.
A174

Postmarks, stamps: 1500 l, Karpas, Cyprus #131.
2500 l, Gazi Magusa (Famagusta), #71. 5000 l, Bey
Keuy, Cyprus #150. 7000 l, Aloa, Cyprus, #179.
8500 l, Pyla, Cyprus #152.

Perf. 13¹/₂

		1994, Aug. 15	Litho.	Wmk. 390	
372	A174	1500 l multicolored		15	15
373	A174	2500 l multicolored		20	20
374	A174	5000 l multicolored		40	40
375	A174	7000 l multicolored		55	55
376	A174	8500 l multicolored		70	70
		Nos. 372-376 (5)		2.00	2.00

Sea Shells — A175

			Wmk. 390		
		1994, Nov. 15	Litho.	Perf. 14	
377	A175	2500 l Charonia tritonis		15	15
378	A175	12,500 l Tonna galea		70	35
379	A175	12,500 l Cypraea talpa		70	35
		Nos. 377-379 (3)		1.55	85

Nos. 307, 309
Surcharged   2500 TL ****

1994, Dec. 12   Perfs., etc. as Before
380	A136	1500 l on 250 l multi	15	15
381	A135	2500 l on 250 l multi	15	15
		Set value	22	22

Size and location of surcharge varies.

European Nature Conservation
Year — A176

Designs: 2000 l, Donkeys on mountain top.
3500 l, Shoreline. 15,000 l, Donkeys in field.

				Wmk. 390	
		1995, Feb. 10	Litho.	Perf. 14	
382	A176	2000 l multicolored		15	15
383	A176	3500 l multicolored		22	22
384	A176	15,000 l multicolored		1.00	1.00
		Nos. 382-384 (3)		1.37	1.37

Souvenir Sheet

Peace and Freedom — A177

Europa: a, Globe, dove. b, Doves over Europe.
Illustration reduced.

Perf. 13¹/₂x14

		1995, Apr. 20	Litho.	Wmk. 390	
385	A177	15,000 l Sheet of 2, #a.-b.		1.50	1.50

Nos. 275 & 290 Surcharged   ***
                                    2000 TL

1995, Apr. 21   Perfs., etc. as Before
386	A123	2000 l on 900 l #275	15	15
387	A130	3500 l on 300 l #290	22	22

Size and location of surcharge varies.

TURKMENISTAN

LOCATION — Southern Asia, bounded by Kazakhstan, Uzbekistan, Iran and Afghanistan
GOVT. — Independent republic, member of the Commonwealth of Independent States
AREA — 188,417 sq. mi.
POP. — 3,500,000 (1989)
CAPITAL — Ashkhabad

With the breakup of the Soviet Union on Dec. 26, 1991, Turkmenistan and ten former Soviet republics established the Commonwealth of Independent States.

100 Kopecks = 1 Ruble
Manat (1994)

Catalogue values for all unused stamps in this country are for Never Hinged items.

Dagdan Necklace, 19th Century — A1

Designs: No. 3, Girl in traditional costume, horiz. No. 4, Akhaltekin horse and rider in native riding dress. No. 5, Mollanepes Theater, horiz. 15r, National arms. No. 7, Pres. Saparmurad Niyazov at left, national flag, horiz. No. 8, Niyazov at right, flag, horiz. No. 9, Map of Turkmenistan.

		1992	Litho.	Perf. 12x12½	
1	A1	50k multicolored			80
			Perf. 12½		
2	A1	10r multicolored			85
3	A1	10r multicolored			85
4	A1	10r multicolored			85
5	A1	10r multicolored			15
6	A1	15r multicolored			1.30
7	A1	25r multicolored			2.15
8	A1	25r multicolored			2.15
		Nos. 1-8 (8)			9.10

Size: 112x79mm
Imperf
9	A1	10r multicolored	3.50

Issued: 50k, 1992; #8, Dec. 8; others, Aug. 27.

Nos. 4, 6 Ovptd. with Horse's Head
1992, Dec. 12
Color of Overprint

10	A1	10r black	85
11	A1	10r brown	85
12	A1	10r red	85
13	A1	10r vermilion	85
14	A1	10r carmine	85
15	A1	10r green	85
16	A1	15r black	1.30
17	A1	15r brown	1.30
18	A1	15r red	1.30
19	A1	15r pink	1.30
20	A1	15r blue	1.30
21	A1	15r yellow	1.30
		Nos. 10-21 (12)	12.90

1992 Summer Olympics, Barcelona A2

Designs: a, 1r, Weight lifting. b, 3r, Equestrian. c, 5r, Wrestling. d, 10r, Rowing. e, 15r, Emblem of Turkmenistan Olympic Committee.
No. 23, Flags, symbols for equestrian, weight lifting, rowing, gymnastics.

1992, Dec. 15 Photo. Perf. 10½x10
22	A2	Strip of 5, #a.-e.	6.20

Imperf
Size: 108x82mm
23	A2	15r multicolored	4.90

For surcharge see No. 33.

Musical Instruments — A3

Photo. & Engr.
1992, Sept. 13 Perf. 12x11½
28	A3	35k buff, red brn, gold & black	18

Horse — A4

1992, Aug. 9 Photo. Perf. 12
29	A4	20k shown	15
30	A4	40k Snake, vert.	30

A5

1992, Nov. 29 Litho. Perf. 12x11½
31	A5	1r multicolored	20

US Pres. Bill Clinton, Pres. Saparmurad Niyazov A6

Designs dated: a. 21.30.93. b. 22.03.93. c, 23.03.93. d, 24.03.93. e, 25.03.93.

1993, Mar. 21 Litho. Perf. 10½
32	A6	100r Strip of 5, #a.-e.	5.25

Pres. Niyazov's visit to New York City & Washington DC.

No. 22 Surcharged

25,0 ≡

1993, Apr. 1 Photo. Perf. 10½x10
33	A2	Strip of 5	10.50
a.		25r on 1r	2.25
b.		10r on 3r	85
c.		15r on 5r	1.30
d.		15r on 10r	1.30
e.		50r on 15r	4.50

Size of surcharge varies.

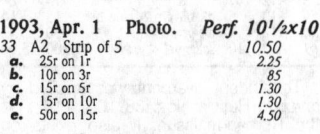

Phoca Caspica A7

Designs: a, 25r, Facing right. b, 500r, Facing left.

1993 Litho. Perf. 13½
34	A7	Pair #a.-b.	1.10

World Wildlife Fund — A8

Phoca caspica: 15r, Lying in snow. 50r, On rocks. 100r, Mother and young. 150r, Swimming.
1993
35	A8	15r multicolored	15
36	A8	50r multicolored	15
37	A8	100r multicolored	20
38	A8	150r multicolored	30

Formation of Tovarishch Society for Exploitation of Turkmen Oil Fields, 115th Anniv. — A9

Designs: 1m, Two men viewing oil field. 1.5m, Early tanker Turkmen. 2m, Oil well. 3m, Alfred Nobel, Ludwig Nobel, Robert Nobel, Petr Bilderling, vert. 5m, Early oil field.

1994 Litho. Perf. 13
39	A9	1m multicolored	65
40	A9	1.5m multicolored	95
41	A9	2m multicolored	1.25
42	A9	5m multicolored	1.90
a.		Miniature sheet of 8 + label	15.00

Souvenir Sheet
43	A9	5m multicolored	2.00

See Azerbaijan Nos. 416-419.

Repetek Natl. Park — A10

Designs: 3m, Repetek Institute. No. 45, Desert, camels. No. 46, Echus carinatus. No. 47, Varanus griseus. 20m, Testudo horsfieldi.
No. 49, Haloxylon ammodendron.

1994, Dec. 11 Litho. Perf. 13
44	A10	3m multicolored	1.90
45	A10	5m multicolored	2.00
46	A10	5m multicolored	2.00
a.		Miniature sheet of 8 + label	16.00
47	A10	15m multicolored	4.00
48	A10	20m multicolored	8.00
		Nos. 44-48 (5)	17.90

Souvenir Sheet
49	A10	10m multicolored	4.00

Intl. Olympic Committee, Cent. A11

1994, Dec. 30 Litho. Perf. 14
50	A11	11.25m multicolored	2.25

Souvenir Sheet
51	A11	20m multicolored	4.25

UBANGI-SHARI
(UBANGI-SHARI-CHAD)

LOCATION — In Western Africa, north of the equator
GOVT. — A former French Colony
AREA — 238,767 sq. mi.
POP. — 833,916
CAPITAL — Bangui

In 1910 French Congo was divided into the three colonies of Gabon, Middle Congo and Ubangi-Shari and officially named "French Equatorial Africa." Under that name in 1934 the group, with the territory of Chad included, became a single administrative unit. See Gabon.

100 Centimes = 1 Franc

Stamps of Middle Congo Overprinted in Black

OUBANGUI-CHARI-TCHAD

1915-22 Unwmk. Perf. 14x13½
Chalky Paper
1	A1	1c ol gray & brn	15	15
a.		Double overprint	90.00	
b.		Imperf.	22.50	
2	A1	2c vio & brn	15	15
3	A1	4c bl & brn	15	15
4	A1	5c dk grn & bl	15	15
5	A1	5c yel & bl ('22)	22	22
6	A1	10c car & bl	28	28
7	A1	10c dp grn & bl grn ('22)	18	18
8	A1	15c brn vio & rose	40	40
9	A1	20c brn & bl	80	80

No. 8 is on ordinary paper.

Overprinted | OUBANGUI-CHARI-TCHAD

10	A2	25c bl & grn	35	35
11	A2	25c bl grn & gray ('22)	22	22
12	A2	30c scarlet & grn	28	28
13	A2	30c dp rose & rose ('22)	22	22
14	A2	35c vio brn & bl	1.75	1.75
15	A2	40c dl grn & brn	1.75	1.75
16	A2	45c vio & red	1.75	1.75
17	A2	50c bl grn & red	2.75	2.75
18	A2	50c bl & grn ('22)	22	22
19	A2	75c brn & bl	4.50	4.50
20	A3	1fr dp grn & vio	4.50	4.50
21	A3	2fr vio & gray grn	4.50	4.50
22	A3	5fr blue & rose	14.00	14.00
		Nos. 1-22 (22)	39.27	39.27

For surcharges see Nos. B1-B2.

Types of Middle Congo, 1907-22, Overprinted in Black or Red

OUBANGUI-CHARI

1922
23	A1	1c vio & grn	15	15
a.		Overprint omitted	70.00	
b.		Imperf.	14.00	
24	A1	2c grn & salmon	18	18
25	A1	4c ol brn & brn	25	25
a.		Overprint omitted	70.00	
26	A1	5c indigo & rose	35	35
27	A1	10c dp grn & gray grn	48	48
28	A1	15c lt red & dl bl	55	55
29	A1	20c choc & salmon	2.00	2.00

Overprinted | OUBANGUI CHARI

30	A2	25c vio & salmon	1.75	1.75
31	A2	30c rose & pale rose	1.00	1.00
32	A2	35c vio & grn	2.00	2.00
33	A2	40c ind & vio (R)	1.75	1.75
34	A2	45c choc & vio	1.75	1.75
35	A2	50c dk bl & pale bl	1.00	1.00
36	A2	60c on 75c vio, pnksh	1.00	1.00
37	A2	75c choc & sal	2.00	2.00
38	A3	1fr grn & dl bl (R)	2.00	2.00
a.		Overprint omitted		
39	A3	2fr grn & salmon	3.00	3.00
40	A3	5fr grn & ol brn	5.75	5.75
		Nos. 23-40 (18)	26.96	26.96

Stamps of 1922 Issue with Additional Overprint in Black, Blue or Red

AFRIQUE EQUATORIALE FRANÇAISE

1924-33
41	A1	1c vio & grn (Bl)	15	15
a.		"OUBANGUI CHARI" omitted	55.00	
42	A1	2c grn & sal (Bl)	15	15
a.		"OUBANGUI CHARI" omitted	57.50	
b.		Double overprint	62.50	

43	A1	4c ol brn & brn (Bl)	15	15
a.		Double overprint (Bl + Bk)	90.00	
b.		"OUBANGUI CHARI" omitted	90.00	
44	A1	5c ind & rose	15	15
a.		"OUBANGUI CHARI" omitted	62.50	
45	A1	10c dp grn & gray grn	15	15
46	A1	10c red org & bl ('25)	16	16
47	A1	15c sal & dl bl	25	25
48	A1	15c sal & dl bl (Bl) ('26)	25	25
49	A1	20c choc & sal (Bl)	24	24

On Nos. 41-49 the color in ( ) refers to the overprint "Afrique Equatoriale Francaise."

AFRIQUE EQUATORIALE FRANÇAISE

50	A2	25c vio & salmon (Bl)	16	16
a.		Imperf.		
51	A2	30c rose & pale rose (Bl)	15	15
52	A2	30c choc & red ('25)	16	16
a.		"OUBANGUI CHARI" omitted	65.00	
53	A2	30c dk grn & grn ('27)	35	35
54	A2	35c vio & grn (Bl)	15	15
a.		"OUBANGUI CHARI" omitted		
55	A2	40c ind & vio (Bl)	20	20
56	A2	45c choc & vio (Bl)	24	24
57	A2	50c dk bl & pale bl (R)	15	15
58	A2	50c gray & bl vio ('25) (R)	42	42
59	A2	60c on 75c dk vio, pnksh (R)	15	15
60	A2	65c org brn & bl ('28)	45	45
61	A2	75c choc & sal (Bl)	24	24
62	A2	75c dp bl & lt bl ('25) (R)	16	16
a.		"OUBANGUI CHARI" omitted	65.00	
63	A2	75c rose & dk brn ('28)	45	45
64	A2	90c brn red & pink ('30)	1.90	1.90
65	A3	1fr grn & ind (Bl + Bl)	20	20
66	A3	1fr grn & ind (R + Bl)	16	16
67	A3	1.10fr bister & bl ('28)	65	65
68	A3	1.25fr mag & lt grn ('33)	1.90	1.90
69	A3	1.50fr ultra & bl ('30)	2.00	2.00
70	A3	1.75fr dk brn & dp buff ('33)	2.75	2.75
71	A3	2fr grn & red	30	30
a.		"OUBANGUI CHARI" omitted	550.00	375.00
72	A3	3fr red vio ('30)	1.90	1.90
73	A3	5fr grn & ol brn (Bl)	1.25	1.25
		Nos. 41-73 (33)	18.09	18.09

On Nos. 65, 66 the first overprint color refers to OUBANGUI CHARI
For surcharges see Nos. 74-81.

Types of 1924 Issue Surcharged with New Values in Black or Red

1925-26

74	A3	65c on 1fr vio & ol	60	55
a.		"65" omitted	50.00	
75	A3	85c on 1fr vio & ol	60	55
a.		"AFRIQUE EQUATORIALE FRANÇAISE" omitted	57.50	
b.		Double surcharge	65.00	
76	A3	1.25fr on 1fr dk bl & ultra (R) ('26)	40	35
a.		"1f25" omitted	65.00	65.00

Bars cover old denomination on No. 76.

Types of 1924 Issue Surcharged with New Values and Bars

1927

77	A2	90c on 75c brn red & rose red	55	45
78	A3	1.50fr on 1fr ultra & bl	42	45
79	A3	3fr on 5fr org brn & dl red	90	70
80	A3	10fr on 5fr ver & vio	7.00	6.50
81	A3	20fr on 5fr vio & gray	10.00	9.00
		Nos. 77-81 (5)	18.87	17.10

Colonial Exposition Issue
Common Design Types

1931 Engr. Perf. 12½
Name of Country Typo. in Black

82	CD70	40c deep green	1.50	1.50
83	CD71	50c violet	1.50	1.50
84	CD72	90c red orange	1.50	1.50
a.		Imperf.	37.50	
85	CD73	1 50fr dull blue	1.50	1.50

SEMI-POSTAL STAMPS

Regular Issue of 1915 **5c.**
Surcharged

1916 Unwmk. Perf. 14x13½
Chalky Paper

B1	A1	10c + 5c car & blue	90	90
a.		Inverted surch.	40.00	40.00
b.		Double surcharge	40.00	40.00
c.		"OUBANGUI CHARI" omitted	55.00	55.00
d.		Double surcharge, one inverted	40.00	40.00
e.		Vertical surcharge	40.00	40.00
		No period under "C"	5.75	5.75

Regular Issue of 1915 **5c**
Surcharged in Carmine

B2	A1	10c + 5c car & blue	28	28

POSTAGE DUE STAMPS

OUBANGUI-CHARI

A. E. F.

Postage Due Stamps of France Overprinted

1928 Unwmk. Perf. 14x13½

J1	D2	5c light blue	48	48
J2	D2	10c gray brown	48	48
J3	D2	20c olive green	48	48
J4	D2	25c bright rose	48	48
J5	D2	30c light red	48	48
J6	D2	45c blue green	48	48
J7	D2	50c brown violet	65	65
J8	D2	60c yellow brown	90	90
J9	D2	1fr brown	1.00	1.00
J10	D2	2fr orange red	1.50	1.50
J11	D2	3fr bright violet	1.50	1.50
		Nos. J1-J11 (11)	8.43	8.43

Landscape — D3   Emile Gentil — D4

1930 Typo.

J12	D3	5c dp bl & olive	30	30
J13	D3	10c dk red & brn	40	40
J14	D3	20c grn & brn	50	50
J15	D3	25c lt bl & brn	50	50
J16	D3	30c bis brn & Prus bl	75	75
J17	D3	45c Prus bl & ol	1.00	1.00
J18	D3	50c red vio & brn	2.00	2.00
J19	D3	60c gray lil & bl blk	2.25	2.25
J20	D4	1fr bis brn & bl blk	90	90
J21	D4	2fr vio & brown	1.25	1.25
J22	D4	3fr dp red & brn	2.25	2.25
		Nos. J12-J22 (11)	12.10	12.10

Stamps of Ubangi-Shari were replaced in 1936 by those of French Equatorial Africa.

UKRAINE

LOCATION — In southeastern Europe, bordering on the Black Sea
GOVT. — Republic
AREA — 170,998 sq. mi.
POP. — 51,940,426 (1992)
CAPITAL — Kiev

Following the collapse of the Russian Empire, a national assembly met at Kiev and formed the Ukrainian National Republic. On July 6, 1923, Ukraine joined the Soviet Union and since that time the postage stamps of the Soviet Union have been in use.

With the breakup of the Soviet Union on Dec. 26, 1991, Ukraine and ten former Soviet republics established the Commonwealth of Independent States.

200 Shahiv = 100 Kopiyok (Kopecks) = 1 Karbovanets (Ruble)
100 Shahiv = 1 Hryvnia
100 Kopecks = 1 Ruble (1992)
100 Kopiyok = 1 Karbovanets (1992)

Catalogue values for unused stamps in this country are for Never Hinged items, beginning with Scott 100 in the regular postage section, and Scott B9 in the semi-postal section.

Republic's Trident Emblem—A1

Ukrainian Peasant — A2

Watermark

Wmk. 116- Crosses and Circles

Stamps of Russia Overprinted in Violet, Black, Blue, Red, Brown or Green

This trident-shaped device was taken from the arms of the Grand Duke Volodymyr and adopted as the device of the Ukrainian Republic. The overprint was handstamped, typographed or lithographed. It was applied in various cities in the Ukraine and there are numerous types. Values are for the most common types.

On Stamps of 1902-03

1918 Wmk. 168 Perf. 13½

1	A12	3½r black & gray	13.00	16.00
2	A12	7r black & yellow	10.00	13.00

On Stamps of 1909-18
Lozenges of Varnish on Face
Perf. 14, 14½x15
Unwmk.

3	A14	1k orange	15	15
4	A14	2k green	15	15
5	A14	3k red	15	15
6	A15	4k carmine	15	15
7	A14	5k claret	15	15
8	A14	7k light blue	15	15
9	A14	10k dark blue	15	15
10	A11	14k blue & rose	15	25
11	A11	15k red brn & bl	15	15
12	A8	20k blue & car	15	15
13	A11	25k grn & gray vio	25	30
14	A11	35k red brn & grn	15	15
15	A8	50k violet & grn	15	15
16	A11	70k brown & org	15	15

Perf. 13½

17	A9	1r lt brn, brn & org	15	30
18	A12	3½r mar & lt grn	32	85
19	A13	5r dk bl, grn & pale bl	6.50	20.00
20	A12	7r dk grn & pink	2.75	4.50
21	A13	10r scar, yel & gray	4.50	6.00
		Nos. 3-21 (19)	16.42	34.10

On Stamps of 1917
Perf. 14, 14½x15

41	A14	10k on 7k light blue	15	15
42	A11	20k on 14k bl & rose	15	15
		Set value	25	15

On Stamps of 1917-18
Imperf

43	A14	1k orange	15	15
44	A14	2k gray green	15	15
45	A14	3k red	15	15
46	A14	4k carmine	15	15
47	A14	5k claret	20	35
51	A11	15k red brn & bl	15	15
52	A8	20k bl & car	20	60
54	A11	35k red brn & grn	15	15
55	A8	50k violet & grn	16	32
56	A11	70k brown & org	15	15
57	A9	1r pale brn, brn & red org	15	15
58	A12	3½r mar & lt grn	15	60
59	A13	5r dk bl, grn & pale bl	15	16
60	A12	7r dk grn & pink	30	42
61	A13	10r scar, yel & gray	13.00	13.00

The trident overprint was applied by favor to Russia Nos. 88-104, 110-111, the Romanov issue. It also exists on Russia No. 127, the 25k of 1917.
For surcharges see Russian Offices in the Turkish Empire Nos. 320-339.

Ukrainian Girl — A3   Trident — A4

Inscription of Value — A5

1918 Thin Paper Typo. Imperf.

62	A1	10sh buff	15	25
63	A2	20sh brown	15	25
64	A3	30sh ultra	15	25
a.		30sh blue	65	1.25
65	A4	40sh green	15	25
66	A5	50sh red	15	25
		Nos. 62-66 (5)	75	1.25

The stamps of this issue exist perforated or pin-perforated unofficially.

Thin Cardboard
Inscriptions on Back

1918 Perf. 11½

67	A1	10sh buff	4.00	
68	A2	20sh brown	4.00	
69	A3	30sh ultra	4.00	
70	A4	40sh green	4.00	
a.		Imperf.	150.00	
71	A5	50sh red	4.00	
a.		Imperf.	35.00	

Nos. 67-71 were intended to be used as paper money but they were occasionally used for postage.

Nos. 62 and 66 Surcharged **35 к.**

1919 Unwmk. Imperf.

72	A1	35k on 10sh buff	5.00	6.50
73	A5	70k on 50sh red	15.00	20.00
a.		Surcharge inverted	32.50	

Some authorities state that Nos. 72-73 were issued by the Soviets in the Ukraine in April 1919. Excellent forged surcharges exist.

A6

1919 Litho.

74	A6	20hr red & green	3.50	15.00

Кур'єрсько польова Пошта. 10 Гривень
a   b

Nos. 62-66 surcharged "a" and "b" are of private origin.

Югъ Россіи.

Ukraine stamps of 1918-10, 20, 30 and 50sh-overprinted diagonally as above ("South Russia") are believed to be of private origin.

Р.О.П.и Т.

This overprint (in two sizes) was privately applied to stamps of Russian Offices in Turkey. The overprinted stamps were not issued.

A lithographed set of 14 stamps (1hr-200hr) of these types, perf. 11½, was prepared in 1920, but never placed in use. Value, set $2.

All values exist imperf., some with inverted centers.

For German stamps overprinted "Ukraine" see Russia Nos. N29-N48.

Catalogue values for unused stamps in this section, from this point to the end of the section, are for Never Hinged items.

Cossacks in Ukraine, 500th Anniv. — A20

Design: No. 101, Ukrainian emigrants to Canada.

1992, Mar. 1   Litho.   Perf. 12
100 A20 15k multicolored   75
101 A20 15k multicolored   75

Ukrainian emigration to Canada, centennial (No. 101). Dated 1991.

Mykola V. Lysenko (1842-1912), Composer A21

1992, Mar. 22   Perf. 13
102 A21 1r multicolored   1.00

Numerous trident overprints exist on recent Soviet stamps. These may be locals. Their status is being investigated.

Ukrainian Girl — A22

1992   Litho.   Perf. 12x12½
118 A22 50k bright blue   15
119 A22 70k bister   15
121 A22 1kb yellow green   15
122 A22 2kb purple   28
124 A22 5kb blue   70
126 A22 10kb red   1.40

---

128 A22 20kb green   2.75
130 A22 50kb brown   7.00
    Nos. 118-130 (8)   12.58

Issued: Nos. 124, 126, 128, 130, 5/16; 118-119, 121-122, 6/17.

Mykola I. Kostomarov (1817-1885), Writer — A23

1992, May 16   Photo.   Perf. 12x11½
133 A23 20k olive green   25

1992 Summer Olympics, Barcelona
A24   A25

1992, July 25   Litho.   Perf. 13
134 A24 3kb yel green & multi   38
135 A25 4kb multicolored   50
136 A24 5kb buff & multi   65

World Forum of Ukrainians, Kiev — A26

1992, Aug. 19   Litho.   Perf. 13
137 A26 2kb multicolored   28

Declaration of Independence from the Soviet Union — A27

1992, Aug. 19   Perf. 13½x13
138 A27 2kb multicolored   28

Souvenir Sheet

Union of Ukrainian Philatelists, 25th Anniv. — A28

1992, Aug. 21   Perf. 12
139 A28 2kb multicolored   38

Intl. Letter Writing Week — A29

1992, Oct. 4   Perf. 13x13½
140 A29 5kb multicolored   30

World Congress of Ukrainian Lawyers, Kiev — A30

1992, Oct. 18   Litho.   Perf. 13
141 A30 15kb multicolored   58

Ukrainian Diaspora in Austria — A31

Perf. 13½x14½
1992, Nov. 27   Litho.
142 A31 5kb multicolored   38

Embroidery — A32

1992, Nov. 16   Litho.   Perf. 11½x12
143 A32 50k black & orange   15

Mohyla Academy, Kiev, 360th Anniv. — A33

1992, Nov. 27   Litho.   Perf. 12x12½
144 A33 1.50kb multicolored   18

Souvenir Sheet

Ukrainian Medal Winners, 1992 Summer Olympics, Barcelona — A34

1992, Dec. 14   Litho.   Perf. 14
145 A34 10kb multicolored   1.25

Coats of Arms — A35

1993   Litho.   Perf. 14x13½
148 A35 3kb Lviv   95
150 A35 5kb Kiev   1.65

Issue date: 3kb, 5kb, Feb. 15.
Numbers have been reserved for additional values in this set.

Cardinal Joseph Slipij (1892-1984) — A36

1993, Feb. 17   Litho.   Perf. 14x13½
166 A36 15kb multicolored   1.25

1st Vienna-Cracow-Lviv-Kiev Air Mail Flight, 75th Anniv. — A37

1993, Mar. 31   Perf. 13½x14
167 A37 35kb Biplane   1.00
168 A37 50kb Jet   1.50

Easter — A39

1993, Apr. 8   Litho.   Perf. 13½
169 A39 15kb multicolored   2.00

UN Declaration of Human Rights, 45th Anniv. — A40

Design: 5kb, Country Wedding in Lower Austria, by Ferdinand Georg Waldmuller.

Perf. 14½x13½
1993, June 11   Litho.
170 A40 5kb multicolored   1.65

A41

A41a   A41b   A41c

A41d   A41e   A41f

A41g   A41h

Villagers at Work: 50kb, #177, Reaper with scythe. 100kb, #185, Ox carts. #173A, 200kb, 500kb, Reaper with sickle. #173B, Farmer with oxen. 150kb, 300kb, #184, Shepherd. #183, Bee keeper. #184A, Fisherman. #186, Potter. (Illustrations A41a-A41h help identify the Cyrillic characters, not the designs.)

Perf. 12x12¹/₂, 14 (#173B, 183, 184A, 186)

1993-94			Litho.
171	A41	50kb green	15
173	A41	100kb blue	15
173A	A41a	(100kb) brown	15
173B	A41b	(100kb) magenta	15
174	A41	150kb red	15
176	A41	200kb orange	15
177	A41c	(250kb) green	15
179	A41	300kb violet	15
182	A41	500kb brown	25
183	A41d	(1800kb) org brn	15
184	A41e	(5000kb) red	80
184A	A41f	(5300kb) blue	18
185	A41g	(10,000kb) blue	1.50
186	A41h	(17,000kb) red brn	55
		Set value	3.90

Issued: 50, 100, 150, 200, 300, 500kb, 12/18/93; #184, 185, 5/28/94; #173A, 177, 7/2/94; #173B, 184A, 10/15/94; #183, 186, 11/12/94.

Famine Deaths, 60th Anniv. — A42

1993, Sept. 12   Litho.   Perf. 12
188 A42 75kb brown   22

First Ukrainian Postage Stamp, 75th Anniv. — A43

1993, Oct. 9
189 A43 100kb blue & brown   30

Stamp Day.

Liberation of Kiev, 50th Anniv. — A44

1993, Nov. 6   Litho.   Perf. 12
190 A44 75kb multicolored   22

A45   A46

1994, Jan. 15   Litho.   Perf. 12
191 A45 200kb black & red   38

Ahapit, Kievan Rus physician, Middle Ages.

1994, Feb. 19   Perf. 12x12¹/₂
Endangered species: No. 192, Erythronium dens, canis. No. 193, Cypripedium calceolus.

192 A46 200kb multicolored   18
193 A46 200kb multicolored   18

Independence Day — A47

Illustration reduced.

1994, Sept. 3   Litho.   Imperf.
194 A47 5000kb multicolored   1.00

No. 194 has simulated perforations.

Liberation of Russian Areas, 50th Anniv. A48

Battle maps and: a, Katyusha rockets, liberation of Russia. b, Russian fighter planes, liberation of Ukraine. c, Combined offensive, liberation of Belarus.

1994, Oct. 8   Litho.   Perf. 12¹/₂x12
195 A48 500kb Block of 3 + label   45

See Russia No. 6213, Belarus No. 78.

City of Uzhgorod, 1100th Anniv. — A53

1995, Jan. 28   Litho.   Perf. 12
200 A53 5000kb multicolored   18

Ivan Franko (1856-1916), Writer A54

Ivan Pulyny (Johann Puluj) (1845-1918), Physicist — A55

Design: No. 203, Lessia Ukrainka (1871-1913), poet.

1995, Feb. 2   Perf. 13¹/₂
201 A54 3000kb multicolored   15
202 A55 3000kb multicolored   15
203 A54 3000kb multicolored   15
       Set value   35

SEMI-POSTAL STAMPS

Ukrainian Soviet Socialist Republic

"Famine" — SP1

Taras H. Shevchenko SP2

"Death" Stalking Peasant — SP3   "Ukraine" Distributing Food — SP4

Perf. 14¹/₂x13¹/₂, 13¹/₂x14¹/₂

1923, June		Litho.	Unwmk.	
B1	SP1	10k + 10k gray bl & blk	32	1.25
B2	SP2	20k + 20k vio brn & org brn	32	1.25
B3	SP3	90k + 30k db & blk, *straw*	32	1.25
B4	SP4	150k + 50k red brn & blk	32	1.25

Imperf., Pairs

B1a	SP1	10k + 10k	50.00	75.00
B2a	SP2	20k + 20k	50.00	75.00
B3a	SP3	90k + 30k	50.00	75.00
B4a	SP4	150k + 50k	50.00	75.00

The values of these stamps are in karbovanets, which are the rubles of the Ukraine

Wmk. 116
Same Colors

B5	SP1	10k + 10k	25.00	40.00
B6	SP2	20k + 20k	25.00	40.00
a.		Imperf., pair		
B7	SP3	90k + 30k	25.00	40.00
B8	SP4	150k + 50k	25.00	40.00

> Catalogue values for unused stamps in this section, from this point to the end of the section, are for Never Hinged items.

Mercy and Health Fund — SP5

1994, Jan. 15   Litho.   Perf. 12
B9   SP5 150kb +20kb multi   32

UMM AL QIWAIN

LOCATION — Oman Peninsula, Arabia, on Arabian Gulf
GOVT. — Sheikdom under British protection
AREA — 300 sq. mi.
POP. — 5,700

Umm al Qiwain is one of six Persian Gulf sheikdoms to join the United Arab Emirates which proclaimed independence Dec. 2, 1971. See United Arab Emirates.

100 Naye Paise = 1 Rupee
100 Dirham = 1 Riyal (1967)

> Catalogue values for all unused stamps in this country are for Never Hinged items.

Sheik Ahmed bin Rashid al Mulla and Gazelles — A1

Photogravure and Lithographed
1964, June 29   Unwmk.   Perf. 14
Size: 35x22mm

1	A1	1np shown	15	15
2	A1	2np Snake	15	15
3	A1	3np Hyena	15	15
4	A1	4np Conspicuous trigger-fish	15	15
5	A1	5np Fish	15	15
6	A1	10np Silver andgelfish	15	15
7	A1	15np Palace	15	15
8	A1	20np Umm al Qiwain	15	15
9	A1	30np Tower	15	15

Size: 42x26mm

10	A1	40np as 1np	15	15
11	A1	50np as 2np	15	15
12	A1	70np as 3np	15	15
13	A1	1r as 4np	20	15
14	A1	1.50r as 4np	30	15
15	A1	2r as 10np	40	15

Size: 52x33mm

16	A1	3r as 15np	60	20
17	A1	5r as 20np	1.00	25
18	A1	10r as 30np	2.00	50
		Set value	5.00	1.60

National Stadium, Tokyo, and Discobolus — A2

Designs: 1r, 2r, National Stadium, Tokyo. 1.50r, Indoor swimming arena. 3r, Komazawa Gymnasium. 4r, Stadium entrance.

1964, Nov. 25   Photo.   Perf. 14

19	A2	50np multi		15	15
20	A2	1r multi		20	15
21	A2	1.50r multi		30	15
22	A2	2r multi		40	15
23	A2	3r multi		60	15
24	A2	4r multi		80	20
25	A2	5r multi		1.00	25
		Nos. 19-25 (7)		3.45	
		Set value			85

18th Olympic Games, Tokyo, Oct. 10-25, 1964. Perf. and imperf. souvenir sheets contain 4 stamps similar to #22-25 in changed colors. Size: 145x115mm.

A3   A4

Designs: 10np, Pres. Kennedy's funeral cortege leaving White House. 15np, Mrs. Kennedy with children, and Robert Kennedy following coffin. 50np, Horse-drawn caisson. 1r, Presidents Truman and Eisenhower, and Margaret Truman Daniels. 2r, Pres. Charles de Gaulle, Emperor Haile Selassie, Chancellor Ludwig Erhart, Sir Alec Douglas-Home and King Frederick IX. 3r, Kennedy family on steps of St. Matthew's Cathedral. 5r, Honor guard at tomb. 7.50r, Portrait of Pres. John F. Kennedy.

Perf. 14½

1965, Jan. 20   Unwmk.   Photo.
Black Design with Gold Inscriptions
Size: 29x44mm

26	A3	10np pale blue		15	15
27	A3	15np pale yellow		15	15
28	A3	50np pale green		15	15
29	A3	1r pale pink		20	15
30	A3	2r pale green		40	15

Size: 33x51mm

31	A3	3r pale gray		60	20
32	A3	5r pale blue		1.00	30
33	A3	7.50r pale yellow		1.50	50
		Nos. 26-33 (8)		4.15	
		Set value			1.25

Pres. John F. Kennedy. A souvenir sheet contains 2 stamps similar to Nos. 32-33 with pale green (5r) and pale salmon (7.50r) backgrounds, size: 29x44mm. Size of sheet: 114x70mm.

1969, Nov. 19   Litho.   Perf. 14½

Designs: 10d, Astronaut on Moon. 20d, Landing module approaching moon. 30d, Apollo XII on launching pad. 50d, Commanders Charles Conrad, Jr., Alan L. Bean, Richard F. Gordon, Jr., earth and moon, horiz. 75d, Earth and Apollo XII, horiz. 1r, Sheik Ahmed, rocket and lunar landing module, horiz.

34	A4	10d multi		25
35	A4	20d multi		25
36	A4	30d multi		30
37	A4	50d emerald & multi		40
38	A4	75d purple & multi		60
39	A4	1r dk bl & multi		75
		Nos. 34-39 (6)		2.55

US Apollo XII moon landing mission, 11/14-24/69.

Two imperf. souvenir sheets of 3 exist, containing stamps similar to Nos. 34-36 and Nos. 37-39.

A5   A7

A6

1970, May 29   Litho.   Perf. 14

40	A5	10d James A. Lovell		15
41	A5	30d Fred W. Haise, Jr.		15
42	A5	50d John L. Swigert, Jr.		20
a.		Souv. sheet of 3, #40-42		40
		Set value		36

Safe return of the crew of Apollo 13.

1970, Aug. 14   Litho.   Perf. 13½x14

Designs: 5d, 1.25r, EXPO '70 Emblem. 10d, 20d, Japanese Pavilion.

43	A6	5d yellow & multi		15
44	A6	10d blue & multi		15
45	A6	20d red & multi		15
48	A6	1.25r red & multi		25
		Set value		40

EXPO '70 Intl. Exhib., Osaka, Japan, Mar. 15-Sept. 13, 1970.

A 40d and 1r, showing the Emperor and Empress of Japan, and a souvenir sheet containing these and Nos. 43-45, 48 were prepared, but not issued.

1970, Oct. 12   Litho.   Perf. 14½x14

Uniforms: 10d, Private, North Lancashire Regiment. 20d, Royal Navy seaman. 30d, Officer, North Lancashire (Loyal) Regiment. 50d, Private, York and Lancaster Regiment. 75d, Royal Navy officer. 1r, Officer, York and Lancaster Regiment.

49	A7	10d multi		16
50	A7	20d multi		28
51	A7	30d multi		40
a.		Souv. sheet of 3, #49-51		1.50
52	A7	50d buff & multi		70
53	A7	75d multi		1.00
54	A7	1r buff & multi		1.50
a.		Souv. sheet of 3, #52-54		3.50
		Nos. 49-54 (6)		4.04

British landings on the Trucial Coast, 150th anniv.

Stamps of Umm al Qiwain were replaced in 1972 by those of United Arab Emirates.

AIR POST STAMPS

Type of Regular Issue, 1964
Photogravure and Lithographed
1965   Unwmk.   Perf. 14
Size: 42x26mm

C1	A1	15np as #1		15	15
C2	A1	25np as #2		15	15
C3	A1	35np as #3		15	15
C4	A1	50np as #4		15	15
C5	A1	75np as #5		15	15
C6	A1	1r as #6		20	15

Size: 52x33mm

C7	A1	2r as #7		40	15
C8	A1	3r as #8		60	20
C9	A1	5r as #9		1.00	32
		Set value		2.60	90

Issued: #C7-C9, Nov. 6; others, Oct. 18.

AIR POST OFFICIAL STAMPS

Type of Regular Issue, 1964
Photogravure and Lithographed
1965, Dec. 22   Unwmk.   Perf. 14
Size: 42x26mm

CO1	A1	75np as #6		15	15

Size: 52x33mm

CO2	A1	2r as #7		40	15
CO3	A1	3r as #8		60	20
CO4	A1	5r as #9		1.00	32
		Nos. CO1-CO4 (4)		2.15	
		Set value			68

OFFICIAL STAMPS

Type of Regular Issue, 1964
Photogravure and Lithographed
1965, Dec. 22   Unwmk.   Perf. 14
Size: 42x26mm

O1	A1	25np as #1		15	15
O2	A1	40np as #2		15	15
O3	A1	50np as #3		15	15
O4	A1	75np as #4		15	15
O5	A1	1r as #5		20	15
		Set value		58	25

UNITED ARAB EMIRATES

LOCATION — Arabia, on Arabian Gulf
GOVT. — Federation of sheikdoms
AREA — 32,300 sq. mi.
POP. — 1,175,000 (est. 1982)
CAPITAL — Abu Dhabi

The UAE was formed Dec. 2, 1971, by the union of Abu Dhabi, Ajman, Dubai, Fujeira, Sharjah and Umm al Qiwain. Ras al Khaima joined in Feb. 1972.

1,000 Fils = 1 Dinar
100 Fils = 1 Dirham (1973)

> Catalogue values for all unused stamps in this country are for Never Hinged items.

Abu Dhabi Nos. 56-67 Overprinted

دولة الامارات العربية المتحدة

UAE

1972, Aug.   Litho.   Unwmk.   Perf. 14

1	A10	5f multicolored		
2	A10	10f multicolored		
3	A10	25f multicolored		
4	A10	35f multicolored		
5	A10	50f multicolored		
6	A10	60f multicolored		
7	A10	70f multicolored		
8	A10	90f multicolored		
9	A11	125f multicolored		
10	A11	150f multicolored		
11	A11	500f multicolored		
12	A11	1d multicolored		
		Nos. 1-12 (12)		275.00

The overprint differs.
#1-12 were used in Abu Dhabi. #2-3 were placed on sale later in Dubai & Sharjah.

Map and Flag of UAE — A1

Almagta Bridge, Abu Dhabi A2

Designs: 10f, Like 5f. 15f, 35f, Coat of arms of UAE (eagle). 75f, Khor Fakkan, Sharjah. 1d, Steel Clock Tower, Dubai. 1.25d, Buthnah Fort, Fujeira. 2d, Alfalaj Fort, Umm al Qiwain. 3d, Khor Khwair, Ras al Khaima. 5d, Palace of Sheik Rashid bin Humaid al Nuaimi, Ajman. 10d, Sheik Zaid bin Sultan al Nahayyan, Abu Dhabi.

1973, Jan. 1   Unwmk.   Perf. 14½
Size: 41x25mm

13	A1	5f multicolored		15	15
14	A1	10f multicolored		15	15
15	A1	15f blue & multi		25	25
16	A1	35f olive & multi		55	55

Perf. 14x15
Size: 45x29½mm

17	A2	65f multicolored		1.00	1.00
18	A2	75f multicolored		1.25	1.25
19	A2	1d multicolored		1.50	1.50
20	A2	1.25d multicolored		2.75	2.75
21	A2	2d multicolored		32.50	8.00
22	A2	3d multicolored		4.75	4.75
23	A2	5d multicolored		8.00	8.00
24	A2	10d multicolored		16.00	16.00
		Nos. 13-24 (12)		68.85	44.35

For surcharge see No. 68.

Festival Emblem — A3

1973, Mar. 27   Litho.   Perf. 13½x14

25	A3	10f shown		3.50	15
26	A3	1.25d Trophy		9.00	6.50

National Youth Festival, Mar. 27.

Pedestrian Crossing in Dubai — A4

Designs: 35f, Traffic light and school crossing sign, vert. 1.25d, Traffic policemen with car and radio, vert.

1973, Apr. 1   Perf. 13½x14, 14x13½

27	A4	35f green & multi		2.00	1.10
28	A4	75f blue & multi		4.00	2.00
29	A4	1.25d violet & multi		6.75	3.00

Traffic Week, Apr. 1-7.

Human Rights Flame and People — A5

1973, Dec. 10   Litho.   Perf. 14½x14

30	A5	35f blue, blk & org		1.25	50
31	A5	65f red, blk & org		2.00	1.00
32	A5	1.25d olive, blk & org		3.25	1.90

25th anniversary of the Universal Declaration of Human Rights.

UPU and Arab Postal Union Emblems — A6

1974, Aug. 5   Litho.   Perf. 14x14½
33	A6	25f multicolored	95	40
34	A6	60f emerald & multi	1.90	75
35	A6	1.25d lt brown & multi	3.75	1.75

Centenary of Universal Postal Union.

Health Care — A7

Education — A8

Designs: 65f, Construction. 1.25d, UAE flag, UN and Arab League emblems.

1974, Dec. 2   Litho.   Perf. 13½
36	A7	10f multicolored	90	15
37	A8	35f multicolored	1.75	65
38	A8	65f blue & brown	2.50	1.25
39	A8	1.25d multicolored	4.75	3.00

Third National Day.

Arab Man and Woman Holding Candle over Book — A9

Man and Woman Reading Book — A10

Perf. 14x14½, 14½x14
1974, Dec. 27
40	A9	35f deep ultra & multi	1.25	40
41	A10	65f orange brn & multi	1.75	75
42	A10	1.25d gray & multi	3.50	1.50

World Literacy Day.

Oil De-gassing Station — A11

Designs: 50f, Off-shore drilling platform. 100f, Underwater storage tank. 125f, Oil production platform.

1975, Mar. 10   Litho.   Perf. 13x13½
43	A11	25f multicolored	90	30
44	A11	50f multicolored	1.25	60
45	A11	100f multicolored	2.50	1.40
46	A11	125f multicolored	3.25	1.50
a.		Souvenir sheet of 4, #43-46	7.50	5.25

9th Arab Petroleum Conference.

Three stamps to commemorate the 2nd Gulf Long Distance Swimming Championship were prepared in June, 1975, but not issued.

Jabal Ali Earth Station A12

Jabal Ali Earth Station: 35f, 65f, Communications satellite over globe.

1975, Nov. 8   Litho.   Perf. 13
47	A12	15f multicolored	70	18
48	A12	35f multicolored	1.25	50
49	A12	65f multicolored	1.75	85
50	A12	2d multicolored	4.25	2.50

Various Scenes — A13   Sheik Hamad, Fujeira Ruler — A14

Supreme Council Members (Sheikdom rulers): 60f, Sheik Rashid bin Humaid al Naimi, Ajman. 80f, Sheik Ahmed bin Rashid al Mulla, Umm al Qiwain. 90f, Sheik Sultan bin Mohammed al Qasimi, Sharjah. 1d, Sheik Saqr bin Mohammed al Qasimi, Ras al Khaima. 140f, Sheik Rashid bin Said al Maktum, Dubai. 5d, Sheik Zaid bin Sultan al Nahayan, Abu Dhabi.

1975, Dec. 2   Litho.   Perf. 14
51	A13	10f multicolored	32	24
52	A14	35f multicolored	1.25	95
53	A14	60f multicolored	1.90	1.65
54	A14	80f multicolored	2.50	2.25
55	A14	90f multicolored	3.00	2.25
56	A14	1d multicolored	3.25	2.50
57	A14	140f multicolored	4.50	3.50
58	A14	5d multicolored	18.00	14.00
		Nos. 51-58 (8)	34.72	27.34

Fourth National Day.

Students and Lamp of Learning — A15

Arab Literacy Day: 15f, Lamp of learning. 3d, like 50f.

1976, Feb. 8   Litho.   Perf. 14
59	A15	15f orange & multi	50	16
60	A15	50f ultra & multi	85	58
61	A15	3d multicolored	5.00	3.25

Road and Traffic Lights — A16

Traffic Week: 15f, Traffic lights and signals, vert. 140f, Children crossing street.

Perf. 14½x14, 14x14½
1976, Apr. 1   Litho.
62	A16	15f brt blue & multi	50	50
63	A16	80f blue & multi	2.50	2.50
64	A16	140f ocher & multi	4.50	4.50

Waves and Ear Phones, ITU Emblem, Coat of Arms — A17

1976, May 17   Litho.   Perf. 14
65	A17	50f gray green & multi	85	42
66	A17	80f pink & multi	1.65	65
67	A17	2d tan & multi	3.50	1.65

International Telecommunications Day.

No. 18 Surcharged

═══   ═══

50   ٥٠

1976   Litho.   Perf. 14x15
68	A2	50f on 75f multi	20.00	5.00

Coat of Arms — A18

1976, Aug. 15   Litho.   Perf. 11½
69	A18	5f dull rose	15	15
70	A18	10f golden brown	15	15
71	A18	15f orange	32	22
72	A18	35f dull red brn	60	40
73	A18	50f bright lilac	75	50
74	A18	60f bister	85	60
75	A18	80f yellow green	1.10	80
76	A18	90f ultra	1.25	90
77	A18	1d blue	1.75	1.10
78	A18	140f olive green	2.25	1.40
79	A18	150f rose violet	2.25	1.65
80	A18	2d slate	3.00	2.00
81	A18	5d blue green	7.75	5.25
82	A18	10d lilac rose	15.00	10.50
		Nos. 69-82 (14)	37.17	25.62

See Nos. 91-104.

Sheik Zaid — A19

1976, Dec. 12   Litho.   Perf. 13
83	A19	15f rose & multi	1.50	25
84	A19	140f blue & multi	3.75	2.50

5th National Day.

Symbolic Falcon and Globe — A20

1976, Dec. 15   Perf. 14x13½
85	A20	80f yellow & multi	1.65	80
86	A20	2d red & multi	3.75	2.25

International Falconry Congress, Abu Dhabi, Dec. 1976.

A21   A22

1976, Dec. 30   Litho.   Perf. 13
87	A21	50f multicolored	2.75	1.00
88	A21	80f multicolored	3.00	1.65

Mohammed Ali Jinnah (1876-1948), 1st Governor General of Pakistan.

1977, Apr. 12   Litho.   Perf. 13½x14

APU emblem, members' flags.
89	A22	50f multicolored	2.00	1.10
90	A22	80f multicolored	3.00	1.50

Arab Postal Union, 25th anniversary.

Arms Type of 1976

1977, July 25   Litho.   Perf. 11½
91	A18	5f dull rose & blk	15	15
92	A18	10f gldn brn & blk	15	15
93	A18	15f dull org & blk	15	15
94	A18	35f lt brown & blk	65	50
95	A18	50f brt lilac & blk	45	35
96	A18	60f bister & blk	1.00	75
97	A18	80f yel grn & blk	65	50
98	A18	90f ultra & blk	80	60
99	A18	1d blue & blk	1.00	70
100	A18	140f ol grn & blk	1.65	1.25
101	A18	150f rose vio & blk	1.65	1.25
102	A18	2d slate & blk	2.00	1.50
103	A18	5d bl grn & blk	4.75	3.75
104	A18	10d lil rose & bl	10.00	7.25
		Nos. 91-104 (14)	25.05	18.85

Man Reading Book, UAE Arms, UN Emblem — A23

1977, Sept. 8   Litho.   Perf. 14x13½
105	A23	50f green, brn & gold	80	35
106	A23	3d blue & multi	3.50	2.00

International Literacy Day.

A set of three stamps for the 6th Natl. Day was withdrawn from sale on the day of issue, Dec. 2, 1977.

Post Horn and Sails — A24

1979, Apr. 14 Photo. *Perf. 12x11½*
107 A24 50f multicolored 48 30
108 A24 5d multicolored 4.75 3.00

Gulf Postal Organization, 2nd Conf., Dubai.

Arab
Achievements
A25

1980, Mar. 22 Litho. *Perf. 14x14½*
109 A25 50f multicolored 35 35
110 A25 140f multicolored 1.00 1.00
111 A25 3d multicolored 2.25 2.25

9th National Day — A26

1980, Dec. 2 Litho. *Perf. 13½*
112 A26 15f multicolored 55 20
113 A26 40f multicolored 1.40 55
114 A26 80f multicolored 1.90 90
115 A26 150f multicolored 2.75 1.75

Souvenir Sheet
Perf. 13½x14
116 A26 3d multicolored 7.50 5.00

Family on
Graph — A27

Hegira (Pilgrimage
Year) — A28

1980, Dec. 15
117 A27 15f shown 45 25
118 A27 80f Symbols 1.75 1.00
119 A27 90f like #118 2.25 1.25
120 A27 2d like #117 4.50 2.50

1980 population census.

1980, Dec. 18 *Perf. 14x13½*
121 A28 15f multicolored 25 15
122 A28 80f multicolored 1.00 50
123 A28 90f multicolored 1.25 90
124 A28 140f multicolored 1.65 90

Souvenir Sheet
125 A28 3d multicolored 6.50 3.50

No. 125 contains one 36x57mm stamp.

OPEC
Emblem
A29

1980, Dec. 21 *Perf. 14*
126 A29 50f Men holding OPEC emblem, vert. 65 48
127 A29 80f like #126 1.00 85
128 A29 90f shown 1.10 90
129 A29 140f like #128 1.75 1.40

Souvenir Sheet
130 A29 3d like #128 9.00 4.50

Traffic Week — A30

Designs: 15f, 80f, Crossing guard, students, traffic light. 50f, 5d, Crossing guard, traffic light and signs.

1981, Mar. 26 Litho. *Perf. 14½*
131 A30 15f multicolored 32 32
132 A30 50f multicolored 65 65
133 A30 80f multicolored 1.25 1.25
134 A30 5d multicolored 5.25 5.25

Size of Nos. 131 and 133: 25½x35mm.

10th Natl.
Day — A31

1981, Dec. 2 Litho. *Perf. 15x14*
135 A31 25f Cogwheel 35 18
136 A31 150f Soldiers 2.50 1.10
137 A31 2d UN emblem 3.00 1.50

Intl. Year of the
Disabled — A32

Perf. 14½x14, 14x14½
1981, Dec. 26 Litho.
138 A32 25f Couple 48 32
139 A32 45f Man in wheelchair, vert. 80 55
140 A32 150f like #139 2.75 2.00
141 A32 2d like #138 4.00 3.00

Natl. Arms — A33

1982-86
142 A33 5f multicolored 15 15
143 A33 10f multicolored 15 15
144 A33 15f multicolored 15 15
145 A33 25f multicolored 18 18
145A A33 35f multicolored 20 20
146 A33 50f multicolored 36 36
147 A33 75f multicolored 55 55
148 A33 100f multicolored 75 75
149 A33 110f multicolored 85 85
150 A33 125f multicolored 95 95
151 A33 150f multicolored 1.10 1.10
151A A33 175f multicolored 95 95

Size: 23x27mm
Perf. 13
152 A33 2d multicolored 1.35 1.35
152A A33 250f multicolored 1.40 1.40
153 A33 3d multicolored 2.00 2.00
154 A33 5d multicolored 3.35 3.35
155 A33 10d multicolored 6.75 6.75
156 A33 20d multicolored 13.50 13.50
157 A33 50d multicolored 27.00 27.00
Nos. 142-157 (19) 61.69 61.69

Issue dates: 35f, 175f, 250f, Dec. 15, 1984. 50d, Feb. 6, 1986. Others, Mar. 7, 1982.

6th Arab Gulf Soccer
Championships — A34

1982, Apr. 4 Litho. *Perf. 14*
167 A34 25f Emblem, flags 32 32
168 A34 75f Eagle, soccer ball, stadium, vert. 95 95
169 A34 125f Players, vert. 1.65 1.65
170 A34 3d like 75f, vert. 3.75 3.75

2nd Disarmament
Meeting — A35

1982, Oct. 24 Litho. *Perf. 13x13½*
171 A35 25f multicolored 32 25
172 A35 75f multicolored 1.00 80
173 A35 125f multicolored 1.75 1.40
174 A35 150f multicolored 1.90 1.65

11th Natl.
Day — A36

Designs: 25f, 150f, Skyscraper, communications tower, natl. crest, castle turret, open book, flag. 75f, 125f, Sun, bird, vert.

1982, Dec. 2 Litho. *Perf. 14½*
175 A36 25f multicolored 40 26
176 A36 75f multicolored 1.25 75
177 A36 125f multicolored 2.00 1.25
178 A36 150f multicolored 2.25 1.75

A37 A38

1983, Dec. 20 Litho. *Perf. 14x14½*
179 A37 25f multicolored 28 28
180 A37 150f multicolored 1.75 1.75
181 A37 2d multicolored 2.25 2.25
182 A37 3d multicolored 3.25 3.25

World Communications Year.

1983, Jan. 8 Litho. *Perf. 14½*
Arab Literacy Day: 25f, 75f, Oil lamp, open Koran. 35f, 3d, Scribe.
183 A38 25f multicolored 11.00
184 A38 35f multicolored 30 30
185 A38 75f multicolored 16.00
186 A38 3d multicolored 2.25 2.25

Nos. 183 and 185 withdrawn from sale on day of issue because of an error in Koranic inscription.

INTELSAT, 20th Anniv. — A39

1984, Nov. 24 Litho. *Perf. 14½*
187 A39 2d multicolored 3.00 3.00
188 A39 2.50d multicolored 4.00 4.00

13th Natl.
Day — A40

Flag, portrait of an Emir and building or view from each capital.

1984, Dec. 2 *Perf. 14½x13½*
189 A40 1d Building, pavilion 1.65 1.65
190 A40 1d Fortress, cannon 1.65 1.65
191 A40 1d Port, boats 1.65 1.65
192 A40 1d Fortress 1.65 1.65
193 A40 1d Oil refinery 1.65 1.65
194 A40 1d Building, garden 1.65 1.65
195 A40 1d Oil well, palace 1.65 1.65
Nos. 189-195 (7) 11.55 11.55

Tidy Week — A41 A42

1985, Mar. 15 *Perf. 12½*
196 A41 5d multicolored 7.00 4.50

1985, Sept. 10 *Perf. 13½x14½*
197 A42 2d multicolored 2.50 1.75
198 A42 250f multicolored 3.50 2.00

World Junior Chess Championships, Sharjah, Sept. 10-27.

14th Natl.
Day — A43

1985, Dec. 2 *Perf. 14x13½*
199 A43 50f multicolored 65 30
200 A43 3d multicolored 4.00 1.75

Population
Census — A44

1985, Dec. 16
201 A44 50f multicolored 55 32
202 A44 1d multicolored 1.25 60
203 A44 3d multicolored 3.25 1.75

Intl. Youth
Year
A45

1985, Dec. 23   *Perf. 14¹/₂*
204 A45 50f Silhouettes, sapling,
              vert.   65   35
205 A45 175f Globe, open book   1.90 1.10
206 A45 2d Youth carrying world,
              vert.   2.25 1.50

Women and Family
Day — A46

1986, Mar. 21   *Perf. 13¹/₂*
207 A46 1d multicolored   1.00   90
208 A46 3d multicolored   3.00 2.50

General Postal
Authority, 1st
Anniv. — A47

Designs: 50f, 250f, Posthorn, map, natl. flag,
globe. 1d, 2d, Emblem, globe, vert.

1986, Apr. 1
209 A47 50f multicolored   40   38
210 A47 1d multicolored   90   75
211 A47 2d multicolored   1.75 1.50
212 A47 250f multicolored   2.00 1.75

United Arab
Shipping Co.,
10th
Anniv. — A48

1986, Aug. 20   *Perf. 13x13¹/₂*
213 A48 2d shown   2.50 1.50
214 A48 3d Ship's bow, vert.   3.00 2.25

A49   A51

 Hawk — A50

1986, Sept. 1   *Perf. 13¹/₂x13*
215 A49 250f multicolored   2.50 1.65
216 A49 3d multicolored   3.00 1.90

Emirates Telecommunications Corp., Ltd., 10th
anniv.

1986, Sept. 9   Photo.   Perf. 15x14
Background Color
217 A50 50f pale green   60   60
218 A50 75f pink   95   95
219 A50 125f gray   1.50 1.50
   a. Bklt. pane of 4 (2 50f, 75f, 125f)   4.50

Nos. 217-219 issued in booklets only.

1986, Oct. 25   *Perf. 13¹/₂*
220 A51 50f Jet, camel   65   65
221 A51 175f Jet   2.50 2.50

Emirates Airlines, 1st anniv.

State Crests,
GCC Emblem
A52

1986, Nov. 2   *Perf. 13*
222 A52 50f shown   55   55
222A A52 175f like no. 223   1.90 1.90
223 A52 3d Tree, emblem   3.25 3.25

Gulf Cooperation Council supreme council 7th
session, Abu Dhabi, Nov. 1986. No. 222A incorrectly inscribed "1.75f."

15th Natl.
Day — A53

1986, Dec. 2   Litho.   Perf. 13¹/₂
224 A53 50f shown   50   50
225 A53 1d like 50f   1.00 1.00
226 A53 175f Flag, emblem   1.75 1.75
227 A53 2d like 175f   2.00 2.00

27th Chess Olympiad, Dubai — A54

1986, Nov. 14   *Perf. 12¹/₂*
228 A54 50f Skyscraper, vert.   60   60
229 A54 2d shown   2.25 2.25
230 A54 250f Tapestry, diff.   3.00 3.00
   a. Souv. sheet of 3, #228-230, perf. 13 7.75 7.75

No. 230a exists imperf.

Arab Police
Day — A55

1986, Dec. 18   *Perf. 13¹/₂*
231 A55 50f multicolored   70   70
232 A55 1d multicolored   1.25 1.25

A56   A57

1987, Mar. 15
233 A56 50f multicolored   70   70
234 A56 1d multicolored   1.25 1.25

Municipalities and Environment Week.

1987, Apr. 10
235 A57 200f multicolored   2.50 2.50
236 A57 250f multicolored   3.00 3.00

UAE Flight Information Region, 1st anniv.

A58   A59

1987, May 25
237 A58 50f Water   55   55
238 A58 2d Solar energy, oil well   2.25 2.25

Conservation.

1987, June 23
239 A59 1d multicolored   1.10 1.10
240 A59 3d multicolored   3.25 3.25

United Arab Emirates University, 10th anniv.

Arab Palm Tree and
Date Day — A61

1987, July 4   *Perf. 13*
241 A60 50f Oil rig   60   60
242 A60 1d Drilling well, vert.   1.10 1.10
243 A60 175f Crew, drill   2.00 2.00
244 A60 2d Oil tanker   2.25 2.25

1st Shipment of Crude Oil from Abu
Dhabi, 25th Anniv. — A60

1987, Sept. 15   Litho.   Perf. 14x15
245 A61 50f shown   65   65
246 A61 1d Tree, fruit, diff.   1.25 1.25

A62   A63

1987, Nov. 21   Litho.   Perf. 13x13¹/₂
247 A62 2d multicolored   1.75 1.75
248 A62 250f multicolored   2.25 2.25

Intl. Year of Shelter for the Homeless.

1987, Dec. 15   *Perf. 13¹/₂*
249 A63 1d multicolored   95   95
250 A63 2d multicolored   1.90 1.90

Salim Bin Ali Al-Owais (b. 1887), poet.

UN Child
Survival
Campaign
A64

Abu Dhabi Intl.
Airport, 6th Anniv.
A65

1987, Oct. 25   Litho.   Perf. 13
251 A64 50f Growth monitoring   42   42
252 A64 1d Immunization   85   85
253 A64 175f Oral rehydration ther-
              apy   1.65 1.65
254 A64 2d Breast feeding, horiz.   1.75 1.75

1988, Jan. 2
255 A65 50f Control tower   50   50
256 A65 50f Terminal interior   50   50
257 A65 100f Aircraft over airport   1.00 1.00
258 A65 100f Aircraft at gates   1.00 1.00

Natl. Arts
Festival
A66

1988, Mar. 21   Litho.   Perf. 13¹/₂
259 A66 50f multicolored   60   60
260 A66 250f multicolored   2.50 2.50

Youth Cultural
Festival
A67

Winning children's drawings of a design contest
sponsored by the Ministry of Education and the
Sharjah Cultural and Information Department.

Perf. 13x13¹/₂, 13¹/₂x13
1988, May 25   Litho.
261 A67 50f Net fisherman   45   45
262 A67 1d Woman   1.00 1.00
263 A67 1.75d Youth as flower   1.65 1.65
264 A67 2d Recreation   1.90 1.90

Palestinian
Uprising — A68

1988, June 28   Litho.   Perf. 13¹/₂
265 A68 2d multicolored   2.25 2.25
266 A68 250f multicolored   2.75 2.75

Banks

A69   A70

1988, July 16   Litho.   *Perf. 13½*
267 A69   50f multicolored   90   90
268 A70   50f multicolored   90   90

Abu Dhabi Natl. Bank, Ltd., 20th anniv. (No. 267); Natl. Bank of Dubai, Ltd., 25th anniv. (No. 268).

Port Rashid, Dubai, 16th Anniv. — A71

1988, Aug. 31   Litho.   *Perf. 13½*
269 A71   50f Ground transportation   42   42
270 A71   1d Piers   85   85
271 A71   175f Ship at dock   1.50 1.50
272 A71   2d Ship, unloading cranes 2.00 2.00

1988 Summer Olympics, Seoul
A72   A73

1988, Sept. 17   *Perf. 15x14½*
273 A72   2d Swimming   1.65 1.65
274 A73   250f Cycling   2.00 2.00

Ras Al Khaima Natl. Museum, 1st Anniv. — A74

1988, Nov. 19   Litho.   *Perf. 14*
275 A74   50f Vase, vert.   32   32
276 A74   3d Gold crown   2.25 2.25

18th Arab Scout Conference, Nov. 29-Dec. 3, Abu Dhabi — A75

1988, Nov. 29   *Perf. 12½*
277 A75   1d multicolored   80   80

10th Arbor Day — A76

Perf. 13½x13, 13x13½
1989, Mar. 6   Litho.
278 A76   50f Ghaf, vert.   40   40
279 A76   100f Palm   75   75
280 A76   250f Dahlia blossom   1.90 1.90

Sharjah Intl. Airport, 10th Anniv. — A77

1989, Apr. 21   Litho.   *Perf. 13½*
281 A77   50f multicolored   40   40
282 A77   100f multicolored   80   80

Postal Service, 80th Anniv. — A78

1989, Aug. 19   Litho.   *Perf. 13x13½*
283 A78   50f Seaplane   42   42
284 A78   3d Ship   2.75 2.75

Al-Ittihad Newspaper, 20th Anniv. — A79

1989, Oct. 20   Litho.   *Perf. 13½*
285 A79   50f shown   40   40
286 A79   1d Al Ittihad Press   80   80

Gulf Investment Corporation, 5th Anniv. A80

1989, Nov. 25
287 A80   50f multicolored   40   40
288 A80   2d multicolored   1.65 1.65

Child on Crutches, Hands — A81   Bank Building — A82

Designs: 2d, Crouched youth, cracked earth, bread in hand, horiz.

1989, Dec. 5   *Perf. 15x14, 14x15*
289 A81   2d multicolored   1.65 1.65
290 A81   250f shown   2.00 2.00

Intl. Volunteer's Day, Red Crescent Soc.

1989, Dec. 20   *Perf. 13½*
291 A82   50f Emblem, architecture 58   58
292 A82   1d shown   1.15 1.15

Commercial Bank of Dubai, Ltd., 20th Anniv.

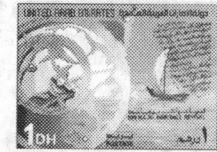

Astrolabe, Manuscript Page and Ship of Bin Majid, 15th Cent. Navigator and Writer
A83

Perf. 13x13½, 13½x13
1989, Dec. 25
293 A83   1d shown   75   75
294 A83   3d Ship, page, vert.   2.25 2.25

Heritage revival.

A84   Falcon — A85

1990, Jan. 17   *Perf. 13½*
295 A84   50f multicolored   58   58
296 A84   1d multicolored   1.15 1.15

3rd Al Ain festival.

1990, Feb. 17   Litho.   *Perf. 11½*
Granite Paper
297 A85   5f multicolored   15   15
298 A85   20f multicolored   15   15
299 A85   25f multicolored   15   15
301 A85   50f multicolored   30   30
302 A85   100f multicolored   65   65
303 A85   150f multicolored   90   90
304 A85   175f multicolored   1.10 1.10

Size: 21x26mm
Perf. 11½x12
306 A85   2d multicolored   1.25 1.25
307 A85   250f multicolored   1.50 1.50
309 A85   3d multicolored   1.75 1.75
310 A85   5d multicolored   3.00 3.00
311 A85   10d multicolored   6.00 6.00
312 A85   20d multicolored   12.00 12.00
313 A85   30d multicolored   30.00 30.00
          Nos. 297-313 (14)   58.90 58.90

A86   A87

1990, Mar. 10   Litho.   *Perf. 13½*
316 A86   50f multicolored   42   42
317 A86   250f multicolored   2.00 2.00

Children's cultural festival.

1990, Aug. 5   Litho.   *Perf. 14x15*
318 A87   175f shown   1.40 1.40
319 A87   2d Starving child   1.65 1.65

Red Crescent Society.

Dubai Chamber of Commerce and Industry, 25th Anniv. — A88

1990, July 1   *Perf. 13*
320 A88   50f multicolored   40   40
321 A88   1d multicolored   1.00 1.00

World Cup Soccer Championships, Italy — A89

UAE emblem, character trademark and: 1d, Leaning Tower of Pisa, desert, vert. 2d, Soccer ball, vert. 250f, Circle of flags. 3d, Map, vert.

1990, June 8   *Perf. 13½*
322 A89   50f multicolored   38   38
323 A89   1d multicolored   80   80
324 A89   2d multicolored   1.50 1.50
325 A89   250f multicolored   1.90 1.90

Souvenir Sheet
Perf. 12½
326 A89   3d multicolored   3.00 3.00

A90   A91

1990, Sept. 22   Litho.   *Perf. 13½*
327 A90   50f shown   35   35
328 A90   1d Emblem, 30 years   75   75
329 A90   175f Emblem, drop of oil 1.25 1.25

Organization of Petroleum Exporting Countries (OPEC), 30th anniv.

1990, Aug. 25   *Perf. 14x14½*

Flowers.
330 A91   50f Argyrolobeum roseum 40   40
331 A91   50f Lamranthus roseus   40   40
332 A91   50f Centavrea pseudo sinaica 40   40
333 A91   50f Calotropis procera   40   40
  a.   Souvenir sheet of 4, #330-333 1.65 1.65
334 A91   50f Nerium oleander   40   40
335 A91   50f Catharanthus roseus 40   40
336 A91   50f Hibiscus rosa sinensis 40 40
337 A91   50f Bougainvillea glabra 40   40
  a.   Souvenir sheet of 4, #334-337 1.65 1.65
          Nos. 330-337 (8)   3.20 3.20

A92   A93

1990, Oct. 8   **Litho.**   *Perf. 13*
338 A92 50f Water pollution   38   38
339 A92 3d Air pollution   2.25 2.25

Environmental pollution.

1990, Dec. 2   *Perf. 13¹/₂*
340 A93 50f shown   35 35
341 A93 175f Bank building, horiz.   1.40 1.40

Central Bank, 10th anniv.

Intl. Conference on
High Salinity Tolerant
Plants — A94

1990, Dec. 8   *Perf. 13x13¹/₂*
342 A94 50f Tree   38 38
343 A94 250f Water, trees   2.00 2.00

Grand Mosque,
Abu
Dhabi — A95

Design: 2d, Al Jumeirah Mosque, Dubai, vert.

Perf. 13¹/₂x13, 13x13¹/₂
1990, Nov. 26
344 A95 1d multicolored   80 80
345 A95 2d multicolored   1.65 1.65

A96   A98

A97

1991, Jan. 16   **Litho.**   *Perf. 13x13¹/₂*
346 A96 50f multicolored   42 42
347 A96 2d multicolored   1.75 1.75

Abu Dhabi Intl. Fair.

1991, May 17   **Litho.**   *Perf. 14x13¹/₂*
348 A97 2d multicolored   1.50 1.50
349 A97 3d multicolored   2.25 2.25

World Telecommunications Day.

1991, June 18   *Perf. 13¹/₂*
350 A98 1d Sheikh Saqr Mosque   80 80
351 A98 2d King Faisal Mosque   1.65 1.65

Children's
Paintings
A99

Designs: 50f, Celebration. 1d, Women waving
flags. 175f, Women playing blind-man's buff. 250f,
Women dancing for men.

1991, July 15   **Litho.**   *Perf. 14x13¹/₂*
352 A99 50f multicolored   35 35
353 A99 1d multicolored   75 75
354 A99 175f multicolored   1.40 1.40
355 A99 250f multicolored   1.90 1.90

Fish
A100

1991, Aug. 5   **Litho.**   *Perf. 13¹/₂x14*
356 A100 50f Yellow marked butterfly-
     lyfish   35 35
357 A100 50f Golden trevally   35 35
358 A100 50f Two banded porgy   35 35
359 A100 50f Red snapper   35 35
360 A100 1d Three banded grunt   75 75
361 A100 1d Rabbit fish   75 75
362 A100 1d Black bream   75 75
363 A100 1d Greasy grouper   75 75
   a.   Min. sheet of 8, #356-363   4.75 4.75
     Nos. 356-363 (8)   4.40 4.40

A101   A103

A102

Intl. Aerospace Exhibition, Dubai: 175f, Jet
fighter over Dubai Intl. Airport. 2d, Fighter silhouette over airport.

1991, Nov. 3   **Litho.**   *Perf. 13¹/₂*
364 A101 175f multicolored   1.25 1.25
365 A101 2d multicolored   1.50 1.50

1991, Oct. 7   *Perf. 13*

Sheikh Rashid Bin Saeed Al Maktoum (1912-90),
Ruler of Dubai and: 50f, Airport, vert. 175f, City
skyline, vert. 2d, Waterfront, satellite dish.

366 A102 50f multicolored   35 35
367 A102 1d multicolored   75 75
368 A102 175f multicolored   1.25 1.25
369 A102 2d multicolored   1.50 1.50

1991, Oct. 8   **Litho.**   *Perf. 13¹/₂*
370 A103 50f multicolored   45 45
371 A103 1d multicolored   90 90

Civil Defense Day.

A104

A105

A106

20th Natl. Day — A107

Designs: No. 374, Emir at left, fortress, cannon.
No. 377, Fortress on rocky outcropping. No. 378,
Emir at right, fortress, cannon. 3d, Sheikh Said bin
Sultan an-Nahayan, Defense Forces.

1991, Dec. 2   **Litho.**   *Perf. 13*
372 A104 75f multicolored   58 58
373 A105 75f multicolored   58 58
374 A105 75f multicolored   58 58
375 A106 75f multicolored   58 58
376 A107 75f multicolored   58 58
377 A107 75f multicolored   58 58
378 A107 75f multicolored   58 58

Imperf
Size: 70x90mm
378A A107 3d multicolored   4.00 4.00
     Nos. 372-378A (8)   8.06 8.06

On Nos. 372-378 portions of the design were
applied by a thermographic process producing a
shiny, raised effect.

A108   A109

1991, Nov. 16   *Perf. 13¹/₂*
379 A108 50f lt green & multi   35 35
380 A108 3d orange & multi   2.25 2.25

Gulf Cooperaton Council, 10th anniv.

1992, Jan. 15   **Litho.**   *Perf. 13¹/₂*
381 A109 175f pink & multi   1.10 1.10
382 A109 250f lt blue & multi   1.60 1.60

Abu Dhabi National Oil Company, 20th anniv.

Al-Jahli Castle
Al-Ain
A110

1992, Apr. 20   **Litho.**   *Perf. 13¹/₂*
383 A110 2d multicolored   1.25 1.25
384 A110 250f multicolored

Expo '92, Seville.
No. 384 was withdrawn because of poor rendi-
tion of Arabic word for "postage."

A111   A112

Mosques: 50f, Sheikh Rashid Bin Humaid Al
Nuaimi, Ajman. 1d, Sheikh Ahmed Bin Rashid Al
Mualla, Umm Al Quwain.

1992, Mar. 26   *Perf. 14x13¹/₂*
385 A111 50f multicolored   32 32
386 A111 1d multicolored   65 65

See Nos. 417-418.

1992, Apr. 20   *Perf. 13¹/₂x13*
387 A112 1d shown   65 65
388 A112 3d Ear with hearing aid   1.90 1.90

Week of the deaf child.

Zayed
Seaport,
20th
Anniv.
A113

1992, June 28   **Litho.**   *Perf. 13¹/₂*
389 A113 50f Aerial view   32 32
390 A113 1d Cargo transport   65 65
391 A113 175f Ship docked   1.10 1.10
392 A113 2d Map   1.30 1.30

1992 Summer
Olympics,
Barcelona — A114

1992, July 25   **Litho.**   *Perf. 14x13¹/₂*
393 A114 50f Yachting   32 32
394 A114 1d Running   65 65
395 A114 175f Swimming   1.10 1.10
396 A114 250f Cycling   1.60 1.60

Souvenir Sheet
396A A114 3d Equestrian   2.00 2.00

Children's
Paintings — A115

1992, Aug. 15   *Perf. 13¹/₂x14*
397 A115 50f Playing soccer   32 32
398 A115 1d Playing in field   65 65
399 A115 2d Playground   1.25 1.25
400 A115 250f Children among trees   1.60 1.60

Intl. Bank of
United Arab
Emirates, 15th
Anniv. — A116

Design: 175f, Bank emblem.

Litho. & Embossed
1992, Sept. 9   *Perf. 11*
401 A116 50f gold & multi   32 32

Size: 35x41mm
Perf. 11¹/₂
402 A116 175f lake, gold & vio   1.10 1.10

Traditional
Musical
Instruments
A116a

1992, Oct. 17   Litho.   Perf. 13½
402A	A116a	50f	Tambourah, vert.	32 32
402B	A116a	50f	Oud, vert.	32 32
402C	A116a	50f	Rababah, vert.	32 32
402D	A116a	1d	Mizmar, shindo	65 65
402E	A116a	1d	Tabel, hibban	65 65
402F	A116a	1d	Marwas, duff	65 65
			Nos. 402A-402F (6)	2.91 2.91

Camels
A117

Designs: 50f, Race. 1d, Used for transportation, vert. 175f, Harnessed for obtaining water from well. 2d, Roaming free, vert.

1992, Dec. 23   Litho.   Perf. 13½
403	A117	50f	multicolored	32 32
404	A117	1d	multicolored	65 65
405	A117	175f	multicolored	1.10 1.10
406	A117	2d	multicolored	1.25 1.25

A118   A119

1992, Dec. 21
407	A118	50f	multicolored	32 32
408	A118	2d	yellow & multi	1.25 1.25

Gulf Cooperation Council, 13th session.

1993, Jan. 28   Litho.   Perf. 13½
409	A119	2d	shown	1.25 1.25
410	A119	250f	Building, fishing boat	1.60 1.60

Dubai Creek Golf and Yacht Club.

Tourism — A120

1993, Jan. 16
411	A120	50f	Golf, horiz.	32 32
412	A120	1d	Fishing	65 65
413	A120	2d	Boating, horiz.	1.25 1.25
414	A120	250f	Motor vehicle touring, horiz.	1.60 1.60

Natl. Youth
Festival — A121

1993, Mar. 27   Litho.   Perf. 14x13½
415	A121	50f	violet & multi	32 32
416	A121	3d	red brown & multi	1.90 1.90

Mosque Type of 1992

1993, Feb. 16   Perf. 13½
Designs: 50f, Thabit Bin Khalid Mosque, Fujeira. 1d, Sharq Al Morabbah Mosque, Al Ain.
417	A111	50f	multicolored	32 32
418	A111	1d	multicolored	65 65

Shells
A122

1993, Apr. 3   Litho.   Perf. 13
419	A122	25f	Conus textile	16 16
420	A122	50f	Pinctada radiata	32 32
421	A122	100f	Murex scolopax	65 65
422	A122	150f	Natica pulicaris	95 95
423	A122	175f	Lambis truncata sebae	1.10 1.10
424	A122	200f	Cardita bicolor	1.25 1.25
425	A122	250f	Cypraea grayana	1.55 1.55
426	A122	300f	Cymatium trilineatum	1.90 1.90
			Nos. 419-426 (8)	7.88 7.88

Campaign
Against
Drugs — A123

Design: 1d, Skull, drugs, vert.

1993, Aug. 21   Litho.   Perf. 13½
427	A123	50f	multicolored	32 32
428	A123	1d	multicolored	65 65

Natl. Bank of Abu
Dhabi, 25th
Anniv. — A124

Designs: 50f, Abu Dhabi skyline, bank emblem. 1d, Bank emblem. 175f, Bank building, emblem. 2d, Skyline, emblem, diff.

1993, Sept. 15   Litho. & Typo.   Perf. 11½
429	A124	50f	silver & multi	32 32
430	A124	1d	silver & multi	65 65
431	A124	175f	silver & multi	1.10 1.10
432	A124	2d	silver & multi	1.25 1.25

Dubai Ports
Authority — A125

Designs: 50f, Aerial view of port. 1d, Loading cargo. 2d, Aerial view, diff. 250f, Globe.

1993, Nov. 10   Litho.   Perf. 13½
433	A125	50f	purple & multi	32 32
434	A125	1d	green & multi	65 65
435	A125	2d	orange & multi	1.25 1.25
436	A125	250f	pink & multi	1.50 1.50

Natl.
Day — A126

Children's paintings: 50f, Soldiers saluting flag. 1d, Two women sitting, one standing, flag, vert. 175f, Flag, boat. 2d, Flags atop castle tower.

1993, Dec. 2   Litho.   Perf. 13½
437	A126	50f	multicolored	32 32
438	A126	1d	multicolored	65 65
439	A126	175f	multicolored	1.10 1.10
440	A126	2d	multicolored	1.25 1.25

Archaeological Discoveries — A127

Designs: 50f, Tomb. 1d, Rectangular artifact. 175f, Animal-shaped artifact. 250f, Bowl.

1993, Dec. 15   Perf. 14x13½
441	A127	50f	multicolored	32 32
442	A127	1d	multicolored	65 65
443	A127	175f	multicolored	1.10 1.10
444	A127	250f	multicolored	1.50 1.50

10th Childrens'
Festival,
Sharjah
A128

Children's paintings: 50f, Children with balloons, flags. 1d, Children playing, three trees. 175f, Child with picture, girls with balloons. 2d, House, children playing outdoors.

1994, Mar. 19   Litho.   Perf. 13x13½
445	A128	50f	green & multi	32 32
446	A128	1d	blue & multi	65 65
447	A128	175f	red violet & multi	1.10 1.10
448	A128	2d	carmine & multi	1.25 1.25

Arabian
Horses
A129

Designs: 50f, Brown horse on hind feet, vert. 1d, White horse. 175f, Head of brown horse, vert. 250f, Head of white and brown horse.

Perf. 13x13½, 13½x13
1994, Jan. 25
449	A129	50f	multicolored	32 32
450	A129	1d	multicolored	65 65
451	A129	175f	multicolored	1.10 1.10
452	A129	250f	multicolored	1.50 1.50

10th
Conference of
Arab Towns,
Dubai
A130

Perf. 13x13½, 13½x13
1994, May 15   Litho.
453	A130	50f	Map, city, vert.	32 32
454	A130	1d	shown	65 65

Pilgrimage to
Mecca — A131

1994, Apr. 29   Litho.   Perf. 13x13½
455	A131	50f	shown	32 32
456	A131	2d	Holy Ka'aba	1.25 1.25

Intl. Year of
the Family
A132

Intl. Olympic
Committee,
Cent. — A133

Arab Housing
Day — A134

Writers Assoc., 10th
Anniv. — A135

1994, June 15   Perf. 13x13½
457	A132	1d	multicolored	65 65
458	A133	1d	multicolored	65 65

Perf. 13½x13
459	A134	1d	multicolored	65 65
460	A135	1d	multicolored	65 65

Archaeological
Finds, Al
Qusais, Dubai
A136

Designs: 50f, Lidded pitcher, vert. 1d, Pointed-handle pitcher. 175f, Pitcher, arm-shaped handle. 250f, Short round vase.

1994, Aug. 16   Litho.   Perf. 13½
461	A136	50f	multicolored	32 32
462	A136	1d	multicolored	65 65
463	A136	175f	multicolored	1.10 1.10
464	A136	250f	multicolored	1.50 1.50
			Nos. 461-464 (4)	3.57 3.57

Environmental Protection — A137

Designs: 50f, Arabian leopard. 1d, Gordon's wildcat. 2d, Caracal. 250f, Sand cat.

1994, Oct. 10   Litho.   Perf. 13½
465	A137	50f	multicolored	32 32
466	A137	1d	multicolored	65 65
467	A137	2d	multicolored	1.25 1.25
468	A137	250f	multicolored	1.50 1.50
			Nos. 465-468 (4)	3.72 3.72

12th Arab Gulf Soccer Championships, Abu Dhabi — A138

1994, Nov. 3   Litho.   Perf. 13½
469 A138 50f Ball, emblem, vert. 32 32
470 A138 3d Soccer players 2.00 2.00

Birds
A139   50 FILS

Designs: 50f, Merops orientalis. 175f, Halcyon chloris. 2d, Dromas ardeola. 250f, Coracias benghalensis.
3d, Phoenicopterus ruber, vert.

1994, Dec. 12
471 A139 50f multicolored 32 32
472 A139 175f multicolored 1.10 1.10
473 A139 2d multicolored 1.25 1.25
474 A139 250f multicolored 1.50 1.50
    Nos. 471-474 (4) 4.17 4.17
Souvenir Sheet
475 A139 3d multicolored 2.00 2.00

Archaeological Finds, Mulaiha, Sharjah — A140

Designs: 50f, Front of carved horse, vert. 175f, Ancient coin, vert. 2d, Inscription on metal, vert. 250f, Inscription on stone.

1995, Jan. 25   Litho.   Perf. 13½
476 A140 50f multicolored 32 32
477 A140 175f multicolored 1.10 1.10
478 A140 2d multicolored 1.25 1.25
479 A140 250f multicolored 1.50 1.50
    Nos. 476-479 (4) 4.17 4.17

Natl. Dances
A141   50 FILS

1995, Feb. 14
480 A141 50f Al-Naashat 32 32
481 A141 175f Al-Ayaalah 1.10 1.10
482 A141 2d Al-Shahhoh 1.25 1.25
    Nos. 480-482 (3) 2.67 2.67

UPPER SENEGAL AND NIGER

LOCATION — In Northwest Africa, north of French Guinea and Ivory Coast
GOVT. — A former French Colony
AREA — 617,600 sq. mi.
POP. — 2,474,142
CAPITAL — Bamako

In 1921 the name of this colony was changed to French Sudan and postage stamps so inscribed were placed in use.

100 Centimes = 1 Franc

Gen. Louis   Oil
Faidherbe — A1   Palms — A2

Dr. N. Eugène
Ballay — A3

Perf. 14x13½
1906-07   Unwmk.   Typo.
Name of Colony in Red or Blue
1 A1 1c slate 60 60
2 A1 2c brown 60 60
3 A1 4c brn, gray bl 60 60
4 A1 5c green 1.40 1.00
5 A1 10c car (B) 1.40 70
6 A1 15c vio ('07) 1.40 1.10
7 A2 20c bluish gray 1.75 1.75
8 A2 25c bl, pnksh 5.75 1.40
9 A2 30c vio brn, pnksh 2.25 1.75
10 A2 35c blk, yellow 1.40 1.10
11 A2 40c car, az (B) 2.50 2.25
12 A2 45c brn, grnsh 3.25 3.00
13 A2 50c dp vio 3.00 2.25
14 A2 75c bl, org 3.50 3.50
15 A3 1fr blk, green 9.00 5.50
16 A3 2fr bl, pink 17.50 16.00
17 A3 5fr car, straw (B) 40.00 30.00
    Nos. 1-17 (17) 95.90 73.10

Camel with Rider — A4

1914-17   Perf. 13½x14
18 A4 1c brn vio & vio 15 15
19 A4 2c gray & brn vio 15 15
20 A4 4c blk & bl 15 15
21 A4 5c yel grn & bl grn 15 15
22 A4 10c red org & rose 65 52
23 A4 15c choc & org ('17) 40 18
24 A4 20c brn vio & blk 40 18
25 A4 25c ultra & bl 40 30
26 A4 30c ol brn & brn 40 26
27 A4 35c car rose & vio 80 52
28 A4 40c gray & car rose 42 30
29 A4 45c bl & ol brn 42 35
30 A4 50c blk & grn 42 35
31 A4 75c org & ol brn 52 42
32 A4 1fr brn & brn vio 65 52
33 A4 2fr grn & bl 80 80
34 A4 5fr vio & blk 3.75 2.75
    Nos. 18-34 (17) 10.63 8.05

For surcharge see No. B1.

SEMI-POSTAL STAMP

 5ᶜ

Regular Issue of 1914
Surcharged in Red

1915   Unwmk.   Perf. 13½x14
B1 A4 10c + 5c red orange & rose 40 40

POSTAGE DUE STAMPS

Natives — D1   D2

1906   Unwmk.   Typo.   Perf. 14x13½
J1 D1 5c green, greenish 1.10 90
J2 D1 10c red brown 2.75 2.00
J3 D1 15c dark blue 3.75 3.00
J4 D1 20c black, yellow 4.25 2.25
J5 D1 50c violet 8.25 7.75
J6 D1 60c black, buff 5.00 5.00
J7 D1 1fr black, pinkish 12.50 11.00
    Nos. J1-J7 (7) 37.60 31.90

1914
J8 D2 5c green 35 35
J9 D2 10c rose 35 35
J10 D2 15c gray 40 40
J11 D2 20c brown 40 40
J12 D2 30c blue 70 70
J13 D2 50c black 40 40
J14 D2 60c orange 2.00 2.00
J15 D2 1fr violet 2.00 2.00
    Nos. J8-J15 (8) 6.60 6.60

Stamps of Upper Senegal and Niger were superceded in 1921 by those of French Sudan.

UPPER SILESIA

LOCATION — Formerly in eastern Germany and prior to World War I a part of Germany.

A plebiscite held under the terms of the Treaty of Versailles failed to determine the status of the country, the voting resulting about equally in favor of Germany and Poland. Accordingly, the League of Nations divided the territory between Germany and Poland.

100 Pfennig = 1 Mark
100 Fennigi = 1 Marka

Plebiscite Issues

A1

Perf. 14x13½
1920, Feb. 20   Typo.   Unwmk.
1 A1 2½pf slate 32 40
2 A1 3pf brown 32 40
3 A1 5pf green 15 22
4 A1 10pf dull red 35 45
5 A1 15pf violet 15 22
6 A1 20pf blue 15 22
a. Imperf., pair 165.00 175.00
7 A1 50pf violet brn 3.75 4.00
8 A1 1m claret 3.50 3.75
9 A1 5m orange 3.50 3.75
    Nos. 1-9 (9) 12.19 13.41

Black Surcharge

5 5 5 5
Pf. Pf. Pf. Pf.
I II III IV

10 A1 5pf on 15pf vio (I) 9.00 14.00
a. Type II 10.00 20.00
b. Type III 10.00 20.00
c. Type IV 9.00 14.00
11 A1 5pf on 20pf blue (I) 15 22
a. Type II 20 50
b. Type III 20 40
c. Type IV 15 50

Red Surcharge

10 10 10 10
Pf. Pf. Pf. Pf.
I II III IV

12 A1 10pf on 20pf bl (I) 15 22
a. Type II 15 22
b. Type III 15 22
c. Type IV 15 22
d. Imperf. 25.00

Black Surcharge

50 50 50 50 50
Pf. Pf. Pf. Pf. Pf.
I II III IV V

13 A1 50pf on 5m org (I) 14.00 22.50
a. Type II 14.00 22.50
b. Type III 14.00 22.50
c. Type IV 14.00 22.50
d. Type V 25.00 40.00

Nos. 10-13 are found with many varieties including surcharges inverted, double and double inverted.

Dove with Olive Branch Flying over Silesian Terrain — A2

A3

1920, Mar. 26   Typo.   Perf. 13½x14
15 A2 2½pf gray 18 15
16 A2 3pf red brown 20 15
17 A2 5pf green 15 15
18 A2 10pf dull red 15 15
19 A2 15pf violet 15 15
20 A2 20pf blue 15 15
21 A2 25pf dark brown 18 15
22 A2 30pf orange 15 15
23 A2 40pf olive green 15 15
    Perf. 14x13½
24 A3 50pf gray 15 15
25 A3 60pf blue 20 15
26 A3 75pf deep green 65 35
27 A3 80pf red brown 52 30
28 A3 1m claret 30 15
29 A3 2m dark brown 30 20
30 A3 3m violet 52 20
31 A3 5m orange 1.25 75
    Nos. 15-31 (17) 5.35
    Set value 2.65

Nos. 18-28 Overprinted in Black or Red

Plébiscite 20 mars 1921.

1921, Mar. 20
32 A2 10pf dull red 1.90 4.50
33 A2 15pf violet 1.90 4.50
34 A2 20pf blue 2.75 7.25
35 A2 25pf dk brn (R) 4.75 12.00
36 A2 30pf orange 4.75 12.00
37 A2 40pf olive grn (R) 4.75 12.00

Overprinted

Plébiscite 20 mars 1921.

38 A3 50pf gray (R) 4.75 12.00
39 A3 60pf blue 6.75 12.00
40 A3 75pf deep green 6.75 14.00
41 A3 80pf red brown 6.75 17.00
42 A3 1m claret 10.00 22.50
    Nos. 32-42 (11) 55.80 129.75

Inverted or double overprints exist on Nos. 32-33, 35-40. Counterfeit overprints exist.

Type of 1920 and Surcharged   **10 M**

1922, Mar.
45 A3 4m on 60pf ol grn 60 85
46 A3 10m on 75pf red 90 1.50
47 A3 20m on 80pf orange 4.50 8.00

Stamps of the above design were a private issue not recognized by the Inter-Allied Commission of Government.

OFFICIAL STAMPS

German Stamps of 1905-20 Handstamped in Blue

1920, Feb. Wmk. 125 *Perf. 14, 14½*
On Stamps of 1906-19

O1	A22	2pf gray	1.10	1.25
O3	A22	2½pf gray	55	65
O4	A16	3pf brown	55	65
O5	A16	5pf green	55	65
O6	A22	7½pf orange	55	65
O7	A16	10pf car rose	55	65
O8	A16	15pf dk violet	55	65
O9	A16	20pf blue violet	55	65
O10	A16	25pf org & blk, *yel*	5.25	6.50
O11	A16	30pf org & blk, *buff*	55	65
O12	A22	35pf red brown	55	65
O13	A16	40pf lake & blk	55	65
O14	A16	50pf vio & blk, *buff*	55	65
O15	A16	60pf magenta	55	65
O16	A16	75pf green & blk	55	65
O17	A16	80pf lake & blk, *rose*	6.50	8.00
O18	A17	1m car rose	1.10	1.25
O19	A21	2m gray blue	5.25	6.50

On National Assembly Stamps of 1919-20

O25	A23	10pf car rose	90	1.10
O26	A24	15pf choc & bl	1.65	2.00
O27	A25	25pf green & red	3.25	4.00
O28	A25	30pf red vio & red	2.50	3.00

On Semi-Postal Stamps of 1919

O30	A22	10pf + 5pf carmine	6.50	8.00
O31	A22	15pf + 5pf dk vio	6.50	8.00
		Nos. O1-O31 (24)	47.65	58.05

Red Handstamp

O5a	A16	5pf	10.00	14.00
O8a	A22	10pf	6.50	10.00
O9a	A16	20pf	6.50	10.00
O13a	A16	40pf	20.00	30.00
O16a	A16	75pf	20.00	30.00
O26a	A24	15pf	15.00	

Values of Nos. O1-O31 are for reprints made with a second type of handstamp differing in minor details from the original (example: period after "S" is round instead of the earlier triangular form). Originals are scarce. Counterfeits exist.

Germany No. 65C with this handstamp is considered bogus by experts.

Local Official Stamps **C. G. H. S.** of Germany, 1920, Overprinted

1920, Apr. *Perf. 14*

O32	LO2	5pf green	18	24
O33	LO3	10pf carmine	18	24
O34	LO4	15pf violet brn	18	24
O35	LO5	20pf deep ultra	18	24
O36	LO6	30pf orange, *buff*	18	24
O37	LO7	50pf violet, *buff*	40	40
O38	LO8	1m red, *buff*	4.00	5.75
		Nos. O32-O38 (7)	5.30	7.35

Same Overprint on Official Stamps of Germany, 1920-21

1920-21

O39	O1	5pf green	65	1.65
O40	O2	10pf carmine	15	15
O41	O3	15pf violet brn	15	15
O42	O4	20pf deep ultra	15	15
O43	O5	30pf orange, *buff*	15	15
O44	O6	40pf carmine rose	15	15
O45	O7	50pf violet, *buff*	15	15
O46	O8	60pf red brown	15	15
O47	O9	1m red, *buff*	15	15
O48	O10	1.25m dk blue, *yel*	15	15
O49	O11	2m dark blue	3.50	5.50
O50	O12	5m brown, *yel*	15	15

1922, Feb.   **Wmk. 126**

O51	O11	2m dark blue	15	15
		Set value, #O39-		
		O51	4.60	

This overprint is found both horizontal and vertical, reading up or down. It also exists on most values inverted, double and double, one inverted.

URUGUAY

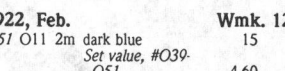

LOCATION — South America, between Brazil and Argentina and bordering on the Atlantic Ocean
GOVT. — Republic
AREA — 72,172 sq. mi.
POP. — 2,991,341 (est. 1983)
CAPITAL — Montevideo

120 Centavos = 1 Real
8 Reales = 1 Peso
100 Centesimos = 1 Peso (1859)
1000 Milesimos = 1 Peso (1898)

Watermarks

Wmk. 187- R O in Diamond

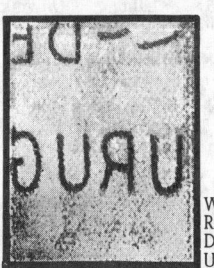

Wmk. 188- REPUBLICA O. DEL URUGUAY

Wmk. 189- Caduceus

Wmk. 227- Greek Border and REPUBLICA O. DEL URUGUAY in Alternate Curved Lines

Wmk. 327- Coat of Arms

Wmk. 332- Large Sun and R O U

Values of early Uruguay stamps vary according to condition. Quotations for Nos. 1-17 are for fine copies. Very fine to superb specimens sell at much higher prices, and inferior or poor copies sell at reduced prices, depending on the condition of the individual specimen.

Catalogue values for unused stamps in this country are for Never Hinged items, beginning with Scott 534 in the regular postage section, Scott B5 in the semi-postal section, Scott C113 in the airpost section, Scott CB1 in the airpost semi-postal section, Scott E9 in the special delivery section, and Scott Q64 in the parcel post section.

Carrier Issues
Issued by Atanasio Lapido, Administrator-General of Posts

"El Sol de Mayo"
A1   A1a

1856, Oct. 1 Unwmk. Litho. *Imperf.*

1	A1	60c blue	250.	
a.		60c deep blue	400.	
b.		60c indigo	700.	
2	A1	80c green	225.	
a.		80c deep green	250.	
3	A1	1r vermilion	200.	
a.		1r carmine vermilion	250.	

1857, Oct. 1

3B	A1a	60c blue	*1,500.*	
c.		60c pale blue	*1,000.*	
d.		60c dark blue	*1,600.*	

As Nos. 1-3d were spaced closely on the stone, four-margin copies are unusual. Most genuinely used specimens are pen canceled.
See Nos. 410-413, 771A.

A2

1858, Mar.

4	A2	120c blue	175.00	150.00
a.		120c deep blue	175.00	150.00
b.		120c greensh blue	175.00	150.00
c.		Tête bêche pair	7,500.	
5	A2	180c green	50.00	75.00
a.		180c deep green	100.00	200.00
b.		Thick paper	100.00	100.00
c.		Tête bêche pair	10,000.	
6	A2	240c dull ver	50.00	*300.00*
a.		240c deep vermilion	62.50	
b.		240c brown red	150.00	
c.		180c dl ver in stone of 240c		
d.		Thick paper (dull ver)	50.00	

Government Issues

A3

A4

1859, June 26
Thin Numerals

7	A3	60c lilac	20.00	17.50
a.		60c gray lilac	21.00	17.50
8	A3	80c yellow	175.00	32.50
a.		80c orange	250.00	42.50
9	A3	100c brown lake	50.00	37.50
a.		100c brown rose	50.00	37.50
10	A3	120c blue	32.50	12.50
a.		120c slate blue	42.50	15.00
11	A3	180c green	12.50	15.00
12	A3	240c vermilion	45.00	45.00

1860
Thick Numerals

13	A4	60c dull lilac	12.50	4.00
a.		60c gray lilac	15.00	4.00
b.		60c brown lilac	15.00	6.00
c.		60c red lilac	15.00	6.00
d.		As "a," fine impression (1st printing)	62.50	37.50
14	A4	80c yellow	17.50	10.00
a.		80c orange	40.00	12.50
15	A4	100c rose	42.50	20.00
a.		100c carmine	42.50	20.00
16	A4	120c blue	20.00	8.00
17	A4	180c yellow grn	110.00	75.00
a.		180c deep green	125.00	87.50

No. 13 was first printed (1860) in sheets of 192 (16x12) containing 24 types. The impressions are very clear; paper is whitish and of better quality than that of the later printings. In the 1861-62 printings, the layout contains 12 types and the subjects are spaced farther apart.

Coat of Arms — A5

1864, Apr. 13

18	A5	6c rose	7.50	4.75
a.		6c carmine	12.50	10.00
b.		6c red	14.00	14.00
c.		6c brick red	17.50	17.50
20	A5	6c salmon	75.00	
21	A5	8c green	12.50	12.50
a.		Tête bêche pair	325.00	
22	A5	10c yellow	17.50	12.00
a.		10c ocher	17.50	12.00
23	A5	12c blue	7.50	6.00
a.		12c dark blue	10.00	8.00
b.		12c slate blue	12.50	10.00

No. 20, which is on thicker paper, was never placed in use.

Stamps of 1864 Surcharged in Black

1866, Jan. 1

24	A5	5c on 12c blue	12.50	25.00
a.		5c on 12c slate blue	20.00	35.00
b.		Inverted surcharge	37.50	
c.		Double surcharge	20.00	
d.		Pair, one without surcharge		
e.		Triple surcharge	42.50	
25	A5	10c on 8c brt grn	12.50	25.00
a.		10c on 8c dl grn	12.50	25.00
b.		Tête bêche pair	150.00	
c.		Double surcharge	25.00	
26	A5	15c on 10c ocher	15.00	37.50
a.		15c on 10c yellow	15.00	37.50
b.		Inverted surcharge	42.50	
c.		Double surcharge	22.50	
27	A5	20c on 6c rose	17.50	37.50
a.		20c on 6c rose red	25.00	37.50
b.		Inverted surcharge	45.00	
c.		Double surcharge	25.00	
d.		Pair, one without surcharge		
28	A5	20c on 6c brick red	*100.00*	
a.		Double surcharge		

Many counterfeits exist.
No. 28 was not issued.

Coat of Arms and Numeral of Value — A7

A8

A8a

A8b   A8c

ONE CENTESIMO:
Type I - The wavy lines behind "CENTESIMO" are clear and distinct. Stamps 4mm apart.
Type II - The wavy lines are rough and blurred. Stamps 3mm apart.

1866, Jan. 10   *Imperf.*

29	A7	1c black (type II)	1.25	2.00
a.		1c black (type I)	1.25	2.00
30	A8	5c blue	2.00	1.10
a.		5c dull blue	2.00	1.00
b.		5c ultramarine	17.50	3.75
c.		Numeral with white flag	15.00	5.50
d.		"ENTECIMOS"	15.00	8.75
e.		"CENTECIMO"	15.00	8.75
f.		"CENTECIMOS" with small "S"	8.75	3.75
g.		Pelure paper	12.50	7.00
h.		Thick paper	17.50	7.00
31	A8a	10c yellow green	7.00	3.00
a.		10c blue green	10.00	3.00
b.		"I" of "CENTECIMOS" omitted	22.50	8.75
c.		"CENIECIMOS"	22.50	8.75
d.		"CENTRCIMOS"	22.50	8.75
32	A8a	15c orange yel	12.00	4.75
a.		15c yellow	12.00	4.75
33	A8c	20c rose	14.00	4.75
a.		20c lilac rose	14.00	5.00
b.		Thick paper	22.50	6.75

See Nos. 34-38. For overprint see No. O11.
Engraved plates were prepared for Nos. 30 to 33 but were not put in use. The stamps were printed from lithographic transfers from the plate. In 1915 a few reprints of the 15c were made from the engraved plate by a California philatelic society, each sheet being numbered and signed by officers of the society; then the plate was defaced.

1866-67   *Perf. 8½ to 13½*

34	A7	1c black	3.00	3.00
35	A8	5c blue	2.50	45
a.		5c dark blue	2.50	45
b.		Numeral with white flag	9.00	6.25
c.		"ENTECIMOS"	10.00	2.50
d.		"CENTECIMO"	10.00	2.50
e.		"CENTECIMOS" with small "S"	10.00	1.50
f.		Pelure paper	7.50	2.00
36	A8a	10c green	5.00	42
a.		10c yellow green	5.00	42
b.		"CENIECIMOS"	12.50	2.50
c.		"I" of "CENTECIMOS" omitted	12.50	2.50
d.		"CENTRCIMOS"	12.50	2.50
e.		Pelure paper	12.50	6.25
37	A8b	15c orange yel	2.50	1.75
a.		15c yellow	2.50	1.75
b.		Pelure paper	14.00	6.25
38	A8c	20c rose	6.00	1.50
a.		20c brown rose	6.00	1.50
b.		Pelure paper	20.00	7.50
c.		Thick paper	11.00	3.00
		Nos. 34-38 (5)	19.00	7.12

A9   A10

A11   A12

1877-79   *Engr.*   *Rouletted 8*

39	A9	1c red brown	35	25
40	A10	5c green	40	20
a.		Thick paper	2.50	90
41	A11	10c vermilion	52	20
42	A11	20c bister	75	30
43	A11	50c black	4.00	1.50
43A	A12	1p blue ('79)	22.50	7.00
		Nos. 39-43A (6)	28.52	9.45

The first printing of the 1p had the coat of arms smaller with quarterings reversed. These "error" stamps were not issued, and all were ordered burned. A copy is known to have been in a celebrated Uruguayan collection and a few others exist.
See No. 44. For overprints and surcharges see Nos. 52-53, O1-O8, O10, O19.

1880, Nov. 10   *Litho.*   *Rouletted 6*

44	A9	1c brown	15	15
a.		Imperf., pair	8.75	
b.		Rouletted 12½	1.75	

Joaquin Suárez — A13

1881, Aug. 25   *Perf. 12½*

45	A13	7c blue	1.00	90
a.		Imperf., pair	7.50	7.50

For overprint see No. O9.

Devices from Coat of Arms
A14   A14a

1882, May 15

46	A14	1c green	50	50
a.		1c yellow green	1.75	90
b.		Imperf., pair	10.00	
47	A14a	2c rose	45	45
a.		Imperf., pair	12.50	

These stamps bear numbers from 1 to 100 according to their position on the sheet.
Counterfeits of Nos. 46 and 47 are plentiful.
See Nos. 1132-1133. For overprints see Nos. 54, O12-O13, O20.

Coat of Arms
A15   A16

Gen. Máximo   General José
Santos — A17   Artigas — A18

Perf. 12, 12x12½, 12x13, 13x12
1883, Mar. 1

48	A15	1c green	65	38
49	A16	2c red	75	50
50	A17	5c blue	1.00	75
51	A18	10c brown	1.50	1.00

Imperf., Pairs

48a	A15	1c	5.50
49a	A16	2c	5.50
50a	A17	5c	5.00
51a	A18	10c	9.00

For overprints see Nos. O14-O18.

1883

No. 40 Overprinted in Black

Provisorio

1883, Sept. 24   *Rouletted 8*

52	A10	5c green	50	38
a.		Double overprint	11.25	11.25
b.		Overprint reading down	4.00	4.00
c.		"Provisorio" omitted	6.00	6.00
d.		"1883" omitted	4.00	4.00

No. 52 with overprint in red is a color essay.

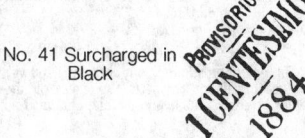

No. 41 Surcharged in Black

1884, Jan. 15

53	A11	1c on 10c ver	18	18
a.		Small figure "1"	2.50	1.75
b.		Inverted surcharge	2.50	1.75
c.		Double surcharge	5.00	3.00

No. 47 Overprinted in Black

PROVISORIO
1884

Perf. 12½

54	A14a	2c rose	38	38
a.		Double overprint	11.25	
b.		Imperf., pair	20.00	

A22   A23

Thick Paper
1884, Jan. 25   *Litho.*   *Unwmk.*

55	A22	5c ultra	1.25	50
a.		Imperf., pair	6.00	3.50

Thin Paper
Perf. 12½, 13 and Compound

56	A23	5c blue	60	30
a.		Imperf., pair	12.50	

For overprints see Nos. O21-O22.

A24   A24a

A24b

Artigas   Santos
A25   A26

A27   A28

1884-88   *Engr.*   *Rouletted 8*

57	A24	1c gray	54	30
58	A24	1c olive	42	25
59	A24	1c green	25	15
60	A24	2c vermilion	25	16
60A	A24a	2c rose ('88)	25	15
61	A24b	5c deep blue	50	20
61A	A24b	5c blue, *blue*	1.25	50
62	A24b	5c vio ('86)	20	15
63	A24b	5c lt bl ('88)	25	15
64	A25	7c dk brown	1.25	55

65	A25	7c org ('88)	75	38
66	A26	10c olive brn	25	15
67	A27	20c red violet	1.00	30
68	A27	20c bis brn ('88)	75	38
69	A28	25c gray violet	1.75	65
70	A28	25c ver ('88)	1.40	50
		Nos. 57-70 (16)	11.06	4.92

Water dissolves the blue in the paper of No. 61A.
For overprints see Nos. 73, 98-99, O23-O34, O36-O39, O61.

A29   A30

1887, Oct. 17   *Litho.*   *Rouletted 9*

71	A29	10c lilac	90	50
a.		10c gray lilac	90	50

For overprint see No. O40.

1888, Jan. 1   *Engr.*   *Rouletted 8*

72	A30	10c violet	30	18

For overprint see No. O35.

No. 62 Overprinted in **Provisorio** Black

1889, Oct. 14

73	A24b	5c violet	20	20
a.		Inverted overprint	5.00	3.00
b.		Inverted "A" for "V" in "Provisorio"	3.00	

No. 73 with overprint in red is a color essay.

Coat of   Numeral of
Arms — A32   Value — A33

A34   A35

A36   A37

Justice   Mercury
A38   A39

A40

Perf. 12½ to 15½ and Compound
1889-1901   *Engr.*

74	A32	1c green	25	15
a.		Imperf., pair	9.00	
75	A32	1c dull bl ('94)	25	15
76	A33	2c rose	25	15
77	A33	2c red brn ('94)	32	18
78	A33	2c org ('99)	25	18
79	A34	5c dp blue	25	15
80	A34	5c rose ('94)	38	15
81	A35	7c bister brn	50	20
82	A35	7c green ('94)	3.50	1.50
83	A35	7c car ('00)	3.00	1.25

84	A36 10c blue grn	2.00	50
a.	Printed on both sides	15.00	
85	A36 10c org ('94)	2.00	38
86	A37 20c orange	1.50	38
87	A37 20c brown ('94)	3.50	1.00
88	A37 20c lt blue ('00)	1.50	20
a.	20c greenish blue	1.75	20
89	A38 25c red brown	2.00	45
90	A38 25c ver ('94)	4.50	2.00
91	A38 25c bis brn ('01)	2.50	30
92	A39 50c lt blue	4.50	1.50
93	A39 50c lilac ('94)	8.00	3.00
94	A39 50c car ('01)	4.50	38
95	A40 1p lilac	11.00	2.50
96	A40 1p lt blue ('94)	14.00	3.75
97	A40 1p dp grn ('01)	14.00	1.00
a.	Imperf., pair	22.50	
	Nos. 74-97 (24)	84.45	21.40

For surcharges and overprints see Nos. 100-101, 142, 180, 185, C1-C3, O41-O60, O89-O91, O108-O109.

Nos. 59 and 62 Overprinted in Red

Provisorio 1892
a

Provisorio 1891
b

1891-92   **Rouletted 8**

98	A24 (a) 1c green ('92)	25	25
a.	Inverted overprint	4.25	3.75
b.	Double overprint	5.50	5.00
c.	Double ovpt, one invtd.	3.00	2.50
d.	"PREVISORIO"	2.75	2.50
99	A24b (b) 5c violet	15	15
a.	"1391"	2.50	1.75
b.	Double overprint	2.50	1.75
c.	Inverted overprint	2.50	1.75
d.	Double ovpt, one invtd.	5.00	3.00

Nos. 86 and 81 Surcharged in Black or Red

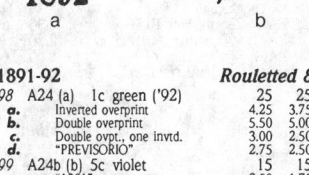

UN Centésimo Provisorio 1892
c

CINCO Centésimos Provisorio 1892
d

Perf. 12½ to 15½ and Compound
1892

100	A37 (c) 1c on 20c org (Bk)	20	15
a.	Inverted surcharge	3.00	3.00
101	A35 (d) 5c on 7c bis brn (R)	20	15
a.	Inverted surcharge	1.00	1.00
b.	Double surcharge, one inverted	3.00	3.00
c.	Double surcharge	3.00	3.00
d.	Vertical surcharge	10.00	
e.	"PREVISORIO"	2.00	2.00
f.	"Cinco" omitted	4.50	

No. 101 with surcharge in green is a color essay. Several surcharge errors of date and misspelling of "Centésimos" exist. Value $12.50.

A45   A46

Arms A47   Peace A48

1892   **Engr.**

102	A45 1c green	25	15
103	A46 2c rose	25	15
104	A47 5c blue	25	15
105	A48 10c orange	1.10	50

Issued: 1c, 2c, Mar. 9; 5c, Apr. 19; 10c, Dec. 15.

Liberty A49   Arms A50

1894, June 2

106	A49 2p carmine	15.00	9.00
107	A50 3p dull violet	15.00	9.00

Gaucho A51   Solis Theater A52

Locomotive A53   Bull's Head A54

Ceres — A55   Sailing Ship — A56

Liberty A57   Mercury A58

Coat of Arms — A59

Montevideo Fortress — A60   Cathedral in Montevideo — A61

Perf. 12 to 15½ and Compound
1895-99

108	A51 1c bister	25	15
109	A51 1c slate bl ('97)	25	15
a.	Printed on both sides	14.00	
110	A52 2c blue	25	15
111	A52 2c claret ('97)	25	15
112	A53 5c red	25	15
113	A53 5c green ('97)	38	15
a.	Imperf., pair	3.50	
114	A53 5c grnsh bl ('99)	30	15
115	A54 7c deep green	5.00	1.25
116	A54 7c orange ('97)	2.50	65
117	A55 10c brown	1.10	25
118	A56 20c green & blk	4.00	55
119	A56 20c cl & blk ('97)	3.00	45
120	A57 25c red brn & blk	3.50	65
a.	Center inverted		1,500.
121	A57 25c pink & bl ('97)	2.00	38
122	A58 50c blue & blk	4.50	2.00
123	A58 50c grn & brn ('97)	3.50	65
124	A59 1p org brn & blk	7.00	2.50
125	A59 1p yel brn & bl ('97)	6.00	1.75
126	A60 2p violet & grn	15.00	10.00
127	A60 2p bis & car ('97)	6.00	1.00
128	A61 3p carmine & blue	15.00	8.00
129	A61 3p lil & car ('97)	5.50	1.50
	Nos. 108-129 (22)	85.53	32.63

All values of this issue exist imperforate but they were not issued in that form.

For overprints and surcharges see Nos. 138-140, 143, 145, 147, O62-O78.

President Joaquin Suárez A62   A63

Statue of President Suárez — A64

Perf. 12½ to 15 and Compound
1896, July 18

130	A62 1c brown vio & blk	20	15
131	A63 5c pale bl & blk	20	15
132	A64 10c lake & blk	60	30

Dedication of Pres. Suárez statue.
For overprints and surcharge see Nos. 133-135, 144, 146, 152, O79-O81.

Same Overprinted in Red:

PROVISORIO 1897
e

PROVISORIO 1897
f

1897, Mar. 1

133	A62 (e) 1c brn vio & blk	30	20
a.	Inverted overprint	3.50	3.00
134	A63 (e) 5c pale blue & blk	30	20
a.	Inverted overprint	6.00	4.00
135	A64 (f) 10c lake & blk	65	45
a.	Inverted overprint	8.50	7.50
b.	Double overprint	7.50	

"Electricity" — A68

1897-99   **Engr.**

136	A68 10c red	1.10	30
137	A68 10c red lilac ('99)	38	25

For overprints see Nos. 141, O82-O83.

PAZ 1897

Regular Issues Overprinted in Red or Blue

1897, Sept. 26

138	A51 1c slate bl (R)	50	38
a.	Inverted overprint	3.00	3.00
139	A52 2c claret (Bl)	75	75
a.	Inverted overprint	2.50	2.50
140	A53 5c green (Bl)	1.10	1.00
a.	Inverted overprint	5.00	5.00
b.	Double overprint		
141	A68 10c red (Bl)	1.75	1.75
a.	Inverted overprint	10.00	10.00

Commemorating the Restoration of Peace at the end of the Civil War.
Issue for use only on the days of the National Fête, Sept. 26-28, 1897.

Regular Issues Surcharged in Black, Blue or Red

PROVISIONAL 1/2 CENTESIMO

1898, July 25

142	A32 ½c on 1c bl (Bk)	20	20
a.	Inverted surcharge	3.00	3.00
143	A51 ½c on 1c bis (Bl)	20	20
a.	Inverted surcharge	3.00	
b.	Double surcharge	2.50	
144	A62 ½c on 1c brn vio & blk (R)	20	20
145	A52 ½c on 2c blue (Bk)	20	20
146	A63 ½c on 5c pale bl & blk	20	20
a.	Double surcharge	6.25	
147	A54 ½c on 7c dp grn (R)	20	20
	Nos. 142-147 (6)	1.20	1.20

The 2c red brown of 1894 (No. 77) was also surcharged like Nos. 142 to 147 but was not issued.

Liberty — A69   Statue of Artigas — A70

1898-99   **Litho.**   **Perf. 11, 11½**

148	A69 5m rose	15	18
149	A69 5m purple ('99)	20	20

1899-1900   **Engr.**   **Perf. 12½, 14, 15**

150	A70 5m lt blue	15	15
151	A70 5m orange ('00)	15	15
	Set value	24	15

1900

No. 135 With Additional Surcharge in Black

5 CENTESIMOS

1900, Dec. 1

152	A64 5c on 10c lake & blk	30	20
a.	Black bar covering "1897" omitted	15.00	

Cattle — A72   Girl's Head — A73

Shepherdess — A74

Perf. 13½ to 16 and Compound
1900-10   **Engr.**

153	A72 1c yellow green	25	15
154	A73 5c dull blue	50	15
155	A73 5c slate grn ('10)	50	15
156	A74 10c gray violet	60	15
	Set value		46

For surcharges and overprints see Nos. 179, 184, O84, O86, O88, O106-O107.

Eros and
Cornucopia
A75

Basket of Fruit
A76

1901, Feb. 11
157 A75 2c vermilion   35 15
158 A76 7c brown orange   1.10 20

For surcharges and overprints see Nos. 197-198, O85, O87, O105.

General
Artigas — A78

Cattle — A79

Eros — A80

Cow — A81

Shepherdess
A82

Numeral
A83

Justice — A84

1904-05   Litho.   Perf. 11½
160 A78 5m orange   25 15
  a.   5m yellow   20 15
161 A79 1c green   38 15
  a.   Imperf., pair   3.50
162 A80 2c dp orange   18 15
  a.   2c orange red   15 15
  b.   Imperf., pair   3.00
163 A81 5c blue   50 15
  a.   Imperf., pair   3.50
164 A82 10c dk violet ('05)   30 15
165 A83 20c gray grn ('05)   1.75 30
166 A84 25c olive bis ('05)   2.00 50
     Nos. 160-166 (7)   5.36
     Set value   1.30

For overprints see Nos. 167-169, O92-O98, O101-O103.

Overprinted
Diagonally in
Carmine or Black

Paz 1904

1904, Oct. 15
167 A79 1c green (C)   38 20
168 A80 2c deep orange (Bk)   42 25
169 A81 5c dark blue (C)   75 38

Commemorating the end of the Civil War of 1904. In the first overprinting, "Paz 1904" appears at a 50-degree angle; in the second, at a 63-degree angle.

A85

A86

1906, Feb. 23   Litho.   Unwmk.
170 A85 5c dark blue   65 15
  a.   Imperf., pair   6.00

1906-07
171 A86 5c deep blue   15 15
172 A86 7c orange brn ('07)   30 18
173 A86 50c rose   3.00 50

Cruiser "Montevideo" — A87

1908, Aug. 23   Typo.   Rouletted 13
174 A87 1c carmine & dk grn   65 65
175 A87 2c green & dk grn   65 65
176 A87 5c orange & dk grn   65 65

Center Inverted
174a A87 1c   225.00 225.00
175a A87 2c   225.00 225.00
176a A87 5c   225.00 225.00

Imperf., Pairs
174b A87 1c   20.00
175b A87 2c   20.00
176b A87 5c   20.00

Independence of Uruguay, declared Aug. 25, 1825. Counterfeits exist.
For surcharges and overprints see Nos. 186, O99-O100, O104, O110.

View of the
Port of
Montevideo
A88

Perf. 11½
1909, Aug. 24   Engr.   Wmk. 187
177 A88 2c lt brown & blk   1.00 1.00
178 A88 5c rose red & blk   1.00 1.00

Issued to commemorate the opening of the Port of Montevideo, Aug. 25, 1909.

8
Centésimos

Nos. 156, 91
Surcharged

Provisorio

Perf. 14 to 16
1909, Sept. 13   Unwmk.
179 A74 8c on 10c dull vio   50 15
  a.   "Centesimos"   2.00 1.10
180 A38 23c on 25c bis brn   1.00 38

Centaur — A89

Perf. 11½
1910, May 22   Wmk. 187   Engr.
182 A89 2c carmine red   40 25
183 A89 5c deep blue   40 25

Cent. of Liberation Day, Aug. 25, 1810.
The 2c in deep blue and 5c in carmine red were prepared for collectors.

Stamps of 1900-06 Surcharged

PROVISORIO
5
MILESIMOS
—1910—
a

PROVISORIO
5
Centesimos
-1910-
b

PROVISORIO
5
CENTÉSIMOS
—1910—
c

Perf. 14 to 16, 11½
1910, Oct. 6   Unwmk.
Black Surcharge
184 A72 (a) 5m on 1c yel grn   15 15
  a.   Inverted surcharge   4.50 3.75
Dark Blue Surcharge
185 A39 (b) 5c on 50c dull red   20 15
  a.   Inverted surcharge   4.50 4.50
Blue Surcharge
186 A86 (c) 5c on 50c rose   50 38
  a.   Double surcharge   20.00
  b.   Inverted surcharge   10.00 8.75

Artigas
A90

"Commercial
Progress"
A91

1910, Nov. 21   Engr.   Perf. 14, 15
187 A90 5m dk violet   15 15
188 A90 1c dp green   15 15
189 A90 2c orange red   15 15
190 A90 5c dk blue   15 15
191 A90 8c gray blk   30 15
192 A90 20c brown   50 15
193 A91 23c dp ultra   1.50 30
194 A91 50c orange   2.00 75
195 A91 1p scarlet   6.00 50
     Nos. 187-195 (9)   10.90
     Set value   2.00

See Nos. 199-210. For overprints see Nos. 211-213, O118-O124.

Symbolical of the
Posts — A92

1911, Jan. 6   Wmk. 187   Perf. 11½
196 A92 5c rose car & blk   45 35

1st South American Postal Cong., at Montevideo, Jan. 1911.

ARTIGAS
5
CENTÉSIMOS
1811-1911

No. 158 Surcharged
in Red or Dark Blue

Perf. 14 to 16
1911, May 17   Unwmk.
197 A76 2c on 7c brn org (R)   25 20
198 A76 5c on 7c brn org (Bl)   25 15
  a.   Inverted surcharge   6.00

Centenary of the battle of Las Piedras, won by the forces under Gen. Jose Gervasio Artigas, May 8, 1811.

Types of 1910

FOUR AND FIVE CENTESIMOS.
Type I - Large numerals about 3mm high.
Type II - Small numerals about 2¼mm high.

1912-15   Typo.   Perf. 11½
199 A90 5m violet   15 15
  a.   5m purple   15 15
200 A90 5m magenta   15 15
  a.   5m dull rose   15 15
201 A90 1c green ('13)   15 15
202 A90 2c brown org   15 15
203 A90 2c rose red ('13)   15 15
  a.   2c deep red ('14)   15 15
204 A90 4c org (I) ('14)   15 15
  a.   4c orange (II) ('15)   15 15
  b.   4c yellow (II) ('13)   15 15
205 A90 5c dull bl (I)   20 15
  a.   5c blue (II)   20 15
206 A90 8c ultra ('13)   30 15
207 A90 20c brown ('13)   90 15
  a.   20c chocolate   90 15
208 A91 23c dk blue ('15)   2.50 50
209 A91 50c orange ('14)   2.50 80
210 A91 1p vermilion ('15)   6.00 65
     Nos. 199-210 (12)   13.30
     Set value   2.45

CENTENARIO
DE LAS
INSTRUCCIONES
DEL
AÑO XIII

Stamps of 1912-15
Overprinted

1913, Apr. 4
211 A90 2c brown orange   40 30
  a.   Inverted overprint   5.00 4.50
212 A90 4c yellow   40 30
213 A90 5c blue   40 30

Cent. of the Buenos Aires Cong. of 1813.

Liberty Extending
Peace to the
Country — A93

1918, Jan. 3   Litho.
214 A93 2c green & red   45 30
215 A93 5c buff & blue   45 30

Promulgation of the Constitution.

Statue of
Liberty, New
York Harbor
A94

Harbor of
Montevideo
A95

Perf. 14, 15, 13½
1919, July 15   Engr.
217 A94 2c carmine & brn   25 15
218 A94 4c orange & brn   38 15
219 A94 5c blue & brn   45 15
220 A94 8c org brn & ind   65 25
221 A94 20c ol bis & blk   1.75 50
222 A94 23c green & blk   2.50 90
     Nos. 217-222 (6)   5.98 2.10

Peace at end of World War I.
Perf 13½ used only on 2c, 20c, 23c.

1919-20   Litho.   Perf. 11½
225 A95 5m violet & blk   15 15
226 A95 1c green & blk   15 15
227 A95 2c red & blk   15 15
228 A95 4c orange & blk   20 15
229 A95 5c ultra & slate   25 15
230 A95 8c gray bl & lt brn   32 15

231	A95	20c brown & blk	1.10	20
232	A95	23c green & brn	1.75	42
233	A95	50c brown & blue	3.50	1.25
234	A95	1p dull red & bl	5.25	2.00
		Nos. 225-234 (10)	12.82	4.77

For overprints see Nos. O125-O131.

José Enrique
Rodó
A96

Mercury
A97

1920, Feb. 28   Engr.   *Perf. 14, 15*
235	A96	2c car & blk		45	35
236	A96	4c org & bl		50	40
237	A96	5c bl & brn		65	45

Issued to honor José Enrique Rodó, author. For surcharges see Nos. P2-P4.

1921-22   Litho.   *Perf. 11½*
238	A97	5m lilac	15	15
239	A97	5m gray blk ('22)	15	15
240	A97	1c lt grn	15	15
241	A97	1c vio ('22)	18	15
242	A97	2c fawn	35	15
243	A97	2c red ('22)	35	15
244	A97	3c bl grn ('22)	50	15
245	A97	4c orange	35	15
246	A97	5c ultra	35	15
247	A97	5c choc ('22)	50	15
248	A97	12c ultra ('22)	1.50	38
249	A97	36c ol grn ('22)	6.00	2.00
		Nos. 238-249 (12)	10.53	
		Set value		2.95

See Nos. 254-260. For overprint and surcharge see Nos. E1, P1.

Dámaso A. Larrañaga
(1771-1848), Bishop,
Writer, Scientist and
Physician — A98

1921, Dec. 10   Unwmk.
250	A98	5c slate	1.00	75

Mercury Type of 1921-22

1922-23   Wmk. 188
254	A97	5m gray blk	15	15
255	A97	1c violet ('23)	18	15
a.		1c red violet	18	15
256	A97	2c pale red	25	15
257	A97	2c deep rose ('23)	30	15
259	A97	5c yel brn ('23)	50	15
260	A97	8c salmon pink ('23)	75	65
		Nos. 254-260 (6)	2.13	
		Set value		90

Equestrian Statue of
Artigas — A99

1923, Feb. 26   Unwmk.
Engr.   *Perf. 14*
264	A99	2c car & sepia	20	15
265	A99	5c vio & sepia	20	15
266	A99	12c blue & sepia	30	15
		Set value		35

Southern
Lapwing — A100

Perf. 12½, 11½x12½
1923, June 25   Litho.   Wmk. 189
Size: 18x22½mm
267	A100	5m gray	15	15
268	A100	1c org yel	15	15
269	A100	2c lt vio	15	15
270	A100	3c gray grn	25	15
271	A100	5c lt bl	25	15
272	A100	8c rose red	40	20
273	A100	12c dp bl	55	20
274	A100	20c brn org	90	20
275	A100	36c emerald	2.00	85
276	A100	50c orange	3.75	1.25
277	A100	1p brt rose	16.00	10.00
278	A100	2p lt grn	16.00	10.00
		Nos. 267-278 (12)	40.55	23.45

See #285-298, 309-314, 317-323, 334-339. For surcharges and overprints see Nos. 345-348, O132-O148, P5-P7.

Battle of Sarandi
Monument — A101

1923, Oct. 12   Wmk. 188   *Perf. 11½*
279	A101	2c dp grn	45	35
280	A101	5c scarlet	45	35
281	A101	12c dk bl	45	35

Unveiling of the Sarandi Battle Monument by José Luis Zorrilla, Oct. 12, 1923.

Olympic Games Issue

"Victory of Samothrace" — A102

Unwmk.
1924, July 29   Typo.   *Perf. 11*
282	A102	2c rose	11.00	8.00
283	A102	5c mauve	11.00	8.00
284	A102	12c brt bl	11.00	8.00

Sheets of 20 (5x4).
Five hundred sets of these stamps were printed on yellow paper for presentation purposes. They were not on sale at post offices. Value for set, $225.

Lapwing Type of 1923
First Redrawing
Imprint: "A. BARREIRO Y RAMOS"
Perf. 12½, 11½

1924, July 26   Litho.
Size: 17¼x21½mm
285	A100	5m gray blk	15	15
286	A100	1c fawn	15	15
287	A100	2c rose lil	30	15
288	A100	3c gray grn	20	15
289	A100	5c chalky blue	15	15
290	A100	8c pink	35	20
291	A100	10c turq blue	30	15
292	A100	12c slate blue	38	25
293	A100	15c lt vio	38	20
294	A100	20c brown	75	30
295	A100	36c salmon	3.00	70
296	A100	50c greenish gray	3.75	1.00
297	A100	1p buff	6.25	2.25
298	A100	2p dl vio	12.50	6.50
		Nos. 285-298 (14)	28.61	12.30

Landing of the 33 "Immortals" Led by
Juan Antonio Lavalleja
A103

Perf. 11, 11½
1925, Apr. 19   Wmk. 188
300	A103	2c salmon pink & blk	75	75
301	A103	5c lilac & blk	75	75
302	A103	12c blue & blk	75	75

Cent. of the landing of the 33 Founders of the Uruguayan Republic.

Legislative
Palace
A104

Perf. 11½
1925, Aug. 24   Unwmk.   Engr.
303	A104	5c vio & blk	75	50
304	A104	12c bl & blk	75	50

Dedication of the Legislative Palace.

General Fructuoso
Rivera — A105

Wmk. 188
1925, Sept. 24   Litho.   *Perf. 11*
305	A105	5c light red	30	30

Centenary of Battle of Rincón. See No. C9.

Battle of
Sarandí
A106

1925, Oct. 12   *Perf. 11½*
306	A106	2c bl grn	75	70
307	A106	5c dl vio	75	70
308	A106	12c dp bl	1.00	80

Centenary of the Battle of Sarandi.

Lapwing Type of 1923
Second Redrawing
Imprint: "Imprenta Nacional"

1925-26   *Perf. 11, 11½, 10½*
Size: 17½x21¾mm
309	A100	5m gray blk	50	15
310	A100	1c dl vio	65	15
311	A100	2c brt rose	65	15
312	A100	3c gray grn	65	25
313	A100	5c dl bl ('26)	75	15
314	A100	12c slate blue	3.00	25
		Nos. 309-314 (6)	6.20	
		Set value		70

The design differs in many small details from that of the 1923-24 issues. These stamps may be readily identified by the imprint and perforation.

Lapwing Type of 1923
Third Redrawing
Imprint: "Imp. Nacional" at center

1926-27   *Perf. 11, 11½, 10½*
Size: 17½x21¾mm
317	A100	5m gray	20	15
318	A100	1c lt vio ('27)	1.00	20
319	A100	2c red	75	15
320	A100	3c gray grn	1.00	30
321	A100	5c lt bl	75	15
322	A100	8c pink ('27)	1.50	38
323	A100	36c rose buff	6.00	2.50
		Nos. 317-323 (7)	11.20	3.83

These stamps may be distinguished from preceding stamps of the same design by the imprint.

Philatelic Exhibition Issue

Post Office at
Montevideo — A107

Unwmk.
1927, May 25   Engr.   *Imperf.*
330	A107	2c green	2.00	2.00
a.		Sheet of 4	10.00	10.00
331	A107	5c dull red	2.00	2.00
a.		Sheet of 4	10.00	10.00
332	A107	8c dark blue	2.00	2.00
a.		Sheet of 4	10.00	10.00

Printed in sheets of 4 and sold at the Montevideo Exhibition. Lithographed counterfeits exist.

Lapwing Type of 1923
Fourth Redrawing
Imprint: "Imp. Nacional" at right
Perf. 11, 11½

1927, May 6   Litho.   Wmk. 188
Size: 17¾x21¾mm
334	A100	1c gray vio	15	15
335	A100	2c vermilion	15	15
336	A100	3c gray grn	40	15
337	A100	5c blue	25	15
338	A100	8c rose	2.00	32
339	A100	20c gray brn	2.50	80
		Nos. 334-339 (6)	5.45	
		Set value		1.40

The design has been slightly retouched in various places. The imprint is in italic capitals and is placed below the right numeral of value.

Inauguración
Ferrocarril
SAN CARLOS
a ROCHA
14/1/928
5 cts. 5

No. 292 Surcharged in
Red

1928, Jan. 13   Unwmk.   *Perf. 11½*
345	A100	2c on 12c slate blue	1.10	1.10
346	A100	5c on 12c slate blue	1.10	1.10
347	A100	10c on 12c slate blue	1.10	1.10
348	A100	15c on 12c slate blue	1.10	1.10
		Nos. 345-348 (4)	4.40	4.40

Issued to celebrate the inauguration of the railroad between San Carlos and Rocha.

General
Rivera — A108

1928, Apr. 19   Engr.   *Perf. 12*
349	A108	5c car rose	25	15

Centenary of the Battle of Las Misiones.

Artigas (7 dots in panels
below portrait.) — A109

Imprint:
"Waterlow & Sons. Ltd., Londres"
***Perf. 11, 12½, 13x13½, 12½x13,
13x12½***

1928-43
Size: 16x19½mm
350	A109	5m black	15	15
350A	A109	5m org ('43)	15	15
351	A109	1c dk vio	15	15
352	A109	1c brn vio ('34)	15	15
352A	A109	1c vio bl ('43)	15	15
353	A109	2c dp grn	15	15
353A	A109	2c brn red ('43)	15	15
354	A109	3c bister	15	15
355	A109	3c dp grn ('32)	15	15
355A	A109	3c brt grn ('43)	15	15
356	A109	5c red	15	15
357	A109	5c ol grn ('33)	15	15
357A	A109	5c dl pur ('43)	15	15
358	A109	7c car ('32)	15	15
359	A109	8c dk bl	15	15
360	A109	8c brn ('33)	15	15
361	A109	10c orange	22	15
362	A109	10c red org ('32)	42	25
363	A109	12c dp bl ('32)	20	15
364	A109	15c dl bl	35	15
365	A109	17c dk vio ('32)	50	15
366	A109	20c ol brn	42	15
367	A109	20c red brn ('33)	65	35
368	A109	24c car rose	90	35
369	A109	24c yel ('33)	50	25
370	A109	36c ol grn ('33)	90	30
371	A109	50c gray	2.25	1.25

372	A109	50c blk ('33)	3.00	1.10
373	A109	50c blk brn ('33)	2.25	90
374	A109	1p yel grn	5.25	2.00
		Nos. 350-374 (30)	20.21	
		Set value		8.00

1929-33   *Perf. 12½*
Size: 22 to 22½x28½ to 29½mm

375	A109	1p ol brn ('33)	3.50	2.00
376	A109	2p dk grn	6.50	3.50
377	A109	2p dl red ('32)	14.00	10.00
378	A109	3p dk bl	9.00	6.50
379	A109	3p blk ('32)	9.00	8.00
380	A109	4p violet	14.00	11.00
381	A109	4p dk ol grn ('32)	14.00	10.00
382	A109	5p car brn	17.50	14.00
383	A109	5p red org ('32)	14.00	10.00
384	A109	10p lake ('33)	50.00	35.00
385	A109	10p dp ultra ('33)	50.00	35.00
		Nos. 375-385 (11)	201.50	145.00

See Nos. 420-423, 462. See type A135.

Equestrian Statue of
Artigas — A110

1928, May 1

386	A110	2p Prus bl & choc	6.50	3.50
387	A110	3p dp rose & blk	8.00	8.00

Symbolical of Soccer Victory — A111   Gen. Eugenio Garzón — A112

1928, July 29

388	A111	2c brn vio	6.00	5.00
389	A111	5c dp red	6.00	5.00
390	A111	8c ultra	6.00	5.00

Uruguayan soccer victories in the Olympic Games of 1924 and 1928. Printed in sheets of 20, in panes of 10 (5x2).

1928, Aug. 25   *Imperf.*

391	A112	2c red	1.00	1.00
	a.	Sheet of 4	5.00	5.00
392	A112	5c yel grn	1.00	1.00
	a.	Sheet of 4	5.00	5.00
393	A112	8c dp bl	1.00	1.00
	a.	Sheet of 4	5.00	5.00

Dedication of monument to Garzon. Issued in sheets of 4. Lithographed counterfeits exist.

Black River Bridge — A113

Gauchos Breaking a Horse — A114

Peace A115   Montevideo A116

Liberty and Flag of Uruguay A117

Liberty with Torch and Caduceus A118   Statue of Artigas A124

Artigas Dictating Instructions for 1813 Congress — A119

Seascape A120

Montevideo Harbor, 1830 — A121

Liberty and Coat of Arms — A122

Montevideo Harbor, 1930 — A123

1930, June 16   *Perf. 12½, 12*

394	A113	5m gray blk	15	15
395	A114	1c dk brn	15	15
396	A115	2c brn rose	15	15
397	A116	3c yel grn	18	15
398	A117	5c dk bl	18	15
399	A118	8c dl red	22	15
400	A119	10c dk vio	35	22
401	A120	15c bl grn	40	35
402	A121	20c indigo	55	40
403	A122	24c red brn	75	40
404	A123	50c org red	2.00	1.25
405	A124	1p black	3.75	2.00
406	A124	2p bl vio	9.00	5.75
407	A124	3p dk red	13.00	9.00
408	A124	4p red org	15.00	11.00
409	A124	5p lilac	22.50	13.00
		Nos. 394-409 (16)	68.33	44.27

Cent. of natl. independence and the promulgation of the constitution.

Type of 1856 Issue
Values in Centesimos
Wmk. 227

1931, Apr. 11   *Litho.*   *Imperf.*

410	A1	2c gray blue	1.65	1.65
	a.	Sheet of 4	8.00	8.00
411	A1	8c dull red	1.65	1.65
	a.	Sheet of 4	8.00	8.00
412	A1	15c blue black	1.65	1.65
	a.	Sheet of 4	8.00	8.00

Wmk. 188

413	A1	5c light green	1.65	1.65

Issued in sheets containing four stamps each, in commemoration of the Philatelic Exhibition at Montevideo, April 11-15, 1931. The stamps were on sale during the five days of the exhibition only.

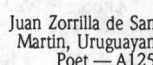

Juan Zorrilla de San Martin, Uruguayan Poet — A125

1932, June 6   *Unwmk.*   *Perf. 12½*

414	A125	1½c brown violet	15	15
415	A125	3c green	18	15
416	A125	7c dk blue	22	15
417	A125	12c lt blue	40	22
418	A125	1p deep brown	12.00	8.00
		Nos. 414-418 (5)	12.95	8.67

1 1/2

Semi-Postal Stamp No. B2
Surcharged

2/1 1

1932, Nov. 1   *Perf. 12*

419	SP1	1½c on 2c + 2c dp grn	20	15

Artigas Type of 1928
Imprint: "Imprenta Nacional" at center

1932-35   *Litho.*   *Perf. 11, 12½*
Size: 15¾x19¼mm

420	A109	5m lt brown ('35)	15	15
421	A109	1c pale violet ('35)	15	15
422	A109	15m black	18	15
423	A109	5c bluish grn ('35)	30	15
		Set value	64	32

Gen. J. A. Lavalleja A126   Flag of the Race and Globe A127

1933, July 12   *Engr.*   *Perf. 12½*

429	A126	15m brown lake	15	15

Perf. 11, 11½, 11x11½

1933, Aug. 3   *Litho.*

430	A127	3c blue green	20	15
431	A127	5c rose	25	18
432	A127	7c lt blue	25	15
433	A127	8c dull red	75	40
434	A127	12c deep blue	30	20
435	A127	17c violet	1.00	50
436	A127	20c red brown	2.00	1.25
437	A127	24c yellow	2.50	1.25
438	A127	36c orange	3.00	1.50
439	A127	50c olive gray	3.50	1.75
440	A127	1p bister	10.00	4.50
		Nos. 430-440 (11)	23.75	11.83

Raising of the "Flag of the Race" and of the 441st anniv. of the sailing of Columbus from Palos, Spain, on his first voyage to America.

Sower — A128   Juan Zorrilla de San Martin — A129

1933, Aug. 28   *Unwmk.*   *Perf. 11½*

441	A128	3c blue green	15	15
442	A128	5c dull violet	25	18
443	A128	7c lt blue	20	15
444	A128	8c deep red	50	30
445	A128	12c ultra	1.00	60
		Nos. 441-445 (5)	2.10	1.38

3rd Constituent National Assembly.

1933, Nov. 9   *Engr.*   *Perf. 12½*

446	A129	7c slate	15	15

Albatross Flying over Map of the Americas — A130

1933, Dec. 3   *Typo.*   *Perf. 11½*

447	A130	3c green, blk & brn	1.40	1.40
448	A130	7c turq bl, brn & blk	80	60
449	A130	12c dk bl, gray & ver	1.25	1.00
450	A130	17c ver, gray & vio	2.75	2.75
451	A130	20c yellow, bl & grn	3.00	3.00
452	A130	36c red, blk & yel	4.00	4.00
		Nos. 447-452 (6)	13.20	12.75

7th Pan-American Conf., Montevideo. Issued in sheets of 6. For overprints see Nos. C61-C62.

General Rivera — A131

1934, Feb.   *Engr.*   *Perf. 12½*

453	A131	3c green	15	15

Stars Representing the Three Constitutions — A132

1934, Mar. 23   *Typo.*

454	A132	3c yellow grn & grn	30	20
455	A132	7c orange red & red	30	20
456	A132	12c ultra & blue	80	40

Perf. 11½

457	A132	17c brown & rose	1.00	90
458	A132	20c yellow & gray	1.25	1.00
459	A132	36c dk vio & bl grn	1.25	1.25
460	A132	50c black & blue	3.25	2.50
461	A132	1p dk car & vio	8.00	5.25
		Nos. 454-461 (8)	16.15	11.70

First Year of Third Republic.

Artigas Type of 1928
Imprint: "Barreiro & Ramos S. A."

1934, Nov. 28   *Litho.*

462	A109	50c brown black	2.50	1.00

"Uruguay" and "Brazil" Holding Scales of Justice A133   Florencio Sánchez A134

1935, May 30   *Unwmk.*   *Perf. 11*

463	A133	5m brown	38	22
464	A133	15m black	20	20
465	A133	3c green	22	18
466	A133	7c orange	25	15
467	A133	12c ultra	65	38
468	A133	50c yellow green	2.50	2.00
		Nos. 463-468 (6)	4.20	3.13

Visit of President Vargas of Brazil.

1935, Nov. 7

469	A134	3c green	15	15
470	A134	7c brown	15	15
471	A134	12c blue	40	15
		Set value		38

Florencio Sanchez (1875-1910), author.

Artigas (6 dots in panels below portrait) — A135

Imprint: "Imprenta Nacional" at center
1936-44 Perf. 11, 12½
474	A135	5m orange brn ('37)	15	15
475	A135	5m lt brown ('39)	15	15
476	A135	1c lt violet ('37)	15	15
477	A135	2c dk brown ('37)	15	15
478	A135	2c green ('39)	15	15
479	A135	5c brt brown ('37)	15	15
480	A135	5c bluish grn ('39)	20	15
481	A135	12c dull blue ('38)	20	15
482	A135	20c fawn	75	25
482A	A135	20c rose ('44)	50	20
483	A135	50c brown black	1.50	38

Size: 21½x28½mm
483A	A135	1p brown	4.00	1.75
483B	A135	2p blue	7.50	7.00
483C	A135	3p gray black	11.25	9.00
	Nos. 474-483C (14)	26.80	19.78

See Nos. 488, 576. See type A109.

Power Dam on Black River — A136

1937-38
484	A136	1c dull violet	15	15
485	A136	10c blue	25	15
486	A136	15c rose	1.00	38
487	A136	1p choc ('38)	4.00	1.50

Imprint: "Imprenta Nacional" at right
1938
|488|A135|1c bright violet|15|15|

International Law Congress, 1889 — A137

1939, July 16 Litho. Perf. 12½
489	A137	1c brown orange	15	15
490	A137	2c dull green	18	15
491	A137	5c rose ver	18	15
492	A137	12c dull blue	38	25
493	A137	50c lt violet	1.50	1.00
	Nos. 489-493 (5)	2.39	1.70

50th anniversary of the Montevideo Congress of International Law.

Artigas A138 A138a

1939-43 Litho. Unwmk.
Size: 15¾x19mm
494	A138	5m dl brn org ('40)	15	15
495	A138	1c lt blue	15	15
496	A138	2c lt violet	15	15
497	A138	5c violet brn	15	15
498	A138	8c rose red	15	15
499	A138	10c green	20	15
500	A138	15c dull blue	50	20

Size: 24x29½mm
501	A138	1p dull brn ('41)	1.65	40
502	A138	2p dl rose vio ('40)	4.00	1.65
503	A138	4p orange ('43)	4.75	2.00
504	A138	5p ver ('41)	8.00	3.25
	Nos. 494-504 (11)	19.85	8.40

See No. 578.

Redrawn: Horizontal lines in portrait background
1940-44
Size: 17x21mm
505	A138a	5m brn org ('41)	15	15
506	A138a	1c lt blue	15	15
507	A138a	2c lt violet ('41)	15	15

508	A138a	5c violet brn	15	15
509	A138a	8c salmon pink ('44)	15	15
510	A138a	10c green ('41)	15	15
511	A138a	50c olive bis ('42)	3.75	80
511A	A138a	50c yellow grn ('44)	2.75	1.00
	Nos. 505-511A (8)	7.45	
	Set value		2.05

See Nos. 568-575, 577, 601, 632, 660-661. For surcharges see Nos. 523, 726.

Juan Manuel Blanes, Artist A139 / Francisco Acuna de Figueroa A140

1941, Aug. 11 Engr. Perf. 12½
512	A139	5m ocher	15	15
513	A139	1c henna brown	15	15
514	A139	2c green	15	15
515	A139	5c rose carmine	38	15
516	A139	12c deep blue	75	35
517	A139	50c dark violet	3.50	2.75
	Nos. 512-517 (6)	5.08	3.70

1942, Mar. 18 Unwmk.
518	A140	1c henna brown	15	15
519	A140	2c deep green	15	15
520	A140	5c rose carmine	20	15
521	A140	12c deep blue	75	40
522	A140	50c dark violet	2.25	2.00
	Nos. 518-522 (5)	3.50	2.85

Issued in honor of Francisco Acuna de Figueroa, author of the National anthem.

No. 506 Surcharged in Red
Valor $ 0.005

1943, Jan. 27
|523|A138a|5m on 1c lt bl|15|15|

Coat of Arms A141 / Clio A142

1943, Mar. 12 Litho.
524	A141	1c on 2c dl vio brn (R)	15	15
525	A141	2c on 2c dl vio brn (V)	15	15
a.		Inverted surcharge	12.50	12.50
	Set value		15

Nos. 524-525 are unissued stamps surcharged. See Nos. 546-555, Q67, Q69, Q74-Q76.

1943, Aug. 24
526	A142	5m lt violet	15	15
527	A142	1c lt ultra	15	15
528	A142	2c brt rose	25	15
529	A142	5c buff	25	15
	Set value		35

100th anniversary of the Historic and Geographic Institute of Uruguay.

Swiss Colony Monument A143 / YMCA Seal A144

Overprinted "1944" and Surcharged in Various Colors
1944, May 18
530	A143	1c on 3c dull grn (R)	15	15
531	A143	5c on 7c brn red (B)	15	15
532	A143	10c on 12c dk bl (Br)	30	18
	Set value		30

50th anniversary of the founding of the Swiss Colony.

1944, Sept. 8
|533|A144|5c blue|15|15|

100th anniv. of the YMCA.

> Catalogue values for unused stamps in this section, from this point to the end of the section, are for Never Hinged items.

"La Educación del Pueblo" A145 / José Pedro Varela A146

Monument A147 A148

Perf. 11½
1945, June 13 Litho. Unwmk.
534	A145	5m brt green	15	15
535	A146	1c dp brown	15	15

Perf. 12½
536	A147	2c rose red	15	15
537	A148	5c blue	20	15
a.		Perf. 11½	16	15
	Set value	55	25

Centenary of the birth of José Pedro Varela, author.

Santiago Vazquez — A149 / Silvestre Blanco — A150

Eduardo Acevedo — A151 / Bruno Mauricio de Zabala — A152

José Pedro Varela — A153 / José Ellauri — A154

Gen. Luis de Larrobla — A155

Engraved (5m, 5c, 10c); Lithographed
1945-47 Perf. 10½, 11, 11½, 12½
538	A149	5m purple ('46)	15	15
539	A150	1c yel brn ('46)	15	15
540	A151	2c brown vio	15	15
541	A152	3c grn & dp grn ('47)	15	15
542	A153	5c brt carmine	16	15
543	A154	10c ultra	32	15
544	A155	20c dp grn & choc ('47)	85	38
	Set value	1.65	80

No. C86A Surcharged in Blue

CORREO INAUGURACIÓN DICIEMBRE, 1945 20 CENTS

1946, Jan. 9 Perf. 12½
|545|AP7|20c on 68c pale vio brn|85|45|

Inauguration of the Black River Power Dam. See No. C120.

Type A141 Overprinted **0.02**

1946-51 Unwmk. Litho. Perf. 12½
546	A141	5m orange ('49)	15	15
a.		Inverted overprint		
547	A141	2c dl vio brn ('47)	15	15
548	A141	3c green	15	15
549	A141	5c ultra ('51)	15	15
550	A141	10c orange brn	16	15
551	A141	20c dk green	48	15
552	A141	50c brown	1.40	50
553	A141	3p lilac rose	5.50	3.00
	Nos. 546-553 (8)	8.14	
	Set value		3.85

Type A141 Surcharged

1947-48
554	A141	2c on 5c ultra ('48)	15	15
555	A141	3c on 5c ultra	15	15
	Set value	20	15

Statue of Ariel — A158 / Bas-relief — A160

Bust of José Enrique Rodó — A159 / Bas-relief — A161

Perf. 12½
1948, Jan. 30 Unwmk. Engr.
Center in Orange Brown
556	A158	1c grnsh gray	15	15
557	A159	2c purple	15	15
558	A160	3c green	15	15

559 A161	5c red violet		16	15
560 A160	10c dp orange		20	15
561 A161	12c ultra		28	15
562 A158	20c rose violet		55	25
563 A159	50c dp carmine		2.00	90
	Nos. 556-563 (8)		3.64	
	Set value			1.50

Dedication of the Rodó monument.

View of the
Port, Paysandú
A162

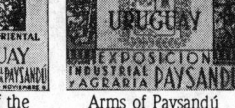

Arms of Paysandú
A163

1948, Oct. 9   **Litho.**

564 A162	3c blue green		16	15
565 A163	7c ultra		28	15
	Set value			16

Issued to publicize the Exposition of Industry and Agriculture, Paysandú, October-November 1948.

Santa Lucia
River Highway
Bridge — A164

1948, Dec. 10

566 A164	10c dark blue		40	15
567 A164	50c green		1.65	65

Redrawn Artigas Types of 1940, 1936, 1939

1948-51   **Litho.**   **Perf. 12½**

568 A138a	5m gray ('49)		15	15
569 A138a	1c rose vio ('50)		15	15
570 A138a	2c orange		15	15
571 A138a	2c choc ('50)		15	15
572 A138a	3c blue green		15	15
572A A138a	7c violet blue		15	15
573 A138a	8c rose car ('49)		20	15
574 A138a	10c orange brn ('51)		15	15
575 A138a	12c blue ('51)		15	15
576 A135	20c violet		32	15
577 A138a	20c rose pink ('51)		55	15

Size: 18x21¾mm

578 A138	1p lilac rose ('51)		1.10	25
	Set value		2.85	85

Nos. 571-572A also exist perf. 11.

Plowing
A165

Mounted
Cattle
Herder
A166

1949, Apr. 29   **Unwmk.**   **Perf. 12½**

579 A165	3c green		15	15
580 A166	7c blue		20	15
	Set value			15

4th Regional American Conf. of Labor, 1949.

Cannon, Rural and
Urban Views — A167

Symbolical of
Soccer
Matches — A168

1950, Oct. 11   **Litho.**

581 A167	1c lilac rose		15	15
582 A167	3c green		15	15
583 A167	7c deep blue		15	15
	Set value		28	15

200th anniv. of the founding of Cordón, a district of Montevideo.

1951, Mar. 20

584 A168	3c green		50	15
585 A168	7c violet blue		1.00	25

4th World Soccer Championship, Rio de Janeiro.

Gen. José
Artigas — A169

Flight of the
People
A170

Designs: 1c, 2c, 5c, Various equestrian portraits of Artigas. 7c, Dictating instructions. 8c, In congress. 10c, Artigas' flag. 14c, At the citadel. 20c, Arms of Artigas. 50c, In Paraguay. 1p, Bust.

Engraved and Photogravure

1952, Jan. 7   **Unwmk.**   **Perf. 13½**

586 A169	5m slate		15	15
587 A169	1c bl & blk		15	15
588 A169	2c pur & red brn		15	15
589 A170	3c aqua & dk brn		15	15
590 A169	5c red org & blk		15	15
591 A170	7c ol & blk		16	15
592 A170	8c car & blk		25	15
593 A170	10c choc, brt ultra & crim		28	15
594 A169	14c dp bl		28	15
595 A169	20c org yel, dp ultra & car		40	15
596 A169	50c org brn & blk		85	32
597 A169	1p bl gray & cit		2.25	90
	Nos. 586-597 (12)		5.22	
	Set value			1.80

Centenary (in 1950) of the death of Gen. José Artigas.

Plane and
Stagecoach
A171

1952, Oct. 9   **Photo.**   **Perf. 13½x13**

598 A171	3c bl grn		15	15
599 A171	7c blk brn		15	15
600 A171	12c ultra		16	15
	Set value		16	

75th anniv. (in 1949) of the UPU.

Redrawn Artigas Type of 1940-44

1953, Feb. 23   **Litho.**   **Perf. 11**
Size: 24x29½mm

601 A138a	2p fawn		4.50	2.00

Franklin D.
Roosevelt — A172

1953, Apr. 9   **Engr.**   **Perf. 13½**

602 A172	3c green		15	15
603 A172	7c ultra		15	15
604 A172	12c blk brn		24	15
	Set value		45	20

5th Postal Congress of the Americas and Spain.

Ceibo, Natl.
Flower — A173

Horse
Breaking — A174

Legislature
Building
A175

"Island of Seals"
(Southern Sea Lions)
A176

Fair Entrance
A177

Designs: 2c, 10c, 5p, Ombu tree. 3c, 50c, Passion Flower. 7c, 3p, Montevideo fortress. 12c, 2p, Outer gate, Montevideo.

Perf. 13x13½, 13½x13, 12½x13, 13x12½

Photo. (5m, 3c, 20c, 50c); Engr.

1954, Jan. 14   **Unwmk.**

605 A173	5m multi		15	15
606 A174	1c car & blk		15	15
607 A174	2c brn & grn		15	15
608 A173	3c multi		15	15
609 A175	5c pur & red brn		15	15
610 A173	7c brn & grn		15	15
611 A176	8c car & ultra		25	15
612 A174	10c org & grn		18	15
613 A175	12c dp ultra & dk brn		15	15
614 A174	14c rose lil & blk		15	15
615 A173	20c grn, brn, gray & car		35	15
616 A173	50c car & multi		70	15
617 A175	1p car & red brn		1.25	40
618 A175	2p car & blk brn		2.50	80
619 A173	3p lil & grn		2.75	80
620 A176	4p dp brn & dp ultra		7.25	3.25
621 A174	5p vio bl & grn		6.50	2.50
	Nos. 605-621 (17)		22.93	
	Set value			8.25

For surcharges see Nos. 637-639, 750, C299.

1956, Jan. 19   **Litho.**   **Perf. 11**

622 A177	3c pale olive green		15	15
623 A177	7c blue		15	15
	Set value		15	15

Issued to publicize the First Exposition of National Products. See Nos. C166-C168.

José Batlle y
Ordonez — A178

Design: 7c, Full length portrait.

Perf. 13½

1956, Dec. 15   **Wmk. 90**   **Photo.**

624 A178	3c rose red		15	15
625 A178	7c sepia		16	15
	Set value			15

Centenary of the birth of President José Batlle y Ordonez. See Nos. C169-C172.

Same Surcharged with New Values

1957-58

626 A178	5c on 3c ('58)		15	15
627 A178	10c on 7c		16	15
a.	Surcharge inverted		17.00	17.00
	Set value			15

Diver — A179

Eduardo
Acevedo — A180

Design: 10c, Swimmer at start (horiz.).

Perf. 10½, 11½

1958, Feb. 15   **Litho.**   **Unwmk.**

628 A179	5c brt bl grn		16	15
629 A179	10c brt bl		32	15
	Set value			18

14th South American swimming meet, Montevideo.

1958, Mar. 19   **Perf. 11½, 10½**

630 A180	5c lt ol grn & blk		15	15
631 A180	10c ultra & blk		20	15

Issued to commemorate the centenary of the birth of Eduardo Acevedo (1856-1948), lawyer, legislator, minister of foreign affairs.

Artigas Type of 1940-44

1958, Sept. 25   **Litho.**   **Perf. 11**

632 A138a	5m blue		15	15

Baygorria
Hydroelectric
Works
A181

1958, Oct. 30   **Unwmk.**   **Perf. 11**

633 A181	5c yel grn & blk		15	15
634 A181	10c brn org & blk		15	15
635 A181	1p bl gray & blk		32	15
636 A181	2p rose & blk		75	30
	Set value		1.20	60

Nos. 608, 610 and 605
Surcharged Similarly to

Photogravure and Engraved

1958-59   **Perf. 13x13½**

637 A173	5c on 3c multi ('59)		15	15
638 A173	10c on 7c brn & grn		15	15
639 A173	20c on 5m multi		15	15
	Set value		22	16

Gabriela Mistral
A182

Carlos Vaz
Ferreira
A183

Perf. 11½

1959, July 6   Litho.   Wmk. 327
640 A182 5c green   15 15
641 A182 10c dark blue   15 15
642 A182 20c red   15 15
  Set value   25 15

Gabriela Mistral, Chilean poet and educator.

1959, Sept. 3   Perf. 11
643 A183 5c blk & lt bl   15 15
644 A183 10c blk & ocher   15 15
645 A183 20c blk & ver   15 15
646 A183 50c blk & vio   24 15
647 A183 1p blk & grn   40 15
  Set value   80 35

Ferreira (1872-1958), educator and author.

A184

A185

Wmk. 332
1960, May 16   Litho.   Perf. 12
648 A184 3c red lil & blk   15 15
649 A184 5c dp vio & blk   15 15
650 A184 10c brt bl & blk   15 15
651 A184 20c choc & blk   15 15
652 A184 1p gray & blk   24 15
653 A184 2p org & blk   50 15
654 A184 3p ol grn & blk   85 30
655 A184 4p yel brn & blk   1.40 70
656 A184 5p brt red & blk   1.65 70
  Nos. 648-656 (9)   5.24
  Set value   2.10

Dr. Martin C. Martinez (1859-1940), statesman.

1960, June 6   Wmk. 332   Perf. 12
657 A185 10c Uprooted oak emblem   15 15

Issued to publicize World Refugee Year, July 1, 1959-June 30, 1960. See No. C207.

Revolutionists
and Cabildo,
Buenos Aires
A186

1960, Nov. 4   Litho.   Perf. 12
658 A186 5c bl & blk   15 15
659 A186 10c bl & ocher   15 15
  Set value, #658-659,
  C208-C210   60 40

150th anniversary of the May Revolution of 1810.

Artigas Type of 1940-44

1960-61   Wmk. 332   Perf. 11
660 A138a 2c gray   15 15
661 A138a 50c brn ('61)   15 15
  Set value   15 15

Gen. Manuel Oribe
(1796?-1857),
Revolutionary Leader,
Pres. of Uruguay (1835-38) — A187

1961, Mar. 4   Litho.   Perf. 12
671 A187 10c brt bl & blk   15 15
672 A187 20c bis & blk   15 15
673 A187 40c grn & blk   15 15
  Set value   26 18

Cavalry
Charge
A188

1961, June 12   Wmk. 332   Perf. 12
674 A188 20c bl & blk   15 15
675 A188 40c emer & blk   24 15
  Set value   15

150th anniversary of the revolution.

Welfare, Justice and
Education — A189

Gen. José
Fructuoso
Rivera — A190

1961, Aug. 14   Wmk. 322   Perf. 12
676 A189 2c bis & lil   15 15
677 A189 5c bis & org   15 15
678 A189 10c bis & scar   15 15
679 A189 20c bis & yel grn   15 15
680 A189 50c bis & lt vio   15 15
681 A189 1p bis & blue   20 15
682 A189 2p bis & citron   52 20
683 A189 3p bis & gray   70 48
684 A189 4p bis & lt bl   1.10 60
685 A189 5p bis & choc   1.25 75
  Nos. 676-685 (10)   4.52
  Set value   2.45

Inter-American Economic and Social Conference of the Organization of American States, Punta del Este, August, 1961. See Nos. C233-C244.

Wmk. 332
1962, May 29   Litho.   Perf. 12
686 A190 10c brt red & blk   15 15
687 A190 20c bis & blk   15 15
688 A190 40c grn & blk   16 15
  Set value   30 18

Issued to honor Gen. José Fructuoso Rivera (1790-1854), first President of Uruguay.

Spade, Grain, Swiss
"Scarf" and
Hat — A191

Bernardo
Prudencio
Berro — A192

1962, Aug. 1   Wmk. 332   Perf. 12
689 A191 10c bl, blk & car   15 15
690 A191 20c lt grn, blk & car   15 15
  Set value   15 15

Issued to commemorate the centenary of the Swiss Settlement in Uruguay. See Nos. C245-C246.

1962, Oct. 22   Litho.   Perf. 12
691 A192 10c grnsh bl & blk   15 15
692 A192 20c yel brn & blk   15 15
  Set value   15 15

Pres. Bernardo P. Berro (1803-1868).

Damaso
Larrañaga
A193

1963, Jan. 24   Wmk. 332   Perf. 12
693 A193 20c lt bl grn & dk brn   15 15
694 A193 40c tan & dk brn   15 15

Damaso Antonio Larranaga (1771-1848), teacher, writer and founder of National Library.

Rufous-bellied Thrush — A194

Birds: 50c, Rufous ovenbird. 1p, Chalkbrowed mockingbird. 2p, Rufous-collared sparrow.

1963, Apr. 1   Wmk. 332   Perf. 12
695 A194 2c rose, brn & blk   15 15
696 A194 50c lt brn & blk   32 15
697 A194 1p tan, brn & blk   50 20
698 A194 2p lt brn, blk & gray   1.40 38
  Set value   70

Thin frame on No. 696, no frame on No. 698.

UPAE
Emblem
A195

1963, May 31   Litho.
699 A195 20c ultra & blk   15 15

50th anniv. of the founding of the Postal Union of the Americas and Spain, UPAE. See Nos. C252-C253. For surcharge see No. C321.

Wheat
Emblem — A196

Anchors — A197

1963, July 8   Wmk. 332   Perf. 12
700 A196 10c grn & yel   15 15
701 A196 20c brn & yel   15 15
  Set value   15 15

FAO "Freedom from Hunger" campaign. See Nos. C254-C255.

1963, Aug. 16
702 A197 10c org & vio   15 15
703 A197 20c dk red & gray   15 15
  Set value   15 15

Voyage around the world by the Uruguayan sailing vessel "Alferez Campora," 1960-63. See Nos. C256-C257.

Large Intestine,
Congress
Emblem — A198

1963, Dec. 9   Litho.
704 A198 10c lt grn, blk & dk car   15 15
705 A198 20c org, yel, blk & dk car 15 15
  Set value   15 15

Issued to commemorate the First Uruguayan Proctology Congress, Montevideo, Dec. 9-15.

Red Cross
Centenary
Emblem
A199

Imprint: "Imp. Nacional"

1964, June 5   Wmk. 332   Perf. 12
706 A199 20c blue & red   15 15
707 A199 40c gray & red   16 15
  Set value   16 15

Centenary of International Red Cross. No. 706 exists with imprint missing.

Luis Alberto
de Herrera
A200

1964, July 22   Litho.   Unwmk.
708 A200 20c dl grn, bl & blk   15 15
709 A200 40c lt bl, bl & blk   15 15
710 A200 80c yel org, bl & blk   15 15
711 A200 1p lt vio, bl & blk   16 15
712 A200 2p gray, bl & blk   28 18
  Set value   65 42

Herrera (1873-1959), leader of Herrerista party and member of National Government Council.

Nile Gods
Uniting
Upper and
Lower Egypt
(Abu Simbel)
A201

1964, Oct. 30   Wmk. 332   Perf. 12
713 A201 20c multi   15 15

UNESCO world campaign to save historic monuments in Nubia. See Nos. C266-C267 and souvenir sheet No. C267a.

Pres. John F.
Kennedy
A202

1965, Mar. 5   Wmk. 327   Perf. 11½
714 A202 20c gold, emer & blk   15 15
  a. Gold omitted
715 A202 40c gold, redsh brn & blk   15 15
  a. Gold omitted
  Set value   15 15

Issued in memory of Pres. John F. Kennedy (1917-63). See Nos. C269-C270.

Tete Beche
Pair of
1864, No.
21a
A203

1965, Mar. 19   Wmk. 332   *Perf. 12*
716 A203 40c blk & grn   15 15

1st Rio de la Plata Stamp Show, sponsored jointly by the Argentine and Uruguayan philatelic associations, Montevideo, Mar. 19-28. See No. C271.

Benito Nardone
A204

Design: 40c, Benito Nardone before microphone, vert.

1965, Mar. 25   Litho.
717 A204 20c blk & emer   15 15
718 A204 40c blk & emer   15 15
              Set value   15 15

1st anniversary of the death of Benito Nardone, president of the Council of Government.

Artigas
Quotation
A205

Designs: 40c, Artigas bust and quotation. 80c, José Artigas.

**   *Perf. 12x11½***
1965, May 17   Litho.   Wmk. 327
719 A205 20c bl, yel & red   15 15
720 A205 40c vio bl, cit & blk   15 15
721 A205 80c brn, yel, red & bl   15 15
              Set value, #719-721,   32 20
              C273-C275   60 40

José Artigas (1764-1850), leader of the independence revolt against Spain.

Soccer
A206

Designs: 40c, Basketball. 80c, Bicycling. 1p, Woman swimmer.

1965, Aug. 3   Litho.   Wmk. 327
722 A206 20c grn, org & blk   15 15
723 A206 40c hn brn, cit & blk   15 15
724 A206 80c gray, red & blk   15 15
725 A206 1p bl, yel grn & blk   15 15
              Set value   32 20

18th Olympic Games, Tokyo, Oct. 10-25, 1964. See Nos. C276-C281.

No. 572A Surcharged in
Red   **10c**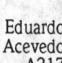

1965   Unwmk.   *Perf. 12½*
726 A138a 10c on 7c vio bl   15 15

No. B5 Surcharged:

4c.

CINCUENTENARIO
Sociedad Arquitectos
del Uruguay

1966, Jan. 25   Wmk. 327   *Perf. 11½*
727 SP2 4c on 5c + 10c grn & org   15 15

Association of Uruguayan Architects, 50th anniv.

Winston
Churchill
A207

Wmk. 332
1966, Apr. 29   Litho.   *Perf. 12*
728 A207 40c car, dp ultra & brn   15 15

Sir Winston Spencer Churchill, statesman and World War II leader. See No. C284.

Arms of Rio de
Janeiro and
Sugar Loaf
Mountain
A208

1966, June 9   Litho.   Wmk. 332
729 A208 40c emer & brn   15 15

400th anniversary of the founding of Rio de Janeiro. See No. C285.

Army   Daniel Fernandez
Engineer — A209   Crespo — A210

1966, June 17   Litho.
730 A209 20c blk, red, vio bl & yel   15 15

50th anniversary of the Army Engineers Corps.

1966, Sept. 16   Wmk. 332   *Perf. 12*
Portraits: No. 732, Washington Beltran. No. 733, Luis Batlle Berres.

731 A210 20c lt bl & blk   15 15
732 A210 20c lt bl & dk brn   15 15
733 A210 20c brick red & blk   15 15
              Set value   36 30

Issued to honor political leaders.

Old Printing
Press — A211

1966, Oct. 14   Photo.   *Perf. 12*
734 A211 20c tan, grnsh gray & dk brn 15 15

50th anniversary of State Printing Office.

Fireman
A212

1966   Litho.
735 A212 20c red & blk   28 15

Issued to publicize fire prevention. Printed with alternating red and black label inscribed: "Prevengase del fuego! Del pueblo y para el pueblo."

No. 716 Overprinted in Red: "Segunda Muestra y / Jornadas Rioplatenses / de Filatelia / Abril 1966 / Centenario del Sello / Escudito Resellado"

1966, Nov. 4
736 A203 40c blk & grn   15 15

2nd Rio de la Plata Stamp Show, Buenos Aires, Apr. 1966, and cent. of Uruguay's 1st surcharged issue. See No. C298.

General Leandro
Gomez — A213

Designs: No. 738, Gen. Juan Antonio Lavalleja. No. 739, Aparicio Saravia, revolutionary, on horseback, horiz.

Wmk. 332
1966, Nov. 24   Litho.   *Perf. 12*
737 A213 20c slate, blk & dp bl   15 15
738 A213 20c red, blk & bl   15 15
739 A213 20c blue & blk   15 15
              Set value   30 22

Montevideo
Planetarium
A214

1967, Jan. 13   Wmk. 332   *Perf. 12*
740 A214 40c pink & blk   28 15

10th anniv. of the Montevideo Municipal Planetarium. See No. C301.

Sunflower, Cow   Church of San
and   Carlos — A216
Emblem — A215

1967, Jan. 13   Litho.
741 A215 40c dk brn & yel   28 15

20th anniversary of the Young Farmers' Movement.

1967, Apr. 17   Wmk. 332   *Perf. 12*
742 A216 40c lt bl, blk & dk red   16 15

Bicentenary of San Carlos.

Eduardo
Acevedo
A217

1967, Apr. 17
743 A217 20c grn & brn   15 15
744 A217 40c org & grn   15 15
              Set value   24 15

Issued to honor Eduardo Acevedo, lawyer, legislator and Minister of Foreign Affairs.

Arms of   José Enrique Rodó
Carmelo   A219
A218

1967, Aug. 11   Litho.   *Perf. 12*
745 A218 40c lt & dk bl & ocher   16 15

150th anniversary of the founding of Carmelo.

1967, Oct. 6   Wmk. 332   *Perf. 12*
Design: 2p, Portrait of Rodó and sculpture, horiz.

746 A219 1p gray, brn & blk   15 15
747 A219 2p rose cl, blk & tan   15 15
              Set value   22 15

50th anniversary of the death of José Enrique Rodó, author.

Senen M.
Rodriguez and
Locomotive
A220

1967, Oct. 26   Litho.   *Perf. 12*
748 A220 2p ocher & dk brn   28 15

Centenary of the founding of the first national railroad company.

Child and Map   Cocoi Heron
of Americas   A222
A221

1967, Nov. 10   Wmk. 332   *Perf. 12*
749 A221 1p vio & red   16 15

40th anniversary of the Inter-American Children's Institute.

No. 610 Surcharged
in Red

1.00 PESO

Perf. 13x13½
1967, Nov. 10   Engr.   Unwmk.
750 A173 1p on 7c brn & grn   15 15

1968-70 Wmk. 332 Litho. Perf. 12

Birds: 1p, Great horned owl. 3p, Brown-headed gull, horiz. No. 754, White-faced tree duck, horiz. No. 754A, Black-tailed stilts. 5p, Wattled jacanas, horiz. 10p, Snowy egret, horiz.

751	A222	1p dl yel & brn	15	15
752	A222	2p bl grn & blk	15	15
753	A222	3p org, gray & blk ('69)	15	15
754	A222	4p brn, tan & blk	24	15
754A	A222	4p ver & blk ('70)	24	15
755	A222	5p lt red brn, blk & yel	25	15
756	A222	10p lil & blk	60	15
		Nos. 751-756 (7)	1.78	
		Set value		50

Concord Bridge, Presidents of Uruguay, Brazil
A223

1968, Apr. 3
757 A223 6p brown   16 15

Opening of Concord Bridge across the Uruguay River by Presidents Jorge Pacheco Areco of Uruguay and Arthur Costa e Silva of Brazil.

Soccer Player and Trophy — A224

1968, May 29   Litho.
758 A224 1p blk & yel   24 15

Victory of the Penarol Athletic Club in the Intercontinental Soccer Championships of 1966.

St. John Bosco, Symbols of Education and Industry
A225

1968, July 31   Wmk. 332   Perf. 12
759 A225 2p brn & blk   16 15

75th anniv. of the Don Bosco Workshops of the Salesian Brothers.

Sailors' Monument, Montevideo
A226

Designs: 6p, Lighthouse and buoy, vert. 12p, Gunboat "Suarez" (1860).

1968, Nov. 12   Litho.   Perf. 12

760	A226	2p gray ol & blk	15	15
761	A226	6p lt grn & blk	15	15
762	A226	12p brt bl & blk	16	15
		Set value, #760-762,		
		C340-C343	85	48

Sesquicentennial of National Navy.
For surcharge see No. Q101.

Oscar D. Gestido — A227

1968, Dec. 6   Wmk. 332   Perf. 12
763 A227 6p brn, dp car & bl   16 15

Issued to commemorate the first anniversary of the death of President Oscar D. Gestido.

Gearwheel, Grain and Two Heads — A228

1969, Mar. 17   Litho.   Perf. 12
764 A228 2p blk & ver   16 15

25th anniversary of Labor University.

Bicyclists A229

1969, Mar. 21   Wmk. 332
765 A229 6p dk bl, org & emer   28 15

1968 World Bicycle Championships. See No. C347.

Gymnasts and Club Emblem A230

1969, May 8   Wmk. 332   Perf. 12
766 A230 6p blk & ver   28 15

75th anniversary of L'Avenir Athletic Club.

Baltasar Brum (1883-1933) — A231

Former presidents: No. 768, Tomas Berreta (1875-1947).

1969   Litho.   Perf. 12

767	A231	6p rose red & blk	16	15
768	A231	6p car rose & blk	16	15
		Set value		16

Fair Emblem — A232

1969, Aug. 15   Wmk. 332   Perf. 12
769 A232 2p multi   16 15

Issued to publicize the 2nd Industrial World's Fair, Montevideo, 1970.

Diesel Locomotive A233

Design: No. 771, Old steam locomotive and modern railroad cars.

1969, Sept. 19   Litho.   Wmk. 332

770	A233	6p car, blk & ultra	28	15
771	A233	6p car, blk & ultra	28	15
e.		Pair, #770-771	56	30

Centenary of Uruguayan railroads. No. 771e has continuous design and label between pairs.
For surcharges see Nos. Q102-Q103.

Souvenir Sheet

Diligencia Issue, 1856 — A233a

1969, Oct. 1   Imperf.

771A	A233a	Sheet of 3	3.00	3.00
b.		60p blue	65	65
c.		80p green	85	85
d.		100p red	1.00	1.00

Stamp Day 1969. No. 771A contains stamps similar to No. 1-3, with denominations in pesos.
No. 771A was re-issued Apr. 15, 1972, with black overprint for 15th anniv. of 1st Lufthansa flight from Uruguay to Germany and the Munich Olympic Games.

"Combat" and Sculptor Belloni — A234

1969, Oct. 22   Wmk. 332   Perf. 12
772 A234 6p olive, slate grn & blk   16 15

José L. Belloni (1882-), sculptor.

Reserve Officers' Training Center Emblem A235

Design: 2p, Training Center emblem, and officer in uniform and as civilian.

1969, Nov. 5   Litho.

773	A235	1p yel & dk bl	15	15
774	A235	2p dk brn & lt bl	20	15
		Set value		15

Reserve Officers' Training Center, 25th anniv.

Map of Americas and Sun — A236

Stylized Pine — A237

1970, Apr. 20   Wmk. 332   Perf. 12
775 A236 10p dp bl & gold   20 20

11th meeting of the governors of the Inter-American Development Bank, Punta del Este.

1970, May 14
776 A237 2p red, blk & brt grn   15 15

2nd National Forestry and Wood Exhibition.

Artigas' Ancestral Home in Sauce A238

1970, June 18   Wmk. 332   Perf. 12
777 A238 15p ver, ultra & blk   24 24

Map of Uruguay, Sun and Sea — A239

1970, July 8   Litho.
778 A239 5p greenish blue   15 15

Issued for tourist publicity.

EXPO '70 Emblem, Mt. Fuji and Uruguay Coat of Arms — A240

EXPO '70 Intl. Exhibition, Osaka, Japan, 3/15-9/13: No. 780, Geisha. No. 781, Sun Tower. No. 782, Youth pole.

1970, Aug. 5   Wmk. 332   Perf. 12

779	A240	25p grn, slate bl & yel	28	28
780	A240	25p org, slate bl & grn	28	28
781	A240	25p yel, slate bl & pur	28	28
782	A240	25p pur, slate bl & org	28	28
a.		Block of 4, #779-782	1.15	1.15

Cobbled Street in
Colonia del
Sacramento
A241

Mother and Son
by Edmundo Prati
in Salto
A242

1970, Oct. 21   Litho.   Perf. 12
783 A241 5p blk & multi   15 15

290th anniv. of the founding of Colonia del Sacramento, the 1st European settlement in Uruguay.

1970, Nov. 4   Litho.
784 A242 10p grn & blk   28 28

Issued to honor mothers.

URUEXPO
Emblem
A243

1970, Dec. 9   Wmk. 332   Perf. 12
785 A243 15p bl, brn org & vio   28 28

URUEXPO '70, National Philatelic Exposition, Montevideo, Sept. 26-Oct. 4.

Children Holding Hands, and UNESCO
Emblem — A244

Children's Drawings: No. 786, Two girls holding hands, vert. No. 788, Boy sitting at school desk, vert. No. 789, Astronaut and monster.

1970, Dec. 29   Litho.   Perf. 12½
786 A244 10p multi   16 16
787 A244 10p multi   16 16
788 A244 10p dp car & multi   16 16
789 A244 10p bl & multi   16 16
a.   Block of 4, #786-789 + 2 labels   75 75

International Education Year.

Alfonso Espinola (1845-
1905), Physician,
Professor and
Philanthropist — A245

1971, Jan. 13   Wmk. 332   Perf. 12
790 A245 5p dp org & blk   15 15

Exposition Poster — A246

1971   Litho.   Perf. 12
791 A246 15p multi   20 20

Uruguay Philatelic Exposition, 1971, Montevideo, March 26-Apr. 19.

5c Coin of
1840,
Obverse
A247

Design: #793, 1st coin of Uruguay, reverse.

1971, Apr. 16   Wmk. 332   Perf. 12
792 A247 25p bl, brn & blk   38 38
793 A247 25p bl, brn & blk   38 38
a.   Pair, #792-793   80 80

Numismatists' Day.

Domingo Arena,
Lawyer and
Journalist — A248

1971, May 3   Wmk. 332   Perf. 12
794 A248 5p dk car   15 15

National
Anthem
A249

1971, May 19   Litho.
795 A249 15p bl, blk & yel   30 30

José F. Arias,
Physician — A250

1971, May 25   Wmk. 332   Perf. 12
796 A250 5p sepia   15 15

Eduardo
Fabini, Bar
from
"Campo"
A251

1971, June 2   Litho.
797 A251 5p dk car rose & blk   30 30

Eduardo Fabini (1882-1950), composer, and 40th anniversary of first radio concert.

José E. Rodó,
UPAE Emblem
A252

1971, July 15   Wmk. 332   Perf. 12
798 A252 15p ultra & blk   20 20

José Enrique Rodó (1871-1917), writer, first Uruguayan delegate to Congress of the Postal Union of the Americas and Spain.

Water Cart
and Faucet
A253

1971, July 17
799 A253 5p ultra & multi   15 15

Centenary of Montevideo's drinking water system.

Sheep and
Cloth
A254

Design: 15p, Sheep, cloth and bale of wool.

1971, Aug. 7
800 A254 5p grn & gray   15 15
801 A254 15p dk bl, grnsh bl & gray 20 20

Wool Promotion.

José Maria
Elorza and
Merilin
Sheep
A255

1971, Aug. 10
802 A255 5p lt bl, grn & blk   15 15

José Maria Elorza, developer of the Merilin sheep.

Criollo
Horse — A256

1971, Aug. 11
803 A256 5p blk, gray bl & org   15 15

Bull and
Ram
A257

1971, Aug. 13
804 A257 20p red, grn, blk & gold   30 30

Centenary of Rural Association of Uruguay; 19th International Cattle Breeding Exposition, and 66th National Cattle Championships at Prado, Aug. 1971.

Symbol of
Liberty and
Order
A258

Design: 20p, Policemen, flag of Uruguay and emblem.

1971
805 A258 10p gray, blk & bl   15 15
806 A258 20p dk bl, blk, lt bl & gold 25 25

To honor policemen killed on duty. Issue dates: 10p, Sept. 9; 20p, Nov. 4.

10p Banknote of 1896 — A259

Design: No. 808, Reverse of 10p note.

1971, Sept. 23
807 A259 25p dl grn, gold & blk   30 30
808 A259 25p dl grn, gold & blk   30 30

75th anniversary of Bank of the Republic. Printed se-tenant in sheets of 20 stamps and 5 labels.

Farmer and
Arms of
Durazno
A260

1971, Oct. 11
809 A260 20p gold, bl & blk   20 20

Sesquicentennial of the founding of Durazno.

Emblem and Laurel — A261

1971, Oct. 20
810 A261 10p vio bl, gold & red   15 15

Winners of Liberator's Cup, American Soccer Champions, 1971.
For surcharge see No. 825.

Voter Casting
Ballot — A262

Design: 20p, Citizens voting, horiz.

1971, Nov. 22   Wmk. 332   Perf. 12
811 A262 10p bl & blk   15 15
812 A262 20p bl & blk   20 20

Universal, secret and obligatory franchise.

Map of Uruguay on Globe — A263

1971, Dec. 23
813 A263 20p lt bl & vio brn   25 25

7th Littoral Expo., Paysandu, Mar. 26-Apr. 11.

URUGUAY Juan Lindolfo Cuestas — A264

1971, Dec. 27
814 A264 10p shown   15 15
815 A264 10p Julio Herrera y Obes   15 15
816 A264 10p Claudio Williman   15 15
817 A264 10p José Serrato   15 15
818 A264 10p Andres Martinez Truebá   15 15
a.   Horiz. strip of 5, #814-818   55 55
       Set value   40 40

Presidents of Uruguay.

Souvenir Sheet

Uruguay No. 4, Cathedral of Montevideo and Plaza de la Constitucion — A265

1972, Jan. 17   *Imperf.*
819 A265 120p brn, bl & dp rose   50 50

Stamp Day 1971 (release date delayed). See Nos. 834-835, 863.

Bartolomé Hidalgo   Missa Solemnis,
A266   by Beethoven
                      A267

1972, Feb. 28   *Perf. 12*
820 A266 5p lt brn, blk & red   15 15

Bartolomé Hidalgo (1788-1822), Uruguayan-Argentine poet.

1972, Apr. 20   Litho.   Wmk. 332
822 A267 20p lil, emer & blk   15 15

12th Choir Festival of Eastern Uruguay.

Dove and   Columbus Arch,
Wounded   Colon — A269
Bird — A268

1972, May 9
823 A268 10p ver & multi   15 15

To honor Dionision Disz (age 9), who died saving his sister.

1972, June 21
824 A269 20p red, bl & blk   15 15

Centenary of Colon, now suburb of Montevideo.

No. 810 Surcharged in Silver

(Surcharge 69mm wide)

1972, June 30
825 A261 50p on 10p multi   25 25

Winners of the 1971 Intl. Soccer Cup.

Tree   "Collective
Planting — A270   Housing" — A271

1972, Aug. 5   Wmk. 332   Perf. 12
826 A270 20p grn & blk   15 15

Afforestation program.

1972, Sept. 30   *Litho.*
827 A271 10p dp bl & multi   15 15

Publicity for collective housing plan.

Amethyst
A272

Uruguayan Gem Stones: 9p, Agate. 15p, Chalcedony.

1972, Oct. 7
828 A272 5p gray & multi   15 15
829 A272 9p gray bl & multi   15 15
830 A272 15p gray grn & multi   25 25

Uniform of 1830 — A273

Design: 20p, Lancer.

1972, Nov. 21   *Litho.*
831 A273 10p multi   15 15
832 A273 20p rose red & multi   25 25

Red Cross and Map of Uruguay A274

1972, Dec. 11   Wmk. 332   Perf. 12
833 A274 30p multi   25 25

75th anniv. of the Uruguayan Red Cross.

Stamp Day Type of 1972
Souvenir Sheets

Designs: 200p, Coat of arms type of 1864 similar to Nos. 18, 20-21, but 60p, 60p and 80p. 220p, Similar to Nos. 22-23, but 100p and 120p.

1972, Dec. 20   *Imperf.*
834 A265 200p multi   55 55
835 A265 220p multi   70 70

Stamp Day 1972. 1st printed cancellations, 200th anniv,. #834; Decree establishing regular postal service, cent., #835.

Scales of Justice, Olive Branch A275

1972, Dec. 27   Wmk. 332   Perf. 12
836 A275 10p gold, dk & lt bl   15 15

Civil Rights Law for Women, 25th anniv.

Gen. José   Hand Holding Cup; Grain,
Artigas   Map of Americas
A276   A277

1972-74   Wmk. 332   Litho.   Perf. 12
837 A276 5p yel ('74)   15 15
838 A276 10p dk bis ('74)   15 15
839 A276 15p emer ('74)   15 15
840 A276 20p lilac ('73)   15 15
841 A276 30p lt bl ('73)   15 15
842 A276 40p dp org ('73)   15 15
843 A276 50p ver ('73)   15 15
844 A276 75p ap grn ('73)   15 15
845 A276 100p emerald   16 16
846 A276 150p choc ('73)   20 20
847 A276 200p dk bl ('73)   35 35
848 A276 250p pur ('73)   40 40
849 A276 500p gray ('73)   75 75
849A A276 1000p blue ('73)   1.40 1.40
       Set value   3.90 3.90

For surcharges see Nos. 929-932.

1973, Jan. 9
850 A277 30p rose red, yel & blk   15 15

Intl. Institute for Agricultural Research, 39th anniv.

Elbio Fernandez and José P. Varela — A278

1973, Jan. 16
851 A278 10p dl grn, gold & blk   15 15

Society of Friends of Public Education, cent.

Map of Americas, "1972" and Columbus A279

1973, Jan. 30
852 A279 50p purple   15 15

Tourist Year of the Americas 1972.

Carlos Maria Ramirez, Scales and Books A280

1973, Feb. 15
853 A280 10p shown   15 15
854 A280 10p Justino Jimenez de
            Arechaga   15 15
855 A280 10p Juan Andres Ramirez   15 15
856 A280 10p Justino E. Jimenez de
            Arechaga   15 15
a.   Horiz. strip of 4, #853-856 + label 50 50
       Set value   40 40

Professorship of Constitutional Rights, cent.

Provincial Map of Uruguay A281

1973, Feb. 27   Litho.   Perf. 12½x12
857 A281 20p bl & multi   18 18

See No. 1167.

Francisco de los Santos A282

1973, May 16   Wmk. 332   Perf. 12
858 A282 20p grn & blk   18 18

Soldiers' Day and Battle of Piedras. Santos was a courier who went through enemy lines.

No. C319 Surcharged with New Value and: "HOMENAJE AL 4 CENTENARIO DE CORDOBA . ARGENTINA . 1973"

1973, May 9   Litho.   Imperf.
Souvenir Sheet
859 AP57 100p on 5p multi   65 65

Founding of Cordoba in Argentina, 400th anniv.

Friar, Indians,
Church — A283

1973, July 25 **Perf. 12**
860 A283 20p lt ultra, pur & blk 15 15

Villa Santo Domingo Soriano, first Spanish settlement in Uruguay.

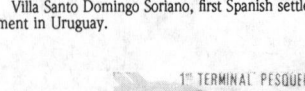

Symbolic
Fish — A284

1973, Aug. 15
861 A284 100p bl & multi 30 30

First station of Oceanographic and Fishery Service, Montevideo.

A285 Herrera — A286

Sun over flower in Italian colors.

1973, Sept.
862 A285 100p multi 20 20

Italian Chamber of Commerce of Uruguay.

Stamp Day Type of 1972
Souvenir Sheet

Design: 240p, Thin numeral sun type of 1859 and street scene.

Wmk. 332
1973, Oct. 1 **Litho.** **Imperf.**
863 A265 240p grn, org & blk 75 75

Stamp Day 1973.

1973, Nov. 12 **Perf. 12**
866 A286 50p gray, brn & dk brn 15 15

Centenary of the birth of Luis Alberto de Herrera.

Emblem of Social
Coordination
Volunteers
A287

Wmk. 352
1973, Nov. 19 **Litho.** **Perf. 12**
867 A287 50p bl & multi 15 15

Festival of Nations, Montevideo.

Arm with
Arteries and
Heart — A288

1973, Nov. 22
868 A288 50p blk, red & pink 15 15

3rd Cong. of the Pan-American Federation of Blood Donors, Montevideo, Nov. 23-25.

Madonna, by Rafael
Perez
Barradas — A289

1973, Dec. 10 **Litho.** **Wmk. 332**
869 A289 50p grn, gray & yel grn 15 15

Christmas 1973.

Nicolaus Copernicus — A290

1973, Dec. 26 **Litho.**
870 A290 50p grn & multi 15 15

500th anniversary of the birth of Nicolaus Copernicus (1473-1543), Polish astronomer.

Praying Hands and
Andes — A291

Design: 75p, Statue of Christ on mountain, and flower.

1973, Dec. 26 **Litho.**
871 A291 50p blk, lt grn & ultra 15 15
872 A291 75p bl, blk & org 15 15

Survival and rescue of victims of airplane crash.

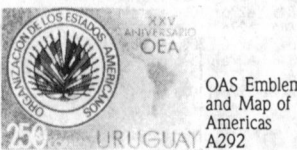

OAS Emblem
and Map of
Americas
A292

1974, Jan. 14 **Wmk. 332** **Perf. 12**
873 A292 250p gray & multi 50 50

25th anniversary of the Organization of American States (OAS).

Scout
Emblems and
Flame
A293

1974, Jan. 21
874 A293 250p multi 50 50

1st Intl. Boy Scout Games, Montevideo, 1974.

Hector Suppici
Sedes and
Car — A294

1974, Jan. 28 **Perf. 12**
875 A294 50p sep, grn & blk 15 15

70th anniversary of the birth of Hector Suppici Sedes (1903-1948), automobile racer.

Three
Gauchos — A295

1974, Mar. 20 **Litho.** **Wmk. 332**
876 A295 50p multi 15 15

Centenary of the publication of "Los Tres Gauchos Orientales" by Antonio D. Lussich.

Rifle, Target
and Swiss
Flag — A296

1974, Apr. 2
877 A296 100p multi 20 20

Centenary of the Swiss Rifle Association.

Map of
Uruguay and
Compass
Rose — A297

1974, Apr. 23 **Litho.**
878 A297 50p multi 15 15

Military Geographical Service.

Montevideo Stadium
Tower — A298

Design: 75p, Soccer player, Games' emblem, horiz. 1000p, similar to 75p.

1974, May 7 **Wmk. 332** **Perf. 12**
879 A298 50p multi 15 15
880 A298 75p multi 15 15
881 A298 1000p multicolored

World Cup Soccer Championship, Munich, June 13-July 7.
No. 881 had limited distribution. A souvenir sheet of one No. 881 was not valid for postage.

Tourism — A299

Wmk. 332
1974, June 6 **Litho.** **Perf. 12**
882 A299 1000p multicolored

No. 882 had limited distribution.

Old and New
School and
Founders
A300

1974, May 21
883 A300 75p black & bister 15 15

Centenary of the Osimani-Llerena Technical School at Salto, founded by Gervasio Osimani and Miguel Llerena.

Gardel and
Score — A301

Volleyball and
Net — A302

Wmk. 332
1974, June 24 **Litho.** **Perf. 12**
884 A301 100p multi 30 30

Carlos Gardel (1887-1935), singer and motion picture actor. See No. 1173.

1974, July 11 **Wmk. 332** **Perf. 12**
885 A302 200p lil, yel & blk 30 30

First anniversary of Women's Volleyball championships, Montevideo, 1973.

"Protect your Heart" — A303

Portrait and Statue — A304

1974, July 24 **Litho.**
886 A303 75p ol grn, yel & red 15 15

Heart Foundation publicity.

1974, Aug. 5
887 A304 75p dk & lt bl 15 15

Centenary (in 1973) of the founding of San José de Mayo by Eusebio Vidal.

A305 A306

Artigas statue, Buenos Aires, flags of Uruguay and Argentina.

1974, Aug. 13 **Perf. 12½**
888 A305 75p multi 15 15

Unveiling of Artigas monument, Buenos Aires.

1974, Sept. 24 **Wmk. 332** **Perf. 12**
889 A306 100p Radio tower and waves 15 15

50th anniv. of Broadcasting in Uruguay.

URUEXPO 74 Emblem — A307

URUEXPO Emblem and Old Map of Montevideo Bay — A308

1974
890 A307 100p blk, dk bl & red 15 15
891 A308 300p sepia, red & grn 38 38

URUEXPO 74 Philatelic Exhibition, 10th anniversary of Philatelic Circle of Uruguay (100p) and 250th anniversary of fortification of Montevideo. Issue dates: 100p, Oct. 1; 300p, Oct. 19.

Letters and UPU Emblem A309

UPU Cent.: 200p, UPU emblem, letter, and globe.

1974, Oct. 9
892 A309 100p lt bl & multi 15 15
893 A309 200p lil, blk & gold 15 15
 Set value 20 20

A 1000p souvenir sheet was not valid for postage. See Nos. C395-C396.

Artigas Statue and Map of Lavalleja A310

1974, Oct. 17 **Perf. 12**
894 A310 100p ultra & multi 15 15

Unveiling of Artigas statue in Minas, Lavalleja.

Ship in Dry Dock, Arsenal's Emblem A312

1974, Nov. 15 **Litho.** **Wmk. 332**
896 A312 200p multi 30 30

Centenary of Naval Arsenal, Montevideo.

Globe Hydrogen Balloon — A313

1974, Nov. 20
897 A313 100p shown 15 15
898 A313 100p Farman biplane 15 15
899 A313 100p Castaibert monoplane 15 15
900 A313 100p Bleriot monoplane 15 15
 a. Strip of 4, #897-900 60 60
901 A313 150p Military and civilian pilots' emblems 18 18
902 A313 150p Nieuport biplane 18 18
903 A313 150p Breguet-Bidon fighter 18 18
904 A313 150p Caproni bomber 18 18
 a. Strip of 4, #901-904 72 72
 Nos. 897-904 (8) 1.32 1.32

Aviation pioneers.

Sugar Loaf Mountain and Summit Cross — A314

1974, Nov. 30
905 A314 150p multi 18 18

Cent. of the founding of Sugar Loaf City.

Adoration of the Kings — A315

1974 **Perf. 12**
906 A315 100p shown 15 15
907 A315 150p Three Kings 15 15
 Set value 15 15

Christmas 1974. See Nos. C400-C401. Issue dates: 100p, Dec. 17; 150p, Dec. 19.

Nike, Fireworks, Rowers and Club Emblem — A316

1975, Jan. 27 **Litho.** **Wmk. 332**
908 A316 150p gray & multi 15 15

Centenary of Montevideo Rowing Club.

Treaty Signing, by José Zorilla de San Martin — A317

1975, Feb. 12 **Perf. 12**
909 A317 100p multi 15 15

Commercial Treaty between Great Britain and Uruguay, 1817.

New issue listings, plus the most interesting read in the hobby, characterize the "Scott Stamp Monthly". For more information, please call 1-800-488-5351.

Rose — A318

1975, Mar. 18 **Litho.** **Wmk. 332**
910 A318 150p multi 15 15

Bicentenary of city of Rosario.

"The Oath of the 33," by Juan M. Blanes — A319

1975, Apr. 16 **Perf. 12**
911 A319 150p gold & multi 15 15

Sesquicentennial of liberation movement.

Ship, Columbus and Ancient Map — A320

1975, Oct. 9 **Litho.** **Wmk. 332**
912 A320 1p gray & multi 80 80

Hispanic Stamp Day.

Leonardo Olivera and Santa Teresa Fort — A321

Artigas as Young and Old Man — A322

1975 **Litho.** **Wmk. 332** **Perf. 12**
913 A321 10c org & multi 15 15
914 A322 50c vio bl & multi 50 50

Sesquicentennial of the capture of Fort Santa Teresa (10c) and of Uruguay's declaration of independence (50c). Issue dates: 10c, Oct. 20; 50c, Oct. 17.

Battle of Rincon, by Diogenes
Hequet — A323

Designs: No. 916, Artigas' Home, Ibiray, Paraguay. 25c, Battle of Sarandi, by J. Manuel Blanes.

1975   **Litho.**
915 A323 15c ol & blk   15 15
916 A323 15c ol & multi   15 15
917 A323 25c ol & multi   30 30

Uruguayan independence. Nos. 915 and 917,
150th anniversary of Battles of Rincon and Sarandi.
No. 916, 50th anniversary of school at Artigas
mansion.
Issue dates: No. 915, Oct. 23; No. 916, Nov. 18;
No. 917, Nov. 28.

"En Familia,"
by Sanchez
A324

Florencio
Sanchez
A325

Designs (Plays by Sanchez): No. 919, Barranca
Abajo. No. 920, M'Hijo el Doctor. No. 921,
Canillita.

1975, Oct. 31   Wmk. 332   Perf. 12
918 A324 20c gray, red & blk   20 20
919 A324 20c bl, grn & blk   20 20
920 A324 20c red, bl & blk   20 20
921 A324 20c grn, gray & blk   20 20
922 A325 20c multi   20 20
   a. Block of 5 stamps + 4 labels   1.50

Florencio Sanchez (1875-1910), dramatist, birth
centenary. Nos. 918-922 printed se-tenant in sheets
of 30 stamps and 20 labels.

Maria Eugenia
Vaz Ferreira
A326

Design: No. 924, Julio Herrera y Reissig.

1975
923 A326 15c yel, blk & brn   15 15
924 A326 15c org, blk & maroon   15 15

Maria Eugenia Vaz Ferreira (1875-1924), poet-
ess, and Julio Herrera y Reissig (1875-1910), poet,
birth anniversaries.
Issue dates: #923, Dec. 9; #924, Dec. 29.

Virgin and Child
A327   A328

Fireworks — A329

1975
925 A327 20c bl & multi   25 25
926 A328 30c blk & multi   38 38
927 A329 60c multi   50 50

Christmas 1975.
Issue dates: 20c, Dec. 16; 30c, Dec. 15; 60c,
Dec. 11.

Col. Lorenzo Latorre
(1840-1916), Pres. of
Uruguay (1876-
80) — A330

1975, Dec. 30   Perf. 12
928 A330 15c multi   15 15

Nos. 840, 842-843, 849A   **N$**
Surcharged   **0,10**

1975
929 A276 10c on 20p lilac   15 15
930 A276 15c on 40p orange   15 15
931 A276 50c on 50p ver   25 25
932 A276 1p on 1000p blue   50 50
   Set value   88 88

Ariel, Stars,
Book and
Youths
A331

1976, Jan. 12   Litho.   Wmk. 332
933 A331 15c grn & multi   15 15

75th anniversary of publication of "Ariel," by
Jose Enrique Rodo (1872-1917), writer.

Water Sports
A332

Telephone
A333

1976, Mar. 12   Litho.   Wmk. 332
934 A332 30c multi   15 15

23rd South American Swimming, Diving and
Water Polo Championships.

1976, Apr. 9   Perf. 12
935 A333 83c multi   42 42

Centenary of first telephone call by Alexander
Graham Bell, Mar. 10, 1876.

"Plus Ultra" and
Columbus'
Ships — A334

Wmk. 332
1976, May 10   Litho.   Perf. 12
936 A334 63c gray & multi   40 40

Flight of Dornier "Plus Ultra" from Spain to
South America, 50th anniversary.

A335   A336

Dornier "Wal" and Boeing 727, hourglass.

1976, May 24
937 A335 83c gray & multi   42 42

Lufthansa German Airline, 50th anniv.

1976, June 3   Perf. 11½

Designs: 10c, Olympics. 15c, Telephone, cent.
25c, UPU, cent., UN #2. 50c, World Cup Soccer
Championships, Argentina, 1978.

938 A336 10c shown
939 A336 15c multicolored
940 A336 25c multicolored
941 A336 50c multicolored

Nos. 938-941 had limited distribution.
A souvenir sheet containing one each, Nos. 938-
941, was not valid for postage.

Louis Braille
A340

1976, June 7
942 A340 60c blk & brn   35 35

Sesquicentennial of the invention of the Braille
system of writing for the blind by Louis Braille
(1809-1852).

Signing of US
Declaration of
Independence
A341

1976, June 21
943 A341 1.50p multi   1.65 1.25

American Bicentennial.

Freeing of
the Slaves,
by P. Figari
A342

Wmk. 332
1976, July 29   Litho.   Perf. 12
944 A342 30c ultra & multi   15 15

Abolition of slavery, sesquicentennial.

Gen.
Fructuoso
Rivera Statue
A343

1976, Aug. 2
945 A343 5p on 10p multi   2.50 1.25

No. 945 was not issued without surcharge.

General
Accounting
Office
A344

Wmk. 332
1976, Aug. 24   Litho.   Perf. 12
946 A344 30c bl, blk & brn   22 22

National General Accounting Office,
sesquicentennial.

Old Pump, Emblem
and Flame — A345

1976, Sept. 6
947 A345 20c red & blk   15 15

First official fire fighting service, centenary.

Southern
Lapwing — A346

Mburucuya
Flower — A347

Spearhead — A348

Figurine — A349

La Yerra, by J. M. Blanes — A350

The Gaucho, by Blanes — A351

Artigas — A352

Designs: 15c, Ceibo flower.

1976-79 Litho. Wmk. 332 Perf. 12

948	A346	1c violet	15	15
949	A347	5c lt grn	15	15
950	A347	15c car rose	15	15
951	A348	20c gray	15	15
952	A349	30c gray blue	15	15
953	A352	45c brt bl ('79)	15	15
954	A350	50c grnsh bl ('77)	20	15
955	A351	1p dk brn ('77)	40	20
956	A352	1p brt yel ('79)	16	16
957	A352	1.75p bl grn ('79)	30	30
958	A352	1.95p gray ('79)	32	32
959	A352	2p dl grn ('77)	90	90
960	A352	2p lil rose ('79)	40	35
961	A352	2.65p vio ('79)	42	42
962	A352	5p dk bl	2.50	2.50
963	A352	10p brn ('77)	4.25	2.50
		Nos. 948-963 (16)	10.75	8.70

"Diligencia" Uruguay No. 1 A353

Wmk. 332

1976, Sept. 26 Litho. Perf. 12

964 A353 30c bis, red & bl 15 15

Philatelic Club of Uruguay, 50th anniv.

Games' Emblem — A354

1976, Oct. 26 Litho. Perf. 12

965 A354 83c gray & multi 40 40

5th World University Soccer Championships.

World Cup Soccer Championships, Argentina — A355

Anniversaries and Events: 30c, 1976 Summer Olympics, Montreal. 50c, Viking spacecraft. 80c, Nobel prizes, 75th anniv.

1976, Nov. 12 Perf. 12

966	A355	10c multicolored	
967	A355	30c multicolored	
968	A355	50c multicolored	
969	A355	80c multicolored	

Nos. 966-969 had limited distribution. See Nos. C424-C425.

Eye and Spectrum A356

1976, Nov. 24

970 A356 20c blk & multi 16 16

Foresight prevents blindness.

Map of Montevideo, 1748 — A357

Designs: 45c, Montevideo Harbor, 1842. 70c, First settlers, 1726. 80c, Coin with Montevideo arms, vert. 1.15p, Montevideo's first coat of arms, vert.

Wmk. 332

1976, Dec. 30 Litho. Perf. 12

971	A357	30c multi	15	15
972	A357	45c multi	20	20
973	A357	70c multi	35	35
974	A357	80c multi	38	38
975	A357	1.15p multi	45	45
		Nos. 971-975 (5)	1.53	1.53

Founding of Montevideo, 250th anniversary.

Symbolic of Flight A358

1977, May 7 Litho. Perf. 12

976 A358 80c multi 50 50

50th anniversary of Varig airlines.

Artigas Mausoleum A359

1977, June 17 Litho. Perf. 12

977 A359 45c multi 30 30

A360

A361

1977, July 5 Wmk. 332

978 A360 45c Map of Uruguay and arch 30 30

Centenary of Salesian Brothers' educational system in Uruguay.

1977, July 21

Anniversaries and events: 20c, Werner Heisenberg, Nobel Prize for Physics. 30c, World Cup Soccer Championships, Uruguay Nos. 282, 390. 50c, Lindbergh's trans-Atlantic flight, 50th anniv. 1p, Rubens 400th birth anniv.

979	A361	20c shown	
980	A361	30c multicolored	
981	A361	50c multicolored	
982	A361	1p multicolored	
a.		Strip, 2 each #979-982 + 2 labels	

Nos. 979-982 had limited distribution.
A souvenir sheet containing Nos. 979-982, imperf., was not valid for postage. It sold for 8p. See Nos. C426-C427.

Children — A362

Windmills — A364

"El Sol de Mayo" A363

1977, Aug. 10 Litho. Perf. 12

983 A362 45c multi 30 30

Interamerican Children's Institute, 50th anniversary.

1977, Oct. 1 Litho. Perf. 12

984 A363 45c multi 20 20

Stamp Day 1977.

1977, Sept. 29 Wmk. 332

985 A364 70c yel, car & blk 35 35

Spanish Heritage Day.

Souvenir Sheet

View of Sans (Barcelona), by Barradas — A365

1977, Oct. 7 Litho. Perf. 12

986	A365	Sheet of 2	3.00 3.00
a.-b.		5p, single stamp	1.40

ESPAMER '77 Philatelic Exhibition, Barcelona, Oct. 7-13.

Planes, UN Emblem, Globe A366

1977, Oct. 17

987 A366 45c multi 15 15

30th anniv. of Civil Aviation Organization.

Holy Family — A367

Santa Claus A368

1977, Dec. 1 Wmk. 332

988 A367 45c multi 15 15
989 A368 70c blk, yel & red 20 20

Christmas 1977.

Map of Rio Negro Province A369

1977, Dec. 16

990 A369 45c multi 15 15

Rio Negro Dam; development of argiculture, livestock and beekeeping. See Nos. 1021-1033.

Mail Collection — A370

1977, Dec. 21

991	A370	50c shown	15	15
992	A370	50c Mail truck	15	15
993	A370	50c Post office counter	15	15
994	A370	50c Postal boxes	15	15
995	A370	50c Mail sorting	15	15
996	A370	50c Pigeonhole sorting	15	15
997	A370	50c Route sorting (seated carriers)	15	15
998	A370	50c Home delivery	15	15
999	A370	50c Special delivery (motorcyclists)	15	15
1000	A370	50c Airport counter	15	15
a.		Strip of 10, #991-1000	1.50	1.50
		Nos. 991-1000 (10)	1.50	1.50

150th anniversary of Uruguayan postal service.

Edison's Phonograph, 1877 — A371

1977, Dec. 30

1001 A371 50c vio brn & yel 15 15

Centenary of invention of the phonograph.

"R", Rainbow
and Emblem
A372

1977, Dec. 30   **Wmk. 332**
1002 A372 50c multi   15 15

World Rheumatism Year.

Emblem and
Diploma
A373

1978, Mar. 27   **Litho.**   **Perf. 12**
1003 A373 50c multi   15 15

50th anniversary of Military College.

Erhard Schon
by Albrecht
Durer (1471-
1528)
A374

Painting: 50c, Self-Portrait by Peter Paul Rubens (1577-1640).

1978, June 13   **Perf. 12½**
1004 A374 25c blk & brn
1005 A374 50c brn & blk

Nos. 1004-1005 had limited distribution.
See Nos. C430-C432.

Map and
Arms of
Artigas
Department
A375

Wmk. 332
1978, June 16   **Litho.**   **Perf. 12**
1006 A375 45c multi   16 16

Souvenir Sheet

Anniversaries — A376

Designs: 2p, Papilio thoas. No. 1007b, "100." No. 1007c, Argentina '78 emblem and globes. 5p, Model T Ford.

Wmk. 332
1978, Aug. 24   **Litho.**   **Perf. 12**
1007 A376 Sheet of 4   4.25 4.25
  b. 2p multi   50 50
  b. 4p multi   85 85
  c. 4p multi   85 85
  d. 5p multi   1.25 1.25

75th anniv. of 1st powered flight; URUEXPO '78 Phil. Exhib.; Parva Domus social club, cent.; 11th World Cup Soccer Championship, Argentina, June 1-25; Ford motor cars, 75th anniv.

Visiting
Angels, by
Solari
A377

Designs (Details from No. 1008b): No. 1008a, Second angel. No. 1008c, Third angel.

1978, Sept. 13   **Unwmk.**
1008 Strip of 3   1.00 1.00
  a. A377 1.50p, 19x30mm   32 32
  b. A377 1.50p, 38x30mm   32 32
  c. A377 1.50p, 19x30mm   32 32

Solari, Uruguayan painter.

Bernardo
O'Higgins
A378

Design: No. 1010, José de San Martin and monument.

1978   **Wmk. 332**
1009 A378 1p multi   20 20
1010 A378 1p multi   20 20

Benardo O'Higgins (1778-1842) and José de San Martin (1778-1850), South American liberators. Issued: No. 1009, Sept. 13; No. 1010, Oct. 10.

Telephone
Dials
A379

1978, Sept. 25
1011 A379 50c multi   15 15

Automation of telephone service.

Symbolic
Stamps
A380

Iberian Tile
Pattern — A381

1978, Oct. 31
1012 A380 50c multi   15 15
1013 A381 1p multi   20 20

Stamp Day (50c) and Spanish heritage (1p).

Boeing
727 — A382

1978, Nov. 27
1014 A382 50c multi   15 15

Inauguration of Boeing 727 flights by PLUNA Uruguayan airlines, Nov. 1978.

Angel Blowing Horn — A383

1978, Dec. 7
1015 A383 50c multi   15 15
1016 A383 1p multi   20 20

Christmas 1978.

A384   A385

1978, Dec. 15   **Perf. 12½**
1017 A384 1p Flag flying on Plaza of the
   Nation   20 20

Wmk. 332
1978, Dec. 27   **Litho.**   **Perf. 12**
1018 A385 1p blk, red & yel   20 20

Horacio Quiroga (1868-1928), short story writer.

Arch,
Olympic
Rings, Lake
Placid and
Moscow
Emblems
A386

Design: 7p, Olympic Rings and Lake Placid '80 emblem.

1979, Apr. 28   **Litho.**   **Perf. 12**
1019 A386 5p multi   1.10 1.10
1020 A386 7p multi   1.65 1.65

81st Session of Olympic Organizing Committee, Apr. 3-8 (5p), and 13th Winter Olympic Games, Lake Placid, NY, Feb. 12-24.

Souvenir Sheets
1021 Sheet of 4
  a. A386 3p similar to #1019
  b. A386 5p Olympic rings
  c. A386 7p Rider looking back
  d. A386 10p Rider facing forward
1022 Sheet of 4
  a. A386 3p similar to #1020
  b. A386 5p Uruguay '79

---

  c. A386 7p World Chess Olympics '78
  d. A386 10p Sir Rowland Hill, Great Britain stamp

No. 1022d shows Great Britain No. 836, but with 11p denomination. No. 1021c-1021d have continuous design.
Nos. 1021-1022 had limited distribution. Except for No. 1022d, singles were sold for postal use in 1980. Nos. 1021-1022 exist imperf.

Map and
Arms of
Paysandu
A387

Map and Arms of
Maldonado — A388

1979-81
1023 A387 45c shown   15 15
1024 A387 45c Salto   15 15
1025 A388 45c shown   15 15
1026 A387 45c Cerro Largo   15 15
1027 A387 50c Treinta y Tres   15 15
1028 A387 50c Durazno ('80)   15 15
1020 A388 2p Rocha ('81)   35 35
1030 A388 2p Flores   35 35
   Set value   1.25 1.25

See No. 990.

Sapper with Pickax,
1837 — A389

Army Day: No. 1039, Artillery man with cannon, 1830.

1979, May 18   **Litho.**   **Perf. 12**
1038 A389 5p multi   1.10 1.10
1039 A389 5p multi   1.10 1.10

Madonna and
Child by
Durer
A390

Anniversaries and events: 80c, World Cup Soccer Championships, Spain. 1.30p, Sir Rowland Hill, Greece No. 117.

1979, June 18   **Perf. 12**
1040 A390 70c brn & gray
1041 A390 80c multicolored
1042 A390 1.30p multicolored

Nos. 1040-1042 had limited distribution.
Issued in sheets of 24 containing 6 blocks of 4 with margin around. See #C437-C438.

Salto
Dam
A391

1979, June 19
1043 A391 2p multi   42 42

Crandon
Institute
Emblem,
Grain
A392

1979, July 19
1044 A392 1p vio bl & bl   16 16

Crandon Institute (private Methodist school),
centenary.

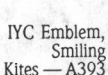

IYC Emblem,
Smiling
Kites — A393

Cinderella — A394

1979
1045 A393 2p multi   35 35
1046 A394 2p multi   35 35

International Year of the Child. Issue dates: No.
1045, July 23; No. 1046, Aug. 29.

Uruguay Coat of Arms 150th
Anniversary — A395

1979, Sept. 6
1047 A395 8p multi   1.40 1.40

Virgin and Child
A396

Symbols, by Torres-
Garcia
A397

Wmk. 332
1979, Nov. 19   **Litho.**   *Perf. 12*
1048 A396 10p multi   1.65 1.65

Christmas 1979; Intl. Year of the Child.

1979, Nov. 12
1049 A397 10p yel & blk   1.65 1.65

J. Torres-Garcia (1874-1948), painter.

UPU and Brazilian Postal
Emblems — A398

1979, Oct. 11
1050 A398 5p multi   90 80

18th UPU Congress, Rio, Sept.-Oct.

Dish Antenna and Sun — A400

Perf. 12x11½
1979, Nov. 26   **Litho.**   **Wmk. 332**
1052 A400 10p multi   1.25 1.10

Telecom '79, 3rd World Telecommunications
Exhibition, Geneva, Sept. 20-26.

Spanish Heritage
Day — A401

1979, Dec. 3   *Perf. 12*
1053 A401 10p multi   1.65 1.65

Silver Coin
Centenary
A402

Designs: Obverse and reverse of coins in denominations matching stamps.

Wmk. 332
1979, Dec. 26   **Litho.**   *Perf. 12*
1054 A402 10c multi   15 15
1055 A402 20c multi   15 15
1056 A402 50c multi   15 15
1057 A402 1p multi   25 25
        Set value   50 50

Souvenir Sheet

Security
Agent — A403

1980, Jan. 10
1058   Sheet of 4   2.00 2.00
   a. A403 1p Police emblem   16 16
   b. A403 2p shown   35 35
   c. A403 3p Policeman, 1843   50 50
   d. A403 4p Cadet, 1979   75 75

Police force sesquicentennial.

Light
Bulb,
Thomas
Edison
A404

1980, Jan. 18
1059 A404 2p multi   42 42

Centenary of electric light (1979).

Bass and
Singer — A405

1980, Jan. 30
1060   Sheet of 4   1.75 1.75
   a. A405 2p Radio waves   40 40
   b. A405 2p shown   40 40
   c. A405 2p Ballerina   40 40
   d. A405 2p Television waves   40 40

Performing Arts Society, 50th anniversary.

Stamp Day — A406

La Leyenda
Patria — A407

1980, Feb.
1061 A406 1p multi   16 16

1980, Feb. 26
1062 A407 1p multi   16 16

Printers'
Association, 50th
Anniversary
A408

1980, Feb.
1063 A408 1p multi   16 16

Lufthansa Cargo Container Service
Inauguration — A409

1980, Apr. 12   **Unwmk.**   *Perf. 12½*
1064 A409 2p multi   35 35

Conf. Emblem,
Banners — A410

Man, Woman and
Birds — A411

1980, Apr. 28   **Wmk. 332**   *Perf. 12*
1065 A410 2p multi   35 35

8th World Hereford Conf., Punta del Este and
Livestock Exhib., Prado/Montivideo.

1980   **Litho.**   *Perf. 12*
1066 A411 1p multi   16 16

International Year of the Child (1979).

Latin-American Lions, 9th Forum — A412

1980, May 6   **Wmk. 332**   *Perf. 12*
1067 A412 1p multi   20 20

Souvenir Sheet

Rifleman,
1814 — A413

1980, May 16
1068   Sheet of 4   1.65 1.65
   a. A413 2p shown   40 40
   b. A413 2p Cavalry officer, 1830   40 40
   c. A413 2p Private Liberty Dragoons,
       1826   40 40
   d. A413 2p, Artigas Militia officer, 1815   40 40

Army Day, May 18.

Arms of
Colonia — A414

Colonia,
1680
A415

1980, June 17   **Litho.**   *Perf. 12*
1069 A414   50c multi   15   15
Souvenir Sheet
1070   Sheet of 4   85   85
a.   A415 1p shown   20   20
b.   A415 1p 1680, diff.   20   20
c.   A415 1p 1980   20   20
d.   A415 1p 1980, diff.   20   20

Colonia, 300th anniversary.

Rotary Emblem on   Hand Putting Out
Globe — A416   Cigarette — A417

1980, July 8
1071 A416   5p multi   90   90

Rotary International, 75th anniversary.

1980, Sept. 8   **Photo.**
1072 A417   1p multi   16   16

World Health Day and anti-smoking campaign.

Artigas   Christmas 1980
A418   A419

         Perf. 12½
1980-85   **Litho.**   **Wmk. 332**
1073 A418   10c blue ('81)   15   15
1074 A418   20c orange   15   15
1075 A418   50c red   15   15
1076 A418   60c yellow   15   15
1077 A418   1p gray   16   16
1078 A418   2p brown   35   35
1079 A418   3p brt grn   50   50
1080 A418   4p brt bl ('82)   65   65
1081 A418   5p green ('82)   25   25
1082 A418   6p brt org ('85)   15   15
1083 A418   7p lil rose ('82)   1.25   75
1084 A418   10p blue ('82)   55   35
1085 A418   12p blk ('85)   20   20
1086 A418   15.50p emer ('85)   22   22
1087 A418   20p dk vio ('82)   1.10   1.10
1088 A418   30p lt brn ('82)   1.65   1.65
1089 A418   50p gray bl ('82)   2.50   2.50
    Nos. 1073-1089 (17)   10.13   9.43

1980, Dec. 15   **Litho.**   *Perf. 12*
1090 A419   2p multi   35   35

Constitution
Title
Page — A420

1980, Dec. 23   *Perf. 12½*
1091 A420   4p brt bl & gold   65   65

Sesquicentennial of Constitution.

A421   A422

1980, Dec. 30   *Perf. 12*
1092 A421   5p Montevideo Stadium   65   65
1093 A421   5p Soccer gold cup   65   65
          Size: 25x79mm
1094 A421   10p Flags   1.40   1.40
a.   Souv. sheet of 3, #1092-1094   3.00   3.00

Soccer Gold Cup Championship, Montevideo.

1981, Jan. 27
1095 A422   2p multi   35   18

Spanish Heritage Day.

UPU
Membership
Centenary
A423

1981, Feb. 6
1096 A423   2p multi   35   18

Alexander von
Humboldt (1769-
1859), German
Explorer and
Scientist — A424

1981, Feb. 19
1097 A424   2p multi   40   25

Intl.
Education
Congress and
Fair,
Montevideo
(1980)
A425

1981, Mar. 31
1098 A425   2p multi   35   18

Hand Holding   Eighth Notes on
Gold   Map of
Cup — A426   Americas — A427

1981, Apr. 8
1099 A426   2p multi   35   18
1100 A426   5p multi   80   40

1980 victory in Gold Cup Soccer Championship.

1981, Apr. 28
1101 A427   2p multi   35   18

Inter-American Institute of Musicology, 40th
anniv.

World
Tourism
Conference,
Manila, Sept.
27, 1980
A428

1981, June 1   **Litho.**   *Perf. 12*
1102 A428   2p multi   35   18

Inauguration of PLUNA Flights to
Madrid — A429

1981, May 12
1103 A429   2p multi   35   18
1104 A429   5p multi   80   40
1105 A429   10p multi   1.65   85

Army   Natl. Atomic
Day — A430   Energy
                Commission,
                25th
                Anniv. — A431

1981, May 18   **Litho.**   *Perf. 12*
           Wmk. 332
1106 A430   2p Cavalry soldier, 1843   35   18
1107 A430   2p Infantryman, 1843   35   18

1981, July 20
1108 A431   2p multi   35   18

Europe-South
American
Soccer
Cup — A432

1981, Aug. 4
1109 A432   2p multi   35   18

Stone Tablets,
Salto Grande
Excavation
A433

1981, Sept. 10
1110 A433   2p multi   35   18

10th Lavalleja
Week — A434

1981, Oct. 3
1111 A434   4p multi   65   35

Intl. Year of
the Disabled
A435

1981, Oct. 26   **Litho.**   *Perf. 12*
           Wmk. 332
1112 A435   2p multi   35   18

UN
Environmental
Law Meeting
Montevideo,
Oct. 28-Nov.
6 — A436

1981, Oct. 28
1113 A436   5p multi   80   40

A437   A439

1981, Oct. 13
1114 A437   2p multi   35   18

   50th anniv. of ANCAP (Natl. Administration of
Combustible Fuels, Alcohol and Cement).

1981, Dec. 5   *Perf. 12*
1116 A439   2p multi   35   18

   Topographical Society sesquicentennial. See No.
1407.

Bank of Uruguay, 85th Anniv. — A440

1981, Dec. 17   *Perf. 12½*
1117 A440   2p multi   35   18

Palmar
Dam
A441

1981, Dec. 22   *Perf. 12*
1118 A441   2p multi   35   18

Christmas
1981
A442

1981, Dec. 23
1119 A442 2p multi 35 18

Pres. Joaquin Suarez
Bicentenary — A443

1982, Mar. 15
1120 A443 5p multi 80 40

Artillery Captain,
1872, Army
Day — A444

Cent. (1981) of
Pinocchio, by Carlo
Collodi — A445

Wmk. 332
1982, May 18 Litho. *Perf. 12*
1121 A444 3p shown 50 25
1122 A444 3p Florida Battalion, 1865 50 25

See Nos. 1136-1137.

1982, June 17
1123 A445 2p multi 35 18

2nd UN
Conference on
Peaceful Uses of
Outer Space,
Vienna, Aug. 9-
21 — A446

1982, June 3
1124 A446 3p multi 80 50

World Food
Day
A447

1982
1125 A447 2p multi 35 18

25th Anniv. of Lufthansa's Uruguay-
Germany Flight — A448

1982, Apr. 14 **Unwmk.** *Perf. 12½*
1126 A448 3p Lockheed L-1049-G
Super Constellation 50 35
1127 A448 7p Boeing 747 1.20 65

American Air Forces
Cooperation
System — A449

1982, Apr. 14 **Wmk. 332** *Perf. 12*
1128 A449 10p Emblem 1.60 80

Juan Zorilla
de San
Martin
(1855-1931),
Painter
A450

1982, Aug. 18 *Perf. 12½*
1129 A450 3p Self-portrait 50 35

165th
Anniv.
of Natl.
Navy
A451

1982, Nov. 15 *Perf. 12*
1130 A451 3p Navy vessel Capitan Miranda 16 15

Natl. Literacy
Campaign
A452

Stamp Day
A453

1982, Nov. 30
1131 A452 3p multi 16 15

1982, Dec. 23 *Perf. 12½*
1132 A453 3p like #46 30 15
1133 A453 3p like #47 30 15
a. Pair, #1132-1133 65 40

These stamps bear numbers from 1 to 100
according to their position on the sheet.

Christmas 1982 — A454

1983, Jan. 4 *Perf. 12*
1134 A454 3p multi 45 22

Eduardo
Fabini (1882-
1950),
Composer
A455

1983, May 10
1135 A455 3p gold & brn 45 22

Army Day Type of 1982

1983, May 18
1136 A444 3p Military College cadet,
1885 45 22
1137 A444 3p 2nd Cavalry Regiment officer, 1885 45 22

Visit of King Juan Carlos and Queen Sofia
of Spain, May
A456

1983, May 20 **Unwmk.**
1138 A456 3p Santa Maria, globe 50 25
1139 A456 7p Profiles, flags 1.25 60

Size of No. 1138: 29x39mm.

Brasiliana '83
Emblem — A457

80th Anniv. of
First Automobile
in
Uruguay — A458

Opening of UPAE
Building,
Montevideo
A459

Jose Cuneo (1887-
1977), Painter
A460

1982 World
Cup — A461

Graf Zeppelin
Flight Over
Montevideo,
50th Anniv.
(1984)
A462

J.W. Goethe (1749-1832), 150th Death
Anniv. — A463

First Space
Shuttle Flight
A464

1983 **Litho.** **Wmk. 332** *Perf. 12*
1140 A457 3p multi 45 22
1141 A458 3p multi 45 22
1142 A459 3p multi 45 22
1143 A460 3p multi 45 22
a. Souvenir sheet of 4 1.50 1.50
1144 A461 7p multi 85 42
1145 A462 7p multi 85 42
1146 A463 7p multi 85 42
1147 A464 7p multi 85 42
a. Souvenir sheet of 4 3.75 3.75
Nos. 1140-1147 (8) 5.20 2.56

No. 1143a contains stamps similar to Nos. 1140-
1143. No. 1147a stamps similar to Nos. 1144-
1147. Nos. 1143a and 1147a for URUEXPO '83
and World Communications Year.
Issue dates: No. 1142, June 8; Nos. 1143, 1146,
Sept. 29; Nos. 1143a, 1147a, June 9; No. 1140,
July 22; Nos. 1144, Dec. 13; No. 1146, Sept. 20;
No. 1145, Dec. 8.

Bicentenary of City of
Minas — A465

Wmk. 332
1983, Oct. 17 Litho. *Perf. 12*
1148 A465 3p Founder 25 15

World Communications Year — A466

1983, Nov. 30
1149 A466 3p multi 25 15

*The Scott International album pro-
vides spaces for an extensive representative collection of the world's
postage stamps.*

Garibaldi Death
Centenary
URUGUAY   N$ 7 A467

1983, Dec. 5
1150 A467 7p multi   60   30

Christmas
1983
A468

Lithographed and Embossed (Braille)
1983, Dec. 21   *Perf. 12¹/₂*
1151 A468 4.50p multi   35   18

50th Anniv.
of Automatic
Telephones
A469

1983, Dec. 27   *Perf. 12*
1152 A469 4.50p multi   35   18

Simon
Bolivar,
Battle Scene
A470

Wmk. 332
1984, Mar. 28   Litho.   *Perf. 12*
1153 A470 4.50p brn & gldn brn   35   18

Gen. Leandro
Gomez — A471

1984, Jan. 2
1154 A471 4.50p multi   35   18

American
Women's
Day — A472

Reunion
Emblem — A473

1984, Feb. 18
1155 A472 4.50p Flags, emblem   35   18

1984, Mar. 23
1156 A473 10p multi   85   42

Intl. Development Bank Governors, 25th annual
reunion, Punta del Este.

50th Anniv.
of Radio Club
of Uruguay
(1983)
A474

1984, Apr. 11
1157 A474 7p multi   60   30

A475   A476

1984, Feb. 7   Litho.   *Perf. 12*
1158 A475 4.50p multi   35   18
Intl. Maritime Org., 25th anniv.

1984, May 2   Litho.   *Perf. 12*
1159 A476 4.50p multi   35   18
1930 World Soccer Championships, Montevideo.

Department
of San Jose
de Mayo,
200th Anniv.
A477

1984, May 9   Litho.   *Perf. 12*
1160 A477 4.50p multi   35   18

Tourism,
50th Anniv.
A478

1984, May 15   Litho.   *Perf. 12*
1161 A478 4.50p multi   35   18

Military
Uniforms — A479

Artigas on the
Plains — A480

1984, June 19   Litho.   *Perf. 12*
1162 A479 4.50p Artillery Regiment,
        1895   35   18
1163 A479 4.50p Cazadores, 2nd battal-
        ion   35   18

1984, July 2   Litho.   *Perf. 12*
1164 A480 4.50p bl & blk   35   18
1165 A480 8.50p bl & redsh brn   68   35

A. Penarol
Soccer Club
A481

1984, Aug. 21   Litho.   *Perf. 12*
1166 A481 4.50p Championship trophy 35   18

Provincial Map Type of 1973
1984, Sept. 21   Litho.   *Perf. 12*
1167 A281 4.50p multi   35   18

Childrens
Council,
50th Anniv.
A482

1984, Oct. 11   Litho.   *Perf. 12*
1168 A482 4.50p multi   35   18

Christmas — A483   A484

1984   Litho.   *Perf. 12*
1169 A483 6p multi   48   25

1985, Feb. 13   Litho.   *Perf. 12*
1170 A484 4.50p multi   35   18
1st Jr. World Basketball Championships.

Don Bruno Mauricio
de Zabala, 300th
Birth Anniv. — A485

1985, Apr. 16   Litho.   *Perf. 12*
1171 A485 4.50p multi   28   15

Intl.
Olympic
Committee,
90th Anniv.
A486

Design: Olympic rings, Los Angeles and Sarajevo
1984 Games emblems.

1985, May 22   *Perf. 12¹/₂*
1172 A486 12p multi   70   35

Carlos Gardel, (1890-
1935),
Entertainer — A487

Catholic Circle of
Workers,
Cent. — A488

1985, June 21   *Perf. 12*
1173 A487 6p lt gray, red brn & bl 35 18

Wmk. 332
1985, June 21   Litho.   *Perf. 12*
1174 A488 6p Cross, clasped hands   15 15

Icarus, by
Hans Erni
A489

1985, July   Photo.   Wmk. 332
1175 A489 4.50p multi   15   15
Intl. Civil Aviation Org., 40th anniv.

American Air Forces
Cooperation System,
25th Anniv. — A490

1985, July
1176 A490 12p Emblem, flags   30   15

FUNSA, Natl.
Investment
Funds Corp.,
50th Anniv.
A491

1985, July 31   Litho.   Wmk. 332
1177 A491 6p multi   15   15

Intl. Youth
Year — A492

1985, Aug. 28
1178 A492 12p mar & blk   30 15

Installation of Democratic
Government — A493

1985, Aug. 30
1179 A493 20p brt pur, yel ocher & dk
grnsh bl   48 24

Intl. Book Fair — A494

1985
1180 A494 20p multi   48 24

Military
School,
Cent.
A495

1985, Nov. 29   Litho.   Perf. 12
1181 A495 10p multi   25 15

Department of   Day of Hispanic
Flores,   Solidarity — A498
Cent. — A496

Christmas
1985
A497

1985, Dec. 9
1182 A496 6p Map, arms   15 15

1985, Dec. 23
1183 A497 10p multi   25 15
1184 A497 22p multi   52 25

1985, Dec. 27
1185 A498 12p Isabel Monument   30 15

3rd Inter-American Agricultural
Congress — A499

Wmk. 332
1986, Jan. 7   Photo.   Perf. 12
1186 A499 12p blk, dl yel & red   30 15

UPU
Day — A500

1986, Jan. 14   Litho.   Perf. 12
1187 A500 15.50p multi   38 20

1985 Census
A501

1986, Jan. 21
1188 A501 10p multi   25 15

Conaprole,
50th Anniv.
A502

1986, Jan. 25
1189 A502 10p gold, brt ultra & bl   25 15

UN, 40th
Anniv.
A503

Wmk. 332
1986, Feb. 26   Litho.   Perf. 12
1190 A503 20p multi   38 20

Brokers and
Auctioneers Assoc.,
50th Anniv. — A504

1986, Mar. 19
1191 A504 10p multi   16 15

Gen. Manuel Ceferino
Oribe (1792-1857),
President — A505

Portraits: Nos. 1196, 1200, 2p, 7p, 15p, 20p,
Oribe. Nos. 1195, 1209, 1211, 3p, Lavalleja. Nos.
1199, 1208, 1210, 30p, 100p, 200p, Artigas. No.
1198, 17p, 22p, 26p, 45p, 75p, Rivera.

1986-89   Perf. 12½

1192	A505	1p dl grn	15	15
1193	A505	2p scarlet	15	15
1194	A505	3p ultra	15	15
1195	A505	5p dark blue	15	15
1196	A505	5p violet blue	15	15
1197	A505	7p tan	15	15
1198	A505	10p lilac rose	20	20
1199	A505	10p brt green	15	15
1200	A505	10p bluish green	15	15
1201	A505	15p dull blue	15	15
1202	A505	17p deep blue	20	20
1203	A505	20p light brown	15	15
1204	A505	22p violet	22	22
1205	A505	26p olive blk	30	30
1206	A505	30p pale org	30	30
1207	A505	45p dark red	32	32
1208	A505	50p dp bis	50	50
1209	A505	50p bright pink	15	15
1210	A505	60p dark gray	70	70
1211	A505	60p orange	15	15
1211A	A505	75p red orange	15	15
1211B	A505	100p dl red brn	1.00	1.00
1211C	A505	200p brt yel grn	1.45	1.45
		Set value	6.25	6.25

The 22p is airmail.
Issue dates: 1p, 7p, Apr. 18. No. 1195, 30p, June
16. No. 1198, 22p, Sept. 24. No. 1208, Aug. 5.
100p, July 2. 2p, June 16, 1987. 3p, No. 1210,
Aug. 14, 1987. No. 1199, 17p, Aug. 4, 1987. 26p,
Sept. 2, 1987. 15p, Sept. 9, 1988. 45p, Dec. 20,
1988. 200p, Oct. 19, 1988. No. 1211A, May 19,
1989. No. 1211, July 27, 1989. Nos. 1196, 1203,
Aug. 15, 1989. No. 1209, Dec. 12, 1989. No.
1200, 1989.
See Nos. 1321-1329.

Italian
Chamber
of
Commerce
in Uruguay
A506

1986, May 5   Perf. 12
1212 A506 20p multi   32 16

A507   A508

1986, May 28   Photo.   Perf. 12
1213 A507 20p multi   38 20

1986 World Cup Soccer Championships, Mexico.

Wmk. 332
1986, May 19   Litho.   Perf. 12
1214 A508 10p multi   15 15

Genocide of the Armenian people, 71st anniv.

A509   A510

1986, June 16
1215 A509 10p multi   15 15

El Dia Newspaper, cent.

1986, July 14
1216 A510 20p Garcia, Peruvian flag   20 20

State visit of Pres. Alan Garcia of Peru.

Simon
Bolivar, Gen.
Sucre,
Map — A511

1986, July 24
1217 A511 20p multi   20 20

State visit of Pres. Jaime Lusinchi of Venezuela.

State Visit of Pres.   Zelmar Michelini,
Jose Sarney of   Assassinated Liberal
Brazil — A512   Senator — A513

1986, July 31
1218 A512 20p multi   20 20

1986, Aug. 21
1219 A513 10p vio bl & rose lake   15 15

B'nai B'rith
of Uruguay,
50th Anniv.
A514

1986, Sept. 10
1220 A514 10p red, gold & red brn   15 15

General Agreement on Tariffs & Trade
(GATT) Committee Meeting, Punta del
Este
A515

1986, Sept. 15
1221 A515 10p multi   15 15

Scheduled Flights between Uruguay and Spain, 40th Anniv. A516

1986, Sept. 22
1222 A516 20p multi   20 20

Fish Exports A517

1986, Oct. 1
1223 A517 20p multi   20 20

Wool Exports A518

1986, Oct. 15
1224 A518 20p multi   20 20

Pres. Blanco, Natl. and Dominican Flags A519

1986, Oct. 29
1225 A519 20p multi   20 20

State visit of Pres. Salvador Jorge Blanco of the Dominican Republic.

State Visit of Pres. Sandro Pertini of Italy — A520

State Visit of Pres. Raul Alfonsin of Argentina — A521

1986, Oct. 31
1226 A520 20p grn & buff   20 20

1986, Nov. 10
1227 A521 20p multi   20 20

Hispanic Solidarity Day — A522

Design: Felipe and Santiago, the patron saints of Montevideo, and cathedral.

Wmk. 332
1987, Jan. 12   Litho.   Perf. 12
1228 A522 10p rose lake & blk   15 15

JUVENTUS, 50th Anniv. (in 1986) A523

1987, Jan. 28
1229 A523 10p brt yel, blk & ultra   15 15

Juventus, a Catholic sports, culture and leisure organization.

Hector Gutierrez Ruiz (1934-1976), Politician A524

Intl. Symposium on Science and Technology A525

1987, Feb. 23
1230 A524 10p brn & deep mag   15 15
1231 A525 20p multi   22 22

Ruiz represented Uruguay at an earlier science and technology symposium.

Visit of Pope John Paul II to La Plata Region — A526

Dr. Jose F. Arias (1885-1985), Founder of the University of Crafts — A527

1987, Mar. 31
1232 A526 50p blk & deep org   58 58

1987, Apr. 28
1233 A527 10p multi   15 15

Jewish Community in Uruguay, 70th Anniv. — A528

1987, July 8
1234 A528 10p blk, org & brt blue   15 15

Pluna Airlines, 50th Anniv. (in 1986) A529

1987, Sept. 16
1235 A529 10p Dragon Fly   15 15
1236 A529 20p Douglas DC-3   22 22
1237 A529 25p Vickers Viscount   28 28
1238 A529 30p Boeing 707   35 35

Artigas Antarctic Station A530

1987, Sept. 28
1239 A530 20p multi   22 22

Uruguay Mortgage Bank, 75th Anniv. A531

1987, Oct. 14
1240 A531 26p multi   30 30

Exports — A532

1987, Oct. 28
1241 A532 51p Beef   52 52
1242 A532 51p Milk products   52 52

Christmas 1987 A533

1987, Dec. 21
1243 A533 17p Nativity, vert.   18 18
1244 A533 66p shown   70 70

State Visit of Jose Napoleon Duarte, President of El Salvador — A534

VARIG Airlines, 60th Anniv. (in 1987) — A535

1988, Jan. 12
1245 A534 20p brt olive grn & Prus blue   22 22

1988, Feb. 9
1246 A535 66p blk, blue & brt yel   65 65

Post Office Stamp Foundation — A536

Wmk. 332
1988, Feb. 9   Litho.   Perf. 12
1247 A536 30p on 10+5p brt blue, blk & yel   22 22

No. 1247 not issued without surcharge.

Intl. Peace Year A537

1988, Feb. 11
1248 A537 10p multi   15 15

Euskal Erria, 75th Anniv. (in 1987) — A538

1988, Mar. 9
1249 A538 66p multi   55 55

Basque-Uruguayan diplomatic relations.

Air Force, 75th Anniv. — A539

1988, Mar. 11
1250 A539 17p multi   18 15

Interamerican Children's Institute, 60th Anniv. — A540

Wmk. 332
1988, Mar. 28   Litho.   Perf. 12
1251 A540 30p apple grn, blk & grn   28 28

State Hydroelectric Works (UTE), 75th Anniv. A541

1988, Apr. 20
1252 A541 17p shown   15 15
1253 A541 17p Baygorria Dam   15 15
1254 A541 51p Gabriel Terra Dam   42 42
1255 A541 51p Constitucion Dam   42 42
1256 A541 66p Dams on map   55 55
    Nos. 1252-1256 (5)   1.69 1.69

Dated 1987.

Postal Union of America and Spain (UPAE), 75th Anniv. (in 1987) A542

1988, May 10
1257 A542 66p multi 55 55

Israel, 40th Anniv. A543

1988, May 17
1258 A543 66p lt ultra & blk 55 55

Postal Messenger of Peace — A544

1988, May 24
1259 A544 66p multi 55 55

Portrait, *La Cumparsita* Tango — A545

Firemen, Cent. — A546

1988, June 7
1260 A545 17p Parade, horiz. 15 15
1261 A545 51p Score 38 38

Gerardo H. Matos Rodrigues, composer.

1988, June 21
1262 A546 17p Pablo Banales, founder 15 15
1263 A546 26p Fireman, 1900 20 20
1264 A546 34p Emblem, horiz. 25 25
1265 A546 51p Merry Weather fire engine, 1907, horiz. 38 38
1266 A546 66p Fire pump, 1888, horiz. 50 50

Size: 44x24½mm
1267 A546 100p Ladder truck, 1921 80 80
Nos. 1262-1267 (6) 2.28 2.28

Capitan Miranda Trans-world Voyage, Cent. — A547

1988, July 28
1268 A547 30p multi 25 25

Exports A548

1988
1269 A548 30p Citrus fruit 25 25
1270 A548 45p Rice 35 35
1271 A548 55p Footwear 45 45
1272 A548 55p Leather and furs 45 45

Issue dates: 30p, No. 1272, Sept. 14; 45p, No. 1271, Aug. 23.

Natl. Museum of Natural History, 150th Anniv. — A549

Designs: 30p, *Usnea densirostra* fossil. 90p, *Toxodon platensis* bone, Quaternary period. Printed setenant.

1988, Sept. 20
1273 A549 30p blk, yel & red brn 25 25
1274 A549 90p blk, ultra & beige 75 75

Battle of Carpinteria, 150th Anniv. (in 1986) — A550

1988, Nov. 23
1275 A550 30p multi 20 20

Horiz. row contains two stamps, label, then two more stamps.

Christmas — A551   A552

1988, Dec. 21
1276 A551 115p multi 70 70

1988, Dec. 27

Paintings: a, *Manolita Pina, 1920*, by J. Torres Garcia. b, *78 Squares and Rectangles*, by J.P. Costigliolo. c, Print publicizing an exhibition of works by Pedrero Figari, 1945. d, *Self-portrait, 1947*, by J. Torres Garcia.

1277 Block or strip of 4 + label 2.75 2.75
a.-d. A552 115p any single 65 65

No. 1277 can be collected as a vert. or horiz. strip of 4, or block of 4, with label.

Spanish Heritage Day — A553

1989, Jan. 9
1278 A553 90p multi 55 55
1279 A553 115p multi 65 65

Armenian Organization Hnchakian, Cent. — A554

Wmk. 332
1989, June 7   Litho.   Perf. 12
1280 A554 210p red, yel & blue 38 38

French Revolution, Bicentennial — A555

1989, July 3
1281 A555 50p Plumb line, frame 15 15
1282 A555 50p Liberty tree 15 15
1283 A555 210p Eye in sunburst 38 38
1284 A555 210p Liberty 38 38

Use Postal Codes A556

1989, July 25
1285 A556 50p Montevideo Dept. map 15 15
1286 A556 210p National map, vert. 38 38

3rd Pan American Milk Congress — A557

1989, Aug. 24
1287 A557 170p sky blue & ultra 30 30

A558   A559

Wmk. 332
1989, Aug. 29   Photo.   Perf. 12
1288 A558 170p multicolored 38 38

Joaquin Jose da Silva Xavier.

1989, Aug. 31
1289 A559 210p blk, red & bl 46 46

Inter-Parliamentary Union Conf., London.

FAO Emblem, Map, Citrus Slice — A560

1989, Sept. 11
1290 A560 180p multicolored 40 40

8th Conf., Intergovernmental Group on Citrus Fruits.

UN Decade for the Disabled A561

1989, Oct. 4
1291 A561 50p shown 15 15
1292 A561 210p Disabled people 48 48

America Issue — A562

Nacurutu artifact and UPAE emblem.

1989, Oct. 11   Perf. 12½
1293 A562 60p multicolored 15 15
1294 A562 180p multicolored 40 40

City of Pando, Bicentennial — A563

1989, Dec. 27   Litho.   Perf. 12
1295 A563 60p multicolored 15 15

Christmas A564

1989, Dec. 19

1296	A564	70p Virgin of Trienta y Tres	15	15
1297	A564	210p Barradas, horiz.	38	38

Charity Hospital, Bicent. (in 1988) — A565

1990, Jan. 23   Wmk. 332
1298	A565	60p multicolored	55	55

Provincial Arms and Maps — A566

1990
1299	A566	70p Soriano	24	24
1300	A566	70p Florida, vert.	24	24
1301	A566	90p Canelones	30	30
1302	A566	90p Lavalleja, vert.	30	30
1303	A566	90p San Jose, vert.	30	30
1304	A566	90p Rivera	30	30
		Nos. 1299-1304 (6)	1.68	1.68

Dated 1989.

Writers — A567

Designs: a, Luisa Luisi (1883-1940). b, Javier de Viana (1872-1926). c, Delmira Agustini (1886-1914). d, J. Zorrilla de San Martin (1855-1931). e, Alfonsina Storni (1892-1938). f, Julio Casal (1889-1954). g, Juana de Ibarbourou (1895-1979). h, Carlos Roxlo (1861-1926).

1990, Mar. 20
1320		Block of 8 + 2 labels	3.50	3.50
a.-b.	A567	60p any single	20	20
c.-d.	A567	75p any single	25	25
e.-f.	A567	170p any single	55	55
g.-h.	A567	210p any single	68	68

Printed in sheets of 4 blocks of 4 separated by vert. and horiz. rows of 5 labels. Position of denomination varies to form border around each block. Dated 1989.

Portraits Type of 1986

Designs: 25p, 30p, Lavalleja. 60p, 90p, Rivera. 100p, 150p, 300p, 500p, 1000p, Artigas.

1990   Litho.   Wmk. 332   Perf. 12½
1321	A505	25p orange	15	15
1322	A505	30p ultra	15	15
1323	A505	60p purple	15	15
1324	A505	90p org red	30	30
1325	A505	100p brown	36	36
1326	A505	150p dk blue green	45	45
1327	A505	300p blue	75	75
1328	A505	500p orange red	1.65	1.65
1329	A505	1000p red	2.50	2.50
		Nos. 1321-1329 (9)	6.46	6.46

Issued: 30p, 60p, 7/17; 90p, 3/24; 150p, 6/22; 300p, 7/5; 500p, 3/22; 1000p, 7/24.

A568   A569

1990, Apr. 3   Perf. 12
1346	A568	70p multicolored	22	22

City of Mercedes, bicent. Dated 1989.

1990, Apr. 24
1347	A569	210p multicolored	68	68

Intl. Agricultural Development Fund, 10th anniv.. Dated 1989.

Traffic Safety A570

Designs: a, Bus, car. b, Don't drink and drive. c, Cross on the green light. d, Obey traffic signs.

1990, May 28
1348	A570	70p Block of 4, #a.-d.	88	88

General Artigas — A571

1990, June 18
1349	A571	60p red & blue	18	18

A572   A573

1990, June 26
1350	A572	70p multicolored	22	22

Intl. Mothers' Day. Dated 1989.

1990, July 10

Treaty of Montevideo, 1889: a, Gonzalo Ramirez. b, Ildefonso Garcia. c, Flags at left. d, Flags at right.

1351	A573	60p Block of 4, #a.-d.	72	72

Nos. 1351c-1351d printed in continuous design. Dated 1989.

Microphone, Tower — A574

Designs: b, Newspaper boy. c, Television camera. d, Books.

1990, Sept. 26
1352	A574	70p Block of 4, #a.-d.	88	88

Carlos Federico Saez (1878-1901) — A575

Portraits: b, Pedro Blanes Viale (1879-1926). c, Edmundo Prati (1889-1970). d, Jose L. Zorrilla de San Martin (1891-1975).

1990, Dec. 26
1353		Block of 4	2.00	2.00
a.-b.	A575	90p any single	30	30
c.-d.	A575	210p any single	68	68

Prevent Forest Fires — A576

Wmk. 332
1990, Oct. 26   Litho.   Perf. 12
1354	A576	70np multicolored	88	88

America Issue — A577

1990, Nov. 6
1355	A577	120p Odocoileus bezoarticus	36	36
1356	A577	360p Peltophorum dubium, vert.	1.10	1.10

Army Corps of Engineers, 75th Anniv. — A578

1991, Jan. 21
1357	A578	170p multicolored	50	50

The Nativity by Brother Juan B. Maino — A579

1990, Dec. 24
1358	A579	170p bis & multi	50	50
1359	A579	830p sil & multi	2.50	2.50

Organization of American States, Cent. (in 1989) — A580

Wmk. 332
1991, Mar. 21   Litho.   Perf. 12
1360	A580	830p bl, blk & yel	2.50	2.50

Prevention of AIDS — A581

1991, Mar. 8
1361	A581	170p bl & multi	50	50
1362	A581	830p grn & multi	2.50	2.50

Carnival — A582

1991, Feb. 19
1363	A582	170p multicolored	50	50

Education — A583

Expanding youth's horizons: a, Stone ax, megalithic monument. b, Wheel, pyramids. c, Printing press, solar system. d, Satellite, diagram.

Wmk. 332
1991, Apr. 23   Litho.   Perf. 12
1364		Block of 4	1.50	1.50
a.-b.	A583	120p any single	20	20
c.-d.	A583	330p any single	55	55

Natl. Cancer Day A584

1991, June 17
1365 A584 360p red & black   60   60

A585

Exports of Uruguay — A586

Perf. 12¹/₂x13, 13x12¹/₂
1991   Litho.   Wmk. 332
1366 A585 120p Textiles   22   22
1367 A586 120p Clothing   22   22
1368 A585 400p Semiprecious
              stones, granite   70   80

Issue dates: No. 1366, 400p, Apr. 23. No. 1367, June 26.

7th Pan American Maccabiah Games A587

1991, July 4   Perf. 12¹/₂x13
1369 A587 1490p multicolored   2.35 2.35

Dornier Wal, Route Map — A588

1991, July 5   Perf. 12
1370 A588 1510p multicolored   2.50 2.50

Espamer '91.

Entrance to Sacramento Colony A589

Railroads and Trains: 540p, 825p, First locomotive, 1869. 600p, like 360p. 800p, Entrance to Sacramento Colony. 1510p, 2500p, Horse-drawn streetcar.

1991-93 Litho. Wmk. 332   Perf. 12
1378 A589 360p ol bis & yel   55   55
1378A A589 540p dk bl & gray   85   85
1379 A589 600p brn, yel & blk   70   70
1379A A589 800p grn & yel grn   70   70
1379B A589 825p bl, gray & blk   1.00 1.00
1380 A589 1510p ol bis & emer   2.50 2.50

1382 A589 2500p ol bis, emer &
              blk   2.65 2.65
      Nos. 1378-1382 (7)   8.95 8.95

Issued: 360p, 540p, 1510p, July 19; 825p, Feb. 11, 1991; 2500p, May 29, 1002; 600p, June 18, 1992; 800p, Feb. 9, 1993.
This is an expanding set. Numbers will change.

Sagrada Family College, Cent. — A590

College of the Immaculate Heart of Mary, Cent. — A591

Wmk. 332
1991, June 26   Litho.   Perf. 12
1383 A590 360p multicolored   55   55
1384 A591 1370p multicolored   2.15 2.15

Constitutional Oath — A592

1991, July 17
1385 A592 360p multicolored   55   55

Swiss Confederation, 700th Anniv. — A593

1991, Aug. 1   Perf. 13x12¹/₂
1386 A593 1510p multicolored   3.35 3.35
Souvenir Sheet
Perf. 12
1387 A593 3000p multicolored   6.65 6.65

Photography, 150th Anniv. A594

Perf. 12¹/₂x13
1991, Sept. 12   Litho.   Wmk. 332
1388 A594 1370p multi   1.95 1.95

Actors Society of Uruguay, 50th Anniv. — A595

1991, Aug. 24   Perf. 12
1389 A595 450p blk & red   65   65

CREA (Agriculture Association), 25th Anniv. A596

1991, Sept. 14   Perf. 12¹/₂x13
1390 A596 450p multicolored   65   65

Whitbread Around the World Race — A597

1991, Aug. 20   Perf. 13x12¹/₂
1391 A597 1510p multicolored   2.25 2.25

Amerigo Vespucci (1454-1512) — A598

America Issue: 450p, First landing at River Plate, 1602, vert.

1991, Oct. 11   Perf. 12
1392 A598 450p yel & brn   65   65
1393 A598 1740p ol & brn   2.40 2.40

Automobiles A599

Designs: 350p, Gladiator, 1902. 1370p, E.M.F., 1909. 1490p, Renault, 1912. 1510p, Clement-Bayard, 1903, vert.

Perf. 12¹/₂x13, 13x12¹/₂
1991, Oct. 18
1394 A599 360p multicolored   50   50
1395 A599 1370p multicolored   1.95 1.95
1396 A599 1490p multicolored   2.00 2.00
1397 A599 1510p multicolored   2.25 2.25

Natl. Soccer Team, Winners of Toyota and Europe-South America Cups — A600

Wmk. 332
1991, Nov. 8   Litho.   Perf. 12
1398 A600 450p shown   65   65
1399 A600 450p Emblem, trophy,
              vert.   65   65

Margarita Xirgu (1888-1969), Actress — A601

1991, Oct. 4
1400 A601 360p yel & brn   52   52

INTERPOL, 60th Congress — A602

1991, Oct. 30
1401 A602 1740p multicolored   2.35 2.35

Maria Auxiliadora Institute, Cent. — A603

1991, Nov. 11
1402 A603 450p multicolored   65   65

Technological Laboratory, 25th Anniv. — A604

1991, Nov. 11
1403 A604 1570p dk bl & lt bl   2.00 2.00

The Table by Zoma Baitler — A605

1991, Oct. 18
1404 A605 360p multicolored   52   52

World Food Day — A606

1991, Oct. 16   *Perf. 12½x13*
1405 A606 1740p multicolored   2.35   2.35

Ships — A607

Designs: a, Steam yacht, Gen. Rivera. b, Coast Guard cutter, Salto. c, Cruiser, Uruguay. d, Tanker, Pte. Oribe.

Wmk. 332
1991, Oct. 4   **Litho.**   *Perf. 12*
1406   Block of 4   5.50   5.50
a.-b. A607 450p any single   60   60
c.-d. A607 1570p any single   2.05   2.05

Topographical Society Type of 1981

1991, Dec. 3   *Perf. 12½*
1407 A439 550p multi   72   72

Topographical Society, 160th anniv.

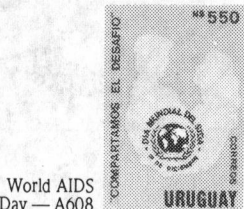

World AIDS Day — A608

1991, Dec. 1
1408 A608 550p bl, blk & brt yel   72   72
1409 A608 2040p lt grn, blk & lil   2.60   2.60

Export Industies A609

1991, Mar. 20   **Litho.**   *Perf. 12½*   **Wmk. 332**
1410 A609 120p multicolored   16   16

Christmas   CORREOS
A610   URUGUAY   N$ 550

1991, Dec. 24   *Perf. 12*
1411 A610 550p Angel   70   70
1412 A610 2040p Adoration of the
      Angels   2.50   2.50

Muscians A611

Designs: No. 1413a, Francisco Canaro. No. 1413b, Anibal Troilo. No. 1414a, Juan de Dios Filiberto. No. 1414b, Pintin Castellanos.

Wmk. 332
1992, Jan. 20   **Photo.**   *Perf. 12*
1413 A611 450p Pair, #a.-b.   1.10   1.10
1414 A611 450p Pair, #a.-b.   1.10   1.10

Patricio Aylwin, Pres. of Chile — A612

Perf. 11½x12
1992, Mar. 23   **Litho.**   **Unwmk.**
1415 A612 550p multicolored   65   65

Penarol, Winners of Liberator's Cup in Club Soccer — A612a   La Paz City, 120th Anniv. — A612b

Perf. 13x12½
1992, May 29   **Litho.**   **Wmk. 332**
1415A A612a 600p yellow & black   70   70

Souvenir Sheet
Perf. 12
1415B A612a 3000p yellow & black   3.50   3.50

1992, May 25   *Perf. 13x12½*
1415C A612b 550p multicolored   65   65

World No-Smoking Day — A613

Wmk. 332
1992, May 31   **Litho.**   *Perf. 12*
1416 A613 2500p multicolored   2.65   2.65

United Nations World Health Day A614

Wmk. 332
1992, July 28   **Litho.**   *Perf. 13*
1417 A614 2500p bl, lt bl & red   2.75   2.75

Mercosur A615

1992, Aug. 5   **Photo.**   *Perf. 12*
1418 A615 2500p multicolored   2.75   2.75

Olymphilex '92, Barcelona — A616

Wmk. 332
1992, Aug. 8   **Photo.**   *Perf. 12*
1419 A616 2900p multicolored   3.00   3.00

Discovery of America, 500th Anniv. A617

Perf. 11½x12, 12x11½
1992, Oct. 10   **Litho.**   **Unwmk.**
1420 A617 700p Ship, masts, vert.   65   65
1421 A617 2900p Globe, ship   2.75   2.75

Jose Pedro Varela Natl. Teachers College, 50th Anniv. A618

1992, Oct. 22   *Perf. 12x11½*
1422 A618 700p multicolored   65   65

22nd Regional FAO Conference A619

Designs: 2500p, Emblems. 2900p, Emblems, children with food basket.

1992, Sept. 28
1423 A619 2500p multicolored   2.35   2.35
1424 A619 2900p multicolored   2.75   2.75

Intl. Conf. on Nutrition, Rome, Italy (#1424).

Cesar Vallejo (1892-1938), Poet — A620

1992, Sept. 30
1425 A620 2500p brn & dk brn   2.35   2.35

A621   A622

1992, Oct. 26   *Perf. 11½x12*
1426 A621 700p gray, red & black   65   65

Assoc. of Wholesalers and Retailers, cent.

Perf. 11½x12
1992, Oct. 10   **Litho.**   **Unwmk.**
1427 A622 700p black, blue & grn   65   65

Monument to Columbus, cent.

A623   A624

Ruins and lighthouse, Colonia del Sacramento.

1992, Oct. 10
1428 A623 700p multicolored   65   65

Discovery of America, 500th anniv.

1992, Oct. 19
1429 A624 700p red lil, rose lil & blk   65   65

Columbus Philanthropic Society, cent.

N•E•W

Scott Supplement
Pages for

Uruguay

are now available

A625   A626

1992, Oct. 19
1430 A625 2900p multicolored   2.75 2.75

Judaism in the Americas, 500th anniv.

1992, Oct. 30
1431 A626 2900p multicolored   2.75 2.75

Lebanon Society of Uruguay, 50th anniv.

Pan American Health Organization, 90th
Anniv. — A627

Perf. 12x11½
1992, Dec. 15   Litho.   Unwmk.
1432 A627 3200p blk, bl & yel   2.75 2.75

22nd Lions
Club Forum
for Latin
America and
the
Caribbean
A628

1992, Dec. 2
1433 A628 2700p multicolored   2.30 2.30

Christmas — A629

1992, Dec. 1   Perf. 11½x12
1434 A629 800p Nativity scene   70 70
1435 A629 3200p Star in sky   2.70 2.70

General
Manuel
Oribe,
Birth
Bicent.
A630

Designs: No. 1436, Oribe, Oriental College. No. 1437, Oribe in military dress uniform, vert.

Perf. 12x11½, 11½x12
1992, Dec. 8   Litho.   Unwmk.
1436 A630 800p multicolored   70 70
1437 A630 800p multicolored   70 70

Logosofia,
60th
Anniv.
A631

1992, Dec. 29   Perf. 12x11½
1438 A631 800p blue & yellow   70 70

Immigrants'
Day — A632

1992, Dec. 4   Perf. 11½x12
1439 A632 800p black & green   70 70

ANDEBU,
70th
Anniv.
A633

Caritas of
Uruguay,
30th Anniv.
A634

1992, Dec. 22   Photo.   Perf. 12x11½
1440 A633 2700p Satellite   2.20 2.20
1441 A634 3200p Map, huts by
water   2.65 2.65

A635   A636

1992, Dec. 18   Perf. 11½x12
1442 A635 800p brown & yellow   70 70

Jose H. Molaguero S. A., 50th anniv.

Perf. 11½x12
1993, Mar. 1   Litho.   Unwmk.
1443 A636 80c multicolored   65 65

Wilson Ferreira Aldunate.

Economic Science and Accountancy
College, Cent. — A637

Perf. 12x11½
1993, Apr. 15   Photo.   Unwmk.
1444 A637 1p multicolored   80 80

Souvenir Sheet

Polska '93, Intl. Philatelic
Exhibition — A638

Designs: a, Lech Walesa. b, Pope John Paul II.

1993, May 3   Perf. 11½x12
1445 A638 2p Sheet of 2, #a.-b.   3.00 3.00

Mail Truck — A639

A639a   A639b

Designs: No. 1448, Mail truck. No. 1450, Express Mail motorscooter. Nos. 1451, 1453, Stylized gull. No. 1452, Arrows. No. 1454, Letter box, 1879.

1993-94   Litho.   Wmk. 332   Perf. 12
1448 A639   1p orange yellow &
blue   80 80
1450 A639a   1p orange & blue   55 55
1451 A639b (1.40p) green   65 65
1452 A639b   1.40p yellow & blue   65 65
1453 A639b (1.60p) red   1.00 1.00
1454 A639b   1.80p blue & yellow   1.10 1.10
Nos. 1448-1454 (6)   4.75 4.75

Issued: #1448, 4/15/93; #1450, 10/3/94; #1451, 12/1/93; #1452, 1/4/94; #1453, 4/4/94; #1454, 8/9/94.
This is an expanding set. Numbers may change.

Interior Fire
Service, 50th
Anniv. — A640

15th Congress of
UPAEP — A641

Perf. 11½x12
1993, May 28   Litho.   Unwmk.
1466 A640 1p multicolored   75 75

1993, June 21
1467 A641 3.50p multicolored   2.50 2.50

Uruguayan
Navy,
175th
Anniv.
A642

Design: 1p, Sailing ship, Pedro Campbell, first admiral.

Perf. 12x11½
1993, June 28   Litho.   Wmk. 332
1468 A642 1p multicolored   75 75

Intl.
University
Society,
25th Anniv.
A643

1993, July 2
1469 A643 1p multicolored   75 75

Automobile
Club of
Uruguay,
75th Anniv.
A644

1993, July 19   Photo.   Unwmk.
1470 A644 3.50p 1910 Hupmobile   2.50 2.50

Uruguay Battalion in UN Peacekeeping
Force, Cambodia — A645

Perf. 12x11½
1993, Aug. 6   Litho.   Unwmk.
1471 A645 1p multicolored   75 75

Souvenir Sheet

Brasiliana '93 — A646

World Cup Soccer Champions: a, Uruguay, 1930, 1950. b, Brazil, 1958, 1962, 1970.

1993, July 28   Perf. 11½x12
1472 A646 2.50p Sheet of 2, #a.-b.   3.75 3.75

State
Television
Channel
5, 30th
Anniv.
A647

1993, Aug. 19   Perf. 12x11½
1473 A647 1.20p multicolored   90 90

ANDA, 60th
Anniv.
A648

Perf. 12½
1993, Sept. 24   Litho.   Unwmk.
1474 A648 1.20p multicolored   85   85

Natl. Police
Academy,
50th Anniv.
A649

1993, Sept. 24
1475 A649 1.20p multicolored   90   90

Newspaper Diario El
Pais, 75th
Anniv. — A650

Perf. 12½
1993, Sept. 30   Litho.   Unwmk.
1476 A650 1.20p multicolored   85   85

Latin American Conference on Rural
Electrification — A651

1993, Oct. 11
1477 A651 3.50p multicolored   2.50 2.50

B'nai B'rith,
150th Anniv.
A652

1993, Oct. 13
1478 A652 3.70p multicolored   2.75 2.75

A653   Fauna — A654

1993 Photo.   Wmk. 332   Perf. 12½
1482 A653 20c Seriema bird   15   15
1484 A653 30c Dragon bird   20   20
1486 A653 50c Anteaters, horiz.   35   35
1492 A654 1.20p Giant armadillo   90   90

Issued: 1.20p, 8/3/93; 20c, 30c, 50c, 10/22/93.
This is an expanding set. Numbers may change.

America
Issue
A655

Perf. 12½
1993, Oct. 6   Litho.   Unwmk.
1504 A655 1.20p Caiman latirostris   85   85
1505 A655 3.50p Athene cunicularia,
vert.   2.50 2.50

Souvenir Sheet

Whitbread Trans-Global Yacht
Race — A656

1993, Oct. 22   Perf. 11½x12
1506 A656 5p multicolored   3.50 3.50

Beatification of   Intl. Year of
Mother Francisca   Indigenous
Rubatto — A657   People — A658

1993, Oct. 29   Wmk. 332   Perf. 12
1507 A657 1.20p multicolored   85   85

Perf. 13x12½
1993, Oct. 29   Unwmk.
1508 A658 3.50p multicolored   2.50 2.50

Rotary Club of
Montevideo, 75th
Anniv. — A658a

Perf. 12½
1993, Nov. 10   Litho.   Unwmk.
1508A A658a 3.50p dk bl & bis   2.50 2.50

Rhea Americana
A659

1993, Dec. 20   Litho.   Perf. 12
1509 A659 20c shown   15   15
1510 A659 20c With chicks   15   15
1511 A659 50c Head   35   35
1512 A659 50c Two walking   35   35

World Wildlife Fund.

Children's
Rights Day
A660

1994, Jan. 4   Perf. 12½
1513 A660 1.40p multicolored   95   95

Independence of Lebanon, 50th
Anniv. — A661

1993, Nov. 22
1514 A661 3.70p multicolored   2.50 2.50

Eduardo Victor
Haedo — A662

1993, Nov. 24
1515 A662 1.20p multicolored   85   85

Christmas — A663   Intl. AIDS
Day — A664

1993, Dec. 7
1516 A663 1.40p shown   90   90
1517 A663 4p Nativity, diff.   2.75 2.75

1993, Dec. 1
1518 A664 1.40p multicolored   95   95

Souvenir Sheets

URUGUAY CORREOS $1
Anniversaries & Events — A665

Designs: No. 1519a, Switzerland #3L1, 1913
Swiss private air mail stamp. b, Germany #C40,
Uruguay #C426c. c, Uruguay #C372, US #C76. d,
Uruguay #C282a, US #C104.
No. 1520a, Switzerland Types A1, A2. b, Swit-
zerland #B541.

1993, Nov. 18
1519 A665   1p Sheet of 4, #a.-d.   2.00 2.00
1520 A665 2.50p Sheet of 2, #a.-b.   2.50 2.50

Swiss postage stamps, 150th anniv. (#1519a,
1520). Dr. Hugo Eckener, 125th anniv. of birth
(#1519b). First man on moon, 25th anniv.
(#1519c). 1994 World Cup Soccer Championships,
US (#1519d).
Nos. 1519-1520 exist imperf.

17th Inter-American Naval
Conference — A666

1994, Mar. 21   Litho.   Perf. 12½
1521 A666 3.70p multicolored   2.50 2.50

A667   A668

1994, Mar. 11   Perf. 12½
1522 A667 4p multicolored   2.75 2.75

5th World Sports Congress, Punta del Este.

Unwmk.
1994, Apr. 4   Litho.   Perf. 12
1523 A668 3.90p multicolored   2.50 2.50

Latin America Youth Organization, 7th
conference.

A669   A670

1994, Apr. 18
1524 A669 4.30p multicolored   2.75 2.75

4th World Congress on Merino Wool.

1994, Apr. 28   Perf. 12½
1525 A670 4.30p multicolored   2.75 2.75

ILO, 75th anniv.

Miniature Sheet

1994
Winter
Olympic
Medal
Winners
A671

Designs: a, Katja Seizinger. b, Markus Wasmeier.
c, Vreni Schneider. d, Gustav Weder.

1994, May 6   Perf. 12
1526 A671 1.25p Sheet of 4, #a.-d.   6.25 6.25

No. 1526 exists demonitized and imperf on
paper with watermark 322. This item was sold with
No. 1526 and has a matching serial number.

Miniature Sheet

1994 World Cup Soccer Championships, US — A672

Designs: a, Soccer ball, flags of Uruguay, Brazil. b, Ball, flags of Italy, Argentina. c, Ball, flags of Germany, Great Britain. d, Olympic Rings.

1994, May 16
1527 A672 1.25p Sheet of 4, #a.-d. 6.25 6.25

Uruguay, Olympic soccer gold medalists, 1924-1928 (#1527d).
See note after No. 1526.

Clemente Estable (1894-1976), Biologist — A673

1994, May 23   Litho.   Perf. 12½
1528 A673 1.60p olive & black 1.00 1.00

Electoral Court, 70th Anniv. — A674

1994, June 7
1529 A674 1.60p multicolored 1.00 1.00

Natl. Commission to Prevent Tapeworms — A675

Perf. 12½
1994, June 17   Litho.   Unwmk.
1530 A675 1.60p multicolored 95 95

Souvenir Sheet

Cesareo L. Berisso, First Aviator to Land at Natl. Airport, Carrasco — A676

1994, June 21   Perf. 12
1531 A676 5p multicolored 3.00 3.00

Intl. Cooperatives, 150th Anniv. — A677

1994, July 1   Perf. 12½
1532 A677 4.30p multicolored 2.50 2.50

Commission on Integration of Regional Electricity, 30th Anniv. — A678

1994, July 8
1533 A678 1.60p multicolored 95 95

Abate Pierre A679

Perf. 12½
1994, Aug. 5   Litho.   Unwmk.
1534 A679 4.80p multicolored 2.75 2.75

Intl. Year of the Family A680

1994, July 28
1535 A680 4.80p multicolored 2.75 2.75

The Man of Lugano, by Goffredo Sommavilla (1850-1944) A681

Perf. 12½
1994, Aug. 15   Litho.   Unwmk.
1536 A681 4.80p multicolored 2.75 2.75

First Manned Moon Landing, 25th Anniv. A682

1994, July 20
1537 A682 3p multicolored 1.75 1.75

Intl. Olympic Committee, Cent. — A683

1994, Aug. 23
1538 A683 4.80p multicolored 2.75 2.75

Elbio Fernandez School, 125th Anniv. A684

Perf. 12½
1994, Aug. 29   Litho.   Unwmk.
1539 A684 1.80p multicolored 1.00 1.00

A685   A686

1994, Sept. 10   Perf. 12
1540 A685 1.80p black & blue 1.00 1.00

Gral. Aparicio Saravia, 90th Death Anniv.

1994, Sept. 30   Perf. 12½
1541 A686 4.80p multicolored 2.50 2.50

6th Latin American Urban Congress.

General Assoc. of Uruguayan Authors, 65th Anniv. — A687

Perf. 12½
1994, Sept. 26   Litho.   Unwmk.
1542 A687 1.80p multicolored 95 95

America Issue A688

1994, Oct. 10
1543 A688 1.80p Stagecoach 95 95
1544 A688 4.80p Paddle steamer 2.75 2.75

A689   A690

Perf. 12½
1994, Oct. 28   Litho.   Unwmk.
1545 A689 2p multicolored 1.10 1.10

Assoc. of Directors of Marketing, 50th anniv.

1994, Nov. 25
1546 A690 2p multicolored 1.10 1.10

YMCA in Uruguay, 85th anniv.

Lottery, 55th Anniv. A691

1994, Nov. 21
1547 A691 2p multicolored 1.10 1.10

First Intl. Seminar to Promote Roads in Uruguay, Punta del Este A692

1994, Oct. 14
1548 A692 2p multicolored 1.10 1.10

Uruguayan Press Assoc., 50th Anniv. A693

1994, Oct. 24
1549 A693 2p multicolored 1.10 1.10

Miniature Sheet

Natl. Mint, 150th Anniv. A694

Portions of old coin press and: a, Mint building. b, 1844 Copper coin. c, 1844 Silver coin. d, Montevideo silver peso.

1994, Oct. 17   Perf. 12
1550 A694 1.50p Sheet of 4, #a.-d. 3.25 3.25

No. 1550 exists demonitized and imperf. on paper with watermark 322. This item was sold with No. 1550 and has matching serial numbers.

Miniature Sheet

Natl. Navy
URUGUAY CORREOS $1.50 A695

Ships: a, ROU Uruguay, ROU Artigas. b, ROU Fortuna. c, ROU Uruguay. d, ROU Cte. Pedro Campbell.

1994, Nov. 15
1551 A695 1.50p Sheet of 4, #a.-d. 3.25 3.25

Latin American Peace Movement, 25th Anniv. A696

1994, Nov. 15   Perf. 12½
1552 A696 4.30p multicolored   2.25 2.25

4th Conference of the Latin American and Caribbean Organization of High Fiscal Entities, Montevideo — A697

1994, Dec. 5
1553 A697 5.50p multicolored   3.00 3.00

Christmas — A698

1994, Dec. 2
1554 A698 2p shown   1.10 1.10
1555 A698 5.50p Star, tree, house   3.00 3.00

Uruguayan Red Cross & Red Crescent Societies, 75th Anniv. A699

1994, Dec. 20   Perf. 12½   Litho.   Unwmk.
1556 A699 5p multicolored   2.50 2.50

A700

1995   Litho.   Wmk. 332   Perf. 12
1557 A700 20c yellow green   22 22

Issued: 20c, 1/11/95. This is an expanding set. Number may change.

Naval Aviation, 70th Anniv. A704

1995, Feb. 7   Perf. 12½   Litho.   Unwmk.
1567 A704 2p multicolored   1.10 1.10

World Tourism Organization — A705

Designs: No. 1568, Ranch house, sheep herders. No. 1569, Water recreation park. No. 1570, Native wildlife. No. 1571, Beach resort.

1995, Feb. 13
1568 A705 5p multicolored   2.50 2.50
1569 A705 5p multicolored   2.50 2.50
1570 A705 5p multicolored   2.50 2.50
1571 A705 5p multicolored   2.50 2.50
Nos. 1568-1571 (4)   10.00 10.00

17th World Conference of Lifeguard Services — A706

1995, Feb. 15
1572 A706 5p multicolored   2.50 2.50

Rotary Intl., 90th Anniv. A707

1995, Feb. 22
1573 A707 5p multicolored   2.50 2.50

ICAO, 50th Anniv. A708

1995, Mar. 14
1574 A708 5p multicolored   2.50 2.50

SEMI-POSTAL STAMPS

Indigent Old Man — SP1

Unwmk.
1930, Nov. 13   Engr.   Perf. 12
B1 SP1 1c + 1c dark violet   18 18
B2 SP1 2c + 2c deep green   20 20
B3 SP1 5c + 5c red   25 25
B4 SP1 8c + 8c gray violet   25 25

The surtax on these stamps was for a fund to assist the aged.
For surcharge see No. 419.

> Catalogue values for unused stamps in this section, from this point to the end of the section, are for Never Hinged items.

Dam, Child and Rising Sun — SP2

1959, Sept. 29   Wmk. 327   Perf. 11½   Litho.
B5 SP2 5c + 10c green & org   15 15
B6 SP2 10c + 10c dk bl & org   15 15
B7 SP2 1p + 10c purple & org   25 25
Set value   40 38

National recovery. See Nos. CB1-CB2. For surcharges see Nos. 727, Q100.

AIR POST STAMPS

No. 91 Overprinted in Dark Blue, Red or Green

1921-22   Unwmk.   Perf. 14
C1 A38 25c bis brn (Bl)   7.50 6.00
  a. Black overprint   450.00 450.00
C2 A38 25c bis brn (R)   2.50 1.90
  a. Inverted overprint   60.00 60.00
C3 A38 25c bis brn (G) ('22)   2.50 1.90

This overprint also exists in light yellow green.
No. C1a was not issued. Some authorities consider it an overprint color trial.

AP2

Perf. 11½
1924, Jan. 2   Litho.   Wmk. 188
C4 AP2 6c dk bl   1.00 1.00
C5 AP2 10c scarlet   1.50 1.50
C6 AP2 20c dp grn   2.50 2.50

Heron — AP3

1925, Aug. 24   Perf. 12½
Inscribed "MONTEVIDEO"
C7 AP3 14c bl & blk   20.00 10.00
Inscribed "FLORIDA"
C8 AP3 14c bl & blk   20.00 10.00

These stamps were used only on Aug. 25, 1925, the cent. of the Assembly of Florida, on letters intended to be carried by airplane between Montevideo and Florida, a town 60 miles north. The stamps were not delivered to the public but were affixed to the letters and canceled by post office clerks. Later uncanceled copies came on the market.
One authority believes Nos. C7-C8 served as registration stamps on these two attempted special flights.

Gaucho Cavalryman at Rincón AP4

1925, Sept. 24   Perf. 11
C9 AP4 45c blue green   6.00

Centenary of Battle of Rincon. Used only on Sept. 24. No. C9 was affixed and canceled by post office clerks.

Albatross — AP5

1926, Mar. 3   Wmk. 188   Imperf.
C10 AP5 6c dk bl   70 70
C11 AP5 10c vermilion   1.00 1.00
C12 AP5 20c bl grn   1.40 1.40
C13 AP5 25c violet   1.40 1.40

Excellent counterfeits exist.

1928, June 25   Perf. 11
C14 AP5 10c green   1.00 90
C15 AP5 20c orange   1.50 1.10
C16 AP5 30c indigo   1.50 1.10
C17 AP5 38c green   2.25 2.00
C18 AP5 40c yellow   2.75 2.50
C19 AP5 50c violet   3.00 3.00
C20 AP5 76c orange   5.50 5.50
C21 AP5 1p red   4.50 4.50
C22 AP5 1.14p indigo   13.00 11.50
C23 AP5 1.52p yellow   20.00 20.00
C24 AP5 1.90p violet   24.00 22.50
C25 AP5 3.80p red   65.00 57.50
Nos. C14-C25 (12)   144.00 132.10

Counterfeits of No. C25 exist.

1929, Aug. 23   Unwmk.
C26 AP5 4c olive brown   1.90 1.90

The design was redrawn for Nos. C14-C26. The numerals are narrower, "CENTS" is 1mm high instead of 2½mm and imprint letters touch the bottom frame line.

Pegasus — AP6

1929-43   Engr.   Perf. 12½
Size: 34x23mm
C27 AP6 1c red lil ('30)   16 16
C28 AP6 1c dk bl ('32)   16 16
C29 AP6 2c yellow ('30)   16 16
C30 AP6 2c ol grn ('32)   16 16
C31 AP6 4c Prus bl ('32)   28 24
C32 AP6 4c car rose ('32)   28 24
C33 AP6 6c dl vio ('30)   30 24
C34 AP6 6c red brn ('32)   30 24
C35 AP6 8c red org   1.40 1.40
C36 AP6 8c gray ('30)   1.65 1.40
C36A AP6 8c brt grn ('43)   20 16
C37 AP6 16c indigo   1.40 1.00
C38 AP6 16c rose ('30)   1.40 1.40
C39 AP6 24c claret   1.25 1.25
C40 AP6 24c brt vio ('30)   1.65 1.40
C41 AP6 30c bister   1.40 1.40
C42 AP6 30c dk grn ('30)   80 40
C43 AP6 40c dk brn   2.50 2.50
C44 AP6 40c yel org ('30)   2.50 2.25
C45 AP6 60c bl grn   2.25 1.65
C46 AP6 60c emer ('30)   3.75 3.00
C47 AP6 60c dp org ('31)   1.25 80
C48 AP6 80c dk ultra   4.00 3.75
C49 AP6 80c grn ('30)   6.50 5.25
C50 AP6 90c light blue   3.75 2.75
C51 AP6 90c dk ol grn ('30)   6.50 5.25
C52 AP6 1p car rose ('30)   3.00 2.50
C53 AP6 1.20p ol grn   9.00 9.00
C54 AP6 1.20p dp car ('30)   14.00 12.00
C55 AP6 1.50p red brn   9.00 7.25
C56 AP6 1.50p blk brn ('30)   5.00 4.50
C57 AP6 3p dp red   15.00 14.00
C58 AP6 3p ultra ('30)   10.00 10.00
C59 AP6 4.50p black   26.00 24.00

C60	AP6	4.50p vio ('30)	18.00 16.00
C60A	AP6	10p dp ultra ('43)	9.00 7.25
		Nos. C27-C60A (36)	163.95 145.11

See Nos. C63-C82. For surcharges see Nos. C106-C112, C114.

Nos. 450, 452
Overprinted in Red

1934, Jan. 1   *Perf. 11½*

C61	A130	17c ver, gray & vio	10.00 8.00
a.		Sheet of 6	87.50
b.		Gray omitted	100.00
c.		Double overprint	100.00
C62	A130	36c red, blk & yel	10.00 8.00
a.		Sheet of 6	87.50

7th Pan-American Conference, Montevideo.

Pegasus Type of 1929

1935   Engr.   *Perf. 12½*
  Size: 31½x21mm

C63	AP6	15c dl yel	1.25 1.00
C64	AP6	22c brick red	75 65
C65	AP6	30c brn vio	1.25 1.00
C66	AP6	37c gray lil	65 50
C67	AP6	40c rose lake	1.00 65
C68	AP6	47c rose	2.00 1.75
C69	AP6	50c Prus bl	65 38
C70	AP6	52c dp ultra	2.00 1.75
C71	AP6	57c grnsh bl	1.00 90
C72	AP6	62c olive grn	90 40
C73	AP6	87c gray grn	2.75 2.25
C74	AP6	1p olive	1.75 1.10
C75	AP6	1.12p brn red	1.75 1.10
C76	AP6	1.20p bis brn	6.00 4.75
C77	AP6	1.27p red brn	6.00 5.00
C78	AP6	1.62p rose	4.00 4.00
C79	AP6	2p brn rose	6.50 5.75
C80	AP6	2.12p dk sl grn	6.50 5.75
C81	AP6	3p dl bl	4.00
C82	AP6	5p orange	20.00 20.00
		Nos. C63-C82 (20)	72.70 64.43

Counterfeits exist.

Power Dam on Black River — AP7

Imprint: "Imp. Nacional" at center

1937-41   Litho.

C83	AP7	20c lt grn ('38)	1.75 1.50
C84	AP7	35c red brn	2.75 2.50
C85	AP7	62c bl grn ('38)	30 15
C86	AP7	68c yel org ('38)	75 52
C86A	AP7	68c pale vio brn ('41)	60 24
C87	AP7	75c violet	2.75 80
C88	AP7	1p dp pink ('38)	1.00 75
C89	AP7	1.38p rose ('38)	9.00 8.00
C90	AP7	3p dk bl ('40)	5.00 1.00
		Nos. C83-C90 (9)	23.90 15.46

Imprint at left

C91	AP7	8c pale brn ('39)	25 20
C92	AP7	20c lt grn ('38)	1.00 65

For surcharge and overprint see Nos. 545, C120.

Plane over Sculptured Oxcart — AP8

1939-44   *Perf. 12½*

C93	AP8	20c slate	18 15
C94	AP8	20c lt vio ('43)	28 30
C95	AP8	20c blue ('44)	22 15
C96	AP8	35c red	35 28
C97	AP8	50c brn org	35 15
C98	AP8	75c dp pink	40 15
C99	AP8	1p dp bl ('40)	1.10 15
C100	AP8	1.38p brt vio	2.00 80
C101	AP8	1.38p yel org ('44)	1.75 1.65
C102	AP8	2p blue	3.00 55
a.		Perf. 11	3.00 40
C103	AP8	5p rose lilac	3.75 80
C104	AP8	5p bl grn ('44)	5.00 2.00
C105	AP8	10p rose ('48)	30.00 20.00
		Nos. C93-C105 (13)	48.38 27.13

Counterfeits exist.
For surcharges see Nos. C116-C119.

Nos. C68, C71, C75, C73, C77-C78, C80 Surcharged in Red or Black   **$0.79**

1944, Nov. 22

C106	AP6	40c on 47c	30 24
C107	AP6	40c on 57c (R)	40 30
C108	AP6	74c on 1.12p	40 30
C109	AP6	79c on 87c	1.40 1.00
C110	AP6	79c on 1.27p	2.00 1.65
C111	AP6	1.20p on 1.62p	1.10 80
C112	AP6	1.43p on 2.12p (R)	1.40 1.00
		Nos. C106-C112 (7)	7.00 5.29

> Catalogue values for unused stamps in this section, from this point to the end of the section, are for Never Hinged items.

Legislature Building — AP9

Unwmk.
1945, May 11   Engr.   *Perf. 11*

C113	AP9	2p ultra	1.65 65

Type of 1929, Surcharged in Violet

1945, Aug. 14   *Perf. 12½*

C114	AP6	44c on 75c brown	65 30

Allied Nations' victory in Europe.

"La Eolo" AP10

1945, Oct. 31   *Perf. 11*

C115	AP10	8c green	60 20

Nos. C97 and C101 Surcharged in Violet, Black or Blue

1945-46   *Perf. 12½*

C116	AP8	14c on 50c (V) ('46)	32 20
a.		Inverted surcharge	37.50
C117	AP8	23c on 1.38p	40 25
a.		Inverted surcharge	75.00
C118	AP8	23c on 50c	50 30
a.		Inverted surcharge	75.00
C119	AP8	1p on 1.38p (Bl)	2.75 1.50
a.		Inverted surcharge	75.00

Victory of the Allied Nations in WWII.

No. C85 Overprinted in Black
INAUGURACION
DICIEMBRE, 1945

1946, Jan. 9

C120	AP7	62c blue green	65 35

Issued to commemorate the inauguration of the Black River Power Dam.

AP11

Black Overprint
1946-49   Litho.

C121	AP11	8c car rose	15 15
a.		Inverted overprint	40 20
C122	AP11	50c brown	40 20
a.		Double overprint	25.00
C123	AP11	1p lt bl	65 25
C124	AP11	2p ol ('49)	3.00 1.50
C125	AP11	3p lil rose	3.00 1.50
C126	AP11	5p rose car	6.00 4.00
		Nos. C121-C126 (6)	13.20 7.60

Four-Motored Plane — AP12

National Airport AP13

1947-49 *Perf. 11½, 12½*

C129	AP12	3c org brn ('49)	15 15
C130	AP12	8c car rose ('49)	15 15
C131	AP12	14c ultra	16 15
C132	AP12	23c emerald	20 15
C133	AP13	1p car & brn ('49)	1.00 24
C134	AP13	3p ultra & brn ('49)	2.25 1.25
C135	AP13	5p grn & brn ('49)	5.00 2.50
C136	AP13	10p lil rose & brn	5.25 3.75
		Nos. C129-C136 (8)	14.16 8.34

Counterfeits exist. See Nos. C145-C164. For surcharges see Nos. C206, Q94.

AP14   School of Architecture, University of Uruguay — AP15

Black Overprint
1948, June 9   *Perf. 12½*

C137	AP14	12c blue	16 15
C138	AP14	24c Prus grn	28 15
C139	AP14	36c slate blue	40 18
		Set value	32

1949, Dec. 7

Designs: 27c, Medical School. 31c, Engineering School. 36c, University.

C141	AP15	15c carmine	15 15
C142	AP15	27c chocolate	16 15
C143	AP15	31c dp ultra	28 15
C144	AP15	36c dull green	30 15
		Set value	35

Issued to commemorate the centenary of the founding of the University of Uruguay.

Plane Type of 1947-49

1952-59   Unwmk.   *Perf. 11, 12½*

C145	AP12	10c blk ('54)	15 15
C146	AP12	10c lt red ('58)	15 15
a.		Imperf. pair	30.00
C147	AP12	15c org brn	15 15
a.		Vert. pair, imperf. between	42.50

C148	AP12	20c lil rose ('54)	15 15
C149	AP12	21c purple	16 15
C150	AP12	27c yel grn ('57)	16 15
C151	AP12	31c chocolate	28 15
C152	AP12	36c ultra	20 15
C153	AP12	36c blk ('58)	20 15
C154	AP12	50c lt bl ('57)	32 18
C155	AP12	50c bl blk ('58)	24 15
C156	AP12	62c dl sl bl ('53)	40 18
C157	AP12	65c rose ('53)	40 18
C158	AP12	84c org ('59)	48 30
C159	AP12	1.08p vio brn	85 32
C160	AP12	2p Prus bl	1.40 50
C161	AP12	3p red org	1.65 65
C162	AP12	5p dk gray grn	3.25 1.50
C163	AP12	5p gray ('57)	2.00 1.00
C164	AP12	10p dp grn ('55)	8.25 4.50
		Nos. C145-C164 (20)	20.84 10.81

Planes and Show Emblem AP16

Unwmk.
1956, Jan. 5   Litho.   *Perf. 11*

C166	AP16	20c ultra	32 30
C167	AP16	31c olive grn	40 20
C168	AP16	36c car rose	60 25

First Exposition of National Products.

Type of Regular Issue and

José Batlle y Ordonez AP17

Designs: 10c, Full-face portrait without hand. 36c, Portrait facing right.

Perf. 13½
1956, Dec. 15   Wmk. 90   Photo.

C169	A178	10c magenta	15 15
C170	A178	20c grnsh blk	16 15
C171	AP17	31c brown	28 16
C172	AP17	36c bl grn	32 16
		Set value	45

Issued to commemorate the centenary of the birth of President José Batlle y Ordonez.

Stamp of 1856 and Stagecoach AP18

1956, Dec. 15   Litho.

C173	AP18	20c grn, bl & pale yel	48 20
C174	AP18	31c brn, bl & lt bl	52 22
C175	AP18	36c dp claret & bl	65 35

Issued to commemorate the centenary of the first postage stamps of Uruguay.

Flags of 21 American Nations AP19   Men and Torch of Freedom AP20

Perf. 11, 11½ (No. C177)
1958, June 19   Unwmk.

C176	AP19	23c blue & blk	20 15
C177	AP19	34c green & blk	30 15
C178	AP19	44c cerise & blk	48 20

10th anniversary of the Organization of American States.

1958, Dec. 10   Perf. 11

C179 AP20	23c blk & blue	20 15
C180 AP20	34c blk & yel grn	28 15
C181 AP20	44c blk & org red	52 25
	Set value	46

10th anniversary of the signing of the Universal Declaration of Human Rights.

"Flight" from Monument to Fallen Aviators — AP21

1959   Litho.   Perf. 11
Size: 22x37½mm

C182 AP21	3c bis brn & blk	15 15
C183 AP21	8c brt lil & blk	15 15
C184 AP21	38c black	15 15
C185 AP21	50c citron & blk	15 15
C186 AP21	60c vio & blk	15 15
C187 AP21	90c ol grn & blk	22 15
C188 AP21	1p blue & blk	26 15
C189 AP21	2p ocher & blk	90 40
C190 AP21	3p grn & blk	1.10 65
C191 AP21	5p vio brn & blk	1.50 1.10
C192 AP21	10p dp rose car & blk	5.00 3.25
	Nos. C182-C192 (11)	9.73 6.45

See Nos. C211-C222. For surcharge see No. Q97.

Alberto Santos-Dumont — AP22

1959, Feb. 13   Wmk. 327   Perf. 11½

C193 AP22	31c multi	20 15
C194 AP22	36c multi	20 15
	Set value	20

Airplane flight of Alberto Santos-Dumont, Brazilian aeronaut, in 1906 in France.

Girl and Waves AP23

Designs: 38c, 60c, 1.05p, Compass and map of Punta del Este.

1959, Mar. 6   Perf. 11½

C195 AP23	10c ocher & lt bl	15 15
C196 AP23	38c grn & bis	20 15
C197 AP23	60c lilac & bister	28 16
C198 AP23	90c red org & grn	32 20
C199 AP23	1.05p blue & bister	40 30
	Nos. C195-C199 (5)	1.35
	Set value	78

50th anniv. of Punta del Este, seaside resort.

Torch, YMCA Emblem and Chrismon AP24

Perf. 11½
1959, Dec. 22   Wmk. 327   Litho.

C200 AP24	38c emer, blk & gray	28 18
C201 AP24	50c bl, blk & gray	30 15
C202 AP24	60c red, blk & gray	35 35

50th anniv. of the YMCA in Uruguay.

José Artigas and George Washington AP25

Refugees and WRY Emblem AP26

1960, Mar. 2   Perf. 11½x12

C203 AP25	38c red & blk	16 16
C204 AP25	50c brt bl & blk	20 20
C205 AP25	60c dp grn & blk	24 24

Issued to commemorate Pres. Dwight D. Eisenhower's visit to Uruguay, Feb. 1960.

No. C204 exists imperforate, but was not regularly issued in this form.

No. C150 Surcharged **20 c**

1960, Apr. 8   Unwmk.   Perf. 11

C206 AP12	20c on 27c yel grn	15 15
a.	Perf. 12½	16 15

1960, June 6   Wmk. 332
Size: 24x35mm

C207 AP26	60c brt lil rose & blk	24 18

Issued to publicize World Refugee Year, July 1, 1959-June 30, 1960.

Type of Regular Issue, 1960
Wmk. 332
1960, Nov. 4   Litho.   Perf. 12

C208 A186	38c bl & ol grn	15 15
C209 A186	50c bl & ver	16 15
C210 A186	60c bl & pur	24 15
	Set value	30

Type of 1959 Redrawn with Silhouette of Airplane Added

1960-61   Litho.   Perf. 12

C211 AP21	3c blk & pale vio	15 15
C212 AP21	20c blk & crimson	15 15
C213 AP21	38c blk & pale bl	15 15
C214 AP21	50c blk & buff	15 15
C215 AP21	60c blk & dp grn	15 15
C216 AP21	90c blk & rose	20 15
C217 AP21	1p blk & gray	22 15
C218 AP21	2p blk & yel grn	42 18
C219 AP21	3p blk & red lil	52 25
C220 AP21	5p blk & org ver	80 50
C221 AP21	10p blk & yel	1.40 85
C222 AP21	20p blk & dk bl ('61)	3.25 1.65
	Nos. C211-C222 (12)	7.56
	Set value	3.90

Pres. Gronchi and Flag Colors AP27

1961, Apr. 17   Wmk. 332   Perf. 12

C223 AP27	90c multi	24 15
C224 AP27	1.20p multi	28 20
C225 AP27	1.40p multi	32 25

Issued to commemorate the visit of President Giovanni Gronchi of Italy to Uruguay, April, 1961.

Carrasco National Airport — AP28

1961, May 16   Wmk. 332   Perf. 12
Building in Gray

C226 AP28	1p lt vio	16 15
C227 AP28	2p ol gray	32 15
C228 AP28	3p orange	48 20
C229 AP28	4p purple	70 25
C230 AP28	5p aqua	80 40
C231 AP28	10p lt ultra	1.50 60
C232 AP28	20p maroon	2.50 1.65
	Nos. C226-C232 (7)	6.46 3.40

Type of Regular "CIES" Issue, 1961

1961, Aug. 3   Litho.   Wmk. 332

C233 A189	20c blk & org	15 15
C234 A189	45c blk & grn	15 15
C235 A189	50c blk & gray	15 15
C236 A189	90c blk & plum	15 15
C237 A189	1p blk & dp rose	16 15
C238 A189	1.40p blk & lt vio	22 15
C239 A189	2p blk & bister	25 16
C240 A189	3p blk & lt bl	42 24
C241 A189	4p blk & yellow	52 38
C242 A189	5p blk & blue	70 50
C243 A189	10p blk & yel grn	1.40 90
C244 A189	20p blk & dp pink	2.50 1.90
	Nos. C233-C244 (12)	6.77 4.98

Swiss Flag, Plow, Wheat Sheaf AP29

1962, Aug. 1   Wmk. 332   Perf. 12

C245 AP29	90c car, org & blk	24 15
C246 AP29	1.40p car, bl & blk	30 30

Cent. of the Swiss Settlement in Uruguay.

Red-crested Cardinal — AP30

Birds: 45c, White-capped tanager, horiz. 90c, Vermilion flycatcher. 1.20p, Great kiskadee, horiz. 1.40p, Fork-tailed flycatcher.

1962, Dec. 5   Litho.   Perf. 12

C247 AP30	20c gray, blk & red	15 15
C248 AP30	45c multi	24 18
C249 AP30	90c crim rose, blk & lt brn	50 15
C250 AP30	1.20p lt bl, blk & yel	65 18
C251 AP30	1.40p blue & sepia	1.00 25
	Nos. C247-C251 (5)	2.54
	Set value	78

No frame on No. C248, thin frame on No. C251. See Nos. C258-C263.

Type of Regular UPAE Issue, 1963

1963, May 31   Wmk. 332   Perf. 12

C252 A195	45c bluish grn & blk	15 15
C253 A195	90c magenta & blk	24 18
	Set value	22

Freedom from Hunger
Type of Regular Issue

1963, July 9   Wmk. 332   Perf. 12

C254 A196	90c red & yel	16 15
C255 A196	1.40p violet & yel	20 15
	Set value	22

"Alferez Campora" — AP31

1963, Aug. 16   Litho.

C256 AP31	90c dk grn & org	15 15
C257 AP31	1.40p ultra & yel	28 15
	Set value	20

Voyage around the world by the Uruguayan sailing vessel "Alferez Campora," 1960-63.

Bird Type of 1962

Birds: 1p, Glossy cowbird (tordo). 2p, Yellow cardinal. 3p, Hooded siskin. 5p, Sayaca tanager. 10p, Blue and yellow tanager. 20p, Scarlet-headed marsh-bird. All horizontal.

1963, Nov. 15   Wmk. 332   Perf. 12

C258 AP30	1p vio bl, blk & brn org	32 20
C259 AP30	2p lt brn, blk & yel	65 25
C260 AP30	3p yel, brn & blk	1.00 38
C261 AP30	5p emer, bl grn & blk	1.65 50
C262 AP30	10p multi	3.25 1.00
C263 AP30	20p gray, org & blk	7.00 4.50
	Nos. C258-C263 (6)	13.87 6.83

Frame on Nos. C260-C263.

Pres. Charles de Gaulle — AP32

Design: 2.40p, Flags of France and Uruguay.

1964, Oct. 9   Litho.   Perf. 12

C264 AP32	1.50p multi	32 18
C265 AP32	2.40p multi	65 32

Charles de Gaulle, Pres. of France, Oct. 1964.

Submerged Statue of Ramses II — AP33

Design: 2p, Head of Ramses II.

1964, Oct. 30   Litho.   Wmk. 332

C266 AP33	1.30p multi	
C267 AP33	2p bis, red brn & brt bl	60 30
a.	Souv. sheet of 3, #713, C266-C267, imperf.	1.25 1.10

UNESCO world campaign to save historic monuments in Nubia.

National Flag AP34

1965, Feb. 18   Wmk. 332   Perf. 12

C268 AP34	50p gray, dk bl & yel	4.75 3.00

Kennedy Type of Regular Issue

1965, Mar. 5   Wmk. 327   Perf. 11½

C269 A202	1.50p gold, lil & blk	16 15
C270 A202	2.40p gold, brt bl & blk	28 18

Issue of 1864, No. 23 — AP35

Designs: 6c, 8c and 10c denominations of 1864 issue.

Wmk. 332

1965, Mar. 19   Litho.   *Perf. 12*
C271   Sheet of 10   1.10 1.10

"URUGUAY" at bottom

a.	AP35 1p blue & black	15	15
b.	AP35 1p brick red & black	15	15
c.	AP35 1p green & black	15	15
d.	AP35 1p ocher & black	15	15
e.	AP35 1p carmine & black	15	15

"URUGUAY" at top

f.	AP35 1p blue & black	15	15
g.	AP35 1p brick red & black	15	15
h.	AP35 1p green & black	15	15
i.	AP35 1p ocher & black	15	15
j.	AP35 1p carmine & black	15	15

1st Rio de la Plata Stamp Show, sponsored jointly by the Argentine and Uruguayan philatelic associations, Montevideo, Mar. 19-28. No. C271 contains two horizontal rows of stamps and two rows of labels; Nos. C271a-C271e are in first row, Nos. C271f-C271j in second row. Adjacent labels in top and bottom rows.
For overprint see No. C298.

National Arms — AP36

Artigas Monument — AP37

1965, Apr. 30   Wmk. 332   *Perf. 12*
C272   AP36 20p multi   1.40 75

Type of Regular Issue and AP37.

Designs: 1.50p, Artigas and wagontrain. 2.40p, Artigas quotation.

Perf. 11¹/₂x12, 12x11¹/₂

1965, May 17   Litho.   Wmk. 327
C273	AP37	1p multi	15	15
C274	A205	1.50p multi	16	15
C275	A205	2.40p multi	24	15
		Set value	45	28

José Artigas (1764-1850), leader of the independence revolt against Spain.

Olympic Games Type of Regular Issue

Designs: 1p, Boxing. 1.50p, Running. 2p, Fencing. 2.40p, Sculling. 3p, Pistol shooting. 20p, Olympic rings.

1965, Aug. 3   Litho.   *Perf. 12x11¹/₂*
C276	A206	1p red, gray & blk	15	15
C277	A206	1.50p emer, bl & blk	15	15
C278	A206	2p dk car, bl & blk	16	15
C279	A206	2.40p lt ultra, org & blk	20	15
C280	A206	3p lil, yel & blk	24	15
C281	A206	20p dk vio bl, pink & lt bl	72	45
		Nos. C276-C281 (6)	1.62	
		Set value		95

Souvenir Sheet

Designs: 5p, Stamp of 1924, No. 284. 10p, Stamp of 1928, No. 389.

C282	Sheet of 2	1.40	1.40
a.	5p buff, blue & black	40	40
b.	10p blue, black & rose red	65	65

18th Olympic Games, Tokyo, Oct. 10-25, 1964.

ITU Emblem and Satellite AP38

1966, Jan. 25   Wmk. 332   *Perf. 12*
C283   AP38 1p bl, bluish blk & ver   15 15

Cent. of the ITU (in 1965).

Winston Churchill — AP39

1966, Apr. 29   Wmk. 332   *Perf. 12*
C284   AP39 2p car, brn & gold   15 15

Rio de Janeiro Type of Regular Issue

1966, June 9   Wmk. 332   *Perf. 12*
C285   A208 80c dp org & brn   15 15

International Cooperation Year Emblem AP40

1966, June 9   Litho.
C286   AP40 1p bluish grn & blk   15 15

UN International Cooperation Year.

President Zalman Shazar of Israel — AP41

1966, June 21   Wmk. 327
C287   AP41 7p multi   42 25

Visit of Pres. Zalman Shazar of Israel.

Crested Screamer — AP42

1966, July 7   Wmk. 327   *Perf. 12*
C288   AP42 100p bl, blk, red & gray   3.25 1.65

Jules Rimet Cup, Soccer Ball and Globe — AP43

1966, July 11   Litho.
C289   AP43 10p dk pur, org & lil   55 25

Issued to commemorate the World Cup Soccer Championship, Wembley, England, July 11-30.

Bulls AP44

1966   Wmk. 327, 332 (10p)
C290	AP44	4p Hereford	15	15
C291	AP44	6p Holstein	20	15
C292	AP44	10p Shorthorn	28	20
C293	AP44	15p Aberdeen Angus	40	20
C294	AP44	20p Norman	65	40
C295	AP44	30p Jersey	1.00	50
C296	AP44	50p Charolais	1.65	1.00
		Nos. C290-C296 (7)	4.33	2.60

Issued to publicize Uruguayan cattle. Dates of issue: 4p, 50p, Aug. 13; 6p, 30p, Aug. 29; 10p, 15p, 20p, Sept. 26.

Boiso Lanza, Early Plane and Space Capsule AP45

1966, Oct. 14   Litho.   *Perf. 12*
C297   AP45 25p ultra, blk & lt bl   65 45

Issued to honor Capt. Juan Manuel Boiso Lanza, pioneer of military aviation.

No. C271 Overprinted: "CENTENARIO DEL SELLO / ESCUDITO RESELLADO"

1966, Nov. 4   Wmk. 332
C298   Sheet of 10   1.10 1.10

"URUGUAY" at bottom

a.	AP35 1p blue & black	15	15
b.	AP35 1p brick red & black	15	15
c.	AP35 1p green & black	15	15
d.	AP35 1p ocher & black	15	15
e.	AP35 1p carmine & black	15	15

"URUGUAY" at top

f.	AP35 1p blue & black	15	15
g.	AP35 1p brick red & black	15	15
h.	AP35 1p green & black	15	15
i.	AP35 1p ocher & black	15	15
j.	AP35 1p carmine & black	15	15

2nd Rio de la Plata Stamp Show, Buenos Aires, Apr. 1966, sponsored by the Argentine and Uruguayan philatelic associations, and commemorating the for of Uruguay's 1st surcharged issue. The addition of black numerals makes the designs resemble the surcharged issue of 1866, Nos. 24-28.
Labels in top row are overprinted "SEGUNDA MUESTRA 1966," in bottom row "SEGUNDAS JORNADAS 1966" and "CENTENARIO DEL SELLO / ESCUDITO RESELLADO" in both rows. One label each in top and bottom rows is overprinted "BUENOS AIRES / ABRIL 1966."

No. 613 Surcharged in Dark Blue

40 ANIVERSARIO
Club Filatélico del Uruguay

$ 1.00 aéreo

Perf. 12¹/₂x13

1966, Dec. 17   Engr.   Unwmk.
C299   A175 1p on 12c   16 15

Philatelic Club of Uruguay, 40th anniv.

Dante Alighieri AP46

Planetarium Projector AP47

Wmk. 332
1966, Dec. 27   Litho.   *Perf. 12*
C300   AP46 50c sepia & bister   15 15

Dante Alighieri (1265-1321), Italian poet.

1967, Jan. 13   Wmk. 332   *Perf. 12*
C301   AP47 5p dl bl & blk   40 20

Montevideo Municipal Planetarium, 10th anniv.

Archbishop Makarios and Map of Cyprus — AP48

1967, Feb. 14   Wmk. 332   *Perf. 12*
C302   AP48 6.60p rose lil & blk   20 15

Visit of Archbishop Makarios, president of Cyprus, Oct. 21, 1966.

Dr. Albert Schweitzer Holding Fawn — AP49

1967, Mar. 31   Litho.   Wmk. 332
C303   AP49 6p grn, blk, brn & sal   20 15

Albert Schweitzer (1875-1965), medical missionary.

Corriedale Ram AP50

Various Rams: 4p, Ideal. 5p, Romney Marsh. 10p, Australian Merino.

1967, Apr. 5
C304	AP50	3p red org, blk & gray	15	15
C305	AP50	4p emer, blk & gray	16	15
C306	AP50	5p ultra, blk & gray	20	15
C307	AP50	10p yel, blk & gray	35	20
		Set value		38

Uruguayan sheep raising.

Flag of Uruguay and Map of the Americas AP51

1967, Apr. 8
C308   AP51 10p dk gray, bl & gold   30 16

Meeting of American Presidents, Punta del Este, Apr. 10-12.

Numeral Stamps of 1866, Nos. 30-31 — AP52

Design: 6p, Nos. 32-33; diff. frame.

Wmk. 332
1967, May 10   Litho.   *Perf. 12*
C309	AP52	3p bl, yel grn & blk	16	15
a.		Souvenir sheet of 4	65	65
C310	AP52	6p bis, dp rose & blk	32	20
a.		Souvenir sheet of 4	1.50	1.50

Cent. of the 1866 numeral issue. Nos. C309a-C310a each contain 4 stamps similar to Nos. C309 and C310 respectively (the arrangement of colors differs in the souvenir sheets).

Ansina, Portrait by
Medardo
Latorre — AP53

1967, May 17
C311 AP53 2p gray, dk bl & red   15 15

Issued to honor Ansina, servant of Gen. José
Artigas.

Plane Landing
AP54

1967, May 30
C312 AP54 10p red, bl, blk & yel   32 18

30th anniv. (in 1966) of PLUNA Airline.

Shooting for
Basket — AP55

Basketball Game — AP56

Basketball Players in Action: No. C314, Driving
(ball shoulder high). No. C315, About to pass (ball
head high). No. C316, Ready to pass (ball held
straight in front). No. C317, Dribbling with right
hand.

1967, June 9
C313 AP55 5p multi   16 15
C314 AP55 5p multi   16 15
C315 AP55 5p multi   16 15
C316 AP55 5p multi   16 15
C317 AP55 5p multi   16 15
  a.   Strip of 5, Nos. C313-C317   85 50
        Nos. C313-C317 (5)   80
        Set value   42

Souvenir Sheet
C318 AP56 10p org, brt grn & blk   55 50

5th World Basketball Championships, Montevideo, May 1967.
For overprint see No. C349.

José Artigas, Manuel Belgrano, Flags of
Uruguay and Argentina — AP57

Wmk. 332
1967, June 19   Litho.   Imperf.
C319 AP57 5p bl, grn & yel   50 40

3rd Rio de la Plata Stamp Show, Montevideo,
Uruguay, June 18-25.
For surcharge see No. 859.

Nos. C248 and C252 Surcharged in Gold
1967, June 22   Perf. 12
C320 AP30 5.90p on 45c multi   20 20
C321 A195 5.90p on 45c multi   20 20

Don Quixote and Sancho Panza, Painted
by Denry Torres — AP58

1967, July 10
C322 AP58 8p bis brn & brn   20 20

Issued in honor of Miguel de Cervantes Saavedra
(1547-1616), Spanish novelist.
For surcharge see No. C356.

Stone
Axe — AP59

Railroad
Crossing — AP60

Designs: 15p, Headbreaker stones. 20p, Spear-
head. 50p, Birdstone. 75p, Clay pot. 100p,
Ornitholite (ritual sculpture), Balizas, horiz. 150p,
Lasso weights (boleadores). 200p, Two spearheads.

1967-68   Wmk. 332   Perf. 12
C323 AP59 15p gray & blk   15 15
C324 AP59 20p gray & blk   16 15
C325 AP59 30p gray & lt gray   35 15
C326 AP59 50p gray & blk   50 16
C327 AP59 75p brn & blk   80 30
C328 AP59 100p gray & blk   1.10 45
C329 AP59 150p gray & blk ('68)   1.40 52
C330 AP59 200p gray & blk ('68)   2.00 1.10
     Nos. C323-C330 (8)   6.46 2.98

1967, Dec. 4
C331 AP60 4p blk, yel & red   15 15

10th Pan-American Highway Congress,
Montevideo.

Lions Emblem and Map
of South
America — AP61

1967, Dec. 29
C332 AP61 5p pur, yel & emer   30 15

50th anniversary of Lions International.

Boy
Scout — AP62

1968, Jan. 24   Litho.
C333 AP62 9p sep & brick red   40 18

Issued in memory of Robert Baden-Powell,
founder of the Boy Scout organization.

Sun, UN
Emblem and
Transportation
Means
AP63

1968, Feb. 29   Wmk. 332   Perf. 12
C334 AP63 10p gray, yel, lt & dk bl   16 15

Issued for International Tourist Year.

Octopus
AP64

Marine Fauna: 20p, Silversides. 25p, Characin.
30p, Catfish, vert. 50p, Squid, vert.

1968   Wmk. 332   Perf. 12
C335 AP64 15p lt grn, bl & blk   20 15
C336 AP64 20p brn, grn & bl   20 15
C337 AP64 25p multi   28 15
C338 AP64 30p bl, grn & blk   32 16
C339 AP64 50p dp org, grn & dk bl   50 25
     Nos. C335-C339 (5)   1.50 86

Issued: 30p, 50p, 10/10; 15p, 20p, 25p, 11/5.

Navy Type of Regular Issue

Designs: 4p, Naval Air Force. 6p, Naval arms.
10p, Signal flags, vert. 20p, Corsair (chartered by
General Artigas).

1968, Nov. 12   Litho.
C340 A226 4p bl, blk & red   15 15
C341 A226 6p multi   15 15
C342 A226 10p lt ultra, red & yel   16 15
C343 A226 20p ultra & blk   28 15
     Set value   54 25

Rowing — AP65

1969, Feb. 11   Wmk. 332   Perf. 12
C344 AP65 30p shown   35 16
C345 AP65 50p Running   55 28
C346 AP65 100p Soccer   95 45

19th Olympic Games, Mexico City, 10/12-
27/68.

Bicycling Type of Regular Issue
Designs: 20p, Bicyclist and globe, vert.

1969, Mar. 21   Wmk. 332   Perf. 12
C347 A229 20p bl, pur & yel   28 15

"EFIMEX 68"
and
Globe — AP66

1969, Apr. 10   Wmk. 332   Perf. 12
C348 AP66 20p dk grn, red & bl   28 15

EFIMEX '68, International Philatelic Exhibition,
Mexico City, Nov. 1-9, 1968.

No. C318 Overprinted with Names of
Participating Countries, Emblem, Bars, etc.
and "CAMPEONATO MUNDIAL DE
VOLEIBOL"
1969, Apr. 25   Souvenir Sheet
C349 AP56 10p org, brt grn & blk   24 20

Issued to commemorate the World Volleyball
Championships, Montevideo, Apr. 1969.

Book, Quill and
Emblem
AP67

Automobile Club
Emblem
AP68

1969, Sept. 16   Litho.   Perf. 12
C350 AP67 30p grn, org & blk   40 20

10th Congress of Latin American Notaries.

1969, Oct. 7   Wmk. 332   Perf. 12
C351 AP68 10p ultra & red   16 15

50th anniv. (in 1968) of the Uruguayan Automobile Club.

ILO Emblem
AP69

1969, Oct. 29   Litho.   Perf. 12
C352 AP69 30p dk bl grn & blk   32 15

50th anniv. of the ILO.

Exhibition
Emblem — AP70

1969, Nov. 15   Wmk. 332   Perf. 12
C353 AP70 20p ultra, yel & grn   24 15

ABUEXPO 69 Philatelic Exhibition, San Pablo,
Brazil, Nov. 15-23.

Rotary Emblem and Hemispheres AP71

1969, Dec. 6 — *Perf. 12*
C354 AP71 20p ultra, bl & bis — 50 15

South American Regional Rotary Conference and the 50th anniv. of the Montevideo Rotary Club.

Dr. Luis Morquio — AP72

1969, Dec. 22 — *Litho.* — *Wmk. 332*
C355 AP72 20p org red & brn — 22 15

Centenary of the birth of Dr. Luis Morquio, pediatrician.

No. C322 Surcharged "FELIZ AÑO 1970 / 6.00 / PESOS"

1969, Dec. 24
C356 AP58 6p on 8p bis brn & brn — 16 15

Issued for New Year 1970.

Mahatma Gandhi and UNESCO Emblem AP73

1970, Jan. 26 — *Wmk. 332* — *Perf. 12*
C357 AP73 100p lt bl & brn — 1.10 1.10

Mohandas K. Gandhi (1869-1948), leader in India's fight for independence.

Evaristo C. Ciganda AP74 — Giuseppe Garibaldi AP75

1970, Mar. 10 — *Litho.*
C358 AP74 6p brt grn & brn — 16 16

Centenary of the birth of Evaristo C. Ciganda, author of the first law for teachers' pensions.

1970, Apr. 7 — *Unwmk.* — *Perf. 12*
C359 AP75 20p rose car & pink — 15 15

Centenary of Garibaldi's command of foreign legionnaires in the Uruguayan Civil War.

Fur Seal — AP76

Designs: 20p, Rhea, vert. 30p, Common tegu (lizard). 50p, Capybara. 100p, Mulita armadillo. 150p, Puma. 200p, Nutria.

1970-71 — *Wmk. 332* — *Perf. 12*
C361 AP76 20p pur, emer & blk — 24 16
C362 AP76 30p emer, yel & blk — 28 20
C363 AP76 50p dl yel & brn — 50 40
C365 AP76 100p org, sep & blk — 80 65
C366 AP76 150p emer & brn — 1.25 1.25
C367 AP76 200p brt rose, brn & blk ('71) — 1.65 1.65
C368 AP76 250p gray, bl & blk — 2.00 2.00
Nos. C361-C368 (7) — 6.72 6.31

Soccer and Mexican Flag — AP77

1970, June 2 — *Litho.* — *Perf. 12*
C369 AP77 50p multi — 60 60

9th World Soccer Championships for the Jules Rimet Cup, Mexico City, May 30-June 21.

"U N" and Laurel — AP78

1970, June 26 — *Wmk. 332* — *Perf. 12*
C370 AP78 32p dk bl & gold — 30 30

25th anniversary of the United Nations.

Eisenhower and US Flag — AP79

1970, July 14 — *Litho.*
C371 AP79 30p gray, vio bl & red — 28 28

Issued in memory of Gen. Dwight David Eisenhower, 34th Pres. of US (1890-1969).

Neil A. Armstrong Stepping onto Moon — AP80

1970, July 21
C372 AP80 200p multi — 1.90 1.90

1st anniversary of man's 1st landing on the moon.

Flag of the "Immortals" AP81

1970, Aug. 24 — *Wmk. 332* — *Perf. 12*
C373 AP81 500p bl, blk & red — 4.50 4.50

The 145th anniversary of the arrival of the 33 "Immortals," the patriots, who started the revolution for independence.

Congress Emblem with Map of South America AP82

1970, Sept. 16 — *Unwmk.* — *Perf. 12*
C374 AP82 30p bl, dk bl & yel — 28 28

Issued to publicize the 5th Pan-American Congress of Rheumatology, Punta del Este.

Souvenir Sheet

Types of First Air Post Issue — AP83

1970, Oct. 1 — *Wmk. 332* — *Perf. 12½*
C375 AP83 Sheet of 3 — 1.50 1.50
a. 25p brown (Bl) — 48 48
b. 25p brown (R) — 48 48
c. 25p brown (G) — 48 48

Stamp Day. #C375 contains 3 stamps similar to #C1-C3, but with denominations in pesos.

Flags of ALALC Countries — AP84

1970, Nov. 23 — *Litho.* — *Perf. 12*
C376 AP84 22p multi — 28 20

For the Latin-American Association for Free Trade (Asociación Latinoamericana de Libre Comercio).

Yellow Fever, by J. M. Blanes AP85

1971, June 8 — *Wmk. 332* — *Perf. 12*
C377 AP85 50p blk, dk red brn & yel — 40 40

Juan Manuel Blanes (1830-1901), painter.

Racial Equality, UN Emblem AP86

1971, June 28 — *Litho.*
C378 AP86 27p blk, pink & bis — 25 25

Intl. Year Against Racial Discrimination.

Congress Emblem with Maps of Americas AP87

1971, July 6 — *Wmk. 332* — *Perf. 12*
C379 AP87 58p dl grn, blk & org — 45 45

12th Pan-American Congress of Gastroenterology, Punta del Este, Dec. 5-10, 1971.

Committee Emblem — AP88

1971, Nov. 29
C380 AP88 30p bl, blk & yel — 25 25

Inter-governmental Committee for European Migration.

Llama and Mountains — AP89 — Munich Olympic Games Emblem — AP90

1971, Dec. 30
C381 AP89 37p multi — 45 35

EXFILIMA '71, Third Inter-American Philatelic Exposition, Lima, Peru, Nov. 6-14.

1972, Feb. 1 — *Perf. 11½x12*
Designs (Munich '72 Emblem and): 100p, Torchbearer. 500p, Discobolus.

C382 AP90 50p blk, red & org — 15 15
C383 AP90 100p multi — 30 30
C384 AP90 500p multi — 1.50 1.50

20th Olympic Games, Munich, Aug. 26-Sept. 11.

Retort and WHO Emblem — AP91 — Ship with Flags Forming Sails — AP92

1972, Feb. 22 — *Perf. 12*
C385 AP91 27p multi — 15 15

50th anniversary of the discovery of insulin by Frederick G. Banting and Charles H. Best.

1972, Mar. 6 — *Wmk. 332*
C386 AP92 37p multi — 15 15

Stamp Day of the Americas.

1924 and 1928 Gold Medals,
Soccer — AP93

Design: 300p, Olympic flag, Motion and Munich emblems, vert.

1972, June 12   Litho.   Perf. 12
C387 AP93 100p bl & multi   30   30
C388 AP93 300p multi   90   90

20th Olympic Games, Munich, Aug. 26-Sept. 11.

Cross — AP94

1972, Aug. 10
C389 AP94 37p vio & gold   15   15

Dan A. Mitrione (1920-70), slain US official.

Interlocking Squares and UN Emblem — AP95

1972, Aug. 16
C390 AP95 30p gray & multi   15   15

3rd UN Conf. on Trade and Development (UNCTAD III), Santiago, Chile, Apr.-May 1972.

Brazil's "Bull's-eye," 1843 — AP96

Wmk. 332
1972, Aug. 26   Litho.   Perf. 12
C391 AP96 50p grn, yel & bl   15   15

4th Inter-American Philatelic Exhibition, EXFIL-BRA, Rio de Janeiro, Aug. 26-Sept. 2.

Map of South America, Compass Rose — AP97

1972, Sept. 28
C392 AP97 37p multi   15   15

Uruguay's support for extending territorial sovereignty 200 miles into the sea.

Adoration of the Kings and Shepherds, by Rafael Perez Barradas — AP98

1972, Oct. 12
C393 AP98 20p lemon & multi   20   20

Christmas 1972 and first biennial exhibition of Uruguayan painting, 1970. Setenant with label inscribed with name of painter and painting.

WPY Emblem
AP99

Wmk. 332
1974, Aug. 20   Litho.   Perf. 12
C394 AP99 500p gray & red   70   70

World Population Year 1974.

Soccer, Olympics and UPU Emblems — AP100

Anniversaries and events: No. C398a, 17th UPU Congress, Lausanne. No. C398b, World Soccer Federation, 1st South American president. No. C398c, 1976 Summer and Winter Olympics, Innsbruck and Montreal.

1974, Aug. 30
C395 AP100 200p grn & multi   50   50
C396 AP100 300p org & multi   65   65
C397 AP100 500p multicolored

Souvenir Sheet
C398   Sheet of 3
a.-c.   AP100 500p any single

Centenary of Universal Postal Union. Nos. C397-C398 had limited distribution.

Mexico No. O1 and Mexican Coat of Arms AP101

Wmk. 332
1974, Oct. 15   Litho.   Perf. 12
C399 AP101 200p multi   16   16

EXFILMEX '74 5th Inter-American Philatelic Exhibition, Mexico City, Oct. 26-Nov. 3.

Christmas Type of 1974

Design: 240p, Kings following star. 2500p, Virgin and Child.

1974
C400 A315 240p multi   16   16
Miniature Sheet
C401 A315 2500p multi   2.25 2.25

Issue dates: 240p, Dec. 27; 2500p, Dec. 31.

Spain No. 1, Colors of Spain and Uruguay — AP102

1975, Mar. 4
C402 AP102 400p multi   30   30

Espana 75, International Philatelic Exhibition, Madrid, Apr. 4-13.

Souvenir Sheet

Nos. C253, 893 and C402 — AP103

Wmk. 332
1975, Apr. 4   Litho.   Perf. 12
C403 AP103   Sheet of 3   3.00 3.00
a.   1000p No. C253   90   90
b.   1000p No. 893   90   90
c.   1000p No. C402   90   90

Espana 75 Intl. Phil. Exhib., Madrid, Apr. 4-13.

1976 Summer & Winter Olympics, Innsbruck & Montreal — AP104

1975, May 16   Perf. 12
C404 AP104 400p shown
C405 AP104 600p Flags, Olympic rings

Souvenir Sheets
C406   Sheet of 2
a.   AP104 500p Montreal emblem
b.   AP104 1000p Innsbruck emblem
C407   Sheet of 2
a.   AP104 500p Emblems, horiz.
b.   AP104 1000p Flags, horiz.

Nos. C404-C407 had limited distribution.

Floor Design for Capitol, Rome AP105

1975, Aug. 15
C408 AP105 1p multi   75   75

500th birth anniversary of Michelangelo Buonarroti (1475-1564), Italian sculptor, painter and architect.

Apollo-Soyuz Space Mission, USA & Uruguay Independence — AP106

Anniversaries and events: 15c, Apollo-Soyuz spacecraft. 20c, Apollo-Soyuz spacecraft. 25c, Artigas monument, vert. 30c, George Washington, Pres. Artigas. No. C412, Early Aircraft, vert. No. C413a, Apollo spacecraft, astronauts. No. C413b, US and Uruguayan Declarations of Independence. No. C413c, Modern aircraft. No. C413d, UN Secretaries General. No. C414c, Boiso Lanza, aviation pioneer. 1p, Flags of UN and Uruguay.

1975, Sept. 29
C409 AP106 10c multicolored
C410 AP106 15c multicolored
C411 AP106 25c multicolored
C412 AP106 50c multicolored

Souvenir Sheets
C413   Sheet of 4
a.-d.   AP106 40c any single
C414   Sheet of 4
a.   AP106 20c multicolored
b.   AP106 30c multicolored
c.   AP106 50c multicolored
d.   AP106 1p multicolored

Nos. C409-C414 had limited distribution.

Sun, Uruguay No. C59 and other Stamps — AP108

Wmk. 332
1975, Oct. 13   Litho.   Perf. 12
C415 AP108 1p blk, gray & yel   90   90

Uruguayan Stamp Day.

Montreal Olympic Emblem and Argentina '78 AP109

Flags of US and Uruguay AP110

UPU and UPAE Emblems — AP111

Perf. 11½
1975, Oct. 14   Litho.   Wmk. 332

C416	AP109	1p multi	52	52
C417	AP110	1p multi	52	52
C418	AP111	1p multi	52	52
a.		Souvenir sheet of 3	7.00	

EXFILMO '75 and ESPAMER '75 Stamp Exhibitions, Montevideo, Oct. 10-19. No. C418a contains 3 stamps similar to Nos. C416-C418, 2p each.

Ocelot
AP112

Orchid: #C416, Oncidium bifolium.

1976, Jan.   Litho.   Perf. 12

C419	AP112	50c vio bl & multi	35	30
C420	AP112	50c emer & multi	35	30

Souvenir Sheets

Olympics, Soccer, Telecommunications and UPU — AP113

1976, June 3   Perf. 11½

C422	Sheet of 3	
a.	AP113 30c Soccer player	
b.	AP113 70c Alexander Graham Bell	
c.	AP113 1p UPU emblem, UN #5	
C423	Sheet of 3	
a.	AP113 40c Discus thrower	
b.	AP113 60c Telephone, cent.	
c.	AP113 2p UPU emblem, UN #11	

Nos. C422-C423 had limited distribution.

Anniversaries and Events Type of 1976
Souvenir Sheets

Designs: 20c, Frederick Passy, Henri Dunant. 35c, Nobel prize, 75th anniv. 40c, Viking spacecraft. 60c, 1976 Summer Olympics, Montreal. 75c, US space missions. 90c, 1976 Summer Olympics, diff.
World Cup Soccer Championships, Argentina: 1p, Uruguay, 1930 champions. 1.50p, Uruguay, 1950 champions.

1976, Nov. 12   Perf. 12

C424	Sheet of 4	
a.	A355 20c multicolored	
b.	A355 40c multicolored	
c.	A355 60c multicolored	
d.	A355 1.50p multicolored	
C425	Sheet of 4	
a.	A355 35c multicolored	
b.	A355 75c multicolored	
c.	A355 90c multicolored	
d.	A355 1p multicolored	

Nos. C424-C425 had limited distribution.

Nobel Prize Type of 1977
Souvenir Sheets

Anniversaries and events: 10c, World Cup Soccer Championships. 40c, Victor Hess, Nobel Prize in Physics. 60c, Max Plank, Nobel Prize in Physics. 80c, Graf Zeppelin, Concorde. 90c, Virgin and Child by Rubens. 1.20p, World Cup Soccer Championships, diff. 1.50p, Eduardo Bonilla, Count von Zeppelin. 2p, The Nativity by Rubens.

1977, July 21

C426	Sheet of 4	
a.	A361 10c multicolored	
b.	A361 60c multicolored	
c.	A361 80c multicolored	
d.	A361 2p multicolored	
C427	Sheet of 4	
a.	A361 40c multicolored	
b.	A361 90c multicolored	
c.	A361 1.20p multicolored	
d.	A361 1.50p multicolored	

Nos. C426-C427 had limited distribution.

Uruguay Natl. Postal System, 150th Anniv. AP114

1977, July 27

C428	AP114 8p multicolored	

Souvenir Sheet

C429	AP114 10p multicolored	

No. C428, imperf., was not valid for postage. Souvenir sheets sold in the package with No. C429 were not valid for postage.
For overprint see No. C435.

Paintings Type of 1978

Paintings: 1p, St. George Slaying Dragon by Durer. 1.25p, Duke of Lerma by Rubens. No. 432a, Madonna and Child by Durer. No. 432b, Holy Family by Rubens. No. 432c, Flight from Egypt by Francisco de Goya (1746-1828).

1978, June 13   Perf. 12½

C430	A374	1p brn & blk		
C431	A374	1.25p blk & brn		

Souvenir Sheet

C432	Sheet of 3	
a.-c.	A374 1p any single	

Nos. C430-C432 had limited distribution.

Souvenir Sheet

ICAO, 30th Anniv. and 1st Powered Flight, 75th Anniv. — AP115

Designs: a, Concorde, Dornier DO-x. b, Graf Zeppelin, Wright Brothers' Flyer. c, Space shuttle and De Pinedo's plane.

1978, June 13

C433	Sheet of 3	
a.-c.	AP115 1p any single	

No. C433 had limited distribution.

Souvenir Sheet

World Cup Soccer Championships, Argentina — AP116

1978, June 13   Perf. 12

C434	Sheet of 3	
a.	AP116 50c multicolored	
b.	AP116 1.50p multicolored	
c.	AP116 2p multicolored	

No. C434 had limited distribution.

No. C428 Overprinted in Black

1978, Aug. 28

C435	AP114 8p multicolored	

No. C435 had limited distribution.

Boiso Lanza, Wright Brothers AP117

75th anniv. of powered flight.

1979, June 18   Perf. 12½

C437	AP117 1.80 multicolored	

No. C437 had limited distribution.
Issued in sheet of 24 containing 6 blocks of 4r with margin around. See Nos. 1040-1042.

Souvenir Sheet

1982 World Cup Soccer Championships, Spain — AP118

1979, June 18   Perf. 12

C438	Sheet of 3	
a.	AP118 50c Jules Rimet cup	
b.	AP118 2.50p Uruguay flag	
c.	AP118 3p Espana '82	

No. C438 had limited distribution.

AIR POST SEMI-POSTAL STAMPS

Catalogue values for unused stamps in this section are for Never Hinged items.

Type of Semi-Postal Stamps, 1959
Perf. 11½
1959, Dec. 29   Wmk. 327   Litho.

CB1	SP2	38c + 10c brown & org	20	20
CB2	SP2	60c + 10c gray grn & org	25	25

Issued for national recovery.

SPECIAL DELIVERY STAMPS

No. 242 Overprinted **MENSAJERIAS**

1921, Aug.   Unwmk.   Perf. 11½

E1	A97	2c fawn	45	15
a.		Double overprint	3.25	

Caduceus — SD1

Imprint: "IMP. NACIONAL."
1922, Dec. 2   Litho.   Wmk. 188
Size: 21x27mm

E2	SD1	2c light red	25	15

1924, Oct. 1

E3	SD1	2c pale ultra	25	15

1928   Unwmk.   Perf. 11

E4	SD1	2c light blue	30	15

Imprint: "IMPRA. NACIONAL."
1928-36   Wmk. 188
Size: 16½x19½mm.

E5	SD1	2c black, green	15	15

Unwmk.

E6	SD1	2c blue green ('29)	15	15

Perf. 11½, 12½

E7	SD1	2c blue ('36)	15	15
		Set value, #E5-E7		15

1944, Oct. 23   Perf. 12½

E8	SD1	2c salmon pink	16	15

Catalogue values for unused stamps in this section, from this point to the end of the section, are for Never Hinged items.

1947, Nov. 19

E9	SD1	2c red brown	15	15

No. E9 Surcharged with New Value
1957, Oct. 30

E10	SD1	5c on 2c red brown	15	15

LATE FEE STAMPS

Galleon and Modern Steamship — LF1

Wmk. Crossed Keys in Sheet
1936, May 18   Litho.   Perf. 11

I1	LF1	3c green	15	15
I2	LF1	5c violet	15	15
I3	LF1	6c blue green	15	15
I4	LF1	7c brown	18	18
I5	LF1	8c carmine	35	35
I6	LF1	12c deep blue	50	50
		Set value	1.30	1.30

POSTAGE DUE STAMPS

D1

1902   Unwmk.   Engr.   Perf. 14 to 15
Size: 21¼x18½mm

J1	D1	1c blue green	30	15
J2	D1	2c carmine	35	15
J3	D1	4c gray violet	45	15
J4	D1	10c dark blue	75	25
J5	D1	20c ocher	1.10	60
		Nos. J1-J5 (5)	2.95	1.30

PROVISORIO
Surcharged in Red
UN cent'mo.

1904

J6	D1	1c on 10c dk bl	60	60
a.		Inverted surcharge	6.00	6.00

1913-15 Litho. Perf. 11½
Size: 22½x20mm

J7	D1	1c lt grn	35	15
J8	D1	2c rose red	35	18
J9	D1	4c dl vio	50	18
J10	D1	6c dp prem	60	25

Size: 21¼x19mm

J11	D1	10c dl bl	60	25
		Nos. J7-J11 (5)	2.40	1.01

Imprint: "Imprenta Nacional"

1922
Size: 20x17mm

J12	D1	1c bl grn	20	15
J13	D1	2c red	20	15
J14	D1	3c red brn	30	25
J15	D1	4c brn vio	20	15
J16	D1	5c blue	38	20
J17	D1	10c gray grn	38	20
		Nos. J12-J17 (6)	1.66	1.10

1926-27 Wmk. 188 Perf. 11
Size: 20x17mm

J18	D1	1c bl grn ('27)	18	15
J19	D1	3c red brn ('27)	30	20
J20	D1	5c slate blue	30	20
J21	D1	6c light brown	35	30

1929 Unwmk. Perf. 10½, 11

J22	D1	1c blue green	18	15
J23	D1	10c gray green	25	18

Figure of Value Redrawn
(Flat on sides)

1932 Wmk. 188

J24	D1	6c yel brn	35	25

Imprint: "Casa A. Barreiro Ramos S. A."

1935 Unwmk. Litho. Perf. 12½
Size: 20x17mm

J25	D1	4c violet	30	20
J26	D1	5c rose	30	20

Type of 1935
Imprint: "Imprenta Nacional" at right

1938

J27	D1	1c blue green	15	15
J28	D1	2c red brown	15	15
J29	D1	3c deep pink	15	15
J30	D1	4c light violet	15	15
J31	D1	5c blue	15	15
J32	D1	8c rose	15	15
		Set value	48	48

OFFICIAL STAMPS

Regular Issues
Handstamped in Black,
Red or Blue — a

Many double and inverted impressions exist of the handstamped overprints on Nos. O1-O83. Prices are the same as for normal stamps or slightly more.

On Stamps of 1877-79

1880-82 Unwmk. Rouletted 8

O1	A9	1c red brn	1.50	1.50
O2	A10	5c green	40	40
O3	A11	20c bister	1.25	1.25
O4	A11	50c black	8.00	8.00
O5	A12	1p blue	8.00	8.00
		Nos. O1-O5 (5)	19.15	19.15

On No. 44
Rouletted 6

O6	A9	1c brown ('81)	90	90

On Nos. 43-43A
Rouletted 8

O7	A11	50c black (R)	9.00	9.00
O8	A12	1p blue (R)	9.00	9.00

On Nos. 45, 41, 37a
Perf. 12½

O9	A13	7c blue (R) ('81)	2.00	2.00

Rouletted 8

O10	A11	10c ver (Bl)	90	90

Perf. 13½

O11	A8b	15c yellow (Bl)	2.50	2.50

On Nos. 46-47

1883 Perf. 12½

O12	A14	1c green	2.50	2.50
O13	A14a	2c rose	5.00	4.00

On Nos. 50-51
Perf. 12½, 12x12½, 13

O14	A17	5c bl (R)	1.50	1.10
a.		Imperf., pair	3.00	
O15	A18	10c brn (Bl)	3.50	1.75
a.		Imperf., pair	4.50	

No. 48 Handstamped

1884 Perf. 12½

O16	A15	1c green	17.50	15.00

Overprinted Type "a" in Black
On Nos. 48-49

1884 Perf. 12, 12x12½, 13

O17	A15	1c green	15.00	15.00
O18	A16	2c red	5.00	5.00

On Nos. 53-56
Rouletted 8

O19	A11	1c on 10c ver	75	75
a.		Small "1" (No. 53a)	5.00	

Perf. 12½

O20	A14a	2c rose	3.00	3.00
O21	A22	5c ultra	2.50	2.50
O22	A23	5c blue	1.25	90

On Stamps of 1884-88

1884-89 Rouletted 8

O23	A24	1c gray	5.00	2.50
O24	A24	1c grn ('88)	1.00	50
O25	A24	1c olive grn	1.50	75
O26	A24a	2c vermilion	60	30
O27	A24a	2c rose ('88)	90	55
O28	A24b	5c slate blue	90	50
O29	A24b	5c slate bl, bl	2.00	1.10
O30	A24b	5c vio ('88)	2.00	1.50
O31	A24b	5c lt bl ('89)	1.75	1.75
O32	A25	7c dk brn	1.50	75
O33	A25	7c org ('89)	1.50	1.00
O34	A26	10c ol brn	75	42
O35	A30	10c vio ('89)	7.50	4.00
O36	A27	20c red vio	1.50	75
O37	A27	20c bis brn ('89)	7.50	3.00
O38	A28	25c gray vio	1.50	75
O39	A28	25c ver ('89)	7.50	3.00
		Nos. O23-O39 (17)	44.90	23.12

The OFICIAL handstamp, type "a," was also applied to No. 73, the 5c violet with "Provisorio" overprint, but it was not regularly issued.

On No. 71

1887 Rouletted 9

O40	A29	10c lilac	3.00	

No. O40 was not regularly issued.

On Stamps of 1889-1899
Perf. 12½ to 15 and Compound

1890-1900

O41	A32	1c green	50	18
O43	A32	1c blue ('95)	1.10	1.10
O44	A33	2c rose	50	18
O45	A33	2c red brn ('95)	1.50	1.50
O46	A33	2c org ('00)	65	30
O47	A34	5c dp bl	1.00	1.00
O48	A34	5c rose ('95)	2.00	2.00
O49	A35	7c bis brn	75	50
O50	A35	7c grn ('95)	18.50	
O51	A36	10c bl grn	75	65
O52	A36	10c org ('95)	18.50	
O53	A37	20c orange	75	65
O54	A37	20c brn ('95)	18.50	
O55	A38	25c red brn	75	65
O56	A38	25c ver ('95)	37.50	
O57	A39	50c lt bl	3.50	3.50
O58	A39	50c lilac ('95)	4.00	4.00
O59	A40	1p lilac	4.00	3.50
O60	A40	1p lt bl ('95)	27.50	

Nos. O50, O52, O54, O56 and O60 were not regularly issued.

On No. 99

1891 Rouletted 8

O61	A24b	5c violet	1.00	1.00
a.		"1391"	9.00	

On Stamps of 1895-99
Perf. 12½ to 15 and Compound

1895-1900

O62	A51	1c bister	15	15
O63	A51	1c slate bl ('97)	45	28
O64	A52	2c blue	15	15
O65	A52	2c claret ('97)	75	50
O66	A53	5c red	50	35
O67	A53	5c green ('97)	75	45
O68	A53	5c grnsh bl ('00)	75	65
O69	A54	7c dp grn	35	35
O70	A55	10c brown	35	35
O71	A56	20c grn & blk	50	50
O72	A56	20c cl & blk ('97)	3.00	1.50
O73	A57	25c red brn & blk	55	55
O74	A57	25c pink & bl ('97)	3.00	1.50
O75	A58	50c blue & blk	75	75
O76	A58	50c grn & brn ('97)	4.00	1.50
O77	A59	1p org brn & blk	3.50	3.50
O78	A59	1p yel brn & bl ('97)	6.00	4.00
a.		Inverted overprint		
		Nos. O62-O78 (17)	25.50	17.03

On Nos. 133-135

1897, Sept.

O79	A62	1c brn vio & blk	75	50
O80	A63	5c pale bl & blk	90	65
O81	A64	10c lake & blk	1.25	75

On Nos. 136-137
Perf. 12½ to 15 and Compound

1897-1900

O82	A68	10c red	2.50	1.50
O83	A68	10c red lilac ('00)	1.25	1.25

Regular Issue of 1900-01
Overprinted

1901 Perf. 14 to 16

O84	A72	1c yel grn	25	15
O85	A75	2c vermilion	30	15
O86	A73	5c dull blue	30	15
O87	A76	7c brn org	40	40
O88	A74	10c gray vio	45	45
O89	A37	20c lt bl	4.00	3.00
O90	A38	25c bis brn	75	65
O91	A40	1p dp grn	5.00	4.00
a.		Inverted overprint	9.00	7.00
		Nos. O84-O91 (8)	11.45	8.95

Most of the used official stamps of 1901-1928 have been punched with holes of various shapes, in addition to the postal cancellations.

Regular Issue of 1904-05
Overprinted

1905 Perf. 11½

O92	A79	1c green	25	15
O93	A80	2c org red	25	15
O94	A81	5c dp bl	25	15
O95	A82	10c dk vio	50	35
O96	A83	20c gray grn	1.50	90
a.		Inverted overprint		
O97	A84	25c ol bis	1.00	60
		Nos. O92-O97 (6)	3.75	2.30

Regular Issues of 1904-07
Overprinted

1907, Mar.

O98	A79	1c green	15	15
O99	A86	5c dp bl	15	15
O100	A86	7c org brn	15	15
O101	A82	10c dk vio	15	15
O102	A83	20c gray grn	30	25
a.		Inverted overprint	4.00	
O103	A84	25c ol bis	35	30
O104	A86	50c rose	60	50
		Nos. O98-O104 (7)	1.85	1.65

Regular Issues of 1900-10
Overprinted

1910, July 15 Perf. 14½ to 16

O105	A75	2c vermilion	5.00	3.00
O106	A73	5c slate grn	3.00	2.50
O107	A74	10c gray vio	1.50	90
O108	A37	20c grnsh bl	1.50	90
O109	A38	25c bis brn	2.50	1.75

Perf. 11½

O110	A86	50c rose	3.25	1.75
a.		Inverted overprint	15.00	10.00
		Nos. O105-O110 (6)	16.75	10.80

Peace — O1

1911, Feb. 18 Litho.

O111	O1	2c red brn	35	20
O112	O1	5c dk bl	35	15
O113	O1	8c slate	35	15
O114	O1	20c gray brn	50	25
O115	O1	23c claret	75	35
O116	O1	50c orange	1.00	60
O117	O1	1p red	2.50	90
		Nos. O111-O117 (7)	5.80	2.60

Regular Issue of 1912-15
Overprinted

1915, Sept. 16

O118	A90	2c carmine	50	35
O119	A90	5c dk bl	50	35
O120	A90	8c ultra	50	35
O121	A90	20c dk brn	1.10	45
O122	A91	23c dk bl	3.00	2.50
O123	A91	50c orange	5.00	2.50
O124	A91	1p vermilion	6.00	2.50
		Nos. O118-O124 (7)	16.60	8.00

Regular Issue of
1919 Overprinted

1919, Dec. 25

O125	A95	2c red & blk	75	20
a.		Inverted overprint	3.50	
O126	A95	5c ultra & blk	90	35
O127	A95	8c gray bl & lt brn	90	35
a.		Inverted overprint	3.50	
O128	A95	20c brn & blk	1.75	60
O129	A95	23c grn & brn	1.75	60
O130	A95	50c brn & bl	2.50	1.25
O131	A95	1p dl red & bl	6.50	2.00
a.		Double overprint	12.50	
		Nos. O125-O131 (7)	15.05	5.35

Regular Issue of 1923
Overprinted

1924 Wmk. 189 Perf. 12½

O132	A100	2c violet	20	15
O133	A100	5c light blue	20	15
O134	A100	12c deep blue	30	15
O135	A100	20c buff	35	15
O136	A100	36c bl grn	1.25	90
O137	A100	50c orange	2.75	1.90
O138	A100	1p pink	4.50	3.50
O139	A100	2p lt grn	8.00	6.50
		Nos. O132-O139 (8)	17.55	13.40

Same Overprint on Regular Issue of 1924

1926-27 Unwmk. Imperf.

O140	A100	2c rose lilac	35	15
O141	A100	5c pale blue	50	15
O142	A100	8c pink ('27)	55	15
O143	A100	12c slate blue	75	15
O144	A100	20c brown	1.25	35
O145	A100	36c dull rose	2.50	75
		Nos. O140-O145 (6)	5.90	1.70

Regular Issue of 1924
Overprinted

1928 Perf. 12½

O146	A100	2c rose lilac	1.25	75
O147	A100	8c pink	1.25	30
O148	A100	10c turq blue	1.75	30

Since 1928, instead of official stamps, Uruguay has used envelopes with "S. O." printed on them, and stamps of many issues which are punched with various designs such as star or crescent.

NEWSPAPER STAMPS

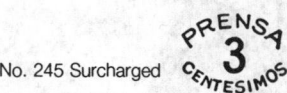

No. 245 Surcharged

1922, June 1 Unwmk. Perf. 11½
P1	A97	3c on 4c orange	25	25
a.		Inverted surcharge	6.00	6.00
b.		Double surcharge	2.50	2.50

Nos. 235-237 Surcharged

1924, June 1 Perf. 14½
P2	A96	3c on 2c car & blk	30	25
P3	A96	6c on 4c red org & bl	30	25
P4	A96	9c on 5c bl & brn	30	25

Nos. 288, 291, 293 Overprinted or Surcharged in Red:

PRENSA   PRENSA   9 CENTESIMOS

1926 Imperf.
P5	A100	3c gray green	50	20
a.		Double overprint	1.00	1.00
P6	A100	9c on 10c turq bl	60	35
a.		Double surcharge	1.00	1.00
P7	A100	15c light violet	75	40

PARCEL POST STAMPS

Mercury — PP1

Imprint: "IMPRENTA NACIONAL"
Perf. 11½
1922, Jan. 15 Litho. Unwmk.
Size: 20x29½mm
Inscribed "Exterior"
Q1	PP1	5c grn, straw	15	15
Q2	PP1	10c grn, bl gray	30	15
Q3	PP1	20c grn, rose	1.50	45
Q4	PP1	30c grn, grn	1.40	15
Q5	PP1	50c grn, blue	2.50	20
Q6	PP1	1p grn, org	3.50	90
		Nos. Q1-Q6 (6)	9.35	2.00

Inscribed "Interior"
Q7	PP1	5c grn, straw	20	15
Q8	PP1	10c grn, bl gray	20	15
Q9	PP1	20c grn, rose	65	18
Q10	PP1	30c grn, grn	1.10	20
Q11	PP1	50c grn, blue	1.50	25
Q12	PP1	1p grn, org	4.00	75
		Nos. Q7-Q12 (6)	7.65	1.68

Imprint: "IMP. NACIONAL"
Inscribed "Exterior"
1926, Jan. 20 Perf. 11½
Q13	PP1	20c grn, rose	1.75	50

Inscribed "Interior"
Perf. 11
Q14	PP1	5c grn, yellow	30	15
Q15	PP1	10c grn, bl gray	35	15
Q16	PP1	20c grn, rose	90	20
Q17	PP1	30c grn, bl grn	1.25	25
		Nos. Q13-Q17 (5)	4.55	
		Set value		1.10

Inscribed "Exterior"
1926 Perf. 11½
Q18	PP1	5c blk, straw	25	15
Q19	PP1	10c blk, bl gray	40	15
Q20	PP1	20c blk, rose	1.10	15

Inscribed "Interior"
Q21	PP1	5c blk, straw	25	15
Q22	PP1	10c blk, bl gray	30	15
Q23	PP1	20c blk, rose	60	15
Q24	PP1	30c blk, bl grn	1.10	20
		Nos. Q18-Q24 (7)	4.00	
		Set value		82

PP2

PP3

Perf. 11, 11½
1927, Feb. 22 Wmk. 188
Q25	PP2	1c dp bl	15	15
Q26	PP2	2c lt grn	15	15
Q27	PP2	4c violet	15	15
Q28	PP2	5c red	15	15
Q29	PP2	10c dk brn	25	15
Q30	PP2	20c orange	35	18
		Set value	1.00	42

See Nos. Q35-Q38, Q51-Q54.

1928, Nov. 20 Perf. 11
Size: 15x20mm
Q31	PP3	5c blk, straw	15	15
Q32	PP3	10c blk, gray blue	15	15
Q33	PP3	20c blk, rose	30	15
Q34	PP3	30c blk, green	50	15
		Set value		22

Type of 1927 Issue
1929-30 Unwmk. Perf. 11, 12½
Q35	PP2	1c violet	15	15
Q36	PP2	1c ultra ('30)	15	15
Q37	PP2	2c bl grn ('30)	15	15
Q38	PP2	5c red ('30)	15	15
		Set value	32	19

Nos. Q35-Q38, and possibly later issues, occasionally show parts of a papermaker's watermark.

PP4

1929, July 27 Wmk. 188 Perf. 11
Q39	PP4	10c orange	20	15
Q40	PP4	15c slate blue	20	15
Q41	PP4	20c ol brn	32	25
Q42	PP4	25c rose red	45	30
Q43	PP4	50c dark gray	1.25	60
Q44	PP4	75c violet	5.00	5.00
Q45	PP4	1p gray green	3.50	1.75
		Nos. Q39-Q45 (7)	10.92	8.20

For overprints see Nos. Q57-Q63.

Ship and Train — PP5

Numeral of Value — PP6

1938-39 Unwmk. Perf. 12½
Q46	PP5	10c scarlet	35	15
Q47	PP5	20c dk bl	50	15
Q48	PP5	30c lt vio ('39)	75	15
Q49	PP5	50c green	1.10	15
Q50	PP5	1p brn org	1.75	15
		Nos. Q46-Q50 (5)	4.45	
		Set value		32

See #Q70-Q73, Q80, Q88-Q90, Q92-Q93, Q95.

Type of 1927 Redrawn
1942-55? Litho. Perf. 12½
Q51	PP2	1c vio ('55)	15	15
Q52	PP2	2c bl grn	15	15
Q54	PP2	5c lt red ('44)	15	15
		Set value, Nos. Q52, Q54	18	15

The vertical and horizontal lines of the design have been strengthened, the "2" redrawn, etc. No. Q51 has oval "O" in CENTESIMO, 2¼mm from frame line at right; No. Q35 has round "O" 1¾mm from frame line.

1943, Apr. 28 Engr.
Q55	PP6	1c dk car rose	15	15
Q56	PP6	2c grnsh blk	15	15
		Set value	15	15

AÑO 1943
Parcel Post Stamps of 1929 Overprinted in Black

1943, Dec. 15 Wmk. 188 Perf. 11
Q57	PP4	10c orange	16	15
Q58	PP4	15c slate blue	16	16
Q59	PP4	20c olive brn	25	18
Q60	PP4	25c rose red	45	25
Q61	PP4	50c dk gray	90	45
Q62	PP4	75c violet	1.75	1.25
Q63	PP4	1p gray grn	2.25	1.75
		Nos. Q57-Q63 (7)	5.92	4.19

> Catalogue values for unused stamps in this section, from this point to the end of the section, are for Never Hinged items.

Bank of the Republic — PP7

University — PP8

Perf. 12½
1945, Sept. 5 Litho. Unwmk.
Q64	PP7	1c green	15	15
Q65	PP8	2c brt vio	15	15
		Set value	15	15

See Nos. Q77-Q79, Q84.

Custom House — PP9

No. Q67

1946, Dec. 11 Perf. 11½
Q66	PP9	5c yel brn & bl	15	15

Red Overprint
1946, Dec. 27 Perf. 12½
Q67	A141	1p light blue	70	15

See Nos. Q69, Q76.

Mail Coach — PP11

A141

1946, Dec. 23
Q68	PP11	5p red & ol brn	9.00	3.00

Black Overprint
1947
Q69	A141	2c dull violet brn	15	15

See Nos. Q74-Q75.

Type of 1938
1947-52 Unwmk. Perf. 12½
Q70	PP5	5c brown org ('52)	15	18
Q71	PP5	10c violet	20	15
Q72	PP5	20c vermilion	25	18
Q73	PP5	30c blue	50	15
		Set value		46

Types of 1946-47
Black Overprint
1948-49
Q74	A141	1c rose lilac ('49)	15	15
Q75	A141	5c ultra	15	15
Q76	A141	5p rose carmine	3.25	1.25

Types of 1945
1950
Q77	PP8	1c vermilion	15	15
Q78	PP7	2c chalky blue	15	15
		Set value	15	15

1952 Perf. 11
Q79	PP7	10c blue green	15	15

Type of 1938-39
1954 Perf. 12½
Q80	PP5	20c carmine	20	20

Custom House — PP13

Design: 1p, State Railroad Administration Building.

1955 Unwmk. Litho. Perf. 12½
Q81	PP13	5c brown	15	15
Q82	PP13	1p light ultra	2.00	1.50

See Nos. Q83, Q85-Q86, Q96. For surcharge see No. Q87.

Types of 1945 and 1955
Design: 20c, Solis Theater.

1956-57 Perf. 11
Q83	PP13	5c gray ('57)	32	15
Q84	PP7	10c lt olive grn	15	15
Q85	PP13	20c yellow	15	15
Q86	PP13	20c lt red brn ('57)	16	15
		Set value	62	20

No. Q83 Surcharged with New Value in Red
1957
Q87	PP13	30c on 5c gray	16	15

Type of 1938-39
1957-60 Wmk. 327 Perf. 11
Q88	PP5	20c lt blue ('59)	15	15

Unwmk.
Q89	PP5	30c red lilac	20	20

Perf. 12½
Q90	PP5	1p dk blue ('60)	25	25

Nos. Q88 and Q93 are in slightly larger format-17¼x21mm instead of 16x19½mm.

National Printing Works — PP14

1960, Mar. 23 Wmk. 327 Perf. 11
Q91	PP14	30c yellow green	15	15

Type of 1938-39
1962-63 Wmk. 332 Perf. 11
Q92	PP5	50c slate green	20	15

Perf. 10½
Q93	PP5	1p blue grn ('63)	40	40
		Set value		45

$ 5.00

No. C158 Surcharged

ENCOMIENDAS

1965 Unwmk. Perf. 11
Q94	AP12	5p on 84c orange	28	15

For use on regular and air post parcels.

Types of 1938-55

Design: 1p, State Railroad Administration Building.

1966   **Litho.**   **Perf. 10½**
Q95 PP5 10c blue green   15   15

Wmk. 327
Q96 PP13 1p brown   15   15
     Set value   15   15

ENCOMIENDAS

No. C184
Surcharged in Red

1.00
PESO

1966   **Unwmk.**   **Perf. 11**
Q97 AP21 1p on 38c black   15   15

Plane and
Bus — PP15

Design: 20p, Plane facing left and bus; "Encomiendas" on top.

Wmk. 332
1969, July 8   **Litho.**   **Perf. 12**
Q98 PP15 10p blk, crim & bl grn   15   15
Q99 PP15 20p bl, blk & yel   30   16
     Set value   22

Encomiendas

No. B7 Surcharged   **$ 0.60**

1971, Feb. 3   **Wmk. 327**   **Perf. 11½**
Q100 SP2 60c on 1p + 10c   60   60

No. 761 Surcharged in Red

IMPUESTOS A ENCOMIENDAS $0.60

1971, Nov. 12   **Wmk. 332**   **Perf. 12**
Q101 A226 60c on 6p lt grn & blk   25   22

Nos. 770-771 Surcharged

$1
IMPUESTO A
ENCOMIENDAS

1972, Nov. 6   **Litho.**   **Perf. 12**
Q102 A233 1p on 6p multi (#770)   30   30
Q103 A233 1p on 6p multi (#771)   30   30
   a.   Pair, #Q102-Q103   60   60

See note after No. 771.

Parcels and
Arrows — PP16

Old Mail
Truck
PP17

Designs: Early means of mail transport.

1974   **Wmk. 332**   **Litho.**   **Perf. 12**
Q104 PP16 75p shown   15   15
Q105 PP17 100p shown   25   18
Q106 PP17 150p Steam engine   25   25
Q107 PP17 300p Side-wheeler   60   45
Q108 PP17 500p Plane   1.00   75
     Nos. Q104-Q108 (5)   2.25   1.78

Issue dates: 75p, Feb. 13. Others, Mar. 6.

UZBEKISTAN

LOCATION — Central Asia, bounded by Kazakhstan, Turkmenistan, Tadjikistan and Kyrgyzstan
GOVT. — Independent republic, member of the Commonwealth of Independent States
AREA — 172,700 sq. mi.
POP. — 19,900,000 (1989)
CAPITAL — Tashkent

With the breakup of the Soviet Union on Dec. 26, 1991, Uzbekistan and ten former Soviet republics established the Commonwealth of Independent States.

100 Kopecks = 1 Ruble
100 Tiyin = 1 Sum

Catalogue values for all unused stamps in this country are for Never Hinged items.

A1

Perf. 11½x12
1992, May 7   **Unwmk.**   **Photo.**
1   A1   20k multicolored   65

Melitaea
Acreina — A2

1992, Aug. 31   **Litho.**   **Perf. 12**
2   A2   1r multicolored   15

Independence
from Soviet
Union, 1st
Anniv. — A3

1992   **Photo.**   **Perf. 12**
3   A3   1r multicolored   30

Khiva Mosque,
19th
Cent. — A4

1992   **Perf. 11½**
4   A4   50k multicolored   20

Samarkand — A5

1992   **Litho.**   **Perf. 13x13½**
5   A5   10r multicolored   36

Winner of 1992 Aga Khan Award for Architecture.

Samovar, 19th
Cent. — A6

1992   **Perf. 12x11½**
6   A6   50k multicolored   15

Fauna — A7

Designs: 1r, Teratoscincus scincus. No. 8, Naja oxiana. No. 9, Ondatra zibethica, vert. 3r, Pandion haliaetus, vert. 5r, Remiz pendulinus, vert. 10r, Dryomys nitedula, vert. 15r, Varanus griseus. 20r, Cervus elaphus baktrianus.

1993, Mar. 12   **Litho.**   **Perf. 12**
7   A7   1r multicolored   15
8   A7   2r multicolored   15
9   A7   2r multicolored   15
10   A7   3r multicolored   22
11   A7   5r multicolored   38
12   A7   10r multicolored   75
13   A7   15r multicolored   1.10
     Nos. 7-13 (7)   2.90

Souvenir Sheet
14   A7   20r multicolored   1.50

Flag and Coat of
Arms — A8

Perf. 12x12½, 11½x12 (#33)
1993   **Litho.**
30   A8   8r multicolored   15
31   A8   15r multicolored   15
33   A8   50r multicolored   45
34   A8   100r multicolored   90

No. 33 is 19x26½mm.

Flowers — A9

1993   **Perf. 12**
38   A9   20r Dianthus uzbekistanicus   28
39   A9   20r Colchicum kesselringii   28
40   A9   25r Crocus alatavicus   35
41   A9   25r Salvia bucharica   35
42   A9   30r Tulipa kaufmanniana   42
43   A9   30r Tulipa greigii   42
     Nos. 38-43 (6)   2.10

Souvenir Sheet
44   A9   50r Tulip   70

Coat of Arms — A10

1994   **Litho.**   **Perf. 11½x12**
50   A10   75s claret   15

This is an expanding set. Number may change.

Bakhouddin,
675th Anniv.
A11

1994   **Perf. 12½x12**
55   A11   100s multicolored   32

No. 55 printed se-tenant with label.

Souvenir Sheet

President's Cup Intl. Tennis Tournament,
Tashkent — A12

1994   **Perf. 12x12½**
56   A12   500s multicolored   1.00

Ulugh Beg (1394-
1449),
Astronomer — A13

Designs: 30t, Portals of Samarkand. 35t, Portal of Bukhara. 40t, Globe, astrolabe. 45t, Statue. 60t, Portrait.

Stamps of Uzbekistan can be mounted in the annual Scott Russia and Commonwealth of Independent States supplement.

1994, Sept. 15 Litho. Perf. 12x12½

57	A13	30t multicolored	15
58	A13	35t multicolored	15
59	A13	40t multicolored	16
60	A13	45t multicolored	18
		Nos. 57-60 (4)	64

Souvenir Sheet

61	A13	60t multicolored	23

Nos. 57-59 are printed se-tenant with label.

VATICAN CITY

LOCATION — Western Italy, directly outside the western boundary of Rome

GOVT. — Independent state subject to certain political restrictions under a treaty with Italy

AREA — 108.7 acres

POP. — 1,000 (est.)

100 Centesimi = 1 Lira

Catalogue values for unused stamps in this country are for Never Hinged items, beginning with Scott 68 in the regular postage section, Scott C1 in the airpost section, Scott E3 in the special delivery section, and Scott J7 in the postage due section.

Watermarks

Wmk. 235 - Crossed Keys

Wmk. 277 - Winged Wheel

Papal Arms — A1

Pope Pius XI — A2

Unwmk.

1929, Aug. 1 Engr. Perf. 14

Surface-Colored Paper

1	A1	5c dk brown & pink	15	15
2	A1	10c dk grn & lt grn	20	20
3	A1	20c violet & lilac	55	32
4	A1	25c dk bl & lt bl	55	35
5	A1	30c indigo & yellow	70	52
6	A1	50c indigo & sal buff	70	52
7	A1	75c brown car & gray	1.00	70

Photo.

White Paper

8	A2	80c carmine rose	52	28
9	A2	1.25 l dark blue	1.25	70
10	A2	2 l olive brown	3.75	1.50
11	A2	2.50 l red orange	3.00	2.50
12	A2	5 l dk green	4.50	9.25
13	A2	10 l olive blk	6.50	11.00
		Nos. 1-13,E1-E2 (15)	37.12	38.24
		Set, never hinged	170.00	

The stamps of Type A1 have, in this and subsequent issues, the words "POSTE VATICANE" in rows of colorless letters in the background.

For surcharges and overprints see Nos. 14, 35-40, 61-67, J1-J6, Q1-Q13.

No. 5 Surcharged in Red

C. 25

1931, Oct. 1

14	A1	25c on 30c ind & yel	2.25	1.00
		Never hinged	4.25	

Arms of Pope Pius XI — A5

Vatican Palace and Obelisk — A6

Vatican Gardens — A7

Pope Pius XI — A8

St. Peter's Basilica A9

1933, May 31 Engr. Wmk. 235

19	A5	5c copper red	15	15
a.		Imperf., pair	225.00	350.00
20	A6	10c dk brown & blk	15	15
21	A6	12½c dp green & blk	15	15
22	A6	20c orange & blk	15	15
a.		Vertical pair imperf. between and at bottom	175.00	175.00
23	A6	25c dk olive & blk	15	15
a.		Imperf., pair	150.00	165.00
24	A7	30c black & dk brn	15	15
25	A7	50c violet & dk brn	15	15
26	A7	75c brn red & dk brn	15	15
27	A7	80c rose & dk brn	15	15
28	A8	1 l violet & blk	3.00	60
29	A8	1.25 l dk bl & blk	10.50	3.25
30	A8	2 l dk brown & blk	25.00	18.00
31	A8	2.75 l dk vio & blk	27.50	30.00
32	A9	5 l blk brn & dk grn	15	22
33	A9	10 l dk blue & dk grn	15	35
34	A9	20 l black & dp grn	15	60
		Nos. 19-34,E3-E4 (18)	68.10	54.93
		Set, never hinged	175.00	

Nos. 8-13 Surcharged in Black ≡ 40 ≡

1934, June 16 Unwmk.

35	A2	40c on 80c	1.10	3.25
36	A2	1.30 l on 1.25 l	95.00	47.50
a.		Small figures "30" in "1.30"	1,250.	1,500.
37	A2	2.05 l on 2 l	125.00	10.50
a.		No comma btwn. 2 & 0	210.00	32.50
38	A2	2.55 l on 2.50 l	95.00	150.00
a.		No comma btwn. 2 & 5	150.00	150.00
39	A2	3.05 l on 5 l	300.00	300.00
40	A2	3.70 l on 10 l	300.00	575.00
a.		No comma btwn. 3 & 7	525.00	425.00
		Nos. 35-40 (6)	916.10	1,086.
		Set, never hinged	2,600.	

A second printing of Nos. 36-40 was made in 1937. The 2.55 l and 3.05 l of the first printing and 1.30 l of the second printing sell for more. Forged surcharges of Nos. 35-40 are plentiful.

Tribonian Presenting Pandects to Justinian I A10

Pope Gregory IX Promulgating Decretals A11

1935, Feb. 1 Photo.

41	A10	5c red orange	20	55
42	A10	10c purple	20	55
43	A10	25c green	1.65	3.50
44	A11	75c rose red	22.50	14.00

45	A11	80c dk brown	19.00	10.00
46	A11	1.25 l dk blue	22.50	10.00
		Nos. 41-46 (6)	66.05	38.60
		Set, never hinged	475.00	

Intl. Juridical Congress, Rome, 1934.

Doves and Bell — A12

Allegory of Church and Bible — A13

St. John Bosco — A14

St. Francis de Sales — A15

1936, June 22

47	A12	5c blue green	22	65
48	A13	10c black	22	28
49	A14	25c yellow green	14.00	4.50
50	A12	50c rose violet	22	55
51	A13	75c rose red	25.00	22.50
52	A14	80c orange brn	38	1.10
53	A15	1.25 l dark blue	70	1.65
54	A15	5 l dark brown	45	3.50
		Nos. 47-54 (8)	41.19	34.73
		Set, never hinged	300.00	

Catholic Press Conference, 1936.

Crypt of St. Cecilia in Catacombs of St. Calixtus A16

Basilica of Sts. Nereus and Achilleus in Catacombs of St. Domitilla A17

1938, Oct. 12 Perf. 14

55	A16	5c bister brown	28	15
56	A16	10c deep orange	40	28
57	A16	25c deep green	40	28
58	A17	75c deep rose	4.75	6.25
59	A17	80c violet	18.00	12.50
60	A17	1.25 l blue	16.00	12.50
		Nos. 55-60 (6)	39.83	31.96
		Set, never hinged	110.00	

Intl. Christian Archaeological Congress, Rome, 1938.

Interregnum Issue

Nos. 1-7 Overprinted in Black

SEDE VACANTE MCMXXXIX

1939, Feb. 20 Perf. 14

61	A1	5c dk brn & pink	27.50	10.00
62	A1	10c dk grn & lt grn	65	48
63	A1	20c violet & lilac	65	48
64	A1	25c dk bl & lt bl	1.90	10.00
65	A1	30c indigo & yellow	70	1.00
a.		Pair, one without ovpt.	750.00	

66	A1	50c indigo & sal buff	70	70
67	A1	75c brn car & gray	70	70
		Nos. 61-67 (7)	32.80	23.36
		Set, never hinged	92.50	

Catalogue values for unused stamps in this section, from this point to the end of the section, are for Never Hinged items.

Coronation of Pope Pius XII — A18

1939, June 2 Photo.

68	A18	25c green	2.75	42
69	A18	75c rose red	16	15
70	A18	80c violet	4.50	3.00
71	A18	1.25 l deep blue	16	15

Coronation of Pope Pius XII, Mar. 12, 1939.

Arms of Pope Pius XII — A19

Vatican

We Buy!

We buy all Vatican and Italian Area including quantity material to date.

Top Prices Paid!

Especially needed: Collections, Rarities, Covers, Zeppelin Flights, Errors.

We Sell!

Large stock of top quality material at realistic prices.

Free Price List

Year Units, Individual sets NH & H. Postal Stationery and Specialized material. Western European Country price lists also available.

For buying or selling Vatican City and all other U.S. & Worldwide call

1-800-9-4-STAMP

(1-800-947-8267)

VISA   MasterCard   DISCOVER   AMERICAN EXPRESS

Henry Gitner Philatelists, Inc.

P.O. Box 3077-S
Middletown, NY 10940
Tel: 914-343-5151
Fax: 914-343-0068

Philately - The Quiet Excitement!

Pope Pius XII

A20   A21

Wmk. 235

1940, Mar. 12   Engr.   *Perf. 14*
72	A19	5c dark carmine	15	15
73	A20	1 l purple & blk	25	18
74	A21	1.25 l slate bl & blk	15	15
a.		Imperf., pair	350.00	550.00
75	A20	2 l dk brown & blk	1.40	1.10
76	A21	2.75 l dk rose vio & blk	1.75	1.50
		Nos. 72-76 (5)	3.70	3.08

See Nos. 91-98.

A22   A23

Picture of Jesus inscribed "I have Compassion on the Multitude."

1942, Sept. 1   Photo.   Unwmk.
77	A22	25c dk blue green	15	15
78	A22	80c chestnut brown	15	15
79	A22	1.25 l deep blue	28	25
		Set value	40	40

See Nos. 84-86, 99-101.

1942, Jan. 16

Consecration of Archbishop Pacelli by Pope Benedict XV.

80	A23	25c myr grn & gray grn	15	15
81	A23	80c dk brn & yel grn	15	15
82	A23	1.25 l sapphire & vio bl	15	15
a.		Name and value panel omitted		
83	A23	5 l vio blk & gray blk	52	35
		Set value	75	63

25th anniv. of the consecration of Msgr. Eugenio Pacelli (later Pope Pius XII) as Archbishop of Sardes.

Type of 1942
Inscribed MCMXLIII

1944, Jan. 31
84	A22	25c dk blue green	15	15
85	A22	80c chestnut brown	15	15
86	A22	1.25 l deep blue	30	15
		Set value	48	27

Raphael Sanzio — A24

Designs: 80c, Antonio da Sangallo. 1.25 l, Carlo Maratti. 10 l, Antonio Canova.

1944, Nov. 21   Wmk. 235   Photo.
87	A24	25c olive & green	15	15
88	A24	80c claret & rose vio	16	15
a.		Dbl. impression of center	600.00	
89	A24	1.25 l bl vio & dp bl	42	15
a.		Imperf., pair	700.00	1,000
90	A24	10 l bister & ol brn	2.00	1.25

400th anniv. of the Pontifical Academy of the Virtuosi of the Pantheon.

Types of 1940

1945, Mar. 5   Engr.   Unwmk.
91	A19	5c gray	15	15
a.		Imperf., pair	200.00	
92	A19	30c brown	15	15
a.		Imperf., pair	120.00	

93	A19	50c dark green	15	15
94	A21	1 l brown & blk	15	15
95	A21	1.50 l rose car & blk	15	15
a.		Imperf., pair	325.00	
96	A21	2.50 l dp ultra & blk	15	15
97	A20	5 l rose vio & blk	16	15
98	A20	20 l gray grn & blk	22	15
		Nos. 91-98,E5-E6 (10)	2.15	
		Set value		1.30

Nos. 91-96 exist in pairs imperf. between, some vertical, some horizontal. Value, each $125.
Pair imperf. vertically exist of 30c and 50c (value $60), and of 5 lire (value $90).

Type of 1942
Inscribed MCMXLIV
Wmk. 277

1945, Sept. 12   Photo.   *Perf. 14*
99	A22	1 l dk blue green	15	15
100	A22	3 l dk carmine	15	15
a.		Jesus image omitted	100.00	100.00
101	A22	5 l deep ultra	32	20
		Set value	45	32

Nos. 99-101 exist in pairs imperf. between, both horizontal and vertical. Value, each $100.
Pairs imperf. horizontally exist of 3 lire (value $30) and 5 lire (value $125).

Nos. 91 to 98 Surcharged with New Values and Bars in Black or Blue

Two types of 25c on 30c:
I - Surcharge 16mm wide.
II - Surcharge 19mm wide.

Two types of 1 l on 50c:
I - Surcharge bars 5mm wide.
II - Bars 4mm wide.

1946, Jan. 9   Unwmk.   *Perf. 14*
102	A19	20c on 5c	20	15
103	A19	25c on 30c (I)	20	15
a.		Type II	40	15
b.		Inverted surcharge (II)	275.00	275.00
104	A19	1 l on 50c (I)	20	15
a.		Type II	11.00	4.50
105	A21	1.50 l on 1 l (Bl)	20	15
a.		Double surcharge	175.00	
106	A21	3 l on 1.50 l	20	15
107	A21	5 l on 2.50 l	48	16
108	A20	10 l on 5 l	75	24
109	A20	30 l on 20 l	4.25	1.65
		Nos. 102-109,E7-E8 (10)	14.98	6.10

Nos. 102, 105-109 exist in horizontal pairs, imperf. between. Value, each $110.
Vertical pairs imperf. between exist of Nos. 102, 106-107 (value, each $150) and of No. 104a (value $225).
Nos. 102, 104-108 exist in pairs imperf. vertically or horizontally, or both. Value $40 to $60.
Nos. 102-108 exist in pairs, one without surcharge. Value, Nos. 102-105, each $150; Nos. 106-108, each $200.

St. Vigilio Cathedral,   St. Angela
Trent — A28   Merici — A29

Designs: 50c, St. Anthony Zaccaria. 75c, St. Ignatius of Loyola. 1 l, St. Cajetan Thiene. 1.50 l, St. John Fisher. 2 l, Christoforo Cardinal Madruzzi. 2.50 l, Reginald Cardinal Pole. 3 l, Marcello Cardinal Cervini. 4 l, Giovanni Cardinal del Monte. 5 l, Emperor Charles V. 1 l, Pope Paul III.

Perf. 14, 14x13½
1946, Feb. 21   Photo.   Unwmk.
Centers in Dark Brown
110	A28	5c olive bister	15	15
111	A29	25c purple	15	15
112	A29	50c brown orange	15	15
113	A29	75c black	15	15
114	A29	1 l dk violet	15	15
115	A29	1.50 l red orange	15	15
116	A29	2 l yellow green	15	15
117	A29	2.50 l deep blue	15	15
118	A29	3 l brt carmine	15	15
119	A29	4 l ocher	15	15
120	A29	5 l brt ultra	60	15
121	A29	10 l dp rose car	60	15
		Nos. 110-121,E9-E10 (14)	3.10	
		Set value		1.00

400th anniv. of the Council of Trent (1545-63).
Vertical pairs imperf. between exist of Nos. 110-111, 114, 116-117 (value, each $150); Nos. 113,

---

119 (value, each $100); Nos. 115, 118 (value, each $75).
Horizontal pairs imperf. between exist of No. 121 (value $150); Nos. 113, 117 (value $100).

Basilica of St. Agnes — A40

Basilica of the Holy Cross in Jerusalem A41

Basilica of the Holy Cross in Jerusalem
A41

Pope Pius XII
A42

Basilicas: 3 l, St. Clement. 5 l, St. Prassede. 8 l, St. Mary in Cosmedin. 6 l, St. Sebastian. 25 l, St. Lawrence. 35 l, St. Paul. 40 l, St. Mary Major.

Perf. 14, 14x13½, 13½x14
1949, Mar. 7   Photo.   Wmk. 235
122	A40	1 l dark brown	15	15
123	A40	3 l violet	15	15
124	A40	5 l deep orange	20	15
a.		Perf. 14x13½	21.00	4.50
125	A40	8 l dp blue grn	15	15
126	A41	13 l dull green	5.50	3.50
127	A41	16 l dk olive brn	40	18
a.		Perf. 14	75	28
128	A41	25 l car rose	7.00	50
129	A41	35 l red violet	37.50	7.75
a.		Perf. 13½x14	52.50	8.25
130	A41	40 l blue	30	15
a.		Perf. 14x13½	1.90	32

Engr.
Perf. 14
131	A42	100 l sepia	4.75	2.75
		Nos. 122-131,E11-E12 (12)	84.10	24.93

Jesus Giving St.   Cathedrals of St.
Peter the Keys to   Peter, St. Paul, St.
Heaven — A43   John Lateran and
                       St. Mary
                       Major — A44

Pope Boniface VIII   Pope Pius XII in
Proclaiming Holy   Ceremony of
Year in   Opening the Holy
1300 — A45   Door — A46

Wmk. 277
1949, Dec 21   Photo.   *Perf. 14*
132	A43	5 l red brn & brn	15	15
133	A44	6 l ind & yel brn	15	15
134	A45	8 l ultra & dk grn	60	45
135	A46	10 l green & slate	15	15
136	A43	20 l dk grn & red brn	60	25
137	A44	25 l sepia & dp blue	32	25

138	A45	30 l grnsh blk & rose lil	2.75	85
139	A46	60 l blk brn & brn rose	2.00	1.65
		Nos. 132-139 (8)	6.72	3.90

Holy Year, 1950.

Palatine Guard and Statue of St. Peter — A47

1950, Sept. 12
140	A47	25 l sepia	10.00	6.50
141	A47	35 l dark green	4.00	3.75
142	A47	55 l red brown	2.25	2.00

Centenary of the Palatine Guard.

Pope Pius XII   Crowd at the
Making   Basilica of St. Peter
Proclamation   A49
A48

1951, May 8   Unwmk.
143	A48	25 l chocolate	2.50	1.10
144	A49	55 l brt blue	13.00	7.50

Proclamation of the Roman Catholic dogma of the Assumption of the Virgin Mary, Nov. 1, 1950.

Pope Pius X
A50   A51

Perf. 14x13½
1951, June 3   Photo.   Wmk. 235
Background of Medallion in Gold
145	A50	6 l purple	15	15
146	A50	35 l Prus green	35	22
147	A51	60 l blue	9.50	5.75
148	A51	115 l brown	12.00	6.50

Council of Chalcedon
A52

Pope Leo I
Remonstrating
with Attila
the
Hun — A53

1951, Oct. 31   Engr.   *Perf. 14x13½*
149	A52	5 l dk gray green	45	40
a.		Pair, imperf. horiz.	350.00	
150	A53	25 l red brown	3.00	2.50
		Horiz. pair, imperf. btwn.	700.00	700.00

151 A52	35 l carmine rose	8.00	5.50
152 A53	60 l deep blue	22.50	12.50
153 A52	100 l dark brown	30.00	21.00
	Nos. 149-153 (5)	63.95	41.90

Council of Chalcedon, 1500th anniv.

No. 126 Surcharged with New Value and Bars in Carmine

1952, Mar. 15   *Perf. 14*

154 A41	12 l on 13 l dull grn	2.25	1.25
a.	Perf. 13½x14	2.25	1.25
b.	Pair, one without surcharge	375.00	450.00

Roman States Stamp and Stagecoach A54

1952, June 9   Engr.   *Perf. 13*

155 A54	50 l sep & dp bl, cr	6.50	4.50
a.	Souvenir sheet	125.00	85.00

Centenary of the 1st stamp of the Papal States. #155a contains 4 stamps similar to #155, with papal insignia and inscription in purple. Singles from the souvenir sheet differ slightly from #155. The colors are closer to black and blue, and the cream tone of the paper is visible on the back.

St. Maria Goretti — A55   St. Peter — A56

Perf. 13½x14

1953, Feb. 12   Photo.   Wmk. 235

156 A55	15 l dp brown & vio	5.50	3.00
157 A55	35 l dp rose & brn	4.50	3.00

Martyrdom of St. Maria Goretti, 50th anniv.

Perf. 13½x13, 14

1953, Apr. 23   Engr.

Designs: 5 l, Pius XII and Roman sepulcher. 10 l, St. Peter and Tomb of the Apostle. 12 l, Sylvester I and Constantine Basilica. 20 l, Julius II and Bramante's plans. 25 l, Paul III and the Apse. 35 l, Sixtus V and dome. 45 l, Paul V and facade. 60 l, Urban VIII and the canopy. 65 l, Alexander VII and colonnade. 100 l, Pius VI and the sacristy.

158 A56	3 l dk red brn & blk	15	15
159 A56	5 l slate & blk	15	15
160 A56	10 l dk green & blk	15	15
161 A56	12 l chestnut & blk	15	15
162 A56	20 l violet & blk	45	35
163 A56	25 l dk brown & blk	15	15
164 A56	35 l dk carmine & blk	15	15
165 A56	45 l olive brn & blk	45	35
166 A56	60 l dk blue & blk	15	15
167 A56	65 l car rose & blk	45	35
168 A56	100 l rose vio & blk	15	15
	Set value, #158-168, E13-E14	2.75	2.10

St. Clare of Assisi — A57   Peter Lombard Medal — A59

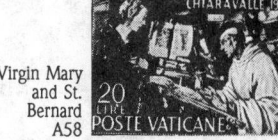

Virgin Mary and St. Bernard A58

Unwmk.

1953, Aug. 12   Photo.   *Perf. 13*

169 A57	25 l aqua, yel brn & vio brn	3.00	1.10
170 A57	35 l brn red, yel brn & vio brn	15.00	10.50

Death of St. Clare of Assisi, 700th anniv.

1953, Nov. 10

171 A58	20 l ol grn & dk vio brn	1.10	75
172 A58	60 l brt bl & ol grn	11.00	5.50

Death of St. Bernard of Clairvaux, 800th anniv.

1953, Dec. 29

173 A59	100 l lil rose, bl, dk grn & yel	35.00	22.50

Peter Lombard, Bishop of Paris 1159.

Pope Pius XI and Vatican City — A60

1954, Feb. 12   Wmk. 235

174 A60	25 l bl, red brn & cr	2.00	1.25
175 A60	60 l yel brn & dp bl	3.50	2.75

Signing of the Lateran Pacts, 25th anniv.

Pope Pius IX A61

Portraits: (At left) - 6 l, 20 l, Pope Pius IX. (At right) - 4 l, 12 l, 35 l, Pope Pius XII.

1954, May 26   Engr.   *Perf. 13*

176 A61	3 l violet	15	15
177 A61	4 l carmine	15	15
178 A61	6 l plum	15	15
179 A61	12 l blue green	1.25	20
180 A61	20 l red brown	1.10	85
181 A61	35 l ultra	2.75	2.75
	Nos. 176-181 (6)	5.55	4.25

Marian Year; centenary of the dogma of the Immaculate Conception.

St. Pius X — A62

1954, May 29   Photo.
Colors (except background): Yellow and Plum

182 A62	10 l dark brown	15	15
183 A62	25 l violet	3.50	95
184 A62	35 l dk slate gray	4.25	3.75

Canonization of Pope Pius X, May 20, 1954. Nos. 182-184 exist imperf. Value, each pair $800.

Basilica of St. Francis of Assisi — A63

1954, Oct. 1   Photo.   *Perf. 14*

185 A63	20 l dk vio gray & cr	3.50	1.90
186 A63	35 l dk brown & cream	2.50	1.75

Consecration of the Basilica of St. Francis of Assisi, 200th anniv.

St. Augustine A64

1954, Nov. 13

187 A64	35 l blue green	1.65	1.10
188 A64	50 l redsh brown	3.25	1.90

1600th birth anniv. of St. Augustine.

Madonna of the Gate of Dawn, Vilnius — A65

1954, Dec. 7

189 A65	20 l pink & multi	1.40	80
190 A65	35 l blue & multi	7.00	4.00
191 A65	60 l multicolored	13.00	6.00

Issued to mark the end of the Marian Year.

St. Boniface and Fulda Abbey — A66

1955, Apr. 28   Engr.   *Perf. 13*

192 A66	10 l grnsh gray	15	15
193 A66	35 l violet	95	70
a.	Imperf., pair	300.00	
194 A66	60 l brt blue green	95	70

1200th death anniv. of St. Boniface.

Pope Sixtus II and St. Lawrence A67   Pope Nicholas V A68

Wmk. 235

1955, June 27   Photo.   *Perf. 14*

195 A67	50 l carmine	6.25	3.50
196 A67	100 l deep blue	2.75	1.50

Fra Angelico (1387-1455), painter. Design is from a Fra Angelico fresco.

1955, Nov. 28

197 A68	20 l grnsh bl & ol brn	28	18
198 A68	35 l rose car & ol brn	55	38
199 A68	60 l yel grn & ol brn	1.40	75

Death of Pope Nicholas V, 500th anniv.

St. Bartholomew and Church of Grottaferrata A69   Capt. Gaspar Roust A70

1955, Dec. 29

200 A69	10 l brown & gray	16	15
201 A69	25 l car rose & gray	1.10	60
202 A69	100 l dk green & gray	2.75	2.25

900th death anniv. of St. Bartholomew, abbot of Grottaferrata.

1956, Apr. 27   Engr.   *Perf. 13*

Designs: 6 l, 50 l, Guardsman. 10 l, 60 l, Two drummers.

203 A70	4 l dk carmine rose	15	15
204 A70	6 l deep orange	15	15
205 A70	10 l deep ultra	15	15
206 A70	35 l brown	85	60
207 A70	50 l violet	1.40	95
208 A70	60 l blue green	1.75	1.40
	Nos. 203-208 (6)	4.45	3.40

450th anniv. of the Swiss Papal Guard.

St. Rita of Cascia — A71   Pope Paul III Confirming Society of Jesus — A72

1956, May 19   Photo.   *Perf. 14*

209 A71	10 l gray green	15	15
210 A71	25 l olive brown	95	60
211 A71	35 l ultra	65	40

500th death anniv. of St. Rita of Cascia.

1956, July 31   Engr.   *Perf. 13*

212 A72	35 l dk red brown	70	65
213 A72	60 l blue gray	1.40	1.10

400th death anniv. of St. Ignatius of Loyola, founder of the Society of Jesus.

St. John of Capistrano — A73

1956, Oct. 30   *Perf. 14*

214 A73	25 l slate blk & grn	2.75	1.90
215 A73	35 l dk brn car & blue	1.25	95

5th centenary of the death of St. John of Capistrano, leader in the war against the Turks.

Footnotes near stamp listings often refer to other stamps of the same design.

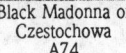

Black Madonna of
Czestochowa
A74

St. Domenico
Savio
A75

1956, Dec. 20
216	A74	35 l dk blue & blk	35	28
217	A74	60 l green & ultra	80	65
218	A74	100 l brn & dk car rose	1.40	1.00

300th anniv. of the proclamation of the Madonna of Czestochowa as "Queen of Poland."

1957, Mar. 21 Wmk. 235 Perf. 13½
Design: 6 l, 60 l, Sts. Domenico Savio and John Bosco.

219	A75	4 l red brown	15	15
220	A75	6 l brt carmine	15	15
221	A75	25 l green	20	15
222	A75	60 l ultra	1.90	1.50

Death cent. of St. Domenico Savio.

Cardinal
Capranica and
College
A76

Design: 10 l, 100 l, Pope Pius XII.

1957, June 27 Engr. Perf. 13
223	A76	5 l dk carmine rose	15	15
224	A76	10 l pale brown	15	15
225	A76	35 l grnsh black	32	22
226	A76	100 l ultra	1.10	70
		Set value	1.50	1.05

500th anniv. of Capranica College, oldest seminary in the world.

Pontifical
Academy of
Science — A77

1957, Oct. 9 Photo. Perf. 14
227	A77	35 l dk blue & green	75	65
228	A77	60 l brown & ultra	1.00	65

Pontifical Academy of Science, 20th anniv.

Mariazell
A78

High
Altar — A79

1957, Nov. 14 Engr. Perf. 13½
229	A78	5 l green	15	15
230	A79	15 l slate	15	15
231	A78	60 l ultra	52	28
232	A79	100 l violet	1.75	85

Mariazell shrine, Austria, 800th anniv.

Apparition of the
Virgin Mary — A80

Designs: 10 l, 35 l, Sick man and basilica. 15 l, 100 l, St. Bernadette.

1958, Feb. 21 Wmk. 235 Perf. 13x14
233	A80	5 l dark blue	15	15
234	A80	10 l blue green	15	15
235	A80	15 l redsh brown	15	15
236	A80	25 l rose carmine	15	15
237	A80	35 l gray brown	15	15
238	A80	100 l violet	15	15
		Set value	50	35

Centenary of apparition of the Virgin Mary at Lourdes and the establishment of the shrine.

Pope
Pius XII — A81

Statue of Pope
Clement XIII by
Canova — A82

Design: 60 l, 100 l, Vatican pavilion at Brussels fair.

1958, June 19 Engr. Perf. 13
239	A81	35 l claret	45	45

Perf. 13x14
240	A81	60 l fawn	70	55
241	A81	100 l violet	2.50	1.90
242	A81	300 l ultra	1.90	1.40
a.	Souvenir sheet of 4, #239-242		22.50	20.00

Universal and Intl. Exposition, Brussels.

1958, July 2 Perf. 14
Statues: 10 l, Clement XIV. 35 l, Pius VI. 100 l, Pius VII.

243	A82	5 l brown	15	15
244	A82	10 l carmine rose	15	15
245	A82	35 l blue gray	28	22
246	A82	100 l dark blue	1.75	1.00
		Set value		1.30

Antonio Canova (1757-1822), sculptor.

Interregnum Issue

St. Peter's
Keys and Papal
Chamberlain's
Insignia
A83

Wmk. 235
1958, Oct. 21 Photo. Perf. 14
247	A83	15 l brn blk, *yel*	1.90	1.10
248	A83	25 l brown black	15	15
249	A83	60 l brn blk, *pale vio*	15	15

Pope John
XXIII — A84

Pope
Pius XI — A85

Design: 35 l, 100 l, Coat of Arms.

1959, Apr. 2 Photo. Perf. 14
250	A84	25 l car rose, bl & buff	15	15
251	A84	35 l multicolored	15	15
252	A84	60 l rose car, bl & ocher	15	15
253	A84	100 l multicolored	15	15
		Set value	38	30

Coronation of Pope John XXIII, Nov. 4, 1958.

1959, May 25 Wmk. 235 Perf. 14
254	A85	30 l brown	15	15
255	A85	100 l violet blue	30	15
		Set value		18

Lateran Pacts, 30th anniversary.

St. Lawrence
A86

Radio Tower and
Archangel Gabriel
A87

Portraits of Saints: 25 l, Pope Sixtus II. 50 l, Agapitus. 60 l, Filicissimus. 100 l, Cyprianus. 300 l, Fructuosus.

1959, May 25
256	A86	15 l red, brn & yel	15	15
257	A86	25 l lilac, brn & yel	15	15
258	A86	50 l Prus bl, blk & yel	65	40
259	A86	60 l ol grn, brn & bis	38	25
260	A86	100 l maroon, brn & yel	28	25
261	A86	300 l bis brn & dk brn	75	45
		Nos. 256-261 (6)	2.36	1.65

Martyrs of Emperor Valerian's persecutions.

1959, Oct. 27 Photo. Perf. 14
262	A87	25 l rose, org yel & dk brn	15	15
263	A87	60 l multicolored	16	15

2nd anniv. of the papal radio station, St. Maria di Galeria.

St. Casimir,
Palace and
Cathedral,
Vilnius
A88

1959, Dec. 14 Engr. Wmk. 235
264	A88	50 l brown	15	15
265	A88	100 l dull green	30	15
		Set value		24

500th anniv. (in 1958) of the birth of St. Casimir, patron saint of Lithuania.

Nativity by
Raphael — A89

1959, Dec. 14 Engr. Perf. 13½
266	A89	15 l dark gray	15	15
267	A89	25 l magenta	15	15
268	A89	60 l bright ultra	32	15
		Set value	52	30

St.
Antoninus — A90

Transept of Lateran
Basilica — A91

Designs: 25 l, 110 l, St. Antoninus preaching.

1960, Feb. 29 Wmk. 235 Perf. 13x14
269	A90	15 l ultra	15	15
270	A90	25 l turquoise	15	15
271	A90	60 l brown	32	25
272	A90	110 l rose claret	60	40
		Set value		78

5th cent. of death of St. Antoninus, bishop of Florence.

1960, Feb. 29 Photo. Perf. 14
273	A91	15 l brown	15	15
274	A91	60 l black	42	42
		Set value		30

Roman Diocesan Synod, February, 1960.

Flight into Egypt by
Fra
Angelico — A92

Cardinal Sarto's
Departure from
Venice — A93

Designs: 10 l, 100 l, St. Peter Giving Alms to the Poor, by Masaccio. 25 l, 300 l, Madonna of Mercy by Piero della Francesca.

1960, Apr. 7 Wmk. 235 Perf. 14
275	A92	5 l green	15	15
276	A92	10 l gray brown	15	15
277	A92	25 l deep carmine	15	15
278	A92	60 l lilac	20	15
279	A92	100 l ultra	1.90	1.50
280	A92	300 l Prus green	65	30
		Nos. 275-280 (6)	3.20	2.40

World Refugee Year. July 1, 1959-June 30, 1960.

1960, Apr. 11 Engr. Perf. 13½
Designs: 35 l, Pope John XXIII praying at coffin of Pope Pius X. 60 l, Body of Pope Pius X returning to Venice.

281	A93	15 l brown	25	20
282	A93	35 l rose carmine	60	60
283	A93	60 l Prus green	1.25	80

Return of the body of Pope Pius X to Venice.

Feeding the
Hungry
A94

"Acts of Mercy," by Della Robbia: 10 l, Giving drink to the thirsty. 15 l, Clothing the naked. 20 l, Sheltering the homeless. 30 l, Visiting the sick. 35 l, Visiting prisoners. 40 l, Burying the dead. 70 l, Pope John XXIII.

1960, Nov. 8 Photo. Perf. 14
Centers in Brown
284	A94	5 l red brown	15
285	A94	10 l green	15
286	A94	15 l slate	15
287	A94	20 l rose carmine	15
288	A94	30 l violet blue	15
289	A94	35 l violet brown	15
290	A94	40 l red orange	15
291	A94	70 l ocher	15
		Set value, #284-291,	
		E15-E16,	72

Holy Family by Gerard van Honthorst A95

1960, Dec. 6 — Wmk. 235 — Perf. 14

292	A95	10 l slate grn & slate blk	15	15
293	A95	15 l sepia & ol blk	15	15
294	A95	70 l grnsh bl & dp bl	28	18
		Set value	46	34

St. Vincent de Paul — A96   St. Meinrad — A97

Designs: 70 l, St. Louisa de Marillac. 100 l, St. Louisa and St. Vincent.

1960, Dec. 6

295	A96	40 l dull violet	15	15
296	A96	70 l dark gray	30	16
297	A96	100 l dk red brown	70	32

Death of St. Vincent de Paul, 300th anniv.

1961, Feb. 28 — Perf. 14

Designs: 40 l, Statue of Our Lady of Einsiedeln. 100 l, Einsiedeln monastery, horiz.

298	A97	30 l dark gray	45	15
299	A97	40 l lt violet	1.50	40
300	A97	100 l brown	1.50	85

Death of St. Meinrad, 1,100th anniv.; Einsiedeln Abbey, Switzerland.

Pope Leo the Great Defying Attila — A98

Wmk. 235
1961, Apr. 6 — Photo. — Perf. 14

301	A98	15 l rose brown	15	15
302	A98	70 l Prus green	26	26
303	A98	300 l brown black	1.75	55

Death of Pope Leo the Great (St. Leo Magnus), 1,500th anniv. The design is from a marble bas-relief in St. Peter's Basilica.

St. Paul Arriving in Rome, 61 A.D. — A99

Designs: 10 l, 30 l, Map showing St. Paul's journey to Rome. 20 l, 200 l, First Basilica of St. Paul, Rome.

1961, June 13 — Wmk. 235 — Perf. 14

304	A99	10 l Prus green	15	15
305	A99	15 l dl red brn & gray	15	15
306	A99	20 l red org & gray	15	15
307	A99	30 l blue	16	15
308	A99	75 l org brn & gray	30	32
309	A99	200 l blue & gray	1.65	1.10
		Nos. 304-309 (6)	2.56	
		Set value		1.70

Arrival of St. Paul in Rome, 1,900th anniv.

1861 and 1961 Mastheads A100

Designs: 70 l, Editorial offices. 250 l, Rotary press.

1961, July 4

310	A100	40 l red brn & blk	18	15
311	A100	70 l blue & blk	42	28
312	A100	250 l yellow & blk	1.90	1.10

Centenary of L'Osservatore Romano, Vatican's newspaper.

St. Patrick's Purgatory, Lough Derg — A101   Arms of Roncalli Family — A102

Design: 10 l, 40 l, St. Patrick, marble sculpture.

Wmk. 235
1961, Oct. 6 — Photo. — Perf. 14

313	A101	10 l buff & slate grn	15	15
314	A101	15 l blue & sepia	15	15
315	A101	40 l yellow & bl grn	22	16
316	A101	150 l Prus bl & red brn	70	50
		Set value		80

Death of St. Patrick, 1,500th anniv.

1961, Nov. 25

Designs: 25 l, Church at Sotto il Monte. 30 l, Santa Maria in Monte Santo, Rome. 40 l, Church of San Carlo al Corso, Rome (erroneously inscribed with name of Basilica of Sts. Ambrosius and Charles, Milan). 70 l, Altar, St. Peter's, Rome. 115 l, Pope John XXIII.

317	A102	10 l gray & red brn	15	15
318	A102	25 l ol bis & sl grn	15	15
319	A102	30 l vio bl & pale pur	15	15
320	A102	40 l lilac & dk blue	15	15
321	A102	70 l gray grn & org brn	32	15
322	A102	115 l choc & slate	70	45
		Set value	1.30	75

80th birthday of Pope John XXIII.

"The Adoration" by Lucas Chen — A103   Draining of Pontine Marshes Medal by Pope Sixtus V, 1588 — A104

1961, Nov. 25
Center Multicolored

323	A103	15 l bluish green	15	15
324	A103	40 l gray	15	15
325	A103	70 l pale lilac	30	15
		Set value	50	28

Christmas.

1962, Apr. 7 — Wmk. 235 — Perf. 14

Design: 40 l, 300 l, Map of Pontine Marshes showing 18th century drainage under Pope Pius VI.

326	A104	15 l dark violet	15	15
327	A104	40 l rose carmine	15	15
328	A104	70 l brown	18	15
329	A104	300 l dull green	65	35
		Set value		62

WHO drive to eradicate malaria.

"The Good Shepherd" — A105   Wheatfield (Luke 10:2) — A106

1962, June 2 — Photo.

330	A105	10 l lilac & black	15	15
331	A105	15 l blue & ocher	15	15
332	A105	70 l lt green & blk	24	30
333	A106	115 l fawn & ocher	1.25	1.10
334	A105	200 l brown & black	2.00	1.40
		Nos. 330-334 (5)	3.79	3.10

Issued to honor the priesthood and to stress its importance as a vocation.

"The Good Shepherd" is a fourth-century statue in the Lateran Museum, Rome.

St. Catherine of Siena — A107   Paulina M. Jaricot — A108

1962, June 12

335	A107	15 l brown	15	15
336	A107	60 l brt violet	32	25
337	A107	100 l blue	60	42

Canonization of St. Catherine of Siena, 500th anniv. The portrait is from a fresco by Il Sodoma, Church of St. Dominic, Siena.

1962, July 5
Portrait Multicolored

338	A108	10 l pale violet	15	15
339	A108	50 l dull green	18	15
340	A108	150 l gray	80	48

Paulina M. Jaricot (1799-1862), founder of the Society for the Propagation of the Faith.

Sts. Peter and Paul — A109

Design: 40 l, 100 l, "The Invincible Cross," relief from sarcophagus.

Wmk. 235
1962, Sept. 25 — Photo. — Perf. 14

341	A109	20 l lilac & brown	15	15
342	A109	40 l lt brown & blk	15	15
343	A109	70 l bluish grn & brn	15	15
344	A109	100 l salmon pink & blk	20	15
		Set value	45	32

6th Congress of Christian Archeology, Ravenna, Sept. 23-28.

"Faith" by Raphael — A110

Designs: 10 l, "Hope." 15 l, "Charity." 25 l, Arms of Pope John XXIII and emblems of the Four Evangelists. 30 l, Ecumenical Congress meeting in St. Peter's. 40 l, Pope John XXIII on throne. 60 l, Statue of St. Peter. 115 l, The Holy Ghost as a dove (symbolic design).

Photo.; Center Engr. on 30 l
1962, Oct. 30

345	A110	5 l brt blue & blk	15	15
346	A110	10 l green & blk	15	15
347	A110	15 l ver & sepia	15	15
348	A110	25 l ver & slate	15	15
349	A110	30 l lilac & blk	15	15
350	A110	40 l dk carmine & blk	15	15
351	A110	60 l dk green & dp org	15	15
352	A110	115 l crimson	15	15
		Set value	50	50

Vatican II, the 21st Ecumenical Council of the Roman Catholic Church, which opened Oct. 11, 1962. Nos. 345-347 show "the Three Theological Virtues" by Raphael.

Ethiopian Nativity Scene — A111

1962, Dec. 4
Center Multicolored

353	A111	10 l gray	15	15
354	A111	15 l brown	15	15
355	A111	90 l dull green	28	15
		Set value	42	25

Miracle of the Loaves and Fishes by Murillo — A112   Pope John XXIII — A113

Design: 40 l, 200 l, "The Miraculous Catch of Fishes" by Raphael.

Wmk. 235
1963, Mar. 21 — Photo. — Perf. 14

356	A112	15 l brn & dk brn	15	15
357	A112	40 l rose red & blk	15	15
358	A112	100 l blue & dk brn	15	15
359	A112	200 l bl grn & blk	18	15
		Set value	42	30

FAO "Freedom from Hunger" campaign.

1963, May 8

360	A113	15 l red brown	15	15
361	A113	160 l black	42	18
		Set value		24

Awarding of the Balzan Peace Prize to Pope John XXIII.

Interregnum Issue

Keys of St. Peter and Papal Chamberlain's Insignia — A114

1963, June 15 — Wmk. 235 — Perf. 14

362	A114	10 l dk brown	15	15
363	A114	40 l dk brown, yel	15	15
364	A114	100 l dk brown, vio	15	15
		Set value	30	20

788 VATICAN CITY

Pope Paul VI — A115   St. Cyril — A116

Design: 40 l, 200 l, Arms of Pope Paul VI.

1963, Oct. 16   Engr.   *Perf. 13x14*

365	A115	15 l black	15	15
366	A115	40 l carmine	15	15
367	A115	115 l redsh brown	22	15
368	A115	200 l slate blue	40	22
		Set value	75	45

Coronation of Pope Paul VI, June 30, 1963.

Wmk. 235
1963, Nov. 22   Photo.   *Perf. 14*

Designs: 70 l, Map of Hungary, Moravia and Poland, 16th century. 150 l, St. Methodius.

369	A116	30 l violet black	15	15
370	A116	70 l brown	30	15
371	A116	150 l rose claret	42	18
		Set value		36

1100th anniv. of the beginning of missionary work among the Slavs by Sts. Cyril and Methodius. The pictures of the saints are from 16th century frescoes in St. Clement's Basilica, Rome.

African Nativity Scene — A117   Church of the Holy Sepulcher, Jerusalem — A118

1963, Nov. 22

372	A117	10 l brn & pale brn	15	15
373	A117	40 l ultra & brown	15	15
374	A117	100 l gray olive & brn	26	15
		Set value	40	25

The design is after a sculpture by the Burundi artist Andreas Bukuru.

1964, Jan. 4   Wmk. 235   *Perf. 14*

Designs: 15 l, Pope Paul VI. 25 l, Nativity Church, Bethlehem. 160 l, Well of the Virgin Mary, Nazareth.

375	A118	15 l black	15	15
376	A118	25 l rose brown	15	15
377	A118	70 l brown	15	15
378	A118	160 l ultra	15	15
		Set value	38	28

Visit of Pope Paul VI to the Holy Land, Jan. 4-6.

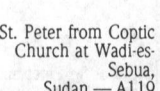

St. Peter from Coptic Church at Wadi-es-Sebua, Sudan — A119

Design: 20 l, 200 l, Trajan's Kiosk, Philae.

1964, Mar. 10   Photo.

379	A119	10 l ultra & red brn	15	15
380	A119	20 l multicolored	15	15
381	A119	70 l gray & red brn	15	15
382	A119	200 l gray & multi	15	15
		Set value	36	26

UNESCO world campaign to save historic monuments in Nubia.

Pietà by Michelangelo A120   Isaiah by Michelangelo A121

Designs: 15 l, 100 l, Pope Paul VI. 250 l, Head of Mary from Pietà.

1964, Apr. 22   Wmk. 235   *Perf. 14*

383	A120	15 l violet blue	15	15
384	A120	50 l dark brown	15	15
385	A120	100 l slate blue	15	15
386	A120	250 l chestnut	16	15
		Set value	40	26

New York World's Fair, 1964-65.

1964, June 16   Engr.   *Perf. 13¹/₂x14*

387	A121	10 l Michelangelo, after Jacopino del Conte	15	15
388	A121	25 l Isaiah	15	15
389	A121	30 l Delphie Sibyl	15	15
390	A121	40 l Jeremiah	15	15
391	A121	150 l Joel	15	15
		Set value	36	30

Michelangelo Buonarroti (1475-1564). Designs of Nos. 387-391 are from Sistine Chapel.

The Good Samaritan A122

Perf. 14x13¹/₂
1964, Sept. 22   Engr.   Wmk. 235

392	A122	10 l red brown & red	15	15
393	A122	30 l dark blue & red	15	15
394	A122	300 l gray & red	22	15
		Set value	40	20

Cent. (in 1963) of the founding of the Intl. Red Cross.

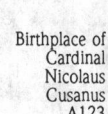

Birthplace of Cardinal Nicolaus Cusanus A123

Design: 200 l, Cardinal's sepulcher, Church of San Pietro in Vincoli, Rome.

1964, Nov. 16   Wmk. 235

395	A123	40 l dull blue grn	15	15
396	A123	200 l rose red	28	16
		Set value		22

German cardinal Nicolaus Cusanus (Nicolaus Krebs of Kues) (1401-1464).

Japanese Nativity Scene by Kimiko Koseki — A124   Pope Paul VI and Map of India and Southeast Asia — A125

1964, Nov. 16   Photo.   *Perf. 14*

397	A124	10 l multicolored	15	15
a.		Yellow omitted		

398	A124	15 l black & multi	15	15
399	A124	135 l bister & multi	26	15
		Set value	36	22

1964, Dec. 2

Designs: 15 l, Pope Paul VI at prayer. 25 l, Eucharistic Congress altar, Bombay, horiz. 60 l, Gateway of India, Bombay. horiz.

400	A125	15 l dull violet	15	15
401	A125	25 l green	15	15
402	A125	60 l brown	15	15
403	A125	200 l dull violet	15	15
		Set value	40	24

Trip of Pope Paul VI to India, Dec. 2-5, 1964.

Uganda Martyrs — A126   Dante by Raphael — A127

Designs: Various groups of Martyrs of Uganda.

Perf. 13¹/₂x14
1965, Mar. 16   Engr.   Wmk. 235

404	A126	15 l Prus green	15	15
405	A126	20 l brown	15	15
406	A126	30 l ultra	15	15
407	A126	75 l black	15	15
408	A126	100 l rose red	15	15
409	A126	160 l violet	15	15
		Set value	45	30

Canonization of 22 African martyrs, Oct. 18, 1964.

Photogravure and Engraved
1965, May 18   *Perf. 13¹/₂x14*

Designs: 40 l, Dante and the 3 beasts at entrance to the Inferno. 70 l, Dante and Virgil at entrance to Purgatory. 200 l, Dante and Beatrice in Paradise. (40 l, 70 l, 200 l, by Botticelli)

410	A127	10 l bis brn & dk brn	15	15
411	A127	40 l rose & dk brn	15	15
412	A127	70 l lt grn & dk brn	15	15
413	A127	200 l pale bl & dk brn	20	15
		Set value	38	28

Birth of Dante Alighieri, 700th anniv.

St. Benedict by Perugino A128   Pope Paul VI Addressing UN Assembly A129

Design: 300 l, View of Monte Cassino.

1965, July 2   Photo.   *Perf. 14*

414	A128	40 l brown	15	15
415	A128	300 l dark green	30	15
		Set value		18

Conferring of the title Patron Saint of Europe upon St. Benedict by Pope Paul VI; restoring of the Abbey of Monte Cassino.

1965, Oct. 4   Wmk. 235   *Perf. 14*

Designs: 30 l, 150 l, UN Headquarters and olive branch.

416	A129	20 l brown	15	15
417	A129	30 l sapphire	15	15
418	A129	150 l olive green	15	15
419	A129	300 l rose violet	26	15
		Set value	48	24

Visit of Pope Paul VI to the UN, New York City, Oct. 4.

Peruvian Nativity Scene A130   Cartographer A131

1965, Nov. 25   Engr.   *Perf. 13¹/₂x14*

420	A130	20 l rose claret	15	15
421	A130	40 l red brown	15	15
422	A130	200 l gray green	18	15
		Set value	30	20

1966, Mar. 8   Photo.   *Perf. 14*

Designs: 5 l, Pope Paul VI. 10 l, Organist. 20 l, Painter. 30 l, Sculptor. 40 l, Bricklayer. 55 l, Printer. 75 l, Plowing farmer. 90 l, Blacksmith. 130 l, Scholar.

423	A131	5 l sepia	15	15
424	A131	10 l violet	15	15
425	A131	15 l brown	15	15
426	A131	20 l gray green	15	15
427	A131	30 l brown red	15	15
428	A131	40 l Prus green	15	15
429	A131	55 l dark blue	15	15
430	A131	75 l dk rose brown	15	15
431	A131	90 l carmine rose	15	15
432	A131	130 l black	15	15
		Set value, #423-432,		
		E17-E18	1.00	90

The Pope's portrait is from a bas-relief by Enrico Manfrini; the arts and crafts designs are bas-reliefs by Mario Rudelli from the chair in the Pope's private chapel.

King Mieszko I and Queen Dabrowka A132

Designs: 25 l, St. Adalbert (Wojciech) and Cathedrals of Wroclaw and Gniezno. 40 l, St. Stanislas, Skalka Church, Wawel Cathedral and Castle, Cracow. 50 l, Queen Jadwiga (Hedwig), Holy Gate with Our Lady of Mercy, Vilnius, and Jagellon University Library, Cracow. 150 l, Black Madonna of Czestochowa, cloister and church of Bright Mountain, Czestochowa, and St. John's Cathedral, Warsaw. 220 l, Pope Paul VI blessing students and farmers.

Perf. 14x13¹/₂
1966, May 3   Engr.   Wmk. 235

433	A132	15 l black	15	15
434	A132	25 l violet	15	15
435	A132	40 l brick red	15	15
436	A132	50 l claret	15	15
437	A132	150 l slate blue	15	15
438	A132	220 l brown	15	15
		Set value	45	40

Millenium of Christianization of Poland.

Pope John XXIII Opening Vatican II Council A133   Nativity, Sculpture by Scorzelli A134

Designs: 15 l, Ancient Bible on ornate display stand. 55 l, Bishops celebrating Mass. 90 l, Pope Paul VI greeting Patriarch Athenagoras I. 100 l, Gold ring given to participating bishops. 130 l, Pope Paul VI carried in front of St. Peter's.

1966, Oct. 11   Photo.   *Perf. 14*

439	A133	10 l	red & black	15 15
440	A133	15 l	brown & green	15 15
441	A133	55 l	blk & brt rose	15 15
442	A133	90 l	slate grn & blk	15 15
443	A133	100 l	green & ocher	15 15
444	A133	130 l	orange brn & brn	15 15
			Set value	40 40

Conclusion of Vatican II, the 21st Ecumenical Council of the Roman Catholic Church, Dec. 8, 1965.

1966, Nov. 24   Wmk. 235   *Perf. 14*

445	A134	20 l	plum	15 15
446	A134	55 l	slate green	15 15
447	A134	225 l	yellow brown	15 15
			Set value	30 20

St. Peter, Fresco, Catacombs, Rome — A135

Cross, People and Globe — A136

Designs: 20 l, St. Paul, fresco from Catacombs, Rome. 55 l, Sts. Peter and Paul, glass painting, Vatican Library. 90 l, Baldachin by Bernini, St. Peter's, Rome. 220 l, Interior of St. Paul's, Rome.

Perf. 13¹/₂x14

1967, June 15   Photo.   Unwmk.

448	A135	15 l	multi	15 15
449	A135	20 l	multi	15 15
450	A135	55 l	multi	15 15
451	A135	90 l	multi	15 15
452	A135	220 l	multi	15 15
			Set value	42 36

Martyrdom of the Apostles Peter and Paul, 1,900th anniv.

1967, Oct. 13   Wmk. 235   *Perf. 14*

453	A136	40 l	carmine rose	15 15
454	A136	130 l	brt blue	20 15
			Set value	28 20

3rd Congress of Catholic Laymen, Rome, Oct. 11-18.

Sculpture of Shepherd Children of Fatima — A137

Nativity, 9th Century Painting on Wood — A138

Designs: 50 l, Basilica at Fatima. 200 l, Pope Paul VI praying before statue of Virgin of Fatima.

1967, Oct. 13   *Perf. 13¹/₂x14*

455	A137	30 l	multi	15 15
456	A137	50 l	multi	15 15
457	A137	200 l	multi	15 15
			Set value	30 24

Apparition of the Virgin Mary to 3 shepherd children at Fatima, 50th anniv.

Christmas Issue

1967, Nov. 28   Photo.   Unwmk.

458	A138	25 l	purple & multi	15 15
459	A138	55 l	gray & multi	15 15
460	A138	180 l	green & multi	15 15
			Set value	30 24

Pope Paul VI A139

Holy Infant of Prague A140

Designs: 55 l, Monstrance from fresco by Raphael. 220 l, Map of South America.

1968, Aug. 22   Wmk. 235   *Perf. 14*

461	A139	25 l	blk & dk red brn	15 15
462	A139	55 l	blk, gray & ocher	15 15
463	A139	220 l	blk, lt bl & sep	15 15
			Set value	32 24

Visit of Pope Paul VI to the 39th Eucharistic Congress in Bogotá, Colombia, Aug. 22-25.

Engraved and Photogravure

1968, Nov. 28   *Perf. 13¹/₂x14*

464	A140	20 l	plum & pink	15 15
465	A140	50 l	vio & pale vio	15 15
466	A140	250 l	dk bl & lt bluish gray	15 15
			Set value	32 24

The Resurrection, by Fra Angelico de Fiesole — A141

Pope Paul VI with African Children — A142

Easter Issue

Perf. 13¹/₂x14

1969, Mar. 6   Engr.   Wmk. 235

467	A141	20 l	dk carmine & buff	15 15
468	A141	90 l	green & buff	15 15
469	A141	180 l	ultra & buff	15 15
			Set value	30 22

Europa Issue
Common Design Type

Perf. 13¹/₂x14

1969, Apr. 28   Photo.   Wmk. 235
Size: 36¹/₂x27mm

470	CD12	50 l	gray & lt brn	15 15
471	CD12	90 l	vermilion & lt brn	15 15
472	CD12	130 l	olive & lt brn	15 15
			Set value	38 28

Perf. 13¹/₂x14

1969, July 31   Photo.   Wmk. 235

Designs: 55 l, Pope Paul VI and African bishops. 250 l, Map of Africa with Kampala, olive branch and compass rose.

473	A142	25 l	bister & brown	15 15
474	A142	55 l	dk red & brown	15 15
475	A142	250 l	multicolored	18 15
			Set value	35 26

Visit of Pope Paul VI to Uganda, July 31-Aug. 2.

Pope Pius IX — A143

Mt. Fuji and EXPO '70 Emblem — A144

Designs: 50 l, Chrismon, emblem of St. Peter's Circle. 220 l, Pope Paul VI.

Perf. 13¹/₂x14

1969, Nov. 18   Engr.   Wmk. 235

476	A143	30 l	red brown	15 15
477	A143	50 l	dark gray	15 15
478	A143	220 l	deep plum	18 15
			Set value	34 28

Centenary of St. Peter's Circle, a lay society dedicated to prayer, action and sacrifice.

1970, Mar. 16   Photo.   Unwmk.

EXPO '70 Emblem and: 25 l, EXPO '70 emblem. 40 l, Osaka Castle. 55 l, Japanese Virgin and Child, by Domoto in Osaka Cathedral. 90 l, Christian Pavilion.

479	A144	25 l	gold, red & blk	15 15
480	A144	40 l	red & multi	15 15
481	A144	55 l	brown & multi	15 15
482	A144	90 l	gold & multi	15 15
483	A144	110 l	blue & multi	20 15
			Set value	50 35

EXPO '70 Intl. Exhibition, Osaka, Japan, Mar. 15-Sept. 13.

Centenary Medal, Jesus Giving St. Peter the Keys — A145

Designs: 50 l, Coat of arms of Pope Pius IX. 180 l, Vatican I Council meeting in St. Peter's, obverse of centenary medal.

Engr. & Photo.; Photo. (50 l)

1970, Apr. 29   *Perf. 13x14*

484	A145	20 l	orange & brown	15 15
485	A145	50 l	multicolored	15 15
486	A145	180 l	ver & brn	30 22
			Set value	45 36

Centenary of the Vatican I Council.

Christ, by Simone Martini A146

Designs: 25 l, Christ with Crown of Thorns, by Rogier van der Weyden. 50 l, Christ, by Albrecht Dürer. 90 l, Christ, by El Greco. 180 l, Pope Paul VI.

1970, May 29   Photo.   *Perf. 14x13*

487	A146	15 l	gold & multi	15 15
488	A146	25 l	gold & multi	15 15
489	A146	50 l	gold & multi	15 15
490	A146	90 l	gold & multi	15 15
491	A146	180 l	gold & multi	22 15
			Set value	50 42

Ordination of Pope Paul VI, 50th anniv.

Adam, by Michelangelo; UN Emblem — A147

Pope Paul VI — A148

UN Emblem and: 90 l, Eve, by Michelangelo. 220 l, Olive branch.

1970, Oct. 8   Photo.   *Perf. 13x14*

492	A147	20 l	multi	15 15
493	A147	90 l	multi	18 15
494	A147	220 l	multi	28 20
			Set value	50 34

25th anniversary of the United Nations.

1970, Nov. 26   Photo.   Unwmk.

Designs: 55 l, Holy Child of Cebu, Philippines. 100 l, Madonna and Child, by Georg Hamori, Darwin Cathedral, Australia. 130 l, Cathedral of Manila. 220 l, Cathedral of Sydney.

495	A148	25 l	multi	15 15
496	A148	55 l	multi	15 15
497	A148	100 l	multi	15 15
498	A148	130 l	multi	16 15
499	A148	220 l	multi	25 18
			Set value	70 50

Visit of Pope Paul VI to the Far East, Oceania and Australia, Nov. 26-Dec. 5.

Angel Holding Lectern — A149

Madonna and Child by Francesco Ghissi — A150

Sculptures by Corrado Ruffini: 40 l, 130 l, Crucified Christ surrounded by doves. 50 l, like 20 l.

1971, Feb. 2   *Perf. 13x14*

500	A149	20 l	multicolored	15 15
501	A149	40 l	dp orange & multi	15 15
502	A149	50 l	purple & multi	15 15
503	A149	130 l	multicolored	22 15
			Set value	42 30

Intl. year against racial discrimination.

1971, Mar. 26   Photo.   *Perf. 14*

Paintings: Madonna and Child, 40 l, by Sassetta (Stefano di Giovanni); 55 l, Carlo Crivelli; 90 l, by Carlo Maratta. 180 l, Holy Family, by Ghisberto Ceracchini.

504	A150	25 l	gray & multi	15 15
505	A150	40 l	gray & multi	15 15
506	A150	55 l	gray & multi	15 15
507	A150	90 l	gray & multi	15 15
508	A150	180 l	gray & multi	20 15
			Set value	60 46

St. Dominic, Sienese School — A151

St. Stephen, from Chasuble, 1031 — A152

Portraits of St. Dominic: 55 l, by Fra Angelico. 90 l, by Titian. 180 l, by El Greco.

1971, May 25   Unwmk.   *Perf. 13x14*

509	A151	25 l	multi	15 15
510	A151	55 l	multi	15 15
511	A151	90 l	multi	15 15
512	A151	180 l	multi	26 15
			Set value	60 36

St. Dominic de Guzman (1170-1221), founder of the Dominican Order.

1971, Nov. 25

Design: 180 l, Madonna as Patroness of Hungary, 1511.

513	A152	50 l	multi	15 15
514	A152	180 l	black & yellow	32 20

Millenium of the birth of St. Stephen (975?-1038), king of Hungary.

Bramante — A153

Designs: 25 l, Bramante's design for dome of St. Peter's. 130 l, Design for spiral staircase.

1972, Feb. 22 Engr. *Perf. 13¹/₂x14*

515	A153	25 l dull yellow & blk	15	15
516	A153	90 l dull yellow & blk	18	15
517	A153	130 l dull yellow & blk	24	15
		Set value	48	30

Bramante (real name Donato d'Agnolo; 1444-1514), architect.

St. Mark in Storm, 12th Century Mosaic A154

Map of Venice, 1581 — A155

Design: 180 l, St. Mark's Basilica, Painting by Emilio Vangelli.

Unwmk.

1972, June 6 Photo. *Perf. 14*

518	A154	25 l lt brown & multi	15	15
519	A155	Block of 4	1.00	60
a.-d.		50 l, UL, UR, LL, LR, each	22	15
520	A154	180 l lt blue & multi	1.10	65
a.		Souvenir sheet, #518-520	2.50	2.50

UNESCO campaign to save Venice.

Gospel of St. Matthew, 13th Century, French A156

Illuminated Initials from: 50 l, St. Luke's Gospel, Biblia dell'Aracoeli 13th century, French. 90 l, Second Epistle of St. John, 14th century, Bologna. 100 l, Apocalypse of St. John, 14th century, Bologna. 130 l, Book of Romans, 14th century, Central Italy.

1972, Oct. 11 *Perf. 14x13¹/₂*

521	A156	30 l multi	15	15
522	A156	50 l multi	15	15
523	A156	90 l multi	15	15
524	A156	100 l multi	15	15
525	A156	130 l multi	38	22
		Set value	75	50

Intl. Book Year. Illustrations are from illuminated medieval manuscripts.

Luigi Orione A157

Design: 180 l, Lorenzo Perosi and music from "Hallelujah."

1972, Nov. 28 Photo. *Perf. 14x13¹/₂*

526	A157	50 l rose, lilac & blk	18	15
527	A157	180 l orange, grn & blk	32	18

Secular priests Luigi Orione (1872-1940), founder of CARITAS, Catholic welfare organization; and Lorenzo Perosi (1872-1956), composer.

Cardinal Bessarion — A158

Eucharistic Congress Emblem — A159

Designs: 40 l, Reading Bull of Union between the Greek and Latin Churches, 1439, from bronze door of St. Peter's. 130 l, Coat of arms from tomb, Basilica of Holy Apostles, Rome.

Perf. 13x14

1972, Nov. 28 Wmk. 235 Engr.

528	A158	40 l dull green	15	15
529	A158	90 l carmine	22	15
530	A158	130 l black	20	18

Johannes Cardinal Bessarion (1403?-1472), Latin Patriarch of Constantinople, who worked for union of the Greek and Latin Churches. Portrait by Cosimo Rosselli in Sistine Chapel.

1973, Feb. 27 Photo. Unwmk.

Designs: 75 l, Head of Mary (Pietá), by Michelangelo. 300 l, Melbourne Cathedral.

531	A159	25 l violet & multi	15	15
532	A159	75 l olive & multi	15	15
533	A159	300 l multicolored	48	42
		Set value	65	58

40th Intl. Eucharistic Congress, Melbourne, Australia, Feb. 18-25.

St. Teresa A160

Copernicus A161

Designs: 25 l, St. Teresa's birthplace, Alençon. 220 l, Lisieux Basilica.

1973, May 23 Engr. & Photo.

534	A160	25 l black & pink	15	15
535	A160	50 l black & yellow	15	15
536	A160	220 l black & lt blue	40	25
		Set value	60	42

St. Teresa of Lisieux and of the Infant Jesus (1873-1897), Carmelite nun.

1973, June 19 Engr. *Perf. 14*

Designs: 20 l, 100 l, View of Torun.

537	A161	20 l dull green	15	15
538	A161	50 l brown	15	15
539	A161	100 l lilac	18	15
540	A161	130 l dark blue	32	18
		Set value	64	42

Nicolaus Copernicus (1473-1543), Polish astronomer.

Vatican City stamps can be mounted in the annually supplemented Scott Vatican City album.

St. Wenceslas A162

1973, Sept. 25 Photo. *Perf. 14*

541	A162	20 l shown	15	15
542	A162	90 l Arms of Prague Diocese	15	15
543	A162	150 l Spire of Prague Cathedral	22	15
544	A162	220 l St. Adalbert	38	15
		Set value		36

Millenium of Prague Latin Episcopal See.

St. Nerses Shnorali — A163

Designs: 25 l, Church of St. Hripsime. 90 l, Armenian khatchkar, a stele with cross and inscription.

Engr. & Litho.

1973, Nov. 27 *Perf. 13x14*

545	A163	25 l tan & dk brown	15	15
546	A163	90 l lt violet & blk	20	15
547	A163	180 l lt green & sepia	35	18
		Set value	60	32

Armenian Patriarch St. Nerses Shnorali (1102-1173).

Noah's Ark, Rainbow and Dove (Mosaic) — A164

Design: 90 l, Lamb drinking from stream, and Tablets of the Law (mosaic).

1974, Apr. 23 Litho. *Perf. 13x14*

548	A164	50 l gold & multi	20	15
549	A164	90 l gold & multi	30	15

Centenary of the Universal Postal Union.

"And There was Light" — A165

St. Thomas Aquinas Teaching — A166

Designs: 25 l, Noah's Ark, horiz. 50 l, The Annunciation. 90 l, Nativity (African). 180 l, Hands holding grain (Spanish inscription: The Lord feeds his people), horiz. Designs chosen through worldwide youth competition in connection with 1972 Intl. Book Year.

Perf. 13x14, 14x13

1974, Apr. 23 Photo.

550	A165	15 l brown & multi	15	15
551	A165	25 l yellow & multi	15	15
552	A165	50 l blue & multi	15	15
553	A165	90 l green & multi	16	15
554	A165	180 l rose & multi	28	15
		Set value	65	46

"The Bible: the Book of Books."

Engr. & Litho.

1974, June 18 Unwmk. *Perf. 13x14*

Designs: 50 l, Students (left panel). 220 l, Students (right panel). Designs from a painting in the Convent of St. Mark in Florence, by an artist from the School of Fra Angelico.

Sizes: 50 l, 220 l, 20x36mm, 90 l, 26x36mm

555	A166	50 l dk brown & gold	15	15
556	A166	90 l dk brown & gold	15	15
557	A166	220 l dk brown & gold	42	24
a.		Strip of 3, #555-557	70	55
		Set value		44

St. Thomas Aquinas (1225-1274), scholastic philosopher.

St. Bonaventure — A167

Woodcuts: 40 l, Civita Bagnoregio. 90 l, Tree of Life (13th century).

1974, Sept. 26 Photo. *Perf. 13x14*

558	A167	40 l gold & multi	15	15
559	A167	90 l gold & multi	22	15
560	A167	220 l gold & multi	30	20
		Set value		42

St. Bonaventure (Giovanni di Fidanza; 1221-1274), scholastic philosopher.

Christ, St. Peter's Basilica — A168

Pope Paul VI Giving his Blessing — A169

Holy Year 1975: 10 l, Christus Victor, Sts. Peter and Paul. 30 l, Christ. 40 l, Cross surmounted by dove. 50 l, Christ enthroned. 55 l, St. Peter. 90 l, St. Paul. 100 l, St. Peter. 130 l, St. Paul. 220 l, Arms of Pope Paul VI. Designs of 10 l, 25 l, are from St. Peter's; 30 l, 40 l, from St. John Lateran; 50 l, 55 l, 90 l, from St. Mary Major; 100 l, 130 l, from St. Paul outside the Walls.

1974, Dec. 19 Photo. *Perf. 13x14*

561	A168	10 l multi	15	15
562	A168	25 l multi	15	15
563	A168	30 l multi	15	15
564	A168	40 l multi	15	15
565	A168	50 l multi	15	15
566	A168	55 l multi	15	15
567	A168	90 l multi	15	15
568	A168	100 l multi	16	15
569	A168	130 l multi	15	15
570	A169	220 l multi	25	18
571	A169	250 l multi	30	25
		Set value	1.25	1.00

Pentecost, by El Greco — A170

1975, May 22   Engr.   Perf. 13x14
572 A170 300 l car rose & org   60 40

Fountain, St. Peter's Square — A171

Fountains of Rome: 40 l, Piazza St. Martha, Apse of St. Peter's. 50 l, Borgia Tower and St. Peter's. 90 l, Belvedere Courtyard. 100 l, Academy of Sciences. 200 l, Galleon.

Litho. & Engr.

1975, May 22   Perf. 14
573 A171 20 l buff & blk   15 15
574 A171 40 l pale violet & blk   15 15
575 A171 50 l salmon & blk   15 15
576 A171 90 l pale citron & blk   15 15
577 A171 100 l pale green & blk   15 15
578 A171 200 l pale blue & blk   30 25
            Set value   85 68

European Architectural Heritage Year.

Miracle of Loaves and Fishes, Gilt Glass — A172

Designs: 150 l, Painting of Christ, from Comodilla Catacomb. 200 l, Raising of Lazarus. All works from 4th century.

Perf. 14x13½
1975, Sept. 25   Photo.   Unwmk.
579 A172 30 l multi   15 15
580 A172 150 l brown & multi   28 20
581 A172 200 l green & multi   45 30

9th Intl. Congress of Christian Archaeology.

Investiture of First Librarian Bartolomeo Sacchi by Pope Sixtus IV A173

Designs: 100 l, Pope Sixtus IV and books in old wooden press, from Latin Vatican Codex 2044, vert. 250 l, Pope Sixtus IV visiting Library, fresco in Hospital of the Holy Spirit. Design of 70 l is from fresco by Melozzo di Forli in Vatican Gallery.

Perf. 14x13½, 13½x14
1975, Sept. 25   Litho. & Engr.
582 A173 70 l gray & lilac   15 15
583 A173 100 l lt yellow & grn   25 15
584 A173 250 l gray & red   50 30

Founding of the Vatican Apostolic Library, 500th anniv.

Mt. Argentario Monastery A174

St. Paul of the Cross, by Giovanni Della Porta — A175

Design: 300 l, Basilica of Sts. John and Paul and burial chapel of Saint.

1975, Nov. 27   Photo.   Perf. 14x13½
585 A174 50 l multi   15 15
586 A175 150 l multi   22 20
587 A174 300 l multi   48 28
            Set value   54

Bicentenary of death of St. Paul of the Cross, founder of the Passionist religious order in 1737.

Praying Women, by Fra Angelico — A176

International Women's Year: 200 l, Seated women, by Fra Angelico.

1975, Nov. 27   Perf. 13½x14
588 A176 100 l multi   20 18
589 A176 200 l multi   40 22

Virgin and Child in Glory, by Titian — A177

Design: 300 l, The Six Saints, by Titian. Designs from "The Madonna in Glory with the Child Jesus and Six Saints."

1976, May 13   Engr.   Perf. 14x13½
590 A177 100 l rose magenta   22 15
591 A177 300 l rose magenta   52 40
  a.   Pair, #590-591   75 60

Titian (1477-1576), painter.

A178   A179

Designs: 150 l, Eucharist, wheat and globe. 200 l, Hands Holding Eucharist. 400 l, Hungry mankind reaching for the Eucharist.

1976, July 2   Photo.   Perf. 13½x14
592 A178 150 l gold, red & bl   18 18
593 A178 200 l gold & blue   25 22
594 A178 400 l gold, grn & brn   42 40

41st Intl. Eucharistic Congress, Philadelphia, PA, Aug. 1-8.

Details from Transfiguration by Raphael: 30 l, Moses Holding Tablets. 40 l, Transfigured Christ. 50 l, Prophet Elijah with book. 100 l, Apostles John and Peter. 150 l, Group of women. 200 l, Landscape.

595 A179 30 l ocher & multi   15 15
596 A179 40 l red & multi   15 15
597 A179 50 l violet & multi   15 15
598 A179 100 l multicolored   18 15
599 A179 150 l green & multi   28 20
600 A179 200 l ocher & multi   35 22
            Set value   1.00 70

St. John's Tower A180

Roman Views: 100 l, Fountain of the Sacrament. 120 l, Fountain at entrance to the gardens. 180 l, Basilica, Cupola of St. Peter's and Sacristy. 250 l, Borgia Tower and Sistine Chapel. 300 l, Apostolic Palace and Courtyard of St. Damasius.

Litho. & Engr.
1976, Nov. 23   Perf. 14
601 A180 50 l gray & black   15 15
602 A180 100 l salmon & dk brn   15 15
603 A180 120 l citron & dk grn   16 15
604 A180 180 l pale gray & blk   15 15
605 A180 250 l yellow & brn   28 20
606 A180 300 l pale lilac & mag   32 25
  Nos. 601-606 (6)   1.21
            Set value   90

The Lord's Creatures A181

Designs: 70 l, Brother Sun. 100 l, Sister Moon and Stars. 130 l, Sister Water. 170 l, Praise in infirmities and tribulations. 200 l, Praise for bodily death. Designs are illustrations by Duilio Cambellotti for "The Canticle of Brother Sun," by St. Francis.

1977, Mar. 10   Photo.   Perf. 14x13½
607 A181 50 l multi   15 15
608 A181 70 l multi   15 15
609 A181 100 l multi   15 15
610 A181 130 l multi   18 15
611 A181 170 l multi   20 15
612 A181 200 l multi   25 16
            Set value   95 65

St. Francis of Assisi, 750th death anniv.

Sts. Peter and Paul — A182

Dormition of the Virgin — A183

Design: 350 l, Pope Gregory XI and St. Catherine of Siena. Designs are after fresco by Giorgio Vasari.

1977, May 20   Engr.   Perf. 14
613 A182 170 l black   30 18
614 A182 350 l black   50 30
  a.   Pair, #613-614   85 60

Return of Pope Gregory XI from Avignon, 600th anniv.

1977, July 5   Photo.   Perf. 13½x14
Design: 400 l, Virgin Mary in Heaven. Both designs after miniatures in Latin manuscripts, Vatican Library.

615 A183 200 l multi   32 20
616 A183 400 l multi   52 32

Feast of the Assumption.

The Nile Deity, Roman Sculpture — A184

Sculptures: 120 l, Head of Pericles. 130 l, Roman Couple Joining Hands. 150 l, Apollo Belvedere, head. 170 l, Laocoon, head. 350 l, Apollo Belvedere, torso.

1977, Sept. 29   Perf. 14x13½
617 A184 50 l multi   15 15
618 A184 120 l multi   16 15
619 A184 130 l multi   16 15
620 A184 150 l multi   16 15
621 A184 170 l multi   20 15
622 A184 350 l multi   32 30
  Nos. 617-622 (6)   1.15 1.05

Classical sculptures in Vatican Museums.

Creation of Man and Woman — A185

Designs: 70 l, Three youths in the furnace. 100 l, Adoration of the Kings. 130 l, Raising of Lazarus. 200 l, The Good Shepherd. 400 l, Chrismon, Cross, sleeping soldiers (Resurrection). Designs are bas-reliefs from Christian sarcophagi, 250-350 A.D., found in Roman excavations.

1977, Dec. 9   Photo.   Perf. 14x13½
623 A185 50 l multi   15 15
624 A185 70 l multi   15 15
625 A185 100 l multi   15 15
626 A185 130 l multi   16 18
627 A185 200 l multi   18 20
628 A185 400 l multi   38 25
            Set value   1.00 92

Madonna with the Parrot and Rubens Self-portrait — A186

1977, Dec. 9   Perf. 13½x14
629 A186 350 l multi   50 50

Peter Paul Rubens (1577-1640).

Pope Paul VI, by Lino Bianchi Barriviera A187

Design: 350 l, Christ's Face, by Pericle Fazzini and arms of Pope Paul VI.

1978, Mar. 9   Photo.   Perf. 14
630 A187 350 l multi   50 32
631 A187 400 l multi   50 40

80th birthday of Pope Paul VI.

Pope Pius IX (1792-1878)
A188

Designs: 130 l, Arms of Pope Pius IX. 170 l, Seal of Pius IX, used to sign definition of Dogma of Immaculate Conception.

Litho. & Engr.

1978, May 9   Perf. 13x14
632 A188 130 l multi   20 15
633 A188 170 l multi   30 15
634 A188 200 l multi   35 20

Interregnum Issues

Keys of St. Peter and Papal
Chamberlain's Insignia
A189   A190

1978, Aug. 23   Photo.   Perf. 14
635 A189 120 l purple & lt green   32 15
636 A189 150 l purple & salmon   32 15
637 A189 250 l purple & yellow   32 15

1978, Oct. 12   Photo.   Perf. 14
638 A190 120 l black & multi   22 15
639 A190 200 l black & multi   22 15
640 A190 250 l black & multi   22 15

Pope John Paul I,
Pope from Aug. 26 to
Sept. 28,
1978 — A191

Pope John Paul I: 70 l, Sitting on his throne. 250 l, Walking in Vatican garden. 350 l, Giving blessing, horiz.

1978, Dec. 11   Perf. 13x14, 14x13
641 A191 70 l multi   15 15
642 A191 120 l multi   28 28
643 A191 250 l multi   28 28
644 A191 350 l multi   40 40

Arms of Pope
John Paul II
A192

Designs: 250 l, Pope John Paul II raising hand in blessing. 400 l, Jesus giving keys to St. Peter.

Litho. & Engr.

1979, Mar. 22   Perf. 14x13
645 A192 170 l black & multi   25 25
646 A192 250 l black & multi   32 32
647 A192 400 l black & multi   52 48

Inauguration of pontificate of Pope John Paul II.

Martyrdom of   St. Basil the Great
St. Stanislas   Instructing Monk
A193   A194

Designs: 150 l, St. Stanislas appearing to the people. 250 l, Gold reliquary, 1504, containing saint's head. 500 l, View of Cracow Cathedral.

1979, May 18   Photo.   Perf. 14
648 A193 120 l multi   18 18
649 A193 150 l multi   20 16
650 A193 250 l multi   38 32
651 A193 500 l multi   75 65

900th anniversary of martyrdom of St. Stanislas (1030-1079), patron saint of Poland.

Engr. & Photo.

1979, June 25   Perf. 13¹/₂x14
St. Basil the Great, 16th cent. of Death: 520 l, St. Basil the Great visiting the sick.

652 A194 150 l multi   18 15
653 A194 520 l multi   85 70

Father Secchi, Solar Protuberance,
Spectrum and Meteorograph — A195

Father Angelo Secchi (1818-1878), astronomer, solar protuberance, spectrum and: 220 l, Spectroscope. 300 l, Telescope.

Perf. 14x13¹/₂

1979, June 25   Litho. & Engr.
654 A195 180 l multi   28 24
655 A195 220 l multi   38 28
656 A195 300 l multi   42 30

Vatican
City — A196

Papal Arms and Portraits: 70 l, Pius XI. 120 l, Pius XII. 150 l, John XXIII. 170 l, Paul VI. 250 l, John Paul I. 450 l, John Paul II.

1979, Oct. 11   Photo.   Perf. 14x13¹/₂
657 A196 50 l multi   15 15
658 A196 70 l multi   15 15
659 A196 120 l multi   16 16
660 A196 150 l multi   20 16
661 A196 170 l multi   22 22
662 A196 250 l multi   32 28
663 A196 450 l multi   70 50
     Nos. 657-663 (7)   1.90 1.62

Vatican City State, 50th anniversary.

Infant, by Andrea
Della Robbia, IYC
Emblem — A197

IYC Emblem and Della Robbia Bas Reliefs, Hospital of the Innocents, Florence.

Engr. & Photo.

1979, Nov. 27   Perf. 13¹/₂x14
664 A197 50 l multi   15 15
665 A197 120 l multi   18 15
666 A197 200 l multi   30 18
667 A197 350 l multi   52 35
     Set value   70

International Year of the Child.

Abbot Desiderius Giving Codex to St.
Benedict — A198

Illuminated Letters and Illustrations, Codices, Vatican Apostolic Library: 100 l, St. Benedict writing the Rule. 150 l, Page from the Rule. 220 l, Death of St. Benedict. 450 l, Montecassino (after painting by Paul Bril).

1980, Mar. 21   Photo.   Perf. 14x13¹/₂
668 A198 80 l multi   15 15
669 A198 100 l multi   15 15
670 A198 150 l multi   22 22
671 A198 220 l multi   30 28
672 A198 450 l multi   60 55
     Nos. 668-672 (5)   1.42 1.35

St. Benedict of Nursia (patron saint of Europe), 1500th birth anniversary.

Bernini,
Medallion
Showing
Baldacchino
in St. Peter's
A199

Gian Lorenzo Bernini (1598-1680), Architect (Self-portrait and Medallion): 170 l, St. Peter's Square with third wing (never built). 250 l, Bronze chair, Doctors of the Church. 350 l, Apostolic Palace stairway.

1980, Oct. 16   Litho.   Perf. 14x13¹/₂
673 A199 80 l multicolored   15 15
674 A199 170 l multicolored   26 22
675 A199 250 l multicolored   35 32
676 A199 350 l multicolored   55 38

St. Albertus Magnus
on Mission of
Peace — A200

1980, Nov. 18   Litho.   Perf. 13¹/₂x14
677 A200 300 l shown   40 30
678 A200 400 l As bishop   55 42

St. Albertus Magnus, 700th death anniv.

Communion of
the
Saints — A201

1980, Nov. 18   Perf. 14x13¹/₂
679 A201 250 l shown   32 25
680 A201 500 l Christ and saints   65 60

Feast of All Saints.

Guglielmo
Marconi and
Pope Pius XI,
Vatican Radio
Emblem,
Vatican
Arms — A202

Designs: 150 l, Microphone, Bible text. 200 l, St. Maria di Galeria Radio Center antenna, Archangel Gabriel statue. 600 l, Pope John Paul II.

1981, Feb. 12   Photo.   Perf. 14x13¹/₂
681 A202 100 l shown   15 15
682 A202 150 l multicolored   24 20
683 A202 200 l multicolored   32 28
684 A202 600 l multicolored   80 65

Vatican Radio, 50th anniversary.

Virgil Seated at Podium, Vergilius
Romanus — A203

1981, Apr. 23   Litho.   Perf. 14
685 A203 350 l multicolored   85 70
686 A203 600 l multicolored   1.50 1.25

2000th birth anniversary of Virgil.
Issued in sheets of 16 stamps plus 9 labels.

Congress
Emblem
A204

Congress Emblem and: 150 l, Virgin appearing to St. Bernadette. 200 l, Pilgrims going to Lourdes. 500 l, Bishop and pilgrims.

1981, June 22   Photo.
687 A204 80 l multicolored   15 15
688 A204 150 l multicolored   22 22
689 A204 200 l multicolored   30 30
690 A204 500 l multicolored   60 60

42nd Intl. Eucharistic Congress, Lourdes, France, July 16-23.

Intl. Year of
the Disabled
A205

1981, Sept. 29   Photo.   Perf. 14x13¹/₂
691 A205 600 l multicolored   90 80

Jan van
Ruusbroec,
Flemish Mystic,
500th Birth
Anniv. — A206

Perf. 13¹/₂x14

1981, Sept. 29   Litho. & Engr.
692 A206 200 l shown   35 35
693 A206 300 l Portrait   45 45

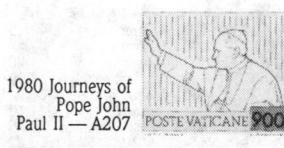

1980 Journeys of
Pope John
Paul II — A207

Perf. 13¹/₂x14¹/₂
1981, Dec. 3 **Photo.**
694	A207	50 l	Papal arms	15	15
695	A207	100 l	Map of Africa	15	15
696	A207	120 l	Crucifix	15	15
697	A207	150 l	Communion	18	18
698	A207	200 l	African bishop	22	22
699	A207	250 l	Visiting sick	30	30
700	A207	300 l	Notre Dame, France	38	38
701	A207	400 l	UNESCO speech	50	50
702	A207	600 l	Christ of the Andes, Brazil	90	90
703	A207	700 l	Cologne Cathedral, Germany	1.00	1.00
704	A207	900 l	John Paul II	1.10	1.10
	Nos. 694-704 (11)			5.03	5.03

700th Death Anniv.
of St. Agnes of
Prague — A208

Designs: 700 l, Handing order to Grand Master of the Crosiers of the Red Star. 900 l, Receiving letter from St. Clare.

1982, Feb. 16 **Photo.** **Perf. 13¹/₂x14**
705	A208	700 l	multicolored	1.00	1.00
706	A208	900 l	multicolored	1.10	1.10

Pueri Cantores
A209

St. Teresa of Avila
(1515-1582)
A210

Luca Della Robbia (1400-1482), Sculptor: No. 708, Pueri Cantores, diff. No. 709, Virgin in Prayer (44x36mm).

Photo. & Engr.
1982, May 21 **Perf. 14**
707	A209	1000 l	multicolored	1.25	1.10
708	A209	1000 l	multicolored	1.25	1.10
709	A209	1000 l	multicolored	1.25	1.10
a.	Strip of 3, #707-709			4.00	3.50

1982, Sept. 23 **Photo.**

Sketches of St. Teresa by Riccardo Tommasi-Ferroni.

710	A210	200 l	multicolored	28	28
711	A210	600 l	multicolored	85	85
712	A210	1000 l	multicolored	1.40	1.40

Christmas
A211

Nativity Bas-Reliefs: 300 l, Wit Stwosz, Church of the Virgin Mary, Cracow. 450 l, Enrico Manfrini.

Photo. & Engr.
1982, Nov. 23 **Perf. 14**
713	A211	300 l	multicolored	45	45
714	A211	450 l	multicolored	65	65

400th Anniv. of
Gregorian
Calendar — A212

Sculpture Details, Tomb of Pope Gregory XIII, Vatican Basilica.

1982, Nov. 23 **Engr.** **Perf. 13¹/₂x14**
715	A212	200 l	Surveying the globe	26	26
716	A212	300 l	Receiving Edict of Reform	42	42
717	A212	700 l	Presenting edict	90	90
a.	Souvenir sheet of 3, #715-717			3.00	3.00

Souvenir Sheets

Greek Vase — A213

1983, Mar. 10 **Litho.** **Perf. 13¹/₂x14**
718		Sheet of 6		3.25	2.00
a.	A213	100 l	shown	16	16
b.	A213	200 l	Italian vase	35	22
c.	A213	250 l	Female terra-cotta bust	48	32
d.	A213	300 l	Marcus Aurelius bust	55	35
e.	A213	350 l	Bird fresco	65	45
f.	A213	400 l	Pope Clement VIII vestment	75	45

1983, June 14 **Litho.** **Perf. 13¹/₂x14**
719		Sheet of 6		3.50	3.50
a.	A213	100 l	Horse's head, Etruscan terra cotta	15	15
b.	A213	200 l	Horseman, Greek fragment	22	15
c.	A213	300 l	Male head, Etruscan	32	15
d.	A213	400 l	Apollo Belvedere head	48	26
e.	A213	500 l	Moses, Roman fresco	55	35
f.	A213	1000 l	Madonna and Child, by Bernardo Daddi	1.25	70

1983, Nov. 10 **Litho.** **Perf. 13¹/₂x14**
720		Sheet of 6		4.00	4.00
a.	A213	150 l	Greek cup, Oedipus and the Sphinx	22	15
b.	A213	200 l	Etruscan bronze statue of a child	28	15
c.	A213	350 l	Emperor Augustus marble statue	42	28
d.	A213	400 l	Good Shepherd marble statue	55	32
e.	A213	500 l	St. Nicholas Saving a ship by G. da Fabriano	70	40
f.	A213	1200 l	The Holy face by G. Rouault	1.50	1.00

Vatican Collection: The Papacy and Art - US 1983 exhibition, New York, Chicago, San Francisco.

Extraordinary Holy
Year, 1983-84
(1950th Anniv. of
Redemption)
A214

Sketches by Giovanni Hajnal.

1983, Mar. 10 **Photo. & Engr.**
721	A214	300 l	Crucifixion	45	30
722	A214	350 l	Christ the Redeemer	55	38
723	A214	400 l	Pope	45	45
724	A214	2000 l	Holy Spirit	2.75	2.75

Theology, by
Raphael (1483-
1517)
A215

St. Casimir of
Lithuania (1458-
1484)
A217

Gregor
Johann
Mendel
(1822-1884),
Biologist
A216

Allegories, Room of the Segnatura.

1983, June 14
725	A215	50 l	shown	15	15
726	A215	400 l	Poetry	60	60
727	A215	500 l	Justice	70	70
728	A215	1200 l	Philosphy	1.75	1.75

Photo. & Engr.
1984, Feb. 28 **Perf. 14x13¹/₂**

Phases of pea plant hybridization.

729	A216	450 l	multicolored	60	45
730	A216	1500 l	multicolored	2.00	1.50

1984, Feb. 28 **Perf. 14**
731	A217	550 l	multicolored	90	55
732	A217	1200 l	multicolored	2.00	1.25

Pontifical Academy of Sciences — A218

1984, June 18 **Litho. & Engr.**
733	A218	150 l	shown	22	18
734	A218	450 l	Secret Archives	65	55
735	A218	550 l	Apostolic Library	80	65
736	A218	1500 l	Observatory	2.25	1.75

Papal
Journeys — A218a

1984-85 **Photo.** **Perf. 13¹/₂x14¹/₂**
737	A218a	50 l	Pakistan	15	15
738	A218a	100 l	Philippines	22	15
739	A218a	150 l	Guam	32	20
740	A218a	250 l	Japan	52	32
741	A218a	300 l	Alaska	65	55
742	A218a	400 l	Africa	90	50
743	A218a	450 l	Portugal	1.00	60
a.	Bkt. pane of 16 + 4 labels (4 each, #738, 741-743) ('85)			12.00	
744	A218a	550 l	Gt. Britain	1.25	70
745	A218a	1000 l	Argentina	2.25	1.40
746	A218a	1500 l	Switzerland	3.25	1.90
747	A218a	2500 l	San Marino	4.50	3.25
748	A218a	4000 l	Spain	9.00	5.25
	Nos. 737-748 (12)			24.01	14.97

St. Damasus I
(b.
304) — A219

St. Damasus I and: 200 l, Sepulchre of Sts. Marcellinus and Peter. 500 l, Epigraph of St. Januarius. 2000 l, Basilica, Church of the Martyrs Simplicius, Faustinus and Beatrice.

1984, Nov. 27 **Photo.** **Perf. 14x13¹/₂**
749	A219	200 l	multicolored	35	24
750	A219	500 l	multicolored	85	60
751	A219	2000 l	multicolored	3.75	2.25

St. Methodius (d.
885) — A220

St. Methodius and: 500 l, Madonna and Christ. 600 l, St. Cyril, carrying the body of St. Clement I. 1700 l, Sts. Benedict and Cyril, patrons of Europe.

Photo. & Engr.
1985, May 7 **Perf. 13¹/₂x14**
752	A220	500 l	multicolored	90	48
753	A220	600 l	multicolored	1.10	60
754	A220	1700 l	multicolored	3.25	1.65

St. Thomas
More (1477-
1535)
A221

St. Thomas More (from a portrait by Hans Holbein) and: 250 l, map of British Isles. 400 l, Frontispiece of Utopia. 2000 l, Frontispiece of Domenico Regi's biography of More.

Perf. 14x13¹/₂
1985, May 7 **Litho. & Engr.**
755	A221	250 l	multicolored	45	24
756	A221	400 l	multicolored	75	42
757	A221	2000 l	multicolored	3.75	2.00

St. Gregory VII
(c. 1020-85)
A222

Designs: 150 l, Eagle from Byzantine door, St. Paul's Basilica, Rome. 450 l, St. Gregory blessing. 2500 l, Sarcophagus.

Perf. 13¹/₂x14, 14x13¹/₂
1985, June 18 **Photo.**
758	A222	150 l	multi, vert.	24	15
759	A222	450 l	multi, vert.	75	45
760	A222	2500 l	multicolored	4.00	2.50

43rd Intl. Eucharistic
Congress — A223

Emblem, host, cross and: 100 l, Outline map of Africa. 400 l, Altar and Assembly of Bishops. 600 l, African chalice. 2300 l, African Christian family.

Photo. & Engr.
1985, June 18 **Perf. 13¹/₂x14**
761	A223	100 l	multicolored	15	15
762	A223	400 l	multicolored	60	38
763	A223	600 l	multicolored	90	55
764	A223	2300 l	multicolored	3.50	2.00

Concordat
Agreement
Ratification
A224

1985, Oct. 15   Photo.   Perf. 14x13½
765 A224 400 l Papal arms, map of Italy   65   35

Coaches
A225

1985, Oct. 15   Litho. & Engr.
766 A225 450 l dp lil rose & int bl   75   38
767 A225 1500 l brt bl & dp lil rose   2.00 1.40
  a.   Souvenir sheet of 2, #766-767, perf.
       13½x12½   3.25 3.25

Italia '85.

Intl. Peace
Year
1986 — A226

Vatican City — A227

Biblical and gospel texts: 50 l, Isaiah 2:4. 350 l,
Isaiah 52:7. 450 l, Matthew 5:9. 650 l, Luke 2:14.
2000 l, Message for World Peace, speech of Pope
John Paul II, Jan. 1, 1986.

1986, Apr. 14   Photo.   Perf. 14
768 A226   50 l multicolored   15   15
769 A226 350 l multicolored   55   32
770 A226 450 l multicolored   80   40
771 A226 650 l multicolored   1.10   60
772 A226 2000 l multicolored   3.50 2.00
       Nos. 768-772 (5)   6.10 3.47

1986, Apr. 14   Perf. 13½x14
773   Block of 6   6.75 3.00
  a.-f. A227 550 l, any single   1.10   50

UNESCO World Heritage Campaign. No. 773
has continuous design.

Patron Saints of the
Sick — A228

Conversion of St.
Augustine (354-
430) in
387 — A230

Pontifical
Academy of
Sciences,
50th Anniv.
A229

Designs: No. 774, St. Camillus de Lellis rescuing
invalid during Tiber flood, by Pierre Subleyras
(1699-1749). No. 775, St. John of God with
invalids, by Gomez Moreno (1834-1918). 2000 l,
Pope John Paul II visiting the sick.

Perf. 13½x14
1986, June 12   Litho. & Engr.
774 A228 700 l multicolored   1.25   60
775 A228 700 l multicolored   1.25   60
776 A228 2000 l multicolored   3.50 1.90

Perf. 14x13½
1986, Oct. 2   Litho. & Engr.
  School of Athens (details), by Raphael: 1500 l,
Scribes. 2500 l, Students learning math.
777 A229 1500 l multicolored   2.75 1.50
778 A229 2500 l multicolored   4.25 2.50

1987, Apr. 7   Photo.   Perf. 13½x14
  Religious art: 300 l, St. Augustine reading St.
Paul's Epistles, fresco by Benozzo Gozzoli (1420-
1498), Church of St. Augustine, San Gimignano.
400 l, Baptism of St. Augustine, painting by
Bartolomeo di Gentile (1470-1534), Vatican Art
Gallery. 500 l, Ecstasy of St. Augustine, fresco by
Benozzo Gozzoli, Church of St. Augustine. 2200 l,
St. Augustine, detail of Disputa del Sacramento,
fresco by Raphael (1483-1520), Room of the
Segnatura, Apostolic Palace.
779 A230 300 l multicolored   52   32
780 A230 400 l multicolored   70   45
781 A230 500 l multicolored   85   52
782 A230 2200 l multicolored   3.75 2.25

Christianization Anniversaries
A231   A232

  Seals: 700 l, Church of Riga, 1234-1269. 2400 l,
Marian Basilica of the Assumption, Aglona, 1780.

1987, June 2   Photo.   Perf. 13½x14
783 A231 700 l multicolored   1.40   95
784 A231 2400 l multicolored   4.75 3.25

Christianization of Latvia, 800th anniv.

1987, June 2   Perf. 13½x14
  Designs: 200 l, Christ, statue in the Lithuanian
Chapel, Vatican Crypt. 700 l, Two Angels and Our
Lady Holding the Body of Christ, by a Lithuanian
artist. 3000 l, Lithuanian shrine.
785 A232 200 l multicolored   30   22
786 A232 700 l multicolored   1.10   70
787 A232 3000 l multicolored   4.50 3.00

Christianization of Lithuania, 600th anniv.

OLYMPHILEX '87,
Rome, Aug. 29-Sept.
9 — A233

  Details of mosaic from the Baths of Caracalla:
400 l, Judge. 500 l, Athlete. 600 l, Athlete, diff.
2000 l, Athlete, diff.

Litho. & Engr.
1987, Aug. 29   Perf. 14
788 A233 400 l multicolored   65   45
789 A233 500 l multicolored   85   55
790 A233 600 l multicolored   1.00   65
791 A233 2000 l multicolored   3.25 2.25

Souvenir Sheet
792   Sheet of 4 + 4 labels   5.75 5.75
  a. A233 400 l like No. 788   65   65
  b. A233 500 l like No. 789   80   80
  c. A233 600 l like No. 780   1.00 1.00
  d. A233 2000 l like No. 791   3.25 3.25

Stamps from souvenir sheet have a Greek border
in blue surrounding vignettes (pictured). Nos. 788-
791 have single line border in blue. No. 792 has 4
labels picturing the papal arms, a goblet, a crown
and the exhibition emblem.

Inauguration
of the
Philatelic and
Numismatic
Museum
A235

  Designs: 400 l, Philatelic department, Vatican
City, No. 1. 3500 l, Numismatic department, 1000-
lire coin of 1986.

1987, Sept. 29   Photo.   Perf. 14x13½
793 A235 400 l multicolored   60   42
794 A235 3500 l multicolored   5.50 3.75

Journeys of
Pope John
Paul II,
1985-86
A236

  Designs: 50 l, Venezuela, Peru, Ecuador and
Trinidad & Tobago, 1985. 250 l, The Netherlands,
Luxembourg, Belgium, 1985. 400 l, Togo, Ivory
Coast, Cameroun, Central Africa, Zaire, Kenya and
Morocco, 1985. 500 l, Liechtenstein, 1986. 4000 l,
Bangladesh, Singapore, Fiji, New Zealand, Australia
and Seychelles, 1986.

1987, Oct. 27   Photo.   Perf. 14x13½
795 A236   50 l multicolored   15   15
796 A236 250 l multicolored   65   45
797 A236 400 l multicolored   1.10   70
798 A236 500 l multicolored   1.25   85
799 A236 600 l multicolored   1.65 1.00
800 A236 700 l multicolored   1.90 1.25
801 A236 2500 l multicolored   6.75 4.50
802 A236 4000 l multicolored   11.00 7.25
       Nos. 795-802 (8)   24.45 16.15

A237   A238

  Transfer of St. Nicholas Relics from Myra to Bari,
900th anniv.: 500 l, Arrival of relics at Bari. 700 l,
Act of charity, three improverished women. 3000 l,
Miraculous rescue of ship.

1987, Dec. 3   Perf. 13½x14
803 A237 500 l multicolored   2.00 1.25
804 A237 700 l multicolored   3.00 2.00
805 A237 3000 l multicolored   12.50 8.00

  St. Nicholas of Bari (c. 270-352), bishop of Myra.
Legend of Santa Claus originated because of his
charitable works. Printed in sheets of 8 + 16 se-
tenant labels picturing Santa Claus.

1988, Apr. 19   Photo.
  Children and: 500 l, Sister of the Institute of the
Daughters of Mary Help of Christians. 1000 l, St.
John Bosco. 2000 l, Salesian lay brother. Printed in
a continuous design.
806   Strip of 3   5.25 4.00
  a. A238 500 l multicolored   70   50
  b. A238 1000 l multicolored   1.50 1.00
  c. A238 2000 l multicolored   3.00 2.00

St. John Bosco (1815-1888), educator.

A239   A240

1988, June 16   Photo.   Perf. 13½x14
807 A239   50 l Annunciation   15   15
808 A239 300 l Nativity   42   25
809 A239 500 l Pentecost   70   40
810 A239 750 l Assumption   1.10   60
811 A239 1000 l Mother of the
                Church   1.40   80
812 A239 2400 l Refuge of Sinners 3.25 1.90
       Nos. 807-812 (6)   7.02 4.10

Marian Year, 1987-88.

1988, June 16
  Baptism of the Rus' of Kiev, Millennium: 450 l,
"Prince St. Vladimir the Great," from a 15th cent.
icon. 650 l, Cathedral of St. Sophia, Kiev. 2500 l,
"Mother of God in Prayer," from a mosaic at the
cathedral.
813 A240 450 l multicolored   75   45
814 A240 650 l multicolored   1.00   65
815 A240 2500 l multicolored   3.75 2.25

Paintings by Paolo Veronese (1528-
1588) — A241

  Designs: 550 l, Marriage of Cana (Madonna and
Christ) the Louvre, Paris. 650 l, Self-portrait of the
Artist, Villa Barbaro of Maser, Treviso. 3000 l, Mar-
riage of Cana (woman and two men).

Perf. 13½x14, 14x13½
1988, Sept. 29   Photo. & Engr.
816 A241 550 l multicolored   80   48
817 A241 650 l multi, horiz.   95   55
818 A241 3000 l multicolored   4.25 2.50

Christmas — A242

  Luke 2:14 and: 50 l, Angel facing LR. 400 l,
Angel facing UR. 500 l, Angel facing LL. 550 l,
Shepherds. 850 l, Nativity. 1500 l, Magi.

1988, Dec. 12   Photo.   Perf. 13½x14
819 A242   50 l multicolored   15   15
820 A242 400 l multicolored   60   28
821 A242 500 l multicolored   70   35
822 A242 550 l multicolored   80   40
823 A242 850 l multicolored   1.25   60
824 A242 1500 l multicolored   2.25 1.00
       Nos. 819-824 (6)   5.75 2.78

Souvenir Sheet
825   Sheet of 6   5.75 5.75
  a. A242 50 l gold & multi   15   15
  b. A242 400 l gold & multi   60   28
  c. A242 500 l gold & multi   70   35
  d. A242 550 l gold & multi   80   40
  e. A242 850 l gold & multi   1.25   60
  f. A242 1500 l gold & multi   2.25 1.00

No. 825 has continuous design.

Feast of the
Visitation, 600th
Anniv. — A243

Illuminations: 550 l, The Annunciation. 750 l, The Visitation (Virgin and St. Elizabeth). 2500 l, Mary, Elizabeth and infants.

1989, May 5   Photo.   Perf. 13¹/₂x14

826	A243	550 l multicolored	80 40
827	A243	750 l multicolored	1.10 55
828	A243	2500 l multicolored	3.75 1.90

Souvenir Sheet

Gregorian Egyptian Museum, 150th Anniv. — A244

Designs: 400 l, Apis. 650 l, Isis and Apis dicephalous bust. 750 l, Statue of the physician Ugiahorresne. 2400 l, Pharaoh Mentuhotep.

Perf. 14x13¹/₂

1989, May 5   Litho. & Engr.

829		Sheet of 4	6.00 6.00
a.	A244	400 l multicolored	55 28
b.	A244	650 l multicolored	90 48
c.	A244	750 l multicolored	1.10 55
d.	A244	2400 l multicolored	3.25 1.75

A245   A246

Birds from engravings by Eleazar Albin in *Histoire Naturelle des Oiseaux*, 1750.

1989, June 13   Photo.   Perf. 12
Granite Paper

830	A245	100 l Parrot	15 15
831	A245	150 l Green woodpecker	20 15
832	A245	200 l Crested and common wrens	25 15
833	A245	350 l Kingfisher	45 22
834	A245	500 l Red grosbeak of Virginia	65 32
835	A245	700 l Bullfinch	90 45
836	A245	1500 l Lapwing plover	2.00 1.00
837	A245	2500 l French teal	4.00 2.00
		Nos. 830-837 (8)	8.60 4.44

Photo. & Engr.

1989, Sept. 29   Perf. 13¹/₂x14

Symbols of the Eucharist.

838	A246	550 l shown	80 40
839	A246	850 l multi, diff.	1.25 65
840	A246	1000 l multi, diff.	1.50 75
841	A246	2500 l multi, diff.	3.75 1.90

44th Intl. Eucharistic Congress, Seoul, Oct. 5-8.

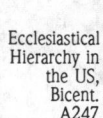

Ecclesiastical Hierarchy in the US, Bicent. A247

Designs: 450 l, Basilica of the Assumption of the Blessed Virgin Mary, Baltimore. 1350 l, John Carroll (1735-1815), 1st bishop of Baltimore and the US. 2400 l, Cathedral of Mary Our Queen, Baltimore.

1989, Nov. 9   Photo.   Perf. 12

842	A247	450 l multicolored	65 40
843	A247	1350 l multicolored	2.00 1.25
844	A247	2400 l multicolored	3.50 2.00

Papal Journeys 1988 — A248

Papal arms, Pope John Paul II and maps: 50 l, Uruguay, Bolivia, Peru and Paraguay, May 7-19. 550 l, Austria, June 23-27. 800 l, Zimbabwe, Botswana, Lesotho, Swaziland and Mozambique, Sept. 10-19. 1000 l, France, Oct. 8-11. 4000 l, Pastoral visits in Italy, 1978-1988.

1989, Nov. 9   Perf. 14x13¹/₂

845	A248	50 l multicolored	15 15
846	A248	550 l multicolored	80 48
847	A248	800 l multicolored	1.10 70
848	A248	1000 l multicolored	1.50 90
849	A248	4000 l multicolored	5.75 3.50
		Nos. 845-849 (5)	9.30 5.73

St. Angela Merici (c. 1474-1540) — A249

Designs: 700 l, The vision of the mystical stair, Prophecy of the Ursulines. 800 l, Evangelical counsel. 2800 l, Ursulines mission continued.

1990, Apr. 5   Photo.   Perf. 13¹/₂x14

850	A249	700 l multicolored	1.25 85
851	A249	800 l multicolored	1.40 95
852	A249	2800 l multicolored	4.75 3.25

Caritas Intl., 40th Anniv. — A250

Designs: 450 l, Abraham. 650 l, Three visitors. 800 l, Abraham and Sarah. 2000 l, Three visitors at Abraham's table.

1990, June 5   Photo.   Perf. 12x11¹/₂
Granite Paper

853	A250	450 l multicolored	75 50
854	A250	650 l multicolored	1.10 70
855	A250	800 l multicolored	1.25 85
856	A250	2000 l multicolored	3.25 2.00

Souvenir Sheet

857		Sheet of 4	6.00 6.00
a.	A250	450 l like #853	65 48
b.	A250	650 l like #854	1.00 65
c.	A250	800 l like #855	1.25 85
d.	A250	2000 l like #856	3.00 2.00

Nos. 853-856 have a single line border in gold. Nos. 857a-857d have no border line.

A251   A252

1990, June 5   Perf. 13¹/₂x14

858	A251	300 l Ordination of St. Willibrord	48 32
859	A251	700 l Stay in Antwerp	1.10 70
860	A251	3000 l Leaving belongings, death	4.75 3.15

1300th anniv. of ministry of St. Willibrord.

1990, Oct. 2

Diocese of Beijing-Nanking, 300th Anniv.: 500 l, Lake Beijing. 750 l, Church of the Immaculate Conception, Beijing, 1650. 1500 l, Lake Beijing, diff. 2000 l, Church of the Redeemer, Beijing, 1703.

861	A252	500 l multicolored	70 45
862	A252	750 l multicolored	1.10 70
863	A252	1500 l multicolored	2.25 1.40
864	A252	2000 l multicolored	2.75 1.90

Christmas A253

Details from painting by Sebastiano Mainardi.

1990, Nov. 27   Photo.   Perf. 13

865	A253	50 l Choir of Angels	15 15
866	A253	200 l St. Joseph	32 32
867	A253	650 l Holy Child	1.10 1.10
868	A253	750 l Madonna	1.25 1.25
869	A253	2500 l Nativity scene, vert.	4.00 4.00
		Nos. 865-869 (5)	6.82 6.82

Paintings of the Sistine Chapel — A254

Different details from lunettes: 50 l, 100 l, Eleazar. 150 l, 250 l, Jacob. 350 l, 400 l, Josiah. 500 l, 650 l, Asa. 800 l, 1000 l, Zerubbabel. 2000 l, 3000 l, Azor.

1991, Apr. 9   Photo.   Perf. 11¹/₂
Granite Paper

870	A254	50 l multicolored	15 15
871	A254	100 l multicolored	15 15
a.		Booklet pane of 6	75
872	A254	150 l multicolored	20 20
a.		Booklet pane of 6	1.25
873	A254	250 l multicolored	35 35
874	A254	350 l multicolored	45 45
875	A254	400 l multicolored	52 52
876	A254	500 l multicolored	70 70
877	A254	650 l multicolored	90 90
a.		Booklet pane of 6	5.50
878	A254	800 l multicolored	1.00 1.00
879	A254	1000 l multicolored	1.40 1.40
880	A254	2000 l multicolored	2.75 2.75
881	A254	3000 l multicolored	4.00 4.00
		Nos. 870-881 (12)	12.57 12.57

Encyclical Rerum Novarum, Cent. A255

Arms of Pope Leo XIII and: 600 l, Title page of Encyclical. 750 l, Allegory of Church's interest in workers, employers. 3500 l, Pope Leo XIII (1878-1903).

1991, May 23   Engr.   Perf. 14x13¹/₂

882	A255	600 l blue & dk grn	90 90
883	A255	750 l sage grn & rose car	1.10 1.10
884	A255	3500 l brt pur & dk bl	5.25 5.25

Vatican Observatory, Cent. — A256   Canonization of St. Bridget, 600th Anniv. — A257

Designs: 750 l, Astrograph for making photographic sky map, 1891. 1000 l, Zeiss Double Astrograph, Lake Castelgandolfo, 1935, horiz. 3000 l, New telescope, Vatican Observatory, Mt. Graham, Arizona, 1991.

Perf. 11¹/₂x12, 12x11¹/₂
1991, Oct. 1   Photo.
Granite Paper

885	A256	750 l multicolored	1.10 1.10
886	A256	1000 l multicolored	1.50 1.50
887	A256	3000 l multicolored	4.50 4.50

1991, Oct. 1   Perf. 12¹/₂x13

Designs: 1500 l, Receiving Madonna's revelations. 2000 l, Receiving Christ's revelations.

888	A257	1500 l multicolored	2.25 2.25
889	A257	2000 l multicolored	3.25 3.25

Journeys of Pope John Paul II, 1990 — A258

Pope John Paul II and: 200 l, Cathedral of Immaculate Conception, Ouagadougou, Burkina Faso. 550 l, St. Vitus' Cathedral, Prague. 750 l, Our Lady of Guadaloupe's Basilica, Mexico. 1500 l, Ta' Pinu Sanctuary, Gozo. 3500 l, Cathedral of Christ the King, Gitega, Burundi.

Perf. 13¹/₂x14
1991, Nov. 11   Litho. & Engr.

890	A258	200 l green & multi	30 30
891	A258	550 l org brn & multi	85 85
892	A258	750 l claret & multi	1.10 1.10
893	A258	1500 l dk brn & multi	2.25 2.25
894	A258	3500 l grn bl & multi	5.50 5.50
		Nos. 890-894 (5)	10.00 10.00

West Africa, Jan. 25-Feb. 1 (200 l); Czechoslovakia, Apr. 21-22 (550 l); Mexico, Curacao, May 6-14 (750 l); Malta, May 25-27 (1500 l); Tanzania, Burundi, Rwanda, Ivory Coast, Sept. 1-10 (3500 l).

A259   A260

Special Assembly for Europe of Synod of Bishops: 300 l, Colonnade of St. Peter's Basilica. 500 l, St. Peter's Basilica and Square. 4000 l, Colonnade of St. Peter's Basilica, Apostolic Palace.

1991, Nov. 11   Engr.   Perf. 12¹/₂x13

895	A259	300 l olive & blk	45 45
896	A259	500 l olive & blk	80 80
897	A259	4000 l olive & blk	6.00 6.00
a.		Strip of 3, #895-897	8.00 8.00

No. 897a has continous design.

1992, Mar. 24   Photo.   Perf. 11¹/₂x12

Discovery and Evangelization of America, 500th Anniv.: 500 l, Christopher Columbus. 600 l, Saint Peter Claver. 850 l, La Virgen de los Reyes Catolicos. 1000 l, Bishop Bartolome de las Casas. 2000 l, Father Junipero Serra.

No. 903a, Chart of New World. b, Chart of Old World.

Granite Paper

898	A260	500 l multicolored	75 75
899	A260	600 l multicolored	90 90
900	A260	850 l multicolored	1.25 1.25
901	A260	1000 l multicolored	1.50 1.50
902	A260	2000 l multicolored	3.00 3.00
		Nos. 898-902 (5)	7.40 7.40

Souvenir Sheet
Perf. 12

903	A260	Sheet of 2	6.00 6.00
a.		1500 l multicolored	2.25 2.25
b.		2500 l multicolored	3.75 3.75

VATICAN CITY

BUYING AND SELLING,
QUALITY STAMPS OF
VATICAN CITY
MINT NH OR LH ALSO
USED, SOME FDC's.
THE ITALIAN AREA,
INCLUDING SAN MARINO,
TRIESTE A & B -
Whether buying or selling,
my prices are very reasonable.

EUROPE

From Andorre to Turkey,
including
The English Area,
Mint Never Hinged Sets.

My buy-sell price list contains well over
12,000 sets, all kinds of topicals, where
you will find my selling prices, and the
price I pay for each set that I need.

**SEND A #10 55¢ SASE
TODAY FOR YOUR FREE
COPY OF OUR PRICE LIST!
You will be glad you did.**

F. COPPOLA
P.O. Box 181022
Utica, MI 48318-1022

Piero Della
Francesca (d.
1492), Painter
A261

St. Giuseppe
Benedetto
Cottolengo (1786-
1842)
A262

Frescoes: 300 l, 750 l (detail), Our Lady of Child-
birth. 1000 l, 3000 l (detail), Resurrection.

VATICAN CITY SPECIALIST

We service everything for the New Issue collector.

We carry a complete line of...
- **MINT AND CANCELED SETS**
- **FDCs • MAXIMUM CARDS • ACTAS**
... for Past as well as New Issues.
We also carry Papal Trips commemorative cover sets

"Since 1912"

PENNY BLACK STAMP CO.
P.O. BOX 3486, BETHLEHEM, PA 18017
E – Mail = pnnyblck@fast.net

VPS

★ **Send for our complete pricelist!** ★

1992, May 15   Photo.   *Perf. 13½x14*

904	A261	300 l	multicolored	42	42
905	A261	750 l	multicolored	1.10	1.10
906	A261	1000 l	multicolored	1.40	1.40
907	A261	3000 l	multicolored	4.25	4.25

1992, May 15   *Perf. 11½x12*

St. Giuseppe Benedetto Cottolengo: 650 l, Com-
forting the sick. 850 l, With Little House of Divine
Providence.

Granite Paper

908	A262	650 l	multicolored	1.00	1.00
909	A262	850 l	multicolored	1.40	1.40

A263   A264

Plants of the New World: a, Frumentum
indicum. b, Solanum pomiferum. c, Opuntia. d,
Cacaos, cacavifera. e, Solanum tuberosum, capsi-
cum, mordens. f, Ananas sagitae folio.

1992, Sept. 15   Photo.   *Perf. 11½x12*
Granite Paper

910		Block of 6	7.50	7.50
a.-f.	A263	850 l any single	1.25	1.25

1992, Oct. 12   *Perf. 12½x13*

911	A264	700 l	multicolored	1.05	1.05

4th General Conference of the Latin American
Episcopacy.

Christmas
A265

Mosaics from Basilica of St. Maria Maggiore,
Rome: 600 l, The Annunciation. 700 l, Nativity.
1000 l, Adoration of the Magi. 1500 l, Presentation
to the Temple.

1992, Nov. 24   Photo.   *Perf. 11½*
Granite Paper

912	A265	600 l	multicolored	90	90
913	A265	700 l	multicolored	1.00	1.00
914	A265	1000 l	multicolored	1.45	1.45
915	A265	1500 l	multicolored	2.15	2.15

St. Francis Healing
Man from Ilerda, by
Giotto di Bondone
(1266-1337) — A266

1993, Jan. 9   Litho.   *Perf. 13½x14*

916	A266	1000 l	multicolored	1.25	1.25

Prayer Meeting for Peace in Europe, Assisi. No.
916 printed se-tenant with label.

Architecture of
Vatican City and
Rome — A267

Buildings: 200 l, St. Peter's Basilica, Vatican City.
300 l, St. John Lateran Basilica, Rome. 350 l, St.
Mary Major's Basilica, Rome. 500 l, St. Paul's Basil-
ica, Rome. 600 l, Apostolic Palace, Vatican. 700 l,
Lateran Apostolic Palace, Rome. 850 l, Papal Pal-
ace, Castel Gandolfo. 1000 l, Chancery Palace,
Rome. 2000 l, Palace of the Propagation of the
Faith, Rome. 3000 l, St. Calixtus Palace, Rome.

1993, Mar. 23   Photo.   *Perf. 12x11½*
Granite Paper

917	A267	200 l	multicolored	28	28
a.		Booklet pane of 4	1.15	
918	A267	300 l	multicolored	40	40
a.		Booklet pane of 4	1.60	
919	A267	350 l	multicolored	48	48
a.		Booklet pane of 4	2.00	
920	A267	500 l	multicolored	68	68
a.		Booklet pane of 4	2.75	
921	A267	600 l	multicolored	80	80
922	A267	700 l	multicolored	95	95
923	A267	850 l	multicolored	1.15	1.15
924	A267	1000 l	multicolored	1.40	1.40
925	A267	2000 l	multicolored	2.75	2.75
926	A267	3000 l	multicolored	4.10	4.10
		Nos. 917-926 (10)	12.99	12.99

45th Intl. Eucharistic
Congress,
Seville — A268

Congress emblem, Vatican arms and: 500 l,
Cross, grape vines. 700 l, Cross, hands breaking
bread. 1500 l, Hands lifting chalice. 2500 l, Wheat,
banner.

1993, May 22   Litho.   *Perf. 14x13½*

927	A268	500 l	multicolored	62	62
928	A268	700 l	multicolored	90	90
929	A268	1500 l	multicolored	1.85	1.85
930	A268	2500 l	multicolored	3.10	3.10

Ascension Day,
May 20 — A269

Traditio Legis Sarcophagus, St. Peter's Basilica: a,
200 l, Sacrifice of Isaac. b, 750 l, Apostle Peter
receiving law from Jesus, Apostle Paul. c, 3000 l,
Christ watching servant pouring water on Pilate's
hands.

1993, May 22   Engr.   *Perf. 13½x14*

931	A269	Triptych, #a.-c.	5.00	5.00

Contemporary
Art — A270

Europa: 750 l, Crucifixion, by Felice Casorati
(1886-1963). 850 l, Rouen Cathedral, by Maurice
Utrillo (1883-1955).

1993, Sept. 29   Photo.   *Perf. 13*

932	A270	750 l	multicolored	95	95
933	A270	850 l	multicolored	1.00	1.00

Death of St. John of
Nepomuk, 600th
Anniv. — A271

Designs: 2000 l, Buildings in Prague, Charles
Bridge.

1993, Sept. 29   Litho.   *Perf. 13½x14*

934	A271	1000 l	multicolored	1.25	1.25
935	A271	2000 l	multicolored	2.50	2.50

Travels of
Pope John
Paul
II — A272

Visits to: 600 l, Senegal, Gambia, Guinea. 1000 l,
Angola, St. Thomas and Prince. 5000 l, Dominican
Republic.

1993, Nov. 23   Photo.   *Perf. 12x11½*
Granite Paper

936	A272	600 l	multicolored	70	70
937	A272	1000 l	multicolored	1.25	1.25
938	A272	5000 l	multicolored	5.75	5.75

Hans Holbein the
Younger (1497?-
1543),
Painter — A273

Details or entire paintings: 700 l, 1000 l,
Madonna of Solothurn. 1500 l, Self-portrait.

**   *Perf. 13½x14***
1993, Nov. 23   Litho. & Engr.

939	A273	700 l	multicolored	85	85
940	A273	1000 l	multicolored	1.25	1.25
941	A273	1500 l	multicolored	1.75	1.75

Synod of
Bishops,
Special
Assembly for
Africa
A274

Designs: 850 l, Stylized crosier, dome with cross, vert. 1000 l, Crucifix, dome of St. Peter's Basilica, crosiers, African landscape.

Perf. 12¹/₂x13, 13x12¹/₂

			1994, Apr. 8		Photo.
942	A274	850 l multicolored	1.10	1.10
943	A274	1000 l multicolored	1.25	1.25

The Restored Sistine Chapel A275

Frescoes, by Michelangelo: Creation of the Sun and Moon: No. 944, Sun. No. 945, God pointing toward moon. Creation of Man: No. 946, Adam, No. 947, God. Original Sin: No. 948, Adam, Eve taking apple from serpent. No. 949, Adam, Eve forced from Garden of Eden. The Flood: No. 950, People on dry ground. No. 951, People on stone outcropping.

4000 l, Detail of Last Judgment, Christ and the Virgin.

1994, Apr. 8   Photo.   Perf. 11¹/₂

944	A275	350 l multicolored	42	42
945	A275	350 l multicolored	42	42
a.		Pair, #944-945	85	85
946	A275	500 l multicolored	60	60
947	A275	500 l multicolored	60	60
a.		Pair, #946-947	1.25	1.25
948	A275	1000 l multicolored	1.25	1.25
949	A275	1000 l multicolored	1.25	1.25
a.		Pair, #948-949	2.50	2.50
950	A275	2000 l multicolored	2.50	2.50
951	A275	2000 l multicolored	2.50	2.50
a.		Pair, 950-951	5.00	5.00
		Nos. 944-951 (8)	9.54	9.54

Souvenir Sheet
Perf. 12

952	A275	4000 l multicolored	5.00	5.00

No. 952 contains one 36x54mm stamp.

European Inventions, Discoveries — A276

Europa: 750 l, Progress from wheel to atom traced by white thread. 850 l, Galileo in center of solar system, scientific instruments.

1994, May 31   Litho.   Perf. 13x13¹/₂

953	A276	750 l multicolored	95	95
954	A276	850 l multicolored	1.10	1.10

Intl. Year of the Family — A277

Stained glass: 400 l, God creating man and woman. 750 l, Family under names of four Evangelists. 1000 l, Parents teaching son. 2000 l, Young man conforting elderly couple.

1994, May 31   Photo.   Perf. 13x14

955	A277	400 l multicolored	50	50
956	A277	750 l multicolored	95	95
957	A277	1000 l multicolored	1.25	1.25
958	A277	2000 l multicolored	2.50	2.50

Giovanni da Montecorvino (1247-1328), Missionary — A278

1994, Sept. 27   Litho.   Perf. 14

959	A278	1000 l multicolored	1.40	1.40

Evangelization of China, 700th anniv.

13th Intl. Convention of Christian Archaeology, Split, Croatia — A279

Mosaics from Euphrasian Basilica, Parentium, Croatia, 6th Cent.: 700 l, Bishop Euphrasius, Archdeacon Claudius, Claudius' son. 1500 l, Madonna and Child, two angels. 3000 l, Christ, Apostles Peter & Paul.

1994, Sept. 27   Perf. 13x14

960	A279	700 l multicolored	1.00	1.00
961	A279	1500 l multicolored	2.00	2.00
962	A279	3000 l multicolored	4.25	4.25
		Nos. 960-962 (3)	7.25	7.25

Travels of Pope John Paul II — A280

Designs: 600 l, Benin, Uganda, Sudan. 700 l, Albania. 1000 l, Spain. 2000 l, Jamaica, Mexico, US. 3000 l, Lithuania, Latvia, Estonia.

1994, Nov. 18   Engr.   Perf. 13

963	A280	600 l multicolored	85	85
964	A280	700 l multicolored	1.00	1.00
965	A280	1000 l multicolored	1.40	1.40
966	A280	2000 l multicolored	2.75	2.75
967	A280	3000 l multicolored	4.25	4.25
		Nos. 963-967 (5)	10.25	10.25

Christmas A281

The Nativity, by Il Tintoretto: 700 l, The Holy Family. No. 969, The Holy Family, two women. No. 970, Adoration of the shepherds.

1994, Nov. 18   Photo.   Perf. 11¹/₂
Granite Paper

968	A281	700 l multicolored	1.00	1.00

Size: 45x27mm

969	A281	1000 l multicolored	1.40	1.40
970	A281	1000 l multicolored	1.40	1.40
a.		Pair, #969-970	2.80	2.80
		Nos. 968-970 (3)	3.80	3.80

Peace and Freedom A282

1995, Mar. 25   Photo.   Perf. 14x13

971	A282	750 l shown	90	90
972	A282	850 l Hands clasp, dove	1.00	1.00

Europa.

Shrine of Loreto, 700th Anniv. — A283

Details of artworks from vaults of Sacristy: 600 l, St. Mark's, Angel with chalice, by Melozzo da Forli. 700 l, St. Mark's, Angel with lamb, by da Forli. 1500 l, 2500 l, St. John's, Music making angels, by Luca Signorelli.

No. 977, Marble carving showing Holy House of Loreto.

1995, Mar. 25   Perf. 11¹/₂

973	A283	600 l multicolored	70	70
974	A283	700 l multicolored	80	80
975	A283	1500 l multicolored	1.75	1.75
976	A283	2500 l multicolored	3.00	3.00
		Nos. 973-976 (4)	6.25	6.25

Souvenir Sheet

977	A283	3000 l multicolored	3.50	3.50

No. 977 contains one 36x36mm stamp.

Year Sets

Year set values are determined from price lists offering complete sets for each year. Not all dealers offer these sets. Values may be lower or higher than the total value of the individual stamps. Contents of the sets being offered may differ.

1959	#250-268, C35-C44	3.50
1960	#269-297, E15-E16	7.00
1961	#298-325	11.00
1962	#326-355, C45-C46	8.75
1963	#356-374	2.25
1964	#375-403	2.75
1965	#404-422	1.50
1966	#423-447, E17-E18	1.65
1967	#448-460, C47-C52	2.00
1968	#461-466, C53-C54, J19-J24	3.75
1969	#467-478	1.25
1970	#479-499	2.25
1971	#500-514, C55-C58	4.50
1972	#515-530, 520a	6.00
1973	#531-547	2.25
1974	#548-571, C59	5.25
1975	#572-589	3.00
1976	#590-606, C60-C62	8.00
1977	#607-629	4.25
1978	#630-644, C63-C65	10.00
1979	#645-667	6.00
1980	#668-680, C66-C72	14.00
1981	#681-704	10.50
1982	#705-717a	12.50
1983	#718-728, C73-C74	26.00
1984	#729-751	37.50
1985	#752-767a	27.50
1986	#768-778, C75-C82	50.00
1987	#779-805	70.00
1988	#806-825, C83-C87	46.00
1989	#826-849	40.00
1990	#850-869, C88-C91	47.50
1991	#870-897	42.50

SEMI-POSTAL STAMPS

Holy Year Issue

Cross and Orb
SP1   SP2

1933   Unwmk.   Engr.   Perf. 13x13¹/₂

B1	SP1	25c + 10c grn	4.25	2.25
B2	SP1	75c + 15c scar	9.50	4.50
B3	SP2	80c + 20c red brn	14.00	14.00
B4	SP2	1.25 l + 25c ultra	6.50	8.75
		Set, never hinged	100.00	

AIR POST STAMPS

Catalogue values for unused stamps in this section are for Never Hinged items.

FILATELIA RIVA RENO
PAYING TOP PRICES • SERIOUS BUYER...
TRIESTE ZONE A – ZONE B
VATICAN, SAN MARINO and ITALY
Collections, Lots, Accumulations, Postal History & Covers
- A.M.G. - Italian Social Republic - Italian Offices Abroad

BEFORE SELLING, ASK US!

Don't hesitate! Call or fax for our...top buying prices and quick payment in US funds!

NEW ISSUE SERVICE!

• Special Conditions for Dealers •

Filatelia Riva Reno di Luciano Morselli
Via Galliera, 23 - 40121 Bologna - Italy
FAX +39-51-232180 • TEL +39-51-237480

american philatelic society
feder. nazion. comm. filatelici italiani-roma
borsa filatelica nazionale milano
philatelic traders' society
verband des deutschen briefm. handels
american stamp dealers' association

Statue of St.
Peter — AP1

Dove of Peace
over
Vatican — AP2

Elijah's Ascent
into
Heaven — AP3

Our Lady of Loreto
and Angels Moving the
Holy House — AP4

Wmk. 235

1938, June 22   Engr.   Perf. 14

C1	AP1	25c brown	18	15
C2	AP2	50c green	18	15
C3	AP3	75c lake	18	15
C4	AP4	80c dark blue	18	15
C5	AP1	1 l violet	70	48
C6	AP2	2 l ultra	85	60
C7	AP3	5 l slate blk	1.90	1.50
C8	AP4	10 l dk brown vio	2.75	1.90
		Nos. C1-C8 (8)	6.92	5.08

Dove of Peace Above
St. Peter's
Basilica — AP5

House of Our
Lady of
Loreto — AP6

Birds Circling
Cross — AP7

1947, Nov. 10   Photo.

C9	AP5	1 l rose red	15	15
C10	AP6	4 l dark brown	15	15
C11	AP5	5 l brt ultra	15	15
C12	AP7	15 l brt purple	2.50	65
C13	AP6	25 l dk blue green	3.25	65
C14	AP7	50 l dk gray	9.00	1.75
C15	AP7	100 l red orange	14.00	2.00
		Nos. C9-C15 (7)	29.20	5.50

Nos. C13-C15 exist imperf. Value, each pair $1,000.

Archangel
Raphael and
Young
Tobias — AP8

1948, Dec. 28   Engr.   Perf. 14

C16	AP8	250 l sepia	13.00	4.75
C17	AP8	500 l ultra	450.00	235.00

Angels and
Globe — AP9

1949, Dec. 3

C18	AP9	300 l ultra	27.50	8.25
C19	AP9	1000 l green	110.00	50.00

UPU, 75th anniversary.

Franciscus
Gratianus
AP10

Dome of St. Peter's
Cathedral
AP11

1951, Dec. 20   Perf. 14x13

C20	AP10	300 l deep plum	200.00	140.00
C21	AP10	500 l deep blue	42.50	15.00

Publication of unified canon laws, 800th anniv.

1953, Aug. 10   Perf. 13

C22	AP11	500 l chocolate	22.50	3.00
C23	AP11	1000 l deep ultra	62.50	7.50

See Nos. C33-C34.

Archangel Gabriel
by Melozzo da
Forli — AP12

Obelisk of St. John
Lateran — AP13

Archangel Gabriel: 10 l, 35 l, 100 l, Annunciation by Pietro Cavallini. 15 l, 50 l, 300 l, Annunciation by Leonardo da Vinci.

1956, Feb. 12   Wmk. 235

C24	AP12	5 l gray black	15	15
C25	AP12	10 l blue green	15	15
C26	AP12	15 l deep orange	15	15
C27	AP12	25 l dk car rose	15	15
C28	AP12	35 l carmine	50	42
C29	AP12	50 l olive brown	15	15
C30	AP12	60 l ultra	4.50	3.50
C31	AP12	100 l orange brown	15	15
C32	AP12	300 l deep violet	50	42
		Nos. C24-C32 (9)	6.40	5.24

Type of 1953

1958   Perf. 13½

C33	AP11	500 l grn & bl grn	9.00	5.50
a.		Perf. 14	650.00	350.00
C34	AP11	1000 l dp magenta	1.00	1.00
a.		Perf. 14	1.00	1.00

1959, Oct. 27   Engr.   Perf. 13½x14

Obelisks, Rome: 10 l, 60 l, St. Mary Major. 15 l,
100 l, St. Peter. 25 l, 200 l, Piazza del Popolo. 35 l,
500 l, Trinita dei Monti.

C35	AP13	5 l dull violet	15	15
C36	AP13	10 l blue green	15	15
C37	AP13	15 l dk brown	15	15
C38	AP13	25 l slate grn	15	15
C39	AP13	35 l ultra	16	15
C40	AP13	50 l yellow grn	15	15
C41	AP13	60 l rose carmine	15	15
C42	AP13	100 l bluish black	16	15
C43	AP13	200 l brown	28	15
C44	AP13	500 l orange brn	55	25
		Set value	1.50	90

Archangel Gabriel
by Filippo
Valle — AP14

Jet over St. Peter's
Cathedral — AP15

1962, Mar. 13   Wmk. 235

C45	AP14	1000 l brown	1.00	60
C46	AP14	1500 l dark blue	2.50	1.40

1967, Mar. 7   Photo.   Perf. 14

Designs: 40 l, 200 l, Radio tower and statue of
Archangel Gabriel (like A87). 90 l, 500 l, Aerial
view of St. Peter's Square and Vatican City.

C47	AP15	20 l brt violet	15	15
C48	AP15	40 l black & pink	15	15
C49	AP15	90 l sl bl & dk gray	15	15
C50	AP15	100 l black & salmon	15	15
C51	AP15	200 l vio blk & gray	22	15
C52	AP15	500 l dk brn & lt brn	50	30
		Set value	1.00	70

Archangel Gabriel by
Fra Angelico — AP16

1968, Mar. 12   Engr.   Perf. 13½x14

C53	AP16	1000 l dk car rose, *cr*	1.00	85
C54	AP16	1500 l black, *cr*	2.00	1.65

St. Matthew,
by Fra
Angelico
AP17

The Evangelists, by Fra Angelico from Niccolina
Chapel: 300 l, St. Mark. 500 l, St. Luke. 1000 l, St.
John.

**Engr. & Photo.
Perf. 14x13½**

1971, Sept. 30   Unwmk.

C55	AP17	200 l black & pale grn	26	20
C56	AP17	300 l black & bister	35	30
C57	AP17	500 l black & salmon	1.40	1.00
C58	AP17	1000 l black & pale lil	70	52

AP18   AP19

Seraph, mosaic from St. Mark's Basilica, Venice.

Litho. & Engr.

1974, Feb. 21   Perf. 13x14

C59	AP18	2500 l multicolored	3.00	2.50

Litho. & Engr.

1976, Feb. 19   Perf. 13x14

Last Judgment, by Michelangelo: 500 l, Angel
with Trumpet. 1000 l, Ascending figures. 2500 l,
Angels with trumpets.

C60	AP19	500 l sal, bl & brn	1.90	1.65
C61	AP19	1000 l sal, bl & brn	80	75
C62	AP19	2500 l sal, bl & brn	2.75	2.25

Radio
Waves,
Antenna,
Papal Arms
AP20

1978, July 11   Engr.   Perf. 14x13

C63	AP20	1000 l multicolored	85	70
C64	AP20	2000 l multicolored	3.00	2.25
C65	AP20	3000 l multicolored	3.25	2.50

10th World Telecommunications Day.

Pope John
Paul II Shaking
Hands, Arms
of Dominican
Republic
AP21

1980   Litho. & Engr.   Perf. 14x13½

C66	AP21	200 l shown	25	25
C67	AP21	300 l Mexico	32	32
C68	AP21	500 l Poland	65	65
C69	AP21	1000 l Ireland	1.25	1.25
C70	AP21	1500 l US	1.90	1.90
C71	AP21	2000 l UN	2.25	2.25
C72	AP21	3000 l with Dimitrios I,		
		Turkey	3.75	3.75
		Nos. C66-C72 (7)	10.37	10.37

Issue dates: 3000 l, Sept. 18; others June 24.

World Communications Year — AP22

Designs: 2000 l, Moses Explaining The Law to
the People by Luca Signarelli. 5000 l, Paul Preaching in Athens, Tapestry of Raphael design.

1983, Nov. 10   Perf. 14

C73	AP22	2000 l multicolored	3.25	3.25
C74	AP22	5000 l multicolored	7.50	7.50

Journeys of
Pope John
Paul II,
1983-84
AP23

Designs: 350 l, Central America, the Caribbean,
1983. 450 l, Warsaw Cathedral, Our Lady of Czestochowa, Poland, 1983. 700 l, Statue of Our
Lady, Lourdes, France, 1983. 1000 l, Mariazell
Sanctuary, St. Stephen's Cathedral, Austria, 1983.
1500 l, Asia, the Pacific, 1984. 2000 l, Einsiedeln
Basilica, St. Nicholas of Flue, Switzerland, 1984.
2500 l, Quebec's Notre Dame Cathedral, five
crosses of the Jesuit martyrs, Canada, 1984.
5000 l, Saragossa, Spain, Dominican Republic and
Puerto Rico, 1984.

1986, Nov. 20   Photo.   Perf. 14x13½

C75	AP23	350 l multicolored	55	55
C76	AP23	450 l multicolored	70	70
C77	AP23	700 l multicolored	1.10	1.10
C78	AP23	1000 l multicolored	1.65	1.65
C79	AP23	1500 l multicolored	2.50	2.50
C80	AP23	2000 l multicolored	3.50	3.50
C81	AP23	2500 l multicolored	4.25	4.25
C82	AP23	5000 l multicolored	8.50	8.50
		Nos. C75-C82 (8)	22.75	22.75

Papal Journeys Type of 1986

Designs: 450 l, Horseman, shepherdess, St.
Peter's Basilica, Cathedral of Santiago in Chile, and
the Sanctuary of Our Lady of Lujan, Argentina.
650 l, Youths and the Cathedral of Speyer, Federal
Republic of Germany. 1000 l, St. Peter's Basilica,
Altar of Gdansk, flowers and thorns. 2500 l, Crowd
and American skyscrapers. 5000 l, Tepee at Fort
Simpson, Canada, and American Indians.

1988, Oct. 27   Photo.   Perf. 14x13½

C83	AP23	450 l multicolored	65	65
C84	AP23	650 l multicolored	95	95
C85	AP23	1000 l multicolored	1.50	1.50
C86	AP23	2500 l multicolored	3.50	3.50
C87	AP23	5000 l multicolored	7.25	7.25
		Nos. C83-C87 (5)	13.85	13.85

Uruguay, Chile and Argentina, Mar. 30-Apr. 14,
1987 (450 l); Federal Republic of Germany, Apr.
30-May 4, 1987 (650 l); Poland, June 8-14, 1987
(1000 l); US, Sept. 10-19, 1987 (2500 l); and
Canada, Sept. 20, 1987 (5000 l).

VATICAN CITY (continued)

Journeys of Pope John Paul II, 1989 — AP24

1990, Nov. 27 Photo. Perf. 12
Granite Paper

C88	AP24	500 l	Africa	80 80
C89	AP24	1000 l	Scandinavia	1.65 1.65
C90	AP24	3000 l	Santiago de Compostela, Spain	5.00 5.00
C91	AP24	5000 l	Asia	8.00 8.00

Madagascar, Reunion, Zambia and Malawi, Apr. 28-May 6 (500 l); Norway, Iceland, Finland, Denmark and Sweden, June 1-10 (1000 l); Korea, Indonesia and Mauritius, Oct. 6-16 (5000 l).

Travels of Pope John Paul II, 1991 — AP25

1992, Nov. 24 Photo. Perf. 14

C92	AP25	500 l	multicolored	70 70
C93	AP25	1000 l	multicolored	1.45 1.45
C94	AP25	4000 l	multicolored	5.75 5.75
C95	AP25	6000 l	multicolored	8.50 8.50

Portugal, May 10-13 (500 l); Poland, June 1-9 (1000 l); Poland, Hungary, Aug. 13-20 (4000 l); Brazil, Oct. 12-21 (6000 l).

SPECIAL DELIVERY STAMPS

Pius XI — SD1

Unwmk.
1929, Aug. 1 Photo. Perf. 14

E1	SD1	2 l	carmine rose	8.00 5.75
E2	SD1	2.50 l	dark blue	5.75 4.50

For overprints see Nos. Q14-Q15.

Catalogue values for unused stamps in this section, from this point to the end of the section, are for Never Hinged items.

Aerial View of Vatican City SD2

1933 Wmk. 235 Engr.

E3	SD2	2 l	rose red & brn	15 28
E4	SD2	2.50 l	dp blue & brn	15 28
			Set value	22

1945 Unwmk.

E5	SD2	3.50 l	dk car & ultra	35 25
E6	SD2	5 l	ultra & green	52 30

Nos. E5 and E6 Surcharged with New Values and Bars in Black

1946, Jan. 9

E7	SD2	6 l on 3.50 l	dk car & ultra	4.25 1.65
E8	SD2	12 l on 5 l	ultra & grn	4.25 1.65

Vertical pairs imperf. between exist of No. E7 (value $150) and No. E8 (value $200).

Bishop Matteo Giberti SD3

Design: 12 l, Gaspar Cardinal Contarini.

1946, Feb. 21 Photo.
Centers in Dark Brown

E9	SD3	6 l	dark green	18 15
E10	SD3	12 l	copper brown	22 15
			Set value	20

See note after No. 121.
Nos. E9-E10 exist imperf. and part perforate.

Basilica of St. Peter — SD5

Design: 80 l, Basilica of St. John.

1949 Wmk. 235 Perf. 14

E11	SD5	40 l	slate gray	11.00 3.50
a.		Perf. 13½x14		17.00 4.50
E12	SD5	80 l	chestnut brown	17.00 6.00
a.		Perf. 13½x14		19.00 9.00

St. Peter and His Tomb — SD6

Design: 85 l, Pius XII and Roman sepulcher.

Perf. 13½x13, 14
1953, Apr. 23 Engr.

E13	SD6	50 l	blue grn & dk brn	16 15
E14	SD6	85 l	dp orange & dk brn	50 38

Arms of Pope John XXIII — SD7

1960 Photo. Perf. 14

E15	SD7	75 l	red & brown	15 15
E16	SD7	100 l	dk blue & brown	15 15
			Set value	24 24

Pope Paul VI by Enrico Manfrini — SD8

Design: 150 l, Papal arms.

1966, Mar. 8 Wmk. 235 Perf. 14

E17	SD8	150 l	black brown	15 15
E18	SD8	180 l	brown	20 16

POSTAGE DUE STAMPS

Regular Issue of 1929 Overprinted in Black and Brown

1931 Unwmk. Perf. 14

J1	A1	5c	dk brown & pink	15 15
a.		Double frame		
J2	A1	10c	dk grn & lt grn	15 15
a.		Frame omitted		400.00
J3	A1	20c	violet & lilac	6.00 2.00

Surcharged

J4	A1	40c on 30c	indigo & yel	1.50 4.00

Surcharged

J5	A2	60c on 2 l	olive brn	35.00 18.00
J6	A2	1.10 l on 2.50 l	red org	3.25 16.00
		Nos. J1-J6 (6)		46.05 40.30
		Set, never hinged		110.00

In addition to the surcharges, #J4-J6 are overprinted with ornamental frame as on #J1-J3.

Catalogue values for unused stamps in this section, from this point to the end of the section, are for Never Hinged items.

Papal Arms

D1   D2

1945 Unwmk. Typo. Perf. 14

J7	D1	5c	black & yellow	15 15
J8	D1	20c	black & lilac	15 15
J9	D1	80c	black & salmon	15 15
J10	D1	1 l	black & green	15 15
J11	D1	2 l	black & blue	15 15
J12	D1	5 l	black & gray	15 15
a.		Imperf., pair		125.00 125.00
		Set value		60 36

A second type of Nos. J7-J12 exists, in which the colored lines of the background are thicker.
The 20c and 5 lire exist in horizontal pairs imperf. vertically. Value, each $30.
The 20c exists in horizontal pairs imperf. between. Value $80.

Perf. 13½x13
1954 Wmk. 235 Engr.

J13	D2	4 l	black & rose	15 15
J14	D2	6 l	black & green	30 30
J15	D2	10 l	black & yellow	15 15
J16	D2	20 l	black & blue	45 30
J17	D2	50 l	black & ol brn	15 15
J18	D2	70 l	black & red brn	15 15
		Nos. J13-J18 (6)		1.35
		Set value		1.05

Papal Arms — D3

Photo. & Engr.
1968, May 28 Wmk. 235 Perf. 14

J19	D3	10 l	black, grysh bl	15 15
J20	D3	20 l	black, pale bl	15 15
J21	D3	50 l	black, pale lil rose	15 15
J22	D3	60 l	black, gray	15 15

J23	D3	100 l	black, dull yel	15 15
J24	D3	180 l	black, bluish lil	22 22
			Set value	58 58

PARCEL POST STAMPS

Regular Issue of 1929 **PER PACCHI** Overprinted

1931 Unwmk. Perf. 14

Q1	A1	5c	dk brown & pink	38 30
Q2	A1	10c	dk grn & lt grn	38 30
Q3	A1	20c	violet & lilac	4.75 5.50
Q4	A1	25c	dk bl & lt bl	6.25 4.25
Q5	A1	30c	indigo & yel	9.25 4.25
Q6	A1	50c	indigo & sal buff	9.25 4.25
Q7	A1	75c	brn car & gray	2.75 2.75

Overprinted **PER PACCHI**

Q8	A2	80c	carmine rose	1.65 1.90
Q9	A2	1.25 l	dark blue	2.75 2.00
Q10	A2	2 l	olive brown	55 85
a.		Inverted overprint		325.00 475.00
Q11	A2	2.50 l	red orange	55 85
a.		Double overprint		225.00
b.		Inverted overprint		500.00
Q12	A2	5 l	dark green	55 85
Q13	A2	10 l	olive black	55 85
a.		Double overprint		325.00

Special Delivery Stamps of 1929 **PER PACCHI** Overprinted Vertically

Q14	SD1	2 l	carmine rose	55 85
Q15	SD1	2.50 l	dark blue	55 85
		Nos. Q1-Q15 (15)		40.71 30.60
		Set, never hinged		95.00

VENEZUELA

LOCATION — Northern coast of South America, bordering on the Caribbean Sea
GOVT. — Republic
AREA — 352,143 sq. mi.
POP. — 15,260,000 (est. 1984)
CAPITAL — Caracas

100 Centavos = 8 Reales = 1 Peso
100 Centesimos = 1 Venezolano (1879)
100 Centimos = 1 Bolivar (1880)

Watermark

Wmk. 346

Catalogue values for unused stamps in this country are for Never Hinged items, beginning with Scott 743 in the regular postage section, Scott B2 in the semi-postal section, Scott C709 in the airpost section, and Scott E1 in the special delivery section.

Values of early Venezuela stamps vary according to condition. Quotations for Nos. 1-21 are for fine copies. Very fine to superb specimens sell at much higher prices, and inferior or poor copies sell at reduced prices, depending on the condition of the individual specimen.

Coat of Arms — A1

Arms — A2

Eagle — A3

Fine Impression
No Dividing Line Between Stamps
1859, Jan. 1 Unwmk. Litho. *Imperf.*

1	A1	½r yellow	17.50	7.00
a.		½r orange	20.00	8.00
b.		Greenish paper	200.00	
2	A1	1r blue	250.00	16.00
3	A1	2r red	32.50	11.00
a.		2r dull rose red	40.00	13.00
b.		Half used as 1r on cover		200.00
c.		Greenish paper	200.00	125.00

Coarse Impression
1859-62
Thick Paper

4	A1	½r orange ('61)	8.00	3.00
a.		½r yellow ('59)	425.00	20.00
b.		½r olive yellow	650.00	30.00
c.		Bluish paper	525.00	
d.		½r dull rose (error)		
5	A1	1r blue ('62)	14.00	8.75
a.		1r pale blue	25.00	9.25
b.		1r dark blue	25.00	9.25
c.		Half used as ½r on cover		200.00
d.		Bluish paper	175.00	
6	A1	2r red ('62)	22.50	12.50
a.		2r dull rose	27.50	14.00
b.		Tête bêche pair	4,500.	3,250.
c.		Half used as 1r on cover		165.00
d.		Bluish paper	200.00	

In the fine impression, the background lines of the shield are more sharply drawn. In the coarse impression, the shading lines at each end of the scroll inscribed "LIBERTAD" are usually very heavy. Stamps of the coarse impression are closer together, and there is usually a dividing line between them.

Nos. 1-3 exist on thick paper and on bluish paper. Nos. 1-6 exist on pelure paper.

The greenish paper varieties (Nos. 1b and 3c) and the bluish paper varieties were not regularly issued.

🏛 🏛 🏛 🏛 🏛 🏛 🏛

VENEZUELA
MINT & USED

WANT LISTS INVITED
FOR ALL SINGLES, 19th & 20th CENTURY COVERS, ERRORS, AND LOCAL STAMPS.

NEW ISSUE SERVICE AVAILABLE!
• YEAR UNITS •

WE ALSO BUY BETTER ITEMS!

FILATELIA P.M.
ADDRESS...USA:
P.O. BOX 402187
Miami Beach, Florida 33140
Phone: 305-633-7500

VENEZUELA:
C.C.C.T. Apartado 64825
Chuao - Caracas 1064
Phone: 011-58-2-959-1203,
011-59-2-959-6651
FAX: 011-58-2-959-5230

🏛 🏛 🏛 🏛 🏛 🏛 🏛

1862　　　　　　　　　　　**Litho.**

7	A2	¼c green	14.00	80.00
8	A2	½c dull lilac	22.50	150.00
9	A2	1c gray brown	32.50	170.00

Counterfeits are plentiful. Forged cancellations abound on Nos. 7-17.

1863-64

10	A3	½c pale red ('64)	40.00	65.00
a.		½c red	45.00	100.00
11	A3	1c slate ('64)	45.00	75.00
12	A3	½r orange	5.50	2.50
13	A3	1r blue	13.00	6.00
a.		1r pale blue	22.50	10.00
b.		Half used as ½r on cover		100.00
14	A3	2r green	18.00	16.00
a.		2r deep yellow green	22.50	16.00
b.		Quarter used as ½r on cover		200.00
c.		Half used as 1r on cover		150.00

Counterfeits exist.

Redrawn
1865

15	A3	½r orange	3.00	1.75
a.		½r yellow	3.00	1.75

The redrawn stamp has a broad "N" in "FEDER-ACION." "MEDIO REAL" and "FEDERACION" are in thin letters. There are 52 instead of 49 pearls in the circle.

The status of No. 15 has been questioned.

A4

Simón Bolívar — A5

1865-70

16	A4	½c yel grn ('67)	165.00	250.00
17	A4	1c bl grn ('67)	165.00	200.00
18	A4	½r brn vio (thin paper)	6.50	1.50
19	A4	½r lil rose ('70)	6.50	2.00
a.		½r brownish rose	6.50	3.50
b.		Tête bêche pair	90.00	125.00
20	A4	1r vermilion	32.50	12.00
a.		Half used as ½r on cover		100.00
21	A4	2r yellow	110.00	60.00
a.		Half used as 1r on cover		300.00
b.		Quarter used as ½r on cover		350.00

This issue is known unofficially rouletted. Postal forgeries exist of the ½r. For overprints see Nos. 37-48.

Overprinted in Very Small Upright Letters
"Bolivar Sucre Miranda - Decreto de 27 de Abril de 1870",
or "Decreto de 27 de Junio 1870" in Slanting Letters

(The "Junio" overprint is continuously repeated, in four lines arranged in two pairs, with the second line of each pair inverted.)

Un	1	Siete	7
Dos	2	Nueve	9
Tres	3	Quince	15
Cuatro	4	Veinte	20
Cinco	5	Cincuenta	50

1871-76　　　　　　　　　　**Litho.**

22	A5	1c yellow	75	25
a.		1c orange	1.25	42
b.		1c brown orange ('76)	1.25	25
c.		1c pale buff ('76)	1.25	38
d.		Laid paper	2.50	50
23	A5	2c yellow	1.25	38
a.		2c orange	3.50	38
b.		2c brown orange	3.00	65
c.		2c pale buff ('76)	3.00	38
d.		Laid paper	3.00	50
e.		Frame inverted	4,000.	3,000.
24	A5	3c yellow	2.00	50
a.		3c orange	2.50	1.25
b.		3c pale buff ('76)	4.50	1.50
25	A5	4c yellow	2.50	50
a.		4c orange	4.00	1.10
b.		4c brown orange ('76)	4.00	1.10
c.		4c buff ('76)	4.00	1.10
26	A5	5c yellow	2.50	50
a.		5c orange	2.50	75
b.		5c pale buff ('76)	2.50	75
c.		Laid paper	5.50	75

27	A5	1r rose	2.50	38
a.		1r pale red	2.50	38
b.		Laid paper	4.50	75
28	A5	2r rose	4.00	65
a.		2r pale red	4.00	65
b.		Laid paper	10.00	2.00
29	A5	3r rose	4.50	65
a.		3r pale red	4.50	65
30	A5	5r rose	4.50	85
a.		5r pale red	4.50	85
31	A5	7r rose	5.50	2.00
a.		7r pale red	5.50	2.00
32	A5	9r green	14.00	3.75
a.		9r olive green	14.00	5.00
33	A5	15r green	27.50	7.50
a.		15r gray green ('76)	27.50	7.50
b.		Frame inverted	8,000.	6,500.
34	A5	20r green	65.00	12.50
a.		Laid paper	100.00	32.50
35	A5	30r green	300.00	100.00
a.		30r gray green ('76)	575.00	150.00
b.		Double overprint		
36	A5	50r green	1,000.	275.00
a.		50r gray green ('76)		

These stamps were made available for postage and revenue by official decree, and were the only stamps sold for postage in Venezuela from Mar., 1871 to Aug., 1873.

Due to lack of canceling stamps, the majority of specimens were canceled with pen marks. Fiscal cancellations were also made with the pen. The values quoted are for pen-canceled copies.

Different settings were used for the different overprints. Stamps with the upright letters were issued in 1871. Those with the slanting letters in one double line were issued in 1872-73. Specimens with the slanting overprint in two double lines were issued starting in 1874 from several different settings, those of 1877-78 showing much coarser impressions of the design than the earlier issues. The 7r and 9r are not known with this overprint. Stamps on laid paper (1875) are from a separate setting.

Stamps and Types of 1866-67
Overprinted in Two Lines of Very Small Letters Repeated Continuously
Overprinted "Estampillas de Correo - Contrasena"

1873, July 1

37	A4	½r pale rose	55.00	10.00
a.		½r rose	55.00	10.00
b.		Inverted overprint	115.00	42.50
c.		Tête bêche pair	2,500.	1,900.
38	A4	1r vermilion	65.00	17.50
a.		Inverted overprint	375.00	160.00
39	A4	2r yellow	125.00	62.50
a.		Inverted overprint	375.00	160.00

Overprinted "Contrasena - Estampillas de Correo"

1873, Nov.

40	A4	1c gray lil	22.50	25.00
a.		Inverted overprint	5.50	15.00
41	A4	2c green	85.00	70.00
a.		Inverted overprint	32.50	42.50
42	A4	½r rose	55.00	10.00
a.		Inverted overprint	22.50	3.00
b.		½r pink	50.00	9.25
43	A4	1r vermilion	65.00	17.50
a.		Inverted overprint	27.50	7.50
44	A4	2r yellow	225.00	100.00
a.		Inverted overprint	95.00	40.00

Overprinted "Contrasena - Estampilla de Correos"

1875

45	A4	½r rose	65.00	7.50
a.		Inverted overprint	110.00	20.00
b.		Double overprint	145.00	80.00
46	A4	1r vermilion	95.00	12.00
a.		Inverted overprint	175.00	70.00
b.		Tête bêche pair	3,250.	2,750.

Overprinted "Estampillas de correo - Contrasena"

1876-77

47	A4	½r rose	65.00	7.50
a.		½r pink	65.00	7.50
b.		Inverted overprint	65.00	7.50
c.		Both lines of overprint read "Con-trasena"	75.00	17.50
d.		Both lines of overprint read "Es-tampillas de correo"	75.00	17.50
e.		Double overprint	125.00	35.00
48	A4	1r vermilion ('77)	75.00	20.00
a.		Inverted overprint	85.00	24.00
b.		Tête bêche pair	2,250.	2,500.

On Nos. 47 and 48 "correo" has a small "c" instead of a capital. Nos. 45 and 46 have the overprint in slightly larger letters than the other stamps of the 1873-76 issues.

Simón Bolívar
A6　　　　　A7

Overprinted "Decreto de 27 Junio 1870" Twice, One Line Inverted

1879

49	A6	1c yellow	2.50	20
a.		1c orange	3.50	20
b.		1c olive yellow	4.00	1.00
50	A6	5c yellow	3.50	50
a.		5c orange	2.50	75
b.		Double overprint	20.00	10.00
51	A6	10c blue	5.00	50
52	A6	30c blue	6.25	1.00
53	A6	50c blue	7.50	1.00
54	A6	90c blue	30.00	6.25
55	A7	1v rose red	65.00	8.75
56	A7	3v rose red	110.00	35.00
57	A7	5v rose red	190.00	65.00

In 1879 and the early part of 1880 there were no regular postage stamps in Venezuela and the stamps inscribed "Escuelas" were permitted to serve for postal as well as revenue purposes. Postally canceled copies are extremely scarce. Values quoted are for stamps with cancellations of banks or business houses or with pen cancellations. Copies with pen marks removed are sometimes offered as unused stamps, or may have fraudulent postal cancellations added.

Nos. 49-57 exist without overprint. These probably are revenue stamps.

A8　　　　　A9

1880　　　　　　　　　　　**Perf. 11**

58	A8	5c yellow	1.25	15
a.		5c orange	1.25	20
b.		Printed on both sides	150.00	85.00
59	A8	10c yellow	2.00	20
a.		10c orange	2.00	20
60	A8	25c yellow	1.75	25
a.		25c orange	2.00	32
b.		Printed on both sides	110.00	52.50
c.		Impression of 5c on back	175.00	90.00
61	A8	50c yellow	3.50	30
a.		50c orange	4.00	32
b.		Half used as 25c on cover		18.00
c.		Printed on both sides	150.00	90.00
d.		Impression of 25c on back	150.00	90.00
62	A9	1b pale blue	8.75	75
63	A9	2b pale blue	14.00	85
64	A9	5b pale blue	32.50	75
a.		Half used as 2½b on cover		200.00
65	A9	10b rose red	165.00	52.50
66	A9	20b rose red	1,000.	165.00
67	A9	25b rose red	4,250.	500.00

See note on used values below No. 57.

Bolívar — A10

1880　　　**Litho.**　　　**Perf. 11**
Thick or Thin Paper

68	A10	5c blue	7.50	4.00
a.		Printed on both sides	200.00	125.00
69	A10	10c rose	12.50	7.50
a.		10c carmine	12.50	7.50
b.		Double impression	80.00	65.00
c.		Horiz. pair, imperf. btwn.	65.00	65.00
70	A10	10c scarlet	15.00	8.00
a.		Horiz. pair, imperf. btwn.	65.00	65.00
71	A10	25c yellow	7.50	4.00
b.		Thick paper	20.00	10.00
72	A10	50c brown	40.00	20.00
a.		50c deep brown	40.00	20.00
b.		Printed on both sides	200.00	125.00
73	A10	1b green	60.00	30.00
a.		Horiz. pair, imperf. btwn.	250.00	250.00
		Nos. 68-73 (6)	142.50	73.50

Nos. 68 to 73 were used for the payment of postage on letters to be sent abroad and the Escuelas stamps were then restricted to internal use.

Counterfeits of this issue exist in a great variety of shades as well as in wrong colors. They are on thick and thin paper, white or toned, and imperf. or perforated 11, 12 and compound. They are also found tête bêche. Counterfeits of Nos. 68 to 72 inclusive often have a diagonal line across the "S" of "CENTS" and a short line from the bottom of that letter to the frame below it. Originals of No. 73 show parts of a frame around "BOLIVAR."

Simón Bolívar
A11   A12

A13   A14

A15

1882, Aug. 1	Engr.	Perf. 12	
74	A11	5c blue	50	20
75	A12	10c red brown	50	20
76	A13	25c yellow brown	65	25
a.		Printed on both sides	50.00	27.50
77	A14	50c green	1.50	40
78	A15	1b violet	2.50	1.00
		Nos. 74-78 (5)	5.65	2.05

Nos. 75-78 exist imperf. Value, set $32.50.
See Nos. 88, 92-95. For surcharges and overprints see Nos. 100-103, 108-112.

A16   A17

A18   A19

A20   A21

A22   A23

1882-88

79	A16	5c blue green	15	15
80	A17	10c brown	15	15
81	A18	25c orange	15	15
82	A19	50c blue	15	15
83	A20	1b vermilion	15	15
84	A21	3b dull vio ('88)	15	15

85	A22	10b dark brn ('88)	50	50
86	A23	20b plum ('88)	65	65
		Set value	1.75	1.50

By official decree, dated Apr. 14, 1882, stamps of types A11 to A15 were to be used for foreign postage and those of types A16 to A23 for inland correspondence and fiscal use.
Issue date: Nos. 79-83, Aug. 1.
See Nos. 87, 89-91, 96-99. For surcharges and overprints see Nos. 104-107, 114-122.

1887-88		Litho.	Perf. 11	
87	A16	5c gray green	25	18
88	A13	25c yel brown	42.50	15.00
89	A18	25c orange	38	32
90	A20	1b org red ('88)	3.50	75
		Perf. 14		
91	A16	5c gray green	70.00	22.50

Stamps of type A16, perf. 11 and 14, are from a new die with "ESCUELAS" in smaller letters. Stamps of the 1887-88 issue, perf. 12, and a 50c dark blue, perf. 11 or 12, are believed by experts to be from printer's waste.
Counterfeits of No. 91 have been made by perforating printers waste of No. 96.

		Rouletted 8		
92	A11	5c blue	30.00	15.00
93	A13	25c yel brown	12.00	7.50
94	A14	50c green	12.00	7.50
95	A15	1b purple	24.00	15.00

1887-88				
96	A16	5c green	15	15
97	A18	25c orange	15	15
98	A19	50c dark blue	38	38
99	A21	3b purple ('88)	1.90	1.90

The so-called imperforate varieties of Nos. 92 to 99, and the pin perforated 50c dark blue, type A19, are believed to be from printer's waste.

Stamps of 1882-88 Handstamp Surcharged in Violet

1892			Perf. 12	
100	A11	25c on 5c blue	30.00	30.00
101	A12	25c on 10c red brn	12.00	12.00
102	A13	1b on 25c yel brn	12.00	12.00
103	A14	1b on 50c grn	13.50	13.50

See note after No. 107.

1892				
104	A16	25c on 5c bl grn	10.00	6.00
105	A17	25c on 10c brown	10.00	6.00
106	A18	1b on 25c orange	12.50	7.00
107	A19	1b on 50c blue	17.50	7.00

Counterfeits of this surcharge abound.

Stamps of 1882-88 Overprinted in Red or Black:

1893				
108	A11	5c blue (R)	50	20
a.		Inverted overprint	3.25	3.25
b.		Double overprint	16.00	16.00
109	A12	10c red brn (Bk)	65	65
a.		Inverted overprint	4.00	4.00
b.		Double overprint	16.00	16.00
110	A13	25c yel brn (R)	50	25
a.		Inverted overprint	5.25	5.25
b.		Double overprint	16.00	16.00
c.		25c yel brn (Bk)	250.00	250.00
111	A14	50c green (R)	65	40
a.		Inverted overprint	5.25	5.25
b.		Double overprint	27.50	27.50
112	A15	1b pur (R)	1.50	60
a.		Inverted overprint	10.00	10.00
		Nos. 108-112 (5)	3.80	2.10

1893				
114	A16	5c bl grn (R)	15	15
a.		Inverted overprint	3.25	3.25
b.		Double overprint	5.25	5.25

115	A17	10c brn (R)	15	15
a.		Inverted overprint	3.25	3.25
116	A18	25c org (R)	15	15
a.		Inverted overprint	3.25	3.25
117	A18	25c org (Bk)	2.25	2.00
a.		Inverted overprint	8.25	5.00
118	A19	50c blue (R)	15	15
a.		Inverted overprint	3.25	3.25
119	A20	1b ver (Bk)	45	22
a.		Inverted overprint	4.00	4.00
120	A21	3b dl vio (R)	60	30
a.		Double overprint	8.25	8.25
121	A22	10b dk brn (R)	1.75	1.50
a.		Double overprint	10.00	10.00
b.		Inverted overprint	20.00	20.00
122	A23	20b plum (Bk)	1.50	1.50
a.		Double overprint	10.00	20.00
b.		Inverted overprint		
		Nos. 114-122 (9)	7.15	6.12

Counterfeits exist.

Simón Bolívar
A24   A25

1893			Engr.	
123	A24	5c red brn	60	15
124	A24	10c blue	2.50	60
125	A24	25c magenta	12.00	32
126	A24	50c brn vio	2.50	40
127	A24	1b green	3.25	60
		Nos. 123-127 (5)	20.85	2.07

Many shades exist in this issue, but their values do not vary.

1893				
128	A25	5c gray	15	15
129	A25	10c green	15	15
130	A25	25c blue	15	15
131	A25	50c orange	15	15
132	A25	1b red vio	20	15
133	A25	3b red	35	15
134	A25	10b dl vio	65	50
135	A25	20b red brn	2.00	1.75
		Nos. 128-135 (8)	3.80	
		Set value		2.60

By decree of Nov. 28, 1892, the stamps inscribed "Correos" were to be used for external postage and those inscribed "Instruccion" were for internal postage and revenue purposes.
For surcharge see No. 230.

After July 1, 1895, stamps inscribed "Escuelas" or "Instruccion" were no longer available for postage.

Landing of Columbus
A26

1893			Perf. 12	
136	A26	25c magenta	8.00	50

4th cent. of the discovery of the mainland of South America, also participation of Venezuela in the Intl. Exhib. at Chicago in 1893.

Map of Venezuela
A27

1896			Litho.	
137	A27	5c yel grn	2.50	2.00
a.		5c apple green	2.50	2.00
138	A27	10c blue	2.50	2.00
139	A27	25c yellow	3.00	4.00
a.		25c orange	3.00	4.00
140	A27	50c rose red	40.00	20.00
a.		Tête bêche pair	40.00	40.00
b.		50c red	40.00	40.00
c.		Tête bêche pair	100.00	100.00
141	A27	1b violet	30.00	20.00
		Nos. 137-141 (5)	78.00	48.00

Gen. Francisco Antonio Gabriel de Miranda (1752-1816).
These stamps were in use from July 4 to Nov. 4, 1896. Later usage is known.

Bolívar — A28

There are many forgeries of this issue. They include faked errors, imperforate stamps and many tête bêche. The paper of the originals is thin, white and semi-transparent. The gum is shiny and crackled. The paper of the reprints is often thick and opaque. The gum is usually dull, smooth, thin and only slightly adhesive.

1899-1901			Engr.	
142	A28	5c dk grn	75	20
143	A28	10c red	1.00	25
144	A28	25c blue	1.20	40
145	A28	50c gray blk	1.50	75
146	A28	50c org ('01)	1.20	38
147	A28	1b yel grn	25.00	12.50
149	A28	2b orange	300.00	190.00
		Nos. 142-147,149 (7)	330.65	204.48

Stamps of 1899 Overprinted in Black

1900				
150	A28	5c dk grn	75	20
a.		Inverted overprint	4.00	4.00
151	A28	10c red	75	25
a.		Inverted overprint	5.25	5.25
b.		Double overprint	10.50	10.50
152	A28	25c blue	5.00	75
a.		Inverted overprint	10.50	10.50
153	A28	50c gray blk	2.50	38
a.		Inverted overprint	9.25	9.25
154	A28	1b yel grn	1.00	50
a.		Double overprint	13.00	13.00
b.		Inverted overprint	9.25	9.25
155	A28	2b orange	1.75	1.25
a.		Inverted overprint	27.50	27.50
b.		Double overprint	32.50	32.50
		Nos. 150-155 (6)	11.75	3.33

Initials are those of R. T. Mendoza.
Counterfeit overprints exist, especially of inverted and doubled varieties.

Bolivar Type of 1899-1903 **1900** Overprinted

1900				
156	A28	5c dk grn	150.00	150.00
157	A28	10c red	150.00	150.00
158	A28	25c blue	300.00	150.00
159	A28	50c yel orange	18.00	1.00
160	A28	1b slate	1.00	75
a.		Without overprint	4,000.	

Overprinted

1900, Aug. 14				
161	A28	5c green	5.00	35
162	A28	10c red	4.00	65
163	A28	25c blue	5.00	60
		Inverted Overprint		
161a	A28	5c	8.00	5.25
162a	A28	10c	8.00	5.25
163a	A28	25c	10.00	5.25

Overprint exists on each value without "Castro" or without "1900."

Type of 1893 Surcharged

CORREOS Vale B 0,05 1904

1904, Jan.   Perf. 12
230	A25	5c on 50c green	50	40
a.		"Vele"	18.00	18.00
b.		Surcharge reading up	75	35
c.		Double surcharge	18.00	18.00

Gen. José de   Pres. Cipriano
Sucre — A35   Castro — A37

1904-09   Engr.
231	A35	5c bl grn	25	15
232	A35	10c carmine	32	15
233	A35	15c violet	55	16
234	A35	25c dp ultra	4.00	16
235	A35	50c plum	55	25
236	A35	1b plum	60	25
		Nos. 231-236 (6)	6.27	1.12

Issue date: 15c, Dec. 1909. Others, July 1, 1904.

1905, July 5   Litho.   Perf. 11½
245	A37	5c vermilion	2.50	2.50
a.		5c carmine	3.75	3.75
246	A37	10c dk bl	4.00	3.25
247	A37	25c yellow	1.25	1.00

National Congress. Issued for interior postage
only. Valid only for 90 days.
Various part-perforate varieties of Nos. 245-247
exist. Value, $15-$30.

Liberty — A38

1910, Apr. 19   Engr.   Perf. 12
249	A38	25c dark blue	10.00	55

Centenary of national independence.

Francisco de   Rafael
Miranda   Urdaneta
A39   A40

Bolívar — A41

1911   Litho.   Perf. 11½x12
250	A39	5c dp grn	30	15
251	A39	10c carmine	30	15
252	A40	15c gray	4.00	25
253	A40	25c dp bl	2.00	38
a.		Imperf., pair	40.00	50.00
254	A41	50c purple	2.50	30
255	A41	1b yellow	2.50	1.25
		Nos. 250-255 (6)	11.60	2.48

The 50c with center in blue was never issued
although copies were postmarked by favor.
The centers of Nos. 250-255 were separately
printed and often vary in shade from the rest of the
design. In a second printing of the 5c and 10c, the
entire design was printed at one time.

Redrawn

1913
255A	A40	15c gray	2.50	1.65
255B	A40	25c deep blue	1.25	45
255C	A41	50c purple	1.25	45

The redrawn stamps have two berries instead of
one at top of the left spray; a berry has been added
over the "C" and "S" of "Centimos"; and the lowest leaf at the right is cut by the corner square.

Simón Bolívar
A42   A43

1914, July   Engr.   Perf. 13½, 14, 15
256	A42	5c yel grn	24.00	30
257	A42	10c scarlet	21.00	25
258	A42	25c dark blue	4.00	15

Printed by the American Bank Note Co.
Different frames.

1915-23   Perf. 12
259	A43	5c green	3.25	20
260	A43	10c vermilion	7.75	38
261	A43	10c claret ('22)	7.75	70
262	A43	15c dull ol grn	7.50	42
263	A43	25c ultra	5.00	20
a.		25c blue	10.00	50
264	A43	40c dull green	17.50	7.50
265	A43	50c dp violet	4.50	50
266	A43	50c ultra ('23)	11.00	3.75
267	A43	75c lt blue	45.00	15.00
		75c greenish blue	45.00	15.00
268	A43	1b dark gray	20.00	4.00
		Nos. 259-268 (10)	129.25	32.65

See Nos. 269-285. For surcharges see Nos. 307,
309-310.

Type of 1915-23 Issue
Printed by Waterlow & Sons, Ltd.
Re-engraved

1924-39   Perf. 12½
269	A43	5c orange brn	40	15
a.		5c yellow brown	40	15
b.		Horiz. pair, imperf. between	25.00	40.00
270	A43	5c green ('39)	7.50	80
271	A43	7½c yel grn ('39)	75	25
272	A43	10c dk green	15	15
273	A43	10c dk car ('39)	2.50	20
274	A43	15c olive grn	1.50	35
275	A43	15c brown ('27)	25	15
276	A43	25c ultra	1.50	15
277	A43	25c red ('28)	15	15
a.		Horiz. pair, imperf. btwn.	50.00	85.00
278	A43	40c dp blue ('25)	40	15
279	A43	40c slate bl ('39)	5.00	75
280	A43	50c dk blue	40	15
281	A43	50c dk pur ('39)	6.00	70
282	A43	1b black	40	20
283	A43	3b yel org ('25)	1.25	70
284	A43	3b red org ('39)	10.00	3.25
285	A43	5b dull vio ('25)	12.00	6.50
		Nos. 269-285 (17)	50.15	14.75

Perf. 14
269c	A43	5c	5.25	1.25
272a	A43	10c	5.25	1.25
274a	A43	15c	6.50	2.00
276a	A43	25c	8.00	3.00
280a	A43	50c	25.00	8.50
282a	A43	1b	32.50	20.00

The re-engraved stamps may readily be distinguished from the 1915 issue by the perforation and
sometimes by the colors. The designs differ in
many minor details which are too minute for illustration or description.

Bolívar and
Sucre
A44

Perf. 11½x12, 12
1924, Dec. 1   Litho.
286	A44	25c grayish blue	2.25	40

Redrawn
286A	A44	25c ultra	2.75	65

Centenary of the Battle of Ayacucho.
The redrawn stamp has a whiter effect with less
shading in the faces. Bolívar's ear is clearly visible
and the outline of his aquiline nose is broken.

A45   A46

Revenue Stamps Surcharged in Black or Red
1926   Perf. 12, 12½
287	A45	5c on 1b ol grn	50	25
a.		Double surcharge	8.00	8.00
b.		Pair, one without surcharge	12.00	12.00
c.		Inverted surcharge	8.00	8.00
288	A46	25c on 5c dk brn (R)	50	30
a.		Inverted surcharge	8.00	8.00
b.		Double surcharge	8.00	8.00

View of Ciudad
Bolívar and
General J.V.
Gómez — A47

1928, July 21   Litho.   Perf. 12
289	A47	10c deep green	65	40
a.		Imperf., pair	40.00	

25th anniversary of the Battle of Ciudad Bolívar
and the foundation of peace in Venezuela.

Simón Bolívar
A48   A49

1930, Dec. 9
290	A48	5c yellow	75	30
291	A48	10c dark blue	75	20
292	A48	25c rose red	75	20

Imperf., Pairs
290a	A48	5c	5.25	5.25
291a	A48	10c	6.50	6.50
292a	A48	25c	10.50	10.50

Death centenary of Simón Bolívar (1783-1830),
South American liberator.
Nos. 290-292 exist part-perforate, including pairs
imperf. between, imperf. horiz., imperf. vert. Value
range, $6-12.

Various Frames
Bluish Winchester Security Paper
1932-38   Engr.   Perf. 12½
293	A49	5c violet	24	15
294	A49	7½c dk green ('37)	60	24
295	A49	10c green	32	15
296	A49	15c yellow	80	16
297	A49	22½c dp car ('38)	2.00	40
298	A49	25c red	65	15
299	A49	37½c ultra ('36)	2.50	1.25
300	A49	40c indigo	2.50	16
301	A49	50c olive grn	2.50	24
302	A49	1b lt blue	3.25	52
303	A49	3b brown	25.00	10.00
304	A49	5b yellow brn	32.50	13.00
		Nos. 293-304 (12)	72.86	26.42

For surcharges see Nos. 308, 318-319, C223.

Arms of Bolívar — A50

1933, July 24   Litho.   Perf. 11
306	A50	25c brown red	2.00	1.50
a.		Imperf., pair	32.50	32.50

150th anniv. of the birth of Simón Bolívar. Valid
only to Aug. 21.

1933

Stamps of 1924-32
Surcharged in
Black: (Blocks of
Surcharge in Color
of stamps)

7½

1933
307	A43	7½c on 10c grn	40	20
a.		Double surcharge	2.50	2.50
b.		Inverted surcharge	3.25	3.25
308	A49	22½c on 25c (#298)	1.40	70
309	A43	22½c on 25c (#277)	1.25	1.25
a.		Double surcharge	10.00	10.00
310	A43	37½c on 40c dp bl	1.50	75
a.		Double surcharge	11.50	11.50
b.		Inverted surcharge	8.25	8.25

Nurse and   River
Child — A51   Scene — A52

Gathering   Cattle Raising — A54
Cacao
Pods — A53

Plowing
A55

Perf. 11, 11½ or Compound
1937, July 1   Litho.
311	A51	5c deep violet	40	28
312	A52	10c dk slate grn	40	15
313	A53	15c yellow brn	80	40
314	A51	25c cerise	80	24
315	A54	50c yellow grn	5.00	3.25
316	A55	3b red orange	8.75	6.00
317	A51	5b lt brown	18.00	12.00
		Nos. 311-317 (7)	34.15	22.32

Nos. 311-317 exist imperforate. Value for set
$75. Nos. 311-315 exist in pairs, imperf. between;
value range, $20-$30.
For overprints and surcharges see Nos. 321-324,
345, 376-377, 380-384.

1937

No. 300
Surcharged in
Black

VALE POR
25

1937, July   Perf. 12½
318	A49	25c on 40c indigo	5.00	65
a.		Double surcharge	16.00	16.00
a.		Double surcharge	16.00	16.00
b.		Inverted surcharge	13.00	13.00
c.		Triple surcharge	32.50	32.50

1937

Surcharged

VALE POR
25

319	A49	25c on 40c indigo	325.00	275.00
a.		Double surcharge		

A56

1937, Oct. 28   Litho.   Perf. 10½
320 A56 25c blue   1.00 40

Acquisition of the Port of La Guaira by the Government from the British Corporation, June 3, 1937. Exists imperf. See Nos. C64-C65.
A redrawn printing of No. 320, with top inscription beginning "Nacionalización . . ." was prepared but not issued. Value, $40.
For surcharge see No. 385.

Teresa Carreño
A60

1938, June 12   Perf. 11½x12
343 A60 25c blue   4.00 40

Teresa Carreno, Venezuelan pianist, whose remains were repatriated Feb. 14, 1938.
For surcharge see No. 386.

Stamps of 1937 Overprinted in Black

RESELLADO
1937-1938

1937, Dec. 17   Perf. 11, 11½
321 A51   5c deep violet   3.75 2.00
322 A52 10c dk slate grn   1.00   50
 a.   Inverted overprint   13.00 13.00
323 A51 25c cerise   75   42
 a.   Inverted overprint   16.00 16.00
324 A55   3b red orange   150.00 75.00

Part-perforate pairs exist of Nos. 321-322 and 324. Value range, $12.50 to $125.
See Nos. C66-C78.

Gathering Coffee Beans — A57

Simón Bolívar — A58

Post Office, Caracas — A59

1938   Engr.   Perf. 12
325 A57   5c green   30   15
326 A57   5c deep green   30   15
327 A58 10c car rose   50   15
328 A58 10c dp rose   50   15
329 A59 15c dk violet   1.00   20
330 A59 15c olive grn   65   20
331 A58 25c lt blue   30   15
332 A58 25c dk blue   30   15
333 A58 37½c dk blue   6.00 2.50
334 A58 37½c lt blue   2.00   65
335 A59 40c sepia   15.00 4.00
336 A59 40c black   12.50 4.00
337 A57 50c olive grn   20.00 4.00
338 A57 50c dull violet   7.00 4.00
339 A58   1b dp brown   8.25 4.00
340 A58   1b black brown   12.50 1.00
341 A57   3b orange   70.00 26.00
342 A59   5b black   8.75 4.00
      Nos. 325-342 (18)   165.85 52.10

See Nos. 400 and 412.

Teresa Carreño
A60

1938, July 24   Perf. 12
344 A61 25c dark blue   4.50 42

"The Day of the Worker."
For surcharge see No. 387.

VALE
Type of 1937 Surcharged in Black
Bs. 0,40
1938

1938   Litho.   Perf. 11, 11½
345 A51 40c on 5b lt brn   7.00 3.00
 a.   Inverted surcharge   21.00 21.00

Gen. José I. Paz Castillo, Postmaster of Venezuela, 1859 — A62

1939, Apr. 19   Engr.   Perf. 12½
348 A62 10c carmine   1.75 40

80th anniv. of the first Venezuelan stamp.

View of Ojeda — A63

1939, June 24   Photo.
349 A63 25c dull blue   6.50 50

Founding of city of Ojeda.

Cristóbal Mendoza
A64

Diego Urbaneja
A65

1939, Oct. 14   Engr.   Perf. 13
350 A64   5c green   32   16
351 A64 10c dk car rose   32   16
352 A64 15c dull lilac   80   24
353 A64 25c brt ultra   65   16
354 A64 37½c dark blue   12.00 6.00
355 A64 50c lt olive grn   12.00 4.00
356 A64   1b dark brown   5.00 3.25
      Nos. 350-356 (7)   31.09 13.97

Cristóbal Mendoza (1772-1839), postmaster general.

1940-43   Perf. 12
357 A65   5c Prus green   35   15
357A A65 7½c dk bl grn ('43)   50   18
358 A65 15c olive   65   20
359 A65 37½c deep blue   1.00   50

360 A65 40c violet blue   75   20
361 A65 50c violet   4.00 1.00
362 A65   1b dk violet brn   2.00   65
363 A65   3b scarlet   6.00 2.50
      Nos. 357-363 (8)   15.25 5.38

See Nos. 399, 408, 410 and 411. For surcharges see Nos. 396, C226.

Battle of Carabobo, 1821 — A67

1940, June 13
365 A67 25c blue   4.50 40

150th anniversary of the birth of General José-Antonio Páez.

"Crossing the Andes" by Tito Salas — A68

1940, June 13
366 A68 25c dark blue   4.50 40

Death cent. of General Francisco Santander.

Monument and Urn containing Ashes of Simón Bolívar — A69

Bed where Simón Bolívar was Born — A70

Designs: 15c, "Christening of Bolivar" by Tito Salas. 20c, Bolivar's birthplace, Caracas. 25c, "Bolivar on Horseback" by Salas. 30c, Patio of Bolivar House, Caracas. 37½c, Patio of Bolivar's Birthplace. 50c, "Rebellion of 1812" by Salas.

1940-41
367 A69   5c turq green   22   15
368 A70 10c rose pink   22   15
369 A69 15c olive   50   15
370 A70 20c blue ('41)   85   15
371 A69 25c lt blue   50   15
372 A70 30c plum ('41)   1.25   18
373 A70 37½c dk blue   2.50   85
374 A70 50c purple   1.50   38
      Nos. 367-374 (8)   7.54
      Set value   1.80

110th anniv. of the death of Simón Bolívar.
See Nos. 397, 398, 403, 405-407 and 409. For surcharges see Nos. 375, 401-402, C224, C237-C238.

HABILITADO
1941
VALE
BS. 0,20
No. 371 Surcharged In Black

1941
375 A69 20c on 25c lt blue   50   15
 a.   Inverted surcharge   10.00 10.00

HABILITADO
Nos. 311-312 Overprinted in Black
1940

1941   Perf. 11½
376 A51   5c deep violet   1.50   38
 b.   Double overprint   10.00 10.00
 c.   Vert. pair, imperf. btwn. 14.00 14.00
 c.   Inverted overprint   20.00 10.00
377 A52 10c dk slate grn   85   25
 a.   Double overprint   13.00 13.00

Symbols of Industry
A77

Caracas Cathedral
A78

1942, Dec. 17   Litho.   Perf. 12
378 A77 10c scarlet   75   18
 a.   Imperf., pair   22.50 22.50

Grand Industrial Exposition, Caracas.

1943   Engr.
379 A78 10c rose carmine   50   15

See No. 404.

Stamps of 1937 Overprinted in Black
Resellado
1943

1943   Perf. 11, 11½
380 A51   5c deep violet   9.00 5.00
381 A52 10c dk slate grn   3.50 2.00
382 A54 50c yellow green   4.75 2.50
383 A55   3b red orange   20.00 11.00

Nos. 380 to 383 were issued for sale to philatelists and sold only in sets.

Habilitado
Stamps of 1937-38 Surcharged in Black
Vale
Bs. 0.20

1943   Perf. 11½, 10½, 12
384 A51 20c on 25c cerise   18.00 18.00
385 A56 20c on 25c blue   50.00 40.00
386 A60 20c on 25c dk blue   10.00 10.00
387 A61 20c on 25c dk blue   10.00 10.00
 a.   Inverted surcharge   25.00 25.00

Nos. 384-387 were issued for sale to philatelists and sold only in sets.

Souvenir Sheet

A79

1944, Aug. 22   Litho.   Perf. 12
Flags in Red, Yellow, Blue & Black
388 A79   Sheet of 4   16.00 16.00
 a.   5c Prussian green   3.00   80
 b.   10c rose   3.25   80
 c.   20c ultramarine   3.25 1.65
 d.   1b rose lake   4.00 2.50

80th anniv. of Intl. Red Cross and 37th anniv. of Venezuela's joining.
No. 388 exists imperf. Value $50.

Antonio José de Sucre — A80

1945, Mar. 3   Engr.   Unwmk.
389 A80   5c orange yellow   90   30
390 A80 10c dark blue   1.25   60
391 A80 20c rose pink   1.50   60
      Nos. 389-391,C206-C215 (13) 15.03 8.14

Birth of Antonio de Sucre, 150th anniv.

Andrés   Gen. Rafael
Bello — A81   Urdaneta — A82

1946, Aug. 24
392 A81 20c deep blue   65 25
393 A82 20c deep blue   65 25

80th anniversary of the death of Andrés Bello
(1780?-1865), educator and writer, and the centenary of the death of Gen. Rafael Urdaneta.
See Nos. C216-C217.

Allegory of the
Republic — A83

1946, Oct. 18   Litho.   Perf. 11½
394 A83 20c greenish blue   65 25
    Nos. 394,C218-C221 (5)   4.05 2.60

Anniversary of Revolution of October, 1945.
Exists imperf.
See Nos. C218-C221.

Anti-tuberculosis
Institute,
Maracaibo — A84

1947, Jan. 12
395 A84 20c ultra & yellow   60 25
    Nos. 395,C228-C231 (5)   4.80 3.59

12th Pan-American Health Conf., Caracas, Jan.
1947. Exists imperf. and part perf.

J. R. G.

No. 362 Surcharged in   **CORREOS**
Green   **Vale Bs. 0.15**
                          1946

396 A65 15c on 1b dk vio brn   65 25
  a. Inverted surcharge   6.00 5.00

See Nos. C223-C227.

Types of 1938-40

1947   Engr.
397 A69 5c green   15 15
398 A70 30c black   60 40
399 A65 40c red violet   40 15
400 A59 5b deep orange   32.50 16.00

R1

In 1947 a decree authorized the use of
5c and 10c revenue stamps of the above
type for franking correspondence. Other
denominations were also used unofficially.
For surcharges see Nos. 876-883.

CORREOS
Nos. 398 and 373   **Vale Bs. 0.05**
Surcharged in Red   **1947**

1947   Unwmk.   Perf. 12
401 A70 5c on 30c black   30 15
  a. Inverted surcharge   5.00 5.00

402 A70 5c on 37½c dk bl   35 15
  a. Inverted surcharge   5.00 5.00
      Set value   15

Types of 1938-43

1947-48
403 A69 5c brt ultra   15 15
404 A78 10c red   15 15
405 A69 15c rose car   38 15
406 A69 25c violet   30 15
407 A70 30c dk vio brn ('48)   38 15
408 A65 40c orange ('48)   38 15
409 A70 50c olive green   65 18
410 A65 1b deep blue   1.25 18
411 A65 3b gray   2.50 65
412 A59 5b chocolate   11.00 4.25
    Nos. 403-412 (10)   17.14 6.16

M. S.
Republica de
Venezuela
A85

Imprint: "American Bank Note Company"

1948-50   Engr.   Perf. 12
413 A85 5c blue   15 15
414 A85 7½c red org ('49)   42 22
  a. Booklet pane of 20
415 A85 10c car rose   32 15
  a. Booklet pane of 10
416 A85 15c gray ('50)   32 15
417 A85 20c sepia   20 15
418 A85 25c violet ('49)   32 15
419 A85 30c orange ('50)   2.25 1.10
420 A85 37½c brown ('49)   1.00 80
421 A85 40c olive ('50)   1.50 1.00
422 A85 50c red violet ('49)   40 15
423 A85 1b gray green   1.00 30
    Nos. 413-423 (11)   7.88 4.32

Grand Colombian Merchant Fleet. See Nos. 632-
634, C256-C271, C554-C556. For surcharges see
Nos. 450-451.

Santos   Christopher
Michelena — A86   Columbus — A87

1949, Apr. 25   Perf. 12½
424 A86 5c ultra   15 15
425 A86 10c carmine   30 15
426 A86 20c sepia   1.25 40
427 A86 1b green   4.00 1.90
    Nos. 424-427,C272-C277 (10)   11.60 5.30

Centenary of the death of Santos Michelena,
Finance Minister, and the 110th anniversary of the
Postal Convention of Bogota.

1949-50   Engr.
428 A87 5c deep ultra   25 15
429 A87 10c carmine   1.00 30
430 A87 20c dark brown   1.25 40
431 A87 1b green   3.00 1.50
    Nos. 428-431,C278-C283 (10)   11.42 4.53

450th anniversary (in 1948) of Columbus' discovery of the American mainland.
Issue dates: 5c, 10c, 1949. 20c, 1b, Jan. 1950.

Arms of
Venezuela
A88

1948
432 A88 5c blue   1.25 65
433 A88 10c red   1.50 75

The 20c and 1b, type A88, and six similar air
post stamps were prepared but not issued. Value,
set of 8, about $125.

Gen. Francisco de
Miranda — A89

1950, Mar. 28   Unwmk.   Perf. 12
434 A89 5c blue   15 15
435 A89 10c green   35 15
436 A89 15c sepia   70 30
437 A89 1b rose carmine   3.25 1.50

Bicentenary of birth of General Francisco de
Miranda.

Map and   Alonso de
Population   Ojeda — A91
Chart — A90

1950, Sept. 1
438 A90 5c blue   15 15
439 A90 10c gray   15 15
440 A90 15c sepia   18 15
441 A90 25c green   28 15
442 A90 30c red   40 15
443 A90 50c violet   80 30
444 A90 1b red brown   2.00 1.00
    Nos. 438-444 (7)   3.96
      Set value   1.80

Issued to publicize the 8th National Census of
the Americas. See Nos. C302-C310.

1950, Dec. 18   Photo.   Perf. 11½
445 A91 5c deep blue   18 15
446 A91 10c deep red   25 15
447 A91 15c slate gray   30 15
448 A91 20c ultra   1.25 50
449 A91 1b blue green   5.00 2.50
    Nos. 445-449 (5)   6.98 3.45

450th anniversary (in 1949) of the discovery of
the Gulf of Maracaibo.
See Nos. C316-C321.

Nos. 414 and 420 Surcharged in Black
RESELLADO
"5 CENTIMOS"

1951   Unwmk.   Perf. 12
450 A85 5c on 7½c red org   25 15
451 A85 10c on 37½c brn   25 15
  a. Inverted surcharge   16.00 16.00
      Set value   24

Telegraph Stamps   **Habilitado**
Surcharged in Black   **Correos**
or Red   **25 Centimos**

1951, June   Engr.
        Grayish Security Paper
452   5c on 5c brown   15 15
453   10c on 10c green   25 15
454   20c on 1b blk (R)   50 15
455   25c on 25c carmine   65 25
456   30c on 2b ol grn (R)   85 65
    Nos. 452-456 (5)   2.40
      Set value   1.15

The 5c and 10c surcharges include quotation
marks on each line and values are expressed "Bs.
0.05" etc.

Bolivar Statue,
New
York — A92

1951, July 13   Perf. 12
457 A92 5c green   20 15
458 A92 10c car rose   40 15
459 A92 20c ultra   40 15
460 A92 30c slate gray   52 24
461 A92 40c deep green   70 24
462 A92 50c red brown   1.50 52
463 A92 1b gray black   4.75 2.50
    Nos. 457-463 (7)   8.47 3.95

Relocation of the equestrian statue of Simon Bolivar in NYC, Apr. 19, 1951. See Nos. C322-C329.

Arms of Carabobo and
"Industry" — A93

1951   Unwmk.   Photo.   Perf. 11½
464 A93 5c green   15 15
465 A93 10c red   15 15
466 A93 15c brown   24 15
467 A93 20c ultra   35 16
468 A93 25c orange brn   40 20
469 A93 30c blue   85 35
470 A93 35c purple   3.25 2.75
    Nos. 464-470 (7)   5.39 3.91

Issue dates: 5c, 10c, Oct. 8. Others, Oct. 29.

Arms of Zulia and "Industry"
471 A93 5c green   15 15
472 A93 10c red   30 15
473 A93 15c brown   65 30
474 A93 20c ultra   85 45
475 A93 50c brown org   5.25 3.75
476 A93 1b dp gray grn   1.75 65
477 A93 5b rose violet   3.75 2.50
    Nos. 471-477 (7)   12.70 7.95

Issue dates: 5c, 10c, Sept. 8. Others, Sept. 20.

Arms of Anzoategui and Globe
478 A93 5c green   15 15
479 A93 10c red   15 15
480 A93 15c brown   65 30
481 A93 20c ultra   1.10 20
482 A93 40c red orange   2.25 1.10
483 A93 45c rose violet   6.75 3.75
484 A93 3b blue gray   2.50 1.25
    Nos. 478-484 (7)   13.55 6.90

Issue date: Nov. 9.

Arms of Caracas and Buildings
485 A93 5c green   38 15
486 A93 10c red   50 15
487 A93 15c brown   1.25 30
488 A93 20c ultra   2.50 30
489 A93 25c orange brn   3.75 65
490 A93 30c blue   3.25 75
491 A93 35c purple   32.50 19.00
    Nos. 485-491 (7)   44.13 21.30

Issue dates: 5c, 10c, June 20. Others, Aug. 6.

**Arms of Tachira and Agricultural
Products**
492 A93 5c green   15 15
493 A93 10c red   38 15
494 A93 15c brown   75 25
495 A93 20c ultra   1.75 45
496 A93 50c brown org   110.00 14.00
497 A93 1b dp gray grn   1.75 65
498 A93 5b dull purple   4.50 2.50
    Nos. 492-498 (7)   119.28 18.15

Issue date: Aug. 9.

**Arms of Venezuela and Statue of
Simon Bolivar**
499 A93 5c green   30 15
500 A93 10c red   22 15
501 A93 15c brown   2.25 45
502 A93 20c ultra   2.25 30
503 A93 25c orange brn   3.75 85
504 A93 30c blue   3.75 85
505 A93 35c purple   20.00 15.00
    Nos. 499-505 (7)   32.52 17.75

Issue date: Aug. 6.

1952
Arms of Miranda and Agricultural Products

506	A93	5c green	15	15
507	A93	10c red	18	15
508	A93	15c brown	45	15
509	A93	20c ultra	50	20
510	A93	25c orange brn	65	32
511	A93	30c blue	1.10	50
512	A93	35c purple	6.50	4.50
		Nos. 506-512 (7)	9.53	5.97

Arms of Aragua and Stylized Farm

513	A93	5c green	15	15
514	A93	10c red	20	15
515	A93	15c brown	40	15
516	A93	20c ultra	35	16
517	A93	25c orange brn	90	25
518	A93	30c blue	90	40
519	A93	35c purple	5.00	3.75
		Nos. 513-519 (7)	7.90	5.01

Issue date: 20c, 30c, Mar. 24.

Arms of Lara, Agricultural Products and Rope

520	A93	5c green	15	15
521	A93	10c red	15	15
522	A93	15c brown	24	16
523	A93	20c ultra	60	20
524	A93	25c orange brn	70	52
525	A93	30c blue	1.25	40
526	A93	35c purple	5.25	3.75
		Nos. 520-526 (7)	8.34	5.33

Issue date: 20c, 30c, Mar. 24.

Arms of Bolivar and Stylized Design

527	A93	5c green	15	15
528	A93	10c red	15	15
529	A93	15c brown	30	15
530	A93	20c ultra	65	20
531	A93	40c red orange	2.50	85
532	A93	45c rose violet	6.50	4.50
533	A93	3b blue gray	3.00	2.00
		Nos. 527-533 (7)	13.25	8.00

Issue date: 20c, Mar. 24.

Arms of Sucre, Palms and Seascape

534	A93	5c green	15	15
535	A93	10c red	15	15
536	A93	15c brown	75	15
537	A93	20c ultra	75	15
538	A93	40c red orange	2.50	65
539	A93	45c rose violet	9.00	5.50
540	A93	3b blue gray	2.25	1.50
		Nos. 534-540 (7)	15.55	8.25

Arms of Trujillo Surrounded by Stylized Tree

541	A93	5c green	15	15
542	A93	10c red	15	15
543	A93	15c brown	90	16
544	A93	20c ultra	90	25
545	A93	50c brown orange	5.00	3.00
546	A93	1b dp gray green	1.25	55
547	A93	5b dull purple	3.00	1.90
		Nos. 541-547 (7)	11.35	6.16

1953-54
Map of Delta Amacuro and Ship

548	A93	5c green	15	15
549	A93	10c red	15	15
550	A93	15c brown	30	15
551	A93	20c ultra	50	20
552	A93	40c red orange	1.65	1.00
553	A93	45c rose violet	7.50	4.50
554	A93	3b blue gray	2.00	1.50
		Nos. 548-554 (7)	12.25	7.65

Arms of Falcon and Stylized Oil Refinery

555	A93	5c green	15	15
556	A93	10c red	15	15
557	A93	15c brown	40	15
558	A93	20c ultra	40	15
559	A93	50c brown orange	2.00	1.00
560	A93	1b dp gray grn	1.25	80
561	A93	5b dull purple	3.75	2.00
		Nos. 555-561 (7)	8.10	4.40

Issue date: 20c, Feb. 13.

Arms of Guarico and Factory

562	A93	5c green	15	15
563	A93	10c red	15	15
564	A93	15c brown	35	16
565	A93	20c ultra	40	20
566	A93	40c red orange	1.90	1.40
567	A93	45c rose violet	4.50	2.75
568	A93	3b blue gray	1.90	1.25
		Nos. 562-568 (7)	9.35	6.06

Issue date: 20c, Feb. 13.

Arms of Merida and Church

569	A93	5c green	15	15
570	A93	10c red	15	15
571	A93	15c brown	25	16
572	A93	20c ultra	65	16
573	A93	50c brown orange	3.00	1.25
574	A93	1b dp gray green	80	55
575	A93	5b dull purple	3.00	1.65
		Nos. 569-575 (7)	8.00	4.07

Issue date: 20c, Feb. 2.

Arms of Monagas and Horses

576	A93	5c green	15	15
577	A93	10c red	15	15
578	A93	15c brown	30	20
579	A93	20c ultra	45	25
580	A93	40c red orange	2.00	75
581	A93	45c rose violet	6.25	3.75
582	A93	3b blue gray	2.50	2.00
		Nos. 576-582 (7)	11.80	7.25

Arms of Portuguesa and Forest

583	A93	5c green	15	15
584	A93	10c red	15	15
585	A93	15c brown	24	15
586	A93	20c ultra	52	15
587	A93	50c brown org	2.75	1.75
588	A93	1b dp gray grn	70	30
589	A93	5b dull purple	3.00	2.00
		Nos. 583-589 (7)	7.51	4.65

Issue date: 5c, 10c, Feb. 2.

Map of Amazonas and Orchid

590	A93	5c green	50	15
591	A93	10c red	50	15
592	A93	15c brown	1.10	15
593	A93	20c ultra	3.00	30
594	A93	40c red orange	3.50	1.00
595	A93	45c rose violet	5.50	2.75
596	A93	3b blue gray	8.00	3.00
		Nos. 590-596 (7)	22.10	7.50

Issue date: Jan. 1954.

Arms of Apure, Horse and Bird

597	A93	5c green	15	15
598	A93	10c red	15	15
599	A93	15c brown	30	15
600	A93	20c ultra	1.75	20
601	A93	50c brown org	2.25	1.75
602	A93	1b dp gray grn	75	65
603	A93	5b dull purple	4.50	2.50
		Nos. 597-603 (7)	9.85	5.55

Issue date: Jan. 1954.

Arms of Barinas, Cow and Horse

604	A93	5c green	15	15
605	A93	10c red	15	15
606	A93	15c brown	26	15
607	A93	20c ultra	1.75	24
608	A93	50c brown org	2.00	1.25
609	A93	1b dp gray grn	52	24
610	A93	5b dull purple	4.50	2.25
		Nos. 604-610 (7)	9.33	4.43

Issue date: Jan. 1954.

Arms of Cojedes and Cattle

611	A93	5c green	15	15
612	A93	10c red	15	15
613	A93	15c brown	15	15
614	A93	20c ultra	16	15
615	A93	25c orange brown	90	24
616	A93	30c blue	1.40	40
617	A93	35c purple	1.75	1.10
		Nos. 611-617 (7)	4.66	2.34

Issue date: Dec, 17, 1953.

Arms of Nueva Esparta and Fish

618	A93	5c green	15	15
619	A93	10c red	15	15
620	A93	15c brown	45	20
621	A93	20c ultra	50	15
622	A93	40c red orange	2.25	85
623	A93	45c rose vio	5.50	3.25
624	A93	3b blue gray	2.50	1.75
		Nos. 618-624 (7)	11.50	6.50

Issue date: Jan. 1954.

Arms of Yaracuy and Tropical Foliage

625	A93	5c green	38	15
626	A93	10c red	15	15
627	A93	15c brown	32	15
628	A93	20c ultra	45	20
629	A93	25c orange brn	65	30
630	A93	30c blue	75	25
631	A93	35c purple	1.75	1.10
		Nos. 625-631 (7)	4.45	2.30
		Nos. 464-631 (168)	412.39	177.38

Issue date: Jan. 1954.
See Nos. C338-C553.

Ship Type of 1948-50, Redrawn
Coil Stamps
Imprint: "Courvoisier S.A."

1952 Unwmk. Photo. Perf. 11½x12

632	A85	5c green	65	15
633	A85	10c car rose	1.10	15
634	A85	15c gray	3.75	15
		Set value		36

See Nos. C554-C556.

Juan de Villegas and Cross of Father Yepez — A94

Virgin of Coromoto and Child — A95

1952, Sept. 14   Perf. 11½

635	A94	5c green	20	15
636	A94	10c red	40	15
637	A94	20c dk gray bl	65	25
638	A94	40c dp org	3.00	1.50
639	A94	50c brown	1.65	80
640	A94	1b violet	3.00	1.00
		Nos. 635-640 (6)	8.90	3.85

400th anniversary of the founding of the city of Barquisimeto by Juan de Villegas. See Nos. C557-C564.

1952-53   Perf. 11½x12
Size: 17x26mm

641	A95	1b rose pink	5.00	80

Size: 26½x41mm

642	A95	1b rose pink ('53)	3.75	80

Size: 36x55mm

643	A95	1b rose pink ('53)	1.65	65

300th anniv. of the appearance of the Virgin Mary to a chief of the Coromoto Indians.
Issue date: No. 641, Oct. 6.

Correos
Telegraph Stamps Surcharged in Black or Red

Exposición Objetiva Nacional 1948 - 1952

5c.

1952, Nov. 24   Engr.   Perf. 12
Grayish Security Paper

644	5c on 25c car	25	15
645	10c on 1b blk (R)	25	15
	Set value		15

CORREOS
HABILITADO
Surcharged
1952
Bs. 0,50

1952, Dec.

646	20c on 25c car	30	15
647	30c on 2b ol grn	1.90	1.25
648	40c on 1b blk (R)	75	38
649	50c on 3b red org	2.50	1.50

Post Office, Caracas — A96

1953-54   Perf. 13x12½

			Unwmk.	Photo.
650	A96	5c green	15	15
a.		Bklt. pane of 10		
651	A96	7½c brt green	38	25
652	A96	10c rose carmine	25	15
a.		Bklt. pane of 10		
653	A96	15c gray	38	15
654	A96	20c ultra	25	15
655	A96	25c magenta	38	15
656	A96	30c blue	1.90	25
657	A96	35c brt red vio	85	25
658	A96	40c orange	1.25	38
659	A96	45c violet	1.90	65
660	A96	50c red orange	1.25	38
		Nos. 650-660 (11)	8.94	
		Set value		2.50

Issue dates: 20c, 30c, 45c, Mar. 11. 7½c, 25c, 50c, June, 1953. 5c, 10c, Feb. 1954. 15c, 1954.
See Nos. C565-C575, C587-C589.

Type of 1953-54 Inscribed "Republica de Venezuela"
1955

661	A96	5c green	15	15
662	A96	10c rose car	15	15
663	A96	15c gray	18	15
664	A96	20c ultra	25	15
665	A96	30c blue	65	38
666	A96	35c brt red vio	65	15
667	A96	40c orange	1.00	25
668	A96	45c violet	1.25	50
		Nos. 661-668 (8)	4.28	
		Set value		1.45

See Nos. C597-C606.

Arms of Valencia and Industrial Scene — A97

Coat of Arms — A98

1955, Mar. 26   Engr.   Perf. 12

669	A97	5c brt grn	18	15
670	A97	20c ultra	38	15
671	A97	25c reddish brn	65	15
672	A97	50c vermilion	1.00	25
		Nos. 669-672,C590-C596 (11)	4.63	
		Set value		1.35

400th anniv. of the founding of Valencia del Rey.

1955, Dec. 9   Unwmk.   Perf. 11½

673	A98	5c green	30	15
674	A98	20c ultra	1.00	15
675	A98	25c rose car	80	15
676	A98	50c orange	1.00	15
		Nos. 673-676,C607-C612 (10)	5.41	
		Set value		90

1st Postal Convention, Caracas, Feb. 9-15, 1954.

Book and Map of the Americas — A99

Simon Bolivar — A100

1956   Photo.   Perf. 11½
Granite Paper

677	A99	5c lt grn & bluish grn	15	15
678	A99	10c lil rose & rose vio	15	15
679	A99	20c ultra & dk bl	18	15
680	A99	25c gray & lil gray	25	15
681	A99	30c lt bl & bl	25	15
682	A99	40c bis brn & brn	38	18
683	A99	50c ver & red brn	65	25
684	A99	1b lt pur & vio	1.00	50
		Nos. 677-684 (8)	3.01	
		Set value		1.30

Issued for the Book Festival of the Americas, Nov. 15-30, 1956. See Nos. C629-C635.

Engraved, Center Embossed
1957-58   Unwmk.   Perf. 13½

685	A100	5c brt bl grn	15	15
686	A100	10c red	15	15
687	A100	20c lt slate bl	38	15
688	A100	25c rose lake	38	15
689	A100	30c vio blue	50	15
690	A100	40c red orange	75	18
691	A100	50c orange yel	1.00	50
		Nos. 685-691 (7)	3.31	
		Set value		1.10

150th anniv. of the Oath of Monte Sacro and the 125th anniv. of the death of Simon Bolivar (1783-1830).
Issued: 10c, 50c, 1958; others, Nov. 15, 1957.
See Nos. C636-C642.

Hotel
Tamanaco,
Caracas
A101

1957-58 Engr. Perf. 13
602 A101 5c green 15 15
693 A101 10c carmine 15 15
694 A101 15c black 24 15
695 A101 20c dark blue 30 15
696 A101 25c dp claret 30 15
697 A101 30c dp ultra 52 20
698 A101 35c purple 30 15
699 A101 40c orange 40 15
700 A101 45c rose violet 52 20
701 A101 50c yellow 70 30
702 A101 1b dk slate grn 1.00 40
Nos. 692-702 (11) 4.58
Set value 1.70

Issued: 5c, 10c, Oct. 10, 1957; others, 1958.
See Nos. C643-C657. For surcharge see No.
878.

Main Post Office,
Caracas — A102

1958, May 14 Litho. Perf. 14
703 A102 5c emerald 15 15
704 A102 10c rose red 15 15
705 A102 15c gray 15 15
706 A102 20c lt bl 15 15
707 A102 35c red lilac 18 15
708 A102 45c brt vio 1.25 85
709 A102 50c yellow 30 15
710 A102 1b lt ol grn 75 38
Nos. 703-710 (8) 3.08
Set value 1.60

See Nos. 748-750, C658-C670, C786-C792.
For surcharges see Nos. 865, C807, C856-C861.

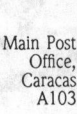

Main Post
Office,
Caracas
A103

Coil Stamps

1958, Nov. 17 Engr. Perf. 11½x12
711 A103 5c green 25 15
712 A103 10c rose red 38 15
713 A103 15c black 50 15
Nos. 711-713,C671-C673 (6) 2.26
Set value 40

Arms of
Merida — A104

1958, Oct. 9 Photo. Perf. 14x13½
714 A104 5c green 15 15
715 A104 10c brt red 15 15
716 A104 15c grnsh gray 15 15
717 A104 20c blue 15 15
718 A104 25c magenta 40 15
719 A104 30c violet 20 15
720 A104 35c lt pur 24 15
721 A104 40c orange 60 20
722 A104 45c dp rose lil 30 15
723 A104 50c brt yel 52 20
724 A104 1b gray grn 1.52 52
Nos. 714-724 (11) 4.38
Set value 1.50

400th anniversary of the founding of the city of
Merida. See Nos. C674-C689. For surcharge see
No. 873.

Arms of Trujillo, Bolivar
Monument and Trujillo
Hotel — A105

1959, Nov. 17 Unwmk. Perf. 14
725 A105 5c emerald 15 15
726 A105 10c rose 15 15
727 A105 15c gray 15 15
728 A105 20c blue 15 15
729 A105 25c brt pink 25 15
730 A105 30c lt ultra 38 15
731 A105 35c lt pur 42 18
732 A105 45c rose lilac 50 25
733 A105 50c yellow 50 20
734 A105 1b lt ol grn 1.25 65
Nos. 725-734 (10) 3.90
Set value 1.70

400th anniversary of the founding of the city of
Trujillo. See Nos. C690-C700.

Stadium
A106

1959 Mar. 10 Litho. Perf. 13½
735 A106 5c brt grn 15 15
736 A106 10c rose pink 15 15
737 A106 20c blue 40 20
738 A106 30c dk bl 52 24
739 A106 50c red lilac 80 20
Nos. 735-739 (5) 2.02
Set value 78

8th Central American and Caribbean Games,
Caracas, Nov. 29-Dec. 14, 1958. See #C701-C705.
#735-739 exist imperf. Value, pair $25.

Stamp of
1859,
Mailman and
José Ignacio
Paz Castillo
A107

Stamp of 1859 and: 50c, Mailman on horseback
and Jacinto Gutierrez. 1b, Plane, train and Miguel
Herrera.

1959, Sept. 15 Engr. Perf. 13½x14
740 A107 25c org yel 30 15
741 A107 50c blue 52 20
742 A107 1b rose red 1.00 40
Nos. 740-742 (6) C706-C708 3.45 1.57

Centenary of Venezuelan postage stamps.

Catalogue values for unused
stamps in this section, from this
point to the end of the section, are
for Never Hinged items.

Alexander von
Humboldt
A108

Newspaper, 1808,
and View of Caracas,
1958
A109

1960, Feb. 9 Unwmk. Perf. 13½
743 A108 5c grn & yel grn 35 15
744 A108 30c vio bl & vio 95 18
745 A108 40c org & brn org 1.25 40
Nos. 743-745,C709-C711 (6) 5.25
Set value 1.20

Centenary of the death of Alexander von Humboldt, German naturalist and geographer.

Post Office Type of 1958

1960, July Litho. Perf. 14
748 A102 25c yellow 20 15
749 A102 30c light blue 24 15
750 A102 40c fawn 48 15
Set value 26

1960, June 6 Litho. Perf. 14
751 A109 10c rose & blk 42 15
752 A109 20c lt blue & blk 65 18
753 A109 35c lilac & blk 1.00 70
Nos. 751-753,C712-C714 (6) 6.47 2.70

150th anniv. (in 1958) of the 1st Venezuelan
newspaper, Gazeta de Caracas.

Agustin
Codazzi — A110

National
Pantheon — A111

1960, June 15 Engr. Unwmk.
754 A110 5c brt green 15 15
755 A110 15c gray 65 15
756 A110 20c blue 52 15
757 A110 45c purple 65 32
Nos. 754-757,C715-C720 (10) 5.59
Set value 1.85

Centenary (in 1959) of the death of Agustin
Codazzi, geographer.
For surcharges see Nos. 869, C884.

1960, May 9 Litho.

Pantheon in Bister

758 A111 5c emerald 15 15
759 A111 20c brt blue 52 15
760 A111 25c light olive 80 18
761 A111 30c dull blue 95 20
762 A111 40c fawn 1.40 38
763 A111 45c lilac 1.40 38
Nos. 758-763 (6) 5.22 1.44

See Nos. C721-C734.
For surcharges see Nos. C894-C895.

Andres Eloy Blanco,
Poet (1896-1955)
A112

1960, May 21 Unwmk. Perf. 14
Portrait in Black
764 A112 5c emerald 20 15
765 A112 30c dull blue 32 15
766 A112 50c yellow 65 25
Nos. 764-766,C735-C737 (6) 4.02
Set value 1.10

For surcharge see No. C874.

Independence Meeting of April 19, 1810,
Led by Miranda — A113

1960, Aug. 19 Litho. Perf. 13½
Center Multicolored
767 A113 5c brt green 50 15
768 A113 20c dull blue 1.00 25
769 A113 30c violet blue 1.25 38
Nos. 767-769,C738-C740 (6) 6.25 1.72

150th anniversary of Venezuela's Independence.
See Nos. 812-814, C804-C806. For surcharge
see No. C893.

Drilling for
Oil — A114

1960, Aug. 26 Engr. Perf. 14
770 A114 5c grn & slate grn 1.65 65
771 A114 10c dk car & brn 65 25
772 A114 15c gray & dull pur 85 30
Nos. 770-772,C741-C743 (6) 5.50 2.06

Issued to publicize Venezuela's oil industry.

Luisa Cáceres de
Arismendi — A115

Unwmk.
1960, Oct. 21 Litho. Perf. 14
Center Multicolored
773 A115 20c light blue 1.25 35
774 A115 25c citron 1.00 38
775 A115 30c dull blue 1.40 52
Nos. 773-774,C744-C746 (5) 6.70 2.33

94th anniversary of the death of Luisa Cáceres de
Arismendi.

José Antonio
Anzoategui — A116

1960, Oct. 29 Engr.
776 A116 5c emerald & gray ol 28 15
777 A116 15c ol gray & dl vio 65 15
778 A116 20c blue & gray vio 70 15
Nos. 776-778,C747-C749 (6) 3.48
Set value 1.15

140th anniversary (in 1959) of the death of General José Antonio Anzoategui.

Antonio José de
Sucre — A117

Unwmk.
1960, Nov. 18 Litho. Perf. 14
Center Multicolored
779 A117 10c deep rose 48 15
780 A117 15c gray brown 60 20
781 A117 20c rose blue 80 30
Nos. 779-781,C750-C752 (6) 5.13 1.88

130th anniversary of the death of General
Antonio José de Sucre.

Bolivar Peak,
Merida — A118

Designs: 15c, Caroni Falls, Bolivar. 35c,
Cuacharo caves, Monagas.

1960, Mar. 22   *Perf. 14*
782 A118   5c emerald & grn   80   80
783 A118   15c gray & dk gray   2.75   2.75
784 A118   35c rose lil & lil   2.25   2.25
   Nos. 782-784,C753-C755 (6)   11.50   11.50

Buildings and People — A119

1961   Litho.   Unwmk.
Building in Orange
785 A119   5c emerald   15   15
786 A119   10c carmine   15   15
787 A119   15c gray   15   15
788 A119   20c blue   16   15
789 A119   25c lt red brown   24   15
790 A119   30c dull blue   24   15
791 A119   35c red lilac   32   15
792 A119   40c fawn   48   16
793 A119   45c brt violet   65   24
794 A119   50c yellow   48   15
   Nos. 785-794 (10)   3.02
   Set value   95

1960 national census. See #C756-C770. For surcharge see No. 866.

Rafael Maria Baralt — A120   Yellow-headed Parrot — A121

1961, Mar. 11   Engr.   *Perf. 14*
795 A120   5c grn & slate grn   15   15
796 A120   15c gray & dull red brn   40   15
797 A120   35c rose lilac & lt vio   60   20
   Nos. 795-797,C771-C773 (6)   3.47
   Set value   1.30

Issued to commemorate the centenary of the death of Rafael Maria Baralt, statesman.

1961, Sept. 6   Litho.   *Perf. 14¹/₂*
798 A121   30c shown   60   30
799 A121   40c Snowy egret   80   30
800 A121   50c Scarlet ibis   1.65   60
   Nos. 798-800,C776-C778 (6)   5.70   3.00

Juan J. Aguerrevere A122

1961, Oct. 21   Unwmk.   *Perf. 14*
801 A122   25c dark blue   20   15
   a. Souvenir sheet, imperf.   1.40   1.40

Centenary of the founding of the Engineering Society of Venezuela, Oct. 28, 1861.
No. 801a sold for 1b.
No. 801a exists with "Valor: Bs 1,00" omitted at lower left corner. Value, $3.50.

Battle of Carabobo, 1821 — A123

1961, Dec. 1   *Perf. 14*
Center Multicolored
802 A123   5c emerald & blk   15   15
803 A123   40c brown & blk   60   22
   Nos. 802-803,C779-C784 (8)   12.45   4.77

140th anniversary of Battle of Carabobo.

Oncidium Papilio Lindl. — A124

Orchids: 10c, Caularthron bilamellatum. 20c, Stanhopea Wardii Lodd. 25c, Catasetum pileatum. 30c, Masdevallia tovarensis. 35c, Epidendrum Stamfordianum Batem, horiz. 50c, Epidendrum atropurpureum Willd. 3b, Oncidium falcipetalum Lindl.

Perf. 14x13¹/₂, 13¹/₂x14
1962, May 30   Litho.   Unwmk.
Orchids in Natural Colors
804 A124   5c black & orange   15   15
805 A124   10c black & brt grnsh bl   15   15
806 A124   20c black & yel grn   30   15
807 A124   25c black & lt blue   42   15
808 A124   30c black & olive   50   15
809 A124   35c black & yellow   55   18
810 A124   50c black & gray   65   25
811 A124   3b blk & vio   3.75   2.00
   Nos. 804-811 (8)   6.47
   Set value   2.80

See Nos. C794-C803. For surcharges see Nos. C885-C887.

Independence Type of 1960
Design: Signing Declaration of Independence.

1962, June 11   *Perf. 13¹/₂*
Center Multicolored
812 A113   5c emerald   22   15
813 A113   20c blue   45   15
814 A113   25c yellow   65   30
   a. Souvenir sheet of 3, #812-814, imperf.   2.50   2.50
   Nos. 812-814,C804-C806 (6)   4.89   1.80

150th anniv. of the Venezuelan Declaration of Independence, July 5, 1811.
No. 814a sold for 1.50b.

Shot Put A125

1962, Nov. 30   Litho.   *Perf. 13x14*
815 A125   5c shown   15   15
816 A125   10c Soccer   16   15
817 A125   25c Swimming   30   15
   a. Souvenir sheet of 3, #815-817, imperf.   2.25   2.25
   Nos. 815-817,C808-C810 (6)   3.13   1.64

1st Natl. Games, Caracas, 1961. The stamps are arranged so that two pale colored edges of each stamp join to make a border around blocks of four.
No. 817a sold for 1.40b.
For surcharge see No. C899.

Vermilion Cardinal — A126

Malaria Eradication Emblem, Mosquito and Map — A127

Birds: 10c, Great kiskadee. 20c, Glossy black thrush. 25c, Collared trogons. 30c, Swallow tanager. 40c, Long-tailed sylph. 3b, Black-necked stilt.

1962, Dec. 14   *Perf. 14x13¹/₂*
Birds in Natural Colors, Black Inscription
818 A126   5c brt yellow grn   15   15
819 A126   10c violet blue   20   15
820 A126   20c lilac rose   40   15
821 A126   25c dull brown   48   18
822 A126   30c lemon   60   20
823 A126   40c lilac   80   30
824 A126   3b fawn   5.00   3.00
   Nos. 818-824 (7)   7.63   4.13

See Nos. C811-C818. For surcharges see Nos. 868, C880-C882.

Lithographed and Embossed
Perf. 13¹/₂x14
1962, Dec. 20   Wmk. 346
825 A127   50c brown & black   60   22

WHO drive to eradicate malaria. See Nos. C819-C819a.

White-tailed Deer — A128

Designs: 10c, Collared peccary. 35c, Collared titi (monkey). 50c, Giant Brazilian otter. 1b, Puma. 3b, Capybara.

Perf. 13¹/₂x14
1963, Mar. 13   Litho.   Unwmk.
Multicolored Center; Black Inscriptions
826 A128   5c green   15   15
827 A128   10c orange   15   15
828 A128   35c red lilac   20   15
829 A128   50c blue   40   15
830 A128   1b rose brown   2.00   1.00
831 A128   3b yellow   4.00   2.00
   Nos. 826-831 (6)   6.90   3.60

See Nos. C820-C825. For surcharges see Nos. 870-871, C888-C889.

Fisherman and Map of Venezuela A129

Cathedral of Bocono A130

1963, Mar. 21
832 A129   25c pink & ultra   24   15

FAO "Freedom from Hunger" campaign. See Nos. C826-C827.

1963, May 30   Wmk. 346
833 A130   50c brn, red & grn, *buff*   55   15

400th anniversary of the founding of Bocono. See No. C828.

St. Peter's Basilica, Rome — A131

1963, June 11   *Perf. 14x13¹/₂*
834 A131   35c dk bl, brn & buff   32   15
835 A131   45c dk grn, red brn & buff   40   15

Vatican II, the 21st Ecumenical Council of the Roman Catholic Church. See Nos. C829-C830.

National Flag — A132

1963, July 29   Unwmk.   *Perf. 14*
836 A132   30c gray, red, yel & bl   28   15

Centenary of Venezuela's flag and coat of arms. See No. C831.

Lake Maracaibo Bridge — A133   Map, Soldier and Emblem — A134

Perf. 13¹/₂x14
1963, Aug. 24   Wmk. 346
837 A133   30c blue & brown   35   15
838 A133   35c bluish grn & brn   42   18
839 A133   80c blue grn & brn   80   32
   Nos. 837-839,C832-C834 (6)   5.07   1.93

Opening of bridge over Lake Maracaibo. For surcharge see No. 875.

1963, Sept. 10   Unwmk.
840 A134   50c red, bl & grn, *buff*   52   18

25th anniversary of the armed forces. See No. C835. For surcharge see No. C862.

Dag Hammarskjold and World Map — A135

Perf. 14x13¹/₂
1963, Sept. 25   Unwmk.
841 A135   25c dk bl, bl grn & ocher   24   15
842 A135   55c grn, grnsh bl & ocher   90   32

Issued to commemorate the "First" anniversary of the death of Dag Hammarskjold, Secretary General of the United Nations, 1953-61. See Nos. C836-C837a. For surcharges see Nos. 867, C875-C876.

Dr. Luis Razetti — A136   Dr. Francisco A. Risquez — A137

1963, Oct. 10   Litho.
843 A136 35c blue, ocher & brn   48 18
844 A136 45c mag, ocher & brn   65 18

Centenary of the birth of Dr. Luis Razetti, physician. See Nos. C838-C839.

1963, Dec. 31   Perf. 11¹/₂x12

Design: 20c, Dr. Carlos J. Bello.

845 A137 15c multicolored   20 15
846 A137 20c multicolored   25 15
     Set value   15

Cent. of the Intl. Red Cross. See #C840-C841.

Oil Field
Workers — A138

Pedro
Gual — A139

Designs: 10c, Oil refinery. 15c Crane and building construction. 30c, Cactus, train and truck. 40c, Tractor.

1964, Feb. 5   Litho.   Perf. 14x13¹/₂
847 A138 5c multi   15 15
848 A138 10c multi   16 15
849 A138 15c multi   24 15
850 A138 30c multi   32 15
851 A138 40c multi   50 18
     Nos. 847-851 (5)   1.37
     Set value   45

Centenary of the Department of Industrial Development. See Nos. C842-C846.

1964, Mar. 20   Unwmk.   Perf. 14
852 A139 40c lt olive green   50 18
853 A139 50c lt red brown   55 20

Centenary of the death (in 1862) of Pedro Gual, statesman. See Nos. C847-C848.

Carlos
Arvelo — A140

1964, Apr. 17   Engr.   Perf. 14x13¹/₂
854 A140 1b dull bl & gray   1.25 45

Centenary of the death of Dr. Carlos Arvelo (1784-1862), chief physician of Bolivar's revolutionary army, director of Caracas Hospital, rector of Central University and professor of pathology. For surcharge see No. 874.

Foundry Ladle
and Molds
A141

1964, May 22   Perf. 14x13¹/₂
855 A141 20c multicolored   28 15
856 A141 50c multicolored   52 20
     Set value   28

Orinoco Steel Mills. See Nos. C849-C850.

Romulo Gallegos,
Novelist, 80th
Birthday — A142

1964, Aug. 3   Unwmk.   Litho.   Perf. 12
857 A142 5c dk & lt green   15 15
858 A142 10c bl & pale bl   15 15
859 A142 15c dk & lt red lil   28 15
     Nos. 857-859,C852-C854 (6)   2.23
     Set value   88

Angel Falls,
Bolivar
State — A143

Tourist Publicity: 10c, Tropical landscape, Sucre State. 15c, San Juan Peaks, Guarico. 30c, Net fishermen, Anzoategui. 40c, Mountaineer, Merida.

1964, Oct. 22   Perf. 13¹/₂x14
860 A143 5c multi   15 15
861 A143 10c multi   16 15
862 A143 15c multi   20 15
863 A143 30c multi   40 15
864 A143 40c multi   60 15
     Nos. 860-864 (5)   1.51
     Set value   45

RESELLADO

Issues of 1958-64
Surcharged in Black,
Dark Blue or Lilac

VALOR

Bs. 0,05

1965
865 A102 5c on 1b (#710)   42 15
866 A119 10c on 45c (#793)   16 15
867 A135 15c on 55c (#842)   15 15
868 A126 20c on 3b (#824)   20 15
869 A110 25c on 45c (#757) (DB)   20 15
870 A128 25c on 3b (#830)   22 15
871 A128 25c on 3b (#831)   28 15
872 A124 25c on 3b (#811) (L)   20 15
873 A104 30c on 1b (#724)   22 15
874 A140 40c on 1b (#854)   60 18
875 A133 60c on 80c (#839)   75 22
     Nos. 865-875 (11)   3.40
     Set value   1.40

Lines of surcharge arranged variously; old denomination obliterated with bars on Nos. 867, 870-872. See Nos. C856-C899.

CORREOS
RESELLADO
VALOR
Bs. 0,05

Revenue Stamps of
1947 Surcharged in
Red or Black

Imprint: "American Bank Note Co."

1965 Engr.   Perf. 12, 13¹/₂ (No. 882)
876 R1 5c on 5c emerald   15 15
877 R1 5c on 20c red brn   15 15
878 R1 10c on 10c brn ol   15 15
879 R1 15c on 40c grn   15 15
880 R1 20c on 3b dk bl (R)   28 15
881 R1 25c on 5b vio bl (R)   60 22
882 R1 25c on 5b vio bl (R) (Imprint: "Bundesdruckerei Berlin")   28 15
883 R1 60c on 3b dk bl (R)   75 26
     Nos. 876-883 (8)   2.51
     Set value   95

Type R1 is illustrated above No. 401.

John F.
Kennedy and
Alliance for
Progress
Emblem
A144

1965, Aug. 20 Photo.   Perf. 12x11¹/₂
884 A144 20c gray   35 15
885 A144 40c bright lilac   52 20

Issued in memory of President John F. Kennedy (1917-1963). See Nos. C900-C901.

Map of Venezuela
and Guiana by
Codazzi,
1840 — A145

Protesilaus
Leucones — A146

Maps of Venezuela and Guiana: 15c, by Juan M. Restrepo, 1827, horiz. 40c, by L. de Surville, 1778.

1965, Nov. 5   Litho.   Perf. 13¹/₂
886 A145 5c multi   15 15
887 A145 15c multi   28 15
888 A145 40c multi   55 15
 a.   Souv. sheet of 3, #886-888, imperf.   1.90 1.90
     Nos. 886-888,C905-C907 (6)   2.60
     Set value   84

Issued to publicize Venezuela's claim to part of British Guiana.
No. 888a sold for 85c.

1966, Jan. 25   Litho.   Perf. 13¹/₂x14
Various Butterflies in Natural Colors
Black Inscriptions
889 A146 20c lt olive grn   28 15
890 A146 30c lt yellow grn   40 15
891 A146 50c yellow   65 20
     Nos. 889-891,C915-C917 (6)   4.43 1.66

Ship and Map
of Atlantic
Ocean
A147

1966, Mar. 10   Litho.   Perf. 13¹/₂x14
892 A147 60c brown, bl & blk   1.25 45

Bicentenary of the first maritime mail.

"El Carite" Dance — A148

Various Folk Dances

Perf. 14x13¹/₂

1966, Apr. 5   Litho.   Unwmk.
893 A148 5c gray & multi   15 15
894 A148 10c orange & multi   15 15
895 A148 15c lemon & multi   22 15
896 A148 20c lilac & multi   28 15
897 A148 25c brt pink & multi   45 16
898 A148 35c yel grn & multi   52 22
     Nos. 893-898 (6)   1.77
     Set value   70

See Nos. C919-C924.

Type of Air Post Stamps and

Arturo
Michelena,
Self-portrait
A149

Paintings: 1b, Penthesileia, battle scene. 1.05b, The Red Cloak.

Perf. 12¹/₂x12, 12x12¹/₂

1966, May 12   Litho.   Unwmk.
899 A149 95c sepia & buff   85 45
900 AP74 1b multi   90 45
901 AP74 1.05b multi   1.00 45
     Nos. 899-901,C927-C929 (6)   5.40 2.70

Arturo Michelena (1863-1898), painter. Miniature sheets of 12 exist.

Construction Worker
and Map of
Americas — A150

Designs: 20c, as 10c. 30c, 65c, Labor monument. 35c, Machinery worker and map of Venezuela. 50c, Automobile assembly line.

1966, July 6   Litho.   Perf. 14x13¹/₂
902 A150 10c yellow & blk   15 15
903 A150 20c lt grnsh bl & blk   24 15
904 A150 30c lt blue & vio   20 15
905 A150 35c lemon & olive   30 15
906 A150 50c brt rose & claret   50 18
907 A150 65c salmon pink & brn   65 25
     Nos. 902-907 (6)   2.04
     Set value   75

2nd Conference of Ministers of Labor of the Organization of American States.

Velvet Cichlid
A151

1966, Aug. 31   Litho.   Perf. 13¹/₂x14
908 A151 15c shown   20 15
909 A151 25c Perch cichlid   28 15
910 A151 45c Piranha   75 28
     Nos. 908-910,C933-C935 (6)   4.53 1.78

Nativity — A152

Rubén
Dario — A154

Satellite, Radar,
Globe, Plane and
Ship — A153

1966, Dec. 9   Litho.   Perf. 13¹/₂x14
911 A152 65c violet & blk   80 28

Christmas 1966.

1966, Dec. 28   Perf. 13¹/₂x14
912 A153 45c multi   60 22

30th anniv. of the Ministry of Communications.

1967   Litho.
913 A154 70c gray bl & dk bl   1.00 45

Rubén Dario (pen name of Felix Rubén Garcia Sarmiento, 1867-1916), Nicaraguan poet, newspaper correspondent and diplomat.

Old Building
and Arms,
University of
Zulia — A155

Perf. 13¹/₂x14

1967, Apr. 21   Litho.   Unwmk.
914 A155 80c gold, blk & car   1.00   45

Founding of the University of Zulia, 75th anniv.

Front Page and
Printing
Press — A156

1968, June 27   Photo.   Perf. 14x13¹/₂
915 A156 1.50b emer, blk & brn   1.50   60

Newspaper Correo del Orinoco, 150th anniv.

Boll
Weevil
A157

Insect Pests: 20c, Corn borer, vert. 90c, Tobacco caterpillar.

Perf. 14x13¹/₂, 13¹/₂x14
1968, Aug. 30   Litho.
916 A157 20c multicolored   35   15
917 A157 75c olive & multi   75   28
918 A157 90c multicolored   95   35
  Nos. 916-918,C989-C991 (6)   2.83
      Set value   1.05

Guayana
Substation — A158

Designs: 45c, Guaira River Dam, horiz. 50c, Macagua Dam and power plant, horiz. 80c, Guri River Dam and power plant.

1968, Nov. 8   Litho.
919 A158 15c fawn & multi   20   15
920 A158 45c dl yel & multi   52   20
921 A158 50c bl grn & multi   75   22
922 A158 80c blue & multi   1.10   50

Electrification program.

House and
Piggy
Bank — A159

1968, Dec. 6   Litho.   Perf. 13¹/₂x14
923 A159 45c blue & multi   60   22

National Savings System.

Nursery
and Child
Planting
Tree
A160

Designs: 15c, Child planting tree (vert.; this design used as emblem on entire issue). 30c, Waterfall, vert. 45c, Logging, vert. 55c, Fields and village, vert. 75c, Palambra (fish).

Perf. 14x13¹/₂, 13¹/₂x14
1968, Dec. 19   Litho.
924 A160 15c multicolored   15   15
925 A160 20c multicolored   20   15
926 A160 30c multicolored   28   15
927 A160 45c multicolored   35   15
928 A160 55c multicolored   75   28
929 A160 75c multicolored   55   20
  Nos. 924-929 (6)   2.28
      Set value   85

Issued to publicize nature conservation. See Nos. C1000-C1005.

Colorada
Beach,
Sucre — A161

Designs: 45c, Church of St. Francis of Yare, Miranda. 90c, Stilt houses, Zulia.

1969, Jan. 24   Perf. 13¹/₂x14
930 A161 15c multicolored   20   15
931 A161 45c multicolored   55   15
932 A161 90c multicolored   80   50
  Nos. 930-932,C1006-C1008 (6)   2.51
      Set value   1.12

Tourist publicity. For souvenir sheet see No. C1007a.

Bolivar Addressing Congress of
Angostura — A162

1969, Feb. 15   Litho.   Perf. 11
933 A162 45c multicolored   60   22

Issued to commemorate the sesquicentennial of the Congress of Angostura (Ciudad Bolivar).

Martin Luther King,
Jr. — A163

1969, Apr. 1   Litho.   Perf. 13¹/₂
934 A163 1b bl, red & dk brn   80   30

Rev. Dr. Martin Luther King, Jr. (1929-1968), American civil rights leader and recipient of the Nobel Peace Prize, 1964.

Tabebuia
A164

Trees: 65c, Erythrina poeppigiana. 90c, Platymiscium.

1969, May 30   Litho.   Perf. 13¹/₂x14
935 A164 50c multicolored   55   20
936 A164 65c gray & multi   75   28
937 A164 90c pink & multi   1.10   40
  Nos. 935-937,C1009-C1011 (6)   3.18
      Set value   1.15

Issued to publicize nature conservation.

Still Life
with
Pheasant,
by Rojas
A165

Paintings by Cristobal Rojas (1858-1890): 25c, On the Balcony, vert. 45c, The Christening. 50c, The Empty Place (family). 60c, The Tavern. 1b, Man's Arm, vert.

Perf. 14x13¹/₂, 13¹/₂x14
1969, June 27   Litho.   Unwmk.
Size: 32x42mm, 42x32mm
938 A165 25c gold & multi   24   15
939 A165 35c gold & multi   42   18
940 A165 45c gold & multi   65   28
941 A165 50c gold & multi   80   30
942 A165 60c gold & multi   1.00   35

Perf. 11
Size: 26x53mm
943 A165 1b gold & multi   1.50   60
  Nos. 938-943 (6)   4.61   1.86

ILO Emblem
A166

1969, July 28   Perf. 13¹/₂
944 A166 2.50b fawn & blk   2.00   1.25

50th anniv. of the ILO.

Charter and
Coat of Arms
A167

Industrial
Complex
A168

1969, Aug. 26   Litho.   Perf. 13¹/₂
945 A167 45c ultra & multi   65   22
946 A168 1b multicolored   1.00   35

Industrial development.

House with Arcade,
Carora — A169

Designs: 25c, Ruins of Pastora Church. 55c, Chapel of the Cross. 65c, House of Culture.

1969, Sept. 8   Perf. 13x14¹/₂
947 A169 20c multicolored   20   15
948 A169 25c multicolored   28   15
949 A169 55c multicolored   75   28
950 A169 65c multicolored   95   32
      Set value   76

400th anniversary of city of Carora.

Simon Bolivar in
Madrid — A170

Designs: 10c, Bolivar's wedding, Madrid, 1802, horiz. 35c, Bolivar monument. Madrid.

Perf. 13¹/₂x14, 14x13¹/₂
1969, Oct. 28   Litho.
951 A170 10c multicolored   15   15
952 A170 15c brn red & blk   28   15
953 A170 35c multicolored   42   15
  a. Souvenir sheet of 2   1.25   95
      Set value   28

Bolivar's sojourn in Spain. No. 953a contains 2 imperf. stamps similar to Nos. 952-953 with simulated perforation. Sold for 75c.

"Birds in the Woods" — A171

Design: 45c, "Children in Summer Camp." Both designs are after children's paintings.

1969, Dec. 12   Litho.   Perf. 12¹/₂
954 A171 5c emerald & multi   15   15
955 A171 45c red & multi   65   28
      Set value   34

Issued for Children's Day.

Map of Great
Colombia
A172

1969, Dec. 16   Litho.   Perf. 11¹/₂
956 A172 45c multicolored   55   20

150th anniversary of the founding of the State of Great Colombia.

St. Anthony's,
Clarines
A173

Churches: 30c, Church of the Conception, Caroni. 40c, St. Michael's, Burbusay. 45c, St. Anthony's, Maturin. 75c, St. Nicholas, Moruy. 1b, Coro Cathedral.

810 VENEZUELA

1970, Jan. 15 *Perf. 14*
957 A173 10c pink & multi 15 15
958 A173 30c emerald & multi 28 15
959 A173 40c yellow & multi 55 20
960 A173 45c gray bl & multi 75 28
a. Souvenir sheet of 1, imperf. 1.50 1.50
961 A173 75c yellow & multi 95 32
962 A173 1b orange & multi 1.10 40
Nos. 957-962 (6) 3.78 1.50

Colonial architecture.
No. 960a sold for 75c.

A174

A175

Design: Seven Hills of Valera.

1970, Feb. 13 Litho. *Perf. 13x14½*
963 A174 95c multicolored 1.00 35

Sesquicentennial of the city of Valera.

1970, July 29 Litho. *Perf. 14x13½*
Flowers: 20c, Monochaetum Humboldtianum.
25c, Symbolanthus vasculosis. 45c, Cavedishia
splendens. 1b, Befaria glauca.
964 A175 20c multicolored 28 15
965 A175 25c multicolored 55 15
966 A175 45c multicolored 75 28
967 A175 1b multicolored 1.10 40
Nos. 964-967,C1049-C1052 (8) 5.16 1.96

Battle of Boyaca, by Martin Tovar y Tovar — A176

1970, Aug. 7 *Perf. 13½x14*
968 A176 30c multicolored 35 15

150th anniversary of Battle of Boyaca.

Our Lady of Belén de San Mateo — A177

Designs: 35c, Pastoral Cross of Archbishop Silvestre Guevara y Lira, 1867. 40c, Our Lady of Valle. 90c, Virgin of Chiquinquira. 1b, Our Lady of Socorro de Valencia.

1970, Sept. 1 *Perf. 14x13½*
969 A177 35c gray & multi 42 15
970 A177 40c gray & multi 55 20
971 A177 60c gray & multi 80 30
a. Souvenir sheet of 1, imperf. 1.25 1.25
972 A177 90c gray & multi 95 40
973 A177 1b gray & multi 1.25 50
Nos. 969-973 (5) 3.97 1.55

The designs are from sculptures and paintings in various Venezuelan churches.
No. 971a sold for 75c.

Venezuela No. 22 and EXFILCA Emblem — A178

Designs: 20c, EXFILCA emblem and flags of participating nations, vert. 70c, Venezuela No. C13 and EXFILCA emblem, vert.

1970, Nov. 28 Litho. *Perf. 11*
974 A178 20c yellow & multi 28 15
975 A178 25c dk blue & multi 35 15
976 A178 70c brown & multi 75 28
a. Souvenir sheet of 1, imperf. 1.40 1.40
Set value 45

Issued to publicize EXFILCA 70, 2nd Interamerican Philatelic Exhibition, Caracas, Nov. 27-Dec. 6. No. 976a is a hexagon with each side 50mm long. Sold for 85c.

Guardian Angel, by Juan Pedro Lopez — A179

1970, Dec. 1 Litho. *Perf. 14½x13½*
977 A179 45c dull yel & multi 55 20

Christmas 1970.

Jet and 1920 Plane A180

1970, Dec. 10 *Perf. 13x14*
978 A180 5c blue & multi 15 15

Venezuelan Air Force, 50th anniversary.

Question Mark Full of Citizens — A181

1971, Apr. 30 Litho. *Perf. 14x13½*
Light Green, Red & Black
979 Block of 4 2.50 1.40
a. A181 30c frame L & T 60 25
b. A181 30c frame T & R 60 25
c. A181 30c frame L & B 60 25
d. A181 30c frame B & R 60 25

National Census, 1971. Sheet of 20 contains 5 No. 979 and 5 blocks of 4 labels. See No. C1054.

Battle of Carabobo A182

1971, June 21 *Perf. 13½x14*
980 A182 2b blue & multi 1.40 80

Sesquicentennial of Battle of Carabobo.

Map of Federal District A183

Designs: State maps. 25c, 55c, 85c, 90c, vert.

1971 Litho. *Perf. 13½x14, 14x13½*
981 A183 5c shown 15 15
982 A183 15c Monagas 15 15
983 A183 20c Nueva Esparta 15 15
984 A183 25c Portuguesa 18 15
985 A183 45c Sucre 25 15
986 A183 55c Tachira 35 18
987 A183 65c Trujillo 45 20
988 A183 75c Yaracuyo 55 28
989 A183 85c Zulia 70 28
990 A183 90c Amazonas 1.10 32
991 A183 1b Federal Dependencies 1.40 55
Nos. 981-991 (11) 5.43
Set value 2.15

Issue dates: 5c, July 15; 15c, 20c, Aug. 16; 25c, 45c, Sept. 15; 55c, 65c, Oct. 15; 75c, 85c, Nov. 15; 90c, 1b, Dec. 15.
See Nos. C1035-C1048.

Madonna and Child A184

Luis Daniel Beauperthuy A185

Design: #993, Madonna & Jesus in manger.

1971, Dec. 1 *Perf. 11*
992 A184 25c multicolored 30 15
993 A184 25c multicolored 30 15
a. Pair, #992-993 60 50

Christmas 1971. Printed checkerwise.

1971, Dec. 10 *Perf. 14x13½*
994 A185 1b vio bl & multi 75 35

Dr. Luis Daniel Beauperthuy, scientist.

Globe in Heart Shape — A186

Flags of Americas and Arms of Venezuela — A187

1972, Apr. 7 Litho. *Perf. 14x13½*
995 A186 1b red, ultra & blk 75 45

"Your heart is your health," World Health Day 1972.

1972, May 16 Litho. *Perf. 14x13½*
Designs: 4b, Venezuelan flag. 5b, National anthem. 10b, Araguaney, national tree. 15b, Map, North and South America. All show flags of American nations in background.
996 A187 3b multicolored 2.25 1.00
997 A187 4b multicolored 2.75 1.65
998 A187 5b multicolored 3.25 2.00
999 A187 10b multicolored 6.75 3.00
1000 A187 15b multicolored 10.00 4.00
Nos. 996-1000 (5) 25.00 11.65

"Venezuela in America."

Parque Central Complex A188

Designs: No. 1002, Front view ("Parque Central" on top). No. 1003, Side view ("Parque Central" at right).

1972, July 25 *Perf. 11½*
1001 A188 30c yellow & multi 20 15
1002 A188 30c blue & multi 20 15
1003 A188 30c red & multi 20 15
a. Strip of 3, #1001-1003 95 95

Completion of "Parque Central" middle-income housing project, Caracas.

Mahatma Gandhi A189

1972, Oct. 2 Litho. *Perf. 13½x14*
1004 A189 60c multicolored 60 30

103rd birthday of Mohandas K. Gandhi (1869-1948), leader in India's fight for independence, advocate of non-violence.

Children Playing Music — A190

Christmas: #1006, Children roller skating.

1972, Dec. 5 Litho. *Perf. 13½x14*
1005 A190 30c multicolored 20 15
1006 A190 30c multicolored 20 15
a. Pair, #1005-1006 50 50

Indigo Snake — A191

Snake: 15c, South American chicken snake. 25c, Venezuelan lance-head. 30c, Coral snake. 60c, Casabel rattlesnake. 1b, Boa constrictor.

1972, Dec. 15 Litho. *Perf. 13½x14*
1007 A191 10c black & multi 15 15
1008 A191 15c black & multi 15 15
1009 A191 25c black & multi 30 15
1010 A191 30c black & multi 35 18
1011 A191 60c black & multi 60 30
1012 A191 1b black & multi 90 45
Nos. 1007-1012 (6) 2.45
Set value 1.20

Copernicus A192

Sun A193

Designs: 5c, Model of solarcentric system. 15c, Copernicus' book "De Revolutionibus."

1973, Feb. 19   Litho.   Perf. 13½x14

1013 A192	5c multicolored	15	15
1014 A192	10c multicolored	25	15
1015 A192	15c multicolored	35	15
a.	Strip of 3, #1013-1015	75	45
	Set value		20

500th anniversary of the birth of Nicolaus Copernicus (1473-1543), Polish astronomer.

1973   Litho.   Perf. 13½

Designs: Planetary system.

Size: 26½x29mm

1016 A193	5c shown	15	15
1017 A193	5c Earth	15	15
1018 A193	20c Mars	45	15
1019 A193	20c Saturn	30	15
1020 A193	30c Asteroids	35	15
1021 A193	40c Neptune	45	18
1022 A193	50c Venus	60	30
1023 A193	60c Jupiter	75	35
1024 A193	75c Uranus	90	45
1025 A193	90c Pluto	1.10	50
1026 A193	90c Moon	1.25	60
1027 A193	1b Mercury	1.50	75

Size: 27x55mm
Perf. 12

1028 A193	10c Orbits and Saturn	18	15
1029 A193	15c Sun, Mercury, Venus, Earth	30	15
1030 A193	15c Jupiter, Uranus, Neptune, Pluto	35	15
a.	Strip of 3, #1028-1030	90	90
	Nos. 1016-1030 (15)	8.78	
	Set value		3.70

10th anniversary of Humboldt Planetarium. No. 1030a has continuous design showing solar system. Issue dates: Nos. 1016, 1018, 1021, 1023-1025, Mar. 15; others Mar. 30.

OAS Emblem, Map of Americas — A194

1973, Apr. 30   Litho.   Perf. 13½x14

1031 A194	60c multicolored	45	22

25th anniversary of the Organization of American States.

José Antonio Paez — A195

Street of the Lancers, Puerto Cabello — A196

Designs: 10c, Paez in uniform. 30c, Paez and horse, from old print. 2b, Paez at Battle of Centauro, horiz. 10c, 2b are after contemporary paintings.

1973   Perf. 14x13½, 13½x14

1032 A195	10c gold & multi	15	15
1033 A195	30c red, blk & gold	22	15
1034 A195	50c bl, vio bl & dk brn	45	22
1035 A196	1b multicolored	90	45
1036 A195	2b gold & multi	1.50	90
	Nos. 1032-1036 (5)	3.22	1.87

Gen. José Antonio Paez (1790-1873), leader in War of Independence, President of Venezuela. The 1b for the sesquicentenary of the fall of Puerto Cabello.
Issue dates: Nos. 1033-1034, May 6; Nos. 1032, 1036, June 13; No. 1035, Nov. 8.

José P. Padilla, Mariano Montilla, Manuel Manrique — A197

Designs: 1b, Naval battle. 2b, Line-up for naval battle.

1973, July 27   Litho.   Perf. 12½

1037 A197	50c multicolored	32	18
1038 A197	1b multicolored	70	32
1039 A197	2b multicolored	1.40	70

150th anniv. of the Battle of Maracaibo.

Bishop Ramos de Lora — A198

Plane, Ship, Margarita Island — A199

1973, Aug. 1   Photo.   Perf. 14x13½

1040 A198	75c gold & dk brn	50	22

Sesquicentennial of the birth of Ramos de Lora (1722-1790), first Bishop of Merida de Maracaibo and founder of the Colegio Seminario, the forerunner of the University of the Andes.

1973, Sept. 8   Litho.   Perf. 14x13½

1041 A199	5c multicolored	18	15

Establishment of Margarita Island as a free port.

Map of Golden Road and Waterfall — A200

Designs (Road Map and): 10c, Scarlet macaw. 20c, Church ruins. 50c, 60c, Indian mountain sanctuary. 90c, Colonial church. 1b, Flags of Venezuela and Brazil.

1973, Oct. 1   Litho.   Perf. 13

1042 A200	5c black & multi	15	15
1043 A200	10c black & multi	15	15
1044 A200	20c black & multi	25	15
1045 A200	50c black & multi	65	22
1046 A200	60c black & multi	65	22
1047 A200	90c black & multi	95	30
1048 A200	1b black & multi	1.10	42
	Nos. 1042-1048 (7)	3.90	
	Set value		1.35

Completion of the Golden Road from Santa Elena de Uairen, Brazil, to El Dorado, Venezuela. Issue dates: 50c, 60c, Oct. 30; others Oct. 1.

Gen. Paez Dam and Power Station — A201

1973, Oct. 14   Perf. 14x13½

1049 A201	30c multicolored	25	15

Opening of the Gen. José Antonio Paez Dam and Power Station.

Child on Slide — A202

Designs: No. 1051, Fairytale animals. No. 1052, Children's book. No. 1053, Children disembarking from plane for vacation.

1973, Dec. 4   Litho.   Perf. 12

1050 A202	10c multicolored	22	15
1051 A202	10c multicolored	22	15
1052 A202	10c multicolored	22	15
1053 A202	10c multicolored	22	15
	Set value		24

Children's Foundation Festival.

King Following Star — A203

Christmas: No. 1055, Two Kings.

1973, Dec. 5   Litho.   Perf. 14x13½

1054 A203	30c multicolored	35	15
1055 A203	30c multicolored	35	15
a.	Pair, #1054-1055	85	85

Regional Map of Venezuela A204

1973, Dec. 13   Perf. 13½x14

1056 A204	25c multicolored	22	15

Introduction of regionalization.

Handicraft — A205

Designs: 35c, Industrial park. 45c, Cog wheels and chimney.

1973, Dec. 18   Perf. 14x13½

1057 A205	15c blue & multi	15	15
1058 A205	35c multicolored	30	15
1059 A205	45c yellow & multi	45	18
	Set value		32

Progress in Venezuela and jobs for the handicapped.

Map of Carupano and Revelers — A206

1974, Feb. 22   Perf. 13½x14

1060 A206	5c multicolored	15	15

10th anniversary of Carupano Carnival.

Congress Emblem — A207

1974, May 20   Litho.   Perf. 13½

1061 A207	50c multicolored	45	15

9th Venezuelan Engineering Congress, Maracaibo, May 19-25.

Waves and "M" A208

Designs: Under-water photographs of deep-sea fish and marine life.

1974, June 20   Litho.   Perf. 12½

1062 A208	15c multicolored	15	15
1063 A208	35c multicolored	20	15
1064 A208	75c multicolored	50	22
1065 A208	80c multicolored	55	32
	Set value		70

3rd UN Conference on the Law of the Sea, Caracas, June 20-Aug. 29.

Pupil and New School — A209

"Pay your Taxes" Campaign: 10c, 15c, 20c, like 5c. 25c, 30c, 35c, 40c, Suburban housing development. 45c, 50c, 55c, 60c, Highway and overpass. 65c, 70c, 75c, 80c, Playing field (sport). 85c, 90c, 95c, 1b, Operating room. All designs include Venezuelan coat of arms, coins and banknotes.

1974   Perf. 13½

1066 A209	5c blue & multi	15	15
1067 A209	10c ultra & multi	15	15
1068 A209	15c violet & multi	15	15
1069 A209	20c lilac & multi	15	15
1070 A209	25c multicolored	15	15
1071 A209	30c multicolored	40	20
1072 A209	35c multicolored	20	15
1073 A209	40c olive & multi	32	15
1074 A209	45c multicolored	32	15
1075 A209	50c green & multi	32	15
1076 A209	55c multicolored	55	30
1077 A209	60c multicolored	42	20
1078 A209	65c bister & multi	1.00	50
1079 A209	70c multicolored	45	20
1080 A209	75c multicolored	50	22
1081 A209	80c brown & multi	50	22
1082 A209	85c ver & multi	50	22

1083	A209	90c multicolored	65 24
1084	A209	95c multicolored	1.25 65
1085	A209	1b multicolored	65 32
		Nos. 1066-1085 (20)	8.78
		Set value	4.00

Bolivar at Battle of Junin A210

1974, Aug. 6   Litho.   Perf. 13¹/₂x14
1086 A210 2b multicolored   1.50 75

Sesquicentennial of the Battle of Junin.

Globe and UPU Emblem — A211

Design: 50c, Postrider, sailing ship, steamer and jet.

1974, Oct. 9   Perf. 12
1087 A211 45c dk blue & multi   32 15
1088 A211 50c black & multi   40 20

Centenary of Universal Postal Union.

Rufino Blanco-Fombona A212

Designs: Portraits of Blanco-Fombona and his books.

1974, Oct. 16   Litho.   Perf. 12¹/₂
1089 A212 10c gray & multi   15 15
1090 A212 30c yellow & multi   20 15
1091 A212 45c multicolored   30 15
1092 A212 90c buff & multi   50 22
            Set value   52

Centenary of the birth of Rufino Blanco-Fombona (1874-1944), writer.

Children — A213

1974, Nov. 29   Litho.   Perf. 13¹/₂
1093 A213 70c blue & multi   50 24

Children's Foundation Festival.

General Sucre — A214

Globe with South American Map and Flags — A215

Battle of Ayacucho — A216

Design: 1b, Map of South America with battles marked.

1974, Dec. 9   Perf. 14x13¹/₂, 13¹/₂x14
1094 A214 30c multicolored   20 15
1095 A215 50c multicolored   30 22
1096 A215 1b multicolored   65 32
1097 A215 2b multicolored   1.25 65

Sesquicentennial of the Battle of Ayacucho.

Adoration of the Shepherds, by J. B. Mayno
A217   A218

1974, Dec. 16   Photo.   Perf. 14x13¹/₂
1098 A217 30c gold & multi   22 15
1099 A218 30c gold & multi   22 15
   a. Pair, #1098-1099   70 70

Christmas 1974.

Road Building, 1905 and El Ciempies Overpass, 1972 — A219

Designs: 20c, 1b, Jesus Muñoz Tebar, first Minister of Public Works. 25c, Bridges on Caracas-La Guaira Road, 1912 and 1953. 40c, View of Caracas, 1874 and 1974. 70c, Tucacas Railroad Station, 1911, and projected terminal, 1974. 80c, Anatomical Institute, Caracas, 1911, and Social Security Hospital, 1969. 85c, Quininari River Bridge, 1804, and Orinoco River Bridge, 1967.

1974, Dec. 18   Litho.   Perf. 12¹/₂
1100 A219 5c ultra & multi   15 15
1101 A219 20c ocher & blk   22 15
1102 A219 25c blue & multi   25 15
1103 A219 40c yellow & multi   22 15
1104 A219 70c green & multi   85 22

1105	A219	80c multicolored	1.00 30
1106	A219	85c orange & multi	1.25 32
1107	A219	1b red & black	1.65 50
		Nos. 1100-1107 (8)	5.59
		Set value	1.65

Centenary of the Ministry of Public Works.

Women and IWY Emblem — A220

1975, Oct. 8   Litho.   Perf. 13¹/₂x14
1108 A220 90c multicolored   50 32

International Women's Year.

Scout Emblem and Tents A221

1975, Nov. 11   Litho.   Perf. 13¹/₂x14
1109 A221 20c multicolored   15 15
1110 A221 80c multicolored   42 25
            Set value   32

14th World Boy Scout Jamboree, Lille-hammer, Norway, July 29-Aug. 7.

Adoration of the Shepherds
A222   A223

1975, Dec. 5   Litho.   Perf. 13¹/₂x14
1111 A222 30c multicolored   20 15
1112 A223 30c multicolored   20 15
   a. Pair, #1111-1112   70 70
            Set value   20

Christmas 1975.

Bolivar's Tomb — A224

Design: 1.05b, National Pantheon.

1976, Feb. 2   Engr.   Perf. 14x13¹/₂
1113 A224 30c gray & ultra   15 15
1114 A224 1.05b sepia & car   50 22
            Set value   28

Centenary of National Pantheon.

Bolivia Flag Colors A225

1976, Mar. 22   Litho.   Perf. 13¹/₂
1115 A225 60c multicolored   35 15

Sesquicentennial of Bolivia's independence.

Aerial Map Survey — A226

1976, Apr. 8   Perf. 13¹/₂x12¹/₂
1116 A226 1b black & vio bl   50 22

Natl. Cartographic Institute, 40th anniv.

Gen. Ribas' Signature A227

José Felix Ribas A228

1976, Apr. 26   Photo.   Perf. 12¹/₂x13
1117 A227 40c red & green   24 15
                        Perf. 13¹/₂
1118 A228 55c multicolored   35 15

Gen. José Felix Ribas (1775-1815), independence hero, birth bicentenary.

Musicians of the Chacao School, by Armandio Barrios — A229

Lamas's Colophon A230

1976, May 13   Litho.   Perf. 13¹/₂
1119 A229 75c multicolored   35 22

                Photo.   Perf. 12¹/₂x13
1120 A230 1.25b buff, red & gray   60 35

José Angel Lamas (1775-1814), composer, birth bicentenary.

Bolivar, by José Maria
Espinoza — A231

1976		Engr.	Perf. 12

Size: 18x22½mm

1121	A231	5c green	15	15
1122	A231	10c lilac rose	15	15
1123	A231	15c brown	15	15
1124	A231	20c black	15	15
1125	A231	25c yellow	15	15
1126	A231	30c violet bl	15	15
1127	A231	45c dk purple	15	15
1128	A231	50c orange	16	15
1129	A231	65c blue	20	15
1130	A231	1b vermilion	30	25

Size: 26x32mm
Perf. 12x11½

1131	A231	2b gray	60	25
1132	A231	3b violet blue	80	40
1133	A231	4b yellow	1.00	55
1134	A231	5b orange	1.50	75
1135	A231	10b dull purple	2.75	1.40
1136	A231	15b blue	4.25	2.00
1137	A231	20b vermilion	5.50	2.75
		Nos. 1121-1137 (17)	18.11	9.70

Issued: 5c-1b, May 17. 2b-20b, July 15.

Coil Stamps
1978, May 22   Perf. 13½ Horiz.
Size: 18x22½mm

1138	A231	5c green	15	15
1139	A231	10c lilac rose	15	15
1140	A231	15c brown	15	15
1141	A231	20c black	15	15
1142	A231	25c yellow	15	15
1143	A231	30c violet blue	15	15
1144	A231	45c dk purple	20	15
1144A	A231	50c orange	22	15
1144B	A231	65c blue	25	15
1144C	A231	1b vermilion	42	15
		Set value	1.60	72

Black control number on back of every fifth stamp.
See Nos. 1305-1307, 1362-1366, 1401-1409, 1482, 1484, 1487, 1490. Compare with types A405-A406.

Maze
A232

Central
University
A233

Faculty
Emblems
A234

1976, June 1   Litho.   Perf. 12½x13
1145	A232	30c multicolored	15	15
1146	A233	50c yel, org & blk	24	15
1147	A234	90c black & yellow	52	35

Central University of Venezuela, 250th anniv.

"Unity" — A235

Washington, US Bicent.
Emblem — A236

Designs: 45c, 1.25b, similar to 15c.

1976, June 29   Litho.   Perf. 12½
1148	A235	15c multicolored	15	15
1149	A235	45c multicolored	24	15
1150	A235	1.25b multicolored	55	35
		Set value		46

Amphictyonic Cong. of Panama, Sesqui.

1976, July 4   Engr.   Perf. 14
US Bicentennial Emblem and: No. 1152, Jefferson. No. 1153, Lincoln. No. 1154, F. D. Roosevelt. No. 1155, J. F. Kennedy.

1151	A236	1b red brn & blk	52	32
1152	A236	1b green & blk	52	32
1153	A236	1b purple & blk	52	32
1154	A236	1b blue & blk	52	32
1155	A236	1b olive & blk	52	32
		Nos. 1151-1155 (5)	2.60	1.60

American Bicentennial.

Valve — A237

Ornament — A239

Nativity, by
Barbaro
Rivas — A238

Designs: Computer drawings of valves and pipelines.

1976, Nov. 8   Photo.   Perf. 12⅓x14
1156	A237	10c multicolored	15	15
1157	A237	30c multicolored	15	15
1158	A237	35c multicolored	15	15
1159	A237	40c multicolored	15	15
1160	A237	55c multicolored	24	15
1161	A237	90c multicolored	45	24
		Nos. 1156-1161 (6)	1.29	
		Set value		68

Nationalization of the oil industry.

1976, Dec. 1   Litho.   Perf. 13x14
| 1162 | A238 | 30c multicolored | 35 | 15 |

Christmas 1976.

Lithographed and Embossed
1976, Dec. 15   Perf. 14x13½
| 1163 | A239 | 60c yellow & blk | 35 | 15 |

Declaration of Bogota (economic agreements of Andean countries), 10th anniv.

Coat of Arms of Barinas — A240

1977, May 25   Photo.   Perf. 12½x13
| 1164 | A240 | 50c multicolored | 35 | 15 |

400th anniv. of the founding of Barinas.

Crucified Christ,
Patron Saint of La
Grita — A241

1977, Aug. 6   Litho.   Perf. 13
| 1165 | A241 | 30c multicolored | 20 | 15 |

400th anniv. of the founding of La Grita (in 1976).

Symbolic
City — A242

1977, Aug. 26   Litho.   Perf. 13½
| 1166 | A242 | 1b multicolored | 50 | 22 |

450th anniversary of the founding of Coro.

Communications Symbols — A243

1977, Sept. 30   Litho.   Perf. 13½x14
| 1167 | A243 | 85c multicolored | 50 | 15 |

9th Interamerican Postal and Telecommunications Staff Congress, Caracas, Sept. 26-30.

Cable Connecting with
TV, Telephone and
Circuit Box — A244

1977, Oct. 12   Litho.   Perf. 14
| 1168 | A244 | 95c multicolored | 50 | 15 |

Inauguration of Columbus underwater cable linking Venezuela and the Canary Islands.

"Venezuela"
A245

Designs: "Venezuela" horizontal on 50c, 1.05b; reading up on 80c, 1.25b; reading down on 1.50b.

1977, Nov. 26   Photo.   Perf. 13½x13
1169	A245	30c brt yel & blk	15	15
1170	A245	50c dp org & blk	22	15
1171	A245	80c gray & blk	42	15
1172	A245	1.05b red & blk	50	20
1173	A245	1.25b yel & blk	55	20
1174	A245	1.50b gray & blk	70	24
		Nos. 1169-1174 (6)	2.54	
		Set value		95

Iron industry nationalization, 1st anniv.

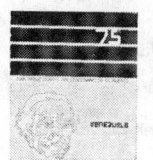

Juan Pablo
Duarte — A246

Nativity, Colonial
Sculpture — A247

1977, Dec. 8   Engr.   Perf. 11x13
| 1175 | A246 | 75c black & lilac | 40 | 15 |

Duarte (1813-76), leader in liberation struggle.

1977, Dec. 15   Litho.   Perf. 13
| 1176 | A247 | 30c green & multi | 18 | 15 |

Christmas 1977.

OPEC
Emblem — A248

1977, Dec. 20
| 1177 | A248 | 1.05b brt & lt bl & blk | 50 | 15 |

50th Conference of Oil Producing and Exporting Countries, Caracas.

Racing
Bicyclists
A249

1978, Jan. 16   Litho.   Perf. 13½x13
1178	A249	5c shown	15	15
1179	A249	1.25b Bicyclist	55	20
		Set value	60	25

World Bicycling Championships, San Cristobal, Tachira, Aug. 22-Sept. 4.

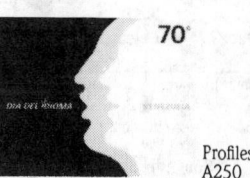

Profiles
A250

1978, Apr. 21   Litho.   Perf. 13½x14
| 1180 | A250 | 70c blk, gray & lil | 32 | 15 |

Language Day.

Magnetic
Computer Tape
and
Satellite — A251

1978, May 17   Litho.   Perf. 14
| 1184 | A251 | 75c violet blue | 35 | 20 |

10th World Telecommunications Day.

The first value column gives the catalogue value of an unused stamp, the second that of a used stamp.

"1777-1977"
A252

Goya's Carlos III as
Computer Print
A253

1978, June 23   Litho.   Perf. 12
1185 A252 30c multicolored   15 15
1186 A253 1b multicolored   50 15
        Set value   22

200th anniversary of Venezuelan unification.

Bolivar Bicentenary

Juan Vicente Bolivar y Ponte, Father of
Simon Bolivar
A254

The Oath on Monte Sacro, Rome, by Tito
Salas — A255

Designs: 30c, Bolivar as infant in nurse-maid's
arms (detail from design of No. 1189). No. 1189,
Baptism of the Liberator, by Tito Salas, 1929.
Illustration A255 is reduced.

1978, July 24   Engr.   Perf. 12½
1187 A254 30c emerald & blk   15 15
1188 A254 1b multicolored   50 22

Souvenir Sheet
Litho.
Perf. 14
1189 A255   Sheet of 5   13.00 13.00
  a.   50c, single stamp   1.25 1.25

1978, Dec. 17   Engr.   Perf. 12½

Designs: 30c, Bolivar at 25. 1b, Simon Rodriguez
(Bolivar's tutor).

1190 A254 30c multicolored   15 15
1191 A254 1b rose red & blk   32 15
        Set value   22

Souvenir Sheet
Litho.
Perf. 14
1192 A255   Sheet of 5   1.00 1.00
  a.   50c, single stamp   15   15

Size of souvenir sheet stamps: 20x24mm. Size of
No. 1189: 154x130mm. Size of No. 1192:
130x155mm.

1979, July 24   Engr.   Perf. 12½

Designs: 30c, Alexandre Sabes Petion, president
of Haiti. 1b, Bolivar's signature.
No. 1195a, Partial map of Jamaica, horiz. b, Partial map of Jamaica, vert. c, Bolivar, 1816. d, Luis
Brion. e, Petion.

1193 A254 30c org, vio & blk   15 15
1194 A254 1b red org & blk   32 15
        Set value   22

Souvenir Sheet
Litho.
Perf. 14
1195 A255   Sheet of 5   2.00 2.00
  a.-e. 50c, any single   15   15

Size of souvenir sheet stamps: 26x20, 20x26mm.

1979, Dec. 17   Engr.   Perf. 12½

Designs: 30c, Bolivar. 1b, Slave. No. 1198, Freeing of the Slaves, by Tito Salas. (30c, 1b, details
from design of No. 1198.)

1196 A254 30c multicolored   15 15
1197 A254 1b multicolored   32 15
        Set value   22

Souvenir Sheet
Litho.
Perf. 14
1198 A255   Sheet of 5   1.00 1.00
  a.   50c, single stamp   15   15

Simon Bolivar, birth centenary. Size of souvenir
sheet stamps: 22x28mm.
See Nos. 1228-1230, 1264-1266, 1276-1284,
1294-1296, 1317-1322.

"T" and
"CTV" — A256

Symbolic
Design — A257

Designs: Different arrangement of letters "T" and
"CTV" for "Confederacion de Trabajeros
Venezolanos."

1978, Sept. 27 Photo.   Perf. 13x13½
1199   Strip of 5   52 52
  a. A256 30c, single stamp   15 15
1200   Strip of 5   1.50 1.50
  a. A256 95c, single stamp   25 15

Workers' Day.

1978, Oct. 3   Litho.   Perf. 14
1201 A257 50c dark brown   50 22

Rafael Rangel, physician and scientist, birth
centenary.

Drill Head,
Tachira Oil Field
Map — A258

"P" as Pipeline
A259

1978, Nov. 2   Litho.   Perf. 13½
1202 A258 30c multicolored   15 15
1203 A259 1.05b multicolored   50 22
        Set value   28

Centenary of oil industry.

Star — A260

1978, Dec. 6   Litho.   Perf. 14
1204 A260 30c multicolored   18 15

Christmas 1978.

"P T" — A261

1979, Feb. 8   Litho.   Perf. 12½
1205 A261 75c black & red   24 15

Creation of Postal and Telegraph Institute.

"Dam Holding
Back
Water" — A262

1979, Feb. 15   Photo.   Perf. 13½
1206 A262 2b silver, gray & blk   65 32

Guri Dam, 10th anniversary.

San
Martin,
by E. J.
Maury
A263

Designs: 60c, San Martin, by Mercedes. 70c,
Monument, Guayaquil. 75c, San Martin's
signature.

1979, Feb. 25   Perf. 12½x13
1207 A263 40c blue, blk & yel   15 15
1208 A263 60c blue, blk & yel   22 15
1209 A263 70c blue, blk & yel   30 15
1210 A263 75c blue, blk & yel   32 20
        Set value   52

José de San Martin (1778-1850), South American liberator.

"Rotary" — A264

1979, Aug. 7   Litho.   Perf. 14x13½
1211 A264 85c gold & blk   28 15

Rotary Club of Caracas, 50th anniversary.

Our Lady of
Coromoto
Appearing to
Children — A265

Engraved and Lithographed
1979, Aug. 23   Perf. 13
1212 A265 55c black & dp org   18 15

25th anniversary of the canonization of Our Lady
of Coromoto.

London
Residence,
Coat of
Arms,
Miranda
A266

1979, Oct. 23   Litho.   Perf. 14½x14
1213 A266 50c multicolored   15 15

Francisco de Miranda (1750-1816), Venezuelan
independence fighter.

O'Leary,
Maps of
South
America
and United
Kingdom
A267

1979, Nov. 6
1214 A267 30c multicolored   15 15

Daniel O'Leary (1801-1854), writer.

A268

A269

IYC Emblem and: 79c, Boy holding nest. 80c,
Boys in water, bridge.

1979, Nov. 20   Litho.   Perf. 14½x14
1215 A268 70c lt blue & blk   22 15
1216 A268 80c multicolored   25 15
        Set value   24

International Year of the Child.

1979, Dec. 1   Litho.   Perf. 13
1217 A269 30c multicolored   18 15

Christmas 1979.

Caudron
Bomber,
EXFILVE
Emblem
A270

EXFILVE Emblem and: No. 1219, Stearman
biplane. No. 1220, UH-1H helicopter. No. 1221,
CF-5 jet fighter.

1979, Dec. 15   Perf. 11x11½
1218 A270 75c multicolored   24 15
1219 A270 75c multicolored   24 15
1220 A270 75c multicolored   24 15
1221 A270 75c multicolored   24 15
  a. Block of 4, #1218-1221   1.00 60
        Set value   48

Venezuelan Air Force, 59th anniv.; EXFILVE 79,
3rd Natl. Philatelic Exhibition, Dec. 7-17.

IPOSTEL
Emblem,
World
Map — A271

1979, Dec. 27   Perf. 11½
1222 A271 75c multicolored   24 15

Postal and Telegraph Institute, introduction of
new logo.

Queen
Victoria,
Hill
A272

1980, Feb. 13   Litho.   Perf. 12½
1223 A272 55c multicolored   18 15
Sir Rowland Hill (1795-1879), originator of
penny postage.

Dr. Augusto
Pi Suner,
Physiologist,
Birth
Centenary
A273

1980, Mar. 14   Litho.   Perf. 11½
1224 A273 80c multicolored   25 15

Spanish Seed   Juan Lovera (1778-
Leaf — A274   1841),
                         Artist — A275

Lithographed and Engraved
1980, Mar. 27   Perf. 13
1225 A274 50c multicolored   18 15
Pedro Loefling (1729-56), Swedish botanist.

1980, May 25   Litho.   Perf. 13½
1226 A275 60c blue & dp org   20 15
1227 A275 75c violet & org   24 15
           Set value   22

Bolivar Bicentenary Type of 1978

Designs: 30c, Signing of document. 1b, House of
Congress. No. 1230, Angostura Congress, by Tito
Salas.

1980, July 24   Engr.   Perf. 12½
1228 A254 30c multicolored   15 15
1229 A254 1b multicolored   32 15
           Set value   22

Souvenir Sheet
Litho.
Perf. 14
1230 A255   Sheet of 5   1.75 1.00
 a.   50c, single stamp   15 15
Simon Bolivar (1783-1830), revolutionary. Size
of souvenir sheet stamps: 25x20mm, 20x25mm.

Dancing Girls, by   Bernardo
Armando   O'Higgins — A277
Reveron — A276

1980, Aug. 17   Litho.   Perf. 13
1231 A276 50c shown   15 15
Size: 25x40mm
1232 A276 65c Portrait   42 22
           Set value   30
Armando Reveron (1889-1955), artist.

Lithographed and Engraved
1980, Aug. 22   Perf. 13x14
1233 A277 85c multicolored   55 25
Bernardo O'Higgins (1776-1842), Chilean soldier
and statesman.

School Ship
Simon
Bolivar — A278

Frigate
Mariscal
Sucre
A279

Perf. 11½ (#1234), 11x11½
1980, Sept. 13   Litho.
1234 A278 1.50b shown   75 24
1235 A279 1.50b shown   75 24
1236 A279 1.50b Submarine Picuda   75 24
1237 A279 1.50b Naval Academy   75 24
"Picuda" is misspelled on stamp.

Workers
Holding OPEC
Emblem
A280

20th Anniversary of OPEC (Organization of
Petroleum Exporting Countries): No. 1239,
Emblem.

1980, Sept. 14   Litho.   Perf. 12x11½
1238 A280 1.50b multicolored   50 24
1239 A280 1.50b multicolored   50 24

Death of
Simon
Bolivar
A281

1980, Dec. 17   Litho.   Perf. 11x11½
1240 A281 2b multicolored   65 32
Simon Bolivar, 150th anniversary of death.

A282   A283

Lithographed and Engraved
1980, Dec. 17   Perf. 13x12½
1241 A282 2b multicolored   65 32
Gen. José Antonio Sucre, 150th anniv. of death.

1980, Dec. 19   Litho.   Perf. 14x13½
1242 A283 1b Nativity by Rubens   25 15
Christmas 1980.

Helen Keller's Initials (Written and
Braille) — A284

Lithographed and Embossed
1981, Feb. 12   Perf. 12½
1243 A284 1.50b multicolored   40 20
Helen Keller (1880-1968), blind and deaf writer
and lecturer.

John Baptiste de   San Felipe City,
la Salle — A285   250th
                       Anniv. — A286

1981, May 15   Litho.   Perf. 11½x11
1244 A285 1.25b multicolored   32 15
Christian Brothers' 300th anniv.

1981, May 1   Perf. 11½
1245 A286 3b multicolored   65 32

Municipal
Theater of
Caracas
Centenary
A287

1981, June 28   Litho.   Perf. 12
1246 A287 1.25b multicolored   32 15

A288   A290

A289

1981, Sept. 15   Litho.   Perf. 11½
1247 A288 2b multicolored   40 20
UPU membership centenary.

1981, Oct. 14   Litho.
1248 A289 1b multicolored   25 15
11th natl. population and housing census.

1981, Dec. 3   Litho.   Perf. 11½
1249 A290 95c multicolored   25 15
9th Bolivar Games, Barquismeto.

19th Cent.
Bicycle
A291

1981, Dec. 5   Photo.   Perf. 13x14
1250 A291   1b shown   25 15
1251 A291   1.05b Locomotive, 1926   25 15
1252 A291   1.25b Buick, 1937   32 15
1253 A291   1.50b Coach   40 20
See Nos. 1289-1292, 1308-1311.

Christmas
1981 — A292

1981, Dec. 21   Litho.   Perf. 11½
1254 A292 1b multicolored   25 15

50th Anniv. of Natural
Science Society — A293

1982, Jan. 21   Perf. 11½
1255 A293   1b Mt. Autana   25 15
1256 A293   1.50b Sarisarinama   40 20
1257 A293   2b Guacharo Cave   50 22

20th Anniv.
of
Constitution
A294

1982, Jan. 28   Photo.   Perf. 13x13½
1258 A294 1.85b gold & blk   50 22

A295   A296

1982, Feb. 19   Litho.   Perf. 13½
1259 A295 3b multicolored   85 32

20th anniv. of agricultural reform.

1982, Mar. 12   Litho.   Perf. 13½
1260 A296 1b blue & dk blue   15 15

Jules Verne (1828-1905), science fiction writer.

Natl. Anthem Centenary (1981) A297

1982, Mar. 26   Perf. 11½
1261 A297 1b multicolored   15 15

1300th Anniv. of Bulgaria A298   6th Natl. 5-Year Plan, 1981-85 A299

1982, June 2   Litho.   Perf. 13½
1262 A298 65c multicolored   15 15

1982, June 11
1263 A299 2b multicolored   25 15

Bolivar Types of 1978

1982, July 24   Engr.   Perf. 12½
1264 A254 30c Juan José Rondon   15 15
1265 A254 1b José Antonio Anzoategui   15 15
Set value   18 15

Souvenir Sheet
Litho.
Perf. 14
1266 A255 Sheet of 5   40 40
a.-e.   50c, any single   15 15

Single stamps of No. 1266 show details from Battle of Boyaca, by Martin Tovar y Tovar. Size of souvenir sheet stamps: 19x26mm, 26x19mm.

Cecilio Acosta (1818-1881), Writer — A299a

1982, Aug. 13   Litho.   Perf. 11½
1266F A299a 3b multicolored   40 20

Aloe A300

1982, Oct. 14   Photo.   Perf. 13
1267 A300 1.05b shown   30 15
1268 A300 2.55b Tortoise   85 20
1269 A300 2.75b Tara armilla tree   90 20
1270 A300 3b Guacharo bird   1.00 22

Andres Bello (1781-1865), Statesman and Reformer A301

1982, Nov. 20   Litho.   Perf. 12
1271 A301 1.05b multicolored   20 15
1272 A301 2.55b multicolored   55 20
1273 A301 2.75b multicolored   60 20
1274 A301 3b multicolored   65 22

Christmas 1982 — A302

Design: Holy Family creche figures by Francisco J. Cardozo, 18th cent.

Photogravure and Engraved
1982, Dec. 7   Perf. 13½
1275 A302 1b multicolored   18 15

Bolivar Types of 1978

1982-83   Engr.   Perf. 12½
1276 A254 30c Victory Monument, Carabobo 16 15
1277 A254 30c Monument to the Meeting plaque 16 15
1278 A254 30c Antonio de Sucre   16 15
1279 A254 1b Jose Antonio Paez   35 15
1280 A254 1b Sword hilt, 1824   35 15
1281 A254 1b Guayaquil Monument   35 15
Nos. 1276-1281 (6)   1.53
Set value   35

Souvenir Sheets
Litho.
Perf. 14
1282 A255 Sheet of 5   1.50 65
a.-e.   50c, any single   15 15
1283 A255 Sheet of 5   1.50 65
a.-e.   50c, any single   15 15
1284 A255 Sheet of 5   1.50 65
a.-e.   50c, any single   15 15

No. 1282: Battle of Carabobo by Martin Tovar y Tovar; No. 1283, Monument to the Meeting; No. 1284, Battle of Ayacucho, by Martin Tovar y Tovar. Issue dates: Nos. 1276-1277, 1279, 1281-1283, Dec. 17; others, Apr. 18, 1983.

Gen. Jose Francisco Bermudez — A303

Antonio Nicolas Briceno, Liberation Hero A304

Perf. 13x13½, 15x14
1982, Dec. 23   Litho.
1285 A303 3b multicolored   40 20
1286 A304 3b multicolored   40 20

25th Anniv. of 1958 Reforms A305

1983, Jan. 23   Perf. 10½x10
1287 A305 3b multicolored   40 20

A306   A307

1983, Mar. 20 Photo. Perf. 13½x13
1288 A306 4b olive & red   50 25

25th anniv. of Judicial Police Technical Dept.

Transportation Type of 1981
Perf. 13½x14½
1983, Mar. 28   Photo.
1289 A291 75c Lincoln, 1923   22 15
1290 A291 80c Locomotive, 1889   25 15
1291 A291 85c Willys truck, 1927   30 15
1292 A291 95c Cleveland motorcycle, 1920 30 15
Nos. 1289-1292 (4)   1.07
Set value   26

1983, May 17 Photo. Perf. 13x12½
1293 A307 2.85b multicolored   32 20

World Communications Year.

Bolivar Type of 1978

Designs: 30c; Flags of Colombia, Peru, Chile, Venezuela, and Buenos Aires. 1b; Equestrian Statue of Bolivar.

Photo. & Engr. (#1294), Engr. (#1295)
1983, July 25   Perf. 12½
1294 A254 30c multicolored   15 15
1295 A254 1b multicolored   15 15
Set value   16 15

Souvenir Sheet
Litho.
Perf. 14
1296 A255 Sheet of 5   50 40
a.-e.   50c, any single   15 15

Single stamps of No. 1296 show details of "The Liberator on the Silver Mountain of Potosi" Size of souvenir sheet stamps, 20x25mm.

9th Pan-American Games
A308   A309

Designs: #1303a, baseball. b, cycle wheel. c, boxing glove. d, soccer ball. e, target.

Lithographed and Engraved
1983, Aug. 25   Perf. 13
1297 A308 2b shown   25 15
1298 A308 2b Swimming   25 15
1299 A308 2.70b Cycling   32 15
1300 A308 2.70b Fencing   32 15
1301 A308 2.85b Runners   42 16
1302 A308 2.85b Weightlifting   42 16
Nos. 1297-1302 (6)   1.98 92

Souvenir Sheet
1303   Sheet of 5
a.-e.   A309 1b, any single

No. 1303 issued for Copan '83. Size: 167x121mm.

25th Anniv. of Cadafe (State Electricity Authority) — A310

1983, Oct. 27   Litho.   Perf. 14
1304 A310 3b multicolored   80 40

Bolivar Type of 1976
1983, Sept. 29   Engr.   Perf. 12
Size: 26x32mm
1305 A231 25b blue green   5.25 2.75
1306 A231 30b brown   6.50 3.25
1307 A231 50b brt rose lilac   10.50 5.25

Transportation Type of 1981

Various views of Caracas Metro.

1983, Dec. Photo. Perf. 13½x14½
1308 A291 55c multicolored   15 15
1309 A291 75c multicolored   15 15
1310 A291 95c multicolored   20 15
1311 A291 2b multicolored   52 25
Set value   50

Christmas 1983 A311

1983, Dec. 1   Litho.   Perf. 13x14
1312 A311 1b Nativity   15 15

Scouting Year (1982) A312

Lithographed and Engraved
1983, Dec. 14   Perf. 12½x13
1313 A312 2.25p Pitching tent   22 15
1314 A312 2.55b Planting tree   28 15
1315 A312 2.75b Mountain climbing   30 15
1316 A312 3b Camp site   32 15

Bolivar Type of 1976

Designs: No. 1317, Title page of "Opere di Raimondo Montecuccoli" (most valuable book in Caracas University Library). No. 1318, Pedro Gual, Congress of Panama delegate, 1826. No. 1319, Jose Maria Vargas (b. 1786), University of Caracas pres. No. 1320, José Faustino Sanchez Carrion, Congress of Panama delegate, 1826.

1984   Engr.   Perf. 12½
1317 A254 30c multicolored   15 15
1318 A254 30c multicolored   15 15
1319 A254 1b multicolored   15 15
1320 A254 1b multicolored   15 15
Set value   30 26

Souvenir Sheets
Litho.
Perf. 14
1321 A255 Sheet of 5   65
a.-e.   50c, any single   15
1322 A255 Sheet of 5   65
a.-e.   50c, any single   15

Single stamps of No. 1321 show details of Arts, Science and Education, fresco by Hector Poleo;

1322, Map of South America, 1829. Size of souvenir sheet stamps: 20x30mm; 27x20mm.
   Issue dates: Nos. 1317, 1319, 1321, Jan. 19. Others, Jan. 20.

Radio Waves — A313

Intelligentsia for Peace — A314

1984, Jan. 30   Litho.   Perf. 14x13
1323 A313 2.70b multicolored   32 15
   Radio Club of Venezuela, 50th anniv.

1984, Jan. 31
1324 A314   1b Doves   15 15
1325 A314 2.70b Profile   30 15
1326 A314 2.85b Flower, head   32 15
      Set value   36

President Romulo Gallegos (1884-1969)
A315

Gallegos: No. 1327, Portrait as a young man in formal dress. No. 1328, Portrait, 1948.

1984-85   Litho.   Perf. 11½
1327 A315 1.70b royal bl, dl bl, beige &
                   blk   25 15
1328 A315 1.70b ocher, org brn & buff 25 15
      Set value   24

   Issue dates: No. 1327, Oct. 12, 1984; No. 1328, Jan. 18, 1985. See Nos. 1335-1336.

Pan-American Union of Engineering Associations, 18th Convention — A316

1984, Oct. 28
1329 A316 2.55b pale buff, dk bl   40 15

Christmas 1984
A317

1984, Dec. 3
1330 A317 1b multicolored   18 15

Pope John Paul II, Statue of the Virgin of Caracas
A318

1985, Jan. 26   Litho.   Perf. 12
1331 A318 1b multicolored   25 15
      Papal visit, 1985.

Pascua City Bicent.
A319

1985, Feb. 10
1332 A319 1.50b multicolored   20 15

Dr. Mario Briceno-Iragory (b. 1897), Historian — A320

1985, Oct.   Litho.   Perf. 12
1333 A320 1.25b silver & ver   18 15

Natl. St. Vincent de Paul Soc., Cent. — A321

1985, July
1334 A321 1b dk ol bis, ver & buff   20 15

   Gallegos Memorial Type of 1984-85

   Designs: Gallegos, diff.

1985, Aug. 8
1335 A315 1.70b gray grn, dk gray grn
                   & dl gray grn   24 15
1336 A315 1.70b grn, sage grn & dl grn 24 15
      Set value   24

      Dated 1984.

Latin American Economic System, 10th Anniv.
A322

1985, Aug. 15
1337 A322 4b black & red   1.10 45

Miniature Sheet

Virgin Mary, Birth Bimillennium
A323

   Statues: a, Virgin of the Divine Shepherd. b, Chiquinquira Madonna. c, Coromoto Madonna. d, Valley Madonna. e, Virgin of Perpetual Succor. f, Virgin of Peace. g, Immaculate Conception Virgin. h, Soledad Madonna. i, Virgin of Consolation. j, Nieves Madonna.

1985, Sept. 9
1338   Sheet of 10   3.50 1.10
a.-j. A323 1b, any single   35   15

OPEC, 25th Anniv.
A324

1985, Sept. 13
1339 A324 6b multicolored   80 40

Opening of the Museum of Contemporary Art, Caracas — A325

1985, Oct. 24   Perf. 13½
1340 A325 3b multicolored   40 20
      Dated 1983.

UN, 40th Anniv.
A326

1985, Nov. 15   Perf. 12
1341 A326 10b brt blue & ver   1.25 65

Intl. Youth Year — A327

1985, Nov. 26
1342 A327 1.50b multicolored   20 15

Christmas 1985
A328

   Nativity: a, Sheperds. b, Holy Family, Magi. Setenant in a continuous design.

1985, Dec. 2
1343   Pair   1.00 25
a.-b. A328 2b, any single   50 15

Dr. Luis Maria Drago (b. 1859), Politician
A329

1985, Dec. 20   Perf. 13½
1344 A329 2.70b tan, ver & sepia   35 18
      Dated 1984.

Miniature Sheet

Natl. Oil Industry, 10th Anniv.
A330

   Designs: a, Industry emblem. b, Isla Oil Refinery. c, Bariven oil terminal. d, Pequiven refinery. e, Corpoven drilling rig. f, Maraven offshore rig. g, Intevep labs. h, Meneven refinery. i, Lagoven refinery. j, Emblem, early drilling rig.

1985, Dec. 13   Perf. 12
1345   Sheet of 10   6.00 2.00
a.-b. A330 1b multi   18   15
c.-d. A330 2b multi   35   15
e.-f. A330 3b multi   60   20
g.-h. A330 4b multi   75   25
i.-j. A330 5b multi   95   32

Simon Bolivar Memorial Coins — A331

1985, Dec. 18
1346 A331   2b multicolored   25 15
1347 A331 2.70b multicolored   35 18
1348 A331   3b multicolored   40 20

      Dated 1984.

Guayana Development Corp., 25th Anniv. — A332

1985, Dec. 27
1349 A332 2b Guayana City   25 15
1350 A332 3b Orinoco Steel Mill   40 20
1351 A332 5b Raul Leoni-Guri Hydro-
             electric Dam   65 32

Miniature Sheet

Bicentenario del Nacimiento del Dr. José María Vargas

VENEZUELA Bs.   A333

Dr. Jose Vargas (1786-1854) — A334

Designs: No. 1352a, Handwriting and signature. b, Portrait, 1874, by Martin Tovar y Tovar. c, Statue, Palace of the Academies. d, Flags, EXFILBO '86 emblem. e, Vargas do Caracas Hospital. f, Frontispiece of lectures manual, 1842. g, Portrait, 1986, by Alirio Palacios. h, Gesneria vargasii. i, Bolivar-Vargas commemorative medal, 1955, 6th Natl. Medical Sciences Cong. j, Portrait, anonymous, 19th cent.

No. 1353a, Portrait, facing front. b, Portrait, facing left, Nos. 1352a, 1352d, 1352e, 1352h and 1352i have horizontal vignettes.

1986, Mar. 10   Litho.   Perf. 12
1352   Sheet of 10   2.25 1.25
a.-j.   A333 3b, any single   22   15
Souvenir Sheet
Imperf
1353   Sheet of 2   7.75 1.25
a.-b.   A334 15b, any single   3.75   60

EXFILBO '86, Mar. 10-17, Caracas, 1st Bolivarian exhibition.

VENEZUELA BS.

Youths Painting School Wall — A335

1986, May 12   Perf. 12
1354 A335 3b shown   42   15
1355 A335 5b Repairing desk   70   18

Founding and maintenance of educational institutions.

Bs 1.05   Francisco Miranda's Work for American Liberation, Bicent. (1981) A336

Lithographed and Engraved
1986, Apr. 18   Perf. 13
1356 A336 1.05b multicolored   15   15

Dated 1983.

INDULAC, 45th Anniv. A337

1986, June 27   Litho.   Perf. 12
1357 A337 2.55b Milk trucks, vert. 20   15
1358 A337 2.70b Map, vert.   22   15
1359 A337 3.70b Milk processing plant 30 15
                     Set value   36

Industria Lactea (INDULAC), Venezuelan milk processing company.

Miniature Sheet

Viasa Venezuelan Airlines, 25th Anniv. A338

Designs: a, Commemorative coin. b, Douglas DC-8 ascending. c, DC-10 taxiing. d, Boeing 737 in flight. No. e, Jet tails. f, Map of hemispheres. g, DC-9 taking off. h, Engine, wing, jet. i, DC-10 in flight. j, Crew in cockpit.

1986, Aug. 11   Litho.   Perf. 12
1360   Sheet of 10   5.00 1.65
a.-e.   A338 3b, any single   32   15
f.-j.   A338 3.25b, any single   35   15

Miniature Sheet

VENEZUELA Bs.2.70

Romulo Betancourt (1908-1981), President — A339

Designs: a, i, Portrait with natl. flag. b, j, Seated in armchair, smoking pipe. c, h, Wearing hat, text. d, f, Wearing sash of office. e, g, Reading.

1986, Sept. 28
1361   Sheet of 10   4.00 1.10
a.-e.   A339 2.70b, any single   25   15
f.-j.   A339 3b, any single   30   15

Redrawn Bolivar Type of 1976
1986, Sept. 29   Litho.   Perf. 12½
1362 A231 25c red   15   15
1363 A231 50c blue   15   15
1364 A231 75c pink   15   15
1365 A231 1b orange   16   15
1366 A231 2b brt yellow grn   28   15
           Nos. 1362-1366 (5)   89
                     Set value   28

Nos. 1362-1366 inscribed Armitano. For surcharges see Nos. 1453-1464.

VENEZUELA Bs.2.70

Re-opening of Zulia University, 40th Anniv. — A340

1986, Sept. 29
1367 A340 2.70b shown   20   15
1368 A340 2.70b Library entrance   20   15
a.   Pair, #1367-1368   40   20
                     Set value   20

Bs. 1,40

11th Congress of Architects, Engineers and Affiliated Professionals A341

1986, Oct. 3
1369 A341 1.40b multicolored   15   15
1370 A341 1.55b multicolored   15   15
a.   Pair, #1369-1370   30   20
                     Set value   16

Bs. 0,70   1983

VENEZUELA Fauna and Flora A342

1986, Sept. 12   Photo.   Perf. 13½
1371 A342 70c Priodontes maximus   15   15
1372 A342 85c Espeletia angustifolia 15   15
1373 A342 2.70b Crocodylus intermedius 15 15
1374 A342 3b Brownea grandiceps   18   15
                     Set value   46   26

Miniature Sheet

Bs. 1.00

VENEZUELA

S.S. Juan Pablo II

State Visit of Pope John Paul II — A343

1986, Oct. 22   Perf. 12
1375   Sheet of 10   3.50 1.65
a.   A343 1b Pope, mountains   15   15
b.   A343 2b Bridge   22   15
c.   A343 3b Kissing the ground   30   15
d.   A343 3b Statue of Our Lady   30   15
e.   A343 4b Crosier, buildings   45   15
f.   A343 5.25b Waterfall   60   20

#1375 contains 2 each #1375a-1375b, 1375e-1375f and one each #1375c-1375d.

Miniature Sheet

VENEZUELA

20 AÑOS Bs. FUNDACION DEL NIÑO 2.55

Children's Foundation, 20th Anniv. A344

Children's drawings: a, Three children. b, Hearts, children, birds. c, Child, animals. d, Animals, house. e, Landscape. f, Child, flowers on table. g, Child holding ball. h, Children, birds. i, Lighthouse, port. j, Butterfly in flight.

1986, Nov. 10
1376   Sheet of 10   3.00 1.25
a.-e.   A344 2.55b, any single   28   15
f.-j.   A344 2.70b, any single   30   15

Christmas A345

Creche figures carved by Eliecer Alvarez.

1986, Nov. 10
1377 A345 2b shown   20   15
1378 A345 2b Virgin and child   20   15
a.   Pair, #1377-1378   40   25
                     Set value   15

No. 1378a has a continuous design.

VENEZUELA Bs 2.70

City Police, 25th Anniv. A346

Emblem and: a, Emergency medical aid, helicopter. b, Security at sporting event. c, Bar code. d, Cadets in front of police academy. e, Motorcycle police.

1986, Dec. 10
1379   Strip of 5   1.50 50
a.-e.   A346 2.70b, any single   30   15

Folk Art — A347

VENEZUELA Bs. 2

Lithographed and Engraved
1987, Jan. 31   Perf. 13
1380 A347 2b Musical instrument   22   15
1381 A347 2b Fabric   22   15
1382 A347 3b Ceramic pot   32   15
1383 A347 3b Basket work   32   15
                     Set value   40

Dated 1983. Nos. 1380, 1382 show Pre-Hispanic art.

VENEZUELA

Discovery of the Tubercle Bacillus by Robert Koch, Cent. (in 1982) A348

Lithographed and Engraved
1987, Feb. 27   Perf. 14x14½
1384 A348 2.55b multicolored   45   15

Dated 1983.

Miniature Sheet

Easter 1987 A349

Paintings and sculpture: a, Arrival of Jesus in Jerusalem. b, Christ at the Column. c, Jesus of Nazareth. d, The Descent. e, The Solitude. f, The Last Supper. g, Christ Suffering. h, The Crucifixion. i, Christ Entombed. j, The Resurrection.

1987, Apr. 2   Litho.   Perf. 12
1385   Sheet of 10   2.75 90
a.-e.   A349 2b, any single   25   15
f.-j.   A349 2.25b, any single   28   15

VENEZUELA Bs. 3.00

NEUROQUIMICA '87

CONGRESO MUNDIAL

World Neurochemistry Congress — A350

Designs: 3b, Bolivar and Bello, outdoor sculpture by Marisol Escobar. 4.25b, Retinal neurons.

1987, May 8   Litho.   Perf. 12
1386 A350 3b multicolored   35   15
1387 A350 4.25b multicolored   48   15

Miniature Sheet

Tourism
A351

Hotels: a, f, Barquisimeto Hilton. b, g, Lake Hotel Intercontinental, Maracaibo. c, h, Macuto Sheraton, Caraballeda. d, i, Melia Caribe, Caraballeda. e, j, Melia, Puerto la Cruz.

1987, May 29   Litho.   Perf. 12
1388	Sheet of 10	4.50	1.75
a.-e.	A351 6b, any single	40	15
f.-j.	A351 6.50b, any single, diff.	40	18

Natl. Institute of Canalization, 35th Anniv. A352

1987, June 25   Litho.   Perf. 12
1389	A352	2b Map of Amazon territory waterways	15	15
1390	A352	4.25b Apure and Bolivar states waterways	22	15
a.		Pair, #1389-1390	40	30
		Set value		20

Vincente Emilion Sojo (1887-1974), Composer — A352a

Designs: 2b, Academy of Fine Arts, Caracas. 4b, Sojos directing choir. 5b, Hymn to Bolivar score. 6b, Sojo, score on blackboard. 7b, Portrait, signature.

1987, July 1   Litho.   Perf. 12
1390A	Strip of 5	1.65	85
b.	A352a 2b tan & sepia	15	15
c.	A352a 4b tan & sepia	25	15
d.	A352a 5b tan & sepia	32	15
e.	A352a 6b tan & sepia	40	20
f.	A352a 7b tan & sepia	48	24

Printed in sheets of 10 containing two strips of five, black control number (UR).

Simon Bolivar University, 20th Anniv. A353

Designs: a, Bolivar statue by Roca Rey, 1973. b, Outdoor sculpture of solar panels by Alejandro Otero, 1972. c, Rectory, 1716. d, Laser. e, Owl, sculpture, 1973.

1987, July 9   Litho.   Perf. 12
1391	Strip of 5	1.00	50
a.	A353 2b multicolored	15	15
b.	A353 3b multicolored	15	15
c.	A353 4b multicolored	20	15
d.	A353 5b multicolored	24	15
e.	A353 6b multicolored	30	15

Miniature Sheet

Ministry of Transportation and Communication — A354

Designs: a, Automobiles. b, Ship. c, Train, Cathedral. d, Letters, telegraph key. e, Communication towers. f, Highway. g, Airplane. h, Locomotive, rail caution signs. i, Satellite dish. j, Satellite in orbit.

1987, July 16
1392	Sheet of 10	1.10	52
a.-e.	A354 2b any single	15	15
f.-j.	A354 2.25b any single	15	15

Nos. 1392a and 1392f, 1392b and 1392g, 1392c and 1392h, 1392d and 1392i, 1392e and 1392j have continuous designs.

Miniature Sheet

Venezuela Navigation Company, 70th Anniv. A355

Designs: a, Corporate headquarters. b, Fork lift. c, Ship's Superstructure. d, Engine room. e, The Zulia. f, The Guarico. g, Ship's officer on the bridge. h, Bow of supertanker. i, Loading dock. j, Map of sea routes.

1987, July 31   Litho.   Perf. 12
1393	Sheet of 10	2.00	1.00
a.-b.	A355 2b, any single	15	15
c.-d.	A355 3b, any single	15	15
e.-f.	A355 4b, any single	20	15
g.-h.	A355 5b, any single	24	15
i.-j.	A355 6b, any single	30	15

Nos. 1393a, 1393c, 1393e, 1393g and 1393i in vertical strip; No. 1393b, 1393d, 1393f, 1393h and 1393j in vertical strip.

Miniature Sheet

Natl. Guard, 50th Anniv. A356

Designs: a, f, Air-sea rescue. b, g, Traffic control. c, h, Environment and nature protection. d, i, Border control. e, j, Industrial security.

1987, Aug. 6
1394	Sheet of 10	2.25	1.15
a.-e.	A356 2b, any single	15	15
f.-j.	A356 4b, any single	30	15

Discovery of America, 500th Anniv. (in 1992) A357

20th cent. paintings (details): 2b, Departure from Port of Palos, by Jacobo Borges. 7b, Discovery of America, by Tito Salas. 11.50b, El Padre de las Casas, Protector of the Indians, by Salas. 12b, Trading in Venezuela at the Time of the Conquest, by Salas. 12.50b, Defeat of Guaicaipuro, by Borges.

1987, Oct.   Litho.   Perf. 12
1395	Strip of 5	3.30	1.65
a.	A357 2b multi	15	15
b.	A357 7b multi	50	25
c.	A357 11.50b multi	85	42
d.	A357 12b multi	88	45
e.	A357 12.50b multi	90	45

Christmas 1987 — A358

Paintings and sculpture representing the Spanish Colonial School, 18th cent.: 2b, The Annunciation, by Juan Pedro Lopez (1724-1787). 3b, Nativity, by Jose Francisco Rodriguez (1767-1818). 5.50b, Adoration of the Magi, anonymous. 6b, Flight into Egypt, by Lopez.

1987, Nov. 17   Litho.   Perf. 12
1396	Block of 4	1.35	68
a.	A358 2b multi	16	15
b.	A358 3b multi	24	15
c.	A358 5.50b multi	45	22
d.	A358 6b multi	48	25

Miniature Sheet

Sidor Mills, 25th Anniv. — A359

Natl. steel production: a-d, Exterior view of steel plant (in a continuous design). e, Tower bearing the SIDOR emblem. f, Furnaces and molten steel flowing down gutters. g, Pooring steel rods. h, Slab mill. i, Steel rod production, diff. j, Anniv. emblem.

1987, Nov. 23
1397	Sheet of 10	6.25	3.15
a.	A359 2b multi	16	15
b.	A359 6b multi	48	25
c.	A359 7b multi	58	28
d.	A359 11.50b multi	92	45
e.	A359 12b black	98	50
f.	A359 2b multi	16	15
g.	A359 6b multi	48	25
h.	A359 7b multi	58	28
i.	A359 11.50b multi	92	45
j.	A359 12b multi	98	50

Meeting of 8 Latin American Presidents, 1st Anniv. A360

1987, Nov. 26
| 1398 | A360 6b multi | 48 | 25 |

Pequiven Petrochemical Co., 10th Anniv. — A361

1987, Dec. 1
1399	Strip of 5	3.15	1.55
a.	A361 2b Plastics	16	15
b.	A361 6b Refined oil products	48	25
c.	A361 7b Fertilizers	58	28
d.	A361 11.50b Installations	92	45
e.	A361 12b Expansion	98	50

St. John Bosco (1815-88) A362

Portrait of Bosco and: 2b, Map, children. 3b, National Church, Caracas. 4b, Vocational training (printer's apprentice). 5b, Church of Mary Auxiliadora. 6b, Missionary school (nun teaching children).

1987, Dec. 8
1400	Strip of 5	1.60	80
a.	A362 2b multi	16	15
b.	A362 3b multi	24	15
c.	A362 4b multi	32	16
d.	A362 5b multi	40	20
e.	A362 6b multi	48	24

Redrawn Bolivar Type of 1976

1987, Dec. 31   Litho.   Perf. 12½
1401	A231	3b emerald grn	24	15
1402	A231	4b gray	32	16
1403	A231	5b vermilion	40	20
1404	A231	10b dark olive bister	80	40
1405	A231	15b rose claret	1.20	60
1406	A231	20b bright blue	1.60	80
1407	A231	25b olive bister	2.00	1.00
1408	A231	30b dark violet	2.40	1.20
1409	A231	50b carmine	4.00	2.00
	Nos. 1401-1409 (9)		12.96	6.51

Nos. 1401-1409 inscribed Armitano.

29th Assembly of Inter-American Development Bank Governors — A363

1988, Mar. 18   Litho.   Perf. 12
| 1410 | A363 11.50b multi | 90 | 45 |

Miniature Sheet

Republic Bank, 30th Anniv. A364

Bank functions and finance projects: a, Personal banking at branch. b, Capital for labor. c, Industrial projects. d, Financing technology. e, Exports and imports. f, Financing agriculture. g, Fishery credits. h, Dairy farming development. i, Construction projects. j, Tourism trade development.

1988, Apr. 11
1411	Sheet of 10	3.00	1.50
a.-e.	A364 2b any single	15	15
f.-j.	A364 6b any single	45	22

No. 1411 contains two strips of five.

Anti-Polio Campaign Day of Victory, May 25 — A365

Design: Polio victims pictured on bronze relief, Rotary and campaign emblems.

1988, May 20   Litho.   Perf. 12
| 1412 | A365 11.50b multi | 78 | 40 |

Carlos Eduardo Frias (1906-1986),
Founder of the Natl. Publicity
Industry — A366

1988, May 27   **Litho.**   **Perf. 12**
1414	A366	Pair	98 50
a.	4b multi		28 15
b.	10b multi		70 35

Publicity Industry, 50th anniv.

Venalum Natl.
Aluminum Corp.,
10th
Anniv. — A367

Designs: 2b, Factory interior. 6b, Electric
smelter. 7b, Aluminum pipes. 11.50b, Aluminum
blocks moved by crane. 12b, Soccer team, aluminum equipment on playing field.

1988, June 10
1415	Strip of 5		2.75 1.35
a.	A367 2b multi		15 15
b.	A367 6b multi		42 20
c.	A367 7b multi		50 25
d.	A367 11.50b multi		82 40
e.	A367 12b multi		85 42

Nature
Conservation
A368

Birds: 2b, Carduelis cucullata. 6b, Eudocimus
ruber. 11.50b, Harpia harpyja. 12b, Phoenicopterus
ruber ruber. 12.50b, Pauxi pauxi.

1988, June 17   **Litho.**   **Perf. 12**
1416	Strip of 5		3.00 1.50
a.	A368 2b multi		15 15
b.	A368 6b multi		40 20
c.	A368 11.50b multi		78 40
d.	A368 12b multi		80 40
e.	A368 12.50b multi		85 42

Army
Day — A369

Military uniforms: a, Simon Bolivar in dress uniform, 1828. b, Gen.-in-Chief Jose Antonio Paez in
dress uniform, 1821. c, Liberation Army division
gen., 1810. d, Brig. gen., 1820. e, Artillery corpsman, 1836. f, Alferez Regiment parade uniform,
1988. g, Division Gen. No. 1 dress uniform, 1988.
h, Line Infantry Regiment, 1820. i, Promenade
Infantry, 1820. j, Light Cavalry, 1820.

1988, June 20
1417	Sheet of 10		5.50 2.75
a., f.	A369 2b multi		15 15
b., g.	A369 6b multi		42 20
c., h.	A369 7b multi		50 25
d., i.	A369 11.50b multi		82 40
e., j.	A369 12b multi		85 42

Scabbard,
Sword and
Signature
A370

Paintings by Tito Salas: 4.75b, *The General's
Wedding.* 6b, Portrait. 7b, *Battle of Valencia.* 12b,
Retreat from San Carlos.

1988, July 1   **Litho.**   **Perf. 12**
1418	Strip of 5		2.25 1.10
a.	A370 2b shown		15 15
b.	A370 4.75b multi		35 16
c.	A370 6b multi		42 20
d.	A370 7b multi		48 24
e.	A370 12b multi		85 42

General Rafael Urdaneta (b. 1788).

General Santiago
Marino (b. 1788),
by Martin Tovar y
Tovar — A371

1988, July
1419	A371 4.75b multi		35 16

1988 Summer
Olympics,
Seoul — A372

1988, Aug. 2
1420	A372 12b multi		85 42

Electric
Industry,
Cent.
A373

Buildings, 1888: 2b, 1st Office. 4.75b, Jaime Car-
rillo and electrical plant. 10b, Bolivar Plaza. 11.50b,
Baralt Theater. 12.50b, Central Thermoelectric
Plant, Ramon Lagoon, 1988.

1988, Oct. 25   **Litho.**   **Perf. 12**
1421	Strip of 5		2.75 1.40
a.	A373 2b multi		15 15
b.	A373 4.75b multi		32 16
c.	A373 10b multi		68 35
d.	A373 11.50b multi		78 40
e.	A373 12.50b multi		85 42

Christmas
A374

Designs: 4b, Nativity (left side), by Tito Salas,
1936. 6b, Christ child, anonymous, 17th cent. 15b,
Nativity (right side).

1988, Dec. 9
1422	A374	4b multi	28 15
1423	A374	6b multi	40 20
1424	A374	15b multi	1.05 52

Nos. 1422 and 1424 se-tenant in a continuous
design. Nos. 1422-1424 printed in strips of 5 containing No. 1423 flanked by pairs of Nos. 1422,
1424.

Miniature Sheet

Marian
Year — A375

Icons: a, Our Lady of Copacabana, Bolivia. b,
Our Lady of Chiquinquira, Colombia. c, Our Lady
of Coromoto, Venezuela. d, Our Lady of the
Clouds, Ecuador. e, Our Lady of Antigua, Panama.
f, Our Lady of the Evangelization, Peru. g, Our Lady
of Lujan, Argentina. h, Our Lady of Altagracia,
Dominican Republic. i, Our Lady of Aparecida, Brazil. j, Our Lady of Guadalupe, Mexico.

1988, Aug. 15   **Litho.**   **Perf. 12**
1425	Sheet of 10		3.85 1.90
a.-e.	A375 4.75b any single		35 18
f.-j.	A375 6b any single		42 20

Juan Manuel
Cagigal
Observatory,
Cent.
A376

Designs: 2b, Bardou refracting telescope. 4.75b,
Universal theodolite AUZ-27. 6b, Bust of Cagigal.
11.50b, Boulton cupola and night sky over Caracas
in September. 12b, Satellite photographing Hurri-
cane Allen.

1989, Sept. 5
1426	Strip of 5		2.90 1.45
a.	A376 2b multicolored		16 15
b.	A376 4.75b muiticolored		38 20
c.	A376 6b multicolored		48 25
d.	A376 11.50b multicolored		90 45
e.	A376 12b multicolored		95 48

Comptroller-General's
Office, 50th
Anniv. — A377

1988, Oct. 14   **Litho.**   **Perf. 12**
1427	A377 10b multi		70 35

Portrait of
Founder Juan
Pablo Rojas Paul,
by Cristobal
Rojas,
1890 — A378

1989, Oct. 21   **Litho.**   **Perf. 12**
1428	A378	6b Commemorative medal	40 20
1429	A378	6.50b shown	45 22
a.	Pair, #1428-1429		90 60

Natl. History Academy, cent.

Portrait of
Ricardo
A379

Paintings: No. 1430, Simon Bolivar and Dr.
Mordechay Ricardo. No. 1430A, The Octagon.
Nos. 1430-1430A printed in continuous design
completing the painting *The Liberator in Curacao,*
by John de Pool.

1989, Jan. 27   **Litho.**   **Perf. 12**
1430	A379	10b multi	75 37
1430A	A379	10b multi	75 37
1430B	A379	11.50b shown	90 45
c.	Strip of 5 (2 each #1430-1430A, #1430B)		4.00 2.00

Convention with
Holy See, 25th
Anniv. — A380

Designs: a, Raul Leoni, constitutional president,
1964-69. b, Cardinal Quintero, archbishop of
Caracas, 1960-80. c, Arms of Cardinal Lebrun,
archbishop of Caracas since 1980. d, Arms of
Luciano Storero, titular archbishop of Tigimma. e,
Pope Paul VI.

1989, May 4   **Litho.**   **Perf. 12**
1431	Strip of 5		3.30 1.65
a.-b.	A380 4b any single		28 15
c.-d.	A380 12b any single		82 40
e.	A380 16b any single		1.10 55

Bank of
Venezuela,
Cent.
A381

Designs: a, *Cocoa Harvest,* by Tito Salas, 1946.
b, *Teaching a Boy How to Grow Coffee,* by Salas,
1946. c, Bank headquarters, Caracas. d, Archive of
the Liberator, Caracas. e, Aforestation campaign
(seedling). f, Aforestation campaign (five youths
planting seedlings). g, 50-Bolivar bank note (left
side). h, 50-Bolivar bank note (right side). i, 500-
Bolivar bank note (left side). j, 500-Bolivar bank
note (right side).

1989, Aug. 1
1432	Sheet of 10		3.90 2.00
a.-f.	A381 4b any single		28 15
g.-j.	A381 8b any single		55 28

Nos. 1432g-1432h and 1432i-1432j printed in
continuous designs.

America
Issue — A382

UPAE emblem and pre-Columbian votive bisque
artifacts: 6b, Vessel. 24b, Statue of a man.

1989
1433	A382	6b multicolored	40 20
1434	A382	24b multicolored	2.40 1.20
a.	Pair, #1433-1434		3.00 2.00

Christmas
A383

Designs: 1435a, Shepherds, sheep. b, Angel appears to 3 shepherds. c, Holy Family. 12b, Two witnesses. 15b, Adoration of the kings.

1989	Litho.	Perf. 12	
1435	Strip of 5	3.10	1.55
a.	A383 5b shown	35	18
b.-c.	A383 6b any single	42	20
d.	A383 12b multicolored	85	42
e.	A383 15b multicolored	1.05	52

Miniature Sheets

Bank of
Venezuela, 20th
Anniv. — A384

Tree and arms: No. 1436: a, Tabebuia chrysantha, national. b, Ceiba pentandra, Federal District. c, Myrospermum frutescens, Anzoategui. d, Pithecellobium saman, Aragua. e, Cedrela odorata, Barinas. f, Diptenyx punctata, Bolivar. g, Licania pyrofolia, Apure. h, Sterculia apetala, Carabobo.

No. 1437: a, Tabebuia rosea, Cojedes. b, Prosopis juliflora, Falcon. c, Copernicia tectorum, Guarico. d, Erythrina poeppigiana, Merida. e, Brawnea leucantha, Miranda. f, Mauritia flexuosa, Monagas. g, Malpighia glabra, Lara. h, Guaicum officinale, Nueva Esparta.

No. 1438: a, Swietenia macrophylla, Portuguesa. b, Platymiscium diadelphum, Sucre. c, Prumnopitys montana de Laub, Tachira. d, Roystonea venezuelana, Yaracuy. e, Cocos nucifera, Zulia. f, Hevea benthamiana, Federal Territory of Amazonas. g, Erythrina fusca, Trujillo. h, Rhizophora mangle, Territory of the Amacuro Delta.

1990, June 27	Litho.	Perf. 12	
1436	Sheet of 8 + 2 labels	7.50	3.75
a.-f.	A384 10b any single	50	25
g.	A384 40b multicolored	2.00	1.00
h.	A384 50b multicolored	2.50	1.25
1437	Sheet of 8 + 2 labels	7.50	3.75
a.-f.	A384 10b any single	50	25
g.	A384 40b multicolored	2.00	1.00
h.	A384 50b multicolored	2.50	1.25
1438	Sheet of 8 + 2 labels	7.50	3.75
a.-f.	A384 10b any single	50	25
g.	A384 40b multicolored	2.00	1.00
h.	A384 50b multicolored	2.50	1.25

Central Bank
of Venezuela,
50th Anniv.
A385

Designs: a, Santa Capilla Headquarters, 1943. b, Headquarters, 1967. c, Left half of 500b Bank Note, 1940. d, Right half of 500b Bank Note, 1940. e, Sun of Peru decoration, 1825. f, Medals Ayacucho, 1824, Boyaca, 1820 and Liberators of Quito, 1822. g, Swords of Peru, 1825. h, Cross pendant, Bucaramanga, 1830. i, Medallion of George Washington, 1826. j, Portrait of Gen. O'Leary.

1990, Oct. 15			
1439	Sheet of 10	9.00	4.50
a.-f.	A385 10b any single	50	25
g.-h.	A385 15b any single	72	35
i.	A385 40b multicolored	2.00	1.00
j.	A385 50b multicolored	2.50	1.25

University of
Zulia, Cent.
A386

Designs: a, Dr. Francisco Ochoa, founder. b, Dr. Jesus E. Lossada, President, 1946-47. c, Soil conservation. d, Developing alternative automotive fuels. e, Organ transplants.

1990, Sept. 18	Litho.	Perf. 12	
1440	Strip of 5	3.40	1.70
a.-b.	A386 10b any single	50	25
c.-d.	A386 15b any single	70	35
e.	A386 20b multicolored	1.00	50

Christmas
A387

Paintings: a, St. Joseph and Child by Juan Pedro Lopez. b, The Nativity by Lopez. c, The Return from Egypt by Matheo Moreno. d, The Holy Family by unknown artist. e, The Nativity (oval painting) by Lopez.

1990, Nov. 25			
1441	Strip of 5	3.50	1.75
a.-c.	A387 10b any single	50	25
d.-e.	A387 20b multicolored	1.00	50

OPEC, 30th
Anniv. — A388

Designs: a, Globe. b, Square emblem. c, Circular emblem. d, Diamond emblem. e, Flags.

1990, Dec. 21	Litho.	Perf. 12	
1442	Strip of 5	5.00	2.50
a.-b.	A388 10b any single	50	25
c.	A388 20b multicolored	1.00	50
d.	A388 30b multicolored	1.50	75
e.	A388 40b multicolored	2.00	1.00

AMERICA Issue — A389

1990, Dec. 12	Litho.	Perf. 12	
1443	A389 10b Lake dwelling	50	25
1444	A389 40b Coastline	1.90	95
a.	Pair, #1443-1444	2.40	1.20

N·E·W

Scott Supplement Pages for
Venezuela
are now available

Exfilve '90, Caracas — A389a

Designs: 40b, Bank of Venezuela 1000b note. 50b, Bank of Caracas 100b note.

1990, Nov. 16	Litho.	Imperf.	
1444B	A389a 40b multicolored	1.90	85
1444C	A389a 50b multicolored	2.35	1.20

No. 1444B, Bank of Venezuela, cent. No. 1444C, Bank of Caracas, cent.

St. Ignatius of
Loyola (1491-
1556)
A390

Designs: a, Jesuit quarters, Caracas. b, Death mask. c, Statue by Francisco de Vergara, 18th century. d, Statue of Our Lady of Montserrat, 11th century.

1991, Apr. 12	Litho.	Perf. 12	
1445	Strip of 4 + label	5.25	2.65
a.-b.	A390 12b any single	55	28
c.	A390 40b multicolored	1.85	92
d.	A390 50b multicolored	2.30	1.15

Venezuelan-American Cultural Center,
50th Anniv. — A391

Designs: a, Elisa Elvira Zuloaga (1900-1980), painter & engraver. b, Gloria Stolk (1912-1979), writer. c, Caroline Lloyd (1924-1980), composer. d, Jules Waldman (1912-1990), publisher. e, William Coles (1908-1978), attorney.

1991, July 4	Litho.	Perf. 12	
1446	Strip of 5	5.85	2.95
a.-c.	A391 12b any single	55	28
d.	A391 40b multicolored	1.85	95
e.	A391 50b multicolored	2.30	1.15

Miniature Sheet

Orchids
A392

Designs: No. 1447a, 12b, Acineta alticola. b, 12b, Brassavola nodosa. c, 12b, Brachionidium brevicaudatum. d, 12b, Bifrenaria maguirei. e, 12b, Odontoglossum spectatissimum. f, 12b, Catasetum macrocarpum. g, 40b, Mendocella jorisiana. h, 40b, Cochleanthes discolor. i, 50b, Maxillaria splendens. j, 50b, Pleurothallis dunstervillei. No. 1448, Cattleya violacea.

1991, Aug. 22	Litho.	Perf. 12	
1447	A392 Sheet of 10, #a.-j.	10.00	5.00

Souvenir Sheet

1448	A392 50b multicolored	2.00	1.00

No. 1448 contains one 42x37mm stamp.

See Nos. 1508-1509, type A407.

Democratic
Action Party,
50th Anniv.
A393

Designs: a, People voting. b, Agricultural reform. c, Students and teachers. d, Nationalization of the petroleum industry.

1991, Sept. 13	Litho.	Perf. 12	
1449	A393 12b Block of 4, #a.-d.	1.75	88

America
Issue — A394

1991, Oct. 24			
1450	A394 12b Terepaima Chief	45	22
1451	A394 40b Paramaconi Chief	2.00	1.00
a.	Pair, #1450-1451	2.45	1.22

Children's
Foundation,
25th Anniv.
A395

Children's drawings: a, 12b, Children in house. b, 12b, Playground. c, 12b, Carnival. d, 12b, Woman and girl walking by pond. e, 12b, Boy in hospital. f, 12b, Five children around tree. g, 40b, Two girls in colorful room. h, 40b, Classroom. i, 50b, Three children. j, 50b, Four children dancing.

1991, Oct. 31	Litho.	Perf. 12	
1452	A395 Sheet of 10, #a.-j.	11.65	5.85

Nos. 1362-1364
Surcharged

1991	Litho.	Perf. 12½	
1453	A231 5b on 25c red	20	15
1454	A231 5b on 75c pink	20	15
1455	A231 10b on 25c red	40	20
1456	A231 10b on 75c pink	40	20
1457	A231 12b on 50c blue	48	24
1458	A231 12b on 75c pink	48	24
1459	A231 20b on 50c blue	80	40
1460	A231 20b on 75c pink	80	40
1461	A231 40b on 50c blue	1.60	80
1462	A231 40b on 75c pink	1.60	80
1463	A231 50b on 50c blue	2.00	1.00
1464	A231 50b on 75c pink	2.00	1.00
	Nos. 1453-1464 (12)	10.96	5.58

Christmas
A396

Children's art work: a, 10b, Wise men. b, 12b, Holy Family. c, 20b, Statues of Holy Family. d, 25b, Shepherds. e, 30b, Holy Family, cow, donkey.

1991, Nov. 14　Litho.　Perf. 12
1465 A396　Strip of 5, #a.-e.　　3.50 1.75

Souvenir Sheet

Exfilve '91, Caracas — A397

1991, Nov. 29　Litho.　Perf. 12
1466 A397 50b No. 136　　2.00 1.00

Discovery of America, 500th Anniv. (in 1992) — A398

Designs: a, 12b, Coat of arms of Columbus. b, 12b, Santa Maria. c, 12b, Map by Juan de la Cosa. d, 12b, Sighting land. e, 50b, Columbus with Queen Isabella and King Ferdinand II.

1991, Dec. 12　Litho.　Perf. 12
1468 A398　Strip of 5, #a.-e.　　4.60 2.30

1992, Mar. 15

Designs: No. 1469a, 12b, Emblem for discovery of America Commission. b, 12b, Venezuelan pavilion, Expo '92. c, 12b, 15th century map of Spain. d, 12b, Portrait of Columbus, by Susy Dembo. e, 12b, Encounter, by Ivan Jose Rojas. f, 12b, 0x500 America, by Annella Armas. g, 40b, Imago-Mundi, by Alessandro Grechi. h, 40b, Long Journey, by Gloria Fiallo. i, 50b, Playa Dorado, by Carlos Riera. j, 50b, Irminaoro, by Erasmo Sanches Cedeno. No. 1470, Untitled work, by Muaricio Sanchez.

1469 A398　　Sheet of 10, #a.-j.　11.65 5.80
1470 A398 50b multicolored　　2.30 1.15

Expo '92, Seville. No. 1470 contains one 38x42mm stamp.

Protection of Nature A399

Turtles: No. 1471a, Geochelone carbonaria, facing left. b, Geochelone carbonaria, facing right. c, Podocnemis expansa, facing left. d, Podocnemis expansa, swimming.

1992, June 12　Litho.　Perf. 12
1471 A399 12b Block of 4, #a.-d.　2.25 1.15

World Wildlife Fund.

Miniature Sheet

Beatification of Josemaria Escriva — A400

Designs: a, 18b, Teaching in Venezuela, 1975. b, 18b, Celebrating mass. c, 18b, Parents, Jose Escriva

and Dolores Albas. d, 18b, Text with autograph. e, 18b, Kissing feet of Madonna. f, 18b, Commemorative medallion. g, 60b, With Pope Paul VI. h, 60b, At desk, writing. i, 75b, Portrait. j, 75b, Portrait in St. Peter's Square, 1992.

1992, Oct. 2　Litho.　Perf. 12
1472 A400　Sheet of 10, #a.-j.　12.00 6.00

Electrification of Southern Regions A401

Designs: a, 12b, Roof of native hut. b, 12b, Transmission lines and towers. c, 12b, Horses running through pond. d, 40b, Workmen under tower. e, 50b, Baskets, crafts.

1992, July 15　Litho.　Perf. 12
1473 A401　Strip of 5, #a.-e.　　2.10 1.05

Miniature Sheet

Artwork, by Mateo Manaure — A402

Color of background: a, 12b, Red. b, 12b, Red violet. c, 12b, Gray. d, 12b, Violet brown. e, 40b, Brown. f, 40b, Blue. g, 50b, Blue violet. h, 50b, Black.

1993, July 23
1474 A402　Sheet of 8, #a.-h. + 2 labels　　5.75 2.75

Bank of Maracaibo, 110th anniv.

Discovery of America, 500th Anniv. — A403

Paintings: a, 18b, The Third Trip, by Elio Caldera. b, 60b, Descontextura, by Juan Pablo Nascimiento.

1992, Nov. 20　Litho.　Perf. 12
1476 A403　Pair, #a.-b.　　2.25 1.10

Christmas — A404

Artwork by Lucio Rivas: a, 18b, Adoration of the Shepherds. b, 75b, Adoration of the Magi. 100b, Flight into Egypt.

1992, Dec. 3　Litho.　Perf. 12
1477 A404　Pair, #a.-b.　　2.60 1.30

Souvenir Sheet

1478 A404 100b multicolored　2.75 2.75

No. 1478 contains one 42x38mm stamp.

Redrawn Bolivar Type of 1976 and

A405　　　A406

Designs: 5b, Natl. Pantheon. 10b, Victory Monument, Carabobo. 20b, Jose Antonio Paez. 25b, Luisa Caceres de Arismendi. 35b, Ezequiel Zamora. 40b, Cristobal Mendoza. #1490, Central University. #1491, Jose Felix Ribas. #1494, Manuel Piar. 200b, Simon Bolivar.

1993-94　Litho.　Perf. 12½
Size: 18x22mm

1479	A405	1b silver	15	15
1480	A405	2b greenish blue	15	15
1482	A231	5b red	15	15
1484	A231	10b violet	28	15
1487	A231	20b olive green	55	28
1488	A405	25b red brown	30	15
1488A	A405	35b brt yellow green	42	20
1489	A405	40b lt blue	48	25
1490	A231	50b orange	1.38	65
1491	A405	50b lilac rose	90	45
1493	A406	100b brown	2.75	1.38
1494	A405	100b dark blue	1.25	60
1496	A405	200b brown	2.50	1.25
		Nos. 1479-1496 (13)	11.26	5.81

Nos. 1479-1493 inscribed Armitano. This is an expanding set. Numbers may change.

Miniature Sheet

Orchids A407

Designs: a, 20b, Cattleya percivaliana. b, 20b, Anguloa ruckeri. c, 20b, Chondrorhyncha flaveola. d, 20b, Stenia pallida. e, 20b, Zygosepalum lindeniae. f, 20b, Maxillaria triloris. g, 80b, Stanhopea wardii. h, 80b, Oncidium papilio. i, 100b, Oncidium hastilabium. j, 100b, Sobralia cattleya. 150b, Polycycnis muscifera.

1993, Apr. 1　Litho.　Perf. 12
1499 A407　Sheet of 10, #a.-j.　13.00 6.50
Souvenir Sheet
1500 A407 150b multicolored　2.00 1.00

Miniature Sheet

Settlement of Tovar Colony, 150th Anniv. — A408

Designs: a, 24b, Woman. b, 24b, Children. c, 24b, Catholic Church, 1862. d, 24b, Statue of St. Martin of Tours, 1843. e, 24b, Fruits and vegetables. f, 24b, School, 1916. g, 80b, Home of founder, Augustin Codazzi, 1845. h, 80b, House of colony director, Alexander Benitz, 1845. i, 100b, Breidenbach Mill, 1860. j, 100b, Parade.

1993, Apr. 12　Litho.　Perf. 12
1501 A408　Sheet of 10, #a.-j.　12.50 6.25

Miniature Sheet

19th Pan-American Railways Conference A409

Designs: a, 24b, Tucacas steam locomotive, 1813. b, 24b, Halcon steam locomotive on Las Mostazas Bridge, 1894. c, 24b, Maracaibo locomotive. d, 24b, Tender, rail cars, Palo Grande Station.

e, 24b, Fiat diesel locomotive, 1957. f, 24b, GP-9-L diesel locomotive, 1957. g, 80b, GP-15-L diesel locomotive, 1982. h, 80b, Metro subway train, Caracas. i, 100b, Electric locomotive. j, 100b, Passenger cars of electric train.

1993, May 25　Litho.　Perf. 12
1502 A409　Sheet of 10, #a.-j.　15.00 7.50

Nos. 1502c-1502d, 1502i-1502j are continuous designs.

A410　　　　　A411

World Day to Stop Smoking: a, 24b, Shown. b, 80b, "No smoking" emblem.

1993, May 27　Litho.　Perf. 12½x12
1503 A410　Pair, #a.-b.　　2.75 1.40

1993, Oct. 7　Litho.　Perf. 12

America Issue: a, 24b, Amazona barbadensis. b, 80b, Ara macao.

1504 A411　Pair, #a.-b.　　4.75 2.50

Miniature Sheets

Native Indians — A412　　Christmas — A413

Designs: No. 1505a, 1b, Two Yanomami children with painted bodies, spear. b, 1b, Yanomami woman preparing food. c, 40b, Two Panare children performing in Katyayinto ceremony. d, 40b, Panare man with nose flute. e, 40b, Taurepan man in canoe. f, 40b, Taurepan girl weaving. g, 40b, Piaroa woman with infant. h, 40b, Piaroa dancers wearing war masks. i, 100b, Hoti man blowing flute. j, 100b, Hoti woman carrying baby, basket over back. 150b, Child blowing traditional whistle.

1993, Nov. 25　Litho.　Perf. 12
1505 A412　　Sheet of 10, #a.-j.　9.25 4.75
Souvenir Sheet
1506 A412 150b multicolored　3.25 1.50

1993, Nov. 30

Nativity scene: a, f, 24b, Joseph. b, g, 24b, Madonna and Child. c, h, 24b, Shepherd boy, wise man holding gift, lambs. d, i, 80b, Wise man with hands folded, boy. e, j, 100b, Wise man presenting gift, boy with hands folded.

1507 A413　Sheet of 10, #a.-j.　10.50 5.25

Nos. 1507f-1507j are black, magenta & buff.

Orchid Type of 1991
Miniature Sheet

Designs: a, 35b, Chrysocycnis schlimii. b, 35b, Galeandra minax. c, 35b, Oncidium falcipetalum. d, 35b, Oncidium lanceanum. e, 40b, Sobralia violacea linden. f, 40b, Sobralia infundibuligera. g, 80b, Mendoncella burkei. h, 80b, Phragmipedium caudatum. i, 100b, Phragmipedium kaieteurum. j, 200b, Stanhopea grandiflora. 150b, Epidendrum elongatum.

1994, May 19　Litho.　Perf. 12
1508 A392　Sheet of 10, #a.-j.　12.00 6.00
Souvenir Sheet
1509 A392 150b multicolored　2.50 1.25

No. 1509 contains one 42x37mm stamp.

Miniature Sheet of 10

FEDECAMARAS (Federal Council of Production & Commerce Associations), 50th Anniv. — A414

Designs: a, 35b; f, 80b, Anniversary emblem. b, 35b; e, 80b, Luis Gonzalo Marturet (1914-64), first president. c, 35b; d, 80b, FEDECAMARAS emblem.

1994, July 17	Litho.	Perf. 12
1510 A414	#c, f, 2 each #a-b, d-e	5.00 2.50

Judicial Service — A415

1994	Litho.	Perf. 12
1511 A415	100b multicolored	1.25 60

Miniature Sheet

Christmas A416

Paintings: a, 35b, g, 80b, The Nativity, by follower of Jose Lorenzo de Alvarado. b, 35b, h, 80b, The Nativity, 19th cent. c, 35b, i, 80b, The Nativity, diff., by follower of Jose Lorenzo de Alvarado. d, 35b, j, 80b, Adoration of the Magi, 17th cent.. e, 35b, f, 80b, Birth of Christ, by School of Tocuyo.

1994		
1512 A416	Sheet of 10, #a.-j.	6.75 3.50

Miniature Sheet

Antonio Jose de Sucre (1795-1830) A417

Designs: No. 1513a, 25b, Portrait. b, 25b, Dona Mariana Carcelen Y Larrea Marquesa de Solanda. c, 35b, Top of equestrian monument. d, 35b, Bottom of monument. e, 40b, Painting of Battle of Pichincha, mountains at top. f, 40b, Painting of Battle of Pichincha, battle scent. g, 80b, Painting of Battle of Ayacucho, soldiers on horseback. h, 80b, Painting of Battle of Ayacucho, dead soldiers. i, 100b, Painting of Surrender at Ayacucho, general signing document. j, 100b, Painting of Surrender at Ayacucho, seated general at right.

150b, Portion of mural, Carabobo, by Pedro Centeno Vallenilla.

1995		
1513 A417	Sheet of 10, #a.-j.	6.50 3.25

Souvenir Sheet

1514 A417	150b multicolored	1.75 90

SEMI-POSTAL STAMPS

A 5c green stamp of the Cruzada Venezolana Sanitaria Social portraying Simon Bolivar was overprinted "EE. UU. DE VENEZUELA CORREOS" in 1937.

It is stated that 50,000 copies without control numbers on back were sold by post offices and 147,700 with control numbers on back were offered for sale by the Society at eight times face value.

Bolívar Funeral Carriage SP1

Unwmk.

1942, Dec. 17	Engr.	Perf. 12
B1 SP1	20c + 5c blue	4.00 40

Cent. of the arrival of Simón Bolívar's remains in Caracas. The surtax was used to erect a monument to his memory. See Nos. CB1-CB2.

> Catalogue values for unused stamps in this section, from this point to the end of the section, are for Never Hinged items.

Red Cross Nurse — SP2

1975, Dec. 15	Litho.	Perf. 14
B2 SP2	30c + 15c multi	30 15
B3 SP2	50c + 25c multi	45 22

Surtax for Venezuelan Red Cross.

Carmen América Fernandez de Leoni — SP3

Children in Home — SP4

1976, June 7	Litho.	Perf. 13½
B4 SP3	30c + 15c multi	22 15
B5 SP4	50c + 25c multi	40 22

Surtax was for the Children's Foundation, founded by Carmen América Fernandez de Leoni in 1966.

Patient — SP5

1976, Dec. 8	Litho.	Perf. 14
B6 SP5	10c + 5c multi	15 15
B7 SP5	30c + 10c multi	22 15
	Set value	20

Surtax was for Anti-tuberculosis Society.

AIR POST STAMPS

Air post stamps of 1930-42 perforated "GN" (Gobierno Nacional) were for official use.

Airplane and Map of Venezuela
AP1   AP2

1930	Unwmk.	Litho.	Perf. 12	
C1	AP1	5c bister brn	15	15
C2	AP1	10c yellow	15	15
a.		10c salmon	32.50	32.50
C3	AP1	15c gray	15	15
C4	AP1	25c lilac	15	15
C5	AP1	40c olive grn	15	15
a.		40c slate blue	40.00	
b.		40c slate green	40.00	
C6	AP1	75c dp red	25	15
C7	AP1	1b indigo	32	15
C8	AP1	1.20b blue grn	50	22
C9	AP1	1.70b dk blue	65	28
C10	AP1	1.90b blue grn	75	35
C11	AP1	2.10b dk blue	1.25	45
C12	AP1	2.30b vermilion	1.25	35
C13	AP1	2.50b dk blue	1.25	35
C14	AP1	3.70b blue grn	1.25	55
C15	AP1	10b dull vio	3.00	1.40
C16	AP1	20b gray grn	5.00	3.00
		Nos. C1-C16 (16)	16.22	8.00

Nos. C1-C16 exist imperforate or partly perforated. See Nos. C119-C126.
Issue dates: 10b, June 8. 20b, June 16. Others, Apr. 5.

Bluish Winchester Security Paper

1932, July 12	Engr.	Perf. 12½	
C17	AP2	5c brown	25	15
C18	AP2	10c org yel	25	15
C19	AP2	15c gray lilac	25	15
C20	AP2	25c violet	32	15
C21	AP2	40c ol grn	50	15
C22	AP2	70c rose	42	15
C23	AP2	75c red org	75	15
C24	AP2	1b dk bl	85	15
C25	AP2	1.20b green	1.50	65
C26	AP2	1.70b red brn	3.00	45
C27	AP2	1.80b ultra	1.50	28
C28	AP2	1.90b green	3.75	2.75
C29	AP2	1.95b blue	4.25	2.25
C30	AP2	2b blk brn	3.00	1.75
C31	AP2	2.10b blue	6.25	4.50
C32	AP2	2.30b red	3.00	1.75
C33	AP2	2.50b dk bl	3.75	1.10
C34	AP2	3b dk vio	3.75	65
C35	AP2	3.70b emerald	5.00	4.50
C36	AP2	4b red org	3.75	1.10
C37	AP2	5b black	5.00	1.65
C38	AP2	8b dk car	10.00	3.50
C39	AP2	10b dk vio	20.00	5.75
C40	AP2	20b grnsh slate	42.50	16.00
		Nos. C17-C40 (24)	123.59	49.83

Pairs imperf. between exist of the 1b (value $150); the 25c and 4b (value $300 each).

Air Post Stamps of 1932 Surcharged in Black

```
   1937
VALE POR
  -5-
CENTIMOS
```

1937, June 4		
C41	AP2	5c on 1.70b red brn	9.00 5.50
C42	AP2	10c on 3.70b emer	9.00 5.50
C43	AP2	15c on 4b red org	4.00 2.75
C44	AP2	25c on 5b blk	4.00 2.75
C45	AP2	1b on 8b dk car	3.00 2.75
C46	AP2	2b on 2.10b bl	24.00 18.00
		Nos. C41-C46 (6)	53.00 37.25

Various varieties of surcharge exist, including double and triple impressions. No. C43 exists in pair imperf. between; value $30 unused, $50 used.

Allegory of Flight — AP3

Allegory of Flight — AP4

National Pantheon at Caracas AP5

Airplane — AP6   AP7

Perf. 11, 11½ and Compound

1937, July 1		Litho.	
C47	AP3	5c brn org	25	22
C48	AP4	10c org red	20	15
C49	AP5	15c gray blk	50	22
C50	AP6	25c dk vio	50	22
C51	AP4	40c yel grn	85	30
C52	AP3	70c red	85	22
C53	AP3	75c bister	2.00	80
C54	AP3	1b dk gray	1.25	30
C55	AP4	1.20b pck grn	5.00	2.25
C56	AP3	1.80b dk ultra	2.50	1.10
C57	AP5	1.95b lt ultra	7.50	4.50
C58	AP6	2b chocolate	3.00	1.75
C59	AP6	2.50b gray bl	8.75	5.75
C60	AP4	3b lt vio	5.00	2.75
C61	AP6	3.70b rose red	7.00	6.00
C62	AP5	10b red vio	19.00	7.75
C63	AP3	20b gray	20.00	14.00
		Nos. C47-C63 (17)	84.15	48.28

All values except 3.70b exist imperf. and part-perf.
Counterfeits exist.
For overprints and surcharges see Nos. C66-C78, C114-C118, C164-C167, C169-C172, C174-C180.

1937, Oct. 28			Perf. 11	
C64	AP7	70c emerald	1.10	45
C65	AP7	1.80b ultra	1.75	80

Acquisition of the Port of La Guaira by the Government from the British Corporation, June 3, 1937. Exist imperf.
A redrawn printing of Nos. C64-C65, with lower inscription beginning "Nacionalización . . ." was prepared but not issued. Price, $40 each.
For overprints see Nos. C168, C173.

Air Post Stamps of 1937 Overprinted in Black

```
RESELLADO
1937-1938
```

1937, Dec. 17			Perf. 11, 11½	
C66	AP4	10c org red	80	55
a.		Inverted overprint	13.00	10.00
C67	AP6	25c dk vio	1.50	75
C68	AP4	40c yel grn	1.65	1.10
C69	AP3	70c red	1.25	75
a.		Inverted overprint	13.00	11.50
b.		Double overprint	20.00	16.00
C70	AP3	1b dk gray	1.65	1.10
a.		Inverted overprint	16.00	13.00
b.		Double overprint	13.00	
C71	AP4	1.20b pck grn	24.00	15.00
a.		Inverted overprint	65.00	
C72	AP3	1.80b dk ultra	4.00	1.90
C73	AP5	1.95b lt ultra	6.00	3.50
a.		Inverted overprint	50.00	30.00
C74	AP6	2b chocolate	40.00	18.00
a.		Inverted overprint	100.00	90.00
b.		Double overprint	82.50	82.50
C75	AP6	2.50b gray bl	40.00	15.00
a.		Double overprint	70.00	
b.		Inverted overprint	105.00	82.50
C76	AP4	3b lt vio	24.00	9.25
C77	AP5	10b red vio	57.50	30.00
C78	AP3	20b gray	65.00	37.50
a.		Double overprint	145.00	145.00
		Nos. C66-C78 (13)	267.35	134.40

Counterfeit overprints exist on #C77-C78.

View of La Guaira AP8

National Pantheon AP9

Oil Wells AP10

1938-39   Engr.   Perf. 12

C79	AP8	5c green	70	40
C80	AP8	5c dk grn	15	15
C81	AP9	10c car rose	1.00	65
C82	AP9	10c scarlet	15	15
C83	AP8	12½c dull vio	45	38
C84	AP10	15c slate vio	2.25	80
C85	AP8	15c dk bl	65	15
C86	AP8	25c dk bl	2.25	80
C87	AP8	25c bis brn	20	15
C88	AP10	30c vio ('39)	1.50	15
C89	AP9	40c dk vio	2.50	90
C90	AP9	40c redsh brn	1.75	15
C91	AP8	45c Prus grn ('39)	75	15
C92	AP9	50c blue ('39)	85	15
C93	AP10	70c car rose	65	22
C94	AP8	75c bis brn	5.00	1.40
C95	AP8	75c ol bis	1.00	15
C96	AP10	90c red org ('39)	75	15
C97	AP9	1b ol & bis	5.00	1.75
C98	AP9	1b dk vio	85	15
C99	AP10	1.20b orange	15.00	4.50
C100	AP10	1.20b green	1.50	35
C101	AP8	1.80b ultra	1.50	35
C102	AP9	1.90b black	3.75	2.25
C103	AP10	1.95b lt bl	3.00	2.00
C104	AP8	2b ol gray	32.50	10.50
C105	AP8	2b car rose	1.25	55
C106	AP9	2.50b red brn	32.50	12.50
C107	AP9	2.50b orange	8.00	2.25
C108	AP10	3b bl grn	15.00	3.75
C109	AP10	3b ol gray	3.75	1.40
C110	AP8	3.70b gray blk	5.50	3.50
C111	AP10	5b red brn ('39)	5.50	1.40
C112	AP9	10b vio brn	16.00	1.75
C113	AP10	20b red org	45.00	20.00
		Nos. C79-C113 (35)	218.15	76.00

See Nos. C227a, C235-C236, C254-C255.
For surcharge see No. C227.

1938
VALE
CINCO
CÉNTIMOS

Nos. C51, C56, C58-C59, C61 Surcharged

1938, Apr. 15   Perf. 11, 11½

C114	AP3	5c on 1.80b	70	38
a.		Inverted surcharge	14.00	7.50
C115	AP6	10c on 2.50b	2.50	75
a.		Inverted surcharge	12.00	7.50
C116	AP6	15c on 2b	1.25	75
C117	AP4	25c on 40c	1.40	85
C118	AP6	40c on 3.70b	2.75	1.50
		Nos. C114-C118 (5)	8.60	4.23

Plane & Map Type of 1930
White Paper; No Imprint

1938-39   Engr.   Perf. 12½

C119	AP1	5c dk grn ('39)	20	15
C120	AP1	10c org yel ('39)	45	15
C121	AP1	12½c rose vio ('39)	90	65
C122	AP1	15c dp bl	80	15
C123	AP1	25c brown	90	15
C124	AP1	40c olive ('39)	2.25	15
a.		Imperf., pair	40.00	
C125	AP1	70c rose car ('39)	16.00	6.25
C126	AP1	1b dk bl ('39)	5.00	2.50
		Nos. C119-C126 (8)	26.50	10.35

Monument to Sucre — AP11

Monuments at Carabobo
AP12   AP13

1938, Dec. 23   Perf. 13½

C127	AP11	20c brn blk	32	18
C128	AP12	30c purple	45	18
C129	AP13	45c dk bl	65	15
C130	AP11	50c lt ultra	55	15
C131	AP13	70c dk car	10.00	5.50
C132	AP12	90c red org	90	35
C133	AP13	1.35b gray blk	1.10	55
C134	AP11	1.40b slate gray	4.50	1.75
C135	AP12	2.25b green	2.25	1.25
		Nos. C127-C135 (9)	20.72	10.06

For surcharge see No. C198.

Simón Bolívar and Carabobo Monument AP14

1940, Mar. 30   Perf. 12

C136	AP14	15c blue	32	15
C137	AP14	20c olive bis	25	15
C138	AP14	25c red brn	1.65	18
C139	AP14	40c blk brn	1.25	15
C140	AP14	1b red lilac	2.75	28
C141	AP14	2b rose car	5.00	45
		Nos. C136-C141 (6)	11.22	
		Set value		1.15

"The Founding of Grand Colombia" AP15

1940, June 13

C142	AP15	15c copper brown	75	38

50th anniv. of the founding of the Pan American Union.

Statue of Simón Bolívar, Caracas — AP16

1940-44

C143	AP16	5c dk green ('42)	15	15
C144	AP16	10c scarlet ('42)	15	15
C145	AP16	12½c dull purple	55	16
C146	AP16	15c blue ('43)	30	15
C147	AP16	20c bister brn ('44)	30	15
C148	AP16	25c bister brn ('42)	30	15
C149	AP16	30c dp violet ('43)	30	15
C150	AP16	40c black brn ('43)	40	15
C151	AP16	45c turq grn ('43)	40	15
C152	AP16	50c blue ('44)	40	15
C153	AP16	70c rose pink	1.25	16
C154	AP16	75c olive bis ('43)	5.00	90
C155	AP16	90c red org ('43)	80	16
C156	AP16	1b dp red lil ('42)	40	15
C157	AP16	1.20b dp yel grn ('43)	1.65	45
C158	AP16	1.35b gray blk ('42)	6.50	3.00
C159	AP16	2b rose pink ('43)	1.25	15
C160	AP16	3b olive blk ('43)	2.00	45
C161	AP16	4b black	1.65	45
C162	AP16	5b red brn ('44)	13.00	4.75
		Nos. C143-162 (20)	36.75	12.13

See Nos. C232-C234, C239-C253. For surcharges see Nos. C225, C873.

Resellado 1943
Nos. C48, C50-C65 Overprinted

Perf. 11, 11½ & Compound
1943, Dec. 21

C164	AP4	10c orange red	1.00	65
C165	AP6	25c dk violet	1.00	75
C166	AP6	40c yellow grn	1.25	75
C167	AP3	70c red	1.00	75
C168	AP7	70c emerald	1.25	75
C169	AP5	75c bister	1.40	90
C170	AP3	1b dk gray	1.40	90
C171	AP4	1.20b peacock grn	2.00	1.10
C172	AP3	1.80b dk ultra	1.75	90
C173	AP7	1.80b dk ultra	2.50	1.25
C174	AP5	1.95b lt ultra	2.75	1.40
C175	AP6	2b chocolate	2.75	2.25
C176	AP6	2.50b gray blue	3.25	2.25
C177	AP4	3b lt violet	4.00	2.50
C178	AP6	3.70b rose red	45.00	32.50
C179	AP5	10b red violet	16.00	10.00
C180	AP3	20b gray	26.00	20.00
		Nos. C164-C180 (17)	114.30	79.60

Issued for sale to philatelists. Nos. C164-C169 were sold only in sets.
Nearly all are known with invtd. ovpt.

Flags of Venezuela and the Red Cross — AP17   Baseball Players — AP18

1944, Aug. 22   Litho.   Perf. 12
Flags in red, yellow, blue and black

C181	AP17	5c gray green	15	15
C182	AP17	10c magenta	15	15
C183	AP17	20c brt blue	15	15
C184	AP17	30c violet bl	25	15
C185	AP17	40c chocolate	38	15
C186	AP17	45c apple green	1.10	45
C187	AP17	90c orange	1.00	38
C188	AP17	1b gray black	1.50	28
		Nos. C181-C188 (8)	4.68	
		Set value		1.40

80th anniv. of the Intl. Red Cross and 37th anniv. of Venezuela's joining the organization. Nos. C181-C188 exist imperf. and part perf.

1944, Oct. 12
"AEREO" in dark carmine

C189	AP18	5c dull vio brn	25	16
a.		"AEREO" double		8.25
C190	AP18	10c gray green	30	16
C191	AP18	20c ultra	38	22
C192	AP18	30c dull rose	50	35
C193	AP18	45c rose violet	1.25	55
C194	AP18	90c red orange	2.25	1.10
C195	AP18	1b dark gray	2.50	1.10
C196	AP18	1.20b yellow grn	7.50	5.75
a.		"AEREO" inverted	15.00	13.00
C197	AP18	1.80b ocher	10.00	7.75
		Nos. C189-C197 (9)	24.93	17.14

7th World Amateur Baseball Championship Games, Caracas.
Nos. C189-C197 exist imperf., and all but 1b exist part perf.

Habilitado
1944
VALE
Bs. 0.30

No. C134 Surcharged in Black

1944, Nov. 17   Perf. 13½

C198	AP11	30c on 1.40b	45	45
a.		Double surcharge	32.50	32.50
b.		Inverted surcharge	13.00	13.00

Charles Howarth AP19   Antonio José de Sucre AP20

1944, Dec. 21   Unwmk.   Perf. 12

C199	AP19	5c black	16	15
C200	AP19	10c purple	16	15
C201	AP19	20c sepia	35	22
C202	AP19	30c dull green	45	22
C203	AP19	1.20b bister	2.00	1.75
C204	AP19	1.80b deep ultra	3.50	2.25
C205	AP19	3.70b rose	4.50	3.75
		Nos. C199-C205 (7)	11.12	8.49

Cent. of founding of 1st cooperative shop in Rochdale, England, by Charles Howarth.
Nos. C199-C205 exist imperf. and part perf.

1945, Mar. 3   Engr.

C206	AP20	5c orange	15	15
C207	AP20	10c violet	18	15
C208	AP20	20c grnsh blk	28	16
C209	AP20	30c brt green	42	28
C210	AP20	40c olive	65	45
C211	AP20	45c black brn	85	45
C212	AP20	90c redsh brn	1.50	55
C213	AP20	1b dp red lil	1.10	45
C214	AP20	1.20b black	2.50	2.25
C215	AP20	2b yellow	3.75	1.75
		Nos. C206-C215 (10)	11.38	6.64

150th birth anniv. of Antonio Jose de Sucre, Grand Marshal of Ayacucho.

Type of 1946
1946, Aug. 24   Perf. 12

C216	A81	30c Bello	50	20
C217	A82	30c Urdaneta	50	20

Allegory of Republic — AP23

Perf. 11½
1946, Oct. 18   Litho.   Unwmk.

C218	AP23	15c dp violet bl	25	16
C219	AP23	20c bister brn	30	16
C220	AP23	30c dp violet	35	28
C221	AP23	1b brt rose	2.50	1.75

Anniversary of the Revolution of October, 1945. Exist imperf. and part perf.

J. R. G.
AEREO
Vale Bs.0.15
1946

Nos. 297, 371, C152 and 362 Surcharged in Black

1947, Jan.   Perf. 12

C223	A49	10c on 22½c dp car	15	15
a.		Inverted surcharge	4.00	4.00
C224	A69	15c on 25c lt bl	30	15
C225	AP16	20c on 50c blue	28	15
a.		Inverted surcharge	5.00	5.00
C226	A65	70c on 1b dk vio brn	60	40
a.		Inverted surcharge	4.00	4.00

J. R. G.
AEREO
Vale Bs. 20
1946

Type of 1938 Surcharged in Black

C227	AP10	20b on 20b org red	21.00	11.00
a.		Surcharge omitted	85.00	25.00
		Nos. C223-C227 (5)	22.33	11.85

"J. R. G." are the initials of "Junta Revolucionaria de Gobierno."
Also exist: 20c on #C143, 10c on #371.

Anti-tuberculosis Institute, Maracaibo — AP24

1947, Jan. 12   **Litho.**
Venezuela Shown on Map in Yellow

C228	AP24	15c dark blue	40	30
C229	AP24	20c dark brown	40	24
C230	AP24	30c violet	40	30
C231	AP24	1b carmine	3.00	2.50

12th Pan-American Health Conf., Caracas, Jan. 1947.
Nos. C228-C231 exist imperf., part perf. and with yellow omitted.

Types of 1938-40

1947, Mar. 17   **Engr.**

C232	AP16	75c orange	3.25	1.90
C233	AP16	1b brt ultra	40	16
C234	AP16	3b red brown	8.00	3.00
C235	AP10	5b scarlet	9.00	1.90
C236	AP9	10b violet	13.00	3.75
		Nos. C232-C236 (5)	33.65	10.71

On Nos. C235 and C236 the numerals of value are in color on a white table.

AEREO
No. 370
Surcharged in
Black
Vale Bs. 0.05
1947

1947, June 20

C237	A70	5c on 20c blue	25	15
C238	A70	10c on 20c blue	25	15
a.		Inverted surcharge	5.00	5.00
		Set value		20

Types of 1938-44

1947-48   **Engr.**

C239	AP16	5c orange	15	15
C240	AP16	10c dk green	15	15
C241	AP16	12½c bister brn	28	20
C242	AP16	15c gray	15	15
C243	AP16	20c violet	15	15
C244	AP16	25c dull green	15	15
C245	AP16	30c brt ultra	25	15
C246	AP16	40c green ('48)	15	15
C247	AP16	45c vermilion	38	15
C248	AP16	50c red violet	18	15
C249	AP16	70c dk car	65	35
C250	AP16	75c purple ('48)	35	18
C251	AP16	90c black	55	25
C252	AP16	1.20b red brn ('48)	80	55
C253	AP16	3b dp blue	1.25	45
C254	AP16	5b olive grn	4.00	1.65
C255	AP9	10b yellow	5.00	2.00
		Nos. C239-C255 (17)	14.59	6.98

On Nos. C254 and C255 the numerals of value are in color on a white table.
Issue dates: 5c, 10c, Oct. 8. 15c, Dec. 2, 40c, 75c, 1.20b, May 10, 1948. Others, Oct. 27, 1947.

M. S. Republica
de Venezuela
AP25

Santos Michelena
AP26

Imprint: "American Bank Note Company"

1948-50   **Unwmk.**   **Perf. 12**

C256	AP25	5c red brown	15	15
C257	AP25	10c deep green	15	15
C258	AP25	15c brown	15	15
C259	AP25	20c violet brn	15	15
C260	AP25	25c brown black	15	15
C261	AP25	30c olive green	15	15
C262	AP25	45c blue green	32	15
C263	AP25	50c gray black	40	18
C264	AP25	70c orange	80	18
C265	AP25	75c brt ultra	1.65	25
C266	AP25	90c car lake	80	55
C267	AP25	1b purple	1.00	35
C268	AP25	2b gray	1.25	55
C269	AP25	3b emerald	4.00	1.40
C270	AP25	4b deep blue	2.25	1.40
C271	AP25	5b orange red	8.00	2.75
		Nos. C256-C271 (16)	21.37	8.66

Issued to honor the Grand-Colombian Merchant Fleet. See Nos. C554-C556.
Issue dates: 5c, 10c, 15c, 25c, 30c, 1b, July 9, 1948. 45c, 75c, 5b, May 11, 1950. Others, Mar. 9, 1949.
For surcharges see Nos. C863-C864.

1949, Apr. 25

C272	AP26	5c orange brn	15	15
C273	AP26	10c gray	15	15
C274	AP26	15c red orange	35	20
C275	AP26	25c dull green	75	35
C276	AP26	30c plum	75	35
C277	AP26	1b violet	3.75	1.50
		Nos. C272-C277 (6)	5.90	2.70

See note after No. 427.

Christopher
Columbus
AP27

1948-49   **Unwmk.**   **Perf. 12½**

C278	AP27	5c brown ('49)	18	15
C279	AP27	10c gray	24	15
C280	AP27	15c orange ('49)	35	15
C281	AP27	25c green ('49)	75	28
C282	AP27	30c red vio ('49)	90	35
C283	AP27	1b violet ('49)	3.50	1.10
		Nos. C278-C283 (6)	5.92	2.18

See note after No. 431.

AP28   AP29

Symbols of global air mail.

1950   **Perf. 12**

C284	AP28	5c red brown	15	15
C285	AP28	10c dk green	15	15
C286	AP28	15c olive brn	15	15
C287	AP28	25c olive gray	32	22
C288	AP28	30c olive grn	45	25
C289	AP28	50c black	28	15
C290	AP28	60c brt ultra	90	45
C291	AP28	90c carmine	1.25	55
C292	AP28	1b purple	1.40	55
		Nos. C284-C292 (9)	5.05	
		Set value		2.05

75th anniv. of the UPU.
Issue dates: 5c, Jan. 28. Others, Feb. 19.

1950, Aug. 25   **Photo.**   **Perf. 11½**

Araguaney, Venezuelan national tree.

Foliage in Yellow

C293	AP29	5c orange brn	18	15
C294	AP29	10c blue grn	15	15
C295	AP29	15c deep plum	45	20
C296	AP29	25c dk gray grn	3.00	1.25
C297	AP29	30c red orange	3.25	1.65
C298	AP29	50c dark gray	1.75	40
C299	AP29	60c deep blue	3.00	80
C300	AP29	90c red	5.50	1.65
C301	AP29	1b rose violet	6.50	2.00
		Nos. C293-C301 (9)	23.78	8.25

Issued to publicize Forest Week, 1950.

Census Type of 1950

1950, Sept. 1   **Engr.**   **Perf. 12**

C302	A90	5c olive gray	15	15
C303	A90	10c green	15	15
C304	A90	15c olive green	18	15
C305	A90	25c gray	30	28
C306	A90	30c orange	45	24
C307	A90	50c lt brown	28	15
C308	A90	60c ultra	28	18
C309	A90	90c rose carmine	1.10	45
C310	A90	1b violet	1.75	1.40
		Nos. C302-C310 (9)	4.64	3.15

Signing Act of Independence — AP31

1950, Nov. 17

C311	AP31	5c vermilion	18	15
C312	AP31	10c red brown	18	15
C313	AP31	15c violet	35	18
C314	AP31	30c brt blue	55	28
C315	AP31	1b green	3.00	1.40
		Nos. C311-C315 (5)	4.26	2.16

200th anniversary of the birth of Gen. Francisco de Miranda.

Alonso de Ojeda Type of 1950

1950, Dec. 18   **Photo.**   **Perf. 11½**

C316	A91	5c orange brn	16	15
C317	A91	10c cerise	22	15
C318	A91	15c black brn	30	15
C319	A91	25c violet	55	28
C320	A91	30c orange	1.10	45
C321	A91	1b emerald	4.50	2.25
		Nos. C316-321 (6)	6.83	3.43

Bolivar Statue Type of 1951

1951, July 13   **Engr.**   **Perf. 12**

C322	A92	5c purple	22	15
C323	A92	10c dull green	32	15
C324	A92	20c olive gray	32	15
C325	A92	25c olive green	35	15
C326	A92	30c vermilion	45	30
C327	A92	40c lt brown	45	32
C328	A92	50c gray	1.40	55
C329	A92	70c orange	2.25	1.40
		Nos. C322-C329 (8)	5.76	3.17

Queen Isabella I — AP34

1951, Oct. 12   **Photo.**   **Perf. 11½**

C330	A34	5c dk green & buff	30	15
C331	A34	10c dk red & cream	30	15
C332	A34	20c dp blue & gray	52	15
C333	A34	30c dk blue & gray	52	15
a.		Souv. sheet of 4, #C330-C333	3.00	2.75
		Set value		40

500th anniv. of the birth of Queen Isabella I of Spain.

Bicycle
Racecourse
AP35

1951, Dec. 18   **Engr.**   **Perf. 12**

C334	AP35	5c green	65	16
C335	AP35	10c rose carmine	75	18
C336	AP35	20c redsh brown	85	22
C337	AP35	30c blue	1.10	30
a.		Souv. sheet of 4, #C334-C337	11.00	11.00

3rd Bolivarian Games, Caracas, Dec. 1951.

Arms of Carabobo and
"Industry" — AP36

1951   **Photo.**   **Perf. 11½**

C338	AP36	5c blue grn	15	15
C339	AP36	7½c gray grn	32	32
C340	AP36	10c carmine rose	15	15
C341	AP36	15c dark brown	25	15
C342	AP36	20c gray blue	35	15
C343	AP36	30c deep blue	1.25	22
C344	AP36	45c magenta	55	25
C345	AP36	60c olive brown	1.10	55
C346	AP36	90c rose brown	3.00	1.75
		Nos. C338-C346 (9)	7.12	3.69

Issue date: Oct. 29.

Arms of Zulia and "Industry"

C347	AP36	5c blue green	35	15
C348	AP36	10c carmine rose	15	15
C349	AP36	15c dk brown	40	16
C350	AP36	30c dp blue	3.00	1.25

C351	AP36	60c olive brown	1.65	40
C352	AP36	1.20b brown car	7.00	5.00
C353	AP36	3b blue gray	1.75	80
C354	AP36	5b purple brn	3.00	2.00
C355	AP36	10b violet	5.00	4.00
		Nos. C347-C355 (9)	22.30	13.91

Issue dates: 5b, Sept. 8. 5c, 3b, 10b, Oct. 8. Others, Oct. 29.

Arms of Anzoategui

C356	AP36	5c blue green	15	15
C357	AP36	10c carmine rose	15	15
C358	AP36	15c dk brown	32	15
C359	AP36	25c sepia	40	15
C360	AP36	30c deep blue	1.10	80
C361	AP36	50c henna brn	1.10	40
C362	AP36	60c olive brn	1.65	24
C363	AP36	1b purple	2.00	80
C364	AP36	2b violet gray	3.75	1.75
		Nos. C356-C364 (9)	10.62	4.59

Issue date: Nov. 9.

Arms of Caracas and Buildings

C365	AP36	5c blue green	50	15
C366	AP36	7½c gray green	1.90	75
C367	AP36	10c car rose	30	15
C368	AP36	15c dk brown	4.50	50
C369	AP36	20c gray blue	3.00	50
C370	AP36	30c deep blue	5.00	1.00
C371	AP36	45c magenta	3.00	65
C372	AP36	60c olive brn	10.00	1.25
C373	AP36	90c rose brn	6.00	5.00
		Nos. C365-C373 (9)	34.20	9.95

Issue date: Aug. 6.

Arms of Tachira and Agricultural Products

C374	AP36	5c blue green	20	15
C375	AP36	10c car rose	15	15
C376	AP36	15c dk brown	65	15
C377	AP36	30c deep blue	9.00	1.10
C378	AP36	60c olive brn	7.00	1.10
C379	AP36	1.20b brown car	7.00	5.00
C380	AP36	3b blue gray	1.75	90
C381	AP36	5b purple brn	4.00	2.00
C382	AP36	10b violet	5.75	4.00
		Nos. C374-C382 (9)	35.50	14.55

Issue date: Aug. 9.

Arms of Venezuela and Bolivar Statue

C383	AP36	5c blue green	30	15
C384	AP36	7½c gray grn	85	65
C385	AP36	10c car rose	20	15
C386	AP36	15c dk brown	2.00	65
C387	AP36	20c gray blue	2.75	50
C388	AP36	30c deep blue	5.00	1.10
C389	AP36	45c magenta	2.25	45
C390	AP36	60c olive brn	11.00	2.25
C391	AP36	90c rose brn	7.00	5.00
		Nos. C383-C391 (9)	31.35	10.90

Issue date: Aug. 6.

1952
Arms of Miranda and Agricultural Products

C392	AP36	5c blue green	15	15
C393	AP36	7½c gray grn	32	32
C394	AP36	10c car rose	15	15
C395	AP36	15c dark brown	40	15
C396	AP36	20c gray blue	65	25
C397	AP36	30c deep blue	1.10	40
C398	AP36	45c magenta	90	20
C399	AP36	60c olive brn	2.25	55
C400	AP36	90c rose brn	12.00	8.00
		Nos. C392-C400 (9)	17.92	10.17

Issue date: 7½c, 15c, 20c, 30c, Mar. 24.

Arms of Aragua and Stylized Farm

C401	AP36	5c blue green	40	15
C402	AP36	7½c gray grn	32	32
C403	AP36	10c car rose	15	15
C404	AP36	15c dk brown	1.00	25
C405	AP36	20c gray blue	55	25
C406	AP36	30c deep blue	1.65	30
C407	AP36	45c magenta	1.40	25
C408	AP36	60c olive brn	2.75	40
C409	AP36	90c rose brn	14.00	8.00
		Nos. C401-C409 (9)	22.22	10.07

Issue date: 7½c, 15c, 20c, 30c, Mar. 24.

Arms of Lara, Agricultural Products and Rope

C410	AP36	5c blue green	40	15
C411	AP36	7½c gray grn	32	32
C412	AP36	10c car rose	15	15
C413	AP36	15c dk brown	65	15
C414	AP36	20c gray blue	90	20
C415	AP36	30c deep blue	2.25	40
C416	AP36	45c magenta	90	35
C417	AP36	60c olive brn	2.25	65
C418	AP36	90c rose brn	13.00	10.00
		Nos. C410-C418 (9)	20.82	12.37

Issue date: 7½c, 15c, 20c, Mar. 24.

Arms of Bolivar and Stylized Design

C419	AP36	5c blue green	3.00	32
C420	AP36	10c car rose	15	15
C421	AP36	15c dark brown	35	15
C422	AP36	25c sepia	28	15
C423	AP36	30c deep blue	1.75	90

C424	AP36	50c henna brn	1.25	40
C425	AP36	60c olive brn	2.25	55
C426	AP36	1b purple	1.75	40
C427	AP36	2b violet gray	3.75	1.75
		Nos. C419-C427 (9)	14.53	4.77

Issue date: 15c, 30c, Mar. 24.

Arms of Sucre, Palms and Seascape

C428	AP36	5c blue green	30	15
C429	AP36	10c car rose	15	15
C430	AP36	15c dk brown	38	15
C431	AP36	25c sepia	8.50	20
C432	AP36	30c deep blue	2.75	85
C433	AP36	50c henna brn	1.25	30
C434	AP36	60c olive brn	1.65	65
C435	AP36	1b purple	2.00	50
C436	AP36	2b violet gray	4.50	2.25
		Nos. C428-C436 (9)	21.48	5.20

Issue date: 15c, 30c, Mar. 24.

Arms of Trujillo Surrounded by Stylized Tree

C437	AP36	5c blue green	4.50	35
C438	AP36	10c car rose	15	15
C439	AP36	15c dk brown	1.10	15
C440	AP36	30c deep blue	5.00	1.10
C441	AP36	60c olive brn	4.00	1.00
C442	AP36	1.20b rose red	3.75	2.40
C443	AP36	3b blue gray	1.65	1.00
C444	AP36	5b purple brn	3.75	1.75
C445	AP36	10b violet	6.00	4.00
		Nos. C437-C445 (9)	29.90	11.90

Issue date: 5c, 30c, Mar. 24.

1953-54
Map of Delta Amacuro and Ship

C446	AP36	5c blue green	30	15
C447	AP36	10c car rose	15	15
C448	AP36	15c dk brown	45	20
C449	AP36	25c sepia	65	30
C450	AP36	30c deep blue	2.25	65
C451	AP36	50c henna brn	1.10	30
C452	AP36	60c olive brn	1.75	50
C453	AP36	1b purple	2.25	75
C454	AP36	2b violet gray	3.75	2.75
		Nos. C446-C454 (9)	12.65	5.75

Issue date: 15c, 30c, Feb. 13.

Arms of Falcon and Stylized Oil Refinery

C455	AP36	5c blue green	50	20
C456	AP36	10c car rose	15	15
C457	AP36	15c dk brown	45	15
C458	AP36	30c deep blue	3.75	90
C459	AP36	60c olive brn	2.75	65
C460	AP36	1.20b rose red	3.50	3.00
C461	AP36	3b blue gray	3.75	2.00
C462	AP36	5b purple brn	6.00	4.00
C463	AP36	10b violet	6.00	4.50
		Nos. C455-C463 (9)	26.85	15.55

Issue date: 10c, 15c, 30c, Feb. 13.

Arms of Guarico and Factory

C464	AP36	5c blue grn	30	15
C465	AP36	10c car rose	20	15
C466	AP36	15c dk brown	45	15
C467	AP36	25c sepia	65	30
C468	AP36	30c deep blue	2.50	1.00
C469	AP36	50c henna brn	1.25	45
C470	AP36	60c olive brn	1.50	65
C471	AP36	1b purple	2.50	65
C472	AP36	2b vio gray	3.75	2.00
		Nos. C464-C472 (9)	13.10	5.50

Issue date: 15c, 30c, Feb. 13.

Arms of Merida and Church

C473	AP36	5c blue green	25	15
C474	AP36	10c car rose	15	15
C475	AP36	15c dk brown	40	15
C476	AP36	30c deep blue	3.75	80
C477	AP36	60c olive brn	1.65	40
C478	AP36	1.20b rose red	3.00	2.00
C479	AP36	3b blue gray	1.65	80
C480	AP36	5b purple brn	3.75	2.00
C481	AP36	10b violet	5.00	3.25
		Nos. C473-C481 (9)	19.60	9.70

Issue date: 10c, Feb. 2.

Arms of Monagas and Horses

C482	AP36	5c blue green	25	15
C483	AP36	10c car rose	15	15
C484	AP36	15c dk brown	40	15
C485	AP36	25c sepia	32	15
C486	AP36	30c deep blue	3.00	90
C487	AP36	50c henna brn	1.10	40
C488	AP36	60c olive brn	1.40	40
C489	AP36	1b purple	2.00	55
C490	AP36	2b vio gray	2.75	1.65
		Nos. C482-C490 (9)	11.37	4.50

Issue date: 10c, Feb. 2.

Arms of Portuguesa and Forest

C491	AP36	5c blue green	1.10	30
C492	AP36	10c car rose	20	15
C493	AP36	15c dk brown	50	20
C494	AP36	30c deep blue	3.50	1.50
C495	AP36	60c olive brn	2.50	50
C496	AP36	1.20b rose red	6.25	3.75
C497	AP36	3b blue gray	2.00	1.00

C498	AP36	5b purple brn	3.75	2.00
C499	AP36	10b violet	5.50	4.50
		Nos. C491-C499 (9)	25.30	13.90

Issue date: 5c, 10c, 30c, Feb. 2.

Map of Amazonas and Orchid

C500	AP36	5c blue green	85	15
C501	AP36	10c car rose	20	15
C502	AP36	15c dk brown	85	20
C503	AP36	25c sepia	1.75	20
C504	AP36	30c deep blue	4.50	45
C505	AP36	50c hn brn	3.50	75
C506	AP36	60c olive brn	4.50	75
C507	AP36	1b purple	17.50	2.50
C508	AP36	2b vio gray	7.00	3.00
		Nos. C500-C508 (9)	40.65	8.15

Issue date: Jan. 1954

Arms of Apure, Horse and Bird

C509	AP36	5c blue green	40	15
C510	AP36	10c car rose	15	15
C511	AP36	15c dk brown	40	15
C512	AP36	30c deep blue	2.00	80
C513	AP36	60c olive brn	1.90	40
C514	AP36	1.20b brown car	3.00	2.00
C515	AP36	3b blue gray	1.90	80
C516	AP36	5b purple brn	3.75	1.65
C517	AP36	10b violet	5.25	3.75
		Nos. C500-C517 (9)	18.75	9.85

Issue date: Jan. 1954.

Arms of Barinas, Cow and Horse

C518	AP36	5c blue green	20	15
C519	AP36	10c car rose	15	15
C520	AP36	15c dk brown	75	20
C521	AP36	30c dp blue	2.50	1.00
C522	AP36	60c olive brn	2.50	50
C523	AP36	1.20b brn car	3.50	1.90
C524	AP36	3b blue gray	2.25	1.00
C525	AP36	5b purple brn	3.75	1.25
C526	AP36	10b violet	5.50	4.00
		Nos. C518-C526 (9)	21.10	10.15

Issue date: Jan. 1954.

Arms of Cojedes and Cattle

C527	AP36	5c blue green	2.50	38
C528	AP36	7½c gray grn	65	38
C529	AP36	10c car rose	15	15
C530	AP36	15c dk brown	20	15
C531	AP36	20c gray blue	50	15
C532	AP36	30c dp blue	3.50	50
C533	AP36	45c magenta	1.25	30
C534	AP36	60c olive brn	2.50	45
C535	AP36	90c rose brn	3.00	1.75
		Nos. C527-C535 (9)	14.25	4.21

Issue date: Dec.

Arms of Nueva Esparta and Fish

C536	AP36	5c blue green	38	15
C537	AP36	10c car rose	15	15
C538	AP36	15c dk brown	65	15
C539	AP36	25c sepia	1.10	25
C540	AP36	30c deep blue	2.25	50
C541	AP36	50c henna brn	2.25	50
C542	AP36	60c olive brn	2.25	30
C543	AP36	1b purple	3.25	75
C544	AP36	2b vio gray	4.50	2.25
		Nos. C536-C544 (9)	16.78	5.00

Issue date: Jan. 1954.

Arms of Yaracuy and Tropical Foliage

C545	AP36	5c blue green	45	15
C546	AP36	7½c gray grn	6.00	6.00
C547	AP36	10c car rose	15	15
C548	AP36	15c dk brown	45	15
C549	AP36	20c gray blue	85	15
C550	AP36	30c deep blue	1.75	50
C551	AP36	45c magenta	1.25	30
C552	AP36	60c olive brn	1.25	50
C553	AP36	90c rose brn	3.50	2.50
		Nos. C545-C553 (9)	15.65	10.40
		Nos. C338-C553 (216)	504.01	214.73

Issue date: Jan. 1954.

Ship Type of 1948-50 Redrawn
Coil Stamps
Imprint: "Courvoisier S.A."

1952   Unwmk.   Perf. 12x11½

C554	AP25	5c rose brn	90	15
C555	AP25	10c org red	1.40	15
C556	AP25	15c ol brn	1.75	15
		Set value		18

Barquisimeto Type of 1952

1952, Sept. 14   Photo.   Perf. 11½

C557	A94	5c blue green	20	15
C558	A94	10c car rose	15	15
C559	A94	20c dk blue	32	15
C560	A94	25c black brn	40	15
C561	A94	30c ultra	55	15
C562	A94	40c brown org	3.00	1.50
C563	A94	50c dk ol grn	1.00	40
C564	A94	1b purple	4.00	2.00
		Nos. C557-C564 (8)	9.62	4.65

Caracas Post Office Type of 1953-54

1953, Mar. 11   Perf. 12½

C565	A96	7½c yellow grn	15	15
C566	A96	15c dp plum	15	15
C567	A96	20c slate	15	15
C568	A96	25c sepia	35	15
C569	A96	40c plum	35	15
C570	A96	45c rose vio	35	15
C571	A96	50c red orange	55	15
C572	A96	70c dk sl grn	1.10	55
C573	A96	75c dp ultra	3.75	80
C574	A96	90c brown org	90	45
C575	A96	1b violet blue	90	45
		Nos. C565-C575 (11)	8.70	
		Set value		2.75

See Nos. C587-C589, C597-C606.

Simon Rodriguez
AP39

Quotation from Bolivar's Manifesto of 1824
AP40

1954, Feb. 28   Perf. 11½

C576	AP39	5c blue green	22	15
C577	AP39	10c car rose	35	15
C578	AP39	20c gray blue	45	15
C579	AP39	45c magenta	65	22
C580	AP39	65c gray green	2.25	1.00
		Nos. C576-C580 (5)	3.92	
		Set value		1.35

Issued to commemorate the centenary of the death of Simon Rodriguez, scholar and tutor of Bolivar.

1954, Mar. 1   Unwmk.

C581	AP40	15c blk & brn buff	15	15
C582	AP40	25c dk red brn & gray	65	15
C583	AP40	40c dk red brn & red org	45	15
C584	AP40	65c black & blue	1.10	55
C585	AP40	80c dk red brn & rose	90	45
C586	AP40	1b pur & rose lil	1.75	35
		Nos. C581-C586 (6)	5.00	
		Set value		1.60

Issued to publicize the 10th Inter-American Conference, Caracas, Mar. 1954.

P.O. Type of 1953

1954, Feb.   Photo.   Perf. 12½

C587	A96	5c orange	15	15
C588	A96	30c red brown	1.90	1.00
C589	A96	60c bright red	1.90	1.25

Valencia Arms Type of 1955

1955, Mar. 26   Engr.   Perf. 12

C590	A97	5c blue green	15	15
C591	A97	10c rose pink	15	15
C592	A97	20c ultra	15	15
C593	A97	25c gray	16	15
C594	A97	40c violet	45	22
C595	A97	50c vermilion	45	22
C596	A97	60c olive green	90	22
		Nos. C590-C596 (7)	2.42	
		Set value		85

P.O. Type of 1953 Inscribed: "Republica de Venezuela"

1955   Photo.   Perf. 12½

C597	A96	5c orange	15	15
C598	A96	10c olive brn	15	15
C599	A96	15c deep plum	15	15
C600	A96	20c slate	15	15
C601	A96	30c red brn	25	15
C602	A96	40c plum	75	25
C603	A96	45c rose violet	75	38
C604	A96	70c dk slate grn	1.90	85
C605	A96	75c deep ultra	1.25	50
C606	A96	90c brown org	65	25
		Nos. C597-C606 (10)	6.25	
		Set value		2.45

Caracas Arms Type of 1955

1955, Dec. 9   Unwmk.   Perf. 11½

C607	A98	5c yellow org	15	15
C608	A98	15c claret brn	18	15
C609	A98	25c violet blk	18	15
C610	A98	40c red	45	15
C611	A98	50c red orange	45	16
C612	A98	60c car rose	90	35
		Nos. C607-C612 (6)	2.31	
		Set value		75

University Hospital, Caracas — AP43

Designs: 5c, 10c, 15c, 70c, O'Leary School, Barinas. 25c, 30c, 80c, University Hospital, Caracas. 40c, 45c, 50c, 1b, Caracas-La Guaira Highway. 60c, 65c, 75c, 2b, Towers of Simon Bolivar Center.

1956, Nov. 5   Unwmk.   Perf. 11½

C613	AP43	5c orange	15	15
C614	AP43	10c sepia	15	15
C615	AP43	15c claret brn	15	15
C616	AP43	20c dk blue ('56)	15	15
C617	AP43	25c gray blk	15	15
C618	AP43	30c henna brn	28	15
C619	AP43	40c brt crimson	35	15
C620	AP43	45c brown vio	25	15
C621	AP43	50c dp orange ('56)	45	15
C622	AP43	60c olive grn ('56)	45	15
C623	AP43	65c brt blue	70	20
C624	AP43	70c blue green	75	28
C625	AP43	75c ultra	80	35
C626	AP43	80c car rose	90	18
C627	AP43	1b plum	55	25
C628	AP43	2b dk car rose	1.10	75
		Nos. C613-C628 (16)	7.33	
		Set value		2.75

Book and Flags of American Nations — AP44

1956-57
Granite Paper

C629	AP44	5c orange & brn	15	15
C630	AP44	10c brn & pale brn	15	15
C631	AP44	20c blue & sapphire	15	15
C632	AP44	25c gray vio & gray	22	15
C633	AP44	40c rose red & pale pur	35	15
C634	AP44	45c vio brn & gray brn	45	15
C635	AP44	60c olive & gray ol	90	45
		Nos. C629-C635 (7)	2.37	
		Set value		88

Issued for the Book Festival of the Americas, Nov. 15-30, 1956.

Issued: 5c, 40c, Nov. 15; others, Feb. 7, 1957.

Bolivar Type of 1957-58
Engraved; Center Embossed

1957-58   Unwmk.   Perf. 13½

C636	A100	5c orange	15	15
C637	A100	10c olive gray	15	15
C638	A100	20c blue	55	15
C639	A100	25c gray black	60	16
C640	A100	40c rose red	55	15
C641	A100	45c rose lilac	65	25
C642	A100	65c yellow brn	1.10	45
		Nos. C636-C642 (7)	3.75	
		Set value		1.20

Issued: 45c, 1958; others, Nov. 15, 1957.

Tamanaco Hotel Type of 1957-58

1957-58   Engr.   Perf. 13

C643	A101	5c dull yellow	15	15
C644	A101	10c brown	15	15
C645	A101	15c chocolate	16	15
C646	A101	20c gray blue	15	15
C647	A101	25c sepia	15	15
C648	A101	30c violet bl	20	15
C649	A101	40c car rose	22	15
C650	A101	45c claret	30	15
C651	A101	50c red org	30	15
C652	A101	60c yellow grn	55	15
C653	A101	65c orange brn	1.50	75
C654	A101	70c slate	80	35
C655	A101	75c grnsh blue	90	45
C656	A101	1b dk claret	90	45
C657	A101	2b dk gray	1.50	55
		Nos. C643-C657 (15)	7.93	
		Set value		3.35

Issue dates: 5c, 10c, Oct. 10. Others, 1958.
For surcharge see No. C878.

Post Office Type of 1958

1958, May 14   Litho.   Perf. 14

C658	A102	5c dp yellow	15	15
C659	A102	10c brown	15	15
C660	A102	15c red brn	15	15
C661	A102	20c lt blue	15	15
C662	A102	25c lt gray	15	15

C663	A102	30c lt ultra	15	15
C664	A102	40c brt yel grn	15	15
C665	A102	50c red orange	15	15
C666	A102	60c rose pink	16	15
C667	A102	65c red	25	15
C668	A102	90c violet	35	18
C669	A102	1b lilac	45	18
C670	A102	1.20b bister brn	5.50	3.75
		Nos. C658-C670 (13)	7.91	
		Set value		4.70

See Nos. C786-C792. For surcharges see Nos. C856-C861.

Post Office Type of 1958
Coil Stamps

1958		**Engr.**	**Perf. 11½x12**	
C671	A103	5c deep yellow	25	15
C672	A103	10c brown	38	15
C673	A103	15c dark brown	50	15
		Set value		22

Merida Type of 1958

1958, Oct. 9		**Photo.**	**Perf. 13½**	
C674	A104	5c orange yellow	15	15
C675	A104	10c gray brown	15	15
C676	A104	15c dull red brn	15	15
C677	A104	20c chalky blue	15	15
C678	A104	25c brown gray	28	15
C679	A104	30c violet bl	22	15
C680	A104	40c rose car	35	15
C681	A104	45c brt lilac	35	15
C682	A104	50c red orange	45	22
C683	A104	lt olive grn	35	16
C684	A104	65c henna brn	1.10	45
C685	A104	70c gray black	65	35
C686	A104	75c brt grnsh bl	1.25	65
C687	A104	80c brt vio bl	80	35
C688	A104	90c blue green	80	38
C689	A104	1b lilac	90	45
		Nos. C674-C689 (16)	8.10	
		Set value		3.50

Trujillo Type of 1959

1958, Nov. 17		**Photo.**	**Perf. 14**	
C690	A105	5c orange yel	15	15
C691	A105	10c lt brown	15	15
C692	A105	15c redsh brown	15	15
C693	A105	20c lt blue	16	15
C694	A105	25c pale gray	22	15
C695	A105	30c lt vio blue	22	15
C696	A105	40c brt yel grn	28	15
C697	A105	50c red orange	30	15
C698	A105	60c lilac rose	45	22
C699	A105	65c vermilion	1.40	65
C700	A105	1b lilac	90	28
		Nos. C690-C700 (11)	4.38	
		Set value		1.90

Emblem — AP45

1959, Mar. 10		**Litho.**	**Perf. 13½**	
C701	AP45	5c yellow	15	15
C702	AP45	10c red brown	18	15
C703	AP45	15c orange	22	15
C704	AP45	30c gray	45	28
C705	AP45	50c green	52	35
		Nos. C701-C705 (5)	1.52	
		Set value		90

8th Central American and Caribbean Games, Caracas, Nov. 29-Dec. 14, 1958. Exist imperf. Value, pair $25.

Stamp Centenary Type of 1959

Stamp of 1859 and: 25c, Mailman and José Ignacio Paz Castillo. 50c, Mailman on horseback and Jacinto Gutierrez. 1b, Plane, train and Miguel Herrera.

1959, Sept. 15		**Engr.**	**Perf. 13½**	
C706	A107	25c orange yel	28	15
C707	A107	50c blue	45	22
C708	A107	1b rose red	90	45

> Catalogue values for unused stamps in this section, from this point to the end of the section, are for Never Hinged items.

Alexander von Humboldt Type of 1960

1960, Feb. 9			**Unwmk.**	
C709	A108	5c ocher & brn	35	15
C710	A108	20c brt bl & turq bl	95	15
C711	A108	40c ol & ol grn	1.40	38
		Set value		58

Newspaper Type of 1960

1960, June 11		**Litho.**	**Perf. 14**	
C712	A109	5c yellow & blk	1.90	80
C713	A109	15c lt red brn & blk	1.00	32
C714	A109	65c salmon & blk	1.50	55

Agustin Codazzi Type of 1960

1960, June 15			**Engr.**	
C715	A110	5c yel org & brn	15	15
C716	A110	10c brn & dk brn	20	15
C717	A110	25c gray & blk	42	15
C718	A110	30c vio bl & sl	55	15
C719	A110	50c org brn & brn	90	32
C720	A110	70c gray ol & ol gray	1.40	55
		Nos. C715-720 (6)	3.62	
		Set value		1.20

For surcharge see No. C884.

National Pantheon Type of 1960

1960, May 9			**Litho.**	
		Pantheon in Bister		
C721	A111	5c dp bister	15	15
C722	A111	10c red brown	22	15
C723	A111	15c fawn	30	15
C724	A111	20c lt blue	45	15
C725	A111	25c gray	1.40	22
C726	A111	30c lt vio bl	1.50	40
C727	A111	40c brt yel grn	45	15
C728	A111	45c lt violet	70	15
C729	A111	60c deep pink	90	28
C730	A111	65c salmon	90	28
C731	A111	70c gray	1.10	40
C732	A111	75c chalky blue	2.25	70
C733	A111	80c lt ultra	1.90	60
C734	A111	1.20b bister brn	2.25	85
		Nos. C721-C734 (14)	14.47	4.63

For surcharges see Nos. C894-C895.

Andres Eloy Blanco Type of 1960

1960, May 21			**Perf. 14**	
		Portrait in Black		
C735	A112	20c blue	40	15
C736	A112	75c grnsh blue	1.25	30
C737	A112	90c brt violet	1.20	30

For surcharge see No. C874.

Independence Type of 1960

1960, Aug. 19		**Litho.**	**Perf. 13½**	
		Center Multicolored		
C738	A113	50c orange	85	24
C739	A113	75c brt grnsh blue	1.25	40
C740	A113	90c purple	1.40	30

Oil Refinery — AP46

			Unwmk.	
1960, Aug. 26			**Engr.**	**Perf. 14**
C741	AP46	30c dk bl & sl bl	50	18
C742	AP46	40c yel grn & ol	85	30
C743	AP46	50c org & red brn	1.00	38

Issued to publicize Venezuela's oil industry.

Luisa Cáceres de Arismendi Type of 1960

1960, Oct. 21		**Litho.**	**Perf. 14**	
		Center Multicolored		
C744	A115	5c bister	95	35
C745	A115	10c redsh brown	1.25	55
C746	A115	60c rose carmine	2.25	70

José Antonio Anzoategui Type of 1960

1960, Oct. 29			**Engr.**	
C747	A116	25c gray & brown	55	20
C748	A116	40c yel grn & ol gray	55	40
C749	A116	45c rose cl & dl pur	75	30

Antonio José de Sucre Type of 1960

			Unwmk.	
1960, Nov. 18		**Litho.**	**Perf. 14**	
		Center Multicolored		
C750	A117	25c gray	75	28
C751	A117	30c violet blue	1.10	40
C752	A117	50c brown orange	1.40	55

Type of Regular Issue, 1960

Designs: 30c, Bolivar Peak. 50c, Caroni Falls. 65c, Cuacharo caves.

1960, Mar. 22			**Perf. 14**	
C753	A118	30c vio bl & blk bl	1.90	1.90
C754	A118	50c brn org & brn	1.90	1.90
C755	A118	65c red org & red brn	1.90	1.90

Cow's Head, Grain, Man and Child
AP47

Arms of San Cristobal
AP48

1961, Feb. 6		**Litho.**	**Unwmk.**	
		Cow and Inscription in Black		
C756	AP47	5c yellow	15	15
C757	AP47	10c brown	15	15
C758	AP47	15c redsh brn	15	15
C759	AP47	20c dull blue	15	15
C760	AP47	25c gray	16	15
C761	AP47	30c violet bl	20	15
C762	AP47	40c yellow grn	28	15
C763	AP47	45c lilac	30	15
C764	AP47	50c orange	32	15
C765	AP47	60c cerise	40	15
C766	AP47	65c red orange	52	20
C767	AP47	70c gray	80	32
C768	AP47	75c brt grnsh bl	70	25
C769	AP47	80c brt violet	70	20
C770	AP47	1.10b violet	1.10	40
		Nos. C756-C770 (15)	6.08	
		Set value		2.25

9th general census and 3rd agricultural census. Issue dates: 5c, 10c, 15c, 30c, 60c, 65c, 75c, 80c, Feb. 6. Others, Apr. 6.
For surcharges see Nos. C865-C866.

Rafael Maria Baralt Type of 1961

1961, Mar. 11			**Engr.**	**Perf. 14**
C771	A120	25c gray & sepia	65	28
C772	A120	30c dk blue & vio	72	32
C773	A120	40c yel grn & ol grn	95	40

1961, Apr. 10				**Litho.**
		Arms in Original Colors		
C774	AP48	5c orange & blk	15	15
C775	AP48	55c yel grn & blk	65	24
		Set value		30

400th anniversary of San Cristobal.
For surcharge see No. C879.

Bird Type of 1961

Birds: 5c, Troupial. 10c, Golden cock of the rock. 15c, Tropical mockingbird.

1961, Sept. 6		**Unwmk.**	**Perf. 14½**	
C776	A121	5c multicolored	1.25	85
C777	A121	10c multicolored	60	45
C778	A121	15c multicolored	80	50

Charge, Battle of Carabobo — AP49

1961, Dec. 1		**Litho.**	**Perf. 14**	
		Center Multicolored		
C779	AP49	50c black & ultra	65	15
C780	AP49	1.05b black & org	1.40	50
C781	AP49	1.50b black & lil rose	1.65	50
C782	AP49	1.90b black & lilac	2.25	1.00
C783	AP49	2b black & gray	2.50	1.00
C784	AP49	3b black & grnsh bl	3.25	1.25
		Nos. C779-C784 (6)	11.70	4.40

140th anniversary of Battle of Carabobo.
For surcharges see Nos. C867-C870.

Arms of Cardinal Quintero — AP50

Archbishop Rafael Arias Blanco — AP51

1962, Mar. 1			**Unwmk.**	
C785	AP50	5c lilac rose	15	15
a.		Souv. sheet of 1, imperf.	1.65	1.25

1st Venezuelan Cardinal, José Humberto Quintero.
No. C785a, issued Mar. 23, sold for 1b.

Post Office Type of 1958

1962, Apr. 12		**Litho.**	**Perf. 13½x14**	
C786	A102	35c citron	28	15
C787	A102	55c gray olive	42	18
C788	A102	70c bluish green	65	22
C789	A102	75c brown orange	80	18
C790	A102	80c fawn	80	30
C791	A102	85c deep rose	1.25	45
C792	A102	95c lilac rose	85	42
		Nos. C786-C792 (7)	5.05	1.90

For surcharges see Nos. C856-C861.

1962, May 10			**Perf. 10½**	
C793	AP51	75c red lilac	80	30

4th anniversary (in 1961) of the anti-communist pastoral letter of the Archbishop of Caracas, Rafael Arias Blanco.

Orchid Type of 1962

Orchids: 5c, Oncidium volvox. 20c, Cycnoches chlorochilon. 25c, Cattleya Gaskelliana. 30c, Epidendrum difforme, horiz. 40c, Catasetum callosum Lindl, horiz. 50c, Oncidium bicolor Lindl. 1b, Brassavola nodosa Lindl, horiz. 1.05b, Epidendrum lividum Lindl. 1.50b, Schombgrkla undulata Lindl. 2b, Oncidium zebrinum.

		Perf. 14x13½, 13½x14		
1962, May 30		**Litho.**	**Unwmk.**	
		Orchids in Natural Colors		
C794	A124	5c black & lt grn	15	15
C795	A124	20c black	15	15
C796	A124	25c black & fawn	35	15
C797	A124	30c black & pink	25	15
C798	A124	40c black & yel	35	15
C799	A124	50c black & lil	45	16
C800	A124	1b blk & pale rose	75	32
C801	A124	1.05b blk & dp org	2.00	1.00
C802	A124	1.50b blk & pale vio	2.25	1.10
C803	A124	2b blk & org brn	2.75	1.65
		Nos. C794-C803 (10)	9.45	4.98

For surcharges see Nos. C885-C887.

Independence Type of 1960

Design: Signing Declaration of Independence.

1962, June 11			**Perf. 13½**	
		Center Multicolored		
C804	A113	55c olive	52	15
C805	A113	1.05b brt rose	1.65	55
C806	A113	1.50b purple	1.40	50
a.		Souv. sheet of 3, #C804-C806, imperf.	4.00	4.00

No. C806a, issued Oct. 13, sold for 4.10b. A buff cardboard folder exists with impressions of Nos. 812-814, C804-C806. Perforation is simulated. Sold for 5.60b. Value $3.
For surcharge see No. C893.

No. 710 Surcharged in Rose Carmine: "BICENTENARIO DE UPATA 1762-1962 RESELLADO AEREO VALOR Bs. 2,00"

1962, July 7			**Perf. 13½x14**	
C807	A102	2b on 1b lt ol grn	2.00	90

200th anniversary of Upata, a village in the state of Bolivar.

National Games Type of 1962

			Perf. 13x14	
1962, Nov. 30		**Unwmk.**	**Litho.**	
C808	A125	40c Bicycling	42	22
C809	A125	75c Baseball	60	32
C810	A125	85c Woman athlete	1.50	65
a.		Souv. sheet of 3, #C808-C810 imperf.	3.00	3.00

See note after No. 817.
No. C810a sold for 3b.
For surcharge see No. C899.

Bird Type of 1962

Birds: 5c, American kestrel. 20c, Black-bellied tree duck, horiz. 25c, Amazon kingfisher. 30c, Rufous-tailed chachalaca. 50c, Black-and-yellow troupial. 55c, White-naped nightjar. 2.30b, Red-crowned woodpecker. 2.50b, Black-moustached quail-dove.

Perf. 14x13½, 13½x14

1962, Dec. 14

Birds in Natural Colors; Black Inscription

C811	A126	5c car rose	16	15
C812	A126	20c brt blue	35	15
C813	A126	25c lt gray	42	15
C814	A126	30c lt olive	50	16
C815	A126	50c violet	80	30
C816	A126	55c dp orange	1.40	50
C817	A126	2.30b dl red brn	4.00	2.25
C818	A126	2.50b orange yel	4.00	2.50
		Nos. C811-C818 (8)	11.63	6.16

For surcharges see Nos. C880-C882.

Malaria Eradication
Emblem, Mosquito
and Map — AP52

Lithographed and Embossed
Perf. 13½x14

1962, Dec. 20   **Wmk. 346**

C819	AP52	30c green & blk	55	22
a.		Souv. sheet of 2, #825, C819, imperf.	3.00	3.00

WHO drive to eradicate malaria. No. C819a sold for 2b.

Animal Type of Regular Issue

Designs: 5c, Spectacle bear, vert. 40c, Paca. 50c, Three-toed sloths. 55c, Great anteater. 1.50b, South American tapirs. 2b, Jaguar.

Perf. 14x13½, 13½x14

1963, Mar. 13   **Litho.**   **Unwmk.**

Multicolored Center; Black Inscriptions

C820	A128	5c yellow	22	15
C821	A128	40c brt green	65	22
C822	A128	50c lt violet	90	32
C823	A128	55c brown olive	1.10	40
C824	A128	1.50b gray	3.25	1.65
C825	A128	2b ultra	5.25	2.50
		Nos. C820-C825 (6)	11.37	5.24

For surcharges see Nos. C888-C889.

Freedom from Hunger Type of 1963

Designs: 40c, Map and shepherd. 75c, Map and farmer.

1963, Mar. 21

C826	A129	40c lt yel grn & dl red	52	28
C827	A129	75c yellow & brown	35	40

Arms of
Bocono — AP53

1963, May 30   **Wmk. 346**

C828	AP53	1b multicolored	1.40	38

400th anniversary of the founding of Bocono. For surcharge see No. C892.

Papal and
Venezuelan
Arms — AP54

1963, June 11   *Perf. 14x13½*

Arms Multicolored

C829	AP54	80c light green	1.00	32
C830	AP54	90c gray	1.00	38

Vatican II, the 21st Ecumenical Council of the Roman Catholic Church.
For surcharges see Nos. C871-C872.

Arms of
Venezuela — AP55

1963, July 29   **Unwmk.**   *Perf. 14*

C831	AP55	70c gray, red, yel & bl	95	40

Centenary of Venezuela's flag and coat of arms.
For surcharge see No. C883.

Lake
Maracaibo
Bridge
AP56

Wmk. 346

1963, Aug. 24   **Litho.**   *Perf. 14*

C832	AP56	90c grn, brn & ocher	1.25	40
C833	AP56	95c blue, brn & ocher	1.25	48
C834	AP56	1b ultra, brn & ocher	1.00	40

Opening of bridge over Lake Maracaibo.
For surcharges see Nos. C897-C898.

Armed Forces Type of 1963

1963, Sept. 10   **Unwmk.**

C835	A134	1b red & bl, *buff*	1.65	75

For surcharge see No. 862.

Hammarskjold Type of 1963

1963, Sept. 25   **Unwmk.**   *Perf. 14*

C836	A135	80c dk bl, lt ultra & ocher	95	40
C837	A135	90c dk bl, bl & ocher	1.25	55
a.		Souv. sheet of 4, #841-842, C836-C837, imperf.	3.50	3.50

No. C837a sold for 3b.
For surcharges see Nos. C875-C876.

Dr. Luis Razetti,
Physician, Birth
Cent. — AP57

1963, Oct. 10   **Engr.**

C838	AP57	95c dk blue & mag	1.40	60
C839	AP57	1.05b dk brown & grn	1.50	75

For surcharges see Nos. C890-C891.

Red Cross Type of 1963

Designs: 40c, Sir Vincent K. Barrington. 75c, Red Cross nurse and child.

1963, Dec. 31   **Litho.**   *Perf. 11½x12*

C840	A137	40c multicolored	42	28
C841	A137	75c multicolored	75	40

Development Type of 1964

Designs: 5c, Loading cargo. 10c, Tractor and corn. 15c, Oil field workers. 20c, Oil refinery. 50c, Crane and building construction.

1964, Feb. 5   **Unwmk.**   *Perf. 14x13½*

C842	A138	5c multi	15	15
C843	A138	10c multi	15	15
C844	A138	15c multi	16	15
C845	A138	20c multi	20	15
C846	A138	50c multi	50	25
		Set value	1.00	48

Cent. of the Dept. of Industrial Development and to publicize the Natl. Industrial Expo.

Pedro Gual Type of 1964

1964, Mar. 20   *Perf. 14x13½*

C847	A139	75c dull blue grn	65	25
C848	A139	1b brt pink	85	30

Blast Furnace and
Map of Venezuela
AP58

Arms of Ciudad
Bolivar
AP59

1964, May 22   **Litho.**   *Perf. 13½x14*

C849	AP58	80c multi	90	32
C850	AP58	1b multi	1.25	40

Issued to publicize the Orinoco steel mills.

1964, May 22   *Perf. 10½*

C851	AP59	1b multi	1.25	70

Bicentenary of Ciudad Bolivar.

AP60

AP61

1964, Aug. 3   **Unwmk.**   *Perf. 11½*

C852	AP60	30c bister brn & yel	35	15
C853	AP60	40c plum & pink	55	20
C854	AP60	50c brn & tan	75	28

Issued to commemorate the 80th birthday of novelist Romulo Gallegos.

1964, Nov. 11   **Litho.**   *Perf. 14x13½*

C855	AP61	1b orange & dk vio	1.10	48

Issued to honor Eleanor Roosevelt and the 15th anniversary (in 1963) of the Universal Declaration of Human Rights.
For surcharge see No. C896.

Issues of 1947-64 Surcharged
in Black, Dark Blue, Red, Carmine or Lilac
with New Value and: "RESELLADO / VALOR"

1965

C856	A102	5c on 55c (#C787)	15	15
C857	A102	5c on 55c (#C788)	15	15
C858	A102	5c on 80c (#C790)	15	15
C859	A102	5c on 85c (#C791)	15	15
C860	A102	5c on 90c (#C668)	15	15
C861	A102	5c on 95c (#C792)	15	15
C862	A134	5c on 1b (#C835)	40	20
C863	AP25	10c on 3b (#C269) (C)	15	15
C864	AP25	10c on 4b (#C270) (C)	52	20
C865	AP47	10c on 70c (#C767) (C)	25	15
C866	AP47	10c on 90c (#C770) (C)	20	15
C867	AP49	10c on 1.05b (#C780)	40	15
C868	AP49	10c on 1.90b (#C782)	20	15
C869	AP49	10c on 2b (#C783)	25	15
C870	AP49	10c on 3b (#C784)	25	15
C871	AP54	10c on 80c (#C829)	15	15
C872	AP54	10c on 90c (#C830)	15	15
C873	AP16	15c on 3b (#C253)	25	15
C874	A112	15c on 90c (#C737)	20	15
C875	A135	15c on 80c (#C836)	20	15
C876	A135	15c on 90c (#C837)	20	15
C877	AP59	15c on 1b (#C851)	25	15
C878	A101	20c on 2b (#C657) (R)	35	15
C879	AP48	20c on 55c (#C775) (DB)	25	15
C880	A126	20c on 55c (#C816)	40	15
a.		25c on 55c (#C816)		
C881	A126	20c on 2.30b (#C817)	28	15
C882	A126	20c on 2.50b (#C818)	40	15
C883	AP55	20c on 70c (#C831)	40	20
C884	A110	20c on 70c (#C720) (DB)	45	15
C885	A124	25c on 1.05b (#C801) (L)	28	15
C886	A124	25c on 1.50b (#C802) (L)	28	15
C887	A124	25c on 2b (#C803) (L)	40	15
C888	A128	25c on 1.50b (#C824)	40	15
C889	A128	25c on 2b (#C825)	40	15
C890	AP57	25c on 95c (#C838)	35	15
C891	AP57	25c on 1b (#C839)	40	15
C892	AP53	30c on 1b (#C828)	55	20
C893	A113	40c on 1.05b (#C805) (DB)	40	15
C894	A111	50c on 65c (#C730) (DB)	20	15
C895	A111	50c on 1.20b (#C734) (DB)	55	20
C896	AP61	50c on 1b (#C855)	28	15

C897	AP56	60c on 90c (#C832)	85	32
C898	AP56	60c on 95c (#C833)	65	20
C899	A125	75c on 85c (#C810)	75	30
		Nos. C856-C899 (44)	14.19	
		Set value		6.20

Lines of surcharge arranged variously on Nos. C856-C899. Old denominations obliterated with bars on Nos. C862, C871-C873, C875-C877, C883, C885-C887, C889, C892, C896-C898. Vertical surcharge on Nos. C865-C866, C871-C872, C874, C878, C896.

Kennedy Type of 1965

1965, Aug. 20   **Photo.**   *Perf. 12x11½*

C900	A144	60c lt grnsh bl	75	28
C901	A144	80c red brn	90	32

Medical Federation
Emblem — AP62

1965, Aug. 24   **Litho.**   *Perf. 13½x14*

C902	AP62	65c red org & blk	1.10	55

20th anniversary of the founding of the Medical Federation of Venezuela.

Unisphere and
Venezuela
Pavilion
AP63

1965, Aug. 31   *Perf. 14x13½*

C903	AP63	1b multi	1.00	32

New York World's Fair, 1964-65.

Andrés Bello (1780?-
1865), Educator and
Writer — AP64

Perf. 14x13½

1965, Oct. 15   **Litho.**   **Unwmk.**

C904	AP64	80c dk brn & org	1.10	55

Map Type of 1965

Maps of Venezuela and Guiana: 25c, Map of Venezuela and Guiana by J. Cruz Cano, 1775. 40c, Map stamp of 1896 (No. 140). 75c, Map by the Ministry of the Exterior, 1965 (all horiz.).

1965, Nov. 5   *Perf. 13½*

C905	A145	25c multi	35	15
C906	A145	40c multi	52	15
C907	A145	75c multi	75	28
a.		Souv. sheet of 3, #C905-C907, imperf.	2.75	2.75

#C907a, issued June 7, 1966, sold for 1.65b.

ITU Emblem
and Telegraph
Poles — AP65

1965, Nov. 19   **Litho.**   *Perf. 13½x14*

C908	AP65	75c blk & ol grn	75	28

Cent. of the ITU.

Simon Bolivar and
Quotation — AP66

1965, Dec. 9   *Perf. 14x13½*
C909 AP66 75c lt bl & dk brn   75 28
Sesquicentennial of Bolivar's Jamaica letter, Sept.
6, 1815.

Children Riding
Magic Carpet and
Three Kings on
Camels — AP67

Fermin
Toro — AP68

1965, Dec. 16   *Perf. 13½x14*
C910 AP67 70c yel & vio bl   1.10 55
Children's Festival, 1965 (Christmas).

1965, Dec. 22   *Perf. 14x13½*
C911 AP68 1b blk & org   90 32
Death centenary of Fermin Toro (1808-1865),
statesman and writer.

Winston
Churchill
AP69

1965, Dec. 29   *Perf. 14½x13*
C912 AP69 1b lil & blk   1.10 40
Sir Winston Spencer Churchill (1874-1965),
statesman and World War II leader.

ICY Emblem,
Arms of
Venezuela and
UN Emblem
AP70

1965, Dec. 30   *Perf. 13½x14*
C913 AP70 85c gold & vio blk   1.10 40
International Cooperation Year, 1965.

OAS Emblem and
Map of
America — AP71

Farms of 1936 and
1966 — AP72

1965, Dec. 31   *Perf. 14x13½*
C914 AP71 50c bl, blk & gold   90 32
Organization of American States, 75th anniv.

Butterfly Type of 1966
1966, Jan. 25 Litho. Perf. 13½x14
**Various Butterflies in Natural Colors;
Black Inscriptions**
C915 A146 65c lilac   75 28
C916 A146 85c blue   1.10 40
C917 A146 1b salmon pink   1.25 48

1966, Mar. 1   *Perf. 14x13½*
C918 AP72 55c blk, yel & emer   80 30
Issued to commemorate the 30th anniversary of
the Ministry for Agriculture and Husbandry.

Dance Type of 1966
Various folk dances.

1966, Apr. 5   Litho.   Perf. 14
C919 A148 40c bl & multi   60 24
C920 A148 50c multi   75 28
C921 A148 60c vio & multi   45 15
C922 A148 70c multi   1.00 42
C923 A148 80c red & multi   1.10 45
C924 A148 90c ocher & multi   1.40 60
    Nos. C919-C924 (6)   5.30 2.14

Title Page
"Popule Meus"
AP73

1966, Apr. 15   *Perf. 13½x14*
C925 AP73 55c yel grn, blk & bis   55 28
C926 AP73 95c dp mag, blk & bis   75 40
150th anniversary (in 1964) of the death of José
Angel Lamas, composer of national anthem.

Circus Scene, by Michelena — AP74

Paintings by Michelena: 1b, Miranda in La Car-
raca. 1.05b, Charlotte Corday.

Perf. 12x12½
1966, May 12   Litho.   Unwmk.
C927 AP74 95c multi   75 45
C928 AP74 1b multi   90 45
C929 AP74 1.05b multi   1.00 45
Centenary of the birth of Arturo Michelena
(1863-1898), painter. Miniature sheets of 12 exist.
See Nos. 900-901.

Abraham
Lincoln — AP75

1966, May 31   *Perf. 13½x14*
C930 AP75 1b gray & blk   90 55

Dr. José
Gregorio
Hernandez
AP76

1966, July 29 Litho. Perf. 14x13½
C931 AP76 1b brt bl & vio bl   1.25 48
Centenary (in 1964) of the birth of Dr. José Gre-
gorio Hernandez, physician.

Dr. Manuel
Dagnino and
Hospital
AP77

1966, Aug. 16 Litho. Perf. 13½x14
C932 AP77 1b sl grn & yel grn   1.10 40
Issued to commemorate the centenary of the
founding of Chiquinquira Hospital.

Fish Type of 1966
Fish: 75c, Pearl headstander, vert. 90c, Sword-
tail characine. 1b, Ramirez's dwarf cichlid.

Perf. 14x13½, 13½x14
1966, Aug. 31
C933 A151 75c multi   1.10 40
C934 A151 90c grn & multi   1.10 40
C935 A151 1b multi   1.10 40

Rafael Arevalo
Gonzalez — AP78

Simon Bolivar,
1816 — AP79

1966, Sept. 13 Litho. Perf. 13½x14
C936 AP78 75c yel bis & blk   1.00 40
Centenary of the birth of Rafael Arevalo Gonza-
lez, journalist.

Imprint: "Bundesdruckerei Berlin 1966"
Bolivar Portraits: 25c, 30c, 35c, by José Gil de
Castro, 1825. 40c, 50c, 60c, Anonymous painter,
1825. 80c, 1.20b, 4b, Anonymous painter, c.
1829.

1966
Multicolored Center
C937 AP79 5c lem & blk   15 15
C938 AP79 10c lt ol grn & blk   15 15
C939 AP79 20c grn & blk   15 15
C940 AP79 25c salmon & blk   15 15
C941 AP79 30c pink & blk   20 15
C942 AP79 35c dl rose & blk   24 15
C943 AP79 40c bis brn & blk   20 15
C944 AP79 50c org brn & blk   35 15
C945 AP79 60c brn red & blk   35 15
C946 AP79 80c brt bl & blk   75 28
C947 AP79 1.20b dl bl & blk   1.10 55
C948 AP79 4b vio bl & blk   3.75 2.25
    Nos. C937-C948 (12)   7.54
    Set value   3.75
Issued to honor Simon Bolivar.
Issue dates: Nos. C937-C939, Aug. 15. Nos.
C940-C942, Sept. 29. Others, Oct. 14.

See Nos. C961-C972.

"Justice" — AP80

1966, Nov. 3 Litho. Perf. 14x13½
C949 AP80 50c pale lil & red lil   75 28
Issued to commemorate the 50th anniversary of
the Academy of Political and Social Sciences.

Angostura Bridge, Orinoco River — AP81

1967, Jan. 6 Litho. Perf. 13½x14
C950 AP81 40c multi   32 18
Issued to commemorate the opening of the
Angostura Bridge over the Orinoco River.

Pavilion of
Venezuela
AP82

1967, Apr. 28 Litho. Perf. 11x13½
C951 AP82 1b multi   90 32
EXPO '67, International Exhibition, Montreal,
Apr. 28-Oct. 27, 1967.

Statue of Chief
Guaicaipuro
AP83

Constellations over Caracas, 1567 and
1967 — AP84

Designs: 45c, Captain Francisco Fajardo. 55c,
Diego de Losada, the Founder. 65c, Arms of
Caracas. 90c, Map of Caracas, 1578. 1b, Market
on Plaza Mayor, 1800.

1967 Litho. Perf. 14x13½, 13½x14
C952 AP83 15c multi   15 15
C953 AP83 45c gold, car & brn   35 15
C954 AP83 55c multi   45 18
C955 AP84 60c blk, ultra & sil   52 20
C956 AP83 65c multi   65 24
C957 AP84 90c multi   80 30
C958 AP84 1b multi   90 35
    Nos. C952-C958 (7)   3.82 1.57
400th anniv. of the founding of Caracas (1st
issue). See Nos. C977-C982 (2nd issue).

Two souvenir sheets each contain single stamps similar to Nos. C952-C953, but with simulated perforation. Sold for 1b each. Size: 80x119mm. Value $45 each.
Issued: 55c, 65c, July 28; others, July 12.

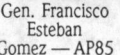

Gen. Francisco Esteban Gomez — AP85

Juan Vicente González — AP86

1967, July 31   Litho.   Perf. 14x13¹/₂
C959 AP85 90c multi   90   40

150th anniversary, Battle of Matasiete.

1967, Oct. 18   Litho.   Perf. 14x13¹/₂
C960 AP86 80c ocher & blk   90   32

Centenary of the death (in 1866) of Juan Vicente González, journalist.

Bolivar Type of 1966
Imprint: "Druck Bruder Rosenbaum. Wien"

1967-68   Litho.   Perf. 13¹/₂x14
Multicolored Center

C961	AP79	5c lemon & blk	15	15
C962	AP79	10c lemon & blk	15	15
C963	AP79	20c grn & blk	30	15
C964	AP79	25c salmon & blk	25	15
C965	AP79	30c pink & blk	30	15
C966	AP79	35c dl rose & blk	30	15
C967	AP79	40c bis brn & blk	50	15
C968	AP79	50c org brn & blk	90	32
C969	AP79	60c brn red & blk	1.75	80
C970	AP79	80c brt bl & blk	1.00	40
C971	AP79	1.20b dl bl & blk	1.50	32
C972	AP79	4b vio bl & blk	4.00	1.65
		Nos. C961-C972 (12)	11.10	4.54

Issue dates: 20c, 30c, 50c, Nov. 24. 5c, 25c, 40c, Feb. 5, 1968. Others, Aug. 28, 1967.

Child with Pinwheel — AP87

1967, Dec. 15   Litho.   Perf. 14x13¹/₂
C973	AP87	45c multi	50	18
C974	AP87	75c multi	65	25
C975	AP87	90c multi	85	32

Children's Festival.

Madonna with the Rosebush, by Stephan Lochner — AP88

1967, Dec. 19
C976 AP88 1b multi   1.25   55

Christmas 1967.

Palace of the Academies, Caracas — AP89

Views of Caracas: 50c, St. Theresa's Church, vert. 70c, Federal Legislature. 75c, University City. 85c, El Pulpo highways crossing. 2b, Avenida Libertador.

Perf. 13¹/₂x14, 14x13¹/₂
1967, Dec. 28
C977	AP89	10c multi	15	15
C978	AP89	50c lil & multi	35	15
C979	AP89	70c multi	65	20
C980	AP89	75c multi	75	24
C981	AP89	85c multi	75	28
C982	AP89	2b multi	2.25	80
		Nos. C977-C982 (6)	4.90	1.82

400th anniv. of Caracas (2nd issue).

Dr. José Manuel Nuñez Ponte (1870-1965), Educator — AP90

1968, Mar. 8   Litho.   Perf. 14
C983 AP90 65c multi   55   28

De Miranda and Printing Press — AP91

Designs (Miranda Portraits and): 35c, Parliament, London. 45c, Arc de Triomphe, Paris. 70c, Portrait, vert. 80c, Portrait bust and Venezuelan flags, vert.

Perf. 13¹/₂x14, 14x13¹/₂
1968, June 20   Litho.
C984	AP91	20c yel brn, grn & brn	24	15
C985	AP91	35c multi	42	15
C986	AP91	45c lt bl & multi	75	28
C987	AP91	70c multi	90	24
C988	AP91	80c multi	1.10	40
		Nos. C984-C988 (5)	3.41	1.22

General Francisco de Miranda (1750?-1816), revolutionist, dictator of Venezuela.

Insect Type of 1968

Insect Pests: 5c, Red leaf-cutting ant, vert. 15c, Sugar cane beetle, vert. 20c, Leaf beetle.

Perf. 14x13¹/₂, 13¹/₂x14
1968, Aug. 30   Litho.
C989	A157	5c multi	15	15
C990	A157	15c multi	28	15
C991	A157	20c gray & multi	35	15
		Set value		28

Three Keys — AP92

1968, Oct. 17   Litho.   Perf. 14x13¹/₂
C992 AP92 95c yel, vio & dk grn   95   35

30th anniv. of the National Comptroller's Office.

Fencing AP93

Designs: 5c, Pistol shooting, vert. 15c, Running. 75c, Boxing. 5b, Sailing, vert.

Perf. 14x13¹/₂, 13¹/₂x14
1968, Nov. 6   Litho.   Unwmk.
C993	AP93	5c vio, bl & blk	15	15
C994	AP93	15c multi	30	15
C995	AP93	30c yel grn, dk grn & blk	45	15
C996	AP93	75c multi	90	32
C997	AP93	5b multi	4.50	1.65
		Nos. C993-C997 (5)	6.30	2.42

Issued to commemorate the 19th Olympic Games, Mexico City, Oct. 12-27.

Holy Family, by Francisco José de Lerma — AP94

Dancing Children and Stars — AP95

1968, Dec. 4   Litho.   Perf. 14x13¹/₂
C998 AP94 40c multi   55   20

Christmas 1968.

1968, Dec. 13   Litho.   Perf. 14x13¹/₂
C999 AP95 80c vio & org   75   28

Issued for the 5th Children's Festival.

Conservation Type of 1968

Designs: 15c, Marbled wood-quail, vert. 20c, Water birds, vert. 30c, Woodcarvings and tools, vert. 90c, Brown trout. 95c, Valley and road. 1b, Red-eyed vireo feeding young bronzed cowbird.

Perf. 13¹/₂x14, 14x13¹/₂
1968, Dec. 19   Litho.
C1000	A160	15c multi	15	15
C1001	A160	20c multi	20	15
C1002	A160	30c multi	28	15
C1003	A160	90c multi	75	28
C1004	A160	95c multi	1.25	48
C1005	A160	1b multi	90	32
		Nos. C1000-C1005 (6)	3.53	
		Set value		1.25

Tourist Type of 1969

Designs: 15c, Giant cactus and desert, Falcon. 30c, Hotel Humboldt, Federal District. 40c, Cable car and mountain peaks, Merida.

1969, Jan. 24   Perf. 13¹/₂x14
C1006	A161	15c multi	24	15
C1007	A161	30c multi	24	15
a.		Souv. sheet of 2, #931, C1007, imperf.	1.40	1.40
C1008	A161	40c multi	48	20
		Set value		42

Tree Type of 1969

Trees: 5c, Cassia grandis. 20c, Triplaris caracasana. 25c, Samanea saman.

1969, May 30   Litho.   Perf. 13¹/₂x14
C1009	A164	5c lt grn & multi	15	15
C1010	A164	20c org & multi	28	15
C1011	A164	25c lt vio & multi	35	15
		Set value		28

Alexander von Humboldt, by Joseph Stieler — AP96

Map of Maracaibo, 1562 — AP97

1969, Sept. 12   Photo.   Perf. 14
C1012 AP96 50c multi   60   20

Alexander von Humboldt (1769-1859), naturalist and explorer.

Perf. 13¹/₂x13, 13x13¹/₂
1969, Sept. 30   Litho.

Designs: 20c, Ambrosio Alfinger, Alfonso Pacheco and Pedro Maldonado, horiz. 40c, Maracaibo coat of arms. 70c, University Hospital. 75c, Monument to the Indian Mara. 1b, Baralt Square, horiz.

C1013	AP97	20c lil & multi	24	15
C1014	AP97	25c org & multi	28	15
C1015	AP97	40c multi	35	18
C1016	AP97	70c grn & multi	75	28
C1017	AP97	75c brn & multi	90	32
C1018	AP97	1b multi	1.10	40
		Nos. C1013-C1018 (6)	3.62	1.48

400th anniversary of Maracaibo.

Astronauts Neil A. Armstrong, Edwin E. Aldrin, Jr., Michael Collins and Moonscape AP98

1969, Nov. 18   Litho.   Perf. 12¹/₂
C1019	AP98	90c multi	1.25	48
a.		Souv. sheet of 1, imperf.	1.90	1.90

See note after US No. C76.

Virgin with the Rosary, 17th Century — AP99

Christmas: 80c, Holy Family, Caracas, 18th Century.

1969, Dec. 1   Litho.   Perf. 12¹/₂
C1020	AP99	75c gold & multi	75	28
C1021	AP99	80c gold & multi	90	32
a.		Pair, #C1020-C1021	1.40	1.40

Simon Bolivar, 1819, by M. N. Bate — AP100

Bolivar Portraits: 45c, 55c, like 15c. 65c, 70c, 75c Drawing by Francois Roulin, 1828. 85c, 90c, 95c, Charcoal drawing by José Maria Espinoza, 1828. 1b, 1.50b, 2b, Drawing by Espinoza, 1830.

1970, Mar. 16   Litho.   Perf. 14x13½

C1022	AP100	15c multi	15	15
C1023	AP100	45c bl & multi	30	15
C1024	AP100	55c org & multi	45	15
C1025	AP100	65c multi	45	15
C1026	AP100	70c bl & multi	55	25
C1027	AP100	75c org & multi	65	28
C1028	AP100	85c multi	75	30
C1029	AP100	90c bl & multi	80	32
C1030	AP100	95c org & multi	90	32
C1031	AP100	1b multi	90	32
C1032	AP100	1.50b bl & multi	1.10	40
C1033	AP100	2b multi	2.25	1.10
		Nos. C1022-C1033 (12)	9.25	3.89

Issued to honor Simon Bolivar (1783-1830), liberator and father of his country.

General Antonio Guzmán Blanco and Dr. Martin J. Sanabria AP101

1970, June 26   Litho.   Perf. 13

C1034	AP101	75c brt grn & multi	65	30

Issued to commemorate the centenary of free obligatory elementary education.

Map of Venezuela with Claim to Part of Guyana — AP102

Designs: State map and arms. 55c, 90c, vert.

Perf. 13½x14, 14x13½

1970-71   Litho.

C1035	AP102	5c shown	15	15
C1036	AP102	15c Apure	20	15
C1037	AP102	20c Aragua	24	15
C1038	AP102	20c Anzoategui	28	15
C1039	AP102	25c Barinas	28	15
C1040	AP102	25c Bolivar	28	15
C1041	AP102	45c Carabobo	48	18
C1042	AP102	55c Cojedes	55	20
C1043	AP102	65c Falcon	60	20
C1044	AP102	75c Guárico	75	22
C1045	AP102	85c Lara	90	28
C1046	AP102	90c Mérida	90	32
C1047	AP102	1b Miranda	90	40
C1048	AP102	2b Delta Amacuro Territory	2.25	95
		Nos. C1035-C1048 (14)	8.76	
		Set value		3.15

Issue dates: 5c, July 15. 5c, No. C1037, Jan. 18. Nos. C1038-C1039, Feb. 15, 1971. No. C1040, 45c, Mar. 15, 1971. 55c, 65c, Apr. 15. 75c, 85c, May 15, 1971. 90c, 1b, June 15, 1971. 2b, July 15, 1971.

Flower Type of 1970

Flowers: 20c, Epidendrum secundum. 25c, Oyedaea verbesinoides. 45c, Heliconia villosa. 1b, Macleania nitida.

1970, July 29   Litho.   Perf. 14x13½

C1049	A175	20c multi	28	15
C1050	A175	25c multi	35	15
C1051	A175	45c multi	75	28
C1052	A175	1b multi	1.10	40

Caracciolo Parra Olmedo — AP104

1970, Nov. 16   Photo.   Perf. 12½

C1053	AP104	20c bl & multi	28	15

Sesquicentennial of birth of Caracciolo Parra Olmedo (1819-1900), professor of law, rector of University of Merida.

Census Chart AP105

1971, Apr. 30   Litho.   Perf. 13½x14

C1054		Block of 4	4.50	2.25
a.	AP105	70c, frame L & T	80	28
b.	AP105	70c, frame T & R	80	28
c.	AP105	70c, frame L & B	80	28
d.	AP105	70c, frame B & R	80	28

See note after No. 979.

Cattleya Gaskelliana AP106

Orchids: 20c, Cattleya percivaliana, vert. 75c, Cattleya mossiae, vert. 90c, Cattleya violacea. 1b, Cattleya lawrenciana.

Perf. 14x13½, 13½x14

1971, Aug. 25

C1055	AP106	20c blk & multi	28	15
C1056	AP106	25c blk & multi	35	18
C1057	AP106	75c blk & multi	70	32
C1058	AP106	90c blk & multi	80	40
C1059	AP106	1b blk & multi	95	45
		Nos. C1055-C1059 (5)	3.08	1.50

40th anniversary of Venezuelan Society of Natural History. Issued in sheets of 5 stamps and one label with Society emblem in blue.

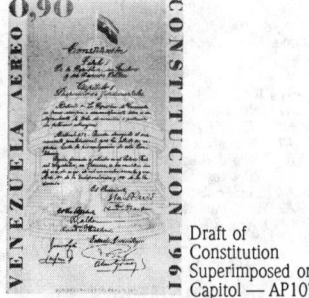

Draft of Constitution Superimposed on Capitol — AP107

1971, Dec. 29   Litho.   Perf. 13½

C1060	AP107	90c multi	80	40

Anniversary of 1961 Constitution.

AIR POST SEMI-POSTAL STAMPS

King Vulture — SPAP1

1942, Dec. 17   Unwmk.   Engr.   Perf. 12

CB1	SPAP1	15c + 10c org brn	1.40	55
CB2	SPAP1	30c + 5c violet	1.40	70

See note after No. B1.

SPECIAL DELIVERY STAMPS

Catalogue values for unused stamps in this section are for Never Hinged items.

SD1   SD2

Perf. 12½

1949, Mar. 9   Unwmk.   Engr.

E1	SD1	30c red	38	16

Perf. 13½

1961, Apr. 7   Wmk. 116   Litho.

E2	SD2	30c orange	42	18

REGISTRATION STAMPS

Bolívar — R1

1899, May   Unwmk.   Engr.   Perf. 12

F1	R1	25c yellow brown	2.50	1.90

No. F1 Overprinted like Nos. 150-155

1900

F2	R1	25c yellow brown	1.50	1.50
a.		Inverted overprint	22.50	22.50
b.		Double overprint	30.00	30.00

Counterfeit overprints exist, especially of the varieties.

OFFICIAL STAMPS

Coat of Arms
O1   O3

Lithographed, Center Engraved

1898, May 1   Unwmk.   Perf. 12

O1	O1	5c bl grn & blk	38	35
O2	O1	10c rose & blk	75	70
O3	O1	25c bl & blk	1.00	90

O4	O1	50c yel & blk	1.90	1.75
O5	O1	1b vio & blk	1.90	1.75
		Nos. O1-O5 (5)	5.93	5.45

1899

Nos. O4 and O5 Handstamp Surcharged in Magenta or Violet

5 Cms. - 5

1899, Nov.

O6	O1	5c on 50c yel & blk	3.50	3.25
O7	O1	5c on 1b vio & blk	14.00	12.50
O8	O1	25c on 50c yel & blk	14.00	12.50
O9	O1	25c on 1b vio & blk	8.25	7.50

Inverted Surcharge

O6a	O1	5c on 50c	13.00	13.00
O7a	O1	5c on 1b	32.50	32.50
O8a	O1	25c on 50c	27.50	27.50
O9a	O1	25c on 1b	27.50	27.50

Nos. O6-O9 exist with double surcharge. Value each $18.50-$37.50.

Many of the magenta overprints have become violet. There are intermediate shades.

Counterfeit overprints exist.

1900   Litho., Center Engr.

O14	O3	5c bl grn & blk	25	22
O15	O3	10c rose & blk	32	30
O16	O3	25c bl & blk	32	30
O17	O3	50c yel & blk	38	35
O18	O3	1b dl vio & blk	42	48
		Nos. O14-O18 (5)	1.69	1.65

O4   No Stars Above Shield — O5

Imprint: "American Bank Note Co., N.Y."

1904, July   Engr.

O19	O4	5c emerald & blk	18	16
O20	O4	10c rose & blk	38	35
O21	O4	25c blue & blk	38	35
O22	O4	50c red brn & blk	2.50	2.25
a.		50c claret & black	2.50	2.25
O23	O4	1b red brn & blk	1.25	1.10
a.		1b claret & black	1.25	1.10
		Nos. O19-O23 (5)	4.69	4.21

1912   Lithographed in Caracas

O24	O5	5c grn & blk	18	16
O25	O5	10c car & blk	18	16
O26	O5	25c dk bl & blk	18	16
O27	O5	50c pur & blk	25	22
a.		Center double	19.00	
O28	O5	1b yel & blk	50	45
		Nos. O24-O28 (5)	1.29	1.15

Perforated Initials

After 1925, Venezuela's official stamps consisted of regular postage stamps, some commemoratives and air post stamps of 1930-42 punched with "GN" (Gobierno Nacional) in large perforated initials.

LOCAL STAMPS FOR THE PORT OF CARUPANO

In 1902 Great Britain, Germany and Italy, seeking compensation for revolutionary damages, established a blockade of La Guaira and seized the custom house. Carúpano, a port near Trinidad, was isolated and issued the following provisionals. A treaty effected May 7, 1903, referred the dispute to the Hague Tribunal.

A1

A2

1902 Typeset Imperf.

1	A1	5c purple, *orange*	19.00
2	A2	10c black, *orange*	30.00
a.		Tête bêche pair	82.50
3	A1	25c purple, *green*	25.00
4	A1	50c green, *yellow*	47.50
5	A1	1b blue, *rose*	60.00

A3

1902

6	A3	1b black, *yellow*	135.00
a.		Tête bêche pair	

A4

1903 Handstamped

7	A4	5c carmine, *yellow*	19.00	19.00
8	A4	10c green, *yellow*	60.00	60.00
9	A4	25c green, *orange*	25.00	25.00
10	A4	50c blue, *rose*	25.00	25.00
11	A4	1b violet, *gray*	25.00	25.00
12	A4	2b carmine, *green*	25.00	25.00
13	A4	5b violet, *blue*	25.00	25.00

Dangerous counterfeits exist of Nos. 1-13.

LOCAL STAMPS FOR THE STATE OF GUAYANA

Revolutionary Steamship "Banrigh" — A1

Control Mark

1903 Typo. Perf. 12

1	A1	5c black, *gray*	19.00	19.00
2	A1	10c black, *orange*	47.50	47.50
3	A1	25c black, *pink*	19.00	19.00
4	A1	50c black, *blue*	30.00	30.00
5	A1	1b black, *straw*	25.00	25.00
		Nos. 1-5 (5)	140.50	140.50

Nos. 1-5 can be found with or without the illustrated control mark which covers four stamps.

Counterfeits include the 10c and 50c in red and are from different settings from the originals. They are on papers differing in colors from the originals. All 5c on granite paper are bogus.

Coat of Arms A2

1903

11	A2	5c black, *pink*	40.00
12	A2	10c black, *orange*	47.50
13	A2	25c black, *gray blue*	40.00
a.		25c black, *blue*	40.00
14	A2	50c black, *straw*	40.00
15	A2	1b black, *gray*	30.00
		Nos. 11-15 (5)	197.50

Postally used examples are very scarce, and are specimens having 9 ornaments in horizontal borders. Nos. 11-15 pen canceled sell for same values as unused.

See note on controls after No. 5.

Counterfeits exist of Nos. 11-15. Stamps with 10 ornaments in horizontal borders are counterfeits.

Nos. 1-5, 11-15 were issued by a group of revolutionists and had a limited local use. The dates on the stamps commemorate the declaration of Venezuelan independence and a compact with Spain against Joseph Bonaparte.

VIET NAM

LOCATION — In eastern Indo-China
GOVT. — Kingdom
AREA — 123,949 sq. mi.
CAPITAL — Hanoi

Viet Nam, which included the former French territories of Tonkin, Annam and Cochin China, became an Associated State of the French Union in 1949. The Communist Viet Minh obtained control of Northern Viet Nam in 1954, and the republic of South Viet Nam was established in October, 1955.

100 Cents (Xu) = 1 Piaster (Dong)

Catalogue values for all unused stamps in this country are for Never Hinged items.

Bongour Falls, Dalat — A1   Emperor Bao-Dai — A2

Designs: 20c, 2pi, 10pi, Imperial palace, Hué. 30c, 15pi, Lake, Hanoi. 50c, 1pi, Temple, Saigon.

Perf. 13x13½, 13½x13

1951, Aug. 16 Photo. Unwmk.

1	A1	10c olive green	20	15
2	A1	20c deep plum	20	15
3	A1	30c blue	32	15
4	A1	50c red	52	15
5	A1	60c brown	42	15
6	A1	1pi chestnut brn	42	15
7	A2	1.20pi yellow brn	2.25	1.65
8	A1	2pi purple	85	18
9	A2	3pi dull blue	2.25	20
10	A1	5pi green	3.00	32
11	A1	10pi crimson	7.75	42
12	A1	15pi red brown	42.50	3.00
13	A2	30pi blue green	25.00	3.50
		Nos. 1-13 (13)	85.68	10.17

Souvenir booklets exist comprising five gummed sheets containing a single copy each of Nos. 1, 2, 6, 9, and 12, together with commemorative inscriptions.

Empress Nam-Phuong A3

Globe and Lightning Bolt A4

1952, Aug. 15 Perf. 12½

14	A3	30c dk pur, yel & brn	35	30
15	A3	50c blue, yel & brn	75	55
16	A3	1.50pi ol grn, yel & brn	1.50	25

For surcharge see No. B1.

1952, Aug. 24 Engr. Perf. 13

17	A4	1pi greenish blue	3.00	1.40

Viet Nam's admission to the ITU, 1st anniv.

Coastal Scene and UPU Emblem A5

1952, Sept. 12

18	A5	5pi red brown	3.00	1.00

Viet Nam's admission to the UPU, 1st anniv.

Bao-Dai and Pagoda of Literature, Hanoi — A6

1952, Nov. 10 Perf. 12

19	A6	1.50pi rose violet	2.50	50

39th birthday of Emperor Bao-Dai.

Crown Prince Bao-Long in Annamite Costume — A7

Designs: 70c, 80c, 100pi, Prince in Annamite costume. 90c, 20pi, 50pi, Prince in Western uniform.

1954, June 15 Perf. 13

20	A7	40c aqua	15	15
21	A7	70c claret	28	25
22	A7	80c black brown	32	32
23	A7	90c dark green	80	80
24	A7	20pi rose pink	3.00	3.00
25	A7	50pi violet	7.75	8.00
26	A7	100pi blue violet	13.00	13.00
		Nos. 20-26 (7)	25.30	25.52

SOUTH VIET NAM

(Viet Nam Cong Hoa)

GOVT. — Republic
AREA — 66,280 sq. mi.
POP. — 19,600,000 (est. 1973)
CAPITAL — Saigon

Mythological Turtle — A8

Unwmk.

1955, July 20 Engr. Perf. 13

27	A8	30c claret	1.00 15
28	A8	50c dark green	2.75 60
29	A8	1.50pi brt blue	2.00 25

Refugees on Raft — A9

1955, Oct. 11

30	A9	70c crimson rose	60	15
31	A9	80c brown violet	1.90	35
32	A9	10pi indigo	3.75	50
33	A9	20pi vio, red brn & org	11.00	75
34	A9	35pi dk bl, blk brn & yel	22.50	3.75
35	A9	100pi dk grn, brn vio & org	50.00	6.75
		Nos. 30-35 (6)	89.75	12.25

1st anniv. of the flight of the North Vietnamese. No. 34 is inscribed "Chiên-Dich-Huynh-Dê" (Operation Brotherhood) below design. See No. 54.

Post Office, Saigon — A10

Pres. Ngo Dinh Diem — A11

1956, Jan. 10 Perf. 12

36	A10	60c bluish green	1.25 22
37	A10	90c violet	2.25 38
38	A10	3pi red brown	3.75 60

5th anniv. of independent postal service.

1956 Engr. Perf. 13x13½

39	A11	20c orange ver	15 15
40	A11	30c rose lilac	15 15
41	A11	50c brt carmine	16 15
42	A11	1pi violet	26 15
43	A11	1.50pi violet	52 15
44	A11	3pi black brown	60 15
45	A11	4pi dark blue	85 15
46	A11	5pi red brown	1.50 20
47	A11	10pi blue	2.25 25
48	A11	20pi gray black	4.25 48
49	A11	35pi green	13.00 1.10
50	A11	100pi brown	17.50 4.25
		Nos. 39-50 (12)	41.19 7.33

Nos. 36-38 Overprinted   Công-thự Bưu-điện

1956, Aug. 6 Perf. 12

51	A10	60c bluish green	60 15
52	A10	90c violet	1.00 15
53	A10	3pi red brown	1.75 30

The overprint reads: "Government Post Office Building."

No. 34 with Black Bar over Inscription below Design

1956, Aug. 6

54	A9	35pi dk bl, blk brn & yel	4.50 90

Bamboo — A12

Children — A13

1956, Oct. 26   Litho.   Perf. 13x13½

55	A12	50c scarlet	42	15
56	A12	1.50pi rose violet	85	15
57	A12	2pi brt green	1.10	15
58	A12	4pi deep blue	2.75	22
		Set value		48

1st anniv. of the Republic.

1956, Nov. 7   Engr.   Perf. 13½x14

59	A13	1pi lilac rose	40	15
60	A13	2pi blue green	52	15
61	A13	6pi purple	95	15
62	A13	35pi violet blue	5.00	1.25

"Operation Brotherhood."

Hunters on
Elephants
A14

Loading Cargo
A15

Design: 90c, 2pi, 3pi, Mountain dwelling.

1957, July 7   Photo.   Perf. 13

63	A14	20c yellow grn & pur	32	15
64	A14	30c bister & dp magenta	40	15
65	A14	90c yel grn & dk brn	45	15
66	A14	2pi green & ultra	60	16
67	A14	3pi blue vio & brn	75	30
		Nos. 63-67 (5)	2.52	
		Set value		75

1957, Oct. 21   Perf. 13½x13

68	A15	20c rose violet	15	15
69	A15	40c lt olive grn	15	15
70	A15	50c lt carmine rose	20	15
71	A15	2pi ultra	70	15
72	A15	3pi brt green	90	15
		Nos. 68-72 (5)	2.10	
		Set value		35

9th Colombo Plan Conference, Saigon.

Torch, Map and
Constitution
A16

Farmers, Tractor
and Village
A17

1957, Oct. 26   Litho.   Perf. 13x13½

73	A16	50c black, green & sal	15	15
74	A16	80c black, brt bl & mag	20	15
75	A16	1pi black, bl grn & brt car	32	15
76	A16	4pi black, ol grn & fawn	45	15
77	A16	5pi black, grnsh bl & cit	60	22
78	A16	10pi black, ultra & rose	1.25	42
		Nos. 73-78 (6)	2.97	
		Set value		1.00

Republic of South Viet Nam, 2nd anniv.

1958, July 7   Engr.   Perf. 13½

79	A17	50c yellow green	26	15
80	A17	1pi deep violet	35	15
81	A17	2pi ultra	60	15
82	A17	10pi brick red	1.50	45
		Set value		70

4th anniv. of the government of Ngo Dinh Diem.

Girl and
Lantern — A18

A19

1958, Sept. 27

83	A18	30c yellow	22	15
84	A18	50c dk carmine rose	22	15
85	A18	2pi dp carmine	25	15
86	A18	3pi blue green	60	15
87	A18	4pi lt olive green	95	15
		Nos. 83-87 (5)	2.24	
		Set value		42

Children's Festival.

1958, Oct. 26   Perf. 13½

88	A19	1pi dull red brown	15	15
89	A19	2pi bluish green	20	15
90	A19	4pi rose carmine	30	15
91	A19	5pi rose lilac	60	25
		Set value		48

Issued for United Nations Day.

> Most South Viet Nam stamps from 1958 onward exist imperforate in issued and trial colors, and also in small presentation sheets in issued colors.

UNESCO Building,
Paris — A20

Torch and UN
Emblem — A21

1958, Nov. 3   Perf. 12½x13

92	A20	50c ultra	24	15
93	A20	2pi bright red	26	15
94	A20	3pi lilac rose	52	15
95	A20	6pi violet	75	18
		Set value		45

Opening of UNESCO Headquarters in Paris, Nov. 3.

1958, Dec. 10   Engr.   Perf. 13½

96	A21	50c dark blue	15	15
97	A21	1pi brown carmine	22	15
98	A21	2pi yellow green	32	15
99	A21	6pi rose violet	70	24
		Set value		50

Signing of the Universal Declaration of Human Rights, 10th anniv.

Cathedral of
Hué — A22

Thien Mu Pagoda,
Hué — A23

National
Museum — A24

Design: 50c, 2pi, Palace of Independence, Saigon.

1958-59   Perf. 13½

100	A22	10c dk blue gray	20	15
101	A23	30c green ('59)	38	15
102	A24	40c dk green ('59)	38	15
103	A24	50c green ('59)	38	15
104	A24	2pi grnsh blue ('59)	1.10	15
105	A23	4pi dull purple ('59)	1.25	22
106	A24	5pi dk carmine ('59)	1.40	22
107	A22	6pi orange brown	1.90	30
		Nos. 100-107 (8)	6.99	
		Set value		1.20

Trung Sisters on
Elephants — A25

1959, Mar. 14   Photo.   Perf. 13

108	A25	50c multicolored	35	15
109	A25	2pi ocher, grn & bl	1.00	15
110	A25	3pi emerald, vio & bis	1.50	16
111	A25	6pi multicolored	2.75	30
		Set value		65

Sisters Trung Trac and Trung Nhi who resisted a Chinese invasion in 40-44 A.D.

Symbols of
Agrarian
Reforms
A26

1959, July 7   Engr.   Perf. 13

112	A26	70c lilac rose	15	15
113	A26	2pi dk grn & Prus bl	20	15
114	A26	3pi olive	35	15
115	A26	6pi dark red & red	80	25
		Set value		48

5th anniv. of Ngo Dinh Diem's presidency.

Diesel Engine and Map
of North and South
Viet Nam — A27

1959, Aug. 7

116	A27	1pi lt violet & grn	55	15
117	A27	2pi gray & green	65	15
118	A27	3pi grnsh bl & grn	80	15
119	A27	4pi maroon & grn	1.50	15
		Set value		40

Re-opening of the Saigon-Dongha Railroad.

Volunteer Road
Workers
A28

1959, Oct. 26

120	A28	1pi org brn, ultra & grn	50	15
121	A28	2pi violet, org & grn	60	15
122	A28	4pi dk bl, bl & bis	1.40	28
123	A28	5pi bister, brn & ocher	1.50	38
		Set value		70

4th anniv. of the constitution, stressing communal development.

Boy Scout — A29

1959, Dec.   Engr.   Perf. 13

124	A29	3pi brt yellow grn	32	15
125	A29	4pi deep lilac rose	55	15
126	A29	8pi dk brn & lil rose	90	32
127	A29	20pi Prus bl & brt grn	2.25	70
		Nos. 124-127 (4)	4.02	1.32

National Boy Scout Jamboree.

Symbols of
Family and
Justice — A30

1960

128	A30	20c emerald	20	15
129	A30	30c brt grnsh blue	20	15
130	A30	2pi orange & maroon	55	15
131	A30	6pi car & rose vio	2.00	35
		Set value		55

Issued to commemorate the family code.

Refugee Family
and WRY
Emblem
A31

1960, Apr. 7   Engr.   Perf. 13

132	A31	50c brt lilac rose	15	15
133	A31	3pi brt green	42	15
134	A31	4pi scarlet	52	16
135	A31	5pi dp violet blue	65	20
		Set value		55

World Refugee Year, July 1, 1959-June 30, 1960.

Buying & Selling Stamps and Covers of...
Vietnam ★ Thailand ★ Laos
All China ★ Hong Kong
Japan ★ Korea ★ Cambodia
• WANT LISTS SERVICED •
Buying Worldwide! Write, Call or Send Insured For Our Top Offer!

PACIFIC MIDWEST CO.
(Our 29th year)

China
Stamp Soc.
P.O. Box 1696, Daly City, CA 94014
Ph. 415-994-1117 • FAX 415-994-7439
• We accept Visa, MasterCard, Diner's Card, Carte Blanche •

Soc. Thai.
Philately

Henri Dunant — A32

1960, May 8
Cross in Carmine

136	A32 1pi dark blue	40	15
137	A32 3pi green	1.10	16
138	A32 4pi crimson rose	1.10	15
139	A32 6pi dp lilac rose	1.50	28

Centenary (in 1959) of the Red Cross idea.

Model Farm — A33

1960, July 7 *Perf. 13*

140	A33 50c ultra	22	15
141	A33 1pi dark green	30	15
142	A33 3pi orange	60	15
143	A33 7pi bright pink	1.10	28
	Set value		60

Establishment of communal rice farming.

Girl With Basket of Rice and Rice Plant — A34

1960, Nov. 21

144	A34 2pi emerald & green	32	15
145	A34 4pi blue & ultra	70	28

Conf. of the UN FAO, Saigon, Nov. 1960.

Map and Flag of Viet Nam — A35

1960, Oct. 26 **Engr.** *Perf. 13*

146	A35 50c grnsh bl, car & yel	25	15
147	A35 1pi ultra, car & yel	30	15
148	A35 3pi purple, car & yel	55	15
149	A35 7pi yel grn, car & yel	90	15
	Set value		40

Fifth anniversary of the Republic.

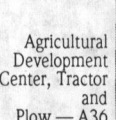

Agricultural Development Center, Tractor and Plow — A36

1961, Jan. 3 *Perf. 13*

150	A36 50c red brown	20	15
151	A36 70c rose lilac	32	15
152	A36 80c rose red	35	15
153	A36 10pi bright pink	1.65	22
	Set value		40

Plant and Child — A37

Pres. Ngo Dinh Diem — A38

1961, Mar. 23 *Perf. 13*

154	A37 70c light blue	22	15
155	A37 80c ultra	25	15
156	A37 4pi olive bister	38	15
157	A37 7pi grnsh bl & yel grn	80	20
	Set value		38

Child protection.

1961, Apr. 29 *Perf. 13*

158	A38 50c brt ultra	32	15
159	A38 1pi red	55	15
160	A38 2pi lilac rose	1.10	15
161	A38 4pi brt violet	2.25	15

Second term of Pres. Ngo Dinh Diem.

Boy, Girl and Flaming Torch — A39

1961, July 7 **Engr.** *Perf. 13*

162	A39 50c red	15	15
163	A39 70c bright pink	20	15
164	A39 80c ver & maroon	28	15
165	A39 8pi dp claret & magenta	70	20
	Set value		35

Issued for Youth Day.

Saigon-Bien Hoa Highway Bridge — A40

1961, July 28

166	A40 50c yellow green	26	15
167	A40 1pi orange brown	30	15
168	A40 2pi dark blue	52	15
169	A40 5pi brt red lilac	90	15
	Set value		35

Opening of Saigon-Bien Hoa Highway.

Alexandre de Rhodes — A41

1961, Sept. 5

170	A41 50c rose carmine	20	15
171	A41 1pi claret	22	15
172	A41 3pi bister brown	28	15
173	A41 6pi emerald	80	15
	Set value		32

Alexandre de Rhodes (1591-1660), Jesuit missionary who introduced Roman characters to express the Viet Nam language.

Young Man with Torch, Sage, Pagoda A42

Temple Dedicated to Confucius A43

1961, Oct. 26 *Perf. 13*

174	A42 50c orange ver	16	15
175	A42 1pi brt green	32	15
176	A42 3pi rose red	40	15
177	A42 8pi rose lilac & brn	1.25	30
	Set value		50

Moral Rearmament of Youth Movement.

1961, Nov. 4 **Engr.**

178	A43 1pi brt green	24	15
179	A43 2pi rose red	28	15
180	A43 5pi olive	1.00	15
	Set value		24

15th anniversary of UNESCO.

Earth Scraper Preparing Ground for Model Village — A44

Man Fighting Mosquito and Emblem — A45

1961, Dec. 11 *Perf. 13*

181	A44 50c dark green	15	15
182	A44 1pi Prus bl & car lake	24	15
183	A44 2pi olive grn & brn	32	15
184	A44 10pi Prus blue	1.25	32
	Set value		55

Agrarian reform program.

1962, Apr. 7 *Perf. 13*

185	A45 50c brt lilac rose	22	15
186	A45 1pi orange	35	15
187	A45 2pi emerald	42	15
188	A45 6pi ultra	1.00	15
	Set value		50

WHO drive to eradicate malaria.

Postal Check Center, Saigon — A46

Madonna of Vang — A47

1962, May 15 **Engr.** *Perf. 13*

189	A46 70c dull green	15	15
190	A46 80c chocolate	15	15
191	A46 4pi lilac rose	65	18
192	A46 7pi rose red	1.50	32
	Set value		65

Inauguration of postal checking service.

1962, July 7

193	A47 50c violet & rose red	15	15
194	A47 1pi red brn & indigo	18	15
195	A47 2pi brown & rose car	38	15
196	A47 8pi green & dk blue	1.75	26
	Set value		50

Catholic shrine of the Madonna of Vang.

Armed Guards and Village — A48

1962, Oct. 26

197	A48 50c bright red	15	15
198	A48 1pi yellow green	32	15
199	A48 1.50pi lilac rose	40	15
200	A48 7pi ultra	1.10	28
	Set value		50

"Strategic village" defense system.

Gougah Waterfall, Dalat — A49

Trung Sisters' Monument and Vietnamese Women — A50

1963, Jan. 3

201	A49 60c orange red	38	15
202	A49 1pi bluish black	52	15
	Set value		20

62nd birthday of Pres. Ngo Dinh Diem; Spring Festival.

1963, Mar. 1 **Engr.**

203	A50 50c green	15	15
204	A50 1pi dk carmine rose	25	15
205	A50 3pi lilac rose	32	16
206	A50 8pi violet blue	75	32
	Set value		65

Issued for Women's Day.

Farm Woman with Grain — A51

1963, Mar. 21 *Perf. 13*

207	A51 50c red	28	15
208	A51 1pi dk car rose	32	15
209	A51 3pi lilac rose	48	15
210	A51 5pi violet	80	15
	Set value		35

FAO "Freedom from Hunger" campaign.

Common Defense Emblem — A52

Emblem — A53

1963, July 7 **Engr.** *Perf. 13*

211	A52 30c bister	30	15
212	A52 50c lilac rose	38	15
213	A52 3pi brt green	60	15
214	A52 8pi red	95	24
	Set value		50

Common defense effort. The inscription says: "Personalism-Common Progress."

1963, Oct. 26 *Perf. 13*

215	A53 50c rose red	18	15
216	A53 1pi emerald	25	15
217	A53 4pi purple	55	15
218	A53 5pi orange	1.00	35
	Set value		60

The fighting soldiers of the Republic.

Centenary Emblem and Map — A54

1963, Nov. 17   **Engr.**
Cross in Deep Carmine
219 A54 50c Prus blue   22 15
220 A54   1pi deep carmine   32 15
221 A54 3pi orange yellow   45 15
222 A54 6pi brown   1.00 28
         Set value   55

Centenary of International Red Cross.

Book and Scales — A55

1963, Dec. 10   *Perf. 13*
223 A55 70c orange   20 15
224 A55   1pi brt rose   32 15
225 A55 3pi green   42 15
226 A55 8pi ocher   1.00 32
         Set value   60

15th anniv. of the Universal Declaration of Human Rights.

Danhim Hydroelectric Station A56

1964, Jan. 15   **Engr.**
227 A56 40c rose red   30 15
228 A56   1pi bister brown   30 15
229 A56 3pi violet blue   45 16
230 A56 8pi olive green   95 35
         Set value   60

Inauguration of the Danhim Hydroelectric Station.

Atomic Reactor — A57

1964, Feb. 3   *Perf. 13*
231 A57 80c olive   24 15
232 A57 1.50pi brown orange   26 15
233 A57 3pi chocolate   40 15
234 A57 7pi brt blue   75 24
         Set value   55

Peaceful uses of atomic energy.

Compass Rose, Barograph and UN Emblem — A58

South Vietnamese Gesturing to North Vietnamese; Map — A59

1964, Mar. 23
235 A58 50c bister   15 15
236 A58   1pi vermilion   28 15
237 A58 1.50pi rose claret   32 15
238 A58 10pi emerald   1.00 35
         Set value   60

4th World Meteorological Day, Mar. 23.

1964, July 20   *Perf. 13*
239 A59 30c dk grn, ultra & mar 45 15
240 A59 50c dk car rose, yel & blk 50 15
241 A59 1.50pi dk bl, dp org & blk 75 20
         Set value   25

10th anniv. of the Day of National Grief, July 20, 1954, when the nation was divided into South and North Viet Nam.

Hatien Beach — A60

1964, Sept. 7   **Engr.**   *Perf. 13½*
242 A60 20c bright ultra   15 15
243 A60 3pi emerald   65 25
         Set value   32

Revolutionists and "Nov. 1" — A61

Designs: 80c, Soldier breaking chain. 3pi, Broken chain and date: "1-1 1963," vert.

1964, Nov. 1   **Engr.**   *Perf. 13*
244 A61 50c red lilac & ind   35 15
245 A61 80c violet & red brn   40 15
246 A61 3pi dk blue & red   75 40
         Set value   60

Anniv. of November 1963 revolution.

Temple, Saigon — A62

Designs: 1pi, Royal tombs, Hué. 1.50pi, Fishermen and sailboats at Phan-Thiet beach. 3pi, Temple, Gia-Dhin.

1964-66   *Perf. 13*
              Size: 35½x26mm
247 A62 50c fawn, grn & dl vio   22 15
248 A62   1pi olive bis & ind   45 15
249 A62 1.50pi ol gray & dk sl grn 52 18
250 A62 3pi vio, dk sl grn & cl 1.25 38
         Set value   65
              Coil Stamp
              Size: 23x17mm
250A A62 1pi ol bis & ind ('66) 4.75 1.00

Issue date: Nos. 247-250, Dec. 2, 1964.

Hung Vuong and Au Co with their Children A63

1965, Apr.   **Engr.**   *Perf. 13*
251 A63 3pi car lake & org red   80 25
252 A63 100pi brown vio & vio   8.75 1.75

Mythological founders of Viet Nam, c. 2000 B.C.

 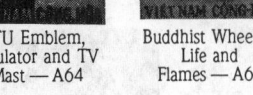

ITU Emblem, Insulator and TV Mast — A64

Buddhist Wheel of Life and Flames — A65

1965, May 17   **Engr.**
253 A64 1pi olive, dp car & bis 38 15
254 A64 3pi henna brn, car & lil 1.00 22
         Set value   30

ITU, centenary.

1965, May 15   *Perf. 13*
Designs: 1.50pi, Wheel, lotus blossom and world map, horiz. 3pi, Wheel and Buddhist flag.

         Inscribed: "Phat-Giao" (Buddhism)
255 A65 50c dark carmine   55 15
256 A65 1.50pi dk blue & ocher 1.40 15
257 A65 3pi org brn & dk brn   1.50 20
         Set value   40

Anniversary of Buddha's birth.

ICY Emblem and Women of Various Races — A66

Ixora — A67

1965, June 26
258 A66 50c bluish blk & bis   24 15
259 A66   1pi dk brn & brn   48 15
260 A66 1.50pi dark red & gray   60 20
         Set value   40

International Cooperation Year.

1965, Sept. 10   **Engr.**   *Perf. 13*
Flowers: 80c, Orchid. 1pi, Chrysanthemum. 1.50pi, Lotus, horiz. 3pi, Plum blossoms.
261 A67 70c grn, sl grn & red   18 15
262 A67 80c dk brn, lil & sl grn 22 15
263 A67   1pi dk blue & yellow   28 15
264 A67 1.50pi sl grn, dl grn & gray 42 15
265 A67 3pi slate grn & org   85 15
         Nos. 261-265 (5)   1.95
         Set value   40

Student, Dormitory and Map of Thu Duc — A68

1965, Oct. 15   *Perf. 13*
266 A68 50c dark brown   15 15
267 A68   1pi bright green   18 15
268 A68 3pi crimson   48 20
269 A68 7pi dark blue violet   1.40 45
         Set value   80

Issued to publicize higher education.

Farm Boy and Girl, Pig and 4-T Emblem A69

Design: 4pi, Farm boy with chicken, village and 4-T flag.

1965, Nov. 25   **Engr.**   *Perf. 13*
270 A69 3pi emerald & dk red   52 18
271 A69 4pi dull violet & plum   70 25

10th anniv. of the 4-T Clubs and the National Congress of Young Farmers.

Basketball A70

Designs: 1pi, Javelin. 1.50pi, Hand holding torch, athletic couple. 10pi, Pole vault.

1965, Dec. 14   **Engr.**   *Perf. 13*
272 A70 50c dk car & brn org   24 15
273 A70   1pi brn org & red brn   42 15
274 A70 1.50pi brt green   60 15
275 A70 10pi red lil & brn org 1.75 60
         Set value   75

Radio Tower — A71

Loading Hook and Globe — A72

Design: Radio tower, telephone dial and map of Viet Nam.

1966, Apr. 24   **Engr.**   *Perf. 13*
276 A71 3pi brt blue & brn   32 15
277 A71 4pi purple, red & blk   42 20

Saigon microwave station.

1966, June 22   **Engr.**   *Perf. 13*
278 A72 3pi gray & dk car rose   24 15
279 A72 4pi olive & dk purple   30 16
280 A72 6pi brt grn & dk blue   48 25

Appreciation of the help given by the free world.

Hands Reaching for Persecuted Refugees A73

1966, July 20
281 A73 3pi brn, vio brn & ol   32 15
282 A73 7pi cl, vio brn & dk pur 70 16
         Set value   25

Refugees from communist oppression.

Paper Soldiers, Votive Offering A74

Designs: 1.50pi, Man and woman making offerings. 3pi, Floating candles in paper boats. 5pi, Woman burning paper offerings.

1966, Aug. 30   **Engr.**   *Perf. 13*
283 A74 50c red, blk & bis brn   15 15
284 A74 1.50pi brown, emer & grn 45 15
285 A74 3pi rose red & lake   95 16
286 A74 5pi org brn, bis & dk brn 1.50 25
         Set value   55

Wandering Souls Festival.

Oriental Two-string Violin — A75

Vietnamese Instruments: 3pi, Woman playing 16-string guitar. 4pi, Musicians playing two-string guitars. 7pi, Woman and boy playing flutes.

1966	Engr.		Perf. 13	

Size: 35½x26mm

287	A75	1pi brown red & brn	18	15
288	A75	3pi rose lilac & pur	55	15
289	A75	4pi rose brown & brn	75	18
290	A75	7pi dp blue & vio bl	1.40	35

Coil Stamp
Size: 23x17mm

| 290A | A75 | 3pi rose lil & pur | 5.00 | 50 |
| | b. | Booklet pane of 5 | 30.00 | |

Nos. 287-290 were issued Sept. 28. No. 290b contains a vertical strip of 5 with selvage at either end. These strips were also sold loose without booklet cover.

WHO Building, Geneva, and Flag — A76

Designs: 50c, WHO Building and emblem, horiz. 8pi, WHO flag and building.

1966, Oct. 12				
291	A76	50c purple & carmine	15	15
292	A76	1.50pi red brn, vio bl & blk	20	15
293	A76	8pi grnsh bl, vio bl & brn	1.00	50
		Set value		65

Opening of WHO Headquarters, Geneva.

Hand Holding Spade, and Soldiers A77

Soldier and Workers — A78

Designs: 1.50pi, Flag, workers, tractor and soldier. 4pi, Soldier and cavalryman.

1966, Nov. 1	Engr.		Perf. 13	
294	A77	.80c dull brn & red brn	22	15
295	A77	1.50pi car rose, yel & brn	45	15
296	A78	3pi brown & slate grn	90	15
297	A78	4pi lilac, black & brn	1.25	16
		Set value		35

3rd anniv. of the revolution against the government of Pres. Ngo Dinh Diem.

Symbolic Tree and UNESCO Emblem — A79

Designs: 3pi, Globe and olive branches. 7pi, Symbolic temple, horiz.

1966, Dec. 15	Engr.		Perf. 13	
298	A79	1pi pink, brn & dk org	20	15
299	A79	3pi dp bl, grn & brn org	65	15
300	A79	7pi grnsh bl, dk bl & red	1.25	22
		Set value		40

20th anniv. of UNESCO.

Bitter Melon — A80

1967, Jan. 12	Engr.		Perf. 13	
301	A80	50c Cashew, vert.	20	15
302	A80	1.50pi shown	55	15
303	A80	3pi Sweetsop	1.10	15
304	A80	20pi Areca nuts	4.50	24
		Set value		40

Phan-Boi-Chau — A81

Designs: 20pi, Phan-Chau-Trinh portrait and addressing crowd.

1967, Mar. 24	Engr.		Perf. 13	
305	A81	1pi mar, red brn & dk brn	22	15
306	A81	20pi vio, slate grn & blk	1.10	45
		Set value		50

Issued to honor Vietnamese patriots.

Woman Carrying Produce A82

Labor Day: 1pi, Market scene. 3pi, Two-wheeled horse cart. 8pi, Farm scene with water buffalo.

1967, May 1	Engr.		Perf. 13	
307	A82	50c vio bl, dk bl & ultra	15	15
308	A82	1pi sl grn & dull pur	15	15
309	A82	3pi dk carmine	38	15
310	A82	8pi brt car rose & pur	75	16
		Set value		30

Potter, Vases and Lamp — A83

Weavers and Potters A84

Designs: 1.50pi, Vase and basket. 35d, Bag and lacquerware.

1967, July 22	Engr.		Perf. 13	
311	A83	50c red brn, grn & ultra	15	15
312	A83	1.50pi grnsh bl, car & blk	28	15
313	A84	3pi red, vio & org brn	32	15
314	A83	35pi bis brn, blk & dk red	2.25	60
		Set value		85

Issued to publicize Vietnamese handicrafts.

Wedding Procession A85

1967, Sept. 18	Engr.		Perf. 13	
315	A85	3pi rose claret, dk vio & red	75	22

Symbols of Stage, Music and Art — A86

Litho. & Engr.

1967, Oct. 27			Perf. 13	
316	A86	10pi bl gray, blk & red	75	15

Issued to publicize the Cultural Institute.

"Freedom and Justice" — A87

Balloting — A88

"Establishment of Democracy" A89

1967, Nov. 1			Photo.	
317	A87	4pi magenta, brn & ocher	48	15
318	A88	5pi brown, yel & blk	50	15
319	A89	30pi dl lil, indigo & red	2.50	40
		Set value		52

National Day; general elections.

Pagoda and Lions Emblem — A90

1967, Dec. 5		Photo.	Perf. 13½x13	
320	A90	3pi multicolored	1.00	20

50th anniversary of Lions International.

Teacher with Pupils and Globe — A91

1967, Dec. 10		Perf. 13x13½	
321	A91	3pi tan, blk, yel & car	75	20

International Literacy Day, Sept. 8, 1967.

Tractor and Village — A92

Rural Construction Program: 9pi, Bulldozer and home building. 10pi, Wheelbarrow, tractor and new building. 20pi, Vietnamese and Americans working together.

1968, Jan. 26		Photo.	Perf. 13½	
322	A92	1pi multicolored	15	15
323	A92	9pi lt blue & multi	80	15
324	A92	10pi multicolored	1.25	15
325	A92	20pi yel, red lil & blk	1.65	25
		Set value		60

WHO Emblem — A93

1968, Apr. 7		Photo.	Perf. 13½	
326	A93	10pi gray grn, blk & yel	80	25

WHO, 20th anniversary.

Flags of Viet Nam's Allies — A94

Designs: 1.50pi, Flags surrounding SEATO emblem. 3pi, Flags, handclasp, globe and map of Viet Nam. 50pi, Flags and handclasp.

1968, June 22		Photo.	Perf. 13½	
327	A94	1pi multicolored	60	15
328	A94	1.50pi multicolored	75	15
329	A94	3pi multicolored	1.00	15
330	A94	50pi multicolored	4.50	70
		Set value		95

Issued to honor Viet Nam's allies.

Three-wheeled Truck and Tractor — A95

Private Property Ownership: 80c, Farmer, city man and symbols of property. 2pi, Three-wheeled cart, taxi and farmers. 30pi, Taxi, three-wheeled cart and tractor in field.

Inscribed: "HUU-SAN-HOA CONG-NHAN VA NONG-DAN"

1968, Nov. 1		Photo.	Perf. 13½	
331	A95	80c multicolored	15	15
332	A95	2pi steel blue & multi	20	15
333	A95	10pi orange brn & multi	90	15
334	A95	30pi gray blue & multi	2.75	38
		Set value		60

Human Rights
Flame — A96

Men of Various
Races — A97

1968, Dec. 10   Photo.   Perf. 13½
335 A96 10pi multicolored   42 15
336 A97 16pi purple & multi   90 18

International Human Rights Year.

UNICEF Emblem, Mother and
Child — A98

UNICEF: 6pi, Children flying kite with UNICEF
emblem.

1968, Dec. 11
337 A98 6pi multicolored   35 15
338 A98 16pi multicolored   80 28

Workers and
Train — A99

Design: 1.50pi, 3pi, Crane, train and map of Viet
Nam.

1968, Dec. 15
339 A99 1.50pi multicolored   60 15
340 A99 3pi org, vio bl & grn   70 15
341 A99 9pi multicolored   95 16
342 A99 20pi multicolored   1.75 30

Reopening of Trans-Viet Nam Railroad.

Farm
Woman — A100

Vietnamese Women: 1pi, Merchant. 3pi, Nurses,
horiz. 20pi, Three ladies.

1969, Mar. 23   Engr.   Perf. 13
343 A100 50c vio bl, lil & ocher   15 15
344 A100 1pi grn, bis & dk brn   15 15
345 A100 3pi brown, blk & bl   28 15
346 A100 20pi lilac & multi   1.40 30
          Set value   52

Soldiers and
Civilians
A101

Family
Welcoming
Soldier — A102

1969, June 1   Photo.   Perf. 13
347 A101 2pi multicolored   15 15
348 A102 50pi multicolored   2.25 38

Pacification campaign.

Man Reading
Constitution,
Scales of
Justice — A103

Voters, Torch
and
Scales — A104

1969, June 9
349 A103 1pi yel org, yel & blk   20 15
350 A104 20pi multicolored   2.00 18

Constitutional democracy. Phrase on both
stamps: "Democratic and Governed by Law."

Mobile Post
Office — A105

Mobile Post Office: 3pi, Window service. 4pi,
Child with letter. 20pi, Crowd at window and postmark: "15, 12, 67."

1969, July 10
351 A105 1pi multicolored   16 15
352 A105 3pi multicolored   42 15
353 A105 4pi multicolored   52 15
354 A105 20pi ocher & multi   1.10 28
          Set value   55

Installation of the first mobile post office in Viet
Nam.

Mnong-gar
Woman — A106

Designs: 1pi, Djarai woman. 50pi, Bahnar man.

1969, Aug. 29   Photo.   Perf. 13
355 A106 1pi brt pink & multi   22 15
356 A106 6pi sky blue & multi   70 15
357 A106 50pi gray & multi   5.00 35
          Set value   48

Ethnic minorities in Viet Nam.

Civilians
Becoming
Soldiers
A107

General Mobilization: 3pi, Bayonet training. 5pi,
Guard duty. 10pi, Farewell.

1969, Sept. 20
Inscribed: "TONG BONG VIEN"
358 A107 1.50pi orange & multi   42 15
359 A107 3pi purple & multi   85 15
360 A107 5pi black, red & ocher   1.00 15
361 A107 10pi pink & multi   1.65 15
          Set value   35

ILO Emblem and
Globe — A108

1969, Oct. 29   Photo.   Perf. 13
362 A108 6pi blue grn, blk & gray   30 15
363 A108 20pi red, blk & gray   90 16
          Set value   22

ILO, 50th anniversary.

Pegu
House
Sparrow
A109

Birds: 6pi, Moluccan munia. 7pi, Great hornbill.
30pi, Old world tree sparrow.

1970, Jan. 15   Perf. 12½x14
364 A109 2pi blue & multi   48 15
365 A109 6pi orange & multi   1.25 15
366 A109 7pi org brn & multi   1.75 16
367 A109 30pi blue & multi   6.50 50

Burning House and Family — A110

Design: 20pi, Family fleeing burning house and
physician examining child.

1970, Jan. 31   Photo.   Perf. 13
368 A110 10pi multicolored   55 15
369 A110 20pi multicolored   1.25 25

Mau Than disaster, 1968.

Vietnamese Costumes — A111

Traditional Costumes: 1pi, Man, woman and
priest, vert. 2pi, Seated woman with fan. 100pi,
Man and woman.

Inscribed: "Y-PHUC CO TRUYEN"
1970, Mar. 15   Photo.   Perf. 13
370 A111 1pi lt brown & multi   15 15
371 A111 2pi pink & multi   15 15
372 A111 3pi ultra & multi   15 15
373 A111 100pi multicolored   4.50 90
          Set value   1.10

Issued for the Trung Sisters' Festival.

Building
Workers,
Pagodas and
Bridge — A112

Rebuilding of Hué: 20pi, Concrete mixers and
scaffolds.

1970, June 10   Litho. & Engr.
374 A112 6pi multicolored   38 15
375 A112 20pi rose lil, brn & bis   1.10 24
          Set value   30

Plower in Rice
Field — A113

1970, Aug. 29   Perf. 13
376 A113 6pi multicolored   75 15

"Land to the Tiller" agricultural reform program.

New Building
and
Scaffold — A114

Construction
Work — A115

1970, Sept. 15   Engr.   Perf. 13
377 A114 8pi pale ol & brn org   45 15
378 A115 16pi brn, indigo & yel   90 22
          Set value   30

Reconstruction after 1968 Tet Offensive.

Productivity Year
Emblem — A116

1970, Oct. 3
379 A116 10pi multicolored   50 15

Asian Productivity Year.

Nguyen-Dinh-Chieu
A117

Education Year
Emblem
A118

1970, Nov. 16   Engr.   Perf. 13½
380 A117 6pi dull vio, red & brn   38 15
381 A117 10pi grn, red & dk brn   60 18
          Set value   25

Nguyen-Dinh-Chieu (1822-1888), poet.

Litho. & Engr.
1970, Nov. 30   Perf. 13
382 A118 10pi pale brn, yel & blk   70 16

International Education Year.

Parliament Building
A119

Dancers
A120

Design: 6pi, Senate Building.

1970, Dec.
383 A119 6pi lt bl, cit & dk brn   38   15
384 A119 10pi multicolored   75   15

No. 383 issued Dec. 8 for the 6th Congress and No. 384 issued Dec. 9 for the 9th General Assembly of the Asian Interparliamentary Union.

1971, Jan. 12
Designs: Various Vietnamese dancers and musicians. 6pi and 7pi horizontal.

385 A120 2pi ultra & multi   28   15
386 A120 6pi pale green & multi   75   15
387 A120 7pi pink & multi   95   16
388 A120 10pi brown org & multi   1.00   20
     Set value   50

For surcharge see No. 500.

Farmers and Law — A121

Agrarian Reform Law: 3pi, Tractor and law, dated 26.3.1970. 16pi, Farmers, people rejoicing and law book.

1971, Mar. 26   Engr.   Perf. 13
389 A121 2pi vio bl, dk brn & dl org   18   15
390 A121 3pi pale grn, brn & dk bl   25   15
391 A121 16pi multicolored   1.10   16
     Set value   25

For surcharge see No. 482.

Courier on Horseback A122

Design: 6pi, Mounted courier with flag.

Engr. & Photo.
1971, June 6   Perf. 13
392 A122 2pi violet & multi   30   15
393 A122 6pi tan & multi   1.25   18
     Set value   25

Postal history.

Military and Naval Operations on Vietnamese Coast — A123

1971, June 19
394 A123 3pi multicolored   35   15
395 A123 40pi multicolored   3.25   40
     Set value   45

Armed Forces Day. Narrow vertical yellow and red label inscribed "Mung Ngay Quan Luc / 19.6.1971" is se-tenant with each stamp.

Deer — A124   Rice Harvest — A125

1971, Aug. 20   Engr.
396 A124 9pi shown   80   15
397 A124 30pi Tiger   2.50   35

Litho. & Engr.
1971, Sept. 28   Perf. 13
Designs: 30pi, Threshing and winnowing rice and rice plants. 40pi, Bundling and carrying rice.

398 A125 1pi multicolored   15   15
399 A125 30pi sal pink, dk pur & blk   1.65   26
400 A125 40pi sepia, yel & grn   1.90   32

For surcharge see No. 496.

Inauguration of UPU Building, Bern — A126

1971, Nov. 9   Engr.   Perf. 13
401 A126 20pi green & multi   1.10   25

Fish — A127

Various Fish; 2pi vertical.

1971, Nov. 16   Photo. & Engr.
402 A127   2pi multicolored   20   15
403 A127 10pi violet & multi   90   15
404 A127 100pi lilac & multi   8.00   1.00
     Set value   1.10

Mailman and Woman on Water Buffalo — A128

Rural Mail: 10pi, Bird carrying letter. 20pi, Mailman with bicycle delivering mail to villagers.

1971, Dec. 20   Engr.   Perf. 13
Inscribed: "PHAT TRIEN BUU-CHINH NONG THON"

405 A128 5pi multicolored   32   15
406 A128 10pi multicolored   60   16
407 A128 20pi multicolored   1.10   28
     Set value   50

Trawler Fishermen, and Fish — A129

Publicity for Fishing Industry: 7pi, Net fishing from boat. 50d, Trawler with seine.

1972, Jan. 2   Engr.   Perf. 13
408 A129 4pi pink, blk & blue   25   15
409 A129 7pi lt blue, blk & red   38   15
410 A129 50pi multicolored   2.00   50
     Set value   65

King Quang Trung (1752-1792) — A130

1972, Jan. 28   Perf. 13½
411 A130 6pi red & multi   55   15
   a.   Booklet pane of 10   35.00
412 A130 20pi black & multi   1.65   32

No. 411a is imperf. horizontally.

Road Workers — A131

1972, Feb. 4
413 A131 3pi multicolored   22   15
414 A131 8pi multicolored   85   15
     Set value   15

Community development.

Rice Farming — A132

1972, Mar. 26   Engr.   Perf. 13½
415 A132 1pi shown   15   15
416 A132 10pi Wheat farming   95   15
     Set value   15

Farmers' Day.

Plane over Dalat — A133

1972, Apr. 18   Engr. & Photo.
417 A133 10pi shown   1.65   15
418 A133 10pi over Ha-tien   1.65   15
419 A133 10pi over Hue   1.65   15
420 A133 10pi over Saigon   1.65   15
   a.   Block of 4, #417-420   6.75   40
421 A133 25pi like No. 417   3.50   25
422 A133 25pi like No. 418   3.50   25
423 A133 25pi like No. 419   3.50   25
424 A133 25pi like No. 420   3.50   25
   a.   Block of 4, #421-424   17.00   1.20
     Nos. 417-424 (8)   20.60
     Set value   1.30

20 years Air Viet Nam.

Scholar — A134

Designs: 20pi, Teacher and pupils. 50pi, Scholar and scroll.

1972, May 5   Engr. & Litho.
425 A134 5pi multicolored   28   15

Engr.
426 A134 20pi lt green & multi   75   15
427 A134 50pi pink & multi   2.50   30

Ancient letter writing art.

Armed Farmer — A135

Designs: 6pi, Civilian rifleman and Self-defense Forces emblem, horiz. 20pi, Man and woman training with rifles.

Engr. & Litho.
1972, June 15   Perf. 13
428 A135 2pi brt rose & multi   40   15
429 A135 6pi multicolored   95   15
430 A135 20pi lt violet & multi   2.75   20
     Set value   32

Civilian Self-defense Forces.

Hands Holding Safe — A136

1972, July 10
431 A136 10pi lt blue & multi   55   15
432 A136 25pi lt green & multi   1.25   20
     Set value   26

Treasury Bonds campaign.

Frontier Guard — A137   Soldier Helping Wounded Man — A138

Designs: 10pi, 3 guards and horse, horiz. 40pi, Marching guards, horiz.

Engr. & Litho.
1972, Aug. 14   Perf. 13
433 A137 10pi olive & multi   52   15
434 A137 30pi buff & multi   1.40   22
435 A137 40pi lt blue & multi   1.90   35

Historic frontier guards.

1972, Sept. 1
Designs: 16pi, Soldier on crutches and flowers. 100pi, Veterans' memorial, map and flag.

436 A138   9pi olive & multi   48   15
437 A138 16pi yellow & multi   70   15
438 A138 100pi lt blue & multi   3.75   80
     Set value   90

For surcharge see No. 483.

Tank, Memorial, Flag and Map — A139   Soldiers and Map of Viet Nam — A140

1972, Nov. 25   Litho.   Perf. 13
439 A139 5pi multicolored   55   15
440 A140 10pi ultra & multi   1.40   15
     Set value   15

Victory at Binh-Long.

Book Year Emblem and Globe — A141

Designs: 4pi, Emblem, books circling globe. 5pi, Emblem, books and globe.

1972, Nov. 30
441 A141 2pi dp carmine & multi   38   15
442 A141 4pi blue & multi   65   15
443 A141 5pi yellow bis & multi   95   15
     Set value   15

International Book Year.

Liberated Vietnamese Family — A142

Soldiers Raising Vietnamese Flag — A143

1973, Feb. 18   Litho.   Perf. 13
444 A142 10pi yellow & multi   1.10 15

To celebrate the 200,000th returnee.

1973, Feb. 24   Litho.   Perf. 13

Design: 10pi, Victorious soldiers and map of demilitarized zone, horiz.

445 A143 3pi lilac & multi   85 15
446 A143 10pi yellow grn & multi   1.25 15
          Set value   15

Victory at Quang Tri.

Satellite, Storm over Viet Nam—A144

1973, Mar. 23   Litho.   Perf. 12½x12
447 A144 1pi lt blue & multi   80 15

World Meteorological Day.
For surcharge see No. 497.

Farmers with Tractor, Symbol of Law—A145

Farmer Plowing with Water Buffalos—A146

Pres. Thieu Holding Agrarian Reform Law—A147

1973, Mar. 26   Litho.   Perf. 12½x12
448 A145 2pi lt green & multi   1.90 15
449 A146 5pi orange & multi   1.90 15
          Perf. 11
450 A147 10pi blue & multi   45.00 5.00

3rd anniv. of the agrarian reform law; 5-year plan for rural development. See No. 475.

INTERPOL Emblem and Headquarters A148

Designs: 2pi, INTERPOL emblem. 25pi, INTERPOL emblem and side view of Headquarters.

1973, Apr. 8   Litho.   Perf. 12½x12
451 A148 1pi olive & multi   15 15
452 A148 2pi yellow & multi   16 15
453 A148 25pi ocher, lilac & brn   1.90 16
          Set value   26

Intl. Criminal Police Org., 50th anniv.
For surcharge see No. 498.

ITU Emblem and Waves — A149

Designs: 2pi, Globe and waves. 3pi, ITU emblem.

1973, May 17
454 A149 1pi dull blue & multi   24 15
455 A149 2pi brt blue & multi   50 15
456 A149 3pi orange & multi   75 15
          Set value   15

World Telecommunications Day.
For surcharge see No. 499.

Globe, Hand Holding House — A150

Men Building Pylon — A151

Design: 10pi, Fish in net, symbols of agriculture, industry and transportation.

1973, Nov. 6   Litho.   Perf. 12x12½
457 A150 8pi gray & multi   48 15
458 A150 10pi vio bl, blk & gray   60 15
459 A151 15pi blk, org & lil rose   95 15
          Set value   15

National development.
For surcharge see No. 514.

Water Buffalos—A152

1973, Dec. 20   Litho.   Perf. 12x12½
460 A152 5pi shown   70 15
461 A152 10pi Water buffalo   1.00 20
          Set value   30

Human Rights Flame, Three Races—A153

Design: 100pi, Human Rights flame, scales and people, vert.

Perf. 12½x12, 12x12½
1973, Dec. 29
462 A153 15pi ultra & multi   60 15
463 A153 100pi green & multi   2.00 28
          Set value   35

25th anniv. of Universal Declaration of Human Rights.

"25" and WHO Emblem—A154

Design: 15pi, WHO emblem (different).
1973, Dec. 31   Perf. 12½x12
464 A154 8pi orange, bl & brn   52 15
465 A154 15pi lt brn, bl & brt pink 80 15
          Set value   15

25th anniversary of WHO.
For surcharge see No. 515.

Sampan Ferry—A155

Design: 10pi, Sampan ferry (different).

1974, Jan. 13   Litho.   Perf. 14x13½
466 A155 5pi lt blue & multi   80 15
467 A155 10pi yellow grn & multi   1.25 15
          Set value   15

Sampan ferry women.

Soldiers of 7 Nations — A156

American War Memorial — A157

Map of South Viet Nam and Allied Flags — A158

Design: No. 469, Soldiers and flags of South Viet Nam, Korea, US, Australia New Zealand, Thailand and Philippines. Same flags shown on 8pi and 60pi.

Perf. 12½x12, 12x12½
1974, Jan. 28
468 A156 8pi multicolored   35 15
469 A156 15pi lt brown & multi   75 15
470 A157 15pi multicolored   75 15
471 A158 60pi multicolored   2.25 20
          Set value   40

In honor of South Viet Nam's allies.
For surcharge see No. 516.

Trung Sisters on Elephants Fighting Chinese — A159

1974, Feb. 27   Litho.   Perf. 12½x12
472 A159 8pi green, cit & blk   18 15
473 A159 15pi dp orange & multi   35 15
474 A159 80pi ultra, pink & blk   1.75 20
          Set value   32

Trung Trac and Trung Nhi, queens of Viet Nam, 39-43 A.D. Day of Vietnamese Women.

Pres. Thieu Type of 1973 and

Farmers Going to Work — A160

Woman Farmer Holding Rice — A161

1974, Mar. 26   Litho.   Perf. 14
475 A147 10pi blue & multi   1.50 15
          Perf. 12½x12, 12x12½
476 A160 20pi yellow & multi   42 15
477 A161 70pi blue & multi   1.10 30
          Set value   48

Agriculture Day. Size of No. 475 is 31x50mm, No. 450 is 34x54mm and printed on thick paper. No. 475 has been extensively redrawn and first line of inscription in bottom panel changed to "26 THANG BA."

Hung Vuong with Bamboo Tallies A162

Flag Inscribed: Hung Vuong, Founder of Kingdom A163

1974, Apr. 2   Perf. 14x13½
478 A162 20pi yellow & multi   80 15
479 A163 100pi olive & multi   2.75 40

Hung Vuong, founder of Vietnamese nation and of Hông-Bang Dynasty (2879-258 B.C.).

National Library A164

New National Library Building: 15pi, Library, right facade and Phoenix.

1974, Apr. 14
480 A164 10pi orange, brn & blk   65 15
481 A164 15pi multicolored   85 15
          Set value   25

Nos. 391 and 437 Surcharged with New Value and Two Bars in Red

1974   Perf. 13
482 A121 25pi on 16pi multi   1.00 15
483 A138 25pi on 16pi multi   1.00 15

Memorial Tower, Saigon — A165

Globe, Crane Lifting Crate — A167

Crane with Flags, Globe and Map of Viet Nam — A166

Perf. 12x12½, 12½x12½
1974, June 22   Litho.
484 A165 10pi blue & multi   45 15
485 A166 20pi multicolored   1.10 15
486 A167 60pi yellow & multi   3.50 20
          Set value   32

International Aid Day.

Sun and Views of Saigon, Dalat Hué — A168

Cau-Bong Bridge, Nha Trang A169

Thien-Mu Pagoda, Hué — A170

Perf. 14x13½, 13½x14

1974, July 12
487	A168	5pi blue & multi	75	15
488	A169	10pi blue & multi	75	15
489	A170	15pi yellow & multi	1.25	15
		Set value		34

Tourist publicity.

Rhynchostylis Gigantea A171

Orchids: 20pi, Cypripedium caliosum, vert. 200pi, Dendrobium nobile.

1974, Aug. 18
490	A171	10pi blue & multi	26	15
491	A171	20pi yellow & multi	32	15
492	A171	200pi bister & multi	4.25	90
		Set value		1.00

Hands Passing Letter, UPU Emblem — A172

UPU Emblem and Woman — A173

UPU Cent.: 30pi, World map, bird, UPU emblem.

Perf. 12½x12, 12x12½

1974, Oct. 9   Litho.
493	A172	20pi ultra & multi	30	15
494	A172	30pi orange & multi	48	15
495	A173	300pi gray & multi	3.25	80
		Set value		94

Nos. 398, 447, 451, 454, 387 Surcharged with New Value and Two Bars in Red

1974-75
496	A125	25pi on 1pi multi	6.50
497	A144	25pi on 1pi multi	6.50
498	A148	25pi on 1pi multi	6.50
499	A149	25pi on 1pi multi	9.25
500	A120	25pi on 7pi multi	9.25
		Nos. 496-500 (5)	38.00

Issue dates: Nos. 497, 499-500, Nov. 18, 1974. Others, Jan. 1, 1975.

Hien Lam Pavilion, Hué — A174

Throne, Imperial Palace, Hué — A175

Water Pavilion, Hué — A176

1975, Jan. 5   Litho.   Perf. 14x13½
501	A174	25pi multicolored	65	15
502	A175	30pi multicolored	80	15
503	A176	60pi multicolored	1.65	16
		Set value		28

Historic sites.

Symbol of Youth, Children Holding Flower — A177

Family and Emblem — A178

1975, Jan. 14   Perf. 11½
504	A177	20pi blue & multi	45	15

Perf. 12½x12
505	A178	70pi yellow & multi	1.50	22
		Set value		28

Intl. Conf. on Children and National Development.

Unicorn Dance A179

Boy Lighting Firecracker — A180

Bringing New Year Gifts and Wishes — A181

Perf. 14x13½, 13½x14

1975, Jan. 26   Litho.
506	A179	20pi multicolored	55	15
507	A180	30pi blue & multi	70	15
508	A181	100pi bister & multi	1.25	15
		Set value		25

Lunar New Year, Tet.

A182

A183   A184

Designs: 25pi, Military chief from play "San Hau." 40pi, Scene from "Tam Ha Nam Duong." 100pi, Warrior Luu-Kim-Dinn.

1975, Feb. 23
509	A182	25pi rose & multi	75	15
510	A183	40pi lt green & multi	95	15
511	A184	100pi violet & multi	2.25	15
		Set value		22

National theater.

Produce, Map of Viet Nam, Ship — A185

Irrigation Project — A186

1975, Mar. 26   Litho.   Perf. 12½x12
512	A185	10pi multicolored	40	15
513	A186	50pi multicolored	2.75	16
		Set value		20

Agriculture Day; 5th anniv. of Agrarian Reform Law.

Nos. 457, 464, 468 Surcharged with New Value and Two Bars in Red

1975
514	A150	10pi on 8pi multi	12.00	1.40
515	A154	10pi on 8pi multi	7.50	55
516	A156	25pi on 8pi multi	7.50	1.20

In the 1980's a number of South Viet Nam stamps appeared on the market. These apparently had been printed before the collapse of the Republic but saw no postal use. These include, but are not limited to, sets of two for western electric and for rural electric, one each for history, library, New Years and cows, a set of three for transportation and a set of four for economic development.

SEMI-POSTAL STAMPS

Type of 1952 Surcharged in Carmine

✚

+50ᶜ

Perf. 12x12½

1952, Nov. 10   Unwmk.
B1	A3	1.50pi + 50c bl, yel & brn	3.25	3.25

The surtax was for the Red Cross.

Sabers and Flag — SP1

1952, Dec. 21   Engr.   Perf. 13
B2	SP1	3.30pi + 1.70pi dp claret	1.25	1.25

The surtax was for the Wounded Soldiers' Aid Organization.

X-ray Camera and Patient — SP2

1960, Aug. 1   Perf. 13
B3	SP2	3pi + 50c bl grn & red		85 85

The surtax was for the Anti-Tuberculosis Foundation.

AIR POST STAMPS

AP1

AP2

Perf. 13½x12½

1952-53   Unwmk.   Photo.
C1	AP1	3.30pi dk brn red & pale yel grn	80	15
C2	AP1	4pi brown & yellow	1.10	15
C3	AP1	5.10pi dk vio bl & sal pink	1.00	16
C4	AP2	6.30pi yellow & car	1.00	20

Issue dates: No. C2, Nov. 24, 1953. Others, Mar. 8, 1952.

Dragon AP3

Fish — AP4

1952, Sept. 3   Engr.   Perf. 13
C5	AP3	40c red	85	30
C6	AP3	70c green	1.25	30
C7	AP3	80c ultra	1.25	35
C8	AP3	90c brown	1.25	40
C9	AP4	3.70pi deep magenta	2.75	38
		Nos. C5-C9 (5)	7.35	1.73

Nos. C5-C9 exist imperforate in a souvenir booklet.

South Viet Nam

Phoenix — AP5

1955, Sept. 7

C10	AP5	4pi violet & lil rose	1.65 15

Crane Carrying Letter — AP6

1960, Dec. 20.   *Perf. 13*

C11	AP6	1pi olive	55 15
C12	AP6	4pi green & dk blue	1.10 18
C13	AP6	5pi ocher & purple	1.40 24
C14	AP6	10pi deep magenta	2.50 50

POSTAGE DUE STAMPS

Temple Lion D1

Dragon D2

Perf. 13x13½

1952, June 16   Typo.   Unwmk.

J1	D1	10c red & green	20 15
J2	D1	20c green & yellow	32 15
J3	D1	30c purple & orange	42 15
J4	D1	40c dk grn & sal rose	52 15
J5	D1	50c dp carmine & gray	70 15
J6	D1	1pi blue & silver	1.25 20
		Nos. J1-J6 (6)	3.41
		Set value	50

South Viet Nam

1955-56

J7	D2	2pi red vio & org	32 15
J8	D2	3pi violet & grnsh bl	45 16
J9	D2	5pi violet & yellow	50 16
J10	D2	10pi dk green & car	70 20
J11	D2	20pi red & brt grn ('56)	1.25 50
J12	D2	30pi brt grn & yel ('56)	1.75 80
J13	D2	50pi dk red brn & yel ('56)	4.00 1.50
J14	D2	100pi purple & yel ('56)	8.00 3.50
		Nos. J7-J14 (8)	16.97 6.97

Nos. J11-J14 inscribed "BUU-CHINH" instead of "TIMBRE-TAXE."

Atlas Moth — D3

Design: 3pi, 5pi, 10pi, Three butterflies.

1968, Aug. 20 Photo.   *Perf. 13½x13*

J15	D3	50c multicolored	60 15
J16	D3	1pi multicolored	60 15
J17	D3	2pi multicolored	1.25 15
J18	D3	3pi multicolored	1.75 15
J19	D3	5pi multicolored	3.00 15
J20	D3	10pi multicolored	4.00 20
		Nos. J15-J20 (6)	11.20
		Set value	55

Nos. J15-J18 Surcharged with New Value and Two Bars in Red

1974, Oct. 1

J21	D3	5pi on 3pi multi	1.60
J22	D3	10pi on 50c multi	1.60
J23	D3	40pi on 1pi multi	5.00
J24	D3	60pi on 2pi multi	6.25

MILITARY STAMPS

Soldier Guarding Village — M1

Rouletted 7½

1961, June   Unwmk.   Litho.

M1	M1	ocher, brn, dk grn & blk	3.75 1.00

1961, Sept.   Typo.

M2	M1	org yel, dk grn & brn	3.50 1.00

Bottom inscription on No. M1 is black, brown on No. M2.

Battle and Refugees M2

1969, Feb. 22   Litho.   *Imperf.*

M3	M2	red & green	60.00
a.		Booklet pane of 10	600.00

NORTH VIET NAM

LOCATION — In eastern Indo-China.
GOVT. — Republic
AREA — 61,293 sq. mi.
POP. — 18,800,000 (1968 est.)
CAPITAL — Hanoi

Beginning in 1946, the Communist Viet Minh fought the French in a guerrilla war that ended with the French defeat at Dien Bien Phu in 1954. In an agreement signed in Geneva on July 21, 1954, Viet Nam was partitioned at the 17th parallel. The government in Hanoi controlled the north, and engaged in another protracted military campaign against American and South Vietnamese forces that led to the official reunification of the country under Communist control on July 2, 1976.

100 Cents = 1 Dong
100 Xu = 1 Dong (1959)

All stamps are without gum unless otherwise indicated. Values for stamps with gum are for Never Hinged items.

Watermark

Wmk. 376- "R de C"

The editors are developing listings of regional issues from 1945-1954. Anyone wishing to supply stamps and information may contact the catalogue editor.

Ho Chi Minh, Map of Vietnam A1

1951-55   Unwmk.   Litho.   *Imperf.*

1	A1	100d brown	
a.		Perf. 11 ('55)	
2	A1	100d green	
a.		Perf. 11 ('55)	

Perf. 11

3	A1	200d red	
a.		Imperf. ('55)	

Nos. 1-3 printed on thin semi-transparent paper.

Blacksmith — A2

1953-55   *Perf. 11*

4-5	A2	100d, 500d, set of 2	10.00

Issued: 100d, 6/53. 500d, 2/55.

Georgi Malenkov, Ho Chi Minh, Mao Tse-tung and Flags A3

1954-55   *Perf. 11*

6	A3	50d brown & red, *brnish*	
7	A3	100d red	
8	A3	100d yellow & red, *brnish*	
		Nos. 6-8 (3)	70.00

Issued: 50d, 10/54; #7, 1/54; #8, 4/55. No. 7 printed on thin, white paper.

Nos. 9-16 have been reserved for a group of surcharges released during Oct. 1954. The editors would like to examine these issues.

Victory at Dien Bien Phu — A4

1954-56   *Perf. 11*

17-19	A4	10d, 50d, 150d, set of 3	37.50
17a-19a		Imperf.	

Issued: #17a-19a, 10/54; others, 1956. See #O5.

VIETNAM 1945 TO DATE

BUYING AND SELLING
Singles to Complete Collections

Fast Service & Fair Pricing!

WE ALSO STOCK:
BHUTAN • CHINA (PRC)
CAMBODIA • INDONESIA
LAOS • THAILAND
FRENCH COLONIES
Specializing in...
Afars & Issas, New Caledonia, Polynesia, Fr. So. Antarctic, Wallis & Futuna, and St. Pierre & Miquelon.

Albany Stamp Co.
P.O. Box 30398
Charleston, S.C. 29417-0398
Phone (803) 766-6396
FAX
(803) 766-2235
MasterCard   VISA

Liberation of Hanoi A5

1955, Jan. 1   *Perf. 11½*

20-22	A5	10d, 50d, 150d, set of 3	60.00

Land Reform A6

LET US HELP YOU BUILD A GREAT NORTH VIETNAM COLLECTION —— TODAY!

FOR EXAMPLE / MICHEL CAT. FOOTNOTE UNDER #683-688 / 30xu UNISSUED PROOF.   SPECIAL $49.50

SEND TO:
M & W BROOKS
P.O. Box 630218 / Kappock St. / Spuyten Duyvil Station
Riverdale, New York 10463 Phone or Fax: 718-548-4297

TERMS: 1) Payment with order / U.S. check or money order only. 2) N.Y.S. residents add 8¼% sales tax.
3) Orders under $50 add $3.00 for postage and insurance. We guarantee service. Best stamp quality, knowledge, reliability and satisfaction.

1955-56   *Perf. 11*
23-27 A6 5d, 10d, 20d, 50d,
      100d, set of 5   100.00

Issued: 100d, 12/55; 20d, 50d, 2/56; others, 6/56. See Nos. O8-O9.

Return of Government to Hanoi — A7

Denominations: 1000d, 1500d, 2000d, 3000d.

1956, Mar. 1   *Perf. 11*
28-31 A7 Set of 4   200.00

Re-opening of Hanoi-China Railroad — A8

Denominations: 100d, 200d, 300d, 500d.

1956, Mar. 1
32-35 A8 Set of 4   125.00 110.00

Nos. 36-38 are reserved for three surcharges released in May 1956. The editors would like to see these stamps.

Tran Dang Ninh
(1910-55),
Guerrilla
Leader — A9

1956, July   Litho.   *Perf. 11½x11*
39-42 A9 5d, 10d, 20d, 100d, set
      of 4   25.00 10.00

Mac Thi Buoi
(1927-51),
Guerrilla
Leader — A10

Denominations: 1000d, 2000d, 4000d, 5000d.

1956, Nov. 3   *Perf. 11½*
43-46 A10 Set of 4   400.00 160.00

Bai Thuong
Dam — A11

Denominations: 100d, 200d, 300d.

1956-58   *Perf. 11*
47-49 A11 Set of 3   37.50 25.00
47a-49a   Set of 3, perf. 13   40.00 40.00

Issued: #47-49, 12/15/56; #47a-49a, 1958.

Ho Chi
Minh — A12

1956, Dec.   Typo.   *Rough Perf. 7*
50 A12 50d on 5d red, *brnish*   80.00 100.00

No. 50 is printed on rough handmade paper.

Cotton
Mill — A13

1957, Mar.   Litho.   *Perf. 12½*
51-53 A13 100d, 200d, 300d, set
      of 3   21.50 21.50

Ho Chi Minh — A14

1957   *Perf. 12½*
54-57 A14 20d, 60d, 100d, 300d,
      set of 4   30.00 10.00

Issued: 20d, 60d, 12/13; others, 5/19.

Fourth World
Trade Union
Congress,
Leipzig — A15

1957, Aug. 1   *Perf. 12½*
58 A15 300d red violet   7.50 3.25

Democratic
Republic, 12th
Anniv. — A16

1957, Sept. 2   *Perf. 13*
59-60 A16 20d, 100d, set of 2   10.00 6.50

Presidents
Voroshilov,
Ho Chi
Minh
A17

1957, Nov. 7   *Perf. 12½*
61-63 A17 100d, 500d, 1000d, set
      of 3   40.00

Russian revolution, 40th anniv.

Education
Campaign
A18

1958, Jan. 6   *Perf. 12½*
64-66 A18 50d, 150d, 1000d, set
      of 3   27.50 24.00

A19   A20

1958, Mar. 8
67-68 A19 150d, 500d, set of 2   32.50 30.00

Physical education.

1958, May 1
69-70 A20 50d, 150d, set of 2   10.00 7.50

May Day.

Fourth Intl.
Congress of
Democratic
Women,
Vienna — A21

1958, May   *Typo.*
71 A21 150d blue   7.50 7.00

A22   Arts & Crafts Fair,
            Hanoi — A22a

Designs: No. 72 (150d), 2000d, Basket, lace & cup, vert. No. 73 (150d), 1000d, Potter.

1958   *Litho.*
72-75 A22, A22a Set of 4   27.50 25.00

Issued: Nos. 72, 75, 6/26; others, 8/19.

Building the
Reunification
Railway
A23

1958, July 20
76-77 A23 50d, 150d, set of 2   6.00 4.00

August
Revolution,
13th
Anniv. — A24

1958, Aug. 19
78-79 A24 150d, 500d, set of 2   7.50 7.50

Resistance
Movement in
South Viet
Nam, 13th
Anniv. — A25

1958, Sept. 23
80-81 A25 50d, 150d, set of 2   11.50 6.00

Tran Hung Dao (1253-
1300) — A26

1958, Oct.
82 A26 150d greenish bl & blk   3.00 2.00

Hanoi Engineering
Plant — A27

1958, Nov. 7   Engr.   *Perf. 11½*
83 A27 150d brown   3.00 1.25

Mutual Aid
Teams — A28

1958, Nov. 7
84-85 A28 150d, 500d, set of 2   12.50 6.00

Ngoc Son Temple
(Temple of
Jade) — A29

1958, Dec. 1   Photo.   *Perf. 12*
86-87 A29 150d, 2000d, set of 2   35.00 12.50

Rattanware
Cooperative
A30

1958, Dec. 31
88 A30 150d greenish blue   3.00 1.00

Ha Long
Bay — A31

1959, Feb. 8
89-90 A31 150d, 350d, set of 2   8.00 4.00

Cam Pha Coal
Mines — A32

1959, Mar. 3 Engr. *Perf. 11½*
91 A32 150d blue 3.00 80

Trung Sisters — A33

1959, Mar. 14 Litho. *Perf. 11*
92-93 A33 5xu, 8xu, set of 2 7.50 6.00

World Peace Movement, 10th
Anniv. — A34

1959, Apr. 15
94 A34 12xu purple, *rose* 3.50 70

Xuan
Quang
Dam
A35

1959, May 1
95-96 A35 6xu, 12xu, set of 2 10.00 2.00

Phu Loi
Massacre
A36

1959, May 15
97-98 A36 12xu, 20xu, set of 2 7.00 2.00

Hien Luong
Bridge — A37

1959, July 20
99 A37 12xu black & carmine 4.00 1.75

Me Tri Radio
Station — A38

1959, Aug. 10
100-101 A38 3xu, 12xu, set of 2 4.50 1.25

Sports
A39

Designs: 1xu, Shooting. 6xu, Swimming. 12xu,
Wrestling.

1959, Sept. 2
102-104 A39 Set of 3 7.50 3.50
Size of No. 103 is 43x31mm.

People's Republic of
China, 10th
Anniv. — A40

1959, Oct. 1
105 A40 12xu multicolored 5.00 50

Fruits — A41

Designs: 3xu, Coconuts. 12xu, Bananas. 30xu,
Pineapple.

1959, Nov. 20
106-108 A41 Set of 3 14.00 5.50

People's
Army, 15th
Anniv.
A42

1959, Dec. 22
109 A42 12xu multicolored 3.00 2.00

A43 A44

1960, Jan. 6
110-111 A43 2xu, 12xu, set of 2 6.00 3.00
Vietnamese Workers' Party, 30th Anniv.

1960, Jan. 6
Ethnic costumes: 2xu, Ede. 10xu, Meo. No. 114,
12xu, Tay. No. 115, 12xu, Thai.
112-115 A44 Set of 4 10.00 7.50

Census
A45

Designs: 1xu, People. 12xu, Transmitting tower,
dam, buildings, workers.

1960, Feb. 20
116-117 A45 Set of 2 4.50
No. 117 is 37x26mm.

Intl. Women's
Day, 50th
Anniv. — A46

1960, Mar. 8
118 A46 12xu multicolored 2.50

A47 A48

1960, Apr. 5
119-120 A47 4xu, 12xu, set of 2 75.00 50.00
Hung Vuong Temple.

1960, Apr. 22
121-122 A48 5xu, 12xu, set of 2 8.00
121a Souv. sheet of 1, olive brown &
blue, imperf. .75.00
Lenin. No. 121a exists on brownish paper.

Election of National
Assembly
Delegates — A49

1960, May 3 *Perf. 11*
123 A49 12xu multicolored, *rose* 1.50 50

A50 A51

1960, May 8
124-125 A50 8xu, 12xu, set of 2 6.00
Viet Nam Red Cross.

1960, May 19
Ho Chi Minh, 70th Birthday: Nos. 128, 130, Ho
with children.
126 A51 4xu green & purple
127 A51 12xu pink & brown
128 A51 12xu multicolored
Nos. 126-128 (3) 10.00 3.00
Souvenir Sheets
Imperf
129 A51 10xu yellow bister &
brown, *rose* 8.00
130 A51 10xu multicolored 6.00
No. 128 is 25x39mm.

New
Constitution
A52

1960, July 7
131 A52 12xu lemon & gray 2.50 1.25

National
Day, 15th
Anniv.
A53

1960, Sept. 2
132-133 A53 4xu, 12xu, set of 2 7.50

Development — A54

Designs: No. 134, Classroom. No. 135, Plowing.
No. 136, Factory.

1960, Sept. 2
134-136 A54 12xu Set of 3 10.50

3rd
Vietnamese
Communist
Party
Congress
A55

1960, Sept. 4
137-138 A55 1xu, 12xu, set of 2 8.00 2.50

World Federation of Trade Unions, 15th Anniv. — A56

1960, Oct. 3
139 A56 12xu black & vermilion 6.00 5.00

Hanoi, 950th Anniv. — A57

1960, Oct. 10   **Litho.**   *Perf. 11*
140-141 A57 8xu, 12xu, set of 2   8.50 4.00
141a   Souv. sheet of 1, imperf.   13.50

No. 141a exists on brownish paper.

15 Years' Achievements Exhibition A58

1960, Oct. 20
142-143 A58 2xu, 12xu, set of 2   4.50 2.25

World Federation of Democratic Youth, 15th Anniv. — A59

1960, Nov. 10
144 A59 12xu multicolored   3.50

Trade Unions, 2nd Natl. Congress A60

1961, Feb. 10
145 A60 12xu multicolored, *rose*   2.50 1.25

Vietnamese Women's Union, 3rd Natl. Congress — A61

1961, Mar. 8   **Tinted Paper**
146-147 A61 6xu, 12xu, set of 2   5.75 1.75

Animals — A62   Ly Tu Trong — A63

Designs: 12xu, Rusa unicolor. 20xu, Helarctos malynus. 50xu, Elephas maximus. 1d, Hylobates leucogenys.

1961, Mar. 8
148-151 A62   Set of 4   27.50 16.00
   Imperf., #148-151   25.00

1961, Mar. 18
152-153 A63 2xu, 12xu, set of 2   3.50 2.00

Youth Labor Union, 3rd Congress.

Young Pioneers, 20th Anniv. A64

1961, May 2
154-155 A64 1xu, 12xu, set of 2   6.50 2.75

Intl. Red Cross — A65

1961, May 8
156-157 A65 6xu, 12xu, set of 2   7.00 3.50

Intl. Children's Day — A66

1961, June 1   *Perf. 11*
158-159 A66 4xu, 12xu, set of 2   5.50 2.75

Yuri Gagarin's Space Flight — A67

1961, June 15
160-161 A67 6xu, 12xu, set of 2   30.00 13.00
   Imperf., #160-161   35.00

Hanoi, Hue and Saigon — A68

1961, July 20
162-163 A68 12xu, 3d, set of 2   25.00 17.50

A69   A70

1961, July 20
164-165 A69 12xu, 2d, set of 2   10.00 2.50
   Imperf., #164-165

Reunification campaign.

1961, Aug. 21
166-167 A70 2xu, 12xu, set of 2   6.00 2.00

Geological exploration.

Savings Campaign A71

1961, Aug. 21
168-169 A71 3xu, 12xu, set of 2   6.00 1.75

Ancient Towers — A72   Gherman Titov's Space Flight — A73

Designs: 6xu, Thien Mu, Hue. 10xu, Pen Brush, Bac Ninh. No. 172, 12xu, Binh Son, Vinh Phuc. No. 173, 12xu, Cham, Phan Rang.

1961, Sept. 12
170-173 A72   Set of 4   9.00 3.75
   Imperf., #170-173

1961, Oct. 17
174-175 A73 6xu, 12xu, set of 2   7.00 4.00
   Imperf., #174-175   8.00

A74   A76

Port of Haiphong A75

1961, Oct. 17
176 A74 12xu vermilion & black   3.50 2.00

22nd Communist Party Congress, Moscow.

1961, Nov. 7
177-178 A75 5xu, 12xu, set of 2   9.00 3.50

1961, Nov. 18   *Perf. 13½*
Musicians: No. 179, 12xu, Flutist. No. 180, 12xu, Cymbalist. 30xu, Dancer with fan. 50xu, Guitarist.

179-182 A76   Set of 4   14.00 14.00
   Imperf., #179-182   17.50
182a   Souvenir sheet of 4, #179-182   65.00

Stamps on No. 182a are se-tenant and perfed on outside edges of the strip of 4.

5th World Trade Union Congress, Moscow A77

1961, Dec. 4   *Perf. 11*
183 A77 12xu deep red lilac & gray   2.50 1.00

Natl. Resistance, 15th Anniv. — A78

1961, Dec. 4
184-185 A78 4xu, 12xu, set of 2   2.50

Tet Holiday — A79

Designs: 6xu, Sow, piglets. 12xu, Poultry.

1962, Jan. 16   **Litho.**
186-187 A79   Set of 2   7.50

Tet Tree-Planting Festival — A80

1962, Jan. 16
188-189 A80 12xu, 40xu, set of 2   5.00

Crops — A81

Designs: 2xu, Camellia sinensis. 6xu, Illicium verum. No. 192, 12xu, Coffea arabica. No. 193, 12xu, Ricinus communis. 30xu, Rhus succedanea.

1962, Mar. 1
190-194 A81   Set of 5   17.50 8.00

Folk Dances — A82

Designs: No. 195, 12xu, Rong Chieng. No. 196, 12xu, Bamboo. 30xu, Hat. 50xu, Parasol.

1962, Mar. 20 Photo. Perf. 11½x12
195-198 A82 Set of 4   20.00 5.00
       Imperf., #195-198   25.00
Souvenir Sheet
199 A82 30xu like #195   30.00

First Five Year Plan — A83

Designs: 1xu, Kim Lien Apartments, Hanoi. 3xu, State farm. 8xu, Natl. Institute of Hydraulics.

1962, Apr. 10 Litho. Perf. 11
200-202 A83 Set of 3   4.00

A84   A85

Flowers: No. 203, 12xu, Hibiscus rosa sinensis. No. 204, 12xu, Plumeria acutifolia. 20xu, Chrysanthemum indicum. 30xu, Nelumbium nuciferum. 50xu, Ipomoea pulchella.

Perf. 12½x11½
1962, Apr. 10   Photo.
203-207 A84 Set of 5   27.50
       Imperf., #203-207   35.00
206a   Souvenir sheet of 1   15.00

1962, May 4 Litho. Perf. 11
208 A85 12xu multicolored   3.50

3rd Natl. Heroes of Labor Congress.

Harrow A86

Dai Lai Lake A87

1962, May 25
209-210 A86-A87 6xu, 12xu, set of 2   5.00

Visit by Gherman Titov — A88

Titov: 12xu, Waving at children. 20xu, Receiving medal from Ho Chi Minh. 30xu, Wearing space suit.

1962, June 12
211-213 A88 Set of 3   8.00 8.00
       Imperf., #211-213   8.00

Anti-Malaria Campaign A89

1962, July 9
214-216 A89 8xu, 12xu, 20xu, set of 3   7.50 3.50

War for Reunification — A90

1962, July 20
217 A90 12xu multicolored   2.50 1.25

Ba Be Lake — A91

Design: No. 219, Ban Gioc Falls, vert.

1962, Aug. 14
218-219 A91 12xu Set of 2   3.50

A stamp picturing a weight lifter exists, but was not released.

King Quang Trung (1752-92) A92   Nguyen Trai (1380-1442) A93

1962, Sept. 16
220-221 A92 3xu, 12xu, set of 2   3.50

1962, Sept. 19
222-223 A93 3xu, 12xu, set of 2   3.50

Food Crops — A94

Designs: 1xu, Peanuts. 4xu, Beans. 6xu, Sweet potatoes. 12xu, Corn. 30xu, Cassava.

1962, Oct. 10
224-228 A94 Set of 5   10.00 5.00
       Imperf., #224-228

Animal Husbandry A95

Designs: 2xu, Feeding poultry. No. 230, 12xu, Feeding pigs. No. 231, 12xu, Cattle grazing. No. 232, 12xu, Tending water buffalo.

1962, Nov. 28
229-232 A95 Set of 4   5.50

A stamp commemorating the 45th anniversary of the Russian Revolution exists, but was not issued.

First Five Year Plan — A96

Designs: No. 233, Evening classes. No. 234, Clearing land.

1962, Dec. 28
233-234 A96 12xu Set of 2   5.00

Flights of Vostok 3 and 4 — A97

Designs: 12xu, Pavel Popovich, Vostok 4. 20xu, Andrian Nikolayev, Vostok 3. 30xu, Rockets lifting-off, vert.

1962, Dec. 28   Perf. 11
235-237 A97 Set of 3   6.50 3.25
       Imperf., #235-237   12.00

Guerrilla A98   Hoang Hoa Tham (1846-1913) A99

1963, Jan. 15
238-239 A98 5xu, 12xu, set of 2   2.75

1963, Feb. 10
240-241 A99 6xu, 12xu, set of 2   2.50

A100

First Five Year Plan — A100a

Designs: No. 242, Fertilizing rice paddy. No. 243, Lam Thao superphosphate plant.

1963, Feb. 25
242-243 A100-A100a 12xu Set of 2   3.50

Karl Marx — A101

1963, Mar. 14
244-245 A101 3xu, 12xu, set of 2   3.25

Nos. 244-245 are printed on greenish and rose toned paper respectively.

Fidel Castro, Vietnamese Soldiers — A102

1963, Apr. 17
246 A102 12xu multicolored   1.50 80

May Day A103

1963, May 8
247 A103 12xu multicolored   1.50 80

Intl. Red Cross, Cent.
A104   A105

Design: No. 249, Child, syringe.

1963, May 8
248 A104 12xu green, black & red
249 A104 12xu green, red & black
250 A105 20xu multicolored
       Nos. 248-250 (3)   6.00

Fishing Industry A107

Designs: No. 255, Trawler, offshore fish. No. 256, Freshwater fish.

1963, July 3
255-256 A107 12xu Set of 2   10.00

Ho Chi Minh, Nguyen Van Hien — A108

1963, July 20
257 A108 12xu multicolored   2.50

Flights of Vostok 3, 4 — A109

Designs: 12xu, Rockets in orbit. 20xu, Nikolayev. 30xu, Popovich.

261-262 A110 Set of 2   3.00

Fish A111

Designs: No. 263, 12xu, Cyprinus carpio. No. 264, 12xu, Myloharyngodon piceus. No. 265, 12xu, Hypophthalmichthys molitrix. 20xu, Ophiocephalus caqua. 30xu, Tilapia mossambica.

1963, Sept. 10
263-267 A111 Set of 5   13.00
    Imperf., #263-267   22.50

Birds — A112

Designs: No. 268, 12xu, Francolinus stephenson. No. 269, 12xu, Acridotheres cristatellus. No. 270, 12xu, Halcyon smyrneusis. 20xu, Diardigallus diardi, horiz. 30xu, Egretta. 40xu, Psittacula alexandri.

Perf. 11½x12, 12x11½
1963, Oct. 15   *Photo.*
268-274 A112 Set of 6   35.00 17.50
    Imperf., #268-274

Souvenir Sheet
274A A112 50xu Sheet of 1, like #273
                                       50.00

World Federation of Trade Unions Congress for Viet Nam — A113

1963, Oct. 20   *Litho.*   *Perf. 11*
275 A113 12xu multicolored   1.50

GANEFO Games A114

Designs: No. 276, 12xu, Swimming. No. 277, 12xu, Volleyball, vert. No. 278, 12xu, Soccer, vert. 30xu, High jump.

1963, Nov. 10
276-279 A114 Set of 4   5.00 5.00
    Imperf., #276-279   6.00

A115   A116

Flowers: 6xu, Rauwolfia verticillata. No. 281, 12xu, Sophora japonica. No. 282, 12xu, Fibraurea tinctoria. No. 283, 12xu, Chenopodium ambrosioides. 20xu, Momordica cochinchinensis.

1963, Dec. 3
280-284 A115 Set of 5   8.50 4.00
    Imperf., #280-284   12.00

1963, Dec. 20
285 A116 12xu multicolored   2.50

World Day for Viet Nam.

A117

First Five-Year Plan — A118

Designs: 6xu, Molten cast iron. No. 287, 12xu, Thai Nguyen Steel and Iron Works. No. 288, 12xu, Power lines.

1964, Jan. 25   *Litho.*
286-288 A117-A118 Set of 3   4.50 1.75

Intl. Quiet Sun Year — A119

1964, Jan. 25
289-290 A119 12xu, 50xu, set of 2   5.00
    Imperf., #289-290   20.00

Flights of Vostok 5 and 6 A120

Designs: No. 291, 12xu, Rockets in orbit. No. 292, 12xu, Valery Bykovsky. 30xu, Valentina Tereshkova.

1964, Mar. 25
291-293 A120 Set of 3   6.00 6.00
    Imperf., #291-293   12.00

A stamp commemorating the anniversary of the founding of the People's Democratic Republic of Korea was printed but not issued.

A121   A122

Flowers: No. 294, 12xu, Persica vulgaris. No. 295, 12xu, Hibiscus mutabilis. No. 296, 12xu, Passiflora hispida. No. 297, 12xu, Saraca dives. 20xu, Michelia champaca. 30xu, Camellia amplexicaulis.

1964, Apr. 10   *Perf. 11½x12*
294-299 A121 Set of 6   15.00 6.50
    Imperf., #294-299   15.00

1964, Apr. 27   *Perf. 11*
Costumes: 6xu, Peasant, 19th cent. No. 301, 12xu, Woman wearing large hat, 19th cent. No. 302, 12xu, Woman carrying hat.

300-302 A122 Set of 3   6.00 3.25

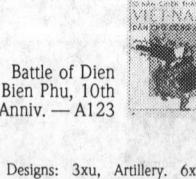

Battle of Dien Bien Phu, 10th Anniv. — A123

Designs: 3xu, Artillery. 6xu, Machine gun emplacement. Nos. 305, 307c, Bomb disposal. Nos. 306, 307d, Farmer on tractor.

1964, May 7
303 A123 3xu red & black
304 A123 6xu blue & black
305 A123 12xu yellow orange & black
306 A123 12xu red lilac & black
    Nos. 303-306 (4)   6.50 6.00
    Imperf., #303-306   10.00

Souvenir Sheet
Imperf
307   Sheet of 4   12.00
  a. A123 3xu orange & black
  b. A123 6xu yellow green & black
  c. A123 12xu red, black & orange
  d. A123 12xu blue & black

Ham Rong Bridge — A124

1964, May 17
308 A124 12xu multicolored   1.75 80

Wild Animals A125

Designs: No. 309, 12xu, Panthera tigris, vert. No. 310, 12xu, Pseudaxis axis, vert. No. 311, 12xu, Tapirus indicus. 20xu, Bubalus bubalis. 30xu, Rhinoceros bicornis. 40xu, Bibos banteng.

1964, June 2   *Perf. 10½*
309-314 A125 Set of 6   17.50
    Imperf., #309-314   20.00

A126

Geneva Agreement on Viet Nam, 10th Anniv. — A127

1964, July 20   *Perf. 11*
315-316 A126-A127 12xu Set of 2   2.50 1.60

Nam Bac Ninh Pumping Station A128

1964, Aug. 25
317 A128 12xu blue gray & black   1.50 80

Liberation of Hanoi, 10th Anniv. A129

Designs: 6xu, People cheering soldiers in truck. 12xu, Construction, hammerhead crane.

1964, Oct. 10
318-319 A129 Set of 2   3.50 2.50

Natl. Defense Games A130

Designs: 5xu, Rowing. No. 321, 12xu, Parachuting, vert. No. 322, 12xu, Gliders, vert. No. 323, 12xu, Shooting.

1964, Oct. 18
320-323 A130 Set of 4   6.50 2.50

Fruits — A131

Designs: No. 324, 12xu, Mangifera indica. No. 325, 12xu, Guarcinia mangostana. No. 326, 12xu, Nephelium litchi. 20xu, Anona squamosa. 50xu, Citrus medica.

1964, Oct. 31   Photo.   *Perf. 11½x12*
324-328 A131 Set of 5   12.50 5.25
    Imperf., #324-328   15.00

World Solidarity Conference A132

Designs: a, Ba Dinh Hall. b, Vietnamese soldier shaking hands with foreign people. c, Fist, planes, submarine.

1964, Nov. 25   Litho.   *Perf. 11*
329 A132 12xu Strip of 3, #a.-c.   4.50

People's Army, 20th Anniv. A133

Designs: No. 330, Soldiers, flag. No. 331a, Coast guards. No. 331b, Mounted border guards, vert.

1964, Dec. 22
330 A133 12xu multicolored
331 A133 12xu Pair, #a.-b.
    Nos. 330-331 (2)   5.00 1.25

Cuban Revolution, 6th Anniv. — A134

Designs: a, Vietnamese, Cuban flags. b, Cuban revolutionaries.

1965, Jan. 1
332 A134 12xu Pair, #a.-b.   4.50 3.25

Economic & Cultural Development of Mountain Region — A135

Designs: 2xu, 3xu, Women pollinating corn. 12xu, Girls walking to school.

1965, Jan. 1
333-335 A135 Set of 3   3.00 2.50
    Imperf., #333-335

A136

Vietnamese Worker's Party, 35th Anniv. A137

Politicians: No. 336a, Le Hong Phong. b, Tran Phu. c, Hoang Van Thu. d, Ngo Gia Tu. e, Nguyen Van Cu.
No. 337a, Party flag. b, Worker, soldier.

1965   Litho.   *Perf. 11*
336 A136 6xu Strip of 5, #a.-e.
337 A137 12xu Pair, #a.-b.
    Nos. 336-337 (2)   5.00
   Issued: No. 336, 2/3; No. 337, 1/30.

Transportation Ministers Conference, Hanoi A138

Design: 12xu, 30xu, Nguyen Van Troi, locomotive.

1965, Mar. 23
338-339 A138 Set of 2   6.00 2.00
    Imperf., #338-339

Vignette on No. 339 is mirror image of No. 338.

Flight of Voskhod 1 A139

Designs: 20xu, Cosmonauts Komarov, Feoktistov, Yegorov, rocket, globe. 1d, Cosmonauts, rocket.

1965, Mar. 30
340-341 A139 Set of 2   8.50
    Imperf., #340-341   13.00

Lenin, Soldier — A140

1965, Apr. 22   Litho.
342-343 A140 8xu, 12xu, set of 2   4.00

A141   A142

1965, May 19
344-345 A141 6xu, 12xu, set of 2   2.00
   Ho Chi Minh, 75th birthday.

1965, May 19
346 A142 12xu multicolored   2.50
   Afro-Asian Conference, 10th anniv.

Trade Union Conference, Hanoi — A143

Designs: No. 347, Workers solidarity. No. 348, Soldiers, vert. No. 349, Naval battle.

1965, June 2
347-349 A143 12xu Set of 3   3.50

Wild Animals — A144

Designs: No. 350, 12xu, Martes flavigula. No. 351, 12xu, Chrotogale owstoni. No. 352, 12xu, Manis pentadactyla. No. 353, 12xu, Presbytis delacouri, vert. 20xu, Petaurista lylei, vert. 50xu, Nycticebus pygmaeus, vert.

1965, June 24   Photo.   *Perf. 12*
350-355 A144 Set of 6   19.00 6.00
    Imperf., #350-355   25.00

A145   A146

1965, July 1   *Perf. 11½x11*
356 A145 12xu multicolored   3.50 40
   6th Socialist Postal Ministers Conference.

1965, July 20   Litho.   *Perf. 11*
  Nguyen Van Troi (1940-64). Denominations: 12xu, 50xu, 4d.
357-359 A146 Set of 3   9.00 6.00

Insects
A147   A148

Designs: No. 360, 12xu, Tessaratoma papillosa. No. 361, 12xu, Rhynchocoris humeralis. No. 362, 12xu, Poeciliocoris latus.
No. 363, 12xu, Tosena melanoptera. 20xu, Cicada. 30xu, Fulgora candelaria.

1965, July 24   Photo.
360-362 A147 Set of 3
363-365 A148 Set of 3
    Nos. 360-365 (6)   12.00 8.00
    Imperf., #360-365   15.00

August Revolution, 20th Anniv. — A149

1965, Aug. 19   Litho.
366-367 A149 6xu, 12xu, set of 2   2.50 1.60

Marine Life A150

Designs: No. 368, 12xu, Penaeus indicus. No. 369, 12xu, Scylla serrata. No. 370, 12xu, Metapenaeus joyneri. No. 371, 12xu, Neptunus. 20xu, Palinurus japonicus. 50xu, Uca marionis.

1965, Aug. 19'
368-373 A150 Set of 6   22.50 8.00
    Imperf., #368-373   20.00

500th US Warplane Shot Down — A151

1965, Aug. 30
374 A151 12xu gray green & lilac   6.00 6.00

Completion of 1st Five-Year Plan
A152   A153

Designs: No. 375, Foundry worker. No. 376, Electricity, irrigation. No. 377, Public health, education. No. 377, Students, children playing. No. 378, Factory worker. No. 379, Rice paddy.

1965
375-377   A152   12xu   Set of 3   3.50   1.75
378-380   A153   12xu   Set of 3   3.50   1.75
      Imperf., #375-380
Issued: Nos. 375-377, 9/2; Nos. 378-380, 12/25.

Nghe An, Ha Tinh Uprising, 35th
Anniv. — A154

1965, Sept. 12
381-382   A154   10xu, 12xu, set of 2   2.50   1.75
      Imperf., #381-382

Friendship Between Viet Nam, People's
Republic of China, 16th Anniv.
A155

Designs: No. 383, Youth holding flags, Friendship
Gate. No. 384, Children waving flags, walking
through Gate, vert.

1965, Oct. 1
383-384   A155   12xu   Set of 2   10.00   1.75

Flight of
Voskhod 2
A156

Designs: No. 385, 12xu, Konstantin Tsiolkovsky,
Sputnik I. No. 386, 12xu, Voskhod 2, A. Leonov, P.
Belyayev. No. 387, 50xu, Yuri Gagarin. No. 388,
50xu, Leonov walking in space.

1965, Oct. 5
385-388   A156   Set of 4   8.00   4.00
      Imperf., #385-388

A157   A158

Norman R. Morrison, US anti-war demonstration.

1965, Nov. 22
389   A157   12xu   black & red   2.50   1.25

1965, Nov. 25
    Nguyen Du (1765-1820), poet: No. 390, 12xu,
Birthplace. No. 391, 12xu, Museum. 20xu, Volume
of poems entitled Kieu. 1d, Scene from Kieu.

390-393   A158   Set of 4   6.00   5.75

A159

Designs: No. 394, 12xu, Ho Chi Minh. No. 395,
12xu, Karl Marx. No. 396, 12xu, Lenin. 50xu,
Frederich Engels.

Litho. & Engr. (#394), Litho.
1965, Nov. 28   *Perf. 11½*
394-397   A159   Set of 4   5.00   5.00
    Nos. 395-397 have white border.

Butterflies — A160

Designs: No. 398, 12xu, Cethosia cyane. No.
399, 12xu, Zelides sarpedon. No. 400, 12xu,
Cethosia. No. 401, 12xu, Apatura ambica. 20xu,
Papilio paris. 30xu, Tros aristolochiae.

1965, Nov. 28   **Litho.**   *Perf. 11*
398-403   A160   Set of 6   24.00   7.50
      Imperf., #398-403   55.00

South Viet Nam Natl. Liberation Front, 5th
Anniv. — A161

1965, Dec. 20
404   A161   12xu lilac   2.50   1.25
   Imperf.

1st General
Elections,
20th
Anniv.
A162

1966, Jan. 6
405   A162   12xu   black & red   2.50   1.25

A163   A164

Orchids: No. 406, 12xu, Vanda teres. No. 407,
12xu, Dendrobium meschatum. No. 408, 12xu,
Dendrobium nobile. No. 409, 12xu, Dendrobium
crystallinum. 20xu, Vandopsis gigantea. 30xu,
Dendrobium.

1966, Jan. 10   *Perf. 12*
406-411   A163   Set of 6   10.00   5.00
      Imperf., #406-411

1966, Jan. 18   *Perf. 11*
412   A164   12xu multicolored   2.50   1.25
    Imperf.

    New Year 1966 (Year of the Horse).

Reptiles — A165

Designs: No. 413, 12xu, Physignathus
cocincinus. No. 414, 12xu, Gekko gecko. No. 415,
12xu, Trionyx sinensis. No. 416, 12xu, Testudo
elongata. 20xu, Varanus salvator. 40xu,
Eretmochelys imbricata.

1966, Feb. 25   *Perf. 12x11½*
413-418   A165   Set of 6   10.00   5.00
      Imperf., #413-418   20.00

Natl. Sports
A166

Designs: No. 419, Archery. No. 420, Wrestling.
No. 421, Spear fighting.

1966, Mar. 25   *Perf. 11*
419-421   A166   12xu   Set of 3   5.00

    6xu, 12xu, 1d stamps for running,
swimming and shooting were printed but
not issued.

Youth Labor Union,
35th Anniv. — A167

1966, Mar. 26
422   A167   12xu multicolored   1.50

1000th US Warplane Shot Down — A168

1966, Apr. 29
423   A168   12xu multicolored   5.00   4.00

    May Day — A169

1966, May 1
424   A169   6xu multicolored   1.50   50

Defending
Con Co
Island
A170

1966, June 1
425   A170   12xu multicolored   2.50

A171   A172

1966, June 1
426   A171   12xu   red & black   1.50
    Young Pioneers, 25th anniv.

1966, July 1
    Designs: 3xu, View of Yenan. 12xu, Ho Chi
Minh, Mao Tse-Tung.

427-428   A172   Set of 2   4.50   1.75
      Imperf., #427-428

    Chinese Communist Party, 45th anniv.

A173   A174

    Luna 9: 12xu, Flight path to moon. 50xu, In
lunar orbit.

1966, Aug. 5
429-430   A173   Set of 2   7.50   3.25
      Imperf., #429-430   9.00

1966, Oct. 10
431   A174   12xu multicolored   3.25
With Additional Inscription: "NGAY
14.10.1966"
431A   A174   12xu multicolored   3.75
      Imperf., #431-431A

    1500th US warplane shot down.

Victory in
Dry Season
Campaign
A175

Designs: 1xu, 12xu (No. 433), Woman guerrilla
carrying guns. 12xu (No. 434), Soldier escorting
prisoners of war.

1966, Oct. 15
432-434 A175 Set of 3   3.25 1.75
  Imperf., #432-434

Vietnamese
Women's
Union, 20th
Anniv.
A176

1966, Oct. 20
435 A176 12xu orange & black   1.00   80
  Imperf.

Birds
A177

Designs: No. 436, 12xu, Pitta moluccensis. No.
437, 12xu, Psarisomus dolhousiae. Nos. 438,
12xu, Alcedo atthis, vert. No. 439, 12xu, Oriolus
chinensis, vert. 20xu, Upupa epops, vert. 30xu,
Oriolus traillii.

Perf. 12x12½, 12½x12
1966, Oct. 31
436-441 A177 Set of 6   13.00
  Imperf., #436-441   30.00

GANEFO Asian
Games — A178

Designs: No. 442, Soccer. No. 443, Shooting.
No. 444, Swimming. No. 445, Running.

1966, Nov. 25   **Perf. 1**
442-445   Set of 4   5.00
  Imperf., #442-445   7.50
443a   A178 12xu Pair, #442-443
445a   A178 30xu Pair, #444-445
  Nos. 443A, 445A (4)   8.50

Ho Chi Minh's
Appeal for
Natl.
Resistance,
20th Anniv.
A179

Designs: No. 446, Flags, workers. No. 447,
Soldiers, workers, ships.

1967, Jan. 30
446-447 A179 12xu Set of 2   2.50

  See Nos. 501-504.

Rice
Harvest
A180

1967, Jan. 30
448 A180 12xu multicolored   1.50

Bamboo — A181

Designs: No. 449, 12xu, Bambusa arundinaceu.
No. 450, 12xu, Arundinaria rolleana. No. 451,
12xu, Arundinaria racemosa. No. 452, 12xu,
Bambusa bingami. 30xu, Bambusa nutans. 50xu,
Dendrocalamus petellaris.

1967, Feb. 2   **Perf. 12x11½**
449-454 A181 Set of 6   9.00
  Imperf., #449-454   10.00

Wild
Animals
A182

Designs: No. 455, 12xu, Cuon rutilans. No. 456,
12xu, Arctictis binturong. No. 457, 12xu, Arctonyx
collaris. 20xu, Viverra zibetha. 40xu, Macaca speciosa. 50xu, Neofelis nebulosa.

1967, Mar. 26   **Litho.**   **Perf. 12**
455-460 A182 Set of 6   11.00 6.00
  Imperf., #455-460   14.00

Fish
A184

Designs: No. 463, 12xu, Saurida filamentosa.
No. 464, 12xu, Scomberomorus niphonius. No.
465, 12xu, Haplogenys mucronatus. 20xu,
Lethrinus haematopterus. 30xu, Formio niger.
50xu, Lutianus erythropterus.

1967, July 25   **Perf. 12**
463-468 A184 Set of 6   11.00 11.00
  Imperf., #463-468   14.00

A185   A186

Launch of 1st Chinese ballistic missile: 12xu,
Missile, flag, agricultural scene. 30xu, Missile, Gate
of Heavenly Peace.

1967, July 25   **Perf. 11**
469-470 A185 Set of 2   7.50 3.00
  Imperf., #469-470

1967, Oct. 15
Russian October Revolution, 50th anniv.: 6xu,
Lenin, revolutionary soldiers. No. 472a, 12xu,
Lenin, armed mob. No. 472b, 12xu, Lenin, Marx,
Vietnamese soldiers. 20xu, Cruiser Aurora.

471-473 A186 Set of 4   4.00 3.00

  No. 472 is printed se-tenant.

2500th US
Warplane
Shot Down
A187

Design: No. 475, Plane in flames, vert.

1967, Nov. 6
474-475 A187 12xu Set of 2   8.00 8.00

1st Chinese
Hydrogen
Bomb Test
A188

Designs: 12xu, Atomic symbol, Gate of Heavenly
Peace. 20xu, Chinese lantern, atomic symbol, dove.

1967, Nov. 20
476-477 A188 Set of 2   5.00 3.00
  Imperf., #476-477   35.00

  No. 477 is 30x35mm.

A189

Designs: No. 478, 12xu, Rifle fire from trenches.
No. 479, 12xu, Militia with captured US pilot. No.
480, 12xu, Factory anti-aircraft unit. No. 481,
12xu, Naval anti- aircraft unit. 20xu, Aerial dog-
fight. 30xu, Heavy anti-aircraft battery.

1967, Dec. 19   **Perf. 12**
478-483 A189 Set of 6   6.00 6.00

Chickens — A190

Designs: No. 484, 12xu, White spotted cock,
hen. No. 485, 12xu, Black hens. No. 486, 12xu,
Bantam cock, hen. No. 487, 12xu, Bantam cock.
20xu, Fighting cocks. 30xu, Exotic hen. 40xu,
Hen, chicks from Ho region. 50xu, Dong Cao's
cock, hen.

1968, Feb. 29
484-491 A190 Set of 8   13.00 6.75
  Imperf., #484-491   17.50

Victories of
1966-67
A191

No. 492a, Soldier attacking US tank. b, Gunner
firing on US ships. c, Burning village. d, Soldier
firing mortar.
No. 493a, Attacking US artillery. b, Escorting US
prisoners. c, Interrogating refugees. d, Civilian
demonstration.

1968, Mar. 5   **Perf. 11**
492-493 A191 12xu, 2 blocks of 4   6.00 6.00
  Imperf., #492-493

Maxim Gorki (1868-1936) — A192

1968, Mar. 5
494 A192 12xu brown & black   1.50   80
  Imperf.

Roses — A193

Designs: No. 495, 12xu, Pale red. No. 496,
12xu, Orange. No. 497 12xu, Pink. 20xu, Yellow,
30xu, Dark red. 40xu, Lilac.

1968, Apr. 25 Photo.   **Perf. 11½x12**
495-500 A193 Set of 6   12.00 12.00
  Imperf., #495-500   16.00

Ho Chi Minh's Appeal for Resistance Type
of 1967

Values and colors: No. 501, 6xu, greenish blue
and yellow. No. 502, 12xu, vermilion. No. 503,
12xu, bright blue. No. 504, 12xu, brownish lilac.

1968, Apr. 25   Litho.   **Perf. 11**
Size: 25x17mm
501-504 A179 6xu, 12xu Set of 4   6.00 3.00
  Imperf., #501-504

Ho Chi Minh,
Flag — A195

1968, May 19
505 A195 12xu brown & red   2.00   50
  Imperf.

Karl Marx — A196

1968, May 19
506 A196 12xu olive green & black 1.75 25

3000th US Warplane Shot Down A197

No. 507a, 12xu, Anti-aircraft machine gunners. b, 12xu, Women firing anti-aircraft gun. No. 508a, 40xu, Vietnamese plane shooting down US plane. b, 40xu, Anti-aircraft missile.

1968, May 19
507-508 A197 Set of 2 pairs 12.00 12.00
Imperf., #507-508 15.00

Handicrafts — A198

Designs: 6xu, Rattan products. No. 510, 12xu, Ceramics. No. 511, 12xu, Bamboo products. 20xu, Ivory carving. 30xu, Lacquerware. 40xu, Silverware.

1968, July 5 *Perf. 12*
509-514 A198 Set of 6 6.50 6.50
Imperf., #509-514 15.00

Martial Arts — A199

Designs: No. 515, 12xu, Fencing. No. 516, 12xu, Stick fighting. No. 517, 12xu, Dagger fighting. 30xu, Unarmed combat. 40xu, Scimitar fighting. 50xu, Duel with swords, shields.

1968, Nov. 1
515-520 A199 Set of 6 10.00 10.00
Imperf., #515-520 17.50

Architecture — A200

Designs: No. 521, 12xu, Khue Van tower, vert. No. 522, 12xu, Bell tower, Keo pagoda, vert. 20xu, Covered bridge, Thay pagoda. 30xu, One-pillar

pagoda, Hanoi, vert. 40xu, Gateway, Ninh Phuc pagoda. 50xu, Tay Phuong pagoda.

1968, Nov. 5
521-526 A200 Set of 6 6.00 6.00
Imperf., #521-526 12.50

Foreign Solidarity with Viet Nam A201

Designs: No. 527, 12xu, Latin American guerrilla, vert. No. 528, 12xu, Cuban, Vietnamese militia. 20xu, Asian, African, Latin American soldiers, vert.

**1968, Dec. 15 Wmk. 376 *Perf. 12½*
With Gum**
527-529 A201 Set of 3 4.50 3.00

Scenes of War A202

Artworks: No. 530, 12xu, Defending the mines. No. 531, 12xu, Plowman with rifle, vert. 30xu, Repairing railway track. 40xu, Wreckage of US aircraft.

**1968, Dec. 15 Wmk. 376 *Perf. 12½*
With Gum**
530-533 A202 Set of 4 4.50 4.00

Victories in South Viet Nam A203

Designs: No. 534, 12xu, Tay Nguyen throwing grenade. No. 535, 12xu, Gun crews, Tri Thien. No. 536, 12xu, Nam Ngai shooting down US aircraft. 40xu, Insurgents, Tay Ninh, destroyed US armor. 50xu, Guerrillas preparing bamboo spike booby traps.

**1969, Feb. 16 Unwmk. *Perf. 11½*
534-538 A203 Set of 5 6.00 6.00

Timber Industry A204

Designs: 6xu, Loading timber trucks. No. 540, 12xu, Log raft running rapids. No. 541, 12xu, Launch towing log raft. No. 542, 12xu, Elephant hauling timber. No. 543, 12xu, Forest protection. 20xu, Water buffalo hauling log. 30xu, Hauling logs by overhead cable.

1969, Apr. 10
539-545 A204 Set of 7 9.00 9.00
Imperf., #539-545 10.00

Scenes of War — A205

Designs: No. 546, 12xu, Young guerrilla. No. 547, 12xu, Scout on patrol. 20xu, Female guerrilla, vert. 30xu, Halt at way station. 40xu, After a skirmish. 50xu, Liberated hamlet.

Perf. 12½x11½, 11½x12½

1969, July 20
546-551 A205 Set of 6 8.00 8.00
Imperf., #546-551 10.00

Tet Offensive Victories A206

Designs: 8xu, 12xu (No. 553), Ben Tre. No. 554, 12xu, Mortar crew, Khe Sanh, vert. No. 555, 12xu, Two soldiers, flag, Hue, vert. No. 556, 12xu, Soldier running toward US Embassy, Saigon, vert.

1969, July 31 *Perf. 11*
552-556 A206 Set of 5 3.50 3.25
Imperf., #552-556

Liberation of Hanoi, 15th Anniv. A207

Designs: No. 557, Soldier with flamethrower. No. 558, Children constructing toy buildings.

1969, Oct. 10
557-558 A207 12xu Set of 2 3.50 1.75
Imperf., #557-558

A208 A209

1969, Oct. 10
559 A208 12xu brown, black & red 2.50 80
Imperf.

Bertrand Russell Intl. War Crimes Tribunal, Stockholm and Roskilde.

1969, Nov. 20 *Perf. 12*

Fruits: No. 560, 12xu, Papaya. No. 561, 12xu, Grapefruit. 20xu, Tangerines. 30xu, Oranges. 40xu, Lychee nuts. 50xu, Persimmons.

560-565 A209 Set of 6 5.50 2.75
Imperf., #560-565 11.50

Viet Nam Labor Party, 40th Anniv. A210

Designs: No. 566, Nguyen Ai Quoc. No. 567, Chi Minh. No. 568, Le Hong Phong. No. 569, Tran Phu. No. 570, Nguyen Van Cu.

1970, Feb. 3 *Perf. 11*
566-570 A210 12xu Set of 5 4.00 4.00
Imperf., #566-570

Nos. 568-570 are 40x25mm. Nos. 566-567 issued in vertical se-tenant pairs. Nos. 568-570 issued in horizontal strips of 3.

Children's Activities — A211

Designs: No. 571, 12xu, Playing with toys. No. 572, 12xu, Three boys at kindergarten. No. 573, 20xu, Tending a garden. No. 574, 20xu, Tending water buffaloes. 30xu, Feeding chickens. 40xu, Piano, violin duet. 50xu, Flying model airplane. 60xu, Walking to school.

1970, Mar. 8 *Perf. 12*
571-578 A211 Set of 8 8.00 8.00

For overprints see Nos. 2181-2188.

Lenin A212

Designs: 12xu, Making speech. 1d, Portrait.

1970, Apr. 22 *Perf. 11*
579-580 A212 Set of 2 4.50 3.75
Imperf., #579-580

Shells A213

Designs: No. 581, 12xu, On con lon. No. 582, 12xu, Oc xa cu. 20xu, Oc tien. 1d, Oc tu va.

1970, Apr. 26 *Perf. 12½x12*
581-584 A213 Set of 4 6.50 6.50
Imperf., #581-584 10.00

Ho Chi Minh — A214

Designs: 12xu (Nos. 585, 588c, 588g), In 1930 (full face, no beard). 12xu (Nos. 586, 588b, 588f), In 1945 (facing right, beard). 2d, 6xu, Nos. 587, 588a, 588e), In 1969 (full face, beard).

1970, May 19   *Perf. 11*
585-587 A214   Set of 3   4.75   4.75
    Imperf., #585-587
Souvenir Sheets of 3
Imperf
588   Types of #585-587, #a.-c., or-   5.50
    ange background
588D   Types of #585-587, #e.-g.,   5.50
    pale lilac background

Stamps in souvenir sheets have white backgrounds. The 6xu stamp is larger than the 2d
stamp. Nos. 588a and 588e, 588c and 588g are
different colors.

Vietcong Flag A215

1970, June 6
589 A215 12xu multicolored   1.50   80
   Formation of Revolutionary Provisional Government of South Viet Nam, 1st anniv.

Fruits and Vegetables — A216

   Designs: No. 590, 12xu, Watermelon. No. 591,
12xu, Pumpkin. 20xu, Cucumber. 50xu, Zucchini.
1d, Melon.

1970, July 15   *Perf. 12*
590-594 A216   Set of 5   6.00   6.00
    Imperf., #590-594   13.00

Consumer Industries — A217

   Designs: No. 595, Coal miners, truck. No. 596,
Power linesman, vert. No. 597, Hands winding
thread on bobbin, vert. No. 597, Stoker, power
plant, vert.

    Perf. 12x11½, 11½x12
1970, Aug. 25   *Litho. & Engr.*
595-598 A217 12xu Set of 4   4.00   3.25

Agriculture — A218

1970, Aug. 25   *Litho.*   *Perf. 11*
599 A218 12xu multicolored   2.50   80

Democratic Republic of Viet Nam, 25th Anniv. A219

Famous people: No. 600, 12xu, Vo Thi Sau facing firing squad. No. 601, 12xu, Nguyen Van Troi,
captors. No. 602, 12xu, Phan Din Giot attacking
pillbox. No. 603, 12xu, Ho Chi Minh. 20xu,
Nguyen Viet Xuan, troops in battle. 1d, Nguyen Van
Be attacking tank with mine.

1970, Sept. 2
600-605 A219   Set of 6   4.50   4.00
    Imperf., #600-605
   No. 603 is 41x28mm.

Indo-Chinese People's Summit Conf. — A220

1970, Oct. 25
606 A220 12xu multicolored   2.50   80
    Imperf.

Bananas — A221

   Designs: No. 607, 12xu, Tay. No. 608, 12xu,
Tieu. 50xu, Ngu. 1d, Mat.

1970, Oct. 25   *Perf. 12*
607-610 A221   Set of 4   7.00   4.75
    Imperf., #607-610   10.00

Friedrich Engels A222

1970, Nov. 28   *Perf. 11*
611-612 A222 12xu, 1d, set of 2   3.25   3.25

Snakes A223

   Designs: 12xu, Akistrodon ciatus. 20xu, Calliophis macclellandii. 50xu, Bungarus faciatus. 1d,
Trimeresurus gramineus.

1970, Nov. 30   *Photo.*   *Perf. 12x11½*
613-616 A223   Set of 4   6.00
    Imperf., #613-616   20.00

Natl. Liberation Front of South Viet Nam, 10th Anniv. A224

   Design: 6xu, Mother and child, flag, vert.

1970, Dec. 20   *Litho.*   *Perf. 11*
617-618 A224   Set of 2   2.50   1.75
    Imperf., #617-618

Launching of 1st Chinese Satellite, 1st Anniv. A225

1971, Apr. 10
619-620 A225 12xu, 50xu Set of 2   2.00   2.00
    Imperf., #619-620

Ho Chi Minh A226

   Denominations: 1xu, 3xu, 10xu, 12xu.

1971, May 19
621-624 A226   Set of 4   1.75   1.75
    Imperf., #621-624
624a   Souvenir sheet of 1, imperf.
   No. 624a contains one 52x52mm stamp.

Tay Son Uprising, Bicent. — A227

1971, June 1
625-626 A227 6xu, 12xu, set of 2   1.75   1.75
    Imperf., #625-626

Marx, Music for The Internationale A228

1971, June 20   *Perf. 12½*
627 A228 12xu orange, black & red   75   75
    Imperf.
   Paris Commune, cent.

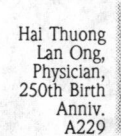
Hai Thuong Lan Ong, Physician, 250th Birth Anniv. A229

1971, July 1
628-629 A229 12xu, 50xu Set of 2   3.50   2.00
    Imperf., #628-629

Statues from Tay Phuong Pagoda — A230

   Designs: No. 630, 12xu, Vasumitri. No. 631,
12xu, Kapimala. No. 632, 12xu, Dhikaca. No. 633,
12xu, Sangkayasheta. 30xu, Bouddha Nandi. 40xu,
Rahulata. 50xu, Sangha Nandi. 1d, Cakyamuni.

1971, July 30   *Photo.*   *Perf. 12*
630-637 A230   Set of 8   11.00   11.00
    Imperf., #630-637   17.00

Ho Chi Minh Working Youth Union, 40th Anniv. — A231

1971, Sept. 7   *Litho.*   *Perf. 11*
638 A231 12xu multicolored   1.50   80
    Imperf.

Flight of Luna 16 — A232

   Luna 16: No. 639a, 12xu, Return from Moon.
No. 639b, 12xu, Flight to Moon. 1d, On Moon.

1971, Sept. 17
639-640 A232   Set of 3   4.00   4.00
    Imperf., #639-640   12.00

Flight of Luna 17 A233

   Designs: No. 641, 12xu, Landing on Moon, vert.
No. 642 12xu, On Moon. 1d, Lunakhod 1 crossing
lunar crevasse.

1971, Oct. 15
641-643 A233   Set of 3   4.00   4.00
    Imperf., #641-643   20.00

Five Tigers — A234

   Folk paintings: No. 644, 12xu, White tiger. No.
645, 12xu, Red tiger. No. 646, 12xu, Yellow tiger.
40xu, Green tiger. 50xu, Black tiger. 1d, Five
tigers.

1971, Nov. 25   *Perf. 12*
644-649 A234   Set of 6   10.00   7.00
    Imperf., #644-649   12.50
    Size: 90x119mm
    Imperf
650 A234 1d multicolored   12.00

Chinese Communist Party, 50th Anniv. A235

1971, Dec. 1   *Perf. 11*
651 A235 12xu multicolored   1.50   40

Mongolian People's Republic, 50th Anniv. — A236

1971, Dec. 25
652 A236 12xu multicolored   1.50   40

Folk Engravings from Dong Ho — A237

Designs: No. 653a, 12xu, Traditional wrestling. No. 653b, 12xu, Drum procession. No. 654a, 12xu, Gathering coconuts, vert. No. 654b, 12xu, Jealousy, vert. 40xu, Wedding of mice. 50xu, Frog school.

1972, Jan. 30
653-656 A237   Set of 6   10.00 10.00
     Imperf., #653-656   7.50

No. 653 is tete-beche.

3rd Natl. Trade Unions Congress A238

Designs: 1xu, Workers facing right. 12xu, Workers facing left.

1972, May 1
657-658 A238   Set of 2   2.50 1.75
     Imperf., #657-658

Natl. Resistance, 25th Anniv. — A239

Designs: No. 659, Munitions worker. No. 660, Soldier in battle. No. 661, Woman in rice paddy. No. 662, Text of Ho Chi Minh's appeal.

1972, May 5
659-662 A239 12xu Set of 4   3.50 1.75
     Imperf., #659-662

Ho Chi Minh's Birthplace A240

Design: No. 664, Home in Hanoi.

1972, May 19
663-664 A240 12xu Set of 2   2.50 1.75
     Imperf., #663-664

A241   A242

1972, June 20
665-666 A241 12xu Set of 2   5.00 2.50
     Imperf., #665-666

3500th US warplane shot down. Added inscription on No. 666 reads "NGAY 20.4.1972."

1972, Aug. 15
Georgi Dimitrov (1882-1949), Bulgarian politician: No. 668, Dimitrov at Leipzig Court, 1933.

667-668 A242 12xu Set of 2   2.50 1.75
     Imperf., #667-668

Birds — A243

Designs: No. 669, 12xu, Lobivanellus indicus. No. 670, 12xu, Anas falcata. 30xu, Bubulcus ibis. 40xu, Gallicrex cinerea. 50xu, Prophyria porphyrio. 1d, Leptoptilos dubius.

1972, Oct. 12   *Perf. 12*
669-674 A243   Set of 6   10.00 8.00
     Imperf., #669-674

A244   A245

4000th US warplane shot down: No. 676, Gunner holding shell.

1972, Oct. 19   *Perf. 11*
675-676 A244 12xu Set of 2   6.00 1.75
     Imperf., #675-676

1972, Dec. 1   *Perf. 12*
Tay Nguyen folk dances: No. 677, 12xu, Drum. No. 678, 12xu, Umbrella. No. 679, 12xu, Shield.

20xu, Horse. 30xu, Ca Dong. 40xu, Rice pounding. 50xu, Gong. 1d, Cham rong.

677-684 A245   Set of 8   9.00 9.00
     Imperf., #677-684   12.50

Flight of Soyuz 11 A246

Designs: 12xu, Soyuz 11 docking with Salyut laboratory. 1d, Soyuz 11 cosmonauts.

1972, Dec. 30   *Perf. 11*
685-686 A246 Set of 2   3.50 2.75
     Imperf., #685-686   20.00

Wild Animals A247

Designs: 12xu, Cuon alpinus. 30xu, Panthera pardus. 50xu, Felis bengalensis. 1d, Lutra lutra.

1973, Feb. 15   *Perf. 12½*
687-690 A247   Set of 4   7.00 5.00
     Imperf., #687-690

Copernicus A248

Copernicus and: No. 691a, 12xu, Armillary sphere. No. 691b, 12xu, Sun. 30xu, Signature, vert.

1973, Feb. 17   *Perf. 11*
691-692 A248   Set of 3   3.50 3.00
     Imperf., #691-692

Engravings on Ngoc Lu Bronze Drums — A249

Designs: No. 693, Drummers (Nha Danh Trong). No. 694, Pounding rice (Nha Gia Gao). No. 695, Dancers (Mua). No. 696, War canoe (Thuyen). No. 697, Birds (Chim, Thu).

1973, Apr. 12
693-697 A249 12xu Set of 5   4.00 4.00
     Imperf., #693-697

Wild Animals — A250

Designs: 12xu, Tragulus javanicus. 30xu, Capricornis sumatraensis. 50xu, Sus scrofa. 1d, Moschus moschiferus.

1973, May 25   *Perf. 12x12½*
698-701 A250 Set of 4   5.00 5.00
     Imperf., #698-701   9.00

Birds — A251

Designs: No. 702, 12xu, Pycnonotus jocosus. No. 703, 12xu, Megalurus palustris. 20xu, Capsychus saularis. 40xu, Rhipidura albicollis. 50xu, Parus major. 1d, Zosterops japonica.

1973, July 15   *Perf. 12*
702-707 A251   Set of 6   7.00 7.00
     Imperf., 702-707   10.00

Disabled Soldiers
A252   A252a

1973, July 27   *Perf. 11*
708-709 A252, A252a 12xu Set of 2   2.25
     Imperf., #708-709

Three Readiness Youth Movement A253

Designs: No. 710, Road building. No. 711, Open-air class. No. 712, On the march.

1973, Sept. 2
710-712 A253 12xu Set of 3   2.50 1.25
     Imperf., #710-712

Democratic People's Republic of Korea, 25th Anniv. A254

1973, Sept. 9
713 A254 12xu multicolored   1.50 40
     Imperf.

4181st US Warplane Shot Down — A255

Designs: No. 714, 12xu, US B-52 hit by air attack. No. 715, 12xu, US B-52, fighter crashing over Haiphong Harbor. No. 716, 12xu, Anti-aircraft battery. 1d, Aircraft wreckage caught in fishing net.

1973, Oct. 10
714-717 A255 Set of 4   7.00 3.75
     Imperf., #714-717

Flowers — A256

Designs: 6xu, 12xu (No. 719), Chrysanthemum (Cuc), No. 720, 12xu, Rose. No. 721, 12xu, Dahlia. No. 722, 12xu, Chrysanthemum (Bach mi). No. 723, 12xu, Chrysanthemum (Dai doa).

1974, Jan. 15
718-723 A256 Set of 6   50.00
   Imperf., #718-723

No. 718 may not have been officially released.

Elephants
A257

Designs: No. 724, 12xu, Hauling logs. No. 725, 12xu, War elephant. 40xu, Setting logs in place. 50xu, Circus elephant. 1d, Carrying war supplies.

1974, Feb. 10   *Perf. 11½*
724-728 A257 Set of 5   7.50   7.00
  Imperf., #724-728   12.00

Victory at Dien Bien Phu, 20th Anniv. — A258

Designs: a, Dien Bien Phu soldier's badge. b, Soldier waving victory flag.

1974, May 7   *Perf. 11*
729 A258 12xu Pair, #a.-b.   2.50   80
 Imperf.

Three Responsibilities Women's Movement — A259

Designs: a, Armed worker, peasant. b, Female textile worker.

1974, June 1
730 A259 12xu Pair, #a.-b.   2.50
 Imperf.

A260   A261

Chrysanthemums: No. 731, 12xu, Brown. No. 732, 12xu, Yellow (Vang). 20xu, Ngoc Khong Tuoc. 30xu, White. 40xu, Kim. 50xu, Hong mi. 60xu, Gam. 1d, Lilac.

1974, June 20   *Perf. 12x12½*
731-738 A260 Set of 8   8.00   4.00
  Imperf., #731-738   11.00

1974, Aug. 15   *Perf. 11*
Industrial plants: No. 739, 12xu, Corchorus capsularis. No. 740, 12xu, Cyperus tojet jormis. 30xu, Morus alba.

739-741 A261 Set of 3   4.50   2.75
  Imperf., #739-741

Liberation of Hanoi, 20th Anniv. — A262

Designs: a, Woman laying bricks. b, Soldier holding child waving flag.

1974, Oct. 10
742 A262 12xu Pair, #a.-b.   2.50   80

  Imperf., #743-744

Marine Life A264

Designs: No. 745, 12xu, Rhizostoma. No. 746, 12xu, Loligo. 30xu, Haleotis. 40xu, Pteria martensii. 50xu, Sepia officinalis. 1d, Palinurus japonicus.

1974, Oct. 25   *Perf. 12½*
745-750 A264 Set of 6   7.00   2.50
  Imperf., #745-750   12.00

People's Republic of Albania, 30th Anniv. — A265

Designs: a, Natl. arms. b, Albanian, Vietnamese flags, women.

1974, Nov. 29   *Perf. 11*
752 A265 12xu Pair, #a.-b.   2.25   80
 Imperf.

Paris Agreement on Vietnam, 2nd Anniv. — A266

Designs: No. 753, Intl. Conference on Viet Nam in session, 5-line inscription. No. 754, Signing of Paris Agreement, 4-line inscription.

1975, Jan. 27
753-754 A266 12xu Set of 2   2.50   80
 Imperf.

Medicinal Plants — A267

Designs: No. 755, 12xu, Costus speciosus. No. 756, 12xu, Curcuma zedoaria. No. 757, 12xu, Rosa laevigata. 30xu, Erythrina indica. 40xu, Lilium brownii. 50xu, Hibiscus sagittifolius. 60xu, Papaver somniferum. 1d, Belamcanda chinensis.

1975, Feb. 2   *Perf. 11½x12*
755-762 A267 Set of 8   8.00   8.00
  Imperf., #755-762   12.50

Vietnamese Labor Party, 45th Anniv. A268

Designs: No. 763, 12xu, Tran Phu. No. 764, 12xu, Le Hong Phong. No. 765, 12xu, Nguyen Van Cu. No. 766, 12xu, Ngo Gia Tu. 60xu, Ho Chi Minh in 1924, vert.

1975, Feb. 3   *Perf. 11*
763-767 A268 Set of 5   2.75   2.00
  Imperf., #763-767

Fruit — A269

Designs: No. 768, 12xu, Achras sapota. No. 769, 12xu, Persica vulgaris. 20xu, Eugenia jambos. 30xu, Chrysophyllum cainito. 40xu, Lucuma mamosa. 50xu, Prunica granitum. 60xu, Durio ziberthinus. 1d, Prunus salicina.

1975, Apr. 25   *Perf. 12x12½*
768-775 A269 Set of 8   7.50   6.00
  Imperf., 768-775   12.00

Ho Chi Minh, 85th Birthday — A270

1975, May 19   *Perf. 11*
776-777 A270 12xu, 60xu, set of 2   3.50   1.25
  Imperf., #776-777

People's Republic of Poland, 30th Anniv. A271

1975, July 5
778-781 A271   1xu, 2xu, 3xu, 12xu, set of 4   3.00
  Imperf., #778-781

Flags — A272

Natl. Arms — A273

Flag of North Viet Nam and: No. 782, Draped flag. No. 783, Flag with star & cresent. No. 784, DDR flag and handshake.

1975
782-785 A272-A273 12xu Set of 4   8.00
  Imperf., #782-784

People's Republic of China, 25th anniv. (#782), Republic of Algeria, 20th anniv. (#783), German Democratic Republic, 25th anniv. (#784), liberation of Hungary, 30th anniv. (#785).
Issued: No. 782, 7/5. Nos. 783-785, 8/15.

Independence, 30th Anniv. — A274

Designs: No. 786, Flag. No. 787, Natl. arms. Nos. 788-789, Ho Chi Minh proclaiming independence.

1975, Sept. 2
786-788 A274 12xu Set of 3   3.50   1.25
      Souvenir Sheet
        Imperf
789   A274 20xu multicolored

No. 789 contains one 45x30mm stamp.

Reptiles — A275

Designs: No. 790, 12xu, Dermochelys coriacea. No. 791, 12xu, Physignathus cocincinus. 20xu, Hydrophis brookii. 30xu, Platysternum megacephalum. 40xu, Leiolepis belliana. 50xu, Python molurus. 60xu, Naja hannah. 1d, Draco maculatus.

1975, Nov. 25   *Perf. 12*
790-797 A275 Set of 8   8.00   7.00
  Imperf., #790-797

Butterflies
A276

Designs: No. 798, 12xu, Pathysa antiphates. No. 799, 12xu, Danaus plexippus. 20xu, Cynautocera papilionaria. 30xu, Maenas salaminia. 40xu, Papilio machaon. 50xu, Ixias pyrene. 60xu, Eusemia vetula. 1d, Eriboea.

1976, Jan. 6
798-805 A276 Set of 8   9.00 9.00
    Imperf., #798-805

No. 799 misspelled "Danais."

Lan Hoang Thao
Orchid — A277

1976, Jan. 25   *Perf. 11*
806-807 A277 6xu, 12xu, set of 2   4.00 1.75

Wild
Animals — A278

Designs: No. 808, 12xu, Callosciurus erythraeus. No. 809, 12xu, Paguma larvata. 20xu, Macaca mulatta. 30xu, Hystrix hodgsoni. 40xu, Nyctereutes procyonoides. 50xu, Selenarctos thibetanus. 60xu, Panthera pardus. 1d, Cynocephalus variegatus.

1976, Mar. 20   *Perf. 12*
808-815 A278 Set of 8   7.00 2.50
    Imperf., #808-815   12.00

1st Elections
to Unified
Natl. Assembly
A279

Designs: 6xu (No. 816), Map, hand placing ballot in ballot box. 6xu (No. 817), 12xu, Map, voters.

1976, Apr. 10   *Perf. 11*
816-818 A279 Set of 3   3.50 1.25
    Imperf., #816-818

Size of Nos. 817-818 is 35x22mm.

Unified Natl.
Assembly, 1st
Session
A280

Design: 12xu, Inscribed "Doc Lap Thong Nhat Chu Nghia Xa Hoi."

1976, June 24
819-820 A280 6xu, 12xu, set of 2   2.50 80

Reunification of Viet
Nam — A281

1976, June 24   *Perf. 12x12½*
821 A281 12xu multicolored   1.50   40

Orchids — A282

Designs: No. 822, 12xu, Habenaria rhodocheila. No. 823, 12xu, Dendrobium devonianum. 20xu, Dendrobium tortile. 30xu, Doritis pulcherrima. 40xu, Dendrobium farmeri. 50xu, Dendrobium aggregatum. 60xu, Eria pannea. 1d, Paphiopedilum concolor.

1976, June 24   *Perf. 12*
822-829 A282 Set of 8   8.00 2.00
    Imperf., #822-829   12.00

Socialist Republic of Viet Nam

AREA—127,246 sq. mi.
POP.—73,104,000
CAPITAL—Hanoi

Fish — A284

Designs: No. 831, 12xu, Lutjanus sebae. No. 832, 12xu, Dampieria melanotaenia. 20xu, Therapon theraps. 30xu, Amphiprion bifasciatus. 40xu, Abudefduf sexfasciatus. 50xu, Heniochus acuminatus. 60xu, Amphiprion macrostoma. 1d, Symphorus spilurus.

1976, Aug. 15   *Perf. 12*
831-838 A284 Set of 8   6.00 6.00
    Imperf., #831-838   11.00

Viet Nam
Worker's
Party, 4th
Natl.
Congress
A285

1976, Nov. 12   *Perf. 11*
839-844 A285 2xu, 3xu, 5xu, 10xu,
    12xu, 20xu, set of
    6   3.50 2.50

Viet Nam Communist Party, 4th Natl.
Congress — A286

Designs: a, Agriculture, industry. b, Ho Chi Minh, worker, farmer, soldier, scientist.

1976, Dec. 10
845 A286 12xu Pair, #a.-b.   2.50   80
    Imperf.

See Nos. 951-954.

Unification of Viet
Nam — A287

1976, Dec. 14
846-847 A287 6xu, 12xu, set of 2   2.50   80
    Imperf., #846-847

General
Offensive,
1975
A288

Designs: 2xu, 50xu, Liberation of Buon Me Thuot. 3xu, 1d, Tanks liberating Da Nang. 6xu, 2d, Tank, soldiers liberating Presidential palace, Saigon.

1976, Dec. 14
848-853 A288 Set of 6   4.50 4.50

Dragonflies
A289

Designs: No. 856, 12xu, Ho. No. 857, 12xu, Bao. 20xu, Canh dom. 30xu, Nuong. 40xu, Suoi. 50xu, Canh vang. 60xu, Canh khoang. 1d, Canh den.

1977, Jan. 25   *Perf. 12*
856-863 A289 Set of 8   7.00 1.50
    Imperf., #856-863   16.00

Rare
Birds — A290

Designs: 12xu (No. 864), 60xu, Buceros bicornis. 12xu (No. 865), Ptilolaemus tickelli. 20xu, Berenicornis comatus. 30xu, Aceros undulatus. 40xu, Anthracoceros malabaricus. 50xu, Anthracoceros malayanus. 1d, Aceros nipalensis.

1977, Apr. 15
864-871 A290 Set of 8   6.00 2.25
    Imperf., #864-871   9.00

Natl. Assembly General
Elections, 1st
Anniv. — A291

Bronze drum and: 4xu, Thang Long Tower. 5xu, Map. 12xu, Lotus blossom. 50xu, Flag.

1977, Apr. 25   *Perf. 11*
872-875 A291 Set of 4   4.50 2.00
    Imperf., #872-875

Beetles
A292

Designs: No. 876, 12xu, Black-spotted (Dom den). No. 877, 12xu, Yellow-spotted (Lang vang). 20xu, Veined (Van gach). 30xu, Green (Nhung xanh). 40xu, Green-spotted (Hoa xanh). 50xu, Black (Van den). 60xu, Leopard skin (Da bao). 1d, Nine-spotted (Chin cham).

1977, June 15   *Perf. 12½x12*
876-883 A292 Set of 8   7.00 1.75
    Imperf., #876-883   16.00

Wildflowers — A293

Designs: No. 884, 12xu, Thevetia peruviana. No. 885, 12xu, Broussonetia papvrifera. 20xu, Aleurites montana. 30xu, Cerbera manghes. 40xu, Cassia multijuga. 50xu, Cassia nodosa. 60xu, Hibiscus schizopetalus. 1d, Lagerstroesnia speciosa.

1977, Aug. 19   *Perf. 12x12½*
884-891 A293 Set of 8   5.00 1.75
    Imperf., #884-891   10.00

A294   A295

Dahlias: 6xu (No. 892), 12xu (No. 894), Pink. 6xu (No. 893), 12xu (No. 895), Orange cactus.

1977, Sept. 10   *Perf. 11*
892-895 A294 Set of 4   4.50 1.75

See Nos. 921-924.

Goldfish — A296

Designs: No. 901, 12xu, Dong nai. No. 902, 12xu, Velvet (Hoa nhung). 20xu, Blue Chinese (Tau xanh). 30xu, Dragon-eyed (Mat bong). 40xu, Cam trang. 50xu, Five-colored (Ngu sac). 60xu, Dong nai. 1d, Thap cam.

1977, Oct. 20   *Perf. 12*
901-908 A296 Set of 8   7.50 1.75
   Imperf., #901-908   14.50

A297   A298

Russian October Revolution, 60th anniv.: 12xu (No. 909, olive background), 12xu (No. 910, blue background), Ho Chi Minh, Lenin banner. 50xu, Mother holding child with flag. 1d, Workers, farmers, Moscow Kremlin, cruiser Aurora.

1977, Nov. 7
909-912 A297 Set of 4   3.00 2.50

1978, Jan. 25

Songbirds: 12xu, Gracula religiosa. No. 914, 20xu, Garrulax canorus. No. 915, 20xu, Streptopelia chinensis. 30xu, Linius schach. 40xu, Garrulax formosus. 50xu, Garrulax chinensis. 60xu, Acridotheres cristatellus. 1d, Garrulax yersini.

913-920 A298 Set of 8   6.00 1.75
   Imperf., #913-920   12.00

Cultivated Flower Type of 1977

Designs: 5xu, 10xu, Sunflower. 6xu, 12xu, Pansy.

1978, Mar. 20   *Perf. 11*
921-924 A294 Set of 4   3.50 2.00

Intl. Children's Day (June 1977) — A299

1978, Mar. 20
925 A299 12xu multicolored   1.50 40

Sports — A300

Designs: No. 926, 12xu, Discus. No. 927, 12xu, ng jump. 20xu, Hurdles. 30xu, Hammer throw. xu, Shot put. 50xu, Javelin. 60xu, Running. 1d, h jump.

78, Apr. 10   *Perf. 11½*
926-933 A300 Set of 8   4.50 1.75
   Imperf., #926-933   10.00

A301   A302

4th Viet Nam Trade Union Congress: No. 934, Trade Union emblem. No. 935, Ho Chi Minh, workers.

1978, May 1   *Perf. 11*
934-935 A301 10xu Set of 2   2.50 80

1978, May 15

Designs: 10xu, Ho Chi Minh conducting orchestra. 12xu, Ho Chi Minh's mausoleum, horiz.

936-937 A302 Set of 2   2.50 80

No. 937 is 39x23mm.

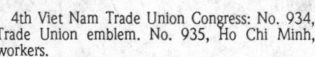

Young Pioneers' Cultural Palace, Hanoi — A303

1978, May 29
938 A303 10xu multicolored   1.50 40

Intl. Children's Day.

Sculptures from Tay Phuong Pagoda — A304

Designs: No. 939, 12xu, Sanakavasa. No. 940, 12xu, Parsva. No. 941, 12xu, Punyasas. No. 942, 20xu, Kumarata. No. 943, 20xu, Nagarjuna. 30xu, Yayata. 40xu, Cadiep. 50xu, Ananda. 60xu, Buddhamitra. 1d, Asvagmosa.

1978, July 1   *Perf. 12*
939-948 A304 Set of 10   9.50 2.00
   Imperf., #939-948   25.00

Cuban Revolution, 25th Anniv. — A305

1978, July 20   *Perf. 11*
949-950 A305 6xu, 12xu Set of 2   2.50 80

Types of 1976

Designs: 6xu (No. 951), 12xu (No. 953), like #845a. 6xu (No. 952), 12xu (No. 952), like #845b.

1978, Aug. 15
951-954 A286 Set of 4   4.00 2.00

Space Exploration, 20th Anniv. — A306

Designs: No. 955, 12xu, Sputnik. No. 956, 12xu, Venus 1. 30xu, Spacecraft docking. 40xu, Molniya 1. 60xu, Soyuz. 2d, Cosmonauts Gubarev, Grechko.

1978, Aug. 28   *Perf. 12½x12*
955-960 A306 Set of 6   5.00 1.50
   Imperf., #955-960

World Telecommunications Day — A307

Designs: a, Printed circuit. b, ITU emblem.

1978, Sept. 25   *Perf. 11*
962 A307 12xu Pair, #a.-b.   2.50 80
   Imperf.   20.00

20th Congress of Socialist Postal Ministers — A308

1978, Sept. 25
963 A308 12xu multicolored   1.50 40

Chrysanthemums A309

Designs: No. 964, 12xu, Tim. No. 965, 12xu, Kim tien. 20xu, Hong. 30xu, Van tho. 40xu, Vang. 50xu, Thuy tim. 60xu, Vang mo. 1d, Nau do.

1978, Oct. 1   *Perf. 12*
964-971 A309 Set of 8   5.50 1.75
   Imperf., #964-971   12.00

Dinosaurs A310

Designs: No. 972, 12xu, Plesiosaurus. No. 973, 12xu, Brontosaurus. 20xu, Iguanodon. 30xu, Tyrannosaurus rex. 40xu, Stegosaurus. 50xu, Mosasaurus. 60xu, Triceratops. 1d, Pteranodon.

1979, Jan. 1   Litho.   *Perf. 11½*
972-979 A310 Set of 8   11.00 1.50
   Imperf., #972-979   20.00

No. 977 misspelled "Mozasaurus."

A311   A312

1979, Jan. 1   *Perf. 11*
980 A311 12xu multicolored   1.50 40
   Imperf.

Socialist Republic of Cuba, 20th anniv.

1979, Feb. 1

Quang Trung's victory over the Chinese, 190th Anniv.: No. 981, Battle plan. No. 982, Quang Trung.

981-982 A312 12xu Set of 2   2.50 80
   a.   Perf 12, #981-982

Albert Einstein, Physicist — A313

Designs: 983, 12xu, Einstein. 60xu, Equation, sun, planets.

1979, Mar. 14
983-984 A313 12xu, 60xu, set of 2   3.00 1.50

Domestic Animals A314

Designs: 10xu, Ram. 12xu, Ox. 20xu, Ewe, lamb. 30xu, White buffalo, vert. 40xu, Cow. 50xu, Goat. 60xu, Water buffalo, calf. 1d, Young goat, vert.

1979, Mar. 20   *Perf. 12*
985-992 A314 Set of 8   7.50 1.50
   Imperf., #985-992   10.00

Five Year Plan (1976-80) — A315

Designs: Nos. 993, 998, Map, emblem. Nos. 994, 999, Factory worker. Nos. 995, 1000, Peasant woman, tractor. Nos. 996, 1001, Soldier. Nos. 997, 1002, Man, atom, compass.

1979   *Perf. 11*
993-997 A315 6xu set of 5
998-1002 A315 12xu Set of 5
1000a   Perf. 12
   Nos. 993-1002 (10)   10.00

Issued: Nos. 993-997, 5/1. Nos. 998-1002, 6/1. No. 993, 996-1002 on toned paper.

Philaserdica
'79, Intl.
Stamp
Exhibition,
Sofia, Bulgaria
A316

1979, May 27　　　　**Perf. 12**
1003-1004 A316　12xu, 30xu, set of
2　　　　　　　　　　　2.50　80

Intl. Year of the
Child — A317

Designs: 12xu, Ho Chi Minh, children. 20xu,
Nurse, mother, child. 50xu, Children with glider,
painting supplies. 1d, Girls of different races.

1979, June 1　　　　**Perf. 11**
1005-1008 A317　Set of 4　　　4.00　3.00

Ornamental Birds — A318

Designs: No. 1009, 12xu, Lophura diardi. No.
1010, 12xu, Tragopan temminckii. 20xu, Pha-
sianus colchicus. 30xu, Lophura edwardsi. 40xu,
Lophura nycthemera, vert. 50xu, Polyplectron
germaini, vert. 60xu, Rheinartia ocellata, vert. 1d,
Pavo muticus, vert.

1979, June 16　　　　**Perf. 12**
1009-1016 A318　Set of 8　　　6.50　1.75
　　　　Imperf., #1009-1016　　　12.50

Orchids
A319

Designs: No. 1017, 12xu, Dendrobium hetero-
cacpum. No. 1018, 12xu, Cymbidium hybridum.
20xu, Rhynchostylis gigantea. 30xu, Dendrobium
mobile. 40xu, Aerides falcatum. 50xu, Paphiopedilum callosum. 60xu, Vanda teres. 1d, Dendrobium phalaenopsis.

1979, Aug. 10　　　　**Perf. 12**
1017-1024 A319　Set of 8　　　6.50　1.75
　　　　Imperf., #1017-1024　　　13.00

Cats
A320

Designs: No. 1025, 12xu, Meo tam the. No.
1026, 12xu, Meo muop, vert. 20xu, Meo khoang,
vert. 30xu, Meo dom van. 40xu, Meo muop dom,
vert. 50xu, Meo vang, vert. 60xu, Meo xiem. 1d,
Meo van am.

1979, Nov. 10
1025-1032 A320　Set of 8　　　6.50　5.75
　　　　Imperf., #1025-1032　　　13.00

Vietnamese
People's
Army, 25th
Anniv.
A321

Designs: a, People greeting soldiers. b, Frontier
guards.

1979, Dec. 22　　　　**Perf. 11**
1033 A321　12xu Pair, #a.-b.　　80　80

Roses — A322

Designs: 1xu, 12xu (No. 1036), Red, pink roses.
2xu, 12xu (No. 1037), Single pink rose.

1980, Jan. 1
1034-1037 A322　Set of 4　　　3.50　1.75
　　　　See Nos. 1084-1085.

Aquatic
Flowers — A323

Designs: No. 1038, 12xu, Nelumbium
nuciferum. No. 1039, 12xu, Nymphala stellata.
20xu, Ipomola reptans. 30xu, Nymphoides
indicum. 40xu, Jussiala repens. 50xu, Eichhornia
crassipes. 60xu, Monochoria voginalis. 1d,
Nelumbo nucifera.

1980, Jan. 15　　　　**Perf. 12½**
1038-1045 A323　Set of 8　　　5.00　1.50
　　　　Imperf., #1038-1045　　　9.00

Vietnamese Communist Party, 50th
Anniv. — A324

Designs: No. 1046a, Ho Chi Minh proclaiming
independence, 1945. No. 1046b, Peasants with
banner, improvised weapons. No. 1047a, Map,
soldiers, tanks storming palace. No. 1047b, Soldiers
waving flag at Dien Bien Phu. 2d, Ho Chi Minh,
soldiers and workers.

1980, Feb. 3　　　　**Perf. 11**
1046 A324　12xu Pair, #a.-b.
1047 A324　20xu Pair, #a.-b.
1048 A324　　2d multicolored
　　　Nos. 1046-1048 (5)　　3.50　3.50

Lenin,
110th
Anniv. of
Birth
A325

1980, Apr. 22　　　　**Perf. 12**
1049-1051 A325　6xu, 12xu, 1d, set
　　　of 3　　　　　　　　3.25　2.00

1980
Summer
Olympics,
Moscow
A326

Designs: No. 1052, 12xu, Hurdles. No. 1053,
12xu, Running. 20xu, Team handball. 30xu, Soccer. 40xu, Wrestling. 50xu, Gymnastics, horiz.
60xu, Swimming, horiz. 1d, Sailing, horiz.

1980, May 1　**Perf. 12x12½, 12½x12**
1052-1059 A326　Set of 8　　　5.00　1.50
　　　　Imperf., #1052-1059　　　10.00

A327　　　　　　　　A328

Ho Chi Minh, 90th anniv. of birth: 12xu, In
1924. 40xu, As president.

1980, May 19　　　　**Perf. 11**
1060-1061 A327　Set of 2　　　2.00　1.25

1980, June 15
1062 A328　5xu multicolored　　1.00　40

Intl. Children's Day.

Designs: No. 1070, 12xu, Rhincodon typus. No.
1071, 12xu, Galeocerdo cuvier. 20xu, Orectolobus
japonicus. 30xu, Heterodontus zebra. 40xu, Dasy-
atis uarnak. 50xu, Pristis microdon. 60xu, Sphyrna
lewini. 1d, Myliobatis tobijei.

Saltwater Fish — A330

1980, Aug. 1　　　　**Perf. 12**
1070-1077 A330　Set of 8　　　6.00　1.75
　　　　Imperf., #1070-1077　　　11.50

A331　　　　　　　A332

Post and Telecommunications Office, 35th
Anniv.: 12xu, Ho Chi Minh reading newspaper.
20xu, Ho Chi Minh talking on telephone. 50xu,
Kim Dong carrying bird in cage. 1d, Dish antenna.

1980, Aug. 15　**Litho.**　**Perf. 12½**
1078-1081 A331　Set of 4　　　4.00　3.75

1980, Aug. 25　**Perf. 11, 12 (#1083)**
Natl. Telecommunications Day: No. 1082, Telephone switchboard operator. No. 1083, Train, map.

1082-1083 A332　12xu Set of 2　　2.25　1.60

Rose Type of 1980

Roses: No. 1084, Pink. No. 1085, Red and pink.

1980, Aug. 25　　　　**Perf. 11**
　　　　Size: 20x24mm
1084-1085 A322　12xu Set of 2　　2.00　1.40

For surcharge see No. 1385.

Republic of Vietnam,
35th Anniv. — A333

Designs: No. 1086, 12xu, Ho Chi Minh. No.
1087, 12xu, Natl. arms. 40xu, Pac Bo Cave. 1d,
Source of Lenin River, horiz.

1980, Sept. 2　　　　**Perf. 12½**
1086-1089 A333　Set of 4　　　5.00　5.00

A334　　　　　　　A335

Natl. emblems: 6xu, Arms. No. 1091, 12xu,
lag, horiz. No. 1092, 12xu, Anthem.

1980, Sept. 20　　　　**Perf. 12**
1090-1092 A334　Set of 3

1980, Oct. 6　　　　**Perf. 11**
Nguyen Trai, 600th birth anniv.: 12xu, Nguyen
Trai. 50xu, Books, horiz. 1d, Ho Chi Minh reading
commemorative stele, Con Son.

1093-1095 A335　Set of 3　　　5.00　5.00

For surcharge see No. 1386.

A336   A337

H
w

1
l

1

N
Pe
Th
tic
spe

1
10   5.50 1.40
                       10.00

Ornamental
Fish
A338

Designs: No. 1106, 12xu, Betta splendens. No. 1107, 12xu, Symphysodon aequifasciata. 20xu, Poecilobrycon eques. 30xu, Gyrinocheilus aymonieri. 40xu, Barbus tetrazona. 50xu, Pterophyllum eimekei. 60xu, Xiphophorus helleri. 1d, Trichopterus sumatranus.

1981, Jan. 15   *Perf. 12*
1106-1113 A338 Set of 8   5.50 5.50
   Imperf., #1106-1113   10.00

26th Soviet
Communist Party
Congress — A339

Designs: 20xu, Rocket, book. 50xu, Young people, flag.

1981, Feb. 23   *Perf. 11*
1114-1115 A339 Set of 2   2.50 2.00

Animals from Cuc Phuona Natl.
Forest — A340

Designs: No. 1116, 12xu, Hylobates concolor. No. 1117, 12xu, Macaca speciosa. 20xu, Selenarctos thibetanus. 30xu, Cuon alpinus. 40xu, Sus scrofa. 50xu, Cervus unicolor. 60xu, Panthera pardus. 1d, Panthera tigris.

1981, Apr. 10   *Perf. 12¹/₂x12*
1116-1123 A340 Set of 8   8.00 1.75
   Imperf., #1116-1123   10.00

Doves
A341

Designs: No. 1124, 12xu, Treron sieboldi. No. 1125, 12xu, Ducula aenea, vert. 20xu, Streptopelia tranquebarica, vert. 30xu, Macropygia unchall, vert. 40xu, Ducula badia, vert. 50xu, Treron apicauda. 60xu, Chalcophaps indica. 1d, Seimun n seimundi.

1, June 5   *Perf. 12*
-1131 A341 Set of 8   8.00 6.00
   Imperf., #1124-1131   11.00

Nectar-sucking Birds — A342

Designs: No. 1132, 20xu, Aethopyga siparaja. No. 1133, 20xu, Anthreptes singalensis. 30xu, Aethopyga saturata. 40xu, Aethopyga gouldiae. 50xu, Nectarinia chalcostetha. No. 1137, 50xu, Nectarinia hypogrammica. 60xu, Nectarinia sperata. 1d, Aethopyga nipalensis.

1981, Aug. 5   *Perf. 12¹/₂x12*
1132-1139 A342 Set of 8   6.50 1.75
   Imperf., #1132-1139   10.00

A343   A343a

1981, Aug. 5   *Perf. 11*
1140 A343 12xu Lotus flower

1981, Aug. 5

Design: Factory militiawoman.
1140A A343a 12xu yellow & multi 20.00

See Nos. M30-M31.

A344   A345

Fruit: No. 1141, 20xu, Elaeagnus latifolia. No. 1142, 20xu, Fortunella japonica. 30xu, Nephelium lappaceum. 40xu, Averrhoa bilimbi. No. 1145, 50xu, Ziziphus mauritiana. No. 1146, 50xu, Fragaria vesca. 60xu, Bouea oppositifolia. 1d, Syzygium aqueum.

1981, Oct. 12   *Perf. 12*
1141-1148 A344 Set of 8   5.75 1.75
   Imperf., #1141-1148   10.00

1981, Nov. 15   *Perf. 11*

Planting trees: No. 1149, Ho Chi Minh. No. 1150, Three people.

1149-1150 A345 30xu Set of 2   1.75 1.00

Tree planting festival.

Bulgaria,
1300th
Anniv.
A346

1981, Dec. 9   *Perf. 11*
1151-1153 A346 30xu, 50xu, 2d,
   set of 3   5.50 5.50

Wild Animals — A347

Designs: No. 1154, 30xu, Orangutan. No. 1155, 30xu, Bison bonasus. No. 1156, 40xu, Kangaroo. No. 1157, 40xu, Hippopotamus. No. 1158, 50xu, Rhinoceros sondaicus. No. 1159, 50xu, Giraffe. 60xu, Zebra. 1d, Lion.

1981, Dec. 9   *Perf. 12¹/₂x12*
1154-1161 A347 Set of 8   6.00 2.00
   Imperf., #1154-1161   10.00

A348   A349

World Food Day: 30xu, 50xu, Woman holding sheaf of rice. 2d, FAO emblem, horiz.

1982, Jan. 26   *Perf. 11*
1162-1164 A348 Set of 3   3.50

1982, Feb. 19
1165-1166 A349 50xu, 5d, set of 2 4.75 4.75

10th World Trade Unions Congress, Havana, Cuba.

5th Vietnamese Communist Party
Congress — A350

Designs: No. 1167, 30xu, Ho Chi Minh. No. 1168, 30xu, Hammer, sickle. No. 1169, 30xu, Worker, dam. 50xu, Women harvesting rice.

1982, Feb. 15
1167-1170 A350 Set of 4   4.00 2.00

Bees
A351

Designs: No. 1172, 20xu, Ong bove. No. 1173, 20xu, Ông van xanh. 30xu, To vo nau. 40xu, Ong vang. No. 1176, 50xu, Ong dau nau. No. 1177, 50xu, To vo xanh. 60xu, Ong bau. 1d, Ong mat.

1982, Feb. 25   *Perf. 12*
1172-1179 A351 Set of 8   5.00 2.00
   Imperf., #1172-1179   10.00

Soccer
A352

Designs: No. 1180, 30xu, 3 players. No. 1181, 30xu, 2 players. No. 1182, 40xu, Striped background. No. 1183, 40xu, grass background. No. 1184, 50xu, Vertically striped background. No. 1185, 50xu, Horizonally striped background. 60xu, Various soccer scenes.

1982, Apr. 15
1180-1187 A352 Set of 8   6.00 1.75
   Imperf., #1180-1187   10.00

For overprints see Nos. 2142-2149.

A353   A354

Vietnamese Red Cross, 35th Anniv.: 1d, Red Cross emblem.

1982, May 15   *Perf. 11*
1188-1189 A353 Set of 2   2.50

1982, May 19   *Perf. 12*

5th Natl. Women's Congress: No. 1191, Congress emblem, three women.

1190-1191 A354 12xu Set of 2   2.00

A355   A356

Birds of Prey: No. 1192, 30xu, Microhierax melanoleucos. No. 1193, 30xu, Falco tinnunculus. 40xu, Aviceda leuphotes. No. 1195, 50xu, Icthyophaga nana. No. 1196, 50xu, Milvus korschun. 60xu, Neohierax harmandi, horiz. No. 1198, 1d, Elanus caeruleus, horiz. No. 1199, 1d, Circaetus gallicus.

1982, June 1
1192-1199 A355 Set of 8   8.00 2.25
   Imperf., #1192-1199   12.00

1982, June 1   *Perf. 11*
1200-1201 A356 30xu, 3d, set of 2 5.00

Georgi Dimitrov (1882-1949), Bulgarian Communist leader.

Dahlias — A357

Designs (last word or two of Vietnamese inscription): No. 1202, 30xu, Da cam. No. 1203, 30xu, Do. 40xu, Canh se. No. 1205, 50xu, Do nhung. No. 1206, 50xu, Vang. 60xu, Do tuoi. No. 1208, 1d, Bien. No. 1209, 1d, Trang. Various flowers.

1982, July 15   **Perf. 12x12½**
1202-1209 A357   Set of 8   7.00   2.25
    Imperf., #1202-1209   12.00

1982 World Cup Soccer Championships, Spain — A358

Designs: No. 1210, 50xu, Ball at bottom right. No. 1211, 50xu, Ball at right in air. No. 1212, 50xu, Ball at bottom center. No. 1213, 1d, 1 player. No. 1214, 1d, 3 players. 2d, 2 players.

1982, July 15   **Perf. 12x12½**
1210-1215 A358   Set of 6   8.00   8.00
    Imperf., #1210-1215   11.50

A359   A360

1982, July 25   **Perf. 11**
1216 A359 30xu Natl. defense   1.50   80
    See No. M32.

1982, Aug. 15
1217 A360 30xu multicolored   1.50
Cuban victory at Giron (Bay of Pigs), 20th anniv.

World Environment Day — A361

Design: No. 1219, Ho Chi Minh, children planting tree.

1982, Aug. 15
1218-1219 A361 30xu Set of 2   2.00

A362   A363

1982, Sept. 20
1220 A362 30xu multicolored   1.50   80
Rabindranath Tagore (1861-1941), poet.

1982, Sept. 25   **Perf. 12x12½**
Insects: No. 1221, 30xu, Catacanthus incarnatus. No. 1222, 30xu, Sycanus falleni. 40xu, Nezara viridula. No. 1224, 50xu, Lohita grandis.

No. 1225, 50xu, Helcomeria spinosa. 60xu, Chrysocoris stollii. No. 1227, 1d, Pterygamia srayi. No. 1228, 1d, Tiarodes ostentans.

1221-1228 A363   Set of 8   6.75   2.25
    Imperf., #1221-1228   11.50

Russian Revolution, 65th Anniv. — A364

Design: No. 1230, Lenin, workers.

1982, Nov. 7   **Perf. 11**
1229-1230 A364 30xu Set of 2   1.75

Fish A366

Designs: No. 1235, 30xu, Samaris cristatus. No. 1236, 30xu, Tephrinectes sinensis. No. 1237, 40xu, Psettodes erumei. No. 1238, 40xu, Zebrias zebra. No. 1239, 50xu, Cynoglossus puncticeps. No. 1240, 50xu, Pardachirus pavoninus. 60xu, Brachirus orientalis. 1d, Psettina iijimae.

1982, Dec. 15   **Perf. 12**
1235-1242 A366   Set of 8   6.00   1.75
    Imperf., #1235-1242   10.00

Socialist Ideals — A367

Designs: No. 1243, 30xu, Agriculture. No. 1244, 30xu, Industry. 1d, Natl. defense. 2d, Health and education.

1982, Dec. 25   **Perf. 11**
1243-1246 A367 Set of 4   5.50

Founding of Soviet Union, 60th Anniv. A368

1982, Dec. 30
1247 A368 30xu multicolored   2.50   80

Sampans — A369

Designs: 30xu, Docked. 50xu, With striped sails. 1d, Sampans on Red River. 3d, With white sails. 5d, With patched sail. 10d, Fast sampan, horiz.

1983, Jan. 10   **Perf. 12½**
1248-1253 A369   Set of 6   7.50
    Imperf., #1248-1253   12.50

Locomotives — A370

Designs: 30xu, Class 231-300. 50xu, Class 230-000. 1d, Class 140-601. 2d, Class 241-000. 3d, Class 141-500. 5d, Class 150-000. 8d, Class 40-300.

1983, Feb. 20   **Perf. 13**
1254-1260 A370   Set of 7   7.50
    Imperf., #1254-1260   12.50

1st Manned Balloon Flight, Bicent. A371

Balloons: 30xu, Montgolfier. 50xu, Yellow. 1d, CA-11. 2d, Hot-air. 3d, Over harbor. 5d, Le Geant. 8d, Ascending. 10d, Montgolfier, diff.

1983, Mar. 25   **Litho.**   **Perf. 12½**
1261-1267 A371   Set of 7   8.00
    Imperf., #1261-1267   15.00
    Souvenir Sheet
    Perf. 13
1268 A371 10d Sheet of 1   4.00
No. 1268 contains one 32x40mm stamp.

Discovery of Tubercle Bacillus, Cent. A372

1983, Mar. 25   **Perf. 11**
1269 A372 5d multicolored   3.00

Laos-Cambodia-Viet Nam Summit — A373

1983, Mar. 25
1270-1271 A373 50xu, 5d Set of 2   2.75

Cosmonauts — A374

Designs: 30xu, Gubarev, Remek. No. 1273, 50xu, Klimuk, Hermaszewski. No. 1274, 50xu, Bykovsky, Jahn. No. 1275, 1d, Rukavishnikov, Ivanov. No. 1276, 1d, Farcas, Kubasov. No. 1277, 2d, Mendez, Romanenko. No. 1278, 2d, Gorbatko, Tuan. 5d, Dzhanibekov, Gurragcha. 8d, Popov, Prunariu. No. 1281, Gagarin.

1983, Apr. 1   **Perf. 12½x12**
1272-1280 A374   Set of 9   9.00
    Imperf., #1272-1280   14.00
    Souvenir Sheet
1281 A374 10d multicolored   5.00
No. 1281 contains one 36x28mm stamp.

Reptiles A375

Designs: No. 1282, 30xu, Teratolepis fasciata. No. 1283, 30xu, Chamaeleo jacksoni. No. 1284, 50xu, Uromastyx acanthinurus. No. 1285, 80xu, Heloderma suspectum. 1d, Cameleo menle. 2d, Amphibolurus barbatus. 5d, Chlamydosaurus kingi. 10d, Phrynosoma coronatum.

1983, Apr. 5   **Perf.**
1282-1289 A375   Set of 8   7.50
    Imperf., #1282-1289   13.00

Raphael (1483-1520), Painter — A375a

Designs: 30xu, Virgin Mother Seated on Chair. 50xu, Granduca, the Virgin Mother. 1d, Sistine Madonna. 2d, Marriage of Maria. 3d, The Gardener. 5d, Woman with Veil. 8d, 10d, Self-Portrait.

1983, Apr. 30   **Perf. 12½**
1289A-1289G A375a Set of 7   6.00
    Souvenir Sheet
    Perf. 13
1289H A375a 10d multicolored   6.50

Chess Pieces — A376

Designs: 30xu, Vietnamese pawns. 50xu, Indian elephant. 1d, Scottish knight, bishop. 2d, Indian elephant, diff. 3d, Knight. 5d, Sailing ship. 8d, Jester, elephant. 10d, Modern pawns.

1983, May 9   *Perf. 13*
1290-1296 A376 Set of 7   7.00
     Imperf., #1290-1296   12.00
Souvenir Sheet
1297 A376 10d multicolored   6.00

No. 1297 contains one 28x36mm stamp.

Souvenir Sheet

TEMBAL '83 World Stamp Exhibition, Basel — A377

1983, May 21   *Perf. 13*
1298 A377 10d multicolored   5.00 5.00

1984 Summer Olympics, Los Angeles — A378

Designs: 30xu, Long jump. 50xu, Running. 1d, Javelin. 2d, High jump, horiz. 3d, Hurdles, horiz. 5d, Shot put. 8d, Pole vault. 10d, Discus.

1983, June 13   **Litho.**   *Perf. 13*
1299-1305 A378 Set of 7
Souvenir Sheet
1306 A378 10d Sheet of 1

No. 1306 contains one 32x40mm stamp. The issuance of this set has been questioned.

Find what you're looking for in the "Scott Stamp Monthly". New issue and topical listings, as well as fascinating features, are found in each issue. Please call 1-800-488-5351 for more information.

Souvenir Sheet

Brasiliana '83, Rio de Janeiro — A379

1983, July 20   *Perf. 13*
1307 A379 10d Rhamphastos toco   6.00 6.00

Butterflies — A380

Designs: No. 1308, 30xu, Leptocircus meges. No. 1309, 30xu, Terias hecabe. No. 1310, 40xu, Zetides agamemnon. No. 1311, 40xu, Nyctalemon patroclus. No. 1312, 50xu, Papilio chaon. No. 1313, 50xu, Precis almana. 60xu, Thauria lathyi. 1d, Kallima inachus.

1983, July 30   **Litho.**   *Perf. 12*
1308-1315 A380 Set of 8   7.00
     Imperf., #1308-1315   10.00

Souvenir Sheet

Bangkok '83 — A381

1983, Aug. 4   *Perf. 13*
1316 A381 10d multicolored   10.00 10.00

Karl Marx (1818-1883) A382

1983, Oct. 10   *Perf. 11*
1317-1318 A382 50xu, 10d, set of 2   5.00
     Imperf., #1317-1318   50.00

Phu Dong Sports Festival A383

1983, Oct. 10
1319-1320 A383 30xu, 1d, set of 2   2.00

World Food Day — A384

Design: 50xu, Infant, fish. 4d, Family.

1983, Oct. 10   *Perf. 12½*
1321-1322 A384 Set of 2   2.50
     Imperf., #1321-1322   5.00

Mushrooms — A385

Designs: No. 1323, 50xu, Flammulina velutipes. No. 1324, 50xu, Pleurotus ostreatus. No. 1325, 50xu, Cantharellus cibarius. No. 1326, 50xu, Coprinus atramentarius. 1d, Volvariella volvacea. 2d, Agaricus silvaticus. 5d, Morchella esculenta. 10d, Amanita caesarea.

1983, Oct. 10   *Perf. 12x12½*
1323-1330 A385 Set of 8   9.00 9.00
     Imperf., #1323-1330   15.00

For overprints see Nos. 2150-2157.

World Communications Year — A386

Designs: 50xu, Letter carrier. 2d, Mail sorting room. 8d, Switchboard operators. No. 1334, 10d, Radio operator, antenna. No. 1335, 10d, Telephone, letter, dish antenna, ship.

1983, Oct. 30   *Perf. 12½*
1331-1334 A386 Set of 4   4.50
Souvenir Sheet
     Perf. 13
1335 A386 10d Sheet of 1   3.00

5th Natl. Trade Unions Congress A387

Designs: 50xu, Woman with flowers, Vietnam-Soviet Union Friendship Cultural Building. 2d, 30d, Welder.

1983, Nov. 16   *Perf. 11*
1336-1338 A387 Set of 3   7.50

Water Birds — A388

Designs: No. 1339, 50xu, Ciconia nigra. No. 1340, 50xu, Ardea cinerea. No. 1341, 50xu, Ardea purpurea. No. 1342, 50xu, Ibis leucocephalus. 1d, Grus grus. 2d, Platalea minor. 5d, Nycticorax nycticorax. 10d, Anastomus oscitans.

1983, Nov. 20   A388   Set of 8   *Perf. 12x12½*
1339-1346 A388 Set of 8   9.00 5.00
     Imperf., #1339-1346   14.00

No. 1343 inscribed "Grus grue."

World Peace Conference, Prague — A389

Designs: 50xu, Shown. 3d, 5d, 20d, Hands, globe, dove.

1984, Jan. 15   *Perf. 11*
1347-1350 A389 Set of 4   9.00

1984 Winter Olympics, Sarajevo, Yugoslavia — A390

Designs: No. 1351, 50xu, Cross-country skiing, vert. No. 1352, 50xu, Biathlon, vert. 1d, Speed skating, vert. 2d, Bobsled, vert. 3d, Hockey. 5d, Ski jumping. 6d, Slalom skiing. 10d, Pairs figure skating.

1984, Jan. 30   *Perf. 12½*
1351-1357 A390 Set of 7   6.00
     Imperf., #1351-1357   12.00
Souvenir Sheet
1358 A390 10d multicolored   4.00

No. 1358 contains one 40x32mm stamp.

Soviet Union-Vietnamese Projects, 1978-83 — A391

Designs: 20xu (No. 1359), 4d, Hoa Binh Hydro-electric project. 20xu (No. 1360), Vietnamese-Soviet Cultural Palace. 50xu, Thang Long Bridge.

1984, Jan. 31   *Perf. 11*
With Gum
1359-1362 A391 Set of 4   55.00

Endangered Animals — A392

Designs: No. 1363, 50xu, Felis marmorata. No. 1364, 50xu, Panthera tigris. No. 1365, 50xu, Panthera pardus. No. 1366, 1d, Hylobates lar. No. 1367, 1d, Nycticebus coucang. No. 1368, 2d, Elephas indidus. No. 1369, 2d, Bos gaurus.

1984, Feb. 26   Perf. 12½x12
1363-1369 A392 Set of 7   5.00
   Imperf., #1363-1369   14.00

Wildflowers — A393

Designs: No. 1370, 50xu, Banhinia variegata. No. 1371, 50xu, Caesalpinia pulcherrima. 1d, Cassia fistula. 2d, Delonix regia. 3d, Artagotrys uncinatus. 5d, Corchorus olitorius. 8d, Banhinia grandiflora.

1984, Mar. 15   Perf. 12x12½
1370-1376 A393 Set of 7   6.50
   Imperf., #1370-1376   12.50
Souvenir Sheet
1377 A393 10d Delonix regia   3.75

Location of inscriptions differs on Nos. 1373, 1377.

Orchids — A394

Designs: No. 1378, 50xu, Cymbidium. N 1379, 50xu, Brasse cattleya. 1d, Cattleya Dia 2d, Cymbidium, diff. 3d, Cymbidium hybridu 5d, Phoenix winged orchids. 8d, Yellow Que orchids.

1984, Mar. 28   Perf.
1378-1384 A394 Set of 7   7.00
   Imperf., #1378-1384   10.00

Nos. 1085, 1093 Surcharged

50xu
a

50xu
b

1984, Apr. 25   Perfs. as before
1385 A322(a) 50xu on 12xu #1085
1386 A335(b) 50xu on 12xu #1093

Souvenir Sheet

Espana '84, Madrid — A395

1984, Apr. 27   Perf. 12½
1387 A395 10d Ciconia ciconia   4.50

Victory at Dien Bien Phu, 30th Anniv. A396

Designs: No. 1388, 50xu, Ho Chi Minh, generals, battle map. No. 1389, 50xu, Troops, truck. 1d, Civilians carrying provisions. 2d, Man-hauling artillery. 3d, Anti-aircraft battery. 5d, Troops attacking enemy base. 8d, Troops waving flag.

1984, May 7   Perf. 12½
1388-1394 A396 Set of 7   5.00

No. 1395 has been reserved for a souvenir sheet with this set.

Souvenir Sheet

Fish
A398

Designs: No. 1397, 30xu, Cypselurus spilopterus. No. 1398, 30xu, Ostracion cornutus. 50xu, Diodon hystrix. 80xu, Chelmon rostratus. 1d, Antennarius tridens. 2d, Pterois russelli. 5d, Mola mola. 10d, Minous monodactylus.

1984, June 25   Litho.   Perf. 12
1397-1404 A398 Set of 8   7.50
   Imperf., #1397-1404   12.00

Ornamental Fish
A399

Designs: No. 1405, 50xu, Trichogaster trichopterus. No. 1406, 50xu, Brachydanio rerio. 1d, Macropodus opercularis. 2d, Gymnocorymbus ternetzi. 3d, Hyphessobrycon serpae. 5d, Labeo bicolor. 8d, Batta splendens.

1984, June 29   Perf. 12½
1405-1411 A399 Set of 7   6.00
   Imperf., #1405-1411   10.00

Minh visiting factory. 3d, Hanoi Mechanical Engineering plant. 5d, Intl. trade union movement.

1984, July 20   Perf. 11
1412-1416 A400 Set of 6   3.75
Souvenir Sheet
Imperf
1417   A400 2d like #1414   10.00

No. 1412 printed se-tenant. No. 1417 contains one 45x38mm stamp.

Rock Formations, Ha Long Bay — A401

Designs: No. 1418, 50xu, Hang-Bo Nau. No. 1419, 50xu, Nui Yen Ngua. No. 1420, 50xu, Hon Dua. No. 1421, 50xu, Hang Con Gai. No. 1422, 1d, Hon Coc. No. 1423, 1d, Hon Ga Choi. 2d, Hon Dinh Huong. 3d, Hon Su Tu. 5d, Hon Am. 8d, Nui Bai Tho.

1984, July 30   Perf. 12½x12
1418-1427 A401 Set of 10   7.00
   Imperf., #1418-1427   12.50

Dinosaurs — A402

Designs: No. 1428, 50xu, Styracosaurus. No. 1429, 50xu, Diplodocus. No. 1430, 1d, Corythosaurus. No. 1431, 1d, Rhamphyorhynchus. 2d, Seymouria. 3d, Allosaurus. 5d, Dimetrodon. 8d, Brachiosaurus.

1984, Aug. 30
1428-1435 A402 Set of 8   15.00
   Imperf., #1428-1435   20.00

Viet Nam-Laos-Cambodia Friendship — A403

1984, Aug. 30   Perf. 11
1436-1437 A403 50xu, 10d, set of 2   5.00

Souvenir Sheet

Ausipex '84, Melbourne, Australia — A404

1984, Sept. 20   Perf. 13
1438 A404 10d Koala   10.00

Viet Nam-Cambodia Friendship Agreement, 5th Anniv. — A405

Designs: 50xu, 3d, People, pagoda, statue. 50d, Dancers.

1984, Sept. 30   Perf. 11
1439-1441 A405 Set of 3   13.00

Liberation of Hanoi, 30th Anniv. A406

Designs: 50xu, Thang Long Bridge. 1d, Khue Van Gateway. 2d, Ho Chi Minh mausoleum.

1984, Oct. 5
1442-1444 A406 Set of 3   3.50

Vintage Automobiles — A407

Designs: No. 1445, 50xu, Vis-a-Vis, vert. No 1446, 50xu, Duc. 1d, Tonneau. 2d, Double phae ton. 3d, Landalet. 5d, Torpedo. 6d, Coupe de Ville.

Perf. 12¹/₂x13, 13x12¹/₂
1984, Oct. 30
1445-1451 A407 Set of 7   5.00
    Imperf., #1445-1451   11.50

Lenin (1870-
1924)
A408

Paintings of Lenin: 50xu, At his desk. 1d, Standing with revolutionaries. 3d, Speaking at factory.
5d, Meeting with farmers.

1984, Nov. 15   **Perf. 12x12¹/₂**
1452-1455 A408 Set of 4   3.50
    Imperf., #1452-1455   8.00

UNICEF
A409

Paintings: 30xu, Woman, soldiers. 50xu,
Mother, children. 1d, Miner, family. 3d, Young girl,
vert. 5d, Children playing on ground. 10d, Women,
child, vert.

1984, Dec. 7   **Perf. 12**
1456-1461 A409 Set of 6   5.50
    Imperf., #1456-1461   10.00

A410   A411

Denominations: 50xu, 30d. Frontier Forces, 25th
anniv.

1984, Dec. 15   **Perf. 11**
1462-1463 A410 Set of 2   11.00
    Imperf., #1462-1463
See No. M39.

1984, Dec.   **Perf. 12¹/₂x12**
Flora and Fauna: 20xu, Bubalus bubalis. 30xu,
Felis marmorata. No. 1466, 50xu, Hibiscus rosa-
sinensis. No. 1467, 50xu, Allurus fulgens. No.
1468, 50xu, Rosa centifolia. No. 1469, 50xu, Betra
splendens. No. 1470, 1d, Chrysanthemum sinense.
No. 1471, 1d, Nymphaea ampla. No. 1472, 1d,
Pelecanus onocrotalus. No. 1473, 1d, Panthera
tigris. No. 1474, 2d, Nycticebus coucang. No.
1475, 2d, Macaca fascicularis. No. 1476, 2d, Dalia
coccinea. 5d, Gekko gecko. 10d, Rhytidoceros
bicornis.

1464-1478 A411 Set of 15   12.50
    Imperf., #1464-1478   15.00

No. 1466 inscribed "Hybiscus." No. 1470
inscribed "Chrysanthemun."

A412   A413

1985   **Perf. 11**
1479-1480 A412 3d, 5d, set of 2   3.50
    Imperf., #1479-1480   30.00
New Year 1985 (Year of the Buffalo).
Issued: 3d, 1/21; 5d, 4/30.

1985, Apr. 26   **Perf. 11**
1481 A413 2d Ho Chi Minh   1.00
Vietnamese Communist Party, 55th anniv.

Military
Victory in
South Viet
Nam, 10th
Anniv.
A414

Designs: 1d, Soldiers advancing forward. 2d,
10d, Ho Chi Minh, tank, soldiers. 4d, Construction
worker. 5d, Map, women.

1985, Apr. 30   **Perf. 12¹/₂**
1482-1485 A414 Set of 4   3.75
    Souvenir Sheet
    Perf. 13
1486 A414 10d multicolored   3.75

Cactus — A415

Designs: No. 1487, 50xu, Echinocereus knippe-
lianus. No. 1488, 50xu, Lemaireocereus thurberi.
1d, Notocactus haselbergii. 2d, Parodia chrysacan-
thion. 3d, Pelecyphora pseudopectinata. 5d, Rebu-
tia frebrighii. 8d, Lobivia aurea.

1985, Apr. 30   **Perf. 11¹/₂**
1487-1493 A415 Set of 7   7.25
    Imperf., #1487-1493   15.00

Vietnamese People's Army, 40th
Anniv. — A416

Designs: No. 1494, 50xu, Ho Chi Minh. No.
1495, 50xu, Taking oath on flag. 1d, Anti-aircraft
missile. 2d, Soldiers, civilians working together. 3d,
Tank entering grounds of presidential palace, Saigon. 5d, Soldier demonstrating use of rifle. 8d,
Officers, soldiers, map.

1985, May 6   **Perf. 12¹/₂**
1494-1500 A416 Set of 7   6.00
No. 1501 reserved for souvenir sheet with this
set.

A417   A418

End of World War II, 40th Anniv.: 1d, 10d, Victory Monument. 2d, Vietnamese soldier. 4d, Dove,
falling American eagle. 5d, Child, doves.

1985, May 7   **Perf. 12x12¹/₂**
1502-1505 A417 Set of 4   3.75
    Imperf., #1502-1505   12.50
    Souvenir Sheet
1506 A417 10d multicolored   3.50

1985, May 13   **Perf. 11**
Liberation of Haiphong, 30th anniv.: 2d, Long
Chau Lighthouse. 5d, An Duong Bridge, horiz. 10d,
To Hieu (1912-44), vert.
1507-1508 A418 Set of 2   2.50
    Souvenir Sheet
    Imperf
1509 A418 10d multicolored   3.00

Ho Chi
Minh,
95th
Birth
Anniv.
A419

Ho Chi Minh: 1d, At battlefield. 2d, Reading. 4d,
10d, Portrait, vert. 5d, Writing.

1985, May 19   **Perf. 12¹/₂**
1510-1513 A419 Set of 4   5.00
    Souvenir Sheet
    Perf. 13
1514 A419 10d multicolored   3.50
No. 1514 contains one 30x36mm stamp.

Motorcycles, Cent. — A420

Designs: No. 1515, 1d, 1895, Germany. No.
1516, 1d, 1898 tricycle, France. No. 1517, 2d,
1913 Harley-Davidson, US. No. 1518, 2d, 1918
Cleveland, US. 3d, 1935 Simplex, US. 4d, 1984
Minarelli, Italy. 6d, 1984 Honda, Japan. 10d, 1984
Honda racing bike.

1985, June 28   **Perf. 13**
1515-1521 A420 Set of 7   6.00
    Imperf., #1515-1521   14.00
    Souvenir Sheet
1522 A420 10d multicolored   7.50
No. 1522 contains one 32x40mm stamp.

Argentina '85, Buenos Aires — A421

Wild animals: No. 1523, 1d, Aptenodytes pen-
nati, vert. No. 1524, 1d, Dolichotis patagonum,
vert. No. 1525, 2d, Panthera onca. No. 1526, 2d,

Hydrochoerys capibara. 3d, Peterocnemia pennata,
vert. 4d, Priodontes giganteus. 6d, Voltur gryphus.
10d, Lama glama, horiz.

1985, July 5   **Perf. 12¹/₂**
1523-1529 A421 Set of 7   12.00
    Imperf., #1523-1529   16.00
    Souvenir Sheet
    With Gum
    Perf. 13
1530 A421 10d multicolored   8.00
No. 1530 contains one 40x32mm stamp.

12th World
Youth and
Students
Festival,
Moscow

Marine
Life — A423

Designs: No. 1536, 30xu, Nadoa tuberculata.
No. 1537, 30xu, Luidia maculata. No. 1538, 30xu,
Stichopus chloronotus. No. 1539, 30xu, Holothuria
monacaria. No. 1540, 40xu, Astropyga radiata. No.
1541, 40xu, Astropecten scoparius. No. 1542,
40xu, Linckia laevigata.

1985, July 30   **Perf. 12**
1536-1542 A423 Set of 7   10.00
    Imperf., #1536-1542   17.50

2d

Socialist Republic
of Viet Nam, 40th
Anniv. — A424

Designs: 2d, Construction. 3d, Hands shaking,
doves. 5d, Flag, military forces. No. 1567, 10d,
Flag, Ho Chi Minh.

1985, Aug. 28   **Perf. 12¹/₂**
1543-1546 A424 Set of 4   5.00
    Imperf., #1543-1546   17.50
    Souvenir Sheet
    Perf. 13
1547 A424 10d like #1543   4.50
No. 1547 contains one 32x40mm stamp.

Vietnamese
Police Force,
40th Anniv.
A425

1985, Aug. 30   **Perf. 11**
1548 A425 10d multicolored   4.50
See No. M41.

1st Natl. Sports Festival A426

Designs: 5d, Gymnastics. 10d, Gymnastics, running, swimming.

1985, Aug. 30
1549-1550 A426 Set of 2   6.25

German Railways, 150th Anniv. — A427

Various locomotives: No. 1551, 1d, Facing left. No. 1552, 1d, Facing right. No. 1553, 2d, Facing left. No. 1554, 2d, Facing right. 3d, 4d, 6d.

1985, Sept. 13   *Perf. 12½*
1551-1557 A427 Set of 7   8.00
    Imperf., #1551-1557   10.00
Souvenir Sheet
With Gum
Perf. 13
1558 A427 10d multicolored   4.00
No. 1558 contains one 32x40mm stamp.

Vietnamese Geological Survey, 30th Anniv. A428

Designs: No. 1559, Drilling rigs. No. 1560, Aerial survey.

1985, Oct. 5   *Perf. 11*
1559-1560 A428 1d Set of 2   2.25

Italia '85 A429

Vintage Italian cars: No. 1561, 1d, 1922 Alfa Romeo. No. 1562, 1d, 1932 Bianchi Berlina. No. 1563, 2d, 1912 Itala. No. 1564, 2d, 1928 Isotta Fraschini. No. 1565, 2d, 1930 Bugatti. 4d, 1934 Lancia Augusta. 6d, 1927 Fiat Convertable (top up). 10d, 1927 Fiat Convertable (top down).

1985, Oct. 25   *Perf. 13*
1561-1567 A429 Set of 7   7.50
    Imperf., #1561-1567   12.50
Souvenir Sheet
With Gum
1568 A429 10d multicolored   5.50
No. 1568 contains one 40x32mm stamp.

Whales A430

Designs: No. 1569, 1d, Balaenoptera musculus. No. 1570, 1d, Balaena borealis. No. 1571, 2d, Orcinus orca. No. 1572, 2d, Delphinus. 3d, Megaptera boops. 4d, Balaenoptera physalus. 6d, Eubalaena glacialis.

1985, Nov. 15
1569-1575 A430 Set of 7   10.50
    Imperf., #1569-1575   15.00

1988 World Cup Soccer Championships, Mexico City — A431

Various soccer plays: No. 1576, 1d, From behind goal. No. 1577, 1d, Goalie from side. No. 1578, 2d, From behind goal. No. 1579, 2d, From in front of goal, vert. 3d, vert. 4d, vert. 6d, vert.

1985, Nov. 30
1576-1582 A431 Set of 7   5.00
    Imperf., #1576-1582   10.00
Souvenir Sheet
Perf. 13
1583 A431 10d multicolored   3.75
No. 1583 contains one 40x32mm stamp.

People's Democratic Republic of Laos, 10th Anniv. — A432

Designs: a, Woman, dove. b, Woman dancing, natl. arms.

1985, Dec. 2   *Perf. 11*
1584 A432 1d Pair, #a.-b.   2.50

Traditional Musical Instruments A433

Designs: No. 1585, 1d, Stone chimes. No. 1586, 1d, Large bronze drum. No. 1587, 2d, Flutes. No. 1588, 2d, Large red drum. 3d, Monochord. 4d, Moon-shaped lute. 6d, Vietnamese two-string violin.

1985, Dec. 5   *Perf. 12½x12*
1585-1591 A433 Set of 7   6.25

A434   A435

Socialist Republic of Viet Nam, 40th Anniv.: No. 1592, 10d, Industry. No. 1593, 10d, Agriculture. 20d, Public health. 30d, Education.

1985, Dec. 15   *Perf. 11*
1592-1595 A434 Set of 4   40.00

1986, Jan. 6   Litho.   *Perf. 11*
1596-1597 A435 50xu, 1d Set of 2   2.00
1st Natl. Elections, 40th anniv.

A436   A437

1986, Jan. 6
1598 A436 1d multicolored   1.50
UN 40th anniv.

1986, Feb. 24   *Perf. 12½*
Halley's Comet: No. 1599, 2d, Edmond Halley. No. 1600, 2d, Isaac Newton. 3d, Rocket, flags. 5d, Comet.

1599-1602 A437 Set of 4   5.25
    Imperf., #1599-1602   9.00

A438   A439

Soviet Communist Party, 27th Congress: 50xu, Kremlin, map. 1d, Lenin banner.

1986, Feb. 25   *Perf. 11*
1603-1604 A438 Set of 2   2.25

1986, Mar. 1
1605 A439 1d Map of Battle of Xuong Giang   1.25
Le Loi, 600th birth anniv.

1986 World Cup Soccer Championships, Mexico City — A440

Various soccer players in action: No. 1606, 1d, Viet Nam at left. No. 1607, 1d, Viet Nam at right. 2d, Viet Nam at left. No. 1609, 3d, Viet Nam at left. No. 1610, 3d, Viet Nam at right. No. 1611, 5d, Viet Nam at left. No. 1612, 5d, Viet Nam at right.

1986, Mar. 3   *Perf. 12½*
1606-1612 A440 Set of 7   5.50
    Imperf., #1606-1612   9.00
Souvenir Sheet
Perf. 13
1613 A440 10d multicolored   5.50
No. 1613 contains one 40x32mm stamp.

1st Manned Space Flight, 25th Anniv. A441

Designs: No. 1614, 1d, Konstantin Tsiolkovsky. No. 1615, 1d, Rocket on transporter. 2d, Yuri Gagarin. No. 1617, 3d, Valentina Tereshkova, vert. No. 1618, 3d, Alexei Leonov. No. 1619, 5d, Apollo-Soyuz, crews. No. 1620, 5d, Soyuz, Salut space station. 10d, Cosmonauts, vert.

1986, Apr. 12   *Perf. 13*
1614-1620 A441 Set of 7   5.50
    Imperf., #1614-1620   10.00
Souvenir Sheet
1621 A441 10d multicolored   5.50
No. 1621 contains one 32x40mm stamp.

Ernst Thalmann (1886-1944), German Politician A442

1986, Apr. 16   *Perf. 11*
1622 A442 2d red & black   1.50

May Day — A443

1986, May 1
1623-1624 A443 1d, 5d, set of 2   3.00

Vancouver Expo '86 — A444

Airplanes: No. 1625, 1d, Hawker Hart. No. 1626, 1d, Curtiss Jenny. 2d, PZL-P23. No. 1628, 3d, Yakovlev Yak-11. No. 1629, 3d, Fokker Dr.1. No. 1630, 5d, Boeing P-12 (1920). No. 1631, 5d, Nieuport-Delage NiD.29C1 (1929).

1986, May 12   *Perf. 13*
1625-1631 A444 Set of 7   5.50
    Imperf., #1625-1631   9.00

Dam-Strengthening Committee, 40th Anniv. — A445

1986, May 22   *Perf. 11*
1632 A445 1d carmine   1.50

Bonsai — A446

Designs: No. 1633, 1d, Ficus glomerata. No. 1634, 1d, Ficus benjamina. 2d, Ulmus tonkinensis. No. 1636, 3d, Persica vulgaris. No. 1637, 3d, Streblus asper. No. 1638, 5d, Pinus khasya. No. 1639, 5d, Podocarpus macrophyllus. 10d, Serissa foetida, horiz.

1986, June 16   **Perf. 12x12½**
1633-1639 A446 Set of 7   7.00
   Imperf., #1633-1639   11.00
Souvenir Sheet
Perf. 12½x12

1640 A446 10d multicolored   5.00

Domestic Cats — A447

Various cats (Background colors): No. 1641, 1d,
blue green. No. 1642, 1d, red. 2d, blue. No. 1644,
3d, brown. No. 1645, 3d, blue. No. 1646, 5d,
violet. No. 1647, 5d, red, vert.

Perf. 13x12½, 12½x13
1986, June 16
1641-1647 A447 Set of 7   8.00
   Imperf., #1641-1647   14.00

Traditional
Houses
A448

Designs: No. 1648, 1d, Thai den. No. 1649, 1d,
Nung. 2d, Thai trang. No. 1651, 3d, Tay. No.
1652, 3d, Hmong. No. 1653, 5d, Dao. No. 1654,
5d, Tay nguyen, vert.

Perf. 12½x12, 12x12½
1986, June 20
1648-1654 A448 Set of 7   7.00
   Imperf., #1648-1654   12.50
Souvenir Sheet
Perf. 12x12½

1655 A448 10d like #1654   4.00

Postal Service, 40th
Anniv. — A449

Designs: No. 1656, 2d, Telecommunications.
No. 1657, 2d, Map, letter carrier. 4d, Soldiers,
Nguyen Thi Nghia. 5d, Dish antenna.

1986, Aug. 15   **Perf. 13**
1656-1659 A449 Set of 4   2.50
   Imperf., #1656-1659   15.00

A450   A451

Birds: No. 1660, 1d, Merops apiaster. No. 1661,
1d, Cissa chinensis. 2d, Pteruthius erythropterus.
No. 1663, 3d, Garrulax leucolophus. No. 1664, 3d,
Psarisomus dalhousiae, horiz. No. 1665, 5d, Cya-
nopica cyanus, horiz. No. 1666, 5d, Motacilla alba.
No. 1666, 5d, Copsychus malabaricus.

1986, Aug. 28   **Perf. 13**
1660-1666 A450 Set of 7   6.00
   Imperf., #1660-1666   11.50
Souvenir Sheet
Perf. 12½

1667 A450 10d multicolored   5.00

No. 1667 contains one 32x40mm stamp.
Stockholmia '86.

1986, Sept. 15   **Perf. 12x12½**
Domestic fowl: No. 1668, 1d, Plymouth Rock.
No. 1669, 1d, Maleagris gallopavo. No. 1670, 2d,
Ri. No. 1671, 2d, White Plymouth rock. No. 1672,
3d, Leghorn. No. 1673, 3d, Rhode Island red. No.
1674, 3d, Rhode ri. 5d, Gray Plymouth rock hen.

1668-1675 A451 Set of 8   7.00
   Imperf., #1668-1675   12.50

11th Intl.
Trade
Unions
Congress
A452

1986, Sept. 16   **Perf. 12½**
1676 A452 1d blue & red   1.50

Artifacts,
Hung-Voung
Period
A453

Designs: No. 1677, 1d, Seated figure, vert. No.
1678, 1d, Knife hilt in form of female figure, vert.
2d, Bronze axe. No. 1680, 3d, Bronze axe, diff. No.
1681, 3d, Bronze bowl. No. 1682, 5d, Bronze pot
(round). No. 1683, 5d, Bronze vase (open top).

Perf. 12x12½, 12½x12
1986, Oct. 15
1677-1683 A453 Set of 7   5.50
   Imperf., #1677-1683   10.00
Souvenir Sheet
Perf. 12x12½

1684 A453 10d like #1677   5.00

Vietnamese Red
Cross, 40th
Anniv. — A454

1986, Oct. 20   **Perf. 12½**
1685 A454 3d rose & greenish blue   1.50

Sailing
Ships
A455

Various sail and oar-powered ships (sail colors):
No. 1686, 1d, blue, green, yellow. No. 1687, 1d,
orange. 2d, yellow. No. 1689, 3d, purple & red. No.
1690, 3d, blue. No. 1691, 5d, blue, brown, orange.
No. 1692, 5d, orange.

Perf. 12½x12, 12½x13 (#1688)
1986, Oct. 20
1686-1692 A455 Set of 7   5.75

No. 1688 is 38x47mm.

Butterflies — A456

Designs: No. 1693, 1d, Catopsilia scylla. No.
1694, 1d, Euploea midamus. 2d, Appias nero. No.
1696, 3d, Danaus chrysippus. No. 1697, 3d,
Papilio polytes stichius. No. 1698, 5d, Euploea
diocletiana. No. 1699, 5d, Charaxes polyxena.

1986, Nov. 11   **Perf. 12½**
1693-1699 A456 Set of 7   7.00
   Imperf., #1693-1699   15.00

No. 1696 misspelled "Danais."

Vietnamese Communist Party, 6th
Congress — A457

Designs: 1d, Construction projects. 2d, Natl.
defense. 4d, Ho Chi Minh. 5d, Intl. cooperation.

1986, Nov. 20   **Perf. 11**
1700-1703 A457 Set of 4   3.50
  a. Perf. 12½, #1700-1703
1702b   Perf. 11x12½
Souvenir Sheet
Imperf

1704 A457 10d like #1700   4.50

Insects
A458

Designs: No. 1705, 1d, Poecilocoris nepalensis.
No. 1706, 1d, Bombus americanorum. 2d, Romalea
microptera. No. 1708, 3d, Chalcocoris rutilans. No.
1709, 3d, Chrysocoris sellatus. No. 1710, 5d,
Paranthrene palmi. No. 1711, 5d, Crocisa crucifera.
10d, Anabrus simplex.

1986, Nov. 30   **Perf. 12½**
1705-1711 A458 Set of 7   5.75
   Imperf., #1705-1711   12.50
Souvenir Sheet

1712 A458 10d multicolored   5.50

No. 1712 contains one 32x40mm stamp.

Intl. Peace
Year — A459

1986, Dec. 7   **Perf. 11**
1713-1714 A459 1d, 3d, set of 2   2.25

Handicrafts — A460

Designs: No. 1715, 1d, Round dish. No. 1716,
1d, Rattan handbag. 2d, Rattan foot stool. No.
1718, 3d, Bamboo hand basket. No. 1719, 3d,
Muong pannier. No. 1720, 5d, Rattan basket with
shoulder straps. No. 1721, 5d, Rattan basket with
lid. 10d, Tall rattan basket.

1986, Dec. 10   **Perf. 11½**
1715-1721 A460 Set of 7   7.50
   Imperf., #1715-1721   10.00
Souvenir Sheet

1722 A460 10d multicolored   3.50

A461   A462

1986, Dec. 18   **Perf. 11**
1723 A461 2d blue green & fawn   1.50

Natl. Resistance, 40th anniv.

1986, Dec. 26   **Perf. 12x12½**
Endangered flora: No. 1724, 1d, Fokienia hodg-
insii. No. 1725, 1d, Amentotaxus yunnanensis. 2d,
Pinus kwangtungensis. No. 1727, 3d, Taxus
chinensis. No. 1728, 3d, Cupressus torulosa. No.
1729, 5d, Ducampopinus krempfii. No. 1730, 5d,
Tsuga yunnanensis. 10d, Abies nukiangensis.

1724-1230 A462 Set of 7   6.00
   Imperf., #1724-1730   13.00
Souvenir Sheet

1731 A462 10d multicolored   4.25

Elephants
A463

Designs: No. 1732, 1d, Two elephants. No.
1733, 1d, Female, calf. No. 1734, 3d, Elephant.
No. 1735, 1d, Elephant facing, vert. No. 1736, 5d,
Man riding elephant, vert. No. 1737, 5d, Four
elephants.

1986, Dec. 30   **Perf. 12½**
1732-1737 A463 Set of 6   7.00
   Imperf., #1732-1737   12.00

No. 1737 is 68x27mm.

Vietnamese
Legends
A464

Designs: a, Son Tinh. b, My Nuong. c-e, Battle between Mountain Genie and Water Genie. f-h, Celebration.

1987, Jan. 20   *Perf. 12*
1738 A464 3d Strip of 8, #a.-h.   7.50
         Imperf.   12.50

New Year 1987 (Year
of the Cat) — A465

1987, Jan. 25   *Perf. 11*
1739 A465 3d red lilac   1.50

Natl. Events
A466

Ho Chi Minh and: 10d, August revolution, Aug. 19, 1945. 20d, Proclaiming independence, Sept. 9, 1945. 30d, Victory at Dien Bien Phu, July 7, 1954. 50d, Capture of Saigon, Apr. 30, 1975.

1987, Apr. 10   *Perf. 11*
1740-1743 A466 Set of 4   4.50

A467   A468

Champa art: 3d, Temple, Da Nang. 10d, Tower, Na Trang. 15d, Temple, Da Nang (side view). 20d, Dancing girl. 25d, Bust of woman. 30d, Girl playing flute. 40d, Dancing girl, diff.

1987, June 30   *Perf. 12x12½*
1744-1750 A467 Set of 7   7.50
         Imperf., #1744-1750   9.50
         Souvenir Sheet
1751 A467 50d like #1749   5.00

1987, July 10   *Perf. 12½*
Various flowering cacti: 5d, 10d, 15d, 20d, 25d, 30d, 40d.

1752-1758 A468 Set of 7   5.00
         Souvenir Sheet
                    Perf. 13
1759 A468 50d multicolored   6.00

Global Population Reaches 5
Billion — A469

1987, July 11   *Perf. 13*
1760 A469 5d multicolored   1.50

World Wildlife
Fund — A470

Designs: No. 1761, 5d, Concolor gibbon. No. 1762, 5d, Douc monkeys. 15d, Black concolor gibbon. 40d, Douc monkey.

1987, July 15   *Perf. 12½*
1761-1764 A470 Set of 4   9.00
         Imperf., #1761-1764   40.00

A471   A472

Western high plateau costumes: 5d, Male Bana. No. 1766, 20d, Female Bana. No. 1767, 20d, Female Gia Rai. No. 1768, 30d, Male Gia Rai. No. 1769, 30d, Male Ede. 40d, Female Ede.

1987, July 25   *Perf. 12x12½*
1765-1770 A471 Set of 6   7.00
         Imperf., #1765-1770   10.00

1987, July 27   *Perf. 13*
1771 A472 5d multicolored   1.50

Day of the Invalids, 40th anniv.

Postal
Trade
Union,
40th
Anniv.
A473

Designs: 5d, Letter carrier, jet, truck, train. 30d, Switchboard operator.

1987, Aug. 30
1772-1773 A473 Set of 2   1.75

A474   3d

Paintings by Picasso: No. 1774, 3d, Trio. No. 1775, 20d, War. No. 1776, 20d, Peace. No. 1777, 30d, Child with Dove, vert. No. 1778, 30d, Portrait of Gertrude Stein, vert. 40d, Guernica. 50d, Child as Harlequin.

1987, Oct. 1   *Perf. 12½*
1774-1779 A474 Set of 6   6.00
         Imperf., #1774-1779   12.00
         Souvenir Sheet
1780 A474 50d multicolored   5.00

No. 1779 is 44x27mm. No. 1780 contains one 40x32mm stamp.

VIỆT NAM Coral — A475

Designs: 5d, Epanouis. 10d, Acropora. 15d, Rhizopsammia. 20d, Acropora, diff. 25d, Alcyone, 30d, Corollum. 40d, Cristatella.

1987, Oct. 3   *Perf. 12x12½*
1781-1787 A475 Set of 7   8.00
         Imperf., #1781-1787   12.50

Russian
Revolution, 70th
Anniv. — A477

Designs: 5d, 65d, Industry, agriculture. 20d, Lenin. 30d, Construction. 50d, Ho Chi Minh.

1987, Oct. 6   *Perf. 13*
1789-1792 A477 Set of 4   3.75
         Souvenir Sheet
1793 A477 65d multicolored   6.00

Hafnia
'87
A478   HAFNIA 87

Seaplanes: 5d, PBY-5. 10d, LeO H-246. 15d, Dornier DO-18. 20d, Short Sunderland. 25d, Rohrbach Rostra. 30d, Chetverikov ARK-3. 40d, CANT Z-509. 50d, Curtiss H-16.

1987, Oct. 12   *Perf. 13*
1794-1800 A478 Set of 7   5.50
         Souvenir Sheet
1801 A478 50d multicolored   4.50

No. 1801 contains one 40x32mm stamp.

Czechoslovakia-Viet Nam Friendship
Agreement, 10th Anniv. — A479

Designs: 10d, Handshake. 50d, Flags, buildings.

1987, Oct. 31
1802-1803 A479 Set of 2   4.00
         Imperf., 1802-1803   17.50

Viet Nam-
Soviet Union
Cooperation
A480

Designs: 5d, Industry. 50d, Buildings.

1987, Nov. 3
1804-1805 A480 Set of 2   4.00

Mushrooms
A481

Designs: 5d, Polyporellus squamosus. 10d, Clitocybe geotropa. 15d, Tricholoma terreum. 20d, Rusula aurata. 25d, Collybia fusipes. 30d, Cortinarius violaceus. 40d, Boletus aereus.

987, Nov. 10   *Perf. 12½*
1806-1812 A481 Set of 7   6.00
         Imperf., #1806-1812   11.00

Peace
A482

1987, Nov. 30   *Perf. 13*
1813 A482 10d multicolored   1.50

Afro-Asian Solidarity Committee (AAPSO),
30th Anniv. — A483

Designs: 10d, Hands, dove. 30d, Map, hands, vert.

1987, Nov. 30
1814-1815 A483 Set of 2   2.25
         Imperf., #1814-1815   20.00

Victory Over US
Bombing Campaign,
15th Anniv. — A484

Designs: 10d, B-52 wreckage. 30d, Children with flowers, wreckage.

1987, Dec. 26
1816-1817 A484 Set of 2   2.00
         Imperf., #1816-1817   20.00

Productivity
A485

Designs: 5d, Consumer goods. 20d, Agriculture. 30d, Export products.

1987, Dec. 30
1818-1820 A485 Set of 3   4.00

Hoang Sa, Truong Sa Islands
A486

Designs: 10d, Ship, sailor. 100d, Maps.

1988, Jan. 19
1821-1822 A486 Set of 2   6.00

Tropical Fish
A488

Designs: 5d, Red betta splendens. 10d, Labeo bicolor. 15d, Puntis tetrazona. 20d, Brachydania albolineatus. 25d, Puntis conchonius. 30d, Betta splendens, diff. 40d, Botia lecontei.

1988, Jan. 20   *Perf. 13*
1831-1837 A488 Set of 7   5.50
        Imperf., #1831-1837   10.00

Intl. Red Cross, Red Crescent, 125th Anniv. — A489

1988, Feb. 17
1838 A489 10d multicolored   1.40

Battle of Bach Dang, 700th Anniv.
A490

Designs: 80d, Fleet of ships. 200d, Battle scene.

1988, Apr. 8
1839-1840 A490 Set of 2   5.00

Tourism
A491

Designs: 5d, One-pillar pagoda. 10d, Bach Dang River. 15d, Thien Mu Tower, Hue. 20d, Hgu Hanh Mountain, Da Nang. 25d, Nha Trang beach. 30d, Pren Waterfalls. 40d, Market, Ben Thanh. 50d, Cleft Rocks, Quang Ninh.

1988, Apr. 20   *Perf. 12¹/₂x12*
1841-1847 A491 Set of 7   7.00 7.00
        Imperf., #1841-1847   10.00
            Souvenir Sheet
1848 A491 50d multicolored   5.50

Water Lilies — A492

Designs: 5d, Nymphaea lotus. No. 1850, 10d, Nymphaea pubescens. No. 1851, 10d, Nymphaea nouchali. No. 1852, 20d, Nymphaea rubra. No. 1853, 20d, Nymphaea gigantea. 30d, Nymphaea laydekeri. 50d, Nymphaea capensis.

1988, Apr. 20   *Perf. 12x12¹/₂*
1849-1855 A492 Set of 7   6.50
        Imperf., #1849-1855   12.50

Offshore Oil Drilling — A493

1988, Apr. 28   *Perf. 13*
1856 A493 1000d multicolored   8.50

A494

Parrots: No. 1857, 10d, Ara araruna. No. 1858, 10d, Psittacula himalayana. No. 1859, 20d, Aprosmictus erythropterus. No. 1860, 20d, Ara chloroptera. No. 1861, 30d, Ara militaris. No. 1862, 30d, Psittacula alexandri. 50d, Loriculus vernalis. 80d, Ara chloroptera, diff.

1988, May 5   *Perf. 12x12¹/₂*
1857-1863 A494 Set of 7   7.00
        Imperf., #1857-1863   11.00
            Souvenir Sheet
1864 A494 80d multicolored   4.00

A495   A496

Membership in Council of Mutual Economic Assistance, 10th Anniv.: 200d, Map. 300d, Headquarters building.

1988, May 29   *Perf. 13*
1865-1866 A495 Set of 2   5.50

1988, June 1
1867 A496 60d multicolored   1.25

Vaccinations against disease.

Problems of Peace and Socialism Magazine, 30th Anniv. — A497

1988, July 20
1868 A497 20d multicolored   1.25

A498   A499

1988, Aug. 20
1869 A498 150d multicolored   2.00

Pres. Ton Duc Thang, birth cent.

1988, Aug. 28

6th Vietnamese Trade Union Congress: 50d, Emblem. 100d, Workers.

1870-1871 A499 Set of 2   2.50

Children's Paintings
A500

Designs: No. 1872, 10d, My Family. No. 1873, 10d, My House. No. 1874, 20d, Fishing. No. 1875, 20d, Flying Kites. No. 1876, 30d, Girl playing guitar, animals. No. 1877, 30d, Children in rain, vert. 50d, Girl holding dove, vert. 80d, Family, diff., vert.

                                    Perf. 12¹/₂x12, 12x12¹/₂
1988, Sept. 25
1872-1878 A500 Set of 7   6.50 6.50
                                    10.00
            Souvenir Sheet
                                    Perf. 12x12¹/₂
1879 A500 80d multicolored   5.00

Hydroelectric Plants — A501

Designs: 2000d, Tri An. 3000d, Hoa Binh.

1988, Sept. 27   *Perf. 13*
1880-1881 A501 Set of 2   12.00

A502   A503

1988, Nov. 3   *Perf. 13¹/₂x13*
1882 A502 50d multicolored   1.25

Viet Nam-USSR Friendship Agreement, 10th anniv.

1988, Dec. 27

Designs: 100d, Fidel Castro. 300d, Flags, Vietnamese, Cuban people.

1883-1884 A503 Set of 2   2.25

Cuban revolution, 30th anniv.

Wild Animals
A504

Designs: No. 1885, 10d, Bos banteng. No. 1886, 10d, Bos gaurus. No. 1887, 20d, Axis porcinus. No. 1888, 20d, Tapirus indicus. No. 1889, 30d, Capricornis sumatrensis. No. 1890, 30d, Sus scrofa. 50d, Bubalus bubalus. 80d, Rhinoceros sodaicus.

1988, Dec. 30   *Perf. 12¹/₂*
1885-1891 A504 Set of 7   6.50
        Imperf., #1885-1891   12.50
            Souvenir Sheet
1892 A504 80d multicolored   6.50

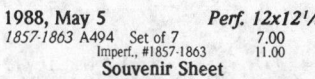

Locomotives — A505

Designs: No. 1893, 20d, Kiha 80, Japan. No. 1894, 20d, LRC, Canada. No. 1895, 20d, Hitachi, Japan. No. 1896, 20d, BL-85, USSR. No. 1897, 30d, RC-1, Sweden. No. 1898, 30d, DR-1A, USSR. 50d, T3-136, USSR. 80d, SCNF Z6400.

1988, Dec. 30   *Perf. 13*
1893-1899 A505 Set of 7   6.00
    Imperf., #1893-1899   12.50
Souvenir Sheet
1900 A505 80d multicolored   4.50

No. 1900 contains one 40x32mm stamp.

A506   A507

Fruits, vegetables: No. 1901, 10d, Lagenaria siceraria. No. 1902, 10d, Momordica charantia. No. 1903, 20d, Solanum melongena. No. 1904, 20d, Cucurbita moschata. No. 1905, 30d, Luffa cylindrica. No. 1906, 30d, Benincasa hispida. 50d, Lycopercicon esculentum.

1988, Dec. 30   *Perf. 12x12½*
1901-1907 A506 Set of 7   6.00
    Imperf., #1901-1907   12.50

1988, Dec. 30   *Perf. 13*
Various project spacecraft: No. 1908, 10d, Mars. No. 1909, 10d, Moon. No. 1910, 20d, Saturn. No. 1911, 20d, Inter-planetary. No. 1912, 30d, Venus. No. 1913, 30d, Earth orbital space station. 50d, Cosmos house. 80d, Lander docking with orbiter.

1908-1914 A507 Set of 7   6.00
Souvenir Sheet
1915 A507 80d multicolored   5.00
Cosmos Day.
No. 1915 contains one 32x40mm stamp.

Shells
A508

Designs: No. 1916, 10d, Conus miles. No. 1917, 10d, Strombus lentiginosus. No. 1918, 20d, Nautilus. No. 1919, 20d, Bursa rana. No. 1920, 30d, Turbo petholatus. No. 1921, 30d, Oliva erythros. 50d, Mitra eriscopalis. 80d, Tonna tessellata.

1988, Dec. 30   *Perf. 12½x12*
1916-1922 A508 Set of 7   6.00
    Imperf., #1916-1922   12.50
Souvenir Sheet
1923 A508 80d multicolored   4.50

India
'89
A509

Butterflies: No. 1924, 50d, Anaea echemus. No. 1925, 50d, Ascia monuste. No. 1926, 50d, Juniona evarete. No. 1927, 100d, Phoebis avellaneda. No. 1928, 100d, Eurema proterpia. 200d, Papilio palamedes. 300d, Danaus plexippus. 400d, Parides gundlachiamus.

1989, Jan. 7   *Perf. 12½*
1924-1930 A509 Set of 7   6.50
    Imperf., #1924-1930   10.00
Souvenir Sheet
1931 A509 400d multicolored   4.50

No. 1931 contains one 40x32mm stamp. Nos. 1924-1930 printed with se-tenant label.

Natl. Day of Cambodia, 10th Anniv. A510

Designs: 100d, Soldiers, women working in field. 500d, Viet Nam-Cambodia friendship.

1989, Jan. 7   *Perf. 13x13½*
1932-1933 A510 Set of 2   2.25
    Imperf., #1932-1933   20.00

India '89 — A511

Designs: No. 1934, 100d, Science, technology. No. 1935, 100d, Agriculture, industry. 300d, Asoka pillar. 600d, Nehru (1889-1964).

1989, Jan. 20   *Perf. 13*
1934-1937 A511 Set of 4   3.50

Battle of Dong Da, Bicent. A512

Designs: 100d, Festival. 1000d, Quang Trung defeating Qing invaders.

1989, Feb. 10   *Perf. 13*
1938-1939 A512 Set of 2   3.00

Inter-Parliamentary Union, Cent. — A513

Designs: 100d, Vietnamese membership, 10th anniv. 200d, Centennial emblem.

1989, Mar. 1
1940-1941 A513 Set of 2   2.50

Fishing Boats — A513a

Boats from: No. 1942, 10d, Quang Nam. No. 1943, 10d, Quang Tri. No. 1944, 20d, Thua Thien. No. 1945, 20d, Da Nang (sail furled). No. 1946, 30d, Da Nang (under sail). No. 1947, 30d, Quang Tri (under sail). 50d, Hue.

1989, Mar. 20   *Perf. 12½x12*
1942-1948 A513a Set of 7   6.50
    Imperf., #1942-1948   10.00

Helicopters
A514

Designs: No. 1949, 10d, Kamov KA-26. No. 1950, 10d, Boeing Vertol 234. No. 1951, 20d, Mil MI-10(V10). No. 1952, 20d, MBB BO 105. No. 1953, 30d, Kawasaki Hughes 369HS. No. 1954, 30d, Bell 206B Jet Ranger, 50d, Mil MI-8. 80d, Puma SA330.

1989, Apr. 12   *Perf. 12½*
1949-1955 A514 Set of 7   5.50
    Imperf., #1949-1955   11.50
Souvenir Sheet
1956 A514 80d multicolored   5.00

No. 1956 contains one 40x32mm stamp.

Bicycles
A515

Designs: No. 1957, 10d, Bowden Spacelander. No. 1958, 10d, Rabasa Derbi. No. 1959, 20d, Huffy. No. 1960, 20d, Rabasa Derbi. No. 1961, 30d, VMX-PL. No. 1962, 30d, Premier. 50d, Columbia RX5.

1989, May 1   *Perf. 13*
1957-1963 A515 Set of 7   6.00
    Imperf., #1957-1963   10.00

Turtles — A516

Designs: No. 1964, 10d, Cuora trifasciata. No. 1965, 10d, Testudo elegans. No. 1966, 20d, Eretmochelys imbricata. No. 1967, 20d, Platysternon megacephalum. No. 1968, 30d, Dermochelys coriacea. No. 1969, 30d, Chelonia mydas. 50d, Caretta caretta. 80d, Caretta caretta, diff.

1989, May 1   *Perf. 12½*
1964-1970 A516 Set of 7   6.00
    Imperf., #1964-1970   11.50
Souvenir Sheet
1971 A516 80d multicolored   4.00
Finlandia '89 (#1971).

Poisonous Snakes
A517

Designs: No. 1972, 10d, Trimeresurus popeorum. No. 1973, 10d, Trimeresurus mucrosquamatus. No. 1974, 20d, Bungarus fasciatus. No. 1975, 20d, Bungarus candidus. No. 1976, 30d, Calliophis maclellandii. No. 1977, 30d, Ancistrodon acutus. 50d, Ophiophagus hannah, vert.

1989, May 1
1972-1978 A517 Set of 7   6.50
    Imperf., #1972-1978   12.50

Pairs Figure Skating — A518

Various figure skaters: No. 1979, 10d, "Viet Nam" at left. No. 1980, 10d, "Viet Nam" at right. No. 1981, 20d, "Viet Nam" at left. No. 1982, 20d, "Viet Nam" at right, horiz. No. 1983, 30d, "Viet Nam" at left. No. 1984, 30d, "Viet Nam" at right, horiz. 50d, "Viet Nam" at left, horiz.

1989, May 29   *Perf. 13*
1979-1985 A518 Set of 7   5.50
    Imperf., #1979-1985   10.00
Souvenir Sheet
With Gum
1986 A518 80d multi, horiz.   4.00

No. 1986 contains one 40x32mm stamp.

A519   A520

1989, June 5   *Perf. 13*
1987 A519 100d buff   1.50

Post & Telecommunications.

1989, July 1   *Perf. 12*
Ceramics, Li-Tran Period: 50d, Pitcher. No. 1989, 100d, Bowl. No. 1990, 100d, Jug. 200d, Jug, diff. 300d, Vase.

1988-1992 A520 Set of 5   4.00
    Imperf., #1988-1992   8.00

Legend of Giong
A521

Designs: 50d, Mother nursing infant. No. 1994, 100d, Giong meets imperial messenger. No. 1995, 100d, Giong riding iron horse, people following. 200d, Giong pulling up bamboo trees. 300d, Giong flying into sky.

1989, July 1   *Perf. 12½x12*
1993-1997 A521 Set of 5   4.00
    Imperf., #1993-1997   7.50

French Revolution, Bicent. — A522

Designs: 100d, Emblem. 500d, Liberty leading the people, after Delacroix.

1989, July 14   *Perf. 13½x13*
1998-1999 A522 Set of 2   2.25

VIETNAM 50d

PHILEXFRANCE '89 — A523

Paintings: No. 2000, 50d, Oath of the Tennis Court, by David. No. 2001, 50d, Capture of Louis XVI, horiz. No. 2002, 50d, Liberty, Equality, Fraternity, horiz. No. 2003, 100d, Storming the Bastille. No. 2004, 100d, Death of Marat, by David. 200d, Child and Rabbit, by Prud'hon. 300d, Slave Market, by Gerome, horiz. 400d, Liberty Leading the People, by Delacroix.

1989, July 14   *Perf. 13*
2000-2006 A523   Set of 7   5.50
   Imperf., #2000-2006   10.00
     Souvenir Sheet
2007 A523 400d multicolored   3.50

No. 2007 contains one 33x44mm stamp.

1990 World Cup Soccer Championships, Italy — A524

Soccer plays: No. 2008, 50d, Dribbling. No. 2009, 50d, Tackling. No. 2010, 50d, Goalie. No. 2011, 100d, Dribbling, diff. No. 2012, 100d, Dribbling, diff., vert. 200d, Preparing to kick, vert. 300d, Heading ball, vert. 400d, Heading ball, diff., vert.

    Perf. 13x12¹⁄₂, 12¹⁄₂x13
2008-2014 A524   Set of 7   5.00
   Imperf., #2008-2014   11.00
     Souvenir Sheet
     Perf. 13
2015 A524 400d multicolored   5.00

No. 2015 contains one 32x40mm stamp.

Dogs A525

Designs: No. 2016, 50d, Dachshund. No. 2017, 50d, Beagle. No. 2018, 50d, English setter, vert. No. 2019, 100d, German short-haired pointer, vert. No. 2020, 100d, Basset hounds. 200d, German sheperd, vert. 300d, Beagle, diff.

1989, Aug. 20   *Perf. 12¹⁄₂*
2016-2022 A525   Set of 7   6.00
   Imperf., #2016-2022   10.00

No. 2020 is 68x28mm.

Horses A526

Designs: No. 2023, 50d, Tennessee Walking. No. 2024, 50d, Appaloosa. No. 2025, 50d, Tersky. No. 2025, 100d, Kladruber. No. 2026, 100d, Welsh cob. 200d, Pinto. 300d, Pony and bridle.

1989, Sept. 23   *Perf. 13*
2023-2029 A526   Set of 7   5.50
   Imperf., #2023-2029   10.00

No. 2029 is 68x28mm.

Flowers — A527

Designs: No. 2030, 50d, Paphiopedilum siamense. No. 2031, 50d, Fuchsia fulgens. No. 2032, 100d, Hemerocallis fulva. No. 2033, 100d, Gloriosa superba. 200d, Strelitzia reginae. 300d, Iris.

1989, Sept. 23   *Perf. 12¹⁄₂*
2030-2035 A527   Set of 6   6.00
   Imperf., #2030-2035   11.00

German Democratic Republic, 40th Anniv. A528

1989, Oct. 7   *Perf. 13*
2036 A528 200d multicolored   1.50

Immunization Campaign — A529

Designs: No. 2037, Woman receiving vaccination. No. 2038, Child receiving oral vaccine. No. 2039, Clinic.

1989, Oct. 20
2037-2039 A529 100d Set of 3   2.25

Drawings of Everyday Life, 19th Cent. — A530

Designs: 50d, Assembling plow. No. 2041, 100d, Harrowing. No. 2042, 100d, Irrigating. 200d, Fertilizing. 300d, Harvesting.

1989, Oct. 28   *Perf. 12x12¹⁄₂*
2040-2044 A530   Set of 5   4.50
   Imperf., #2040-2044   7.50

Horse Paintings, by Tu Bi Hong (1895-1953) A531

Various horses: 100d, 200d, 300d, 500d horiz., 800d, 1000d, 1500d.

1989, Dec. 22   *Perf. 13*
2045-2051 A531   Set of 7   5.00
   Imperf., #2045-2051   11.00
     Imperf
    Size: 117x72mm
2052 A531 2000d multicolored   5.00

Vietnamese Communist Party, 60th Anniv. A532

Designs: 100d, Ho Chi Minh, tank. 500d, Workers, refinery, field.

1990, Feb. 3   **Litho.**   *Perf. 13*
2053-2054 A532   Set of 2   3.00
   Imperf., #2053-2054   6.50

Ducks A533

Designs: a, 100d, Anas platyrhynchos hybrid. b, 300d, Anas penelope. c, 500d, Anas platyrhynchos. d, 1000d, Anas erythrorhyncha. e, 2000d, Anas platyrhynchos, diff. f, 3000d, Anas undulata.

1990, Feb. 15
2055 A533 Block of 6, #a.-f.   5.00

Trucks A534

Designs: 100d, Mack. 200d, Volvo F89. 300d, Tatra 915 S1. 500d, Hino KZ30000. 1000d, Iveco. 2000d, Leyland DAF Super Comet. 3000d, Kamaz 53212.

1990, Feb. 20
2056-2062 A534   Set of 7   4.00
   Imperf., #2056-2062   6.50

Architectural Sites, Hue — A535

Designs: No. 2063, 100d, Tu Duc's Mausoleum. No. 2064, 100d, Hien Nhon Arch. 200d, Ngo Mon Gate. 300d, Thien Mu Temple. 400d, Palace, gateway.

1990, Feb. 20   *Perf. 12¹⁄₂x12*
2063-2066 A535   Set of 4   3.00
     Souvenir Sheet
2067 A535 400d multicolored   4.00

Goldfish — A536   Paintings — A537

Designs: 100d, Bulging-eyed, horiz. 200d, Telescopic-eyed, horiz. 500d, Red-headed, horiz. 1000d, Double-tailed. 2000d, Rainbow. 3000d, Comet.

1990, Mar. 20   *Perf. 13*
2068-2073 A536   Set of 6   4.75
   Imperf., #2068-2073   8.00

1990 World Cup Soccer Championships, Italy — A538

Various soccer players in action: 100d, 200d, 300d, 500d, 1000d, 2000d, 3000d.

1990, Apr. 19
2082-2088 A538   Set of 7   4.00
     Souvenir Sheet
2089 A538 3500d multicolored   3.25

No. 2089 contains one 32x40mm stamp. For overprints see Nos. 2189-2196.

Cats — A539   Dogs — A540

Various cats: 100d, horiz., 200d, 300d, horiz., 500d, 1000d, horiz., 2000d, 3000d.

1990, May 5
2090-2096 A539   Set of 7   4.75
     Souvenir Sheet
2097 A539 3500d multicolored   3.25

No. 2097 contains one 44x33mm stamp. Belgica '90 (#2097).

1990, May 15

Various dogs: 100d, 200d, 300d, 500d, 1000d, 2000d, 3000d.

2098-2104 A540   Set of 7   4.50
     Souvenir Sheet
2105 A540 3500d Collies   3.50

    New Zealand '90.

Ho Chi Minh
(1890-1969)
A541

Ho Chi Minh and: 100d, Lenin. 300d, Soldiers
waving flag. 500d, Hand holding rifle, dove. 1000d,
Map. 2000d, Child, dove. 3000d, Stylized globe.
3500d, Flag.

1990, May 17   Perf. 13
2106-2111 A541 Set of 6   4.50
          Imperf., #2106-2111   7.50
                 Souvenir Sheet
                  Perf. 12¹⁄₂x13
2112 A541 3500d multicolored   4.50

No. 2112 contains one 33x44mm stamp.

Dinosaurs
A542

Designs: 100d, Gorgosaurus. 500d, Cer-
atosaurus. 1000d, Ankylosaurus. 2000d,
Ankylosaurus, diff. 3000d, Edaphosaurus.

1990, June 1   Perf. 13
2113-2117 A542 Set of 5   5.25

Columbus' Discovery of America, 500th
Anniv. — A543

Designs: 50d, Fleet. No. 2119, 100d, Columbus
presenting gifts to natives. No. 2120, 100d, Columbus, priest at Rabida. No. 2121, 100d, Columbus at
Court of Ferdinand, Isabella. No. 2122, 200d, Map
of Caribbean. No. 2123, 200d, Columbus, arms.
300d, Map of Atlantic. 500d, Teotihuacan pot.

1990, June 10   Perf. 12¹⁄₂
2118-2124 A543 Set of 7   5.00
                 Souvenir Sheet
2125 A543 500d multicolored   4.00

No. 2125 contains one 40x32mm stamp. For
overprints see Nos. 2313-2320.

Sailing
Ships
A544

Designs: 100d, Viking longship. 500d, Caravel.
No. 2128, 1000d, Carrack, 14th-15th cent. No.
2129, 1000d, Flit. No. 2130, 1000d, Carrack, 15th
cent., vert. 2000d, Galleon, vert. 3000d, Galleon,
diff. 4200d, Egyptian barge.

1990, June 10   Perf. 13
2126-2132 A544 Set of 7   4.25
          Imperf., #2126-2132   7.50
                 Souvenir Sheet
                  Perf. 13x12¹⁄₂
2133 A544 4200d multicolored   7.50

No. 2133 contains one 44x33mm stamp.

11th Asian Games,
Beijing — A545

Designs: 100d, High jump. 200d, Basketball.
300d, Table tennis. 500d, Volleyball. 1000d, Rhythmic gymnastics. 2000d, Tennis. 3000d, Judo.
3500d, Hurdles.

1990, June 20   Perf. 13
2134-2140 A545 Set of 7   6.00
          Imperf., #2134-2140   7.50
                 Souvenir Sheet
                  Perf. 12¹⁄₂x13
2141 A545 3500d multicolored   4.50

No. 2141 contains one 33x44mm stamp.

Nos. 1180-1187 Ovptd. in
Red, Green and Black

1990, June 22   Perf. 12
2142-2149 A352 Set of 8   5.25

1990 World Cup Soccer Championships, Italy.

Nos. 1323-1330 Ovptd. in
Black and Red

1990, June 22   Perf. 12x12¹⁄₂
2150-2157 A385 Set of 8   5.50
                      Tourism.

Modern
Ships
A546

Designs: 100d, Freighter. 300d, Container ship.
500d, Cruise ship. 1000d, Liquified natural gas
tanker. 2000d, Ro-Ro ship. 3000d, Ferry.

1990, July 20   Perf. 13
2158-2163 A546 Set of 6   4.00
          Imperf., #2158-2163   5.00

Post & Telecommunications Dept., 45th
Anniv. — A547

Designs: 100d, Dove, ship, plane. 1000d, Satellite antenna.

1990, Aug. 15   Perf. 13x13¹⁄₂
2164-2165 A547 Set of 2   2.25
          Imperf., #2164-2165   4.50

Socialist Republic of
Viet Nam, 45th
Anniv. — A548

Designs: 100d, Flag, construction projects. 500d,
Map, tank, soldiers. 1000d, "VI," ship, communica-
tions network. 3000d, Workers, oil rigs. 3500d, Ho
Chi Minh.

1990, Sept. 1   Perf. 13
2166-2169 A548 Set of 4   4.00
          Imperf., #2166-2169   6.00
                 Souvenir Sheet
                  Perf. 12¹⁄₂x13
2170 A548 3500d multicolored   3.00

No. 2170 contains one 33x44mm stamp. Sixth
Vietnamese Communist Party Congress (#2168).

Airships
A549

Designs: 100d, Henry Gifford, 1871. 200d,
Lebandy, 1910. 300d, Graf Zeppelin. 500d, R-101,
1930. 1000d, Soviet, 1936. 2000d, Tissandier,
1883. 3000d, US Navy. 3500d, "Zodiac," 1931.

1990, Sept. 10   Perf. 12¹⁄₂
2171-2177 A549 Set of 7   3.75
                 Souvenir Sheet
2178 A549 3500d multicolored   3.50

No. 2178 contains one 40x32mm stamp.
Helvetia '90, Stamp World London '90.

Fable of Thach
Sanh — A550

Designs: a, 100d, Thach Sanh carrying bundles
of wood. b, 300d, Ly Thong. c, 500d, Thach Sanh
killing python. d, 1000d, Thach Sanh shooting
arrow at eagle. e, 2000d, Thach Sanh in prison. f,
3000d, Thach Sanh, princess.

1990, Sept. 20   Perf. 13
2179 A550 Block of 6, #a.-f.   4.00

Asian-Pacific
Postal
Training
Center, 20th
Anniv.
A551

1990, Sept. 25
2180 A551 150d multicolored   1.00

Nos. 571-578 Ovptd. with
Red Cross in Red and
"FOR THE FUTURE GENERATION" in
various Languages in Black

Language: No. 2181, 12xu, Japanese. No. 2182,
12xu, Italian. No. 2183, 20xu, German. No. 2184,
20xu, Vietnamese. 30xu, English. 40xu, Russian.
50xu, French. 60xu, Spanish.

1990, Sept. 25   Perf. 12
2181-2188 A211 Set of 8   5.50

Position of overprint varies.
Use of these stamps at stated face value is
unlikely.

Nos. 2082-2089 Ovptd.   1 GERMANY
                           2 ARGENTINA
                           3 ITALY

1990, Sept. 25   Perf. 13
2189-2195 A538 Set of 7   6.00
                 Souvenir Sheet
2196 A538 3500d multicolored   2.50

Vietnamese
Women's
Federation,
60th Anniv.
A552

Designs: 100d, Woman carrying rifle. 500d,
Women working in field, laboratory.

1990, Oct. 10
2197-2198 A552 Set of 2   1.00
          Imperf., #2197-2198   2.00

Correggio (1494-
1534),
Painter — A553

Various paintings of the Madonna and Child: No.
2199, 50xu, shown. No. 2200, 50xu, diff. 1d, 2d,
3d, 5d, 6d.

1990, Nov. 13   Perf. 12¹⁄₂
2199-2205 A553 Set of 7   4.50
                 Souvenir Sheet
2206 A553 10d multicolored   4.50

No. 2206 contains one 32x40mm stamp.
Dated "1984." Use of these stamps at stated face
value is unlikely.

Protection of Forests — A554

Designs: 200d, Water conservation, healthy forest. 1000d, SOS, prevent forest fires.

1990, Nov. 15   Perf. 13
2207-2208 A554 Set of 2   1.00

A555   A555a

Poisonous mushrooms: 200d, Amanita pantherina. 300d, Amanita phalloides. 1000d, Amanita
virosa. 1500d, Amanita muscaria. 2000d, Russula
emetica. 3000d, Boletus satanas.

1991, Jan. 21
2209-2214 A555 Set of 6   4.25
          Imperf., #2209-2214   7.00

1991, Jan. 31

1992 Summer Olympics, Barcelona: 200d, Sailing. 300d, Boxing. 400d, Cycling. 1000d, High

jump. 2000d, Equestrian. No. 2220, 3000d, Judo. No. 2221, 3000d, Wrestling, horiz. 5000d, Soccer, horiz.

| 2215-2221 A555a | Set of 7 | 4.50 |
| | Imperf., #2215-2221 | 7.00 |

Souvenir Sheet

| 2222 A555a 5000d multicolored | 2.25 |
| Imperf., #2222 | 5.00 |

No. 2222 contains one 44x33mm stamp.

Nguyen Binh Khiem (1491-1585), Writer — A556

1991, Feb. 15

| 2223 A556 200d multicolored | 1.25 |
| Imperf. | 2.00 |

Discovery of America, 500th Anniv. A557

Sailing ships: 200d, Marisiliana. No. 2225, 400d, Venetian. No. 2226, 400d, Cromster, vert. No. 2227, 2000d, Nina. No. 2228, 2000d, Pinta. 3000d, Howker, vert. 5000d, Santa Maria. 6500d, Portrait of Columbus.

1991, Feb. 22

| 2224-2230 A557 | Set of 7 | 5.00 |
| | Imperf., #2224-2230 | 6.00 |

Souvenir Sheet

| 2231 A557 6500d multicolored | 4.00 |
| Imperf. | 6.00 |

Sharks A559

Designs: 200d, Carcharhinus melanopterus. 300d, Carcharhinus amblyrhynchos. 400d, Triakis semifasciata. 1000d, Sphyrna mokarran. 2000d, Triaenodon abesus. No. 2241, 3000d, Carcharias laurus. No. 2242, 3000d, Carcharhinus leucas.

1991, Apr. 6

| 2236-2242 A559 | Set of 7 | 4.00 |
| | Imperf., #2236-2242 | 7.50 |

Endangered Birds — A560

World Wildlife Fund: 200d, Grus vipio. 300d, Grus antigone chick, vert. 400d, Grus japonensis, vert. 1000d, Grus antigone, adults, vert. 2000d, Grus nigricollis, vert. No. 2248, 3000d, Balearica regulorum, vert. No. 2249, 3000d, Bugeranus leucogerranus.

1991, Apr. 20

| 2243-2249 A560 | Set of 7 | 6.00 |
| | Imperf., #2243-2249 | 6.00 |

Shellfish A561

Designs: 200d, 1000d, 2000d, Palinurus, all diff. 300d, Alpheus bellulus. 400d, Periclemenes brevicarpalis. No. 2255, 3000d, Astacus. No. 2256, 3000d, Palinurus, diff.

1991, Apr. 20

| 2250-2256 A561 | Set of 7 | 4.00 |
| | Imperf., #2250-2256 | 7.00 |

Young Pioneers, 50th Anniv. — A562

Designs: 200d, shown. 400d, UN Convention on Children's Rights.

1991, May 15

| 2257-2258 A562 | Set of 2 | 2.00 |
| | Imperf., #2257-2258 | 4.00 |

Rally Cars A563

Designs: No. 2259, 400d, Lada. No. 2260, 400d, Nissan. 500d, Ford Sierra RS Cosworth. 1000d, Suzuki. 2000d, Mazda 323 4WD. No. 2264, 3000d, Lancia. No. 2265, 3000d, Peugeot 405.

1991, May 24

| 2259-2265 A563 | Set of 7 | 4.00 |
| | Imperf., #2259-2265 | 5.00 |

Souvenir Sheet

| 2266 A563 5000d multicolored | 2.50 |
| Imperf. | 5.00 |

No. 2266 contains one 44x33mm stamp.

Locomotives — A564

Designs: No. 2267, 400d, Puffing Billy, 1811, vert. No. 2268, 400d, Fusee, 1829, vert. 500d, Stevens, 1825. 1000d, Crampton No. 80, 1852. 2000d, Locomotion, 1825. No. 2272, 3000d, Saint-Lo, 1844. No. 2273, 3000d, Coutances, 1855. 5000d, Atlantic, 1843.

1991, May 25

| 2267-2273 A564 | Set of 7 | 5.00 |
| | Imperf., #2267-2273 | 8.00 |

Souvenir Sheet

| 2274 A564 5000d multicolored | 3.00 |
| Imperf. | 6.00 |

No. 2274 contains one 33x44mm stamp.

Frogs — A565

World Wildlife Fund: 200d, Dendrobates leucomelas. 400d, Rana esculenta. 500d, Mantella aurantiaca. 1000d, Dendrobates tinctorius. 2000d, Hyla halowelli. No. 2280, 3000d, Agalychnis callidryas. No. 2281, 3000d, Hyla aurea.

1991, June 12

| 2275-2281 A565 | Set of 7 | 6.00 |
| | Imperf., #2275-2281 | 6.00 |

7th Vietnamese Communist Party Congress A566

Designs: 200d, Ho Chi Minh, buildings. 300d, Workers. 400d, Mother, children.

1991, June

| 2282-2284 A566 | Set of 3 | 2.25 |
| | Imperf., #2282-2284 | 4.50 |

Vietnamese Communist Party, 60th Anniv. — A566a

1991, June 24   Litho.   *Perf. 13*

| 2284A A566a 100d red | 1.25 |

1992 Winter Olympics, Albertville A567

Designs: 200d, Speed skating, vert. 300d, Freestyle skiing, vert. 400d, Bobsled. 1000d, Biathlon. 2000d, Slalom skiing. No. 2290, 3000d, Crosscountry skiing, vert. No. 2291, 3000d, Ice dancing, vert. 5000d, Hockey, vert.

1991, July 15

| 2285-2291 A567 | Set of 7 | 4.00 |
| | Imperf., #2285-2291 | 5.00 |

Souvenir Sheet

| 2292 A567 5000d multicolored | 2.50 |
| Imperf. | 5.00 |

No. 2292 contains one 33x44mm stamp.

Prehistoric Animals A568

Designs: a, 200d, Arsinoitherium zitteli. b, 500d, Elephas primigenius. c, 1000d, Baluchitherium. d, 2000d, Deinotherium giganteum. e, 3000d, Brontops. f, 3000d, Uinatherium.

1991, July 26

| 2293 A568 Block of 6, #a.-f. | 4.50 |

A569   A570

Golden Heart Charity: 200d, Eye, folded hands. 3000d, Tennis player in wheelchair.

1991, July 27

| 2294-2295 A569 Set of 2 | 1.25 |

1991, Aug. 20

Chess pieces: 200d, Pawn. 300d, Knight. 1000d, Rook. 2000d, Queen. No. 2300, 3000d, Bishop. No. 2301, 3000d, King. 5000d, Pawn, Knight, King.

| 2296-2301 A570 | Set of 6 | 4.25 |
| | Imperf., #2296-2301 | 5.00 |

Souvenir Sheet

| 2302 A570 5000d multicolored | 2.50 |
| Imperf. | 5.00 |

No. 2302 contains one 33x44mm stamp.

PHILANIPPON '91 — A571

Butterflies: 200d, Attacus atlas. 400d, Morpho cypris. 500d, Troides rothschildi. No. 2306, 1000d, Papilio demetrius. No. 2307, 1000d, Vanessa atalanta. 3000d, Papilio weiskei. 5000d, Apatura ilia substituta. 5500d, Heliconius melpomene.

1991, Aug. 29

| 2303-2309 A571 | Set of 7 | 4.50 |
| | Imperf., #2303-2309 | 5.00 |

Souvenir Sheet

| 2310 A571 5500d multicolored | 2.50 |
| Imperf. | 5.00 |

No. 2310 contains one 44x33mm stamp.

Post and Telecommunications Research Institute, 25th Anniv. — A572

1991, Aug.
2311 A572 200d multicolored   1.25
    Imperf.   2.00

Souvenir Sheet
2312 A572 3500d Communications
                   network, horiz.   2.50
    Imperf.   5.00

No. 2312 contains one 44x33mm stamp.

Nos. 2118-2125 Ovptd. in
Red

1992, Jan. 15   *Perf. 12½*
2313-2319 A543 Set of 7   6.50
Souvenir Sheet
2320 A543 500d multicolored   4.00

7th Vietnamese
Communist Party
Congress — A574

Designs: 200d, Workers, industry, agriculture, atomic energy symbol. 2000d, Map of Asia, hands clasped.

1992, Feb. 3   Litho.   *Perf. 13*
2322-2323 A574 Set of 2   1.00

1992 Winter Olympics, Albertville — A575

Designs: 200d, Biathlon. 2000d, Hockey. 4000d, Slalom skiing. 5000d, Pairs figure skating. 6000d, Downhill skiing.

1992, Feb. 5
2324-2328 A575 Set of 5   4.50

Miniature Sheet

Columbus' Discovery of America, 500th
Anniv. — A576

Designs: a, 4000d, Columbus, flag. b, 6000d, Columbus, natives. c, 8000d, Aboard ship. d, 3000d, Two sailing ships. e, 400d, Columbus' fleet setting sail.
11,000d, Columbus with Ferdinand and Isabella.

1992, Feb. 12
2329 A576 #a.-f. + label   6.00
Imperf
Size: 102x70mm
2330 A576 11,000d multicolored   5.00

Việt Nam 400d Airplanes
                 A577

Designs: 400d, Tupelov TU-154M. 500d, Concorde. 1000d, Airbus A-320. 3000d, Airbus A340-300. 4000d, Boeing Dash 8-400. 5000d, Boeing 747-200. 6000d, McDonnell-Douglas MD-11CF.

1992, Mar. 6   *Perf. 13*
2331-2337 A577 Set of 7   5.00

Intl. Decade for
Natural Disaster
Reduction — A578

Designs: 400d, Storm system, weather forecasting equipment. 4000d, Man taking water depth readings.

1992, Mar. 23
2338-2339 A578 Set of 2   1.00

1992 Summer
Olympics,
Barcelona — A579

Designs: 400d, Archery. 600d, Volleyball. 1000d, Wrestling. 3000d, Fencing. 4000d, Running. 5000d, Weight lifting. 6000d, Field hockey. 10,000d, Basketball.

1992, Mar. 28
2340-2346 A579 Set of 7   4.50
Souvenir Sheet
2347 A579 10,000d multicolored   3.00

No. 2347 contains one 32x43mm stamp.

Motorcycles — A580

Designs: 400d, 5000d, Suzuki 500F. 500d, Honda CBR 600F. 1000d, Honda HRC 500F. 3000d, Kawasaki 250F, vert. 4000d, Suzuki RM 250F, vert. 6000d, BMW 1000F. 10,000d, Suzuki RM 250F, diff.

1992, Apr. 8
2348-2354 A580 Set of 7   5.00
Souvenir Sheet
2355 A580 10,000d multicolored   4.50

No. 2355 contains one 33x44mm stamp.

Intl.
Space
Year
A581

Designs: 400d, Space shuttle launch, vert. 500d, Launch of shuttle Columbia, vert. 3000d, Columbia in space. 4000d, Space station, shuttle Hermes. 5000d, Shuttle Hermes. 6000d, Astronauts, Hubble space telescope, vert.

1992, Apr. 12
2356-2361 A581 Set of 6   5.00

Saigon Post
Office, Cent.
A582

Designs: 200d, Main entrance. 10,000d, Facade.

1992, Apr. 30   *Perf. 13*
2362 A582 200d multicolored   1.00
Souvenir Sheet   *Perf. 13½*
2363 A582 10,000d multicolored   2.50

No. 2363 contains one 43x32mm stamp.

European Cup Soccer
Championships
A583

Various soccer players in action: 200d, 2000d, 4000d, 5000d, 6000d.

1992, May 14   *Perf. 13*
2364-2368 A583 Set of 5   5.00
Souvenir Sheet
2369 A583 9000d multicolored   4.00

No. 2369 contains one 44x33mm stamp.

Spanish
Paintings
A584

Designs: 400d, Portrait of a Girl, by Zurbaran. 500d, Woman with a Jug, by Murillo. 1000d, Portrait of Maria Aprickaia, by Velazquez. 3000d, Holy Family with St. Katherine, by de Ribera. 4000d, Madonna and Child with Saints Agnes and Thekla, by El Greco. 5000d, Woman with a Jug, by Goya. 6000d, The Naked Maja, by Goya, horiz. 10,000d, Three Women, by Picasso, horiz.

1992, May 30
2370-2376 A584 Set of 7   5.00
Souvenir Sheet
2377 A584 10,000d multicolored   4.00

No. 2377 contains one 44x33mm stamp. Expo '92, Seville (#2377).

UN Conference on Environmental
Protection, 20th Anniv. — A585

Designs: 200d, Clean, polluted water. 4000d, Graph comparing current development pattern with environmentally safe pattern.

1992, June 1
2378-2379 A585 Set of 2   1.00

A586   Flowers — A587

Lighthouses: 200d, Cu Lao Xanh. 3000d, Can Gio. 5000d, Vung Tau. 6000d, Long Chau.

1992, June 14   *Perf. 13½x13*
2380-2383 A586 Set of 4   4.50
Genoa '92.

1992, June 28   *Perf. 13*
Designs: 200d, Citrus maxima. 2000d, Nerium indicum. 3000d, Ixora coccinea. 5000d, Cananga oborata. 6000d, Cassia surattensis.
2384-2388 A587 Set of 5   4.00

Birds — A588   Rodents — A589

Designs: 200d, Ducula spilorrhoa. 2000d, Petrophassa ferruginea. 4000d, Columba livia. 5000d, Lopholaimus antarcticus. 6000d, Streptopelia senegalensis, horiz.

1992, July 3
2389-2393 A588 Set of 5   4.50

1992, July 26
Designs: 200d, 500d, Cavia porcellus, horiz. 3000d, Hystrix indica, horiz. 4000d, Gerbillus gerbillus. 5000d, Petaurista petaurista. 6000d, Oryctolagus cuniculus.
2394-2399 A589 Set of 6   5.00

Disabled
Soldiers Day,
45th
Anniv. — A590

1992, July 27
2400 A590 200d multicolored   50

3rd Phu
Dong
Games
A591

1992, Aug. 1
2401 A591 200d multicolored   50

Betta
Splendens
A592

Various fish: 200d, 500d, 3000d, 4000d, 5000d, 6000d.

1992, Aug. 15
2402-2407 A592 Set of 6   5.00

Fable of Tam
Cam — A598

Designs: 200d, Returning from river. 800d, ...sion of old man by goldfish pool. 1000d, With ...old rice at market. 3000d, Trying on slipper for ...ince. 4000d, Rising from lotus flower. 10,000d, ...oyal couple.

...993, Jan. 18
...121-2426 A598   Set of 6   4.50

..., ...u 10000, Anniv. emblem, map.

1992, Oct. 1
2408-2409 A593   Set of 2   1.00

Hanoi
Medical
School,
90th
Anniv.
A594

Designs: 200d, Medical students. 5000d, Alexandre Yersin, school.

1992, Nov. 20
2410-2411 A594   Set of 2   1.25

SOS Children's
Villages — A595

Designs: 200d, Adult sheltering child. 5000d, Women, children inside house.

1992, Dec. 22
2412-2413 A595   Set of 2   1.50

17th
Southeast
Asian
Games,
Singapore
A596

1993, Jan. 1
2414 A596 200d multicolored   50

Bees
A597

Designs: 200d, Apis dorsata. 800d, Apis koschevnikovi. 1000d, Apis laboriosa. 2000d, Apis cerana japonica. 5000d, Apis cerana cerana. 10,000d, Apis mellifera, vert.

1993, Jan. 15
2415-2420 A597 Set of 6   5.00

New Year
1993 (Year of
the Rooster)
A599

Designs: 200d, 5000d, Rooster, hen and chicks.

1993, Jan. 20
2427-2428 A599   Set of 2   2.50

Medicinal
Plants — A600

Designs: 200d, Atractylodes macrocephala. No. 2430, 1000d, Lonicera japonica. No. 2431, 1000d, Quisqualis indica. 3000d, Rehmannia glutinosa. 12,000d, Gardenia jasminoides.

1993, Feb. 27
2429-2433 A600   Set of 5   4.00

Communications
A601

Designs: 200d, Map, communications equipment. 2500d, Map, Hong Kong-Sri Racha Cable route.

1993, Mar. 1
2434-2435 A601   Set of 2   75

Asian
Animals
Gấu trúc Ailuropoda melanoleuca A602

Designs: 200d, Ailuropoda melanoleuca. 800d, Panthera tigris. 1000d, Elephas maximus. 3000d, Rhinoceros unicornis. 4000d, Hylobates leucogenys. No. 2441, 10,000d, Neofelis nebulosa. No. 2442, 10,000d, Box sauveli.

1993, Mar. 10
2436-2441 A602   Set of 6   4.50
Souvenir Sheet
Perf. 13½
2442 A602 10,000d multicolored   2.50

1994 World Cup Soccer Championships,
US — A603

Various soccer players in action.

1993, Mar. 30   *Perf. 13*
2443-2445 A603   200d, 1500d,
7000d, set of 3   2.00

Transportation — A604

Designs: 200d, Wheelbarrow. 800d, Buffalo cart. 1000d, Rickshaw, top up. 2000d, Rickshaw with passenger. 5000d, Rickshaw, top down. 10,000d, Horse-drawn carriage.

1993, Apr. 6
2446-2451 A604   Set of 6   4.50

500Kv Electricity
Lines — A605

1993, May 1
2452-2453 A605   300d, 400d, set of
2   60

Polska
'93 — A606

Paintings: 200d, Sunflowers, by Van Gogh. No. 2455, 1000d, Young Woman, by Mogidliani. No. 2456, 1000d, Couple in Forest, by Rousseau. 5000d, Harlequin with Family, by Picasso. No.

2458, 10,000d, Female Model, by Matisse, horiz. No. 2459, 10,000d, Portrait of Dr. Gachet, by Van Gogh.

1993, May 15   *Perf. 13*
2454-2458 A606   Set of 5   2.50
Souvenir Sheet
Perf. 12½
2459 A606 10,000d multicolored   2.50

No. 2459 contains one 32x43mm stamp.

Da Lat,
Cent.
A607

Orchids: 400d, Paphiopedilum hirsutissimum. No. 2461, 1000d, Paphiopedilum malipoense. No. 2462, 1000d, Paphiopedilum gratrixianum. 12,000d, Paphiopedilum hennisianum.

1993, June 21   *Perf. 13*
2460-2463 A607   Set of 4   3.50

Asian Architecture — A608

Landmark buildings from: 400d, Thailand, vert. 800d, Indonesia, vert. 1000d, Singapore, vert. No. 2467, 2000d, Malaysia. No. 2468, 2000d, Cambodia. 6000d, Laos. 8000d, Brunei.

1993, July 10
2464-2470 A608   Set of 7   4.75

No. 2471 has been reserved for a souvenir sheet with this set.

Crabs — A609

Designs: 400d, Scylla serrata. 800d, Portunus sanguinotentus. 1000d, Charybdis bimaculata. 2000d, Paralithodes brevipes. 5000d, Portunus pelagicus. 10,000d, Lithodes turritus.

1993, July 30
2472-2477 A609   Set of 6   4.50

Stamp
Day — A610

Designs: 400d, shown. 5000d, Hand holding stamped envelope.

1993, Aug. 15
2478-2479 A610   Set of 2   1.25

VIETNAM— ALL AREAS

★ BUYING ★
PAYING TOP PRICES
FOR ALL PERIODS!
CALL NOW FOR OUR UP-
TO-THE-MINUTE QUOTES!!!

★ SELLING ★
EXCELLENT STOCK OF
CLASSIC TO MODERN!
SATISFACTION GUARANTEED!
SEND FOR FREE PRICE LIST!

THE PROFESSIONAL PHILATELIC SERVICE RESPECTED WORLDWIDE

Marlen Stamps & Coins Ltd.

156B Middle Neck Road
Great Neck, N.Y. 11021

Phone: 516-482-8404
FAX: 516-482-8437
Toll Free 1-800-831-STAR

VISA · AMERICAN EXPRESS

Miniature Sheet

Tennis — A611

Women tennis players: a, 400d. c, 1000d.
Male tennis players: b, 1000d. d, 12,000d.

1993, Sept. 20
2480 A611 #a.-d. + 2 labels　　3.50

A613　　　　A614

Costumes: 400d, Lo Lo. 800d, Thai. 1000d, Dao
Do. 2000d, H'mong. 5000d, Kho Mu. No. 2488,
10,000d, Kinh.
No. 2489, 10,000d, Precious gem stones.

VIETNAM AT FACE VALUE
Collect The Colorful Stamps of Vietnam!
· SEND FOR FREE PRICE LIST ·
VIETNAM STAMP AGENCY NORTH AMERICA
703 Market Street, Suite 811,
SAN FRANCISCO, CA 94103
FAX 415-957-0214 · PHONE 415-957-0344

1993　　　　　　　　　**Perf. 13**
2483-2488 A613　Set of 6　　2.50
　　　Souvenir Sheet
　　　　Perf. 13½
2489 A613 10,000d multicolored　2.50

Bangkok '93. Issued: Nos. 2483-2488, 10/1/93.
No. 2489, 10/10/93.
No. 2489 contains one 43x32mm stamp.

1994, Jan. 1
New Year 1994 (Year of the Dog): Various dogs.
2490-2491 A614　400d, 6000d, set
　　　　　　　of 2　　　1.75
　　Imperf., #2490-2491　　4.00

Flowers
A615

Designs: 400d, Prunus persica. 15,000d, Delonix
regia.

1994
2492-2493 A615　Set of 2　　3.75

Issued: 400d, 1/4/94. 15,000d, 4/3/94.
Nos. 2494-2495 are reserved for two additional
values in this set.

Chess
A616

Designs: 400d, Anatoly Karpov. 1000d, Gary
Kasparov. 2000d, Bobby Fischer. 4000d, Emanuel
Lasker. No. 2500, 10,000d, Jose Capablanca.
No. 2501, 10,000d, King.

1994, Jan. 20
2496-2500 A616　Set of 5　　4.50
　　Imperf., #2496-2500　　8.00
　　　Souvenir Sheet
2501 A616 10,000d multicolored　2.75
　　Imperf.　　　　　　4.75

Hong Kong
'94 — A617

Festivals: 400d, Hoi Lim. 800d, Cham. 1000d,
Tay Nguyen. 12,000d, Nam Bo.

1994, Feb. 18
2502-2505 A617　Set of 4　　4.00
　　Imperf., #2502-2505　　6.75

A618　　　　　A619

Various opera masks: 400d, 500d, 2000d,
3000d, 4000d, 7000d.

1994, Mar. 15
2506-2511 A618　Set of 6　　4.75
　　Imperf., #2506-2511　　8.50

1994, Mar. 30
Various gladiolus hybridus: 400d, 2000d, 5000d,
8000d.
2512-2515 A619　Set of 4　　3.75
　　Imperf., #2512-2515　　6.75

Japanese Paintings — A620

Paintings by: 400d, Utamaro. 500d, Harunobu.
1000d, Hokusai. 2000d, Hiroshige. 3000d,
Hokusai, diff. 4000d, Utamaro, diff. 8000d, Choki.

1994, Apr. 9
2516-2522 A620　Set of 7　　5.25
　　Imperf., #2516-2522　　9.25

Insects — A621

Designs: 400d, Cicindela aurulenta. 1000d, Har-
monia octomaculata. 6000d, Cicindela tennipes.
7000d, Collyris.

1994, Apr. 20
2523-2526 A621　Set of 4　　3.75
　　Imperf., #2523-2526　　6.75

Victory at
Dien Bien
Phu, 40th
Anniv.
A622

Designs: 400d, Soldiers dragging equipment.
3000d, Celebration.

1994, Apr.
2527-2528 A622　Set of 2　　90
　　Imperf., #2527-2528　　1.25

Newspaper
"Young
Pioneers," 40th
Anniv. — A623

1994, May 15　　　**Perf. 13x13½**
2529 A623　400d red & black　　45

Crocodiles
A625

Designs: 400d, Crocodylus paresus. 600d, Alligator mississippiensis. 2000d, Crocodylus niloticus.
3000d, Alligator sinensis. 4000d, Caiman yacare.
9000d, Crocodylus johnsoni.
10,000d, Caiman crocodilus.

1994, June 1　　　**Perf. 13x13½**
2532-2537 A625　Set of 6　　5.00
　　Imperf., #2532-2537　　8.75
　　　Souvenir Sheet
　　　　Perf. 13½
2538 A625 10,000d multicolored　2.75
　　Imperf.　　　　　　4.75

No. 2538 contains one 43x32mm stamp.

1994 World Cup
Soccer
Championships,
US — A626

Various soccer players in action: 400d, 600d,
1000d, 2000d, 3000d, 11,000d.

1994, June 15　　　**Perf. 13**
2539-2544 A626　Set of 6　　4.75
　　Imperf., #2539-2544　　8.25
　　　Souvenir Sheet
　　　　Perf. 13½
2545 A626 10,000d multicolored　2.75
　　Imperf.　　　　　　4.75

No. 2545 contains one 32x43mm stamp.

Yersin's
Discovery of
Plague Bacillus,
Cent. — A627

1994, June　　　**Perf. 13x13½**
2546 A627　400d multicolored　　45

UPU, 120th Anniv. A629

Designs: 400d, UPU emblem, "120." 5000d, World map. 10,000d, UPU emblem, "P," vert.

1994, Aug. 1   *Perf. 13*
2551-2552 A629 Set of 2   1.40
Souvenir Sheet
Perf. 14x13¹/₂
2553 A629 10,000d multicolored   2.75

PHILAKOREA '94 — A630

Birds: 400d, Numenius arquata. 600d, Oceanites oceanicus. 1000d, Fregata minor. 2000d, Morus capensis. 3000d, Lunda cirrhata. 11,000d, Larus belcheri.
10,000d, Collocalia fuciphaga.

1994, Aug. 16   *Perf. 13x13¹/₂*
2554-2559 A630 Set of 6   4.75
Souvenir Sheet
Perf. 13¹/₂
2560 A630 10,000d multicolored   2.75

No. 2560 contains one 43x32mm stamp.

A631   A632

Bamboo: 400d, Bambusa blumeana. 1000d, Phyllostachys aurea. 2000d, Bambusa vulgaris. 4000d, Tetragonocalamus quadrangularis. 10,000d, Bambusa venticosa.

1994, Aug. 17   *Perf. 13¹/₂x13*
2561-2565 A631 Set of 5   4.50
Singpex '94.

1994, Sept. 20   *Perf. 13x13¹/₂*
Various bridges: 400d, 900d, 8000d.
2566-2568 A632 Set of 3   2.25

Children's Future — A634

Designs: 400d+100d, Boy helping girl in wheelchair with kite. 2000d, Children dancing, vert.

1994, Oct. 2   Litho.   *Perf. 13*
2572-2573 A634 Set of 2   80

A636   A637

People's Army, 50th Anniv.: 400d, People in formation. 1000d, Soldiers, battle map. 2000d, Ho Chi Minh, child. 4000d, Anti-aircraft battery.

1994, Dec. 22
2576-2579 A636 Set of 4   2.00

1994   *Perf. 13*
Intl. Olympic Committee, Cent.: 400d, Flags. 6000d, Pierre de Coubertin.
2580-2581 A637 Set of 2   1.90

ICAO, 50th Anniv. A638

Jets: 400d, In flight. 3000d, On ground.

1994
2582-2583 A638 Set of 2   90

SEMI-POSTAL STAMPS

World Communications Year — SP1

Designs: No. B1, Hands holding envelope with ITU emblem. No. B2, Satellite dish antenna.

1983, Nov. 1   **Unwmk.**
                Litho.   *Perf. 11*
B1-B2 SP1 50xu +10xu Set of 2   3.75

AIR POST STAMPS

AP1

1959, Nov. 20   **Unwmk.**
                Litho.   *Perf. 11*
C1 AP1 20xu blue & black   10.00

MILITARY STAMPS

M1

                Perf. 12¹/₂
1958, May 1   Litho.   Unwmk.
M1 M1 multicolored   10.00 5.00

Invalids in Rice Paddy M2

1959-60   Litho.   *Perf. 11*
M2 M2 org brn & brown
M3 M3 grey blue & olive
  Nos. M2-M3 (2)   7.50 3.00
Issued: No. M2, 3/14/59. No. M3, 7/27/60.

Soldier, Train — M3

1959, July 1
M4 M3 bluish green   4.00 1.75

Frontier Guard — M4

1961, Jan. 3
M5 M4 multicolored   12.50 8.00

Naval Patrol — M5

1962, June 15
M6 M5 multicolored   4.00 2.00

Military Medal, Invalid's Badge — M6

1963, Sept. 10
M7 M6 12xu multicolored   4.00 4.00

Rifleman — M7

1964, Aug.
M8 M7 multicolored   4.00 4.00

Rifleman Jumping Wall — M8

1965
M9 M8 red & black
M10 M8 yellow green & black
  Nos. M9-M10 (2)   5.00 4.00
Issued: No. M9, 7/1. No. M10, 12/25.

Soldier, Guerrilla Woman M9

1966, Sept. 25
M11 M9 greenish blue & vio bl   5.00 4.00

Badge of People's Army — M10

1967, Oct. 7
M13 M10 multicolored   2.25 80

M11

1968, Nov. 10
M14 M11 lilac   3.50 80

M12

1969, Nov. 15
M15 M12 red & brown red   2.50 1.25

M13

1971, Apr. 27
M16 M13 yellow, brown & red   3.00 1.25

Nguyen Van Be — M14

Design: No. M18, Nguyen Viet Xuan.

1971, Oct. 30 *Perf. 11*
M17 M14 multicolored 2.25 1.10
Perf. 12½
M18 M14 black, pink & buff 2.25 1.10

 M15

 M16

1973, Dec. 20 *Perf. 11*
M20 M15 blue, black & buff
a. Perf. 12½
M22 M16 olive, red & black
a. Perf. 12½
Nos. M20, M22 (2) 4.00

Disabled Veteran in Factory — M17

Design: No. M24, Invalid's Badge, open book, vert.

1976, July 27
M23-M24 M17 Set of 2 3.50 1.75

 Soldier, Map — M18

 Pilot — M19

1976, Oct. 21
M25 M18 red & black

1978
Designs: No. M27, Tank driver. No. M28, Seaman.
M26-M28 M19 Set of 3 4.00 1.25
Issued: No. M26, 6/3; others, 10/10.

 M20

Designs: a, Pilot. b, Badge of People's Army.

1979, Dec. 22
M29 M20 Vertical pair, #a.-b.

Types A343a, A359 and

 Ho Chi Minh — M21

Designs: No. M30, Factory militiawoman. No. M31, Soldier, woman pointing. No. M32, Militiawoman.

1981, Aug. 5
M30 A343a salmon & multi
M31 A343a green & multi
M32 A359 blue & multi
M33 M21 blue & tan
Nos. M30-M33 (4) 4.50 2.25
Size of No. M32: 13x18mm.

 M22

1982, Nov. 9
M34 M22 pink & greenish blue 1.25 80

 M23

1983, Apr. 30
M35 M23 multicolored 2.25 1.10

Victory at Dien Bien Phu, 30th Anniv. — M24

1984, May 5 *Litho.*
M37 M24 multicolored 1.25

Disabled Soldier Teaching Class — M25

1984, Nov. 10
M38 M25 tan & brown 1.25

Frontier Forces Type of 1984
1984, Dec. 15
M39 A410 multicolored

 M26

1984, Dec. 22
M40 M26 multicolored 2.50

Policemen and Women M27

1985, Aug. 30
M41 M27 multicolored

 M28

1986, Oct. 1
M42 M28 olive brown & black 1.50 75

 M29

1987, Sept. 23
M43 M29 carmine and tan 2.00 1.00

OFFICIAL STAMPS

Harvesting Rice — O1

Denominations in grams or kilograms of rice: 600g, 1k, 2k, 5k. Dated 1953.

1953, July Litho. Unwmk. *Perf. 11*
O1-O4 O1 Set of 4 45.00 35.00

Dien Bien Phu Type of 1954
1954-56 *Perf. 11*
O5 A4 600g sepia & ocher 10.00
a. Perf. 6
b. Imperf
Issued: No. O5, 10/54. No. O5a, 12/54. No. O5b, 1956.

Ho Chi Minh — O2

1955 Typo. *Perf. 7*
O6-O7 O2 100g on 2d, 100g on 5d, set of 2 300.00
Nos. O6-O7 were surcharged on rough hand-made brown paper stamps issued in Tonkin in 1948.

Land Reform Type of 1955-56 Inscribed "SU VU" Above Value
1955 Litho. *Perf. 11*
O8-O9 A6 40d, 80d, set of 2 27.50 27.50

Cu Chinh Lan (1930-1952) O3

Denominations: 20d, 80d, 100d, 500d, 1000d, 2000d, 3000d.

1956, June Litho. *Perf. 11½*
O10-O16 O3 Set of 7 200.00 200.00

4th World Trade Union Congress Type of 1957
Inscribed "SU VU" Above Value
1957, Aug. 1 *Perf. 12½*
O17-O20 A15 20d, 40d, 80d, 100d, set of 4 16.00 16.00

One-Pillar Pagoda — O4

1957-58
O21 O4 150d green and brown
O22 O4 150d orange and slate
Nos. O21-O22 (2) 17.50 7.50
Nos. O21-O22 exist with and without imprint and designer's name. Issued: No. O21, 12/22/57; No. O22, 3/12/58.

Craft Fair, Hanoi — O5

1958, May 30
O23-O24 O5 150d, 200d, set of 2 4.00 3.00

1st World Congress of Young Workers, Prague — O6

1958, June 26
O25 O6 150d lt olive green & red 2.50 1.25

Soldier, Factory, Crops — O7

1958, Aug. 19
O26-O28 O7 50d, 150d, 200d, set of 3 7.50 4.00

Opening of New Hanoi Stadium O8

1958, Dec. 31
O29-O32 O8 10d, 20d, 80d, 150d, set of 4 7.00 3.00

Planting Rice — O9

1962, Sept. 1 *Perf. 11*
O33-O35 O9 3xu, 6xu, 12xu, set of 3 2.50 2.50

Rural Mail
Service
O10

1966, July 1   *Perf. 11*
O36-O37 O10 3xu, 6xu, set of 2   2.50 2.50

WALLIS AND FUTUNA ISLANDS

LOCATION — Group of islands in the South Pacific Ocean, northeast of Fiji
GOVT. — French Overseas Territory
AREA — 106 sq. mi.
POP. — 13,000 (est. 1984)
CAPITAL — Mata-Utu, Wallis Island

100 Centimes = 1 Franc

Catalogue values for unused stamps in this country are for Never Hinged items, beginning with Scott 127 in the regular postage section, Scott B9 in the semi-postal section, Scott C1 in the airpost section, and Scott J37 in the postage due section.

New Caledonia Stamps of 1905-28 Overprinted in Black or Red

ILES WALLIS et FUTUNA

1920-28   **Unwmk.**   *Perf. 14x13¹/₂*
1	A16	1c black, *green*	15	15
a.		Double overprint	25.00	
2	A16	2c red brown	15	15
3	A16	4c blue, *org*	15	15
4	A16	5c green	15	15
5	A16	5c dull blue ('22)	15	15
6	A16	10c rose	15	15
7	A16	10c green ('22)	15	15
8	A16	10c red, *pink* ('25)	26	26
9	A16	15c violet	15	15
10	A17	20c gray brown	15	15
11	A17	25c blue, *grn*	18	18
12	A17	25c red, *yel* ('22)	18	18
13	A17	30c brown, *org*	28	28
14	A17	30c dp rose ('22)	18	18
15	A17	30c red orange ('25)	18	18
16	A17	30c lt green ('27)	38	38
17	A17	35c black, *yel* (R)	15	15
18	A17	40c rose, *grn*	18	18
19	A17	45c violet brn, *pnksh*	22	22
20	A17	50c red, *org*	18	18
21	A17	50c dark blue ('22)	18	18
22	A17	50c dark gray ('25)	35	35
23	A17	65c deep blue ('28)	90	90
24	A17	75c olive green	42	42

ILES WALLIS et FUTUNA

Overprinted
25	A18	1fr blue, *yel grn*	85	85
a.		Triple overprint	42.50	
26	A18	1.10fr orange brn ('28)	70	70
27	A18	2fr carmine, *bl*	1.25	1.25
28	A18	5fr black, *org* (R)	2.25	2.25
		Nos. 1-28 (28)	10.62	10.62

No. 9 Surcharged New Value and Bars in Various Colors **0,01**

1922
29	A16	0.01c on 15c violet (Bk)	15	15
30	A16	0.02c on 15c violet (Bl)	15	15
31	A16	0.04c on 15c violet (G)	15	15
32	A16	0.05c on 15c violet (R)	15	15

Stamps and Types of 1920 Surcharged with New Values and Bars in Black or Red

1924-27
33	A18	25c on 2fr car, *bl*	18	18
34	A18	25c on 5fr black, *org*	18	18
35	A17	65c on 40c rose red, *grn* ('25)	22	22
36	A17	85c on 75c ol grn ('25)	22	22

37	A17	90c on 75c dp rose ('27)	35	35
38	A18	1.25fr on 1fr dp bl (R; '26)	18	18
39	A18	1.50fr on 1fr dp bl, *bl* ('27)	52	52
a.		Double surcharge	60.00	
b.		Surcharge omitted	82.50	
40	A18	3fr on 5fr red vio ('27)	1.00	1.00
a.		Surcharge omitted	82.50	
b.		Double surcharge	65.00	
41	A18	10fr on 5fr ol, *lav* ('27)	6.00	6.00
42	A18	20fr on 5fr vio rose, *yel* ('27)	9.50	9.50
		Nos. 33-42 (10)	18.35	18.35

New Caledonia Stamps and Types of 1928-40 Overprinted as in 1920

1930-40   *Perf. 13¹/₂, 14x13, 14x13¹/₂*
43	A19	1c brn vio & indigo	15	15
a.		Double overprint	30.00	
44	A19	2c dk brn & yel grn	15	15
45	A19	3c brn vio & ind ('40)	15	15
46	A19	4c org & Prus grn	15	15
47	A19	5c Prus bl & dp ol	15	15
48	A19	10c gray lil & dk brn	15	15
49	A19	15c yel brn & dp bl	15	15
50	A19	20c brn red & dk brn	15	15
51	A19	25c dk grn & dk brn	15	15
52	A20	30c gray grn & bl grn	15	15
53	A20	35c Prus grn & dk grn ('38)	15	15
a.		Without overprint	82.50	
54	A20	40c brt red & olive	15	15
55	A20	45c dp bl & red org	15	15
56	A20	45c bl grn & dl grn ('40)	15	15
57	A20	50c vio & brn	15	15
58	A20	55c bl vio & rose red ('38)	42	42
59	A20	60c vio bl & car ('40)	15	15
60	A20	65c org brn & bl	30	30
61	A20	70c dp rose & brn ('38)	15	15
62	A20	75c Prus bl & ol gray	45	45
63	A20	80c dk cl & grn ('38)	15	15
64	A20	85c grn & brn	85	85
65	A20	90c dp red & brt red	32	32
66	A20	90c ol grn & rose red ('39)	15	15
67	A21	1fr dp ol & sal red	85	85
68	A21	1fr rose red & dk car ('38)	35	35
69	A21	1fr brn red & grm ('40)	15	15
70	A21	1.10fr dp grn & brn	7.00	7.00
71	A21	1.25fr brn red & grn ('33)	45	45
72	A21	1.25fr rose red & dk car ('39)	15	15
73	A21	1.40fr dk bl & red org ('40)	20	20
74	A21	1.50fr dp bl & bl	15	15
75	A21	1.60fr grn & brn ('40)	24	24
76	A21	1.75fr dk bl & red org ('33)	3.00	3.00
77	A21	1.75fr vio bl ('38)	45	45
78	A21	2fr red org & brn	30	30
79	A21	2.25fr vio bl ('39)	20	20
80	A21	2.50fr brn & lt brn ('40)	25	25
81	A21	3fr mag & brn	30	30
82	A21	5fr dk bl & brn	30	30
83	A21	10fr vio & brn, *pnksh*	42	42
84	A21	20fr red & brn, *yel*	75	75
		Nos. 43-84 (42)	20.70	20.70

For overprints see Nos. 94-126.

Colonial Exposition Issue
Common Design Types
1931, Apr. 13   **Engr.**   *Perf. 12¹/₂*
Name of Country Typo. in Black
85	CD70	40c dp grn	1.50	1.50
86	CD71	50c violet	1.50	1.50
87	CD72	90c red org	1.50	1.50
88	CD73	1.50fr dull blue	1.50	1.50

Colonial Arts Exhibition Issue
Common Design Type
Souvenir Sheet
1937   *Imperf.*
89   CD78   3fr red violet   1.75 1.75

New York World's Fair Issue
Common Design Type
1939, May. 10   **Engr.**   *Perf. 12¹/₂x12*
90	CD82	1.25fr carmine lake	50	50
91	CD82	2.25fr ultramarine	50	50

Petain Issue
New Caledonia Nos. 216A-216B Overprinted "WALLIS ET FUTUNA" in Lilac or Red
1941   **Engr.**   *Perf. 12¹/₂x12*
92	A21a	1fr bluish grn (L)	16	
93	A21a	2.50fr dk bl (R)	16	

Nos. 92-93 were issued by the Vichy government and were not placed on sale in the dependency.
Six stamps of New Caledonia types A19 and A21 without "RF" were overprinted "ILES WALLIS ET FUTUNA" by the Vichy government and issued in 1944, but were not placed on sale in the dependency.

Nos. 43-69, 71, 74, 77-78, 80-84 with Additional Overprint in Black

France Libre
1941-43   *Perf. 14x13¹/₂*
94	A19	1c	18	18
95	A19	2c	18	18
96	A19	3c	42.50	42.50
97	A19	4c	18	18
98	A19	5c	18	18
99	A19	10c	18	18
100	A19	15c	18	18
101	A19	20c	32	32
102	A19	25c	32	32
103	A20	30c	32	32
104	A20	35c	18	18
105	A20	40c	32	32
106	A20	45c #55	32	32
107	A20	45c #56	40.00	40.00
108	A20	50c	22	22
109	A20	55c	22	22
110	A20	60c	40.00	40.00
111	A20	65c	22	22
112	A20	70c	22	22
113	A20	75c	65	65
114	A20	80c	35	35
115	A20	85c	65	65
116	A20	90c #65	55	55
117	A21	1fr #68	65	65
118	A21	1.25fr #71	65	65
119	A21	1.50fr	45	45
120	A21	1.75fr #77	45	45
121	A21	2fr	65	65
122	A21	2.50fr	80.00	80.00
123	A21	3fr	45	45
124	A21	5fr	1.75	1.75
125	A21	10fr	22.50	22.50
126	A21	20fr	40.00	40.00
		Nos. 94-126 (33)	275.99	275.99

Catalogue values for unused stamps in this section, from this point to the end of the section, are for Never Hinged items.

Ivi Poo, Bone Carving in Tiki Design A1

1944   **Unwmk.**   **Photo.**   *Perf. 11¹/₂x12*
127	A1	5c lt brown	15	15
128	A1	10c dp gray blue	15	15
129	A1	25c emerald	15	15
130	A1	30c dull orange	15	15
131	A1	40c dk slate grn	25	25
132	A1	80c brown red	20	20
133	A1	1fr red violet	15	15
134	A1	1.50fr red	15	15
135	A1	2fr gray black	15	15
136	A1	2.50fr brt ultra	20	20
137	A1	4fr dark purple	20	20
138	A1	5fr lemon yellow	20	20
139	A1	10fr chocolate	32	32
140	A1	20fr deep green	45	45
		Set value	2.40	2.40

Nos. 127, 129 and 136 Surcharged with New Values and Bars in Black or Carmine

1946
141	A1	50c on 5c lt brown	30	30
142	A1	60c on 5c lt brown	30	30
143	A1	70c on 5c lt brown	16	16
144	A1	1.20fr on 5c lt brown	16	16
145	A1	2.40fr on 25c emerald	16	16
146	A1	3fr on 25c emerald	16	16
147	A1	4.50fr on 25c emerald	42	42
148	A1	15fr on 2.50fr (C)	45	45
		Nos. 141-148 (8)	2.11	2.11

Military Medal Issue
Common Design Type
Engraved and Typographed
1952, Dec. 1   *Perf. 13*
149   CD101   2fr multicolored   1.00 1.00

Wallis Islander — A2

Unwmk.
1957, June 11   **Engr.**   *Perf. 13*
150	A2	3fr dk purple & lil rose	42	42
151	A2	9fr bl, dl lil & vio brn	70	70

Imperforates
Most Wallis and Futuna stamps from 1957 onward exist imperforate in issued and trial colors, and also in small presentation sheets in issued colors.

Flower Issue
Common Design Type
Design: 5fr, Montrouziera, horiz.
1958, July 7   **Photo.**   *Perf. 12¹/₂x12*
152   CD104   5fr multicolored   1.25 90

Human Rights Issue
Common Design Type
1958, Dec. 10   **Engr.**   *Perf. 13*
153   CD105   17fr brt bl & dk bl   1.65 1.65

Women Making Tapa Cloth — A3

Kava Ceremony A4

Designs: 17fr, Dancers. 19fr, Dancers with paddles.

1960, Oct. 19   **Engr.**   *Perf. 13*
154	A3	5fr dk brown, grn & org brn	30	30
155	A4	7fr dk brown & Prus grn	42	42
156	A4	17fr ultra, claret & grn	65	65
157	A3	19fr claret & slate	90	90

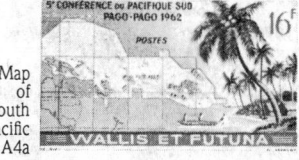

Map of South Pacific A4a

1962, July 19   **Photo.**   *Perf. 13x12*
158   A4a   16fr multicolored   1.75 1.75
5th South Pacific Conference, Pago Pago, 1962.

Sea Shells — A5

1962-63   **Engr.**   *Perf. 13*
Size: 22x36mm
159	A5	25c Triton	18	18
160	A5	1fr Mitra episcopalis	18	18
161	A5	2fr Cypraecassis rufa	24	24
162	A5	4fr Murex tenuspina	48	48
163	A5	10fr Oliva erythrostoma	1.40	1.40
164	A5	20fr Cyprae tigris	2.00	2.00
		Nos. 159-164,C18 (7)	8.48	7.98

Red Cross Centenary Issue
Common Design Type
1963, Sept. 2   **Unwmk.**   *Perf. 13*
165   CD113   12fr red lil, gray & car   1.20 1.20

Human Rights Issue
Common Design Type

		Engr.	
1963, Dec. 10			
166 CD117 29fr dk red & ocher		2.50	2.50

Philatec Issue
Common Design Type

		Unwmk.	*Perf. 13*
1964, Apr. 15			
167 CD118 9fr dk sl grn, grn & red		1.25	1.25

Queen Amelia and Ship "Queen Amelia" — A6

		Photo.	*Perf. 12½x13*
1965, Feb. 15			
168 A6 11fr multicolored		2.25	2.25

WHO Anniversary Issue
Common Design Type

		Engr.	*Perf. 13*
1968, May 4			
169 CD126 17fr bl grn, org & lil		2.00	2.00

Human Rights Year Issue
Common Design Type

		Engr.	*Perf. 13*
1968, Aug. 10			
170 CD127 19fr dk pur, org brn & brt mag		1.40	1.40

Outrigger Canoe — A7

		Photo.	*Perf. 13*
1969, Apr. 30			
171 A7 1fr multicolored		40	40
Nos. 171,C31-C35 (6)		12.80	6.90

ILO Issue
Common Design Type

		Engr.	*Perf. 13*
1969, Nov. 24			
172 CD131 9fr orange, brn & bl		1.10	1.10

UPU Headquarters Issue
Common Design Type

		Engr.	*Perf. 13*
1970, May 20			
173 CD133 21fr lil rose, ind & ol bis		1.25	1.25

No. 157 Surcharged with New Value and Two Bars

		Engr.	*Perf. 13*
1971			
174 A3 12fr on 19fr		50	50

Weight Lifting — A8

1971, Oct. 25			
175 A8 24fr shown		1.90	1.90
176 A8 36fr Basketball		2.25	2.25

4th South Pacific Games, Papeete, French Polynesia, Sept. 8-19. See Nos. C37-C38.

De Gaulle Issue
Common Design Type

Designs: 30fr, Gen. de Gaulle, 1940. 70fr, Pres. de Gaulle, 1970.

		Engr.	*Perf. 13*
1971, Nov. 9			
177 CD134 30fr blue & black		1.65	1.10
178 CD134 70fr blue & black		3.50	2.25

Child's Outrigger Canoe — A9

Designs: 16fr, Children's canoe race. 18fr, Outrigger racing canoe.

		Photo.	*Perf. 13x12½*
1972, Oct. 16			
		Size: 35½x26½mm	
179 A9 14fr dk green & multi		65	45
180 A9 16fr dk plum & multi		65	45
181 A9 18fr blue & multi		1.00	70

Outrigger sailing canoes. See No. C41.

Rhinoceros Beetle — A10

Insects: 25fr, Cosmopolites sordidus (beetle). 35fr, Ophideres fullonica (moth). 45fr, Dragonfly.

		Photo.	*Perf. 13*
1974, July 29			
182 A10 15fr olive & multi		70	55
183 A10 25fr olive & multi		90	60
184 A10 35fr gray blue & multi		1.50	90
185 A10 45fr multicolored		2.00	1.40

Georges Pompidou (1911-74), Pres. of France — A11

		Engr.	*Perf. 13*
1975, Dec. 1			
186 A11 50fr ultra & slate		2.25	1.75

Battle of Yorktown and George Washington — A12

American Bicentennial: 47fr, Virginia Cape Battle and Lafayette.

		Engr.	*Perf. 13*
1976, June 28			
187 A12 19fr blue, red & olive		70	50
188 A12 47fr blue, red & maroon		1.65	1.40

For overprints see Nos. 205-206.

Conus Ammiralis — A13

Sea Shells: 23fr, Cyprae assellus. 43fr, Turbo petholatus. 61fr, Mitra papalis.

		Engr.	*Perf. 13*
1976, Oct. 1			
189 A13 20fr multicolored		65	60
190 A13 23fr multicolored		80	60
191 A13 43fr multicolored		2.00	1.20
192 A13 61fr ultra & multi		2.50	1.90

Father Chanel and Poi Church — A14

Design: 32fr, Father Chanel and map of islands.

		Litho.	*Perf. 12*
1977, Apr. 28			
193 A14 22fr multicolored		60	38
194 A14 32fr multicolored		80	55

Return of the ashes of Father Chanel, missionary.

Bowl, Mortar and Pestle — A15

Handicrafts: 25fr, Wooden bowls and leather bag. 33fr, Wooden comb, club, and boat model. 45fr, War clubs, Futuna. 69fr, Lances.

		Litho.	*Perf. 12½*
1977, Sept. 26			
195 A15 12fr multicolored		35	24
196 A15 25fr multicolored		60	38
197 A15 33fr multicolored		75	45
198 A15 45fr multicolored		1.10	70
199 A15 69fr multicolored		1.65	1.00
Nos. 195-199 (5)		4.45	2.77

Post Office, Mata Utu — A16

Designs: 50fr, Sia Hospital, Mata Utu. 57fr, Administration Buildings, Mata Utu. 63fr, St. Joseph's Church, Sigave. 120fr, Royal Palace, Mara Utu.

		Litho.	*Perf. 13*
1977, Dec. 12			
200 A16 27fr multicolored		38	35
201 A16 50fr multicolored		75	55
202 A16 57fr multicolored		90	60
203 A16 63fr multicolored		1.00	90
204 A16 120fr multicolored		2.00	1.40
Nos. 200-204 (5)		5.03	3.80

Nos. 187-188 Overprinted: "JAMES COOK / Bicentenaire de la / découverte des Iles / Hawaii 1778-1978"

		Engr.	*Perf. 13*
1978, Jan. 22			
205 A12 19fr multicolored		1.40	1.25
206 A12 47fr multicolored		2.75	1.75

Bicentenary of the arrival of Capt. Cook in the Hawaiian Islands.

Cruiser Triomphant — A17

Warships: 200fr, Destroyers Cap des Palmes and Chevreuil. 280fr, Cruiser Savorgnan de Brazza.

		Photo.	*Perf. 13x12½*
1978, June 18			
207 A17 150fr multicolored		4.50	3.50
208 A17 200fr multicolored		6.00	4.50
209 A17 280fr multicolored		8.00	6.00

Free French warships serving in the Pacific, 1940-1944.

Solanum Seaforthianum A18

Flowers: 24fr, Cassia alata. 29fr, Gloriosa superba. 36fr, Hymenocallis littoralis.

		Photo.	*Perf. 13*
1978, July 11			
210 A18 16fr multicolored		38	28
211 A18 24fr multicolored		45	35
212 A18 29fr multicolored		50	45
213 A18 36fr multicolored		90	65

Gray Egret — A19

Birds: 18fr, Red-footed booby. 28fr, Brown booby. 35fr, White tern.

		Photo.	*Perf. 13*
1978, Sept. 5			
214 A19 17fr multicolored		50	35
215 A19 18fr multicolored		50	35
216 A19 28fr multicolored		60	50
217 A19 35fr multicolored		1.20	80

Traditional Patterns — A20

Designs: 55fr, Corpus Christi procession. 59fr, Chief's honor guard.

1978, Oct. 3			
218 A20 53fr multicolored		1.00	65
219 A20 55fr multicolored		1.25	75
220 A20 59fr multicolored		1.40	90

Human Rights Flame — A21

		Litho.	*Perf. 12½*
1978, Dec. 10			
221 A21 44fr multicolored		80	45
222 A21 56fr multicolored		1.40	75

30th anniversary of Universal Declaration of Human Rights.

Fishing Boat — A22

Designs: 30fr, Weighing young tuna. 34fr, Stocking young tunas. 38fr, Measuring tuna. 40fr, Angler catching tuna. 48fr, Adult tuna.

1979, Mar. 19   Litho.   Perf. 12
223	A22	10fr multicolored	32	25
224	A22	30fr multicolored	55	45
225	A22	34fr multicolored	65	55
226	A22	38fr multicolored	90	65
227	A22	40fr multicolored	1.10	90
228	A22	48fr multicolored	1.25	1.10

a. Souv. sheet of 6, #223-228 + 3 labels   8.00 8.00
Nos. 223-228 (6)   4.77 3.90

Tuna tagging by South Pacific Commission.
For surcharge see No. 261.

Boy with Raft and IYC Emblem — A23

Design: 58fr, Girl on horseback.

1979, Apr. 9   Photo.   Perf. 13
229 A23 52fr multicolored   1.00 80
230 A23 58fr multicolored   1.25 90

International Year of the Child.

Bombax Ellipticum — A24

Designs: 64fr, Callophyllum. 76fr, Pandanus odoratissimus.

1979, Apr. 23   Litho.   Perf. 13
231 A24 50fr multicolored   75 65
232 A24 64fr multicolored   1.25 75
233 A24 76fr multicolored   1.40 90

Green and Withered Landscapes — A25

1979, May 28   Photo.   Perf. 13
234 A25 22fr multicolored   45 38

Anti-alcoholism campaign.

Flowers — A26

1979, July 16   Photo.   Perf. 12½x13
235 A26 20fr Crinum   42 35
236 A26 42fr Passiflora   85 60
237 A26 62fr Canna indica   1.10 80

See Nos. 279-281.

Swimming — A27

1979, Aug. 27   Engr.   Perf. 13
238 A27 31fr shown   90 75
239 A27 39fr High jump   1.10 90

6th South Pacific Games, Suva, Fiji, Aug. 27-Sept. 8.

Flower Necklaces — A28

Design: 140fr, Coral necklaces.

1979, Aug. 27   Litho.
240 A28 110fr multicolored   2.25 1.50
241 A28 140fr multicolored   3.00 2.00

Trees and Birds, by Sutita — A29

Paintings by Local Artists: 65fr, Birds and Mountain, by M. A. Pilioko, vert. 78fr, Festival Procession, by Sutita.

1979, Oct. 8   Perf. 13x12½, 12½x13
242 A29 27fr multicolored   65 50
243 A29 65fr multicolored   1.25 80
244 A29 78fr multicolored   1.60 1.20

Marine Mantis A30

Marine Life: 23fr, Hexabranchus sanguineus. 25fr, Spondylus barbatus. 43fr, Gorgon coral. 45fr, Linckia laevigata. 63fr, Tridacna squamosa.

1979, Nov. 5   Photo.   Perf. 13x12½
245 A30 15fr multicolored   35 30
246 A30 23fr multicolored   50 38
247 A30 25fr multicolored   60 38
248 A30 43fr multicolored   70 55
249 A30 45fr multicolored   80 60
250 A30 63fr multicolored   1.20 1.00
Nos. 245-250 (6)   4.15 3.21

See Nos. 294-297.

Transportation Type of 1979
1980, Feb. 29   Litho.   Perf. 13
251 AP32 1fr like No. C87   15 15
252 AP32 3fr like No. C88   15 15
253 AP32 5fr like No. C89   15 15
Set value   26 15

Radio Station and Tower — A31

1980, Apr. 21   Litho.   Perf. 13
254 A31 47fr multicolored   95 55

Radio station FR3, 1st anniversary.

Jesus Laid in the Tomb, by Maurice Denis — A32

1980, Apr. 28   Perf. 13x12½
255 A32 25fr multicolored   65 50

Easter 1980.

Gnathodentex Mossambicus A33

1980, Aug. 25   Litho.   Perf. 12½x13
256 A33 23fr shown   55 40
257 A33 27fr Pristipomoides filamentosus   60 55
258 A33 32fr Etelis carbunculus   60 55
259 A33 51fr Cephalopholis wallisi   1.00 80
260 A33 59fr Aphareus rutilans   1.40 1.20
Nos. 256-260 (5)   4.15 3.50

Nos. 256-260 se-tenant.

No. 228 Surcharged:

═ 50ᶠ   SYDPEX 80

29 Septembre

1980   Litho.   Perf. 12
261 A22 50fr on 48fr multi   1.00 70

Sydpex 80 Philatelic Exhibition, Sydney.

13th World Telecommunications Day — A34

1981, May 17   Litho.   Perf. 12½
262 A34 49fr multicolored   80 60

Pierre Curie and Laboratory Equipment — A35

1981, May 25   Litho.   Perf. 13
263 A35 56fr multicolored   1.00 70

Pierre Curie (1859-1906), discoverer of radioactivity.

Conus Textile — A36

Designs: Marine life.

1981, June 22   Perf. 12½x13
264 A36 28fr Favites   40 35
265 A36 30fr Cyanophyces   55 40
266 A36 31fr Ceratium vultur   55 40
267 A36 35fr Amphiprion frenatus   55 50
268 A36 40fr shown   65 65
269 A36 55fr Comatule   1.10 90
Nos. 264-269 (6)   3.80 3.10

Also exists in se-tenant strips of 6 from sheet of 24.

60th Anniv. of Anti-tuberculin Vaccine (Developed by Calmette and Guerin) — A37

1981, July 28   Litho.   Perf. 13
270 A37 27fr multicolored   45 40

Intl. Year of the Disabled — A38

1981, Aug. 17
271 A38 42fr multicolored   75 45

No. 245 Surcharged in Red

1981, Sept.   Photo.   Perf. 13x12½
272 A30 5fr on 15fr multi   15 15

Thomas Edison (1847-1931) and his Phonograph, 1878 — A39

1981, Sept. 5   Engr.   Perf. 13
273 A39 59fr multicolored   1.00 70

Battle of Yorktown, 1781 (American Revolution) — A40

1981, Oct. 19 Engr.   Perf. 13
274 A40 66fr Admiral de Grasse   65 60
275 A40 74fr Sea battle, vert.   1.20 90

200-Mile Zone Surveillance — A41

1981, Dec. 4 Litho.   Perf. 13
276 A41 60fr Patrol boat Dieppoise 60 45
277 A41 85fr Protet   80 65

TB Bacillus Centenary — A42

1982, Mar. 24 Litho.   Perf. 13
278 A42 45fr multicolored   60 50

Flower Type of 1979 in Changed Colors
1982, May 3 Photo.   Perf. 12½x13
279 A26 1fr like No. 235   15 15
280 A26 2fr like No. 236   15 15
281 A26 3fr like No. 237   15 15
   Set value   15 15

PHILEXFRANCE '82 Intl. Stamp Exhibition, Paris, June 11-21 — A43

1983, May 12 Engr.   Perf. 13
282 A43 140fr No. 25   2.00 1.40

Acanthe Phippium A44

Orchids and rubiaceae (83fr).

1982, May 24 Litho.   Perf. 12½x13
283 A44 34fr shown   55 50
284 A44 68fr Acanthe phippium, diff. 1.00 90
285 A44 70fr Spathoglottis pacifica 1.10 90
286 A44 83fr Mussaenda raiateensis 1.40 1.20

Scouting Year — A45

1982, June 21   Perf. 12½
287 A45 80fr Baden-Powell   1.00 80

Cypraea Talpa — A46

Porcelaines shells.

1982, June 28   Perf. 12½x13
288 A46 10fr shown   15 15
289 A46 15fr Cypraea vitellus 22 16
290 A46 25fr Cypraea argus   32 30
291 A46 27fr Cypraea carneola 38 30
292 A46 40fr Cypraea mappa   55 40
293 A46 50fr Cypraea tigris 60 45
   Nos. 288-293 (6)   2.22 1.76

Marine Life Type of 1979
1982, Oct. 1 Photo.   Perf. 13x12½
294 A30 32fr Gorgones milithea 30 26
295 A30 35fr Linckia laevigata 38 30
296 A30 46fr Hexabranchus sanguineus 45 35
297 A30 63fr Spondylus barbatus 65 50

St. Teresa of Jesus of Avila (1515-1582) A48

1982, Nov. 8 Engr.   Perf. 13
298 A48 31fr multi   40 32
See No. 315.

Traditional House — A49

1983, Jan. 20 Litho.   Perf. 13
299 A49 19fr multi   22 15

Gustave Eiffel (1832-1923), Architect — A50

1983, Feb. 14 Engr.   Perf. 13
300 A50 97fr multi   1.25 1.00

A51   A52

1983, June 28 Engr.   Perf. 13
301 A51 92fr Thai dancer, 19th cent. 1.00 75
BANGKOK '83 Intl. Stamp Show, Aug. 4-13.

1983, Aug. 23 Litho.   Perf. 13x13½
302 A52 20fr multi   25 15
World Communications Year.

Cone Shells — A53

1983-84 Litho.   Perf. 13½x13
303 A53 10fr Conus tulipa   15 15
304 A53 17fr Conus capitaneus   25 16
305 A53 21fr Conus virgo   30 25
306 A53 22fr Strombus lentiginosus 30 20
307 A53 25fr Lambis chiragra   38 28
308 A53 35fr Strombus dentatus 45 35
309 A53 39fr Conus vitulinus   55 45
310 A53 43fr Lambis scorpius   60 45
311 A53 49fr Strombus aurisdianae 62 55
312 A53 52fr Conus marmoreus   65 55
313 A53 65fr Conus leopardus   90 65
314 A53 76fr Lambis crocata   1.10 80
   Nos. 303-314 (12)   6.25 4.84

Issue dates: 22fr, 25fr, 35fr, 43fr, 49fr, 76fr, Mar. 23, 1984; others, Oct. 14, 1983.

No. 298 Redrawn with Espana '84 Emblem
1984, Apr. 27 Engr.   Perf. 13
315 A48 70fr multi   1.00 65

Denis Diderot (1713-1784), Philosopher — A54

1984, May 11
316 A54 100fr Portrait, encyclopedia title page   1.10 90

Nature Protection (Whale) A55

1984, June 5 Litho.   Perf. 13x12½
317 A55 90fr Orcina orca   1.00 80

4th Pacific Arts Festival — A56

1984, Nov. 30 Litho.   Perf. 13
318 A56 160fr Islanders   1.20 80

Lapita Pottery — A57

Ethno-Archaeological Museum: Excavation site, reconstructed ceramic bowl.

1985, Jan. 16 Litho.   Perf. 13
319 A57 53fr multi   40 25

Seashells A58

1985, Feb. 11
320 A58 2fr Nautilus pompilius 15 15
321 A58 3fr Murex bruneus   15 15
322 A58 41fr Casmaria erinaceus 35 20
323 A58 47fr Conus vexillum   42 25
324 A58 56fr Harpa harpa   48 28
325 A58 71fr Murex ramosus   60 38
   Nos. 320-325 (6)   2.15
   Set value   1.20

Victor Hugo, Author (1802-1885) — A59   Bat — A60

1985, Mar. 7   Engr.
326 A59 89fr multi   90 45

1985, Apr. 29   Litho.
327 A60 38fr multi   40 20

Intl. Youth Year — A61

1985, May 20 Litho.   Perf. 12½x13
328 A61 64fr European, Malaysian children   60 32

UN, 40th Anniv. — A61a

1985, July 12   Engr.   Perf. 13
328A A61a 49fr Prus grn, dk ultra & red   50 25

Pierre de Ronsard (1524-1585), Poet — A62

1985, Sept. 16   Engr.   Perf. 13
329 A62 170fr brt bl, sep & brn   1.65 70

Dr. Albert Schweitzer — A63

1985, Nov. 22   Engr.   Perf. 13
330 A63 50fr blk, dk red lil & org brn   50 25

World Food Day — A64

1986, Jan. 23   Litho.   Perf. 12½x13
331 A64 39fr Breadfruit   48 25

Flamboyants — A65

1986, Feb. 13   Perf. 13x12½
332 A65 38fr multi   48 28

Seashells — A66

1986, Apr. 24   Litho.   Perf. 13½x13
333 A66   4fr Lambis truncata   15 15
334 A66   5fr Charonia tritonis   15 15
335 A66 10fr Oliva miniacea   15 15
336 A66 18fr Distorsio anus   28 15
337 A66 25fr Mitra mitra   38 20
338 A66 107fr Conus distans   1.60 80
    Nos. 333-338 (6)   2.71
    Set value   1.30

Also exists in se-tenant strips of 6 from sheet of 24.

1986 World Cup Soccer Championships, Mexico — A67

1986, May 20   Perf. 13x12½
339 A67 95fr multi   1.45 72

UNICEF.

Discovery of Horn Islands, 370th Anniv. — A68

Designs: No. 340a, 8fr, William Schouten, ship. No. 340b, 9fr, Jacob LeMaire, ship. No. 340c, 155fr, Map of Alo and Alofi.

1986, June 19   Engr.   Perf. 13
340   Strip of 3, #a.-c.   2.65 1.35

James Watt (1736-1819), Inventor, and Steam Engine — A69

1986, July 11
341 A69 74fr blk & dk red   1.10 55

La Lorientaise Patrol Boat — A70

1986, Aug. 7
342 A70   6fr shown   15 15
343 A70   7fr Commandant Blaison   15 15
344 A70 120fr Balny escort ship   1.80 90
    Set value   1.00

Rose Laurel — A71

1986, Oct. 2   Litho.   Perf. 13x12½
345 A71 97fr multi   1.50 75

Virgin and Child, by Sandro Botticelli A72

1986, Dec. 12   Litho.   Perf. 12½x13
346 A72 250fr multi   3.75 1.90

Christmas.

Butterflies — A73

1987, Apr. 2   Litho.   Perf. 12½
347 A73   2fr Papilio montrouzieri   15 15
348 A73 42fr Belenois java   62 30
349 A73 46fr Delias ellipsis   70 35
350 A73 50fr Danaus pumila   75 38
351 A73 52fr Luthrodes cleotas   78 40
352 A73 59fr Precis villida   90 45
    Nos. 347-352 (6)   3.90 2.03

World Wrestling Championships — A74

1987, May 26   Litho.   Perf. 12½
353 A74 97fr multi   1.50 75

For overprint see No. 360.

Seashells A75

1987, June 24   Litho.   Perf. 13
354 A75   3fr Cymatium pileare   15 15
355 A75   4fr Conus textile   15 15
356 A75 28fr Cypraea mauritiana   45 22
357 A75 44fr Bursa bubo   70 35
358 A75 48fr Cypraea testudinaria   75 38
359 A75 78fr Cypraecassis rufa   1.25 62
    Nos. 354-359 (6)   3.45 1.87

Also exists in se-tenant strips of 6 from sheet of 24.

No. 353 Overprinted OLYMPHILEX '87 ROME

1987, Aug. 29   Litho.   Perf. 12½
360 A74 97fr multi   2.00 1.00

OLYMPHILEX '87, Rome.

Bust of a Girl, by Auguste Rodin (1840-1917) — A76

1987, Sept. 15   Engr.   Perf. 13
361 A76 150fr plum   2.25 1.15

World Post Day A77

1987, Oct. 9   Litho.   Perf. 13
362 A77 116fr multi   2.40 1.20

Birds — A78

1987, Oct. 28   Perf. 13x12½
363 A78   6fr Anas superciliosa   15 15
364 A78 19fr Pluvialis dominica   40 20
365 A78 47fr Gallicolumba stairi   1.00 50
366 A78 56fr Arenaria interpres   1.20 60
367 A78 64fr Rallus philippensis   1.40 70
368 A78 68fr Limosa lapponica   1.50 75
    Nos. 363-368 (6)   5.65 2.90

Francis Carco (1886-1958), Painter — A79

Design: Carco and views of the Moulin de la Galette and Place du Tertre, Paris.

1988, Jan. 29   Litho.   Perf. 13
369 A79 40fr multi   82 40

Jean-Francois de Galaup, Comte de La Perouse, Explorer — A80

Design: Ships L'Astrolabe and La Boussole, portrait of La Perouse.

1988, Mar. 21   Engr.   Perf. 13
370 A80 70fr org brn, dark blue & olive grn   1.40 70

Intl. Red Cross and Red Crescent Organizations, 125th Anniv. — A81

1988, July 4   Engr.   Perf. 13
371 A81 30fr blk, dark red & brt
     blue grn   55   28

1988 Summer Olympics, Seoul — A82

1988, Sept. 1   Engr.   Perf. 13
372 A82 11fr Javelin   20   15
373 A82 20fr Women's volleyball   35   18
374 A82 60fr Windsurfing   1.05   52
375 A82 80fr Yachting   1.40   70
  a. Souv. sheet of 4, #372-375 + 2 la-
      bels, gutter between   3.00 3.00

Intl. Maritime Organization Emblem and Packet *Escorteur* F727 — A83

1989, Jan. 26   Litho.   Perf. 13
376 A83 26fr multi   48   25

Jean Renoir (1894-1979), Film Director, and Scene from *The Grand Illusion* — A84

1989, Feb. 16   Engr.   Perf. 13
377 A84 24fr brt lil rose, dark vio
     brn & brt org   45   22

Antoine Becquerel (1788-1878), Physicist A85

Perf. 13x12¹⁄₂
1988, Nov. 9   Engr.   Unwmk.
378 A85 18fr blk & dark ultra   38   20

Futuna Hydroelectric Plant — A86

Perf. 13¹⁄₂
1989, Apr. 13   Litho.   Wmk. 385
379 A86 25fr multi   50   25

A87   A88

Unwmk.
1988, Oct. 26   Litho.   Perf. 13
380 A87 17fr multi   35   18

World Post Day.

1989, May 17   Perf. 12¹⁄₂x13
381 A88 21fr multi   42   21

World Telecommunications Day.

Fresco — A89

1989, June 8   Perf. 12¹⁄₂
382 A89 22fr multi   45   22

PHILEXFRANCE '89 — A90

Declaration of Human Rights and Citizenship, Bicent. — A91

1989, July 7   Litho.   Perf. 13
383 A90 29fr multi   52   25
384 A91 900fr multi   15.75 7.85
  a. Souv. sheet of 2, #383-384 + la-
      bel   17.50 17.50

No. 384 is airmail. No. 384a sold for 1000fr.

World Cycling Championships — A92

1989, Sept. 14   Engr.   Perf. 13
385 A92 10fr blk, red brn & emerald 22   15

World Post Day — A93

Unwmk.
1989, Oct. 18   Litho.   Perf. 13
386 A93 27fr multicolored   48   25

Landscape — A94

1989, Nov. 23   Litho.   Perf. 13
387 A94 23fr multicolored   40   20

Star of Bethlehem A95

1990, Jan. 9   Litho.   Perf. 12¹⁄₂
388 A95 44fr multicolored   88   45

Fossilized Tortoise A96

1990, Feb. 15   Litho.   Perf. 12¹⁄₂x13
389 A96 48fr multicolored   95   48

Sculpture by Auguste Rodin (1840-1917) — A97

1990, Mar. 15   Engr.   Perf. 13
390 A97 200fr royal blue   3.90 1.95

1990 World Cup Soccer Championships, Italy — A98

1990, Apr. 16   Litho.
391 A98 59fr multicolored   1.15   58

Orchids A99

1990, May 17   Litho.   Perf. 12¹⁄₂
392 A99 78fr multicolored   1.50   75

Mother's Day

Phaeton — A100

1990, July 16   Perf. 13
393 A100 300fr multicolored   6.75 3.35
394 A100 600fr Island   13.00 6.50

Moana II — A101

1990, Aug. 16   Engr.   Perf. 13
395 A100 40fr shown   80   40
396 A100 50fr Moana III   1.00   50

Native Huts — A102

1990, Sept. 17   Litho.   Perf. 13x12¹⁄₂
397 A102 28fr multicolored   70   35

Stamp Day — A103

1990, Oct. 16   Litho.   Perf. 12¹⁄₂
398 A103 97fr multicolored   2.40 1.20

Wallis Island Pirogue — A104

1990, Nov. 16   Litho.   Perf. 13x12¹⁄₂
399 A104 46fr multicolored   1.15   60

Best Wishes — A105

1990, Dec. 17   Litho.   *Perf. 13x12 1/2*
400 A105 100fr multicolored   2.10 1.05

Patrol Boat La Glorieuse — A106

1991   Engr.   *Perf. 13*
401 A106 42fr La Moqueuse   95   50
402 A106 52fr shown   1.25   65

Issue dates: 42fr, Jan. 7; 52fr, Mar. 4.

A107

1991, Feb. 4   Litho.   *Perf. 13*
403 A107 7fr Breadfruit picker   22   15
404 A107 54fr Taro planter   1.15   60
405 A107 62fr Spear fisherman   1.35   70
406 A107 72fr Native warrior   1.75   90
407 A107 90fr Kailao dancer   2.10 1.05
a.   Souv. sheet of 5, #403-407   7.00 3.50
     Nos. 403-407 (5)   6.57 3.40

Issue dates: 7fr, Sept. 2; 54fr, ; 62fr, Apr. 1; 72fr, Feb. 4; 90fr, Nov. 4.
No. 407a sold for 300fr.

Doctors Without Borders, 20th Anniv. A108

1991, Feb. 18   Litho.   *Perf. 13 1/2*
408 A108 55fr multicolored   1.25   65

Ultralight Aircraft — A108a

1991, June 24
409 A108a 85fr multicolored   1.80   95

Portrait of Jean by Auguste Renoir (1841-1919)
A109

1991, July 8   Photo.   *Perf. 12 1/2x13*
410 A109 400fr multicolored   8.30 4.25
            Litho.
            Die Cut
            Self-Adhesive
411 A109 400fr multicolored   8.30 4.25

Overseas Territorial Status, 30th Anniv. — A110

1991, July 29   Litho.   *Perf. 13*
412 A110 102fr multicolored   2.20 1.20

Feast of the Assumption — A111

1991, Aug. 15   *Perf. 13x12 1/2*
413 A111 30fr multicolored   65   35

Amnesty Intl., 30th Anniv. A113

1991, Oct. 7   *Perf. 13x12 1/2*
414 A113 140fr bl, vio & yel   3.10 1.55

Central Bank for Economic Cooperation, 50th Anniv. — A114

1991, Dec. 2   Litho.   *Perf. 13*
415 A114 10fr multicolored   22   15

Flowers
A115

Designs: 1fr, Monette allamanda cathartica. 4fr, Hibiscus rosa sinensis, vert. 80fr, Ninuphar.

1991, Dec. 2   *Perf. 12 1/2x13, 13x12 1/2*
416 A115 1fr multicolored   15   15
417 A115 4fr multicolored   15   15
418 A115 80fr multicolored   1.75   90
           Set value   96

Christmas — A116

1991, Dec. 16   Litho.   *Perf. 13*
419 A116 60fr multicolored   1.45   75

Maritime Surveillance — A117

1992, Jan. 20   Litho.   *Perf. 13*
420 A117 48fr multicolored   1.15   58

1992 Winter Olympics, Albertville — A118

1992, Feb. 17   Litho.   *Perf. 13*
421 A118 150fr multicolored   3.50 1.75

Canada '92, Intl. Philatelic Exposition, Montreal — A119

Illustration reduced.

1992, Mar. 25   Engr.   *Perf. 13*
422 A119 35fr blk, violet & red   80   40

1992 Summer Olympics, Barcelona — A120

1992, Apr. 15   Engr.   *Perf. 13*
423 A120 106fr bl grn, grn & bl   2.30 1.15

Granada '92, Intl. Philatelic Exposition — A121

Illustration reduced.

1992, Apr. 17   Engr.   *Perf. 12 1/2x12*
424 A121 100fr multicolored   2.25 1.10

Expo '92, Seville — A122

1992, Apr. 20   *Perf. 13*
425 A122 200fr bl grn, ol & red brn 4.50 2.25

Chaetodon Ephippium — A123

Designs: 22fr, Chaetodon auriga. 23fr, Heniochus monoceros. 24fr, Pygoplites diacanthus. 25fr, Chaetodontoplus conspicillatus. 26fr, Chaetodon unimaculatus. 27fr, Siganus punctatus. 35fr, Zebrasoma veliferum. 45fr, Paracanthurus hepatus. 53fr, Siganus vulpinus.

1992-93   *Perf. 13*
426 A123 21fr multicolored   48   24
427 A123 22fr multicolored   55   28
428 A123 23fr multicolored   55   28
429 A123 24fr multicolored   58   30
430 A123 25fr multicolored   60   30
431 A123 26fr multicolored   60   30
432 A123 27fr multicolored   60   30
433 A123 35fr multicolored   75   38
434 A123 45fr multicolored   1.00   50
435 A123 53fr multicolored   1.25   60
           Nos. 426-435 (10)   6.96 3.48

Issued: 21fr, 26fr, May 18; 22fr, July 22; 25fr, July 27; 23fr, 24fr, Sept. 14; 35fr, 45fr, June 21, 1993; 27fr, 53fr, Sept. 6, 1993.

Natives
A125

Designs: a, Three warriors. b, Two warriors. c, Warrior, two boats. d, Two spear fisherman. e, Three fisherman.

1992, June 15   Litho.   *Perf. 12*
436 A125 70fr Strip of 5, #a.-e.   8.50 4.25
f.   Souvenir sheet of 5, #a.-e. 10.50 5.25

No. 436 has continuous design. No. 436f sold for 450fr.

Support Ship, "La Garonne" A126

1992, Oct. 12   Litho.   Perf. 12
437 A126 20fr multicolored   48   24

L'Idylle D'Ixelles, by Auguste Rodin (1840-1917) A127

1992, Nov. 17   Engr.   Perf. 13
438 A127 300fr lilac & dk blue   6.75 3.40

Miribilis Jalapa A128

1992, Dec. 7   Litho.   Perf. 12½
439 A128 200fr multicolored   4.50 2.25

Maritime Forces of the Pacific — A129

1993, Jan. 25   Litho.   Perf. 13x12½
440 A129 130fr multicolored   2.85 1.45

School Art A130

1993, Feb. 22   Litho.   Perf. 12
441 A130 56fr multicolored   1.30 65

See Nos. 451-452.

Birds — A131

Designs: 50fr, Rallus philippensis swindellsi. 60fr, Porphyrio porphyrio. 110fr, Ptilinopus greyi.

1993, Mar. 20   Perf. 13½
442 A131 50fr multicolored   1.15 58
443 A131 60fr multicolored   1.35 68
444 A131 110fr multicolored   2.50 1.25

Mother's Day — A132

1993, May 30   Litho.   Perf. 12½
445 A132 95fr Hibiscus   2.00 1.00
446 A132 120fr Siale   2.50 1.25

Admiral Antoine d'Entrecasteaux (1737-1793), French Navigator — A133

1993, July 12   Engr.   Perf. 13
447 A133 170fr grn bl, red brn & blk 3.75 1.90

Taipei '93 A134

1993, Aug. 14   Litho.   Perf. 13x12½
448 A134 435fr multicolored   9.00 4.50

Churches — A135

1993, Aug. 15   Perf. 13
449 A135 30fr Tepa, Wallis   65   32
450 A135 30fr Vilamalia, Futuna   65   32

School Art Type of 1993

1993 Litho.   Perf. 13x13½, 13½x13
451 A130 28fr Stylized trees   60   30
452 A130 52fr Family, vert.   1.10 55

Issue dates: 28fr, Oct. 18. 52fr, Nov. 8.

Christmas — A136

1993, Dec. 6   Perf. 13
453 A136 80fr multicolored   1.65 85

Traditional Arts and Crafts Exhibition A137

1994, Mar. 24   Litho.   Perf. 12½
454 A137 80fr multicolored   1.75 90

Liberation of Paris, 50th Anniv. — A138

1994, Apr. 21   Engr.   Perf. 13
455 A138 110fr black, blue & red   2.75 1.40

Satellite Communications — A139

1994, June 23   Litho.
456 A139 10fr multicolored   28   15

1994 World Cup Soccer Championships, US — A140

1994, June 23
457 A140 105fr multicolored   2.50 1.25

Princesses Ouveennes, 1903 — A141

1994, July 21   Engr.   Perf. 13
458 A141 90fr blue grn, blk & red   2.25 1.10

Symbols of Playing Cards Suits — A142

1994, Aug. 25   Litho.   Perf. 13
459 A142 40fr multicolored   1.00 50

Ultra-Light Aircraft — A143

1994
460 A143 5fr multicolored   16   15

Coconut — A144

1994, Oct. 13   Litho.   Perf. 13
461 A144 36fr multicolored   95   45

Grand Lodge of France, Cent. — A146

1994, Nov. 24   Engr.   Perf. 13
463 A146 250fr multicolored   6.25 3.00

SEMI-POSTAL STAMPS

French Revolution Issue
Common Design Type
Unwmk.

1939, July 5   Photo.   Perf. 13
Name and Value Typo. in Black
B1 CD83 45c + 25c green   3.25 3.25
B2 CD83 70c + 30c brown   3.25 3.25
B3 CD83 90c + 35c red org   3.25 3.25
B4 CD83 1.25fr + 1fr rose pink 3.25 3.25
B5 CD83 2.25fr + 2fr blue   3.25 3.25
     Nos. B1-B5 (5)   16.25 16.25

New Caledonia Nos. B10 and B12 Overprinted "WALLIS ET FUTUNA" in Blue or Red, and Common Design Type

1941   Photo.   Perf. 13½
B6 SP2   1fr + 1fr red   45
B7 CD86 1.50fr + 3fr maroon   45
B8 SP3   2.50fr + 1fr dark blue   45

Nos. B6-B8 were issued by the Vichy government and were not placed on sale in the dependency.
In 1944 Nos. 92-93 were surcharged "OEUVRES COLONIALES" and surtax (including change of denomination of the 2.50fr to 50c). These were issued by the Vichy government and not placed on sale in Wallis and Futuna.

Catalogue values for unused stamps in this section, from this point to the end of the section, are for Never Hinged items.

Red Cross Issue
Common Design Type
1944   Photo.   Perf. 14½x14
B9 CD90 5fr + 20fr red orange   60 60

The surtax was for the French Red Cross and national relief.

AIR POST STAMPS

Catalogue values for unused stamps in this section are for Never Hinged items.

Victory Issue
Common Design Type
Perf. 12½

		Unwmk.	Engr.
1946, May 8
C1 CD92 8fr dk vio — 38 38

Chad to Rhine Issue
Common Design Types
1946
C2 CD93 5fr dk vio 28 28
C3 CD94 10fr dk slate grn 28 28
C4 CD95 15fr vio brn 28 28
C5 CD96 20fr brt ultra 40 40
C6 CD97 25fr brn org 60 60
C7 CD98 50fr carmine 75 75
Nos. C2-C7 (6) 2.59 2.59

Types of New Caledonia Air Post Stamps of 1948, Overprinted in Blue:

WALLIS ET FUTUNA

1949, July 4 Perf. 13x12½, 12½x13
C8 AP2 50fr yel & rose red 2.25 2.25
C9 AP3 100fr yel & red brn 3.75 3.75

The overprint on No. C9 is in three lines.

UPU Issue
Common Design Type
1949, July 4 Engr. Perf. 13
C10 CD99 10fr multi 2.00 2.00

Liberation Issue
Common Design Type
1954, June 6
C11 CD102 3fr sepia & vio brn 2.00 2.00

Father Louis Marie Chanel — AP1

1955, Nov. 21 Unwmk. Perf. 13
C12 AP1 14fr dk grn, grnsh bl & ind 1.10 65

Issued in honor of Father Chanel, martyred missionary to the Islands.

View of Mata-Utu, Queen Amelia and Msgr. Bataillon — AP2

Design: 33fr, Map of islands and sailing ship.

1960, Sept. 19 Engr. Perf. 13
C13 AP2 21fr bl, brn & grn 1.50 1.10
C14 AP2 33fr ultra, choc & bl grn 2.75 2.25

Shell Diver AP3

1962, Sept. 20 Unwmk. Perf. 13
C16 AP3 100fr bl, grn & dk red brn 10.00 7.00

Telstar Issue
Common Design Type
1962, Dec. 5
C17 CD111 12fr dk pur, mar & bl 1.40 1.40

Sea Shell Type of Regular Issue, 1962
Design: 50fr, Harpa ventricosa.

1963, Apr. 1 Engr.
Size: 26x47mm
C18 A5 50fr lil rose, Prus grn & red brn 4.00 3.50

Javelin Thrower — AP4

1964, Oct. 10 Engr. Perf. 13
C19 AP4 31fr emer, ver & vio brn 8.00 6.25

18th Olympic Games, Tokyo, Oct. 10-25.

ITU Issue
Common Design Type
1965, May 17 Unwmk. Perf. 13
C20 CD120 50fr multi 9.00 6.50

Mata-Utu Wharf — AP5

1965, Nov. 26 Engr. Perf. 13
C21 AP5 27fr brt bl, sl grn & red brn 1.65 1.00

French Satellite A-1 Issue
Common Design Type

Designs: 7fr, Diamant rocket and launching installations. 10fr, A-1 satellite.

1966, Jan. 17 Engr. Perf. 13
C22 CD121 7fr crim, red & car lake 1.75 1.75
C23 CD121 10fr car lake, red & crim 1.75 1.75
a. Strip of 2, #C22-C23 + label 4.00 4.00

French Satellite D-1 Issue
Common Design Type
1966, June 2 Engr. Perf. 13
C24 CD122 10fr lake, bl grn & red 1.40 1.40

WHO Headquarters, Geneva, and Emblem AP6

1966, July 5 Photo. Perf. 12½x13
C25 AP6 30fr org, mar & bl 1.50 1.50

New WHO Headquarters, Geneva.

Girl and Boy Reading; UNESCO Emblem — AP7

1966, Nov. 4 Engr. Perf. 13
C26 AP7 50fr grn, org & choc 2.00 1.75

20th anniv. of UNESCO.

Athlete and Pattern AP8

Design: 38fr, Woman ballplayer and pattern.

1966, Dec. 8 Engr. Perf. 13x12½
C27 AP8 32fr bl, dp car & blk 1.50 1.25
C28 AP8 38fr emer & brt pink 1.65 1.40

2nd South Pacific Games, Nouméa, Dec. 8-18.

Samuel Wallis' Ship and Coast of Wallis Island — AP9

1967, Dec. 16 Photo. Perf. 13
C29 AP9 12fr multi 2.75 2.00

Bicentenary of the discovery of Wallis Island.

Concorde Issue
Common Design Type
1969, Apr. 17 Engr. Perf. 13
C30 CD129 20fr blk & plum 5.00 4.00

Man Climbing Coconut Palm — AP10

Designs: 32fr, Horseback rider. 38fr, Men making wooden stools. 50fr, Spear fisherman and man holding basket with fish. 100fr, Women sorting coconuts.

1969, Apr. 30 Photo. Perf. 13
C31 AP10 20fr multi 90 45
C32 AP10 32fr multi 1.75 90
C33 AP10 38fr multi 1.75 90
C34 AP10 50fr multi 2.75 1.50
C35 AP10 100fr multi 5.25 2.75
Nos. C31-C35 (5) 12.40 6.50

No. C14 Surcharged with New Value and Three Bars

1971 Engr. Perf. 13
C36 AP2 21fr on 33fr multi 1.50 1.50

Pole Vault AP11

1971, Oct. 25 Engr. Perf. 13
C37 AP11 48fr snown 2.25 1.50
C38 AP11 54fr Archery 3.00 2.25

4th South Pacific Games, Papeete, French Polynesia, Sept. 8-19.

South Pacific Commission Headquarters, Noumea — AP12

1972, Feb. 5 Photo. Perf. 13
C39 AP12 44fr bl & multi 1.90 1.50

South Pacific Commission, 25th anniv.

Round House and Festival Emblem — AP13

1972, May 15 Engr. Perf. 13
C40 AP13 60fr dp car, grn & pur 2.25 1.50

South Pacific Festival of Arts, Fiji, May 6-20.

Canoe Type of Regular Issue
Design: 200fr, Outrigger sailing canoe race, and island woman.

1972, Oct. 16 Photo. Perf. 13x12½
Size: 47½x28mm
C41 A9 200fr multi 9.00 6.25

La Pérouse and "La Boussole" — AP14

Explorers and their Ships: 28fr, Samuel Wallis and "Dolphin." 40fr, Dumont D'Urville and "Astrolabe." 72fr, Bougainville and "La Boudeuse."

1973, July 20 Perf. 13
C42 AP14 22fr brn, sl & car 70 50
C43 AP14 28fr sl grn, dl red & bl 1.00 70
C44 AP14 40fr brn, ind & ultra 1.40 90
C45 AP14 72fr bl & pur 2.50 1.90

Charles de Gaulle — AP15

1973, Nov. 9 Engr. Perf. 13
C46 AP15 107fr brn org & dk brn 4.00 3.25

Pres. Charles de Gaulle (1890-1970).

Red Jasmine
AP16

Designs: Flowers from Wallis.

1973, Dec. 6   Photo.   Perf. 13
C47 AP16 12fr shown   60   40
C48 AP16 17fr Hibiscus tiliaceus   65   40
C49 AP16 19fr Phaeomeria magnifi-
              ca   80   60
C50 AP16 21fr Hibiscus rosa sinen-
              sis   80   60
C51 AP16 23fr Allamanda cathartica   1.10 70
C52 AP16 27fr Barringtonia   1.10 70
C53 AP16 39fr Flowers in vase   2.25 1.75
     Nos. C47-C53 (7)   7.30 5.15

UPU Emblem and
Symbolic
Design — AP17

1974, Oct. 9   Engr.   Perf. 13
C54 AP17 51fr multi   1.50 1.50

Centenary of Universal Postal Union.

Holy Family,
Primitive
Painting
AP18

1974, Dec. 9   Photo.   Perf. 13
C55 AP18 150fr multi   4.00 3.25

Christmas 1974.

Tapa
Cloth
AP19

Designs (Tapa Cloth): 24fr, Village scene. 36fr, Fish and marine life. 80fr, Marine life, map of islands, village scene.

1975, Feb. 3   Photo.   Perf. 13
C56 AP19 3fr multi   25   20
C57 AP19 24fr multi   95   52
C58 AP19 36fr multi   1.10 75
C59 AP19 80fr multi   2.50 1.90

DC-7 in   Volleyball — AP21
Flight — AP20

1975, Aug. 13   Engr.   Perf. 13
C60 AP20 100fr multi   2.75 2.25

First regular air service between Nouméa, New Caledonia, and Wallis.

1975, Nov. 10   Photo.   Perf. 13
C61 AP21 26fr shown   70   45
C62 AP21 44fr Soccer   1.00 70
C63 AP21 56fr Javelin   1.50 1.10
C64 AP21 105fr Spear fishing   3.25 2.75

5th South Pacific Games, Guam, Aug. 1-10.

Lalolalo Lake, Wallis — AP22

Landscapes: 29fr, Vasavasa, Futuna. 41fr, Sigave Bay, Futuna. 68fr, Gahi Bay, Wallis.

1975, Dec. 1   Litho.   Perf. 13
C65 AP22 10fr grn & multi   38   35
C66 AP22 29fr grn & multi   95   60
C67 AP22 41fr grn & multi   1.25 80
C68 AP22 68fr grn & multi   1.90 1.40

Concorde, Eiffel Tower and Sugar Loaf
Mountain — AP23

1976, Jan. 21   Engr.   Perf. 13
C69 AP23 250fr multi   9.50 7.75

1st commercial flight of supersonic jet Concorde from Paris to Rio, Jan. 21.
For overprint see No. C73.

Hammer Throw and Stadium — AP24

Design: 39fr, Diving, Stadium and maple leaf.

1976, Aug. 2   Engr.   Perf. 13
C70 AP24 31fr multi   90   60
C71 AP24 39fr multi   1.25 90

21st Olympic Games, Montreal, Canada, July 17-Aug. 1.

De Gaulle
Memorial — AP25

Photogravure and Embossed
1977, June 18   Perf. 13
C72 AP25 100fr gold & multi   2.75 2.25

5th anniversary of dedication of De Gaulle Memorial at Colombey-les-Deux-Eglises.

No. C69 Overprinted in Dark Brown:
"PARIS NEW-YORK / 22.11.77 / 1er
VOL COMMERCIAL"
1977, Nov. 22   Engr.   Perf. 13
C73 AP23 250fr multi   6.25 5.25

Concorde, 1st commercial flight, Paris-NY.

Balistes Niger — AP26

Fish: 35fr, Amphiprion akindynos. 49fr, Pomacanthus imperator. 51fr, Zanclus cornutus.

1978, Jan. 31   Litho.   Perf. 13
C74 AP26 26fr multi   60   45
C75 AP26 35fr multi   90   65
C76 AP26 49fr multi   1.50 1.20
C77 AP26 51fr multi   1.60 1.40

Map of Futuna and Alofi Islands — AP27

Design: 500fr, Map of Wallis and Uvea Islands, vert.

1978, Mar. 7   Engr.
C78 AP27 300fr vio bl & grnsh bl   9.00 6.25
C79 AP27 500fr multi   12.50 10.00

Father Bataillon, Churches on Wallis and
Futuna Islands — AP28

Design: 72fr, Monsignor Pompallier, map of Wallis, Futuna and Alofi Islands, outrigger canoe.

1978, Apr. 28   Litho.   Perf. 13x12½
C80 AP28 60fr multi   1.10 75
C81 AP28 72fr multi   1.50 1.10

First French missionaries on Wallis and Futuna Islands.

ITU Emblem — AP29

1978, May 17   Litho.   Perf. 13
C82 AP29 66fr multi   1.50 85

10th World Telecommunications Day.

Nativity and Longhouse — AP30

1978, Dec. 4   Photo.   Perf. 13
C83 AP30 160fr multi   3.25 2.25

Christmas 1978.

Popes Paul VI and John Paul I, St. Peter's,
Rome — AP31

Designs: 37fr, Pope Paul VI, vert. 41fr, Pope John Paul I, vert.

Perf. 12½x13, 13x12½
1979, Jan. 31   Litho.
C84 AP31 37fr multi   70   50
C85 AP31 41fr multi   1.10 75
C86 AP31 105fr multi   3.00 1.65

In memory of Popes Paul VI and John Paul I.

Monoplane of
UTA
Airlines — AP32

Designs: 68fr, Freighter Muana. 80fr, Hihifo Airport.

1979, Feb. 28   Perf. 13x12½
C87 AP32 46fr multi   90   55
C88 AP32 68fr multi   1.20 90
C89 AP32 80fr multi   1.60 1.10

Inter-Island transportation.
See Nos. 251-253.

France No. 67 and Eole Weather
Satellite — AP33

Designs: 70fr, Hibiscus and stamp similar to No. 25, vert. 90fr, Rowland Hill and Penny Black. 100fr, Birds, Kano School, Japan 17th century, and Japan No. 9.

1979, May 7   **Photo.**   *Perf. 13*
C90 AP33 5fr multi   22   15
C91 AP33 70fr multi   90   65
C92 AP33 90fr multi   1.25   70
C93 AP33 100fr multi   1.50 1.00
Sir Rowland Hill (1795-1879), originator of penny postage.

Cross of Lorraine and People — AP34

1979, June 18   **Engr.**   *Perf. 13*
C94 AP34 33fr multi   75   55

Map of Islands, Arms of France AP35

1979, July 19   **Photo.**   *Perf. 13*
C95 AP35 47fr multi   1.00   60
Visit of Pres. Valery Giscard d'Estaing of France.

Capt. Cook, Ships and Island — AP36

1979, July 28
C96 AP36 130fr multi   2.50 1.75
Bicentenary of the death of Capt. James Cook (1728-1779).

Telecom Emblem, Satellite, Receiving Station — AP37

1979, Sept. 20   **Litho.**   *Perf. 13*
C97 AP37 120fr multi   2.00 1.50
3rd World Telecommunications Exhibition, Geneva, Sept. 20-26.

Virgin and Child, by Albrecht Durer AP38

1979, Dec. 17   **Engr.**   *Perf. 13*
C98 AP38 180fr red & blk   4.25 3.50
Christmas 1979.

Rotary International, 75th Anniversary — AP39

1980, Feb. 29   **Litho.**   *Perf. 13*
C99 AP39 86fr multi   2.00 1.60

Rochambeau and Troops, US Flag, 1780 — AP40

1980, May 27   **Engr.**   *Perf. 13*
C100 AP40 102fr multi   1.90 1.40
Rochambeau's landing at Newport, RI (American Revolution), bicentenary.

National Day, 10th Anniversary — AP41

1980, July 15   **Litho.**   *Perf. 13*
C101 AP41 71fr multi   1.10   65

Transatlantic Airmail Flight, 50th Anniversary — AP42

1980, Sept. 22   **Engr.**   *Perf. 13*
C102 AP42 122fr multi   2.25 1.60

Fleming, Penicillin Bacilli — AP43

1980, Oct. 20
C103 AP43 101fr multi   1.65   90
Alexander Fleming (1881-1955), discoverer of penicillin, 25th death anniversary.

Charles De Gaulle, 10th Anniversary of Death — AP44

1980, Nov. 9   **Engr.**   *Perf. 13*
C104 AP44 200fr sep & dk ol grn   3.50 2.50

Virgin and Child with St. Catherine, by Lorenzo Lotto — AP45

1980, Dec. 20   **Litho.**   *Perf. 13x12½*
C105 AP45 150fr multi   2.50 2.00
Christmas 1980.

Alan B. Shepard and Spacecraft — AP46

20th Anniversary of Space Flight: 44fr, Yuri Gagarin.

1981, May 11   **Litho.**   *Perf. 13*
C106 AP46 37fr multi   45   40
C107 AP46 44fr multi   50   45

Vase of Flowers, by Paul Cezanne (1839-1906) AP47

Design: 135fr, Harlequin, by Pablo Picasso.

1981, Oct. 22   **Litho.**   *Perf. 12½x13*
C108 AP47 53fr multi   80   70
C109 AP47 135fr multi   2.50 1.50

Espana '82 World Cup Soccer — AP48

1981, Nov. 16   **Engr.**   *Perf. 13*
C110 AP48 120fr blk, brn & grn   1.65   95
See No. C110A. For overprint see No. C115.

1982, May 13
C110A AP48 120fr lil, brn & ol grn   1.60 1.50

Christmas 1981 — AP49

1981, Dec. 21   **Litho.**   *Perf. 12½*
C111 AP49 180fr multi   2.50 1.75

Tapestry, by Pilioho Aloi — AP50

1982, Feb. 22   **Litho.**   *Perf. 12½x13*
C112 AP50 100fr multi   1.50 1.25

Boats at Collioure, by George Braque (1882-1963) AP51

1982, Apr. 13   **Litho.**   *Perf. 12½x13*
C113 AP51 300fr multi   4.00 3.25

Alberto Santos-Dumont (1873-1932), Aviation Pioneer — AP52

1982, July 24
C114 AP52 95fr multi   1.50 1.20

No. C110 Overprinted with Winner's
Name in Blue

1982, Aug. 26   Engr.   Perf. 13
C115 AP48 120fr multi   1.65 1.10

Italy's victory in 1982 World Cup.

French Overseas Possessions Week, Sept.
18-25 — AP53

1982, Sept. 17   Litho.
C116 AP53 105fr Beach   1.10 90

Day of the
Blind — AP54

1982, Oct. 18   Engr.
C117 AP54 130fr red & blue   1.40 1.10

Christmas
1982
AP55

Design: Adoration of the Virgin, by Correggio.

1982, Dec. 20   Litho.   Perf. 12¹/₂x13
C118 AP55 170fr multi   2.25 1.60

Wind Surfing (1984
Olympic
Event) — AP56

1983, Mar. 4   Litho.   Perf. 13
C119 AP56 270fr multi   3.50 3.00

World
UPU
Day
AP57

1983, Mar. 30   Litho.   Perf. 13
C120 AP57 100fr multi   1.50 1.20

Manned Flight
Bicentenary — AP58

1983, Apr. 25   Litho.   Perf. 13
C121 AP58 205fr Montgolfiere   3.00 2.25

Cat, 1926, by
Foujita (d.
1968) — AP59

1983, May 20   Litho.   Perf. 12¹/₂x13
C122 AP59 102fr multi   1.50 1.10

Pre-Olympic
Year — AP60

1983, July 5   Engr.   Perf. 13
C123 AP60 250fr Javelin   2.75 1.90

Alfred Nobel (1833-1896) — AP61

1983, Aug. 1   Engr.   Perf. 13
C124 AP61 150fr multi   1.75 1.10

Nicephore Niepce (1765-1833),
Photography Pioneer — AP62

1983, Sept. 20   Engr.   Perf. 13
C125 AP62 75fr dk grn & rose vio   1.00 70

Raphael
(1483-1520),
500th Birth
Anniv.
AP63

1983, Nov. 10   Litho.   Perf. 12¹/₂x13
C126 AP63 167fr The Triumph of
Galatea   2.00 1.60

Pandanus
AP64

1983, Nov. 30   Litho.   Perf. 13
C127 AP64 137fr multi   1.50 90

Christmas
1983 — AP65

1983, Dec. 22   Litho.   Perf. 12¹/₂x13
C128 AP65 200fr Sistine Madonna,
by Raphael   2.50 2.00

Steamer Commandant Bory — AP66

1984, Jan. 9   Perf. 13
C129 AP66 67fr multi   90 65

1984 Summer Olympics — AP67

1984, Feb. 3   Litho.   Perf. 13
C130 AP67 85fr Weight lifting   1.00 90

Frangipani
Blossoms
AP68

1984, Feb. 28   Perf. 12¹/₂
C131 AP68 130fr multi   1.10 75

Easter
1984 — AP69

1984, Apr. 17   Litho.   Perf. 12¹/₂x13
C132 AP69 190fr Descent from the
Cross   2.50 1.90

Homage to
Jean Cocteau
AP70

1984, June 30   Litho.   Perf. 13
C133 AP70 150fr Portrait   1.90 1.60

Soano Hoatau Tiki
Sculpture
AP71

Portrait of Alice, by
Modigliani (1884-
1920)
AP72

1984, July 26
C134 AP71 175fr multi   2.00 1.60

1984, Aug. 20
C135 AP72 140fr multi   1.75 1.50

N·E·W
Scott Supplement Pages for
**Wallis &
Futuna Islands**
are now available

WALLIS AND FUTUNA ISLANDS

887

Ausipex
'84 — AP73

1984, Sept. 21 Litho. Perf. 12¹/₂x13
C136 AP73 180fr Pilioko Tapestry   2.25 1.90

Se-tenant with label showing exhibition emblem.

Local Dances, by Jean Michon — AP74

1984, Oct. 11 Photo. Perf. 13
C137 AP74 110fr multi   1.25 1.00

Altar — AP75

1984, Nov. 5 Litho. Perf. 13x12¹/₂
C138 AP75 52fr Mount Lulu Chapel   50 40

Christmas 1984 — AP76

1984, Dec. 21 Litho. Perf. 13x12¹/₂
C139 AP76 260fr Tropical Nativity   3.00 2.00

Pilioko Tapestry — AP77

1985, Apr. 3 Litho. Perf. 13x12¹/₂
C140 AP77 500fr multi   5.50 4.00

The Post in
1926, by
Utrillo
AP78

1985, June 17 Litho. Perf. 12¹/₂x13
C141 AP78 200fr multi   1.50 70

Wallis Island Pirogue — AP79

1985, Aug. 9 Perf. 13
C142 AP79 350fr multi   3.00 1.40

Ship Jacques
Cartier — AP80

1985, Oct. 2 Engr. Perf. 13x13¹/₂
C143 AP80 51fr Prus bl, brt bl & dk bl   55 22

Portrait of a
Young Woman,
by Patrice
Nielly — AP81

1985, Oct. 28 Litho. Perf. 12¹/₂x13
C144 AP81 245fr multi   2.25 1.20

Nativity, by
Jean Michon
AP82

1985, Dec. 19 Litho. Perf. 12¹/₂x13
C145 AP82 330fr multi   2.50 1.20

Halley's Comet — AP83

1986, Mar. 6 Litho. Perf. 13
C146 AP83 100fr multi   1.40 70

Cure of Ars, Birth
Bicent. — AP84

1986, Mar. 28 Litho. Perf. 12¹/₂x13
C147 AP84 200fr multi   2.50 1.40

French Overseas Territory Status, 25th
Anniv. — AP85

1986, July 29 Engr. Perf. 13
C148 AP85 90fr Queen Amelia   1.35 68
C149 AP85 137fr July 30 Law, Journal of the Republic   2.05 1.05
a. Strip of 2, #C148-C149 + label   3.50 3.50

Queen Amelia's request to France for protection, cent.

World Post Day — AP86

1986, Oct. 9 Litho. Perf. 13
C150 AP86 270fr multi   3.25 1.65

Statue of Liberty,   Poi Basilica, 1st
Cent. — AP87   Anniv. — AP88

1986, Oct. 31 Engr.
C151 AP87 205fr multi   3.00 1.50

1987, Apr. 30 Litho. Perf. 13
C152 AP88 230fr Fr. Chanel, basilica   3.50 1.75

Telstar Transmitting to Pleumeur-Bodou,
France — AP89

1987, May 17 Engr. Perf. 13
C153 AP89 200fr gray, brt bl & brn
      org   3.00 1.50

World Communications Day, 25th anniv. of
Telstar.

Piccard, Bathyscaphe
Trieste and
Stratospheric
Balloon — AP90

1987, Aug. 21 Engr. Perf. 13
C154 AP90 135fr brt ol grn, dk bl &
      brt bl   2.75 1.40

Auguste Piccard (1884-1962), physicist.

Arrival of First Missionary, 150th
Anniv. — AP91

Design: 260fr, Monsignor Bataillon's arrival in
1837, ship and the islands.

1987, Nov. 8 Engr. Perf. 13
C155 AP91 260fr brt blue, blk &
      blue grn   5.50 2.25

Christmas 1987 — AP92

1987, Dec. 15 Litho. Perf. 13x12¹/₂
C156 AP92 300fr multi   6.00 3.00

Garros and Bleriot Aircraft — AP93

1988, Feb. 18 Engr. Perf. 13
C157 AP93 600fr multi   12.50 6.25

Roland Garros (1888-1918), aviator and tennis
player.

Self-portrait with Lace Cravat, by Maurice Quentin de La Tour (1704-88) AP94

1988, Apr. 8   Litho.
C158 AP94 500fr multi   10.00 5.00

World Telecommunications Day — AP95

1988, May 5   Litho.   Perf. 12¹/₂x13
C159 AP95 100fr multi   2.00 1.00

South Pacific Episcopal Conference — AP96

1988, June 1   Litho.   Perf. 13
C160 AP96 90fr Map, bishop   1.65 82

Christmas — AP97

Unwmk.
1988, Dec. 15   Litho.   Perf. 13
C161 AP97 400fr multi   7.25 3.65

Royal Throne — AP98

1989, Mar. 11
C162 AP98 700fr multi   11.90 6.00

The Virgin of the Crescent Moon, by Albrecht Dürer AP99

1989, Dec. 21   Engr.   Perf. 13¹/₂x13
C163 AP99 800fr plum   15.50 7.75

Clement Ader (1841-1926), Aviation Pioneer — AP100

1990, June 9   Engr.   Perf. 13
C164 AP100 56fr multicolored   1.25 65
First anniversary of Wallis-Tahiti air link.

Gen. Charles de Gaulle (1890-1979) AP101

1990, Nov. 22   Perf. 12¹/₂x13
C165 AP101 1000fr multi   24.00 12.00

Father Louis Marie Chanel, 150th Death Anniv. — AP102

1991, Apr. 28   Litho.   Perf. 13
C166 AP102 235fr multicolored   5.15 2.60

French Open Tennis Championships, Cent. — AP103

Illustration reduced.

1991, May 24   Engr.   Perf. 13x12¹/₂
C167 AP103 250fr blk, grn & org 5.00 2.50

Wolfgang Amadeus Mozart, Death Bicent. AP104

1991, Sept. 23   Engr.   Perf. 13
C168 AP104 500fr multicolored   11.50 5.75

World Columbian Stamp Expo '92, Chicago — AP105

1992, May 22   Litho.   Perf. 13x12¹/₂
C169 AP105 100fr multicolored   2.50 1.25

1992, July 15   Perf. 13
C170 AP105 800fr multicolored   20.00 10.00
Genoa '92.

First French Republic, Bicent. — AP106

1992, Aug. 17   Engr.   Perf. 13
C171 AP106 350fr blk, bl & red   8.00 4.00

Louvre Museum, Bicent. — AP107

1993, Apr. 12   Engr.   Perf. 13
C172 AP107 315fr blue, dk blue & red   7.25 3.75

Nicolaus Copernicus, Heliocentric Solar System — AP108

1993, May 7   Engr.   Perf. 13
C173 AP108 600fr multicolored   13.25 6.60
Polska '93.

Second Year of First French Republic, Bicent. — AP109

1993, Sept. 22   Engr.   Perf. 13
C174 AP109 400fr blue, black & red 8.75 4.50

Wallis Island Landscape — AP110

1994, Jan. 26   Litho.   Perf. 13
C175 AP110 400fr multicolored   8.50 4.25

Hong Kong '94 — AP111

1994, Feb. 18   Litho.   Perf. 14x13¹/₂
C176 AP111 700fr multicolored   15.00 7.50

South Pacific Geography Day — AP112

1994, May 4   Litho.   Perf. 13
C177 AP112 85fr multicolored   2.10 1.00
See New Caledonia No. C259.

European Stamp Salon, Paris — AP113

1994, Sept. 22   Litho.   Perf. 13
C178 AP113 300fr multicolored   8.75 4.50

Antoine de Saint-Exupery (1900-44),
Aviator, Author — AP114

1994, Oct. 27   Engr.   Perf. 13
C179 AP114 800fr multicolored   20.00 10.00

Christmas
AP115

1994, Dec. 15   Litho.   Perf. 13
C180 AP115 150fr multicolored   3.75 1.90

AIR POST SEMI-POSTAL STAMPS
Stamps of New Caledonia type V5
overprinted "Wallis et Futuna" and type
of Cameroun V10 inscribed "Wallis et
Futuna" were issued in 1942 by the
Vichy Government, but were not placed
on sale in the dependency.

POSTAGE DUE STAMPS

Postage Due Stamps
of New Caledonia,
1906, Overprinted in
Black or Red

ILES WALLIS et FUTUNA

1920   Unwmk.   Perf. 13¹/₂x14
J1 D2 5c ultra, azure   22 22
J2 D2 10c brn, buff   22 22
J3 D2 15c grn, grnsh   22 22
J4 D2 20c blk, yel (R)   28 28
a. Double overprint   35.00
J5 D2 30c car rose   28 28
J6 D2 50c ultra, straw   45 45
J7 D2 60c olive, azure   60 60
a. Double overprint   35.00
J8 D2 1fr grn, cream   90 90
    Nos. J1-J8 (8)   3.17 3.17

Type of 1920 Issue Surcharged   2f

1927
J9 D2 2fr on 1fr brt vio   3.50 3.50
J10 D2 3fr on 1fr org brn   3.50 3.50

Postage Due Stamps of New Caledonia,
1928, Overprinted as in 1920

1930
J11 D3 2c sl bl & dp brn   15 15
J12 D3 4c brn red & bl grn   15 15
J13 D3 5c red org & bl blk   15 15
J14 D3 10c mag & Prus bl   15 15
J15 D3 15c dl grn & scar   15 15
J16 D3 20c maroon & ol grn   15 15
J17 D3 25c bis brn & sl bl   15 15
J18 D3 30c bl grn & ol grn   26 26
J19 D3 50c lt brn & dk red   15 15
J20 D3 60c mag & brt rose   40 40
J21 D3 1fr dl bl & Prus grn   22 22
J22 D3 2fr dk red & ol grn   28 28
J23 D3 3fr vio & brn   32 32
    Set value   2.00 2.00

Postage Due Stamps of   **FRANCE**
1930 with Additional   **LIBRE**
Overprint in Black

1943
J24 D3 2c sl bl & dp brn   11.00 11.00
J25 D3 4c brn red & bl grn   11.00 11.00
J26 D3 5c red org & bl blk   11.00 11.00
J27 D3 10c mag & Prus bl   13.00 13.00
J28 D3 15c dl grn & scar   13.00 13.00
J29 D3 20c mar & ol grn   13.00 13.00
J30 D3 25c bis brn & sl bl   13.00 13.00
J31 D3 30c bl grn & ol grn   13.00 13.00
J32 D3 50c lt brn & dk red   13.00 13.00
J33 D3 60c mag & brt rose   13.00 13.00
J34 D3 1fr dl bl & Prus grn   15.00 15.00
J35 D3 2fr dk red & ol grn   15.00 15.00
J36 D3 3fr vio & brn   15.00 15.00
    Nos. J24-J36 (13)   169.00 169.00

Catalogue values for unused
stamps in this section, from this
point to the end of the section, are
for Never Hinged items.

Thalassoma
Lunare — D1

Fish: 1fr, Zanclus cornutus, vert. 5fr,
Amphiprion percula.

Perf. 13x13¹/₂
1963, Apr. 1   Typo.   Unwmk.
J37 D1 1fr yel org, bl & blk   40 40
J38 D1 3fr red, grnsh bl & grn   60 60
J39 D1 5fr org, bluish grn & blk   1.00 1.00

WESTERN UKRAINE

LOCATION — In Eastern Central Europe
GOVT. — A former short-lived independent State

A provisional government was established
in 1918 in the eastern part of Austria-Hungary but the area later came under Polish
administration.

100 Shahiv (Sotykiv) = 1 Hryvnia
100 Heller = 1 Krone

Forgeries of almost all Western
Ukraine stamps are plentiful.
Used values are for stamps canceled
to order.

Kolomyya Issue
Укр. Н. Р.

Austria Nos. 168,
145, 147, 149
Surcharged

5

1918   Unwmk.   Perf. 12¹/₂
1 A42 5sh on 15h dl red   30.00 50.00
2 A37 10sh on 3h vio   30.00 50.00
3 A37 10sh on 6h dp org   950.00 700.00
4 A37 10sh on 12h lt bl   950.00 700.00

Nos. 1-4 exist with surcharge inverted or double.

Lviv Issue

Austria Nos. 134, 146,
148, 169 Overprinted

1918
5 A37 3h bright violet
6 A37 5h light green
7 A37 10h magenta
8 A42 20h dark green

Nos. 5-8 exist with surcharge inverted. Red or
green overprints are proofs.
These stamps, the first Western Ukraine issue,
were used in Lviv for only two days. After the fall of

---

the city they were used in Khodoriv, Stanislav and
Kolomyya.

Stanislav Issue
Пошта
Укр.Н.Рен.

Austrian Stamps of
1916-18 Surcharged
in Shahiv (shown) and
Hryvnia Currency

waris
*   *

1919
11 A37 3sh brt vio   10.00 10.00
12 A37 5sh lt grn   10.00 10.00
13 A37 6sh dp org   20.00 20.00
14 A37 10sh magenta   20.00 20.00
15 A37 12sh lt bl   20.00 20.00
16 A42 15sh dl red   20.00 20.00
17 A42 20sh dp grn   20.00 20.00
18 A42 30sh dl vio   100.00 100.00
19 A39 40sh ol grn   20.00 20.00
20 A39 50sh dk grn   20.00 20.00
21 A39 60sh dp bl   20.00 20.00
22 A39 80sh org brn   20.00 20.00
23 A39 1hr car, yel   30.00 30.00
24 A40 2hr lt bl   22.50 22.50
25 A40 3hr car rose   40.00 40.00
a.   3hr claret   2,500. 2,000.
26 A40 4hr yel grn   30.00 30.00
a.   4hr deep green   200.00 200.00
27 A40 10hr dp vio   475.00 750.00

The overprint exists inverted on 12sh and 80sh,
double on 12sh and 10hr.
The 25sh, type A42, with this overprint is considered bogus.

Granite Paper
28 A40 3hr car rose   30.00 30.00

**Same Surcharged on Austrian
Military Semipostal Stamps of 1918**
Perf. 12¹/₂x13
31 MSP7 10sh gray grn   70.00 70.00
32 MSP8 20sh magenta   55.00 55.00
33 MSP7 45sh blue   40.00 40.00

The overprint exists inverted on Nos. 31-33,
double on No. 32.

**Same Surcharge on Austrian Military
Stamps of 1917**
Perf. 12¹/₂
34 M3 1sh grnsh bl   650.00 650.00
35 M3 2sh red org   65.00 65.00
36 M3 3sh ol gray   140.00 140.00
37 M3 5sh ol grn   225.00 225.00
38 M3 6sh violet   115.00 115.00
39 M3 10sh org brn   750.00 650.00
40 M3 12sh blue   450.00 450.00
41 M3 15sh brt rose   450.00 450.00
42 M3 20sh red brn   10.50 11.50
43 M3 25sh ultra   2,750. 3,250.
44 M3 30sh slate   775.00 900.00
45 M3 40sh ol bis   650.00 650.00
46 M3 50sh dp grn   6.50 6.50
47 M3 60sh car rose   600.00 600.00
48 M3 80sh dl bl   40.00 40.00
49 M3 90sh dk vio   800.00 650.00
50 M4 2hr rose, straw   13.00 18.00
51 M4 3hr bl, grn   20.00 22.50
52 M4 4hr rose, grn   20.00 22.50
53 M4 10hr dl vio, gray

The overprint exists double on 2sh, 3sh and
20sh, inverted on 12sh, 50sh and 4hr.

**Same Surcharge on Austrian Postage
Due Stamps of 1916**
54 D5 1hr ultra   65. 80.
55 D5 5hr ultra   1,000. 1,500.

**Surcharged on Austrian Postage Due
Stamps of 1917
with two bars over "PORTO"**
57 A38 15sh on 36h vio   275. 275.
58 A38 50sh on 42h choc   5,000. 5,000.

Shahiv is in two parts in the overprint: wa and
rib.

**Same Surcharge on Postage Due
Stamps of Bosnia, 1904**
61 D1 1sh blk, red & yel   20.00 20.00
62 D1 2sh blk, red & yel   6.50 11.00
63 D1 3sh blk, red & yel   6.50 11.00
64 D1 4sh blk, red & yel   65.00 65.00
65 D1 5sh blk, red & yel   2,750. 3,000.
66 D1 6sh blk, red & yel   140.00 140.00
67 D1 7sh blk, red & yel   11.50 14.00
68 D1 8sh blk, red & yel   14.00 18.00
69 D1 10sh blk, red & yel   850.00 1,100.
70 D1 15sh blk, red & yel   325.00 325.00
71 D1 20sh blk, red & yel   5,000. 5,000.
72 D1 50sh blk, red & yel   140.00 140.00

Two types of surcharge on No. 61: Shahiv in
singular (wara) and in plural (warib). Value the
same.

The overprint exists inverted on #61, 64, 66-68.

A2

Black Surcharge on Austrian Military
Stamps of 1917-18.

1919
75 A2 2hr on 2k rose, straw   7.00 9.00
76 A2 3hr on 2k rose, straw   7.00 10.00
77 A2 3hr on 3k green, blue   70.00 140.00
78 A2 4hr on 2k rose, straw   7.00 10.00
79 A2 4hr on 4k rose, grn   1,000. 1,500.
80 A2 5hr on 2k rose, straw   7.00 10.00
a. Inverted surch.   250.00
81 A2 10hr on 50h dp grn (Aus-
    tria type M3)   10.00 27.50

З. У.
Н. Р.

Austrian Stamps of
1916-18 Overprinted

1919, May
85 A37 3h bright vio   50 1.25
86 A37 5h light grn   50 1.25
87 A37 6h deep org   50 1.25
88 A37 10h magenta   50 1.25
89 A37 12h light blue   50 1.25
90 A42 15h dull red   50 1.25
91 A42 20h deep green   50 1.25
92 A42 25h blue   50 1.25
93 A42 30h dull vio   50 1.25
94 A39 40h olive green   65 1.50
95 A39 50h dark green   65 1.50
96 A39 60h deep blue   65 1.50
97 A39 80h org brn   75 1.75
98 A39 90h red violet   75 2.00
99 A39 1k car, yel   1.00 5.00
100 A40 2k light blue   1.75 7.50
101 A40 3k car rose   2.25 7.50
102 A40 4k yel green   9.00 12.00
103 A40 10k deep violet   11.00 50.00
    Nos. 85-103 (19)   32.95

The four letters in the overprint are the initials of
Ukrainian words equivalent to "Western Ukrainian
National (or Peoples) Republic." The country was
formed from the eastern part of Galicia, formerly a
province of the Austro-Hungarian Empire.
Forged cancellations abound.

REGISTRATION STAMPS

Kolomyya Issue

Укр. Н. Р.
П
50 сот.
RS1

1919   Unwmk.   Typeset   Imperf.
F1 RS1 30sot blk, rose   100.00 48.00
F2 RS1 50sot blk, dp rose   22.50 27.50

OCCUPATION STAMPS

Romanian Occupation of Pokutia

Austrian Stamps
Surcharged in Dark Blue
Black

C.M.T.
60 h.

1919   **Unwmk.**   *Perf. 12½*

On Stamps of 1916-18

N3	A37	40h on 5h lt grn
N10	A39	1k 20h on 50h dk grn
N11	A39	1k 20h on 60h dp bl
N14	A39	1k 20h on 1k car, *yel*

On Stamps of 1917-18

N15	A42	60h on 15h dl red
N16	A42	60h on 20h dp grn
N17	A42	60h on 25h blue
N18	A42	60h on 30h dl vio

Surcharge in colors other than dark blue black are bogus or proofs. Surcharges on other stamps are bogus.

———

POSTAGE DUE STAMPS

Austrian Postage Due Stamps Surcharged like Regular Issues

1919   **Unwmk.**   *Perf. 12½*

On Stamps of 1916

NJ1	D4	40h on 5h rose red
NJ5	D4	1k 20h on 25h rose red
NJ6	D4	1k 20h on 30h rose red

On Stamp of 1917

NJ13	A38	1k 20h on 50h on 42h choc

WEST IRIAN

(Irian Barat)
(West New Guinea)

LOCATION — Western half of New Guinea, southwest Pacific Ocean
GOVT. — Province of Indonesia
AREA — 162,927 sq. mi.
POP. — 923,440 (1973)
CAPITAL — Djajapura (formerly Hollandia)

The former Netherlands New Guinea became a territory under the administration of the United Nations Temporary Executive Authority on Oct. 1, 1962.

The territory came under Indonesian administration on May 1, 1963.

100 Cents = 1 Gulden

100 Sen = 1 Rupiah

(1 rupiah = 1 former Netherlands New Guinea gulden)

> Catalogue values for all unused stamps in this country are for Never Hinged items.

Issued Under United Nations Temporary Executive Authority

Netherlands New Guinea Stamps of 1950-60 Overprinted **UNTEA**

Perf. 12½x12, 12½x13½

1962   **Photo.**   Unwmk.

1	A4	1c vermilion & yel	55	55
2	A1	2c deep orange	70	70
3	A4	5c choc & yel	65	65
4	A5	7c org red, bl & brn vio	70	70
5	A4	10c aqua & red brn	65	65
6	A5	12c grn, bl & brn vio	70	70
7	A4	15c dp yel & red brn	90	90
8	A5	17c brn vio & bl	90	90
9	A4	20c lt bl grn & red brn	90	90
10	A6	25c red	55	55
11	A6	30c deep blue	70	70
12	A6	40c deep orange	1.00	1.00
13	A6	45c dark olive	2.75	2.75
14	A6	55c slate blue	2.25	2.25
15	A6	80c dl gray vio	12.00	12.00
16	A6	85c dk vio brn	4.50	4.50
17	A6	1g plum	3.75	3.75

Engr.

18	A3	2g reddish brn	12.00	12.00
19	A3	5g green	15.00	15.00
		Nos. 1-19 (19)	61.15	61.15

The overprint exists in four types: (1.) Size 17½mm. Applied locally and sold in West New Guinea. Top of "N" is slightly lower than the "U," and the base of the "T" is straight, or nearly so. (2.) Size 17½mm. Applied in the Netherlands and sold by the UN in New York. Top of the "N" is slightly higher than the "U," and the base of the "T" is concave. (3.) Size 14mm. Exists on eight values. (4.) Size 19mm. Exists on 1c and 10c.

Types 3 and 4 were applied in West New Guinea and it is doubtful whether they were regularly issued.

West Irian

Indonesia Nos. 454, 456, 494-501, 387, 390, 392 and 393 Surcharged or Overprinted: "IRIAN BARAT"

Perf. 12½x13½

1963, May 1   **Photo.**   Unwmk.

20	A63	1s on 70s org ver	15	15
21	A63	2s on 90s yel grn	15	15

Perf. 12x12½

22	A76	5s gray	15	15
23	A76	6s on 20s ocher	15	15
24	A76	7s on 50s dp bl	15	15
25	A76	10s red brn	15	15
26	A76	15s plum	15	15
27	A76	25s brt bl grn	15	15
28	A76	30s on 75s scar	20	20
29	A76	40s on 1.15r plum	22	22

Perf. 12½x12

30	A55	1r purple	60	60
31	A55	2r green	1.10	1.10
32	A55	3r dk bl	1.25	1.25
33	A55	5r brown	2.25	2.25
		Nos. 20-33 (14)	6.82	6.82

"Indonesia's Flag from Sabang to Merauke" — A1

Designs: 20s, 50s, Parachutist landing in New Guinea. 60s, 75s, Bird of paradise and map of New Guinea.

1963, May 1

34	A1	12s org brn, blk & red	15	15
35	A1	17s org brn, blk & red	15	15
36	A1	20s multi	15	15
37	A1	50s multi	30	30
38	A1	60s multi	42	42
39	A1	75s multi	55	55
		Nos. 34-39 (6)	1.72	1.72

Liberation of West New Guinea.

Maniltoa Gemmipara — A2

Designs: 15s, Dendrobium lancifolium (orchid). 30s, Gardenia gjellerupii. 40s, Maniltoa flower. 50s, Phalanger. 75s, Cassowary. 1e, Kangaroo. 3r, Crowned pigeons.

1968, Aug. 17   **Photo.**   *Perf. 12½x12*

40	A2	5s dl grn & vio blk	15	15
41	A2	15s emer & dk pur	25	25
42	A2	30s org & dp grn	45	45
43	A2	40s lemon & brt pur	45	45
44	A2	50s rose car & blk	45	45
45	A2	75s dl bl & blk	60	60
46	A2	1r brn org & blk	1.25	1.25
47	A2	3r apple grn & blk	2.00	2.00
		Nos. 40-47 (8)	5.60	5.60

Man, Map of Indonesia and Torches — A3

1968, Aug. 17

48	A3	10s ultra & gold	22	22
49	A3	25s crimson & gold	45	45

Issued to publicize the pledge of the people of West Irian to remain unified and integrated with the Republic of Indonesia.

Carving, Mother and Child — A4   Black-capped Lory — A5

West Irian Wood Carvings: 6s, Shield with 3 human figures. 7s, Child atop filigree carving. 10s, Drum. 25s, Seated man. 30s, Drum (3-tiered base). 50s, Carved bamboo. 75s, Man-shaped ornament. 1r, Shield. 2r, Seated man (hands raised).

1970   **Photo.**   *Perf. 12½x12*

50	A4	5s multi	15	15
51	A4	6s multi	15	15
52	A4	7s multi	15	15
53	A4	10s multi	15	15
54	A4	25s multi	15	15
55	A4	30s multi	15	15
56	A4	40s multi	15	15
57	A4	75s multi	20	20
58	A4	1r multi	42	42
59	A4	2r multi	70	70
		Set value	1.75	1.75

Issued: Nos. 50-54, Apr. 30; Nos. 55-59, Apr. 15.

1970, Oct. 26   **Photo.**   *Perf. 12x12½*

60	A5	5r shown	70	70
61	A5	10r Bird of paradise	1.40	1.40

POSTAGE DUE STAMPS

Type of Indonesia Overprinted: "IRIAN BARAT"

Perf. 13½x12½

1963, May 1   **Litho.**   Unwmk.

J1	D8	1s light brown	15	15
J2	D8	5s light gray olive	15	15
J3	D8	10s light blue	15	15
J4	D8	25s gray	15	15
J5	D8	40s salmon	30	30
J6	D8	100s bister	70	75
		Set value	1.40	1.40

Type of Indonesia Dated "1968" and Overprinted: "IRIAN BARAT"

1968   **Photo.**   *Perf. 13½x12½*

J7	D9	1s blue & lt grn	15	15
J8	D9	5s grn & pink	15	15
J9	D9	10s red & gray	15	15
J10	D9	25s grn & yel	15	15
J11	D9	40s vio brn & pale grn	30	30
J12	D9	100s org & bister	75	75
		Set value	1.40	1.40

YEMEN

LOCATION — Arabian Peninsula, south of Saudi Arabia and bordering on the Red Sea
GOVT. — Republic
AREA — 73,300 sq. mi.
CAPITAL — San'a

40 Bogaches = 1 Imadi

40 Bogaches = 1 Riyal (1962)

100 Fils = 1 Riyal (1978)

> Catalogue values for unused stamps in this country are for Never Hinged items, beginning with Scott 44 in the regular postage section, Scott C1 in the airpost section.

Watermarks

Wmk. 127- Quatrefoils   Wmk. 258- Arabic Characters and Y G Multiple

---

Wmk. 277- Winged Wheel

For Domestic Postage

Crossed Daggers and Arabic Inscriptions
A1   A2

1926   **Unwmk.**   **Typo.**   *Imperf.*
Laid Paper
Without Gum

1	A1	2½b black	16.00	12.50
2	A1	2½b black, *orange*	16.00	12.50
3	A2	5b black	19.00	12.50

No. 2 is known rouletted 7½ or 9.
Type A1 differs from A2 primarily in the inscription in the left dagger blade.
All come on wove paper.

For Foreign and Domestic Postage

Arabic Inscriptions
A3   A4

1930-31   **Wmk. 127**   *Perf. 14*

7	A3	½b org ('31)	15	15
8	A3	1b green	30	25
9	A3	1b yel grn ('31)	15	15
10	A3	2b ol grn	35	30
11	A3	2b ol brn ('31)	20	15
12	A3	3b dl vio ('31)	30	15
13	A3	4b red	60	45
14	A3	4b deep rose ('31)	50	15
15	A3	5b slate gray ('31)	75	50
16	A4	6b dull blue	1.25	75
17	A4	6b dp ultra ('31)	70	45
18	A4	8b lil rose ('31)	1.00	60
19	A4	10b lt brn	1.75	1.00
20	A4	10b brn org ('31)	1.25	1.00
21	A4	20b yel grn ('31)	3.50	2.25
22	A4	1i red brn & lt bl	8.75	6.50
23	A4	1i lil rose & yel grn ('31)	8.75	6.00
		Nos. 7-23 (17)	30.25	20.80

Some values exist imperforate.
For surcharges and overprints see Nos. 30, 59-62, 166-167, 169-171, 174-176.

Flags of Saudi Arabia, Yemen and Iraq — A5

1939 Litho. Wmk. 258 Perf. 12½

24	A5	4b dl rose & ultra	30	30
25	A5	6b slate bl & ultra	40	40
26	A5	10b fawn & ultra	70	70
27	A5	14b olive & ultra	1.00	1.00
28	A5	20b yel grn & ultra	1.75	1.75
29	A5	1i claret & ultra	3.50	3.50
		Nos. 24-29 (6)	7.65	7.65

2nd anniv. of the Arab Alliance. Nos. 24-29 exist imperforate.

For overprints see Nos. C29-C29D.

No. 7 Handstamped in Black

a-b-c

Three types of surcharge:
a. 11½x16mm
b. 13-13½x15½mm
c. 12x16mm

Values of surcharged stamps are for ordinary copies. Clear, legible surcharges command a premium.

1939 Wmk. 127 Perf. 14

30	A3	4b on ½b orange	5.00	2.00

See Nos. 44-48, 59-67, 82, 86-87.

A6

A7

1940 Wmk. 258 Litho. Perf. 12½

31	A6	½b ocher & ultra	15	15
32	A6	1b lt grn & rose red	15	15
33	A6	2b bis brn & vio	15	15
34	A6	3b dl vio & ultra	15	15
35	A6	4b rose & yel grn	20	20
36	A6	5b dk gray grn & bis brn	25	25
37	A7	6b ultra & yel org	20	20
38	A7	8b claret & dl bl	38	38
39	A7	10b brn org & yel grn	35	32
40	A7	14b gray grn & vio	42	32
41	A7	18b emer & blk	75	75
42	A7	20b yel ol & cerise	1.10	1.00
43	A7	1i vio rose, yel grn & brn red	2.50	1.60
		Nos. 31-43 (13)	6.75	5.62

No. 36 was used as a 4b stamp in 1957.

For surcharges see Nos. 44-47.

> Catalogue values for unused stamps in this section, from this point to the end of the section, are for Never Hinged items.

Nos. 31-34, 36 Handstamped Type "b" in Black

1946-51 Perf. 12½

44	A6	4b on ½b ('51)	1.60	1.00
45	A6	4b on 1b ('49)	1.50	80
46	A6	4b on 2b ('49)	1.20	65
47	A6	4b on 3b ('49)	1.40	80

1945-48 Handstamp Type "a"

44a	A6	4b on ½b	3.50	1.50
45a	A6	4b on 1b ('48)	4.00	1.75
46a	A6	4b on 2b ('48)	3.00	1.50
47a	A6	4b on 3b ('48)	3.50	1.75
48	A6	4b on 5b ('46)	3.50	1.75

Forged surcharges exist.

A8

1946

Frames in Emerald

49	A8	4b black	1.00	1.00
50	A8	6b lilac rose	1.40	90
51	A8	10b ultra	1.60	1.60
52	A8	14b olive green	3.00	1.60

Opening of Mutawakkili Hospital. Exist imperforate.

For overprints see Nos. 168, 172-173.

Mocha Coffee Tree — A9

Palace, San'a — A10

1947-58 Unwmk. Engr. Perf. 12½

53	A9	½b yel brn	15	15
54	A9	1b purple	38	16
55	A9	2b ultra	65	38
56	A10	4b red	60	30
57	A9	5b gray blue	38	25
58	A9	6b yel grn ('58)	1.00	65
		Nos. 53-58 (6)	3.16	1.89

No. 58 was printed in 1947 but not officially issued until June, 1958.

Additional values, prepared but not issued, were 10b, 20b and 1i, with views of palaces superimposed on flag, and palace square. These were looted from government storehouses during the 1948 revolution and a number of copies later reached collectors.

For surcharges see Nos. 63-65.

Nos. 9, 11, 12 and 15 Handstamped Type "a" in Black

1949 Wmk. 127 Perf. 14

59	A3	4b on 1b yel grn	1.60	1.20
60	A3	4b on 2b ol brn	15.00	7.50
61	A3	4b on 3b dl vio	2.50	1.50
62	A3	4b on 5b slate gray	2.50	1.50

Handstamped type "b" are bogus.

Nos. 53-55 Handstamped Type "b" and "a"

1949 Unwmk. Perf. 12½

63	A9(b)	4b on ½b yel brn	2.00	2.00
64	A9(a)	4b on 1b purple	2.00	2.00
a.		Handstamp type "b"	2.00	2.00
65	A9(a)	4b on 2b ultra	4.00	3.75
a.		Handstamp type "b"	4.00	3.50
b.		Handstamp 13x15mm		

Nos. J1-J2 Handstamped Type "b" in Black

1953 Wmk. 258

66	D1	4b on 1b org & yel grn	6.00	5.00
67	D1	4b on 2b org & yel grn	6.00	5.00
a.		Handstamp type "c"		

Three minor types of this handstamped 4b surcharge exist. Types "a" and "b" exist inverted, double or horizontal.

Forged surcharges exist.

Parade Ground, San'a — A13

Mosque, San'a — A14

Designs: 5b, Flag of Yemen. 6b, Flag & eagle. 8b, Mocha coffee branch. 14b, Walled city of San'a. 20b, 1i, Ta'iz & its citadel.

1951 Wmk. 277 Photo. Perf. 14

68	A13	1b dk brn	15	15
69	A13	2b red brn	18	15
70	A13	3b lilac rose	25	15
71	A14	4b bl & red	38	15
72	A13	6b dk pur & red	50	15
73	A13	8b dk bl & gray grn	50	15
74	A14	10b rose lilac	65	25
75	A14	14b blue green	1.00	38
76	A14	20b rose red	1.50	65
77	A14	1i violet	2.50	1.25
		Nos. 68-77 (10)	7.61	
		Set value		3.00

No. 71 was used as a 4b stamp in 1956. See Nos. C3-C9. For surcharges see Nos. 82, 86-87, .

Palace of the Rock, Wadi Dhahr — A15

Design: 20b, Walls of Ibb.

Engraved and Photogravure

1952 Unwmk. Perf. 14½, Imperf.

78	A15	12b choc, bl & dl grn	5.00	5.00
79	A15	20b dp car, bl & brn	7.00	7.00

See Nos. C10-C11.

Flag and View of San'a (Palace in Background) — A16

1952

80	A16	1i red brn, car & gray	8.50	8.50

4th anniv. of the accession of King Ahmed, Feb. 18, 1948. See Nos. 81, C12-C13.

Palace in Foreground

1952

81	A16	30b red brn, car & dk grn	6.00	6.00

Victory of Mar. 13, 1948. See No. C13.

No. 69 Handstamped Type "b" in Black

1951 (?) Wmk. 277 Perf. 14

82	A13	4b on 2b red brown	1.40	65

Forged surcharges exist. See Nos. 86-87.

Leaning Minaret, Mosque of Ta'iz — A17

Yemen Gate, San'a — A18

1954 Photo. Unwmk.

83	A17	4b dp org	40	16
84	A17	6b dp bl	60	35
85	A17	8b bl grn	80	40
		Nos. 83-85,C14-C16 (6)	3.58	2.21

Accession of King Ahmed I, 5th anniv.

Nos. 68 and 70 Handstamped Type "b" in Black

1955 Wmk. 277 Perf. 14

86	A13	4b on 1b dk brn	2.00	1.90
a.		Handstamp type "c"		1.60
87	A13	4b on 3b lil rose	2.25	2.25

1956-57 Wmk. 277 Perf. 14

87A	A18	1b lt brn	25	15
87B	A18	5b bl grn	25	15
87C	A18	10b dk bl ('57)	50	50

Nos. 87A-87C were prepared for official use, but issued for regular postage. The 1b and 5b were used as 4b stamps. A 20b and 1-imadi of type A18 were not issued.

Arab Postal Union Issue

Globe — A19

Perf. 13½x13

1957-58 Wmk. 195 Photo.

88	A19	4b yel brn	1.00	90
89	A19	6b green ('58)	1.40	1.10
90	A19	16b violet ('58)	2.00	1.50

Issued to commemorate the founding of the Arab Postal Union, July 1, 1954.

Telecommunications Issue

Globe, Radio and Telegraph A20

1959, Mar. Wmk. 318 Perf. 13x13½

91	A20	4b vermilion	35	35

Arab Union of Telecommunications.

United Arab States Issue

Flags of UAR and Yemen A21

1959, Mar. 13

92	A21	1b dl red brn & blk	16	16
93	A21	2b dk bl & blk	25	25
94	A21	4b sl grn, car & blk	30	30
		Nos. 92-94,C17-C19 (6)	2.24	1.79

First anniversary of United Arab States.

Arab League Center Issue

Arab League Center, Cairo A22

Perf. 13x13½

1960, Mar. 22 Wmk. 328

95	A22	4b dl grn & blk	40	35

Opening of the Arab League Center and the Arab Postal Museum in Cairo.

Refugees Pointing to Map of Palestine
A23

1960, Apr. 7   Photo.
96 A23 4b brown   70   70
97 A23 6b yellow green   1.00 1.00

Issued to publicize World Refugee Year, July 1, 1959-June 30, 1960.
In 1961 a souvenir sheet was issued containing a 4b gray and 6b sepia in type A18, imperf. Black marginal inscription, "YEMEN 1960," repeated in Arabic. Size: 103x85mm. Value $15.

Torch and Olympic Rings A24

1960, Dec.   Unwmk.   Perf. 14x14½
98 A24 2b blk & lil rose   15   15
99 A24 4b blk & yel   20   20
100 A24 6b blk & org   32   32
101 A24 8b brn blk & bl grn   52   52
102 A24 20b dk bl, org & vio   1.00   65
     Nos. 98-102 (5)   2.19 1.84

Issued to commemorate the 17th Olympic Games, Rome, Aug. 25-Sept. 11.
An imperf. souvenir sheet exists, containing one copy of No. 99. Size: 100x60 mm. Value $50.

Alabaster Funerary Mask — A27

Imam's New Palace, San'a — A28

Designs (ancient sculptures from Marib, Sheba): 2b, Horned animal's head, symbolizing Moon God (limestone). 4b, Bronze head of an Emperor 1st or 2nd century. 8b, Statue of Emperor Dhamar Ali. 10b, Statue of a child, 2nd or 3rd century (alabaster). 12b, Stairs in court of Temple of the Moon God. 20b, Alabaster relief, boy riding monster. 1i, Woman with grapes, relief.

1961, Oct. 14   Photo.   Perf. 11½
Granite Paper
113 A27 1b sal, blk & gray   15   15
114 A27 2b pur & gray   15   15
115 A27 4b pale brn, gray & blk   15   15
116 A27 8b brt pink & blk   20   20
117 A27 10b yel & blk   35   35
118 A27 12b lt vio bl & blk   50   50
119 A27 20b gray & blk   60   60
120 A27 1i gray ol & blk   1.20 1.20
   Nos. 113-120, C20-C21 (10)   3.87 3.87

For overprints see Nos. 144-145, 147, 151, 153, 156-158, C24, C25.

1961, Nov. 15   Unwmk.
Designs: 8b, Side view of Imam's palace, San'a, horiz. 10b, Palace of the Rock (Dar al-Hajar).
121 A28 4b blk & lt bl grn   16   16
122 A28 8b blk, brt pink & grn   35   35
123 A28 10b blk, sal & grn   42   42
   Nos. 121-123, C22-C23 (5)   1.51 1.51

Exist imperf.
For overprints see #148, 152, 154, C24A, C25A.

Hodeida-San'a Road — A29

1961, Dec. 25   Litho.   Perf. 13½x13
124 A29 4b multicolored   40   20
125 A29 6b multicolored   60   30
126 A29 10b multicolored   1.00   50

Opening of the Hodeida-San'a highway. A miniature sheet exists containing one each of Nos. 124-126, imperf. Size: 159x129mm. Value $2.
For overprints see Nos. 178-179.

Cranes and Ship, Hodeida A26

1961, June   Litho.   Perf. 13x13½
110 A26 4b multi   22   15
111 A26 6b multi   45   30
112 A26 20b brown   85   70

Opening of deepwater port at Hodeida.
An imperf. souvenir sheet exists, containing one each of Nos. 110-112. Size: 160x130mm. Value $2.50.
For overprints see Nos. 177, 180.

UN Emblem Breaking Chains A25

1961   Unwmk.   Perf. 14x14½
103 A25 1b violet   15   15
104 A25 2b green   15   15
105 A25 3b grnsh bl   15   15
106 A25 4b brt ultra   16   16
107 A25 6b brt lil   20   20
108 A25 14b rose brn   52   50
109 A25 20b brown   1.00   80
    Nos. 103-109 (7)   2.33 2.11

15th anniversary (in 1960) of UN.
An imperf. souvenir sheet exists, containing one copy of No. 106. Blue marginal inscription. Size: 100x60mm. Value $9.
For overprints see Nos. 137-143.

Trajan's Kiosk, Philae, Nubia — A30

1962, Mar. 1   Photo.   Perf. 11x11½
127 A30 4b dk red brn   70   50
128 A30 6b blue green   1.60 1.00

Issued to publicize UNESCO's help in safeguarding the monuments of Nubia.
A souvenir sheet exists, containing one each of #127-128, imperf. Size: 100x88½mm. Value $4.

Arab League Building, Cairo, and Emblem — A31

1962, Mar. 22   Perf. 13½x13
129 A31 4b dk grn   30   25
130 A31 6b dp ultra   45   38

Arab League Week, Mar. 22-28.
A souvenir sheet exists, containing one each of Nos. 129-130, imperf. Size: 94x80mm. Value $1.25.
For overprints see Nos. 164-165.

Nurses, Mother and Child — A32

Malaria Eradication Emblem — A33

Designs: 4b, Nurse weighing child. 6b, Vaccination. 10b, Weighing infant.

1962, June 20   Unwmk.   Perf. 11½
131 A32 2b multi   20   20
132 A32 4b multi   25   25
133 A32 6b multi   38   38
134 A32 10b multi   50   50

Issued for Child Welfare.
For overprints see Nos. 146, 149-150, 155.

1962, July 20   Perf. 13½x13
135 A33 4b blk & dp org   25   16
136 A33 6b dk brn & grn   50   35

WHO drive to eradicate malaria. An imperf. souvenir sheet contains one each of Nos. 135-136. Size: 95x79mm. Value $12.50.
No. 136 has laurel leaves added and inscription rearranged.
For overprints see Nos. 189-190.

Nos. 103-109 Overprinted

١٩٦٢-١٩٤٥

1945-1962

1962 Photo. Unwmk. Perf. 14x14½
137 A25 1b vio
138 A25 2b grn
139 A25 3b greenish blue
140 A25 4b brt ultra
141 A25 6b brt lil
142 A25 14b rose brn
143 A25 20b brn

Nos. 113-123 and 131-134 Ovptd. in Dark Green or Dark Red

الجمهورية العربية اليمنية
١٩٦٢/٩/٢٧-١٣٨٢/٤/٢٨
Y. A. R. 27.9.1962
a

الجمهورية العربية اليمنية
١٩٦٢/٩/٢٧ - ١٣٨٢/٤/٢٨
Y.A.R. 27.9.1962
b

1963, Jan. 1   Perf. 11½
144 A27 (a) 1b No. 113 (G)
145 A27 (a) 2b No. 114
146 A32 (a) 2b No. 131
147 A27 (a) 4b No. 115 (G)
148 A28 (a) 4b No. 121
149 A32 (a) 4b No. 132 (G)
150 A32 (a) 6b No. 133
151 A27 (a) 8b No. 116
152 A28 (a) 8b No. 122 (G)
153 A27 (a) 10b No. 117
154 A28 (a) 10b No. 123
155 A32 (a) 10b No. 134 (G)
156 A27 (a) 12b No. 118
157 A27 (a) 20b No. 119
158 A27 (a) 1i No. 120

For overprints see Nos. C24-C25A.

Proclamation of the Republic — A34

UN Freedom From Hunger Campaign — A35

1963, Mar. 15   Perf. 11x11½
159 A34 4b shown
160 A34 6b Flag, tank

See Nos. C26-C28.

Perf. 11½x11, 11x11½
1963, Mar. 21
162 A35 4b Milk cow, horiz.   90
163 A35 6b shown   1.25

An imperf. souvenir sheet of 2 exists containing one each Nos. 162-163.
For overprints see Nos. 219-220.

الجمهورية العربية اليمنية   Y.A.R.

Nos. 129-130 Ovptd. in Dark Red

١٩٦٢/٩/٢٧ - ١٣٨٢/٤/٢٨
27-9-1962

1963, Sept. 1   Perf. 13½x13
164 A31 4b dark grn
165 A31 6b deep ultra

Nos. 15-16, 18-23, 50-52 Ovptd. in Black

بريد اليمن

الجمهورية العربية اليمنية
١٣٨٢/٤/٢٨
١٩٦٢/٩/٢٧
Y. A. R.
27. 9. 1962
بريد اليمن
a

الجمهورية العربية اليمنية
١٣٨٢/٤/٢٨
١٩٦٢/٩/٢٧
Y. A. R.
27. 9. 1962
b

1963, Sept. 1
166 A3 (a) 5b No. 15
167 A4 (a) 6b No. 16
168 A8 (b) 6b No. 50
169 A4 (a) 8b No. 18
170 A4 (a) 10b No. 19
171 A4 (a) 10b No. 20
172 A8 (b) 10b No. 51
173 A8 (b) 14b No. 52

174 A4 (a) 20b No. 21
175 A4 (a) 1i No. 22
176 A4 (a) 1i No. 23

Nos. 111-112 and 125-126 Ovptd. in Black

━━━━━━━━

الجمهورية العربية اليمنية
١٣٨٢-٤-٢٧ — ١٩٦٢-٩-٢٧
Y. A. R.   27. 9 1962

Perf. 13x13½, 13½x13
1963, Sept. 1   Litho.   Unwmk.
177 A26 6b No. 111
178 A29 6b No. 125
179 A29 10b No. 126
180 A26 16b No. 112

On Nos. 178-179 the bars eliminate old inscription with text of overprint positioned below and to the right of them, on Nos. 177 and 180, the text is slightly left below the bars.
Imperf. souvenir sheets of 2 exist containing Nos. 177 and 180 or Nos. 178-179.

1st Anniv. of the Revolution A36

Perf. 11½x11, 11x11½
1963, Sept. 26   Photo.
186 A36 2b Flag, torch, candle, vert.
187 A36 4b shown
188 A36 6b Flag, grain, chain, vert.

Imperf. souvenir sheets of 3 exist containing one each Nos. 186-188.

Red Cross Centenary. Set of six. ¼, ⅓, ½, 4, 8, 20b. Imperf. souv. sheet of two, 4, 8b. Oct. Nos. 6301-6307.

━━━━━━━━

الجمهورية العربية اليمنية

Nos. 135-136 Ovptd. in Black   ١٣٨٢/٤/٢٨
١٩٦٢/٩/٢٧
Y. A. R.
27. 9. 1962

1963, Nov. 25   *Perf. 13½x13*
189 A33 4b blk & deep org
190 A33 6b dark brn & grn

UN Declaration of Human Rights, 15th Anniv. A37

1963, Dec. 10   *Perf. 13½*
191 A37 4b org & dark brn vio   90
192 A37 6b blue grn & blk   1.25

An imperf. souvenir sheet of 2 exists containing one each Nos. 191-192.

1964
Olympic Sports. Set of eight, ¼, ⅓, ½, 1, 1½b, airmail 4, 20b, 1r. Imperf. souv. sheet, 4b. Mar. 30. Nos. 6401-6409.

Bagel Spinning and Weaving Factory Inauguration — A38

Perf. 11x11½, 11½x11
1964, Apr. 10
193 A38 2b Factory, bobbin, spool, cloth
194 A38 4b Loom machine
195 A38 6b Factory, spool, bolt of cloth
196 A38 16b shown

Nos. 193-195 vert. An imperf. souvenir sheet of one exists containing No. 195.
No. 196 is air mail.

Hodeida Airport Inauguration — A39

1964, Apr. 30   *Perf. 11½x11*
197 A39 4b Runway
198 A39 6b Runway, terminal
199 A39 10b Aircraft, terminal, ship at sea

An imperf. souvenir sheet of one exists containing No. 199.

New York World's Fair. Set of seven, ¼, ⅓, ½, 1, 4b, airmail 16, 20b. Imperf. souv. sheet, 20b. May 10. Nos. 6410-6417.
Summer Olympics, Tokyo. Set of nine, ¼, ⅓, ½, 1, 1½b, airmail, 4, 6, 12, 20b. Imperf. souv. sheet, 20b. June 1. Nos. 6418-6427.
Boy Scouts. Set of nine, ¼, ⅓, ½, 1, 1½b, airmail, 4, 6, 16, 20b. Two souvenir sheets, 16b, perf.; 20b, imperf. June 20. Nos. 6428-6438.
Animals. Set of eleven, ¼, ⅓, ½, 1, 1½b, airmail, 4, 12, 20b, postage due, 4, 12, 20b. Aug. 15. Nos. 6439-6449.
Flowers. Set of eight, ¼, ⅓, ½, 1, 1½b, airmail, 4, 12, 20b. Sept. 1. Nos. 6450-6457.

San'a Intl. Airport Inauguration — A40

1964, Oct. 1
200 A40 1b shown
201 A40 2b Terminal, runway, aircraft
202 A40 4b like 2b
203 A40 8b like 1b

An imperf. souvenir sheet of two exists containing one each Nos. 202 and C30.
See No. C30.

Arab Postal Union, 10th Anniv. A41

2nd Arab Summit Conference A42

1964, Oct. 15   *Perf. 13½*
204 A41 4b multicolored
See No. C31.

1964, Nov. 30
205 A42 4b shown
206 A42 6b Conference emblem, map

An imperf. souvenir sheet of 2 exists containing one each Nos. 205-206.
For overprints see Nos. 221-222.

2nd Anniv. of the Revolution A43

Deir Yassin Massacre A44

1964, Dec. 30
207 A43 2b Torch, map
208 A43 4b Revolutionary
209 A43 6b Flag, 2 candles, map

An imperf. souvenir sheet of one exists containing No. 209.

1965
Birds. Set of eleven, ¼, ½, ¾, 1, 1½, 4b, airmail, 6, 8, 12, 20b, 1r. Imperf. souv. sheet, 20b. Jan. 30. Nos. 6501-6512.

1965, Apr. 30   *Perf. 11x11½*
210 A44 4b red lil & deep blue   90
See No. C32.

Intl. Telecommunications Union (ITU), Cent. — A45

Perf. 11x11½, 11½x11
1965, May 17
211 A45 4b red & pale blue, vert.   90
212 A45 6b org brn & grn   1.25

A souvenir sheet of 1 exists containing #212.

Burning of Algiers Library, 3rd Anniv. A46

1965, July 7   *Perf. 11½x11*
214 A46 4b sepia, red & grn
See No. C33.

3rd Anniv. of the Revolution A47

1965, Sept. 26
215 A47 4b Tractor, corn, grain
216 A47 6b Tractor, tower, buildings

An imperf. souvenir sheet of one exists containing No. 216.

Intl. Cooperation Year — A48

1965, Oct. 15   *Perf. 11x11*
217 A48 4b shown
218 A48 6b UN building, New York

An imperf. souvenir sheet of one exists containing No. 218.

John F. Kennedy Memorial. Set of eight, 3x¼, ⅓, ½, 4b, airmail, 8, 12b. Two imperf. souv. sheets, 4, 8b. Nov. 29. Nos. 6513-6522.
Space Exploration. Set of eight, 3x¼, ⅓, ½b, airmail, 4, 8, 16b. Imperf. souv. sheet, 16b. Dec. 29. Nos. 6523-6531.

Nos. 162-163 Overprinted in Black

مكافحة الدرن
١٩٦٥
Tuberculous Campaign
1 9 6 5

مكافحة الدرن
١٩٦٥
TUBERCULOUS CAMPAIGN
1965

Perf. 11½x11, 11x11½
1966, Jan. 15
219 A35 4b sal rose & golden brn
220 A35 6b brt pur & yel

An imperf. souvenir sheet of two exists containing Nos. 219-220.

Communications. Set of eight, 3x¼, ⅓, ½b, airmail, 4, 6, 20b. Imperf. airmail souv. sheet, 20b. Jan. 29. Nos. 6601-6609.
Animals issue of 1965 overprinted in black or red "Prevention of Cruelty to Animals" in English and Arabic. Set of eleven. Souv. sheet, 20b. Mar. 5. Nos. 6610-6621.

مؤتمر القمة العربي
الثالث ـ ١٩٦٥
Nos. 205-206 Ovptd. in Red or Black
3rd. Arab SummitConference
1965

1966, Mar. 20   *Perf. 13½*
221 A42 4b dark grn (R)
222 A42 6b org brn

An imperf. souvenir sheet of two exists containing Nos. 221-222 ovptd. in bright pink (4b) or black (6b) with additional inscription at bottom "CASABLANCA / 1965."

Builders of World Peace. Set of nine, 3x¼, ⅓, ½, 4b, airmail, 6, 10, 12b. Two imperf. souvenir sheets, 4, 8b. Mar. 25. Nos. 6622-6632.
Domestic Animals. Set of six, 3x¼, ⅓, ½, 4b. Imperf. souv. sheet, 22b. May 5. Nos. 6633-6639.
Space Exploration issue of 1965 overprinted "Luna IX / 3 February 1966" in English and Arabic. Set of eight. Imperf. souvenir sheet. Nos. 6640-6648.
World Cup Soccer Championship. Set of eight, 3x¼, ⅓, ½b, airmail, 4, 5, 20b. Imperf. souvenir sheet, 20b. May 29. Nos. 6649-6657.

Traffic Day — A49

1966, June 30   *Perf. 11x11½*
223 A49 4b grn & ver
224 A49 6b grn & ver

Space Exploration issue of 1965 overprinted "Surveyor 1 / 2 June 1966" in English and Arabic. Set of five, 3x1b on ⅛b, 3b on ⅓b, 4b on ½b. Aug. 15. Nos. 6658-6662.

Revolution, 4th Anniv. Set of three, 2, 4, 6b. Imperf. souv. sheet of 2; 4, 6b. Sept. Nos. 6663-6666.

World's Fair issue of 1964 overprinted "1965 Sana'a." Set of seven. Imperf. souvenir sheet. Nos. 6667-6674.

WHO Headquarters Inauguration. Set of six, 3x¼b, airmail, 4, 8, 16b. Imperf. souvenir sheet, 16b. Nov. 1. Nos. 6675-6681.

Gemini 6-7. Set of eight, 3x¼, ⅓, ½, 2b, airmail, 8, 12b. Imperf. souvenir sheet, 12b. Dec. 1. Nos. 6682-6690.

Gemini 6-7 issue overprinted in red "Gemini IX / Cernan-Stafford / June 1966" in English and Arabic. Set of eight. Imperf. souvenir sheet. Dec. 25. Nos. 6691-6699.

1967
Fruit. Set of thirteen, 3x¼, ⅓, ½, 2, 4b, airmail, 6, 8, 10b, postage due, 6, 8, 10b. Feb. 10. Nos. 6701-6713.

Arab League, 25th Anniv. A56

1970, Oct. 5   Photo.   *Perf. 11½x11*
276 A56 5b org, grn & dark pur
277 A56 7b blue, grn & brn
278 A56 16b dark olive grn, grn & chalky blue

An imperf souvenir sheet of one exists containing No. 278.

UN, 25th Anniv. A60

1971, Apr. 4   Photo.   *Perf. 11½x11*
282 A60 5b dark olive grn, grn & dark vio
283 A60 7b blue, grn & dark blue

Souvenir Sheet
Imperf
284 A60 16b multi

10th anniv. of Revolution — A80

1972, Nov. 25   Photo.   *Perf. 13*
301 A80   7b lt bl, blk & multi   65   50
302 A80 10b gray, blk & multi   1.00   65

See No. C40. For surcharge see No. 318.

25th Anniv. of WHO — A81

1972, Dec. 1   Litho.
303 A81   2b lt yel grn & multi   50   35
304 A81 21b sky bl & multi   1.40   1.20
305 A81 37b red lil & multi   2.25   2.00

Burning of Al-Aqsa Mosque, 2nd Anniv. — A82

1972, Jan. 1   Photo.   *Perf. 13½*
306 A82   7b lt bl, blk & multi   1.50   60
307 A82 18b lt bl, blk & multi   2.50   1.10

See No. C41. For surcharges see Nos. 319, 341.

25th Anniv. of UNICEF — A83

1973, Jan. 15   Photo.   *Perf. 13*
308 A83   7b lt bl, blk & multi   1.00   65
309 A83 10b lt bl, blk & multi   1.40   80

See No. C42. For surcharge see No. C46.

UPU Cent. — A84   10th World Hunger Program — A85

1974, Nov. 20   Photo.   *Perf. 14*
310 A84 10b multi   75   40
311 A84 30b multi   2.25   1.50
312 A84 40b multi   3.25   1.90

1975, Feb. 5   Litho.   *Perf. 13½*
313 A85 10b multi   25   25
314 A85 30b multi   70   70
315 A85 63b multi   1.20   1.20

12th Anniv. of Revolution A86

1975, Sept. 25
316 A86 25f Janad Mosque   50   35
317 A86 75f Althawra Hospital   1.00   65

Nos. 301, 306 surcharged in Black with New Values and Bars

1975, Nov. 15   Photo.   *Perf. 13½*
318 A80   75f on 7b   2.00   65
319 A82 278f on 7b   3.50   1.20
    Nos. 318-319,C46-C48 (5)   9.05   4.00

Telephone Cent. — A87   Coffee Bean Branch — A88

1976, Mar. 10   Litho.   *Perf. 14½*
320 A87 25f brt pink & blk   25   25
321 A87 75f lt grn & blk   60   60
322 A87 160f lt bl & blk   1.20   1.20
   a.   Souvenir sheet of 1

No. 322a exists both perf. and imperf.

1976, Apr. 25   *Perf. 14*
323 A88   1f dull lilac   15   15
324 A88   3f pale gray   15   15
325 A88   5f lt bl grn   15   15
326 A88 10f bis brn   15   15
327 A88 25f golden brn   22   22
328 A88 50f brt plum   42   42
329 A88 75f dull pink   70   60

Size: 22x30mm
Perf. 14½
330 A88   1r sky blue   1.25   70
331 A88 1.50r red lilac   1.90   1.40
332 A88   2r light grn   2.25   1.40
333 A88   5r yel org   5.00   3.00
    Nos. 323-333 (11)   12.34   8.34

For surcharges see Nos. 403-407, 592.

2nd Anniv. of Reformation Movement — A89

1976, June 13   Photo.   *Perf. 12x12½*
334 A89   75f Industrial Park   70   50
335 A89 135f Forestry   1.00   70

Souvenir Sheet
336 A89 135f Forestry   2.00   2.00

No. 336 contains one stamp (32x47mm).

14th Anniv. of Revolution — A90   3rd Anniv. of Correction Movement — A91

Designs: 25f, Natl. Institute of Public Administration. 75f, Housing and population census. 160f, Sanaa University emblem.

1976, Sept. 26   Photo.   *Perf. 12x12½*
337 A90 25f buff & multi   25   25
338 A90 75f yel bis & multi   60   60

---

339 A90 160f pale grn & multi   1.20   1.20
Souvenir Sheet
340 A90 160f pale grn & multi   2.25   2.25

No. 340 contains one stamp (33x49mm).

No. 306 Surcharged in Black with New Value and Bars

1976
341 A82 75f on 7b   1.00   65

1977   Photo.   *Perf. 14*
342 A91 25f Dish antenna   20   15
343 A91 75f Computer, technician   60   30
   a.   Miniature sheet of 1   1.50   1.50

15th Anniv. of September Revolution — A92

1977   Photo.   *Perf. 13½*
344 A92 25f Sa'ada-San'a Road   25   20
345 A92 75f Television, Transmitting tower   50   30
346 A92 160f like 25f   1.00   70
   a.   Souvenir sheet of 1   2.25   2.25

25th Anniv. of Arab Postal Union — A93   Pres. Hamdi — A94

1978   *Perf. 14*
347 A93 25f lt yel grn & multi   40   25
348 A93 60f bis & multi   90   60
   a.   Miniature sheet of 1   2.25   2.25

1978   *Perf. 11½*
349 A94 25f dk grn & blk   16   15
350 A94 75f ultra & blk   40   20
351 A94 160f brn & blk   80   50
   a.   Miniature sheet of 1   15.00   6.50

30th Anniv. of ICAO (1977) A95

1979, Nov. 15   Photo.   *Perf. 13½*
352 A95   75f multi   60   40
353 A95 135f multi   1.40   90
   a.   Miniature sheet of 1   2.00   2.00

Book, World Map, Arab Achievements — A96

1979, Dec. 1   *Perf. 14*
354 A96 25f multi   35   18
355 A96 75f multi   90   60
   a.   Souvenir sheet of 1   2.00   2.00

A97   A98

1980, Jan. 1
356 A97 75f multi   60   40
357 A97 135f multi, horiz.   1.40   90
a.   Miniature sheet of 1   2.00 2.00

12th World Telecommunications Day, May 17, 1979.

1980   Photo.   Perf. 14

Dome of the Rock.

358 A98 5f brt bl & multi   50   35
359 A98 10f yel & multi   1.00   65

Palestinian fighters and their families.

Argentina World Cup — A99

Designs: World Cup emblem and various players.

1980, Mar. 30
360 A99 25f gold & multi   38   38
361 A99 30f gold & multi   40   30
362 A99 35f gold & multi   50   38
363 A99 50f gold & multi   70   50
Nos. 360-363,C49-C52 (8)   6.48 4.76

Issued in sheets of 8.

International Year of the Child — A100

1980, Apr. 1   Perf. 13½
364 A100 25f Girl, bird   65   50
365 A100 50f Girl, bird, diff.   1.20   80
366 A100 75f Boy, butterfly, flower 1.60 1.20
Nos. 364-366,C53-C55 (6)   9.95 6.10

Issued in sheets of 6.

World Scouting Jamboree — A101

1980, May 1   Perf. 13½x14
367 A101 25f Fishing   40   20
368 A101 35f Troup, aircraft   55   30
369 A101 40f Mounted bugler, flag   65   38
370 A101 50f Telescope, night sky   80   40
Nos. 367-370,C56-C58 (7)   6.80 3.43

Issued in sheets of 6.

Argentina 1978 World Cup
Winners — A102

Designs: World cup emblem and various soccer players.

1980, June 1   Perf. 14
371 A102 25f gold & multi   45   25
372 A102 30f gold & multi   60   30
373 A102 35f gold & multi   60   38
374 A102 50f gold & multi   90   40
Nos. 371-374,C59-C62 (8)   8.05 4.28

Hegira,
1500th
Anniv.
A102A

Designs: 160f, Outside view.

1980, July 1   Perf. 13½
375 A102a 25f blk & multi   30   18
376 A102a 75f car rose & multi   90   60
377 A102a 160f blk & multi   1.90   75
a.   Miniature sheet of 1   4.00 4.00

17th Anniv. of
September
Revolution
A103

A104

1980, Sept. 26   Perf. 13½
378 A103 25f multi   35   22
379 A104 75f multi   1.10   65
Souvenir Sheet
380   100f multi   3.75 3.75

No. 380 contains one stamp combining designs A103 and A104 (42x34mm).

Al Aqsa Mosque
A105

Mosques: 25f, Al-Rawda entrance. 100f, Al-Nabwi. 160f, Al-Haram.

1980, Nov. 6   Photo.   Perf. 13½
381 A105 25f multi   20   16
382 A105 75f multi   60   50
383 A105 100f multi   1.40   65
384 A105 160f multi   1.75 1.00
Souvenir Sheet
385   160f multi   4.50 3.25

Islamic Postal Systems Week and Hegira. No. 385 contains one stamp (109x47mm) combining designs of Nos. 382-384.

Intl. Palestinian
Solidarity
Day — A106

1980, Nov. 29
386 A106 25f lt bl & multi   40   22
387 A106 75f ver & multi   1.10   90

Inscribed 1979.

9th Arab Archaeological
Conference — A107

1981, Mar. 1   Perf. 13½
388 A107 75f Al Aamiriya Mosque   1.10   60
389 A107 125f Al Hadi Mosque   1.75   85
a.   Souvenir sheet of 2, #388-389 3.25 3.25

1980 World
Tourism
Conference,
Manila
A108

1981, Apr. 1
390 A108 25f shown   20   15
391 A108 75f Mosque, houses   60   30
392 A108 100f Columns, horiz.   80   45
393 A108 135f Bridge   1.10   60
394 A108 160f Vuiew of San'a,
                 horiz.   1.40   60
a.   Miniature sheet of 1   4.50 4.50
Nos. 390-394 (5)   4.10 2.10

Sir Rowland Hill (1795-1879), Postage
Stamp Inventor — A109

1981, Sept. 15   Litho.   Perf. 14
395 A109 25f Portrait, UPU em-
                 blem   16
396 A109 30f Emblem, stamp of
                 1963   20
397 A109 50f Portrait, stamps   35
398 A109 75f Portrait, globe, jet   50
399 A109 100f Portrait, stamp collec-
                 tion   65
400 A109 150f Jets, No. 322   1.00
Nos. 395-400 (6)   2.86
Souvenir Sheets
401 A109 200f Portrait, vert.   4.00
Imperf
402 A109 200f Portrait, diff.   4.00

Nos. 398-402 are airmail.

Nos. 323-327 Surcharged

1981
403 A88 125f on 1f   80
404 A88 150f on 3f   1.00
405 A88 325f on 5f   2.00
406 A88 350f on 10f   2.25
407 A88 375f on 25f   2.50

20th
Anniv.
of
Yemen
Airways
A110

1983, Apr. 1   Litho.   Perf. 14
408 A110 75f yel & multi   50   50
409 A110 125f red & multi   80   80
410 A110 325f bl & multi   2.00 2.00

Folk Costumes — A111

1983, May 1
411 A111 50f Woman carrying
                 waterjar   35
412 A111 50f Women, sheep   35
413 A111 50f Man, donkeys   35
414 A111 50f Man in town square   35
415 A111 75f Women, child, well   50
416 A111 75f Scholar   50
417 A111 75f Woman on beach   50
418 A111 75f Camel-drawn plow   50
Nos. 411-418 (8)   3.40
Souvenir Sheets
419 A111 200f Woman
Imperf
420 A111 200f Man

#411-414 vert. #415-420 are airmail.

Sept. 26th
Revolution,
20th Anniv.
(1982)
A112

1983, Sept. 26   Litho.   Perf. 14
421 A112 100f Communications
422 A112 150f Literacy
423 A112 325f Educational development
a.   Souvenir sheet of 2, #422, 423
424 A112 400f Independence

World Communications Year — A113

1983, Dec. 15
425 A113 150f lt bl & multi
426 A113 325f lt grn & multi
  a. Souvenir sheet of 1

Sept. 26
Revolution,
21st Anniv.
A114

1984, Apr. 1   Litho.   Perf. 14
427 A114 100f shown
428 A114 150f Fist, statue
429 A114 325f Gate, tank
  a. Souvenir sheet of 1

Israel Aggression
Day — A115

1984, Sept. 7
430 A115 150f multi   1.00
431 A115 325f multi   2.00

Size: 91x120mm
Imperf
432 A115 325f multi   5.00

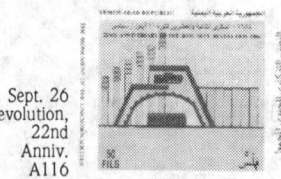

Sept. 26
Revolution,
22nd
Anniv.
A116

1985, Oct. 1
433 A116 50f Triumphal Arch
434 A116 150f San'a Castle walls
435 A116 325f Stadium, Govt. Palace, San'a
  a. Souvenir sheet of 1

Intl. Anti-Apartheid
Year (1978) — A117

1985, Jan. 1
436 A117 150f dp ver & multi
437 A117 325f grn & multi
  a. Souvenir sheet of 1

Intl. Civil
Aviation
Org., 40th
Anniv.
A118

1985, Sept. 20
438 A118 25f multi
439 A118 50f multi
440 A118 325f multi
  a. Souvenir sheet of 1

Arabsat
Satellite, 1st
Anniv.
A119

1986, Apr. 15   Litho.   Perf. 14
442 A119 150f multi
443 A119 325f multi
  a. Souvenir sheet of 1

World Telecommunications, 120th
Anniv. — A120

1986, May 1
444 A120 150f multi
445 A120 325f multi
  a. Souvenir sheet of 1

General
People's
Conference,
2nd Anniv.
A121

1986, May 1
446 A121 150f multi
447 A121 325f multi
  a. Souvenir sheet of 1

A122   A123

1986, July 1
448 A122 150f multi
449 A122 325f multi
  a. Souvenir sheet of 1

15th Islamic Foreign Ministers' Conference,
San'a, Dec. 18-22, 1984.

1986, Oct. 1
450 A123 150f multi
451 A123 325f multi
  a. Souvenir sheet of 1

UN 40th anniv.

Arab
League,
39th Anniv.
A124

1986, Nov. 15
452 A124 150f multi
453 A124 325f multi

Natl. Arms
A125

1987, Sept. 26   Litho.   Perf. 14
454 A125 100f multi
455 A125 150f multi
456 A125 425f multi
  a. Souvenir sheet of 1
457 A125 450f multi

Sept. 26th Revolution, 25th anniv.
For surcharge see No. 593.

Intl. Youth
Year (1985)
A126

1987, Oct. 15   Perf. 13x13¹/₂
458 A126 150f multi
459 A126 425f multi
  a. Souvenir sheet of 1

For surcharge see No. C150.

Drilling of
the
Republic's
First Oil
Well, 1984
A127

1987, Nov. 1   Perf. 14
460 A127 150f Oil derrick
461 A127 425f Derrick, refinery
  a. Souvenir sheet of 1

For surcharge see No. C151.

General
Population
and Housing
Census, 1986
A128

1987, Dec. 1
462 A128 150f multi
463 A128 425f multi
  a. Souvenir sheet of 1

For surcharge see No. C152.

1986 World Cup Soccer Championships,
Mexico — A129

Designs: 100f, 150f, Match scenes, vert. 425f,
Match scene and Pique, character trademark.

1988, Jan. 1   Litho.   Perf. 14
464 A129 100f multi
465 A129 150f multi, diff.
466 A129 425f multi
  a. Souvenir sheet of 1

For surcharge see No. C153.

17th Scouting
Conference,
San'a — A130

1988, Mar. 1   Litho.   Perf. 14
467 A130 25f Skin diving
468 A130 30f Table tennis
469 A130 40f Tennis
470 A130 50f Two scouts, flag
471 A130 60f Volleyball
472 A130 100f Tug-of-war
473 A130 150f Basketball
474 A130 425f Archery

Souvenir Sheet
475 A130 425f Scout, emblem, hand
          sign
For surcharge see No. C154.

San'a
Preservation
A131

1988, May 1   Litho.   Perf. 14
476 A131 25f multicolored
477 A131 50f multicolored
478 A131 100f multicolored
479 A131 150f multicolored
480 A131 425f multicolored
  a. Souvenir sheet of 1

For surcharge see No. 594.

Battle of
Hattin, 800th
Anniv. in
1987
A132

1988   Litho.   Perf. 14
482 A132 150f multicolored
483 A132 425f multicolored
  a. Souvenir sheet

For surcharge see No. C155.

Arab Telecommunication Day,
1987 — A133

1988
484 A133 100f multicolored
485 A133 150f multicolored
486 A133 425f multicolored
  a. Souvenir sheet

For surcharge see No. C156.

A134

Sept. 26 Revolution,
26th
Anniv. — A134a

1989, Sept. 30
487 A134 300f multicolored
488 A134 375f multicolored
489 A134a 850f multicolored
490 A134a 900f multicolored

For surcharges see Nos. 595, 605.

A135

October 14
Revolution, 25th
Anniv. — A135a

1989, Oct. 14
491 A135 300f multicolored
492 A135 375f multicolored
493 A135a 850f multicolored
494 A135a 900f multicolored

For surcharges see Nos. 596, 606..

1988 Summer
Olympics,
Seoul — A136

Game emblem and various events: 300f, Table tennis, basketball, track, boxing. 375f, Soccer game. 850f, Soccer, judo, vert. 900f, Torch bearer.

1989, Nov. 10 Litho. Perf. 13x13½
495 A136 300f multicolored
496 A136 375f multicolored
a. Souvenir sheet
497 A136 850f multicolored
498 A136 900f multicolored

For surcharges see Nos. 597, 607.

Palestinian
Uprising
A137

1989, Dec. 9 Perf. 13x13½, 13½x13
499 A137 300f shown
500 A137 375f Flag raising, vert.
a. Souvenir sheet of 1
501 A137 850f Burning barricades
502 A137 900f Man waving flag, vert.

For surcharges see Nos. 598, 608.

Arab
Cooperation
Council
A138

1990 Litho. Perf. 13x13½
504 A138 300f multicolored
505 A138 375f multicolored
a. Souvenir sheet
506 A138 850f multicolored
507 A138 900f multicolored

For surcharges see Nos. 599, 609.

First
Exported
Oil — A139

1990, Mar. 15 Perf. 14
508 A139 300f multicolored
509 A139 375f multicolored
a. Souvenir sheet
510 A139 850f multi, diff.
511 A139 900f like 850f

For surcharges see Nos. 600, 610.

Arab Scout
Movement,
75th Anniv.
A140

1990, June 15 Litho. Perf. 13x13½
512 A140 300f Scouts holding globe
513 A140 375f like No. 512
a. Souvenir sheet of 1
514 A140 850f Oil rig, scouts, globe
515 A140 900f like No. 514

For surcharges see Nos. 601, 611.

Arab Board for
Medical
Specializations, 10th
Anniv. — A141

1990, Apr. 15 Photo. Perf. 13½x13
516 A141 300f brt grn & multi
517 A141 375f lt bl & multi
a. Sheet of 1, perf. 12½
518 A141 850f lt org & multi
519 A141 900f lt vio & multi

For surcharges see Nos. 602, 612.

Immunization
Campaign
A142

Design: 300f, 375f, Mother feeding infant, vert.

Perf. 13½x13, 13x13½
1990, May 15
520 A142 300f lt bl & multi
521 A142 375f lt org & multi
a. Sheet of 1, perf. 12½
522 A142 850f lt bl grn & multi
523 A142 900f lt lake & multi

No. 521a contains one 26x37mm stamp.
For surcharges see Nos. 603, C157.

UN Development
Program, 40th
Anniv. — A144

1990 Litho. Perf. 12
532 A144 150f multicolored

For surcharge see No. 622.

Ducks
A145

1990, Sept. 18 Litho. Perf. 12
533 A145 10f Pintail swimming
534 A145 20f Wigeon
535 A145 25f Ruddy shelduck
536 A145 40f Gadwall
537 A145 75f Shelduck, male
538 A145 150f Shoveler
539 A145 600f Teal

Souvenir Sheet
540 A145 460f Pintail in flight

For surcharge see No. 623.

Moths and
Butterflies
A146

1990, Nov. 3 Perf. 12½x12
541 A146 5f Dirphia multicolor
542 A146 20f Automeris io
543 A146 25f Papilio machaon
544 A146 40f Bhutanitis lidderdalii
545 A146 55f Prepona demophon muson
546 A146 75f Agarista agricola
547 A146 700f Attacus edwardsii

Souvenir Sheet
Perf. 12x12½
548 A146 460f Daphnis nerii, vert.

Prehistoric
Animals
A147

Perf. 12x12½, 12½x12
1990, Nov. 27
549 A147 5f Protembolotherium, vert.
550 A147 10f Diatryma, vert.
551 A147 35f Mammuthus
552 A147 40f Edaphosaurus
553 A147 55f Dimorphodon
554 A147 75f Phororhacos
555 A147 700f Ichthyosaurus, vert.

Size: 61x90mm
Imperf
556 A147 460f Tyrannosaurus, vert.

A148   A149

Various domestic cats.

1990, Dec. 26 Perf. 12x12½
557 A148 5f multicolored
558 A148 15f multicolored
559 A148 35f multicolored
560 A148 55f multicolored
561 A148 60f multicolored
562 A148 150f multicolored
563 A148 600f multicolored

Size: 70x90mm
Imperf
564 A148 460f multicolored

1991, Mar. 18 Litho. Perf. 12x12½
Mushrooms.

565 A149 50f Boletus aestivalis
566 A149 60f Suillus luteus
567 A149 80f Gyromitra esculenta
568 A149 100f Leccinum scabrum
569 A149 130f Amanita muscaria
570 A149 200f Boletus erythropus
571 A149 300f Leccinum testaceos-cabrum

Size: 70x90mm
Imperf
572 A149 460f Stropharia aeruginosa

Unified
Yemen
Republic, 1st
Anniv.
A150

Designs: 300f, 375f, Eagle crest. 850f, 900f, Hand holding flag, map, sun.

1991, May 22 Perf. 13x13½
573 A150 300f pink & multi
574 A150 375f grn bl multi
a. Sheet of 1, perf. 12½
575 A150 850f lt bl & multi
576 A150 900f bl grn & multi

No. 574a contains one 37x27mm stamp.
For surcharges see Nos. 604, 613, 624, 627.

Unity Agreement
Signed Nov. 30,
1989 — A151

Designs: 300f, 375f, 850f, Fist, flag, map.

1991, May 22 Perf. 13½x13
577 A151 225f multicolored
578 A151 300f multicolored
579 A151 375f multicolored
a. Sheet of 1, perf. 12½
580 A151 650f multicolored
581 A151 850f multiccolored

No. 579a contains one 27x37mm stamp.
For surcharges see Nos. 614, 625.

World Anti-
Smoking
Day — A153

Designs: 300f, 375f, 850f, Man facing skull smoking cigarette.

1991, May 31   *Perf. 13x13¹/₂*
582 A153 225f multicolored
583 A153 300f multicolored
584 A153 375f multicolored
  a.   Sheet of 1, perf. 12¹/₂
585 A153 650f multicolored
586 A153 850f multicolored

No. 584a contains one 36x26mm stamp.
For surcharges see Nos. 615, 626.

United
Nations, 45th
Anniv.
A154

1991, June 26   *Perf. 13x13¹/₂*
587 A154 5f multicolored
588 A154 8f multicolored
589 A154 10f multicolored
590 A154 12f multicolored

Souvenir Sheet
Perf. 12¹/₂

591 A154 6f multicolored

No. 591 contains one 37x28mm stamp.

Nos. 329, 456, 480, 489-490, 493-494,
497-498, 501-502, 506-507, 510-511,
514-515, 518-519, 523, 575-576, 581, &
586 Surcharged

1993, Jan. 1   *Perfs., Etc. as Before*
592 A88   5r on 75f #329
593 A125   8r on 425f #456
594 A131   8r on 425f #480
595 A134a 10r on 900f #490
596 A135a 10r on 900f #494
597 A136   10r on 900f #498
598 A137   10r on 900f #502
599 A138   10r on 900f #507
600 A139   10r on 900f #511
601 A140   10r on 900f #515
602 A141   10r on 900f #519
603 A142   10r on 900f #523
604 A150   10r on 900f #576
605 A134a 12r on 850f #489
606 A135a 12r on 850f #493
607 A136   12r on 850f #497
608 A137   12r on 850f #501
609 A138   12r on 850f #506
610 A139   12r on 850f #510
611 A140   12r on 850f #514
612 A141   12r on 850f #518
613 A150   12r on 850f #575
614 A151   12r on 850f #581
615 A153   12r on 850f #586

Size and location of surcharge varies.

Yemen Republic Nos. 532, 538, 573-574,
579, & 584 Surcharged

50
R

a

1993, Sept. 1   *Perfs., Etc. as Before*
622 A144(a) 50r on 150f #532
623 A145(a) 50r on 150f #538
624 A150(a) 50r on 375f #574
625 A151(a) 50r on 375f #579
626 A153(a) 50r on 375f #584
627 A150(a) 100r on 300f #573

Size and location of surcharge varies.

Yemen People's Democratic Republic Nos.
75, 84B, 204, 208, 216, 232, 235, 244,
267, 335-336, 347, 425, 436-437, & 439
Surcharged Type a and

b

1993, Sept. 1   *Perfs., Etc. as Before*
628 A25(a)   8r on 100f #84B
629 A63(a)   8r on 110f #204
630 A64(a)   8r on 110f #208
631 A66(a)   8r on 110f #216
632 A72(a)   8r on 110f #232

633 A74(a)   8r on 110r #235
634 A76(a)   8r on 110r #244
635 A86(a)   8r on 110r #267
636 A105(a) 100r on 2d #347
637 A137(a) 100r on 300f #439
638 A24(a)   200r on 5f #75
639 (b)   200r on 15f
640 A105(b) 200r on 15f #335
641 (b)   200r on 20f
642 A105(b) 200r on 20f #336
643 A131(a) 200r on 20f #425
644 A134(a) 200r on 75f #436
645 A135(a) 200r on 250f #437

Size and location of surcharge varies.
Nos. 639, 641 without surcharge have not been
listed in the Scott Catalogue.

Yemen Unity, 4th
Anniv. — A155

Various views of govt. building, San'a.

1994, Sept. 27 Litho.   *Perf. 13¹/₂x14*
646 A155 3r multicolored
647 A155 6r multicolored
648 A155 8r multicolored
649 A155 20r multicolored

Souvenir Sheet
650 A155 20r multi, diff.

1994 World Cup
Soccer
Championships,
US — A156

Designs: 2r, Player in yellow shirt dribbling ball,
vert. 6r, Player in striped shirt dribbling, vert. 10r,
Goal keeper. No. 654, Heading ball, vert.
No. 655, Tackling.

1994, Oct. 1 Perf. 14x13¹/₂, 13¹/₂x14
651 A156 2r multicolored
652 A156 6r multicolored
653 A156 10r multicolored
654 A156 12r multicolored

Souvenir Sheet
655 A156 12r multicolored

The Yemen Arab Republic and the
People's Republic of Yemen planned a
30-month unification process scheduled
for completion by November 1992.
While government ministries merged,
both currencies remained valid. At the
current time the two areas are at war.

———————

AIR POST STAMPS

Catalogue values for unused
stamps in this section are for Never
Hinged items.

Plane over
San'a — AP1

1947 Unwmk. Engr.   *Perf. 12¹/₂*
C1 AP1 10b bright blue   4.50 4.50
C2 AP1 20b olive green   6.50 6.50

6
BOGACHES   View of
San'a — AP2

Palace of the Rock,
Wadi Dhahr — AP3

Designs: 10b, Mocha coffee branch. 16b, Palace,
Ta'iz. 20b, 1i, Parade Ground, San'a.

1951 Wmk. 277 Photo.   *Perf. 14*
C3 AP2 6b blue   15   15
C4 AP2 8b dark brown   20   15
C5 AP2 10b dark green   25   15
C6 AP3 12b dark blue   28   20
C7 AP2 16b lilac rose   35   28
C8 AP3 20b orange brown 55   42
C9 AP3 1i dark red   1.10 75
    Nos. C3-C9 (7)   2.88 2.10

Nos. C3 and C4 were used provisionally in 1957
for registry and foreign ordinary mail.

Type of Regular Issue, 1952

Designs: 12b, Palace of the Rock, Wadi Dhahr.
20b, Walls of Ibb.

Engraved and Photogravure
1952 Unwmk.   *Perf. 14¹/₂*
C10 A15 12b grnsh blk, bl & brn   2.75 2.75
C11 A15 20b indigo, bl & brn   3.75 3.75

Flag-and-View Type of Regular Issue, 1952
1952
C12 A16 1i dk brn, car & brt ultra 5.50 5.50

Palace in Foreground
1952
C13 A16 30b yel grn, car & gray   3.75 3.75

Leaning Minaret,
Mosque of
Ta'iz — AP6

1954 Photo.   *Perf. 14*
C14 AP6 10b scarlet   38   25
C15 AP6 12b dull blue   50   40
C16 AP6 20b olive bister 90   65

Accession of King Ahmed I, 5th anniv.

Type of Regular Issue, 1959
1959 Wmk. 318   *Perf. 13x13¹/₂*
C17 A21 6b orange & blk   38 25
C18 A21 10b red & blk   50 38
C19 A21 16b brt violet & red 65 45

Antiquities of Marib Type of 1961
Designs: 6b, Columns, Temple of the Moon
God. 16b, Control tower and spillway of 2,700-
year-old dam of Marib.

Perf. 11¹/₂
1961, Oct. 14 Unwmk. Photo.
C20 A27 6b lt bl grn & blk   15 15
C21 A27 16b lt blue & blk   42 42

For overprints see Nos. C24, C25.

Buildings Type of Regular Issue
Design: 6b, Bab al-Yemen, main gate of San'a,
horiz. 16b, Palace of the Rock (Dar al-Hajar).

1961, Nov. 15
C22 A28 6b blk, lt bl & grn   20 20
C23 A28 16b blk, rose & grn   38 38

For overprints see Nos. C24A, C25A.

Nos. C20-C23 Ovptd. Like Nos. 144-158
in Dark Red or Black
Perf. 11¹/₂
1963, Jan. 1 Photo. Unwmk.
C24   A27 (a) 6b No. C20
C24A A28 (b) 6b No. C22
C25   A27 (a) 16b No. C21
C25A A28 (b) 16b No. C23 (B)

Proclamation of the Republic Type
Perf. 11x11¹/₂, 11¹/₂x11
1963, Mar. 15
C26 A34 8b Bayonette, torch
C27 A34 10b Jet, torch, tank
C28 A34 16b Flag, chain, torch

Nos. C27-C28 horiz.

Nos. 25-29
Ovptd. in
Black

Perf. 12¹/₂
1963, Sept. 1 Litho. Wmk. 258
C29   A5 6b slate blue & ultra
C29A A5 10b fawn & ultra
C29B A5 14b olive & ultra
C29C A5 20b yel grn & ultra
C29D A5 1i claret & ultra

Astronauts. Set of five airmail, ¹/₄, ¹/₃,
¹/₂, 4, 20b. Airmail imperf. souvenir
sheet, 20b. Dec. 5. Nos. 63C01-63C06.
1964
Astronauts issue of 1963 overprinted
in black or red brown "John F. Kennedy /
1917 / 1963" in English or Arabic. Set of
five airmail. May 5. Nos. 64C01-64C05.

San'a Intl. Airport Type of 1964
Perf. 11¹/₂x11
1964, Oct. 1 Photo. Unwmk.
C30 A40 6b Sun, buildings, aircraft

See note after No. 203.

APU 10th Anniv. Type of 1964
1964, Oct. 15   *Perf. 13¹/₂*
C31 A41 6b blue grn & blk

An imperf. souvenir sheet of one exists containing No. C31.

Deir Yassin Massacre Type of 1965
1965, Apr. 30   *Perf. 11x11¹/₂*
C32 A44 6b ver & brt org   1.25

Library Type of 1965
1965, July 7   *Perf. 11¹/₂x11*
C33 A46 6b sepia, red & int blue

An imperf. souvenir sheet of one exists containing No. C33.

1966
Butterflies. Set of four airmail, 6, 8, 10,
16b. May 5. Nos. 66C01-66C04.

Lenin's Birth
Centenary — AP7

1970, Aug. 15   Litho.   Perf. 12x12½
C34 AP7 6b Public speech
C35 AP7 16b Meeting with Arab delegates

8th Anniv. of the Revolution — AP8

1971, Jan. 24   Perf. 13
C36 AP8 5b Country estate
C37 AP8 7b Workers
C38 AP8 16b Handshake, flag, flowers,
          open book

A souv. sheet of 1 exists containing No. C38.

Revolution Type of 1972
1972, Nov. 25   Photo.   Perf. 13
C40 A80 21b lilac, blk & multi   5.00 3.50

Al-Aqsa Mosque Type of 1973
1973, Jan. 1   Photo.   Perf. 13½
C41 A82 24b lt bl, blk & multi   2.00 1.40
a.   Min. sheet of 1, imperf.

UNICEF Type of 1973
1973, Jan. 15   Photo.   Perf. 13
C42 A83 18b lt bl, blk & multi   70 65
a.   Min. sheet of 1, imperf.   80 80

For surcharge see No. C46.

11th Anniv.
of Revolution
AP10

1973, Sept. 26   Photo.   Perf. 14
C43 AP10 7b Bank   38 20
C44 AP10 10b Cement factory   60 32
C45 AP10 18b Hospital   1.10 60

For surcharges see Nos. C47-C48.

Nos. C42, C43, C45 Surcharged in Black
with New Value and Bars
1975, Nov. 15
C46 A83   75f on 18b lt bl, blk &
               multi   80 60
C47 AP10 90f on 7b multi   1.25 75
C48 AP10 120f on 18b multi   1.50 80
a.   Overprinted in red

Argentina 1978 World Cup Type of 1980
Designs: World cup emblem and various soccer
players.

1980, Mar. 30   Photo.   Perf. 14
C49 A99 60f gold & multi   80 60
C50 A99 75f gold & multi   1.00 70
C51 A99 80f gold & multi   1.20 90
C52 A99 100f gold & multi   1.50 1.00

Two 225f souvenir sheets exist.

IYC Type of 1980
1980, Apr. 1   Perf. 13½
C53 A100 80f Girl, bird   1.60 1.00
C54 A100 100f Boy, butterfly, flower 1.90 1.20
C55 A100 150f Boy, butterfly, flower,
              diff.   3.00 1.40

Two 200f souvenir sheets exist.

Scouting Type of 1980
1980, May 1   Photo.   Perf. 13½x14
C56 A101 60f Bicycling   1.00 50
C57 A101 75f Fencing   1.40 65
C58 A101 120f Butterfly catching   2.00 1.00

Two 300f souvenir sheets exist.

Argentina 1978 Winners' Type of 1980
Designs: World cup emblem and various soccer
players.

1980, June 1   Photo.   Perf. 14
C59 A102 60f gold & multi   1.00 50
C60 A102 75f gold & multi   1.40 65
C61 A102 80f gold & multi   1.50 70
C62 A102 100f gold & multi   1.60 1.10

Two 225f souvenir sheets exist.

19th Anniv. of
Sept. 26th
Revolution
(1981) — AP11

1982, Jan. 25   Litho.   Perf. 14
C63 AP11 75f Map   45 25
C64 AP11 125f Map in sunset   70 40
C65 AP11 325f Dove in natl. colors   2.00 1.20
a.   Souvenir sheet of 1   5.00 5.00
C66 AP11 400f Jets   2.25 1.40

Al-Hasan Ibn Al-Hamadani, Writer — AP12

1982, Feb. 1
C67 AP12 125f green & multi   1.25 60
C68 AP12 325f blue & multi   2.75 1.40

Souvenir Sheet
C69 AP12 375f multi   3.50 3.50

No. C69 contains one stamp (36x46mm).
For surcharge see No. C138.

World
Food
Day
AP13

Designs: No. C76a, Eggplants. No. C76b, Tomatoes. No. C76c, Beets, peas. No. C76d, Cauli-
flower, carrots. No. C77a, Dove. No. C77b, Water
birds. No. C77c, Fish. No. C77d, Geese.

1982, Mar. 1   Litho.   Perf. 14
C70 AP13 25f Rabbits   50
C71 AP13 50f Rooster, Hens   1.00
C72 AP13 60f Turkeys   1.25
C73 AP13 75f Sheep   1.50
C74 AP13 100f Cattle   2.00
C75 AP13 125f Deer   2.50
       Nos. C70-C75 (6)   8.75

Souvenir Sheets
C76   Sheet of 4   2.00
a.-d.   AP13 100f, any single   50
C77   Sheet of 4   2.50
a.-d.   AP13 125f, any single   60

For surcharges see Nos. C139, C144.

1980 Summer
Olympics,
Moscow
AP14

1982, Apr. 1
C78 AP14 25f Gymnastics
C79 AP14 50f Pole vault
C80 AP14 60f Javelin
C81 AP14 75f Running
C82 AP14 100f Basketball
C83 AP14 125f Soccer

Two souvenir sheets of 4 exist: 100f, picturing
boxing, wrestling, canoeing, swimming, and 125f,
picturing weight lifting, discus, long jump, fencing.
For surcharges see Nos. C140, C145.

Aviation — AP15

Various space and aircraft.

1982, May 21
C86 AP15 25f multi
C87 AP15 50f multi
C88 AP15 60f multi
C89 AP15 75f multi
C90 AP15 100f multi
C91 AP15 125f multi

Two souvenir sheets of 4 exist, 100f and 125f,
picturing various aircraft and satellites.
For surcharges see Nos. C141, C146.

Intl. Year of the Disabled — AP16

Designs: Nos. C94-C99, Diff. flowers.
No. C100a, Emblem, natl. flag. b, Emblem on
globe. c, Natl. colors, UN emblems. d, Disabled
man, gifts, nurse.
No. C101a, Flags, globe and nurse. b, UN
emblems, natl. flag. c, Emblem, disabled man. d,
UN emblem, nurse.

1982, June 1
C94 AP16 25f multi
C95 AP16 50f multi
C96 AP16 60f multi
C97 AP16 75f multi
C98 AP16 100f multi
C99 AP16 125f multi

Souvenir Sheets
C100   Sheet of 4
a.-d.   AP16 100f, any single
C101   Sheet of 4
a.-d.   AP16 125f, any single

For surcharge see No. C147.

Telecommunications Progress — AP17

Designs: 25f, FNRR communication center. 50f,
Dish receivers, satellite, globe. 60f, Broadcast towers, dish receivers. 75f, Receivers, birds over plain.
100f, Receivers, satellite, telegraph key. No. C107,
Receivers, passenger jet, Earth.
No. C108a, Receivers, Earth. b, Earth, television,
flag and camera. c, Computer. d, Skyscraper, Earth,
telephone.
No. C109a, Receivers, satellite, ship. b, Communication center, bolts of energy, receivers. c, Receivers, jet, ship, train, car, carriage. d, Radar.

1982, July 1   Litho.   Perf. 14
C102 AP17 25f multi
C103 AP17 50f multi
C104 AP17 60f multi
C105 AP17 75f multi
C106 AP17 100f multi
C107 AP17 125f multi

Souvenir Sheets
C108   Sheet of 4
a.-d.   AP17 100f any single
C109   Sheet of 4
a.-d.   AP17 125f any single

For surcharges see Nos. C142, C148.

TB Bacillus Centenary — AP18

1982   Litho.   Perf. 14
C110 AP18 25f multi
C111 AP18 50f multi
C112 AP18 60f multi
C113 AP18 75f multi
C114 AP18 100f multi
C115 AP18 125f multi

Souvenir Sheets
C116   Sheet of 4, Fruit
a.   AP18 100f, any single
C117   Sheet of 4, Flowers
a.   AP18 125f, any single

For surcharges see Nos. C143, C149.

1982 World Cup Soccer Championships,
Spain — AP19

Various soccer plays.

1982, Sept. 1   Perf. 14
C118 AP19 25f multi
C119 AP19 50f multi
C120 AP19 60f multi
C121 AP19 75f multi
C122 AP19 100f multi
C123 AP19 125f multi

Palestinian Children's Day — AP20

1982, Oct. 20
C126 AP20 75f Boy
C127 AP20 125f Girl
C128 AP20 325f Boy and girl
a.   Souvenir sheet of 1

Arab
Postal
Union,
30th
Anniv.
AP21

1982, Dec. 1

C129	AP21	75f yellow & multi	
C130	AP21	125f green & multi	
C131	AP21	325f magenta & multi	
a.	Souvenir sheet of 1		

1984 Summer Olympics, Los
Angeles — AP22

1984, Nov. 15

C132	AP22	20f Wrestling
C133	AP22	30f Boxing
C134	AP22	40f Running
C135	AP22	60f Hurdling
C136	AP22	150f Pole vault
C137	AP22	325f Javelin throw

Two souvenir sheets of four 75f stamps exist
picturing water sports, gymnastics, weightlifting,
shot put and discus throwing.

No. C67 Surcharged

Nos. 459, 461, 463, 466, 474, 483, 486,
522, C73, C75, C81, C83, C89, C91,
C97, C105, C107, C113 & C115
Surcharged with New Value and "AIR
MAIL"

1993, Jan. 1   *Perfs, etc. as Before*

C138	AP12	3r on 125f #C67
C139	AP13	3r on 125f #C75
C140	AP14	3r on 125f #C83
C141	AP15	3r on 125f #C91
C142	AP17	3r on 125f #C107
C143	AP18	3r on 125f #C115
C144	AP13	5r on 75f #C73
C145	AP14	5r on 75f #C81
C146	AP15	5r on 75f #C89
C147	AP16	5r on 75f #C97
C148	AP17	5r on 75f #C105
C149	AP18	5r on 75f #C113
C150	A126	8r on 425f #459
C151	A127	8r on 425f #461
C152	A128	8r on 425f #463
C153	A129	8r on 425f #466
C154	A130	8r on 425f #474
C155	A132	8r on 425f #483
C156	A133	8r on 425f #486
C157	A142	12r on 850f #522

Size and location of surcharge varies.

POSTAGE DUE STAMPS

D1

1942   Litho.   Wmk. 258   Perf. 12½

J1	D1	1b org & yel grn	15	15
J2	D1	2b org & yel grn	15	15
J3	D1	4b org & yel grn	20	20
J4	D1	6b org & brt ultra	30	30
J5	D1	8b org & brt ultra	40	40
J6	D1	10b org & brt ultra	50	50
J7	D1	12b org & brt ultra	60	60
J8	D1	20b org & brt ultra	1.00	1.00
		Nos. J1-J8 (8)	3.30	3.30

Yemen had no postage due system. Nos. J1-J8
were used for regular postage.
See Nos. 66-67 for surcharges.

YEMEN, PEOPLE'S DEMOCRATIC REPUBLIC OF

LOCATION — Southern Arabia
GOVT. — Republic
AREA — 111,074 sq. mi.
POP. — 2,030,000 (est. 1981)
CAPITAL — Aden

The People's Republic of Southern Yemen
was proclaimed Nov. 30, 1967, when the

Federation of South Arabia achieved independence. It consisted of the former British
colony of Aden and the protectorates. The
name was changed to People's Democratic
Republic of Yemen on Nov. 30, 1970. See
South Arabia, Volume 1B.

1,000 Fils = 1 Dinar

> Catalogue values for all unused
> stamps in this country are for Never
> Hinged items.

People's Republic of Southern Yemen
South Arabia Nos. 3-16 Overprinted in
Red or Blue

PEOPLE'S REPUBLIC
OF SOUTHERN YEMEN
Nos. 1-10

PEOPLE'S REPUBLIC
OF SOUTHERN YEMEN
Nos. 11-14

Perf. 14½x14

1968, Apr. 1   Photo.   Unwmk.

1	A1	5f blue	15	15
2	A1	10f lt vio bl	15	15
3	A1	15f bl grn	15	15
4	A1	20f green	15	15
5	A1	25f org brn (B)	15	15
6	A1	30f lemon	20	15
7	A1	35f red brn (B)	20	16
8	A1	50f rose red (B)	25	22
9	A1	65f lt yel grn	30	30
10	A1	75f rose car (B)	45	40
11	A2	100f multi (B)	60	50
12	A2	250f multi	1.20	1.00
13	A2	500f multi (B)	2.25	2.00
14	A2	1d vio & multi	6.25	5.00
		Nos. 1-14 (14)	12.45	10.48

Globe
and Flag
A1

Designs: 15f, Revolutionist with broken chain
and flames, vert. 50f, Aden Harbor. 100f, Cotton
picking.

1968, May 25   Litho.   Perf. 13x12½

15	A1	10f multi	15	15
16	A1	15f multi	15	15
17	A1	50f multi	30	30
18	A1	100f multi	65	65

Independence Day, Nov. 30, 1967.

Girl Scouts
at Campfire
A2

Designs: 25f, Three Girl Scouts, vert. 50f, Three
Girl Scout leaders.

Perf. 13½

1968, Sept. 21   Litho.   Unwmk.

19	A2	10f ultra & sepia	20	20
20	A2	25f org brn & Prus bl	32	32
21	A2	50f yel, bl & brn	75	75

Girl Scout movement in Southern Yemen, established 1966 (in Aden).

Revolutionary — A3

"Freedom-   King of Ausan,
Socialism-Unity"   Alabaster Statue
A4   A5

Design: 30f, Radfan Mountains where first revolutionary fell.

1968, Oct. 14   Unwmk.   Perf. 13

22	A3	20f brn & lt bl	16	16
23	A3	30f grn & brn	20	20
24	A4	100f ver & yel	65	65

Issued for Revolution Day, commemorating the
revolution of Oct. 14, 1963.

1968, Dec. 28   Litho.   Perf. 13

Antiquities of Southern Yemen: 35f, African-type
sculpture of a man. 50f, Winged bull, Assyrian-type
bas-relief, horiz. 65f, Bull's head (Moon God), alabaster plaque, 230 B.C., horiz.

25	A5	5f olive & bister	15	15
26	A5	35f maroon & lt bl	25	25
27	A5	50f bister & blue	40	40
28	A5	65f lt grnsh bl & lilac	50	50

A6   A7

Martyr Monument, Steamer Point, Aden.

1969, Feb. 11   Litho.   Perf. 13

29	A6	15f yellow & multi	15	15
30	A6	35f emerald & multi	20	20
31	A6	100f orange & multi	60	60

Issued for Martyr Day.

1969, June 1   Litho.   Perf. 13

Albert Thomas Monument, Geneva, and ILO
emblem.

32	A7	10f brt grn, blk & lt brn	15	15
33	A7	35f car rose, blk & lt brn	25	25
		Set value	32	32

50th anniv. of the ILO, and to honor founder
Albert Thomas.

Classroom — A8

1969, Sept. 8   Litho.   Perf. 13

34	A8	35f orange & multi	25	25
35	A8	100f yellow & multi	70	70

International Literacy Day, Sept. 8.

Mahatma
Gandhi — A9

1969, Sept. 27   Litho.   Perf. 13

36	A9	35f lt ultra & vio brn	25	25

Mohandas K. Gandhi (1869-1948), leader in
India's fight for independence.

Family
A10

1969, Oct. 1

37	A10	25f lt grn & multi	20	20
38	A10	75f car rose & multi	60	60

Issued for Family Day.

UN Headquarters, NYC — A11

1969, Oct. 24   Perf. 13

39	A11	20f rose red & multi	15	15
40	A11	65f emer & multi	42	42

Issued for United Nations Day.

Map and
Flag of
Southern
Yemen
A12

Design: 40f, 50f, Tractors and flag (agricultural
progress).

1969, Nov. 30   Litho.   Unwmk.
Size: 41x24½mm

41	A12	15f multi	15	15
42	A12	35f multi	20	20

Size: 37x37mm

43	A12	40f blue & multi	25	25
44	A12	50f brown & multi	38	38

Second anniversary of independence.

Map of
Arab
League
Countries,
Flag and
Emblem
A13

1970, Mar. 22   Unwmk.   Perf. 13

45	A13	35f lt bl & multi	25	25

25th anniversary of the Arab League.

Lenin — A14

Fighter — A15

1970, Apr. 22   Litho.   Perf. 13
46   A14 75f multi   50 50

Lenin (1870-1924), Russian communist leader.

1970, May 15

Designs: 35f, Underground soldier and plane destroyed on ground. 50f, Fighting people hailing Arab liberation flag, horiz.

47   A15 15f grn, red & blk   16 15
48   A15 35f grn, bl, red & blk   42 35
49   A15 50f grn, blk & red   55 45

Issued for Palestine Day.

UPU Headquarters, Bern — A16

1970, May 22   Litho.   Perf. 13
50   A16 15f org & brt grn   15 15
51   A16 65f yel & car rose   40 40

New UPU Headquarters in Bern.

Yemeni Costume — A17

Regional Costumes: 15f, 20f, Women's costumes. 50f, Three men of Aden.

1970, July 2   Litho.   Perf. 13
52   A17 10f yel & multi   15 15
53   A17 15f lt lil & multi   15 15
54   A17 20f lt bl & multi   16 16
55   A17 50f multi   30 30

Camel and Calf — A18

Designs: 25f, Goats. 35f, Arabian oryx. 65f, Socotra dwarf cows.

1970, Aug. 31   Litho.   Perf. 13
56   A18 15f dk brn & multi   20 20
57   A18 25f car rose & multi   32 32
58   A18 35f ultra & multi   60 60
59   A18 65f brt grn & multi   90 90

A19

Designs: 35f, National Front Organization Headquarters. 50f, Farm worker, 1970, and battle scene, 1963.

1970, Oct. 14   Litho.   Perf. 13
        Size: 41½x29½mm
60   A19 25f multi   20 20
        Size: 56½x27mm
61   A19 35f multi   30 30
        Size: 41x24½mm
62   A19 50f multi   38 38

7th anniversary of Oct. 14 Revolution.

UN Headquarters, Emblem — A20

1970, Oct. 24   Litho.   Perf. 13
63   A20 10f org & bl   15 15
64   A20 65f brn & bl   45 45
        Set value   52 52

25th anniversary of the United Nations.

People's Democratic Republic of Yemen

Temples at Philae — A21

1971, Feb. 1   Litho.   Perf. 13½x13
65   A21 5f violet & multi   15 15
66   A21 35f blue & multi   25 25
67   A21 65f green & multi   55 55

UNESCO campaign to save the monuments in Nubia.

Scales, Book and Sword A22

1971, Mar. 1   Perf. 13x12½
68   A22 10f brt pink & multi   15 15
69   A22 15f brt grn & multi   16 16
70   A22 35f lt ultra & multi   30 30
71   A22 50f rose & multi   40 40

First Constitution, 1971.

Men of 3 Races, Human Rights Emblem A23

1971, Mar. 21
72   A23 20f lt bl & multi   15 15
73   A23 35f grn & multi   30 30
74   A23 75f lt vio & multi   55 55

Intl. year against racial discrimination.

Map and Flag — A24

"Brothers' Blood" Tree, Socotra Island A25

1971-77   Litho.   Perf. 13½
75   A24 5f yel & multi   15 15
76   A24 10f grn & multi   15 15
77   A24 15f yel & multi   15 15
78   A24 20f org & multi   15 15
79   A24 25f bl & multi   15 15
80   A24 35f red org & multi   15 15
81   A24 40f vio & multi   15 15
82   A24 50f yel grn & multi   30 30
82A   A24 60f red & multi   22 22
83   A24 65f pale vio & multi   38 38
84   A24 80f org brn & multi   45 45
84A   A24 90f ol & multi   35 35

        Perf. 13
84B   A25 110f brn & multi   40 40
85   A25 125f ultra & multi   80 80
86   A25 250f org & multi   1.25 1.25
87   A25 500f multi   2.50 2.25
88   A25 1d grn & multi   5.00 4.25
        Nos. 75-88 (17)   12.70 11.70

Issue dates: Nos. 82A, 84A-84B, Oct. 17, 1977. Others, Apr. 1, 1971.
        See Nos. 332-333. For surcharges see Yemen Nos. 628, 638.

Machine Gun and Map — A26

Arms with Wrench and Cogwheel — A27

Designs: 45f, Woman fighter and flame, horiz. 50f, Fighter, factories and rainbow.

1971, June 9   Litho.   Perf. 12½x13
89   A26 15f multi   15 15
90   A26 35f green & multi   30 30
91   A26 50f multi   45 45

Armed revolution in the Arabian Gulf.

1971, June 22

Designs: 25f, Torch, factories, symbols. 65f, Windmill.

92   A27 15f blue & multi   35 25
93   A27 25f multi   1.20 1.00
94   A27 65f multi   1.40 1.20

2nd anniversary of the revolution of June 22, 1969 (Corrective Move).
    A 20f picturing a fighter holding rifle and flag, with flag colors transposed, was withdrawn on day of issue.

Revolutionary Emblem — A28

Design: 40f, Map of southern Arabia and flag of republic.

1971, Sept. 26
95   A28 10f yellow & multi   15 15
96   A28 40f grn & multi   30 30
        Set value   36 36

9th anniv. of the revolution of Sept. 26.

Gamal Abdel Nasser — A29

UNICEF Emblem, Children of the World — A30

1971, Sept. 28   Litho.   Perf. 12½x13
97   A29 65f multi   40 40

First anniversary of the death of Gamal Abdel Nasser (1918-1970), President of Egypt.

1971, Dec. 11   Perf. 13x13½
98   A30 15f org, car & blk   15 15
99   A30 40f lt ultra, car & blk   20 20
100   A30 50f yel grn, car & blk   38 38

25th anniv. of UNICEF.

Pigeons — A31

Birds: 40f, Partridge. 65f, Partridge and guinea fowl. 100f, European kite.

1971, Dec. 22   Perf. 13½x13
101   A31 5f bl, blk & car   15 15
102   A31 40f salmon & multi   20 20
103   A31 65f brt grn, blk & car   38 38
104   A31 100f yel, blk & car   60 60

Dhow under Construction A32

Design: 80f, Dhow under sail, vert.

**   Perf. 13½x13, 13x13½**
1972, Feb. 15
105   A32 25f bl, brn & yel   20 20
106   A32 80f lt bl & multi   80 60

Band A33

Designs: 25f, 40f, 80f, Various folk dances.

1972, Apr. 8   Litho.   Perf. 13
107   A33 10f lt grn & multi   15 15
108   A33 25f org & multi   15 15
109   A33 40f red & multi   30 30
110   A33 80f blue & multi   60 60
        Set value   1.00 1.00

Palestinian Fighter and Barbed Wire A34

1972, May 15
111 A34	5f emerald & multi	35	16
112 A34	20f blue & multi	50	35
113 A34	65f org ver & multi	65	50

Struggle for Palestine liberation.

Policemen on Parade
A35

Design: 80f, Militia women on parade.

1972, June 20   Litho.   Perf. 13½
114 A35	25f lt bl & multi	15	15
115 A35	80f bl grn & multi	50	50
a.	Souv. sheet of 2, #114-115	1.50	1.50

Police Day. No. 115a sold for 150f.

Start of Bicycle Race — A36

Designs: 15f Parade of young women. 40f, Yemeni Guides and Scouts on parade. 80f, Acrobats, vert.

1972, July 20   Litho.   Perf. 13½
116 A36	10f lt bl & multi	15	15
117 A36	15f multi	20	15
118 A36	40f buff & multi	40	40
119 A36	80f lt ultra & multi	1.00	50
	Set value		85

Turtle A37

1972, Sept. 2   Litho.   Perf. 13
120 A37	15f Shown	45	15
121 A37	40f Sailfish	50	35
122 A37	65f Kingfish	65	45
123 A37	125f Spiny lobster	80	80

Book Year Emblem A38

1972, Sept. 9
| 124 A38 | 40f red, ultra & yel | 30 | 30 |
| 125 A38 | 65f org, ultra & yel | 50 | 50 |

International Book Year 1972.

Farm Couple and Fields A39

1972, Nov. 23   Litho.   Perf. 13
126 A39	10f orange & multi	15	15
127 A39	25f rose lilac & multi	16	16
128 A39	40f red & multi	30	30
	Set value	52	52

Lands Day, publicizing land reforms.

Militia A40

Designs: 20f, Soldier guarding village. 65f, Industrial, agricultural and educational progress, vert.

1972, Dec. 2   Litho.   Perf. 13
129 A40	5f multi	15	15
130 A40	20f multi	16	16
131 A40	65f multi	45	45
a.	Souv. sheet of 3, #129-131, imperf.	70	70

5th anniversary of independence.

Census Chart — A41

1973, Apr. 3   Litho.   Perf. 12½x13½
| 132 A41 | 25f org, emer & ol | 16 | 16 |
| 133 A41 | 40f rose, bl & vio | 35 | 35 |

Population census 1973.

WHO Emblem and "25" — A42

1973, Apr. 7   Perf. 14x12½, 12½x14
134 A42	5f "25" and WHO emblem, vert	15	15
135 A42	20f Shown	16	16
136 A42	125f "25" and WHO emblem	65	65

25th anniv. of the WHO.

Elephant Bay A43

Tourist Publicity: 20f, Taweels Tanks Reservoir, vert. 25f, Shibam Town. 100f, Al-Mohdar Mosque, Tarim.

1973, June 9   Litho.   Perf. 13
137 A43	20f multi	15	15
138 A43	25f multi	16	16
139 A43	40f multi	30	30
140 A43	100f multi	55	55

Office Buildings and Slum, Aden A44

Design: 80f, Intersection, Aden, vert.

1973, Aug. 4   Litho.   Perf. 13
| 141 A44 | 20f multi | 15 | 15 |
| 142 A44 | 80f multi | 50 | 50 |

Nationalization of buildings.

People's Army A45

People's Army: 20f, Four marching soldiers. 40f, Sailors on parade. 80f, Tanks.

Army Unit A45

1973, Sept. 1
143 A45	10f multi	15	15
144 A45	20f multi	15	15
145 A45	40f multi	30	30
146 A45	80f multi	50	50
	Set value	95	95

FAO Emblem, Loading Food A46

Design: 80f, Workers and grain sacks.

1973, Dec. 19   Litho.   Perf. 13
| 147 A46 | 20f blue & multi | 15 | 15 |
| 148 A46 | 80f blue & multi | 50 | 50 |

World Food Program, 10th anniversary.

Letter and UPU Emblem A47

UPU Emblem and Yemeni Flag — A48

Map of Yemen, UPU Emblem — A49

UPU cent.: 20f, "100" formed by people, and UPU emblem.

1974, Oct. 9   Litho.   Perf. 12½x13½
149 A47	5f multi	15	15
150 A47	15f multi	15	15
151 A48	40f multi	35	35
152 A49	125f multi	60	60

Irrigation System — A50

Progress in Agriculture: 20f, Bulldozer pushing soil. 100f, Tractors plowing field.

1974   Litho.   Perf. 13
153 A50	10f multi	15	15
154 A50	20f multi	15	15
155 A50	100f multi	50	50

Lathe Operator — A51

Industrial progress: 40f, Printers. 80f, Women textile workers, horiz.

1975, May 1   Litho.   Perf. 13
156 A51	10f multi	15	15
157 A51	40f multi	30	30
158 A51	80f multi	50	50

Yemeni Woman — A52

Designs: Various women's costumes.

1975, Nov. 15   Litho.   Perf. 11½x12
159 A52	5f blk & ocher	15	15
160 A52	10f blk & vio	15	15
161 A52	15f blk & olive	15	15
162 A52	25f blk & rose lil	25	25
163 A52	40f blk & Prus bl	42	42
164 A52	50f blk & org brn	60	60
	Nos. 159-164 (6)	1.72	1.72

Women Factory Workers, IWY Emblem A53

1975, Dec. 30   Litho.   Perf. 12x11½
| 165 A53 | 40f blk & salmon | 25 | 25 |
| 166 A53 | 50f blk & yel grn | 38 | 38 |

International Women's Year 1975.

Soccer Player and Field — A54

Designs: Different scenes from soccer.

1976, Apr. 1   Litho.   Perf. 11½x12
167 A54	5f lt bl & brn	15	15
168 A54	40f yel & green	30	30
169 A54	80f salmon & vio	50	50

Rocket Take-off from Moon — A55

Designs: 15f, Alexander Satalov. 40f, Lunokhod on moon, horiz. 65f, Valentina Tereshkova and rocket.

Perf. 11¹/₂x12, 12x11¹/₂
1976, Apr. 17   Litho.
170	A55	10f multi	15 15
171	A55	15f multi	15 15
172	A55	40f multi	38 38
173	A55	65f multi	55 55
		Set value	1.05 1.05

Soviet cosmonauts and space program.

Traffic Policemen A56

1977, Apr. 16   Litho.   **Perf. 14**
174	A56	25f red & blk	30 30
175	A56	60f yel & blk	60 60
176	A56	75f grn & blk	75 75
177	A56	110f dp bl & blk	1.00 1.00

Traffic change to right side of road.

APU Emblem — A57

1977, Apr. 12   Litho.   **Perf. 13¹/₂**
178	A57	20f lt bl & multi	15 15
179	A57	60f gray & multi	42 42
180	A57	70f lt grn & multi	50 50
181	A57	90f bl grn & multi	55 55

Arab Postal Union, 25th anniversary.

Congress Decree and Red Star — A58

Designs: 25f, Pres. Salim Rubi'a Ali, Council members Ali Nasser Muhamed and Abdul Farta Ismail. 65f, Women's militia on parade. 95f, Aerial view of textile mill.

1977, May   Photo.   **Perf. 13**
182	A58	25f grn, gold & dk brn	16 16
183	A58	35f red, gold & lt bl	25 25
184	A58	65f bl, gold & lil	38 38
185	A58	95f org, gold & grn	45 45

Unification Congress, 1st anniversary.

Afrivoluta Pringlei A59

Shells: 60f, Festilyria duponti, vert. 110f, Conus splendidulus. 180f, Cypraea 4broderipii.

1977, July 16   Litho.   **Perf. 13¹/₂**
186	A59	60f multi	40 28
187	A59	90f multi	60 30
188	A59	110f multi	1.00 60
189	A59	180f multi	1.40 1.00

Emblem and Flag — A60

Designs: 20f, Man with broken chain. 90f, Pipeline, agriculture and industry. 110f, Flag, symbolic tree and hands holding tools.

1977, Nov. 30   Litho.   **Perf. 13¹/₂**
190	A60	5f blk & multi	15 15
191	A60	20f blk & multi	15 15
192	A60	90f blk & multi	30 20
193	A60	110f blk & multi	50 25
		Set value	90 90

10th anniversary of independence.

Dome of the Rock — A61

1978, May 15   **Perf. 12**
194	A61	5f multi	65 35

Palestinian fighters & families. See #264A.

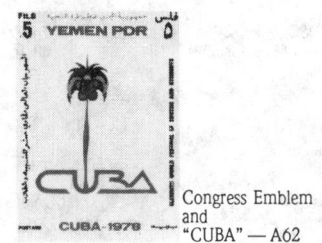

Congress Emblem and "CUBA" — A62

Designs: 60f, Congress emblem. 90f, Festival emblem as flower. 110f, Festival emblem, dove, young man and woman.

1978, June 22   Litho.   **Perf. 14**
195	A62	5f multi	15 15
196	A62	60f multi	55 35
197	A62	90f multi	70 40
198	A62	110f multi	90 60

11th World Youth Festival, Havana.

Silver Ornaments A63

Designs: Various silver ornaments.

1978, July 22   Litho.   **Perf. 13¹/₂**
199	A63	10f blk & multi	15 15
200	A63	15f blk & multi	15 15
201	A63	20f blk & multi	15 15
202	A63	60f blk & multi	20 16
203	A63	90f blk & multi	38 25
204	A63	110f blk & multi	50 30
		Set value	1.25 90

For surcharge see Yemen No. 629.

Yemeni Musical Instruments — A64

1978, Aug. 26   **Perf. 14**
205	A64	35f Almarfaai	15 15
206	A64	60f Almizmar	25 16
207	A64	90f Alqnboos	30 20
208	A64	110f Simsimiya	50 30

For surcharge see Yemen No. 630.

"V" for Vanguard — A65   Man with Palm, Factories — A66

1978, Oct. 11   Litho.   **Perf. 14**
209	A65	5f multi	15 15
210	A65	20f multi	15 15
211	A65	60f multi	25 15
212	A65	180f multi	50 30
		Set value	85 55

1st Conf. of Vanguard Party, Oct. 11-13.

1978, Oct. 14

Designs: 10f, Palm branches, broken chains, horiz. 60f, Candle and "15." 110f, Woman and man with rifle, "15."
213	A66	10f multi	15 15
214	A66	35f multi	20 15
215	A66	60f multi	40 20
216	A66	110f multi	70 40

15th Revolution Day.
For surcharge see Yemen No. 631.

Child, Map of Arabia and IYC Emblem — A67

1979, Mar. 20   Litho.   **Perf. 13¹/₂**
217	A67	15f multi	15 15
218	A67	20f multi	15 15
219	A67	60f multi	25 15
220	A67	110f multi	38 20
		Set value	75 44

International Year of the Child.

Sickle, Star, Tractor, Wheat and Dove — A68

Designs: 35f, Pylon, star, compass, wheat and hammer. 60f, Students, worker and clock. 90f, Woman with raised arms, doves and star.

1979, June 22   Litho.   **Perf. 14**
221	A68	20f multi	15 15
222	A68	35f multi	15 15
223	A68	60f multi	25 15
224	A68	110f multi	38 20
		Set value	80 44

Corrective Move, 10th anniversary.

Yemen #52, Hill A69

Hill and: 110f, Yemen #56. 250f, Aden #12.

1979, Aug. 27   Litho.   **Perf. 14**
225	A69	90f multi	30 20
226	A69	110f multi	38 25

Souvenir Sheet
227	A69	250f multi	1.00 1.00

Sir Rowland Hill (1795-1879), originator of penny postage.

Book, World Map, Arab Achievements A70

1979, Sept. 26   Litho.   **Perf. 14**
228	A70	60f multi	25 15

Party Emblem — A71   Cassia Adenesis — A72

1979, Oct. 13   **Perf. 14¹/₂x14**
229	A71	60f multi	25 15

Yemeni Socialist Party, 1st anniversary.

1979, Nov. 30   Litho.   **Perf. 13¹/₂**

Flowers: 90f, Nerium oleander. 110f, Calligonum comosum. 180f, Adenium obesium.
230	A72	20f multi	16 15
231	A72	90f multi	65 35
232	A72	110f multi	1.00 50
233	A72	180f multi	1.20 65

For surcharge see Yemen No. 632.

First Anniv. of Iranian Revolution — A73

1980, Feb. 12   Litho.   **Perf. 13¹/₂**
234	A73	60f multi	22 22

Dido — A74

1980, Mar. 5   Litho.   Perf. 13½
235 A74 110f shown   65   28
236 A74 180f Anglia   90   40
237 A74 250f India   1.25   52

For surcharge see Yemen No. 633.

Basket Maker,
London 1980
Emblem — A75

1980, May 6   Litho.   Perf. 14
238 A75   60f shown   20   15
239 A75   90f Hubble bubble pipe mak-
          er   30   16
240 A75 110f Weaver   38   25
241 A75 250f Potter   90   50

London 1980 Intl. Stamp Exhib., May 6-14.

Hemprich's
Skink
A76

1980, May 8   Litho.   Perf. 14
242 A76   20f shown   20   15
243 A76   35f Mole viper   28   15
244 A76 110f Carter's day gecko   75   32
245 A76 180f Cobra   1.25   60

For surcharge see Yemen No. 634.

Misha and
Olympic
Emblem — A77

Farmers
Armed — A78

1980, July 19   Litho.   Perf. 12½x12
246 A77 110f multi   50   28

For overprint see No. 287.

1980, Oct. 17   Perf. 13½
247 A78   50f Armed farmers working,
          horiz.   30   15
248 A78   90f shown   45   30
249 A78 110f Sickle (wheat) and fist 60   38

10th anniversary of farmers' uprising.

110th Birth
Anniversary of
Lenin — A79

1980, Nov. 7   Litho.   Perf. 12
250 A79   35f multi   15   15

Douglas
DC-3
A80

1981, Mar. 11   Litho.   Perf. 13½
251 A80   60f shown   20   15
252 A80   90f Boeing 707   38   20
253 A80 250f DHC Dash 7   1.00   50

Democratic Yemen Airlines, 10th anniv.

Ras Boradli
Earth Satellite
Station
A82

1981, June 22   Litho.   Perf. 12
257 A82   60f multi   40   32

Conocarpus
Lancifolius — A83

Supreme People's
Council, 10th
Anniv. — A84

1981, Aug. 1   Litho.   Perf. 12
258 A83   90f shown   30   16
259 A83 180f Ficus vasta   65   40
260 A83 250f Maerua crassifolia 1.00   65

1981, Aug. 18   Litho.   Perf. 15x14½
261 A84 180f multi   65   40

Desert Fox — A85

1981, Sept. 26   Litho.   Perf. 14½
262 A85   50f shown   30   15
263 A85   90f South Arabian leopard 60   30
264 A85 250f Ibex   1.40   75

No. 194 Redrawn

1981, Oct. 15   Litho.   Perf. 12
Size: 25x27mm
264A A61   5f multi   15   15

Denomination in upper right.

Tephrosia
Apollinea — A86

1981, Nov. 30   Litho.   Perf. 13½
265 A86   50f shown   20   15
266 A86   90f Citrullus colocynthis 30   16
267 A86 110f Aloe sqarrosa   40   16
268 A86 250f Lawsonia inermis   1.00   60

For surcharge see Yemen No. 635.

Intl. Year of
the
Disabled
A87

1981, Dec. 12   Litho.   Perf. 14½
269 A87   50f multi   16   15
270 A87   90f multi   38   16
271 A87 150f multi   60   38

TB
Bacillus
Centenary
A88

1982, Mar. 24   Litho.   Perf. 14½
272 A88   50f multi   30   16

30th Anniv.
of Arab
Postal Union
A89

1982, Apr. 12   Litho.   Perf. 14
273 A89 100f multi   50   30

1982
World Cup
A90

Designs: Various soccer players.

1982, June 13   Litho.   Perf. 14
274 A90   50f multi   25   15
275 A90 100f multi   50   30
276 A90 150f multi   70   45
277 A90 200f multi   1.00   60
  a. Souv. sheet of 4, #274-277 2.50 1.50

For overprints see Nos. 281-284.

60th Anniv.
of USSR
A93

1982, Dec. 22   Litho.   Perf. 12½x12
280 A93   50f Flags, arms   50   35

Nos. 274-277, 277a Ovptd. with Emblem
and "WORLD CUP / WINNERS / 1982 /
1st ITALY / 2nd W-GERMANY / 3rd
POLAND / 4th FRANCE" in Blue
1982, Dec. 30   Litho.   Perf. 14
281 A90   50f multi   20   20
282 A90 100f multi   40   40
283 A90 150f multi   60   60
284 A90 200f multi   70   70
  a. Souvenir sheet of 4, #281-284 2.00 2.00

Palestinian
Solidarity
A94

1983, Apr. 10   Perf. 13½x14½
285 A94   50f Yasser Arafat   20   20
286 A94 100f Arafat, Dome of the Rock 40   40
  a. Souvenir sheet of 1, imperf. 50   50

No. 246 Ovptd. with TEMBAL '83
Emblem in Yellow
1983, May 21   Perf. 12½x12
287 A77 110f multi   42   42

World Communications Year — A95

Designs: 50f, Correspondent, postrider, ship.
100f, Postman, coach, telegraph. No. 290, Telephones, bus. 200f, Telecommunications. No. 292,
Montage.

1983, June 10   Perf. 13x13½
288 A95   50f blk & brt bl   20   20
289 A95 100f multi   40   40
290 A95 150f multi   60   60
291 A95 200f multi   70   70

Souvenir Sheet
292 A95 150f multi   60   60

Pablo Picasso
(1881-1973),
Painter
A96

Paintings: No. 293, The Poor Family, 1903. No.
294, Woman with Crow. No. 295a, The Gourmet.
No. 295b, Woman with Child on Beach. No. 295c,
Sitting Beggar. No. 296, The Solar Family, horiz.

1983, July 25   Perf. 14
293 A96   50f multi   20   20
294 A96 100f multi   40   40

Souvenir Sheets
295   Sheet of 3   1.20 1.20
  a. A96 50f multi   20   20
  b. A96 100f multi   40   40
  c. A96 150f multi   60   60
296 A96 150f multi   60   60

23rd Pre-Olympics Games, 1984 — A97

1983, July 30
297	A97	25f Show jumping	15	15
298	A97	50f Show jumping, diff.	20	20
299	A97	100f Three-day event	40	40

Souvenir Sheets
300		Sheet of 4	80	80
a.	A97	20f Bay, vert.	15	15
b.	A97	40f Gray, vert.	15	15
c.	A97	60f Bay, diff., vert.	22	22
d.	A97	80f Arabian	32	32
301	A97	200f Show jumping, diff., vert.	70	70

Locomotives — A98

1983, Aug. 24   Perf. 14½x15
302	A98	25f P8 steam engine, 1905	15	15
303	A98	50f 880 steam, 1915	20	20
304	A98	100f GT 2-4-4, 1923	40	40

Souvenir Sheets
305		Sheet of 3	80	80
a.	A98	40f D51 steam, 1936	15	15
b.	A98	60f 45 Series, 1937	22	22
c.	A98	100f PT 47, 1948	40	40
306	A98	200f P36, 1950	80	80

Natl. Revolution, 20th Anniv. A100

1983, Oct. 15   Litho.   Perf. 13½x13
312	A100	50f shown	20	20
313	A100	100f Flag, freedom fighter	40	40

1st Manned Flight, Bicent. — A101

Balloons: 100f, La Montgolfiere prototype. No. 316a, Lunardi's. No. 316b, Charles and Robert's. No. 316c, Wiseman's. No. 316d, Blanchard and Jeffries's. 200f, Five-balloon craft.

1983, Oct. 25   Perf. 14
314	A101	50f shown	20	20
315	A101	100f multi	40	40

Souvenir Sheets
316		Sheet of 4	80	80
a.	A101	20f multi	15	15
b.	A101	40f multi	15	15
c.	A101	60f multi	20	20
d.	A101	80f multi	32	32
317	A101	200f multi	80	80

1984 Winter Olympics, Sarajevo A102

1983, Dec. 28   Litho.   Perf. 14
318	A102	50f Men's downhill skiing	20	20
319	A102	100f Two-man bobsled	40	40

Souvenir Sheets
320		Sheet of 2	40	40
a.	A102	40f Ski jumping	15	15
b.	A102	60f Figure skating	20	20
321	A102	200f Ice hockey	80	80

1984 Summer Olympics, Los Angeles — A103

1984, Jan. 24
322	A103	25f Fencing	15	15
323	A103	50f Fencing, diff.	20	20
324	A103	100f Fencing, diff.	40	40

Souvenir Sheets
325		Sheet of 4	80	80
a.	A103	20f Gymnastics	15	15
b.	A103	40f Water polo	15	15
c.	A103	60f Wrestling	20	20
d.	A103	80f Show jumping	32	32
326	A103	200f Show jumping, diff.	80	80

Nos. 83 and 84B Surcharged with Black Squares

1984, May 26   Litho.   Perf. 13½, 13
332	A24	50f on 65f multi	
333	A25	100f on 110f multi	

Fish — A105

1984, Nov. 25   Litho.   Perf. 11½
334	A105	10f Abalistes stellaris	15	15
335	A105	15f Caranx speciocus	15	15
336	A105	20f Pomadasys maculatus	15	15
337	A105	25f Chaetodon fasciatus	15	15
338	A105	35f Pomacanthus imperator	15	15
339	A105	50f Rastrelliger kanagurta	20	20
340	A105	100f Euthynnus affinis	40	40
341	A105	150f Heniochus acuminatus	60	60
342	A105	200f Pomacanthus maculosus	80	80
343	A105	250f Pterois russellii	1.00	1.00
344	A105	400f Argyrops spinifer	1.60	1.60
345	A105	500f Dasyatis uarnak	2.00	2.00
346	A105	1d Epinephalus chlorostigma	3.75	3.75
347	A105	2d Drepane longimana	8.00	8.00
		Nos. 334-347 (14)	19.10	19.10

For surcharges see Yemen Nos. 636, 640, 642.

Natl. Literacy Campaign A106

1985, Feb. 27   Perf. 12
350	A106	50f Girls writing	20	20
351	A106	100f Hand, fountain pen, vert.	40	40

Victory Parade, Red Square, Moscow, 1945 — A107

12th World Youth and Students Festival — A108

1985, May 9   Perf. 12x12½
352	A107	100f multi	40	40

Defeat of Nazi Germany, end of World War II, 40th anniv.

1985, Aug. 3   Perf. 12
353	A108	50f Emblem	20	20
354	A108	100f Hand holding emblem	40	40

UNESCO World Heritage Campaign A109

Natl. Socialist Party, 3rd Gen. Cong. A110

1985, Aug. 29
355	A109	50f Shibam city	20	20
356	A109	50f Close-up of buildings	20	20
357	A109	100f Windows	40	40
358	A109	100f Door	40	40

Nos. 355-357 horiz.

1985, Oct. 10
359	A110	25f Energy	15	15
360	A110	50f Industry	20	20
361	A110	100f Agriculture	40	40

UN Child Survival Campaign A111

World Food Day A112

1985, Nov. 28
362	A111	50f Mother feeding child	20	20
363	A111	50f Holding child	20	20
364	A111	100f Feeding child, diff.	40	40
365	A111	100f Breastfeeding	40	40

1986, Jan. 30
366	A112	20f Almihdar Mosque, Aden	15	15
367	A112	180f Palm trees	1.05	1.05

UN Food and Agriculture Org., 40th anniv.

Lenin, Red Square, Moscow A113

1986, Feb. 25   Perf. 12x12½
368	A113	75f multi	45	45
369	A113	250f multi	1.45	1.45

27th Soviet Communist Party Cong., Moscow.

Costumes Worn at the 1984 Brides Dance Festival — A114

Designs: No. 370, Bride wearing red and green costume, face markings. No. 371, Violet costume. No. 372, Veiled bride. No. 373, Unveiled bride. No. 374, Groom holding dagger. No. 375, Groom holding rifle.

1986, Feb. 27
370	A114	50f multi	30	30
371	A114	50f multi	30	30
372	A114	50f multi	30	30
373	A114	100f multi	58	58
374	A114	100f multi	58	58
375	A114	100f multi	58	58
		Nos. 370-375 (6)	2.64	2.64

Revolution Martyrs A115

1986, Oct. 15   Litho.   Perf. 12
376	A115	75f Abdul Fattah Ismail	45	45
377	A115	75f Ali Shayaa Hadi	45	45
378	A115	75f Saleh Musleh Kasim	45	45
379	A115	75f Ali Ahmed N. Antar	45	45

UN Child Survival Campaign A116

Infant Immunization Program.

1987, Apr. 7   Litho.   Perf. 12
380	A116	20f Immunizing pregnant woman	15	15
381	A116	75f Immunizing infant	45	45
382	A116	140f Oral immunization	85	85
383	A116	150f Infant, girl, pregnant woman	90	90

1st Socialist Party General Conference A117

1987, July 30   Litho.   Perf. 12
384	A117	75fr multi	45	45
385	A117	150fr multi	90	90

October Revolution, Russia, 70th Anniv. — A118

Monuments, Ancient City of Shabwa — A119

1987, Nov. 7   Litho.   Perf. 12¹/₂x12
386 A118 250f multi   1.50 1.50

1987, Nov. 18   Perf. 12
387 A119 25f Royal palace and court   15   15
388 A119 75f Palace, diff.   45   45
389 A119 140f Winged lion bas-relief on
                stone capital   85   85
390 A119 150f The Moon, legend on
                bronze tablet   90   90

Nos. 387-388 horiz.

Natl. Independence, 20th Anniv. A120

Designs: 5f, Students walking to school. 75f, Family, apartments. 140f, Workers, oil derrick, thermal plant. 150f, Workers, soldier, Workers' Party headquarters.

1987, Nov. 29   Perf. 12x12¹/₂
391 A120 25f multi   15   15
392 A120 75f multi   45   45
393 A120 140f multi   85   85
394 A120 150f multi   90   90

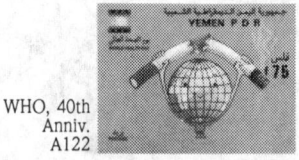

September 26th Revolution, 25th Anniv. A121

1988, Feb. 27   Litho.   Perf. 13
395 A121 75f Revolution monument,
                San'a   45   45

WHO, 40th Anniv. A122

1988, Apr. 7   Litho.   Perf. 12
396 A122 40f Sanitary public water
                supply, vert.   25   25
397 A122 75f No smoking   45   45
398 A122 140f Child immunization   85   85
399 A122 250f Health care for all by
                the year 2000   1.55 1.55

1988 Summer Olympics, Seoul — A125

1988, Sept. 17   Litho.   Perf. 12x12¹/₂
406 A125 40f Weight lifting   25   25
407 A125 75f Running   45   45
408 A125 140f Boxing   85   85
409 A125 150f Soccer   90   90

1st Freedom Fighter Killed at the Liberation Front, Radfan Mountains A126

Perf. 12¹/₂x12, 12x12¹/₂
1988, Oct. 12   Litho.
410 A126 25f Freedom fighters,
                flag, vert.   18   18
411 A126 75f shown   45   45
412 A126 300f Anniv. emblem, vert.   1.85 1.85

October 14th Revolution, 25th anniv.

Indigenous Birds — A127

1988, Nov. 5   Perf. 12x12¹/₂, 12¹/₂x12
413 A127 40f Treron waalia   25   25
414 A127 50f Coracias caudatus lor-
                ti, vert.   32   32
415 A127 75f Upupa epops, vert.   45   45
416 A127 250f Chlamydotis undulata
                macqueenii   1.55 1.55

Handicrafts — A128

Designs: 25f, Incense brazier. 75f, Cage-shaped dress form. 150f, Shell and wicker lidded basket. 250f, Wicker basket.

1988, Nov. 29   Litho.   Perf. 12¹/₂x12
417 A128 25f multi   18   18
418 A128 75f multi   45   45
419 A128 150f multi   90   90
420 A128 250f multi   1.55 1.55

Aden Harbor and Yemen Port Authority, Cent. — A129

1988, Dec. 5   Perf. 12x12¹/₂
421 A129 75f Old harbor facility   65   65
422 A129 300f New facility   2.75 2.75

Preservation of San'a City, a Site on the UNESCO World Heritage List — A130

Perf. 12x12¹/₂, 12¹/₂x12
1988, Dec. 15
423 A130 75f shown   45   45
424 A130 250f City view, diff., vert. 1.55 1.55

World Wildlife Fund — A131

1989, May 18   Litho.   Perf. 12¹/₂x12
425 A131 20f Sand cat   15   15
426 A131 25f Cat's head   15   15
427 A131 50f Fennec fox   30   30
428 A131 75f Fox's head   45   45

For surcharge see Yemen No. 643.

Military Forces — A132

Abdul Fattah Ismail — A133

Developments of the corrective movement.

1989, Aug. 15   Perf. 12x12¹/₂
429 A132 25f shown   15   15
430 A132 35f Industry   22   22
431 A132 40f Agriculture   25   25

June 22 Corrective Movement, 20th anniv.

1989, Aug. 28
432 A133 75f multi   45   45
433 A133 150f multi   90   90

50th Birthday of Abdul Fattah Ismail, 1st secretary-general of the natl. Socialist Party.

Ali Anter Yemeni Pioneer Organization, 15th Anniv. — A134

Perf. 12x12¹/₂, 12¹/₂x12
1989, Sept. 29   Litho.
434 A134 10f Drawing by Abeer
                Anwer   15   15
435 A134 25f Girl in pioneer uniform   15   15
436 A134 75f Parade, Aden   45   45
                Set value   65   65

Nos. 434-435 vert.
For surcharge see Yemen No. 644.

Nehru and the Taj Mahal — A135

1989, Nov. 14   Photo.   Perf. 14
437 A135 250f blk & golden brn   1.50 1.50

Jawaharlal Nehru, 1st prime minister of independent India.
For surcharge see Yemen No. 645.

Seventy-Day Siege of San'a, 1967-68 — A136

Coffee Plant — A137

1989, Oct. 25   Litho.   Perf. 12x12¹/₂
438 A136 150f multicolored   90   90

1989, Dec. 20
439 A137 300f multicolored   1.75 1.75

For surcharge see Yemen No. 637.

Seera Rock, Aden, and the Arc de Triomphe, Paris A138

1989, Dec. 29   Litho.   Perf. 12¹/₂x12
440 A138 250f multicolored   1.50 1.50

French Revolution, bicent.

World Cup Soccer Championships, Italy — A139

Character trademark, soccer plays and flags of participants: 5f, US, Belgium, 1930. 10f, Switzerland, Holland, 1934. 20f, Italy, France, 1938. 35f, Sweden, Spain, 1950. 50f, Federal Republic of Germany, Austria, 1954. Brazil, England, 1958. 500f, Russia, Uruguay, 1962. No. 448, Soccer game.

1990, Apr. 30   Perf. 12¹/₂x12
441 A139 5f multicolored   15   15
442 A139 10f multicolored   15   15
443 A139 20f multicolored   15   15
444 A139 35f multicolored   22   22
445 A139 50f multicolored   30   30
446 A139 60f multicolored   36   36
447 A139 500f multicolored   3.00 3.00
        Nos. 441-447 (7)   4.33 4.33
                Souvenir Sheet
448 A139 340f multicolored   2.05 2.05

The Yemen Arab Republic and the People's Republic of Yemen are in the middle of a 30-month unification process scheduled for completion by November 1992. While government ministries have merged, both currencies are still valid. To the BEST OF OUR KNOWLEDGE both Yemen Arab Republic and the People's Republic of Yemen are issuing postage stamps that have validity throughout the new country. At the current time the two areas are at war.

YUGOSLAVIA

LOCATION — Southern Europe, bordering on the Adriatic Sea
GOVT. — Republic
AREA — 98,766 sq. mi.
POP. — 22,850,000 (est. 1983)
CAPITAL — Belgrade

On December 1, 1918, Bosnia and Herzegovina, Croatia, Dalmatia, Montenegro, Serbia and Slovenia united to form a kingdom which was later called Yugoslavia. A republic was proclaimed November 29, 1945. Other listings may be found under all.

100 Heller = 1 Krone
(Bosnia & Herzegovina)
100 Filler = 1 Krone
(Croatia-Slavonia)
100 Paras = 1 Dinar (General Issues)

Catalogue values for unused stamps in this country are for Never Hinged items, beginning with Scott 410 in the regular postage section, Scott C50 in the airpost section, Scott J67 in the postage due section, Scott RA1 in the postal tax section, and Scott RAJ1 in the postal tax due section.

Counterfeits exist of most of the 1918-19 overprints for Bosnia and Herzegovina, Croatia-Slavonia and Slovenia.

BOSNIA AND HERZEGOVIA

Stamps of Bosnia and Herzegovina, 1910, Overprinted or Surcharged in Black or Red

DRŽAVA S.H.S.

1918   **1918**

Bosna i Hercegovina
a
ДРЖАВА С.Х.С.

1918   **1918**

Босна и Херцеговина
b
**DRŽAVA
S. H. S.**

1918   **1918**
c

Bosna i Hercegovina

1918	Unwmk.		Perf. 12½	
1L1	A4(a)	3h olive green	40	70
1L2	A4(b)	5h dark green (R)	15	15
1L3	A4(a)	10h carmine	15	15
1L4	A4(a)	20h dark brown (R)	15	15
1L5	A4(b)	25h deep blue (R)	15	15
1L6	A4(b)	30h green	15	20
1L7	A4(b)	40h orange	15	15
1L8	A4(b)	45h brown red	15	15
1L9	A4(b)	50h dull violet	15	18
1L10	A4(a)	60h on 50h dl vio	15	18
1L11	A4(a)	80h on 6h org brown	15	32
1L12	A4(a)	90h on 35h myr green	15	15
1L13	A5(c)	2k gray green	15	32
1L14	A4(a)	3k on 3h ol grn	80	1.25
1L15	A4(a)	4k on 1k maroon	1.40	1.90
1L16	A4(b)	10k on 2h vio	2.25	2.50
	Set value			5.85

Inverted and double overprints and assorted varieties exist on the stamps for Bosnia and Herzegovina.

Bosnian Girl — A1

1918	Typo.		Perf. 11½	
1L17	A1	2h ultramarine	15	22
1L18	A1	6h violet	55	1.90
1L19	A1	10h rose	18	20
1L20	A1	20h green	18	20

Imperforate stamps of this type (A1) are newspaper stamps of Bosnia.
See Nos. 1L21-1L22, 1L43-1L45.

Bosnia and Herzegovina Nos. P1-P2 (Nos. 1L17-1L18, Imperf.) Surcharged

1918			Imperf.	
1L21	A1	3h on 2h ultra	15	15
a.	Double surcharge		14.00	
1L22	A1	5h on 6h violet	15	15
a.	Double surcharge		14.00	
	Set value			18

Stamps of Bosnia and Herzegovina, 1906-17, Overprinted or Surcharged in Black or Red:

КРАЉЕВСТВО

d
C. X. C.

KRALJEVSTVO

e
S. H. S.

KRALJEVSTVO
f
S. H. S.

1919			Perf. 12½	
1L25	A23(d)	3h claret	16	48
1L26	A23(e)	5h green	15	16
1L27	A23(e)	10h on 6h dark gray	15	15
1L28	A24(e)	20h on 35h myr green	15	16
1L29	A23(e)	25h ultra	15	16
1L30	A23(d)	30h orange red	48	90
1L31	A24(d)	45h olive brn	35	45
1L32	A27(e)	45h on 80h org brown	15	16
a.	Perf. 11½		3.25	4.00
1L33	A24(e)	50h slate blue	20.00	24.00
1L34	A24(e)	50h on 72h dk blue (R)	15	16
1L35	A24(d)	60h brown violet	15	16
1L36	A27(e)	80h orange brown	20	24
a.	Perf. 11½		24.00	30.00
1L37	A27(e)	90h dark violet	16	20
a.	Perf. 11½		2.25	2.75
1L38	A17(f)	2k gray green	20	24
a.	Imperf.		27.50	
b.	Perf. 9½		4.50	5.00
1L39	A26(d)	3k car, green	80	90
1L40	A28(e)	4k car, green	1.75	2.50
1L41	A26(d)	5k dk vio, gray	1.75	2.75
1L42	A28(e)	10k dk vio, gray	2.00	2.75
	Nos. 1L25-1L42 (18)		28.90	36.52

Nos. 1L32, 1L36, 1L37, 1L40 and 1L42 have no bars in the overprint.
Nos. 1L25 to 1L42 exist with inverted overprint or surcharge.

Bosnia and Herzegovina Nos. P2-P4 (Nos. 1L18-1L20, Imperf.) Surcharged

1920			Imperf.	
1L43	A1	2h on 6h violet	50.00	70.00
1L44	A1	2h on 10h rose	20.00	40.00
1L45	A1	2h on 20h green	1.10	2.75

SEMI-POSTAL STAMPS ISSUES FOR BOSNIA AND HERZEGOVINA

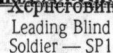
Leading Blind Soldier — SP1

Wounded Soldier — SP2

Semi-Postal Stamps of Bosnia and Herzegovina, 1918 Overprinted

1918	Unwmk.		Perf. 12½, 13	
1LB1	SP1	10h greenish bl	65	1.00
a.	Overprinted as No. 1LB2		27.50	37.50
1LB2	SP2	15h red brown	1.75	1.75
a.	Overprinted as No. 1LB1		27.50	37.50

Bosnian Semi-Postal Stamps of 1916 Overprinted like No. 1LB2

1918				
1LB3	SP1	5h green	130.00	140.00
a.	Overprinted as No. 1LB1		235.00	300.00
1LB4	SP2	10h magenta	75.00	95.00

Inverted and double overprints exist on Nos. 1LB1-1LB4.

Mail Wagon SP3

Bridge at Mostar SP4

Scene near Sarajevo — SP5

Regular Issue of Bosnia, 1906 Surcharged in Black

1919				
1LB5	SP3	10h + 10h on 40h org red	1.75	1.90
1LB6	SP4	20h + 10h on 20h dk brown	60	60
1LB7	SP5	45h + 15h on 1k mar	2.50	2.75

Nos. 1LB5-1LB7 exist with surcharge inverted. Value each $7.50.

SPECIAL DELIVERY STAMPS ISSUES FOR BOSNIA AND HERZEGOVINA

Lightning
SD1   SD2

Bosnian Special Delivery Stamps Overprinted in Black

1918	Unwmk.		Perf. 12½, 13	
1LE1	SD1	2h vermilion	4.75	5.00
a.	Inverted overprint		32.50	
b.	Overprinted as No. 1LE2		30.00	35.00
1LE2	SD2	5h deep green	1.40	1.50
a.	Inverted overprint		18.00	
b.	Overprinted as No. 1LE1		30.00	35.00

POSTAGE DUE STAMPS ISSUES FOR BOSNIA AND HERZEGOVINA

Postage Due Stamps of Bosnia and Herzegovina, 1916, Overprinted in Black or Red:

**ДРЖАВА С.Х.С.
БОСНА И
ХЕРЦЕГОВИНА**
a

хелера

**DRŽAVA S.H.S.
BOSNA I
HERCEGOVINA**
b

HELERA

1918	Unwmk.		Perf. 12½, 13	
1LJ1	D2 (a)	2h red	15	15
1LJ2	D2 (b)	4h red	24	65
1LJ3	D2 (b)	5h red	15	15
1LJ4	D2 (b)	6h red	30	40
1LJ5	D2 (a)	10h red	15	15
1LJ6	D2 (b)	15h red	4.00	4.75
1LJ7	D2 (a)	20h red	15	15
1LJ8	D2 (b)	25h red	24	70
1LJ9	D2 (a)	30h red	24	70
1LJ10	D2 (b)	40h red	15	15
1LJ11	D2 (a)	50h red	55	80

**DRŽAVA S.H.S.
BOSNA I
HERCEGOVINA**
c

KRUNA

**ДРЖАВА С.Х.С.
Босна и
ХЕРЦЕГОВИНА**
d

круна

1LJ12	D2 (c)	1k dark blue (R)	28	28
1LJ13	D2 (d)	3k dark blue (R)	18	18
	Nos. 1LJ1-1LJ13 (13)		6.78	9.21

Nos. 1LJ1-1LJ13 exist with overprint double or inverted. Value $3 to $7.
Nos. 1LJ1-1LJ11 exist with type "b" overprint instead of type "a," and vice versa. Value, each $10.

Stamps of Bosnia and Herzegovina, 1900-04, Surcharged

ПОРТО   PORTO

5 x   20h
e   f

1919				
1LJ14	A2 (e)	2h on 35h blue	28	1.10
1LJ15	A2 (e)	5h on 45h grnsh bl	42	85
1LJ16	A2 (e)	10h on 10 red	15	15
1LJ17	A2 (e)	15h on 40h org	18	80
1LJ18	A2 (f)	20h on 5h green	15	15
1LJ19	A2 (f)	25h on 20h pink	18	50
1LJ20	A2 (f)	30h on 30h bis brn	18	45
1LJ21	A2 (e)	1k on 50h red lil	15	15
1LJ22	A2 (e)	3k on 25h blue	20	28

Postage Due Stamps of Bosnia and
Herzegovina, 1904 Surcharged:

КРАЉЕВСТВО СРБА, ХРВАТА И СЛОВЕНАЦА **40**

KRALJEVSTVO SRBA, HRVATA I SLOVENACA **50**

40 хелера 40
g

50 helera 50
h

1LJ23	D1 (g)	40h on 6h blk, red & yel	15	20
1LJ24	D1 (h)	50h on 8h blk, red & yel	15	18
1LJ25	D1 (h)	200h blk, red & grn	2.50	2.50
1LJ26	D1 (h)	4k on 7h blk, red & yel	18	32
	Nos. 1LJ14-1LJ26 (13)		4.87	7.63

Nos. 1LJ14-1LJ26 exist with overprint double or
inverted. Value, $3 to $6.

CROATIA-SLAVONIA

Stamps of Hungary Overprinted in Blue

A1

1918	**Wmk. 137**	**Perf. 15**	
On Stamps of 1913			
2L1	A1	6f olive green	1.10 2.00
2L2	A1	50f lake, *blue*	85 1.75

A2

A3

On Stamps of 1916

2L3	A2	10f violet	20.00 27.50
2L4	A3	15f red	20.00 27.50

A4

On Hungary Nos. 106-107
White Numerals

2L4A	A4	10f rose	240.00 300.00
2L5	A4	15f violet	22.50 27.50
a.	Inverted overprint		125.00

On Stamps of 1916-18
Colored Numerals

2L6	A4	2f brown orange	15 15
2L7	A4	3f red lilac	15 15
2L8	A4	5f green	15 15
2L9	A4	6f greenish blue	15 24
2L10	A4	10f rose red	1.65 2.75
2L11	A4	15f violet	15 15
2L12	A4	20f gray brown	15 28
2L13	A4	25f dull blue	15 15
2L14	A4	35f brown	15 20
2L15	A4	45f olive green	20 48

The overprints and surcharges for Croatia-Slavonia exist inverted, double, double inverted, in
wrong colors, on wrong stamps, on back, in pairs
with one lacking overprint, etc.

A5

A6

2L16	A5	50f red vio & lilac	15	15
2L17	A5	75f brt bl & pale bl	15	24
2L18	A5	80f grn & pale grn	15	16
2L19	A6	1k red brown & cl	15	15
2L20	A6	2k olive brn & bis	15	16
2L21	A6	3k dark vio & ind	40	1.00
2L22	A6	5k dk brn & lt brn	2.00	4.00
2L23	A6	10k vio brn & vio	7.50	14.00

Stamps of Hungary Overprinted in Blue,
Black or Red

A7

A8

2L24	A7	10f scarlet (Bl)	15	15
2L25	A7	20f dark brown (Bk)	15	15
2L26	A7	25f deep blue (R)	80	2.50
2L27	A8	40f olive green (Bl)	15	16
	Nos. 2L6-2L27 (22)		14.95	27.52

Many other stamps of the 1913-18 issues of Hungary, the Semi-Postal Stamps of 1915-16 and Postage Due Stamps were surreptitiously overprinted
but were never sold through the post office.

Freedom of Croatia-
Slavonia — A9

1918	**Unwmk. Litho.**	**Perf. 11½**	
2L28	A9	10f rose	1.00 1.00
2L29	A9	20f violet	1.25 1.25
2L30	A9	25f blue	2.50 2.50
2L31	A9	45f greenish blk	24.00 24.00

Independence of Croatia, Slavonia and Dalmatia.
#2L28-2L31 exist imperforate, but were not offi-
cially issued in this condition.
Excellent counterfeits of #2L28-2L31 exist.

Allegory of
Freedom
A10

Youth with
Standard
A11

Falcon, Symbol of
Liberty — A12

1919		**Perf. 11½**	
2L32	A10	2f brn orange	15 15
2L33	A10	3f violet	15 15
2L34	A10	5f green	15 15
2L35	A11	10f red	15 15
2L36	A11	20f black brown	15 15
2L37	A11	25f deep blue	15 15
2L38	A11	45f dark ol grn	15 15
2L39	A12	1k carmine rose	15 15
2L40	A12	3k dark violet	35 35
2L41	A12	5k deep brown	85 70
	Set value		1.90 1.75

		Perf. 12½	
2L32a	A10	2f	1.25 1.25
2L33a	A10	3f	1.25 1.25
2L34a	A10	5f	40.00 52.50
2L35a	A11	10f	35 35
2L36a	A11	20f	28 25
	Nos. 2L32a-2L36a (5)		43.13 55.60

#2L32-2L41 exist imperf. Value, set $25.

SEMI-POSTAL STAMPS ISSUES FOR CROATIA-SLAVONIA

SP1

SP2

SP3

1918	**Wmk. 137**	**Perf. 15**	
2LB1	SP1	10f + 2f rose red	30 2.75
2LB2	SP2	15f + 2f dull violet	15 40
2LB3	SP3	40f + 2f brn carmine	15 85

SPECIAL DELIVERY STAMP ISSUE FOR CROATIA-SLAVONIA

SD1

Hungary No. E1 Overprinted in Black

1918	**Wmk. 137**	**Perf. 15**	
2LE1	SD1	2f gray green & red	15 15

POSTAGE DUE STAMPS ISSUES FOR CROATIA-SLAVONIA

D1

Postage Due Stamps of Hungary
Overprinted in Blue

1918	**Wmk. Crown (136)**	**Perf. 15**	
2LJ1	D1	50f green & blk	175.00 175.00
	Wmk. Double Cross (137)		
2LJ2	D1	1f green & red	6.25 6.25
a.	Inverted overprint		22.50 22.50
2LJ3	D1	2f green & red	75 75
2LJ4	D1	10f green & red	55 55
2LJ5	D1	12f green & red	25.00 25.00
2LJ6	D1	15f green & red	45 45
2LJ7	D1	20f green & red	45 45
2LJ8	D1	30f green & red	1.10 1.10
2LJ9	D1	50f green & red	7.75 7.75
	Nos. 2LJ2-2LJ9 (8)		42.30 42.30

NEWSPAPER STAMPS ISSUES FOR CROATIA-SLAVONIA

N1

N2

Hungary No. P8 Overprinted in Black

1918	**Wmk. 137**	**Imperf.**	
2LP1	N1	(2f) orange	15 30

1919	**Litho.**	**Unwmk.**	
2LP2	N2	2f yellow	15 50

SLOVENIA

Chain Breaker
A1   A2

3, 5, 10, 15f: Chain on right wrist is short,
extending only about half way to the frame.
10f: Numerals are 8½mm high.
20, 25, 30, 40f: Distant mountains show faintly
between legs of male figure.
40f: Numerals 7mm high. The upright strokes of
the "4" extend to the same height; the "0" is 3mm
wide.

1919	**Unwmk.**	**Perf. 11½**	
Lithographed at Ljubljana			
Fine Impression			
3L1	A1	3f violet	15 15
3L2	A1	5f green	15 15
3L3	A1	10f carmine rose	15 15
3L4	A1	15f blue	15 15
3L5	A2	20f brown	20 15
3L6	A2	25f blue	18 15
3L7	A2	30f lilac rose	18 15
3L8	A2	40f bister	18 15
	Set value		1.12 48

Various stamps of this series exist imperforate
and part perforate. Many shades exist.
See Nos. 3L9-3L17, 3L24-3L28. For surcharges
see Nos. 3LJ15-3LJ32.

Allegories of Freedom
A3   A4

King Peter I — A5

3, 5, 15f: The chain on the right wrist touches
the bottom tablet.
10f: Numerals are 7½mm high.
15f: Curled end of loin cloth appears above letter
"H" in the bottom tablet.
20, 25, 30, 40f: The outlines of the mountains
have been redrawn and they are more distinct than
on the lithographed stamps.
40f: Numerals 8mm high. The left slanting stroke
of the "4" extends much higher than the main
vertical stroke. The "0" is 2½mm wide and
encloses a much narrower space than on the lithographed stamp.

1919-20		**Perf. 11½**	
Typographed at Ljubljana and Vienna			
Coarse Impression			
3L9	A1	3f violet	15 15
3L10	A1	5f green	15 15
3L11	A1	10f red	18 15
3L12	A1	15f blue	20 15
3L13	A2	20f brown	20 15
3L14	A2	25f blue	18 15
3L15	A2	30f carmine rose	20 15
3L16	A2	30f dp red	2.75 90
3L17	A2	40f orange	24 15
3L18	A3	50f green	30 15
a.	50f dark green		28 15
b.	50f olive green		3.50 1.10
3L19	A3	60f dark blue	45 15
a.	60f violet blue		85 20
3L20	A4	1k vermilion	28 15
a.	1k red orange		45 18
3L21	A4	2k blue	30 15
c.	2k dull ultramarine		90 20

3L22	A5	5k brown lake		45	15
a.		5k lake		12.00	1.65
b.		5k dull red		60	15
3L23	A5	10k deep ultra		2.75	90
		Nos. 3L9-3L23 (15)		8.78	
		Set value			3.00

Nos. 3L9-3L23 exist imperf. Value, set $90.
Many of the series exist part perforate.
Many shades exist of lower values.
See Nos. 3L29-3L32, 3L40-3L41.

Serrate Roulette 13½

3L24	A1	5f light grn	15	15
3L25	A1	10f carmine	15	15
3L26	A1	15f slate blue	15	15
3L27	A2	20f dark brown	30	15
a.		Serrate x straight roul.	55	15
3L28	A2	30f car rose	20	15
a.		Serrate x straight roul.	60	18
3L29	A3	50f green	28	15
3L30	A3	60f dark blue	45	15
a.		60f violet blue	2.25	1.10
3L31	A4	1k vermilion	65	15
a.		1k rose red	65	15
3L32	A4	2k blue	13.00	1.50
		Nos. 3L24-3L32 (9)	15.33	
		Set value		2.30

Roulette x Perf. 11½

3L24a	A1	5f	130.00	145.00
3L25a	A1	10f	45.00	47.50
3L26a	A1	15f	140.00	155.00
3L28b	A2	30f	45.00	47.50
3L29a	A3	50f	5.25	4.00
3L30b	A3	60f	45.00	47.50
3L31b	A4	1k	45.00	47.50

Thick Wove Paper

1920   Litho.   *Perf. 11½*

3L40	A5	15k gray green	4.00	5.25
3L41	A5	20k dull violet	1.00	2.00

On Nos. 3L40-3L41 the horizontal lines have been removed from the value tablets. They are printed over a background of pale brown wavy lines.

Chain Breaker A7

Freedom A8

King Peter I — A9

Dinar Values:
Type I - Size: 21x30½mm.
Type II - Size: 22x32½mm.

Thin to Thick Wove Paper

1920   *Serrate Roulette 13½*

3L42	A7	5p olive green	15	15
3L43	A7	10p green	15	15
3L44	A7	15p brown	15	15
3L45	A7	20p carmine	75	1.00
3L46	A7	25p chocolate	30	30
3L47	A8	40p dark violet	15	15
3L48	A8	45p yellow	15	15
3L49	A8	50p dark blue	15	15
3L50	A8	60p red brown	15	15
3L51	A9	1d dark brown (I)	15	15

Perf. 11½

3L52	A9	2d gray vio (II)	15	15
3L53	A9	4d grnsh black (I)	30	30
3L54	A9	6d olive brn (II)	15	25
3L55	A9	10d brown red (II)	30	30
		Set value	2.10	2.70

The 2d and 6d have a background of pale red wavy lines, the 10d of gray lines.
Counterfeits exist of No. 3L45.

POSTAGE DUE STAMPS ISSUES FOR SLOVENIA

D1

1919   Litho.   Unwmk.   *Perf. 11½*
Ljubljana Print
Numerals 9½mm high

3LJ1	D1	5f carmine	15	15
3LJ2	D1	10f carmine	15	15
3LJ3	D1	20f carmine	15	15
3LJ4	D1	50f carmine	20	15

Nos. 3LJ1-3LJ4 were also printed in scarlet and dark red.

Numerals 8mm high

3LJ5	D1	1k dark blue	45	32
3LJ6	D1	5k dark blue	65	50
3LJ7	D1	10k dark blue	90	75
		Nos. 3LJ1-3LJ7 (7)	2.65	
		Set value		1.90

1920

Vienna Print
Numerals 11 to 12 mm high

3LJ8	D1	5f red	15	15
3LJ9	D1	10f red	15	15
3LJ10	D1	20f red	22	15
3LJ11	D1	50f red	1.25	85

Numerals 7mm high

3LJ12	D1	1k Prussian blue	1.10	70
a.		1k dark blue	5.00	4.50
3LJ13	D1	5k Prussian blue	1.65	1.25
a.		5k dark blue	8.00	6.75
3LJ14	D1	10k Prussian blue	3.75	3.25
a.		10k dark blue	14.00	15.00
		Nos. 3LJ8-3LJ14 (7)	8.27	6.50

Nos. 3LJ8-3LJ14 exist imperf. Value, set $40.

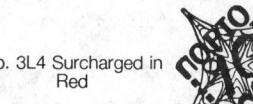

No. 3L4 Surcharged in Red

1920   *Perf. 11½*
On Litho. Stamps

3LJ15	A1	5p on 15f blue	15	15
3LJ16	A1	10p on 15f blue	60	60
3LJ17	A1	20p on 15f blue	15	15
3LJ18	A1	50p on 15f blue	15	15

Nos. 3L7, 3L12, 3L26, 3L28, 3L28a Surcharged in Dark Blue

3LJ19	A2	1d on 30f lil rose	15	15
3LJ20	A2	3d on 30f lil rose	22	15
3LJ21	A2	8d on 30f lil rose	1.10	55
		Set value	2.20	1.50

On Typographed Stamps
Perf. 11½

3LJ22	A1	5p on 15f pale bl	12.00	2.50
3LJ23	A1	10p on 15f pale bl	27.50	22.50
3LJ24	A1	20p on 15f pale bl	11.00	4.00
3LJ25	A1	50p on 15f pale bl	6.00	7.00

Serrate Roulette 13½

3LJ26	A1	5p on 15f slate bl	2.75	50
3LJ27	A1	10p on 15f slate bl	8.50	3.25
3LJ28	A1	20p on 15f slate bl	2.75	50
3LJ29	A1	50p on 15f slate bl	2.75	50
3LJ30	A2	1d on 30f dp rose	2.75	50
a.		Serrate x straight roulette	7.00	4.50
3LJ31	A2	3d on 30f dp rose	5.75	1.75
a.		Serrate x straight roulette	8.00	5.50

3LJ32	A2	8d on 30f dp rose	95.00	6.50
a.		Serrate x straight roulette	90.00	7.50
		Nos. 3LJ26-3LJ32 (7)	120.25	13.65

The para surcharges were printed in sheets of 100, ten horizontal rows of ten. There were: 5p three rows, 10p one row, 20p three rows, 50p three rows. The dinar surcharges were in a setting of 50, arranged in vertical rows of five. There were: 1d five rows, 3d three rows, 8d two rows.

NEWSPAPER STAMPS ISSUES FOR SLOVENIA

Eros — N1

1919   Unwmk.   Litho.   *Imperf.*
Ljubljana Print

3LP1	N1	2f gray	15	15
3LP2	N1	4f gray	15	15
3LP3	N1	6f gray	3.25	4.00
3LP4	N1	10f gray	15	15
3LP5	N1	30f gray	15	15
		Nos. 3LP1-3LP5 (5)	3.85	4.60

See Nos. 3LP6-3LP13. For surcharges see Nos. 3LP14-3LP23, 4LB1-4LB5.

1920

Vienna Print

3LP6	N1	2f gray	15	15
3LP7	N1	4f gray	6.50	10.00
3LP8	N1	6f gray	1.75	2.75
3LP9	N1	10f gray	14.00	21.00
3LP10	N1	2f blue	22	32
3LP11	N1	4f blue	15	15
3LP12	N1	6f blue	90.00	115.00
3LP13	N1	10f blue	15	15
		Nos. 3LP6-3LP13 (8)	112.92	149.52

Nos. 3LP1, 3LP10 Surcharged:

On Ljubljana Print

3LP14	N1 (a)	2p on 2f gray	25	40
3LP15	N1 (a)	4p on 2f gray	25	40
3LP16	N1 (a)	6p on 2f gray	42	65
3LP17	N1 (b)	10p on 2f gray	65	80
3LP18	N1 (b)	30p on 2f gray	65	85

On Vienna Print

3LP19	N1 (a)	2p on 2f blue	15	15
3LP20	N1 (a)	4p on 2f blue	15	15
3LP21	N1 (a)	6p on 2f blue	15	15
3LP22	N1 (b)	10p on 2f blue	15	20
3LP23	N1 (b)	30p on 2f blue	15	15
		Nos. 3LP14-3LP23 (10)	2.97	4.00

The five surcharges were arranged in a setting of 100, in horizontal rows of ten. There were: 2p three rows, 4p three rows, 6p two rows, 10p one row and 30p one row. The sheets were perforated 11½ horizontally between the groups of the different values.

SEMI-POSTAL STAMPS ISSUE FOR CARINTHIA PLEBISCITE

SP1

Nos. 3LP2, 3LP1 Surcharged With Various Designs in Dark Red

1920

4LB1	SP1	5p on 4f gray	15	15
4LB2	SP1	15p on 4f gray	15	15
4LB3	SP1	25p on 4f gray	15	15
4LB4	SP1	45p on 2f gray	15	20
4LB5	SP1	50p on 2f gray	15	15
4LB6	SP1	2d on 2f gray	1.25	1.65
		Nos. 4LB1-4LB6 (6)	2.00	2.45

Nos. 4LB1 to 4LB6 have a different surcharge on each stamp but each includes the letters "K.G.C.A." which signify Carinthian Governmental Commission, Zone A.
Sold at three times face value for the benefit of the Plebiscite Propaganda Fund.

GENERAL ISSUES

For Use throughout the Kingdom

King Alexander A1   King Peter I A2

Unwmk.
1921, Jan. 16   Engr.   *Perf. 12*

1	A1	2p olive brown	15	15
2	A1	5p deep green	15	15
3	A1	10p carmine	15	15
4	A1	15p violet	15	15
5	A1	20p black	15	15
6	A1	25p dark blue	15	15
7	A1	50p olive green	15	15
8	A1	60p vermilion	15	15
9	A1	75p purple	15	15
10	A2	1d orange	15	15
11	A2	2d olive bister	25	15
12	A2	4d dark green	40	15
13	A2	5d carmine rose	2.00	20
14	A2	10d red brown	4.00	50
		Set value	7.25	1.25

Exist imperf. Value, set $22.50.
For surcharge see No. 27.

Nos. B1-B3 Surcharged in Black, Brown, Green or Blue:

a   дин. 1 din.

b   дин. 8 din.

1922-24

15	SP1(a)	1d on 10p	15	15
16	SP2(b)	1d on 15p ('24)	15	15
17	SP3(a)	1d on 25p (Br)	15	15
18	SP2(b)	1d on 15p (G)	70	15
a.		Blue surcharge	1.65	15
19	SP2(b)	8d on 15p (G)	1.25	15
a.		Double surcharge	32.50	30.00
b.		9d on 15p (error)	100.00	
20	SP2(b)	20d on 15p	6.00	1.00
21	SP2(b)	30d on 15p (Bl)	12.00	2.50
		Nos. 15-21 (7)	20.40	4.25

A3

1923, Jan. 23   **Engr.**

22	A3	1d red brown	65	15
23	A3	5d carmine	3.25	15
24	A3	8d violet	6.25	24
25	A3	20d green	16.00	75
26	A3	30d red orange	42.50	2.00
		Nos. 22-26 (5)	68.65	3.29

For surcharge see No. 28.

Nos. 8 and 24
Surcharged in Black or
Blue

napa 20 para

1924, Feb. 18

27	A1	20p on 60p ver	24	15
28	A3	5d on 8d violet (Bl)	4.75	60

The color of the surcharge on No. 28 varies,
including blue, blue black, greenish black and
black.

A4   A5

1924, July 1   **Perf. 14**

29	A4	20p black	90	15
30	A4	50p dark brown	90	15
31	A4	1d carmine	38	15
32	A4	2d myrtle green	75	15
33	A4	3d ultramarine	60	15
34	A4	5d orange brown	2.50	15
35	A5	10d dark violet	8.50	15
36	A5	15d olive green	5.00	20
37	A5	20d vermilion	4.50	15
38	A5	30d dark green	4.50	1.10
		Nos. 29-38 (10)	28.53	
		Set value		2.00

No. 33 Surcharged **П 50 Р**

1925, June 5

39	A4	25p on 3d ultramarine	15	15
40	A4	50p on 3d ultramarine	15	15
		Set value	20	16

King Alexander
A6   A7

1926-27   **Typo.**   **Perf. 13**

41	A6	25p deep green	15	15
42	A6	50p olive brown	20	15
43	A6	1d scarlet	30	15
44	A6	2d slate black	30	15
45	A6	3d slate blue	42	15
46	A6	4d red orange	2.00	15
47	A6	5d violet	1.50	15
48	A6	8d black brown	3.75	15
49	A6	10d olive brown	3.50	15
50	A6	15d brown ('27)	6.75	15
51	A6	20d dark vio ('27)	8.25	20
52	A6	30d orange ('27)	25.00	45
		Nos. 41-52 (12)	52.12	
		Set value		1.25

For overprints and surcharges see Nos. 53-62,
87-101, B5-B16.

Semi-Postal Stamps of 1926 Overprinted
over the Red Surcharge

XXXX

1928, July

53	A6	1d scarlet	1.25	15
a.		Surcharge "0.50" inverted		
54	A6	2d black	4.00	15
55	A6	3d deep blue	3.00	32
56	A6	4d red orange	9.25	40
57	A6	5d bright vio	3.00	15

58	A6	8d black brown	4.50	65
59	A6	10d olive brown	6.00	15
60	A6	15d brown	35.00	2.00
61	A6	20d violet	18.00	2.00
62	A6	30d orange	40.00	4.00
		Nos. 53-62 (10)	124.00	9.97

With Imprint at Foot

1931-34   **Perf. 12 1/2**

63	A7	25p black	70	15
64	A7	50p green	60	15
65	A7	75p slate green	15	15
66	A7	1d red	65	15
67	A7	1.50d pink	32	15
68	A7	1.75d dp rose ('34)	55	35
69	A7	3d slate blue	3.50	15
70	A7	3.50d ultra ('34)	1.10	28
71	A7	4d deep orange	2.00	15
72	A7	5d purple	2.00	15
73	A7	10d dark olive	5.50	15
74	A7	15d deep brown	5.50	15
75	A7	20d dark violet	9.25	15
76	A7	30d rose	6.00	45
		Nos. 63-76 (14)	37.82	
		Set value		1.80

Type of 1931 Issue
Without Imprint at Foot

1932-33

77	A7	25p black	15	15
78	A7	50p green	32	15
79	A7	1d red	65	15
80	A7	3d slate bl ('33)	1.65	15
81	A7	4d deep org ('33)	3.50	15
82	A7	5d purple ('33)	5.25	15
83	A7	10d dk olive ('33)	17.00	15
84	A7	15d deep brn ('33)	21.00	15
85	A7	20d dark vio ('33)	32.50	15
86	A7	30d rose ('33)	37.50	35
		Nos. 77-86 (10)	119.52	
		Set value		1.10

See Nos. 102-115.

ЈУГОСЛАВИЈА

Nos. 41 to 52
Overprinted

JUGOSLAVIJA

1933, Sept. 5   **Perf. 13**

87	A6	25p deep green	15	15
88	A6	50p olive brown	15	15
89	A6	1d scarlet	40	15
90	A6	2d slate black	1.75	70
91	A6	3d slate blue	1.65	15
92	A6	4d red orange	1.10	15
93	A6	5d violet	1.65	15
94	A6	8d black brown	4.75	1.00
95	A6	10d olive brown	6.75	15
96	A6	15d brown	8.25	1.75
97	A6	20d dark violet	15.00	15
98	A6	30d orange	13.00	65
		Nos. 87-98 (12)	54.60	
		Set value		5.00

Semi-Postal Stamps of 1926 Overprinted
like Nos. 87 to 98 and Four Bars over the
Red Surcharge of 1926

1933, Sept. 5

99	A6	25p green	50	15
100	A6	50p olive brown	60	15
101	A6	1d scarlet	1.25	40

Nos. 99-101 exist with double impression of
bars. Value, each $5.50 unused, $4.50 used.

King Alexander Memorial Issue
Type of 1931-34 Issues
Borders in Black

1934, Oct. 17

102	A7	25p black	15	15
103	A7	50p green	15	15
104	A7	75p slate green	15	15
105	A7	1d red	15	15
106	A7	1.50d pink	15	15
107	A7	1.75d deep rose	15	15
108	A7	3d slate blue	20	15
109	A7	3.50d ultramarine	25	15
110	A7	4d deep orange	35	15
111	A7	5d purple	42	15
112	A7	10d dark olive	1.65	15
113	A7	15d deep brown	3.00	15
114	A7	20d dark violet	4.50	15
115	A7	30d rose	3.00	20
		Nos. 102-115 (14)	14.27	
		Set value		1.15

King Peter II — A10

1935-36   **Perf. 13x12 1/2**

116	A10	25p brown black	15	15
117	A10	50p yel orange	15	15
118	A10	75p turq green	15	15
119	A10	1d brown red	15	15
120	A10	1.50d scarlet	15	15
121	A10	1.75d cerise	15	15
122	A10	2d magenta ('36)	15	15
123	A10	3d brn orange	15	15
124	A10	3.50d ultramarine	15	15
125	A10	4d yellow grn	75	15
126	A10	4d slate blue ('36)	15	15
127	A10	10d bright vio	35	15
128	A10	15d brown	60	20
129	A10	20d bright blue	2.25	15
130	A10	30d rose pink	1.50	25
		Nos. 116-130 (15)	6.95	
		Set value		1.30

The abbreviation "Din." is in Cyrillic characters
on Nos. 116, 118, 120, 123, 125, 126, 128 and
130.
For overprints see Nos. N12, 14, N29.

King Alexander   Nikola Tesla
A11   A12

1935, Oct. 9   **Perf. 12 1/2x11 1/2, 11 1/2**

131	A11	75p turq green	20	20
132	A11	1.50d scarlet	20	20
133	A11	1.75d dark brown	70	1.00
134	A11	3.50d ultramarine	70	1.00
135	A11	7.50d rose carmine	70	1.00
		Nos. 131-135 (5)	2.50	3.40

Death of King Alexander, 1st anniv.

Perf. 12 1/2x11 1/2

1936, May 28   **Litho.**

136	A12	75p yel grn & dk brn	15	15
137	A12	1.75d dl bl & indigo	22	20

80th birthday of Nikola Tesla (1856-1943), electrical inventor.
Lettering at side in Roman, at bottom in Serbian
on No. 136. This arrangement is reversed on No.
137.

Memorial   Coats of Arms of
Church,   Yugoslavia, Greece,
Oplenac   Romania and Turkey
A13   A14

1937, July 1

138	A13	3d Prussian grn	60	20
a.		Perf. 12 1/2	6.50	5.00
139	A13	4d dark blue	60	20

"Little Entente," 16th anniversary. "Yugoslavia"
in Cyrillic characters on No. 138.

Perf. 11, 11 1/2, 12 1/2

1937, Oct. 29   **Photo.**

140	A14	3d peacock grn	35	15
141	A14	4d ultramarine	45	32

Balkan Entente. "Yugoslavia" in Latin characters
on No. 141.

King Peter II — A16

1939-40   **Typo.**   **Perf. 12 1/2**

142	A16	25p black ('40)	15	15
143	A16	50p orange ('40)	15	15
144	A16	1d yellow grn	15	15
145	A16	1.50d red	15	15
146	A16	2d dp mag ('40)	15	15
147	A16	3d dull red brn	15	15
148	A16	4d ultra	15	15
148A	A16	5d dk blue ('40)	15	15
148B	A16	5.50d dk vio brn ('40)	22	15
149	A16	6d slate blue	42	15
150	A16	8d sepia	42	15
151	A16	12d bright vio	70	15
152	A16	16d dull violet	1.00	12
153	A16	20d blue ('40)	1.00	20
154	A16	30d brt pink ('40)	2.25	32
		Nos. 142-154 (15)	7.21	
		Set value		1.50

For overprints and surcharges see Nos. N1-N11,
N13, N15-N28, N30-N35, Croatia 1-25.

Arms of Yugoslavia, Greece, Romania
and Turkey
A17   A18

1940, June 1

155	A17	3d ultramarine	60	32
156	A18	3d ultramarine	60	32
a.		Pair, #155-156	2.00	2.00
157	A17	4d dark blue	60	32
158	A18	4d dark blue	60	32
a.		Pair, #157-158	2.00	2.00

Balkan Entente.

Bridge at
Obod — A19

1940, Sept. 29   **Litho.**

159	A19	5.50d slate grn & dull grn	1.50	1.75

Zagreb Phil. Exhib.; 500th anniv. of Johann
Gutenberg's invention of printing. The first press in
the Yugoslav area was located at Obod in 1493.

Issues for Federal Republic
Types of Serbia, 1942-43, Surcharged in
Green or Vermilion

Демократска
Федеративна
Југославија

+2

1944, Dec.   **Unwmk.**   **Perf. 11 1/2**
Overprinted with Pale Green Network

159A	OS4	5d (3d + 2d) rose pink	15	25
159B	OS4	10d (7d + 3d) dk sl grn (V)	15	25
		Set value		20

Similar Surcharge on Serbia Nos. 2N37-
2N39

1945, Jan. 24   **Without Network**

159C	OS4	5d (3d + 2d) rose pink	15	25
159D	OS4	10d (7d + 3d) dk sl grn (V)	15	25
159E	OS4	25d (4d + 21d) ultra (Bk)	15	25
		Set value		30

Marshal Tito (Josip Broz) — A20

Prohor Pcinski Monastery — A21

1945 **Photo.** **Perf. 12½**
160 A20 25p bright bl grn   32   15
161 A20 50p deep green   25   15
162 A20 1d crimson rose   1.25   15
163 A20 2d dark car rose   32   15
164 A20 4d deep blue   50   15
165 A20 5d deep green   15   40
166 A20 6d dark purple   40   15
167 A20 9d orange brown   50   20
168 A20 10d deep rose   15   40
169 A20 20d orange   2.50   25
170 A20 25d dark purple   17   60
171 A20 30d deep blue   20   70
Nos. 160-171 (12)   6.71 3.45

1945, Aug. 2 **Typo.** **Perf. 11½**
172 A21 2d red   60   15

Formation of the Popular Antifascist Chamber of Deputies of Macedonia, Aug. 2, 1944.

Partisans
A22   A23

Marshal Tito — A24   City of Jajce — A25

Partisan Girl and Flag — A26

1945, Oct. 10 **Litho.** **Perf. 12½**
173 A22 50p olive gray   15   15
174 A22 1d blue green   15   15
175 A23 1.50d orange brown 15   15
176 A24 2d scarlet   15   15
177 A25 3d red brown   65   15
178 A24 4d dark blue   15   15
179 A25 5d dark yel grn   65   15
180 A26 6d black   25   15
181 A26 9d deep plum   25   15
182 A23 12d ultramarine   40   15
183 A22 16d blue   40   15
184 A23 20d orange ver   1.00   20
Nos. 173-184 (12)   4.35
Set value   98

See Nos. 211-214. For surcharges and overprints see Nos. 202-203, 273-292, 286-289, Istria 42, 44, 46, 48, 50, Trieste 5-14.

"Labor" and "Agriculture"
A27   A28

1945, Nov. 29 **Photo.** **Perf. 12**
185 A27 2d brn carmine   2.25 2.00
186 A28 2d brn carmine   2.25 2.00
187 A27 4d deep blue   2.25 1.65
188 A28 4d deep blue   2.25 1.65

189 A27 6d dk slate grn   2.25 1.65
190 A28 6d dk slate grn   2.25 1.65
191 A27 9d red orange   2.25 1.65
192 A28 9d red orange   2.25 1.65
193 A27 16d bright ultra   2.25 1.65
194 A28 16d bright ultra   2.25 1.65
195 A27 20d dark brown   2.25 1.65
  a. Souv. sheet of 5, #191-195, perf. 11½   9.25 13.00
196 A28 20d dark brown   2.25 1.65
  a. Souv. sheet of 2, #192, 196, perf. 11½   9.25 13.00
Nos. 185-196 (12)   27.00 20.50
Se-tenant pairs, #185-196 (6) 30.00 30.00

Constitution for the Democratic Federation of Yugoslavia, Nov. 29, 1945.

Parade of Armed Forces
A31   Svetozar Markovic A32

1946, May 9 **Unwmk.** **Perf. 12½**
199 A31 1.50d org yel & red 30   22
200 A31 2.50d cerise & red   45   28
201 A31 5d blue & red   1.25   90

Victory over fascism, 1st anniv.

Type of 1945 Surcharged with New Values in Black

1946, Apr. 1
202 A26 2.50d on 6d bright red 90   15
203 A26 8d on 9d orange   95   15
Set value   15

1946, Sept. 22
204 A32 1.50d blue green   75   38
205 A32 2.50d dp red lilac 85   50

Markovic, Serbian socialist, birth cent. Latin and Cyrillic spellings of Yugoslavia are transposed on No. 205.

People's Theater, Sofia — A33

Sigismund Monument, Warsaw — A35

Designs: 1d, Prague. 2½d, Victory Monument, Belgrade. 5d, Spassky Tower, Kremlin.

1946, Dec. 8 **Litho.** **Perf. 11½**
206 A33 ½d dk brn & yel brn 15   15
207 A33 1d grnsh blk & emer 15   15
208 A35 1½d dk car rose & rose 15 15
209 A35 2½d hn brn & brn org 18 15
210 A35 5d dark bl & blue   32   20
Set value   72   55

Pan-Slavic Congress, Belgrade, Dec. 1946.

Types of 1945

1947, Jan. 15 **Litho.** **Perf. 12½**
211 A26 2.50d red orange   35   15
212 A25 3d dull red   35   15
213 A25 5d dark blue   1.10   15
214 A26 8d orange   90   15
Set value   38

Gorski Vijenac A38   Peter P. Nyegosh A39

1947, June 8 **Typo.**
215 A38 1.50d Prus grn & blk 15   15
216 A39 2.50d ol bis & dk car 25   20
217 A38 5d blue & black   25   22

Centenary of the Montenegrin national epic "Gorski Vijenac" (Wreath of Mountains) by Nyegosh.

Girls' Physical Training Classes — A40

Girl Runner — A41

Physical Culture Parade A42

1947, June 15 **Litho.** **Perf. 11**
218 A40 1.50d brown   16   16
219 A41 2.50d red   25   25
220 A42 4d violet blue   42   35

Natl. sports meet, Belgrade, June 15-22, 1947.

Map and Star — A43

1947, Sept. 16 **Typo.**
231 A43 2.50d dp car & dark bl 15 15
232 A43 5d org brn & dk grn   15 15

Annexation of Julian Province.

Music and One-string Gusle A44   Vuk Karadzic A45

1947, Sept. 27 **Perf. 11½x12, 12½**
233 A44 1.50d green   25   25
234 A45 2.50d orange red   25   25
235 A44 5d violet blue   25   25

Centenary of Serbian literature.

Symbols of Industry and Agriculture, Map and Flag — A46   Danube River Scene — A47

1948, Apr. 8 **Litho.** **Perf. 12½**
236 A46 1.50d grn, bl & salmon 15   15
237 A46 2.50d red brn, bl & sal 15   15
238 A46 5d dk bl, bl & sal   15   15
Set value   36   36

International Fair, Zagreb, May 8-17.

1948, July 30 **Unwmk.**
239 A47 2d green   2.50 1.40
240 A47 3d carmine   2.50 1.40
241 A47 5d blue   2.50 1.40
242 A47 10d brown orange   2.50 1.40

Danube Conference, Belgrade.

Marchers with Party Flag — A48   Laurent Kosir — A49

1948, July 21 **Perf. 11½, 12½**
243 A48 2d dark green   15   15
244 A48 3d dark red   24   18
245 A48 10d dark blue vio   35   20

5th Congress of the Communist Party in Yugoslavia, July 21, 1948. Commemorative inscription in Latin characters on No. 245.

1948, Aug. 21 **Perf. 12½**
246 A49 3d claret   15   15
247 A49 5d blue   18   15
248 A49 10d red orange   15   15
249 A49 12d dull green   18   15
Set value   54   42

80th death anniv. of Laurent Kosir, recognized by Yugoslavia as inventor of the postage stamp.

Arms of Bosnia and Herzegovina A50   Arms of Yugoslavia A51

1948, Nov. 29 **Perf. 12½, 12x11½**
Arms of Yugoslav Peoples Republics
250 A50 3d green   32   32
251 A50 3d rose lil (Macedonia) 32 32
252 A50 3d gray bl (Serbia) 32   32
253 A50 3d gray (Montenegro) 32   32
254 A50 3d rose (Croatia)   32   32
255 A50 3d orange (Slovenia) 32   32
256 A51 10d deep carmine   1.40 1.40
Nos. 250-256 (7)   3.32 3.32

The Cyrillic and Latin inscriptions are transposed on Nos. 252, 253 and 255.

Franc
Presern — A52

1949, Feb. 8   **Photo.**   *Perf. 11½*
257 A52   3d dark blue   32   15
258 A52   5d brown orange   32   15
259 A52   10d olive black   32   15

Death cent. of Franc Presern, poet.

Ski Jump,   Ski
Planica — A53   Jumper — A54

Perf. 12½x11½
1949, Mar. 20   **Litho.**
260 A53   10d magenta   85   55
261 A54   12d slate gray   85   55

Intl. Ski Championships, Planica, Mar. 13-20.

Soldiers — A55   Farmers — A56

Arms and Flags of
Macedonia and
Yugoslavia — A57

1949, Aug. 2   *Perf. 12½*
262 A55   3d carmine rose   20   22
263 A56   5d dull blue   20   22
264 A57   12d red brown   2.00   2.75

Liberation of Macedonia, 5th anniv.
It is reported that No. 264 was not sold to the
public at post offices.
For overprints see Nos. C30-C32.

Postal
Communications
A58

UPU, 75th anniversary: 5d, Plane, locomotive
and stagecoach, horiz.

1949, Sept. 8   **Unwmk.**
265 A58   3d red   1.25   1.25
266 A58   5d blue   30   30
267 A58   12d brown   30   30

For overprints see Trieste Nos. 15-16.

Locomotives
ФНРЈУГОСЛАВИЈА A60

1949, Dec. 15   **Photo.**
269 A60   2d Early steam   90   20
270 A60   3d Modern steam   90   20
271 A60   5d Diesel   2.50   28
272 A60   10d Electric   8.75   5.50

Centenary of Yugoslav railroads.
For overprints see Trieste Nos. 17-20.

Official Stamps
Nos. O7 and O8
Surcharged:

1949   **Typo.**
272A O1   3d on 8d chocolate   15   15
272B O1   3d on 12d violet   20   15
     Set value   18

Stamps of 1945 and 1947 Overprinted or
Surcharged in Black:

1949   **Litho.**
273 A22 (a)   50p olive gray   15   15
274 A22 (a)   1d blue green   15   15
275 A24 (b)   2d scarlet   15   15
276 A26 (c)   3d on 8d orange   15   15
277 A25 (d)   3d dull red   15   15
278 A25 (d)   5d dark blue   15   15
279 A23   10d on 20d org ver   24   15
280 A23   12d ultramarine   35   15
281 A23   16d blue   60   15
282 A23   20d orange ver   45   15
     Set value   2.15   75

On No. 279 the surcharge includes a rule below
"JUGOSLAVIJA" and "D 10" with two bars over
"20D."
See Nos. 286-289.

Surveying for
Highway — A61

Bridge, Map and
Automobile
A62

Highway
Completion
Symbolized
A63

1950, Jan. 16   **Photo.**   *Perf. 12½*
283 A61   2d blue green   35   35
284 A62   3d rose brown   15   15
285 A63   5d violet blue   80   80

Completion of Belgrade-Zagreb highway, Dec.
1949.

Types of 1945 Overprinted in Black
1950   **Unwmk.**   *Perf. 12½*
286 A22 (a)   1d brownish org   15   15
287 A24 (b)   2d blue green   15   15
288 A25 (d)   3d rose pink   15   15
289 A25 (d)   5d blue   25   15
     Set value   48   20

Marshal   Child
Tito — A64   Eating — A65

1950, Apr. 30   **Engr.**
290 A64   3d red   70   32
291 A64   5d dull blue   70   32
292 A64   10d brown   4.50   3.25
293 A64   12d olive black   1.25   70

Labor Day, May 1.

1950, June 1   **Photo.**
294 A65   3d brown red   25   15

Issued to publicize Children's Day, June 1.

Boy and Model   Map and Chess
Plane — A66   Symbols — A67

Designs: 3d, Glider aloft. 5d, Parachutists. 10d,
Aviatrix. 20d, Glider on field.

1950, July 2   **Engr.**
295 A66   2d dark green   65   32
296 A66   3d brown red   65   32
297 A66   5d violet   65   32
298 A66   10d chocolate   65   32
299 A66   20d ultramarine   5.50   4.00
     Nos. 295-299 (5)   8.10   5.28

Third Aviation Meet, July 2-11.

1950, Aug. 20   **Photo.**   *Perf. 11½*

Designs: 3d, Rook and ribbon. 5d, Globe and
chess board. 10d, Allegory of international chess.
20d, View of Dubrovnik, knight and ribbon.

300 A67   2d red brn & rose
         brown   45   35
301 A67   3d blk brn, gray brn &
         dl yellow   45   35
302 A67   5d dk grn, bl & buff   75   48
303 A67   10d cl, bl & org yel   1.10   60
304 A67   20d dk bl, bl & org yel-
         low   7.75   5.00
     Nos. 300-304 (5)   10.50   6.78

Intl. Chess Matches, Dubrovnik, Aug. 1950.

Electrification   Coal and Logs for
A68   Export
     A69

Designs: 50p, Metallurgy. 2d, Agriculture. 3d,
Construction. 5d, Fishing. 7d, Mining. 10d, Fruit-
growing. 12d, Lumbering. 16d, Gathering sunflowers. 20d, Livestock raising. 30d, Book manufacture. 50d, Loading ship.

1950-51   **Unwmk.**   **Engr.**   *Perf. 12½*
305 A68   50p dk brn ('51)   15   15
306 A68   1d blue green   15   15
307 A68   2d orange   15   15
308 A68   3d rose red   15   15
309 A68   5d ultramarine   30   15
310 A68   7d gray   30   15

---

311 A68   10d chocolate   50   15
312 A68   12d vio brn ('51)   1.25   15
313 A68   16d vio bl ('51)   1.75   30
314 A68   20d ol grn ('51)   1.75   25
314A A68   30d red brn ('51)   3.50   1.00
315 A68   50d violet ('51)   21.00   12.00
     Nos. 305-315 (12)   30.95   14.75

See Nos. 343-354, 378-384A. For overprints see
Trieste Nos. 68-75, 90-92.

1950, Sept. 23   **Photo.**
316 A69   3d red brown   32   15

Zagreb International Fair, 1950.

Early Sailing Vessel   Partisans with
"Dubrovnik" — A70   Flag — A71

Designs: 3d, Partisans in boat. 5d, Loading
freighter. 10d, Transatlantic ship "Zagreb." 12d,
Sailboats. 20d, Naval gun and ship.

1950, Nov. 29
317 A70   2d brown violet   15   15
318 A70   3d orange brown   15   15
319 A70   5d dull green   20   15
320 A70   10d chalky blue   32   20
321 A70   12d dark blue   70   32
322 A70   20d red brown   2.00   1.10
     Nos. 317-322 (6)   3.52   2.07

Yugoslav navy. Inscriptions on Nos. 318, 320
and 322 are in Cyrillic characters.

1951, Mar. 27   **Engr.**
323 A71   3d red & red brn   2.75   1.50

Yugoslavia's resistance to Nazi Germany, 10th
anniv.

Stane
Rozman — A72

Design: 5d, Post-boy during Slovene
insurrection.

1951, Apr. 27   **Photo.**
324 A72   3d brown red   35   24
325 A72   5d dark blue   60   42

Slovene insurrection, 10th anniv.

Children
Painting — A73

1951, June 3
326 A73   3d red   60   20

Issued to publicize Children's Day, June 3.

Zika   Serbian
Jovanovich — A74   Revolutionists — A75

1951, July 7
327 A74 3d brown red   45 25
328 A75 5d deep blue   70 42

Serbian insurrection, 10th anniv.

Sava Kovacevich
A76

Kovacevich Leading
Revolutionists
A77

1951, July 13
329 A76 3d rose pink   70 25
330 A77 5d light blue   1.00 42

Montenegrin insurrection, 10th anniv.

Monument to Marko
Oreskovich — A78

1951, July 27
331 A78 3d shown   45 25
332 A78 5d Monument to wounded   70 42

Croatian insurrection, 10th anniv.

Sium Bolaj
A79

Revolutionists of
Bosnia and
Herzegovina
A80

1951, July 27
333 A79 3d rose brown   35 18
334 A80 5d blue   75 42

Revolution in Bosnia and Herzegovina, 10th anniv.

Primoz
Trubar — A81

National
Handicrafts — A82

Portraits: 12d, Marko Marulic. 20d, Tsar Stefan Duschan.

1951, Sept. 9   Engr.
335 A81 10d slate gray   42 25
336 A81 12d brown orange   42 25
337 A81 20d violet   2.50 2.00

Yugoslav cultural anniversaries.
No. 337 is inscribed in Cyrillic.
For overprints see Trieste Nos. 40-41.

1951, Sept. 15 Litho. Perf. 11½
338 A82 3d multicolored   1.75 45

Zagreb International Fair, 1951.

Mirce
Acev — A83

Monument at
Skopje — A84

1951, Oct. 11
339 A83 3d deep plum   55 30
340 A84 5d indigo   1.10 65

Macedonian insurrection, 10th anniv.

Soldier and
Emblem — A85

Peter P.
Nyegosh — A86

1951, Dec. 22 Photo. Perf. 12½
341 A85 15d deep carmine   48 15

Army Day. See No. C54.

1951, Nov. 29   Engr.
342 A86 15d deep claret   2.00 55

Death centenary of Nyegosh. See note after No. 217.

Types of 1950-51
1951-52   Engr.

Designs: 15d, Gathering sunflowers. 25d, Agriculture. 35d, Construction. 75d, Lumbering. 100d, Metallurgy.

343 A68 1d gray ('52)   15 15
344 A68 2d rose car ('52)   24 15
345 A68 5d orange ('52)   1.10 15
346 A68 10d emerald ('52)   4.25 15
347 A68 15d rose car ('52)   9.50 1.50
348 A68 20d purple   2.00 15
349 A68 25d yel brn ('52)   6.25 18
350 A68 30d blue   1.10 15
351 A68 35d red brn ('52)   1.50 15
352 A68 50d greenish bl   1.10 15
353 A68 75d purple ('52)   1.75 18
354 A68 100d sepia ('52)   2.75 24
Nos. 343-354 (12)   31.69
Set value   2.50

Marshal Tito
A87   A88

1952, May 25 Photo. Perf. 11½
355 A87 15d shown   45 45
356 A88 28d shown   1.00 90
357 A87 50d Tito facing left   7.75 7.75

60th birthday of Marshal Tito

Child with
Ball — A89

1952, June 1 Litho. Perf. 12½
358 A89 15d bright rose   3.50 1.00

Issued to publicize Children's Day, June 1.

For overprint see Trieste No. 60.

Girl
Gymnast — A90

Split,
Dalmatia — A91

1952, July 10   Perf. 12½
359 A90 5d shown   50 35
360 A90 10d Runner   50 35
361 A90 15d Swimmer   50 35
362 A90 28d Boxer   50 35
363 A90 50d Basketball   4.00 2.00
364 A90 100d Soccer   8.50 6.25
Nos. 359-364 (6)   14.50 9.65

15th Olympic Games, Helsinki, 1952.
Nos. 360, 362 and 364 are inscribed in Cyrillic characters.
Nos. 359-364 exist imperf. Value $250.
For overprints see Trieste Nos. 51-56.

1952, Sept. 10   Litho.
365 A91 15d shown   1.10 1.10
366 A91 28d Naval scene   1.75 1.75
367 A91 50d St. Stefan   6.75 6.75

Yugoslav navy, 10th anniv.
For overprints see Trieste Nos. 57-59.

Belgrade, 16th
Century
A92

1952, Sept. 14 Engr. Perf. 11½
368 A92 15d violet brn   6.00 5.00

1st Yugoslav Phil. Exhib., Sept. 14-20. Sold only at the exhibition.

Marching Workers
and Congress
Flag — A93

1952, Nov. 2   Perf. 11½
369 A93 15d red brown   1.25 1.10
370 A93 15d dark vio blue   1.25 1.10
371 A93 15d dark brown   1.25 1.10
372 A93 15d blue green   1.25 1.10

6th Yugoslav Communist Party Congress, Zagreb.
For overprints see Trieste Nos. 61-64.

Nikola
Tesla — A94

Woman Pouring
Water — A95

1953, Jan. 7   Unwmk.
373 A94 15d brown carmine   65 15
374 A94 30d chalky blue   2.00 35

Death of Nikola Tesla, 10th anniv.
For overprints see Trieste Nos. 66-67.

1953, Mar. 24 Litho. Perf. 11½

Designs: 30d, Hands holding two birds. 50d, Woman holding Urn.

375 A95 15d dk olive green   90 32
376 A95 30d chalky blue   90 32
377 A95 50d henna brown   6.00 1.65

Issued to honor the United Nations.
See Nos. RA19 and RAJ16. For overprints see Trieste Nos. 76-78.

Types of 1950-52
1953-55 Litho. Perf. 12½

Designs: 8d, Mining. 17d, Livestock raising.

378 A68 1d dull gray   70 15
379 A68 2d carmine   2.50 15
380 A68 5d orange   3.50 15
381 A68 8d blue   2.50 15
382 A68 10d yellow green   5.50 15
383 A68 12d lt vio brown   25.00 20
384 A68 15d rose red   11.00 15
384A A68 17d vio brn ('55)   2.00 15
Nos. 378-384A (8)   52.70
Set value   78

For overprints see Trieste Nos. 68-75, 90-92.

Automobile Climbing
Mt. Lovcen — A96

Designs: 30d, Motorcycle and auto at Opatija. 50d, Racers leaving Belgrade. 70d, Auto near Mt. Triglav.

1953, May 10 Photo. Perf. 12½
385 A96 15d sal & dp plum   20 15
386 A96 30d bl & dark blue   28 15
387 A96 50d ocher & choc   45 16
388 A96 70d lt bl grn & ol grn   1.90 45
Set value   78

Intl. Automobile & Motorcycle Races, 1953.

President
Tito — A97

Star and Flag-
encircled
Globe — A98

1953, June 28 Engr. Unwmk.
389 A97 50d deep purple   4.25 1.25

Marshal Tito's election to the presidency, Jan. 14, 1953.
For overprint see Trieste No. 83.

1953, July 25 Engr.; Star Typo.
390 A98 15d gray & green   2.50 2.00

38th Esperanto Congress, Zagreb, July 25-Aug. 1.
For overprint see Trieste No. 84.

Macedonian
Revolutionary
A99

Nicolas Karev
A100

1953, Aug. 2   Litho.
391 A99 15d dark red brown   85 65
392 A100 30d dull green   3.00 1.75

Macedonian Insurection of 1903, 50th anniv.

Family — A101

Branko Radicevic — A102

1953, Sept. 6   **Photo.**
393 A101 15d deep green   10.00 2.50

Liberation of Istria and the Slovene coast, 10th anniv.
For overprint see Trieste No. 85.

1953, Oct. 1   **Engr.**
394 A102 15d lilac   4.25 1.50

10th death anniv. of Branko Radicevic, poet.
For overprint see Trieste No. 86.

View of Jajce — A103

Designs: 30d, First meeting place. 50d, Marshal Tito addressing Assembly.

1953, Nov. 29   **Perf. 12½x12**
395 A103 15d dark green   1.40 70
396 A103 30d rose car   1.90 1.10
397 A103 50d dark brown   7.75 7.00

2nd Assembly of the Natl. Republic of Yugoslavia, 10th anniv.
For overprints see Trieste Nos. 87-89.

Ground Squirrel A104

Lammergeier A105

1954, June 30   **Photo.**   **Perf. 11½**
398 A104   2d shown   22 15
399 A104   5d Lynx   20 15
400 A104 10d Red deer   20 15
401 A104 15d Brown bear   32 15
402 A104 17d Chamois   32 15
403 A104 25d White pelican   50 25
404 A105 30d shown   50 25
405 A105 35d Black beetle   50 25
406 A105 50d Bush cricket   4.00 1.65
407 A105 65d Adriatic lizard   8.25 3.50
408 A105 70d Salamander   7.25 3.50
409 A105 100d Trout   12.00 10.00
    Nos. 398-409 (12)   34.26 20.15

See Nos. 497-505. For overprints see Trieste Nos. 93-104.

> Catalogue values for unused stamps in this section, from this point to the end of the section, are for Never Hinged items.

Ljubljana, 17th Century A106

1954, July 29   **Engr.**
410 A106 15d vio blk, dk grn & dk brn   11.00 10.50

2nd Yugoslav Phil. Exhib., July 29-Aug. 8. Sold for 50d, which included admission to the exhibition.

Revolutionary Flag — A107

Engr. & Typo.

1954, Oct. 3   **Perf. 12½**
411 A107 15d shown   2.00 45
412 A107 30d Cannon   2.75 80
413 A107 50d Revolutionary seal   6.00 1.10
414 A107 70d Karageorge   22.50 4.75

1st Serbian insurrection, 150th anniv.
For overprints see Trieste Nos. 105-108.

Vatroslav Lisinski — A108

Portraits: 30d, Andrea Kacic-Miosic. 50d, Jure Vega. 70d, Jovan Jovanovic-Zmaj. 100d, Philip Visnic.

1955, Dec. 25   **Engr.**
415 A108   15d dark green   2.75 1.00
416 A108   30d chocolate   2.75 1.65
417 A108   50d dp claret   3.75 3.00
418 A108   70d indigo   7.50 7.00
419 A108 100d purple   19.00 19.00
    Nos. 415-419 (5)   35.75 31.65

Scene from "Robinja" — A109

"A Midsummer Night's Dream" — A110

1955   **Photo.**   **Perf. 12x11½, 12½**
Glazed Paper
420 A109 15d brown lake   90 55
421 A110 30d dark blue   3.25 1.65

Festival at Dubrovnik.

Dragon Emblem of Ljubljana — A111

1955   **Engr.**   **Perf. 12½**
422 A111 15d dk grn & brn   3.00 95

1st Intl. Exhib. of Graphic Arts, Ljubljana, July 3-Sept. 3.

Symbol of Sign Language — A112

Hops — A113

1955, Aug. 23
423 A112 15d rose lake   2.00 48

2nd World Congress of Deaf Mutes, Zagreb, Aug. 23-27.

1955, Sept. 24   **Photo.**   **Perf. 11½**

Medicinal Plants.

424 A113   5d shown   15 15
425 A113 10d Tobacco   15 15
426 A113 15d Poppy   15 15
427 A113 17d Linden   15 15
428 A113 25d Chamomile   15 15
429 A113 30d Salvia   30 15
430 A113 50d Dog rose   4.00 1.50
431 A113 70d Gentian   5.00 1.90
432 A113 100d Adonis   9.00 2.50
    Nos. 424-432 (9)   19.05 6.80

"Peace" Statue, New York — A114

Woman and Dove — A115

1955, Oct. 24   **Litho.**   **Perf. 12½**
433 A114 30d lt bl & blk   1.90 1.10

United Nations, 10th anniversary.

1955, Nov. 29   **Engr.**
434 A115 15d dull violet   65 20

10th anniv. of the "New Yugoslavia."

St. Donat, Zadar — A116

Cornice, Cathedral at Sibenik — A117

Yugoslav Art: 10d, Relief of a King, Split. 15d, Griffin, Studenica Monastery. 20d, Figures, Trogir Cathedral. 25d, Fresco, Sopocani Monastery. 30d, Tombstone, Radimlje. 40d, Ciborium, Kotor Cathedral. 50d, St. Martin from Tryptich, Dubrovnik. 70d, Figure, Belec Church. 100d, Rihard Jakopic, self-portrait. 200d, "Peace" Statue, New York.

1956, Mar. 24   **Photo.**   **Perf. 11½**
435 A116   5d blue vio   32 15
436 A116 10d slate grn   32 20
437 A116 15d olive brn   40 20
438 A116 20d brown car   40 30
439 A116 25d black brn   50 32
440 A116 30d dp claret   50 32
441 A117 35d olive grn   1.00 45
442 A117 40d red brown   1.25 52
443 A116 50d olive brn   2.75 45
444 A116 70d dk green   6.50 3.25
445 A116 100d dark pur   16.00 8.25
446 A116 200d deep blue   27.50 20.00
    Nos. 435-446 (12)   57.44 34.41

13th Century Tower, Zagreb A118

1956, Apr. 20   **Engr.**   **Perf. 11½**
Chalky Paper
447 A118 15d vio brn, bis brn & gray   40 20
    a.   Miniature sheet of 4   4.00 1.65

3rd Yugoslavia Phil. Exhib. (JUFIZ III), Zagreb, May 20-27. No. 447a was sold at the exhibition, tipped into a folder, for 75 dinars.
See No. C56.

Induction Motor — A119

Perf. 11½x12½

1956, July 10   **Photo.**
448 A119 10d shown   24 15
449 A119 15d Transformer   30 15
450 A119 30d Electronic controls   55 24
451 A119 50d Nikola Tesla   1.90 1.00

Birth cent. of Nikola Tesla, inventor.

Sea Horse — A120

Paper Nautilus — A121

Designs: 20d, European rock lobster. 25d, "Sea Prince." 30d, Sea perch. 35d, Red mullet. 50d, Scorpion fish. 70d, Wrasse. 100d, Dory.

1956, Sept. 10   **Perf. 11½**
Granite Paper
Animals in Natural Colors
452 A120 10d bright grn   15 15
453 A121 15d ultra & blk   15 15
454 A121 20d deep blue   18 15
455 A121 25d violet blue   24 15
456 A121 30d brt grnsh bl   28 15
457 A121 35d dk bl green   45 16
458 A121 50d indigo   2.00 70
459 A121 70d slate grn   3.00 80
460 A121 100d dark blue   8.50 3.50
    Nos. 452-460 (9)   14.95 5.91

Nos. 453, 455, 457 and 459 are inscribed in Cyrillic characters.

Runner A122

Centaury A123

Designs: 15d, Paddling kayak. 20d, Skiing. 30d, Swimming. 35d, Soccer. 50d, Water polo. 70d, Table tennis. 100d, Sharpshooting.

1956, Oct. 24   **Litho.**   **Perf. 12½**
Design and Inscription in Bister
461 A122 10d dk carmine   15 15
462 A122 15d dark blue   15 15
463 A122 20d ultramarine   15 15
464 A122 30d olive grn   18 15
465 A122 35d dark brown   25 15
466 A122 50d green   65 15
467 A122 70d brn violet   2.00 1.10
468 A122 100d dark red   4.75 2.25
    Nos. 461-468 (8)   8.28 4.25

16th Olympic Games, Melbourne, 11/22-12/8.
Nos. 462, 464, 466 and 468 have Latin characters at the top and Cyrillic characters at the bottom.

1957, May 25   Photo.   *Perf. 11½*

Medicinal Plants: 15d, Belladonna. 20d, Autumn crocus. 25d, Marsh mallow. 30d, Valerian. 35d, Woolly Foxglove. 50d, Aspidium. 70d, Green Winged Orchid. 100d, Pyrethrum.

Granite Paper
Flowers in Natural Colors

469	A123	10d dk bl & grn	15	15
470	A123	15d violet	15	15
471	A123	20d lt grn & brn	15	15
472	A123	25d dp cl & dk bl	24	15
473	A123	30d lilac rose & claret	38	15
474	A123	35d dk gray & dl pur	60	15
475	A123	50d dp grn & choc	1.00	32
476	A123	70d pale brn & grn	1.90	65
477	A123	100d gray & brown	5.75	1.25
		Nos. 469-477 (9)	10.32	
		Set value		2.60

See #538-546, 597-605, 689-694, 772-777.

Hand Holding
Factory — A124

1957, June 25   Engr.   *Perf. 12½*

478	A124	15d dark car rose	35	15
479	A124	30d violet blue	1.40	35

Congress of Workers' Councils, Belgrade, June 25. No. 479 inscribed in Cyrillic characters.

2nd Gymnastic Meet,
Zagreb, July 10-
14 — A125

Various gymnastic positions.

1957, July 1   Photo.

480	A125	10d ol grn & blk	25	15
481	A125	15d brn red & blk	25	15
482	A125	30d Prus bl & blk	55	15
483	A125	50d brn & black	2.25	1.25
		Set value		1.40

Montenegro
A126

Natl. Costumes: 15d, Macedonia. 30d, Croatia. 50d, Serbia. 70d, Bosnia and Herzegovina. 100d, Slovenia. 50d, 70d, 100d vert.

1957, Sept. 24   Typo.   *Perf. 12½*
Background in Bister Brown

484	A126	10d dk brn, ultra & red	15	15
485	A126	15d dk brn, blk & red	18	15
486	A126	30d dk brn, grn & red	22	15
487	A126	50d dk brn & green	55	22
488	A126	70d dk brn & black	65	38
489	A126	100d dk brn, grn & red	3.75	1.90
		Nos. 484-489 (6)	5.50	2.95

Revolutionists   Simon Gregorcic
A127   A128

Lithographed and Engraved
1957, Nov. 7   *Perf. 11½x12½*

490	A127	15d ocher & red	55	42

Russian Revolution, 40th anniv.

1957, Dec. 3   Engr.   *Perf. 12½*

Famous Yugoslavs: 30d, Anton Linhart, dramatist and historian. 50d, Oton Kucera, physicist. 70d, Stevan Mokranjac, composer. 100d, Jovan Sterija Popovic, writer

491	A128	15d sepia	48	15
492	A128	30d indigo	60	15
493	A128	50d reddish brn	1.25	15
494	A128	70d dl violet	4.25	1.60
495	A128	100d olive grn	14.00	12.00
		Nos. 491-495 (5)	20.58	13.95

"Young Man on   Stylized
Fire" — A129   Bird — A130

1958, Apr. 22   Photo.

496	A129	15d deep plum	38	15

Union of Yugoslav Communists, 7th congress, Ljubljana, Apr. 22.

Types of 1954

Game birds.

1958, May 25   *Perf. 11½*
Granite Paper
Birds in Natural Colors

497	A104	10d Mallard	15	15
498	A104	15d Capercaillie	15	15
499	A104	20d Ring-necked pheasant	15	15
500	A104	25d Coot	16	15
501	A104	30d Water rail	35	15
502	A104	35d Great bustard	45	15
503	A104	50d Rock partridge	1.90	50
504	A104	70d Woodcock	3.00	90
505	A105	100d Eurasian crane	6.50	2.25
		Nos. 497-505 (9)	12.81	
		Set value		4.00

1958, June 14   Engr.   *Perf. 12½*

506	A130	15d bluish black	50	22

Opening of Postal Museum, Belgrade.

Flag and
Laurel — A131

1958, July 1   Unwmk.

507	A131	15d brn carmine	38	15

15th anniv. of victory over Germans at Sutjeska, Bosnia.

Onufrio Well,
Dubrovnik — A132

1958, Aug. 10   Litho.   *Perf. 12½*

508	A132	15d black & brn	65	30

Marin Drzic, dramatist, 450th birth anniv.

Sisak Steel   Titograd Hotel and
Works   Open-Air Theater
A133   A134

Industrial Progress Designs: 2d, Crude oil production. 5d, Shipbuilding. 10d, Sisak steel works. 15d, Jablanica hydroelectric works. 17d, Lumber industry. 25d, Overpass, Zagreb-Ljubljana highway. 30d, Litostroy turbine factory. 35d, Lukavac coke plant. 50d, Bridge at Skopje. 70d, Railroad station, Sarajevo. 100d, Triple bridge, Ljubljana. 200d, Mestrovic station, Zagreb. 500d, Parliament, Belgrade.

1958   Typo.   *Perf. 12½ Horiz.*

509	A133	10d green	7.50	3.00
510	A133	15d orange ver	7.50	3.00

Engr.   *Perf. 12½*

511	A133	2d olive	15	15
512	A133	5d brown red	15	15
513	A133	10d green	15	15
514	A133	15d orange ver	16	15
515	A133	17d deep claret	15	15
516	A133	25d slate	16	15
517	A133	30d blue black	16	15
518	A133	35d rose red	16	15
519	A134	40d car rose	24	15
520	A134	50d bright bl	28	15
521	A134	70d orange ver	45	15
522	A134	100d green	2.25	15
523	A134	200d red brown	2.00	16
524	A134	500d intense bl	3.75	32
		Nos. 511-524 (14)	10.21	
		Set value		1.00

Nos. 509-510 are coil stamps. See #555-562, 627-645, 786-789, 830-840.

Ocean
Exploration — A135

1958, Oct. 24   Unwmk.

525	A135	15d brown violet	50	25

Intl. Geophysical Year, 1957-58. See #C58.

White and Black
Hands Holding
Scales — A136

1958, Dec. 10   *Perf. 12½*

526	A136	30d steel blue	55	30

Universal Declaration of Human Rights, 10th anniv.

Dubrovnik   Red Flags
A137   A138

Tourist attractions: No. 528, Bled. No. 529, Postojna grotto. No. 530, Ohrid. No. 531, Opatija. No. 532, Plitvice National Park. No. 533, Split. No. 534, Sveti Stefan. No. 535, Exhibition Hall, Belgrade.

1959, Feb. 16   Litho.   *Perf. 12½*

527	A137	10d crim rose & cit	15	15
528	A137	10d lt grn & lt vio bl	15	15
529	A137	15d grnsh bl & pur	15	15
530	A137	15d grn & bright bl	15	15
531	A137	20d lt grn & grnsh bl	15	15
532	A137	20d ol bis & brt grn	15	15
533	A137	30d yel org & purple	70	15
534	A137	30d lt vio bl & gray ol	70	15
535	A137	70d gray & grnsh bl	2.25	1.10
		Nos. 527-535 (9)	4.55	
		Set value		1.40

Nos. 527, 530, 532 and 534 are inscribed in Cyrillic characters. See #650-658, 695-700.

1959, Apr. 20   Unwmk.   *Perf. 12½*

536	A138	20d multicolored	22	15

Yugoslav Communist Party, 40th anniv.

Dubrovnik,
15th Century
A139

1959, May 24   Engr.   *Perf. 11½*

537	A139	20d yel grn, dk grn & bl	85	75

4th Yugoslavia Phil. Exhib. (JUFIZ IV), Dubrovnik.

Type of 1957

Medicinal Plants: 10d, Lavender. 15d, Black Alder. 20d, Scopolia. 25d, Monkshood. 30d, Bilberry. 35d, Juniper. 50d, Primrose. 70d, Pomegranate. 100d, Jimson weed.

1959, May 25   Photo.
Granite Paper
Flowers in Natural Colors

538	A123	10d lt bl & dk blue	15	15
539	A123	15d brt yel & car	15	15
540	A123	20d dk ol bis & mar	15	15
541	A123	25d ap grn & dk pur	15	15
542	A123	30d pink & dk bl	15	15
543	A123	35d bis brn & vio bl	38	18
544	A123	50d brn & green	95	30
545	A123	70d yel & ocher	1.25	45
546	A123	100d lt brn & brn	2.50	1.10
		Nos. 538-546 (9)	5.83	
		Set value		2.30

Tug of
War — A140

Sports: 15d, High jump and runners. 20d, Ring and parallel bar exercises. 35d, Women gymnasts. 40d, Sailors doing gymnastics. 55d, Field ball and basketball. 80d, Swimming. 100d, Festival emblem, vert.

1959, June 26   Litho.   *Perf. 12½*

547	A140	10d dk sl grn & ocher	15	15
548	A140	15d vio bl & sepia	15	15
549	A140	20d ol bis & dl lil	15	15
550	A140	35d deep cl & gray	15	15
551	A140	40d violet & gray	15	15
552	A140	55d sl grn & ol bis	16	15
553	A140	80d indigo & olive	75	38
554	A140	100d pur & bister	1.75	1.00
		Set value	2.95	1.70

Physical Culture Festival.

Types of 1958; Designs as before

Designs: 8d, Lumber industry. 15d, Overpass, Zagreb-Ljubljana highway. 20d, Jablanica hydroelectric works. 40d, Titograd Hotel. 55d, Bridge at Skopje. 80d, Railroad Station, Sarajevo.

1959   Typo.   *Perf. 12½ Horizontally*

555	A133	15d green	2.50	1.10
556	A133	20d orange ver	3.00	1.10

Engr.   *Perf. 12½*

557	A133	8d deep claret	25	15
558	A133	15d green	35	15
559	A133	20d orange ver	60	15
560	A134	40d bright blue	1.40	15
561	A134	55d carmine rose	2.25	15
562	A134	80d orange ver	3.75	15
		Nos. 557-562 (6)	8.60	
		Set value		30

Nos. 555-556 are coil stamps.

Fair
Emblem — A141

Athletics — A142

1959, Sept. 5   Litho.   Unwmk.
563 A141 20d lt vio bl & blk   55   20

50th International Fair at Zagreb.

1960, Apr. 25   Perf. 12½

564 A142	15d shown	15	15
565 A142	20d Swimming	15	15
566 A142	30d Skiing	15	15
567 A142	35d Wrestling	15	15
568 A142	40d Bicycling	16	15
569 A142	55d Yachting	24	15
570 A142	80d Horseback riding	60	35
571 A142	100d Fencing	80	48
Nos. 564-571 (8)		2.40	
Set value			1.25

17th Olympic Games.

Hedgehog
A143

1960, May 25   Photo.   Perf. 12x11½
Animals in Natural Colors

572 A143	15d shown	15	15
573 A143	20d Red squirrel	15	15
574 A143	25d Pine marten	15	15
575 A143	30d Hare	15	15
576 A143	35d Red fox	16	15
577 A143	40d Badger	20	15
578 A143	55d Wolf	40	28
579 A143	80d Roe deer	65	32
580 A143	100d Wild bear	1.40	1.00
Nos. 572-580 (9)		3.41	
Set value			2.05

"Yugoslavia" in Latin letters on Nos. 573, 575, 577, 579.

See Nos. 663-671.

Lenin, 90th Birth
Anniv.
A144

Atomic Accelerator
A145

1960, June 22   Engr.   Perf. 12½
581 A144 20d dk grn & slate grn   15   15

1960, Aug. 23   Unwmk.

582 A145	15d shown	15	15
583 A145	20d Generator	15	15
584 A145	40d Nuclear reactor	30	15
Set value		50	22

Nuclear energy exposition, Belgrade.

Serbian National
Theater, Novi
Sad — A146

Ivan Cankar,
Writer — A147

Designs: 20d, Woman from Croatian play. 40d, Edward Rusijan and early plane. 55d, Symbolic hand holding fruit. 80d, Atom and UN emblem.

1960, Oct. 24   Perf. 12½

585 A146	15d gray black	15	15
586 A146	20d brown	15	15
587 A146	40d dark gray blue	15	15
588 A146	55d dull claret	15	15
589 A146	80d dark green	30	15
Set value		70	35

Serbian Natl. Theater, Novi Sad, cent. (#585); Croatian Natl. Theater, Zagreb, cent. (#586); 1st flight in Yugoslavia, 50th anniv. (#587); 15th anniv. of the Yugoslav Republic (#588); UN, 15th anniv. (#589).

1960, Dec. 24   Engr.   Perf. 12½

Famous Yugoslavs: 20d, Silvije Strahimir Kranjcevic, poet. 40d, Paja Jovanovic, painter. 55d, Dura Jaksic, writer and painter. 80d, Mihajlo Pupin, electro-technician. 100d, Ruder Boskovic, mathematician.

590 A147	15d dark green	15	15
591 A147	20d henna brown	15	15
592 A147	40d olive bister	15	15
593 A147	55d magenta	18	15
594 A147	80d dark blue	30	15
595 A147	100d Prussian bl	60	30
Set value		1.30	60

International
Atomic Energy
Commission
Emblem
A148

Victims'
Monument,
Kragujevac
A149

Engr. & Litho.
1961, May 15   Perf. 12½
596 A148 25d multicolored   22   15

Intl. Nuclear Electronic Conf., Belgrade.

Flower Type of 1957

Medicinal plants: 10d, Yellow foxglove. 15d, Marjoram. 20d, Hyssop. 25d, Scarlet haw. 40d, Rose mallow. 50d, Soapwort. 60d, Clary. 80d, Blackthorn. 100d, Marigold.

1961, May 25   Photo.   Perf. 11½
Granite Paper
Flowers in Natural Colors

597 A123	10d lt bl & grnsh bl	15	15
598 A123	15d gray & chnt	15	15
599 A123	20d buff & green	24	15
600 A123	25d lt vio & vio	25	15
601 A123	40d lt ultra & ultra	40	15
602 A123	50d lt bl & blue	45	25
603 A123	60d beige & dk car rose	60	25
604 A123	80d lt grn & green	75	40
605 A123	100d redsh brn & choc	2.00	95
Nos. 597-605 (9)		4.99	
Set value			2.10

1961, July 3   Perf. 12x12½

Monuments: 15d, Stevan Filipovic, Valjevo. 20d, Relief from Insurrection, Bozansko Grahovo. 60d, Victory, Nova Gradiska. 100d, Marshal Tito, Titovo Uzice.

Granite Paper
Gold Frames and Inscriptions

606 A149	15d crimson & brn	15	15
607 A149	20d brn & ol bis	15	15
608 A149	25d bl grn & gray olive	15	15
609 A149	60d violet	28	15
610 A149	100d indigo & black	55	40
Set value		1.10	65

Souvenir Sheet
Imperf
611 A149 500d indigo & black   60.00 60.00

Natl. Insurrection, 20th anniv.

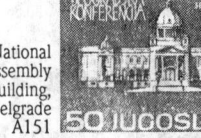
Men of Five
Races
A150

National
Assembly
Building,
Belgrade
A151

1961, Sept. 1   Litho.   Perf. 11½
613 A150 25d brown   15   15
Engr.
614 A151 50d blue green   20   15
Set value   15

Miniature Sheet
Imperf
615 A150 1000d claret   12.00 12.00

Conference of Non-aligned Nations, Belgrade, Sept. 1961. See Nos. C59-C60.

St. Clement, 14th
Century Wood
Sculpture — A152

1961, Sept. 10   Engr.   Perf. 12½
616 A152 25d sepia & olive   22   15

12th Intl. Congress for Byzantine Studies.

Serbian
Women — A153

Regional Costumes: 25d, Montenegro. 30d, Bosnia and Herzegovina. 50d, Macedonia. 65d, Croatia. 100d, Slovenia.

1961, Nov. 28   Litho.

617 A153	15d beige, brn & red	15	15
618 A153	25d beige, red brn & black	15	15
619 A153	30d beige, brn & dk red	15	15
620 A153	50d multicolored	15	15
621 A153	65d brn, red & yel	24	15
622 A153	100d multicolored	90	24
Set value		1.50	60

Luka
Vukalovic — A154

Hands with Flower
and Rifle — A155

1961, Dec. 15   Engr.
623 A154 25d slate blue   20   15

Centenary of Herzegovina insurrection.

1961, Dec. 22
624 A155 25d red & vio blue   20   15

20th anniversary of Yugoslav army.

Miladinov
Brothers — A156

1961, Dec. 25   Litho.
625 A156 25d buff & claret   20   15

Centenary of Macedonian folksong "Koder;" Dimitri and Konstantin Miladinov, brothers who collected and published folksongs. Monument is at Struga.

Types of 1958; Designs as Before

Designs: 5d, Shipbuilding. 8d, Lumber industry. 10d, Sisak steel works. 15d, Overpass. 20d, Jablanica hydroelectric works. 25d, Cable factory, Svetozarevo. 30d, Litostroy turbine factory. 40d, Lukavac coke plant. 50d, Zenica steel works. 65d, Sevojno copper works. 100d, Crude oil production. 150d, Titograd hotel. 200d, Bridge, Skoplje. 300d, Railroad station, Sarajevo. 500d, Triple bridge, Ljubljana. 1000d, Mestrovic station, Zagreb. 2000d, Parliament, Belgrade.

1961-62   Typo.   Perf. 12½ Horiz.

627 A133	10d dark red brn	3.00	52
628 A133	15d emerald	5.25	28

Engr.   Perf. 12½

629 A133	5d dull orange	15	15
630 A133	8d gray	15	15
631 A133	10d dk red brn	15	15
632 A133	15d emerald	15	15
633 A133	20d violet blue	15	15
634 A133	25d vermilion	15	15
635 A133	30d red brown	15	15
636 A133	40d dp cl ('62)	15	15
637 A133	50d gray blue	24	15
638 A133	65d green	15	15
639 A133	100d yel olive	1.75	15
640 A134	150d car ('62)	42	15
641 A134	200d sl grn ('62)	42	15
642 A134	300d olive ('62)	90	15
643 A134	500d dl violet	90	15
644 A134	1000d bister brn	2.00	18
645 A134	2000d claret	4.50	30
Nos. 629-645 (17)		12.48	
Set value			1.10

Nos. 627-628 are coil stamps. For surcharges see Nos. 786, 789.

Isis of
Kalabsha — A157

Joy of Motherhood
by Frano
Krsinic — A158

Design: 50d, Ramses II, Abu Simbel.

1962, Apr. 7   Engr.   Perf. 12½
646 A157 25d grnsh blk, cream   16   15
647 A157 50d brown, buff   35   15
Set value   15

15th anniv. (in 1961) of UNESCO.

1962, Apr. 7
648 A158 50d black, cream   32   15

15th anniv. (in 1961) of UNICEF.

Anopheles
Mosquito — A159

1962, Apr. 7   Unwmk.
649 A159 50d black, gray   30   15

WHO drive to eradicate malaria.

Scenic Type of 1959

Tourist attractions: No. 650, Portoroz. No. 651, Jajce. No. 652, Zadar. No. 653, Popova Sapka. No. 654, Hvar. No. 655, Bay of Kotor. No. 656, Danube, Iron Gate. No. 657, Rab. No. 658, Zagreb.

1962, Apr. 24   **Litho.**

650	A137	15d ol & chlky bl	15	15
651	A137	15d blue grn & bis	15	15
652	A137	25d blue & red brn	15	15
653	A137	25d dk bl & pale bl	15	15
654	A137	30d blue & brn org	20	15
655	A137	30d gray & chlky bl	30	15
656	A137	50d ol & grnsh bl	65	15
657	A137	50d blue & olive	65	15
658	A137	100d dk grn & gray bl	3.00	40
		Nos. 650-658 (9)	5.40	
		Set value		85

Nos. 651, 653, 655 and 656 are inscribed in Cyrillic characters.

Marshal Tito, by Augustincic
A160

Pole Vault
A161

Design: 50d, 200d, Sideview of bust by Antun Augustincic.

1962, May 25   **Engr.**   *Perf. 12½*

659	A160	25d dark green	15	15
660	A160	50d dark brown	15	15
661	A160	100d dark blue	60	30
662	A160	200d greenish blk	2.50	90
a.		Souv. sheet of 4, #659-662, imperf.	12.00	12.00
		Set value		1.30

70th birthday of Pres. Tito (Josip Broz).

Animal Type of 1960

Designs: 15d, Crested newt. 20d, Fire salamander. 25d, Yellow-bellied toad. 30d, Pond frog. 50d, Pond turtle. 65d, Lizard. 100d, Emerald lizard. 150d, Leopard snake. 200, European viper (adder).

1962, June 8 **Photo.** *Perf. 12x11½*
Animals in Natural Colors

663	A143	15d green	15	15
664	A143	20d purple	15	15
665	A143	25d chocolate	15	15
666	A143	30d violet blue	15	15
667	A143	50d dark red	20	15
668	A143	65d bright grn	32	15
669	A143	100d black	52	30
670	A143	150d brown	1.40	60
671	A143	200d car rose	3.00	1.25
		Nos. 663-671 (9)	6.04	
		Set value		2.50

Latin inscription on Nos. 666-669.

1962, July 10   **Litho.**   *Perf. 12½*

Sports: 25d, Woman discus thrower, horiz. 30d, Long distance runners. 50d, Javelin thrower, horiz. 65d, Shot put. 100d, Women runners, horiz. 150d, Hop, step and jump. 200d, High jump, horiz.

Athletes in Black

672	A161	15d blue	15	15
673	A161	25d magenta	15	15
674	A161	30d emerald	15	15
675	A161	50d red	15	15
676	A161	65d vio blue	18	15
677	A161	100d green	55	15
678	A161	150d orange	65	30
679	A161	200d orange brn	1.25	60
		Nos. 672-679 (8)	3.23	
		Set value		1.25

7th European Athletic Championships, Belgrade, Sept. 12-16. See No. C61.

Child at Play — A162

Litho. & Engr.
1962, Oct. 1   *Perf. 12½*

680	A162	25d red & black	32	15

Issued for Children's Week.

Gold Mask, Trebeniste, 5th Century B.C.
A163

Bathing the Infant Christ, Fresco, Decani Monastery
A164

Yugoslav Art Treasures: 25d, Horseman and bird, bronze vase (5th cent. B.C.). 50d, God Kairos, marble relief. 65d, "The Pigeons of Nerezi," fresco (12th cent.). 150d, Archangel Gabriel, icon (14th cent.).

1962, Nov. 28   **Photo.**

681	A163	25d Prus bl, blk & gold	15	15
682	A163	30d gold, saph & blk	15	15
683	A164	50d dk grn, brn & gold	18	15
684	A164	65d multicolored	35	22
685	A164	100d multicolored	48	60
686	A163	150d multicolored	1.90	1.10
		Nos. 681-686 (6)	3.21	2.37

Latin letters on Nos. 681, 683-684, 686.

Parched Earth and Wheat — A165

Dr. Andrija Mohorovicic and UN Emblem — A166

1963, Mar. 21   **Engr.**   *Perf. 12½*

687	A165	50d dark brn, *tan*	25	15

FAO "Freedom from Hunger" campaign.

1963, Mar. 23   **Unwmk.**

688	A166	50d dk blue, *gray*	25	15

UN 3rd World Meteorological Day, Mar. 23. Dr. Mohorovicic (1857-1936) was director of the Zagreb meteorological observatory.

Flower Type of 1957

Medicinal Plants: 15d, Lily of the valley. 25d, Iris. 30d, Bistort. 50d, Henbane. 65d, St. John's wort. 100d, Caraway.

1963, May 25   **Photo.**   *Perf. 11½*
Granite Paper
Flowers in Natural Colors

689	A123	15d gray grn & grn	15	15
690	A123	25d lt bl, ultra & pur	15	15
691	A123	30d gray & black	15	15
692	A123	50d redsh brn & red brn	15	15
693	A123	65d pale brn & brn	35	15
694	A123	100d slate & blk	1.00	35
		Set value	1.70	65

Scenic Type of 1959

Tourist attractions: 15d, Pula. 25d, Vrnjacka Banja. 30d, Crikvenica. 50d, Korcula. 65d, Durmitor mountain. 100d, Ljubljana.

1963, June 6   **Litho.**   *Perf. 12½*

695	A137	15d multicolored	15	15
696	A137	25d multicolored	15	15
697	A137	30d multicolored	15	15
698	A137	50d multicolored	15	15
699	A137	65d multicolored	15	15
700	A137	100d multicolored	85	25
		Set value	1.30	60

Nos. 696 and 699 are inscribed in Cyrillic characters.

Partisans on the March, by Djordje Andrejevic-Kun
A167

Sutjeska (Gorge)
A168

Design: No. 702A, As 15d, but inscribed "Vis 1944-1964." 50d, Partisans in battle.

Engr. & Litho.; Litho. (No. 702)
1963-64   *Perf. 12½, 11½*

701	A167	15d gray & dk sl grn	15	15
702	A168	25d dark slate grn	15	15
702A	A167	25d gray & dark car rose	15	15
703	A167	50d tan & purple	20	15
		Set value	48	20

20th anniv. of the Partisan Battle of Sutjeska (Nos. 701, 702-703); 20th anniv. of the arrival of the Yugoslav General Staff on the island of Vis (No. 702A).

Issue dates: No. 702A, July 27, 1964. Others, July 3, 1963.

Gymnast on Vaulting Horse — A169

Mother, by Ivan Mestrovic — A170

1963, July 6   **Litho.**   *Perf. 12½*

704	A169	25d shown	15	15
705	A169	50d Parallel bars	20	15
706	A169	100d Rings	55	38
		Set value	62	52

5th Gymnastics Europa Prize.

1963, Sept. 28   **Engr.**

Sculptures by Mestrovic (1883-1962): 50d, "Reminiscences" (woman). 65d, Head of Kraljevic Marko. 100d, Indian on Horseback.

707	A170	25d brown, *buff*	15	15
708	A170	50d sl green, *grnsh*	15	15
709	A170	65d grnsh blk, *grysh*	70	30
710	A170	100d black, *grayish*	1.00	60
				1.05

Children with Toys — A171

1963, Oct. 5   **Litho.**

711	A171	25d multicolored	35	15

Issued for Children's Week.

Soldier with Gun and Flag — A172

Litho. & Engr.
1963, Oct. 20   *Perf. 12½*

712	A172	25d ver, tan & gold	15	15

Yugoslavian Democratic Federation, 20th anniv.

Relief from Tombstone, Herzegovina
A173

Dositej Obradovic
A174

Art through the centuries: 30d, Horseback trio, Split Cathedral, horiz. 50d, King and queen on horseback, Beram Church, Istria, horiz. 65d, Archangel Michael, Dominican monastery, Dubrovnik. 100d, Man pouring water, fountain, Ljubljana. 150d, Archbishop Eufrasie, mosaic, Porec Basilica, Istria.

1963, Nov. 29   **Photo.**

713	A173	25d multicolored	15	15
714	A173	30d multicolored	15	15
715	A173	50d multicolored	15	15
716	A173	65d multicolored	24	15
717	A173	100d multicolored	32	24
718	A173	150d multicolored	1.25	80
		Nos. 713-718 (6)	2.26	
		Set value		1.25

Issued for the Day of the Republic.

1963, Dec. 10   **Engr.**

Famous Yugoslavians: 30d, Vuk Stefanovic Karadzic, reformer of Serbian language. 50d, Franc Miklosic, Slovenian philologist. 65d, Ljudevit Gaj, reformer of Croatian language. 100d, Peter Petrovich Nyegosh, Montenegrin prince, bishop and poet.

Variously Toned Paper

719	A174	25d black	15	15
720	A174	30d black	15	15
721	A174	50d black	15	15
722	A174	65d black	42	20
723	A174	100d black	70	50
		Nos. 719-723 (5)	1.57	
		Set value		88

Vanessa Io — A175

Fireman Rescuing Child — A176

Designs (Butterflies and Moths): 30d, Vanessa antiopa. 40d, Daphnis nerii. 50d, Parnassius apollo. 150d, Saturnia pyri. 200d, Papilio machaon.

1964, May 25   **Photo.**   *Perf. 12½*

724	A175	25d multicolored	15	15
725	A175	30d multicolored	15	15
726	A175	40d multicolored	15	15
727	A175	50d multicolored	15	15
728	A175	150d multicolored	45	30
729	A175	200d multicolored	75	40
		Nos. 724-729 (6)	1.80	
		Set value		85

1964, June 14   **Litho.**

730	A176	25d red & black	25	15

Centenary of voluntary firemen.

Runner — A177

1964, July 1   **Unwmk.**   *Perf. 12½*

731	A177	25d shown	15	15
732	A177	30d Boxing	15	15
733	A177	40d Rowing	15	15
734	A177	50d Basketball	15	15
735	A177	150d Soccer	45	24
736	A177	200d Water polo	75	35
		Set value	1.50	75

18th Olympic Games, Tokyo, Oct. 10-25.

UN Flag over
Scaffolding — A178

Design: 25d, Upheaval of the earth and scaffolding.

1964, July 26   **Engr.**
737 A178 25d red brown   15 15
738 A178 50d blue   20 15
Set value   26 15

Earthquake at Skopje; 1st anniv.

Serbian
Women — A179

Friedrich
Engels — A180

Regional Costumes: 30d, Slovenia. 40d, Bosnia and Herzegovina. 50d, Croatia. 150d, Macedonia. 200d, Montenegro.

1964, Aug. 5   **Litho.**
Costumes Multicolored
740 A179 25d violet & brn   15 15
741 A179 30d slate & green   15 15
742 A179 40d redsh brn & blk   15 15
743 A179 50d blue & black   15 15
744 A179 150d dl grn & sepia   52 24
745 A179 200d tan, red & brn   65 45
Set value   1.50 85

Litho. & Engr.
1964, Sept. 27   **Perf. 11½**
746 A180 30d shown   15 15
747 A180 50d Karl Marx   20 15
Set value   15

1st Socialist Intl., London, Sept. 28, 1864.

Children at
Play — A181

1964, Oct. 4   **Litho.**   **Perf. 12½**
748 A181 25d ver, pink & gray grn   35 15

Issued for Children's Week.

The Victor by Ivan
Mestrovic — A182

1964, Oct. 20   **Engr.**   **Perf. 11½**
749 A182 25d gold & blk, pnksh   15 15

Liberation of Belgrade, 20th anniv.

Initial from
Evangel of
Hilandar
A183

Hand, "Liberty
and Equality"
A184

Art through the centuries: 30d, Initial from Evangel of Miroslav (musician). 40d, Detail from Cetigne octavo, 1494 (saint with scroll). 50d, Miniature from Evangel of Trogir, 13th cent. (female saint). 150d, Miniature from Hrovoe Missal, 15th cent. (knight on horseback). 200d, Miniature from 14th cent. manuscript (symbolic fight), horiz.

Perf. 11½x12, 12x11½
1964, Nov. 29   **Photo.**   **Unwmk.**
750 A183 25d multicolored   15 15
751 A183 30d multicolored   15 15
752 A183 40d multicolored   15 15
753 A183 50d multicolored   15 15
754 A183 150d multicolored   42 24
755 A183 200d multicolored   90 42
Set value   1.60 85

Issued for Day of the Republic.

1964, Dec. 7   **Perf. 12**
Designs: 50d, Dove over factory, "Peace and Socialism." 100d, Smokestacks, "Building Socialism."
756 A184 25d multicolored   15 15
757 A184 50d multicolored   18 15
758 A184 100d multicolored   40 25
Set value   38

Yugoslav Communist League, 8th congress.

Table Tennis
Player — A185

Titograd — A186

1965, Apr. 15   **Litho.**   **Perf. 12½**
759 A185 50d shown   18 15
760 A185 150d Player at left   40 25
Set value   32

28th Table Tennis Championships, Ljubljana, Apr. 15-25.

1965, May 8   **Engr.**
761 A186 25d shown   15 15
762 A186 30d Skopje   15 15
763 A186 40d Sarajevo   15 15
764 A186 50d Ljubljana   15 15
765 A186 150d Zagreb   30 15
766 A186 200d Belgrade   65 40
Set value   1.30 75

Liberation of Yugoslavia from the Nazis, 20th anniv.

Young
Pioneer — A187

ITU Emblem and
Television
Tower — A188

1965, May 10   **Litho. & Engr.**
767 A187 25d blk & tan, buff   15 15
Young Pioneer Games "20 Years of Freedom."

1965, May 17   **Engr.**
768 A188 50d dark blue   15 15
ITU, centenary.

Iron Gate,
Danube
A189

Arms of Yugoslavia and Romania and
Djerdap Dam — A190

Design: 50d (55b), Iron Gate hydroelectric plant and dam.

1965, May 20   **Litho.**   **Perf. 12½x12**
769 A189 25d (30b) lt bl & grn   15 15
770 A189 50d (55b) lt bl & dk red   24 15
Set value   28 15

Miniature Sheet
Perf. 13½x13
771 A190   Sheet of 4   2.50 2.50
   a.   100d multicolored   35 35
   b.   150d multicolored   70 70

Nos. 769-771 were issued simultaneously by Yugoslavia and Romania to commemorate the start of the construction of the Iron Gate hydroelectric plant. Nos. 769-770 were valid for postage in both countries.
No. 771 contains one each of Nos. 771a, 771b and Romania Nos. 1747a and 1747b. Only Nos. 771a and 771b were valid in Yugoslavia. Sold for 500d.
See Romania Nos. 1745-1747.

Flower Type of 1957
Medicinal Plants: 25d, Milfoil. 30d, Rosemary. 40d, Inula. 50d, Belladonna. 150d, Mint. 200d, Foxglove.

1965, May 25   **Photo.**   **Perf. 11½**
Granite Paper
Flowers in Natural Colors
772 A123 25d deep carmine   15 15
773 A123 30d olive bister   15 15
774 A123 40d red brown   15 15
775 A123 50d dark blue   18 15
776 A123 150d violet blue   42 25
777 A123 200d purple   90 70
Nos. 772-777 (6)   1.95
Set value   1.10

Intl. Cooperation
Year
Emblem — A191

1965, June 26   **Litho.**   **Perf. 12½**
778 A191 50d dk bl & dull bl   18 15

Sibenik — A192

Cat — A193

1965, July 6   **Unwmk.**   **Perf. 12½**
779 A192 25d Rogaska Slatina   15 15
780 A192 30d shown   15 15
781 A192 40d Prespa Lake   15 15
782 A192 50d Prizren   15 15
783 A192 150d Scutari   35 16
784 A192 200d Sarajevo   70 55
Set value   1.35 85

1965, Oct. 3   **Litho.**   **Perf. 12½**
785 A193 30d maroon & brt yel   65 15

Issued for Children's Week.

**Nos. 630 and 634 Surcharged in Maroon
and Type of 1958**

Designs: 20d, Jablanica hydroelectric works. 30d, Litostroy turbine factory.

1965   **Engr.**   **Perf. 12½**
786 A133 5d on 8d gray   60 15
787 A133 20d emerald   52 15
788 A133 30d red orange   80 15
789 A133 50d on 25d vermilion   60 15
Set value   20

Branislav
Nusic — A194

Marshal
Tito — A195

Famous Yugoslavs: 50d, Antun Gustav Matos, poet. 60d, Ivan Mazuranic, writer. 85d, Fran Levstik, writer. 200d, Josif Pancic, physician and botanist. 500d, Dimitrije Tucovic, political writer.

1965, Nov. 28   **Engr.**
Variously Toned Paper
790 A194 30d dull red   15 15
791 A194 50d indigo   15 15
792 A194 60d brown   15 15
793 A194 85d dark blue   15 15
794 A194 200d dk olive grn   24 16
795 A194 500d deep claret   75 55
Set value   1.25 90

1966, Feb. 4   **Litho.**   **Perf. 12½**
796 A195 20p bluish grn   48 15
797 A195 30p rose pink   65 15
Set value   15

Rowing — A196

Designs: 30p, Long jump. 50p, Ice hockey. 3d, Hockey sticks and puck. 5d, Oars and scull.

1966, Mar. 1   Engr.

798	A196	30p dk car rose	15 15
799	A196	50p dk purple	15 15
800	A196	1d gray green	15 15
801	A196	3d dk red brn	42 15
802	A196	5d dark blue	75 60
		Set value	1.40 85

25th Balkan Games; World ice hockey championship; 2nd rowing championships.

"T" from 15th Century Psalter — A197   Radio Amateurs' Emblem — A198

Art through the Centuries (Initials from Medieval Manuscripts): 50p, Cyrillic "V," Divosh Evangel, 14th century. 60p, "R," Gregorius I, Libri moralium, 12th century. 85p, Cyrillic "P," Miroslav Evangel, 12th century. 2d, Cyrillic "B," Radomir Evangel, 13th century. 5d, "F," Passional, 11th century.

1966, Apr. 25   Photo.   Perf. 12

803	A197	30p multicolored	15 15
804	A197	50p multicolored	15 15
805	A197	60p multicolored	15 15
806	A197	85p multicolored	15 15
807	A197	2d multicolored	40 20
808	A197	5d multicolored	80 60
		Set value	1.50 90

1966, May 23   Engr.   Perf. 12½x12

809	A198	85p dark blue	18 15

Union of Yugoslav Radio Amateurs, 20th anniv.; Intl. Congress of Radio Amateurs, Opatija, 5/23-28.

Stag Beetle — A199   Serbia No. 2, 1866 — A200

Beetles: 50p, Floral beetle. 60p, Oil beetle. 85p, Ladybird. 2d, Rosalia alpina. 5d, Aquatic beetle.

1966, May 25   Photo.   Perf. 12x12½

810	A199	30p gray, blk & bis	15 15
811	A199	50p gray, emer & blk	15 15
812	A199	60p bluish blk, sl grn & gray	15 15
813	A199	85p dl org, dp org & black	15 15
814	A199	2d gray, ultra & blk	28 15
815	A199	5d tan, brn & blk	48 45
		Set value	1.05 75

Litho. & Engr.
1966, June 25   Perf. 12½

816	A200	30p shown	15 15
817	A200	50p No. 3	15 15
818	A200	60p No. 4	15 15
819	A200	85p No. 5	24 15
820	A200	2d No. 6	60 38
		Set value	1.10 70

Souvenir Sheet
Imperf

821	A200	10d No. 1	2.50 2.50

Serbia's first postage stamps, cent.

Leather Shield with Farmer, Soldier and Woman — A201   Bishop Strossmayer and Franjo Racki — A202

1966, July 2   Perf. 12½

822	A201	20p pale grn, gold & red brown	15 15
823	A201	30p buff, gold & dp mag	15 15
824	A201	85p lt gray, gold & Prus bl	15 15
825	A201	2d lt bl, gold & vio	24 24
		Set value	42 40

25th anniversary of National Revolution.

1966, July 15

826	A202	30p dl ol, blk & buff	15 15

Centenary of Academy of Arts and Sciences, founded by Bishop Josip Juraj Strossmayer with Racki as first president.

Mostar Bridge, Neretva River — A203

1966, Sept. 24   Engr.   Perf. 12½

827	A203	30p rose claret	2.00 25

400th anniversary of Mostar Bridge.

Medieval View of Sibenik — A204

1966, Sept. 24

828	A204	30p deep plum	40 15

900th anniversary of Sibenik.

Girl A205   Shipbuilding A206

1966, Oct. 2   Litho.

829	A205	30p ultra, org, red & blk	1.00 15

Issued for Children's Week.

1966   Engr.   Perf. 12½

Designs: 10p, Sisak steel works. 15p, Overpass. 20p, Jablonica hydroelectric works. 30p, Litostroy turbine factory. 40p, Lukavac coke factory. 50p, Zenica steel works. 60p, Cable factory, Svetozarevo. 65p, Sevojno copper works. 85p, Lumber industry. 1d, Crude oil production.

830	A206	5p dull orange	15 15
831	A206	10p brown	15 15
832	A206	15p vio blue	15 15
833	A206	20p emerald	30 15
834	A206	30p vermilion	1.10 15
835	A206	40p dp claret	18 15
836	A206	50p gray blue	24 15
837	A206	60p red brown	28 15
838	A206	65p green	35 15
839	A206	85p dl purple	55 15
840	A206	1d yel olive	80 15
		Nos. 830-840 (11)	4.25
		Set value	50

Issued: 5, 15p, June 10. 10, 40, 50p, June 8. 20, 30p, Apr. 28. 60, 65, 85p, May 12. 1d, June 18. For surcharge see No. 1322.

UNESCO Emblem — A207   Santa Claus — A208

1966, Nov. 4   Litho.

841	A207	85p violet blue	22 15

20th anniversary of UNESCO.

1966, Nov. 25   Litho.   Perf. 12½

Designs: 15p, Stylized winter landscape. 30p, Stylized Christmas tree.

842	A208	15p org & dk bl	15 15
843	A208	20p org & purple	15 15
844	A208	30p org & sl grn	15 15

1966, Dec. 23   Photo.   Perf. 12½

845	A208	15p gold & dk bl	30 22
846	A208	20p gold & red	30 22
847	A208	30p gold & green	30 22
		Set value, #842-847	1.12 75

Nos. 842-847 issued for New Year, 1967.

Wolf's Head Coin of Durad I, 1373 — A209

Medieval Coins: 50p, ½d of King Stefan, c. 1461 (arms of Bosnia). 60d, Dinar of Serbia (portrait of Durad Brankovic). 85p, Dinar of Ljubljana, c. 1250 (heraldic eagle). 2d, Dinar of Split, c. 1403-1413 (shield with arms of Duke Hrvoje Vukcic). 5d, Dinar of Emperor Stefan Dusan, c. 1346-1355 (Emperor on horseback).

1966, Nov. 28   Photo.
Coins in Silver, Gray and Black

848	A209	30p ver & blk	15 15
849	A209	50p ultra & blk	15 15
850	A209	60p magenta & blk	15 15
851	A209	85p violet & blk	15 15
852	A209	2d dk ol bis & blk	25 15
853	A209	5d brt grn & blk	65 35
			1.20 65

Medicinal Plants — A210   Marshal Tito — A211

1967, May 25   Photo.   Perf. 11½
Granite Paper

854	A210	30p Arnica	15 15
855	A210	50p Flax	15 15
856	A210	85p Oleander	15 15
857	A210	1.20d Gentian	15 15
858	A210	3d Laurel	25 15
859	A210	5d African rue	70 32
		Set value	1.25 60

Youth Day, May 25.

1967, May 25   Engr.   Perf. 12½
Size: 20x27½mm

860	A211	5p orange	15 15
861	A211	10p dk red brown	15 15
862	A211	15p dk vio blue	15 15
863	A211	20p green	15 15
864	A211	30p vermilion	15 15
865	A211	40p black	15 15
866	A211	50p Prussian grn	15 15
867	A211	60p lilac	15 15
868	A211	85p deep blue	22 15
869	A211	1d lilac	15 15
		Set value	1.00 60

75th birthday of Pres. Tito. Sheets of 15. Nos. 860-869 were reissued in 1967 with slight differences including thinner paper and slightly darker shades.
See #924-939. For surcharge see #1414.

Coil Stamps

1968-69   Photo.   Perf. 12½ Horiz.

869A	A211	20p green	32 15
869B	A211	40p vermilion	42 15
869C	A211	50p vermilion ('69)	32 15
		Set value	15

EXPO Emblem, Sputnik 1 and Explorer 1 — A212   ITY Emblem, St. Tripun's Church, Kotor — A213

Spacecraft: 50p, Tiros, Telstar and Molniya. 85p, Luna 9 and lunar satellite. 1.20d, Mariner 4, and Venus 3. 3d, Vostok, Gemini and Agena Rocket. 5d, Astronaut walking in space.

1967, June 26   Photo.   Perf. 11½

870	A212	30p ultra & multi	15 15
871	A212	50p yel & multi	15 15
872	A212	85p slate & multi	15 15
873	A212	1.20d multicolored	20 15
874	A212	3d vio & multi	38 35
875	A212	5d blue & multi	60 60
		Nos. 870-875 (6)	1.63
		Set value	1.10

EXPO '67, Montreal, Apr. 28-Oct. 27; 18th Congress of the Intl. Astronautical Federation, Belgrade.

1967, July 17   Engr.

Designs (ITY Emblem and): 50p, Municipal Building, Maribor. 85p, Cathedral, Trogir. 1.20d, Fortress gate, Nis. 3d, Drina Bridge, Visegrad. 5d, Daut-pasha's Bath, Skopje.

876	A213	30p slate bl & lt ol	15 15
877	A213	50p brn & dl vio	15 15
878	A213	85p dk bl & dp claret	15 15
879	A213	1.20d dp claret & brn	15 15
880	A213	3d brn & slate grn	40 15
881	A213	5d slate grn & brn	60 55
		Set value	1.40 1.00

Issued for International Tourist Year, 1967.

Partridge — A214

1967, Sept. 22   Photo.   Perf. 14

882	A214	30p shown	15 15
883	A214	50p Pike	15 15
884	A214	1.20d Red deer	22 20
885	A214	5d Peregrine falcon	75 70

Intl. Fishing and Hunting Exposition and Fair, Novi Sad.

Congress Emblem with Sputnik 1 A215

Litho. & Engr.
1967, Sept. 25   *Perf. 12½*
886 A215 85p dk bl, lt bl & gold   22 15

18th Congress of the Intl. Astronautical Federation, Belgrade, Sept. 25-30.

Old Theater and Castle, Ljubljana — A216   Child's Drawing: Winter Scene — A217

1967, Sept. 29   Engr.   *Perf. 12½*
887 A216 30p sepia & dk grn   20 15

Centenary of Slovene National Theater.

1967, Oct. 2   Litho.
888 A217 30p multicolored   80 15

International Children's Week, Oct. 2-8.

Lenin by Mestrovic A218   4-Leaf Clover A219

1967, Nov. 7   Engr.   *Perf. 12½*
889 A218 30p dark purple   15 15
890 A218 85p olive gray   25 15
   Set value   32 15

Souvenir Sheet
Imperf
891 A218 10d magenta   3.75 3.00

Russian October Revolution, 50th anniv.

1967, Nov. 15   Photo.   *Perf. 14*

Designs: 30p, Chimney sweep. 50p, Horseshoe and flower.

Dated "1968"
892 A219 20p shown   15 15
893 A219 30p Chimney sweep   15 15
894 A219 50p Horseshoe, flower   15 15
   Set value   25 16

New Year 1968. See Nos. 957-959.

The Young Sultana, by Vlaho Bucovac — A220

Paintings: 85p, The Watchtower, by Dura Jaksic, vert. 2d, Visit to the Family, by Josip Petkovsek. 3d, The Cock Fight, by Paja Jovanovic. 5d, "Spring" (woman and children), by Ivana Kobilca, vert.

Perf. 11½x12, 12x11½
1967, Nov. 28   Engr. & Litho.
895 A220 85p multicolored   15 15
896 A220 1d multicolored   16 15
897 A220 2d multicolored   40 28

---

898 A220 3d multicolored   55 40
899 A220 5d multicolored   1.10 70
   Nos. 895-899 (5)   2.36 1.68

Issued for the Day of the Republic, Nov. 29. See Nos. 942-946, 995-1000.

Ski Jump A221   Annunciation A222

Sport: 1d, Figure skating pair. 2d, Downhill skiing. 5d, Ice hockey.

1968, Feb. 5   Engr.   *Perf. 12½*
900 A221 50p dk bl & dk pur   15 15
901 A221 1d brn & sl green   15 15
902 A221 2d sl grn & lake   24 15
903 A221 5d sl grn & dk bl   70 35
   Set value   62

10th Winter Olympic Games, Grenoble, France, Feb. 6-18.

1968, Apr. 20   Photo.   *Perf. 13½*
Medieval Icons: 50p, Madonna, St. George's Church, Prizren. 1.50d, St. Sava and St. Simeon. 2d, Christ's descent into hell, Ohrid. 3d, Crucifixion, St. Clement's Church, Ohrid. 5d, Madonna, Church of Our Lady of the Bell Tower, Split.

906 A222 50p gold & multi   15 15
907 A222 1d gold & multi   16 15
908 A222 1.50d gold & multi   24 15
909 A222 2d gold & multi   48 28
910 A222 3d gold & multi   65 40
911 A222 5d gold & multi   1.50 1.00
   Nos. 906-911 (6)   3.18
   Set value   1.85

European Bullfinch A223   800-meter Race for Women A224

Finches: 1d, Goldfinch. 1.50d, Chaffinch. 2d, European greenfinch. 3d, Red crossbill. 5d, Hawfinch.

1968, May 25   Photo.   *Perf. 11½*
Birds in Natural Colors
912 A223 50p bister   15 15
913 A223 1d rose lake   15 15
914 A223 1.50d gray blue   20 15
915 A223 2d deep orange   28 15
916 A223 3d olive green   52 24
917 A223 5d pale violet   80 52
   Nos. 912-917 (6)   2.10
   Set value   1.00

Issued for Youth Day.

Litho. & Engr.
1968, June 28   *Perf. 12½*
Sports: 1d, Basketball. 1.50d, Gymnast on vaulting horse. 2d, Rowing. 3d, Water polo. 5d, Wrestling.
918 A224 50p dk brn & dk red brown   15 15
919 A224 1d Prus bl & blk   15 15
920 A224 1.50d slate & dk brn   15 15
921 A224 2d bis & sl grn   22 15
922 A224 3d blk brn & ind   28 20
923 A224 5d dk grn & vio blk   65 45
   Nos. 918-923 (6)   1.60
   Set value   90

19th Olympic Games, Mexico City, Oct. 12-27.

Tito Type of 1967
1968-72   Engr.   *Perf. 12½*
Size: 20x27½mm
924 A211 20p dark blue   15 15
925 A211 25p lake   15 15
926 A211 30p green   15 15
927 A211 50p vermilion   20 15
928 A211 70p black   30 15
929 A211 75p slate grn   40 15
930 A211 80p olive   40 15
930A A211 80p red org ('72)   35 15
931 A211 90p olive   30 15
932 A211 1.20d dark blue   52 15
932A A211 1.20d sl grn ('72)   42 15
933 A211 1.25d deep blue   45 15
934 A211 1.50d slate grn   40 15
Size: 20x30½mm
935 A211 2d sepia   65 15
936 A211 2.50d Prussian grn   1.65 15
937 A211 5d deep plum   1.40 15
938 A211 10d violet blk   3.00 35
939 A211 20d bluish black   4.25 40
   Nos. 924-939 (18)   15.14
   Set value   1.75

The shading of the background of Nos. 924-939 has been changed from the 1967 issue to intensify the contrast around the portrait.

Cannon and Laurel Wreath — A225   Mother Nursing Twins, Fresco by Jan of Kastav — A226

1968, Aug. 2   Photo.   *Perf. 12½*
940 A225 50p org brn & gold   20 15

65th anniversary of the Ilinden uprising.

1968, Sept. 9   Litho.
941 A226 50p black & multi   15 15

Annexation of Istria and the Slovene Coast to Yugoslavia, 25th anniv.

Painting Type of 1967
Paintings: 1d, Lake Klansko, by Marko Pernhart. 1.50d, Bavarian Landscape, by Milan Popovic. 2d, Porta Terraferma, Zadar, by Ferdo Quiquerez. 3d, Mt. Triglav seen from Bohinj, by Anton Karinger. 5d, Studenica Monastery, by Djordje Krstic.

Perf. 14x13½
1968, Oct. 3   Engr. & Litho.
942 A220 1d gold & multi   15 15
943 A220 1.50d gold & multi   15 15
944 A220 2d gold & multi   25 15
945 A220 3d gold & multi   40 15
946 A220 5d gold & multi   1.00 70
   Nos. 942-946 (5)   1.95
   Set value   1.05

Aleksa Santic (1868-1924), Poet — A227   "Going for a Walk" — A228

1968, Oct. 5   Engr.   *Perf. 12½*
947 A227 50p dark blue   20 15

1968, Oct. 6   Litho.
948 A228 50p multicolored   22 15

Issued for Children's Week.

Karl Marx (1818-1883), by N. Mitric — A229   Old Theater and Belgrade Castle — A230

1968, Oct. 11   Engr.
949 A229 50d dk car rose   20 15

1968, Nov. 22   Engr.   *Perf. 12½*
950 A230 50p ol brn & sl grn   20 15

Serbian National Theater, Belgrade, cent.

Hasan Brkic — A231   The Family, by J. Soldatovic — A232

Portraits: 75p, Ivan Milutinovic. 1.25d, Rade Koncar. 2d, Kuzman Josifovski. 2.50d, Tone Tomsic. 5d, Mosa Pijade.

1968, Nov. 28   Engr.   *Perf. 12½*
951 A231 50p violet black   15 15
952 A231 75p black   15 15
953 A231 1.25d red brown   25 15
   a. Souv. sheet, 2 each #951-953   13.00 13.00
954 A231 2d bluish black   35 15
955 A231 2.50d slate green   55 25
956 A231 5d claret   1.25 85
   a. Souv. sheet, 2 each #954-956   13.00 13.00
   Nos. 951-956 (6)   2.70
   Set value   1.45

2nd Assembly of the National Republic of Yugoslavia, 25th anniv.

Type of New Year's Issue, 1967
1968, Nov. 25   Photo.   *Perf. 14*
Dated "1969"
957 A219 20p Four-leaf clover   15 15
958 A219 30p Chimney sweep   15 15
959 A219 50p Horseshoe, flower   15 15
   Set value   26 18

Issued for New Year 1969.

1968, Dec. 10   Engr.   *Perf. 12½*
960 A232 1.25d dark blue   25 15

International Human Rights Year.

ILO Emblem — A233   Dove, Hammer and Sickle Emblem — A234

Litho. & Engr.
1969, Jan. 27   *Perf. 12½*
961 A233 1.25d red & black   25 15

ILO, 50th anniv.

Engr. & Photo.
1969, Mar. 11   *Perf. 12½*
Designs: 75p, Graffiti "TITO" and five-pointed star. 1.25d, Five-pointed crystal. 10d, Marshal Tito in 1943.
962 A234 50p black & red   15 15
963 A234 75p ol bis & blk   20 15

| 964 | A234 1.25d red & black | 35 | 20 |

Souvenir Sheet

| 964A | | Sheet of 9 | 5.50 | 5.50 |
| b. | A234 10d brown, engr. | | 3.00 | 3.00 |

Communist Federation of Yugoslavia, 50th anniv.; 9th party congress. No. 964A contains 4 #962, 2 each #963-964, 964b.

St. Nikita, from Manasija Monastery — A235

Frescoes from Monasteries: 75p, Apostles, Zakopani. 1.25d, Crucifixion, Studenica. 2d, Wedding at Cana, Kalenic. 3d, Angel at the Grave, Milseva. 5d, Pietá, Nerezi.

1969, Apr. 7		**Photo.**	**Perf. 13½**
965	A235	50p gold & multi	15	15
966	A235	75p gold & multi	15	15
967	A235	1.25d gold & multi	15	15
968	A235	2d gold & multi	24	15
969	A235	3d gold & multi	55	45
970	A235	5d gold & multi	1.50	90
		Nos. 965-970 (6)	2.74	
		Set value		1.60

Roman Memorial and View of Ptuj — A236

1969, Apr. 23		**Engr.**	**Perf. 11½**
971	A236 50p violet brown	15	15

1900th anniv. of Ptuj, the Roman Petovio. Issued in sheets of 9 (3x3).

Vasil Glavinov — A237   Thin-leafed Peony — A238

1969, May 8			**Perf. 12x12½**
972	A237 50p ocher & rose lilac	15	15

Vasil Glavinov, Macedonian socialist, birth cent.. Issued in sheets of 9 (3x3).

1969, May 25		**Photo.**	**Perf. 11½**

Medicinal Plants: 75p, Coltsfoot. 1.25d, Primrose. 2d, Hellebore. 2.50d, Violets. 5d, Anemones.

Flowers in Natural Colors

973	A238	50p yellow brn	15	15
974	A238	75p dull purple	15	15
975	A238	1.25d blue	15	15
976	A238	2d brown	25	15
977	A238	2.50d plum	30	20
978	A238	5d green	90	70
		Nos. 973-978 (6)	1.90	
		Set value		1.15

See Nos. 1056-1061, 1140-1145.

Eber, by Vasa Ivankovic — A239

Paintings of Sailing Ships: 1.25d, Tare, by Franasovic. 1.50d, Brig Sela, by Vasa Ivankovic. 2.50d, Dubrovnik galleon, 16th century. 3.25d, Madre Mimbelli, by Antoine Roux. 5d, The Virgin Saving Seamen from Disaster, 16th century ikon.

1969, July 10		**Photo.**	**Perf. 11½**
979	A239	50p gold & multi	15	15
980	A239	1.25d gold & multi	20	15
981	A239	1.50d gold & multi	32	15
982	A239	2.50d gold & multi	50	25
983	A239	3.25d gold & multi	85	45
984	A239	5d gold & multi	2.00	1.00
		Nos. 979-984 (6)	4.02	2.15

Dubrovnik Summer Festival, 20th anniv.

11th World Games for the Deaf, Belgrade, Aug. 9-16 — A240

1969, Aug. 9		**Engr.**	**Perf. 12½**
985	A240 1.25d dp claret & dl vio	38	15

Lipice Horse — A241

Horses: 75p, Bosnian mountain horse. 3.25d, Ljutomer trotter. 5d, Half-breed.

1969, Sept. 26		**Photo.**	**Perf. 11½**
986	A241	75p multicolored	15	15
987	A241	1.25d olive & multi	15	15
988	A241	3.25d brn & multi	30	15
989	A241	5d multicolored	75	75
		Set value		1.00

Zagreb Veterinary College, 50th anniv.

Children and Birds, by Tanja Vucanik, 13 years — A242

1969, Oct. 5		**Litho.**	**Perf. 12½**
990	A242 50p org, blk & gray	20	15

Issued for Children's Week.

Arms of Belgrade — A243   Josip Smodlaka — A244

Coats of Arms: No. 992, Skopje (bridge and mountain). No. 993, Titograd (bridge and fortifications).

1969		**Litho.**	**Perf. 12½**
991	A243	50p gold & multi	18	15
992	A243	50p gold & multi	18	15
993	A243	50p gold & multi	18	15
		Set value		15

Liberation of capitals of the Federated Republics, 25th anniv. See Nos. 1017-1020.

1969, Nov. 9			**Engr.**
994	A244 50p dark blue	15	15

Smodlaka (1869-1956), leader in Yugoslavia's fight for independence.

Painting Type of 1967

Paintings of Nudes: 50p, The Little Gypsy with the Rose, by Nikola Martinoski, vert. 1.25d, Girl on a Red Chair, by Sava Sumanovic, vert. 1.50d, Woman Combing her Hair, by Marin Tartaglia, vert. 2.50d, Olympia, by Miroslav Kraljevic. 3.25d, The Bather, by Jovan Bijelic, vert. 5d, Woman on a Couch, by Matej Sternen.

Photo. & Engr.

1969, Nov. 29			**Perf. 13½**
995	A220	50p multi	15	15
996	A220	1.25d multi	42	15
997	A220	1.50d multi	55	20
998	A220	2.50d multi	70	52
999	A220	3.25d multi	1.40	90
1000	A220	5d multi	2.50	2.00
		Nos. 995-1000 (6)	5.72	3.92

University of Ljubljana, 50th Anniv. — A245

1969, Dec. 9		**Engr.**	**Perf. 11½**
1001	A245 50p slate grn	15	15

Seal of Zagreb University — A246   Jovan Cvijic, Geographer — A247

Photo. & Engr.

1969, Dec. 17			**Perf. 12½**
1002	A246 50p gold, bl & brn	15	15

University of Zagreb, 300th anniv.

Europa Issue, 1969
Common Design Type

1969, Dec. 20		**Photo.**	**Perf. 11½**
1003	CD12	1.25d grnsh gray, buff & brn	3.25	3.25
1004	CD12	3.25d rose lil, gray & dk bl	12.00	12.00

Yugoslavia's admission to CEPT.

1970, Feb. 16		**Engr.**	**Perf. 12½**

Famous Yugoslavs: 1.25d, Dr. Andrija Stampar, hygienist. 1.50d, Joakim Krcovski, author. 2.50d, Marko Miljanov, Montenegrin patriot-hero. 3.25d, Vaca Pelagic, socialist. 5d, Oton Zupancic, Slovenian poet.

1005	A247	50p reddish brn	15	15
1006	A247	1.25d brnsh black	15	15
1007	A247	1.50d lilac	22	15
1008	A247	2.50d slate grn	28	15
1009	A247	3.25d reddish brn	28	24
1010	A247	5d blue vio	52	45
		Nos. 1005-1010 (6)	1.60	
		Set value		1.00

Common Design Types pictured in section at front of book.

Punishment of Dirce, Pulj — A248

Mosaics from the 1st-4th Centuries: 1.25d, Cerberus, Bitola, horiz. 1.50d, Angel of the Annunciation, Porec. 2.50d, Hunters, Gamzigard. 3.25d, Bull and cherry tree, horiz. 5d, Virgin and Child enthroned, Porec.

1970, Mar. 16		**Photo.**	**Perf. 13½**
1011	A248	50p gold & multi	15	15
1012	A248	1.25d gold & multi	15	15
1013	A248	1.50d gold & multi	20	15
1014	A248	2.50d gold & multi	40	25
1015	A248	3.25d gold & multi	65	38
1016	A248	5d gold & multi	1.25	1.10
		Nos. 1011-1016 (6)	2.80	
		Set value		1.90

Arms Type of 1969

Coats of Arms: No. 1017, Sarajevo (arcade). No. 1018, Zagreb (castle). No. 1019, Ljubljana (dragon and tower). No. 1020a, Yugoslavia (embossed coat of arms.)

1970		**Litho.**	**Perf. 12½**
1017	A243	50p gold & multi	15	15
1018	A243	50p gold & multi	15	15
1019	A243	50p gold & multi	15	15
		Set value		30

Souvenir Sheet

| 1020 | | Sheet of 7 | 6.00 | 6.00 |
| a. | A243 12d gold & black | | 2.00 | 2.00 |

Liberation of Yugoslavia, 25th anniv. No. 1020 contains one each of Nos. 991-993, 1017-1019, one No. 1020a and 2 labels with commemorative inscriptions.

Issued: #1017, Apr. 6; #1018, May 8; #1019, May 9; #1020, May 15.

Lenin (1870-1924), by S. Stojanovic — A249   Basketball — A250

Design: 1.25d, Lenin sculpture facing left.

1970, Apr. 22			**Engr.**
1021	A249	50p rose lilac	15	15
1022	A249	1.25d blue gray	20	15
		Set value		15

1970, Apr. 25			
1023	A250 1.25d plum	28	15

6th World Basketball Championships, Ljubljana, May 10-23.

Europa Issue, 1970
Common Design Type

1970, May 4		**Photo.**	**Perf. 11½**
		Size: 32½x23mm		
1024	CD13	1.25d lt bl, dk bl & lt grnsh bl	50	50
1025	CD13	3.25d rose lil, plum & gray	1.00	1.00

Istrian Shorthaired Hound — A251

Yugoslav Breeds of Dogs: 1.25d, Yugoslav tricolor hound. 1.50d, Istrian hard-haired hound. 2.50d, Balkan hound. 3.25d, Dalmatian. 5d, Shara mountain dog.

1970, May 25   Photo.   Perf. 11½
Granite Paper

1026	A251	50p	tan & multi	15	15
1027	A251	1.25d	ol & multi	15	15
1028	A251	1.50d	vio & multi	15	15
1029	A251	2.50d	slate & multi	25	15
1030	A251	3.25d	multi	45	20
1031	A251	5d	multi	65	60
			Set value	1.50	1.00

Telegraph
Circuit — A252

Stylized
Gymnast — A254

Bird — A253

1970, June 20   Litho.   Perf. 12½
1032 A252 50p hn brn, gold & blk   15 15

Telegraph service in Montenegro, cent.

1970, Oct. 5
1033 A253 50p multicolored   20 15

Issued for Children's Week, Oct. 5-11.

1970, Oct. 22   Engr.
1034 A254 1.25d car & slate   20 15

17th World Gymnastics Championships, Ljubljana, Oct. 22-27.

UN Emblem
and Hand
Holding Dove,
by Makoto
A255

Litho. & Engr.
1970, Oct. 24   Perf. 11½
1035 A255 1.25d dk brn, blk & gold   28 15

25th anniversary of the United Nations.

Ascension, by
Teodor D.
Kracum
A256

Baroque Paintings: 75p, Abraham's Sacrifice, by Federiko Benkovic. 1.25d, Holy Family, by Francisek Jelovsek. 2.50d, Jacob's Ladder, by Hristofor Zefarovic. 3.25d, Baptism of Christ, by unknown Serbian painter. 5.75d, The Coronation of Mary, by Tripo Kokolja.

Engr. & Photo.
1970, Nov. 28   Perf. 13½x14

1036	A256	50p	gold & multi	15	15
1037	A256	75p	gold & multi	15	15
1038	A256	1.25d	gold & multi	16	15
1039	A256	2.50d	gold & multi	28	16
1040	A256	3.25d	gold & multi	52	28
1041	A256	5.75d	gold & multi	1.00	80
		Nos. 1036-1041 (6)	2.26	
		Set value		1.35

Alpine
Rhododendron
A257

European Nature Protection Year emblem and: 3.25d, Bearded vulture.

1970, Dec. 14   Photo.   Perf. 11½
1042 A257 1.25d multi   3.50 3.50
1043 A257 3.25d multi   11.00 8.50

Sheets of 9.

Frano
Supilo — A258

British, French,
Canadian, Italian
Satellites — A259

Litho. & Engr.
1971, Jan. 25   Perf. 12½
1044 A258 50p black & buff   15 15

Supilo (1870-1917), Croat leader for independence from Austria-Hungary. Sheets of 9.

1971, Feb. 8   Photo.   Perf. 13½

Designs: 75p, Satellite. 1.25d, Automated moon exploration. 2.50d, Various spacecraft, horiz. 3.25d, First experimental space station, horiz. 5.75d, Astronauts on moon, horiz.

1045	A259	50p	bl & multi	15	15
1046	A259	75p	multi	18	15
1047	A259	1.25d	multi	38	15
1048	A259	2.50d	brn & multi	1.00	45
1049	A259	3.25d	multi	1.40	95
1050	A259	5.75d	multi	3.25	2.50
		Nos. 1045-1050 (6)	6.36	4.35

"Space in the service of science." Sheets of 9.

Proclamation of the Commune, Town Hall, Paris — A260

Litho. & Engr.
1971, Mar. 18   Perf. 11½
1051 A260 1.25d bis brn & gray brn   30 15

Centenary of the Paris Commune.

Europa Issue, 1971
Common Design Type

1971, May 4   Photo.   Perf. 11½
Size: 33x23mm
1052 CD14 1.50d Prus bl, pale grn & dk bl   50 50
1053 CD14 4d mag, pink & dk mag   1.10 1.10

Circles — A261

Prince Lazar,
Fresco, Lazarica
Church — A262

1971, May 5   Perf. 13½
1054 A261 50p shown   52 22
1055 A261 1.25d 20 circles   1.50 80

2nd Congress of Managers of Autonomous States.

Flower Type of 1969

Medicinal Plants: 50p, Common mallow. 1.50d, Common buckthorn. 2d, Water lily. 2.50d, Poppy. 4d, Wild chicory. 6d, Physalis.

1971, May 25   Photo.   Perf. 11½
Flowers in Natural Colors

1056	A238	50p	lt ultra	15	15
1057	A238	1.50d	olive bis	15	15
1058	A238	2d	dull blue	18	15
1059	A238	2.50d	dark car	38	22
1060	A238	4d	dp bister	48	25
1061	A238	6d	org brown	80	60
		Nos. 1056-1061 (6)	2.14	
		Set value		1.25

1971, June 28   Photo.   Perf. 13½
1062 A262 50p gray & multi   15 15

600th anniversary of founding of Krusevac by Prince Lazar Hrebeljanovic (1329-1389).

View of Krk — A263

Views: 5p, Krusevac. 10p, Castle and church, Gradacac. 20p, Church and bridge, Bohinj. 35p, Shore and mountains, Omis. 40p, Peje. 50p, Memorial column, Krusevac. 60p, Logar Valley. 75p, Bridge and church, Bohinj. 80p, Church, Piran. 1d, Street, Bitolj. 1.20d, Minaret, Pocitelj. 1.25d, 1.50d, Gate tower, Hercegnovi. 2d, Cathedral and City Hall Square, Novi Sad. 2.50d, Crna River.

1971-73   Engr.   Perf. 13

1063	A263	5p	orange ('73)	15	15
1064	A263	10p	brown ('72)	15	15
1065	A263	20p	vio blk ('73)	15	15
1066	A263	30p	ol gray ('72)	15	15
a.		30p green		90	15
1067	A263	35p	brn car ('73)	15	15
1068	A263	40p	black ('72)	15	15
1069	A263	50p	vermilion	1.25	15
1070	A263	50p	green ('72)	15	15
1071	A263	60p	purple ('72)	24	15
1072	A263	75p	slate green	28	15
1073	A263	80p	rose red ('72)	1.25	15
1073A	A263	1d	violet brn	1.25	48
1073B	A263	1.20d	sl grn ('72)	1.65	20
1073C	A263	1.25d	deep blue	1.00	15
1073D	A263	1.50d	bluish blk ('73)	28	15
1073E	A263	2d	blue ('72)	90	15
1073F	A263	2.50d	dl pur ('73)	90	18
		Nos. 1063-1073F (17)	10.05	
		Set value		1.75

Issued with and without fluorescent bars. See type A323. See Nos. 1482-1486, 1599-1600, 1602-1603, 1717. For surcharges see Nos. 1413, 1711-1712, 1765-1766, 1769.

Emperor
Constantine, 4th
Century — A264

UNICEF Emblem,
Children in
Balloon — A265

Tourist Issue

Antique Bronzes excavated in Yugoslavia: 1.50d, Boy with fish. 2d, Hercules, replica after Lysippus. 2.50d, Satyr. 4d, Head of Aphrodite. 6d, Citizen of Emona, 1st century tomb.

1971, Sept. 20   Photo.   Perf. 13½

1074	A264	50p	rose & multi	15	15
1075	A264	1.50d	multicolored	15	15
1076	A264	2d	multicolored	15	15
1077	A264	2.50d	lem & multi	38	18
1078	A264	4d	ocher & multi	48	30
1079	A264	6d	multicolored	1.10	80
		Nos. 1074-1079 (6)	2.41	
		Set value		1.45

Sheets of 9.

1971, Oct. 4   Litho.   Perf. 13x13½
1080 A265 50p multicolored   35 15

Children's Week, Oct. 3-10.

Woman in
Serbian
Costume, by
Katarina
Ivanovic
A266

Portraits, 19th Century: 1.50d, The Merchant Ivanisevic, by Anastasije Bocaric. 2d, Ana Kresic, by Vjekoslav Karas. 2.50d, Pavle Jagodic, by Konstantin Danil. 4r, Luiza Pesjakova, by Mihael Stroj. 6d, Old Man and view of Ljubljana, by Matevz Langus.

Engraved and Photogravure
1971, Nov. 29   Perf. 13½x14

1081	A266	50p	gold & multi	15	15
1082	A266	1.50d	gold & multi	15	15
1083	A266	2d	gold & multi	16	15
1084	A266	2.50d	gold & multi	32	16
1085	A266	4d	ocher & multi	45	32
1086	A266	6d	gold & multi	1.25	90
		Nos. 1081-1086 (6)	2.48	
		Set value		1.50

See Nos. 1120-1125.

Letter with Postal
Code, Map of
Yugoslavia
A267

Damjan Gruev
(1871-1906),
Macedonian
Revolutionist
A268

1971, Dec. 15   Photo.   Perf. 13½x14
1087 A267 50p ultra & multi   15 15

Introduction of postal code system.

1971, Dec. 22   Engr.   Perf. 12½
1088 A268 50p dark blue   15 15

11th Winter
Olympic
Games,
Sapporo,
Japan, Feb. 3-
13 — A269

Engr. & Typo.
1972, Feb. 3   Perf. 11½
1089 A269 1.25d Speed skating   1.10 70
1090 A269 6d Slalom   4.75 3.00

Sheets of 9.

First Page of
Statute of
Dubrovnik
A270

Lithographed and Engraved
1972, Mar. 15   *Perf. 13½*
1091 A270 1.25d gold & multi   30   15

700th anniversary of the Statute of Dubrovnik, a
legal code given by Prince Marko Justiniani.

Ski Jump Track,   Water Polo and
Planica — A271   Olympic
                Rings — A272

1972, Mar. 21   *Perf. 11½*
1092 A271 1.25d blk, lt bl & grn   25   15

World Ski Jump Championships, Planica, Mar.
22-26.

1972, Apr. 17   Litho.   *Perf. 12½x12*
1093 A272   50p shown   15   15
1094 A272   1.25d Basketball   15   15
1095 A272   2.50d Butterfly stroke   18   18
1096 A272   3.25d Boxing   40   15
1097 A272   5d Running   65   30
1098 A272   6.50d Yachting   1.25   80
      Nos. 1093-1098 (6)   2.78 1.73

20th Olympic Games, Munich, Aug. 26-Sept. 10.
Sheets of 9.

Europa Issue 1972
Common Design Type
1972, May 4   Photo.   *Perf. 11½*
1100 CD15 1.50d bl, grn & yel   1.00 1.00
1101 CD15   5d brt rose, mag &   org   2.50 2.50

Wall   Marshal Tito, by
Creeper — A275   Bozidar
                 Jakac — A276

Birds: 1.25d, Little bustard. 2.50d, Red-billed
chough. 3.25d, Spoonbill. 5d, Eagle owl. 6.50d,
Rock ptarmigan.

1972, May 8
Birds in Natural Colors
1102 A275   50p gray violet   15   15
1103 A275   1.25d ocher   15   15
1104 A275   2.50d gray olive   16   16
1105 A275   3.25d light plum   35   20
1106 A275   5d red brown   60   32
1107 A275   6.50d violet   1.25   80
      Nos. 1102-1107 (6)   2.66 1.78

Nature protection.

1972, May 25   Litho.   *Perf. 12½*
1108 A276   50p cr & dk brn   16   15
1109 A276   1.25d gray & ind   65   25

Souvenir Sheet
Imperf
1110 A276   10d gray & blk brn   3.25 3.25

80th birthday of Pres. Tito. Sheets of 9. No.
1110 printed in blocks of 4.

First Locomotive
Built in Serbia,
1882 — A277

Design: 5d, Modern Yugoslavian electric
locomotive.

1972, June 12   Photo.   *Perf. 11½*
1111 A277   1.50d multicolored   16   15
1112 A277   5d multicolored   85   30
          Set value   38

Intl. Railroad Union, 50th anniv.

Glider — A278

1972, July 8   Photo.   *Perf. 12½*
1113 A278   2d bl gray, gold & blk   22   15

13th World Gliding Championships, Vrsac Airport, July 9-23. Sheets of 9.

Pawn on
Chessboard — A279

Design: 6d, Chessboard, emblems of King and
Queen.

1972, Sept. 18   *Perf. 11½*
1114 A279   1.50d multi   30   15
1115 A279   6d multi   1.10   70

20th Men's and 5th Women's Chess Olympiad,
Skopje, Sept.-Oct. Sheets of 9.

Boy on Rocking   Goce
Horse — A280   Delchev — A281

1972, Oct. 2   Litho.   *Perf. 12½*
1116 A280   80p org & multi   22   15

Children's Week, Oct. 2-8.

1972, Oct. 16   *Perf. 13*
1117 A281   80p yel grn & blk   15   15

Delchev (1872-1903), Macedonian freedom
fighter.

Grga Martic, by
Ivan Mestrovic
A282

1972, Nov. 3   *Perf. 12½*
1118 A282   80p red, yel grn & blk   15   15

Brother Grga Martic (1822-1905), Franciscan
administrator, educator and poet.

Serbian
National
Library,
Belgrade
A283

1972, Nov. 25   Engr.   *Perf. 11½x12*
1119 A283   50p chocolate   15   15

140th anniversary of the Serbian National Library
and opening of new building.

Painting Type of 1971

Still-Life Paintings: 50p, by Milos Tenkovic,
horiz. 1.25d, by Jozef Pekovsek. 2.50d, by Katarina Jovanovic, horiz. 3.25d, by Konstantin Danil,
horiz. 5d, by Nikola Masic. 6.50d, by Celestin
Medovic, horiz.

     Perf. 14x13½, 13½x14
1972, Nov. 28   Engr. & Photo.
1120 A266   50p gold & multi   15   15
1121 A266   1.25d gold & multi   15   15
1122 A266   2.50d gold & multi   16   15
1123 A266   3.25d gold & multi   38   15
1124 A266   5d gold & multi   50   32
1125 A266   6.50d gold & multi   75   52
      Nos. 1120-1125 (6)   2.09
          Set value   1.20

Battle of Stubica, by Krsto
Hegedusic — A284

Design: 6d, Battle of Krsko, by Gojmir Anton
Kos.

1973, Jan. 29   Photo.   *Perf. 11½*
1126 A284   2d gold & multi   40   15
1127 A284   6d gold & multi   1.50   70

Croatian-Slovenian Rebellion, 400th anniv. (2d);
Beginning of the peasant rebellions in Slovenia,
500th anniv. (6d). Sheets of 9.

Radoje Domanovic
(1873-1908), Serbian
Writer — A285

1973, Feb. 3   Litho.   *Perf. 12½*
1128 A285   80p tan & brn   40   15

      Sheets of 9.

 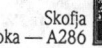

Skofja
Loka — A286

1973, Feb. 15   *Perf. 11½*
1129 A286   80p brown & buff   30   15

Millennium of the founding of Skofja Loka.
Sheets of 9.

Novi Sad, by
Peter
Demetrovic
A287

Old Engravings: 1.25d, Zagreb, by Josef Szeman.
2.50d, Kotor, by Pierre Mortier. 3.25d, Belgrade,
by Mancini. 5d, Split, by Louis-Francois Cassas.
6.50d, Kranj, by Matthaus Merian.

Engraved and Photogravure
1973, Mar. 15   *Perf. 13½*
1130 A287   50p gold, buff & blk   15   15
1131 A287   1.25d gold, gray & black   15   15
1132 A287   2.50d gold & blk   18   15
1133 A287   3.25d gold & blk   24   20
1134 A287   5d gold, buff & blk   38   30
1135 A287   6.50d gold & blk   60   45
      Nos. 1130-1135 (6)   1.70
          Set value   1.20

Championship
Poster — A288

1973, Apr. 5   Litho.   *Perf. 13½x13*
1136 A288   2d multicolored   35   15

32nd Intl. Table Tennis Championships, Sarajevo,
Apr. 5-15. Sheets of 9.

Europa Issue, 1973
Common Design Type
1973, Apr. 30   Photo.   *Perf. 11½*
     Size: 32½x23mm
1138 CD16   2d dk bl, lil & lt grn   80   80
1139 CD16   5.50d pur, cit & sal pink   2.50 2.50

      Sheets of 9.

Flower Type of 1969

Medicinal Plants: 80p, Birthwort. 2d, Globe
thistles. 3d, Olive branch. 4d, Corydalis. 5d,
Mistletoe. 6d, Comfrey.

1973, May 25   Photo.   *Perf. 11½*
Flowers in Natural Colors
1140 A238   80p orange & grn   15   15
1141 A238   2d dl bl & blue   24   15
1142 A238   3d olive & blk   35   20
1143 A238   4d yel grn & grn   55   24
1144 A238   5d org & sepia   85   42
1145 A238   6d lilac & grn   1.65   70
      Nos. 1140-1145 (6)   3.79 1.86

Anton Jansa (1734-
1773), Teacher,
Apiculturist and
Bee — A291

1973, Aug. 25   Engr.   *Perf. 12½*
1147 A291   80p black   15   15

      Sheets of 9.

Championship
Badge — A292

1973, Sept. 1   Litho.   Perf. 13½x13
1148 A292 2d multicolored   30 15

World water sport championships (swimming,
water polo, water jumps, figure swimming), Belgrade, Sept. 1-9. Sheets of 9.

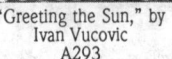

"Greeting the Sun," by   Post Horn
Ivan Vucovic   A294
A293

1973, Oct. 1   Perf. 12½
1149 A293 80p multicolored   35 15

Children's Week, Oct. 1-7. Sheets of 9.

Coil Stamps

1973-77   Photo.   Perf. 14½x14
1150 A294 30p brown   15 15
1151 A294 50p gray blue   15 15
1152 A294 80p rose red ('74)   20 15
1153 A294 1d yel grn ('77)   15 15
1154 A294 1.20d pink ('74)   30 15
1155 A294 1.50d rose ('77)   15 15
      Set value   90 35

Juraj Dalmatinac,
Sculptor, Architect,
500th Anniv. of
Death — A295

1973, Oct. 8   Litho.   Perf. 12½
1158 A295 80p grnsh gray & ol blk 15 15

Sheets of 9.

Nadezda
Petrovic (1873-
1915), Self-
Portrait
A296

Lithographed and Engraved
1973, Oct. 12   Perf. 11½
1159 A296 2d gold & multi   30 15

Sheets of 9.

Interior, by Marko Celebonovic — A297

Paintings of Interiors by Yugoslav artists: 2d, St.
Duja, by Emanuel Vidovic. 3d, Room with Slovak
Woman, by Marino Tartaglia. 4d, Painter with
Easel, by Miljenko Stancic. 5d, Studio, by Milan
Konjovic. 6d, Tavern in Stara Loka, by France
Slana.

1973, Oct. 20   Photo.   Perf. 13½
1160 A297 80p gold & multi   15 15
1161 A297 2d gold & multi   15 15
1162 A297 3d gold & multi   15 15
1163 A297 4d gold & multi   24 15
1164 A297 5d gold & multi   48 28
1165 A297 6d gold & multi   65 40
      Set value   1.60 1.00

Sheets of 9.

Dragojlo
Dudic — A298

Lithographed and Engraved
1973, Nov. 29   Perf. 12½
Gray and Indigo

1166 A298 80p shown   15 15
1167 A298 80p Strahil Pindzur   15 15
1168 A298 80p Boris Kidric   15 15
1169 A298 80p Radoje Dakic   15 15

Gray and Plum

1170 A298 2d Josip Mazar-Sosa   28 28
1171 A298 2d Zarko Zrenjanin   28 28
1172 A298 2d Emin Duraku   28 28
1173 A298 2d Ivan-Lola Ribar   28 28
      Nos. 1166-1173 (8)   1.72 1.72

Republic Day, Nov. 29, honoring national heroes
who perished during WWII. Nos. 1166-1173
printed se-tenant in sheets of 8 (4x2).

Memorial, by O.   Winged Globe, by
Boljka,   D. Dzamonja, at
Ljubljana — A299   Podgaric — A300

Sculptures: 4.50d, Tower by D. Dzamonja, at
Kozara. 5d, Memorial, by B. Grabulovski, at
Belcista. 10d, Abstract, by M. Zivkovic, at Sutjeska.
50d, Stone "V," by Zivkovic, at Kragujevac.

1974   Engr.   Perf. 12½
1174 A299 3d slate grn   1.25 15
1175 A299 4.50d brn lake   1.90 15
1176 A299 5d dark vio   1.90 15
   b.   Perf. 13½   1.90 15
1177 A300 10d slate grn   2.25 35
1178 A300 20d dull pur   2.75 48
1179 A300 50d indigo   5.75 1.50
      Nos. 1174-1179 (6)   15.80 2.78

1978-82   Litho.
1176a A299 5d   1.90 24
1177a A300 10d ('81)   1.90 48
1178a A300 20d ('81)   2.75 48
1179a A300 50d ('82)   3.00 75

Metric Measure
A301

1974, Jan. 10   Litho.   Perf. 13
1180 A301 80p plum & multi   15 15

Centenary of introduction of metric system.

European Ice Skating
Championships, Jan.
29-Feb. 2,
Zagreb — A302

1974, Jan. 29
1181 A302 2d multicolored   65 25

Diligence,
1874 — A303

Litho. & Engr.
1974, Feb. 25   Perf. 11½
1182 A303 80p shown   15 15
1183 A303 2d New UPU headquar-
           ters   16 15
1184 A303 8d Jet plane   1.10 75
      Set value   90

Centenary of the Universal Postal Union.

Montenegro No.
1 — A304

Litho. & Engr.
1974, Mar. 11   Perf. 13
1185 A304 80p shown   15 15
1186 A304 6d Montenegro No. 7   42 24
      Set value   30

Centenary of first Montenegrin postage stamps.

Marshal   Lenin, by Nandor
Tito — A305   Glid — A306

1974   Litho.   Perf. 13
1193 A305 50p green   15 15
   a.   Perf. 13x12½
1196 A305 80p vermilion   25 15
1198 A305 1.20d slate green   30 15
1201 A305 2d gray blue   30 15
   a.   Perf. 13x12½
      Set value   26

Issued with and without fluorescence.
For surcharge, see No. 1415.

1974, Apr. 20   Litho.   Perf. 13
1204 A306 2d blk & silver   25 15

50th death anniv. of Lenin.

Lepenski Vir
Statue, c. 4950
B.C. — A307

Europa: 6d, Widow and Child, by Ivan
Mestrovic.

1974, Apr. 29   Photo.   Perf. 11½
1205 A307 2d multicolored   75 70
1206 A307 6d multicolored   2.75 2.50

Great   Congress
Tit — A308   Poster — A309

1974, May 25   Photo.   Perf. 11½
1207 A308 80p shown   22 15
1208 A308 2d Rose   55 22
1209 A308 6d Cabbage butterfly   1.40 1.10

Youth Day. Issued in sheets of 9.

1974, May 27   Litho.   Perf. 11½
1210 A309 80p gold & multi   15 15
1211 A309 2d silver & multi   16 15
1212 A309 6d ocher & multi   55 55
      Set value   70

10th Congress of Yugoslav League of Communists, Belgrade, May 27-30.

Radar Ground   Games Emblem
Station,   and Soccer
Ivanjica — A311   Cup — A312

1974, June 7   Engr.   Perf. 13
1214 A311 80p shown   16 15
1215 A311 6d Intelsat IV   1.25 52

Opening of first satellite ground station in Yugoslavia at Ivanjica. Sheets of 9.

1974, June 13   Litho.   Perf. 13
1216 A312 4.50d vio bl & multi   1.40 1.00

World Cup Soccer Championship, Munich, June
13-July 7. Sheets of 9.

Klek Mountain,
Edelweiss,
Mountaineers'
Emblem
A313

1974, June 15
1217 A313 2d grn & multi   22 15

Mountaineering in Yugoslavia, cent. Sheets of 9.

Children's Dance, by Jano
Knjazovic — A314

Paintings: 2d, "Crucified Rooster," by Ivan
Generalic, vert. 5d, Laundresses, by Ivan Lackovic,
vert. 8d, Dance, by Janko Brasic.

1974, Sept. 9   Photo.   Perf. 11½
1218 A314 80p multi   16 15
1219 A314 2d multi   22 15
1220 A314 5d multi   85 60
1221 A314 8d multi   2.50 1.00

Yugoslav primitive art.

Cock and Flower, by Kaca Milinojsin A315

Designs (Children's Paintings): 3.20d, Girl and Boy, by Ewa Medrzecka, vert. 5d, Cat and Kitten, by Jelena Anastasijevic.

1974, Oct. 7   Litho.   Perf. 13
1222	A315	1.20d multi	15	15
1223	A315	3.20d multi	22	15
1224	A315	5d multi	85	18
		Set value	28	

Children's Week, Oct. 1-7, and Joy of Europe meeting in Belgrade. Sheets of 9.

Library and Primoz Trubar Statue — A316

1974, Oct. 21   Engr.   Perf. 13
1225	A316	1.20d black	15	15

Natl. University Library, Ljubljana, 200th anniv.

White Peonies, by Petar Dobrovic A317

Paintings of Flowers by Yugoslav artists: 2d, Carnations, by Vilko Gecan. 3d, Flowers, still-life, by Milan Konjovic. 4d, White Vase, by Sava Sumanovic. 5d, Larkspur, by Stane Kregar. 8d, Roses, by Petar Lubarda.

1974, Nov. 28   Photo.   Perf. 11¹/₂
1226	A317	80p gold & multi	15	15
1227	A317	2d gold & multi	15	15
1228	A317	3d gold & multi	20	20
1229	A317	4d gold & multi	32	20
1230	A317	5d gold & multi	45	22
1231	A317	8d gold & multi	85	35
		Nos. 1226-1231 (6)	2.12	1.27

Sheets of 9.

Title Page and View of Belgrade A318

1975, Jan. 8   Litho.   Perf. 13
1232	A318	1.20d citron	15	15
a.		Perf. 12¹/₂		

Sesquicentennial of the first publication of Matica Srpska, literary journal.

Map of Europe and Dove — A319

Svetozar Markovic, by Stevan Bodnarov — A321

Gold-plated Bronze Earring — A320

1975, Jan. 30   Perf. 12x11¹/₂
1233	A319	3.20d bl & multi	65	24
1234	A319	8d multi	2.00	90

Interparliamentary Union for European Cooperation and Security, 2nd Conference, Belgrade, Jan. 31-Feb. 6.

1975, Feb. 25   Photo.   Perf. 14x13

Antique jewelry in Yugoslav museums: 2.10d, Silver bracelet, 18th cent. 3.20d, Silver gilt belt buckle, 18th cent. 5d, Silver ring with Nike cameo, 14th cent. 6d, Silver necklace, 17th cent. 8d, Bronze gilt bracelet, 14th cent.
1235	A320	1.20d multi	15	15
1236	A320	2.10d multi	15	15
1237	A320	3.20d multi	18	15
1238	A320	5d multi	42	24
1239	A320	6d multi	80	35
1240	A320	8d multi	1.00	75
		Nos. 1235-1240 (6)	2.70	1.79

1975, Feb. 26   Engr.   Perf. 13
1241	A321	1.20d blue blk	15	15

Markovic (1846-1975), writer and poet.

Fettered Woman, by Frano Krsinic A322

Street, Ohrid A323

1975, Mar. 8   Photo.   Perf. 14¹/₂x14
1242	A322	3.20d gold & sepia	30	16

International Women's Year.

1975-77   Litho.   Perf. 13

Views: 25p, Budva. 75p, City Hall, Rijeka (Fiume). Nos. 1245, 1246, Street, Ohrid. 1.50d, Church, Bihac. 2.10d, Street and fountain, Hvar. 3.20d, Skofja Loka. 3.40d, Main Square, Vranje. 4.90d, Mosque, Perast.

No Inscription at Bottom
1243	A323	25p carmine ('76)	15	15
1244	A323	75p purple ('76)	15	15
1245	A323	1d dull purple	24	15
1246	A323	1d dl grn ('76)	16	15
a.		Perf. 13x12¹/₂		
1247	A323	1.50d rose red ('76)	28	15
a.		Perf. 13x12¹/₂		
1248	A323	2.10d gray green	50	15
1249	A323	3.20d dull blue	70	15
1250	A323	3.40d gray grn ('77)	28	15
a.		Perf. 13x12¹/₂		
1251	A323	4.90d dl bl ('76)	55	15
		Nos. 1243-1251 (9)	3.01	
		Set value	60	

See Nos. 1487-1491, 1598, 1601, 1603A, 1713, 1718-1719. For surcharges see Nos. 1382-1383, 1481, 1502, 1545, 1550, 1594-1597A, 1764, 1767-1768, 1770-1771, 1964, 1973.

Europa Issue 1975

Still Life with Eggs, by Mosa Pijade — A325

Painting: 8d, Three Graces, by Ivan Radovic.

1975, Apr. 28
1252	A325	3.20d gold & multi	32	32
1253	A325	8d gold & multi	1.65	1.65

Srem Front Fighters' Monument, by Dusan Dzamonja A326

1975, May 9   Litho.   Perf. 13¹/₂
1254	A326	3.20d red & multi	30	15

Victory over Fascism in WWII; liberation of Yugoslavia, 30th anniv.

Garland Flower — A327

Kayak — A328

1975, May 24   Photo.   Perf. 14x14¹/₂
1255	A327	1.20d shown	15	15
1256	A327	2.10d Garden balsam	15	15
1257	A327	3.20d Rose mallow	26	18
1258	A327	5d Geranium	48	30
1259	A327	6d Crocus	65	38
1260	A327	8d Oleander	1.00	75
		Nos. 1255-1260 (6)	2.69	1.91

Youth Day.

1975, June 20   Litho.   Perf. 13¹/₂
1261	A328	3.20d grnsh bl & multi	25	15

9th World Championship of Wild Water Racing, Radika River, June 24-25, and 14th World Championship of Canoe-Slalom, Treska River, June 28-29.

Ambush, Herzegovinian Insurgents, by Ferdo Quiquerez — A329

1975, July 9   Photo.   Perf. 13¹/₂x14¹/₂
1262	A329	1.20d gold & multi	15	15

Bosnian & Herzegovinian Uprising, cent.

Stjepan Mitrov Ljubisa (1824-1878) — A330

Yugoslav writers: 2.10d, Ivan Prijatelj (1875-1937). 3.20d, Jakov Ignjatovic (1824-1889). 5d, Dragojla Jarnevic (1824-1889). 6d, Svetozar

Corovic (1875-1919). 8d, Ivana Brlic-Mazuranic (1874-1938).

1975, Sept. 16   Litho.   Perf. 13
1263	A330	1.20d brick red & blk	15	15
1264	A330	2.10d dl grn & blk	16	15
1265	A330	3.20d ol bis & blk	26	15
1266	A330	5d brn org & blk	38	15
1267	A330	6d yel grn & blk	45	15
1268	A330	8d Prus bl & blk	60	35
		Nos. 1263-1268 (6)	2.00	
		Set value	65	

"Joy of Europe" Children's Meeting, Oct. 2-7, Belgrade — A331

Children's drawings.

1975, Oct. 1   Litho.   Perf. 13¹/₂
1269	A331	3.20d Young Lion	45	15
1270	A331	6d Baby Carriage	1.90	65

Peace Dove — A332

1975, Oct. 10
1271	A332	3.20d multi	30	15
1272	A332	8d multi	1.10	45

European Security and Cooperation Conference, Helsinki, July 30-Aug. 1.

Red Cross, "100", Map of Yugoslavia A333

Design: 8d, Red Cross, people seeking help.

1975, Nov. 1   Litho.   Perf. 13¹/₂x13
1273	A333	1.20d red & multi	16	15
1274	A333	8d red & multi	80	30
		Set value	35	

Centenary of Red Cross in Yugoslavia.

Soup Kitchen, by Dorde Andrejevic-Kun A334

Social paintings by 20th century Yugoslav artists: 2.10d, People at the Door, by Vinko Grdan. 3.20d, Drunks in Coach, by Marijan Detoni, horiz. 5d, Workers' Lunch, by Tone Kralj, horiz. 6d, Water Wheel, by Lazar Licenoski. 8d, The Hanging, by Krsto Hegedusic.

Perf. 14¹/₂x13¹/₂, 13¹/₂x14¹/₂
1975, Nov. 28   Photo.
1275	A334	1.20d gold & multi	15	15
1276	A334	2.10d gold & multi	15	15
1277	A334	3.20d gold & multi	18	18
1278	A334	5d gold & multi	30	20
1279	A334	6d gold & multi	40	32
1280	A334	8d gold & multi	70	65
		Nos. 1275-1280 (6)	1.88	1.65

Sheets of 9.

Diocletian's
Palace, 304
A.D. — A335

Designs: 3.20d, House of Ohrid, 19th century, vert. 8d, Gracanica Monastery, Kosovo, 1321.

1975, Dec. 10　Engr.　Perf. 13½
1281	A335	1.20d dark brown	15	15
1282	A335	3.20d bluish black	32	15
1283	A335	8d dk vio brown	80	35
		Set value		52

European Architectural Heritage Year 1975. Sheets of 9.

12th Winter
Olympic Games,
Feb. 4-15,
Innsbruck,
Austria — A336

1976, Feb. 4　Engr.　Perf. 13½
1284	A336	3.20d Ski jump	28	15
1285	A336	8d Pair figure skating	85	52

Red
Flag — A337

1976, Feb. 14　　　　Litho.
1286	A337	1.20d red & multi	15	15

"Red Flag" workers demonstration, Kragujevac, Feb. 15, 1876.

Svetozar Miletic
(1826-1901),
Lawyer, Founder
of United Serbian
Youth — A338

1976, Feb. 23　　　Perf. 13½x13
1287	A338	1.20d grnsh gray & dl grn	15	15

Borislav "Bora"
Stankovic, (1876-
1927),
Writer — A339

1976, Mar. 31　Litho.　Perf. 13½x13
1288	A339	1.20d lem, ol & mar	15	15

Sheets of 9.

Europa Issue 1976

King Matthias, by
Jakob Pogorelec,
1931 — A340

1976, Apr. 26　Photo.　Perf. 11½
1289	A340	3.20d shown	22	22
1290	A340	8d Bowl, 14th cent	75	75

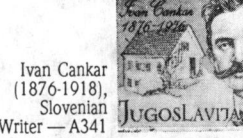

Ivan Cankar
(1876-1918),
Slovenian
Writer — A341

1976, May 8　Litho.　Perf. 13½x13
1291	A341	1.20d orange & plum	15	15

Train on Viaduct
in
Bosnia — A342

Design: 8d, Train on viaduct in Montenegro.

1976, May 15　Engr.　Perf. 13½
1292	A342	3.20d deep magenta	26	15
1293	A342	8d deep blue	75	35

Inauguration of the Belgrade-Bar railroad.

Hawker
Dragonfly
A343

Fresh-water Fauna: 2.10d, Winkle. 3.20d, Rudd. 5d, Green frog. 6d, Ferruginous duck. 8d, Muskrat.

1976, May 25　　　　Litho.
1294	A343	1.20d yel & multi	15	15
1295	A343	2.10d bl & multi	15	15
1296	A343	3.20d vio & multi	16	16
1297	A343	5d multicolored	38	30
1298	A343	6d multicolored	45	38
1299	A343	8d multicolored	75	52
		Nos. 1294-1299 (6)	2.04	1.66

Youth Day.

Vladimir Nazor,
Croatian Writer, Birth
Cent. — A344

1976, May 29　　　　Perf. 13
1300	A344	1.20d pale lil & dl bl	15	15

Battle of
Vucji
Dol,
1876
A345

1976, June 16　Litho.　Perf. 13
1301	A345	1.20d gold, brn & buff	15	15

Liberation of Montenegro from Turkey, cent.

Serbian
Pitcher — A346

Water Pitchers: 2.10d, Slovenia. 3.20d, Bosnia-Herzegovina. 5d, Vojvodina 6d, Macedonia. 8d, Kosovo.

1976, June 22　Photo.　Perf. 14x13
1302	A346	1.20d dk car & multi	15	15
1303	A346	2.10d olive & multi	15	15
1304	A346	3.20d red & multi	18	16
1305	A346	5d brown & multi	38	24
1306	A346	6d dk grn & multi	45	35
1307	A346	8d dk bl & multi	1.00	42
		Nos. 1302-1307 (6)	2.31	1.47

Tesla
Monument,
Belgrade, and
Niagara
Falls — A347

1976, July 10　Engr.　Perf. 13
1308	A347	5d slate grn & indigo	50	15

Nikola Tesla (1856-1943), electrical engineer and inventor. Sheets of 9.

21st Olympic
Games, July 17-
Aug. 1,
Montreal,
Canada,
A348

1976, July 17
1309	A348	1.20d Long jump	15	15
1310	A348	3.20d Soccer	25	15
1311	A348	5d Target shooting	38	20
1312	A348	8d Single scull rowing	65	40
		Set value		78

Sheets of 9.

World Map
and Peace
Dove — A349

1976, Aug. 16　Litho.　Perf. 13
1313	A349	4.90d multi	30	15

5th Summit Conference of Non-Aligned Countries, Colombo, Sri Lanka, Aug. 9-19. Sheets of 9.

Children's
Train — A350

Children's drawings: 4.90d, Navy Day (submarine).

1976, Oct. 2　　Litho.　Perf. 13
1314	A350	4.90d multi	42	15
1315	A350	8d multi	1.00	35
		Set value		42

"Joy of Europe" Children's Meeting, Belgrade, Oct. 2-7.

Herzegovinian Fugitives, by Uros
Predic — A351

Historical paintings by 19th-20th century Yugoslav painters: 1.20d, Battle of the Montenegrins, by

Djura Jaksic, vert. 2.10d, Nikola S. Zrinjski at Siget, by Oton Ivekovic, vert. 5d, Uprising at Razlovci, by Borko Lazeski. 6d, Enthroning of Slovenian Duke at Gospovetsko Field, by Anton Gojmir Kos. 8d, Break-through at Solun Front, by Veljko Stanojevic.

Perf. 13½x12½, 12½x13½

1976, Nov. 29　　　　　　Photo.
1316	A351	1.20d gold & multi	15	15
1317	A351	2.10d gold & multi	16	15
1318	A351	3.20d gold & multi	22	16
1319	A351	5d gold & multi	32	28
1320	A351	6d gold & multi	60	38
1321	A351	8d gold & multi	80	52
		Nos. 1316-1321 (6)	2.25	1.64

Sheets of 9.

No. 839 Surcharged with New Value and
3 Bars in Rose

1976, Dec. 8　Engr.　Perf. 12½
1322	A206	1d on 85p dl pur	15	15

Mateja
Nenadovic
A352
　　　　Rajko Zinzifov
　　　　A353

1977, Feb. 4　Photo.　Perf. 13½x14
1323	A352	4.90d multicolored	30	16

Prota Mateja Nenadovic (1777-1854), Serbian Duke, archbishop and writer.

1977, Feb. 10　Litho.　Perf. 13x13½
1324	A353	1.50d brn & sepia	15	15

Rajko Zinzifov (1839-1877), writer.

Phlox — A354
　　　　Alojz
　　　　Kraigher — A356

Croatian Music Institute, Zagreb, 150th
Anniv. — A355

Flowers: 3.40d, Lily. 4.90d, Bleeding heart. 6d, Zinnia. 8d, Spreading marigold. 10d, Horseshoe geranium.

1977, Mar. 8　　　　Perf. 13½x13
1325	A354	1.50d multi	15	15
1326	A354	3.40d multi	25	15
1327	A354	4.90d multi	35	15
1328	A354	6d multi	40	15
1329	A354	8d multi	60	15
1330	A354	10d multi	95	55
		Nos. 1325-1330 (6)	2.70	
		Set value		98

1977, Apr. 4　Engr.　Perf. 13
1331	A355	4.90d bl & sepia	30	15

1977, Apr. 11　Litho.　Perf. 13½
1332	A356	1.50d lemon & brn	15	15

Kraigher (1877-1959), Slovenian writer.

Boka Kotorska,
by Milo
Milunovic
A357

Europa: 10d, Zagorje in November, by Ljubo Babie.

1977, May 4   Photo.   Perf. 11½
1333 A357 4.90d gold & multi   30   30
1334 A357 10d gold & multi   1.10 1.10

Issued in sheets of 9.

Marshal Tito, by Omer Mujadzic — A358

Mountain Range and Gentian — A359

1977, May 25   Perf. 11½x12
1335 A358 1.50d gold & multi   15   15
1336 A358 3.40d gold & multi   38   30
1337 A358 8d gold & multi   75   52

85th birthday of Pres. Tito. Sheets of 9.

1977, June 6   Litho.   Perf. 13x13½
Design: 10d, Plitvice Lakes Falls, trees, robin and environmental protection emblem.
1338 A359 4.90d multicolored   40   15
1339 A359 10d multicolored   90   65

World Environment Day.

Petar Kocic (1877-1916), Writer — A360

1977, June 15   Perf. 13½
1340 A360 1.50d pale grn & brn   15   15

Map of Europe and Peace Dove — A361

1977, June 15   Litho.   Perf. 13½
1341 A361 4.90d multi   1.10 1.10
1342 A361 10d multi   4.75 4.75

Security and Cooperation Conference, Belgrade, June 15.

Child on Float — A362

Children's drawings: 10d, Fruit picking.

1977, Oct. 3   Litho.   Perf. 13½
1343 A362 4.90d multi   48   15
1344 A362 10d multi   1.25 55

"Joy of Europe" Children's Meeting.

Sava Congress Center, Belgrade A363

1977, Oct. 4   Litho.   Perf. 13½
1345 A363 4.90d bl & multi   65   45
1346 A363 10d car & multi   4.50 3.50

European Security and Cooperation Conference, Belgrade.

Exhibition Emblem — A364

1977, Oct. 20   Litho.   Perf. 13½
1347 A364 4.90d gold & multi   30   15

Balkanfila 1977, 6th Intl. Phil. Exhib. of Balkan Countries, Belgrade, Oct. 24-30.

Double Flute and Shepherd A365

Designs (Landscape and Musician): 3.40d, 4.90d, 6d, Various string instruments. 8d, Bagpipes. 10d, Panpipes.

1977, Oct. 25   Engr.   Perf. 13½
1348 A365 1.50d ocher & red brown   15   15
1349 A365 3.40d green & brn   26   15
1350 A365 4.90d dk brn & yel   30   15
1351 A365 6d bl & red brn   45   16
1352 A365 8d brick red & sep   70   25
1353 A365 10d sl grn & bis   1.00 28
    Nos. 1348-1353 (6)   2.86
    Set value   1.00

Musical instruments from Belgrade Ethnographical Museum.

Ivan Vavpotic, Self-portrait A366

Self-portraits of Yugoslav artists: 3.40d, Mihailo Vukotic. 4.90d, Kosta Hakman. 6d, Miroslav Kraljevic. 8d, Nikola Martinovski. 10d, Milena Pavlovic-Barili.

Perf. 13½x12½
1977, Nov. 26   Photo.
1354 A366 1.50d gold & multi   15   15
1355 A366 3.40d gold & multi   25   15
1356 A366 4.90d gold & multi   35   15
1357 A366 6d gold & multi   45   15
1358 A366 8d gold & multi   70   18
1359 A366 10d gold & multi   95   65
    Nos. 1354-1359 (6)   2.85
    Set value   1.10

Festival of Testaccio, by Klovic — A367

Julija Klovic, by El Greco — A368

1978, Jan. 14   Photo.   Perf. 13½
1360 A367 4.90d multicolored   20   15
1361 A368 10d multicolored   50   45

Julija Klovic (1498-1578), Croat miniaturist.

Stampless Cover, Banaviste to Kubin, 1869 — A369

Designs: 3.40d, Mailbox. 4.90d, Ericsson telephone, 1900. 10d, Morse telegraph, 1844.

1978, Jan. 28   Perf. 13x14
1362 A369 1.50d multicolored   15   15
1363 A369 3.40d multicolored   24   15
1364 A369 4.90d multicolored   35   15
1365 A369 10d multicolored   70   42
    Set value   62

Post Office Museum, Belgrade.

Battle of Pirot A370

1978, Feb. 20   Litho.   Perf. 13½
1366 A370 1.50d gold, blk & sl grn   20   15

Centenary of Serbo-Turkish War.

Airplanes A371

1978, Apr. 24   Litho.   Perf. 13½
1367 A371 1.50d S-49A, 1949   15   15
1368 A371 3.40d Galeb, 1961   25   15
1369 A371 4.90d Utva-75, 1976   38   15
1370 A371 10d Orao, 1974   95   45
    Set value   65

Aeronautical Day.

Europa Issue

View of Golubac — A372

1978, May 3   Photo.   Perf. 11½
1371 A372 4.90d shown   75   75
1372 A372 10d St. Naum Monastery, Ohrid   1.90 1.90

Boxing Glove A373

Honeybee A374

1978, May 5   Litho.   Perf. 13½
1373 A373 4.90d multicolored   45   15

Amateur Boxing Championships.

1978, May 25   Photo.   Perf. 11½
Bees of Yugoslavia: 3.40d, Halictus scabiosae. 4.90d, Blue carpenter bee. 10d, Large earth bumblebee.
1374 A374 1.50d multi   15   15
1375 A374 3.40d multi   28   20
1376 A374 4.90d multi   40   28
1377 A374 10d multi   1.00 70

Filip Filipovic (1878-1938), Radovan Radovic (1878-1906), Revolutionaries A375

1978, June 19   Litho.   Perf. 13½
1378 A375 1.50d dk pur & dl ol   15   15

Marshal Tito — A376

Congress Emblem — A377

1978, June 20
1379 A376 2d red & multi   16   15
1380 A377 4.90d red & multi   60   15
    Set value   16

Souvenir Sheet
Imperf
1381 A376 15d red & multi   5.50 3.75

11th Congress of Yugoslav League of Communists, Belgrade, June 20-23.

Nos. 1246, 1248 Surcharged with New Value and Two Bars in Brown
1978   Litho.   Perf. 13
1382 A323 2d on 1d   25   15
1383 A323 3.40d on 2.10d   28   15
    Set value   15

Issue dates: #1382, July 17; #1383, Aug. 1.

Get free stamps every month! A subscription to the "Scott Stamp Monthly" entitles you to write in for each month's free offer. The value of the free stamps more than offsets the subscription cost. For more information, please call 1-800-488-5351.

Conference Emblem over Belgrade A378

Championship Emblem A379

1978, July 25   Photo.   Perf. 13¹/₂
1384 A378 4.90d bl & lt blue   30   15
Conference of Foreign Ministers of Nonaligned Countries, Belgrade, July 25-29.

1978, Aug. 10   Litho.   Perf. 13¹/₂x13
1385 A379 4.90d multicolored   30   15
14th Kayak and Canoe Still Water Championships, Lake Sava, Aug. 10-14.

Mt. Triglav, North Rock — A380

Black Lake, Mt. Durmitor — A381

1978, Aug. 26   Photo.   Perf. 14
1386 A380 2d multicolored   20   15
Bicentenary of first ascent of Mt. Triglav by Slovenian climbers.

1978, Sept. 20
1387 A381 4.90d shown   35   15
1388 A381 10d Tara River   75   38
Protection of the environment.

Night Sky A382

1978, Sept. 30   Litho.   Perf. 13x12¹/₂
1389 A382 4.90d bl blk, blk & gold   30   15
29th Congress of International Astronautical Federation, Dubrovnik, Oct. 1-8.

People in Forest — A383

Children's drawings: 10d, Family around pond.

1978, Oct. 2   Perf. 13¹/₂x13
1390 A383 4.90d multi   45   15
1391 A383 10d multi   1.00   45
"Joy of Europe" Children's Meeting.

Seal on Insurrection Declaration A384

1978, Oct. 5   Perf. 13¹/₂
1392 A384 2d gold, brn & blk   20   15
Centenary of Kresna uprising.

Teachers' Training Institute, Sombor, Bicent. A385

1978, Oct. 16
1393 A385 2d multicolored   20   15

Croatian Red Cross, Cent. — A386

1978, Oct. 21
1394 A386 2d lt bl, blk & red   20   15

Metallic Sculpture XXII, by Dusan Dzamonja A387

Modern Sculptures: 3.40d, Circulation in Space I, by Vojin Bakic, vert. 4.90d, Tectonic Octopode, by Olga Jevric, vert. 10d, Tree of Life, by Drago Trsar.

Perf. 13¹/₂x13, 13x13¹/₂
1978, Nov. 4   Litho.
1395 A387 2d multicolored   15   15
1396 A387 3.40d multicolored   22   15
1397 A387 4.90d multicolored   32   22
1398 A387 10d multicolored   80   48

Crossing of Neretva Pass, by Ismet Mujezinovic A388

1978, Nov. 10   Litho.   Perf. 13
1399 A388 2d multicolored   20   15
35th anniversary of Battle of Neretva.

Workers Leaving Factory, by Marijan Detoni A389

Larch Cone A390

Engravings: 3.40d, Workers, by Maksim Sedej. 4.90d, Lumberjacks, by Daniel Ozmo. 6d, Meal Break, by Pivo Karamatijevic. 10d, Hanged Man and Raped Woman, by Djordje Andrejevic Kun.

1978, Nov. 28   Photo.   Perf. 14x13¹/₂
1400 A389 2d gold, blk & buff   16   15
1401 A389 3.40d gold & black   24   15
1402 A389 4.90d gold, yel & blk   32   22

1403 A389 6d gold, buff & blk   48   30
1404 A389 10d gold, cr & blk   80   60
    Nos. 1400-1404 (5)   2.00 1.42
Republic day.

1978, Dec. 11   Photo.   Perf. 13x12¹/₂
1405 A390 1.50d shown   20   15
1406 A390 1.50d Red squirrel   20   15
1407 A390 2d Sycamore leaves   25   15
1408 A390 2d Red deer   25   15
    a. Bklt. pane of 8   1.25
1409 A390 3.40d Alder leaves   40   15
1410 A390 3.40d Partridge   40   15
1411 A390 4.90d Oak leaves   50   15
1412 A390 4.90d Grouse   50   15
    a. Bklt. pane of 8   3.50
    Nos. 1405-1412 (8)   2.70
    Set value   78
New Year 1979. Nos. 1405-1412 printed se-tenant in sheets of 25.
No. 1408a contains 4 each of Nos. 1407-1408; No. 1412a 2 each of Nos. 1409-1412, with background colors changed.

Nos. 1064, 868, 1198 Surcharged with New Value and Bars
1978   Engr.; Litho.   Perf. 12¹/₂, 13¹/₂
1413 A263 35p on 10p brown   15   15
1414 A211 60p on 85p dp bl   15   15
1415 A305 80p on 1.20d sl grn   15   15
    Set value   28   15

First Masthead of Politika — A391

1979, Jan. 25   Litho.   Perf. 13¹/₂
1416 A391 2d gold & black   20   15
Politika daily newspaper, 75th anniv.

Red Flags and Emblem A392

Child and IYC Emblem A393

1979, Feb. 15
1417 A392 2d red & gold   20   15
11th Meeting of Self-managers, Kragujevac, Feb. 15-16.

1979, Mar. 1   Photo.   Perf. 11¹/₂x12
1418 A393 4.90d gold vio & bl   65   30
International Year of the Child.

Sabre, Mace, Koran Pouch A394

Old Weapons: 3.40d, Pistol and ramrod, Montenegro. 4.90d, Short carbine and powder horn, Slovenia and Croatia. 10d, Oriental rifle and cartridge pouch.

1979, Mar. 26   Photo.   Perf. 14
1419 A394 2d multicolored   18   15
1420 A394 3.40d multicolored   24   15
1421 A394 4.90d multicolored   30   20
1422 A394 10d multicolored   65   52

5-Pointed Star, Hammer and Sickle — A395

1979, Apr. 20   Photo.   Perf. 13¹/₂
1423 A395 2d multicolored   18   15
1424 A395 4.60d multicolored   45   15
    Set value   15
Communist and Communist Youth Leagues, 60th anniversary.

Cyril and Methodius University and Emblem A396

1979, Apr. 24   Litho.
1425 A396 2d multicolored   20   15
Sts. Cyril and Methodius University, Skopje, 30th anniv.

19th Century Belgrade, by C. Goebel — A397

Europa: 10d, Postilion and Ljubljana, 17th century, by Jan van der Heyden.

1979, Apr. 30   Photo.   Perf. 11¹/₂
1426 A397 4.90d multicolored   30   30
1427 A397 10d multicolored   1.10 1.10

Blue Sow Thistles A398

Milutin Milankovic, by Paja Jovanovic A399

Flowers: 3.40d, Anemones. 4.90d, Astragalus. 10d, Alpine trifolium.

1979, May 25   Photo.   Perf. 13¹/₂
1428 A398 2d multicolored   15   15
1429 A398 3.40d multicolored   20   15
1430 A398 4.90d multicolored   42   15
1431 A398 10d multicolored   85   35
    Set value   65

1979, May 28
1432 A399 4.90d multi   45   20
Milutin Milankovic (1879-1958), scientist.

Kosta Abrasevic (1879-1898), Poet — A400

1979, May 29   Litho.   Perf. 13¹/₂x13
1433 A400 2d org, blk & gray   20   15

Eight-Oared Shell — A401

1979, Aug. 28   Litho.   Perf. 13
1434 A401 4.90d multicolored   50   25
9th World Rowing Championship, Lake Bled.

8th Mediterranean Games, Sept. 15-29, Split — A402

1979, Sept. 10
1435 A402   2d Games Emblem   16   15
1436 A402   4.90d Mascot   42   16
1437 A402   10d Map, Flags   85   45

Seal, 15th Century — A403

1979, Sept. 14   Perf. 12½
1438 A403 2d multicolored   20   15
Zagreb Postal Service, 450th anniversary.

Lake Palic — A404

Environment Protection: 10d, Lakefront, Prokletije Mountains.

1979, Sept. 20   Photo.   Perf. 14x13½
1439 A404 4.90d multicolored   42   15
1440 A404 10d multicolored   85   50

Bank and Fund Emblems A405

Engr. & Photo.
1979, Oct. 1   Perf. 13½
1441 A405 4.90d multicolored   45   15
1442 A405 10d multicolored   90   45
Meeting of the World Bank and International Monetary Fund, Belgrade, Oct. 2-5.

"Joy of Europe" A406

Children's drawings.

1979, Oct. 2   Litho.
1443 A406 4.90d shown   48   15
1444 A406 10d Child in yard   1.00   55

Mihailo Pupin (1854-1935), Physicist, Inventor — A407

1979, Oct. 9   Perf. 13x13½
1445 A407 4.90d multicolored   50   20

Marko Cepenkov — A408

Radovan Portal, Trogir Cathedral — A410

1979, Nov. 15   Litho.   Perf. 13½
1446 A408 2d multicolored   25   15
Cepenkov (1829-1920), Macedonian folklorist.

Pristina University, 10th Anniversary A409

1979, Nov. 17
1447 A409 2d multicolored   25   15

1979, Nov. 28   Photo.
Romanesque Sculptures: 3.40d, Choir stall, Cathedral of Split. 4.90d, Triforium, Church of the Resurrection, Decani. 6d, Buvina Portal, Cathedral of Split. 10d, Western portal, Church of Our Lady, Studenica.

1448 A410   2d multi   18   15
1449 A410   3.40d multi   30   15
1450 A410   4.90d multi   42   20
1451 A410   6d multi   50   25
1452 A410   10d multi   95   40
   Nos. 1448-1452 (5)   2.35 1.15

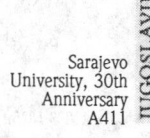
Sarajevo University, 30th Anniversary A411

1979, Dec. 1   Litho.
1453 A411 2d multicolored   25   15

Duro Dakovic and Nikola Hecimovic, Communist Revolutionaries, 50th Death Anniv. — A412

1979, Dec. 10
1454 A412 2d multicolored   25   15

Sidewheeler Deligrad, 1862-1914 — A413

1979, Dec. 14
1455 A413 4.90d shown   1.00 1.00
1456 A413 10d Sidewheeler Serbia, 1917-72   2.25 2.25
Danube Conference.

Milton Manaki and Camera — A414

Edward Kardelj, by Zdenko Kalin — A415

1980, Jan. 21   Litho.   Perf. 13½
1457 A414 2d dp bis & plum   20   15
Manaki (1880-1964), photographer and documentary film maker.

1980, Jan. 26
1458 A415 2d multicolored   20   15
Kardelj (1910-1979), labor movement leader.

No. 1458 Overprinted in Red

1980, Jan. 26
1459 A415 2d multicolored   32   15
Ploce renamed Kardeljevo.

13th Winter Olympic Games, Feb. 12-24, Lake Placid, NY — A416

1980, Feb. 13
1460 A416 4.90d Speed skating   40   30
1461 A416 10d Cross-country skiing 1.10 60

University of Belgrade, 75th Anniversary A417

1980, Feb. 27
1462 A417 2d multicolored   20   15

22nd Summer Olympic Games, July 19-Aug. 3, Moscow A418

1980, Apr. 21
1463 A418   2d Fencing   15   15
1464 A418   3.40d Bicycling   32   32
1465 A418   4.90d Field hockey   42   42
1466 A418   10d Archery   85   85

PLOĆE 1980 KARDELJEVO

Marshal Tito, by Antun Augustincic A419

Europa: 13d, Tito, by Djordje Prudnikov.

1980, Apr. 28   Photo.   Perf. 11½
Granite Paper
1467 A419 4.90d multi   1.10   90
1468 A419 13d multi   4.00 2.75

Marshal Tito, by Bozidar Jakac — A420

1980, May 4   Litho.   Perf. 13½
1469 A420 2.50d purplish blk   35   35
  a.   Perf. 10½   40   35
1470 A420 4.90d gray black   4.75 4.75
Marshal Tito (1892-1980) memorial. Issued in sheets of 8 plus label.

Sava Kovacevic (1905-1943), Revolutionary A421

1980, May 11   Litho.   Perf. 13½
1471 A421 2.50d multicolored   25   18

Wood Baton and Letter — A422

1980, May 14
1472 A422 2d multicolored   20   15
1st Tito Youth Relay Race, 35th anniv.

Flying Gunard — A423

Emperor Trajan Decius Coin, 3rd Cent. — A424

1980, May 24   Photo.   Perf. 12
1473 A423   2d shown   15   15
1474 A423   3.40d Loggerhead turtle 50   18
1475 A423   4.90d Sea swallow   38   28
1476 A423   10d Dolphin   75   60

1980, June 10
3rd Century Roman Coins (Illyrian Emperors): 3.40d, Aurelianus. 4.90d, Probus. 10d, Diocletianus.
1477 A424   2d multicolored   15   15
1478 A424   3.40d multicolored   32   18
1479 A424   4.90d multicolored   40   22
1480 A424   10d multicolored   80   50

No. 1247 Surcharged with New Value and Bars

1980, June 17   Litho.   Perf. 13½
1481 A323 2.50d on 1.50d   20   15

Types of 1971-77

Views: 5p, Krusevac. 10p, Gradacac. 30p, Krk. 35p, Omis. 40p, Pec. 2.50d, Kragujevac. 3.50d, Vrsac. 5.60d, Travnik. 8d, Dubrovnik.

Perf. 13½, 13½x12½ (#1487)

1980-81

1482	A263	5p dp orange	15	15
1483	A263	10p brown	24	15
1483A	A263	20p purple ('78)	15	15
1484	A263	30p olive gray	20	15
1485	A263	35p brown red	15	15
1486	A263	40p gray	16	15
1487	A323	2.50d rose red	16	15
1488	A323	2.50d bl gray ('81)	16	15
1489	A323	3.50d red org ('81)	30	15
1490	A323	5.60d gray grn ('81)	38	15
1491	A323	8d gray ('81)	50	20
	Nos. 1482-1491 (11)		2.55	
	Set value			80

No. 1483A has all three numerals in denomination the same size. On No. 1065 "20" is taller than first "0."

Perf. 13x12½

1482a	A263	5p
1485a	A263	35p
1487a	A323	2.50d
1488a	A323	2.50d
1489a	A323	3.50d
1490a	A323	5.60d
1491a	A323	8d

400th Anniversary of Lipica Stud Farm A425

1980, June 25

1493	A425	2.50d black	25	15

A426   A427

1980, June 27   **Perf. 13½**

1494	A426	2.50d mag & red	25	15

Tito, Basic Law of Self-management, 30th anniv.

1980, June 28   **Perf. 13**

1495	A427	2.50d light green	25	15

University of Novi Sad, 20th anniv.

Mljet National Park — A428   Minerals — A429

1980, Sept. 5   Photo.   Perf. 14

1496	A428	4.90d shown	28	18
1497	A428	13d Galicica Natl. Park	80	48

European Nature Protection Year.

1980, Sept. 10   Litho.   Perf. 13½

1498	A429	2.50d Pyrrhotine	15	15
1499	A429	3.40d Dolomite	26	16
1500	A429	4.90d Sphalerite	35	20
1501	A429	13d Wulfenite	75	52

No. 1244 Surcharged with New Value and Bars

1980, Oct. 15   Litho.   Perf. 13

1502	A323	5d on 75p pur	35	15

View of Kotor, UNESCO Emblem A430

1980, Sept. 23   **Perf. 13½**

1503	A430	4.90d multicolored	40	15

21st UNESCO General Conf., Belgrade,

Children in Garden — A431

Joy of Europe Children's Festival: 13d, Three faces.

1980, Oct. 2   **Perf. 13½x13**

1504	A431	4.90d multi	35	25
1505	A431	13d multi	90	52

Dove over Madrid Meeting Hall — A432

Lithographed and Engraved

1980, Nov. 11   **Perf. 13½**

1506	A432	4.90d dk grn & bl grn	38	32
1507	A432	13d dk brn & yel brown	1.40	90

European Security Conference, Madrid.

Federal Flag of Yugoslavia A433

Republic Day: Socialist Republic flags. Nos. 1508-1515 se-tenant. No. 1511 has Latin letters.

1980, Nov. 28   Litho.   Perf. 12½

1508	A433	2.50d Bosnia & Herzegovina	15	15
1509	A433	2.50d Croatia	15	15
1510	A433	2.50d shown	15	15
1511	A433	2.50d Yugoslavia	15	15
1512	A433	2.50d Macedonia	15	15
1513	A433	2.50d Montenegro	15	15
1514	A433	2.50d Serbia	15	15
1515	A433	2.50d Slovenia	15	15
	Nos. 1508-1515 (8)		1.20	
	Set value			72

Woman with Straw Hat — A434

Paintings: 3.40d, Atelier No. 1, by Gabriel Stupica. 4.90d, To the Glory of the Sutjeska Fighters, by Ismet Mujezinovic. 8d, Serenity, by Marino Tartaglia, vert. 13d, Complaint, by Milos Vuskovic, vert.

1980, Dec. 16   **Perf. 13½**

1516	A434	2.50d multi	15	15
1517	A434	3.40d multi	22	15
1518	A434	4.90d multi	30	20
1519	A434	8d multi	45	35
1520	A434	13d multi	75	55
	Nos. 1516-1520 (5)		1.87	1.40

Ivan Ribar (1881-1968), Politician — A435

1981, Jan. 21   Litho.   Perf. 13½

1521	A435	2.50d rose red & blk	25	25

Cementusa Hand Bomb A436

Partisan Weapons: 5.60d, Rifle. 8d, 52-mm Cannon. 13d, Man-powered tank.

1981, Feb. 16

1522	A436	3.50d brick red & blk	22	15
1523	A436	5.60d grn & blk	32	20
1524	A436	8d bis brn & blk	42	25
1525	A436	13d rose vio & blk	70	40

Monastery of the Virgin, Eleousa, 900th Anniversary A437

1981, Mar. 3

1526	A437	3.50d multicolored	25	15

36th World Table Tennis Championship, Novi Sad, Apr. 14-26 — A438

1981, Apr. 14   Litho.   Perf. 13½

1527	A438	8d multicolored	45	25

Europa Issue

Wedding in Herzegovina, by Nikola Arsenovic A439

Paintings by Nikola Arsenovic (1823-1885): 13d, Witnesses at a Wedding.

**1981, May 5   Photo.   Perf. 12
Granite Paper**

1528	A439	8d multicolored	50	50
1529	A439	13d multicolored	85	85

Dimitrije Tucovic and Slavija Square, Belgrade A440

1981, May 13   Litho.   Perf. 13½

1530	A440	3.50d bl vio & red	25	20

Tucovic (1881-1914), Socialist leader.

Marshal Tito, by Milivoje Unkovic — A441

**1981, May 25   Photo.   Perf. 11½x12
Granite Paper**

1531	A441	3.50d gold & dk brn	1.00	1.00

Marshal Tito's 89th birth anniversary.

Sunflower A442   3rd Autonomous Enterprises Cong. A443

**1981, May 28   Photo.   Perf. 11½
Granite Paper**

1532	A442	3.05d shown	20	15
1533	A442	5.60d Hops	26	18
1534	A442	8d Corn	38	30
1535	A442	13d Wheat	65	48

1981, June 16   Litho.   Perf. 13½

1536	A443	3.50d multicolored	25	20

Djordje Petrov (1864-1921), Macedonian Revolutionary A444

1981, June 22

1537	A444	3.50d bister & blk	25	20

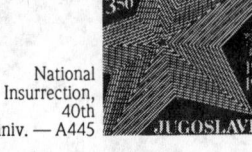

National Insurrection, 40th Anniv. — A445

1981, July 4   **Perf. 12½**

1538	A445	3.50d red org & tan	20	15
1539	A445	8d red org & tan	40	22
	Set value			30

**Souvenir Sheet
Imperf**

1540	A445	30d Lenin monument	1.65	1.40

800th Anniv. of Varazdin A446

1981, Aug. 20   Litho.   Perf. 13½

1541	A446	3.50d multicolored	25	20

Parliament Building, Belgrade — A447

1981, Sept. 1
1542 A447 8d red & blue 45 30
Belgrade Conference of Non-Aligned Countries, 20th anniv.

Serbian Printing Office, 150th Anniv. — A448

1981, Sept. 15
1543 A448 3.50d pale rose & dk bl 25 20

Fran Levstik (1831-1887), Writer — A449

1981, Sept. 28 *Perf. 12x11½*
1544 A449 3.50d dl red & gray 25 20

No. 1251 Surcharged with New Value and Bars

1981, Oct. *Perf. 13*
1545 A323 5d on 4.90d dl bl 35 20
a. Perf. 13x12½

Joy of Europe Children's Festival A450

1981, Oct. 2
1546 A450 8d Barnyard 35 35
1547 A450 13d Skiers 65 45

125th Anniv. of European Danube Commission — A451

1981, Oct. 28 *Litho. Perf. 13½*
1548 A451 8d Tugboat Karlovac 35 35
1549 A451 13d Train hauling boat, Sip Canal 65 45

No. 1250a Surcharged with New Value and Bars

1981, Oct. 9 *Litho. Perf. 13x12½*
1550 A323 3.50d on 3.40d gray grn 38 20
a. on #1250

Savings Bank of Yugoslavia, 60th Anniv. A452

Intl. Inventions Conference A453

1981, Oct. 31 *Perf. 11½x12*
1551 A452 3.50d multicolored 20 20

1981, Nov. 4 *Perf. 13½*
1552 A453 8d red & gold 35 35

Nature Protection A454

1981, Nov. 14
1553 A454 8d Plant, Ruguvo Ravine 35 35
1554 A454 13d Lynx, Prokletjie Mountains 55 55

August Senoa (1838-1881), Writer — A455

1981, Dec. 12 *Perf. 11½x12*
1555 A455 3.50d dl gray vio & gldn brn 20 20

Still Life with a Fish, by Jovan Bijelic (1886-1964) — A456

Paintings of Animals: 5.60d, Raven, by Milo Milunovic (1897-1967). 8d, Bird on Blue Background, by Marko Celebonovic (b. 1902). 10d, Horses, by Peter Lubarda (1907-1974). 13d, Sheep, by Nikola Masic (1852-1902).

1981, Dec. 29 *Photo. Perf. 13½*
1556 A456 3.50d multi 18 18
1557 A456 5.60d multi 25 25
1558 A456 8d multi 32 32
1559 A456 10d multi 42 42
1560 A456 13d multi 55 55
Nos. 1556-1560 (5) 1.72 1.72

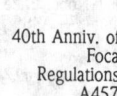

40th Anniv. of Foca Regulations A457

1982, Jan. 14 *Litho. Perf. 13½*
1561 A457 3.50d Mosa Pijade 20 20

60th Anniv. of Communist Newspaper Borba — A458

1982, Feb. 19 *Litho.*
1562 A458 3.50d red & blk 20 20

500th Anniv. of City of Cetinje — A459

1982, Mar. 10
1563 A459 3.50d dull red brn 20 20

Capt. Ivo Visin (1806-1868), Boka Kotorska's Map — A460

1982, May 5 *Photo. Perf. 11½*
1564 A460 8d shown 32 32
1565 A460 15d Ship Splendido 55 55
Europa, 1st Yugoslavian circumnavigation, 1852-1859.

Male House Sparrow — A461

1982, May 24 *Litho. Perf. 13½*
1566 A461 3.50d shown 16 16
1567 A461 5.60d Female house sparrow 28 28
1568 A461 8d Male field sparrow 40 40
1569 A461 15d Female field sparrow 70 70
See Nos. 1687-1690.

90th Birth Anniv. of Marshal Tito — A462

1982, May 25 *Photo. Perf. 11½x12*
Granite Paper
1570 A462 3.50d multicolored 20 20

1982 World Cup — A463

Designs: Soccer ball in various positions.

1982, June 12 *Perf. 11½*
Granite Paper
1571 Sheet of 4 1.40 1.40
a. A463 3.50d multicolored 15 15
b. A463 5.60d multicolored 16 16
c. A463 8d multicolored 30 30
d. A463 15d multicolored 55 55

12th Congress of Yugoslavian Communists' League, Belgrade, June 26-29 — A464

1982 June 26 *Litho. Perf. 13½*
1572 A464 3.50d orange & red 15 15
1573 A464 8d gray & red 28 28

Souvenir Sheet
Perf. 12½
1574 Sheet of 2 1.40 1.40
a. A464 10d like 3.50d 45 45
b. A464 20d like 8d 85 85

Dura Jaksic (1832-1878), Writer, Painter — A465

1982, July 27 *Litho. Perf. 14*
1575 A465 3.50d Self-portrait 20 20

1982 World Championships Held in Yugoslavia A466

1982, July 30 *Perf. 13½*
1576 A466 8d Gymnastics 32 32
1577 A466 8d Kayak 32 32
1578 A466 8d Weightlifting 32 32

Ivan Zajc (1832-1914), Composer and Conductor — A467

1982, Aug. 3
1579 A467 4d brown 20 20

Breguet XIX and Potez XXV — A468

1982, Sept. 1 *Litho. Perf. 13½*
1580 A468 4d shown 16 16
1581 A468 6.10d Super Galeb G-4 20 20
1582 A468 8.80d Armed boat 35 35
1583 A468 15d Rocket gun boat 50 50

40th anniv. of Air Force/Anti-aircraft Defense and Navy.

Spruce Branch, Tara Natl. Park A469

1982, Sept. 3
1584 A469 8.80d shown   35 35
1585 A469 15d Mediterranean monk seal, Kornati   55 55

14th Joy of Europe Children's Festival A470

1982, Oct. 2
1586 A470 8.80d Traffic   35 35
1587 A470 15d In the Bath   55 55

Small Onofrio's Fountain, 15th Cent. — A471

1982, Oct. 23
1588 A471 8.80d multi   32 32

16th Universal Federation of Travel Agents' Assoc. Cong., Dubrovnik, Oct. 24-30.

600th Anniv. of Hercegnovi A472

1982, Oct. 28
1589 A472 4d multicolored   20 20

14th Winter Olympic Games, Sarajevo, Feb. 8-19, 1984 — A473

1982, Nov. 20   *Perf. 12½*
1590 A473 4d Bridge, Miljacka River   15 15
1591 A473 6.10d Minaret, Mosque   18 18
1592 A473 8.80d Evangelical Church   30 30
1593 A473 15d Street   45 45

Nos. 1488a and 1489a Surcharged In Red, Blue, Black or Red Violet with Two Bars or Shield

1982-83   **Litho.**   *Perf. 13x12½*
1594 A323 30p on 2.50d (R)   15 15
1595 A323 50p on 2.50d (Bl)   15 15
1596 A323 60p on 2.50d ('83)   15 15
1597 A323 1d on 3.50d   15 15
1597A A323 2d on 2.50d (RV)   15 15
    Set value   30 25

Perf. 13
1594a A323 30p on #1488
1595a A323 50p on #1488
1596a A323 60p on #1488
1597b A323 1d on #1489

Types of 1971-77

Designs: 3d, Skofja Loka. 4d, Pocitelj. 5d, Osijek. 6.10d, like 2.10d. 8.80d, Hercegnovi. 10d, Sarajevo. 16.50d, Ohrid.

1982-83   **Litho.**   *Perf. 13x12½*
1598 A323 3d gray bl   15 15
1599 A263 4d red org   16 15
1600 A263 5d grnsh bl ('83)   20 15
1601 A323 6.10d olive grn   28 15

1602 A263 8.80d gray   52 15
    Perf. 13½
1603 A263 10d red lil ('83)   52 15
1603A A323 16.50d dl bl ('83)   80 25
    Nos. 1598-1603A (7)   2.63
    Set value   90

Type styles of Nos. 1600, 1603-1603A differ somewhat from illustrations.

Perf. 13
1598a A323 3d
1599a A323 4d
1600a A323 5d
1601a A323 6.10d
1602a A323 8.80d
1603b A323 10d
1603c A323 16.50d

40th Anniv. of Anti-Fascist Council A474

1982, Nov. 26   *Perf. 13½*
1604 A474 4d Bihac, 1942   15 15

The Manuscript, by Janez Bernik (b. 1933) — A475

Designs: 4d, Prophet on Golden Background, by Joze Ciuha (b. 1924). 6.10d, Journey to the West, by Andrej Jemec (b. 1934). 8.80d, Black Comb with Red Band, by Riko Debenjak (b. 1908). 15d, The Vitrine, by Adriana Maraz (b. 1931). 4d, 6.10d, 8.80d vert.

1982, Nov. 27
1605 A475 4d multi   15 15
1606 A475 6.10d multi   15 15
1607 A475 8.80d multi   22 22
1608 A475 10d multi   25 22
1609 A475 15d multi   40 30
    Nos. 1605-1609 (5)   1.17 1.04

Uros Predic (1857-1953), Painter — A476

1982, Dec. 7
1610 A476 4d multicolored   15 15

Union of Pioneers, 40th Anniv. — A477

1982, Dec. 27   *Perf. 12*
1611 A477 4d multicolored   15 15

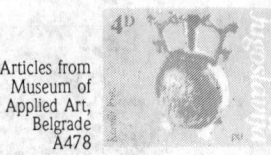

Articles from Museum of Applied Art, Belgrade A478

Designs: 4d, Lead pitcher, Gnjilane, 16th cent. 6.10d, Silver-plated jug, Macedonia, 18th cent. 8.80d, Goblet, 16th cent., Dalmatia. 15d, Mortar, 15th cent., Kotor.

1983, Feb. 19
1612 A478 4d multicolored   15 15
1613 A478 6.10d multicolored   15 15
1614 A478 8.80d multicolored   22 22
1615 A478 15d multicolored   40 30

Mount Jalovec — A479

Serbian Telephone Service Centenary — A480

1983, Feb. 26
1616 A479 4d blue & lt bl   15 15

Slovenian Mountaineering Soc., 90th anniv.

1983, Mar. 15
1617 A480 3d Ericsson phone   15 15

25th Anniv. of Intl. Org. for Maritime Navigation (OMI) — A481

1983, Mar. 17   *Perf. 13½x14*
1618 A481 8.80d multi   30 30

Edible Mushrooms A482

1983, Mar. 21   *Perf. 14*
1619 A482 4d Agaricus campestris   15 15
1620 A482 6.10d Morchella vulgaris   16 16
1621 A482 8.80d Boletus edulis   24 24
1622 A482 15d Cantharellus cibarius   40 32

Rijeka Railway, 110th Anniv. — A483

Boro and Ramiz Monument, Landovica — A484

1983, Apr. 5
1623 A483 4d Steam engine series 401   15 15
1624 A483 23.70d on 8.80d Thyristor locomotive 442   38 38
    Set value   44

No. 1624 not issued without surcharge.

1983, Apr. 10
1625 A484 4d multi   15 15

Boro Vukmirovic and Ramiz Sadiku, revolutionary martyrs, 40th death anniv.

Europa Issue

Ivo Andric (1892-1975), Poet, 1961 Nobel Prize Winner — A485

1983, May 5   **Photo.**   *Perf. 11½*
    Granite Paper
1626 A485 8.80d Medal, Travnik Chronicle text   25 25
1627 A485 20d Portrait, Bridge, Drina River   55 50

50th Intl. Agricultural Fair, Novi Sad — A486

1983, May 13   **Litho.**   *Perf. 14*
1628 A486 4d Combine harvester   15 15

40th Anniv. of Battle of Sutjeska — A487

1983, May 14   *Perf. 12½*
1629 A487 3d Assault, by Pivo Karamatijevic   15 15

A488   A489

1983, May 25   *Perf. 13½*
1630 A488 4d Tito, Parliament   15 15
a.   Perf. 12½

30th anniv. of election of Pres. Tito.

1983, May 27
1631 A489 4d First mail and passenger car   15 15
1632 A489 16.50d Mountain road, Kotor   38 18
    Set value   24

80th anniv. of automobile service in Montenegro.

A490   A491

1983, June 5   *Perf. 14*
1633 A490 23.70d multi   60 30

UN Conference on Trade and Development, 6th session, Belgrade, June 6-30.

1983, June 7   *Perf. 12½*
1634 A491 4d Engraving by Valvasor   15 15

Town of Pazin millenium.

Triumphal Arch, Titograd A492

1983, June 9   *Perf. 12½*
1635 A492 100d Memorial to F. Filipovic, Valjevo, vert.   2.25 1.10
a.   Perf. 13x13½
1636 A492 200d shown   4.50 2.25
a.   Perf. 13½x13

Skopje Earthquake, 20th Anniv. — A493

1983, July 26   **Litho.**   *Perf. 12½*
1637 A493 23.70d dp mag   55 25
a.   Perf. 13½

For surcharge, see No. 1715.

Sculpture by Ivan Mestrovic A494   Joy of Europe A496

European Nature Protection — A495

1983, Aug. 15
1638 A494 6d multicolored   15 15

1983, Sept. 10   **Litho.**   *Perf. 13*

Designs: 16.50d, Gentian, Kopaonik National Park. 23.70d, Chamois, Perucica Gorge.

1639 A495 16.50d multi   32 15
1640 A495 23.70d multi   52 25

See Nos. 1685-1686.

1983, Oct. 3   **Litho.**   *Perf. 13½*

Children's Paintings: 16.50d, Bride and Bridegroom by Verna Paunkonik. 23.70d, Andres and his Mother by Marta Lopez-Ibor.

1641 A496 16.50d multi   38 18
1642 A496 23.70d multi   52 25

A497   — A498

1983, Oct. 17   **Litho.**   *Perf. 12½*
1643 A497 5d multicolored   15 15

Kragujevac High School sesquicentenary.

1983, Oct. 17   **Litho.**   *Perf. 13½*
1644 A498 5d multicolored   15 15

Timok Uprising centenary.

14th Winter Olympic Games, Sarajevo, Feb. 8-19, 1984 — A499

1983, Nov. 25   **Engr.**   *Perf. 13½*
1645 A499   4d   Ski jump   15 15
1646 A499   4d   Slalom   15 15
1647 A499 16.50d Bobsledding   42 22
1648 A499 16.50d Downhill skiing   42 22
1649 A499 23.70d Speed skating   60 30
1650 A499 23.70d Hockey   60 30
Nos. 1645-1650 (6)   2.34
Set value   1.15

Souvenir Sheet
Imperf
1651 A499 50d Emblem   1.40 60

Jovan Jovanovic Zmaj (1833-1904), Poet, Neven Masthead A500

1983, Nov. 24   **Litho.**   *Perf. 12½*
1652 A500 5d multicolored   15 15

Peasant Wedding, by Pieter Brueghel — A501

Paintings: No. 1654, Susanna with the Old Men, No. 1655, Allegory of Wisdom and Strength, by Paolo Veronese (1528-1588). No. 1656, Virgin Mary from Salamanca, by Robert Campin (1375-1444). No. 1657, St. Ann with Madonna and Jesus, by Albrecht Dürer (1471-1528).

1983, Nov. 26   *Perf. 14*
1653 A501   4d multi   15 15
1654 A501 16.50d multi   40 20
1655 A501 16.50d multi   40 20
1656 A501 23.70d multi   55 28
1657 A501 23.70d multi   55 28
Nos. 1653-1657 (5)   2.05 1.11

View of Jajce — A502   Koco Racin (1908-1943), Writer — A504

World Communications Year — A503

1983, Nov. 28   *Perf. 13x12½*
1658 A502 5d multicolored   15 15

Souvenir Sheet
Imperf
1659 A502 30d Tito   1.25 60

40th anniv. of Second Session of the Antifascist Council of the Natl. Liberation of Yugoslavia, Jajce, Nov. 29-30.

1983, Dec. 10   *Perf. 13½*
1660 A503 23.70d multi   .50 25

1983, Dec. 22
1661 A504 5d multicolored   15 15

Politika Front Page, Oct. 28, 1944 — A505

1984, Jan. 25   **Litho.**   *Perf. 12½*
1662 A505 5d red & black   15 15

80th anniv. of Politika newspaper and 40th anniv. in Yugoslavia.

Veljko Petrovic (1884-1967), Poet — A506

1984, Feb. 4   **Litho.**   *Perf. 13½*
1663 A506 5d multicolored   15 15

1984 Winter Olympics A507

1984, Feb. 8
1664 A507   4d   Biathlon   15 15
1665 A507   4d   Giant slalom   15 15
1666 A507   5d   Bobsledding   15 15
1667 A507   5d   Slalom   15 15
1668 A507 16.50d Speed skating   45 22
1669 A507 16.50d Hockey   45 22
1670 A507 23.70d Ski jumping   65 35
1671 A507 23.70d Downhill skiing   65 35
Nos. 1664-1671 (8)   2.80
Set value   1.40

Souvenir Sheets
Imperf
1672 A507   50d Flame, rings   1.40 70
1673 A507 100d Flame, map   2.75 1.40

Natl. Heroines A508

Designs: a, Marija Bursac (1902-43). b, Jelena Cetkovic (1916-43). c, Nada Dimic (1923-42). d, Elpida Karamandi (1920-42). e, Toncka Cec Olga (1896-1943). f, Spasenija Babovic Cana (1907-77). g, Jovanka Radivojevic Kica (1922-43). h, Sonja Marinkovic (1916-41).

1984, Mar. 8   **Litho.**   *Perf. 14*
1674   A508   Sheet of 8 + label   1.00 75
a.-h.   A508 5d any single   15 15

Slovenia Monetary Institute, 40th Anniv. — A509

1984, Mar. 12   *Perf. 12½*
1675 A509 5d Bond, note   15 15

Railroad Service in Serbia (Belgrade-Nis) Centenary A510

1984, Apr. 9   *Perf. 13*
1676 A510 5d Train, Central Belgrade Station   15 15

The values of stamps in very fine to superb condition are greater than catalogue value.

Jure Franko, Giant Slalom Silver Medalist, 1984 — A511

1984, Apr. 28
1677 A511 23.70d multi   85 35

Yugoslavia's first Winter Olympic medalist.

Europa (1959-84) A512

1984, Apr. 30   *Perf. 13½*
1678 A512 23.70d multi   55 24
1679 A512   50d multi   1.10 52

5d 1984 Summer Olympics, Los Angeles — A513

1984, May 14
1680 A513   5d   Basketball   15 15
1681 A513 16.50d Diving   40 18
1682 A513 23.70d Equestrian   55 25
1683 A513   50d Running   1.25 55

Marshal Tito — A514

1984, May 25   *Perf. 13*
1684 A514 5d brown red   15 15

Nature Type of 1983

Designs: 26d, Centaurea gloriosa (flower), Biokovo Mountain Park. 40d, Anophthalmus (insect), Pekel Cave, Savinja Valley.

1984, June 11   **Litho.**   *Perf. 13½*
1685 A495 26d multicolored   32 15
1686 A495 40d multicolored   50 22

Bird Type of 1982

1984, June 28
1687 A461   4d   Great black-backed gull   15 15
1688 A461   5d   Black-headed gull   15 15
1689 A461 16.50d Herring gull   30 15
1690 A461 40d   Common tern   35 18
Set value   82 46

19th Cent. Cradles — A515

1984, Sept. 1   **Litho.**   *Perf. 12½*
1691 A515   4d Bosnia & Herzegovina   15 15
1692 A515   5d Montenegro   15 15
1693 A515 26d Macedonia   25 15
1694 A515 40d Serbia   40 20
Set value   82 46

Olive Tree, Mirovica
A516

1984, Sept. 1
1695 A516 5d multi   15 15

Joy of Europe — A517   Map, Concentric Waves — A519

City of Virovitica, 750th Anniv. — A518

Children's Drawings.

1984, Oct. 2 Litho. Perf. 14
1696 A517 26d Traditional costumes   32 15
1697 A517 40d Girl with doll carriage   48 22

1984, Oct. 4 Perf. 13½
1698 A518 5d Engraving, 17th cent.   15 15

1984, Oct. 10
1699 A519 6d Prus bl & brt grn   15 15

Radio and telegraph service in Montenegro, 80th anniv.

Veterans Conference
A520

1984, Oct. 18
1700 A520 26d multicolored   32 15
1701 A520 40d multicolored   48 22

Conference of Veterans on Security, Disarmament and Cooperation in Europe, Belgrade, Oct. 18-20.

Liberation of Belgrade, 40th Anniv. — A521   Miloje Milojevic (1884-1946), Composer — A522

1984, Oct. 20
1702 A521 6d "40," arms   15 15

1984, Oct. 27
1703 A522 6d Portrait, score   15 15

Medals Events, 1984 Summer Olympics — A522a

Designs: a, Wrestling. b, Running. c, Field hockey. d, Shot put. e, Soccer. f, Basketball. g, Netball. h, Rowing.

1984, Nov. 14 Litho. Perf. 13½
1704   Sheet of 8   2.75 2.50
a.-h.   A522a 26d any single   32 24

The Tahitians, by Gauguin
A523

Paintings by Foreign Artists in Yugoslav Museums: 6d, Portrait of Madame Tatichek, by Ferdinand Waldmuller (1793-1865). No. 1706, The Bathers, by Renoir (1841-1919). No. 1707, At the Window, by Henri Matisse (1869-1954). 40d, Ballerinas, by Edgar Degas (1834-1917). Nos. 1705-1707 vert.

Perf. 13½x14, 14x13½

1984, Nov. 15
1705 A523 6d multicolored   15 15
1706 A523 26d multicolored   40 30
1707 A523 26d multicolored   40 20
1708 A523 38d multicolored   58 30
1709 A523 40d multicolored   60 30
  Nos. 1705-1709 (5)   2.13 1.25

Nova Macedonia Newspaper, 40th Anniv.
A523a

1984, Nov. 29 Perf. 13½
1710 A523a 6d 1st & recent editions   15 15

Nos. 1602, 1599 and 1637 Surcharged with Three Bars in Red Brown or Black, Types of 1975 and

Exhibition Center, Zagreb — A524

Bird, Jet, Landscape
A525

Designs: 6d, Kikinda. 26d, Korcula. 38d, Maribor. 70d, Trumpeter monument, riverside buildings in Zagreb.

Perf. 13½x12½, 13 (#1713, 1717), 12½ (#1715)

1984-86   **Litho.**
1711 A263 2d on 8.80d   15 15
a.   on #1602a
1712 A263 6d on 4d (RBr)   15 15
a.   on #1599a
1713 A323 6d lt red brn   15 15
a.   Perf. 13x12½
1715 A493 20d on 23.70d   22 15
1717 A263 26d dp ultra   30 15
  a.   Perf. 13x12½
1718 A323 38d dp lil rose   42 22
  a.   Perf. 13
1719 A323 70d brt ultra ('85)   40 30
  b.   Perf. 13

Perf. 14
1719A A524 100d brt org yel & vio   65 45

Perf. 12½
1720 A525 500d redsh brn & multi ('85)   3.25 2.25
1721 A525 1000d org brn & multi ('85)   6.50 4.50
  a.   Perf. 13½
  Nos. 1711-1721 (10)   12.19 8.47

Type styles for Nos. 1717-1718 differ somewhat from illustration.

Museum Exhibits - Fossils — A526

1985, Feb. 4 Litho. Perf. 12½
1722 A526 5d Aturia aturi   15 15
1723 A526 6d Pachyophis woodwardi   15 15
1724 A526 33d Chaetodon hoeferi   22 15
1725 A526 60d Homo sapiens neanderthalensis   40 20
  Set value   72 40

40th Anniv., Monument Protection
A527

1985, Feb. 20 Litho. Perf. 12½
1726 A527 6d Hopovo church   15 15

Ski Jumping at Planica, 50th Anniv.
A528   European Nature Conservation
A529

1985, Mar. 15 Litho. Perf. 13½
1727 A528 6d Three herons in flight   15 15

1985, Mar. 30 Perf. 14
1728 A529 42d Pandion haliaetus   32 15
1729 A529 60d Upupa epops   48 20

Audubon birth bicentenary, European Information Center for Nature Protection.

A530   A531

Fresco of St. Methodius, St. Naum Monastery, Ohrid.

1985, Apr. 6 Litho. Perf. 11½x12
1730 A530 10d multicolored   15 15

St. Methodius (d. 885), archbishop of Pannonia and Moravia.

1985, Apr. 16 Litho. Perf. 12½
1731 A531 6d Clasped hands   15 15

Osimo Agreements, 10th anniv. Yugoslavia-Italy political and economic cooperation.

Josip Slavenski (1896-1955), Composer
A532

Europa: 60d, Portrait, block flute, darabukka. 80d, Balkanophonia score, signature.

1985, Apr. 29 Perf. 14
1732 A532 60d multi   42 20
1733 A532 80d multi   60 24

Joachim Vujic, by Dimitrije Avramovic (1815-1855)
A533

1985, May 8 Perf. 12x11½
1734 A533 10d multi   15 15

Joachim Vujic Theater, Kragujevac, 150th anniv.

Liberation from German Occupation Forces, 40th Anniv. — A534

1985, May 9 Perf. 13½
1735 A534 10d shown   15 15
1736 A534 10d Order of Natl. Liberation   15 15
  Set value   20 15

Franjo Kluz (1912-1944), Rudi Cajavec (1911-1942), Breguet-19 Fighter — A535

1985, May 21 Perf. 13x12½
1737 A535 10d multi   15 15

Air Force Day.

Pres. Tito (1892-1980)
A536   Cres-Losinj Municipal Tourism Bureau, Cent.
A537

1985, May 25 Perf. 13½
1738 A536 10d Portrait   15 15

1985, June 12
1739 A537 10d Map, town arms, villa   15 15

UN 40th Anniv. — A538   Rowing — A539

1985, June 26 Litho. Perf. 12½
1740 A538 70d Emblem, rainbow   55 25

1985, June 29   Litho.   Perf. 13½
1741 A539 70d multicolored   55 25
Souvenir Sheet
1742 A539 100d Course map, arms   75 38
Intl. European-Danube Rowing Regatta, 30th anniv.

Nautical Tourism — A540

1985, July 1   Litho.
1743 A540 8d Sailboat   15 15
1744 A540 10d Windsurfing   15 15
1745 A540 50d Sailboat, diff.   35 18
1746 A540 70d Sailboat, diff.   48 25
Set value   52

F1B Class Motorized Model Plane — A541

1985, Aug. 10   Litho.   Perf. 12½x13
1747 A541 70d multicolored   45 35
Free Flight World Championships, Livno, Aug. 12-18.

Algae — A542

1985, Sept. 20   Perf. 14
1748 A542 8d Corallina officinalis   15 15
1749 A542 10d Desmarestia viridis   15 15
1750 A542 50d Fucus vesiculosus   30 22
1751 A542 70d Padina pavonia   40 30
Set value   82 62

Intl. Federation of Stomatologists, 73rd Congress, Belgrade, Sept. 21-28 — A543

1985, Sept. 21   Perf. 12x11½
1752 A543 70d multicolored   45 30

Children's Drawings — A544

Designs: 50d, Children in a Horse-drawn Cart, by Branka Lukic, age 14, Yugoslavia. 70d, Children in Field, by Suzanne Straathof, age 9, Netherlands.

1985, Oct. 2   Perf. 14
1753 A544 50d multicolored   30 22
1754 A544 70d multicolored   40 30

Croatian Natl. Theater, Zagreb, 125th Anniv. — A545

1985, Nov. 23   Perf. 12½
1755 A545 10d Facade detail   15 15

Miladin Popovic A546 — Natl. Coat of Arms A547

1985, Nov. 26   Perf. 11½x12
1756 A546 10d Portrait   15 15
Popovic (1910-1945), revolutionary.

1985, Nov. 28   Perf. 13½
1757 A547 10d multicolored   15 15
Souvenir Sheet
Imperf
1758 A547 100d multicolored   65 45
Socialist Federal Republic of Yugoslavia, 40th anniv. No. 1758 contains one stamp 18x27mm.

Royal Procession, by Iromie Wijewardena, Sri Lanka — A548

Paintings from the Art Gallery of Non-aligned Countries, Titograd: 10d, Return from Hunting, by Mama Cangare, Mali. No. 1761, Drum of Coca, by Agnes Ovando Sanz De Franck, Bolivia. No. 1762, The Cock, by Mariano Rodriguez, Cuba. 70d, Three Women, by Quamrul Hassan, Bangladesh.

1985, Dec. 2   Perf. 14
1759 A548 8d multicolored   15 15
1760 A548 10d multicolored   15 15
1761 A548 50d multicolored   30 22
1762 A548 50d multicolored   30 22
1763 A548 70d multicolored   40 30
Set value   1.10 82

Nos. 1243, 1482, 1485a, 1490, 1491, 1713a, 1717a, 1603A and 1718 Surcharged in Light Red Brown, Brown or Dark Brown
Perf. 13½, 13½x12½
1985-86   Litho.
1764 A323 1d on 25p (B)   15 15
1765 A263 2d on 5p (DB)   15 15
  a.   on #1482a
1766 A263 3d on 35p (DB)   15 15
  a.   on #1485a
1767 A323 4d on 5.60d (B)   15 15
  b.   on #1490
1767A A323 5d on 8d (B)   15 15
  c.   on #1491a
1768 A323 8d on 6d   15 15
  a.   on #1713
1769 A263 20d on 26d   16 15
  a.   on #1717
1770 A323 50d on 16.50d (B)   40 30
  a.   on #1603c
1771 A323 70d on 38d   55 42
Set value   1.35 1.05
Issue dates: No. 1767A, Mar. 17, 1986. Others, Dec. 1985.

Natl. Automobile Assoc., 40th Anniv. — A549

1986, Feb. 25   Perf. 12½
1772 A549 10d Car   15 15
1773 A549 70d Helicopter   40 32
Set value   38

Tara River, Montenegro A550

1986, Mar. 3   Perf. 14
1774 A550 100d Canyon   55 42
1775 A550 150d Bridge   95 60
European nature protection. Sheets of 9.

Studenica Monastery, 800th Anniv. — A551

1986, Mar. 15   Perf. 13½
1776 A551 10d Chapel of Our Lady   15 15

 A552

Various soccer plays.

1986, Apr. 5   Litho.   Perf. 14
1777 A552 70d multi   35 28
1778 A552 150d multi   75 55
1986 World Cup Soccer Championships, Mexico.

Arrival of St. Clement in Ohrid, 1100th Anniv. — A553

1986, Apr. 12   Perf. 12½
1779 A553 10d Township model   15 15

Europa Issue

Brain, Mushroom Cloud — A554

1986, Apr. 28   Perf. 14
1780 A554 100d shown   48 35
1781 A554 200d Injured deer   1.00 70

European Men's Senior Judo Championships, Belgrade, May 8-11 — A555

1986, May 7   Perf. 12½
1782 A555 70d multi   35 28

Natl. Costumes A556 — Yachts, Moscenika Draga Bay A557

Designs: a, Slovenia. b, Vojvodina. c, Croatia. d, Macedonia. e, Serbia. f, Montenegro. g, Kosovo. h, Bosnia & Herzegovina.

1986, May 22   Litho.   Perf. 12x13
1783   Bklt. pane of 8   2.25
  a.-h. A556 50d any single   28 15
Issued in booklets only.

1986, May 23   Perf. 14
1784 A557 50d multi   26 15
1785 A557 80d multi, diff.   40 18
Souvenir Sheet
Imperf
1786 A557 100d multi   55 52
European Sailing Championships, Croatia, May 29-June 7, Flying Dutchman Class. No. 1786 contains one stamp 22x28mm.

Marshal Tito — A557a

1986, May 24   Perf. 13x12½
1787 A557a 10d multicolored   15 15

Moths and Butterflies A558

1986, May 26   Perf. 14
1788 A558 10d Eudia pavonia   15 15
1789 A558 20d Inachis io   15 15
1790 A558 50d Parnassius apollo   24 15
1791 A558 100d Apatura iris   48 24
Set value   90 48

Ancient Manuscripts A558a

Designs: 10d, Evangelical, 18th cent. 20d, Leontijevo Evangelical, 16th cent. 50d, Astrological, Mesopotamia, 15th cent. 100d, Hebrew Haggadah, Spain, 14th cent.

1986, June 12　　Litho.　　Perf. 14

1792	A558a	10d multicolored	15	15
1793	A558a	20d multicolored	15	15
1794	A558a	50d multicolored	30	15
1795	A558a	100d multicolored	60	30
		Set value		56

A559

A560

Designs: 20d, Postman on motorcycle. 30d, Postman, resident. 40d, Forklift, mail pallets. 50d, Mail train. 60d, Man posting letters in mailbox. 93d, Open envelope and greetings telegram form. 100d, Postman, mail van. No. 1803, Computer operator facing right. No. 1804, 140d, Computer operator facing left. 120d, Woman sending love letter. 200d, Freighter in high seas. 500d, Postal employee sorting mail. 1000d, Woman at telephone station. 2000d, Aircraft, hemispheres on world map. 30d, 60d, 93d, 106d, 120d, 140d, 500d, 1000d vert.

Perf. 13¹/₂, 12¹/₂x13¹/₂ (20d, 40d, 50d), 14 (100d)

1986-88　　　　　　　　Litho.

1796	A559	20d brt pink	15	15
a.		Perf. 14		
1797	A559	30d lt brn vio	20	15
a.		Perf. 13x12¹/₂		
1798	A559	40d brt red	25	15
1799	A559	50d violet	30	15
a.		Perf. 14		
1800	A559	60d lt sage grn	25	15
1801	A559	93d ultra	25	15
1802	A559	100d dl magenta	65	32
1803	A559	106d rose red	30	15
1804	A559	106d brn org	18	15
1805	A559	120d dull blue grn	15	15
1806	A559	140d dull rose	16	15
1807	A559	200d greenish bl	1.20	60
a.		Perf. 12¹/₂		
b.		Perf. 12¹/₂x13¹/₂		
1808	A559	500d deep blue & beige	72	35
1809	A559	500d chalky blue & yel	58	28
1810	A559	1000d vio & blue grn	1.15	58
b.		Perf. 12¹/₂		
1810A	A560	2000d brt blue, red & brt vio	2.30	1.15
		Nos. 1796-1810A (16)	8.79	4.78

Size of No. 1802: 19¹/₂x18mm.

Issue dates: 20d, Mar. 17. 50d, 200d, June 4. 40d, July 17. 100d, June 12. 30d, July 26. 60d, June 5, 1987. #1803, Dec. 10, 1987. 93d, Dec. 16, 1987. #1804, Jan. 22, 1988. #1808, Apr. 29, 1988. 1000d, July 21, 1988. 120d, 140d, 2000d, #1809, Sept. 5, 1988.

See Nos. 1935-1945. For surcharges see Nos. 1877, 1912-1913, 1947-1948, 1972, 1974-1975, 2004-2007, 2013-2015, 2017, 2019, 2048-2051, 2053.

13th Communist Federations Congress (SKJ) — A561

1986, June 25　　　　　Perf. 12¹/₂

1811	A561	10d shown	15	15
1812	A561	20d Star	15	15
		Set value		18	15

Souvenir Sheet
Imperf

1813	A561	100d Tito	48	24

Trubar, Abecedarian Manuscript Title Page — A562

1986, June 28　　Litho.　　Perf. 12¹/₂x13

1814	A562	20d multi	15	15

Primoz Trubar (1508-1568), Slovenian philologist and religious reformer.

Serbian Natl. Theater, Novi Sad, 125th Anniv. — A563

1986, July 28　　　　　Perf. 14

1815	A563	40d Thalia	20	15

Rugovo Dance, Kosovo Province — A564

1987 Universiade Games, Zagreb, July 8-19 — A565

1986, Sept. 10

1816	A564	40d multi	20	15

1986, Sept. 22　　　　　Perf. 13¹/₂

1817	A565	30d Volleyball	15	15
1818	A565	40d Canoeing	20	15
1819	A565	100d Gymnastics	45	22
1820	A565	150d Fencing	65	32
		Set value		72

18th Joy of Europe Youth Conference — A566

Children's drawings: 100d, Dove, by Tanja Faletic, 14. 150d, Buildings, by Johanna Kraus, 12, DDR.

1986, Oct. 2　　　　　Perf. 14

1821	A566	100d multicolored	45	22
1822	A566	150d multicolored	70	32

Rotary Switching Apparatus, Village of Bled A567

1986, Oct. 4　　　　　Perf. 13¹/₂

1823	A567	40d multicolored	20	15

Telephone exchanges connected with automatic switching equipment, 50th anniv.

INTERPOL 55th General Assembly, Belgrade, Oct. 6-13 — A568

Intl. Brigades, 50th Anniv. — A569

1986, Oct. 6　　　　　Perf. 14

1824	A568	150d multicolored	65	32

1986, Oct. 21　　　　　Perf. 13¹/₂

1825	A569	40d multicolored	20	15

Intl. Peace Year — A570

1986, Nov. 20

1826	A570	150d multicolored	65	30

Serbian Academy of the Arts and Sciences, Cent. — A571

1986, Nov. 1　　Photo.　　Perf. 13¹/₂

1827	A571	40d multicolored	20	15

Paintings by Foreign Artists in the Museum of Contemporary Art, Skopje — A572

Designs: No. 1828, Still Life, by Frantisek Muzika, Czechoslovakia. No. 1829, Disturance, by Rafael Canogar, England. No. 1830, Iol, by Victor Vasarely, France, vert. No. 1831, Portrait, by Bernard Buffet, France, vert. No. 1832, Woman's Head, by Pablo Picasso, Spain, vert.

1986, Dec. 10　　Litho.　　Perf. 14

1828	A572	30d multi	16	15
1829	A572	40d multi	22	15
1830	A572	100d multi	52	25
1831	A572	100d multi	52	25
1832	A572	150d multi	78	40
		Nos. 1828-1832 (5)	2.20	1.20

Wildlife Conservation A573

Designs: 30d, Lutra lutra. 40d, Ovis musimon. 100d, Cervus elaphus. 150d, Ursus arctos.

1987, Jan. 22　　Litho.　　Perf. 13¹/₂x14

1833		Strip of 4 + label	1.40	65
a.	A573	30d multi	15	15
b.	A573	40d multi	18	15
c.	A573	100d multi	40	20
d.	A573	150d multi	65	32

Label pictures nature reserve.

Ruder Boskovic (1711-1787), Scientist, and Solar Eclipse over Brera Observatory, Italy — A574

1987, Feb. 13　　　　　Perf. 14

1834	A574	150d multicolored	65	32

European Nature Protection A575

1987 World Alpine Skiing Championships, Crans Montana A576

1987, Mar. 9

1835	A575	150d shown	65	32
1836	A575	400d Triglav glacial lake	1.65	85

1987, Mar. 20　　Litho.　　Perf. 14

1837	A576	200d multicolored	80	40

No. 1837 printed in sheets of 8 plus center label.

Natl. Civil Aviation, 60th Anniv. A577

1987, Mar. 20　　　　　Perf. 14

1838	A577	150d POTEZ-29	70	35
1839	A577	400d DC-10	1.75	90

Each printed in sheets of 8 plus center label.

Kole Nedelkovski (1912-1941), Poet, Revolutionary A578

1987, Apr. 2　　　　　Perf. 13¹/₂

1840	A578	40d multicolored	22	15

Liberation of Montenegro from Turkey, 125th Anniv. — A579

1987, Apr. 16　　　　　Perf. 13¹/₂

1841	A579	40d Battle flags, folk guitar	22	15

Slovenian Communist Party, Cebine, 50th Anniv. — A580

1987, Apr. 18   *Perf. 14*
1842 A580 40d multicolored   22 15

Europa Issue

Tito Bridge, Krk — A581

1987, Apr. 30   **Litho.**   *Perf. 14*
1843 A581 200d shown   90 38
1844 A581 400d Bridges over canal   1.75 75

Fruit Trees — A582   Tito, 1930, by Mosa Pijade — A583

1987, May 15   **Litho.**   *Perf. 14*
1845 A582 60d Almond   16 15
1846 A582 150d Pear   40 18
1847 A582 200d Apple   52 25
1848 A582 400d Plum   1.10 48

1987, May 25
1849 A583 60d multi   15 15

50th anniv. of Tito's assumption of Yugoslavian communist party leadership.

Vuk Stefanovik Karadzic (1787-1864), Linguist and Historian A584

Designs: 60d, Bust by Petar Ubavkic, his Trsic residence and Vienna. 200d, Portrait by Uros Knezevic, and alphabet from Karadzic's Serbian Dictionary, 1818.

1987, June 10
1850 A584 60d multi   15 15
1851 A584 200d multi   52 24

Zrenjanin Postal Service, 250th Anniv. — A585

1987, June 22   *Perf. 13½*
1852 A585 60d multi   15 15

UNIVERSIADE '87, Zagreb, July 8-19 — A586

1987, July 8   **Litho.**   *Perf. 13½*
1853 A586 60d Hurdling   15 15
1854 A586 150d Basketball   35 16
1855 A586 200d Balance beam   45 24
1856 A586 400d Swimming   1.00 45

Each printed in sheets of eight plus label.

Fire Fighting A587   Monument, Anindol Park, Samobor A588

1987, July 20   *Perf. 14*
1857 A587 60d Canadair CL-215 spraying forest   15 15
1858 A587 200d Fire boat   48 24
    Set value   32

Each printed in sheets of eight plus label.

1987, Aug. 1   *Perf. 13½*
1859 A588 60d multi   15 15

Communist Party of Croatia, 50th anniv.

Sabac High School, 150th Anniv. — A589

1987, Sept. 10   **Litho.**   *Perf. 13½*
1860 A589 80d multi   20 20

Exhibition Emblem, Balkan Peninsula, Flowers A590

Clock Tower, Petrovaradin Fortress and Novi Sad — A591

1987, Sept. 19   *Perf. 14*
1861 A590 250d multi   50 25

Souvenir Sheet
Imperf
1862 A591 400d multi   90 80

BALKANFILA XI, Novi Sad, Sept. 19-26.

19th Joy of Europe Conference A592   Bridges A593

Children's drawings: 250d, Girls in forest, by Bedic Aranka, Juguoslavia. 400d, Scarecrow, by Schaffer Ingeborg, Austria.

1987, Oct. 2   **Litho.**   *Perf. 14*
1863 A592 250d multi   65 32
1864 A592 400d multi   1.00 50

Printed in sheets of nine.

1987, Oct. 15
1865 A593 80d Arslanagica, Trebinje, 16th cent.   22 15
1866 A593 250d Terzija, Djakovica, 15th cent.   68 35

Ship, Dunav-Tisa Channel A594

1987, Oct. 20   *Perf. 13½*
1867 A594 80d multi   22 15

City of Titov Vrbas, 600th anniv.

Astronomical and Meteorological Observatory, Belgrade, Cent. — A595

1987, Nov. 21   *Perf. 14*
1868 A595 80d multi   22 15

St. Luke the Evangelist, by Raphael — A596

Paintings by foreign artists in national museums: 200d, Infanta Maria Theresa, by Velazquez. 250d, Nicholas Rubens, Painter's Son, by Rubens. 400d, Louis Laure Sennegon, Painter's Niece, by Jean-Baptiste-Camille Corot (1796-1875).

1987, Nov. 28
1869 A596 80d shown   22 15
1870 A596 200d multi   55 28
1871 A596 250d multi   68 35
1872 A596 400d multi   1.10 55

Traditional Competitions A597

Designs: 80d, Bull fighting. 200d, Ljubicevo Horse Games. 250d, Moresca game. 400d, Sinj iron ring.

1987, Dec. 10
1873 A597 80d multi   22 15
1874 A597 200d multi   55 28
1875 A597 250d multi   68 35
1876 A597 400d multi   1.10 55

No. 1800 Surcharged 80≡

1987, Sept. 22   *Perf. 13½*
1877 A559 80d on 60d multi   18 15

Vinodol Codex, City of Vinodolski, Coat of Arms A598

1988, Jan. 6   **Litho.**   *Perf. 14*
1878 A598 100d multi   25 15

Vinodol Codex, 700th anniv.

Intl. Women's Golden Fox Skiing Championships, 25th Anniv. — A599

1988, Jan. 30
1879 A599 350d Slalom, emblem, Mirobor City   85 42

Printed in sheets of eight plus center label.

World Wildlife Fund — A600

Brown bears (Ursus arctos).

1988, Feb. 1
1880 A600 70d Cub   20 15
1881 A600 80d Cubs   22 15
1882 A600 200d Adult, head   55 28
1883 A600 350d Adult   1.00 50

1988 Winter Olympics, Calgary — A601

1988, Feb. 13   *Perf. 14x13½*
1884 A601 350d Slalom   85 42
1885 A601 1200d Ice hockey   3.00 1.50

Each printed in sheets of 8 plus center label.

Souvenir Sheet

Map of Europe Highlighting Balkan Nations — A602

1988, Feb. 24　Litho.　Imperf.
1886 A602 1500d multi　　　　3.00 3.00

Congress of Foreign Affairs Ministers from the Balkan Countries, Belgrade, Feb. 24-26.

1988 Summer Olympics, Seoul — A603

South Korean Landscape — A604

1988, Mar. 21　　　Perf. 14x13½
1887 A603 106d Basketball　　22　15
1888 A603 450d High jump　　　90　45
1889 A603 500d Pommel horse　1.00　50
1890 A603 1200d Boxing　　　2.40 1.20

Souvenir Sheet
Imperf
1891 A604 1500d multi　　　2.75 2.75

Nos. 1887-1890 printed in sheets of 8 plus center label.

Europa Issue

Telecommunications — A605

1988, Apr. 30　Litho.　Perf. 13½x14
1892 A605 450d shown　　　　68　35
1893 A605 1200d Transportation　1.75　88

Sea Shells — A606

1988, May 14
1894 A606 106d Gibbula magus　　15　15
1895 A606 550d Pecten jacobaeus　75　35
1896 A606 600d Tonna galea　　　80　40
1897 A606 1000d Argonauta argo　1.25　65

Trial of Tito and Five Comrades, 60th Anniv. — A607

1988, May 25
1898 A607 106d black & brn　　18　15

Palace of Princess Ljubica of Serbia, 1st University Building A608

1988, June 14　Litho.　Perf. 13½
1899 A608 106d multi　　　　18　15

Belgrade University, 150th anniv.

Flowers — A609　　Esperanto, Cent. — A610

1988, July 2　　　　　Perf. 14
1900 A609 600d Phelypaea boissieri　60　30
1901 A609 1000d Campanula formanekiana　　　1.00　50

Council of Europe.

1988, July 14　　　　Perf. 13½
1902 A610 600d dull vio & ol grn　60　30

Printed in sheets of 8 plus center label.

Cargo Ships — A611

Map of the Danube Basin — A612

1988, Aug. 18　Litho.　Perf. 14
1903 A611 1000d multi　　　80　40

Souvenir Sheet
Imperf
1904 A612 2000d multi　　　1.55 1.55

Danube Conference, 40th anniv.

13th European Junior Basketball Championships, Aug. 21-28 — A613

1988, Aug. 20　　　Perf. 14
1905 A613 600d multi　　　48　24

1st Horse Race in Belgrade, 125th Anniv. — A614

1988, Aug. 27
1906 A614 140d Thoroughbred racing　15　15
1907 A614 600d Steeplechase　　48　24
1908 A614 1000d Harness racing　80　40

Museum of Bosnia and Herzegovina, Sarajevo, Cent. — A615

1988, Sept. 10　　　Perf. 13½
1909 A615 140d Museum, Bosnian bell-flower　　　　　15　15

Anti-Cancer and AIDS Campaigns A616

1988, Sept. 24　　　Perf. 14
1910 A616 140d Arm, lobster claw　15　15
1911 A616 1000d Blood, scream　80　40
　　　　　　Set value　　　　　46

Nos. 1801 and 1804 Surcharged

1988, July　Litho.　Perf. 13½
1912 A559 120d on 93d ultra　18　15
1913 A559 140d on 106d brn org　20　15
　　　　　　Set value　　　　　18

Joy of Europe Youth Conference — A617

Portraits of girls by: 1000d, P. Ranosovic. 1100d, Renoir.

1988, Oct. 1　　Litho.　Perf. 14
1914 A617 1000d multi　　　80　40
1915 A617 1100d multi　　　88　45

See Nos. 1987-1988.

Slovenski Academy, 50th Anniv. A618

1988, Oct. 13　Litho.　Perf. 14
1916 A618 200d multi　　　15　15

Museum Exhibits and Places of Origin A618a

Designs: 200d, Wood bassinet, traditional wedding (Galicka), vert. No. 1918, Embroidery, man and woman wearing folk costumes of Vojvodina. No. 1919, Scimitar, flintlock, man and woman wearing folk costumes of Kotor (Bokelji), vert. 1100d, Masks (Kurenti).

1988, Oct. 18
1917 A618a 200d multi　　　15　15
1918 A618a 1000d shown　　68　35
1919 A618a 1000d multi　　68　35
1920 A618a 1100d multi　　75　38

Woman with Lyre, 4th Cent. B.C. — A618b

Grecian terra cotta figurines: No. 1922, Eros and Psyche, 2nd cent. B.C. No. 1923, Seated woman, 3rd cent. B.C. 1100d, Woman by Stele, 3rd cent. B.C.

1988, Oct. 28
1921 A618b 200d multi　　　15　15
1922 A618b 1000d multi　　45　22
1923 A618b 1000d multi　　45　22
1924 A618b 1100d multi　　50　25

Peter II (1813-1851), Prince Bishop and Poet — A618c

Portraits and: 200d, Cetinje Monastery and frontispiece of his principle work. 1000d, Njegos Mausoleum.

1988, Nov. 1
1925	A618c	200d multi	15	15
1926	A618c	1000d multi	80	40

Postal Service Types of 1986 and

Telephone Receiver and Telephone Card — A619

Bird, Posthorn, Simulated Stamp — A620

Propeller Plane, Two Arrows and Map — A621

Designs: 170d, 300d, Flower, envelope, mailbox and simulated stamp. 220d, PTT emblem on simulated stamp, mail coach. 800d, Postman on motorcycle. No. 1941, Postman, resident. No. 1942, Mail train. No. 1943, Envelopes, satellite dish. No. 1944, Earth, telecommunications satellite. 100,000d, Bird, open envelope, flower. 170d, 220d, 300d, 2000d, 5000d, No. 1941 vert.

1988-89 Litho. Perf. 13½
1935	A559	170d dl grn	15	15
1936	A559	220d brn org	15	15
1937	A559	300d ver	15	15
1938	A559	800d brt ultra	15	15
1939	A619	2000d multi	24	15
1940	A620	5000d dk red & ultra	2.10	1.05

Perf. 12½
1937a	A559	300d		
1938a	A559	800d		
1939a	A619	2000d		
1940a	A620	5000d		
1941	A559	10,000d org & brt lil	36	18
a.		Perf. 13½		
1942	A559	20,000d lt ol grn & lt red brn	60	30

Perf. 13½
1943	A560	10,000d multi	2.80	1.40
1944	A560	20,000d multi	2.35	1.15
1944A	A621	50,000d org & dl bl	2.30	1.15
1945	A560	100,000d org & dl grn	3.15	1.55
		Nos. 1935-1945 (12)	14.50	7.53

Issued: 1988 - 170d, Nov. 17; 220d, Dec. 6; 1989 - 300d, May 11; 800d, 2000d, July 20; 5000d, Jan. 20; #1941, Nov. 28; #1942, Dec. 8; #1943, Mar. 20; #1944, July 19; 50,000d, Nov. 8; 100,000d, Dec. 4.
See Nos. 2008-2009, 2017, 2052. For surcharges see Nos. 1972, 1974, 2048.

Yugoslavia, 70th Anniv. — A622

1988, Dec. 1 Litho. Perf. 14
1946 A622	200d Krsmanovic Hall, Belgrade	15	15

Nos. 1805-1806 Surcharged

1988 Litho. Perf. 13½
1947	A559	170d on 120d	15	15
1948	A559	220d on 140d	15	15
		Set value	24	15

Issue dates: #1947, Dec. 21. #1948, Dec. 15.

Miniature Sheet

Victory of Yugoslavian Athletes at the 1988 Summer Olympics, Seoul — A623

Medals and events: a, Women's air pistol. b, Team handball. c, Table tennis. d, Wrestling. e, Double sculls. f, Basketball. g, Water polo. h, Boxing.

1988, Dec. 31 Litho. Perf. 14
1949	Sheet of 8 + label	1.80	88
a.-h.	A623 500d any single	22	15

Ivan Gundulic (1589-1638), Poet — A624

1989, Jan. 7 Perf. 13½
1950 A624	220d multi	16	15

World Wildlife Fund — A625

Ducks.

1989, Feb. 23 Litho. Perf. 14
1951		Strip of 4 + label	4.00	2.00
a.	A625	300d Anas platyrhynchos	15	15
b.	A625	2100d Anas crecca	1.25	62
c.	A625	2200d Anas acuta	1.30	65
d.	A625	2200d Anas clypeata	1.30	65

Printed in sheets of 20+5 labels. Label pictures WWF emblem.

Publication of The Glory of the Duchy of Kranjska, by Johann Valvasor (1641-1693), 300th Anniv. — A626

1989, Mar. 10 Perf. 13½
1952 A626	300d Portrait	22	15

Flowering Plants — A627

1989, Mar. 20 Perf. 14
1953 A627	300d Bulbocodium vernum	15	15
1954 A627	2100d Nymphaea alba	1.25	62
1955 A627	2200d Fritillaria degeniana, vert.	1.30	65
1956 A627	3000d Orchis simia, vert.	1.75	90

6th World Air-Gun Championships, Sarajevo, Apr. 27-30 — A628

1989, Apr. 26
1957 A628	3000d multi	1.75	90

Europa 1989 — A629

1989, Apr. 29
1958 A629	3000d shown	1.75	90
1959 A629	6000d Marbles	3.50	1.80

15th European Trophy for Natl. Athletic Club Champions, Belgrade, June 3-4 — A630

1989, June 1 Litho. Perf. 13½
1960 A630	4000d Pole vault	68	35

Printed in sheets of 8+label picturing flags of participating nations.

Yugoslavia Motorcycle Grand Prix, Rijeka, June 9-11 — A631

Various race scenes.

1989, June 9 Perf. 14
1961 A631	500d multi	15	15
1962 A631	4000d multi	60	30
	Set value		35

Souvenir Sheet
Perf. 14x13½
1963 A631	6000d multi	90	45

No. 1963 contains one 54x35 stamp.

No. 1246 Surcharged
1989, Apr. 6 Litho. Perf. 13
1964 A323	100d on 1d dull grn	15	15
a.	Perf. 13x12½		

Tito — A632

1989, May 25 Perf. 13½x14
1965 A632	300d multi	15	15

Early Adriatic Ships — A633

Designs: a, Ancient Greek galley. b, Roman galley. c, Crusade galleon, 13th cent. d, Nava of Dubrovnik, 16th cent. e, French ship, 17th cent. f, Vessels, 18th cent. 3000d, View of Dubrovnik seaport, called Ragusa in Italian, from a 17th cent. engraving.

1989, June 10 Perf. 13½
1966	Block of 6	90	48
a.-f.	A633 1000d any single	15	15

Souvenir Sheet
1967 A633	3000d multi	45	22

No. 1967 contains one 75x32mm stamp. Nos. 1966-1967 printed se-tenant and sold folded in booklet cover.

26th European Basketball Championships A634

Map of Europe, basketball and flags of: No. 1968, France, Yugoslavia, Greece, Bulgaria. No. 1969, Netherlands, Italy, Russia, Spain.

1989, June 20 Litho. Perf. 13½x14
1968 A634	2000d multi	28	15
1969 A634	2000d multi	28	15

Defeat of the Serbians at the Battle of Kosovo, 1389 A635

1989, June 28
1970 A635	500d multi	15	15

Danilovgrad Library, Cent. — A636

1989, July 15 Litho. Perf. 13½
1971 A636	500d multi	15	15

Nos. 1797, 1719, 1935, 1936 Surcharged
1989
1972 A559	400d on 30d lt brn vio	15	15
1973 A323	700d on 70d brt ultra	15	15
1974 A559	700d on 170d dull green	15	15
1975 A559	700d on 220d brn org	15	15
	Set value	26	20

Issue dates: #1975, July 19. #1974, Aug. 10. #1972, Aug. 23. #1973, Dec. 13.

Kulin Ban Charter, 800th Anniv. A638

1989, Aug. 29 Litho. Perf. 14
1976 A638	500d multi	15	15

World Rowing Championships A639

1989, Sept. 2 Perf. 13½
1977 A639	10,000d multi	80	40

Interparliamentary Union, Cent. — A640

Architecture: No. 1978, Parliament, London (emblem at R). No. 1979, Notre Dame Cathedral (emblem at L).

1989, Sept. 4   *Perf. 13¹/₂x14*
1978 A640 10,000d multi   78 40
1979 A640 10,000d multi   78 40

A641

View of Belgrade and Maps BEOGRAD '89 — A642

Architecture and antiquities of exhibition host cities: No. 1980, Belgrade '61, Cairo '64. No. 1981, Lusaka '70, Algiers '73. No. 1982, Colombo '76, Havana '79. No. 1983, New Delhi '83, Harare '76.

1989, Sept. 4
1980 A641 10,000d multi   78 40
1981 A641 10,000d multi   78 40
1982 A641 10,000d multi   78 40
1983 A641 10,000d multi   78 40

Souvenir Sheet
Perf. 14
1984 A642 20,000d multi   1.60 1.60

European Nature Protection A643

Designs: 8000d, Paeonia officinalis, Brezovica-Jazinac Lake. 10,000d, Paeonia corallina, Mirusa Canyon.

1989, Sept. 11   *Perf. 14*
1985 A643 8000d multi   58 30
1986 A643 10,000d multi   70 40

Joy of Europe Type of 1988

Portraits of children: No. 1987, Child with Lamb, by Jovan Popovic. No. 1988, Girl Feeding Dog, by Albert Cuyp (1620-1691).

1989, Oct. 2   **Litho.**   *Perf. 14*
1987 A617 10,000d multi   62 30
1988 A617 10,000d multi   62 30

Karpos Uprising, 300th Anniv. — A644

1989, Oct. 20   **Litho.**   *Perf. 13¹/₂*
1989 A644 1200d ver & dark brn   15 15

No. 1833c, Cancellation, Quill Pen, Wax Seals and Seal Device on Parchment A645

1989, Oct. 31   *Perf. 14*
1990 A645 1200d multicolored   15 15

Stamp Day.

Museum Exhibits A646

1989, Nov. 2
1991 A646 1200d Pack-saddle maker   15 15
1992 A646 14,000d Cooper   68 34
1993 A646 15,000d Winegrower   72 35
1994 A646 30,000d Weaver   1.45 72

Religious Paintings A647

Designs: 2100d, Apostle Matthew, vert. 21,000d, St. Barbara, vert. 30,000d, The Fourth Day of Creation. 50,000d, The Fifth Day of Creation.

1989, Nov. 28   **Litho.**   *Perf. 14*
1997 A647 2100d multicolored   15 15
1998 A647 21,000d multicolored   72 35
1999 A647 30,000d multicolored   1.05 52
2000 A647 50,000d multicolored   1.75 88

A648

League of Communists 14th Congress — A649

1990, Jan. 20   **Litho.**   *Perf. 13¹/₂x14*
2001 A648 10,000d Star   18 15
2002 A648 50,000d Computer   82 40

Souvenir Sheet
Imperf
2003 A649 100,000d Star, diff.   1.65 1.65

Postal Service Types of 1986-88

Designs: 10p, Man posting letters in mailbox. 20p, Postal employee sorting mail. 30p, Postman, resident. 40p, Woman at telephone station. 1d, Mail train. 2d, Ship and envelope. 3d, Flower, mailbox, envelope and simulated stamp. 10d, Bird, open envelope, flower. 20d, Woman at telephone station.

10p, 20p, 30p, 40p, 3d, 5d vert.

1990   *Perf. 12¹/₂*
2004 A559 10p br yel grn & vio   15 15
2005 A559 20p red vio & org   15 15
2006 A559 30p org & yel grn   15 15
    a.   Perf. 13¹/₂
2007 A559 40p blue grn & red vio   15 15
2008 A620 50p pur & blue grn   15 15
2009 A619 60p red org & brt vio   15 15
2013 A559 1d rose lil & greenish bl   18 15
2014 A559 2d red lil & blue   35 18
    a.   Perf. 13¹/₂
2015 A559 3d org & dl blue   52 25
2017 A621 5d ultra & grnsh blue   85 42
2019 A559 10d red org & vio bl   1.80 90

Perf. 13¹/₂
2021 A559 20d car rose & org   30 15
    Nos. 2004-2021 (12)   4.90
    Set value   2.10

Issue dates: 10p, 20p, Feb. 9; 30p, 40p, Jan. 24; 50p, Jan. 29; 60p, Feb. 6; 2d, Feb. 14; 3d, Feb. 22; 5d, Jan. 31. 1d, May 24. 10d, June 12. Jan. 27, 1992.

For surcharges see Nos. 2049-2053.

This is an expanding set. Numbers will change if necessary.

Anti-smoking Campaign A650

1990, Jan. 31   **Litho.**   *Perf. 13¹/₂x13*
2034 A650 10d gry & yel brn   1.70 85

Protected Fish — A651

1990, Feb. 15   *Perf. 13¹/₂*
2035   Strip of 4 + label   5.30 2.65
    a. A651 1d *Esox lucius*   15 15
    b. A651 5d *Silurus glanis*   85 42
    c. A651 10d *Lota lota*   1.70 85
    d. A651 15d *Perca fluviatilis*   2.60 1.30

Zabljak Fortress, Illuminated Manuscript, Coat of Arms A652

1990, Mar. 9   *Perf. 14x13¹/₂*
2036 A652 50p multicolored   15 15

Enthronement of Djuradj Crnojevic, 500th anniv.

ITU, 125th Anniv. A653

1990, Mar. 23
2037 A653 6.50d Telegrapher, computer   1.10 55

1990 World Cup Soccer Championships, Italy — A654

1990, Apr. 16
2038 A654 6.50d shown   1.10 55
2039 A654 10d multi, diff.   1.70 85

Europa 1990 — A655

Post offices: 6.50d, PTT Central, Skopje. 10d, Telecommunications Central, Belgrade.

1990, Apr. 23   *Perf. 13¹/₂x14*
2040 A655 6.50d multicolored   1.10 55
2041 A655 10d multicolored   1.70 85

A656   A657

1990, Apr. 30   **Litho.**   *Perf. 13¹/₂*
2042 A656 6.50d multicolored   1.25 62

Labor Day, cent.

1990, May 5   *Perf. 14x13¹/₂*

Eurovision Song Contest: 10d, Conductor, musical score.

2043 A657 6.50d multicolored   1.25 62
2044 A657 10d multicolored   1.80 90

Tennis — A658

1990, May 15   **Litho.**   *Perf. 14*
2045 A658 6.50d multicolored   1.25   62
2046 A658 10d multicolored   1.90   95

Tito — A659

1990, May 25   *Perf. 13¹/₂x14*
2047 A659 50p multicolored   15   15

Nos. 1938, 2005-2007 Surcharged

1990   **Litho.**   *Perf. 13¹/₂*
2048 A559 50p on 800d #1938   15   15

       Perf. 12¹/₂
2049 A559 50p on 20p red vio & org   15   15
2050 A559 1d on 30p org & yel grn   20   15
2051 A559 2d on 40p bl grn & red vio, I   40   20
    a.   Type II, perf. 13¹/₂   40   20
    b.   Type I, perf. 13¹/₂
       Set value   78   40

Type II surcharge has 3 instead of 2 bars obliterating old value, new denomination is at bottom of stamp.
Issue dates: No. 2048, May 24. No. 2049, Sept. 18; No. 2050, Aug. 8.
This is an expanding set. Numbers will change if necessary.

Nos. 2004, 2009 Surcharged

10

5 ═══

1991   **Litho.**   *Perf. 12¹/₂*
2052 A619 5d on 60p   15   15
2053 A559 10d on 10p   15   15
       Set value   18   15

Issued: No. 2052, Dec. 7; No. 2053, Dec. 12.

Public Postal Service in Serbia, 150th Anniv. A660

1990, May 25
2056 A660 50p multicolored   15   15

Pigeons — A661

1990, June 8   *Perf. 13¹/₂*
2057 A661 50p multicolored   15   15
2058 A661 5d multicolored   90   45
2059 A661 6.50d multi, vert.   1.25   62
2060 A661 10d multi, vert.   1.80   90

Mercury Mine at Idrija, 500th Anniv. — A662

Designs: 50p, Idrija.

1990, June 22   *Perf. 13¹/₂x14*
2061 A662 50p multicolored   15   15
2062 A662 6.50d multicolored   1.25   62
       Set value   66

Newspaper "Vjesnik," 50th Anniv. — A663

1990, June 23   *Perf. 13¹/₂*
2063 A663 60p multicolored   15   15

Serbian Migration, 300th Anniv. — A664

1990, Sept. 20   *Perf. 14*
2064 A664 1d shown   20   15
2065 A664 6.50d Caravan   1.30   65

European Track & Field Championships, Split — A665

1990, Aug. 27   *Perf. 13¹/₂*
2067 A665 1d Start of race   18   15
2068 A665 6.50d Runners' feet   1.25   62
       Souvenir Sheet
2069 A665 10d Runners   1.80   90

No. 2069 contains one 54x35mm stamp. A 50p exists but no information on its postal category is available.

Joy of Europe — A666

Paintings: 6.50d, Children by I. Kobilca. 10d, William III of Orange as a Child by A. Hanneman, vert.

1990, Oct. 2   **Litho.**   *Perf. 14*
2070 A666 6.50d multicolored   1.40   70
2071 A666 10d multicolored   2.25   1.10

Souvenir Sheets

29th Chess Olympics, Novi Sad — A667

1990, Oct. 2   *Perf. 11¹/₂*
       Granite Paper
2072   Sheet of 4   4.50   4.50
   a. A667 1d shown   20   20
   b. A667 5d Rook, bishop, knight   1.00   1.00
   c. A667 6.50d King, bishop, knght, pawn   1.30   1.30
   d. A667 10d Chess pieces   2.00   2.00
       Imperf
2073   Sheet of 4   4.50   4.50
   a. A667 1d like No. 2072a   20   20
   b. A667 5d like No. 2072b   1.00   1.00
   c. A667 6.50d like No. 2072c   1.30   1.30
   d. A667 10d like No. 2072d   2.00   2.00

No. 2073 has blue margin inscriptions. Emblems on Nos. 2072a-2072d are in silver, those on Nos. 2073a-2073d are in gold.

Stamp Day A668

1990, Oct. 2   *Perf. 14*
2074 A668 2d multicolored   40   20

150th anniv. of the Penny Black.

Environmental Protection A669

1990, Nov. 16   **Litho.**   *Perf. 14*
2075 A669 6.50d Vransko Lake   1.30   1.30
2076 A669 10d Gyps fulvus   2.00   2.00

Frescoes A670

Designs: 2d, King Milutin, Monastery of Our Lady, Ljeviska. 5d, Saint Sava, Mileseva Monastery. 6.50d, Saint Elias, Moraca Monastery. 10d, Jesus Christ, Sopocani Monastery.

1990, Nov. 28
2077 A670 2d multicolored   40   40
2078 A670 5d multicolored   1.00   1.00
2079 A670 6.50d multicolored   1.30   1.30
2080 A670 10d multicolored   2.00   2.00

Dr. Bozo Milanovic (1890-1980), Religious and Political Leader — A671

1990, Dec. 20   **Litho.**   *Perf. 13¹/₂*
2081 A671 2d multicolored   40   40

Religious Carvings A672

Designs: 2d, Christ in the temple. 5d, Nativity scene. 6.50d, Flight from Egypt, horiz. 10d, Entry into Jerusalem, horiz.

     Perf. 13¹/₂x14, 14x13¹/₂
1990, Dec. 24
2082 A672 2d gld, brn, & blk   40   40
2083 A672 5d gld, brn, & blk   1.05   1.05
2084 A672 6.50d gld, brn, & blk   1.35   1.35
2085 A672 10d gld, brn, & blk   2.10   2.10

Protected Birds — A673   Flora — A674

1991, Jan. 31   **Litho.**   *Perf. 14x13¹/₂*
2086   Strip of 4 + label   4.90   4.90
   a. A673 2d Vanellus vanellus   40   40
   b. A673 5d Lanius senator   1.05   1.05
   c. A673 6.50d Grus grus   1.35   1.35
   d. A673 10d Mergus merganser   2.10   2.10

1991, Feb. 20
2087 A674 2d Crocus kosaninii   40   40
2088 A674 6d Crocus scardicus   1.20   1.20
2089 A674 7.50d Crocus rujanesis   1.55   1.55
2090 A674 15d Crocus adamii   3.15   3.15

Bishop Josip J. Strossmayer (1815-1905), Founder of Academy of Arts and Sciences — A675

1991, Mar. 4   **Litho.**   *Perf. 13¹/₂x14*
2091 A675 2d multicolored   30   30

Academy of Arts and Sciences, 125th Anniv.

Wolfgang Amadeus Mozart, Composer A676

1991, Mar. 20   *Perf. 14*
2092 A676 7.50d multicolored   1.05   1.05

Otto Lilienthal's First Glider Flight, Cent. — A677

Designs: 7.50d, Edvard Rusjan (1886-1911), pilot, aircraft designor. 15d, Otto Lilienthal (1848-1896), aviation pioneer.

1991, Apr. 1
2093 A677 7.50d multicolored   1.00 1.00
2094 A677 15d multicolored   2.00 2.00

Printed in sheets of 8 plus label.

Lhotse I, Himalayas, South Face First Climbed by Tomo Cesen, 1990 A678

1991, Apr. 24   *Perf. 14x13¹/₂*
2095 A678 7.50d multicolored   1.00 1.00

Europa — A679

Designs: 7.50d, Telecommunications satellite. 15d, Satellite, antenna, telephone.

1991, May 6   *Perf. 14*
2096 A679 7.50d multicolored   1.00 1.00
2097 A679 15d multicolored   2.00 2.00

Franciscan Monastery, Trsat, 700th Anniv. — A680

1991, May 10   Litho.   *Perf. 13¹/₂x14*
2098 A680 3.50d multicolored   38 38

Governments of Danube River Region Conf., Belgrade — A681

Designs: 15d, Danube River shipping. 20d, Course of Danube, landmarks, regional animals.

1991, May 15   *Perf. 13¹/₂*
2099 A681 7.50d multicolored   65 65
2100 A681 15d multicolored   1.30 1.30

Souvenir Sheet

2101 A681 20d multicolored   1.75 1.75

No. 2101 contains one 55x35mm stamp.

Opening of Karavanke Tunnel A682

Designs: 4.50d, Passage Over Karavanke by J. Valvasor, 17th century. 11d, Entrance to new Karavanke Tunnel.

1991, June 1   *Perf. 14x13¹/₂*
2102 A682 4.50d multicolored   40 40
2103 A682 11d multicolored   95 95

Basketball, Cent. — A683

1991, June 15   *Perf. 13¹/₂x14*
2104 A683 11d shown   95 95
2105 A683 15d Nets, "100"   1.30 1.30

Yugoslavian Insurrection, 50th Anniv. — A684   Tin Ujevic (1891-1955), Writer — A685

Designs: 4.50d, Partisan Memorial Medal, 1941. 11d, Medal for Courage.

1991, July 4   Litho.   *Perf. 14*
2106 A684 4.50d multicolored   40 40
2107 A684 11d multicolored   95 95

Yugoslav Natl. Army, 50th Anniv.

1991, July 5   *Perf. 13¹/₂*
2108 A685 4.50d multicolored   40 40

Jacobus Gallus (1550-1591), Composer A686

1991, July 18
2109 A686 11d multicolored   95 95

Lighthouses of Adriatic and Danube A687

Designs: a, Savudrija, 1818. b, Sveti Ivan na pucini, 1853. c, Porer, 1833. d, Stoncica, 1865. e, Olipa, c. 1842. f, Glavat, 1884. g, Veli rat, 1849. h, Vir, 1881. i, Tajerske sestrice, 1876. j, Razanj, 1875. k, Derdap-Danube. l, Tamis-Danube.

1991, July 25   Litho.   *Perf. 13¹/₂*
2110 A687 10d Bklt. pane of 12, #a.-l.   10.80 10.80

Sremski Karlovci High School, Bicent. A688

1991, Sept. 12   Litho.   *Perf. 14*
2111 A688 4.50d multicolored   40 40

European Nature Protection A689

1991, Sept. 24   *Perf. 13¹/₂x14*
2112 A689 11d Palingenia longicauda   95 95
2113 A689 15d Phalacrocorax pygmaeus   1.30 1.30

Town of Subotica, 600th Anniv. — A690

1991, Sept. 28   *Perf. 14*
2114 A690 4.50d multicolored   40 40

Joy of Europe — A691

Paintings: 15d, Little Dubravka, by Jovan Bijelic (1886-1964). 30d, Little Girl with a Cat by Mary Cassatt (1845-1926).

1991, Oct. 2
2115 A691 15d multicolored   1.30 1.30
2116 A691 30d multicolored   2.60 2.60

33rd Intl. Apicultural Congress, APIMONDIA '91 — A692

1991, Sept. 28   Litho.   *Perf. 13¹/₂x14*
2117 A692 11d multicolored   1.00 1.00

Stamp Day, Monument to Prince Michael Obrenovich, Serbia #1 A693

1991, Oct. 31   *Perf. 14*
2118 A693 4.50d multicolored   40 40

First Serbia Postage Stamps, 125th Anniv.

Museum Exhibits — A694

Flags and medals: 20d, Vucjido battle flag, medal for courage. 30d, Grahovac battle flag and medal. 40d, Montenegrin state flag, medal for bravery. 50d, Montenegrin court flag, medal of Petrovich Nyegosh Dynasty.

1991, Nov. 28   *Perf. 13¹/₂x14*
2119 A694 20d multicolored   1.75 1.75
2120 A694 30d multicolored   2.75 2.75
2121 A694 40d multicolored   3.50 3.50
2122 A694 50d multicolored   4.50 4.50

Illustrations from Ancient Manuscripts A695

Designs: 20d, Angel carrying Sun around Earth, 17th cent. 30d, Celnica Gospel, menology for April, 14th cent. 40d, Angel from the Annunciation, 13th cent. 50d, Mary Magdalene, 12th cent.

1991, Dec. 12
2123 A695 20d multicolored   1.75 1.75
2124 A695 30d multicolored   2.75 2.75
2125 A695 40d multicolored   3.50 3.50
2126 A695 50d multicolored   4.50 4.50

Gotse Deltchev (1872-1903), Macedonian Revolutionary A696

1992, Jan. 29   Litho.   *Perf. 13¹/₂*
2127 A696 5d multicolored   15 15

Red Star, European and World Soccer Champions A697

1992, Jan. 29   Litho.   *Perf. 14x13¹/₂*
2128 A697 17d multicolored   25 15

A698   A699

1992, Feb. 8   *Perf. 14x13¹/₂*
2129 A698 80d Ski jumping   1.15 58
2130 A698 100d Freestyle skiing   1.45 72

1992 Winter Olympics, Albertville.

1992, Mar. 10   Litho.   *Perf. 14*

Protected Animals: a, 50d, Lepus europaeus. b, 60d, Pteromys volans. c, 80d, Dryomys nitedula. d, 100d, Cricetus cricetus.

2131 A699 Strip of 4 + label   3.75 1.90

Madonna and Child, 14th century, Pec — A700

1992, Mar. 14   *Perf. 13¹/₂x14*
2132 A700 80d multicolored   1.05   50
Promotion of Breastfeeding.

Ski Association of Montenegro A701

1992, Mar. 25   *Perf. 14x13¹/₂*
2133 A701 8d multicolored   15   15
Skiing in Montenegro, cent.

1860 Fountain, Belgrade — A702

Designs: 100d, Fisherman Fountain, Belgrade.

1992   Litho.   *Perf. 13¹/₂*
2137 A702 50d violet   75   38
2139 A702 100d dk grn & lt grn   65   32
Issued: 50d, Apr. 1; 100d, May 6.
This is an expanding set. Numbers may change.

Sinking of the Titanic, 80th Anniv. — A703

1992, Apr. 14   *Perf. 14*
2152 A703 150d multicolored   2.25   1.10

Expo '92, Seville A704

1992, Apr. 20
2153 A704 150d multicolored   2.25   1.10

Discovery of America, 500th Anniv. — A705

1992, May 5   Litho.   *Perf. 13¹/₂x14*
2154 A705 300d Columbus, ship   2.00   1.00
2155 A705 500d Columbus' fleet   3.25   1.65

Souvenir Sheet
Perf. 14x13¹/₂
2156 A705 1200d Ships in port   7.80   7.80
Europa. No. 2156 contains one 54x34mm stamp.

1992 Summer Olympics, Barcelona — A706

1992, May 20   *Perf. 14x13¹/₂*
2157 A706 500d Pistol shooting   3.25   1.65
2158 A706 500d Water polo   3.25   1.65
2159 A706 500d Tennis   3.25   1.65
2160 A706 500d Handball   3.25   1.65

Importation Prohibited
Stamps from Yugoslavia (Serbia and Montenegro) issued after No. 2160 have not been valued because the embargo on trade with Serbia and Montenegro, proclaimed May 30, 1992 by President Bush prohibits the importation from any country of stamps of Yugoslavian origin, used or unused.

European Soccer Championships A707

Various soccer plays.

1992, June 1   *Perf. 13¹/₂*
2161 A707 1000d shown
2162 A707 1000d multicolored

Domestic Cats — A708

Designs: No. 2163, Red Persian. No. 2164, White Persian. No. 2165, Yellow tabby. No. 2166, British blue short-hair.

1992, June 25   Litho.   *Perf. 13¹/₂x14*
Background Color
Cyrillic Letters
2163 A708 1000d blue
2164 A708 1000d purple
Latin Letters
2165 A708 1000d dark purple
2166 A708 1000d brown

Steam Locomotives A709

Designs: a, JDZ 162. b, JDZ 151. c, JDZ 73. d, JDZ 83. e, JDZ 16. f, Prince Nicholas' coach.

1992, July 3   Litho.   *Perf. 14*
2167 A709 1000d Booklet pane of 6, #a.-f.

SEMI-POSTAL STAMPS

Giving Succor to Wounded — SP1

Wounded Soldier — SP2

Symbolical of National Unity — SP3

1921, Jan. 30   Unwmk.   Engr.   *Perf. 12*
B1 SP1 10p carmine   15   15
B2 SP2 15p violet brown   15   15
B3 SP3 25p light blue   15   15
Set value   22   24
Nos. B1-B3 were sold at double face value, the excess being for the benefit of invalid soldiers. For surcharges see Nos. 15-21.

U.R.I.
This overprint was applied to 500,000 copies of No. B1 in 1923 and they were given to the Society for Wounded Invalids (Uprava Ratnih Invalida) which sold them for 2d apiece. These overprinted stamps had no franking power, but some were used through ignorance.

Regular Issue of 1926-27 Surcharged in Dark Red   **+0·25**

1926, Nov. 1   *Perf. 13*
B5 A6 25p + 25p green   15   15
B6 A6 50p + 50p olive brn   15   15
B7 A6 1d + 50p scarlet   20   15
B8 A6 2d + 50p black   60   15
B9 A6 3d + 50p slate blue   50   15
B10 A6 4d + 50p red org   1.40   20
B11 A6 5d + 50p brt vio   75   20
B12 A6 8d + 50p black brn   1.90   60
B13 A6 10d + 1d olive brn   1.75   60
B14 A6 15d + 1d brown   5.00   1.00
B15 A6 20d + 1d dark vio   4.50   75
B16 A6 30d + 1d orange   15.00   1.90
a. Double surcharge
Nos. B5-B16 (12)   31.90   6.00
The surtax on these stamps was intended for a fund for relief of sufferers from floods. For overprints see Nos. 99-101.

Cathedral at Duvno SP4

King Tomislav SP6

Kings Tomislav and Alexander SP5

1929, Nov. 1   Typo.
B17 SP4 50p (+ 50p) ol green   24   24
B18 SP5 1d (+ 50p) red   24   24
B19 SP6 3d (+ 1d) blue   1.25   1.10
Millenary of the Croatian kingdom. The surtax was used to create a War Memorial Cemetery in France and to erect a monument to Serbian soldiers who died there.

View of Dobropolje — SP7

War Memorial — SP8

View of Kajmaktchalan SP9

1931, Apr. 1   *Perf. 12¹/₂, 11¹/₂*
B20 SP7 50p + 50p blue grn   15   15
B21 SP8 1d + 1d scarlet   15   15
B22 SP9 3d + 3d deep blue   15   15
Set value   28   30
The surtax was added to a fund for a War Memorial to Serbian soldiers who died in France during World War I.

SP10

SP12

SP11

Black Overprint
1931, Nov. 1   *Perf. 12¹/₂, 11¹/₂x12*
B23 SP10 50p (+ 50p) olive grn   15   28
B24 SP11 1d (+ 50p) red   15   30
B25 SP12 3d (+ 1d) blue   18   35
Set value   34
Surtax for War Memorial fund.

Rower on Danube at Smederevo SP13

Bled Lake — SP14

Danube near Belgrade SP15

View of Split
Harbor
SP16

Zagreb
Cathedral — SP17

Prince
Peter — SP18

1932, Sept. 2   Litho.   Perf. 11½

B26	SP13	75p + 50p dl grn & lt blue	45	1.00
B27	SP14	1d + ½d scar & lt blue	45	1.10
B28	SP15	1½d + ½d rose & green	45	1.10
B29	SP16	3d + 1d bl & lt bl	75	2.00
B30	SP17	4d + 1d red org & lt blue	4.25	10.00
B31	SP18	5d + 1d dl vio & lilac	4.25	8.50
		Nos. B26-B31 (6)	10.60	23.70

European Rowing Championship Races, Belgrade.

+ 0·25
XI int. kongres
Pen-Klubova
u Dubrovniku 1933.
King Alexander
SP19

Prince Peter
SP20

1933, May 25   Typo.   Perf. 12½

B32	SP19	50p + 25p black	3.50	5.25
B33	SP19	75p + 25p yel grn	3.50	5.25
B34	SP19	1.50d + 50p rose	3.50	5.25
B35	SP19	3d + 1d bl vio	3.50	5.25
B36	SP19	4p + 1d dk grn	3.50	5.25
B37	SP19	5d + 1d orange	3.50	5.25
		Nos. B32-B37 (6)	21.00	31.50

11th Intl. Congress of P.E.N. (Poets, Editors and Novelists) Clubs, Dubrovnik, May 25-27.

The labels at the foot of the stamps are printed in either Cyrillic or Latin letters and each bears the amount of a premium for the benefit of the local P.E.N. Club at Dubrovnik.

1933, June 28

B38	SP20	75p + 25p slate grn	20	25
B39	SP20	1½d + ½d deep red	20	25

60th anniv. meeting of the National Sokols (Sports Associations) at Ljubljana, July 1.

Eagle Soaring
over
City — SP22

Athlete and
Eagle — SP23

1934, June 1   Perf. 12½

B40	SP22	75p + 25p green	1.90	1.10
B41	SP22	1.50d + 50p car	4.00	1.65
B42	SP22	1.75d + 25p brown	6.00	2.25

20th anniversary of Sokols of Sarajevo.

1934, June 1

B43	SP23	75p + 25p Prus grn	2.00	90
B44	SP23	1.50d + 50p car	4.00	1.75
B45	SP23	1.75d + 25p choc	6.50	2.50

60th anniversary of Sokols of Zagreb.

Mother and Children
SP24   SP25

Perf. 12½x11½

1935, Dec. 25   Photo.

B46	SP24	1.50d + 1d dk brn & brown	70	55
a.		Perf. 11½	11.50	11.50
B47	SP25	3.50d + 1.50d bright ultra & bl	1.25	1.00

The surtax was for "Winter Help."

Queen
Mother
Marie
SP26

Prince Regent
Paul
SP27

1936, May 3   Litho.

B48	SP26	75p + 25p grnsh bl	45	45
B49	SP26	1.50d + 50p rose pink	52	52
B50	SP26	1.75d + 75p brown	75	75
B51	SP26	3.50d + 1d brt bl	60	60

Nos. B48 and B50 are printed in Cyrillic, others in Latin letters.

1936, Sept. 20   Typo.

B52	SP27	75p + 50p turq grn & red	22	6.25
B53	SP27	1.50d + 50p cer & red	16	4.00

Surtax for the Red Cross.

Princes Tomislav and Andrej
SP28   SP29

Perf. 11½x12½, 12½x11½

1937, May 1

B54	SP28	25p + 25p red brn	15	20
B55	SP28	75p + 75p emerald	20	24
B56	SP29	1.50d + 1d org red	24	30
B57	SP29	2d + 1d magenta	28	30

Souvenir Sheet

National
Costumes
SP30

1937, Sept. 12   Perf. 14

B57A	SP30	Sheet of 4	1.75	2.75
b.		1d blue green	25	32
c.		1.50d bright violet	25	32
d.		2d rose red	25	32
e.		4d dark blue	25	32

1st Yugoslavian Phil. Exhib., Belgrade. Sold only at the exhibition post office at 15d each.

SP31   SP32

Perf. 11½x12½, 12½x11½

1938, May 1   Photo.

B58	SP31	50p + 50p dark brn	25	28
B59	SP32	1d + 1d dk green	30	32
B60	SP31	1.50d + 1.50d scar	35	40
B61	SP32	2d + 2d magenta	42	45

Surtax for the benefit of Child Welfare. For overprints see Nos. B75-B78.

Bridge and Anti-aircraft
Lights — SP33

1938, May 28   Perf. 11½x12½

B62	SP33	1d + 50p dk grn	24	24
B63	SP33	1.50d + 1d scarlet	35	35
a.		Perf. 11½	17.50	17.50
B64	SP33	2d + 1d rose vio	48	48
a.		Perf. 11½	14.00	14.00
B65	SP33	3d + 1.50d dp bl	55	55

Intl. Aeronautical Exhib., Belgrade.

Cliff at Demir-
Kapiya
SP34

Modern
Hospital
SP35

Runner Carrying
Torch — SP36

Alexander
I — SP37

Perf. 11½x12½, 12½x11½

1938, Aug. 1

B66	SP34	1d + 1d slate grn & dp grn	48	60
B67	SP35	1.50d + 1.50d scar	60	75
B68	SP36	2d + 2d claret & dp rose	75	85
B69	SP37	3d + 3d dp bl	75	85

The surtax was to raise funds to build a hospital for railway employees.

Runner
SP38

Shot-Putter
SP41

Hurdlers
SP39

Pole
Vaulter
SP40

1938, Sept. 11

B70	SP38	50p + 50p org brn	80	80
B71	SP39	1d + 1d sl grn & dp grn	1.00	1.00
B72	SP40	1.50d + 1.50d rose & dk mag	1.00	1.00
B73	SP41	2d + 2d dk blue	1.50	1.50

Ninth Balkan Games.

Stamps of 1938 Overprinted in Black

SALVATE   SALVATE
PARVULOS   PARVULOS
a   b

1938, Oct. 1

B75	SP31(a)	50p + 50p dk brn	40	40
B76	SP32(b)	1d + 1d dk grn	45	45
B77	SP31(a)	1.50d + 1.50d scar	45	48
B78	SP32(b)	2d + 2d mag	60	60

Surtax for the benefit of Child Welfare.

Postriders
SP43

Designs: 1d+1d, Rural mail delivery. 1.50d+1.50d, Mail train. 2d+2d, Mail bus. 4d+4d, Mail plane.

1939, Mar. 15   Photo.   Perf. 11½

B79	SP43	50p + 50p buff, bis & brown	45	55
B80	SP43	1d + 1d sl grn & dp green	60	75
B81	SP43	1.50d + 1.50d red, cop red & brn car	65	90
B82	SP43	2d + 2d dp plum & rose lilac	75	1.10
B83	SP43	4d + 4d ind & sl bl	1.40	1.50
		Nos. B79-B83 (5)	3.85	4.80

Centenary of the present postal system in Yugoslavia. The surtax was used for the Railway Benevolent Association.

The Cyrillic and Latin inscriptions are transposed on Nos. B82 and B83.

Child Eating
SP48

Children at
Seashore — SP49

Children in
Crib — SP51

Boy Planing
Board — SP50

1939, May 1 Perf. 12½
B84	SP48	1d + 1d blk & dp bl green	1.25	1.40
B85	SP49	1.50d + 1.50d org brn & sal	55	1.25
a.		Perf. 11½	40.00	22.50
B86	SP50	2d + 2d mar & vio rose	1.10	1.40
B87	SP51	4d + 4d ind & royal blue	1.40	1.90

The surtax was for the benefit of Child Welfare.

Czar Lazar of
Serbia — SP52

Milosh
Obilich — SP53

1939, June 28 Perf. 11½
B88	SP52	1d + 1d sl grn & bl grn	55	70
B89	SP53	1.50d + 1.50d mar & brt car	55	70

Battle of Kosovo, 550th anniversary.

Training Ship
"Jadran"
SP54

Designs: 1d+50p, Steamship "King Alexander." 1.50d+1d, Freighter "Triglan." 2d+1.50d, Cruiser "Dubrovnik."

1939, Sept. 6 Engr.
B90	SP54	50p + 50p brn org	60	70
B91	SP54	1d + 50p dull grn	80	95
B92	SP54	1.50d + 1d dp rose	70	80
B93	SP54	2d + 1.50d dark bl	80	1.10

Yugoslav Navy and Merchant Marine. The surtax aided a Marine Museum.

Motorcycle and
Sidecar
SP58

Motorcycle
SP60

Racing
Car — SP59

Racing
Car — SP61

1939, Sept. 3 Photo.
B94	SP58	50p + 50p brn, red org & yel	65	75
B95	SP59	1d + 1d blk, bl grn & pck grn	75	85
B96	SP60	1.50d + 1.50d choc & cop red	85	1.00
B97	SP61	2d + 2d ind, dk bl & ultra	1.50	1.75

Automobile and Motorcycle Races, Belgrade. The surtax was for the Race Organization and the State Treasury.

Unknown
Soldier
Memorial
SP62

1939, Oct. 9 Perf. 12½
B98	SP62	1d + 50p sl grn & green	65	85
B99	SP62	1.50d + 1d red & rose red	70	90
B100	SP62	2d + 1.50d dp cl & vio rose	85	1.00
B101	SP62	3d + 2d dp bl & bl	85	1.00

Assassination of King Alexander, 5th anniv. The surtax was used to aid World War I invalids.
The Cyrillic and Latin inscriptions are transposed on Nos. B99 and B101.

Postman
Delivering
Mail — SP64

Postman Emptying
Mail Box — SP65

Parcel Post
Delivery
Wagon
SP66

Parcel
Post — SP67

Repairing Telephone
Wires — SP68

1940, Jan. 1
B102	SP64	50p + 50p brn & deep org	50	55
B103	SP65	1d + 1d sl grn & blue grn	55	70
B104	SP66	1.50d + 1.50d red brn & scar	70	85
B105	SP67	2d + 2d dl vio & red lilac	85	1.40
B106	SP68	4d + 4d sl bl & bl	1.40	1.75
		Nos. B102-B106 (5)	4.00	5.25

The surtax was used for the employees of the Postal System in Belgrade.

Croats' Arrival
at Adriatic in
640 — SP69

King
Tomislav — SP70

Death of Matija
Gubec — SP71

Anton and
Stjepan
Radic — SP72

Map of
Yugoslavia
SP73

1940, Mar. 1 Typo. Perf. 11½
B107	SP69	50p + 50p brn org	28	30
B108	SP70	1d + 1d green	28	30
B109	SP71	1.50d + 1.50d brt red	30	30
B110	SP72	2d + 2d dk cerise	38	45
B111	SP73	4d + 2d dark blue	42	50
		Nos. B107-B111 (5)	1.66	1.85

The surtax was used for the benefit of postal employees in Zagreb.

Children
Playing in
Snow — SP74

Children at
Seashore — SP75

Perf. 11½, 12½
1940, May 1 Photo.
B112	SP74	50p + 50p brn org & org yellow	24	32
B113	SP75	1d + 1d sl grn & dk green	32	40
B114	SP74	1.50d + 1.50d brn red & scarlet	24	32
B115	SP75	2d + 2d mar & vio rose	35	42

The surtax was for Child Welfare.

Nos. C11-C14
Surcharged in
Carmine

Perf. 11½x12½, 12½x11½
1940, Dec. 23
B116	AP6	50p + 50p on 5d	30	30
B117	AP7	1d + 1d on 10d	30	30
B118	AP8	1.50d + 1.50d on 20d	35	40
B119	AP9	2d + 2d on 30d	35	40

The surtax was used to fight tuberculosis.
For surcharges see Nos. NB1-NB4.

St. Peter's
Cemetery,
Ljubljana
SP76

Croatian, Serbian
and Slovenian
SP77

Chapel at
Kajmaktchalan
SP78

Memorial
at Brezje
SP79

1941, Jan. 1 Perf. 12½
B120	SP76	50p + 50p gray grn & yel green	30	35
B121	SP77	1d + 1d brn car & dl rose	30	35
B122	SP78	1.50d + 1.50d myr grn & bl green	35	45
B123	SP79	2d + 2d gray bl & pale lilac	42	55

Surtax for the Ljubljana War Veterans Assoc.

Kamenita Gate,
Zagreb — SP80

13th Century
Cathedral,
Zagreb — SP81

1941, Mar. 16 Engr. Perf. 11½
B124	SP80	1.50d + 1.50d choc	40	80
B125	SP81	4d + 3d blue blk	40	80

2nd Philatelic Exhibition of Croatia, at Zagreb, Mar. 16-27.
Nos. B124-B125 exist perf. 9½ on right side. Value, each $25.

1941, Apr.
B126	SP80	1.50d + 1.50d bl black	8.50	9.50
B127	SP81	4d + 3d choc	8.50	9.50

Regional philatelic exhibition at Slavonski Brod. Nos. B126-B127 with gold overprint, "Nezavisna Drzava Hrvatska," are Croatia Nos. B1-B2.
Nos. B126-B127 exist perf. 9½ on right side. Value, each $55 unused, $70 used.

Issues for Federal Republic

Carrying Wounded Soldier — SP82

Child — SP83

1945, Sept. 15   Typo.   Perf. 11½

B131	SP82	1d + 4d deep ultra	75	75
B132	SP83	2d + 6d scarlet	75	75

The surtax was for the Red Cross.

Russia, Yugoslavia Flags — SP84

1945, Oct. 20   Photo.   Unwmk.

B133	SP84	2d + 5d multi	85	85

Liberation of Belgrade, 1st anniv.

Communications Symbols — SP85

1946, May 10   Perf. 12½

B134	SP85	1.50d + 1d emer	2.75	2.50
B135	SP85	2.50d + 1.50d car rose	2.75	2.50
B136	SP85	5d + 2d gray bl	2.75	2.50
B137	SP85	8d + 3.50d dl brn	2.75	2.50

1st PTT Congress since liberation, May 10. Inscription in lower panel on Nos. B135 and B136 is in Latin characters.

Flag and Young Laborers SP86

Handstand on Horizontal Bar SP87

1946, Aug. 1   Litho.
Flag in Red or Carmine and Deep or Dark Blue

B138	SP86	50p + 50p brn & buff	2.50	1.40
B139	SP86	50p + 50p dk grn & lt green	2.50	1.40
B140	SP86	2.50d + 2d rose vio & rose lilac	2.50	1.40
B141	SP86	5d + 3d gray bl & blue	2.50	1.40

Inscription at top differs on each denomination and the Cyrillic and Latin spellings of Yugoslavia are transposed on Nos. B139 and B141.
The surtax aided railroad reconstruction carried out by Yugoslav youths.

1947, Sept. 5   Perf. 11½

B142	SP87	1.50d + 50p dark grn	18	18
B143	SP87	2.50d + 50p carmine	20	20
B144	SP87	4d + 50p brt blue	24	24

1947 Balkan Games, Sept. 5-7, Ljubljana.

Young Railway Laborers SP88

1947, Sept. 25   Typo.   Perf. 11½x12

B145	SP88	1d + 50p orange	16	15
B146	SP88	1.50d + 1d yel green	16	15
B147	SP88	2.50d + 1.50d car lake	16	15
B148	SP88	5d + 2d deep blue	16	15

The surtax was for youth brigades employed in the construction of the Samac-Sarajevo railway.

Symbolizing Protection of "B.C.G." Vaccine — SP89

Dying Serpent — SP91

"Illness" and "Recovery" — SP90

1948, Apr. 1   Litho.   Perf. 12½

B149	SP89	1.50d + 1d sl blk & red	22	16
B150	SP90	2.50d + 2d grnsh gray, ol blk & red	22	16
B151	SP91	5d + 3d dk bl & car	22	16

Fight against tuberculosis. The surtax was for the Yugoslav Red Cross.

Juro Danicic — SP92

Shot Put — SP93

Portraits: 2.50d+1d, Franjo Racki. 4d+2d, Josip J. Strossmayer.

1948, July 28   Perf. 11

B152	SP92	1.50d + 50p blk green	25	20
B153	SP92	2.50d + 1d dark red	25	20
B154	SP92	4d + 2d dark blue	25	20

Yugoslav Academy of Arts and Sciences, Zagreb, 80th anniv. The surtax was for the Academy. "JUGOSLAVIJA" (Latin characters) on No. B153.

1948, Sept. 10   Perf. 12½

B155	SP93	2d + 1d shown	30	30
B156	SP93	3d + 1d Hurdles	30	30
B157	SP93	5d + 2d Pole vault	30	30

Balkan and Central Europe Games, 1948. Latin and Cyrillic spellings of Yugoslavia transposed on No. B156. On sale 4 days.

AIR POST STAMPS

Dubrovnik AP1

Lake Bled AP2

Falls of Jaice — AP3

Church at Oplenac — AP4

Bridge at Mostar — AP5

Perf. 12½
1934, June 15   Typo.   Unwmk.

C1	AP1	50p violet brown	15	15
C2	AP2	1d green	15	15
C3	AP3	2d rose red	45	15
C4	AP4	3d ultramarine	50	24
C5	AP5	10d vermilion	1.50	1.40
		Nos. C1-C5 (5)	2.75	2.09

King Alexander Memorial Issue
1935, Jan. 1
Border in Black

C6	AP4	3d ultramarine	1.50	1.25

St. Naum Convent — AP6

Sarajevo — AP8

Port of Rab — AP7

Ljubljana — AP9

Perf. 12½, 11½x12½, 12½x11½
1937, Sept. 12   Photo.

C7	AP6	50p brown	15	15
C8	AP7	1d yellow grn	15	15
C9	AP8	2d blue gray	15	15
C10	AP9	2.50d rose red	15	15
C11	AP6	5d brn violet	15	15
C12	AP7	10d brown lake	20	20
C13	AP8	20d dark green	32	32
C14	AP9	30d ultramarine	70	60
		Nos. C7-C14 (8)	1.97	1.87

For surcharges see Nos. B116-B119, NB1-NB4, NC1-NC8.

Cathedral of Zagreb AP10

Bridge at Belgrade AP11

1940, Aug. 15   Litho.   Perf. 12½

C15	AP10	40d Prus grn & pale green	95	1.40
C16	AP11	50d sl bl & gray bl	1.10	1.40

For overprints see Nos. NC9-NC10.

Issues for Federal Republic

Plane over Terrace of Kalimegdan, Belgrade AP12

Plane over Dubrovnik AP13

1947, Apr. 21   Typo.   Perf. 11½
Cyrillic Inscription at Top

C17	AP12	50p ol gray & brn vio	15	15
C18	AP13	1d mag & ol gray	18	15
C19	AP12	2d blue & black	22	15
C20	AP13	5d green & gray	30	15
C21	AP12	10d olive bis & choc	38	22
C22	AP13	20d ultra & olive	75	35

Roman Inscription at Top

C23	AP12	50p ol gray & brn vio	15	15
C24	AP13	1d mag & ol gray	18	15
C25	AP12	2d blue & black	22	15
C26	AP13	5d green & gray	30	15
C27	AP12	10d olive bis & choc	38	22
C28	AP13	20d ultra & olive	75	35
		Nos. C17-C28 (12)	3.96	
		Set value		1.85

Sheets of each denomination contain alternately stamps with Cyrillic or Roman inscription at top. Value, 6 se-tenant pairs, $35.

Laurent Kosir and Birthplace AP14

1948, Aug. 27   Engr.

C29	AP14	15d red violet	1.00	80

Kosir, recognized by Yugoslavia as inventor of the postage stamp, 80th death anniv. Issued in sheets of 25 stamps and 25 labels.

Nos. 262 to 264 Overprinted in Blue or Carmine

AVIONSKA POSTA

1949, Aug. 25   Unwmk.   Perf. 12½

C30	A55	3d carmine rose	1.10	2.50
C31	A56	5d dull blue (C)	1.10	2.50
C32	A57	12d red brown	1.10	2.50

Liberation of Macedonia, 5th anniv.
It is reported that No. C32 was not sold to the public at the post office.

Souvenir Sheet

Electric Train — AP15

Perf. 11½x12½
1949, Dec. 15   Photo.

C33	AP15	10d lilac rose	35.00	19.00
a.		Imperf.	35.00	19.00

Centenary of Yugoslav railroads.
For overprint see Trieste No. C17.

Iron Gate, Derdap — AP16

Belgrade AP17

Marshal Tito, Tank, Factory and Planes — AP20

1951, Dec. 22 Unwmk.
C54 AP20 150d deep blue   5.25 3.50

Army Day, Dec. 22; 10th anniv. of the formation of the 1st military unit of "New" Yugoslavia.

Star and Flag-encircled Globe — AP21

1953, July 30 Engr.
C55 AP21 300d bl & grn   165.00 165.00

38th Esperanto Congress, Zagreb, July 25-Aug. 1. For overprint see Trieste No. C21.

Designs: 2d, Cascades, Plitvice. 3d, Carolina. 6d, Roman bridge, Mostar. 10d, Ohrid. 20d, Gulf of Kotor. 30d, Dubrovnik. 50d, Bled.

Perf. 12½
1951, June 16 Unwmk. Engr.
C34 AP16	1d deep org	15	15
C35 AP16	2d dk green	15	15
C36 AP16	3d dark red	18	15
C37 AP16	6d ultra	3.00	3.50
C38 AP16	10d dark brn	24	15
C39 AP16	20d grnsh blk	30	15
C40 AP16	30d dp claret	50	15
C41 AP16	50d dk purple	90	15
C42 AP17	100d dk gray bl	16.00	2.50
Nos. C34-C42 (9)		21.42	7.05

Souvenir Sheet
Imperf
C43 AP17 100d red brn   65.00 65.00

See Nos. C50-C53. For overprints see Nos. C44, C49, Trieste C22-C32.

Roman Bridge Type of 1951
Overprinted "ZEFIZ 1951" in Carmine
1951, June 16 Perf. 12½
C44 AP16 6d dark green   90 70

Nos. C43-C44 were issued for Zagreb Philatelic Exhibition, June 16-26.

13th Century Tower, Zagreb AP22

1956, May 20 Perf. 11½
Chalky Paper
C56 AP22 30d gray, vio bl & org red 1.65 90

Yugoslav Intl. Phil. Exhib., JUFIZ III, Zagreb, May 20-27.

View on Mt. Kapaonik AP18

Plane and Parachutists AP19

Perf. 12½
1951, July Unwmk. Photo.
C45 AP18	3d shown	90	65
C46 AP18	5d Mt. Triglav	90	65
C47 AP18	20d Mt. Kalnik	35.00	27.50

Intl. Union of Mountaineers, 12th Assembly, Bled, July 13-18.

1951, Aug. 16 Engr.
C48 AP19 6d carmine   2.25 1.10

Type of 1951
Overprinted in Carmine
C49 AP16 50d blue   35.00 25.00

First World Parachute Championship, Bled, Aug. 16-20.

Catalogue values for unused stamps in this section, from this point to the end of the section, are for Never Hinged items.

Types of 1951
Designs: 5d, Cascades, Plitvice. 100d, Carniola. 200d, Roman bridge, Mostar.

1951-52
C50 AP16	5d yel brn ('52)	15	15
C51 AP16	100d green	15	15
C52 AP16	200d deep car ('52)	1.00	30
C53 AP17	500d blue vio ('52)	2.25	65
Set value			1.05

Workers and Cogwheel — AP23

Moon and Earth with Satellites — AP24

1956, June 15 Photo.
Glossy Paper
C57 AP23 30d car rose & blk   1.65 1.65

10th anniversary of technical education.

1958, Oct. 24 Engr. Perf. 12½
C58 AP24 300d dark blue   4.75 2.00

Intl. Geophysical Year, 1957-58.

Types of Regular Issue, 1961
1961, Sept. 1 Perf. 11½
C59 A150	250d dark purple	90	48
C60 A151	500d violet blue	2.50	1.75

Type of Athletic Regular Issue, 1962
Souvenir Sheet
Design: Army Stadium, Belgrade.

1962, Sept. 12 Litho. Imperf.
C61 A161 600d vio & blk   3.25 2.50

7th European Athletic Championships, Belgrade, Sept. 12-16.

POSTAGE DUE STAMPS

King Alexander — D1

1921 Typo. Unwmk. Perf. 11½
Red or Black Surcharge
J1 D1	10p on 5p green (R)	15	15
J2 D1	30p on 5p green (Bk)	15	15
Set value			20

D2

D3

1921-22 Typo. Perf. 11½
J3 D2	10p rose	15	15
J4 D2	30p yellow green	20	15
J5 D2	50p violet	30	15
J6 D2	1d brown	32	15
J7 D2	2d blue	35	15
J8 D3	5d orange	7.50	40
J9 D3	10d violet brown	9.25	45
a.	Cliche of 10p in sheet of 10d	75.00	100.00
J10 D3	25d pink	30.00	2.00
J11 D3	50d green	27.50	1.65
Nos. J3-J11 (9)		75.57	5.25

1924 Perf. 9, 10½, 11½
J12 D3	10p rose red	15	15
J13 D3	30p yellow green	45	35
J14 D3	50p violet	15	15
J15 D3	1d brown	32	15
J16 D3	2d deep blue	55	15
J17 D3	5d orange	9.25	15
J18 D3	10d violet brown	21.00	15
J19 D3	25d pink	42.50	1.00
J20 D3	50d green	57.50	85
Nos. J12-J20 (9)		131.87	
Set value			2.65

Nos. J19-J20 Surcharged **10**

1928
J21 D3	10d on 25d pink	3.25	24
J22 D3	10d on 50d green	3.25	24
a.	Inverted surcharge	30.00	18.00

A second type of "1" in surcharge has flag projecting horizontally. Value, each $15 unused, $3 used.

Coat of Arms — D4

Numeral of Value — D5

1931 Typo. Perf. 12½
With Imprint at Foot
J23 D4	50p violet	1.10	20
J24 D4	1d deep magenta	2.00	15
J25 D4	2d deep blue	5.00	15
J26 D4	5d orange	2.00	20
J27 D4	10d chocolate	6.75	70
Nos. J23-J27 (5)		16.85	1.40

For overprints see Nos. NJ1-NJ13, Croatia 26-29, J1-J5.

1932
Without Imprint at Foot
J28 D4	50p violet	15	15
J29 D4	1d deep magenta	15	15
J30 D4	2d deep blue	15	15
J31 D4	5d orange	15	15
J32 D4	10d chocolate	22	15
Set value		48	32

1933 Perf. 9, 10½, 11½
Overprint in Green, Blue or Maroon
J33 D5	50p vio (G)	15	15
J34 D5	1d brown (Bl)	20	15
a.	Perf. 10½	3.25	85
J35 D5	2d blue (M)	40	15
a.	Perf. 10½	1.65	52
J36 D5	5d orange (Bl)	1.25	15
J37 D5	10d violet brn (Bl)	6.00	1.00
Nos. J33-J37 (5)		8.00	
Set value			1.40

Issues for Federal Republic

Redrawn Type OD5, German Occupation of Serbia, Overprinted in Black

1945 Unwmk. Perf. 12½
J37A OD5	10d red	32	32
J37B OD5	20d ultramarine	32	32

In the redrawn design the eagle is replaced by a colorless tablet.

Coat of Arms — D6

Torches and Star — D7

1945 Litho. Perf. 12½
Numerals in Black
J38 D6	2d brown violet	15	25
J39 D6	3d violet	15	25
J40 D6	5d green	15	25
J41 D6	7d orange brown	15	25
J42 D6	10d rose lilac	15	25
J43 D6	20d blue	15	25
J44 D6	30d light bl grn	18	38
J45 D6	40d rose red	18	38

Numerals in Color of Stamp
J46 D6	1d blue green	15	15
J47 D6	1.50d blue	20	15
J48 D6	2d vermilion	20	15
J49 D6	3d violet brown	20	15
J50 D6	4d rose violet	20	15
Set value		1.75	2.50

For overprints see Nos. J64-J66.

1946-47 Typo. Unwmk.
J51 D7	50p dp orange ('47)	15	15
J52 D7	1d orange	15	15
J53 D7	2d dark blue	15	15
J54 D7	3d yellow green	15	15
J55 D7	5d bright purple	15	15
J56 D7	7d crimson	30	15
J57 D7	10d brt pink ('47)	55	15
J58 D7	20d rose lake ('47)	75	24
Set value		2.10	60

Latin inscription at top, Cyrillic at bottom on 50p, 2d, 5d and 10d.
See Nos. J67-J79. For overprints see Trieste Nos. J1-J5, J11-J18.

ФНР ЈУГОСЛАВИЈА

Nos. J47, J49 and J50 Overprinted in Black

FNR JUGOSLAVIJA

1950 Litho.
J64 D6	1.50d blue	15	15
J65 D6	3d violet brown	15	15
J66 D6	4d rose violet	20	15
Set value		36	30

Catalogue values for unused stamps in this section, from this point to the end of the section, are for Never Hinged items.

Type of 1946-47

1951-52 **Typo.** *Perf. 12½*

J67	D7	1d brown ('52)	15	15
J68	D7	2d emerald	15	15
J69	D7	5d blue	32	15
J70	D7	10d scarlet	1.65	15
J71	D7	20d purple	1.65	15
J72	D7	30d org yel ('52)	2.75	15
J73	D7	50d ultramarine	6.00	25
J74	D7	100d dp plum ('52)	6.25	42
		Nos. J67-J74 (8)	18.92	1.57

Latin inscription at top, Cyrillic at bottom on 2d, 5d and 10d.

For overprints see Istria Nos. J20-J24, Trieste J11-J18.

1962 **Litho.** *Perf. 12½*

J75	D7	10d red orange	2.75	15
J76	D7	20d purple	2.75	15
J77	D7	30d orange	4.25	15
J78	D7	50d ultramarine	10.50	52
J79	D7	100d rose lake	8.75	70
		Nos. J75-J79 (5)	29.00	1.67

Latin inscription at top, Cyrillic at bottom on 10d.

OFFICIAL STAMPS

Issues for Federal Republic

Arms of the Federated People's Republic — O1

1946, Nov. 1 **Unwmk.** *Perf. 12½* **Typo.**

O1	O1	50p orange	15	15
O2	O1	1d blue green	15	15
O3	O1	1.50d olive green	22	15
O4	O1	2.50d red	22	15
O5	O1	4d yellow brown	35	15
O6	O1	5d deep blue	48	15
O7	O1	8d chocolate	80	15
O8	O1	12d violet	95	25
		Nos. O1-O8 (8)	3.32	
		Set value		65

The Cyrillic and Latin inscriptions are transposed on Nos. O2, O4, O6 and O8.

For surcharges see Nos. 272A-272B, Istria 43, 45, 47, 49, 51.

POSTAL TAX STAMPS

Catalogue values for unused stamps in this section are for Never Hinged items.

The tax was for the Red Cross or The Olympic Fund unless otherwise noted.

Red Cross Emblem PT1

Dr. Vladen Djordjevic PT2

1933, Sept. 17 **Litho.** *Perf. 13* **Unwmk.**

RA1 PT1 50p dark blue & red 32 15

Obligatory on inland letters during "Red Cross Week," Sept. 17-23.

1936, Sept. 20 **Typo.** *Perf. 12*

RA2 PT2 50p brn blk & red 35 15

Obligatory on inland letters during "Red Cross Week," Sept. 20-26.

Aiding the Wounded PT3

1938, Sept. 18 **Litho.** *Perf. 12½*

RA3 PT3 50p dk bl, red, yel & grn 35 15

1940, Sept. 15 **Redrawn**

RA4 PT3 50p slate blue & red 1.10 20

The inscription at the upper right of this stamp and the numerals of value are in smaller characters. Obligatory on all letters during the second week of September.

Issues for Federal Republic

Ruined Dwellings PT4

Red Cross Nurse PT5

1947, Jan. 1 **Litho.** *Perf. 12½*

RA5 PT4 50p brn & scarlet 15 15

See No. RAJ2. For overprints see Trieste Nos. RA1, RAJ1.

1948, Oct. 1

RA6 PT5 50p dk vio bl & red 15 15

See No. RAJ3.

Nurse and Child — PT6

Nurse Holding Book — PT7

1949, Nov. 5

RA7 PT6 50p red & brown 15 15

See No. RAJ4. For overprints see Trieste Nos. RA2, RAJ2.

1950, Oct. 1

RA8 PT7 50p dark green & red 15 15

Obligatory Oct. 1-8, 1950. See No. RAJ6.

Hands Raising Red Cross Flag — PT8

Nurse — PT9

1951, Oct. 7

RA9 PT8 50p vio bl & red 15 15

Obligatory Oct. 7-14. For overprints see Trieste Nos. RA3, RAJ3.

1952, Oct. 5 **Photo.** *Perf. 12½*

RA10 PT9 50p gray & carmine 15 15

For overprint see Trieste No. RA4.

Child Receiving Blood Transfusion PT10

Youths Carrying Flags PT11

1953, Oct. 25 **Litho.**

RA11 PT10 2d red vio & red 18 15

See No. RAJ8. For overprints see Trieste Nos. RA5, RAJ5.

1954, Nov. 1

RA12 PT11 2d gray grn & red 18 15

See Nos. RAJ9.

Infant — PT11a

1954, Oct. 4

RA12A PT11a 2d brn & salmon 60 1.25

The tax was for Children's Week.

Girl — PT12

Nurse Opening Window — PT13

1955, Oct. 2 **Unwmk.** *Perf. 12½*

RA13 PT12 2d dull red 15 15

The tax was for child welfare. See No. RAJ10.

1955, Oct. 31

RA14 PT13 2d vio blk & red 18 15

See No. RAJ11.

Ruins in the Snow — PT14

Children and Goose — PT15

1956, May 6 *Perf. 12½*

RA15 PT14 2d sepia & red 15 15

See No. RAJ12.

1956, Sept. 30

RA16 PT15 2d gray green 15 15

The tax was for child welfare. See No. RAJ13.

Plane over Temporary Shelter — PT16

1957, May 5 **Litho.**

RA17 PT16 2d lt bl, blk & car 15 15

See No. RAJ14.

Girl and Boy Pioneers — PT17

1957, Sept. 30 **Unwmk.** *Perf. 12½*

RA18 PT17 2d rose & gray 15 15

Children's Week. Obligatory Oct. 2-6. See No. RAJ15.

Redrawn Type of Regular Issue, 1953

1958, May 4 *Perf. 12½x12*

RA19 A95 2d multicolored 15 15

On No. RA19 the UN emblem has been left out, Cyrillic inscriptions at left added, country name in Latin letters.

Playing Children — PT18

Helping Hand and Family — PT19

1958, Oct. 5 **Litho.** *Perf. 12½*

RA20 PT18 2d brt yel & black 15 15

Children's Week, Oct. 5-11.

1959, May 3

RA21 PT19 2d blue vio & red 15 15

Red Cross centenary. Obligatory May 3-9. See No. RAJ18.

Blackboard, Flower and Fish PT20

"Reconstruction" PT21

1959, Oct. 5 **Unwmk.**

RA22 PT20 2d ocher & Prus grn 15 15

Children's Week. Obligatory on domestic mail, Oct. 5-11. See No. RAJ19.

1960, May 8 *Perf. 12½*

RA23 PT21 2d slate & red 15 15

Obligatory May 8-14. See No. RAJ20.

Girl and Toys — PT22

Blood Donor Symbolism — PT23

1960, Oct. 2   Litho.   Perf. 12½
RA24 PT22 2d red   15 15

Issued for Children's Week. Obligatory on domestic mail Oct. 2-8. See No. RAJ21.

1961, May 7
RA25 PT23 2d multicolored   15 15

Obligatory May 7-13. Exists imperf. Value $12.50. See No. RAJ22.

Bird Holding Flower — PT24

1961, Oct. 1
RA26 PT24 2d orange & violet   15 15

Children's Week. Obligatory on domestic mail, Oct. 1-7. See No. RAJ23.

Bandages and Symbols of Home, Industry, Weather, Transportation, Fire and Flood — PT25

1962, Apr. 30   Perf. 12½
RA27 PT25 5d red brn, gray & red   15 15

Obligatory on domestic mail May 6-12. See No. RAJ24.

Centenary Emblem — PT26

Parachute Drop of Supplies, Yugoslav Flag — PT27

1963, May 5   Unwmk.   Perf. 12½
RA28 PT26 5d dl yel, red & gray   15 15

Intl. Red Cross, centenary. Obligatory on all domestic mail during Red Cross Week, May 5-11. See No. RAJ25.

1964, Apr. 27   Litho.
RA29 PT27 5d blue, rose & dk bl   15 15

Obligatory on domestic mail, May 3-9.

JUGOSLAVIJA Children in Circle — PT28

1965, May 2   Litho.   Perf. 12½
RA30 PT28 5d tan & red   15 15

Obligatory on domestic mail, May 2-8.

Arrows — PT29

1966, Apr. 28   Litho.   Perf. 12½
RA31 PT29 5p gray & multi   15 15

Obligatory on domestic mail, May 1-7.

Crosses and Flower — PT30

1967, Apr. 28   Litho.   Perf. 12½
RA32 PT30 5p vio, red & yel grn   15 15

Honeycomb and Red Cross — PT31

Aztec Calendar Stone and Olympic Rings — PT32

1968, Apr. 30   Litho.   Perf. 12
RA33 PT31 5p multicolored   15 15

Obligatory on all domestic mail May 5-11.

1968, Oct. 12   Perf. 12½
RA34 PT32 10p black & multi   15 15

Red Cross, Hands and Globe — PT33

Globe, Olympic Torch and Rings — PT34

1969, May 18   Litho.   Perf. 12
RA35 PT33 20p red org, dl red & blk 15 15

1969, Nov. 24   Litho.   Perf. 11
RA36 PT34 10p gold & multi   15 15

Yugoslav Olympic Committee, 50th anniv.

Symbolic Flower and People — PT35

1970, Apr. 27   Litho.   Perf. 13
RA37 PT35 20p vio bl, org & red   15 15

Olympic Flag — PT36

Olympic Rings and Disk — PT38

Red Cross Encircling Globe — PT37

1970, June 10   Litho.   Perf. 13x13½
RA38 PT36 10p multicolored   15 15

1971, Apr. 26   Litho.   Perf. 12½
RA39 PT37 20p biue, yel & red   15 15

1971, June 15   Litho.   Perf. 12½
RA40 PT38 10p blue & black   15 15

Red Cross and Hemispheres PT39

1972, Apr. 27   Perf. 13½x13
RA41 PT39 20p red & multi   15 15

Olympic Rings, TV Tower, Munich and Sapporo Emblems — PT40

1972, May   Perf. 13x13½
RA42 PT40 10p ultra & multi   15 15

Red Cross, Crescent and Lion Emblems — PT41

Globe and Olympic Rings — PT42

1973, Apr. 24   Litho.   Perf. 13x13½
RA43 PT41 20p blue & multi   15 15

1973, June 1   Litho.   Perf. 13x13½
RA44 PT42 10p multicolored   15 15

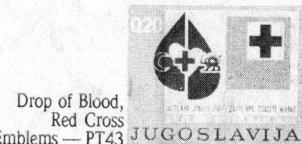
Drop of Blood, Red Cross Emblems — PT43

1974, Apr. 25   Litho.   Perf. 13
RA45 PT43 20p red & multi   15 15

Olympic Rings — PT44

1974, June 1   Litho.   Perf. 13
RA46 PT44 10p blue & multi   15 15

Red Cross, Hands — PT45

1975, Apr. 23   Photo.   Perf. 11½
RA47 PT45 20p blue, car & blk   15 15

Olympic Rings — PT46

1975, June 2   Litho.   Perf. 13½
RA48 PT46 10p multicolored   15 15

Ruin and Clock — PT47

1975, July 26   Litho.   Perf. 13x13½
RA49 PT47 30p blk & dk bl   15 15

Solidarity Week, July 26-Aug. 1. See Nos. RA61-RA62.

Red Crescent, Red Cross, Red Lion — PT48

1976, May 8   Photo.   Perf. 12½x13
RA50 PT48 20p multicolored   85 50

Olympics — PT49

1976, July 26   Litho.   Perf. 13½
RA51 PT49 10p intense blue   30 15

Fight Tuberculosis,
Red Cross — PT50

1977, Sept. 14   **Photo.**
RA52 PT50 50p multicolored   5.25 5.25
RA53 PT50 1d multicolored   80   80

1984 Olympics
PT51

1977, Dec. 17   *Perf. 13¹/₂x13*
RA54 PT51 10p multicolored   22 15

Red Crescent,
Red Cross, Red
Lion — PT52

1978, May 7   **Litho.**   *Perf. 13¹/₂*
RA55 PT52 20p on 1d bl & red   70 38
RA56 PT52 1d blue & red   28 15

1984 Olympics
PT53

1978, Sept.
RA57 PT53 30p multicolored   32 25

8th
Mediterranean
Games, Split,
Sept. 15-
29 — PT54

1979, Mar. 1   **Photo.**   *Perf. 13¹/₂x13*
RA58 PT54 1d violet   25 25
RA59 PT54 1d greenish blue   25 25

Red Cross
Week — PT55

1979, May 6   *Perf. 13¹/₂*
RA60 PT55 1d multicolored   25 25

Ruin and Clock Type of 1975 Inscribed
"1.-7.VI"

1979, June 1
RA61 PT47 30p blk & intense bl   32 22

Solidarity Week.

Ruin and Clock Type of 1975 Inscribed
"1.-7.VI"

1980, June 1   **Litho.**   *Perf. 13x13¹/₂*
RA62 PT47 1d black & blue   25 25

Solidarity Week, June 1-7.

Olympic
Week — PT57

1979, Oct. 15   **Photo.**   *Perf. 14*
RA63 PT57 30p blue & red   25 25

Sculpture, Red
Cross — PT58

Olympic
Week — PT59

1980, May 4   **Litho.**   *Perf. 13¹/₂*
RA64 PT58 1d multicolored   30 30

1980, Oct. 20   *Perf. 14*
RA65 PT59 50p multicolored   25 25

SPENS '81,
Novi
Sad — PT60

1980, Dec. 20   *Perf. 13¹/₂*
RA66 PT60 1d multicolored   22 15

Red Cross — PT61

Fight Tuberculosis,
Red Cross — PT62

1981, May 4   **Photo.**
RA67 PT61 1d multicolored   22 15

1981, Sept. 14
RA68 PT62 1d multicolored   22 15

Handshake — PT63

Fight Tuberculosis,
Red Cross — PT65

Robert
Koch — PT64

1982, May   **Litho.**   *Perf. 13*
RA69 PT63 1d black & red   20 20

1983, Sept. 18   **Litho.**   *Perf. 13*
RA70 PT64 1d multicolored   20 20

For surcharge see No. RA76.

1983, Sept. 14   **Litho.**   *Perf. 13¹/₂*
RA71 PT65 1d bluish grn, blk & red   22 15
RA72 PT65 2d bluish grn, blk & red   22 15

1984 Winter
Olympics,
Sarajevo — PT66

1983, Oct. 20   **Litho.**   *Perf. 12¹/₂*
RA73 PT66 2d greenish blue   20 20

PLANICA
50 — PT67

1985, Apr. 1   **Photo.**   *Perf. 14*
RA74 PT67 2d brt ultra & blue   16 15

Ruin, Clock and Red
Cross — PT68

1987, June 1   **Litho.**   *Perf. 10*
RA75 PT68 30d multicolored   16 15

Solidarity Week, June 1-7.

No. RA70 Surcharged in Silver

1988, Sept. 14   **Litho.**   *Perf. 13*
RA76 PT64 12d on 1d multi   15 15

Intl. Red Cross, 125th
Anniv. — PT69

1989, May 8   **Litho.**   *Perf. 12x11*
Without Gum
RA77 PT69 20d bl, sil & red   15 15
RA78 PT69 80d bl, sil & red   15 15
RA79 PT69 150d bl, sil & red   15 15
RA80 PT69 160d bl, sil & red   15 15
            Set value   26 26

Souvenir folders with perf. or imperf. miniature
sheets of 4 sold for 3200d.

Ruin, Clock and
Red
Cross — PT70

Building, Clock and
Red Cross — PT71

1989, June 1   *Perf. 10*
Without Gum
RA81 PT70 250d red & silver   15 15
           Roulette 10
RA82 PT71 400d brt bl gray & red   18 15
            Set value   15

Souvenir folders with perf. or imperf. miniature
sheets containing one 45x65mm stamp like RA81
sold for 3200d.

Fight Tuberculosis, Red
Cross — PT72

1989, Sept. 14   *Rough Perf. 10¹/₂*
Without Gum
RA83 PT72   20d black & red   15 15
RA84 PT72 200d black & red   15 15
RA85 PT72 250d black & red   15 15
RA86 PT72 400d black & red   15 15
RA87 PT72 650d black & red   15 15
           Set value   50 50

Red Cross — PT73

1990, May 8   *Perf. 13¹/₂*
Without Gum
RA88 PT73 10d green & red   15 15
RA89 PT73 20d green & red   15 15
RA90 PT73 30d green & red   22 15
           Set value   44 22

Flowers — PT74

Macedonian Red
Cross, 45th
Anniv. — PT75

1990, May 8   *Perf. 10*
Without Gum
RA91 PT74 20p shown   15 15
RA92 PT74 20p multi, diff.   15 15
RA93 PT75 20p multicolored   15 15
    a.   Block of 3 + label, #RA91-RA93   45 45
           Set value   20

Souvenir folders with perf. or imperf. miniature
sheets of 3 + label sold for 4d.

PT76

PT77

1990, Sept. 14   **Litho.**   *Perf. 10*
Without Gum
RA94 PT76 20p blue, org & red   15 15
RA95 PT76 25p blue, yel & red   18 15
RA96 PT76 50p blue, yel & red   38 18
           Set value   35

Fight tuberculosis, Red Cross.

1991, Sept. 14   **Litho.**   *Perf. 12¹/₂*
Without Gum
RA97 PT77 1.20d dk bl, yel & red   68 35

Postal Tax Stamps for use in a particular republic or republics fall beyond the scope of this catalogue and are not listed. These stamps, issued since 1977, were not intended for nationwide use. Some of these issues have designs which are similar to stamps used nationwide, most notably those using variations of the Ruin and Clock (PT47) design. Most others show the Red Cross or the Tuberculosis Cross.

POSTAL TAX DUE STAMPS

Catalogue values for unused stamps in this section are for Never Hinged items.

The tax of Nos. RAJ1-RAJ9, RAJ11-RAJ12, RAJ14 and RAJ18 was for the Red Cross.

Postal Tax Due stamps are inscribed "PORTO."

Red Cross Emblem — PTD1   Cross and Map of Yugoslavia — PTD2

1933	Unwmk.	Litho.	Perf. 13		
RAJ1	PTD1	50p dull grn & red		80	15

Type of Postal Tax Stamp of 1947

1947			Perf. 12½		
RAJ2	PT4	50p blue grn & scar		75	15

For surcharge see Trieste No. RAJ1.

Type of Postal Tax Stamp of 1948

1948					
RAJ3	PT5	50p dark grn & red		75	15

Type of Postal Tax Stamp of 1949

1949					
RAJ4	PT6	50p red & violet		1.10	15

For overprint see Trieste No. RAJ2.

1950	Unwmk.		Perf. 12½		
RAJ5	PTD2	50p red brown & red		42	15

Type of Postal Tax Stamp of 1951

1951					
RAJ6	PT8	50p emerald & red		48	15

For overprint see Trieste No. RAJ3.

Red Cross — PTD3

1952	Unwmk.	Photo.	Perf. 12½		
RAJ7	PTD3	50p gray & car		60	15

For overprint see Trieste No. RAJ4.

Type of Postal Tax Stamp of 1953

1953			Litho.		
RAJ8	PT10	2d yel brown & red		80	15

For overprint see Trieste No. RAJ5.

Type of Postal Tax Stamp of 1954

1954					
RAJ9	PT11	2d lilac & red		80	15

Type of Postal Tax Stamp of 1955

1955					
RAJ10	PT12	2d yellow green		70	15

Type of Postal Tax Stamp of 1955

1955					
RAJ11	PT13	2d dk vio brn & red		90	15

Type of Postal Tax Stamp of 1956

1956					
RAJ12	PT14	2d blue grn & red		38	15

Type of Postal Tax Stamp of 1956

1956					
RAJ13	PT15	2d violet brn		70	15

Type of Postal Tax Stamp of 1957

1957					
RAJ14	PT16	2d gray, blk & car		65	15

Type of Postal Tax Stamp, 1957

1957					
RAJ15	PT17	2d lt bl, bis & grn		48	15

Redrawn Type of Regular Issue, 1953

1958			Perf. 12½x12		
RAJ16	A95	2d multicolored		35	15

Child With Toy — PTD4

1958		Litho.	Perf. 12½		
RAJ17	PTD4	2d lt ultra & blk		28	15

Issued for Children's Week, Oct. 5-11.

Type of Postal Tax Stamp, 1959

1959					
RAJ18	PT19	2d yel org & red		32	15

Type of Postal Tax Stamp, 1959

Design: Tree, cock and wheat.

1959					
RAJ19	PT20	2d ocher & mar		38	15

Type of Postal Tax Stamp, 1960

1960					
RAJ20	PT21	2d vio brn & red		48	15

Type of Postal Tax Stamp, 1960

Design: Boy, tools and ball.

1960					
RAJ21	PT22	2d Prussian blue		42	15

Type of Postal Tax Stamp, 1961

1961, May 7					
RAJ22	PT23	2d multicolored		55	15

Type of Postal Tax Stamp, 1961

1961, Oct. 1					
RAJ23	PT24	2d apple grn & brn		28	15

Type of Postal Tax Stamp, 1962

1962, Apr. 30					
RAJ24	PT25	5d brn red, bl & red		25	15

Type of Postal Tax Stamp, 1963

1963, May 5					
RAJ25	PT26	5d red org, red & gray		28	15

OFFICES ABROAD

King Peter II — A1

Type of Postal Tax Stamp of 1955

1943	Unwmk.	Typo.	Perf. 12½		
1K1	A1	2d dark blue		15	4.00
1K2	A1	3d slate		15	4.00
1K3	A1	5d carmine		15	4.00
1K4	A1	10d black		20	4.00

For surcharges see Nos. 1KB1-1KB4.

V. Vodnik — A2   Peter Nyegosh — A3

Designs: 3d, Ljudovit Gaj. 4d, Vuk Stefanovic Karadzic. 5d, Bishop Joseph Strossmayer. 10d, Karageorge.

1943, Dec. 1		Engr.	Perf. 12½x13		
1K5	A2	1d red org & black		32	8.25
1K6	A3	2d yel green & blk		35	8.50
1K7	A2	3d dp ultra & blk		35	8.75
1K8	A3	4d dk pur & brn blk		40	9.25
1K9	A2	5d brn vio & brn blk		42	9.75
1K10	A3	10d brn & brown blk		45	10.00
		Nos. 1K5-1K10 (6)		2.29	54.50

Souvenir Sheet
Perf. 13½
Center in Black

1K11		Sheet of 6, #1K5-1K10		6.75	

25th anniv. of the Union of Liberated Yugoslavia. Valid on ships of the Yugoslav Navy and Mercantile Marine.

Nos. 1K5-1K10 overprinted diagonally "1945" in London were not issued. In 1950, they were sold by the Yugoslav Government without postal validity. Later they appeared with the additional overprint of the outline of a plane at upper left in carmine or black.

OFFICES ABROAD SEMI-POSTAL STAMPS

Nos. 1K1-1K4 Surcharged in Orange or Black   **CRVENI KRST + 12.50**

1943	Unwmk.		Perf. 12½		
1KB1	A1	2d + 12.50d dk bl		65	8.25
1KB2	A1	3d + 12.50d slate		65	8.25
1KB3	A1	5d + 12.50d car (Bk)		65	8.25
1KB4	A1	10d + 12.50d black		65	8.25

The surtax was for the Red Cross.

LJUBLJANA

(Lubiana, Laibach)

Italian Occupation

Under Italian occupation in 1941, the western half of Slovenia was known as the Province of Ljubljana (Lubiana to the Italians, Laibach to the Germans) and a quisling administration was set up under the profascist General Rupnik.

100 Centesimi = 1 Lira

Yugoslavia Nos. 127, 128, 142-154 Overprinted in Black   **Co. Ci.**

1941	Unwmk.		Perf. 12½, 13x12½		
N1	A16	25p black		15	20
N2	A16	50p orange		15	20
N3	A16	1d yellow grn		15	20
N4	A16	1.50d red		15	20
N5	A16	2d dp magenta		15	20
N6	A16	3d dl red brn		15	20
N7	A16	4d ultra		15	20
N8	A16	5d dark blue		15	20
N9	A16	5.50d dk vio brn		15	20
N10	A16	6d slate blue		18	25
N11	A16	8d sepia		24	32
N12	A10	10d bright vio		30	42
N13	A10	12d brt violet		32	55
N14	A10	15d brown		60.00	85.00

N15	A16	16d dl violet		32	60
N16	A16	20d blue		1.50	2.50
N17	A16	30d brt pink		10.50	14.00
		Nos. N1-N17 (17)		74.71	105.44

Yugoslavia Nos. 127, 142-154 Overprinted in Black

R. Commissariato Civile Territori Sloveni occupati LUBIANA

N18	A16	25p black		15	20
N19	A16	50p orange		15	20
N20	A16	1d yellow grn		15	20
N21	A16	1.50d red		15	20
N22	A16	2d dp magenta		15	20
N23	A16	3d dl red brn		15	20
N24	A16	4d ultra		15	20
N25	A16	5d dark blue		24	45
N26	A16	5.50d dk vio brn		15	20
N27	A16	6d slate blue		15	20
N28	A16	8d sepia		18	30
N29	A10	10d brt violet		65	1.00
N30	A16	12d bright vio		18	30
N31	A16	16d dl violet		65	1.00
N32	A16	20d blue		1.25	2.00
N33	A16	30d brt pink		32.50	42.50

Yugoslavia Nos. 145, 148 Surcharged in Black

R. Commissariato Civile Territori Sloveni occupati LUBIANA
Din

N34	A16	50p on 1.50d red		15	18
N35	A16	1d on 4d ultra		15	18
		Nos. N18-N35 (18)		37.30	49.71

German Occupation

Stamps of Italy, 1929-42, Overprinted or Surcharged in Blue, Carmine, Black or Green

a   b

c

L 2.55

1944	Wmk. 140		Perf. 14		
N36	A90(a)	5c ol brown		15	1.25
N37	A92(a)	10c dark brn		15	1.25
N38	A93(a)	15c sl grn (C)		15	1.25
N39	A91(b)	20c rose red		15	1.25
N40	A94(a)	25c dp grn (C)		15	1.25
N41	A95(b)	30c ol brown		15	1.25
N42	A93(a)	35c dp bl (C)		20	1.25
N43	A95(b)	50c purple (C)		20	2.00
N44	A94(a)	75c rose red		15	2.75
N45	A91(b)	1 l deep vio		20	2.75
N46	A94(a)	1.25 l dp bl (C)		15	1.65
N47	A92(b)	1.75 l red org		85	8.50
N48	A93(a)	2 l car lake		20	2.00
N49	A90(c)	2.55 l on 5c ol brn (Bk)		52	4.00
N50	A94(a)	5 l on 25c dp grn		40	4.00
N51	A93(b)	10 l purple		2.75	16.00
N52	A91(a)	20 l on 20c rose red (G)		2.75	16.00
N53	A93(b)	25 l on 2 l car lake (G)		2.75	27.50
N54	A92(a)	50 l on 1.75 l red org (C)		6.50	50.00
		Nos. N36-N54 (19)		18.52	145.90

Krizna Jama — A1   Cerknica Lake — A2

Designs: 20c, Railroad Bridge, Borovnica. 25c, Landscape near Ljubljana. 50c, Church, Ribnica. 75c, View, Ljubljana. 1 l, Old Castle, Ljubljana. 1.25 l, Kocevje (Gottschee). 1.50 l, Borovnica Falls. 2 l, Castle, Konstanjevnica. 2.50 l, Castle, Turjak. 3 l, Castle, Zuzemperk. 5 l, View of Krk. 10 l, View of Otolac. 20 l, Farm, Carniola. 30 l, Castle and church, Tabor.

Perf. 10½x11½, 11½x10½

1945			Photo.		Unwmk.
N55	A1	5c black		18	1.25
N56	A2	10c red orange		18	1.25
N57	A2	20c brn carmine		18	1.65
N58	A2	25c dk sl green		18	1.65
N59	A1	50c deep violet		18	1.65
N60	A2	75c vermilion		18	1.65
N61	A2	1 l dark ol grn		18	1.65
N62	A1	1.25 l dark blue		18	3.25
N63	A1	1.50 l olive black		18	3.25
N64	A2	2 l ultramarine		24	5.00
N65	A2	2.50 l brown		24	5.00
N66	A1	3 l brt red vio		52	8.25
N67	A2	5 l dk red brn		65	8.25
N68	A2	10 l slate green		1.10	16.00
N69	A2	20 l sapphire		6.25	60.00
N70	A1	30 l rose pink		35.00	475.00
		Nos. N55-N70 (16)		45.62	594.75

SEMI-POSTAL STAMPS

Italian Occupation
Yugoslavia Nos. B116-B119 with Additional Overprint in Black

R.Commissariato
Civile
Territori Sloveni
occupati
LUBIANA

Perf. 11½x12½, 12½x11½

1941			Unwmk.
NB1	AP6	50p + 50p on 5d	6.50	9.75
NB2	AP7	1d + 1d on 10d	6.50	9.75
NB3	AP8	1.50d + 1.50d on 20d	6.50	9.75
NB4	AP9	2d + 2d on 30d	6.50	9.75

German Occupation
Italy Nos. E14 and E15 Surcharged in Red:

1944			Wmk. 140
NB5	SD4	1.25 l + 50 l green	11.50	115.00
NB6	SD4	2.50 l + 50 l dp grn	11.50	115.00

The surtax aided the Red Cross.

Same, Surcharged in Blue or Green:

NB7	SD4	1.25 l + 50 l grn (B)	11.50	115.00
NB8	SD4	2.50 l + 50 l dp org	11.50	115.00

The surtax aided the Homeless Relief Fund. The German and Slovenian inscriptions in the surcharges are transposed on Nos. NB6 and NB8.

Italy Nos. C12-C14, C16-C18 Surcharged "DEN WAISEN," "SIROTAM," Heraldic Eagle and Surtax in Blue or Red

1944			Wmk. 140
NB9	AP4	25c + 10 l dk grn	5.25	40.00
NB10	AP3	50c + 10 l ol brn	5.25	40.00
NB11	AP5	75c + 20 l org brn	5.25	40.00
NB12	AP5	1 l + 20 l purple	5.25	40.00
NB13	AP6	2 l + 20 l dp bl (R)	5.25	40.00
NB14	AP5	5 l + 20 l dp org	5.25	40.00
		Nos. NB9-NB14 (6)	31.50	240.00

The surcharge aided orphans.

Same, Surcharged "WINTERHILFE," "ZIMSKA POMOC," Heraldic Eagle and Surtax in Blue or Red

NB15	AP4	25c + 10 l dk grn	5.25	40.00
NB16	AP3	50c + 10 l ol brn	5.25	40.00
NB17	AP5	75c + 20 l org brn	5.25	40.00
NB18	AP5	1 l + 20 l purple	5.25	40.00
NB19	AP6	2 l + 20 l dp bl (R)	5.25	40.00
NB20	AP5	5 l + 20 l dk grn	5.25	40.00
		Nos. NB15-NB20 (6)	31.50	240.00

The surcharge was for winter relief.

AIR POST STAMPS

Italian Occupation
Yugoslavia Nos. C7-C16 Ovptd. like Nos. NB1-NB4

Perf. 12½, 12½x11½, 11½x12½

1941			Unwmk.
NC1	AP6	50p brown	40	85
NC2	AP7	1d yel grn	40	85
NC3	AP8	2d bl gray	55	1.10
NC4	AP9	2.50d rose red	55	1.10
NC5	AP6	5d brn vio	1.00	1.65
NC6	AP7	10d brn lake	1.00	1.65
NC7	AP8	20d dark grn	8.25	10.00
NC8	AP9	30d ultra	22.50	22.50
NC9	AP10	40d Prus grn & pale grn	70.00	70.00
NC10	AP11	50d sl bl & gray bl	45.00	45.00
a.		Inverted overprint	200.00	
		Nos. NC1-NC10 (10)	149.65	154.70

German Occupation
Italy Nos. C12-C14, C16-C19 Overprinted Types "a" and "b" in Carmine, Green or Blue

1944			Wmk. 140		Perf. 14
NC11	AP4(a)	25c dk grn (C)		1.10	6.25
NC12	AP3(b)	50c ol brn (C)		4.00	30.00
NC13	AP5(a)	75c org brn (G)		1.25	8.75
NC14	AP5(b)	1 l pur (C)		5.00	24.00
NC15	AP6(a)	2 l dp bl (Bl)		2.75	20.00
NC16	AP3(b)	5 l dk grn (C)		2.75	24.00
NC17	AP3(a)	10 l dp car (G)		2.25	32.50
		Nos. NC11-NC17 (7)		19.10	145.50

AIR POST SPECIAL DELIVERY STAMP

German Occupation
Italy #CE3 Ovptd. Type "b" in Blue

1944			Wmk. 140		Perf. 14
NCE1	APSD2	2 l gray blk		3.75	15.00

SPECIAL DELIVERY STAMP

German Occupation
Italy #E14 Ovptd. Type "b" in Green

1944			Wmk. 140		Perf. 14
NE1	SD4	1.25 l green		95	5.00

POSTAGE DUE STAMPS

Italian Occupation
Yugoslavia Nos. J28-J32 Overprinted in Black Like Nos. N1-N17

1941			Unwmk.		Perf. 12½
NJ1	D4	50p violet		18	35
NJ2	D4	1d rose		18	35
NJ3	D4	2d deep blue		18	35
NJ4	D4	5d orange		1.25	2.00
NJ5	D4	10d chocolate		1.25	2.00
		Nos. NJ1-NJ5 (5)		3.04	5.05

Same Overprinted in Black

R.Commissariato
Civile
Territori Sloveni
occupati
LUBIANA

NJ6	D4	50p violet		15	20
NJ7	D4	1d rose		15	20
NJ8	D4	2d deep blue		24	40
NJ9	D4	5d orange		10.00	12.00
NJ10	D4	10d chocolate		2.00	3.25
		Nos. NJ6-NJ10 (5)		12.54	16.05

Same Overpainted in Black

R. Commissariato
Civile
Territori Sloveni
occupati
LUBIANA

NJ11	D4	50p violet	25	50
NJ12	D4	1d rose	45	70
NJ13	D4	2d deep blue	9.25	11.50

German Occupation
Postage Due Stamps of Italy, 1934, Overprinted or Surcharged in Various Colors

d   e
f   g

1944			Wmk. 140		Perf. 14
NJ14	D6(d)	5c brown (Br)		1.10	13.00
NJ15	D6(e)	10c blue (Bl)		1.10	13.00
NJ16	D6(d)	20c rose red (R)		20	52
NJ17	D6(e)	25c green (G)		20	52
NJ18	D6(f)	30c on 50c vio (Bk)		20	52
NJ19	D6(g)	40c on 5c brn (Bl)		20	52
NJ20	D6(d)	50c violet (V)		20	52
NJ21	D7(e)	1 l red orange (R)		1.10	6.50
NJ22	D7(d)	2 l green (Bl)		1.10	6.50
		Nos. NJ14-NJ22 (9)		5.40	41.60

Fiume-Kupa Zone
Italian Occupation

ZONA
OCCUPATA
FIUMANO
KUPA

O.N.M.I.

Four issues of 1941-42 consist of overprints on Yugoslav stamps of 1939-41: (a.) 14 stamps overprinted "ZONA OCCUPATO FIUMANO KUPA" and "ZOFK ZOFK ZOFK." (b.) 3 stamps overprinted as illustrated. (c.) 1 stamp surcharged "MEMENTO AVDERE SEMPER." "L1," etc. (d.) 3 stamps overprinted in arch: "Pro Maternite e Infanzia."

ISSUES FOR ISTRIA AND THE SLOVENE COAST (ZONE B)

Grapes — A1   Olive Branch — A2

Sailboat, Pola — A3

Designs: 50c, Donkey. Nos. 25-26, Ruined home. 2 l, Duino Castle. 5 l, Birthplace of Vladimir Gortan. 10 l, Plowing. Nos. 33-34, Tuna. 30 l, Viaduct at Solkan, Soca River.

Perf. 11½, 12, 10½x11½

1945-46			Photo.
23	A1	25c dark green	85	1.00
24	A1	50c red brown	15	15
25	A1	1 l green	15	15

26	A1	1 l red	15	15
27	A2	1.50 l olive brown	15	20
28	A2	2 l dk Prus grn	15	15
29	A3	4 l red	15	15
30	A3	4 l bright blue	30	40
31	A3	5 l gray black	15	15
32	A3	10 l brown	15	15
33	A3	20 l blue	1.65	85
34	A3	20 l dark violet	4.50	4.00
35	A3	30 l magenta	1.25	60
		Nos. 23-35 (13)	9.75	8.10

The first (Ljubljana) printing is perf. 10½x11½ and consists of Nos. 23-24, 26-28, 30-32, 34-35. The second (Zagreb) printing is perf. 12 and consists of Nos. 23-25, 27-29, 31-33, 35. The third (Belgrade) printing is perf. 11½ and consists of Nos. 25, 28, 40-41.
See Nos. 40-41. For surcharges see Nos. 36-37, J1-J19.

Nos. 33 and 35 Surcharged with New Values and Bars in Black

1946			Unwmk.		Perf. 11½
36	A3	1 l on 20 l blue		70	32
37	A3	2 l on 30 l magenta		65	32

Types of 1945

Design: 3 l, Duino Castle

1946, Nov. 30			
40	A2	3 l crimson	15	15
41	A3	6 l ultra	15	15
		Set value	20	15

Types of Yugoslavia and of Official Stamps of 1946 Surcharged in Black

On A26   **VOJNA UPRAVA JUGOSLAVENSKE ARMIJE**   **L 1**

On O1   **VOJNA UPRAVA JUGOSLAVENSKE ARMIJE**   **L 1.50**

1947			Unwmk.		Perf. 12½
42	A26	1 l on 9d lilac rose		15	15
43	O1	1.50 l on 9d lilac rose		15	15
44	A26	2 l on 9d lilac rose		15	15
45	O1	3 l on 50p blue		15	15
46	A26	5 l on 9d lilac rose		15	15
47	O1	6 l on 50p blue		15	15
48	A26	10 l on 9d lilac rose		15	15
49	O1	15 l on 50p blue		15	15
50	A26	35 l on 9d lilac rose		15	15
51	O1	50 l on 50p blue		20	20
		Set value		70	70

POSTAGE DUE STAMPS

PORTO 1.- Lit.

Nos. 23, 24 34 and 35 Surcharged in Black

1945			Unwmk.		Perf. 10½x11½
J1	A3	50c on 20 l dk vio		50	1.25
J2	A1	1 l on 25c dk grn		2.75	3.50
J3	A3	2 l on 30 l magenta		40	1.00
J4	A1	4 l on 50c red brn		30	20
J5	A1	8 l on 50c red brn		22	15
J6	A1	10 l on 50c red brn		3.00	1.65
J7	A1	20 l on 50c red brn		3.00	1.65
		Nos. J1-J7 (7)		10.17	9.40

Lira 1.-
PORTO

Nos. 25 and 35 Surcharged in Black

1945					Perf. 12
J8	A1	1 l on 1 l green		15	15
J9	A1	2 l on 1 l green		15	15
J10	A1	4 l on 1 l green		22	15
J11	A3	10 l on 30 l magenta		55	35

J12 A3 20 l on 30 l magenta 3.00 1.50
J13 A3 30 l on 30 l magenta 3.00 1.50
Nos. J8-J13 (6) 7.07 3.80

The surcharges are arranged to fit the designs of the stamps.

No. 23 Surcharged in Black

1946
J14 A1 1 l on 25c dark green 60 70
J15 A1 2 l on 25c dark green 85 1.00
J16 A1 4 l on 25c dark green 1.00 1.10

No. 33 Surcharged in Black

PORTO Lira 10.-

J17 A3 10 l on 20 l blue 3.00 50
J18 A3 20 l on 20 l blue 5.50 4.00
J19 A3 30 l on 20 l blue 6.75 5.00
Nos. J14-J19 (6) 17.70 12.30

Type of Yugoslavia Postage Due Stamps, 1946, Surcharged in Black

Vojna Uprava Jugoslavenske Armije   L 1

1947
J20 D7 1 l on 1d brt blue grn 15 15
J21 D7 2 l on 1d brt blue grn 15 15
J22 D7 6 l on 1d brt blue grn 15 15
J23 D7 10 l on 1d brt blue grn 15 15
J24 D7 30 l on 1d brt blue grn 32 40
Set value 74 90

TRIESTE, ZONE A
See listing under Italy, Vol. 3.

TRIESTE

A free territory (1947-1954) on the Adriatic Sea between Italy and Yugoslavia. In 1954 the territory was divided, Italy acquiring the northern section and seaport, Yugoslavia the southern section (Zone B).

Catalogue values for all unused stamps in this country are for Never Hinged items.

ZONE B

Issued by the Yugoslav Military Government
100 Centesimi = 1 Lira
100 Paras = 1 Dinar (1949)

See Istria and the Slovene Coast (Zone B) for preceding issues of 1945-47.

Stylized Gymnast and Arms of Trieste — A1

1948 Unwmk. Litho. Perf. 10½x11
Inscriptions in:
1 A1 100 l Italian 2.25 1.90
2 A1 100 l Croatian 2.25 1.90
3 A1 100 l Slovene 2.25 1.90
a. Strip of 3, #1-3 10.00 17.50
May Day.

Clasped Hands, Hammer and Sickle — A2

1949 Photo. Perf. 11½x12½
4 A2 10 l grnsh blk & ol grn 42 38
Labor Day, May 1, 1949.
"V.U.J.A. S.T.T." are the initials of "Vojna Uprava Jugoslovenske Armije, Slobodna Teritorija Trsta" (Military Administration Yugoslav Army, Free Territory of Trieste).

Stamps of Yugoslavia, 1945-47 Overprinted in Carmine or Ultramarine   **STT VUJA**

1949, Aug. 15   Perf. 12½
5 A22 50p ol gray 24 25
6 A22 1d bl grn 24 25
7 A24 2d scar (U) 24 25
8 A25 3d dl red (U) 55 55
9 A24 4d dk bl 24 25
10 A25 5d dk bl 24 25
11 A26 9d rose vio (U) 55 55
12 A23 12d ultra 2.00 2.25
13 A22 16d blue 1.90 1.90
14 A23 20d org ver (U) 3.00 3.50
Nos. 5-14 (10) 9.20 10.00

The letters of the overprint are set closer and in one line on Nos. 7 and 9.

Yugoslavia Nos. 266 and 267 Overprinted **VUJA - STT** in Carmine

Burelage in Color of Stamp
1949
15 A58 5d blue 7.50 10.50
16 A58 12d brown 7.50 10.50
75th anniv. of the UPU.

Yugoslavia, Nos. 269 to 272, Overprinted in Carmine **VUJA - STT**

1950
17 A60 2d bl grn 40 38
18 A60 3d car rose 80 75
19 A60 5d blue 2.00 1.90
20 A60 10d dp org 6.00 5.75

Workers Carrying Tools and Flag — A3   Peasant on Ass — A4

1950, May 1   Photo.
21 A3 3d violet 42 38
22 A3 10d carmine 85 75
Labor Day, May 1, 1950.

1950 Unwmk. Perf. 12½
Designs: 1d, Cockerel. 2d, Goose. 3d, Bees and honeycomb. 5d, Oxen. 10d, Turkey. 15d, Goats. 20d, Silkworms.
23 A4 50p dk gray 15 15
24 A4 1d brn car 15 15
25 A4 2d dp bl 15 15
26 A4 3d org brn 25 35
27 A4 5d aqua 28 75
28 A4 10d brown 50 55
29 A4 15d violet 5.00 5.75
30 A4 20d dk grn 2.00 2.25
Nos. 23-30 (8) 8.48 10.10

1951
31 A4 1d orange brown 15 25
32 A4 3d rose brown 15 25

Worker — A5

1951, May 1
33 A5 3d dark red 60 55
34 A5 10d brown olive 1.00 95
Labor Day.

Pietro Paolo Vergerio — A7   Bicycle Race — A8

1951, Oct. 21   Litho.
37 A7 5d blue 65 55
38 A7 10d claret 65 60
39 A7 20d sepia 65 60

Types of Yugoslavia, 1951, Overprinted "STT VUJA"
1951, Nov.
40 A81 10d brn org (V) 90 75
41 A81 12d grnsh blk (C) 90 75

1952   Photo.
42 A8 5d shown 22 25
43 A8 10d Soccer 22 25
44 A8 15d Rowing 22 25
45 A8 28d Sailing 70 55
46 A8 50d Volleyball 1.50 1.10
47 A8 100d Diving 4.00 4.50
Nos. 42-47 (6) 6.86 6.90

Marshal Tito
A9   A10

1952, May 25   Perf. 11½
48 A9 15d dk brn 1.75 1.50
49 A10 28d red brn 1.75 1.50
50 A9 50d dk gray grn 1.75 1.50
60th birthday of Marshal Tito.

Types of Yugoslavia 1952 Overprinted in Carmine "STT VUJNA"
1952, July 26   Perf. 12½
51 A90 5d dk brn & sal, cr 38 38
52 A90 10d dk grn & grn 38 38
53 A90 15d dk brn & bl, lil 38 38
54 A90 28d dk brn & buff, cr 1.50 1.50
55 A90 50d dk brn & buff, yel 6.75 6.75
56 A90 100d ind & lil, pink 15.00 15.00
Nos. 51-56 (6) 24.39 24.39
15th Olympic Games, Helsinki, 1952. Nos. 52, 54, 56 inscribed in Cyrillic characters. The added "N" in "VUJNA" stands for "Narodna" (Peoples'). See note after No. 4. Nos. 51-56 exist imperf. Value of set, $375.

Yugoslavia Nos. 365 to 367 Overprinted in Carmine "STT VUJNA"
1952, Sept. 13
57 A91 15d deep claret 55 55
58 A91 28d dark brown 75 75
59 A91 50d gray 3.00 3.00
10th anniv. of the formation of the Yugoslav navy.

Yugoslavia No. 358 Overprinted "STT VUJA" in Blue
1952, June 22
60 A89 15d bright rose 90 95
Children's Week.

Yugoslavia Nos. 369-372 Overprinted "VUJNA STT" in Blue or Carmine
1952, Nov. 4
61 A93 15d red brn (Bl) 50 75
62 A93 15d dk vio bl 50 75
63 A93 15d dk brn 50 75
64 A93 15d bl grn 50 75
Issued to publicize the 6th Yugoslavia Communist Party Congress, Zagreb, 1952.

Anchovies and Starfish A11

1952 Unwmk. Photo. Perf. 11x11½
65 A11 15d red brown 1.25 1.65
a. Souvenir sheet, imperf. 8.75 15.00
Capodistria Phil. Exhib., Nov. 29-Dec. 7. No. 65a contains a 50d dark blue green stamp. Sold for 85d.

Stamps or Types of Yugoslavia Overprinted "STT VUJNA" in Various Colors
1953, Feb. 3   Perf. 12½
66 A94 15d brn carmine (Bl) 32 38
67 A94 30d chalky blue (R) 85 55
10th anniv. of the death of Nikola Tesla.

1953
68 A68 1d gray 2.25 2.50
69 A68 2d car (V) 45 48
70 A68 3d rose red (R) 45 48
71 A68 5d orange 45 48
72 A68 10d emerald (G) 45 48
73 A68 15d rose red (V) 90 1.10
74 A68 30d blue (Bl) 1.90 2.00
75 A68 50d grnsh bl (Bl) 3.50 4.00
Nos. 68-75 (8) 10.35 11.52

Nos. 69, 71 and 73 are lithographed. See Nos. 90-92.

1953, Apr. 21   Perf. 11½
76 A95 15d dk ol grn (O) 35 38
77 A95 30d chalky blue (O) 35 38
78 A95 50d henna brown 1.10 1.10
Issued in honor of the United Nations.

Automobile Climbing Mt. Lovcen — A12

1953, June 2   Perf. 12½
79 A12 15d ocher & choc 35 18
80 A12 30d lt bl grn & ol grn 35 38
81 A12 50d salmon & dp plum 35 38
82 A12 70d bl & dk brn 70 75
Issued to publicize the International Automobile and Motorcycle Races, 1953.

Keep up to date with all new stamp issues by subscribing to the "Scott Stamp Monthly". Please call 1-800-488-5351 for more information.

Stamps or Types of Yugoslavia Overprinted
"STT VUJNA" in Various Colors

			Engr.	
1953, July 8				
83	A97	50d grnsh gray (C)	1.90	1.50

Issued to commemorate Marshal Tito's election to the presidency, January 14, 1953.

1953, July 31

84	A98	15d gray & grn (C)	2.00	1.90

38th Esperanto Cong., Zagreb, July 25-Aug. 1, 1953. See No. C21.

1953, Sept. 5

85	A101	15d blue (C)	3.25	2.25

10th anniv. of the liberation of Istria and the Slovene coast.

1953, Oct. 3

86	A102	15d gray	1.40	1.50

Cent. of the death of Branko Radicevic, poet.

1953, Nov. 29　　　　　Perf. 12¹/₂x12

87	A103	15d gray vio (V)	45	38
88	A103	30d claret (Br)	65	55
89	A103	50d dl bl grn (Dk Bl)	1.00	95

10th anniv. of the 1st republican legislative assembly of Yugoslavia.

1954, Mar. 5　　　　　Perf. 12¹/₂

90	A68	5d org (V)	50	50
91	A68	10d yel grn (C)	35	28
92	A68	15d rose red (G)	50	38

Overprinted in Carmine

1954	**Photo.**		Perf. 11¹/₂	
93	A104	2d red brn, sl & cr	15	25
94	A104	5d gray & dk yel brn	15	25
95	A104	10d ol grn & dk org brn	15	25
96	A104	15d dp bl grn & dk org brn	15	25
97	A104	17d gray brn, dk brn & cr	15	25
98	A104	25d bis, gray bl & org yel	15	25
99	A105	30d lil & dk brn	15	25
100	A105	35d rose vio & bl blk	30	50
101	A105	50d yel grn & vio brn	45	75
102	A105	65d org brn & gray blk	2.25	3.50
103	A105	70d bl & org brn	4.50	7.50
104	A105	100d brt bl & blk brn	15.00	25.00
		Nos. 93-104 (12)	23.55	39.00

Overprinted in Various Colors

1954, Oct. 8		Perf. 12¹/₂	
105	A107	15d mar, red, ocher & dk bl (Bk)	35	38
106	A107	30d dk bl, grn, sal buff & choc (G)	35	38
107	A107	50d brn, bis & red (G)	55	55
108	A107	70d dk grn, gray grn & choc (R)	1.40	1.25

150th anniv. of the 1st Serbian insurrection.

AIR POST STAMPS

AP1

Perf. 12¹/₂x11¹/₂

1948, Oct. 17	**Photo.**	**Unwmk.**	
C1	AP1	25 l gray	75	75
C2	AP1	50 l orange	75	75

Economic Exhib. at Capodistria, Oct. 17-24.

Fishermen — AP2　　　Farmer and Pack Mule — AP3

Mew over Chimneys
AP4

1949, June 1			Perf. 11¹/₂	
C3	AP2	1 l grnsh bl	22	15
C4	AP3	2 l red brn	22	15
C5	AP3	5 l blue	22	15
C6	AP3	10 l purple	1.25	85
C7	AP2	25 l brown	1.65	90
C8	AP3	50 l ol grn	1.65	90
C9	AP4	100 l dk vio brn	2.25	1.50
		Nos. C3-C9 (7)	7.46	4.60

Italian inscriptions on Nos. C5 and C6, Croatian on No. C7, Slavonic on No. C8.
Nos. C3-C4 exist imperf. Value, each $135.

Nos. C3-C9 Surcharged "DIN," or New Value and "DIN" in Various Colors

1949, Nov. 5				
C10	AP2	1d on 1 l (Bk)	20	18
C11	AP3	2d on 2 l (Br)	20	18
C12	AP2	5d on 5 l (Bl)	20	18
C13	AP3	10d on 10 l (V)	40	38
C14	AP2	15d on 25 l (Br)	4.75	4.50
C15	AP3	20d on 50 l (Gr)	1.65	1.50
C16	AP4	30d on 100 l (Bk)	1.65	1.50
		Nos. C10-C16 (7)	9.05	8.42

On Nos. C14 and C15 the original value is obliterated by a framed block, on No. C16 by four parallel lines.

Yugoslavia No. C33 Overprinted in Carmine and Lilac Rose Network

VUJA - STT

Souvenir Sheet

1950			Perf. 11¹/₂x12¹/₂	
C17	AP15	10d lilac rose	50.00	57.50
a.		Imperf.	50.00	57.50

Main Square,　　　Lighthouse,
Capodistria — AP5　　Pirano — AP6

Design: 25d, Hotel, Portorose.

1952	**Unwmk.**	**Photo.**	Perf. 12¹/₂	
C18	AP5	5d brown	7.50	7.00
C19	AP6	15d brt bl	4.75	5.50
C20	AP5	25d green	4.75	5.50

75th anniv. (in 1949) of the UPU.

Type of Yugoslavia, 1953 Overprinted "STT VUJNA" in Carmine

1953, July 31				
C21	AP21	300d vio & grn	185.00	165.00

38th Esperanto Cong., Zagreb, July 25-Aug. 1. Sheets of 12 (12,000 stamps) and sheets of 8 (3,000 stamps in light violet and green).
A private red overprint was applied marginally to 250 sheets of 8: "Esperantski Kongres - 38 - a Universala Kongreso de Esperanto - Congreso del Esperanto."

Air Post Stamps of Yugoslavia in New Colors Overprinted "STT VUJNA" in Various Colors

1954			Engr.	
C22	AP16	1d dp pur gray	15	15
C23	AP16	2d brt grn (G)	15	15
C24	AP16	3d red brn (Br)	15	15
C25	AP16	5d chocolate	15	15
C26	AP16	10d bl grn	15	15
C27	AP16	20d brn (Br)	26	38
C28	AP16	30d blue	26	38
C29	AP16	50d olive blk	38	55
C30	AP16	100d scar (R)	1.10	1.50
C31	AP16	200d dk bl vio (Bl)	2.75	3.75
		Perf. 11x11¹/₂		
C32	AP17	500d orange (Br)	8.50	12.00
		Nos. C22-C32 (11)	14.00	19.31

POSTAGE DUE STAMPS

Yugoslavia Nos. J51 to J55 Overprinted "S T T VUJA" in Two Lines in Ultramarine or Carmine

1949		**Unwmk.**	Perf. 12¹/₂	
J1	D7	50p dp org	55	55
J2	D7	1d orange	55	55
J3	D7	2d dk bl (C)	55	55
J4	D7	3d yel grn (C)	55	55
J5	D7	5d brt pur (C)	1.10	1.10
		Nos. J1-J5 (5)	3.30	3.30

Croakers　　　　Anchovies
D1　　　　　　　D2

1950			**Photo.**	
J6	D1	50p brn org	22	22
J7	D1	1d dp ol grn	90	95
J8	D2	2d dk grnsh bl	90	95
J9	D2	3d dk vio bl	90	95
J10	D2	5d plum	4.50	4.25
		Nos. J6-J10 (5)	7.42	7.32

Yugoslavia Nos. J67-J74 Overprinted "STT VUJNA" in Blue or Carmine

1952				
J11	D7	1d brown (Bl)	15	15
J12	D7	2d emerald	15	15
J13	D7	5d blue	15	15
J14	D7	10d scar (Bl)	15	15
J15	D7	20d purple	15	15
J16	D7	30d org yel (Bl)	15	15
J17	D7	50d ultra	15	15
J18	D7	100d dp plum (Bl)	3.00	4.50
		Nos. J11-J18 (8)	4.05	5.55

POSTAL TAX STAMPS

Yugoslavia No. RA5 Surcharged in Blue

V U J A
S. T. T.
2 L

1948	**Unwmk.**	Perf. 12¹/₂	
RA1	PT4	2 l on 50p brn & scar	6.50	10.00

Obligatory on all mail from May 22-30.

Yugoslavia No. RA7 Overprinted "VUJA STT" in Black

1950, July 3				
RA2	PT6	50p red & brn	35	40

Yugoslavia No. RA9 Overprinted in Black "STT VUJA"

1951				
RA3	PT8	50p vio bl & red	6.50	10.00

Yugoslavia No. RA10 Overprinted "STT VUJNA" in Carmine

1952				
RA4	PT9	50p gray & carmine	18	20

Type of Yugoslavia, 1953, Overprinted "STT VUJNA" in Blue

1953				
RA5	PT10	2d org brn & red	18	30

The tax of Nos. RA1-RA5 was for the Red Cross.

POSTAL TAX DUE STAMPS

Yugoslavia No. RAJ2 Surcharged Like No. RA1 in Scarlet

1948	**Unwmk.**	Perf. 12¹/₂	
RAJ1	PT4	2 l on 50p bl grn & scar	100.00	140.00

Yugoslavia No. RAJ4 Overprinted "VUJA STT" in Black

1950, July 3				
RAJ2	PT6	50p red & vio	85	1.25

Yugoslavia No. RAJ6 Overprinted in Black "STT VUJA"

1951				
RAJ3	PT8	50p emer & red	85.00	115.00

Yugoslavia No. RAJ7 Overprinted "STT VUJNA" in Carmine

1952				
RAJ4	PTD3	50p gray & car	50	60

Type of Yugoslavia, 1953, Overprinted "STT VUJNA" in Blue

1953				
RAJ5	PT10	2d lilac rose & red	50	60

ZAIRE
(formerly Congo Democratic Republic)

LOCATION — Central Africa
GOVT. — Republic
AREA — 905,365 sq. mi.
POP. — 31,944,000 (est. 1983)
CAPITAL — Kinshasa

Congo Democratic Republic changed its name to Republic of the Zaire in November 1971. Issues before that date are listed in Vol. 2 under Congo Democratic Republic.

100 Sengi = 1 Li-Kuta
100 Ma-Kuta = 1 Zaire

> **Catalogue values for all unused stamps in this country are for Never Hinged items.**

UNICEF Emblem, Child Care — A143

UNICEF Emblem and: 14k, Map of Africa showing Zaire. 17k, Boy in African village.

Perf. 14x13¹/₂

1971, Dec. 18			**Unwmk.**	
750	A143	4k gold & multi	42	20
751	A143	14k lt bl, gold, red & grn	1.10	65
752	A143	17k gold & multi	1.65	60

25th anniv. of UNICEF. For surcharge see No. 1327.

Pres. Mobutu, MPR Emblem
A144

1972   Photo.   *Perf. 11¹/₂*

753 A144	4k multi	4.25	2.75
754 A144	14k multi	4.25	2.75
755 A144	22k multi	4.25	2.75

5th anniversary of the People's Revolutionary Movement (MPR). For surcharge see No. 1308.

Zaire Arms — A145   Pres. Joseph D. Mobutu — A146

1972   Litho.   *Perf. 14*

756 A145	10s red org & blk	15	15
757 A145	40s brt bl & multi	15	15
758 A145	50s citron & multi	15	15

Perf. 13

759 A146	1k sky bl & multi	15	15
760 A146	2k org & multi	15	15
761 A146	3k multi	15	15
762 A146	4k emer & multi	15	15
763 A146	5k multi	18	15
764 A146	6k multi	20	15
765 A146	8k cit & multi	32	15
766 A146	9k multi	42	18
767 A146	10k lt lil & multi	42	20
768 A146	14k multi	60	24
769 A146	17k multi	65	30
770 A146	20k yel & multi	75	42
771 A146	50k multi	1.90	95
772 A146	100k fawn & multi	4.25	1.75
Nos. 756-772 (17)		10.74	
Set value			4.75

For surcharges and overprints see Nos. 860, 1328, O1-O11.

Same, Denominations in Zaires

1973, Feb. 21

773 A146	0.01z sky bl & multi	15	15
774 A146	0.02z org & multi	15	15
775 A146	0.03z multi	18	15
776 A146	0.04z multi	24	15
777 A146	0.10z multi	55	25
778 A146	0.14z multi	85	35
Set value			90

Inga Dam A147

1973, Jan. 25   Litho.   *Perf. 13¹/₂*

790 A147	0.04z multi	16	15
791 A147	0.14z pink & multi	52	30
792 A147	0.18z yel & multi	70	45

Completion of first section of Inga Dam Nov. 24, 1972.

World Map A148

1973, June 23   Photo.   *Perf. 12¹/₂x12*

793 A148	0.04z lil & multi	20	15
794 A148	0.07z multi	32	16
795 A148	0.18z multi	1.00	35

3rd Intl. Fair at Kinshasa, June 23-July 8. The dark brown ink of the inscription was applied by a thermographic process and varnished, producing a shiny, raised effect.

Hand and INTERPOL Emblem — A149

1973, Sept. 28   Litho.   *Perf. 12¹/₂*

796 A149	0.06z multi	42	16
797 A149	0.14z multi	85	38

50th anniversary of International Criminal Police Organization.

Leopard with Soccer Ball on Globe A150

1974, July 17   Photo.   *Perf. 11¹/₂x12*

798 A150	1k multi	15	15
799 A150	2k multi	25	15
800 A150	3k multi	38	15
801 A150	4k multi	48	15
802 A150	5k multi	60	18
803 A150	14k multi	1.50	48
Nos. 798-803 (6)		3.36	
Set value			1.00

World Cup Soccer Championship, Munich, June 13-July 7.

Foreman-Ali Fight — A151

1974, Nov. 9   Litho.   *Perf. 12x12¹/₂*

804 A151	1k multi	15	15
805 A151	4k multi	20	15
806 A151	6k multi	30	15
807 A151	14k multi	60	20
808 A151	20k multi	80	30
Nos. 804-808 (5)		2.05	
Set value			75

World Heavyweight Boxing Championship match between George Foreman and Muhammad Ali, Kinshasa, Oct. 30 (postponed from Sept. 25).

Same, Type of 1974, Denominations in Zaires and Inscribed in Various Colors

1975, Aug.   Litho.   *Perf. 12x12¹/₂*

809 A151	0.01z multi (R)	15	15
810 A151	0.04z multi (Br)	20	15
811 A151	0.06z multi (Bk)	30	16
812 A151	0.14z multi (G)	80	38
813 A151	0.20z multi (Bk)	1.10	40
Nos. 809-813 (5)		2.55	
Set value			1.10

Judge, Lawyers, IWY Emblem A152

1975, Dec.   Photo.   *Perf. 11¹/₂*

814 A152	1k dull blk & multi	15	15
815 A152	2k dp rose & multi	25	15
816 A152	4k dull grn & multi	50	18
817 A152	14k violet & multi	1.25	60

International Women's Year 1975.

Waterfall A153   Okapis A154

1975   Photo.   *Perf. 11¹/₂*

818 A153	1k multicolored	16	15
819 A153	2k lt blue & multi	30	16
820 A153	3k multicolored	45	25
821 A153	4k salmon & multi	65	32
822 A153	5k green & multi	65	40
Nos. 818-822 (5)		2.21	1.28

12th General Assembly of the Intl. Union for Nature Preservation (U.I.C.N.), Kinshasa, Sept. 1975.

1975

823 A154	1k blue & multi	18	15
824 A154	2k yellow grn & multi	38	20
825 A154	3k brown red & multi	55	30
826 A154	4k green & multi	85	40
827 A154	5k yellow & multi	95	45
Nos. 823-827 (5)		2.91	1.50

Virunga National Park, 50th anniversary.

Siderma Maluku Industry — A155

Designs: 1k, Sozacom apartment building, vert. 3k, Matadi flour mill, vert. 4k, Women parachutists. 8k, Pres. Mobutu visiting Chairman Mao, vert. 10k, Soldiers working along the Salongo. 14k, Pres. Mobutu addressing UN Gen. Assembly, Oct. 1974. 15k, Celebrating crowd.

1975

828 A155	1k ocher & multi	15	15
829 A155	2k yel grn & multi	15	15
830 A155	3k multi	20	15
831 A155	4k multi	28	15
832 A155	8k dk brn & multi	55	25
833 A155	10k sep & multi	65	35
834 A155	14k bl & multi	90	45
835 A155	15k org & multi	1.10	55
Nos. 828-835 (8)		3.98	
Set value			1.85

10th anniversary of new government.

Tshokwe Mask — A156   Map of Zaire, UPU Emblem — A157

Designs: 2k, 4k, Seated woman, Pende. 7k, like 5k. 10k, 14k, Antelope mask, Suku. 15k, 18k, Kneeling woman, Kongo. 20k, 25k, Kuba mask.

1977, Jan. 8   Photo.   *Perf. 11¹/₂*

836 A156	2k multi	15	15
837 A156	4k multi	15	15
838 A156	5k gray & multi	15	15
839 A156	7k multi	18	15
840 A156	10k multi	25	15
841 A156	14k multi	35	20
842 A156	15k multi	40	22
843 A156	18k multi	48	28
844 A156	20k multi	95	32
845 A156	25k vio & multi	1.00	40
Nos. 836-845 (10)		4.06	2.17

Wood carving and masks of Zaire.

1977, Apr.   Litho.   *Perf. 13¹/₂*

846 A157	1k org & multi	15	15
847 A157	4k dk bl & multi	22	18
848 A157	7k ol grn & multi	38	38
849 A157	50k brn & multi	4.75	4.75

Cent. of UPU (in 1974).

Congo Stamps of 1968-1971 Surcharged with New Value, Bars and "REPUBLIQUE DU ZAIRE"

1977

850 A126	1k on 10s (#642)	15	15
851 A122	2k on 9.6k (#618)	15	15
852 A140	10k on 10s (#735)	25	18
853 A134	25k on 10s (#703)	65	45
854 A127	40k on 9.6k (#652)	1.10	70
855 A135	48k on 10s (#713)	1.40	90
Nos. 850-855 (6)		3.70	2.53

Congo Nos. 644, 643, 635, 746 Surcharged with New Value, Bars and "REPUBLIQUE DU ZAIRE" in Black or Carmine, Zaire No. 757 Surcharged

1977

856 A126	5k on 30s	22	15
857 A126	10k on 15s (C)	22	15
858 A124	20k on 9.60k	50	22
859 A141	30k on 12k	95	35
860 A145	100k on 40s (C)	2.75	1.50
Nos. 856-860 (5)		4.64	2.37
Nos. 850-860 (11)		8.34	4.90

Souvenir Sheet

Adoration of the Kings, by Rubens — A158

1977, Dec. 19   Photo.   *Perf. 13¹/₂*

861 A158	5z multi	20.00	16.00

Christmas 1977.

Pantodon Buchholzi A159   Soccer Game, Argentina-France A160

Fish: 70s, Aphyosemion striatum. 55, Ctenopoma fasciolatum. 8k, Malapterurus electricus. 10k, Hemichromis bimaculatus. 30k, Marcusenius isidori. 40k, Synodontis nigriventris. 48k, Julidochromis ornatus. 100k, Nothobranchius brieni. 250k, Micralestes interruptus.

1978, Jan. 23   Litho.   *Perf. 14*

862 A159	30s multi	15	15
863 A159	70s multi	15	15
864 A159	5k multi	16	15
865 A159	8k multi	22	15
866 A159	10k multi	22	15
867 A159	30k multi	70	42
868 A159	40k multi	90	55
869 A159	48k multi	1.10	70
870 A159	100k multi	3.25	1.40
Nos. 862-870 (9)		6.85	3.82

Souvenir Sheet

Perf. 13¹/₂

871 A159	250k multi	5.50	5.50

No. 871 contains one 46x35mm stamp. For surcharges see Nos. 1294, 1311.

1978, Aug. 7   Litho.   *Perf. 12¹/₂*

Various Soccer Games and Jules Rimet Cup: 3k, Austria-Brazil. 7k, Scotland-Iran. 9k, Netherlands-Peru. 10k, Hungary-Italy. 20k, Fed. Rep. of Germany-Mexico. 50k, Tunisia-Poland. 100k, Spain-Sweden. 500k, Rimet Cup, Games' emblem and cartoon of soccer player, horiz.

872	A160	1k multi	15	15
873	A160	3k multi	15	15
874	A160	7k multi	15	15
875	A160	9k multi	15	15
876	A160	10k multi	16	15
877	A160	20k multi	32	20
878	A160	50k multi	85	50
879	A160	100k multi	1.65	1.00
		Nos. 872-879 (8)	3.58	
		Set value		2.00

Souvenir Sheets

880	A160	500k bl & multi	11.00	8.50
881	A160	500k red & multi	11.00	8.50

11th World Cup Soccer Championship, Argentina, June 1-25. Nos. 880-881 contain one stamp each (47x36mm). Stamp of No. 880 has blue frameline. Stamp of No. 881 has red frame line.
For surcharge see No. 1259.

Mama Mobutu — A161

Pres. Joseph D. Mobutu — A162

1978, Oct. 23   Photo.   *Perf. 12*

882	A161	8k multi	20	15

Mama Mobutu (1941-1977), wife of Pres. Mobutu.

1978   Photo.   *Perf. 12*
Granite Paper

883	A162	2k multi	15	15
884	A162	5k multi	15	15
885	A162	6k multi	15	15
886	A162	8k multi	15	15
887	A162	10k multi	15	15
888	A162	25k multi	20	16
889	A162	48k multi	50	32
890	A162	1z multi	95	70
		Set value	2.00	1.40

See Nos. 1053, 1055-1056. For surcharges see Nos. 1313, 1333-1336.

Souvenir Sheet

Elizabeth II in Westminster Abbey — A163

1978, Dec. 11   Photo.   *Perf. 13¹/₂*

891	A163	5z multi	10.50	10.50

Coronation of Queen Elizabeth II, 25th anniv.

Souvenir Sheet

Albrecht Dürer, Self-portrait A164

1978, Dec. 18   *Perf. 13*

892	A164	5z multi	10.50	10.50

Albrecht Dürer (1471-1528), German painter and engraver.

Leonardo da Vinci and his Drawings A165

History of Aviation: 70s, Planes of Wright Brothers, 1905, and Santos Dumont, 1906. 1k, Bleriot XI, 1909, and Farman F-60, 1909. 5k, Junkers G-38, 1929, and Spirit of St. Louis, 1927. 8k, Sikorsky S-42B, 1934 and Macchi-Castoldi MC-72, 1934. 10k, Boeing 707, 1960, and Fokker F-VII, 1935. 50k, Apollo XI, 1969, and Concorde, 1976. 75k, Helicopter and Douglas DC-10, 1971. 5z, Giffard's balloon, 1852, and Hindenburg LZ 129, 1936.

1978, Dec. 28   Litho.   *Perf. 13*

893	A165	30s multi	15	15
894	A165	70s multi	15	15
895	A165	1k multi	15	15
896	A165	5k multi	16	16
897	A165	8k multi	22	22
898	A165	10k multi	28	28
899	A165	50k multi	1.40	1.40
900	A165	75k multi	1.90	1.90
		Nos. 893-900 (8)	4.41	4.41

Souvenir Sheet
Perf. 11¹/₂

901	A165	5z multi	11.00	11.00

For overprint and surcharges see Nos. 993, 1173-1181, 1291, 1295.

Pres. Mobutu, Map of Zaire, N'tombe Dancer A166

Designs (Pres. Mobutu and Map): 3k, Bird. 4k, Elephant. 10k, Diamond and cotton boll. 14k, Hand holding torch. 17k, Leopard's head and Victoria Regia lily. 25k, Finzia waterfall. 50k, Wagenia fishermen.

1979, Feb.   Litho.   *Perf. 14x13¹/₂*

902	A166	1k multicolored	15	15
903	A166	3k multicolored	15	15
904	A166	4k multicolored	15	15
905	A166	10k multicolored	15	15
a.		Souvenir sheet of 4, #902-905	1.75	1.25
906	A166	14k multicolored	22	16
907	A166	17k multicolored	30	20
908	A166	25k multicolored	45	32
909	A166	50k multicolored	90	65
a.		Souvenir sheet of 4, #906-909	10.00	7.00
		Nos. 902-909 (8)	2.47	1.93

Zaire (Congo) River expedition.

Phylloporus Ampliporus — A167

Phylloporus ampliporus

Mushrooms: 5k, Engleromyces goetzei. 8k, Scutellinia virungae. 10k, Pycnoporus sanguineus. 30k, Cantharellus miniatescens. 40k, Lactarius phlebonemus. 48k, Phallus indusiatus. 100k, Ramaria moelleriana.

1979, Mar.   Photo.   *Perf. 13¹/₂x13*

910	A167	30s multicolored	15	15
911	A167	5k multicolored	16	15
912	A167	8k multicolored	25	16
913	A167	10k multicolored	35	20
914	A167	30k multicolored	1.10	60
915	A167	40k multicolored	1.25	85
916	A167	48k multicolored	1.65	1.10
917	A167	100k multicolored	3.00	2.25
		Nos. 910-917 (8)	7.91	5.46

For surcharges see Nos. 1296, 1298, 1312, 1361-1362, 1365-1366, 1368-1369, 1372, 1375.

Souvenir Sheets

Pope John XXIII (1881-1963) A168

Popes: No. 919, Paul VI (1897-1978). No. 920, John Paul I (1912-78).

1979, June 25   Litho.   *Perf. 11¹/₂*

918	A168	250k multi	2.75	1.50
919	A168	250k multi	2.75	1.50
920	A168	250k multi	2.75	1.50

Boy Beating Drum — A169

IYC Emblem on Map of Zaire and: 10k, 20k, Girl, diff. 50k, Boy. 100k, Boys. 300k, Mother and child. 10z, Mother and children, horiz.

1979, July 23   Litho.   *Perf. 12¹/₂*

921	A169	5k multi	15	15
922	A169	10k multi	15	15
923	A169	20k multi	24	16
924	A169	50k multi	60	35
925	A169	100k multi	1.25	70
926	A169	300k multi	3.50	1.65
		Nos. 921-926 (6)	5.89	3.16

Souvenir Sheet

927	A169	10z multi	12.00	9.25

International Year of the Child.
For surcharges see Nos. 997, 999, 1299, 1306.

Globe and Drummer A170

1979, July 23

928	A170	1k multi	15	15
929	A170	9k multi	15	15
930	A170	90k multi	90	45
931	A170	100k multi	1.00	50

Souvenir Sheet

932	A170	500k multi	4.75	2.75

6th International Fair, Kinshasa. No. 932 contains one 52x31mm stamp.
For overprint and surcharge see Nos. 996, 1320.

Globe and School Desk — A171

1979, Dec. 24   Litho.   *Perf. 13*

933	A171	10k multi	15	15

Intl. Bureau of Education, Geneva, 50th anniv.

Adoration of the Kings, by Memling — A172

1979, Dec. 24   *Imperf.*

934	A172	5z multi	5.00	2.50

Christmas 1979.

"Puffing Billy," 1814, Gt. Britain A173

1980, Jan. 14   Litho.   *Perf. 13¹/₂x13*

935	A173	50s shown	15	15
936	A173	1.50k Buddicom No. 33, 1843, France	15	15
937	A173	5k "Elephant," 1835, Belgium	15	15
938	A173	8k No. 601, 1906, Zaire	15	15
939	A173	50k "Slieve Gullion 440," Ireland	40	20
940	A173	75k "Black Elephant," Germany	60	32
941	A173	2z Type 1-15, Zaire	1.65	85
942	A173	5z "Golden State," US	4.00	2.00
		Nos. 935-942 (8)	7.25	3.97

Souvenir Sheet

943	A173	10z Type E.D.75, Zaire	8.50	5.50

For overprints and surcharges see Nos. 991-992, 994, 1325.

Hill, Belgian Congo No. 257 — A174

1980, Jan. 28   *Perf. 13¹/₂x14*

944	A174	2k No. 5	15	15
945	A174	4k No. 13	15	15
946	A174	10k No. 24	15	15
947	A174	20k No. 38	16	15
948	A174	40k No. 111	30	16
949	A174	150k No. B29	1.10	60
950	A174	200k No. 198	1.40	75
951	A174	250k shown	1.75	95
		Nos. 944-951 (8)	5.16	3.06

Souvenir Sheet

952	A174	10z No. 198	7.50	5.00

Sir Rowland Hill (1795-1879), originator of penny postage.
For overprint and surcharge see Nos. 998, 1329.

The Scott International album provides spaces for an extensive representative collection of the world's postage stamps.

Albert Einstein
(1879-1955),
Theoretical
Physicist — A175

1980, Feb. 18   *Perf. 13*
953	A175	40s multi	15	15
954	A175	2k multi	15	15
955	A175	4k multi	15	15
956	A175	15k multi	15	15
957	A175	50k multi	45	25
958	A175	300k multi	2.00	1.00
		Nos. 953-958 (6)	3.05	
		Set value		1.40

Souvenir Sheet
959	A175	5z multi, diff.	4.00	2.50

For surcharges see Nos. 1285, 1290, 1304.

Salvation Army Brass Players — A176

Emblem and: 50s, Booth Memorial Hospital, NYC. 4.50k, Commissioner George Railton sailing for US mission. 10k, Mobile dispensary, Masina. 20k, Gen. Evangeline Booth, officer holding infant, vert. 75k, Outdoor well-baby clinic. 1.50z, Disaster relief. 2z, Parade, vert. 10z, Gen. and Mrs. Arnold Brown.

1980, Mar. 3   *Perf. 11*
960	A176	50s multi	15	15
961	A176	4.50k multi	15	15
962	A176	10k multi	15	15
963	A176	20k multi	18	15
964	A176	40k multi	35	15
965	A176	75k multi	55	25
966	A176	1.50z multi	1.10	55
967	A176	2z multi	1.65	80
		Nos. 960-967 (8)	4.28	
		Set value		2.00

Souvenir Sheet
968	A176	10z multi	7.50	5.00

Salvation Army cent. in US. No. 968 contains one 53x38mm stamp and 2 labels.

Souvenir Sheets

Pope John
Paul II — A177

1980, May 2   **Litho.**   *Perf. 11½*
969	A177	10z multi	6.00	3.25

Visit of Pope John Paul II to Zaire, May.

Baia Castle, by Antonio Pitloo — A178

1980, May 5
970	A178	10z multi	5.50	3.00

20th International Philatelic Exhibition, Europa '80, Naples, Apr. 26-May 4.

A179

Perf. 12½x13, 13x12½

1980, May 24   **Litho.**
971	A179	50k Woman, line-drawing	22	15
972	A179	100k Plutiarch	48	28
973	A179	500k Kneeling man, sculpture, vert.	2.50	1.40
a.		Souvenir sheet of 3	3.25	2.00

Rotary Intl., 75th anniv. No. 973a contains 3 stamps similar to Nos. 971-973, size: 55x35, 35x55mm. Exists imperf.
For surcharge see No. 1313.

Tropical Fish — A180

1980, Oct. 20   **Litho.**   *Perf. 14x13½*
974	A180	1k Chaetodon collaris	15	15
975	A180	5k Zebrasoma veliferum	15	15
976	A180	10k Euxiphipops xanthometapon	15	15
977	A180	20k Pomazcanthus annularis	15	15
978	A180	50k Centropyge oriculus	32	16
979	A180	150k Oxymonacanthus longirostris	75	45
980	A180	200k Balistoides niger	1.00	55
981	A180	250k Rhinecanthus aculeatus	1.25	70
		Nos. 974-981 (8)	3.92	
		Set value		2.00

Souvenir Sheet
981A	A180	5z Baliste ondule	2.50	1.10

For surcharge see No. 1307.

Exhibition
Emblem,
Congo
#365
A181

1980, Dec. 6   **Litho.**   *Perf. 13*
982		Block of 4	2.00	1.40
a.	A181	1z, UR shown	45	30
b.	A181	1z, UL Belgium #511	45	30
c.	A181	1z, UR like #982b	45	30
d.	A181	1z, UL like #982a	45	30
983		Block of 4	4.00	2.25
a.	A181	2z, UR Congo #432	90	55
b.	A181	2z, UL Belgium # B835	90	55
c.	A181	2z, UR like #983b	90	55
d.	A181	2z, UL like #983a	90	55
984		Block of 4	6.00	3.50
a.	A181	3z, UR Zaire #755	1.40	80
b.	A181	3z, UL Belgium # B878	1.40	80
c.	A181	3z, UR like #984b	1.40	80
d.	A181	3z, UL like #984a	1.40	80

985		Block of 4	8.00	4.50
a.	A181	4z, UR Congo #572	1.75	1.00
b.	A181	4z, UL Belgium # B996	1.75	1.00
c.	A181	4z, UR like #985b	1.75	1.00
d.	A181	4z, UL like #985a	1.75	1.00

PHIBELZA, Belgium-Zaire Phil. Exhib. Nos. 982-985 can be collected as strips of 4. For surcharge see No. 1342.

Map of
Africa, King
Leopold I
A182

Belgian independence sesquicentennial: 75k, Stanley expedition, Leopold II. 100k, Colonial troops, Albert I. 270k, protected animals, Leopold III. Visit of King Baudouin and Queen Fabiola.

1980, Dec. 13   **Photo.**   *Perf. 14*
986	A182	10k multi	15	15
987	A182	75k multi	55	30
988	A182	100k multi	65	38
989	A182	145k multi	90	55
990	A182	270k multi	1.65	90
		Nos. 986-990 (5)	3.90	2.28

For surcharges see Nos. 1326, 1331, 1345, 1357, 1408-1412, 1426.

Nos. 935, 936, 898, 939, 900, 931, 925, 951, Overprinted in Red, Silver or Black: 20e Anniversaire-Independence / 1960-1980

1980, Dec. 13   **Litho.**
991	A173	50s multi	15	15
992	A173	1.50k multi	15	15
993	A165	10k multi	15	15
994	A173	50k multi	28	16
995	A165	75k multi	40	22
996	A170	100k multi (S)	55	35
997	A169	1z on 5z on 100k multi (B)	65	35
998	A174	250k multi	1.40	75
999	A169	5z on 100k multi (B)	2.75	1.50
		Nos. 991-999 (9)	6.48	3.78

20th anniversary of independence. For surcharges see Nos. 1300, 1316.

Nativity
A183

1980, Dec. 24   *Perf. 13*
1000	A183	10k Shepherds and angels	15	15
1001	A183	75k Flight into Egypt	48	28
1002	A183	80k Three kings	48	28
1003	A183	145k shown	80	48

Souvenir Sheet
1004	A183	10z Church, nativity	5.50	3.00

Christmas 1980. No. 1004 contains one 49x33mm stamp. Exists imperf. For surcharges see Nos. 1301, 1317-1318.

Postal Clerk
Sorting Mail,
by Norman
Rockwell
A184

Designs: Saturday Evening Post covers by Norman Rockwell.

1981, Apr. 27   **Litho.**   *Perf. 14*
1005	A184	10k multi	15	15
1006	A184	20k multi	15	15
1007	A184	50k multi	28	20
1008	A184	80k multi	48	28
1009	A184	100k multi	55	35
1010	A184	125k multi	65	40
1011	A184	175k multi	95	55
1012	A184	200k multi	1.10	60
		Nos. 1005-1012 (8)	4.31	2.68

For surcharges see Nos. 1262, 1265, 1269, 1275, 1281, 1354.

First
Anniv. of
Visit of
Pope
John
Paul II
A185

Designs: Scenes of Pope's visit. 50k, 500k, vert.

1981, May 2   *Perf. 13*
1013	A185	5k multi	15	15
1014	A185	10k multi	15	15
1015	A185	50k multi	35	16
1016	A185	100k multi	60	35
1017	A185	500k multi	2.75	1.75
1018	A185	800k multi	5.00	2.75
		Nos. 1013-1018 (6)	9.00	5.31

For surcharges see Nos. 1190-1194, 1292, 1302, 1343.

Soccer Players — A186

Designs: Soccer scenes.

1981, July 6   **Litho.**   *Perf. 12½*
1019	A186	2k multi	15	15
1020	A186	10k multi	15	15
1021	A186	25k multi	15	15
1022	A186	90k multi	50	30
1023	A186	2z multi	1.00	55
1024	A186	3z multi	1.50	80
1025	A186	6z multi	3.00	1.75
1026	A186	8z multi	4.50	2.50
		Nos. 1019-1026 (8)	10.95	6.35

Souvenir Sheet
1027		Sheet of 2	5.25	2.75
a.	A186	5z like #1019	2.50	1.25
b.	A186	5z like #1025	2.50	1.25

ESPANA '82 World Cup Soccer Championship. For surcharges see Nos. 1287, 1303, 1309, 1321.

Intl. Year of the Disabled — A187

1981, Nov. 2   **Litho.**   *Perf. 14x14½*
1028	A187	2k Archer	15	15
1029	A187	5k Ear, sound waves	15	15
1030	A187	10k Amputee	15	15
1031	A187	18k Cane braille, sunglasses	15	15
1032	A187	50k Boy with leg braces	16	15
1033	A187	150k Sign language	52	30
1034	A187	500k Hands	1.90	1.00
1035	A187	800k Dove	2.75	1.75
		Nos. 1028-1035 (8)	5.93	
		Set value		3.40

For surcharges see Nos. 1288, 1293, 1305, 1314.

Birth Sesqui. of
Heinrich von Stephan,
UPU Founder — A188

Christmas
1981 — A189

Photogravure and Engraved
1981, Dec. 21   *Perf. 11¹/₂x12*
1036 A188 15z purple   4.75 2.75

1981, Dec. 21   Litho.   Perf. 14

Designs: 25k, 1z, 1.50z, 3z, 5z, Various children. 10z, Holy Family, horiz.

1037 A189	25k multi		15	15
1038 A189	1z multi		45	20
1039 A189	1.50z multi		55	32
1040 A189	3z multi		1.25	65
1041 A189	5z multi		2.00	1.00
	Nos. 1037-1041 (5)		4.40	2.32

Souvenir Sheet

1042 A189 10z multi   4.00 2.00

13th World Telecommunications Day
(1981) — A190

Designs: Symbols of communications and health care delivery.

1982, Feb. 8   Litho.   Perf. 13

1043 A190	1k multi		15	15
1044 A190	25k multi		15	15
1045 A190	90k multi		32	16
1046 A190	1z multi		38	18
1047 A190	1.70z multi		60	30
1048 A190	3z multi		1.10	55
1049 A190	4.50z multi		1.65	75
1050 A190	5z multi		1.75	85
	Nos. 1043-1050 (8)		6.10	3.09

For surcharges see Nos. 1270, 1282.

Pres. Mobutu Type of 1978

1982   Photo.   Perf. 12
Granite Paper

1053 A162	50k multi		16	15
1055 A162	2z multi		65	35
1056 A162	5z multi		1.60	80

20th Anniv. of African Postal Union
(1981) — A191

1982, Mar. 8   Litho.   Perf. 13
1057 A191 1z yel grn & gold   40 18

For surcharges see Nos. 1348, 1352.

1982
World
Cup
A192

Designs: Flags and players of finalists.

1982

1058 A192	2k multi		15	15
1059 A192	8k multi		15	15
1060 A192	25k multi		15	15
1061 A192	50k multi		18	15
1062 A192	90k multi		32	16
1063 A192	1z multi		38	18
1064 A192	1.45z multi		50	24
1065 A192	1.70z multi		60	30
1066 A192	3z multi		1.10	55
1067 A192	3.50z multi		1.25	60
1068 A192	5z multi		1.75	85
1069 A192	6z multi		2.25	1.10
	Nos. 1058-1069 (12)		8.78	4.58

Souvenir Sheet

1070 A192 10z multi   4.50 2.00

Issued: #1058-1069, July 6; #1070, Sept. 21.
For surcharges see #1289, 1315, 1322, 1344.

9th Conference of Heads of State of Africa
and France, Kinshasa, Oct. — A193

1982, Oct. 8   Litho.   Perf. 13

1071 A193	75k multi		22	15
1072 A193	90k multi		30	15
1073 A193	1z multi		35	16
1074 A193	1.50z multi		50	25
1075 A193	3z multi		1.00	50
1076 A193	5z multi		1.60	80
1077 A193	8z multi		2.50	1.40
	Nos. 1071-1077 (7)		6.47	3.41

For surcharge see Nos. 1268, 1271, 1280, 1283, 1347, 1351.

Animals from Virunga Natl. Park — A194

1982, Nov. 5

1078 A194	1z Lions		38	16
1079 A194	1.70z Buffalo		60	30
1080 A194	3.50z Elephants		1.25	60
1081 A194	6.50z Antelope		2.50	1.45
1082 A194	8z Hippopotamus		2.75	1.50
1083 A194	10z Monkeys		3.75	1.65
1084 A194	10z Leopard		3.75	1.65
	Nos. 1078-1084 (7)		14.98	7.11

#1083-1084 se-tenant with label showing map.
For surcharge see No. 1430.

Scouting
Year — A195

1982, Nov. 29   Photo.   Perf. 11¹/₂
Granite Paper

1085 A195	90k Camp		40	16
1086 A195	1.70z Campfire		75	35
1087 A195	3z Scout		1.40	65

1088 A195	5z First aid		2.00	1.10
1089 A195	8z Flag signals		3.25	1.90
	Nos. 1085-1089 (5)		7.80	4.16

Souvenir Sheet

1090 A195 10z Baden-Powell   4.50 2.00

For surcharges see Nos. 1207-1214.

Local
Birds — A196

1982, Dec. 6   Litho.   Perf. 13

1091 A196	25k Quelea quelea		15	15
1092 A196	50k Ceyx picta		18	15
1093 A196	90k Tauraco persa		32	18
1094 A196	1.50z Charadrius tricollaris		55	28
1095 A196	1.70z Cursorius temminckii		60	30
1096 A196	2z Campethera bennetii		70	38
1097 A196	3z Podiceps ruficollis		1.10	55
1098 A196	3.50z Kaupifalco monogrammicus		1.25	60
1099 A196	5z Limnocorax flavirostris		1.75	85
1100 A196	8z White-headed vulture		2.75	1.50
	Nos. 1091-1100 (10)		9.35	4.94

All except 3.50z, 8z horiz.
For surcharges see Nos. 1263, 1266, 1272, 1276, 1278, 1284, 1425, 1432.

Souvenir Sheet

Christmas — A197

1982, Dec. 20   Photo.   Perf. 13¹/₂
1101 A197 15z Adoration of the
Magi, by van der
Goes   6.50 3.25

Quartz — A198

1983, Feb. 13   Photo.   Perf. 11¹/₂
Granite Paper

1102 A198	2k Malachite, vert.		15	15
1103 A198	45k shown		25	15
1104 A198	75k Gold		25	15
1105 A198	1z Uraninite		40	18
1106 A198	1.50z Bournonite, vert.		55	28
1107 A198	3z Cassiterite		1.10	55
1108 A198	6z Dioptase, vert.		2.25	1.10
1109 A198	8z Cuprite, vert.		2.75	1.65
	Nos. 1102-1109 (8)		7.70	4.21

Souvenir Sheet

1110 A198 10z Diamonds   4.50 4.50

For surcharges see Nos. 1324, 1330, 1332, 1346.

TB Bacillus
Centenary
A199

1983, Feb. 21   Litho.   Perf. 13

1111 A199	80k multi		25	15
1112 A199	1.20z multi		40	20
1113 A199	3.60z multi		1.20	60
1114 A199	9.60z multi		3.25	1.60

For surcharges see Nos. 1319, 1356, 1358, 1360, 1433.

Kinshasa Monuments — A200

1983, Apr. 25

1115 A200	50k Zaire Diplomat, vert.		16	15
1116 A200	1z Echo of Zaire		35	16
1117 A200	1.50z Messengers, vert.		50	25
1118 A200	3z Shield of Revolution, vert.		1.00	50
1119 A200	5z Weeping Woman		1.60	80
1120 A200	10z Militant, vert.		3.50	1.60
	Nos. 1115-1120 (6)		7.11	3.46

For surcharges see Nos. 1267, 1279, 1349-1350.

ITU Plenipotentiaries Conference, Nairobi,
Sept. 1982 — A201

Various satellites, dish antennae and maps.

1983, June 13   Litho.   Perf. 13

1121 A201	2k multi		15	15
1122 A201	4k multi		15	15
1123 A201	25k multi		15	15
1124 A201	1.20z multi		40	20
1125 A201	2.05z multi		65	35
1126 A201	3.60z multi		1.20	60
1127 A201	6z multi		2.00	1.00
1128 A201	8z multi		2.50	1.40
	Nos. 1121-1128 (8)		7.20	4.00

For surcharges see Nos. 1260-1261, 1264, 1273-1274, 1277, 1355, 1359, 1429, 1434.

Christmas
1983 — A202

Raphael Paintings; No. 1129: a, Virgin and Child. b, Holy Family. c, Esterhazy Madonna. d, Sistine Madonna. No. 1130: a, La Belle Jardiniere. b, Virgin of Alba. c, Holy Family, diff. d, Virgin and Child, diff.

1983, Dec. 26   Photo.   Perf. 13¹/₂x13

1129	Sheet of 4		3.50	3.50
a.-d.	A202 10z, any single		85	85
1130	Sheet of 4		5.25	5.25
a.-d.	A202 15z, any single		1.25	1.25

Garamba Park — A203

1984, Apr. 2   Litho.   Perf. 13
1131	A203	10k Darby's Eland	15	15
1132	A203	15k Eagles	15	15
1133	A203	3z Servals	22	22
1134	A203	10z White rhinocer-		
		os	75	75
1135	A203	15z Lions	1.10	1.10
1136	A203	37.50z Warthogs	2.75	2.75
1137	A203	40z Koris bustards	3.00	3.00
1138	A203	40z Crowned		
		cranes	3.00	3.00
		Nos. 1131-1138 (8)	11.12	11.12

Nos. 1137-1138 are se-tenant and narrower (size 49x34mm), with design continuing to the side perforations. An attached label shows park location on map of Zaire.
For surcharge see No. 1428.

World Communications Year — A204

Designs: 10k, Computer operator, Congo River ferry. 15k, Communications satellite. 8.50z, Engineer, Congo River Bridge. 10z, Satellite, ground receiving station. 15z, TV camerawoman filming crowed crane. 37.50z, Satellite, dish antennas. 80z, Switchboard operator, bus.

1984, May 14   Litho.   Perf. 13x12½
1139	A204	10k multi	15	15
1140	A204	15k multi	15	15
1141	A204	8.50z multi	60	60
1142	A204	10z multi	65	65
1143	A204	15z multi	1.00	1.00
1144	A204	37.50z multi	2.50	2.50
1145	A204	80z multi	5.50	5.50
		Nos. 1139-1145 (7)	10.55	10.55

Hypericum
Revolutum — A205

Local flowers: 15k, Borreria dibrachiata. 3z, Disa erubescens. 8.50z, Scaevola plumieri. 10z, Clerodendron thompsonii. 15z, Thumbergia erecta. 37.50z, Impatiens niamniamensis. 100z, Canarina eminii.

1984, May 28   Photo.   Perf. 14x13½
1146	A205	10k multi	15	15
1147	A205	15k multi	15	15
1148	A205	3z multi	20	20
1149	A205	8.50z multi	70	70
1150	A205	10z multi	75	75
1151	A205	15z multi	1.10	1.10
1152	A205	37.50z multi	2.75	2.75
1153	A205	100z multi	7.75	7.75
		Nos. 1146-1153 (8)	13.55	13.55

1984 Summer
Olympics — A206

Manned Flight
Bicent. — A207

1984, June 5   Litho.   Perf. 13
1154	A206	2z Basketball	15	15
1155	A206	3z Equestrian	22	22
1156	A206	10z Running	75	75
1157	A206	15z Long jump	1.10	1.10
1158	A206	20z Soccer	1.50	1.50
		Nos. 1154-1158 (5)	3.72	3.72

Souvenir Sheet
Perf. 11½
1159	A206	50z Kayak	4.00	4.00

No. 1159 contains one 31x49mm stamp.
For surcharge see No. 1427.

1984, June 28   Litho.   Perf. 14
1160	A207	10k Montgolfiere,		
		1783	15	15
1161	A207	15k Charles & Rob-		
		ert, 1783	15	15
1162	A207	3z Gustave, 1783	22	22
1163	A207	5z Santos-Dumont		
		III, 1899	38	38
1164	A207	10z Stratospheric		
		balloon, 1934	75	75
1165	A207	15z Zeppelin LZ-		
		129, 1936	1.10	1.10
1166	A207	37.50z Double Eagle		
		II, 1978	2.75	2.75
1167	A207	80z Hot air bal-		
		loons	6.00	6.00
		Nos. 1160-1167 (8)	11.50	11.50

For surcharges see Nos. 1413-1420.

Okapi — A208

1984, Oct. 15   Litho.   Perf. 13
1168	A208	2z Grazing	15	15
1169	A208	3z Resting	16	16
1170	A208	8z Mother and young	50	50
1171	A208	10z In water	65	65

Souvenir Sheet
Perf. 11½
1172	A208	50z like 10z	3.25	3.25

World Wildlife Fund. No. 1172 contains one 36x51mm stamp, margin continues the design of the 10z without emblem.

Nos. 893, 896, 894-895, 898, 897, 900, 899 Ovptd. with Black Bar, Silver Emblem and Surcharged on Stamp and Margin: 60e ANNIVERSAIRE/1re LIASON AERIENNE/BRUXELLES-KINSHASAL/PAR EDMOND THIEFFRY in 3 or 5 Lines

1985, Feb. 19   Perf. 13, 11½
1173	A165	2.50z on 30s multi	18	18
1174	A165	5z on 5k multi	38	38
1175	A165	6z on 70s multi	42	42
1176	A165	7.50z on 1k multi	60	60
1177	A165	8.50z on 10k multi	60	60
1178	A165	10z on 8k multi	75	75
1179	A165	12.50z on 75k multi	95	95
1180	A165	30z on 50k multi	2.25	2.25
		Nos. 1173-1180 (8)	6.13	6.13

Souvenir Sheet
1181	A165	50z on 5z multi	14.00	14.00

OLYMPHILEX '85, Lausanne — A209

1985, Apr. 19   Perf. 13
1182	A209	1z Swimming	15	15
1183	A209	2z Soccer, vert.	15	15
1184	A209	3z Boxing	18	18
1185	A209	4z Basketball, vert.	25	25
1186	A209	5z Equestrian	38	38
1187	A209	10z Volleyball, vert.	75	75
1188	A209	15z Running	1.25	1.25
1189	A209	30z Cycling, vert.	2.50	2.50
		Nos. 1182-1189 (8)	5.61	5.61

Nos. 1013-1018, 969 Ovptd. and Surcharged with 1 or 2 Gold Bars and "AOUT 1985" in Gold or Black

1985, Aug. 15   Perf. 13, 11½
1190	A185	2z on 5k	16	16
1191	A185	3z on 10k	25	25
1192	A185	5z on 50k	40	40
1192A	A185	10z on 100k	80	80
1192B	A185	15z on 500k	1.25	1.25
1193	A185	40z on 800k	3.50	3.50
		Nos. 1190-1193 (6)	6.36	6.36

Souvenir Sheet
1194	A177	50z on 10z (B)	4.50	4.50

Second visit of Pope John Paul II.

Audubon Birth Bicent. — A210

Illustrations of North American bird species by John Audubon.

1985, Oct. 1   Perf. 13
1195	A210	5z Great egret	24	24
1196	A210	10z Yellow-beaked duck	48	48
1197	A210	15z Small heron	75	75
1198	A210	25z White-fronted duck	1.25	1.25

For surcharges see Nos. 1421-1424.

Natl. Independence,
25th Anniv. — A211

1985, Oct. 23   Photo.
Granite Paper   Perf. 12
1200	A211	5z multi	22	22
1201	A211	10z multi	45	45
1202	A211	15z multi	70	70
1203	A211	20z multi	1.10	1.10

Souvenir Sheet
Perf. 11½
1204	A211	50z multi	2.00	2.00

UN, 40th
Anniv.
A212

1985, Nov. 26
1205	A212	10z Flags, vert.	50	50
1206	A212	50z Emblem, UN build-		
		ing	2.50	2.50

Nos. 1087-1088, 1085-1086, 1089-1090 Surcharged with 7 Green Bars and IYY Emblem

1985, Dec. 2   Perf. 11½
Granite Paper
1207	A195	3z on 3z multi	16	16
1208	A195	5z on 5z multi	24	24
1209	A195	7z on 90k multi	32	32
1210	A195	10z on 90k multi	48	48
1211	A195	15z on 1.70z multi	75	75
1212	A195	20z on 8z multi	95	95
1213	A195	50z on 90k multi	2.50	2.50
		Nos. 1207-1213 (7)	5.40	5.40

Souvenir Sheet
1214	A195	50z on 10z multi	2.50	2.50

Intl. Youth Year.

Souvenir Sheet

Virgin and
Child, by
Titian
A213

Photogravure and Engraved
1985, Dec. 23   Perf. 13½
1215	A213	100z brown	4.50	4.50

Christmas 1985.

Natl.
Transit
Authority,
50th
Anniv.
A214

1985, Dec. 31   Perf. 13
1216	A214	7z Kokolo mail ship	25	25
1217	A214	10z Steam locomotive	38	38
1218	A214	15z Luebo ferry	55	55
1219	A214	50z Stanley locomotive	1.90	1.90

Postage
Stamp,
Cent.
A215

Stamps on stamps: 7z, Belgian Congo No. 30. 15z, Belgian Congo No. B28. 20z, Belgian Congo No. 226. 25z, Zaire No. 1059. 40z, Zaire No. 1152. 50z, Zaire No. 883 and Belgium No. 1094.

1986, Feb. 23   Perf. 13
1220	A215	7z multi	35	35
1221	A215	15z multi	75	75
1222	A215	20z multi	1.00	1.00
1223	A215	25z multi	1.25	1.25
1224	A215	40z multi	2.00	2.00
		Nos. 1220-1224 (5)	5.35	5.35

Souvenir Sheet
Perf. 11½
1225	A215	50z multi	2.50	2.50

No. 1225 contains one 50x35mm stamp.

Beatification of Sister Anuarite Nengapeta,
Aug. 15, 1985 — A216

1986, Feb. 21   Litho.   Perf. 13
1226	A216	10z Pope John Paul II	35	35
1227	A216	15z Sr. Anuarite	55	55
1228	A216	25z Both portraits	90	90

Souvenir Sheet
Imperf
1229	A216	100z Both portraits, trian-		
		gular	3.75	3.75

Nos. 1226-1227 vert. No. 1229 contains one quadrilateral stamp, size: 30x36x60mm.
For surcharges see Nos. 1370, 1373, 1376-1377.

Congo Stamp
Cent. — A217

1986, Feb. 22   Litho.   Perf. 13
1230 A217 25z Belgian Congo No. 3   1.00   1.00

See Belgium No. 1236.

Indigenous
Reptiles — A218

1987, Feb. 11   Litho.   Perf. 13
1231 A218 2z Dasypeltis scaber   15   15
1232 A218 5z Agama agama   15   15
1233 A218 10z Python regius   25   25
1234 A218 15z Chamaeleo dilepis   40   40
1235 A218 25z Dendroaspis jamesoni   65   65
1236 A218 50z Naja nigricolis   1.30   1.30
Nos. 1231-1236 (6)   2.90   2.90

Christmas
1987 — A219

Paintings (details) by Fra Angelico: 50z, Virgin
and Child, center panel of the Triptych of Cortona,
1435. 100z, The Nativity. 120z, Virgin and Child
with Angels and Four Saints, Fiesole Retable. 180z,
Virgin and Child with Six Saints, Annalena Retable.

1987, Dec. 24   Litho.   Perf. 13
1237 A219 50z multi   78   78
1238 A219 100z multi   1.55   1.55
1239 A219 120z multi   1.90   1.90
1240 A219 180z multi   2.80   2.80

French Revolution, Bicent. — A220

Designs: 50z, Declaration of the Rights of Man
and Citizen. 100z, Abstract art. 120z, Globe showing Africa, South America.

1989   Litho.   Perf. 13¹/₂x14¹/₂
1241 A220 40z multicolored   45   45
1242 A220 50z multicolored   55   55
1243 A220 100z multicolored   1.10   1.10
1244 A220 120z multicolored   1.40   1.40

REGIDESCO, 50th Anniv. — A221

1989
1245 A221 40z Administration bldg.   40   40
1246 A221 50z Modern factory   50   50
1247 A221 75z Water works   75   75
1248 A221 120z Woman drawing
water   1.20   1.20

Fight Against AIDS — A222

Designs: 40z, Bowman firing arrow through
SIDA. 80z, "SIDA" on Leopard. 150z, World map
with AIDS symbols.

1989
1249 A222 30z multicolored   50   50
1250 A222 40z multicolored   65   65
1251 A222 80z multicolored   1.40   1.40

Souvenir Sheet
Perf. 14
1252 A222 150z multicolored   2.50   2.50

Tourist Attractions — A223

1990   Litho.   Perf. 13¹/₂x14¹/₂
1253 A223 40z Waterfalls of Venus   55   55
1254 A223 60z Rural village   85   85
1255 A223 100z Kivu Lake   1.40   1.40
1256 A223 120z Niyara Gongo Volcano   1.70   1.70

Souvenir Sheet
Perf. 14¹/₂
1257 A223 300z Kisantu Botanical
Gardens, vert.   4.25   4.25

Souvenir Sheet

Christmas — A224

Illustration reduced.

1990   Litho.   Perf. 14
1258 A224 500z muiticolored   3.40   3.40

20 Z

Various 1971-1983
Stamps
Surcharged in Gold

1990   Perfs., Etc. as Before
1259 A160 20z on 20k #877   40   40
1260 A201 40z on 2k #1121   40   40
1261 A201 40z on 4k #1122   40   40
1262 A184 40z on 10k #1005   40   40
1263 A196 40z on 25k #1091   40   40
1264 A201 40z on 25k #1123   40   40
1265 A184 40z on 50k #1007   40   40
1266 A196 40z on 50k #1092   40   40
1267 A200 40z on 50k #1115   40   40
1268 A193 40z on 75k #1071   40   40
1269 A184 40z on 80k #1008   40   40
1270 A190 40z on 90k #1045   40   40
1271 A193 40z on 90k #1072   40   40
1272 A196 40z on 90k #1093   40   40
1273 A201 80z on 2k #1121   80   80
1274 A201 80z on 4k #1122   80   80
1275 A184 80z on 10k #1005   80   80
1276 A196 80z on 25k #1091   80   80
1277 A201 80z on 25k #1123   80   80
1278 A196 80z on 50k #1092   80   80
1279 A200 80z on 50k #1115   80   80
1280 A193 80z on 75k #1071   80   80
1281 A184 80z on 80k #1008   80   80
1282 A190 80z on 90k #1045   80   80
1283 A193 80z on 90k #1072   80   80
1284 A196 80z on 90k #1093   80   80
1285 A175 100z on 40s #953   1.00   1.00
1287 A186 100z on 2k #1019   1.00   1.00
1288 A187 100z on 2k #1028   1.00   1.00
1289 A192 100z on 2k #1058   1.00   1.00
1290 A175 100z on 4k #955   1.00   1.00
1291 A165 100z on 5k #896   1.00   1.00
1292 A185 100z on 5k #1013   1.00   1.00
1293 A187 100z on 5k #1029   1.00   1.00
1294 A159 100z on 8k #865   1.00   1.00
1295 A165 100z on 8k #897   1.00   1.00
1296 A167 100z on 8k #912   3.00   3.00
1298 A169 100z on 10k #913   1.00   1.00
1299 A169 100z on 10k #922   1.00   1.00
1300 A165 100z on 10k #993   5.00   5.00
1301 A183 100z on 10k #1000   5.00   5.00
1302 A185 100z on 10k #1014   1.00   1.00
1303 A186 100z on 10k #1020   1.00   1.00
1304 A175 100z on 15k #956   1.00   1.00
1305 A169 100z on 18k #1031   1.00   1.00
1306 A169 100z on 20k #923   1.00   1.00
1307 A180 100z on 20k #977   1.00   1.00

1308 A144 100z on 22k #755   1.00   1.00
1309 A186 100z on 25k #1021   1.00   1.00
1311 A159 100z on 48k #869   1.00   1.00
1312 A167 100z on 48k #916   3.00   3.00
1313 A179 100z on 50k #971   1.00   1.00
1314 A187 100z on 50k #1032   1.00   1.00
1315 A192 100z on 50k #1061   1.00   1.00
1316 A165 100z on 75k #995   1.00   1.00
1317 A183 100z on 75k #1001   1.90   1.00
1318 A183 100z on 80k #1002   2.00   2.00
1319 A199 100z on 80k #1111   1.00   1.00
1320 A170 100z on 90k #930   1.00   1.00
1321 A186 100z on 90k #1022   1.00   1.00
1322 A192 100z on 90k #1062   40   40
1324 A198 300z on 2k #1102   3.00   3.00
1325 A173 300z on 8k #938   3.00   3.00
1326 A182 300z on 10k #986   3.00   3.00
1327 A143 300z on 14k #751   3.00   3.00
1328 A146 300z on 17k #769   3.00   3.00
1329 A174 300z on 20k #947   3.00   3.00
1330 A198 300z on 45k #1103   3.00   3.00
1331 A182 300z on 75k #987   3.00   3.00
1332 A198 300z on 75k #1104   3.00   3.00
1333 A162 500z on 8k #886   5.00   5.00
1334 A162 500z on 10k #887   2.00   2.00
1335 A162 500z on 25k #888   2.00   2.00
1336 A162 500z on 48k #889   2.00   2.00
Nos. 1259-1336 (74)   100.60   100.60

Size and location of surcharge varies. Some
surcharges show "z" before numeral. Numbers
have been reserved for additional values in this set.

Various 1980-1983 Stamps Surcharged

1991   Perfs., Etc., as Before
1342 A181 1000z on 1z #982a-
982d   1.40   1.40
1343 A185 1000z on 100k
#1016   35   35
1344 A192 1000z on 1z #1063   35   35
1345 A182 2000z on 100k #988   70   70
1346 A198 2000z on 1z #1105   70   70
1347 A193 2500z on 1z #1073   82   82
1348 A191 3000z on 1z #1057   1.05   1.05
1349 A200 4000z on 1z #1116   1.40   1.40
1350 A200 4000z on 1z #1116   1.65   1.65
1351 A193 10,000z on 1z #1073   3.30   3.30
1352 A191 15,000z on 1z #1057   5.00   5.00
Nos. 1342-1352 (11)   16.72   16.72

Size and location of surcharge varies.

Nos. 989, 1010, 1112, 1124 Surcharged

50.000 Z.

1992   Perfs., Etc. as Before
1354 A184 50th z on 125k #1010   20   20
1355 A201 100th z on 1.20z #1124   38   38
1356 A199 150th z on 1.20z #1112   60   60
1357 A182 200th z on 145k #989   75   75
1358 A199 250th z on 1.20z #1112   95   95
1359 A201 300th z on 1.20z #1124   1.10   1.10
1360 A199 500th z on 1.20z #1112   1.90   1.90
Nos. 1354-1360 (7)   5.88   5.88

Size and location of surcharge varies. Numbers
have been reserved for additional values in this set.

500.000ᶻ   **1 MILLION Z**
#1361-1366   #1368-1374

1993   Photo.   Perf. 13¹/₂x13
1361 A167 500th z on 30s #910   20   20
1362 A167 500th z on 5k #911   20   20
1365 A167 750th z on 8k #912   30   30
1366 A167 750th z on 10k #913   30   30
1368 A167 1 mil z on 30k #914   40   40
1369 A167 1 mil z on 40k #915   40   40
1372 A167 5 mil z on 48k #916   2.00   2.00
1375 A167 10 mil z on 100k #917   4.00   4.00
Nos. 1361-1375 (8)   7.80   7.80

Nos. 1226-1229 Surcharged

CAMPO RODAN

RUE DU LOMBARD 9
1000 BRUSSELS, BELGIUM
PHONE: 011-32-2-514-5292
FAX: 011-32-2-514-5415

Specialists in...
BELGIUM

and former
territories:

CONGA - ZAIRE
KATANGA
SOUTH KASAI
RUANDA
URUNDI
RWANDA
BURUNDI
LUXEMBOURG
EUROPE

Charge it! We accept:

3 MILLIONS Z

1993		Litho.	Perf. 13	
1370	A216	3 mil z on 10z #1226	1.25	1.25
1373	A216	5 mil z on 15z #1227	2.00	2.00
1376	A216	10 mil z on 25z #1228	4.00	4.00

Souvenir Sheet

| 1377 | A216 | 10 mil z on 100z #1229 | 4.00 | 4.00 |

Size and location of surcharge varies.

Natl. Game
Parks, 50th
Anniv.
A225

1994		Litho.	Perf. 13	
1403	A225	30k Cape eland	15	15
1404	A225	50k Elephants	15	15
1405	A225	1.50z Giant eland	32	32
1406	A225	3.50z White rhinoceros	75	75
1407	A225	5z Bongo	1.10	1.10
		Nos. 1403-1404 (2)	30	30

For surcharge see No. 1431.

Nos. 986-900 Surcharged   **30 NK**

1994		Photo.	Perf. 14	
1408	A182	30k on 10k	22	22
1409	A182	50k on 75k	38	38
1410	A182	1.50z on 100k	1.10	1.10
1411	A182	3.50z on 145k	2.75	2.75
1412	A182	5z on 270k	3.75	3.75
		Nos. 1408-1412 (5)	8.20	8.20

Nos. 1160-1167 Surcharged

1994		Litho.	Perf. 14	
1413	A207	30k on 10k	22	22
1414	A207	50k on 15k	38	38
1415	A207	1.50z on 3z	1.10	1.10
1416	A207	2.50z on 5z	1.90	1.90
1417	A207	3.50z on 10z	2.75	2.75
1418	A207	5z on 15z	3.75	3.75
1419	A207	7.50z on 37.50z	5.75	5.75
1420	A207	10z on 80z	7.75	7.75
		Nos. 1413-1420 (8)	23.60	23.60

Nos. 1195-1198
Surcharged   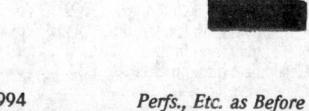 **50 NK**

1994		Litho.	Perf. 13	
1421	A210	50k on 5z	30	30
1422	A210	1.50z on 10z	90	90
1423	A210	3.50z on 15z	2.00	2.00
1424	A210	5z on 25z	3.00	3.00

Nos. 990, 1079, 1094, 1097, 1113, 1125-
1126, 1133, 1155, & 1404 Surcharged in
Gold

20 NZ

1994		Perfs., Etc. as Before	
1425	A196	20z on 3z #1097	15	15
1426	A182	40z on 270k #990	15	15
1427	A206	45z on 3z #1155	15	15
1428	A203	50z on 3z #1133	15	15
1429	A201	100z on 2.05z #1125	28	28
1430	A194	150z on 1.70z #1079	42	42
1431	A225	200z on 50k #1404	55	55
1432	A196	250z on 1.50z #1094	70	70
1433	A199	300z on 3.60z #1113	85	85
1434	A201	500z on 3.60z #1126	1.40	1.40
		Nos. 1425-1434 (10)	4.80	4.80

Size and location of surcharge varies.

OFFICIAL STAMPS

Nos. 756-772 Overprinted   (SP)

1975		Litho.	Perf. 14	
O1	A145	10s red org & blk	15	15
O2	A145	40s multi	15	15
O3	A145	50s multi	15	15
			Perf. 13	
O4	A146	1k multi	15	15
O5	A146	2k multi	15	15
O6	A146	3k multi	18	15
O7	A146	4k multi	24	15
O8	A146	5k multi	30	16
O9	A146	6k multi	42	18
O10	A146	8k multi	48	24
O11	A146	9k multi	48	30
O12	A146	10k multi	70	30
O13	A146	14k multi	95	48
O14	A146	17k multi	1.25	48
O15	A146	20k multi	1.25	65
O16	A146	50k multi	3.00	1.50
O17	A146	100k multi	8.25	3.00
		Nos. O1-O17 (17)	18.25	8.34

"SP" are the initials of "Service Public."

ZAMBEZIA

LOCATION — A former district of the
Mozambique Province in Portuguese East
Africa

GOVT. — Part of the Portuguese East
Africa Colony

The districts of Quelimane and Tete were
created from Zambezia. Eventually stamps
of Mozambique came into use. See Quelimane and Tete.

1000 Reis = 1 Milreis

King Carlos
A1   A2

Perf. 11½, 12½, 13½

1894		Typo.	Unwmk.	
1	A1	5r yellow	40	38
2	A1	10r red violet	50	38
3	A1	15r chocolate	1.00	85
a.		Perf. 12½	27.50	19.00
4	A1	20r lavender	1.25	1.00
5	A1	25r blue green	1.50	1.40
a.		Perf. 11½		
6	A1	50r lt blue	1.75	1.50
7	A1	75r carmine	5.00	5.25
a.		Perf. 11½	50.00	35.00
8	A1	80r yellow grn	3.50	5.50
9	A1	100r brown, buff	3.50	4.00
10	A1	150r car, rose	4.00	6.25
11	A1	200r dk blue, bl	4.00	5.25
a.		Perf. 11½	200.00	150.00
b.		Perf. 13½	42.50	32.50
12	A1	300r dk bl, salmon	10.00	10.50
a.		Perf. 11½	25.00	20.00

For surcharges and overprints see Nos. 36-47,
73-74, 77-81, 84-88.

1898-1903			Perf. 11½	
		Name and Value in Black or Red (500r)		
13	A2	2½r gray	40	20
14	A2	5r orange	40	20
15	A2	10r lt green	40	20
16	A2	15r brown	2.00	1.50
17	A2	15r gray grn ('03)	2.00	1.00
18	A2	20r gray violet	1.00	60
19	A2	25r sea green	1.00	60
20	A2	25r carmine ('03)	1.50	70
21	A2	50r blue	2.50	1.00
22	A2	50r brown ('03)	3.50	3.75
23	A2	65r dull bl ('03)	9.00	9.50
24	A2	75r rose	9.00	6.00
25	A2	75r lilac ('03)	3.50	4.25
26	A2	80r violet	11.00	5.00
27	A2	100r dk bl, bl	2.50	2.75
28	A2	115r org brn, pink ('03)	9.00	12.50
29	A2	130r brn, straw ('03)	12.00	10.00
30	A2	150r brn, buff	7.50	5.50
31	A2	200r red vio, pnksh	6.50	5.50
32	A2	300r dk bl, rose	7.00	6.00
33	A2	400r dull bl, straw ('03)	15.00	12.00
34	A2	500r blk, bl ('01)	10.50	9.50
35	A2	700r vio, yelsh ('01)	13.00	12.00
		Nos. 13-35 (23)	130.20	111.25

For surcharges and overprints see Nos. 49-68,
72, 82-83, 93-107.

Stamps of 1894
Surcharged   **65 RÉIS**

1902			Perf. 11½, 12½	
36	A1	65r on 10r red vio	5.00	6.00
37	A1	65r on 15r choc	5.00	6.00
38	A1	65r on 20r lav	5.00	6.00
39	A1	65r on 300r bl, sal	5.00	6.00
40	A1	115r on 5r yel	5.00	7.00
41	A1	115r on 25r bl grn	5.00	6.00
42	A1	115r on 80r yel grn	5.00	6.00
43	A1	130r on 75r car	5.00	6.00
44	A1	130r on 150r car, rose	4.50	5.25
45	A1	400r on 50r lt bl	2.00	3.25
46	A1	400r on 100r brn, buff	2.00	3.50
47	A1	400r on 200r bl, bl	2.00	3.50

Same Surcharge on No. P1

| 48 | N1 | 130r on 2½r brn | 5.00 | 6.00 |
| | | Nos. 36-48 (13) | 55.50 | 70.50 |

Stamps of 1898
Overprinted   *PROVISORIO*

1902			Perf. 11½	
49	A2	15r brown	1.75	1.50
50	A2	25r sea green	1.75	1.50
51	A2	50r blue	1.75	1.50
52	A2	75r rose	5.00	3.75

No. 23 Surcharged in
Black   **50 RÉIS**

1905				
53	A2	50r on 65r dull blue	5.00	5.50

Stamps of 1898-1903
Overprinted in
Carmine or Green   *REPUBLICA*

1911				
54	A2	2½r gray	20	20
55	A2	5r orange	20	20
56	A2	10r light green	20	20
a.		Inverted overprint	12.50	12.50
57	A2	15r gray green	30	30
58	A2	20r gray violet	40	30
59	A2	25r carmine (G)	90	50
60	A2	50r brown	50	2.75
61	A2	75r lilac	1.00	2.75
62	A2	100r dk bl, bl	1.00	2.75
63	A2	115r org brn, pink	1.00	2.75
64	A2	130r brown, straw	1.00	2.75
65	A2	200r red vio, pnksh	1.00	2.75
66	A2	400r dull bl, straw	1.65	2.00
67	A2	500r blk & red, bl	1.65	1.40
68	A2	700r violet, yelsh	1.75	4.00
		Nos. 54-68 (15)	12.75	25.60

Stamps of 1902-05
Overprinted in
Carmine or Green   *REPUBLICA*

1914				
		Without Gum		
72	A2	50r on 65r dl bl	575.00	575.00
73	A1	115r on 5r yellow	1.00	1.50
74	A1	115r on 25r bl grn	1.00	1.50
75	A1	115r on 80r yel grn	1.00	1.50
76	N1	130r on 2½r brn (G)	1.00	1.50
a.		Carmine overprint	22.50	22.50
77	A1	130r on 75r car	1.50	1.50
a.		Perf. 12½	5.50	7.00
78	A1	130r on 150r car, rose	1.50	1.50
a.		Perf. 12½	11.00	11.00
79	A1	400r on 50r lt bl	2.00	3.00
80	A1	400r on 100r brn, buff	2.00	2.50
81	A1	400r on 200r bl, bl	2.00	2.50

On Nos. 51-52

82	A2	50r blue	1.25	1.50
83	A2	75r rose	1.25	1.50
		Nos. 73-83 (11)	15.00	20.00

Preceding Issues
Overprinted in
Carmine   *REPUBLICA*

1915				
		On Provisional Issue of 1902		
84	A1	115r on 5r yellow	50	45
85	A1	115r on 25r bl grn	50	45
86	A1	115r on 80r lt grn	50	45
87	A1	130r on 75r carmine	50	45
a.		Perf. 12½	4.50	2.25
88	A1	130r on 150r car, rose	50	45
92	N1	130r on 2½r (down)	50	45
		On Nos. 51, 53		
93	A2	50r blue	50	50
a.		"Republica" inverted		
94	A2	50r on 65r dull bl	3.50	4.50
		Nos. 84-94 (8)	7.00	7.70

Stamps of 1898-
1903 Overprinted
Locally in Carmine   *REPUBLICA*

1917				
		Without Gum		
95	A2	2½r gray	1.50	3.00
96	A2	5r orange	6.00	6.50
97	A2	10r light green	6.50	6.00
98	A2	15r gray green	5.75	6.50
99	A2	20r gray violet	6.75	6.50
100	A2	25r sea green	12.00	15.00
101	A2	100r blue, blue	2.50	2.75
102	A2	115r org brn, pink	2.25	2.50
103	A2	130r brown, straw	2.25	2.50
104	A2	200r red vio, pnksh	2.25	2.50
105	A2	400r dull bl, straw	3.25	3.50
106	A2	500r blk & red, bl	3.25	3.50
107	A2	700r vio, yelsh	6.00	4.50
		Nos. 95-107 (13)	60.25	65.25

NEWSPAPER STAMP

N1

1894		Unwmk.	Typo.	Perf. 12½
P1	N1	2½r brown		45	25

For overprints and surcharges see Nos. 76, 92.

N·E·W

Scott Supplement
Pages for

Zaire

will be available in

November

Index and Identifier

Illustrated Identifier

This section pictures stamps or parts of stamp designs that will help identify postage stamps that do not have English words on them.

Many of the symbols that identify stamps of countries are shown here as well as typical examples of their stamps.

See the Index and Identifier on the previous pages for stamps with inscriptions such as "sen," "posta," "Baja Porto," "Helvetia," "K.S.A.", etc.

Linn's Stamp Identifier is now available. The 144 pages include more 2,000 inscriptions and over 500 large stamp illustrations. Available from Linn's Stamp News, P.O. Box 29, Sidney, OH 45365-0029.

HEADS, PICTURES AND NUMERALS

GREAT BRITAIN

Great Britain stamps never show the country name, but, except for postage dues, show a picture of the reigning monarch.

Victoria

Edward VII   George V   Edward VIII

George VI

Elizabeth II

Silhouette (sometimes facing right, generally at the top of stamp)

The silhouette indicates this is a British stamp. It is not a U.S. stamp.

VICTORIA

Queen Victoria

INDIA

Other stamps of India show this portrait of Queen Victoria and the words "Service" and "Annas."

AUSTRIA

YUGOSLAVIA

(Also BOSNIA & HERZEGOVINA if imperf.)

BOSNIA & HERZEGOVINA

Denominations also appear in top corners instead of bottom corners.

HUNGARY

Another stamp has posthorn facing left

BRAZIL

AUSTRALIA

 Kangaroo and Emu

NEW ZEALAND

GERMANY

Mecklenburg-Vorpommern

SWITZERLAND

ORIENTAL INSCRIPTIONS

CHINA

Any stamp with this one character is from China (Imperial, Republic or People's Republic).

中 中

Some Chinese stamps show the Sun

Most stamps of Republic of China show this series of characters.

Stamps with the China character and this character are from People's Republic of China. 人

Calligraphic form of People's Republic of China

Chinese stamps without China character

REPUBLIC OF CHINA

PEOPLE'S REPUBLIC OF CHINA

Mao Tse-tung

MANCHUKUO

Temple   The first 3 characters   Emperor
are common to many   Pu-Yi
Manchukuo stamps.

The last 3 characters are common to
other Manchukuo stamps

Orchid Crest

Manchukuo
stamp with-
out these
elements

JAPAN

Chrysanthemum Crest   Country Name

Japanese stamps without these elements

RYUKYU ISLANDS

Country Name

PHILIPPINES
(Japanese Occupation)

Country Name

NORTH BORNEO
(Japanese Occupation)

Indicates Japanese   Country
Occupation   Name

MALAYA
(Japanese Occupation)

Indicates Japanese Occupation

 Country Name

BURMA
(Japanese Occupation)

Indicates Japanese Occupation

シヤン   Country Name

Other Burma Japanese Occupation stamps
without these elements

Burmese Script

KOREA

These two characters, in any order, are common
to stamps from the Republic of Korea (South
Korea) or the unlisted stamps of the People's
Democratic Republic of Korea (North Korea)

This series of four characters can be found
on the stamps of both Koreas.

Yin Yang appears on some stamps

Indicates Republic of Korea (South Korea)

THAILAND

Country Name

King Prajadhipok and Chao P'ya Chakri

CENTRAL AND EASTERN ASIAN INSCRIPTIONS

INDIA - FEUDATORY STATES

Alwar   Bhor

Bundi

Similar stamps come with
different designs in corners
and differently drawn daggers
(at center of circle)

Faridkot

Hyderabad

 Similar stamps exist with
straight line frame around
stamp, and also with different
central design which is
inscribed "Postage" or "Post
& Receipt."

Indore   Jammu
                          & Kashmir

Jhalawar   Nowanuggur

Rajpeepla   Soruth

BANGLADESH

NEPAL

Similar stamps are smaller, have squares in
upper corners and have five or nine
characters in central bottom panel

TANNU TUVA   ISRAEL

GEORGIA

ARMENIA

The four characters are found somewhere
on pictorial stamps. On some stamps only
the middle two are found.

ARABIC INSCRIPTIONS

AFGHANISTAN

Many early Afghanistan stamps show Tiger's head, many of these have ornaments protruding from outer ring, others show inscriptions in black

Arabic Script

Mosque Gate & Crossed Cannons

BAHRAIN

EGYPT

IRAN

Country Name

Note Crown

Lion with Sword

JORDAN

LEBANON

Similar types have
denominations at top and
slightly different design

LIBYA

Country Name in various styles

Other Libya stamps show Eagle and Shield (head
facing either direction) or Red, White and Black
Shield (with or without eagle in center).

SAUDI ARABIA

Note Tughra (Central design)

20 H

Palm Tree and Swords

SYRIA

THRACE   YEMEN

PAKISTAN - Bahawalpur

Country Name in top panel,
star and crescent

TURKEY

Star & Crescent

 Tughra (similar tughras can be
found on stamps of Afghanistan
and Saudi Arabia)

Mohammed V

Mustafa Kemal

Plane, Star
and Crescent

TURKEY IN ASIA

Other Turkey in Asia pictorials show
star & crescent

GREEK INSCRIPTIONS

GREECE

Country Name in various styles
(Some Crete stamps overprinted with the Greece
country name are listed in Crete.)

Lepta

ΔΡΑΧΜΗ ΔΡΑΧΜΑΙ ΛΕΠΤΟΝ
Drachma   Drachmas   Lepton

Abbreviated Country Name ΕΛΛ

Other forms of Country Name

No country name

CRETE

Country Name

These words are on other stamps

Grosion

Crete stamps with a surcharge that have the year "1922" are listed under Greece.

EPIRUS
Country Name

IONIAN ISLANDS

CYRILLIC INSCRIPTIONS

RUSSIA
Postage Stamp

Imperial Eagle

Postage in various styles

Abbreviation for Kopeck

 Abbreviation for Ruble

Россія Russia

Abbreviation for Russian Soviet Federated Socialist Republic

Abbreviation for Union of Soviet Socialist Republics

RUSSIA - Army of the North

"ОКСА"

RUSSIA - Wenden

RUSSIAN OFFICES IN THE TURKISH EMPIRE

These letters appear on other stamps of the Russian offices.

The unoverprinted version of this stamp and a similar stamp were overprinted by various countries (see below).

ARMENIA

FAR EASTERN REPUBLIC
Country Name

SOUTH RUSSIA
Country Name

FINLAND

Circles and Dots
on stamps similar
to Imperial
Russia issues

BATUM

Forms of Country Name

TRANSCAUCASIAN
FEDERATED REPUBLICS

Abbreviation for
Country Name

KAZAKHSTAN

Country Name

KYRGYZSTAN   ROMANIA

КЫРГЫЗСТАН
Counrty Name

TADJIKISTAN

Counrty Name & Abbreviation

UKRAINE

Country Name in various forms

The trident
appears on many
stamps, usually
as an overprint.

Abbreviation for
Ukrainian Soviet
Socialist Republic

WESTERN UKRAINE

Abbreviation for
Country Name

AZERBAIJAN

Country Name

ACCP

Azerbaijan Soviet
Socialist Republic

MONTENEGRO

ЦРНА ГОРА

Country Name in various forms

Abbreviation for   No country name
country name   (A similar Montene-
             gro stamp without
             country name has
             same vignette.)

SERBIA

Country Name in various forms

Abbreviation for country name

YUGOSLAVIA

Showing
country name

No Country Name

MACEDONIA

Country Name

BULGARIA

Country Name   Postage

Stotinka   Abbreviation for Stotinki

Stotinki (plural)

Country Name in various forms and styles

НР България

No country name

Abbreviation for
Lev, leva

MONGOLIA

Country name in
one word

Tugrik in Cyrillic

Country name
in two words

Mung in Cyrillic

Mung
in Mongolian

Tugrik
in Mongolian

Arms

No Country Name

INDEX TO ADVERTISERS – 1996 VOLUME 5

MENTION SCOTT WHEN RESPONDING TO ADVERTISEMENTS!

SCOTT...GIVES YOU THE... **AMERICAN MARKET AND AN EVER INCREASING WORLD MARKET!**

SCOTT ADVERTISING OPPORTUNITIES!

DEALERS...present your Buying or Selling Messages, Services, Auctions, Topicals, FDC's, etc., to Serious Collectors by placing your advertisements in Scott Products!!!

1997 SCOTT CATALOGUES
Call now to reserve ad space and to receive advertising information. If you're interested in specific positions...call or write as soon as possible.

SCOTT STAMP MONTHLY
Whether you're buying or selling, our readership of active mail-order collectors offers you a perfect opportunity for increased sales and contacts.

SCOTT U.S. FDC CATALOGUE
If you want to reach active First Day Cover collectors and beginning First Day Cover collectors who purchase this excellent annual catalogue, call now for ad information.

SCOTT U.S. POCKET CATALOGUE
If you deal in U.S. material, an ad in this popular annual catalogue can bring you many new customers. Thousands are sold each year to active and beginning collectors.

**FOR COMPLETE INFORMATION ON THESE ADVERTISING OPPORTUNITIES...
CALL 513-498-0832, FAX 513-498-0807 OR WRITE...**

SCOTT PUBLISHING CO.
P.O. Box 828
Sidney, OH 45365-0828 U.S.A.

1996
Volume 5
DEALER DIRECTORY
YELLOW PAGE LISTINGS

This section of your Scott Catalogue contains
advertisements to help you conveniently find
what you need,
when you need it...!

Accessories

H & S ROGG
P.O. Box 1076
Port Richey, FL 34673-1076
813-848-7697

FREEWAY STAMP SUPPLIES
635 S. Raymond Ave.
Suite D
Fullerton, CA 92631
714-447-8100 or 800-447-8105
714-447-8100 FAX

Albums

VIDIFORMS COMPANY INC.
Showgard House
110 Brenner Drive
Congers, NY 10920
914-268-4005
914-268-5324 FAX

Albums & Accessories

THE KEEPING ROOM
P.O. Box 257
Trumbull, CT 06611-0257
203-372-8436

Appraisals

APX
P.O. Box 952
Yakima, WA 98907
509-452-9517

**FOUNTAIN SQUARE STAMP &
COIN INC.**
27 Fountain Square Plaza
Cincinnati, OH 45202
513-621-6696
513-621-3901 FAX

UNIQUE ESTATE APPRAISALS
1937 NE Broadway
Portland, OR 97232
503-287-4200

Approvals

THE STAMP ACT
Rt. 1 P.O. Box 93
East Orland, ME 04431
800-743-7832

Approvals - Personalized

THE KEEPING ROOM
P.O. Box 257
Trumbull, CT 06611-0257
203-372-8436

Approvals - Sweden

WEST NISSOURI STAMP CO.
P.O. Box 4641-A
London, Ontario N5W 5L7
CANADA
519-432-0080 or 519-432-0286

Approvals - Topicals

STUART KATZ
P.O. Box 656 SM
Middleton, MA 01949
508-777-2327

Approvals - Worldwide

49ER STAMP CO.
P.O. Box 416
Lebanon, NH 03766

M & H DAVISON
Box 510 - T
South Sutton, NH 03273-0510

WEST NISSOURI STAMP CO.
P.O. Box 4641-A
London, Ontario N5W 5L7
CANADA
519-432-0080 or 519-432-0286

ROSS WETREICH INC.
P.O. Box 1300
Valley Stream, NY 11582-1300
516-825-8974

Accessories

Showgard Mounts

The time proven hingeless method for protecting stamp values!

• AT STAMP DEALERS EVERYWHERE •

Sample on request from:

VIDIFORMS CO., INC.
110 Brenner Drive, Congers, NY 10920 U.S.A.

THE LEADING DISTRIBUTOR
OF ALL MAJOR NORTH AMERICAN & EUROPEAN
STAMP & COIN LINES
NOW OFFERS...

COMPLETE 160-PAGE STAMP AND COIN
ACCESSORIES CATALOGUE!

Send $2.50 to cover shipping & handling costs.
(refundable with first purchase)

UNITRADE ASSOCIATES
99 FLORAL PARKWAY, DEPT. SC5, TORONTO, ONTARIO M6L 2C4 CANADA

FREE 80 PAGE DISCOUNT CATALOG

$1 POSTAGE APPRECIATED

SCOTT - MINKUS - HARRIS
LIGHTHOUSE - KABE - SAFE
LINDNER - ELBE - G&K

America's Largest Discount Stamp Company

ALL MAJOR BRANDS OF:
ALBUMS, MOUNTS,
REFERENCE BOOKS, ACCESS.,
STAMPS, PACKETS,
& ALL COIN SUPPLIES

SUBWAY STAMP SHOP, INC.

2121 BEALE AVENUE, ALTOONA, PA 16601
PHONE: 800-221-9960

Approvals – Worldwide

1,000 STAMPS $2.95
GUARANTEED WORTH OVER $30 AT INTERNATIONAL CATALOG PRICES!

Save These Valuable Postage Stamps *NOW* While They Last!

Reward yourself now — a great opportunity to increase the value of your present collection or to start a new one. You get 1,000 all-different postage stamps from over 55 countries *Plus Big Illustrated Collectors' Catalog* — Everything to Enjoy the World's Most Rewarding Hobby!   *GREAT FAMILY FUN!*

YOURS FREE! "FINDER'S GUIDE TO RARE AND VALUABLE POSTAGE STAMPS!" This fascinating illustrated booklet will enable you to tell at a glance **how to recognize rare stamps — stamps once considered relatively common and now worth up to hundreds and thousands of dollars each**!

Also, selections of other sensational stamps from our 10-Day Free Examination Shop-At-Home Approval Service. Buy any or none — return balance — cancel Service anytime. Send $2.95 NOW!

90-DAY MONEY-BACK GUARANTEE IF NOT DELIGHTED!
KENMORE, Milford OP-124, N.H. 03055

Asia

ALLKOR STAMP COMPANY
Box 1346
Port Washington, NY 11050
516-883-3296 PHONE & FAX

REGENCY STAMPS, LTD.
Le Chateau Village #106
10411 Clayton Road ,
St. Louis, MO 63131
800-782-0066
314-997-2231 FAX

MICHAEL ROGERS, INC.
199 E. Welbourne Ave.
Winter Park, FL 32789
407-644-2290
407-645-4434 FAX

Auction House

B TRADING CO.
114 Quail Street
Albany, NY 12206
518-465-3497 PHONE & FAX

REGENCY PHILATELIC AUCTIONS, LTD.
LeChateau Village #106
10411 Clayton Road
St. Louis, MO 63131
800-782-0066
314-997-2231 FAX

Auctions

Schiff Auctions

Buyers, Auctioneers & Appraisers of U.S. & Worldwide Stamps & Covers

We have been catering to the individual buyer and seller since 1947. Let us put our expertise to work for you when selling your stamps, covers or your collection. Whether consigning to public auction or selling outright, call us first. Contact us before sending stamps. Be sure to include your address and telephone number.

CATALOG SUBSCRIPTIONS	N. AMERICA	OVERSEAS
1 Year with Realizations	$10.00	$18.00
1 Year Catalog Only	$7.50	$15.00
1 Catalog with Realizations	$1.50	$2.50
1 Catalog Only	$1.00	$1.50

JACQUES C. SCHIFF, JR., INC.

195 Main St., Ridgefield Park, NJ 07660 USA
Telephone 201-641-5566 from NYC 662-2777
FAX 201-641-5705

OFFICIAL AUCTIONEERS:
AMERIPEX 1986.
WORLD STAMP EXPO 1989.
WORLD COLUMBIAN STAMP EXPO 1992.
YEARLY: COMPEX-CHICAGO.

QUALIFIED AUCTIONEER

Approvals – Worldwide

Direct from Moscow...

Historic First Year Set of Independent Russia

It's no surprise this <u>complete</u> 1992 Russia mint stamp set is in great demand worldwide. These amazingly beautiful stamps chronicle the tremendous turmoil and historic rebirth of Russia.

Collectors and non-collectors alike are captivated by unfolding events in Moscow. Each day brings amazing news, with Yeltsin's influence rising and falling like the stock market.

This complete mint collection of stamps is never-hinged. Includes 76 stamps, 14 extremely scarce miniature sheets issued in small quantities, and 3 souvenir sheets. Includes the new Russian flag, joint issue space stamps, the beloved Nutcracker Ballet, religious icons, cathedrals and the discovery of America.

The entire set is yours for only $35.95, half the normal Mystic retail! Germany's *Michel* catalog values the stamps at $156.00! The Mystic price offers an exceptionally good value.

This set will sell out... we expect worldwide demand to be tremendous. There is no more affordable way to own authentic artifacts of this most historic time! It's history you hold in your hands.

Mystic has created a 19-page album supplement picturing the 1992 Russia stamps. This high quality special supplement is a $5 value, and it's yours free with each collection ordered. Limit one set, please.

Your satisfaction is guaranteed. Order the Mint 1992 Russia set today and also receive special collectors information along with other Russian stamps on approval.

YES Send the First Stamps of Independent Russia plus my special bonus album supplement.

Mail coupon with $35.95 to:
Mystic Stamp Company, Dept. CA936, Camden, NY 13316

Check or money order enclosed _____

Charge my Visa, MC or American Express _____

Card # _____

Expiration Date _____

Name _____

Street _____

City/State/Zip _____

Mystic Stamp Company
America's Leading Stamp Dealer

Auctions

CEE-JAY STAMP AUCTIONS,INC.
P.O. Box 321
Waldorf, MD 20604
301-843-2022
301-705-7255 FAX

CHARLES G. FIRBY AUCTIONS
6695 Highland Road Suite #107
Waterford, MI 48327
810-666-5333
810-666-5020 FAX

HARMER-SCHAU AUCTION GALLERIES INC.
617A Second Street
Petaluma, CA 94952
707-778-6454
707-763-6772 FAX

STAMP CENTER/DUTCH COUNTRY AUCTIONS
4115 Concord Pike
Wilmington, DE 19803
302-478-8740
302-478-8779 FAX

Automatic Album Update Service

DELAWARE VALLEY STAMP CO.
69 Strasburg Road
Atglen, PA 19310
610-593-6684

Booklets – Worldwide

HENRY GITNER PHILATELISTS INC.
P.O. Box 3077-S
Middletown, NY 10940
914-343-5151/800-947-8267
914-343-0068 FAX

Collections

GAYLAND BIRD
Box 8073
Dept. S
Asheville, NC 28814
704-645-6949 PHONE & FAX

HENRY GITNER PHILATELISTS INC.
P.O. Box 3077-S
Middletown, NY 10940
914-343-5151/800-947-8267
914-343-0068 FAX

Covers

JUDNICK POSTCARDS & COVERS
P.O. Box 12248
Columbus, OH 43212-0248
614-278-9399

Covers – Asia

MICHAEL ROGERS, INC.
199 E. Welbourne Ave.
Winter Park, FL 32789
407-644-2290
407-645-4434 FAX

Call or write for the new full color

1995 SCOTT PRODUCT GUIDE

TO GET YOUR FREE COPY CALL 1-800-572-6885

Featuring more than 1,400 products!

To see the fine line of Scott products first hand, contact your local dealer.
If you're not sure where a dealer may be located in your area,
let us know and we'll help you find one.

S·C·O·T·T®

Collections

★ ★ ★ **STOP** ★ ★ ★
WORLDWIDE COLLECTIONS AT LOW, LOW PRICES!
• • • • • • •
If you spend over $25.00 per month you should subscribe to the "Money's Worth" list.
For 3 free issues, write or call:

WARREN A. WASSON
DALLAS STAMP GALLERY
1002 N. Central, Suite 501, Richardson, TX 75080
═══ Call TOLL FREE 1-800-759-9109 ═══

Covers - Worldwide

MICHAEL ROGERS, INC.
199 E. Welbourne Ave.
Winter Park, FL 32789
407-644-2290
407-645-4434 FAX

Covers - Zeppelins

MICHAEL ROGERS, INC.
199 E. Welbourne Ave.
Winter Park, FL 32789
407-644-2290
407-645-4434 FAX

Dead Countries

MICHAEL ROGERS, INC.
199 E. Welbourne Ave.
Winter Park, FL 32789
407-644-2290
407-645-4434 FAX

Discount Supplies

VERUS DISCOUNT STAMP CO.
P.O. Box 187
West Chicago, IL 60186
708-896-8938

Duck Stamps

TRENTON STAMP & COIN CO.
1804 RT. 33
Trenton, NJ 08690
800-446-8664
609-587-8664 FAX

Europe

REGENCY STAMPS, LTD.
Le Chateau Village #106
10411 Clayton Road
St. Louis, MO 63131
800-782-0066
314-997-2231 FAX

Inverted Centers - World

MARTIN SELLINGER
Box 47
White Plains, NY 10602
914-948-4246
914-682-7384 FAX

Latin America

BROOKSIDE STAMPS
P.O. Box 412
Worthington, OH 43085
614-436-0524

Lots & Collections

DAVE ALLEGO
P.O. Box 13
Ambridge, PA 15003-0013
412-266-4255

GAYLAND BIRD
Box 8073
Dept. S
Asheville, NC 28814
704-645-6949 PHONE & FAX

Mail Bid Sales

CONNEXUS
P.O. Box 453
Guilford, CT 06437
203-453-4298
203-458-2220 FAX

JUNO STAMPS
1765 Juno Avenue
St. Paul, MN 55116
800-714-3469
612-699-2510 FAX

QUEST INTERNATIONAL
P.O. Box 139A,
Thames Ditton,
Surrey, KT7 OER, UNITED KINGDOM
44-181-398-7740
44-181-398-4661 FAX

Mail Order

B & D HOBBIES
P.O. Box 4
Gladstone, OR 97027
503-656-3149

BOB BECK
Box 3209 Harbourtown Station
Hilton Head Island, SC 29928
803-671-3241

LOG HOUSE PHILATELIST
Box 267 Harju Road
Grand Marais, MI 49839

Middle East - Arab

THE PERFECT PERF
P.O. Box 16127
Pittsburgh, PA 15242
412-429-1618
412-561-0660 FAX

Monaco

E. JOSEPH Mc CONNELL INC.
P.O. Box 683
Monroe, NY 10950
914-496-5916
914-782-0347 FAX

Mounts

VIDIFORMS COMPANY INC.
Showgard House
110 Brenner Drive
Congers, NY 10920
914-268-4005
914-268-5324 FAX

New Issues

DAVIDSON'S STAMP SERVICE
P.O. Box 20502
Indianapolis, IN 46220
317-255-9408

New Issues - Retail

BOMBAY PHILATELIC CO., INC.
P.O. Box 7719
Delray Beach, FL 33484-7719
407-499-7990
407-499-7553 FAX

GERSON'S INT'L INC.
520 SW Yamhill Street
Suite 402
Portland, OR 97204
503-228-5233
503-228-5288 FAX

HERRICK STAMP CO.
P.O. Box 219
Lawrence, NY 11559
516-569-3959
516-569-7093 FAX

STANLEY M. PILLER
3351 Grand Ave.
Oakland, CA 94610
510-465-8290
510-465-7121 FAX

New Issues - Scandinavia

NORDICA
P.O. Box 284
Old Bethpage, NY 11804
516-931-3485 PHONE & FAX

New Issues - Wholesale

THE NEW ISSUE CLUB
P.O. Box 1926
Beavertown, OR 97075

Philatelic Societies

AMERICAN PHILATELIC SOCIETY
Dept TZ P.O. Box 8000
State College, PA 16803
814-237-3803
814-237-6128 FAX

SOCIETY FOR CZECHOSLO-VAK PHILATELY, INC.
Tom Cossaboom, SCP Secretary
Box 25332
Scott Air Force Base, IL 62225 (USA)

Postcards

AURORA BOREALIS STAMP & SUPPLY
2273 S. 65th Street
Milwaukee, WI 53219
800-362-1010
414-543-0340 FAX

JUDNICK POSTCARDS & COVERS
P.O. Box 12248
Columbus, OH 43212-0248
614-278-9399

Proofs & Essays

HENRY GITNER PHILATELISTS INC.
P.O. Box 3077-S
Middletown, NY 10940
914-343-5151/800-947-8267
914-343-0068 FAX

New Issues

SPECTACULAR
NEW ISSUE SERVICE
Extensive Coverage - New Issues from the Entire World
Remember Our Specialty:
All Topicals and New Issues
Want Lists for Older Issues Serviced
Top Prices Paid for Collections & Accumulations
FREE ILLUSTRATED TOPICAL MONTHLY NEW ISSUE LIST
COUNTY STAMP CENTER
P.O. Box 3373, Annapolis, MD 21403
PH. 410-757-5800 • FAX 410-573-0025

Publications / Collector

GLOBAL STAMP NEWS
P.O. Box 97
Sidney, OH 45365-0097
513-492-3183
513-492-6514 FAX

MEKEEL'S WEEKLY STAMP NEWS
Box 5050-sy
White Plains, NY 10602
800-MEKEEL-1
914-997-7261 FAX

Romania

GEORGE ARGHIR
Detunata 17-27 P.O. Box 521
RO-3400 Cluj-Napoca 9
ROMANIA
+40-64-414036 PHONE/FAX

HUNGARIA STAMP EXCHANGE
P.O. Box 3024
Andover, MA 01810
508-682-0242
508-794-2567 FAX

Russia

FRANK GEIGER PHILATELISTS
242 W. Saddle River Road
Suite 5
Upper Saddle River,
NJ 07458-2620
201-236-8122
201-236-8133 FAX

SHARI'S STAMPS
104-3 Old Highway 40 #130
O'Fallon, MO 63366
800-382-3597

THE STAMP GALLERY
10335 Main Street
Bellevue, WA 98004
206-455-3781 PHONE & FAX

Russia - Ducks

METROPOLITAN STAMP CO. of CHICAGO, INC.
P.O. Box 1133
Chicago, IL 60690-1133
815-439-0142
815-439-0143 FAX

Russia - New Issues

RUSSIA STAMP AGENCY IN NORTH AMERICA
One Unicover Center
Cheyenne, WY 82008-0012
800-443-4225
800-628-3123 FAX

Ryukyus

MICHAEL ROGERS, INC.
199 E. Welbourne Ave.
Winter Park, FL 32789
407-644-2290
407-645-4434 FAX

Saar

R. SCHNEIDER
Box 23049
Belleville, IL 62223
618-277-8543
618-277-1050 FAX

JOE HARRIS
P.O. Box 13430
Baltimore, MD 21203
410-732-4791

Safes - Stamps

KINGSBERY MANUFACTURING CORP.
715 West Zavala Street
Crystal City, TX 78839
800-445-0763

St. Pierre et Miquelon

E. JOSEPH Mc CONNELL INC.
P.O. Box 683
Monroe, NY 10950
914-496-5916
914-782-0347 FAX

San Marino

FRANK GEIGER PHILATELISTS
242 W. Saddle River Road
Suite 5
Upper Saddle River,
NJ 07458-2620
201-236-8122
201-236-8133 FAX

Saudi Arabia

HENRY GITNER PHILATELISTS INC.
P.O. Box 3077-S
Middletown, NY 10940
914-343-5151/800-947-8267
914-343-0068 FAX

Scandinavia

ICE BEAR STAMPS
P.O. Box 40068-C
Eugene, OR 97404
503-461-0890

Slovakia

SOCIETY FOR CZECHOSLO-VAK PHILATELY INC.
Tom Cossaboom, SCP
Secretary
Box 25332
Scott Air Force Base, IL 62225
(USA)

Slovenia

FRANK GEIGER PHILATELISTS
242 W. Saddle River Road
Suite 5
Upper Saddle River,
NJ 07458-2620
201-236-8122
201-236-8133 FAX

Southeast Asia

MICHAEL ROGERS, INC.
199 E. Welbourne Ave.
Winter Park, FL 32789
407-644-2290
407-645-4434 FAX

Spain

FRANK GEIGER PHILATELISTS
242 W. Saddle River Road
Suite 5
Upper Saddle River,
NJ 07458-2620
201-236-8122
201-236-8133 FAX

JOE HARRIS
P.O. Box 13430
Baltimore, MD 21203
410-732-4791

IF YOU COLLECT UNITED STATES, SPAIN AND WORLDWIDE...
Early Issues and big
Complete MINT SETS...
ask for our
FREE
SALE CATALOGS
AND MAIL AUCTIONS
Write...
FILATELIA LLACH, S.L.
"Stamp Dealers Since 1915"
489 Diagonal Avenue
08029 BARCELONA
SPAIN
Fax +34-3-4194728

Spanish Colonies

JOE HARRIS
P.O. Box 13430
Baltimore, MD 21203
410-732-4791

Stamp Accessories

BROOKLYN GALLERY COIN & STAMP
8725 4th Avenue
Brooklyn, NY 11209
718-745-5701
718-745-2775 FAX

Stamp Packets

AURORA BOREALIS STAMP & SUPPLY
2273 S. 65th Street
Milwaukee, WI 53219
800-362-1010
414-543-0340 FAX

Stamp Shows

BEACH PHILATELICS
P.O. Box 150
Virginia Beach, VA 23458-0150
804-425-8566 PHONE & FAX

HIGHTSTOWN SECOND SATURDAY BOURSE
Monmouth St.(RTE.633) opposite Ramada Inn
Exit 8 New Jersey Turnpike
Hightstown, NJ 08520

AL SOTH
P.O. Box 22081
Milwaukie, OR 97269
503-794-0956

STAMP STORES

Arizona

B.J.'S STAMPS / BARBARA J. JOHNSON
6342 W. Bell Road
Glendale, AZ 85308
602-878-2080
602-412-3456 FAX

California

ASHTREE STAMP & COIN
2410 N. Blackstone
Fresno, CA 93703
209-227-7167

BROSIUS STAMP & COIN
2105 Main Street
Santa Monica, CA 90405
310-396-7480

FISCHER - WOLK PHILATELICS
24771 "G" Alicia Parkway
Laguna Hills, CA 92653
714-837-2932

HERB'S STAMP CENTER
11748 Washington Place
West Los Angeles, CA 90066
310-397-3883

KENRICH CO.
9418-A Las Tunas Drive
Temple City, CA 91780
818-286-3888
818-286-6035 FAX

NATICK STAMPS & HOBBIES
405 S. Myrtle Avenue
Monrovia, CA 91016
818-305-7333
818-305-7335 FAX

STANLEY M. PILLER
3351 Grand Ave.
Oakland, CA 94610
510-465-8290
510-465-7121 FAX

THE STAMP GALLERY
1515 Locust Street
Walnut Creek, CA 94596
510-944-9111

STAMP STORES

Colorado

ACKLEY'S ROCKS & STAMPS
3230 N. Stone Ave.
Colorado Springs, CO 80907
719-633-1153

SHOWCASE STAMPS
3865 Wadsworth Blvd.
Wheat Ridge, CO 80033
303-425-9252
303-425-7410 FAX

Connecticut

J&B STAMPS & COLLECTIBLES
41 Colony Street
Meriden, CT 06451
203-235-7634

MILLER'S STAMP SHOP
41 New London Turnpike
Uncasville, CT 06382
203-848-0468 PHONE & FAX

Washington, D.C.

WOODWARD & LOTHROP STAMP DEPT.
11th & G St. NW
Washington, DC 20013
202-879-8028

Florida

BEACH STAMP & COIN
971 E. Eau Gallie Blvd.
and Highway A1A Suite G
Melbourne Beach, FL 32937
407-777-1666

ARLINGTON STAMP & COIN CO.
1350 University Blvd., North
Jacksonville, FL 32211-5226
904-743-1776

HAUSER'S COIN & STAMP
3425 S. Florida Ave.
Lakeland, FL 33803
813-647-2052
813-644-5738 FAX

HUGO'S STAMP EMPORIUM
P.O. Box 5527
Lake Worth, FL 33466
407-966-7517

Florida

INTERCONTINENTAL/ RICARDO DEL CAMPO
7379 Coral Way
Miami, FL 33155-1402
305-264-4983
305-262-2919 FAX

JACK'S COINS & STAMPS
801 Northlake Blvd.
North Palm Beach, FL 33408
407-844-7710

JERRY SIEGEL/STAMPS FOR COLLECTORS
1920 E. Hallandale Beach Blvd.
Suite 507
Hallandale, FL 33009
305-457-0422 PHONE & FAX

NEW ENGLAND STAMP
4987 Tamiami Trail East
Village Falls Professional Ctr
Naples, Fl 33962
941-732-8000
941-732-7701 FAX

ST. JOHN'S STAMP SHOP
2 Aviles Street
St. Augustine, FL 32084
904-829-9673

SARASOTA STAMP DEPOT
1564 Main Street
Sarasota, FL 34236
813-365-5415

THE STAMP PLACE
576 First Avenue North
St. Petersburg, FL 33701
813-894-4082

WINTER PARK STAMP SHOP
199 E. Welbourne Ave.
Suite 201
Winter Park, FL 32789
800-845-1819
407-628-0091 FAX

Georgia

STAMPS UNLIMITED OF GEORGIA
133 Carnegie Way
Room 250
Atlanta, GA 30303
404-688-9161

Georgia

BLUE RIDGE STAMP CO.

801 E. MAIN STREET
POST OFFICE BOX 2230
BLUE RIDGE, GA 30513
1-800-61-STAMP
FAX 706-632-3908

WE OFFER A FULL LINE OF STAMPS & SUPPLIES FOR THE BEGINNER AND THE ADVANCED COLLECTOR.

WE OFFER A NEW ISSUE SERVICE UNIQUE FROM OTHERS: NO MINIMUMS AND WE STOCK THE COUNTRIES WE SERVICE.

Our 4000 Sq. Ft. Store Is Located In The N. Georgia Mtns. Surrounded By Antique, Craft, and Specialty Shops.

G.P.S.   B.I.A. CSA

Illinois

DON CLARK'S STAMPS
937 1/2 W. Galena Blvd.
Aurora, IL 60506
708-896-4606

H.C. STAMP & COIN CO.
10 Crystal Lake Plaza
Crystal Lake, IL 60014
815-459-3940

MARSHALL FIELD'S STAMP DEPT.
111 N. State Street
Chicago, IL 60602
312-781-4237

STAMP KING / RICHARD E. DREWS AUCTIONS
7139 W. Higgins Road
Chicago, IL 60656
312-775-2100
312-792-9116 FAX

Indiana

J & J COINS & STAMPS
7019 Calumet Avenue
Hammond, IN 46324
219-932-5818

KNIGHT STAMP & COIN COMPANY
301 Main Street
Hobart, IN 46342
800-634-2646

VILLAGE STAMP AND COIN
40 E. Cedar
Zionsville, IN 46077
317-873-6762

Kentucky

COLLECTORS STAMPS LTD.
4012 DuPont Circle #313
Louisville, KY 40207
502-897-9045

TREASURE ISLAND COINS & STAMPS
232 W. Broadway
Louisville, KY 40202
502-583-1222

Louisiana

LIVINGSTON STAMP & RARE BOOK CO.
13595 Henry Drive
Denham Springs, LA 70726
504-665-7815

Maryland

BALTIMORE COIN & STAMP EXCHANGE INC.
10194 Baltimore National Pike
Unit 104
Ellicott City, MD 21042
410-418-8282
410-418-4813 FAX

BULLDOG STAMP CO.
4641 Montgomery Ave.
Bethesda, MD 20814
301-654-1138

DELMARVA STAMPS & COLLECTIBLES
23 Salisbury Mall
Civic Avenue
Salisbury, MD 21801
410-742-7077

STAMP & COIN WORLD
511-A Delaware Avenue
Towson, MD 21286
410-828-4465 or 800-452-4560

Massachusetts

BATTLE GREEN STAMP COMPANY
4 Muzzey Street
Lexington, MA 02173
617-862-2330

FALMOUTH STAMP & COIN
11 Town Hall Square
Falmouth, MA 02540
508-548-7075 or 800-341-3701

J & N FORTIER
484 Main Street
Worcester, MA 01608
508-757-3657

Florida

WHEN VISITING CENTRAL FLORIDA BE SURE TO STOP BY...

Send 32¢ long SASE for our MONTHLY NEWSLETTER of stamps for sale!

Michael Rogers - Alvin Hintz

WINTER PARK STAMP SHOP

199 E. Welbourne Ave., 2nd floor, Winter Park, FL 32789
Phone 407-628-1120 • FAX 407-628-0091
1-800-845-1819

Open Mon. through Fri. 10am-6pm • Sat. 10am-3pm (4 miles North of Orlando)

THERE'S A [
INSIDE THE
SCOTT STA

FREE MAGAZINE

SCOTT STAMP MONTHLY IS PACKED WITH STAMP STORIES YOU WON'T READ ANYWHERE ELSE! EACH MONTH YOU'RE TREATED TO NEW WRITERS, NEW FEATURES, NEW SUBJECTS AND ALWAYS A FEW SURPRISES. FOR A FREE LOOK AT STAMP COLLECTING'S MOST ENTERTAINING AND INFORMATIVE MAGAZINE, SIMPLY CALL OUR TOLL-FREE NUMBER 1-800-488-5351.

WAYNE YOUNGBLOOD
EDITOR

Since taking over as editor of Scott Stamp Monthly, Wayne has been busy redesigning the magazine. Under his tenure, a number of new departments have been introduced to meet the needs and desires of our readers. Wayne's efforts have paid off, Scott Stamp Monthly is the only major philatelic publication that is consistently growing in paid circulation.

TO ERR IS DIVINE

A lighthearted, full-color look at design discrepancies and historical inaccuracies on stamps. Philatelic entertainment at its best, showing goofs and gaffes that will make you howl.

FREE FOR ALL
IT'S YOUR CHANCE TO
GET FREE STAMPS
EVERY MONTH!

The stamps are not automatically sent to all subscribers, but are available to all who want them. All you need to do is send a

stamped, addressed envelope and follow the instructions in the "Free For All" column. The stamps given away each month more than cover the subscription price.

FEATURE ARTICLES

You'll enjoy articles ranging from topical interest to light research. Each month you'll discover fascinating, often obscure facts and gain new insight into the stamps of the world.

T GOING ON
PAGES OF
MONTHLY

PRIVATE VIEWING

A full-color, two page spread showcasing some of the world's most beautiful and intriguing stamps.

CATALOGUE UPDATE

The most authoritative new issue listing of its kind, showing more stamps in more detail than other philatelic publications. Every

AMAZING STAMP STORIES

A full-color story page done in the classic illustrated style of Ripley's "Believe It or Not." There's a new story each month dealing with some of the world's greatest issues, remarkable stamp discoveries and the people associated with them.

SCOTT

JUST HISTORY

An entertaining glimpse of the people, places and events behind the stamps. In this age of high speed stamp production and computer generated images, Just History is a refreshing change of pace.

month more than 800 stamps are catalogued and identified from hundreds of countries. The listings are presented in the same format as the Scott Catalogue, complete with Scott numbers and illustrations.

FREE LOOK NO COST AND NO OBLIGATION

FOR A FREE LOOK AT SCOTT STAMP MONTHLY, CALL 1-800-488-5351. IF YOU DECIDE TO SUBSCRIBE YOU'LL RECEIVE 11 MORE ISSUES FOR THE LOW RATE OF $17.95. IF YOU DECIDE NOT TO SUBSCRIBE, WRITE CANCEL ON THE BILL AND RETURN IT AND OWE NOTHING. THE FREE ISSUE IS YOURS TO KEEP!

STAMP STORES

Massachusetts

KAPPY'S COINS & STAMPS
534 Washington St.
Norwood, MA 02062
617-762-5552
617-762-3292 FAX

ARLINGTON WARREN COLLECTIBLES
89 Warren St.
Arlington, MA 02174
617-641-1640
617-641-0870 FAX

Michigan

AMERICA'S STAMP STOP
23333 Orchard Lake Rd.
Farmington, MI 48334
810-474-4460

BIRMINGHAM COIN AND JEWELRY
1287 S. Woodward
Birmingham, MI 48009
810-642-1234
810-642-4207 FAX

MEL COON STAMPS
3833 Twelve Mile
Berkley, MI 48072
810-398-6085
810-398-4549 FAX

LIBERTY COINS & STAMPS
300 Frandor Avenue
Lansing, MI 48912
517-351-4720

THE MOUSE AND SUCH
696 N. Mill Street
Plymouth, MI 48170
313-454-1515

Minnesota

CROSSROADS STAMP SHOP
2211 West 54th Street
Minneapolis, MN 55419-1515
612-928-0119

JW STAMP COMPANY
5300 250th Street
Saint Cloud, MN 56301
612-252-2996

Missouri

KNIGHT'S COINS & STAMPS
323 South Ave.
Springfield, MO 65806
417-862-3018

REGENCY STAMPS, LTD.
Le Chateau Village #106
10411 Clayton Road
St. Louis, MO 63131
800-782-0066
314-997-2231 FAX

Nebraska

TUVA ENTERPRISES
209 So. 72nd Street
Omaha, NE 68114
402-397-9937

New Hampshire

BRUNELLE STAMPS & COINS
25 East Broadway
Derry, NH 03038
603-432-2658
603-437-7279 FAX

New Jersey

AALLSTAMPS
38 North Main Street
Box 249
Milltown, NJ 08850
908-247-1093
908-247-1094 FAX

A.D.A STAMP CO., INC.
910 Boyd Street
Toms River, NJ 08753
908-240-1131
908-240-2620 FAX

BERGEN STAMPS & COLLECTABLES
717 American Legion Dr.
Teaneck, NJ 07666
201-836-8987

CHARLES STAMP SHOP
47 Old Post Road
Edison, NJ 08817
908-985-1071
908-819-0549 FAX

COLONIAL COINS & STAMPS
1865 Rt. #35
Wall Township, NJ 07719
908-449-4549

FAIRIDGE STAMP INC.
447 Broadway
Westwood, NJ 07675
201-666-8869

RON RITZER STAMPS & COLLECTIBLES
Millburn Mall
2933 Vauxhall Road
Union, NJ 07088
908-687-0007 PHONE & FAX

TRENTON STAMP & COIN CO.
1804 RT. 33
Trenton, NJ 08690
800-446-8664
609-587-8664 FAX

New Mexico

THE CLASSIC COLLECTOR
7102 Menaul Blvd. NE
Albuquerque, NM 87110
505-884-9516

New York

B.B.C. STAMP & COIN INC.
185 East Main St.
P.O. Box 2141
Setauket, NY 11733-0715
516-751-5662

JOHN'S COINS, CARDS & STAMPS INC.
36 West 34th Street
2nd Floor
New York, NY 10001
212-244-2646

LINCOLN COIN & STAMP
33 West Tupper Street
Buffalo, NY 14202
716-856-1884

New York

SUBURBAN STAMPS, COINS AND COLLECTIBLES
120 Kreischer Road
North Syracuse, NY 13212
315-452-0593

VILLAGE STAMPS & COINS
22 Oriskany Blvd.
Yorkville Plaza
Yorkville, NY 13495
315-736-1007 or 800-490-1007

North Dakota

THE COLLECTORS DEN/ L.V. FISCHER
P.O. Box 9303
Fargo, ND 58106-9303
701-241-7747 PHONE & FAX

Ohio

CROWN & EAGLE
5303 N. High Street
Columbus, OH 43214
614-436-2042

HILLTOP STAMP SERVICE
P.O. Box 626
Wooster, OH 44691
216-262-5378

J L F STAMP STORE
3041 E. Waterloo Road
Akron, OH 44312
216-628-8343

LAZARUS STAMP DEPT.
141 S. High St.
5th Floor
Columbus, OH 43215
614-463-3214

THE LINK STAMP CO.
3461 E. Livingston Ave.
Columbus, OH 43227
614-237-4125 or 800-546-5726

NEWARK STAMP COMPANY
49 North Fourth Street
Newark, OH 43055
614-349-7900

Oregon

AL'S STAMP & COIN
2132 West 6th
Eugene, OR 97402
503-343-0091

D'S TOYS & HOBBIES
3312 N. Highway 97
Bend, OR 97701
503-389-1330

UNIQUE ESTATE APPRAISALS
1937 NE Broadway
Portland, OR 97232
503-287-4200

Pennsylvania

KAUFMANN'S STAMP DEPT.
400 Fifth Ave.
Pittsburgh, PA 15219
412-232-2598

LARRY LEE STAMPS
322 S. Front Street
Wormleysburg, PA 17043
717-763-7605

Pennsylvania

PENNSYLVANIA STAMP CO.
229 Sixth Street
McKeesport, PA 15132
800-545-6604

PHILLY STAMP & COIN CO. INC.
1804 Chestnut Street
Philadelphia, PA 19103
215-563-7341
215-563-7382 FAX

WORLD OF STAMPS & COINS
Route 611
Fountain Court Mall
Bartonsville, PA 18321
717-688-9829

Rhode Island

PODRAT COIN EXCHANGE INC.
769 Hope Street
Providence, RI 02906
401-861-7640
401-272-3032 FAX

South Carolina

THE STAMP OUTLET
Oakbrook Center #9
Summerville, SC 29484
803-873-4655

Tennessee

HERRON HILL, INC.
5007 Black Road
Suite 140
Memphis, TN 38117-4505
901-683-9644

Texas

ALAMO HEIGHTS STAMP SHOP
1201 Austin Hwy
Suite 128
San Antonio, TX 78209
210-826-4328

ARTEX STAMPS FOR COLLECTORS
3216 W. Park Row
Suite M
Arlington, TX 76013
817-265-8645

AUSTIN STAMP & COIN
13107 F M 969
Austin, TX 78724
512-276-7793

DALLAS STAMP GALLERY
1002 North Central
Expressway
Suite 501
Richardson, TX 75080
800-759-9109
214-669-4742 FAX

METROPLEX STAMP CO.
11811 Preston Road At
Forest Lane
Dallas, TX 75230
214-490-1330

Utah

HIGHLAND STAMP SHOP
4835 S. Highland Dr. #1346
Salt Lake City, UT 84117
801-272-1141

STAMP STORES

Virginia

CENTURY STAMPS & COINS
6436 Brandon Ave.
Springfield, VA 22150
703-569-0739

KENNEDY'S STAMPS & COINS
7059 Brookfield Plaza
Springfield, VA 22150
703-569-7300

LATHEROW & CO. INC.
5054 Lee Highway
Arlington, VA 22207
703-538-2727

PRINCE WILLIAM STAMP & COIN CO.
14011-H St. Germain Dr.
Centreville, VA 22020
703-830-4669

Washington

HIDDEN TREASURES INC.
9960 N.W. Silverdale Way #11
Silverdale, WA 98383
360-692-1999

PEOPLE'S STAMP SERVICE
4132 F. Street
West Bremerton, WA 98312
360-377-1210

RAINIER PHILATELIC INC.
15405 First Avenue South
Burien, WA 98148
206-248-2367

TACOMA MALL BLVD. COIN & STAMP
5225 Tacoma Mall Blvd. E-101
Tacoma, WA 98409
206-472-9632

THE STAMP & COIN PLACE
1310 Commercial
Bellingham, WA 98225
360-676-8720
360-647-6947 FAX

THE STAMP GALLERY
10335 Main Street
Bellevue, WA 98004
206-455-3781 PHONE & FAX

Wisconsin

AURORA BOREALIS STAMP & SUPPLY
2273 S. 65th Street
Milwaukee, WI 53219
800-362-1010
414-543-0340 FAX

HERITAGE STAMPS
11400 W. Bluemound Rd.
Milwaukee, WI 53226
800-231-6080
414-369-0741 FAX

JIM LUKES' STAMP & COIN
815 Jay Street
P.O. Box 1780
Manitowoc, WI 54221
414-682-2324

Supplies

FREEWAY STAMP SUPPLIES
635 S. Raymond Ave.
Suite D
Fullerton, CA 92631
714-447-8100 or 800-447-8105
714-447-8100 FAX

VIDIFORMS COMPANY INC.
Showgard House
110 Brenner Drive
Congers, NY 10920
914-268-4005
914-268-5324 FAX

Supplies & Accessories

BEACH PHILATELICS
P.O. Box 150
Virginia Beach, VA 23458-0150
804-425-8566 PHONE & FAX

GLOBAL STAMP & COIN
460 Ridge Street
Lewiston, NY 14092
800-368-4328
715-754-8513 FAX

Supplies - Mail Order

GOPHER SUPPLY CO.
2499 Rice St. Suite 132
Roseville, MN 55113
612-486-8007
612-486-8441 FAX

STAMPCRAFT
P.O. Box 2425
Santa Clara, CA 95055
800-245-5389
408-241-4440 FAX

Supplies - Protective Sleeves

HOBBY HOUSE DISTRIBUTING
P.O. Box 18025
Indianapolis, IN 46218
317-547-1372

Supplies - Stamps & Coins

GOLD COAST COIN & STAMP SUPPLIES
1007 NE 43rd Street
Ft. Lauderdale, FL 33334
305-565-4688
305-565-4689 FAX

M.A. STORCK CO.
652 Congress Street
Portland, ME 04104
800-734-7271

Supplies - U.S. Stamps

CALUMET STAMPS
P.O. Box 83
Griffith, IN 46319
219-924-4836

Surinam

FRANK GEIGER PHILATELISTS
242 W. Saddle River Road
Suite 5
Upper Saddle River,
NJ 07458-2620
201-236-8122
201-236-8133 FAX

Sweden

FRANK GEIGER PHILATELISTS
242 W. Saddle River Road
Suite 5
Upper Saddle River,
NJ 07458-2620
201-236-8122
201-236-8133 FAX

JOE HARRIS
P.O. Box 13430
Baltimore, MD 21203
410-732-4791

ICE BEAR STAMPS
P.O. Box 40068-C
Eugene, OR 97404
503-461-0890

Sweden - New Issues

SWEDEN STAMP AGENCY IN NORTH AMERICA
One Unicover Center
Cheyenne, WY 82008-0008
800-443-4225
800-628-3123 FAX

Switzerland

AMERICAN COIN & STAMP EXCHANGE
330 So. Gallatin Road
Madison, TN 37115
615-865-8791

FRANK GEIGER PHILATELISTS
242 W. Saddle River Road
Suite 5
Upper Saddle River,
NJ 07458-2620
201-236-8122
201-236-8133 FAX

HENRY GITNER PHILATELISTS INC.
P.O. Box 3077-S
Middletown, NY 10940
914-343-5151/800-947-8267
914-343-0068 FAX

JOE HARRIS
P.O. Box 13430
Baltimore, MD 21203
410-732-4791

Sweden

FRANK GEIGER PHILATELISTS
242 W. Saddle River Road
Suite 5
Upper Saddle River,
NJ 07458-2620
201-236-8122
201-236-8133 FAX

Thailand

MICHAEL ROGERS, INC.
199 E. Welbourne Ave.
Winter Park, FL 32789
407-644-2290
407-645-4434 FAX

Tibet

MICHAEL ROGERS, INC.
199 E. Welbourne Ave.
Winter Park, FL 32789
407-644-2290
407-645-4434 FAX

Topicals

FRANK GEIGER PHILATELISTS
242 W. Saddle River Road
Suite 5
Upper Saddle River,
NJ 07458-2620
201-236-8122
201-236-8133 FAX

CHARLES P. SCHWARTZ
P.O. Box 165
Mora, MN 55051
612-679-4705

Topicals - Columbus

MR. COLUMBUS
Box 1492
Frankenmuth, MI 48734

Topicals - Middle East

THE PERFECT PERF
P.O. Box 16127
Pittsburgh, PA 15242
412-429-1618
412-561-0660 FAX

Topicals – French S & A Territories

TOPICALS in Award Winning Varieties PROOFS, ESSAYS, ERRORS
• ENGRAVINGS •
FRENCH S. ANTARCTICA

• DIE PROOFS • PLATE PROOFS • IMPERFS
• TRIAL COLORS • DELUXE SHEETS
• SEPIA INSPECTION SHEETS • COLLECTIVE SHEETS

Write or call today and discuss your personal interests.
E. Joseph McConnell, Inc.

P.O. Box 683, Monroe, NY 10950
Phone 914-496-5916 • FAX: 914-782-0347

Scott Specialty Album Pages

Collections housed in Scott albums bring a better price when it comes time to sell. Make a lifetime investment in collecting pleasure. Here are a few of the features that distinguish genuine Scott albums from the rest.

- High quality, chemically neutral paper.
- Pages printed on one side only.
- All spaces identified with Scott numbers and illustrations.
- All pages have matching borders.
- Spaces provided for every major variety stamp within each country or specialty area.
- All pages and binders are interchangeable.
- Pages contain all general postage issues, as well as complete back-of-the-book material.

SCOTT®

See your authorized Scott Dealer or order direct from:
Scott Publishing Co., P.O. Box 828, Sidney, OII 45365-0828